LAST LINES
An Index to the Last Lines of Poetry

LAST LINES
An Index to the Last Lines of Poetry

Volume 2

Author Index • **Keyword Index**

Victoria Kline

Facts On File
New York • Oxford

Last Lines: An Index to the Last Lines of Poetry

Copyright © 1991 by Victoria Kline

Facts On File, Inc. Facts On File Limited
460 Park Avenue South Collins Street
New York NY 10016 Oxford OX4 1XJ
USA United Kingdom

Library of Congress Cataloging-in-Publication Data
Kline, Victoria K.
 Last lines.
  1. Poetry—Indexes. 2. English poetry—Indexes
3. Closure (Rhetoric)—Indexes. I. Title.
PN1022.K55 1989 016.80881 88-30948
ISBN 0-8160-1265-2 (set)
ISBN 0-8160-2763-3 (Vol. 1)
ISBN 0-8160-2764-1 (Vol. 2)

A British CIP catalogue record for this book is available from the British Library.

Facts On File books are available at special discounts when purchased in bulk quantities for businesses, associations, institutions or sales promotions. Please contact our Special Sales Department in New York at 212/683-2244 (dial 800/322- 8755 except in NY, AK, or HI) or in Oxford at 865/728399.

Composition by Logidec
Manufactured by Arcata Graphics/Kingsport Press
Printed in the United States of America

10 9 8 7 6 5 4 3 2 1

This book is printed on acid-free paper.

LAST LINES

An Index to the Last Lines of Poetry

Volume 2

Author Index • Keyword Index

AUTHOR INDEX

A

A Becket, Gilbert Abbott
A Holiday Task.
Aal, Katharyn Machan
Ants.
He Says He Wrote by
Moonlight.
Aaronson, Leonard
The Homeward Journey.
Pesci Misti.
Abbe, George
Horizon Thong.
New York City.
The Passer.
Abbey, Henry
Donald.
Faith's Vista.
In Memory of General Grant.
What Do We Plant?
Winter Days.
Abbott, Anthony S.
Out of Mourning.
Abbott, Clifton
Just Keep On.
Abbott, Keith
Blue Mason Jars.
French Desire.
Good News Bad News.
Persephone.
To an Old San Francisco
Poet.
Abbott, Steve
Reading Today's Newspaper.
Abbott, Wenonah Stevens
A Soul's Soliloquy.
Abd-ar-Rahman I
The Palm Tree.
Abeita, Louise *See* **E-Yeh-Shure**
Abelard, Peter
David's Lament for Jonathan.
Good Friday: The Third
Nocturn.
Hymn for the Close of the
Week.
Rumor Laetalis.
To Gabriel of the
Annunciation.
Abercrombie, Lascelles
All Last Night...
Balkis.
Ceremonial Ode Intended for
a University.
Emblems of Love: Epilogue.
Epitaph.
The Fear.
The Fools' Adventure: The
Seeker.
Hope and Despair.
Hymn to Love.
Mary and the Bramble.
Small Fountains.
The Stream's Song.
Vashti.
Witchcraft: New Style.
Aberg, William
Dividing the Field.
The Harvest.
Poem for John My Brother.
The Sleepers.
The Weight.

Abhau, Elliot
Indecsion Means Flexibility.
Abrahams, Peter
Lonely Road.
Me, Colored.
Abrahams, William
In the Henry James Country.
The Museum.
Poem in Time of War.
Seance.
Abramovitch, Henry
Psalm of the Jealous God.
Abrams, Robert J.
Two Poems.
Abrams, Sam
Cakewalkman.
Not the Arms Race.
The United States of America
We.
What the Sixties Were Really
Like.
The World Is with Me Just
Enough.
Abse, Dannie
After the Release of Ezra
Pound.
Angels.
Down the M4.
Duality.
Florida.
Inscription on the Flyleaf of a
Bible.
Letter to Alex Comfort.
The Mountaineers.
Near the Border of Insanities.
Pantomime Diseases.
Peachstone.
Poem and Message.
Portrait of a Marriage.
Public Library.
The Second Coming.
Song for Dov Shamir.
The Stethoscope.
Tales of Shatz.
The Trial.
Verses at Night.
The Victim of Aulis.
Watching a Cloud.
Words Spoken Alone.
Absher, Tom
Hunting with My Father.
Abu Bakr
The Sword.
Abu Dharr
The Oranges.
Abu Dolama
Humorous Verse: "The caliph
shot a gazelle."
Abu Khalid. Fawziyya
Mother's Inheritance.
Abu-l-Ala al-Maarri
Aweary Am I.
The Cryptic Streets.
The Draught of Life.
Summum Bonum.
This World.
Abu Nuwas
An Escape.
The Great Offence.
Abu Zakariya
Bubbling Wine.
Abu'l-Atahija
The Atheist Buries His Son.

For Haroun al Raschid.
Abutsu
The Diary of the Waning
Moon (excerpt).
Acharya, Ananda
My Faith.
Realization.
The Witness.
Ackerley, J. R.
After the Blitz, 1941.
Ackerly, W. C.
Prayer of an Unemployed
Man.
Ackerman, Diane
A Fine, a Private Place.
Ice Dragons.
In the Silks.
Ode to the Alien.
Patrick Ewing Takes a Foul
Shot.
Space Shuttle.
Spiders.
St. Augustine Contemplating
the Bust of Einstein.
Ackerson, Duane
Rip the Apple Seller Awakes;
or, after 50 Years, the Great
Depression.
Stone and the Obliging Pond.
When Daddy Died.
Acorn, Milton
Blackfish Poem.
The Fights.
Ghostly Story.
I'd Like to Mark Myself.
I've Gone and Stained with
the Color of Love.
I've Tasted My Blood.
Knowing I Live in a Dark
Age.
Lover That I Hope You Are.
Monument.
Offshore Breeze.
On Saint-Urbain Street.
Poem for a Singer.
Poem in June.
Saint-Henri Spring.
You Growing.
Acosta, Teresa
My Mother Pieced Quilts.
Acton, Ellen M. V.
Exodus from a Renaissance
Gallery.
Adaios
Epigram: "If you see someone
beautiful."
Adair, Ivan
Real Presence.
Adali-Mortti, G.
Palm Leaves of Childhood.
Adam, Helen
The House o' the Mirror.
I Love My Love.
Adam of St. Victor
The Eagle Swift.
Hail, Mother of the Savior.
Lux Advenit Veneranda.
Adame, Leonard
Black and White.
Song for My Little Friends.
Adams, Anna
Her Dancing Days.
Unrecorded Speech.

Adams, Arthur H.
The Australian.
Adams, Bill
The Ballad of the Ivanhoe.
The Homeward Bound.
Peg-Leg's Fiddle.
Shore Roads of April.
Stowaway.
Adams, Charles Follen
John Barley-Corn, My Foe.
Misplaced Sympathy.
My Infundibuliform Hat.
Prevalent Poetry.
Repartee.
To Bary Jade.
Yaw, Dot Is So!
Yawcob Strauss.
Adams, F. J.
There Is a Tavern in the
Town.
Adams, Francis Lauderdale
Evening Hymn in the Hovels.
Hagar.
Jesus.
To the Christians.
William Wallace.
Adams, Franklin Pierce
("F.P.A.")
Ad Persephonen.
A Ballade of Lawn Tennis.
Ballade of Schopenhauer's
Philosophy.
Baseball Note.
Baseball's Sad Lexicon.
Christopher Columbus.
Composed in the Composing
Room.
The Double Standard.
February 14, 22 B. C.
A Garland of Recital
Programs.
Georgie Porgie (parody).
Happy Lifetime to You.
If Mr. H.W. Longfellow Had
Written Miss Millay's.
Life.
Lines Where Beauty Lingers.
Maud Muller Mutatur
(parody).
Persicos Odi.
Poetry and Thoughts on
Same.
The Reconciliation: A Modern
Version Odes of Horace III,
9.
Regarding (1) the U. S. and
(2) New York.
The Rich Man.
De Senectute.
Song: "Don't Tell Me What
You Dreamt Last Night."
Such Stuff as Dreams.
Those Two Boys.
Thoughts on the Cosmos.
To a Lady Troubled by
Insomnia.
To a Thesaurus.
To a Young Woman on the
World Staff.
To the Polyandrous Lydia.
Tonight.
The Translated Way.
Us Potes.

Adams, Georgia B.
The Family Altar.
A Helping Hand.
The Hour of Prayer.
The Secret Place of Prayer.
Thank Thee, Lord.
Adams, Georgine M.
That Did in Luve So Lively
Write.
Adams, Helen Baker
No Doubt.
Adams, Henry
Prayer to the Virgin of
Chartres.
Adams, James Barton
At a Cowboy Dance.
Billy, He's in Trouble.
The Cowboy's Life.
The Dust of the Overland
Trail.
The Ruin of Bobtail Bend.
A Tough Cuss from Bitter
Creek.
Adams, Jean
A Dream, or the Type of the
Rising Sun.
Adams, John Coleman
We Praise Thee, God, for
Harvests Earned.
Adams, John G.
Heaven Is Here.
Adams, John Quincy
The Lip and the Heart.
Send Forth, O God, Thy
Light and Truth.
To Sally.
The Wants of Man.
Adams, Léonie
Alas, Kind Element.
April Mortality.
Bell Tower.
Caryatid.
Counsel to Unreason.
Country Summer.
Death and the Lady.
Early Waking.
The Font in the Forest.
Ghostly Tree.
Grapes Making.
A Gull Goes Up.
Home-Coming.
The Horn.
Kingdom of Heaven.
Light at Equinox.
Lullaby.
The Mount.
Night-Piece.
The People in the Park.
The Reminder.
The River in the Meadows.
The Runner with the Lots.
Send Forth the High Falcon.
Song from a Country Fair.
Sundown.
This Measure.
Those Not Elect.
Thought's End.
Twilit Revelation.
Words for the Raker of
Leaves.
Adams, Marguerite Janvrin
They Who Possess the Sea.
Adams, Mary Mathews
Dead Love.
Adams, Nehemiah
Saints in Glory, We Together.
Adams, Oscar Fay
At Lincoln.
On a Grave in Christ-Church,
Hants.
Adams, Perseus
The Murder Trial.

My Grandmother.
Thieves.
The Woman and the Aloe.
Adams, Samuel Hopkins
The Centipede.
Adams, Sarah Flower
The Mourners Came at Break
of Day.
Nearer, My God, to Thee.
Adams, William Henry
Davenport
The Last Voyage of the
Fairies.
Adamson, Robert
Action Would Kill It/A
Gamble.
My House.
The Ribbon-Fish.
Sail away.
Sonnet to Be Written from
Prison.
Things Going out of My Life.
Adawiyya, Rabi'a al-
Two Prayers.
Adcock, Arthur St. John
By Deputy.
Adcock, Betty
Poetry Workshop in a Reform
School.
The Sixth Day.
Adcock, Fleur
Blue Glass.
Christmas Dawn.
The Ex-Queen among the
Astronomers.
Instead of an Interview.
Note on Propertius 1.5.
Addiego, John
The Berkeley Pier.
Addison, Joseph
Blenheim.
The Campaign.
Cato's Soliloquy.
Italy and Britain.
A Letter from Italy.
Ode: "How are thy Servants
blest, O Lord!"
Pastoral Hymn.
The Play-House.
Song: "Oh the charming
month of May!"
The Spacious Firmament on
High.
To a Rogue.
When All Thy Mercies.
Addison, Medora C.
Some Day.
The Spell.
Addison, William
Shadows among the Ettrick
Hills.
Addleshaw, Percy
The Happy Wanderer.
Ade, George
Il Janitoro.
The Microbe's Serenade.
R-E-M-O-R-S-E.
Adeane, Louis
Four Poems for April.
The Night Loves Us.
Poem on Hampstead Heath.
Adee, Lucy A. K.
Our Lady of Good Voyage.
"Adeler, Max" (Charles Heber
Clark)
In Memoriam.
Obituary.
Out of the Hurly-Burly.
Adkin, Will S.
If I Only Was the Fellow.

Adler, Felix
Hail! The Glorious Golden
City.
Adler, Friedrich
By the Waterfall.
Adler, Hans
Protect Me.
Ulster.
Adler, Lucile
The Traveling Out.
Adler, Mortimer J.
The Fearless.
Adnan, Etel
The Beirut–Hell Express.
Adoff, Arnold
Dry July.
Adolphus, Gustavus
Battle Hymn.
Ady, Endre
The Last Boats.
Aeschylus
Agamemnon.
Prometheus Bound.
Salamis.
The Seven against Thebes.
The Wail of Prometheus
Bound.
Aesop
The Ass in the Lion's Skin.
The Boy and the Wolf.
The Frogs Who Wanted a
King.
The Greedy Fox and the
Elusive Grapes.
The Mountain in Labor.
The Shepherd-Boy and the
Wolf.
The Swan and the Goose.
The Vine and the Goat.
Agate, James
The Eumenides at Home
(parody).
Agathias
Dialogue.
Not Such Your Burden.
Plutarch.
Rhodanthe.
The Swallows.
Agee, James
Description of Elysium.
The Happy Hen.
In Heavy Mind I Strayed the
Field.
Lyrics.
Millions Are Learning How.
Permit Me Voyage.
Rapid Transit.
So It Begins.
Song with Words.
Sonnets, II: "Our doom is in
our being."
Sonnets, XIX: "Those former
loves wherein our lives have
run."
Sonnets, XX: "Now stands
our love on that still verge of
day."
Sunday: Outskirts of
Knoxville, Tennessee.
Two Songs on the Economy
of Abundance.
Agnew, Edith
Ambition.
Los Pastores.
Progress.
Summer Comes.
Agnew, Joan
Sons of the Kings.
Agnew, Marjorie L.
On Going Home.
Agostinho da Cruz
To Our Saviour.

Agricola
The Daventry Wonder.
Aguila, Pancho
Birthing: 2000.
Nuclear Racial Lockdowns.
St. Valentine.
The Turnaround for
Higherground.
Woman Guard.
Agustini, Delmira
Blindness.
From Far away.
Aharoni, Ada
To a Captain in Sinai.
Ahmed-Ud-Din, Feroz
Cinderella.
"Ai"
29 (A Dream in Two Parts).
Abortion.
Almost Grown.
The Anniversary.
Child Beater.
Conversation.
Cuba, 1962.
Everything: Eloy, Arizona,
1956.
Guadalajara Hospital.
Hangman.
Ice.
I Have Got to Stop Loving
You.
Immortality.
One Man Down.
Pentecost.
She Didn't Even Wave.
The Sweet.
Twenty-Year Marriage.
Why Can't I Leave You?
Woman.
Woman to Man.
Winter in Another Country.
Ai Shih-te
The Human Mind.
Aicard, Jean
In Provence.
Aïdé, Hamilton
Remember or Forget.
When We Are Parted.
Aidoo, Christine Ama Ata
Cornfields in Accra.
Prelude.
Aig-Imoukhuede, Frank
One Wife for One Man.
Aiken, Conrad
The Accomplices.
A Is for Alpha: Alpha Is for
A.
All Lovely Things.
And Already the Minutes.
And in the Hanging Gardens.
Annihilation.
At a Concert of Music.
Beloved, Let Us Once More
Praise the Rain.
Bend as the Bow Bends.
Blind Date.
But How It Came from Earth.
The Calyx of the Oboe
Breaks.
Chiaroscuro: Rose.
The Cicada (excerpt).
Cloister.
The Coming Forth by Day of
Osiris Jones: The Nursery.
The Crab.
Dear Uncle Stranger.
Discordants.
Doctors' Row.
Elder Tree.
Evening Song of Senlin.
Evensong.
Farewell Voyaging World!

The First Note, Simple; the
 Second Note, Distinct.
Goya.
The Habeas Corpus Blues.
Hatteras Calling.
Herman Melville.
The House of Dust: Portrait
 of One Dead.
If Man, That Angel of Bright
 Consciousness.
Improvisations: Light and
 Snow (excerpt).
Keep in the Heart the
 Journal.
The Kid: The Awakening
 (excerpt).
King Borborigmi.
A Letter from Li Po (excerpt).
Limerick: "Animula vagula
 blandula."
Limerick: "It's time to make
 love: douse the glim."
Limerick: "On the deck of a
 ship called the Masm."
Limerick: "There once was a
 wonderful wizard."
The Lovers.
Mayflower.
Miracles.
Morning Dialogue.
Multitudes Turn in Darkness.
The Nameless Ones.
Nocturne of Remembered
 Spring.
North Infinity Street.
Nothing to Say, You Say?
Nuit Blanche: North End.
Obituary in Bitcherel.
One Star Fell and Another.
Preludes for Memnon.
Preludes to Definition: Time
 in the Rock (excerpt).
Priapus and the Pool.
Proem to "The Kid."
The Quarrel.
Queen Cleopatra.
The Return.
The Road.
The Room.
Samadhi.
Sea Holly.
Senlin.
Shaemus.
Sighed a Dear Little
 Shipboard Divinity.
Sleep: and between the Closed
 Eyelids of Sleep.
Snowflake on Asphodel.
The Soldier.
A Sonnet.
Sound of Breaking.
The Sounding.
South End.
The Stepping Stones.
Stone Too Can Pray.
Summer.
Systole and Diastole.
Tetelestai.
Then Came I to the Shoreless
 Shore of Silence.
There Once Was a Wicked
 Young Minister.
The Things.
Three Star Final.
The Time Has Come, the
 Clock Says Time Has Come.
The Unknown Soldier.
The Vampire.
Variations (excerpt).
The Walk in the Garden.
Watch Long Enough, and
 You Will See.

The Wedding.
When the Tree Bares.
Who Shapes a Balustrade?
The Window.
You Went to the Verge, You
 Say, and Came Back Safely?
Aiken, Joan
 Down Below.
 Fable.
 The Fisherman Writes a
  Letter to the Mermaid.
 In the Old House.
 John's Song.
 Night Landscape.
 Rhyme for Night.
Aiken, John
 Picturesque; a Fragment.
Aiken, Lucy
 The Beggar Man.
 The Swallow.
Aikin, John
 Tit for Tat: A Tale.
Ainger, A. C.
 God Is Working His Purpose
  Out.
Ainger, Alfred
 On Taine.
 On the Triumph of
  Rationalism.
Ainslee, Hew
 The Ingle-Side.
Ainslie, Douglas
 Apprehension.
 The Archer.
 The Stirrup Cup.
Ainslie, Hew
 Willie and Helen.
Ainsworth, Henry
 Except the Lord, That He for
  Us Had Been.
 Fire in My Meditation
  Burned.
 Give Ear, O Heavens, to That
  Which I Declare.
 How Long, Jehovah?
 I Minded God.
 I Spread Out unto Thee My
  Hand.
 In the Distress upon Me.
 To God Our Strength Shout
  Joyfully.
 Unto Jehovah Sing Will I.
 With All My Heart, Jehovah,
  I'll Confess.
Aisha bint Ahmad
 I Am a Lioness.
Aist, Dietmar von
 The Linden Tree.
Akahito (Yamabe no Akahito)
 I passed by the beach.
 I Wish I Could Lend a Coat.
 Love, that dwarfs our life.
 The men of valor.
 The mists rise over.
 The Plum-Blossom.
 Two Poems.
Akazome Emon
 I, who cut off my sorrows.
 In My Heart's Depth.
Akenside, Mark
 Amoret.
 Benevolence.
 The Complaint.
 Early Influences.
 England, Unprepared for War.
 For a Statue of Chaucer at
  Woodstock.
 Hymn to Science.
 Inscription for a Grotto.
 Nature's Influence on Man.
 The Nightingale.
 Ode I: Allusion to Horace.

Ode on a Sermon against
 Glory.
Ode to the Evening Star.
On Leaving Holland (excerpt).
The Pleasures of Imagination.
The Poet: A Rhapsody.
Poets.
Song: "The shape alone let
 others prize."
Akers, Elizabeth
 Bringing Our Sheaves.
 Left Behind.
 Little Feet.
 Lost Light.
 Sea-Birds.
 Snow.
 Until Death.
Akers, Garfield
 Dough Roller Blues.
Akesson, Sonja
 Autobiography.
 Ears.
 Evening Walk.
Akhmadulina, Bella
 At Night.
 Autumn.
 The Bride.
 A Dream.
 Fifteen Boys, or Perhaps Even
  More.
 Goodbye.
 In the Emptied Rest Home.
 The Names of Georgian
  Women.
 Silence.
 Sleepwalkers.
 Small Aircraft.
 The Sound of Rain.
 Volcanoes.
 Winter.
 Words Spoken by Pasternak
  during a Bombing.
Akhmatova, Anna
 Alone.
 Broad Gold.
 Each Day Is Anxious.
 Everything is Plundered.
 The Grey-Eyed King.
 Hands Clenched under My
  Shawl...
 He loved three things in life.
 How can you look at the
  Neva.
 I Taught Myself to Live
  Simply and Wisely.
 I wrung my hands under my
  dark veil...
 July 1914.
 A Land Not Mine.
 Lot's Wife.
 Requiem 1935-1940.
 Summer Garden.
 Tashkent Breaks into
  Blossom.
 There Is In Human Closeness
  a Sacred Boundary.
 Voronezh.
 What's worse than this past
  century?
 The White Bird.
 You Are Always New.
 Your lynx-eyes, Asia.
Akhnaton (Amenhotep IV)
 Hymn to the Sun.
 Thy Rising Is Beautiful.
Akhyaliyya, Laila
 Camel.
 Laila Boasting.
 Lamenting Tauaba.
Akin, Guften
 Ellas and the Statues.

Akins, Zoë
 Conquered.
 First Rain.
 I Am the Wind.
 Norah.
 Rain, Rain.
 This Is My Hour.
 The Wanderer.
Akjartoq
 An Old Woman's Song.
 Remembering.
Al-Aswad, Son of Ya'fur
 Old Age.
Al-Fituri, Muhammad
 I Am a Negro.
 The Knell.
Al-Hallaj
 The Ecstasy.
 There Is a Selfhood in My
  Nothingness.
Al-Harizi, Judah
 Heavy-Hearted.
 Love Song.
 Song of the Flea.
 The Song of the Pen.
 Under Leafy Bowers.
 The Unhappy Lover.
 Within My Heart.
Al-Khansa
 Elegy for Her Brother Sakhr.
 In Death's Field.
 The Night.
 Rain to the Tribe.
 Sleepless.
Al-Khirniq
 Lament after Her Husband
  Bishr's Murder.
Al-Mahdi
 The Preacher.
Al Mutanabbi
 Shame Hitherto.
 Written in Flight from His
  Royal Patron.
Alabaster, William
 Incarnatio Est Maximum
  Donum Dei.
 On the Reed of Our Lord's
  Passion.
 Sonnet I.
 Sonnet II.
 Sonnet XV.
 Sonnet XVI.
 Sonnet XIX.
 Sonnet XXIV.
 Sonnet XXXII.
 Sonnet XXXIII.
 Sonnet XXXVII.
 Sonnet XLIV.
 Sonnet XLVI.
 Sonnet LVI.
 Sonnet LXVI.
 Sonnet LXX.
 Sonnet LXXI.
 Sonnet LXXIV.
 Upon the Crucifix.
 Upon the Ensignes of Christes
  Crucifyinge.
Alamanni
 Satires.
Alba, Nanina
 Be Daedalus.
 For Malcolm X.
Albee, John
 At the Grave of
  Champernowne.
 Bos'n Hill.
 Dandelions.
 Landor.
 Music and Memory.
 A Soldier's Grave.
Albert, Samuel L.
 After a Game of Squash.

All of Her.
Honeymoon.
Near the Base Line.
One, Two, Three.
Rebuff.
Street-Walker in March.
Alberti, Rafael
Chaplin's Sad Speech.
Madrigal to a Streetcar
Token.
Albiach, Anne-Marie
Etat (excerpt).
He accepts the circle, speech
and so.
Albizzi, degli Niccolo
Prolonged Sonnet: When the
Troops Were Returning from
Milan.
Albrecht von Johannsdorf
The Pilgrimage.
Albright, Mary E.
Let Me Go Back.
Alcaeus
An Armoury.
Epigram: "Nicander, ooh..."
Let Us Drink.
The Storm.
Two Drinking Songs.
Alcman
No More, O Maidens.
On the Mountains.
Sleep upon the World.
Alcock, Mary
The Chimney-Sweeper's
Complaint.
Written in Ireland.
Alcosser, Sandra
A Fish to Feed All Hunger.
Alcott, Amos Bronson
Bartol.
Channing.
Emerson.
Garrison.
Hawthorne.
Margaret Fuller.
Thoreau.
Wendell Phillips.
Alcott, Louisa May
In Memorium.
A Little Kingdom I Possess.
Love's Resurrection Day.
Our Little Ghost.
Thoreau's Flute.
Alcuin
Lament for the Cuckoo.
Aldan, Daisy
Stones: Avesbury.
Aldana, Francisco de
The Image of God.
Alden, Henry Mills
The Magic Mirror.
Aldington, Hilda Doolittle *See*
Doolittle, Hilda (H. D.)
Aldington, Richard
After Two Years.
At the British Museum.
Barrage.
Battlefield.
Bombardment.
Choricos.
Epilogue.
Evening.
Fatigues.
The Faun Sees Snow for the
First Time.
Her Mouth.
Images.
In the Trenches.
Lesbia.
Loss.
On the March.
The Poplar.

Possession.
Prelude.
Reserve.
A Ruined House.
Soliloquy I.
Soliloquy II.
Three Little Girls.
Vicarious Atonement.
Aldis, Dorothy
The Balloon Man.
Blum.
Brooms.
Clouds.
Feet.
First Winter's Day.
For Christmas.
Fourth of July Night.
Hands.
Hiding.
I Have to Have It.
Ice.
In Spring in Warm Weather.
Kick a Little Stone.
Little.
My Brother.
Names.
Night and Morning.
Our Little Calf.
Our Silly Little Sister.
Radiator Lions.
Riddle: What Am I?
Setting the Table.
Snow.
Somersault.
The Story of the Baby
Squirrel.
Then.
The Twins.
What They Are For.
When I Was Lost.
Windy Wash Day.
Aldis, Mary
Barberries.
The Happening.
The Other One Comes to Her.
She Remembers.
She Thinks of the Faithful
One.
They Meet Again.
The Wandering One Makes
Music.
Aldiss, Brian W.
Progression of the Species.
Tom Wedgwood Tells.
Aldrich, Anne Reeve
April—And Dying.
A Crowned Poet.
Death at Daybreak.
The Eternal Justice.
Fanny.
Fraternity.
In November.
A Little Parable.
Love's Change.
Music of Hungary.
Recollection.
A Song About Singing.
Suppose.
Aldrich, Henry
Christ Church Bells.
Five Reasons for Drinking.
Aldrich, James
A Death-Bed.
Aldrich, Thomas Bailey
Alec Yeaton's Son.
Andromeda.
Appreciation.
At a Reading.
Baby Bell.
Before the Rain.
The Bells at Midnight.
By the Potomac.

Circumstance.
L'Eau Dormante.
Enamored Architect of Airy
Rhyme.
The Face against the Pane.
Fannie.
The Flight of the Goddess.
Forever and a Day.
Fredericksburg.
Guilielmus Rex.
Heredity.
A Hint from Herrick.
Identity.
Kriss Kringle.
Lady of Castlenoire.
Maple Leaves.
Masks.
Memories.
The Menu.
Nocturne.
An Ode: "Not with slow,
funereal sound."
On an Intaglio Head of
Minerva.
On Reading–.
Originality.
Outward Bound.
Palabras Carinosas.
A Petition.
Prescience.
Quits.
Realism.
Reminiscence.
Sargent's Portrait of Edwin
Booth at "The Players".
A Shadow of the Night.
Sleep.
Tennyson.
Thalia.
Tiger-Lilies.
To Hafiz.
A Turkish Legend.
The Undiscovered Country.
Unguarded Gates.
Untimely Thoughts.
When the Sultan Goes to
Ispahan.
The World's Way.
Aldridge, Richard
By Return Mail.
A Matter of Life and Death.
The Pine Bough.
A Serendipity of Love.
Spring Night.
To Himself.
Weeping Willow.
Alegria, Claribel
Disillusionment.
Loneliness and July Ninth.
Search.
Small Country.
Aleichem, Sholom
Epitaph.
Sleep, My Child.
Aleixandre, Vicente
After Love.
Aleqaajik
Great Grief Came over Me.
Alexander, A. L.
This, Too, Shall Pass Away.
Alexander, Bonnie L.
Lapidary.
Alexander, Cecil Frances
The Adoration of the Wise
Men.
All Things Bright and
Beautiful.
The Beggar Boy.
The Burial of Moses.
A Christmas Hymn.
Dreams.
Evening Song.

The Fieldmouse.
Once in Royal David's City.
St. Simon and St. Jude's Day.
There Is a Green Hill.
We May Not Know.
Alexander, Frances
The Breastplate of St. Patrick.
The Contentment of
Willoughby.
His Are the Thousand
Sparkling Rills.
Alexander, John T.
The Winning of the TV West.
Alexander, Joseph Addison
The Doomed Man.
The Hidden Line.
Alexander, Lewis
Africa.
The Dark Brother.
Day and Night.
Dream Song.
Enchantment.
Japanese Hokku.
Negro Woman.
Nocturne Varial.
Tanka I–VIII.
Transformation.
Alexander, Lilla M.
There Is Never a Day So
Dreary.
Alexander, S. J.
To San Francisco.
Alexander, Sidney
The Castle.
Lenox Avenue.
Alexander, Texas
98 Degree Blues.
Levee Camp Moan.
No More Women Blues.
Alexander, Sir William *See*
**Stirling, William Alexander,
Earl of**
Alexander, William
The Birthday Crown.
Frost-Morning.
Robert Burns.
A Vision of Oxford (excerpt).
Alexis
Hangover Cure.
Alfieri, Vittorio
To Dante.
Alford, Henry
The Gypsy Girl.
Harvest Home.
Ten Thousand Times Ten
Thousand.
You and I.
Alford, Janie
Mother Love.
Thanks Be to God.
Alford, John
Glory, Glory to the Sun.
Alfred, William
Mary Lifted from the Dead.
Alger, Horatio, Jr
John Maynard.
Alhamisi, Ahmed Legraham
The Black Narrator.
Ali Ben Abu Taleb
Make Friends.
"Alice"
The Story of the Rose.
Aliesan, Jody
Arachne.
On a Wednesday.
Radiation Leak.
Sutra Blues or, This Pain Is
Bliss.
This Fall.

Alighieri, Dante *See* **Dante Alighieri**
Aliger, Margarita
  House in Meudon.
  To a Portrait of Lermontov.
  Two.
Alishan, Leo
  Easter Song.
Alkabez, Solomon H
  Come, O Friend, to Greet the Bride.
Alkaios *See* **Alcaeus**
Allah, Fareedah
  Funky Football.
  The Generation Gap.
  Lawd, Dese Colored Chillum.
  You Made It Rain.
Allan, Edwin
  The Ass.
Allan, James Alexander
  Breaking.
Allan, M.
  Echo Poem.
Allan, Thomas H.
  Leave the Miracle to Him.
Allana, Gudam Ali
  The Spectre Is on the Move.
Allen, Alice E.
  Life's Common Things.
  My Mother's Garden.
Allen, Dick
  Green Pastures.
  Mime.
Allen, Edward
  The Best Line Yet.
Allen, Elizabeth
  Verse for Vestigials.
Allen, Elizabeth Akers
  Endurance.
  In a Garret.
  The Last Landlord.
  My Dearling.
  Rock Me to Sleep.
  A Toad.
Allen, Ernest Bourner
  I Am With Thee.
Allen, George Leonard
  Portrait.
  To Melody.
Allen, Glen
  The Woman I Am.
Allen, Grace Elisabeth
  Pinkletinks.
Allen, Hervey
  Carolina Spring Song.
  Moments.
  Refuge.
  Saga of Leif the Lucky (excerpt).
  Shadow to Shadow.
  Southward Sidonian Hanno.
  Upstairs Downstairs.
  Walls.
  Whim Alley.
Allen, John Alexander
  Admiral.
Allen, Jonathan
  Sinners, Will You Scorn the Message?
Allen, Leslie Holdsworth
  The Reaper.
Allen, Lyman Whitney
  The Coming of His Feet.
  The People's King.
  The Star of Sangamon.
Allen, Marie Louise
  First Snow.
  Five Years Old.
  The Mitten Song.
  My Zipper Suit.
  Sneezing.
  What Is It?

Allen, Paula Gunn
  The Beautiful Woman Who Sings.
  Catching One Clear Thought Alive.
  Coyote's Daylight Trip.
  Donna.
  Grandmother.
  Kopis'taya.
  Madonna of the Hills.
  Pocahontas to her English husband, John Rolfe.
  Poem for Pat.
  Powwow 79, Durango.
  Rain for Ka-waik.
  Recuerdo.
  Robin.
  (San Ysidro, Cabezon).
  Snowgoose.
  Star Child Suite.
  Suicid/ing Indian Women.
  The Trick Is Consciousness.
  Womanwork.
Allen, Richard
  The God of Bethel Heard Her Cries.
Allen, Samuel ("Paul Vesey")
  American Gothic.
  Dylan, Who Is Dead.
  If the Stars Should Fall.
  Love Song.
  A Moment Please.
  My Friend.
  Nat Turner.
  Ski Trail.
  The Staircase.
  To Satch.
  View from the Corner.
  What Bright Pushbutton?
Allen, Sara Van Alstyne
  Marble Statuette Harpist.
  Walk on a Winter Day.
  The Zoo in the City.
Allen, William S.
  The Erie Canal.
Allen, Willis Boyd
  Thalatta.
Allerton, Ellen Palmer
  Beautiful Things.
Alline, Henry
  Amazing Sight! The Saviour Stands.
  Christ Inviting Sinners to His Grace (excerpt).
  Hard Heart of Mine.
  Turn, Turn, Unhappy Souls, Return.
Alling, Kenneth Slade
  Beauty.
  Dead Wasp.
  Dr. Donne.
  Duality.
  First World War.
  Monsoon.
  On the Park Bench.
  Onion Skin in Barn.
  Rain.
  The Unscarred Fighter Remembers France.
Allingham, William
  Abbey Asaroe.
  The Abbot of Inisfalen.
  Adieu to Belashanny.
  Aeolian Harp.
  After Sunset.
  Among the Heather.
  Amy Margaret.
  At Ballyshannon, Co. Donegal.
  Blowing Bubbles.
  Death Deposed.
  The Dream.

  Earth's Night.
  An Evening.
  Everything Passes and Vanishes.
  Express.
  The Fairies.
  The Fairy King.
  Four Ducks on a Pond.
  Fragment: "Near where the riotous Atlantic surge."
  Fragment: "The wing'd seeds with decaying wings."
  Fragment: "–you see."
  George Levison.
  The Girl's Lamentation.
  Girls Going to the Fair.
  Homeward Bound.
  In a Spring Grove.
  In Snow.
  Irish History.
  Kate o' Belashanny.
  Late Autumn.
  Laurence Bloomfield in Ireland.
  The Lion and the Wave.
  The Lough.
  Lovely Mary Donnelly.
  The Lover and Birds.
  The Lupracaun, or Fairy Shoemaker.
  The Maids of Elfin-Mere.
  Meadowsweet.
  Midsummer.
  The Milkmaid.
  A Mill.
  The Mowers.
  Nanny's Sailor Lad.
  The Nobleman's Wedding.
  Riding.
  Robin Redbreast.
  The Ruined Chapel.
  Ruins at Sunset.
  The Sailor.
  Song–Across the Sea.
  Song: "I walk'd in the lonesome evening."
  Song: "O spirit of the Summertime!"
  Spring.
  Sunday Bells.
  A Swing Song.
  Three Fragments.
  Up the Airy Mountain.
  A Wealthy Man.
  Wild Rose.
  The Winding Banks of Erne.
  Windlass Song.
  Wishing.
  The Witch-Bride.
  Writing.
Allison, Drummond
  The Brass Horse.
  Dedication.
  King Lot's Envoys.
  No Remedy.
  O Sheriffs.
Allison, John
  Okeechobee.
  Reflection: After Visiting Old Friends.
"Allison, Joy" (Mary A. Cragin)
  Which Loved Best?
Allison, William Talbot
  O Amber Day, Amid the Autumn Gloom.
Allison, Young Ewing
  Derelict.
Allman, John
  You Owe Them Everything.
Allott, Kenneth
  Cheshire Cat.
  Departure Platform.

  Lament for a Cricket Eleven.
  Prize for Good Conduct.
  The Statue.
Allston, Washington
  On the Late S. T. Coleridge.
  Rosalie.
  To Benjamin West.
Allston, William
  America to Great Britain.
Allwood, Brian
  No Laws.
Allwood, Martin Samuel
  Gethsemane, Illinois.
Alma-Tadema, Laurence
  If No One Ever Marries Me.
  Playgrounds.
  Strange Lands.
Alohikea, Alfred
  The Glory of Hanalei Is Heavy Rain.
Alonso, Ricardo
  Tiempo Muerto.
Alphonsus Liguori, Saint
  Madonna's Lullaby.
Alqamah
  The Mufaddaliyat: His Camel.
Alquit, B. (Eliezer Blum)
  The Light of the World.
  Wandering Chorus.
Alsop, George
  The Author to His Book.
  Be Just (Domestick Monarchs) unto Them.
  Could'st Thou (O Earth) Live Thus Obscure.
  Heavens Bright Lamp, Shine Forth Some of Thy Light.
  Lines on a Purple Cap Received as a Present from My Brother.
  Poor Vaunting Earth, Gloss'd with Uncertain Pride.
  'Tis Said the Gods Lower Down That Chain Above.
  To My Cosen Mris. Ellinor Evins.
  Trafique Is Earth's Great Atlas.
Alston, Joseph Blynth
  Stack Arms!
Alta
  After Reading Sylvia Plath:...
  The Art of Enforced Deprivation.
  Bitter Herbs.
  Daily Courage Doesnt Count.
  Euch, Are You Having Your Period?
  First Pregnancy.
  He Said, Lying There.
  Hunger for Me.
  I Don't Have No Bunny Tail on My Behind.
  I Never Saw a Man in a Negligee.
Alterman, Nathan
  From All Peoples (excerpt).
  Poem About Your Face.
  Saul.
  The Spinning Girl.
  Tammuz.
  This Night.
  To the Elephants.
Altgood, Laurence
  Song of the Brave.
Altman, Shalom
  Vine and Fig Tree.
Altolaguirre, Manuel
  To a Cloud.
Altrocchi, Julia Cooley
  The Pigeon-Feeders in Battery Park.

Alurista
Get Stuffed.
In the Barrio.
Must Be the Season of the
   Witch.
Alvarez, Alfred
A Cemetery in New Mexico.
Dying.
The Fortunate Fall.
Lost.
Mourning and Melancholia.
Operation.
Alver, Betti
Iron Heaven.
The Painter in the Lion Cage.
A Tailor Called Sorrow.
The Titans.
Alyea, Dorothy
Keepsake from Quinault.
Amabile, George
Snowfall: Four Variations.
Twink Drives Back, in a Bad
   Mood, from a Party in
   Massachusetts.
Amarou
He Drunken Rose.
Ambapali, Basham
Black and Glossy as a Bee
   and Curled Was My Hair.
Ambrose of Milan, Saint
Hymn: "Framer of the earth
   and sky."
Verbum Supernum.
Amen, Grover
The Cot.
Amergin
The Incantation.
Invocation to Ireland.
Ames, A. S.
Abraham Lincoln.
Ames, Evelyn
Because I Live.
Two Solitudes.
Ames, Jay
On Corwen Road.
Amichai, Yehuda
Advice.
God Has Pity on
   Kindergarten Children.
I Am a Leaf.
I Am Sitting Here.
I Think of Oblivion.
In the Old City.
Jerusalem, Port City.
Lament.
Lay Your Head on My
   Shoulder.
My Mother Once Told Me.
Not Like a Cypress.
Of Three or Four in a Room.
On the Day of Atonement.
On the Wide Stairs.
A Painful Love Song.
A Pity. We Were Such a
   Good Invention.
Quick and Bitter.
Shadow of the Old City.
Since Then.
Sodom's Sister City.
Song of Resignation.
The Town I Was Born In.
We Did It.
"Amini, Johari" (Jewel C.
Latimore)
Before/and After...
Brother...
Childhood.
Positives.
Saint Malcolm.
Signals.
A Sun Heals.
To a Poet I Knew.

Utopia.
Amir, Aharon
Cock.
Nothingness.
Amiri, Akhtar
I Am a Woman (excerpt).
Amis, Kingsley
After Goliath.
Against Romanticism.
Alternatives.
Autobiographical Fragment.
Beowulf.
A Bookshop Idyll.
Departure.
A Dream of Fair Women.
The Evans Country.
An Ever-Fixed Mark.
The Helbatrawss.
The Last War.
Masters.
New Approach Needed.
A Note on Wyatt.
Nothing to Fear.
Ode to Me.
On a Portrait of Mme.
   Rimsky-Korsakov.
A Poet's Epitaph.
Reborn.
Science Fiction.
Shitty.
Sight Unseen.
The Silent Room.
St. Asaph's.
Terrible Beauty.
A Tribute to the Founder.
Amis, Lewis R.
Jehovah, God, Who Dwelt of
   Old.
Ammianus
Epitaph of Nearchos.
Ammonides
Secret Weapon.
Ammons, Archie Randolph
80-Proof.
Apologia pro Vita Sua.
The Arc Inside and Out.
Auto Mobile.
Ballad.
Bay Bank.
Bonus.
Bridge.
Cascadilla Falls.
Chasm.
Christmas Eve.
The City Limits.
Clarity.
Classic.
Cleavage.
Close-Up.
The Confirmers.
Conserving the Magnitude of
   Uselessness.
The Constant.
Coon Song.
Corsons Inlet.
Coward.
Cut the Grass.
Dark Song.
Dinah.
Diner.
Easter Morning.
The Eternal City.
First Carolina Said-Song.
Grace Abounding.
Gravelly Run.
Hardweed Path Going.
He Held Radical Light.
Hope's Okay.
Hymn.
Imperialist.
Kind.
Laser.

Life in the Boondocks.
Loss.
Mechanism.
Mirrorment.
Model.
Mountain Talk.
Needs.
Periphery.
Pet Panther.
Play.
Plunder.
Poetics.
Prospecting.
The Put-Down Come On.
Reflective.
Rivulose.
Rocking.
Runoff.
Satisfaction.
Second Carolina Said-Song.
Self-Projection.
Silver.
Sitting down, Looking up.
Small Song.
So I Said I Am Ezra.
Sphere (excerpt).
Spring Coming.
Terrain.
The Unifying Principle.
Time's Times Again.
Transaction.
Treaties.
Triphammer Bridge.
Unsaid.
Upland.
Viable.
Visit.
The Wide Land.
Windy Trees.
Winter Saint.
Winter Scene.
Working with Tools.
The Yucca Moth.
Amner, John
A Motet.
Amon-Re
Hymn of Victory: Thutmose
   III.
Amorosi, Ray
Note in a Sanitorium.
Nothing Inside and Nothing
   Out.
Amoss, Harry
Pedagogical Principles.
Riding.
Amphis
Hangover Cure.
Amprimoz, Alexandre L.
The Final Fall.
Ana, Marcos
To the Faithful.
Anacreon
Design for a Bowl.
Heat.
The Picture.
The Thracian Filly.
To Dionysus.
To Eros.
To Himself.
To His Young Mistress.
Woman's Arms.
Anatolius, Saint
Great and Mighty Wonder.
Jesus, Deliverer.
Andal
Cuckoo, noisy among the
   Shenbaka flowers.
O people who live in the
   world.
To Krishna Haunting the
   Hills.

Andersen, Astrid Hjertenaes
Before the sun goes down.
Andersen, Hans Christian
The Pearl.
Anderson, Alexander
("Surfaceman")
Cuddle Doon.
Jenny wi' the Airn Teeth.
Langsyne, When Life Was
   Bonnie.
Anderson, Bill
Letter from a Black Soldier.
Outbreak.
Anderson, David Earle
With the Nuns at Cape May
   Point.
Anderson, Don
Have You Thanked a Green
   Plant Today.
Anderson, Ethel
Afternoon in the Garden.
Bucolic Eclogues: Waking,
   Child, While You Slept.
Kunai-Mai-Pa Mo.
Migrants.
Anderson, Forrest
The Beach Homos.
Anderson, Gordon
The First Hunt.
Anderson, Jack
Aesthetics of the Moon.
Another Letter to Joseph
   Bruchac.
Commanding a Telephone to
   Ring.
Face in a Mirror.
Faces.
A Garden of Situations.
Going to Norway.
The Invention of New Jersey.
Ode to Pornography.
Reading Sign.
Visit to the Hermitage.
Anderson, James
When Father Slept.
Anderson, John
The Blue Animals.
Clipper Ships.
Shadows of Sails.
Anderson, Jon
American Landscape with
   Clouds & a Zoo.
Falling in Love.
Homage to Robert Bresson.
In Autumn.
In Sepia.
John Clare.
Lives of the Saints.
The Milky Way.
The Parachutist.
The Photograph of Myself.
Refusals.
Rosebud.
The Secret of Poetry.
Witness.
Ye Bruthers Dogg.
Years.
Anderson, Kenneth L.
Hope.
Anderson, Margaret Steele
The Breaking.
Anderson, Maxwell
Judith of Minnewaulken:
   Judith Remembers.
Lafayette to Washington.
Lucifer.
Parallax.
Toll the Bell for Damon.
Anderson, Patrick
Camp.
Canoe.
Capital Square.

Drinker.
Houses Burning: Quebec.
My Bird-Wrung Youth.
Poem on Canada: Cold
  Colloquy.
Sestina in Time of Winter.
Sleighride.
Anderson, S. E.
Junglegrave.
A New Dance.
The Sound of Afroamerican
  History Chapt I.
The Sound of Afroamerican
  History Chapt II.
Anderson, Sherwood
The Lame One.
A Visit.
Anderson, Teresa
Delphine.
Our People.
Anderson, Violet
The Cloak.
Through the Barber Shop
  Window.
Andrade, Jorge Carrera
Augusto Ngangula.
Fourth Poem.
Walnut.
André, John
The Cow-Chace.
André, Michael
1,000 Illustrations & a
  Complete Concordance.
My Regrets.
**Andresen, Sophia de Mello
Breyner**
Camoes and the Debt.
The Dead Men.
Dionysus.
The Mirrors.
The Small Square.
The Young Girl and the
  Beach.
Andrew, Prudence
Whippet.
Andrew of Wynton
Macbeth's Dream.
Andrewes, Francis
Shepherdess' Valentine.
Andrews, Charlton
Our Modest Doughboys.
Andrews, Harvey
Unaccompanied.
Andrews, John
The Anatomy of Baseness: To
  The Detracted.
Andrews, John Williams
La Madonna di Lorenzetti.
**Andrews, Mary Raymond
Shipman**
A Call to Arms.
Andrews, Robert
Mercury. On Losing my
  Pocket Milton...
Urania.
Andriello, Amelia
Autumn Even.
Aneirin
The Lovely Youth.
Aneirin [(or Aneurin)]
The Gododdin (excerpt).
Angell, Walter Foster
To New Haven and Boston.
Angelou, Maya
Africa.
Chicken-Licken.
My Arkansas.
On Diverse Deviations.
Pickin Em Up and Layin Em
  Down.
Remembering.
Sepia Fashion Show.

Song for the Old Ones.
Southeast Arkanasia.
Still I Rise.
They Went Home.
To a Husband.
Woman Me.
Woman Work.
**"Angelus Silesius" (Johannes
Scheffler)**
The Cherubic Pilgrim.
In Thine Own Heart.
Nothing Fair on Earth I See.
The Rose.
Song of Praise to Mary.
The Tree of the Cross.
Angermayer, Frances
Conversion.
Anghelaki-Rooke, Katrina
The Body Is the Victory and
  the Defeat of Dreams.
Notes on My Father.
Angiolieri, Cecco da Siena
Sonnet: He Argues His Case
  with Death.
Sonnet: He Is Past All Help.
Sonnet: He Rails Against
  Dante...
Sonnet: He Will Not Be Too
  Deeply in Love.
Sonnet: In Absence from
  Becchina.
Sonnet: Of All He Would Do.
Sonnet: Of Becchina in a
  Rage.
Sonnet: Of Becchina, the
  Shoemaker's Daughter.
Sonnet: Of Love, in Honor of
  His Mistress Becchina.
Sonnet: Of Love in Men and
  Devils.
Sonnet: Of the 20th June
  1291.
Sonnet: Of Why He Is
  Unhanged.
Sonnet: Of Why He Would Be
  a Scullion.
Sonnet: To Dante Alighieri
  (He Writes to Dante...).
Sonnet: To Dante Alighieri
  (On the Last Sonnet of the
  Vita Nuova).
Angoff, Charles
God Is Here Again.
Litany.
A Little Girl.
What Has Happened.
Angulo, Hector
Dopefiends Trip.
Angus, Marion
Alas! Poor Queen.
Foxgloves and Snow.
Mary's Song.
Annan, Annie Rankin
Dandelion.
Annand, J. K.
Arctic Convoy.
O Aa the Manly Sports.
On the Croun o Bidean.
What Finer Hills?
Annensky
Black Spring.
Annett, David
The Wreck of the
  Deutschland (parody).
Ansari of Herat
I Live Only to Do Thy Will.
Anselm, Saint
To Our Lord in the
  Sacrament.
Ansen, Alan
Fatness.

A Fit of Something against
  Something.
Tennyson.
"Ansky, S." (Solomon Rapport)
Emigrant Song.
The Tailor.
Anson, John Seller
The Lighthouse.
Proverbial.
Anstadt, Henry
A Little Rhyme and a Little
  Reason.
Anster, John
Sonnet: "If I might choose
  where my tired limbs shall
  lie."
Anstey, Christopher
Burglar Bill.
Letter Containing a Panegyric
  on Bath.
The New Bath Guide.
The ordinary valour only
  works.
Ant, Howard
Bucket of Sea-Serpents.
Antar [(or Antana)]
Abla.
The Mu'Allaqa of Antar.
Antella, Simone dall'
Prolonged Sonnet.
Anthony, Edward
The Bloodhound.
College Song.
The Collies.
The Dachshund.
From Oddity Land.
I Know a Barber.
Anthony, George
Autumn Evening.
Anthony, Florence See "Ai"
Anthony of Padua, Saint
Death-Bed Hymn of Saint
  Anthony of Padua.
Antin, David
The Passengers.
Radical Coherency.
Antipater of Sidon
Aristeides.
Erinna.
Never Again, Orpheus.
Pindar.
Undying Thirst.
Antiphilus of Byzantium
A Freshet.
Antokolsy
Hate!
Antoninus, Brother See also
Everson, William
Advent.
A Canticle to the Waterbirds.
I Am Long Weaned.
The Song of the Body
  Dreamed in the Spirit's Mad
  Behest.
The South Coast.
What Birds Were There.
Year's End.
Antrobus, John
The Cowboy.
Anyte [(or Anytes)]
I am Hermes.
I, Hermes, Have Been Set Up.
Alive, this man was Manes, a
  common slave.
A Shepherd's Gift.
Lounge in the shade of the
  luxuriant laurel's/beautiful
  foliage.
Ap Gwillym, Dafydd
The Rattle Bag.
Aphek, Edna
Sarah.

The Story of Abraham and
  Hagar.
Apolebieji, Odeniyi
Salute to the Elephant.
Apollinaire, Guillaume
Calligram, 15 May 1915.
The Little Car.
The Mirabeau Bridge.
Moonlight.
Poem to Lou.
Shadow.
War.
Zone.
Apollinaris, Sidonius
Invitation to the Dance.
Appel, Benjamin
The Talker.
Appleman, Philip
Amurrika! (parody).
East Hampton: The Structure
  of Sound.
In the Gazebo (parody).
Is There a Voice (parody).
It Is Enough (parody).
Maples (parody).
Memo to the 21st Century.
La Misere (parody).
More (parody).
My Friend (parody).
On a Morning Full of Sun.
Peace with Honor.
So What (parody).
Try (parody).
Waiting for the Fire.
When (parody).
Winding down the War.
Appleton, Everard Jack
The Fighting Failure.
The Woman Who
  Understands.
Applewhite, James
Bordering Manuscript.
My Grandfather's Funeral.
The Ravine.
Red Wing Hawk.
To Earth.
Aragon, Louis
Dirge.
The Lilacs and the Roses.
Aratus of Soli
Praise of Zeus.
Arbuthnot, John
Colonel Chartres.
Epitaph on Colonel Francis
  Chartres.
Archer, Kate Rennie
The Lairdless Place.
Archer, Nuala
Flies Love Me.
Archestratus
Gastrology (excerpt).
Hare.
Archias
Sea Dirge.
Archibald, Esther
In My Place.
Archilochus
Decks Awash.
Like Odysseus under the
  Ram.
May He Lose His Way on the
  Cold Sea.
The Poet's Shield.
This Island.
Tossed on a Sea of Trouble.
Archpoet of Cologne
The Confession of Golias
  (abridged).
Arden, John
The Lobster Pot.
Arden, R. P.
On Dr. Samuel Ogden.

Ardinger, Richard
At 85.
Arensberg, Walter Conrad
About an Allegory.
Chryseis.
The Inner Significance of the
Statues Seated Outside the
Boston...
The Masterpiece.
Out of Doors.
To a Poet.
Voyage a L'Infini.
Arensberg, William
To Hasekawa.
Aretino, Pietro
Brother Astolfo Sated
Appetite.
Stragglers.
**Argensola, Bartolome Leonardo
de**
To Mary Magdalen.
Argentarius, Marcus
A Blackbird.
The Old Story.
Rumoresque Senum
Severiorum.
Arguelles, Ivan
The Spanish Girls.
Aridjis, Umberto
Sun Set.
Ariosto, Lodovico
Can I Believe.
Orlando Furioso.
Song for the Third Marriage
of Lucrezia Borgia (excerpt).
Aristophanes
The Birds.
The Clouds.
Lysistrata.
The Peace: Midst the Free
Green Fields.
The Thesmophoriazusae:
Women Speak Out in
Defense of Themselves.
Arkell, Reginald
A Public Nuisance.
Rumors.
Arkwright, John Stanhope
The Supreme Sacrifice.
Armand, Octavio
Possible Love Poem to the
Usurer.
Armattoe, R. E. G.
Deep Down the Blackman's
Mind.
Armitage, Jennifer
To Our Daughter.
Armknecht, Richard F.
Crow's Nest.
Armour, Richard
Deus Ex Machina.
Epitaph: "Insured for every
accident."
Fish Story.
Good Sportsmanship.
Hiding Place.
Horses.
Money.
One Down.
Travelling Companions.
Armstrong, Frankie
The Collier Lass.
Month of January.
Out of the Darkness.
Women of My Land.
Armstrong, Hamilton Fish
Lines for the Hour.
Armstrong, J. A.
Another Reply to In Flanders
Fields.
Armstrong, John
The Advantages of Washing.

The Art of Preserving Health
(excerpt).
Blest Winter Nights.
The Dangers of Sexual Excess.
The Home of the Naiads.
The Oeconomy of Love
(excerpt).
Armstrong, Margaret D.
Invocation for the New Year.
Armstrong, Martin
The Buzzards.
On a Little Bird.
To a Jilt.
Armstrong, Peter
Butterfly.
Armstrong, Thomas
The Row between the Cages.
Arnatkoak
Personal Song.
Arnaut, Daniel
Canzo of Bird-Songs and
Love.
Arndt, Ernst Moritz
The German Fatherland.
Arnett, Carroll
Anadarko John.
Ayohu Kanogisdi Death Song.
Bio-Poetic Statement:
Instruction to Warriors on
Security.
Drunk.
Land.
Last May.
Look Back.
The Old Man Said.
Removal: Last Part.
Rock Painting.
Something for Supper.
Song of the Breed.
The Story of My Life.
You.
Arnold, George
Alone by the Hearth.
Beer.
Farewell to Summer.
The Golden Fish.
In the Dark.
The Jolly Old Pedagogue.
Jubilate.
September.
Sweet September.
Youth and Age.
Arnold, Gertrude Thomas
Desert Bloom.
Arnold, Irene
Pray!
Arnold, Kokomo
Mean Old Twister.
Arnold, Lila
The Paisley Ceiling.
Arnold, Matthew
Austerity of Poetry.
Bacchanalia (excerpt).
Below the Surface-Stream,
Shallow and Light.
The Better Part.
The Buried Life.
Cadmus and Harmonia.
Calais Sands.
A Caution to Poets.
Courage.
The Death of Sohrab.
Desire.
Destiny.
Dover Beach.
A Dream.
East London.
Empedocles on Etna.
Epilogue to Lessing's
Laocoon.
The Forsaken Merman.
The Future.

Geist's Grave.
Growing Old.
Haworth Churchyard
(excerpt).
The Hayeswater Boat
(excerpt).
The Hymn of Empedocles
(excerpt).
Immortality.
In Harmony with Nature.
In Utrumque Paratus.
Kaiser Dead.
The Lake.
The Last Word.
Life and Thought.
Lines Written in Kensington
Gardens.
Longing.
Matthias (excerpt).
Memorial Verses.
A Memory-Picture.
Morality.
Mycerinus.
A Nameless Epitaph.
Obermann Once More.
Palladium.
Persistency of Poetry.
Philomela.
Poor Matthias.
The Progress of Poesy.
Quiet Work.
Requiescat.
Resignation.
The River.
Rugby Chapel–November,
1857.
S. S. "Lusitania."
Scenes from Carnac.
The Scholar-Gipsy.
The Second Asgard.
Self-Deception.
Self-Dependence.
Separation.
Shakespeare.
Sohrab and Rustum.
Stanzas from the Grande
Chartreuse.
Stanzas in Memory of the
Author of "Obermann".
The Strayed Reveller.
A Summer Night.
Switzerland.
Thyrsis.
To a Friend.
To a Republican Friend.
Urania.
We Cannot Kindle.
West London.
A Wish.
Written in Butler's Sermons.
The Youth of Nature:
Wordsworth's Country.
Youth's Agitations.
Arnold, Mrs. Major
The End which Comes.
He and She.
The Light of Asia (excerpt).
The Musmee.
Somewhere.
Thank God for the Country!
To a Pair of Egyptian
Slippers.
Arnold, Sir Edwin
After Death in Arabia.
Almond Blossom.
Darien.
Destiny.
The Light of Asia.
She and He.
Arnstein, Flora J.
Timers.

Aronsten, Joan
Ad Infinitum.
Arowa
Dirge for Fajuyi.
Arp, Hans
The Domestic Stones.
I Am a Horse.
Two Little Arabs Adult and
Arabesque.
When It Burns before the
Harps and Freezes behind
the Easels.
Arp, Jean
What the Violins Sing in
Their Baconfat Bed.
Arrabey, Salaan
To a Faithless Friend.
Arrivi, Francisco
Song for a Day (excerpt).
Song for a Transformation
(excerpt).
Arrowsmith, Pat
Christmas Story (1980).
Political Activist Living
Alone.
Arsenault, Joel
Windfall.
Arudra
Poeti-c Art.
Arvey, Michael
Concert.
Follower.
Arvey, Verna
All That I Am.
Asayasu
Across clear drops of dew.
Asbaje, Juana de See **Juana Ines
de la Cruz, Sister**
Asch, Frank
Leaves.
Play.
Summer.
Sunflakes.
Asclepiades
Desire Knows.
Epitaph of a Courtesan.
Eumares.
Poems from the Greek
Anthology (excerpt).
Rain, Night, and Wine.
To a Recalcitrant Virgin.
Asgrimsson, Eysteinn
Author's Entreaty for His
Lay.
Ash, Sarah Leeds
Changeless Shore.
Ashbery, John
An Additional Poem.
And Ut Pictura Poesis Is Her
Name.
Around the Rough and
Rugged Rocks the Ragged
Rascal Rudely Ran.
As One Put Drunk into the
Packet-Boat.
At North Farm.
A Blessing in Disguise.
A Boy.
The Bungalows.
But What Is the Reader to
Make of This?
The Chateau Hardware.
City Afternoon.
Civilisation and Its
Discontents.
Decoy.
Down by the Station, Early in
the Morning.
Drunken Americans.
The Ecclesiast.
Europe.
Evening in the Country.

Everyman's Library.
Farm Implements and Rutabagas in a Landscape.
Faust.
Fear of Death.
For John Clare.
Friends.
Glazunoviana.
Grand Abacus.
The Grapevine.
He.
How Much Longer Will I Be Able to Inhabit the Divine Sepulcher...
The Ice-Cream Wars.
Idaho.
If the Birds Knew.
De Imagine Mundi.
The Instruction Manual.
Landscapeople.
Last Month.
A Last World.
Leaving the Atocha Station.
Le Livre Est sur la Table.
A Love Poem.
A Man of Words.
Many Wagons Ago.
Marchenbilder.
Melodic Trains.
Mixed Feelings.
My Erotic Double.
Never Seek to Tell Thy Love.
On Autumn Lake.
The One Thing That Can Save America.
The Ongoing Story.
Our Youth.
The Painter.
Pantoum.
Paradoxes and Oxymorons.
The Picture of Little J.A. in a Prospect of Flowers.
Poem: "While we were walking under the top."
Pyrography.
Rivers and Mountains.
Self-Portrait in a Convex Mirror.
Some Trees.
Soonest Mended.
Spring Day.
Street Musicians.
Syringa.
The Tennis Court Oath.
Tenth Symphony.
These Lacustrine Cities.
They Dream Only of America.
Thoughts of a Young Girl.
The Ticket.
To Redoute.
Two Scenes.
Two Sonnets.
Variations, Calypso and Fugue on a Theme of Ella Wheeler Wilcox.
A Vase of Flowers.
Wet Casements.
What Is Poetry.
White Roses.
Worsening Situation.
The Wrong Kind of Insurance.
Years of Indiscretion.
The Young Price and the Young Princess.

Ashburton, Robert Offley
A Harrow Grave in Flanders.

Ashby, Cliff
Latter Day Psalms.
A Stranger in This Land.

Ashby-Sterry, Joseph
Kindness to Animals.
The King of the Cradle.
A Portrait.

Ashe, Thomas
The City Clerk.
Corpse-Bearing.
A Machine Hand.
Meet We No Angels, Pansie?
No and Yes.
To Two Bereaved.

Ashley, Nova Trimble
Humiliation Revisited.

Ashley, Paul David
Beauty.
Prison.
The Ritual.
Song from the Unfinished Man.
Sounds.

Askenazy, Ludvik
The Wall.

Asklepiades See Asclepiades
"Asmus" See Claudius, Matthius
Asphodel
Full Moon in Malta.
On the Pilgrim's Way in Kent, as It Leads to the Coldrum Stones.
Winter Solstice–For Frank.

Asquith, Herbert
Birthday Gifts.
Eggs.
The Elephant.
The Frowning Cliff.
The Hairy Dog.
The Mare.
A Ship Sails up to Bideford.
Skating.
The Volunteer.

Assisi, Saint Francis of See
Francis of Assisi, Saint
Astley, Thea
Droving Man.

Astor, Susan
Dame.
Four Spacious Skies.
The Road the Crows Own.

Astra
Bloody Pause.
Daughters.
Now or Never.

Asya (Asya Gray)
Celan.
The Deer.
A Grain of Moonlight.
My Strawlike Hair.
My True Memory.
Pause a Moment.

At Taliq
I Took Leave of My Beloved One Evening.

Atchity, Kenneth John
A Delicate Impasse.

Atharva Veda
An Imprecation Against Foes and Sorcerers.

Athenogenes, Saint
Hymn for the Lighting of the Lamps.

Atherstone, Edwin
Sunrise at Sea.

Atherton, John
Tank Town.

Atimantiyar
Nowhere, Not among the Warriors at Their Festival.

Atkins, Russell
At War.
Christophe.
Dangerous Condition: Sign on Inner-City House.

Dark Area.
Editorial Poem on an Incident of Effects Far-Reaching.
Inner-City Lullaby.
Irritable Song.
It's Here In The.
Narrative.
New Storefront.
Night and a Distant Church.
On the Fine Arts Garden, Cleveland.
Probability and Birds.

Attar, Samar
The Return of the Dead (excerpt).
The Sun of My Perfection Is a Glass.

Attey, John
Madrigal: "Flow forth, abundant tears."
Madrigal: "Vain Hope, adieu."

Atwell, Roy
Some Little Bug.

Atwood, Margaret
The accident has occurred.
After the Agony in the Guest Bedroom.
Against Still Life.
The Animals in That Country.
At First I Was Given Centuries.
At the Tourist Center in Boston.
Daguerreotype Taken in Old Age.
Death of a Young Son by Drowning.
Dream 2: Brian the Still-Hunter.
Dufferin, Simcoe, Grey.
Elegy for the Giant Tortoises.
Five Poems for Dolls.
Game after Supper.
Habitation.
I Can Change Myself.
Interview with a Tourist.
It Is Dangerous to Read Newspapers.
Landcrab.
Lying Here, Everything In Me.
Marrying the Hangman.
A Night in the Royal Ontario Museum.
Notes towards a Poem That Can Never Be Written.
November.
Pig Song.
Provisions.
Songs of the Transformed: Siren Song.
Spelling.
There Is Only One of Everything.
They Eat Out.
This Is a Photograph of Me.
This Year I Intended Children.
Variation on the Word Sleep.
We Are Standing Facing Each Other.
Woman Skating.
You Begin.
You Fit into Me.
You Refuse to Own.
You Take My Hand And.
You Want to Go Back.
Your Back Is Rough.

Aua
Bear Hunting.
Morning Prayer.
Walrus Hunting.

Aubert, Alvin
Blood to Blood.
Levitation.
One More Time.
There Were Fierce Animals in Africa.
When the Wine Was Gone.

Aubert, Rosemary
Love Poem.

Aubigne, Theodore Agrippa d'
A Portrait of Henri III.

Auchterlonie, Dorothy
Apopemptic Hymn.
Meditation of a Mariner.
The Tree.
Waiting for the Post.

Audelay, John
Be True to Your Condition in Life.
Dread of Death.
The Fairest Flower.
In His Utter Wretchedness.
The Love of God.
What Tidings?

Auden, W. H.
The Aesthetic Point of View.
After Reading a Child's Guide to Modern Physics.
The Airman's Alphabet.
Alonso to Ferdinand.
Always the Following Wind.
Amor Loci.
Another Time.
Anthem for St. Cecilia's Day.
As He Is.
At Last the Secret Is Out.
At Lucky Moments We Seem on the Brink.
At the Grave of Henry James.
At the Manger.
At the Party.
Atlantis.
August 1968.
August for the People.
Autumn 1940.
Ballad: "O what is that sound which so thrills the ear."
The Ballad of Barnaby.
Base Words Are Uttered.
Before This Loved One.
Behold the Manly Mesomorph.
Brussels in Winter.
Canzone.
Carry Her over the Water.
Casino.
Chorale.
City without Walls.
The Composer.
Consider This and in Our Time.
Crisis.
The Cultural Presuppostion.
Dear, though the night is gone.
The Decoys.
Dialogue between Mary and Gabriel.
The Diaspora.
The Dog Beneath the Skin.
Doggerel by a Senior Citizen.
Edward Lear.
Epigram: "Private faces in public places."
Epitaph for the Unknown Soldier.
Epitaph on a Tyrant.
Epithalamion.
Et In Arcadia Ego.
The Exiles.
Fairground.
The Fall of Rome.

Far from the Heart of
Culture.
First Things First.
For The Time Being.
For What As Easy.
From Scars Where Kestrels
Hover.
Gare du Midi.
Get There If You Can and
See the Land.
Good-Bye to the
Mezzogiorno.
A Happy New Year (excerpt).
A Healthy Spot.
Hearing of Harvest Rotting in
the Valleys.
Henry Adams.
Herman Melville.
The History of Truth.
Horae Canonicae (excerpt).
The Horatians.
Hunting Season.
I Am Not a Camera.
I'm Beginning to Lose
Patience.
If, on Account of the Political
Situation.
In Due Season.
In Memory of Ernst Toller.
In Memory of Sigmund
Freud.
In Memory of W. B. Yeats.
In Praise of Limestone.
In Time of War.
The Island Cemetery.
It's No Use Raising a Shout.
James Honeyman.
Journey to Iceland.
Jumbled in the Common Box.
The Labyrinth.
Lady, Weeping at the
Crossroads.
Lakes.
Lauds.
Law Like Love.
Lay Your Sleeping Head, My
Love.
Let the Florid Music Praise.
The Letter.
Letter to Lord Byron.
Look, Stranger.
Lost.
The Love Feast.
The Managers.
Many Happy Returns.
Marginalia (excerpt).
May with Its Light Behaving.
Miss Gee.
Missing.
Moon Landing.
The More Loving One.
Mountains.
Mundus et Infans.
Musee des Beaux Arts.
New Year Letter.
Night Falls on China.
Night Mail.
No Change of Place.
Nones.
Note on Intelligence.
Now the Leaves Are Falling
Fast.
Now through Night's
Caressing Grip.
Numbers and Faces (excerpt).
O For Doors to Be Open.
O Where Are You Going?
Objects.
Ode: To My Pupils.
Ode to Terminus.
Ode to the Medieval Poets.
Oly.

On Installing an American
Kitchen in Lower Austria.
On the Circuit.
On This Island.
Once for Candy Cook Had
Stolen.
Our Bias.
Our Hunting Fathers.
Over the Heather the Wet
Wind Blows.
Parable.
Paysage Moralise.
Perhaps.
Petition.
Pick a Quarrel, Go to War.
Plains.
Poem: "He watched with all
his organs of concern."
Poem: "O who can ever praise
enough."
Powers and Times Are Not
Gods.
Preface.
Prime.
Progress?
Prologue.
The Proof.
The Question.
Refugee Blues.
The Riddle.
Rimbaud.
Roman Wall Blues.
Runner.
The Sea and the Mirror.
September 1, 1939.
The Shield of Achilles.
The Silly Fool.
Since.
Sir Rider Haggard.
Sob, Heavy World.
The Soldier Loves His Rifle.
Something Is Bound to
Happen.
Song: "As I walked out one
evening."
Song: "Fish in the unruffled
lakes."
Song for St. Cecilia's Day.
Song for the New Year.
Song: "Make this night
loveable."
Song: "So large a morning, so
itself, to lean."
Song: Stop All the Clocks.
Sonnets from China (excerpt).
Spain 1937.
Spring 1940.
A Starling and a Willow-
Wren.
The Strings' Excitement.
A Summer Night.
T. S. Eliot.
Taller To-Day.
Thanksgiving for a Habitat.
That Night When Joy Began.
Their Lonely Betters.
There Will Be No Peace.
This Lunar Beauty.
The Traveller.
The Trial.
The Truest Poetry Is the Most
Feigning; or, Ars Poetica for
Hard Times.
Uncle Henry.
Under Sirius.
Under Which Lyre.
The Unknown Citizen.
Unpredictable but
Providential.
Up There.
Vespers.
Villanelle.

Voltaire at Ferney.
The Walking Tour.
Watch Any Day.
The Watershed.
When Statesmen Gravely Say
"We Must Be Realistic."
Who's Who.
Who Will Endure.
With What Conviction the
Young Man Spoke.
Woods.

Auerbach, Ephraim
Seismograph.
Augustine, Saint
The Joys of Paradise.
Take My Heart.
Thou Hast Made Us for
Thyself.
Augustini, Delmira
Vision.
Ault, Norman
Clouds.
Father Time.
Wishes.
Auringer, O. C.
April.
The Ballad of Oriskany.
The Flight of the War-Eagle.
Aus of Kuraiza
Apostasy.
Auslander, Joseph
Abraham Lincoln.
A Blackbird Suddenly.
Cesar Franck.
Elegy.
If We Break Faith–.
Internal.
A Prayer for Thanksgiving.
Sunrise Trumpets.
Three Things.
Wings at Dawn.
Auslander, Rose
Father.
Hasidic Jew from Sadagora.
In Chagall's Village.
Jerusalem.
The Lamed-Vow.
My Nightingale.
Passover.
Phoenix.
Ausonius, Decimus Magnus
Epigram: "Glad youth had
come thy sixteenth year to
crown."
Epigram: "Reincarnating
Pythagoras, say."
Epigrams, CXVIII.
Evening on the Moselle.
Idyll of the Rose.
On the Sicilian Strand a Hare
Well Wrought.
Poems from a Greek
Anthology (excerpt).
To His Wife.
Auster, Paul
Covenant.
Hieroglyph.
Scribe.
Song of Degrees.
Austin, A. G.
Chez-Nous.
Austin, Alfred
Agatha.
The Human Tragedy
(excerpt).
Is Life Worth Living?
The Last Redoubt.
Love's Trinity.
The Lover's Song.
The Maiden of the Smile.
Primroses.
Prince Lucifer: Mother-Song.

The Thrush.
To America.
To Beatrice Stuart Wortley:
Aetat 2.
Winter Is Gone, and Spring Is
Over.
Austin, John
Fain Would My Thoughts.
Hark, My Soul.
Austin, Mary
At Carmel.
The Beggar Wind.
The Brown Bear.
Caller of the Buffalo.
Elf Owl.
A Feller I Know.
The Grass on the Mountain.
Grizzly Bear.
The Heart's Friend.
Lament of a Man for His Son.
A Little Song of Spring.
Prairie-Dog Town.
Riddle: "First I am frosted."
Riddle: "I come more softly
than a bird."
Riddle: "I have no wings, but
yet I fly."
Riddle: "I never speak a
word."
San Francisco.
The Sandhill Crane.
Song for the Newborn.
Song of a Passionate Lover.
Song of a Woman Abandoned
by the Tribe...
A Song of Greatness.
Texas Trains and Trails.
Warrior's Song.
Western Magic.
Winter in the Sierras.
Austin, Regina M.
Still Life.
Austin, William
Chanticleer.
To a Musician.
Automedon
Epigram: "I dined with
Demetrios."
Auvaiyar
Shall I Charge Like a Bull.
You Stand and Hold the Post
of My Small House.
Auxier, Sylvia
Breaking Point.
Ava, Frau
I am yours.
Avane
The Ageing Hunter.
Avery, Richard K.
And the Cock Begins to
Crow.
Avison, Margaret
The Butterfly.
Butterfly Bones; or, Sonnet
against Sonnets.
Civility a Bogey; or, Two
Centuries of Canadian Cities.
The Dumbfounding.
For Dr. and Mrs. Dresser.
For Tinkers Who Travel on
Foot.
Hiatus.
In a Season of
Unemployment.
Janitor Working on
Threshold.
Knowledge of Age.
A Lament.
Meeting Together of Poles &
Latitudes: in Prospect.
Mordent for a Melody.
A Nameless One.

New Year's Poem.
The Party.
Person, or A Hymn on and to the Holy Ghost.
Perspective.
Rigor Viris.
Snow.
Stray Dog, near Ecully.
The Swimmer's Moment.
Tennis.
Transit.
The Two Selves.
Unspeakable.
Water and Worship: An Open-Air Service on the Gatineau River.
Watershed.
Avrett, Robert
Renaissance.
Awad, Joseph
Generations.
In a World of Change.
Awoonor, Kofi (George Williams)
Rediscovery.
The Sea Eats the Land at Home.
Axelrod, David B.
Once in a While a Protest Poem.
Smell My Fingers.
Axelrod, Susan
The Home.
Axford, Roger
Victory.
Axionicus
Sausage.
Ayer, Ethan
Like a Whisper.
Ayer, Frederick Fanning
The Indictment (excerpt).
Ayer, William Ward
Be Still.
Ayers, Vivian
Instantaneous.
Ayloffe, John
Britannia and Raleigh.
Marvell's Ghost.
Oceana and Britannia.
The Parliament Dissolved at Oxford.
The Tune to the Devonshire Cant.
Aymrich, Angela
Women at the Market.
Ayre, Anna Chandler
Jack O'Lantern.
Ayres, Philip
Cynthia on Horseback.
Describes the Place Where Cynthia Is Sporting Herself.
An Epigram on Woman.
Ever Present.
Fair and Softly.
The Fly.
Invites His Nymph to His Cottage.
On a Fair Beggar.
On Lydia Distracted.
To Love A Sonnet.
To the Nightingale.
To the Winds. A Song.
"Ayton" [(or Aytoun)] Sir Robert
The Biter Bit.
The Broken Pitcher.
Comfort in Affliction.
Edinburgh after Flodden (excerpt).
The Exercise of Affection.
Hermontimus.
I Loved Thee Once.

Inconstancy Reproved.
The Island of the Scots (excerpt).
The Massacre of the Macpherson.
The Old Scottish Cavalier.
On a Woman's Inconstancy.
Sonnet to Britain.
To an Inconstant One.
To His Forsaken Mistress.
Upon a Diamond Cut in Forme of a Heart...
Upone Tabacco.
When Thou Didst Think I Did Not Love.
Aytoun, William
The Execution of Montrose.
The Laureate (parody).
The Lay of the Levite.
La Mort d'Arthur (parody).

B

"B, C. B."
Because You Prayed.
"B, R. K."
Limerick: "You remember that pastoral frolic."
"B, R. L."
Silly Willy.
Baba Kuhi of Shiraz
Illumination and Ecstasy.
Babcock, Donald Campbell
Adios.
America.
The Anthill.
Discourse Heard One Day.
In a Garden.
Meditation by Mascoma Lake.
The Migrant.
Neoplatonic Soliloquy.
O God, in Whom the Flow of Days.
Program Note on Sibelius.
Two Things.
Vacation Trip.
Babcock, Maltbie Davenport
Be Strong.
Companionship.
Death.
Give Us This Day Our Daily Bread.
Not to Be Ministered To.
This Is My Father's World.
Babcock, William Henry
Bennington.
Baca, Jimmy Santiago
Ancestor.
The County Jail.
Dreaming about Freedom.
I Am Sure of It.
It Started.
The New Warden.
Bacchylides
Peace on Earth.
Song and Wine.
Bachar, Eli
A Dawn of Jaffa Pigeons.
Houses, Past and Present.
Room Poems.
Bacheller, Irving
Whisperin' Bill.
Bachmann, Ingeborg
Curriculum Vitae.
Days in White.
Every Day.
The Firstborn Land.
The Great Freight.

Out of the corpse-warm vestibule of heaven steps the sun.
The Respite.
Songs in Flight (excerpt).
To the Sun.
You want the summer lightning, throw the knives.
Backus, Bertha Adams
Then Laugh.
Bacmeister, Rhoda Warner
Bridges.
Galoshes.
Stars.
Bacon, Barbara
In Between the Curve.
Bacon, Francis
The Life of Man.
The World.
Bacon, Josephine Dodge Daskam
Brother, Lift Your Flag with Mine.
Motherhood.
An Omar for Ladies.
The Sleepy Song.
Bacon, Leonard
An Afternoon in Artillery Walk.
Chorus from a Tragedy.
Flyfisherman in Wartime.
Hail, Tranquil Hour of Closing Day.
Horatian Variation.
The Pilgrim Fathers.
The Reason.
Richard Tolman's Universe.
Wake the Song of Jubilee.
Bacon, Peggy
Darkness.
Token.
Baden-Powell, Sir Robert
Man, matron, maiden.
Baer, William
Books.
Bagg, Robert
Ballad in Blonde Hair Foretold.
For Her on the First Day Out.
Oracle at Delphi.
Ronald Wyn.
See That One?
Soft Answers.
Speak This Kindly to Her.
Baggesen, Jens
Childhood.
"Bagritsky, Edward" (Edward Dzyubin)
He Tries out the Concords Gently.
My Honeyed Languor.
A Piece of Black Bread.
Baha Ad-din Zuhayr
On a Blind Girl.
Bahe, Liz Sohappy
And What of Me?
Farewell.
Grandmother Sleeps.
Once Again.
Printed Words.
The Ration Card.
Talking Designs.
Baildon, Henry Bellyse
A Moth.
Bailey, Alfred Goldsworthy
Algonkian Burial.
Border River.
Colonial Set.
Miramichi Lightning.
Off Saguenay.
The Question, Is It?

Shrouds and Away.
Tao.
Bailey, Alice Morrey
The Defiant One.
Bailey, Anthony
The Green and the Black.
Bailey, H. Sewall
Sailor Man.
Bailey, Lansing C.
Eight Volunteers.
Bailey, Liberty Hyde
Farmer.
The Miracle.
Bailey, Margaret
A Prayer.
Bailey, Philip James
The Aim of Life: A Country Town.
Festus: Proem to the Third Edition.
My Lady.
Baillie, Joanna
The Blackcock.
A Child to His Sick Grandfather.
The Country Inn: Song: "Though richer swains thy love pursue."
A Disappointment.
The Horse and His Rider.
A Mother to Her Waking Infant.
The Outlaw's Song.
Song of the Outlaws.
Wake, Lady!
Baillie, Lady Grizsel
Werena My Heart Licht I Wad Dee.
Bainbridge, Philip
Achilles in Scyros (excerpt).
Bairam at Tunisie
An Autobiography.
Baird, Martha
Effortlessly Democratic Santa Fe Trail.
Baker, Alison
Custer (1).
Custer (2).
Baker, Carlos
A Chinese Mural.
On a Landscape of Sestos.
Baker, David
8-Ball at the Twilite.
Caves.
Hermit.
Ice River.
Persimmon Trees, She Remembers, Not Far Away.
Running the River Lines.
The Wrecker Driver Foresees Your Death.
Baker, Donald W.
Formal Application.
Baker, Edna L. S.
Child of the World.
Baker, George Augustus
Thoughts on the Commandments.
Baker, George Henry
A Ballad of Sir John Franklin.
Baker, Howard
Ode to the Sea.
Baker, Isaac W.
The San Francisco Company.
Baker, J. G.
My Trundle Bed.
Baker, John C.
The Burman Lover.
Baker, Julia Aldrich
Mizpah.
Baker, Karle Wilson
Beauty's Hands Are Cool.

Burning Bush.
Creeds.
Days.
Good Company.
I Shall Be Loved as Quiet Things.
Let Me Grow Lovely.
Morning Song.
The Ploughman.
Poet Songs.
Pronouns.
Rondel for September.
A Silver Lantern.
Baker, Kathleen Leland
The Baby Hilary, Sir Edmund.
Honey Moon.
Baker, Leon
All Night !
Cap'n & Me.
Getting Back to Work.
Jackson State Prison.
On Youth, the Warden & Solitary!
Baker, Olaf
Little Saling.
Baker, Sir Henry William
Christ the Consoler.
The Declaimer.
The King of Love.
Love.
The Rapture.
Baker, T.
The Steam-Engine (parody) (excerpt).
Baker, Theodore
Prayer of Thanksgiving.
Baker, Thomas
The Electric Telegraph.
Means of Propulsion for Steam-Ships.
Watt's Improvements to the Steam Engine.
Baker, Willie
No No Blues.
Bakewell, John
Hail, Thou Once Despised Jesus!
Balaban, John
After Our War.
The Guard at the Binh Thuy Bridge.
Balakian, Peter
The Blue Church.
Father Fisheye.
Homage to Hart Crane.
In the Turkish Ward.
Jersey Bait Shack.
Balazs, Mary
Incident at Mossel Bay.
Pregnant Teenager on the Beach.
Balch, Emily Greene
The Flag Speaks.
Baldenegro, Salomon R., Jr.
Man, I Felt Like Running All Night.
Balderston, Jean
RIP.
Baldwin, Deirdra
Remembering the Automobile.
Baldwin, Mary Newton
Lonely Are the Fields of Sleep.
Baldwin, Michael
Death on a Live Wire.
Baldwin, Tama
Hooking the Rainbow.
Baldwin, Thomas
From Whence Doth This Union Arise?

Baldwin, William
Christ, My Beloved.
Christ to His Spouse.
How Collingbourne Was Cruelly Executed for Making a Foolish Rhyme.
The Spouse to the Beloved.
The Spouse to the Younglings.
Bales, C. O.
Discipleship.
Balfour, Mary
The Dew Each Trembling Leaf Inwreath'd.
In Ringlets Curl'd Thy Tresses Flow.
Balhurst, W.H.
Unshrinking Faith.
Ball, Arthur
Above Ben Loyal.
The Tall Sky.
Ball, William
Praise to Jesus!
Ballantine, James
Castles in the Air.
Creep Afore Ye Gang.
Its Ain Drap o' Dew.
Muckle-Mou'd Meg.
Ballantyne, Deirdre
The Long Word.
Ballard, C. R.
The Pacific Highway.
Ballard, Charles G.
During the Pageant at Medicine Lodge.
Grandma Fire.
Memo.
Now the People Have the Light.
Sand Creek.
The Speaker.
The Spirit Craft.
Their Cone-Like Cabins.
The Winds of Change.
You Northern Girl.
Ballard, Harlan Hoge
In the Catacombs.
Ballard, Rae
Father of the Victim.
Ballou, Silas
Almighty God in Being Was.
While I Am Young.
Ballou I, Hosea
Dear Lord, Behold Thy Servants.
In God's Eternity.
When God Descends with Men to Dwell.
Ballou II, Hosea
Ye Realms Below the Skies.
Balsdon, Dacre
Endurance Test.
Bamberger, Augustus Wright
Each a Part of All.
Out of the Vast.
Bampfylde, John Codrington
On a Frightful Dream.
On a Wet Summer.
Sonnet: "As when, to one who long hath watched, the morn."
To the Evening.
Bancks, John
A Description of London.
A Fragment.
Bancroft, Charles
Tadoussac.
Bancroft, James Henry
Brother, Though from Yonder Sky.
Banda, Innocent
Lindedi Singing.
Malawi.

May Bright Mushrooms Grow.
That There Should Be Laughter.
Where Is the Fruit.
Bangham, Mary Dickerson
Come, Holy Babe!
Bangs, Edward
Yankee Doodle.
The Yankee's Return from Camp.
Bangs, Janet Norris
Design for Peace.
Bangs, John Kendrick
Blind.
"Don't Care" and "Never Mind."
The Dreadful Fate of Naughty Nate.
The Hired Man's Way.
I Never Knew a Night So Black.
If.
Lincoln's Birthday.
The Little Elf.
May 30, 1893.
My Dog.
On File.
A Philosopher.
Philosophy.
Teddy's Wonderings.
Thanksgiving Day.
To a Withered Rose.
Today.
What hundred books are best.
Banim, John
He Said That He Was Not Our Brother.
The Irish Mother in the Penal Days.
Soggarth Aroon.
Banker, William, Jr
The Battle of Queenstown.
Banks, George Linnaeus
My Aim.
What I Live For.
Bannerman, Frances
An Upper Chamber.
Banning, Kendall
Once on a Time.
Banning, Lex
Apocalypse in Springtime.
Captain Arthur Phillip and the Birds.
Epitaph for a Scientist.
Bantock, Gavin
Bard.
Dirge.
Joy.
Banus, Maria
Eighteen.
Gift Hour.
The New Notebook.
Baraka, Imamu Amiri *See* **Jones, LeRoi**
Barba, Sharon
Dykes in the Garden.
Barbauld, Anna Laetitia
Come, Says Jesus' Voice.
Life! I Know Not What Thou Art.
The Mouse's Petition.
The Rights of Women.
To Mr. S. T. Coleridge.
Barbee, John Henry
Six Week Old Blues.
Barbeitos, Arlindo
In the Forest of Your Eyes.
A Man of Rain.
Many Years Ago.
O Night Flower.

Barber, Frances
Play-Acting.
Barber, J.
The White Steed of the Prairies.
Barber, Mary
On Seeing an Officer's Widow Distracted.
Written for My Son...at His First Putting on Breeches.
Barber, Melanie Gordon
Sonnet for My Son.
Barber, William
Explanation.
Barberino, Francesco da
Of Caution.
A Virgin Declares Her Beauties.
Barbour, George Hurlbut
Decoration Day.
Barbour, John
The Battle of Bannockburn.
The Bruce.
Bruce Addresses His Army.
Bruce Consults His Men.
Bruce Meets Three Men with a Wethe.
Prologue to the Avowis of Alexander.
Barclay, Alexander
Egloge V (excerpt).
Preachment for Preachers.
The Ship of Fools.
Barclay, Edwin
Human Greatness.
Barclay, Robert
Hic Liber Ad Me Pertinet.
Bardeen, C. W.
The Birds' Ball.
Bardsley, Alice
Storm Warning.
Barford, John
Eric.
Serve Her Right.
Sundered.
Toleration.
Whom Jesus Loved.
Barham, Richard Harris
As I Laye A-Thynkynge.
The Confession.
The Cynotaph.
Eheu Fugaces.
Hon. Mr. Sucklethumbkin's Story.
The Ingoldsby Legends: The Jackdaw of Rheims.
Last Lines.
The Lay of St. Cuthbert (excerpt).
A Lay of St. Gengulphus (excerpt).
Lines Left at Mr. Theodore Hook's House in June, 1834.
Misadventures at Margate.
Not a Sou Had He Got (parody).
Baring, Maurice
Ballad.
Diffugere Nives, 1917.
The Dying Reservist.
I Dare Not Pray to Thee.
I.M.H.
In Memoriam, A. H. 1916.
Julian Grenfell.
Leiroessa Kalyx.
Baring-Gould, Sabine
For Evening.
Now the Day Is over.
The Olive Tree.
Onward, Christian Soldiers.
Through the Night of Doubt and Sorrow.

Barker, David
Lispy Bails Out.
Matisse Tits.
Packard.
View from the Planetarium.
Zoo Dream.
Barker, Edward D.
Go Sleep, Ma Honey.
Barker, Elsa
Caresses.
Confession.
Consummation.
Fulfilment.
I Know.
The Inscription.
Love's Immortality.
When I Am Dead and Sister
to the Dust.
Barker, George
Allegory of the Adolescent
and the Adult.
Calamiterror, VI.
Channel Crossing.
The Crystal.
The Death of Yeats.
Dog, Dog in My Manger.
Elegy V.
Elegy on the Eve.
Epitaph for the Poet.
Evening Star.
First Cycle of Love Poems.
For the Fourth Birthday of
My Daughter.
He Comes among.
Holy Poems.
The House I Go to in My
Dream.
In Memory of a Friend.
In Memory of David Archer
(excerpt).
The Leaping Laughers.
Letter to a Young Poet.
Love Poem: "Less the dog
begged to die in the sky."
Memorial Couplets for the
Dying Ego.
Munich Elegy No 1.
My Joy, My Jockey, My
Gabriel.
News of the World.
Not in the Poet.
O Golden Fleece.
O Tender under Her Right
Breast.
The Oak and the Olive.
Ode against St. Cecilia's Day.
On First Hearing Beethoven.
Pacific Sonnets.
Resolution of Dependence.
Sacred Elegy V.
Satan Is on Your Tongue.
Sequence.
Shut the Seven Seas against
Us.
Sonnet of Fishes.
Sonnet to My Mother.
Sonnets of the Triple-Headed
Manichee: II.
A Sparrow's Feather.
Summer Idyll.
Summer Song I.
The Three Dead and the
Three Living.
Three Memorial Sonnets.
To Any Member of My
Generation.
To My Son (excerpt).
Triumphal Ode
MCMXXXIX.
The True Confession of
George Barker.

Turn on Your Side and Bear
the Day to Me.
Verses for a First Birthday.
Verses for the 60th Birthday
of T. S. Eliot.
The Village Coddled in the
Valley.
Wild Dreams of Summer
What Is Your Grief?
The Wraith-Friend.
Barker, Jane
Epitaph on the Secretary to
the Muses.
To Her Lover's Complaint.
Barker, Shirley
Sonnets from a Sequence.
Barker, Squire Omar
Code of the Cow Country.
Fine!
Hot Ir'n!
Jackrabbits.
The Law West of the Pecos.
Rodeo Days.
The Sheep Beezness.
Tall Men Riding.
To a Jack Rabbit.
When Billy the Kid Rides
Again.
Barker, Thomas
Baits for Various Fish.
How to Catch a Trout.
Methods of Cooking Trout.
Barks, Coleman
Adam's Apple.
Brain.
Bruises.
Downy Hair in the Shape of a
Flame Moving up the
Stomach...
Finger of Necessity.
Goosepimples.
The Mule.
Semen.
Barksdale, Clement
To My Nephew, J.B.
Barley, William
Madrigal: "Short is my rest."
Barlow, George
The Dead Child.
Mellowness & Flight.
The Soul.
Spiritual Passion.
Sweet Diane.
Barlow, Jane
Christmas Rede.
Out of Hearing.
Barlow, Joel
Advice to a Raven in Russia
December 1812.
Along the Banks.
The Columbiad: One Centred
System.
The First American Congress.
Freedom.
The Hasty Pudding.
Judge Me, O God.
O God of My Salvation, Hear.
On the Discoveries of Captain
Lewis.
A Song.
**Barnard, Charlotte Allington
("Claribel")**
Come Back to Erin.
Take Back the Heart.
Barnard, John
Nations That Long in
Darkness Walked.
Thrice Blest the Man.
Barnard, Katherine R.
The Voice of God.

Barnard, Lady Anne *See also*
Lindsay, Lady Anne
Auld Robin Gray.
My Heart Is a Lute.
Barnard, Mary
The Pleiades.
Shoreline.
The Solitary.
Barnby, Joseph
Sweet and Low.
Barnefieldi, Richard *See*
Barnfield, Richard
Barnes, Barnabe
Ah Sweet Content, where Is
Thy Mylde Abode?
Content.
God's Virtue.
Jove for Europaes Love Tooke
Shape of Bull.
The Life of Man.
O Powers Celestial, with
What Sophistry.
Ode: "Why doth heaven bear
a sun."
Parthenope.
To the Most Beautiful Lady,
the Lady Bridget Manners.
Barnes, Djuna
Transfiguration.
Barnes, Jeanette
Absence.
Barnes, Jim
Accident at Three Mile
Island.
Autobiography, Chapter XII.
Autobiography, Chapter
XVII.
Autobiography: Last Chapter.
Bone Yard.
Camping Out on Rainy
Mountain.
The Captive Stone.
A Choctaw Chief Helps Plan
a Festival...
Comcomly's Skull.
Descent to Bohannon Lake.
Four Choctaw Songs.
Four Things Choctaw.
Halcyon Days.
Last Look at La Plata,
Missouri.
Lying in a Yuma Saloon.
Old Soldiers Home at
Marshalltown, Iowa.
Paiute Ponies.
Sweating It Out on Winding
Stair Mountain.
These Damned Trees Crouch.
Tracking Rabbits: Night.
Wolf Hunting near Nashoba.
Barnes, Jo
Clinic Day.
Barnes, Kate
Hector the Dog.
A Mare.
Barnes, William
Air an' Light.
All Still.
The Bean Vield.
Black an' White.
The Blackbird.
Blackmwore Maidens.
Burncombe Hollow.
The Bwoat.
The Child an' the Mowers.
Childhood.
The Clote.
Come!
Come an' Meet Me wi' the
Childern on the Road.
Day's Work A-Done.
Dobbin Dead.

Dock-Leaves.
Easter Zunday.
Eclogue.
Evening, and Maidens.
The Fall.
False Friends-Like.
The Girt Woak Tree That's in
the Dell.
Green.
The Head-Stone.
Heedless o' My Love.
In the Spring.
Jay A-Pass'd.
Jenny's Ribbons.
Leady-Day, an' Ridden
House.
Leaves.
Liady-Day an' Ridden House.
Light or Sheade.
The Lost Little Sister.
Lowshot Light.
Lullaby.
Lwonesomeness.
Mater Dolorosa.
May.
The May Tree.
Melhill Feast.
Musings.
My Love's Guardian Angel.
My Orcha'd in Linden Lea.
The Oak-Tree.
The Old House.
Polly Be-En Upzides Wi'
Tom.
Readen Ov a Head-Stwone.
Rings.
Rustic Childhood.
The Rwose in the Dark.
Seasons and Times.
Sheep in the Sheade.
Shellbrook.
Shop O' Meat-Weare.
Slow to Come, Quick A-Gone.
Sonnet: "In every dream thy
lovely features rise."
Sonnet: Leaves.
The Spring.
The Storm-Wind.
The Stwonen Steps.
Times o' Year.
To Me.
Tokens.
Troubles of the Day.
The Turnstile.
Uncle an' Aunt.
The Vaices That Be Gone.
The Vield Path.
The Vierzide Chairs.
Vo'k a-Comen into Church.
Walken Hwome at Night.
When We That Now Ha'
Childern Wer Childern.
Which Road?
White an' Blue.
Whitsuntide an' Club Walken.
The Wife A-Lost.
The Wind at the Door.
A Winter Night.
A Witch.
With you first shown to me.
Withstanders.
Woak Hill.
The Woodlands.
The Young Rhymer Snubbed.
The Zilver-Weed.
A Zong.
Zummer Stream.
Zummer Thoughts in Winter
Time.
The Zun A-Lighten Eyes A-
Shut.
Zun-Zet.

Barnett, Anthony
The Book of Mysteries.
Celan.
Cloisters.
Crossing.
A Marriage.
Barnett, Ratcliffe
For Summer's Here.
Barnett, Stella
Evening in the Suburbs.
Barney, William D.
Caught in the Pocket.
Nearly Everybody Loves
Harvey Martin.
A Post Card out of Panama.
The Rasslers.
Barnfield, Richard
The Affectionate Shepherd
(excerpt).
A Comparison of the Life of
Man.
Daphnis to Ganymede.
The Nightingale.
An Ode: "As it fell upon a
day."
Philomel.
A Shepherd's Complaint.
Sonnets, I: "Sporting at fancie,
setting light by love."
Sonnets, IV: "Two stars there
are in one faire firmament."
Sonnets, VI: "Sweet Corrall
lips, where Nature's treasure
lies."
Sonnets, VII: "Sweet Thames
I honour thee."
Sonnets, VIII: "Sometimes I
wish that I his pillow were."
Sonnets, X: "Thus was my
love, thus was my
Ganymed."
Sonnets, XI: "Sighing, and
sadly sitting by my Love."
Sonnets, XII: "Some talke of
Ganymede th' Idalian Boy."
Sonnets, XIV: "Here, hold
this glove."
Sonnets, XVII: "Cherry-Lipt
Adonis in his snowie shape."
Sonnets, XIX: "Ah no; nor I
my selfe: though my pure
love."
Sonnets, XX: "But now my
Muse toyled with continuall
care."
To His Friend Master R.L., in
Praise of Music and Poetry.
Vergidemiarum: Prologue: "I
first adventure, with
foolhardy might."
Barnie, John
The Dog in Us.
Barnstone, Aliki
A Letter from the Hotel.
Mating the Goats.
To a Friend's Child.
Windows in Providence.
Barnstone, Willis
Borges.
Changsha Shoe Factory.
The Eyes of Cantonese
Schoolmasters Remembered
in Hong Kong.
Gas Lamp.
The Good Beasts.
Grandfather.
Milos Radnoti.
Paradise.
Rooftop.
Stained Glass.
With Schoolchildren.
The Worm.

Baro, Gene
Cherry.
For Hani, Aged Five, That
She Be Better Able to
Distinguish a Villain.
The Horsemen.
Judges, Judges.
The Ladder.
Lament for Better or Worse.
A Northern Spring.
Northwind.
The Street.
Travelling Backward.
Under the Boughs.
Baron, Mary
For an Egyptian Boy, Died c.
700 B.C.
Letters for the New England
Dead.
Barr, Alice M.
Guard Thy Tongue.
Barr, G. W.
The U-S-U Range.
Barr, Isabel Harriss
Madaket Beach.
Barr, John
The Bonny Harvest Moon.
New Zealand Comforts.
Rise Oot Your Bed.
There's Nae Place Like Otago
Yet.
To My Auld Dog Dash.
Barr, Matthias
Moon, So Round and Yellow.
Only a Baby Small.
Barratt, Ken
Burke and Wills.
Barrax, Gerald William
Black Narcissus.
Christmas 1959 et Cetera.
Efficiency Apartment.
For Malcolm: After Mecca.
Fourth Dance Poem.
If She Sang.
Slow Drivers.
To a Woman Who Wants
Darkness and Time.
Your Eyes Have Their
Silence.
Barreno, Maria Isabel See
Marias, The Three
Barret, Pringle
A Hint to the Wise.
Barrett, Alfred Joseph
Chant of Departure.
A Martyr's Mass.
Mary's Assumption.
The Rosebush and the Trinity.
Unearth.
Barrett, Eaton Stannard
Woman.
Barrett, Rowena
Thanksgiving Magic.
Barrett, Wilton Agnew
A New England Church.
Barrie, Hugh
When I Am Dead.
Barrington, Patrick
The Air Sentry.
I Had a Duck-billed Platypus.
I Had a Hippopotamus.
I Was a Bustle-Maker Once,
Girls.
Barrington, Pauline B.
A White Iris.
Barrios, Gregorio
Crazy Movie.
Barrios, Miguel de
Epitaph: "Daniel and
Abigail."

Barrow, Jedediah
You Call That a Ts'ing: A
Letter (parody).
Barrows, Anita
The Ancestors.
Avenue Y.
Emigration.
Letter to a Friend in an
Unknown Place.
Reflections.
Barry, H. H.
He Leadeth Me.
Barson, Alfred
On the Death of Parents.
Barstow, Henry H.
If Easter Be Not True.
Barth, John
The Minstrel's Last Lay.
Barth, R. L.
Waking Early.
Bartlett, Elizabeth
999 Call.
After the Storm.
Behold This Dreamer.
The Cage.
Charlotte, Her Book.
Contre Jour.
Dark Angel.
In Days of New.
The Question Is Proof.
Bartlett, I.
The Town of Don't-You-
Worry.
Bartlett, Ruth Fitch
Belief.
Bartole, Genevieve
Canadian Farmer.
Barton, Bernard
Bruce and the Spider.
Not Ours the Vows.
Walking in the Light.
Barton, David
Solutions.
Barton, Fred
The Death of the Sailor's
Wife.
Barton, Joan
The Mistress.
Baruch, Dorothy Walter
Automobile Mechanics.
Barber's Clippers.
Cat.
Different Bicycles.
I would Like to be–A Bee.
Lawn-Mower.
Merry-Go-Round.
The Popcorn-Popper.
Rabbits.
The Skunk.
Stop-Go.
Baruch of Worms
Elegy.
Bary, Anna Bunston de
As Rivers of Water in a Dry
Place.
The Snowdrop.
Bas-Quercy
Carol of the Birds.
Bashford, Herbert
Alice.
Along Shore.
The Arid Lands.
By the Pacific.
Morning in Camp.
Mount Rainier.
The Song of the Forest
Ranger.
Sunset.
Bashford, Sir Henry Howarth
The Good Day.
Lullaby in Bethlehem.
Parliament Hill.

To Petronilla Who Has Put
Up Her Hair.
Where Do the Gipsies Come
From?
Basho (Matsuo Basho)
Beauty.
Cicada-Shell.
Friend Sparrow.
Haiku: "Fish shop..."
Haiku: "Green weeds of
summer."
Haiku: "In the old stone
pool."
Haiku: "Moor:".
Haiku: "On a withered
branch."
Haiku: "On this road."
Haiku: "So the spring has
come?"
Haiku: "The lightning
flashes!"
Harbingers.
In My New Clothing.
A Lonely Pond in Age-Old
Stillness Sleeps.
The Monkey's Raincoat.
Old Men, White-Haired,
beside the Ancestral Graves.
The Old Pond.
Play about, Do.
Plum Blossoms.
Quick-Falling Dew.
Three Poems.
Wake Up! Wake Up!
Bass, Ellen
Celia.
I am the sorrow in the wheat
fields.
In Celebration.
Partly to My Cat.
September 7.
Bass, Tom
Spring Sunday on Quaker
Street.
Basse, William
The Anglers Song.
Elegy on Shakespeare.
A Memento for Mortality.
Bassen, Lois
Brain Coral.
Bassett, A. A.
Twice Fed.
Bassett, Lee
Wires.
Bastard, Thomas
Ad Henricum Wottonem.
Epitaph: Iohannis Sande.
In Gaetam.
De Naevo in Facie Faustinae.
On a Child Beginning to Talk.
De Puero Balbutiente.
Bat-Miriam, Yocheve
Distance Spills Itself.
The Monasteries Lift Gold
Domes.
Bate, John
Cologne.
Bates, Arlo
Conceits.
The Cyclamen.
In Paradise.
Like to a Coin.
On the Road to Chorrera.
A Rose.
A Shadow Boat.
The Torch-Bearers: America.
The Watchers.
A Winter Twilight.
Bates, Charlotte Fiske
Andre.
A Character.
The Clue.

Delay.
The Living Book.
Woodbines in October.
Bates, Clara Doty
At Grandfather's.
Gray Thrums.
Thistle-Down.
Who Likes the Rain?
Bates, David
Speak Gently.
Bates, Esther and Brainard
Ipswich Bar.
Bates, G. E.
Pentagonia (parody).
Bates, Herbert
The Heavens Are Our Riddle.
Prairie.
Bates, Katharine Lee
America the Beautiful.
The Changing Road.
Christmas Island.
Despised and Rejected.
Earth Listens.
For Deeper Life.
Gypsy-Heart.
In His Steps.
The Kings of the East.
The Little Knight in Green.
The New Crusade.
Robin's Secret.
Sarah Threeneedles.
A Song of Riches.
A Song of Waking.
Thou Knowest.
Wild Weather.
Youth.
Bates, Scott
Fable of the Talented
Mockingbird.
Whales.
Bateson, Thomas
Madrigal: "I heard a noise."
Bathgate, Dave
For Tony, Dougal, Mick,
Bugs, Nick et al.
Rock Leader.
Bathurst, William Hiley
The Triumphs of Thy
Conquering Power.
Batterham, Eric N.
Once.
Baudelaire, Charles
The Abyss.
The Accursed.
The Albatross.
Anywhere Out of the World.
At One O'Clock in the
Morning.
The Balcony.
Be Drunken.
La Beaute.
The Blind.
A Carrion.
The Cat.
Condemned Women.
Correspondences.
Crowds.
Damned Women.
Don Juan in Hell.
Elevation.
Epilogue.
Evening Twilight.
The Giantess.
Harmonie du Soir.
Her Hair.
Les Hiboux.
The Ideal.
Ill Luck.
The Injured Moon.
Intimate Associations.
The Jewels.
Litany to Satan.

The Lovers' Death.
Metamorphoses of the
Vampire.
Mists and Rain.
The Music.
Parfum Exotique.
Parisian Dream.
De Profundis Clamavi.
The Sadness of the Moon.
The Seven Old Men.
Sois Sage O Ma Douleur.
Spleen.
The Stranger.
The Swan.
To a Madonna.
To a Passer-By.
To Azrael.
To Beauty.
To One Who Is Too Gay.
To the Reader.
Voyage to Cythera.
Women Damned.
You'd Take the Entire
Universe to Bed with You.
Bauer, Grace
Spring and All.
Bauer, Steven
Stopped in Memphis.
Baugh, Sue
Seal Rock.
Baughan, Blanche Edith
In Exile.
The Old Place.
The Ship and the Sea.
Baum, Peter
Horror.
Psalms of Love.
Bax, Sir Arnold *See* "O'Byrne,
Dermot"
Bax, Clifford
Turn Back, O Man.
Baxter, Carolyn
Houston Street, N.Y.
Lower Court.
Masochistic Tendencies.
Toilet Bowl Congregation.
Warden's Day.
Baxter, Elizabeth
In Your Absence.
Baxter, James Keir
The Apple Tree.
Autumn Testament (excerpt).
The Buried Stream.
Cressida.
A Dentist's Window.
East Coast Journey.
Elegy for an Unknown
Soldier.
Evidence at the Witch Trials.
A Family Photograph 1939.
He Waiata mo Te Kare.
Hermit.
High Country Weather.
Homecoming.
How to Fly by Standing Still
(excerpt).
The Ikons.
The Inflammable Woman.
Jerusalem Sonnets.
Lament for Barney Flanagan.
Mandrakes for Supper.
Mill Girl.
Never No More.
New Zealand.
News from a Pacified Area.
Poem by the Clock Tower,
Summer.
Poem in the Matukituki
Valley.
Rocket Show.
A Rope for Harry Fat.
Seraphion.

Tarras Moon.
To a Print of Queen Victoria.
To My Father.
Tunnel Beach.
Wild Bees.
Baxter, Richard
Entering by His Door.
Lord, It Belongs Not to My
Care.
Love Breathing Thanks and
Praise (excerpt).
A Psalm of Praise (excerpt).
Baxter, Ron
Moon Mission.
Winter: The Abandoned Nest.
Bayldon, Arthur
Marlowe.
Sunset.
Baylebridge, William
The Ampler Circumscription.
Life's Testament.
Love Redeemed.
Moreton Miles, LIV.
Sextains.
Bayles, James C.
In the Gloaming.
Bayley, Thomas Haynes
Gaily the Troubadour.
Bayliss, John
Apocalypse and Resurrection.
October.
Seven Dreams.
Bayly, Thomas Haynes
Do You Remember.
I'd Be a Butterfly.
Long, Long Ago.
The Mistletoe Bough.
Oh, No! We Never Mention
Her.
Oh! Where Do Fairies Hide
Their Heads?
She Wore a Wreath of Roses.
Beach, Joseph Warren
Dropping Your Aitches.
Horatian Ode.
Beach, Seth Curtis
Mysterious Presence! Source
of All.
Thou One in All, Thou All in
One.
Beaglehole, J. C.
Considerations on Certain
Music of J.S. Bach (excerpt).
Beard, Cathy
Any April.
Beardsley, Aubrey
The Ballad of a Barber.
The Three Musicians.
Beatles, The *See also* Lennon,
John
A Day in the Life.
Eleanor Rigby.
The Fool on the Hill.
I Am the Walrus.
Beatrice de Dia
Handsome Friend, Charming
and Kind.
My True Love Makes Me
Happy.
Beattie, J. H.
On the Author of the Treatise
of Human Nature.
Beattie, James
An Epitaph.
The Minstrel.
Nature and the Poets.
Nature's Charms.
The Question.
Solitude.
To Mr. Alexander Ross.
Beatty, Pakenham
When Will Love Come?

Beaumont, Francis
The Examination of His
Mistress' Perfections.
Fie on Love.
The Indifferent.
A Letter to Ben Jonson.
The Masque of the Inner-
Temple and Gray's Inne.
Mr. Francis Beaumont's
Letter to Ben Johnson...
On the Marriage.
On the Tombs in Westminster
Abbey.
Pining for Love.
Three Songs.
True Beauty.
Upon Master Edmund
Spenser, the Famous Poet.
**Beaumont, Francis and John
Fletcher**
Aspatia's Song.
Away Delight.
Cupid's Revenge.
Hold Back Thy Hours.
I Died True.
The Knight of the Burning
Pestle.
Lullaby: "Come sleep, and
with the sweet deceiving".
Song: "Hence all you vaine
Delights."
Song: "Hold back thy hours,
dark night, till we have
done."
Song: "O faire sweet face, O
eyes celestiall bright."
Song: "Take, oh take those
Lips away."
Song: "Turn, turn thy
beauteous face away."
The Woman-Hater.
Beaumont, Joseph
The Ascension.
Biothanatos.
The Garden.
The Gentle Check.
The Gnat.
Home.
Love.
A Morning Hymn.
Purification of the Blessed
Virgin.
Whit Sunday.
Whiteness, or Chastity.
Beaumont, Sir John
The Assumption.
Bosworth Field: Richard III's
Speech.
An Epitaph upon My Dear
Brother, Francis Beaumont.
O Thou Who Art Our Author
and Our End.
Of My Dear Son, Gervase
Beaumont.
Of Sir Philip Sidney.
Of True Liberty.
The Relish of the Muse.
To His Late Majesty
Concerning the True Form
of English Poetry.
Upon a Funeral.
Beauvais, Phyllis
Outside.
Under Your Voice, among
Legends.
Beauveau, Marie
Air: Sentir Avec Ardeur.
Beaver, Bruce
Cow Dance.
The Entertainer.
Letters to Live Poets.

Beccadelli, Antonio
Epitaph on Pegasus, a
Limping Gay.
To Corydon.
Bechtel, Louise Seaman
Grandfather Frog.
Beck
Bless, Dear Saviour, This
Child.
Beck, Victor E.
Sifting.
Becker, Charlotte
The Door-Bell.
Becker, Edna
Reflections.
Becker, John
Feather or Fur.
For Maria at Four.
Becket, Thomas a
Columbia the Gem of the
Ocean.
Beckett, Samuel
Alba.
Cascando.
Dieppe.
Enueg.
Gnome.
I Would Like My Love to
Die.
Malacoda.
My Way Is in the Sand
Flowing.
Saint-Lo.
Watt (excerpt).
What Would I Do without
This World Faceless
Incurious.
Whoroscope.
Words and Music (excerpt).
Beckford, William
Ode: "To orisons, the
midnight bell."
Becquer, Gustavo Adolfo
Rimas.
Shadowy Swallows.
They Closed Her Eyes.
Three Rimas.
The Waiting Harp.
Beddo, Frank
Jeff Buckner.
Beddoes, Thomas Lovell
Alpine Spirit's Song.
Ballad of Human Life.
A Beautiful Night.
Bona de Mortuis.
The Bride's Tragedy: Poor
Old Pilgrim Misery.
Death's Jest-Book.
Death Sweet.
Dirge: "If thou wilt ease thy
heart."
Dirge Written for a Drama.
Do Not Minute.
Dream-Pedlary.
L'Envoi.
Fragment.
Grief-In-Idleness.
Has no one seen my heart of
you?
Her Kisses.
Hist, oh hist.
Humble Beginnings.
I'll Be As True.
The Ivory Gate: Stanzas.
A Lake.
The Lily of the Valley.
Lines: "How lovely is the
heaven of this night."
Lines: "I followed once a fleet
and mighty serpent."
Lord Alcohol.
The Lost Man: A Crocodile.

Love-In-Idleness.
Man's Anxious, but
Ineffectual Guard Against
Death.
Mandrake's Song.
The New Cecilia.
The Old Ghost.
The Oviparous Tailor.
The Phantom-Wooer.
The Reason Why.
Resurrection Song.
The Second Brother.
Silenus in Proteus.
Song from the Waters.
Song: "Hither haste, and
gently strew."
Song: "How many times do I
love thee, dear?"
Song of the Stygian Naiades.
Song on the Water.
Song: "Strew not earth with
empty stars."
Sonnet: To Tartar, a Terrier
Beauty.
Threnody.
To Night.
To Sea.
Wolfram's Dirge.
Wolfram's Song.
Beddome, Benjamin
The Glorious Gift of God.
**"Bede, Cuthbert" (Edward
Bradley)**
Entrance Exams.
In Immemoriam.
Limerick: "There was a queer
fellow named Woodin."
Bede, The Venerable
A Hymn: "A hymn of glory
let us sing."
Bedingfield, Thomas
The Lover's Choice.
Beebe, Lucius
I Am Weary of These Times
and Their Dull Burden.
Beecham, Audrey
Exile.
Beecham, Sir Thomas
Hark the Herald Angels Sing.
Beecher, John
Aztec Figurine.
Desert Holy Man.
To Live and Die in Dixie
(excerpt).
Beeching, Henry Charles
Accidia.
Bicycling Song.
The Blackbird.
A Boy's Prayer.
First Come I; My Name Is
Jowett.
Going Down Hill on a
Bicycle.
Knowledge after Death.
The Masque of Balliol
(excerpt).
On Solomon Lazarus Lee,
Exhibitioner of Balliol.
Prayers.
Beeching, Jack
1944—On the Invasion Coast.
Beedome, Thomas
The Broken Heart.
The Choyce.
To His Mistresse on Her
Scorne.
To the Noble Sir Francis
Drake.
Beeler, Janet
The Photographer's Wife.
Beenen, Jennivien-Diana
Morning Poem.

Be'er, Hayim
Love Song.
The Sequence of Generations.
Tabernacle of Peace.
Beer, Henry
The Babe of Bethlehem.
Beer, Morris Abel
The Church in the Heart.
Manhattan.
Beer, Patricia
Birthday Poem from Venice.
Christmas Carols.
Christmas Eve.
The Christmas Tree.
Creed of Mr. Nicholas
Culpeper.
Dilemma.
The Fifth Sense.
Gallery Shepherds.
In a Country Museum.
In the Cathedral.
Jane Austen at the Window.
Leaping into the Gulf.
The Letter.
Lion Hunts.
Middle Age.
The Postilion Has Been
Struck by Lightning.
Witch.
Beer-Hofmann, Richard
An Evil Man.
Jacob's Destiny.
Lullaby for Miriam.
Beerbohm, Max
Addition to Kipling's "The
Dead King (Edward VII),
1910."
Ballade Tragique a Double
Refrain.
Brave Rover.
Elegy on Any Lady by
George Moore.
Epitaph for G. B. Shaw.
Lines on a Certain Friend's
Remarkable Faculty...
The Lost History Plays:
Savanarola (parody).
A Luncheon.
On the Imprint of the First
English Edition of....
Police Station Ditties.
The Road to Zoagli.
Thomas Hardy and A. E.
Housman.
Vague Lyric by G.M.
Beers, Ethel Lynn
All.
The Picket-Guard.
Weighing the Baby.
Which Shall It Be?
Beers, Henry Augustin
Biftek aux Champignons.
Ecce in Deserto.
On a Miniature.
Posthumous.
The Singer of One Song.
Beesly, A. H.
Andre's Ride.
Beeton, Douglas Ridley
Autumn.
Beevers, John
Atameros.
Beghtol, Charles
Hopi Lament.
Hopi Prayer.
In Old Tucson.
Behemb, M.
I Shall Be Satisfied.
Behm, Richard
Cleaning Fish.
The Collector.
The Hunt of the Poem.

Return to Lake Emily
Chequamegon National
Forest.
Trout Fishing: A Sign.
Behn, Aphra
Amyntas Led Me to a Grove.
And Forgive Us Our
Trespasses.
Beneath a Cool Shade.
The Coquette.
The Defiance.
The Disappointment.
The Dream.
Love in Fantastic Triumph.
Love's Witness.
The Lucky Chance: Song.
Not to sigh and to be tender.
O What Pleasure 'Tis to Find.
On Her Loving Two Equally.
Sir Patient Fancy: Epilogue
(excerpt).
Song in the Same Play, by the
Wavering Nymph.
Song. Love Arm'd.
Song: "When maidens are
young, and in their spring."
That Beauty I Ador'd Before.
A Thousand Martyrs I Have
Made.
To the Fair Clarinda, Who
Made Love to Me, Imagin'd
More than Woman.
Westminster Drollery, 1671.
When Damon First Began to
Love.
When you Love, or speak of
it.
The Willing Mistress.
Behn, Harry
Adventure.
A Christmas Carol.
Christmas Morning.
Curiosity.
Easter Snowfall.
Evening.
Follow the Leader.
The Gnome.
Growing Up.
Hallowe'en.
Invitation.
The Kite.
Lesson.
Mr. Pyme.
Others.
Spring.
Spring Rain.
Surprise.
This Happy Day.
Trees.
Visitors.
Waiting.
Windy Morning.
Behrend, Alice
Snowflakes.
Behune, Lebert
A Juju of My Own.
Beidler, Martha
Mohammed Ibrahim Speaks.
Beissel, Henry
The Boar and the Dromedar.
Beissel, Johann Conrad
The Sun Now Risen.
Beker, Ruth
Don't Show Me.
**"Belasco, F." See also
Rosenfield, Monroe F.**
Johnny Get Your Gun.
Belford, Ken
Beside the Road.
Blueline.
Branches Back Into.
Carrier Indians.

Dusk.
For Kelley.
Glove Glue.
Hunchbacked and Corrected.
New Potatoes.
Peanuts.
Stove.
Turn (a poem in 4 parts).

Belfrage, Sally
Progress.

Belisle, Eugene L.
At 21.

Belitt, Ben
Battery Park, High Noon.
Charwoman.
Late Dandelions.
Papermill Graveyard.
The Sand Painters.
View from the Gorge.
Winter Pond.
Xerox.

Belknap, Jeremy
Far from Our Friends.
Thus Spake the Saviour.

Bell, Birdie
I Have Always Found It So.

Bell, Charles Dent
Solemn Rondeau.

Bell, Charles G.
Banana.
Baptism.
The Blue-Hole.
Diretro al Sol.
The Fire.
The Flood.
From Le Havre.
The Gar.
Girl Walking.
Heraclitus in the West.
Island Dogs.
Love in Age.
On a Baltimore Bus.
Termites.
This Little Vigil.
Two Families.
Windowed Habitations.
Woodbird.

Bell, Ed
Frisco Whistle Blues.
Hambone Blues.
Tooten Out Blues.

Bell, Henry Glassford
Mary, Queen of Scots.

Bell, John Jay
On the Quay.

Bell, Julian
Pluviose.
The Redshanks.
Woods and Kestrel.

Bell, Martin
Footnote to Enright's
"Apocalypse."
The Songs.
Ultimate Anthology.
Winter Coming On.

Bell, Marvin
3 Stanzas about a Tree.
Acceptance Speech.
A Cabin in Minnesota.
Communication on His
Thirtieth Birthday.
Coralville, in Iowa.
The Extermination of the
Jews.
Fresh News from the Past.
Garlic.
Gemwood.
Getting Lost in Nazi
Germany.
Here.
The Hole in the Sea.
The Home Front.

Impotence.
Iowa Land.
The Israeli Navy.
Little Father Poem.
A Memory.
The Music of the Spheres.
The Mystery of Emily
Dickinson.
The New Formalists.
New Students.
Obsessive.
Origin of Dreams.
The Parents of Psychotic
Children.
The Perfection of Dentistry.
Reflexes.
Residue of Song.
Stars Which See, Stars Which
Do Not See.
These Green-Going-to-Yellow.
Things We Dreamt We Died
For.
To Dorothy.
Treetops.
A True Story.
Two Pictures of a Leaf.
What Is There.
What They Do to You in
Distant Places.
Who's in Charge Here?

Bell, Maurice
The Alabama.

Bell, Robert Mowry
The Second Volume.
The Tutelage.

Bell, Walker Meriwether
Jefferson Davis.

Bell, William
The Coolin Ridge.
Elegy.
On a Dying Boy.
On a Ledge.
Sonnet: "You waken slowly.
In your dream you're
straying."
To a Lady on Her Marriage.
A Young Man's Song.

Bellamann, Henry
A Charleston Garden.
Cups of Illusion.
The Deeper Seas.
The Gulf Stream.

Bellamy, Peter
Sweet Loving Friendship.

Belle, John Cross
Secret Prayer.

Belleau, Remy
April.

Bellenden, John
A Starscape.

Bellerby, Frances
Bereaved Child's First Night.
A Clear Shell.
An Inconclusive Evening.
It Is Not Likely Now.

Bellg, Albert
Raincoats for the Dead.
Watertower.

Belli, Giuseppe Gioacchino
Campidoglio.
The Confessor.
Death with a Coda.
Good Weather.
Judgment Day.
Sanct Christopher II.

Belloc, Hilaire
Almighty God, Whose Justice
Like a Sun.
Another on the Same.
B Stands for Bear.
Ballade of Hell and of Mrs.
Roebeck.

Ballade of Illegal Ornaments.
Ballade of the Heresiarchs.
Ballade to Our Lady of
Czestochowa.
Because My Faltering Feet.
The Big Baboon.
Birds in Their Little Nests
Agree.
The Bison.
The Camelopard.
Courtesy.
Crusade.
Cuckoo!
Dedication on the Gift of a
Book to a Child.
Dedicatory Ode: They Say
That in the Unchanging
Place.
Discovery.
Duncton Hill.
The Early Morning.
The Elephant.
Epigram: "First in his pride
the orient sun's display."
Epitaph: On the Favourite
Dog of a Politician.
Epitaph on the Politician
Himself.
Epitaph upon Himself.
The False Heart.
Fatigue.
The Fragment.
Franklin Hyde.
The Frog.
G.
The Game of Cricket.
The Garden Party.
George.
The Gnu.
Godolphin Horne.
Grandmamma's Birthday.
Ha'nacker Mill.
Habitations.
Henry King.
Her Faith.
Heretics All.
The Hippopotamus.
In a Boat.
Jack and His Pony, Tom.
"Jim, Who Ran Away from
His Nurse and Was Eaten by
a Lion."
Juliet.
The Justice of the Peace.
The Leader.
Lines for a Christmas Card.
Lines to a Don.
The Lion.
The Llama.
Lord Abbott.
Lord Epsom.
Lord Finchley.
Lord Heygate.
Lord High-Bo.
Lord Lucky.
Lord Lundy.
Matilda.
A Moral Alphabet (excerpt).
The Night.
Noel.
On a Dead Hostess.
On a General Election.
On a Hand.
On a Puritan.
On a Sundial.
On Another.
On His Books.
On Hygiene.
On Jam.
On Lady Poltagrue, a Public
Peril.
On Mundane Acquaintances.

On Noman, a Guest.
On Paunch, A Parasite.
On the Same.
On Two Ministers of State.
On Vital Statistics.
Our Lord and Our Lady.
The Pacifist.
The Prophet Lost in the Hills
at Evening.
The Python.
Rebecca, Who Slammed
Doors for Fun and Perished
Miserably.
The Rebel.
Sarah Byng.
The Scorpion.
Season's Greetings.
The Song Called "His Hide Is
Covered with Hair."
Song of Duke William.
Song: "You wear the morning
like your dress."
Sonnet: "The world's a stage."
Sonnet: "We will not whisper,
we have found the place."
The South Country.
Stanzas Written on Battersea
Bridge during a
Southwesterly Gale.
The Statesman.
The Statue.
Tarantella.
The Telephone.
They Say, and I am Glad
They Say.
To Dives.
Various Beasts.
The Vulture.
West Sussex Drinking Song.
The Yak.

Bellows, Isabel Frances
Limerick: "C is for Curious
Charlie."
Limerick: "G is for dear little
Gustave."
Limerick: "I is for Ignorant
Ida."
Limerick: "N is for naughty
young Nat."
Limerick: "O's Operatic
Olivia."

Bellows, Silence Buck
Last Cargo.

Belsham, R. A.
Christ for Everything.

Belvin, William
Palermo, Mother's Day, 1943.

Beman, Nathan S. S.
Jesus, I Come to Thee.

Ben Abun, Simeon
All the Hosts of Heaven.
I Come to Supplicate.

Ben Isaac, Mordecai
Fair Thou Art.
Rock of My Salvation.

Ben Jacob, Menahem
The Harvesting of the Roses.
A Martyr's Death.

Ben Judah, Daniel
The Living God.

Ben Judah, Kalonymos
Although Tormented.

Ben Kalir, Eleazar
O Hark to the Herald.
Palms and Myrtles.
Prayer for Dew.
The Prophet Jeremiah and the
Personification of Israel.
The Terrible Sons.
To Him Who Is Feared.

Ben Kalonymos, Kalonymos
The Hypocrite.

The Unfortunate Male.
The Yoke.
Ben Makhir
How Sweet Thy Precious Gift
of Rest.
Ben Moses, Kalonymos
His Sovereignty.
Ben Samuel, Isaac
His Hand Shall Cover Us.
Ben Shefatiah, A.
Hymn of Weeping.
Ben Yeshaq, Yosef D.
The Rusted Chain.
Ben-Yitzhak, A.
Blessed Are Those Who Sow
and Do Not Reap.
I Didn't Know My Soul.
Psalm.
Benbow, Margaret
The Old Biograph Girl.
Bender, Debra Woolard
World within a World.
Bendo, Brian
The Dream.
Benedict, Hester A.
Good-Night.
Benedikt, Michael
Clement Attlee.
Divine Love.
The European Shoe.
The Eye.
Fate in Incognito.
Fraudulent Days.
The Future.
The Grand Guignols of Love.
The Life of Particles.
The Meat Epitaph.
Of How Scientists Are Often
Ahead of Others in
Thinking...
Some Feelings.
Some Litanies.
Thoughts.
Benediktsson, Einar
Rain.
Benet, Laura
Adventure.
Mountain Convent.
Peter.
The Rowers.
She Wandered after Strange
Gods...
The Thrush.
Benet, Mayster
The Alphabet of Aristotle.
Benet, Rosemary
Johnny Appleseed.
To an Unknown Neighbor at
the Circus.
**Benét, Rosemary and Stephen
Vincent**
Abraham Lincoln.
Benjamin Franklin.
Daniel Boone, 1735-1820.
George Washington.
Hernando de Soto.
Jesse James.
John Adams.
Lewis and Clark.
Nancy Hanks.
Negro Spirituals.
Southern Ships and Settlers,
1606-1732.
Thomas Jefferson.
Western Wagons.
Benét, Stephen Vincent
Aaron Burr.
American Muse.
American Names.
Andrew Jackson.
The Ballad of William
Sycamore.

Dulce Ridentem.
For All Blasphemers.
For City Spring.
The General Public.
Going Back to School.
Hymn in Columbus Circle.
The Innovator.
John Brown's Body.
John Quincy Adams
1767-1848.
King David.
Listen to the People:
Independence Day, 1941
(excerpt).
Litany For Dictatorships.
Metropolitan Nightmare.
The Mountain Whippoorwill.
Nightmare at Noon.
Nightmare Number Three.
Nightmare, with Angels.
A Nonsense Song.
Portrait of a Boy.
Rain after a Vaudeville Show.
The Retort Discourteous.
Three Elements.
To Rosemary.
Western Star (excerpt).
Winged Man.
Written in a Time of Crisis.
Benet, William Rose
Bast.
Brazen Tongue.
Debutantrum.
Eternal Masculine.
The Falconer of God.
The Fancy.
The Fawn in the Snow.
Gaspara Stampa.
Her Way.
The Horse Thief.
How to Catch Unicorns.
Inscription for a Mirror in a
Deserted Dwelling.
Jesse James.
Judgment.
The Light in the Temple.
Mad Blake.
Merchants from Cathay.
Night.
The Old Adam.
Old Bill's Memory Book.
On Sunday in the Sunlight.
Pearl Diver.
Sagacity.
Song Under Shadow.
The Strong Swimmer.
Subversive.
There Lived a Lady in Milan.
Tricksters.
Whale.
The Woodcutter's Wife.
The Words of Jesus.
The World's Desire.
Beneveni, Girolamo
Lauda.
Beneyto, Maria
Nocturne in the Women's
Prison.
Benford, Lawrence
The Beginning of a Long
Poem on Why I Burned the
City.
Benjacob, Isaac
An Epitaph.
Benjamin, Park
The Old Sexton.
To Arms.
Benjamin, Paul L.
We Who Are Dead.
Benjamin, Saul Hillel
At Summer's End.

Benjamin, Virginia Sarah
A Puzzling Example.
Benlowes, Edward
Theophila: Cynthia.
Benn, Gottfried
Beautiful Youth.
Poplar.
A Weightless Element.
Bennard, George
The Old Rugged Cross.
Bennett, Alan
Place-Names of China.
Bennett, Anna Elizabeth
Candle Song.
Hush Thee, Princeling.
Bennett, Arnold
Limerick: "There was a young
man of Montrose."
A Love Affair.
Bennett, Benjamin K.
Paradox.
Bennett, Bruce
The Bad Apple.
Early.
Poetry Is...
The Stick.
Success Story.
The True Story of Snow
White.
Villanelle with a Line by
Yeats.
Bennett, Gertrude Ryder
Diary of a Raccoon.
Bennett, Gwendolyn B.
Advice.
Fantasy.
Hatred.
Heritage.
Lines Written at the Grave of
Alexander Dumas.
Nocturne.
Quatrains.
Secret.
Song: "I am weaving a song
of waters."
Sonnet: "He came in silvern
armor, trimmed with black."
Sonnet: "Some things are very
dear to me."
To A Dark Girl.
To Usward.
Your Songs.
Bennett, Henry
Saint Patrick.
St. Patrick Was a Gentleman.
Bennett, Henry Holcomb
The Flag Goes By.
Bennett, John
The Abbot of Derry.
God Bless You, Dear, To-
Day!
Her Answer.
In a Rose Garden.
Master Skylark.
Pentecost.
The Song of the Spanish
Main.
A Tiger's Tale.
Bennett, Joseph
Autumnall.
Complaint.
Earthly Love.
Headsong.
On the Nativity of Christ Our
Lord.
Quatrina.
To Eliza, Duchess of Dorset.
Bennett, Lerone Jr.
And Was Not Improved.
Blues and Bitterness.
Bennett, Murray
Funeral.

Bennett, Paula
To a Young Poet.
Bennett, Peggy
A Mother Is a Sun.
Parable.
Shut Up, I Said.
A Snap Judgement on the
Llama.
Bennett, Rowena Bastin
April Puddle.
Boats.
Christmas Brownie.
Come, Ride with Me to
Toyland.
Conversation between Mr. and
Mrs. Santa Claus.
Conversation with an April
Fool.
End-of-Summer Poem.
Four Seasons.
Golden Cobwebs.
If I Were a Pilgrim Child.
Meeting the Easter Bunny.
A Modern Dragon.
Motor Cars.
Picture People.
Remembering the Winter.
Sunrise.
Umbrellas.
Vacation Time.
Witch Cat.
Bennett, S. Fillmore
Sweet By and By.
Bennett, Will
New Jersey.
Nod.
Poor Movies.
Bennett, William C.
Baby May.
Invocation to Rain in
Summer.
Lullaby, O Lullaby.
To a Cricket.
A Wife's Song.
Benoit, Pierre
Diaduminius.
Bensel, James Berry
Ahmad.
Bensko, John
Mail Call.
Mowing the Lawn.
The Night-Blooming Cactus.
A Veteran of the Great War.
Bensley, Connie
Charity.
Desires.
Benson, Arthur Christopher
Amen.
Knapweed.
Land of Hope and Glory.
Lord Vyet.
The Phoenix.
Prelude.
Benson, Gerard
Horse.
Leavings (parody).
The Probatioun Officeres Tale.
Benson, Louis F.
Far Trumpets Blowing.
O Love That Lights the
Eastern Sky.
O Risen Lord upon the
Throne.
O Thou Whose Feet Have
Climbed Life's Hill.
O Thou Whose Gracious
Presence Blest.
Why Linger Yet upon the
Strand?
Benson, Margaret
Once on a Time.

Benson, Mary Josephine
Smoking Flax.
Benson, Nathaniel A.
Holy Night.
Year's End.
Benson, Robert Hugh
At High Mass.
The Priest's Lament.
The Teresian Contemplative.
Benson, Stella
Frost.
Now I Have Nothing.
Bental, Anath
The Angel Michael.
Jerusalem in the Snow.
Bentley, Beth
Bridges and Tunnels.
The Gnomes.
The Lesson.
Temple of the Muses.
The Therapeutist.
Bentley, Edmund Clerihew
Adam Smith.
Ballade of Liquid
Refreshment.
Clerihews.
George the Third.
Liszt.
Savonarola.
Sir Christopher Wren.
Sir Humphry Davy.
When Alexander Pope.
The Younger Van Eyck.
Bentley, Nicolas
On Mrs. W–.
Bentley, Richard
A Reply to an Imitation of
the Second Ode....of Horace.
Verses.
Benton, Frank
Old Buck's Ghost.
Benton, Joel
At Chappaqua.
Grover Cleveland.
The Poet.
The Scarlet Tanager.
Benton, Myron B.
The Mowers.
Benton, Patricia
Desert River.
Benton, Walter
Summary of the Distance
between the Bomber and the
Objective.
This Is My Beloved (excerpt).
With the Most Susceptible
Element, the Mind, Already
Turned...
Benveniste, Asa
The Alchemical Cupboard.
Benvenuta, Sister Mary
Mater Incognita.
Beranger, Pierre Jean de
The King of Yvetot.
Berceo, Gonzalo de
The Life of San Millan
(excerpt).
San Miguel De La Tumba.
Berenberg, David P.
Two Sonnets.
Bereng, David Granmer T.
The Birth of Moshesh.
Berenguer, Amanda
Housework.
Berg, Sharon
Tongues.
Berg, Stephen
The Animals.
Between Us.
Desnos Reading the Palms of
Men on Their Way to the
Gas Chambers.

Don't Forget.
Dreaming with a Friend.
Entering the Body: The
Survivor.
A Glimpse of the Body Shop.
Gooseberries.
The Holes.
Ollie, Answer Me.
People Trying to Love.
To My Friends.
A Wife Talks to Herself.
Berge, Carol
Chiaroscuro.
Bergengren, Ralph W.
The Dirigible.
The Worm.
Berger, Bruce
False Cadence.
Berggolts, Olga
Infidelity.
To My Sister.
To Song.
Bergman, Alexander
The Chronicler.
Letter.
Bergman, David
Eclogue.
Why I Am Offended By
Miracles.
Bergonzi, Bernard
Anemones for Miss Austen.
Bergquist, Beatrice
The Song of the Robin.
Bering, Betsy
Still Life.
Berke, Judith
The Red Room.
Berkeley, George
Verses on the Prospect of
Planting Arts and Learning
in America.
Berkeley, Sir William
Song: "Where did you borrow
that last sigh."
Berkson, Bill
Baby's Awake Now.
Blind Geronimo.
Blue Is the Hero...
Bubbles.
Call It Goofus.
Christmas Eve.
Dream with Fred Astaire.
Familiar Music.
February.
A Fixture.
Fourth Street, San Rafael.
Ivesiana.
Leave Cancelled.
October.
Ode: "Midnight moonlight
mobbed Dante's bridge."
Oscar.
Out There.
Russian New Year.
Sound from Leopardi.
Stanky.
Star Motel.
Strawberry Blond.
Surabaja.
Berkson, Lee L.
Bogey.
Berlin, Irving
God Bless America.
Berlind, Bruce
Fragment.
Period Piece.
Berman, Ruth
The Blessing.
Snow Queen's Portrait.
Bernadine
It Begins Softly.
A Letter from When.

An Open-Letter-Poem-Note to
Vincent Van G.
Bernard, Artis
Snowfall.
Bernard de Ventadour
Canzo: "Can l'erba fresch'elh
folha par."
The Lark.
No Marvel Is It.
Troubadour Song.
Bernard of Clairvaux, Saint
Hail, Thou Head!
Jesu Dulcis.
Jesus, Thou Joy of Loving
Hearts.
Thy Kingdom Come.
Wide Open Are Thy Hands.
Bernard of Cluny
Jerusalem, the Golden.
Mariale (excerpt).
Bernard of Morlas
Contempt for the World, III.
Bernhardt, Clara
A Sailor's Wife.
Bernhardt, Suzanne
In a Dream Ship's Hold.
The Unveiling.
Bernheimer, Alan
Passing Strange.
Portrait of a Man.
Specimen of an Induction to a
Poem.
Word of Art.
Bernstein, Charles
The Harbor of Illusion.
The Kiwi Bird in the Kiwi
Tree.
Live Acts.
Of Time and the Line.
Special Pleading.
The Voyage of Life.
Bernstein, Harriet
Gladioli for My Mother.
Berrigan, Daniel
Almost Everybody Is Dying
Here: Only a Few Actually
Make It.
The Beautiful Ruined
Orchard.
Great God Paused among
Men.
Handicapped.
The News Stand.
On the Birth of Dan
Goldman.
Patience, Hard Virtue.
Rehabilitative Report: We Can
Still Laugh.
Somewhere the Equation
Breaks Down.
A Typical 6:00 P.M. in the
Fun House.
We Were Permitted to Meet
Together in Prison to
Prepare for Trial.
Berrigan, Ted
Bean Spasms.
Cranston near the City Line.
For You.
Frank O'Hara.
How to Get to Canada.
III.
Lady.
Last Poem.
LI.
LII.
LIII.
Living with Chris.
Love.
LV.
LXX.

LXXII A Sonnet for Dick
Gallup.
LXXIV.
LXXVI.
People of the Future.
People Who Died.
Personal Poem #7.
Personal Poem #8.
Real Life.
Resolution.
The Sonnets.
Things to Do in New York
(City).
Things to Do in Providence.
Today's News.
Whitman in Black.
Words for Love.
XXXVI.
**Berrigan, Ted and Anne
Waldman**
Memorial Day: A
Collaboration.
Berry, D. C.
Alluding to the One-Armed
Bandit (parody).
Also Watches (parody).
Cosmogony (parody).
Dog (parody).
Faces (parody).
Foots It (parody).
Forehead Dead-Ends Half-
Way through the Poem
(parody).
Godiva (parody).
Having Eaten Breakfast
(parody).
If Love's a Yoke.
In Blue (parody).
Leaps over the Aisle of
Syllogism (parody).
Listens, Too (parody).
On Reading Poems to a
Senior Class at South High.
Up against the Wall (parody).
Berry, Eleanor
Multiplicity.
Berry, Francis
Gudveig.
Berry, Fred
Silica Carbonate Rock.
Berry, Martyn
Cairngorm, November 1971.
Berry, Wendell
9 Verses of the Same Song.
Ascent.
The Barn.
The Buildings.
Canticle.
Earth and Fire.
For the Rebuilding of a
House.
The Gift of Gravity.
The Grandmother.
Grief.
The Guest.
In Rain.
Independence Day.
Inland Passages, I: The Long
Hunter.
The Lilies.
A Man Walking and Singing.
May Song.
A Music.
My Great-Grandfather's
Slaves.
November Twenty-Sixth
Nineteen Hundred and Sixty-
Three.
The Peace of Wild Things.
Poem for J.
Reverdure.
September 2.

The Slip.
The Snake.
The Springs.
The Stones.
To Know the Dark.
To My Children, Fearing for
  Them.
The Way of Pain.
The Wheel.
The Wild.
Berryman, John
1 September 1939.
Alcoholic.
American Lights, Seen from
  Off Abroad.
Apollo 8.
The Ball Poem.
The Black Book.
The Cage.
Canto Amor.
Certainty before Lunch.
Cloud and Flame.
College of Flunkeys, and a
  Few Gentlemen.
Conversation.
Desires of Men and Women.
The Dispossessed.
Dream Songs.
Eleven Addresses to the Lord.
Gislebertus' Eve.
Go, ill-sped book.
He Resigns.
Hello.
Henry's Understanding.
His Toy, His Dream, His
  Rest.
Homage to Mistress
  Bradstreet.
Keep your eyes open when
  you kiss.
King David Dances.
Lauds.
The Moon and the Night and
  the Men.
New Year's Eve.
Note to Wang Wei.
Of Suicide.
Our Sunday morning when
  dawn-priests were applying.
Parting as Descent.
The Poet's Final Instructions.
A Prayer for the Self.
A Professor's Song.
Sigh as It Ends.
The Song of the Demented
  Priest.
The Song of the Tortured
  Girl.
Sonnet.
The Soviet Union.
The Statue.
A Sympathy, a Welcome.
Three Around the Old
  Gentleman.
The Traveller.
Washington in Love.
We Were in the 8th Grade.
Whether There Is Sorrow in
  the Demons.
Winter Landscape.
A Winter-Piece to a Friend
  Away.
Your Birthday in Wisconsin
  You Are 140.
Bersohn, Robert
The Dignity of Labor.
Berssenbrugge, Mei-Mei
Book of the Dead, Prayer 14.
Chronicle.
Farolita.
The Membrane.
Sleep.

Spring Street Bar.
The Translation of Verver.
Bertken, Sister
Love Wears Roses' Elegance.
When I went into my garden.
Bertolino, James
The Night Was Smooth.
Bertram, James
Epitaph for an American
  Bomber.
Is It Well-Lighted, Papa?
Rondeau in Wartime.
Bertrand
A Perigord pres del Muralh.
Planh for the Young English
  King.
Protestation.
A War Song.
Bertrand, Sister Mary
Our Lady of Mercy.
Berwick, Thurso
Idleset (2).
Besant, Walter
To Daphne.
Best, Charles
The Moon.
A Sonnet of the Moon.
Best, Susie M.
Thanksgiving.
Betham-Edwards, Matilda
Gethsemane.
A Valentine.
Bethell, Mary Ursula
Detail.
The Long Harbour.
Looking Down on
  Mesopotamia.
Pause.
Response.
Spring Snow and Tui.
Time.
Warning of Winter.
Weather.
Bethune, George Washington
The Blessed Name.
He Died for Me.
It is Not Death to Die.
Jesus, Shepherd of Thy Sheep.
O for the Happy Hour.
O Jesus! When I Think of
  Thee.
There Is No Name So Sweet
  on Earth.
Bethune, Lebert
Blue Tanganyika.
Bwagamoyo.
Harlem Freeze Frame.
A Juju of My Own.
To Strike for Night.
Betjeman, Sir John
Advent 1955.
The Archaeological Picnic.
The Arrest of Oscar Wilde at
  the Cadogan Hotel.
Arrogance Repressed.
Before Invasion, 1940.
Before the Anaesthetic; or, A
  Real Fright.
Beside the Seaside.
Bristol and Clifton.
A Child Ill.
Christmas.
The City.
The Cottage Hospital.
Crematorium.
Death in Leamington.
Death of King George V.
Diary of a Church Mouse.
East Anglian Bathe.
Executive.
Felixstowe, or The Last of
  Her Order.

For Patrick, Aetat: LXX.
For the Queen Mother.
Great Central Railway,
  Sheffield Victoria to Banbury.
The Heart of Thomas Hardy.
How to Get On in Society.
Hunter Trials.
Huxley Hall.
Hymn: "The Church's
  Restoration." (parody).
In a Bath Teashop.
In Memoriam: A.C., R.J.O.,
  K.S.
In Memory of Basil, Marquess
  of Dufferin and Ava.
In Memory of George
  Whitby, Architect.
In the Public Gardens.
In Westminster Abbey.
An Incident in the Early Life
  of Ebenezer Jones, Poet,
  1828.
Indoor Games near Newbury.
Inevitable.
Invasion Exercise on the
  Poultry Farm.
Ireland with Emily.
Late-Flowering Lust.
The Licorice Fields at
  Pontefract.
Longfellow's Visit to Venice.
Lord Cozens Hardy.
Matlock Bath.
The Metropolitan Railway.
  Baker Street Station Buffet.
Middlesex.
Myfanwy.
New King Arrives in His
  Capital by Air...
Norfolk.
NW5 & N6.
The Old Liberals.
The Olympic Girl.
On a Portrait of a Deaf Man.
Parliament Hill Fields.
The Planster's Vision.
Potpourri from a Surrey
  Garden.
Remorse.
Seaside Golf.
Senex.
A Shropshire Lad.
Slough.
The Small Towns of Ireland.
St. Saviour's, Aberdeen Park,
  Highbury, London, N.
A Subaltern's Love-Song.
Summoned by Bells: Cornwall
  in Childhood.
Sunday Afternoon Service in
  St. Enodoc Church,
  Cornwall.
Sunday Morning, King's
  Cambridge.
The Town Clerk's Views.
Trebetherick.
Tregardock.
Upper Lambourne.
Westgate-on-Sea.
Youth and Age on Beaulieu
  River, Hants.
Betts, Craven Langstroth
Don Quixote.
The Hollyhocks.
To the Moonflower.
Betts, Frank
The Pawns.
Bevington, Helen
Academic Moon.
The Cataract at Lodore
  (parody).
The Company of Scholars.

Herrick's Julia (parody).
The Man from Porlock.
Mr. Rockefeller's Hat.
Mrs. Trollope in America.
Nature Study, after Dufy.
Penguins in the Home.
Report from the Carolinas.
Talk with a Poet.
The Teacher.
Turner's Sunrise.
Bevington, Louisa S.
Afternoon.
Am I to Lose You?
Egoisme a Deux.
Love and Language.
Twilight.
Bewe
Actaeon.
Beyer, Evelyn
Jump or Jiggle.
Beyer, Richard
Second Reading.
Beyer, Tony
A Comfort Stop.
Cornwallis.
Cut Lilac.
The Seventies.
Bezruc, Petr
Ostrava.
Bezymensky, A.
Village and Factory.
Bhaird, Laoiseach Mac an
Civil Irish and Wild Irish.
Bhanot, V.
I Am Alone.
Bhartrihari
The Angler.
Dilemma.
In former days we'd both
  agree.
Love in Moonlight.
Peace.
Round Robin.
She who is always in my
  thoughts prefers.
The Sign.
Time.
Bhasa
The Dream Queen: Dialogue.
The Moon.
Bhavabhuti
Deep in Love.
Bhushan, V. N.
Creation.
Bialik, Chaim Nachman
The Dead of the Wilderness.
The Mathmid.
Night.
Songs of the People.
Bialik, Hayim N.
Place Me under Your Wing.
Bialik, Hayim Nahman
After My Death.
Alone.
Beneath Thy Wing.
Blessing over Food.
The City of Slaughter.
The Dance of Despair.
The Death of David.
Footsteps of Spring.
The Grasshopper's Song.
The Graveyard.
I Didn't Find Light by
  Accident.
I Know on a Night Overcast.
I Scattered My Sighs to the
  Wind.
If Thou Wouldst Know.
Midnight Prayer.
My Song.
Night.
Queen Sabbath.

The Sea of Silence Exhales
Secrets.
Should I Be a Rabbi?
The Stars Are Lit.
Summer Night.
Sunset.
The Talmud Student.
Throbs the Night with Mystic
Silence.
When the Days Grow Long.
Whence and Whither.
The Young Acacia.
Biasotti, Raymond
City.
Bibbs, Hart Leroi
Six Sunday.
Bible, N.T., St. Matthew
God Provides.
Bickerstaffe, Isaac
An Expostulation.
Love in a Village (excerpt).
The Recruiting Serjeant
(excerpt).
Song: "How happy were my
days, till now."
What Are Outward Forms.
**Bickersteth, Edward Henry,
Bishop of Exeter**
O God, the Rock of Ages.
Peace, Perfect Peace.
The Prince of Peace.
Bickston, Diane
As All Things Pass.
Collect Calls.
For Chicle & Justina.
For Zorro.
Pipe Dreams.
Bidart, Frank
Another Life.
Elegy (excerpt).
Happy Birthday.
Herbert White.
Self-Portrait, 1969.
Bieiris de Romans
Lady Maria, in You Merit
and Distinction.
Bierbaum, Otto Julius
Blacksmith Pain.
Jeannette.
Kindly Vision.
Oft in the Silent Night.
Bierce, Ambrose
Advice.
Another Way.
An Attorney General.
Beneath This Mound.
Black Bart, P08.
The Bride.
By Plain Analogy We're Told.
Commonwealth.
Compliance.
Condone.
The Convicts' Ball.
Covet.
Creation.
The Death of Grant.
The Devil's Dictionary.
Doctor Blenn.
Don't Steal.
Epitaph: "Here lies the
remains of great Senator
Vrooman."
Epitaph: "We mourn the
loss."
Here Huntington's Ashes
Long Have Lain.
Montefiore.
My Country 'Tis of Thee.
Presentiment.
Sheriff.
Sir Francis Bacon.
T.A.H.

Undertakers.
Bierds, Linda
Elegy for 41 Whales Beached
in Florence, Ore., June, 1979.
Mid-Plains Tornado.
Big Eagle, Duane
Birthplace.
Elegy.
My Grandfather Was a
Quantum Physicist.
Recollection.
Wind and Impulse.
Bigelow, J. S.
The Bat and the Scientist.
Bigg, J. Stanyan
An Irish Picture.
Biggar, H. Howard
Your Neighbor.
Bigger, Duff
The Comedian Said It.
It Is When the Tribe Is Gone.
Biggs, Maurice
Spring Offensive, 1941.
Bignold, Thomas Frank
The Holiday.
Bilal
Muhammedan Call to Prayer.
Bilderdijk, Willem
Prayer.
Bilhana
Black Marigolds.
Bill, Barefoot
Big Rock Jail.
From Now On.
My Crime.
Squabbling Blues.
Billings, Josh
Explanation.
Thrice Is He Armed That
Hath His Quarrel Just.
Billings, Robert
Beast Enough.
Billings, William
Chester.
David's Lamentation.
Let Tyrants Shake Their Iron
Rod.
When Jesus Wept.
Bily-Hurd, Michael
Woman in an Abandoned
House.
Bingham, G. Clifton
Love's Old Sweet Song.
Binney, Thomas
Eternal Light!
Binns, Elsie
Christmas Is Remembering.
The Smallest Angel.
Binyon, Laurence
Amasis.
August.
Bab-Lock-Hythe.
Beauty.
The Belfry.
The Burning of the Leaves.
Day's End.
The Dray.
Eleonora Duse as Magda.
Ezekiel.
Ferry Hinksey.
Fetching the Wounded.
Fog.
For the Fallen.
A Glimpse of Time.
The House That Was.
Hunger.
In Misty Blue.
Invocation to Youth.
John Winter.
Lament.
The Little Dancers.
Little Hands.

Magnets.
Nothing Is Enough.
November.
O World, Be Nobler.
A Song.
The Sower.
The Statues.
Tristram's End.
Virgil's Farewell to Dante.
Winter Sunrise (excerpt).
Ypres.
Bion
A Dream of Venus.
Lament for Adonis.
Biondi, Clemente
For a Blind Beggar's Sign.
Biran, Paddy
Paddy Biran's Song.
Birch, Harry
Reuben and Rachel.
Bird, Bessie Calhoun
Proof.
Bird, Dolly
Can I Say.
Bird, Edward
To His Coy Mistress (parody).
Bird, Robert
The Fairy Folk.
Bird, Stephen Moylan
May.
The Silent Ranges.
Birdseye, George
Paradise: A Hindoo Legend.
Birkenhead, Sir John
The Four-Legg'd Elder.
Birnbaum, Henry
A Room I Once Knew.
When Silence Divests Me.
Birney, Earle
Anglosaxon Street.
The Bear on the Delhi Road.
Birthday.
Bushed.
Can. Hist.
Can. Lit.
Charite Esperance et Foi.
Christchurch, N.Z.
Christmas Comes...
Damnation of Vancouver:
Speech of the Salish Chief.
David.
El Greco: Espolio.
For Steve.
From the Hazel Bough.
Hot Springs.
Irapuato.
Mappemounde.
Monody on a Century.
Museum of Man.
My Love Is Young.
On Going to the Wars.
Pacific Door.
Poet-Tree.
The Road to Nijmegen.
Sinaloa.
Slug in Woods.
A Small Faculty Stag for the
Visiting Poet.
There Are Delicacies.
This Page My Pigeon.
Twenty-Third Flight.
Vancouver Lights.
A Walk in Kyoto.
World Winter.
Birnie, Patrick
The Auld Man's Mear's Dead.
Bishop, Elissa
At Nine O'Clock in the
Spring.
Bishop, Elizabeth
12 O'Clock News.
The Armadillo.

Arrival at Santos.
At the Fishhouses.
The Bight.
Brazil, January 1, 1502.
The Burglar of Babylon.
Cape Breton.
Casabianca.
Cirque d'Hiver.
A Cold Spring.
The Colder the Air.
Cootchie.
Crusoe in England.
Faustina, or Rock Roses.
Filling Station.
First Death in Nova Scotia.
The Fish.
Florida.
From the Country to the City.
From Trollope's Journal.
House Guest.
The Imaginary Iceberg.
In the Waiting Room.
Insomnia.
Invitation to Miss Marianne
Moore.
Jeronimo's House.
Large Bad Picture.
Late Air.
Letter to N. Y.
Little Exercise.
Love Lies Sleeping.
The Man-Moth.
Manners.
Manuelzinho.
The Map.
A Miracle for Breakfast.
The Monument.
The Moose.
North Haven.
One Art.
Over 2000 Illustrations and a
Complete Concordance.
Poem: "About the size of an
old-style dollar bill."
The Prodigal.
Questions of Travel.
The Riverman.
Roosters.
Sandpiper.
Seascape.
Sestina.
The Shampoo.
Sleeping on the Ceiling.
Some Dreams They Forgot.
Songs for a Colored Singer.
Squatter's Children.
A Summer's Dream.
Two Mornings and Two
Evenings.
The Unbeliever.
Under the Window: Ouro
Preto.
Varick Street.
View of the Capitol from the
Library of Congress.
Visits to St. Elizabeths.
Wading at Wellfleet.
The Weed.
While Someone Telephones.
The Wit.
Bishop, G. E.
The Bigger Day.
Bishop, John Peale
Always, from My First
Boyhood.
The Ancestors.
Apparition.
The Birds of Paradise.
Boys, By Girls Held in Their
Thighs.
Colloquy with a King-Crab.
The Dream.

Fiametta.
Four Years Were Mine at Princeton.
A Frieze.
A Green and Pleasant Land.
The Hours.
The Hunchback.
Hunger and Thirst.
In the Dordogne.
An Interlude.
John Donne's Statue.
Metamorphoses of M.
O Pioneers!
Ode: "Why will they never sleep."
Percy Shelley.
Perspectives Are Precipices.
The Return.
Saint Francis.
Speaking of Poetry.
The Statue of Shadow.
The Submarine Bed.
This Dim and Ptolemaic Man.
The Triumph of Doubt.
Why They Waged War.
Your Chase Had a Beast in View.

Bishop, Morris
Ambition.
The Anatomy of Humor.
Bishop Orders His Tomb in St. Praxed's.
The Complete Misanthropist.
Dementia Praecox.
Diogenes.
Drinking Song for Present-Day Gatherings.
Early Morning.
Ecclesiastes.
Epitaph for a Funny Fellow.
For the Opening of the Hunting Season.
Gas and Hot Air.
How to Treat Elves.
I Hear America Griping.
The Immoral Arctic.
It Rolls On.
Limerick: "A bull-voiced young fellow of Pauling."
Limerick: "A chap has a shark up in Sparkill."
Limerick: "A Clergyman out in Dumont."
Limerick: "A ghoulish old fellow in Kent."
Limerick: "A strong-minded lady of Arden."
Limerick: "At a modernist school in Park Hill."
Limerick: "I have heard," said a maid of Montclair."
Limerick: "Said a girl from beyond Pompton Lakes."
Limerick: "Said old Peeping Tom of Fort Lee."
Limerick: "There's a lady in Washington Heights."
Limerick: "There's a sensitive man in Toms River."
Limerick: "There's a vaporish maiden in Harrison."
The Maladjusted: A Tragedy (excerpt).
Merry Old Souls (excerpt).
The Naughty Preposition.
A New Hampshire Boy.
Ozymandias Revisited.
The Perforated Spirit.
Public Aid for Niagara Falls.
Sales Talk for Annie.
Settling Some Old Football Scores.

Sing a Song of the Cities.
Song of the Pop-Bottlers.
Sonnet and Limerick.
The Tales the Barbers Tell.
There's Money in Mother and Father.
A Tonversaton with Baby.
We Have Been Here Before.
What Hath Man Wrought Exclamation Point.
Who'd Be a Hero (Fictional)?
A Winter Madrigal.
The Witch of East Seventy-Second Street.

Bishop, Roy
The Inefficacious Egg.

Bishop, Samuel
At Newmarket.
Epigrams: "Need from excess– excess from folly growing."
To His Wife on the Fourteenth Anniversary of Her Wedding-Day...
The Touch-Stone.

Bishop, Verna
Choose.

Bishop, Wendy
Family History.

Bissert, Ellen Marie
Another.
The Most Beautiful Woman at My Highschool Reunion.

Bisset, James
Ramble of the Gods through Birmingham (excerpt).

Bissett, Bill
Christ i wudint know normal if i saw it when.
Dont Worry Yr Hair.
Th Wundrfulness uv th Mountees Our Secret Police.

Biton, Erez
Beginnings.
A Bird's Nest.
Buying a Shop on Dizengoff.

Bitton, W. Nelson
Resurgam.

Bixler, W. A.
Beautiful.

Bjornson, Bjornstjerne
The Boy and the Flute.
Fatherland Song.
Synnove's Song.
The Tree.

Bjornvig, Thorkild
The Owl.

Black, Austin
Soul.

Black, Charles
All Too Little on Pictures.
The Reach of Silence.

Black, Isaac J.
Roll Call: A Land of Old Folk and Children.
Talking to the Townsfolk in Ideal, Georgia.

Black, Jack
Awake! (parody).

Black, James M.
When the Roll Is Called up Yonder.

Black, MacKnight
Corliss Engine-Wheel.
Heart.
Rock, Be My Dream.

Black, Theodore
Bard.

Black Bart
I've Labored Long and Hard for Bread.

Blackburn, Alexander
What Makes a Nation Great.

Blackburn, Paul
17. IV. 71.
The Assassination of President McKinley.
The Assistance.
Banalbufar, A Brazier, Relativity, Cloud Formations...
Clickety-Clack.
The Continuity.
The Crossing.
El Camino Verde.
The Encounter.
Getting a Job.
Good Morning Love!
Hot Afternoons Have Been in West 15th Street.
In Winter.
Invitation Standing.
The Letter.
Meditation on the BMT.
Mother, in the 45 cent Bottle.
Night Song for Two Mystics.
The Once-Over.
The One-Night Stand: An Approach to the Bridge.
Park Poem.
Phone Call to Rutherford.
Plaza Real with Palmtrees.
The Problem.
The Proposition.
The Purse–Seine.
The Routine.
The Sign.
Sirventes.
The Slogan.
Song of the Hesitations.
The Stone.
Sunflower Rock.
Three Part Invention.
The Tides.
The Watchers.
The Yawn.

Blackburn, Thomas
An Aftermath.
Families.
Felo Da Se.
Ganga.
Hospital for Defectives.
The Lucky Marriage.
Oedipus.
Song for the Infant Judas.

Blackie, John Stuart
How Small Is Man.
My Loves.
Ye Simple Men.

Blackmore, Richard Doddridge
Dominus Illuminatio Mea.
Yes.

Blackmore, Sir Richard
The Circulation of the Blood.
A Satire against Wit.

Blackmur, Richard P.
Before Sentence Is Passed.
The Dead Ride Fast.
Half-Tide Ledge.
The Rape of Europa.
Resurrection.
Scarabs for the Living.
Sea Island Miscellany.
Sonnet: "Three silences made him a single word."
Views of Boston Common and Nearby.

Blackstock, Walter
Old Voyager.

Blackwell, Harriet Gray
Forest.
Hill People.

Blackwell, Will H.
Tides.

Bladen, Peter
Coronation Day at Melrose.

Blair, Lee
Limerick: "A careless young driver, McKissen."
Limerick: "Here is the reply made by Benny."
Limerick: "I must eat an apple," said Link."

Blair, Robert
Friendship.
The Grave.

Blake, Blind
Diddie Wa Diddie.

Blake, Felicia
A Woman's Answer to the Vampire.

Blake, Howard
Argent Solipsism.

Blake, James Vila
In Him.

Blake, James W.
The Sidewalks of New York.

Blake, Marie
Barter.

Blake, Mary Elizabeth
The Dawning o' the Year.

Blake, William
Abstinence Sows Sand All Over.
Ah, Sun-Flower.
America A Prophecy.
And Did Those Feet in Ancient Time.
The Angel.
An Answer to the Parson.
Auguries of Innocence.
The Bard.
The Birds.
Blind-Man's Buff.
The Blossom.
The Book of Thel.
The Caverns of the Grave I've Seen.
Children of a Future Age.
The Chimney Sweeper.
The Clod and the Pebble.
A Compliment to the Ladies (parody).
Cradle Song.
Cromek.
The Crystal Cabinet.
The Divine Image.
A Dream.
Earth's Answer.
The Echoing Green.
Epigram: "Give pensions to the Learned Pig."
Epigram: "Grown old in Love from seven till Seven times Seven."
Epigram: "Some people admire the work of a Fool."
Epigram: "The Hebrew Nation did not write it."
Epigram: "The only Man that e'er I knew."
Epigram: To English Connoisseurs.
Epigram: "To forgive enemies Hayley does pretend."
Epigram: To Hunt.
Epitaph: "Come knock your heads against this stone."
Epitaph: "Here lies John Trot, the friend of all mankind."
Epitaph: "I was buried near this dyke."
Eternity.
The Everlasting Gospel.
The Fly.

For the Sexes: The Gates of
 Paradise.
The Four Zoas.
The French Revolution.
The Garden of Love.
Gnomic Verses.
The Golden Net.
Great Things.
He Has Observ'd the Golden
 Rule.
He Who Binds to Himself a
 Joy.
Hear the Voice of the Bard!
Her Whole Life is an
 Epigram.
Holy Thursday.
How Sweet I Roam'd.
The Human Abstract.
I Asked a Thief to Steal Me a
 Peach.
I Heard an Angel Singing.
I Laid Me Down upon a
 Bank.
I Saw a Chapel All of Gold.
If You Trap the Moment.
The Immortal.
In Deadly Fear.
Infant Joy.
Infant Sorrow.
Is This a Holy Thing to See.
An Island in the Moon.
It Is Not So with Me.
Jerusalem.
The Lamb.
The Land of Dreams.
The Lark's Song.
Laughing Song.
Letters: With Happiness
 Stretchd Across the Hills.
The Little Black Boy.
The Little Boy Found.
Little Boy Lost.
The Little Girl Found.
The Little Girl Lost.
The Little Vagabond.
London.
Love's Secret.
Love to Faults Is Always
 Blind.
Mad Song.
The Marriage of Heaven and
 Hell.
The Marriage Ring.
The Mayors.
The Mental Traveler.
Milton.
Mock On, Mock On, Voltaire,
 Rousseau.
Mockery.
Morning.
Mr. Cromek to Mr. Stothard.
My Pretty Rose Tree.
My Silks and Fine Array.
My Spectre around Me Night
 & Day.
Never Seek to Tell Thy Love.
Night.
Night the Ninth Being the
 Last Judgment.
Nurse's Song.
O Lapwing, Thou Fliest
 around the Heath.
O Why Was I Born with a
 Different Face?
An Old Maid Early.
On Another's Sorrow.
Orator Prigg.
Piping Down the Valleys
 Wild.
The Poet's Voice.
A Poison Tree.
The Prince of Love.

Proverbs of Hell.
The Question Answer'd.
Riches.
The Schoolboy.
The Secrets of the Earth.
The Shepherd.
The Sick Rose.
Silent, Silent Night.
Sir Joshua Reynolds.
Sleep! Sleep! Beauty Bright.
The Smile.
Soft Snow.
A Song of Liberty.
Spring.
The Sword and the Sickle.
Thel's Motto.
Three Things to Remember.
The Tiger.
To Autumn.
To Flaxman.
To God.
To Hayley.
To Morning.
To Mrs. Ann Flaxman.
To My Friend Butts I Write.
To My Mirtle.
To Nobodaddy.
To See a World in a Grain of
 Sand.
To Spring.
To Summer.
To the Evening Star.
To the Muses.
To the Queen.
To Tirzah.
To Winter.
Vala; or, The Four Zoas.
The Vision of Beulah.
Visions.
Visions of the Daughters of
 Albion.
A War Song.
A War Song to Englishmen.
When a Man Has Married a
 Wife.
When Klopstock England
 Defied.
Where to Seek Love.
Why Should I Care for the
 Men of Thames?
The Wild Flower's Song.
With Happiness Stretched
 Across the Hills.
Blakely, Henry
 H. Rap Brown.
 Morning Song.
Blakely, Roger
 Winslow Homer, Prisoners
 from the Front.
Blakeney, Lena Whittaker
 The Covered Wagon.
Blaker, Margaret
 Pippa Passes, but I Can't Get
 around This Truck.
Blamire, Susanna
 The Siller Croun.
 Stoklewath; or, The Cymbrian
 Village.
Blanchard, Edward Laman
 Vilikins and His Dinah.
Blanchard, Ferdinand Q.
 O Child of Lowly Manger
 Birth.
 Word of God, Across the
 Ages.
Blanchard, Laman
 Nell Gwynne's Looking-Glass.
 Ode to the Human Heart.
Bland, James A.
 Carry Me Back to Old
 Virginny.

In the Evening by the
 Moonlight.
 Oh, Dem Golden Slippers.
 Old Virginny.
Blanden, Charles G.
 Quatrain.
 The Rose Is a Royal Lady.
 A Song the Grass Sings.
 The Songs I Sing.
Blandiana, Ana
 The Couple.
 I need only fall asleep.
Blanding, Don
 Aloha Oe.
 Hollywood.
 Soldier, What Did You See?
 Vagabond House.
Blankner, Frederika
 Remainder.
Blaser, Robin
 A 4 Part Geometry Lesson.
 The Faerie Queene.
 Herons.
 Image-Nation (the Poesis).
 Image-Nation 3.
 Image-Nation 13 (the
 Telephone).
 The Park.
 Poem.
 Poem by the Charles River.
 Sophia Nichols.
 Suddenly.
Blasing, Randy
 Horse.
Blauner, Laurie
 Billiards.
Blaustein, Rachel
 His Wife.
Blazek, Douglas
 Eichmann.
 Greed.
 My Definition of Poetry.
Blenkhorn, Ada
 The Heavenly Stranger.
Blessing, Richard
 The Eagle.
Blewett, Jean
 At Quebec.
Blicher, Steen Steensen
 The Heather.
Blight, John
 Becalmed.
 The Cat-o-Nine-Tails.
 The Coral Reef.
 Cormorants.
 Crab.
 Death of a Whale.
 Down from the Country.
 Evolution.
 The Gate's Open.
 The Letter.
 Mangrove.
 Morgan.
 The Oyster-Eaters.
 Pearl Perch.
 Stonefish and Starfish.
 Tenant at Number 9.
Blind, Mathilde
 The After-Glow.
 April Rain.
 Dare Quam Accipere.
 The Dead.
 Hymn to Horus.
 Internal Firesides.
 Lassitude.
 Love in Exile.
 Manchester by Night.
 Mourning Women.
 On a Forsaken Lark's Nest.
 Reapers.
 Rest.
 The Sakiyeh.

Soul-Drift.
 The Sower.
Blishen, Edward
 Abroad Thoughts.
Bliss, H. W.
 Understanding.
Bliss, Philip
 Almost Persuaded.
 Hold the Fort.
Blitzstein, Marc
 Art for Art's Sake.
Bliven, Bruce
 Not Lost in the Stars.
Blixen, Karen See "**Dinesen,
 Isak**"
Bloch, Alice
 Six Years.
Bloch, Chana
 The Converts.
 The Death of the Bronx.
 Deer in the Bush.
 Exile.
 Furniture.
 Goodbye.
 A Life.
 Noah.
 Paradise.
 The Sacrifice.
 Yom Kippur.
Bloch, Jean-Richard
 Idea of a Swimmer.
Block, Allan
 Causeway.
Block, Louis James
 Fate.
 The Final Struggle.
 The Garden Where There is
 No Winter.
 Tuberose.
 Work.
Block, Ron
 Ballade of the Back Road.
Blockcolski, Lew
 The 49 Stomp.
 After the First Frost.
 The Flicker.
 The Flint Hills.
 Indian Love Song.
 Langston Hughes.
 My Dream.
 Peyote Vision.
 Playing Pocahontas.
 Powwow Remnants.
 Reservation Special.
 The Urban Experience.
 Wisga.
 The Woyi.
Blocklyn, Paul
 The Days.
Blodgett, E. D.
 Fossil.
 Snails.
Bloede, Gertrude
 My Father's Child.
 Night after Night.
 Soul, Wherefore Fret Thee?
Blok, Alexander
 Dances of Death.
 I Planted My Bright Paradise.
 Little Catkins.
 A Red Glow in the Sky.
 Russia.
 The Scythians.
 She Came out of the Frost.
 The Twelve.
Blood, Henry Ames
 Comrades.
 Shakespeare.
Bloom, Barbara
 From the Ice Age.
Bloomfield, Robert
 The Coracle Fishers.

The Farmer's Boy.
Meandering Wye.
Moonlight...Scattered Clouds.
Shooter's Hill.

Blossom, Henry
Because You're You.
Kiss Me again.
The Streets of New York.

Blount, Charles
A Dialogue between King William and the Late King James...

Blount, Edward Augustus, Jr.
A Crew Poem.

Blount, Roy, Jr.
Against Broccoli.
For the Record.
Gryll's State.
Limerick: "A certain old party of Moultrie."
Limerick: "A hearty old cook of Lithonia."
Limerick: "A lady track star from Toccoa."
Limerick: "A vigorous matron of Baxter."

Blouz, Hovhannes
The Caravan.

Blue Cloud, Peter
Composition.
Coyote, Coyote, Please Tell Me.
Death Chant.
Dogwood Blossoms.
Elderberry Flute Song.
Hawk Nailed to a Barn Door.
Sweat Song.
To-ta Ti-om.
Untitled.
Wolf.

Blue-Swartz, Janice
Return to Prinsengracht.

Blum, Etta
When You Reach the Hilltop the Sky Is on Top of You.

Blumenthal, Michael C.
Abandoning Your Car in a Snowstorm: Rosslyn, Virginia.
Back from the Word Processing Course, I Say to My Old Typewriter.
The Flirtation.
I Have Lived This Way for Years and Do Not Wish to Change.
In Assisi.
Mushroom Hunting in Late August, Peterborough, N.H.
On the Edge at Santorini.
Squid.
Today I Am Envying the Glorious Mexicans.
Washington Heights, 1959.
Wishful Thinking.

Blumenthal, Walter Hart
Da Silva Gives the Cue.

Blumenthal-Weiss, I.
A Jewish Child Prays to Jesus.

Blumgarten (Yehoash), Solomon
Angelus.
An Old Song.

Blumstein, Rachel *See "Rachel"*

Blundell of Crosby, William
England's Prayer.

Blunden, Edmund Charles
1916 Seen from 1921.
Almswomen.
At the Great Wall of China.
The Barn.
Behind the Line.

Bleue Maison.
The Cottage at Chigasaki.
A Country God.
Departure.
Eastern Tempest.
Festubert: The Old German Line.
Forefathers.
The Giant Puffball.
The Gods of the Earth Beneath.
Les Halles d'Ypres.
The Hurrying Brook.
In Festubert.
An Infantryman.
Into the Salient.
Late Light.
Lonely Love.
The March Bee.
The May Day Garland.
The Memory of Kent.
The Midnight Skaters.
Mole Catcher.
The New Moon.
Old Homes.
The Pike.
The Poor Man's Pig.
A Psalm.
The Recovery.
Reliques.
Report on Experience.
Sheepbells.
Sheet Lightning.
Shepherd.
The Sighing Time.
The Sunlit Vale.
The Survival.
Thiepval Wood.
Thoughts of Thomas Hardy.
Threshold.
Trees on the Calais Road.
Two Voices.
Uneasy Peace.
The Veteran.
A View of the Present State of Ireland.
Vlamertinghe: Passing the Chateau.
The Waggoner.
What Is Winter?
Wild Cherry Tree.
Winter: East Anglia.
Zillebeke Brook.
The Zonnebeke Road.

Blunt, Hugh Francis
What No Man Knoweth.

Blunt, Wilfrid Scawen
As to His Choice of Her.
Depreciating Her Beauty.
The Desolate City.
Esther.
The Falcon.
Farewell to Juliet.
Fear Has Cast Out Love.
Gibraltar.
He Has Fallen from the Height of His Love.
Honour Dishonoured.
How Shall I Build.
An Idler's Calendar: January.
In Answer to a Question.
In Vinculis: The Deeds That Might Have Been.
Joy's Treachery.
The Mockery of Life.
A Nocturne.
The Oasis of Sidi Khaled.
The Old Squire.
On the Nature of Love.
The Pleasures of Love.
The Same Continued.
The Sinner-Saint.

Song: "Oh fly not, Pleasure, pleasant-hearted Pleasure."
St. Valentine's Day.
A Storm in Summer.
To a Happy Warrior.
To Manon.
To Manon, Comparing Her to a Falcon.
To Manon, on His Fortune in Loving Her.
To One on Her Waste of Time.
To One Who Would Make a Confession.
The Wisdom of Merlyn.
Written at Florence.

Bluwstein, Rachel
Kinnereth.

Bly, Robert
After Drinking All Night with a Friend...
After Long Busyness.
After the Industrial Revolution, All Things Happen at Once.
After Working.
Afternoon Sleep.
Andrew Jackson's Speech.
Asian Peace Offers Rejected without Publication.
At a March against the Vietnam War.
At Mid-Ocean.
At the Funeral of Great-Aunt Mary.
August Rain.
Awakening.
Barnfire during Church.
Black Pony Eating Grass.
A Busy Man Speaks.
Christmas Eve Service at Midnight at St. Michael's.
The Clear Air of October.
Come with Me.
Counting Small-Boned Bodies.
The Dead Seal near McClure's Beach.
Depression.
A Dream of Suffocation.
Driving through Minnesota during the Hanoi Bombings.
Driving to Town Late to Mail a Letter.
Driving toward the Lac Qui Parle River.
Ducks.
Evolution from the Fish.
The Executive's Death.
Fishing on a Lake at Night.
For My Son Noah, Ten Years Old.
Getting Up Early.
The Great Society.
Hatred of Men with Black Hair.
Hearing Men Shout at Night on MacDougal Street.
A Hollow Tree.
Hunting Pheasants in a Cornfield.
Hurrying away from the Earth.
In a Mountain Cabin in Norway.
In a Train.
Johnson's Cabinet Watched by Ants.
Late at Night during a Visit of Friends.
A Late Spring Day in My Life.
Laziness and Silence.

Leonardo's Secret.
A Long Walk before the Snows Began.
Looking at a Dead Wren in My Hand.
Looking at a Dry Canadian Thistle Brought in from the Snow.
Looking at New-Fallen Snow from a Train.
Looking at Some Flowers.
Looking into a Face.
Looking into a Tide Pool.
Love Poem.
The Man Whom the Sea Kept Awake.
Melancholia.
A Missouri Traveller Writes Home: 1830.
Mourning Pablo Neruda.
My Father's Wedding 1924.
Night.
November Day at McClure's.
Old Boards.
The Origin of the Praise of God.
Poem against the British.
Poem against the Rich.
Poem in Three Parts.
The Possibility of New Poetry.
The Puritan on His Honeymoon.
Reading in Fall Rain.
Romans Angry about the Inner World.
Shack Poem.
Silence.
Six Winter Privacy Poems.
Sleet Storm on the Merritt Parkway.
A Small Bird's Nest Made of White Reed Fiber.
Snowbanks North of the House.
Snowfall in the Afternoon.
Solitude Late at Night in the Woods.
Summer, 1960, Minnesota.
Sunday in Glastonbury.
Surprised by Evening.
The Teeth Mother Naked at Last.
Thinking of "The Autumn Fields."
Those Being Eaten by America.
Three Presidents: Andrew Jackson.
Three Presidents: John F. Kennedy.
Three Presidents: Theodore Roosevelt.
Turning away from Lies.
Visiting Emily Dickinson's Grave with Robert Francis.
Waking from Sleep.
War and Silence.
Watching Television.
Water under the Earth.
Watering the Horse.
When the Dumb Speak.
Where We Must Look for Help.
Written Forty Miles South of a Spreading City.
Written in Dejection near Rome.

Blyton, Carey
The Manatee.

Boake, Barcroft Henry
An Allegory.
At Devlin's Siding.

The Digger's Song.
Where the Dead Men Lie.
Boas, Guy
The Underground.
The Vet.
Bobango, Gerald
The Educational
Administration Professor's
Prayer.
Boccaccio, Giovanni
Apology for Love.
Fiammetta.
The Queen of the Angels.
A Tribute to Dante.
Bock, Frederick
Aubade: The Desert.
Big, Fat Summer–and the
Lean and Hard.
A Return from the Wars.
Bode, John E.
To the End.
Bodecker, N. M.
The Island of Yorrick.
Miss Bitter.
Mr 'Gater.
Bodenheim, Maxwell
Advice to a Blue-Bird.
Advice to a Forest.
City Girl.
Death.
Forgetfulness.
Here Is Your Realism.
Hill-Side Tree.
Interlude.
Jack Rose.
Lynched Negro.
Metaphysical Poem.
Minna.
Negroes.
New York City.
Poem: "O men, walk on the
hills."
Poem to Negro and Whites.
Poet to His Love.
Rear Porches of an
Apartment Building.
Soldiers.
To an Enemy.
Upper Family.
Bodker, Cecil
Calendar.
Fury's Field.
Self-Portrait.
Boer, James Den
Spring in Washington.
Boethius
The Consolation of
Philosophy.
O Thou Whose Pow'r.
This Discord in the Pact of
Things.
Bogan, Jim
The Discriminations: Virtuous
Amusements and Wicked
Demons.
Bogan, Louise
After the Persian.
The Alchemist.
Animal, Vegetable and
Mineral.
Baroque Comment.
Betrothed.
Cartography.
Cassandra.
The Changed Woman.
Chanson un Peu Naive.
Come, Break with Time.
The Crossed Apple.
The Crows.
The Daemon.
Decoration.
The Dragonfly.

The Dream.
Evening in the Sanitarium.
Exhortation.
Fiend's Weather.
The Frightened Man.
Henceforth, from the Mind.
Hypocrite Swift.
I Saw Eternity.
Juan's Song.
July Dawn.
Knowledge.
Last Hill in a Vista.
Late.
M., Singing.
Man Alone.
March Twilight.
The Mark.
Masked Woman's Song.
Medusa.
The Meeting.
Men Loved Wholly Beyond
Wisdom.
Musician.
Night.
Old Countryside.
Packet of Letters.
Portrait.
Putting to Sea.
Question in a Field.
Roman Fountain.
Several Voices out of a Cloud.
Simple Autumnal.
Single Sonnet.
The Sleeping Fury.
Song for a Lyre.
Song for a Slight Voice.
Song for the Last Act.
Spirit's Song.
Statue and Birds.
Summer Wish.
To an Artist, to Take Heart.
To Be Sung on the Water.
To My Brother.
Train Tune.
Variation on a Sentence.
Winter Swan.
Women.
Zone.
Bogardus, Edgar
Eastward to Eden.
Bogart, Elizabeth
He Came Too Late.
Bogin, George
Abraham.
Alone in the House.
Troopship for France, War II.
The Visitor.
Bogle, Eric
The Band Played Waltzing
Matilda.
No Man's Land.
Now I'm Easy.
Bohanan, Otto Leland
The Dawn's Awake!
The Washer-Woman.
Boiarski, Phil
Still Wrestling.
Boileau-Despreaux, Nicholas
L'Art poetique.
Satires.
Boilleau, Joan
I Saw a Ghost.
Boimwall, Rachel
At Night.
Diaspora Jews.
Lifelong.
Round.
Boker, George Henry
The Battle of Lookout
Mountain.
Before Vicksburg.
The Black Regiment.

Countess Laura.
The Crossing at
Fredericksburg.
The Cruise of the Monitor.
Dirge for a Soldier.
The Ferry.
God to Thee We Humbly
Bow.
Hooker's Across.
Lincoln.
On Board the Cumberland.
Sonnets: A Sequence on
Profane Love.
To England.
To My Lady.
Upon the Hill before
Centreville.
The Varuna.
Zagonyi.
Boland, Eavan
Athene's Song.
Child of Our Time.
The Famine Road.
New Territory.
Song: "Where in blind files."
The War Horse.
Boland, Patrick
Mandala.
Bold, Alan
Graffiti.
The Malfeasance.
That's Life?
Bold, Henry
Song: "Chloris, forbear a
while."
Song: "Fire, fire."
Boleyn, Anne
O Death, Rock Me Asleep.
Boleyn, George
O Death, Rock Me Asleep.
Bolles, Matthew
Here, Lord, Retired, I Bow in
Prayer.
Bolton, Edmund
A Carol.
A Palinode.
To Favonius.
Bolton, Sarah Knowles
The Inevitable.
Paddle Your Own Canoe.
Bolz, Jody
Migration as a Passage in
Time.
Bomze, Nahum
City of Light.
Pshytik.
Bonar, Horatius
Abide with Us.
Be True.
Beyond the Smiling and the
Weeping.
Bless the Blessed Morn.
Blessing, and Honor.
Christ Is All.
Cross and Throne.
The Fairest He.
The First and the Last.
He Liveth Long Who Liveth
Well.
He Took My Place.
His Glory Tell.
How We Learn.
I Heard the Voice of Jesus
Say.
I Lay My Sines on Jesus.
I Was a Wandering Sheep.
It Is Finished.
Lost But Found.
Love Is of God.
The Master's Touch.
More of Thee.
My Prayer.

The Same Forever.
This Do in Remembrance of
Me.
Thy Way, Not Mine.
The Voice from Galilee.
The Work That Saves!
Bonaventure, Saint
Adeste Fideles.
Psalter of the Blessed Virgin
Mary.
Boncho
Haiku: "The long, long river."
Bond, Carrie Jacobs
I Love You Truly.
A Perfect Day.
Bond, Harold
The Glove.
Letters from Birmingham.
Swallowing.
Bond, Julian
The Bishop of Atlanta: Ray
Charles.
Habana.
Look at That Gal.
Rotation.
Bone, Edith
On Myself.
Bone, Florence
A Prayer for a Little Home.
Bonefonius
All Those I Love Die Young.
Boner, John Henry
The Light'ood Fire.
Poe's Cottage at Fordham.
Remembrance.
We Walked among the
Whispering Pines.
Bonham, Thomas
In Praise of Ale.
Bonn, John Louis
Madonna: 1936.
Bonnell, Otto
The Cat Came Back.
Bontemps, Arna
A Black Man Talks of
Reaping.
Blight.
Close Your Eyes!
Dark Girl.
The Daybreakers.
Gethsemane.
God Give to Men.
Golgotha Is a Mountain.
Homing.
Idolatry.
Lancelot.
Length of Moon.
Miracles.
Nocturne at Bethesda.
Nocturne of the Wharves.
A Note of Humility.
Reconnaissance.
The Return.
Southern Mansion.
To a Young Girl Leaving the
Hill Country.
A Tree Design.
Boodson, Alison
Carol: "Fire is what's precious
now..."
Night Alert.
Poem: "He lying spilt like
water from a bowl."
Poem: "I do not want to be
your weeping woman."
Book of the Dead
Adoration of the Disk by
King Akhn-Aten and
Princess Nefer Neferiu..
The Dead Man Ariseth and
Singeth a Hymn to the Sun.

He Approacheth the Hall of
Judgment.
He Asketh Absolution of
God.
He Biddeth Osiris to Arise
from the Dead.
He Cometh Forth into the
Day.
He Commandeth a Fair Wind.
He Defendeth His Heart
against the Destroyer.
He Embarketh in the Boat of
Ra.
He Entereth the House of the
Goddess Hathor.
He Establisheth His Triumph.
He Holdeth Fast to the
Memory of His Identity.
He Is Declared True of Word.
He Is Like the Lotus.
He Is Like the Serpent Saka.
He Kindleth a Fire.
He Knoweth the Souls of the
East.
He Maketh Himself One with
Osiris.
He Maketh Himself One with
the God Ra.
He Maketh Himself One with
the Only God, Whose Limbs
Are the Many God.
He Overcometh the Serpent of
Evil in the Name of Ra.
He Prayeth for Ink and
Palette That He May Write.
He Singeth a Hymn to Osiris,
the Lord of Eternity.
He Singeth in the
Underworld.
He Walketh by Day.
The Other World.
Booker, Betty
David in April.
Booker, Stephen Todd
Flash.
Look away/Look away.
Lynched.
No Fig.
Paperweight Escape.
Booth, Barton
Song: "Sweet are the Charms
of her I love."
Booth, Eva Gore
Crucifixion.
Harvest.
Booth, Philip
Adam.
Animal Fair.
Barred Islands.
Big Dog.
Catwise.
Cold Water Flat.
The Countershadow.
Crossing.
Crows.
The Day the Tide.
Deer Isle.
Dreamscape.
Ego.
Elegy for a Diver.
First Lesson.
Fisherman.
Great Farm.
Green Song.
Hard Country.
Heron.
How to See Deer.
If It Comes.
The Incredible Yachts.
Instruction in the Art.
Jake's Wharf.
A Late Spring: Eastport.

Lines from an Orchard Once
Surveyed by Thoreau.
Maine.
Marin.
The Misery of Mechanics.
Nightsong.
North.
Offshore.
Old Man.
One Man's Wife.
Photographer.
The Round.
Rout.
Seeing Auden off.
Siasconset Song.
Stove.
Thanksgiving.
These Men.
The Tower.
Twelfth Night.
Vermont: Indian Summer.
Was a Man.
The Wilding.
Boothby, Sir Brooke
Sonnet on Life.
Boothroyd, John Basil
And Now...
Best of Two Worlds.
Holy Order.
Please Excuse Typing.
Sanctuary.
Borawski, Walta
Normal as Two Ships in the
Night.
Borenstein, Emily
Grandfather Yoneh.
Life of the Letters.
Borges, Jorge Luis
Afterglow.
The Dagger.
Hengest Cyning.
Ode Written in 1966.
Plainness.
Things That Might Have
Been.
Borgese, Giuseppe Antonio
Dream of a Decent Death.
Easter Sunday, 1945.
Borie, Lysbeth Boyd
Five-in-June.
Five Years Old.
GraceAnAnne.
Boring, Mollie
September Butterfly.
Borregaard, Ebbe
Each Found Himself at the
End of...
Some Stories of the Beauty
Wapiti.
Borrell, D. E.
Another Death.
Borson, Roo
Abundance.
Flowers.
Gray Glove.
In the Cafe.
Jacaranda.
Just before Dawn.
Now and Again.
October, Hanson's Field.
Talk.
This Is the Last Night.
The Transparence of
November.
Borst, Terry
Random Wheels,.
Borthwick, Jane
Light Shining Out of
Darkness.
Borum, Memphis Willie
Bad Girl Blues.

Boscan, Juan
The Quarry.
Bose, Buddhadeva
The Burden of Everyday.
Bosman, Herman Charles
Learning Destiny.
Old I Am.
Seed.
Bossert, Shirley
At Arm's Length.
Bossidy, John Collins
Boston.
A Boston Toast.
Bost, Marcia Inzer
Mountain Born.
Bostwick, Grace G.
Pep.
Bostwick, Helen Barron
Little Dandelion.
Boswell, Arthur
Roughchin, the Pirate.
Boswell, James
Journal of a Tour through the
Courts of Germany (excerpt).
Boswell, Margie B.
The Texas Ranger.
Bosworth, Martha
Angle of Vision.
Botrel, Theodore
Little Gregory.
Botsford, S. B.
Sonneteering Made Easy.
Bottomley, Gordon
"L'Apparition" of Gustave
Moreau.
Blanid's Song.
Dawn.
Eager Spring.
The End of the World.
A Hymn of Form.
A Hymn of Touch.
Netted Strawberries.
L'Oiseau Bleu.
Suilven and the Eagle
(excerpt).
To Iron-Founders and Others.
Bottoms, David
Coasting toward Midnight at
the Southeastern Fair.
The Copperhead.
The Desk.
Faith Healer Come to Rabun
County.
In a U-Haul North of
Damascus.
In the Black Camaro.
Sign for My Father, Who
Stressed the Bunt.
Stumptown Attends the
Picture Show.
The Traveler.
Under the Boathouse.
Wrestling Angels.
Writing on Napkins at the
Sunshine Club Macon,
Georgia 1971.
Bottrall, Ronald
Darkened Windows.
Icarus.
Mating Answer.
Proserpine at Enna.
Rondeau: "Homage to change
that scatters the poppy seed."
Botwood, Edward
Hot Stuff.
Bouflers, Marquise de
An A B C for Grown
Gentlemen.
Boulton, Harold
All through the Night.
Boumi-Pappas, Rita
The Crow.

Boundy, Rex
A Virile Christ.
Boundzekei-Dongala, Emmanuel
Fantasy Under the Moon.
Bourdillon, Francis William
Aucassin and Nicolete.
Eurydice.
A Lost God (excerpt).
The night has a thousand
eyes.
A Violinist.
Where Runs the River?
Bourinot, Arthur Stanley
Dark Flows the River.
Johnny Appleseed.
A Legend of Paul Bunyan.
Nicolas Gatineau.
Only Silence.
Snow Anthology.
Sonnets to My Mother.
Tom Thomson.
What Far Kingdom.
Winter Sketch.
Bourke, Sharon
Sopranosound, Memory of
John.
Bourne, David
Parachute Descent.
Bourne, Nina
Where the Single Men Go in
Summer.
Bourne, Vincent
The Cricket.
The Housekeeper.
The Snail.
Bouvard, Marguerite
White.
Bouve, Thomas Tracy
The Shannon and the
Chesapeake.
Bovshover, Joseph
To the Laggards.
Bowden, James H.
At the Spa.
Bowden, Samuel
The Paper Kite (excerpt).
Bowditch, Nathaniel Ingersoll
A World Beyond.
Bowen, Charles, Baron
The rain it raineth on the just.
Bowen, Donna
The Little Searcher.
Bowen, Edward Ernest
Forty Years On.
Shemuel.
Bowen, James K.
The Edge.
Bowering, George
The Beach at Veracruz.
Circus Maximus.
Dobbin.
The Egg.
The Envies.
Grandfather.
Grass, Grass.
The House.
In the Forest.
My Atlas Poet.
Smoking Drugs with
Strangers.
Solid Mountain.
Summer Solstice.
Under.
Winter's Dregs.
Bowering, Marilyn
And If I Turn.
The Journey of the Suicides.
Love Poem for Lin Fan.
Part Winter.
Peter Rabbit Sex Poem.
Russian Asylum.
Seeing Oloalok.

St. Augustine's Pear Tree.
Wishing Africa.

Bowers, Edgar
Adam's Song to Heaven.
Aix-la-Chappelle, 1945.
The Astronomers of Mont
Blanc.
The Centaur Overheard.
Dark Earth and Summer.
From William Tyndale to
John Frith.
Grove and Building.
The Mirror.
The Mountain Cemetery.
The Prince.
Le Reve.
The Stoic: for Laura von
Courten.
To the Contemporary Muse.
Two Poems on the Catholic
Bavarians.
The Virgin Mary.
The Wise Men.

Bowers, Neal
Archetypes.
Unplanned Design.

Bowie, Beverly
To My New Mistress.

Bowie, Walter Russell
God of the Nations.
O Holy City Seen of John.

Bowie, William C.
Before the Statue of a
Laughing Man.

Bowker, Richard Rogers.
Thomas a Kempis.

Bowker, Tom
Eagle.

Bowles, Paul Frederic
Extract.

Bowles, William Lisle
At Dover Cliffs, July 20,
1787.
The Butterfly and the Bee.
An Egyptian Tomb.
Hope.
Sonnet at Dover Cliffs.
Sonnet. At Ostend, July 22,
1787.
Sonnet: "Evening, as slow thy
placid shades descend."
Sonnet: "O Time! who
know'st a lenient hand to
lay."
Time and Grief.
To the River Itchin, near
Winton.

Bowman, Gladys M.
Only One Life.

Bowman, Louise Hollingsworth
The Quiet Hour.

Bowman, Louise Morey
Sea Lavender.
She Plans Her Funeral.

Bowman, P. C.
Homing.
Route 95 North: New Jersey.

Bowndheri, Ilmi
As Camels Who Have Become
Thirsty...The Poet's Lament.

Bowring, John
God Is Love.
Towering O'er the Wrecks of
Time.
Watchman, Tell us of the
Night.

Bowsher, Kathryn
Thy Nail-Pierced Hands.

Bowsher, Kathryn T.
My Hiding Place.

Box, Earl Gene
Aunt Beulah's Wisdom.

Butch Is Back.
Midwife.
Old Man Con.
Trash.

Boyajian, Aram
American Commencement.
Blok Let Me Learn the Poem.
The Death of the Epileptic
Poet Yesenin.
George Washington Goes to a
Girlie Movie.
The Hairs in My Nose.
Poetry Is in the Darkness.
The World Is Really a
Sugarplum House in the
Forest.

Boyars, Arthur
Initial.

Boyd, Bruce
Sanctuary.
This Is What the Watchbird
Sings, Who Perches in the
Lovetree.
Venice Recalled.

Boyd, Marion M.
To One Older.
White Dusk.

Boyd, Mark Alexander
Fra Bank to Bank.

Boyd, Melba Joyce
Beer Drops.
Sunflowers and Saturdays.
Why?

Boyd, Nancy
I Like Americans.

Boyd, Thomas
The Heath.
The King's Son.
Love on the Mountain.
To the Leanan Shee.

Boyden, Polly Chase
Mud.
New Mexico.

Boye, Karin
A Dedication.
A Sword.

Boyer, Jill Witherspoon
Detroit City.
Dream Farmer.
King Lives.
When Brothers Forget.

Boyeson, Hjalmar Hjorth
Thoralf and Synnov.

Boyle, Kay
A Communication to Nancy
Cunard.
Flying Foxes and Others.
For James Baldwin.
For Marianne Moore's
Birthday.
Funeral in Hungary.
The Invitation in It.
Monody to the Sound of
Zithers.
To a Seaman Dead on Land.

Boyle, Sarah Roberts
The Voice of the Grass.

Boyle, Virginia Frazer
I Know That My Redeemer
Liveth.
Tennessee.

Boynton, H. W.
The Golfer's Rubaiyat
(parody).

Bozanic, Nick
The Crane's Ascent.

Brabant, Suzanne
Morgans in October.
Two at Showtime.

Brabazon, Francis
Victoria Market.

Bracey, Ishman
Leaving Town Blues.
Saturday Blues.

Bracken, Thomas
Not Understood.

Bracker, Milton
Limerick: "An unusual thing
called a Troupial."
P Is for Paleontology.
The Umpire.
Where, O Where?

Brackett, Anna Callender
Benedicite.
In Hades.

Bradbury, Bianca
Nor'Easter.

Bradby, Godfrey Fox
In Hoc Signo.

Bradby, H. C.
Comfort for the Sleepless.

Bradford, Gamaliel
Ardor.
Exit God.
God.
Hope.
My Delight.

Bradford, William
And Truly It Is a Most
Glorious Thing.
Epitaphium Meum.
New England's Growth.
Of Boston in New England.
A Word to New England.

Bradley, Edward *See* "Bede,
Cuthbert"

Bradley, George
In Bed with a River.
Swing One, Swing All.

Bradley, Katherine *See* "Field,
Michael"

Bradley, Mary Emily
Beyond Recall.
A Chrysalis.
In Death.
A Spray of Honeysuckle.

Bradley, Sam
Casual Meeting.

Bradley, William Aspenwall
To Little Renee on First
Seeing Her Lying in Her
Cradle.

Bradstreet, Anne
Another.
Another Letter to Her
Husband, Absent upon
Publick Employment.
As Spring the Winter Doth
Succeed.
As Weary Pilgrim, Now at
Rest.
The Author to Her Book.
Before the Birth of One of
Her Children.
Childhood.
Contemplations.
Deliverance from a Fit of
Fainting.
The Flesh and the Spirit.
The Four Seasons of the Year.
Four Seasons of the Year:
Spring.
In Honour of That High and
Mighty Princess Queen
Elizabeth...
In Memory of My Dear
Grandchild Elizabeth
Bradstreet.
In Reference to Her Children,
23. June, 1656.
In Thankful Remembrance
for My Dear Husband's Safe
Arrivall....

A Letter to Her Husband,
Absent upon Public
Employment.
O Thou Most High Who
Rulest All.
On My Dear Grand-Child
Simon Bradstreet...
The Prologue.
Some Verses Upon the
Burning of Our House, July
10th, 1666.
To My Dear and Loving
Husband.
The Vanity of All Worldly
Things.

Bradstreet, Samuel
An Almanack for the Year of
Our Lord, 1657.

Brady, Charles A.
Dimidium Animae Meae.

Brady, Edwin James
A Ballad of the Captains.
A Capstan Chantey.
The Coachman's Yarn.
Lost and Given Over.
The Whaler's Pig.

Brady, George M.
The Autumn House.
The Day.
The Garden.
The Generations.
The Hosts.
Land-Fall.
Old Michael.
The Settled Men.

Brady, June
Far Trek.

**Brady, Nicholas and Nahum
Tate**
Lord, Who's the Happy Man.

Bragdon, Claude
The Point, the Line, the
Surface and Sphere.

Bragg, Linda Brown
Our Blackness Did Not Come
to Us Whole.
A Poem about Beauty,
Blackness, Poetry.

Brainard, E. M.
Compensation.

Brainard, John Gardiner Calkins
The Captain.
The Deep.
The Fall of Niagara.
I Saw Two Clouds at
Morning.
Mr. Merry's Lament for
"Long Tom".
On the Death of Commodore
Oliver H. Perry.
Sonnet to the Sea Serpent.
Stanzas.
To Thee, O God, the
Shepherd Kings.

Brainard, Mary Gardiner
Not Knowing.

Braisted, Harry
She Was Bred in Old
Kentucky.
You're Not the Only Pebble
on the Beach.

Braithwaite, William Stanley
Del Cascar.
Golden Moonrise.
The House of Falling Leaves.
Hymn for the Slain in Battle.
I Am Glad Daylong.
If I Could Touch.
In a Grave-Yard.
Ironic:LL.D.
It's a Long Way.
October XXIX, 1795.

Rhapsody.
Rye Bread.
Sandy Star.
Scintilla.
Sea Lyric.
Sic Vita.
To —.
Turn Me to My Yellow
  Leaves.
Twenty Stars to Match His
  Face.
Two Questions.
The Watchers.
White Magic: An Ode.
Braley, Berton
Business Is Business.
Do It Now.
The Hills.
Limerick: "Said a fellow from
  North Philadelphia."
Limerick: "When twins came,
  their father, Dan Dunn."
Loyalty.
Opportunity.
A Prayer.
Start Where You Stand.
That's Success!
The Thinker.
Bramston, James
The Art of Politics.
The Man of Taste.
Time's Changes.
Branch, Anna Hempstead
Ere the Golden Bowl is
  Broken.
Grieve Not, Ladies.
I Think of Him as One Who
  Fights.
Mathematics or the Gift of
  Tongues.
The Monk in the Kitchen.
A Song for My Mother–Her
  Hands.
A Song for My Mother–Her
  Stories.
A Song for My Mother–Her
  Words.
To a New York Shop-Girl
  Dressed for Sunday.
An Unbeliever.
The Warrior Maid.
Branch, Mary Bolles
The Petrified Fern.
The Petrified Leaf.
Schmaltzenor.
Brand, Millen
All One.
Clausa Germanis Gallia.
The Last Families in the
  Cabins.
Longing for the Persimmon
  Tree.
Lost.
Thirty Childbirths.
Brandi, John
How to Get to New Mexico.
Brandling, Charles
To a Lady, with a Present of
  a Fan.
Brant, Beth
For all my Grandmothers.
Native Origin.
Ride the Turtle's Back.
Brant, LeRoy V.
Green Plumes of Royal
  Palms.
Oh, Day of Days.
Brantingham, Philip
Sarentino–South Tyrol.
Brasch, Charles
Crossing the Straits.
The Discovery.

The Estate: "Waking by
  Night".
Henley on Taieri.
I Think of Your Generation.
In Memory of Robin Hyde,
  1906-39.
Night Cries, Wakari Hospital.
On Mt. Iron.
Poland, October.
Tempora Mutantur.
The View of Rangitoto.
Watch-Dog.
The Way up Is the Way
  down.
Winter Anemones.
A Word to Peter Olds.
Brasfield, James
The Stringer.
Brasfield, Philip
Censorship.
Inebriates.
An Interview.
Rune.
Trouble.
Brashers, Charles
Poem after a Speech by Chief
  Seattle, 1855.
Brasier, Virginia
Primer of Consequences.
Psychological Prediction.
Song for a Lost Art.
Time of the Mad Atom.
Brass, Perry
I Think the New Teacher's a
  Queer.
Brathwaite, Edward Kamau
Cherries: "So when the
  hammers of the witnesses of
  heaven.."
Brathwaite, Richard
The Nightingale.
A Strappado for the Devil: Of
  Maids' Inconstancy.
Braude, Michael
Curtain Speech.
Braun, Richard Emil
Domestic Duties.
Goose.
Niagara.
Brautigan, Richard
All Watched over by
  Machines of Loving Grace.
The Day They Busted the
  Grateful Dead.
Gee, You're So Beautiful That
  It's Starting to Rain.
Haiku Ambulance.
In a Cafe.
Late Starting Dawn.
Brawley, Benjamin
Chaucer.
My Hero.
Braxton, Jodi
Sometimes I Think of
  Maryland...
Bray, J. J.
The Execution of Madame du
  Barry.
Braybrooke
Memoria Technica for the
  Books of the Bible.
Brazelton, Ethel M. C.
Poor Lil' Brack Sheep.
Brecht, Bertolt
The Burning of Books.
Children's Crusade, 1939.
Coal for Mike.
Difficult Times.
The First Psalm.
The God of War.
In Memory of Marie A.

Of Swimming in Lakes and
  Rivers.
Time's Mutability.
The Wheel Change.
Breck, Mrs. Frank A.
A Christmas Thought.
They Two.
Breed, Eleanor D.
Scapegoats.
Breeser, Bettye
Nature at Three.
Bregy, Katherine
I Thirst...
The Maid.
Bremser, Ray
Blood.
Poem of Holy Madness, IV.
Brenan, Gerald
My Sailor of Seven.
Brenan, Joseph
Come to Me, Dearest.
Brennan, Christopher John
Because She Would Ask Me
  Why I Loved Her.
Come Out, Come Out, Ye
  Souls That Serve.
I Cry to You as I Pass Your
  Windows.
I Saw My Life as Whitest
  Flame.
Interlude: The Casement.
Lilith: Adam to Lilith.
Lilith on the Fate of Man.
Lilith: The Anguish'd Doubt
  Broods over Eden.
My Heart Was Wandering.
O Desolate Eves.
Pauca Mea: I Said, This
  Misery Must End.
The Quest of Silence: Fire in
  the Heavens, and Fire Along
  the Hills.
Sweet Silence after Bells!
Towards the Source: Let Us
  Go Down, the Long Dead
  Night Is Done.
The Twilight of Disquietude:
  The Years That Go to Make
  Me Man.
The Wanderer.
We Woke Together.
What Do I Know?
Brennan, Eileen
Evening on Howth Head.
May Evening.
One Kingfisher and One
  Yellow Rose.
Thoughts at the Museum.
Brennan, Gerald
The Mornin's Mornin'.
Brennan, J. Keirn
Let the Rest of the World Go
  By.
Brennan, John Michael
Air Is.
Brennan, Joseph Payne
The Cat!
Raccoon on the Road.
Brennan, Matthew
Noon Glare.
Seeing in the Dark.
Brenner, Summer
Fata Morgana.
Natural Selection.
Brent, Hally Carrington
I Think I Know No Finer
  Things Than Dogs.
Brentano, Clemens
Bridal Song.
Prelude.
Brereton, John Le Gay
Buffalo Creek.

Cling to Me.
Unborn.
Bretherton, C. H.
In Winter.
Breton, Andre
Dreams.
Freedom of Love.
Postman Cheval.
The Spectral Attitudes.
Sunflower.
Breton, Nicholas
Aglaia.
An Assurance.
Come, Little Babe.
A Cradle Song.
The Happy Countryman.
His Wisdom.
I have neither plums nor
  cherries.
An Invective Against the
  Wicked of the World.
An Odd Conceit.
Olden Love-Making.
The Passionate Shepherd.
A Pastoral.
Phyllida and Corydon.
Phyllis.
Pretty Twinkling Starry Eyes.
Rare News.
A Report Song in a Dream,
  between a Shepherd and His
  Nymph.
Shepherd and Shepherdess.
A Supplication.
A Sweet Lullaby.
To His Muse.
Upon a Dainty Hill Sometime.
Brett, Peter
Night Teeth.
Pickers.
Brett, Reginald, Viscount Esher
At Swindon.
Brettell, Noel Harry
Autumn Song.
Brew, Kwesi
Ancestral Faces.
The Lonely Traveller.
A Plea for Mercy.
The Search.
Brewer, Ebenezer Cobham
The Signs of the Zodiac.
Brews, Margery
Unto My Valentine.
Brewster, Elizabeth
Anti-Love Poems.
Death by Drowning.
East Coast–Canada.
The Egoist Dead.
Eviction.
Great-Aunt Rebecca.
If I Could Walk out into the
  Cold Country.
In the Library.
Playing the Bones.
The Princess Addresses the
  Frog Prince.
River Song.
Brewster, Martha
The Stately Structure of This
  Earth.
Brice, Andrew
Freedom: A Poem, Written in
  Time of Recess...
Brick, Norman
Of Snow.
Bricuth, John
Song of the Darkness.
"Bridges, Madeline"
Friend and Lover.
Life's Mirror.

Bridges, Matthew
Rise, Glorious Conqueror!
Rise.
Bridges, Robert
The Affliction of Richard.
Angel Spirits of Sleep.
April 1885.
Awake, My Heart.
Cheddar Pinks.
The Cliff-Top.
The Clouds Have Left the
Sky.
Dear Lady, When Thou
Frownest.
Dejection.
Elegy: On a Lady, Whom
Grief for the Death of Her
Betrothed Killed.
Epistle II: To a Socialist in
London.
Eros.
The Evening Darkens Over.
First Spring Morning.
Flycatchers.
For Beauty Being the Best of
All We Know.
Fortunatus Nimium.
Founder's Day.
The Garden in September.
Gheluvelt.
The Growth of Love: O
Weary Pilgrims.
The Hill Pines Were Sighing.
A Hymn of Nature.
I Have Loved Flowers.
I Heard a Linnet Courting.
I Love All Beauteous Things.
I Never Shall Love the Snow
Again.
I Praise the Tender Flower.
I Will Be What God Made
Me, Nor Protest.
I Will Not Let Thee Go.
The Idle Flowers.
The Idle Life I Lead.
Indolence.
James McCosh.
Johannes Milton, Senex.
Laus Deo.
The Linnet.
London Snow.
Long Are the Hours the Sun
Is Above.
Low Barometer.
Melancholia.
Muse and Poet.
My Delight and Thy Delight.
Nightingales.
Nimium Fortunatus.
Noel: Christmas Eve, 1913.
The North Wind Came Up
Yesternight.
North Wind in October.
November.
On a Dead Child.
Our Lady.
The Palm Willow.
A Passer-By.
Pater Filio.
The Philosopher to His
Mistress.
Poor Poll.
The Psalm.
Riding Adown the Country
Lanes.
Say Who Is This with Silvered
Hair.
Screaming Tarn.
Since to Be Loved Endures.
Since We Loved.
The Snow Lies Sprinkled on
the Beach.

So Sweet Love Seemed.
Song: "I love my lady's eyes."
A Song of My Heart.
The South Wind.
Spirits.
Spring Goeth All in White.
Spring Hath Her Own Bright
Days of Calm and Peace.
The Storm Is Over.
The Testament of Beauty.
Thanksgiving Day.
Thou Didst Delight My Eyes.
To the United States of
America.
A Toast to Our Native Land.
Triolet.
The Unillumined Verge.
The Upper Skies Are Palest
Blue.
A Useless Burden upon the
Earth.
A Water-Party.
Weep Not To-Day.
When Death to Either Shall
Come.
When My Love Was Away.
Who Has Not Walked Upon
the Shore.
The Whole World Now Is but
the Minister.
The Winnowers.
Winter Nightfall.
Bridges-Adams, W.
Fragment from the
Elizabethans.
Brierre, Jean
Harlem.
Briggs, Olga Hampel
Brief History.
Brigham, Besmilr
Tell Our Daughters.
The Will's Love.
Bright, Verne
Revelation.
Brigid, Saint
The Feast of Saint Brigid of
Kildare.
The Heavenly Banquet.
Brine, Mary Dow
Hearts and Flowers.
Somebody's Mother.
Bringhurst, Robert
Deuteronomy.
Notes to the Reader.
These Poems, She Said.
Brininstool, Earl Alonzo
Back to Arizona.
The Range Rider's Soliloquy.
The Stampede.
Brinnin, John Malcolm
Angel Eye of Memory.
The Ascension: 1925.
At the Airport.
At the Band Concert.
At the Museum.
Cape Ann: A View.
Carmarthen Bar.
Dachau.
The End of My Sister's
Guggenheim.
Every Earthly Creature.
Flight 539.
Girl in a White Coat.
Heavy Heavy Heavy.
Hotel Paradiso e
Commerciale.
Islands: A Song.
John without Heaven.
Letter from an Island.
Letter to Statues.
Love in Particular.
My Father, My Son.

Nuns at Eve.
Roethke Plain.
Saul, afterward, Riding East.
Skin Diving in the Virgins.
A Thin Facade for Edith
Sitwell.
Views of the Favorite
Colleges.
The Wind Is Ill.
Winter Term.
With a Posthumous Medal.
The Worm in the Whirling
Cross.
Brisby, Stewart
The Artist.
Attica Is.
The Cyclone.
Poem for Edie Sedgwick.
Public School 168.
Brissenden, R. F.
Verandahs.
Walking down Jalan Thamrin.
Bristol, Augusta Cooper
The Pysidanthera.
Bristol, John Digby, Earl of
Grieve Not, Dear Love.
Britt, Alan
After Spending All Day at the
National Museum of Art.
Serenade.
Bro, Margueritte Harmon
Prayer.
Broaddus, Andrew
Help Thy Servant.
Brock, Edwin
Catastrophe.
The Curtain Poem.
Five Ways to Kill a Man.
To His Love in Middle-Age.
To My Mother.
Turn the Key Deftly.
Brock, Van K.
Lying on a Bridge.
The Sea Birds.
Brockerhoff, Hans
Pygmalion.
Brockman, Zoe Kincaid
The Grapevine.
Brod, Max
Goldfish on the Writing Desk.
Hebrew Lesson.
Brode, Anthony
Breakfast with Gerard Manley
Hopkins.
Calypsomania.
Obituary.
Unromantic Song.
Brodey, Jim
Expansion to Aveline's.
From Vice, 1966.
Homeward Bound.
Identikit.
Little Light.
Mswaki.
Noh Play.
Poem.
Poem ("Woke This A.M.").
Rosewood Vision.
To Guillaume Appollinaire.
Vision of Turtle (One).
Brodie, Hugh
A Sergeant's Prayer.
Brodsky, Joseph
Etude.
A Jewish Cemetery Near
Leningrad.
Monument to Pushkin.
Pilgrims.
Six Years Later.
Soho.
To a Tyrant.

Verses on Accepting the
World.
Brodsky, Louis Daniel
Ancestry.
Buffalo.
Death Comes to the Salesman.
My Flying Machine.
Sitting in Bib Overalls,
Workshirt, Boots on the
Monument to Liberty.
Weeding in January.
Brody, Alter
The Cry of the Peoples.
A Family Album.
Ghetto Twilight.
Lamentations.
Broker, George Henry
The Ballad of New Orleans.
Broley, Jim
Poem, to Jane Wilson on
Television.
Brome, Alexander
The Anti-Politician.
The Contrary.
The Counsel.
Courtship.
Drinking Song.
Love's without Reason.
The Pastoral on the King's
Death. Written in 1648.
Plain Dealing.
The Resolve.
The Riddle.
The Royalist.
To a Painted Lady.
To His Friend J. H.
Bromley, Beatrice Marion
Camp Fire.
Bromley, Isaac H.
The Passenjare.
Bromwich, David
From the Righteous Man
Even the Wild Beasts Run
away.
Wandsworth Common.
Bronk, William
After the Spanish Chroniclers.
Aspects of the World Like
Coral Reefs.
The Body.
The Continuance.
The Feeling.
Go Ahead; Goodbye; Good
Luck; and Watch Out.
March, Upstate.
The Mask the Wearer of the
Mask Wears.
Metonymy as an Approach to
a Real World.
A Postcard to Send to Sumer.
What Form the World Has.
Bronson, Daniel Ross
Cleaning Up, Clearing Out.
Bronte, Anne
The Doubter's Prayer.
He Doeth All Things Well.
If This Be All.
A Prayer.
Bronte, Charlotte
The Autumn Day Its Course
Has Run.
Home-Sickness.
The House Was Still–The
Room Was Still.
I Now Had Only to Retrace.
Mementos.
The Nurse Believed the Sick
Man Slept.
On the Death of Anne Bronte.
Bronte, Emily
Ah! Why, Because the
Dazzling Sun.

All Hushed and Still Within
  the House.
And When Thy Heart Is
  Resting.
Anticipaton.
At Castle Wood.
At Such a Time, in Such a
  Spot.
Come, the wind may never
  again.
Come, Walk with Me.
A Day Dream.
Death.
A Dream.
A. E.
Enough of Thought,
  Philosopher.
The Evening Sun.
Fall, Leaves, Fall.
D.G.C. to J.A.
God of Visions.
Had There Been Falsehood in
  My Breast.
Hope.
How Still, How Happy!
I Am the Only Being Whose
  Doom.
I Die; But When the Grave
  Shall Press.
I Gazed upon the Cloudless
  Moon.
I Gazed Within.
I Know Not How It Falls on
  Me.
I'll Come When Thou Art
  Sadder.
I'm Happiest When Most
  Away.
I Saw Thee, Child, One
  Summer's Day.
If Grief for Grief Can Touch
  Thee.
It Is Too late to Call Thee
  Now.
It's Over Now; I've Known It
  All.
It Will Not Shine Again.
Julian M. and A.G. Rochelle.
Ladybird! Ladybird!
The Linnet in the Rocky
  Dells.
A Little While, a Little While.
Long Neglect Has Worn
  away.
Love and Friendship.
Mild the Mist upon the Hill.
The Night Is Darkening
  Round Me.
The Night Wind.
No Coward Soul Is Mine.
O Come with Me, Thus Ran
  the Song.
O Dream, Where Art Thou
  Now?
Often Rebuked, Yet Always
  Back Returning.
Oh, for the Time When I
  Shall Sleep.
The Old Stoic.
Plead for Me.
The Prisoner.
Redbreast, Early in the
  Morning.
Remembrance.
Shall Earth No More Inspire
  Thee?
She Dried Her Tears.
Sleep Brings No Joy.
Sleep Not, Dream Not.
Stanzas.
Stanzas to—-.
The Sun Has Set.

Sympathy.
Tell Me, Tell Me, Smiling
  Child.
That Wind.
There Let Thy Bleeding
  Branch Atone.
To Imagination.
The Two Children.
Upon Her Soothing Breast.
The Visionary.
The Wanderer from the Fold.
Warning and Reply.
What Winter Floods, What
  Showers of Spring.
Why Do I Hate That Lone
  Green Dell?

Brooke, Fulke Greville, Lord
  O Wearisome Condition.
Brooke, Henry
  Jack the Giant Queller. An
  Antique History.
Brooke, Jocelyn
  Three Barrows Down.
Brooke, Rupert
  The Busy Heart.
  A Channel Passage.
  The Chilterns.
  Clouds.
  Colloquial.
  Day That I Have Loved.
  The Dead.
  Dining-Room Tea.
  Doubts.
  Dust.
  Failure.
  The Fish.
  Fragment.
  The Funeral of Youth:
    Threnody.
  The Great Lover.
  Heaven.
  The Hill.
  In Freiburg Station.
  A Letter to a Live Poet.
  Love.
  Mary and Gabriel.
  A Memory.
  Menelaus and Helen.
  Mummia.
  Mutability.
  The Night Journey.
  The Old Vicarage,
    Grantchester.
  The One before the Last.
  One Day.
  Peace.
  Pine Trees and the Sky:
    Evening.
  Safety.
  Second Best.
  The Soldier.
  The Song of the Pilgrims.
  Song: "Oh! Love," they said,
    "is King of Kings."
  Sonnet: "Oh! Death will find
    me, long before I tire."
  Sonnet Reversed.
  Success.
  There's Wisdom in Women.
  Thoughts on the Shape of the
    Human Body.
  Tiare Tahiti.
  Wagner.
  Waikiki.
  The Wayfarers.
Brooke, Stopford Augustus
  Courage.
  The Earth and Man.
  Lines.
  A Moment.
Brookhouse, Christopher
  For Stephen.

The Man in the Ocelot Suit.
Brooks, Charles Timothy
  The Great Voices.
  A Plea for Flood Ireson.
Brooks, Edwin
  Tulips from Their Blood.
Brooks, Francis
  Down the Little Big Horn.
  On the Plains.
  Tennessee.
Brooks, Fred Emerson
  Barnyard Melodies.
  Foreigners at the Fair.
  Kissing.
Brooks, Gwendolyn
  Andre.
  The Anniad.
  Appendix to the Anniad.
  An Aspect of Love, Alive in
    the Ice and Fire.
  The Bean Eaters.
  Beverly Hills, Chicago.
  The Birth in a Narrow Room.
  A Black Wedding Song.
  The Blackstone Rangers.
  Boy Breaking Glass.
  Boys. Black.
  Bronzeville Man with a Belt
    in the Back.
  But Can See Better There,
    and Laughing There.
  A Catch of Shy Fish.
  The Chicago Defender Sends
    a Man to Little Rock, Fall,
    1957.
  The Children of the Poor.
  Cynthia in the Snow.
  The Egg Boiler.
  The Empty Woman.
  Estimable Mable.
  Eunice in the Evening.
  First Fight. Then Fiddle.
  Five Men Against the Theme
    "My Name is Red Hot....."
  Flags.
  Friend.
  Horses Graze.
  Jessie Mitchell's Mother.
  Kitchenette Building.
  The Last Quatrain of the
    Ballad of Emmet Till.
  The Life of Lincoln West.
  Loam Norton.
  A Lovely Love.
  The Lovers of the Poor.
  Malcolm X.
  Martin Luther King Jr.
  Medgar Evers.
  The Mother.
  The Murder.
  My Dreams, My Works, Must
    Wait Till after Hell.
  Narcissa.
  Negro Hero.
  Of De Witt Williams on His
    Way to Lincoln Cemetery.
  Of Robert Frost.
  The Old-Marrieds.
  Old People Working (Garden,
    Car).
  Old Tennis Player.
  Otto.
  Paul Robeson.
  A Penitent Considers Another
    Coming of Mary.
  Pete at the Zoo.
  Piano after War.
  Riot.
  The Rites for Cousin Vit.
  Rudolph Is Tired of the City.
  Sadie and Maud.

The Second Sermon on the
  Warpland.
The Sermon on the Warpland.
A Song in the Front Yard.
The Sonnet-Ballad.
Steam Song.
Still Do I Keep My Look, My
  Identity...
A Street in Bronzeville:
  Southeast Corner.
A Street in Bronzeville: The
  Ballad of Chocolate Mabbie.
Strong Men, Riding Horses.
A Sunset of the City.
To Be in Love.
Two Dedications, I: The
  Chicago Picasso.
Two Dedications: The Wall.
The Vacant Lot.
Vern.
Way-Out Morgan.
We Real Cool.
What Shall I Give My
  Children?
When You Have Forgotten
  Sunday: The Love Story.
The Womanhood.
Young Heroes, III: Walter
  Bradford.
Brooks, Helen Morgan
  Plans.
  Words.
  A Young David: Birmingham.
Brooks, Jonathan Henderson
  And One Shall Live in Two.
  The Last Quarter Moon of the
    Dying Year.
  Muse in Late November.
  My Angel.
  Paean.
  The Resurrection.
  She Said...
Brooks, Maria Gowen
  Farewell to Cuba.
  Song of Egla.
  Zophiel: Palace of the
    Gnomes.
Brooks, Phillips
  A Christmas Carol.
  Christmas Everywhere.
  O Little Town of Bethlehem.
  Our Burden Bearer.
  The Unfailing One.
  A Wish for the New Year.
Brooks, Shirley
  For A' That and A' That
    (parody).
  I paints and paints.
  New Proverb.
  The Philosopher and Her
    Father.
  Poem by a Perfectly Furious
    Academician.
  A "Prize" Poem.
  To Disraeli.
  What Jenner Said on Hearing
    in Elysium That Complaints
    Had Been Made..
Brooks, Walter R.
  From the Ballad of Two-Gun
    Freddy.
Brooks, William E.
  Inasmuch!
  Memorial Day.
  Three Wise Kings.
Broome, Frederick Napier
  A Leave-Taking.
  To the Soul.
Broome, William
  The Rose-Bud To a Young
    Lady.

Broomell, Myron H.
Prayer for the Age.
Broonzy, Big Bill
I'm Gonna Move to the
Outskirts of Town.
Looking Up at Down.
Brophy, Liam
Assumpta est Maria.
Brosman, Catharine Savage
Route 29.
Brotherton, Alice Williams
The Blazing Heart.
The First Thanksgiving.
My Enemy.
Brough, Robert Barnabas
An Early Christian.
The Marquis of Carabas.
My Lord Tomnoddy.
Sir Menenius Agrippa, the
Friend of the People.
Brougham, Lord
The Orator's Epitaph.
Broughton, James Richard
Afterword: Song of Song.
The Birds of America.
Feathers or Lead?
Genesis of Vowels.
It Was the Worm.
The Lighthouse Keeper's
Offspring.
The Psalm of St. Priapus.
Psyche to Cupid: Her Ditty.
Those Old Zen Blues.
Broughton, T. Alan
My Father Dragged by
Horses.
Thaw.
Broumas, Olga
Backgammon.
Cinderella.
Elegy.
Epithalamion.
Landscape with Leaves and
Figure.
Landscape with Next of Kin.
Leda and Her Swan.
Little Red Riding Hood.
Rapunzel.
Snow White.
Brown, Abbie Farwell
The Fairy Book.
The Fisherman.
Friends.
Grandser.
Limerick: "There once was a
peach on a tree."
The Lost Playmate.
On Opening a New Book.
Pirate Treasure.
Somebody's Birthday.
Brown, Alex J.
The Wickedest Man in
Memphis.
Brown, Alice
The Artisan.
A Benedictine Garden.
Candlemas.
Cloistered.
Edwin Booth.
A Farewell.
Hora Christi.
Life.
Limerick: "There once was a
sensitive cat."
Pagan Prayer.
The Road to Castaly:
Revelation.
Seaward Bound.
Sleep.
Sunrise on Mansfield
Mountain.
Trilby.

The West-Country Lover.
Brown, Allan
Girl in a Black Bikini.
Brown, Audrey Alexandra
Amber Beads.
The Dark Cat.
The Goldfish.
Museum-Piece.
Night Boat.
Reveille.
The Strangers.
Brown, Beatrice Curtis
Anniversary in September.
The Apple Tree.
Jonathan Bing.
A New Song to Sing about
Jonathan Bing.
Brown, Bruce Bennett
The Return.
Brown, Catherine Bernard
A Prayer for Pentecost.
Brown, Charles O.
The History of Arizona: How
It Was Made and Who Made
It.
Brown, Frank London
Jazz.
Brown, George Mackay
Beachcomber.
Carpenter.
The Death of Peter Esson.
December Day, Hoy Sound.
The Desertion of the Women
and Seals.
Dream of Winter.
The Five Voyages of Arnor.
Harald, the Agnostic Ale-
Loving Old Shepherd...
The Keeper of the Midnight
Gate.
The Lodging.
Old Fisherman with Guitar.
The Old Women.
Our Lady of the Waves.
Roads.
The Seven Houses.
Stars.
Tea Poems: Afternoon Tea.
Tea Poems: Chinaman.
Tea Poems: Smugglers.
Trout Fisher.
Unlucky Boat.
Wedding.
Brown, Hamish
Aye, There's Hills.
Beyond Feith Buidhe.
Footprints.
The Harlot.
In the Rut.
Pitch Seven.
Ronas Hill.
Weather Rhymes.
Wind.
Brown, Harry
The Drill.
Incident on a Front Not Far
from Castel di Sangro.
Brown, Henry
Skin Man.
Titanic Blues.
Brown, Horatio
Bored.
A Kodak; Tregantle.
Brown, Irene Fowler
The Rear Guard.
Brown, Isabella Maria
Another Day.
Prayer.
Brown, John
Night.
A Rhapsody, Written at the
Lakes in Westmorland.

Brown, John Eliot
The Man Who Rode to
Conemaugh.
Brown, Joseph Brownlee
Thalatta! Thalatta!
Brown, Kate Louise
The Christmas Candle.
Brown, Margaret Wise
Little Black Bug.
The Secret Song.
Brown, Melvin Douglass
Boxer Shorts Named
Champion.
The Dirt Doctor.
A Message from Reverend Fat
Back Made Possible by...
The Nuclear Family.
The Steelworker.
Brown, Oliver Madox
Laura's Song.
Brown, Palmer
The Spangled Pandemonium.
Brown, Phoebe Hinsdale
I Love to Steal Awhile Away.
Private Devotion.
Welcome, Ye Hopeful Heirs
of Heaven.
Brown, Rabbit
James Alley.
Brown, Rita Mae
Aristophanes' Symposium.
Canto Cantare Cantavi
Cantatum.
Dancing the Shout to the
True Gospel.
The Disconnection.
Fire Island.
The New Litany.
Sappho's Reply.
Brown, Robert Adger
Gloaming.
Brown, Robert Carlton
I Am Aladdin.
Running Vines in a Field.
Brown, Solyman
Artificial Teeth.
Caries.
Tartar.
The Value of Dentistry.
Brown, Spencer
In an Old House.
Brown, Sterling A.
After Winter.
Challenge.
Crispus Attucks McCoy.
Effie.
Foreclosure.
Long Gone.
Maumee Ruth.
Memphis Blues.
Old Lem.
An Old Woman Remembers.
Remembering Nat Turner.
Return.
Salutamus.
Sister Lou.
Slim Greer.
Slim in Hell.
Southern Cop.
Southern Road.
Strange Legacies.
Strong Men.
To a Certain Lady, in Her
Garden.
When de Saints Go Ma'chin'
Home.
Brown, Stewart
Anthropology: Cricket at
Kano.
Brown, Sydney
Maple Leaf Rag.

Brown, Theron
His Majesty.
Brown, Thomas Edward
Between Our Folding Lips.
Braddan Vicarage.
The Bristol Channel.
Catherine Kinrade.
Dartmoor: Sunset at
Chagford.
Disguises.
High Overhead My Little
Daughter.
I Bended unto Me.
Ibant Obscurae.
In the Coach: Conjergal
Rights.
Jessie.
Lynton Verses.
My Garden.
Opifex.
The Organist in Heaven.
Pain.
The Parsons.
Peggu's Wedding.
Preparation.
Roman Women.
Salve!
A Sermon at Clevedon.
Social Science.
To K. H.
Vesper.
The Voices of Nature.
The Well.
Wesley in Heaven.
When Love Meets Love.
Brown, Thomas (Tom)
Epigram: "Our fathers took
oaths as of old they took
wives."
An Epitaph upon That
Profound and Learned
Casuist...
His Own Epitaph.
Horse Guards Parade.
Non Amo Te.
A Satire upon the French
King.
To That Most Senseless
Scoundrel, the Author of
Legion's Humble...
Upon the Anonymous Author
of Legion's Humble Address
to the Lords.
Brown, William Goldsmith
A Hundred Years to Come.
Mother, Home, Heaven.
Brown, Willie
Future Blues.
M & O Blues.
**Browne, Albert H. and Seymour
Rice**
You Tell Me Your Dream, I'll
Tell You Mine.
Browne, Cecil
But Not So Odd.
Browne, Francis Fisher
Santa Barbara.
Under the Blue.
Browne, Irving
At Shakespeare's Grave.
Man's Pillow.
My New World.
Browne, Isaac Hawkins
Blest Leaf! Whose Aromatic
Gales Dispense (parody).
Boy! Bring an Ounce of
Freeman's Best (parody).
The Fire Side. A Pastoral
Soliloquy.
A Pipe of Tobacco.

"Browne, Matthew" *See* **Rands, William Brightly**
Browne, Michael Dennis
The Delta.
Hallowe'en 1971.
Iowa.
Iowa, June.
The King in May.
Lamb.
The Man.
News from the House.
Paranoia.
Peter.
The Plants.
Power Failure.
The Roof of the World.
The Visitor.
Warrior with Shield.
The Wife of Winter's Tale.
Browne, Moses
The Shrimp.
A Survey of the
Amphitheatre.
Browne, Patrick
The Green Autumn Stubble.
Browne, Sir Thomas
A Colloquy with God.
In Yellow Meadows I Take
No Delight.
One in the Gout Wishing for
King Pyrrhus His Toe...
Browne, Sir William
Britannia's Pastorals.
The Complete Lover.
Epitaph on the Countess
Dowager of Pembroke.
Epitaph on the Countesse
Dowager of Pembroke.
In Obitum M.S., X° Maii
1614.
Love Who Will, for I'll Love
None.
Lydford Journey.
Memory.
An Ode: "Awake, faire Muse;
for I intend."
On a Rope Maker Hanged.
On the Countess Dowager of
Pembroke.
Oxford & Cambridge.
The Rose.
A Round.
Shall I Love Again.
The Shepherd's Pipe: Dawn of
Day.
Since She Is Gone.
Son of Erebus and Night.
Song: "Choose now among
this fairest number."
Song: "Love, that looks still
on your eyes."
Song of the Sirens.
To Pyrrha.
Underneath This Sable Herse.
Visions.
A Welcome.
**Browne (Aunt Effie), Jane
Euphemia**
The Great Brown Owl.
Little Raindrops.
Pleasant Changes.
The Rooks.
Brownell, Florence Kerr
Coin in the Fist.
Brownell, Henry Howard
Abraham Lincoln.
The Battle of Charlestown.
The Bay Fight.
The Burial of the Dane.
Bury Them.
The Eagle of Corinth.
From "The River-Fight."

The Lawyer's Invocation to
Spring.
Night Quarters.
The Old Cove.
The River Fight.
The Sphinx.
Sumter.
Browning, Elizabeth Barrett
Adequacy.
Aurora Leigh.
The Best.
Bianca among the
Nightingales.
A Child's Thought of God.
Comfort.
Confessions.
Convinced by Sorrow.
A Court Lady.
Cowper's Grave.
The Cry of the Children.
A Curse for a Nation.
The Dead Pan.
A Denial.
The Deserted Garden.
Died.
Farewells from Paradise.
Flush or Faunus.
Grief.
Hiram Powers' "Greek Slave."
Hugh Stuart Boyd: His
Blindness.
Hymn.
If Thou Must Love Me.
Inclusions.
Lady Geraldine's Courtship.
The Lady's Yes.
Lament for Adonis.
Lessons from the Gorse.
The Look.
Lord Walter's Wife.
The Mask.
The Meaning of the Look.
The Mediator.
Mother and Poet.
A Musical Instrument.
My Doves.
My Heart and I.
My Kate.
Mystery.
The North and the South.
On a Portrait of Wordsworth
by B. R. Haydon.
Out in the Fields with God.
Patience Taught by Nature.
The Pet Name.
The Poet.
A Portrait.
Praise of Earth.
De Produndis (excerpt).
Reward of Service.
Romance of the Swan's Nest.
Rosalind's Scroll.
Round Our Restlessness.
The Runaway Slave at
Pilgrim's Point.
The Sea-Mew.
The Sleep.
A Song for the Ragged
Schools of London.
Sonnets from the Portuguese.
The Soul's Expression.
The Soul's Travelling
(excerpt).
Substitution.
Summing Up in Italy.
To George Sand: A Desire.
A Valediction.
The Virgin Mary to the Child
Jesus.
A Vision of Poets (excerpt).
The Weakest Thing.
A Woman's Shortcomings.

Browning, Frederick G.
Amen.
Browning, Ophelia Guyon
Pray Without Ceasing.
Sometime–Somewhere.
Browning, Robert
Abt Vogler.
Adam, Lilith, and Eve.
After.
All Service Ranks the Same
with God.
The Ancient Doctrine.
And What Sordello Would
See There.
Andrea Del Sarto.
Andromeda.
Any Wife to Any Husband.
Apparent Failure.
Appearances.
Artemis Prologizes.
Asolando.
At Ecelin.
Bad Dreams.
Bishop Blougram's Apology.
The Bishop Orders His Tomb
at Saint Praxed's Church.
By the Fire-Side.
Caliban upon Setebos.
The Cardinal and the Dog.
Cavalier Tunes.
Childe Roland to the Dark
Tower Came.
Christmas Eve (excerpt).
Cleon.
The Confessional.
Confessions.
Count Gismond.
Cristina.
David's Song.
A Death in the Desert.
Development.
Dis Alitr Visum; or, le Byron
de nos Jours.
Dramatis Personae: Epilogue.
Earl Mertoun's Song.
The Englishman in Italy.
An Epistle.
Evelyn Hope.
A Face.
Faith.
Fame.
Fifine at the Fair, XCIII
(excerpt).
The Flight of the Duchess.
Fra Lippo Lippi.
Garden Fancies.
A Grammarian's Funeral.
The Guardian Angel.
De Gustibus–.
The Heretic's Tragedy.
Herve Riel.
Holy-Cross Day.
Home Thoughts From
Abroad.
Home-Thoughts, from the
Sea.
House.
How a Poet's Soul Comes
Into Play.
How It Strikes a
Contemporary.
How They Brought the Good
News From Ghent to Aix.
In a Gondola.
In A Year.
In the Doorway.
Inapprehensiveness.
Incident of the French Camp.
Instans Tyrannus.
The Italian in England.
Johannes Agricola in
Meditation.

The Laboratory.
The Last Ride Together.
Life in a Love.
A Light Woman.
A Likeness.
The Lost Leader.
The Lost Mistress.
Love.
Love Among the Ruins.
Love in a Life.
Love's Pursuit.
Magical Nature.
Master Hugues of Saxe-Gotha.
May and Death.
Meeting at Night.
Memorabilia.
Misconceptions.
A Moon Rainbow.
Muckle-Mouth Meg.
My Last Duchess.
My Star.
Natural Magic.
Ned Bratts.
Never the Time and the Place.
Now.
O Never Star Was Lost.
Oh, The Wild Joy of Living.
Old Pictures in Florence.
The Old Pope is Comforted
by the Thought of the Young
Pompilia.
One Way of Love.
One Word More.
Orpheus and Eurydice.
Pacchiarotto and Other
Poems: Epilogue.
Pan and Luna.
Paracelsus.
Parleyings with Certain People
of Importance in Their Day.
Parting at Morning.
The Patriot.
A Pearl, a Girl.
Phases of the Moon.
Pictor Ignotus.
The Pied Piper of Hamelin.
Pippa Passes.
Popularity.
Porphyria's Lover.
Prospice.
Rabbi Ben Ezra.
Respectability.
Rhyme for a Child Viewing a
Naked Venus in a Painting...
The Ring and the Book.
Rudel to the Lady of Tripoli.
Saul.
Service.
Shelley.
Shop.
Soliloquy of the Spanish
Cloister.
Song: "Give her but a least
excuse to love me!"
Song: "Nay but you, who do
not love her."
Song: "The moth's kiss, first!"
Sordello's Birth-Place.
The Statue and the Bust.
Summum Bonum.
Thamuris Marching.
Through the Metidja to Abd-
el-Kadr.
To Edward Fitzgerald.
A Toccata of Galuppi's.
Transcendentalism: A Poem in
Twelve Books.
Tray.
Two in the Campagna.
Up at a Villa–Down in the
City.

A Vault inside the Castle at
 Goito.
Waring.
Water and Air.
When I Vexed You.
Why I Am a Liberal.
A Woman's Last Word.
Women and Roses.
The Year's at the Spring.
You'll Love Me Yet!
Youth and Art.
Brownjohn, Alan
Class Incident from Graves.
Elephant.
In This City.
Of Dancing.
The Train.
"Brownjohn, John"
The School-Master and the
 Truants.
Brownlie, W. S.
On First Looking into
 Chapman's Homer (parody).
Brownstein, Michael
Against the Grain.
Behind the Wheel.
Big City.
Children, It's Time.
Clean & Clear.
Declaration of Independence.
Driving through Belgium.
Floating.
For Them.
I Am Not the Constant
 Reader.
Kites.
Lily Flower.
Lost in a Corridor of Power.
Nations.
No Empty Hands.
Pounds and Ounces.
Something Else.
Spiral Landscape.
Triplets.
Waitress.
War.
Bruce, Charles
Back Road Farm.
Biography.
The Fisherman's Son.
The Flowing Summer.
Words Are Never Enough.
Bruce, George
The Fisherman.
A Gateway to the Sea–St.
 Andrews.
Kinnaird Head.
My House.
Robins.
The Singers.
Sumburgh Heid.
Tom on the Beach.
Bruce, John
The Pike.
Bruce, Lennart
Poem: "I met Mother on the
 street."
Bruce, Michael
Elegy: In Spring.
Ode: To the Cuckoo.
Bruce, Richard
Cavalier.
Shadow.
Bruce, Wallace
Our Nation Forever.
Parson Allen's Ride.
Two Argosies.
Bruchac, Joseph
City.
Coming Back.
Coots.
Elegy for Jack Bowman.

For a Winnebago Brave.
Frozen Hands.
The Grandmother Came down
 to Visit Us.
Hiking.
IV.
A Meeting at the Crossroads.
Migration.
The Narrows.
Open.
Passive Resistance.
Poem for Jan.
Second Skins–A Peyote Song.
Stone Giant.
Sunlight.
Three Poems for the Indian
 Steelworkers in a Bar...
Bruck, Edith
Birth.
Childhood.
Equality, Father!
Go, Then.
Let's Talk, Mother.
Sister Zahava.
Why Would I Have Survived?
You Hide.
Brucker, H. P.
Praise Now Your God.
Brudne, Eva
A Farewell Ballad of Poppies.
Memento Vivendi.
Brummels, J. V.
Jeans.
Bruner, Margaret E.
An Angry Word.
Atonement.
The Beggar.
Beyond the Grave.
Casual Meeting.
The Clown.
A Dog's Vigil.
The Dreaded Task.
Epitaph for a Cat.
For One Lately Bereft.
For One Who Is Serene.
The Gift.
God's Ways Are Strange.
Good-By.
The Greater Gift.
If Lincoln Should Return.
The Lonely Dog.
Midwinter.
On City Streets.
Plea For Tolerance.
Prayer for Strength.
Rebirth.
Remembrance.
Selfishness.
The Sinner.
Time's Hand is Kind.
Wedding Anniversary.
Whom the Gods Love.
Brunini, John Gilland
The Assumption.
Repeated Pilgrimage.
To Mary at Christmas.
Bruno, Giordano
The Philosophic Flight.
Bruns, John Dickson
The Foe at the Gates.
Brush, Thomas
The Happy Poem.
Letter from the Street.
Brutus, Dennis
The Beauty of My Land Peers
 Warily.
Blood River Day.
Letter #8.
On the Island.
Somehow We Survive.
The Sounds Begin Again.

Bryan, Elizabeth Mabel
Father of the Man.
Bryan, Sharon
Big Sheep Knocks You
 About.
Corner Lot.
Hollandaise.
Lunch with Girl Scouts.
Bryan, Vincent
In My Merry Oldsmobile.
Bryant, F. J.
The Languages We Are.
Bryant, Helen
Lost Companions.
Bryant, John Frederick
On a Piece of Unwrought
 Pipeclay.
Bryant, John H.
At the Lincoln Tomb.
Bryant, William Cullen
Abraham Lincoln.
The African Chief.
America.
The Antiquity of Freedom.
Autumn Woods.
The Battle-Field.
Centennial Hymn.
The Conqueror's Grave.
Dante.
The Death of Lincoln.
The Death of Slavery.
The Death of the Flowers.
Dedication.
Earth.
An Evening Revery.
The Evening Wind.
The Flood of Years.
A Forest Hymn.
The Forest Maid.
The Gladness of Nature.
The Green Mountain Boys.
Green River.
The Holy Star.
The Hunter of the Prairies.
Hymn of the City.
A Hymn of the Sea.
Hymn of the Waldenses.
"I Broke the Spell That Held
 Me Long."
In Memory of John Lothrop
 Motley.
An Indian at the Burial-Place
 of His Fathers.
Inscription for the Entrance to
 a Wood.
June.
March.
The May Sun Sheds an
 Amber Light.
A Meditation on Rhode
 Island Coal.
Mighty One, Before Whose
 Face.
Monument Mountain.
The Mother's Hymn.
My Autumn Walk.
O Fairest of the Rural Maids.
Oh Mother of a Mighty Race.
Other Sheep I Have, Which
 Are Not of This Fold.
Our Country's Call.
The Past.
The Path.
The Planting of the Apple-
 Tree.
The Poet.
The Prairies.
Robert of Lincoln.
Seventy-Six.
The Snow-Shower.
Song of Marion's Men.
The Stream of Life.

Summer Wind.
Thanatopsis.
The Tides.
To a Mosquito.
To a Waterfowl.
To Cole, the Painter,
 Departing for Europe.
To the Fringed Gentian.
Truth, the Invincible.
The Twenty-Second of
 December.
The White-footed Deer.
A Winter Piece.
The Yellow Violet.
Bryant, Jr., F. J.
Cathexis.
Patience of a People.
Brydges, Sir Samuel Egerton
And Jesus Wept.
Lines Written Immediately
 after Parting from a Lady.
Bryher, Winifred
Hellenics: Blue Sleep.
Three Songs: Thessalian.
Brynes, Edward
Oration on the Toes.
Bryusov, Valery
Radiant Ranks of Seraphim.
Buber, Martin
The Fiddler.
I Consider the Tree.
Buchan, John
Leap in the Smoke.
Buchan, Tom
The Invitation.
Buchanan, Dugald
The Day of Judgment.
Omnia Vanitas.
Buchanan, George
Neaera When I'm There Is
 Adamant.
The Pope from Penance
 Purgatorial.
Buchanan, Robert Williams
The Blind Linnet.
The Churchyard.
The Faery Reaper.
The Green Gnome.
Judas Iscariot.
Langley Lane.
The Little Milliner.
The Pilgrim and the Herdboy.
Spring Song in the City.
The Starling.
Tom Dunstan, or, The
 Politician.
Buchwald, Emilie
Still Lives.
Buck, Byron
Song from a Two-Desk Office.
Buck, Richard Henry
Dear Old Girl.
Kentucky Babe.
Buckaway, C. M.
Saskatchewan Dusk.
Buckham, James
A Child of To-Day.
The Heart's Proof.
Buckham, John Wright
Hills of God, Break Forth in
 Singing.
O God, Above the Drifting
 Years.
**Buckingham, George Villiers,
Duke of**
To His Mistress.
**Buckingham, John Sheffield,
Duke of** *See* Sheffield, John
Duke of Buckingham
Buckley, Christopher
The Letters of Summer.
Light Rain.

Buckley, R. Bishop
Wait for the Wagon.
Buckley, Vincent
Ghosts, Places, Stories, Questions.
Good Friday and the Present Crucifixion.
Korea.
Late Tutorial.
No New Thing.
Parents.
Return of a Popular Statesman.
Various Wakings.
Buckmaster, Charles
Vanzetti.
Buckner, Samuel O.
Do It Right.
Budbill, David
Antoine and I Go Fishing.
New York in the Spring.
Budenz, Julia
Crockery.
Budzynski, Joe
Have Faith in God.
Buist, A. A.
The Hills of God.
Bukowski, Charles
3:16 and One Half...
Another Academy.
Eddie and Eve.
For Jane.
Hell Hath No Fury...
Letters.
My Style.
Short Order.
Style.
The Sun Wields Mercy.
The Tragedy of the Leaves.
The Trash Men.
Vegas.
Bulcke, Karl
There Is an Old City.
Bulfinch, Stephen Greenleaf
Hail to the Sabbath Day.
Bulkeley, Peter, the Younger
Like to the Grass That's Green Today.
Bull, Arthur J.
Eve.
Bullen, Arthur
The Whisperer.
Buller, A. H. Reginald
Limerick: "There was a young lady named Bright."
Buller, Marguerite
Proud Hollyhock.
Bullett, Gerald
Carol: "We saw him sleeping in his manger bed."
The Church Mouse.
Footnote to Tennyson.
Bullins, Ed
When Slavery Seems Sweet.
Bullis, Jerald
Revelation.
Bullock, J.
Fear Not.
Bullock, Mark
Be Thankful.
Bullock, Mary
Blessed Nearness.
Bullokar, William
To His Child.
Bullwinkle, Marcia
There's a Feeling.
Bulwer-Lytton, Edward Robert
See "Meredith, Owen"
Bumble Bee Slim
No Woman No Nickel.
Bunin, Ivan
Flax.

Bunker, John
The Old Woman.
Petition of Youth before Battle.
Bunn, Alfred
I Dreamt I Dwelt in Marble Halls.
When Other Lips and Other Hearts.
Bunner, Alice Learned
Immustabilis.
Separation.
Bunner, Freda Newton
Country Cemetery.
Bunner, Henry Cuyler
The Appeal to Harold.
Behold the Deeds!
Candor.
The Chaperon.
Da Capo.
Deaf.
Feminine.
Grandfather Watts's Private Fourth.
The Heart of the Tree.
Home, Sweet Home.
J.B.
Les Morts Vont Vite.
The Old Flag.
On Reading a Poet's First Book.
One, Two, Three!
A Pitcher of Mignonette.
Poetry and the Poet.
Shake, Mulleary and Go-ethe.
She Was a Beauty.
Strong as Death.
To a June Breeze.
The Way to Arcady.
Yes?
Bunting, Basil
Briggflatts.
Chomei at Toyama.
Coda.
The Complaint of the Morpethshire Farmer.
Darling of Gods and Men, beneath the Gliding Stars.
Fearful Symmetry.
Fishermen.
Gin the Goodwife Stint.
On the Fly-Leaf of Pound's Cantos.
The Orotava Road.
To Violet.
What the Chairman Told Tom.
The Word.
Bunyan, John
Neither Hook nor Line.
Of the Boy and Butterfly.
Of the Child with the Bird at the Bush.
Of the Cuckoo.
Of the Going Down of the Sun.
The Pilgrim's Progress.
The Shepherd's Song.
Time and Eternity.
Upon a Ring of Bells.
Upon a Snail.
Upon the Horse and Rider.
Upon the Lark and the Fowler.
Upon the Snail.
Upon the Swallow.
Upon the Weathercock.
Burbank, Carol
Call to Order.
Surgery.
Burbidge, Thomas
She Bewitched Me.

Burden, Jean
Lost Word.
Sabbath.
Words.
Burder
Christ, the Conqueror.
Burdette, Robert Jones
Christ.
Limerick: "Oh, King of the fiddle, Wilhelmj."
Limerick: "There was a young man of Cohoes."
Orphan Born.
Soldier, Rest!
When My Ship Comes In.
Burdick, Arthur J.
Washington's Birthday.
Burford, William
A Christmas Tree.
The Fire.
On the Apparition of Oneself.
The Tomboy.
Burge, Maureen
The Diet.
Disillusion.
Burgess, Anthony
Lines Inspired by the Controversy on the Value...of Old English...
Burgess, Charles
Albatross.
Five Serpents.
Lady and Crocodile.
Two Garden Scenes.
Burgess, Gelett
Abstemia.
Abstrosophy.
Adolphus Elfinstone.
Ah, Yes, I Wrote "The Purple Cow."
An Alphabet of Famous Goops.
Ballad of the Hyde Street Grip.
Ego Sum.
Felicia Ropps.
I Wish That My Room Had a Floor.
The Invisible Bridge.
The Jilted Funeral.
Lament.
The Lazy Roof.
Limerick: "I don't give a...."
Limerick: "There is little in afternoon tea."
A Low Trick.
My Feet.
My Feet They Haul Me 'Round the House.
My Legs Are So Weary.
On Digital Extremities.
Parisian Nectar.
The Protest of the Illiterate.
Psycholophon.
The Purple Cow.
Remarkable Art.
The Sunset.
Table Manners.
Tardiness.
Trapping Fairies in West Virginia.
Willy and the Lady.
The Window Has Four Little Panes.
A Woman's Reason.
Burgess, George
The Harvest Dawn Is Near.
While O'er the Deep Thy Servants Sail.
Burgh, Hugh de
Punchinello.

Burgin, Richard
Concertmaster.
Burgon, John William
Pedra.
Written on the Plain of Thebes.
Burgos, Julia de
Call Out My Number.
Nothing.
Pentachromatic.
Poem of the Intimate Agony.
Poem to My Death.
Poem with the Final Tune.
Rio Grande de Loiza.
To Julia de Burgos.
Burgoyne, Arthur G.
"Everybody Works but Father" as W. S. Gilbert Would Have Written It.
Burke, Daniel
Ash Wednesday.
The Teacher to Heloise (After Waddell).
Burke, Francis
The Mediatix of Grace.
A Sequence with Strophes in Paraphrase Thereof.
Burke, Kenneth
Civil Defense.
Frigate Jones, the Pussyfooter.
Heavy, Heavy–What Hangs Over?
If All the Thermo-Nuclear Warheads.
Know Thyself.
Nursery Rhyme.
Burke, Thomas
Piccadilly.
Burket, Gail Brook
Columbus Never Knew.
February 12, 1809.
From Countless Hearts.
House in Springfield.
Noel.
So Touch Our Hearts with Loveliness.
Thought for a New Year.
Burkhard von Hohenfels
A Dance Song.
Burkholder, Clarence M.
Easter Beatitudes.
Burleigh, William Cecil, Lord
To Mistress Anne Cecil.
Burleigh, William Henry
Abide Not in the Realm of Dreams.
Lead Us, O Father, in the Paths of Peace.
The Weaver.
Burnand, Sir Francis Cowley
Fishing for Sticklebacks, with Rod and Line.
His Heart Was True to Poll.
Oh, My Geraldine.
Shakespearean Soliloquy in Progress: "Tubby or not tubby–" (parody).
Burnat-Provins, Marguerite
The fruits you give me are more savory than others.
Sylvius, your hands near my mouth are heady flowers.
You told me: "I am not worthy of you."
Burnes, Carol
Long-Distance.
Burnet, Dana
Marching Song.
The Road to Vagabondia.
Song: "Love's on the highroad."
Wayfarers.

Burnett, Olive H.
The Best for Us.
Burnham, Maud
The Barnyard.
The Five Little Fairies.
Burns, Diane
Big Fun.
DOA in Dulse.
For Carole.
Gadoshkibos.
Houston and Bowery, 1981.
Our People.
Sure You Can Ask Me a
Personal Question.
Burns, Jim
The End Bit.
Burns, Ralph
Only One.
Burns, Richard
Angels.
Mandelstam.
Burns, Robert
Address to a Haggis.
Address to a Lady.
Address to the Deil.
Address to the Unco Guid, or
the Rigidly Righteous.
Addressed to a Gentleman at
Table Who Kept Boasting...
Ae Fond Kiss.
Afton Water.
Anna.
Auld Lang Syne.
Ay Waukin O.
The Banks o' Doon.
Bess and Her Spinning-Wheel.
The Birks of Aberfeldy.
Blooming Nelly.
Bonnie Doon.
Bonnie Lesley.
Bonnie Wee Thing.
The Bookworms.
The Brigs of Ayr.
Ca' the Yowes.
Charlie He's My Darling.
A Child's Grace.
Chloe.
Comin' Thro' the Rye.
Composed in Spring.
Contented wi' Little.
Corn Rigs Are Bonnie.
The Cotter's Saturday Night.
Could You Do That?
The Daisy.
The Day Returns.
The De'il's awa' wi' the
Exciseman.
Death and Doctor Hornbook.
A Dedication to G****
H******* Esq.
A Dream: "Guid-mornin to
your majesty."
Duncan Gray.
Elegy on Captain Matthew
Henderson.
Epigram: "A head pure,
sinless quite of brain or
soul."
Epigram: "No more of your
titled acquaintances boast."
Epigram on Elphinstone's
Translation of Martial's
Epigrams.
Epigram: The Parson's Looks.
Epistle to a Young Friend.
Epistle to Davie, a Brother
Poet.
Epistle to Dr. Blacklock.
Epistle to James Smith.
Epitaph for William Nicol.
Epitaph: "Here cursing
swearing Burton lies."

Epitaph: "Lo worms enjoy the
seat of bliss."
Epitaph on a Schoolmaster.
Epitaph on John Dove.
The Exciseman.
False Love.
For a' That and a' That.
For the Sake O' Somebody.
Gie the Lass Her Fairin'.
The Gloomy Night Is
Gath'ring Fast.
Godly Girzie.
The Gowden Locks of Anna.
Grace after Dinner.
Grace at Kirkudbright.
Green Grow the Rashes.
Halloween.
Hark! the Mavis.
Here's a Health to Them
That's Awa'.
Highland Harry Back Again.
Highland Mary.
The Holy Fair.
Holy Willie's Prayer.
How Can I Keep My
Maidenhead.
How Daur Ye Call Me Owlet
Face.
The Humble Petition of Bruar
Water to the Noble Duke of
Athole.
Hunting Song.
I Do Confess Thou Art Sae
Fair.
I Hae a Wife O' My Ain.
I'll Aye Ca' in By Yon Town.
I'm O'er Young to Marry Yet.
I Murder Hate by Field or
Flood.
I Once Was a Maid.
The Inventory.
It Was a' for Our Rightfu'
King.
Jean.
John Anderson My Jo.
John Barleycorn.
Johnnie, Cock up Your
Beaver.
The Jolly Beggars.
The Keekin' Glass.
The Kirk's Alarm.
Lament for Culloden.
The Lass and the Friar.
The Lass That Made the Bed
for Me.
Last May a Braw Wooer.
The Lea Rig.
Lines on the Author's Death.
Lord Galloway.
Love and Liberty. A Cantata.
The Lovely Lass o' Inverness.
Luath.
Macpherson's Farewell.
A Man's a Man for A' That.
Man's Inhumanity to Man.
Man was Made to Mourn, A
Dirge.
Mary Morison.
A Mother's Lament for the
Death of Her Son.
Muirland Meg.
My Ain Kind Dearie, O.
My Bonnie Highland Laddie.
My Heart's in the Highlands.
My Love, She's but a Lassie
Yet.
My Luve's Like a Red, Red
Rose.
My Nannie's Awa'.
My Wife's a Winsome Wee
Thing.
Nine Inch Will Please a Lady.

No Cold Approach.
Nobody.
The Nut-Gathering Lass.
O'er the Water to Charlie.
O, for Ane-and-Twenty.
O Mally's Meek, Mally's
Sweet.
O Merry Hae I Been Teethin'
a Heckle.
O, Open the Door to Me, O!
O Were My Love Yon Lilac
Fair.
O Wert Thou in the Cauld
Blast.
Of A' the Airts the Wind Can
Blaw.
Oh Wert Thou in the Cauld
Blast.
On a Dog of Lord Eglinton's.
On a Noisy Polemic.
On a Wag in Mauchline.
On Andrew Turner.
On James Grieve, Laird of
Boghead, Tarbolton.
On Lord Galloway.
On Mr. Pitt's Hair-Powder
Tax.
On Scaring Some Waterfowl
in Loch Turit...
On Seeing the Royal Palace at
Stirling in Ruins.
On the Birth of a Posthumous
Child, Born in Peculiar
Circumstances...
On W. R—, Esq.
On William Graham, Esq., of
Mossknowe.
Open the Door to Me, O.
The Patriarch.
The Plowman.
A Poet's Grace.
The Poet's Welcome to His
Illegitimate Child.
A Poet's Welcome to His
Love-Begotten Daughter.
A Prayer in the Prospect of
Death.
Prayer under the Pressure of
Violent Anguish.
The Rantin Dog the Daddie
O't.
Rantin, Rovin Robin.
A Red Red Rose.
The Rigs o' Barley.
Scots Wha Hae.
Second Epistle to Robert
Graham.
She'll Do It.
Sic a Wife as Willie Had.
The Silver Tassie.
Somebody.
Song: "Again rejoicing Nature
sees."
Such a Parcel of Rogues in a
Nation.
Suppertime.
Tam Glen.
Tam O'Shanter.
Tam Samson's Elegy.
Thou Lingering Star.
The Thrusting of It.
To a Field Mouse.
To a Louse.
To a Mountain Daisy.
To a Mouse.
To an Artist.
To Miss Ferrier.
To Mr. E— on His Translation
of and Commentaries on
Martial.
To Ruin.

To Terraughty, on His Birth-
Day.
To William Simpson,
Ochiltree.
The Toad-Eater.
Tommie Makes My Tail
Toddle.
The Tree of Liberty.
Twa Bonny Lads.
The Twa Dogs.
Up in the Morning Early.
Verses Intended to Be Written
below a Noble Earl's Picture.
The Vision.
Wee Willie Gray.
Wha Is That at My Bower-
Door?
Whistle an' I'll Come to Ye,
My Lad.
Whistle O'er the Lave o't.
Willie Brew'd a Peck o' Maut.
Winter.
A Winter Night.
Ye Flowery Banks.
Burnshaw, Stanley
Bread.
End of the Flower-World
(A.D. 2300).
House in St. Petersburg.
Isaac.
Strange.
Talmudist.
Burr, Amelia Josephine
Battle-Song of Failure.
Certainty Enough.
Gorgio Lad.
Joyce Kilmer.
My Mother.
New Life.
Nocturne.
Pershing at the Tomb of
Lafayette.
Perugia.
Rain in the Night.
Romany Gold.
A Song of Living.
Surrender.
To Her–Unspoken.
Where Love Is.
Where You Passed.
Burr, Gray
The Butterfly.
The Epistemological Rag.
Eye.
Garden Puzzle.
A Glance at the Album.
Indian Summer.
A Play of Opposites.
Robin Hood.
Sailing, Sailing.
A Skater's Waltz.
What We Listened for in
Music.
Burrell, Sophia
Epigram on Two Ladies.
Burrington, E. H.
Serio-Comic History of
Bridgwater.
Burroughs, Alethea S.
Savannah.
Burroughs, John
Waiting.
Burroughs, Margaret Goss
Black Pride.
Everybody but Me.
Only in This Way.
To Soulfolk.
Burroway, Jan
Owed to Dickens, 1956.
Song: "With whomsoever I
share the spring."

Burroway, Janet
The Scientist.
Burrowes, Elizabeth
O God, Send Men.
Burrows, E. G.
The Admiral's Daughter.
Dear Country Cousin.
Hidden Valley.
Bursk, Chris
A Handful of Small Secret
Stones.
Burstein, Abraham
The Love of Hell.
Burt, Bates G.
O God of Youth.
Burt, Della
A Little Girl's Dream World.
On the Death of Lisa Lyman.
Spirit Flowers.
Burt, Don
The Poolhall.
Burt, J.F.A.
Southward Bound.
Burt, Lucile
Sleeping at the Beach.
Burt, Nathaniel
Out.
Burt, Struthers
Fifty Years Spent.
I Know a Lovely Lady Who
Is Dead.
The Land.
Resurgam.
Burton, Henry K.
Jesus Himself.
Pass It On.
There's a Light upon the
Mountains.
Burton, John
Do I Really Pray?
Holy Bible, Book Divine.
Burton, Richard
Across the Fields to Anne.
The Authors Abstract of
Melancholy.
Black Sheep.
The City of the Dead.
The Comfort of the Stars.
Deserted Farms.
Do What Thy Manhood Bids
Thee Do.
Extras.
The First Song.
The Forefather.
The Glorious Game.
God's Garden.
Idols.
Love Is Strong.
Of Those Who Walk Alone.
The Old Santa Fe Trail.
On a Ferry Boat.
The Polar Quest.
Rhyme for Remembrance of
May.
Roll a Rock Down.
Sealed Orders.
The Song of the Unsuccessful.
An Unpraised Picture.
Wood Witchery.
Burton, Richard E.
Song of the Sea.
Burton, Sir Richard Francis
The Kasidah.
Burwell, Rex
Depression.
Busch, Ernst
Hans Beimler.
Bush, Barney
Another Old Song.
Blood.
It Is Finished.
Voice in the Blood.

Whose Voice.
Bush, Jocelyn
The Little Red Sled.
Bushby, D. Maitland
Drifting.
Bushnell, Amy
Retreat.
Bushnell, Frances Louisa
In the Dark.
Unfulfilment.
World Music.
Buson (Taniguchi Buso)
Conversation.
Haiku: "Deep in a windless."
Haiku: "Plum-viewing..."
Haiku: "Spring rain! And as
yet."
Haiku: "The halo of the
moon."
The Piercing Chill I Feel.
The Short Night.
The Whale.
Spring Scene.
Busse, Carl
In the Night of the Full
Moon.
The Quiet Kingdom.
Buster, Marjorie Lorene
My Friend.
Butler, Alpheus
Death of a Fair Girl.
Butler, Arthur Gray
Edith and Harold.
Two Long Vacations:
Grasmere.
Butler, Derek
Man's World Dissolving.
Parole Board.
Pigeons in Prison.
School Days/Rule Days.
Tryst.
Butler, Guy
Cape Coloured Batman.
Common Dawn.
Giotto's Campanile.
Myths.
Stranger to Europe.
Surveyor.
Butler, Lynne
The Man in the Dream Is
Death.
Butler, Samuel (1612-80)
Burlesque Translation of Lines
from Lope de Vega's
"Arcadia".
Description of Holland.
Epigram.
Epigram: "The greatest saints
and sinners have been
made."
Epigram: "What makes all
subjects discontent."
Epitaph: "A great philosopher
did choke."
Godly Casuistry.
Hudibras.
Inventions.
The Law.
Love.
On William Prynne.
Presbyterian Church
Government.
Presbyterian Knight and
Independent Squire.
A Psalm of Montreal.
Religion.
The Metaphysical Sectarian.
The Religion of Hudibras.
These Things to Come.
Satire upon the Licentious
Age of Charles II.

Sidrophel, the Rosicrucian
Conjurer.
Butler, Samuel (1835-1902)
O God! O Montreal!
The Righteous Man.
Butler, William Allen
All's Well!
The Gathering on the Plains.
Incognita of Raphael.
Nothing to Wear.
Butler-Andrews, C.
That Little Hatchet.
Butler the Second, Samuel
A Prayer.
Butterfield, Frances Westgate
Time Out.
**Butterfield, James, and George
W. Johnson**
When You and I Were
Young, Maggie.
Butterworth, Hezekiah
The Bird with a Broken Wing.
The Church of the
Revolution.
The Death of Jefferson.
Five Kernels of Corn.
The Fountain of Youth.
Garfield's Ride at
Chickamauga.
The Legend of Waukulla.
Ortiz.
Roger Williams.
The Thanksgiving for
America.
The Thanksgiving in Boston
Harbor.
Verazzano.
Whitman's Ride for Oregon.
Buttle, Myra
Sweeney in Articulo (parody).
The Sweeniad (parody).
Butts, Antony
Massenet/Never wrote a Mass
in A.
Butts, Mary Frances
The Christmas Trees.
In Galilee.
A Million Little Diamonds.
That's July.
That's June.
Today.
Trot, Trot!
Buzea, Constanta
I'm not here never was.
Byatt, Howard
Death.
Byer, B. L.
The Ageless Christ.
Byers, Samuel H. M.
Sherman's March to the Sea.
With Corse at Allatoona.
Byfield, Bruce
Stood-Up.
Byles, Mather
Great God, How Frail a
Thing Is Man.
Great God, Thy Works.
To Thee the Tuneful Anthem
Soars.
When Wild Confusion Wrecks
the Air.
**Bynner, Witter ("Emanuel
Morgan")**
An Adobe House.
Aged Fisherman.
An Autumn Walk.
Beforehand.
Captain's Table.
Charioteer.
Chariots.
Correspondent.
A Dance for Rain.

The Day.
Defeat.
Dream.
Driftwood.
During a Chorale by Cesar
Franck.
Ecce Homo.
A Fortune-Teller.
Ganymede.
Ghost.
God's Acre.
The Golden Heart.
Grieve Not for Beauty.
Haskell.
I Change.
I Need No Sky.
Inscriptions on Chinese
Paintings: Lines To Do With
Youth.
Jeremiah.
Lightning.
Lotuses.
A Masque of Life and Death.
The Mystic.
New Mexican Desert.
The New World: The New
God.
Out of the Sea.
Pittsburgh.
The Poet.
Prayer.
Prepare.
Republic to Republic.
The Sandpiper.
Sentence.
Shasta.
Songs Ascending.
Spouse.
To a Phoebe-Bird.
To a President.
Vinegaroon.
Byrd, John
Old Timbrook Blues.
Byrd, William
A Carol for Christmas Day.
Lulla La, Lulla Lulla Lullaby.
Madrigal: "Come, woeful
Orpheus."
Madrigal: "Is Love a boy?"
Madrigal: "Penelope, that
longed for the sight."
Madrigal: "What is life."
Madrigal: "When younglings
first."
The Quiet Life.
Song: "Let not the sluggish
sleep."
Byrne, William A.
The Bog Lands.
Byrom, John
Careless Content.
Contentment: or, The Happy
Workman's Song.
The Desponding Soul's Wish.
Epigram on Handel and
Bononcini.
Extempore Verses upon a
Trial of Skill....
A Full and True Account of a
Horrid and Barbarous
Robbery.
Hymn for Christmas Day.
An Hymn on the
Omnipresence.
A Jacobite Toast.
My Dog Tray.
On Clergymen Preaching
Politics.
On the Origin of Evil.
On Trinity Sunday.
A Pastoral.

The Salutation of the Blessed
Virgin.
The Soul's Tendency Towards
Its True Centre.
To Henry Wright of
Mobberley, Esq. on Buying
the Picture...
Tom the Porter.
Two Monopolists.
Byron, George Gordon, Lord
The Age of Bronze: Rent,
Rent, Rent!
All Is Vanity, Saith the
Preacher.
And Angling, Too.
Answer to—'s Professions of
Affection.
The Archangel.
At the Gate of Heaven.
The Battle of Waterloo.
Beppo; a Venetian Story.
The Bride of Abydos.
Bright Be the Place of Thy
Soul!
By the Deep Sea.
Childe Harold's Pilgrimage.
The Coliseum.
The Cornelian.
Darkness.
The Destruction of
Sennacherib.
Don Juan.
The Dream.
The Dying Gladiator.
Elegy.
Elegy on Thyrza.
English Bards and Scotch
Reviewers.
Epigram.
Epilogue (parody).
Epistle to Augusta.
Epistle to Mr. Murray.
Epitaph.
Epitaph for William Pitt.
Epitaph to a Dog.
Fare Thee Well!
Farewell! If Ever Fondest
Prayer.
Farewell to Malta.
The Fatal Spell.
The First Kiss of Love.
For Music.
A Fragment.
Friendship Is Love without
His Wings.
From the Turkish.
George the Fourth in Ireland.
George the Third.
Haidee.
The Highlands' Swelling Blue.
Hours of Idleness.
I Would I Were a Careless
Child.
The Immortal Mind.
Invocation.
The Isolation of Genius.
Italy Versus England.
Know Ye the Land?
Lachin Y Gair.
Lake Leman.
Lara.
Last Words on Greece.
Lines on Hearing That Lady
Byron Was Ill.
Lines to Mr. Hodgson.
Lines Written beneath a
Picture.
The Lisbon Packet.
Love and Death.
The Lovers.
Maid of Athens, Ere We Part.
Manfred: An Incantation.

Mazeppa.
My Days of Love Are Over.
Newstead Abbey.
The Night before the Battle of
Waterloo.
Ode to a Lady Whose Lover
Was Killed by a Ball...
An Ode to the Framers of the
Frame Bill.
Ode to Venice.
Oh! Weep for Those.
On John Adams, of Southwell.
On Jordan's Bank.
On My Thirty-Third Birthday
January 22, 1821.
On the Bust of Helen by
Canova.
On This Day I Complete My
Thirty-sixth Year.
The Poet and the World.
The Prisoner of Chillon.
Prometheus.
The Prophecy of Dante.
Remember thee! remember
thee!
She Walks in Beauty.
The Siege of Corinth.
A Sketch.
So, We'll Go No More a
Roving.
Song of the Corsairs.
Sonnet on Chillon.
Sonnet to the Prince Regent.
Stanzas for Music.
Stanzas to a Lady, with the
Poems of Camoens.
Stanzas to Augusta.
Stanzas to the Po.
Stanzas Written on the Road
between Florence and Pisa.
Sun of the Sleepless.
Sunset over the Aegean.
That Idiot, Wordsworth.
To Ianthe.
To Mr. Murray.
To My Son.
To Thomas Moore.
To Woman.
The Two Foscari: Swimming.
Vision of Belshazzar.
The Vision of Judgment.
The Vision of Judgment.
The Waltz: Hail, Spirit-
Stirring Waltz.
Washington.
When a Man Hath No
Freedom to Fight for at
Home.
When We Two Parted.
Who Kill'd John Keats?
William Lisle Bowles.
The World Is a Bundle of
Hay.
Written After Swimming
From Sestos to Abydos.
Youth and Age.
Byron, H. J.
An Adage.
Rural Simplicity.
Byron, Mary C. G.
The Adventurers.
The Fairy Thrall.
The Pageant of Seaman.
The Storm-Child.

C

"C, E."
Emaricdulfe.
"C, J."
The Frailty of Beauty.
"C, R."
Limerick: "A merchant
addressing a debtor."
Cabalquinto, Luis
The Big One.
Blue Tropic.
Eating Lechon, with my
Brothers and Sisters.
The Flower Vendor.
Hometown.
Cabell, James Branch
Alone in April.
Easter Eve.
Garden-Song.
Retractions.
Story of the Flowery
Kingdom.
Cable, Franklin
Tree-Building.
Cable, George Washington
The New Arrival.
Written in the Visitors' Book
at the Birthplace of Robert
Burns.
Cabral, Olga
Another Late Edition
(excerpt).
At the Jewish Museum.
The Factory.
Hokusai's Wave.
Lillian's Chair.
Mother and Sister of the
Artist.
On the Death of Neruda.
Picasso's Women.
Cader, Teresa D.
On the Edge of a Safe Sleep.
Cadnum, Michael
Skull of a Neandertal.
Cadsby, Heather
Poem for a Song.
Reunion.
Caedmon
Caedmon's Hymn.
Far and Wide She Went.
Genesis: The Approach of
Pharaoh.
Hymn: "Now we must praise
heaven-kingdom's Guardian."
The Hymn of the World's
Creator (excerpt).
Caesar, Irving
Tea for Two.
Cahucer, Geoffrey
The Former Age.
Cain, John
At the Nursing Home.
Cain, Seymour
Due Date.
My Son, My Son...
Cairncross, Thomas S.
Grey Galloway.
Calder, Dave
At Kirk Yetholm.
Calderon de la Barca, Pedro
The Cross.
The Demon Speaks.
The Dream Called Life.
The Holy Eucharist.
Life Is a Dream.
Thou Art of All Created
Things.
Caldwell, Arthur I.
The Stampede.

Caldwell, John
The Mule-Skinners.
Caldwell, William Warner
Robin's Come!
Calenberg, Connie
I Love Thee, Lord.
Take My Hand, O Blessed
Master.
Calicott, Joe
Fare Thee Well Blues.
Calkins, Clinch
The Dead City.
Call, Frank Oliver
Blue Homespun.
An Old Habitant.
Call, Wathen Mark Wilks
Hymn.
The People's Petition.
Renunciation.
Callaghan, Gertrude
Sorrow's Ladder.
Callanan, Jeremiah Joseph
Dirge of O'Sullivan Bear.
The Girl I Love.
Lines to the Blessed
Sacrament.
The Outlaw of Loch Lene.
Pure is the Dewy Gem.
Serenade.
Song: "Awake thee, my Bessy,
the morning is fair."
To * * * * *.
When Each Bright Star Is
Clouded.
Written to a Young Lady.
Callimachus
Crethis.
Elegy on Herakleitos.
His Son.
The One Who Runs Away.
Saon of Acanthus.
Sopolis.
Timon's Epitaph.
To Archinus.
Callinus
A Call to Action.
Calverley, Charles Stuart
The Alphabet.
Arcades Ambo (parody).
The Auld Wife.
Beer.
Changed.
The Cock and the Bull.
Companions, a Tale of a
Grandfather...
Contentment.
Disaster (parody).
Dover to Munich.
Epitaph of Cleonicus.
Epitaph of Hipponax.
First Love.
Forever.
Gemini and Virgo.
Hic Vir, Hic Est.
In the Gloaming.
Lines on Hearing the Organ.
Lines Suggested By the
Fourteenth of February.
Love.
Lovers, and a Reflection.
Morning.
Motherhood.
Ode to Tobacco.
On the Beach.
Ortho's Epitaph.
Peace.
Precious Stones.
Proverbial Philosophy: Of
Reading.
Sad Memories.
The Schoolmaster Abroad
with His Son.

Striking.
Wanderers.
Calvert, George Henry
Bunker Hill.
Calvin, John
Salutation to Jesus Christ.
Cambridge, Ada
Faith.
Fashion.
The Future Verdict.
On Australian Hills.
The Virgin Martyr.
Cambridge, Richard Owen
The Fakir.
Camden, William
On a Puritanicall Lock-Smith.
Camerino, Aldo
Calm.
Fear.
For a Voice That Is Singing.
Mother.
Night.
Recluse.
Cameron, C. C.
Success.
Cameron, Don
Drilling Missed Holes.
Song of the Leadville Mine
 Boss.
Cameron, George Frederick
Ah Me! The Mighty Love.
The Future.
In After Days.
My Political Faith.
Relics.
Standing on Tiptoe.
Cameron, Norman
Bear in Mind, O Ye
 Recording Angels.
The Compassionate Fool.
The Dirty Little Accuser.
The Disused Temple.
Fight with a Water-Spirit.
The Firm of Happiness,
 Limited.
For the Fly-Leaf of a School-
 Book.
Forgive Me, Sire.
From a Woman to a Greedy
 Lover.
Green, Green is El Aghir.
A Hook for Leviathan.
In the Queen's Bedroom.
She and I.
Shepherdess.
The Thespians at
 Theermopylae.
The Unfinished Race.
The Verdict.
The Winter House.
Camille, Roussan
Nocturne.
Camoens, Luì de
Babylon and Sion (Goa and
 Lisbon).
Dear gentle soul, who went so
 soon away.
The Luciad.
On the Death of Catarina de
 Attayda.
Sonnet: "Leave me, all sweet
 refrains my lip hath made."
Sonnet: "Time and the mortal
 will stand never fast."
Waterspout.
Camp, James
Bruckner.
The Figure in the Carpet.
Campana, Dino
Night Character.
Campanella, Tomasso
The People.

Campbell, A. Y.
Animula Vagula.
The Dromedary.
Murie Sing (parody).
Campbell, Alistair
At the Fishing Settlement.
The Dark Lord of Savaiki.
Hut Near Desolated Pines.
Images.
Lie on the Sand.
Narcissus.
Now He Is Dead.
Now Sleeps the Gorge.
O Catch Miss Daisy Pinks.
Campbell, Anne
Before and After Marriage.
Shabby Old Dad.
There Is Always a Place for
 You.
To My Friend.
Campbell, Calder
Ossian's Serenade.
Campbell, David
Ariel.
The Australian Dream.
Beach Queen.
Duchesses.
The End of Exploring.
Fox.
Harry Pearce.
Hear the Bird of Day.
Heart of Light.
Men in Green.
The Monaro.
Mothers and Daughters.
Mr. Hughes.
Night Sowing.
On Frosty Days.
Pallid Cuckoo.
Soldier's Song.
Song for the Cattle.
Speak With the Sun.
Ulinda.
Campbell, Donald
Hauf-Roads Up Schiehallion.
Campbell, Gene
Robbing and Stealing Blues.
Campbell, James Edwin
Compensation.
De Cunjah Man.
Negro Serenade.
Ol' Doc' Hyar.
Uncle Eph's Banjo Song.
When Ol' Sis' Judy Pray.
Campbell, Jane M.
We Plough the Fields.
Campbell, Joseph
Ad Limina.
The Antiquary.
As I Came over the Grey,
 Grey Hills.
The Besom-Man.
Blanaid's Song.
The Blind Man at the Fair.
Butterfly in the Fields.
Chesspieces.
The Dancer.
Darkness.
A Fighting-Man.
Go, Ploughman, Plough.
The Gombeen.
Harvest Song.
Herb-Leech.
The Hills of Cualann.
I Am the Gilly of Christ.
I Am the Mountainy Singer.
I Will Go with My Father A-
 Ploughing.
Ideal and Reality.
The Ninepenny Fidil.
O Glorious Childbearer.
Old Age Pensioner.

The Old Woman.
On Waking.
The Poet Loosed a Winged
 Song.
Three Colts Exercising in a
 Six-Acre.
The Tinkers.
Unfrocked Priest.
Campbell, Marion
Levavi Oculos.
Campbell, Marjorie Freeman
Only the Heart.
Vigil.
Campbell, Nancy
The Apple-Tree.
Campbell, Robert Bhain
Final Poem.
The Task.
Campbell, Roy
African Moonrise.
Autumn.
Ballad of Don Juan Tenorio
 and the Statue of the
 Comendador.
Buffel's Kop.
Choosing a Mast.
Christ in the Hospital.
Driving Cattle to Casas
 Buenas.
Fishing Boats in Martigues.
The Flaming Terrapin.
The Georgiad.
Georgian Spring.
The Golden Shower.
A Good Resolution.
Heartbreak Camp.
Hialmar.
Horses on the Camargue.
Limerick: "He died in
 attempting to swallow."
Luis de Camoes.
Mass at Dawn.
Mazeppa.
On Lisa's Golden Hair.
On Professor Drennan's Verse.
On Some South African
 Novelists.
On the Death of a Journalist.
On the Same.
The Palm.
Poets in Africa.
Pomegranates.
Rounding the Cape.
The Secret Muse.
The Serf.
The Sisters.
The Snake.
Talking Bronco.
The Theology of Bongwi, the
 Baboon.
To a Pet Cobra.
To the Sun.
Toledo.
Tristan da Cunha.
Upon a Gloomy Night.
A Veld Eclogue: The
 Pioneers.
The Wayzgoose.
The Zebras.
The Zulu Girl.
Campbell, Thomas
The Battle of the Baltic.
The Beatific Sea.
The Beech Tree's Petition.
Caroline, II.
The Dead Eagle.
Epistle, from Algiers, to
 Horace Smith.
Exile of Erin.
Florine.
Freedom and Love.
Glenara.

Hallowed Ground.
The Harper.
Hohenlinden.
The Jilted Nymph.
The Last Man.
Lines on Leaving a Scene in
 Bavaria.
Lochiel's Warning.
Lord Ullin's Daughter.
The Maid of Neidpath.
Margaret and Dora.
Mighty Sea! Cameleon-Like
 Thou Changest.
Napoleon and the British
 Sailor.
Ode to Winter.
The Parrot.
The Pilgrim of a Day.
The Pleasures of Hope.
The River of Life.
The Soldier's Dream.
Song to the Evening Star.
To the Rainbow.
Ye Mariners of England.
**Campbell, Wilfred (William
Wilfred Campbell)**
Bereavement of the Fields.
The Hills and the Sea.
How One Winter Came in the
 Lake Region.
Indian Summer.
Morning on the Shore.
Vapour and Blue.
The Winter Lakes.
With Cortez in Mexico.
Campion, Thomas
And Would You See My
 Mistress' Face?
Are You What Your Faire
 Lookes Expresse?
Author of Light, Revive My
 Dying Spright.
Awake, Awake!
Bar Not the Door.
Basia.
Be Thou Then by Beauty
 Named.
Be Wise, and Fly Not.
Beauty Is But A Painted Hell.
Beauty, Since You So Much
 Desire.
Blame Not My Cheeks.
Breake Now My Heart and
 Dye!
Come, Chearfull Day, Part of
 My Life, to Mee.
Come, Follow Me.
Come, Let Us Sound with
 Melody, the Praises.
Come, O Come.
Come, You Pretty False-Eyed
 Wanton.
Content.
Corinna.
The Cypress Curtain of the
 Night.
The Dance.
Dear If I with Guile.
Devotion.
Dido.
Dismissal.
An Elegye.
Fain Would I Wed a Fair
 Young Man.
First Love.
Follow, Follow.
Follow Your Saint.
Fortunati Nimium.
Give Beauty All Her Right.
Harden Now Thy Tired
 Heart.

Hark, All You Ladies That Do Sleep.
Her Fair Inflaming Eyes.
Her Sacred Bower.
The Hours of Sleepy Night.
I Care Not for These Ladies.
I Must Complain, Yet Doe Enjoy My Love.
In Praise of Neptune.
It Fell on a Summer's Day.
Jack and Joan.
Just Beguiler.
Kind Are Her Answers.
Kisses.
A Lamentation.
Love-Charms.
Love Me or Not.
A Lover's Plea.
A Maid's Complaint.
The Man of Life Upright.
Mistress, Since You So Much Desire.
My Life's Delight.
My Sweetest Lesbia.
Neptune.
Never Love.
Never Weather-Beaten Sail.
Now while the night her sable veil hath spread.
O Sweet Delight.
Of Corinna's Singing.
Oft have I sigh'd for him that heares me not.
Out of My Soul's Depth.
The Peaceful Western Wind.
Raving Warre, Begot.
Rose-Cheeked Laura.
Roses.
A Secret Love or Two I Must Confess.
Seek the Lord.
Shall I Come, If I Swim? Wide Are the Waves, You See.
Shall I Come, Sweet Love, to Thee.
Shall I Then Hope When Faith Is Fled?
Sic Transit.
Sing a Song of Joy!
Sleep, Angry Beauty.
So Quicke, So Hot, So Mad Is Thy Fond Sute.
So Tir'd Are All My Thoughts.
Some Hot, Some Cold.
Song: "Follow thy fair sun, unhappy shadow."
Song: To the Masquers Representing Stars.
There Is a Garden in Her Face.
There Is None, O None But You.
Think'st Thou to Seduce Me Then.
Thou Art Not Fair.
Thou Joy'st, Fond Boy.
Though You Are Young.
Though Your Strangenesse Frets My Hart.
Thrice Toss These Oaken Ashes in the Air.
Thus I Resolve.
To Musicke Bent.
Turn All Thy Thoughts.
Turn Back, You Wanton Flyer.
Vain Men, Whose Follies.
View Me, Lord, a Work of Thine.

Were My Hart as Some Mens Are.
What Fair Pomp Have I Spied of Glittering Ladies.
What Harvest Half So Sweet Is.
What If a Day.
What Then Is Love But Mourning.
When Thou Must Home.
When to Her Lute Corinna Sings.
When We Court and Kiss.
Where Are All Thy Beauties Now, All Hearts Enchaining?
Whether Men Do Laugh or Weep.
Winter Nights.
The Writer to His Book.
Young and Simple Though I Am.
Your Fair Looks Inflame My Desire.

Canan, Janine
Dear Body.
Diagnosis.
I Turned On the Hot Water.
She Is Carefully Stepping over the Important Communications.

Cane, Melville
Alpine View.
Dawn Has Yet to Ripple in.
Each to Each.
A Harvest to Seduce.
Hymn to Night.
Operatic Note.
Park Pigeons.
Presence of Snow.
Rural Dumpheap.
Snow Toward Evening.
Sun and Cloud.
Tree in December.

Canfield, Harry Clifford
On the Loss of U.S. Submarine S4 (excerpt).

Cannady, Criss E.
In the Sitting Room of the Opera.
Sunlight in a Cafeteria.

Cannan, May Wedderburn
Rouen.

Canning, Effie I.
Rock-a-Bye Baby.

Canning, George
Ballynahinch.
The Candid Friend.
The Dutch.
The Elderly Gentleman.
Inscription for the Door of the Cell in Newgate...
Ipecacuanha.
A Political Despatch.
The Progress of Man.
The Rovers: Rogero's Song.
To Mrs. Leigh Upon Her Wedding Day.

Cannon, Edward
An Unsuspected Fact.

Cannon, Hughie
Bill Bailey.

Cannon, Margery
Venite Adoremus.

Cannon, Melissa
Crippled Child at the Window.

Cannon, Jr., David Wadsworth
Freedom in Mah Soul.
Western Town.

Canterbury, George
New Mexico and Arizona.

Canton, William
Carol: "When the herds were watching."
The Crow.
Day-Dreams.
Laus Infantium.
A New Poet.

Cantus, Eleanor Hollister
Fame.

Canzoneri, Robert
Two.

Capetanakis, Demetrios
Abel.
The Isles of Greece.

Capp, Joseph
Generalization.

Caragher, Mary E.
Tree Tag.

Carb, Alison B.
An Israeli Soldier's Nightmare.

Carbell, E. T.
The Frogs' Singing-School.

"Carbery, Ethna" (Anna Johnston MacManus)
Hills o' My Heart.
The Love-Talker.
Mea Culpa.
The Shadow House of Lugh.

Cardenal, Ernesto
Epitaph for the Tomb of Adolfo Baez Bone.

Cardenas, Reyes
Lowriders #2.

Cardiff, Gladys
Carious Exposure.
Combing.
Dragon Skate.
Grey Woman.
Leaves Like Fish.
Long Person.
Outer Space, Inner Space.
Owl and Rooster.
Simples.
Swimmer.
Tlanusi'yi, the Leech Place.
To Frighten a Storm.
Tsa'lagi Council Tree.
Where Fire Burns.

Cardona-Hine, Alvaro
Geo-Politics.

Carducci, Giosue
Fantasy.
Petrarch.
Primo Vere.
Snowfall.

Careme, Maurice
You Can Get Despondent.

Carenza, Iselda
Tenson.

Carew
He That Loves a Rosy Cheek.

Carew, Lady Elizabeth
Miriam: Chorus.

Carew, Richard
Survey of Cornwall.

Carew, Thomas
Another.
Ask Me No More.
A Beautifull Mistress.
Boldness in Love.
Celia Bleeding, to the Surgeon.
Celia Singing.
The Comparison.
The Complement.
A Cruell Mistris.
A Deposition from Love.
Disdain Returned.
A Divine Mistris.

An Elegy upon the Death of the Dean of St. Paul's, Dr. John Donne.
Epitaph on Maria Wentworth.
Epitaph on the Lady Mary Villiers.
Eternity of Love Protested.
An Excuse of Absence.
A Fly That Flew into My Mistress's Eye.
For a Picture Where a Queen Laments over the Tomb of a Slain Knight.
Good Counsel to a Young Maid.
Her Sweet Voice.
An Hymeneal Song on the Nuptials of the Lady Anne Wentworth and...
An Hymeneall Dialogue.
I Will Enjoy Thee Now.
In Answer of an Elegiacall Letter upon the Death of the King of Sweden.
Ingratefull Beauty Threatned.
The Inscription on the Tombe of the Lady Mary Wentworth.
A Lady's Prayer to Cupid.
A Looking-Glass.
Love's Courtship.
Love's Force.
The Lover Consults with Reason.
A Lover, upon an Accident Necessitating His Departure....
Maria Wentworth, Thomae Comitis Cleveland...
Mediocrity in Love Rejected.
Murdering Beauty.
A New-Year's Sacrifice.
Now That the Winter's Gone.
Obsequies to the Lady Anne Hay.
On a Damaske Rose Sticking upon a Ladies Breast.
On His Mistress Looking in a Glass.
On Sight of a Gentlewoman's Face in the Water.
On the Death of Donne.
On the Marriage of T. K. and C. C. the Morning Stormy.
A Pastorall Dialogue.
Persuasions to Enjoy.
Persuasions to Love.
A Prayer to the Wind.
The Primrose.
The Protestation, A Sonnet.
A Rapture.
Red, and White Roses.
The Second Rapture.
Secrecy Protested.
Song: "Would you know what's soft?"
The Spring.
The Tinder.
To A. L.
To a Lady That Desired I Would Love Her.
To Ben. Johnson. Upon Occasion of His Ode of Defiance.
To Celia, upon Love's Ubiquity.
To Her Againe, She Burning in a Feaver.
To Her in Absence.
To His Inconstant Mistress.
To My Cousin, (C.R.) Marrying My Lady (A.).

To My Friend G. N. from
  Wrest.
To My Inconstant Mistress.
To My Mistress in Absence.
To My Mistris, I Burning in
  Love.
To My Mistris Sitting by a
  River's Side. An Eddy.
To My Worthy Friend Master
  George Sands....
To One That Desired to
  Know My Mistris.
To Saxham.
To T. H., a Lady Resembling
  My Mistress.
To the King, at His Entrance
  into Saxham.
To the New Year.
To the Reader of Master
  William Davenant's Play,
  The Wits.
The Unfading Beauty.
Upon a Mole in Celia's
  Bosom.
Upon a Ribband.
Upon Master Walter
  Montagu's Return from
  Travel.
Upon My Lord Chief Justice's
  Election of My Lady Anne
  Wentworth...
Upon Some Alterations in My
  Mistress, after My Departure
  into France.
The Willing Prisoner to His
  Mistress.
Carey, Henry
The Ballad of Sally in our
  Alley.
A Drinking-Song.
God Save the King.
Happy Myrtillo.
Harry Carey's General
  Reply...
The Huntsman's Rouse.
A Lilliputian Ode on Their
  Majesties' Accession.
A Maiden's Ideal of a
  Husband.
Namby-Pamby.
Roger and Dolly.
Sally in Our Alley.
Sally Sweetbread.
Carey, Patrick
Hymn: Crucifixus Pro Nobis.
Carleton, Sara King
Late October.
Carleton, Will
Across the Delaware.
Betsey and I Are Out.
The Country Doctor.
Cuba to Columbia.
Death-Doomed.
The Doctor's Story.
"Flash:" The Fireman's Story.
Johnny Rich.
The Litttle Black-Eyed Rebel.
The New Church Organ.
Out of the Old House, Nancy.
Over the Hill to the Poor-
  House.
The Prize of the Margaretta.
The Victory Wreck.
Carleton, William
Sir Turlough; or, The
  Churchyard Bride.
Carlile, Henry
Dodo.
Flying.
Grandmother.
The Grief of Our Genitals.
Havana Blues.

Listening to Beethoven on the
  Oregon Coast.
Spider Reeves.
Carlin, Francis
Ballad of Douglas Bridge.
Before I Stumbled.
Beyond Rathkelly.
The Gray Plume.
Hope's Song.
Mac Diarmod's Daughter.
The Market Town.
Perfection.
Plea for Hope.
The Virgin's Slumber Song.
Virgins.
Carlson, Randolph
Rapture.
Carlyle, Jane Welsh
To a Swallow Building under
  Our Eaves.
Carlyle, Thomas
Adieu.
Cui Bono?
The Sower's Song.
To-Day.
Carman, Bliss
An April Morning.
Arnold, Master of the Scud.
An Autumn Garden.
The Choristers.
A Christmas Eve Choral.
Christmas Song.
Daffodil's Return.
The Daisies.
Daphne.
The Deserted Pasture.
Envoy.
The Grave-Tree.
The Gravedigger.
Hack and Hew.
Hem and Haw.
The Heretic.
I Loved Thee, Atthis, in the
  Long Ago.
In a Copy of Browning.
In October.
In Philistia.
In the House of Idiedaily.
The Joys of the Road.
Lord of My Heart's Elation.
Lord of the Far Horizons.
Low Tide on Grand-Pre.
The Man of Peace.
Marian Drury.
The Mendicants.
Moment Musicale.
A More Ancient Mariner.
Morning in the Hills.
Mr. Moon.
A Northern Vigil.
The Old Grey Wall.
Over the Wintry Threshold.
Overlord.
Roadside Flowers.
Sappho.
A Sea Child.
A Seamark.
The Ships of Saint John.
The Ships of Yule.
A Son of the Sea.
Song: "Love, by that loosened
  hair."
Songs of the Sea-Children.
Spring Song.
Threnody for a Poet.
Trees.
Triumphalis.
A Vagabond Song.
Veni Creator.
Vestigia.
Where Is Heaven?
Why.

Winter Streams.
Carmer, Carl
Black Boy.
Carmi, T.
The Author's Apology.
The Condition.
Carmichael, Amy
Comforted.
Deliver Me.
Do We Not Hear Thy
  Footfall?
The Evening Star.
For All in Pain.
Have We Not Seen Thy
  Shining Garment's Hem.
Hope.
The Last Defile.
Lord, Thou Hast Suffered.
Tune Thou My Harp.
Yet Listen Now.
Carmichael, Waverly Turner
Keep Me, Jesus, Keep Me.
Winter is Coming.
Carnegie, James
The Flitch of Dunmow.
Carnevali, Emanuel
His Majesty the Letter-
  Carrier.
In This Hotel.
Queer Things.
Serenade.
Walt Whitman.
Carney, Julia A. Fletcher
Little Things.
Carolan, Turlough
Why, Liquor of Life?
Carossa, Hans
Mysterious Landscape.
Caroutch, Yvonne
Child of silence and shadow.
I come to you with the
  vertigoes of the source.
The limb of forests rises up.
Night opens like an almond.
When We Are Like Two
  Drunken Suns.
Carpenter, Amelia Walstein
Old Flemish Lace.
Recollection.
The Ride to Cherokee.
Carpenter, Edward
Among the Ferns.
Have Faith.
Love's Vision.
A Mightier Than Mammon.
Over the Great City.
The Songs of the Birds.
The Stupid Old Body.
Towards Democracy.
The Wandering Lunatic Mind.
Carpenter, Henry Bernard
The Reed.
Carpenter, Joseph Edward
Do They Think of Me at
  Home.
Carpenter, Lis R.
At His Feet.
Carpenter, Margaret Haley
September Afternoon.
Carpenter, Maurice
To S. T. C. on His 179th
  Birthday, October 12th,
  1951.
Carpenter, Rhys
Beggars.
The Master Singers.
Who Bids Us Sing?
Carpenter, William
Autumn.
Fire.
The Keeper.

Carpenter, William Boyd
Before Thy Throne.
Carphyllides
A Happy Man.
Carr, Alan J.
Old Man.
Carr, Frank
Frankenstein Gets His Man.
Carr, John
Derwent: An Ode.
Carr, Leroy
Mean Mistreater Mama.
Take a Walk around the
  Corner.
Carr, Mary Jane
The Big Swing-Tree Is Green
  Again.
The Birthday of the Lord.
The Castle in the Fire.
Pirate Wind.
Shop of Dreams.
Six Birthday Candles Shining.
The West Wind's Secret.
When a Fellow's Four.
When a Ring's Around the
  Moon.
Carr, Robert V.
Bill Haller's Dance.
Comin' to Town.
The Commission Man.
The Cowboy and the Stork.
Cowboy's Salvation Song.
Enlightenment.
Goody-by, Steer.
Home.
The Old Cowboy's Lament.
Prairie Wolves.
The Rattlesnake.
Remember the Promise,
  Dakotah.
Romance of the Range.
The Roundup Cook.
Silhouette in Sepia.
The War Dance.
The Western Trail.
When Dutchy Plays the
  Mouth Harp.
Carr, Sir John
Sonnet upon a Swedish
  Cottage.
Carrera Andrade, Jorge
The Perfect Life.
Carrier, Constance
Black Water and Bright Air.
Colonel B.
Fugue.
Lisa.
Party.
Peter at Fourteen.
Pro Patria.
Seminary.
Transformation Scene.
Carrier, Warren
What I Saw in October.
Carrington, John William
The Second Coming.
Carrington, N. T.
On Seeing a Fine Frigate at
  Anchor in a Bay off Mount
  Edgecumbe.
Carroll, Jim
The Distances.
**"Carroll, Lewis" (Charles
Lutwidge Dodgson)**
The Aged Aged Man
  (parody).
Alice's Recitation.
Brother and Sister.
Disillusioned.
Doll Song.
The Duchess's Lullaby.

Evidence Read at the Trial of the Knave of Hearts.
Facts.
Father William.
Fragment of a Song.
Fury Said to a Mouse.
Hiawatha's Photographing.
Hit or Miss.
How Doth the Little Crocodile.
Humpty Dumpty's Recitation.
The Hunting of the Snark.
In Winter, When the Fields Are White.
Jabberwocky.
The King-Fisher Song.
Limerick: "There was a young lady of station."
Lions and Gruel and Uncles.
Little Birds.
The Lobster Quadrille.
The Mad Gardener's Song.
The Mad Hatter's Song.
The Manlet (parody).
Melancholetta.
Melodies.
My Fairy.
My Fancy.
The Palace of Humbug.
A Pig-Tale.
Poeta Fit, non Nascitur.
A Quotation from Shakespeare with Slight Improvements.
Rules and Regulations.
A Sea Dirge.
She's All My Fancy Painted Him.
A Song of Love.
Speak Roughly to Your Little Boy.
Sylvie and Bruno.
Tema con Variazioni.
The Three Badgers.
The Three Voices (parody).
"The Time Has Come," the Walrus Said.
To the Looking-Glass World It Was Alice That Said (parody).
Turtle Soup.
Tutor's Dignity.
A Visitor.
The Voice of the Lobster.
The Walrus and the Carpenter.
The Wasp's Song.
The White Knight's Song.
Carroll, Paul
Father.
Carrothers, James David
In the Matter of Two Men.
Carruth, Hayden
The Asylum, II.
Bouquet in Dog Time.
Contra Mortem.
The Cows at Night.
Dornroschen.
Emergency Haying.
Fear and Anger in the Mindless Universe.
Five Short-Shorts.
The Insomniac Sleeps Well for Once and.
Keraunograph.
Late Sonnet.
Loneliness: An Outburst of Hexasyllables.
Mending the Adobe.
My Dog Jock.
New Orleans.

On a Certain Engagement South of Seoul.
Once More.
Our Tense and Wintry Minds.
A Paragraph.
Privation.
Rimrock, Where It Is.
Salt Lake City.
Sonnet: "Cry, crow."
Speaking for Them.
Summer's Early End at Hudson Bay.
This Decoration.
Twilight Comes.
When Howitzers Began.
Carruth, William Herbert
Dreamer of Dreams.
Each in His Own Tongue.
Carryl, Charles Edward
An Alphabet.
My Recollectest Thoughts.
The Plaint of the Camel.
Robinson Crusoe.
The Sleepy Giant.
The Song in the Dell.
The Walloping Window-Blind.
Carryl, Guy Wetmore
The Arrogant Frog and the Superior Bull.
A Ballad (parody).
The Domineering Eagle and the Inventive Bratling.
The Embarrassing Episode of Little Miss Muffet.
The Harmonious Heedlessness of Little Boy Blue.
How a Girl Was Too Reckless of Grammar.
How Jack Found that Beans May Go Back on a Chap.
How the Helpmate of Blue-Beard Made Free with a Door.
The Inhuman Wolf and the Lamb Sans Gene.
Little Boy Blue.
Little Red Riding Hood.
The Opportune Overthrow of Humpty Dumpty.
The Singular Sangfroid of Baby Bunting.
The Sycophantic Fox and the Gullible Raven.
When the Great Gray Ships Come in.
Carsley, Sara E.
The Little Boats of Britain.
Portrait of a Very Old Man.
Carson, Ciaran
The Bomb Disposal.
The Car Cemetery.
The Insular Celts.
St. Ciaran and the Birds.
Visiting the Dead.
Carson, E. J.
November Snow.
Carson, Joseph
As I Grow Older and Fatten on Myself.
Carson, Mary Newland
My "Patch of Blue."
Carter, Aline Badger
Give Our Conscience Light.
Carter, Bo
All Around Man.
Old Devil.
Carter, Charlotte Osgood
Limerick: "Said the elephant to the giraffe."
Carter, Elizabeth
Ode to Wisdom.

Carter, Hodding
In the Jury Room.
Slave Story.
Carter, Jared
At the Sign-Painter's.
For Jack Chatham.
The Measuring.
Carter, John Marshall
Turn on the Footlights: The Perils of Pedagogy.
Carter, Sydney
The Faith Came First.
The First of My Lovers.
Lord of the Dance.
Carter, William Lorenzo
Young Charlottie.
Cartwright, Peter
Our Bondage It Shall End.
Where Are the Hebrew Children?
Cartwright, William
Come, my sweet, whiles every strain.
The Dead Sparrow.
Falsehood.
A New-Years-Gift to Brian Lord Bishop of Sarum...
No Platonique Love.
On a Virtuous Young Gentlewoman That Died Suddenly.
On the Queens Return from the Low Countries.
The Siege: Seal Up Her Eyes, O Sleep.
A Song of Dalliance.
To Chloe, Who Wished Herself Young Enough For Me.
Upon the Dramatick Poems of Mr. John Fletcher.
A Valediction.
Women.
Carus, Titus Lucretius
The Origins of Life.
Caruthers, Mazie V.
Prayer of Any Husband.
Carvalho, Ronald de
Per Amica Silentia Lunae.
Carver, Mabel MacDonald
Codicil.
Carver, Raymond
Bobber.
Forever.
Looking for Work.
Marriage.
Photograph of My Father in His Twenty-Second Year.
Poem for Hemingway & W. C. Williams.
Prosser.
Wes Hardin: From a Photograph.
You Don't Know What Love Is (parody).
Your Dog Dies.
Cary, Alice
Among the Beautiful Pictures.
Balder's Wife.
Dying Hymn.
The Gray Swan.
Her Mother.
Make Believe.
My Creed.
Nobility.
November.
An Order for a Picture.
To Mother Fairie.
Cary, Patrick
And Now a Fig for the Lower House.

Whilst I Beheld the Neck o' th' Dove.
Cary, Phoebe
"The Day is Done" (Parody on Longfellow)..
Jacob.
Keep a Stiff Upper Lip.
The Leak in the Dike.
A Legend of the Northland.
The Lovers.
Nearer Home.
One Sweetly Solemn Thought.
Our Heroes.
Peace.
Ready.
Samuel Brown.
Suppose.
Thaddeus Stevens.
True Love.
When Lovely Woman.
Cary, Thomas
On His Mistresse Going to Sea.
Caryll, John
The Hypocrite.
Naboth's Vineyard.
Casa, Giovanni della
To Sleep.
Casal, Julian del
The Friar.
Casas, Jose Joaquin
The Secret.
Case, Elizabeth York
There Is No Unbelief.
Case, John
From One of Case's Pill-Boxes.
Over Case's Door.
To Saffold's Customers.
Case, Lizzie York
There Is No Unbelief.
Case, Phila H.
Nobody's Child.
Casement, Roger
In the Streets of Catania.
Lost Youth.
Casewit, Curtis W.
End of the Affair.
Casey, John Keegan
Maire My Girl.
The Rising of the Moon A.D. 1798.
Casey, Michael
Driving While under the Influence.
Casey, Peter
The Merry Jovial Beggar.
Casey, Thomas F.
Drill Ye Tarriers, Drill.
Casillas, Rick
Yaqui Women: Three Generations.
Caskey, Noelle
Ripening.
Casone, Girolamo
Time Recover'd.
Cassel, Irwin M.
I Love Life.
Cassian, Nina
All Night Long.
The Blood.
Cripples.
Hills picking up the moonlight.
Knowledge.
Lady of Miracles.
Like Gulliver.
Ordeal.
Self-Portrait.
Vegetable Destiny.
Cassity, Turner
L'Aigle a Deux Jambes.

Calvin in the Casino.
Chronology.
The Gardens of Proserpine.
Grace at the Atlanta Fox.
Links.
Pacelli and the Ethiop.
Technique on the Firing Line.
Wine from the Cape.
Castelete, Rachael
When I Came to London.
Castellânos, Rosario
Foreign Woman.
Silence Concerning an Ancient
Stone.
Three Poems.
Useless Day.
Casterline, Helen Annis
God Cares.
Castillejo, Cristobal de
Some Day, Some Day.
Castillo, Ana
Napa, California.
Castle, Sandie
The Blake Mistake.
Hand-Jive.
Mother's Day.
Casto, Robert Clayton
Classical Autumn.
The Salt Pork.
Castro, Michael
Grandfathers.
Percolating Highway.
Castro, Rosalia de
Crickets and Locusts, Cicadas.
How Placidly Shine.
In the Sky, Clearest Blue.
Long May.
Now all that sound of
laughter, sound of singing.
Plants Don't Talk, People
Say.
Castro de Murguia, Rosalia
The Carillon.
Castro Rios, Andres
For Nothing.
Words to Remind Me of
Grandmother.
Caswall, Edward
Light of the Soul.
Sleep, Holy Babe.
Catacalos, Rosemary
Homecoming Celebration.
Cater, Catherine
Here and Now.
Cather, Willa
L'Envoi.
The Hawthorn Tree.
A Likeness.
The Palatine.
Spanish Johnny.
Cather, Willa Sibert
Grandmither, Think Not I
Forget.
Catlin, Ellen Weston
Childlike Heart.
Cato, Nancy
Independence.
Cattafi, Bartola
Patience.
Catton, Bruce
Names From the War.
Catullus, Caius Valerius
Attis.
Carmina.
Cataclysm.
Catullus Talks to Himself.
Cominus, You Reprobate Old
Goat.
Counting Kisses.
The Dead Sparrow.
The Death of Lesbia's Bird.

A Debate on Marriage versus
Virginity.
Dialogue with a Door.
Dianae Sumus in Fide.
Egnatius, Because His Teeth
Are White.
Expect No Thanks.
Farewell to Lesbia.
Flavius, If Your Girl Friend.
Gellius, What Reason Can
You Give.
Hendecasyllables, Help!
Hymeneal.
Hymn to Diana.
Hymn to Marriage, for
Manlius and Junia.
I Entrust My All to You,
Aurelius.
I Have Something for You to
Laugh at, Cato.
I'll Have You by the Short
and Curly Hair.
If I Could Go On Kissing
Your Honeyed Eyes.
An Invitation to an Invitation.
Juventius, Could You Not
Find in This Great Crowd of
Men.
Juventius, My Honey.
Lesbia loads me night & day
with her curses.
Lesbia Railing.
Letter to Manlius Torquatus.
Love and Death.
Love Is All.
My Woman.
Naso, You're All Men's Man.
Ode: Acme and Septimius.
Of All Our Bath-House
Thieves the Cleverest One.
Of You, If Anyone, It Can Be
Said.
On the Burial of His Brother.
Phyllis Corydon clutched to
him.
Prayer against Love.
Return to Sirmio.
Sappho.
Sirmio.
So Help Me God.
Spring.
They Make a Pretty Pair of
Debauchees.
To Himself.
To Lesbia.
To Naso.
To Varus.
Transformation.
Two Poems against His Rival,
II.
Veranius, My Dear Friend.
Whom Lesbia Loved.
World without End.
The Yacht.
Your Catullus Is Depressed.
"Caudwell, Christopher"
(Christopher St. John Sprigg)
Classic Encounter.
The Progress of Poetry.
Causley, Charles
Angels' Song.
The Animals' Carol.
Armistice Day.
At Candlemas.
At the British War Cemetery,
Bayeux.
Autobiography.
A Ballad for Katharine of
Aragon.
Betjeman, 1984.
Chief Petty Officer.
Colonel Fazackerley.

Cowboy Song.
Death of a Poet.
Death of an Aircraft.
Envoi.
For an Ex-Far East Prisoner
of War.
H.M.S. Glory at Sydney.
I Saw a Jolly Hunter.
Infant Song.
Innocent's Song.
King's College Chapel.
Loss of an Oil Tanker.
Mary's Song.
Nursery Rhyme of Innocence
and Experience.
On Seeing a Poet of the First
World War on the Station at
Abbeville.
On the Thirteenth Day of
Christmas.
Ou Phrontis.
Recruiting Drive.
Riley.
Sailor's Carol.
The Seasons in North
Cornwall.
The Song of Samuel Sweet.
Ten Types of Hospital Visitor.
A Visit to Van Gogh.
Cavafy, Constantine P.
Alexander Jannai.
Days of 1896.
He Asked about the Quality.
In Despair.
Ithaca.
The Mirror in the Front Hall.
The Next Table.
On the Street.
One of the Jews.
Return.
Their Beginning.
To Remain.
The Twenty-Fifth Year of His
Life.
Two Young Men, 23 to 24
Years Old.
Walls.
The Window of the Tobacco
Shop.
Cavalcanti, Guido
Ballata: Concerning a
Shepherd-Maid.
Ballata: He Reveals, in a
Dialogue, His Increasing
Love for Mandetta.
Ballata: In Exile at Sarzana.
Ballata: Of a Continual Death
in Love.
Ballata: Of His Lady among
Other Ladies.
Ballata of Love's Power.
Ballata V: "Light do I see
within my Lady's eyes."
Canzone: Donna Mi Priegha.
The Effigy.
Love's Assize.
Sonnet: A Rapture
Concerning His Lady.
Sonnet: Guido Cavalcanti to
Dante.
Sonnet: He Compares All
Things with His Lady, and
Finds Them Wanting.
Sonnet: He Speaks of a Third
Love of His.
Sonnet: Of an Ill-Favored
Lady.
Sonnet: Of His Pain from a
New Love.
Sonnet: Of the Eyes of a
Certain Mandetta, of
Toulouse...

Sonnet: On the Detection of a
False Friend.
Sonnet: To a Friend Who
Does Not Pity His Love.
Sonnet: To Dante Alighieri
(He Reports in a Feigned
Vision).
Sonnet: To His Lady Joan, of
Florence.
Sonnetto VII: "Who is she
that comes."
Sonnetto XXXV: "My Lady's
face it is they worship
there."
Cavanass, J. M.
By the Waters of Minnetonka.
Cavendish, Margaret *See*
Newcastle, Margaret
Cavendish, Dutchess of
Cavendish William *See*
Newcastle, William Cavendish,
Duke of
Cawein, Madison
Attainment.
Ballad of Low-Lie-Down.
Comradery.
The Creek-Road.
Death.
Deserted.
Dirge.
Enchantment.
Flight.
Here Is the Place Where
Loveliness Keeps House.
Ku Klux.
The Man Hunt.
Mene, Mene, Tekel, Upharsin.
The Miracle of Dawn.
Morning Serenade.
Mosby at Hamilton.
The Old Home.
Old Man Rain.
Opportunity.
Proem.
The Rain-Crow.
The Soul.
To a Wind-Flower.
The Wind in the Pines.
Cawthorn, James
Of Taste; An Essay.
Cayley, George John
An Epitaph.
Cedering, Sir *See* **Fox, Sir**
Cedering
Ceile De, Oengus
The Time Is Ripe and I
Repent.
Ceitinn, Seathrun
At the News from Fal's High
Plain I Cannot Sleep.
O Lady Full of Guile.
Celan, Paul
Ash-Glory.
Cello Entry.
Corona.
Etched away From.
Fugue of Death.
Hut Window.
In Egypt.
In Prague.
Irish.
The Jugs.
Just Think.
Leap-Centuries.
Over Three Nipple-Stones.
...Plashes the Fountain.
Psalm.
A Speck of Sand.
Tenebrae.
Thread Suns.
Turn Blind.
Your Hand Full of Hours.

Zurich, zum Storchen.
Cennick, John
Be Present at Our Table, Lord.
Children of the Heavenly King.
Centamputan, Maturai Eruttalan
What She Said.
Ceravolo, Joseph
The Book of Wild Flowers.
Dangers of the Journey to the Happy Land.
Don't Break It.
Drunken Winter.
Fill and Illumined.
Happiness in the Trees.
Ho Ho Ho Caribou.
In My Crib.
Route.
A Song of Autumn.
Spring of Work Storm.
A Story from the Bushmen.
Wild Provoke of the Endurance Sky.
The Wind Is Blowing West.
Cerenio, Virginia
Manong Benny.
Pick-up at Chef Rizal Restaurant.
Pinay.
You Lovely People.
Cernuda, Luis
Birds in the Night.
Cervantes, Lorna Dee
Beneath the Shadow of the Freeway.
Poem for the Young White Man Who Asked Me How I, an Intelligent...
Visions of Mexico While at a Writing Symposium in Port Townsend...
The Woman in My Notebook.
Cervantes Saarvedra, Miguel de
Sonnet: "When I was marked for suffering, love forswore."
Cetina, Gutierre de
Madrigal: "Eyes that are clear, serene."
Ceu, Sor Violante do
Voice of a Dissipated Woman inside a Tomb...
Cha Liang-cheng
Hungry China.
There Is No Nearer Nearness.
Chace, Jean Valentine
Visit to a Hospital.
Chadwick, Jerah
The Runner.
Chadwick, John
Hymn.
O Love, That Dost with Goodness Crown.
Chadwick, John White
The Abiding Love.
Auld Lang Syne.
Full Cycle.
The Golden-Robin's Nest.
His Mother's Joy.
The Making of Man.
Mugford's Victory.
Recognition.
The Rise of Man.
Starlight.
A Wedding-Song.
Chaet, Eric
A Letter Catches Up with Me.
Yom Kippur.
Chaffee, Eleanor Alletta
The Cobbler.
The Difference.

Chaffin, Lillie D.
Haiku, for Cinnamon.
Tourism.
Chaibrera, Gabriello
Epitaph: "O flower of all that springs from gentle blood."
Chaikin, Miriam
Light Another Candle.
One-Upmanship.
Chalfi, Abraham
My Father.
Chalfi, Raquel
A Childless Witch.
Like a Field Waiting.
A Witch Going Down to Egypt.
Chalkhill, John
The Angler.
Coridon's Song.
Rhotus on Arcadia.
Chalmers, Patrick Reginald
The Cuckoo.
The Gardener's Cat.
Hold.
In an Old Nursery.
Lavender's for Ladies.
My Woodcock.
Pan-Pipes.
Puk-Wudjies.
The Road.
The Tortoiseshell Cat.
The Visitor.
When Mary Goes Walking.
Chalmers, Stephen
Home.
The New Physician.
Chalpin, Lila
Curse of a Fisherman's Wife.
Chamberlain, Brenda
Dead Ponies.
First Woman's Lament.
Give No White Flower.
Lament.
Poem: "You, who in April laughed, a green god in the sun."
Second Woman's Lament.
Song: "Bone-aged is my white horse."
Song: "Heron is harsh with despair."
Song–Talysarn.
Chamberlain, Enola
After the Dark.
Chamberlain, Richard
To the Much Honoured R. F. Esq.
Chamberlain, Robert
In Praise of Country Life.
Chamberlayne, Sir James
Dedication.
Chambers, Jane
Woman.
Chambers, Robert William
The Grey Horse Troop.
Officer Brady.
The Recruit.
To Nature Seekers.
Chan Fang-sheng
Sailing Homeward.
Chandler, Elsie Williams
Christmas Singing.
Chandler, Janet Carncross
Leave the Top Plums.
To Drift Down.
Chandler, Len
I Would Be a Painter Most of All.
Chandonnet, Ann
The Edge.
Chandra, G. S. Sharat
In Praise of Blur.

Chang, Diana
Artists East and West.
Cannibalism.
Codes.
The Horizon Is Definitely Speaking.
Once and Future.
Second Nature.
Trying to Stay.
Chang Heng
The Bones of Chuang Tzu.
Chanler, Isaac
Awake My Soul, Betimes Awake.
Thrice Welcome First and Best of Days.
Channing, William Ellery
The Barren Moors.
Edith.
A Poet's Hope.
A Prayer.
Tears in Spring.
Channing, II, William Ellery
The Earth-Spirit.
Hymn of the Earth.
Channing-Stetson, Grace Ellery
England.
Judgment.
A Song of Arno.
War.
Chantikian, Kosrof
Love Song.
Your Eyes.
Chao Li-hua
Farewell.
Chao Luan-luan
Slender Fingers.
Chao Ying-Tou
The Decress of God.
Chapin, Carol Earle
Highway Construction.
Chapin, Edwin Hubbell
Hark! Hark! With Harps of Gold.
O Thou, Who Didst Ordain the Word.
Chapin, Henry
Easy Does It.
Helpmate.
A Quality of Air.
Threes.
Chapin, Katherine Garrison
Love Beleagured.
On a Sea-Grape Leaf.
The Other Journey.
Plain-Chant for America.
Portrait in Winter.
Chaplin, Ralph
The Commonwealth of Toil.
Mourn Not the Dead.
Solidarity Forever.
To France.
Chapman, Arthur
Beecher Island.
The Blanket Injun.
The Dead Prospector.
Last Drift.
Little Papoose.
Pete's Error.
The Santa Fe Trail.
The Sheep-Herder's Lament.
The Sheriff's Report.
Chapman, George
Bussy d'Ambois.
Caesar and Pompey.
The Conspiracy of Charles, Duke of Byron.
A Coronet for His Mistress Philosophy.
Descend, Fair Sun!

The Epistle Dedicatory to Chapman's Translation of the Iliad.
Eugenia: Presage of Storme.
Euthymiae Raptus.
De Guiana, Carmen Epicum.
Hero and Leander.
Homeric Hymn to Neptune.
A Hymne to Our Saviour on the Cross.
Learning.
The Master Spirit.
Ovid's Banquet of Sense.
The Pilot.
The Poet Questions Peace.
Praise of Homer.
Repentance.
Rich Mine of Knowledge.
The Shadow of Night.
Shadow of Night: Hymnus in Noctem.
Song: "O come, soft rest of cares! come, Night!"
Such Love Is Like a Smoky Fire.
To Mars.
The Wedding of Alcmane and Mya.
Chapman, John Alexander
Gipsy Queen.
Chapman, John Jay
Clouds.
Lines on the Death of Bismarck.
Song: "Old Farmer Oats and his son Ned."
Toil Away.
Chapone, Hester
To Stella.
Chappell, Fred
Guess Who.
The Lost Carnival.
My Grandfather's Church Goes Up.
My Mother Shoots the Breeze (excerpt).
Northwest Airlines.
Rimbaud Fire Letter to Jim Applewhite.
Spitballer.
Chappell, George S.
Innocence.
Chappell, Jeannette
Newton to Einstein.
Char, Rene
True Night.
Charasson, Henriette
Ave Maria.
Charles, Dorthi
Concrete poem: Concrete Cat.
Charles, Elizabeth Rundle
The Child on the Judgment Seat.
Charles, Mary Grant
Flood.
Charles, Robert E.
A Roundabout Turn.
Charles of Orleans See Orleans, Charles Duc d'
Chartier, Alain
I turn you out of doors.
Chartres, Vidame de
April.
Chase, Edith Newlin
The New Baby Calf.
Passenger Train.
Tiger-Cat Tim.
Work Horses.
Chase, Frank
The Tale of the Dixie-Belle.
Chase, Victoria
The Birthday Cake.

Chasin, Helen
City Pigeons.
Falling Out.
Joy Sonnet in a Random
  Universe.
Looking Out.
Mythics.
Photograph at the Cloisters:
  April 1972.
The Poetess Ko Ogimi.
The Recovery Room: Lying-
  in.
The Word Plum.
Chatain, Robert
World of Darkness.
Chatt, George
At Elsdon.
Chatterton, Thomas
The Accounte of W.
  Canynge's Feast.
An African Song.
Bristowe Tragedie.
The Copernican System.
Elinoure and Juga.
An Excelente Balade of
  Charitie.
Goddwyn: Ode to Liberty.
If Wishing for the Mystic Joys
  of Love.
Last Verses.
The Minstrel's Song.
My Love Is Dead.
Mynstrelles Songe.
O Sing unto my Roundelay.
Ode to Miss Hoyland
  (parody).
Resignation.
Sentiment.
Chattopadhyaya, Harindranath
Imagery.
Chaucer, Geoffrey
An A.B.C.
Against Women Unconstant.
And As For Me.
Arcite's Farewell.
Ballade of Good Counsel
  (modern version).
Ballade to Rosamund.
The Birds' Rondel (modern
  version).
The Book of the Duchess.
But Whan the Cok: Troilus
  and Criseide.
The Canterbury Tales.
The Complaint of Chaucer to
  His Empty Purse.
The Complaint of Troilus.
Controlling the Tongue.
Death and the Three
  Revellers.
The Dream of the Romaunt
  of the Rose.
L'Envoy de Chaucer a
  Scogan.
Envoy (To King Henry IV).
Gentilesse.
The Good Parson.
The House of Fame: Jove's
  Eagle Carries Chaucer into
  Space.
The House of Fame: The
  Eagle Converses with
  Chaucer.
Hyd, Absolon, Thy Gilte
  Tresses Clere.
Lak of Stedfastnesse.
The Legend of Good Women.
The Love Unfeigned.
Madam Eglantine.
Merciless Beauty.
The Murder in the Cathedral:
  The Cook's Tale (parody).

O Blisful Light: Troilus and
  Criseide.
Parlement of Foules.
Patient Griselda.
Prayer to Venus.
La Priere de Nostre Dame.
Proem to the Parlement of
  Foules.
A Rondel of Merciless Beauty.
The Shipman.
A Song to His Purse for the
  King.
Three Roundels of Love
  Unreturned.
To Rosamond.
Troilus and Criseyde.
Two Invocations of the
  Virgin.
Unto Adam, His Own
  Scriveyn.
Welcome, Summer.
Young Woman.
Chaudhari, Kirti
Inertia.
Chavez, Fray Angelico
Esther.
Lady of Lidice.
Lady of Peace: Cathedral:
  Honolulu..
Mary.
Mulier Amicta Sole.
Sea-Birds.
Chawner, George F.
A Prayer.
Chayat, Juliet
Stone.
Chear, Abraham
To My Youngest Kinsman, R.
  L.
Chedid, Andrée
The Future and the Ancestor.
What Are We Playing At?
Cheever, George Barrell
Blest Be the Wondrous Grace.
Cheke, Henry
Of Perfect Friendship.
Ch'en Yun
Twilight.
Cheney, Ednah D.
The Larger Prayer.
Prayer–Answer.
Cheney, Elizabeth
Overheard in an Orchard.
There Is a Man on the Cross.
Cheney, John Vance
Evening Songs.
Every One to His Own Way.
The Golden Age.
The Happiest Heart.
Lincoln.
The Man with the Hoe: A
  Reply.
On a Picture of Lincoln.
San Francisco.
The Skilful Listener.
The Strong.
Unto Our God Most High We
  Sing.
The Way of It.
Whither.
Cheng Min
Student.
Chenier, Andre Marie de
Elegies.
Iambes VIII.
When I Was Small.
Cherbury, Edward Herbert See
  **Herbert of Cherbury, Edward,
  Lord**
Cherner, Anne
Everglade.

To Helen Frankenthaler of
  Circe, 1974.
To Mark Rothko of Untitled
  (Blue, Green), 1969.
To Morris Louis of the Blue
  Veil 1958-9.
Window.
Chernin, Kim
Eve's Birth.
Chernoff, Maxine
Breasts.
How Lies Grow.
A Name.
Utopia TV Store.
Cherry, Andrew
The Green Little Shamrock of
  Ireland.
Cherry, Edith E.
Kept for Jesus.
Cherry, Kelly
A Scientific Expedition in
  Siberia, 1913.
Cherwinski, Joseph
Forsythia Is the Color I
  Remember.
Manhattan Menagerie.
Chester, Anson G.
The Tapestry Weaver.
Chester, Laura
28 VIII 69.
Bees Inside Me.
Correspondence.
Far Be It.
Go Round.
The Good Time Is Now.
In a Motion.
Last Breath.
Moved Towards a Future.
On the Wallowy.
Pavane for the Passing of a
  Child.
Returning to the World.
Simply.
Trellis.
We Heart.
Chester, Sir Robert
Ditty.
Her Hair.
**Chesterfield, Philip Stanhope,
  Earl of**
Advice to a Lady in Autumn.
Impromptu Lines on Being
  Asked by Sir Thomas
  Robinson...
On Miss Eleanor Ambrose, A
  Celebrated Beauty in Dublin.
On Mr. Nash's Present of His
  Own Picture at Full
  Length...
Song: "Whenever, Chloe, I
  begin."
To a Lady on Reading
  Sherlock upon Death.
To Miss Eleanor Ambrose...
Chesterman, Hugh
Yesterday.
Chesterton, Frances
Alle Vogel Sind Schon Da.
How Far Is It to Bethlehem.
To Felicity Who Calls Me
  Mary.
Chesterton, Gilbert Keith
Antichrist; or, The Reunion of
  Christendom: An Ode.
A Ballad of Abbreviations.
The Ballad of the White
  Horse.
Ballade d'une Grande Dame.
A Ballade of Suicide.
The Beatific Vision.
The Black Virgin.
By the Babe Unborn.

A Christmas Carol.
Citizenship.
The Convent.
A Dedication.
The Donkey.
Ecclesiastes.
Elegy in a Country
  Churchyard.
Fantasia.
The Fat White Woman
  Speaks (parody).
The Feast of the Snow.
Feast on Wine or Fast on
  Water.
Femina Contra Mundum.
For a War Memorial.
Glencoe.
Gold Leaves.
The Good Rich Man.
The Happy Man.
The Holy of Holies.
The House of Christmas.
Hymn for the Church
  Militant.
A Hymn–O God of Earth and
  Altar.
King Alfred Answers the
  Danes.
Lepanto.
The Logical Vegetarian.
The Myth of Arthur.
Old King Cole (parody).
The Old Song.
On a Prohibitionist Poem.
On the Dangers Attending
  Altruism on the High Seas.
The Oneness of the
  Philosopher with Nature.
Portmanteau Parodies: After
  Algernon Charles Swinburne.
Portmanteau Parodies: After
  W.B. Yeats.
Portmanteau Parodies: After
  Walt Whitman.
The Praise of Dust.
Prayer.
A Prayer in Darkness.
Regina Angelorum.
The Return of Eve.
The Rolling English Road.
The Secret People.
The Skeleton.
The Song against Grocers.
The Song Against Songs.
The Song of Quoodle.
The Song of the Strange
  Ascetic.
Songs of Education.
The Songs of Guthrum and
  Alfred.
Sonnet: "High on the wall
  that holds Jerusalem."
The Sword of Surprise.
To F. C. in Memoriam
  Palestine.
To M. E. W.
To the Unknown Warrior.
Triolet.
Variations of an Air.
Variations on an Air
  Composed on Having to
  Appear in a Pageant...
The Wild Knight.
Wine and Water.
The World State.
Chestre, Thomas
Sir Launfal.
Chettle, Henry
Aeliana's Ditty.
Chettur, G. K.
World's End.

Chevalier, Albert
My Old Dutch: A Cockney Song.
Chew, Beverly
Old Books Are Best.
Cheyney, Ralph
Comrade Jesus.
No Armistice in Love's War.
Toward a True Peace.
Ch'i, Kao
Written on Seeing the Flowers, and Remembering My Daughter.
Chiabrera, Gabriello
Epitaph.
Chiang, Fay
A Letter to Peter.
Snow.
Voices That Have Filled My Day.
Chicken, Edward
The Collier's Wedding.
Ch'ien Wen-ti, Emperor
Lo-Yang.
Child, A. C.
Wishes.
Child, Lydia Maria
Apple-Seed John.
Thanksgiving Day.
The World I Am Passing Through.
Child, Philip
The Basilisk.
Dancing Partners.
Descent for the Lost.
Lyric.
Macrocosm.
Oak.
Childe, Wilfred Rowland
The Last Abbot of Gloucester.
Our Lady with Two Angels.
The Shepherd of Meriador.
Childers, David C.
Another One for the Devil.
Childress, W. L.
The Beautiful World.
Childress, William
Korea Bound, 1952.
The Metamorphosis of Aunt Jemima.
Chima, Richard Augustine
Chronique Scandaleuse.
In This Shanty Shebeen without You.
Why?
Chimako, Tada
Mirror.
Chimedza, Polycarp
The Factory Hands.
Raid on the Market.
Chimombo, Steve
Four Ways of Dying.
Chimsoro, Samuel
The Change.
The Curfew Breakers.
I Love.
The Laborer.
To Come Back Home.
Chin, Marilyn
A Chinaman's Chance.
Grandmother Poems.
The Landlord's Wife.
We Are a Young Nation, Uncle.
Write, Do Write.
Ch'in Chia
To His Wife.
Ching, Laureen
Memorial Day.
Chipasula, Frank Mkalawile
A Hanging.

A Love Poem for My Country.
Those Makheta Nights.
Chipp, Elinor
Before Dawn.
Doubt.
Lullaby.
Wild Geese.
Chisoku
The Dragonfly.
Chittenden, William Lawrence
The Cowboys' Christmas Ball.
Ode to the Norther.
Texas Types–"The Bad Man."
Chitty, Cordelia
Galloping.
Ch'iu Chin
A Call to Action.
How many wise men and heroes.
Chivers, Thomas Holley
Avalon.
Chinese Serenade for the Ut-Kam and Tong-Koo.
Lily Adair.
The Moon of Mobile.
Railroad Song.
To Allegra Florence in Heaven.
The Voice of Thought.
Chiyo
Haiku: "After a long winter, giving."
Haiku: "Don't dress for it."
Haiku: "Hardly Spring, with ice."
Haiku: "Once my parents were older."
Cho Wen-chun
Song of Snow-White Heads.
Chock, Eric
For the Field.
The Mango Tree.
Papio.
Pulling Weeds.
Termites.
Cholmondeley, Hester H.
Betrayal.
Cholmondeley-Pennell, Henry
The Bloated Biggaboon.
I've Lost My—.
Lay of the Deserted Influenzaed.
Our Traveller.
What the Prince of I Dreamt.
Chorley, Henry Fothergill
The Brave Old Oak.
Chorley, Josiah
A Metrical Index to the Bible.
Chorny, Sasha
A Vilna Puzzle.
Choyce, A. Newberry
Come Michaelmas.
Let Me Love Bright Things.
Oblation.
Christensen, Inger
Men's Voices.
Christgau, Ferdinand G.
Limerick: "A bright little maid in St. Thomas."
Limerick: "A guy asked two jays at St. Louis."
Christian, Marcus B.
The Craftsman.
Dialect Quatrain.
Drums of Haiti.
McDonogh Day in New Orleans.
Song of Hannibal: Rome.
Christiansen, Avis B.
Yes, I Have Been to Calvary.

Christina, Martha
Couplets for WCW.
Christine de Pisan *See* **Pisan, Christine de**
Christopher, Nicholas
Big City Glissando.
The Driver in Italy.
John Garfield.
The Track.
Walt Whitman at the Reburial of Poe.
Chu Ching-Yu
The Toilette.
Chu Hsi
The Boats Are Afloat.
Chu-i, Po
Madly Singing in the Mountains.
Chu Shu-chen
Alone.
Hysteria.
Lost.
Morning.
The Old Anguish.
Plum Blossoms.
Sorrow.
Stormy Night in Autumn.
Chu Yuan
The Battle.
The Great Summons.
The Lord of the East.
Chubb, Ralph
The Book of God's Madness.
Song of My Soul.
The Sun Spirit.
Chubb, Thomas Caldecot
At the Edge of the Bay.
Praise of New England.
Chudleigh, Mary Lee, Lady
The Resolve.
To the Ladies.
Chuilleanain, Eilean Ni
Dead Fly.
Letter to Pearse Hutchinson.
Lucina Schynning in Silence of the Night...
Old Roads.
Site of Ambush: Narration.
Swineherd.
Wash.
Church, Hubert
Favonius.
A Fugue.
New Zealand.
Retrospection.
Church, Peggy Pond
Ultimatum.
Church, Richard
The Alchemist.
Be Frugal.
The Cat.
Edward Millington.
Hay's Wharf.
The Londoner in the Country.
The Man Without Faith.
The Mountain Lake.
Nocturne.
On Hearing the First Cuckoo.
A Road in the Weald.
Something in Common.
Thinking of a Master.
Twentieth Century Love-Song.
The Woodpecker.
Churchill, Charles
Against Education.
The Apology Addressed to the Critical Reviewers.
The Author.
Conscience.
A Critical Fribble.
The Dedication to the Sermons.

The Duellist.
The Farewell.
The Ghost.
Gotham.
Hogarth.
Night: an Epistle to Robert Lloyd.
On Himself.
The Prophecy of Famine.
The Rosciad.
The Times.
What Is't to Us?
Churchyard, Thomas
A Farewell to a Fondling.
Old-Time Service.
Chute, Marchette
Birthdays.
Cats.
Christmas.
Dandelions.
Day before Christmas.
Drinking Fountain.
Easter Parade.
Food.
Fourth of July.
My Dog.
My Plan.
One Night.
Presents.
Sliding.
Spring.
Spring Rain.
Tracks in the Snow.
Chute, Robert M.
Snow White.
Chworowsky, Karl M.
Motherhood.
Ciardi, John
About the Teeth of Sharks.
After Sunday Dinner We Uncles Snooze.
An Apology for a Lost Classicism.
At My Father's Grave.
Back through the Looking Glass to This Side.
Ballad of the Icondic.
Birthday.
Camptown.
Captain Spud and His First Mate, Spade.
The Cat Heard a Cat-Bird.
Censorship.
Children When They're Very Sweet.
Composition for a Nativity.
Counting on Flowers.
Dan Dunder.
Dawn of the Space Age.
Death's the Classic Look.
The Dollar Dog.
Elegy Just in Case.
Epitaph: "Here, time concurring (and it does)."
The Evil Eye.
Exit Line.
Faces.
First Snow on an Airfield.
For My Twenty-Fifth Birthday in Nineteen Forty-One.
The Gift.
Goodmorning with Light.
Goodnight.
The Happy Family.
Home Revisited: Midnight.
Homecoming–Massachusetts.
How to Tell the Top of a Hill.
I Took a Bow and Arrow.
In Place of a Curse.
In the Hole.

In the Year of Many
  Conversions and the Private
  Soul.
Journal.
Letter from a Death Bed.
Limerick: "A pointless old
  miser named Quince."
Limerick: "There was a young
  fellow named Shear."
A Magus.
The Man from the Woods.
The Man in the Onion Bed.
The Man Who Sang the
  Sillies.
Men Marry What They Need.
I Marry You.
Minus One.
Morning in the Park.
Most Like an Arch This
  Marriage.
My Father's Watch.
Mystic River.
No White Bird Sings.
Ode for the Burial of a
  Citizen.
On a Photo of Sgt. Ciardi a
  Year Later.
On Being Much Better Than
  Most and Yet Not Quite
  Good Enough.
On Evolution.
On Learning to Adjust to
  Things.
The Pilot in the Jungle.
The Pinwheel's Song.
Plea.
Poem for My Thirty-Second
  Birthday.
Polo Match.
Prattle.
Rain Sizes.
The Reason for the Pelican.
The River Is a Piece of Sky.
Romping.
Seven Sharp Propeller Blades.
Some Sound Advice from
  Singapore.
Someone.
Song for an Allegorical Play.
Song: "The bells of Sunday
  rang us down."
The Stranger in the Pumpkin.
Suburban.
Suzie's New Dog.
That Summer's Shore.
To a Reviewer Who Admired
  My Book.
To Judith Asleep.
Two Egrets.
V-J Day.
Vale.
What Will You Learn about
  the Brobinyak.
Cibber, Colley
  The Blind Boy.
Cille, Colum
  If I Owned All of Alba.
  Mary Mild, Good Maiden.
  My Claw Is Tired of Scribing!
  O Son of God, It Would Be
    Sweet.
  Three Places Most Loved I
    Have Left.
Cino da Pistoia
  Canzone: His Lament for
    Selvaggia.
  Madrigal: To His Lady
    Selvaggia Vergiolesi...
  Sonnet: A Trance of Love.
  Sonnet: Death Is Not without
    but within Him.

  Sonnet: Of the Grave of
    Selvaggia, on the Monte della
    Sambuca.
  Sonnet: To Love, in Great
    Bitterness.
Citeku Ndaaya
  Ndaaya's Kasala (excerpt).
Citino, David
  Last Rites.
  Map Reading.
Ciullo d'Alcamo
  Dialogue: Lover and Lady.
Clairmont, Robert
  The Answers.
  When Did the World Begin.
Clampitt, Amy
  Agreeable Monsters.
  Amphibian.
  Beach Glass.
  Berceuse.
  Camouflage.
  The Cormorant in Its
    Element.
  A Curfew: December 13,
    1981.
  The Kingfisher.
  Mysterious Britain.
  On the Disadvantages of
    Central Heating.
  A Procession at Candlemas.
  What the Light Was Like.
  The Woodlot.
Clamurro, William
  The Edge of Town.
Clancy, Joseph P.
  Boxer.
Clancy, Liam P.
  Christmas Eve.
  A Gaelic Christmas.
Clanvowe, Thomas
  The Cuckoo and the
    Nightingale.
Clapp, Ross B.
  Mother's Love.
Clapper, Merl A.
  When Nobody Prays.
Clar, Clarence E.
  In His Service.
Clare, John
  Address to Plenty.
  An Anecdote of Love.
  The Ants.
  Autumn.
  Autumn Birds.
  Autumn Change.
  The Autumn Wind.
  The Badger Grunting on His
    Woodland Track.
  Beans in Blossom.
  Birds' Lament.
  Birds' Nests.
  Bits of Straw.
  Black Absence Hides upon the
    Past.
  Bonny Lassie O!
  Break of Day.
  Child Harold: Ballad.
  Clock-a-clay.
  Come Hither, My Dear One.
  The Cottager.
  Country Letter.
  The Crow Sat on the Willow.
  Crows in Spring.
  Death.
  December.
  Deluge.
  Dewdrops.
  The Dying Child.
  Early Nightingale.
  Emmonsail's Heath in Winter.
  The Eternity of Nature.
  Evening.

  Evening Primrose.
  Evening Schoolboys.
  A Faithless Shepherd.
  The Fallen Elm.
  Farewell.
  The Fear of Flowers.
  Field Path.
  The Firetail's Nest.
  First Love.
  Firwood.
  The Flitting.
  The Fox.
  Fragment: "Some pretty face
    remembered in our youth."
  The Frightened Ploughman.
  Gipsies.
  Graves of Infants.
  The Hailstorm in June 1831.
  The Happy Bird.
  Hares at Play.
  The Hedgehog.
  Hen's Nest.
  Hesperus.
  Honey Dew Falls from the
    Tree.
  Hymn to the Creator.
  I Am.
  I Feel I Am.
  I Lost the Love of Heaven.
  I Love the Blue Violet.
  I saw her crop a rose.
  I've Had Many an Aching
    Pain.
  I Went My Sunday Mornings
    Rounds.
  I Wish I Was Where I Would
    Be.
  Invitation to Eternity.
  Joys of Childhood.
  The Landrail.
  Language Has Not the Power
    to Speak What Love Indites.
  The Lark's Nest.
  Lines Written on a Very
    Boisterous Day in May,
    1944.
  Little Trotty Wagtail.
  Lord, Hear My Prayer.
  The Lout.
  Love, Meet Me in the Green
    Glen.
  Love's Emblem.
  Love's Memories Haunt My
    Footsteps Still.
  Love's Pains.
  The Lover's Invitation.
  The Maid o' the West.
  The Maple Hangs Its Green
    Bee Flowers.
  The Martin Cat Long Shaged
    of Courage Good.
  Meet Me in the Primrose
    Lane.
  The Milking Shed.
  The Missel-Thrush's Nest.
  The Mist Rauk Is Hanging.
  The Mole.
  The Mother's Lullaby.
  Mouse's Nest.
  My Early Home.
  Nature.
  Nature's Hymn to the Deity.
  No Single Hour Can Stand for
    Naught.
  Noon.
  The Old Cottagers.
  The Old Year.
  One Careless Look.
  The Passing of a Dream.
  Pastoral Poesy.
  The Peasant Poet.
  Peggy Said Good Morning.

  The Pettichap's Nest.
  Pleasant Sounds.
  The Ploughboy.
  Poets Love Nature.
  Proposals for Building a
    Cottage.
  Remember Dear Mary.
  Remembrances.
  The Sand Martin.
  Schoolboys in Winter.
  A Sea Boy on the Giddy
    Mast.
  The Secret.
  Secret Love.
  She Tied Up Her Few Things.
  Sheep in Winter.
  The Shepherd Boy.
  The Shepherd's Calendar.
  Signs of Winter.
  Silent Love.
  The Sleep of Spring.
  Snowstorm.
  Soft Falls the Sweet Evening.
  Solitude.
  Song.
  Song's Eternity.
  A Spring Morning.
  Stanzas.
  The Stranger.
  Sudden Shower.
  Summer.
  Summer Images.
  Summer Morning.
  Sunrise in Summer.
  Swordy Well.
  There Is a Charm in Solitude
    That Cheers.
  The Thunder Mutters Louder
    and More Loud.
  To an Infant Daughter.
  To Harriett.
  To Mary: I Sleep with Thee,
    and Wake with Thee.
  To Mary: It Is the Evening
    Hour.
  To Miss B.
  To the Ivy.
  To the Snipe.
  To Wordsworth.
  A Vision.
  The Vixen.
  We Passed by Green Closes.
  Well, Honest John.
  What Is Love?
  Where She Told Her Love.
  Winter.
  Winter in the Fens.
  Winter Winds Cold and Blea.
  The Winters Spring.
  With Garments Flowing.
  The Wood-Cutter's Night
    Song.
  A World for Love.
  Written in a Thunder Storm
    July 15th 1841.
  Written in Prison.
  The Yellowhammer.
  Young Lambs.
Clare, Josephine
  Fine Body.
"Claribel" *See* **Barnard,**
Charlotte Allington
Clark, Badger
  Cottonwood Leaves.
  The Glory Trail.
  Pioneers.
  The Smoke-Blue Plains.
Clark, Carl
  Allegory in Black.
  Conundrum.
  No More.
  Ode to a Beautiful Woman.

The Second Coming.
Thoughts from a Bottle.
Clark, Charles Heber
Mr. Slimmer's Funeral Verses for the Morning Argus.
Clark, Constance
Morning Rush.
Clark, David R.
Asylum.
Clark, Duane
Bonner's Ferry Beggar.
Clark, Eunice
Fallow Land.
The People Has No Obituary.
Clark, John Pepper
Agbor Dancer.
Fulani Cattle.
Ibadan.
Clark, Kevin
Death Comes for the Old Cowboy.
Clark, Leonard
November the Fifth.
The Walk.
Clark, Leslie Savage
Beacon Light.
In the Time of Trouble.
Litany for Peace.
The Way.
Clark, Lewis Gaylord
The Flamingo.
Clark, Martha Haskell
Red Geraniums.
Clark, Charles Heber *See* "**Adeler, Max**"
Clark, Naomi
Tables.
Clark, Preston
Faith.
Youth.
Clark, Robert
Generations.
Clark, Stephen
Summer Visitors.
Clark, Thomas Curtis
Abraham Lincoln, the Master.
Apparitions.
At Mount Vernon.
Blow, Bugle!
The Call.
Challenge.
Common Blessings.
Faith for Tomorrow.
Farewell and Hail!
For Those Who Died.
The Forgotten Star.
Friends.
The Glory of Lincoln.
He Shall Speak Peace.
I Am Still Rich.
Keep Love in Your Life.
Lincoln, Come Back.
The Message of the Bells.
Mother.
My Country, Right!
On a World War Battlefield.
Sons of Promise.
Take Time to Live.
This Is America.
The Touch of Human Hands.
Trees.
Trust the Great Artist.
Wanderers.
We Thank Thee.
Clark, Tom
Alpha November Golf Sierra Tango.
And You Are There.
Arc.
Baseball.
Climbing.
Comanche.

Crows.
Daily News.
A Difference.
Dispersion and Convergence.
Doors.
Eyeglasses.
Final Farewell.
Going to School in France or America.
The Greeks.
I'm on an Island.
The Knot.
The Lake: Coda.
Like Musical Instruments.
Penmanship.
Poem: "The tiny new emotions."
Rec Room in Paradise.
Sonnet.
Sunglasses.
Superballs.
To Bert Campaneris.
The Ty Cobb Story.
The X of the Unknown.
The Yearbook.
You.
Clark, Walter
After Snow.
Free Will.
The Morning After.
Uncle Death.
Clark, Jr., Charles Badger
The Legend of Boastful Bill.
The Night Herder.
Ridin'.
The Sheep-Herder.
Clarke, Andrew S. C.
Prayer: "Bless Thou this year, O Lord!"
Clarke, Austin
Aisling.
Anacreontic.
Ancient Lights.
The Blackbird of Derrycairn.
Burial of an Irish President.
Celebrations.
Civil War.
Cypress Grove.
Dirge.
Early Unfinished Sketch.
The Envy of Poor Lovers.
The Fair at Windgap.
Gracey Nugent.
Her Voice Could Not Be Softer.
Inscription for a Headstone.
Intercessors.
Irish-American Dignitary.
Japanese Print.
The Jest.
The Jewels.
The Last Republicans.
Living in Sin.
The Loss of Strength.
The Lost Heifer.
The Lucky Coin.
Marriage.
Martha Blake at Fifty-One.
Miss Marnell.
Mnemosyne Lay in Dust.
Night and Morning.
Penal Law.
Pilgrimage.
The Pill.
The Planter's Daughter.
Respectable People.
A Sermon on Swift.
The Straying Student.
A Strong Wind.
Tenebrae.
Three Poems about Children.
Tiresias (excerpt).

Usufruct.
The Vengeance of Finn: The Awakening of Dermuid.
The Young Woman of Beare.
Clarke, C. R.
Song of the Mariner's Needle.
Clarke, F.W.
The Rhyme of the Rain Machine.
Clarke, George Frederick
The Saint John.
Clarke, George Herbert
Fog-Horn.
Halt and Parley.
Over Saleve.
Santa Maria del Fiore.
Clarke, Gillian
Baby-Sitting.
A Journal from France: Seamstress at St. Leon.
Clarke, James Freeman
Brother, Hast Thou Wandered Far.
Dear Friend, Whose Presence in the House.
Rabia.
White-Capped Waves.
Clarke, John Cooper
Evidently Chicken Town.
Clarke, John Henrik
Determination.
Sing Me a New Song.
Clarke, Joseph Ignatius Constantin
The Fighting Race.
Pro Libra Mea.
The Way of the Cross.
Clarke, Marcus
The Wail of the Waiter.
Clarke, Peter
In Air.
Play Song.
Young Shepherd Bathing His Feet.
Clarke, Rose Terry
The Death of Goody Nurse.
Clarke, Thomas Curtis
Bugle Song of Peace.
The Poet's Call.
The Search.
Clarke, Willis Gaylord
A Remembrance.
Clarkson, M. J.
The Secret of the Cross.
Clason, Isaac
Don Juan. Canto XVII.
Claudel, Alice Moser
Southern Season.
Claudel, Paul
Fourth Station.
Our Lady, Help of Christians.
Seventh Station.
Shadows.
Claudian
Epithalamium for Honorius and Maria: Palm Tree Mates with Palm.
The Hairdresser's Art.
Preparing for the Wedding.
Sing, Woods and Rivers All.
Thorns Arm the Rose.
Claudian (Claudius Claudianus)
Epitaph.
The Lonely Isle.
The Old Man of Verona.
Claudius, Matthis ("Asmus")
The Most Acceptable Gift.
Clayre, Alasdair
Professor Drinking Wine.
Clayton, Arnold
Pity the Down-Trodden Landlord.

Claytor, Gertrude
Grant at Appomattox.
Cleanthes
God Leads the Way.
Hymn to Zeus.
Cleaveland, C. L.
November.
Cleaveland, Elizabeth H. Jocelyn
No Sect in Heaven.
Cleavland, Benjamin
O Could I Find from Day to Day.
Cleghorn, Sarah N.
Come, Captain Age.
Comrade Jesus.
Contented at Forty.
Dorothea.
Emilia.
The Golf Links.
Hemlock Mountain.
The Incentive.
Saint R. L. S.
The Survival of the Fittest.
Vermont.
Cleland, William
Hallo My Fancy.
Clemens, Samuel *See* "**Twain, Mark**"
Clement of Alexandria (Titus Flavius Clemens)
The Earliest Christian Hymn.
Hymn to Christ the Saviour.
Clementelli, Elena
Etruscan Notebook.
Clements, John R.
God's Trails Lead Home.
Clemmons, Carole Gregory
Ghetto Lovesong–Migration.
I'm Just a Stranger Here, Heaven Is My Home.
Love from My Father.
Migration.
Spring.
Clemo, Jack R.
The Burnt Bush.
A Calvinist in Love.
Charlotte Nicholls.
Christ in the Clay-Pit.
Growing in Grace.
Mould of Castile.
Neither Shadow of Turning.
On the Death of Karl Barth.
The Water-Wheel.
The Winds.
Clephane, Elizabeth Cecilia
There Were Ninety and Nine.
Clerk, John
Fane Wald I Luve.
O Merry May the Maid Be.
Clerke, William
So, So.
Cleveland, John
The Antiplatonick.
The Author's Mock-Song to Mark Anthony.
An Elegy on Ben. Jonson.
Epitaph on the Earl of Strafford.
A Fair Nymph Scorning a Black Boy Courting Her.
Fuscara or the Bee Errant.
The General Eclipse.
The Hecatomb to His Mistress.
The King's Disguise (excerpt).
Mark Anthony.
On Scotland.
On the Memory of Mr. Edward King Drown'd in the Irish Seas.
The Rebel Scot.

Square-Cap.
To the State of Love.
Upon an Hermaphrodite.
Upon Phillis Walking in a
  Morning before Sun-rising.
Whenas the Nightingale.
A Young Man to an Old
  Woman Courting Him.

Cleveland, Philip Jerome
By Night.
I Yield Thee Praise.
There Is a Love.

Clewell, David
After the Seance.

Clifford, Carrie Williams
The Black Draftee from Dixie.

Clifford, Ethel
The Dark Road.
The Harp of Sorrow.
The Last Hour.

**Clifford, George, Earl of
Cumberland**
My Thoughts Are Winged
  with Hopes.
To Cynthia.

Clifford, John
The Anvil of God's Word.
God's Word.

Clifton, Lucille
The 1st.
Admonitions.
Africa.
At Last We Killed the
  Roaches.
Confession.
Daddy.
Eviction.
Explanations.
For deLawd.
Forgiving My Father.
Friends Come.
God Send Easter.
Good Times.
Her Love Poem.
Holy Night.
I Once Knew a Man.
I Went to the Valley.
If I Stand in My Window.
If Something Should Happen.
In Populated.
In Salem.
In the Inner City.
Incandescence.
Let There Be New Flowering.
The Light That Came.
Listen Children.
The Lost Baby Poem.
Love Rejected.
Malcolm.
Miss Rosie.
Mother, I Am.
My Mama Moved among the
  Days.
Perhaps.
The Poet.
The Raising of Lazarus.
Salt.
Still.
Testament.
The thirty eighth year.
This Morning.
Those Boys That Ran
  Together.
To Bobby Seale.
To Joan.
Untitled.

Clive, Caroline
Conflict.

Clockadale, Jill
Change of Venue.

Close, John
In Respectful Memory of Mr.
  Yarker.

Clothier, Cal
Soaring.

Cloud, Frederick
Hands.

Cloud, Virginia Woodward
The Ballad of Sweet P.
Care.
The Mother's Song.
An Old Street.
What the Lord High
  Chamberlain Said.
Youth.

Clough, Arthur Hugh
Actaeon.
All Is Well.
Ambarvalia.
Amours de Voyage.
As I Sat at the Cafe.
The Bothie of Tober-na-
  Vuolich.
Columbus.
Come Back.
Come Home, Come Home!
Currente Calamo.
Darkness.
Dipsychus.
Easter Day I.
Easter Day II.
The Engagement.
The Grasses Green of Sweet
  Content.
Green Fields of England.
Here Have I Been These One
  and Twenty Years.
Hope Evermore and Believe.
I Dreamed a Dream.
I Have Seen Higher, Holier
  Things Than These.
In a London Square.
Is It True, Ye Gods, Who
  Treat Us.
It Fortifies My Soul to Know.
It Is Not Sweet Content, Be
  Sure.
Ite Domum Saturae, Venit
  Hesperus.
Keeping On.
The Latest Decalogue.
A Letter from Rome.
Life is Struggle.
Look You, My Simple Friend.
Mari Magno.
My Wind Is Turned to Bitter
  North.
Natura Naturans.
O Thou Whose Image.
Peschiera.
Put Forth Thy Leaf, Thou
  Lofty Plane.
Qua Cursum Ventus.
Qui Laborat, Orat.
Reply to Dipsychus.
Resignation–To Faustus.
Say Not the Struggle Nought
  Availeth.
Serve in Thy Post.
Sic Itur.
Spectator Ab Extra.
The Spirit's Song.
That There Are Powers above
  Us I Admit.
"There Is No God," the
  Wicked Saith.
To Spend Uncounted Years of
  Pain.
Les Vaches.
Whate'er You Dream with
  Doubt Possest.

When the Dews Are Earliest
  Falling.
Where Lies the Land?
With Whom Is No
  Variableness, Neither
  Shadow of Turning.
Would That I Were.

Clouts, Sydney
Animal Kingdom.
Dawn Hippo.
Earth, Sky.
Firebowl.
The Grave's Cherub.
Of Thomas Traherne and the
  Pebble outside.
Poetry is Death Cast Out.
The Portrait of Prince Henry.
Prince Henry the Navigator.
The Sea and the Eagle.
The Sleeper.

Cluysenaar, Anne
Epithalamium.

Coalman, Horace
A Black Soldier Remembers.

Coan, Titus Munson
The Crystal.
A Dream of Flowers.
The Love-Knot.
Nihil Humani Alienum.
Riding Down.
Who Knows?

Coates, Carol
Choral Symphony Conductor.
The Circle.
Country Reverie.
Light.

Coates, Florence Earle
The Angelus.
Be Thou My Guide.
Buffalo.
By the Conemaugh.
Columbus.
Death.
Dream the Great Dream.
A Hero.
His Face.
The House of Pain.
The Morning-Glory.
The New Mars.
Per Aspera.
Perdita.
Pilgrim Song.
Requiem for a Young Soldier.
A Seeker in the Night.
Song: "For me the jasmine
  buds unfold."
Song: "If love were but a little
  thing."
Suppliant.
Survival.
Tennyson.
Thanksgiving.
Tomorrow.
The World Is Mine.

Coats, Adelbert Sumpter
The Common Lot.
Pentecost.

Coatsworth, Elizabeth Jane
All Goats.
April Fool.
August Smiles.
The Axe Has Cut the Forest
  Down.
The Bad Kittens.
The Barn.
Bread the Holy.
Calling in the Cat.
Candle and Star.
The Circus-Postered Barn.
Cold Winter Now Is in the
  Wood.
Conquest.

Counters.
Daniel Webster's Horses.
Down the Rain Falls.
Easter.
Eerily Sweet.
Ever Since.
Footnote to History.
He Who Has Never Known
  Hunger.
A Horse Would Tire.
How Gray the Rain.
January.
Labor of Fields.
The Lady.
A Lady Comes to an Inn.
Lullaby.
March.
The Mouse.
The Navajo.
No Shop Does the Bird Use.
No Snake in Springtime.
Nosegay.
November.
The Old Mare.
On a Night of Snow.
The Open Door.
Pirates.
The Pleiades.
The Rabbits' Song outside the
  Tavern.
Roosters.
Saint John.
The Sea Gull Curves His
  Wings.
Sleigh Bells at Night.
Snow.
Sometimes a Little House Will
  Please.
Song for a Little Cuckoo
  Clock.
Song for Midsummer Night.
Song of the Rabbits Outside
  the Tavern.
The Storm.
Straws.
Sunday.
This Air That Blows in from
  the Sea.
This Is the Hay That No Man
  Planted.
Twelfth Night.
Violets, Daffodils.
The Warm of Heart Shall
  Never Lack a Fire.
The Ways of Trains.
Whale at Twilight.
What Could Be Lovelier Than
  to Hear.
"Who Are You?" Asked the
  Cat of the Bear.
Wilderness Rivers.
Winter Rune.

Cobb, Alice S.
Angela Davis.
The Searching.

Cobb, Ann
Kivers.

Cobb, Charlie
Containing Communism.
For Sammy Younge.
Nation.
To Vietnam.

Cobb, Will
School Days.

Cobb, Will D.
School Days.
Waltz Me Around Again,
  Willie.

Coblentz, Catherine Cate
The Housewife.
Our History.

Coblentz, Stanton A.
Calm.
History of the Modern World.
Land's End.
The Last Trail.
On Some Trees Needlessly
Slain.
Prayer for Light.
We Who Build Visions.
Coburn, Wallace D.
Cow-Boy Fun.
The Cowboy's Fate.
The Stampede.
Coccimiglio, Vic
Visit.
Cochrane, Alfred
The Eight-Day Clock.
Omnia Vincit.
Upon Lesbia–Arguing.
Cochrane, Frances
Face to Face.
Cochrane, Shirley G.
Dream of a Father.
Leaving Home.
"Cockatoo Jack"
The Numerella Shore.
Cockburn, Alison
The Flowers of the Forest.
Cocke, Zitella
Miss Nancy's Gown.
My Cross.
Cockrell, Doug
Field Work.
Fist Fight.
His Lunch Bucket.
Hunting at Dusk.
Cocteau, Jean
Leoun.
Plain Song.
Poem of Circumstance.
To a Sleeping Friend.
Codish, Edward
A Juggle of Myrtle Twigs.
Yetzer ha Ra.
Codrescu, Andrei
Against Meaning.
Au Bout du Temps.
En Passant.
A Grammar.
The Imagination of Necessity.
The Inner Source.
A Petite Histoire of Red
Fascism.
Poetry Paper.
De Rerum Natura.
The Threat.
Work.
Cody, H. A.
The Old Figurehead Carver.
Old Ship Riggers.
Coe, Alice Rollit
The Turn of the Road.
Coe, Peter
The Wizard of Alderley Edge.
Coffey, Brian
Advent.
H E A D R O C K.
Missouri Sequence: Nightfall.
Muse, June, Related.
The Nicest Phantasies Are
Shared.
Odalisque.
Coffin, Charles
Glad Tidings from the King
of Kings.
Coffin, Robert P.T.
Getting Through.
New Englanders Are Maples.
Coffin, Robert P. Tristram
Alexander Graham Bell Did
Not Invent the Telephone.
America Was Schoolmasters.

Christening-Day Wishes for
My God-Child Grace Lane
Berkley II.
Covered Bridge.
Cows Are Coming Home in
Maine.
The Fog.
Golden Falcon.
Graveyard.
Hound on the Church Porch.
The Jelly Fish.
Little Boys of Texas.
Lonely Lover.
Old Farmer Alone.
The Pheasant.
The Ram.
The Secret Heart.
The Skunk.
The Spider.
Square-Toed Princes.
The Starfish.
Thunder Pools.
Tree-Sleeping.
Where I Took Hold of Life.
Yankee Cradle.
The Young Calves.
Coghill, Mary
Knowing.
Coghill, Rhoda
The Bright Hillside.
Dead.
In Wicklow.
The Plough-Horse.
Poem: "Is to love, this–to
nurse a name."
Runaway.
Spring Doggerel.
The Young Bride's Dream.
Cogswell, Fred
A Christmas Carol.
Cohan, George M.
Forty-Five Minutes from
Broadway.
Give My Regards to
Broadway.
Life's a Funny Proposition
after All.
Mary's a Grand Old Name.
The Yankee Doodle Boy.
You're a Grand Old Flag.
Cohen, Jacob
The Eternal Jew.
The Harp of David.
Surely My Soul...
Cohen, Leonard
Another Night with
Telescope.
As the Mist Leaves No Scar.
Ballad: "My lady was found
mutilated."
The Bus.
Celebration.
Credo.
Elegy.
For Anne.
For E.J.P.
Gift.
Heirloom.
I Have Not Lingered in
European Monasteries.
I Wonder How Many People
in This City.
If It Were Spring.
"The killers that run..."
A Kite Is a Victim.
The Music Crept by Us.
The Only Tourist in Havana
Turns His Thoughts
Homeward.
Poem for Marc Chagall.
Poem: "I heard of a man."
Prayer for Messiah.

Queen Victoria and Me.
The Sleeping Beauty.
Story of Isaac.
Suzanne Takes You Down.
What I'm Doing Here.
You Do Not Have to Love
Me.
You Have the Lovers.
Cohen, Robert David
The Bones of Incontention.
Day on Kind Continent.
The Storm.
The Street of Named Houses.
Cohen, Shlomit
The Same Dream.
Wife of Kohelet.
Cohn, Myra
Sliding.
Coignard, Gabrielle
Prayer.
Cokayne, Sir Aston
Epitaph on a Great Sleeper.
Funeral Elegy on the Death of
His Very Good Friend Mr.
Michael Drayton.
Of a Mistress.
To Plautia.
Colaizzi, Randall
Telemachus and the Bow.
Colby, Joan
Equestrienne.
How the Sky Begins to Fall.
The Magician.
The Old Nudists.
Rose Red to Snow White.
Colby, Vine
The Rainbow.
Colclough, Phil and June
Blood on the Sails.
Song for Ireland.
Colcord, Lincoln
The Fishing Fleet.
Cole, Barry
The Men Are Coming Back!
Cole, Bob
Under the Bamboo Tree.
Cole, E. R.
Oh, You Wholly Rectangular.
Cole, G. D. H.
Civil Riot.
Cole, Harriet
The End of the Way.
Cole, James
The Wheel.
Cole, Joanna
Happy New Year, Anyway.
Hippopotamus.
Cole, Samuel Valentine
Abraham Lincoln.
Hammer and Anvil.
Satisfied.
The Trees.
Cole, Thomas
By the Beautiful Sea.
La Grande Jatte: Sunday
Afternoon.
The Landscape of Love.
The Life of Hubert, I
(excerpt).
My Lady Takes the Sunlight
for Her Gown.
Old Woman's Song.
Praise to Light.
Spider.
The Tray.
Variations on a Still Morning.
Cole, Timothy
The Year's End.
Cole, William
Alma Mater, Forget Me.
Back Yard, July Night.

Clerihew: "The Saturday
Review."
Epitaph on a Career Woman.
Geeandess.
Have I Got Dogs!
Hypnopompic Poem.
Just Dropped In.
Lost Contact.
Marriage Couplet.
Mutual Problem.
Mysterious East.
Oh, Noa, Noa!
Poor Kid.
A Question.
Time Piece.
Undersea Fever.
War Horses.
What a Friend We have in
Cheeses!
What Could It Be?
Coleman, Elliott
Sirens.
Winter over Nothing.
Coleman, Emily Holmes
The Liberator.
Coleman, Helena
As Day Begins to Wane.
More Lovely Grows the
Earth.
Coleman, Herbert T. J.
Cockle-Shell and Sandal-
Shoon.
The Poet Confides.
Coleman, Horace
Poem for a "Divorced"
Daughter.
Remembrance of Things Past.
Coleman, Jaybird
No More Good Water.
Coleman, Lucile
With Lilacs in My Eye.
Coleman, Mary Joan
Grandfather.
Coleman, Victor
Day Twenty-Three.
How the Death of a City Is
Never More Than the Sum
of the Deaths...
Coleman the Younger, George
Gluggity Glug.
Coleridge, Derwent
And So Men Say, I Love
Thee!
Coleridge, Hartley
Address to Certain Gold
Fishes.
Butter's Etymological Spelling
Book, &c.
Death-Bed Reflections of
Michel-Angelo.
Dedicatory Sonnet to S. T.
Coleridge.
Early Death.
Fie on Eastern Luxury!
From Country to Town.
Full Well I Know.
Hast Thou Not Seen an Aged
Rifted Tower.
He Lived amidst th'
Untrodden Ways.
How Shall a Man Fore-
Doomed.
If I Have Sinn'd in Act.
Lines.
Long Time a Child.
May, 1840.
"Multum Dilexit."
Night.
November.
On the Death of Echo.
Poietes Apoietes.
Prayer.

Reply.
Rydal.
She Is Not Fair to Outward View.
The Solitary-Hearted.
Song: "'Tis sweet to hear the merry lark."
Summer Rain.
To a Cat.
To a Deaf and Dumb Little Girl.
To a Friend.
To a Lofty Beauty, from Her Poor Kinsman.
What Is Young Passion.
Whither Is Gone the Wisdom and the Power.

Coleridge, Mary Elizabeth
After Reading Certain Books.
After St. Augustine.
As I Went Singing over the Earth.
Awake.
Blue and White.
Change.
A Clever Woman.
Companionship.
Cut It Down.
Death.
A Dedication.
Depart from Me.
The Deserted House.
Egypt's Might is Tumbled Down.
From My Window.
Gibberish.
Gifts.
Gone.
Good Friday in My Heart.
He Knoweth Not That the Dead Are Thine.
A Huguenot.
I Saw a Stable.
In Dispraise of the Moon.
An Insincere Wish Addressed to a Beggar.
Jealousy.
The King.
Lord of the Winds.
Marriage.
Mortal Combat.
My True Love Hath My Heart and I Have His.
The Nurse's Lament.
L'Oiseau Bleu.
On Such a Day.
The Other Side of a Mirror.
Our Lady.
Punctilio.
There.
There Was No Place Found.
Three Helpers in Battle.
To Memory.
Unwelcome.
Veneta.
We Never Said Farewell.
Where a Roman Villa Stood, above Freiburg.
The White Women.
Whither Away?
The Witch.
The Witches' Wood.

Coleridge, Samuel Taylor
The Aeolian Harp.
Answer to a Child's Question.
Apologia Pro Vita Sua.
The Ballad of the Dark Ladie.
A Child's Evening Prayer.
Christabel.
A Christmas Carol.
Cologne.
Constancy to an Ideal Object.

The Death of the Starling.
Dejection.
The Delinquent Travellers.
The Desired Swan-Song.
The Destiny of Nations.
The Devil's Thoughts.
The Dungeon.
The Eolian Harp.
Epigram: "Truth I pursued, as Fancy sketch'd the way."
Epitaph on Himself.
The Exchange.
La Fayette.
Fears in Solitude.
France: An Ode.
Frost at Midnight.
The Fruit Plucker.
Glycine's Song.
The Good Great Man.
Hear, Sweet Spirit.
The Homeric Hexameter, Described and Exemplified.
Human Life: On the Denial of Immortality.
Hymn before Sunrise, in the Vale of Chamouni.
I Asked My Fair, One Happy Day.
I Mix in Life.
If I Had but Two Little Wings.
Inscription for a Fountain on a Heath.
The Knight's Tomb.
Koskiusko.
Kubla Khan.
Lesson for a Boy.
Lewti.
Life.
Limbo.
Lines Written in the Album at Elbingerode, in the Hartz Forest.
A Little Child, a Limber Elf.
Love.
Love's Apparition and Evanishment.
A Mathematical Problem.
Metrical Feet.
Modern Critics.
My Baptismal Birthday.
Ne Plus Ultra.
The Netherlands.
The Nightingale.
Ode on the Departing Year.
On a Bad Singer.
On a Discovery Made Too Late.
On a Lord.
On a Ruined House in a Romantic Country.
On Donne's Poem "To a Flea."
On Donne's Poetry.
On Imitation.
On My Joyful Departure from the City of Cologne.
Or Wren or Linnet.
The Ovidian Elegiac Metre, Described and Exemplified.
The Pains of Sleep.
Pantisocracy.
Phantom.
Phantom or Fact.
Psyche.
The Raven.
Recollections of Love.
Reflections.
Religious Musings.
A Rhymester.
The Rime of the Ancient Mariner.

The Scars Remaining.
Sea-Ward, White Gleaming through the Busy Scud.
Self-Knowledge.
Song: "A sunny shaft did I behold."
Songs of the Pixies.
Sonnet: Oft o'er My Brain.
Sonnet to a Friend...
Sonnet: To the River Otter.
The Spruce and Limber Yellow-Hammer.
A Sunset.
This Lime-Tree Bower My Prison.
Time, Real and Imaginary.
To a Young Ass.
To a Young Friend.
To Nature.
To the Reverend W.L. Bowles.
To William Wordsworth.
A Tombless Epitaph.
A Voice Sings.
W. H. Eheu!
What Is an Epigram?
What is Life?
"What? Rise Again with All One's Bones."
Work without Hope.
Youth and Age.

Coleridge, Sara
The Garden Year.
He Came Unlook'd For.
I Was a Brook.
The Mother.
O Sleep, My Babe, Hear Not the Rippling Wave.
Trees.

Coles, Don
Natalya Nikolayevna Goncharov.
Photograph in a Stockholm Newspaper for March 13, 1910.

Colesworthy, Daniel C.
While We Lowly Bow Before Thee.

College, Stephen
A Raree Show.
Truth Brought to Light; or, Murder Will Out.

Collier, Edward A.
After the Rain.

Collier, John
The Pluralist and Old Soldier.

Collier, Mary
The Woman's Labour.

Collier, Michael
Counting.

Collier, Thomas Stephen
Cleopatra Dying.
Compensation.
Disappointment.
Infallibility.
Power.
The Spectre Ship.
Time.

Collin, William Edwin
Monserrat.
Sancho.

Collins, Emanuel
The Fatal Dream; or, The Unhappy Favourite.

Collins, Helen Johnson
To an Avenue Sport.

Collins, John
The Chapter of Kings.
Tomorrow.

Collins, Leslie Morgan
Creole Girl.
Stevedore.

Collins, Martha
Retreat.
The Story We Know.

Collins, Mortimer
Ad Chloen, M.A.
If.
Kate Temple's Song.
Lotos Eating.
Martial in London.
My Thrush.
Queen and Slave.
Salad.
To F. C.

Collins, Ruth
The Song of a Factory Worker.

Collins, Sam
The Jailhouse Blues.
Slow Mama Slow.

Collins, W. F.
The Lincoln Statue.

Collins, William
Captain Molly.
How Sleep the Brave!
The Lookout.
Ode Occasioned by the Death of Mr. Thomson.
Ode on the Poetical Character.
An Ode on the Popular Superstitions of the Highlands of Scotland...
Ode to Evening.
Ode to Fear.
Ode to Mercy.
Ode to Pity.
Ode to Simplicity.
The Passions.
Persian Eclogues, II.
A Song from Shakespeare's "Cymbeline".
Sonnet: "When Phoebe form'd a wanton smile."
The Stormy Hebrides.

Collinson, Laurence
The Sea and the Tiger.

Collom, Jack
Phone Number.
Sidonie.

Collop, John
The Leper Cleansed.
To the Soul.

Collyer, Robert
Saxon Grit.
Under the Snow.

Collymore, Frank A.
The Zobo Bird.

Colman, Benjamin
Another to Urania.
A Hymn of Praise, on a Recovery from Sickness.
A Poem on Elijahs Translation....
A Quarrel with Fortune.
To "Philomela."
To Urania on the Death of Her First and Only Child.

Colman, George
On Sir Nathaniel Wraxall the Historian.

Colman, George the Younger
The Maid of the Moor, or The Water-Fiends.
My Muse and I, Ere Youth and Spirits Fled.
Unfortunate Miss Bailey.

Colman, Mary Elizabeth
We Men Are of Two Worlds.

Colman, Saint
Hymn Against Pestilence.
To Colman Returning.

Colombo, John Robert
Riverdale Lion.
What Pablo Picasso Did in
"Les Demoiselles
d'Avignon".
Colonna, Vittoria da
As when Some Hungry
Fledgling Hears and Sees.
I live on this depraved and
lonely cliff.
O What Transparent Waves,
What a Tranquil Sea.
When the Orient Is Lit by the
Great Light.
When the Troubled Sea Swells
and Surrounds.
Colony, Horatio
Ghost Pet.
Colquitt, Betsy
Photographing the Facade–
San Miguel de Allende.
Colton, Arthur
Allah's Tent.
Harps Hung Up in Babylon.
Phillis and Corydon.
Sometime It May Be.
A Song with a Discord.
To Faustine.
Colton, Walter
A Leap for Life.
Colum, Mary M.
Dirge of the Lone Woman.
Colum, Padraic
Across the Door.
After Speaking of One Dead a
Long Time.
Asses.
At Ferns Castle.
The Ballad of Downal Baun.
Belfast: High Street.
The Book of Kells.
The Burial of Saint Brendan.
Catalpa Tree.
Condors Flying.
A Cradle Song.
Dahlias.
David Ap Gwillam's Mass of
the Birds.
A Drover.
Dublin: The Old Squares.
Fourth Sation.
Fuchsia Hedges in Connacht.
Garadh.
Garland Sunday.
Her Skin Is So White as a
Lily.
I Saw the Wind To-Day.
I Shall Not Die for Thee.
Interior.
Irises.
The Knitters.
Lilies.
Lullaby, O Men from the
Fields.
Monkeys.
No Child.
An Old Man Said.
Old Soldier.
An Old Woman of the Roads.
Olive Trees.
On Not Hearing the Birds
Sing in Ireland.
Peach Tree with Fruit.
The Plougher.
The Poor Girl's Meditation.
A Poor Scholar of the
'Forties.
Poplar Tree.
The Puppet Play.
River-Mates.
The Sea Bird to the Wave.

Shall I Go Bound and You
Go Free?
She Moved through the Fair.
Spider.
The Stations of the Cross.
The Terrible Robber Men.
The Tin-Whistle Player.
The Toy-Maker.
Tulips.
The Wall of China.
Wild Ass.
Young Girl: Annam.
Columcille, Saint
A Boat Song.
Clamour of the Wind Making
Music.
Columcille's Greeting to
Ireland.
Columcille the Scribe.
Farewell to Ireland.
A Hedge before Me.
My Hand Has a Pain.
On His Exile to Iona.
The Praise of Derry.
Combe, William
The Tour of Dr. Syntax: In
Search of the Picturesque.
Combs, Tram
Ars Poetica About Ultimates.
I Flung up My Arm Half
from Sleep.
Just after Noon with Fierce
Shears.
Cometas
Country Gods.
Comfort, Alex
After Shakespeare.
After You, Madam.
The Atoll in the Mind.
Epitaph.
Fear of the Earth.
Haste to the Wedding.
Hoc Est Corpus.
Love Poem.
The Lovers.
Notes for My Son.
Pick upon Pick...
The Postures of Love.
Song for the Heroes.
Sublimation.
A Wartime Exchange: As One
Non-Combatant to Another.
A Wartime Exchange: Letter
to an American Visitor.
Comfort, Florence Crocker
Make Way!
Comyn, Michael
Oisin in the Land of Youth.
Conant, Isabel Fiske
Emergency.
Many Wings.
Conant-Bissell, Jane
Milton's Wife on Her Twenty-
Third Birthday.
Conard, Audrey
Clinic: Examination.
A Vegetarian Sings.
Concanen, Matthew
Heaps on Heaps.
Conder, Josiah
Bread of Heaven, on Thee We
Feed.
Day by Day the Manna Fell.
Trust in Jesus.
Cone, Helen Gray
Arraignment.
The Common Street.
The Contrast.
The Dandelions.
Fair England.
Heartbreak Road.
The Last Cup of Canary.

Narcissus in Camden
(parody).
The Ride to the Lady.
The Spring Beauties.
Thisbe.
A Yellow Pansy.
Confucius
Airs of Pei.
Chou and the South.
Deer Song.
Shao and the South.
Songs of Ch'en.
Songs of Cheng.
Songs of T'ang.
Wei Wind.
Yung Wind.
Congdon, Kirby
Daredevil.
Conger, Marion
Fall Days.
Congreve, William
Amoret.
The Better Bargain.
Doris.
False Though She Be to Me.
A Hue and Cry after Fair
Amoret.
Jack Frenchman's Defeat.
Lesbia.
Letter to Viscount Cobham.
The Mourning Bride.
Nil Admirari.
A Nymph and a Swain.
A Soldier and a Sailor.
Song: Ah Stay.
Song: "Pious Selinda goes to
prayers."
Song: "See, see, she wakes!
Sabina wakes!"
Song: "With my frailty don't
upbraid me."
Conkling, Grace Hazard
After Sunset.
The Goatherd.
I Have Cared for You, Moon.
A Letter to Elsa.
The Little Rose Is Dust, My
Dear.
Nightingales.
The Road to the Pool.
The Snail.
The Star.
Tampico.
To a New-Born Baby Girl.
Victory Bells.
The Whole Duty of Berkshire
Brooks.
The Wind's Way.
Conkling, Hilda
Butterfly.
Chickadee.
Dandelion.
Fairies.
I Am.
Little Snail.
Loveliness.
Moon Song.
Moonbeam.
Mouse.
Poems.
Spring Song.
Water.
Weather.
Conley, Robert J.
The Hills of Tsa la gi.
Ned Christie.
The Rattlesnake Band.
Tom Starr.
Untitled.
Wili Woyi, Shaman, also
known as Billy Pigeon.

Conn, Stewart
Marriage on a Mountain
Ridge.
Under Creag Mhor.
Connell, Charles
Wyvern.
Connell, F. Norreys
Requiem.
Connell, Hugh
A Dream.
Erris Coast, 1943.
The Mountain Tree.
Connell, James
The Red Flag.
Connell, Jim
New Words to the Tune of
"O'Donnel Abu."
Connellan, Leo
Watching Jim Shoulders.
Conniff, Richard
Dublin Doggerel.
Misogynist.
Connolly, Francis X.
No More Destructive Flame.
Connolly, Myles
Lament for a Poor Poet.
Quo Vadis?
Said the Innkeeper.
Connor, Tony
Apologue.
Elegy for Alfred Hubbard.
Lancashire Winter.
Last of the Poet's Car.
Connor, Torrey
The Old Casa.
Conolly, Luke Aylmer
The Enchanted Island.
Conover, Carl
Nude Reclining at Word
Processor, in Pastel.
Conquest, Robert
747 (London–Chicago).
Adriatic.
The Agents.
Aids to Composition.
Appalachian Convalescence.
Art and Civilization.
By Rail through Istria.
Excerpt from a Report to the
Galactic Council.
Generalities.
Guided Missiles Experimental
Range.
Horror Comic.
Lake Success.
Man and Woman.
The Motives of Rhythm.
Near the Death of Ovid.
On the Danube.
The Rokeby Venus.
Seal Rocks: San Francisco.
Semantic.
To Be a Pilgrim.
Conrad, May Ricker
What Does Easter Mean to
You?
Conrard, Harrison
Dead on the Desert.
A Hopi Prayer.
In Old Tucson.
Constable, Henry
Damelias' Song to His
Diaphenia.
Diana.
Love's Franciscan.
Needs Must I Leave, and Yet
Needs Must I Love.
O Gracious Shepherd.
Of the Nativity of the Lady
Rich's Daughter.
On the Death of Sir Philip
Sidney.

Sonnet: "If ever Sorrow spoke
from soul that loves."
To God the Father.
To God the Son.
To His Flocks.
To Live in Hell, and Heaven
to Behold.
To Our Blessed Lady.
To Saint Catherine.
To Saint Margaret.
To Saint Mary Magdalen.
To the Blessed Sacrament.
Whilst Eccho Cryes, What
Shall Become of Mee.
Constable, Thomas
Old October.
Constantine, David
Watching for Dolphins.
Constantine of Rhodes
Before the Ikon of the Mother
of God.
Constanzo, Gerald
The Meeting.
Contardo, Luis Felipe
The Calling.
Contoski, Victor
Broken Treaties: Teeth.
Dream 1971.
Invitation.
The Mailman.
Money.
Moonlit Night in Kansas.
Nocturne for the U.S.
Congress.
The Suicides of the Rich.
Those I Love.
Contractus, Hermanus
Alma Redemptoris Mater.
Converse, Florence
Rune of Riches.
Conway, Jack
Clothes Make the Man.
Conway, Katherine Eleanor
Annunciation Night.
The Heaviest Cross of All.
Saturninus.
Conway, Margaret Devereaux
The Annunciation.
Conyus
The Great Santa Barbara Oil
Disaster OR:.
He's Doing Natural Life.
San Francisco County Jail
Cell B-6.
Six Ten Sixty-Nine.
Untitled Requiem for
Tomorrow.
Upon Leaving the Parole
Board Hearing.
Coogler, J. Gordon
Alas! Carolina!
Alas! for the South!
Byron.
In Memorial.
A Mustacheless Bard.
Poor South! Her Books Get
Fewer and Fewer.
A Pretty Girl.
To Amy.
Cook
Duty.
Cook, Clarence Chatham
On One Who Died in May.
Cook, Edmund Vance
Fin De Siecle.
Rags.
Cook, Eliza
The Englishman.
The Indian Hunter.
The Mouse and the Cake.
My Old Straw Hat.
No!

Old Arm-Chair.
The Sailor's Grave.
Song of the Seaweed.
They All Belong to Me.
Three Little Kittens.
Where There's a Will There's
a Way.
Cook, Harold Lewis
Warning.
Cook, Joseph
Rhyme for a Chemical Baby.
Rhyme for a Geological Baby.
Rhyme for Astronomical
Baby.
Rhyme for Botanical Baby.
Cook, Mike
Bootie Black and the Seven
Giants All Sipping Chili...
Cook, Mrs. M. A. W.
In Some Way or Other the
Lord Will Provide.
Cook, Paul H.
Driving through the Pima
Indian Reservation.
Cook, R. L.
Tonight the City.
Cook, Russell Sturgis
Just As Thou Art.
Cook, Stanley
Christmas Tree.
Cook, Warren F.
Revelation.
Cook, William W.
Hudson Hornet.
Cooke, Edmund Vance
Born Without a Chance.
How Did You Die?
The Moo-Cow-Moo.
Off Manilly.
The Perfect Gift.
Cooke, John Esten
The Band in the Pines.
Cooke, Michael G.
An Unseen Fire.
Cooke, Philip Pendleton
Florence Vane.
Cooke, Rose T.
Arachne.
Bluebeards's Closet.
Done For.
In Vain.
Lise.
Segovia and Madrid.
Cooke, Rose Terry
The Snow-Filled Nest.
Then.
The Two Villages.
Coolbrith, Ina Donna
From Russian Hill.
Fruitionless.
Helen Hunt Jackson.
The Mariposa Lily.
Cooley, Peter
Alternatives.
The Confession.
Frog Hunting.
Naked Poetry.
The Other.
Such Comfort as the Night
Can Bring to Us.
To a Wasp Caught in the
Storm Sash...
Vanishing Point.
Coolidge, Clark
Back Aways.
Disturbing the Sallies Forth.
Fed Drapes.
Ghost.
The Hammer.
High Pitched Whale.
Mangrove in Crome.
Movies.

Of the Confident Stranger.
Remove the Predicate.
Risen Matters.
Rome Once Alone.
Styro.
To Mind.
Coolidge, Grace
The Open Door.
**"Coolidge, Susan" (Sarah
Chauncey Woolsey)**
Bind-Weed.
Calvary and Easter.
Charlotte Bronte.
A Child's Thought of Harvest.
Commonplace.
An Easter Song.
Edenhall.
Gulf Stream.
Helen.
How the Leaves Came Down.
Measles in the Ark.
Time to Go.
When.
Coon, Jeanette Saxton
A Mother's Prayer.
Cooper, Alice Cecilia
San Juan Capistrano.
Cooper, Belle
A Street Melody.
The Vintage.
Cooper, Charles
Dreams.
Honky.
Idle Chatter.
Rubin.
Cooper, Dennis
Being Aware.
Hustlers.
My Past.
Cooper, Edith See **"Field,
Michael"**
Cooper, George
Baby-Land.
Bob White.
October's Party.
Only One Mother.
Sweet Genevieve.
What Robin Told.
While the Days Are Going
By.
Why Did They Dig Ma's
Grave So Deep?
Cooper, James Fenimore
A Fable for Critics.
My Brigantine.
Cooper, Jane
The Builder of Houses.
Childhood in Jacksonville,
Florida.
A Circle, a Square, a Triangle
and a Ripple of Water.
Dispossessions.
El Sueno de la Razon.
The Faithful.
For a Very Old Man, on the
Death of His Wife.
For Thomas Hardy.
The Graveyard.
House Poem.
In the House of the Dying.
In the Last Few Moments
Came the Old German
Cleaning Woman.
The Knowledge That Comes
Through Experience.
Morning on the St. John's.
My Young Mother.
Obligations.
A Poem with Capital Letters.
Praise.
Rent.
Rock Climbing.

The Sundial.
Waiting.
The Weather of Six Mornings.
Cooper, John
Madrigal: "Oft thou hast with
greedy ear."
Cooper, John Gilbert
The Temper of Aristippus.
Cooper, Julian
A Warm Winter Day.
Cooper, Junius
Jabberwocky.
Cooper, Leonard
Rhyming Prophecy for a New
Year.
Cooper, Roger
To See the Cross at
Christmas.
Cooper, Jr., James Fenimore
Fate.
To a Friend.
Cooperman, Hasye
The Mists Are Rising Now.
Cooperman, Robert
All Up and Down the Lines.
Cooperman, Stanley
Redemption.
Cope, Jack
The Flying Fish.
If You Come Back.
Rock Painting.
Sappho.
Sons.
Cope, Wendy
Budgie Finds His Voice
(parody).
Depression.
Limerick: "A Phoenician
called Phlebas forgot."
Limerick: "In April one
seldom feels cheerful."
Limerick: "No water. dry
rocks and dry throats."
Limerick: "She sat in a
mighty fine chair."
Limerick: "The Thames runs,
bones rattle, rats creep."
Mr Strugnell (parody).
A Policeman's Lot.
Copeland, Benjamin
Christ's Life Our Code.
Our Fathers' God.
Copeland, Josephine
The Zulu King: New Orleans.
Copenhaver, Laura S.
Heralds of Christ.
Coppard, Alfred Edgar
The Apostate.
Epitaph.
The Horse.
Mendacity.
The Unfortunate Miller.
Coppee, Francois
Promenades and Interiors.
Coppinger, Matthew
A Song.
To Clelia.
Corbet, Richard
Certain True Woords Spoken
Concerning One Benet
Corbett.
The Distracted Puritan.
An Elegie.
An Epitaph on Doctor Donne,
Deane of Pauls.
The Fairies' Farewell.
Farewell to the Fairies.
Great Tom.
Like to the Thundering Tone.
Little Lute.
A Non Sequitor.
Nonsense.

On Mr. Francis Beaumont
(then newly dead).
To His Son, Vincent.
Upon Faireford Windowes.
Corbett, Elizabeth T.
A Misspelled Tail.
A Tail of the See.
The Three Wise Couples.
Three Wise Old Women.
Corbett, Mrs. E. R.
The Inventor's Wife.
Corbiere, Tristan
Cries Out of Blindness.
Epitaph.
The Gangrel Rymour and the
Pairdon of Sanct Anne.
Litany of Sleep.
Paris at Night.
Rhapsody of the Deaf Man.
To My Mouse-Colored Mare.
To the Eternal Feminine.
The Toad.
Corbin, Alice
Buffalo Dance.
Courtship.
Echoes of Childhood.
The Green Corn Dance.
Indian Death.
Juan Quintana.
Listening.
Love Me at Last.
Parting.
Sand Paintings.
Two Voices.
What Dim Arcadian Pastures.
Where the Fight Was.
The Wind.
Corbin, Lloyd M., Jr. *See*
Djangatolum
Corcos, Francine
I Suppose Her Mother Told
Her.
Corder, W.
The Murder of Maria Marten.
Core, Arthur Cleveland
Iona.
Coren, Alan
By the Klondike River.
Corey, Del
Hypodermic Release.
Corgo, Emanuel
Against Negritude.
Corinna
Fragments.
I Disapprove Even of
Eloquent Myrtis.
"Corinna"
Sehnsucht, or, What You
Will.
Corke, Hilary
Any Man to His Secretary.
Calm Winter Sleep.
Chair, Dog, and Clock.
The Choice.
Destroying Angel.
The Ghost.
November Poppies.
Poem at Equinox.
The Snake.
A Storm of Love.
Waiting.
The Waltz.
Corkery, Daniel
The Call.
No Miracle.
Corkine, William
Madrigal: "My dearest
mistress."
Madrigal: "Shall a frown."
Madrigal: "Sweet Cupid, ripen
her desire."
Sweet, Let Me Go.

Cormac Mac Cuilenan
The Heavenly Pilot.
Instructions of King Cormac.
Cormack, Barbara Villy
Reprieve.
Corman, Cid
Big Grave Creek.
Blessings Are.
Call It a Louse.
Cincinnati.
The Container.
Deceased.
The Desk.
The Detail.
I Have Come Far to Have
Found Nothing.
I'm a Baby.
I Promessi Sposi.
It's Food.
The Locus.
The Old Men.
The Old Pines.
The Poppy.
La Selva.
So Little Wanted.
There Are Things to Be Said.
This Is the Non-Existent
Beast.
Three Tiny Songs.
The Tortoise.
The Toy.
Without You.
Cormican, P. J.
True Son of God, Eternal
Light.
Corn, Alfred
Darkening Hotel Room.
Deception.
The Documentary on Brazil.
Dreambooks.
Fifty-Seventh Street and Fifth.
Fire: The People.
Grass.
Moving: New York–New
Haven Line.
Remembering Mykenai.
Tokyo West.
Corneille, Pierre
The Cid: Two Lovers in the
Toils of Honor.
Epitaph for Elizabeth
Ranquet.
Stanzas.
Cornelius, Maxwell N.
Some Time We'll Understand.
Cornelius, Peter
The Christmas Tree.
Cornell, Annette Patton
Sailor's Woman.
Cornford, Frances
After the Party.
All Souls' Night.
At Night.
Autumn Morning at
Cambridge.
Childhood.
The Coast: Norfolk.
The Corner of the Field.
The Country Bedroom.
Daybreak.
Epitaph for a Timid Lady.
Feri's Dream.
For M. S. Singing
Fruhlingsglaube in 1945.
For Nijinsky's Tomb.
A Glimpse.
The Guitarist Tunes Up.
The Herd.
The Hills.
In France.
In the Backs.

Inscription for a Wayside
Spring.
Lincolnshire Remembered.
London Despair.
Near an Old Prison.
Night Song.
On the Beach.
Parting in Wartime.
Preexistence.
The Princess and the Gypsies.
A Recollection.
The Scholar.
She Warns Him.
The Single Woman.
Summer Beach.
Susan to Diana.
To a Fat Lady Seen from the
Train.
The Unbeseechable.
Village before Sunset.
A Wasted Day.
The Watch.
Weekend Stroll.
Youth.
Cornford, John
Full Moon at Tierz: Before
the Storming of Huesca.
Huesca.
A Letter from Aragon.
Corning, Howard McKinley
These People.
Cornish, Sam
April 68.
A Black Man.
Death of Dr. King.
Dory Miller.
Frederick Douglass.
Home.
Lenox Christmas Eve 68.
Montgomery.
One Eyed Black Man in
Nebraska.
Panther.
Ray Charles.
The River.
Sam's World.
Sooner or Later.
To a Single Shadow without
Pity.
When My Grandmother Died.
Your Mother.
Cornish, William
Desire.
Pleasure It Is.
**"Cornwall, Barry" (Bryan
Waller Procter)** *See also*
Procter, Bryan Waller
The Blood Horse.
The Fate of the Oak.
The Hunter's Song.
Is My Lover on the Sea?
The Sea.
The Sea–in Calm.
Sit Down, Sad Soul.
The Stormy Petrel.
Cornwallis, Kinahan
The Battle of Murfreesboro.
Cornwell, Henry Sylvester
Jefferson D.
May.
The Sunset City.
Corpi, Lucha
Dark Romance.
Corpman, Izora
The Photos from Summer
Camp.
Corretjer, Juan Antonio
The Convoy.
In Jail.
Corrie, Joe
The Image o' God.
Miners' Wives.

Corrigan, Paul
The Boss Machine-Tender
after Losing a Son.
Corrothers, James David
At the Closed Gate of Justice.
Dream and the Song.
An Indignation Dinner.
The Negro Singer.
Paul Laurence Dunbar.
The Road to the Bow.
Corsellis, Timothy
Engine Failure.
Repression.
They Have Taken It from Me.
The Thrush.
To Stephen Spender.
Corso, Gregory
Birthplace Revisited.
Body Fished from the Seine.
But I Do Not Need Kindness.
Dear Girl.
Dialogue–2 Dollmakers.
A Difference of Zoos.
Dream of a Baseball Star.
A Dreamed Realization.
Eastside Incidents.
From Another Room.
God Is a Masturbator.
Hello.
I Am 25.
I Held a Shelley Manuscript.
I Met This Guy Who Died.
In the Fleeting Hand of Time.
Italian Extravagance.
The Last Warmth of Arnold.
The Mad Yak.
Marriage.
New York City–1935.
Notes after Blacking Out.
Paranoia in Crete.
Paris.
Poets Hitchhiking on the
Highway.
Reflection in a Green Arena.
Requiem for "Bird" Parker.
Seed Journey.
Spontaneous Requiem for the
American Indian.
Uccello.
The Vestal Lady on Brattle.
Vision of Rotterdam.
Waterchew!
Writ on the Eve of My 32nd
Birthday.
You, Whose Mother's Lover
Was Grass.
Zizi's Lament.
Cortez, Jayne
For Real.
Grinding Vibrato.
I Am New York City.
In the Morning.
Initiation.
Lead.
Orange Chiffon.
Orisha.
Phraseology.
So Long.
So Many Feathers.
Under the Edge of February.
**Cortissoz, Ellen Mackay
Hutchinson**
April Fantasie.
The Bride's Toilette.
A Cry from the Shore.
Harvest.
Moth-Song.
On Kingston Bridge.
Pamela in Town.
Praise-God Barebones.
Quaker Ladies.
The Quest.

Sea-Way.
So Wags the World.
Corwin, Norman
Man Unto His Fellow Man.
Corwin, Philip
Achilles.
Cory, David
Miss You.
Cory, William Johnson
Anteros.
The Bride's Song.
Eton Boating Song.
Europa.
Heraclitus.
An Invocation.
Mimnermus in Church.
Mortem, Quae Violat Suavia, Pellit Amor.
Notes of an Interview.
Oh, Earlier Shall the Rosebuds Blow.
Remember.
A Separation.
The Two Captains.
Cosier, Tony
Not This Leaf Haunts Me.
Cosmas, Saint
Nativity Ode.
The Purification.
Costa, Maria Velho da *See* **Marias, The Three**
Costanzo, Gerald
Braille.
Introduction of the Shopping Cart.
Jeane Dixon's America.
The Man Who Invented Las Vegas.
Nobody Lives on Arthur Godfrey Boulevard.
Coste, Marie Ravenal de la
Somebody's Darling.
Costello, Tomas
From a Lament for Una.
Cothi, Lewis Glyn
On the Death of His Son.
Cottam, Samuel Elsworth
To G.R.
Cotter, Joseph Seamon, Jr.
And What Shall You Say?
An April Day.
The Band of Gideon.
The Deserter.
Is It Because I Am Black?
A Prayer.
Rain Music.
Supplication.
The Tragedy of Pete.
The Way-Side Well.
Cotter, Jr, Joseph Seaman
Sonnet to Negro Soldiers.
Cotterill, Sarah
Cutting Redbud: An Accidental Death.
Cottle, Joseph
Malvern Hills.
Cotton, Charles
Les Amours.
The Angler's Ballad.
Clepsydra.
An Epitaph on M.H.
Epitaph on Mistress Mary Draper.
Epitaph on Mr. Robert Port.
Evening Quatrains.
The Joys of Marriage.
Laura Sleeping.
The Litany.
Madrigal: "To be a whore, despite of grace."
The New Year.
Noon Quatrains.

Ode: "Good night, my Love, may gentle rest."
Ode to Chloris.
Ode to Cupid.
Ode: "Without the evening dew and showers."
Old Tityrus to Eugenia.
On My Pretty Marten.
On Tobacco.
Resolution in Four Sonnets.
The Retreat.
Song: "Join once again, my Celia, join."
Song. Set by Mr. Coleman.
Sonnet: "Chloris, whilst thou and I were free."
The Tempest.
To Celia.
To Mr. Izaak Walton.
The Winter Glass.
Cotton, Elizabeth
Oh, Babe, It Ain't No Lie.
Cotton, John
Fragments.
In Saram.
Old Movies.
Pigs.
Pumpkins.
A Thankful Acknowledgment of God's Providence.
To My Reverend Dear Brother, M. Samuel Stone...
Toad.
Upon the Death of G: B.
Cotton, Nathaniel
The Bee, the Ant, and the Sparrow.
Contentment.
Early Thoughts of Marriage.
Marriage.
To a Child Five Years Old.
Coulette, Henri
Antony and Cleopatra.
At the Telephone Club.
The Attic.
The Black Angel.
The Blue-Eyed Precinct Worker.
Emeritus, n.
The Family Goldschmitt.
Intaglio.
The Junk Shop.
Night Thoughts.
The Sickness of Friends.
The War of the Secret Agents.
Coulter, John
Morning Bus.
Council, Floyd
Don't Want No Hungry Woman.
Councilman, Emily Sargent
Between the Tides.
Coupey, Pierre
Study No. X.
Coursen, H. R.
Fall Again.
Suburban.
Court, Wesli
Academic Curse: An Epitaph.
Courthope, W. J.
The Trail of the Bird.
Courtney, Margaret
Be Kind.
Cousens, Mildred
American Vineyard.
Cousins, James
A Starling's Spring Rondel.
Cousins, James H.
Behind the Plough.
The Corncrake.
A Curse on a Closed Gate.
High and Low.

Omens.
The Wings of Love.
Coutts, Francis
On a Wife.
Coward, Noel
Any Part of Piggy.
A Bar on the Piccola Marina.
The Boy Actor.
He Never Did That to Me.
I've Been to a Marvellous Party.
Irish Song: Rosie O'Grady.
The Little Ones' A.B.C.
Mad Dogs and Englishmen.
The Stately Homes of England (parody).
There Are Bad Times Just Around the Corner.
To Noel Coward.
What's Going to Happen to the Tots?
Cowdery, Mae V.
I Sit and Wait for Beauty.
Cowen, Joseph R.
Recessional for the Class of 1959...
Cowing, Sheila
The Hinge.
Cowley, Abraham
Against Hope.
Age.
All-Over Love.
Anacreontics.
Beauty.
But Since I Know Thy Falsehood and Thy Pride.
The Change.
The Chronicle.
Clad All in White.
The Country Mouse.
Davideis.
Destinie.
Dialogue after Enjoyment.
The Dissembler.
Drinking.
The Duel.
The Epicure.
Epitaph of Pyramus and Thisbe.
The Extasie.
The Frailty.
The Grasshopper.
Honour.
Hymn, to Light.
Leaving Me, and Then Loving Many.
Life and Fame.
The Motto.
My Diet.
Ode of Wit.
Ode upon Doctor Harvey.
Of Solitude.
On the Death of Mr. Crashaw.
On the Death of Mr. William Hervey.
Platonic Love.
The Praise of Pindar in Imitation of Horace His Second Ode, Book 4.
The Prophet.
Reason. The Use of It in Divine Matters.
The Request.
The Soul.
The Spring.
The Swallow.
The Thief.
This Only Grant Me.
The Thraldome.
To His Mistress.
To Mr. Hobbes.

To Sir William Davenant.
To the Royal Society.
The Welcome.
The Wish.
Written in Juice of Lemmon.
Cowley, Malcolm
Blue Juniata: The Streets of Air.
Danny.
For St. Bartholomew's Eve.
Here and There: Nocturnal Landscape.
The Hill Above the Mine.
The Long Voyaage.
Piney Woods.
Stone Horse Shoals.
Tumbling Mustard.
The Urn.
William Wilson.
Cowper, William
Absence of Occupation.
The Acquiescence of Pure Love.
Addressed to a Young Lady.
Beau's Reply.
Boadicea.
Capability Brown.
The Castaway.
A Comparison.
The Contrite Heart.
The Diverting History of John Gilpin.
The Dog and the Water-lily.
England.
Epigram on the Refusal of the University of Oxford to Subscribe...
An Epistle to Robert Lloyd, Esq.
An Epitaph: "My name–my country–what are they to thee?"
Epitaph on a Free but Tame Redbreast.
Epitaph on a Hare.
Epitaph on Johnson.
Evening.
Exhortation to Prayer.
The Faithful Friend.
Fragment.
The Golden Mean.
Hope.
Human Frailty.
I Will Praise the Lord at All Times.
In His Mental Illness, William Cowper Finds He Is Not Alone.
The Jackdaw.
Jehovah Our Righteousness.
Jehovah-Rophi.
Joy and Peace in Believing.
The Light and Glory of the World.
Light Shining Out of Darkness.
Lines on a Bill of Mortality, 1790.
Lines Written during a Period of Insanity.
Lines Written on a Window-Shutter at Weston.
Love Constraining to Obedience.
Lovest Thou Me?
The Man That Hails You Tom or Jack.
The Monarch.
My Former Hopes Are Fled.
My Soul Thirsts for God.
The Nightingale and Glow-Worm.

O Lord, My Best Desire
  Fulfil.
An Ode: Secundum Artem.
Old-Testament Gospel.
Olney Hymns.
On a Similar Occasion for the
  Year 1792.
On a Spaniel Called Beau
  Killing a Young Bird.
On Friendship.
On His Portrait.
On the Death of Mrs.
  Throckmorton's Bullfinch.
On the Ice Islands Seen
  Floating in the German
  Ocean.
On the Loss of the "Royal
  George."
On the Queen's Visit to
  London.
On the Receipt of My
  Mother's Picture Out of
  Norfolk.
Pernicious Weed.
Playthings.
The Poplar Field.
The Progress of Error.
Prudent Simplicity.
A Reflection on the Foregoing
  Ode.
The Retired Cat.
Retirement.
A Riddle.
The Rights of Women.
The Robin in Winter.
Self-Acquaintance.
The Shrubbery.
Simple Faith.
Slaves Cannot Breathe in
  England.
Sonnet to William
  Wilberforce, Esq.
The Sower.
The Spirit's Light.
Squirrel in Sunshine.
Stanzas Subjoined to the
  Yearly Bill of Mortality.
The Statesman in Retirement.
The Stricken Deer.
Sweet Meat Has Sour Sauce.
Table Talk.
The Task.
Temptation.
Tirocinium; or, A Review of
  Schools.
To a Young Lady.
To Mary.
To Mary Unwin.
To Mr. Newton on His
  Return from Ramsgate.
To the Immortal Memory of
  the Halibut on Which I
  Dined This Day.
To the Rev. Mr. Newton.
Truth.
The Valley of the Shadow of
  Death.
Verses Supposed to be Written
  by Alexander Selkirk.
Walking with God.
The Woodman's Dog.
Yardley-Oak.
Cox, C. C.
  I Love Thee, Gracious Lord.
Cox, Eleanor Rogers
  The Dream of Aengus Og.
  Dreaming of Cities Dead.
  The Return.
  Three White Birds of Angus.
  To a Portrait of Whistler in
    the Brooklyn Art Museum.

Cox, Elizabeth
  Mask.
Cox, Kenyon
  The Bumblebeaver.
  The Kangarooster.
  Limerick: "His figure's not
    noted for grace."
  The Octopussycat.
  Work.
Cox, Leo
  The Bells of Ste. Anne des
    Monts.
  Cornfield.
  Easter Thought.
Cox, Palmer
  The Brownies' Celebration.
  The Lazy Pussy.
  The Mouse's Lullaby.
Cox, Samuel K.
  Lord, Thou Hast Promised.
Coxe, Arthur Cleveland
  America.
  Body of Jesus.
  Father, Who Mak'st Thy
    Suff'ring Sons.
  In the Silent Midnight
    Watches.
  The Present Age.
  Saviour, Sprinkle Many
    Nations.
  We Are Living, We Are
    Dwelling.
  Ye Shall Live Also.
Coxe, Louis O.
  Dead Marine.
  From the Window Down.
  The Lake.
  Nightsong.
  Pin-Up Girl.
  Red Right Returning.
  Squaring the Circle.
  The Veteran.
  Winter Night.
  The World As Wave and
    Idea.
Coxon, Philip
  April, Glengarry.
Coxon, William W.
  The Flash Colonial Barman.
Crabbe, George
  The Ancient Mansion.
  An Ancient Virgin.
  Books.
  The Borough.
  The Caroline.
  Crusty Critics.
  The Dean's Lady.
  Delay Has Danger.
  The Frank Courtship.
  Frenzy.
  Inebriety (parody).
  The Lady of the Manor.
  Late Wisdom.
  Life.
  A Marriage Ring.
  Meeting.
  My Birthday.
  The Newspaper.
  The Parish Register.
  Peter Grimes.
  Phoebe Dawson.
  Resurrection.
  Rural Life.
  The Sad Lover.
  Sailing upon the River.
  Sir Eustace Grey.
  A Slum Dwelling.
  Tales of the Hall.
  Truth in Poetry.
  The Vicar.
  The Village.
  The Whistling Boy.

The Winter Storm at Sea.
  Young Paris.
Craddle, W.
  Egoism.
Cradock, Thomas
  What Glorious Vision.
  Ye Scattered Nations.
Cragin, Mary A. *See* "Allison,
  Joy"
Craig, Alexander
  Hillside.
  Sonnet: "Go you, O winds
    that blow from north to
    south."
Craig, David
  One Thousand Feet of
    Shadow.
  One Way Down.
Craig, John
  O Hear My Prayer, Lord.
  O Lord, That Art My God
    and King.
Craig, Maurice James
  Ballad to a Traditional
    Refrain.
  Fable.
  From Burton the Anatomist.
  Love Poem.
  Poem: "High on a ridge of
    tiles."
  Winter.
Craig, Norma
  Question.
Craik, Dinah Maria Mulock
  Four Years.
  Friendship.
  Green Things Growing.
  In Our Boat.
  Lettice.
  The New Year.
  Now and Afterwards.
  Philip, My King.
  Plighted.
  Too Late.
Cramer, Steven
  Two Women with Mangoes.
Cranch, Christopher Pearse
  After the Centennial.
  The Bear and the Squirrels.
  The Bobolinks.
  Gnosis.
  I in Thee, and Thou in Me.
  An Old Cat's Confession.
  The Pines and the Sea.
  So Far, So Near.
  Stanza from an Early Poem.
  Thought.
Crandall, Charles Henry
  The Human Plan.
  Stella.
  Three Trees.
  With Lilacs.
Crane, Carl
  The Reader Writes.
Crane, Elizabeth Green
  Gentian.
Crane, Frank
  Because You Care.
Crane, Hart
  The Air Plant.
  At Melville's Tomb.
  Atlantis.
  Ave Maria.
  The Bathers.
  Black Tambourine.
  The Bridge: Indiana.
  The Bridge: Three Songs.
  The Broken Tower.
  Cape Hatteras.
  Carrier Letter.
  Chaplinesque.
  Cutty Sark.

The Dance.
Emblems of Conduct.
For the Marriage of Faustus
  and Helen.
The Harbor Dawn.
The Hurricane.
Imperator Victus.
In Shadow.
Island Quarry.
Key West.
Legend.
March.
My Grandmother's Love
  Letters.
A Name for All.
National Winter Garden.
North Labrador.
O Carib Isle!
Paraphrase.
Passage.
The Phantom Bark.
Praise for an Urn.
Purgatorio.
Quaker Hill.
Recitative.
Repose of Rivers.
The River.
Royal Palm.
The Sea.
Sunday Morning Apples.
To Brooklyn Bridge.
To Emily Dickinson.
To Potapovitch.
The Tunnel.
The Urn.
Van Winkle.
Voyages.
The Wine Menagerie.
Crane, Nathalia
  The Blind Girl.
  The Janitor's Boy.
  The Moon of Brooklyn.
  Spooks.
  The Vestal.
Crane, Orin L.
  Slow Me Down, Lord!
Crane, Stephen
  Ancestry.
  Behold, the Grave.
  The Black Riders.
  The Blades of Grass.
  The Book of Wisdom.
  The Candid Man.
  Charity, Thou Art a Lie.
  Content.
  Do Not Weep, Maiden, for
    War Is Kind.
  Epigram: "A man said to the
    universe."
  God Fashioned the Ship of
    the World Carefully.
  A God in Wrath.
  The Heart.
  Hymn.
  I Explain.
  I Saw a Man Pursuing the
    Horizon.
  I Stood Upon a High Place.
  I Walked in a Desert.
  If I Should Cast Off This
    Tattered Coat.
  In the Desert.
  It Was Wrong to Do This,
    Said the Angel.
  A Learned Man.
  The Livid Lightnings Flashed
    in the Clouds.
  A Man Adrift on a Slim Spar.
  A Man Said.
  Many Red Devils.
  Many Workmen.
  The Ocean Said to Me Once.

On the Desert.
The Peaks.
A Row of Thick Pillars.
'Scaped.
Should the Wide World Roll
  Away.
A Slant of Sun on Dull
  Brown Walls.
Tell Me Not in Joyous
  Numbers.
Ten Poems.
There Is a Grey Thing That
  Lives in the Tree-Tops.
There Was a Crimson Clash
  of War.
There Was a Man with a
  Tongue of Wood.
There Was One I Met upon
  the Road.
Think as I Think.
Three Poems.
The Trees in the Garden
  Rained Flowers.
War Is Kind.
The Wayfarer.
When a People Reach the Top
  of a Hill.
Why?
A Youth in Apparel That
  Glittered.

Crane, Walter
The Crocus.
A Seat for Three: Written on
  a Settle.

Cranston, Claudia
In the Name of Jesus Christ.

Crapsey, Adelaide
Amaze.
Cinquain: A Warning.
Cradle-Song.
Dirge.
For Lucas Cranach's Eve.
The Guarded Wound.
The Lonely Death.
Moon Shadows.
Night Winds.
November Night.
On Seeing Weather-Beaten
  Trees.
Roma Aeterna.
Rose-Marie of the Angels.
Snow.
Song: "I make my shroud but
  no one knows."
Susanna and the Elders.
To Man Who Goes Seeking
  Immortality, Bidding Him
  Look Nearer Home.
Triad.
Vendor's Song.
The Warning.

Crase, Douglas
Heron Weather.
Summer.

Crashaw, Richard
And He Answered Them
  Nothing.
An Apologie for the Precedent
  Hymnes on Teresa.
An Apology for the Foregoing
  Hymn....
Charitas Nimia, or the Deare
  Bargain.
Christ Crucified.
The Coming Child.
Death's Lecture at the
  Funeral of a Young
  Gentleman.
An Epitaph upon Doctor
  Brook.

An Epitaph upon Husband
  and Wife Who Died and
  Were Buried Together.
An Epitaph upon Mr. Ashton
  a Conformable Citizen.
Epithalamium.
The Flaming Heart.
For Hope.
The Hymn of Saint Thomas
  in Adoration of the Blessed
  Sacrament.
A Hymn to the Name and
  Honour of the Admirable
  Saint Teresa.
A Hymne for the Epiphanie.
  Sung as by the Three Kings.
I Am the Door.
In Memory of the Vertuous
  and Learned Lady Madre de
  Teresa.
In the Glorious Epiphanie of
  Our Lord God.
In the Holy Nativity of Our
  Lord God.
In the Holy Nativity of Our
  Lord: Shepherds' Hymn.
A Letter to the Countess of
  Denbigh.
Love's Horoscope.
Love's Nightingale.
Luke 11: "Blessed be the paps
  which Thou hast sucked".
M. Crashaws Answer for
  Hope.
Music's Duel.
New Year's Day.
An Ode Which was Prefixed
  To a Prayer Booke.
On a Prayer Book Sent to
  Mrs. M. R. (excerpt).
On Dives.
On Hope.
On Marriage.
On Mr. G. Herbert's Book.
On Our Crucified Lord,
  Naked and Bloody.
On the Baptized Aethiopian.
On the Bleeding Wounds of
  Our Crucified Lord.
On the Blessed Virgin's
  Bashfulness.
On the Glorious Assumption
  of Our Blessed Lady.
On the Miracle of Loaves.
On the Name of Jesus.
Out of Catullus.
Out of the Italian.
Quaerit Jesum suum Maria.
Qui Perdiderit Animam Suam.
Saint Mary Magdalene.
Samson to His Delilah.
A Song: "Lord, when the
  sense of thy sweet grace."
Sospetto d'Herode.
St. Peter's Shadow.
The Tear.
Temperance or the Cheap
  Physitian upon the
  Translation of Lessius.
To a Young Gentle-Woman,
  Councel Concerning Her
  Choice.
To Our Blessed Lord upon
  the Choice of His Sepulchre.
To Our Lord, upon the Water
  Made Wine.
To the Infant Martyrs.
To the Name Above Every
  Name, the Name of Jesus A
  Hymn.

To the Noblest and Best of
  Ladies, the Countess of
  Denbigh.
Two Went up to the Temple
  to Pray.
Upon Bishop Andrewes His
  Picture before His Sermons.
Upon Ford's Two Tragedies...
Upon Lazarus His Teres.
Upon the Bleeding Crucifix.
Upon the Death of a
  Gentleman.
Upon the Holy Sepulchre.
Upon the Infant Martyrs.
Upon Venus Putting on Mars
  His Armes.
The Weeper.
The Widow's Mites.
Wishes to His Supposed
  Mistress.

Craster, Mrs. Edward
Quandary.

Craveirinha, Jose
Black Cry.
Mamana Saquina.
Mamano.
Mamparra M'gaiza.
Ode to a Lost Cargo in a Ship
  Called Save.
Poem of the Future Citizen.
Song of the Negro on the
  Ferry.

Crawford, Dan
Jesus and I.

Crawford, Francis Marion
New National Hymn.

Crawford, Isabella Valancy
The Axe of the Pioneer.
A Battle.
The Camp of Souls.
The Canoe.
The City Tree.
The Dark Stag.
Gisli, the Chieftain: The Song
  of the Arrow.
Laughter.
The Lily Bed.
Love Me, Love My Dog.
Love's Land.
Malcolm's Katie.
Said the Canoe.
The Song of the Arrow.
True and False.

Crawford, John Wallace (Jack)
Broncho Versus Bicycle.
The Death of Custer.

Crawford, Louisa Macartney
Kathleen Mavourneen.

Crawford, Tom
Phone Call.

Crawford, Vesta Pierce
Pioneer Woman.

Creekmore, Hubert
Concert at Sea.
Dividends.
Music in the Rec Hut.
Pocket Guide for Servicemen.

Creeley, Robert
The Act of Love.
After Lorca.
Air: Cat Bird Singing.
Air: "The Love of a Woman."
All That Is Lovely in Men.
America.
And.
Anger.
The Awakening.
Ballad of the Despairing
  Husband.
The Business.
The City.
The Conspiracy.

A Counterpoint.
The Cracks.
The Crisis.
The Crow.
Damon & Pythias.
The Death of Venus.
Distance.
The Door.
The End of the Day.
Fancy.
The Figures.
The Fire.
The Flower.
For Fear.
For Love.
For My Mother: Genevieve
  Jules Creeley.
For No Clear Reason.
For the New Year.
A Form of Adaptation.
A Form of Women.
The Gift.
A Gift of Great Value.
Hart Crane.
Here.
Heroes.
The Hill.
The House.
I Keep to Myself Such
  Measures.
I Know a Man.
If You.
The Immoral Proposition.
The Innocence.
The Invoice.
Just Friends.
The Kind of Act of.
Kore.
The Language.
Like They Say.
Love Comes Quietly.
The Man.
A Marriage.
The Mechanic.
The Memory.
Moment.
The Moon.
The Mountains in the Desert.
The Name.
Naughty Boy.
Oh No.
On Vacation.
The Operation.
The People.
The Pool.
Prayer to Hermes.
Quick-Step.
The Rain.
A Reason.
The Rescue.
The Rhyme.
The Rhythm.
The Rose.
The Saints.
She Went to Stay.
A Sight.
The Signboard.
Sing Song.
The Snow.
Something.
Somewhere.
Song: "Those rivers run from
  that land."
Song: "What I took in my
  hand."
Sounds.
The Statue.
The Three Ladies.
The Tiger.
Time.
A Token.
The Turn.

Wait for Me.
Waiting.
The Warning.
The Way.
The Whip.
A Wicker Basket.
The Wife.
The Wind.
The Window.
The World.
Creelman, Josephine Rice
My Mother.
Creighton, Alan
Pastoral.
Return of a Reaper.
Spring Workman.
Cresson, Abigail
Cloak of Laughter.
Market Day.
Cresswell, D'Arcy
The Impatient Poet.
Lyttelton Harbor.
Time Lags Abed.
To L–.
Crew, Helen Coale
In a Low Rocking-Chair.
Crewe, Jennifer
Visitations.
Crewe, Robert, Marquess of
Seven Years.
Crews, Jacquelyne
Auguries for Three Women.
Crews, Judson
Declaration at Forty.
Love Poem.
Oh Beach Love Blossom.
"Crichton, John" (Norman Gregor Guthrie)
A Bed of Campanula.
Crinagoras
Epitaph on an Infant.
Sepulchral Imprecation.
This Torch, Still Burning in My Hand.
Cripps, Arthur Shearly
Les Belles Roses sans Mercie.
To the Veld.
Criswell, Cloyd Mann
The Newlyweds.
Crites, Lucile
Folks and Me.
"Critics, The"
Grey October.
Crocker, Henry
Evangelize!
Croffut, William Augustus
A Dirge.
A Living Memory.
Croft, Roy
Love.
Why Do I Love You?
Croker, T. F. Dillon
Shakespearean Soliloquy in Progress: "To shave, or not to..." (parody).
Croly, George
An Aestuary.
Approach of Evening.
Death and Resurrection.
The Death of Leonidas.
A Fauxbourg.
The Genius of Death.
Leonidas.
Cromwell, Gladys
The Crowning Gift.
Folded Power.
The Mould.
The Quest.
Renewal.
Cronin, Anthony
Anarchist.
Apology.

Autumn Poem.
Baudelaire in Brussels.
The Elephant to the Girl in Bertram Mills' Circus.
For a Father.
R.M.S. Titanic.
Surprise.
Crooke, Sheila Jane
The Statue of Liberty.
Crooker, Barbara
Kneading.
Moving.
Cros, Charles
The Smoked Herring.
Crosby, Ernest
Choir Practice.
In the Garden.
Rebels.
The Search.
The Soul of the World.
The Tournament of Man.
Crosby, Fanny J.
The Best of All.
Blessed Assurance, Jesus Is Mine.
Blind but Happy.
Jesus, Keep Me Near the Cross.
Keep Thou My Way, O Lord.
There's Music in the Air.
Unseen.
Crosby, Harry
Firebrand.
Telephone Directory.
Crosby, Ranice Henderson
Poem about a Seashell.
Thoughts for You (when She Came back from the Mountains).
Crosland, T. W. H.
Slain.
Cross, Allen Eastman
The Gray Hills Taught Me Patience.
Though Fatherland Be Vast.
Young and Radiant, He Is Standing.
Cross, Zora
Elegy on an Australian Schoolboy.
Love Sonnets.
When I Was Six.
Crossley-Holland, Kevin
Postcards from Kodai.
Crossman, Samuel
I Said Sometimes with Tears.
Love Unknown.
My Song Is Love Unknown.
Croswell, William
The Clouds.
Lord! Lead the Way the Saviour Went.
Crouch, Nathaniel
David and Goliath.
The Tower of Babel.
Crouch, Pearl Riggs
The Snowstorm.
A Story in the Snow.
Crouch, Stanley
After the Rain.
Albert Ayler: Eulogy for a Decomposed Saxophone Player.
Blackie Thinks of His Brothers.
Chops Are Flyin.
No New Music.
Riding across John Lee's Finger.
Crow, Mary
Foreign Streets.
Rain-in-the-Face.

Crowe, Ronald
Guns.
Crowe, William
Lewesdon Hill.
Crowell, Albert
The Joy of Incompleteness.
Crowell, Grace Noll
Because of Thy Great Bounty.
The Common Tasks.
Courage to Live.
Definition.
Eternal Values.
I Have Found Such Joy.
I Think That God Is Proud.
Let Us Keep Christmas.
The Poet Prays.
Prayer for a Day's Walk.
Quiet Things.
Crowell, Norman H.
My Candidate.
Crowley, Aleister
The Lesbian Hell.
Crowne, John
Kind Lovers, Love On.
Untitled.
Croxall, Samuel
Sylvia.
Crozier, Lorna
The Child Who Walks Backwards.
Consummation.
Fishing in Air.
Indigo.
Morgain Le Fay.
South Dakota Refuge.
The Weather.
Woman from the West Coast.
Crudup, Arthur ("Big Boy")
Death Valley Blues.
Cruickshank, Helen B.
Caenlochan.
Comfort in Puirtith.
Schiehallion.
Shy Geordie.
The Wishin' Well.
Crummy, Biddy
A Fragrant Prayer.
Cruz, San Juan de la *See* **Juana Ines de la Cruz, Sister**
Cruz, Victor Hernandez
224 Stoop.
African Things.
Bring the Soul Blocks.
California #2.
Carmen.
Cities #8.
Confusion.
The Electric Cop.
Energy.
Going Uptown to Visit Miriam.
Listening to the Music of Arsenio Rodriguez Is Moving Closer...
Man I Thought You Was Talking Another Language That Day.
The Physics of Ochun.
Sometimes on My Way Back Down to the Block.
Spirits.
The Story of Zeros.
Today Is a Day of Great Joy.
Urban Dream.
You Gotta Have Your Tips on Fire.
Csoori, Sandor
It Must Be Summer.
Cudahy, Sheila
Heroes of the Strip.
Cudjoe, Seth D.
Transmigration.

Cuelho, Art
My Own Brand.
Culhane, Charles
The Ancient One.
Death Row.
Green Haven Halls.
The Straw Men.
There Isn't Enough Bread.
Cullen, Cornelius C.
Battle of Somerset.
Cullen, Countee
Any Human to Another.
Black Magdalens.
Black Majesty.
Brown Boy to Brown Girl.
A Brown Girl Dead.
For a Lady I Know.
For a Mouthy Woman.
For a Pessimist.
For a Poet.
For Amy Lowell.
For John Keats, Apostle of Beauty.
For My Grandmother.
For Paul Laurence Dunbar.
From the Dark Tower.
Fruit of the Flower.
Heritage: What Is Africa to Me?
I Have a Rendezvous with Life.
In Memory of Colonel Charles Young.
Incident.
Judas Iscariot.
Lines to Our Elders.
The Litany of the Dark People.
Magnets.
Mary, Mother of Christ.
Only the Polished Skeleton.
Protest.
Red.
Saturday's Child.
Scottsboro, Too, Is Worth Its Song.
Simon the Cyrenian Speaks.
Song in Spite of Myself.
A Song of Praise.
Tableau.
That Bright Chimeric Beast.
A Thorn Forever in the Breast.
Three Epitaphs: For a Virgin Lady.
Timid Lover.
To Certain Critics.
To John Keats, Poet, at Springtime.
To Lovers of Earth: Fair Warning.
Uncle Jim.
Under the Mistletoe.
The Unknown Color.
The Wakeupworld.
The Wise.
Yet Do I Marvel.
Youth Sings a Song of Rosebuds.
Cullen, Paula B.
Cousins.
Cullum, J. W.
Roses, Revisited, in a Paradoxical Autumn.
Cumberland, George Clifford, Earl of *See* **Clifford, George, Earl of Cumberland**
Cumberland, Richard
The Benefits and Abuse of Alcohol.
Cumbie, Richard
New Jersey Turnpike.

Cumbo, Kattie M.
Black Sister.
Ceremony.
Dark People.
Domestics.
I'm a Dreamer.
Malcolm.
The Morning after...Love.
Nocturnal Sounds.
Washiri (Poet).
Cummings, Alison Elizabeth
To a Little Sister, Aged Ten.
Cummings, David
Emily's Haunted Housman (parody).
From the Brothers Grimm to Sister Sexton to Mother Goose (parody).
Sweeney, Old and Phthisic, among the Hippopotami (parody).
Cummings, Edward Estlin
2 Little Whos.
72: wild(at our first)beasts uttered human words.
All Ignorance Toboggans into Know.
"All in green went my love riding".
All Which Isn't Singing Is Mere Talking.
Always Before Your Voice My Soul.
Annie died the other day.
Anyone Lived in a Pretty How Town.
As Freedom Is a Breakfastfood.
As Is the Sea Marvelous.
As Joe Gould Says In.
Being to Timelessness as It's to Time.
Buffalo Bill's.
But.
Buy Me an Ounce and I'll Sell You a Pound.
The Cambridge Ladies.
Chanson Innocent.
Come,Gaze with Me upon This Dome.
Darling! Because My Blood Can Sing.
Dive for Dreams.
Doll's Boy's Asleep.
Dominic Has a Doll.
Enter No (Silence is the Blood Whose Flesh.
Epigram: "IN)/all those who got".
Faithfully Tinying at Twilight Voice.
The First of All My Dreams.
Flotsam and Jetsam.
For Prodigal Read Generous.
Four III "here's a little mouse."
Gee I Like to Think of Dead.
Goodby Betty, Don't Remember Me.
A Great.
The Greedy the People.
La Guerre.
A He as O.
Her careful distinct sex whose sharp lips comb.
Hist Whist.
The Hours Rise Up.
How Many Moments Must(Amazing Each.
I am a little church (no great cathedral).
I Am So Glad and Very.

I go to this window.
I like my body when it is with your.
I Sing of Olaf Glad and Big.
I Thank You God for Most This Amazing.
I Was Sitting in McSorley's.
I Will Be.
If Everything Happens That Can't Be Done.
If I Have Made, My Lady, Intricate.
If i should sleep with a lady called death.
If in Beginning Twilight.
If There Are Any Heavens.
If(Touched by Love's Own Secret)We,Like Homing.
If You Can't Eat You Got To.
(Im)c-a-t(mo).
Impossibly, motivated by midnight.
Impressions, Number III.
In Heavenly Realms of Hellas Dwelt.
In Just-.
Is 5.
It Is at Moments after I Have Dreamed.
It Is So Long Since My Heart Has Been with Yours.
It May Not Always Be So.
It's Over a(See Just.
It Was a Goodly Co.
ITEM.
Jake Hates All the Girls.
Jehovah Buried, Satan Dead.
Ladies and Gentlemen This Little Girl.
Life Is More True.
Listen.
Little Joe Gould Has Lost His Teeth and Doesn't Know Where.
Little tree.
Love Is a Place.
Love Is More Thicker Than Forget.
Maggie and milly and molly and may.
A Man Who Had Fallen Among Thieves.
May I Feel Said He.
May My Heart Always.
Me Up at Does.
Meet Mr. Universe.
Might These Be Thrushes.
The Moon Is Hiding in.
Mr U Will Not Be Missed.
My Father Moved through Dooms of Love.
My Love.
My Specialty Is Living Said.
My sweet old etcetera.
Next to of Course God America I.
No Man, If Men Are Gods.
No Thanks.
No Time Ago.
Nobody Loses All the Time.
Noone and a Star Stand, Am to Am.
"Noone" Autumnal This Great Lady's Gaze.
Notice the Convulsed Orange Inch of Moon.
Now Does Our World Descend.
O By the By.
O Sweet Spontaneous.

O Thou to Whom the Musical White Spring.
Of Nicolette.
Old Age Sticks.
(One!).
One Times One.
One Winter Afternoon.
One X.
Paris: This April Sunset Completely Utters.
Pity this busy monster, manunkind.
Plato Told.
Poem; or, Beauty Hurts Mr. Vinal.
A Politician.
Ponder, Darling, These Busted Statues.
Portrait.
A Pretty a Day.
Purer Than Purest Pure.
Q:dwo.
R-P-O-P-H-E-S-S-A-G-R.
Raise the Shade.
A Salesman Is an It That Stinks Excuse.
The Season 'Tis, My Lovely Lambs.
Serene Immediate Silliest and Whose.
She being Brand.
Silence.
Since Feeling Is First.
Slightly before the Middle of Congressman Pudd.
Somewhere I Have Never Travelled, Gladly Beyond.
Song: "All in green went my love riding."
Song: "Thy fingers make early flowers."
Songs.
Sonnet: "A wind has blown the rain away."
Sonnet Entitled How to Run the World.
Sonnets–Actualities.
Sonnets–Unrealities.
Space Being(Don't Forget to Remember)Curved.
Spring Is Like a Perhaps Hand.
Spring Omnipotent Goddess.
Sunset.
Sweet Spring Is Your.
Than(By Yon Sunset's Wintry Glow.
Thanksgiving (1956).
This Is the Garden.
This little bride & groom are.
Twentyseven Bums.
Two X "16 heures l'Etoile."
The Way to Hump a Cow.
What a Proud Dreamhorse.
What If a Much of a Which of a Wind.
What Is.
When Any Mortal.
When Faces Called Flowers.
When God Lets My Body Be.
When Life Is Quite Through With.
When Serpents Bargain for the Right to Squirm.
When the spent day begins to frail.
When What Hugs Stopping Earth Than Silent Is.
Wherelings Whenlings.
White Guardians of the Universe of Sleep.
Who Are You, Little I.

Who Knows if the Moon's.
Who's Most Afraid of Death?
Why Did You Go.
Why from This Her and Him.
You Are Like the Snow Only.
You Shall Above All Things Be Glad and Young.
Your Birthday Comes to Tell Me This.
Your Little Voice.
Cummins, Evelyn Atwater
I Know Not Where the Road Will Lead.
Cumpian, Carlos
Cuento.
Cuney, Waring
Burial of the Young Love.
Conception.
Crucifixion.
The Death Bed.
Dust.
Finis.
I Think I See Him There.
My Lord, What a Morning.
No Images.
O. T.'s Blues.
The Radical.
Threnody.
A Triviality.
Troubled Jesus.
True Love.
Wake Cry.
Cunningham
Calvary's Cry.
Cunningham, Allan
Gone Were but the Winter Cold.
Hame, Hame, Hame.
John Grumlie.
Loyalty.
The Mariner.
A Sea Song.
The Spring of the Year.
The Sun Rises Bright in France.
A Wet Sheet.
Cunningham, J. V.
The Aged Lover Discourses in the Flat Style.
Agnosco Veteris Vestigia Flammae.
All in Due Time.
And What Is Love? Misunderstanding, Pain.
Ars Amoris.
The Chase.
Choice.
Coffee.
Dark Thoughts Are My Companions.
Dear Child Whom I Begot.
Doctor Drink.
Elegy for a Cricket.
Envoi.
Epigram: "Dear, my familiar hand in love's own gesture."
Epigram: "Good Fortune, when I hailed her recently."
Epigram: "The man who goes for Christian resignation."
Epigram: "This is my curse, Pompous, I pray."
Epigram: "You ask me how Contempt who claims to sleep."
Five Epigrams.
For a College Yearbook.
For My Contemporaries.
Friend, on This Scaffold Thomas More Lies Dead.
The Helmsman: An Ode.
Here Lies My Wife.

History of Ideas.
Horoscope.
I Had Gone Broke.
I Married in My Youth a
  Wife.
In Innocence.
In the Thirtieth.
Interview with Doctor Drink.
It Was in Vegas.
The Judge is Fury: Epigraph.
Lady, of Anonymous Flesh
  and Face.
Lector Aere Perennior.
Life Flows to Death as Rivers
  to the Sea.
Meditation on a Memoir.
Meditation on Statistical
  Method.
The Metaphysical Amorist.
Miramar Beach.
Modern Love.
Montana Fifty Years Ago.
Montana Pastoral.
A Moral Poem.
Motto for a Sun Dial.
Nescit Vox Missa Reverti.
A Periphrastic Insult, Not a
  Banal.
The Phoenix.
The Pick-Up.
Some Twenty Years of
  Marital Agreement.
Sonnet on a Still Night.
This Humanist Whom No
  Beliefs Constrained.
Three Epigrams.
To a Friend, on Her
  Examination for the
  Doctorate in English.
To the Reader.
To What Strangers, What
  Welcome.
To Whom It May Concern.
Trivial, Vulgar, and Exalted:
  19.
Uncollected Poems and
  Epigrams, 2.
Vegas.
Cunningham, James (Olumo)
The City Rises.
The Covenant.
A Footnote to a Gray Bird's
  Pause.
For Cal.
From a Brother Dreaming in
  the Rye.
From the Narrator's Trance.
Happy Day.
High-Cool/2.
Incidental Pieces to a Walk:
  for Conrad.
Lee-ers of Hew...
Leg-acy of a Blue Capricorn.
A Plea to My Sister Carolyn
  Cunningham: the Artist.
Rapping along with Ronda
  Davis.
Slow Riff for Billy.
Solitary Visions of a
  Kaufmanoid...
St. Julien's Eve: For Dennis
  Cross.
A Street in Kaufman-Ville: or
  a Note Thrown to Carolyn...
Tambourine.
A Welcome for Etheridge.
While Cecil Snores: Mom
  Drinks Cold Milk.
Cunningham, Jim
A Portrait of Rudy.
Cunningham, John
Day: A Pastoral.

An Epigram: "A member of
  the modern great."
Kate of Aberdeen.
A Landscape.
The Miller.
Morning.
On a Certain Alderman.
Sent to Miss Bell H--, with a
  Pair of Buckles.
The Virtuous Fox and the
  Self-Righteous Cat.
Cunningham, Julia
Hymn to Joy.
Curnow, Allen
At Dead Low Water.
Attitudes of a New Zealand
  Poet.
A Balanced Bait in Handy
  Pellet Form.
Bring Your Own Victim.
Country School.
Crash at Leithfield.
Elegy on My Father.
An Excellent Memory.
House and Land.
An Incorrigible Music.
Landfall in Unknown Seas.
Magellan.
Not in Narrow Seas.
Out of Sleep.
A Reliable Service.
Stratagem.
This Beach Can Be
  Dangerous.
Time.
Trees, Effigies, Moving
  Objects.
The Unhistoric Story.
Wild Iron.
You Will Know When You
  Get There.
Curran, Edwin
Autumn.
The Clod.
First Frost.
The Painted Hills of Arizona.
Curran, John Philpot
Cushla Ma Chree.
The Deserter's Lamentation.
Curran, Mary Doyle
No Fear.
Currey, Ralph Nixon
Children Waking: Indian Hill
  Station.
Cock-Crow.
Halo.
In Memoriam Roy Campbell.
Jersey Cattle.
Landscape of Violence.
Marrakech.
Remembering Snow.
Song: "There is no joy in
  water apart from the sun."
Ultimate Exile IV.
Unseen Fire.
Volubilis, North Africa.
Currie, Robert
Brothers.
Forget about It.
The Home Place.
July the First.
The Musician at His Work.
Rope and Drum.
What He Saw.
Currier, John
Electricity Is Funny!
Curtis, Christine Turner
Villa Sciarra: Rome.
Curtis, George William
Ebb and Flow.
Egyptian Serenade.

Curtis, Simon
Satie, at the End of Term.
Curtis, Thelma
God's Will Is Best.
Curtis, Tony
To My Father.
Curtright, Wesley
The Close of Day.
Four-Leaf Clover.
Heart of the Woods.
Curzon, Colin
Not Tonight, Josephine.
**Curzon, George Nathanial,
Marquis**
On an Insignificant Fellow.
Cuscaden, R. R.
In Detroit.
Cushing, William O.
We Are Watching, We Are
  Waiting.
Cushman, Charlotte
God's Work.
Cushman, Ralph Spaulding
The Secret.
Sheer Joy.
Cust, Henry
Non Nobis.
Custance, Olive
The Parting Hour.
Twilight.
Cuthbertson, D. C.
A Picture.
Cuthbertson, James L.
A Racing Eight.
Cutler, Bruce
Results of a Scientific Survey.
Cutler, Elbridge Jefferson
The Volunteer.
Cutler, Julian S.
Through the Year.
Cutting, Edith E.
Against Gravity.
Cutting, Sewall Sylvester
God of the World, Thy
  Glories Shine.
Gracious Saviour, We Adore
  Thee.
Cutts, John, Lord
The Innocent Gazer.
Song: "Only tell her that I
  love."
Cybulski, Walter
Museum with Chinese
  Landscapes.
Cynewulf
Christ.
Christ 2.
Death of Saint Guthlac.
The Dream of the Rood.
Elene.
Fates of the Apostles.
Helena Embarks for Palestine.
Juliana.
Czamanske, W. M.
The Higher Calling.

D

"D., D."
Limerick: "A Boston boy
  went out to Yuma."
"d, e"
A Word Made Flesh Is
  Seldom.
"D., H." *See* Doolittle, Hilde
Da, Sousa, Noemia
Appeal.

Dabney, Betty Page
Earth's Bondman.
Dabydeen, Cyril
Folklore.
Lives.
Posterity.
Rehearsal.
Rhapsodies.
Dacey, Philip
The Amputee Soldier.
The Animals' Christmas.
Another Stone Poem.
The Birthday.
The Black Death.
Edward Weston in Mexico
  City.
Form Rejection Letter.
How I Escaped from the
  Labyrinth.
Jack, Afterwards.
Jill, Afterwards.
The Obscene Caller.
One of the Boys.
The Poem as Striptease.
Prisms (Altea).
The Ring Poem: A Husband
  Loses His Wedding Band...
Rondel.
Small Dark Song.
Thumb.
The Way It Happens.
Dacre, Harry
Daisy Bell (A Bicycle Built
  for Two).
Da Cruz, Viriato
Black Mother.
Dadie, Bernard
Dry Your Tears, Africa!
I Give You Thanks My God.
Dadu
Bani.
Dafydd ap Gwilym
A Reproach to Morvyth.
Da Gama, Luis
Who I Am.
Dahl, Roald
Little Red Riding Hood and
  the Wolf.
Snow White and the Seven
  Dwarfs.
Dahlberg, Edward
Kansas City West Bottoms.
Daiches, David
Notes for a History of Poetry.
To Kate, Skating Better Than
  Her Date.
Ulysses' Library.
Winter Song.
Daigaku, Horiguchi
The Muddy Rat.
Daigon, Ruth
Like an Ideal Tenant.
Night Flight.
Daihaku, Princess
How Will You Manage.
Daiken, Leslie
Bohernabreena.
June Song of a Man Who
  Looks Two Ways.
Larch Hill.
Lines to My Father.
Lines Written in a Country
  Parson's Orchard.
Nostalgie d'Automne.
Spring, St. Stephen's Green.
Dailey, Joel
Everyone in the World.
Good Night.
Joie de Vivre.
Known.
Meanwhile.
Revving Up La Reve.

Dakin, Laurence
Pyramus and Thisbe.
Dalcour, Pierre
Verse Written in the Album
of Mademoiselle--.
Dale, Edward Everett
The Prairie Schooner.
Dale, Peter
The Fragments.
The Rite.
Daley, Edith
Praise.
Daley, Victor J.
The Ascetic.
The Dove.
Dreams.
Faith.
In a Wine Cellar.
Lachesis.
Mother Doorstep.
Narcissus and Some Tadpoles.
Night.
Tall Hat.
Tamerlane.
When London Calls.
The Woman at the Washtub.
Dali, Salvador
The Art of Picasso.
Dallas, Mary Kyle
He'd Nothing But His Violin.
Dallas, Ruth
Farmyard.
Grandmother and Child.
Milking Before Dawn.
Roads.
World's Centre.
Dallas, Sir George
The India Guide....
Dallman, Elaine
From the Dust.
Dalmon, Charles
Ballad of the Epiphany.
Early Morning Meadow Song.
A Legend of Cherries.
O What if the Fowler.
Dalton, Annie Charlotte
For an Eskimo.
The Neighing North.
The Robin's Egg.
The Sounding Portage.
To the Young Man Jesus.
Dalton, John
A Descriptive Poem,
Addressed to Two Ladies....
"Dalton, Power" (Harold Caleb
Dalton)
Finite.
Flail.
Dalven, Rae
My Father.
Daly, Eugene Howell
Alpheus and Arethusa.
Daly, James
The Eagle.
Daly, James J.
In Coventry.
The Latin Tongue.
Nox Ignatiana.
Daly, John
A Toast to the Flag.
Daly, Thomas Augustin
A Child's Christmas Song.
Da Leetla Boy.
Leetla Giorgio Washeenton.
The Man's Prayer.
Mia Carlotta.
The Peaceable Race.
Pennsylvania Places.
The Sanctum.
The Tides of Love.
To a Thrush.

Dalziel, Kathleen
He Could Have Found His
Way.
Damagetus
The Spartan Wrestler.
Damas, Leon
Put Down.
They Came This Evening.
D'Ambrosio, Vinnie-Marie
The Grace of Cynthia's
Maidenhood.
Moon as Medusa.
On the Fifth Anniversary of
Bluma Sach's Death.
Da Modena, Leone
Epitaph.
Damon, S. Foster
Bridge.
Dana, Mary Stanley Bunce
O Sing to Me of Heaven.
Dana, Richard Henry
The Buccaneer: The Island.
The Chanting Cherubs - A
Group by Greenough.
Immortality.
The Little Beach-Bird.
The Moss Supplicateth for the
Poet.
Dana, Robert Patrick
Horses.
Mineral Point.
Notes on a Child's Coloring
Book.
The Way We Live Now.
A Winter's Tale.
Dance, James
Cricket. An Heroic Poem.
Dancer, John
The Variety.
Dandridge, Danske
The Dead Moon.
On the Eve of War.
The Spirit of the Fall.
Dandridge, Ray Garfield
De Drum Majah.
'Ittle Touzle Head.
Sprin' Fevah.
Time To Die.
Zalka Peetruza.
Dane, Barbara
Bring 'Em Home.
**Dane, Barbara and Jack
Warshaw**
The Kent State Massacre.
Danforth, John
A Few Lines to Fill up a
Vacant Page.
The Mercies of the Year,
Commemorated.
On My Lord Bacon.
Pindarick Elegy upon the
Renowned Mr. Samuel
Willard.
A Poem upon the Triumphant
Translation of a Mother in
Our Israel.
Profit and Loss: An Elegy
upon the Decease of Mrs.
Mary Gerrish...
Two Vast Enjoyments
Commemorated.
Danforth, Samuel
Almanac Verse.
Awake Yee Westerne
Nymphs, Arise and Sing.
Danforth II, Samuel
Ad Librum.
An Elegy in Memory of the
Worshipful Major Thomas
Leonard Esq....
Dangel, Leo
Pa.

Plowing at Full Moon.
Dangerfield, George
To Ultima Thule.
Daniel, Arnaut
L'Aura Amara.
Autet e Bas.
Bel M'es Quan Lo Vens
M'Alena.
Mot Eran Dous Miei Cossir.
Daniel, George
Anti-Platonicke.
Ode: "Poor bird, I do no envy
thee."
One Desiring Me to Read, but
Slept It out, Wakening.
Pure Platonicke.
The Robin.
Daniel, H. J.
My Epitaph.
Daniel, John
If I Could Shut the Gate
against My Thoughts.
Daniel, Marky
Crabbing.
Daniel, Robert T.
The Time Will Surely Come.
Daniel, Samuel
The Appeal.
Are They Shadows That We
See?
Care-Charmer, Sleep.
Chorus.
The Civil Wars between the
Two Houses of Lancaster
and York.
Cleopatra: Chorus.
The Complaint of Rosamond.
Constancy.
A Description of Beauty,
Translated out of Marino.
Early Love.
English Poetry.
Enjoy Thy April Now.
Epistle to Henry Wriothesley,
Earl of Southhampton.
Had Sorrow Ever Fitter Place.
The High Mind.
I Once May See when Yeares
Shall Wreck My Wrong.
If So It Hap, This Of-Spring
of My Care.
Let Others Sing of Knights
and Palladines.
Lonely Beauty.
Love Is a Sickness.
Musophilus.
None Other Fame Mine
Unambitious Muse.
O Fearfull, Frowning
Nemesis.
Ode: "Now each creature joys
the other."
A Pastoral of Tasso.
Philotas: Chorus.
Poet and Critic.
Rosamond's Appeal.
Secrecy.
Sonnet: "But love whilst that
thou may'st be loved again."
Sonnet: "Look, Delia, how we
esteem the half-blown rose."
Sorrow.
These Plaintive Verse, the
Postes of My Desire.
To Delia.
To Sir Thomas Egerton.
To the Lady Lucy, Countess
of Bedford.
To the Lady Margaret,
Countess of Cumberland.
To the Reader.

To the Right Worthy Knight
Sir Fulke Greville.
Ulysses and the Siren.
When Men Shall Find.
Daniel. Peter, Ernst. Karl
Freedom.
Daniells, Roy
Buffalo.
Deeper into the Forest.
Farewell to Winnipeg.
Noah.
So They Went Deeper in the
Forest.
Summer Days.
Daniels, Jim
Going Up and Down.
Danks, Hart Pease and Eben E.
Silver Threads among the
Gold.
Danner, Margaret
And Through the Caribbean
Sea.
At Home in Dakar.
Best Loved of Africa.
The Convert.
Dance of the Abakweta.
The Elevator Man Adheres to
Form.
Far from Africa.
Garnishing the Aviary.
Goodbye David Tamunoemi
West.
A Grandson Is a Hoticeberg.
I'll Walk the Tightrope.
The Painted Lady.
The Rhetoric of Langston
Hughes.
Sadie's Playhouse.
The Slave and the Iron Lace.
This Is an African Worm.
D'Annunzio, Gabriele
Morgana.
Danquah, Joseph V. B.
The Way of Life.
Dante Alighieri
Ballata: He Will Gaze upon
Beatrice.
Beatrice Has Gone up into
High Heaven.
Canzone: He Beseeches Death
for the Life of Beatrice.
Canzone: To the Lady Pietra,
of Sienna.
The Celestial Pilot.
Dante's Angels.
Death, Always Cruel.
Divina Commedia.
Even as the Others Mock.
The First Canzone of the
Convito.
Ladies That Have Intelligence
in Love.
Mine Eyes Beheld the Blessed
Pity.
Pier delle Vigne.
Sestina: Of the Lady Pietra
degli Scrovigni.
Sonnet: Of Beatrice de'
Portinari, on All Saints' Day.
Sonnet: Of Beauty and Duty.
Sonnet: On the 9th of June
1290.
Sonnet: To Brunetto Latini.
Sonnet: To Certain Ladies.
Sonnet: To Guido Cavalcanti.
Sonnet: To the Same Ladies;
with Their Answer.
The Vision.
La Vita Nuova.
Danyel, John
Can Doleful Notes to Mesur'd
Accents Set.

Da Ponte, Lorenzo
Giovinette, Che Fate
All'Amore.
To an Artful Theatre
Manager.
Daqiqi
On His Love.
Wine.
D'Arcy, Hugh Antoine
The Face Upon the Floor.
D'Arcy, Jack
The Conservative Shepherd to
His Love.
Darcy, M. M.
Astronaut's Choice.
Dargan, Olive
Duo.
The New Freedom.
Path Flower.
To William Blake.
Dargan, Olive Tilford
Rescue.
Dargan, Vere
City Trees.
Dario, Ruben
Afternoon in the Tropics.
Alleluya.
The Murmur from the Stable.
Nocturne II.
Portico.
Symphony in Gray Major.
The Three Kings.
To Columbus.
Darion, Joe
The Impossible Dream.
Darley, George
The Call of the Morning.
Chorus of Spirits.
Consolation.
Dirge: "Wail! wail ye o'er the
dead!"
The Dove's Loneliness.
The Enchanted Spring.
Errors of Ecstasie.
Ethelstan: O'er the Wild
Gannet's Bath.
The Fallen Star.
Hundred-Gated Thebes.
Hurry Me Nymphs.
It Is Not Beauty I Demand.
Last Night.
Lay of the Forlorn.
Lilian's Song.
Love's Likeness.
The Loveliness of Love.
The Lyre.
Nepenthe.
O Blest Unfabled Incense
Tree.
On the Death of a Recluse.
The Phoenix.
Robin's Cross.
The Sea-Ritual.
Serenade.
Serenade of a Loyal Martyr.
Siren Chorus.
The Solitary Lyre.
Song: "Down the dimpled
green-sward dancing."
Song: "I've taught thee Love's
sweet lesson o'er."
Song: "Sweet in her green dell
the flower of beauty
slumbers."
Song: "The streams that wind
among the hills."
Speckle-Black Toad and
Freckle-Green Frog.
To the Moon.
Wherefore, Unlaurelled Boy.
Winds of the West, Arise!

Darnley, Henry Stewart, Lord
Gife Langour–.
To the Queen.
Darr, Ann
About Motion Pictures.
For Great Grandmother and
Her Settlement House.
Love Is.
Oblique Birth Poem.
The Pot-Bellied Anachronism.
Riding with the Fireworks.
Whatever It Was I Was
Saving for My Old Age.
Darring, Walter
Surprised by Me.
Darwin, Erasmus
The Action of Electricity.
The Action of Invisible Ink.
The Botanic Garden.
Eliza.
Immortal Nature.
The Loves of the Plants.
The Protection of Plants.
Reproduction of Life.
The Temple of Nature.
Vegetable Loves.
Visit of Hope to Sydney Cove,
near Botany-Bay.
Daryush, Elizabeth
Armistice.
Autumn, Dark Wanderer.
Eyes That Queenly Sit.
Farewell for a While.
Fresh Spring.
Frustration.
How on Solemn Fields of
Space.
The Look.
November.
November Sun.
O Strong to Bless.
Still-Life.
Subalterns.
Throw away the Flowers.
Das, Kamala
The House-Builders.
An Introduction.
...With Its Quiet Tongue.
Da Sousa, Noemia
Poem of Distant Childhood.
Daswani, Tilottama
I, Pluto.
Daubeny, Charles
Verses on a Cat.
Dauenhauer, Nora
Breech Birth.
Genocide.
Jessy.
Kelp.
Pregnant Image of
"Exaggerating the Village."
Rookery.
Seal Pups.
Skiing on Russian Christmas.
Voices.
Winter Developing.
Daugherty, James
Texas.
Trail Breakers.
Daugherty, Michael
Buzzard.
Daumal, Rene
The Four Cardinal Times of
Day.
Daunt, John
Daybreak on a Pennsylvania
Highway.
Davenant, Sir William
The Christians Reply to the
Phylosopher.
The Cruel Brother: What Is
Past.

Endimion Porter and Olivia.
Epitaph.
For the Lady Olivia Porter; a
Present upon a New-years
Day.
Gondibert.
The Lark Now Leaves His
Wat'ry Nest.
The Mistress.
My Lodging It Is on the Cold
Ground.
O Thou That Sleep'st.
The Philosopher and the
Lover to a Mistress Dying.
Praise and Prayer.
Song: "Roses and pinks will
be strewn where you go."
The Souldier Going to the
Field.
Storm at Sea.
To the Queen, Entertain'd at
Night by the Countess of
Anglesey.
Under the Willow-Shades.
Wake All the Dead.
Davenport, Guy
The Medusa.
Davenport, Mariana B.
Suspended Moment.
The Widow.
Davenport, R. A.
A Serious Danger.
Davey, Frank
The Piano.
She'd Say.
David, John
What Happiness Can Equal
Mine.
Davidman, Joy
Prayer Against Indifference.
The Princess in the Ivory
Tower.
Davidson, Donald
John Darrow.
Lee in the Mountains.
On a Replica of the
Parthenon.
The Wolf.
Davidson, Gustav
Ambushed by Angels.
Nevertheless.
Somewhere I Chanced to
Read.
Davidson, John
A Ballad in Blank Verse of
the Making of a Poet.
A Ballad of a Nun.
A Ballad of Heaven.
A Ballad of Hell.
Butterflies.
Christmas Eve.
A Cinque Port.
Dedication to the Generation
Knocking at the Door.
Eclogue.
A Frosty Morning.
Holiday.
Imagination.
In Romney Marsh.
In the Isle of Dogs.
Last Journey.
London.
The Merchantman.
A Northern Suburb.
November: Epping Forest.
A Runnable Stag.
Song: "Closes and courts and
lanes."
Song of a Train.
Song: "The boat is chafing at
our long delay."
St. Michael's Mount.

Summer.
The Testament of a Man
Forbid.
The Testament of John
Davidson: The Last Journey.
Thirty Bob a Week.
The Twinkling Earn.
Two Dogs.
The Unknown.
Waiting.
War Song.
The Wasp.
**Davidson, Margaret Gilman
(George)**
Moritura.
Davidson, Peter
Artemis.
Finale: Presto.
Davidson, Thomas
And There Will I Be Buried.
Love's Last Suit.
Davie, Donald
At Knaresborough.
Autumn Imagined.
Barnsley and District.
A Christening.
Corrib. An Emblem.
The Evangelist.
For an Age of Plastics.
Plymouth.
For Doreen.
The Forests of Lithuania.
The Fountain.
G.M.B.
The Garden Party.
Gardens No Emblems.
Having No Ear.
Hearing Russian Spoken.
Heigh-Ho on a Winter
Afternoon.
Homage to William Cowper.
The Life of Service.
A Meeting of Cultures.
The Mushroom Gatherers.
New York in August.
On Bertrand Russell's
"Portraits from Memory".
Orpheus.
The Priory of St Saviour,
Glendalough.
Remembering the Thirties.
Thanks to Industrial Essex.
Time Passing, Beloved.
To a Teacher of French.
The Wind at Penistone.
A Winter Talent.
Woodpigeons at Raheny.
Davieau, Robert Stiles
Arizona Village.
Davies, Arthur
West Paddocks.
Davies, D. H.
The Muse.
Davies, Hugh Sykes
Music in an Empty House.
Poem: "In the stump of the
old tree."
Poem: "It doesn't look like a
finger..."
Davies, Idris
Gwalia Deserta.
High Summer on the
Mountains.
The Lay Preacher Ponders.
Davies, J. R. S.
Cranes.
Davies, Jeffrey
The Washing Machine.
Davies, John, of Hereford
Against Gaudy-Bragging-
Undoughty Daccus.
Against Proud Poor Phryna.

The Author Loving These
  Homely Meats...
Of Astraea.
Of Kate's Baldness.
A Remembrance of My
  Friend Mr. Thomas Morley.
Sonnet: "It is as true as
  strange, else trial feigns."
Sonnet: "So shoots a star as
  doth my mistress glide."
Davies, Mary Carolyn
Be Deferent to Trees.
David.
The Day before April.
The Dead Make Rules.
The Door.
Door-Mats.
Easter.
Feet.
The Gown.
Hunger.
I'll Wear a Shamrock.
If I Had Known.
June.
Let Me Be a Giver.
Love.
A Man's Woman.
Men Are the Devil.
A New Year.
Out of the Earth.
A Prayer for a Marriage.
A Prayer for a Sleeping Child.
A Prayer for Every Day.
Rust.
Six in June.
The Terrible Dead.
To Give One's Life.
Traps.
Tree Birthdays.
A Vow for New Year's.
Davies, Russell
Book Review.
Dear Father Christmas
  (parody).
Davies, Samuel
Eternal Spirit, Source of
  Light.
Lord, I Am Thine.
While O'er Our Guilty Land,
  O Lord.
Davies, Sir John
An Acclamation.
Affliction.
Contention between Four
  Maids...
A Contention betwixt a Wife,
  a Widow, and a Maid.
The Dance of Love.
A Gulling Sonnet.
The Immortality of the Soul.
In Francum.
In Fuscum.
In Librum.
In Rainy-Gloomy Weather.
Kate Being Pleased.
Knowledge and Reason.
Man.
The Mariner's Song.
The Muse Reviving.
Nosce Teipsum: An
  Acclamation.
On a Pair of Garters.
On the Deputy of Ireland's
  Child.
Orchestra.
The Sea Danceth.
Sonnets to Philomel.
The Soul and the Body.
To His Lady.
To His Very Friend, Master
  Richard Martin.

To My Most Gracious Dread
  Sovereign.
To Queen Elizabeth.
To the Nightingale.
To the Prince.
To the Right Noble,
  Valourous, and Learned
  Prince Henry...
To the Rose.
To the Spring.
Who Doth Not See the
  Measure of the Moon?
Davies, Sneyd
A Scene.
A Voyage to Tintern Abbey.
Davies, William Henry
All in June.
Ambition.
The Battle.
The Beautiful.
The Best Friend.
The Bird of Paradise.
Body and Spirit.
Cant.
The Cat.
The Chase.
The Child and the Mariner.
A Child's Pet.
Christ, the Man.
Come, Let Us Find.
Days That Have Been.
Days Too Short.
The Dog.
Dreams of the Sea.
The Dumb World.
Early Morn.
The Elements.
An Epitaph.
The Example.
Eyes.
Facts.
Fancy's Home.
The Flirt.
Flying Blossoms.
The Fog.
Frost.
The Ghost.
A Great Time.
A Greeting.
The Happy Child.
The Heap of Rags.
Her Merriment.
The Hermit.
The Hospital Waiting-Room.
The Hour of Magic.
I Am the Poet Davies,
  William.
In May.
The Inquest.
D Is for Dog.
Jenny Wren.
Joy and Pleasure.
The Kingfisher.
Lamorna Cove.
The Last Years.
Leaves.
Leisure.
Love's Caution.
Loyalty.
A Maiden and Her Hair.
Mangers.
The Mind's Liberty.
Money.
The Moon.
My Garden.
Oh, Sweet Content.
On Hearing Mrs. Woodhouse
  Play the Harpsichord.
One Poet Visits Another.
One Token.
The Poet.
The Pond.

Poor Kings.
The Power of Silence.
The Rabbit.
The Rain.
The Rainbow.
The Rat.
Rich Days.
Robin Redbreast.
The Sailor to His Parrot.
School's Out.
The Sea.
Sheep.
The Sleepers.
The Sluggard.
Songs of Joy.
Speed.
Sweet Stay-at-Home.
A Thought.
Thunderstorms.
To a Butterfly.
To a Lady Friend.
To the Wind at Morn.
The Trick.
Truly Great.
The Truth.
The Two Stars.
The Villain.
The Visitor.
When Diamonds, Nibbling in
  my Ears.
When Yon Full Moon.
The White Horse.
The White Monster.
Wild Oats.
The Wind.
Davis, Abijah
Blest Is the Man Whose
  Tender Breast.
Davis, Blind Gary
Blow Gabriel.
You Got to Go Down.
Davis, Catherine
After a Time.
Insights.
Kindness.
Nausea.
Davis, Daniel Webster
Hog Meat.
'Weh Down Souf.
Davis, Emily
A Song of Winter.
Davis, F. W.
Thankful Heart.
Davis, Fannie Stearns
The Forbidden Lure.
The Moods.
Davis, Florence Boyce
The Three Wise Monkeys.
Davis, Francis
Nanny.
Davis, Frank Marshall
Arthur Ridgewood, M.D.
Dancing Gal.
Flowers of Darkness.
Four Glimpses of Night.
Giles Johnson, Ph.D.
I Sing No New Songs.
Midsummer Morn.
Onward Christian Soldiers!
Rain.
Robert Whitmore.
Snapshots of the Cotton
  South.
Tenement Room: Chicago.
To Those Who Sing America.
Davis, Gloria
To Egypt.
Davis, Glover
The Burial.
Lost Moments.
Davis, Gussie L.
In the Baggage Coach Ahead.

Davis, H.L.
Proud Riders.
To the River Beach: Stalks of
  Wild Hay.
Davis, Helen Bayley
Jack Frost.
Song for a Child.
Davis, J.
The Sun.
Davis, Jack
Day Flight.
Davis, Julia Johnson
Loss.
She Sews Fine Linen.
To My Little Son.
Davis, Katherine
Act II.
Davis, Leasa
The Old Woman Sits.
Davis, Leland
The Ballad of Adam's First.
Davis, Lloyd
Armstrong Spring Creek.
Bad Day on the Boulder.
Last Day of the Trip.
Panic.
Davis, Mary Evelyn Moore
The Battle-Flag.
Counsel.
Davis, Norma L.
Daydreamers.
Davis, Ossie
To a Brown Girl.
Davis, Ozora S.
At Length There Dawns the
  Glorious Day.
We Bear the Strain of Earthly
  Care.
Davis, Pamela Oberon
Why Write Poetry?
Davis, Paul
Afternoon at Cannes.
Davis, Robert A.
Dust Bowl.
Pastorale.
Davis, Ronda
Invitation (To the Night and
  All Other Things Dark).
Parasitosis.
A Personality Sketch: Bill.
Poems about Playmates.
Spacin.
Davis, Thadious M.
Asante Sana, Te Te.
Double Take at Relais de
  l'Espadon.
Honeysuckle Was the Saddest
  Odor of All, I Think.
It's All the Same.
Remembering Fannie Lou
  Hamer.
Davis, Thomas Osborne
The Battle Eve of the Brigade.
Clare's Dragoons.
The Fate of King Dathi.
Fontenoy.
The Geraldines.
The Girl I Left behind Me.
The Irish Hurrah.
Lament for the Death of
  Eoghan Ruadh O'Neill.
My Grave.
My Land.
A Nation Once Again.
O, the Marriage!
Oh! for a Steed.
The Sack of Baltimore.
Tone's Grave.
A Welcome.
The West's Asleep.

Davis, Walter
　I Can Tell by the Way You
　　Smell.
Davis, William Virgil
　The Chandelier as
　　Protagonist.
　To My Son, Not Yet Born.
Davison, Edward
　The Enchanted Heart.
　In This Dark House.
　Nocturne.
　The Novice.
　The Owl.
　Sonnet: "She is so young, and
　　never never before."
Davison, Francis
　Ah Cupid, I mistook thee.
　Are Women Fair?
　Cupid's Pastime.
　Dispraise of Love, and Lovers'
　　Follies.
　His Farewell to His Unkind
　　and Unconstant Mistress.
　How Can the Heart Forget
　　Her.
　I Muse Not.
　In health and ease am I.
　Like to the seely fly.
　Madrigal: "Some there are as
　　fair to see to."
　Madrigal: "The sound of thy
　　sweet name, my dearest
　　treasure."
　My Only Star.
　Song: "Lady, you are with
　　beauties so enriched."
　Sorrow seldom killeth any.
　Three Epitaphs.
　To Cupid.
　Upon His Timorous Silence in
　　Her Presence.
Davison, Francis Douglas
　Bought.
Davison, Peter
　Bed Time.
　The Breaking of the Day.
　The Compound Eye.
　The Cost of Pretending.
　The Firstling.
　Housing Starts.
　The Last Word.
　Lunch at the Coq D'or.
　Magpie.
　The Money Cry.
　Motley.
　The Peeper.
　The Pleaders.
　The Poem in the Park.
　The Star Watcher.
Davison, Walter
　At Her Fair Hands.
　To His Lady, Who Had
　　Vowed Virginity.
Dawe, Bruce
　Abandonment of Autos.
　Americanized.
　At Shagger's Funeral.
　The City: Midnight.
　Drifters.
　Elegy for Drowned Children.
　Homecoming.
　The Not-So-Good Earth.
　Only the Beards Are
　　Different.
　Perpetuum Immobile.
　Suburban Lovers.
Dawe, Gerald
　Lives.
Dawes, Rufus
　Love Unchangeable.
Dawson, Gene
　When a Body.

Dawson, Grace Stricker
　To a Friend.
Dawson, William James
　Deliverance.
　The House of Pride.
　Inspirations.
Day, Beth
　Three Gates.
Day, Clarence
　The Egg.
　Historical Incidents.
　Man Is but a Castaway.
　Might and Right.
　The Parting Injunctions.
　Sad Story.
　Who Drags the Fiery Artist
　　Down?
Day, Dorothea
　My Captain.
Day, George Edward
　The Master of Laborers.
Day, John
　A Ditty.
　The Parliament of Bees.
Day, Lewis, Cecil
　The Double Vision.
　Is It Far to Go.
　My Love Is a Tower.
　The Neurotic.
　Pegasus.
　Statuette: Late Minoan.
　Transitional Poem.
　Two Travelers.
Day, Lucille
　Labor.
　Neural Folds.
　Reject Jell-O.
　Self-Portrait with Hand
　　Microscope.
　Tumor.
　Yom Kippur.
Day, Richard Edwin
　England.
　To Shakespeare.
Day, Thomas Fleming
　The Clipper.
　The Coasters.
　The Main-Sheet Song.
　Making Land.
Day, William
　Mount Vernon, the Home of
　　Washington.
Day-Lewis, Cecil
　The Album.
　Almost Human.
　As One Who Wanders Into
　　Old Workings.
　Birthday Poem for Thomas
　　Hardy.
　Bombers.
　But Two There Are...
　Chiefly to Mind Appears.
　Christmas Eve.
　The Chrysanthemum Show.
　Circus Lion.
　Can the Mole Take.
　Come Up, Methuselah.
　The Committee.
　The Conflict.
　Consider These, For We Have
　　Condemned Them.
　The Dead.
　Departure in the Dark.
　Desire Is a Witch.
　Do Not Expect Again a
　　Phoenix Hour.
　Emily Bronte.
　A Failure.
　Few Things Can More
　　Inflame.
　Flight to Italy.
　The Fox.

　From Feathers to Iron.
　The Great Magicians.
　A Happy View.
　A Hard Frost.
　In Heaven, I Suppose, Lie
　　down Together.
　In Me Two Worlds.
　In the Heart of
　　Contemplation.
　In the Shelter.
　It Is Becoming Now to
　　Declare My Allegiance.
　Jig.
　Let Us Now Praise Famous
　　Men.
　Love Was Once Light as Air.
　The Magnetic Mountain:
　　Condemned.
　Maple and Sumach.
　Marriage of Two.
　A Meeting.
　The Misfit-1939-1945.
　My Mother's Sister.
　The Nabara.
　Nearing Again the Legendary
　　Isle.
　Newsreel.
　Noah and the Waters: Chorus.
　Now I Have Come to Reason.
　Now She Is Like the White
　　Tree-Rose.
　O Dreams, O Destinations.
　Oh Light Was My Head.
　On Not Saying Everything.
　On the Sea Wall.
　One and One.
　Overtures to Death.
　The Poet.
　Reconciliation.
　Rest from Loving and Be
　　Living.
　The Room.
　Seen from the Train.
　Sheepdog Trials in Hyde Park.
　Son and Father.
　The Stand-To.
　The Sun Came Out in April.
　Tempt Me No More.
　Third Enemy Speaks.
　Though Bodies Are Apart.
　A Time to Dance: The Flight.
　The Tourists.
　Two Songs.
　The Unwanted.
　When They Have Lost.
　Where Are the War Poets?
　Winter Night.
　With Me My Lover Makes.
　Word over All.
　You That Love England.
Dayre, Sydney
　Grandma's Lost Balance.
　A Lesson for Mamma.
　Morning Compliments.
Dayton, David
　The Woman Driving the
　　Country Squire.
Dayton, Ebenezer
　Wherein Consists the High
　　Estate.
Dayton, Irene
　Ear Is Not Deaf.
De, Lima, Jorge
　The Bird.
Deacon, Ann
　Certified Copy.
　Man and Wife Is One Flesh.
　There Is No Balm in
　　Birmingham.
Deal, Susan Strayer
　These Trees Are.

Deamer, Dulcie
　Artemis.
Dean, Agnes Louise
　October Night.
Dean, Elma
　Old Men's Ward.
Dean, John
　Schedules.
　Seeing and Doing.
De Andrade, Mario
　Aspiration.
　Rondeau for You.
Deane, Anthony C.
　The Ballad of the Billycock.
　The Cult of the Celtic.
　Here Is the Tale.
　Mary, Mary (parody).
　An Ode: "I sing a song of
　　sixpence, and of rye."
　Rural Bliss.
　A Rustic Song.
Deane, Seamus
　Derry.
　Elegy: Three.
　Fording the River.
　Northern Ireland: Two
　　Comments.
　Osip Mandelstam.
　Return.
　Scholar I.
　Scholar II.
Dearmer, Geoffrey
　The Turkish Trench Dog.
　A Vision.
De Assis, Joaquim M.
　Blue Fly.
De Baca, Marc
　The Lizards of La Brea.
De Bary, Anna
　Under a Wiltshire Apple Tree.
De Bevoise, Arlene
　Good Friday.
　Two Gardens.
De Bolt, William Walter
　Back to the Angels.
　Thesis.
De Botton, Isaac
　Desire.
De Boully, Monny
　Beyond Memory.
de Brebeuf, Jean
　Let Christian Hearts Rejoice
　　Today.
De Brun, Padraig
　In Memoriam.
De Brunne, Robert
　Handling Synne.
DeBurgh, H. J.
　Half Hours with the Classics.
Dec, Frederick
　Bulldozers.
　Class of 19–.
De Carrion, Santob
　A Friend.
　A Jewish Poet Counsels a
　　King.
　Resignation.
　Self-Defense.
De Casseres, Benjamin
　Moth-Terror.
Deck, James G.
　The King in His Beauty.
Decker, Bessie B.
　Disillusion.
De Clue, Charlotte
　Diary. Black Bear's Moon.
　Diary. Moon of the Hiding
　　Doe.
　Diary. Solitary Moon.
　Diary. The Deer Break Their
　　Horns.
　Healing.

Ijajee's Story.
In Memory of the Moon. (A
    Killing.).
Morning Song.
Place-of-Many-Swans.
The Underside of Trees.
Dederick, Robert
Karoo Town.
Robben Island.
Deems, Charles F.
I Shall Not Want: In Deserts
    Wild.
Defoe, Daniel
The Diet of Poland, a Satire.
An Encomium upon a
    Parliament.
The English Race.
A Hymn to the Pillory.
More Reformation.
Reformation of Manners.
The Spanish Descent.
The True-Born Englishman.
The Vision.
Wherever God Erects a House
    of Prayer.
DeFoe, Mark
13 Ways of Eradicating
    Blackbirds (parody).
Euphoria, Euphoria.
On a Photo of a Baby Killed
    in the War.
DeFord, Miriam Allen
Ronsard.
Traveller's Ditty.
We Shall Say.
De Ford, Sara
The Sleeping Beauty.
De Forest, J. W.
The Phantom Ship.
The Sea-Maiden.
DeForest, John William
A National Hymn.
Defrees, Madeline
In the Hellgate Wind.
Letter to an Absent Son.
The Odd Woman.
Pendant Watch.
With a Bottle of Blue Nun to
    All My Friends.
De Gasztold, Carmen
The Prayer of the Donkey.
**Degeyter, Pierre and Eugene
    Potter**
The Internationale.
Degraph, Peter
Poor Ellen Smith.
deGravelles, Charles
The Astrologer Argues Your
    Death.
Night Out, Tom Cat.
De Haan, Jakov
All Is God's.
God's Gifts.
Hanukah.
Sabbath.
Unity.
De Hearn, Nellie
The Shut-In.
Dehmel, Richard
Before the Storm.
Harvest Song.
The Laborer.
My Drinking Song.
The Silent Town.
To—?
A Trysting.
Vigil.
Voice in Darkness.
Dehn, Paul
Alternative Endings to an
    Unwritten Ballad.
Armistice.

At the Dark Hour.
Come Unto These Yellow
    Sands (parody).
Fern House at Kew.
A Game of Consequences.
Government Official.
I Wandered Angry as a Cloud
    (parody).
Jeny Kiss'd Me When We
    Met.
Lament for a Sailor.
A Leaden Treasury of English
    Verse.
Nuclear Wind, When Wilt
    Thou Blow.
Reunion.
Rhymes for a Modern
    Nursery.
Ring-a-Ring o' Neutrons.
St. Aubin d'Aubigne.
Twinkle, Twinkle, Little Star
    (parody).
Whenas in Jeans.
Dei-Anang, Michael
Africa Speaks.
My Africa.
Deissler, Mary Louise
Man of Galilee.
Deitz, Purd E.
Builders.
DeJong, David Cornel
On the Twenty-Fifth of July.
De Kay, Charles
Arcan Sylvarum.
The Draft Riot.
The Tornado.
Ulf of Ireland.
Dekker, Thomas
Art Thou Poor, Yet Hast
    Thou Golden Slumbers?
Bridal Song.
Christ's Coming to Judgment.
Cold's the Wind.
Country Glee.
The Defeat of the Armada.
Drinking Song.
Fortune and Virtue.
Golden Slumbers.
Haymakers, Rakers.
The Honest Whore, I, 1604.
Old Fortunatus.
The Pleasant Comedie of Old
    Fortunatus.
Pleasant Comedie of Patient
    Grissill.
Saint Hugh.
The Shoemaker's Holiday.
Song: "O the month of May,
    the merry month of May."
Song: "Virtue's branches
    wither, virtue pines."
Troll the Bowl!
Troynovant.
Delafield, Harriet L.
No Escape.
De La Mare, Walter
Alas, Alack.
All but Blind.
All That's Past.
Alone.
Alulvan.
Ann and the Fairy Song.
Antiques.
Arabia.
Archery.
Arrogance.
As Soon as Ever Twilight
    Comes.
At Ease.
At Home, Alone with the Cat.
At the Keyhole.
At the Zoo.

Autumn.
Away.
Bah!
A Ballad of Christmas.
The Bandog.
The Barber's.
The Bards.
The Bead Mat.
Berries.
The Bindweed.
The Birthnight: To F.
Bishop Winterbourne.
Bones.
The Bookworm.
The Bottle.
Breughel's Winter.
The Buckle.
Bunches of Grapes.
Buttons.
The Chart.
Chicken.
The Children of Stare.
The Christening.
Clear Eyes.
The Comb.
The Corner.
The Corner Stone.
Corporal Pym.
Crazed.
Crumbs.
The Cupboard.
The Dark Chateau.
Dream-Song.
Drugged.
The Dunce.
Dust to Dust.
Echo.
The Eel.
The Empty House.
An Epitaph.
Eyes.
Faint Music.
False Dawn.
False Gods.
Fare Well.
The Feckless Dinner Party.
A Fiddler.
Five Eyes.
The Fly.
Full Moon.
The Funeral.
The Galliass.
The Ghost.
Go Far, Come Near.
Gone.
Goodbye.
Green.
A Hare.
The Hawthorn Hath a
    Deathly Smell.
The Holly.
Horse in a Field.
The Horseman.
The Hunt.
The Huntsmen.
Hyssop.
I Met at Eve.
Immanent.
In Memory of G. K.
    Chesterton.
In the Dock.
In the Dying of Daylight.
In the Local Museum.
Iron.
It Might Be a Lump of
    Amber.
J. J.
Jim Jay.
John Mouldy.
The Keys of Morning.
Kiph.

The Last Chapter.
The Last Coachload.
Limerick: "There was a young
    lady of Rheims."
Limerick: "There was an old
    man said, 'I fear.'"
The Linnet.
The Listeners.
The Little Bird.
The Little Creature.
The Little Green Orchard.
The Lost Shoe.
Lovelocks.
Lucy.
Maerchen.
Many a Mickle.
March Hares.
The Marionettes.
Martha.
Me.
The Mermaids.
Mima.
The Miracle.
Miss Loo.
Miss Pheasant.
Miss T.
Mistletoe.
The Mocking Fairy.
Moonlight.
The Moth.
Motley.
The Mountains.
Napoleon.
Ned Vaughan.
Never More, Sailor.
Nicholas Nye.
Nod.
Nostalgia.
Nothing.
Off the Ground.
The Old Angler.
The Old Men.
Old Shellover.
The Old Summerhouse.
Old Susan.
The Owl.
Peace.
Polonius.
Ponjoo.
Pooh!
Poor Henry.
A Portrait.
Quack!
The Quartette.
A Queen Wasp.
The Quiet Enemy.
The Railway Junction.
The Rainbow.
Rats.
Reserved.
The Revenant.
The Ride-by-Nights.
A Robin.
Sam.
Santa Claus.
The Scarecrow.
Scholars.
The Scribe.
Seeds.
The Shadow.
She Said.
The Ship of Rio.
Silver.
The Silver Penny.
The Sleeper.
Sleeping Beauty.
Sleepyhead.
Slim Cunning Hands.
Snow.
The Snowflake.
Softly, Drowsily.
Solitude.

Someone.
Somewhere.
A Song of Enchantment.
The Song of Finis.
The Song of Shadows.
The Song of the Mad Prince.
The Song of the Shadows.
The Spotted Flycatcher.
Still Life.
The Stranger.
Summer Evening.
Sunk Lyonesse.
The Sunken Garden.
Supper.
Susannah Prout.
Tartary.
Tat for Tit.
Theologians.
There Blooms No Bud in May.
Things.
Thomas Hardy.
Thomas Logge.
The Three Cherry Trees.
Three Sisters.
Thunder.
Tillie.
Tired Tim.
Titmouse.
To a Candle.
To K.M.
Tom's Angel.
Tom's Little Dog.
The Tomtit.
Trees.
The Truants.
The Vacant Farm House.
Vain Finding.
Vain Questioning.
Virtue.
The Voice.
Voices.
The Waif.
Where.
Why?
A Widow's Weeds.
Winter.
Winter Dusk.
The Wreck.
De La Monnoye, Bernard
Patapan.
Deland, Margaret
Affaire d'Amour.
The Christmas Silence.
The Clover.
Doubt.
The Fairies' Shopping.
Life.
Love and Death.
Love's Wisdom.
Sent with a Rose to a Young Lady.
While Shepherds Watched.
Delaney, John
Golf Ball.
Delano, Alanzo
The Miner's Progress.
Delany, Clarissa Scott
Interim.
Joy.
The Mask.
Solace.
De la Selva, Salomon See **Selva, Salomon de la**
del Castillo, Sister Francisca Josefa
Christmas Carol.
The Holy Eclogue.
De Leeuw, Adele
Auction Sale–Household Furnishings.

De Lemos, Gouveia
Song of Agony.
De Leon, Nephtali
In the Plaza We Walk.
De Lima, Jorge
Papa John.
The Words Will Resurrect.
Delius, Anthony
Brief Farewell.
The Coming.
Deaf-and-Dumb School.
Distance.
Footnote.
The Gamblers.
Intuition.
Lady Anne Bathing.
Shadow.
The Thinker.
Del Medigo, Joseph Solomon
Epigram.
Del Monte, Crescenzo
One Thing to Take, Another to Keep.
A Roman Roman.
Those Zionists.
Deloney, Thomas
A Dialogue between the Lovelorn Sir Hugh and Certain Ladies....
A Joyful New Ballad.
Song: "The primrose in the green forest."
Would God That It Were Holiday!
De Long, Juanita
My Hereafter.
De Longchamps, Joanne
Blind, I Speak to the Cigarette.
Tortoise.
Del Renzio, Toni
Can You Change a Shilling?
Demarest, Mary Lee
My Ain Countree.
Demetriadis, Mary
When Lovely Woman Stoops to Folly (parody).
Demille, A. B.
The Ice King.
De Mille, James
The Gallant Highwayman.
Sweet Maiden of Passamaquoddy.
Deming, A. G.
Who Is Tapping at My Window.
Demodocus
The Snake It Was That Died.
Demon, Andrew
Reflections of a Trout Fisherman.
De Morgan, Augustus
On Fleas.
Dempster, Barry
After Peckinpah.
The Birth of My Father.
Hippies.
Links.
Mary Speaks to Jesus.
Mother.
Seasons.
Three Women.
Dempster, Roland Tombekai
Africa's Plea.
Is This Africa?
DenBoer, James
Charming the Moon.
Denby, Edwin
Aaron.
Air.
Ciampino.
City without Smoke.

The Climate.
Dishonor.
A Domestic Cat.
Forza D'Agro.
Northern Boulevard.
People on Sunday.
A Postcard.
Sant'Angelo D'Ischia.
The Shoulder.
The Silence at Night.
Standing on the Streetcorner.
Summer.
Trastevere.
de Nerval, Gerard See **Nerval, Gerard de**
Denham, Sir John
Against Love.
The Destruction of Troy: Aeneid II.
The Progress of Learning: Preface.
Deniehy, Daniel Henry
To His Wife.
Denman, Annie
For His Sake.
Dennen, Grace Atherton
Gold-of-Ophir Roses.
Denney, Reuel
Fixer of Midnight.
The Laboratory Midnight.
A March with All Drums Muffled.
Tennis in San Juan.
Dennis, C. J.
The growth of Sym.
The Martyred Democrat.
The Play.
The Traveller.
The Triantiwontigongolope.
Dennis, Carl
The Band.
The Chosen.
The Trip.
Dennis, Zelma S.
An Irish Wind.
Denny, Sir Edward
Hope of Our Hearts.
Dennys, John
The Secrets of Angling.
Dent, Tom
The Blue Light.
Come Visit My Garden.
Love.
Mississippi Mornings.
On Dreams and Mexican Songs.
Denwood, Jonathan
Bleeberrying.
Denza, Luigi
Funiculi, Funicula.
De Ponciano, Angelo
Empties Coming Back.
Der Hovanessian, Diana
Poultry.
De Regniers, Beatrice Schenk
Keep a Poem in Your Pocket.
Derian, Vahan
Words at Farewell.
Derleth, August
The Planetary Arc-Light.
Dermody, Thomas
A Decayed Monastery.
John Baynham's Epitaph.
An Ode to Myself.
The Petition of Tom Dermody to the Three Fates in Council Sitting.
The Shepherd's Despair.
De Roche, Joseph
Aunt Laura Moves Toward the Open Grave of Her Father.

Blond.
de Ronsard, Pierre
Pastoral Song for the Nuptials of Charles, Duke of Lorraine...
De Ronsard, Pierre See **Ronsard, Pierre de**
Derosier, Lola
The Last Day.
Derricke, John
The Image of Irelande (excerpt).
Derwood, Gene
After Reading St. John the Divine.
Bird, Bird.
Camel.
Elegy on Gordon Barber.
In Common.
In the Proscenium.
The Innocent.
Mailed to G. B.
N. B., Symmetrians.
Rides.
Shelter.
So, Man?
Spring Air.
Star.
Third Madrigal.
To George Barker.
War's Clown in the Proscenium.
With God Conversing.
Derzhavin
O, Thou Eternal One!
De Saint-Gelais, Mellin See **Saint-Gelais, Mellin de**
Desbordes-Valmore, Marceline
The Roses of Sa'adi.
Deschamps, Eustache
The Knightly Code.
Deshoulieres, A.
Reflections.
de Sille, Nicasius
God Set Us Here.
Desmond, Gerald, Earl of
Against Blame of Woman.
Desnos, Robert
The Day It Was Night.
Desnoues, Lucienne
First Things.
De Sousa, Noemia
If You Want to Know Me.
Magaica.
The Poem of Joao.
Desportes, Philippe
Conquest.
Desprez, Frank
Lasca.
Dessner, Lawrence Jay
Tennis Pro.
Dessus, Ronald James
The Difference between a Lie and the Truth.
Geronimo: Old Man Lives On.
Imagine a World of People.
Ta Wa Nee.
De Tabley, John Byrne Leicester Warren, Lord
Anticipation.
The Churchyard on the Sands.
Fortune's Wheel.
A Frosty Day.
The Knight in the Wood.
Lines to a Lady-Bird.
Medea: Chorus.
Nuptial Song.
The Ocean Wood.
Ode: "Sire of the rising day."
Philoctetes.
The Power of Interval.

A Song of Dust.
The Study of a Spider.
The Two Old Kings.
The Windmill.

de Tocqueville
America Is Great Because...

Detrick, Daisy L.
The Little Johnny Mine.
The Ol' Jinny Mine.

Dett, R. Nathaniel
The Rubinstein Staccato Etude.

Deutsch, Babette
The Aged Woman to Her Sons.
Apocrypha.
A Bull.
Capriccio.
The Dancers.
Dogma.
Earliness at the Cape.
Fireworks.
A Girl.
Homage to the Philosopher.
The Hound.
The Hunt.
In a Museum.
Late Reflections.
Memory.
Morning Workout.
Natural Law.
Need.
New Words for an Old Song.
New York * December * 1931.
No Moon, No Star.
Old Women.
Paradigm.
Piano Recital.
Pity.
The Poem.
Reflections in a Little Park.
Scene with Figure.
Small Colored Boy in the Subway.
Solitude.
Songs.
String Quartet.
Tak for Sidst.
They Came to the Wedding.
To the Moon, 1969.

Devaney, James
Mortality.
Song of the Captured Woman.
Vision.
Winter Westerlies.

Dever, Joseph
Queen of Horizons.

De Vere, Aubrey Thomas
Autumnal Ode.
A Ballad of Sarsfield.
Coleridge.
Dei Genitrix.
The Dirge of Kildare.
Dirge of Rory O'More.
The Divine Presence.
Epilogue.
Epitaph.
Evening Melody.
Festum Nativitatis.
Florence MacCarthy's Farewell to Her English Lover.
Flowers I Would Bring.
The Friendly Blight.
Glauce.
Human Life.
Implicit Faith.
In Ruin Reconciled.
Incompatibility.
Ione.
Lines.

Love's Spite.
May Carols.
Parvuli Ejus.
Religio Novissima.
Roisin Dubh.
The Sacraments of Nature.
Scene in a Madhouse.
The Sea-Watcher.
Serenade.
Song: "He found me sitting among flowers."
Song: "Seek not the tree of silkiest bark."
Song: "Sing the old song, amid the sounds dispersing."
Song: "Softly, O midnight Hours!"
Song: "The little Black Rose shall be red at last!"
Sorrow.
Spring Song.
The Sun God.
The Three Woes.
Troilus and Cressida.
Urania.
Waterloo.
Wedding of the Clans.
Winter.
A Year of Sorrow.

De Vere, Edward, Earl of Oxford
Epigram: "Were I a king, I could command content."
If Women Could Be Fair.
The Judgement of Desire.
Of the Birth and Bringing Up of Desire.
Pains and Gains.
White and Red.
Who Taught Thee First to Sigh?

De Vere, Mary Ainge
A Breath.
Faith Trembling.
A Farewell.
God Keep You.
Poet and Lark.
The Spinner.
When the Most Is Said.
The Wind-Swept.

De Vere, Sir Aubrey
Castleconnell.
The Children Band.
Hymn for the Feast of the Annunciation.
Kilmallock.
The Landrail.
Mater Amabilis.
Reality.
The Right Use of Prayer.
The Rock of Cashel.
Sorrow.

De Vere, William
Walk, Damn You, Walk!

De Vito, Ethel Barnett
Birthday Gift.

Devlin, Denis
Ank'hor Vat.
Anteroom: Geneva.
Ascension.
Ballad of Mistress Death.
The Colours of Love.
Daphne Stillorgan.
Encounter.
Eve in My Legend.
Farewell and Good.
From Government Buildings.
The Heavenly Foreigner.
Jansenist Journey.
The Lancet.
Little Elegy.
Lough Derg.

Memoirs of a Turcoman Diplomat.
The Passion of Christ.
Renewal by Her Element.
The Statue and the Perturbed Burghers.
The Tomb of Michael Collins.
Venus of the Salty Shell.
Welcome My World.
Wishes for Her.

Devries, Peter
Beth Appleyard's Verses.
Christmas Family Reunion.
Mirror.
Sacred and Profane Love, or, There's Nothing New under the Moon Either.
Theme and Variation.
To His Importunate Mistress.
To My Friends.

DeVries, Rachel
Jealousy.

Dewar, A. W.
Life and the Weaver.

Dewdney, Christopher
Coelacanth.
The Drawing out of Colour.
Grid Erectile.
The Lateshow Diorama.
A Natural History of Southwestern Ontario, III.
This My Emissary.
Winter Central.

Dewet, George Washington
Blind Louise.

Dewey, Berenice C.
Conversation.

DeWitt, Samuel A.
Two Sonnets for a Lost Love.

Dexter, R. P.
Shadow Dirge.

Dey, Richard Morris
Fog 9/76.

De Young, Lily A.
I Have a Place.

Dhingra, Baldoon
Day and Night.

Dia, Beatriz de
Estat ai en greu cossirier.

Diamond, David
We Will Not Fear.

Diaper, William
Brent: A Poem to Thomas Palmer, Esq.
Eclogue.
Oppian's Halieuticks (parody).
Sea Eclogue.

Dias, Antonio G.
Song of Exile.

Diaz Miron, Salvador
Nox.

Dibben, Dennis
Some Modern Good Turns.

Dibdin, Charles
The Anchorsmiths.
Blow High! Blow Low!
Captain Wattle and Miss Roe.
Jack's Fidelity.
The Jolly Young Waterman.
The Lady's Diary.
The Leadsman's Song.
Nongtongpaw.
Poor Jack.
A Popular Functionary.
The Sailor's Consolation.
Tom Bowling.

Dibdin, Thomas
A Child That Has a Cold We May Suppose.

Di Caprio, Isabelle
Jabber-Whacky.

Di Castagnola, Alice Fay
Mortal Combat.

Di Cicco, Pier Giorgio
America.
Beyond Labelling Me.
Errore.
The Explosion of Thimbles.
Flying Deeper into the Century.
The Friendship Game.
The Head Is a Paltry Matter.
Male Rage Poem.
The Poem Becomes Canadian.
Relationships.
Words to the Wind.

Dickens, Charles
The Cannibals' Grace Before Meat.
The Fine Old English Gentleman New Version.
The Ivy Green.
The Loving Ballad of Lord Bateman.

Dickenson, George-Therese
Transducing.

Dickenson, John
Tityrus to His Fair Phyllis.

Dickey, James
Adultery.
After the Night Hunt.
Armor.
At Darien Bridge.
The Bee.
The Beholders.
The Being.
Between Two Prisoners.
Birth.
The Birthday Dream.
Bread.
Breath.
Buckdancer's Choice.
Bums, on Waking.
By Canoe through the Fir Forest.
The Call.
The Cancer Match.
The Celebration.
Chenille.
Cherrylog Road.
Coming Back to America.
The Common Grave.
Deborah as Scion.
A Dog Sleeping on My Feet.
The Driver.
Drowning with Others.
The Dusk of Horses.
Encounter in the Cage Country.
Faces Seen Once.
Falling.
Fence Wire.
The Fiend.
The Firebombing.
The Flash.
For Every Last Batch When the Next One Comes Along.
For the Death of Vince Lombardi.
For the Last Wolverine.
For the Nightly Ascent of the Hunter Orion over a Forest Clearing.
For the Running of the New York City Marathon.
Gamecock.
Goodbye to Serpents.
The Heaven of Animals.
Hedge Life.
The Hospital Window.
Hunting Civil War Relics at Nimblewill Creek.
The Ice Skin.

In the Marble Quarry.
In the Mountain Tent.
In the Pocket.
In the Tree House at Night.
Inside the River.
The Island.
The Landfall.
The Leap.
The Lifeguard.
Listening to Foxhounds.
Looking for the Buckhead
  Boys.
Madness.
The Magus.
The Moon Ground.
The Movement of Fish.
On the Hill below the
  Lighthouse.
The Owl King.
The Performance.
The Poet's Farewell to His
  Teeth.
Pursuit from Under.
Reincarnation (I).
The Scratch.
The Shark's Parlor.
The Sheep Child.
Slave Quarters.
Sled Burial, Dream Ceremony.
Springer Mountain.
The Summons.
To Landrum Guy, Beginning
  to Write at Sixty.
Trees and Cattle.
The Underground Stream.
Venom.
Walking on Water.
Winter Trout.
The Zodiac, X.

Dickey, Martha
Studies from Life.

Dickey, R. P.
Early June.
Santo Domingo Corn Dance.
Takes All Kinds.

Dickey, William
The Anniversary.
Another Given: The Last Day
  of the Year.
Canonical Hours.
The Dolls Play at Hansel and
  Gretel.
Face-Paintings of the Caduveo
  Indians.
The Fish Upstairs.
Happiness.
Hope.
Horn, Mouth, Pit, Fire.
Love among the Manichees.
Resolving Doubts.
Spectrum.
Teaching Swift to Young
  Ladies.
Things Kept.
Tutankhamen.
Voyage to the Moon.
What It Means, Living in the
  City.

Dickinson, Blanche Taylor
Four Walls.
Poem.
Revelation.
That Hill.
To an Icicle.
The Walls of Jericho.

Dickinson, Charles Monroe
The Children.

Dickinson, Emily
Afraid? Of whom am I afraid?
After a Hundred Years.
After great pain, a formal
  feeling comes.

Ah, necromancy sweet!
Ah, Teneriffe!
Alter? When the Hills Do.
An altered look about the
  hills.
Although I put away his life.
Ample make this bed.
And This of All My Hopes.
Apparently with No Surprise.
Arcturus Is His Other Name.
As by the dead we love to sit.
As imperceptibly as grief.
At half-past three.
At last, to be identified!
At Least–To Pray–Is Left–Is
  Left.
The auctioneer of parting.
The bat is dun, with wrinkled
  wings.
Beauty–be not caused–it is.
Because I Could Not Stop for
  Death.
Because that you are going.
A bee his burnished carriage.
Bee! I'm Expecting You!
The Bee Is Not Afraid of Me.
Before I got my eye put out.
Behind me–dips eternity–.
Behold This Little Bane.
Belshazzar.
Bereaved of All, I Went
  Abroad.
Besides the autumn poets sing.
The Bible Is an Antique
  Volume.
A bird came down the walk.
Birthday of but a single pang.
Bloom is result.
The Bone That Has No
  Marrow.
The Brain–Is Wider than the
  Sky.
The Brain, Within It's
  Groove.
Bring me the sunset in a cup.
The Bustle in a House.
Called Back.
Choice.
A Clock Stopped.
Color–Caste–Denomination.
Come Slowly–Eden.
Constant.
Could Mortal Lip Divine.
The Cricket Sang.
Crumbling is not an instant's
  act.
Dare You See a Soul at the
  White Heat?
Dear March, come in!
Death is a dialogue.
Delayed till she had ceased to
  know.
Departed–to the Judgment.
Did our best moment last.
Did the Harebell.
The difference between
  despair.
Doubt me, my dim
  companion!
Drama's vitallest expression is
  the common day.
A drop fell on the apple tree.
Drowning is Not so Pitiful.
A drunkard cannot meet a
  cork.
Dying.
A Dying Tiger–Moaned for
  Drink.
Dying! To be afraid of thee.
Elysium is as far as to.
Essential Oils Are Wrung.
Essential Oils–are wrung–675.

Expanse Cannot Be Lost.
Exultation is the going.
A faded boy in sallow clothes.
Faith–is the Pierless Bridge.
Fame is a fickle food.
Farther in summer than the
  birds.
The Fascinating Chill That
  Music Leaves.
Finding Is the First Act.
The first day's night had
  come.
Floss won't save you.
Forbidden Fruit.
Four trees upon a solitary
  acre.
Frigid and sweet her parting
  face.
From all the jails the boys
  and girls.
The Frost Was Never Seen.
Further in Summer Than the
  Birds.
A fuzzy fellow, without feet.
The gentian weaves her
  fringes.
Glass was the street.
Go not too near a house of
  rose.
God Is a Distant–Stately
  Lover.
God is indeed a jealous God.
God Made a Little Gentian.
God's Residence.
Going to her.
The grass so little has to do.
Great Streets of Silence Led
  Away.
Have You Got a Brook.
He ate and drank the precious
  words.
He Fumbles at Your Soul.
He preached upon breadth.
He scanned it, staggered,
  dropped the loop.
He Was Weak.
The Heart Asks Pleasure
  First.
Heart, We Will Forget Him.
Heaven–Is What I Cannot
  Reach!
"Heavenly Father," take to
  thee.
Her breast is fit for pearls.
Her face was in a bed of hair.
Her–"last Poems"–.
Her sweet weight on my heart
  a night.
His mansion in the pool.
Hope Is a Subtle Glutton–.
Hope Is the Thing with
  Feathers.
How Happy Is the Little
  Stone.
How many times these low
  feet staggered.
How the waters closed above
  him.
I am afraid to own a body.
I am alive–I guess.
I asked no other thing.
I breathed enough to take the
  trick.
I can wade grief.
I cannot dance upon my toes.
I Cannot Live With You.
I could bring you jewels–had I
  a mind to.
I Died for Beauty.
I dreaded that first Robin, so.
I Dwell in Possibility.

I envy seas, whereon he rides–
  .
I felt a cleavage in my mind.
I felt a Funeral, in my Brain.
I Found the Phrase.
I Gave Myself to Him.
I Got So I Could Hear His
  Name.
I Had Been Hungry, All the
  Years.
I had no time to hate.
I Had Not Minded Walls.
I Have a King.
I have never seen volcanoes.
I haven't told my garden yet.
I Heard a Fly Buzz–When I
  Died.
I held a jewel in my fingers.
I know a place where summer
  strives.
I know some lonely houses off
  the road.
I Know That He Exists.
I Like a Look of Agony.
I like to see it lap the miles.
I'll Tell You How the Sun
  Rose.
I Lost a World–the Other
  Day!
I'm ceded–I've stopped being
  theirs.
I'm nobody! Who are you?
I'm Wife–I've Finished That.
I Many Times Thought Peace
  Had Come.
I meant to have but modest
  needs.
I measure every grief I meet.
I never hear that one is dead.
I never hear the word
  "escape".
I never lost as much but
  twice.
I never saw a moor.
I Read My Sentence–Steadily.
I reason, earth is short.
I Reckon When I Count at
  All.
I saw no way–the heavens
  were stitched.
I shall know why.
I should have been too glad.
I Should Not Dare to Be So
  Sad.
I started Early–Took my Dog.
I Stepped from Plank to
  Plank.
I taste a liquor never brewed.
I took my power in my hand.
I've Known a Heaven Like a
  Tent.
I've seen a dying eye.
I watched the moon around
  the house.
I Went to Heaven.
I Would Not Paint a Picture.
I Years Had Been from
  Home.
If I Can Stop One Heart from
  Breaking.
If I Could Tell How Glad I
  Was.
If I should die.
If I shouldn't be alive.
If my bark sink.
If recollecting were forgetting.
If You Were Coming in the
  Fall.
Immortal is an ample word.
In lands I never saw, they say.
In Winter in my Room.
Indian Summer.

It Dropped So Low–in My Regard.
It is an honorable thought.
It Makes No Difference Abroad.
It's Easy to Invent a Life.
It's Such a Little Thing to Weep.
It sifts from leaden sieves.
It sounded as if the streets were running.
It struck me every day.
It troubled me as once I was.
It Was Not Death, for I Stood Up.
It would have starved a gnat.
Jesus! Thy crucifix.
Just Lost, When I Was Saved!
Lad of Athens, faithful be.
A lady red upon the hill.
The lamp burns sure, within.
The Last Night That She Lived.
Lest any doubt that we are glad that they were born Today.
A light exists in spring.
Lightly stepped a yellow star.
The lightning is a yellow fork.
Like trains of cars on tracks of plush.
A little madness in the spring.
The Little Toil of Love.
Lonely House.
A long, long sleep.
Love can do all but raise the dead.
Love is that later thing than death.
Love's Stricken "Why."
Many a Phrase Has the English Language–.
The martyr poets–did not tell–.
Me from myself–to banish.
Mine–By the Right of the White Election!
Mine enemy is growing old.
The Moon Is Distant from the Sea.
The moon upon her fluent route.
The moon was but a chin of gold.
The morns are meeker than they were.
The Mountain Sat upon the Plain.
The mountains grow unnoticed.
Much madness is divinest sense.
The Murmur of a Bee.
The Mushroom Is the Elf of Plants–.
Musicians wrestle everywhere.
My country need not change her gown.
My friend must be a Bird.
My life closed twice before its close.
My Life had stood–a Loaded Gun.
My Period Had Come for Prayer.
My portion is defeat–today.
My triumph lasted till the drums.
The name–of it–is "Autumn."
A narrow Fellow in the Grass.
"Nature" Is What We See.

New Feet Within My Garden Go–.
No passenger was known to flee.
No Rack Can Torture Me.
None Can Experience Stint.
Not Any More to Be Lacked.
Not Any Sunny Tone.
Not with a club.
Now I knew I lost her.
Of All the Souls That Stand Create.
Of All the Sounds Despatched Abroad.
Of bronze and blaze.
Of course–I prayed.
Of God We Ask One Favor.
On this wondrous sea.
One blessing had I.
One Crucifixion is Recorded Only.
One dignity delays for all.
One Need Not Be a Chamber–To Be Haunted.
The only ghost I ever saw.
The Only News I Know.
Our Journey Had Advanced.
Our little kinsmen.
Our lives are Swiss.
Our share of night to bear.
Ourselves we do inter with sweet derision.
Ourselves were wed one summer–dear.
The Outer from the Inner.
Over the fence.
The Overtakelessness of Those.
Pain Has an Element of Blank.
Papa above.
Pass to thy Rendezvous of Light.
The pedigree of honey.
Perception of an Object Costs.
Pink, Small and Punctual (Arbutus).
The Poets Light but Lamps.
A Precious–Mouldering Pleasure–'tis–.
Precious to me–she still shall be.
Precious Words.
Presentiment.
Proud of my broken heart since thou didst break it.
Publication Is the Auction.
The Rat Is the Concisest Tenant.
Read, Sweet, How Others Strove.
Rearrange a Wife's Affection?
Remorse–is memory–awake.
Reportless subjects, to the quick.
The Robin Is the One.
A route of evanescence.
Safe in their Alabaster Chambers.
Said death to passion.
Satisfaction–Is the agent.
Savior! I've No One Else to Tell.
A science–so the savans say.
A shady friend for torrid days.
Shall I Take Thee, the Poet Said.
She dealt her pretty words like blades.
She died–this was the way she died.

She lay as if at play.
She Rose to His Requirement–Dropt.
She sweeps with many-colored brooms.
The Show is not the Show.
Simplicity.
The Skies Cant Keep Their Secret!
The sky is low, the clouds are mean.
So proud she was to die.
Softened by time's consummate plush.
A Solemn Thing–It Was–I Said.
Some Keep the Sabbath Going to Church.
Some Things That Fly There Be.
Some we see no more, tenements of wonder.
Some wretched creature, savior take.
The Soul Has Bandaged Moments.
The Soul Selects Her Own Society.
The spider holds a silver ball.
Spring is the Period.
The stars are old, that stood for me.
Step lightly on this narrow spot!
The stimulus beyond the grave.
Struck Was I, Nor Yet by Lightning.
Success is counted sweetest.
Summer Has Two Beginnings.
Surgeons Must Be Very Careful.
Sweet Is the Swamp with Its Secrets.
Tell All the Truth but Tell It Slant.
A Tempest.
That after horror that was Us.
That it will never come again.
That love is all there is.
That such have died enable us.
Their height in heaven comforts not.
There are two mays.
There Came a Day at Summer's Full.
There Came A Wind Like A Bugle.
There is a flower that bees prefer.
There is a languor of the life.
There is a morn by men unseen.
There is a pain–so utter.
There is a shame of nobleness.
There is no frigate like a book.
There is No Trumpet Like the Tomb.
There's a Certain Slant of Light.
There's been a death, in the opposite house.
These are the days when birds come back.
They called me to the window.
They dropped like flakes.
They might not need me.
They say that "Time assuages."

They shut me up in prose.
This dirty little heart.
This Is My Letter to the World.
This quiet dust was gentlemen and ladies.
This Was a Poet.
This World Is Not Conclusion.
Those–Dying Then.
Those Not Live Yet.
Though I get home how late, how late!
Though the Great Waters Sleep.
The thought beneath so slight a film.
A Thought Went Up My Mind.
Through the Straight Pass of Suffering.
A Thunder-Storm.
Tie the strings to my life, my Lord.
The Tint I Cannot Take Is Best.
'Tis not that dying hurts us so.
'Tis so much joy!
'Tis true–they shut me in the cold.
Title divine–Is mine!
To fight aloud is brave.
To flee from memory.
To Hear an Oriole Sing.
To know just how he suffered would be dear.
To learn the transport by the pain.
To make a prairie it takes a clover and one bee.
To My Quick Ear.
To Pile Like Thunder to Its Close.
To see her is a picture.
Too happy time dissolves itself.
A triumph may be of several kinds.
Truth is as old as god.
'Twas Just This Time, Last Year, I Died.
'Twas Like a Maelstrom, with a Notch.
'Twas Warm at First, Like Us.
Two lengths has every day.
Undue significance.
Until the desert knows.
Utterance.
Victory comes late.
The waters chased him as he fled.
The Way I Read a Letter's–This.
We do not play on graves.
We dream–it is good we are dreaming.
We like March–his shoes are purple.
We miss a kinsman more.
We Never Know How High We Are.
We outgrow love, like other things.
We Play at Paste.
We thirst at first.
Went up a year this evening!
What inn is this.
What Is–"Paradise".
What Mystery Pervades a Well!

What soft–cherubic creatures.
When night is almost done.
Where Ships of Purple–Gently Toss.
While we were fearing it.
"Whole gulfs of red and fleets of red".
A Wife–at Daybreak I Shall Be.
Wild nights–wild nights!
Will there really be a morning?
The wind begun to knead the grass.
The wind tapped like a tired man.
"The wind took up the northern things".
Witchcraft was hung, in history.
With a Flower.
With Flowers.
Within my Garden, rides a Bird.
Wonder–Is Not Precisely Knowing.
The world feels dusty.
A wounded deer leaps highest.
Your Thoughts Don't Have Words Every Day.

Dickinson, G. Lowes
I Never Asked for More Than Thou Hast Given.

Dickinson, John
The Liberty Song.

Dickinson, Martha Gilbert
Forgiveness Lane.
Heaven.
Her Music.
A Priest's Prayer.
Reality.
Separation.
Unanswered.

Dickinson, Patric
Advent: A Carol.
The Hounds.
Jodrell Bank.
Lament for the Great Yachts.
Lines for an Eminent Poet and Critic.
On a Female Snob, Surprised.
The Redwing.
St. Stephen's Day.
The Swallows.

Dickinson, Peter
By-Election Idyll.

Dickson, Aimor R.
The Company One Keeps.

Dickson, John
Art Gallery.
Looking Down on West Virginia.

Die, Countess Beatriz de
I Sing a Song Reluctantly.
Lately I've felt a grave concern.

Diego, Gerardo
Seesaw.

Diego Padro, Jose I. de
Epistolary Briefs to Proclus.

Diekmann, Conrad
Winter Trees.

Dienstag, Alan
Audrey.
Nina.
Sylvia.

Diespecker, Dick
Between Two Furious Oceans.

Dietmar von Aist, Sir
A Bird Was Singing.
A Lady Stood.
Parting at Morning.

Dietz, Howard
On the Rising Generation.

Digby, John
One Night away from Day.
Sooner or Later.

Digby, Kenelm H.
The Catholic Faith.
Erin.

Digby, Sir Kenelm
On His Late Espoused Saint.

Dillard, Annie
Arches and Shadows.
Light in the Open Air.
The Windy Planet.

Dillard, R. H. W.
Hats.
How Copernicus Stopped the Sun.
How Einstein Started It Up Again.
Meditation for a Pickle Suite.

Dillenback, John D.
Colorado.

Diller, John Irving
Lullaby Town.

Dillon, Dan
Testing, Testing.

Dillon, George
"April's amazing meaning".
The Constant One.
Elemental.
The Hard Lovers.
A Kind Inn.
No Question.
Remember, Though the Telescope Extend.
Woman Without Fear.
"The world goes turning".

Dillow, H. C.
Confrontions of March.

di Michele, Mary
The Disgrace.
A Fiction of Edvard Munch.
The Food of Love.
The Moon and the Salt Flats.
Patience on a Monument.
Piccante.
Romance of the Cigarette.

Dimmette, Celia
Apology of the Young Scientists.

Dimoff, John
West of Chicago.

Dimond, William
The Mariner's Dream.

"Dinesen, Isak" (Karen Blixen)
Zebra.

Dinis, King of Portugal
Song.

Dinnies, Anna Peyre
The Wife.

Dinnis, Enid
The Cherub-Folk.
A Franciscan Prayer.

Diogenes Laertius
Be Gone Ye Blockheads.
Ecce Quomodo Moritur Justus.

Diop, Birago
Breaths.

Diop, David
Africa.
He Who Has Lost All.
Suffer, Poor Negro.
Those Who Lost Everything.
The Vultures.
Your Presence.

Diotimus
Without the Herdsman.

DiPasquale, Emanuel
Advice.
First Surf.

Incantation to Get Rid of a Sometime Friend.
Rain.

Di Piero, W. S.
Fat Tuesday.
Four Brothers.
Lines to a Friend in Trouble.
A Living.
On Christmas Eve.
Second Horn.

Dipoko, Mbella Sonne
Autobiography.

Di Prima, Diane
Goodbye Nkrumah.
In Memory of My First Chapatis.
The Jungle.
Moon Mattress.
The Practice of Magical Evocation.
The Quarrel.
Revolutionary Letter #19.
Revolutionary Letters.

Di Roma, Immanuel
Elegy.
Happiness Amidst Troubles.
Love.
My Sweet Gazelle!
Oh, Let Thy Teachings.
On the Wall.
Paradise.
Virtue.
What Profit?
The Worthless Heart.

Di Rossi, Azariah
Epitaph.

Disch, Thomas M.
La, La, La!
The Rapist's Villanelle.

Disch, Tom
Homage to the Carracci.
The Vowels of Another Language.

Dismond, Binga
At Early Morn.
Status Quo.

Disraeli, Benjamin
Wellington.

Ditlevsen, Tove
A Man's Love.
Morning.
The Old Folk.
Self Portrait 4.

Ditmars, Rembrandt William B.
Lincoln.

Ditsky, John
Chamber Music.
Epithalamium.
Mainline.

Ditta, J. M.
In the Surgery.

Divine, Charles
At the Lavender Lantern.
Look Not to Me for Wisdom.
Never Will You Hold Me.
Paris: The Seine at Night.
Spanish Song.
We Met on Roads of Laughter.

Divine, Jay
Coal Miner's Grace.

Dix, W.C.
Silver Lamps.

Dix, William Chatterton
As with Gladness Men of Old.
What Child Is This?

Dixon, Alan
Chops.
Song.

Dixon, Henry
The Description of a Good Boy.

Dixon, Maynard
Laguna Perdida.
Navajo Song.
The Plains.

Dixon, Melvin
Man Holding Boy.
Richard, Richard: American Fuel.
Tour Guide: La Maison des Esclaves.

Dixon, Richard Watson
Both Less and More.
By the Sea.
Dawning.
Dream.
Fallen Rain.
Humanity.
The Judgment of the May.
Love's Consolation.
Ode on Advancing Age.
Ode: The Spirit Wooed.
Rapture: An Ode.
Song: "Oh, bid my tongue be still."
Song: "The feathers of the willow."
Unrest.
Winter Will Follow.
The Wizard's Funeral.

Dixon, Sarah
Lines Occasioned by the Burning of Some Letters.

Djabali, Leila
For My Torturer, Lieutenant D–.

Djalparmiwi
The Blowflies Buzz.

Djangatolum
Ali.
Dedication to the Final Confrontation.

Djanikian, Gregory
Michelangelo: "The Creation of Adam."

Djellaladin Pasha, Mahmud
Song: "If you love God, take your mirror between your hands and look."

Djurberaui
All You Others, Eat.

D'Lettuso, Homer
Old Houses.

Doak, H. L.
The Beggar.
The Scarecrow.

Doane, George Washington
Bishop Doane on His Dog.
Evening Contemplation.
Fling Out the Banner!
Life Sculpture.
Once More, O Lord.
Robin Redbreast.
Thou Art the Way.

Doane, William Croswell
Ancient of Days, Who Sittest Throned in Glory.
The Modern Baby.
The Preacher's Mistake.

Dobberstein, Michael
The Engine: A Manual.

Dobbs, Jeannine
Kitchen Song.

Dobbs, Kildare
The Exequy.

Dobell, Bertram
Microcosm.

Dobell, Sydney Thomas
America.
L'Avenir.
Balder.
The Ballad of Keith of Ravelston.

The Botanist's Vision.
A Chanted Calendar.
Daft Jean.
Desolate.
Eden-Gate.
An Even-Song.
The German Legion.
He Loves and He Rides
　Away.
How's My Boy?
Isabel.
Keith of Ravelston.
A Nuptial Eve.
The Orphan's Song.
Perhaps.
Return!
Sonnet: The Army Surgeon.
Sonnet: The Common Grave.
To the Authoress of "Aurora
　Leigh".
Tommy's Dead.
Wind.

Dobson, Henry Austin
A Ballad of Heroes.
The Ballad of Imitation.
A Ballad to Queen Elizabeth.
Before Sedan.
Bidean Nam Bian.
The Child-Musician.
Circle.
A City Flower.
Clean Hands.
The Cure's Progress.
The Dance of Death.
A Dead Letter.
A Dialogue from Plato.
Don Quixote.
Dora versus Rose.
Fame and Friendship.
Fame Is a Food That Dead
　Men Eat.
A Fancy from Fontenelle.
For a Copy of Theocritus.
A Garden Song.
A Gentleman of the Old
　School.
Good-Night, Babette.
A Greek Gift.
Growing Gray.
Henry Wadsworth Longfellow.
In After Days.
Incognita.
A Kiss.
The Ladies of St. James's.
Little Blue Ribbons.
The Maltworm's Madrigal.
The Milkmaid.
On a Fan That Belonged to
　the Marquise De
　Pompadour.
On the Hurry of This Time.
Persicos Odi: Pocket Version.
The Rondeau.
A Song of Angiola in Heaven.
A Song of the Four Seasons.
A Tear.
To a Greek Girl.
To Brander Matthews.
To Lydia Languish.
Urceus Exit: Triolet.
The Wanderer.
When I Saw You Last, Rose.
When There Is Peace.
With Pipe and Flute.

Dobson, John
Robin. A Pastoral Elegy.

Dobson, Rosemary
Across the Straits.
Being Called For.
The Birth.
The Bystander.
Child with a Cockatoo.

Country Press.
Detail from an Annunciation
　by Crivelli.
The Devil and the Angel.
The Edge.
The Fever.
Folding the Sheets.
In a Cafe.
In My End Is My Beginning.
The Missal.
The Raising of the Dead.
The Three Fates.

Dobyns, Stephen
Cemetery Nights.
Counterparts.
The Delicate, Plummeting
　Bodies.
Dream.
Fear.
Getting Up.
Girl in White.
Japanese Girl with Red Table.
Oatmeal Deluxe.
The Triangular Field.
The White Skirt.
The Window.

Dobzynski, Charles
The Fable Merchant.
Memory Air.
The Never Again.
Zealot Without a Face.

Dock, Christopher
O Children, Would You
　Cherish?

Dodat, Francois
Dromedary.

Dodd, Lee Wilson
The Comrade.
The Flower.

Dodd, Leonard
Compel Them to Come In.

Dodd, Wayne
Night Poem.

Doddridge, Philip
Awake, My Soul!
Christ's Resurrection and
　Ascension.
Hear Us, in This Thy House.
How Gentle God's
　Commands.
Hymn.
Jesus, I Love Thy Charming
　Name.
Live while You Live.
Meditations on the Sepulchre
　in the Garden.
Ye Golden Lamps of Heaven.

Dodge, Henry Nehemiah
Spirit of Freedom, Thou Dost
　Love the Sea.
Thrustararorum.

Dodge, Mary Barker
Now.

Dodge, Mary Mapes
Christmas.
Courtesy.
Emerson.
In Trust.
Lazy Lou.
The Letters at School.
Limerick: "There was a brave
　knight of Lorraine."
The Mayor of Scuttleton.
Melons.
The Minuet.
Not Only in the Christmas-
　Tide.
Now the Noisy Winds Are
　Still.
Oh, No!
Once Before.
One and One.

Poor Crow!
Shadow-Evidence.
Snow-Flakes.
The Stars.
Stocking Song on Christmas
　Eve.
The Sweet, Red Rose.
That's What We'd Do.
The Two Mysteries.
When I am Big, I Mean to
　Buy.
Written on the Raod.
The Zealless Xylographer.

Dodge, Ossian E.
Ho! Westward Ho!.

Dodge, Samuel
People Will Talk.

Dodgson, Charles Lutwidge See
　"Carroll, Lewis"

**Dodington, George Bubb, Baron
Melcombe**
Ode: "Love thy Country, wish
　it well."

Dodsley, Robert
Epigram.
An Epistle to My Friend J. B.
The Kings of Europe A Jest.
A Method of Preserving Hay
　from Being Mow-Burnt, or
　Taking Fire.
Song: "Man's a poor deluded
　bubble."

Dodson, Margery
Poem: "Entombed in my
　heart."

Dodson, Owen
Ballad of Badmen.
The Confession Stone.
Counterpoint.
The Decision.
Drunken Lover.
Epitaph for a Negro Woman.
For Edwin R. Embree.
Hymn Written after Jeremiah
　Preached to Me in a Dream.
I Break the Sky.
Job's Ancient Lament.
Mary Passed This Morning.
Miss Packard and Miss Giles.
The Morning Duke Ellington
　Praised the Lord...
Open Letter.
Poems for My Brother
　Kenneth.
Rag Doll and Summer Birds.
Sailors on Leave.
Sickle Pears (For Glidden
　Parker).
Six O'Clock.
Sorrow Is the Only Faithful
　One.
Yardbird's Skull.

Dohl, Reinhard
Concrete poem: Apfel.

Dolben, Digby Mackworth
After Reading Homer.
The April of the Ages.
Come to Me, Beloved.
Flowers for the Altar.
The Garden.
He Would Have His Lady
　Sing.
Heaven.
I Asked for Peace.
A Prayer.
Requests.
The Shrine.
Strange, All-Absorbing Love.
We Hurry On, Nor Passing
　Note.
The World Is Young Today.

Dole, Nathan Haskell
A Russian Fantasy.
To an Imperilled Traveller.

Dolgorukov, Florence
Intersection.
Three Sunrises from Amtrak.

Dollard, James B.
The Fairy Harpers.
Song of the Little Villages.

Dolliver, Clara
No Baby in the House.

Domanski, Don
Deadsong.
Dreamtime.
Graveside.
Hammerstoke.
Ironwood.
Nocturne of Birth and Water.
Sub Rosa.
Three Songs from the Temple.

Domett, Alfred
A Christmas Hymn.
A Glee for Winter.
A Maori Girl's Song.
Ranolf and Amohia.

Domin, Hilde
Birthdays.
Catalogue.
Cologne.
Dreamwater.

Dominici, Giovanni
Mother Most Powerful.

Domino, Ruth
A Sparrow in the Dust.

Donaghy, John Lyle
At My Whisper.
Deathward.
Duck.
Ebb.
The Fossil.
Glenarm.
The Grave.
The Heron.
A Leitrim Woman.
Linota Rufescens.
Portrait.
Seeing.
Voyage.
Where the Dropwort Springs
　up Lithe and Tall.
Winter.

Donaghy, William A.
Fourth Station.
Thirteenth Station.

Donahue, Jack
Brave Donahue.

Donaldson, Islay Murray
Skye Summer.

Donatus
The Land Called Scotia.

Doney, May
Comfort.
The White Dream.

Donian, Mitchell
If Someone Asks You.

Donne, John
Absence.
Air and Angels.
An Anatomy of the World.
　The First Anniversary.
Annunciation.
Annus Mirabilis.
Antiquary.
The Apparition.
Ascension.
At the Round Earth's
　Imagin'd Corners, Blow.
The Autumnal.
The Bait.
The Blossom.
Break of Day.
The Broken Heart.

A Burnt Ship.
But We by a Love, So Much Refined.
The Calm.
The Canonization.
Change.
The Comparison.
The Computation.
Confined Love.
La Corona.
Crucifying.
The Curse.
The Dampe.
Daybreak.
Devotions.
Devout Fits.
The Dissolution.
The Dream.
The Ecstasy.
Elegy on Mistress Boulstred.
Elegy on the L.C.
Epithalamion Made at Lincolnes Inne.
An Epithalamion, or Marriage Song.
The Expiration.
Farewell to Love.
A Fever.
The First Anniversary: The New Philosophy.
The Flea.
For Forgiveness.
For Whom the Bell Tolls.
The Funeral.
Go and Catch a Falling Star.
Going to Bed.
Good Friday, 1613. Riding Westward.
The Good-Morrow.
His Parting from Her.
His Picture.
Holy Sonnets.
A Hymn to Christ at the Author's Last Going into Germany.
Hymn to God My God, in My Sickness.
A Hymn to God the Father.
If Poisonous Minerals.
The Indifferent.
Jealosie.
A Jeat Ring Sent.
A Lame Beggar.
A Lecture Upon the Shadow.
The Legacie.
Letter to Sir H. Wotton at His Going Ambassador to Venice.
The Litanie.
Love's Alchemy.
Love's Deity.
Love's Exchange.
Love's Growth.
Love's Infiniteness.
Love's Progress.
The Message.
Nativitie.
A Nocturnal upon St Lucy's Day, Being the Shortest Day.
The Obsequies of the Lord Harrington.
On His Mistress.
The Paradox.
The Perfume.
Phryne.
The Primrose, Being at Montgomery Castle, upon the Hill...
The Prohibition.
The Relic.
Resurrection.
The Sacrament.

Satire.
The Second Anniversarie.
A Self Accuser.
The Storm.
The Sun Rising.
Sweetest Love, I Do Not Go.
Temple.
To His Mistress Desiring to Travel with Him as His Page.
To Mr C.B.
To Mr. George Herbert, with One of My Seals, of the Anchor and Christ.
To Mr. I. L.
To Mr. R.W.
To Mr. T. W.
To Mr. Tilman after He Had Taken Orders.
To Sir Edward Herbert at Julyers.
To the Countesee of Bedford.
The Triple Fool.
Truth.
Twicknam Garden.
The Undertaking.
A Valediction Forbidding Mourning.
A Valediction: Of My Name in the Window.
A Valediction: of Weeping.
The Will.
Witchcraft by a Picture.
Woman's Constancy.

Donnell, David
The Canadian Prairies View of Literature.
Hotels.
Open Roads.
Potatoes.
Stepfathers.

Donnelly, Charles
The Flowering Bars.
Heroic Heart.
Last Poem.
The Tolerance of Crows.

Donnelly, Dorothy
Blue Flag.
Chinese Baby Asleep.
Consider the Lilies.
Girandole.
Glass World.
Leaflight.
A Prospect of Swans.
Recollection.
Serenade.
Three-Toed Sloth.
Wheels.

Donnelly, Eleanor C.
Mary Immaculate.

Donnelly, Susan
Rilke Speaks of Angels.

Donnelly, Tom
Myself when Young (parody).

Donohue, James J.
Last Antiphon: To Mary.

Donovan, Gregory
The Working Man.

Donovan, Rhoda
No Signal for a Crossing.
Ten Week Wife.

Donzella, Compiuta
To Leave the World Serve God.

Donzella, D. W.
The Last Job I Held in Bridgeport.

Dooher, Muredach J.
Renascence.

Doolittle, Esther Hull
Secret.

Doolittle, Hilda ("H. D.")
Acon.
Adonis.
Ah (You Say), This Is Holy Wisdom.
At Baia.
At Ithaca.
Birds in Snow.
Callypso Speaks.
Centaur Song.
Egypt.
Epigram: "The golden one is gone from the banquets."
Erige Cor Tuum Ad Me In Caelum.
Eurydice.
Evadne.
Evening.
The Flowering of the Rod.
Fragment Thirty-Six.
From Citron-Bower.
The Garden.
Good Frend.
Halcyon.
Helen in Egypt.
The Helmsman.
Hermes of the Ways.
Hippolytus Temporizes.
Holy Satyr.
Hymen: Never More Will the Wind.
In Time of Gold.
An Incident Here and There.
Invisible, indivisible Spirit.
The Islands.
Lais.
Leda.
Let Zeus Record.
Lethe.
The Moon in Your Hands.
Moonrise.
The Mysteries Remain.
Never More Will the Wind.
Not Honey.
O Heart, Small Urn.
Orchard.
Oread.
Pear Tree.
Phaedra.
The Pool.
Pygmalion.
Sagesse.
Sea Gods.
Sea Rose.
Sea Violet.
She Contrasts with Herself Hippolyta.
She Rebukes Hippolyta.
Sheltered Garden.
The Shrine.
Sigil.
Simaetha.
Sitalkas.
Socratic.
Song: "You are as gold."
Songs from Cyprus.
Stars Wheel in Purple.
Storm.
There Is a Spell, for Instance.
Tribute to the Angels.
The Walls Do Not Fall.
We Have Seen Her.
We have seen how the most amiable.
Where Love Is King.
White World.
Wine Bowl.
Winter Love.

Door, Henry R.
Comrades.

Dor, Moshe
Among the Pine Trees.

The Dwelling.
Nightingales Are Not Singing.
Small Bones Ache.

Doran, Louise A.
The Ship.

Dorcey, Mary
First Love.
Sea Flower.

Doreski, William
The Amish.

Dorgan, John Aylmer
The Beautiful.
The Dead Solomon.

D'Orge, Jeanne
The Convent.
The Enchanted Castle.
Portrait.

Doriot, Jeanne
Indian.

Dorman, Sonya
Teacher.

Dorn, Alfred
Challengers.
Symphony.

Dorn, Edward
The Air of June Sings.
Are They Dancing.
The Biggest Killing.
Chronicle.
Eugene Delacroix Says.
For the New Union Dead in Alabama.
From Gloucester Out.
Gunslinger.
The Hide of My Mother.
Home on the Range, February 1962.
Los Mineros.
La Maquina a Houston.
A Morning to Remember; or, E. Pluribus Unum.
Mourning Letter, March 29 1963.
On the Debt My Mother Owed to Sears Roebuck.
Oxford.
The Rick of Green Wood.
A Song.
Sousa.
Thesis.
Vaquero.
When the Fairies.

Dorney, Elizabeth
The Chemistry of Character.

Dorr, Julia Caroline Ripley
The Fallow Field.
The Legend of the Organ-Builder.
No More the Thunder of Cannon.
O Earth! Art Thou Not Weary?
Outgrown.
Two Paths.
With a Rose from Conway Castle.

Dorrance, Dick
Cockpit in the Clouds.

Dorris, Michael
Frost Heaves.

Dorset, Catherine Ann
The Peacock "At Home".

Dorset, Charles Sackville, Earl of See Sackville, Earl of Dorset

Dos Passos, John
Crimson Tent.

Dos Santos, Marcelin
Dream of the Black Mother.
Here We Were Born.
Where I Am.

Doten, Elizabeth
Farewell to Earth.
In a Hundred Years.
Reconciliation.
Doty, M. R.
Sleep.
Doty, Walter G.
The Best Firm.
Doudney, Sarah
The Christian's "Good-
Night".
The Lesson of the Water-Mill.
Doughty, Charles M.
The Dawn in Britain.
The Fairies Feast.
The Gauls Sacrifice.
Hymn to the Sun.
A Roman Officer Writes.
Douglas, Gavin
An Evening and Morning in
June.
An Evening and Morning in
Winter.
King Hart: Hart's Castle.
The Palace of Honor.
Proloug of the Twelft Buik of
the Aenead.
Welcome to the Sun.
Winter.
Douglas, Gilean
Inscription in a Book.
Douglas, Keith
Aristocrats.
Behaviour of Fish in an
Egyptian Tea Garden.
Cairo Jag.
Canoe.
The Deceased.
Desert Flowers.
Enfidaville.
Gallantry.
How to Kill.
Landscape with Figures.
Leukothea.
The Offensive.
On a Return from Egypt.
Oxford.
Poem: "These grasses, ancient
enemies."
Remember Me.
A Round Number.
Russians.
The Sea Bird.
Simplify Me When I'm Dead.
Snakeskin and Stone.
Song: "Do I venture away too
far."
Time Eating.
Vergissmeinicht.
Douglas, Lord Alfred Bruce
The City of the Soul.
The Dead Poet.
The Green River.
Impression de Nuit: London.
Lighten Our Darkness.
A Prayer.
To Olive.
To—, with an Ivory Hand-
Glass.
Two Loves.
The Witch.
"Douglas, Marian" *See also*
Robinson, Annie Douglas
Ant-Hills.
The Snow-Man.
Douglas, William
Annie Laurie.
Douglass, Suzanne
No Holes Marred.
Progress.
Douskey, Franz
Regressing.

Dove, Rita
Adolescence–II.
Champagne.
Dusting.
The Fish in the Stone.
Geometry.
Nigger Song: An Odyssey.
O.
Parsley.
Planning the Perfect Evening.
This Life.
Dovey, Irma
Unwelcome.
Dow, Dorothy
Song: "I could make you
songs."
Things.
To Atalanta.
Unbeliever.
Dow, Philip
Air (parody).
Bottom's Dream.
Doe.
Dried Fruit (parody).
Drunk Last Night with
Friends, I Go to Work
Anyway.
The Duck Pond at Mini's
Pasture, a Dozen Years
Later.
Early Morning.
Elegy.
Fishing.
Ghazal.
Goodby "Hello."
It Comes during Sleep.
Letter.
The Life.
Mother.
The Skunk (parody).
Snow Geese in the Wind.
Song: "What binds the atom
together."
Suite for Celery and Blind
Date (parody).
Sussyissfriin.
Twilight in California.
Dowd, Emma C.
Fun in a Garret.
Dowden, Edward
An Autumn Song.
Burdens.
Communion.
In the Cathedral Close.
Love's Lord.
Mona Lisa.
New Hymns for Solitude.
Oasis.
Renunciants.
Seeking God.
The Singer.
Windle-Straws.
Dowden, Elizabeth Dickinson
Adrift.
Dowding, Walter
I'r hen Iaith A'i Chanedon
(To the Old Tongue and its
Songs).
Dower, E.
The New River Head, a
Fragment.
Dowland, John
Come away, Sweet Love.
Fine Knacks for Ladies.
Madrigal: "Dear, if you
change."
Madrigal: "Flow not so fast."
Madrigal: "Go, nightly
Cares."
Madrigal: "Sleep, wayward
thoughts."
Weep You No More.

Dowling, Allan
I Sought with Eager Hand.
The Joy of Love.
The Miracle.
Dowling, Bartholomew
The Revel.
Dowling, Basil
The Air in Spring.
Autumn Scene.
Canterbury.
The Early Days.
Mortal Love.
Naseby: Late Autumn.
Shunting.
Summer Afternoon.
Walking in Bush.
Downer, Ann
Koko.
Downey, Fairfax
Rise and Fall of Valentines.
Downie, Freda
Elsdon.
Great-Grandfather.
Her Garden.
Miss Grant.
Starlight.
Downing, Ellen Mary Patrick
My Owen.
"Downing, Major Jack" *See*
Smith Seba
Dowson, Ernest Christopher
Ad Domnulam Suam.
Amantium Irae.
De Amore.
April Love.
Autumnal.
Benedictio Domini.
Breton Afternoon.
Carthusians.
The Dead Child.
Dregs.
Envoy.
Epigram: "Because I am
idolatrous and have
besought."
Exchanges.
Exile.
Extreme Unction.
Flos Lunae.
The Garden of Shadow.
Impenitentia Ultima.
Jadis.
A Last Word.
Non Sum Qualis Eram Bonae
Sub Regno Cynarae.
O Mors! Quam Amara Est
Memoria Tua Homini Pacem
Habenti ...
The Princess of Dreams.
Quid Non Speremus,
Amantes?
The Royal Love Scene.
Saint Germain-en-Laye.
Sapientia Lunae.
Spleen.
Terre Promise.
To One in Bedlam.
A Valediction.
Vesperal.
Villanelle of Acheron.
Villanelle of His Lady's
Treasures.
Villanelle of Marguerites.
Villanelle of Sunset.
Villanelle of the Poet's Road.
Vitae Summa Brevis Spem
Nos Vetat Incohare Longam.
Your Hands.
Doxey, W. S.
Cathedrals.
Doyle, Arthur Conan
Cremona.

The Song of the Bow.
Doyle, Kirby
Strange.
Doyle, Lynn
An Ulsterman.
Doyle, Marion
The Golden Month.
The Month of the Thunder
Moon.
Doyle, Sir Francis Hastings
The Epicurean.
The Loss of the Birkenhead.
The Private of the Buffs.
The Red Thread of Honor.
Doyle, Susanne
November Walk.
Drachler, Rose
As I Am My Father's.
The Dark Scent of Prayer.
Isaac and Esau.
The Letters of the Book.
Under the Shawl.
Zippora Returns to Moses at
Rephidim.
Drachmann, Holger
Amber.
Dracontius, Blossius Aemilius
The Birds.
Drake, Albert
1939 Mercury.
Every Saturday He Stands.
Drake, Francis
To the Memory of the
Learned and Reverend, Mr.
Jonathan Mitchell...
Drake, Gaston V.
The Contrary Boy.
**Drake, Joseph R., and Fitz-
Greene Halleck**
The Man Who Frets at
Worldly Strife.
Ode to Fortune.
Drake, Joseph Rodman
The American Flag.
The Culprit Fay.
Drake, Leah Bodine
The Final Green.
The Green Door.
Honey from the Lion.
The Middle Ages: Two Views.
Precarious Ground.
The Rider.
Dransfield, Michael
Bum's Rush.
Epiderm.
Geography.
Loft.
Pas de Deux for Lovers.
Portrait of the Artist as an
Old Man.
Rainpoem.
That Which We Call a Rose.
Draper, A. S.
Indian Summer.
Draper, George
Rink Keeper's Sestina.
Draper, Jane
I Look into the Stars.
Drayton, Michael
Agincourt.
As Love and I, Late
Harbour'd in One Inn.
Batte's Song.
Cassamen and Dowsabell.
Christopher Marlowe.
Cloris and Mertilla.
The Crier.
The Earl of Surrey to
Geraldine.
Eclogue.
Endymion's Convoy.

The Epistle of Rosamond to King Henry the Second.
An Evil Spirit, Your Beauty Haunts Me Still.
Fame and Fortune.
A Fine Day.
First Steps up Parnassus.
Gorbo and Batte.
Hawking.
Henry to Rosamond.
How Many Paltry Foolish Painted Things.
Idea.
Idea's Mirrour.
If He from Heaven That Filched the Living Fire.
King Henry to Rosamond.
Like an Adventurous Sea-Farer Am I.
Lines.
The Moone-Calfe.
The Muses Elizium.
Night and Day.
Nimphidia, the Court of Fayrie.
Noah's Flood.
Nothing but No and I, and I and No.
Nymphidia.
An Ode Written in the Peak.
The Owle.
Pastoral: The Tenth Eclogue.
Phoebe on Latmus.
Piers Gaveston.
Pigwiggin Arms Himself.
The Poets' Paradise.
Polyolbion.
A Roundelay.
Rowland's Rhyme.
The Sacrifice to Apollo.
The Second Nimphall.
Shepheards Sirena: Song to Sirena.
Shepherd's Garland,.
Sirena.
A Skeltoniad.
So Well I Love Thee, as Without Thee I.
The Song of Hannah.
Song to Beta.
Sonnet: "If chaste and pure devotion of my youth."
Sonnet: "Into these loves who but for passion looks."
Sonnet: "Sweet secrecy, what tongue can tell thy worth?"
Sonnet–To the Critic.
Sonnet: "Whilst thus my pen strives to eternise thee."
Sylvia.
The Third Eclogue.
The Thirteenth Song.
To Cupid.
To Himselfe and the Harpe.
To His Coy Love.
To His Valentine.
To My Most Dearely-loved Friend Henery Reynolds Esquire.
To The New Yeere.
To the Virginian Voyage.
Verses Made the Night before He Died.
The Virginian Voyage.
When Heaven Would Strive to Do the Best She Can.
Wrestlers.
You're Not Alone.
Drennan, John Swanick
Epigram: "A golden casket I designed."
Not Gone Yet.

On the Telescopic Moon.
Perdita.
Drennan, William
Aspiration.
Branch of the Sweet and Early Rose.
Eire.
The Wake of William Orr.
Dresbach, Glenn Ward
An Autumn Road.
The Cave.
Desert Song.
Life or Death.
Magic Lariat.
The Old Sailor.
Ship's Bell.
Since Youth Is All for Gladness.
Through the Blowing Leaves.
Yucca in the Moonlight.
Dresser, Paul
Just Tell Them That You Saw Me.
My Gal Sal.
On the Banks of the Wabash, Far Away.
Drewry, Carleton
Evensong.
In This Strange House.
Invocation.
A Small Thought Speaks for the Flesh.
A Song in Humility.
"Drinan, Adam" See **Macleod, Joseph Gordon**
Drinkwater, John
The Bird's Nest.
Birthright.
Bobby Blue.
Christmas Eve.
The Crowning of Dreaming John.
Deer.
The Feckenham Men.
Foundation of Faith.
The Hit.
I Want to Know.
Invocation.
May Garden.
Moonlit Apples.
My Estate.
Petition.
The Plea.
A Prayer.
Reciprocity.
Snail.
The Sun.
Sunrise on Rydal Water.
Tiptoe Night.
Who Were before Me.
Driscoll, Jack
Arm Wrestling with My Father.
Ice.
Middle of the Day.
Driscoll, Louise
Bargain.
Epitaph.
God's Pity.
The Good Hour.
Grace for Gardens.
The Highway.
Hold Fast Your Dreams.
Idol.
July Meadow.
Mid-August.
My Garden Is a Pleasant Place.
November Garden.
Spring Market.
Thanksgiving.

Driver, C. J.
Birthdays.
In Solitary Confinement, Sea Point Police Cells.
To Jann, in Her Absence.
Dromgoole, Will Allen
The Bridge Builder.
Old Ladies.
Dropkin, Celia
A Circus Dancer.
Droste-Hulshoff, Annette von
Gethsemane.
In the Grass.
The Last Day of the Year (New Year's Eve).
Last Words.
On the Tower.
Drummond, William, of Hawthornden
The Angels for the Nativity of Our Lord.
As in a Dusky and Tempestuous Night.
The Baptist.
The Book of the World.
Change Should Breed Change.
Doth Then the World Go Thus, Doth All Thus Move?
Epitaph: "Sanquhar, whom this earth could scarce contain."
For the Baptist.
For the Magdalene.
An Hymne of the Ascension.
I Know That All beneath the Moon Decays.
If Crossed with All Mishaps.
In This World's Raging Sea.
Inexorable.
Ioolas' Epitaph.
The Ivory, Coral, Gold.
A Kiss.
Kisses Desired.
Lament.
Like the Idalian Queen.
Love Vagabonding.
Love Which Is Here a Care.
Madrigal: "Poor turtle, thou bemoans."
Madrigal: The Beautie, and the Life.
No Trust in Time.
Of Phyllis.
On Mary Magdalen.
On the Death of Pym.
Phoebus, Arise.
Phyllis.
Poems.
Saint John the Baptist.
Sleep, Silence' Child, Sweet Father of Soft Rest.
Sleeping Beauty.
A Solitary Life.
Song II: "It Autumne was, and on our Hemispheare."
Sonnet: "I fear to me such fortune be assign'd."
Sonnet VII: "That learned Graecian (who did so exell)."
Sonnet IX.
Sonnet: "A passing glance, a lightning long the skies."
Sonnet: "Dear quirister, who from those shadows sends."
Sonnet: "How that vast heaven intitled First is rolled."
Sonnet: "Sweet Spring, thou turn'st with all thy goodly train."
Sonnet: "What doth it serve to see sun's burning face."

Spring Bereaved.
The Statue of Medusa.
Stolen Pleasure.
Summons to Love.
Tell Me No More.
This Life, Which Seems So Fair.
Thrice Happy He.
To a Nightingale.
To Chloris.
To His Lute.
To Sir William, of Hawthornden Alexander.
The Trojan Horse.
The World a Hunt.
Dryden, John
Absalom and Achitophel.
Achitophel: the Earl of Shaftesbury.
Ah Fading Joy.
Alexander's Feast.
Alexander's Feast, or, the Power of Music.
All for Love.
Amboyna; or, The Cruelties of the Dutch....
Amphitrion.
Annus Mirabilis.
The Art of Poetry.
Astraea Redux.
Aureng-Zebe.
Calm Was the Even.
The Character of a Good Person.
The Church's Testimony.
The Churches of Rome and of England.
Cleopatra and Antony.
Confessio Fidei.
The Conquest of Granada.
Cymon and Iphigenia.
Diana's Hunting-Song.
Epilogue Spoken at Oxford by Mrs. Marshall.
Epilogue Spoken by Mrs. Boutell.
Epilogue to Mithridates, King of Pontus.
Epitaph Intended for His Wife.
An Evening's Love.
The Fable of Acis, Polyphemus, and Galatea.
Fair Iris and Her Swain.
Farewell ungrateful traitor.
The Fear of Death.
Finite Reason.
Happiness.
Happy the Man.
Harvest Home.
Heroique Stanzas, Consecrated to the Glorious Memory...
The Hind and the Panther.
Horat. Ode 29. Book 3. Paraphras'd in Pindarique Verse.
Hourly I Die.
How Happy the Lover.
I Feed a Flame Within.
Incantation to Oedipus.
The Indian Emperor.
The Indian Queen: Song of Aerial Spirits.
Jacob Tonson, His Publisher.
Juvenal's Sixth Satire.
King Arthur.
King James II.
Kiss Me, Dear.
The Lady's Song.
The Latter Part of the Third Book of Lucretius...

Lines Printed under the
  Engraved Portrait of Milton.
London after the Great Fire,
  1666.
Long Betwixt Love and Fear.
Lord Shaftesbury.
Love's Fancy.
The Loyal General: Prologue.
MacFlecknoe.
MacFlecknoe, or a Satire
  upon the True-Blue
  Protestant Poet T.S.
The Medal.
Mercury's Song to Phaedra.
Midnight.
The New London.
No, No, Poor Suffering Heart.
The Oak.
The Ode on St. Cecilia's Day.
An Ode on the Death of Mr.
  Henry Purcell (excerpt).
Of the Pythagorean
  Philosophy.
On Jacob Tonson, His
  Publisher.
On the Death of Mr. Purcell.
Palamon and Arcite, III:
  "Parts of the whole are we;
  but God the whole."
The Popish Plot.
Prologue to Aureng-Zebe.
Prologue to Love Triumphant.
Prologue to The Tempest.
Prologue to the University of
  Oxford, 1673...
Religio Laici.
Rondelay.
The Second Part of Absalom
  and Achitophel.
Secret-Love.
The Secular Masque.
Sigismonda and Guiscardo.
Sir Fopling Flutter.
A Song: "Fair, sweet and
  young, receive a prize."
Song for a Girl.
A Song from the Italian.
The Song of Momus to Mars.
Song to a Fair, Young Lady,
  Going out of the Town in
  the Spring.
Songs from the Secular
  Masque: Diana.
The Spanish Friar.
The State of Innocence.
Sylvia the Fair.
Sylvoe: A Song.
The Third Satire of Juvenal.
Thomas Shadwell the Poet.
To His Sacred Majesty, a
  Panegyrick...
To Mrs. Anne Killigrew.
To My Dear Friend Mr.
  Congreve, on His Comedy...
To My Friend, Dr. Charleton,
  on His Learned and Useful
  Works.
To My Honour'd Kinsman,
  John Driden...
To the Memory of Mr.
  Oldham.
To the Pious Memory of the
  Accomplisht Young Lady
  Mrs. Anne Killigrew.
Troilus and Cressida.
Tyrannic Love.
Upon the Death of the Earl of
  Dundee.
Upon the Death of the Lord
  Hastings.
Upon the Death of the
  Viscount of Dundee.

Veni Crator Spiritus,
  Translated in Paraphrase.
Vox Populi.
What Is the World?
Whilst Alexis Lay Prest.
Why Should a Foolish
  Marriage Vow.
The Zambra Dance.
Zimri.
Dryden, Myrtle May
Just Forget.
Dube, Janet
Autobiography.
So to Tell the Truth.
Du Bellay, Joachim
Antiquitez de Rome.
Heureux Qui, Comme Ulysse,
  A Fait Un Beau Voyage.
Hymn to the Winds.
Pale Is Death.
Returning Home.
Rome.
Ruines of Rome.
Sonnet.
A Sonnet to Heavenly Beauty.
To His Friend in Elysium.
The Visions.
A Vow to Heavenly Venus.
Dubie, Norman
Alehouse Sonnets: The
  Dressing Station.
At Midsummer.
Balalaika.
The Circus Ringmaster's
  Apology to God.
Coleridge Crossing the Plain
  of Jars: 1833.
Comes Winter, the Sea
  Hunting.
The Composer's Winter
  Dream.
Elegy to the Sioux.
Elizabeth's War with the
  Christmas Bear: 1601.
The Everlastings.
February: The Boy Breughel.
The Fox Who Watched for
  the Midnight Sun.
The Funeral.
The Ganges.
The Hours.
In the Dead of the Night.
Monologue of Two Moons,
  Nudes with Crests. 1938.
Norway.
Parish.
Pastoral.
Sacrifice of a Virgin in the
  Mayan Ball Court.
There Is a Dream Dreaming
  Us.
**Du Bois, William Edward
Burghardt**
A litany of Atlanta.
The Song of the Smoke.
Duche, Jacob
Chilled by the Blasts of
  Adverse Fate.
Great Lord of All, Whose
  Work of Love.
Ducic, Jovan
The Clock.
Duck, Stephen
On Mites, To a Lady.
The Thresher's Labour.
Duckett, Alfred A.
Portrait Philippines.
Sonnet: "Where are we to go
  when this is done?"

**Duclaux, Agnes Mary Frances
(Mme Emile Duclaux)** See
**Robinson, Agnes Mary
Frances**
Dudek, Louis
An Air by Sammartini.
Coming Suddenly to the Sea.
Dawn.
The Dead.
Europe.
Garcia Lorca.
I Have Seen the Robins Fall.
The Jungle.
Morning Light.
The Mountains.
Mouths.
Narrative.
Old Song.
The Pomegranate.
A Store-House.
A Street in April.
Dudley, Dorothy
La Rue de la Montagne
  Sainte-Genevieve.
Dudley, Thomas
Verses Found in Thomas
  Dudley's Pocket after His
  Death.
Dudley, William E.
The City, Lord, Where Thy
  Dear Life.
Duemer, Joseph
Curses.
Duer, Caroline
An International Episode.
A Portrait.
A Word to the Wise.
Duerden, Richard
Dance with Banderillas.
Moon Is to Blood.
Musica No.
Duewel, Wesley
On with the Message.
Dufault, Peter Kane
Black Jess.
Evensong.
In an Old Orchard.
A Letter for Allhallows.
Notes on a Girl.
Odysseus' Song to Calypso.
On Aesthetics, More or Less.
Owl.
Possibilities.
Thalamos.
Tour de Force.
Duff, Esther Lilian
Black and White.
Lad's Love.
Not Three–But One.
Of a Certain Green-Eyed
  Monster.
Duff, James L.
Cradle Song.
The Loan of a Stall.
Dufferin, Helen Selina, Lady See
also **Sheridan, Helen Selina**
The Charming Woman.
Duffett, Thomas
To Francelia.
Duffield, Samuel Willoughby
The Willis.
Duffield, Jr., George
Stand Up for Jesus.
Duffy, Charles Gavan
The Irish Rapparees.
Duffy, John
The Annunciation.
Our Lady's Labor.
Ox-Bone Madonna.
Duffy, Maureen
Evesong.

Sonnet: "Afterwards there are
  dogends in the ashtray."
Duffy, Nona Keen
Above the Stable.
Spring Is in the Making.
Dugan, Alan
Actual Vision of Morning's
  Extrusion.
Adultery.
American against Solitude.
Aside.
Dedication for a Building.
Elegy for a Puritan
  Conscience.
Fabrication of Ancestors.
For an Obligate Parasite.
For Masturbation.
From Heraclitus.
From Rome. For More Public
  Fountains in New York City.
Funeral Oration for a Mouse.
How We Heard the Name.
Let Heroes Account to Love.
Love Song: I and Thou.
Memorial Service for the
  Invasion Beach Where the
  Vacation....
Memories of Verdun.
The Mirror Perilous.
Morning Song.
Niagara Falls.
On a Professional Couple in a
  Side-Show.
On a Seven-Day Diary.
On Alexander and Aristotle,
  on a Black-on-Red Greek
  Plate.
On an East Wind from the
  Wars.
On Don Juan del Norte, Not
  Don Juan Tenorio del Sur.
On Hurricane Jackson.
On Rape Unattempted.
On Visiting Central Park Zoo.
On When McCarthy Was a
  Wolf among a Nation of
  Queer-Queers.
Plague of Dead Sharks.
Poem: "The person who can
  do."
Poem: "What's the balm."
Prison Song.
Stutterer.
Thesis, Antithesis, and
  Nostalgia.
To a Red-Headed Do-Good
  Waitress.
A Trial.
Tribute to Kafka for Someone
  Taken.
Untitled Poem.
Wall, Cave, and Pillar
  Statements, After Asoka.
Winter's Onset from an
  Alienated Point of View.
Dugan, Mrs. D. H.
Christ Is Risen!
Duganne, A. J. H.
Bethel.
Dugdale, Norman
Anarchist.
Duggan, Eileen
After the Annunciation.
Ballad of the Bushman.
The Bushfeller.
Contrast.
Epiphany.
Interlude.
Juniper.
The Last Song.
The Milker.
The Musterer.

The Name.
Peasantry.
Pilgrimage.
Presumption.
The Tides Run Up the
  Wairau.
Victory.
Dugmore, H. H.
  A Reminiscence of 1820.
Du Guillet, Pernette
  Chanson: "If they say my
    furred cloak."
  Epigram.
Duke, Richard
  After the fiercest pangs of hot
    desire.
  An Epithalamium upon the
    Marriage of Captain William
    Bedloe.
  A Panegyric upon Oates.
Duke, William
  Hail Our Incarnate God!
"Dum Dum" *See* Kendall, John
  Kaye
Dumas, Alexandre
  The Lady of the Pearls
    (excerpt).
Dumas, Edmund
  Our School Now Closes Out.
Dumas, Henry
  America.
  Black Star Line.
  Black Trumpeter.
  Buffalo.
  Image.
  Knock on Wood.
Du Maurier, George
  A Legend of Camelot.
  Limerick: "A Potsdam, les
    totaux absteneurs."
  Limerick: "Chaque epoque a
    ses grands noms sonores."
  Limerick: "Il etait un
    gendarme a Nanteuil."
  Limerick: "It etait un Hebreu
    de Hambourg."
  A Lost Illusion.
  Music (after Sully
    Prudhomme).
  Trilby.
  Vers Nonsensiques.
Dunann, Louella
  Hot Line.
Dunbar, Paul Laurence
  Accountability.
  After the Quarrel.
  Angelina.
  An Ante-Bellum Sermon.
  A Boy's Summer Song.
  Compensation.
  The Conquerors.
  A Corn-Song.
  Curtain!
  Dawn.
  A Death Song.
  The Debt.
  Differences.
  Encouraged.
  Equipment.
  Ere Sleep Comes down to
    Soothe the Weary Eyes.
  Frederick Douglass.
  Get Somebody Else.
  Harriet Beecher Stowe.
  The Haunted Oak.
  Howdy, Honey, Howdy!
  A Hymn.
  In the Morning.
  Keep A-Pluggin' Away.
  Li'l' Gal.
  Life.
  The Little Black Sheep.

Little Brown Baby.
Lover's Lane.
Lullaby.
The Master-Player.
Misapprehension.
My Sort o' Man.
A Negro Love Song.
Ode to Ethiopia.
The Old Cabin.
On the Road.
The Paradox.
The Party.
Philosophy.
The Poet.
A Prayer.
Precedent.
Retort.
Ships That Pass in the Night.
Soliloquy of a Turkey.
A Song.
Song of Summer.
A Spiritual.
Sympathy.
Theology.
To a Captious Critic.
The Unsung Heroes.
We Wear the Mask.
When a Feller's Itchin' to Be
  Spanked.
When All Is Done.
When de Co'n Pone's Hot.
When Dey 'Listed Colored
  Soldiers.
When Malindy Sings.
Dunbar, William
  The Amendis to the Telyouris
    and Sowtaris...
  Ane Ballat of Our Lady.
  The Ballad of Kynd Kittok.
  The Book of Two Married
    Women and the Widow.
  The Dance of the Seven
    Deadly Sins.
  Done Is a Battell on the
    Dragon Blak.
  Flyting of Dunbar and
    Kennedy.
  Followis How Dumbar Wes
    Desyrd to Be Ane Freir.
  The Golden Targe.
  A Hymn to Mary.
  In Secreit Place This Hyndir
    Nycht.
  Lament for the Makaris.
  The Man of Valour to His
    Fair Lady.
  Manere of the Crying of Ane
    Playe.
  Meditation in Winter.
  O Wretch, Beware.
  On the Nativity of Christ.
  On the Resurrection of Christ.
  The Petition of the Gray
    Horse, Auld Dunbar.
  Quod Dunbar to Kennedy.
  Remonstrance to the King.
  Rorate Coeli Desuper.
  The Testament of Mr. Andro
    Kennedy.
  The Thrissil and the Rois.
  To a Lady.
  To Aberdein.
  To the City of London.
  To the Merchantis of
    Edinburgh.
  The Tretis of the Tua Mariit
    Wemen and the Wedo.
  The Twa Mariit Wemen and
    the Wedo.
Dunbar-Nelson, Alice
  Music.
  Snow in October.

Duncan, Mary L.
  Jesus Tender Shepherd.
Duncan, Rea Lubar
  Juncture.
Duncan, Robert
  An African Elegy.
  After a Passage in Baudelaire.
  As in the Old Days: Passages
    8.
  At Christmas.
  At the Loom.
  The Ballad of Mrs. Noah.
  Bending the Bow.
  Coming out of.
  Correspondences.
  The Dance.
  Dante.
  Dream Data.
  Envoy.
  Eyesight II.
  The Fire.
  Food for Fire, Food for
    Thought.
  Fourth Song the Night Nurse
    Sang.
  Hero Song.
  Homage and Lament for Ezra
    Pound in Captivity.
  Ingmar Bergman's Seventh
    Seal.
  The Interlude.
  The Lover.
  A Morning Letter.
  My Mother Would Be a
    Falconress.
  A New Poem (for Jack
    Spicer).
  Night Scenes.
  Often I Am Permitted to
    Return to a Meadow.
  An Owl Is an Only Bird of
    Poetry.
  A Part-Sequence for Change.
  Passage Over Water.
  Persephone.
  A Poem beginning with a
    Line by Pindar.
  Poetry, a Natural Thing.
  The Question.
  The Reaper.
  Returning to Roots of First
    Feeling.
  Roots and Branches.
  Shelley's Arethusa Set to New
    Measures.
  The Song of the Borderguard.
  Sonnet.
  A Spring Memorandum.
  Strains of Sight.
  Structure of Rime.
  Such Is the Sickness of Many
    a Good Thing.
  The Temple of the Animals.
  These Past Years: Passages 10.
  This Place Rumord to Have
    Been Sodom.
  The Torso: Passages 18.
  Tribal Memories.
  Two Presentations.
  Up Rising.
  What I Saw: Passages 3.
Duncan, Ronald
  Written on a Girl's Table-
    Napkin at Wiesbaden.
Dunetz, Lora
  The Ailing Parent.
  All That Summer.
  And All the While the Sky Is
    Falling...
  Black Cat.
  On the Night Express to
    Madrid.

Treason.
While the Bells Ring.
Winter Nights.
Dunkels, Marjorie
  Faith.
Dunkin, William
  An Epistle to R.
Dunlop, John
  Dinna Ask Me.
  The Year That's Awa'.
Dunn, Alta Booth
  Unknown Soldier.
Dunn, Douglas
  After the War.
  The Clothes Pit.
  A Dream of Judgement.
  Emblems.
  The Estuarial Republic.
  Glasgow Schoolboys, Running
    Backwards.
  Green Breeks.
  The House Next Door.
  The Musical Orchard.
  On Roofs of Terry Street.
  The Patricians.
  Remembering Lunch.
  A Removal from Terry Street.
  Supreme Death.
  War Blinded.
  Warriors.
  Washing the Coins.
Dunn, Gwen
  Journey Back to Christmas.
Dunn, Max
  Flower of Exile.
  I Danced Before I Had Two
    Feet.
  O, Where Were We before
    Time Was.
Dunn, Stephen P.
  Beached Whales Off Margate.
  Building a Person.
  Building in Nova Scotia.
  California, This Is Minnesota
    Speaking.
  Day and Night Handball.
  Fable of the Water Merchants.
  I Come Home Wanting to
    Touch Everyone.
  Looking for a Rest Area.
  On Hearing the Airlines Will
    Use a Psychological Profile...
  Poem for People Who Are
    Understandably Too Busy to
    Read Poetry.
  Prayer of the Young Stoic.
  The Rapist.
  Small Town: The Friendly.
  Tangier.
Dunnam, Ouida Smith
  Prayer of a Beginning
    Teacher.
Dunne, Carol
  Nursing the Hide.
Dunning, Stephen
  Player.
Dunsany, Edward John, Lord
  Bringing Him Up.
  A Call to the Wild.
  The Deserted Kingdom.
  A Heterodoxy.
  The Memory.
  On the Safe Side.
Dupree, Edgar
  The Light of Faith.
Du Priest, Travis
  Experiential Religion.
Durack, Mary
  Red Jack.
Durand, Oswald
  The Black Man's Son.

Durcan, Paul
Combe Florey.
General Vallancey's Waltz.
In Memory of Those
  Murdered in the Dublin
  Massacre, May 1974.
Ireland 1972.
Ireland 1977.
The Kilfenora Teaboy.
Letter to Ben, 1972.
Making Love outside Aras an
  Uachtarain.
Micheal Mac Liammoir.
Nessa.
November 1967.
Sally.
They Say the Butterfly Is the
  Hardest Stroke.
Durem, Ray
Award.
Basic.
Friends.
I Know I'm Not Sufficiently
  Obscure.
Problem in Social Geometry–
  The Inverted Square!
Ultimate Equality.
Vet's Rehabilitation.
You Know, Joe.
D'Urfey, Thomas
Bright Was the Morning.
Chloe Divine.
Dialogue, between Crab and
  Gillian.
The Fisherman's Song.
I'll Sail upon the Dog-star.
The Newmarket Song.
Sawney Was Tall.
Scotch Song.
A Shepherd Kept Sheep on a
  Hill So High.
Solon's Song.
A Song: "Boast no more fond
  Love, thy Power."
The Winchester Wedding.
Durgnat, Raymond
Scrap Iron.
Durham, Richard V.
Dawn Patrol: Chicago.
Durivage, Francis Alexander
Chez Brebant.
Durrell, Lawrence
The Adepts.
Alexandria.
At Epidaurus.
A Ballad of the Good Lord
  Nelson.
Ballad of the Oedipus
  Complex.
Conon in Alexandria.
Coptic Poem.
Cradle Song.
The Death of General
  Uncebunke: A Biography in
  Little.
Delos.
Eight Aspects of Melissa.
Epitaph.
Green Coconuts: Rio.
In Arcadia.
In Crisis.
In the Garden: Villa
  Cleobolus.
Lesbos.
Levant.
Mythology.
Nemea.
On First Looking into Loeb's
  Horace.
On Seeming to Presume.
Owed to America.
Paphos.

Poggio.
Salamis.
Sarajevo.
Seferis.
Stoic.
Swans.
This Unimportant Morning.
To Argos.
To Ping-Ku, Asleep.
Visitations.
A Water-Colour of Venice.
Durston, Georgia Roberts
The Hippopotamus.
The Rabbit.
Duryee, Mary Ballard
Homestead-Winter Morning.
Du Toit, J.D. *See* "Jotius"
Dutt, Aru
Still Barred Thy Doors.
Dutt, Michael Madhusudan
Satan.
Dutt, Toru
Our Casuarina Tree.
Dutton, G. J. F.
February Thaw.
Hut.
Magma.
Of Only a Single Poem.
Dutton, Geoffrey
Burning Off.
A Finished Gentleman.
Fish Shop Windows.
January.
Nightflight and Sunrise.
A Prisoner Freed.
The Stranded Whales.
The Temple by the Sea.
Time of Waiting.
Variations on a Medieval
  Theme.
Duval, Quinton
Absent Star.
I Point Out a Bird.
Morning Fog.
Du Vall, Jack
Metroliner.
Duvar, John Hunter
La Belle Sauvage.
Dwight, Timothy
As Down a Valley.
The Assault on the Fortress.
Columbia.
I Love Thy Kingdom, Lord.
Shall Man, O God of Light.
Sing to the Lord Most High.
The Smooth Divine.
Star of Columbia.
To the Federal Convention.
The Triumph of Infidelity.
Dwyer, Frank
On the Edge.
Dyer, John
British Commerce.
The Enquiry.
The Fleece.
Grongar Hill.
My Ox Duke.
A Nation's Wealth.
The Ruins of Rome.
To Clio. From Rome.
The Wool Trade.
Dyer, Lady Catherine
Epitaph on the Monument of
  Sir William Dyer at
  Colmworth, 1641.
Dyer, Sir Edward
Corydon to His Phyllis.
Cynthia.
Fancy, Farewell.
Lowest Trees Have Tops.
My Mind to Me a Kingdom
  Is.

Where One Would Be.
Dylan, Bob
Dear Mister Congressman.
Desolation Row.
Mister Tambourine Man.
Sad-Eyed Lady of the
  Lowlands.
Subterranean Homesick Blues.
Dyment, Clifford
As a Boy with a Richness of
  Needs I Wandered.
The Axe in the Wood.
The Children.
Fox.
Man and Beast.
Pastoral.
Sea Shanty.
Secret Idiom: Sanctuary.
A Sitch Cut in April.
The Snow.
The Swans.
The Temple.
To London the Train Gallops,
  Its Shrill Steel Hooves'.
Dyson, Edward
Cleaning Up.
A Friendly Game of Football.
The Old Whim Horse.
Dyson, Will
Death Is but Death.
The Trucker.
Dzyubin, Edward *See*
"Bagritsky, Edward"

E

"E-Yeh-Shure" (Louise Abeita)
Beauty.
"Eagle, Solomon" *See* **Squire,
Sir John Collings**
Eakman, Florence
Our Clock.
Earle, Virginia
A Dream as Reported.
Earley, Tom
Jackdaw.
The Moorhen Pond.
Earls, Michael
To a Carmelite Postulant.
"Eastaway, Edward" *See*
Thomas, Edward
Eastburn, James Wallis
O Holy, Holy, Holy Lord.
Easter, Marguerite Elizabeth
My Laddie's Hounds.
Eastman, Barrett
How We Burned the
  Philadelphia.
Joy Enough.
Richard Somers.
Eastman, Charles Gamage
Dirge.
Eastman, Elaine Goodale
Ashes of Roses.
Baby.
A Countrywoman of Mine.
Goldenrod.
Eastman, Jon
Working the Skeet House.
Eastman, Max
Animal.
The April Earth.
At the Aquarium.
Diogenes.
Egrets.
A Hymn to God in Time of
  Stress.
Invocation.

Rainy Song.
We Have Been Happy.
Eastman, Sophie E.
A Spool of Thread.
Eastwick, Ivy O.
Birthday Cake.
Birthday Garden.
Dark Danny.
Elizabeth Ann Peabody.
First Snow.
Hurry Tomorrow.
I'm Glad My Birthday Comes
  in May!
Jack-in-the-Pulpit.
Lucy Lavender.
Mary's Lullaby.
May Mornings.
Mickleham Way.
Midsummer Magic.
Mother and Child.
My True Love.
The Robber.
Seven Today.
Shadow Dance.
Sing a Song of Moonlight.
Sing a Song of Sunshine.
Stay, Christmas!
Timothy Boon.
Waking Time.
Where's Mary?
Winter in the Wood.
Eaton, Anthony
The Dove Apologizes to His
  God for Being Caught by a
  Cat.
**Eaton, Arthur Wentworth
Hamilton**
The Egyptian Lotus.
The Phantom Light of the
  Baie des Chaleurs.
Pray for the Dead.
Eaton, Burnham
Technique.
Eaton, Charles Edward
The Cubistic Lovers.
A Peony for Apollo.
Seascape with Bookends.
Eaton, Evelyn
The Gardener.
Eaton, Walter Prichard
A White-Throat Sings.
The Willows.
Ebberts, Ruth N.
Kitchen Window.
Ebeling, Georgia Moore
The Centuries Are His.
Eberhardt, Richard
Ode to the Chinese Paper
  Snake.
Eberhart, Nelle Richmond
At Dawning.
Eberhart, Richard
The Advantage of the Outside.
Analogue of Unity in
  Multeity.
As If You Had Never Been.
At Lake Geneva.
At Night.
Ball Game.
Burr Oaks: The Attic.
The Cancer Cells.
Chiliasm.
La Crosse at Ninety Miles an
  Hour.
Dam Neck, Virginia.
The Enigma.
Fear Death by Water.
The Fisher Cat.
Flux.
For a Lamb.
The Forgotten Rock.
From Four Lakes' Days.

The Fury of Aerial Bombardment.
Gnat on My Paper.
Go to the Shine That's on a Tree.
The Goal of Intellectual Man.
The Groundhog.
Half-Bent Man.
Hardy Perennial.
The Horse Chestnut Tree.
The Human Being Is a Lonely Creature.
I Walked Out to the Graveyard to See the Dead.
I Walked over the Grave of Henry James.
I Went to See Irving Babbitt.
If I Could Only Live at the Pitch That Is near Madness.
If This Be Love.
Imagining How It Would Be to Be Dead.
In a Hard Intellectual Light.
In After Time.
In the Garden.
The Incomparable Light.
It Is That Bane of Self in Love.
Kaire.
The Largess.
A Legend of Viable Women.
Light, 2.
Long Term Suffering.
A Loon Call.
The Lost Children.
Man Is God's Nature.
A Man of Sense.
Marrakech.
The Matin Pandemoniums.
Maze.
A Meditation.
The Moment of Vision.
Mysticism Has Not the Patience to Wait for God's Revelation.
A New England Bachelor.
New Hampshire, February.
On a Squirrel Crossing the Road in Autumn, in New England.
On Shooting Particles beyond the World.
Passage.
Plain Song Talk.
The Preacher Sought to Find Out Acceptable Words.
Rainscapes, Hydrangeas, Roses, and Singing Birds.
Reading Room, the New York Public Library.
The Recapitulation.
Remember the Source.
The Rich Interior Life.
The Roc.
Rumination.
Sainte Anne de Beaupre.
Sea Bells.
Sea Burial from the Cruiser "Reve."
Sea-Hawk.
Sea-Ruck.
Seals, Terns, Time.
A Ship Burning and a Comet All in One Day.
A Snowfall.
The Soul Longs to Return Whence It Came.
The Spider.
Spring Mountain Climb.
A Stone.
Stone Words for Robert Lowell.

Storm and Quiet.
Things Known: Under the Hill.
To Auden on His Fiftieth.
To Evan.
To the Field Mice.
The Tobacconist of Eighth Street.
Two Loves.
Ur Burial.
Vast Light.
Vision.
When Doris Danced.
The Wisdom of Insecurity.
Words.
World War.

Eberly, Ralph D.
Prodigal's Return.

Ebon
The Easter Bunny Blues; or, All I Want for Xmas Is the Loop.
The Prophet's Warning; or, Shoot to Kill.
Query.
To our First Born.

Ebright, Frederick
Memorial to the Great Big Beautiful Self-Sacrificing Advertisers.

Echeruo, Michael
Melting Pot.

Eckman, Frederick
Aka.
Lullaby.

Economou, George
Poem for a Suicide.
Seventh Georgic.

Eddy, Gary
Fishing with Buddies.
High Field–First Day of Winter.

Eddy, Mary Baker
O'er Waiting Harp-Strings of the Mind.
Shepherd, Show Me How to Go.

Eddy, Zachary
Floods Swell Around Me, Angry, Appalling.
Jesus, Enthroned and Glorified.

Edelman, Elaine
How Beautiful You Are: 3.

Edelman, Katherine
Irish Grandmother.
Saturday Shopping.

Edelstein, Hyman
Indian Night Tableau.
Last Mathematician.
Palimpsest.

Eden, Helen Parry
Four-Paws.
The Poet and the Wood-Louse.
A Prayer for St. Innocent's Day.
Sorrow.
To a Little Girl.
To Betsey-Jane, on Her Desiring to Go Incontinently to Heaven.

Edey, Marion
August Afternoon.
Christmas Eve.
Midsummer Night.
Our Birthday.

Edfelt, Johannes
Life of Life.

Edgar, Marriott
The Lion and Albert.

Edgar, Mary S.
The Camp Hymn.

Edman, Irwin
Advice to a Young Man (of Letters)...
The Curse of Faint Praise.
La Donna e Perpetuum Mobile.
Flower for a Professor's Garden of Verses.
The Kiss-Fest.
The New Hellas.
Peace.
Prayer for All Poets at This Time.
To Harold Jacoby.

Edmeston, James
An Evening Blessing.
Prayer to the Trinity.

Edmond, Lauris
3 A. M.
Commercial Traveller.
A Difficult Adjustment.
Going to Moscow.
Love Poem.
The Names.
The Sums.
Three Women.
Town Ghost.
Wellington Letter: XI.

Edmond, Murray
An Afternoon in the Garden.
My Return to Czechoslovakia.
A Patching Together: The Cell Lay inside Her Body.
Stopping the Heart.
Telephoning It.

Edmondson, Madeleine
Witches' Spells.

Edmunds, William H.
To Be or Not to Be (parody).

Edson, C. L.
Ravin's of Piute Poet Poe (parody).

Edson, Russell
The Automobile.
The Childhood of an Equestrian.
Children.
A Cottage in the Wood.
Counting Sheep.
The Death of an Angel.
The Fall.
In All the Days of My Childhood.
In the Forest.
A Journey through the Moonlight.
The Little Lady.
The Long Picnic.
The Mouse Dinners.
An Old Man's Son.
Out of Whack.
A Performance at Hog Theater.
The Pilot.
The Prophylactic.
The Retirement of the Elephant.
The Wheelbarrow.
When the God Returns.
The Wounded Breakfast.

Edwards, Amelia Blandford
Give Me Three Grains of Corn, Mother.

Edwards, Archie
What Though the Dark!

Edwards, Harry
How to Change the U.S.A.

Edwards, Jeannette Slocomb
Hester Macdonagh.

Edwards, Mathilda Betham
The Pansy and the Prayer-Book.

Edwards, Matilda C.
The Church Walking with the World.

Edwards, Osman
Residential Rhymes (excerpt).

Edwards, Richard
Amantium Irae.
May.
Of Women.

Edwards, Solomon
Brothers.
Dream.
Shoplifter.

Edwards, Thomas
On the Edition of Mr. Pope's Works with a Commentary and Notes.
Sonnet On a Family Picture.

Eedes, Richard
No Love, to Love of Man and Wife.
Of Man and Wife.

Eeinmar von Zweter, Sir
Fortitude.

Egan, Maurice Francis
Columbus the World-Giver.
He Made Us Free.
Madonna of the Empty Arms.
Maurice de Guerin.
The Old Violin.
The Shamrock.
Vigil of the Immaculate Conception.

Egar, J. H.
Sing, Sing for Christmas.

Egemo, Constance
The Great Wave off Kanagwa.

Egerton, Helen Merrill
Sandpipers.

Egerton, Sarah Fyge
The Emulation.

Eggerth, Chuck
Much of Me.

Eglington, Charles
Arrival and Departure.
Buffalo.
Lourenco Marques.
The Lowveld.
The Vanquished.

"Eglinton, John" (William Kirkpatrick Magee)
The Winds.

Eguren, Jose Maria
The Abbey.
The Horse.

Ehrenburg, Ilya
Our Children's Children Will Marvel.
The Sons of Our Sons.
The Tree.
The Trumpet.
War Poem.

Ehrenstein, Albert
Ares.
Home-Coming.
Homer.
Suffering.

Ehrhart, W. D.
Money in the Bank.
To Maynard on the Long Road Home.
Turning Thirty.

Ehrlich, Gretel
Cutting Wood on Shell Creek.
The Orchard.
A Sheerancher Named John.
A Way of Speaking.

Ehrlich, Helen
Love Song to Lucy.

Lucy Answers.
Ehrlich, Shelley
On Linden Street.
Ehrlichman, Lester
On Reading Mr. Ytche
Bashes' Stories in Yiddish.
Ehrmann, Max
Away.
The Hate and the Love of the
World.
I Ponder on Life.
If You Made Gentler the
Churlish World.
Mother.
A Prayer.
Eibel, Deborah
Freethinkers.
Hagar to Ishmael.
The Kabbalist.
Eichendorff, Baron Joseph von
The Old Garden.
Poet-Hearts.
Returning Spring.
Eichenrand, Lazer
From Life.
The Mute City.
Prologue.
Eifuku, Empress
We Dressed Each Other.
Eigner, Larry
After Shiki.
All Intents.
B.
The Bare Tree/Alternate.
Bird Shadows Mounting.
The Closed System.
The Dark Swimmers.
Do It Yrself.
The Dog Yelped.
Don't Go.
Elysee.
Environ S.
A Fete.
Flake Diamond of/the Sea.
Fleche...
From the Sustaining Air.
A Gone.
I Have Felt It as They've
Said.
Keep Me Still, for I Do Not
Want to Dream.
Letter for Duncan.
Noise Grimaced.
Open.
Passages.
Remember Sabbath Days.
The School Bus.
The Shock.
A Sleep.
That the Neighborhood Might
Be Covered.
Unusual.
A Version of a Song of
Failure.
Washing between the
Buildings.
A Weekday.
The Wind Like an Ocean.
Eiseley, Loren C.
The Deserted Homestead.
The Spider.
Winter Sign.
Eisenberg, Emanuel
Reflections in a Hospital.
Eisenberg, Susan
Grandpa Bear.
Eisler, Hans and Bertolt Brecht
United Front.
Ejong, Yityangu ("New")
Long Song.

Ela, David H.
The Chosen Three, on
Mountain Height.
Elam, William C.
The Mecklenburg Declaration.
Eldan, Anadad
Samson Rends His Clothes.
Words That Speak of Death.
Elder, Anne
Carried Away.
Farmer Goes Berserk.
One Foot in the Door.
School Cadets.
Eldridge, Paul
To a Courtesan a Thousand
Years Dead.
Wang Peng's
Recommendation for
Improving the People.
Eleanore, Sister Mary
The Vocation of St. Francis.
Eleazar
Thy Faithful Sons.
Eliot, George
At Set of Sun.
Brother and Sister.
Count That Day Lost.
I Am Lonely.
O May I Join the Choir
Invisible.
The Spanish Gypsy (excerpt).
Stradivarius: Working with
God.
The Tide of Faith.
Two Lovers.
Eliot, Henrietta Robins
Snowflakes.
Eliot, Thomas Stearns
The Ad-dressing of Cats.
Animula.
Ash-Wednesday.
Aunt Helen.
The Boston Evening
Transcript.
Burbank with a Baedeker:
Bleistein with a Cigar.
Cat Morgan Introduces
Himself.
Chorus from the Rock–III.
Conversation Galante.
Cousin Nancy.
The Cultivation of Christmas
Trees.
Death by Water.
A Dedication to My Wife.
The Dove.
East Coker.
Eyes That Last I Saw in
Tears.
La Figlia Che Piange.
Four Quartets.
Fragment of an Agon.
Gerontion.
Growltiger's Last Stand.
Gus: the Theatre Cat.
The Hippopotamus.
The Hollow Men.
Journey of the Magi.
Landscapes.
Lines for an Old Man.
Lines for Cuscuscaraway and
Mirza Murad Ali Beg.
Lines to Ralph Hodgson,
Esqre.
The Love Song of J. Alfred
Prufrock.
Macavity: the Mystery Cat.
Marina.
Morning at the Window.
Mr. Apollinax.
Murder in the Cathedral.
The Naming of Cats.

Portrait of a Lady.
Preludes.
Rhapsody on a Windy Night.
The Rock.
The Rum Tum Tugger.
Salutation.
Skimbleshanks: the Railway
Cat.
A Song for Simeon.
The Song of the Jellicles.
Sweeney Among the
Nightingales.
Sweeney Erect.
There Shall Always Be the
Church.
Triumphal March.
The Waste Land.
Whispers of Immortality.
Why Should Men Love the
Church?
The Wind Sprang up at Four
O'Clock.
Eliyia, Joseph
Dream.
Epilogue.
Rebecca.
Slender Maid.
Your Passing, Fleet Passing.
**Elizabeth, Empress of Austria-
Hungary**
Inscription on a Shrine Near
Ischl.
Elizabeth I, Queen of England
The Doubt of Future Foes.
Limerick: "The daughter of
debate."
On Fortune.
When I Was Fair and Young.
Written in Her French
Psalter.
Written on a Wall at
Woodstock.
Written with a Diamond on
Her Window at Woodstock.
Youth and Cupid.
Elledge, Jim
Running the Trotline.
Ellenbogen, George
The Announcement.
Unter der Linde.
Eller, David
To a God Unknown.
Ellerton, John Lodge
The Day Thou Gavest.
The God of the Living.
Now the Laborer's Task Is
O'er.
Elliot, Gilbert
Amynta.
Elliot, Henry Rutherford
Laugh It Off.
Elliot, Jane
The Flowers of the Forest.
Elliot, Jean
Exercise in a Meadow.
Elliott, Charlotte
The Hour of Prayer.
Just As I Am.
My Soul Shall Cling to Thee.
Watch and Pray.
Elliott, Ebenezer
Battle Song.
Beware of Dogmas.
Caged Rats.
Donought Would Have
Everything.
Drone v. Worker.
Epigram: "Paddy, I have but
stol'n your living."
Epigram: "Prepare to meet the
King of Terrors."
The Four Dears.

The Fox-Hunters.
God Save the People.
How Different!
Inscription.
On a Rose in December.
On Communists.
Plaint.
Song: "Child, Is Thy Father
Dead?"
Song: "When working
blackguards come to blows."
Spirits and Men (excerpt).
The Splendid Village.
Steam (excerpt).
The Tree of Rivelin.
When Wilt Thou Save the
People?
Elliott, George P.
Her Dwarf.
Sayer.
Elliott, Harley
After Picking Rosehips.
Animals That Stand in
Dreams: The Panda.
Blessed and Resting Uncle.
Brothers Together in Winter.
Crazy Horse Returns to South
Dakota.
For the Man Who Stole a
Rose.
Landscape Workers.
The Natural Order of Things.
Numbers.
On a Country Road.
The Planting.
Thinking Twice in the
Laundromat.
Elliott, Mary
Think before You Act.
Ellis, Colin
Adder's Epigrams.
Bungaloid Growth.
An Epitaph.
International Conference.
The Modern World.
The New Vicar of Bray.
The Old Ladies.
On a Gentleman Marrying
His Cook.
The Romantic.
Spaniel's Sermon.
Ellis, Edwin John
Himself (excerpt).
Ellis, George
Rondeau: "Of Eden lost."
Ellis, John
Sarah Hazard's Love Letter.
Ellis, Mary Anne
Sonnet to a Tyrant.
Ellis, Royston
The Cherry Boy (excerpt).
Spiv Song.
Ellis, Vivian Locke
At Common Dawn.
Ellison, Henry
Fall of the Year.
Ellison, Joan Wyrick
A Mountain Heritage.
Ellsworth, Erastus Wolcott
The Mayflower.
What Is the Use? (excerpt).
Ellwanger, William De Lancey
To Jessie's Dancing Feet.
Ellwood, Thomas
Prayer.
Elmslie, Kenward
Another Island Groupage.
Circus Nerves and Worries.
Duo-tang.
The Dustbowl.
Experts at Veneers.
Feathered Dancers.

Flaming Creatures.
Florida Hillocks.
History of France.
Shirley Temple Surrounded by
  Lions.
White Attic.
Work Room.
Elmslie, W. G.
  The Hand That Held It.
Elson, Virginia
  How Stars and Hearts Grow
    in Apples.
  Not Being Wise.
Elspeth
  It's a Fib.
Elton, Charles
  Luriana, Lurilee.
Eluard, Paul
  Curfew.
  From Solitude to Solitude
    towards Life.
  Lady Love.
  Our Movement.
  Through an Embrace.
  You Rise Up.
Elys, Edmund
  My Mind Keeps out the Host
    of Sin.
Elytis, Odysseus
  The Body of Summer.
Emans, Elaine V.
  Birthday.
  For a Birthday.
  Mistakable Identity.
  The Undreamed.
Emanuel, James A.
  Black Muslim Boy in a
    Hospital.
  Church Burning: Mississippi.
  Emmett Till.
  Fishermen.
  For "Mr. Dudley," a Black
    Spy.
  Get Up, Blues.
  Negritude.
  The Negro.
  Nightmare.
  Old Black Men Say.
  Panther Man.
  Son.
  The Treehouse.
  The Voyage of Jimmy Poo.
  Wedding Procession.
  The Young Ones, Flip Side.
Emanuel, Lynn
  Berlin Interior with Jews,
    1939.
  Frying Trout While Drunk.
  Of Your Father's Indiscretions
    and the Train to California.
  The Sleeping.
Embry, Jacqueline
  Tea.
  Unregenerate.
Embury, Emma Catharine
  Love Unsought.
  The Pilgrim.
Emerson, Caroline D.
  A Modern Ballad.
Emerson, Ralph Waldo
  The Adirondacs.
  Alphonso of Castile.
  "America, My Country..."
  And When I Am Entombed.
  Announced by All the
    Trumpets of the Sky.
  The Apology.
  April.
  Art.
  Astraea.
  Atom from Atom.
  Bacchus.

Berrying.
Blight.
The Bohemian Hymn.
Boston.
Boston Hymn.
Brahma.
Character.
Compensation.
Concord Hymn.
Culture.
Days.
Duty.
Each and All.
The Earth.
Eros.
Excelsior.
Experience.
Fable: "The mountain and the
  squirrel."
Fate.
Forbearance.
Forerunners.
Fragments on the Poet and
  the Poetic Gift.
Gardener.
Give All to Love.
Good-bye.
Grace.
Guy.
Hamatreya.
The Heart of All the Scene
  (From "Woodnotes").
Heroism.
The Humble-Bee.
Hush!
Hymn Sung at the Completion
  of the Concord Monument
  April 19, 1836.
The Informing Spirit.
Intellect.
A Letter.
Letters.
Limits.
Love's Nobility.
May-Day: April and May.
Merlin.
Merops.
The Mighty Heart.
The Miracle.
Mithridates.
The Mountain and the
  Squirrel.
Music.
Musketaquid.
Nahant.
A Nation's Strength (excerpt).
Needless Worry.
Nemesis.
Ode Inscribed to W.H.
  Channing.
Ode: "O tenderly the haughty
  day."
Ode Sung in the Town Hall.
Ode to Beauty.
Orator.
Parks and Ponds.
The Past.
The Poet.
Politics.
The Problem.
Prudence.
Quatrain: Poet.
The Rhodora.
The River.
Saadi.
Sacrifice.
Seashore.
Shakespeare.
The Snow-Storm.
Solution.
Song of Nature.

Song of Seyd Nimetollah of
  Kuhistan.
The Sphinx.
Terminus.
The Test.
Thanksgiving.
Thine Eyes Still Shined.
Thought.
Threnody.
To Ellen at the South.
Two Rivers.
The Undersong.
Uriel.
The Visit.
Voluntaries.
Waldeinsamkeit.
Water.
Waves.
We Love the Venerable
  House.
Wealth.
Woodnotes.
The World-Soul.
Xenophanes.
**Emerson, Ida and Joseph E.
Howard**
  Hello, Ma Baby.
Emeruwa, Leatrice W.
  Personals.
Emery, Frances D.
  Long-Billed Gannets.
Emin, Gevorg
  Doesn't It Seem to You.
  Why Has This Ache.
Emmett, Daniel Decatur
  Boatman's Dance.
  Dixie.
  Old Dan Tucker.
Emmons, Dick
  Cold Fact.
  The Grass, Alas.
Emory, Susan A.
  An Old Woman's Answer to a
    Letter from Her Girlhood.
Empson, William
  Arachne.
  Aubade.
  Bacchus.
  The Beautiful Train.
  Camping Out.
  China.
  Courage Means Running.
  Description of a View.
  Dissatisfaction with
    Metaphysics.
  Doctrinal Point.
  Earth Has Shrunk in the
    Wash.
  Flighting for Duck.
  Four Legs, Two Legs, Three
    Legs.
  High Dive.
  Homage to the British
    Museum.
  Ignorance of Death.
  Invitation to Juno.
  Just a Smack at Auden.
  Kingfisher Flat.
  Legal Fiction.
  Let It Go.
  Letter.
  Manchouli.
  Missing Dates.
  Note on Local Flora.
  Part of Mandevil's Travels.
  Reflection from Rochester.
  Rolling the Lawn.
  The Scales.
  Sea Voyage.
  Sonnet: "Not wrongly moved
    by this dismaying scene."
  Success.

The Teasers.
To an Old Lady.
Villanelle.
The World's End.
Emre, Yunus
  The Whole Universe Is Full of
    God.
Ende, Frederick von
  Wynken De Worde.
Endrezze-Danielson, Anita
  Blue Horses: West Winds.
  Night Mare.
  Song-Maker.
  There Are Three Bones in the
    Human Ear.
  Why Stone Does Not Sing by
    Itself.
Endrezze-Probst, Anita
  The Dream Feast.
  The Passion Drinker.
  Raven/Moon.
  Red Rock Ceremonies.
  The Week-End Indian.
Eng, Steve
  Vanished.
Engel, Mary
  Promised Land.
Engels, John
  An Angler's Vade Mecum.
  The Crows.
  The Disconnections.
  The Homer Mitchell Place.
  Moonwalk.
Engels, Norbert
  Ex Maria Virgine.
  One Immortality.
Engels, Vincent David
  At the Last.
Engle, Paul
  America Remembers
    (excerpt).
  American Child.
  Beasts.
  Chameleon.
  Dancer: Four Poems.
  The Ending.
  In a Bar near Shibuya Station,
    Tokyo.
  The Last Whiskey Cup.
  Lord of Each Soul.
  A Modern Romance.
  Moving In.
  The New World.
  Orion.
  You Can't Be Wise.
Engle, Jr, John D.
  Bilogy Lesson.
  Midway.
  Sonnet Sonnet.
Engler, Robert Klein
  Dichterliebe.
English, Maurice
  Form Was the World.
English, Thomas Dunn
  Arnold at Stillwater.
  Assunpink and Princeton.
  The Battle of Monmouth.
  The Battle of New Orleans.
  The Battle of the Cowpens.
  Battle of the King's Mill.
  Ben Bolt.
  Betty Zane.
  The Burning of Jamestown.
  The Charge by the Ford.
  The Fall of Maubila.
  The Old Mill.
  The Sack of Deerfield.
Engman, John
  Rainer Maria Rilke Returns
    from the Dead...
Engonopoulos, Nikos
  The Hydra of Birds.

Enheduanna
Antiphonal Hymn in Praise of Inanna.
Appeal to the Moongod Nanna-Suen to Throw Out Lugalanne...
Banishment from Ur.
Condemning the Moongod Nanna.
Crimes of Lugalanne.
A Curse on Uruk.
Final Prayer.
Inanna and An.
Inanna and Ebih.
Inanna and Enlil.
Inanna and Ishkur.
Inanna and the Anunna.
Inanna and the City of Uruk.
Inanna and the Divine Essences.
Inanna Exalted (excerpt).
The Restoration of Enheduanna to Her Former Station.
Ennius
Annales: "Like a shower of rain."
Ennodius, Saint
How of the Virgin Mother Shall I Sing?
Enright, D. J.
Along the River.
Anecdote from William IV Street.
Apocalypse.
The "Black" Country.
Buy One Now.
Deir El Bahari: Temple of Hatshepsut.
Development.
Dreaming in the Shanghai Restaurant.
Guest.
History of World Languages.
In Cemeteries.
The Interpreters.
The Last Democrat.
The Laughing Hyena, by Hokusai.
Midstream.
The Monuments of Hiroshima.
Names.
No Offence.
The Noodle-Vendor's Flute.
Parliament of Cats.
Poet Wondering What He Is Up To.
R-and-R Centre: An Incident from the Vietnam War.
Royalties.
Since Then.
The Typewriter Revolution.
An Underdeveloped Country.
University Examinations in Egypt.
Unlawful Assembly.
The Verb "To Think".
Waiting for the Bus.
Enslin, Theodore
The Belongings.
Forms, LXXVII.
Landscape with Figures.
On Such a Windy Afternoon.
Stance.
Tangere.
Tansy for August.
Witch Hazel.
Your Need Is Greater Than Mine.
Enzensberger, Hans
Karl Heinrich Marx.

"Ephelia" (Joan Philips)
Song: "Know, Celadon, in vain you use."
Song: "You wrong me, Strephon."
Ephrem, Saint
The Christmas Hymn.
Epstein, Daniel Mark
At the Millinery Shop.
Cash Only, No Refund, No Return.
Climbing.
Don't Anybody Move.
First Precinct Fourth Ward.
The Follies.
Mannequins.
Miami.
Night Song from Backbone Mountain.
Epstein, Elaine
Luck.
Equi, Elaine
Condo Girl.
For Hollis Sigler.
Girl Friday.
Hi-Fashion Girl.
Think Small.
Vampirella.
Erasmus, Desiderius
The Familiar Colloquies: Sweet Temper and Mutual Affection.
Votive Ode.
Erb, Christopher
While Waiting for Kohoutek.
Erdrich, Louise
Balinda's Dance.
Dear John Wayne.
Jacklight.
The Lady in the Pink Mustang.
Painting of a White Gate and Sky.
Snow Train.
The Strange People.
Turtle Mountain Reservation.
Erinna
Baucis.
The Distaff.
Eristi-Aya
A Letter to Her Mother.
Ernst, John F.
O Jesus Christ, True Light of God.
ErPo 06, Anonymous.
Inscription of a Chemise.
Erskine, Francis Robert St. Clair
Bedtime.
Erskine, John
Apparition.
At the Front.
Dialogue.
Kings and Stars.
Modern Ode to the Modern School.
The Shepherd Speaks.
The Song.
Erskine, Thomas Erskine, Lord
On a Judge from Scotland.
On Tom Moore's Translation of Anacreon.
Erskine, William
This House, Where Once a Lawyer Dwelt.
Erulkar, Mary
The Third Continent.
Esbensen, Barbara J.
Postcard from Zamboanga.

Eschenbach, Sir Wolfram von
See Wolfram von Eschenbach, Sir
Escriva, Joan
Song to Death.
Eshleman, Clayton
The Black Hat.
A Very Old Woman.
Espaillat, Rhina P.
From the Rain Down.
Espirito Santo, Alda
The Same Side of the Canoe.
Where Are the Men Seized in This Wind of Madness?
Espy, Willard R.
Gemini Jones.
Singular Singulars, Peculiar Plurals.
Essex, Edwin
Loneliness.
Essex, Robert Devereux, Earl of
Change Thy Mind Since She Doth Change.
Happy Were He.
Esson, Louis
The Shearer's Wife.
Estes, Laurence E.
Contentment.
Estes, Sleepy John
Brownsville Blues.
Everybody Ought to Make a Change.
Floating Bridge.
Lawyer Clark Blues.
Milkcow Blues.
My Black Gal Blues.
Stack o' Dollars.
Street Car Blues.
Working Man Blues.
Esteves, Sandra Maria
From the Commonwealth.
Vanguardia.
E'tesami, Parvin
To His Father on Praising the Honest Life of the Peasant.
Etherege, Sir George
Chloris, 'Tis Not in Your Power.
Ephelia to Bajazet.
A Letter to Lord Middleton.
The Rival.
Silvia.
Song: "If she be not as kind as fair."
Song: "Ladies, though to your Conqu'ring eyes."
Song: "Tell me no more I am deceived."
Song: "Ye happy swains, whose hearts are free."
To a Lady Asking Him How Long He Would Love Her.
To a Very Young Lady.
To Little or No Purpose.
Upon the Downs.
Etter, Dave
Chicken.
The Fighter.
A House by the Tracks.
Old Dubuque.
Romp.
Snow Country.
Euenos, Bishop
To a Swallow.
The Vine to the Goat.
Eugenius III, Pope
Dedication.
Metrum Parhemiacum Tragicum.
Eunaich, Beinn
Winter Climb.

Euripides
Alcestis.
Andromache.
The Bacchai: The Home of Aphrodite.
Bellerophon: There Are No Gods.
The Breed of Athletes.
Chorus of Satyrs, Driving Their Goats.
Cresophontes: Prayer to Peace.
Cyclops.
Earth and Sky.
The Greek Athlete.
Hippolytus.
Iphigeneia in Aulis: Chorus.
Medea: Chorus.
The Nurse's Dole in the Medea.
The Trojan Women: Cassandra's Epithalamium.
Where Shall Wisdom Be Found.
The Worst Horror.
Euwer, Anthony
Gettin' Born.
Limerick: "As a beauty I'm not a great star."
Limerick: "In the wax works of Nature they strike."
Limerick: "No matter how grouchy you're feeling."
Limerick: "Now the ears, so I always had thunk."
Limerick: "Now the sneeze is a joy-vent, I s'pose."
Limerick: "The ankle's chief end is exposiery."
Limerick: "The hands they were made to assist."
Limerick: "With a conscience we're able to see."
My Face.
The True Facts of the Case.
Evald, Johannes
King Christian.
Evans, Abbie Huston
All Those Hymnings Up to God.
By the Salt Margin.
Come to Birth.
Euroclydon.
The Fundament Is Shifted.
In Space-Time Aware–.
On the Curve-Edge.
Primary.
Return to Life.
Sun-Up in March.
This World.
The Wrestling.
Evans, Abel
An Author's Epitaph. Written by Himself.
On Blenheim House.
Tadlow.
To the Reverend Joseph Trapp, on the First Volume...
Evans, David Allan
Bullfrogs.
Ford Pickup.
Neighbors.
Retired Farmer.
The Sound of Rain.
The Story of Lava.
Sunset.
Uncle Claude.
Evans, Donald
Body of the Queen.
Bonfire of Kings.
Dinner at the Hotel de la Tigresse Verte.

En Monocle.
In the Vices.
Evans, F. Gwynne
Little Thomas.
Matilda.
Evans, George Essex
An Australian Symphony.
The Women of the West.
Evans, H. A. C.
The Egotist.
If Not (parody).
The Liftman.
Montgomery.
Evans, Humphrey
And Again (parody).
Evans, Jonathan
It Is Finished.
Evans, Mari E.
The Alarm Clock.
...And the Old Women
Gathered.
Black Jam for Dr. Negro.
Daufuskie.
The Emancipation of George-
Hector (a colored turtle).
How Will You Call Me,
Brother?
I Am a Black Woman.
If There Be Sorrow.
Into Blackness Softly.
Langston.
Marrow of My Bone.
Point of No Return.
The Rebel.
Shrine to What Should Be.
Spectrum.
Status Symbol.
To Mother and Steve.
Uhuru.
Vive Noir!
When in Rome.
Where Have You Gone.
Evans, Mary Ann *See* **Eliot,**
George
Evans, Nathaniel
To Thee, Then, Let All
Beings Bend.
Evans, Patrick
At Morning an Iris.
Green Grass Growing.
Evans, Sebastian
The Fifteen Days of
Judgement.
The Seven Fiddlers.
Evans, Virginia Moran
Window to the East.
Evarts, Prescott, Jr
Hornpout.
Everard, Harrison
The Holloe Menne (parody).
Everett, Alexander H.
The Young American.
Everett, David
Tall Oaks from Little Acorns
Grow.
Everett, Edward
Dirge of Alaric the Visigoth.
Everett, Graham
Thirteen, Full of Life.
Everett, Laura Bell
The Lament of the Voiceless.
Resurgence.
Eversley, Mary
Just To Be Needed.
Everson, Ronald G.
Child with Shell.
Injured Maple.
One-Night Expensive Hotel.
Pauper Woodland.
Rogue Pearunners.
Stranded in My Ontario.
When I'm Going Well.

Everson, William *See also*
Antonius, Brother
A Canticle to the Waterbirds.
First Winter Storm.
The Flight in the Desert.
The Gash.
In All These Acts.
The Making of the Cross.
March.
The Narrows of Birth.
The Poet Is Dead.
The Presence.
The Raid.
The Stranger.
Winter Ploughing.
Zone of Death.
Everts, Lillian
Playmates.
Everwine, Peter
The Brother.
The Burden of Decision.
The Clearing.
Distance.
Drinking Cold Water.
For the Coming Year.
Going.
In the End.
The Marsh, New Year's Day.
Night.
Perhaps It's as You Say.
Routes.
Someone Knocks.
We Meet in the Lives of
Animals.
Ewart, Gavin
A 14-Year-Old Convalescent
Cat in the Winter.
2001: The Tennyson/Hardy
Poem.
The Bofors A.A. Gun.
A Christmas Message.
Cigarette for the Bambino.
The Deceptive Grin of the
Gravel Porters.
The Dell.
Ending.
An Exeter Riddle.
Fiction: A Message.
"For Whom the Bell Tolls".
From V.C. (a Gentleman of
Verona).
Hymn to Proust.
John Betjeman's Brighton
(parody).
Lifelines.
Lines.
Love Song.
The Lovesleep.
Miss Twye.
A New Poet Arrives.
Nymphs and Satyrs.
Officers' Mess.
On First Looking into
Michael Grant's Cities of
Vesuvius.
On the Tercentenary of
Milton's Death.
Pastoral.
Poem: "To go, to leave the
classics and the buildings."
Prayer.
Psychoanalysis.
Sonnet: Dolce Stil Novo.
Sonnet: "The point where
beauty and intelligence
meet."
They Flee from Me That
Sometime Did Me Seek.
Wanting Out.
When a Beau Goes In.
Xmas for the Boys.
Young Blondes.

Ewer, W. N.
The Chosen People.
How Odd.
Ewing, Annemarie
Ballad: "Mother mine, Mother
mine, what do you see?"
Fisherman's Blunder off New
Bedford, Massachusetts.
If the Heart Be Homeless.
The Man Within.
Rhyme from Grandma Goose.
Sleep, Madame, Sleep.
Ewing, Juliana Horatia
The Burial of Linnet.
The Dolls' Wash.
A Friend in the Garden.
Garden Lore.
The Willow-Man.
Excell, Patricia
Forgotten Objects on a Beach.
Exler, Samuel
The Cats.
Eybers, Elisabeth
Hagar.
Narrative.
Rontgen Photograph.
Sleep-Walking Child.
Snail.
Ezekiel, Nissim
Enterprise.
How My Father Died.
Lamentation.
Morning Prayer.
Totem.
Ezekielos
The Exodus from Egypt.
Ezell, Allamae
The Candidate.
Ezobi, Joseph
A Barren Soul.

F

"F. P. A." *See* **Adams, Franklin**
Pierce
Fabbri, Cora
White Roses.
Faber, F. W.
Right Is Right.
Faber, Frederic W.
The Nearest Friend.
Faber, Frederick William
The All-Embracing.
The Cherwell Water Lily.
The Dog.
The Expectation.
Faith of Our Fathers.
He Satisfies.
Jesus, Child and Lord.
Jesus, My God and My All.
Mundus Morosus.
My God, How Wonderful
Thou Art.
O Paradise! O Paradise!
Our Heavenly Father
(excerpt).
Our Lady in the Middle Ages.
Paradise.
The Shadow of the Rock.
Written in a Little Lady's
Little Album.
Faber, Geoffrey
St Mary's Loch.
Fabilli, Mary
Letter to Robert.
The Rock.

Fabio, Sarah Webster
All Day We've Longed for
Night.
Back into the Garden.
Black Man's Feast.
Chromo.
Evil Is No Black Thing.
To Turn from Love.
Fabyan, Robert
Dedication of the Chronicles
of England and France.
Facos, James
Fable.
Fadiman, Clifton
Alimentary.
Henry James.
Theological.
Fagg, Martin
Burialle of the Dede (parody).
Elegy on Thomas Hood
(parody).
Fagg, William Carson
The Book.
Eclipse.
The Leaf.
Portraits.
Reaching.
Fahy, Christopher
Bunny.
Fahy, Christophr
Miss Ada.
Fahy, Francis A.
Little Mary Cassidy.
The Ould Plaid Shawl.
Fainlight, Harry
Morning.
Fainlight, Ruth
Another Full Moon.
Fire-Queen.
God's Language.
The Hebrew Sibyl.
Lilith.
The Other.
Sibyl of the Waters.
Sleep-Learning.
Fair, C. A.
Chinese Poems: Arthur
Waley.
Fairbridge, Kingsley
The Song-Maker.
Fairbridge, W. S.
Consecration of the House.
Fairburn, A. R. D.
Beggar to Burgher.
La Belle Dame sans Merci.
Disquisition on Death
(excerpt).
Down on My Luck.
Epithalamium.
A Farewell.
Full Fathom Five.
The Impetuous Lover.
Landscape with Figures.
Night Song.
One Race, One Flag.
Song at Summer's End.
To a Friend in the Wilderness
(excerpt).
Winter Night.
Yes Please Gentlemen.
Fairchild, B. H.
Late Game.
Fairfax, Edward
Pluto's Council.
A Prayer Brings Rain.
Faiz, Faiz Ahmen
The Day Death Comes.
Falckner, Justus
Rise, Ye Children.
Falco, Edward
Apology to My Lady.

Falconer, Edward
Killarney.
Falconer, Raymond
No Voice of Man.
Falconer, William
All Hands Unmoor!
Description of a Ninety Gun
Ship.
High O'er the Poop the
Audacious Seas Aspire.
The Midshipman.
The Shipwreck.
Shortening Sail.
Faleti, Adebayo
Independence.
Falk, Marcia
Modern Kabbalist.
Shulamit in Her Dreams.
Woman through the Window.
Falke, Gustav
God's Harp.
Strand-Thistle.
Falkenbury, Francis E.
South Street.
Falkner, John Meade
After Trinity.
Arabia.
Christmas Day.
Epilogue.
Fallis, Edwina
Prairie Spring.
Wise Johnny.
Fallis, Edwina H.
September.
Fallon, Padraic
Assumption.
Elegy for a Countryman.
Farmer.
For Paddy Mac.
The Head.
Kiltartan Legend.
Lady Day.
Lakshmi.
Long John.
Mary Hynes.
Mater Dei.
Odysseus.
Out of Soundings.
Painting of my Father.
Pot Shot.
Raftery's Dialogue with the
Whiskey.
The River Walk.
Virgin.
The Waistcoat.
Weir Bridge.
Wisdom.
Writing on the Wall.
The Young Fenians.
Falstaff, Jake
Beautiful Sunday.
The Dick Johnson Reel.
The Elfin Wife.
Fandel, John
The Bee.
Indians.
Fane, Julian
Ad Matrem.
"Fane, Violet"
Afterwards.
In Green Old Gardens.
A May Song.
Fanshawe, Catherine
Fragment in Imitation of
Wordsworth.
A Riddle: The Letter H.
Fanshawe, Sir Richard
Hope.
Ode on His Majesty's
Proclamation, Commanding
the Gentry...

An Ode, upon Occasion of
His Majesties Proclamation
in the Year 1630.
A Rose.
Fanthorpe, U. A.
At the Ferry.
BC : AD.
Father in the Railway Buffet.
Not My Best Side.
Reindeer Report.
Resuscitation Team.
What the Donkey Saw.
Farallon, Cerise
Pride and Hesitation.
The Serpent of God.
Farber, Norma
Beyond the Tapestries.
Bow Down, Mountain.
Crooked Carol.
Dove.
The Hatch.
Hog at the Manger.
How They Brought the Good
News by Sea.
Jubilate Herbis.
Judas, Joyous Little Son.
Ladybug's Christmas.
Nothing Gold Can Stay.
Spider.
Farbstein, W. E.
Double Duty.
Farewell, George
An Adieu to My Landlady.
The Country Man (excerpt).
Molly Moor.
Privy-Love for my Landlady.
Quaere.
There's Life in a Mussel. A
Meditation.
To the Archdeacon.
Fargas, Laura
The Island of Geological
Time.
Natural History.
Rorschach.
Farhi, Musa Moris
God and Nature.
Paths to God.
Smile at Me.
Thirst.
Who Says.
Faricy, Austin
Through Warmth and Light
of Summer Skies.
Farjeon, Annabel
Ode to a Fat Cat.
Farjeon, Eleanor
Alexander to His Horse.
Annar-Mariar's Christmas
Shopping.
Bedtime.
Blackfriars.
Books.
Boys' Names.
C Is for Charms.
Cat!
Cats.
The Children's Bells.
The Children's Carol.
Choosing.
Circus.
City Streets and Country
Roads.
Coach.
Down! Down!
A Dragonfly.
Earth and Sky.
Farewell to the Old Year!
Farm Cart.
For a Dewdrop.
For a Mocking Voice.
For Christmas Day.

For Snow.
For Them.
Geography.
Getting out of Bed.
Girls' Names.
Good Bishop Valentine.
The Great Discovery.
Holly and Mistletoe.
In the Week When Christmas
Comes.
Jill Came from the Fair.
Jim at the Corner.
Joan's Door.
Keeping Christmas.
A Kitten.
Lewis Carroll.
Light the Lamps Up,
Lamplighter.
Meeting Mary.
The Milk-Cart Pony.
Moon-Come-Out.
The Mother's Tale.
Mrs. Malone.
Mrs. Peck-Pigeon.
Music.
News! News!
The Night Will Never Stay.
Now Every Child.
October's Song.
On the Staircase.
The Riding of the Kings.
Sailor.
School-Bell.
The Shopman.
The Sounds in the Morning.
Tailor.
There Are Big Waves.
This Holy Night.
Three Little Puffins.
Through a Shop Window.
The Tide in the River.
Up the Hill, Down the Hill.
Vegetables.
Welcome to the New Year.
Wheelbarrow.
White Horses.
Who'll Buy My Valley Lilies?
Wild Thyme.
William I–1066.
Z Is for Zoroaster.
Farjeon, Eleanor and Herbert
Henry VIII.
Farjeon, Herbert
Apologia.
Farkas, Endre
Erotica.
I Love You.
Old Country Talk.
Poem Proud Papa.
The Scribe.
Tree Planting.
Farley, Blanche
A Sort of Elegy.
Farley, Henry
The Bounty of Our Age.
The Voice of Ardent Zeal
Speaks from the Lollard's
Tower of St. Paul's.
Farley, Robert E.
Thinking Happiness.
Farley, Susan
How to Own Land.
Farmer, Edward
Little Jim.
Farnaby, Giles
Among the Daffadillies.
Farnham, Jessie
Garland for a Storyteller.
Farningham, Marianne
God Cares.
He Careth.
The Last Hymn.

Farnsworth, Robert
Sketch.
Farrar, Janice
A Thought of Marigolds.
Farrar, John
Alone.
Bundles.
Chanticleer.
Choice.
A Comparison.
The Critic.
The Drum.
A Hillside Farmer.
Parenthood.
Song for a Camper.
Threnody.
The Time Is Today.
Victorian Song.
Watching Clouds.
Farrar, John Chipman
Brest Left behind.
Farrar, Winifred Hamrick
Pushed to the Scroll.
Farrell, Bob
Old Zip Coon (Turkey in the
Straw).
Farrell, J. R.
The Bank Thief.
Farren, Robert
All That Is, and Can Delight.
The Beset Wife.
The Cool Gold Wines of
Paradise.
The Finding of the Tain.
Immolation.
The Island Boatman's Love-
Croon.
Joy's Peak.
Lineage.
Mary.
The Mason.
No Woman Born.
The Pets.
To the Bell-Ringer.
Farrington, Harry Webb
I Know Not How That
Bethlehem's Babe.
Farrokhzad, Forugh
Born Again.
In the land of dwarfs.
O Realm Bejewelled.
On Earth.
Once More.
Someone Like No One Else.
Farrokzad, Forugh
I'm Sad.
Fassler, Joan
My Grandpa Died Today.
Fatchen, Max
So Big!
Faubion, Dorothy
Hump, the Escalator.
Wash-Day Wonder.
Faucher, Real
Archaeologists.
Faulkner, Margherita
Suppositions.
Fauset, Jessie Redmond
Christmas Eve in France.
Dead Fires.
Enigma.
Fragment.
Noblesse Oblige.
Oblivion.
Oriflamme.
Rencontre.
The Return.
Touche.
La Vie C'est La Vie.
Words! Words!
Fawcett, Brian
The Hand.

Fawcett, Edgar
Fireflies.
January Is Here.
To an Oriole.
Wild Roses.
Fawcett, John
Blest Be the Tie That Binds.
Fawcett, Joseph
The Art of War (excerpt).
Fawcett, Susan
The Fisherman.
Fawkes, Francis
The Brown Jug.
An Elegy on the Death of
Dobbin, the Butterwoman's
Horse.
Faydi
On the Death of His Child.
Fearing, Kenneth
American Rhapsody.
Any Man's Advice to His
Son.
Aphrodite Metropolis.
C Stands for Civilization.
Confession Overheard in a
Subway.
Cultural Notes.
Dirge.
Elegy in a Theatrical
Warehouse.
End of the Seers' Convention.
Evening Song.
Green Light.
John Standish, Artist.
Love, 20c the First Quarter
Mile.
Lullaby.
Memo.
Minnie and Mrs. Hoyne.
No Credit.
Obituary.
Operative No. 174 Resigns.
Pact.
Pay-Off.
The People vs. the People.
Portrait.
Readings, Forecasts, Personal
Guidance.
Requiem.
Resurrection.
"These are the live."
Thirteen O'Clock.
Tomorrow.
Twentieth-Century Blues.
X Minus X.
Yes, the Agency Can Handle
That.
Federman, Raymond
Concrete Poem: Moon.
Fedo, David
Camping at Thunder Bay.
Feela, David J.
Cut.
Feeney, Leonard
Because of Her Who Flowered
So Fair.
Family Portrait.
Feeney, Thomas Butler
Captain Kelly Lets His
Daughter Go to Be a Nun.
Feild, Rachel
Pushcart Row.
Fein, Cheri
The Obscene Caller.
Feinberg, Harvey
Welcome.
Feinman, Alvin
November Sunday Morning.
Feinstein, Elaine
Against Winter.
Calliope in the Labour Ward.
Coastline.

Dad.
June.
Lais.
The Magic Apple Tree.
The Medium.
Our Vegetable Love Shall
Grow.
Patience.
Survivors.
Under Stone.
Feinstein, Martin
Burning Bush.
Feinstein, Robert N.
Woolly Words.
Feiritear, Piaras
Lay Your Weapons Down,
Young Lady.
Feirstein, Frederick
L'Art.
The Boarder.
"Grandfather" in.
Spring.
Feld, M. D.
Villanelle.
Feldman, Irving
The Ark.
Assimilation.
A Curse.
The Death of Vitellozzo
Vitelli.
The Double.
Flood.
Greenwich Village Saturday
Night.
The Hand.
The Handball Players at
Brighton Beach.
Little Lullaby.
The Lost Language.
My Olson Elegy.
The No-Night.
The Old Men.
Portrait de Femme.
The Pripet Marshes.
Scene of a Summer Morning.
So it Happens.
Wrack.
Feldman, Ruth
Lilith.
Nocturne: Homage to
Whistler.
Feldman, Susan
How the Invalids Make Love.
Intruder.
Lamentations of an Au Pair
Girl.
Sea Legs.
Fell, Alison
Significant Fevers.
Felltham, Owen
Contentment.
On the Duke of Buckingham,
Slain by Felton...
Song: "When, dearest, I but
think of".
The Sun and Wind.
This Ensuing Copy the Late
Printer Hath been Pleased to
Honour...
Fenderson, Mark
Limerick: "Teacher Bruin
said, "Cub, bear in mind."
Feng Chih
For Tu Fu.
On a Puppy.
The Room and the Windows.
Fenner, Cornelius George
Gulf-Weed.
Fenollosa, Mary McNeil
A Drifting Petal.
Flying Fish.
Miyoko San.

Morning Fancy.
Sunrise in the Hills of
Satsuma.
Yuki.
Fenton, Elijah
To a Lady Sitting before Her
Glass.
Fenton, Elizabeth
Masks.
Under the Ladder to Heaven.
Fenton, James
Dead Soldiers.
The Pitt-Rivers Museum,
Oxford.
Ferber, Edna
To William Allen White.
Ferebe, George
The Houseless Downs.
Ferguson, James
Auld Daddy Darkness.
Ferguson, John
A Cock Crowing in a
Poulterer's Shop.
Ferguson, Roy
The Island of Rhum.
Ferguson, Sir Samuel
Abdication of Fergus Mac
Roy.
Aideen's Grave.
At the Polo-Ground.
Bird and Brook.
The Burial of King Cormac.
Ceann Dubh Deelish.
Congal: Simile.
Congal: The Land Is Ours.
The Death of Dermid.
Deidre's Lament for the Sons
of Usnach.
The Fair Hills of Ireland.
The Fairy Thorn.
The Forging of the Anchor.
Hopeless Love.
Lament for the Death of
Thomas Davis.
The Lapful of Nuts.
Molly Asthore.
Paistin Fionn.
Paul Veronese.
The Pretty Girl of Loch Dan.
The Welshmen of Tirawley.
Fergusson, Robert
Auld Reikie.
Braid Claith.
The Daft-Days.
Epigram on a Lawyer's
Desiring One of the Tribe to
Look....
The Farmer's Ingle.
The Ghaists: A Kirk-Yard
Eclogue.
Hallow-Fair.
The Lee Rigg.
My Winsome Dear.
The Rising of the Session.
The Sow of Feeling.
Ferlinghetti, Lawrence
After the Cries of the Birds.
Away Above a Harborful.
Christ Climbed Down.
A Coney Island of the Mind.
Constantly Risking Absurdity.
Crazy to Be Alive in Such a
Strange World.
Dog.
Fortune.
Frightened.
Funny fantasies are never so
real as oldstyle.
He.
I Am Waiting.
In a Surrealist Year.

In Golden Gate Park That
Day.
In Goya's Greatest Scenes.
Lost Parents.
New York–Albany.
One Thousand Fearful Words
for Fidel Castro.
The Pennycandystore beyond
the El.
A Phoenix at Fifty.
Pictures of a Gone World.
Pound at Spoleto.
The Sea and Ourselves at
Cape Ann.
Sometime during Eternity.
Starting from San Francisco.
Tentative Description of a
Dinner to Promote the
Impeachment...
True Confessional.
Underwear.
Wild Dreams of a New
Beginning.
Fernandez, Abraham
If You Happy Would Be.
Fernandez, Raymond Ringo
Cell-Rap #27.
For Mulatto.
Lies and Gossip.
Poem for the Conguero in D-
yard.
Real Deal Revelation.
Ferne, Doris
Nijinsky.
Sounding.
Fero, Gracia L.
Sharing His Cross.
Ferre, Rosario
I Hear You've Let Go.
Ferril, Thomas Hornsby
Always Begin Where You
Are.
Basic Communication.
House in Denver.
Kochia.
Lost Ships.
The Man Who Thought He
Was a Horse.
Morning Star.
Old Men on the Blue.
Something Starting Over.
Swallows.
The Train Butcher.
Waltz against the Mountains.
What Trinkets?
Wood.
Ferriter, Pierce
He Charges Her to Lay Aside
Her Weapons.
Lay Your Arms Aside.
Ferry, David
The Antagonist.
Johnson on Pope.
Lines for a Dead Poet.
On the Way to the Island.
Out of That Sea.
Poem About Waking.
The Unawkward Singers.
Fertig, Nelle
I Have Come to the
Conclusion.
Fessenden, Thomas Green
Ye Sons of Columbia.
Fet, Afanasi *See* Foeth, Afanasy
Afanasyevich
Fetherling, Doug
Bathing with Father.
Dialogue 4 1 Voice Only.
Diseases of the Moon.
Dispatch Number Nine.
Dispatch Number Sixteen.
Dispatch Number Sixty.

Elijah Speaking.
Explorers as Seen by the
  Natives.
Genius Loci of the Morning.
Nights Passed on Ward's
  Island, Toronto Harbour.
Sex Play in Four Acts.
Shacked Up at the Ritz.
She Employed the Familiar
  "Tu" Form.
Your Absence Has Not
  Taught Me.

Fetter, George Griffith
The Name of Mother.

Fewell, Richard
The "Duke" and the "Count."

Fewster, Ernest
The Cliff Rose.
The Pearly Everlasting.

Fey, Harold E.
We Who Are About to Die.

Fey, Isabella
Bad Example.

Fiacc, Padraic
The Boy and the Geese.
Brendan Gone.
Deranged.
Gloss.
Haemorrhage.
The Poet.
The Stolen Fifer.

Fialkowski, Barbara
To Sleep.

Fiamengo, Marya
In Praise of Old Women.

Fiawoo, F. K.
Soliloquy on Death.

Fiche, Arthur Davison
The Young Recruit.

Fichman, Jacob
Abishag.
In the Old City.

Fichman, Jakov
Eve.

Fichman, Yaakov
Samarian Nights.

Ficke, Arthur Davison
Alcibiades to a Jealous Girl.
April Moment.
Don Quixote.
Epitaph for the Poet V.
Fate With Devoted...
Father.
Four Japanese Paintings: III
  The Wave Symphony.
Her Pedigree.
In That Dim Monument
  Where Tybalt Lies.
The Oracle.
Perspective of Co-Ordination.
Sonnets of a Portrait Painter.
Spring Landscape.
Summons.
The Three Sisters.
To the Harpies.
Troubadours.
View from Heights.

Fickert, Kurt J.
The End of a Meaningful
  Relationship.
Sleeping Alone.

Fiedler, Leslie A.
Dumb Dick.
Thou Shalt Surely Die...: No
  Ghost Is True.

Field, Arthur Gordon
America Prays.
Bells of New Year.
The Discoverer.
The Name of Washington.
The New Song.
Perpetual Christmas.

Field, Charles K.
Barriers Burned.

Field, Edward
Both My Grandmothers.
The Bride of Frankenstein.
Curse of the Cat Woman.
Donkeys.
An Event.
The Floor Is Dirty.
For Arthur Gregor.
Frankenstein.
Graffiti.
The Lost, Dancing.
Mae West.
My Polish Grandma.
New York.
Nightmare.
Notes from a Slave Ship.
Ode to Fidel Castro.
The Reservoir.
Roaches.
The Sentimentalist.
The Sleeper.
The Snowfish.
The Statute of Liberty.
The Telephone.
Tulips and Addresses.
Unwanted.
A View of Jersey.
What Grandma Knew.
Writing for Money.

Field, Eugene
At Cheyenne.
Bachelor Hall.
Bethlehem Town.
The Bibliomaniac's Prayer.
The Boy.
Casey's Table d'Hote.
Chipeta.
Christmas Eve.
Christmas Song.
A Christmas Wish.
The Clink of the Ice.
A Colorado Sand Storm.
The Death of Robin Hood.
Dibdin's Ghost.
The Dinkey-Bird.
The Duel.
Echoes from the Sabine Farm.
Epigram.
Horace I.
In the Firelight.
Jessie.
Jest 'Fore Christmas.
Limerick: "'Tis strange how
  the newspapers honor."
Little Boy Blue.
The Little Peach.
The Lyttel Boy.
Mr. Billings of Louisville.
My Sabine Farm.
A New Year Idyl (excerpt).
Nightfall in Dordrecht.
Norse Lullaby.
Our Two Opinions.
A Piazza Tragedy.
The Pioneer.
The Preference Declared.
The Rock-A-By Lady.
Seein' Things.
The Sioux.
Song of the All-Wool Shirt.
Star of the East.
The Sugar-Plum Tree.
The Three Kings.
To Leuconoe.
To Phyllis.
The Truth about Horace.
The Wanderer.
Wynken, Blynken, and Nod.

Field, Greg
Home Cooking Cafe.

Field, James Thomas
On a Watchman Asleep at
  Midnight.

Field, Matt
Farm Wife.
Rondel: Autumn.

**"Field, Michael" (Katherine
  Bradley and Edith Cooper)**
Ah Me, If I Grew Sweet to
  Man.
And on My Eyes Dark Sleep
  by Night.
Aridity.
Bury Her at Even.
Cyclamens.
Depression.
The Dream.
A Dying Viper.
Ebbtide at Sundown.
Gold Is the Son of Zeus:
  Neither Moth Nor Worm
  May Gnaw It.
If They Honoured Me, Giving
  Me Their Gifts.
Noon.
Renewal.
Sweeter Far Than the Harp,
  More Gold Than Gold.
To the Lord Love.
The Tragic Mary Queen of
  Scots.
Variations on Sappho.
A Vision.
Where the Blessed Feet Have
  Trod.
Whym Chow.
The Woods Are Still.

Field, Mildred Fowler
Carpenter Christ.

Field, Nathaniel
Matin Song.
Rise, Lady Mistress, Rise!

Field, Rachel
Almost.
The Animal Store.
Barefoot Days.
A Birthday.
The Busy Body.
A Charm for Spring Flowers.
Chestnut Stands.
A Circus Garland.
City Rain.
The Dancing Bear.
A Dog Day.
Doorbells.
Eighth Street West.
Elfin Town.
The Flower-Cart Man.
For Christmas.
For My Father.
Fourth of July.
General Store.
Good Green Bus.
The Green Fiddler.
I'd Like to Be a Lighthouse.
The Ice-Cream Man.
If Once You Have Slept on an
  Island.
The Little Rose Tree.
Manhattan Lullaby.
New Year's Day.
The Old Wharves.
Picnic Day.
The Pointed People.
The Pretzel Man.
Roads.
The Sampler.
The Seven Ages of Elf-Hood.
Snow in the City.
Some People.
Something Told the Wild
  Geese.

Song for a Blue Roadster.
Spring Signs.
A Summer Morning.
Taxis.
Ticking Clocks.
Vegetables.
Whistles.

Field, Roswell Martin
At the Ball Game.
A Counterblast against Garlic.

Field, Sara Bard
November 2 A.M. Conspiracy.
We Whom the Dead Have
  Not Forgiven.

Fielding, Henry
Hunting Song.
A Letter to Sir Robert
  Walpole.
On a Halfpenny Which a
  Young Lady Gave a
  Beggar...
The Roast Beef of Old
  England.

Fields, Annie
Cedar Mountain.
Little Guinever.
On Waking from a Dreamless
  Sleep.
The Return.
Song, to the Gods, is Sweetest
  Sacrifice.
Theocritus.

Fields, Dorothy
I Can't Give You Anything
  but Love.

Fields, James Thomas
The Alarmed Skipper.
Ballad of the Tempest.
The Captain's Daughter.
Common Sense.
Jupiter and Ten.
Mabel, in New Hampshire.
The Owl Critic.
Song of the Turtle and
  Flamingo.
The Turtle and the Flamingo.
With Wordsworth at Rydal.

Fields, Julia
Aardvark.
Alabama.
Birmingham.
Black Students.
Harlem in January.
High on the Hog.
I Heard a Young Man Saying.
Madness One Monday
  Evening.
No Time for Poetry.
A Poem for Heroes.
Poems: Birmingham
  1962-1964.

Fifer, H. N.
He Lived a Life.

Figgis, Darrell
Bogac Ban.
Inisgallun.

Filicaja, Vincenzo da
Italy.
Providence.

Filip, Raymond
CANDU Can't Do.
The Might Buck, the
  Immigrant Fuck, and
  Melting Pot Luck.
My Sister, My Self.
Never Marry an Artist.
Roof Garden.
Softening to Heaven.

Finch, Anne *See* **Wilchilsea,
  Anne Finch, Countess of**

Finch, Francis Miles
The Blue and the Gray.

Nathan Hale.

Finch, Julia Neely
The Unborn.

Finch, Robert
Alone.
The Crib.
The Effect of Snow.
Egg-and-Dart.
Jardin de la Chapelle
  Expiatoire.
Last Visit.
The Lost Tribe.
The Mountain.
The Network.
Peacock and Nightingale.
A Rhemish Carol.
Scroll-Section.
Silverthorn Bush.
The Statue.
Time's Bright Sand.
Train Window.
Turning.
Words.

Finch, Vivienne
Green Ice.
Inertia.

Finefrock, Margaret
Demonstration.

Fineran, Mary C.
Night Train.

Finerty, John F.
May-Day at Sea.

Finger, Charles J.
The Cowboy's Dream.

Fink, William
Larrie O'Dee.

Finkel, Donald
The Bush on Mount Venus.
Cain's Song.
The Clothing's New Emperor.
Cocteau's Opium: 1.
Cocteau's Opium: 2.
The Cross-Eyed Lover.
An Esthetic of Imitation.
The Father.
Feeding the Fire.
Finders Keepers.
The Flagpole Sitter.
Genealogy.
Gesture.
Give Way.
The Great Wave: Hokusai.
Hands.
How Things Fall.
Hunting Song.
The Husband.
The Imbecile.
A Joyful Noise.
Juan Belmonte, Torero.
King Midas Has Asses' Ears.
Lame Angel.
Letter to My Daughter at the
  End of Her Second Year.
Lilith.
Metaphysic of Snow.
Note in Lieu of a Suicide.
Oedipus at San Francisco.
The Sirens.
Solo for Bent Spoon.
Spring Song.
Target Practice.
They.
Time Out.
When I Was Young I Tried to
  Sing.

Finlay, Ian Hamilton
Bedtime.
Concrete poem: The Horizon
  of Holland.
The Dancers Inherit the
  Party.
Island Moment.

Orkney Interior.
Twice.

Finley, C. Stephen
October Dusk.
To One Far Away, Dancing.

Finley, Jeanne
The Dead of the World.
The Divorce Dress.

Finley, John
Bachelor's Hall.
A Birthday Prayer.
The Road to Dieppe.

Finne, Diderik
Apollo 113.

Finnell, Dennis
Working at a Service Station,
  I Think of Shinkichi
  Takahashi.

Finnin, Mary
The Farm Near Norman's
  Lane.
Sarah Lorton.
Three Trees at Solstice.

Fionn, Flann
Aldfrid's Itinerary Through
  Ireland.

Firdausi
Alas for Youth.
The Dream of Dakiki.
On the Sultan Mahmud.
Reproach.
When the Sword of Sixty
  Comes Nigh His Head.

Firestone, Laya
Crow, Straight Flier, but
  Dark.
For Gabriel.
Listen to the Bird.
Thoughts for My
  Grandmother.

Firkins, Chester
On a Subway Express.

Firsoff, Axel
The Spirit of the Cairngorms.

"Firth"
Britannia Rules of
  Orthography.

Fischer, Helen Field
The Mystic Borderland.

Fischer, Otakar
From the Depths.

Fischer, William J.
A Faded Letter.

Fishback, Margaret
Christmas Pageant.
The Complacent Cliff-Dweller.
Hallowe'en Indignation
  Meeting.
Hell's Bells.
I Stand Corrected.
I Take 'Em and Like 'Em.
In Extremis.
Kerchoo!
Midsummer Melancholy.
Poem for Mother's Day.
Sentimental Lines to a Young
  Man Who Favors Pink
  Wallpaper...
Sitting Pretty.
This Way Out.
Thoughts of Loved Ones.
Triolet on a Dark Day.

Fisher, A. G.
Day by Day.

Fisher, A. Hugh
Ceylon.

Fisher, Aileen
Away We Go.
The Bells of Peace.
Birthday Cake.
But That Was Yesterday.
Cat in the Snow.

Christmas Shoppers.
Christmas Tree.
Cinderella Grass.
Counting Sheep.
December.
Down in the Hollow.
Early, Early Easter Day.
Fall.
Fireflies.
The Flag We Fly.
Halloween Concert.
Holly Fairies.
Houses.
January Snow.
Legends of Christmas.
Light in the Darkness.
Listening.
A Little Bird.
Little Brother.
Mother's Party.
My Puppy.
Newspaper.
November.
On Mother's Day.
Otherwise.
The Outdoor Christmas Tree.
The Package.
A Picnic.
Puppy.
Richer.
The Seed.
Snoring.
The Snowman's Resolution.
Something Very Elegant.
Tummy Ache.
Until We Built a Cabin.
Valentine's Day.
Wearing of the Green.
Winter Circus.
A Wonderful Man.
The Workshop.
The World's So Big.

Fisher, David
Analyst.
The Birds of Arles.
A Child's Christmas without
  Jean Cocteau.
Death of Rimbaud.
The Emergency Room.
Harvest Poem.
A Junkie with a Flute in the
  Rain.
The Keepsake Corporation.
Lost.
The Mutilated Soldier.
Mycenae.
The Old Man.
On the Esplanade des
  Invalides.
The Pastor Speaks Out.
Rehearsal.
The Retarded Class at F.A.O.
  Schwarz's Celebrates
  Christmas.
Spassky at Reykjavik.
The Teacher.
The Vietnamese Girl in the
  Madhouse.
Why Do You Want to Suffer
  Less.

Fisher, Ed
The Talk of The Town.

Fisher, Harrison
The Controls.
White Zombie.

Fisher, Lori
Pentimento.

Fisher, Mahlon Leonard
The Ancient Sacrifice.
As an Old Mercer.
In Cool, Green Haunts.
November.

On a Sculptured Head of the
  Christ.
Realization.
To Nature.

Fisher, Robert
Minotaur.
Monster Alphabet.
The Phoenix.

Fisher, Roy
As He Came Near Death.
The Entertainment of War.

Fishman, Charles
August 12, 1952.
A Fish Story.

Fishman, Rachel
Even If.
In the Beginning.

Fiske, John
Upon the Decease of Mrs.
  Anne Griffin...
Upon the Much-to-Be
  Lamented Desease of the
  Reverend Mr. John Cotton...

Fitch, Anna M.
The Song of the Flume.

Fitch, Eleazar Thompson
By Vows of Love Together
  Bound.
Lord, At This Closing Hour.

Fitch, Robert
High Brow.

Fitger, Arthur
Evening Prayer.

Fitton, Molly
One-Line Poems from a New
  Statesman Competition.
When Fog Come Creepin'
  over Beccles (parody).

Fitts, Dudley
Southwest Passage.
Ya Se Van Los Pastores.

Fitzell, Lincoln
Conflict.

Fitzgeffrey, Charles
The Bee.

Fitzgerald, Edward
Because.
Chivalry at a Discount.
Old Song.
The Rubaiyat of Omar
  Khayyam.
The Three Arrows.

Fitzgerald, F. Scott
The Great Gatsby: Epitaph.
Obit on Parnassus.
There'd Be an Orchestra.

Fitzgerald, Judith
Effectively coming through
  slaughter.
Energy.
Holy water.
Mouth to mouth recitation.
Step father.
Sunday Morning.
Touch of zygosis.

Fitzgerald, Mary Scott
Rendezvous.

Fitzgerald, Robert
Adulescentia.
Before Harvest.
Celestine.
Cobb Would Have Caught It.
Colorado.
Elegy.
Entreaty.
Errantry.
History.
The Imprisoned.
Jesu, Joy of Man's Desiring.
July in Indiana.
Metaphysical.
Metaphysician.

Mise en Scene.
Mutations: Midsummer.
The Painter.
Park Avenue.
The Queens.
Sea Pieces.
The Shore of Life.
Solstitium Saeculare.
Song for September.
Souls Lake.
Windshield.
Winter Night.

FitzGerald, Robert D.
Back from the Paved Way.
Bog and Candle.
Copernicus.
Edge.
Essay on Memory.
The Face of the Waters.
Favour.
Glad World.
Grace before Meat.
Macquarie Place.
The Man from Strathbogie.
Traditional Tune.
The Wind at Your Door.

Fitzgerald, Thomas
Upon an Ingenious Friend,
Over-Vain.

Fitzherbert, Sir Anthony
Memorial Verses for
Travellers.

Fitzpatrick, Susan
More Than.

Fitzsimon, Henry
Swearing.

Fiumi, Lionello
The Man Closes the Shutters.

Fixmer, Clyde
Canal Street, Chicago.

Flaccus, Aulus Persius
Dance of Death.
Epigram: "Just as he is
growing a beard."
First Satire: Prologue.

**Flagg, James M. and Julian
Street**
To Be Continued.

Flagg, James Montgomery
Limerick: "Said the Reverend
Jabez McCotton."
Limerick: "When you turn
down your glass it's a sign."

Flagg, William
The O'Lincon Family.

Flaischlen, Casar
Most Quietly at Times.

Flanders, Jane
Fairy Tales.
Stars Shine So Faithfully.

Flanders, Michael
First and Second Law.

Flanner, Hildegarde
Daphne.
Discovery.
A Farewell.
The Flowers of Apollo.
Memo.
Moon Song.
Prayer for This Day.
Spring's on the Curb.
To One of Little Faith.

Flantz, Richard
Shir Ma'alot/A Song of
Degrees.

Flash, Harry Lyndon
The Flag.

Flash, Henry Lynden
The Gallant Fifty-One.
Stonewall Jackson.
Zollicoffer.

Flatman, Thomas
The Advice.
An Appeal to Cats in the
Business of Love.
The Defiance.
A Dooms-Day Thought Anno
1659.
Nudus Redibo.
On Marriage.
Pastoral Dialogue Castara and
Parthenia.
The Sad Day.
A Thought of Death.
The Unconcerned.

Flax, Hjalmar
Art.
Littoral.

Flecker, J. E.
Ballad of the Londoner.

Flecker, James Elroy
The Ballad of Camden Town.
The Ballad of Hampstead
Heath.
Brumana.
The Dying Patriot.
Epithalamion.
From Grenoble.
Gates of Damascus.
The Golden Journey to
Samarkand.
The Hammam Name.
Hassan's Serenade.
In Hospital.
In Phaeacia.
Inscription for Arthur
Rackham's Rip Van Winkle.
Lord Arnaldos.
No Coward's Song.
November Eves.
Oak and Olive.
The Old Ships.
Oxford Canal.
The Painter's Mistress.
The Parrot.
Prayer.
The Queen's Song.
Rioupéroux.
Saadabad.
Santorin.
A Ship, an Isle, a Sickle
Moon.
Stillness.
Tenebris Interlucentem.
To a Poet a Thousand Years
Hence.
The Town without a Market.
War Song of the Saracens.
The Welsh Sea.

Flecknoe, Richard
Invocation of Silence.
Noble Love.
Silence Invoked.

Fleg, Edmond
The Dead Cities Speak to the
Living Cities.
The End of Sorrow.
The Wandering Jew Comes to
the Wall.

Fleisher, Bernice
The Perfectionist.

Fleming, Archibald
The Destroyers (excerpt).
The Jungle (excerpt).

Fleming, Carrol B.
Boundaries.

Fleming, Elizabeth
In the Mirror.
Who's In.

Fleming, Gerald
Let Go: Once.

Fleming, Marjory
A Melancholy Lay.

Six-Year-Old Marjory Fleming
Pens a Poem.
A Sonnet: "O lovely O most
charming pug."
A Sonnet on a Monkey.

Fleming, Maybury
To Demeter.
To Sleep.
What though the Green Leaf
Grow?

Fletcher, Bob
A Love Dirge to the
Whitehouse (or It Soots You
Right).

Fletcher, Curley W.
The High-Loping Cowboy.
The Strawberry Roan.

Fletcher, Giles the Elder
I Wish Sometimes, Although
a Worthlesse Thing.
Licia (excerpt).
Lyke Memnons Rocke
Toucht, with the Rising
Sanne.
Sonnet: "Like Memnon's rock,
touched with the rising sun."
In Tyme the Strong and
Statlie Turrets Fall.

Fletcher, Giles the Younger
The Celestial City.
Christ's Victory and Triumph.
Easter Morn.
He Is a Path.
The Heavenly Jerusalem.
On the Crucifixion.
Wooing Song.

Fletcher, John
Arm, Arm, Arm, Arm!
Beauty Clear and Fair.
Cast Our Caps and Cares
Away.
Come Hither, You That Love.
Dearest, Do Not You Delay
Me.
Drink To-day.
Drinking Song.
The Faithful Shepherdess.
God Lyaeus.
Hide, O Hide Those Hills of
Snow.
Hymn to Pan.
Into Slumbers.
Love's Emblems.
Music.
O Divine Star of Heavan.
Orpheus I am Come from the
Deeps Below.
The Power of Love.
Song for the Sick Emperor.
Song in the Wood.
The Spanish Curate.
Tell Me, Dearest.
'Tis Late and Cold.
Weep No More.
Women Pleased.
Women's Longing.

Fletcher, John Gould
Before Olympus.
Blue Symphony.
Down the Mississippi.
Elegy on a Nordic White
Protestant.
Green Symphony.
Irradiations.
Last Judgment.
Lincoln.
London Nightfall.
Mexican Quarter.
The Monadnock.
Rain in the Desert.
A Rebel.
The Road.

The Skaters.
Song of the Moderns.
The Windmills.

Fletcher, Louisa
The Land of Beginning Again.

Fletcher, Phineas
The Apollyonists.
Chromis.
Desiderium.
The Divine Wooer.
Drop, Drop, Slow Tears.
Elisa, or an Elegy upon the
Unripe Decease...
Lines Written at Cambridge,
to W. R., Esquire.
The Overthrow of Lucifer.
Piscatorie Eclogues.
The Purple Island.
Sicelides: Woman's
Inconstancy.
Sin, Despair, and Lucifer.
Song: "Fond men! whose
wretched care the life soon
ending."
To My Soul.

Flexner, Hortense
Builders.
Contemporary.
French Clock.
Poets.
Wandering.
When Last Seen.

Flint, Annie Johnson
The Answered Prayer.
Ask, and Ye Shall Receive.
At the Place of the Sea.
The Blessings That Remain.
Carpenter's Son.
The Cross and the Tomb.
Daily with You.
The Everlasting Love.
He Giveth More.
His Will Be Done.
Hitherto and Henceforth.
In Him.
Mary and Martha.
The Name of Jesus.
Not I, But God.
The Old Year and the New.
Our Father's Hand.
Passing Through.
Pray-Give-Go.
The Red Sea Place in Your
Life.
The Sentinel.
The Sepulcher.
Sometimes.
This Moment.
Thou Remainest.
Through the Waters.
Thy Will Be Done.
We See Jesus.
What God Has Promised.
The Word of God.
The World's Bible.

Flint, Frank Stewart
Eau-Forte.
Lilac.
Prayer.

Flint, James
In Pleasant Lands Have
Fallen the Lines.

Flint, Roland
August from My Desk.

Flohr, Natalie
The Martyr.

Flood, John
To His Coy Mistress (parody).

Florence, Nellie
Jacksonville Blues.

Florencia del Pinar
Another Song of the Same Woman, to Some Partridges...
Florio, John
Of Books.
Flower, Robin
At Mass.
He Praises His Wife When She Had Gone from Him.
Say Not That Beauty.
Troy.
Flynn, Desiree
The Collector.
From the Rain Forest.
Flynn, Elizabeth
After Grave Deliberation...
Flynn, Joseph
Down Went McGinty.
Foerster, Richard
Archne.
Nantucket's Widows.
Those Guyana Nights.
Foeth, Afanasy Afanasyevich
I Come Again.
Morning Song.
Fogazzaro, Antonio
The Bells.
Fogel, Ephim G.
Shipment to Maidanek.
Fogle, Richard Harter
A Hawthorne Garland.
Limerick: "Wrote the clergy: "Our Dear Madame Prynne:".
Folcachieri, Folcachiero de'
He Speaks of His Condition through Love.
Foley, James W.
Drop a Pebble in the Water.
The Salvation of Texas Peters.
Scientific Proof.
Folger, Peleg
Praise Ye the Lord, O Celebrate His Fame.
Folk, Pat
Empty Holds a Question.
Senile.
Follansbee, Mitchell D.
I Like to Quote.
Follen, Eliza Lee
The Good Moolly Cow.
Lord, Deliver, Thou Canst Save.
The Moon.
Ringely, Ringely.
Where Are You Going.
Fondane, Benjamin
By the Waters of Babylon.
Hertza.
Lullaby for an Emigrant.
Plain Song.
The Wandering Jew.
Fonte Boa, Maria Amalia
Two Tile Beaks.
Vitality.
Foot, Edward Edwin
Long Live Our Dear and Noble Queen.
Foote, Lucius Harwood
The Derelict.
Don Juan.
El Vaquero.
On the Heights.
Poetry.
Sutter's Fort, Sacramento.
Foote, Samuel
The Great Panjandrum.
Forbes, Calvin
The Chocolate Soldiers.
Gabriel's Blues.
Lullaby for Ann-Lucian.

M.A.P.
The Other Side of This World.
Reading Walt Whitman.
Some Pieces.
Forbes, Ella C.
Glad Earth.
Forbes, John
Four Heads & How to Do Them.
TV.
Forche, Carolyn
Because One Is Always Forgotten.
Burning the Tomato Worms.
City Walk-Up, Winter 1969.
Departure.
Dulcimer Maker.
Endurance.
For the Stranger.
Kalaloch.
The Memory of Elena.
Reunion.
Selective Service.
Taking Off My Clothes.
The Visitor.
Ford, Charles Henri
Baby's in Jail; the Animal Day Plays Alone.
The Bad Habit.
January Wraps up the Wound of His Arm.
The Overturned Lake.
Plaint.
Somebody's Gone.
There's No Place to Sleep in This Bed, Tanguy.
Ford, Corey
When West Comes East.
Ford, Dan
Love Is Loathing & Why.
Ford, Ford Madox
The Cat of the House.
Children's Song.
The Iron Music.
The Old Houses of Flanders.
On Heaven.
Sidera Cadentia.
A Solis Ortus Cardine.
What the Orderly Dog Saw.
When the World Was in Building.
Wisdom.
Ford, Francis Alan
Song of the Gulf Stream.
Ford, Gena
Legacy.
Lines for a Hard Time.
The Nude on the Bathroom Wall.
Ford, John
The Broken Heart.
Dawn.
Dirge.
Love's Martyrs.
The Lovers Melancholy.
Pleasures, Beauty.
Ford, Mary A.
A Hundred Years from Now.
Ford, Michael C.
Mellow Groove Grave Elegy.
Ford, R. A. D.
Back to Dublin.
Earthquake.
Lynx.
Revenge of the Hunted.
Roadside near Moscow.
Sakhara.
Sleeplessness of Our Time.
The Thieves of Love.
Twenty Below.

Ford, Robert
The Bonniest Bairn in a' the Warl'.
Ford, Thomas
The Marigold.
Ford, Walter H.
The Sunshine of Paradise Alley.
Foresman, Rebecca
How to Forget.
Forgaill, Dallan
A Poem in Praise of Colum Cille.
Forker, Greg
And the Gas Chamber Drones in the Distance.
And the Winner Is.
Christ.
Reasons to Go Home.
A Test of Competence.
The Torch.
Forman, Nicole
Labour of the Brain, Ballad of the Body.
Forrest, Frederick
St. Anthony and His Pig. A Cantata.
Forrester, Alfred A.
To My Nose.
Forrester, Fanny
The Weaver.
Forster, William
The Devil and the Governor (excerpt).
Love Has Eyes.
The Poor of London.
Sonnet on the Crimean War.
Forsyth, James
Artillery Shoot.
Soldier's Dove.
To My Wife.
Forsyth, Sarah
My Christmas: Mum's Christmas.
Fort, Paul
Ballade.
Pan and the Cherries.
Forten, Charlotte
A Parting Hymn.
Poem: "In the earnest path of duty."
To W.L.G. on Reading His Chosen Queen.
Fortini, Franco
For Our Soldiers Who Fell in Russia.
The Gutter.
In Memoriam.
Fortunatus *See* **Venantius Fortunatus, Saint**
Fosdick, Harry Emerson
O God, in Restless Living.
The Prince of Peace His Banner Spreads.
Fosdick, W. W.
Aura Lea.
Foss, Sam Walter
The Calf-Path.
The Coming American.
The Higher Catechism.
The House by the Side of the Road.
"Hullo!"
Husband and Heathen.
The Ideal Husband to His Wife.
The Man from the Crowd.
A Philosopher.
Then Ag'in.
W'en you see a man in woe.
Work for Small Men (excerpt).

Foster, Donald
Triad.
Foster, Jeanne Robert
John Butler Yeats.
The King o' Spain's Daughter.
A Pair of Lovers.
The William P. Frye.
Foster, Stephen Collins
Beautiful Dreamer.
Camptown Races.
Come Where My Love Lies Dreaming.
Gwine to Run All Night; or, De Camptown Races.
Jeanie with the Light Brown Hair.
Massa's in de Cold, Cold Ground.
My Old Kentucky Home.
Nelly Bly.
Oh! Susanna.
Old Black Joe.
Old Dog Tray.
Old Folks at Home.
Who Has Our Redeemer Heard.
Foster, William Prescott
Icebergs.
The Sea's Voice.
Foulke, Dudley
The City's Crown.
Life's Evening.
Foulke, William Dudley
Ad Patriam (excerpt).
Land of My Heart.
Foulkes, William H.
Take Thou Our Minds, Dear Lord.
Fowler, Andrew
Awake, My Soul! In Grateful Songs.
O Gracious Jesus, Blessed Lord!
Fowler, E. Kathryn
Secrets.
Fowler, Ellen Thorneycroft
The Wisdom of Folly.
Fowler, Elsie Melchert
Christmas Morning.
If You've Never.
The Miracle.
Fowler, Gene
Vivisection (excerpt).
Fowler, Hazel J.
Prayer.
Fowler, Laurence
Gather Ye Rosebuds (parody).
Fowler, Lona M.
The Middle-Time.
Fowler, Mary B.
The Promise.
Fowler, Russell T.
In Blanco County.
Fowler, William
If When I Die.
In Orknay.
Ship-Broken Men Whom Stormy Seas Sore Toss.
Fowles, John
Barbarians.
Fox, Eldon Ray
The Bumper Sticker on His Pickup Said, "I'm a Lover, I'm a Fighter..."
Fox, Gail
For Anne, Who Doesn't Know.
It is her cousin's death...
Portrait.
She lay wrapped...
Fox, George
The County of Mayo.

Fox, Lucia
Dream of the Forgotten
Lover.
Fox, Moireen
The Fairy Lover.
Fox, Ruth
Another Kind of Burning.
Fox, Siv Cedering
In the Planetarium.
In the Taxidermist's Shop.
Letter from Caroline Herschel
(1750-1848).
Letters from the Astronomers,
I: Nicholas Copernicus
(1473-1543).
Letters from the Astronomers,
II: Johannes Kepler
(1571-1630).
Nightmares.
Poem for My Mother.
A Raccoon.
To the Man Who Watches
Spiders.
Fox-Smith, Cecily
Hastings Mill.
Mules.
Saint George of England.
Foxton, Thomas
On a Little Boy's
Endeavouring to Catch a
Snake.
Upon Boys Diverting
Themselves in the River.
Fraire, Isabel
If night takes the form of a
whale.
France, Judson
An Aristocratic Trio.
Frances, Emmanuel
The Price of Begging.
Frances, Jacob
Song of Hate.
Francescato, Martha Paley
Parody.
Semen.
Francis
They Answer Back: To His
Ever-Worshipped Will from
W. H.
Francis, Colin
Tony O!
Francis, J. G.
Limerick: "An elephant sat on
some kegs."
Limerick: "There was an old
cat named Macduff."
Francis, Marilyn
Neighbors.
Francis, Pat Therese
Poem for a Neighbor.
The Telephone Operator.
Francis, Robert
Apple Peeler.
The Base Stealer.
Beyond Biology.
Blue Jay.
Blue Winter.
Bouquets.
Boy at a Certain Age.
Boy Riding Forward
Backward.
The Bulldozer.
Burial.
The Buzz Plane.
By Night.
Catch.
Cats.
Cold.
Come Out into the Sun.
Cromwell.
The Curse.
Cypresses.

The Dandelion Gatherer.
December.
Delicate the Toad.
Diver.
Eagle Plain.
Edith Sitwell Assumes the
Role of Luna.
Fair and Unfair.
Fall.
Farm Boy after Summer.
A Fear.
Fisherman.
Glass.
Hallelujah: A Sestina.
High Diver.
History.
Hogwash.
The Hound.
The House Remembers.
Hymn: "My God, I love thee,
not because."
Juniper.
Light Casualties.
Like Ghosts of Eagles.
The Mouse Whose Name Is
Time.
Mr. Eliot's Day.
Night Train.
Now That Your Shoulders
Reach My Shoulders.
Paper Men to Air Hopes and
Fears.
Part for the Whole.
Picasso and Matisse.
Pitcher.
Play Ball!
Sailboat, Your Secret.
Seagulls.
The Seed-Eaters.
Sheep.
Silent Poem.
Sing a Song of Juniper.
Skier.
Spell.
Squash in Blossom.
Swimmer.
That Dark Other Mountain.
Though a Fool.
Three Darks Come down
Together.
Two Bums Walk out of Eden.
Two Wrestlers.
Watching Gymnasts.
Waxwings.
Yes, What?
Francis of Assisi, Saint
Cantica: Our Lord Christ.
Canticle of the Sun.
Cantico del Sole.
Prayer of St. Francis of Assisi
for Peace.
Francisco, Edward
Lilith's Child.
Francisco, Nia
Awee'.
Men tell and talk.
Morning and Myself.
The One Who Is Within.
Story Tellers Summer, 1980.
Franck, Johann
Peace and Joy in Jesus Christ.
Franco, Veronica
No More Words! To the
Field, to Arms!
Frank, Florence Kiper
Baby.
The Jew to Jesus.
The Jewish Conscript.
Lincoln.
Now in the Bloom.
Frank, John Frederick
One No. 7.

Frankau, Gilbert
Gun Teams.
Frankel, Doris
Song of the Truck.
Frankenberg, Lloyd
Autumn Song on Perry Street.
Existentialism.
Hide in the Heart.
Letter to the Night.
Roots Go Down.
The Sea.
Franklin, Benjamin
The Downfall of Piracy.
Enough Not One.
Epitaph.
Epitaph on a Worthy
Clergyman.
Jack and Roger.
The Mother Country.
Franklin, Michael
The Scarecrow.
Franklin, William
The Captive.
Gotta' Smoke?
Hunger Strike.
Lawn Order.
My Street Baby's Lament.
Paper Words.
Franzen, John
O God of Stars and Distant
Space.
Fraser, Alexander Louis
By Cobequid Bay.
Fraser, Barclay
Mountain Days.
Fraser, C. Lovat
The Robin's Song.
Fraser, Douglas
Far in the West.
Freedom of the Hills.
Growing Old.
The Lost Leader.
Mountain Vigil.
On Looking at an Old
Climbing Photograph.
The Quiet Glen.
The Spell o' the Hills.
To Alan.
Fraser, G. S.
A Bought Embrace.
Christmas Letter Home.
Crisis.
Elegy.
Flemish Primitive.
Lean Street.
Letter to Anne Ridler.
Nilotic Elegy.
On a Memory of Beauty.
A Poem about Love.
Rostov.
S. S. City of Benares.
Song for Music.
Sonnet: "My simple heart,
bred in provincial
tenderness."
The Time.
To a Scottish Poet.
The Traveller Has Regrets.
Fraser, Hermia
The Copper Song.
The Rousing Canoe Song.
Song of Welcome.
Fraser, John
The Maiden and the Lily.
Fraser, Kathleen
Casa de Pollos.
Change of Address.
Dresses.
How Tuesday Began.
Interior with Mme. Vuillard
and Son.

Joan Brown, about Her
Painting.
Les Jours Gigantesques / The
Titanic Days.
The Know.
Lily, Lois & Flaubert: The
Site of Loss.
Locations.
Medusa's Hair Was Snakes.
Was Thought, Split Inward.
Nuts and Bolts Poem for Mr.
MacAdams, Sr.
Poem in Which My Legs Are
Accepted.
Poem Wondering If I'm
Pregnant.
Poems for the New.
La Reproduction Interdite /
Not to Be Reproduced.
Song (October 1969).
These Labdanum Hours.
What You Need.
Fraser, Olive
Benighted to the Foothills of
the Cairngorms.
Fraser, Ray
The Cry of an Aged One.
Ecole St. Luc.
Flora.
The Grotto.
In an Empty Window.
Lost Picture.
Not Often.
On Learning to Play the
Guitar.
Policemen Laughing.
Souster.
Frate, Frank
Love Poem Investigation for
A.T.
Frayn, Michael
A Life of T. S. Eliot (parody).
Frazee-Bower, Helen
Alien.
Courage.
A Song of Diligence.
Take Time to Talk with God.
Two Married.
Frazier, Robert
Marie Curie Contemplating
the Role of Women
Scientists...
The Supremacy of Bacteria.
Telephone Ghosts.
Frear, Mary Dillingham
The Young Workman.
Fredericks, Leo
The Rain and the Rainbow.
Free, Spencer Michael
The Human Touch.
Freebairn, A. L.
Ride 'Im Cowboy.
Freed, Ray
In an Hour the Sun.
Freedman, William
Benediction.
Formations.
Freeman, Anne Hobson
I'll Tell You What a Flapper
Is.
Freeman, Arthur
Beauty, Sleeping.
The Cat, Caged and
Shrunken.
The Cell of Himself.
Conversation Piece.
Naples Again.
On a Portrait by Copley.
The Zoo of You.
Freeman, Carol [or Carole]
Christmas Morning I.
Do Not Think.

I Saw Them Lynch.
When My Uncle Willie Saw.
Freeman, Enoch W.
Hither We Come, Our
Dearest Lord.
Freeman, Hollis
The Birds of the Air.
Freeman, James
Lord of the Worlds Below!
Freeman, John
Armistice Day.
Asylum.
Black Poplar-Boughs.
Caterpillars.
The Crowns.
Happy Death.
The Hounds.
It Was the Lovely Moon.
Knocking at the Door.
Stone Trees.
To End Her Fear.
Waiting.
The Wakers.
Freeman, Mary E. Wilkins
Blue-Eyed Mary.
Marm Grayson's Guests.
The Ostrich Is a Silly Bird.
A Pretty Ambition.
Freeman, Robert
Braving the Wilds All
Unexplored.
A Soldier's Prayer.
Why.
Freeman, William T.
Chekhov Comes to Mind at
Harvard.
Freeth, John
Botany Bay.
Bunker's Hill; or, the Soldier's
Lamentation.
The Cottager's Complaint.
Freeze, Mary D.
Our Times Are in His Hands.
Freke, John
The History of Insipids.
Frelimo
The Guerrilla.
My Brother.
Poem near the Sea.
Fremont, John Charles
On Recrossing the Rocky
Mountains after Many Years.
French, Frank
Idaho.
French, Mary Blake
Ella of the Cinders.
French, Percy
Are Ye Right There, Michael?
The Queen's Afterdinner
Speech (excerpt).
French, William Percy
Fighting McGuire.
Goosey Goosey Gander.
Freneau, Philip
The Adventures of Simon
Swaugum.
Amanda's Complaint.
The American Soldier.
An Ancient Prophecy.
Barney's Invitation.
The Battle of Lake
Champlain.
The Battle of Stonington on
the Seaboard of Connecticut.
The Beauties of Santa Cruz.
Belief and Unbelief.
The Bonhomme Richard and
Serapis.
The British Prison Ship:
Canto III. The Hospital
Prison Ship.
By Babel's Streams.

Captain Jones' Invitation.
Columbus in Chains.
Columbus to Ferdinand.
Emancipation from British
Dependence.
Epistle to a Desponding Sea-
Man.
Eutaw Springs.
The Fading Rose: Epitaph.
George the Third's Soliloquy.
The House of Night.
Human Frailty.
The Hurricane.
The Indian Burying Ground.
The Indian Convert.
The Indian Student.
Literary Importation.
Occasioned by General
Washington's Arrival in
Philadelphia...
Ode.
On a Honey Bee.
On a Travelling Speculator.
On the British Invasion.
On the British King's Speech.
On the Capture of the
Guerriere.
On the Death of Benjamin
Franklin.
On the Death of Captain
Nicholas Biddle.
On the Departure of the
British from Charleston.
On the Emigration to
America.
On the Religion of Nature.
On the Ruins of a Country
Inn.
On the Uniformity and
Perfection of Nature.
On the Universality and Other
Attributes of the God of
Nature.
The Parting Glass.
Plato To Theon.
The Power of Fancy.
Reflections (excerpt).
The Royal Adventurer.
The Scurrilous Scribe.
Sir Henry Clinton's Invitation
to the Refugees.
Song: "O'er the waste of
waters cruising."
Song of Thyrsis.
Stanzas Occasioned by the
Ruins of a Country Inn.
To a Caty-Did.
To a Noisy Politician.
To a Republican.
To an Author.
To Sir Toby.
To the Memory of the Brave
Americans.
Tobacco.
The Vanity of Existence.
A Warning to America.
The Wild Honey Suckle.
**Frere, John Hookham and
George Canning**
The Friend of Humanity.
Inscription (parody).
The Soldier's Wife (parody).
The Soldiers' Friend (parody).
Frere, John Hookham
The Boy and the Parrot.
The Boy and the Wolf.
A Fable.
The Fable of the Piece of
Glass and the Piece of Ice.
King Arthur and His Round
Table: Bees and Monks.

The Loves of the Triangles
(excerpt).
To a Lady, with a Present of
a Walking-Stick.
Inscription (in Imitation of
Southey).
Friar, Kimon
Greek Transfiguration.
Friebert, Stuart
The Age of the Butcher.
The Apron.
My Father's Heart.
Fried, Barbara
The Good Old Days.
Fried, Elliot
Amtrak.
Charlton Heston.
Daily I Fall in Love with
Waitresses.
I Can't Figure You Out.
The Man Who Owned Cars.
Mental Health.
Fried, Rivka
Sabbath.
Fried, Susannah
Scraps.
To My Father.
Winter Day.
Friedlaender, Violet Helen
Planting Trees.
Friedlander, Ginny
Here Be Dragons.
Friedmann, Pavel
The Butterfly.
Friel, James P.
Revolutionary.
Friend, Robert
The Doll.
Identity.
In the Orchard.
Letter to P.
The Practice of Absence.
The Riders.
The Test.
Friman, Alice R.
Leda and the Swan.
The Reckoning.
Fringell, Dieter
The Hopes.
Frink, A. L.
The Rose Still Grows beyond
the Wall.
Frisch, Anthony
The Convict.
Joan of Arc to the Tribunal.
Frishman, David
The Messiah.
Fritsch, H. S.
How Old Are You?
Frohlicher, John C.
Miners.
Froissart, Jean
Rondel: "Love, love, what wilt
thou with this heart of
mine?"
Frost, Frances
Apple Season.
Apple Song.
Beach Fire.
Blue Smoke.
Christmas Eve Legend.
Christmas in the Wood.
Counting-Out Rhyme for
March.
Cover.
Dandelions.
Easter in the Woods.
Father.
First Departure.
Growing.
Hallowe'en.
Hydrographic Report.

Inquisitive Barn.
Kentucky Birthday.
The Little Whistler.
The Long Night Moon:
December.
Maple Feast.
Night of Wind.
Night Plane.
Nocturne.
Rambunctious Brook.
School Is Out.
Sea Town.
Sniff.
Song for December Thirty-
First.
Spring in Hiding.
Trains at Night.
Valentine for Earth.
Weather Vanes.
White Season.
Winter Feast.
Woman of This Earth
(excerpt).
Frost, Richard
The Last Rite.
Frost, Robert
Acceptance.
Acquainted with the Night.
After Apple-Picking.
The Aim Was Song.
All Revelation.
The Armful.
At Woodward's Gardens.
August (parody).
Away!
The Axe-Helve.
The Bear.
The Bearer of Evil Tidings.
Bereft.
Beyond Words.
Birches.
The Birthplace.
The Black Cottage.
Blue-Butterfly Day.
A Blue Ribbon at Amesbury.
The Bonfire.
A Brook in the City.
Brown's Descent; or, The
Willy-Nilly Slide.
But God's Own Decent.
Choose Something Like a
Star.
Christmas Trees.
The Code.
Come In.
A Considerable Speck.
The Cow in Apple Time.
The Death of the Hired Man.
The Demiurge's Laugh.
Departmental.
Desert Places.
Design.
Directive.
The Draft Horse.
A Drumlin Woodchuck.
Dust of Snow.
Early April.
The Egg and the Machine.
An Empty Threat.
The Fear.
The Fear of God.
Fire and Ice.
Fireflies in the Garden.
The Flower-Boat.
For Allan.
For Once, Then, Something.
For Travelers Going Sidereal.
Forgive, O Lord, My Little
Jokes on Thee.
A Fountain, a Bottle, a
Donkey's Ears and Some
Books.

The Freedom of the Moon.
From Plane to Plane.
Gathering Leaves.
Ghost House.
The Gift Outright.
Going for Water.
Good-by and Keep Cold.
Happiness Makes up in
  Height for What It Lacks in
  Length.
The Hardship of Accounting.
The Hill Wife.
A Hillside Thaw.
Home Burial.
House Fear.
A Hundred Collars.
Hyla Brook.
I Could Give All to Time.
An Importer.
In a Poem.
In Dives' Dive.
In Hardwood Groves.
In Neglect.
In Winter in the Woods
  Alone.
Innate Helium.
The Investment.
John L. Sullivan Enters
  Heaven (parody).
The Kitchen Chimney.
The Last Word of a Bluebird.
A Leaf-Treader.
Leaves Compared with
  Flowers.
The Lesson for Today.
The Line-Gang.
The Lockless Door.
A Lone Striker.
Lost in Heaven.
Love and a Question.
The Lovely Shall Be Choosers.
Lucretius Versus the Lake
  Poets.
A Masque of Reason: God's
  Thanks to Job.
Meeting and Passing.
Mending Wall.
The Middleness of the Road.
A Minor Bird.
A Mood Apart.
Moon Compasses.
The Most of It.
The Mountain.
Mowing.
My November Guest.
The Need of Being Versed in
  Country Things.
Neither Out Far Nor In Deep.
Never Again Would Birds'
  Song Be the Same.
New Hampshire (excerpt).
Not All There.
Not of School Age.
Not to Keep.
Nothing Gold Can Stay.
Now Close the Windows.
The Objection to Being
  Stepped On.
October.
The Oft-Repeated Dream.
An Old Man's Winter Night.
On Looking up by Chance at
  the Constellations.
On the Heart's Beginning to
  Cloud the Mind.
Once by the Pacific.
The Onset.
Our Singing Strength.
"Out, Out–".
The Oven Bird.
Pan with Us.
The Pasture.

A Patch of Old Snow.
Paul's Wife.
The Pauper Witch of Grafton.
A Peck of Gold.
Plowmen.
Pod of the Milkweed.
A Prayer in Spring.
Pride of Ancestry.
Provide, Provide.
Putting in the Seed.
Questioning Faces.
The Rabbit-Hunter.
Range-Finding.
A Record Stride.
Reluctance.
Revelation.
The Road Not Taken.
The Rose Family.
Rose Pogonias.
The Runaway.
Sand Dunes.
The Secret Sits.
A Semi-Revolution.
A Servant to Servants.
The Silken Tent.
A Sky Pair.
A Soldier.
The Sound of the Trees.
The Span of Life.
Spring Pools.
The Star-Splitter.
Stars.
Stopping by Woods on a
  Snowy Evening.
Storm Fear.
The Strong Are Saying
  Nothing.
The Subverted Flower.
The Telephone.
There Are Roughly Zones.
They Were Welcome to Their
  Belief.
A Time to Talk.
To a Young Wretch.
To Earthward.
To the Right Person.
To the Thawing Wind.
Too Anxious for Rivers.
Tree at My Window.
Trespass.
The Tuft of Flowers.
Two Look at Two.
Two Tramps in Mud Time.
U.S. 1946 King's X.
Unharvested.
The Valley's Singing Day.
The Vantage Point.
Waspish.
Were I in Trouble.
West-Running Brook.
What Fifty Said.
The White-Tailed Hornet.
The Witch of Coos.
The Wood-Pile.
A Young Birch.

Frost, Robert Lee
The Birds Do Thus.
Caesar's Lost Transport Ships.
My Butterfly.
The Quest of the Orchis.
There Is a Nook Among the
  Alders.
Warning.

Frost, Thomas
The Death of Colman.
The Guns in the Grass.

Frothingham, Nathaniel Langdon
The Crossed Swords.
O God Whose Presence
  Glows in All.

Frothingham, Octavius Brooks
Thou Lord of Hosts, Whose
  Guiding Hand.

Froude, Richard Hurrell
Weakness of Nature.

Frug, Simeon S.
Sail Peacefully Home.
Song: "The night is an ancient
  sorceress."
The Talmud.

Frumkin, Gene
Meeting Anais Nin's Elena.
The Old Stories.

Fry, Christopher
The Boy with a Cart
  (excerpt).
Rain.

Fry, Herbert
As I'd Nothing Else to Do.

Fry, Nan
Apple.
Snow.

Fry, Susie
Fickle in the Arms of Spring.

Frym, Gloria
Season Ticket.
Training for the Apocalypse.

Fu Hsuan
A Gentle Wind.

Fuertes, Gloria
Autobiography.
Climbing.
Human Geography.
I Think Table and I Say
  Chair.
I Write Poems.
Interior Landscape.
Love Which Frees.
We're OK.
When I Hear Your Name.

Fuest, Milan
Moses' Account.

Fuguet, Dollett
The Blithe Mask.

Fujino, Seiki
Treasure Boat.

Fujiwara Ietaka
Old Scent of the Plum Tree.

Fujiwara no Kamatari
I have got her.

Fuller, Blind Boy
Bye Bye Baby Blues.
Lost Lover Blues.
Mojo Hiding Woman.
Pistol Slapper Blues.

Fuller, Ethel Romig
Diary (excerpt).
Fir Forest.
Mother–a Portrait.
The Pioneer Mother.
Proof.
The Six-Horse Limited Mail.
Today.
What the King Has.
Wind Is a Cat.

Fuller, Hoyt W.
Lost Moment.
Seravezza.

Fuller, Jean Overton
Not Marching away to Be
  Killed.

Fuller, John
Band Music.
Blues.
God Bless America.
In a Railway Compartment.
Morvin.
Owls.
De Sade.
Snapshot.
The Statue.
White Queen.

Fuller, John, and James Fenton
Poem against Catholics.

Fuller, Margaret
Dryad Song.
Jesus a Child His Course
  Begun.
The Passion-Flower.

Fuller, Robin
The Waiting-Room.

Fuller, Roy
Autobiography of a
  Lungworm.
Ballad: "Father, through the
  dark that parts us."
The Barber.
Be a Monster.
Christmas Day.
Consolations of Art.
Crustaceans.
The Dark.
The Day.
Death.
During a Bombardment by V-
  Weapons.
Edmond Halley.
The End of a Leave.
Epitaph on a Bombing Victim.
The Family Cat.
Faust's Servant.
From the Joke Shop.
The Giraffes.
Good-Bye for a Long Time.
The Green Hills of Africa.
The Hittites.
Horrible Things.
The Ides of March.
The Image.
January 1940.
Last Sheet.
Letter to My Wife.
Meetings and Absences.
Memorial Poem.
Metamorphoses.
The Middle of a War.
Mythological Sonnet XVI.
Mythological Sonnets, VIII:
  "Suns in a skein."
Native Working on the
  Aerodrome.
Nino, the Wonder Dog.
November, 1941.
October 1942.
The Other Side.
Outside the Supermarket.
The Perturbations of Uranus.
The Petty Officers' Mess.
Pigeon.
The Plains.
Poem: "Pity, repulsion, love
  and anger."
Reading in the Night.
Sadness, Glass, Theory.
Shop Talk.
Shore Leave Lorry.
Soliloquy in an Air-Raid.
Sonnet: "The crumbled rock
  of London is dripping
  under."
Spring 1942.
Spring 1943.
The Statue.
Those of Pure Origin.
Translation.
The Tribes.
The Unremarkable Year.
Versions of Love.
War Poet.
What Is Terrible.
Winter Night.
A Wry Smile.

Fullerton, Mary Elizabeth ("E")
Adventure.

Communal.
Cubes.
A Dream.
Emus.
The Farmer.
Flesh.
Independence.
Inspiration.
Lichen.
Lion.
Lovers.
A Man's Sliding Mood.
Martyr.
Ninety.
Passivity.
Poetry.
Stupidity.
Unit.
Fulton, Alice
Chain Letters.
Days through Starch and
Bluing.
The Gone Years.
The Great Aunts of My
Childhood.
How to Swing Those
Obbligatos Around.
The Magistrate's Escape.
Fulton, Dorothy R.
Open Your Hand.
Softly, White and Pure.
Fulton, Robin
More Than People.
Stopping by Shadows.
Funaroff, S.
Dusk of the Gods (excerpt).
Funge, Robert
Arcady Revisited.
Funk, Wilfred J.
Hospital.
Rest in Peace.
Funkhouser, Erica
Hammer.
Hand Saw.
Furlong, Alice
The Betrayal.
My Share of the World.
The Triad of Things Not
Decreed.
The Warnings.
Furness, William Henry
Evening Hymn.
In the Morning I Will Pray.
The Light of Stars.
Slowly, By God's Hand
Unfurled.
Fyleman, Rose
The Balloon Man.
The Barge.
The Best Game the Fairies
Play.
Bingo Has an Enemy.
The Birthday Child.
The Boat.
Christmas-Time.
Daddy.
The Dentist.
Fairies.
A Fairy Went A-Marketing.
The Goblin.
Have You Watched the
Fairies?
Husky Hi.
I Don't Like Beetles.
Jonathan.
Mary Middling.
Mice.
Momotara.
Mother.
Mr. Minnitt.
Mrs. Barks.
Mrs. Brown.

My Donkey.
My Policeman.
The New Neighbor.
October.
Regent's Park.
Shop Windows.
Singing-Time.
Sometimes.
The Spring.
Temper.
There Are No Wolves in
England Now.
Very Lovely.
Winnipeg at Christmas.
Yesterday in Oxford Street.
Fynn, Arthur J.
Land Where the Columbines
Grow.

G

G, A.R.
God Forward.
G, E., O.
My Church.
G, G.
To W.J.M.
G, L.
The Quarrelsome Trio.
Gabriel, Charles H.
My Evening Prayer.
Gabriel y Galan, Jose Maria
The Lord.
Gadbury, John
A Ballad upon the Popish
Plot.
Gadsby, Gordon J.
The Lost Valley.
Gaess, Roger
Fall Lightly on Me.
Viewing Russian Peasants
from a Leningrad-Bound
Train.
Gafford, Charlotte
Quills.
Gag, Wanda
The ABC Bunny.
Gaik, Frank
Whatever Is, Is Right.
Galai, Benyamin
To My Generation.
Galbraith, Georgie Starbuck
No Mixed Green Salad for
Me, Thanks.
Gale, Norman
Bartholomew.
Bobby's First Poem.
Child of Loneliness.
Content.
The Country Faith.
Dawn and Dark.
The Fairy Book.
A Pastoral.
A Prayer.
The Question.
The Second Coming.
The Shaded Pool.
Song: "This peach is pink
with such a pink."
Song: "Wait but a little
while."
The Voice.
Gale, Vi
After Illness.
Hurting.
Shore Birds.
Gale, Zona
Credo.

Gal'ed, Zerubavel
Chickory.
Galindez, Bartolome
In the Azure Night.
Gallager, Joseph
John J. Curtis.
Gallagher, Dorothy Hamilton
Morning.
Gallagher, Katharine
Chant for Skippers.
Poison Ivy!
Gallagher, Tess
The Ballad of Ballymote.
Black Money.
Black Silk.
Breasts.
Complicity.
Crepes Flambeau.
Each Bird Walking.
Harmless Streets.
The Horse in the Drugstore.
Instructions to the Double.
Keeping You Alive.
Kidnaper.
The Meeting.
The Ritual of Memories.
The Shirts.
A Short History of the Better
Life.
Skylights.
Some Painful Butterflies Pass
Through.
Stepping Outside.
Tableau Vivant.
To You on the Broken
Iceberg.
Under Stars.
When You Speak to Me.
Women's Tug of War at
Lough Arrow.
Gallagher, William Davis
Autumn in the West.
The Cardinal Bird.
The Mothers of the West.
Gallaudet, Thomas H.
Jesus, in Sickness and in Pain.
Galler, David
Ballade of the Session after
Camarillo.
The Execrators.
The Jersey Marsh.
The Makers.
Narcissus: To Himself.
Walking Around.
Galloway, George
To the Memory of Gavin
Wilson (Boot, Leg and Arm
Maker).
Galloway, Thomas
The Very Old.
Gallup, Dick
40 Acres and a Mule.
After Alcman.
Backing into the Fan Mail
(Unreceived).
La Boheme.
Building a House.
Death and the Maiden.
The Door to the Future.
Ember Grease.
Eskimoes Again.
Fits of Candor.
From the Beaumont Series.
The Furniture Man.
Homer.
Hygiene Sonnet.
On the Meatwheel.
Out-Dated Poem.
Pretty Beads.
Relaxation.
The Return of Philista.
Some Feathers.

Where I Hang My Hat.
Galsworthy, John
Desert Song.
Devon to Me.
Limerick: "An angry young
husband called Bicket."
Past.
Peace in the World.
So Might It Be.
Valley of the Shadow.
Galt, John
Canadian Boat Song.
Galvam, Francisco
To Our Lord.
Galvez, Javier
This Morning.
Galvin, Brendan
Glass.
A Photo of Miners.
Galvin, James J.
Hematite Lake.
Lady of O.
Morning Star.
Ox-Bone Madonna.
Galvin, Martin
Doorman.
Heron's Bay.
Hubert Horatio Humphrey
(1911-1978).
Shooting Gallery.
Gama, Luis da *See* **Da Gama,
Luis**
Gambara, Veronica
When I See the Earth Ornate
and Lovely.
Gamble, William Miller Thomas
Mediaeval Appreciations.
Gambold, John
The Mystery of Life.
Gander, Gregory
The Twelve Months.
Gannett, William Channing
Consider the Lilies.
From Heart to Heart.
He Hides Within the Lily.
The Highway.
Who Wert and Art and
Evermore Shalt Be.
Ganse, Hervey Doddridge
Lord, I Know Thy Grace Is
Nigh Me.
Garabrant, Nellie M.
The Fairy Artist.
Garbutt, Vin
Mr. Gunman.
Garcia Lorca, Federico
Ballad of Luna, Luna.
Ballad of the Spanish Civil
Guard.
Blind Panorama of New York.
Casida of the Rose.
The Faithless Wife.
Guitar.
Half Moon.
It Is True.
The King of Harlem.
Lament for Ignacio Sanchez
Mejias.
Landscape of the Vomiting
Multitudes.
Little Viennese Waltz.
Madrigal de Verano.
Madrigal to the City of
Santiago.
The Moon Rises.
New York.
Ode to Walt Whitman.
Sleepwalkers' Ballad.
Somnambulistic Ballad.
Song of Black Cubans.
Unsleeping City.

Gardiner, Wrey
Dr. Coppelius.
Our True Beginnings.
Poetry Is Happiness.
Walking in London.
Gardner, Alan
On Walking Back to the Bus.
Gardner, Carl
The Dead Man Dragged from the Sea.
Reflections.
Gardner, Edmund
Sonnet Written in Tintern Abbey, Monmouthshire.
Gardner, Gail
Tyin' a Knot in the Devil's Tail.
Gardner, Isabella
At a Summer Hotel.
Gimboling.
In the Museum.
Letter from Slough Pond.
The Masked Shrew.
Mathematics of Encounter.
The Milkman.
Nightmare.
Part of the Darkness.
The Sloth.
That "Craning of the Neck".
That Was Then.
When a Warlock Dies.
Gardner, Jo
Let Me Lift Jesus, Lord.
Lilies of the Valley.
The Only One.
Gardner, Stephen
Another Cross.
The Carpenter's Real Anguish.
Gardner, William Henry
When Love Comes Knocking.
Gardons, S. S.
The Mother.
The Survivors.
To a Child.
Garesche, Edward F.
The Young Priest to His Hands.
Garfinkel, Patricia
Blizzard.
The Tailor.
Garin, Marita
Bar Harbor.
White Spider.
"Garioch, Robert" (Robert Sutherland)"
Elegy.
Embro to the Ploy.
Ghaisties.
Heard in the Cougate.
I Was Fair Beat.
On Seein an Aik-Tree Sprent Wi Galls.
Sisyphus.
Garland, Hamlin
Color in the Wheat.
The Cry of the Age.
A Dakota Wheat-Field.
Do You Fear the Wind?
The Gift of Water.
Goin' Back T'morrer.
The Gold-Seekers.
The Greeting of the Roses.
The Herald Crane.
Horses Chawin' Hay.
In the Grass.
Logan at Peach Tree Creek.
Lost in a Norther.
The Massasauga.
The Meadow Lark.
The Mountains Are a Lonely Folk.

The Passing of the Buffalo.
Pioneers.
Prairie Fires.
The Toil of the Trail.
A Tribute of Grasses.
The Ute Lover.
The Vulture of the Plains.
A Wish.
Garland, Jim
I Don't Want Your Millions, Mister.
Garlick, Phyllis
St. Patrick (excerpt).
Garmon, John
Light Morning Snow, We Wait for a Warmer Season.
Old Trail Town, Cody, Wyoming.
Paths They Kept Barren.
Garnett, Jane
Paris.
Garnett, Louise Ayres
Hello!
The Moon.
Song of Liberty (excerpt).
Garnett, Richard
The Ballad of the Boat.
Epigram.
Fading-Leaf and Fallen-Leaf.
The Fair Circassian.
The Highwayman's Ghost.
I Hardly Ever Ope My Lips.
Marigold.
Nocturne.
Philosopher, Whom Dost Thou Most Affect.
Sonnet–Age.
'Tis Highly Rational, We Can't Dispute.
Garrett, George
Abraham's Knife.
Caedmon.
On Reading the Metamorphoses.
Romantic.
Saints.
Snapshot.
Tiresias.
Garrick, David
David Garrick, the Actor, to Sir John Hill, a Physician...
An Epigram upon a Young Gentleman Refusing to Walk with the Author...
Epitaph on Laurence Sterne.
Heart of Oak.
On a Certain Lord Giving Some Thousand Pounds for a Horse.
On Oliver Goldsmith.
On Sir John Hill, M.D., Playwright.
To Mr. Gray.
When Doctrines Meet with General Approbation.
Garrigue, Jean
Amsterdam.
Amsterdam Letter.
Beside a Fall.
Bleecker Street.
Catch What You Can.
The Circle.
The Clovers.
Cortege for Colette.
Country Villa.
Epitaph for My Cat.
False Country of the Zoo.
Forest.
From Venice Was That Afternoon.
Lightly Like Music Running.
Morality.

The Mouse.
Movie Actors Scribbling Letters Very Fast in Crucial Scenes.
A Note on Master Crow.
Of History More Like Myth.
Primer of Plato.
Remember That Country.
Shore.
Song for "Buvez les Vins du Postillon"–Advt.
The Stranger.
The Unicorn and the Lady.
You Know.
Garrison, Theodosia
April.
The Ballad of the Angel.
The Ballad of the Cross.
The Closed Door.
The Cynic.
The Days.
The Dreamers.
The Free Woman.
The Green Inn.
Ilicet.
John o' Dreams.
The Kerry Lads.
Memorial Day.
Monseigneur Plays.
The Neighbors.
The Poplars.
A Prayer.
The Road's End.
Shade.
The Shepherd Who Stayed.
Sing Thou, My Soul.
Stains.
The Torch.
The Wife.
Garrison, Wendell Phillips
Post-Meridian.
Garrison, William Lloyd
Freedom For the Mind.
Liberty for All.
Garrison, Winfred Ernest
The Book.
Thy Sea So Great.
Garrod, Heathcote William
Thou should'st be living at this hour.
Garstin, Crosbie
The Figure-Head.
Nocturne.
Garth, Sir Samuel
The Dispensary.
What Frenzy Has of Late Possess'd the Brain!
Garthwaite, Jimmy
Being Sick.
Engineers.
The Organ-Grinder.
Run, Kitty, Run!
Garthwaite, Wymond
Night Watchmen.
School after Christmas.
Garvin, Amelia Beers Warnock
See "Hale, Katherine"
Garvin, Margaret Root
To Each His Own.
Gary, Sid
Circuit Breaker.
Pythagorean Razzle-Dazzle.
Gascoigne, George
The Arraignment of a Lover.
The Constancy of a Lover.
Councell Given to Master Bartholmew Withipoll...
Dan Bartholmew's Dolorous Discourses.
The Divorce of a Lover.
A Farewell.
Farewell with a Mischeife.

Fie, Pleasure, Fie!
For That He Looked Not Upon Her.
The Fruits of War (excerpt).
Gascoigne's Good Morrow.
Gascoigne's Lullaby.
Gascoigne's Memories.
Gascoigne's Passion.
Gascoigne's Praise of His Mistress.
Gascoigne's Woodmanship.
Gascoygnes Good Night.
The Green Knight's Farewell to Fancy.
I Could Not Though I Would.
In Praise of a Gentlewoman.
Inscription in a Garden.
The Looks of a Lover Enamoured.
A Lover's Lullaby.
The Praise of Philip Sparrow.
A Sonet Written in Prayse of the Browne Beautie.
The Steele Glas.
A Strange Passion of a Lover.
Why Then (Quod I) Old Proverbs Never Fail.
Gascoyne, David
And the Seventh Dream in the Dream of Isis.
Apologia.
An Autumn Park.
The Cage.
The Cubical Domes.
Ecce Homo.
An Elegy.
The End Is Near the Beginning.
Eve.
Ex Nihilo.
The Gravel-Pit Field.
Jardin du Palais Royal.
Lachrymae.
Landscape.
Megalometropolitan Carnival (excerpt).
Miserere.
On the Grand Canal.
Orpheus in the Underworld.
Rex Mundi.
The Sacred Hearth.
Salvador Dali.
September Sun: 1947.
Spring MCMXL.
A Tough Generation.
The Truth Is Blind.
A Wartime Dawn.
Winter Garden.
Yves Tanguy.
Gasetsu
The Iris.
Gashe, Marina
The Village.
Gaskin, Bob
Letter to My Kinder.
Gasparini, Len
The Accident.
Greasy Spoon Blues.
Kafka's Other Metamorphosis.
Niagara Falls Nocturne.
Valentine.
Written on a Paper Napkin.
Gass, William H.
On Being Photographed.
Gastold, Carmen B.
Noah's Prayer.
Gates, D. Weston
Transformed.
Gates, Ellen M. Huntington
Beautiful Hands.
Home of the Soul.
I Shall Not Cry Return.

Sleep Sweet.
Your Mission.
Gatty, Alfred Scott
The Three Little Pigs.
Gauer, Jim
The Visit.
Gauldin, Sara Saper
Old Argonaut.
Gautier, Theophile
Ars Victrix.
Art.
Clarimonde.
Love at Sea.
Posthumous Coquetry.
Gavenda, Walt
Eco Right.
Gawsworth, John
Skye.
Gay, John
Air XXIII: "Sleep, O sleep."
Air XXXV: "How happy
could I be with either."
Ballad: "Of all the Girls that
e'er were seen."
The Beggar's Opera.
The Birth of the Squire.
Blouzelinda's Funeral.
A Contemplation on Night.
The Council of Horses.
Damon and Cupid.
The Dangers of Foot-Ball.
The Ditty.
An Elegy on a Lap Dog.
Epistle to the Right
Honourable William
Pulteney, Esq.
The Evening.
Fables, sels.
The Fan.
The Farmer's Wife and the
Raven.
Fly-Fishing.
The Fox at the Point of
Death.
Go, Rose.
The Great Frost.
The Hare with Many Friends.
The Highwaymen.
I'm like a skiff on the Ocean
tost.
If the Heart of a Man.
Life Is a Jest, and All Things
Show It.
The Lion and the Cub.
The Modes of the Court.
Molly Mog: or, The Fair
Maid of the Inn.
The Morning.
Mr. Pope's Welcome from
Greece.
My Own Epitaph.
A New Song of New Similes.
An Ode for the New Year.
Of Ballad-Singers.
Of Crossing the Street.
Of Narrow Streets.
Of Pick-Pockets.
Of Watchmen.
On a Miscellany of Poems to
Bernard Lintott.
On His Dog.
The Painter Who Pleased
Nobody and Everybody.
The Pell Mell Celebrated.
The Pleasure of Walking
through an Alley.
Polly.
A Receipt for Stewing Veal.
Rural Sports.
She who hath felt a real pain.
The Shepherd's Week.

Song: "Can love be controll'd
by advice?"
Song: "Love in her Eyes sits
playing."
Song: "O ruddier than the
cherry!"
Song: "Think of dress in every
light."
Song: "Were I laid on
Greenland's coast."
Sweet William's Farewell to
Black-Eyed Susan.
To a Lady.
To a Lady on Her Passion for
Old China.
To a Young Lady, with Some
Lampreys.
To My Ingenious and Worthy
Friend William Lowndes,
Esq.
The Toilette. A Town
Eclogue.
Traditional Charms for
Finding the Identity of One's
True Love.
Trivia.
The Turkey and the Ant.
The Turtle Thus with
Plaintive Crying.
The Wild Boar and the Ram.
Gay, William
The Crazy World.
Gay, Zhenya
I'd Like to Be a Worm.
I Was Lying Still in a Field
One Day.
My Birthday's in Winter.
When a Goose Meets a
Moose.
The World Is Full of
Wonderful Smells.
Gazaeus
Vota Amico Facta, Fol. 160.
Gearhart, Gladys M.
He Is Coming.
Gebirtig, Mordecai
Waiting for Death.
Geddes, Alexander
Epistle to the President, Vice-
President, and
Members...(excerpt).
Satire.
Geddes, Gary
The Inheritors.
Transubstantiation.
Gegna, Suzanne
Relics.
Gehardt, Paul
Give to the Winds Thy Fears.
Geifer, George L.
Who Threw the Overalls in
Mistress Murphy's Chowder.
Geilt, Suibne
Bellower with the Antlers.
I Am in Great Misery
Tonight.
I Am Suibne the Wanderer.
My Fixed Abode Is Glen
Bolcain.
A Rich Tuft of Ivy.
The Starry Frost Descends.
Sweet Voice of the Garb.
Though My Wanderings Are
Many.
Gellert, Chr. Furchtegott
Jesus Lives, and So Shall I.
Gellert, Lawrence
Ah'm Broke an' Hungry.
Ku Kluck Klan.
Look over Yonder.
Gellert, Leon
Anzac Cove.

Before Action.
House-Mates.
In the Trench.
The Jester in the Trench.
These Men.
Gelman, Juan
Customs.
The Knife.
The Stranger.
Genestet, Petrus Augustus de
Such is Holland!
Genet, Jean
The Man Sentenced to Death.
Genser, Cynthia Kraman
Club 82: Lisa.
Geoghegan, Arthur Gerald
After Aughrim.
Georgakas, Dan
The Acrobat from Xanadu
Disdained All Nets.
George, Daniel
Ode to the Fourth of July.
George, Emery
Homage to Edward Hopper.
A House All Pictures.
Solstice.
George, Faye
Welcome to This House.
George, M. A.
Morning.
George, Marguerite
Prisoner.
George, Phil
America's Wounded Knee.
Battle Won Is Lost.
Favorite Grandson Braid.
First Grade.
Moon of Huckleberries.
Morning Vigil.
Name Giveaway.
Old Man, the Sweat Lodge.
Prelude to Memorial Song.
Spokane Falls.
Spring Cleaning.
Spruce.
Sunflower Moccasins.
The Visit.
Wardance.
Wardance Soup.
George, Stefan
After the Festival.
Das Jahr Der Seele (excerpt).
Homecoming.
Invocation and Prelude.
The Lord of the Isle.
The Lyre Player.
My Child Came Home.
Prelude.
Rapture.
Seasong.
Stanzas Concerning Love.
The Tapestry.
To a Young Leader of the
First World War.
Transport.
Georgeou, Markos
Unseen Flight.
Georgia Tom, Hokum Boys:
Hip Shakin' Strut.
Gerald, Baron of Offaly
The Gambler's Repentance.
Gerard, Edwin
Lofty Lane.
Gerard, Jim
The Angora.
Gerard, Richard H.
Sweet Adeline.
Gerber, Dan
Love for Instance.
Gerez, Jozef Habib
Call from the Afterworld.
We Are Acrobats.

We Fooled Ourselves.
Gergely, Agnes
Birth of a Country.
Conjuration.
Crazed Man in Concentration
Camp.
Desert.
Gerhardt, Paul
Courage.
O Sacred Head! Now
Wounded.
Gerin-Lajoie, Antoine
The Canadian Exile.
Gerlach, Lee
For Peter.
The Pilot's Day of Rest.
The Pilot's Walk.
Gernes, Sonia
Practicing.
Gerondi, Abraham
Hymn for the Eve of the New
Year.
Gerrard, John
A Remonstrance.
Gershwin, Ira
Blah, Blah, Blah.
Embraceable You.
Funny Face: The Babbitt and
the Bromide.
An Incident of the
Occupation.
It Ain't Necessarily So.
Gerstler, Amy
Direct Address.
Gessner, Muriel M.
For February Twelfth.
Gezelle, Guido
To the Sun.
Ghai, Gail
Six Divine Circles.
Ghalib, Mirza
Ghazal XII.
Ghazi, A. Rasheed
A Poem on Inter-Uterine
Device.
Ghigna, Charles
Child Bearing.
Ghiselin, Brewster
Answering a Letter from a
Younger Poet.
The Catch.
Credo.
Crotalus Rex.
Dana Point.
Headland. .
Her Mood around Me.
The Known World.
Meridian.
New World.
Of the New Prosody.
Rattler, Alert.
To the South.
Ghitelman, David
Grand Street & the Bowery.
Ghose, Kashiprosad
The Moon in September.
Ghose, Manmohan
London.
Who Is It Talks of Ebony?
Ghose, Sri Aurobindo
A Dream of Surreal Science.
Ghose, Zulfikar
The Crows.
Pheasant.
The Rise of Shivaji.
This Landscape, These People.
Giandi, Paul
Midwestern Man.
Gibb, Robert
The Minotaur.
Gibbon, Monk
The Babe.

The Bees.
Devil's Cauldron.
The Discovery.
Dispossessed Poet.
Forebears.
French Peasants.
From Disciple to Master.
Salt.
The Shawls.
Song: "Singer within the little
streets."
Wiser Than the Children of
Light.
Gibbons, J. J.
The Burro.
Gibbons, James Sloan
Three Hundred Thousand
More.
Gibbons, Orlando
Madrigal: "Lais now old."
Madrigal: "The silver swan."
Gibbons, Reginald
Breath.
The Cedar River.
Eating.
"Luckies".
Make Me Hear You.
Michael's Room.
The Ruined Motel.
Gibbs, Barbara
What You See Is Me.
Gibbs, Elise
Four.
Gibbs, Jessie Wiseman
If We Believed in God.
Gibbs, Opal Leonore
Interceding.
Giber, David
All Thumbs.
Gibran, Kahlil
The Prophet.
Gibson, Barbara
After the Quarrel.
Gibson, Douglas
January.
Gibson, Evelyn K.
Heartsearch.
Gibson, Margaret
Burning the Root.
Catechism Elegy.
Gemini Elegy.
Long Walks in the Afternoon.
October Elegy.
To Speak of Chile.
Gibson, Morgan
Beyond the Presidency.
Gibson, W. W.
Prelude.
Sight.
The Stone.
The White Dust.
Gibson, Walker
Advice to Travelers.
Allergy.
Athletes.
Billiards.
Blues for an Old Blue.
David.
Epistle to the Reader.
Essay in Defense of the
Movies.
Essay on Lunch.
The Game.
In Memory of the Circus Ship
Euzkera, Wrecked in the
Caribbean Sea...
The Killer Too.
Love.
The Mountains.
Soliloquy in a Motel.
Thaw.
The Umpire.

Vacationer.
Gibson, Wilfred Wilson
Back.
Battle: Hit.
Between the Lines.
A Catch for Singing.
The Dancers.
The Drove-Road.
The Fear.
Fisherman's Luck.
Flannan Isle.
The Gorse.
Inspiration.
A Lament.
Luck.
Mark Anderson.
Marriage.
The Messages.
On Hampstead Heath.
The Parrots.
The Question.
Song: "If once I could gather
in song."
Tenants.
To Rupert Brooke.
The Vindictive Staircase or
The Reward of Industry.
The Whisperers.
Gibson, Wilfrid
All Being Well.
Breakfast.
By the Weir.
The Dancing Seal.
Eagles and Isles.
The Fowler.
Henry Turnbull.
Home.
The Ice.
Long Tom.
Old Skinflint.
The Parrot.
The Peak.
The Ponies.
Proem.
Rupert Brooke.
The Witch.
Gibson, William
Circe.
**Gibson ("Ironbark"), George
Herbert**
A Ballad of Queensland (Sam
Holt).
My Mate Bill.
Gidlow, Elsa
For the Goddess Too Well
Known.
Invocation to Sappho.
Gifford, Fannie Stearns
The Narrow Doors.
Souls.
The Turn of the Road.
**Gifford, Humfrey [(or
Humphrey)]**
For Soldiers.
A Prayer.
Song: "A woman's face is full
of wiles."
Gifford, William
The Della Cruscans.
Gil Polo, Gaspar
Diana Enamorada: Ring
Forth, Fair Nymphs, Your
Joyful Songs.
Gilbert, Celia
Portrait of My Mother on Her
Wedding Day.
Gilbert, Christopher
Beginning by Example.
Charge.
Now.
Philonous' Paradox.

Saturday Morning at the
Laundry.
Touching.
Gilbert, Ellen
Prodigal.
Gilbert, Fred
The Man Who Broke the
Bank at Monte Carlo.
The Midnight March.
Gilbert, Jack
The Abnormal Is Not
Courage.
All the Way from There to
Here.
A Bird Sings to Establish
Frontiers.
Burning and Fathering:
Accounts of My Country.
Byzantium Burning.
Don Giovanni on His Way to
Hell.
The Fashionable Heart.
In Dispraise of Poetry.
The Lives of Famous Men.
The Lord Sits with Me Out in
Front.
More Than Fifty.
The Movies.
My Marriage with Mrs.
Johnson.
New York, Summer.
On Growing Old in San
Francisco.
Orpheus in Greenwich Village.
Perspective He Would Mutter
Going to Bed.
Pewter.
Playing House.
Prospero Dreams of Arnaud
Daniel Inventing Love in the
Twelfth Century.
Prospero on the Mountain
Gathering Wood.
Prospero without His Magic.
The Revolution.
Sects.
Susanna and the Elders.
Translation into the Original.
Gilbert, James Stanley
Beyond the Chagres.
Gilbert, Mercedes
Friendless Blues.
Gilbert, Michael William
Exigencies.
Gilbert, Morris
Epitaph on a Madman's
Grave.
Gilbert, Nicolas Joseph Florent
Ode–Imitated from the
Psalms.
Gilbert, Paul
Your Own Version.
Gilbert, Paul T.
Triolet.
Gilbert, R.V.
The Great Victory.
Gilbert, Ruth
And There shall Be No More
Death (excerpt).
The Blossom of the Branches
(excerpt).
Li Po.
Rachel.
Gilbert, Sandra M.
Elegy.
The Fog Dream.
Rissem.
Gilbert, Sir William Schwenck
Anglicized Utopia.
Arac's Song.
Ben Allah Achmet.
The Bishop of Rum-ti-Foo.

The British Tar.
Captain Reece.
The Chancellor's Nightmare.
The Darned Mounseer.
The Disagreeable Man.
The Duke of Plaza-Toro.
Ellen M'Jones Aberdeen.
Emily, John, James, and I.
The Englishman.
Etiquette.
The Fable of the Magnet and
the Churn.
The Family Fool.
Ferdinando and Elvira.
The First Lord's Song.
The Flowers That Bloom in
the Spring.
The Folly of Brown.
General John.
Gentle Alice Brown.
The Grand Inquisitor's Song.
The House of Peers.
I Am the captain of the
Pinafore.
I Am the Monarch of the Sea.
Iolanthe.
The King of Canoodle-Dum.
Limerick: "There was a
professor called Chesterton."
Limerick: "There was a young
man of St. Bees."
Little Buttercup.
The Lost Mr. Blake.
The Mikado.
My Object All Sublime.
A Nightmare.
Oh, Hollow! Hollow! Hollow!
Out of Sorts.
Patience: Bunthorne's
Recitative and Song.
The Perils of Invisibility.
The Philosophic Pill.
The Pirates of Penzance.
The Rival Curates.
The Rover's Apology.
Sing for the Garish Eye.
Sir Roderic's Song.
The Sorcerer: Mr. Wells.
The Story of Prince Agib.
The Suicide's Grave.
The Susceptible Chancellor.
There Lived a King.
Thomas Winterbottom Hance.
To Phoebe.
To Sit in Solemn Silence.
To the Terrestrial Globe.
A Wand'ring Minstrel.
The Yarn of the "Nancy
Bell".
The Yeoman of the Guard
(excerpt).
Gilbert, Thomas
A View of the Town
(excerpt).
Gilbert, Virginia
Finding You.
Gilbert, Zack
For Angela.
For Stephen Dixon.
In Spite of All This Much
Needed Thunder.
My Own Hallelujahs.
O.D.
When I Heard Dat White
Man Say.
Gilboa, Amir
Birth.
Isaac.
Joshua's Face.
Moses.
My Brother Was Silent.
Samson.

Saul.
Seeds of Lead.
Gilburt, S. Gale
Bequest.
Gilchrist, Alan
Assynt.
Gilchrist, Marie
Apples in New Hampshire.
Gilder, Jeanette
My Creed.
Gilder, Joseph B.
The Parting of the Ways.
Gilder, Richard Watson
After-Song.
Ah, Be Not False.
At the President's Grave.
The Birds of Bethlehem.
Call Me Not Dead.
The Celestial Passion.
The Cello.
Charleston.
A Child.
The Christmas Tree in the
Nursery.
The Comfort of the Trees.
Count My Time by Times
That I Meet Thee.
Credo (excerpt).
The Doubter.
Evening in Tyringham Valley.
God of the Strong, God of the
Weak.
Great Nature Is an Army
Gay.
Hast Thou Heard the
Nightingale?
The Heroic Age.
How to the Singer Comes the
Song?
Hymn (excerpt).
The Invisible.
Memorial Day.
A Midsummer Song.
My Love for Thee.
The New Day: Prelude.
Noel.
O, Love Is Not a Summer
Mood.
Ode.
Of One Who Neither Sees
Nor Hears.
On the Life-Mask of Abraham
Lincoln.
Sherman.
Song: "Because the rose must
fade."
The Song of a Heathen.
A Song of Early Autumn.
Songs.
The Sonnet.
Sonnets after the Italian.
To Thee, Eternal Soul, Be
Praise.
The White City.
A Woman's Thought.
Gildner, Gary
After an All-Night Cackle
with Sloth & Co. I Enter the
Mansion...
Around the Kitchen Table.
Comanche.
Digging for Indians.
First Practice.
Geisha.
The House on Buder Street.
Johann Gaertner (1793-1887).
Letter to a Substitute Teacher.
Letters from Vicksburg, XII.
The Life of the Wolf.
Meeting My Best Friend from
the Eighth Grade.

Meeting the Reincarnation
Analyst.
My Father after Work.
Nails.
Poems.
The Porch.
The Runner.
Then.
They Have Turned the
Church Where I Ate God.
Tongue River Psalm.
Gilead, Zerubavel
Absalom.
Flying Letters.
Pomegranate Tree in
Jerusalem.
Gilfillan, Caroline
Lesbian Play on T.V.
There's Been Some Sort of
Mistake.
Gilfillan, Robert
The Exile's Song.
Gilkey, James G.
O God, in Whose Great
Purpose.
Outside the Holy City.
Gill, Brendan
Girls' Voices.
Gill, David
The Kaleidoscope.
Killing a Whale.
Gill, Eric
Mutans Nomen Evae.
Gill, John
As a Child Seeing a Cardinal.
Before the Thaw.
First Hymn.
I Don't Hear Any Melody
Breathing I Hear.
Late Spring.
Poem: "Something broke the
dream".
What Could Be.
Gill, Julia
Christ and the Little Ones.
Gilleland, Anna M.
Give My Heart a Song.
Gillespie, Dan
Abandoned Copper Refinery.
Desert Gulls.
Strip Mining Pit.
Gillespie, Robert
Snow White.
When Both My Fathers Die.
Gillespie, Yetza
Ashes of the Christmas Tree.
Gillespy, Jeannette Bliss
Forgiven?
A Valentine.
Gillett, Gabriel
Years and Years I Have
Loved You.
Gillies, Andrew
The Two Prayers.
Gillies, Valerie
Clouds and Clay.
Gillilan, Strickland
Are You There?
Be Hopeful.
Finnigin to Flannigan.
Lines Written on the
Antiquity of Microbes.
Need of Loving.
The Other Fellow's Job.
The Reading Mother.
Watch Yourself Go By.
Gillman, F. J.
God Send Us Men.
Gillman, Richard
Bones of a French Lady in a
Museum.
Moved by Her Music.

On a Very Young, Very Dead
Soldier.
Snow Fell with a Will.
Gillom, Arthur L.
I Want You.
Gilman, Caroline
Anna Playing in a Graveyard.
The Boat.
The Dead Sister.
**Gilman, Charlotte Perkins
Stetson**
The Beds of Fleur-De-Lys.
A Common Inference.
A Conservative.
Give Way!
The Living God.
Resolve.
Similar Cases.
To Labor.
Tree Feelings.
Two Prayers.
Wedded Bliss.
Gilman, Samuel
O God, Accept the Sacred
Hour.
Gilmore, Anna Neil
February, Tall and Trim.
Gilmore, Joseph Henry
He Leadeth Me.
Gilmore, Mary
The Baying Hounds.
Boolee, the Bringer of Life.
Dedicatory.
The Dice Were Loaded.
The Disinherited, IX.
Eve-Song.
Fourteen Men.
The Harvesters.
Heritage.
The Little Shoes That Died.
The Myall in Prison.
Nationality.
Never Admit the Pain.
Nurse No Long Grief.
Of Wonder.
Old Botany Bay.
The Pear-Tree.
The Saturday Tub.
The Shepherd.
The Song of the Woman-
Drawer.
Swans at Night.
The Tenancy.
The Waradgery Tribe.
**Gilmore, Patrick Sarsfield
(Louis Lambert)**
When Johnny Comes
Marching Home.
Gilpin, Laura
The Two-Headed Calf.
Giltinan, Caroline
The Builder.
Communion.
The Garden.
Overnight, a Rose.
Spring.
Gingell, Dave
In Memoriam.
Older Now.
Ginsberg, Allen
Aether.
America.
American Change.
Bayonne Turnpike to
Tuscarora.
Bop Lyrics.
Cafe in Warsaw.
Chances "R".
Death News.
Death to Van Gogh's Ear.
Dream Record: June 8, 1955.
The End.

Father Death Blues.
First Party at Ken Keseys
with Hell's Angels.
Flashback.
Footnote to "Howl."
Friday the Thirteenth.
Howl.
Hymmnn.
I Am a Victim of Telephone.
Ignu.
In a Moonlit Hermit's Cabin.
In Back of the Real.
In the Baggage Room at
Greyhound.
Kaddish.
Kral Majales.
Last Night in Calcutta.
The Lion for Real.
Love Poem on Theme by
Whitman.
Malest Cornifici Tuo Catullo.
Maybe Love.
Memory Gardens.
Message.
Mugging (excerpt).
My Alba.
My Sad Self.
The Night-Apple.
Old Moon My Eyes Are New
Moon.
On Burroughs' Work.
On Neal's Ashes.
Please Master.
Poem Rocket.
Postcard to D—.
A Prophecy.
Psalm III.
Sather Gate Illumination.
The Shrouded Stranger.
Song: Fie My Fum.
Sunflower Sutra.
A Supermarket in California.
This Form of Life Needs Sex.
Thus Crosslegged on Round
Pillow Sat in Space.
To Aunt Rose.
To Lindsay.
Uptown.
A Vow.
Waking in New York.
Wales Visitation.
Who Be Kind To.
Wichita Vortex Sutra, II.
Ginsberg, Louis
Biography of an Agnostic.
Buttercups.
Clocks.
The Hounds of the Soul.
Hymn to Evil.
Morning in Spring.
Old Ships.
Prices.
Roots.
Song: "I know that any weed
can tell."
Song in Spring.
Soon at Last My Sighs and
Moans.
To My Mother.
Gioia, Dana
The Sunday News.
Sunday Night in Santa Rosa.
Giorno, John
The American Book of the
Dead: Six Selections.
Easy to Grow.
I'm Tired of Being Scared.
I Resigned Myself to Being
Here.
Outlaw.
Paratrooper.
Pornographic Poem.

She Tasted Death.
Gioseffi, Daniela
Buildings.
Giovanni, Nikki
12 Gates to the City.
Adulthood.
Beautiful Black Men.
A Certain Peace.
Concerning One Responsible
 Negro with Too Much
 Power.
Conversation.
Detroit Conference of Unity
 and Art.
Dreams.
Ego Tripping.
For Saundra.
The Funeral of Martin Luther
 King, Jr.
Kidnap Poem.
Knoxville, Tennessee.
Legacies.
Master Charge Blues.
Mother's Habits.
Mothers.
My Poem.
Nikki-Rosa.
Poem for Aretha.
Poem for Black Boys.
Poem for Flora.
Poem for Unwed Mothers.
Poem (No Name No. 2).
Poem of Angela Yvonne
 Davis.
Poetry.
Revolutionary Dreams.
Scrapbooks.
Seduction.
The True Import of Present
 Dialogue: Black vs. Negro.
Woman Poem.
Word Poem.
Giovannitti, Arturo
The Walker.
Gippius, Zinaida
She.
Gira, R. P.
Mouth of the Amazon.
Gisborne, Thomas
Spring (excerpt).
Gitlin, Todd
The Puritan Hacking away at
 Oak.
Gittings, Robert
The Great Moth.
Gitzen, Julian
The Pheasant Hunter and the
 Arrowhead.
Gjellerup, Karl
O, Let Me Kiss—.
A Pair.
Gladden, Washington
O Lord of Life.
O Master, Let Me Walk with
 Thee.
Glaenzer, Richard Butler
A Ballad of Redhead's Day.
Glancy, Diane
Looking for My Old Indian
 Grandmother in the Summer
 Heat of 1980.
Lunar Eclipse.
Mary Ackerman, 1938,
 Eugene Buechel Photograph
 Museum of Modern Art...
There Won't Be Another.
Two Animals, One Flood.
Glang, Gabriele
August Evenings in Hatteras.
Glanz-Leyeles, A.
Deportation.

Glanz-Leyeles. A
Castles.
Madison Square.
White Swan.
Glaser, Elton
Figure and Ground.
Glaser, Michael S.
Initials.
Glasgow, Alex
The Escalator.
Hands.
Little Tommy Yesterday.
Glasgow, J. Scott
The Pipes o' Gordon's Men.
Glass, Malcolm
The Boy; or, Son of Rip-Off
 (parody).
Coming Down to It (parody).
Mullet Snatching.
Staying Ahead.
Glassco, John
Brummell at Calais.
The Burden of Junk.
Deserted Buildings under
 Shefford Mountain.
The Entailed Farm.
For Cora Lightbody, R.N.
One Last Word.
Quebec Farmhouse.
Stud Groom.
Utrillo's World.
Glatstein, Jacob
Back to the Ghetto.
The Bratzlav Rabbi to His
 Scribe.
Evening Bread.
I'll find My Self-Belief.
In a Ghetto.
Like Weary Trees.
Loyal Sins.
Memorial Poem.
Move On, Yiddish Poet.
Mozart.
The Poet Lives.
Rabbi Yussel Luksh of Chelm.
Where the Cedars.
Glaubitz, Grace Ellen
Christmas Birthday.
Walking.
Glaucus
Epigram: "Time was when
 once upon a time."
Glaze, Andrew
Fantasy Street.
The Outlanders.
Zeppelin.
Glazer, Joseph
A Visit Home.
Gleason, Madeline
Once and Upon.
Glen, Duncan
Ane to Anither.
Stanes.
Glen, Emilie
Cat Ballerina Assoluta.
Glenn, Eleanor
"Trade" Rat.
Glick, Hirsch
Silent Is the Night.
We Survive!
Glickman, Susan
Night Song for an Old Lover.
Gloag, John
The Board Meeting.
Glover, Denis
Arawata Bill.
Arrowtown.
The Casual Man.
Drift.
Dunedin Revisited.
For a Child.
Home Thoughts.

I Remember.
In the Township.
Lake, Mountain, Tree.
The Magpies.
Off Banks Peninsula.
Once the Days.
Security.
Songs.
Themes.
Thistledown.
Threnody.
To a Woman.
Waitaki Dam.
Glover, Guy
The Lucifer.
Glover, Jean
Owre the Muir amang the
 Heather.
Glover, R. W.
It Isn't the Town, It's You.
Glover, Richard
Admiral Hosier's Ghost.
Gluck, Louise
All Hallows.
The Apple Trees.
Bridal Piece.
Brooding Likeness.
Cottonmouth Country.
Dedication to Hunger.
Descending Figure.
The Drowned Children.
For Jane Myers.
For My Mother.
The Garden.
The Gift.
Gratitude.
Gretel in Darkness.
Happiness.
Horse.
Jeanne d'Arc.
Lamentations.
The Magi.
Messengers.
The Mirror.
Mock Orange.
Night Song.
Palais des Arts.
Phenomenal Survivals of
 Death in Nantucket.
Poem: "In the early evening,
 as now, a man is bending."
Portrait.
The Racer's Widow.
The School Children.
The Undertaking.
Glynes, Ella Dietz
Unless.
Goba, Ronald J.
Compozishun–To James
 Herndon and Others.
Goch, Llewelyn
Elegy for Lucy Lloyd.
Godeschalk
Sequaire.
Godfrey, John
Errant.
Reveille.
Godfrey, Thomas
The Invitation.
What Was a Cure for Love?
Godfrey the Satirist
To Grosphus.
Godin, Deborah
January.
Godley, Alfred Denis
After Horace.
The College Cat.
Eureka!
Football and Rowing–An
 Eclogue.
Lines on a Mysterious
 Occurrence.

Motor Bus.
On the Motor Bus.
Pensees de Noel.
Switzerland.
Women's Degrees.
Godley, Elizabeth
Extremely Naughty Children.
Godolphin, Sidney
Chorus.
Constancye.
Lord, When the Wise Men
 Came from Far.
On Ben Jonson.
Reply.
Song: "Noe more unto my
 thoughts appeare."
Song: "Or love mee lesse, or
 love mee more."
Song: "'Tis affection but
 dissembled."
Sonnet: "Madam, 'tis true,
 your beauties move."
To the Tune of, In Fayth I
 Cannot Keepe my Fathers
 Sheepe.
Godric, Saint
A Cry to Mary.
Godsey, Edwin
I Hope I Don't Have You
 Next Semester, But.
Godwin, A.
Song for My Lady.
Goedicke, Patricia
After the Second Operation.
At the Center of Everything
 Which Is Dying.
At the Party.
Daily the Ocean between Us.
The Death Balloon.
The Girl in the Foreign
 Movie.
The Great Depression.
On the Night in Question.
One More Time.
The Serious Merriment of
 Women.
Wise Owl.
Young Men You Are So
 Beautiful up There.
Goertz, Berniece
Wondrous Son of God.
Goethe, Johann Wolfgang von
Christ Is Arisen.
Entoptic Colours.
The Erl-King.
Faust.
The Holy Longing.
The Invisible King.
An Irish Lamentation.
Joy and Dream.
The King of Thule.
The Lay of the Captive
 Count.
The Lover is Near.
The Market-Square's
 Admiring Throngs.
Mignon.
The Minstrel.
Nor Will These Tears Be the
 Last.
O Child of Beauty Rare.
On Lavater's Song of a
 Christian to Christ.
The Pariah's Prayer.
Permanence in Change.
The Poet to the Sleeping Saki.
Prometheus.
The Rose.
The Second Poem the Night-
 Walker Wrote.
The Shepherd's Lament.
Symbolum.

The Thought Eternal.
To a Golden Heart, Worn
Round His Neck.
To the Moon.
To the Parted One.
Trance and Transformation.
True Enough: To the Physicist
(1820).
True Rest.
A Voice from the Invisible
World.
The Voice of Experience.
Wanderer's Night Song.
Wedding Song.
West-Easterly Divan, IX
(excerpt).
Who Never Ate with Tears
His Bread.

Goetz, Philip Becker
Whither.

Goetz, E. Ray and Edgar Leslie
For Me and My Gal.

Goffstein, M. B.
On This Day.

Gogarty, Oliver St. John
After Galen.
Anachronism.
Between Brielle and
Manasquan.
Colophon.
The Conquest.
The Crab Tree.
Death May Be Very Gentle.
Dedication.
Exorcism.
Farrell O'Reilly.
The Forge.
Golden Stockings.
The Image-Maker.
Johnny, I Hardly Knew Ye:
Miltonese (parody).
Leda and the Swan.
Marcus Curtius.
Non Dolet.
O Boys! O Boys!
On the Use of Jayshus.
Palinode.
Per Iter Tenebricosum.
The Plum Tree by the House.
Portait with Background.
Ringsend.
To a Boon Companion.
To a Friend in the Country.
To Death.
To Petronius Arbiter.
To the Liffey with the Swans.
To the Maids Not to Walk in
the Wind.
To W.B. Yeats Who Says That
His Castle of Ballylee Is His
Monument.
Verse.
With a Coin from Syracuse.

Going, Charles Buxton
Armistice.
At the Top of the Road.
Spring in England.
They Who Wait.
To Arcady.

Gold, Artie
Alison.
I don't have the energy...
I Have Been Thinking.
Life.
Old Road Song Poem.
The Poem I Am Writing.
R. W.
Relativity of Spring.
Sex at thirty-one.
Sun Filters through My
Window.

Gold, Jiri
In the Cellars.
An Inhabited Emptiness.

Goldbarth, Albert
The Accountings.
All-Nite Donuts.
And Now Farley Is Going to
Sing While I Drink a Glass
of Water!
Before.
Dime Call.
Family/Grove.
A Film.
The Form and Function of
the Novel.
The Greed Song.
A History of Civilization.
A History of Photography.
Joe Gillon Hypnotizes His
Son.
Note from an Exhibition.
Orphan Boy, Fishing.
Pleasures.
The Psychonaut Sonnets:
Jones.
Recipe.
A Theory of Wind.
The Tip.
The World of Expectations.

Goldbeck, Cecil
Waters of the Sea.

Goldberg, Leah
Answer.
The Blade of Grass Sings to
the River.
From My Mother's Home.
A God Once Commanded Us.
Heavenly Jerusalem,
Jerusalem of the Earth.
My Mother's House (excerpt).
Nameless Journey (excerpt).
Observation of a Bee.
Of Myself.
On the Hazards of Smoking.
Our Backs Are to the
Cypress.
The Symposium (excerpt).
Toward Myself.
When You Will Walk in the
Field.

Goldberg, Louis
Jack.
Quarries in Syracuse.

Goldemberg, Isaac
Bar Mitzvah.
The Jews in Hell.

Golden, Renny
For Jeanette Piccard Ordained
at 79.

Goldensohn, Barry
Becoming Real.

Goldensohn, Lorrie
Ambulance Call.

Goldin, Judah
Reading Faust.

Golding, Arthur
Philemon and Baucis.

Golding, Louis
Broken Bodies.
Doom-Devoted.
Is It Because of Some Dear
Grace...
Judaeus Errans.
O Bird, So Lovely.
Ploughman at the Plough.
Prophet and Fool.
Second Seeing.
The Women at the Corners
Stand.

Goldman, Michael
The Crack.

Goldrick, O. J.
Grand Opening of the
People's Theatre.

Goldring, Douglas
Newport Street, E.
She-Devil.
Streets.

Goldring, Maude
The Drowned Seaman.

Goldsmith, Goldwin
The Monkey's Glue.

Goldsmith, Oliver
Blest Retirement.
David Garrick.
A Description of an Author's
Bedchamber.
The Deserted Village.
The Double Transformation.
Edmund Burke.
Edwin and Angelina. A
Ballad.
Elegy on the Death of a Mad
Dog.
An Elegy on the Glory of Her
Sex, Mrs. Mary Blaize.
Emma.
Farewell to Poetry.
France.
A Great Man.
Happiness Dependent on
Ourselves.
The Haunch of Venison, A
Poetical Epistle to Lord
Clare.
Hope.
A New Simile in the Manner
of Swift.
On a Beautiful Youth Struck
Blind with Lightning.
On a Bookseller.
On Edmund Burke.
Parson Gray.
Real Happiness.
Retaliation.
The Rising Village.
She Stoops to Conquer.
The Sister: Epilogue.
Song: "O memory! thou fond
deceiver."
Song: "When lovely woman
stoops to folly."
A Sonnet: "Weeping,
murmuring, complaining."
Sweet Auburn.
The Three Jolly Pigeons.
The Traveller.
The Vicar of Wakefield.

Goldstein, Jonas
On Philosophy.

Goldstein, Roberta B.
Shattered Sabbath.

Golffing, Francis C.
The Higher Empiricism.

Goll, Claire
Prayer.

Goll, Yvan
Clandestine Work.
John Landless Leads the
Caravan.
Lilith.
Neila.
The Pear-Tree.
Raziel.
Song for a Jewess.

Gom, Leona
All.
Arrowheads.

Gomez de Avellaneda, Gertrudis.
On Leaving Cuba, Her Native
Land.

Gomez Restrepo, Antonio
Toledo.

Gongora y Argote, Luis de
The First Solitude.
A Great Favorit Beheaded.
Let Me Go Warm.
The Nativity of Christ.
Not All Sweet Nightingales.
Polifemo y Galatea: The Love
Song of Polyphemus.
The Rose of Life.
The Rosemary Spray.

Gonick, Catherine
The Boys Brushed By.

Gonsalves, Ricardo
And.

Gonzales De Leon, Ulalume
Words.

Gonzales Martinez, Enrique
Then Twist the Neck of This
Delusive Swan.

Gonzalez, Angel
I Look at My Hand.

Good, Ruth
Mountains and Other Outdoor
Things.

Goodale, Dora Read
The Flight of the Heart.
The Judgement.
The Soul of Man.

Goodale, Dora Reed
Ripe Grain.

Goodchild, John Arthur
The Firstborn.

Goodenough, J. B.
Orchard Snow.

Goodge, W. T.
A Bad Break.
Daley's Dorg Wattle.
Federation.
How We Drove the Trotter.

Goodman, Mae Winkler
Image in a Mirror.
Memorial.
Washington.
Your Glory, Lincoln.

Goodman, Mitchell
Coming and Going.
Man and Wife.

Goodman, Paul
April 1962.
A Classical Quatrain.
Don Larsen's Perfect Game.
Dreams Are the Royal Road
to the Unconscious.
Good Riddance to Bad
Rubbish O at Last!
Haiku: "Sprayed with strong
poison."
I Planned to Have a Border of
Lavender.
Kent State, May 4, 1970.
Lines.
Little Ode.
Long Lines.
The Lordly Hudson.
The Messiah-Blower.
Our Lucy.
Poems of My Lambretta.
Saint Harmony My Patroness.
Sonnet 21.
Stanzas.
Surfers at Santa Cruz.
The Weepers Tower in
Amsterdam.
Wellfleet Harbor.

Goodman, Ryah Tumarkin
Silence Spoke with Your
Voice.

Goodreau, William
The Longing.

Goodrich, Samuel Griswold
Lake Superior.

Goodwin, Edward B.
English History in
Rhyme...(excerpt).
Principal British Writers.
Roman History in Rhyme
(excerpt).
Goodwin, Sandra
Traveling on My Knees.
Googe, Barnabe
Coming Homeward Out of
Spain.
An Epitaph of the Death of
Nicholas Grimald.
The Fly.
Going Towards Spain.
Of Mistress D.S.
Of Money.
The Oftener Seen, the More I
Lust.
Once Musing as I Sat.
Out of Sight, Out of Mind.
A Refusal.
To Alexander Neville.
To Doctor Bale.
To Master Edward Cobham.
To Master Henrye Cobham,
of the Most Blessed State of
Lyfe.
To the Translation of
Palingenius.
Goose, Mary
Cornfield Myth.
Friends.
Insight.
Just an Old Man.
Last Night in Sisseton, S. D.
Gopaleen, Myles Na
Literary Criticism.
Gorbanyevskaya, Natalya
And there is nothing at all–
neither fear.
"Don't Touch Me!" I Scream
at Passers-By.
Here, as in a Painting, Noon
Burns Yellow.
In My Own Twentieth
Century.
Love, Love! What Nonsense It
Is.
Not because of you, not
because of me.
This world is amazingly flat.
To I. Lavrentevaya.
Gordett, Marea
Marriage.
Gordon, Adam Lindsay
After the Quarrel.
A Dedication.
Hippodromania; or Whiffs
from the Pipe (excerpt).
How We Beat the Favourite.
Question Not.
The Rhyme of Joyous Garde
(excerpt).
The Sick Stockrider.
Whisperings in Wattle-
Boughs.
Ye Wearie Wayfarer: Sun and
Rain and Dew from Heaven.
Gordon, Armistead Churchill
Kree.
Roses of Memory.
Gordon, Charles F.
The Long Night Home.
Gordon, Coco
Car Episode.
Gordon, Don
Free Fall.
Laocoon.
Sea.
Gordon, James Lindsay
Wheeler at Santiago.

Gordon, James William
Whalan of Waitin' a While.
Gordon, Judah Leib
Simhat Torah.
Gordon, Mary
The Unwanted.
Gordon, Ruth McKee
Summer Sky.
Gordon, W. J. J.
IBM Hired Her.
Gore-Booth, Eva
The Little Waves of Breffny.
The Sad Years.
Goren, Judith
October.
Gorey, Edward
Limerick: "A lady who signs
herself 'Vexed'".
Limerick: "From Number
Nine, Penwiper Mews."
Limerick: "From the bathing
machine came a din."
Limerick: "Some Harvard
men, stalwart and hairy."
Limerick: "The babe, with a
cry brief and dismal."
Limerick: "There was a young
woman named Plunnery."
Gorges, Sir Arthur
Henceforth I Will Not Set My
Love.
Her Face Her Tongue Her
Wit.
She That Holds Me Under the
Laws of Love.
Would I Were Chang'd into
That Golden Shower.
Goring, J. H.
Home.
Gorman, Herbert Sherman
The Barcarole of James Smith.
Chanson de Chateaulaire.
Lese-Majeste.
The Satyrs and the Moon.
Gormley
Gormley's Laments (excerpt).
Gorter, Herman
The Sea.
Gorton, Samuel
A Lover of Peace.....
R. B.
Gosse, Sir Edmund
The Charcoal-Burner.
A Dream of November.
Epithalamium.
Illusion.
Impression.
Labor and Love.
Lying in the Grass.
The Missive.
On a Lute Found in a
Sarcophagus.
On Yes Tor.
Revelation.
The Swan.
Gotlieb, Phyllis
A Bestiary of the Garden for
Children Who Should Know
Better.
A Cocker of Snooks.
Death's Head.
How and When and Where
and Why.
Late Gothic.
The Morning Prayers of the
Hasid, Rabbi Levi Yitzhok.
This One's on Me.
Three-Handed Fugue.
Gottfried von Strasburg
To Mary.
Gottheil, Gustav
Come, O Sabbath Day.

Gottlieb, Ann
Lady Luck.
Gottlieb, Darcy
Who of Those Coming After.
Gottlieb, Frantisek
Between Life and Death.
Just a While.
Gottlieb, Lynn
Eve's Song in the Garden.
Gottschalk, Laura Riding
Body's Head: Head Itself.
Goudge, Elizabeth
In the Stable.
Thanksgiving for the Earth.
Gould, Dorothy
Armistice Day Vow.
The Dreamer.
His Task–and Ours.
In the Name of Our Sons.
Reconsecration.
Gould, Gerald
Compensation.
The Happy Tree.
Lancelot and Guinevere.
Monogamy (excerpt).
The Sea-Captain.
This Is the Horror That,
Night after Night.
Wander-Thirst.
Gould, Hannah F.
The Spider.
Gould, Hannah Flagg
Day of God! Thou Blessed
Day.
The Dying Child's Request.
The Frost.
A Name in the Sand.
The Spider.
Gould, Mona
This Was My Brother.
Gould, Robert
Fair, and Soft, and Gay, and
Young.
The Rival Sisters, III: Song.
Song: The Hopeless Comfort.
Song: Wit and Beauty.
Gould, Wallace
After Tschaikowsky.
Communion.
Drunken Heracles.
Moment Musicale.
Night Song.
Goulder, Dave
January Man.
The Long and Lonely Winter.
Gouraud, George Fauvel
The Little Nipper an' 'Is Ma.
Gourmont, Remy de
Hair.
Govan, Donald D.
Recollection.
Gowar, Mick
Christmas Thank You's.
Gower, Jean Milne
Big Thompson Canon.
The Curtain (Old Tabor
Grand Opera House.).
Gower, John
Adrian and Bardus.
Ceix and Alceone.
Confessio Amantis.
Jason and Medea.
Medea's Magic.
Graddon, Dorothy
The Wind.
Grade, Chaim
The Miracle.
Refugees.
Sodom.
To Life I Said Yes.
Without Me You Won't Be
Able to See Yourself.

Graeme, James
The Mortified Genius.
Grafflin, Margaret Johnston
To My Son.
Grafton, Richard
The Months of the Year.
Graham, Al
Casey's Daughter at the Bat.
Limerick: "A Martian named
Harrison Harris."
Limerick: "By rocket, to visit
the moon."
Limerick: "The ladies
inhabiting Venus."
Graham, Charles
The Picture That Is Turned
toward the Wall.
Graham, D. L.
Soul.
Tony Get the Boys.
The West Ridge Is Menthol-
Cool.
Graham, Harry
Aunt Eliza.
The Bath.
A Children's Don't.
The Cockney of the North.
The Conversational Reformer.
L'Enfant Glace.
The Gourmand (parody).
Impetuous Samuel.
Indifference.
Lord Gorbals.
Misfortunes Never Come
Singly.
Mr. Jones.
My First Love.
Necessity.
Opportunity.
Patience.
The Perils of Obesity.
Poetical Economy.
Quiet Fun.
Some Ruthless Rhymes.
Tact.
Waste.
**Graham, James, Earl of
Montrose**
His Metrical Prayer: Before
Execution.
His Metrical Vow.
I'll Never Love Thee More.
Lines on the Execution of
King Charles I.
Montrose to His Mistress.
My Dear and Only Love.
Graham, Jorie
The Age of Reason.
An Artichoke for
Montesquieu.
At Luca Signorelli's
Resurrection of the Body.
At the Long Island Jewish
Geriatric Home.
Drawing Wildflowers.
Erosion.
The Geese.
History.
How Morning Glories Could
Bloom at Dusk.
In What Manner the Body Is
United with the Soule.
Kimono.
Love.
Mind.
My Garden, My Daylight.
Netting.
On Why I Would Betray You.
Over and Over Stitch.
Reading Plato.
Salmon.
San Sepolcro.

To Paul Eluard.
Two Paintings by Gustav
  Klimt.
Wanting a Child.
Graham, Rachel
  New Hampshire Farm
  Woman.
Graham, Robert
  O Tell Me How to Woo Thee.
Graham, Rudy Bee
  Memorandum.
Graham, Virginia
  Disillusionment.
Graham, W. S.
  Baldy Bane.
  The Beast in the Space.
  The Children of Greenock.
  The Constructed Space.
  The Dark Dialogues, II.
  Definition of My Brother.
  Gigha.
  The Hill of Intrusion.
  Johann Joachim Quantz's Five
    Lessons.
  Letter II.
  Letter V.
  Letter VI.
  Listen. Put on Morning.
  Many without Elegy.
  Night's Fall.
  The Nightfishing (excerpt).
  Poem: "O gentle queen of the
    afternoon."
  The Thermal Stair.
  To My Father.
Grahame, James
  The Birds of Scotland
    (excerpt).
  Sunday Morning.
Grahame, Jenny
  Wedlock.
Grahame, Kenneth
  Duck's Ditty.
  The Song of Mr. Toad.
  Wind in the Willows
    (excerpt).
Grahn, Judy
  Asking for Ruthie.
  Carol, in the Park, Chewing
    on Straws.
  The Common Woman.
  Ella, in a Square Apron, along
    Highway 80.
  Frigga with Hela.
  A History of Lesbianism.
  In the Place Where Her
    Breasts Come Together.
  The Meanings in the Pattern.
  They Say She Is Veiled.
Grainger, James
  How to Fertilize Soil.
  Ode to Solitude (excerpt).
  Solitude.
  The Sugar Cane.
Granade, John A.
  Come All Ye Mourning
    Pilgrims.
  Sweet Rivers of Redeeming
    Love.
Grannis, Anita
  The Poet.
Grannis, S. M.
  Do They Miss Me at Home?
Grano, Paul L.
  Headlined in Heaven.
  In a Chain-Store Cafeteria.
  A New Shirt! Why?
Gransden, K. W.
  An Interview.
Grant, Bobby
  Nappy Head Blues.

Grant, Gordon
  The Last Gloucesterman.
  The Old Quartermaster.
Grant, James Russell
  Africa.
Grant, Lillian
  Lines Written in a
    Mausoleum.
Grant, Richard E.
  Broken Heart, Broken
    Machine.
Grant, Sir Robert
  The Majesty and Mercy of
    God.
Granville, Charles
  Traveller's Hope.
Granville, [or Grenville],
  George, Baron Lansdowne
  Cloe.
  Impatient with Desire.
  Love.
Grapes, Marcus J.
  And This Is My Father.
Grass, Gunter
  Family Matters.
  Gasco; or, The Toad.
  How I Was Her Kitchen-Boy.
Grave, John
  If Thou Wilt Hear.
Graves, Alfred Perceval
  Father O'Flynn.
  An Irish Lullaby.
  The Little Red Lark.
  The Song of the Ghost.
Graves, Charles Larcom
  Horace, Book V, Ode III.
  An Old Song Resung.
Graves, John Woodcock
  John Peel.
Graves, Richard
  Maternal Despotism; or, The
    Rights of Infants.
  On the Death of an Epicure.
Graves, Robert
  Advice to Colonel Valentine.
  Allie.
  The Ambrosia of Dionysus
    and Semele.
  At First Sight.
  At the Savoy Chapel.
  The Avengers.
  Babylon.
  The Bards.
  The Beach.
  Beauty in Trouble.
  The Bedpost.
  Birth of a Great Man.
  The Blue-Fly.
  The Broken Girth.
  Call It a Good Marriage.
  Carol of Patience.
  Cat-Goddesses.
  Certain Mercies.
  Change.
  Children of Darkness.
  The Clearing.
  The Climate of Thought.
  Confess, Marpessa.
  Conversation Piece.
  The Cool Web.
  The Corner Knot.
  Corporal Stare.
  Counting the Beats.
  Cry Faugh!
  Damocles.
  Dead Cow Farm.
  The Death Room.
  Defeat of the Rebels.
  Despite and Still.
  The Devil's Advice to Story-
    Tellers.
  Dialogue on the Headland.

The Door.
Doralicia's Song.
Down, Wanton, Down!
End of Play.
An English Wood.
Epitaph on an Unfortunate
  Artist.
The Eremites.
Escape.
The Eugenist.
The Face in the Mirror.
The Fallen Tower of Siloam.
Finland.
The Florist Rose.
Flying Crooked.
For the Rain It Raineth Every
  Day.
A Forced Music.
The Foreboding.
The Frog and the Golden
  Ball.
From the Embassy.
A Frosty Night.
Full Moon.
The General Elliott.
Gift of Sight.
The Glutton.
The Great-Grandmother.
Grotesque.
Grotesques.
Hag-Ridden.
The Haunted House.
Hedges Freaked with Snow.
Henry and Mary.
The Hero.
Hide and Seek.
A History of Peace.
Homage to Texas.
I'd Love to Be a Fairy's
  Child.
I Will Write.
I Wonder What It Feels Like
  to Be Drowned?
In Broken Images.
In Her Only Way.
In Her Praise.
In Perspective.
In Procession.
In the Beginning Was a
  Word.
In the Wilderness.
In Time.
Intercession in Late October.
Interruption.
It's a Queer Time.
It Was All Very Tidy.
A Jealous Man.
John Skelton.
Kit Logan and Lady Helen.
Lament for Pasiphae.
The Last Post.
The Laureate.
The Legion.
The Legs.
Like Snow.
Lollocks.
Lost Acres.
A Lost Jewel.
Lost Love.
A Lost World.
A Love Story.
Love without Hope.
Lovers in Winter.
Marigolds.
Mid-Winter Walking.
Mirror, Mirror.
My Name and I.
The Naked and the Nude.
The Narrow Sea.
Nature's Lineaments.
Neglectful Edward.
Never Such Love.

New Legends.
The Next War.
Not Dead.
Ogres and Pygmies.
The Oldest Soldier.
The Oleaster.
On Dwelling.
On Portents.
The Persian Version.
The Person from Porlock.
Philatelist Royal.
The Pier-Glass.
A Pinch of Salt.
A Plea to Boys and Girls.
Poets' Corner.
Point of No Return.
The Portrait.
Pot and Kettle.
The Presence.
The Primrose Bed.
The Pumpkin.
Pure Death.
Pygmalion to Galatea.
Queen Mother to New Queen.
The Quiet Glades of Eden.
Read Me, Please!
Recalling War.
Reproach to Julia.
Return of the Goddess
  Artemis.
Richard Roe and John Doe.
Rocky Acres.
Sail and Oar.
Saint.
The Sea Horse.
Sea Side.
The Second-Fated.
The Secret Land.
Sergeant-Major Money.
The Sharp Ridge.
She Is No Liar.
She Tells Her Love while Half
  Asleep.
Sick Love.
Sirocco at Deya.
The Six Badgers.
A Slice of Wedding Cake.
Song: "How can I care?"
Song: Lift Boy.
Song: One Hard Look.
Spoils.
Star-Talk.
The Straw.
The Succubus.
Surgical Ward: Men.
The Survivor.
Symptoms of Love.
Theseus and Ariadne.
The Thieves.
The Three-Faced.
Tilth.
Time.
To an Ungentle Critic.
To Bring the Dead to Life.
To Calliope.
To Juan at the Winter
  Solstice.
To Lucia at Birth.
To Sleep.
To Walk on Hills.
To Whom Else?
Traveler's Curse after
  Misdirection.
The Troll's Nosegay.
Trudge, Body.
Turn of the Moon.
Twins.
Two Fusiliers.
The Two Witches.
Ulysses.
Under the Pot.
Vain and Careless.

Vanity.
Variables of Green.
The Villagers and Death.
Warning to Children.
The Weather of Olympus.
The Wedding.
Wellcome, to the Caves of
Arta!
Welsh Incident.
What Did I Dream?
The White Goddess.
Wigs and Beards.
Wild Strawberries.
The Window Sill.
With a Gift of Rings.
Wm. Brazier.
Woman and Tree.
The Worms of History.
The Wreath.
The Young Cordwainer.
Gray, Alexander
Epitaph on a Vagabond.
The Kings From the East.
Lassie, What Mair Wad You
Hae?
Gray, Asya *See* **Asya**
Gray, Barry
Ships at Sea.
Gray, Darrell
The 20th Century.
Foreplay of the Alphabet.
Moving.
Ode to Food.
Gray, David
The Cross of Gold.
Divided.
The Golden Wedding.
In the Shadows.
My Epitaph.
On Lebanon.
Sonnet I: "If it must be; if it
must be, O God!"
Where the Lilies Used to
Spring.
Gray, Eva
Christ, My Salvation.
It Was for Me.
Light and Love, Hope and
Faith.
My Daily Prayer.
What Is That in Thine Hand?
Gray, John
The Barber.
Battledore.
Crocuses in the Grass.
Les Demoiselles de Sauve.
The Flying Fish.
Lord, If Thou Art Not
Present.
Mishka.
The Night Nurse Goes Her
Round.
Odiham.
On the South Coast of
Cornwall.
Poem: "Geranium, houseleek,
laid in oblong beds."
Spleen.
They Say, in Other Days.
Tobias and the Angel.
The Vines.
Wings in the Dark.
Gray, Pat
The Girl/The Girlie
Magazine.
Gray, Patrick Worth
Beyond the Firehouse.
Bread Loaf to Omaha,
Twenty-Eight Hours.
Lines for My Father.
MACV Advisor.
Robert Lowell Is Dead.

Gray, Robert
5 Poems.
Gray, Sir Alexander
The Deil o' Bogie.
On a Cat, Ageing.
Scotland.
Gray, Stephen
Girl with Doves.
Girl with Long Dark Hair.
Gray, Thomas
The Alliance of Education
and Govenment.
The Bard. A Pindaric Ode.
The Candidate.
The Curse upon Edward.
The Descent of Odin.
Elegy Written in a Country
Churchyard.
Epitaph on Dr. Keene.
Epitaph on Dr. Keene's Wife.
The Fatal Sisters.
Hymn to Adversity.
Ode on a Distant Prospect of
Eton College.
Ode on the Death of a
Favorite Cat, Drowned in a
Tub of Gold Fishes.
Ode on the Pleasure Arising
from Vicissitude.
Ode on the Spring.
On Dr. Keene, Bishop of
Chester.
On Lord Holland's Seat near
Margate, Kent.
The Progress of Poesy.
Satire upon the Heads; or,
Never a Barrel the Better
Herring.
Sketch of his Own Character.
Song: "Thyrsis, when we
parted, swore."
Sonnet on the Death of
Richard West.
Stanzas Cancelled from the
Elegy.
Stanzas to Mr. Bentley.
There Pipes the Wood-Lark.
Tophet.
The Triumphs of Owen.
William Shakespeare to Mrs.
Anne,...
Gray, Victor
Limerick: "A taxi-cab whore
out at Iver."
Limerick: "A young engine-
driver called Hunt."
Limerick: "An old East End
worker called Jock."
Limerick: "Charlotte Bronte
said, "Wow, sister! What a
man!"
Limerick: "One morning old
Wilfrid Scawen Blunt."
Limerick: "There was a young
fellow called Crouch."
Limerick: "When Gauguin
was visiting Fiji."
Limerick: "When our dean
took a pious young spinster."
Limerick: "While visiting
Arundel Castle."
Gray, William B.
She Is More to Be Pitied
Than Censured.
Grayson, Caroline
After.
Grayston, Joan Byers
Dexter.
Unseen Horses.
Graziano, Frank
The Potato Eaters.

Greacen, Robert
The Bird.
Curse.
Cycling to Dublin.
The Far Country.
The Glorious Twelfth.
Michael Walked in the Wood.
To a Faithless Lover.
Written on the Sense of
Isolation in Contemporary
Ireland.
Greeff, Adele
Sonnet XI.
Green, Brenda Heloise
New England Is New England
Is New England.
Green, F. Pratt
The Old Couple.
Green, H. M.
The Cicada.
Green, J. Charles
A Day of Notes.
Departure.
Freedom.
Isolation Cell Poem.
Parole Denial.
Green, Jane
Songs of Divorce.
Green, Joseph
Permit Us, Lord, to
Consecrate.
Green, Judith
The Bush-Fiddle.
Green, L. C.
Remember Way Back.
Green, Mary McBride
Aeroplane.
Green, Matthew
A Cure for the Spleen.
An Epistle.
In Praise of Water-Gruel.
On Barclay's Apology for the
Quakers.
On Even Keel.
The Sparrow and Diamond.
The Spleen.
Green, Rayna
Another Dying Chieftain.
Coosaponakeesa (Mary
Mathews Musgrove
Bosomsworth)...
Mexico City Hand Game.
Nanye'hi (Nancy Ward), the
Last Beloved Woman of the
Cherokees...
Old Indian Trick.
Palace Dancer, Dancing at
Last.
Road Hazard.
When I Cut My Hair.
Green, Roger Lancelyn
On First Looking into the
Dark Future.
Greenaway, Kate
The Alphabet.
The Boat Sails Away.
Five Little Sisters Walking in
a Row.
Higgledy, Piggledy! See How
They Run!
In Go-Cart So Tiny.
Jump–Jump–Jump.
Little Blue Shoes.
Little Phillis.
Little Wind.
The Naughty Blackbird.
Oh, Susan Blue.
Older Grown.
Ring-A-Ring.
School Is over.
Tommy Was a Silly Boy.
Will You Be My Little Wife.

Greenberg, Alvin
So?
Sungrazer.
Greenberg, Barbara L.
The Faithful Wife.
Judge Kroll.
Greenberg, Blu
The Mikveh.
Greenberg, Eliezer
Bear, Cat and Dove.
Dog and Tiger.
Lion and Rabbit.
Parrot, Fish, Tiger and Mule.
Greenberg, Samuel
The Blank Book Letter.
Conduct.
Emblems of Conduct.
Essence.
Essentials.
The Glass Bubbles.
I Cannot Believe That I Am
of Wind.
Immortality.
Killing.
Man.
The Opponent Charm
Sustained.
Peace.
The Philosophic Apology.
Soul's Kiss.
Spirituality.
To Dear Daniel.
The Tusks of Blood.
Greenberg, Uri Z.
The Great Sad One.
The Hour.
How It Is.
Jerusalem the Dismembered.
Like a Woman.
On the Pole.
Song at the Skirts of Heaven.
There Is a Box.
The Valley of Men.
With My God, the Smith.
Greene, Albert Gorton
The Baron's Last Banquet.
Old Grimes.
Greene, Ashton
A Bather in a Painting.
The Church of the Sacred
Heart.
The Lagoon.
The Parade.
Greene, Homer
My Daughter Louise.
What My Lover Said.
Greene, Richard Leighton
Autolycus' Song (parody).
Song to Imogen (parody).
Greene, Robert
Ah Were She Pitiful.
Barmenissa's Song.
Coridon and Phillis.
The Description of Sir
Geoffrey Chaucer.
Doron's Description of
Samela.
Doron's Jigge.
Eurymachus's Fancy.
Fawnia.
Fie, Fie on Blind Fancy!
From his flock stray'd
Coridon.
Hexametra Alexis in Laudem
Rosamundi.
Ideals.
In Praise of His Loving and
Best-Beloved Fawnia.
Infida's Song.
Love and Jealousy.

Madrigal: "The swans, whose
 pens as white as ivory"
 (excerpt).
Maesia's Song.
Mars and Venus.
Menaphon.
Never Too Late: Infida's Song.
Of His Mistress.
A Palinode.
The Palmer's Ode.
Pandosto: In Praise of his
 Loving and Best-Beloved
 Fawnia.
The Penitent Palmer's Ode.
Philomela's Ode in Her
 Arbour.
Philomela's Second Ode.
Samela.
Sephestia's Song to Her Child.
The Shepherd's Ode.
The Shepherd's Wife's Song.
Sitting by a River Side.
Sonnet: "Fair is my love, for
 April is her face."
Verses under a Peacock
 Portrayed in Her Left Hand.
Whereat Erewhile I Wept, I
 Laugh.
Greene, Sarah Pratt McLean
The Lamp.
De Sheepfol'.
Greenfield, Eloise
Moochie.
Greenleaf, Lawrence N.
The Lodge Room over
 Simpkins' Store.
The Pike's Peakers.
Greenwell, Bill
The Lost History Plays: King
 Ethelred the Unready
 (parody).
Greenwell, Dora
The Battle-Flag of Sigurd.
Content.
Home.
The Man with Three Friends.
A Scherzo.
Greenwood, Grace
Illumination for Victories in
 Mexico.
Greenwood, Theresa
Here I Sit in My Infested
 Cubicle.
Greger, Debora
The Armorer's Daughter.
Compline.
The Light Passages.
The Man on the Bed.
Patches of Sky.
The Second Violinist's Son.
Gregg, Linda
Alma to Her Sister.
As When the Blowfish
 Perishing.
The Beckett Kit.
Being with Men.
Children among the Hills.
Choosing the Devil.
The Chorus Speaks Her
 Words as She Dances.
The Color of Many Deer
 Running.
Coming Back.
Death Looks Down.
Euridice Saved.
Eurydice.
The Girl I Call Alma.
Gnostics on Trial.
The Gods Must Not Know
 Us.
Goethe's Death Mask.
Growing Up.

How the Joy of It Was Used
 Up Long Ago.
Lilith.
Marriage and Midsummer's
 Night.
Not Saying Much.
Not Wanting Myself.
The River Again and Again.
Sigismundo.
The Small Lizard.
Summer in a Small Town.
Sun Moon Kelp Flower or
 Goat.
There She Is.
Things Not of This Union.
Trying to Believe.
We Manage Most When We
 Manage Small.
Whole and Without Blessing.
Gregh, Fernand
Doubt.
Gregor, Arthur
At the Trough.
The Beacon.
Enough.
The Guide.
History.
Irreconcilables.
Late Last Night.
The Likeness.
Lyric.
A Nameless Recognition.
Poem: "So many pigeons at
 Columbus Circle."
Spirit-Like before Light.
Spirits, Dancing.
To Emily.
Two Shapes.
Unalterables.
Gregor, Christian
What Splendid Rays.
Gregoria Francisca, Sisteria
Envying a Little Bird.
Gregory, Augusta Gregory, Lady
Cold, Sharp Lamentation.
Come Ride and Ride to the
 Garden.
Grief of a Girl's Heart.
He Meditates on the Life of a
 Rich Man.
I Am Ireland.
The Old Woman Remembers.
A Poem Written in Time of
 Trouble by an Irish Priest...
Will You Be as Hard?
Gregory, Carole C.
A Freedom Song for the
 Black Woman.
The Greater Friendship
 Baptist Church.
Love Letter.
Revelation.
Gregory, Horace
And of Columbus.
Ask No Return.
The Beggar on the Beach.
Chorus for Survival (excerpt).
Death & Empedocles 444 B.C.
Elegy and Flame.
Elizabeth at the Piano.
For You, My Son.
A Foreigner Comes to Earth
 on Boston Common.
Haunted Odysseus: The Last
 Testament.
If It Offend Thee...
Interior: The Suburbs.
Longface Mahoney Discusses
 Heaven.
The Lunchroom Bus Boy
 Who Looked Like Orson
 Welles.

The Night-Walker.
On a Celtic Mask by Henry
 Moore.
Poems for My Daughter.
The Postman's Bell Is
 Answered Everywhere.
Prisoner's Song.
The Rehearsal.
Salvos for Randolph Bourne.
Siege at Stony Point.
Stanzas for My Daughter.
They Found Him Sitting in a
 Chair.
This Is the Place to Wait.
To the Last Wedding Guest.
Tombstone with Cherubim.
The Unwilling Guest: An
 Urban Dialogue.
Valediction to My
 Contemporaries.
Voices of Heroes.
The Woman Who
 Disapproved of Music at the
 Bar.
Gregory, Leona
Silence, an Eloquent
 Applause.
Gregory, Padraic
The Dream-Teller.
Gregory, Yvonne
Christmas Lullaby for a New-
 Born Child.
Gregory of Narek, Saint
The Christ-Child.
Gregory the Great, Saint
Behold, the Shade of Night Is
 Now Receding.
Morning Hymn.
Greiffenberg, C
On the Ineffable Inspiration of
 the Holy Spirit.
Spring-Joy Praising God.
Praise of the Sun.
Why the Resurrection Was
 Revealed to Women.
Greig, Andrew
Marry the Lass?
On Falling.
Greig, D. A.
On a Scooter.
To a Flea in a Glass of
 Water.
Greki, Anna
Before Your Waking.
The Future Is for Tomorrow.
Grenelle, Lisa
Duel in the Park.
Grenfell, Julian
The Hills.
Into Battle.
Grenier, Robert
For Windows.
Prayer for Boom.
Prewar Late October Sea
 Breeze.
Wrath to Sadness.
Grenville, R. H.
Pawnshop Window.
Praise.
Within Us, Too.
Grenville, Sir Richard
In Praise of Seafaring Men, in
 Hopes of Good Fortune.
Gresham, Walter S.
Crowded Ways of Life.
Gresset, Louis
Vert-Vert, the Parrot.
Greville, Fanny Macartney
A Prayer for Indifference.
Greville, Fulke, Lord Brooke
Caelica, sels.
Change.

Chorus Primus: Wise
 Counsellors.
Chorus: Sacerdotum.
Cupid, Thou Naughty Boy.
An Epitaph upon the Right
 Honorable Sir Philip Sidney.
Eternity's Speech against
 Time.
Juno, That on Her Head.
Love and Fortune.
Love and Honour.
Love Is the Peace, whereto
 All Thoughts Doe Strive.
Love's Glory.
Love, the Delight of All Well-
 Thinking Minds.
Merlin, They Say.
More Than Most Fair.
Mustapha.
The Nurse-Life Wheat.
Of His Cynthia.
Of Human Learning.
Satan, No Woman.
Song to His Cynthia.
Sonnet LXXXVII.
Sonnet XCIV.
Sonnet XCVIII.
Sonnet XCIX.
Sonnet C.
Sonnet CV.
When All This All Doth Pass
 from Age to Age.
You Little Stars That Live in
 Skies.
Grew, Gwendolyn
Burning the Letters.
Grey, Francis W.
Knowest Thou Isaac Jogues?
**Grey of Falloden, Pamela Grey,
Viscountess**
Echo.
**Grider, Dorothy and Marion
Edey**
The Ant Village.
The Jolly Woodchuck.
The Little Fox.
Open the Door.
So Many Monkeys.
Trot along Pony.
Grier, Eldon
I Am Almost Asleep.
In Memory of Garcia Lorca.
Kissing Natalia.
Mountain Town–Mexico.
My Winter Past.
On the Subject of Waves...
Quebec.
View from a Window.
Grieve, Christopher Murray *See*
"MacDiarmid, Hugh"
Griffin, Bartholomew
Care-Charmer Sleep.
Fidessa, More Chaste Than
 Kind, XXXVII.
Her Heart.
My Ladies Haire Is Threeds
 of Beaten Gold.
Sonnet: "I have not spent the
 April of my time."
Sonnet: "Fair is my Love that
 feeds among the lilies."
Venus, with Young Adonis.
Youth.
Griffin, George Randall
The World Was Never Real
 to Me.
Griffin, Gerald
Ancient Lullaby.
Eileen Aroon.
Gone! Gone! Forever Gone.
I Love My Love in the
 Morning.

Know Ye Not That Lovely
  River.
Lines Addressed to a Seagull.
Maiden Eyes.
O Brazil, the Isle of the Blest.
A Place in Thy Memory.
Sleep That Like the Couched
  Dove.
Song.
To the Blessed Virgin Mary.
War Song of O'Driscol.

Griffin, Howard
Suppose in Perfect Reason.

Griffin, Susan
The Awful Mother.
The Bad Mother.
Chance Meeting.
Chile.
Distress.
Dogs.
Field.
I Like to Think of Harriet
  Tubman.
Letter to the Revolution.
Love Should Grow Up Like a
  Wild Iris in the Fields.
My Child.
Nineteen Pieces for Love: #
  15.
The Perfect Mother.
Perversity.
Pot of Tea.
Sitting.
Song My.
Teeth.
Three Poems for Women.
Three Shades of Light on the
  Windowsill.
Tissue.
White Bear.
Woman and Nature.
A Woman Defending Herself
  Examines Her Own
  Character Witness.

Griffith, Margaret
When I Consider.

Griffith, William
Aloha.
Canticle.
I, Who Fade with the Lilacs.
Pierrette in Memory.

Griffiths, T.
La Belle Dame sans Merci
  (parody).
On First Looking into
  Chapman's Homer I
  (parody).

Grigg, Joseph
Ashamed of Jesus.

Grigson, Geoffrey
Above the High.
An Adminsitrator.
And Forgetful of Europe.
Before a Fall.
Bibliotheca Bodleiana.
Burial.
By the Road.
Critics and Poets.
Discoveries of Bones and
  Stone.
End of The Affair.
The Four.
Glen Lough.
Hardy's Plymouth.
Heart Burial.
His Swans.
Inside the Cave.
June in Wiltshire.
The Landscape of the Heart.
Lecture Note: Elizabethan
  Period.
May Trees in a Storm.

Meeting by the Gjulika
  Meadow.
On a Birth.
On a Lover of Books.
On the Eve of a Birthday.
On the Relinquishment of a
  Title.
The Professionals.
To Wystan Auden.
Tresco.
Two Are Together.
Uccello on the Heath.
Under the Cliff.

Grilikhes, Alexandra
The Runner.

Grimald, Nicholas
The Garden.
A True Love.
Virtue.

Grimes, John
The Queen of Crete.

Grimes, Willard M.
Piazza Di Spagna.

Grimke, Angelina Weld
At April.
The Black Finger.
Dusk.
The Eyes of My Regret.
For the Candle Light.
Grass Fingers.
Greeness.
Hushed by the Hands of
  Sleep.
I Weep.
A Mona Lisa.
Paradox.
The Puppet Player.
Surrender.
Tenebris.
To Clarissa Scott Delany.
To Keep the Memory of
  Charlotte Forten Grimke.
The Ways O' Men.
When the Green Lies over the
  Earth.
A Winter Twilight.
Your Hands.

Grindal, Edmund
Give Peace in These Our
  Days, O Lord.

Grissom, Arthur
The Artist.

Griswold, Alexander V.
Holy Father, Great Creator.

Groesbeck, Amy
Momist.

Grosholz, Emily
Letter from Germany.
Rodin to Rilke.

Gross, June
The Drivers of Boston.

Gross, Ronald
Barbie-Doll Goes to College.
Yield.

Grossbardt, Andrew
At Pont-Aven, Gauguin's Last
  Home in France.
Jogging at Dusk.
A River in Asia.

Grosseteste, Robert
A Little Song.

Grossman, Allen
By the Pool.
Lilith.

Grossman, Florence
Riding.

Grossman, Martin
The Bread of Our Affliction.
Into the Book.
A Place to Live.

Grossman, Reuben
Therefore, We Thank Thee,
  God.

Grossman, Richard
The Art of Love.

Group, Verda
I Know.

Grove, Matthew
In Praise of His Lady.

Gruber, A. L.
My Neighbor's Roses.

Gruber, Edmund L.
The Caisson Song.

Gruber, Johann A.
Love That's Pure, Itself
  Disdaining.

Grudin, Louis
Citizen.
Dust on Spring Street.

Grundtvig, Nicolai
I Know a Flower So Fair and
  Fine.

Grunewald, Alfred
The Lamp Now Flickers.

Grutzmacher, Harold M.
Knowledge.

Grynberg, Henryk
Anti-Nostalgia.
The Dead Sea.
Listening to a Confucious.
Poplars.

Guarini, Giovanni Battista
Claim to Love.
Il Pastor Fido.
A Ladies Prayer to Cupid.
Spring.
Thus Saith My Chloris Bright.

Gudmundsson, Gudmundur
Lament.

Guebuza, Armando
If You Ask Me Who I Am.
Your Pain.

Guerin, Charles
In My Old Verses.
Partings.

Guernsey, Bruce
The Apple.
Back Road.
June Twenty-First.

Guernsey, Wellington
Alice, Where Art Thou?

Guerzo, di Montecanti
Sonnet: He Is Out of Heart
  with His Time.

Guest, Barbara
Belgravia.
Everything in the Air Is a
  Bird.
The First of May.
Green Revolutions.
The Hero Leaves His Ship.
The Location of Things.
The Luminous.
Parachutes, My Love, Could
  Carry Us Higher.
Parade's End.
Piazzas.
Poem: "Disturbing to have a
  person."
Les Realites.
Red Lilies.
River Road Studio.
Sadness.
Santa Fe Trail.
Sunday Evening.
Wave.

Guest, Edgar A.
All That Matters.
Becoming a Dad.
The Crucible of Life (excerpt).
Equipment.
A Friend's Greeting.

Grace at Evening.
Home.
It Couldn't Be Done.
Just Folks.
The Kindly Neighbor.
Lemon Pie.
Lord, Make a Regular Man
  Out of Me.
Myself.
Out Fishin'.
Prayer for the Home
  (excerpt).
Sausage.
Sittin' on the Porch.
Stick to It.
Success.
The Things That Make a
  Soldier Great.
What's In It For Me?
You.

Guidacci, Margherita
All Saint's Day (excerpt).
At Night.

Guido delle Colonne
Canzone: To Love and to His
  Lady.

Guild, Marilla Merrimar
The Ocotillo in Bloom.

Guillaume de Lorris
The Romance of the Rose.

Guillaume de Poitiers
Count William's Escapade.

Guillen, Jorge
Metropolitan Night.
Names.

Guillen, Nicolas
Dead Soldier.
Guadalupe, W.I.
Proposition.
Sightseers in a Courtyard.
Two Children.

Guillet, Pernette de
Non Que Je Veuille Oter La
  Liberte.

Guiney, Louise Imogen
Carol.
Deo Optimo Maximo.
Five Carols for Christmastide.
A Footnote to a Famous
  Lyric.
In Leinster.
John Brown: A Paradox.
The Kings.
Martyr's Memorial.
Monochrome.
Nam Semen Est Verbum Dei.
Ode for a Master Mariner
  Ashore.
Of Joan's Youth.
On First Entering
  Westminster Abbey.
An Outdoor Litany.
Pax Paganica.
Sanctuary.
A Song from Sylvan.
To a Dog's Memory.
Tryste Noel.
Valse Jeune.
The Wild Ride.

Guinicelli, Guido
Canzone: He Perceives His
  Rashness in Love, but Has
  No Choice.
Canzone: Of the Gentle Heart.
Sonnet: He Will Praise His
  Lady.
Sonnet: Of Moderation and
  Tolerance.

Guinness, Bryan
The Summer Is Coming.
What Are They Thinking...

Guiterman, Arthur
Ain't Nature Commonplace!
Alibi (parody).
The Ambiguous Dog.
Ancient History.
Anthologistics.
Anthony Wayne.
Bears.
Belsnickel.
Brief Essay on Man.
The Call to the Colors.
The Christmas Exchange.
Consolation (parody).
Constitution for a League of
Nations.
Coyote and the Star.
The Dance of Gray Raccoon.
Daniel Boone.
The Dog Parade.
The Dog's Cold Nose.
Eight Oars and a Coxswain.
Elegy.
Ephraim the Grizzly.
Epilogue to a Book of Verse.
Everything in Its Place.
For a Good Dog.
Growing Up.
Haarlem Heights.
Habits of the Hippopotamus.
Harvest Home.
He Leads Us Still.
Heredity.
Hills.
House Blessing.
Husband and Wife.
In Praise of Llamas.
In the Hospital.
Indian Pipe and Moccasin
Flower.
Lament for the Alamo.
The Legend of the First Cam-
u-el.
Little Lost Pup.
Little Ponds.
Local Note.
March.
Mavrone.
Mexican Serenade.
Motto for a Dog House.
Nature Note.
Ode of Odium on Aquariums.
Ode to the Hayden
Planetarium.
Of Certain Irish Fairies.
Of Tact.
An Offer.
On the Vanity of Earthly
Greatness.
The Oregon Trail.
Ornithology in Florida.
The Pioneer.
A Poet's Proverbs.
The Prairie Dog.
Prayer.
Quivira.
Reward of Virtue.
The Rush of the Oregon.
The Scribe's Prayer.
Sea-Chill.
The Shakespearean Bear.
A Skater's Valentine.
Song of Hate for Eels.
The Starlighter.
The Storming of Stony Point.
Strictly Germ-Proof.
The Superstitious Ghost.
Thanksgiving Wishes.
Tradition.
Twist-Rime on Spring.
Under the Goal Posts.
What the Gray Cat Sings.

The Whole Duty of a Poem.
Young Washington.
Guittone d'Arezzo
Lady of Heaven.
Gulick, Alida Carey
On Waking.
Gullans, Charles
Autumn: An Ode.
Autumn Burial: A Meditation.
First Love.
Narcissus.
Poema Morale.
Satyr.
To a Friend.
Gumilev, Nikolai
The Giraffe.
How Could We, Beforehand,
Live in Quiet.
Gummere, Francis Barton
John Bright.
Gunn, Louise D.
Conversation with Rain.
Gunn, Thom
The Allegory of the Wolf Boy.
The Annihilation of Nothing.
Apartment Cats.
Autumn Chapter in a Novel.
Baby Song.
Back to Life.
Before the Carnival.
Black Jackets.
Breakfast.
The Byrnies.
Carnal Knowledge.
The Cherry Tree.
Claus Von Stauffenberg.
Confessions of the Life Artist.
Considering the Snail.
The Corridor.
Das Liebesleben.
The Discovery of the Pacific.
Elegy on the Dust.
Expression.
Faustus Triumphant.
Fever.
From the Highest Camp.
From the Wave.
Hampstead: The Horse
Chestnut Trees.
High Fidelity.
The Idea of Trust.
In Santa Maria Del Popolo.
In the Tank.
Incident on a Journey.
Innocence.
Iron Landscapes (and the
Statue of Liberty).
Jesus and His Mother.
Lights among Redwood.
Loot.
Merlin in the Cave: He
Speculates without a Book.
The Messenger.
A Mirror for Poets.
Misanthropos (excerpt).
Modes of Pleasure.
Moly.
My Sad Captains.
The Nature of an Action.
New York.
No Speech from the Scaffold.
On the Move.
Painkillers.
The Rooftop.
Slow Waker.
St. Martin and the Beggar.
Street Song.
Tamer and Hawk.
To Yvor Winters, 1955.
Touch.
A Trucker.

The Unsettled Motorcyclist's
Vision of His Death.
Vox Humana.
The Wheel of Fortune.
The Wound.
Gunnars, Kristjana
Changeling VIII.
Coalface universe.
The dots of de dondi.
Monkshood.
Wakepick I.
Gunning, Sara Ogan
Girl of Constant Sorrow.
Gurevitch, Zali
Not Going with It.
Short Eulogy.
Guri, Haim
Anath.
And on My Return.
But We Shall Bloom.
Isaac.
A Latter Purification.
My Samsons.
Nine Men out of a Minyan.
Piyyut for Rosh Hashana.
Prayer.
Rain.
Gurley, Edith B.
His Gift and Mine.
Gurney, Dorothy Frances
The Lord God Planted a
Garden.
Gurney, Ivor
After War.
Ballad of the Three Spectres.
The Bohemians.
Canadians.
Dawns I Have Seen.
Elver Fishers.
Epitaph on a Young Child.
The Escape.
The High Hills.
Larches.
The Love Song.
Moments.
On the Night.
Possessions.
Rainy Midnight.
Requiem.
The Silent One.
Song: "Only the wanderer."
Strange Hells.
To His Love.
Tobacco Plant.
Gurney, Lawrence
Nevada.
Gurr, Robin
Creation.
Gustafson, Jim
Ambitious.
The Dance.
The Idea of Detroit.
The Idea of San Francisco.
Nervous Miracles.
No Money in Art.
Gustafson, Ralph
Armorial.
Aspects of Some Forsythia
Branches.
At the Ocean's Verge.
Carta Canadensis.
Columbus Reaches Juana,
1492.
Dedication.
The Fish.
Legend.
The Meaning.
Mothy Monologue.
On the Road to Vicenza.
On the Struma Massacre.
On This Sea-Floor.

Ramble on What in the
World Why.
S.S.R., Lost at Sea–The
Times.
Wednesday at North Hatley.
Guthrie, Charles E.
God's Will.
Guthrie, Norman Gregor *See*
"Crichton, John"
Guthrie, James
Last Song.
Guthrie, Ramon
The Clown: He Dances in the
Clearing by Night.
Noel Tragique.
Postlude: for Goya.
To and on Other Intellectual
Poets....
Guthrie, Thomas Anstey
Burglar Bill.
Limerick: "There was an old
man of Bengal."
Guthrie, Woody
The 1913 Massacre.
Hard Traveling.
I've Got to Know.
Jesus Christ.
The Ludlow Massacre.
Pastures of Plenty.
Plane Wreck at Los Gatos.
Tom Joad.
Union Maid.
Gutierrez, Jose Angel
22 Miles.
Gutierrez Najera, Manuel
In the Depths of Night.
Gutteridge, Bernard
Burma Hills.
Man into a Churchyard.
Namkwin Pul.
Patrol: Buonamary.
Guyon, Jeanne Marie
Adoration.
A Little Bird I Am.
Gwala, Mafika Pascal
From the Outside.
Promise!
The Shebeen Queen.
Sunset.
Gwillim, Joy
The Ritual.
Gwynne, J. Harold
The Good Shepherd.
The Word of God.
Gwynne, Stephen Lucius
Ireland.
Gyles, Althea
Sympathy.

H

"H, B."
Anacreon to the Sophist.
"H, C. G."
The Power of Innocence.
"H—, Captain"
An Imitation of Martial, Book
II Ep. 105.
"H., F. L."
The Father Knows.
"H., M. G."
He Never Will Forget.
Ha-Nagid, Samuel
Proverbs.
Haad, Siraad
Lament for a Dead Lover.
Haaff, Katherine Maurine
Good Thoughts.

Haag, Terri
Truck Drivers.
Habercom, David
The Life Not Given.
Habington, William
Against Them Who Lay
Unchastity to the Sex of
Women.
Castara.
Cogitabo Pro Peccato Meo.
The Compliment.
The Description of Castara.
A Dialogue betweene Araphill
and Castara.
Elegie.
His Muse Speaks to Him.
Melancholy.
Nox Nocti Indicat Scientiam.
Pretty Sport.
Quoniam Ego in Flagella
Paratus Sum.
The Reward of Innocent
Love.
Time! Where Dist Thou Those
Years Inter.
To a Friend, Inviting Him to
a Meeting upon Promise.
To a Wanton.
To Death, Castara Being
Sicke.
To Roses in the Bosom of
Castara.
To the Right Honourable the
Countesse of C.
To the World the Perfection
of Love.
Upon Castara's Absence.
Upon Thought Castara May
Die.
Welcome, Thou Safe Retreat!
What Am I Who Dare.
Hacker, Marilyn
After the Revolution.
Alba: March.
Aube Provencale.
Before the War.
Canzone.
Elektra on Third Avenue.
La Fontaine de Vaucluse.
The Hang-Glider's Daughter.
Lines Declining a
Transatlantic Dinner
Invitation.
Living in the Moment.
Ordinary Women.
Presentation Piece.
Rondeau after a Transatlantic
Telephone Call.
September.
Sonnet Ending with a Film
Subtitle.
Sonnet: "Matte brandy bottle,
adjacent voices, skin."
Under the Arc de Triomphe:
October 17.
Villanelle.
Hackett, Francis
Sea Dawn.
Hackett, J. W.
Haiku: "A bitter morning:".
Hackleman, Kris
Not to March.
Hadden, Maude Miner
Creative Force.
Hadewijch
Ah Yes, When Love Allows.
All Things Confine.
The Eighteenth Song.
Had I Been Mindful of My
High Descent.
Love has seven names.

What Helps It If of Love I
Sing.
Hadley, Lydia
The Four Calls.
**Hadrian, Emperor (Publius
Aelius Hadrianus)**
Animula Vagula, Blandula.
Hadrian's Address to His Soul
When Dying.
My Little Soul, My Vagrant
Charmer.
To His Soul.
Hafen, Ann Woodbury
Mountain Liars.
Hafiz
From the Garden of Heaven.
Lady That Hast My Heart.
The lips of the one I love are
my perpetual pleasure.
Love Is Where the Glory
Falls.
Odes, sels.
A Persian Song of Hafiz.
Slaves of Thy Shining Eyes.
Hafsa bint al-Hajj
Shall I Come There, or You
Here?
Hagarty, Sir John H.
Funeral of Napoleon I.
Hagedorn, Hermann
Doors.
Early Morning at Bargis.
Evening Prayer.
The Eyes of God.
Light.
The Mother in the House.
Noah.
Prayer during Battle.
Solomon.
Song: "Song is so old."
A Troop of the Guard.
Hagedorn, Jessica
Chiqui and Terra Nova.
Listen.
Ming the Merciless.
Motown/Smokey Robinson.
Song for My Father.
The Woman Who Thought
She Was More Than a
Samba.
Hageman, Samuel Miller
Silence.
Hagerup, Inger
Dies Irae.
Emily Dickinson.
Hagg, Esther Lloyd
His Garments.
It Was Not Strange.
Hagiwara, Sakutaro
A Bar at Night.
World of Bacteria.
Hahn, Kimiko
Dance Instructions for a
Young Girl.
Daughter.
A Girl Combs Her Hair.
When You Leave.
Hahn, Oscar
Adolph Hitler Meditates on
the Jewish Problem.
Hahn, Steve
A July Storm: Johnson,
Nemaha Country, Nebraska.
October.
Hai-Jew, Dianne
Days Ago.
Foreign Soil.
Thirst of the Dragon.
This Night.

Haicead, Padraigin
On Hearing It Has Been
Ordered in the
Chapterhouses of Ireland...
Haight, Dorothy
A New Orleans Balcony–1880.
Haines, John
And When the Green Man
Comes.
At Slim's River.
At White River.
Awakening.
The Cauliflower.
Certain Dead.
The Child in the Rug.
Cicada.
The Cloud Factory.
The Color.
Dream of the Lynx.
Dusk of the Revolutionaries.
The End of the Street.
The Flight.
For Daphne at Lone Lake.
Foreboding.
Forest without Leaves
(excerpt).
The Goshawk.
Homage to David Smith.
If the Owl Calls Again.
Into the Glacier.
The Invaders.
The Lake in the Sky.
The Legend of Paper Plates.
Little Cosmic Dust Poem.
Marigold.
Men against the Sky.
The Middle Ages.
The Mole.
Paul Klee.
A Poem Like a Grenade.
Prayer to the Snowy Owl.
Rain.
Ryder.
The Snowbound City.
Snowy Night.
Spilled Milk.
To Turn Back.
To Vera Thompson.
The Train Stops at Healy
Fork.
The Tundra.
Winter News.
Wolves.
Hairston, Brother Will
Alabama Bus.
Hajek, Louise
No Madam Butterfly.
Hajnal, Anna
Dead Girl.
Fear.
The Felled Plane Tree.
Half Past Four, October.
That's All?
Tree to Flute.
Hake, Thomas Gordon
The Snake-Charmer.
Hakutsu
O Pine-Tree Standing.
Halas, Frantisek
Again.
And Then There.
Halbisch, Harry
Warp and Woof.
Haldane, J. B. S.
Cancer's a Funny Thing.
Haldane, Sean
I Meant to Tell You.
Hale, Arthur
Manila Bay.
The Yankee Privateer.
Hale, Edward Everett
Adrian Block's Song.

Alma Mater's Roll.
Anne Hutchinson's Exile.
The Ballad of Bunker Hill.
Columbus.
From Potomac to Merrimac.
The Lamentable Ballad of the
Bloody Brook.
Lend a Hand.
Look Up!
The Marching Song of Stark's
Men.
The Nameless Saints.
New England's Chevy Chase,
April 19, 1775.
Omnipresence.
The One Thousandth Psalm.
Put It Through.
Hale, Janet Campbell
Aaron Nicholas, Almost Ten.
Backyard Swing.
Cinque.
Custer Lives in Humboldt
County.
Desmet, Idaho, March 1969.
Getting Started.
On a Catholic Childhood.
On Death and Love.
Salad La Raza.
Scene from a Dream.
Six Feet Under.
Walls of Ice.
Where Have All the Indians
Gone?
**"Hale, Katherine" (Amelia
Beers Warnock Garvin)**
Eternal Moment.
Giant's Tomb in Georgian
Bay.
Lost Garden.
Portrait of a Cree.
Hale, Oliver
Where Unimaginably Bright.
Hale, Robert Beverly
The Big Nasturtiums.
Denise.
The Ovibos.
Hale, Sarah Josepha
Alice Ray.
Mary's Lamb.
The Mole and the Eagle.
Our Father in Heaven.
The Watcher.
Hales, Thomas of *See* **Thomas of
Hales**
Halevi, Judah
Amid the Myrtles.
Asleep in the Bosom of
Youth.
Awake, My Fair.
The Dove.
The Earth in Spring.
Fortune's Treachery.
God, Whom Shall I Compare
to Thee?
The Grey Hair.
Hymn for Atonement Day.
Immortal Israel.
Israel's Duration.
A Letter to His Friend Isaac.
Longing.
Longing for Jerusalem.
Lord, Where Shall I Find
Thee?
Love Song.
Marriage Song.
Meditation on Communion
with God.
My Heart Is in the East.
Ode to Zion.
On Parting with Moses Ibn
Ezra.
Ophra.

Parted Lovers.
Parting.
The Pride of a Jew.
Sabbath, My Love.
Song of Loneliness.
Three Love Poems.
Time-Servers.
To the Bridegroom.
To the Choice Bridegroom.
To the Western Wind.
To Zion.
Words Wherein Stinging Bees
Lurk.
Haley, Ed
The Fountain in the Park.
While Strolling through the
Park.
Haley, Molly Anderson
And Lo, the Star!
A Christmas Prayer.
He Is Our Peace.
We Have Seen His Star in the
East.
Haley, Vanessa
At the Smithsonian.
Halkin, Shimon
Do Not Accompany Me.
A Drop of Dew.
Hall, Amanda Benjamin
The Great Farewells.
I'll Build My House.
It Seems That God Bestowed
Somehow.
Joe Tinker.
Joy o' Living.
Too Soon the Lightest Feet.
The Wanderer.
A Woman of Words.
Hall, Caroline Breese
Chicken Soup Therapy: Its
Mode of Action.
Hall, Carolyn
Fireflies.
Hall, Charles Sprague
Glory Hallelujah! or John
Brown's Body.
John Brown's Body.
Hall, Donald
Abroad Thoughts from Home.
Afternoon.
An Airstrip in Essex, 1960.
The Alligator Bride.
Apples.
The Beautiful Horses.
The Black Faced Sheep.
The Blue Wing.
The Body Politic.
The Brain Cells.
Breasts.
By the Exeter River.
The Child.
Christ Church Meadows,
Oxford.
Christmas Eve in
Whitneyville, 1955.
The Clown.
Cold Water.
Crew-Cuts.
Detroit.
Exile.
The Farm.
Five Epigrams.
For an Early Retirement.
Gold.
The Henyard Round.
In the Old House.
Je Suis une Table.
The Jealous Lovers.
Kicking the Leaves.
Laocoon.
The Long River.
Marriage: To K.

The Moon.
The Morning Porches.
Munch's Scream.
My Son, My Executioner.
Names of Horses.
New Hampshire.
The Old Pilot.
On a Horse Carved in Wood.
Ox Cart Man.
Philander.
A Poet at Twenty.
Professor Gratt.
Questions ⅛.
The Raisin.
Reclining Figure.
A Second Stanza for Dr.
Johnson.
Self-Portrait, as a Bear.
Sestina.
The Shudder.
Six Poets in Search of a
Lawyer.
The Sleeping Giant.
The Snow.
Sudden Things.
Swan.
T. R.
The Three Movements.
The Town of Hill.
Valentine.
Wedding Party.
Wells.
White Apples.
The Wives.
Woolworth's.
Your Voice on the Telephone.
Hall, Eugene J.
The Engineer's Story.
Hall, Gertrude
Angels.
The Dust.
Mrs. Golightly.
My Old Counselor.
Hall, Gregory
The Voice of the Power of
This World.
Hall, Hattie Vose
Two Temples.
Hall, Hazel
Flight.
Footsteps.
Foreboding.
June Night.
Late Winter.
Maker of Songs.
My Song.
Twilight.
Hall, Henry
A Ballad on the Times.
On Sir John Fenwick.
Upon the King's Return from
Flanders.
Hall, Henry Clay
Who Does Not Love True
Poetry.
Hall, J. C.
The Crack.
Montgomery.
Responsibilities.
The Telescope.
War.
Hall, James Baker
The Mad Farmer Stands Up
in Kentucky for What He
Thinks Is Right.
The Modern Chinese History
Professor Plays Pool Every
Tuesday...
The Old Athens of the West
Is Now a Blue Grass Tour.
The Song of the Mean Mary
Jean Machine.

Stafford in Kansas (parody).
Hall, James Norman
Eat and Walk.
Hall, Jim
Laughing Backwards.
Waking, the Love Poem Sighs.
Hall, Joan Joffe
Graffiti for Lovers.
The Homeless.
Hall, John
The Call.
Dark Shadows.
An Epicurean Ode.
On an Houre-Glasse.
Pastoral Hymn.
Song: "Distil not poison in
mine ears."
To His Tutor.
What need I travel, since I
may.
Hall, Joseph
The Olden Days.
Virgidemiarum.
Hall, Katie V.
The Old Filthy Beer Pail.
Hall, Kay DeBard
Deer in Aspens.
Hall, Margaret S.
Life Is So Short.
Hall, Mary Lee
Turn Again to Life.
Hall, Owen
Tell Me Pretty Maiden.
Hall, R. W.
The Last Longhorn.
Hall, Radclyffe
Forgotten Island.
Hall, Rodney
Black Bagatelles.
Eyewitness.
Journey.
Mrs. Macintosh.
The Owner of My Face.
A Text for These Distracted
Times.
Wedding Day at Nagasaki.
Hall, Sharlot M.
Arizona.
Away Out West.
Cash In.
In Old Tucson.
The Last Camp-Fire.
Road Runner.
The Song of the Colorado.
Two Bits.
Hall, Walter
That Brings Us to the
Woodstove in the Wilds, at
Night.
Hall, William
An Auctioneer's Handbill.
Hall-Evans, Jo Ann
Cape Coast Castle Revisited.
Seduction.
Hall, Vera, Reed, Doc
Death Is Awful.
Hallack, Cecily
The Divine Office of the
Kitchen.
Lord of All Pots and Pans
and Things.
Hallam, Arthur Henry
On the Picture of the Three
Fates in the Palazzo Pitti, at
Florence.
Halleck, Fitz-Greene
Alnwick Castle.
Burns.
Fanny.
The Field of the Grounded
Arms.
Joseph Rodman Drake.

Marco Bozzaris.
On His Friend, Joseph
Rodman Drake.
On the Death of Joseph
Rodman Drake.
Red Jacket.
Song: "There's a barrel of
porter at Tammany Hall."
Hallet, Mary
Calvary.
Halley, Anne
Against Dark's Harm.
Autograph Book/Prophecy.
Housewife's Letter: to Mary.
O Doctor Dear My Love.
A Pride of Ladies.
Hallock, C. Wiles
Braggin' Bill's Fortytude.
Halloran, Laurence Hynes
Animal Magnetism.
Halperin, Mark
Concerning the Dead.
John Clare.
Halpern, Daniel
Arriving.
The Dance.
Direction from Zulu.
Dutch April.
Epithalamium.
The Ethnic Life.
Fish.
The Gossip.
The Hermit.
How to Eat Alone.
The Hunt.
The Landing.
Late.
Nude.
Portoncini dei Morti.
Return, Starting Out.
Snapshot of Hue.
Street Fire.
Summer, 1970.
The Summer Rentals.
Halpern, Moishe Leib
Considering the Bleakness.
Gingilee.
Go Throw Them Out.
Isaac Leybush Peretz.
Just Because.
Memento Mori.
My Portrait.
Restless as a Wolf.
Sacco-Vanzetti.
That's Our Lot.
Who.
Zlotchev, My Home.
Halpine, Charles Graham
Baron Renfrew's Ball.
Irish Astronomy.
Janette's Hair.
Lecompton's Black Brigade.
Mr. Johnson's Policy of
Reconstruction.
Sambo's Right to be Kilt.
The Song of Sherman's Army.
Halsall, Martyn
Return to Ararat.
**"Halsham, John" (G. Forrester
Scott)**
My Last Terrier.
Ham, Marion Franklin
As Tranquil Streams.
O Thou Whose Gracious
Presence Shone.
A Prayer.
Touch Thou Mine eyes.
Hamameiri, Avigdor
The Hut.
Hambleton, Ronald
Comrades As We Rest
Within.

Sockeye Salmon.
That Strain Again.
Hamblin, Robert W.
On the Death of the
Evansville University
Basketball Team...
Hamburger, Michael
At Staufen.
Blind Man.
A Child Accepts.
The Death of an Old Man.
Dostoievsky's Daughters.
The Dual Site.
Epitaph for a Horseman.
Homage to the Weather.
In October....
Instead of a Journey.
Lines on Brueghel's Icarus.
London Tom-Cat.
Man of the World.
Mathematics of Love.
Memory.
The Note-Book of a European
Tramp (excerpt).
Omens.
A Poet's Progress.
The Search.
Security.
A Song about Great Men.
Squares.
Hamelin, Jacques
Stonetalk.
Hamill, Gerry
It Was Far in the Night and
the Barnies Grat (parody).
A Song of the GPO.
To His Coy Mistress (parody).
Hamill, Janet
Autumn Melancholy.
Carravagio.
Hamill, Sam
Gnostology.
Reno, 2 a.m.
The Wakening.
Hamilton, Alfred Starr
Wheat Metropolis.
Hamilton, Ann
Chanson d'Or.
Inscription.
Pause.
Hamilton, Anna E.
The Hem of His Garment.
We Long to See Jesus.
Hamilton, Bobb
America.
Poem to a Nigger Cop.
Hamilton, Cicely
The March of the Women.
Hamilton, Clayton
Lines Written on November
15, 1933 by a Man Born
November 14, 1881...
Hamilton, Elizabeth
My Ain Fireside.
Hamilton, Eugene Lee
What the Sonnet Is.
Hamilton, George Rostrevor
Don's Holiday.
Exchange.
Exile.
The Imperfect Artist.
No Occupation.
The Old Ox.
On a Distant Prospect of an
Absconding Bookmaker.
On a Statue of Sir Arthur
Sullivan.
Schoolmaster.
To the Greek Anthologists.
Hamilton, Harold
The School of Sorrow.

Hamilton, Horace
Before Dawn.
Displacement.
Hamilton, Ian
Complaint.
Now and Then.
Pretending Not to Sleep.
The Recruits.
Hamilton, John
Cold Blows the Wind.
Hamilton, Marion Ethel
Bird at Night.
Hamilton, Robert Browning
Along the Road.
Hamilton, Sir William Rowan
A Prayer.
Hamlet, Frances Crosby
Our Flag.
Hamm, Timothy
Finding a Friend Home.
Hammarskjöld, Dag
Lord–Thine the Day.
Hammerstein, Oscar, II
All the Things You Are.
June Is Bustin' Out All Over.
Kansas City.
Money Isn't Everything!
Ol' Man River.
There Is Nothin' Like a
Dame.
You've Got to be Carefully
Taught.
Hammial, Philip
Russians Breathing.
Hammon, Jupiter
An Address to Miss Phillis
Wheatley (excerpt).
An Evening Thought.
Hammond, Eleanor
April Fool.
From a Street Corner.
A Valentine.
Hammond, Geraldine
Encounter.
Hammond, James
Elegy: On Delia's Being in the
Country.
Elegy: to Delia.
Hammond, Karla M.
Expectancies: The Eleventh
Hour.
Testing Ground.
Hammond, Mac
In Memory of V. R. Lang.
Hammond, William
Husbandry.
Mutual Love.
Tell Me, O Love.
To Her Questioning His
Estate.
To His Sister, Mrs. S. the
Rose.
To the Same Man's Life.
Hammond. "Doc", Judy. Scott
Song: "We came to Tamichi
in 1880."
Hamod, Sam
Anthropology in Fort
Morgan, Colorado.
Hampl, Patricia
An Artist Draws a Peach.
Blue Bottle.
Hamsun, Knut
Tora's Song.
Hanaford, Phoebe A.
Cast Thy Bread upon the
Waters.
Hanbury-Williams, Charles
A Lamentable Case.
Hanby, Benjamin Russel
Darling Nellie Gray.

Hand, Walter
Youth of the Mountain.
Handley, Helen
Deer Hunt, Salt Lake Valley.
Handy, M. P.
Only a Little Thing.
Handy, Nixeon Civille
Girl to Woman.
Handy, W. C.
The Hesitating Blues.
St. Louis Blues.
Handy, Will
Didn't He Ramble.
Hanes, Leigh
Deserts.
Old Fence Post.
Hanim, Leyla
Let's Get Going.
Hanim, Nigar
Tell Me Again.
Hankey, Katherine
I Love to Tell the Story.
**Hankin, St. John Emile
Clavering**
Consolatory!
The Editor's Tragedy.
An Elegy on the Late King of
Patagonia.
De Gustibus.
Soul-Severance (parody).
Hanley, Katherine
After Vacation.
Hann, Isaac
After Reading the Life of Mrs
Catherine Stubbs...
Hanna, Tom
Tree Poem on My Wife's
Birthday.
Hannay, Patrick
A Maid Me Loved.
Philomela, the Nightingale
(excerpt).
Hannigan, Des
Ben Alder 1963-1977.
Hannigan, Paul
The Carnation.
Hanrahan, Agnes I.
Rosies.
**Hansbrough, Mary Berri
(Chapman)**
The Journey.
Hanscombe, Gillian E.
Jezebel: Her Progress
(excerpt).
Hansen, Chadwick
Creator of Infinities.
Hansen, Joseph
Dakota: Five Times Six.
The Loved One.
Hanson, Amos
The Schooner Fred Dunbar.
A Trip to the Grand Banks.
Hanson, Howard G.
As Rocks Rooted.
That Is Not Indifference.
Hanson, Joseph Mills
Laramie Trail.
The Springfield Calibre Fifty.
Hanson, Kenneth O.
Before the Storm.
Bouzouki.
First of All.
Lighting the Night Sky.
Nikos Painting.
Take It from Me.
West Lake.
Hanson, Pauline
And I Am Old to Know.
From Creature to Ghost.
So Beautiful Is the Tree of
Night.

Hanson, Phyllis
Wisdom.
Hanzlicek, C. G.
The One Song.
Hanzlik, Josef
Clap Your Hands for Herod.
Harada, Gail N.
First Winter.
New Year.
Painted Passages.
Pomegranate.
Harbaugh, Henry
The Aloe Plant.
Jesus, I Live to Thee.
Harbaugh, Thomas Chalmers
Trouble in the "Amen
Corner."
Harbord, A. M.
At Euston.
Harburg, E. Y.
Atheist.
Brother, Can You Spare a
Dime?
A Saint...He Ain't.
Hard, Walter
A Health Note.
Medical Aid (parody).
Hardeman, Louise
In Search of a Short Poem for
My Grandmother.
Harden, Verna Loveday
Post Mortem.
When This Tide Ebbs.
**Hardenerg, George Friedrich
Philipp See "Novalis"**
Hardin, Glenn
Fools.
Harding, George
Reply to a Creditor.
Harding, Mike
Christmas 1914.
Harding, Ruth Guthrie
The Call to a Scot.
Daffodils.
From a Car-Window.
Returning.
Surrender.
Threnody.
Harding, Samuel
Of Death.
Hardt, Ernst
The Specter.
Hardy, Arthur Sherburne
Duality.
Immortality.
Iter Supremum.
Hardy, Elizabeth Clark
Some Time at Eve.
Hardy, Elizabeth Stanton
Echo.
Hardy, Evelyn
Certainty.
Hardy, Jane L.
Lincoln.
Hardy, John Edward
Voyeur.
Hardy, R. Wayne
The Lone Biker.
Meeting Halfway.
October Hill.
Poem Written before Mother's
Day for Mrs. Lopez from the
South.
A Wintering Moon.
Hardy, Thomas
The Abbey Mason.
According to the Mighty
Working.
After a Journey.
After the Fair.
After the Last Breath.
After the Visit.

Afterwards.
Agnosto Theo (To an Unknown God).
Ah, Are You Digging on My Grave?
Albuera.
An Ancient to Ancients.
And There Was a Great Calm.
An Anniversary.
Architectural Masks.
At a Hasty Wedding.
At a Watering-Place.
At an Inn.
At Casterbridge Fair.
At Castle Boterel.
At Lulworth Cove a Century Back.
At Tea.
At the Altar-Rail.
At the Drapers.
An August Midnight.
A Backward Spring.
Bags of Meat.
Barthelemon at Vauxhall.
The Beauty.
Beeny Cliff.
Before Life and After.
Bereft.
Beyond the Last Lamp.
A Bird-Scene at a Rural Dwelling.
Birds at Winter Nightfall.
The Blinded Bird.
A Broken Appointment.
Budmouth Dears.
The Bullfinches.
By Her Aunt's Grave.
Cardinal Bembo's Epitaph on Raphael.
Channel Firing.
The Children and Sir Nameless.
The Choirmaster's Burial.
Christmas 1924.
A Christmas Ghost-Story.
A Church Romance.
The Colonel's Soliloquy.
The Comet at Yalbury or Yell'ham.
A Commonplace Day.
Compassion.
The Conformers.
The Contretemps.
The Convergence of the Twain.
The Country Wedding.
The Curate's Kindness.
The Curtains Now Are Drawn.
The Dark-Eyed Gentleman.
The Darkling Thrush.
The Dead and the Living One.
The Dead Quire.
Dead "Wessex" the Dog to the Household.
Domicilium.
The Dream-Follower.
A Drizzling Easter Morning.
Drummer Hodge.
During Wind and Rain.
The Dynasts.
Embarcation.
The Enemy's Portrait.
Epitaph for George Moore.
Epitaph: "I never cared for Life: Life cared for me."
Epitaph on a Pessimist.
Exeunt Omnes.
The Faded Face.
Faintheart in a Railway Train.

The Fallow Deer at the Lonely House.
The Farm-Woman's Winter.
First or Last.
First Sight of Her and After.
The Five Students.
For Life I Had Never Cared Greatly.
Friends Beyond.
The Garden Seat.
God's Education.
God's Funeral.
The Going.
Going and Staying.
Great Things.
Green Slates.
Hap.
The Haunter.
He Abjures Love.
He Never Expected Much.
He Resolves to Say No More.
He Roman Road.
Heiress and Architect.
Her Dilemma.
Heredity.
His Immortality.
Horses Aboard.
The House of Hospitalities.
How Great My Grief.
I Am the One.
I Found Her Out There.
I Look into My Glass.
I Looked Up from My Writing.
I Need Not Go.
I Said to Love.
I Say I'll Seek Her.
I Watched a Blackbird.
If It's Ever Spring Again.
If You Had Known.
The Impercipient.
In a Cathedral City.
In a Museum.
In Childbed.
In Church.
In Death Divided.
In Front of the Landscape.
In Tenebris.
In the Cemetery.
In the Evening.
In the Nuptial Chamber.
In the Old Theatre, Fiesole.
In the Restaurant.
In the Room of the Bride-Elect.
In the Servants' Quarters.
In the Study.
In the Vaulted Way.
In Time of "The Breaking of Nations."
The Ivy-Wife.
Jezreel.
A Jog-Trot Pair.
Julie-Jane.
The Lacking Sense.
The Last Chrysanthemum.
Last Words to a Dumb Friend.
Lausanne.
Let Me Enjoy.
The Levelled Churchyard.
Liddell and Scott.
Lines to a Movement in Mozart's E-Flat Symphony.
The Lodging-House Fuschsias.
Long Plighted.
Looking at a Picture on an Anniversary.
Lying Awake.
A Man Was Drawing Near to Me.
The Marble-Streeted Town.

Men Who March away.
Midnight on the Great Western.
The Minute before Meeting.
Moments of Vision.
The Mound.
Mute Opinion.
My Spirit Will Not Haunt the Mound.
Nature's Questioning.
Near Lanivet, 1872.
A Necessitarian's Epitaph.
The Nettles.
Neutral Tones.
New Year's Eve.
The Newcomer's Wife.
The Night of the Dance.
No Buyers.
Nobody Comes.
O I Won't Lead a Homely Life.
Old Furniture.
On a Fine Morning.
On a Midsummer Eve.
On an Invitation to the United States.
On His 86th Birthday.
On Sturminster Foot-Bridge.
On the Death-Bed.
On the Departure Platform.
On the Doorstep.
On the Portrait of a Woman About to be Hanged.
Once at Swanage.
One We Knew.
Outside the Window.
Over the Coffin.
Overlooking the River Stout.
The Oxen.
The Peace-Offering.
The Pedigree.
The Phantom Horsewoman.
The Pink Frock.
The Pity of It.
A Placid Man's Epitaph.
A Poet.
A Popular Personage at Home.
A Practical Woman.
Proud Songsters.
The Puzzled Game Birds.
Rain on a Grave.
A Refusal.
Regret Not Me.
The Rejected Member's Wife.
The Reminder.
Reminiscences of a Dancing Man.
The Respectable Burgher.
The Roman Road.
Rome.
The Ruined Maid.
The Sacrilege.
The Satin Shoes.
Satires of Circumstance.
The Schreckhorn.
The Self-Unseeing.
The Selfsame Song.
The Shadow on the Stone.
She.
She Hears the Storm.
She, to Him.
A Sheep Fair.
Shelley's Skylark.
The Shiver.
Shut Out That Moon.
A Singer Asleep.
Snow in the Suburbs.
The Souls of the Slain.
The Statue of Liberty,.
The Stranger's Song.
The Subalterns.

The Sunshade.
Surview.
Tess's Lament.
This Summer and Last.
Thoughts of Phena.
A Thunderstorm in Town.
To an Unborn Pauper Child.
To C.F.H. on Her Christening-Day.
To Lizbie Browne.
To Meet, or Otherwise.
To the Moon.
Tolerance.
A Trampwoman's Tragedy.
Transformations.
The Tree and the Lady.
Two Lips.
The Unborn.
Under the Waterfall.
Unkept Good Fridays.
The Voice.
Voices from Things Growing in a Churchyard.
Wagtail and Baby.
Waiting Both.
The Walk.
Weathers.
Well, World, You Have Kept Faith with Me.
Wessex Heights.
A Wet August.
When I Set out for Lyonnesse.
When Oats Were Reaped.
Where the Picnic Was.
Who's in the Next Room?
Why She Moved House.
A Wife in London.
Winter in Durnover Field.
Wives in the Sere.
The Woman I Met.
The Woodlanders: In a Wood.
The Workbox.
The Year's Awakening.
You on the Tower.
The Young Glass-Stainer.
A Young Man's Epigram on Existence.
Your Last Drive.
Zermatt.

Hare, Amory
Life.
Walking at Night.
Wet or Fine.

Hare, Maurice Evan
Limerick:"There once was a man who said: 'Damn!'"

Haresnape, Geoffrey
The African Tramp.

Harford, David K.
From the Batter's Box.

Harford, Lesbia
Beauty and Terror.
Day's End.
Experience.
He Has Served Eighty Masters.
I'm Like All Lovers.
Revolution.
Sometimes I Wish That I Were Helen-Fair.
This Way Only.
When I Was Still a Child.

Haring, Phyllis
The Earth Asks and Receives Rain.
Foetus.
The Forbidden.
Jungle.
Overture to Strangers.
Twin.

Harington, Donald
The Villanelle.

Harington, Henry
The Abbey Church at Bath.
Trust the Form of Airy
Things.
Harington, John (fl. 1550)
Elegy Wrote in the Tower,
1554.
I See My Plaint.
A Sonnet Made on Isabella
Markham.
Harington, Sir John (1561-1612)
Against an Old Lecher.
Angelica and the Ork.
The Author, of His Own
Fortune.
The Author to His Wife, of a
Woman's Eloquence.
Epigram: Of Treason.
Hate and Debate Rome
through the World Hath
Spread.
Health Counsel.
In Roman.
Of a Fair Shrew.
Of a Zealous Lady.
Of an Heroical Answer of a
Great Roman Lady to Her
Husband.
Of Treason.
To His Wife, for Striking Her
Dog.
To My Lady Rogers, the
Authors Wiues Mother...
Harjo, Joy
Anchorage.
The Blanket around Her.
The Blood-Letting.
Conversations between Here
and Home.
Crossing the Border into
Canada.
Cuchillo.
Early Morning Woman.
Fire.
For Alva Benson, and for All
Those Who have Learned to
Speak.
He Told Me His Name Was
Sitting Bull.
I Am a Dangerous Woman.
Ice Horses.
It's the Same at Four A.M.
The Last Song.
Moonlight.
Morning Once More.
New Orleans.
Noni Daylight Remembers the
Future.
Obscene Phone Call #2.
Origins.
Remember.
A Scholder Indian Poem.
She Had Some Horses.
She Was a Pretty Horse.
Someone Talking.
Talking to the Moon #002.
There Are Oceans.
There Was a Dance,
Sweetheart.
Two Horses.
What Music.
The Woman Hanging from
the 13th Floor Window.
Your Phone Call at Eight
A.M.
Harjo, Patty L.
Death.
The Mask.
Taos Winter.
To an Indian Poet.
Where Have You Gone, Little
Boy.

Wishes.
Harkavi, Hedva
It Was Gentle.
Talk to Me, Talk to Me.
Whenever the Snakes Come.
Harkness, Edward
The Man in the Recreation
Room.
Harlow, Samuel Ralph
O Young and Fearless
Prophet.
Harmon, William
Bureaucratic Limerick.
A Dawn Horse.
There.
Harney, Ben
Mister Johnson.
You've Been a Good Old
Wagon, But You've Done
Broke Down.
Harney, W. E.
West of Alice.
Harney, William Wallace
Adonais.
The Stab.
Harnick, Sheldon
The Merry Minuet.
Harper, Frances E. W.
An Appeal to My
Countrywomen.
Bury Me In a Free Land.
The Crocuses.
Deliverance.
A Double Standard.
Learning to Read.
Let the Light Enter.
She's Free!
The Slave Auction.
Vashti.
Harper, Michael S.
American History.
Barricades.
Blue Ruth: America.
Br'er Sterling and the Rocker.
Cannon Arrested.
Come Back Blues.
The Dance of the Elephants.
The Dark Way Home:
Survivors.
Dear John, Dear Coltrane.
Deathwatch.
Debridement: Operation
Harvest Moon: On Repose.
Effendi.
Elvin's Blues.
Grandfather.
Here Where Coltrane Is.
Homage to the New World.
The Ice-Fishing House: Long
Lake, Minnesota.
Kin.
Landfill.
Last Affair: Bessie's Blues
Song.
Love Medley: Patrice
Cuchulain.
Mahalia.
Martin's Blues.
A Mother Speaks: The Algiers
Motel Incident, Detroit.
Newsletter from My Mother.
Nightmare Begins
Responsibility.
Photographs: A Vision of
Massacre.
Poetry Concert.
Reuben, Reuben.
Tongue-Tied in Black and
White.
We Assume: On the Death of
Our Son, Reuben Masai
Harper.

Harpur, Charles
An Aboriginal Mother's
Lament.
A Basket of Summer Fruit.
Bush Justice.
A Coast View (excerpt).
The Creek of the Four Graves
(excerpt).
A Flight of Wild Ducks.
Love Sonnets, VIII.
Marvellous Martin.
A Midsummer Noon in the
Australian Forest.
The Temple of Infamy
(excerpt).
The Tower of the Dream
(excerpt).
Wellington.
Words.
Harr, Barbara
Walking through a Cornfield
in the Middle of Winter...
(parody).
Harri, Hazel Harper
A Sailor's Song.
"Harriet Annie"
Death of Gaudentis.
Harrigan, Ed [(or Ned)]
The Mulligan Guard.
Walking for That Cake.
Harrigan, Edward
My Dad's Dinner Pail.
Harrigan, Stephen
Over to God.
Harriman, Dorothy
Cat on the Porch at Dusk.
Harrington, Edward
The Bushrangers.
Morgan.
My Old Black Billy.
Harrington, Michael
Gazeteer of Newfoundland.
The Second Iron Age
(1939-1945).
Harris, Benjamin
An Account of the Cruelty of
the Papists...
God Save the King, That
King That Sav'd the Land.
Of the French Kings Nativity,
&c.
Harris, Charles K.
After the Ball.
Break the News to Mother.
Harris, Hazel Harper
Gifts.
Harris, Joel Chandler
My Honey, My Love.
Plantation Play-Song.
The Plough-Hands' Song.
Revival Hymn.
Harris, June Brown
Home.
Harris, Louise
You Are Growing into My
Life...
Harris, Marguerite
My Sun-Killed Tree.
Harris, Max
Lullaby.
Martin Buber in the Pub.
Message from a Cross.
The Plowman.
The Tantanoola Tiger.
Harris, Michael
The Ice Castle.
Harris, Norman
Fable.
Harris, Phyllis
Furniture.
Harris, Sydney Justin
I Come to Bury Caesar.

Harris, Thomas Lake
California.
Fledglings.
Sea-Sleep.
Harris, William J.
Bullfrog Blues.
For Bill Hawkins, a Black
Militant.
Frightened Flower.
Give Me Five.
A Grandfather Poem.
Hey Fella Would You Mind
Holding This Piano a
Moment.
An Historic Moment.
Modern Romance.
On Wearing Ears.
Practical Concerns.
Rib Sandwich.
They Live in Parallel Worlds.
The Truth Is Quite Messy.
We Live in a Cage.
Why Would I Want.
Harrison, De Leon
A Collage for Richard Davis–
Two Short Forms.
The Room.
The Seed of Nimrod.
Some Days/Out Walking
above.
Yellow.
Harrison, Eugene M.
The Soul Winner's Prayer.
Harrison, Frances
At St. Jerome.
Harrison, Henry Sydnor
Osculation.
Harrison, James
Easier.
Eve's Version.
Helen.
Harrison, Janet E.
Lament of a Last Letter.
Harrison, Jim
After the Anonymous
Swedish.
Drinking Song.
Fair/Boy Christian Takes a
Break.
Ghazals.
Horse.
Locations.
Poem: "Form Is the woods."
Returning at Night.
Sketch for a Job Application
Blank.
Sound.
Suite to Fathers.
Trader.
Traverse City Zoo.
Harrison, S. Frances
Chateau Papineau.
Harrison, Sam
After the Show.
Chez Madame.
Journey.
Meeting.
Poem: "This room is very old
and very wise."
Rain.
Harrison, Sam G.
The Fisherman.
Harrison, Tony
The Bedbug.
The Hands.
On Not Being Milton.
Prague Spring.
Schwiegermutterlieder.
Sentences (excerpt).
Harrison, Virginia Bioren
Music of the Dawn.
One Gift I Ask.

Harrison, William
In Praise of Laudanum.
Harrod, Elizabeth B.
August Night, 1953.
Calvinist Autumnal.
Sonnet against the Too-Facile
Mystic.
Summer Afternoon.
"Harry"
Feet.
Harsen, Una W.
A Litany for Old Age.
Prayer before Meat.
Harsent, David
Old Photographs.
Hart, Elizabeth Anna
Mother Tabbyskins.
Sweeping the Skies.
Hart, James
Blemishes.
Hart, Joanne
I Walk on the River at Dawn.
When Your Parents Grow
Old.
Hart, John
Confrontation.
Hart, Lorenz
The Blue Room.
The Lady Is a Tramp.
Manhattan.
The Most Beautiful Girl in
the World.
Mountain Greenery.
My Heart Stood Still.
Hart-Smith, William
Baiamai's Never-failing
Stream.
Bathymeter.
Boomerang.
Christopher Columbus
(excerpt).
Columbus Goes West.
Drama.
Golden Pheasant.
Holding-paddock.
The Inca Tupac Upanqui.
Otters.
Rhinoceros.
Shag Rookery.
Shepherd and the Hawk.
When You Touch.
Wild Geese.
**Harte, Bret (Francis Bret
Harte)**
The Aged Stranger.
An Arctic Vision.
At the Hacienda.
The Ballad of the Emeu.
Caldwell of Springfield.
Chicago.
Chiquita.
Colenso Rhymes for Orthodox
Children.
Coyote.
Crotalus.
Dickens in Camp.
Dow's Flat.
Further Language from
Truthful James.
The Ghost That Jim Saw.
Greyport Legend.
Grizzly.
Guild's Signal.
The Heathen Chinee.
Her Letter.
Jessie.
Jim.
John Burns of Gettysburg.
Madrono.
The Mission Bells of
Monterey.
The Mountain Heart's-Ease.

Mrs. Judge Jenkins.
The Personified Sentimental.
Plain Language from Truthful
James.
Ramon.
Relieving Guard.
The Reveille.
San Francisco from the Sea.
Schemmelfennig.
A Second Review of the
Grand Army.
Serenade.
The Society upon the
Stanislow.
The Spelling Bee at Angels.
The Tale of a Pony.
To a Sea-Bird.
What the Bullet Sang.
What the Engines Said.
The Willows.
Harte, Walter
The Enchanted Region: or,
Mistaken Pleasures.
Hartford, John
The Poor Old Prurient
Interest Blues.
Hartigan, Patrick Joseph
The Field of the Cloth of
Gold.
Said Hanrahan.
Tangmalangaloo.
Hartley, Marsden.
Confidence.
The Crucifixion of Noel.
In Robin Hood Cove.
Warblers.
Hartman, Charles O.
Double Mock Sonnet.
Inflation.
A Little Song.
Trading Chicago.
Hartman, Mary R.
Life's Made up of Little
Things.
Hartmann von Aue
None Is Happy.
The Scales of Love.
Hartnett, Michael
All That Is Left.
All the Death-Room Needs...
Death of an Irishwoman.
Domestic Scene.
Enamoured of the Miniscule.
A Farewell to English
(excerpt).
For My Grandmother, Bridget
Halpin.
I Have Exhausted the
Delighted Range...
I Have Heard Them Knock.
I Think Sometimes...
Marban, a Hermit, Speaks.
The Possibility That Has Been
Overlooked Is the Future.
The Retreat of Ita Cagney.
A Small Farm.
Sonnet: "I saw magic on a
green country road."
Hartsough, Lewis
Come, Friends and Neighbors,
Come.
Let Me Go Where Saints Are
Going.
Harvey, Christopher
Comfort in Extremity.
Harvey, Frederick William
Ducks.
November.
Prisoners.
The Sleepers.
Harvey, Gayle Elen
Tonight when You Leave...

We Are Leaning Away.
Harvey, J. E.
Forgetting God.
Harwood, Gwen
At the Sea's Edge.
Carnal Knowledge.
Death Has No Features of
His Own.
Father and Child.
Homage to Ferd. Holthausen.
Hospital Evening.
In the Bistro.
In the Park.
Last Meeting.
The Lion's Bride.
New Music.
Night Thoughts: Baby &
Demon.
Panther and Peacock.
Prize-Giving.
The Second Life of Lazarus.
A Simple Story.
Suburban Sonnet.
Harwood, Lee
The Final Painting.
Rain Journal: London: June
65.
Soft White.
The "Utopia".
The Words.
Harwood, Ruth
The Shoe Factory.
Hashin
Haiku: "Neither earth nor
sky."
No Sky At All.
Hashmi, Alamgir
The Banquet of the Century
in Persepolis.
Haskell, Jefferson
My Latest Sun Is Sinking
Fast.
Haskin, Leslie L.
Christ the Carpenter.
Haskins, M. Louise
The Gate of the Year.
Hass, Robert
After the Gentle Poet
Kobayashi Issa.
Against Botticelli.
The Apple Trees at Olema.
Child Naming Flowers.
Churchyard.
Fall.
The Feast.
The Harbor at Seattle.
In Weather.
January.
Late Spring.
Maps.
Measure.
Meditation at Lagunitas.
Museum.
Old Dominion.
On the Coast near Sausalito.
The Origin of Cities.
Palo Alto: The Marshes.
Paschal Lamb.
The Return of Robinson
Jeffers.
Rusia en 1931.
San Pedro Road.
Song: "Afternoon cooking in
the fall sun."
Songs to Survive the Summer.
Spring Drawing II.
A Story About the Body.
Tall Windows.
Weed.
Hassall, Christopher
Santa Claus in a Department
Store.

Hassan, Mahammed A.
A Denunciation.
To a Friend Going on a
Journey.
Hassler, Donald M.
Fishing Lines.
Haste, Gwendolen
Montana Wives.
Tomorrow Is a Birthday.
Hastings, Fanny de Groot
Late Comer.
Hastings, Maria
A Farmyard Song.
Sing Little Bird.
Hastings, Thomas
Exhortation.
Hail to the Brightness of
Zion's Glad Morning.
In Sorrow.
Jesus, Merciful and Mild!
Now Be the Gospel Banner.
Now from Labor and from
Care.
Hatfield, Edwin Francis
Hallelujah! Praise the Lord.
Hathaway, Baxter
Again My Fond Circle of
Doves.
The Gorilla.
Hathaway, James B.
What the Stone Dreams.
Hathaway, Jeanine
Conversation with God.
Extensions of Linear Mobility.
In Random Fields of Impulse
and Repose.
Reflections on a Womb Which
Is Called "Vacant."
World Enough.
Hathaway, William
The American Poet–"But
Since It Came to Good..."
Apology for E. H.
Coloring Margarine.
Dear Wordsworth.
Rumplestiltskin Poems.
When I Was Dying.
Why That's Bob Hope.
Hatshepsut
The Obelisk Inscriptions
(excerpt).
Hatton, Joseph
Christmas Bills.
Haug, James
The Long Season.
Hauk, Barbara
Getting Older Here.
Hauroa, Matangi
Lament.
Hauser, Samuel
What Ship Is This?
Hausgen, Mattie Lee
Her Favorites.
Hausman, Gerald
Poem for Lorry.
Hausted, Peter
Of His Mistress.
The Rival Friends: Have Pity,
Grief.
Havergal, Frances Ridley
Afterwards.
Another Year Is Dawning.
Behold Your King!
For Every Day.
God Is Faithful.
A Happy Christmas.
Life-Mosaic.
New Year's Wishes.
Reality.
Take My Life and Let It Be.
A Teacher's Prayer.
Thou Art Coming!

The Unfailing One.

Haweis, Hugh Reginald
The Homeland.

Haweis, Thomas
Come and Welcome.
Remember Me!

Hawes, Stephen
Epitaph of La Graunde
Amoure.
A Pair of Wings.
The Pastime of Pleasure.
The True Knight.

Hawker, Robert Stephen
Aishah-Schechinah.
Are They Not All Ministering
Spirits?
Aunt Mary.
A Christ-Cross Rhyme.
A Croon on Hennacliff.
Datur Hora Quieti.
Death Song.
The Doom-Well of St.
Madron.
Featherstone's Doom.
The First Fathers.
"I Am the Resurrection and
the Life," Saith the Lord!
King Arthur's Waes-Hael.
Morwennae Statio.
The Mystic Magi.
Pater Vester Pascit Illa.
Queen Guennivar's Round.
The Quest of the Sangraal:
The Coming of the Sangraal.
The Silent Tower of
Bottreaux.
The Song of the Western
Men.
The Southern Cross.

Hawkes, Clarence
Christmas Still Lives.
The Mountain to the Pine.

Hawkes, Henry Warburton
Amid the Din of Earthly
Strife.

Hawkins, Buddy Boy
Awful Fix.

Hawkins, Henry
The Bee.
Hoc Cygno Vinces.

Hawkins, Lucy
To L. C.

Hawkins, Walter Everette
The Death of Justice.
A Spade Is Just a Spade.

Hawkins, William
To a Worm Which the
Author Accidentally Trode
Upon.

Hawley, Charles B.
My Little Love.

Hawley, Richard A.
January.

Hawley, W. F.
A Love Song.

Hawling, Francis
The Signal; or, A Satire
against Modesty (excerpt).

Hawthorn, John
The Journey and Observations
of a Countryman (excerpt).
On His Writing Verses.

Hawthorne, Alice
Listen to the Mocking Bird.
Whispering Hope.

Hawthorne, Hildegarde
My Rose.
A Song.

Hawthorne, Julian
Were-Wolf.

Hawthorne, Nathaniel
The Star of Calvary.

Hay, Clarence Leonard
Down and Out.

Hay, George Campbell
Flooer o the Gean.
The Smoky Smirr o' Rain.
Song: "Day will rise and the
sun from eastward."
Sonnet: "Beckie, my luve!–
What is't, ye twa-faced tod?–
".
Still Gyte, Man?
The Two Neighbours.

Hay, Helen
Does the Pearl Know?
Love's Kiss.
Sigh Not for Love.
A Woman's Pride.

Hay, John
Aboriginal Sin.
And Grow.
Bird Song.
The Chickadees.
December Storm.
Defend Us, Lord, from Every
Ill.
The Energy of Light.
Life Must Burn.
Music by the Waters.
Natural Architecture.
Old Man of Tennessee.
Railway Station.
Sent Ahead.
The Silver Leaf.
The Song of the Ancient
People.
The Storm.
Town Meeting.
Variations on a Theme.

Hay, John Milton
Christine.
Distich.
The Enchanted Shirt.
Good Luck and Bad.
Jim Bludso of the Prairie
Belle.
Liberty.
Little Breeches.
Miles Keogh's Horse.
Not in Dumb Resignation.
The Pledge at Spunky Point.
Religion and Doctrine.
The Stirrup Cup.
The Surrender of Spain.
The White Flag.
A Woman's Love.

Hay, Sara Henderson
Ballad of the Golden Bowl.
The Benefactors.
Bottle Should Be Plainly
Labeled Poison.
Christmas, the Year One, A.
D.
The Daily Manna.
Daily Paradox.
Interview.
Juvenile Court.
The Marriage.
The Name.
On Being Told That One's
Ideas Are Victorian.
One of the Seven Has
Somewhat to Say.
Prayer in April.
The Princess.
Rapunzel.
The Sleeper.

Hay, W.
To a Poetic Lover.

Hayakawa, S. Ichiye
To One Elect.

Hayden, Joe
A Hot Time in the Old Town.

Hayden, Robert Earl
Aunt Jemima of the Ocean
Waves.
Baha'u'llah in the Garden of
Ridwan.
The Ballad of Nat Turner.
A Ballad of Remembrance.
The Ballad of Sue Ellen
Westerfield.
Beginnings (excerpt).
Crispus Attucks.
The Diver.
El-Hajj Malik El-Shabazz
(Malcolm X).
Frederick Douglass.
Full Moon.
Homage to the Empress of the
Blues.
In the Mourning Time.
Kid.
The Liar.
Locus.
Middle Passage.
Mourning Poem for the Queen
of Sunday.
"Mystery Boy" Looks for Kin
in Nashville.
The Night-Blooming Cereus.
Night, Death, Mississippi.
O Daedalus, Fly Away Home.
Paul Laurence Dunbar.
The Peacock Room.
A Plague of Starlings.
Richard Hunt's Arachne.
A Road in Kentucky.
Runagate Runagate.
Sphinx.
Stars.
Sub Specie Aeternitatis.
Summertime and the Living....
Those Winter Sundays.
Tour 5.
Unidentified Flying Object.
Veracruz.
The Wheel.
The Whipping.
Witch Doctor.
Words in the Mourning Time.

Hayes, Alfred
The City of Beggars.
The Death of the Craneman.
Epistle to the Gentiles.
Joe Hill.
A Nice Part of Town.
The Slaughter-House.

Hayes, Donald Jeffrey
After All.
Alien.
Appoggiatura.
Auf Wiedersehen.
Benediction.
Confession.
Haven.
Inscription.
Night.
Nocturne.
Pastourelle.
Poet.
Prescience.
Threnody.

Hayes, Ednah Proctor (Clarke)
The Dancer.
The Deathless.
A Good-By.
The Mocking-Bird.
To a Wild Rose Found in
October.

Hayes, J. Milton
The Green Eye of the Yellow
God.

Hayes, James M.
Our Lady of the Skies.

Hayes, John Russell
The Old-Fashioned Garden.

Hayes, Nancy M.
The Shiny Little House.

Hayes, Paul Hamilton
The True Heaven.

**Hayford, Gladys May Casely
(Aquah Laluah)**
Baby Cobina.
Nativity.
Rainy Season Love Song.
The Serving Girl.
Shadow of Darkness.

Hayford, James
Horn.
In a Closed Universe.
Overseer of the Poor.
The Resident Worm.
Under All This Slate.

Haygarth, William
Greece.

Hayley, William
A Card of Invitation to Mr.
Gibbon, at Brighthelmstone.

Hayman, Jane
The Murdered Girl Is Found
on a Bridge.

Hayman, Robert
A Mad Answer of a Madman.
Of the Great and Famous
Ever-to-be-Honored Knight,
Sir Francis Drake..
The Pleasant Life in
Newfoundland.
Quodlibets.

Hayne, Paul Hamilton
Aspects of the Pines.
The Battle of Charleston
Harbor.
Between the Sunken Sun and
the New Moon.
Beyond the Potomac.
Butler's Proclamation.
In Harbor.
A Little While I Fain Would
Linger Yet.
Macdonald's Raid.
Pre-Existence.
The Rose and the Thorn.
South Carolina to the States
of the North.
A Storm in the Distance.
The Stricken South to the
North.
Vicksburg.
Yorktown Centennial Lyric.

Hayne, William Hamilton
An Autumn Breeze.
The Charge at Santiago.
A Cyclone at Sea.
Exiles.
Moonlight Song of the
Mocking-bird.
Night Mists.
A Sea Lyric.
Sleep and His Brother Death.
The Southern Snow-Bird.
To a Cherokee Rose.
The Yule Log.

Haynes, Albert
The Law.

Haynes, Carol
Any Wife or Husband.
Aunt Selina.

Haynes, Renee
Ingenious Raconteur.

Hays, H. R.
Age?
The Case.
For One Who Died Young.
January.
Manhattan.

The Sacred Children.
Hays, Lee and Claude Williams.
Roll the Union On.
Hays, Will S.
O'Grady's Goat.
Hayward, Charles W.
King George V.
Hayward, William
Five Birds Rise.
Haywood, Carolyn
Little Clown Puppet.
Hazaken, Elijah
Precepts He Gave His Folk.
Hazard, Caroline
The Great Swamp Fight.
In Shadow.
Hazard, James
To the Carp, and Those Who
Hunt Her.
Hazlewood-Brady, Anne
Closer First to Earth.
The Double Axe.
Hazo, Samuel
After the Hurricane.
Between You and Me.
Challenge.
God and Man.
Maps for a Son Are Drawn as
You Go.
The Next Time You Were
There.
Skycoast.
To a Blind Student Who
Taught Me to See.
Head, Gwen
Slug.
Stinging Nettle.
Healy, Eloise Klein
Dark.
Los Angeles.
My Love Wants to Park.
This Darknight Speed.
What Is Being Forgotten.
Healy, Ian
Poems from the Coalfields.
Healy, Patrick
My Wishes.
Heaney, Seamus
An Advancement of Learning.
At a Potato Digging.
The Badgers.
The Barn.
The Birthplace.
Blackberry-Picking.
Bogland.
Cana Revisited.
Casualty.
Changes.
A Constable Calls.
Death of a Naturalist.
Digging.
The Diviner.
Docker.
A Dream of Jealousy.
A Drink of Water.
The Early Purges.
England's Difficulty.
Exposure.
Field Work.
Follower.
The Forge.
Gifts of Rain.
The Given Note.
Glanmore Sonnets.
The Grauballe Man.
Gravities.
The Guttural Muse.
The Harvest Bow.
A Hazel Stick for Catherine
Ann.
In Memoriam Francis
Ledwidge.

In Small Townlands.
Kinship.
Limbo.
Linen Town.
Mid-Term Break.
Mossbawn: Two Poems in
Dedication.
Mother.
Mother of the Groom.
A New Song.
Night Drive.
A Northern Hoard.
The Other Side.
The Otter.
The Outlaw.
The Peninsula.
Personal Helicon.
The Plantation.
A Postcard from North
Antrim.
Punishment.
Requiem for the Croppies.
Rite of Spring.
Scaffolding.
The Singer's House.
The Skunk.
Sloe Gin.
Song: "A rowan like a
lipsticked girl."
Station Island (excerpt).
Storm on the Island.
The Strand at Lough Beg.
Summer Home.
Sunlight.
Thatcher.
The Tollund Man.
Traditions.
Triptych.
Trout.
Twice Shy.
Valediction.
Viking Dublin: Trial Pieces.
The Wanderer.
Waterfall.
Whatever You Say Say
Nothing.
Widgeon.
The Wife's Tale.
Heap, Jane
Notes: II.
Heard, Lillian G.
Humble Service.
Hearn, Bonnie
Dinosaur.
Hearn, Michael Patrick
In the Library.
Hearst, James
Behind the Stove.
Dragon Lesson.
Hard Way to Learn.
The New Calf.
Pause between Clock Ticks.
Heath
These Women All.
Women.
Heath, Ella
Poetry.
Heath, Gerturde E.
Limerick: "Oh, there once was
a merry crocodile."
Heath, Robert
On Clarastella Singing.
On Clarastella Walking in Her
Garden.
On the Unusual Cold and
Rainie Weather in the
Summer, 1648.
Seeing Her Dancing.
Song in a Siege.
To Clarastella on St.
Valentines Day Morning.
You Say You Love Me.

Heath, William
Cold Feet in Columbus.
Heath-Stubbs, John
Address Not Known.
Artorius.
Beggar's Serenade.
Carol for Advent.
A Charm against the Tooth-
Ache.
Churchyard of St. Mary
Magdalene, Old Milton.
The Dark Planet.
The Death of Digenes Akritas.
December.
An Ecclesiastical Chronicle
(excerpt).
Epitaph.
February.
The Ghost in the Cellarage.
The Gifts.
The History of the Flood.
Ibycus.
January.
The Lady's Complaint.
Mozart.
Not Being Oedipus.
The Old King.
The Parthenon.
The Poet of Bray.
Poetry Today.
Preliminary Poem.
Send for Lord Timothy.
Titus and Berenice.
To a Poet a Thousand Years
Hence.
Two Men in Armour.
The Unpredicted.
Valse Oubliee.
Virgin and Unicorn.
Virgin Martyrs.
Winter Crickets.
Heaton, John Langdon
Sea Irony.
Heavysege, Charles
Count Filippo.
How Great unto the Living
Seem the Dead!
Jephthah's Daughter.
Night.
Saul.
The Winter Galaxy.
Hebbel, Friedrich
The Tree in the Desert.
Heber, Reginald
By Cool Siloam's Shady Rill.
An Evening Walk in Bengal.
From Greenland's Icy
Mountains.
Holy, Holy, Holy.
Hymn: "Brightest and best of
the sons of the morning."
If Thou Wert by My Side, My
Love.
Providence.
The Son of God Goes Forth
to War.
Sympathy.
Who Follows in His Train?
Hebert, Annabelle
Dream about Sunsets.
Hebert, Anne
The Alchemy of Day.
Bread Is Born.
Crown of Happiness.
The Great Fountains.
Life in the Castle.
The Offended.
Our Hands in the Garden.
The Skinny Girl.
Spring over the City.
The Tomb of the Kings.
The Wooden Chamber.

Hebert, Jr, Albert J.
Heart for All Her Children.
Hecht, Anthony
Adam.
Alceste in the Wilderness.
Application for a Grant.
Avarice.
Behold the Lilies of the Field.
Birdwatchers of America.
Clair de Lune.
La Condition Botanique.
The Cost.
Divination by a Cat.
Double Sonnet.
The Dover Bitch.
Drinking Song.
The End of the Weekend.
Epitaph: "Here lies a poet,
briefly known as Hecht."
The Feast of Stephen.
Fifth Avenue Parade.
Firmness.
From the Grove Press.
Fugue for One Voice.
The Ghost in the Martini.
The Gift of Song.
Going the Rounds: A Sort of
Love Poem.
Hallowe'en.
Here Lies Fierce Strephon.
A Hill.
Improvisations on Aesop.
"It Out-Herods Herod, Pray
You Avoid It."
Japan.
Jason.
A Letter.
Lizards and Snakes.
A Lot of Night Music.
The Man Who Married
Magdalene...
"More Light! More Light!"
An Old Malediction.
The Origin of Centaurs.
Ostia Antica.
Paradise Lost: V.
Pig.
The Place of Pain in the
Universe.
Samuel Sewall.
Sestina d'Inverno.
Tarantula or the Dance of
Death.
Third Avenue in Sunlight.
The Transparent Man.
Upon the Death of George
Santayana.
Vice.
The Vow.
Hector, Mary Louise
Whatsoever I Do.
Hedge, Frederic Henry
Paraphrase of Luther's Hymn.
The Questionings.
Sovereign and Transforming
Grace.
Hedge, T. H.
Via Crucis, Via Lucis.
Hedges, Doris
Onwardness.
Poet's Protest.
Prayer.
Hedin, Mary
On Rears.
Hedin, Robert
The Wreck of the Great
Northern.
Hedylos
Girl Betrayed.
Seduced Girl.
Heffernan, Michael
A Colloquy of Silences.

Daffodils.
Kennedy.
Naked War (parody).
Putting on My Shoes I Hear
  the Floor Cry out beneath
  Me (parody).
Sunday Service (parody).
The Table.
Heguri, Lady
  A thousand years, you said.
Heide, Florence Parry
  Rocks.
Heidenstam, Verner von
  Fellow-Citizens.
  Home.
  How Easily Men's Cheeks Are
    Hot.
Heimler, Eugene
  After an Eclipse of the Sun.
  Psalm.
Hein, Piet
  Lilac Time.
  Literary Gruk.
Heine, Heinrich
  Ad Finem.
  And When I Lamented.
  Anno 1829.
  Ashes.
  Auf Meiner Herzliebsten
    Augelein.
  The Azra.
  The Beating Heart.
  The Best Religion.
  Du Bist Wie Eine Blume.
  By the Waters of Babylon.
  The Choir Boys.
  The Coffin.
  Dear Maiden.
  Dearest Friend, Thou Art in
    Love.
  Der Mond Ist Aufgegangen.
  Die Blauen Veilchen Der
    Augelein.
  Die Heimkehr (excerpt).
  Die Lotosblume Angstigt.
  Die Rose, Die Lilie, Die
    Taube.
  Die Welt Ist Dumm, Die Welt
    Ist Blind.
  Enfant Perdu.
  Epilogue.
  Es Fallt Ein Stern Herunter.
  Es Stehen Unbeweglich.
  Farewell.
  Fresco-Sonnets to Christian
    Sethe.
  Good Fortune.
  Healing the Wound.
  I, a Most Wretched Atlas.
  I Close Her Eyes.
  I Crave an Ampler, Worthier
    Sphere.
  I Love but Thee.
  I'm Black and Blue.
  I Met by Chance.
  I Wept as I Lay Dreaming.
  Ich Weiss Nicht Was Soll Es
    Bedeuten.
  If, Jerusalem, I Ever Should
    Forget Thee.
  Im Traum Sah Ich Ein
    Mannchen Klein Und Putzig.
  Katharine.
  Knight Olaf.
  Love's Resume.
  Madchen Mit Dem Rothen
    Mundchen.
  A Maiden Lies in Her
    Chamber.
  Mein Kind, Wir Waren
    Kinder.

Mein Liebchen, Wir Sassen
  Zusammen.
The Message.
Mir Traumte Von Einem
  Konigskind.
Mir Traumte Wieder Der Alte
  Traum.
The Morning After.
Mortal, Sneer Not at the
  Devil.
My Heart, My Heart Is
  Mournful.
My Songs Are Poisoned.
The New Jewish Hospital at
  Hamburg.
Night on the Shore.
The North Sea (excerpt).
Oh Lovely Fishermaiden.
Precaution.
Princess Sabbath.
Proem.
The Quiet Night.
Religion.
Sag', Wo Ist Dein Schones
  Liebchen.
The Sea Hath Its Pearls.
Shadow-Love.
Solomon.
The Song of Songs.
Song of the Vivandiere.
Song: "There stands a lonely
  pine-tree."
A Sonnet to My Mother.
The Storm.
This Mad Carnival of Loving.
This White and Slender Body.
This World and This Life Are
  So Scattered, They Try Me.
Thou Hast Diamonds.
Three Holy Kings from
  Morgenland.
Three Sweethearts.
To a Political Poet.
To Edom.
To My Mother.
Twilight.
The Voyage.
Warum Sind Denn Die Rosen
  So Blass.
The Waves Gleam in the
  Sunshine.
We Cared for Each Other.
Weavers.
When Two Are Parted.
When Young Hearts Break.
Who Was It, Tell Me.
Wie Langsam Kriechet Sie
  Dahin.
The Window-Glance.
The Wise Men Ask the
  Children the Way.
Your Snow-White Shoulder.
Heinrich von Morungen, Sir.
  Dream and Image.
Hejinian, Lyn
  Redo, 1-5.
Helburn, Theresa
  Mother.
"Helen"
  Another Cynical Variation.
Heller, Binem
  Pesach Has Come to the
    Ghetto Again.
Hellman, Geoffrey
  Dynastic Tiff.
Hellman, George Sidney
  Coleridge.
  The Hudson.
  In a China Shop.
Hellyer, Jill
  Calculating Female.

Helmer, Charles D.
  The Battle of Oriskany.
Helmling, Steven
  Two Weeks after an April
    Frost.
Helmore, Thomas
  Christmas Carol.
Helphingtine, Mary J.
  The Blessings of Surrender.
Helsley, Shel
  Christ Alone.
Helton, Roy
  Glimpses.
  In Passing.
  Lonesome Water.
  Old Christmas Morning.
Helwig, David
  Considerations.
  A Dead Weasel.
  Drunken Poem.
  For Edward Hicks.
  One Step from an Old Dance.
  Words from Hell.
Hemans, Felicia Dorothea
  The Agony in the Garden.
  The Brereton Omen (excerpt).
  Casabianca.
  The Child's First Grief.
  The Cid's Rising.
  Corinne at the Capitol.
  Dirge.
  England's Dead.
  Fairy Song.
  The First Grief.
  Foliage.
  The Graves of a Household.
  He Never Smiled Again.
  The Homes of England.
  The Hour of Death.
  Hymn for Christmas.
  Indian Woman's Death-Song.
  The Landing of the Pilgrim
    Fathers.
  The Memorial Pillar.
  The Orange Bough.
  A Prayer.
  Properzia Rossi.
  To the Poet Wordsworth.
  Where Is the Sea?
**Hemenway, Abby Maria
("Maria Josephine")**
  Annunciation Night.
Hemingway, Ernest
  Chapter Heading.
  The Earnest Liberal's Lament.
  Neo-Thomist Poem.
  Valentine.
  Wanderings: Champs
    d'Honneur.
Hemminger, Graham Lee
  Tobacco.
Hemp, Christine E.
  To Build a Poem.
  To My Blood Sister.
Hemschemeyer, Judith
  Best Friends.
  The Dirty-Billed Freeze
    Footy.
  First Love.
  Flight.
  Gift.
  I Remember the Room Was
    Filled with Light.
  My Grandmother Had Bones.
  My Mother's Death.
  The Painters.
  The Settlers.
  Strawberries.
  That Summer.
  This Love.
  We Interrupt This Broadcast.

Hemsley, Stuart
  S. P. C. A. Sermon.
Henchman, Richard
  In Consort to Wednesday,
    Jan. 1st. 1701...
  Vox Oppressi to the Lady
    Phipps.
Henderson, Alice Corbin
  Nodes.
Henderson, Brian
  3rd Migration, Third Series.
  February Margins.
  Investiture.
  Vertigo.
  Walking through the Door.
  A White Wall under the
    Wallpaper.
Henderson, Daniel
  The Homing Heart.
  Hymn for a Household.
  Nantucket Whalers.
  Opium Clippers.
  The Poet of Gardens.
  The Road to France.
  The Scarlet Thread.
  St. Swithin.
  The Stranger.
  The Two Wives.
Henderson, David
  Do Nothing till You Hear
    from Me.
  A Documentary on Airplane
    Glue.
  Downtown-Boy Uptown.
  It Is Not Enough.
  Keep on Pushing.
  The Louisiana Weekly #4.
  Number 5–December.
  Psychedelic Firemen.
  Sketches of Harlem.
  They Are Killing All the
    Young Men.
  Walk with De Mayor of
    Harlem.
  White People.
Henderson, Florence L.
  The Garden That I Love.
Henderson, Hamish
  The D-Day Dodgers.
  Ding Dong Dollar.
  First Elegy for the Dead in
    Cyrenaica.
  The Flyting o' Life and Daith.
Henderson, Jock
  The Martyr and the Army.
Henderson, John
  Of Love and Time.
Henderson, Peggy
  The Serpent Muses.
Henderson, Rose
  Growing Old.
Henderson, Ruth Evelyn
  Boy's Day.
Hendrie, K. G. P.
  Beckon Me, Ye Cuillins.
Hendry, J. F.
  The Constant North.
  Inverberg.
  Orpheus.
  The Ship.
  Tir-Nan-Og.
Henley, Elizabeth
  The Birthday-Cake
    Glockenspiel.
  It Really Happened.
Henley, Samuel
  Verses Addressed to a
    Friend...
Henley, William Ernest
  All in a Garden Green.
  Apparition.

As Like the Woman as You
 Can.
At Queensferry.
Ballade Made in Hot
 Weather.
Ballade of Dead Actors.
Ballade of Ladies' Names.
Ballade of Youth and Age.
The Blackbird.
A Bowl of Roses.
Collige Rosas.
Culture in the Slums.
A Desolate Shore.
Echoes.
England, My England.
Envoy.
Epilogue to Rhymes and
 Rhythms.
Fill a Glass with Golden
 Wine.
The Full Sea Rolls and
 Thunders.
Gulls in an Aery Morrice.
Home.
I Took a Hansom on To-Day.
In Hospital.
In Memoriam.
In the Dials.
Inter Sodales.
Invictus.
Life and Death.
London Voluntaries.
Madam Life.
O Gather Me the Rose.
Orientale.
Out of Tune.
Over the Hills and Far Away.
Rain.
Rhymes and Rhythms:
 Prologue.
Romance.
Rondel: Beside the Idle
 Summer Sea.
So Be My Passing.
So Let Me Hence.
Space and Dread and the
 Dark.
The Spirit of Wine.
Staff-Nurse: New Style.
Stanzas.
There's A Regret.
To A. D.
To Robert Louis Stevenson.
Two Days.
Under a Stagnant Sky.
Vigil.
Villon's Good-night.
Villon's Straight Tip to All
 Cross Coves.
We'll Go No More A-Roving.
What Is to Come.
With Strawberries.
Hennell, Thomas
 A Mermaiden.
 Queen Anne's Musicians.
 Shepherd and Shepherdess.
Hennen, Tom
 Job Hunting.
 Unusual Things.
 Usually an Old Female Is the
  Leader.
 Woods Night.
 Working near Lake Traverse.
Henniker-Heaton, Peter J.
 Post Early For Space.
Henri, Adrian
 Mrs. Albion You've Got a
  Lovely Daughter.
Henri, Raymond
 At the Woodpile.
 The Bridge from Brooklyn
  (excerpt).

The Temple at Segesta.
 View of the Cathedral.
Henrich, Edith
 Protagonist.
Henry, Francis
 The Old Settler's Song.
Henry, Gordon
 Freeze Tag.
 Leaving Smoke's.
 Outside White Earth.
 Pine Point, you are:...
 Waking on a Greyhound.
Henry, James
 Another and Another and
  Another.
 My Stearine Candles.
 Old Man.
 Once on a Time a Thousand
  Different Men.
 Out of the Frying Pan into
  the Fire.
 Pain.
 Two Hundred Men and
  Eighteen Killed.
 Very Old Man.
**Henry, O. (William Sidney
 Porter)**
 Last Fall of the Alamo.
 Options.
 Tamales.
Henry VIII, King of England
 As the Holly Groweth Green.
 Good Company.
 Green Groweth the Holly.
 The Holly.
 Pastime.
 To His Lady.
Henryson, Robert
 The Abbey Walk.
 The Bludy Serk.
 Cresseid's Complaint against
  Fortune.
 The Garment of Good Ladies.
 The Praise of Age.
 The Preiching of the Swallow.
 Robene and Makyne.
 The Taill of the Foxe, That
  Begylit the Wolf...
 The Tale of the Upland
  Mouse and the Burgess
  Mouse.
 The Testament of Cresseid.
 To Our Lady.
Hensley, Sophia Almon
 Because of You.
Henson, Lance
 Among Hawks.
 Anniversary Poem for the
  Cheyennes Who Fell at Sand
  Creek.
 At chadwicks bar and grill.
 Bay Poem.
 Between Rivers and Seas.
 Buffalo marrow on black.
 The Cold.
 Comanche Ghost Dance.
 Crazy Horse.
 Curtain.
 Dawn in January.
 Epitaph: Snake River.
 Flock.
 Grandfather.
 Image of City.
 Last Words, 1968.
 Moon at Three a.m.
 Moth.
 North.
 Old Man Told Me.
 Old Story.
 Other.
 Our Smoke Has Gone Four
  Ways.

Poem for Carroll Descendant
 of Chiefs.
Poem near midway truck stop.
Rain.
Scattered Leaves.
Sitting Alone in Tulsa Three
 A.M.
Sleep Watch.
Sundown at Darlington 1878.
Travels With the Band-Aid
 Army.
Vision song (cheyenne).
Warrior Nation Trilogy.
We Are a People.
Wish.
Wood Floor Dreams.
Henson, Pauline
 On the Edge of the Copper
  Pit.
Henze, Helen Rowe
 Etruscan Warrior's Head.
Hepburn, Thomas Nicoll *See*
 "Setoun, Gabriel"
Heppenstall, Rayner
 Actaeon.
 Consolation in July.
 Fleur de Lys.
 Hagiograph.
 Spring Song.
 St. Stephen's Word.
 Tammuz.
Heraclides
 In Cnidus Born, the Consort I
  Became.
Herbert, George
 Aaron.
 Affliction.
 The Agonie.
 The Altar.
 Ana(Mary-Army)gram.
 The Answer.
 Artillerie.
 Assurance.
 Avarice.
 The Bag.
 The Banquet.
 Be Useful.
 Bitter-Sweet.
 The British Church.
 The Bunch of Grapes.
 Christmas.
 The Church-Floor.
 Church Lock and Key.
 Church-Monuments.
 Church Music.
 The Church-Porch.
 Clasping of Hands.
 The Collar.
 Confession.
 Conscience.
 The Crosse.
 The Dawning.
 Death.
 Decay.
 Denial.
 Dialogue.
 Discipline.
 Dooms-Day.
 Dulnesse.
 Easter.
 Easter Wings.
 The Elixir.
 Employment.
 L'Envoy.
 Even-Song.
 The Familie.
 Finis.
 The Flower.
 The Forerunners.
 Fraility.
 The Glance.
 Grace.

Grieve Not the Holy Spirit.
The H. Communion.
The H. Scriptures. I.
A Heart to Praise Thee.
Heaven.
Holy Baptism.
Hope.
The Invitation.
Jesu.
The Jews.
Judgement.
Life.
Longing.
Love.
Love-Joy.
Love Unknown.
Man.
Man's Medley.
Marie Magdalene.
Mattens.
Miserie.
Mortification.
Nature.
The Odour.
Our Life Is Hid with Christ in
 God.
Paradise.
A Parodie.
Peace.
The Pearl.
Philosophers Have Measured
 Mountains.
The Pilgrimage.
Praise.
Prayer: "Prayer, the Church's
 banquet."
Preparations.
The Priesthood.
The Pulley.
The Quidditie.
The Quip.
The Rain.
Redemption.
Repentance.
The Reprisall.
The Rose.
The Sacrifice.
The Search.
The Second Thanksgiving, or
 The Reprisal.
Sepulchre.
Shall I Be Silent?
Sighs and Groans.
Sin.
Sins' Round.
Sion.
Song (Attributed to the Earl
 of Pembroke).
Song: "Soules joy, now I am
 gone."
The Sonne.
Sonnet: "My God, where is
 that ancient heat towards
 thee."
Sonnets from Walton's Life of
 Herbert, 1670.
The Starre.
The Storm.
Submission.
Sunday.
The Temper.
The Temple.
The Thanksgiving.
Time.
To All Angels and Saints.
Trinity Sunday.
A True Hymn.
The Twenty-Third Psalm.
Unkindness.
Vanity (I).
Virtue.

Whitsunday.
Who Would Have Thought?
The Windows.
The World.
A Wreath.
Herbert, Henry William
Come Back.
Herbert, Moss
A Gentle Park.
Herbert, P. G.
The Farmer and the Farmer's
Wife.
Herbert, Sir Alan
Less Nonsense.
Herbert, Sir Alan Patrick
At the Theater.
Beaucourt Revisited.
The Centipede.
Coals of Fire.
Cupid's Darts.
The Farmer.
Finale.
The Green Estaminet.
Hattage.
"He Didn't Oughter..."
I Can't Think What He Sees
in Her.
I Like Them Fluffy.
I've Got the Giggles.
Inst., Ult., and Prox.: Answer.
Lines for a Worthy Person
Who Has Drifted by
Accident...
Mullion.
"No Quarrel."
The Prodigy.
The Racing-Man.
Saturday Night.
The Snail.
Stop, Science–Stop!
To a Junior Waiter.
Triangular Legs.
Herbert, Zbigniew
Elegy of Fortinbras.
The End of a Dynasty.
From Mythology.
Pan Cogito's Thoughts on
Hell.
The Return of the Proconsul.
**Herbert of Cherbury, Edward,
Lord**
The Brown Beauty.
A Description.
Ditty in Imitation of the
Spanish....
Echo in a Church.
Echo to a Rock.
Elegy for Doctor Dunn.
Elegy over a Tomb.
Epitaph. Caecil. Boulstr.
Epitaph for Himself.
The First Meeting.
La Gialletta Gallante.
The Green-Sickness Beauty.
In a Glass-Window for
Inconstancy.
Inconstancy's the Greatest of
Sins.
Kissing.
Love Speaks at Last.
Loves End.
Madrigal: "Dear, when I did
from you remove."
Madrigal: "How should I love
my best?"
October 14. 1644.
An Ode upon a Question
Moved, Whether Love
Should Continue For Ever?
Parted Souls.
Platonick Love.
A Sinner's Lament.

Sonnet: "Innumerable
Beauties, thou white haire."
Sonnet Made upon the Groves
near Merlou Castle.
Sonnet of Black Beauty.
Tears, Flow No More.
The Thought.
To a Lady Who Did Sing
Excellently.
To Her Eyes.
To his Friend Ben. Johnson,
of his Horace made English.
To His Mistress for Her True
Picture.
To His Watch, When He
Could Not Sleep.
To Mrs. Diana Cecyll.
A Vision.
Herbin, John Frederic
The Diver.
Haying.
Herbkersman, Gretchen
Cosmetic.
Herder, Johann Gottfried von
Esthonian Bridal Song.
Sir Olaf.
Herea, Te Heuheu
A Mourning-Song for
Rangiaho.
Herebert, William
The Devout Man Prays to His
Relations.
My Folk, What Have I Done
Thee?
A Palm-Sunday Hymn.
Who Is This That Cometh
from Edom?
Heredia, Jose-Maria de
The Flute: A Pastoral.
The Laborer.
Herford, Oliver
The Ant.
A Belated Violet.
A Bunny Romance.
The Cat.
Child's Natural History.
The Chimpanzee.
The Cow.
The Crocodile.
The Dog.
The Elf and the Dormouse.
Eve.
The Fall of J. W. Beane.
Gather Kittens While You
May (parody).
The Hen.
The Hippopotamus.
If This Little World Tonight.
Japanesque.
The Last Violet.
The Laughing Willow.
Limerick: "A camel, with
practical views."
Limerick: "A canary, its woe
to assuage."
Limerick: "A heathen named
Min, passing by."
Limerick: "A is the autograph
bore."
Limerick: "A leopard when
told that benzine."
Limerick: "G is a grumbler
gruff."
Limerick: "'I have often been
told,' said the horse."
Limerick: "Once a grasshoper
(food being scant)."
Limerick: "Once a pound-
keeper chanced to impound."
Limerick: "One evening a
goose, for a treat."

Limerick: "Q is a quoter
who'll cite."
Limerick: "Quoth a cat to me
once: Pray relieve."
Limerick: "Quoth the
bookworm, 'I don't care one
bit.'"
Limerick: "Said a lachrymose
Labrador seal."
Limerick: "Said a lady who
wore a swell cape."
Limerick: "Said the crab:
"'Tis not beauty or birth.'"
Limerick: "Said the Lion: 'On
music I dote.'"
Limerick: "Said the mole:
'You would never suppose.'"
Limerick: "Said the spider, in
tones of distress."
Limerick: "There once was a
kind armadillo."
Limerick: "There once was a
sculptor called Phidias."
Limerick: "There once were
some learned MD's."
Limerick: "There was a young
waitress named Myrtle."
Limerick: "There was once a
fastidious yak."
Limerick: "Thre was a young
lady of Twickenham."
Limerick: "W's a well-
informed wight."
Metaphysics.
The Milk Jug.
The Missing Link.
Mrs. Seymour Fentolin.
The Music of the Future.
The Musical Lion.
My Sense of Sight.
A Penguin.
The Platypus.
The Silver Question.
The Smile of the Goat.
The Smile of the Walrus.
Stairs.
Two Smiles.
The Untutored Giraffe.
Why Ye Blossome Cometh
before Ye Leafe.
The Women of the Better
Class.
Herman, Reinhold W.
Now I Set Me.
Hernaes, Gunnar
Trumpet and Flute.
Hernandez Cruz, Victor *See*
Cruz, Victor Hernandez
Hernton, Calvin C.
D Blues.
The Distant Drum.
Elements of Grammar.
Fall Down.
Jitterbugging in the Streets.
Madhouse.
The Patient: Rockland County
Sanitarium.
Herrera, Demetrio
Training.
Herrera, Fernando de
Ideal Beauty.
Herrick, Robert
Againe.
All Things Decay and Die.
The Amber Bead.
Ambition.
Anacreontic.
Another.
Another Charme for Stables.
Another on Her.
Another to the Maids.

The Apparition of His
Mistress Calling Him to
Elysium.
The Apron of Flowers.
The Argument of His Book.
Art above Nature, to Julia.
The Bad Season Makes the
Poet Sad.
The Bag of the Bee.
Barley-Break; or, Last in Hell.
The Beggar to Mab, the Fairie
Queen.
The Bellman.
The Body.
The Bracelet: To Julia.
The Bubble: A Song.
A Canticle to Apollo.
The Captived Bee; or, The
Little Filcher.
A Cat.
The Ceremonies for
Candlemas Day.
Ceremonies for Candlemas
Eve.
Ceremonies for Christmas.
Ceremony upon Candlemas
Eve.
The Changes to Corinna.
Charm: "Bring the holy crust
of Bread."
Charm: "Let the superstitious
wife."
A Charm, or an Allay for
Love.
The Cheat of Cupid: or, The
Ungentle Guest.
Cherry-Pit.
Cherry-Ripe.
Chop-Cherry.
A Christmas Carol.
A Christmas Caroll, Sung to
the King in the Presence at
White-Hall.
Christmas Eve–Another
Ceremony.
Clothes Do But Cheat and
Cozen Us.
Cock-Crow.
Comfort to a Youth That Had
Lost His Love.
The Coming of Good Luck.
A Conjuration, to Electra.
Connubii Flores, or the Well-
Wishes at Weddings.
Corinna's Going A-Maying.
A Country Life: To His
Brother, M. Tho: Herrick.
Crosses.
The Cruel Maid.
Crutches.
The Curse: A Song.
Dean-Bourn, a Rude River in
Devon, by Which Sometimes
He Lived.
The Definition of Beauty.
Delight in Disorder.
The Departure of the Good
Daemon.
Dew Sat on Julia's Hair.
A Dirge upon the Death of
the Right Valiant Lord,
Bernard Stuart.
Discontents in Devon.
Distrust.
Divination by a Daffadil.
Dreams.
The End of His Work.
The Entertainment, or Porch-
Verse, at the Marriage....
Epitaph on Sir Edward Giles
and His Wife.

Epitaph upon a Child That Died.
An Epitaph upon a Sober Matron.
An Epitaph upon a Virgin.
An Epithalamy to Sir Thomas Southwell and His Lady.
Eternity.
The Eye.
Fair Days; or, Dawns Deceitful.
The Fairies.
The Fairy Temple; or, Oberon's Chapel....
Fame.
Fame Makes Us Forward.
Farewell Frost, or Welcome the Spring.
The Four Sweet Months.
Four Things Make Us Happy Here.
Fresh Cheese and Cream.
A Frolic.
The Frozen Heart.
The Frozen Zone; or, Julia Disdainful.
The Funeral Rites of the Rose.
God to Be First Served.
Good Christians.
Good Men Afflicted Most.
The Good-Night or Blessing.
Grace for a Child.
Grace for Children.
The Hag.
Her Legs.
Here a Little Child I Stand.
His Age.
His Cavalier.
His Charge to Julia at His Death.
His Content in the Country.
His Creed.
His Desire.
His Ejaculation to God.
His Fare-well to Sack.
His Grange, or Private Wealth.
His Hope or Sheet-Anchor.
His Lachrimae or Mirth, Turn'd to Mourning.
His Own Epitaph.
His Parting with Mrs. Dorothy Kennedy.
His Poetry His Pillar.
His Prayer for Absolution.
His Prayer to Ben Jonson.
His Request to Julia.
His Return to London.
His Sailing from Julia.
His Saviour's Words, Going to the Cross.
His Tears to Thamasis.
His Winding-Sheet.
His Wish to God.
The Hock-Cart, or Harvest Home.
Holy Numbers Litany to the Holy Spirit (excerpt).
The Hour-Glass.
How Lillies Came White.
How Roses Came Red.
How Violets Came Blue.
A Hymn to Bacchus.
Impossibilities, to His Friend.
In the Dark None Dainty.
The Invitation.
Julia's Petticoat.
The Kisse: A Dialogue.
Kisses Loathesome.
Kissing and Bussing.
A Lady Dying in Childbed.

The Lilly in a Christal.
Lips Tongueless.
Litany to the Holy Spirit (excerpt).
Long and Lazy.
Love Dislikes Nothing.
Love Me Little, Love Me Long.
Love Perfumes All Parts.
Love What It Is.
Lovers How They Come and Part.
A Lyric to Mirth.
Lyrick for Legacies.
The Mad Maid's Song.
Man's Dying-Place Uncertain.
Matins, or Morning Prayer.
The Meddow Verse or Aniversary to Mistris Bridget Lowman.
A Meditation for His Mistress.
Mercy and Love.
Mirth.
Moderation.
Money Gets the Mastery.
Money Makes the Mirth.
More White Than Whitest Lilies.
The Mount of the Muses.
Music.
Neutrality Loathsome.
A New-Year's Gift Sent to Sir Simeon Steward.
The New-Yeeres Gift, Sung to the King in the Presence at White Hall.
The Night-Piece, to Julia.
No Coming to God without Christ.
No Difference in the Dark.
No Fault in Women.
No Loathsomeness in Love.
No Lock Against Lechery.
Not Every Day Fit for Verse.
Not to Love.
Nothing New.
A Nuptial Song, or Epithalamie, on Sir Clipseby Crew and His Lady.
A Nuptial Verse to Mistress Elizabeth Lee Now Lady Tracy.
Oberon's Feast.
Oberon's Palace.
Observation.
An Ode for Ben Jonson.
An Ode on the Birth of Our Saviour.
An Ode to Master Endymion Porter, upon His Brother's Death.
Of Her Breath.
The Old Wives Prayer.
On Himselfe.
Orpheus.
A Panegyric to Sir Lewis Pemberton.
The Parcae, or Three Dainty Destinies: The Armillet.
The Parting Verse, the Feast There Ended.
The Perfume.
The Peter-Penny.
The Pillar of Fame.
The Plaudite, or End of Life.
The Poet Loves a Mistress, But Not to Marry.
Poetry Perpetuates the Poet.
Power and Peace.
The Power in the People.
Prayers Must Have Poise.

The Primrose.
The Rod.
The Rosarie.
Rubies and Pearls.
The Sadness of Things for Sappho's Sickness.
The Scare-Fire.
Science in God.
The Shoe-Tying.
The Silken Snake.
Sins Loathed, and Yet Loved.
So Look the Mornings.
A Sort Hymne to Venus.
The Spell.
The Star-Song: A Carol to the King; Sung at White-Hall.
Steam in Sacrifice.
Supreme Fortune Falls Soonest.
The Suspition upon His Over-Much Familiarity with a Gentlewoman.
Temptation.
A Ternarie of Littles, Upon a Pipkin of Jelly Sent to a Lady.
A Thankful Heart.
Thanksgiving.
A Thanksgiving to God for His House.
This Crosse-Tree Here.
'Tis Hard to Find God.
The Tithe: To the Bride.
To a Bed of Tulips.
To a Child.
To a Gentleman Objecting to Him His Grey Hairs.
To Aenone.
To Anthea, Who May Command Him Anything.
To Blossoms.
To Cherry-Blossomes.
To Critics.
To Crown It.
To Daffodils.
To Dean Bourn, a Rude River in Devon, by Which Sometimes He Lived.
To Death.
To Dianeme.
To Electra.
To Finde God.
To Fortune.
To God.
To God, on His Sickness.
To Groves.
To His Book.
To His Conscience.
To His Dying Brother, Master William Herrick.
To His Ever-Loving God.
To His Friend, on the Untunable Times.
To His Honoured and Most Ingenious Friend, Master Charles Cotton.
To His Honoured Kinsman Sir William Soame.
To His Kinsman, Master Thomas Herrick, Who Desired to Be in His Book.
To His Kinswoman, Mistress Penelope Wheeler.
To His Lovely Mistresses.
To His Maid Prew.
To His Mistress.
To His Mistress Objecting to Him Neither Toying or Talking.
To His Mistresses.
To His Muse.

To His Saviour, a Child; a Present, by a Child.
To His Tomb-Maker.
To Julia.
To Julia, the Flaminica Dialis, or Queen-Priest.
To Keep a True Lent.
To Lar.
To Laurels.
To Live Merrily, and to Trust to Good Verses.
To Master Denham, on His Prospective Poem.
To Master Henry Lawes, the Excellent Composr of Lyrics.
To Meadows.
To Mistress Katherine Bradshaw, the Lovely, That Crowned Him...
To Music.
To Music: A Song.
To Music, to Becalm a Sweet-Sick Youth.
To Music, to Becalm His Fever.
To My Ill Reader.
To Oenone.
To Perilla.
To Phyllis, to Love and Live With Him.
To Primroses Fill'd with Morning-Dew.
To Robin Red-Breast.
To Sycamores.
To the Generous Reader.
To the King, Upon His Comming with His Army into the West.
To the King, Upon his welcome to Hampton-Court.
To the Most Fair and Lovely Mistris, Anne Soame, Now Lady Abdie.
To the Most Learned, Wise, and Arch-Antiquary, M. John Selden.
To the Most Virtuous Mistress Pot, Who Many Times Entertained Him.
To the Reverend Shade of His Religious Father.
To the Rose.
To the Soure Reader.
To the Virgins, To Make Much of Time.
To the Water Nymphs, Drinking at the Fountain.
To the Western Wind.
To the Willow Tree.
To the Yew and Cypress to Grace His Funeral.
To Violets.
To Virgins.
To Vulcan.
To Women, to Hide Their Teeth, if They Be Rotten or Rusty.
The Transfiguration.
A Trapped Fly.
Two Graces.
Upon a Black Twist, Rounding the Arm of the Countess of Carlisle.
Upon a Child That Died.
Upon a Delaying Lady.
Upon a Flie.
Upon a Maid.
Upon a Virgin Kissing a Rose.
Upon a Wife that Dyed Mad with Jealousie.

Upon a Young Mother of
Many Children.
Upon Batt.
Upon Ben Johnson.
Upon Bunce: Epigram.
Upon Fone a School-master.
Epigram.
Upon Glass: Epigram.
Upon Groins: Epigram.
Upon Gryll.
Upon Her Feet.
Upon Her Voice.
Upon Himself.
Upon His Departure Hence.
Upon His Julia.
Upon His Sister-in-Law,
Mistress Elizabeth Herrick.
Upon His Spaniell Tracie.
Upon Jack and Jill. Epigram.
Upon Jone and Jane.
Upon Julia's Breasts.
Upon Julia's Clothes.
Upon Julia's Fall.
Upon Julia's Hair Filled with
Dew.
Upon Julia's Petticoat.
Upon Julia's Recovery.
Upon Julia's Ribband.
Upon Julia's Voice.
Upon Julia Washing Herself
in the River.
Upon Julia Weeping.
Upon Love.
Upon Love, by Way of
Question and Answer.
Upon Lulls.
Upon M. Ben Jonson–
Epigram.
Upon Master Fletchers
Incomparable Playes.
Upon Mistress Elizabeth
Wheeler under the Name of
Amarillis.
Upon Mistress Susanna
Southwell Her Feet.
Upon Moon.
Upon Pagget.
Upon Parson Beanes.
Upon Prudence Baldwin Her
Sickness.
Upon Prue, His Maid.
Upon Rook: Epigram.
Upon Roses.
Upon Scobble. Epigram.
Upon Showbread: Epigram.
Upon Some Women.
Upon Suddes a Laundresse.
Upon Sybilla.
Upon the Death of His
Sparrow an Elegie.
Upon the Losse of His
Mistresses.
Upon the Nipples of Julia's
Breast.
Upon the Same.
Upon the Troublesome Times.
Upon Time.
Upon Umber: Epigram.
The Vine.
The Vision.
The Vision to Electra.
The Weeping Cherry.
The Welcome to Sack.
What Kind of Mistress He
Would Have.
What Shame Forbids to
Speak.
When He Would Have His
Verses Read.
When I Thy Parts Run O'er.
The White Island.
Why Flowers Change Color.

The Willow Garland.
The Wounded Cupid.
Herschberger, Ruth
In Panelled Rooms.
The Lumberyard.
Mulberry Street.
O Terry.
Poem: "Love being what it is,
full of betrayals."
Song: "Sergei's a flower."
Summer Mansions.
Watergate.
Yaddo.
Herschell, W. M.
The Kid Has Gone to the
Colors.
Hersey, Harold
The Lavender Cowboy.
Lay of the Last Frontier.
Hershenson, Miriam
Husbands and Wives.
Love Poem–1940.
Hershon, Robert
A Boy Who Smells Like
Cocoa.
The Cooper & Bailey Great
London Circus.
Four Translations from the
English of Robert Hershon.
How to Walk in a Crowd.
Ireland Lake.
Kelly.
Responses.
Spitting on Ira Rosenblatt.
The Swimming Lesson.
The U.S. Coast and Geodetic
Survey Ship Pioneer.
Hervey, Christopher
Confusion (parody).
Hervey, J. R.
Carnival.
Hydro Works.
John Donne's Defiance.
Man of Crete.
The Man Who Wanted to be
a Seagull.
Neighbour.
Sonnet of Departure.
Threnos.
Two Old Men Look at the
Sea.
Herzberg, Judith
Commentaries on the Song of
Songs.
Kinneret.
Nearer.
On the Death of Sylvia Plath.
Reunion.
Vocation.
The Voice.
Yiddish.
Herzing, Albert
A Small Boy, Dreaming.
Heseltine, Nigel
Microcosmos.
Hesiod
Works and Days.
Hesketh, Phoebe
The Dipper.
Ducks.
The Fox.
Hess, M. Whitcomb
The Vision of St. Bernard.
Hesse, Herman
Sometimes.
Hesse, Hermann
It's Just the Same to Me.
Midsummer.
Night.
Spring Song.

Hester, M. L., Jr.
International Motherhood
Assoc.
Hester, Jr, M. L.
The Second Night.
Hetherington, George
Charles at the Siege.
Palm House, Botanic Gardens.
Sonnet: "Now keep that long
revolver at your side."
Sonnet: "Since I keep only
what I give away."
Hetherington, Graeme
The Man from Changi.
Hetherington, Henry
Jack Sprat (parody).
Hewett, Dorothy
In Moncur Street.
Moon-Man.
Sanctuary.
This Version of Love.
Hewison, R. J. P.
Genius.
Hewitt, Ethel M.
Wild Wishes.
Hewitt, Geof
Behind That Wall My
Roommate Fucks His Girl.
Ben Plays Hide & Seek in the
Deep Woods.
Chickens.
Conversion.
Emergency at 8.
Explanation.
For Bill.
For Randie.
In Like a Lion.
Rip-off #1: Hippie
Capitalism.
Hewitt, John
Because I Paced My Thought.
First Corncrake.
From a Museum Man's
Album.
The Frontier.
Frost.
The Glens.
Ireland.
An Irishman in Coventry.
Leaf.
The Little Lough.
Load.
Lyric.
A Minor Victorian Painter.
O Country People.
Once Alien Here.
Poem in May.
The Ram's Horn.
The Spectacle of Truth.
The Swatche Uncut.
Hewlett, Maurice
Rosa Nascosa.
When She a Maiden Slim.
Hey, Phil
For Sue.
Old Clothes.
Old Men Working Concrete.
Sweetheart.
The True Ballad of the Great
Race to Gilmore City.
Heyduk, Adolf
Three Fields.
Heyen, William
Arrows.
Auction.
The Berries.
Birds and Roses Are Birds
and Roses.
The Children.
The Dark.
Dark in the Reich of the
Blond.

Dog Sacrifice at Lake
Ronkonkoma.
Driving at Dawn.
The Elm's Home.
Existential.
Fires.
I Move to Random
Consolations.
The King's Men.
The Late Show.
Mantle.
The Mill.
Mother and Son.
Poem Touching the Gestapo.
Ram Time.
Riddle.
Ryokan.
The Snapper.
The Spirit of Wrath.
The Stadium.
This Night.
Heym, Georg
Famine.
War.
Heynen, Jim
Tourist Guide: How You Can
Tell for Sure When You're in
South Dakota.
Heyrick, Thomas
Martial.
On a Peacock.
On a Sunbeam.
On an Indian Tomineois, the
Least of Birds.
On the Crocodile.
On the Death of a Monkey.
Heyse, Paul
Rispetti: On the Death of a
Child.
A Young Girl's Song.
Heyward, DuBose
Dusk.
The Equinox.
Gamesters All.
The Mountain Woman.
Porgy, Maria, and Bess.
Heyward, Janie Screven
Autumn Leaves.
The Spirit's Grace.
Heywood, Jasper
Look or You Leap.
The Lookers-On.
Heywood, John
All a Green Willow Is My
Garland.
Art Thou Heywood.
Cardinal Fisher.
The Cock and the Hen.
The "Gloria Patri."
If Love, For Love of Long
Time Had.
Jack and His Father.
Love Continual.
Of a Daw.
Of Birds and Birders.
Of Use.
On Botching.
On the Princess Mary.
The Play of the Four P.P.:
The Palmer.
The Play of the Weather: The
English Schoolboy.
Tybrun and Westminster.
Heywood, Thomas
The Author to His Booke.
The Cherubim (excerpt).
An Epitaph.
The Golden Age: Hymn to
Diana.
Hierarchie of the Blessed
Angels (excerpt).
Jupiter and Ganimede.

The Message.
Pack, Clouds, away, and
  Welcome, Day!
The Passing Bell.
Praise of Ceres.
She That Denies Me.
Ye Little Birds That Sit and
  Sing.
Hickey, Agnes MacCarthy
Old Essex Door.
Hickey, Emily Henrietta
Beloved, It Is Morn.
Song: "Beloved, it is morn!"
Hickey, Mark
The Road along the Thumb
  and Forefinger.
Hickok, Eliza M.
Prayer.
Hickox, Chauncey
Under the Red Cross.
Hicks, Barbecue Bob
Barbecue Blues.
Cold Wave Blues.
Ease It to Me Blues.
She's Gone Blues.
Hicks, Berryman
The Time Is Swiftly Rolling
  On.
Hicks, John V.
Are You There, Mrs. Goose?
Last Rite.
The Trumpet Shall Sound.
Hickson, William E.
Walking Song.
Hicky, Daniel Whitehead
Georgia Towns.
No Friend Like Music.
Nocturne: Georgia Coast.
Okefenokee Swamp.
The River Boats.
The Runaway.
Say That He Loved Old Ships.
When a Man Turns
  Homeward.
Who Pilots Ships.
Wisdom.
Hiebert, Paul
Steeds.
Hiers, Lois Smith
On Laying up Treasure.
Higgins, Annie
Waking.
Higgins, Brian
Analogy.
Baedeker for Metaphysicians.
The Corrupt Man in the
  French Pub.
Genesis.
Higgins, Frederick Robert
The Ballad of O'Bruadir.
The Boyne Walk.
Chinese Winter.
Father and Son.
The Gallows Tree.
The Little Clan.
O You among Women.
An Old Air.
The Old Jockey.
Padraic O'Conaire–Gaelic
  Storyteller.
Song for the Clatter-Bones.
Higginson, Ella
Beggars.
Four-Leaf Clover.
The Lamp in the West.
The Month of Falling Stars.
Moonrise in the Rockies.
Higginson, Mary Thacher
Changelings.
Ghost-Flowers.
In the Dark.
Inheritance.

Higginson, Thomas Wentworth
Decoration.
Ode to a Butterfly.
The Past Is Dark with Sin
  and Shame.
Since Cleopatra Died.
The Snowing of the Pines.
Such Stuff as Dreams Are
  Made Of.
The Things I Miss.
To Duty.
To Thine Eternal Arms, O
  God.
Higgons, Bevil
The Mourners.
Higgs, Barry O.
Deaf.
In Lord Carpenter's Country.
Night Shore.
Parson's Pleasure.
Reversion.
Higgs, Ted
From Mistra: A Prospect.
Higham, Charles
Barnacle Geese.
Highet, Gilbert
Homage to Ezra Pound
  (parody).
Higo, Aig
Hidesong.
Hikmet, Nazim
I Come and Stand at Every
  Door.
Things I Didn't Know I
  Loved.
Hilarova, Dagmar
Questions.
Hilary of Arles, Saint
Thou Bounteous Giver of the
  Light.
Hildegard von Bingen
Like the Honeycomb
  Dropping Honey.
O Crimson Blood.
Hildreth, Charles Lotin
At the Mermaid Inn.
Implora Pace.
To an Obscure Poet Who
  Lives on My Hearth.
Hill, Aaron
Alone in an Inn at
  Southampton, April the 25th,
  1737.
The Lord's Prayer in Verse.
May-Day.
Modesty.
A Strong Hand.
Whitehall Stairs.
Hill, Benjamin Dionysius
To St. Mary Magdalen.
Hill, Chippie
Charleston Blues.
Hill, Clyde Walton
Lincoln.
Hill, Donald L.
The Buzzing Doubt.
Hill, Frank Ernest
Clouds.
The Earth Will Stay the
  Same.
Upper Air.
Hill, Geoffrey
Annunciations.
An Apology for the Revival of
  Christian
  Architecture...(excerpt).
Asmodai.
Christmas Trees.
The Dead Bride.
The Distant Fury of Battle.
Doctor Faustus.

Doctor Faustus: Another Part
  of the Fable.
Domaine Public.
Genesis.
Gideon at the Well.
God's Little Mountain.
The Guardians.
Idylls of the King.
The Imaginative Life.
In Memory of Jane Fraser.
In Piam Memoriam.
Lachrimae Amantis.
Mercian Hymns (excerpt).
Merlin.
Of Commerce and Society.
Orpheus and Eurydice.
Ovid in the Third Reich.
A Pastoral.
The Pentecost Castle
  (excerpt).
Picture of a Nativity.
The Re-Birth of Venus.
Requiem for the Plantagenet
  Kings.
September Song.
A Short History of British
  India.
A Song from Armenia.
To the (Supposed) Patron.
The Turtle Dove.
Two Chorale-Preludes.
Veni Coronaberis.
The White Ship.
Wreaths.
Hill, George
Leila.
Song of the Elfin Steers -
  Man.
Hill, Hyacinthe
Old Emily.
Rebels from Fairy Tales.
Hill, Jeanne
Lines from a Misplaced
  Person.
Hill, Joe
Casey Jones (Union).
The Rebel Girl.
There Is Power.
The Tramp.
Hill, King Solomon
The Gone Dead Train.
Whoopee Blues.
Hill, Leona Ames
Let Him Return.
Hill, Leslie Pinckney
Christmas at Melrose.
"So Quietly".
Summer Magic.
The Teacher.
Tuskegee.
Hill, Nellie
Soup on a Cold Day.
Hill, Pati
On the Beach.
Time Was.
Two Lovers Sitting on a
  Tomb.
Hill, Quentin
Time Poem.
Hill, Roberta
Blue Mountain.
Depot in Rapid City.
Direction.
E Uni Que A The Hi A Tho,
  Father.
Falling Moon.
In the Madison Zoo.
Leap in the Dark.
Lines for Marking Time.
A Nation Wrapped in Stone.
Night along the Mackinac
  Bridge.

Seal at Stinson Beach.
Sleeping with Foxes.
Song for Healing.
Star Quilt.
Steps.
Swamp.
Whispers.
Winter Burn.
A Wish for Waving Goodbye.
Hill, Rowland M.
Idiot Boy.
Hill, Selima
Below Hekla.
A Voice in the Garden.
Hill, Thomas
The Bobolink.
Hill-Abu Ishak, Elton
Theme Brown Girl.
Hille, Peter
Beauty.
The Maiden.
Hillhouse, Augustus Lucas
Trembling Before Thine
  Awful Throne.
Hillhouse, James Abraham
Hadad: The Demon-Lover.
Hillman, Brenda
Ballet.
Hills, Elijah Clarence
To Pikes Peak.
Hillyer, Robert
As One Who Bears beneath
  His Neighbor's Roof.
The Assassination.
The Bats.
Elegy.
Eppur Si Muove?
The Eternal Return.
Familiar Faces, Long
  Departed.
The Ivory Tower.
Letter to a Teacher of
  English.
A Letter to Charles Townsend
  Copeland (excerpt).
A Letter to Robert Frost.
Lullaby.
Mentis Trist.
Moo!
Nocturne.
Over Bright Summer Seas.
Pastoral.
Prothalamion (excerpt).
The Relic.
Rendezvous.
Seven Times One Are Seven.
Sonnets.
Thermopylae.
A Thought in Time.
To a Scarlatti Passepied.
The Untended Field.
Hillyer, Robert Silliman
And When the Prince Came.
In the Shadowy Whatnot
  Corner.
Intermezzo.
Sonnets, I.
Hilton, Arthur Clement
Ding Dong (parody).
The Heathen Pass-ee.
Limerick: "There was a young
  critic of Kings."
Limerick: "There was a young
  genius of Queens."
Limerick: "There was a young
  gourmand of John's".
Limerick: "There was an old
  Fellow of Trinity."
Octopus (parody).
The Vulture and the
  Husbandman.

Hilton, David
The Melmac Year.
The Poet Tries to Turn in His
Jock.
Hilton, John
Madrigal: "My mistress
frowns when she should
play."
Hilton, L. M.
Have Courage, My Boy, to
Say No!
Himel, Margery
My People.
Himmell, Sophie
In the Month of Green Fire.
Hind bint Utba
Fury against the Moslems at
Uhud.
Tambourine Song for Soldiers
Going into Battle.
Hind bint Uthatha
To a Hero Dead at al-Safra.
Hindley, Charles
Mother Shipton's Prophecies.
Hindley, Norman
Charter Boat.
Off Molokai.
Trout.
Wood Butcher.
Hinds, Samuel
Baby Sleeps.
Hine, Daryl
After the Agony in the
Garden.
August 13, 1966.
A Bewilderment at the
Entrance of the Fat Boy into
Eden.
Bluebeard's Wife.
The Doppelganger.
An English Elegy.
Fabulary Satire, IV.
In Praise of Music in Time of
Pestilence.
Lady Sara Bunbury Sacrificing
to the Graces, by Reynolds.
Plain Fare.
Point Grey.
The Survivors.
The Trout.
Untitled.
Vowel Movements.
The Wasp.
The Wave.
Hines, Herbert H.
A Christmas Prayer.
Hines, J. A.
The August Second Syndrome
Poem.
Cancel My Subscription.
For Myself.
Hines, Nellie Womack
Home.
Hines, Jr, Carl Wendell
Two Jazz Poems.
Hinkson, Katharine Tynan *See
also* **Tynan, Katharine**
Aux Carmelites.
The Beloved.
Cuckoo Song.
The Dead Coach.
The Desire.
The Epitaph.
The Flying Wheel.
The Footpath Way.
A Girl's Song.
In Time of Need.
Larks.
The Last Voyage.
The Little Ghost.
Lux in Tenebris.
The Man of the House.

Mater Dei.
Of an Orchard.
The Old Love.
Passiontide Communion.
A Prayer.
The Quiet Nights.
She Asks for New Earth.
Sheep and Lambs.
Turn o' the Year.
The Witch.
Hinshaw, Dawn
Not-Knowing.
Hioki no Ko-okima
On the Shore of Nawa.
Hippisley, John
Sweet Is the Budding Spring
of Love.
Hippius, Zenaida
A Grey Frock.
L'Imprevisibilite.
Hipple, Ted
The Traditional Grammarian
as Poet.
Hirsch, Edward
At Kresge's Diner in
Stonefalls, Arkansas.
A Chinese Vase.
Dawn Walk.
Dino Campana and the Bear.
Factories.
For the Sleepwalkers.
In the Middle of August.
Little Political Poem.
Matisse.
Poor Angels.
Hirsch, Mannie
Cry for a Disused Synagogue
in Booysens.
Hirschfield, Theodore H.
A.M.–P.M.
Hirschman, Jack
NHR.
Zohara.
Hirshbein, Peretz
Captive.
I Shall Weep.
Stars Fade.
Hirst, Henry Beck
The Fringilla Melodia.
The Funeral of Time.
Hitchcock, George
The Call of the Eastern Quail.
The Chauffeur of Lilacs.
Departure.
Distinguishing Ru from Chu.
Figures in a Ruined Ballroom.
May All Earth Be Clothed in
Light.
The One Whose Reproach I
Cannot Evade.
Song of Expectancy.
Three Portraits.
The United States Prepare for
the Permanent Revolution.
Villa Thermidor.
What to Say to the Pasha.
Hitchner, John T.
Remembering Apple Times.
Hitomaro
For My Sister's Sake.
Gossip Grows Like Weeds.
Lines from an Elegy on the
Death of His Wife.
May the Men Who Are Born.
O Boy Cutting Grass.
On the Moor of Kasuga.
Three Poems.
Two Poems.
When.
Hittan of Tayyi
Hamasah: His Children.

Ho Chih-Fang
Let Me Speak of Pure Things.
Ho Nansorhon
A Woman's Sorrow (excerpt).
Ho Xuan Huong
A Buddhist Priest.
Carved on an Areca Nut...
The Jackfruit.
Hoagland, Everett
The Anti-Semanticist.
It's a Terrible Thing!
Love Child–a Black Aesthetic.
The Music.
My Spring Thing.
Night Interpreted.
Hoare, Prince
The Arethusa.
Hoban, Russell
Boy with a Hammer.
The Empty House.
Jigsaw Puzzle.
Maine Sea Gulls.
Soft-Boiled Egg.
Hobbs, Valine
A Change of Heart.
One Day When We Went
Walking.
Hoberman, Mary Ann
The Birthday Bus.
Cockroach.
Combinations.
Comparison.
The Folk Who Live in
Backward Town.
It's Fun to Go out and Buy
New Shoes to Wear.
The Slushy Snow Splashes and
Sploshes.
Hobsbaum, Philip
A Lesson in Love.
Timon Speaks to a Dog.
Hobson, Archie
Base Chapel, Lejeune 4/79.
Hobson, Dorothy
Do What You Will.
Hobson, Geary
Barbara's Land Revisited–
August 1978.
For My Brother and Sister
Southwestern Indian Poets.
Going to the Water.
Lonnie Kramer.
Tiger People.
Hobson, Katherine Thayer
Duality.
Hobson, Rodney
A Man about the Kitchen.
Hoccleve, Thomas
Anxious Thought.
A Description of His Ugly
Lady.
Hoccleve's Humorous Praise
of His Lady.
Lament for Chaucer.
Lament for Chaucer and
Gower.
La Male Regle de T.
Hoccleve.
O Maister Deere and Fader
Reverent!
The Regimen of Princes
(excerpt).
Hoch, Edward Wallis
Good and Bad.
Hochman, Sandra
Clay and Water.
The Couple.
The Elephant.
The Eyes of Flesh.
The Goldfish Wife.
I Want to Tell You.
Postscript.

Hoddis, Jakov van
The Air Vision.
End of the World.
Tohub.
Hodes, Aubrey
A Jew Walks in Westminster
Abbey.
Hodgdon, Florence B.
How Can I Smile?
Hodge, Arthur J.
Five Were Foolish.
Hodge, Marion
True Child.
Hodges, Elizabeth
Blue Ridge.
Persimmons and Plums.
Hodgson, Ralph
After.
Babylon.
The Bells of Heaven.
The Birdcatcher.
The Bride.
The Bull.
Eve.
Ghoul Care.
The Gipsy Girl.
The Great Auk's Ghost.
The Hammers.
The House across the Way.
Hymn to Moloch.
I Love a Hill.
The Journeyman.
The Late, Last Rook.
The Moor.
The Mystery.
The Past.
Reason Has Moons.
The Riddle.
The Sedge-Warbler.
Silver Wedding.
A Song.
A Song of Honor.
Stupidity Street.
Thrown.
Time.
Time, You Old Gipsy Man.
To Deck a Woman, XI
(excerpt).
The Weaving of the Wing.
A Wood Song.
Hodgson, William Noel
Before Action.
Hoeft, Robert D.
Forty Pounds of Blackberries
Equals Thirteen Gallons of
Wine.
Our Annual Return to the
Lake.
To a Little Boy Learning to
Fish.
Hoelderlin, Friedrich
The Blind Singer.
Evening Fantasy.
The Half of Life.
To Nature.
Hoellein, Alma
There Is a Place.
We'll Never Know.
Hoeppner, Ed
From Garvey's Farm: Seneca,
Wisconsin.
Hoey, Allen
Casting at Night.
The Secret Irish.
Walleye.
When the Cows Come down
to Drink.
Hoey, George
Asleep at the Switch.
Hoffenstein, Samuel
Babies Haven't Any Hair.
The Bird.

Birdie McReynolds.
The Calf, the Goat, the Little Lamb.
Cloud.
Cradle Song.
Dry (parody).
A Father's Heart Is Touched.
For Little Boys Destined for Big Business.
I Burned My Candle at Both Ends.
I'd Rather Listen to a Flute.
Invocation (parody).
A Little While to Love and Rave.
Love-Songs, At Once Tender and Informative.
Lullaby.
Madrigal Macabre.
Mamma Sings.
Miss Millay Says Something Too.
Mr. Vachel Lindsay Discovers Radio (parody).
Mr. Walter de la Mare Makes the Little Ones Dizzy (parody).
The Ocean Spills.
Only the Wholesomest Foods You Eat.
The Pansy.
A Poem Intended to Incite the Utmost Depression.
Poems in Praise of Practically Nothing.
Poems of Passion, Carefully Restrained So as to Offend Nobody.
Question and Answer.
Says Something Too (parody).
Sheep.
The Shropshire Lad's Cousin (parody).
Some Folks I Know.
Song, on Reading That the Cyclotron has Produced Cosmic Rays...
Songs about Life and Brighter Things Yet.
Unequal Distribution.
When You're Away.
With Rue My Heart Is Laden (parody).
You Buy Some Flowers for Your Table.
Hoffman, Charles Fenno
The Mint Julep.
Monterey.
Sparkling and Bright.
Hoffman, Daniel Gerard
An Armada of Thirty Whales.
As I Was Going to Saint Ives.
Ballad of No Proper Man.
The Center of Attention.
The City of Satisfaction.
E, the Feasting Florentines.
Exploration.
First Flight.
Flushing Meadows, 1939.
Halflives.
Himself.
How We Logged Katahdin Stream.
In Humbleness.
In the Beginning.
In the Days of Rin-Tin-Tin.
Inviolable.
A Letter to Wilbur Frohock.
Lines Written near Linton, on Exmoor (parody).
A Meeting.
Ode to Joy.

The Outwit Song.
The Princess Casamassima.
The Seals in Penobscot Bay.
Signatures.
Slick.
The Sonnet.
Three Jovial Gentlemen.
Two Hundred Girls in Tights & Halters.
Who Was It Came.
Hoffman, George Edward
December 26.
Victory Parade.
Hoffman, Jill
Evening Ride.
The Stable.
To a Horse.
Hoffman, O. S.
The Five Best Doctors.
Hoffman, Phoebe W.
Pedro.
Hoffman, William M.
Screw Spring.
Hoffmann, Heinrich
Slovenly Peter.
The Story of Augustus Who Would Not Have Any Soup.
The Story of Fidgety Philip.
The Story of Flying Robert.
The Story of Johnny Head-in-Air.
The Story of Little Suck-a-Thumb.
The Story of the Wild Huntsman.
Hoffmann, Roald
Finnair Fragment.
From a Rise of Land to the Sea.
Hofmannsthal, Hugo von
Ballad of the Outer Life.
Experience.
Many Indeed Must Perish in the Keel.
Poem: "We are such stuff as dreams are made of."
The Ship's Cook, a Captive Sings.
Stanzas on Mutability.
Travel Song.
A Venetian Night.
A Vision.
World-Secret.
Hofstein, David
My Thread.
Hogan, Inez
Blanket Street.
Middle-Aged Child.
Hogan, Linda
Black Hills Survival Gathering, 1980.
Blessings.
Calling Myself Home.
Cities behind Glass.
The Diary of Amanda McFadden.
Going to Town.
Heritage.
Leaving.
Nativity.
Oil.
Red Clay.
Saint Coyote.
Song for My Name.
What's Living?
The Women Are Grieving.
The Women Speaking.
Hogan, Michael
Child of Blue.
The Condor.
December 18, 1975.
Fish.

Food Strike.
Indulgences.
O'Neill's War Song.
Parting.
Prison Break.
Rust.
Scrimshaw.
Spring.
Survivors.
Warriors.
Hogg, James
Bonny Kilmeny Gaed up the Glen.
A Boy's Song.
The Flying Tailor (parody).
Isabelle (parody).
James Rigg (parody).
Kilmeny.
Lock the Door, Lariston.
Love Is Like a Dizziness.
McLean's Welcome.
Moggy and Me.
My Love She's But a Lassie Yet.
She's But a Lassie Yet.
The Skylark.
There's Gowd in the Breast.
The Village of Balmaquhapple.
Walsinghame's Song (parody).
When the Kye Comes Hame.
The Witch o' Fife.
The Women Folk.
Hogg, Robert
Song: "The sun is mine."
Hoh, Israel Kafu
The Vulture.
Holborne, Antony and William
Madrigal: "Since Bonny-boots was dead, that so divinely."
Holbrook, David
Coming Home from Abroad.
A Day in France.
Delivering Children.
Drought.
Fingers in the Door.
Living? Our Supervisors Will Do That for Us!
Maternity Gown.
Poor Old Horse.
Holbrook, John
Fishing the Big Hole.
Holbrook, Weare
Varitalk.
Holcroft, Thomas
The Dying Prostitute, An Elegy.
Fool's Song.
Gaffer Gray.
On Shakespeare and Voltaire.
The Seasons.
To Haydn.
Holden, Jonathan
Alone.
An American Boyhood.
Dancing School.
December Sunset.
Driving through Coal Country in Pennsylvania.
First Kiss.
Full Moon, Rising.
Liberace.
Losers.
Night: Landing at Newark.
A Poem for Ed "Whitey" Ford.
Remembering My Father.
Seventeen.
The Swimming Pool.
Washing My Son.
Why We Bombed Haiphong.

Holden, Molly
Giant Decorative Dahlia.
Hare.
Photograph of Haymaker, 1890.
Seaman, 1941.
Holden, Oliver
How Sweet Is the Language of Love.
Weeping Sinner, Dry Your Tears.
Within These Doors Assembled Now.
Holden, Raymond
Storm Over Rockefeller Center.
Holden, Stephen
In Praise of Antonioni.
Holderlin, Friedrich
All the Fruit...
Bread and Wine, Part 7.
Half of Life.
Patmos.
Ripe, Being Plunged into Fire...
The Sanctimonious Poets.
Holland, Henry Fox, Lord
With a China Chamberpot, to the Countess of Hillsborough.
Holland, Hugh
Epitaph on Prince Henry.
Shakespeare Dead.
Holland, Josiah Gilbert
Babyhood.
Bitter-Sweet: Hymn.
A Christmas Carol: "There's a song in the air!"
Daniel Gray.
God, Give Us Men!
Gradatim.
Lullaby.
A Song of Doubt.
A Song of Faith.
To My Dog Blanco.
Where Shall the Baby's Dimple Be?
Holland, Norah M.
A Little Dog-Angel.
Sea-Gulls.
Sea Song.
Holland, Rob
Eve in Old Age.
Holland, Robert
The Fisherman Casts His Line into the Sea.
Holland, Rupert Sargent
When I Grow Up.
Holland, Sir Richard
The Buke of the Howlat.
Hollander, Gad
Axioms.
Fugato (Coda).
In Memoriam Paul Celan.
Hollander, John
Adam's Task.
The Altarpiece Finished.
Appearance and Reality.
Aristotle to Phyllis.
The Bird.
Breadth. Circle. Desert. Monarch. Month. Wisdom.
By the Sea.
The Curse.
Danish Wit.
Digging It Out.
The Fear of Trembling.
The Great Bear.
Hall of Ocean Life.
Helicon.
Heliogabalus.
Historical Reflections.

Hobbes, 1651.
Horas Tempestatis Quoque
  Enumero: The Sundial.
Jefferson Valley.
The Lady of the Castle.
The Lady's-Maid's Song.
Last Quarter.
Last Words.
A Lion Named Passion.
The Lower Criticism.
Movie-Going.
The Night Mirror.
The Ninth of July.
No Foundation.
Non Sum Qualis Eram in
  Bona Urbe Nordica Illa.
Paysage Moralise.
The Russian Soul II.
Skeleton Key.
Slepynge Long in Greet
  Quiete Is Eek a Greet Norice
  to Leccherie.
Something about It.
Sonnets for Roseblush, XVIII.
A State of Nature.
Sunday Evenings.
Swan and Shadow.
To the Lady Portrayed by
  Margaret Dumont.
Under Cancer.
Violet.
West End Blues.
When All of Tem Ran Off.
Wrath.
The Ziz.

Hollander, Robert
Audiences.
Ice Cream in Paradise.
You Too? Me Too–Why Not?
  Soda Pop.

Holley, Horace
The Hill.

Holley, Margaret
Your Woods.

Holliday, Carl
Thus Speak the Slain.

Hollins, Tony
Stamp Blues.

Hollis, Jocelyn
The Meeting.

Hollis, Mark
Careless Talk.
'Twixt Cup and Lip.

Hollo, Anselm
After Verlaine.
Amazing Grace.
Anthropology.
Aubade.
Behaviorally.
Big Dog.
Buffalo–Isle of Wight Power
  Cable.
The Caterpillar.
The Discovery of LSD a True
  Story.
If.
Le Jazz Hot.
The Language.
Lecture.
Manifest Destiny.
No Complaints.
Rain.
T.V. (1).
T.V. (2).
The Terrorist Smiles.
That Old Sauna High.
Troll Chanting.
Wasp Sex Myth (One).
Wasp Sex Myth (Two).

Holloway, John
The Brothers.
Elegy for an Estrangement.

Family Poem.
Journey through the Night.
The Light.
Warning to a Guest.

Holloway, John Wesley
Black Mammies.
Calling the Doctor.
The Corn Song.
Miss Melerlee.

Holloway, Lucy Ariel Williams
Northboun'.

Holm, Saxe
A Song off Clover.

Holman, Bob
One Flight Up.

Holman, Felice
The Clock.
Halloween Witches.
I Can Fly.
Supermarket.
Who Am I?

Holman, Jesse L.
Lord, In thy Presence Here.

Holman, M. Carl
And on This Shore.
Letter Across Doubt and
  Distance.
Mr. Z.
Notes for a Movie Script.
Picnic: The Liberated.
Song: "Dressed up in my
  melancholy."
Three Brown Girls Singing.

Holme, Jamie Sexton
Mountain Evenings.
Timber Line Trees.

Holmes, Abiel
To Thee, O God.
Who Here Can Cast His Eyes
  Abroad.

Holmes, Georgiana
As Thy Days So Shall Thy
  Strength Be.
At Dawn of the Year.
Be Patient.
He Will Give Them Back.

Holmes, John
At a Country Fair.
The Broken One.
Bucyrus.
But Choose.
Carry Me Back.
The Chance.
The Core.
The Eleventh Commandment
  (excerpt).
Evening Meal in the
  Twentieth Century.
The Fear of Dying.
The Flower.
The Fortune Teller.
Good Night! Good Night!
Grass.
Herself.
The Letter.
Map of My Country.
Metaphor for My Son.
Misery.
The New View.
The Overgrown Back Yard.
Peace Is the Mind's Old
  Wilderness.
Poetry Defined.
Pour Down.
Prayer on the Night Before
  Easter.
Questions for the Candidate.
Rhyme of Rain.
The Somerset Dam for
  Supper.
The Spiral.
Take Home This Heart.

Testament.
The Thrifty Elephant.
What Does a Man Think
  About.
A Willing Suspension.

Holmes, John Haynes
God of the Nations, Near and
  Far.
Hymn.
O'er Continent and Ocean.
The Voice of God Is Calling.

Holmes, Oliver Wendell
Additional Verses to Hail
  Columbia.
After a Lecture on Keats.
After the Fire.
Angel of Peace, Thou Hast
  Wandered Too Long.
At the Pantomime.
At the Saturday Club.
Aunt Tabitha.
The Autocrat of the
  Breakfast-Table.
A Ballad of the Boston Tea-
  Party, December 16, 1773.
The Ballad of the Oysterman.
Bill and Joe.
The Boys.
The Broomstick Train.
Brother Jonathan's Lament
  for Sister Caroline.
Cacoethes Scribendi.
The Chambered Nautilus.
Contentment.
The Crooked Footpath.
Daily Trials.
Daniel Webster.
The Deacon's Masterpiece Or,
  The Wonderful "One-Hoss
  Shay."
The Dorchester Giant.
Dorothy Q.
A Familiar Letter.
A Farewell to Agassiz.
The Flower of Liberty.
God Save the Flag.
Grandmother's Story of
  Bunker-Hill Battle.
La Grisette.
The Height of the Ridiculous.
How the Old Horse Won the
  Bet.
Hymn of Trust.
In Thine Arms.
Intramural Aestivation; or,
  Summer in Town, by a
  Teacher of Latin.
The Iron Gate (excerpt).
The Last Leaf.
Lexington.
Limerick: "The Reverend
  Henry War Beecher."
The Living Temple.
Manhood.
Many Things.
The Moral Bully.
My Aunt.
O Love Divine, That Stooped
  to Share.
Ode for a Social Meeting
  (With Slight Alterations by a
  Teetotaler).
Old Ironsides.
The Old Man Dreams.
On Lending a Punch-Bowl.
On the Death of President
  Garfield.
Our Father! While Our Hearts
  Unlearn.
A Parody on A Psalm of Life.
The Peau de Chagrin of State
  Street.

A Poem (excerpt).
A Poem for the Meeting of
  the American Medical
  Association.
The Poet's Lot.
A Sea Dialogue.
The September Gale (excerpt).
Sherman's in Savannah.
The Strong Heroic Line.
A Sun-Day Hymn.
To an Insect.
To the Portrait of "A
  Gentleman."
Two Sonnets: Harvard.
The Two Streams.
Under the Violets.
Unsatisfied.
The Voiceless.
A Welcome to Dr. Benjamin
  Apthorp Gould.
Welcome to the Nations.

Holmes, Theodore
Buddha.
Christ.
The Dysynni Valley (Wales).
The Old Age Home.

Holmes, W. K.
The Old Mountaineer.
On the Heights.

Holmes, Wright
Alley Blues.

Holshouser, W. L.
Turning Point.

Holt, Edgar
Two Sonnets from a Sequence.

Holt, Jessie
Dying.

**Holty, Ludwig Heinrich
  Christoph**
Harvest Song.

Holtz, Barry
Isaac.

Holub, Miroslav
Brief Reflection on the Insect.
A Dog in the Quarry.
Evening in a Lab.
Hominization.
How to Paint a Perfect
  Christmas.
Newborn Baby.
Poem Technology.
Swans in Flight.
Teaching about Arthropods.
Teeth.
Wings.
Zito the Magician.

Holyday, Barten
Ireland.
Pride.
Song: "O harmless feast."

Holz, Arno
Buddha.
A Leave-Taking.
Phantasus.
Roses Red.

Holzapfel, Rudi
The Employee.

Homer
The Battle of the Frogs and
  Mice.
Hymn to Mercury.
The Hymn to Venus: Venus
  Goes After Anchises.
The Iliad.
The Odyssey.
Ulysses Hears the Prophecies
  of Tiresias.

Homer-Dixon, Homera
The New Year.

Honey, Merrill
Pizen Pete's Mistake.

Honeywood, St. John
Darby and Joan.
A Radical Song of 1786.
Hongo, Garrett Kaoru
Hiking up Hieizan with Alam
Lau/Buddha's Birthday
1974.
The Hongo Store 29 Miles
Volcano Hilo, Hawaii.
Off from Swing Shift.
On the Road to Paradise.
What For.
Who among You Knows the
Essence of Garlic?
Yellow Light.
Honig, Edwin
As a Great Prince.
Being Somebody.
Happening.
In Quest to Have Not.
Jane Retreat.
November through a Giant
Copper Beech.
Now, My Usefulness Over.
Some Knots.
The Tall Toms.
Tete-a-Tete.
Through You.
Walt Whitman.
What Changes, My Love.
Who.
Honnamma
Wasn't your mother a
woman?
Honora, Sister Mary
Land of the Free.
Hood, E. P.
God, Who Hath Made the
Daisies.
Hood, Thomas
Address to Mr. Cross, of
Exeter 'Change on the Death
of the Elephant.
All in the Downs.
Answer to Pauper.
Athol Brose.
Autumn.
A Black Job.
The Bridge of Sighs.
The Carelesse Nurse Mayd.
Choosing Their Names.
Death.
The Death Bed.
Domestic Asides; or, Truth in
Parentheses.
Domestic Didactics by an Old
Servant: The Broken Dish.
The Dream of Eugene Aram.
Fair Ines.
Faithless Nellie Gray.
Faithless Sally Brown.
False Poets and True.
Farewell, Life.
Flowers.
Fragment: "Mary, I believ'd
you quick."
A Friendly Address.
Gold.
Good Night.
The Haunted House.
Hero and Leander.
I'm Not a Single Man.
I Remember, I Remember.
If I Had But Two Little
Wings.
The Irish Schoolmaster
(parody).
It Was the Time of Roses.
The Last Man.
The Lay of the Labourer.
Little Piggy.
Mary's Ghost.

Miss Kilmansegg and Her
Precious Leg.
Miss Kilmansegg's Birth.
Miss Kilmansegg's
Honeymoon.
No!
A Nocturnal Sketch.
Ode: Autumn.
Ode on a Distant Prospect of
Clapham Academy.
Ode to the Cameleopard.
Ode to the Moon.
On a Royal Demise.
On Mistress Nicely, a Pattern
for Housekeepers.
On the Death of the Giraffe.
On the Publication of Diaries
and Memoirs.
An Open Question.
Our Village.
A Parental Ode to My Son.
Peter's Tears.
The Plea of the Midsummer
Fairies.
Please to Ring the Belle.
The Poet's Fate.
Poets and Linnets (parody).
Queen Mab.
A Reflection.
Ruth.
A Sailor's Apology for Bow-
Legs.
Sally Simpkin's Lament.
The Sea of Death.
Serenade.
Silence.
Song: "A lake and a fairy
boat."
The Song of the Shirt.
Sonnet: "It is not death, that
sometime in a sigh."
Sonnet to Vauxhall.
The Stars Are with the
Voyager.
Suggestions by Steam.
The Sun Was Slumbering in
the West.
Tim Turpin.
To–.
To Henrietta, on Her
Departure for Calais.
To Minerva.
To the Reviewers.
Tom Tatter's Birthday Ode.
The Two Swans.
The Water Lady.
We Watch'd Her Breathing.
Ye Tourists and Travellers,
Bound to the Rhine.
Hood, Tom (Thomas Hood, Jr.)
The Cannibal Flea (parody).
A Catch.
Confounded Nonsense.
A Few Muddled Metaphors
by a Moore-ose Melodist.
How Singular.
The little tigers are at rest.
Ravings (parody).
Sunset in the Sea.
The Wedding.
Hood-Adams, Rebecca
Family Portrait.
Hooft, Pieter Corneliszoon
Thus Spoke My Love.
Hook, Theodore
Cautionary Verses to Youth of
Both Sexes.
Hooker, Brian
Ballade of the Dreamland
Rose.
From Life.
A Little Person.

Mother of Men.
A Portrait.
Song: "Only a little while
since first we met."
Hooker, John Lee
Black Snake.
Hookham, George
Chamonix.
Hooley, Teresa
Beauty Eternal: To-Day I Saw
a Butterfly.
Hooper, Ellen
Beauty and Duty.
"The Straight Road.
To R.W.E.
Hooper, Ellen S.
Duty.
Hooper, H. S.
Frisco's Defi.
Hooper, Lucy H.
Three Loves.
Hooper, Patricia
Other Lives.
Psalm.
Hooton, Earnest Albert
Ode to a Dental Hygienist.
To Chloe.
Hooton, Harry
A Sweet Disorder in the
Dress.
Hoover, Paul
Barnabooth Enters Russia.
Long History of the Short
Poem.
Ode to the Protestant Poets.
On History.
The School for Objects.
Trumpet Voluntary.
Hope, A. D.
Advice to Young Ladies.
As Well as They Can.
Australia.
The Bed.
A Blason.
The Brides.
Chorale.
Circe.
Coup de Grace.
The Death of the Bird.
The Double Looking Glass.
Dunciad Minor.
E Questo Il Nido in Che la
Mia Fenice?
The Elegy.
An Epistle.
Faustus.
The Female Principle.
The Gateway.
The House of God.
Imperial Adam.
A Letter to David Campbell
on the Birthday of W. B.
Yeats, 1965.
The Lingam and the Yoni.
The Martyrdom of St. Teresa.
Meditation on a Bone.
Moschus Moschiferus.
Observation Car.
On an Engraving by
Casserius.
Parabola.
Paradise Saved.
Prometheus Unbound.
The Pronunciation of Erse.
Pyramis or The House of
Ascent.
The School of Night.
Standardization.
Tiger.
Hope, Francis
Peeping Tom.

Hope, Henry
Now I Have Found a Friend.
Hope, James Barron
John Smith's Approach to
Jamestown.
Hope, Laurence
Ashore.
The Bride.
Kashmiri Song.
Khristna and His Flute.
The Masters.
The Teak Forest: For This Is
Wisdom.
Youth.
Hope, Margaret
Through the Ages.
Hope, T.
Death Again (parody).
Hopegood, Peter
Dithyramb in Retrospect.
Free Martin.
The Protagonist.
Hopes, David
The Hairdresser.
Lament for Turlough
O'Carolan.
Hopkins, Gerard Manley
The Alchemist in the City.
Andromeda.
As Kingfishers Catch Fire,
Dragonflies Draw Flame.
Ashboughs.
At a Welsh Waterfall.
At the Wedding March.
Bad I am, but yet they child.
Barnfloor and Winepress.
The Beginning of the End.
Binsey Poplars.
The Blessed Virgin compared
to the Air we Breathe.
Brothers.
The Bugler's First
Communion.
By Mrs. Hopley, on Seeing
Her Children Say Goodnight
to Their Father.
The Caged Skylark.
The Candle Indoors.
Carrion Comfort.
Cherry Beggar.
The Child Is Father to the
Man.
Christ Speaks.
Duns Scotus's Oxford.
Easter Communion.
Epigram: "Of virtues I most
warmly bless."
Epithalamion.
Felix Randal.
Fragment.
Fragment: The Furl of Fresh-
Leaved Dog-Rose Down.
God's Grandeur.
The Habit of Perfection.
Harry Ploughman.
Heaven-Haven.
Henry Purcell.
How Looks the Night?
Hurrahing in Harvest.
I Am Like a Slip of Comet.
I Wake and Feel the Fell of
Dark.
In Honor of St. Alphonsus
Rodriguez.
In the Valley of the Elwy.
Inversnaid.
The Lantern out of Doors.
The Leaden Echo and the
Golden Echo.
Let Me Be to Thee as the
Circling Bird.

Mark You How the Peacock's Eye.
The May Magnificat.
Moonless Darkness Stands Between.
Moonrise.
My Own Heart Let Me More Have Pity On.
A New Year's Burden.
Not of All My Eyes See.
NTo R. B.
O Deus, Ego Amo Te.
On a Piece of Music.
On a Poetess.
On St. Winefred.
Oxford Bells.
Peace.
Pied Beauty.
The Rainbow.
Rosa Mystica.
The Sea and the Skylark.
She Schools the Flighty Pupils of Her Eyes.
Six Epigrams (excerpt).
The Soldier.
A Soliloquy of One of the Spies Left in the Wilderness.
Sonnet: "No worst, there is none."
Sonnet: "Patience, hard thing! the hard thing but to pray."
Sonnet: "Thou art indeed just, Lord, if I contend."
Spelt from Sibyl's Leaves.
Spring.
Spring and Death.
Spring and Fall.
St. Alphonsus Rodriguez.
The Starlight Night.
The Summer Malison.
That Nature Is a Heraclitean Fire...
Thee, God, I Come from, to Thee Go.
To His Watch.
To Oxford.
To R. B.
To Seem the Stranger Lies My Lot.
Tom's Garland.
The Windhover.
Winter with the Gulf Stream.
The Wreck of the Deutschland.

Hopkins, John
Thou, Lord, Hast Been Our Sure Defense.

Hopkins, Josiah
O Turn Ye, O Turn Ye.

Hopkins, Lightning
Death Bells.
Highway Blues.
Katie May.
Mister Charlie.
She's Mine.
Short Haired Woman.

Hopkins, Tim
Do Not Go Gentle (parody).

Hopkins, Jr, John Henry
Alleluia! Christ Is Risen Today.
God of Our Fathers, Bless This Our Land.
We Three Kings of Orient Are...

Hopkinson, Francis
American Independence.
Arise and See the Glorious Sun.
At Length the Busy Day Is Done.
The Battle of the Kegs.

British Valor Displayed.
The Daughter's Rebellion.
Enraptured I Gaze.
The New Roof.
O Lord, How Lovely Is the Place.
On the Late Successful Expedition against Louisbourg.

Hopkinson, Joseph
Hail! Columbia.

Hoppe, Anna
Consecration.
Precious Child, So Sweetly Sleeping.

Hopper, Edward
Jesus, Saviour, Pilot Me.
They Pray the Best Who Pray and Watch.

Hopper, Nora
The Dark Man.
The Fairy Fiddler.
June.
King of Ireland's Son.
March.
A Marriage Charm.

Hopper, Virginia Shearer
In the Canadian Rockies.

Horace
Ad Leuconoen.
Ad Xanthiam Phoceum.
Albi, Ne Doreas.
Ars Poetica.
The Art of Poetry.
Barine, the Incorrigible.
The Bore.
Carmen Saeculare.
The Death of Cleopatra.
Epistles.
Epodes.
Extremum Tanain.
For Whom, Pyrrha?
Frippery.
The Gift of Song.
Holiday.
The Immortality of Verse.
Integer Vitae.
Invocation.
It Always Happens.
Moderation: Odes.
Odes.
Part of the 9th Ode of the 4th Book of Horace...
The Passing of Lydia.
The Pine Tree for Diana.
The Profane.
Revenge!
Satires.
The Ship of State.
The Teasing Lovers.
Time to Choose a Lover.
To an Ambitious Friend.
To Chloe.
To Faunus.
To Fuscus Aristus.
To Licinius.
To Phidyle.
To Postumus.
To Pyrrha.
To Sally.
To the Fountain of Bandusia.
To the Ship in Which Virgil Sailed to Athens (Odes, I, 3).
To Venus.
Too Young for Love.
Translation of Horace, Odes, IV, VII.
Winter to Spring.
The young bloods come round less often now.
The Young Men Come Less Often–Isn't It So?

Horan, Robert
By Hallucination Visited.
Emblems of Evening.
Farewell to Narcissus.
Little City.

Horder, John
The Sick Image of My Father Fades.

Horgan, Paul
Now Evening Puts Amen to Day.

Horikawa, Lady
How Can One E'er Be Sure.
How Long Will It Last?
Will he always love me?

Horn, Edward Newman
Darling, If You Only Knew.
In the Tub We Soak Our Skin.
Pussycat Sits on a Chair.
The Tiger Stalking in the Night.

Horn, Herschel
Landscape near a Steel Mill.

Horne, Frank
Immortality.
Kid Stuff.
Letters Found near a Suicide.
Mamma!
More Letters Found Near a Suicide.
Nigger.
On Seeing Two Brown Boys in a Catholic Church.
Patience.
Resurrection.
Symphony.
To a Persistent Phantom.
Toast.
Walk.
Young Heroes.

Horne, Herbert P.
If She Be Made of White and Red.
Nancy Dawson.

Horne, Lewis B.
Moving Day.
Muscae Volitantes.
Suppose...

Horne, Richard Henry
Orion.
Pelters of Pyramids.
The Plow.
Solitude and the Lily.

Horner, Joyce
Public Holiday: Paris.

Horovitz, Frances
The Messenger.
Moon.
The Woman's Dream.

Horsburgh, Wilma
The Train to Glasgow.

Horta, Maria Teresa See also
Marias, The Three
Saved.
Swimming Pool.

Horton, George
A Night in Lesbos.

Horton, George Moses
The Eye of Love.
New Fashions.
On Liberty and Slavery.
The Powers of Love.
The Setting Sun.
Snaps for Dinner, Snaps for Breakfast, and Snaps for Supper.
The Swan–Vain Pleasures.
To a Departing Favorite.

Horvitz, Allan Kolski
King Saul.
The Radiance of Extinct Stars.

Hoshi, Sosei See Sosei
Hosking, Arthur Nicholas
Land of the Free.

Hoskins, Katherine
Baucis and Philemon.
The Bee and the Petunia.
The Byfield Rabbit.
Cote d'Azure.
Not Lotte.
Nuit Blanche.

Hoskyns, John
Absence.
The Bellows Maker of Oxford.
Epitaph: "Here lies the man that madly slain."
Epitaph on Sir Walter Pye, Attorney of the Wards...
Epitaph on the Fart in the Parliament House.
His Own Epitaph, When He Was Sick, Being Fellow in New College...
Of the Loss of Time.
On a Contentious Companion.
On a Whore.
On One That Lived Ingloriously.
To His Little Son Benedict from the Tower of London.
Upon a Fool.
Upon One of the Maids of Honour to Queen Elizabeth.

Hosmer, Frederick Lucian
From Age to Age They Gather.
Hear, Hear, O Ye Nations.
The Indwelling God.
My Dead.
O Beautiful My Country.
O Day of Light and Gladness.
The Prophecy Sublime.
Through Unknown Paths.
Through Willing Heart and Helping Hand.
Thy Kingdom Come.
With Self Dissatisfied.

Hosmer, William Henry Cuyler
Song of Texas.

Hoss, E. Embree
O God, Great Father, Lord, and King.

Houck, James A.
Children's Lenten Wisdom.

Hough, Graham
Dark Corner.

Hough, Lindy
Portrait of the Father.

Houghton, Firman
Mr. Frost Goes South to Boston (parody).
She Sees Another Door Opening (parody).

Houghton, George Washington Wright
The Legend of Walbach Tower.
The March Winds.

Houghton, Richard Milnes, Baron See **Milnes, Richard Monkton, Lord Houghton**

House, Son
The Jinx Blues.
My Black Mama.
The Pony Blues.
Preachin' the Blues.

House, Vernal
In Tribute.

Houselander, Caryll
Litany to Our Lady.
The Reed.
Soeur Marie Emilie.

Housman, Alfred Edward
Along the Field as We Came
  By.
Amelia Mixed the Mustard.
As I Gird on for Fighting.
As into the Garden Elizabeth
  Ran.
Astronomy.
Away with Bloodshed.
Because I Liked You Better.
Could Man Be Drunk for
  Ever.
Crossing Alone the Nighted
  Ferry.
The Day of Battle.
The Deserter.
Easter Hymn.
Eight O'Clock.
The Elephant, or The Force
  of Habit.
Epigram: "Some can gaze and
  not be sick."
Epitaph: "Here dead lie we
  because we did not choose."
Epitaph on an Army of
  Mercenaries.
Epithalamium.
The Fairies Break Their
  Dances.
Far in a Western Brookland.
For My Funeral.
Fragment of a Greek Tragedy.
Friends.
From Far, from Eve and
  Morning.
From the Wash the Laundress
  Sends.
G. K. Chesterton on His
  Birth.
Good Creatures, Do You
  Love Your Lives.
Grenadier.
The Grizzly Bear is huge and
  wild.
Half-Way, for One
  Commandment Broken.
Hallelujah!
He Would Not Stay for Me.
Hell Gate.
Her Strong Enchantments
  Failing.
Ho, Everyone That Thirsteth.
Hughley Steeple.
I Did Not Lose My Heart in
  Summer's Even.
I Hoed and Trenched and
  Weeded.
I Knew a Cappadocian.
I to My Perils.
The Immortal Part.
Infant Innocence.
Inhuman Henry or Cruelty to
  Fabulous Animals.
The Isle of Portland.
The Jar of Nations.
The Lads in Their Hundreds.
Lancer.
Last Poems.
The Lent Lily.
Loitering with a Vacant Eye.
Look Not in My Eyes, for
  Fear.
Loveliest of Trees.
March.
The Mill-stream, Now that
  Noises Cease.
The New Mistress.
New Year's Eve.
The Night is Freezing Fast.
O Billows Bounding Far.
O Have You Caught the
  Tiger.

Oh Fair Enough Are Sky and
  Plain.
Oh, See How Thick the
  Goldcup Flowers.
Oh, when I was in love with
  you.
Oh Who Is That Young
  Sinner with the Handcuffs on
  His Wrists?
The Olive.
On Forelands High in
  Heaven.
On Moonlit Heath and
  Lonesome Bank.
Parta Quies.
The Power of Malt.
The Rain, It Streams on
  Stone.
The Rainy Pleiads Wester.
The Recruit.
Revolution.
Say, Lad, Have You Things to
  Do?
The Shades of Night Were
  Falling Fast (parody).
Shot? So Quick, So Clean an
  Ending?
A Shropshire Lad.
The Sigh That Heaves the
  Grasses.
Smooth between Sea and
  Land.
Soldier from the Wars
  Returning.
The Stars Have Not Dealt Me
  the Worst They Could Do.
Stars, I Have Seen Them Fall.
The Street Sounds to the
  Soldiers' Tread.
Tell Me Not Here, It Needs
  Not Saying.
They Say My Verse Is Sad:
  No Wonder.
Think No More, Lad.
'Tis Time, I Think.
To an Athlete Dying Young.
To Stand Up Straight.
To Think That Two and Two
  Are Four.
The True Lover.
Twice a Week the Winter
  Through.
Wake Not for the World-
  Heard Thunder.
We'll to the Woods No More.
The Welsh Marches.
Westward on the High-Hilled
  Plains.
When Adam Day by Day.
When Green Buds Hang.
When Israel out of Egypt
  Came.
When Smoke Stood Up from
  Ludlow.
When Summer's End Is
  Nighing.
When the Bells Justle in the
  Tower.
When the Eye of Day Is Shut.
White in the Moon.
With Rue My Heart Is Laden.
With Seed the Sowers Scatter.
Yonder See the Morning
  Blink.
Housman, Laurence
All Fellows (excerpt).
Comrades.
The Continuing City.
A Dead Warrior.
Dedication.
Deus Noster Ignis
  Consumens.

Farewell to Town.
The Gardener.
God's Mother.
The Settlers.
Spikenard.
Two Loves.
Hovde, A. J.
I Shall Never Go.
Of a Mouse and Men.
On Hearing a Beautiful
  Young Woman Describe Her
  Class...
Hovell-Thurlow, Edward
The Heron.
May.
When in the Woods I Wander
  All Alone.
Hover, Donald H.
The Other Person's Place.
Hovey, Richard
Accident in Art.
At the Crossroads.
At the End of the Day.
Barney McGee.
The Battle of Manila.
The Birth of Galahad: Ylen's
  Song.
The Call of the Bugles.
Chanson de Rosemonde.
Dartmouth Winter-Song.
Eleazar Wheelock.
Envoy.
Hunting-Song.
Immanence.
The Kavanagh.
Laurana's Song.
Love in the Wind.
The Sea Gypsy.
Spring.
A Stein Song.
Taliesin: A Masque: Voices of
  Unseen Spirits.
Transcendence.
The Two Lovers.
Unmanifest Destiny.
The Wander-Lovers.
The Word of the Lord from
  Havana.
How, William Walsham
O Word of God Incarnate.
We Give Thee but Thine
  Own.
Howard, Ben
The Diver.
Lynx.
Winter Report.
Howard, Dorothy S.
Birkett's Eagle.
Howard, Frances Minturn
Heron in Swamp.
Narcissus in a Cocktail Glass.
Prophecy in Flame.
Howard, Henry
Description of Spring.
The Portrait of Henry VIII.
Howard, Henry, Earl of Surrey
See **Surrey, Henry Howard,
Earl of**
Howard, Jim
Boy Trash Picker.
Newspaper Hats.
Howard, Joseph E.
Good Bye, My Lady Love.
Howard, Leonard
The Humours of the King's
  Bench Prison, a Ballad.
Howard, Philip
Hymn.
Howard, Philip, Earl of Arundel
Though Here in Flesh I Be.
Howard, Quentin R.
In the Corn Land.

Howard, Richard
209 Canal.
Again for Hephaistos, the
  Last Time.
Aubade: Donna Anna to Juan,
  Still Asleep.
The Author of Christine.
Bonnard: A Novel.
Compulsive Qualifications
  (excerpt).
Crepuscular.
A Far Cry after a Close Call.
Gaiety: Queer's Song.
Giovanni da Fiesole on the
  Sublime or Fra Angelico's
  "Last Judgment."
Landed: A Valentine.
Lapsus Linguae.
Natural History.
On Arrival.
Oystering.
Personal Values.
Recipe for an Ocean in the
  Absence of the Sea.
Saturday Morning.
Secular Games.
Howard, Sarah Elizabeth
The Round-Up.
Wild Horse Jerry's Story.
Howard, Sir Robert
To the Unconstant Cynthia.
Howard, Vilma
The Citizen.
Howard, Winifred
Fairy Wings.
The Squirrels' Christmas.
White Horses.
Howard-Jones, Stuart
Hibernia.
Howarth, Ellen Clementine
'Tis but a Little Faded
  Flower.
Howarth, Robert Guy
Memoir.
On a Row of Nuns in a
  Cemetery.
Howe, Fanny
The Nursery.
Howe, George
The Sun-Witch to the Sun.
**Howe, John Grubham, and
Henry Hall.**
A Panegyric.
Howe, Joseph
Acadia (excerpt).
The Song of the MicMac.
Howe, Julia Ward
The Battle Hymn of the
  American Republic.
Decoration Day.
J. A. G.
The Message of Peace.
Our Country.
Pardon.
Parricide.
Robert E. Lee.
Howe, Mark A. De Wolfe
Distinction.
The Travellers.
Whom the Gods Love.
Howe, Solomon
Our Kind Creator.
Howe, Susan
Speeches at the Barriers
  (excerpt).
Howe, William Walsham
Funeral Hymn.
Howell, Elizabeth Lloyd
Milton's Prayer for Patience.

Howell, James
Of London Bridge, and the
Stupendous Sight, and
Structure Thereof.
Howell, Peg Leg
Lowdown Rounder's Blues.
Howell, Thomas
Of Misery.
The Rose.
When He Thought Himself
Contemned.
Who Would Have Thought.
Howells, Mildred
Down a Woodland Way.
God's Will.
Going Too Far.
A Moral in Sevres.
Romance.
Howells, William Dean
August.
The Battle in the Clouds.
The Bewildered Guest.
Calvary.
Caprice.
Change.
Company.
The Empty House.
From Generation to
Generation.
Hope.
If.
In Earliest Spring.
Judgment Day.
Labor and Capital:
Impression.
Living.
Lost Beliefs.
A Prayer.
The Song the Oriole Sings.
A Thanksgiving.
Twelve P.M.
The Two Wives.
Vision.
What Shall It Profit?
Howells, Winifred
Forthfaring.
A Mood.
Past.
The Poet and the Child.
A Wasted Sympathy.
Howes, Barbara
At 79th and Park.
Best of Show.
Cardinal.
Cat on Couch.
Chimera.
City Afternoon.
A Conversation.
Death of a Vermont Farm
Woman.
The Don.
The Dressmaker's Dummy as
Scarecrow.
Early Supper.
Flight.
Four Fawns.
Home Leave.
L'Ile du Levant: The Nudist
Colony.
In Autumn.
Indian Summer.
Jim.
Landscape, Deer Season.
A Letter from the Caribbean.
Light and Dark.
Looking Up at Leaves.
Mistral.
Monkey Difference.
On a Bougainvillaea Vine in
Haiti.
On Galveston Beach.
Out Fishing.

Portrait of an Artist.
Portrait of the Boy as Artist.
Returning to Store Bay.
A Rune for C.
Sea School.
Talking to Animals.
The Triumph of Chastity.
The Triumph of Death.
Views of the Oxford Colleges.
Howes, Grace Clementine
Wind of the Prairie.
Winged Mariner.
Howitt, Mary
The Broom Flower.
Buttercups and Daisies.
The Fairies of the Caldon
Low.
The Monkey.
Old Christmas.
The Rose of May.
The Sale of the Pet Lamb.
The Seagull.
The Spider and the Fly.
Howitt, William
The Migration of the Grey
Squirrels.
The Northern Seas.
The Wind in a Frolic.
Howland, Edward
The Condemned.
Howland, Mary Woolsey
In the Hospital.
Howlin' Wolf
Smokestack Lightnin'.
Hoy, Albert L.
The Hour of Prayer.
Hoyem, Andrew
Circumambulation of Mt.
Tamalpais.
Hoyer, Mildred N.
Voice of the Crocus.
Hoyt, Charles Hale
The Bowery.
Hoyt, Charles Sumner
Is This the Time To Sound
Retreat?
Hoyt, Helen
At Daybreak.
Ellis Park.
Golden Bough.
Homage.
In the Park.
Memory.
Reparation.
The Sense of Death.
Hoyt, Henry Martyn
The Land of Dreams.
The Spell.
Hoyt, Ralph
Old.
Hricz, Lucy
Modern American Nursing.
Hroswitha von Grandersheim
In Praise of Virginity.
Paphnutius (excerpt).
Hsi-chun
Lament of Hsi-Chun.
Hsieh Wang-ying See **"Ping
Hsin"**
Hsin Ch'i-chi
Drinking.
Hsu Pen
The Hermit.
Hsueh Feng
A Palace Poem.
Hsueh T'ao
Spring-Gazing Song.
Weaving Love-Knots.
Weaving Love-Knots 2.
Huang-fu Jan
Spring Thoughts.

Huang O
Every morning I get up.
A Farewell to a Southern
Melody.
To the Tune "Red
Embroiderd Shoes'.
To the Tune "Soaring Clouds'.
To the Tune "The Fall of a
Little Wild Goose."
Hubbard, Jake T. W.
Newton's Third.
Hubbard, P. M.
Subjectivity at Sestos.
To Cynthia, Not to Let Him
Read the Ladies' Magazines.
Hubbell, Nelson
Monologue through Bars.
Hubbell, Patricia
The Abandoned House.
The Fairies.
Vermont Conversation.
Huch, Ricarda
Arrival in Hell.
Death Seed.
Music Stirs Me.
Young Girl.
Huckel, Oliver
O Mind of God, Broad as the
Sky.
Huddle, David
Croquet.
The Field.
A History of the Pets.
Icicle.
In White Tie.
Janie Swecker and Me and
Gone with the Wind.
Kitchen Tables.
Mrs. Green.
My Brother, Beautiful
Shinault, That Goat.
My Grandaddy Mostly with
His Knife.
Shooting Crows.
Stopping by Home.
Hudgins, Andrew
Mine.
"Hudibras"
On Calamy's Imprisonment
and Wild's Poetry.
Hudson, Deatt
Some Tips on Watching Birds.
Hudson, Flexmore
Mallee in October.
Hudson, Frederick B.
My Relatives for the Most.
Hueffer, Ford Madox
The Sanctuary.
Huerta, Efrain
The Sounds of Dawn.
Huff, Barbara A.
Afternoon with Grandmother.
Huff, Robert
Although I Remember the
Sound.
The Course.
Getting Drunk with Daughter.
Rainbow.
The Smoker.
Traditional Red.
The Ventriloquist.
Huffstickler, Albert
Prospectus.
Huggins, Peter
Blackberry Winter.
Hughes, Andrew
Cats and Egypt.
Hughes, Dorothy
The Age of Sheen.
The Dusting of the Books.
Strawberries.

Hughes, Henry
Song: "I prithee send me back
my heart."
Hughes, James D.
My Son.
Hughes, John
The Court of Neptune.
Hughes, Langston
Acceptance.
Advice.
Alabama Earth.
American Heartbreak.
Un-American Investigators.
Angola Question Mark.
April Rain Song.
As I Grew Older.
Aunt Sue's Stories.
The Backlash Blues.
Bad Morning.
Ballad of the Landlord.
Be-Bop Boys.
Beale Street.
Birmingham Sunday.
Birth.
The Black Man Speaks.
A Black Pierrot.
Border Line.
Bound No'th Blues.
Brass Spittoons.
Cafe: 3 A.M.
Carol of the Brown King.
Catch.
Children's Rhymes.
Christ in Alabama.
City: San Francisco.
College Formal: Renaissance
Casino.
Color.
Corner Meeting.
Cross.
Cultural Exchange.
Cycle.
Daybreak in Alabama.
Death in Yorkville.
Dinner Guest: Me.
Dive.
Dream Boogie.
Dream Variation.
Dreams.
Dressed Up.
Drum.
Dust Bowl.
Early Evening Quarrel.
Ennui.
Esthete in Harlem.
Fantasy in Purple.
Fire.
Florida Road Workers.
Frederick Douglass:
1817-1895.
Freedom.
Garment.
Go Slow.
Gone Boy.
Hard Daddy.
Harlem Sweeties.
Havana Dreams.
Heaven.
High to Low.
Homesick Blues.
Hope.
A House in Taos.
I Dream a World.
I Thought It Was Tangiers I
Wanted.
I, Too.
Impasse.
In Time of Silver Rain.
Island.
Jazz Band in a Parisian
Cabaret.
Jazzonia.

Juke Box Love Song.
Junior Addict.
Justice.
Ku Klux.
Last Call.
Late Corner.
Late Last Night.
Lenox Avenue Mural.
Let America Be America
  Again.
Life is Fine.
Lincoln Monument:
  Washington.
Little Lyric (of Great
  Importance).
Long Trip.
The Lord Has a Child.
Luck.
Lumumba's Grave.
Ma Lord.
Madam and Her Madam.
Madam and the Minister.
Madam's Past History.
Mama and Daughter.
Me and the Mule.
Merry-Go-Round.
Mexican Market Woman.
Midnight Dancer.
Militant.
Moonlight Night: Carmel.
Morning After.
Mother to Son.
Motto.
Necessity.
Negro Servant.
The Negro Speaks of Rivers.
A New Wind A-Blowin'.
Night Funeral in Harlem.
October 16: The Raid.
Old Walt.
Oppression.
Passing Love.
Peace.
Pennsylvania Station.
Personal.
Po' Boy Blues.
Poem.
Poem: "I loved my friend."
Prayer.
Preference.
Prime.
Puzzled.
Question and Answer.
Refugee in America.
Request for Requiems.
Sailor.
Saturday Night.
Sea Calm.
Seascape.
Share-Croppers.
Shepherd's Song at Christmas.
Situation.
Slave.
The Snail.
Song for a Dark Girl.
Song for a Suicide.
Song to a Negro Wash-
  Woman.
Special Bulletin.
Still Here.
Stony Lonesome.
Suicide's Note.
Sun Song.
Sylvester's Dying Bed.
Testament.
Theme for English B.
Third Degree.
This Little House Is Sugar.
To Midnight Nan at Leroy's.
Today.
Trip: San Francisco.
Troubled Woman.

Trumpet Player.
Two Somewhat Different
  Epigrams.
Undertow.
Vagabonds.
Wake.
Warning.
The Weary Blues.
What?
When Sue Wears Red.
Where? When? Which?
Who but the Lord?
Winter Moon.
Wisdom.
Without Benefit of
  Declaration.
Words Like Freedom.
World War II.
Youth.

Hughes, Richard
Burial of the Spirit.
Explanation, on Coming
  Home Late.
Felo de Se.
Glaucopis.
The Image.
Invocation to the Muse.
Lover's Reply to Good
  Advice.
Old Cat Care.
On Time.
The Ruin.
The Sermon.
Tramp.
The Walking Road.
Winter.

Hughes, Rupert
For Decoration Day:
  1861-1865.
For Decoration Day:
  1898-1899.
The Martyrs of the Maine.
With a First Reader.

Hughes, Ted
After Lorca.
The Bear.
Birth of Rainbow.
The Bull Moses.
Bullfrog.
Cadenza.
Cat and Mouse.
Childbirth.
A Childish Prank.
Christmas Card.
Cleopatra to the Asp.
Crag Jack's Apostasy.
Crow Blacker Than Ever.
Crow's First Lesson.
Crow's Last Stand.
Deaf School.
A Dove.
A Dream of Horses.
Esther's Tomcat.
Examination at the Womb-
  Door.
Famous Poet.
Fern.
Foxgloves.
Full Moon and Little Frieda.
Gnat-Psalm.
The Hawk in the Rain.
Hawk Roosting.
Heptonstall Old Church.
Her Husband.
His Legs Ran About.
The Horses.
The Howling of Wolves.
In Laughter.
The Jaguar.
Kreutzer Sonata.
The Lake.

Law in the Country of the
  Cats.
Leaves.
Ludwig's Death Mask.
Lupercalia.
A March Calf.
Minstrel's Song.
Moon-Witches.
A Motorbike.
My Aunt.
My Brother Bert.
My Sister Jane.
Nessie.
New Year's Song.
November.
An Otter.
A Pause for Breath.
Pennines in April.
Pibroch.
Pike.
Ravens.
The Retired Colonel.
Reveille.
Revenge Fable.
The River in March.
Roarers in a Ring.
Salmon Eggs.
Second Glance at a Jaguar.
Secretary.
September.
Singing on the Moon.
Six Young Men.
Skylarks.
Snowdrop.
Song: "O lady, when the
  tipped cup of the moon
  blessed you."
Song of a Rat.
Stations.
Stealing Trout.
Still-Life.
That Moment.
Theology.
Thistles.
The Thought-Fox.
Thrushes.
To Paint a Water Lily.
Trees.
Truth Kills Everybody.
Two Wise Generals.
Urn Burial.
View of a Pig.
Water.
Wilfred Owen's Photographs.
Wind.
Wino.
Witches.
Wodwo.
You Drive in a Circle.
You Hated Spain.

Hughes, Thomas
The Dolgelley Hotel.

Hugo, Richard
1614 Boren.
Cataldo Mission.
The Church on Comiaken
  Hill.
December 24 and George
  McBride is Dead.
Degrees of Gray in
  Philipsburg.
Dog Lake with Paula.
Drums in Scotland.
The Freaks at Spurgin Road
  Field.
Graves at Elkhorn.
Graves in Queens.
Greystone Cottage.
In Your Bad Dream.
Invasion North.
The Lady in Kicking Horse
  Reservoir.

Landscapes.
Langaig.
Last Days.
Letter to Bell from Missoula.
Letter to Garber from Skye.
Letter to Levertov from Butte.
Letter to Logan from
  Milltown.
Letter to Reed from Lolo.
Letter to Scanlon from
  Whitehall.
Letter to Wagoner from Port
  Townsend.
Letter to Welch from
  Browning.
A Map of Montana in Italy.
Maratea Porto: Saying
  Goodbye to the Vitolos.
Mill at Romesdal.
Museum of Cruel Days.
Napoli Again.
A Night at the Napi in
  Browning.
Open Country.
Places and Ways to Live.
Plans for Altering the River.
Salt Water Story.
Skykomish River Running.
A Snapshot of Uig in
  Montana.
Tahola.
To Women.
Turtle Lake.
The Way a Ghost Dissolves.
What Thou Lovest Well,
  Remains American.
White Center.
With Kathy at Wisdom.

Hugo, Victor
After Six Thousand Years.
The Age Is Great and Strong.
Be Like the Bird.
The Children of the Poor.
The Genesis of Butterflies.
Good Night.
The Grave and the Rose.
Heard on the Mountain.
House and Home.
The Lion at Noon.
More Strong Than Time.
Nocturne.
The Poet's Simple Faith.
The Poor Children.
Russia 1812.
A Sunset.
To Make the People Happy.
The Universal Republic.
Wings.

Huidobro, Vincente
I Am Partly Moon...

Hull, Eleanor
The Soul's Desire.

Hull, John Mervin
The Gates of the Year.

Hulme, Thomas Ernest
Above the Dock.
Autumn.
Conversion.
The Embankment.
Image.
Mana Aboda.

Hultman, J. A.
Thanks to God.

Hume, Alexander
Of Gods Omnipotencie.
Of the Day Estivall.
A Summer's Day.

Hume, Isobel
Home-Coming.
The Sleeper.
Whiteness.

Hume, Tobias
Soldier's Song.
Humes, Harry
The Road of Birds.
Hummer, T. R.
Any Time, What May Hit
You.
The Beating.
Cruelty.
Lifelines.
Love Poem: The Dispossessed.
The Rural Carrier Stops to
Kill a Nine-Foot
Cottonmouth.
What Shines in Winter Burns.
Where You Go When She
Sleeps.
Hummer, Terry
The Naming.
Humphrey, Frances
My Book of Life.
Humphrey, J. Lee
All Things Being Equal.
Humphreys, David
On Disbanding the Army.
Western Emigration.
Humphries, Barry
Edna's Hymn.
Humphries, Rolfe
Aria.
Around Thanksgiving.
Autumnal.
Coming Home.
The Cynneddf.
Dafydd Ap Gwilym Resents
the Winter.
Down the Field.
Frisbee.
Harp Music–.
He Visits a Hospital.
Heresy for a Class-Room.
The Offering of the Heart.
Polo Grounds.
Render unto Caesar.
Runes for an Old Believer.
The Seasons.
Second Night, or What You
Will.
Song from the Gulf.
Static.
The Summer Landscape; or,
The Dragon's Teeth.
Variation on a Theme by
Francis Kilvert.
Wmffre the Sweep.
Hunnis, William
A Nosegay Always Sweet, for
Lovers to Send for Tokens of
Love...
The Shipmen.
Hunt, [James Henry] Leigh
Abou Ben Adhem.
Captain Sword.
Christmas.
Cupid Drowned.
The Dearest Poets.
Epitaph on Erotion.
Fairies' Song.
The Glove and the Lions.
A House and Grounds.
Jaffar.
Jenny Kiss'd Me.
The Nun.
The Nymphs (excerpt).
On Seeing a Pigeon Make
Love.
On the Death of His Son
Vincent.
Places of Nestling Green.
The Royal Line.
Sneezing.

Song of Fairies Robbing an
Orchard (excerpt).
The Story of Rimini.
A Thought of the Nile.
Three Sonnets.
To Hampstead.
To the Grasshopper and the
Cricket.
To the Spirit Great and Good.
Two Heavens.
Ultra-Germano-Criticasterism.
Hunt, Josephine Slocum
You Kissed Me.
Hunt, Sam
April Fool.
Notes from a Journey.
Stabat Mater.
Hunter, Anne
My Mother Bids Me Bind My
Hair.
Hunter, John
Dear Master, in Whose Life I
See.
Hunter, Lost John
Y M & V Blues.
Hunter, William
"Go Bring Me," Said the
Dying Fair.
Joyfully, Joyfully Onward I
Move.
Hunter-Duvar, John
The Emigration of the Fairies.
De Roberval.
Twilight Song.
Huntington, George
International Hymn.
Huntington, William Reed
Authority.
Tellus.
Huntley, Stanley
Annabel Lee (parody).
Hurdis, James
The Favourite Village
(excerpt).
Hurley, Mary Rita
Beach House.
Hurnard, James
Winter.
Hurston, Z. N.
Jonah's Gourd Vine: I Vision
God.
Hurt, Mississippi John
Ain't No Tellin.
Got the Blues, Can't Be
Satisfied.
Spike Driver Blues.
**Husband, John J. and William
Porter Mackay**
Revive Us Again.
Husid, Mordechai
The Cry of Generations.
On the Way.
Windows.
Huss, Avraham
A Classic Idyll.
A Green Refrain.
Nocturnal Thoughts.
Time.
Hussey, Anne
Cinderella Liberated.
Indian Summer, 1927.
Hutchins, Charles L.
Softly through the Mellow
Starlight.
Hutchinson, Abby
Kind Words Can Never Die.
Hutchinson, Barney
Cold Logic.
Hutchinson, Jesse
The Californian.
Hutchinson, M. M.
Ten Little Indian Boys.

Hutchinson, Pearse
Copper-Beech and Butter-
Fingers.
Distortions.
Gaeltacht.
Into Their True Gentleness.
Malaga.
Hutchinson, Robert
Suburban Wife's Song.
Hutchison, A. G.
A'Chuilionn.
Hutchison, Joseph
This Year.
Hutchison, Percy Adams
Columbus.
Methinks the Measure.
Hutton, Joseph
The Tomb of the Brave.
Hutton, Laurence
The Doves of Venice.
Hutton, Mary
The Sleeping Beauty.
Huws, Daniel
Family Evening.
Goodbye to Regal.
Huxley, Aldous
The Canal.
Doors of the Temple.
First Philosopher's Song.
Frascati's.
Male and Female Created He
Them.
Ninth Philosopher's Song.
September.
Villiers de L'Isle-Adam.
Huxley, Thomas Henry
Tennyson.
Hwang Chin-i
The Blue Hill Is My Desire.
I Cut in Two.
Mountains Are Steadfast but
the Mountain Streams.
Hyde, Abby Bradley
And Canst Thou, Sinner,
Slight.
Dear Saviour, If These Lambs
Should Stray.
Hyde, Douglas
The Cooleen.
Evil Prayer.
I Shall Not Die for Thee.
My Grief on the Sea.
The Mystery.
The Red Man's Wife.
Hyde, Lewis
Ants.
Hyde, Robin
The Beaches (excerpt).
Church of the Holy Innocents,
Dunedin.
The English Rider.
The Houses (excerpt).
Journey from New Zealand.
Ku Li.
The People (excerpt).
Sarah.
Sisters.
Hyde, William deWitt
Creation's Lord, We Give
Thee Thanks.
Hyett, Barbara Helfgott
The Last Flight of the Great
Wallenda.

I

"I. V. S. W."
Snowfall.

Ibarbourou, Juana de
The Assignation.
Fleeting Restlessness.
Life-Hook.
The Strong Bond.
Ibbetson, Julius Caesar
Epigram: "O mortal man, that
lives by bread."
Ibn Abi'l-Khayr, Abu Sa'id
Six Rubaiyat.
Ibn Adiya, Al-Samua'al
Are We Not the People.
Oh, Would That I Knew.
Oh, Ye Censurers.
Ibn al-Abbar
You Know Not How Deep
Was the Love Your Eyes
Did Kindle.
Ibn al-Arabi
Ode: "They journeyed."
Ode: "Who can support the
anguish of love?"
When My Beloved Appears.
Ibn al-Rumi
On a Valetudinarian.
Ibn Chasdai, Abraham
Advice to Bores.
The Elusive Maid.
The Meek and the Proud.
The Poor Scholar.
Ibn Darraj, al Andalusi
The Wing of Separation.
Ibn Ezra, Abraham
The Ages of Man.
Far Sweeter Than Honey.
Freedom.
God Everywhere.
The Law.
The Living God.
My Stars.
Out of Luck.
The Song of Chess.
Ibn Ezra, Moses
Awake, My Soul.
The Beauty of the Stars.
Bring Me the Cup.
Drink, Friends.
A Dying Wife to Her
Husband.
Elegy.
The End of Man Is Death.
Four Love Poems.
God That Doest Wondrously.
I Went Out into the Garden.
Joy of Life.
Love-Songs.
Man Is a Weaver.
Men Are Children of This
World.
My Love Sways, Dancing.
On My Sorrowful Life.
Rejoice, O Youth, in the
Lovely Hind.
The Rosy Days Are
Numbered.
Sorrow Shatters My Heart.
To a Plagiarist.
Walk in the Precepts.
Without My Friends the Day
Is Dark.
The Works of God.
The World's Illusion.
The Young Dove.
Ibn Gabirol, Solomon
Almighty! What Is Man?
Defiance.
A Degenerate Age.
From Thee to Thee.
I Have Sought Thee Daily.
In Praise of Wisdom.
Invitation.
Meditations.

Morning Song.
My God.
Night.
Night-Thoughts.
O Soul, With Storms Beset.
Song of the Wind and the
  Rain.
Stanzas.
Water Song.
Wine and Grief.

Ibn Hazm Al-Andalusi
Twice Times Then Is Now.

Ibn Kolthum
The Mu'allaqat: Pour Us
  Wine.

Ibn Maatuk
Perturbation at Dawn.

Ibn Rashiq
Pretences.

Ibn Sabbatai, Judah
The Expensive Wife.

Ibn Tibbon, Judah
A Father's Testament.

Ibn Zaydun
Cordova.

Ibnu'l-Farid
Remembrance.

Ibsen, Henrik
Brand Speaks.
In the Orchard.

Ibycus
Autumn Love.

Idley, Peter
Covetousness.
Sources of Good Counsel.

Igjugarjuk
Musk Oxen.

Ignatius, Sister Mary
Our Lady of the Libraries.

Ignatius Loyola, Saint
Teach Us to Serve Thee,
  Lord.

Ignatow, David
Against the Evidence.
All Quiet.
An Allegory.
And the Same Words.
The Bagel.
Bowery.
The Business Life.
The City.
Come!
Communion.
A Dialogue.
Dilemma.
Dream.
Each Day.
East Bronx.
Elegy.
Epitaph.
The Escapade.
Europe and America.
First Coffin Poem.
For One Moment.
Gardeners.
Get the Gasworks.
He Puts Me to Rest.
The Heart.
How Come?
I'm Here.
In a Dream.
In No Way.
The Inheritance.
The Journey.
Kaddish.
Last Night.
My Own House.
My Place.
News Report.
Night at an Airport.
No Theory.
Notes for a Lecture.

The Paper Cutter.
Park.
The Professional.
Promenade.
Rescue the Dead.
Ritual Three.
Sediment.
Self-Employed.
The Signal.
Simultaneously.
Six Movements on a Theme.
The Sky Is Blue.
The Song.
A Suite for Marriage.
Sunday at the State Hospital.
Their Mouths Full.
Thoughts.
Three in Transition.
Threnody.
A Time of Night.
To Nowhere.
Us.
Waiting Inside.
With the Door Open.
With the Sun's Fire.

Ignoto
Valediction to Life.

Ikan, Ron
Madrid, Iowa.
Manitou.
Two Hopper.
What I Did Last Summer.

Ikeda, Patricia Y.
A Card Game: Kinjiro
  Sawada.
Recovery.
Translations.

Ikinilik
The Song of the Trout Fisher.

Ikhnaton *See* **Akhnaton**

Ilce, Ana
Summer Street.

Image, Selwyn
A Meditation for Christmas.

Iman, Yusef
Love Your Enemy.

Imber, Naphtali
Hatikvah–A Song of Hope.
Zionist Marching Song.

Imbs, Bravig
Sleep.
The Wind Was There.

Imelda, Sister
An Etching.

Imr el Kais
The Assignation.
The Mu'allaqat: Ode.
The Night Long.
The Storm.
Weep Love's Losing.

Inada, Lawson
Since When As Ever More.

Inada, Lawson Fusao
The Discovery of Tradition.
From Our Album.
Making Miso.
Plucking out a Rhythm.

Inber, Vera
The Pulkovo Meridian:
  Leningrad: 1943.

Indian, Telugu E.
Ritual Not Religion.

Ines de la Cruz, Sister Juana
See **Juana Ines de la Cruz,**
Sister

Inez, Colette
Better to Spit on the Whip
  than Stutter Your Love Like
  a Worm.
Crucial Stew.
The Letters of a Name.
Mercedes, Her Aloneness.

Qua Song.
Waiting for the Doctor.
The Woman Who Loved
  Women.

Ingalls, Jeremy
My Head on My Shoulders.

Ingalls, John James
Opportunity.

Ingamells, Rex
The Golden Bird.
The Great South Land
  (excerpt).
Memory of Hills (excerpt).
Sea-Chronicles.
Ship from Thames.

Inge, Charles Cuthbert
Limerick: "A certain young
  gourmet of Crediton."
On Monsieur Coue.

Inge, William Ralph
Limerick: "There was a good
  Canon of Durham."
Limerick: "There was an old
  man of Khartoum."

Ingelow, Jean
Apprenticed.
Child and Boatman (excerpt).
Divided.
Feathers and Moss.
For Exmoor.
The High Tide on the Coast
  of Lincolnshire.
Like a Laverock in the Lift.
The Long White Seam.
The Noble Tuck-Man.
One Morning, Oh! So Early.
Sea-Nurtured.
The Singing-Lesson.
Song of the Old Love.
Songs of Seven.
Sorrows Humanize Our Race.
Sweet Is Childhood.

Ingemann, Bernard S.
Pilgrim's Song.

Ingham, John Hall
Genesis.
George Washington.
A Summer Santuary.

"Ingoldsby, Thomas" *See*
Barham, Richard Harris

Ingram, John Kells
The Memory of the Dead.
National Presage.
The Social Future.

Inib-sarri
A Letter to Her Father.

Inman, Will
108 Tales of a Po'Buckra, No.
  106.
Shaman.

Innes, Guy
It's Three No Trumps.

Innocent III, Pope
The Golden Sequence.
Stabat Mater Dolorosa.

Inoue, Mitsuko
Country Pastor.

Iqbal, Muhammad
An Invocation (excerpt).

Ireland, W. H.
Shakespearean Soliloquy in
  Progress: "To starve, or not
  to..." (parody).

Iremonger, Valentin
Descending.
The Dog.
Going down the Mountain.
Hector.
Icarus.
In New Ross.
In This River.
Invocation.

Spring Stops Me Suddenly.
These Apple Trees.
This Houre Her Vigill.
The Toy Horse.
While the Summer Trees
  Were Crying.

Irihapeti Rangi te Apakura
Reply to a Marriage Proposal.

Irion, Mary Jean
Invocation from a Lawn
  Chair.

Iris, Scharmel
After the Martyrdom.

Irish, Jerry
A Boy Thirteen.

Irvin, Eric
Brother Ass.
Christmas 1942.
Midnight Patrol.

Irvin, Margaret
Chanticleer.

Irving, Minna
Betsy's Battle-Flag.
His Living Monument.
Lincoln Leads.
The Old Year's Prayer.
The Wedding Gift.

Irving, Washington
A Certain Young Lady.

Irwin, Thomas Caulfield
L'Angelo.
Antique Glimpses (excerpt).
Autumn.
December.
Elizabethan Days.
The Faerie's Child.
The Ghost's Promenade.
Glints of the Year–from a
  Window.
Hours I Remember Lonely
  and Lovely to Me.
Imogen–In Wales.
Iphione.
Leaving Troy.
A May Sunday.
Minnie.
Nature's Key-Notes.
The Objects of the Summer
  Scene.
Song: "My dreams were
  doleful and drear."
Sonnets, I: "The rough green
  wealth of wheaten fields that
  sway."
Sonnets, II: "The rainbow o'er
  the sea of afternoon."
Sonnets, III: "Regions of soft
  clear air, of cold green
  leaves."
Sonnets, IV: "Remote from
  smoky cities, aged and grey."
Sonnets, V: "Into the wood at
  close of rainy day."
Sonnets, VI: "Awakened, I
  behold through dewy leaves."
Sonnets, VII: "Upon an
  upland orchard's sunny
  side."
Sonnets, VIII: "The apples
  ripen under yellowing leaves."
Sonnets, IX: "An isle of trees
  full foliaged in a meadow."
Sonnets, X: "When I had
  turned Catullus into rhyme."
Sonnets, XI: "Ye two fair
  trees that I so long have
  known."
Sonnets, XII: "A roadside inn
  this summer Saturday."
Sonnets, XIII: "I walk of grey
  noons by the old canal."

Sonnets, XIV: "Now, winter's
   dolorous days are o'er."
Spring.
The Suire.
Swift.
To a Skull.
Winter Life and Scenery.
Winter Noon in the Woods.
With the Dawn.
Irwin, Wallace
Aunt Nerissa's Muffin.
Blow Me Eyes!
The Constant Cannibal
   Maiden.
The Fate of the Cabbage
   Rose.
A Nautical Extravaganza.
The Powerful Eyes O' Jeremy
   Tait.
Reminiscence.
The Rhyme of the Chivalrous
   Shark.
Science for the Young.
The Sea Serpant.
Sensitive Sydney.
Song for a Cracked Voice.
Such a Pleasant Familee.
The Worried Skipper.
Irwin, William
From Romany to Rome.
A Grain of Salt.
Isaac, Samuel
Advice to Hotheads.
Isaac, Ted
Urban Roses.
Isaacs, Jorge
The Nima.
Isaacson, Jose
Pre-positions.
Isanos, Magda
Apricot Tree.
Isbell, Hugh O.
Crucifixion.
Ise, Lady
Because we suspected.
Correspondence:.
Elegy: Ise Lamenting the
   Death of Empress Onshi.
Even in my dreams.
A flower of waves.
Hanging from the branches of
   a green willow tree.
If I Consider.
If it is you, there.
Like a ravaged sea.
Near a Waterfall at Ryumon.
News of the palace.
Not Even in Dreams.
On Seeing the Field Being
   Singed.
The Rains of Spring.
Seeing the Plum Blossoms by
   the River.
Seeing the Returning Geese.
Since "The Pillow Knows
   All."
Sleeping with Someone Who
   Came in Secret.
They are rebuilding.
When the fifth month comes.
Ise Tayu
The clear water of the
   imperial pond.
The Farmer's Clothes Are
   Soaked Through and Never
   Dried.
Isenhour, Walter E.
Be Friendly.
The Down-Pullers.
Give Us Sober Men.
God Is There.
Going Home with Jesus.

Happiness.
If You're the Man You Ought
   to Be.
It's Wonderful.
Jesus Never Fails.
Keeping Victory.
Some Things You Cannot
   Will to Men.
Ish-Kishor, Sulamith
War.
Isherwood, Christopher
The Common Cormorant.
On His Queerness.
Ishigaki Rin
Clams.
Cocoon.
Ishikawa Takuboku
I picked up my mother.
Isidorus
On a Fowler.
Island, E. H. L.
Penny Whistle Blues.
Isler, Elizabeth
The Little Things.
Issa
Crawl, Laugh.
Haiku: "Death it can bring."
Haiku: "Once upon a time".
Oraga Haru.
The Wren.
Issaia, Nana
Dream.
Sacrifice.
Ita, Saint
Jesukin.
Saint Ita's Fosterling.
Itzin, Charles
Malcom, Iowa.
Ivanov, Vyacheslav
The Holy Rose.
Ivens, Michael
First Day at School.
Ives, George
A Message.
Once.
Ives, Rich
Memory, a Small Brown Bird.
Ivie, Kelly
Gull Lake Reunion.
Iwa no Hime, Empress
Longing for the Emperor.
Iwano, Homei
Sad Love and Sad Song.
Izembo
A Shower.
Izumi Shikibu
After the Death of Her
   Daughter in Childbirth...
As the Rains of Spring.
The Diary of Izumi Shikibu
   (excerpt).
From Darkness.
From That First Night.
I Go out of Darkness.
In the Dusk the Path.
It Is the Time of Rain and
   Snow.
Love.
Never Could I Think.
Recklessly I Cast Myself
   away.

J

"J., W."
A City Eclogue.
J. H., S.,
A New Year's Wish.

J. M.
The Animal Howl.
The Funeral.
Song of a Jewish Boy.
Jabes, Edmond
The Book Rises Out of the
   Fire.
A Circular Cry.
The Condemned.
The Pulverized Screen.
Song of the Last Jewish Child.
Song of the Trees of the Black
   Forest.
Song: "On the side of the
   road."
Water.
Jacinto, Antonio
Letter from a Contract
   Worker.
Monangamba.
The People Went to War.
Punishment for a Wayward
   Train.
Jacinto, Jaime
The Beads.
The Fire Breather, Mexico
   City.
Looking for Buddha.
Reflections on the Death of a
   Parrot.
Jackett, Will
Extraordinary Will.
Jackowska, Nicki
Family Outing–A Celebration.
The Insect Kitchen.
The Meeting.
The Sisters.
Jackson, Ada
I Have a Roof.
In Memoriam.
Jackson, Angela
Blackmen: Who Make
   Morning.
Jackson, Bessie
Stew Meat Blues.
Tired as I Can Be.
Jackson, Bo Weavil
You Can't Keep No Brown.
Jackson, David
Grandmother Jackson.
Jackson, Edgar
The Hunter Sees What Is
   There.
Magic Word.
Self-Portrait.
The Sinew of Our Dreams.
Three Songs.
Jackson, Haywood
The Children Grown.
On the Latest Crisis of
   Confidence.
Jackson, Helen Fiske
Coronation.
Morn.
Jackson, Helen Hunt
A Ballad of the Gold
   Country.
Cheyenne Mountain.
Danger.
Doubt.
Down to Sleep.
A Dream.
Emigravit.
Grab-Bag.
Habeas Corpus.
A Last Prayer.
My Legacy.
October's Bright Blue
   Weather.
Poppies on the Wheat.
September.
September Days Are Here.

Spinning.
That Things Are No Worse,
   Sire.
Jackson, Jim
Old Dog Blue.
Jackson, Kathryn
Being Twins.
The Twins.
Jackson, Kathryn and Byron
Noonday Sun.
Open Range.
Jackson, Leroy F.
All Aboard for Bombay.
Columbus.
Duckle, Duckle, Daisy.
The Hero.
Hippity Hop to Bed.
I've Got a New Book from
   My Grandfather Hyde.
Jelly Jake and Butter Bill.
A Little Pig Asleep.
Old Father Annum.
Polly Picklenose.
Simple Sam.
Jackson, Lil' Son
Charlie Cherry.
Homeless Blues.
Jackson, Mae
The Blues Today.
For Some Poets.
I remember...
I used to wrap my white doll
   up in.
January 3, 1970.
Reincarnation.
Jackson, Maud Frazer
New Years and Old.
Jackson, Michael
Australia.
Mask-Maker.
Neanderthal.
The Red Flag.
Sudan.
Jackson, Richard
Holding On.
Jackson, William
Making an Impression.
Out of the Deepness.
Jacob, Hildebrand
The Alarm.
The Judgement of Tiresias.
To Cloe.
To Geron.
The Writer.
Jacob, Max
It May Be.
To Modigliani to Prove to
   Him That I Am a Poet.
Jacob, Ruth Apprich
Waiting.
Jacob, Sir Hildebrand
On Delia.
Sent to Him, as He
   Whisper'd.
Jacob, Violet
The Gean Trees.
The Last o' the Tinkler.
The Licht Nichts.
Pride.
The Rowan.
Tam i' the Kirk.
The Wild Geese.
Jacobs, A. C.
Isaac.
Painting.
Poem for My Grandfather.
Yiddish Poet.
Jacobs, Bertha
A Ditty.
Jacobs, Catherine Haydon
Autumn Orchard.
Secret.

Jacobs, Elijah L.
High Wheat Country.
Saturday in the County Seat.
Jacobs, Henry
The Avon.
Jacobs, Henry Eyster
Lord Jesus Christ, We
Humbly Pray.
Jacobs, Henry S.
How Goodly Is Thy House.
Jacobs, Maria
Embroidery.
Song of the Intruder.
Jacobs, P. L.
Abbreviated Rumination.
Electrocution Script.
Fish Story.
Obligatory Love Poem.
Old Man Hall.
Safety or Something.
Jacobsen, Josephine
49th & 5th, December 13.
The Animals.
The Class.
Country Drive-In.
The Eyes of Children at the
Brink of the Sea's Grasp.
For Any Member of the
Security Police.
For Murasaki.
The Interrupted.
It Is the Season.
The Matadors.
Mollesse.
The Murmurers.
The Planet.
Power Failure.
Rainy Night at the Writers'
Colony.
Reindeer and Engine.
The Sea Fog.
The Shade-Seller.
Short Short Story.
There Is Good News.
When the Five Prominent
Poets.
Yellow.
Jacobsen, Rolf
Country Roads.
Road's End.
Sunflower.
Jacobson, Ethel
Atomic Courtesy.
Lines Scratched in Wet
Cement.
Jacoby, Grover
Juxta.
Jacopo da Lentino
Canzonetta: He Will Neither
Boast Nor Lament to His
Lady.
Canzonetta: Of His Lady, and
of His Making Her Likeness.
Sonnet: Of His Lady in
Heaven.
Sonnet: Of His Lady's Face.
Jacopone da Todi
Christ and His Mother at the
Cross.
The Highest Wisdom.
The Little Angels.
Nativity Song.
Of Impatience Which Brings
All Our Gains to Nothing.
Stabat Mater.
Jaeger, Lowell
Poem for My Mother.
Jaffe, Dan
The Owl in the Rabbi's Barn.
This One Is about the Others.
Who?
Yahrzeit.

Jaffray, Norman R.
Limerick: "A salmon
remarked to his mate."
Limerick: "There was a young
man with a beard."
Jago, Richard
Absence.
Edge-Hill.
The Goldfinches.
Hamlet's Soliloquy Imitated
(parody).
Shakespearean Soliloquy in
Progress: "To print, or not
to..." (parody).
The Swallows: An Elegy.
Jahan, Empress Nur
The moon of Id came.
Jahin, Salah
Quatrains.
Jahns, T. R.
Song of the Farmworker.
Jallais, Denise
Lullaby for My Dead Child.
Jama, Aqib Abdullahi
Prayer for Rain.
Jamal, Yasmeen
All That Jazz.
Canteen Pimpin'.
Did Ya Hear?
The Gate.
I Bet God Understands about
Givin up Five.
James, Alice Archer (Sewall)
The Butterfly.
Sinfonia Eroica.
James, Clive
Peregrine Prykke's Pilgrimage
(parody).
To Pete Atkin: A Letter from
Paris (excerpt).
Unsolicited Letters to Five
Artists (parody).
James, David
After Your Death.
The Famous Outlaw Stops in
for a Drink.
James, Edward
Carmina Amico.
James, Elizabeth Ann
Artificial Death, II.
James, Jesse
Sweet Patuni.
James, John
Of John Bunyans Life &c.
On the Decease of the
Religious and Honourable
Jno Haynes Esqr....
James, Nicholas
The Complaints of Poetry
(excerpt).
James, Sibyl
Patty Hearst Hoists the
Carbine.
Rock and Roll.
James, Skip
Cypress Grove Blues.
Devil Got My Woman.
Hard Time Killin' Floor
Blues.
James, Thomas
Hunting for Blueberries.
Letter to a Mute.
Letters to a Stranger.
Mummy of a Lady Named
Jemutesonekh XXI Dynasty.
Reasons.
Snakebite.
James I, King of England
Admonition to Montgomerie.
An Epithalamion upon the
Marquis of Huntilies
Marriage.

Sonnet: "The azured vault, the
crystal circles bright."
James I, King of Scotland
Good Counsel.
The Jolly Beggar.
The Kingis Quhair: The
Coming of Love.
The Nightingale's Song.
Spring Song of the Birds.
James V, King of Scotland
Christ's Kirk on the Green.
Jami
The Great Idealist.
The Hidden Truth.
Night.
The Song of Mystic Unity.
Jamil
Buthaina.
Jamison, Roscoe Conkling
The Negro Soldiers.
Jammes, Francis
Alone.
Amsterdam.
The Child Reads an Almanac.
Georgiques Chretiennes
(excerpt).
The Little Donkey.
Love.
Palm Sunday.
Prayer That an Infant May
Not Die.
Prayer to Go to Paradise with
the Asses.
Jana Bai
She was my staff and I am
blind.
Janeczko, Paul B.
After the Rain.
Lesson for Dreamers.
This Poem Is for Nadine.
Janik, Phyllis
In the Field.
Sleeping Peasants.
The Story of Good.
Jankola, Beth
Women Called Bossy
Cowboys.
Janosco, Beatrice
The Garden Hose.
Janowitz, Phyllis
Case.
Minuet in a Minor Key.
The Wait.
Jansen, Annetta
Prayer for Neighborhood
Evangelism.
Janta, Alexander
Psalm of the Singing Grave.
Janvier, Francis DeHaes
God Save Our President.
Janvier, Margaret Thomson
The Clown's Baby.
Little Wild Baby.
The Sandman.
Janvier, Thomas A.
Santiago.
Jaques, Florence Page
A Goblinade.
There Once Was a Puffin.
Jarman, Mark
The Desire of Water.
Jarrell, Randall
2nd Air Force.
90 North.
Aging.
The Angels at Hamburg.
The Augsburg Adoration.
The Author to the Reader.
Bats.
The Bird of Night.
The Black Swan.
The Blind Sheep.

The Breath of Night.
Burning the Letters.
A Camp in the Prussian
Forest.
The Chipmunk's Day.
Cinderella.
Come to the Stone.
A Country Life.
The Cow Wandering in the
Bare Field.
The Dead in Melanesia.
The Dead Wingman.
The Death of the Ball Turret
Gunner.
Eighth Air Force.
The Elementary Scene.
The Emancipators.
Field and Forest.
For an Emigrant.
A Front.
A Game at Salzburg.
A Girl in a Library.
Gunner.
Hope.
The House in the Wood.
A Hunt in the Black Forest.
In and Out the Bushes, Up
the Ivy.
In Galleries.
In Montecito.
In Nature There Is Neither
Right nor Left nor Wrong.
The Islands.
Jerome.
Jews at Haifa.
Jonah.
The Knight, Death, and the
Devil.
Lady Bates.
The Lines.
The Lonely Man.
Losses.
The Lost Children.
A Lullaby.
The Marchen.
The Mockingbird.
Moving.
Nestus Gurley.
Next Day.
An Officers' Prison Camp
Seen from a Troop-Train.
The Orient Express.
A Pilot from the Carrier.
Pilots, Man Your Planes.
Port of Embarkation.
Prisoners.
Protocols.
The Range in the Desert.
The Refugees.
Say Goodbye to Big Daddy.
Seele Im Raum.
A Sick Child.
The Sick Nought.
Siegfried.
The Sleeping Beauty:
Variation of the Prince.
The Snow-Leopard.
Soldier (T. P.).
The Soldier Walks under the
Trees of the University.
A Soul.
The State.
The Subway from New
Britain to the Bronx.
Thinking of the Lost World.
The Truth.
Variations.
A War.
The Ways and the Peoples.
Well Water.
Woman.

The Woman at the
  Washington Zoo.
Jarrett, Emmett
Dear Mother.
For E.C.J.
Hamlet.
Human Relations.
Song: "Help me now."
The Trip.
The Two of Cups.
Jason, Philip K.
Skin.
Jastrun, Mieczyslaw
Encirclement.
The Jews.
Jaszi, Jean
The Clock.
My Horses.
Winter.
Jauss, David
For My Son, Born during an
  Ice Storm.
On Certain Mornings
  Everything Is Sensual.
Sounding.
Javitz, Alexander
The Old Men.
Jayadeva
Gita Govinda.
A Song from the Gita
  Govinda.
Jazz Gillum
Go back to the Country.
Jeffers, Lance
Black Soul of the Land.
Breath in My Nostrils.
How High the Moon.
Love Pictures You as Black
  and Long-Faced.
My Blackness Is the Beauty of
  This Land.
Nina Simone.
On Listening to the Spirituals.
Trellie.
Who Shined Shoes in Times
  Square.
Jeffers, Robinson
Age in Prospect.
Animals.
The Answer.
Ante Mortem.
Antrim.
Apology for Bad Dreams.
An Artist.
Ascent to the Sierras.
Ave Caesar.
The Beaks of Eagles.
The Beauty of Things.
Birds.
Birds and Fishes.
Birth-Dues.
Black-Out.
The Bloody Sire.
Boats in a Fog.
But I am Growing Old and
  Indolent.
Calm and Full the Ocean.
Carmel Point.
Cassandra.
Clouds of Evening.
Compensation.
Continent's End.
Credo.
Cremation.
The Cruel Falcon.
Crumbs or the Loaf.
Divinely Superfluous Beauty.
Eagle Valor, Chicken Mind.
Evening Ebb.
The Excesses of God.
The Eye.
Fawn's Foster-Mother.

Fire on the Hills.
Fourth Act.
Gale in April.
Granite and Cypress.
Gray Weather.
Haunted Country.
The House Dog's Grave.
Hurt Hawks.
I Shall Laugh Purely.
The Inquisitors.
Iona: The Graves of the
  Kings.
Joy.
Let Them Alone.
Life from the Lifeless.
A Little Scraping.
Look, How Beautiful.
Love the Wild Swan.
The Maid's Thought.
May-June, 1940.
My Burial Place.
New Mexican Mountain.
Night.
Noon.
Nova.
November Surf.
Ocean.
Oh, Lovely Rock.
Original Sin.
Pelicans.
Phenomena.
Post Mortem.
Practical People.
Prescription of Painful Ends.
Promise of Peace.
The Purse-Seine.
Rearmament.
Reference to a Passage in
  Plutarch's Life of Sulla.
Return.
Roan Stallion.
Rock and Hawk.
Salmon-Fishing.
Science.
Self-Criticism in February.
Shane O'Neill's Cairn.
Shine, Perishing Republic.
Shine, Republic.
Shiva.
Signpost.
Skunks (excerpt).
The Stars Go over the Lonely
  Ocean.
Still the Mind Smiles.
Summer Holiday.
Tamar: Part III.
To the Stone-Cutters.
Tor House.
The Trumpet: Grass on the
  Cliff.
Vulture.
Watch the Lights Fade.
Wise Men in Their Bad
  Hours.
Woodrow Wilson.
The World's Wonders.
Jefferson, Blind Lemon
Bad Luck Blues.
Big Night Blues.
Black Horse Blues.
Broke and Hungry.
Chock House Blues.
Deceitful Brownskin Blues.
Easy Rider Blues.
Long Distance Moan.
Peach Orchard Mama.
Piney Woods Money Mama.
Pneumonia Blues.
Prison Cell Blues.
Rabbit Foot Blues.
Rising High Water Blues.
Stocking Feet Blues.

That Black Snake Mama.
That Crawling Baby Blues.
Tin Cup Blues.
Wartime Blues.
Jefferson, Joseph
Immortality.
Jefferys, Charles
We Have Lived and Loved
  Together.
Jeffrey, Francis, Lord Jeffrey
Epitaph.
Epitaph in Christ Church,
  Bristol, on Thomas Turner.
Epitaph in St. Olave's Church,
  Southwark, on Mr. Munday.
Epitaph on Peter Robinson.
Jeffrey, Mildred
Death.
Jeffrey, William
Glen Rosa.
On Glaister's Hill: Carlyle on
  Burns.
Stones.
Jeffries, Charles
Jeannette and Jeannot.
Jeannot's Answer.
Jeffries, Christie
Lone Huntsman.
Jeitteles, Alois
To My Distant Beloved.
Jeitteles, Benedict
Epitaph for a Judge.
Jekyll, Joseph
Epitaph: "See, one physician,
  like a sculler, plies."
Jellicoe, S. Charles
Advice to a Lover.
Jemmat, Catherine
The Rural Lass.
Jenkins, Brooks
Loneliness.
Jenkins, Christina
Sunday Morning.
Jenkins, Louis
Library.
My Feet.
Violence on Television.
Jenkins, Oliver
Merry-Go-Round.
A Ship Comes in.
Time Out.
Waterfront.
Jenks, Orville J.
The Dying Mine Brakeman.
Jenks, Tudor
An Accommodating Lion.
The Baby's Name.
Hard to Bear.
On the Road.
Small and Early.
The Spirit of the Maine.
Jenkyn, Pathericke
Love and Respect.
Jenner, Charles
Eclogue IV. The Poet
  (excerpt).
Jenner, Edward
Sent to a Patient, with the
  Present of a Couple of
  Ducks.
Signs of Rain.
Jennett, Sean
And the Dead.
The Barge Horse.
Cycle.
The Island.
Mahoney.
Merchandise.
My Subtle and Proclamant
  Song.
Old Joyce.
Omphalos: The Well.

The Quick.
Jennings, Elizabeth
Afterthought.
Ago.
The Animals' Arrival.
Answers.
Beyond Possession.
A Birthday in Hospital.
The Child and the Shadow.
The Climbers.
Communication.
The Counterpart.
A Death.
Delay.
Disguises.
Escape and Return.
Father to Son.
Florence: Design for a City.
Fountain.
Fragment for the Dark.
Ghosts.
Harvest and Consecration.
Identity.
The Idler.
In a Garden.
In the Night.
Meditation on the Nativity.
Men Fishing in the Arno.
Mirrors.
Music and Words.
Not in the Guide-Books.
Old Man.
One Flesh.
The Parting.
Rembrandt's Late Self-
  Portraits.
The Room.
Song at the Beginning of
  Autumn.
Song for a Birth or a Death.
Song for a Departure.
The Storm.
Teresa of Avila.
Thinking of Love.
To My Mother at 73.
The Unknown Child.
The Visitation.
A Way of Looking.
Weathercock.
Winter Love.
World I Have Not Made.
A World of Light.
The Young Ones.
Jennings, Humphrey
Prose Poem.
Jennings, Kate
Divorce.
Jennings, Leslie Nelson
Belden Hollow.
Jennings, Paula
Lesbian.
Jennison, C. S.
I'm Leery of Firms with Easy
  Terms.
Jennison, Lucy White
A Dream of Death.
Jensen, Jeffry
Western Movies.
Jensen, Johannes V.
A Bathing Girl.
Jensen, Laura
After I Have Voted.
An Age.
The Ajax Samples.
As the Window Darkens.
The Candles Draw Well after
  All.
The Cloud Parade.
House Is an Enigma.
Household.
In the Hospital.
Indian.

Kite.
The Red Dog.
Sleep in the Heat.
Starlings.
Talking to the Mule.
Tapwater.
Winter Evening Poem.
Jenyns, Soame
The Art of Dancing.
An Epistle Written in the
  Country to....
Epitaph on Dr. Johnson.
The Modern Fine Gentleman
  (excerpt).
The Modern Fine Lady.
The Temple of Venus.
Jerome, Judson
Child's Game.
Deer Hunt.
Eve: Night Thoughts.
Plexus and Nexus.
Psychology Today.
Jerome, William
Bedelia.
Jerry the Mule
Timber.
Jesus, Teresa de
All of a Sudden.
They Go By, Go By, Love,
  the Days and the Hours.
Jewett, Eleanore Myers
Down among the Wharves.
Jewett, Ellen A.
Sermon in a Stocking.
Jewett, John H.
Those Rebel Flags.
Jewett, Sarah Orne
A Country Boy in Winter.
Jewett, Sophie
Armistice.
If Spirits Walk.
In the Dark.
The Least of Carols.
A Smiling Demon of Notre
  Dame.
Song.
When Nature Hath Betrayed
  the Heart That Loved Her.
Jewsbury, Maria Jane
Partings.
To a Young Brother.
Jigmed, Chimedin
For the Cultural Campaign.
A Satirical Poem about Drink.
Jiles, Paulette
Paper Matches.
Time to Myself.
The Tin Woodsman.
Windigo.
Jimenez, Juan Ramon
The Conclusive Voyage.
Deep Night.
Fleeting Return.
Full Consciousness.
Galante Garden.
Galante Garden.
I Recognized You Because
  When I Saw the Print.
In the Subway.
The Lamb Was Bleating
  Softly.
New Leaves.
New Spring.
Oceans.
The Shepherd's Star.
Winter Song.
Jito, Empress
Manyoshu: Spring Is Passing.
Jitrik, Noe
Addio a la Mamma.
Joachim, Paulin
Burial.

Joad, C.E.M.
Limerick: "There was a
  professor of Beaulieu."
Joans, Ted
Chickitten Gitten!
It Is Time.
Knee Deep.
Lester Young.
LOVE TIGHT.
Miles' Delight.
My Ace of Spades.
The Protective Grigri.
Scenery.
To Fez Cobra.
The Truth.
Up out of the African.
Voice in the Crowd.
Watermelon.
Zoo You Too!
Johannes Secundus
Basia, VIII.
Epithalamium.
"John."
Ode to the Last Pot of
  Marmalade.
John, Gwen
A Child's Winter Evening.
John of Damascus, Saint
The Dark Night of the Soul.
The Day of Resurrection.
Easter Hymn.
O Flame of Living Love.
The Obscure Night of the
  Soul.
Resurrection.
Risen with Healing in His
  Wings.
Romance VIII.
John of the Cross
Christ and the Soul.
The Search.
Johns, Orrick
The Home Fire.
The Interpreter.
Little Things.
Mothers and Children.
The Sea-Lands.
Shopping Day.
Spring.
The Tree-Toad.
Wild Plum.
Johnson, Alicia Loy
Black Lotus/a Prayer.
A Black Poetry Day.
Johnson, B. S.
All This Sunday Long.
Great Man.
Why Do We Lie.
Johnson, Blind Willie
God Don't Never Change.
I'm Gonna Run to the City of
  Refuge.
If I Had My Way.
Jesus Is Coming Soon.
Jesus Make Up My Dying
  Bed.
Motherless Children.
Johnson, Burges
The Anxious Farmer.
Contentment.
The Gnu Wooing.
My Sore Thumb.
Remarks from the Pup.
A Rondeau of Remorse.
The Service.
Soap, the Oppressor.
Johnson, Charles
Sleeping Beauty.
Johnson, Charles Bertram
A Little Cabin.
Negro Poets.

Johnson, Charles Frederick
The Modern Romans.
Then and Now.
Johnson, Denis
The Boarding.
Minutes.
Passengers.
Sway.
A Woman.
Johnson, Don
Above the Falls at Waimea.
Brainwashing Dramatized.
For Wilma.
Night Dive.
Night Flight.
O White Mistress.
Ripper Collins' Legacy.
The Sergeant.
Tick Picking in the Quetico.
Johnson, Donald
Indian Summer Here, You in
  Honolulu.
Johnson, Dorothy Vena
Epitaph for a Bigot.
Green Valley.
Palace.
Twinkling Gown.
Johnson, E. Pauline
The Song My Paddle Sings.
Johnson, Edward
Good News from New-
  England.
Mr. Eliot, Pastor of the
  Church of Christ at
  Roxbury...
Mr. Roger Harlackenden.
Mr. Thomas Shepheard...Hee
  a Man of a Thousand.
Oh King of Saints, How
  Great's Thy Work, Say We.
Onely the Reverend Grave
  and Godly Mr. Buckly
  Remaines.
The Reverend Mr.
  Higginson...
The Water-Drinker.
Yee Shall Not Misse of a Few
  Lines in Remembrance of
  Thomas Hooker.
Johnson, Edythe
Will God's Patience Hold Out
  for You?
Johnson, [(Emily)] Pauline
The Corn Husker.
The Lost Lagoon.
Lullaby of the Iroquois.
Marshlands.
Ojistoh.
Shadow River.
The Trail to Lillooet.
The Train Dogs.
Johnson, Esther
If It Be True.
Jealousy.
To Dr. Swift on His Birthday,
  30th November 1721.
Johnson, Fenton
Aunt Jane Allen.
The Banjo Player.
Children of the Sun.
Counting.
The Daily Grind.
The Drunkard.
The Lonely Mother.
The Marathon Runner.
The Minister.
A Negro Peddler's Song.
The New Day.
The Old Repair Man.
Puck Goes to Court.
Rulers: Philadelphia.
The Scarlet Woman.

Tired.
The Vision of Lazarus
  (excerpt).
When I Die.
Who Is That A-Walking in
  the Corn?
The World Is a Mighty Ogre.
Johnson, Fred
Arabesque.
Coda.
Fire, Hair, Meat and Bone.
Noises.
Johnson, Geoffrey
All Over the World.
Drought.
Peat-Cutters.
The Windmill.
Johnson, George
Flight.
Frost.
Johnson, Georgia Douglas
Benediction.
Black Woman.
Common Dust.
Conquest.
Credo.
The Dreams of the Dreamer.
Escape.
Guardianship.
The Heart of a Woman.
Hope.
I Closed My Shutters Fast
  Last Night.
I've Learned to Sing.
I Want to Die while You
  Love Me.
Interracial.
Lethe.
Little Son.
Lost Illusions.
Lovelight.
My Little Dreams.
Old Black Men.
The Poet Speaks.
Prejudice.
Proving.
Recessional.
Remember.
The Riddle.
Service.
Smothered Fires.
The Suppliant.
To William Stanley
  Braithwaite.
Tomorrow's Men.
Trifle.
Welt.
What Need Have I for
  Memory?
When I Am Dead.
Your World.
Johnson, H. B.
Stuff.
Johnson, Helene
Bottled.
Fulfillment.
Invocation.
Magalu.
Poem: "Little brown boy."
Remember Not.
The Road.
Sonnet to A Negro in Harlem.
Summer Matures.
Trees at Night.
What Do I Care for Morning.
Johnson, Henry
Derelict.
The Funeral Parlor.
The Journey.
Mask of Stone.
Search for Love.

Johnson, Herbert Clark
A Boy's Need.
Crossing a Creek.
On Calvary's Lonely Hill.
Willow Bend and Weep.
Johnson, Hilda
Ballade of Expansion.
Johnson, James Weldon
Brothers.
The Creation.
Envoy.
Fifty Years.
From the German of Uhland.
The Glory of the Day Was in
  Her Face.
Go Down Death.
God's Trombones: Listen,
  Lord.
Lift Every Voice and Sing.
My City.
O Black and Unknown Bards.
Sence You Went Away.
The White Witch.
Johnson, Joe
Anna.
If I Ride This Train.
Judeebug's Country.
Samurai and Hustlers.
True Love.
Johnson, Josephine
Supplication.
The Unwilling Gypsy.
Johnson, Josephine Winslow
The Betrayal.
Final Autumn.
In This Hour.
The Quiet Flower.
The Temple.
Under All Change.
Johnson, Lil
Never Let Your Left Hand
  Know.
You'll Never Miss Your Jelly.
Johnson, Linton Kwesi
Di Great Insohreckshan.
Johnson, Lionel Pigot
The Age of a Dream.
Bagley Wood.
Beyond.
By the Statue of King Charles
  at Charing Cross.
Cadgwith.
The Church of a Dream.
Comrades.
The Dark Angel.
The Darkness.
Dead.
Doctor Major.
A Friend.
Friends.
In Memory.
Ireland.
Laleham: Matthew Arnold's
  Grave.
Lambeth Lyric.
London Town.
Magic.
Mystic and Cavalier.
Our Lady of France.
Our Lady of the May.
Oxford.
Oxford Nights.
Plato in London.
The Precept of Silence.
The Roman Stage.
Sancta Silvarum.
Songs: "Now in golden glory
  goes."
A Stranger.
Summer Storm.
Te Martyrum Candidatus.
To a Traveler.

To Morfydd.
To the Dead of '98.
Victory.
Ways of War.
Winchester.
Johnson, Lonnie
Careless Love.
Jersey Belle Blues.
Johnson, Louis
Adversaries.
Comedian.
Coming and Going.
Dirge.
Elegy.
How to Measure a Cat.
Poem in Karori.
Sandwich Man.
This Particular Christian.
Johnson, Louise
On the Wall.
Johnson, Margaret
Day Dreams, or Ten Years
  Old.
Johnson, Mary
Virginiana.
Johnson, Michael L.
Nancy, You Dance.
On the Dates of Poets.
Johnson, Nick
The Sleeping Gypsy–a
  Painting by Rousseau.
Johnson, Paul
Because.
Johnson, Rita
The Corner.
Johnson, Robert
Come On in My Kitchen.
Hellhound on My Trail.
I Believe I'll Dust My Broom.
Love in Vain.
Me and the Devil Blues.
Milkcow's Calf Blues.
Preaching Blues.
Stones in My Passway.
Terraplane Blues.
Traveling Riverside Blues.
Walking Blues.
Johnson, Robert Underwood
As a Bell in a Chime.
The Blossom of the Soul.
Browning at Asolo.
Dewey at Manila.
An English Mother.
Hearth Song.
In Tesla's Laboratory.
An Irish Love-Song.
Italian Rhapsody.
Love Once Was Like an April
  Dawn.
Star Song.
To the Returning Brave.
Ursula.
The Voice of Webster
  (excerpt).
The Wistful Days.
Johnson, Ronald
Letters to Walt Whitman.
Johnson, Rossiter
Evelyn.
A Soldier Poet.
Johnson, Samuel
Anacreon's Dove.
As With My Hat.
Ballad: "I put my hat upon
  my head."
Charles XII of Sweden.
The City of God.
Comets and Princes.
Epigram on a Dog.
Epitaph on William Hogarth.

An Epitaph upon the
  Celebrated Claudy Philips,
  Musician...
Father, in Thy Mysterious
  Presence Kneeling.
The Good-Natur'd Man:
  Prologue.
Hermit Hoar...
I Bless Thee, Lord, for
  Sorrows Sent.
If the Man Who Turnips
  Cries.
Inspiration.
Life's Last Scene.
Lines in Ridicule of Certain
  Poems Published in 1777.
London: A Poem in Imitation
  of the Third Satire of Juvenal
  (excerpt).
On the Death of Dr. Robert
  Levet.
Prologue, Spoken by Mr.
  Garrick...
Prologue to Hugh Kelly's "A
  Word to the Wise".
The Scholar's Life.
A Short Song of
  Congratulation.
A Son Lit.
To Miss–.
To Mrs. Thrale on Her
  Thirty-Fifth Birthday.
Translation of Lines by
  Benerade.
Upon the Feast of St. Simon
  and St. Jude.
The Vanity of Human Wishes.
The Winter's Walk.
The Young Author.
Johnson, Siddie Joe
Midnight in Bonnie's Stall.
Johnson, Thomas
The Best Dance Hall in Iuka,
  Mississippi.
Some Scribbles for a
  Lumpfish.
Johnson, Tom
Becoming Is Perfection.
Johnson, Tommy
Big Road Blues.
Canned Heat Blues.
Maggie Campbell Blues.
Johnson, Victoria Saffelle
Dedication.
Johnson, W. Ralph
July.
Johnson, Willard
Indian Song.
Johnson, William
Chiffons!
Johnson, William Cory
Hersilia.
Johnson, William Martin
On Snow-Flakes Melting on
  His Lady's Breast.
Johnson-Cory, William
Amaturus.
Johnson, Jr, Pyke
Me and Samantha.
The Toucan.
Johnston, Bertha
Did You Ever Hear an
  English Sparrow Sing?
Johnston, George
Beside the Sea.
Bliss.
The Bulge.
Cathleen Sweeping.
Eating Fish.
The Huntress.
Indoors.
Music in the Air.

O Earth, Turn!
Rest Hour.
Veterans.
War on the Periphery.
Johnston, Gordon
The Hot Day and Human
  Nature.
Johnston, Martin
Quantum.
Uncertain Sonnets.
Johnston, Sir Charles
Air Travel in Arabia.
Johnstone, Arthur
A Fisher's Apology.
Johnstone, D. V.
Star of the Morning.
**Johnstone, Henry, Lord
Johnstone**
The Fastidious Serpent.
Jonas, Ann Rae
The Cat in the Box.
The Causes of Color.
Jonas, George
Eight Lines for a Script Girl.
Exit Lines.
Five Stanzas on Perfection.
The Glass Eaters.
Let Me Put It This Way.
Once More.
Peace.
Portrait: The Freedom
  Fighter.
Sleep Only with Strangers.
Temporal.
To Christian Montpelier.
We All Have a Bench in the
  Park to Reach.
Women Don't Travel in
  Clubcars.
Jonas, Gerald
The Day the T.V. Broke.
In Passing.
Love.
Night Thought.
Jonas, Rosalie
Ballade des Belles
  Milatraisses.
Brother Baptis' on Woman
  Suffrage.
Jonas, Samuel Alroy
Lines on the Back of a
  Confederate Note.
Jonas, Steve
Poem: "It's a dull poem."
Jones, Amanda T.
Panama.
Jones, Andrew McCord
Escape.
A Morning Kiss.
A Poem of Broken Pieces.
Snowman.
Somewhere West.
Jones, Charles L. S.
Fort Bowyer.
The Hero of Bridgewater.
Jones, Cullen
Now That the Flowers.
Jones, D.G.
After Midnight.
Annunciation.
Boy in the Lamont Poetry
  Room, Harvard.
For Spring.
"From sex, this sea...".
Northern Water Thrush.
On a Picture of Your House.
Poem for Good Friday.
The River.
These Trees Are No Forest of
  Mourners.
Jones, David
A, a, a, Domine Deus.

The Anathemata.
In Parenthesis.
The Wall.
Jones, E.B.C.
Jerked Heartstrings in Town.
Middle-Age.
Jones, Ebenezer
A Development of Idiotcy.
Eyeing the Eyes of One's
Mistress.
The Hand.
High Summer.
When the World is Burning.
Whimper of Awakening
Passion.
A Winter Hymn–to the Snow.
Jones, Edward Smyth
A Song of Thanks.
Jones, Elijah
How Big Was Alexander?
Jones, Ernest Charles
The Song of the Lower
Classes.
Jones, Evan
A Dream.
Noah's Song.
The Point.
Study in Blue.
Jones, Frederick Scheetz
On the Democracy of Yale.
Jones, G. W.
Portrait of the Pornographer
(parody).
Jones, Gayl
Journal, Part IV.
Many Die Here.
Satori.
Tripart.
Jones, Glyn
Esyllt.
Gold.
Night.
Song: "I kept neat my
virginity."
Jones, H. Bedford
How Do You Do?
Jones, Herbert
The True Romance.
Jones, Howard
Fall To.
Jones, John
To Lydia, with a Coloured
Egg, on Easter Monday.
Jones, John P.
Silver Jack's Religion.
Jones, Joshua Henry
To A Skull.
Jones, L. E.
Death.
Epigram on the Unknown
Inventor of Scissors.
Jones, Lawrence M.
I Am the Flag.
**Jones, LeRoi (Imamu Amiri
Baraka)**
An Agony. As Now.
Air.
As a Possible Lover.
At the National Black
Assembly.
Audubon, Drafted.
Babylon Revisited.
Balboa, the Entertainer.
Ballad of the Morning Streets.
Beautiful Black Women...
Biography.
Black Art.
Black Bourgeoisie.
Black Dada Nihilismus.
Black People!
Black People: This Is Our
Destiny.

Bumi.
The Clearing.
Cold Term.
Crow Jane.
The Dance.
Das Kapital.
The Dead Lady Canonized.
The Death of Nick Charles.
Duncan Spoke of a Process.
Each Morning.
The End of Man Is His
Beauty.
Epistrophe.
Evil Nigger Waits for
Lightnin'.
For Hettie.
Funeral Poem.
A Guerrilla Handbook.
Hegel.
Horatio Alger Uses Scag.
Hymn for Lanie Poo. 4. Each
Morning.
I Substitute for the Dead
Lecturer.
In Memory of Radio.
In One Battle.
Incident.
The Insidious Dr. Fu Man
Chu.
The Invention of Comics.
It's Nation Time.
Ka 'Ba.
Leadbelly Gives an
Autograph.
Legacy.
Leroy.
Letter to E. Franklin Frazier.
Like Rousseau.
Lines to Garcia Lorca.
The New World.
Notes for a Speech.
Numbers, Letters.
One Night Stand.
Ostriches & Grandmothers!
The People's Choice: The
Dream Poems II.
Planetary Exchange.
Plenty.
A Poem for Black Hearts.
Poem for Half-White College
Students.
A Poem for Speculative
Hipsters.
A Poem Some People Will
Have to Understand.
Political Poem.
The Politics of Rich Painters.
Preface to a Twenty Volume
Suicide Note.
The Pressures.
Red Light.
Return of the Native.
Snake Eyes.
Song Form.
SOS.
Study Peace.
Three Modes of History and
Culture.
Tight Rope.
To a Publisher...cut-out.
The Turncoat.
W. W.
Way out West.
We Own the Night.
The World Is Full of
Remarkable Things.
Young Soul.
Jones, Little Hat
Kentucky Blues.
Jones, Louise Seymour
Who Loves a Garden.

Jones, M. Keel
Election Reflection.
Jones, Mary Hoxie
The Four Deer.
Jones, Nancy
Running Blind.
Jones, Patricia
14th St./new york.
I Done Got So Thirsty That
My Mouth Waters at the
Thought of Rain.
Why I Like Movies.
Jones, Paul
Native African
Revolutionaries.
Jones, Paul R.
Becoming a Frog.
Jones, Rae Desmond
Age.
Jones, Ralph M.
Bed-Time.
Jones, Richard
Three Car Poems, III.
Jones, Robert
Madrigal: "My love is neither
young nor old."
Madrigal: "O I do love, then
kiss me."
Madrigal: "Shall I look."
These Days.
Jones, Rodney
The First Birth.
For the Eating of Swine.
The Mosquito.
Remembering Fire.
Thoreau.
Jones, Samuel
The Force of Love.
The Ploughman, in Imitation
of Milton.
Poverty, in Imitation of
Milton.
Jones, Sir William
The Baby.
Epigram: "On parent knees, a
naked new-born child."
An Ode in Imitation of
Alcaeus.
A Persian Song of Hafiz.
What Constitutes a State?
Jones, Thomas Gwynn
The Grave.
Jones, Thomas S.
Saint Thomas Aquinas.
Jones, Jr, Bob
Worship.
Jones, Jr, Thomas S.
Akhnaton.
As in a Rose-Jar.
Ave Atque Vale.
Clonard.
Daphne.
Empedocles.
Gautama.
In the Fall o' Year.
Lao-Tse.
The Little Ghosts.
The Path of the Stars.
Pythagoras.
Sometimes.
To Song.
Zarathustra.
Jones-Quartey, K. B.
Stranger, Why Do You
Wonder So?
Jong, Erica
Alcestis on the Poetry Circuit.
Becoming a Nun.
The Buddha in the Womb.
Climbing You.
Dearest Man-in-the-Moon.
Divorce.

For a Marriage.
How You Get Born.
In Praise of Clothes.
In Sylvia Plath Country.
Jubilate Canis.
The Man under the Bed.
Seventeen Warnings in Search
of a Feminist Poem.
Sexual Soup.
Walking through the Upper
East Side.
The Wives of Mafiosi.
The Woman Who Loved to
Cook.
Jonker, Ingrid
25 December 1960.
Begin Summer.
The Child Who Was Shot
Dead by Soldiers at Nyanga.
Dog.
Don't Sleep.
The Face of Love.
I Am with Those.
I Don't Want Any More
Visitors.
I Drift in the Wind.
Journey Round the World.
Lost City.
Pregnant Woman.
This Journey.
Time of Waiting in
Amsterdam.
When You Laugh.
When You Write Again.
Jonson, Ben
Aeglamour's Lament.
The Alchemist, 1610.
An Angel Describes Truth.
Another Birthday.
Another. In Defence of Their
Inconstancie.
Answer to Master Wither's
Song, "Shall I, Wasting in
Despair?"
Apollo's Song.
Ask Not to Know This Man.
Beauties, Have Ye Seen This
Toy.
Ben. Johnsons Sociable Rules
for the Apollo.
"Buzz," Quoth the Blue Fly.
A Celebration of Charis.
Chorus.
Clerimont's Song.
Come, My Celia.
Cynthia's Revels.
Death and Love.
The Devil Is an Ass: So
White, So Soft, So Sweet.
The Dreame.
An Elegie on the Lady Jane
Pawlet, Marchion: of
Winton.
An Epigram: "Great Charles,
among the holy gifts of
grace."
An Epigram to the Queen,
Then Lying In.
An Epistle Answering to One
That Asked to be Sealed of
the Tribe...
An Epistle to a Friend, to
Persuade Him to the Wars.
Epistle to Elizabeth, Countess
of Rutland.
An Epistle to Sir Edward
Sackville, Now Earl of
Dorset.
An Epitaph: On Elizabeth
Chute.
Epitaph on Elizabeth, L. H.

An Epitaph on Master Philip
  Gray.
An Epitaph on Master
  Vincent Corbett.
Epitaph on S.P. a Child of Q.
  El. Chappel.
Epode.
An Execration upon Vulcan.
First Three Verses of an Ode
  to Cary and Morison.
A Fit of Rime against Rime.
Fools, They Are the Only
  Nation.
Fragmentum Petronius
  Arbiter, Translated.
Francis Beaumont's Letter
  from the Country to Jonson.
The Ghyrlond of the Blessed
  Virgin Marie.
Gipsy Song.
The Glove.
Good and Great God!
Have You Seen.
The Hour Glass.
The Humble Petition of Poor
  Ben to the Best of
  Monarchs...
Hymn to Comus.
A Hymne on the Nativitie of
  My Saviour.
A Hymne to God the Father.
I Follow, Lo, the Footing.
In the Person of Woman
  Kind.
Inviting a Friend to Supper.
The Kiss.
The Lady Venetia Digby.
Love.
Love Restored (excerpt).
Love's Triumph.
Mab the Mistress-Fairy.
The Masque of Christmas.
Masque of Cupid: Up, Youths
  and Virgins, Up, and Praise.
Masque of Hymen: Glad Time
  Is at His Point Arrived.
The Masque of Queenes.
Masques.
My Picture Left in Scotland.
Nano's Song.
The New Inn.
New Yeares, Expect New
  Gifts.
A New-Yeares-Gift Sung to
  King Charles, 1635.
The Noble Balm.
The Noble Nature.
A Nymph's Passion.
Oberon, the Fairy Prince: A
  Catch.
Ode: To Sir William Sydney,
  on His Birth-Day.
On Court-Worme.
On Don Surly.
On English Monsieur.
On Giles and Joan.
On Gut.
On Lieutenant Shift.
On Lucy Countesse of
  Bedford.
On Margaret Ratcliffe.
On My First Daughter.
On My First Son.
On Playwright.
On Some-Thing, That Walkes
  Some-Where.
On Spies.
Pans Anniversarie.
A Part of an Ode.
Patrico's Song.
The Picture of Her Mind.

Pleasure Reconciled to Vertue:
  A Masque.
The Poetaster.
The Praises of a Countrie
  Life. (Horace, Epode 2).
Queen Mab.
The Return of Astraea.
The Sad Shepherd.
See the Chariot at Hand Here
  of Love.
The Shadow.
The Silent Woman:
  Clerimont's Song.
Simplex Munditiis.
Song: "If I freely may
  discover."
Song: "O, do not wanton with
  those eyes."
Song: "O, that joy so soon
  should waste!"
A Song: "Oh do not wanton
  with those eyes."
Song: "That women are but
  men's shadows."
Song: To Celia.
Song: "When Love at first did
  move."
A Sonnet, to the Noble Lady,
  the Lady Mary Worth.
To a Weak Gamester in
  Poetry.
To Doctor Empirick.
To Edward Allen.
To Fine Grand.
To Fine Lady Would-Be.
To Fool, or Knave.
To Francis Beaumont.
To Heaven.
To John Donne.
To King James.
To Lucy, Countesse of
  Bedford, with Mr. Donnes
  Satyres.
To My Booke.
To Penshurst.
To Pertinax Cob.
To Sir Henrie Savile.
To Sir Robert Wroth.
To the Ghost of Martial.
To the Immortal Memory and
  Friendship of That Noble
  Pair...
To the Learned Critic.
To the Memory of My
  Beloved the Author Mr.
  William Shakespeare...
To the Reader.
To the Same.
To the World: a Farewell for
  a Gentlewoman, Virtuous
  and Noble.
To Thomas Lord Chancellor.
To William Camden.
To William Earle of
  Pembroke.
To William Roe.
The Triumph of Charis.
Truth.
Underwoods.
Venus' Runaway.
Verses Placed Over the Door
  at the Entrance into the
  Apollo Room...
The Vision of Delight.
Volpone.
Why I Write Not of Love.
The Witches' Charm.
The Witches' Song.
Jordan, A. C.
  You Tell Me to Sit Quiet.
Jordan, Barbara Leslie
  Desert Shipwreck.

Jordan, Charlie
  Hunkie Tunkie.
  Keep It Clean.
Jordan, Charlotte B.
  To Borglum's Seated Statue of
    Abraham Lincoln.
Jordan, David Starr
  Limerick: "There was a young
    lady whose dream."
  Men Told Me, Lord!
  Viverols.
**Jordan, Dorothy and Annie
McVicar**
  The Blue Bells of Scotland.
Jordan, Ethel Blair
  Disarm the Hearts.
Jordan, June
  All the World Moved.
  Cameo No. II.
  Clock on Hancock Street.
  For My Mother.
  Getting down to Get over.
  If You Saw a Negro Lady.
  In Memoriam: Martin Luther
    King, Jr.
  My Sadness Sits Around Me.
  The New Pieta: For the
    Mothers and Children of
    Detroit.
  Nobody Riding the Roads
    Today.
  Okay "Negroes."
  Poem for My Family: Hazel
    Griffin and Victor Hernandez
    Cruz.
  Poem for Nana.
  Poem from the Empire State.
  Poem to My Sister, Ethel
    Ennis....
  Queen Anne's Lace.
  The Reception.
  Sunflower Sonnet Number
    One.
  Sunflower Sonnet Number
    Two.
  Towards a City That Sings.
  Uncle Bull-Boy.
  Unemployment/Monologue.
  What Happens.
  What Would I Do White?
Jordan, Norman
  August 2.
  Black Warrior.
  Cities and Seas.
  Ending.
  Feeding the Lions.
  July 31.
Jordan, Thomas
  The Careless Gallant.
  Coronemus Nos Rosis
    Antequam Marcescant.
  The Epicure Sung by One in
    the Habit of a Town Gallant.
  Pyms Anarchy.
Jordana, Elena
  Tango.
Josa
  Crocuses.
Joseph, Chief
  War.
Joseph, Jenny
  Back to Base.
  Dog Body and Cat Mind.
  The Lost Continent.
  Rose in the Afternoon.
  Warning.
Joseph, Lawrence
  When You've Been Here Long
    Enough.
Joseph, Michael Kennedy
  Braque.
  The Dancing Ploughmen.

  Drunken Gunner.
  For Any Beachhead.
  Mercury Bay Eclogue.
  New Moses.
  Old Montague.
  On the Mountain.
  Secular Litany.
  Vacation Exercise.
  Victory March.
Joseph, Rosemary
  Baking Day.
Joseph of the Studium, Saint
  The Finished Course.
Joslin, Dorothy
  Sonnet for a Loved One.
Joso
  Haiku: "No need to cling."
  Haiku: "That duck, bobbing
    up".
  Haiku: "These branches..."
  The Little Duck.
Josselyn, John
  And the Bitter Storm
    Augments; the Wild Winds
    Wage.
  Description of a New England
    Spring.
  Verses Made Sometime Since
    upon the Picture....
Joyce, James
  Alone.
  Bahnhofstrasse.
  The Ballad of Persse O'Reilly.
  Bid Adieu to Maidenhood.
  Chamber Music.
  Ecce Puer.
  Flood.
  A Flower Given to My
    Daughter.
  Gas from a Burner.
  The Holy Office.
  I Hear an Army.
  A Memory of the Players in a
    Mirror at Midnight.
  Night Piece.
  O Sweetheart, Hear You.
  On Lady Gregory's Search for
    Talent.
  On the Beach at Fontana.
  The Right Heart in the
    Wrong Place.
  She Weeps over Rahoon.
  Simples.
  Sleep Now, O Sleep Now.
  Soil Searcher.
  Song: "O, it was out by
    Donncarney."
  This Heart That Flutters Near
    My Heart.
  Thou Leanest to the Shell of
    Night.
  Though I Thy Mithridates
    Were.
  Tutto e Sciolto.
  Ulysses (excerpt).
  What Counsel Has the
    Hooded Moon.
Joyce, Robert Dwyer
  The Leprahaun.
Joyce, William
  Small Town.
Juan II of Castile
  Cancion.
Juana Ines de la Cruz, Sister
  Coplas about the Soul which
    Suffers with Impatience.
  The Divine Narcissus.
  First Dream (Excerpt).
  Green Enravishment of
    Human Life.
  I Can't Hold You and I Can't
    Leave You.

Ignorant Men, Who Disclaim.
In the Face of Grief.
In Which She Satisfies a Fear
  with the Rhetoric of Tears.
Redondillas.
She Attempts to Refute the
  Praises That Truth...
She Proves the Inconsistency
  of the Desires and Criticism
  of Men...
Stay, Shade of My Shy
  Treasure!
This Coloured Counterfeit
  That Thou Beholdest.
This Evening, My Love, Even
  as I Spoke Vainly.
To Celio.
To Her Portrait.

Judd, Slyvester
  Light of the World.

Judkins, Charles Otis
  The Play.

Judson, Adoniram
  Come Holy Spirit, Dove
    Divine.
  In Spite of Sorrow.
  Our Father, God.

Judson, Emily Chubbuck
  My Bird.
  Watching.

Judson, Sarah
  Proclaim the Lofty Praise.

Juergensen, Hans
  Anne Sexton.

Juhasz, Ferenc
  Birth of the Foal.

Juhasz, Gyula
  The Wilderness.

Juhasz, Suzanne
  ...The Dancer from the Dance.
  Saying Goodbye.

Julal ed-Din Rumi
  A Beauty That All Night
    Long.

Jules-Bois, H. A.
  India the Magic.

Jumper, Will C.
  California Quail in January.

Junge, Carl S.
  The Dinosaur.

Junkins, Donald
  Walden in July.

Justema, William
  Song: "This is the song."

Justice, Donald
  About My Poems.
  Anonymous Drawing.
  Another Song.
  Beyond the Hunting Woods.
  A Birthday Candle.
  Bus Stop.
  But That Is Another Story.
  Childhood.
  Counting the Mad.
  Crossing Kansas by Train.
  A Dancer's Life.
  Dreams of Water.
  An Elegy Is Preparing Itself.
  Elsewheres.
  First Death.
  Girl Sitting Alone at Party.
  The Grandfathers.
  Here in Katmandu.
  Houses.
  In Bertram's Garden.
  In the Attic.
  Incident in a Rose Garden.
  Landscape with Little Figures.
  A Local Storm.
  Love's Stratagems.
  Luxury.
  The Man Closing Up.

Memo from the Desk of X.
Memory of a Porch.
Men at Forty.
The Missing Person.
Ode to a Dressmaker's
  Dummy.
On a Painting by Patient B of
  the Independence State
  Hospital...
On the Death of Friends in
  Childhood.
Party.
Poem: "Time and the weather
  wear away."
Poem to Be Read at 3 a.m.
Sestina.
The Snowfall.
Sonatina in Yellow.
Song: "Morning opened."
Sonnet for My Father.
Southern Gothic.
Tales from a Family Album.
The Thin Man.
To Waken a Small Person.
The Tourist from Syracuse.
Variations for Two Pianos.
Variations on Southern
  Themes.
White Notes.
Women in Love.

Justus, May
  The Dress of Spring.
  Footwear.
  Remember September.
  Winds A-Blowing.
  Witchwood.

**Juvenal (Decimas Junius
  Juvenalis)**
  Against Women.
  Celestial Wisdom.
  Satires.
  The Vanity of Human Wishes.

K

"K., A."
  La Donna E Mobile.

"K., E. H."
  The City Church.

Ka-ehu
  The Leper.

Kaberry, C. J.
  The Indian Elephant.

Kabir
  The Radiance.
  Songs of Kabir.
  Two Songs, II.
  What Form or Shape to
    Describe?

Kadhani, Mudereri
  Rekayi Tangwena.

Kaffka, Margit
  Father.

Kaga no Chiyo
  Haiku: "Autumn's bright
    moon."
  Haiku: On Her Child's Death.
  Haiku: "Spring rain."
  Haiku: "The dew of the
    rouge-flower."
  Haiku: To Her Husband, at
    the Wedding.

Kagawa, Toyohiko
  Love.
  Meditation.

Kageyama, Yuri
  A Day in a Long Hot
    Summer.

Disco Chinatown.
Love Poem.
My Mother Takes a Bath.
Strings/Himo.

Kahn, Gustave
  Homage.
  The Pilgrim from the East.
  Song: "O lovely April, rich
    and bright."
  The Temple.
  The Word.
  You Masks of the
    Masquerade.

Kahn, Hannah
  Signature.
  To Be Black, To Be Lost.

Kaiama
  Song: "Misty and dim, a bush
    in the wilds of Kapa'a."

Kaikini, P. R.
  The Donkey.

Kais, Imr el *See* **Imr el Kais**

Kalar, Joseph
  Invocation to the Wind.
  Paper Mill.

Kalevala
  Prayer for Rain.

Kalidasa
  Aja's Lament over His Dead
    Wife.
  The Cloud-Messenger.
  Nightfall.
  Salutation of the Dawn.
  The Seasons.

Kallman, Chester
  Dead Center.
  Little Epithalamium.
  Night Music.
  Nightmare of a Cook.
  A Romance.
  Tellers of Tales.
  Urban History.

Kalola
  Fathomless Is My Love.

Kamal ud-Din of Isfahan
  O Love, Thy Hair!

Kamenetz, Rodger
  Pilpul.
  Scraps.
  Why I Can't Write My
    Autobiography.

Kaminsky, Marc
  Erev Shabbos.

Kamm, Nancy P.
  Waiting Carefully.

Kammeyer, Virginia Maughan
  Compensation.

Kamzon, Jacob David
  Very Fair My Lot.

Kanabus, Henry
  The Access.
  Accordance.
  The Scythe.

Kanalenstein, Ruben
  Jerusalem.

Kanbara, Yumei
  The Dark-Red Shadow-Spots.

Kandel, Lenore
  Blues for Sister Sally.
  Bus Ride.

Kane, Douglas V.
  Westering.

Kane, Julie
  Cornelia's Window.

Kaneko, Lonny
  Coming Home from Camp.
  Family Album.
  The Secret.
  Violets for Mother.

Kanie, Anoma
  All That You Have Given
    Me, Africa.

Kanik, Orhan and Halman Veli
  Being Sad.
  People.

Kantor, Mackinlay
  Appomattox.

Kaplan, Allan
  Marvelous.

Kaplan, Milton
  Ballet.
  The Circus.
  The Knife.

Kaplan, Rebbekka
  You Are More Than I Need.

Karelli, Zoe
  Presences.

Karibo, Minji
  Superstition.

Kariuki, Joseph E.
  New Life.

Karlen, Arno
  Bury Me in America.

Karlfeldt, Erik Axel
  Imagined Happiness.

Karlfeldt, Erik Axel
  A Vagrant.

Karni, Yehuda
  Chambers of Jerusalem.
  The Four of Them.
  Place Me in the Breach.

Karoniaktatie
  Dead Heroes.
  Elegy.
  Stone Song (Zen Rock) the
    Seer & the Unbeliever.

Karp, Vickie
  The Last Farmer in Queens.

Karsner, Walta
  Xmas Time.

Kasa, Lady
  I dreamed I held.
  I love and fear him.
  Manyoshu: To Love Someone.

Kaschnitz, Marie L.
  Humility.
  Resurrection.

Kasdaglis, Lina
  Traffic Lights.

Kasmuneh
  Overripe Fruit.
  The Timid Gazelle.

Kass, Jerry
  Fidelity.

Kassia
  Epigram: "A woman working
    hard and wisely."
  Epigram: "Poverty? wealth?
    seek neither."
  Epigram: "Wealth covers sin."
  Mary Magdalene.
  Sticheron for Matins,
    Wednesday of Holy Week.

Kastner, Erich
  The Moral Taxi Ride.
  Ragout fin de siecle.
  Rooming-House Melancholy.

Katav, Shalom
  Pleading Voices.

Kates, J.
  Life Story.

Katrovas, Richard
  Elegy for My Mother.

Katz, Menke
  In the Year of Two Thousand.

Katzin, Olga *See* **"Sagittarius"**

Katzman, Allen
  The Rhododendron Plant.

Kauffman, Reginald Wright
  The Call.
  Troia Fuit.
  The Wastrel.

Kauffman, Russell E.
  The Christ of God.

Kaufman, Bob
African Dream.
Afterwards, They Shall
  Dance.
Battle Report.
Benediction.
Blues Note.
Cincophrenicpoet.
Falling.
I Have Folded My Sorrows.
I, Too, Know What I Am
  Not.
Mingus.
Patriotic Ode on
  the...Persecution of Charlie
  Chaplin.
Response.
To My Son Parker, Asleep in
  the Next Room.
Unholy Missions.
Walking Parker Home.
When We Hear the Eye
  Open...
Kaufman, George S.
Advice to Worriers.
Lines to a Man Who Thinks
  That Apple Betty With Hard
  Sauce Is Food..
Kaufman, Herbert
This Is Your Hour.
Kaufman, Shirley
Apples.
Beetle on the Shasta Daylight.
The Burning of the Birds.
Deja Vu.
Dinosaur Tracks in Beit Zayit.
Her Going.
His Wife.
Leah.
Looking at Henry Moore's
  Elephant Skull Etchings in
  Jerusalem...
Looking for Maimonides:
  Tiberias.
Loving.
Mothers, Daughter.
Nechama.
New Graveyard: Jerusalem.
Next Year, in Jerusalem.
Room.
Starting over.
Watts.
Wonders.
Kavanagh, P. J.
Birthday.
Praying.
The Temperance Billiards
  Rooms.
Kavanagh, Patrick
Advent.
Ante-Natal Dream.
Art McCooey.
Auditors In.
Bluebells for Love.
Canal Bank Walk.
Candida.
A Christmas Childhood.
Come Dance with Kitty
  Stobling.
Dear Folks.
Epic.
Father Mat.
A Glut on the Market.
Gold Watch.
The Great Hunger.
The Hospital.
I Had a Future.
If Ever You Go to Dublin
  Town.
Important Statement.
In Memory of My Mother.
Inniskeen Road: July Evening.

Innocence.
Intimate Parnassus.
Is.
Kerr's Ass.
Leave Them Alone.
Lecture Hall.
Lines Written on a Seat on
  the Grand Canal, Dublin.
The Long Garden.
Memory of Brother Michael.
Memory of My Father.
Morning.
October.
On Looking into E. V. Rieu's
  Homer.
The One.
Peace.
Pegasus.
Prelude.
Pursuit of an Ideal.
Question to Life.
The Road to Hate.
Sanctity.
The Self-Slaved.
Shancoduff.
Spraying the Potatoes.
Stony Grey Soil.
Tarry Flynn (excerpt).
Temptation in Harvest.
"Through the Open Door..."
Tinker's Wife.
To Hell with Commonsense.
To the Man after the Harrow.
Kavinoky, Bernice
Poet to Dancer.
Kawai Chigetsu-Ni
Haiku: "Grasshoppers."
Kay, Charles De See De Kay,
Charles
Kay, Ellen de Young
Cante Hondo.
The Magnanimous.
Pathedy of Manners.
Tiresias' Lament.
To a Blue Hippopotamus.
Kay, W. Lowrie
Lancaster County Tragedy.
Kaye-Smith, Sheila
Ascension Day.
Lady Day in Harvest.
Kayper-Mensah, Albert
A Second Birthday.
Kazan, Molly
Thanksgiving, 1963.
Kazantzis, Judith
Arachne.
The Frightened Flier Goes
  North.
In Memory, 1978.
A Woman Making Advances
  Publicly.
Keach, Benjamin
How Glorious Are the
  Morning Stars.
Kearney, Lawrence
Cuba.
The Cyclists.
Kearney, Peadar
Down by the Glenside.
The Soldier's Song.
The Tri-Coloured Ribbon.
Whack Fol the Diddle.
Kearns, Josie
The Planets Line Up for a
  Demonstration.
Kearns, Lionel
Environment.
Foreign Aid.
In-Group.
Insight.
Keary, E.
Old Age.

Keate, George
Ancient and Modern Rome
  (excerpt).
A Burlesque Ode, on the
  Author's Clearing a New
  House...(excerpt).
Keating, Diane
Boxcars.
Fecundity.
Flower Song.
Glory Be to God for Dappled
  Things.
Leda Forgets the Wings of the
  Swan.
Mad Apples.
Mooncalf I.
Summer Solstice.
Summons for the Undead.
Keating, Geoffrey
Keen Thyself, Poor Wight.
Mourn for Yourself.
My Grief on Fal's Proud
  Plain.
O Woman Full of Wile.
Keating, Norma
Never, Never Can
  Nothingness Come.
Keats, John
Addressed to Haydon.
La Belle Dame Sans Merci.
Bright Star (Original version).
Cancelled Stanza of the Ode
  on Melancholy.
Daisy's Song.
Dawlish Fair.
The Day Is Gone.
December.
Dedication, to Leigh Hunt,
  Esq.
Easily onward, thorough
  flowers and weed...
Endymion.
Epistle to George Keats
  (excerpt).
Epistle to John Hamilton
  Reynolds.
The Eve of St. Agnes.
The Eve of St. Mark.
Faery Song.
The Fall of Hyperion.
Fancy.
Fragment of an Ode to Maia.
From a Letter.
Goldfinches.
Happy Insensibility.
He Saw Far in the Concave
  Green of the Sea.
How Fevered Is the Man.
How Many Bards Gild the
  Lapses of Time!
The Human Seasons.
Hyperion.
I cry your mercy–pity–love!–
  aye, love!
I Had a Dove.
I Stood Tip-Toe.
If by Dull Rhymes Our
  English Must Be Chained.
Imitation of Spenser.
Isabella, or The Pot of Basil.
Lamia.
Lines on Seeing a Lock of
  Milton's Hair.
Lines on the Mermaid Tavern.
Lines to Fanny (excerpt).
Meg Merrilies.
Minnows.
Modern Love.
Morning.
Ode: "Bards of Passion and of
  Mirth."
Ode on a Grecian Urn.

Ode on Indolence.
Ode on Melancholy.
Ode to a Nightingale: The
  Nightingale.
Ode to Apollo.
Ode to Fanny.
Ode to Psyche.
On a Dream (after Reading
  Dante's Episode of Paolo and
  Francesca).
On an Engraved Gem of
  Leander.
On Death.
On Fame.
On First Looking into
  Chapman's Homer.
On Mrs. Reynolds's Cat.
On Oxford (parody).
On Seeing the Elgin Marbles.
On Sitting Down to Read
  "King Lear" Once Again.
On the Grasshopper and the
  Cricket.
On the Sonnet.
The Poet.
A Portrait (parody).
A Real Woman.
The Realm of Fancy.
Robin Hood.
Saturn Fallen.
Sharing Eve's Apple.
The Shell's Song.
The Sigh of Silence.
Sleep and Poetry.
Solitude.
A Song About Myself, st. 4.
Sonnet: After Dark Vapors.
Sonnet: "Keen, fitful gusts are
  whisp'ring here and there."
Sonnet on the Sea.
Sonnet to a Young Lady Who
  Sent Me a Laurel Crown.
Sonnet to Byron.
Sonnet to Chatterton.
Sonnet: To Homer.
Sonnet: "To one who has been
  long in city pent."
Sonnet Written at the End of
  "The Floure and the Lefe."
Sonnet Written in Disgust of
  Vulgar Supersitition.
Sonnet Written on a Blank
  Page in Shakespeare's
  Poems....
Sonnet: Written on the Day
  that Mr. Leigh Hunt Left
  Prison.
Sweet Peas.
The Terror of Death.
This Living Hand.
'Tis the Witching Hour of
  Night.
To a Cat.
To Ailsa Rock.
To Autumn.
To Charles Cowden Clarke.
To Fancy.
To Fanny.
To Leigh Hunt, Esq.
To My Brother George.
To My Brothers.
To Psyche.
To Sleep.
To Spenser.
To the Nile.
To the Poets.
What the Thrush Said.
Where Be You Going, You
  Devon Maid?
Where Didst Thou Find,
  Young Bard.
Where's the Poet?

Why Did I Laugh To-night?
Written upon the Top of Ben
   Nevis.
Keble, John
Balaam.
The Effect of Example.
Eleventh Sunday after Trinity.
Evening.
Fill High the Bowl.
Forest Leaves in Autumn
   (excerpt).
Help Us to Live.
Holy Matrimony.
Morning.
Morning Hymn.
November.
Purity of Heart.
Red o'er the Forest.
St. Stephen's Day.
Third Sunday in Lent.
United States.
We Need Not Bid, for
   Cloistered Cell.
Whitsunday.
Keech, Benjamin
Discovery.
Little Words.
Love is Kind.
True to theBest.
Keeler, Charles Augustus
Black Sailor's Chanty.
Camilla.
Cleaning Ship.
An Ocean Lullaby.
Keeler, Greg
American Falls.
Nymphing through Car
   Windows.
Salmon Fly Hatch on Yankee
   Jim Canyon of the
   Yellowstone.
Spring Catch.
Keeling, Mildred
God's World.
Keenan, Deborah
Folds of a White Dress/Shaft
   of Light.
Keene, H. G.
The Taj.
Keens, William
A Place by the River.
Kees, Weldon
Aspects of Robinson.
Back.
The Beach in August.
The Cats.
Colloquy.
The Coming of the Plague.
The Contours of Fixation.
The Conversation in the
   Drawingroom.
Crime Club.
A Distance from the Sea.
Early Winter.
Five.
For My Daughter.
Guide to the Symphony.
The Heat in the Room.
Henry James at Newport.
Homage to Arthur Waley.
The Hourglass.
January.
Midnight.
Obituary.
The Patient Is Rallying.
Problems of a Journalist.
Relating to Robinson.
River Song.
Robinson.
Robinson at Home.
Round.
Saratoga Ending.

Small Prayer.
The Smiles of the Bathers.
Testimonies.
La Vita Nuova.
Wet Thursday.
Keesing, Nancy
Bread.
Old Men.
A Queer Thing.
Revelation.
Reverie of a Mum.
Wandering Jews.
Kefala, Antigone
Saturday Night.
Kegels, Anne-Marie
I write to make you suffer.
Nocturnal Heart.
When I strip.
Keiter, Anne
Past Love.
Sunday Funnies.
Keith, George
How Firm a Foundation.
Keith, Joseph Joel
Definitions.
Immaculate Palm.
In the First House.
She Walks.
Though She Slumbers.
Keithley, George
Black Hawk in Hiding.
Buster Keaton & the Cops.
The Child.
The Donner Party (excerpt).
Mardi Gras.
Morning Star Man.
On Clark Street in Chicago.
A Song for New Orleans.
The Thief's Niece.
To Bring Spring.
Waiting for Winter.
The Woman.
Keizer, Garret
The Tourist.
Kell, Richard
Calypso.
Fishing Harbour towards
   Evening.
The Makers.
Memorandum for Minos.
Pigeons.
Kelleher, D. L.
For C. K.
Its Name Is Known.
Mother.
An Upper Room.
Kelleher, John
Snow.
Keller, David
In the Dream of the Body.
Keller, Helen
In the Garden of the Lord.
Keller, Martha
Andrew Jackson.
Brady's Bend.
Deadfall.
Mountain Meadows.
Kelley, Andrew J. *See* "Mix,
   Parmenas"
Kelley, Parham J.
Heir to Several Yesterdays.
Kelley, Reeve Spencer
Back Again from Yucca Flats.
Rain in the Southwest.
The Sound of Morning in
   New Mexico.
Kelley, Shannon Keith
That Man in Manhattan.
Kellog, Arthur L.
The Hayseed.
Kelly, Blanche Mary
Brother Juniper.

The Gaelic.
The Housewife's Prayer.
The Kingfisher.
The Mirror.
Omniscience.
Silentium Altum.
Kelly, Conor
Nocturne: Lake Huron.
Kelly, Dave
And Then What?
The Day the Beatles Lost One
   to the Flesh-Eating Horse.
Eight Miles South of Grand
   Haven.
Fall Letter.
Kelly, Dennis
Chicken.
Kelly, J.W.
Slide, Kelly, Slide.
Throw Him Down,
   McCloskey.
Kelly, M.
Last Week I Took a Wife.
Kelly, Robert
The Alchemist.
The Boar.
The Boat.
The Book of Persephone.
The Exchanges II.
Going.
Knee Lunes.
Last Light.
Moonshot.
Parallel Texts.
Poem for Easter.
The Process.
Round Dance, & Canticle.
The Sound.
Sun of the Center.
To Her Body, Against Time.
Kelly, Roy
Death, Don't Be Boring
   (parody).
Ode to a Nightingale
   (parody).
Kelly, Thomas
The Head That Once Was
   Crowned with Thorns.
Kelly, Walt
Boston Charlie.
How Low Is the Lowing
   Herd.
Kelpius, Johannes
I Love My Jesus Quite Alone.
Kelso, Ian
Busy Old Fool (parody).
Kemble, Frances Anne
Absence.
Dream Land.
Faith.
Lament of a Mocking-Bird.
Kemp, Harry
Alienation.
Blind.
The Conquerors.
Farewell.
God the Architect.
He Did Not Know.
The Hummingbird.
Joses, the Brother of Jesus.
Literary Love.
Love-Faith.
The Passing Flower.
A Phantasy of Heaven.
A Prayer.
Resurrection.
A Seaman's Confession of
   Faith.
Tell All the World.
The Voice of Christmas.
Kempf, Elizabeth
Before the Dive.

Kempis, Thomas a *See* **Thomas a
   Kempis**
Ken, Thomas
An Anodyne.
Direct This Day.
An Evening Hymn.
Morning Hymn.
Now.
The Priest of Christ.
Kendall, Henry Clarence
Bell-Birds.
Beyond Kerguelen.
Christmas Creek.
Jim the Splitter.
The Last of His Tribe.
Mooni.
Orara.
Prefatory Sonnet.
The Rain Comes Sobbing to
   the Door.
September in Australia.
Kendall, John
The Contented Bachelor.
Kendall, John Kaye
The Cat That Followed His
   Nose.
My Last Illusion.
Kendall, Laura E.
An Evening Prayer.
Kendall, May
Ballad.
The Lay of the Trilobite.
The Seraph and the Snob.
Taking Long Views.
Kendrick, John F.
Christians at War.
Kenji, Miyazawa
Moon, Son of Heaven.
Kennedy, Benjamin Hall
List of Prepositions.
Memorial Lines on the
   Gender of Latin
   Substantives.
On Christopher Wordsworth,
   Master of Trinity.
The Roman Calendar.
Kennedy, Charles W.
I've Worked for a Silver
   Shilling.
Kennedy, Edward D.
Strange, Is It Not.
Kennedy, Edwin O.
A Prayer for Charity.
Kennedy, G. A. Studdert
My Peace I Give unto You.
The Rose.
Waste.
When through the Whirl of
   Wheels.
Work.
Kennedy, Gerta
At the Nadir.
Chesapeake.
Christmas Songs.
Song of January.
Kennedy, Harry
Say "Au Revoir," but Not
   "Good-Bye."
Kennedy, James
The Exile's Reveries.
Kennedy, Leo
Epithalamium.
Mole Talk.
Rite of Spring.
Words for a Resurrection.
Kennedy, Mary
The Indolent Gardener.
The Newborn Colt.
The Unfortunate Mole.
Kennedy, Sara Beaumont
The Prayer Rug.

Kennedy, Terry
  An Easy Poem.
Kennedy, Walter
  Honour with Age.
Kennedy, X. J.
  The Abominable Baseball Bat.
  The Aged Wino's Counsel to
    a Young Man on the Brink
    of Marriage.
  Apocrypha.
  Ars Poetica.
  Artificer.
  At a Low Mass for Two Hot-
    Rodders.
  B Negative.
  Birth Report.
  Brats.
  Consumer's Report.
  Cross Ties.
  The Death of Professor
    Backwards.
  Down in Dallas.
  Driving Cross-Country.
  Ecology.
  Edgar's Story.
  Epitaph for a Postal Clerk.
  Faces from a Bestiary.
  Father and Mother.
  First Confession.
  For the ERA Crusaders.
  From Emily Dickinson in
    Southern California.
  Golgotha.
  Great-Great Grandma, Don't
    Sleep in Your Treehouse
    Tonight.
  The Haunted Oven.
  Hearthside Story.
  Hickenthrift and Hickenloop.
  In a Prominent Bar in
    Secaucus One Day.
  In the Motel.
  Japanese Beetles.
  Keep a Hand on Your
    Dream.
  Lasagna.
  Last Child.
  Last Lines.
  Lilith.
  Little Elegy.
  Loose Woman.
  Mingled Yarns.
  Mother's Nerves.
  Nothing in Heaven Functions
    As It Ought.
  Nude Descending a Staircase.
  Old Men Pitching Horseshoes.
  On a Child Who Lived One
    Minute.
  One A. M.
  One Winter Night in August.
  Overheard in the Louvre.
  Rondel.
  Solitary Confinement.
  Song to the Tune of
    "Somebody Stole My Gal."
  Space.
  To Dorothy on Her Exclusion
    from the Guinness Book of
    World Records.
  To Mercury.
  To the Muse.
  An Unfinished Work
    (Excerpt).
  Vulture.
  A Water Glass of Whisky.
  The Whales off Wales.
  The Witnesses.
Kennelly, Brendan
  The Grip.
  My Dark Fathers.
  Proof.

The Thatcher.
Kenner, Peggy Susberry
  Black Taffy.
  Comments.
  Image in the Mirror.
  No Bargains Today.
  The Round Table.
Kennet, Lord See **Young,
  Edward Hilton**
Kenney, James
  The Green Leaves All Turn
    Yellow.
  The Old Story over Again.
Kennick, T.
  You Naughty, Naughty Men.
Kenny, Maurice
  Corn-Planter.
  December.
  Going Home.
  They Tell Me I Am Lost.
  Wild Strawberry.
Kenny, Nick
  Patty-Poem.
Kenseth, Arnold
  B-52s.
  How They Came from the
    Blue Snows.
  To the Ladies.
Kent, Margaret
  The Stammerers.
Kent, Richard B.
  Summer Storm.
Kent, Rolly
  The Old Wife.
Kenyon, Bernice Lesbia
  Homecoming in Storm.
  Night of Rain.
Kenyon, James Benjamin
  The Bedouins of the Skies.
  Bring Tem Not Back.
  A Challenge.
  Come Slowly, Paradise.
  Death and Night.
  The Play.
  Tacita.
  The Two Spirits.
Kenyon, John
  Champagne Rosee.
Keohler, Thomas
  Night's Ancient Cloud.
Keppel, Caroline
  Robin Adair.
Keppel, David
  Trouble.
Keppel, Frederick
  A Plain Man's Dream.
Ker, L.
  The Death of the Gods. An
    Ode.
Ker, W. P.
  A Song of Degrees.
  Theme and Variations.
  There Is Snowdrift on the
    Mountain.
Kerehoma, Rarawa
  A Sentinel's Song.
Kernahan, Coulson
  I ran for a catch.
Kerner, Justinus
  Home-Sickness.
Kerouac, Jack
  How to Meditate.
  Mexico City Blues.
  My Gang.
  Pull My Daisy.
  The Sea Shroud.
Kerr, Hugh Thomson
  Thy Will Be Done.
"Kerr, Orpheus C." See **Newell,
  Robert Henry**
Kerr, Walter H.
  Curtains for a Spinster.

The Dignity of Man–Lesson
  #1.
The Proud Trees.
Vilanelle.
Kerr, Watson
  The Ancient Thought.
Kersh, Gerald
  A Soldier: His Prayer.
Kessler, Jascha
  Following the Sun.
  The Gardener at Thirty.
  High Summer.
  Looting.
  My Grandmother's Funeral.
  The Nightmare.
  October Flies.
  P.S.
  Requiem for and Abstract
    Artist.
  A Still Life.
  The Technique of Laughter.
  The Technique of Love.
  The Technique of Power.
  Waiting for Lilith.
Ketcham, Howard
  Limerick: "This bird is the
    Keel-billed Toucan."
Ketchum, Annie Chambers
  The Bonnie Blue Flag.
Ketchum, Arthur
  Candle-Lighting Song.
  Countersign.
  The Spirit of the Birch.
  Thanksgiving.
Kethe, William
  Old Hundredth.
  Scotch Te Deum.
  Such as in God the Lord Do
    Trust.
  Thy Mercies, Lord, to Heaven
    Reach.
Kettle, Thomas Michael
  The Lady of Life.
  Parnell.
  To My Daughter Betty, the
    Gift of God.
Key, Francis Scott
  Hymn.
  On a Young Lady's Going
    into a Shower Bath.
  Our Rock.
  The Star-Spangled Banner.
  To My Cousin Mary, for
    Mending My Tobacco
    Pouch.
  Written at the White Sulphur
    Springs.
Keyes, Sidney
  Against a Second Coming:
    The Walking Woman.
  The Anti-Symbolist.
  Death and the Plowman.
  Early Spring.
  Elegy.
  The Foreign Gate (excerpt).
  The Gardener.
  The Grail.
  Greenwich Observatory.
  Holstenwall.
  Moonlight Night on the Port.
  Neutrality.
  Pheasant.
  Plowman.
  Remember Your Lovers.
  Rome Remember.
  The Snow.
  Time Will Not Grant.
  Timoshenko.
  Were I to Mount beyond the
    Field.
  The Wilderness.
  William Wordsworth.

William Yeats in Limbo.
Keysner, Blanche Whiting
  Old River Road.
Kgositsile, Keorapetse
  For Euse, Ayi Kwei & Gwen
    Brooks.
  Ivory Masks in Orbit.
  My Name Is Afrika.
  New Age.
  Origins.
  Requiem for My Mother.
  Spirits Unchained.
Khaketla, B. Makalo
  Lesotho.
Khaketla, N. M.
  The White and the Black.
Khansa
  Elegy for Her Brother, Sakhr.
  Tears.
Kherdian, David
  Dear Mrs. McKinney of the
    Sixth Grade:.
  For My Father: Two Poems.
  Little Sis.
  Melkon.
  That Day.
  Uncle Jack.
  When These Old Barns Lost
    Their Inhabitants....
  Winter, New Hampshire.
Khodasevich, Vladislav
  It Scarcely Seems Worth
    While.
Khoury-Gata, Venus
  The autumn made colors
    burn.
  Your cheeks flat on the sand.
Ki-no-Akimine
  The Beloved Person Must I
    Think.
Kibbs, Henry "Harry"
  Indigo Pete's J. B.
Kibkarjuk
  Song of the Rejected Woman.
Kickham, Charles Joseph
  The Irish Peasant Girl.
  Rory of the Hill.
Kicknosway, Faye
  After Hilary, Age 5.
  Cats Is Wheels.
  Crystal.
  From 2nd Chance Man: The
    Cigarette Poem.
  Gracie.
  The Horse.
  I Wake, My Friend, I.
  In Mysterious Ways.
  Mr. Muscle-On.
  Old Man.
  Rapunzel.
  There Is No.
Kiefer, Rita Brady
  Agent Orange.
Kieffaber, Alan
  Easter Egg.
Kieffer, Paul
  Limerick: "Yes, theirs was a
    love that was tidal."
Kieran, John
  Advice from an Expert.
  To Lou Gehrig.
Kii, Lady
  I Know the Reputation.
Kikaku
  The Butterfly.
Kikurio
  Daffodils.
Kilgore, James C.
  The Gray Oak Twilight.
  She Told Me.
  The White Man Pressed the
    Locks.

Killigrew, Anne
A Farewel to Worldly Joyes.
On Death.
Killigrew, Henry
Song.
Kilmer, Aline
Ambition.
Experience.
I Shall Not Be Afraid.
Light Lover.
The Masquerader.
My Mirror.
Remembrance.
The Stirrup Cup.
Things.
To Aphrodite: With a Mirror.
A Wind Rose in the Night.
Kilmer, Joyce
Ballade of My Lady's Beauty.
A Blue Valentine.
Daw's Dinner.
Easter.
Gates and Doors.
The House with Nobody in It.
The King's Ballad.
Mid-Ocean in War-Time.
The Peacemaker.
Pennies.
Poets.
Prayer of a Soldier in France.
Roofs.
Rouge Bouquet.
Servant Girl and Grocer's
  Boy.
Trees.
The White Ships and the Red.
Kilmer, Kenton
Yellow.
Kilner, Dorothy
Henry's Secret.
Kim Nam-jo
My Baby Has No Name Yet.
Kim Yo-sop
Shooting at the Moon.
Kimball, Hannah Parker
Beyond.
One Way of Trusting.
Soul and Sense.
Kimball, Harriet McEwen
All's Well.
The Blessed Task.
The Guest.
White Azaleas.
Kimball, Jacob
Thy Praise, O God, in Zion
  Waits.
Kimbrough, Lottie
Going Away Blues.
Rolling Log Blues.
Kindig, L. James
Is It Nothing to You?
King, Alfred Castner
The Miner.
The Ruined Cabin.
King, Anna M.
Faith and Sight.
King, B. B.
Why I Sing the Blues.
King, Ben
The Cultured Girl Again.
The Hair-Tonic Bottle.
How Often (parody).
If I Should Die To-Night.
The Mermaid.
The Pessimist.
King, Black Ivory
Flying Crow.
King, E.L.M.
Robin's Song.
King, Edith
The Duck.
The Holly.

The Rabbit.
King, Edward
The Tsigane's Canzonet.
A Woman's Execution.
King, Ethel
Wood Music.
King, Francis
Seance.
King, Georgiana Goddard
A Man Called Dante, I Have
  Heard.
Song: "Something calls and
  whispers, along the city
  street."
King, Harriet Eleanor Hamilton
The Garden of the Holy
  Souls.
The Sermon in the Hospital
  (excerpt).
King, Helen
The Human Touch, 2.
**King, Henry, Bishop of
Chichester**
The Anniverse: An Elegy.
Conjectured to Be upon the
  Death of Sir Walter Ralegh.
A Contemplation upon
  Flowers.
The Departure.
An Elegy Upon My Best
  Friend.
The Exequy. To His
  Matchlesse Never to Be
  Forgotten Freind.
The Farwell.
From an Elegy upon the Most
  Incomparable King Charles
  the First.
The Legacy.
Madam Gabrina, or the Ill-
  Favour'd Choice.
My Midnight Meditation.
Paradox: That Fruition
  Destroys Love (excerpt).
A Renunciation.
The Retreat.
Sic Vita.
Sonnet: "Go, thou that vainly
  dost mine eyes invite."
Sonnet: "Tell me no more
  how fair she is."
Sonnet: The Double Rock.
The Surrender.
That Distant Bliss.
To a Lady Who Sent Me a
  Copy of Verses at My Going
  to Bed.
To His Unconstant Friend.
To My Dead Friend Ben:
  Johnson.
To My Honoured Friend Mr.
  George Sandys.
Upon a Braid of Hair in a
  Heart.
Upon the Death of My Ever
  Desired Friend Doctor
  Donne Dean of Pauls.
The Vow-Breaker.
King, Jenny
I Enter by the Darkened Door
  (parody).
King, Jill
Grief Plucked Me out of
  Sleep.
King, Linda
The Great Poet.
Hooked on the Magic Muscle.
I Wasn't No Mary Ellen.
Whore.
King, Mary
Mary of Bethlehem.

King, Stoddard
Breakfast Song in Time of
  Diet.
Commissary Report.
Crime at Its Best.
The Difference.
Etude Geographique.
Hearth and Home.
Idyll.
Mrs. Brown and the Famous
  Author.
Trombone Solo.
Wasted Ammunition.
King, William
The Art of Cookery.
The Art of Making Puddings.
The Beggar Woman.
Mully of Mountown (excerpt).
Kingsley, Charles
Airly Beacon.
Ballad.
Dolcino to Margaret.
Drifting away.
Easter Week.
A Farewell.
Instruction sore long time I
  bore.
The Invitation.
The Knight's Leap.
The Last Buccaneer.
The Little Doll.
Lorraine Loree.
The Lost Doll.
Margaret to Dolcino.
A Myth.
The Nereids.
Ode to the North-East Wind.
The Old Song.
The Poetry of a Root Crop.
The Sands of Dee.
Sing Heigh-Ho!
Song: "Oh! that we two were
  Maying."
Song: "When I was a
  greenhorn and young."
The Three Fishers.
The Water-Babies.
Kingsley, Henry
Magdalen.
Kingsmill, Hugh
'Tis Summer Time on Bredon
  (parody).
Two Poems after A. E.
  Housman.
What, Still Alive.
Kingston, Jeremy
Distances.
Kinnell, Galway
After Making Love We Hear
  Footsteps.
Angling, a Day.
Another Night in the Ruins.
The Avenue Bearing the
  Initial of Christ into the New
  World.
La Bagarede.
The Bear.
The Book of Nightmares.
Braemar.
Brother of My Heart.
Burning.
The Call across the Valley of
  Not Knowing.
Cells Breathe in the
  Emptiness.
Chicago.
The Correspondence School
  Instructor Says Goodbye...
Crying.
Daybreak.
The Dead Shall Be Raised
  Incorruptible.

Duck-Chasing.
First Song.
Flower Herding on Mount
  Monadnock.
For Robert Frost.
For the Lost Generation.
For William Carlos Williams.
The Fossils.
Freedom, New Hampshire.
Full Moon.
The Fundamental Project of
  Technology.
Getting the Mail.
Goodbye.
The Homecoming of Emma
  Lazarus.
How Many Nights.
In a Parlor Containing a
  Table.
In Fields of Summer.
Island of Night.
Kissing the Toad.
Last Songs.
Leaping Falls.
Little Sleep's-Head Sprouting
  Hair in the Moonlight.
Looking at Your Face.
Middle of the Way.
Near Barbizon.
Night in the Forest.
On Frozen Fields.
On Hardscrabble Mountain.
Passion.
The Poem.
Poems of Night.
The Porcupine.
Promontory Moon.
Reply to the Provinces.
The River That Is East.
Room of Return.
Ruins under the Stars.
Saint Francis and the Sow.
Spindrift.
Spring Oak.
The Supper after the Last.
To Christ Our Lord.
Told by Seafarers.
Under the Williamsburg
  Bridge.
Vapor Trail Reflected in the
  Frog Pond.
A Walk in the Country.
The Wolves.
Kinney, Coates
Rain on the Roof.
Kinney, Elizabeth Clementine
The Blind Psalmist.
A Dream.
Moonlight in Italy.
The Quakeress Bride.
To The Boy.
Kinnick, B. Jo
Fish Story.
Kinon, Victor
Agnus Dei.
Kinsella, Thomas
Ancestor.
Another September.
Baggot Street Deserta.
Ballydavid Pier.
C. G. Jung's First Years.
Chrysalides.
Clarence Mangan.
A Country Walk.
Cover Her Face.
Crab Orchard Sanctuary: Late
  October.
Death Bed.
The Dispossessed.
Downstream.
Fifth Sunday after Easter.
Finistere.

First Light.
Folk Wisdom.
A Hand of Solo.
Hen Woman.
His Father's Hands.
In the Ringwood.
Je T'Adore.
King John's Castle.
Landscape and Figure.
The Laundress.
Leaf-Eater.
Love.
Mask of Love.
Midsummer.
Mirror in February.
Night Songs.
Nightwalker.
An Old Atheist Pauses by the
   Sea.
Pause en Route.
Ritual of Departure.
Sacrifice.
Scylla and Charybdis.
The Secret Garden.
Song: "The engine screams
   and Murphy, isolate."
Tao and Unfitness at
   Inistiogue on the River Nore.
Tear.
A Technical Supplement.
Touching the River.
Westland Row.
Wormwood.
Wyncote, Pennsylvania: A
   Gloss.

Kinwelmersh, Francis
A Carol for Christmas Day.

Kipling, Rudyard
Arithmetic on the Frontier.
An Astrologer's Song.
The Ballad of East and West.
The Ballad of Fisher's
   Boardinghouse.
The Ballad of Minepit Shaw.
The Beasts Are Very Wise.
The Beginnings (1914-1918).
The Betrothed.
Big Steamers.
Boots.
Bridge-Guard in the Karroo.
The Buddha at Kamakura.
By the Hoof of the Wild
   Goat.
The Camel's Hump.
Certain Maxims of Hafiz.
Chant-Pagan.
Cities and Thrones and
   Powers.
The Coastwise Lights.
A Code of Morals.
Cold Iron.
Commonplaces (parody).
The Conundrum of the
   Workshops.
Dane-Geld.
Danny Deever.
A Dedication.
The Deep-Sea Cables.
Delilah.
Departmental Ditties: Prelude.
The Derelict.
The Dove of Dacca.
The Dykes.
The 'Eathen.
Eddi's Service.
Edgehill Fight.
L'Envoi.
Epigram: "He drank strong
   waters and his speech was
   coarse."
Epigram: "Twelve hundred
   million men are spread."

Epitaphs of the War, 1914-18.
Evarra and His Gods.
The Explorer.
The Fabulists.
The Female of the Species.
The Flight of the Bucket
   (parody).
The Flowers.
Follow Me 'Ome.
For All We Have and Are.
For to Admire.
Ford O' Kabul River.
Frankie's Trade.
Fuzzy-Wuzzy.
The Galley-Slave.
Gehazi.
A General Summary.
Gentlemen-Rankers.
Gethsemane.
Giffen's Debt.
The Gipsy Trail.
The Glory of the Garden.
The Gods of the Copybook
   Headings.
Great-Heart.
Gunga Din.
Harp Song of the Dane
   Women.
Heriot's Ford.
Horses.
The Hump.
The Hyaenas.
If.
In Springtime.
In the Neolithic Age.
The Jam-Pot.
Jane Smith (parody).
Janes's Marriage.
The Job That's Crying to Be
   Done.
Jobson's Amen.
The King.
The Ladies.
The Land.
The Last Chantey.
The Last Lap.
The Law of the Jungle.
The Legends of Evil.
Lichtenberg.
The Lie.
Limerick: "There was a young
   boy of Quebec."
The Liner She's a Lady.
Look, You Have Cast Out
   Love!
The Looking-Glass.
Mandalay.
The "Mary Gloster."
McAndrew's Hymn.
Mesopotamia.
Mother o' Mine.
Municipal (parody).
My Rival.
A Nativity.
Non Nobis Domine.
La Nuit Blanche.
O Mary Pierced with Sorrow.
The Old Men.
Our Lady of the Snows.
Pagett, M. P.
Philadelphia.
Pink Dominoes.
Poseidon's Law.
The Post That Fitted.
The Power of the Dog.
Predestination.
Puck's Song.
The Queen's Men.
Rebirth.
Recessional.
The Return.

The Rhyme of the Three
   Captains.
Road-Song of the Bandar-Log.
The Runes on Weland's
   Sword.
Screw-Guns.
The Sea and the Hills.
Seal Lullaby.
The Sergeant's Weddin'.
The Service Man.
Sestina of the Tramp-Royal.
Shillin' a Day.
Skating.
A Smuggler's Song.
Soldier an' Sailor Too.
The Song of the Banjo.
Song of the Galley-Slaves.
The Sons of Martha.
A St. Helena Lullaby.
Stellenbosch.
The Storm Cone.
The Story of Uriah.
Study of an Elevation, in
   Indian Ink.
Supplication of the Black
   Aberdeen.
There Is a Tide.
There Was a Strife 'Twixt
   Man and Maid.
Tomlinson.
Tommy.
Ulster.
The Undertaker's Horse.
The Vampire.
The Voortrekker.
The Way Through the Woods.
When 'omer Smote 'is
   Bloomin' Lyre.
The White Man's Burden.
The Widow at Windsor.
The Widow's Party.
The Winners.

Kipp, Allan F.
Cubist Blues in Poltergeist
   Major.

Kirby, Patrick F.
Compline.
Consecration.
Rain.
Riddles.
Sequel to Finality.
Song for These Days.

Kircher, Pamela
In the Small Boats of Their
   Hands.

Kirillov, Vladimir
We.

Kirkconnell, Watson
The Crow and the Nighthawk.
The Tide of Life.

Kirkup, James
Baby's Drinking Song.
La Bete Humaine.
A Correct Compassion.
Earth Tremor in Lugano.
Gay Boys.
Giving and Taking.
Homage to Vaslav Nijinsky.
In a London Schoolroom.
Japanese Fan.
The Lonely Scarecrow.
The Love of Older Men.
Mortally.
The Nature of Love.
Old Gramophone Records.
The Pavement Artist.
The Poet.
Sumo Wrestlers.
To My Children Unknown,
   Produced by Artificial
   Insemination.
Ursa Major.

The Zen Archer.

Kirkwood, Judith
Last Born.

Kirsch, Olga
Blockhouse.
Wordspinning.

Kirsch, Sarah
Dandelions for Chains.
Sad Day in Berlin.

Kirschenbaum, Leo
Iberia.

Kirstein, Lincoln
Bath.
Das Schloss.
Fall In.
Foresight.
Rank.
Vaudeville.

Kisa'i of Merv
Beauty's Queen.

Kiser, S. E.
A Bargain Sale.
The Fighter.
My Creed.
Unsubdued.
When I Had Need of Him.

Kiss, Jozsef
The New Ahasuerus.

Kistler, William
Letter to Frances.

Kitahara, Hakushu
Impression of a Fountain.

Kitasono, Katue
Green Sunday.

Kitchel, Mary Eva
So Runs Our Song.

Kitchell, Marilyn
Three.

Kito
Haiku: "Seaweed..."

Kittaararter
Take Your Accusation Back!

Kittner, Alfred
Blue Owl Song.
Old Jewish Cemetery in
   Worms.

Kittredge, Walter
Tenting on the Old Camp
   Ground.
We're Tenting To-Night.

Kitzman, Darlene Button
The Doll House.

Kivkarjuk
I Am but a Little Woman.

Kiwus, Karin
All Splendor on Earth.

Kiyowara Fukuyabu
Because river-fog.

Kizer, Carolyn
Afterthoughts of Donna
   Elvira.
Amusing Our Daughters.
The Copulating Gods.
For Jan, in Bar Maria.
The Great Blue Heron.
Hera, Hung from the Sky.
The Intruder.
Lines to Accompany Flowers
   for Eve.
Lovemusic.
A Muse of Water.
One to Nothing.
A Poet's Household.
Postcards from Rotterdam.
Pro Femina.
Semele Recycled.
Singing Aloud.
The Skein.
Summer Near the River.
Through a Glass Eye, Lightly.
To a Visiting Poet in a
   College Dormitiory.

To Li Po from Tu Fu.
To My Friend, behind Walls.
The Ungrateful Garden.
What the Bones Know.
A Widow in Wintertime.
Kizer, Gary Allan
The Boxer Turned Bartender.
Even the Best.
For Laurence Jones.
Oil and Blood.
One Year After.
Skyhook.
Klappert, Peter
Ellie Mae Leaves in a Hurry.
For the Poet Who Said Poets
Are Struck by Lightning
Only...
The Invention of the
Telephone.
J'Accuse.
The Lord's Chameleons.
O'Connor the Bad Traveler.
Poem for L. C.
Klauber, Edgar
On Buying a Dog.
Klauck, Daniel L.
Catwalk.
Chew Mail Pouch.
Dirty Joke.
Einstein's Father.
Eulogy for a Tough Guy.
Inside a Prison Cell at Count
Time.
Myths.
Visits.
Klein, Abraham Moses
And in That Drowning
Instant.
Baal Shem Tov.
Ballad of the Days of the
Messiah.
Bandit.
Bestiary.
Biography.
Bread.
The Break-Up.
Design for Mediaeval
Tapestry.
For the Sisters of the Hotel
Dieu.
Grain Elevator.
Heirloom.
Indian Reservation:
Caughnawaga.
Montreal.
Orders.
Political Meeting.
Portrait of the Poet as
Landscape.
Psalm of the Fruitful Field.
The Psalter of Avram
Haktani.
Quebec Liquor Commission
Store.
Rabbi Yom-Tob of Mayence
Petitions His God.
Rev Owl.
The Rocking Chair.
The Spinning Wheel.
The Still Small Voice.
The Sugaring.
Upon the Heavenly Scarp.
The Venerable Bee.
Klein, Chris
Bright Winter Morning.
Kleiser, Grenville
The Challenge.
The Most Vital Thing in Life.
My Daily Prayer.
You Can't Fool God.
Kline, Betsy W.
Be Still.

Klingle, George See **Holmes,
Georgiana**
Kloefkorn, William
I Love Old Women.
Loony, 29: The Good Folks at
the Camp Meeting.
Loony, 51: During the War.
My Love for All Things
Warm and Breathing.
Otoe County in Nebraska.
Knapp, Shepherd
Lord God of Hosts.
Not Only Where God's Free
Winds Blow.
Knevet, Ralph
The Passion.
Knibbs, Henry Herbert
The Ballad of Billy the Kid.
Boomer Johnson.
The Bosky Steer.
The Cowboy's Ball.
The Desert.
The Long Road West.
The Lost Range.
The Oro Stage.
Out There Somewhere.
Riders of the Stars.
The Shallows of the Ford.
Waring of Sonora-Town.
Knickman, Lester
Could You Spare Some Time
for Jesus?
Knies, Elizabeth
Absence.
Circles.
Knight, Arthur Winfield
Impotence.
Knight, Douglas
Sleeping Beauty: August.
Knight, Etheridge
2 Poems for Black Relocation
Centers.
Another Poem for Me.
Apology for Apostasy?
As You Leave Me.
Cell Song.
Dark Prophesy: I Sing of
Shine.
Feeling Fucked/Up.
For Black Poets Who Think
of Suicide.
For Dan Berrigan.
For Freckle-Faced Gerald.
Haiku: "A bare pecan tree."
Haiku: "Eastern guard tower."
Haiku: "In the August grass."
Haiku: "Making jazz swing
in."
Haiku: "Morning sun slants
cell."
Haiku: "The falling snow
flakes."
Haiku: "The piano man."
Haiku: "To write a blues
song."
Haiku: "Under moon
shadows."
Hard Rock Returns to Prison
from the Hospital for the
Criminal Insane.
He Sees Through Stone.
Huey.
The Idea of Ancestry.
It Was a Funky Deal.
My Life, the Quality of
Which.
A Nickle Bet.
On Watching Politicians
Perform at Martin Luther
King's Funeral.
A Poem to Galway Kinnell.
Portrait of Malcolm X.

Prison Graveyard.
The Sun Came.
To Dinah Washington.
To the Man Who Sidled Up
to Me and Asked: "How
Long You in fer, Buddy?"
Upon Your Leaving.
The Violent Space.
The Warden Said to Me the
Other Day.
Knight, Henry Coggswell
Lunar Stanzas.
Knight, John
Father to the Man.
Knight, Sarah Kemble
Pleasent Delusion of a
Sumpteous Citty.
Resentments Composed
Because of the Clamor of
Town Topers...
Thoughts on Pausing at a
Cottage near the Paukataug
River.
Thoughts on the Sight of the
Moon.
Warning to Travailers Seeking
Accomodations at Mr.
Devills Inn.
Knight-Adkin, J. H.
No-Man's Land.
The Patrol.
Knister, Raymond
Boy Remembers in the Field.
Change.
February's Forgotten Mitts.
Feed.
The Hawk.
Lake Harvest.
The Plowman.
Plowman's Song.
A Row of Stalls.
Stable-Talk.
White Cat.
Knoepfle, John
At the Roadside.
Riverfront, St. Louis.
The Ten-Fifteen Community
Poems (excerpt).
Those Who Come What Will
They Say of Us.
Knoll, Michael
A Dangerous Music.
The Interrogations.
An Overture.
Prison Letter.
To My Sister, from the
Twenty-Seventh Floor.
Vigil.
Vivaldi on the Far Side of the
Bars.
Knott, Bill
Death.
(End) of Summer (1966).
Goodbye.
Hair Poem.
Poem: "After your death."
Poem: "At your light side
trees shy."
(Poem) (Chicago) (The Were-
Age).
Poem: "The only response."
Sleep.
Song: "She was lyin face down
in her face."
Knowles, Frederic Lawrence
L'Envoi.
If Love Were Jester at the
Court of Death.
The Last Word.
Laus Mortis.
Love Triumphant.
A Memory.

Nature: The Artist.
On a Fly-Leaf of Burn's
Songs.
Out of the Depths.
A Pasture.
A Song of Desire.
To Jesus of Nazareth.
To Mother Nature.
Knowles, James D.
O God, Though Countless
Worlds of Light.
Knox, E.G.V.
The Nimble Stag.
To the God of Love.
Knox, Edward Valpy
At the Water Zoo.
Inspiration.
Limerick: "There was a young
curate of Hants."
The Tryst.
Knox, J. Mason
Co-operation.
Knox, John
The Lord Is My Shepherd.
Knox, Ronald Arbuthnott
Absolute and Abitofhell.
"Horace: Book V, Ode III.".
Limerick: "Evangelical Vicar
in want."
Limerick: "There once was a
man who said, 'God'."
Knox, Warren
Man of Letters.
Knox, William
O Why Should the Spirit of
Mortal Be Proud?
Knox ("Evoe"), E. V.
The Last Bus (parody).
Upon Julia's Clothes (parody).
Knut, Dovid
Haifa.
Rosh Pina.
Safed.
Walking Along the Sea of
Galilee.
A Woman from the Book of
Genesis.
Kobayashi Issa
The New Moon.
Kobbe, Gustav
From the Harbor Hill.
To a Little Girl.
Kober, Arthur
Evidence.
Kocan, Peter
Bill.
The Sleepers.
Koch, C. J.
The Boy Who Dreamed the
Country Night.
Shelly Beach.
Koch, Christopher
Half-heard.
Koch, James H.
To a Young Lady Swinging
Upside Down on a Birch
Limb...
Koch, Kenneth
The Art of Love: Happy the
Man Who Has Two Breasts
to Crush.
The Art of Love: Life Is Full
of Horrors and Hormones.
The Artist.
Aus Einer Kindheit.
The Circus.
The Departure from Hydra.
Down at the Docks.
Fresh Air.
Geography.
Locks.
Lunch.

Ma Provence.
Mending Sump.
Permanently.
Poem for My Twentieth
  Birthday.
A Poem of the Forty-Eight
  States.
The Railway Stationery.
Schoolyard in April.
Sleeping with Women.
Taking a Walk with You.
Thank You.
Thanksgiving.
To You.
Variations on a Theme by
  William Carlos Williams.
West Wind.
You Were Wearing.

Kochanowski, Jan
To Sleep.

Kochek, Edvard
Primary Numbers.

Koehler, G. Stanley
Ground Swell.
New Construction: Bath Iron
  Works.
Siciliana: The Landings at
  Gela.

Koehler, Ted
I've Got the World on a
  String.

Koenig, Alma Johanna
Intimations.

Koenig, Robert L.
Isolation Ward.

Koeppel, Fredric
October.

Koertge, Ronald
12 Photographs of
  Yellowstone.
For My Daughter.
Harelip Mary.
He.
The Magic Words.
Please.
Refusing What Would Bind
  You to Me Irrevocably.
Tonto.
What She Wanted.

Koethe, John
Mission Bay.
Picture of Little Letters.

Kogawa, Joy
Ancestors' Graves in
  Kurakawa.
Dream after Touring the
  Tokyo Tokei.
Hiroshima Exit.
On Meeting the Clergy of the
  Holy Catholic Church in
  Osaka.

Kohler, Sandra
The Wedding.

Kohler, Willibald
The Bridge.

Koianimptiwa
Yellow Butterflies.

Koller, James
I Have Cut an Eagle.
O Dirty Bird Yr Gizzard's
  Too Big & Full of Sand.
Some Magic.
The Unreal Song of the Old.

Kolmar, Gertrud
The Jewish Woman.
Out of the Darkness.
Paris.
Sea-Monster.
The Woman Poet.

Komey, Ellis Ayitey
The Damage You Have Done.
Oblivion.

Komunyakaa, Yusef
April Fools' Day.
Copacetic Mingus.
Somewhere Near Phu Bai.
Starlight Scope Myopia.
Stepfather: A Girl's Song.

Konek, Carol
Daring.

Kono, Tenrai
Wedding Celebration.

Konopnicka, Maria
A Vision.

Kook, Rav Abraham I.
The First One Drew Me.
Radiant Is the World Soul.
When I Want to Speak.

Koopman, Harry Lyman
Icarus.
John Brown.
Revealed.
The Satirist.
Sea and Shore.

Kooser, Ted
Abandoned Farmhouse.
Anniversary.
At Midnight.
Beer Bottle.
Camera.
Central.
A Child's Grave Marker.
Christmas Eve.
Counry-Western Music.
Father.
First Snow.
For a Friend.
Fort Robinson.
Gates.
History Lesson for My Son.
In a Country Cemetery in
  Iowa.
In January, 1962.
In the Basement of the
  Goodwill Store.
Late Lights in Minnesota.
My Grandfather Dying.
Myrtle.
Phil.
Pocket Poem.
Poem: "Get your tongue."
A Room in the Past.
Rooming House.
Snow Fence.
Themes for Country-Western
  Singers (excerpt).
Tom Ball's Barn.
Treehouse.
Wild Pigs.

Kopp, Karl
Incident.
The Judge.
Manly Diversion.

Korinna
Although I was her pupil.
I Korinna am here to sing the
  courage.
Kithairon sang of cunning
  Kronos.
When he sailed into the
  harbor.
Will you sleep forever.

Korkut, Dede
The Story of Bamsi Beyrek of
  the Grey Horse.

Korn, Rachel
From Here to There.
I'm Soaked through with You.
Keep Hidden from Me.
A Letter.
Longing.
My Body.
A New Dress.
Put Your Word to My Lips.

Sometimes I Want to Go Up.
The Thirty-One Camels.
Too Late.
With Poems Already Begun.

Korte, Mary Norbert
Ghost Poem Five.

Korzhavin, Naum
Children of Auschwitz.

Koutchak, Nahab
The Snares.

Kovner, Abba
I Don't Know if Mount Zion.
Near.
Observation at Dawn.

Kowit, Steve
Hate Mail.
Home.
It Was Your Song.
Renewal.
A Swell Idea.

Koyama, Tina
Definitions of the Word Gout.
Grape Daiquiri.
Next.
Ojisan after the Stroke: Three
  Notes to Himself.

Kozer, Jose
Cleaning Day.
My Father, Who's Still Alive.
The Store in Havana.

Koziol, Urszula
Alarum.

Kramer, Aaron
Kennedy Airport.
Now, before Shaving.
Portrait by Alice Neel.

Kramer, Arthur
Adventures.
The Inflamed Disciple.

Kramer, Edgar Daniel
Sequence.
Youth's Thankfulness.

Kramer, Larry
Overcoats.

Kramer, Lotte
Genesis.

Krapf, Norbert
Durer's Piece of Turf.
For an Old Friend.
Rural Lines after Breughel.
Village in Snowstorm.

Krasilovsky, Alexis
Sensational Relatives.

Kraus, Karl
Express Train.
On the Threshold.

Krauss, Ruth
End Song.
Song: "I'd much rather sit
  there in the sun."
Song: "Reading about the
  Wisconsin Weeping Willow."

Kraut, Rochelle
My Makeup.
No Regret.
Sheep.
We Laughed.

Kresensky, Raymond
Comrade, Remember.

Kress, George L.
A Parable.

Kretz, Thomas
The Transandean Railway.

Kreymborg, Alfred
Ants.
Arabs.
Ballad of the Common Man.
Ballad of the Lincoln Penny.
Bloom.
Circe.
Convention.
Credo.

Crocus.
Dorothy.
Ego's Dream.
Festoons of Fishes.
Geometry.
Indian Sky.
Less Lonely.
Life.
Madonna di Campagna.
A Man Whom Men Deplore.
Manikin and Minikin.
Nun Snow.
Race Prejudice.
Rain Inters Maggiore.
A Ribbon Two Yards Wide.
Springtime.
Threnody.
To W. C. W. M. D.
The Tree.
Under Glass.
Vista.
Yearning.

Kriebel, Casper
Now Sleep My Little Child So
  Dear.

Kriel, Margot
The Annunciation.

Krige, Uys
Distant View.
Encounter.
Farm Gate.
The Soldier.
Swallows over the Camp.

Kriloff, Ivan Andreevich
The Peasant and the Sheep.

Krinagoras See Crinagoras

Krishnamurti, M.
The Cloth of Gold (excerpt).
The Spirit's Odyssey.

Krmpotic, Vesna
A December Frost.

Kroetsch, Robert
Stone Hammer Poem.

Kroll, Ernest
Mockingbird in Winter.
Pennsylvania Academy of
  Fine Arts.
Telephone Lineman.

Kroll, Judith
Dick & Jane.
I Think of Housman Who
  Said the Poem Is a Morbid
  Secretion...
Not Thinking of America.
Sestina.

Krolow, Karl
White.

Kronthal, Joseph
Be Careful What You Say.

Krows, Jane W.
The Lesson.
Little Satellite.
The Milkman.
My House.
Space Travel.

Kruger, Charlotte M.
Beautiful Savior.

Kruger, Fania
Passover Eve.

Krylov, Ivan Andreyevich
The Wolf in the Kennels.

Krysl, Marilyn
Words Words Words.

Kryss, Tom
And Jesus Don't Have Much
  Use for His Old Suitcase
  Anymore.
Ballad of an Empty Table.
Bell Too Heavy to Ring.
Breaking Ground in Me.
Nothing Strange.
A Suicide.

This Wind.
Kshetrayya
  Dancing-Girl's Song.
Kuapakaa
  The Ocean Is Like a Wreath.
Kubatum
  Love Song to King Shu-Suen.
Kudaka, Geraldine
  Birthright.
  Death Is a Second Cousin
  Dining with Us Tonight.
  Giving Up Butterflies.
  Okinawa Kanashii
    Monogatari.
  On Writing Asian-American
    Poetry.
Kuder, Blanche Bane
  The Blue Bowl.
Kuka, King D.
  Evening.
  February Morning.
  Gallery of My Heart.
  Jackie.
  Janna.
  My Friend the Wind.
  My Song.
  Untitled.
Kulbak, Moishe
  I Just Walk around, around,
    around.
  Spring.
  Summer.
  Two.
  Vilna.
Kumin, Maxine W.
  400-Meter Freestyle.
  After Love.
  Amanda Dreams She Has
    Died and Gone to the
    Elysian Fields.
  Amanda Is Shod.
  The Appointment.
  The Archaeology of a
    Marriage.
  At a Private Showing in 1982.
  At the End of the Affair.
  Creatures.
  The Excrement Poem.
  A Family Man.
  For a Shetland Pony Brood
    Mare Who Died in Her
    Barren Year.
  For My Son on the Highways
    of His Mind.
  Fraulein Reads Instructive
    Rhymes.
  Getting Through.
  Halfway.
  The Hermit Has a Visitor.
  The Hermit Picks Berries.
  The Hermit Wakes to Bird
    Sounds.
  The Horses.
  How It Goes On.
  In the Root Cellar.
  January 25th.
  The Jesus Infection.
  Life's Work.
  The Lunar Probe.
  The Masochist.
  May 10th.
  The Microscope.
  Morning Swim.
  The Mummies.
  Our Ground Time Here Will
    be Brief.
  The Presence.
  Prothalamion.
  The Retrieval System.
  Riding in the Rain.
  Song for Seven Parts of the
    Body, 3.

Song for Seven Parts of the
  Body, 5.
Song for Seven Parts of the
  Body, 7.
The Sound of Night.
Together.
A Voice from the Roses.
Woodchucks.
Kunene, Raymond Mazisi
  The Political Prisoner.
  Thought on June 26.
  To Africa.
  Vengeance.
  Work Song.
  You Are Lying, O Missionary.
Kunitz, Stanley Jasspon
  The Abduction.
  After the Last Dynasty.
  The Approach to Thebes.
  Benediction.
  Between the Acts.
  Careless Love.
  A Choice of Weapons.
  The Dark and the Fair.
  The Daughters of the
    Horseleech.
  End of Summer.
  Father and Son.
  First Love.
  The Flight of Apollo.
  For the Word is Flesh.
  Foreign Affairs.
  Goose Pond.
  He.
  The Hemorrhage.
  I Dreamed That I Was Old.
  The Illumination.
  The Knot.
  The Last Picnic.
  The Layers.
  Lovers Relentlessly.
  The Mulch.
  An Old Cracked Tune.
  The Portrait.
  Prophecy on Lethe.
  Reflection by a Mailbox.
  River Road.
  Robin Redbreast.
  Route Six.
  The Science of the Night.
  The Scourge.
  She Wept, She Railed.
  The Snakes of September.
  A Spark of Laurel.
  The Summing-Up.
  The Testing-Tree.
  The Thief.
  Three Floors.
  Vita Nuova.
  The Waltzer in the House.
  The War against the Trees.
  Welcome the Wrath.
  When the Light Falls.
Kunjufu, Johari M.
  Ceremony.
  On the Naming Day.
  The Promise.
  Return.
Kunze, John C.
  Yoke Soft and Dear.
Kuo, Alex
  A Chinaman's Chance.
  Did You Not See.
  An Early Illinois Winter.
  Loss.
  On a Clear Day I Can See
    Forever.
  Sheltering the Same Needs.
  There Is Something I Want to
    Say.
  Turning on Daytime TV.

Words Most Often
  Mispronouncd in Poetry.
Kurka, Mira Teru
  Crocodiles.
  Fruit and Government.
  Under Which Heading Does
    All This Information Go?
Kuroda, Saburoh
  Afternoon 3.
Kurt, Kim
  Runaway.
  The Sun-Bather.
  Vernal Paradox.
  Woodlore.
Kurtz, Aaron
  Behold the Sea.
Kushner, Alexander
  To Boris Pasternak.
Kushner, Bill
  I Am.
  My Sisters.
  Up.
Kushniroff, Aaron
  Die My Shriek.
Kuskin, Karla
  Catherine.
  The Gold-Tinted Dragon.
  The Question.
  Very Early.
  When I Went out.
  Where Have You Been Dear?
Kuykendall, John M.
  A Veteran Cowboy's
    Ruminations.
Kuykendall, Mabel M.
  Baseball Pitcher.
Kuzma, Greg
  After Sex.
  Along South Inlet.
  Among Friends.
  Crossing Raquette Lake at
    Night.
  Darkness.
  The Dump.
  For My Father on His
    Birthday.
  Hose and Iron.
  In Love with the Bears.
  Journal of the Storm.
  The Monster.
  Night Fishing.
  The Pelican.
  Poetry.
  Somtimes.
  South Inlet.
  The Wolfman.
  The Young Man Who Loved
    the Girl Who Took Care of
    Her Aging Father.
Kwitko, Leib
  Esau.
  Moods.
  My Fiddle.
  You Who Dog My Footsteps.
Kwon, Paula
  Talking across Kansas.
Kyd, Thomas
  Of Fortune.
Kyei, Kojo Gyinaye
  African in Louisiana.
  The Talking Drums.
Kyger, Joanne
  All This Everyday (excerpt).
  And with March a Decade in
    Bolinas.
  August 18.
  Destruction.
  Don't Hope to Gain by What
    Has Preceded.
  I Have No Strength for Mine.
  My Father Died This Spring.
  Not Yet.

Of All Things for You to Go
  Away Mad.
The Pigs for Circe in May.
September.
When I Was Well into Being
  Savored.
Kyorai
  Haiku: "Even in my village..."
  Haiku: "I called to the wind."
Kyozo, Tagaki
  The Winter Moon.

L

"L., C. G."
  The Master.
Labe, Louise
  And If at Last.
  Elegy XXIII.
  Povre Ame Amoureuse.
  Sonnet I: "Not Ulysses, no,
    nor any other man."
  Sonnet II: "O handsome
    chestnut eyes, evasive gaze."
  Sonnet III: "O interminable
    desires, O futile hope."
  Sonnet IV: "From that first
    flash when awful Love took
    flame."
  Sonnet V: "White Venus
    limpid wandering in the
    sky."
  Sonnet VI: "The coming of
    that limpid Star is twice."
  Sonnet VII: "We see each
    living thing finally die."
  Sonnet VIII: "I live, I die, I
    burn myself and drown."
  Sonnet IX: "As soon as I lie
    down in my soft bed."
  Sonnet X: "When I catch
    sight of your fair head."
  Sonnet XI: "O eyes clear with
    beauty, O tender gaze."
  Sonnet XIII: "As long as I
    continue weeping."
  Sonnet XIV: "Although I cry
    and though my eyes still
    shed."
  Sonnet XV: "To honor the
    return of sparkling sun."
  Sonnet XVI: "After an age
    when thunderbolts and hail."
  Sonnet XVII: "I flee the city,
    temples, and each place."
  Sonnet XVIII: "Kiss me
    again, rekiss me, kiss me
    more."
  Sonnet XIX: "After having
    slain very many beasts."
  Sonnet XX: "A seer foretold
    that I would love one day."
  Sonnet XXI: "What grandeurs
    make a man seem
    venerable?"
  Sonnet XXII: "O blazing Sun,
    how happy you are there."
  Sonnet XXIII: "What good is
    it to me if long ago."
  Sonnet XXIV: "Don't scold
    me, Ladies, if I have loved."
LaBombard, Joan
  By the Beautiful Ohio.
  Heart.
  The Sibyl.
  To My Daughter Riding in
    the Circus Parade.

Labriola, Gina
Orgy.
Lacaussade, Auguste
Les Salaziennes (excerpt).
Lacey, E. A.
Abdelfatteh.
Guest.
Meson Brujo.
Ramon.
Lachman, Sol
Sukkot.
Lachmann, Hedwig
Home-Sickness.
A Walk.
Lacy, Rube
Ham Hound Crave.
Laederach, Monique
Penelope.
La Farge, Christopher
From Prologue, Each to the
Other.
Prayer for Living and Dying.
La Farge, Peter
Ballad of Ira Hayes.
La Follette, Melvin Walker
Arrivals and Departures.
The Ballad of Red Fox.
The Blue Horse.
Didactic Sonnet.
Hunt.
I Knew a Boy with Hair Like
Gold.
Love for a Hare.
Saint Stephen in San
Francisco.
The Sleeping Saint.
Spring Landscape.
Summerhouse.
A Valediction.
La Fontaine, Jean de
Aesop's Fable of the Frogs.
Cat into Lady.
The City Rat and the Country
Rat.
The Cock and the Fox.
The Crow and the Fox.
The Cudgelled but Contented
Cuckold.
The Donkey and the Lapdog.
The Eagle and the Beetle.
The Ear-Maker and the
Mould-Mender.
A Fair Exchange.
The Fox and the Crow.
The Gascon Punished.
The Hag and the Slavies.
Love and Folly.
The Man and His Image.
The Rat and the Elephant.
The Superfluous Saddle.
To Promise Is One Thing, To
Perform Is Another.
The Wolf and the Dog.
The Wolf and the Stork.
Laforgue, Jules
Asides from the Clowns, VII.
The Cigarette.
Complaint on the Oblivion of
the Dead.
The End of a Day in the
Provinces.
For the Book of Love.
Legend.
Lightning of the Abyss.
Winter Sunset.
Without the Moon.
Lagerkvist, Par
Beauty Is Most at Twilight's
Close.
The Purple Blemish.
Lagerlof, Selma
The Child of Peace.

La Grone, Oliver
Africland.
Bathed Is My Blood.
For Kinte.
My America.
Remnant Ghosts at Dawn.
This Hour.
Lahpu
Butterfly Maidens.
Laight, Frederick E.
Drought.
Soliloquy.
Laighton, Albert
Under the Leaves.
Laing, Alexander
The Last Romantic.
My Ain Wife.
Original Sin.
Laing, Allan M.
Clerihew: "Instead of blushing
cherry hue."
Family Life.
When They Found Giotto.
Laing, Dilys Bennett
Aubade.
Eros out of the Sea.
The Farm Hands.
The Gentled Beast.
How Music's Made.
Lines on the Sea.
Villanelle.
Laing, Ronald David
A Finger Points to the Moon.
Jill.
Laird, William
A Prayer.
Traumerei at Ostendorff's.
A Very Old Song.
Lake, Paul
An Old Folks Home.
Lake, Richard
Atavism.
"Lakon"
William the Bastard.
Lal, P.
A Song for Beauty.
Lal Ded
I drag a boat over the ocean.
Impermanence.
Lalleswari
Good Repute Is Water
Carried in a Sieve.
I Set Forth Hopeful.
With My Breath I Cut My
Way through the Six Forests.
Lamantia, Philip
Hermetic Bird.
Irrational.
Man Is in Pain.
Morning Light Song.
She Speaks the Morning's
Filigree.
Still Poem 9.
Surrealism in the Middle
Ages.
Terror Conduction.
Violet Star.
Wilderness Sacred Wilderness.
Lamar, Mirabeau Buonaparte
The Daughter of Mendoza.
Lamarre, Hazel Washington
Time and Tide.
**Lamartine, Alphonse Marie
Louis de**
The Cedars of Lebanon.
The Crucifix.
God.
Lamb, Arthur J.
Asleep in the Deep.
A Bird in a Gilded Cage.
The Bird on Nellie's Hat.

Lamb, Charles
Aspiration.
Childhood Fled.
Farewell to Tobacco.
Free Thoughts on Several
Eminent Composers.
Going or Gone (parody).
Hester.
Hypochondriacus (parody).
In My Own Album.
Lines on the Celebrated
Picture by Leonardo Da
Vinci...
Nonsense Verses.
The Old Familiar Faces.
On an Infant Dying as Soon
as Born.
The Snail.
The Triumph of the Whale.
Written at Cambridge.
Lamb, Charles and Mary
Anger.
The Boy and the Snake.
Choosing a Name.
Cleanliness.
Envy.
Feigned Courage.
The First Tooth.
Going into Breeches.
Lamb, George
On the Inconstancy of
Women: From the Latin of
Catullus.
Lamb, Mary Ann
A Child.
Helen.
Maternal Lady with the
Virgin Grace.
The Two Boys.
Lambdin, Sylvia S.
January.
Lambert, Elisabeth
Brave Old World.
Lambert, Louis See Gilmore,
Patrick Sarsfield
Lamdan, Yitzhak
For the Sun Declined.
Massada.
Lamennais, Robert de
The Book of the People.
Lamont, Colin
Rothiemurchus.
LaMoure, S. E.
Wagon Wheels.
Lampell, Millard and Lee Hays
Get Thee Behind Me, Satan.
Talking Union.
Union Train.
Lampman, Archibald
After the Shower.
Among the Millet.
Among the Orchards.
The City of the End of
Things.
Comfort of the Fields.
The Dawn on the Lievre.
Heat.
In November.
A January Morning.
The Largest Life.
Life and Nature.
Midnight.
Morning on the Lievre.
Personality.
A Prayer.
Refuge.
September.
Snow.
Solitude.
A Summer Evening.
A Sunset at Les Eboulements.
Temagami.

A Thunderstorm.
To a Millionaire.
The Truth.
The Violinist.
Winter Evening.
Winter-Solitude.
Lamport, Felicia
Capsule Philosophy.
Eggomania.
Mother, Mother, Are You All
There?
Poll Star.
Progress.
Lamprey, L.
Days of the Leaders, 1925:
The Deaf.
Lancaster, Osbert
Afternoons with Baedeker.
Eireann.
Landau, Ziche
For All That Ever Has Been
Ours.
I Have a Big Favor to Ask
You, Brothers.
The Little Pig.
Of Course I Know.
Parts.
Tuesday.
Landeweer, Elizabeth
Dakota Badlands.
Landles, William
A Border Forecast.
On Ellson Fell.
Landon, Letitia Elizabeth
A Child Screening a Dove
from a Hawk.
The Little Shroud.
The Unknown Grave.
Landor, Robert Eyres
The Impious Feast.
Landor, Walter Savage
Absence.
According to eternal laws.
Advice.
Age.
Alas! 'Tis Very Sad to Hear.
Alciphron and Leucippe.
Around the Child.
Art Thou Afraid the Adorer's
Prayer.
Autumnal Song.
Before a Saint's Picture.
Bourbons.
Called Proud.
A Case at Sessions.
Commination.
A Copy of Verses Sent by
Cleone to Aspasia.
The Crimean Heroes.
A Critic.
Daniel Defoe.
The Dead Marten.
Death of the Day.
Death Stands above Me.
Defiance.
Distribution of Honours for
Literature.
Do You Remember Me?
The Duke of York's Statue.
Dull Is My Verse.
Epigram: "Above all gifts we
most should prize."
Epigram: "Exhausted now her
sighs, and dry her tears."
Epigram: "God scatters
beauty as he scatters
flowers."
Epigram: "Had we two met,
blythe-hearted Burns."
Epigram: "How often, when
life's summer day."

Epigram: "Ireland never was contented."
Epigram: "Lately our poets loiter'd in green lanes."
Epigram: "Neither in idleness consume thy days."
Epigram: "No charm can stay, no medicine can assuage."
Epigram: "Our youth was happy: why repine."
Epigram: "Poet! I like not mealy fruit."
Epigram: "The scentless laurel a broad leaf displays."
Epigram: "There are two miseries in human life."
Epigram: "Various the roads of life."
Epigram: "Why do the Graces now desert the Muse?"
Epigram: "Why should scribblers discompose."
Epitaph: "Here lies Landor."
Faesulan Idyl.
Fame.
Fate! I Have Asked.
The Fault Is Not Mine.
Florence.
For an Epitaph at Fiesole.
A Foreign Ruler.
Garden at Heidelberg.
Gebir.
The Georges.
The Gifts Return'd.
Graceful Acacia.
Have I, This Moment, Led Thee from the Beach.
The Heart's Abysses.
Hearts-Ease.
Helen and Corythos.
The Hellenics.
How to Read Me.
I Know Not Whether I Am Proud.
Ianthe.
Idle Words.
In Clementina's Artless Mien.
Interlude.
Is It No Dream That I Am He.
Izaac Walton, Cotton, and William Oldways.
Joy Is the Blossom.
The Kiss.
The Last Fruit off an Old Tree.
Late Leaves.
Leaf After Leaf.....
Lines to a Dragon-Fly.
Love and Age.
The Loves Who Many Years Held All My Mind.
The Maid's Lament.
Malvolio (parody).
Masar.
Memory.
Mimnermus Incert.
My Hopes Retire; My Wishes as Before.
Night Airs.
No, Thou Hast Never Griev'd but I Griev'd Too.
No Truer Word.
O Fond, but Fickle and Untrue.
O Friends! Who Have Accompanied Thus Far.
O Friendship! Friendship! the Shell of Aphrodite.
Observing a Vulgar Name on the Plinth of an Ancient Statue.

Of Clementina.
On a Child.
On a Quaker's Tankard.
On Catullus.
On Death.
On Himself.
On His Own Agamemnon and Iphigeneia.
On His Seventy-Fifth Birthday.
On Man.
On Music.
On Seeing a Hair of Lucretia Borgia.
On the Dead.
On the Death of M. D'Ossoli and His Wife, Margaret Fuller.
On the Death of Southey.
On the Heights.
On the Smooth Brow and Clustering Hair.
On Thomas Hood.
The One White Hair.
One Year Ago.
Parrot and Dove.
Pericles and Aspasia.
Pigmies and Cranes.
Plays.
Poem: "I cannot tell, not I, why she."
Poems, LVIII: "Twenty years hence my eyes may grow."
Poems, XCIII: "Mother, I cannot mind my wheel."
Poems, XCVIII: "In spring and summer winds may blow."
Poems, CXL: "The burden of an ancient rhyme."
Portrait.
Proem to Hellenics.
Progress of Evening.
La Promessa Sposa.
A Quarrelsome Bishop.
Reflection from Sea and Sky.
Regeneration.
Remain, Ah Not in Youth Alone.
A Reply to Lines by Thomas Moore.
Resignation.
Retired This Hour from Wondering Crowds.
Rose Aylmer.
The Scribblers.
A Sensible Girl's Reply to Moore's.
Silent, You Say, I'm Grown of Late.
So Late Removed from Him She Swore.
So Then, I Feel Not Deeply!
Some of Wordsworth.
Song: "Often I have heard it said."
Sweet Was the Song.
Ternissa! You Are Fled.
The Test.
There Are Sweet Flowers.
Time to Be Wise.
To a Spaniel.
To Age.
To Alfred Tennyson.
To an Old Poet.
To His Verse.
To Miss Arundell.
To My Child Carlino.
To My Ninth Decade I Have Tottered On.
To One Who Quotes and Detracts.

To Our House-Dog Captain.
To Poets.
To Robert Browning.
To Shelley.
To the Poet T. J. Mathias.
To the Sister of Elia.
To Wordsworth.
To Youth.
The Torch of Love Dispels the Gloom.
Under the Lindens.
What News.
When Helen First Saw Wrinkles in Her Face.
Widcombe Churchyard.
William Gifford.
The Yacht.
Ye Walls! Sole Witnesses of Happy Sighs.
Years.
Yes: I Write Verses.
You See the Worst of Love, but Not the Best.
You smiled, you spoke, and I believed.

Landy, Francis
Lament for Azazel.
Midrash on Hamlet.
The Princess Who Fled to the Castle.
Selichos.

Lane, Franklin K.
I Am What You Make Me.

Lane, Joy M.
The Road to School.

Lane, Patrick
At the Edge of the Jungle.
Beware the Months of Fire They Are Twelve and Contain a Year.
Elephants.
Gray Silk Twisting.
If.
Love.
Loving She Stood Apart.
The Measure.
Mountain Oysters.
Passing into Storm.
Sleep on the Fraser.
Stigmata.
Surcease.
Treaty-Trip from Shulus Reservation.
The Water-Truck.

Lane, Pinkie Gordon
Migration.
Nocturne.
On Being Head of the English Department.
Sexual Privacy of Women on Welfare.
Who Is My Brother?

Lane, Randy
Song: "Sometimes in the fast food kitchen."

Lane, Wilmot B.
Owning.

Lang, Andrew
Almae Matres.
Ballade of a Friar.
Ballade of Middle Age.
Ballade of the Primitive Jest.
Brahma (parody).
But now the dentist cannot die.
Changeful Beauty.
Clevedon Church.
Heliodore.
Homeric Unity.
Jubilee before Revolution (parody).
The Last Chance.

Limerick: "There was a young lady of Limerick."
Limerick: "There was an auld birkie ca'ed Milton."
Lost Love.
Man and the Ascidian.
Nightingale Weather.
The Odyssey.
An Old Tune.
A Psalm of Life.
Romance.
Scythe Song.
Twilight on Tweed.
Villon's Ballade.

Lang, Andrew and Edward Burnett Tylor
Double Ballade of Primitive Man.

Lang, John Dunmore
Colonial Nomenclature.

Lang, Jon
Someone Sits at the Harp.

Lang, V. R.
The Suicide.
Waiting and Peeking.

Lange, Art
Confirmation.
History.
Poem: "Some who are uncertain compel me."
Le Tombeau de Frank O'Hara.

Langer, Jiri M.
On the Margins of a Poem.
Riddle of Night.

Langfield, Angela
Living with You.

Langfield, June Mercer
Full Fathom Five Thy Father Lies (parody).

Langford, Dorothy J.
On Top of Troubled Waters.
The Son of Man.

Langhorne, John
Apology for Vagrants.
The Country Justice.
The Evening Primrose.
A Farewell Hymn to the Valley of Irwan.
Owen of Carron.

Langland, Joseph
Aria for Flute and Oboe.
Conversations from Childhood: The Victrola.
Crane.
Ecclesiastes.
A Hiroshima Lullaby.
Hunters in the Snow: Brueghel.
Pruners: Conca di Marini.
Sacrifice of a Red Squirrel.
A Sea-Change: For Harold.
The Serpent.
Upon Hearing His High Sweet Tenor Again.
War.
Willows.
Winter Juniper.

Langland, William
Et Incarnatus Est.
The Harrowing of Hell.
Love.
The Palace of Truth.
The Palmer.
Piers the Ploughman.
Prayer for Rich and Poor.
The Vision of Piers Plowman.

Langley, Eve
Australia.
Native-Born.
This Year, Before It Ends.

Langton, Daniel J.
Expecting.
Langton, Stephen
Hymn to the Holy Spirit.
Langworthy, Yolande
Drifting Sands and a Caravan.
Lanier, Emilia
Eves Apologie.
Lanier, H. Glenn
O Christ of Bethlehem.
Lanier, Sidney
A Ballad of the Trees and the
Master.
The Centennial Ode: Dear
Land of All My Love.
The Cloud.
Corn.
The Cross.
The Crystal.
The Dying Words of
Stonewall Jackson.
Evening Song.
From the Crystal.
From the Flats.
The Harlequin of Dreams.
Hymns of the Marshes:
Sunrise.
Into the Woods My Master
Went.
Land of the Wilful Gospel.
Lexington.
Marsh Song–At Sunset.
The Marshes of Glynn.
The Mocking Bird.
My Springs.
Night and Day.
Opposition.
Owl against Robin.
The Raven Days.
Remonstrance.
Resurrection.
The Revenge of Hamish.
The Ship of Earth.
Song for "The Jaquerie".
Song of the Chattahoochee.
The Stirrup-Cup.
The Story of Vinland.
Struggle.
The Symphony.
Thar's More in the Man Than
Thar Is in the Land.
The Triumph.
Tyranny.
The Waving of the Corn.
Wedding-Hymn.
Lanier, Sidney and Clifford
The Power of Prayer.
Lanigan, George Thomas
Dirge of the Moolla of Kotal.
A Threnody.
Lankford, Frances Stoakley
Required Course.
Lanning, Jane McKay
To Search Our Souls.
**Lansdowne, George Granville,
Baron** *See* **Granville, Goerge,
Baron Lansdowne**
Lansing, Gerrit
Conventicle.
A Ghazel of Absence.
The Heavenly Tree Grows
Downward.
The Malefic Surgeon.
Tabernacles.
The Undertaking.
Lanusse, Armand
Epigram: "Do you not wish to
renounce the Devil?"
Lao Tse [or Lao Tzu]
The P'eng That Was a K'un.
Tao Teh King.

Lapage, Geoffrey
Mr. Giraffe.
Lape, Fred
Going to Town.
Horse Graveyard.
Lambs Frolicking Home.
The Laughing Faces of Pigs.
Midsummer Pause.
Old Grey.
Puppy.
LaPena, Frank
Waiting for a Second Time.
Wrapped Hair Bundles.
The Year of Winter.
Lapidus, Jacqueline
Coming Out.
Laramore, Vivian Yeiser
Talk to Me Tenderly.
Larbaud, Valery
Poet's Wish.
Larcom, Lucy
Apple Blossoms.
The Brown Thrush.
Dumpy Ducky.
Hal's Birthday.
Hannah Binding Shoes.
Hymn.
In the Tree-Top.
Mistress Hale of Beverly.
Nature's Easter Music.
The Nineteenth of April.
Plant a Tree.
The Sinking of the Merrimac.
Spring Whistles.
A Strip of Blue.
A Thanksgiving.
Tolling.
The Trees.
The Volunteer's Thanksgiving.
Lardner, Ring
Abner Silver's "Pu-leeze! Mr.
Hemingway!"
Fragment from "Clemo Uti–
The Water Lilies."
Hail to Thee, Blithe Owl.
Hardly a Man Is Now Alive.
Parodies of Cole Porter's
"Night and Day".
Quiescent, a Person Sits Heart
and Soul.
Larkin, Philip
Absences.
Age.
Ambulances.
Annus Mirabilis.
Arrivals, Departures.
An Arundel Tomb.
As Bad As a Mile.
At Grass.
Aubade.
Born Yesterday.
The Card-Players.
Chuch Going.
Coming.
Cut Grass.
Days.
Deceptions.
The Dedicated.
Dockery and Son.
Dry-Point.
Dublinesque.
The Explosion.
Faith Healing.
Fiction and the Reading
Public.
First Sight.
Going.
Here.
High Windows.
Homage to a Government.
Home Is So Sad.
I Remember, I Remember.

If, My Darling.
Lines on a Young Lady's
Photograph Album.
Love Songs in Age.
Maiden Name.
MCMXIV.
Mr. Bleaney.
Myxomatosis.
Naturally the Foundation Will
Bear Your Expenses.
Next, Please.
Night-Music.
No Road.
Nothing To Be Said.
Places, Loved Ones.
Poetry of Departures.
Posterity.
Reasons for Attendance.
Sad Steps.
Self's the Man.
Send No Money.
So through That Unripe Day
You Bore Your Head.
Spring.
A Study of Reading Habits.
Sunny Prestatyn.
Take One Home for the
Kiddies.
Talking in Bed.
Toads.
Toads Revisited.
Vers de Societe.
Waiting for Breakfast, While
She Brushed Her Hair.
Wants.
Water.
Wedding Wind.
The Whitsun Weddings.
Wild Oats.
Within the Dream You Said.
Larminie, William
Killarney.
The Nameless Doon.
The Sword of Tethra.
Larrabee, Harold A.
Professors.
Larremore, Wilbur
Blossom Time.
Madam Hickory.
Larsen, Carl
The Plot to Assassinate the
Chase Manhattan Bank.
Larsson, R. Ellsworth
Epistle for Spring.
O City, Cities! (excerpt),.
Larsson, Raymond E. F.
To Our Lady, the Ark of the
Covenants.
Lasker-Schuler, E.
Lord, Listen.
Lasker-Schüler, Else
Abel.
Abraham and Isaac.
Always in the Parting Year.
End of the World.
Hagar and Ishmael.
Homesick.
I Have a Blue Piano.
I Know That I Must Die
Soon.
Jacob.
Jacob and Esau.
Love's Flight.
A Love Song.
Moses and Joshua.
My Love-Song.
My People.
Pharaoh and Joseph.
Reconciliation.
The Rock Crumbles.
Saul.
Zebaoth.

Lasnier, Rina
Serenade of Angels.
Lasynys, Elis Wyn o
Death the Great.
**Lathbury, Mary Artemisia
("Aunt Mary")**
Break Thou the Bread of Life.
The Day Is Dying in the
West.
Easter Song.
Song of Hope.
Summer Sunshine.
Lathrop, Adele
Because He Lives.
Lathrop, George Parsons
Charity.
The Child's Wish Granted.
A Feather's Weight.
The Flown Soul.
Keenan's Charge.
Marthy Virginia's Hand.
Remembrance.
South-Wind.
The Sunshine of Thine Eyes.
The Voice of the Void.
Lathrop, Lena
A Woman's Question.
Lathrop, Rose Hawthorne
The Clock's Song.
Dorothy.
Give Me Not Tears.
A Song Before Grief.
Lathrop, Walter
Here Is a Toast That I Want
to Drink.
Latimer, Bette Darcie
For William Edward
Burghardt Du Bois on His
Eightieth Birthday.
Latimore, Jewel C. *See* **Amini,
Johari**
Latino, Juan
Austriad.
La Trobe, John Antes
The Peace of Christ.
Lattimore, Richmond
The Academic Overture.
Anniversary.
Bathtubs.
Collages and Compositions.
December Fragments.
Dislike of Tasks.
Dolphin Seen Alone.
Failure.
The Father.
Game Resumed.
IT.
The Krankenhaus of
Leutkirch.
Max Schmitt in a Single Scull.
Memory of a Scholar.
Monastery on Athos.
North Philadelphia, Trenton,
and New York.
The Phi Beta Kappa Poem.
Remorse.
Report from a Planet.
Reports of Midsummer Girls.
Rise and Shine.
The Shadowgraphs.
Ship Bottom.
A Siding Near Chillicothe.
Sky Diving.
Spider.
The Swarthmore Phi Beta
Kappa Poem.
Tudor Portrait.
Verse.
Western Ways.
Witness to Death.
Lau, Alan Chong
Crossing Portsmouth Bridge.

Day of the Parade.
Father Takes to the Road and
  Lets His Hair down.
Letters from Kazuko (Kyoto,
  Japan–Summer 1980).
Living in the World.
Laube, Clifford James
  At the Battery Sea-Wall.
  To Lizard Head.
Laufer, Calvin W.
  We Thank Thee, Lord.
Laughlin, E. O.
  The Unknown.
Laughlin, James
  A Letter to Hitler.
  The Mountain Afterglow.
  Step on His Head.
  The Summons.
  You Came as a Thought.
Laughton, Freda
  At the Party.
  The Bull.
  Rain on a Cottage Roof.
  To the Spring Sun.
  The Welcome.
  When from the Calyx-Canopy
    of Night.
  When to My Serene Body.
  The Woman with Child.
Laure, Clifford J.
  Ave, Vita Nostra!
Lauren, Joseph
  The Butterfly and the
    Caterpillar.
Laurence, Elsie
  Alone.
Lautermilch, Steven
  Christmas Morning.
  For My Wife.
Lavant, Christine
  Buy Us a Little Grain.
  Do Not Ask.
Lavater, Louis
  The Barrier.
  Faithless.
  Mopoke.
Lavoie, Steven
  Cloud Spots.
  In Mutual Time.
  Make Way.
Law, T. S.
  Wemen's Wather.
Lawder, Douglas
  The Field.
Lawless, Emily
  After Aughrim.
  Clare Coast.
  Dirge of the Munster Forest
    1581.
  Fontenoy. 1745.
  In Spain.
  The Stranger's Grave.
Lawlor, Joanne
  Gray Days.
Lawn, Beverly
  No Difference.
Lawner, Lynne
  In Your Arrogance.
  Possession.
  Rino's Song.
Lawrence, A. H.
  To Be a Nurse.
Lawrence, D. H.
  All I Ask–.
  All Souls.
  Almond Blossom.
  The American Eagle.
  Andraitx–Pomegranate
    Flowers.
  Autumn Rain.
  Aware.
  Baby Running Barefoot.

Baby Tortoise.
Ballad of Another Ophelia.
Bare Almond-Trees.
Bat.
Bavarian Gentians.
Bei Hennef.
Birds.
Birthday.
The Blue Jay.
Bombardment.
The Bride.
Britannia's Baby.
Brooding Grief.
Butterfly.
Cherry Robbers.
City Life.
The Collier's Wife.
Coming Awake.
Cypresses.
The Deepest Sensuality.
Delicate Mother Kangaroo.
Desire Is Dead.
Discord in Childhood.
A Doe at Evening.
Don Juan.
Don'ts.
Dreams Old and Nascent.
Elemental.
The Elephant Is Slow to
  Mate.
Elephants in the Circus.
End of Another Home
  Holiday.
Energetic Women.
The English Are So Nice!
The Enkindled Spring.
Evil Is Homeless.
Fate and the Younger
  Generation.
Figs.
Flowers and Men.
Food of the North.
Fronleichnam.
The Gazelle Calf.
Giorno dei Morti.
Gloire de Dijon.
Glory.
God and the Holy Ghost.
The Gods! The Gods!
Green.
Gross, Coarse, Hideous.
The Hands of God.
Hibiscus and Salvia Flowers.
History.
How Beastly the Bourgeois
  Is–.
Humming-Bird.
Hymn to Priapus.
I Am Like a Rose.
In Trouble and Shame.
Intimates.
It's No Good!
Kangaroo.
Kisses in the Train.
Last Words to Miriam.
Lightning.
Little Fish.
A Living.
Lizard.
Lord Tennyson and Lord
  Melchett.
Love on the Farm.
Lucifer.
Man and Bat.
Medlars and Sorb-Apples.
The Mess of Love.
Middle of the World.
Moonrise.
Morning Work.
The Mosquito.
Mountain Lion.
My Way Is Not Thy Way.

Mystic.
New Heaven and Earth.
New Moon.
New Year's Eve.
The North Country.
Nostalgia.
Nothing to Save.
O! Start a Revolution.
On the Balcony.
Passing Visit to Helen.
Pax.
Peace.
People.
Piano.
Proper Pride.
Quite Forsaken.
Red Geranium and Godly
  Mignonette.
Red-Herring.
Release.
River Roses.
Roses on the Breakfast Table.
Salt of the Earth.
The Sea.
Sea-Weed.
Self-Pity.
Self-Protection.
Shadows.
The Ship of Death.
Sicilian Cyclamens.
Sinners.
Snake.
Snap-Dragon.
Song of a Man Who Has
  Come Through.
Sorrow.
Spray.
Spring Morning.
Stand Up!–.
Suburbs on a Hazy Day.
Sunday Afternoon in Italy.
Suspense.
Swan.
They Say the Sea Is Loveless.
Things Men Have Made–.
To Women, As Far As I'm
  Concerned.
Tommies in the Train.
Tortoise Family Connections.
Tortoise Gallantry.
Tortoise-Shell.
Tortoise Shout.
Trees in the Garden.
Turkey-cock.
Twilight.
The Virgin Mother (excerpt).
Volcanic Venus.
War-Baby.
We Are Transmitters–.
Wedding Morn.
Whales Weep Not!
What Would You Fight For?
When I Read Shakespeare–.
When I Went to the Circus.
When Satan Fell.
When the Ripe Fruit Falls.
When Wilt Thou Teach the
  People—?
Whether or Not.
A White Blossom.
The White Horse.
The Wild Common.
Willy Wet-Leg.
Winter Dawn.
A Winter's Tale.
Work.
A Young Wife.
A Youth Mowing.
Lawrence, J. B.
  I Believe.
Lawrence, Ruth
  Washington's Tomb.

Lawrence, T. E.
  To S.A.
Lawrence, Terry
  The Harvester.
Lawson, David
  No Great Matter.
Lawson, Henry
  Andy's Gone with Cattle.
  Ballad of the Drover.
  The English Queen.
  Faces in the Street.
  Grog-an'-Grumble
    Steeplechase.
  The Horseman on the Skyline.
  The Men Who Come Behind.
  Ned's Delicate Way.
  Ripperty! Kye! Ahoo!
  The Roaring Days.
  The Sliprails and the Spur.
  Song of the Darling River.
  Talbrager.
  The Teams.
  Up the Country.
  When Your Pants Begin to
    Go.
  Will Yer Write It Down for
    Me?
Lawson, James Gilchrist
  All Nature Has a Voice to
    Tell.
  O Lord, I Come Pleading.
  War!
  The World Hymn.
Lawson, Marie A.
  Halloween.
Lawson, Paul
  The Ambassadors.
  Survey.
Lawson, Sylvia
  Trader's Return.
Lawson, Will
  Bill the Whaler.
Lawton, William Cranston
  My Fatherland.
  Song, Youth, and Sorrow.
Laxness, Halldor
  She Was All That You Loved.
Lay, Norma
  Sea Sonnet.
Layamon
  The Brut.
Layton, Irving
  Aran Islands.
  Bacchanal.
  Berry Picking.
  The Birth of Tragedy.
  Boys in October.
  The Bull Calf.
  Butterfly on Rock.
  Cain.
  The Cold Green Element.
  The Comedian.
  Composition in Late Spring.
  Dionysus.
  El Gusano.
  The Fertile Muck.
  For Anna.
  For Mao Tse-Tung: A
    Meditation on Flies and
    Kings.
  For Musia's Grandchildren.
  For My Brother Jesus.
  For Natalya Correia.
  From Colony to Nation.
  Golfers.
  Gothic Landscape.
  Grand Finale.
  The Haunting.
  Hostia.
  The Improved Binoculars.
  Jewish Main Street.
  Keine Lazarovitch.

Letter to a Librarian.
Misunderstanding.
Nausicaa.
Newsboy.
Ohms.
Osip Mandelshtam.
Overheard in a Barbershop.
Party at Hydra.
Song for Naomi.
A Spider Danced a Cosy Jig.
The Swimmer.
A Tall Man Executes a Jig.
To the Girls of My
  Graduating Class.
Two Communist Poets.
Undine.
What Ulysses Said to Circe on
  the Beach of Aeaea.
Woman.
Words without Music.
Layzer, Robert.
Elegy.
The Insult.
The Lawn Roller.
Saint's Parade.
The Sleeping Beauty.
Lazar, David
Doctor Freud.
Lazard, Naomi
In Answer to Your Query.
Ordinance on Winning.
Walking with Lulu in the
  Wood.
Lazarus, Emma
The Banner of the Jew.
Bar Kochba.
The Cranes of Ibycus.
The Crowing of the Red
  Cock.
Echoes.
Epochs.
Gifts.
In Exile.
In Memoriam Rev. J. J.
  Lyons.
Kindle the Taper.
Lines on Carmen Sylva.
Magnetism.
Mater Amabilis.
The New Colossus.
The New Ezekial.
On the Proposal to Erect a
  Monument in England to
  Lord Byron.
Success.
Venus of the Louvre.
The World's Justice.
Lea, Fanny Heaslip
The Dead Faith.
Lea, Sydney
Accident.
Bernie's Quick-Shave (1968).
Coon Hunt, Sixth Month
  (1955).
The Floating Candles.
Issues of the Fall.
Night Trip across the
  Chesapeake and After.
Old Dog, New Dog.
There Should Have Been.
The Train Out.
Leach, Christopher
Blackbird.
Leadbelly
All Out and Down.
Becky Deem.
Packin' Trunk Blues.
Pigmeat.
Roberta.
T. B. Blues.
Leaf, Walter
The Better Way.

Leahy, Jack
How We Built a Church at
  Ashcroft.
Leamy, Edmund
The Ticket Agent.
Visions.
Leapor, Mary
An Epistle to a Lady.
An Essay on Woman.
Mira's Will.
Lear, Edward
After Tennyson: "Spoonmeat
  at Bill Porter's in the Hall."
After Tennyson: "To watch
  the tipsy cripples on the
  beach."
The Akond of Swat.
Alphabet.
C Was Papa's Gray Cat.
Calico Pie.
The Children of the Owl and
  the Pussy-Cat.
The Courtship of the Yonghy-
  Bonghy-Bo.
The Cummerbund.
Dingle Bank.
The Dong with a Luminous
  Nose.
The Duck and the Kangaroo.
Eclogue.
How Pleasant to Know Mr.
  Lear.
Incidents in the Life of My
  Uncle Arly.
The Jumblies.
A Letter to Evelyn Baring.
Limerick: "There was a young
  girl of Majorca."
Limerick: "There was a young
  lady in White."
Limerick: "There was a young
  lady of Corsica."
Limerick: "There was a young
  lady of Hull."
Limerick: "There was a young
  lady of Norway."
Limerick: "There was a young
  lady of Portugal."
Limerick: "There was a young
  lady of Russia."
Limerick: "There was a young
  lady of Ryde."
Limerick: "There was a young
  lady of Sweden."
Limerick: "There was a young
  lady of Tyre."
Limerick: "There was a young
  lady whose bonnet."
Limerick: "There was a young
  lady whose chin."
Limerick: "There was a young
  lady whose eyes."
Limerick: :"There was a
  young lady whose Nose."
Limerick: "There was a young
  person of Crete."
Limerick: "There was a young
  person of Smyrna."
Limerick: "There was an an
  old man of Peru."
Limerick: "There was an old
  lady of Chertsey."
Limerick: "There was an old
  man in a Barge."
Limerick: "There was an old
  man in a boat."
Limerick: "There was an Old
  Man in a pew."
Limerick: "There was an Old
  Man in a tree."
Limerick: "There was an old
  man of Cape Horn."

Limerick: "There was an Old
  Man of Dumbree."
Limerick: "There was an old
  man of Dunblane."
Limerick: "There was an Old
  Man of Dundee."
Limerick: "There was an old
  man of El Hums."
Limerick: "There was an old
  man of Girgenti."
Limerick: "There was an Old
  Man of Hong Kong."
Limerick: "There was an old
  man of Ibreem."
Limerick: "There was an Old
  Man of Kamschatka."
Limerick: "There was an Old
  Man of Leghorn."
Limerick: "There was an Old
  Man of Madras."
Limerick: "There was an Old
  Man of Melrose."
Limerick: "There was an old
  man of Peru."
Limerick: "There was an old
  man of Spithead."
Limerick: "There was an Old
  Man of the Coast."
Limerick: "There was an Old
  Man of the Dee."
Limerick: "There was an old
  man of the East."
Limerick: "There was an Old
  Man of The Hague."
Limerick: "There was an old
  man of the Nile."
Limerick: "There was an old
  man of the West."
Limerick: "There was an Old
  Man of Thermopylae."
Limerick: "There was an old
  man of Three Bridges."
Limerick: "There was an Old
  Man of Vesuvius."
Limerick: "There was an old
  man of West Dumpet."
Limerick: "There was an old
  man of Whitehaven."
Limerick: "There was an Old
  Man on some rocks."
Limerick: "There was an Old
  Man on the Border."
Limerick: "There was an Old
  Man who said: "How."
Limerick: "There was an Old
  Man who said, "Hush!"
Limerick: "There was an old
  man who screamed out."
Limerick: "There was an Old
  Man who supposed."
Limerick: "There was an old
  man whose despair."
Limerick: "There was an Old
  Man with a beard."
Limerick: "There was an old
  man with a gong."
Limerick: "There was an Old
  Man with a poker."
Limerick: "There was an old
  man with a ribbon."
Limerick: "There was an Old
  Person of Anerley."
Limerick: "There was an old
  person of Bar."
Limerick: "There was an old
  person of Basing."
Limerick: "There was an old
  person of Blythe."
Limerick: "There was an old
  person of Bow."
Limerick: "There was an old
  person of Bradley."

Limerick: "There was an Old
  Person of Bromley."
Limerick: "There was an old
  person of Brussels."
Limerick: "There was an old
  person of Burton."
Limerick: "There was an old
  person of Cassel."
Limerick: "There was an old
  person of Cromer."
Limerick: "There was an old
  person of Crowle."
Limerick: "There was an old
  person of Dean."
Limerick: "There was an old
  person of Diss."
Limerick: "There was an old
  person of Dover."
Limerick: "There was an old
  person of Dutton."
Limerick: "There was an old
  person of Ewell."
Limerick: "There was an old
  person of Grange."
Limerick: "There was an Old
  Person of Gretna."
Limerick: "There was an old
  person of Harrow."
Limerick: "There was an old
  person of Hove."
Limerick: "There was an Old
  Person of Ickley."
Limerick: "There was an Old
  Person of Philae."
Limerick: "There was an old
  person of Prague."
Limerick: "There was an old
  person of Putney."
Limerick: "There was an old
  person of Rhodes."
Limerick: "There was an Old
  Person of Shoreham."
Limerick: "There was an old
  person of Twickenham."
Limerick: "There was an Old
  Person of Ware."
Limerick: "There was an old
  person of Wick."
Limerick: "There was an old
  person of Woking."
Limerick: "There was an old
  Person whose habits."
More Scraps of Lear: "Hassall
  irritates me."
Mr. and Mrs. Discobbolos.
Mr. and Mrs. Spikky Sparrow.
Mrs. Jaypher.
Mrs. Jaypher on Lemons.
The New Vestments.
A Nonsense Alphabet.
The Nutcrackers and the
  Sugar-Tongs.
The Owl and the Pussy-Cat.
The Pelican Chorus.
The Pobble Who Has No
  Toes.
The Quangle Wangle's Hat.
Says I to Myself.
She Sits upon Her Bulbul.
A Sonnet.
The Table and the Chair.
Teapots and Quails.
There Was an Old Man, on
  Whose Nose.
To Make an Amblongus Pie.
The Two Old Bachelors.
The Yonghy-Bonghy-Bo.
Lear, Oscar H.
The Wide Open Spaces.
Learmont, John
An Address to the Plebeians.

Learned, Walter
Growing Old.
In Explanation.
The Last Reservation.
On the Fly-Leaf of a Book of
Old Plays.
On the Fly-Leaf of Manon
Lescaut.
The Prime of Life.
Time's Revenge.
To Critics.
With a Spray of Apple
Blossoms.

Learsi, Rufus
Martyrdom.

Leary, Paris
Elegy for Helen Trent.
First Reader.
Love Lifted Me.
Manifesto.
Onan.
Oxford Commination.
September 1, 1965.
Summa Contra Gentiles.
Views of the Oxford Colleges.
What Five Books Would You
Pick To Be Marooned with...

Leax, John
The Fire Burns Low.
Incarnation Poem.
That Day.

Lebensohn, Micah Joseph
Wine.

Lechlitner, Ruth
Aubade.
Kansas Boy.
The Lizard.

Lecky, William Edward
Hartpole
Early Thoughts.
Of an Old Song.

LeClaire, Gordon
Chameleon.
Love.
Miser.
Old Seawoman.

Le Compte, Calvin
The Visitation.

Leconte de Lisle, Charles
Hialmar Speaks to the Raven.

LeCron, Helen Cowles
Little Charlie Chipmunk.

Lederer, Marjorie
Fifth Birthday Gift.

Ledoux, Louis V.
At Sunset.
Fulfilment.
Slumber Song.

Le Dressay, Anne
Roger and Me.
Song in White.

Ledward, Patricia
Evening in Camp.

Ledwidge, Francis
Ardan Mor.
August.
Behind the Closed Eye.
The Death of Ailill.
A Dream of Artemis.
Evening in England.
Fairy Music.
A Fear.
Had I a Golden Pound.
The Herons.
The Homecoming of the
Sheep.
June.
Lament for the Poets: 1916.
Lament for Thomas
MacDonagh.
A Little Boy in the Morning.
A Mother's Song.

My Mother.
The Shadow People.
The Ships of Arcady.
Soliloquy.
Thomas MacDonagh.
To a Linnet in a Cage.
To a Sparrow.
A Twilight in Middle March.

Lee, Agnes
Convention.
The Ilex Tree.
Motherhood.
Old Lizette on Sleep.
A Statue in a Garden.
The Sweeper.

Lee, Al
Among Sharks.
Beside My Grandmother.
The Far Side of Introspection.
In the Yellow Light of
Brooklyn.
Karl Marx.
The Lie.
Maiden Lane.
One Morning We Brought
Them Order.
Poem for the Year Twenty
Twenty.
Weathering the Depths.

Lee, Ann
Your Light.

Lee, Arthur
A Prophecy.

Lee, Bertha
Mind Reader Blues.

Lee, Deborah
Taking Care of It.
Where He Hangs His Hat.
WOMEN OPEN
CAUTIOUSLY.
Words from a Bottle.
You're Sorry, Your Mother Is
Crazy, & I'm a Chinese
Shiksa.

Lee, Dennis
Civil Elegies (excerpt).
The Gods.
The Last Cry of the Damp
Fly.
Windshield Wipers.

Lee, Don L.
African Poems: We're an
Africanpeople.
An Afterword: For Gwen
Brooks.
Assassination.
Awareness.
Back Again, Home.
Big Momma.
Black Sketches. sels.
But He Was Cool.
Change-Up.
Communication in Whi-te.
The Cure All.
Education.
Gwendolyn Brooks.
In the Interest of Black
Salvation.
Judy-One.
Man and Woman.
Man Thinking about Woman.
Mixed Sketches.
Mwilu/ or Poem for the
Living.
The New Integrationist.
Newark, for Now.
Nigerian Unity/or little
niggers killing little niggers.
One Sided Shoot-Out.
A Poem for a Poet.
A Poem Looking for a
Reader.

A Poem to Complement
Other Poems.
Positives for Sterling Plumpp.
The Primitive.
Re-Act for Action.
The Revolutionary Screw.
The Self-Hatred of Don L.
Lee.
Stereo.
Taxes.
To Be Quicker...
Wake-Up Niggers.
We Walk the Way of the New
World.
With All Deliberate Speed.

Lee, Harry
My Master Was So Very
Poor.

Lee, J. B.
Limerick: "A clumsy young
laddie was Mulligan."

Lee, Jack H.
Death Valley.
Idaho Jack.

Lee, Joseph
Requiem.

Lee, Joyce
Firebell for Peace.
My Father's Country.

Lee, Laurie
April Rise.
Autumn Apples.
Boy in Ice.
Christmas Landscape.
Day of These Days.
The Edge of Day.
Field of Autumn.
First Love.
Home from Abroad.
Invasion Summer.
Juniper.
Larch Tree.
Long Summer.
Milkmaid.
A Moment of War.
My Many-Coated Man.
Poem for Easter.
Summer Rain.
Sunken Evening.
Town Owl.
Twelfth Night.
Village of Winter Carols.

Lee, Mary, Lady Chudleigh See
Chudleigh, Mary Lee, Lady

Lee, Muna
After Reading Saint Teresa,
Luis De Leon and Ramon
Lull.
As Helen Once.
Sonnets.

Lee, Nathaniel
Nathaniel Lee to Sir Roger
L'Estrange, Who Visited
Him in His Madhouse.

Lee, Rena
An Old Story.

Lee, Walter M.
Father, Teach Me.

Lee-Hamilton, Eugene
Among the Firs.
The Death of Puck.
Elfin Skates.
Fairy Godmothers.
Idle Charon.
Lost Years.
Mimma Bella.
My Own Hereafter.
Noon's Dream-Song.
A Snail's Derby.
Song: "Under the Winter,
dear."
Sunken Gold.

To My Tortoise.
Wood-Song.

Lees, Edwin
Signs of Christmas.

Lefanu, Joseph Sheridan
A Drunkard to His Bottle.
Hymn: "Hush! oh ye billows."
The Song of the Spirits.

Lefcowitz, Barbara F.
At the Western Wall.
Driftwood Dybbuk.
Emily Dickinson's Sestina for
Molly Bloom.
The Mirrors of Jerusalem.

Le Fevre, Adam
Metal Fatigue.

Lefevre, H. T.
This I Can Do.

Le Fort, Gertrude von
Christmas.
Te Deum.
Vigil of the Assumption.

Lefroy, Edward Cracroft
A Cricket Bowler.
Echoes from Theocritus.
A Football-Player.
On a Spring-Board.

Leftwich, Joseph
The Tailor.

Le Gallienne, Richard
After the War.
All Sung.
A Ballad of London.
A Ballade-Catalogue of Lovely
Things.
Beatus Vir.
Brooklyn Bridge at Dawn.
Called Away.
A Caravan from China
Comes.
Dream Tryst.
An Easter Hymn.
Lady April.
May Is Building Her House.
A Melton Mowbray Pork-Pie
(parody).
An Old Man's Song.
The Passionate Reader to His
Poet.
A Prayer.
The Second Crucifixion.
Song: "She's somewhere in the
sunlight strong."
Song: "Take it, love!"
Songs for Fragoletta.
Spirit of Sadness.
What of the Darkness?
The Wife from Fairyland.
The Wind's Way.
Wood Flower.

Legare, James Matthew
Ahab Mohammed.
Amy.
To a Lily.

LeGear, Laura Lourene
Unbridled Now.

Léger, Alexis Saint-Léger See
"Perse, St.-John"

Legg, Bernice Hall
A Forest Meditation.

Le Guin, Ursula K.
The Mind Is Still.

Lehman, David
For David Shapiro.
In Praise of Robert Penn
Warren.
Ode.
Perpetual Motion.
Towards the Vanishing Point.

Lehmann, Geoffrey
The Last Campaign.
The Pigs.

Ross's Poems.
Saving the Harvest.
Song for Past Midnight.
Lehmann, John
The Ballad of Banners.
A Death in Hospital.
In a London Terminus.
The Last Ascent.
The Sphere of Glass.
The Summer Story.
This Excellent Machine.
Lehmann, Rudolph Chambers
The Bath.
The Bird in the Room.
The Dance.
Middle Age.
A Plea for a Plural.
Singing Water.
Lehmer, Eunice Mitchell
Armistice.
Lehrer, Tom
Alma.
The Elements.
New Maths.
Leib, Mani
Door and Window Bolted
Fast.
From the Crag.
Hush, Hush.
In Little Hands.
A Plum.
Psalmodist.
The Pyre of My Indian
Summer.
Shopkeepers.
They.
When I See Another's Pain.
Winter.
Leifer, Jay
Six-Forty-Two Farm
Commune Struggle Poem.
Leigh, Amy E.
If I But Knew.
Leigh, Fred W.
Waiting at the Church; or,
My Wife Won't Let Me.
Leigh, Henry Sambrooke
Cossimbazar.
Not Quite Fair.
Only Seven (parody).
Rhymes (?).
Saragossa.
'Twas Ever Thus.
The Twins.
Leigh, Richard
The Eccho.
Sleeping on Her Couch.
Thus Lovely Sleep.
Leigh, Robert
Her Window.
Leigh-Fermor, Patrick
Greek Archipelagoes.
Leighton, Louise
Time Is a Fox on Quick,
Velvet Feet.
Leiper, Esther M.
The Black Bottom Bootlegger.
Shaman.
Leipoldt, C. Louis
The Banded Cobra.
On My Old Ramkiekie.
Leiser, Dorothy
The Migrations of People.
Leiser, Joseph
Kol Nidra.
Leitch, Mary Sinton
From Bethlehem Blown.
The Poet.
The River.
Sea Words.
Leithauser, Brad
The Angel.

Between Leaps.
An Expanded Want Ad.
The Ghost of a Ghost.
A Quilled Quilt, a Needle
Bed.
Leitner, Della Adams
Forbearance.
Tomorrow.
Leitner, S. N.
That's Faith.
Leivick, Halper
How Did He Get Here?
I Hear a Voice.
Night, Stars, Glow-Worms.
Through the Whole Long
Night.
Two Times Two Is Four.
Leland, Charles Godfrey
Ballad by Hans Breitmann.
The Ballad of Charity.
Breitmann in Politics.
El Capitan-General.
Hans Breitmann's Party.
The Legend of Heinz Von
Stein.
Out and Fight.
The Story of Samuel Jackson.
The Two Friends.
Leland, John
The Day Is Past and Gone.
Now Behold the Saviour
Pleading.
Lele-io-Hoku
Albatross.
Lem, Carol
Henry Miller: A Writer.
L'Engle, Madeleine
At Communion.
From St. Luke's Hospital.
O Simplicitas.
Lengyel, Cornel
Fool Song.
Lenhart, Gary
Around the World.
The Old Girl.
Satellites.
Lennen, Elinor
His Last Week.
Nor House Nor Heart.
On Entering a Forest.
Pilgrimage.
Praetorium Scene: Good
Friday.
Prayer for a Play House.
Within the Shelter of Our
Walls.
Lenngren, Anna Maria
Other Fabrics, Other Mores!
The Portraits.
Lennon, Florence Becker
Little White Schoolhouse
Blues.
Lennon, John *See also* **Beatles,**
The
The Fat Budgie.
"Lennox"
Neighbors.
Le Noir, Phil
Ol' Dynamite.
Lenowitz, Harris
The Fringes.
Panegyric.
Lenox, Jean
I Don't Care.
Lense, Edward
Waking Up.
Wolf Dream.
Lenski, Hayim
Language of Ancients.
Purity.
Upon the Lake.

Lenski, Lois
Fourth of July Song.
Oh! To Have A Birthday.
Old Santa Is An Active Man.
People.
Lent, Emma A.
Memorial Day.
Unawares.
Lento, Takako U.
Glass.
Leo XIII, Pope
The Return from Egypt.
War Cry: To Mary.
Leon, Luis Ponce de
About the Heavenly Life.
At the Ascension.
The Life of the Blessed.
Love Song.
The Night Serene.
On Leaving Prison.
To Retirement.
The Valley of the Heavens.
Written on the Walls of His
Dungeon.
Leonard, Eddie
Ida, Sweet as Apple Cider.
Leonard, Priscilla
Happiness.
The Tide Will Win.
Leonard, William Ellery
Gilgamesh: The Seduction of
Engadu.
The Image of Delight.
Indian Summer.
Two Lives.
Leong, George
A Sometimes Love Poem.
This Is Our Music.
Leonidas of Tarentum
Cleitagoras.
The Fisherman.
The Last Journey.
Philocles.
Poems from the Greek
Anthology.
The Spinning Woman.
The Tomb of Crethon.
Leonidas of Alexandria
Menodotis.
Leonidas of Tarentum
Epitaph of a Sailor.
Leontius
Plato, a Musician.
Leopardi, Giacomo
The Broom.
The Evening of the Feast-Day.
L'Infinito.
Saturday Night in the Village.
A Se Stesso.
The Setting of the Moon.
Sylvia.
The Terror by Night.
To Italy.
Lepan, Douglas
Black Bear.
Canoe-Trip.
A Country without a
Mythology.
Coureurs de Bois.
An Incident.
Lion, Leopard, Lady.
The Net and the Sword.
The New Vintage.
Nimbus.
One of the Regiment.
Lepkowski, Frank J.
Two Poems Based on Fact.
Lepore, Dominick J.
Northward.
Lermontov, Mikhail Yuryevich
Composed while Under
Arrest.

The Daemon.
Dagger.
Gratitude.
The Mountain.
My Country.
The Reed.
A Sail.
A Thought.
The Triple Dream.
Lerner, Alan Jay
With a Little Bit of Luck.
Lerner, Laurence
14 July 1956.
All Day and All October.
In a Shoreham Garden.
A Meditation upon the
Toothache.
The Poet at Fifty.
Raspberries.
St Enda.
The Way to the Sea.
What's Hard.
A Wish.
Years Later.
Le Roy, Jean
I Feel an Apparition.
Lesemann, Maurice
Cow-Ponies.
A Man Walks in the Wind.
Ranchers.
Leslie, Cy
On Riots.
Leslie, Kenneth
Easter Song.
Escapade.
From Soil Somehow the
Poet's Word.
Halibut Cove Harvest.
Knife and Sap.
My Love Is Sleeping.
Sonnet: "A warm rain
whispers, but the earth
knows best."
Sonnet: "The silver herring
throbbed thick in my seine."
Sudden Assertion.
Leslie, Shane
Fleet Street.
The Four Winds.
Monaghan.
Muckish Mountain (The Pig's
Back).
Prayer for Fine Weather.
Priest Or Poet.
The Two Mothers.
Lesoro, E. A. S.
The Muscovy Drake.
Lesser, Rika
527 Cathedral Parkway.
La Banditaccia, 1979.
Can Zone; or, The Good
Food Guide.
Canopic Jar.
Degli Sposi.
The News & the Weather.
Translation.
Lessing, Gotthold
Mendax.
On Fell.
The Three Kingdoms of
Nature.
Lester, Julius
In the Time of Revolution.
On the Birth of My Son,
Malcolm Coltrane.
Us.
Lestey, George
Fire and Brimstone; or, The
Destruction of Sodom
(excerpt).
L'Estrange, Sir Roger
Loyalty Confin'd.

Le Sueur, Meridel
Dead in Bloody Snow.
I Light Your Streets.
The Village.
Letters, Francis
The Inglorious Milton.
Lettrell, Henry
Advice to Julia: The Peace.
Letts, W.M.
Tim, an Irish Terrier.
Letts, Winifred M.
Boys.
The Children's Ghosts.
The Connaught Rangers.
In Service.
My Blessing Be on Waterford.
Quantity and Quality.
A Soft Day.
Somehow, Somewhere,
Sometime.
The Spires of Oxford.
Synge's Grave.
To Scott.
Wishes for William.
Lettsom, John Coakley
The Candid Physician.
Levendosky, Charles
The Gifts.
The Heart Mountain Japanese
Relocation Camp: 30 Years
Later.
Nova.
Levenson, Christopher
A Prophecy.
Lever, Charles James
Bad Luck to This Marching.
03] Larry M'Hale.
The Man for Galway.
Mickey Free's Song.
The Pope He Leads a Happy
Life.
The Widow Malone.
Leverett, Ernest
S F.
Leveridge, Lilian
A Cry from the Canadian
Hills.
The First Robin.
Leveridge, Richard
A Song in Praise of Old
English Roast Beef.
Levertin, Oscar
At the Jewish Cemetery in
Prague.
Solomon and Morolph, Their
Last Encounter.
Levertov, Denise
The 90th Year.
Abel's Bride.
About Marriage.
The Absence.
The Ache of Marriage.
Adam's Complaint.
Advent 1966.
The Altars in the Street.
The Anteroom.
Autumn Journey.
The Barricades.
Bedtime.
Beyond the End.
Brass Tacks.
The Breathing.
By Rail through the Earthly
Paradise, Perhaps
Bedfordshire.
The Cabdriver's Smile.
Cancion.
The Cat as Cat.
The Charge.
Christmas 1944.
Claritas.
The Closed World.

Come into Animal Presence.
A Common Ground.
Continuum.
A Day Begins.
The Dead Butterfly.
A Defeat.
The Depths.
Despair.
The Dog of Art.
The Dragonfly-Mother.
During the Eichmann Trial
(excerpt).
Earliest Spring.
Earth Psalm.
The Earth Worm.
Else a Great Prince in Prison
Lies.
An Embroidery.
Epilogue.
Everything That Acts Is
Actual.
February Evening in New
York.
The Five-Day Rain.
Folding a Shirt.
From the Roof.
Gathered at the River.
The Goddess.
Goethe's Blues.
The Good Dream.
The Grace-Note.
The Gulf.
The Hands.
Hypocrite Women.
The Illustration–A Footnote.
Illustrious Ancestors.
In Mind.
Intrusion.
Invocation.
The Jacob's Ladder.
Leaving Forever.
Let Us Sing Unto the Lord a
New Song.
Libation.
Life at War.
Like Loving Chekhov.
Living.
Losing Track.
Mad Song.
The Malice of Innocence.
Man Alone.
A Map of the Western Part of
the County of Essex in
England.
Matins.
Merritt Parkway.
Moon Tiger.
Movement.
The Mutes.
The Novel.
The Novices.
O Taste and See.
Obsessions.
The Offender.
The Old Adam.
Olga Poems.
One A.M.
Our Bodies.
Overheard.
Overheard over S.E. Asia.
Overland to the Islands.
Partial Resemblance.
The Peachtree.
The Pilots.
Pleasures.
The Poem Rising by Its Own
Weight.
Poem: "Some are too much at
home in the role of
wanderer."
The Poem Unwritten.
The Postcards: A Triptych.

The Presence.
Psalm Concerning the Castle.
Psalm–People Power at the
Die-In.
A Psalm Praising the Hair of
Man's Body.
Pure Products.
The Quarry Pool.
The Rainwalkers.
The Recognition.
Relearning the Alphabet.
The Resolve.
Scenes from the Life of the
Peppertrees.
The Secret.
Seems Like We Must Be
Somewhere Else.
Shalom.
The Sharks.
Six Variations.
Six Variations (part iii).
A Solitude.
Song for Ishtar.
The Springtime.
Stepping Westward.
Sunday Afternoon.
Tenebrae.
The Third Dimension.
To the Reader.
To the Snake.
Triple Feature.
Two Variations.
The Victors.
The Vigil.
The Way Through.
The Well.
What Were They Like?
What Wild Dawns There
Were.
Williams: An Essay.
The Wings.
With Eyes at the Back of Our
Heads.
Woman Alone.
The World Outside.
Writing to Aaron.
Levi, Adele
The Death of Friends.
Levi, David
The Bible.
Levi, Peter
L'Aurore Grelottante.
He Met Her at the Green
Horse...
In a Corner of Eden...
In Stone Settlements When
the Moon Is Stone.
Life Is a Platform.
Ship-Building Emperors
Commanded...
To My Friends.
Levi, Primo
For Adolf Eichmann.
Lilith.
Shema.
Levi ben Amittai
Kibbutz Sabbath.
Levi Isaac, of Berditshev
Invocation.
Levin, Gabriel
Adam's Death.
Etude for Voice and Hand.
Ishmael.
Levin, Phillis
Everything Has Its History.
Levine, Al
The Bottle.
Levine, Ellen
One Morning.
Levine, Molly Myerowitz
Safed and I.

Levine, Norman
Crabbing.
Levine, Philip
Above It All.
After.
Animals Are Passing from
Our Lives.
Any Night.
Ashes.
At the Fillmore.
Autumn.
Baby Villon.
Blasting from Heaven.
The Businessman of Alicante.
The Cemetery at Academy,
California.
The Children's Crusade.
Clouds.
Coming Home, Detroit, 1968.
Commanding Elephants.
The Cutting Edge.
The Distant Winter.
The Drunkard.
Everything.
For Fran.
Gangrene.
Get Up.
Heaven.
The Helmet.
Here and Now.
The Horse.
In the New Sun.
Late Moon.
The Lost Angel.
Mad Day in March.
The Midget.
Milkweed.
My Angel.
My Life Like Any Other.
My Son and I.
The Negatives.
The Negatives.
New Season.
News of the World.
Night Thoughts over a Sick
Child.
Now It Can Be Told.
On a Drawing by Flavio.
On My Own.
On the Edge.
Passing Out.
The Poem Circling
Hamtramck, Michigan All
Night in Search of You.
Red Dust.
The Reply.
Salami.
The Second Angel.
Sierra Kid.
Silent in America.
Small Game.
Something Has Fallen.
Spring in the Old World.
Standing on the Corner.
Sunday Afternoon.
They Feed They Lion.
To a Child Trapped in a
Barber Shop.
To My God in His Sickness.
The Turning.
Uncle.
Waking an Angel.
The Way Down.
Winter Rains: Cataluna.
Words.
Zaydee.
Levine, Steve
A Gothic Gesture.
Pure Notations.
Tiny Catullus.
Levinson, Fred
No More Than Five.

A Poem against Rats.
Poem: "the country".
Sharks in Shallow Water.
A Translation from....

Levis, Larry
Bat Angels.
Family Romance.
Fish.
For Zbigniew Herbert,
Summer, 1971, Los Angeles.
Irish Music.
Linnets.
The Ownership of the Night.
Picking Grapes in an
Abandoned Vineyard.
The Poem You Asked For.
The Quilt.
Sensationalism.
To a Wall of Flame in a Steel
Mill, Syracuse, New York,
1969.
Weldon Kees.
Whitman.
Winter Stars.

Levy, Amy
The Birch-Tree at Loschwitz.
Epitaph: "This is the end of
him, here he lies."
A London Plane-Tree.
London Poets.
New Love, New Life.
On the Threshold.
Xantippe.

Levy, Louis
The Swallow's Flight.

Levy, Newman
The Ballad of Sir Brian and
the Three Wishes.
The Belle of the Balkans.
Carmen.
I Wonder What Became of
Rand, McNally...
If You Stick a Stock of
Liquor–.
Midsummer Fantasy.
Midsummer Jingle.
The Reporters.
The Revolving Door.
Rigoletto.
Tannhauser.
Thais.
Tristan and Isolda.

Levy, Raphael See **Ryvel**
Levy, Robert J.
Give Us This Day Our Daily
Day.

Levy, Stephen
Freely, from a Song Sung by
Jewish Women of Yemen.
Friday Night after Bathing.
Home Alone These Last
Hours of the Afternoon...
A Judezmo Writer in Turkey
Angry.

Lew, Walter
Fan.
Leaving Seoul: 1953.
Two Handfuls of Waka for
Thelonious Sphere Monk (d.
Feb. 1982).
Urn I: Silent for Twenty-Five
Years, The Father of My
Mother Advises.

Lewandowski, Stephen
Nantucket / Mussels /
October.
Night Fishing.
Opening the Season.

Lewin, Ralph A.
Les Chasse-Neige.

Lewis, Alonzo
Death Song.

Lewis, Alun
All Day It Has Rained.
Bivouac.
Dawn on the East Coast.
Goodbye.
In Hospital: Poona.
In Hospital: Poona.
Jason and Medea.
The Jungle.
The Mahratta Ghats.
The Mountain Over Aberdare.
Must.
The Peasants.
Port of Call: Brazil.
Postscript: For Gweno.
Sacco Writes to His Son.
The Sentry.
Song: "The first month of his
absence."
To a Comrade in Arms.
To Edward Thomas.
Troopship in the Tropics.
The Unknown Soldier.
Water Music.

Lewis, Angelo
America Bleeds.
Clear.

Lewis, Cecil Day See **Day
Lewis, Cecil**
Lewis, Clive Staples
The Apologist's Evening
Prayer.
Aridity.
Awake, My Lute.
Eden's Courtesy.
Epigrams and Epitaphs, VI.
Evensong.
Evolutionary Hymn.
The Late Passenger.
The Naked Seed.
The Nativity.
On a Vulgar Error.
Pilgrim's Problem.
Prayer.
Prelude to Space.
Scazons.
The Small Man Orders His
Wedding.
Sonnet: "The Bible says
Sennacherib's campaign was
spoiled."

Lewis, David
When None Shall Rail.

Lewis, Dominic Bevin Wyndham
Ballade of the Harrowing of
Hell.
Envoi.
Having a Wonderful Time.
Jig for Sackbuts.
Sapphics.
A Shot at Random.

Lewis, Eiluned
We Who Were Born.

Lewis, Furry
Big Chief Blues.
Billy Lyons and Stack O'Lee.
Dry Land Blues.
I Wilp Turn Your Money
Green.
Judge Harsh Blues.
Kassie Jones.

Lewis, Gardner E.
How to Tell Juan Don from
Another.
Poem, Neither Hillaryous
Norgay.

Lewis, J. Patrick
Pelicanaries.

Lewis, Janet
At Carmel Highlands.
The Candle Flame.
For Elizabeth Madox Roberts.

Girl Help.
Helen Grown Old.
In the Egyptian Museum.
Lines with a Gift of Herbs.
Love Poem.
A Lullaby.

Lewis, M. A.
The Caulker.

Lewis, Matthew Gregory
Allan Water.
Alonzo the Brave and Fair
Imogine.
What Triumph Moves on the
Billows So Blue?
A Wife.

"Lewis, Michael" See also
Untermeyer, Louis
Broken Monologue.
Cherry Blossoms.

Lewis, Percy Wyndham
If So the Man You Are.
One-Way Song.
The Song of the Militant
Romance.

Lewis, Robert
If You Had a Friend.

Lewis, Steven
Fort Wayne, Indiana 1964.

Lewis, Thelma
Exceptional.

Lewis, William S.
.Blackfoot Sin-ka-ha.
Flathead and Nez Perce Sin-
ka-ha.

Lewisohn, James
The Automobile.
Basketball.
The Blind Man.
The Children of the State.
Guernica.
Minimum Security.
Poem for Roslyn.

Lewisohn, Ludwig
Heinrich Heine.
Together.

Lewis's, Noah, Jug Band
New Minglewood Blues.

Leybourne, George
Champagne Charlie.
The Man on the Flying
Trapeze.

Leyden, John
Address to My Malay Krees.
Christmas in Penang.
The Lay of the Ettercap
(parody).
Lords of the Wilderness.

L'Heureux, John
Discovering God Is Waking
One Morning.

Li Ch'ing-chao
Clear Bright.
How many evenings in the
arbor by the river.
I let the incense grow cold.
Last night thin rain, gusty
wind.
Light mist, then dense fog.
Melting in thin mist and
heavy clouds.
Poem to the Tune of "Tsui
Hua Yin."
Poem to the Tune of "Yi
Chian Mei."
Rattan bed, paper netting.
Red lotus incense fades on the
jewelled curtain.
Sky links cloud waves.
Tune: Crimson Lips Adorned.
Tune: Endless Union.
Tune: Magnolia Blossom.

Tune: The Butterfly Woos the
Blossoms.
Two Springs.
Warm rain, sunny wind.
A Weary Song to a Slow Sad
Tune.
Year after year I have
watched.

Li Chu
Harvesting Wheat for the
Public Share.

Li Ho
Ninth Moon.

Li Kwang-T'ien
Over the Bridge.

Li Po See also **Rihaku**
Clearing at Dawn.
Drinking Alone with the
Moon.
Exile's Letter.
His Dream of the Sky-Land:
A Farewell Poem (excerpt).
I Am a Peach Tree.
In Spring.
In the Mountains on a
Summer Day.
The Jewel Stairs' Grievance.
Lament of the Frontier
Guard.
The Long War.
The Moon at the Fortified
Pass.
Poem by the Bridge at Ten-
Shin.
The River Merchant's Wife.
Separation on the River
Kiang.
Taking Leave of a Friend.
To Tan Ch'iu.
Two Letters from Chang-Kan.

Li T'ai-po
Drinking Alone in the
Moonlight.

Li Yi
On Hearing a Flute at Night
from the Wall of Shou-
Hsiang.

Liadan
Gain without Gladness.
Liadan Laments Cuirithir.

Liagarang
Snails.
Yellow Cloud.

Liasides, Pavlos
The Fountain.

Libaire, George
Limerick: "A half-baked
potato, named Sue."
Limerick: "There was a young
curate of Salisbury."
Limerick: "These places
abound in the old."

Libbey, Elizabeth
Before the Mountain.
Concerning the Dead Women:
The Munitions Plant
Explosion: June, 1918.
Marceline, to Her Husband.
To Her Dead Mate: Montana,
1966.

Libera, Sharon Mayer
Mother.
Patty, 1949-1961.

Libero, Libero de
Cicada.

Lichfield, Leon
The Printer, to Her Majesty.

Lichtenstein, Alfred
The Journey to the Insane
Asylum.
Repose.

Liddell, Catherine C.
  Jesus the Carpenter.
Liddy, James
  History.
  Paean to Eve's Apple.
  The Republic 1939.
  Thinking of Bookshops.
  The Voice of America 1961.
Lieber, Francis
  The Ship Canal from the
    Atlantic to the Pacific.
Lieberman, Elias
  Classroom in October.
  Heart Specialist.
  I Am an American.
  Notation in Haste.
  Sholom Aleichem.
Lieberman, Laurence
  The Coral Reef.
  Interview.
  My Father Dreams of
    Baseball.
  Orange County Plague:
    Scenes.
  The Osprey Suicides.
  The Unblinding.
Liessin, Abraham
  Spring Nocturne.
Lietz, Robert
  After the Deformed Woman
    Is Made Correct.
Lifshin, Lyn
  Beryl.
  Even There.
  Family 8.
  For a Friend.
  In Spite of His Dangling
    Pronoun.
  Marrakesh Women.
  Martha Graham.
  Not Quite Spring.
  On the New Road.
  Pulling Out.
  Remember the Ladies.
  To Poem.
  Waiting, the Hallways under
    Her Skin Thick with
    Dreamchildren.
  The Way Sun Keeps Falling
    Away from Every Window.
  You Understand the
    Requirements.
Lifson, Martha
  Quiet By Hillsides in the
    Afternoon.
Liggett, Rosy
  The Obsession.
Lighthall, William Douw
  The Caughnawaga Beadwork
    Seller.
Lightman, Alan P.
  First Rainfall.
  Getting Under.
  In Computers.
Lignell, Kathleen
  Calamity Jane Greets Her
    Dreams.
Likelike, Princess
  My Sweetheart in the
    Rippling Hills of Sand.
Lili' u-o-ka-lani, Queen Lydia
  Puna's Fragrant Glades.
Liliencron, Detlev Freiherr von
  After the Hunt.
  Autumn.
  Death in the Corn.
  Who Knows Where.
Lillard, Charles
  Bushed.
  Lobo.
Lilliard, R. W.
  America's Answer.

Lilliat, John
  False Love.
  Song: "When love on time
    and measure makes his
    ground–".
Lillington, Kenneth
  Ballade to My Psychoanalyst.
Lily, John
  The Song in Making of the
    Arrows.
Lim, Genny
  Departure.
  Sweet 'n Sour.
  Visiting Father.
  Wonder Woman.
Lima, Frank
  Glycerin.
  Inventory–to 100th Street.
  The Memory of Boxer Benny
    (Kid) Paret.
  Mom I'm All Screwed Up.
  Mulata–to Skinny.
  News.
  Note.
  Penicillin.
  Poem.
  Primavera.
  Pudgy.
  The Welder.
  The Woman.
Lima, Jorge de *See* **De Lima
  Jorge**
Lima, Robert
  Peripatetic.
Lin Ling
  Footpaths Cross in the Rice
    Field.
Lincoln, Abraham
  America's Task.
  The Bulwark of Liberty.
  The Faith of Abraham
    Lincoln.
  The Gettysburg Address.
  I Am Not Bound to Win.
  Let Us Have Faith That Right
    Makes Might.
  Memory.
Lincoln, Joseph C.
  The Cod-Fisher.
Lincoln, Mary W.
  Kings of France.
Lincoln (Hicks), Charlie
  Chain Gang Trouble.
  Depot Blues.
  If It Looks Like Jelly, Shakes
    Like Jelly, It Must Be Gel-a-
    Tine.
Lindberg, Gene
  The Home Winner.
Lindegren, Erik
  Journey: IV.
  The Man without a Road: X.
Linden, Eddie
  A Sunday in Cambridge.
Lindh, Stewart
  Settler.
Lindner, Carl
  Mismatch.
Lindon, J. A.
  Gilbertian Recipe for a
    Politician.
  Learner.
  A London Sparrow's If.
  More to It Than Riding.
  My Garden.
  A "Twiner."
Lindquist, Ray
  On the Land.
Lindsay, David
  The Complaynt of Schir
    David Lindesay: The
    Childhood of James V.

Lindsay, Forbes
  The Ball and the Club.
Lindsay, Jack
  Angry Dusk.
  Budding Spring.
  Question Time.
  To My Father Norman Alone
    in the Blue Mountains.
Lindsay, Lady Anne *See also*
  Barnard, Lady Anne
  East Coast Lullaby.
Lindsay, Maurice
  At Hans Christian Andersen's
    Birthplace, Odense,
    Denmark.
  The Exiled Heart.
  Highland Shooting Lodge.
  Hurlygush.
  In the Cheviots.
  May Day Demonstrators.
  Picking Apples.
  Shetland Pony.
Lindsay, Sir David
  The Dreme: Of the Realme of
    Scotland.
  The Dreme: The Compleynt
    of the Comoun Weill of
    Scotland.
  The Historie of Squyer
    William Meldrum: Squire
    Meldrum at.....
  The Monarche: After the
    Flood.
  So Young Ane King.
Lindsay, T.
  Limerick: "There was a young
    man of Mauritius."
Lindsay, Vachel
  Abraham Lincoln Walks at
    Midnight.
  Aladdin and the Jinn.
  The Apple-Barrel of Johnny
    Appleseed.
  At Mass.
  The Blacksmith's Serenade.
  The Broncho That Would Not
    Be Broken.
  Bryan, Bryan, Bryan, Bryan.
  The Chinese Nightingale.
  The Congo.
  The Dandelion.
  The Daniel Jazz.
  Dirge for a Righteous Kitten.
  The Dove of New Snow.
  The Eagle That Is Forgotten.
  Euclid.
  An Explanaton of the
    Grasshopper.
  Factory Windows Are Always
    Broken.
  The Flower-Fed Buffaloes.
  The Flute of the Lonely.
  Franciscan Aspiration.
  From the Santa-Fe Trail.
  General William Booth Enters
    into Heaven.
  The Ghosts of the Buffaloes.
  The Golden Whales of
    California.
  The Haughty Snail-King.
  The Horrid Voice of Science.
  How Samson Bore Away the
    Gates of Gaza.
  I Heard Immanuel Singing.
  I Went Down into the Desert
    to Meet Elijah.
  Incense.
  An Indian Summer Day on
    the Prairie.
  The Jazz of This Hotel.
  John Brown.

  Johnny Appleseed's Hymn to
    the Sun.
  The Kallyope Yell.
  The King of Yellow
    Butterflies.
  The Knight in Disguise.
  The Leaden-Eyed.
  The Lion.
  Litany of the Heroes.
  The Little Turtle.
  The Moon's the North Wind's
    Cooky.
  The Mouse That Gnawed the
    Oak-Tree Down.
  My Fathers Came from
    Kentucky.
  The Mysterious Cat.
  Nancy Hanks, Mother of
    Abraham Lincoln.
  A Net to Snare the
    Moonlight.
  On the Building of Springfield.
  An Oration, Entitled "Old,
    Old, Old, Old Andrew
    Jackson."
  The Pontoon Bridge Miracle.
  The Potatoes' Dance.
  Rain.
  Rhymes to Be Traded for
    Bread: Prologue.
  The Scissors-Grinder.
  The Sea Serpent Chantey.
  A Sense of Humour.
  Simon Legree–A Negro
    Sermon.
  The Sorceress!
  The Spider and the Ghost of
    the Fly.
  The Springfield of the Far
    Future.
  Three Hours.
  To a Golden-Haired Girl in a
    Louisiana Town.
  The Traveler.
  Two Old Crows.
  The Unpardonable Sin.
  What Semiramis Said.
  What the Moon Saw.
  When the Mississippi Flowed
    in Indiana.
  Why I Voted the Socialist
    Ticket.
  Would I Might Rouse the
    Lincoln in You All.
Lindsey, Jim
  Blank Verse for a Fat
    Demanding Wife.
Lindsey, Therese
  The Man Christ.
Lindsey, William
  En Garde, Messieurs.
  The Hundred-Yard Dash.
Lindskoog, Kathryn
  Light Showers of Light.
Lingard, William Horace
  Captain Jinks.
Link, Carolyn Wilson
  Elements.
Link, Gordden
  Artist and Ape.
Link, Lenore M.
  Holding Hands.
Linnell, Kathleen
  Two Birds.
Linthicum, John
  April.
Linton, William James
  Faint Heart.
Lipkin, Jean
  Apocalypse.
  Father.
  Pre Domina.

Lipman, Ed
Because Our Past Lives Every Day.
Because San Quentin Killed Two More Today.
Matrix III.
Nights Primarily III.

Lippmann, Julie Mathilde
Love and Life.
The Pines.
Stone Walls.

Lipscomb, Mance
Alabama Bound.
Captain Captain.

Lipshitz, Fay
The Aleph Bet.
Encounter in Jerusalem.
Judean Summer.

Lipsitz, Lou
After Visiting a Home for Disturbed Children.
Bedtime Story.
Brooklyn Summer.
Conjugation of the Verb, "To Hope."
Pancho Villa.
The Pipes.
Prospect Beach.
The Radical in the Alligator Shirt.
The Sirens.
Thaw in the City.
To a Fighter Killed in the Ring.
The Tree Is Father to the Man.
Winter Twilight.

Lipska, Ewa
The Cock.
The Flood.
If God Exists.
Wedding.

Lipton, James
Misericordia!

Lisboa, Henriqueta
Minor Elegy.

Lisle, Leconte de *See* **Leconte de Lisle, Charles**

Lisle, Samuel
When Orpheus Went Down.

Lisle, Thomas
Letter from Smyrna to His Sisters at Crux-Easton, 1733.
The Power of Music.

Lissauer, Ernst
A Chant of Hate against England.

Lister, R. P.
At the Ship.
Beetle Bemused.
Bone China.
Cuckoo.
The Gemlike Flame.
The Human Races.
I Thought I Saw Stars.
Lament of an Idle Demon.
The Musician.
On a Horse and a Goat.
On Becoming Man.
The Revolutionaries.
The Tale of Jorkyns and Gertie; or, Vice Rewarded.
Time Passes.

Listmann, Thomas
The Sixties.

Litchfield, Grace Denio
Good-By.
My Letter.
My Other Me.
To a Hurt Child.

Lithgow, William
A Painted Whore, the Mask of Deadly Sin.
Still This, Still That I Would!

Litsey, Edwin Carlile
The Dreams Ahead.

Little, Arthur J.
Invocation.

Little, Katharine Day
Hazlitt Sups.

Little, Philip Francis
The Three Poplars.

Littlebird, Harold
After the Pow-Wow (excerpt).
Alone Is the Hunter.
A Circle Begins.
Coming Home in March.
Could I Say I Touched You.
For Drum Hadley.
For the Girls 'Cause They Know.
For Tom Numkena, Hopi/Spokane.
Gaa-A-Muna, a Mountain Flower.
Hummingbird.
Hunter's Morning.
If You Can Hear My Hooves.
In a Double Rainbow.
Mother/Deer/Lady.
Oh But It Was Good...
Ole Moke...
Pennsylvania Winter Indian 1974.
Wrap Me in Blankets of Momentary Winds.

Littledale, Freya
When My Dog Died.

Littlefield, Hazel
Not for Its Own Sake...

Littlefield, Milton S.
Come, O Lord, Like Morning Sunlight.
O Son of Man, Thou Madest Known.

Littleton, Edward
The Spider.

Littlewood, W. E.
The Heart of God.

Littlewort, Dorothy
Prayer of a Teacher.

Litvinoff, Emanuel
All Ruin Is the Same.
Garrison Town.
If I Forget Thee.
Note from an Intimate Diary.
Poem for the Atomic Age.
Rededication.
To T. S. Eliot.
War Swaggers.

Litwack, Susan
Creation of the Child.
Havdolah.
Inscape.
Tonight Everyone in the World Is Dreaming the Same Dream.

Liu, Stephen Shu Ning
Adultery at a Las Vegas Bookstore.
I Lie on the Chilled Stones of the Great Wall.
My Father's Martial Art.
On Pali Lookout.
A Pair of Fireflies.
Tours.

Liu Hsi-Chun
Song of Grief.

Livesay, Dorothy
Abracadabra.
The Children's Letters.
The Colour of God's Face.
Contact.
Encounter.
Epilogue to the Outrider.
Fantasia.
Green Rain.
Improvisation on an Old Theme.
The Inheritors.
Interval with Fire.
Lament.
The Leader.
On Looking into Henry Moore.
Pause.
Serenade for Strings.
Signature.
Spain.
The Uninvited.
Waking in the Dark.
Wedding.
Without Benefit of Tape.

Livesay, Florence Randal
Tim, the Fairy.
The Violin Calls.

Livingston, Edna
A Question.

Livingston, Myra Cohn
12 October.
74th Street.
Car Wash.
Conversation with Washington.
Driving.
Father.
German Shepherd.
Grunion.
Halloween.
Limerick: "A young person of precious precocity."
Limerick: "Curiosity's not in me head."
Limerick: "If you don't know the meaning of snook."
Limerick: "If you're apt to be ravenous, look."
Mill Valley.
Old People.
Only a Little Litter.
Pretending.
Silly Dog.
The Tape.

Livingston, William
Ireland Weeping.
Message to the Bard.

Livingstone, Douglas
An Evasion.
The King.
One Time.
Peace Delegate.
Sunstrike.
To a Dead Elephant.

Llewellyn, K. N.
Prairie.

Llorens Torres, Luis
Love without Love.
Maceo.

Lloyd, Arthur
I'll Strike You with a Feather.

Lloyd, Beatrix Demarest
Love and Time.
Night-Wind.
With Roses.

Lloyd, Cecil Francis
March Winds.
Truth.

Lloyd, Charles
An Essay on the Genius of Pope (excerpt).

Lloyd, Donald J.
Bridal Couch.

Lloyd, Evan
The Methodist.

Lloyd, Robert
The Cit's Country Box.
The Critic's Rules.
A Familiar Epistle to J.B. Esq.
Sent to a Lady, with a Seal.
Shakespeare, an Epistle to David Garrick, Esq.

Lloyd, Roseann
Song of the Fisherman's Lover.

Llster, R. P.
Postscript to Die Schone Mullerin.

Lluellyn, Martin
Cock-Throwing!

Llwyd, John Plummer Derwent
The Vestal Virgin.

Llywarch Hen
Tercets.

Llywelyn
Birds.

Lo Yin
The Book-Burning Pit.

Lochore, Robert
Marriage and the Care O't.

Locke, Lawrence
Animal Pictures.
Leaving Mendota, 1956.
River.

Locker, Malka
Clocks.
Drunken Streets.

Locker-Lampson, Frederick
At Her Window.
The Cuckoo.
A Garden Lyric.
The Jester's Plea.
Loulou and Her Cat.
Love, Time and Death.
Mrs. Smith.
My Mistress's Boots.
A Nice Correspondent.
An Old Buffer.
On an Old Muff.
Our Photographs.
A Rhyme of One.
Rotten Row.
The Skeleton in the Cupboard.
St. James's Street.
A Terrible Infant.
To My Grandmother.
The Widow's Mite.

Lockett, Reginald
Good Times & No Bread.

Lockhart, John Gibson
Lament for Captain Paton.
Lines: "When youthful faith hath fled."
Serenade.
The Wandering Knight's Song.

Locklin, Gerald
Bobbie's Cat.
Don't Answer the Phone for Me the Same.
The Dwarf.
Gunfighter.
Pedagogy.
Poop.
Since You Seem Intent...
The Toad.

Lockman, John
The Penitent Nun.

Lockwood, Margo
December Eclipse.
Victorian Grandmother.
Wind Flowers.

Lockwood, Robert
Little Boy Blue.

Lockwood, William A.
Limerick: "There was a trim maiden named Wood."
Lockyer, Milton
Dark Mountains.
Lodge, Edith
Song of the Hill.
Lodge, George Cabot
Day and Dark.
The East Wind.
A Song of the Wave.
Youth.
Lodge, Thomas
Beauty, Alas, Where Wast Thou Born.
A Blith and Bonny Country Lass.
Carpe Diem.
Coridon's Song.
Devoide of Reason, Thrale to Foolish Ire.
The Earth, Late Choked with Showers.
A Fancy.
For Pity, Pretty Eyes, Surcease.
Her Rambling.
I Would in Rich and Golden Coloured Raine.
Love Guards the Roses of Thy Lips.
Love in My Bosom Like a Bee.
Love's Protestation.
Love's Witchery.
Ode: "Now I find thy looks were feigned."
Of Rosalind.
Old Damon's Pastoral.
Phoebe's Sonnet.
Phyllis.
Pluck the Fruit and Taste the Pleasure.
Rosader's Sonnet.
Rosalynde.
The Rose.
Sonnet: "O shady vales, O fair enriched meads."
Truth's Complaint over England.
A Very Phoenix.
Loesser, Frank
Guys and Dolls.
Once in Love with Amy.
Praise the Lord and Pass the Ammunition!
Loewenthal, Tali
Hebrew Script.
Loewinsohn, Ron
Against the Silences to Come.
Goat Dance.
Insomniac Poem.
The Leaves.
Mrs. Loewinsohn &c.
My Sons.
Pastoral.
The Stillness of the Poem.
The Thing Made Real.
The Windows.
Loftin, Elouise
Pigeon.
Virginia.
Weeksville Women.
Woman.
Lofting, Hugh
Betwixt and Between.
Picnic.
Lofton, Blanche De Good
Song of the Seasons.
Lofton, Cripple Clarence
I Don't Know.

Lofton, Willie
Dark Road Blues.
Logan, J. D.
Heliodore.
Logan, John
Achilles and the King.
Believe It.
The Braes of Yarrow.
A Century Piece for Poor Heine.
Concert Scene.
Dawn and a Woman.
The Experiment That Failed.
First Prelude. Dream in Ohio: The Father.
First Reunion in New Orleans: The Father as King of Revels.
Honolulu and Back.
The Library.
Lines for a Friend Who Left.
Lines for a Young Wanderer in Mexico.
Lines for Michael in the Picture.
Lines on His Birthday.
Lines to His Son on Reaching Adolescence.
Love Poem.
The Monument and the Shrine.
Nude Kneeling in Sand.
On the Death of Keats.
On the House of a Friend.
The Pass.
The Picnic.
The Rescue.
San Francisco Poem.
Saturday Afternoon at the Movies.
Shore Scene.
Spring of the Thief.
A Suite of Six Pieces for Siskind.
Three Moves.
Three Poems on Morris Graves' Paintings.
To a Young Poet Who Fled.
A Trip to Four or Five Towns.
White Pass Ski Patrol.
The Zoo.
Logan, William
Debora Sleeping.
Green Island.
Protective Colors.
Summer Island.
Sutcliffe and Whitby.
Tatiana Kalatschova.
Logan. John, Doddridge. Philip
O God of Bethel.
Logan, Jr, George B.
Dawn.
Logau, Friedrich von
Retribution.
Logue, Christopher
Epitaph.
Friday. Wet Dusk.
Letters from an Irishman to a Rat.
New Numbers: Foreword.
The Story of Two Gentlemen and the Gardener.
Loines, Russell Hillard
On a Magazine Sonnet.
Lom, Iain
The Day of Inverlochy.
To Mackinnon of Strath.
Lomax, Pearl Cleage
Glimpse.
Jesus Drum.
Mississippi Born.

Poem.
London, Jonathan
Batches of New Leaves.
Driving Home.
Lonergan, Frank
Cycle.
Loney, Alan
Elegy.
The Eternal Return.
Of Flowers.
Long, Doughtry
Ginger Bread Mama.
Negro Dreams.
One Time Henry Dreamed the Number.
Poem No. 21.
Long, Elizabeth-Ellen
After-Christmas Poem.
Autumn Song.
Christmas Song.
Discarded Christmas Tree.
Mountain Medicine.
Rain Clouds.
Treasure.
Long, Haniel
Butterflies.
The Cause of This I Know Not.
Dead Men Tell No Tales.
The Faun.
Girl Athletes.
The Herd Boy.
The Poet.
Song: "Poppies paramour the girls."
Students.
Long, Peter
Remember Thy Creator Now.
Long, R. H.
Poet and Peasant.
The Skylark's Nest.
Long, Robert
Saying One Thing.
Long, Stewart I.
Was It You?
Long, Virginia
112 at Presidio.
Mares of Night.
Long, Worth
Arson and Cold Lace (or How I Yearn to Burn Baby Burn).
Longchamps, Joanne de See De Longchamps, Joanne
Longfellow, Henry Wadsworth
Aftermath.
"All Things Must Have an End; the World Itself."
The Arrow and the Song.
The Arsenal at Springfield.
Autumn.
Azrael.
A Ballad of the French Fleet.
The Battle of Lovell's Pond.
The Belfry of Bruges.
Belisarius.
The Bells of Lynn.
The Bells of San Blas.
The Birds of Killingworth.
The Bridge.
The Broken Oar.
The Builders.
The Building of the Long Serpent.
The Building of the Ship.
Burial of the Minnisink.
The Challenge.
The Chamber Over the Gate.
Charlemagne.
Chaucer.
The Children's Hour.
Christmas Bells.

The Courtship of Miles Standish.
The Cross of Snow.
The Cumberland.
Curfew.
Dante.
The Day Is Done.
Daybreak.
Decoration Day.
The Discoverer of the North Cape.
Divina Commedia.
The Divine Tragedy: The Fate of the Prophets.
A Dutch Picture.
Eliot's Oak.
Endymion.
Evangeline.
The Evening Star.
Excelsior.
The Expedition to Wessagusset.
The Fiftieth Birthday of Agassiz.
The Fire of Drift-Wood.
The Flight into Egypt.
Flowers.
Follow Me.
From My Arm-Chair.
The Galley of Count Arnaldos.
Gaspar Becerra.
The Ghosts.
Giles Corey of the Salem Farms: Prologue.
Giotto's Tower.
God's-Acre.
The Golden Legend: This Is Indeed the Blessed Mary's Land.
The Golden Mile-Stone.
The Hanging of the Crane.
The Harvest Moon.
Haunted Houses.
Hawthorne.
Hiawatha's Sailing.
Hiawatha's Wooing.
Him Evermore I Behold.
Holidays.
Home Song.
Hymn of the Moravian Nuns of Bethlehem.
Hymn to the Night.
I Heard the Bells on Christmas Day.
In the Churchyard at Cambridge.
It Is Too late!
Jericho's Blind Beggar.
The Jewish Cemetery at Newport.
John Endicott: Prologue.
Jugurtha.
Keats.
Keramos.
Killed at the Ford.
The Ladder of St. Augustine: The Heights.
Let War's Tempests Cease.
The Luck of Edenhall.
Maidenhood.
The Manuscripts of God.
Mezzo Cammin.
Michael Angelo: A Fragment (excerpt).
Midnight Mass for the Dying Year.
Milton.
The Monk of Casal-Maggiore.
Moonlight.
Morituri Salutamus.
My Books.

My Lost Youth.
Nature.
The Norman Baron (excerpt).
Nuremberg.
O Ship of State.
The Old Bridge at Florence.
The Old Clock on the Stairs.
The Phantom Ship.
President Garfield.
The Proclamation.
A Psalm of Life.
Rain in Summer.
The Rainy Day.
The Reaper and the Flowers.
Resignation.
Retribution.
The Revenge of Rain-In-The-
Face.
The Ropewalk.
The Seaside and the Fireside:
Dedication.
Seaweed.
The Secret of the Sea.
Serenade.
Shakespeare.
Ships That Pass in the Night.
Sir Humphrey Gilbert.
A Skeleton in Armor.
The Slave's Dream.
Snow-Flakes.
The Song of Hiawatha.
The Sound of the Sea.
The Spanish Student:
Serenade.
The Spirit of Poetry.
Suspiria.
Tales of a Wayside Inn.
There Was a Little Girl.
Three Friends of Mine.
The Three Kings.
The Three Silences of
Molinos.
Three Sonnets on the Divina
Commedia.
The Tide Rises, the Tide
Falls.
To an Old Danish Song-Book.
To the Driving Cloud.
The Trial.
Twilight.
Ultima Thule.
Venice.
Victor Galbraith.
The Village Blacksmith.
Wapentake.
The War-Token.
The Warden of the Cinque
Ports.
The Warning.
The Windmill.
With Snow White Veil.
The Witnesses.
Woods in Winter.
The Wreck of the Hesperus.
Longfellow, Samuel
Again as Evening's Shadow
Falls.
Beneath the Shadow of the
Cross.
The Christian Life.
The Church Universal.
God of the Earth, the Sky, the
Sea.
God, through All and in You
All.
Holy Spirit, Truth Divine.
O Life That Maketh All
Things New.
Peace on Earth.
The Summer Days Are Come
Again.
'Tis Winter Now.

Longley, Michael
Caravan.
Christopher at Birth.
Desert Warfare.
Emily Dickinson.
Epithalamion.
Fleadh.
Fleance.
In Memoriam.
Irish Poetry.
Kindertotenlieder.
Leaving Inishmore.
Letter to Derek Mahon.
Letter to Seamus Heaney.
A Letter to Three Irish Poets.
The Linen Workers.
The Lodger.
Man Lying on a Wall.
Miscarriage.
No Continuing City.
Peace.
Persephone.
Second Sight.
Skara Brae.
The Small Hotel.
Swans Mating.
The Third Light.
Wounds.
Longman, Doris
Flight 382.
Longstaff, W. D.
Take Time to Be Holy.
Longwell, E. Elizabeth
The Pear Tree.
Lonzano, Menahem
The Gentleman.
Looke, John
A Famous Sea-Fight.
Loomis, Charles Battell
A Classic Ode.
Jack and Jill (parody).
O-U-G-H.
Propinquity Needed.
Timon of Archimedes.
Loomis, Charles H.
Adelina, the Yale Boola Girl.
Yale Boola March.
Lope de Vega Carpio, Felix
At Dawn the Virgin Is Born...
A Christmas Cradlesong.
Clover.
The Good Shepherd.
A Little Carol of the Virgin.
The Lullaby.
Song for the Divine Bride and
Mother.
A Song for the Virgin Mother.
Tomorrow.
Lopez de Ayala, Pero
Song to the Virgin Mary.
Lopez-Penha, Abraham
Dusk.
Lopez Velarde, Ramon
The Ascension and the
Assumption.
Lord, Everett W.
The Legend of the Admen.
Lord, May Carleton
Old Man with a Mowing
Machine.
Prayer.
Lord, Phillips H.
Your Church and Mine.
Lord, William Wilberforce
The Brook.
Ode to England.
On the Defeat of Henry Clay.
To Rosina Pico.
Worship.
Lorde, Audre
And Fall Shall Sit in
Judgment.

And What About the
Children.
Between Ourselves.
A Birthday Memorial to
Seventh Street.
Chain.
Coal.
Eulogy for Alvin Frost.
Father Son and Holy Ghost.
Father, the Year Is Fallen.
For Each of You.
From the House of Yemanja.
Hanging Fire.
Harriet.
Movement Song.
Naturally.
Now That I Am Forever with
Child.
One Year to Life on the
Grand Central Shuttle.
Outside.
Oya.
Pirouette.
A Poem for a Poet.
Recreation.
Rites of Passage.
Summer Oracle.
To Desi as Joe as Smoky the
Lover of 115th Street.
To My Daughter the Junkie
on a Train.
A Trip on the Staten Island
Ferry.
What My Child Learns of the
Sea.
When the Saints Come
Marching In.
The Woman Thing.
The Workers Rose on May
Day or Postscript to Karl
Marx.
Lorentz, Pare
The River.
Loring, Frederick Wadsworth
In the Old Churchyard at
Fredericksburg.
Lorr, Katharine Auchincloss
The Beekeeper's Dream.
Peking Man, Raining.
Lorraine, Lilith
If These Endure.
Let Dreamers Wake.
Without Regret.
Lorris, Guillaume de See
Guillaume de Lorris
Lott, Clarinda Harriss
Living in the Present.
Lougee, David
A Sestina for Cynthia.
Louis, Adrian C.
Captivity Narrative:
September 1981.
Elegy for the Forgotten
Oldsmobile.
The Hemingway Syndrome.
Indian Education.
The Walker River Night.
Louis, Louise
The Wounded.
Lourie, Dick
Ann's House.
The Dream about Junior High
School in America.
Getting a Poem in the Rain.
The Gift.
Pearl Harbor Day 1970.
September 30.
Sharks.
Stumbling.
Telegram.
Thinking of You.

Louthan, Robert
Elegy for My Father.
L'Ouverture, Isaac
Farewell.
Louys, Pierre
The Agonizing Memory.
The Breasts of Mnasidice.
The Complaisant Friend.
Love.
The Meeting.
Penumbra.
The Songs of Bilitis.
Love, Adelaide
Alchemy.
No Sweeter Thing.
Poet's Prayer.
Walk Slowly.
Love, George
The Noonday April Sun.
Love, John, Jr.
Barber, Spare Those Hairs.
Lovejoy, George Newell
Easter Carol.
Lovelace, Abraham
To Sir William Davenant,
Upon His Two First Books
of Gondibert.
Lovelace, Richard
Advice to My Best Brother,
Colonel Francis Lovelace.
Against the Love of Great
Ones.
An Anniversary on the
Hymeneals of My Noble
Kinsman, Thomas Stanley...
Another.
The Ant.
The Apostasy of One and But
One Lady.
La Bella Bona-Roba.
A Black Patch on Lucasta's
Face.
Calling Lucasta from Her
Retirement.
Cupid Far Gone.
The Duel.
Elinda's Glove.
Epigram: "A fool much bit by
fleas put out the light."
The Falcon.
Female Glory.
A Fly about a Glass of Burnt
Claret.
A Fly Caught in a Cobweb.
The Glove.
The Grasshopper.
Gratiana Dauncing and
Singing.
In Allusion to the French
Song, N'entendez Vous Pas
ce Language.
A la Bourbon.
The Lady A. L., My Asylum
in a Great Extremity.
A Lady with a Falcon on Her
Fist.
A Loose Saraband.
Love Enthroned.
Love Made in the First Age.
Lucasta Laughing.
Lucasta's Fan, with a
Looking-Glass in It.
Lucasta's World.
A Mock Charon.
A Mock Song.
Night.
Orpheus to Beasts.
Orpheus to Woods.
Painture.
The Rose.
The Scrutiny.
The Snail.

Song: "In mine own monument I lie."
Song: "Why should you swear I am forsworn."
Strive Not, Vain Lover, to Be Fine.
To a Lady That Desired Me I Would Bear My Part with Her in a Song.
To Althea from Prison.
To Amarantha.
To Dr. F. B. on His Book of Chess.
To Fletcher Reviv'd.
To Lucasta.
To Lucasta, from Prison.
To Lucasta, Going to the Wars.
To Lucasta: Her Reserved Looks.
To Lucasta, on Going Beyond the Seas.
To Lucasta: The Rose.
To My Noble Kinsman, Thomas Stanley, Esquire, on His Lyric Poems...
To My Truly Valiant, Learned Friend....
To My Worthy Friend Master Peter Lely...
Upon the Curtain of Lucasta's Picture It Was Thus Wrought.
Valiant Love.
The Vintage to the Dungeon.

Loveman, Robert
April Rain.
A Diamond.
Hobson and His Men.
March.
Rain Song.
Spring.
A Sunset.

Lover, Samuel
The Angel's Whisper.
Ask and Have.
Barney O'Hea.
The Birth of St. Patrick.
Father Land and Mother Tongue.
Father Molloy or, the Confession.
The Girl I Left behind Me.
The Low-Backed Car.
Paddy O'Rafther.
The Quaker's Meeting.
Rory O'More; or, Good Omens.
St. Kevin.
The War Ship of Peace.
What Will You Do, Love?
Widow Machree.

Loving, Pierre
The Black Horse Rider.

Low, Benjamin R. C.
Due North.
The Little Boy to the Locomotive.
The Locomotive to the Little Boy.
To-Day.
White Violets.

Low, Patricia
The First Day of the Hunting Moon.
Wet Weather.

Low, Samuel
To a Segar.

Lowbury, Edward
In the Old Jewish Cemetery, Prague, 1970.
The Monster.

The Roc.
Swan.
Tree of Knowledge.

Lowe, Julia Ward
Our Orders.

Lowe, Robert
Songs of the Squatters, I.

Lowell, Amy
Apology.
Autumn.
The Book of Hours of Sister Clotilde.
Carrefour.
Chinoiseries.
The City of Falling Leaves.
Crowned.
A Decade.
Desolation.
Dolphins in Blue Water.
Dreams in War Time (excerpt).
Epitaph on a Young Poet Who Died before Having Achieved Success.
The Fisherman's Wife.
Flute-Priest Song for Rain (excerpt).
Four Sides to a House.
Fragment.
Free Fantasia on Japanese Themes.
Fringed Gentians.
From One Who Stays.
The Garden by Moonlight.
Grotesque.
Hippocrene.
Interlude.
Katydids.
A Lady.
Lilacs.
Little Ivory Figures Pulled with String.
Madonna of the Evening Flowers.
Meeting-House Hill.
Merchandise.
Music.
Night Clouds.
On Looking at a Copy of Alice Meynell's Poems.
The Painted Ceiling.
Patterns.
The Poet.
Points of View.
Proportion.
Reaping.
A Roxbury Garden.
The Sea Shell.
Sisters.
Solitaire.
A Sprig of Rosemary.
Streets.
The Taxi.
Texas.
Thorn Piece.
To a Friend.
The Trumpet-Vine Arbour.
Venus Transiens.
Vernal Equinox.
Wind and Silver.
A Year Passes.

Lowell, James Russell
After the Burial.
Aladdin.
America's Gospel.
Auf Wiedersehen.
Auspex.
An Autograph.
Bibliolaters: God Is Not Dumb.
The Biglow Papers.

Birthday Verses Written in a Child's Album.
The Boss.
Careless Seems the Great Avenger.
The Cathedral.
A Christmas Carol.
Columbus.
The Commemoration Ode.
The Darkened Mind.
The Debate in the Sennit.
A Fable for Critics.
The Fatherland.
The First Snowfall.
Fitz Adam's Story.
Flawless His Heart.
For an Autograph (excerpt).
The Fountain.
Hebe.
The Heritage.
His Throne Is with the Outcast.
Hob Gobbling's Song.
In a Copy of Omar Khayyam.
In an Album.
In the Twilight.
Jonathan to John.
Lincoln.
A Misconception.
Monna Lisa.
Mr. Hosea Biglow to the Editor of "The Atlantic Monthly."
My Love.
The New-Come Chief.
Now Is the High-Tide of the Year.
Ode Recited at the Harvard Commemoration.
On Board the '76.
On Receiving a Copy of Mr. Austin Dobson's "Old World Idylls".
An Oriental Apologue.
The Origin of Didactic Poetry.
Our Fathers Fought for Liberty.
P.S.
Palinode.
A Parable.
Praxiteles and Phryne.
The Present Crisis.
The Recall.
Rev. Homer Wilbur's "Festina Lente."
Rhoecus.
She Came and Went.
The Shepherd of King Admetus.
The Singing Leaves.
Sixty-Eighth Birthday.
St. Michael the Weigher.
A Stanza on Freedom.
Stanzas on Freedom.
Stealing.
Sunthin' in the Pastoral Line.
Tempora Mutantur.
'Tis Sorrow Builds the Shining Ladder Up.
To the Dandelion.
True Love.
Under the Old Elm.
Unwasted Days.
Verses.
The Vision of Sir Launfal.
The Washers of the Shroud.
We Will Speak Out.
Without and Within.
Work.

Lowell, Maria White
The Morning-Glory.

An Opium Fantasy.
Song.

Lowell, Robert
1930's.
After the Surprising Conversions.
Alfred Corning Clark.
As a Plane Tree by the Water.
At the Indian Killer's Grave.
Between the Porch and the Altar.
Beyond the Alps.
The Bomber.
Caligula.
Central Park.
Charles the Fifth and the Peasant.
Child's Song.
Children of Light.
Christ Is Here.
Christmas Eve under Hooker's Statue.
Colloquy in Black Rock.
Commander Lowell.
The Dead in Europe.
Death and the Bridge.
Death from Cancer.
The Death of the Sheriff.
Dolphin.
Down the Nile.
The Drunken Fisherman.
End of a Year.
Epilogue.
The Exile's Return.
Eye and Tooth.
Ezra Pound.
Fall 1961.
Falling Asleep Over the Aeneid.
The Fat Man in the Mirror.
Fishnet.
For George Santayana.
For John Berryman I.
For Sale.
For Sheridan.
For the Union Dead.
Ford Madox Ford.
Fourth of July in Maine.
George III.
The Ghost.
Grandparents.
Harriet.
Her Dead Brother.
History.
The Holy Innocents.
Home after Three Months Away.
Identification in Belfast (I.R.A. Bombing).
In Memory of Arthur Winslow.
In the Cage.
July in Washington.
Katherine's Dream.
Lady Ralegh's Lament.
Last Things, Black Pines at 4 a.m.
The Lesson.
Long Summer (excerpt).
A Mad Negro Soldier Confined at Munich.
Man and Wife.
The March 1.
The March 2.
Marriage.
Mary Winslow.
Memories of West Street and Lepke.
Mexico.
Mother Marie Therese.
The Mouth of the Hudson.
Mr. Edwards and the Spider.

My Last Afternoon with
  Uncle Devereux Winslow.
Near the Ocean.
New Year's Day.
New York 1962: Fragment.
Night Sweat.
The North Sea Undertaker's
  Complaint.
Obit.
October and November.
The Old Flame.
On the Eve of the Feast of the
  Immaculate Conception:
  1942.
The Opposite House.
The Picture.
The Public Garden.
The Quaker Graveyard in
  Nantucket.
Reading Myself.
The Relief of Lucknow.
Robert Frost.
Robespierre and Mozart as
  Stage.
Sailing Home from Rapallo.
Saint-Just 1767-93.
Salem.
Shifting Colors.
Skunk Hour.
The Slough of Despond.
Soft Wood.
Stalin.
T. S. Eliot.
This Golden Summer.
Those before Us.
To Delmore Schwartz.
To Speak of Woe That Is in
  Marriage.
Turtle.
Waking Early Sunday
  Morning.
Waking in the Blue.
Watchmaker God.
Water.
Where the Rainbow Ends.
The Withdrawal.
Words for Hart Crane.
**Lowell, Robert and Spence
  Traill**
The After-Comers.
The Brave Old Ship, the
  Orient.
Lowenfels, Walter
Creed.
Speech to the Court.
Lowenstein, Robert
Peek-A-Boo.
Lowenstein, Tom
Horizon without Landscape.
Nausicaa with Some
  Attendants.
Noah in New England.
Lowery, Mike
Nam.
The Smell of Old Newspapers
  Is Always Stronger...
Stroke.
Lowey, Mark
On Living with Children for a
  Prolonged Time.
Lowry, Betty
The Beasts of Boston.
Lowry, Henry Dawson
Holiday.
The Spring Will Come.
Lowry, Malcolm
After the Publication of
  Under the Volcano.
Cain Shall Not Slay Abel
  Today on Our Good
  Ground.

Christ Walks in This Infernal
  District Too.
Delirium in Vera Cruz.
The Drunkards.
For Under the Volcano.
He Liked the Dead.
In Memoriam.
The Lighthouse Invites the
  Storm.
Lupus in Fabula.
Salmon Drowns Eagle.
Lowry, Robert
How Can I Keep from
  Singing? (excerpt).
Shall We Gather at the River?
Where Is My Wandering Boy
  Tonight?
**Lowry, Robert and Fanny J.
  Crosby**
All the Way My Savior Leads
  Me.
Lowther, Pat
Last Letter to Pablo.
A Stone Diary.
Loy, Mina
Apology of Genius.
Der Blinde Junge.
Human Cylinders.
Love Songs.
Lunar Baedeker.
Loyd, Marianne
Llanberis Summer.
Lu Yu
The Wild Flower Man.
Lubke, Bernice W.
The All-Sufficient Christ.
**Lucan (Marcus Annaeus
  Lucanus)**
Pharsalia: The Rivalry
  between Caesar and Pompey.
Lucas, Alice
Prayer before Sleep.
Lucas, Daniel B.
In the Land Where We Were
  Dreaming.
Lucas, Edward Verrall
Clay.
The Conjuror.
Friends.
Mr. Coggs.
The Pedestrian's Plaint.
Lucas, F. L.
Beleaguered Cities.
The Pipe of Peace.
Spain, 1809.
Lucas, Henry N.
But, Still, He.
Lucas, Lawrence A.
Another Meeting.
Lucas, St. John
The Curate Thinks You Have
  No Soul.
Pain.
Luce, Morton
Thysia.
Lucian [or Lucianus]
Artificial Beauty.
A Dead Child.
Luciano, Felipe
You're Nothing but a Spanish
  Colored Kid.
Lucie-Smith, Edward
At the Roman Baths, Bath.
Caravaggio Dying, Porto
  Ercole, July 1610, Aged 36.
The Dodo.
The Fault.
The Giant Tortoise.
The Ladybirds.
The Lesson.
Meeting Myself.

On Looking at Stubbs's
  Anatomy of the Horse.
The Parrot.
Poet in Winter.
Rabbit Cry.
Lucilius [or Lucillius]
Advice to a Prizefighter.
Boxer Loses Face and
  Fortune.
Eutychides.
First in the Pentathlon.
Lean Gaius, Who Was
  Thinner Than a Straw.
Monument to a Boxer.
On an Old Woman.
On Apis the Prizefighter.
The Retired Boxer.
The Sluggard.
Treasure.
A Valentine for a Lady.
The World's Worst Boxer.
Lucina, Sister Mary
Rain.
Luckey, Eunice W.
Babies of the Pioneers.
**Lucretius (Titus Lucretitus
  Carus)**
Address to Venus.
Against the Fear of Death.
Beyond Religion.
Concerning the Nature of
  Love.
No Single Thing Abides.
De Rerum Natura.
Suave Mari Magno.
Lucy, Sean
Longshore Intellectual.
Senior Members.
Supervising Examinations.
Luders, Charles Henry
A Corsage Bouquet.
The Four Winds.
The Haunts of the Halcyon.
Heart of Oak.
The Mountebanks.
An Old Thought.
Ludlow, Fitz Hugh
Socrates Snooks.
Too Late.
Ludlum, William
A Business Man's Prayer.
That Radio Religion.
Ludvigson, Susan
The Child's Dream.
Man Arrested in Hacking
  Death Tells Police He
  Mistook Mother-in-Law...
Motherhood.
On Learning That Certain
  Peat Bogs Contain Perfectly
  Preserved Bodies.
The Widow.
Luff, W.
I Buried the Year.
Luhrmann, Tom
Beyond Belief.
Lui Chi
A Poet Thinks.
Lulham, Habberton
Nested.
Lull, Ramon
The Lover and the Beloved.
The Tree of Love.
**Lully, J. B. and Charles
  Fonteyn Manney**
Au Clair de la Lune.
Lum, Wing Tek
At a Chinaman's Grave.
Chinatown Games.
The Poet Imagines His
  Grandfather's Thoughts on
  the Day He Died.

To the Old Masters.
Translations.
Lummis, Charles F.
John Charles Fremont.
A Poe-'em of Passion.
The Sidewinder.
Lumumba, Patrice Emery
Dawn in the Heart of Africa.
Lunt, George
Requiem.
Luria, Isaac
A Sabbath of Rest.
Lurie, Annie
Dentyne.
Lushington, Franklin
No More Words.
Luther, Martin
All Hail, Thou Noble Guest.
Away in a Manger.
Cradle Hymn.
From Heaven High I Come to
  You.
A Mighty Fortress Is Our
  God.
Luton, Mildred
Hossolalia.
Pliny Jane.
Luttinger, Abigail
The Palace for Teeth.
Luttrell, Henry
Advice to Julia.
Epigram: "O death, thy
  certainty is such."
On a Man Run over by an
  Omnibus.
On a Poet.
Lutz, Gertrude May
Cat of Many Years.
Prisoner of War.
Song for a New Generation.
Lux, Thomas
All the Slaves.
Barn Fire.
Farmers.
Flying Noises.
Graveyard by the Sea.
History and Abstraction.
If You See This Man.
Lament City.
Man Asleep in the Desert.
The Midnight Tennis Match.
Solo Native.
There Were Some Summers.
This Is a Poem for the
  Fathers and for Michael
  Ryan.
Luzi, Mario
Gothic Notebook (excerpts).
Luzzatto, Isaac
Death, Thou Hast Seized Me.
Unto the Upright Praise:
  Chorus.
Lyall, Sir Alfred Comyn
Meditations of a Hindu
  Prince.
A Night in the Red Sea.
Rajpoot Rebels.
Studies at Delhi.
Lydgate, John
Against Women's Fashions.
Balade Simple: "Fairest of
  stars."
Beware of Doubleness.
The Boy Serving at Table.
The Child Jesus to Mary the
  Rose.
The Complaint of the Black
  Knight.
Court of Sapience.
The Dance of Death.
Devotions of the Fowls.
The Duplicity of Women.

Epithalamium for Gloucester.
The Fall of Princes: Epilogue.
Froward Maymond.
Henry Before Agincourt.
Lat Noman Booste of
  Konnyng Nor Vertu.
The Life of Our Lady.
Like a Midsummer Rose.
London Lickpenny.
A Lover's New Year's Gift.
To the Virgin.
Vox Ultima Crucis.

Lydston, Donna R.
The Family.

Lyle, K. Curtis
Lacrimas; or, There Is a Need
  to Scream.
Sometimes I Go to Camarillo
  & Sit in the Lounge.
Songs for the Cisco Kid or
  Singing for the Face.
Songs for the Cisco Kid or
  Singing Song #2.
Terra Cotta.

Lyly, John
Alexander and Campaspe:
  Apelles' Song.
Apollo's Song.
Cupid's Indictment.
A Fairy Song.
Mother Bombie: Fools in
  Love's College.
Pan's Song.
Sapho's Song.
A Serving Men's Song.
Song: "It is all one in Venus'
  wanton school."
Song of Apollo.
A Song of Diana's Nymphs.
Trico's Song.

Lynch, Annette
Bridgework.
Gratitude.

Lynch, Charles
If We Cannot Live as People.
Jam Fa Jamaica.
Memo.
Shade.
Simfunny of Thee Hold
Whorl.

Lynch, John W.
A Woman Wrapped in
  Silence.

Lynch, Richard
Love's Despair.

Lynch, Stanislaus
Blue Peter.

Lynch, Thomas Toke
Lift Up Your Heads, Rejoice.
Reinforcements.
A Thousand Years Have
  Come.

Lynche, Richard
But Thou My Deere Sweet-
  Sounding Lute Be Still.
What Sugred Termes, What
  All-Perswading Arte.

Lynde, Benjamin
Lines Descriptive of
  Thomson's Island.

Lyndsay, Sir David
Ane Satire of the Three
  Estaitis (excerpt).
Ane Supplication in
  Contemptioun of Syde
  Taillis.
Complaint of the Common
  Weill of Scotland.
The Pardoner's Sermon.

Lynskey, Edward C.
No Idle Boast.

Lyon, George Ella
Birth.
Catechisms: Talking with a
  Four-Year-Old.
Cousin Ella Goes to Town.
My Grandfather in Search of
  Moonshine.
A Testimony.

Lyon, Lilian Bowes
Duchess.
The Feather.
A Shepherd's Coat.
The Stars Go By.
The White Hare.

Lyon, Roger H.
Keep on Praying.

Lyons, Richard
The Sisseton Indian
  Reservation.

Lyons, Richard J.
Titus, Son of Rembrandt:
  1665.

Lysaght, Edward
Garnyvillo.

Lysaght, Sidney Royse
A Deserted Home.
First Pathways.
New Horizons.
The Secret of the Deeps.

Lyte, Henry Francis
Abide with Me; Fast Falls the
  Eventide.
Agnes.
Forgiveness.
A Lost Love.
The Unknown God.

Lytle, William Haines
Antony and Cleopatra.
Antony to Cleopatra.
The Siege of Chapultepec.
The Volunteers.

Lyttelton, George, Lord
Ode. In Imitation of Pastor
  Fido Written Abroad, in
  1729.
Tell Me, My Heart, If This Be
  Love.
To Miss Lucy F—, with a
  New Watch.
To the Memory of a Lady.
Written at Mr. Pope's House
  at Twickenham.

Lyttleton, Lucy
Simon the Cyrenean.

**Lytton, Edward Robert Bulwer,
Earl of** See also "Meredith,
Owen"
Absent Yet Present.
Aux Italiens.
The Chess-Board.
Christ's Sympathy.
Going Back Again.
The Last Wish.
Night and Love.
Nydia's Song.
The Portrait.
Since We Parted.

M

"M"
On the Frequent Review of
  the Troops.

Maas, Willard
Letter to R.
No Season for Our Season.
On Reading Gene Derwood's
  "The Innocent".

Mabbe, James
Sweet Trees Who Shade This
  Mould.

Mabuza, Lindiwe
Summer 1970.

MacAdams, Lewis
The Animals.
The Clock Works.
The Dazzling Day.
Have Sky.
In Memorium.
The Italian Air.
Kora for March 5th.
The Lace Curtains.
A Meditation: What is a
  Stocking in Eternity?
Moguls and Monks.
Olive Grove.
Raw Honey.
Trailer Park.
Warm Tea.
The Young Man.

Macainsh, Noel
Kangaroo by Nightfall.

MacAlpine, James
To an Irish Blackbird.

Mac An Bhaird, Laoiseach
A Fond Greeting, Hillock
  There.
A Man of Experience.
Two Sons.

Macarthur, Bessie J. B.
Nocht o' Mortal Sicht.

MacArthur, Gloria
Phineas Pratt.

Macarthy, Harry
The Bonnie Blue Flag.

Macartney, Frederick T.
Desert Claypan.
Early Summer Sea-Tryst.
Kyrielle: Party Politics.
No Less Than Prisoners.

Macaulay, F. E. M.
The Women's Marseillaise.

**Macaulay, Thomas Babington,
Lord**
The Armada: A Fragment.
The Battle of Naseby.
The Country Clergyman's
  Trip to Cambridge.
The Fight at the Bridge.
Horatius.
Ivry.
A Jacobite's Epitaph.
The Last Buccaneer.
A Radical War Song.
Sermon in a Churchyard.

MacBeth, George
Ash.
Bats.
Bedtime Story.
The Compasses.
The Drawer.
The Five-Minute Orlando
  Macbeth.
The Killing.
The Land-Mine.
Marshall.
The Miner's Helmet.
Mother Superior.
The Orlando Commercial.
The Political Orlando.
The Red Herring.
The Return.
Scissor-Man.
Snowdrops.
The Spider's Nest.
A Star.
The Suicides.
The Wasps' Nest.
When I Am Dead.

MacCaig, Norman
Above in Inverkirkaig.
Aspects.
Basking Shark.
Beach Talk.
Betweens.
Birds All Singing.
By Achmelvich Bridge.
Byre.
Celtic Cross.
Close-Ups of Summer.
Cock before Dawn.
The Drowned.
Edinburgh Spring.
Ego.
Family.
Feeding Ducks.
Fetching Cows.
Flooded Mind.
Frogs.
Golden Calf.
Gone Are the Days.
High Up on Suilven.
In My Mind.
Incident.
Innocence.
Milne's Bar.
Moment Musical in Assynt.
Moorings.
Movements.
No Accident.
November Night, Edinburgh.
Nude in a Fountain.
Old Maps and New.
One of the Many Days.
Orgy.
Poem: "There is a Wailing
  Baby Under Every Stone."
Ringed Plover by a Water's
  Edge.
Sheep Dipping.
Sleet.
Space Fiction.
Spate in Winter Midnight.
Starlings.
Stars and Planets.
Street Preacher.
Summer Farm.
Too Bright a Day.
Two Musics.
The Tyrant Apple Is Eaten.
Unposted Birthday Card.
Water Tap.
Wild Oats.
You within Love.

MacCarthy, Denis Florence
The Foray of Con O'Donnell,
  A.D. 1495.
Lament.
Summer Longings.

**MacCarthy, Donal, Earl of
Clancarty,**
The Body's Speech.

MacCarthy, Ethna
Ghosts.
Insomnia.
Viaticum.

MacCawell, Hugh
Christmas Night.

**Mac Coisdealbhaigh, Tomas
"Laidir"**
Una Bhan.

MacColl, Dugal Sutherland
Ballade of Andrew Lange.

MacColl, Ewan
Ballad of Ho Chi Minh.
The Dove.
The First Time Ever I Saw
  Your Face.
Freeborn Man.
Go Down You Murderers.

MacColmain, Rumann
Song of the Sea.
Mac Con Brettan, Blathmac
A Poem to Mary.
MacConglinne
A Vision That Appeared to
Me.
Wheatlet Son of Milklet.
Macconmidhe, Giollabrighde
Childless.
Macconmidhe, Giollabrighde
A Defence of Poetry.
Mac Cuarta, Seamas Dall
The Houses of Corr an Chait
Are Cold.
MacDermott, Martin
Girl of the Red Mouth.
"MacDiarmid, Hugh"
(Christopher Murray Grieve)
After Two Thousand Years.
Another Epitaph on an Army
of Mercenaries.
Antenora.
At My Father's Grave.
At the Cenotaph.
Bagpipe Music.
The Bonnie Broukit Bairn.
Bracken Hills in Autumn.
British Leftish Poetry,
1930-40.
By Wauchopeside.
Cattle Show.
Cloudburst and Soaring
Moon.
Cophetua.
Crowdieknowe.
Crystals Like Blood.
The Day of the Crucifixion.
The Dead Liebknecht.
Deep-Sea Fishing.
A Drunk Man Looks at the
Thistle (excerpt).
The Eemis-Stane.
Empty Vessel.
Facing the Chair.
The Fleggit Bride.
The Glass of Pure Water
(excerpt).
The Glen of Silence.
The Great Wheel.
Harry Semen.
I Heard Christ Sing.
In Memoriam James Joyce
(excerpt).
In the Children's Hospital.
In the Fall.
In the Hedge-Back.
In the Pantry.
The Innumerable Christ.
The Kind of Poetry I Want
(excerpt).
Lament for the Great Music
(excerpt).
The Light of Life.
Love.
The Love-Sick Lass.
The Man in the Moon.
Milk-Wort and Bog-Cotton.
Moonlight among the Pines.
Munestruck.
O Ease My Spirit.
O Jesu Parvule.
O Wha's the Bride?
The Octopus.
Old Wife in High Spirits.
On the Ocean Floor.
On the Oxford Book of
Victorian Verse.
One of the Principal Causes of
War.
Parley of Beasts.
The Parrot Cry.

Perfect.
Prayer for a Second Flood.
De Profundis.
Reflections in a Slum.
Reflections in an Iron Works.
The Royal Stag.
The Sauchs in the Reuch
Heuch Hauch.
The Scarlet Woman.
Scotland Small?
Scunner.
Second Hymn to Lenin.
Sic Transit Gloria Scotia.
The Skeleton of the Future.
The Spanish War.
Stony Limits.
The Storm-Cock's Song.
To a Sea Eagle.
To Nearly Everybody in
Europe To-Day.
The Two Parents.
Up to Date.
Water Music.
The Watergaw.
Wheesht, Wheesht.
With a Lifting of the Head.
With the Herring Fishers.
MacDonagh, Donagh
Charles Donnelly.
Childhood.
Dublin Made Me.
Galway.
Going to Mass Last Sunday.
Hungry Grass.
The Invitation.
Just an Old Sweet Song.
Love's Language.
On the Bridge of Athlone: A
Prophecy.
Prothalamium.
A Revel.
The Veterans.
A Warning to Conquerors.
The Wind Blows.
Macdonagh, Thomas
In Paris.
John-John.
The Man Upright.
The Night Hunt.
Of a Poet Patriot.
Offering.
On a Poet Patriot.
Song.
What Is White?
Wishes for My Son.
The Yellow Bittern.
Macdonald, Agnes Foley
Eternal.
MacDonald, Alexander
Birlinn Chlann-Raghnaill.
Macdonald, Andrew
The Lover's Leap. A Tale.
MacDonald, Cynthia
Accomplishments.
Apartments on First Avenue.
Celebrating the Freak.
Dr. Dimity Is Forced to
Complain.
Dr. Dimity Lectures on
Unusual Cases.
Instruction from Bly.
The Lady Pitcher.
The Late Mother.
Objets d'Art.
The Stained Glass Man.
MacDonald, Elizabeth Roberts
The Summons.
Macdonald, George
Approaches.
Baby.
A Baby-Sermon.
Be with Me, Lord.

The Carpenter.
A Christmas Prayer.
Come Down.
Dorcas.
The Earl O' Quarterdeck.
Epitaph.
Evening Hymn (excerpt).
Here Lie I, Martin
Elginbrodde.
The Hurt of Love.
Little White Lily.
Lost and Found.
A Mammon-Marriage.
My Morning Song.
No End of No-Story.
Obedience.
A Prayer.
The Preacher's Prayer.
Professor Noctutus.
The Shadows.
Shall the Dead Praise Thee?
The Shortest and.
Sir Lark and King Sun: A
Parable.
Song: "Why do the houses
stand."
Sonnet: "This infant world has
taken long to make."
Sweet Peril.
That Holy Thing.
That Thou Art Nowhere to
Be Found.
This Day Be with Me.
To My God.
The Wind and the Moon.
Winter Song.
Within and Without.
MacDonald, Goodridge
Elegy, Montreal Morgue.
The Sailor.
MacDonald, J. E. H.
Gallows and Cross.
The Hanging.
Kitchen Window.
MacDonald, Marie Bruckman
Limerick: "There was a bright
fellow named Peter."
MacDonald, Susan
The Children.
MacDonald, Wilson
Exit.
In a Wood Clearing.
In the Far Years.
John Graydon.
June.
Moonlight on Lake
Sydenham.
The Toll-Gate Man.
MacDonogh, Patrick
Be Still As You Are Beautiful.
Bring Home the Poet.
Dodona's Oaks Were Still.
Escape to Love.
Flowering Currant.
No Mean City.
Now the Holy Lamp of Love.
The River.
She Walked Unaware.
The Snare.
Song for a Proud Relation.
Song: "She spoke to me gently
with words of sweet
meaning."
Soon with the Lilac Fades
Another Spring.
This Morning I Wakened
among Loud Cries of
Seagulls.
Via Longa.
Waking.
The Widow of Drynam.

MacDonough, Glen
Toyland.
Macdougall, Arthur R., Jr.
Bitter Question.
Captain of the Years.
It Isn't Far to Bethlehem.
We Need a King.
MacDuff, Edward
Ed and Sid and Bernard.
MacDuff, John
Jesus, My Saviour, Look on
Me!
Mace, Frances Laughton
Alcyone.
Only Waiting.
The Succession.
MacEwen, Gwendolyn
A Breakfast for Barbarians.
Dark Pines under Water.
The Discovery.
Manzini: Escape Artist.
Sea Things.
The T.E. Lawrence Poems:
The Void.
There Is No Place to Hide.
The Thing Is Violent.
The Virgin Warrior.
MacFayden, H. R.
The Lone Wild Fowl.
Macfie, Ronald Campbell
In Memoriam: John Davidson.
Mac Gearailt, Gearoid Iarla
Woe to Him Who Slanders
Women.
MacGill, Patrick
The Conger Eel.
Death and the Fairies.
It's a Far, Far, Cry.
Slainthe!
Macgillivray, Pittendrigh
The Return.
Macgillivray, W.
The Thrush's Song.
MacGillvray, Arthur
Madonna of the Dons.
Mac Giolla Ghunna, Cathal Bui
The Yellow Bittern.
MacGowan, Liam
Connolly.
Macgowan, Robin
Paros.
MacGowran, Hugh
The Description of an Irish
Feast, or O'Rourk's Frolic.
Macgoye, Marjorie Oludhe
For Miriam.
MacGreevy, Thomas
Aodhy Ruadh O'Domhnaill.
De Civitate Hominum.
Gioconda.
Homage to Hieronymus
Bosch.
Homage to Jack Yeats.
Homage to Marcel Proust.
Nocturne of the Self-Evident
Presence.
Recessional.
Red Hugh.
MacGregor, Malcolm
Rannoch Moor.
MacGregor, Robert C.
With Two Fair Girls.
Machado, Antonio
Autumn Dawn.
Lament of the Virtues and
Verses on Account of the
Death of Don Guido.
Poem: "A frail sound of a
tunic trailing."
Poems.
Rebirth.

Machado, Manuel
On the Annunciation of Fra
Angelico.
Machar, Agnes Maule
Untrodden Ways.
Machel, Josina
This Is the Time.
Machel, Samora M.
Josina, You Are Not Dead.
Machiavelli, Niccolo
Opportunity.
Poem: "I know not if from
uncreated spheres."
Poem: "The haven and last
refuge of my pain."
MacInnes, Tom
Ballade of Faith.
Chinatown Chant.
The Modernists.
The Tiger of Desire.
To Walt Whitman.
The Velvet Sonneteers.
Zalinka.
MacIntosh, Claire Harris
The Barn in Winter.
The Spirit of the "Bluenose."
MacIntyre, C. F.
Monologue of the Rating
Morgan in Rutherford
County.
MacIntyre, Duncan Ban
Last Leave of the Hills.
On Ben Dorain.
The Praise of Ben Dorain.
MacIntyre, Tom
Child.
The Corrs.
On Sweet Killen Hill.
The Yellow Bittern.
Mack, Alexander
I Am the Lord.
Mack, Cecil
Teasing.
Mack, L. V.
Biafra.
Death Songs.
Mackail, J. W.
On Clinton Edward Dawkins,
Commoner of Balliol.
Mackay, Charles
Cynical Ode to an Ultra-
Cynical Public.
The Good Time Coming.
The Holly Bough.
If I Were a Voice.
Little and Great.
Rolling Home.
The Ship.
True Freedom.
Tubal Cain.
Vixi.
MacKay, Isabel Ecclestone
Fires of Driftwood.
Helen–Old.
When as a Lad.
MacKay, Jessie
The Burial of Sir John
McKenzie.
For Love of Appin.
In Galilee.
Maisrie.
The Noosing of the Sun-God.
Mackay, L. A.
Admonition for Spring.
I Wish My Tongue Were a
Quiver.
Look, I Have Thrown All
Right.
Now There Is Nothing Left.
Nunc Scio, Quid Sit Amor.
Propertian.

MacKay, Margaret Mackprang
Asleep in Jesus.
Dog Wanted.
MacKaye, Percy
After Tempest.
The Automobile.
A Prayer of the Peoples.
To Sleep.
Mackellar, Dorothea
Arms and the Woman.
Dusk in the Domain.
Fancy Dress.
Heritage.
My Country.
Mackellar, Thomas
At the Door of Mercy
Sighing.
Jesus First and Jesus Last.
Mackenzie, Compton
The Lilies of the Field.
A Song of Parting.
Mackenzie, Kenneth
Autumn Mushrooms.
Caesura.
Confession.
Earth Buried.
A Fairy Tale.
God! How I Long for You...
Heat.
The Hospital–Retrospections.
Legerdemain.
An Old Inmate.
Pat Young.
Shall Then Another.
The Snake.
The Spider.
Table-Birds.
Two Trinities.
Mackey, Charles
Baby Mine.
Mackey, L. A.
Battle Hymn of the Spanish
Rebellion.
Mackey, Mary
What Do You Say When a
Man Tells You, You Have
the Softest Skin.
Mackey, Nate
New and Old Gospel.
Mackie, Alastair
Passin Ben Dorain.
Mackie, Albert D.
Molecatcher.
A New Spring.
The Young Man and the
Young Nun.
Mackie, Edmund St. Gascoigne
Charmides (excerpt).
MacKinstry, Elizabeth
The Man Who Hid His Own
Front Door.
Mackintosh, Ewart Alan
In Memoriam, Private D.
Sutherland.
Mackintosh, Newton
Fin de Siecle.
Limerick: "Cleopatra, who
thought they maligned her."
Lucy Lake (parody).
Macklin, Elizabeth
Leaving One of the State
Parks after a Family Outing.
Maclagan, Sir Douglas
The Battle of Glentilt (1847).
Maclaren, Hamish
The Dolphins.
Harp in the Rigging.
Sailor and Inland Flower.
Maclaurin, John, Lord Dreghorn
Elegy.
MacLean, Alasdair
Death of a Hind.

Envoy.
Hen Dying.
View from My Window.
MacLean, Crystal
The Good Woman.
MacLean, Sorley
An Autumn Day.
Dain do Eimhir (excerpt).
Dain Eile (excerpt).
I Walked with My Reason.
Kinloch Ainort.
Knightsbridge of Libya.
The Nightmare.
Sgurr Nan Gillean.
To a Depraved Lying Woman.
MacLeish, Archibald
Alien.
America Was Promises.
American Letter.
L'an Trentiesme de Mon
Eage.
Ars Poetica.
Black Humor.
Boy in the Roman Zoo.
Brave New World.
Burying Ground by the Ties.
Calypso's Island.
Captured.
Conquistador.
Cook County.
Corporate Entity.
Critical Observations.
Crossing.
Discovery of This Time.
"Dover Beach"–a Note to
That Poem.
Dr. Sigmund Freud Discovers
the Sea Shell.
Dusk.
Einstein.
Einstein (1929).
Eleven.
Empire Builders.
The End of the World.
Epistle to Be Left in the
Earth.
Ever Since.
Ezry.
The Fall of the City: Voice of
the Studio Announcer.
Frescoes for Mr. Rockefeller's
City. Landscape as a Nude.
Grazing Locomotives.
The Hamlet of A. MacLeish
(excerpt).
Hurricane.
Hypocrite Auteur.
Immortal Autumn.
Invocation to the Social Muse.
J.B. (excerpt).
Land of the Free.
Landscape as a Nude.
Late Abed.
The Learned Men.
Lines for an Interment.
Memorial Rain.
Men.
Mother Goose's Garland.
Music and Drum.
My Naked Aunt.
"Not Marble Nor the Gilded
Monuments".
Oil Painting of the Artist As
the Artist.
Panic.
The Peepers in Our Meadow.
Poem in Prose.
A Poet Speaks from the
Visitors' Gallery.
Pole Star for This Year.
Prologue.
Psyche with the Candle.

Published Correspondence:
Epistle to the Rapalloan.
Reasons for Music.
The Reconciliation.
The Reed-Player.
Reply to Mr. Wordsworth
(excerpt).
Seafarer.
Signature for Tempo.
The Silence.
The Snow Fall.
The Snowflake Which Is Now
and Hence Forever.
Speech to a Crowd.
Speech to Those Who Say
Comrade.
Spring in These Hills.
Survivor.
Theory of Poetry.
The Too-Late Born.
Unfinished History.
Vicissitudes of the Creator.
Voyage to the Moon.
Voyage West.
Weather.
What Must (iii).
What Riddle Asked the
Sphinx.
What the Serpent Said to
Adam.
Where the Hayfields Were.
Winter is Another Country.
Words in Time.
You Also, Gaius Valerius
Catullus.
You, Andrew Marvell.
The Young Dead Soldiers.
MacLellan, Robert
Sang: "There's a reid lowe in
yer cheek."
"Macleod, Fiona" *See also*
Sharp, William
Dream Fantasy.
The Founts of Song.
Madonna Natura.
The Moon-Child.
The Redeemer.
**Macleod, Joseph Gordon
("Adam Drinan")**
The Ecliptic: Cancer; or, The
Crab (excerpt).
Men of the Rocks.
MacLeod, Mairi
A Complaint about Exile.
MacLow, Jackson
10th Dance–Coming on As a
Horn–20 February 1964.
12th Dance–Getting Leather
by Language–21 February
1964.
13th Dance–Matching
Parcels–21 February 1964.
1st Dance–Making Things
New–6 February 1964.
29th Dance–Having an
Instrument–22 March 1964.
2nd Dance–Seeing Lines–6
February 1964.
2nd Light Poem: For Diane
Wakoski.
37th Dance–Banding–22
March 1964.
3rd Dance–Making a
Structure with a Roof or
under a Roof...
Zen Buddhism and
Psychoanalysis
Psychoanalysis and Zen
Buddhism.
MacMahon, Bryan
Corner Boys.

MacManus, Francis
Pattern of Saint Brendan.
MacManus, Anne Johnston *See*
"Carbery, Ethna"
MacManus, Seumas
The Hedge Schoolmasters.
In Dark Hour.
Lullaby.
Shane O'Neill.
MacManus, Theodore F.
Cave Sedem!
MacMarcuis, Aindrais
This Night Sees Ireland
Desolate.
Macmillan, James
Hill Love.
Nightmare on Rhum.
To This Hill Again.
What Are You Thinking
About?
MacMore, Dallan
Carroll's Sword.
The Song of Carroll's Sword.
Mac Muireadach, Niall Mor
Soraidh Slan Don Oidhche
Areir.
MacMurray, Niall
The Vanished Night.
MacNab, Roy
El Alamein Revisited.
Majuba Hill.
The River.
The Road to Bologna.
Seven of the Clock.
Stages.
Macnaghten, Hugh
Idyll.
MacNamara, Brinsley
On Seeing Swift in Laracor.
MacNamara, Francis
A Convict's Tour to Hell.
Diminutivus Ululans.
For the Company
Underground.
A Petition from the Chain
Gang at Newcastle to
Captain Furlong...
MacNamee, Giolla Brighde
To an Anti-poetical Priest.
MacNeice, Louis
Alcohol.
Among These Turf-Stacks.
As in Their Time.
Aubade.
August.
Autobiography.
Autumn Journal.
Autumn Sequel, IV.
Bad Dream.
Bagpipe Music.
Ballade of England.
Bar-Room Matins.
Birmingham.
The Blasphemies.
The Brandy Glass.
The British Museum Reading
Room.
Brother Fire.
Carrickfergus.
Charon.
Christina.
Christmas Shopping.
Circe.
The Closing Album.
Coda.
Conversation.
Corner Seat.
County Sligo.
Cradle Song.
Cradle Song for Miriam.
The Creditor.
Day of Renewal.

The Death of a Cat (excerpt).
The Death-Wish.
Didymus.
Dublin.
The Ear.
Eclogue between the
Motherless.
An Eclogue for Christmas.
Elegy for Minor Poets.
Entirely.
Epitaph for Liberal Poets.
Explorations.
A Fanfare for the Makers.
Figure of Eight.
Flight of the Heart.
For X.
Galway.
The Glacier.
The Grey Ones.
A Hand of Snapshots
(excerpt).
Hold-Up.
Holes in the Sky (excerpt).
Homage to Wren.
Horses.
House on a Cliff.
Il Piccolo Rifiuto.
In Lieu.
The Individualist Speaks.
The Introduction.
Invocation.
Jehu.
Jigsaw III.
June Thunder.
The Kingdom.
Leaving Barra.
Letter to Graham and Anna.
The Libertine.
London Rain.
Mahabalipuram.
Meeting Point.
The Mixer.
Morning Sun.
Museums.
The National Gallery.
Nature Morte.
Nature Notes (excerpt).
Neutrality.
Night Club.
Nostalgia.
Novelettes III: The Gardener.
Nuts in May.
The Old Story.
Passage Steamer.
Perdita.
Perseus.
Pet Shop.
Poussin.
Prayer before Birth.
Prayer in Mid-Passage.
Precursors.
Prognosis.
Ravenna.
Reflections.
Refugees.
River in Spate.
The Sense of Smell.
Sligo and Mayo.
Slow Movement.
Snow.
Soap Suds.
Solitary Travel.
The Springboard.
Star-Gazer.
The Strand.
The Streets of Laredo.
Stylite.
Suicide.
Sunday Morning.
Les Sylphides.
The Taxis.
Thalassa.

Their Last Will and
Testament.
This Is the Life.
Train to Dublin.
Tree Party.
Trilogy for X (excerpt).
The Truisms.
Turf-Stacks.
Under the Mountain.
Valediction.
Variation on Heraclitus.
Visitations: VII (excerpt).
Wessex Guidebook.
Whitmonday.
Wolves.
Woods.
Macneill, Hector
My Boy Tammy.
Macomber, W.
Christ Is Coming.
Macourek, Milos
The Punching Clock.
MacPherson, James
Fingal: an Ancient Epic Poem
(excerpt).
Fragments of Ancient Poetry
(excerpt).
Macpherson, Jay
Ark Anatomical.
Ark Apprehensive.
Ark Artefact.
Ark Articulate.
Ark Astonished.
Ark Overwhelmed.
Ark Parting.
Ark to Noah.
The Beauty of Job's
Daughters.
The Boatman.
Egg.
Eurynome.
Eve in Reflection.
The Fisherman.
Go Take the World.
The Innocents.
A Lost Soul.
The Marriage of Earth and
Heaven.
Sun and Moon.
The Swan.
They Return.
The Way Down: They Return.
The Woods No More.
Macrow, Brenda G.
At the Shelter-Stone.
Climb in Torridon.
In Praise of Ben Avon.
When I Die.
Macuilxochitl
Battle Song.
MacWard, Fearghal Og
The Flight of the Earls, 1607
(excerpt).
MacWard, Owen Roe
The Little Dark Rose.
Roisin Dubh.
Macy, Arthur
The Rollicking Mastodon.
Macy, George
Daphne and Apollo.
Madden, David
Surfaces.
Madden, F.A.V.
Johnsonian Poem in Progress:
"I put my hat upon my
head" (parody).
Maddow, Ben
The City.
Madeleva, Sister Mary
Apology for Youth.
Ballade on Eschatology.
Beech Trees.

Dialogue.
Knights Errant.
Madge, Charles
At War.
The Birds of Tin.
Blocking the Pass.
Delusions VI.
Fortune.
In Conjunction.
Landscape I.
Loss.
Lusty Juventus.
A Monument.
A Nightly Deed.
On One Condition.
Poem: "The walls of the
maelstrom are painted with
trees."
Rumba of the Three Lost
Souls.
Solar Creation.
The Times.
To Make a Bridge.
Madgett, Naomi Long
Alabama Centennial.
Black Woman.
Deacon Morgan.
Dream Sequence, Part 9.
Exits and Entrances.
Her Story.
Midway.
Mortality.
New Day.
Nocturne.
Nomen.
Offspring.
Pavlov.
Quest.
The Race Question.
Refugee.
Simple.
Star Journey.
Woman with Flower.
Madhubuti, Haki R.
Change Is Not Always
Progress.
Madison, Dolly
La Fayette.
Mael-Isu
Deus Meus.
Maeterlinck, Maurice
The Last Words.
Song: "Three little maidens
they have slain."
Magee, Michael
It Is the Stars That Govern
Us.
Magee, Jr, John Gillespie
High Flight.
Magee, William Kirkpatrick *See*
"Eglintan, John"
"Maggie"
The Passionate Encyclopedia
Britannica Reader to His
Love.
Magid, Margo
Night Watch.
Magil, A. B.
They Are Ours.
Maginn, William
The Irishman and the Lady.
The Rime of the Auncient
Waggonere (parody).
St Patrick of Ireland, My
Dear!
Magogo, Princess
Teasing Song.
Magowan, Robin
Days of 1956.
Pastoral.
Susan.
Zeimbekiko.

Magrath, Andrew
Andrew Magrath's Reply to
John O'Tuomy.
Boatman's Hymn.
Lament of the Mangaire
Sugach.
Maguire, Francis
Whale Song.
Maguire, Tom
Bold Robert Emmet.
Mahadevi (Mahadeviyakka)
Like a Silkworm Weaving.
Like an Elephant.
Like Treasure Hidden in the
Ground.
O Brothers, Why Do You
Talk.
Other men are thorn.
People, male and female.
Riding the Blue Sapphire
Mountains.
Till You've Earned.
Would a circling surface
vulture.
Mahaka, Solomon
Building Bridges.
If I Leave Here Alive.
In the Zoo.
Mahapatra, Jayanta
A Rain of Rites.
Mahlmann, Siegfried August
Allah.
Mahodahi
On the holy day of your going
out to war.
Mahon, Derek
Afterlives.
Autobiographies.
The Banished Gods.
Consolations of Philosophy.
Courtyards in Delft.
A Dark Country.
A Departure.
Derry Morning.
A Disused Shed in Co.
Wexford.
Ecclesiastes.
Exit Molloy.
Father-in-Law.
A Garage in Co. Cork.
Girls in Their Seasons.
Glengormley.
Grandfather.
Homage to Malcolm Lowry.
I Am Raftery.
An Image from Beckett.
In Carrowdore Churchyard.
The Last of the Fire Kings.
A Lighthouse in Maine.
Lives.
Matthew V: 29-30.
The Mute Phenomena.
My Wicked Uncle.
Nostalgias.
Poem Beginning with a Line
by Cavafy.
The Poets of the Nineties.
The Snow Party.
The Spring Vacation.
The Studio.
Tractatus.
An Unborn Child.
The Woods.
Mahone, Barbara
Colors for Mama.
A Poem for Positive Thinkers.
Sugarfields.
**Mahony, Francis Sylvester
("Father Prout")**
Ad Leuconoen.

The Attractions of a
Fashionable Irish Watering-
Place.
The Bells of Shandon.
L'Envoy to W. L. H.
Ainsworth, Esq.
In Mortem Venerabilis
Andreae Prout Carmen.
A Panegyric on Geese.
The Red-Breast of Aquitania.
The Sabine Farmer's Serenade.
Solvitur Acris Hiems.
**Mahony, Francis Sylvester
("Father Prout")**
The Piper's Progress.
Mahony, Medb
Shells.
Mahsati
Quatrain: "Better to live as a
rogue and a bum."
Quatrain: "Gone are the
games we played all night."
Quatrain: "Good-looking, I'll
never stoop for you."
Quatrain: "I knew like a song
your vows weren't strong."
Quatrain: "Unless you can
dance through a common
bar."
Maiano, Dante da
Sonnet: He Craves
Interpreting of a Dream of
His.
Maiden, Jennifer
Climbing.
Dew.
Slides.
Mailer, Norman
Devils.
Dr. Hu.
Eternities.
Maillard, Claude
Christmas Mass for a Little
Atheist Jesus.
Maino, Jeannette
Harvest.
Sky Patterns.
Mainwaring, Arthur
An Excellent New Ballad,
Called The Brawn Bishop's
Complaint.
An Excellent New Song
Called "Mat's Peace," or The
Downfall of Trade.
A New Ballad.
The Queen's Speech.
Tarquin and Tullia.
Mair, Alexander
Hesiod, 1908.
Mair, Charles
Dreamland (excerpt).
The Fireflies (excerpt).
The Last Bison: Song.
Tecumseh.
Winter.
Maisel, Carolyn
A Dream of Women.
The Girl in the Willow Tree.
A Letter from a Friend.
Maisun, Lady
She Scorns Her Husband the
Caliph.
Maitland, Sir Richard
Against the Thieves of
Liddesdale.
Solace in Age.
Major, Clarence
Blind Old Woman.
Brother Malcolm: Waste
Limit.
Celebrated Return.
The Design.

Down Wind against the
Highest Peaks.
Dressed to Kill.
Inside Diameter.
Swallow the Lake.
Vietnam.
Vietnam #4.
Major, John
Poem for Thel–the Very Tops
of Trees.
Major, Nadine
Agatha.
Mak, Lev
Eden.
The Flood.
Prayer.
Makai, Emil
The Comet.
Makere
Lament for Taramoana.
Makhfi
The Beauty of the Friend It
Was That Taught Me.
Maksimovic, Desanka
For All Mary Magdalenes.
Mala'ika, Nazik al-
Jamila.
Malam, Charles
Neighbors.
Steam Shovel.
Malancioiu, Ileana
Bear's blood.
Malanga, Gerard
Temperature.
What I Have Done.
Malangatana, Valente
To the Anxious Mother.
Woman.
Malarkey, Susannah P.
Above the Wall.
Maleska, Eugene T.
Assembly: Harlem School.
Countee Cullen.
To a Negro Boy Graduating.
Malikongwa, Albert G.T.K.
A Protest from a Bushman
(Masarwa).
Malins, Joseph
A Fence or an Ambulance.
Mallalieu, H. B.
Cozzo Grillo.
Empedocles on Etna.
Epilogue.
Look for Me on England.
New Year's Eve.
Next of Kin.
Platform Goodbye.
To Naples.
Mallarme, Stephane
The Afternoon of a Faun:
Eclogue.
Album Leaf.
Anguish.
Another Fan Belonging to
Mademoiselle Mallarme.
Flowers.
Funeral Toast.
The Glazier.
Little Air.
Prose for Des Esseintes.
Pure Nails Brightly Flashing.
Saint.
Sea-Wind.
Sigh.
Sonnet: "This virgin, beautiful
and lively day."
The Swan.
Mallet, David
The Birks of Endermay.
William and Margaret.
Malley, Ern
Durer: Innsbruck, 1495.

Malley, Jean
Untitled: "Words do not grow
on the landscape."
Malley, K.
Conversation.
Malloch, Douglas
Ain't It Fine Today!
Be the Best of Whatever You
Are.
A Comrade Rides Ahead.
Family Trees.
If Easter Eggs Would Hatch.
It's Fine Today.
June.
When the Drive Goes Down.
Mallock, William Hurrell
Christmas Thoughts, by a
Modern Thinker.
A Marriage Prospect.
Softly the Evening (parody).
Mally, E. Louise
Moon Rock.
Malon de Chaide, Pedro
The Conversion of the
Magdalene.
Sonnet.
Malone, Walter
He Who Hath Loved.
The Masterpiece.
October in Tennessee.
Opportunity.
Malone, William
The Agnostic's Creed.
Opportunity.
Maloney, J. J.
Beyond the Wall.
City Jail.
Getting Out.
Poems from Prison.
The Prison Guard.
Somewhere Down below Me
Is a Street.
Malouf, David
Asphodel.
At My Grandmother's.
An die Musik.
Early Discoveries.
Guide to the Perplexed.
Snow.
This Day, under My Hand.
Wolf-Boy.
The Year of the Foxes.
Mammone, Ken
Sun and I.
Man, Gill
Mist.
Mandel, Charlotte
I'm Lucky.
Mandel, E. W.
The Fire Place.
Minotaur Poems.
Song: "When the echo of the
last footstep dies."
Mandel, Eli
David.
Envoi.
From the North
Saskatchewan.
Houdini.
Job.
The Madwomen of the Plaza
de Mayo.
Merits of Laughter and Lust.
Metamorphosis.
On the 25th Anniversary of
the Liberation of
Auschwitz...
On the Death of Ho Chi
Minh.
Phaeton.
Rapunzel.

Mandela, Zindzi
Drink from My Empty Cup.
Echo of Mandela.
I Saw as a Child.
Lock the Place in Your Heart.
There's an Unknown River in
Soweto.

Mandelstam, Osip
Ariosto.
Batyushkov.
Bitter Bread.
Concert at the Station.
I Was Washing outside in the
Darkness.
Leningrad.
Like a Young Levite.
Lines Concerning the
Unknown Soldier: "Arteries
juicy with blood."
Mounds of Human Heads Are
Wandering into the Distance.
Not Yet Dead, Not Yet
Alone.
Notre Dame.
Phaedra.
A Reed.
The Stalin Epigram.
This Night.
Twilight of Freedom.

Mandeville, Bernard
The Grumbling Hive: or,
Knaves turn'd Honest.
The Moral.
On Honour.

Manfred, Freya
For a Young South Dakota
Man.
Grandma Shorba and the
Pure in Heart.
Moon Light.

Mangan, James Clarence
Advice against Travel.
And Then No More.
Avran.
Cean-Salla.
Dark Rosaleen.
The Dawning of the Day.
Disaster.
The Dying Enthusiast.
Ellen Bawn.
Enthusiasm.
The Fair Hills of Eire, O!
The Geraldine's Daughter
(excerpt).
Gone in the Wind.
Good Counsel.
Hymn for Pentecost.
The Irish Language.
The Karamanian Exile.
Kathaleen Ny-Houlahan.
Kincora.
King Cahal Mor of the Wine-
Red Hand.
Lament over the Ruins of the
Abbey of Teach Molaga.
A Lamentation.
Love.
The Lover's Farewell.
The Mariner's Bride.
The Nameless One.
The Night Is Falling.
O'Hussey's Ode to the
Maguire.
Rest Only in the Grave.
Shapes and Signs.
Siberia.
A Song from the Coptic.
Song: "O, strew the way with
rosy flowers."
Sonnet: "Bird that discoursest
from yon poplar bough."

St. Patrick's Hymn before
Tara.
The Three Khalandeers.
Three Proverbs.
The Time of the Barmacides.
To Amine.
To My Native Land.
To Sultan Murad II.
To the Ingleezee Khafir,
Calling Himself Djann Bool
Djenkinzun.
A Triplet on the Reign of the
Great Sultan.
Twenty Golden Years Ago.
Vision of Connaught in the
Thirteenth Century.
Volto Sciolto e Pensieri
Stretti.
Welcome to Prince of Ossory.
The Woman of Three Cows.
The World: a Ghazel.

Mangan, Kathy
Absence.
Cold Snap.

Manger, Itzik
Abishag Writes a Letter
Home.
Abraham and Sarah.
Adam and Eve.
Alone.
Autumn.
A Dark Hand.
Dying Thief.
Evening.
Fairy Tales.
I Am the Autumn.
Jealous Adam.
Mother Sarah's Lullaby.
On the Road There Stands a
Tree.
Rachel Goes to the Well for
Water.
The Strange Guest.
Under the Ruins of Poland.

Mangoaela, Z. D.
Boast of Masopha.

Manhire, Bill
The Collection.
The Elaboration.
Last Things.
Party Going.
The Poetry Reading.
Summer.
Wellington.
Wulf.

Manifold, John Streeter
Assignation with a
Somnambulist.
The Bunyip and the Whistling
Kettle.
Camouflage.
Defensive Position.
The Deserter.
L'Embarquement pour
Cythere.
Fencing School.
Fife Tune.
Garcia Lorca Murdered in
Granada.
Griesly Wife.
Heureux Qui Comme Ulysse...
Listening to a Broadcast.
Makhno's Philosophers.
Making Contact.
Night Piece.
Ration Party.
The Sirens.
Song.
Suburban Lullaby.
The Tomb of Lt. John
Learmonth, A.I.F.

Manilius, Marcus
The Times.

Mann, Leonard
The Earth.
Meditation in Winter.

Manner, Eeva-Liisa
Cambrian (excerpt).
The Lunar Games.

Mannes, Marya
Age.
Canticles to Men.
The First.

Manning, Frederic
Leaves.
The Trenches.

Manning, James Harold
What Is Truth? (excerpt).

Manning-Sanders, Ruth
Come Wary One.
The Old City.

Mannix, Mary E.
All Souls' Eve.

**Mannyng, [(or Manning)]
Robert**
The Bishop's Harp.
The Dancers of Colbek.
Praise of Women.
The Round Table.

Manrique, Jorge
The Coplas on the Death of
His Father, the Grandmaster
of Santiago.

Mansel, William Lort
A Stanza Completed.

Mansfield, Katherine
Friendship.
Little Brother's Secret.
Sanary.
To L.H.B.
Two Nocturnes.
Voices of the Air.

Mansfield, Margery
Blessing Mrs. Larkin.

Mansfield, Richard
The Eagle's Song.

Manson, John
At a Ruined Croft.

Mansour, Joyce
Auditory Hallucinations.
Embrace the Bride.
Last night I saw your corpse.
North Express.
Seated on her bed legs spread
open.
The Sun in Capricorn.
Yesterday Evening I Saw
Your Corpse.

Manville, Marion
Lee's Parole.
The Surrender of New
Orleans.

Manyase, L. T.
The Mother Crab and Her
Family.
Vusumzi's Song.

Manzano, Juan F.
My Thirty Years.

Manzoni, Alessandro
The Fifth of May–Napoleon.

Mapanje, Jack A.
Before Chilembwe Tree.
A Marching Litany to Our
Martyrs.
The New Platform Dances.
On His Royal Blindness
Paramount Chief Kwangala.
When This Carnival Finally
Closes.

Mapes, Edith L.
Oh, If They Only Knew!

Mar, Laureen
At Wonder Donut.

Black Rocks.
The Immigration Act of 1924.
My Mother, Who Came from
China, Where She Never
Saw Snow.
The Window Frames the
Moon.

Maragall, Juan
Canto Espiritual.
Night of the Immaculate
Conception.

Marais, Eugene
The Dance of the Rain.
The Desert Lark.
Heart-of-the-Daybreak.
The Sorceress.

Maran, Rene
Human Soul.

Marano, Russell
Now I Am a Man.
Spring Death.

Marcabrun
At the Fountain.

Marcela de Carpio, Sister
Amor Mysticus.

March, Auzias
What Guardian Counsels?

Marchant, John
Little Miss and Her Parrot.
O Lord, Turn Not Away Thy
Face.
Young Master's Account of a
Puppet Show.

Marcus, Adrianne
In a Dream, the Automobile.

Marcus, Mordecai
A Book of Verses.
A Bouquet for Jerry Ford.
An Election.
Proud Resignation.
Survivors.
Two Refugees.

Marcus, Morton
Look Closely.
Watching Your Gray Eyes.

Marcus Argentarious
Epigram: "Hetero-sex is best."

Margaret, Helene
Impiety (excerpt).

Margarido, Manuela
You Who Occupy Our Land.

Margenat, Hugo
Living Poetry.
The Well-Aimed Stare.
Your Air of My Air.

Margetson, George Reginald
The Fledgling Bard and the
Poetry Society. Part I
(excerpt).

Margolin, Anna
Ancient Murderess Night.
Homecoming.
Mother Earth.
My Kin Talk.
Years.

Margolis, Gary
On the Eve of Our
Anniversary.

Margolis, Silvia
Never Ask Me Why.

Marguerite de Navarre
Autant en Emporte le Vent.
The Smell of Death Is So
Powerful.

"Maria Josephine" *See*
Hemenway, Abby Maria

Mariah, Paul
Always We Watch Them.
At Their Place.
Gravel.
Grey Him.
Quarry/Rock.

Walls Breathe.

Mariani, Paul
Coda: Revising History.
The Girl Who Learned to Sing in Crow.
Golden Oldie.
The Lesson.
Lines I Told Myself I Wouldn't Write.
News That Stays News.
The Ring.
Then Sings My Soul.

Marias, The Three (Maria Isabel Barreno and Maria Teresa Horta and Maria Velho da Costa)
Conversation between the Chevalier de Chamilly and Mariana Alcoforado.
Saddle and Cell.

"Marie, Madelaine"
Crucifixion.
The End Is Now.
Foiled Sleep.
Moriturus.
The Unfading.
Vagabonds.

Marie de France
Chartivel: Song.
Goat's-Leaf.
Honeysuckle (Chevrefoil).
The Nightingale.
Song from "Chartivel."
The Two Lovers.
Would I Might Go Far Over Sea.

Marietta, T. Walking Eagle
A Child of Hers.
The House.
A Reflection of Night.
The Two Coyotes.

Marino, Giambattista
The Bed.
Fading Beauty.
Lips and Eyes.
Madrigal XI: "Love now no fire hath left him."
The Massacre of the Innocents: The Devil's Doubts.

Marinoni, Rosa Zagnoni
At Sunrise.
For a New Home.
Who Are My People?

Marion, David
Her Eyes Don't Shine Like Diamonds.

Marion, Jeff Daniel
Out in the Country, Back Home.
Winter Watch.

Maris Stella, Sister
Afternoon in a Tree.
Bay Violets.
Cause of Our Joy.
Grapes.
I Who Had Been Afraid.
It Is the Reed.
Lines for a Feast of Our Lady.
Love Is Not Solace.
Now That Can Never Be Done.
Oxford Bells.
The Pelicans My Father Sees.
San Marco Museum, Florence.
This One Heart-Shaken.
The Voice.

Mark, Diane Mei Lin
And the Old Folks Said.
Kula...A Homecoming.
Liberation.

Rice and Rose Bowl Blues.
Suzie Wong Doesn't Live Here.

Mark, Twain
Shakespearean Soliloquy in Progress: "To be, or not to be..."(parody).

Markham, Edwin
At Little Virgil's Window.
The Avengers.
Brotherhood.
The Christ of the Andes (excerpt).
Conscripts of the Dream (excerpt).
Courage, All.
A Creed.
Duty.
Earth Is Enough.
The Errand Imperious.
The Father's Business.
The Forgotten Man.
A Free Nation.
A Guard of the Sepulcher.
How Shall We Honor Them?
How the Great Guest Came.
How to Go and Forget.
The Invisible Bride.
Joy of the Morning.
The Last Furrow.
Lincoln, the Man of the People.
The Lizard.
A Look into the Gulf.
The Lord of All.
Man-Making.
The Man with the Hoe.
My Comrade.
The Need of the Hour.
The New Trinity.
The Night Moths.
Our Dead, Overseas.
Outwitted.
Peace.
The Place of Peace.
The Poet.
Poetry.
A Prayer.
Preparedness.
Revelation.
The Right Kind of People.
Rules for the Road.
San Francisco Arising.
San Francisco Falling.
Shine on Me, Secret Splendor.
The Task That Is Given to You.
There Is a High Place.
The Third Wonder.
The Toiler (excerpt).
Two at a Fireside.
Victory in Defeat.
Virgilia (excerpt).
The Wharf of Dreams.
Wind and Lyre.
Young Lincoln.
Your Tears.

Markham, Lucia Clark
Bluebells.

Markish, Peretz
In the Last Flicker of the Sinking Sun.
We Reached Out Far.
Your Burnt-Out Body.

Markman, Stephanie
The Rime of the Ancient Feminist (excerpt).

Marks, Edward B.
The Little Lost Child.
My Mother Was a Lady.

Marks, Godfrey
Sailing Sailing.

Marks, Naomi
Come Live with Me (parody).
High Wonders (parody).

Marks, S. J.
How.

Marks, Shirley
Early Warning.

Marlatt, Daphne
Femina.
Steveston: Imagine: A Town.

Marlatt, Earl Bowman
Malachi.
Pax Nobiscum.
Peter.
Spirit of Life, in This New Dawn.
Through the Dark the Dreamers Came.
Zechariah.

Marlowe, Christopher
The Bloody Conquests of Mighty Tamburlaine (excerpt).
Doctor Faustus.
Edward the Second (excerpt).
Faustus Faces His Doom.
Hero and Leander.
The Jew of Malta: The Song of Ithamore.
The Passionate Shepherd to His Love.
The Portents.
Tamburlaine the Great.

Marot, Clément
Friar Lubin.
A Love-Lesson.
Madame D'Albert's Laugh.
The Posy Ring.
Toast to a Departing Duchess.

Marquis, Don (Donald Robert Marquis)
Another Villon-ous Variation.
Archy at the Zoo.
Archy Confesses.
Archys Autobiography.
Archys Last Name.
Artists Shouldn't Have Offspring.
The Awakening.
Ballade of the under Side.
Certain Maxims of Archy.
Chant Royal of the Dejected Dipsomaniac.
Cheerio My Deario.
Confession of a Glutton.
Fat Is Unfair.
The Flattered Lightning Bug.
A Gentleman of Fifty Soliloquizes.
The God-maker, Man.
Grotesques (excerpt).
Heir and Serf.
The Hen and the Oriole.
The honey bee.
A Hot-Weather Song.
In the Bayou.
The Jokesmith's Vacation.
King Cophetua and the Beggar Maid.
Limerick: "There was a young fellow named Sydney."
A Little While.
Mehitabel and Her Kittens.
Mehitabel Sings a Song.
The Name.
Noah an' Jonah an' Cap'n John Smith.
The Old Trouper.
Only Thy Dust...
Pete at the Seashore.
Prohibition.
Reverie.

Savage Portraits.
Small Talk.
The Song of Mehitabel.
Time Time Said Old King Tut.
To a Lost Sweetheart.
The Tom-Cat.
Tristram and Isolt.
Unrest.
The Wail of Archy (excerpt).
Warty Bliggins, the Toad.

Marr, Barbara
Prayer.

Marriot, John
On John Donne's Book of Poems.

Marriott, Anne
As You Come In.
Beaver Pond.
Prairie Graveyard.
Sandstone.
Search.
The Wind of Our Enemy (excerpt).
Woodyards in the Rain.

Marron, Os
Nocturnal.

Marryat, Frederick
The Captain Stood on the Carronade.
Port Admiral.

Mars, Ann
Shadow.

Marsh, Daniel L.
The Greatest Person In the Universe.

Marsh, E. L.
The Magic Piper.

Marshak, Samuel
The Little House in Lithuania.

Marshall, Archibald
Limerick: "There was a young man of Devizes."

Marshall, Austin John
Dancing at Whitsun.

Marshall, Edward
Leave the Word Alone.
Memory as Memorial in the Last.
Sept. 1957.
Two Poems.

Marshall, Jack
Glimmers.
Hitchhiker.

Marshall, James
Oregon Trail: 1851.

Marshall, Lenore G.
Invented a Person.

Marshall, Matt
Wine O Living.

Marshall, Tom
Astrology.
Interior Monolgue #666.
Politics (excerpt).
Summer.

Marshall, William E.
Brookfield (excerpt).
To a Mayflower.

Marsman, Hendrik
The Zodiac: The Valley of Sleep.

Marston, John
Antonio and Mellida (excerpt).
The Malcontent.
The Metamorphosis of Pygmalion's Image (excerpt).
The Nut-Brown Ale.
O Love, How Strangely Sweet.
Prologue to Antonio's Revenge.
Satire.

Marston
Song: "Delicious beauty, that doth lie."
To Detraction I Present My Poesie.
To Everlasting Oblivion.
Marston, Philip Bourke
After.
After Summer.
At the Last.
How My Songs of Her Began.
If You Were Here.
Inseparable.
Not Thou But I.
The Old Churchyard of Bonchurch.
The Rose and the Wind.
Speechless.
Too Late.
The Two Burdens.
Ungathered Love.
Wedded Memories.
Marti, Jose
Guantanamera.
Simple Verses.
Two Countries.
Marti, Kurt
The Unbidden Wedding Guest.
Martial (Marcus Valerius Martialis)
Abnegation.
The Advantages of Learning.
The Antiquary.
A Bad Joke.
Bought Locks.
De Coenatione Micae.
Country Pleasures.
Critics.
Epigram: "Give me a boy whose tender skin."
Epigram: "Me Polytimus vexes and provokes."
Epigram: "Milo's from home; and, Milo being gone."
Epigram: "My better half, why turn a peevish scold."
Epigrams.
Fair, Rich, and Young.
Familiarity Breeds Indifference.
For a Son's Marriage.
Go, Happy Rose.
A Golden Sorrow.
A Hinted Wish.
How to Raise a Son.
I Hear That Lycoris Has Buried.
In a Cell I Am Bunked.
The Incentive.
Insufficient Vengeance.
The Likeness.
Lycoris darling, once I burned for you.
The Mistaken Resolve.
Near Neighbors.
New Love.
On a Slanderer.
On Bassa.
On Hedylus.
On the Death of a Young and Favorite Slave.
Poems from a Greek Anthology (excerpt).
A Riddle.
Roman Presents.
A Roman Thank-You Letter.
Sealed Bags of Ducats.
Sextus the Usurer.
Temperament.
Though You Serve Richest Wines.
To an Old Fraud.

To Charinus, a Catamite.
To Dindymus.
To His Girl.
To Labienus.
To Lygdus.
To Papilus.
To Philaenis.
To Phoebus.
To Polycharmus.
To Sabidius.
Tomorrow You Will Live.
The Too Literal Pupil.
Verses on Blenheim.
What Makes a Happy Life.
Work and Play.
You Read Us Your Verse.
You Serve the Best Wines Always, My Dear Sir.
Martin, Ada Louise
Sleep.
Martin, Bessie June
Let Me Look At Me.
True Riches.
Martin, C. D.
God's Goodness.
Martin, Charles
Leaving Buffalo.
Sharks at the New York Aquarium.
Signs.
Martin, Connie
Progress.
Martin, D. Roger
Hammerin' Hank.
Martin, D. S.
Limerick: "A farmer's boy, starting to plough."
Martin, David
Dreams in German.
Gordon Childe.
I Am a Jew.
Martin, Edward Sandford
Egotism.
A Girl of Pompeii.
Infirm.
A Little Brother of the Rich.
The Sea Is His.
Martin, Herbert
Antigone.
Lines.
A Negro Soldier's Viet Nam Diary.
Martin, I. L.
At the Tennis Clinic.
Dark Eyes at Forest Hills.
Martin, John
God's Dark.
Martin, Julia E.
With Him.
Martin, Margaret Nickerson
Judas Iscariot.
Martin, Michael C.
Guard.
Martin, Philip
In March.
Tongues.
Martin, Richard
Sister Rose.
Martin, Sara
Death Sting Me Blues.
Martin, Sarah Catherine
The Comic Adventures of Old Mother Hubbard and Her Dog.
Martin, Sir Theodore
The Thieves' Anthology (excerpt) (parody).
Martin, Sir Theodore and Aytoun, William E.
The Cry of the Lovelorn.
Eastern Serenade.
The Lay of the Lovelorn.

Martin, William
An Apple Orchard in the Spring.
Martinez, Lorri
A Person, a Mexican.
Slow Death.
Twenty-Two Minutes.
Martinez, Maurice
Suburbia.
Martinson, David
Nineteen Sections from a Twenty Acre Poem (excerpt).
Martinson, Harry
The Sea Wind.
Visual Memory.
Marty, Sid
In the Dome Car of the "Canadian".
Marula
Meeting after Separation.
Marvell, Andrew
Ametas and Thestylis Making Hay-Ropes.
Appleton House (excerpt).
Bermudas.
The Character of Holland.
Clorinda and Damon.
The Coronet.
Damon the Mower.
The Definition of Love.
A Dialogue between the Resolved Soul and Created Pleasure.
A Dialogue between the Soul and Body.
A Dialogue between Thyrsis and Dorinda.
An Epitaph: "Enough; and leave the rest to Fame."
An Epitaph Upon–.
The Execution of King Charles.
Eyes and Tears.
The Fair Singer.
The Gallery.
A Garden.
The Garden of Appleton House, Laid Out by Lord Fairfax...
The Girl Describes Her Fawn.
An Horatian Ode upon Cromwell's Return from Ireland.
The Kingfisher.
The Last Instructions to a Painter.
The Loyal Scot (excerpt).
The Match.
Mourning.
The Mower against Gardens.
The Mower's Song.
The Mower to the Glow-worms.
The Nymph Complaining for the Death of Her Faun.
On a Drop of Dew.
On Mr. Milton's Paradise Lost.
On the Lord Mayor and Court of Aldermen...
The Picture of Little T. C. in a Prospect of Flowers.
A Poem upon the Death of Oliver Cromwell (excerpt).
The Second Advice to a Painter.
Song of the Emigrants in Bermuda.
The Third Advice to a Painter.
To His Coy Mistress.

To His Noble Friend, Mr. Richard Lovelace, upon His Poems.
To His Worthy Friend Doctor Witty....
Upon Appleton House, to My Lord Fairfax.
Upon His Majesty's Being Made Free of the City.
Upon the Death of His Late Highness the Lord Protector (excerpt).
The Vows.
Marx, Anne
The Lacemaker (Vermeer).
"Mary, Aunt" *See* **Lathbury, Mary Artemisia**
Mary, Queen of Scots
Prayer before Execution.
Mary Ada, Sister
Lines.
Mary Angelita, Sister
Signum Cui Contradicetur.
To a Poet.
To the Memory of J. Horace Kimball.
Mary Catherine, Sister
New Testament: Revised Edition.
Mary Dorothy Ann, Sister
Exchange.
Mary Genoveva, Sister
Archers of the King.
Mary Helen, Sister
Identity.
Mary Honora, Sister
After Mardi Gras.
Eighteen.
Mary Immaculate, Sister
Ordination.
Mary John Frederick, Sister
Joculator Domini.
Mary Madeleva, Sister
Design for a Stream-Lined Sunrise.
Gates.
Motif for Mary's Dolors.
New Things and Old.
November Afternoons.
A Nun Speaks to Mary.
Of Wounds.
Peace by Night.
Snow Storm.
Wardrobe.
Mary Philip, Sister
Poet's Bread.
To-Day.
Mary St. Virginia, Sister
The Case of Thomas More.
Convent Cemetery: Mount Carmel.
Mary Therese, Sister
I Send Our Lady.
Maryam bint Abi
What Can You Expect.
Marz, Roy
Vittoria Colonna.
Marzan, Julio
Epitaph.
Friday Evening.
Graduation Day, 1965.
Marzials, Theophile
May Margaret.
A Pastoral.
Song: "There's one great bunch of stars in heaven."
A Tragedy.
Twickenham Ferry.
Masahongva
Corn-Blossom Maidens.
Now from the East.

Masaoka Shiki *See* **Shiki**
Masaveimah, Kavangho
    Flute Song.
Mase, Sidney Warren
    It's Simply Great.
Masefield, John
    August, 1914.
    D'Avalos' Prayer.
    A Ballad of John Silver.
    Being Her Friend.
    Biography (excerpt).
    C. L. M.
    Cape Horn Gospel–I.
    Captain Stratton's Fancy.
    Cargoes.
    The Choice.
    A Consecration.
    A Creed.
    The Crowd.
    Dauber.
    Dawn.
    The Dead Knight.
    Drop Me the Seed.
    An Epilogue.
    The Everlasting Mercy.
    The Golden City of St. Mary.
    Good Friday: The Madman's
      Song.
    Hell's Pavement.
    I Could Not Sleep for
      Thinking of the Sky.
    I Never See the Red Rose
      Crown the Year.
    It May Be So with Us.
    John Fitzgerald Kennedy.
    June Twilight.
    Laugh and Be Merry.
    The Lemmings.
    Lollingdon Downs.
    Midnight.
    An Old Song Re-Sung.
    On Eastnor Knoll.
    On Growing Old.
    One of Wally's Yarns.
    Partridges.
    The Passing Strange.
    Port of Holy Peter.
    Port of Many Ships.
    Prayer for the Royal
      Marriage.
    Reynard the Fox (excerpt).
    The Rider at the Gate.
    Roadways.
    The Rose of the World.
    Roses are Beauty, but I Never
      See.
    Sea-Change.
    Sea-Fever.
    The Seekers.
    The Ship and Her Makers.
    Sonnet: "Flesh, I have
      knocked at many a dusty
      door."
    Sonnet: "How many ways,
      how many times."
    Sonnet: "If I could get within
      this changing I."
    Sonnet: "Is there a great green
      commonwealth of Thought."
    Sonnet: "O little self, within
      whose smallness lies."
    Sonnet: "There is no God, as
      I was taught in youth."
    Sonnet: "There, on the
      darkened deathbed, dies the
      brain."
    Sonnets.
    Sorrow of Mydath.
    Spanish Waters.
    The Tarry Buccaneer.
    Tewkesbury Road.
    Tomorrow.

    Trade Winds.
    The Tragedy of Pompey the
      Great (excerpt).
    Truth.
    Twilight.
    A Valediction (Liverpool
      Docks).
    The Waggon-Maker.
    The "Wanderer."
    A Wanderer's Song.
    The West Wind.
    What Am I, Life?
    Wherever Beauty Has Been
      Quick in Clay.
    The Wild Duck.
    The Wild Geese.
    Wood-Pigeons.
    The Yarn of the Loch
      Achray.
    You.
Mason, Agnes Carter
    Whenever a Little Child Born.
**Mason, Caroline Atherton
Briggs**
    Eventide.
    An Open Secret.
    President Lincoln's Grave.
    Reconciliation.
    When I Am Old.
    Whichever Way the Wind
      Doth Blow.
Mason, Edgar Cooper
    Safe in His Keeping.
    Satisfied.
Mason, Guy
    Adventure.
    Independence.
Mason, Madeline
    Janus.
Mason, Mary Augusta
    My Little Neighbor.
    The Scarlet Tanager.
Mason, Mary J.
    Saviour, Who Died for Me.
Mason, Mason Jordan
    Big Man.
    In War.
    Last Impression of New York.
    Pen Hy Cane.
    Pico della Mirandola.
    Things of the Spirit.
Mason, R. A. K.
    After Death.
    Be Swift O Sun.
    Body of John.
    Ecce Homunculus.
    Footnote to John ii.4.
    Judas Iscariot.
    On the Swag.
    Our Love Was a Grim
      Citadel.
    Poem.
    Prelude.
    Song of Allegiance.
    Sonnet of Brotherhood.
    The Young Man Thinks of
      Sons.
Mason, Ronald
    Self-Congratulatory Ode on
      Mr Auden's Election
      (parody).
Mason, W. L.
    My Airedale Dog.
Mason, Walt
    Football.
Mason, William
    The English Garden (excerpt).
    How to Build a Ha-Ha.
    Landscape.
    Ode to a Friend.

    Sonnet: "A plaintive Sonnet
      flow'd from MILTON's
      pen."
Massey, Gerald
    As Proper Mode of
      Quenching Legal Lust.
    The Diakka.
    England.
    His Banner over Me.
    Little Willie.
    O, Lay Thy Hand in Mine,
      Dear!
    Our Wee White Rose.
    Parting.
    Womankind.
    Young Love.
Massey, Reginald
    The Child.
Massinger, Philip
    Death Invoked.
    The Forest's Queen.
    The Maid of Honour.
    Men May Talk of Country-
      Christmasses.
    The Renegado (Act V, Scene
      I).
    A Song of Pleasure.
Massman, Gordon
    Liard Hot Springs.
**Masson, Tom (Thomas Lansing
Masson)**
    Enough.
    He Took Her.
    My Poker Girl.
    A Tragedy.
    When I Get Time.
Master, Thomas
    The Cat and the Lute.
Masters, Edgar Lee
    Aaron Hatfield.
    Achilles Deatheridge.
    Alfonso Churchill.
    Amanda Barker.
    Anne Rutledge.
    Arlo Will.
    Bert Kessler.
    "Butch" Weldy.
    Carl Hamblin.
    Cassius Hueffer.
    Catherine Ogg.
    Chandler Nicholas.
    The Circuit Judge.
    Cooney Potter.
    Daisy Fraser.
    Davis Matlock.
    Dora Williams.
    Editor Whedon.
    Edmund Pollard.
    Elliott Hawkins.
    Elsa Wertman.
    Emily Sparks.
    English Thornton.
    Father Malloy.
    Fiddler Jones.
    Frank Drummer.
    Hamilton Greene.
    Harry Wilmans.
    Henry C. Calhoun.
    Herman Altman.
    The Hill.
    Howard Lamson.
    In Memory of Bryan Lathrop.
    J. Milton Miles.
    Jacob Godbey.
    John Horace Burleson.
    John Wasson.
    Jonathan Houghton.
    Jonathan Swift Somers.
    Judge Somers.
    Julia Miller.
    Keats to Fanny Brawne.
    Knowlt Hoheimer.

    The Lost Orchard.
    Lucinda Matlock.
    Marx, the Sign Painter.
    Mind Flying Far.
    Mrs. Williams.
    My Dog Ponto.
    The New World (excerpt).
    Perry Zoll.
    Petit, the Poet.
    Portrait of a Poet.
    Reuben Pantier.
    Rhoda Pitkin.
    Rutherford McDowell.
    Scholfield Huxley.
    Seth Compton.
    Sexsmith the Dentist.
    Silence.
    The Spooniad.
    Supplication.
    Thomas Trevelyan.
    Tomorrow Is My Birthday:
      "The thing is sex, Ben."
    Unknown Soldiers.
    The Village Atheist.
    Week-End by the Sea.
    Widows.
    William Jones.
    Willis Beggs.
Masters, Marcia
    Impressions of My Father/I.
    Country Ways.
Mastin, Florence Ripley
    Return to Spring.
Mastoraki, Jenny
    The Bridal Bed.
    The Crusaders knew the Holy
      Places.
    The Death of a Warrior.
    Prometheus.
    Then they paraded Pompey's
      urn.
    Three Poems.
    The Vandals.
    The Wooden Horse then said.
Mastrolia, Lilyan S.
    Golden Gate: The Teacher.
Matchett, William H.
    Aunt Alice in April.
    Cedar Waxwing.
    Head Couples.
    Old Inn on the Eastern Shore.
    Packing a Photograph from
      Firenze.
    Return to Lane's Island.
    Water Ouzel.
Mather, Cotton
    Epitaph.
    Eternal God, How They're
      Increased.
    Go Then, My Dove, but Now
      No Longer Mine.
    I Lift My Eyes Up to the
      Hills.
    My Heart, How Very Hard
      It's Grown!
    O Glorious Christ of God; I
      Live.
    Vigilantius.
    When the Seed of Thy Word
      Is Cast.
Mather, Joseph
    The File-Hewer's
      Lamentation.
    God Save Great Thomas
      Paine.
Mathers, Edward Powys
    English Girl.
Matheson, Annie
    Love's Cosmopolitan.
    A Song of Handicrafts.
Matheson, George
    Christ's Bondservant.

O Love, That Wilt Not Let
  Me Go.
Matheson, Mary
  Afterward.
  Evening.
Matheus, John Frederick
  Requiem.
Mathew, Ray
  At a Time.
  A Good Thing.
  Let us not Pretend.
  Love and Marriage.
  Lover's Meeting.
  'Morning, Morning.
  One Day.
  Picnic.
  Poem in Time of Winter.
  The Poems Come Easier.
  Seeing St. James's.
  Wynyard Sailor.
  Young Man's Fancy.
Mathews, Albert
  To an Autumn Leaf.
Mathews, Cornelius
  The Poet.
Mathews, Esther
  Song: "I can't be talkin' of
    love, dear."
Mathews, Harry
  Comatas.
  The Firing Squad.
  Invitation to a Sabbath.
  The Relics.
  The Ring.
  The Sense of Responsibility.
Mathews, Richard
  Dear Patty Dear Tania.
Mathis, Cleopatra
  Aerial View of Louisiana.
  Celebrating the Mass of
    Christian Burial.
  For Maria.
  Getting Out.
  Mimosa.
  Pine Barrens: Letter Home.
  Ruston, Louisiana: 1952.
  View of Louisiana.
Mathison, Thomas
  The Goff. An Heroi-Comical
    Poem (excerpt).
Mattam, Donald
  In a Town Garden.
  Table Talk.
Mattera, Don
  At Least.
  Of Reason and Discovery.
  Protea.
Matthews, Alice Clear
  Of the Mathematician.
Matthews, Brander
  An American Girl.
Matthews, Harley
  The Return of the Native.
  Women Are Not Gentlemen.
Matthews, T. S.
  The Invisible Man.
  Song for Mother's Day.
Matthews, William
  An Airline Breakfast.
  Bring the War Home.
  Bystanders.
  The Cat.
  Charming.
  Cows Grazing at Sunrise.
  Directions.
  An Elegy for Bob Marley.
  Hello, Hello.
  Housework.
  In Memory of the Utah Stars.
  The Invention of Astronomy.
  Living among the Dead.
  Loyal.

Lust.
Moving.
Moving Again.
Nurse Sharks.
Oh Yes.
On the Porch at the Frost
  Place, Franconia, NH.
Our Strange and Lovable
  Weather.
The Penalty for Bigamy Is
  Two Wives.
Praise.
The Search Party.
Taking the Train Home.
Twins.
Unrelenting Flood.
Whiplash.
Matthias, John
  Evening Song.
  In Columbus, Ohio.
Matusovsky, Mikhail
  Long Roads.
Matuzak, Joseph
  Nystagmus.
  To Sherrie.
Matveyeva, Novella
  The Eggplants Have Pins and
    Needles.
Maunders, Ruth O.
  Eureka.
Maura, Sister
  Annunciation.
  The Blessing of St. Francis.
  Deirdre's Song at Sunrise.
  Our Lady of the Refugees.
  The Rosary.
  A Short History of the
    Teaching Profession.
  To the Queen of Dolors.
  Woman's Liberation.
Maurice, Furnley
  The Agricultural Show,
    Flemington, Victoria.
  Echoes of Wheels.
  The Gully.
  On a Grey-Haired Old Lady
    Knitting at an Orchestral
    Concert...
  The Supreme Sacrifice.
  The Team.
  To God.
  Upon a Row of Old Boots
    and Shoes in a Pawnbroker's
    Window.
  The Victoria Markets
    Recollected in Tranquillity.
  Whenever I Have.
Maurice, Thomas
  An Epistle to the Right Hon.
    Charles James Fox (excerpt).
Mauropus, John
  Our Lady of the Passion.
Mavimbela
  My Money! O, My Money!
Mavity, Nancy Barr
  Prisoners.
Maxson, H. A.
  When It Rains.
Maxton, Hugh
  Cernunnos.
  Dialectique.
  Landscape with Minute
    Wildflowers.
  Mastrim: A Meditation
    (excerpt).
  Waking.
Maxtone, Mary
  Skywriting.
Maxwell, James Clerk
  In Memory of Edward Wilson
    (parody).
  Rigid Body Sings.

Maxwell-Hall, Agnes
  Jamaica Market.
May, Beulah
  The Captain of St. Kitts.
  Deprecating Parrots.
May, Curtis
  Tucking the Baby In.
May, Edward
  Five Things White.
  On a Young Man and an Old
    Man.
  To a Covetous Churl.
  To Barba.
  To Certain Maidens Playing
    with Snow.
  To Her Love.
May, Julia Harris
  Day by Day.
May, Thomas
  Dear, Do Not Your Fair
    Beauty Wrong.
  The Old Couple, III, i: Love's
    Prime.
Mayakovsky, Vladimir
  At the Top of My Voice
    (excerpt).
  Brooklyn Bridge.
  A Cloud in Trousers:
    Prologue.
  Last Statement.
  Our March.
  Spring.
Maybin, Patrick
  April 1940.
  Ballykinlar: May 1940.
  The Fallen Tree.
  The Monks at Ards.
  Thoughts from Abroad.
Mayer, Bernadette
  America.
  An Ancient Degree.
  Booze Turns Men into
    Women.
  The Complete Introductory
    Lectures on Poetry.
  Corn.
  Essay.
  Eve of Easter.
  Index.
  It Moves Across.
  It Was Miss Scarlet with the
    Candlestick in the Billiard
    Room.
  Laundry & School Epigrams.
  Laura Cashdollars.
  Painting by Chimes.
  Poem.
  The Port.
  Sea.
  Sermon.
  Sonnet: Kamikaze.
  Steps.
  The Tragic Condition of the
    Statue of Liberty.
  Warren Phinney.
  Wind Force.
  A Woman I Mix Men Up...
Mayer, Frank H.
  At Timber Line.
Mayer, Gerda
  Dandelions.
  Small Park in East Germany:
    1969.
Mayhall, Jane
  City Sparrow.
  For the Market.
  The Human Animal.
  The Marshes.
  Surfaces.
Maynard, Don
  Athlete.

Maynard, Theodore
  Desideravi.
  The Duel.
  Dwell with Me, Lovely
    Images.
  Faith's Difficulty.
  If I Had Ridden Horses.
  On the Edge of the Pacific.
  Requiem.
  The Ships.
  The World's Miser.
Mayne, Jasper
  The Amorous War: Time.
  To the Memory of Ben
    Johnson (excerpt).
Mayne, John
  Glasgow (excerpt).
  Hallowe'en.
  Logan Braes.
Mayne, Seymour
  Abraham Sutskever.
  Afternoon's Angel.
  Before Passover.
  In the First Cave.
  Locusts of Silence.
  Roots.
  Yehuda Amichai.
Mayo, E. L.
  Anglo-Saxon.
  At the Louvre.
  The D Minor.
  The Diver.
  The Doomed City.
  El Greco.
  En Route.
  Envoi.
  Failure.
  A Fair Warning.
  I Saw My Father.
  In the Web.
  Letter to Karl Shapiro.
  Nausea.
  Note on Modern Journalism
    during the Last Campaign.
  Of Angels.
  On the Night Train from
    Oxford.
  Oracle.
  The Pool.
  The Sleeping Beauty.
  Stone.
  The Stones of Sleep.
  To the Young Rebels.
  The Uninfected.
  Variations on a Line from
    Shakespeare's Fifty-Sixth
    Sonnet.
  Wagon Train.
  We Still Must Follow.
  The Word of Water.
Mayrocker, F.
  Patron of Flawless Serpent
    Beauty.
Mays, Bert
  Oh Oh Blues.
Maze, Mack
  If You See My Mother.
Mazzaro, Jerome
  At Torrey Pines State Park.
  Fall Colors.
M'Baye, Annette
  Silhouette.
Mberi, Antar S. K.
  Nuflo de Olano (Who Sailed
    with Balboa).
McAfee, Thomas
  If There Is a Perchance.
McAleavey, David
  At the Scenic Drive-In.
  Can-Opener.
  Driving; Driven.
  Gate.

Starship.

McAllister, Claire
Aeneid.
July in the Jardin des Plantes.

McAlmon, Robert
Contributions: For Instance.

McAlpine, R. W.
Two Surprises.

McAlpine, Rachel
On the Train.
The Test.
Three Poems for Your Eyes.

McAnally, Mary
Our Mother's Body Is the
Earth.

McArthur, Peter
Earthborn.
Sugar Weather.

McAuley, James Philip
An Art of Poetry.
At Bungendore.
Because.
The Blue Horses.
Canticle.
Convalescence.
The Death of Chiron.
In the Huon Valley.
Jesus.
Late Winter.
A Letter to John Dryden
(excerpt).
Liberal or Innocent by
Definition.
Merry-Go-Round.
Missa Papae Marcelli.
New Guinea.
Pieta.
Terra Australis.
Winter Drive.

McBride, Mekeel
Aubade.
A Blessing.
Over the Phone.
The Will to Live.

McBurney, William B.
The Croppy Boy.

McCabe, Angela
Back.
Blind Adolphus.
Bloom Street.
From Lois in London.
Inside History.

McCabe, Victoria
Reply.

McCabe, William Gordon
Christmas Night of '62.
Dreaming in the Trenches.

McCall, James Edward
The New Negro.

McCann, John E.
The Utmost in Friendship.

McCann, Michael Joseph
O'Donnell Aboo.

McCann, Rebecca
Humane Thought.

McCann, Richard
The Fat Boy's Dream.

McCarriston, Linda
Spring.

McCarroll, James
The Grey Linnet.

McCarthy, Denis Aloysius
Ah, Sweet Is Tipperary.
Christmas Legends.
The Land Where Hate Should
Die.
The Tailor That Came from
Mayo.

McCarthy, Denis Florence
The Dead Tribune.
The Irish Wolf-Hound.
Spring Flowers from Ireland.

McCarthy, Eugene
Dogs of Santiago.
Kilroy.
Tamarack.

McCarthy, Justin Huntly
If I Were King.

McCartney, Mabel E.
Refuge.

**McCartney, Paul and John
Lennon** See also **Beatles, The**
For No One.

McClane, Kenneth A.
The Judge.

McClatchy, J. D.
Late Autumn Walk.
The Pleasure of Ruins.
A Winter without Snow.

McClaurin, Irma
I, Woman.
The Mask.
To a Gone Era.

McClellan, George Marion
A Butterfly in Church.
Dogwood Blossoms.
The Feet of Judas.
The Hills of Sewanee.

McClennan, Tommy
Brown Skin Girl.

McClintock, Charles W.
Everybody Works but Father.

McCloskey, Mark
The Lights Go On.
Too Dark.

McClure, John
Carol.
Carol Naive.
Chanson Naive.
Man to Man.

McClure, Michael
The Aelf-Scin.
Baja—Outside Mexicali.
The Breech.
Canticle.
The Flowers of Politics.
For Artaud.
From the Window of the
Beverly Wilshire Hotel.
Hymn to St. Geryon, I.
The List.
Mad Sonnet 1.
May Morn.
Moire.
Ode for Soft Voice.
Ode to Joy.
Oh Bright Oh Black Singbeast
Lovebeast Catkin Sleek.
Oh Ease Oh Body-Strain Oh
Love Oh Ease Me Not!
Wound-Bore.
Peyote Poem.
Rant Block.
With Tendrils of Poems.

McCombs, Judith
The Dictionary Is an
Historian.
Packing in with a Man.

McCord, David
Afreet.
Any Day Now.
Ascot Waistcoat.
The Axolotl.
Baccalaureate.
Blessed Lord, What It Is to
Be Young.
Books Fall Open.
A Christmas Package: No. 7
(excerpt).
A Christmas Package: No. 8
(excerpt).
Cities and Science.
Cocoon.
Come Christmas.

Conversation.
The Cow Has a Cud.
Crew Cut.
Crickets.
Crows.
Epitaph on a Waiter.
Every Time I Climb a Tree.
Father and I in the Woods.
The Fisherman.
Fred.
The Frost Pane.
Gloss.
Glowworm.
Go Fly a Saucer.
The Grasshopper.
A Hex on the Mexican X.
History of Education.
In Grato Jubilo.
Joe.
The Lacquer Liquor Locker.
Laundromat.
Limerick: "A bigamist born in
Zambezi."
Limerick: "O limerick, Learest
of lyrics."
Limerick: "The British in
branding their betters."
Mantis.
Monday Morning Back to
School.
New Chitons for Old Gods
(excerpt).
The Newt.
Notes on a Track Meet.
Notice.
Our Mr. Toad.
Perambulator Poem.
The Pickety Fence.
Plane Geometer.
Progress.
The Rainbow.
Second Half.
Singular Indeed.
Song of the Train.
The Sportsman.
Thin Ice.
This Is My Rock.
Tiger Lily.
Tiggady Rue.
To a Certain Most Certainly
Certain Critic.
To a Child.
The Walnut Tree.
Watching the Moon.
Weather Words.
Where Is My Butterfly Net?
Who Wants a Birthday?

McCord, Howard
The Bear That Came to the
Wedding.
In Iceland.
Longjaunes His Periplus
(excerpt).
My Cow.

McCormick, Virginia
To One Who Died in
Autumn.
Twilight.

McCoy, Charlie
That Lonesome Train Took
My Baby Away.

McCoy, Jane
View from the Window.

McCoy, (Kansas) Joe
Evil Devil Woman.

McCoy, Samuel
Thompson Street.

McCracken, Kathleen
I Have Seen.

McCrae, Hugh
Ambuscade.
Camden Magpie.

Colombine.
Columbine.
The End of Desire.
Enigma.
Evening.
Fragment.
I Blow My Pipes.
Joan of Arc: Introduction.
June Morning.
Mad Marjory.
The Mimshi Maiden.
Morning.
The Mouse.
Muse-Haunted.
Song of the Rain.
Spring.
The Uncouth Knight.
Winds.

McCrae, John
The Anxious Dead.
The Harvest of the Sea.
In Flanders Fields.
The Song of the Derelict.

McCreery, John Luckey
There Is No Death.

McCuaig, Ronald
L'Apres Midi d'une Fille aux
Cheveux de Lin.
Au Tombeau de Mon Pere.
Betty by the Sea.
The Daily Round.
Is Love Not Everlasting?
Love Me and Never Leave
Me.
Music in the Air.
Recitative.

McCulloch, Margaret
Aftermath.

McCullough, Ken
Voices in the Winter.

McCully, Laura E.
Canoe Song at Twilight.

McCurdy, Harold
August, at an Upstairs
Window.
Petition.

McDonald, Barry
Ingestion.

Mcdonald, Dorothy Nell
A Birthday Wish.

McDonald, L. A.
It's You.

McDonald, Nan
Burragorang.
The Hatters.
The Makers.
Wet Summer: Botanic
Gardens.
The White Eagle.

McDonald, Roger
Bachelor Farmer.
Components.
Flights.
The Hollow Thesaurus.
Two Summers in Moravia.

McDonald, S. P.
Casey—Twenty Years Later.

McDonald, Walter
On Teaching David to Shoot.
With Cindy at Vallecito.

McDougall, Jean
Quarrel.

McDougall, Joseph Easton
The New House.

McDuffee, Franklin
Hakluyt Unpurchased.

McElhaney, Georgia Lee
Conquistador.
Dervish.
Effigy.

McElroy, Colleen J.
Caledonia.

Looking for a Country under
  Its Original Name.
Ruth.
A Woman's Song.
McElroy, David
Before Breakup on the Chena
  outside Fairbanks.
Dragging in Winter.
Making It Simple December
  8, 1969.
Nocturn at the Institute.
Ode to a Dead Dodge.
Report from the
  Correspondent They Fired.
Spawning in Northern
  Minnesota.
McFadden, David
Art's Variety.
The Day of the Pancreas.
Elephant.
The External Element.
The Fiddlehead.
A Form of Passion.
House Plants.
It's a Different Story When
  You're Going Into the Wind.
Kicking from Centre Field.
Lennox Island.
Pop.
Upon Looking at a Book of
  Astrology.
We Love You the Way You
  Are.
McFadden, Roy
Address to an Absolute.
An Aged Writer.
Elegy.
Epithalamium.
Independence.
Mihailovich.
The Orator.
Saint Francis and the Birds.
Virgin Country.
The White Bird.
William Blake Sees God.
McFarland, Ron
Frost Warning.
McFatter, Janet Reed
Cow.
The Drive.
Go Home.
Indian Camp.
Moving.
Sinkholes.
McFee, Michael
Buster Keaton.
Easter Monday.
McGaffey, Ernest
As the Day Breaks.
A California Idyl.
Geronimo.
I Fear No Power a Woman
  Wields.
Little Big Horn.
Mark.
A Rise.
McGaffin, Audrey
At Cambridge.
Avalon.
The Cemetery Is.
Inertia.
Invalid.
A Poor Relation.
McGahey, Jeanne
Oregon Winter.
McGarvey, Margaret
D–Dawn.
McGaugh, Lawrence
Glimpses # xii (excerpt).
To Children.
Two Mornings.
Young Training.

McGavin, Stewart
Kythans.
McGee, Clyde
Gratitude.
Mary at the Cross.
McGee, Thomas D'Arcy
The Celtic Cross.
The Celts.
The Irish Wife.
Jacques Cartier.
The Man of the North
  Countrie.
McGeorge, Alice Sutton
Autumn's Fete.
McGiffert, Gertrude Huntington
The Maine Trail.
McGinley, Phyllis
About Children.
The Adversary.
B's the Bus.
Ballad of Culinary
  Frustration.
Ballade of Lost Objects.
Ballroom Dancing Class.
C Is for the Circus.
A Certain Age.
The Concert.
The Conquerors.
Conversation in Avila.
Country Club Sunday.
Daniel at Breakfast.
The Day after Sunday.
The Demagogue.
Enigma for Christmas
  Shoppers.
Evening Musicale.
Fourteenth Birthday.
A Garland of Precepts.
The Giveaway.
The Good Humor Man.
Home Is the Sailor.
Homework for Annabelle.
How to Start a War.
The Independent.
Intimations of Mortality.
Journey toward Evening.
Lament for Lost Lodgings.
Last Year's Discussion: The
  Nobel Russian.
Literary Landscape with Dove
  and Poet.
Lucy McLockett.
Malediction.
Midcentury Love Letter.
The Muted Screen of Graham
  Greene.
My Six Toothbrushes.
The New Order.
Notes for a Southern Road
  Map.
Occupation: Housewife.
Ode to the End of Summer.
Office Party.
Oh Come, Little Children.
The Old Beauty.
P's the Proud Policeman.
Portrait of a Girl with Comic
  Book.
Primary Education.
Public Journal.
Publisher's Party.
R is for the Restaurant.
Reflections at Dawn.
Reflections outside of a
  Gymnasium.
Saint Francis Borgia or a
  Refutation for Heredity.
The Spanish Lions.
Speaking of Television: Robin
  Hood.
Spectator's Guide to
  Contemporary Art.

The Temptations of Saint
  Anthony.
The Theology of Jonathan
  Edwards.
The Thunderer.
Tirade on Tea.
To a Talkative Hairdresser.
Trinity Place.
Triolet against Sisters.
U is for Umbrellas.
The Velvet Hand.
W's for Windows.
Why, Some of My Best
  Friends Are Women.
McGlennon, Felix
Comrades.
Love, Sweet Love.
McGonagall, William
An Address to the New Tay
  Bridge.
The Albion Battleship
  Calamity.
The Death of Prince Leopold.
The Hen It Is a Noble Beast.
Jottings of New York.
The Newport Railway.
Richard Pigott, the Forger
  (excerpt).
The Tay Bridge Disaster.
McGough, Roger
40–Love.
The Fight of the Year.
Flood.
Goodbat Nightman.
Gruesome.
If Life's a Lousy Picture, Why
  Not Leave before the End.
Mother the Wardrobe Is Full
  of Infantrymen.
My cat and I.
The Newly Pressed Suit.
P.C. Plod Versus the Dale St.
  Dog Strangler.
McGovern, Robert
Christmas Myth, 1973.
Elegy for a Dead Confederate.
Mr. Kurtz.
Perdido, Duke?
McGrath, Thomas
Against the False Magicians.
A Coal Fire in Winter.
Death for the Dark Stranger.
The End of the World.
Jig Tune: Not for Love.
John Carey's Second Song.
A Letter for Marian.
Letter to an Imaginary
  Friend.
A Long Way Outside
  Yellowstone.
Ode for the American Dead in
  Korea.
The Odor of Blood.
Remembering That Island.
The Repeated Journey.
Something Is Dying Here.
Song: "Lovers in ladies'
  magazines."
Travelling Song.
McGrew, A. O.
A Hit at the Times.
McGroarty, John S.
Blow, Bugles, Blow.
Just California.
The King's Highway.
The Port o' Heart's Desire.
McGuckian, Mebdh
The Aphrodisiac.
Aviary.
Champagne.
The Cure.
Felicia's Cafe.

The Flitting.
The Flower Master.
Gateposts.
The Hard Summer.
June.
The Moon Pond.
Mr. McGregor's Garden.
On Not Being Your Lover.
Power-Cut.
The Seed-Picture.
Slips.
Smoke.
The Sofa.
The Standing.
To My Grandmother.
Tobacco Hole.
Tulips.
Venus and the Rain.
McGuire, Harry
Phantoms.
McGuire, Jack
The Streets of Forbes.
McHugh, Heather
Animal Song.
Breath.
Brightness.
Capital.
Corps d'Esprit.
Down, Down, Down.
The Fence.
Form.
Gig at Big Al's.
Having Read Books.
I Knew I'd Sing.
Impressionist.
Language Lesson, 1976.
Lines.
Meantime.
Message at Sunset for Bishop
  Berkeley.
Night Catch.
Note Delivered by Female
  Impersonator.
A Physics.
Squeal.
McHugh, Vincent
Amphimachos the Dandy.
Crawl Blues.
A Deposition by John
  Wilmot.
The Mantis Friend.
The Mice at the Door.
The Natural History of Pliny.
Suite from Catullus.
Talking to Myself.
McInerney, Sally
Domestic Quarrel.
McInnis, Edgar
Fire Burial.
McIntosh, Joan
Are the Sick in Their Beds as
  They Should Be?
McIntyre, James
On the High Cost of Dairy
  Products.
Queen of Cheese.
Shelly.
McKain, David
Four Pictures by Juan, Age 5.
McKay, Claude
Absence.
Africa.
After the Winter.
America.
Baptism.
The Barrier.
Commemoration.
Desolate.
Enslaved.
Exhortation: Summer, 1919.
Flame-Heart.
Flower of Love.

The Harlem Dancer.
Harlem Shadows.
Home Thoughts.
I Know My Soul.
If We Must Die.
In Bondage.
The Lynching.
My House.
My Mother.
The Negro's Tragedy.
North and South.
Outcast.
The Pagan Isms.
A Song of the Moon.
The Spanish Needle.
Spring in New Hampshire.
St. Isaac's Chruch, Petrograd.
Tiger.
The Tired Worker.
To O.E.A.
To the White Fiends.
The Tropics in New York.
Truth.
Two-An'-Six.
When Dawn Comes to the
City: New York.
The White City.
The White House.
The Wild Goat.

McKay, Don
A Barbed Wire Fence
Meditates upon the
Goldfinch.
I Scream You Scream.
March Snow.

McKay, James T.
Cenotaph of Lincoln.
Making Port.

McKay, Lois Weakley
Night.

McKee, Gladys
Spring Cellar.

McKellar, J. A. R.
Football Field: Evening.
Love in a Cottage.
Twelve O'Clock Boat.

McKelway, St. Clair
Boogie-Woogie Ballads.

McKent, Robert J., Jr.
Pre-History Repeats.

McKeown, Tom
1937 Ford Convertible.
Early Morning of Another
World.
The Graveyard Road.
Invitation of the Mirrors.
Lost in Yucatan.
Night Clouds.

McKinney, Laurence
Compromise.
Oboe.
Song to My Love.

McKinnon, Barry
Bushed.
The North.

McKuen, Rod
Spring Song.
Thoughts on Capital
Punishment.

McLachlan, Alexander
A Backwoods Hero (excerpt).
The Emigrant.
God (excerpt).
O! Come to the Greenwood
Shade.
To an Indian Skull (excerpt).
We Live in a Rickety House.
Woman (excerpt).

McLaren, Floris Clark
Frozen Fire.
No More the Slow Stream.
Visit by Water.

McLaughlin, Joe-Anne
Another Mother and Child.

McLaughlin, Kathy
Suicide Pond.

McLaughlin, Laura
Beltway.

McLean, Alan
Lizard.

McLean, William Alfred, Jr.
War.

McLeish, John A. B.
Not without Beauty.

McLellan, Isaac
New England's Dead.

McLeod, Irene Rutherford
April (excerpt).
Is Love, Then, So Simple.
Lone Dog.
A Prayer.
Rebel.
So Beautiful You Are, Indeed.
Song: "How do I love you?"
Sonnet: "Between my love and
me there runs a thread."
Sonnet: "In heaven there is a
star I call my own."
Sonnet: "Shall I be fearful
thus to speak my mind."
Sonnet: "Sweet, when I think
how summer's smallest bird."
Sonnet: "When some men
gather to talk of Love."
Unborn.
When My Beloved Sleeping
Lies.

McLeod, Norman
A Creed.

"McM"
Allegro.

McMahon, M. J.
The Nonpareil's Grave.

McMahon, Michael Beirne
Once upon a Nag.
Trout Fishing in Virginia.

McMahon, Rhoda
Loss! Loss!
Love! Love!

McMaster, Guy Humphreys
Carmen Bellicosum.

McMaster, Rhyll
Profiles of My Father.
A Round Song.
Tanks.

McMichael, James
The Cabin North of It All.
The Great Garret; or, 100
Wheels.
The Inland Lighthouse.
Lutra, the Fisher.
Terce.
The Village of the Presents.

McNabb, Vincent
The Spotless Maid.

McNair, Wesley
The Bald Spot.
Big Cars.

McNall, Sally
Metaphors.

McNally, Leonard
The Lass of Richmond Hill.

McOwan, Rennie
Highland Loves.
The Hillman Looks Back.
The Hooded Crow.
Mountaineering Bus.
The Things of the North.

McPheron, Judith
Water.

McPherson, Sandra
Alleys.
Butchery.

Centerfold Reflected in a Jet
Window.
Children.
A Coconut for Katerina.
Collapsars.
Elegies for the Hot Season.
For Elizabeth Bishop.
Games.
Gnawing the Breast.
His Body.
Lament, with Flesh and
Blood.
Letter with a Black Border.
Lifesaving.
Loneliness.
Marlow and Nancy.
Michael.
Morning Glory Pool.
The Museum of the Second
Creation.
Open Casket.
Page.
Peter Rabbit.
Pisces Child.
Poppies.
Pornography, Nebraska.
Pregnancy.
Resigning from a Job in a
Defense Industry.
Seaweeds.
Sentience.
Sisters.
To an Alcoholic.
Triolet.
Unitarian Easter.
Urban Ode.
Wanting a Mummy.
Wings and Seeds.

McQueen, Cilla
Matinal.
To Ben, at the Lake.
Weekend Sonnets.

McQuilkin, Rennie
New England Greenhouse.
Tree Man.

McRae, George Gordon
Mamba the Bright-Eyed
(excerpt).

McTell, Blind Willie
Drive Away Blues.
Savannah Mama.
Searching the Desert for the
Blues.
Statesboro Blues.
Talking to Myself.
Three Women Blues.
Travelin' Blues.

McTell, Ralph
First and Last Man.

McWebb, Elizabeth Upham
At Mrs. Appleby's.

Meacham, Harry M.
To a Young Poet.

Mead, Margaret
Misericordia.

Mead, Philip
The Chinese Graves in
Beechworth Cemetery.

Mead, Stella
The Merry Man of Paris.

Means, Alex
Wondrous Love.

Mearns, Hughes
The Lady with Technique.
The Little Man Who Wasn't
There.
Me.
The Perfect Reactionary.

Mechain, Gwerfyl
In the Snowfall.
Lady of the Ferry Inn.

Mechtild of Magdeburg
Ah Dearest Love, for How
Long.
Here Too the Spirit Shafts.
Love Flows from God.

Medici, Lorenzo de'
A Lyric: "How can I sing
light-souled."
A Lyric: "Into a little close of
mine I went."
Triumph of Bacchus and
Ariadne.

Meehan, John James
The Race of the Oregon.

Meeker, Marjorie
Memorial Sonnet.

Meeks, Dodie
There Goes a Girl Walking.

Megged, Matti
The Akedah.
The Phoenix.
White Bird.

Mehri
Coming across.

Mei Yao Ch'en
A Friend Advises Me to Stop
Drinking.
On the Death of a New Born
Child.

Meigs, Charles D.
A Home without a Bible
(excerpt).
Others.

Meigs, Mildred Plew See also
Merryman, Mildred Plew
Abraham Lincoln.
Silver Ships.

Meilir ap Gwalchmai
His Delight.

Meiners, R. K.
Marginal Music.

Meinke, Peter
Absence.
Advice to My Son.
The Artist.
Atomic Pantoum.
Byron vs. DiMaggio.
Dear Reader.
Elegy for a Diver.
Everything We Do.
Happy at 40.
The Heart's Location.
Hermann Ludwig Ferdinand
von Helmholtz.
Mendel's Law.
Progress.
Surfaces.
This Is a Poem to My Son
Peter.
To a Daughter with Artistic
Talent.
To an Athlete Turned Poet.

Meir of Rothenburg
The Burning of the Law.

Meireles, Cecilia
Away from You.
Ballad of the Ten Casino
Dancers.
The Dead Horse.
Motive.
Pyrargyrite Metal, 9.
The Roosters Will Crow.
Song: "I placed my dream in
a boat."

Meissner, Bill
1948 Plymouth Abandoned on
the Ice.

Meissner, William
The Coal Mine Disaster's Last
Trapped Man Contemplates
Salvation.
Fishermen at Dawn.

The Photographer Whose
  Shutter Died.
The Slaughterhouse Boys.
The Smell of Fish.
Meleager
Against Mosquitoes.
Busy with love, the bumble
  bee.
Epigram: "And now I,
  Meleager..."
Epigram: "As honey in wine."
Epigram: "At 12 o'clock in
  the afternoon."
Epigram: "Diodorus is nice..."
Epigram: "Drink, unhappy
  lover."
Epigram: "I was thirsty."
Epigram: "It is true that I
  held Thero fair."
Epigram: "Listen, you who
  know the pains of love."
Epigram: "Lo! Beauty flashed
  forth sweetly."
Epigram: "Love brought me
  quietly."
Epigram: "One boy alone."
Epigram: "The boys of Tyre
  are beautiful."
Epigram: "The breath of my
  life."
A Garland for Heliodora.
I'll Twine White Violets.
In the Spring.
The Little Love-God.
Lost Desire.
Love at the Door.
Love's night & a lamp.
A Lover's Curse.
The Message.
O Gentle Ships.
Of Himself.
Of His Death.
Spring.
That Morn Which Saw Me
  Made a Bride.
To Heliodora: A Fretful
  Monody.
To Heliodora, Dead.
Upon a Maid That Died the
  Day She Was Married.
The Wine Cup.
Melendez, Jesus Papoleto
Open Poetry Reading.
Melinescu, Gabriela
Birth.
Fall.
Time of fish dying.
Mellen, Grenville
The Lonely Bugle Grieves.
Mellichamp, Leslie
Epitaph: "Here he lies
  moulding."
Mello, Francisco Manuel de
Death's Apology.
On Ascending a Hill Leading
  to a Convent.
Melly, George
Belle de Jour (parody).
Homage to Rene Magritte.
Melo, David Abenatar
Thanksgiving.
Meltzer, David
The Eyes, the Blood.
Fifteenth Raga/for Bela
  Lugosi.
A Midrash (excerpt).
Prayerwheel/2.
Revelation.
Tell Them I'm Struggling to
  Sing with Angels.
Twelfth Raga/for John
  Wieners.

Meltzer, Richard
A Poem.
Melville, Herman
The Aeolian Harp.
After the Pleasure Party.
America.
The Apparition.
Art.
At the Cannon's Mouth.
The Attic Landscape.
Ball's Bluff.
The Bench of Boors.
The Berg.
Billy Budd: Billy in the
  Darbies.
The Blue-Bird.
Bridegroom Dick (excerpt).
Buddha.
Camoens.
Camoens in the Hospital.
Clarel.
The College Colonel.
Commemorative of a Naval
  Victory.
The Conflict of Convictions.
Crossing the Tropics.
The Cumberland.
A Dirge for McPherson.
The Eagle of the Blue.
The Enthusiast.
The Enviable Isles.
L'Envoi: The Return of the
  Sire de Nesle A.D. 16–.
The Fall of Richmond.
Falstaff's Lament over Prince
  Hal Become Henry V.
Father Mapple's Hymn.
Formerly a Slave.
The Fortitude of the North.
Fragments of a Lost Gnostic
  Poem of the Twelfth
  Century.
Greek Architecture.
The House-Top.
Immolated.
In a Bye-Canal.
In a Garret.
In the Pauper's Turnip-Field.
In the Prison Pen.
Inscription for Marye's
  Heights, Fredericksburg.
John Marr (excerpt).
Lone Founts.
The Lover and the Syringa
  Bush.
Lyon.
The Maldive Shark.
Malvern Hill.
The March into Virginia.
The Martyr.
Memorials: On the Slain at
  Chickamauga.
Misgivings.
Moby Dick: The Whale.
Monody.
My Jacket Old.
The New Ancient of Days.
The Night-March.
Of Rama.
Old Age in His Ailing.
Old Counsel of the Young
  Master of a Wrecked
  California Clipper.
On the Grave of a Young
  Cavalry Officer Killed in the
  Valley...
On the Slain Collegians.
Pebbles.
Pontoosuce.
The Portent.
The Ravaged Villa.

A Requiem for Soldiers Lost
  in Ocean Transport.
Running the Batteries.
Sheridan at Cedar Creek.
Shiloh, A Requiem.
Southern Cross.
The Stone Fleet.
Stonewall Jackson.
The Surrender at
  Appomattox.
The Temeraire.
To Ned.
The Tuft of Kelp.
An Uninscribed Monument on
  One of the Battle-Fields of
  the Wilderness.
A Utilitarian View of the
  Monitor's Fight.
The Victor of Antietam.
Melville, James
Robin at My Window.
Memphis Jug Band
Oh Ambulance Man.
Menai, Huw
The Old Peasant in the
  Billiard Saloon.
Menander
I Hold Him Happiest.
These Stones.
Menashe, Samuel
Winter.
Mendelssohn, Asher
Cordoba.
Mendelssohn, Moses
Love the Beautiful.
Self-Portrait.
Mendes, Catulle
I Go by Road.
The Mother.
Mendes, Moses
The Ass.
On the Death of a Lady's
  Owl.
The Philanderer.
Mendes, Murilo
Psalm.
Mendoza, Inigo de
Chant of the Ninth Order of
  Seraphim.
Menebroker, Ann
In the Half-Point Time of
  Night.
To the Man I Live with.
Menendez y Pelayo, Marcelino
Rome.
Meng Chiao
After Passing the
  Examination.
Failing the Examination.
Menth, Robert
Cry from the Battlefield.
Menzies, G. K.
Poaching in Excelsis.
Mercantini, Luigi
The Garibaldi Hymn.
Mercer, Ernestine
Artist.
Mercer, Johnny
The Glow-Worm.
I'm an Old Cowhand.
Jubilation T. Cornpone.
Mercer, Margaret
Exhortation to Prayer.
Mercer, Thomas
Arthur's Seat (excerpt).
Merchant, Jane
Unless We Guard Them Well.
Mercier, Louis
Notre Dame des Petits.
Meredith, George
Am I Failing?
The Appeasement of Demeter.

Appreciation.
A Ballad of Past Meridian.
Dirge in the Woods.
Empedocles.
A Faith on Trial (excerpt).
The Garden of Epicurus.
Hymn to Colour.
Islet the Dachs.
Juggling Jerry.
Jump-to-Glory Jane.
King Harald's Trance.
The Lark Ascending.
Lines.
Love in the Valley.
Lucifer in Starlight.
Marian.
Meditation under Stars.
Melampus.
Modern Love.
Night of Frost in May.
O briar-scents, on yon wet
  wing.
Ode to the Spirit of Earth in
  Autumn.
The Old Chartist.
On the Danger of War.
The Orchard and the Heath.
Penetration and Trust.
Phoebus with Admetus.
Pictures of the Rhine.
The Promise in Disturbance.
The Question Whither.
Sense and Spirit.
Should Thy Love Die.
Song.
Song in the Songless.
The Sweet o' the Year.
The Test of Manhood
  (excerpt).
The Thrush in February.
To a Skylark.
When I Would Image.
Wind on the Lyre.
Winter Heavens.
Young Reynard.
Meredith, Joseph
Midnight, Walking the
  Wakeful Daughter.
"Meredith, Owen"
Faith.
Aux Italiens.
Last Lines (excerpt).
One Thing.
Tempora Acta.
What We May Live Without.
The White Anemone.
Twins.
Meredith, William
Accidents of Birth.
At the Natural History
  Museum.
Bachelor.
Battle Problem.
A Boon.
The Chinese Banyan.
Consequences.
Country Stars.
The Couple Overhead.
Do Not Embrace Your
  Mind's New Negro Friend.
Earth Walk.
Effort at Speech.
The Fishvendor.
Fledglings.
For Guillaume Apollinaire.
His Plans for Old Age.
Homage to Paul Mellon, I. M.
  Pei, Their Gallery, and
  Washington City.
Iambic Feet Considered as
  Honorable Scars.
The Illiterate.

A Korean Woman Seated by
   a Wall.
Last Things.
Love Letter from an
   Impossible Land.
My Mother's Life.
An Old Field Mowed.
On Falling Asleep by
   Firelight.
On Falling Asleep to
   Birdsong.
The Open Sea.
Parents.
Perhaps the Best Time.
Picture of a Castle.
Poem about Morning.
The Rainy Season.
Rhode Island.
Starlight.
Thoughts on One's Head.
To a Western Bard Still a
   Whoop and a Holler away
   from English Poetry.
To the Thoughtful Reader.
Transport.
Traveling Boy.
Two Masks Unearthed in
   Bulgaria.
A View of the Brooklyn
   Bridge.
Walter Jenks' Bath.
Weather.
Wholesome.
Winter Verse for His Sister.
Meredith, William Tuckey
   Farragut.
Meredyth, Mr.
   To Miss * * * * * on the
   Death of her Goldfish.
Merilaas, Kersti
   Saint.
Meriluoto, Aila
   Still.
Merington, Marguerite
   Hey Nonny No.
Merivale, Herman Charles
   Aetate XIX.
   Darwinity.
   Ready, Ay, Ready.
Merkel, Andrew
   Tallahassee (excerpt).
Mernit, Susan
   The Scholar's Wife.
   Song of the Bride.
Merriam, Eve
   Alligator on the Escalator.
   Ballad of the Double Bed.
   Blue Alert.
   Catch a Little Rhyme.
   A Charm for Our Time.
   Cheers.
   The Coward.
   Direct Song.
   The Fertile Valley of the Nile.
   Finding a Poem.
   Grandmother, Rocking.
   Leaning on a Limerick.
   Love Letters, Unmailed.
   The Love-Making: His and
   Hers.
   The Moment before
   Conception.
   Monogamania.
   Neuteronomy.
   One, Two, Three–Gough!
   Rainbow Writing.
   Reply to the Question: "How
   Can You Become a Poet?"
   Restricted.
   Some Uses for Poetry.
   Teevee.
   Tryst.

Umbilical.
The Wall.
Which Washington.
Merriam, Lillie Fuller
   At the Door.
Merrick, James
   The Chameleon.
   The Ignorance of Man.
Merrill, Arthur Truman
   Spring in the Desert.
Merrill, Herbert
   Courthouse Square.
Merrill, James
   16. ix. 65.
   18 West 11th Street.
   About the Phoenix.
   After Greece.
   Angel.
   The Bed.
   Birthday.
   The Black Mesa.
   The Black Swan.
   The Broken Bowl.
   The Broken Home.
   Childlessness.
   Cloud Country.
   The Country of a Thousand
   Years of Peace.
   The Current.
   Days of 1964.
   Developers at Crystal River.
   Divine Comedies (excerpt).
   The Drowning Poet.
   Foliage of Vision.
   For a Second Marriage.
   The Friend of the Fourth
   Decade.
   The Furnished Room.
   Getting Through.
   The Grand Canyon.
   Hotel de l'Univers et Portugal.
   In Nine Sleep Valley
   (excerpt).
   Kite Poem.
   Laboratory Poem.
   Last Words.
   Lost in Translation.
   The Mad Scene.
   Manos Karastefanis.
   Matinees.
   Mirabell, Book 9 (excerpt).
   Mirror.
   The Octopus.
   Olive Grove.
   The Parrot Fish.
   Part of the Vigil.
   The Power Station.
   A Preface to the Memoirs.
   A Renewal.
   Samos.
   Scenes of Childhood.
   Some Negatives: X. At the
   Chateau.
   Swimming by Night.
   Syrinx.
   Theory of Vision: The Green
   Eye.
   Thistledown.
   The Thousand and Second
   Night.
   A Timepiece.
   Tomorrows.
   Transfigured Bird.
   Upon a Second Marriage.
   An Urban Convalescence.
   Variations: The Air Is
   Sweetest That a Thistle
   Guards.
   The Victor Dog.
   A View of the Burning.
   Voices from the Other World.
   Watching the Dance.

Whitebeard on Videotape.
Willowware Cup.
Merrill, Lynn
   Steady Rain.
Merrill, William Pierson
   The Call to the Strong.
   Festal Song.
   Not Alone for Mighty
   Empire.
   Rise Up, O Men of God.
Merrill, Jr, Boynton
   The Stallion.
Merrill, Jr, Charles Edmund
   Persicos Odi.
Merriman, Brian
   The Midnight Court.
Merritt, Dixon Lanier
   Limerick: "A wonderful bird
   is the pelican."
Merry, Robert
   Sir Roland; a Fragment.
Merryman, Bryan
   The Midnight Court.
Merryman, Mildred Plew See
also Meigs, Mildred Plew
   Johnny Fife and Johnny's
   Wife.
   The Organ Grinders' Garden.
   The Pirate Don Durk of
   Dowdee.
   The Shepherd Left Behind.
   To Chicago at Night.
Mersar
   Allace! So Sobir Is the Micht.
Mertins, Louis
   Rain Chant.
Merton, Thomas
   An Argument–Of the Passion
   of Christ.
   Aubade: Lake Erie.
   A Baroque Gravure.
   The Blessed Virgin Mary
   Compared to a Window.
   Cana.
   The Dark Morning.
   Duns Scotus.
   Elegy for the Monastery Barn.
   The Evening of the Visitation.
   Figure for an Apocalypse.
   For My Brother.
   Lent in a Year of War.
   Original Child Bomb
   (excerpt).
   A Practical Program for
   Monks.
   A Responsory, 1948.
   Seneca.
   St. Malachy.
   Stranger.
   There Has to Be a Jail for
   Ladies.
   To a Severe Nun.
   The Trappist Abbey: Matins.
Merwin, William Stanley
   Air.
   Animula.
   The Annunciation.
   Another Year Come.
   The Approaches.
   The Asians Dying.
   Assembly.
   Avoiding News by the River.
   Backwater Pond: The
   Canoeists.
   Ballad of John Cable and
   Three Gentlemen.
   Ballade of Sayings.
   Birds Waking.
   The Black Plateau.
   Blind Girl.
   The Bones.
   Bread.

The Broken.
Bucolic.
Burning Mountain.
Burning the Cat.
By Day and by Night.
Caesar.
Camel.
Carol of the Three Kings.
The Chaff.
The Child.
Colloquy at Peniel.
Come Back.
Dead Hand.
December among the
   Vanished.
December Night.
December: Of Aphrodite.
The Defeated.
Departure's Girl-Friend.
Despair.
Dictum: For a Masque of
   Deluge.
The Diggers.
The Distances.
Divinities.
Do Not Die.
A Door.
The Drunk in the Furnace.
Dusk in Winter.
Early January.
Elegy.
Exercise.
Eyes of Summer.
February.
The Fields.
Finding a Teacher.
Fly.
Fog-Horn.
Footprints on the Glacier.
For a Coming Extinction.
For Now.
For the Anniversary of My
   Death.
Foreign Summer.
Glass.
The Gods.
Grandfather in the Old Men's
   Home.
Grandmother and Grandson.
Grandmother Watching at
   Her Window.
Habits.
The Hands.
The Herds.
The Highway.
Home for Thanksgiving.
The Horse.
The Hosts.
The Hours of a Bridge.
I Live Up Here.
In the Gorge.
In the Night Field.
In the Winter of My Thirty-
   Eighth Year.
The Indigestion of the
   Vampire.
The Initiate.
It Is March.
John Otto.
The Judgment of Paris.
The Last One.
Lemuel's Blessing.
Letter.
Leviathan.
Looking for Mushrooms at
   Sunrise.
Lost Month.
Low Fields and Light.
Mariners' Carol.
The Master.
The Moths.
The Mountain.

The Native.
Noah's Raven.
Odysseus.
The Old Boast.
The Old Room.
On the Subject of Poetry.
The Owl.
Peasant.
The Place of Backs.
Plea for a Captive.
The Poem.
The "Portland" Going Out.
Resolution.
Reunion.
The River of Bees.
River Sound Remembered.
Road.
The Rock.
The Room.
The Sapphire.
Sea Monster.
Separation.
Sire.
Small Woman on Swallow
  Street.
Snowfall.
Some Last Questions.
Song of Man Chipping an
  Arrowhead.
Song of Three Smiles.
Spring.
St. Vincent's.
The Students of Justice.
Sunset after Rain.
Surf-Casting.
Things.
Thorn Leaves in March.
To the Hand.
Toro.
Trees.
Two Horses.
Variation on a Line by
  Emerson.
Variation on the Gothic
  Spiral.
Views from the High Camp.
The Vineyard.
Vision.
Voice.
Walk-Up.
The War.
Watchers.
The Way to the River.
We Continue.
When I Came from Colchis.
When the War Is Over.
When You Go Away.
Whenever I Go There.
White Goat, White Ram.
White Summer Flower.
The Widow.
The Windows.
Witnesses.
Yesterday.
Mesens, E. L. T.
The Arid Husband.
Messenger, Bill
Carol Took Her Clothes Off.
Messinger, Robert Hinckley
A Winter Wish.
Metastasio, Pietro
Age of Gold.
Metcalf, Richard
These Are Not Lost.
Metcalfe, James J.
Visit the Sick.
Metz, Jerred
Angels in the House.
Divination.
Her True Body.
Speak Like Rain.

Metz, Roberta
Zeyde.
Meung, Jean de
The Romance of the Rose:
  Love vs. Marriage.
Table Manners for the Hostess
  (excerpt).
Mew, Charlotte
Absence.
Again.
Beside the Bed.
The Call.
The Cenotaph.
The Changeling.
Domus Caedet Arborem.
Fame.
The Farmer's Bride.
Here Lies a Prisoner.
I Have Been through the
  Gates.
I So Liked Spring.
In Nunhead Cemetery.
In the Fields.
Madeleine in Church
  (excerpt).
Monsieur Qui Passe.
Moorland Night.
The Narrow Door.
Not for That City.
Old Shepherd's Prayer.
On the Asylum Road.
On the Road to the Sea.
The Pedlar.
The Quiet House.
A Quoi Bon Dire.
The Rambling Sailor.
Rooms.
Le Sacre-Coeur.
Saturday Market.
Sea Love.
Smile, Death.
Song: "Love, Love today, my
  dear."
To a Child in Death.
The Trees Are Down.
Mey, Mildred T.
Quiet Days.
Meyer, Bert
Funeral.
Meyer, Bertha
God's Eye Is on the Sparrow.
Meyer, Conny Hannes
The Beast That Rode the
  Unicorn.
Of the Beloved Caravan.
Meyer, Conrad Ferninand
Wedding Song.
Meyer, Gerard Previn
Rapunzel Song.
S. T. Colerige Dismisses a
  Caller from Porlock.
Meyer, Kuno
The Crucifixion.
The Deserted Home.
The Fort of Rathangan.
Meyer, Lucy R.
He Was Not Willing.
Meyers, Bert
The Dark Birds.
Daybreak.
The Garlic.
Picture Framing.
Pigeons.
Stars Climb Girders of Light.
Suburban Dusk.
When I Came to Israel.
Meyerstein, E. H. W.
Elegy on the Death of Mme.
  Anna Pavlova (excerpt).
Ivy and Holly.
Meynell, Alice
Advent Meditation.

After a Parting.
At Night.
Chimes.
Christ in the Universe.
Cradle-Song at Twilight.
The Crucifixion.
A Dead Harvest.
Easter Night.
A Father of Women.
The Fugitive.
A General Communion.
I Am the Way.
In Early Spring.
In Manchester Square.
In Portugal, 1912.
In Sleep.
The Lady of the Lambs.
The Lady Poverty.
A Letter from a Girl to Her
  Own Old Age.
My Heart Shall Be Thy
  Garden.
The Newer Vainglory.
November Blue.
The October Redbreast.
One Wept Whose Only Child
  Was Dead.
Parentage.
A Poet of One Mood.
The Poet to the Birds.
The Rainy Summer.
Renouncement.
Rivers Unknown to Song.
San Lorenzo Giustiniani's
  Mother.
The Shepherdess.
A Song of Derivations.
Song of the Night at Day-
  Break.
Summer in England, 1914.
Thoughts in Separation.
The Threshing Machine.
A Thrush before Dawn.
To a Daisy.
To the Body.
To the Mother of Christ, the
  Son of Man.
The Two Poets.
Unto Us a Son Is Given.
Veni Creator.
Via, Veritas, et Vita.
The Watershed.
The Wind Is Blind.
The Young Neophyte.
Meynell, Francis
Permanence.
Meynell, Viola
The Frozen Ocean.
Jonah and the Whale.
Meynell, Wilfrid
The Folded Flock.
Joseph Mary Plunkett.
Meyrich, Geraldine
Washington.
Mezey, Robert
After Hours.
Against Seasons.
April Fourth.
Back.
A Bedtime Story.
Being a Giant.
The Celebration.
A Coffee-House Lecture.
A Confession.
Couplets, XX.
Epitaph of a Faithful Man.
An Evening.
The Friendship.
The Funeral Home.
How Much Longer?
I Am Here.
In Defense of Felons.

In the Soul Hour.
In This Life.
The Lovemaker.
My Mother.
New Year's Eve in Solitude.
Night on Clinton.
No Country You Remember.
Reaching the Horizon.
The Salesman.
A Simpler Thing, a Chair.
Song: "All phantoms of the
  day."
Street Scene.
There.
Theresienstadt Poem.
To Her.
To Philip Levine, on the Day
  of Atonement.
Touch It.
The Underground Gardens.
Vetus Flamma.
The Visit.
The Wandering Jew.
White Blossoms.
You Could Say.
Mezquida, Anna Blake
Chinatown.
Hope.
Mhac an tSaoi, Maire
Harvest of the Sea.
Mhone, Guy C. Z.
The Chisizas I.
A Lament to My Mother.
Miccolis, Leila
I wanted to see you.
Till Death Do Us Part.
Michael, Cyril R.
Shirley Temple.
Michael Marie, Sister
Our Lady on Calvary.
Michael of Kildare
Sweet Jesus.
Swet Jesus.
Michaelis, Hanny
Listening.
Under Restless Clouds.
We Carry Eggshells.
Michal, M. L.
From Skye, Early Autumn.
Michaux, Henri
In the Land of Magic.
Michelangelo, Buonarroti
Celestial Love.
Dante.
The Defence of Night.
The Doom of Beauty.
Eternal Lord! Eased of a
  Cumbrous Load.
For Inspiration.
From Thy Fair Face I Learn.
The Garland and the Girdle.
Joy May Kill.
Last Refuge.
Love's Entreaty.
Love's Justification.
Love, the Light-Giver.
On the Brink of Death.
On the Crucifix.
A Prayer for Faith.
A Prayer for Purification.
Ravished by all that to the
  eyes is fair.
The Soul of Dante.
To Luigi del Riccio, after the
  Death of Cecchino Bracci.
To the Marchesana of
  Pescara.
To the Supreme Being.
To Tommaso de' Cavalieri.
To Vittoria Colonna.
The Transfiguration of Beauty.
Waiting in Faith.

Michelson, Max
The Bird.
A Hymn to Night.
O Brother Tree.
Michie, James
Arizona Nature Myth.
Closing Time.
Dooley Is a Traitor.
From the Epigrams of
Martial.
The Ghost of an Education.
Three Dreams.
To My Daughter.
Michinobu, Fujiwara-No-
The Day Will Soon Be Gone.
Michizane, Sugawara
When I have gone away.
Mickiewicz, Adam
The Sages.
To A Polish Mother.
The Year 1812.
Mickle, William Julius
Almada Hill: An Epistle from
Lisbon (excerpt).
Cumnor Hall.
The Mariner's Wife.
The Sailor's Wife.
Sonnet on Passing the Bridge
of Alcantra, Near Lisbon.
Sunset.
A Wild Romantic Dell.
Middlebrook, Diane
The Contagiousness of
Dreams.
For You, Falling Asleep after
a Quarrel.
Middleton, Bill
Cops and Robbers.
Middleton, Christopher
Alba after Six Years.
The Ancestors.
The Dress.
Edward Lear in February.
Herman Moon's Hourbook.
In Some Seer's Cloud Car.
In the Secret House.
Male Torso.
News from Norwood.
Oystercatchers.
Tanker.
Thinking of Holderlin.
The Thousand Things.
Middleton, Jesse Edgar
The Huron Carol.
Jesous Ahatonhia.
Middleton, Richard
Any Lover, Any Lass.
The Carol of the Poor
Children.
Dream Song.
For He Had Great
Possessions.
The Lass That Died of Love.
Love's Mortality.
On a Dead Child.
Pagan Epitaph.
Serenade.
The Song of the King's
Minstrel.
Middleton, Scudder
Jezebel.
The Journey.
The Poets.
Wisdom.
Middleton, Thomas
Blurt: Master Constable: Song:
Love Is Like a Lamb.
A Chaste Maid in Cheapside:
Parting.
The Ghost of Lucrece: To
Vesta.
Midnight.

Song: "In a maiden-time
professed."
Song: "Love for such a cherry
lip."
Trip It Gipsies, Trip It Fine.
A True Love Ditty.
The Witch, V, i.
Midlane, Albert
Above the Bright Blue Sky.
Miegel, Agnes
The Fair Agnete.
Mieko, Kanai
The House of Madam Juju.
Mifflin, Lloyd
The Battle-Field.
The Doors.
Fiat Lux.
The Flight.
Half-Mast.
The Harvest Waits.
He Made the Night.
Milton.
Sesostris.
The Ship.
The Sovereigns.
Theseus and Ariadne.
To a Maple Seed.
To an Old Venetian Wine-
Glass.
To the Milkweed.
Mihri Hatun
At One Glance.
Miidhu
War Dance.
Miklitsch, Robert
As in the Land of Darkness.
Milbauer, Joseph
Interior.
Paris by Night.
Milburn, Ken
Motive for Mercy.
Miles, C. Austin
In the Garden.
Miles, George Henry
Raphael's San Sisto Madonna.
Said the Rose.
Miles, Josephine
Album.
As Difference Blends into
Identity.
Away.
Belief.
Bibliographer.
Bounty.
Care.
Conception.
Conservancies.
The Day the Winds.
The Doctor Who Sits at the
Bedside of a Rat.
Dolor.
Dream.
The Entrepreneur Chicken
Shed His Tail Feathers,
Surplus.
Entry.
Family.
Find.
Forecast.
Government Injunction.
Gypsy.
The Halt.
Housewife.
"I've been going around
everywhere without any
skin."
If You Will.
Local Habitation: On
Inhabiting an Orange.
Made Shine.
Memorial Day.
Merchant Marine.

Midweek.
Monkey.
Moving In.
None.
Officers.
Preliminary to Classroom
Lecture.
Purchase of a Blue, Green, or
Orange Ode.
Reason.
Ride.
Sale.
The Savages.
Sisyphus.
So Graven.
Student.
Summer.
Sunday.
The Sympathizers.
Tally.
Vacuum.
Voyage.
Witness.
Miles, Ron
Lives of the Poet.
Miles, Sara
Portrait in Available Light.
Miles, Susan
He Sports by Himself
(parody).
Microcosmos.
Millard, Bob
Bury Our Faces.
Millard, G. C.
Hospital.
Millard, Gertrude
Nostalgia.
Millay, Edna St. Vincent
Above These Cares.
Afternoon on a Hill.
An Ancient Gesture.
And You As Well Must Die,
Beloved Dust.
Apostrophe to Man.
Ashes of Life.
Autumn Daybreak.
The Ballad of the Harp-
Weaver.
The Bean-Stalk.
The Betrothal.
The Blue-Flag in the Bog.
The Buck in the Snow.
The Cameo.
Childhood Is the Kingdom
Where Nobody Dies.
City Trees.
Conscientious Objector.
Counting-Out Rhyme.
Departure.
Dirge without Music.
Elegy Before Death.
Elegy: "Let them bury your
big eyes."
The End of Summer.
Endymion.
Epitaph for the Race of Man.
Euclid Alone Has Looked on
Beauty Bare.
Even in the Moment of Our
Earliest Kiss.
Exiled.
Fatal Interview.
The Fawn.
Feast.
First Fig.
From a Very Little Sphinx.
God's World.
Huntsman, What Quarry?
I, being born a woman and
distressed.
I Dreamed I Moved among
the Elysian Fields.

I Shall Forget You Presently,
My Dear.
I Shall Go Back.
In the Grave No Flower.
Intention to Escape from
Him.
Journal (excerpt).
Justice Denied in
Massachusetts.
Keen.
Lament.
Lethe.
Look, Edwin!
Memorial to D.C.
Men Working.
Menses.
Modern Declaration.
Moriturus.
Never May the Fruit Be
Plucked.
O God, I Cried, No Dark
Disguise.
Oh, oh, you will be sorry for
that word!
Oh, Sleep Forever in the
Latmian Cave.
Oh, Think Not I Am Faithful
to a Vow!
On Hearing a Symphony of
Beethoven.
On the Wide Heath.
Passer Mortuus Est.
The Pear Tree.
The Penitent.
The Philosopher.
Pity Me Not.
The Plum Gatherer.
The Poet and His Book.
Portrait by a Neighbor.
Ragged Island.
Recuerdo.
Renascence.
Rendezvous.
The Return.
Say That We Saw Spain Die.
Second Fig.
She Is Overheard Singing.
The Singing-Woman from the
Wood's Edge.
The Snow Storm.
Song of a Second April.
Sonnet: "I know I am but
summer to your heart."
Sonnet: "Not with Libations."
Sonnet: "Oh, my beloved,
have you thought of this."
Sonnet: "Say what you will."
Sonnet to Gath.
Sonnet: "Women have loved
before as I love now."
Sonnets. "What lips my lips
have kissed, and where, and
why."
Spring.
Theme and Variations.
This Beast That Rends Me.
Those Hours When Happy
Hours Were My Estate.
Thou Art Not Lovelier Than
Lilacs.
Thursday.
Time Does Not Bring Relief.
To a Calvinist in Bali.
To a Young Poet.
To Jesus on His Birthday.
To the Wife of a Sick Friend.
Travel.
The True Encounter.
Underground System.
The Unexplorer.
Vacation Song.
A Visit to the Asylum.

What Rider Spurs Him from
  the Darkening East?
What's This of Death.
Wild Swans.
Wraith.
Millay, Kathleen
  Relativity.
Miller, Adam David
  Crack in the Wall Holds
    Flowers.
  The Hungry Black Child.
Miller, Albert G.
  Pygmalion.
Miller, Alice Duer
  An American to France.
  Song.
  A Sonnet.
  The White Cliffs.
Miller, Betty
  The Wind.
Miller, Carolyn
  Nocturnal Visitor.
Miller, Chris
  The Blue Flag (parody).
Miller, Emily Huntington
  The Land of Heart's Desire.
  The Wood-Dove's Note.
Miller, Errol
  The Tough Ones.
Miller, Freeman E.
  The Stampede.
Miller, Grace Maddock
  Poetic Tale.
Miller, Heather Ross
  Quail Walk.
Miller, J. Corson
  Epicedium.
  Flying Fish.
  The March of Humanity.
  Roses.
  The Wind in the Elms.
Miller, James
  Italian Opera.
  The Life of a Beau.
Miller, Jane
  May You Always Be the
    Darling of Fortune.
  Time; or, How the Line
    About Chagall's Lovers
    Disappears.
Miller, Jeffrey
  The Day Glo Question of
    Identity.
  Death.
  Jeremy.
  My Fault's Small, About the
    Size of a Pin Prick.
  The Night Was Clear and the
    Moon Was Yellow.
  Quite Shy Actually but
    Obsessed.
  Sexy Food Stamps.
  The Truth Made Breakfast.
  Your Friends Come and Go.
Miller, Jim Wayne
  Aunt Gladys's Home Movie
    No. 31, Albert's Funeral.
  Family Reunion.
  For Richard Chase.
  Growing Wild.
  A House of Readers.
  Living with Children.
  Nostalgia for 70.
  On the Wings of a Dove.
  Rechargeable Dry Cell Poem.
  Spring Storm.
Miller, Joaquin
  Alaska.
  At the Grave of Walker.
  The Bravest Battle.
  By the Pacific Ocean.

Byron: In Men Whom Men
  Condemn as Ill.
Columbus.
Crossing the Plains.
Cuba Libre.
Dead in the Sierras.
The Defence of the Alamo.
Exodus for Oregon.
For Those Who Fail.
The Fortunate Isles.
The Greatest Battle That Ever
  Was Fought.
Juanita.
Kit Carson's Ride.
The Mothers of Men.
Peter Cooper.
Rejoice.
Resurge San Francisco.
San Francisco.
San Francisco Bay.
Song: "There is many a love
  in the land, my love."
Tantalus–Texas.
To Russia.
Vaquero.
The Voice of the Dove.
Westward Ho!
William Brown.
Miller, John N.
  Prince Charming.
Miller, Joseph Dana
  The Hymn of Hate.
Miller, Katherine
  Stevenson's Birthday.
Miller, Lillian
  Dead Drunk Blues.
Miller, Madeleine Sweeny
  How Far to Bethlehem.
Miller, Mary Britton
  Camel.
  Cat.
  Foal.
  Here She Is.
  Shore.
  A Son Just Born.
Miller, May
  Gift from Kenya.
  Not That Far.
Miller, Merlin G.
  Just to Be Glad.
Miller, Nellie Burget
  The Shack.
  The Sun Drops Red.
Miller, Olive Beaupre
  The Circus Parade.
Miller, Ruth
  Birds.
  Cycle.
  It Is Better to Be Together.
  Long Since Last.
  Penguin on the Beach.
  Plankton.
  Sterkfontein.
Miller, Thomas
  Evening.
  The Sea-Deeps.
  The Watercress Seller.
Miller, Vassar
  Accepting.
  Adam's Footprint.
  Apology.
  At a Child's Baptism.
  Autumnal Spring Song.
  Awkward Goodbyes.
  Bout with Burning.
  Ceremony.
  Christmas Mourning.
  A Clash with Cliches.
  Defense Rests.
  Eden Revisited.
  Encounter.
  Epithalamium.

Faintly and from Far away.
The Farm.
The Final Hunger.
Fulfillment.
Homecoming Blues.
How Far?
Invocation.
Joyful Prophecy.
Judas.
A Lesson in Detachment.
Love Song for the Future.
Love Song out of Nothing.
No Return.
On Approaching My
  Birthday.
One Morning.
The One Thing Needful.
Paradox.
The Quarry.
Receiving Communion.
Reciprocity.
The Resolution.
Slump.
Song for a Marriage.
Sophistication.
Spinster's Lullaby.
Though He Slay Me.
The Tree of Silence.
Trimming the Sails.
Without Ceremony.
The Worshiper.
Miller, William
  Spring (excerpt).
  Willie Winkie.
Millett, William
  I Am Ham Melanite.
Milligan, Alice
  The Dark Palace.
  Fainne Gael An Lae.
  A Song of Freedom.
  When I Was a Little Girl.
Milligan, Spike
  A Baby Sardine.
  The Bongaloo.
  Christmas 1970.
  The Gofongo.
  Hipporhinostricow.
  Limerick: "There was a young
    soldier called Edser."
  Little Tiny Puppy Dog.
  Look at All Those Monkeys.
  My Sister Laura.
  A Thousand Hairy Savages.
Millikin, Richard Alfred
  The Groves of Blarney.
Mills, Harry Edward
  Convicted (excerpt).
  The Early Frogs.
  On a Rainy Night (excerpt).
  Punkin Pie.
Mills, Kerry
  At a Georgia Camp Meeting.
Mills, Mary
  Apostasy.
  Fable.
  Garden Party.
  The Library.
  Pedigree.
  Postscript.
  The White Horse.
  The White Peacock.
Mills, Queenie B.
  The Old and the New.
Mills, William
  Unemployment.
Mills, William G.
  Arise, O Glorious Zion.
Mills, Jr, Ralph J.
  Chelsea Churchyard.
  For Years.
  Grasses.
  March Light.

Millward, Pamela
  Just as the Small Waves Came
    Where No Waves Were.
Milman, Henry Hart
  The Beacons.
  The Crucifixion.
  The Holy Field.
Milne, A.(lan) A.(lexander)
  At the Zoo.
  The Ballad of Private Chadd.
  Binker.
  Buckingham Palace.
  The Christening.
  Disobedience.
  The End.
  Forgiven.
  The Four Friends.
  From a Full Heart.
  Furry Bear.
  The Good Little Girl.
  Growing Up.
  Halfway Down.
  Happiness.
  Hoppity.
  If I Were King.
  The King's Breakfast.
  Limerick: "There was a young
    puppy called Howard."
  Lines Written by a Bear of
    Very Little Brain.
  Market Square.
  Miss James.
  Missing.
  The More It Snows.
  The Old Sailor.
  Politeness.
  Puppy and I.
  Rice Pudding.
  Sand-Between-the-Toes.
  Teddy Bear.
  The Three Foxes.
  Us Two.
  Vespers.
Milne, Angela
  The Coconut.
Milne, Ewart
  Could I Believe.
  Deirdre and the Poets.
  Diamond Cut Diamond.
  Dublin Bay.
  Evergreen.
  The Hills of Pomeroy.
  In a Valley of This Restless
    Mind.
  The Martyred Earth.
  Sierran Vigil.
  Tinker's Moon.
  Vanessa Vanessa.
Milne, J. C.
  Dolomites.
  Faur Wid I Dee?
  Feels.
  The Lairig.
  The Patriot.
Milner, E. V.
  Open to Visitors.
Milner-Brown, A. L.
  Who Knows?
**Milnes, Richard Monckton,
  Lord Houghton**
  The Brookside.
  The Burden of Egypt
    (excerpt).
  Columbus and the Mayflower.
  Good Night and Good
    Morning.
  In Memoriam.
  The Ionian Islands (excerpt).
  Lady Moon.
  The Men of Old.
  Our Mother Tongue; or, An
    Envoy to an American Lady.

The Palm-Tree and the Pine.
Shadows.
Sir Walter Scott at the Tomb of the Stuarts in St. Peter's.
Two Angels.
The Venetian Serenade.

Milns, William
The Federal Constitution.

Milosz, Czeslaw
Elegy for N. N.
A Poor Christian Looks at the Ghetto.

Milton, John
L'Allegro.
Arcades: O'er the Smooth Enamelled Green.
The Ark.
At a Solemn Music.
At a Vacation Exercise.
The Blindness of Samson.
Chastity.
Cromwell, Our Chief of Men.
An Epitaph on the Admirable Dramatic Poet, W. Shakespeare.
An Epitaph on the Marchioness of Winchester.
Evening in Paradise.
The First Day of Creation.
Gabriel Meets Satan.
Hail Holy Light.
Hymn on the Morning of Christ's Nativity.
Il Penseroso.
Last Came, and Last Did Go.
Let Us with a Gladsome Mind.
Light.
Lycidas.
A Masque Presented at Ludlow Castle (Comus).
Morning Hymn of Adam and Eve.
On the Detraction which Followed upon My Writing Certain Treatises.
On the Late Massacre in Piedmont.
On the Lord Gen. Fairfax at the Siege of Colchester.
On the New Forcers of Conscience Under the Long Parliament.
On the Oxford Carrier.
On the Same.
On the University Carrier Who Sickn'd in the Time of His Vacancy...
On Time.
Over All the Face of Earth Main Ocean Flowed.
Paradise Lost.
Paradise Regained.
The Plan of Salvation.
Praise the Lord.
Rivers Arise.
Sabrina Fair.
Samson Agonistes.
Sin and Death.
So Sr. Henry Vane the Younger.
Song on May Morning.
Sonnet I: "O Nightingale, that on yon bloomy Spray."
Sonnet XIII: "Harry whose tuneful and well measur'd Song."
Sonnet XIV: "When Faith and Love which parted from thee never."

Sonnet XVIII: "Cyriack, whose Grandsire on the Royal Bench."
Sonnet XX: To Mr. Lawrence.
Sonnet on His Blindness.
Sonnet on His Having Arrived at the Age of Twenty-Three.
Sonnets XIX: "Methought I saw my late espoused Saint."
A Table Richly Spread.
Temperance and Virginity.
Tetrachordon (excerpt).
Their Wedded Love.
To Mr. Cyriack Skinner Upon His Blindness.
To Mr. H. Lawes on His Airs.
To the Lady Margaret Ley.
To the Lord General Cromwell.
When the Assault Was Intended to the City.
With Thee Conversing.

Mimnermus
Elegiac.
The Sun's Golden Bowl.
Youth and Age.

Minard, Michael D.
A Musician Returning from a Cafe Audition.

Minarik, John Paul
Basic Writing 702.
Grandmother.
A Letter from Home.
There's Nothing Polite about a Tank.
To Be in Love While in Prison.

Minck, Peter
Pain Paint.

Minczeski, John
Another Sunset.
Old Ego Song.
Renaissance/A Triptych.

Minde, Henry S.
Thou Who Taught the Thronging People.

Miner, Virginia Scott
Channel Water.
Elegy for Former Students.
Golden Spurs.
Nichols Fountain.

Minnie, Memphis
'Frisco Town.
Killer Diller.
Me and My Chauffeur Blues.
Memphis Minnie-Jitis Blues.
Nothing in Rambling.

Minor, James
Feeling the Quiet Strike.
Lilies for Neal.

Minot, Laurence
The Burgesses of Calais.
Halidon Hill.

Minsky, Nicolai M.
Force.
Immortality.

Minthorn, Phillip Yellowhawk
Daybreak.
The Earth Cycle Dream.
From Which War.
This Earth.
Vigil of the Wounded.

Minty, Judith
Burning against the Wind.
The End of Summer.
The Legacy.
Letters to My Daughters.
Look to the Back of the Hand.
Making Music.
News from Detroit.
Orchids.

Prowling the Ridge.
Spring Sequence.
Wounds.

Mira Bai [(or Mirabai)]
At the Holi festival of color.
The Clouds.
Friend, don't be angry.
Friend, how can I meet my lord?
Hari helps his people.
Hari, look at me a while.
I can't break with the Dark One.
I don't sleep.
Keep Me As Your Servant, O Girdhar.
Let me see you.
Mira is dancing with bells tied.
My eyes are thirsty.
My love is in my house.
O King, I Know You Gave Me Poison.
Rana, I know you gave me poison.
Rana, why do you treat me.
Wake, child.
Wake Up, Dear Boy That Holds the Flute!
Why Mira Can't Go Back to Her Old House.
Yogi, don't go away.

Miranda, Gary
Field Trip.
Horse Chestnut.
Love Poem.
The Magician.

Mirikitani, Janice
Breaking Silence.
Breaking Tradition.
Sing with Your Body.

Misch, Robert J.
To J.S.

Mish, Charlotte
Stray Dog.

Mistral, Frederic
The Aliscamp.
The Cocooning.
The Leaf-Picking.
The Mares of the Camargue.

Mistral, Gabriela (Lucila Godoy Alcayaga)
Ballad: "He passed by with another."
Bread.
Close to Me.
Death Sonnet I.
Drops of Gall.
Dusk.
Everything Is Round.
Midnight.
Night.
Poem of the Son.
Sister.
Sleep Close to Me.
Slow Rain.
To Drink.
To Noel.
To See Him Again.

Mitchell, Adrian
The Accountant in His Bath.
Another Prince Is Born.
Banana.
Beatrix Is Three.
The Beggar.
Calypso's Song to Ulysses.
Celia Celia.
Fifteen Million Plastic Bags.
Giving Potatoes.
Lying in State.
Norman Morrison.
Private Transport.

Quite Apart from the Holy Ghost.
Remember Suez?
Riddle: "Their tongues are knives, their forks are hands and feet."
Telegram One.
To Whom It May Concern.

Mitchell, Archie
Hills of the Middle Distance.

Mitchell, Cyprus R.
The Soul of Jesus Is Restless.

Mitchell, David
Celebrant.
Windfall.

Mitchell, Elma
Thoughts after Ruskin.

Mitchell, James
Gay Epiphany.

Mitchell, John
Reply to In Flanders Fields.

Mitchell, John Hanlon
A City Song.
Farm Wife.
Sea Hunger.

Mitchell, Jonathan
On the Following Work and Its Author.

Mitchell, Joni
Woodstock.

Mitchell, Karen L.
For Michael.

Mitchell, Langdon Elwyn
Carol: "Mary, the mother, sits on the hill."
Fear.
France.
Sweets That Die.
To a Writer of the Day.
Written at the End of a Book.

Mitchell, Lorna
The Hermaphrodite's Song.

Mitchell, Lucy Sprague
The House of the Mouse.
It Is Raining.
The Lost Ball.
My Bed.

Mitchell, Matthew
Printing Jenny.

Mitchell, Noah
The K.K.K. Disco...
Momma's Not Gods Image...
Out of Question & Mind...
Those Not Confused Are Prisoners of War...
A Truth...

Mitchell, Nora
The Fisherman's Wife.

Mitchell, Roger
Cinderella.

Mitchell, Ruth Comfort
The Bride.
The Night Court.
The Travel Bureau.

Mitchell, Sam
Thunderstorm.

Mitchell, Silas Weir
A Decanter of Madeira, Aged 86, to George Bancroft, Aged 86.
Good-Night.
Herndon.
How the Cumberland Went Down.
Idleness.
Kearsarge.
Lincoln.
Of One Who Seemed to Have Failed.
On a Boy's First Reading of "King Henry V".
The Quaker Graveyard.

The Song of the Flags.
To a Magnolia Flower in the
  Garden of the Armenian
  Convent in Venice.
Vespers.
Mitchell, Stephen
  Abraham.
  Adam in Love.
  Jacob and the Angel.
Mitchell, Susan
  From the Journals of the Frog
    Prince.
  The Heart's Low Door.
  The Living Chalice.
Mitchell, Susan L.
  Immortality.
  The Wind Bloweth Where It
    Listeth.
Mitchell, Thomas
  Open Range.
Mitchell, Walter
  The Cheer of the Trenton.
  Reefing Topsails.
  Tacking Ship Off Shore.
Mitchell, William
  Shall We Forget.
Mitchison, Naomi
  The Boar of Badenoch and
    the Sow of Atholl.
  Buachaille Etive Mor and
    Buachaille Etive Beag.
  Wester Ross.
Mitford, Mary Russell
  Rienzi to the Romans.
  Written in July, 1824.
Mitsuhashi Takajo
  Haiku: "The hair ornament of
    the sun."
Mitsui, Jim
  Graffiti in a University
    Restroom...
  Letter to Tina Koyama from
    Elliot Bay Park.
  Mexico City: 150 Pesos to the
    Dollar.
  Shakuhachi.
  When Father Came Home for
    Lunch.
Mitsune (Oshikochi no Mitsune)
  Since I Heard.
  The white chrysanthemum.
**"Mix, Parmenas" (Andrew J.
Kelley)**
  The New Doctor.
Mizer, Ray
  To a Loudmouth Pontificator.
Mkalimoto, Ernie
  Energy for a New Thang.
Mnthali, Felix
  Antonina.
  The Beauty of Dawn.
  Resurrection: Fragments.
  The Riddles of Change.
  Waiting for the Rain.
Mocarski, Timothy P.
  City.
Mockett, Luella Markley
  The Haymow.
Modena, Leone da *See* **Da
Modena, Leone**
Modisane, Bloke
  Black Blues.
  Blue Black.
  Lonely.
  One Thought for My Lady.
Moffat, Gertrude MacGregor
  All Night I Heard.
Moffett, Judith
  Diehard.
  Dirge for Small Wilddeath.
  Evensong.
  Going to Press.

Mezzo Cammin.
Now or Never.
Twinings Orange Pekoe.
Moffi, Larry
  February.
  A Good Start.
  The Word Man.
Moffit, John
  Closing Cadence.
  Presence.
  To Look at Any Thing.
Mohr, Joseph
  Silent Night.
**Moise, Penina and Edward N.
Calishch**
  God Supreme! To Thee We
    Pray.
Mokhomo, M. A.
  When He Spoke to Me of
    Love.
Molesworth, Charles
  Horned Lizard.
Moliere, Jean-Baptiste Poquelin
  To Monsieur de la Mothe le
    Vayer.
Moll, Ernest G.
  After Reading a Book on
    Abnormal Psychology.
  At the Grave of a Land-
    Shark.
  Beware the Cuckoo.
  The Bush Speaks.
  Clearing for the Plough.
  Eagles Over the Lambing
    Paddock.
  A Gnarled Riverina Gum-
    Tree.
  On Having Grown Old.
Mollin, Larry
  As the World Turns.
  Bunky Boy Bunky Boy Who's
    My Little Bunky Boy.
  My Elbow Ancestry.
  Signature.
  Tubes.
  Wash Day.
Mollineux, Mary
  Solitude.
Molloy, James Lyman
  Bantry Bay.
  The Kerry Dance.
**Molodovsky, (or Molodovski)
Kadya, (or Kadia)**
  And Yet.
  God of Mercy.
  In Life's Stable.
  Jerusalem.
  Night Visitors.
  Song of the Sabbath.
Molofsky, Merle
  Reflections.
Momaday, N. Scott
  Angle of Geese.
  The Bear.
  Before an Old Painting of the
    Crucifixion.
  But Then and There the Sun
    Bore Down.
  Carriers of the Dream Wheel.
  The Colors of Night.
  Comparatives.
  The Delight Song of Tsoai-
    Talee.
  The Eagle-Feather Fan.
  Earth and I Gave You
    Turquoise.
  The Fear of Bo-talee.
  Forms of the Earth at
    Abiquiu.
  The Gourd Dancer.
  Pit Viper.
  Plainview: 3.

Rainy Mountain Cemetery.
Simile.
The Story of a Well-Made
  Shield.
To a Child Running with
  Outstretched Arms in
  Canyon de Chelly.
Trees and Evening Sky.
Wide Empty Landscape with
  a Death in the Foreground.
Winter Holding Off the Coast
  of North America.
Mombert, Alfred
  Along the Strand.
  The Chimera.
  Idyl.
  Sleeping They Bear Me.
Moment, John J.
  The Best Treasure.
Monaghan, Patricia
  Christmas at Vail: On Staying
    Indoors.
  The One Who Grew to Be a
    Wolf.
Monat, Donald
  Rhymed Mnemonic of the
    Forty Counties of England.
Monck, Mary
  Masque of the Virtues against
    Love. From Guarini.
  On a Romantic Lady.
Moncrieff, William Thomas
  Waltzing It.
Mondy, Bob
  Canadice Lake.
  Fishing Drunk.
  Trinidad, 1958.
Monette, Paul
  Bathing the Aged.
  Degas.
  Into the Dark.
Money-Coutts, Francis Burdett
  Any Father to Any Son.
  The Dream.
  Empires.
  A Little Sequence (excerpt).
  Mors, Morituri Te Salutamus.
  On a Fair Woman.
Monkhouse, Cosmo
  Any Soul to Any Body.
  A Dead March.
  In Arcady.
  Limerick: "A lady there was
    of Antigua."
  Limerick: "The poor
    benighted Hindoo."
  Limerick: "There once was a
    girl of New York."
  Limerick: "There once was a
    Master of Arts."
  Limerick: "There once was a
    person of Benin."
  Limerick: "There once was an
    old man of Lyme."
  Limerick: "There was a young
    girl of Lahore."
  Limerick: "There was a young
    lady of Niger."
  Limerick: "There was a young
    lady of Wilts."
  Limerick: "There was an old
    man of Tarentum."
  Limerick: "There were three
    young women of
    Birmingham."
  The Night Express.
  A Song of the Seasons.
  To a New-Born Child.
Monkman, Robina
  Sea Burial.
Monks, Arthur W.
  Twilight's Last Gleaming.

Monod, Theodore
  Christ Alone.
  None of Self and All of Thee.
Monro, Harold
  At a Country Dance in
    Provence.
  The Bird at Dawn.
  Bitter Sanctuary.
  Cat's Meat.
  Children of Love.
  City-Storm.
  Clock.
  Dawn: God.
  Dawn of Womanhood.
  Dog.
  The Empty House.
  Every Thing.
  The Foundered Tram.
  The Fresh Air.
  Goldfish.
  Hearthstone.
  The Hurrier.
  Living.
  London Interior.
  Man Carrying Bale.
  Midnight Lamentation.
  Milk for the Cat.
  Natural History (excerpt).
  The Nightingale near the
    House.
  Officers' Mess.
  Overheard on a Saltmarsh.
  Real Property.
  The Rebellious Vine.
  She Was Young and Blithe
    and Fair.
  The Silent Pool.
  Solitude.
  Strange Meetings.
  Street Fight.
  Suburb.
  The Terrible Door.
  Thistledown.
  Week-End Sonnet No. 1.
  The Wind.
  Youth in Arms: IV. Carrion.
Monroe, Arthur W.
  The Cliff Dwelling.
  The Forest Fire.
  Lost in a Blizzard.
  The Man of the Open West.
  The Toll of the Desert.
Monroe, Harriet
  The Blue Ridge.
  Commemoration Ode.
  A Farewell.
  The Fortunate One.
  The Hotel.
  I Love My Life, but Not Too
    Well.
  In High Places.
  In the Beginning.
  The Inner Silence.
  Mountain Song.
  Nancy Hanks.
  The Night-Blooming Cereus.
  Now.
  The Pine at Timber-Line.
  The Romney.
  The Shadow-Child.
  Two Heroes.
  Vernon Castle.
Monsell, John S. B.
  Light of the World.
Mont, Pol de
  Evening Landscape.
Montagu, Charles
  The Story of the Pot and the
    Kettle.
Montagu, Mary Wortley, Lady
  An Answer to a Lady
    Advising Me to Retirement.

Epistle from Mrs. Yonge to Her Husband.
Epitaph on the Stanton Harcourt Lovers.
Good Advice.
Lady M. M—'s Farewel to Bath.
The Lady's Resolve.
The Lover: A Ballad.
On the Death of Mrs. Bowes.
Receipt for the Vapours.
Six Town Eclogues (excerpt).
Such Soft Ideas All My Pains Beguile.
Verses Written in the Chiosk at Pera, Overlooking Constantinople.

Montague, James J.
And When They Fall.
The Same Old Story.
The Sleepytown Express.
The Vamp Passes.

Montague, John
11 Rue Daguerre.
Above the Pool.
All Legendary Obstacles.
A Bright Day.
The Cage.
The Cave of Night.
A Chosen Light.
Clear the Way.
Coming Events.
The Country Fiddler.
Courtyard in Winter.
Dowager.
A Drink of Milk.
Edge.
A Grafted Tongue.
A Graveyard in Queens.
The Hag of Beare.
Herbert Street Revisited.
Hero's Portion.
Lament for the O'Neills.
Last Journey.
The Leaping Fire.
Like Dolmens Round My Childhood, the Old People.
Mad Sweeny.
Mother Cat.
Murphy in Manchester.
A New Siege: An Historical Meditation (excerpt).
Penal Rock: Altamuskin.
The Point.
Poisoned Lands.
Return.
The Road's End.
The Same Gesture.
The Silver Flask.
Soliloquy on a Southern Strand.
Special Delivery.
Summer Storm.
Sunset.
That Room.
Tim.
Time Out.
Tracks.
The Trout.
Walking Late.
The Water Carrier.
A Welcoming Party.
The Wild Dog Rose.
Wild Sports of the West.
Windharp.
Woodtown Manor.

Montale, Eugenio
The Coastguard House.
The Eel.
Life's Evil.
The Magnolia's Shadow.
News from Mount Amiata.

Montalvan, Juan de
The Self-Deceaver.

Montemayor, Carlos
Heth.

Montesquiou-Fezensac, Robert de
The Child's Prayer.

Montgomerie, Alexander
Adieu to His Mistress.
An Admonition to Young Lassies.
Away Vane World.
The Cherry and the Slae (excerpt).
A Description of Tyme.
Hey! Now the Day Dawns.
The Nicht Is Neir Gane.
The Royal Palace of the Highest Heaven.
The Solsequium.
Sweethairt, Rejoice in Mind.
To Henry Constable and Henry Keir.
To His Maistres.
To R. Hudson.

Montgomerie, William
Author Unknown.
Elegy for William Soutar.
Epitaph: For 2nd Officer James Montgomerie...
Estuary.
Glasgow Street.
Kinfauns Castle (excerpt).
Stags.

Montgomery, Carol Artman
Jimmy Bruder on Quincey Street.
The Triangle Ladies.

Montgomery, Carrie Judd
Discerning the Lord's Body.

Montgomery, F.
Mother's Love.

Montgomery, George Edgar
At Night.
A Dead Soldier.
England.
Graham Bell and the Photophone.
To a Child.

Montgomery, Jack
Addict.

Montgomery, James
At Home in Heaven.
Christ Our Example in Suffering.
Come to Calvary's Holy Mountain.
A Field Flower.
An Indian Mother about to Destroy Her Child.
The Inspiration.
The Lust of Gold.
Make Way for Liberty.
Nativity.
Night.
There Is a Land.
What Is Prayer?

Montgomery, James Stuart
The Landlubber's Chantey.
The Swashbuckler's Song.

Montgomery, L. M.
Off to the Fishing Ground.

Montgomery, Little Brother
The First Time I Met You.

Montgomery, Niall
Eyewash.

Montgomery, Robert
The Omnipresence of the Deity.

Montgomery, Roselle Mercier
Armistice Day.
Counsel.

Ulysses Returns.
What Does It Mean to Be American?

Montgomery, Whitney
Death Rode a Pinto Pony.

Montoro, Antonio de
El Ropero.

Montrose, James Graham, Earl of See **Graham, James, Earl of Montrose**

Montoya, Jose
Louie.
Mother.

Montross, Percy
Clementine.

Montross, Lois Seyster
Codes.
Decent Burial.
I Wear a Crimson Cloak To-Night.

Montross, Percy
Oh, My Darling Clementine.

Monzaemon, Chikamatsu
The Love Suicides at Sonezaki (excerpt).

Moodie, Susanna
The Canadian Herd-Boy.
Indian Summer.

Moody, Minnie Hite
Say This of Horses.

Moody, William Vaughn
Of Wounds and Sore Defeats.

Moody, William Vaughn
The Bracelet of Grass.
The Daguerreotype.
Faded Pictures.
The Fire-bringer.
Gloucester Moors.
A Grey Day.
I Stood Within the Heart of God.
The Menagerie.
An Ode in Time of Hesitation: Robert Gould Shaw.
On a Soldier Fallen in the Philippines.
Pandora's Song.
A Prairie Ride.
The Quarry.
The Serf's Secret.
Thammuz.

Moon, Sheila
Existence.

Mooney, Stephen
At the Airport in Dallas.
Water Color.

Moor, George
The Eternale Footeman's Tale (parody).

Moore, Alice
Three Men.

Moore, Bertha
A Child's Thought.

Moore, Charles Leonard
The Book of Day-Dreams.
The Spring Returns.
To England.

Moore, Clement Clarke
Lord of Life, All Praise Excelling.
A Visit from St. Nicholas.

Moore, Edward
Fables for the Female Sex, V: The Poet and His Patron.
The Goose and the Swans (excerpt).
Song the Eighth.
Song the Ninth.
To the Right Hon. Henry Pelham...

Moore, George
The Corpse.

A Parisian Idyl (excerpt).
Rondo.
A Sapphic Dream.
Sonnet: "Idly she yawned, and threw her heavy hair."

Moore, James
Rothko.

Moore, Janice Townley
Below Bald Mountain.
Out of Body.

Moore, Jim
Instead of Features.

Moore, John
A Broken Gull.
Dingman's Marsh.
A Gaggle of Geese, A Pride of Lions.
Squall.

Moore, John Travers
The Last Flower.

Moore, Julia A.
And Now, Kind Friends, What I Have Wrote.
Ashtabula Disaster.
A Departed Friend.
Grand Rapids.
Grand Rapids Cricket Club (excerpt).
Little Libbie.
Sketch of Lord Byron's Life.
Willie's and Nellie's Wish.

Moore, Lilian
Bedtime Stories.
Listen!
Something Is There.
Until I Saw the Sea.

Moore, Marianne
The Animals Sick of the Plague.
Apparition of Splendor.
The Arctic Ox.
Armour's Undermining Modesty.
Arthur Mitchell.
At Rest in the Blast.
Baseball and Writing.
Bird-Witted.
Black Earth.
Carnegie Hall: Rescued.
A Carriage from Sweden.
Charity Overcoming Envy.
Critics and Connoisseurs.
Dock Rats.
Dream.
An Egyptian Pulled Glass Bottle in the Shape of a Fish.
England.
Enough.
A Face.
The Fish.
Four Quartz Crystal Clocks.
The Fox and the Grapes.
The Frigate Pelican.
Glory.
Granite and Steel.
A Grave.
He "Digesteth Harde Yron".
His Shield.
Hometown Piece for Messrs. Alston and Reese.
I May, I Might, I Must.
The Icosasphere.
Imperious Ox, Imperial Dish: The Buffalo.
In Distrust of Merits.
In the Public Garden.
A Jellyfish.
The Jerboa.
Keeping Their World Large.
The Labors of Hercules.
Leonardo Da Vinci's.
Marriage.

Melancthon.
Melchior Vulpius.
The Mind, Intractable Thing.
The Mind Is an Enchanting
Thing.
The Monkeys.
Nevertheless.
New York.
Nine Nectarines and Other
Porcelain.
No Swan So Fine.
O to Be a Dragon.
Old Amusement Park.
The Pangolin.
The Paper Nautilus.
Part of a Novel, Part of a
Poem, Part of a Play: The
Hero.
The Past Is the Present.
Pedantic Literalist.
Peter.
Pigeons.
Poetry.
Propriety.
Rigorists.
Roses Only.
Saint Nicholas,.
See in the Midst of Fair
Leaves.
Silence.
Snakes, Mongooses, Snake-
Charmers and the Like.
Sojourn in the Whale.
Spenser's Ireland.
St. Valentine,.
The Staff of Aesculapius.
The Steeple-Jack.
The Student.
A Talisman.
Tell Me, Tell Me.
That Harp You Play So Well.
Then the Ermine.
Those Various Scalpels.
To a Chameleon.
To a Snail.
To a Steam Roller.
Tom Fool at Jamaica.
Values in Use.
Virginia Britannia.
W. S. Landor.
Walking-Sticks and
Paperweights and
Watermarks.
What Are Years?
When I Buy Pictures.
Moore, Maurice
Easter, Day of Christ Eternal.
Moore, Merrill
And to the Young Man.
The Book of How.
Domestic: Climax.
The Flies.
He Said the Facts.
Hospital Poems: Transfusion.
How She Resolved to Act.
It Is Winter, I Know.
Just Then the Door.
The Noise That Time Makes.
O Mad Spring, One Waits.
Old Men and Old Women
Going Home on the Street
Car.
Pandora and the Moon.
Scientia Vincit Omnia?
Shot Who? Jim Lane!
They Also Stand...
Undergraduate.
Unknown Man in the Morgue.
Village Noon: Mid-Day Bells.
Warning to One.
Moore, Nicholas
Act of Love.

Alcestis in Ely.
Fred Apollus at Fava's.
The Hair's-Breadth.
Incidents in Playfair House.
The Island and the Cattle.
The Little Girl.
Love.
O Rose, O Rainbow.
The Patient.
The Phallic Symbol.
Song: "A little onion lay by
the fireplace."
Untitled: "Fivesucked the
features of my girl by glory."
Why the British Girls Give in
So Easily.
Winter and Red Berries.
Moore, Richard
Busby, Whose Verse No
Piercing Beams, No Rays.
Friends.
Suburb Hilltop.
The Swarm.
Willy.
Moore, Rosalie
Catalogue (excerpt).
Moore, Sir John Henry
The Duke of Benevento.
Song: "Indeed, my Caelia, 'tis
in vain."
Moore, T. Inglis
Comrade in Arms.
Star Drill.
Moore, Thomas
All That's Bright Must Fade.
An Argument: To Any Phillis
or Chloe.
At the Mid Hour of Night.
Believe Me, If All Those
Endearing Young Charms.
Bendemeer.
The Bird, Let Loose in
Eastern Skies.
A Canadian Boat Song.
The Cherries. A Parable.
Child's Song.
Come, Ye Disconsolate.
Common Sense and Genius.
Copy of an Intercepted
Despatch.
Cupid Stung.
Dear Fanny.
Dear Harp of My Country.
Did Not.
The Duke Is the Lad.
Echo.
Epigram.
Epistle of Condolence.
Epitaph on a Tuft-Hunter.
Epitaph on a Well-Known
Poet.
Epitaph on Robert Southey.
Farewell!–but Whenever You
Welcome the Hour.
Fill the Bumper Fair.
Fragment of a Character.
French Cookery.
The Fudge Family in Paris
(excerpt).
Fum and Hum, the Two Birds
of Royalty.
The Glory of God in
Creation.
Go where Glory Waits Thee.
Hark! The Vesper Hymn Is
Stealing.
The Harp That Once through
Tara's Halls.
Has Sorrow Thy Young Days
Shaded?
How Dear to Me the Hour.

How Oft Has the Banshee
Cried.
I Pray You.
I Saw from the Beach.
I Wish I Were by That Dim
Lake.
Ill Omens.
Irish Antiquities.
The Irish Peasant to His
Mistress.
The Journey Onwards.
The Kiss.
The Lake of the Dismal
Swamp.
Lalla Rookh.
Let Erin Remember the Days
of Old.
The Living Dog and the Dead
Lion.
Love Is a Hunter Boy.
Love's Young Dream.
Lying.
The Meeting of the Ships.
Meeting of the Waters.
The Minstrel-Boy.
Miss Biddy Fudge to Miss
Dorothy (excerpt).
My Birth-Day.
Nonsense.
Ode of Anacreon.
Ode to Nea.
Of All the Men.
Oft, in the Stilly Night.
Oh! Blame Not the Bard, If
He Fly to the Bowers.
Oh, Breathe Not His Name.
Oh, Come to Me when
Daylight Sets.
Oh, Thou! Who Dry'st the
Mourner's Tear.
Oh! Where's the Slave So
Lowly.
On a Squinting Poetess.
Paddy's Metamorphosis.
A Pastoral Ballad. By John
Bull.
Peace to the Slumberers.
The Petition of the
Orangemen of Ireland.
Pro Patria Mori.
Quantum Est Quod Desit.
A Recent Dialogue.
Rhymes on the Road
(excerpt).
Row Gently Here.
Scene from a Play, Acted at
Oxford, Called
"Matriculation."
She Is Far from the Land.
The Snake.
Song: "Come, rest in this
bosom, my own stricken
deer."
Song of Fionnuala.
The Song of O'Ruark, Prince
of Breffni.
Song of the Evil Spirit of the
Woods.
Song: "When the heart's
feeling."
Song: "Where is the nymph,
whose azure eye."
Sound the Loud Timbrel.
Sweet Innisfallen.
Take Back the Virgin Page.
A Temple to Friendship.
Thee, Thee, Only Thee.
They May Rail at This Life.
This Life Is All Chequer'd
with Pleasures and Woes.
This World Is All a Fleeting
Show.

Though a Soldier at Present.
Thro' Grief and Thro'
Danger.
The Time I've Lost in
Wooing.
'Tis the Last Rose of Summer.
To–.
To Cara, after an Interval of
Absence.
To Cloe.
To Fanny.
To Ladies' Eyes.
To Miss–.
To My Mother.
To Sir Hudson Lowe.
Tory Pledges.
The Two Streams.
Venetian Air.
What's My Thought Like?
When Eve upon the First of
Men.
When He Who Adores Thee.
When I Loved Thee.
Wreathe the Bowl.
The Young May Moon.
Moore, Thomas Sturge
Before Rereading
Shakespeare's Sonnets.
A Daughter of Admetus.
Days and Nights.
Death in the Home.
A Duet.
The Dying Swan.
The Event.
The Faun Tells of the Rout of
the Amazons.
The Gazelles.
Kindness.
Lubber Breeze.
On Harting Down.
Response to Rimbaud's Latter
Manner.
Sappho's Death: Three
Pictures by Gustave Moreau
(excerpt).
Sent from Egypt with a Fair
Robe of Tissue to a Sicilian
Vinedresser.
Shells.
Summer Lightning.
Titian's "Bacchanal" in the
Prado at Madrid (excerpt).
To Silence.
Tongues.
Variation on Ronsard.
Wind's Work.
Moore, Virginia
To Spring.
Moore, William
One Way Gal.
Moore, William H. A.
Dusk Song.
It Was Not Fate.
Moorman, Charles
Lois in Concert.
Moraes, Dom
The Final Word.
Girl.
Glitter of Pebbles.
John Nobody.
Letter to My Mother.
Lullaby.
Queen.
Santa Claus.
Song: "The gross sun squats
above."
Moraff, Barbara
"Let us suppose the mind."
Moran, Michael
Pharao's Daughter.

Mordaunt, Charles, Earl of Peterborough
Chloe.
I Said to My Heart.
Mordaunt, Thomas Osbert
Sound, Sound the Clarion.
Verses Written during the War 1756–1763.
Morden, Phyllis B.
Godmother.
More, Hannah
A Book.
Conversation.
The Riot; or, Half a Loaf is Better Than No Bread.
Solitude.
More, Helen F.
What's in a Name?
More, Henry
The Argument of Democritus Platonissans.
Eternal Life.
Hymn to Charity and Humility.
Resolution.
More, Sir Thomas
Age.
Childhood.
Consider Well.
Davy, the Dicer.
Death.
Eternal Reward, Eternal Pain.
Eternity.
Fame.
Fortune.
I Am Called Childhood.
Manhood.
A Mery Gest How a Sergeaunt Wolde Lerne to Be a Frere.
Of Fortune.
Pageant Verses.
A Rueful Lamentation on the Death of Queen Elizabeth.
Thomas More to Them That Seek Fortune.
Time.
To Fortune.
The Twelve Properties or Conditions of a Lover.
The Twelve Weapons of Spiritual Battle.
Venus and Cupide.
Moreh, Shmuel
Melody.
The Return.
The Tree of Hatred.
Morejo, Nancy
Central Park Some People (3 P.M.).
The Reason for Poetry.
Moreland, Jane P.
The Argument.
Pony Girl.
Moreland, John Richard
Birch Trees.
Christ Is Crucified Anew.
Faith.
A Grave.
His Hands.
If a Man Die–.
If I Could Grasp a Wave from the Great Sea.
O Years Unborn.
Only One King.
Sand Dunes and Sea.
Song of Thanksgiving.
The Splendid Lover.
Symbols.
A White Tree in Bloom.
Moreland, Wayne
Sunday Morning.

Morgan, Angela
The Awakening.
Choice.
God Does Do Such Wonderful Things!
God Prays.
God, the Artist.
Hail Man!
June Rapture.
Let Us Declare! (excerpt).
The Poet.
Reality.
Song of the New World.
Thanksgiving.
Three Green Trees.
Today.
The Whole Year Christmas.
Work: A Song of Triumph.
Morgan, Bessie
'Spacially Jim.
Morgan, Edwin
Aberdeen Train.
Absence.
Canedolia.
The Computer's First Christmas Card.
Concrete poem: Siesta of a Hungarian Snake.
From the Domain of Arnheim.
In the Snack-Bar.
Instamatic.
King Billy.
Message Clear.
The Second Life.
Strawberries.
To Hugh MacDiarmid.
Morgan, Elizabeth
Caravatt's Junkyard.
"Morgan, Emanuel" *See* **Bynner, Witter**
Morgan, Eva
A Christmas Dawn at Sea.
Morgan, Evan
The Eel.
Morgan, Frederick
Alexander.
Bones.
Castle Rock.
The Choice.
February 11, 1977.
From a Diary.
I Saw My Darling.
Orpheus to Eurydice.
Morgan, James Appleton
Malum Opus.
Morgan, Jean
The Misogynist.
Morgan, John
Our "Civilization."
Then.
Morgan, John Hunt
Similia Similibus.
Morgan, Lady
Kate Kearney.
Morgan, Robert
Brevard Fault.
Bricking the Church.
Buffalo Trace.
Canning Time.
Cedar.
Chant Royal.
Cow Pissing.
Face.
Hay Scuttle.
Horace Kephart.
Jutaculla Rock.
Lightning Bug.
Man and Machine.
Mountain Bride.
Passenger Pigeons.
Pumpkin.

Reuben's Cabin.
Rockingchair.
Secret Pleasures.
Thermometer Wine.
Uncle Robert.
When the Ambulance Came.
White Autumn.
Morgan, Robin
The Invisible Woman.
Lesbian Poem.
The Two Gretels.
Morgan-Browne, L. E.
The Purple, White and Green.
Morgenstern, Christian
The Aesthete Weasel.
The Funnels.
Ghost.
Klabauterwife's Letter.
The Knee on Its Own.
Korf's Clock.
Korf's Enchantment.
Korf's Joke.
The Moonsheep.
On the Planet of Flies.
Philosophy Is Born.
The Picket Fence.
The Salmon.
The Snail's Monologue.
The Twelve-Elf.
The Virus.
The Wooden Fence.
Morgridge, Harriet S.
Jack and Jill.
Simple Simon.
Morhange, Pierre
Jew.
Lullaby in Auschwitz.
Salomon.
Moriarty, Daniel J.
That Pure Place.
Moricke, Eduard
Beauty Rohtraut.
Prayer.
Morin, Edward
The Big One.
Filling Station.
Forecasting the Economy.
Notes on the Post-Industrial Revolution.
Morison, Ted
Aves.
Moritake
Haiku: "The falling flower."
Moritake, Arakida
The fallen flowers seemed.
Moritz, Yunna
In Memory of Francois Rabelais.
Whiteness.
Morley, Christopher
Animal Crackers.
At the Dog Show.
Confession in Holy Week.
The Crib.
Deny Yourself.
Dial Call.
Elegy Written in a Country Coal-Bin.
Epitaph for Any New Yorker.
Epitaph on the Proofreader of the Encyclopedia Britannica.
Forever Ambrosia.
The Gospel of Mr. Pepys.
A Grub Street Recessional.
In Honour of Taffy Topaz.
Nursery Rhymes for the Tender-Hearted.
Of an Ancient Spaniel in Her Fifteenth Year.
The Old Swimmer.
Pennsylvania Deutsch.
The Plumpuppets.

Public Beach (Long Island Sound).
Quickening.
Secret Laughter.
Six Weeks Old.
Smells.
Song for a Little House.
The Sun's over the Foreyard.
Thoughts for St. Stephen.
Thoughts in the Gulf Stream.
Thoughts on Being Invited to Dinner.
To A Child.
To a Post-Office Inkwell.
To the Little House.
Translations from the Chinese.
Translations from the Chinese.
The Trees.
The Tryst.
Washing the Dishes.
Morley, David J.
Climbing Zero Gully.
Morley, Hilda
The Nike of Samothrace.
The Shirt.
Morley, Thomas
Madrigal: "In nets of golden wire."
Madrigal: "Ladies, you see time flieth."
Madrigal: "No, no, Nigella!"
Madrigal: "Sing we and chant it."
Madrigal: "You black bright stars."
Morningstar, Margaret
The Teacher Sees a Boy.
Moronelli da Fiorenza
Canzonetta: A Bitter Song to His Lady.
Morpurgo, Rachel
Song: "Ah, vale of woe, of gloom and darkness moulded."
Sonnet: "My soul surcharged with grief now loud complains."
Morpurgo, Rahel
Woe Is Me, My Soul Says, How Bitter Is My Fate.
Morris, Alice S.
Mrs. Santa Claus' Christmas Present.
Morris, Betty
The Strath of Kildonan.
Morris, Charles
Addressed to Lady ****, Who Asked What the Passion of Love Was?
Country and Town.
A Reason Fair to Fill My Glass.
Morris, George Hornell
A Sailor's Prayer.
Morris, George Pope
Jeannie Marsh.
The Main-Truck; or, A Leap for Life.
My Mother's Bible.
Near the Lake.
Pocahontas.
The Retort.
We Were Boys Together.
Where Hudson's Wave.
Woodman, Spare That Tree.
Morris, Gouverneur
D'Artagnan's Ride.
Morris, Harrison Smith
Destiny.
Fickle Hope.
June.
The Lonely-Bird.

Mohammed and Seid.
A Pine-Tree Buoy.
Separate Peace.
Walt Whitman.

Morris, Harry
Girod Street Cemetery: New
Orleans.

Morris, Herbert
The Brahms.
The North of Wales.
The Road.
Spanish Blue.
This Alice.
Workmen.

Morris, Hilda
November Wears a Paisley
Shawl.

Morris, Ida Goldsmith
Give to the Living.

Morris, J. W.
Collusion between a Alegaiter
and a Water-Snaik.
What I Think of Hiawatha
(parody).

Morris, John N.
A Child's Nativity.
The Fathers.
In the Hamptons.
A Letter from a Friend.
The Mirror.
My Children's Book.
One Snowy Night in
December.
The Right to Life.
Running It Backward.
Shh! The Professor Is
Sleeping.
Thanksgiving.
Three.

Morris, Madge
In the Yucca Land.
Quien Sabe?
To the Colorado Desert.

Morris, Robert
The Level and the Square.

Morris, Sir Lewis
The Beginnings of Faith.
Brotherhood (excerpt).
Christmas 1898 (excerpt).
A Heathen Hymn (excerpt).
On a Thrush Singing in
Autumn.
A Separation Deed.
Song: "Love took my life and
thrill'd it."
To a Child of Fancy.
Tolerance.

Morris, Thomas
Sapphics.

Morris, William
All for the Cause.
An Ancient Castle.
Another for the Briar Rose.
An Apology.
Atalanta's Race.
Autumn on the Upper
Thames.
The Blue Closet.
The Brooding of Sigurd.
The Day is Coming.
The Day of Days.
The Defence of Guenevere.
The Earthly Paradise.
Echoes of Love's House.
The End of May.
L'Envoi.
The Eve of Crecy.
For the Briar Rose.
From Far away.
A Garden by the Sea.
The Gilliflower of Gold.
Golden Wings.

Gunnar's Howe above the
House at Lithend.
The Haystack in the Floods.
The Hollow Land.
In Prison.
Inscription for an Old Bed.
The Judgement of God.
The Life and Death of Jason.
Love Is Enough.
Masters in This Hall.
Meeting in Winter.
The Message of the March
Wind.
Near Avalon.
November.
Ogier the Dane: Song.
Old Love.
Outlanders, Whence Come Ye
Last?
The Pilgrims of Hope:
Sending to the War.
Pomona.
Praise of My Lady.
Riding Together.
The Road of Life.
The Sailing of the Sword.
Shameful Death.
Song: "Christ keep the Hollow
Land."
Song: "Fair is the night, and
fair the day."
Song from the Story of
Acontius and Cydippe.
Song: "Gold wings across the
sea!"
Song of the Argonauts.
The Story of Sigurd the
Volsung (excerpt).
Summer Dawn.
Tapestry Trees.
Thunder in the Garden.
Two Red Roses Across the
Moon.
The Voice of Toil.
The Wind.
Written in a Copy of The
Earthly Paradise.

Morrison, Lillian
Lobster Cove Shindig.
Of Kings and Things.
The Sidewalk Racer.
Surf.

Morrison, M.T.
What the Choir Sang about
the New Bonnet.

Morrison, Margaret
I'm the Police Cop Man, I
Am.

Morrison, Mary
Nobody Knows But Mother.

Morrow, David
Beyond Wars.

Morse, James Herbert
Brook Song.
His Statement of the Case.
Silence.
The Wayside.
The Wild Geese.

Morse, Katharine
To—.

Morse, Madeline
Christmas Prayer.

Morse, Samuel French
Fracture of Light: Song in the
Cold Season.
The Track into the Swamp.

Morse, Sidney Henry
The Way.

Morstein, Petra von
Anthology Poem.
For one who says he feels.
In the Case of Lobsters.

Justice.
Thing Poem.

Mortenson, Alice
Beautiful Lily.
Behold, My Cross Was Gone!
The Bethlehem Star Shines
On!
Christmas Bells.
He's Come! The Saviour Has
Come!
He Wore a Crown of Thorns.
Let Not Your Heart Be
Troubled.
O Christ of Calvary, This
Lent.
O My Saviour and Redeemer.
Oh, No Cross That I May
Carry!
They've Crucified Our Lord.

Mortiz, Yunna
Snow-Girl.

Morton, Bruce
High Plains Harvest.

Morton, David
Acquaintance.
After Storm.
The Dead.
Epitaph in Sirmio.
Fields at Evening.
His Adoration.
Immortalis.
Lover to Lover.
Mariners.
Old Ships.
Petition for a Miracle.
The Schoolboy Reads His
Iliad.
Ships in Harbour.
Symbol.
Touring.
When There Is Music.
Who Walks with Beauty.
Wooden Ships.

Morton, J. B.
Another Canto (parody).
The Dancing Cabman.
Epitaph: "A glassblower lies
here at rest."
Epitaph for a Lighthouse-
Keeper's Horse.
Epitaph: "Let poets praise the
softer winds of spring."
Epitaph on a Warthog.
Epitaph: "Tread softly; bid a
solemn music sound."
Health and Fitness.
On Sir Henry Ferrett, M.P.
Song of the Ballet.
To a Lady.
Tripe.
When We Were Very Silly.

Morton, Sarah Wentworth
To Aaron Burr, under Trial
for High Treason.

Morton, Thomas
Carmen Elegiacum.
Epitaph.
New Canaans Genius:
Epilogus.
New English Canaan, the
Authors Prologue.
The Poem: "I sing th'
adventures of mine worthy
wights."
The Poem: "Rise Oedipeus,
and if thou canst unfould."
The Poem: "What ailes
Pigmalion? Is it Lunacy."
The Songe: "Drinke and be
merry, merry, merry boyes."

Moryson, Fynes
To Thee, Dear Henry
Morison.

Mosby, George, Jr
And "I Know Why the Caged
Bird Sings": A Villanelle.
Birthday: Tara Regina.
Of an Old Con.
The Old.
To Night: To Judith.
Variations on a Late October
Day.

Moschus
Cupid a Plowman.
Idylls.
A Lament for Bion.
The Ocean.
Pan Loved His Neighbour
Echo—but That Child.
When Winds That Move Not
Its Calm Surface Sweep.

Moser, John W.
Room Service.
Sea Food Thought.

Moser, Mrs. J. F.
Would I Be Called a
Christian?

Moses, Daniel David
Fall Song.
The Hands.

Moses, W. R.
American History.
Angina Pectoris.
Big Dam.
Boy at Target Practice: A
Contemplation.
The Impulse of October.
Little-League Baseball Fan.
The Nature of Jungles.
Night Wind in Fall.
Sitting in the Woods: A
Contemplation.

Moskowitz, Lynn
Nightmares: Part Three.

Mosley, Joseph M., Jr.
Black Church on Sunday.

Moss, Howard
Around the Fish: After Paul
Klee.
Arsenic.
At the Algonquin.
A Balcony with Birds.
Burning Love Letters.
Cats and Dogs.
Chalk from Eden.
A Colloquy with Gregory on
the Balcony.
Crossing the Park.
A Dead Leaf.
Elegy for My Father.
Elizabethan Tragedy: A
Footnote.
Finding Them Lost.
Front Street.
A Game of Chance.
Geography: A Song.
The Gift to Be Simple.
Going to Sleep in the
Country.
Great Spaces.
The Hand.
The Hermit.
Horror Movie.
King Midas.
A Lesson from Van Gogh.
The Lie.
Local Places.
Long Island Springs.
The Meeting.
Movies for the Home.
Piano Practice.
A Problem in Morals.

The Pruned Tree.
Rain.
The Refrigerator.
The Roof Garden.
Shall I Compare Thee to a
  Summer's Day?
Stars.
Still Pond, No More Moving.
A Summer Gone.
To the Islands.
Tourists.
Traction: November 22, 1963.
Tragedy.
Underwood.
Venice.
Water Island.
Waterwall Blues.
Winter's End.
Moss, Stanley
Apocrypha.
Central Park West.
Clams.
An Exchange of Hats.
God Poem.
The Hangman's Love Song.
Prayer.
The Return.
Sailing from the United States.
Scroll.
SM.
Squall.
Two Fishermen.
The Valley.
Voice.
Moss, Thomas
The Beggar.
Mossman, Bina
I'm Going to California.
Motaung, Bonisile Joshua
The Garden Boy.
Mother Goose
As Tommy Snooks and Bessy
  Brooks.
Baa, Baa, Black Sheep.
Barber, Barber, Shave a Pig.
Bell Horses, Bell Horses,
  What Time of Day?
Blow, Wind, Blow! and Go,
  Mill, Go.
Bobby Shaftoe's Gone to Sea.
The Bonnie Cravat.
Bow, Wow, Wow!
Bryan O'Lin Had No
  Breeches to Wear.
Bye, Baby Bunting.
Christmas.
Cross Patch.
Curly Locks.
Daffadowndilly.
Dance to Your Daddie.
Deedle, Deedle, Dumpling,
  My Son John.
A Dillar, a Dollar, a Ten
  O'Clock Scholar.
Ding, Dong, Bell.
A Farmer Went Trotting
  upon His Gray Mare.
Fe, Fi, Fo, Fum.
Girls and Boys, Come out to
  Play.
God Made the Bees.
Good King Arthur.
Goosey, Goosey, Gander.
The Grand Old Duke of
  York.
Handy Spandy.
Hark, Hark! The Dogs Do
  Bark.
Hector Protector Was Dressed
  All in Green.
Here Am I, Little Jumping
  Joan.

Here Sits the Lord Mayor.
Hey, Diddle, Diddle.
Hickory, Dickory, Dock.
Higgledy, Piggledy, My Black
  Hen.
Hippety Hop to the Barber
  Shop.
Hot-Cross Buns.
How Many Days Has My
  Baby to Play?
How many miles to Babylon?
How Much Wood Would a
  Wood-Chuck Chuck.
Humpty Dumpty Sat on a
  Wall.
I Asked My Mother for
  Fifteen Cents.
I Had a Little Husband.
I Had a Little Nut Tree.
I Had a Little Pony.
I'll Tell You a Story.
I Saw a Ship A-Sailing.
If all the world were apple-
  pie.
If I had as much money as I
  could/spend.
Intery, Mintery, Cutery Corn.
Jack and Jill.
Jack Be Nimble.
Jack Sprat Could Eat No Fat.
Jack Sprat's Pig.
January Brings the Snow.
Ladybird, Ladybird.
The Lion and the Unicorn.
Little Bo-Peep.
Little Boy Blue.
Little Jack Horner.
Little Jumping Joan.
Little Miss Muffet.
Little Polly Flinders.
Little Sally Waters.
Little Tommy Tucker.
The Man in the Moon.
March Winds.
Mary, Mary, Quite Contrary.
Master I Have, and I Am His
  Man.
Monday's child is fair of face.
Multiplication Is Vexation.
The North Wind Doth Blow.
Nose, Nose, Jolly Red Nose.
The Nut Tree.
Old King Cole Was a Merry
  Old Soul.
Old Mother Hubbard.
One Misty, Moisty Morning.
One, Two, Buckle My Shoe.
Pease Porridge Hot.
Peter, Peter, Pumpkin Eater.
Polly Put the Kettle On.
Pussy-Cat, Pussy-Cat, Where
  Have You Been?
The Queen of Hearts.
Rain, Rain, Go Away.
Riddle: "A hill full, a hole
  full."
Riddle: "A riddle, a riddle, as
  I suppose."
Riddle: "As I was going to St.
  Ives."
Riddle: "As round as an
  apple, as deep as a cup."
Riddle: "Higher than a
  house."
Riddle: "I have a little sister
  they call her 'Peep-peep'."
Riddle: "Little Nancy
  Etticoat."
Riddle: "Lives in winter."
Riddle: "Old Mother Twitchet
  had but one eye."

Riddle: "Runs all day and
  never walks."
Riddle: "Thirty white horses."
Ride a Cockhorse.
Ride away, Ride away.
Ring-Around-a-Rosy.
Rock-a-Bye Baby.
Rub-a-Dub-Dub.
Simple Simon.
Sing a Song of Sixpence.
Six Little Mice Sat Down to
  Spin.
Solomon Grundy.
Spit, Cat, Spit.
Spring Is Showery, Flowery,
  Bowery.
Star-Light, Star-Bright.
There Was a Crooked Man.
There was a little man.
There Was a Little Woman.
There was a man of our town.
There Was an Old Man
  Named Michael Finnegan.
There Was an Old Woman,
  and What Do You Think?
There Was an Old Woman, as
  I've Heard Tell.
There Was an Old Woman
  Who Lived in a Shoe.
There Were Two Blackbirds
  Sitting on a Hill.
Three wise men of Gotham.
Three Young Rats.
To market, to market.
Wash the Dishes, Wipe the
  Dishes.
Wee Willie Winkie.
A Week of Birthdays.
When Jacky's a Very Good
  Boy.
Motherwell, William
The Cavalier's Song.
Jeanie Morrison.
Last Verses.
Sing On, Blithe Bird!
Motokiyo, Seami
Nishikigi: The Love-Cave.
Moton, Cora Ball
Sight.
Mott, Michael
Islanders, Inlanders.
Meadow Grass.
Mott, Randy
Ghazal: Japanese Paintbrush.
Motteux, Peter Anthony
Man Is for Woman Made.
Slaves to London.
The Town-Rakes.
Moul, Keith
Playing Catch.
Moulton, Louise Chandler
Hic Jacet.
The Last Good-By.
Laura Sleeping.
Laus Veneris.
A Painted Fan.
The Shadow Dance.
Shall I Complain?
Somebody's Child.
The Spring Is Late.
A Summer Wooing.
Tonight.
A Tryst.
We Lay Un Down to Sleep.
Moultrie, John
The Fairy Maimoune.
Forget Thee?
Sir Launfal.
Mounsey, Messenger
On the Physician to Chelsea
  Hospital by Himself.

Mountain, G. J.
The Indian's Grave.
Moure, Erin
Doe-Face.
Fantastic World's End.
Post-Modern Literature.
Proceedings of the Wars.
Professional Amnesia.
Tricks.
Mousley, James P.
Prayer.
Movius, Geoffrey
The Work-Out.
Mowrer, Paul Scott
Mozart's Grave.
Moxon, Edward
Moonlight.
The Nightingale.
Similes.
Moyles, Lois
Report from California.
A Tale Told by a Head.
Thomas in the Fields.
Mozeen, Thomas
The Bedlamite.
The Kilruddery Hunt.
Mozeson, Isaac Eichanan
Masada.
Mphahlele, Ezekiel
Exile in Nigeria.
Homeward Bound.
A Poem.
Somewhere.
Mphande, Lupenga
The Dwarf of the Hill Caves.
Song of a Prison Guard.
The Victim.
When the Storms Come.
Mqhayi, S. E. K.
The Black Army.
The Sinking of the Mendi.
Mririda n'Ait Attik
Azouou.
God Hasn't Made Room.
Like Smoke.
Mririda.
Msham, Mwana Kupona
Poem to Her Daughter
  (excerpt).
Mtshali, Mbuyiseni Oswald
Amagoduka at Glencoe
  Station.
The Birth of Shaka.
Nightfall in Soweto.
The Raging Generation.
The Shepherd and His Flock.
Weep Not for a Warrior.
Muchemwa, Kizito Z.
Circular Roads.
My Friends, This Storm.
The Redeemer.
Tourists.
Muddy Waters
Hoochie Coochie.
Mudie, Ian
They'll Tell You About Me.
This Land.
Underground.
Wilderness Theme.
Mueller, Lisel
Alive Together.
Apples.
The Blind Leading the Blind.
Civilizing the Child.
Drawings by Children.
A Farewell, a Welcome.
For a Nativity.
Historical Museum,
  Manitoulin Island.
Life of a Queen.
The Lonesome Dream.

Merce Cunningham and the
   Birds.
Monet Refused the Operation.
Moon Fishing.
Night Song.
Palindrome.
The People at the Party.
Reading the Brothers Grimm
   to Jenny.
Sans Souci.
Small Poem about the Hounds
   and the Hares.
Untitled.
A Voice from out of the
   Night.
The Weaver.
Muhammadji
   Black Hair.
Muhlenberg, William Augustus
   Fulfillment.
   Heaven's Magnificence.
   I Would Not Live Alway.
   Like Noah's Weary Dove.
   Saviour, Who Thy Flock Art
     Feeding.
Muhringer, Doris
   Questions and Answers.
Muir, E. A.
   Gulls.
Muir, Edwin
   Abraham.
   The Absent.
   The Animals.
   The Annunciation.
   Antichrist.
   Ballad of Hector in Hades.
   Ballad of the Flood.
   A Birthday.
   The Brothers.
   The Castle.
   The Child Dying.
   Childhood.
   The Church.
   The Cloud.
   The Combat.
   The Confirmation.
   The Enchanted Knight.
   The Escape.
   The Face.
   The Fathers.
   The Finder Found.
   For Ann Scott-Moncrieff.
   The Gate.
   The Good Man in Hell.
   The Good Town.
   The Great House.
   The Grove.
   The Horses.
   The Human Fold.
   In Love for Long.
   The Interrogation.
   The Island.
   The Killing.
   The Labyrinth.
   The Little General.
   Love in Time's Despite.
   Love's Remorse.
   Merlin.
   The Myth.
   The Mythical Journey.
   Oedipus.
   The Old Gods.
   One Foot in Eden.
   Reading in War Time.
   The Recurrence.
   The Refugees.
   The Return of the Greeks.
   The Rider Victory.
   The Road.
   Robert the Bruce.
   Salem, Massachusetts.
   Scotland, 1941.

Scotland's Winter.
Suburban Dream.
Then.
The Three Mirrors.
Too Much.
The Town Betrayed.
The Transfiguration.
The Trophy.
Troy.
The Usurpers.
Variations on a Time Theme.
The Voyage.
The Way.
The Wayside Station.
The West.
The Wheel.
The Window.
Muir, Henry D.
   The Soldier's Grave.
Muir, John
   From Garden to Garden,
     Ridge to Ridge.
**Muir, Lewis F. and Grant
Clarke**
   Rag Time Cowboy Joe.
Mu'izzi, Amur
   To a Young Lover.
Mukerji, Rana
   Spring Night.
Mukta Bai
   Although he has no form.
   I live where darkness.
Muldoon, Paul
   Anseo.
   Armageddon, Armageddon
     (excerpt).
   Clonfeacle.
   Dancers at the Moy.
   The Field Hospital.
   Hedgehog.
   The Indians on Alcatraz.
   Meeting the British.
   Mules.
Mulgan, Alan
   Golden Wedding (excerpt).
Mulholland, Rosa
   The Irish Franciscan.
   Love and Death.
Mullen, Harryette
   Saturday Afternoon, when
     Chores Are Done.
Muller, Wilhelm
   Whither?
Mulligan, J. B.
   Deja Vu.
Mullins, Cecil J.
   Enemy, Enemy.
Mullins, Helene
   Even in the Darkness.
Mulock, Dinah Maria
   Autumn's Processional.
   Highland Cattle.
Mulock Craik, Dinah Maria
   God Rest You Merry,
     Gentlemen.
Mumford, Erika
   Shaman: For Malcolm.
   Woman Painter of Mithila.
Mumford, Lewis
   Consolation in War.
Mumford, Marilyn R.
   Recollection.
Mumin, Hassan Sheikh
   Women and Men.
Munby, Arthur Joseph
   Doris: A Pastoral.
   One Way of Looking at It.
   Post Mortem.
   The Serving Maid.
   Vestigia Restrorsum: The
     Vales of the Medway.

Munch-Petersen, Gustaf
   To One.
Munday, Anthony
   Beauty Bathing.
   Colin.
   I Serve a Mistress.
   Love.
   Robin Hood's Funeral.
   To Colin Clout.
Mundell, William D.
   The Uninvited.
Mundorf, Frank
   Letter from a State Hospital.
   Remembering Lincoln.
Munger, Robert Louis
   God's Will.
Mungin, Horace
   Blues.
   Of Man and Nature.
Mungoshi, Charles
   If You Don't Stay Bitter for
     Too Long.
   Important Matters.
Munkittrick, Richard Kendall
   At the Shrine.
   A Bulb.
   Ghosts.
   Molasses River.
   Old King Cabbage.
   The Redingote and the
     Vamoose.
   The Song of the Owl.
   To Miguel de Cervantes
     Saavadra.
   Unsatisfied Yearning.
   What's in a Name?
Munro, Bruce Weston
   Grandmother's Apple Pies.
Munro, Deborah
   Sequence for a Young Widow
     Passing.
   Song of the Strange Young
     Duckling.
Munro, Harold
   Week-End.
Munro, Neil
   The Heather.
   Nettles.
Munro, Robin
   Apprentices.
   Hills.
   Shetland, Hill Dawn.
   View.
Munson, C. C.
   A Dead Past.
Munson, Ida Norton
   Assurance.
Mura, David
   The Hibakusha's Letter
     (1955).
   Lan Nguyen: The Uniform of
     Death 1971.
   The Natives.
   A Nisei Picnic.
   Relocation.
Murano, Shiro
   Pole Vault.
Murasaki Shibiku, Lady
   The Tale of Genji (excerpt).
   While I walked in the
     moonlight.
Muratori, Fred
   The Real Muse.
Murchison, Lee
   In the Beginning Was the.
   The Sprinters.
Murger, Henri
   Old Loves.
   Spring in the Students'
     Quarter.
Murguia, Alejandro
   O California.

Small Towns.
Murphey, Joseph Colin
   The Silver Racer.
Murphy, Beatrice M.
   The Letter.
   Signs.
Murphy, E. G.
   The Smiths.
Murphy, R. D.
   Back Lane.
Murphy, Richard
   The Archaeology of Love.
   The Battle of Aughrim.
   The Battle of Aughrim:
     Rapparees.
   Care.
   Casement's Funeral.
   Coppersmith.
   Enigma.
   Epitaph on a Fir-Tree.
   Girl at the Seaside.
   Green Martyrs.
   High Island.
   The Last Galway Hooker.
   Little Hunger.
   Nocturne.
   Orange March.
   Pat Cloherty's Version of the
     Maisie.
   The Philosopher and the
     Birds.
   The Poet on the Island.
   The Reading Lesson.
   Sailing to an Island.
   Seals at High Island.
   Stormpetrel.
   Trouvaille.
   Walking on Sunday.
   Wolfhound.
   The Woman of the House.
Murphy, Jr, George E.
   Conestoga.
Murray, Ada Foster
   Above Salerno.
   Her Dwelling-Place.
   An Old-Fashioned Poet.
   Prevision.
   Unguarded.
Murray, Anne B.
   Drumochter.
   Then and Now.
Murray, Bertram
   I Caught a Fish.
Murray, Charles
   Bennachie.
   In Lythe Strathdon.
   The Whistle.
Murray, G. E.
   California Dead.
   On the Upside.
   Shelby County, Ohio.
   November 1974.
   Shopping for Midnight.
   Sketch for a Morning in
     Muncie, Indiana.
   Southern Exposures.
Murray, Joan
   After the Murder of Jimmy
     Walsh.
   Crocus.
   An Irish Blessing.
   The Lovers.
Murray, John
   Hark! 'Tis the Saviour of
     Mankind.
Murray, Kenton Foster
   Challenge.
Murray, Les A.
   An Absolutely Ordinary
     Rainbow.
   Bagman O'Reilly's Curse.
   Equanimity.

The Names of the Humble.
Once in a Lifetime, Snow.
Portrait of the Autist as a
New World Driver.
The Powerline Incarnation.
The Smell of Coal Smoke.
Telling the Cousins.

Murray, Paul
Rain.

Murray, Pauli
Dark Testament.
Death of a Friend.
For Mack C. Parker.
Harlem Riot, 1943.
Inquietude.
Mr. Roosevelt Regrets.
Ruth.
Song: "Because I know deep
in my own heart."
Without Name.

Murray, Philip
Carrara.
The Cloud of Unknowing.
The Finches.
In the Annals of Tacitus.
A Little Litany to St. Francis.
The Locust Hunt.
The Turning.

Murray, Robert Fuller
Andrew M'Crie.
The City of Golf.
Critic and Poet.
The End of April.
Every Critic in the Town.
The Man from Inversnaid.

Murray, Rona
The Lizard.

Murray, Sir David
Caelia: Sonnet.

Murry, Calvin
The Challenge.
Logic.
On a Summer Day, 1972.
Prisoner Aboard the S.S.
Beagle.
Sisyphus Angers the Gods of
Condescension.

Murton, Jessie Wilmore
Song of the Builders.

Mus, David
The Joy of Cooking:
Conserves.

Musgrave, Susan
The Judas Goat.
Returning to the Town Where
We Used to Live.

Muske, Carol
Child with Six Fingers.
Found.
Hyena.
Rice.
Swansong.

Musser, Benjamin Francis
Der Heilige Mantel Von
Aachen.
The Holy Land of
Walsingham.

Musset, Alfred de
Juana.
On a Dead Lady.
Souvenir.

Mustapaa, P.
Folk Tale.

Mu'tamid, King of Seville,
The Fountain.
The Great Poet.
I Traveled with Them.
A Letter.
Tears of the World.
Thy Garden.
Woo Not the World.

Muth, Eleanor
Night Enchantment.

Mutis, Alvaro
Amen.
Lied in Crete.

Muuse, Abdillaahi
An Elder's Reproof to His
Wife.

Mycall, John
Our States, O Lord.

Myers, Ernest
Achilles.
Fiorentina.

Myers, Frederic William Henry
Evanescence.
Harold at Two Years Old.
The Inner Light.
O God, How Many Years
Ago.
A Prayer.
Saint Paul.
Surrender to Christ.
Teneriffe (excerpt).

Myers, Jack
The Apprentice Painter.
Day of Atonement.
The Minyan.
Mirror for the Barnyard.
Mockingbird, Copy This.
So Long Solon.
Too Many Miles of Sunlight
between Us.
When I Held You to My
Chest, You Fit.

Myles, Eileen
Dawn.
Greedy Seasons.
Medium Poem.
My Cheap Lifestyle.
On the Death of Robert
Lowell.
Poetry Reading.

Myles, Glenn
Percy/68.

Mylonas, Eva
Holidays.

N

"N., A.M."
God's Treasure.

Nabbes, Thomas
On a Mistress of Whose
Affections He Was Doubtful.
Tottenham Court: Song:
"What a dainty life the
milkmaid leads."

Nabokov, Vladimir
The Ballad of Longwood
Glen.
An Evening of Russian
Poetry.
Lines Written in Oregon.
Literary Dinner.
Ode to a Model.
On Discovering a Butterfly.
Rain.
The Room.

Nadaud, Gustave
Carcassonne.

Nadel, Alan
To Summer.

Nadir, Moishe
Adjectives.

Nadson, Semion Y.
The Brother.

Nagase Kiyoko
Mother.

Nagayasu, Syuichi
The Bored Mirror.

Naggid, Hayim
After the War.
Like a Pearl.
My Mother.
A Snow in Jerusalem.

Nagy, Agnes Nemes
Bird.
I Carried Statues.
Storm.
Words to a Song.

Nahman of Bratzlav
Annul Wars.
The Heart of the World.

Nahum
Spring Song.

Naidu, Sarojini
The Coromandel Fishers.
Cradle Song.
Dirge.
The Snake-Charmer.
Transience.

Naigreshel, Mendel
Nation.
What Will Remain after Me?

Nairn, Lady
Will Ye No Come Back
Again?

Nairne, Carolina Oliphant, Lady
The Auld House.
Caller Herrin'.
Heavenward.
The Laird O' Cockpen.
The Land o' the Leal.
The Lass o' Gowrie.
Lullaby.
Rest Is Not Here.
The Rowan Tree.

Najara, Israel
God of the World.
Loved of My Soul.

Nakasuk
The Gull.
Invocation.

Nakatsukasa
If It Were Not for the Voice.
O Nightingale.

Nale Roxlo, Conrado
The Unforeseen.

Nalungiaq
Magic Worlds.

Namanworth, Elaine
The Fishermen's Wives.

Nance, Berta Hart
Cattle.
Moonlight.
The Road to Texas.

Nangolo, Mvula Ya
Contrast.
A Flower.
Guerrilla Promise.
Hunter's Song.

Nannakaiyar, Kaccipetty
My Lover Capable of Terrible
Lies.

Naone, Dana
Girl with the Green Skirt.
Long Distance.
The Presence.
Sleep.
Untitled.

Napa
Darkened in the Soul.

Napier, Felicity
Houseplant.

Napier, George
To a Lady, with a Compass.

Narautjarri, Smiler
The Witch Doctor's Magic
Flight.

Narihira (Ariwara no Narihira)
I am so lost.
I knew quite well that some
day.

Nash, Dorothy
The Road Moves On.

Nash, Ogden
Admiral Byrd.
Adventures of Isabel.
Among the Anthropophagi.
The Anatomy of Happiness.
And Three Hundred and
Sixty-Six in Leap Year.
The Ant.
Autres Betes, Autres Moeurs.
Bankers Are Just Like
Anybody Else, Except
Richer.
The Bat.
Between Birthdays.
The Boy Who Laughed at
Santa Claus.
Calling Spring VII-MMMC.
The Camel.
The Canary.
The Carnival of Animals
(excerpt).
A Carol for Children.
A Caution to Everybody.
Celery.
Columbus.
Confessions of a Born
Spectator.
Consider the Auk.
The Cow.
Decline and Fall of a Roman
Umpire.
Do You Plan to Speak Bantu?
The Dog.
A Dog's Best Friend Is His
Illiteracy.
A Drink with Something in It.
The Duck.
The Eel.
England Expects.
The Evening Out.
Everybody Eats Too Much
Anyhow.
Exit, Pursued by a Bear.
Family Court.
The Firefly.
First Families Move Over!
Funebrial Reflections.
Genealogical Reflection.
The Germ.
Golly, How Truth Will Out!
Goodbye Now, or, Pardon My
Gauntlet.
The Grackle.
Grandpa Is Ashamed.
Ha! Original Sin!
The Hippopotamus.
The Hunter.
I Never Even Suggested It.
Ill Met by Zenith.
An Intoduction to Dogs.
Introspective Reflection.
Invocation.
The Japanese.
Kind of an Ode to Duty.
Kindly Unhitch That Star,
Buddy.
The Kitten.
A Lady Thinks She Is Thirty.
The Lama.
Limerick: "A bugler named
Douglas MacDougal."
Limerick: "A thrifty soprano
of Hingham."
Limerick: "See that senor so
amorous and menacing."

Limerick: "There was a brave
girl of Connecticut."
Limerick: "There was a young
belle of old Natchez."
Limerick: "There was a young
lady from Cork."
Limerick: "There was an old
man in a trunk."
Limerick: "There was an old
man of Calcutta."
Line-Up for Yesterday.
Lines in Dispraise of
Dispraise.
Lines to a World-Famous
Poet...
Lines to Be Embroidered on a
Bib....
The Lion.
Lucy Lake.
Malice Domestic.
A Man Can Complain, Can't
He?
Max Schling, Max Schling,
Lend Me Your Green
Thumb.
Morning Prayer.
Mr. Artesian's
Conscientiousness.
The New Nutcracker Suite
(excerpt).
Notes for the Chart in 306.
The Octopus.
Oh, Please Don't Get Up!
Oh, Stop Being Thankful All
Over the Place.
Old Men.
One from One Leaves Two.
One, Two, Buckle My Shoe.
The Oyster.
The Panther.
The Parsnip.
Peekaboo, I Almost See You.
The Perfect Husband.
The Phoenix.
.Piano Tuner, Untune Me
That Tune.
The Pig.
Portrait of the Artist as a
Prematurely Old Man.
The Poultries.
The Praying Mantis.
The Private Dining Room.
The Purist.
Reflection on Babies.
Reflections on Ice-Breaking.
Reminiscent Reflection.
The Rhinoceros.
The Sea-Gull.
The Seven Spiritual Ages of
Mrs. Marmaduke Moore.
The Shrew.
So That's Who I Remind Me
Of.
Song of the Open Road.
Song to Be Sung by the
Father of Infant Female
Children.
Spring Comes to Murray Hill.
The Squirrel.
Sweet Dreams.
Tableau at Twilight.
Taboo to Boot.
The Tale of Custard the
Dragon.
Tallyho-Hum.
The Termite.
The Terrible People.
That Reminds Me.
There Was a Young Lady of
Rome.
They Don't Speak English in
Paris.

Third Limick.
To a Small Boy Standing on
My Shoes While I Am
Wearing Them.
Traveler's Rest.
The Turtle.
Two and One Are a Problem.
Two Dogs Have I.
Up from the Egg: The
Confessions of a Nuthatch
Avoider.
Up from the Wheelbarrow.
Very Like a Whale.
The Visit.
The Wapiti.
The Wendigo.
What's the Use.
Who Taught Caddies to
Count? or; A Burnt Golfer
Fears the Child.
The Wombat.
A Word to Husbands.
Nashe [(or Nash)] Thomas
Autumn.
Fair Summer Droops.
Harvest.
A Litany in Time of Plague.
A-Maying, A-Paying.
Microcosmus.
Summer's Farewell.
Summer's Last Will and
Testament: Adieu, Farewell
Earths Blisse.
Nason, Elias
A Child's Question.
The Cricket's Story.
Jesus Only.
Nathan, Leonard
The Diver.
Ellora.
Fantasia.
The Fourth Dimension.
Jane Seagrim's Party.
The Likeness.
Nino Leading an Old Man to
Market.
To a Foreign Friend.
Trying.
Yours Truly.
Nathan, Norman
Modern Architecture.
Voting Machine.
Nathan, Robert
At the Symphony.
Beauty Is Ever to the Lonely
Mind.
Bells in the Country.
Christian, Be Up.
Comes Fall.
The Daughter at Evening.
Dunkirk.
Epitaph.
The Mountaineer.
Now Blue October.
The Poet Describes His Love.
Sonnet: "Because my grief
seems quiet and apart."
These Are the Chosen People.
When in the Crowd I
Suddenly Behold.
Will Beauty Come.
Naude, Adele
Africa.
From a Venetian Sequence.
The Idiot.
Portrait.
Return.
The Unpossessed.
Nauen, Elinor
3 More Things.
The History of the Human
Body....

If I Ever Grow Old.
Maine.
Naylor, James Ball
King David and King
Solomon.
Neagle, Dennis
I Caught This Morning at
Dawning.
Neal, John
Men of the North.
Music of the Night.
Neal, Larry
Harlem Gallery: From the
Inside.
James Powell on Imagination.
Malcolm X–An
Autobiography.
Orishas.
Neale, John Mason
Art Thou Weary?
The Celestial Country.
For Thee, O Dear Dear
Country!
Good King Wenceslas.
Jerusalem.
Light's Glittering Morn.
Oh, Give Us Back the Days
of Old.
Nealy, Mary E.
The Maul.
Neaves, Lord Charles
Let Us All Be Unhappy on
Sunday.
Neeld, Judith
Thinning out the Grove.
Neele, Henry
Moan, Moan, Ye Dying
Gales.
Negri, Ada
Make Way!
Neidhart von Reuental
The Bargain.
On the Mountain.
Neidus, Leib
I Love the Woods.
I Often Want to Let My Lines
Go.
In an Alien Place.
Neihardt, John G.
Battle Cry.
The Child's Heritage.
The Death of Crazy Horse.
Easter, 1923.
Envoi.
Let Me Live Out My Years.
Outward.
Prayer for Pain.
Red Cloud.
The Shooting of the Cup.
The Song of Jed Smith
(excerpt).
When I Am Dead.
When I Have Gone Weird
Ways.
Neilson, Francis
Eugenio Pacelli.
Neilson, John Shaw
Break of Day.
I Spoke to the Violet.
May.
The Orange Tree.
Schoolgirls Hastening.
Song Be Delicate.
Stony Town.
'Tis the White Plum Tree.
To a Blue Flower.
To the Red Lory.
Neilson, Shaw
Beauty Imposes.
The Cool, Cool Country.
The Crane Is My Neighbour.
Flowers in the Ward.

In the Street.
Love's Coming.
The Poor Can Feed the Birds.
The Soldier Is Home.
Strawberries in November.
The Sundowner.
Take down the Fiddle, Karl!
To a School-Girl.
The Walking of the Moon-
Women.
You Cannot Go down to the
Spring.
Nekrasov, Nikolai
The Capitals Are Rocked.
A Hymn.
Nelms, Sheryl L.
Edwin A. Nelms.
How About.
Into Fish.
Killing the Rooster.
Married Three Months.
Nelson, Alice Dunbar
I Sit and Sew.
Sonnet: "I had no thought of
violets of late."
Nelson, David
My Days Are Gliding Swiftly
By.
Nelson, Frank Carleton
The Human Heart.
Nelson, Howard
The Cows near the
Graveyard.
Winter Night, Cold Spell.
Nelson, Paula
The House.
Nelson, Rodney
Anabasis.
Nelson, Sharon
Pedlar.
Nelson, Stanley
Immigrants.
Nelson, Starr
The White Rainbow.
Nemerov, Howard
After Commencement.
An Alexandrine Magazine.
Angel and Stone.
The Author to His Body on
Their Fifteenth Birthday
29.ii.80.
The Backward Look.
The Beautiful Lawn Sprinkler.
The Blue Swallows.
The Book of Kells.
Boom!
Brainstorm.
The Brief Journey West.
Carol: "Now is the world
withdrawn all in silence and
night."
Casting.
Central Park.
Ceremony.
The Companions.
Conversing with Paradise.
Dandelions.
The Death of God.
Debate with the Rabbi.
The Dial Tone.
Dialogue.
The Distances They Keep.
The Dragonfly.
The Dream of Flying Comes
of Age.
The Dying Garden.
Easter.
Elegy.
Elegy for a Nature Poet.
Epigram: A Spiral Shell.
Epigram: Absent-Minded
Professor.

Epigram: An Old Story.
Epigram: April.
Epigram: Invocation.
Epigram: Lucilius.
Epigram: Mythological Beast.
Epigram: The Hunt Goes By.
Exit Line.
Extract from Memoirs.
A Fable of the War.
The Fall Again.
Fugue.
Ginkgoes in Fall.
Glass Dialectic.
Going Away.
Goldfish.
The Goose Fish.
Grace to Be Said at the
  Supermarket.
Guide to the Ruins.
The Historical Judas.
History of a Literary
  Movement.
Holding the Mirror up to
  Nature.
Human Things.
I Only Am Escaped Alone to
  Tell Thee.
The Icehouse in Summer.
Learning by Doing.
Life Cycle of Common Man.
Lion & Honeycomb.
The Lives of Gulls and
  Children.
Lot Later.
Make Love Not War.
The Makers.
Manners.
The Mapmaker on His Art.
The Marriage of Heaven and
  Earth.
The May Day Dancing.
Metamorphoses.
Money.
The Most Expensive Picture
  in the World.
Mousemeal.
The Mud Turtle.
The Murder of William
  Remington.
Mystery Story.
A Negro Cemetery Next to a
  White One.
New Year's 1978.
Nixons at Calvary.
An Old Picture.
On Being Asked for a Peace
  Poem.
On Certain Wits.
The Painter Dreaming in the
  Scholar's House.
The Phoenix.
A Picture.
Pockets.
Power to the People.
Praising the Poets of That
  Country.
A Primer of the Daily Round.
The Print-Out.
Redeployment.
Reflexions on the Seizure of
  the Suez....
The Remorse for Time.
Runes.
The Salt Garden.
The Sanctuary.
Santa Claus.
The Scales of the Eyes.
September, the First Day of
  School.
Sestina on Her Portrait.
Sigmund Freud.
A Singular Metamorphosis.

Sleeping Beauty.
Small Moon.
Snowflakes.
The Sparrow in the Zoo.
Speculation.
A Spell before Winter.
The Statues in the Public
  Garden.
Storm Windows.
Style.
Sunday at the End of
  Summer.
The Sweeper of Ways.
The Tapestry.
Thirtieth Anniversary Report
  of the Class of '41.
The Three Towns.
To D—, Dead by Her Own
  Hand.
To David, about His
  Education.
To My Least Favorite
  Reviewer.
To the Rulers.
The Town Dump.
Trees.
Truth.
The Vacuum.
The View.
The View from an Attic
  Window.
Waiting Rooms.
A Way of Life.
The Weather of the World.
The Western Approaches.
What Kind of a Guy Was
  He?
The Winter Lightning for
  Paul.
Writing.
Young Woman.
Nerber, John
Castaway.
Nerses, Saint
The Annunciation.
The Assumption.
Neruda, Pablo
Almeria.
Always.
The Battle of the Jarama.
Drunk as drunk on
  turpentine.
Enigmas.
The Fickle One.
The Ghost of the Cargo Boat.
Girls.
The International Brigade
  Arrives at Madrid.
Lone Gentleman.
Materia Nupcial.
Nothing but Death.
Ode to Salt.
Ode to the Watermelon.
The Queen.
Return of Autumn.
To Silvestre Revueltas of
  Mexico, in His Death.
Tonight I can write the
  saddest lines.
The United Fruit Co.
Walking around.
Nerval, Gerard de
Artemis.
Delfica.
Fantasy.
Golden Lines.
Nervo, Amado
Mystical Poets.
Nesbit, Edith
Among His Books.
Baby Seed Song.
Child's Song in Spring.

The Claim.
The Gray Folk.
Love's Guerdons.
Mr. Ody met a body.
Oh, Baby, Baby, Baby Dear.
Summer Song.
The Things That Matter.
A Tragedy.
Villeggiature.
Nesbit, Wilbur D.
All to Myself.
A Friend or Two.
A Hymn of Thanksgiving.
Let Us Smile.
Who Hath a Book.
Your Flag and My Flag.
Nesmith, James Ernest
The Statue of Lorenso de
  Medici.
Neto, Agostinho
Farewell at the Hour of
  Parting.
Friend Mussunda.
Kinaxixi.
The Marketwoman.
Western Civilization.
Netser, Eli
My Best Clothes.
Nettles, Isaiah
It's Cold in China Blues.
Neufeld, Ernest
At Masada.
Neugroschel, Joachim
Doves.
Eve's Advice to the Children
  of Israel.
Neumeyer, Peter F.
Rope's End.
Neville, Helen
Body's Freedom.
Neville, Mary
Social Studies.
Nevin, Edwin H.
God's Will.
Happy, Saviour, Would I Be.
I Am with You Alway.
When Our Earthly Sun Is
  Setting.
Newbery, Thomas
The Great Merchant, Dives
  Pragmaticus, Cries His
  Wares.
Newbolt, Sir Henry
Admiral Death.
Admirals All.
Cities Drowned.
Clifton Chapel.
Commemoration.
Craven.
Drake's Drum.
The Fighting Temeraire.
The Final Mystery.
Finis.
From Generation to
  Generation.
Hawke.
He Fell Among Thieves.
Imogen.
Ireland, Ireland.
Master and Man.
Messmates.
The Moss-Rose.
The Only Son.
Rilloby-Rill.
Sacramentum Supremum.
Sailing at Dawn.
Song.
St. George's Day–Ypres, 1915.
To a River in the South.
Vitai Lampada.
Yattendon.

Newbury, Colin
Epilogue of the Wandering
  Jew.
Letter from Paparua.
New Wine, Old Bottles.
**Newcastle, Margaret Cavendish,
  Duchess of**
The Hunting of the Hare.
My Cabinets Are Oyster-
  Shells.
Nature's Cook.
O do not grieve, Dear Heart,
  nor shed a tear.
O Love, how thou art.
The Soul's Garment.
Of the Theme of Love.
What Is Liquid.
**Newcastle, William Cavendish,
  Duke of**
Love Play.
Love's Epitaph.
Love's Matrimony.
Song: "We'll, placed in Love's
  triumphant chariot high."
Newcomb, Bobby
The Big Sunflower.
Newcombe, Rosemarie
At Last.
Newell, Catherine Parmenter
Dream House.
Newell, J. R.
Christmas Carol.
Newell, Mike
Prayer.
Newell, Peter
The Educated Love Bird.
Her Dairy.
Her Polka Dots.
Timid Hortense.
Wild Flowers.
Newell, Robert Henry
The American Traveller.
Columbia's Agony.
Dear Father, Look up.
The Editor's Wooing.
The Neutral British
  Gentleman.
O, Be Not Too Hasty, My
  Dearest.
"Picciola".
The Rejected "National
  Hymns".
Tuscaloosa Sam.
When Your Cheap Divorce Is
  Granted.
Newlove, John
America.
The First Time.
Good Company, Fine Houses.
The Grass Is a Reasonable
  Colour.
I Talk to You.
The Pride.
Samuel Hearne in Wintertime.
Succubi.
Verigin 3.
Verigin, Moving in Alone.
The Well-Travelled Roadway.
What Do You Want?
Newman, John Henry, Cardinal
Angelic Guidance.
Chorus of the Elements.
The Discovery.
The Dream of Gerontius.
The Elements.
England.
The Good Samaritan.
Guardian Angel.
Judaism.
Lead, Kindly Light.
Matins–Friday.
Monks.

My Lady Nature and Her
  Daughters.
The Patient Church.
The Pillar of Cloud.
Progress of Unbelief.
The Queen of Seasons.
Rest.
Sensitiveness.
The Sign of the Cross.
Snapdragon.
St. Philip in Himself.
Substance and Shadow.
A Thanksgiving.
The Trance of Time.
Until the Shadows Lengthen.
Valentine to a Little Girl.
Zeal and Love.
The Zeal of Jehu.
Newman, Joseph S.
Baby Toodles.
Hero and Leander.
Limerick: "Annoying Miss
  Tillie McLush."
Limerick: "Said an asp to an
  adder named Rhea."
Newman, Louis I.
The Voice of God.
The World Looks On.
Newman, Michael
Negative Passage.
Newman, Paul Baker
Mr. Cherry.
Newman, Preston
Some Questions to Be Asked
  of a Rajah...
Newsome, Mary Effie Lee
Arctic Tern in a Museum.
The Baker's Boy.
Bats.
The Cotton Cat.
The Cricket and the Star.
Little Birches.
Morning Light.
Morning Light the Dew-Drier.
Pansy.
The Quilt.
Quoits.
Sassafras Tea.
Sky Pictures.
Wild Roses.
Newton, Byron Rufus
Owed to New York.
Newton, Charles
Stanzas (excerpt).
Newton, Douglas
Gaiety of Descendants.
Invasion Weather.
Newton, John
All Our Griefs to Tell.
Amazing Grace.
Glorious Things of Thee Are
  Spoken.
In Evil Long I Took Delight.
In Sweet Communion.
The Name of Jesus.
Nothing to Wish or to Fear.
The Precious Name.
Thou Art Coming to a King.
Zion; or, the City of God.
Newton, Mary Leslie
Queen Anne's Lace.
Neyroud, Gerard
Limerick: "Said a saucy young
  skunk to a gnu."
Nezalhualcoyotl
In Vain Was I Born.
Ngani, A. Z.
Praises of King George VI.
Ngata, Apirana
Canoe-Hauling Chant.
Ngatho, Stella
Footpath.

Ngunaitponi
The Song of Hungarrda.
Ni Chonaill Eibhlin Dhubh *See*
  O'Connell Eibhlin Dubh
Niatum, Duane
After the Death of an Elder
  Klallam.
Ascending Red Cedar Moon.
Chief Leschi of the Nisqually.
Crow's Way.
Digging Out the Roots.
Elegy for Chief Sealth
  (1786–1866).
Homage to Chagall.
Indian Rock, Bainbridge
  Island, Washington.
No One Remembers
  Abandoning the Village of
  White Fir.
The Novelty Shop.
Old Woman Awaiting the
  Greyhound Bus.
On Hearing the Marsh Bird's
  Water Cry.
On Leaving Baltimore.
On Visiting My Son, Port
  Angeles, Washington.
Raven.
Slow Dancer That No One
  Hears but You.
Song from the Maker of
  Totems.
Street Kid.
To Your Question.
Nibbelink, Herman
Untitled.
Nicander
Gourds.
Nicarchos [(or Nicarchus)]
Fortunatus the R. A.
On Marcus the Physician.
The Raven.
Nichol, John
Good Night.
Gorg, a Detective Story.
Two Words: A Wedding.
Nicholas, Michael
Today: The Idea Market.
Nicholas, Virginia Real
South of the Border.
Nicholl, Louise Townsend
Architect.
Ark of the Covenant.
Cigar Smoke, Sunday, after
  Dinner.
Cleavage.
Color Alone Can Speak.
Creation.
The Cruse.
A Different Speech.
Different Winter.
Hymn.
Improvising.
Incense.
The Made Lake.
Ornamental Water.
Pediment: Ballet.
Physical Geography.
Recital (excerpt).
Rondel for Middle Age.
The Shape of the Heart.
Three Persons.
Time in the Sun.
Wild Cherry.
Nicholls, W. Leslie
Clerihew: "Albert Durer."
Nichols, Carrie May
The Boomerang.
Nichols, Kevin
The Feast of Stephen.
Nichols, R.
The Burial in Flanders.

Nichols, Robert
The Assault.
Aurelia.
Battery Moving Up to a New
  Position from Rest Camp:
  Dawn.
By the Wood.
Casualty.
The Day's March.
Don Juan's Address to the
  Sunset.
Fisbo (excerpt).
The Flower of Flame
  (excerpt).
Fulfilment.
The Full Heart.
Harlots' Catch.
I Love a Flower.
The Moon behind High
  Tranquil Leaves.
Our Dead.
The Secret Garden.
Sonnets to Aurelia.
The Sprig of Lime.
Thanksgiving.
To—.
To D'Annunzio: Lines from
  the Sea.
Nicholson, John
On a Calm Summer's Night.
Nicholson, John Gambril
A Chaplet of Southernwood
  (excerpt).
Nicholson, Martha Snell
And His Name Shall Be
  Called Wonderful.
His Plan for Me.
His Promises.
Home.
Look Up.
My Lord.
Suppose That Christ Had Not
  Been Born.
This Easter Day.
What Are You Doing for
  Jesus?
Nicholson, Meredith
From Bethlehem to Calvary.
Nicholson, Norman
The Blackberry.
The Burning Bush.
Caedmon.
Carol for the Last Christmas
  Eve.
Carol: "Mary laid her Child
  among."
Cleator Moor.
Cockley Moor, Dockray,
  Penrith.
The Expanding Universe.
For All Sorts and Conditions.
For the Bicentenary of Isaac
  Watts.
For the New Year.
Glacier.
Michaelmas.
Millom Old Quarry.
The Motion of the Earth.
Now in the Time of This
  Mortal Life.
Old Man at a Cricket Match.
On the Closing of Millom
  Ironworks.
Poem for Epiphany.
The Preachers.
Ravenglass Railway Station,
  Cumberland.
Rockferns.
Shepherds' Carol.
Song at Night.
Thomas Gray in Patterdale.
To a Child Before Birth.

The Undiscovered Planet.
Wales.
Weather Ear.
Nicias
The Fountain at the Tomb.
Nickens, Thomas G.
Jis' Knowin'.
Pacified.
Radcliff, Kentucky.
State Prison 4:00 p.m.
State Prison 5:00 p.m.
Nickerson, Sheila
Complaint of the Fisherman's
  Wife.
The Enchanted Halibut.
In the Fishing Village.
Nicochares
Hangover Cure.
Nicoidski, Clarisse
Breaking Off from Waiting.
Eyes.
Mouth.
Open Earth.
Remembering.
Nicol, Abioseh
African Easter.
The Continent That Lies
  Within Us.
Nicolas, Vidal de
A Wish.
Nicoll, Robert
The Hero.
We Are Brethren A'.
Nicolson, Alexander
A Warning.
Nicolson, J. U.
Old Maid.
Reconciliation.
String Stars for Pearls.
Nicophon
Beware of Figs.
Niditch, B. Z.
Passover Dachau.
Return to Dachau.
Niebuhr, Reinhold
Prayer for Serenity.
Niedecker, Lorine
Lake Superior.
Seven Poems.
Nietzsche, Friedrich Wilhelm
The Solitary.
Star Morals.
To the Unknown God.
Nightingale, Madeline
The Scissor-Man.
The Waits.
Nihoniho, Tuta
Government.
Nijlen, Jan van
The Master of Time.
Nikitin, Ivan Savvich
A Night in a Village.
Niles, John Jacob
In All the Magic of Christmas
  Time.
Niles, Nathaniel
The American Hero.
Why Should Vain Mortals
  Tremble.
Nims, John Frederick
Apocalypse.
La Ci Darem La Mano.
Clock Symphony.
Clock without Hands.
Conclusion.
Dollar Bill.
Elegy for a Bad Poet, Taken
  from Us Not Long Since.
Eminent Critic.
Fairy Tale.
For My Son.
Good Friday.

Love and Death.
Love Poem.
Madrigal.
Midwest.
The Necromancers.
New Year's Eve, 1938.
Non-Euclidean Elegy.
The Observatory Ode.
Parting: 1940.
Perfect Rhyme.
Ribald Romeos Less and Less
  Berattle.
Tide Turning.
Trainwrecked Soldiers.
Visiting Poet.

Ninine
Prayer to St. Patrick.

Nisbet, Eilidh
Three Girls on a Buttress.
To a Midge.

Nist, John
Made to See.
Sings a Bird.
Villanelle.

Nistor, Der
At the Doors.

Nitschmann, Anna
This Flock So Small.

Nitzche, Jane Chance
Shopping.

Niven, Frederick
Indian Dance.

Nizami
He Poet in His Poverty.

No Ch'on-myong
Cricket.
Deer.

Noailles, Anna de
Image.
Poem on Azure.

Noble, Fay Lewis
Prayer for Song.

Noel, Roden
A Casual Song.
I Flung Me Round Him.

**Noel, Roden and Wriothesley
Berkeley**
A Lady to a Lover.
The Old.
The Swimmer.
Vale!
The Water-Nymph and the
  Boy.

Noel, Thomas
Old Winter.
The Pauper's Drive.

Nogar, Rui
Poem of the Conscripted
  Warrior.

Noguchi, Yone
The Poet.

Noguere, Suzanne
Pervigilium Veneris.

Nohomaiterangi
Lullaby.

Nolan, Bertha
My Mother.

Nolan, Edward
"Oxford is a Stage."

Nolan, James
Mardi Gras / Grandmothers
Portrait in Red and Black
  Crayon.
Sum.

Nolan, Michael
Little Annie Rooney.

Nolan, Pat
Doubt.
Exercise.
The Great Pretender.
Home Life.
Senryu.

Stone Age.
Tea for Two.

Noll, Bink
Divorce.
Moving between Beloit and
  Monroe.
The Picador Bit.
Shutting the Curtains.
Wedlock.

Nomberg, David
A Russian Cradle Song.

Nordan, Lewis
He Fishes with His Father's
  Ghost.

Nordbrandt, Henrik
We Separate the Days.

Nordhaus, Jean
Country Singer.
Yahrzeit Candle.

Norman, Charles
Portrait of a Senator.

Norman, Rosemary
Cabbage.
My Son and I.

Norris, Alfred
A Prayer for Faith.

Norris, Gordon W.
Mi Corazon.
Song of the Border.

Norris, John
The Aspiration.
The Choice.
Hymn to Darkness.
The Retirement.

Norris, John W.
Give Peace, O God, the
  Nations Cry.

Norris, Kathleen
Evaporation Poems.
Focus.
Her Application to Elysium.
Memorandum / The
  Accountant's Notebook.
The Middle of the World.
Running through Sleep.
Stomach.

Norris, Ken
The Case.
Here/There.
In Pursuit of Love.
Ode to the Day.
A Short Treatise upon Our
  Failures.
The Trouble with Angels.
You Are Reading This Too
  Fast.

Norris, Leslie
The Ballad of Billy Rose.
Camels of the Kings.
In Black Chasms.
A Man in Our Village.
Merlin and the Snake's Egg.
Mice in the Hay.
The Park at Evening.
The Quiet-Eyed Cattle.
The Shepherd's Dog.
The Stable Cat.

Norse, Harold
Behind the Glass Wall.
Breathing the Strong Smell.
Colosseum.
Island of Giglio.
You Must Have Been a
  Sensational Baby (excerpt).

North, Dudley, Lord
Air: "So full of courtly
  reverence."

North, Frank Mason
The City.
Where Cross the Crowded
  Ways of Life.

North, Jessica Nelson
Balloon Man.
Truth.

North, Susan
What I Have.

NorthSun, Nila
Falling down to bed.
Future generation.
Little red riding hood.
The red road.
The sweat.
Up & out.
The Way & the Way Things
  Are.

Nortje, Arthur
All Hungers Pass Away.
Brief Thunder at Sharpeville.
Letter from Pretoria Central
  Prison.
Midnight.
Soliloquy: South Africa.

Norton, Andrews
Hymn for the Dedication of a
  Church.
My God, I Thank Thee.

**Norton, Carolina Elizabeth
Sarah**
The Arab's Farewell to His
  Steed.
Bingen on the Rhine.
I Do Not Love Thee!
Juanita.
The King of Denmark's Ride.
Love Not.
Not Lost, but Gone Before.

Norton, Eleanor
Chopin Prelude.

Norton, Grace Fallow
Adventure.
Deer on the Mountain.
Little Gray Songs from St.
  Joseph's.
Love Is a Terrible Thing.
O Sleep.
O World, Be Not So Fair.
This Is My Love for You.

Norton, Thomas
Against Women Either Good
  or Bad.
A Man May Live Thrice
  Nestor's Life.

Norton II, John
A Funeral Elogy...

Norvig, Gerda
Desert March.
The Joining.
The Tree of Life is Also a
  Tree of Fire.

Norwood, Eille
Limerick: "A pretty young
  actress, a stammerer."

Norwood, Robert
The Man of Kerioth (excerpt).

Norworth, Jack
Take Me Out to the Ball
  Game.

Notker Balbulus
Cantemus Cuncti Melodum.
Media Vita.

Notley, Alice
After Tsang Chih.
Backyard.
Flowers of the Foothills &
  Mountain Valleys.
I the People.
In Ancient December.
The Night Sits in This Chair.
Poem: "A clitoris is a kind of
  brain."
Poem: "I believe the yellow
  flowers think with me."
World's Bliss.

Nottage, Mary Hastings
My Father's Voice in Prayer.

"Novalis."
Hymn to the Night: II.

**"Novalis" (George Friedrich
Philipp von Hardenerg)**
Aphorisms.
The Second Hymn to the
  Night.
When Geometric Diagrams...

November, Sharyn
Night Driving.

Nowell, M. H.
Of Disdainful Daphne.

Nowlan, Alden
The Anatomy of Angels.
Aunt Jane.
Baptism.
Beets.
Beginning.
The Bull Moose.
Daisies.
The Execution.
For Jean Vincent d'Abbadie,
  Baron St.-Castin.
God Sour the Milk of the
  Knacking Wench.
Great Things Have Happened.
Gypsies.
He Runs into an Old
  Acquaintance.
He Sits down on the Floor of
  a School for the Retarded.
Helen's Scar.
Hens.
I, Icarus.
In the Operating Room.
Kyran's Christening.
The Loneliness of the Long
  Distance Runner.
Marian at the Pentecostal
  Meeting.
The Palomino Stallion.
Party at Bannon Brook.
Porch.
A Psalm of Onan for Harp,
  Flue and Tambourine.
Rivalry.
Semi-Private Room.
Stars.
Subway Psalm.
Suppose This Moment Some
  Stupendous Question.
Therese.
Waiting for Her.
Wasp.

Noyce, Wilfred
Breathless.

Noyes, Alfred
The Admiral's Ghost.
Art.
Assisi.
The Barrel-Organ.
Betsy Jane's Sixth Birthday.
The Blinded Soldier to His
  Love.
Butterflies.
The Call of the Spring
  (excerpt).
Creation.
The Double Fortress.
Drake.
Edinburgh.
Epilogue: The Flower of Old
  Japan.
Forty Singing Seamen.
The Highwayman.
A Hospital.
In the Cool of the Evening.
A Japanese Love-Song.
Kilmeny.
Love's Rosary.

Messages.
The Messenger.
Old Man Mountain.
On the Death of Francis
Thompson.
Pirates.
A Prayer.
The River of Stars.
Sea-Distances.
Seagulls on the Serpentine.
Song.
Song: "I came to the door of
the House of Love."
A Song of Sherwood.
Spring, and the Blind
Children.
The Strong City.
Sunlight and Sea.
Under the Pyrenees.
Unity.
A Victory Dance.
When Spring Comes Back to
England.
You That Sing in the
Blackthorn.

Noyes, Nicholas
A Consolatory Poem.
A Praefatory Poem to the
Little Book, Entituled,
Christianus per Ignem.
The Rev. Nicholas Noyes to
the Rev. Cotton Mather...
To My Worthy Friend, Mr.
James Bayley...

Noyes, Stanley
Nevada.

Noyle, Ken
The Sea.

Nugent, Gerald
A Farewell to Fal.

Nugent, Maude
Sweet Rosie O'Grady.

Nugent, Robert Nugent, Earl
Epigram: "I loved thee
beautiful and kind."
Epigram: "My heart still
hovering round about you."
Epigram: "Since first you
knew my am'rous smart."
Revenge.
To Clarissa.

Nukada, Princess
Manyoshu: Waiting for the
Emperor Tenji.
Manyoshu: When, Loosened
from the Winter's Bonds.

Nunan, Thomas
The Dreamer.

Nunes, Cassiano
Episode.

Nunez de Arce, Gaspar
Miserere.

Nunley, R. W.
Salmon Draught at Inveraray.

Nutter, C. D.
On Time with God.

Nutter, Medora Addison
Mountain Creed.

Nuur, Faarah
The Limits of Submission.
Modern Love Songs.
Our Country Is Divided.

Nweke, Chuba
Moon Song.

Nye, Naomi Shihab
Catalogue Army.
Grandfather's Heaven.
Hugging the Jukebox.
The Little Brother Poem.
Making a Fist.
Music.
New Skills.

Sleeping in a Cave.
The Use of Fiction.
Where Children Live.

Nyhart, Nina
The String of My Ancestors.
Tennis.

O

Oakes, Urian
An Elegie upon the Death of
the Reverend Mr. Thomas
Shepard (excerpt).
To the Reader.

Oakley, Ebenezer S.
The Thoughts That Move the
Heart of Man.

Oakman, John
The Glutton.

Oaks, Gladys
Anatole France at Eighty.

Oandasan, William
The Past.
Round Valley Reflections.
The Song of Ancient Ways.

Oates, Joyce Carol
Acceleration near the Point of
Impact.
Baby.
Back Country.
The Child-Bride.
Children Not Kept at Home.
A City Graveyard.
Dreaming America.
First Dark.
Foetal Song.
Growing Together.
Insomnia.
Lines for Those to Whom
Tragedy Is Denied.
Moving Out.
New Jersey White-Tailed
Deer.
Night.
The Present Tense.
The Stone Orchard.
The Suicide.
The Wasp.

Obi, Dorothy S.
Winds of Africa.

O'Bolger, T. D.
The Counsels of O'Riordan,
the Rann Maker.

O'Brien
The Ghost.

O'Brien, Edward J.
Her Fairness, Wedded to a
Star.
Irish.
The Shepherd Boy.

O'Brien, Fitz-James
Kane.
The Legend of the Easter
Eggs.
Minot's Ledge.
The Second Mate.

O'Brien, Katharine
Spring Song.

O'Brien, R. C.
Poor Grandpa.

O'Brien, Thomas
Always Battling.
International Brigade Dead.
Terror.

O Brolchain, Mael Isu
I Give Thee Thanks, My
King.

My Sins in Their
Completeness.
To an Elderly Virgin.

O Bruadair, David
For the Family of
Cuchonnacht O Dalaigh.
O It's Best Be a Total Boor.
A Shrewish, Barren, Bony,
Nosy Servant.

O Bruadair, David
Adoramus Te, Christe.
The Change.
Eire.
The New Style.

**"O'Byrne, Dermot" (Sir Arnold
Bax)**
A Dublin Ballad - 1916.

Ocampo, Silvina
In Front of the Seine,
Recalling the Rio De La
Plata.
Prisoner between the Panes of
Glass.

O'Carolan, Turlough
The Cup of O'Hara.
Mabel Kelly.
Peggy Browne.

Occleve, Thomas
To Chaucer.

Occom, Samson
Waked by the Gospel's
Powerful Sound.

Ochester, Ed
110 Year Old House.
Among His Effects We Found
a Photograph.
Ed Shreckongost.
A Farewell to the Moon.
For My Daughter.
For Refugio Talamante.
The Gift.
In the Library.
Killing Rabbits.
My Penis.
My Teeth.
The Penn Central Station at
Beacon, N.Y.
Rowing.
Snow White.
Toward the Splendid City.

O'Connell, Eibhlin Dubh
The Lament for Art O
Laoghaire (excerpt).

O'Connell, Richard
Robert Lowell.
Sidewalk Orgy.

O'Connor, Frank
The Angry Poet.
Autumn.
The End of Clonmacnois.
Hope.
Inheritance.
A Learned Mistress.
Love and Hate.
The Old Woman of Beare
Regrets Lost Youth.
On the Death of His Wife.
Prayer for the Speedy End of
Three Great Misfortunes.
Three Old Brothers.

O'Connor, Joseph
The General's Death.
What Was My Dream?

O'Connor, Martin T.
Requiem.

O'Connor, Michael
Reveille.

O'Connor, Patrick
In Pace In Idipsum Dormiam
Et Requiescam.
The Mantle of Mary.

O'Connor, Philip
Fag-End.
Poems (I-XI).
The Raspberry in the
Pudding.
Writing in England Now.

O'Conor, Norreys Jephson
Beside the Blackwater.
In Memoriam: Francis
Ledwidge.
In the Monastery.
In the Moonlight.
To a Child.

O'Cotter, Pat
A Malemute Dog.

O'Crowley, Denis
Washington.

O'Curnain, Diarmad
Love's Despair.

O'Dala, Donnchadh mor
At Saint Patrick's Purgatory.

O Dalaigh, Gofraidh Fionn
A Child in Prison.
Under Sorrow's Sign.

O Dalaigh, Lochlann Og
In Praise of Three Young
Men.

**O Dalaigh, Muireadhach
Albanach**
Last Night My Soul Departed.
Mighty Mary, Hear Me.
On the Death of His Wife.
On the Gift of a Knife.
Young Man of Alien Beauty.

**O Dalaigh, Muireadhach
Albanach**
In the Heart of Jesus.

O'Daly, Carrol
Eileen Aroon.

O'Daly, Carroll
Lover and Echo.

Odell, Jonathan
On Our Thirty-Ninth
Wedding Day.

Oden, Gloria C.
"...As When Emotion Too Far
Exceeds its Cause"–Elizabeth
Bishop.
The Carousel.
Man White, Brown Girl and
All That Jazz.
The Map.
A Private Letter to Brazil.
Review from Staten Island.
The Riven Quarry.
This Child Is the Mother.
The Triple Mirror.
The Way It Is.

O Direain, Mairtin
Homage to John Millington
Synge.

O Domhnaill, Maghnas
A Famished End to My Tale
This Night.
A Heart Made Full of
Thought.
Love, I Think, Is a Disease.

O'Donnell, Charles L.
Address to the Crown.
Cloister.
The Dead Musician.
Process.
Prodigals.
Resolution.
A Rime of the Rood.
A Road of Ireland.
Security.
The Shed.
The Spinner.
Trelawny Lies by Shelley.

O'Donnell, George Marion
Semmes in the Garden.

O'Donnell, Hugh
Dark Rosaleen.
O'Donnell, John Francis
Adare (excerpt).
April.
By the Turnstile.
Drifting.
Geraldine's Garden.
Happy Christmases (excerpt).
In the Twilight (excerpt).
A July Dawn (excerpt).
Lilies.
Limerick Town (excerpt).
May (excerpt).
My Jack.
Ossian (excerpt).
Reminiscences of a Day:
  Wicklow.
A Spinning Song.
The Spring.
O'Donoghue, Gregory
The Web.
O'Dowd, Bernard
Alma Venus (excerpt).
Australia.
The Bush (excerpt).
The Cow.
Cupid.
Love and Sacrifice.
Young Democracy (excerpt).
O'Dugan, Maurice
The Coolun.
O'Egan, Gerry
1867: Last Sounds.
Oehlenschlager, Adam
Freya's Spinning Wheel.
There Is a Charming Land.
Oerke, Andrew
Serengeti Sunset.
The Sun.
O'Flaherty, Charles
The Humours of Donnybrook
  Fair.
O'Gallagher, Alice
Welcome O Great Mary.
Ogarev, Nikolay Platonovich
The Road.
Ogburn, Charlton
Nature in Couplets.
O'Gillan, Angus
Dead at Clonmacnois.
Ogilvie, D. T.
Last Letter to the Western
  Civilization.
Ogilvie, Will H.
The Death of Ben Hall.
From the Gulf.
How the Fire Queen Crossed
  the Swamp.
If I Were Old.
The Kingship of the Hills.
Whaup o' the Rede: The
  Blades of Harden.
Ogle, George
The Banks of Banna.
Mailligh Mo Stor.
Ogmundarson, Cormac
Two Songs in Praise of
  Steingerd, 1.
Two Songs in Praise of
  Steingerd, 2.
O Gnimh, Fear Flatha
After the Flight of the Earls.
The Passing of the Poets.
O'Gnive, Fearflatha
The Downfall of the Gael.
O'Gorman, Ned
Childhood.
The Kiss.
O'Grady, Desmond
Arrival: The Capital.
The Day Concludes Burning.

The Dying Gaul.
The Father.
If I Went Away.
A Mad Male-Hearted Woman
  in a Prouder Age.
Page from a Diary.
The Pitch Piles Up in Part.
The Poet in Old Age Fishing
  at Evening.
The Poet Loves from Afar.
Professor Kelleher and the
  Charles River.
O'Grady, Standish
The Emigrant.
The Emigrant: Winter in
  Lower Canada.
Lough Bray.
Old Nick in Sorel.
O'Grady, Tom
Aubade after the Party.
O'Hagan, Thomas
Woman.
O'Hara, Frank
An Abortion.
Answer to Voznesensky &
  Evtushenko.
Aubade.
Autobiographia Literaria.
Ave Maria.
Biotherm.
Blocks.
Chez Jane.
The Day Lady Died.
Easter.
Les Etiquettes Jaunes.
For James Dean.
For Janice and Kenneth to
  Voyage.
Getting Up Ahead of
  Someone (Sun).
Homosexuality.
Hotel Transylvanie.
How to Get There.
The Hunter.
An Image of Leda.
In Favor of One's Time.
In Memory of My Feelings.
John Button Birthday.
Life on Earth (excerpt).
Les Luths.
Mary Desti's Ass.
Meditations in an Emergency.
Music.
Naphtha.
Ode: "An idea of justice may
  be precious."
Ode: Salute to the French
  Negro Poets.
Ode to Joy.
Ode to Michael Goldberg's
  Birth and Other Births: "I
  don't remember."
On Rachmaninoff's Birthday.
Personal Poem.
Poem: "At night Chinamen
  jump."
Poem: "Hate is only one of
  many responses."
Poem: "I watched an armory
  combing its bronze bricks."
Poem: "I Will Always Love
  You."
Poem: "Khrushchev is coming
  on the right day!"
Poem: "Lana Turner has
  collapsed!"
Poem Read at Joan Mitchell's.
Poem: "The eager note on my
  door said 'Call me'."
Poem: "There I could never
  be a boy."
Poetry.

Princess Elizabeth of
  Bohemia, as Perdita.
Radio.
Rhapsody.
Should We Legalize Abortion?
Sleeping on the Wing.
Song: "Is it dirty."
A Step Away from Them.
Steps.
A Terrestrial Cuckoo.
To Hell with It.
To the Film Industry in
  Crisis.
To the Harbormaster.
To the Poem.
A True Account of Talking to
  the Sun at Fire Island.
Walking.
Why I Am Not a Painter.
You Are Gorgeous and I'm
  Coming.
You at the Pump (History of
  North and South).
O'Hara, John Myers
Atropos.
O'Hara, Theodore
The Bivouac of the Dead.
O'Heffernan, Mahon
My Son, Forsake Your Art.
Who Will Buy a Poem?
O Hehir, Diana
Alone by the Road's Edge.
Anima.
Courtship.
House.
How to Murder Your Best
  Friend.
Infant.
Learning to Type.
Lost Objects.
The Old Lady under the
  Freeway.
Payments.
A Plan to Live My Life
  Again.
The Power to Change
  Geography.
Private Rooms.
Questions and Answers.
The Retarded Children Find a
  World Built Just for Them.
Shore.
Sleeping Pill.
Some of Us Are Exiles from
  No Land.
Summoned.
Tarantula.
Terminal Version.
They Grow Up Too Fast, She
  Said.
O Heigeartaigh, Padraig
My Sorrow, Donncha.
O Heoghusa, Eochaidh
A Change in Style.
Mag Uidhir's Winter
  Campaign.
O Hifearnain, Mathghamhain
I Ask, Who Will Buy a
  Poem?
O'Higgins, Myron
Blues for Bessie.
Sunset Horn.
Two Lean Cats...
Vaticide.
Young Poet.
O'Higgins, Tomas
To Tomas Costello at the
  Wars.
O'Huigin, Sean
Bye Bye.
O'Huiginn, Tadhg Dall
The Difference.

First Vision.
A Present of Butter.
A Satire on the O'Haras.
Second Vision.
A Visit to Enniskillen.
O Huiginn, Tadhg O'g
On the Breaking-Up of a
  School.
O'Hussey, Eochy
Hugh Maguire.
O'Kane, T. C.
My Mother's Prayer.
Okara, Gabriel
The Call of the River Nun.
The Mystic Drum.
Once Upon a Time.
Piano and Drums.
To Adhiambo.
Were I to Choose.
You Laughed and Laughed
  and Laughed.
O'Keefe, John
Air: "A flaxen-headed cow-
  boy, as simple as may be."
Amo, Amas.
The Friar of Orders Gray.
I Want a Tenant: A Satire.
O'Keeffe, Adelaide
Beasts and Birds.
The Butterfly.
The Kite.
Rather Too Good, Little
  Peggy!
To George Pulling Buds.
O'Kelly, Patrick
Blessings on Doneraile.
The Curse of Doneraile.
Okigbo, Christopher
Distances (excerpt).
Lament of the Flutes.
Okita, Dwight
The Art of Holding On.
Crossing with the Light.
In Response to Executive
  Order 9066: ALL
  AMERICANS OF
  JAPANESE...
Parachute.
Okkur Macatti
What Her Girl-Friend Said to
  Her.
What She Said.
Oku, Princess
How will you cross.
Okura
Because He Is Young.
Olcott, Chauncey
My Wild Irish Rose.
Oldenburg, E. W.
In Canterbury Cathedral.
Older, Julia
Georges Bank.
Oldham, G. Ashton
America First!
Oldham, John
The Careless Good Fellow
  Written March 9, 1680.
The Cup.
A Letter from the Country to
  a Friend in Town.
A Quiet Soul.
A Satire.
A Satire Addressed to a
  Friend (excerpt).
A Satire on Samuel Butler
  (excerpt).
Satyrs upon the Jesuits:
  Prologue.
Upon the Author of a Play
  Called Sodom.
Upon the Works of Ben
  Jonson (excerpt).

Oldknow, Antony
Nude with Green Chair.

Oldmixon, John
I Lately Vowed.
Song: "I lately vow'd, but
'twas in haste."

Olds, N. S.
Rivets.

Olds, Sharon
The Death of Marilyn
Monroe.
The End of World War One.
First Love.
The Hostage and His Takers.
Leningrad Cemetery, Winter
of 1941.
The One Girl at the Boys
Party.
Race Riot, Tulsa, 1921.
Rite of Passage.
Sex without Love.
Solitary.
Things That Are Worse Than
Death.
Time-Travel.

Oldys, William
On a Fly Drinking out of His
Cup.
On Himself.

Oles, Carole
The Magician Suspends the
Children.
A Manifesto for the Faint-
Hearted.
Stonecarver.
The Unteaching.

Oleson, Helmer O.
A Ballad of Johnny
Appleseed.

Oliphant, Dave
A Little Something for
William Whipple.
A Mexican Scrapbook.

Olitski, Leib
My Song to the Jewish
People.

Oliver, Louis (LittleCoon)
Empty Kettle.
Indian Macho.
Materialized into an owl.
The Sharpbreasted Snake
(Hokpe Fuske).
Wagon Full of Thunder.

Oliver, Mary
Aunt Elsie's Night Music.
Beaver Moon–The Suicide of
a Friend.
A Letter from Home.
Mussels.
Poem for My Father's Ghost.
Sleeping in the Forest.
Stark County Holidays.
Strawberry Moon.
The Truro Bear.

Oliver, W.H.
Beachcomber.
Death and the Maiden
(excerpt).
Phoenix.
Sleep Will Come Singly.

Oliver, Wade
Ships with Your Silver Nets.

Oliver, Widnes
I'll Have a Collier for My
Sweetheart.

Olsen, Donald D.
Poem: "We used to float the
paper boats in spring."

Olsen, William
Addressing His Deaf Wife,
Kansas, 1916.

Olson, Charles
Across Space and Time.
As the Dead Prey upon Us.
Celestial Evening, October
1967.
La Chute.
Cole's Island.
The Death of Europe.
The Distances.
I, Maximus of Gloucester, to
You.
In Cold Hell, In Thicket.
The Kingfishers.
A Later Note on Letter #15.
Letter 27.
Letter for Melville 1951.
The Librarian.
The Lordly and Isolate Satyrs.
The Maximus Poems.
Merce of Egypt.
The Moon Is the Number 18.
Moonset, Gloucester,
December 1, 1957, 1:58 AM.
A Newly Discovered
"Homeric" Hymn.
The Praises.
La Preface.
The Ring Of.
The River Map and We're
Done.
The Songs of Maximus.
Variations Done for Gerald
Van de Wiele.

Olson, Elder
Childe Roland, etc.
Crucifix.
Essay on Deity.
Ice-Skaters.
In Defense of Superficiality.
In Despair He Orders a New
Typewriter.
Jack-in-the-Box.
Knight, with Umbrella.
Merry Christmas!
The Night There Was
Dancing in the Streets.
Nightfall.
Plot Improbable, Character
Unsympathetic.
Wild Horse.

Olson, Ernst W.
God of Peace, in Peace
Preserve Us.

Olson, Ted
Hawk's Way.
Starlings.
Things That Endure.

Olumo *See* **Cunningham, James**

O'Malley, Charles J.
The Poet's Harvesting.

O'Malley, D. J.
The Horse Wrangler.

O'Malley, Emanuela
False Prophet.

Omar B. Abi Rabi'a
The Damsel.

Omar Khayyam
The Moving Finger.
The Rubaiyat: A book of
verses underneath the bough.
Rubaiyat of Omar Khayyam.
Worldly Wisdom.

Ombres, Rossana
Bella and the Golem.
Flower Ensnarer of Psalms.

O Meallain, Fear
Exodus to Connacht.

O'Meally, Bob
Make Music with Your Life.

O'Mulconry, Peadar
Were Not the Gael Fallen.

Onakatomi Yoshinobu
The deer on pine mountain.
The Deer Which Lives.

Ondaatje, Michael
Bearhug.
Breaking Green.
Burning Hills.
Buying the Dog.
The Cinnamon Peeler.
A Dog in San Francisco.
Gold and Black.
Letters & Other Worlds.
Prometheus, with Wings:.
To a Sad Daughter.
Walking to Bellrock.
When Charlie Bowdre
Married Manuela.

Onderdonk, Henry Ustic
On Zion and on Lebanon.
The Spirit in Our Hearts.
Though I Should Seek.

O'Neil, David
Starvation Peak Evening.
Vernal Showers.

O'Neil, George
The Cobbler in Willow Street.
Events.
Homage.
Socrates Prays a Day and a
Night.
Where It Is Winter.

O'Neill, Lawrence T.
Train to Reflection.

O'Neill, Mary Devenport
Dead in Wars and in
Revolutions.
Galway.
An Old Waterford Woman.
Scene-Shifter Death.
Sound of Water.
The Tramp's Song.
What Is Black?

O'Neill, Moira
Birds.
A Broken Song.
Corrymeela.
The Fairy Lough.
Forgettin'.
The Grand Match.
Her Sister.
Sea Wrack.
A Song of Glenann.

O'Neill, Rose
Faun-Taken.
When the Dead Men Die.

Onitsura
Directions.
Haiku: "Cherry-blossoms,
more."

Ono no Komachi
The color of the flowers.
Doesn't he realize.
If It Were Real.
No Moon, No Chance to
Meet.
Since I've Felt This Pain.
So lonely am I.
A thing which fades.
This Night of No Moon.
When My Love Becomes.

Ono no Takamura
Did I Ever Think.

Ono-no-Yoshiki
My Love.

Opdyke, Oliver
My Road.
A Spring Lay.

Opengart, Bea
Speak.

Opie, Amelia
The Orphan Boy's Tale.

Opitz, Martin
Beauty of This Earth.

Opoku, Andrew Amankwa
River Afram.

Oppen, George
Bahamas.
The Book of Job and a Draft
of a Poem to Praise the
Paths...
Exodus.
Five Poems about Poetry
(excerpt).
The Forms of Love.
If It All Went up in Smoke.
The People, the People.
Population.
Psalm.
Quotations.
Sara in Her Father's Arms.
Some San Francisco Poems.
Street.

Oppenheim, James
Action.
As to Being Alone.
Death.
For Randolph Bourne.
The Future.
A Handful of Dust.
Hebrews.
Immoral.
The Lincoln-Child.
The New God.
Night (excerpt).
The Reason.
The Runner in the Skies.
James.
Saturday Night.
The Slave.

Oppenheimer, J. Robert
Crossing.

Oppenheimer, Joel
The Bath.
Blue Funk.
The Bus Trip.
Cartography.
The Couple.
Father Poem.
The Feeding.
For the Barbers.
The Innocent Breasts.
Leave It to Me Blues.
The Love Bit.
Mare Nostrum.
Mathematics.
Mother Poem.
The Numbers.
The Peaches.
The Torn Nightgown.
An Undefined Tenderness.

Opper, Frederick B.
Limerick: "Sir Bedivere Bors
was a chivalrous knight."

Opperman, D. J.
Christmas Carol.
Fable.
Fable of the Speckled Cow.
Water Whirligigs.

Oppian
Halieutica.

O'Rahilly, Egan
The Brightest of the Bright.
Geraldine's Daughter.
A Grey Eye Weeping.
Inis Fal.
Lament for Banba.
Last Lines.
More Power.
On a Cock Which Was Stolen
from a Good Priest.
On a Pair of Shoes Presented
to Him (excerpt).
Reverie at Dawn.

Sleepless Night.
The Storm (excerpt).
A Time of Change.
O Rathaille, Aogan
Brightness Most Bright I
Beheld on the Way, Forlorn.
The Drenching Night Drags
On.
No Help I'll Call Till I'm Put
in the Narrow Coffin.
Valentine Browne.
The Vision.
Orban, Otto
Computer.
Hymn.
Ray.
Orde, Julian
The Changing Wind.
O'Reilly, Dowell
Sea-Grief.
O'Reilly, John Boyle
An Art Master.
At Best.
At Fredericksburg.
Boston.
A Builder's Lesson.
Chicago.
Constancy.
Crispus Attucks.
The Cry of a Dreamer.
Disappointment.
Experience.
Forever.
The Infinite.
The Lure.
Mayflower.
A Message of Peace.
Midnight–September 19, 1881.
The Ride of Collins Graves.
A Savage.
Song.
To-Day.
Wendell Phillips (excerpt).
What Is Good.
A White Rose.
O'Reilly, Pat
A Wonderful Mother.
Orente, Rose J.
The Master City.
Oresick, Peter
After the Movement.
Elmer Ruiz.
Family Portrait 1933.
"Orestes"
A Sonnet to Opium;
Celebrating Its Virtues.
Origen
He That Is Near Me Is Near
the Fire.
"Orinda" *See* **Philips, Katherine**
O Riordain, Sean
Claustrophobia.
Death.
Ice Cold.
The Moths.
O'Riordan, Conal
Care Is Heavy.
Hymn to the Virgin Mary.
Orleans, Charles d'
Alons au Bois le May Cueillir.
Ballade: "When fresshe
Phebus, day of Seynt
Valentyne."
Come, Death–My Lady Is
Dead.
Confession of a Stolen Kiss.
Dieu Qu'il la Fait.
Go, Sad Complaint.
Lost.
A Lover's Confession.
A Mistress without Compare.
Oft in My Thoughts.

Rondeau.
Rondel: "Strengthen, my
Love, this castle of my
heart."
Roundel: "My ghostly fadir,
Y me confesse."
The Smiling Mouth and
Laughing Eyen Grey.
Spring.
Well, Wanton Eye.
Orlen, Steve
The Aga Khan.
Bar Mitzvah.
Big Friend of the Stones.
The Biplane.
A Common Light.
The Drunken Man.
Family Cups.
In Praise of Beverly.
Life Study.
The Madman's Wife.
My Grandmother and the
Voice of Tolstoy.
Permission to Speak.
Orlock, Carol
Signature.
Orlovitz, Gil
Art of the Sonnet: LVI.
Orlovsky, Peter
Second Poem.
Ormond, John
At His Father's Grave.
To a Nun.
Ormsby, Frank
Amelia Street.
The Child.
Inferno: A New Circle.
Interim.
On Devenish Island.
Ornaments.
The School Hockey Team in
Amsterdam.
O'Rourke, David
For Your Inferiority Complex.
O'Rourke, May
The Stick.
Orozco, Olga
Sphinxes Inclined to Be.
Orpingalik
My Breath.
Orr, Christine
The Road.
Orr, Gregory
An Abandoned, Overgrown
Cemetery in the Pasture near
Our House.
Adolescence.
After a Death.
Beggar's Song.
The Dinner.
The Doll.
Driving Home after a Funeral.
End of August.
Gathering the Bones Together.
The Girl with 18 Nightgowns.
Haitian Suite.
A Last Address to My
Ghosts.
Like Any Other Man.
The Lost Children.
Love Poem.
Morning Song.
On the Lawn at Ira's.
Poem: "This life like no
other."
The Project.
The Room.
Silence.
Song of the Invisible Corpse
in the Field.
Spring Floods.
The Sweater.

Two Lines from the Brothers
Grimm.
The Visitor.
We Must Make a Kingdom of
It.
Orr, Patrick
Annie Shore and Johnnie
Doon.
Orred, Meta
In the Gloaming.
Ort, Daniel
Tho We All Speak.
Orten, Jiri
A Small Elegy.
Ortiz, Simon J.
Bony.
The Creation: According to
Coyote.
Crossing the Colorado River
into Yuma.
Forming Child Poems.
From Sand Creek (excerpt).
Hunger in New York City.
Indian Guys at the Bar.
Juanita, Wife of Manuelito.
My Father's Song.
My Mother and My Sisters.
A New Story.
A Pretty Woman.
A San Diego Poem: January–
February 1973.
The Serenity in Stones.
The Significance of a
Veteran's Day.
A Story of How a Wall
Stands.
Survival This Way.
To Insure Survival.
Waiting for You to Come By.
Washyuma Motor Hotel.
Watching Salmon Jump.
What I Tell Him.
Ortleb, Chuck
Some Boys.
Ortmayer, Constance
Dawn.
Orwell, George
A Dressed Man and a Naked
Man.
The Italian Soldier Shook My
Hand.
The Lesser Evil.
O'Ryan, Edmond
Ah! What Woes Are Mine.
Osadebay, Dennis C.
The African Trader's
Complaint.
Young Africa's Resolve.
Osaki, Mark
Amnesiac.
Contentment.
For Avi Killed in Lebanon.
Icon.
Turista.
Osborn, Laughton
The Death of General Pike.
Osborn, Margot
Always the Melting Moon
Comes.
Osborn, Mary Elizabeth
Alma Mater.
Come Not Near.
Exquisite Lady.
Mid-Century.
Old Man in the Park.
Rural Legend.
Thought for the Winter
Season.
Water-Images.
Osborn, Seeleck
A Modest Wit.

Osborne, Charles
So Fly by Night.
Osborne, Duffield
Ave! Nero Imperator.
Osborne, Edith D.
The Path of the Padres.
Osborne, Gene H.
Thanksgiving.
Osborne, Louis Shreve
Riding down from Bangor.
Osborne, Marian
The Trinity.
White Violet.
Osgood, Flora L.
Come unto Me.
The Cost.
Osgood, Frances Sargent
Calumny.
A Dancing Girl.
On a Dead Poet.
On Sivori's Violin.
Song.
To Sleep.
Osgood, Francis P.
Winter Fairyland in Vermont.
Osgood, Kate Putnam
Driving Home the Cows.
**O'Shaughnessy, Arthur William
Edgar**
The Appointment.
Barcarolle.
Black Marble.
Doom.
The Fair Maid and the Sun.
The Fountain of Tears.
Hath Any Loved You Well,
Down There.
If She but Knew?
The Line of Beauty.
Living Marble.
A Love Symphony.
Ode: "We are the music-
makers."
Silences.
Song: "Has summer come
without the rose."
Song: "I made another
garden, yea."
Song: "I went to her who
loveth me no more."
St. John the Baptist.
O'Shea, Diarmuid
Prayer at Dawn.
O'Sheel, Shaemas
He Whom a Dream Hath
Possessed.
The Lover Thinks of His
Lady in the North.
Mary's Baby.
They Went Forth to Battle,
but They Always Fell.
While April Rain Went By.
O-Shi-O
When I Think of the Hungry
People.
Ostenso, Martha
The Return.
Ostriker, Alicia
Anxiety about Dying.
Old Men.
Ostroff, Anthony
End of the War in Merida.
Love.
The River Glideth in a Secret
Tongue.
So Long Folks, Off to the
War.
The Sparrows at the Airport.
War.
O Suilleabhain, Eoghan Rua
A Magic Mist.

O Suilleabhain
Seamas, Light-Hearted and Loving Friend of My Breast (excerpt).

O'Sullivan, D. J.
Dawn in Inishtrahull.
Drinking Time.
The Glaucous-Gull's Death.
January.
Lament for Sean.
Moschatel.
Nightfall in Inishtrahull.

O'Sullivan, Owen Roe
To the Blacksmith with a Spade.
His Request.
Rodney's Glory.
The Volatile Kerryman.

O'Sullivan, Seumas (James Starkey)
Birds.
A Blessing on the Cows.
The Convent.
Credo.
The Half Door.
In North Great George's Street.
Lament for Sean MacDermott.
The Lamplighter.
The Land War.
Lullaby.
The Milkman.
My Sorrow.
Nelson Street.
The Others.
A Piper.
Praise.
Rain.
The Sedges.
The Sheep.
Sketch.
Splendid and Terrible.
The Starling Lake.
The Twilight People.

O'Sullivan, Vincent
Brother Jonathan, Brother Kafka (excerpt).
Bus Stop.
Further Instructions.
Late Lunch, San Antonio.
Talking to Her.

Otey, Harold LaMont
Birthday on Deathrow.
Haywood.
Lamentation.
Red White & Another Ism.
Tree.

Otomo of Sakanoe, Lady
The Dress That My Brother Has Put on Is Thin.
My brother has on a thin robe.
My Heart, Thinking.
Sent from the Capital to Her Elder Daughter.
Unknown Love.
You Say, "I Will Come."

Otsuji
Haiku: "into a forest."
Haiku: "Winter midnight."

Otto, Heinrich
Lord, Dear God! To Thy Attending.

O'Tuomy, John
O'Tuomy's Drinking Song.

Otway, Thomas
Come, All Ye Youths.
The Enchantment.

Ou-yang Hsiu
The Cicada.
Green Jade Plum Trees in Spring.

Oumar Ba
Drought.

Ousley, Clarence
When the Mint Is in the Liquor.

Ouston, Hugh
The Climber Surveys His Mountain.

Outlaw, Randolph
720 Gabriel St.
Down Home.
Still Life.
Tennesse Crickets.
Visit.
White Whales Specked Black.

Outram, George
The Annuity.
On Hearing a Lady Praise a Certain Reverend Doctor's Eyes.
Strictures on the Economy of Nature.

Overbury, E. J.
The Springtime It Brings on the Shearing.

Overstreet, Bonaro W.
Count Ten.
First Day of Teaching.

Overton, A. M.
He Maketh No Mistake.

Overton, Ron
Sharks.

Ovid (Publius Ovidius Naso)
Amores.
The Art of Love.
Atalanta.
A Captive of Love.
The Complaisant Swain.
Constant Penelope Sends to Thee, Careless Ulysses.
Elegies.
Heroides: Oenone to Paris (excerpt).
Invective against Ibis (excerpt).
Lente, Lente.
Love, as a Warrior Lord.
Metamorphoses.
De Ponto.
Pyramus and Thisbe.
Shameful Impotence: Book III, Elegia VII.
To Cypassis, Corinna's Maid.
To Graecinus, on Loving Two Women at Once.
To His Mistress.
Tristium.
Winter at Tomi.

Owen, Gareth
Winter Days.

Owen, Gronwy
The Invitation (abridged).

Owen, Guy
Poem to a Mule, Dead Twenty Years.
The White Stallion.

Owen, J. Elgar
Maturity.

Owen, Maureen
African Sunday.
For Emily (Dickinson).
A Heart That's Been Broken.
Novembers or Straight Life.
Some Days.
Three Mile Island.

Owen, Sue
Lullaby.
The Owl.

Owen, Wilfred
Antaeus: A Fragment.
Anthem for Doomed Youth.
Apologia Pro Poemate Meo.
Arms and the Boy.
Asleep.
At a Calvary Near the Ancre.
The Chances.
Le Christianisme.
Conscious.
Disabled.
Dulce et Decorum Est.
The End.
Exposure.
Fragment: I Saw His Round Mouth's Crimson...
From My Diary, July 1914.
Futility.
Greater Love.
Hospital Barge at Cerisy.
Insensibility.
Inspection.
Mental Cases.
Miners.
The Next War.
The Parable of the Old Man and the Young.
The Roads Also.
The Send-Off.
The Sentry.
Shadwell Stair.
The Show.
The Sleeping Beauty.
Soldier's Dream.
Song of Songs.
Sonnet to My Friend, with an Identity Disc.
Spring Offensive.
Strange Meeting.
A Terre.
The Unreturning.

Owens, Rochelle
Between the Karim Shahir.
Chugachimute I Love the Name.
Dance & Eye Me (Wicked)ly My Breath a Fixed Sphere.
Evolution.
Man As He Shall Be.
Medieval Christ Speaks on a Spanish Sculpture of Himself.
The Power of Love He Wants Shih (Everything).
Strawberries Mit Cream.
Woman Par Excellence.

Owens, Vilda Sauvage
The Passing of the Unknown Soldier.

Ower, John
Cudworth's Undergraduate Ode to a Bare Behind.
The Gingerbread House.

Owl Woman
Songs for the Four Parts of the Night.

Oxenham, John
After Work.
Art Thou Lonely?
Bide a Wee!
The Christ.
Credo.
The Day–The Way.
Everymaid.
Face to Face with Reality.
For Beauty, We Thank Thee.
The Goal and the Way.
God's Sunshine.
Gratitude for Work.
In Christ.
Influence.
Judgment Day.
The Key.
Life's Chequer-Board.
The Little Poem of Life.
A Little Te Deum of the Commonplace (excerpt).
Live Christ.
Love.
Love's Prerogative.
No East or West.
Paul.
Per Ardua ad Astra.
A Prayer.
The Prince of Life.
Props.
The Sacrament of Sleep.
Seeds.
So Little and So Much.
Some Blesseds.
Thanksgiving.
To Whom Shall the World Henceforth Belong?
The Valley of Decision.
The Ways.
We Thank Thee.
Where Are You Going, Greatheart?
Whirring Wheels.
Your Place.

Oyama, Richard
The Day after Trinity.
Dreams in Progress.
Obon by the Hudson.
This Song Shows Me Pictures: Morningside Drive, New York City...

Ozerov, Lev
Babi Yar.

Ozick, Cynthia
A Riddle.
The Wonder-Teacher.

P

"P., A. B."
Limerick: "Said the mouse with scholastical hat."

"P., F. B."
O Mother Dear, Jerusalem.

"P.S.M."
Dawn.

Pace, Charles Nelson
The Cross.

Pacernick, Gary
Babel.
I Want to Write a Jewish Poem.
Labor Day.

Pacheco, Jose Emilio
Cave.

Pack, Richardson
An Epistle from a Half-Pay Officer in the Country.

Pack, Robert
Adam on His Way Home.
Anecdote of the Sparrow.
A Bird in Search of a Cage.
The Boat.
Chopping Fire-Wood.
Cleaning the Fish.
Departing Words to a Son.
The Departure.
Descending.
Don't Sit under the Apple Tree with Anyone Else but Me!
The Election.
Everything Is Possible.
The Faithful Lover.
Father.
The Frog Prince.
An Idyl in Idleness.
In a Field.
The Kiss.

The Mugger.
On the Seventh Anniversary
of the Death of My Father.
The Pack Rat.
Parable.
Poem for You.
Raking Leaves.
Resurrection.
The Ring.
Self-Portrait.
The Shooting.
Waiting.
The Way We Wonder.
The Weasel.
Packard, Frederick
Balearic Idyll.
Packard, William
Haircut.
Packard, Winthrop
The Shoogy-Shoo.
Paddock, Nancy
That First Gulp of Air We
All Took When First Born.
Padeshah Khatun
Sovereign Queen.
Padgett, Ron
After the Broken Arm.
December.
Detach, Invading.
The Elms Dispatch.
The Farmer's Head.
High Heels.
Homage to Max Jacob.
Joe Brainard's Painting
"Bingo".
Louisiana Perch.
Love Poem.
A Man Saw a Ball of Gold.
Ode to Bohemians.
Orange Jews.
The Sandwich Man.
Some Bombs (excerpt).
Strawberries in Mexico.
Voice.
Paff, Eric W.
On Sitting up Late, Watching
Kittens.
Pagan, Isobel
Ca' the Yowes to the Knowes.
Pagaza, Joaquin A.
Twilight.
Page, B. Sanford
All Songs.
Page, Geoff
Coloratura.
Country Nun.
Page, Irene
Jane, Do Be Careful.
Page, P. K.
Adolescence.
After Rain.
Arras.
A Backwards Journey.
The Bands and the Beautiful
Children.
Brazilian Fazenda.
The Crow.
Cullen.
Element.
Evening Dance of the Grey
Flies.
Landlady.
Man with One Small Hand.
The Permanent Tourists.
Photos of a Salt Mine.
Sailor.
Schizophrenic.
The Snowman.
The Stenographers.
Stories of Snow.
Summer.
Summer Resort.

T-Bar.
Page, Thomas Nelson
Ashcake.
The Dragon of the Seas.
Uncle Gabe's White Folks.
Page, William
Painlessly out of Ourselves.
Paget-Fredericks, J.
Pipings.
Pagis, Dan
Autobiography.
Brothers.
Draft of a Reparations
Agreement.
The Grand Duke of New
York.
Hide and Seek.
Instructions for Crossing the
Border.
The Last Ones.
Scrawled in Pencil in a Sealed
Railway Car.
The Tower.
Pagliarani, Elio
It's Already Autumn.
Pagnucci, Gianfranco
The Death of an Elephant.
Pai Wei
Madrid.
Pain, Barry
Browning at Tea.
Burns at Tea.
Cowper at Tea.
Macaulay at Tea.
Martin Luther at Potsdam.
Oh! Weary Mother.
Poe at Tea.
The Poets at Tea.
Ride a Cock Horse (parody).
Rossetti at Tea.
Swinburne at Tea.
Tennyson at Tea.
Wordsworth at Tea.
Pain, Philip
Meditation.
Meditations for August 1,
1666.
Meditations for July 19, 1666.
Meditations for July 25, 1666.
Meditations for July 26, 1666.
The Porch.
Whilst in This World I Stay.
Paine, Albert Bigelow
The Cooky-Nut Trees (A Tale
of the Pilliwinks).
The Dancing Bear.
The Hills of Rest.
In Louisiana.
The Little Child.
Mis' Smith.
Paine, Carol
Color Blind.
Paine, Robert Treat
Adams and Liberty.
Paine, Theodora L.
Danger.
Paine, Thomas
Liberty Tree.
Painter, John R.
A Bob-Tailed Flush.
Paitzakow, Louis W.
Take Back Your Gold.
Palagyi, Louis
Aimless.
Palea
Piano at Evening.
Palen, Jennie M.
Early Dutch.
To a Race Horse at Ascot.
Palen, John
Missouri Town.

Palés Matos, Luis
Doorway to Time in Three
Voices.
Elegy for the Duke of
Marmalade.
Kalahari.
Neither This Nor That.
San Sabas.
The Well.
Paley, Grace
The Women in Vietnam.
Paley, Morton
Theodore Roethke.
Palfrey, Sarah Hammond
The Pilgrim.
Palgrave, Francis Turner
The City of God.
Crecy.
Eutopia.
God Save Elizabeth!
Trafalgar.
Palladas
Grammar Commences with a
5-line Curse.
Loving the Rituals That Keep
Men Close.
Naked I Came.
On Maurus the Rhetor.
Poems from a Greek
Anthology (excerpt).
Poor Devil That I Am, Being
So Attacked.
Praise of Women.
Racing, Reckoning Fingers
Flick.
This Life a Theater.
Vanity of Vanities.
When You Send Out
Invitations, Don't Ask Me.
Pallen, Conde B.
Christus Triumphans.
Pallottini, Renata
Message.
Palmanteer, Ted D.
Granma's Words.
Pass it on grandson.
Palmer, Alice Freeman
The Butterfly.
A Communion Hymn.
Hallowed Places.
On a Gloomy Easter.
A Spring Journey.
Palmer, David
Plato Instructs a Midwest
Farmer.
Palmer, E. H.
The Parterre.
The Shipwreck.
Palmer, Herbert
Aunt Zillah Speaks.
Ishmael.
Nature in War-Time.
Prayer for Rain.
Rock Pilgrim.
Woodworker's Ballad.
The Wounded Hawk.
Palmer, John E.
The Band Played On.
Palmer, John Williamson
The Fight at San Jacinto.
For Charlie's Sake.
The Maryland Battalion.
Ned Braddock.
Reid at Fayal.
Stonewall Jackson's Way.
Theodosia Burr.
Palmer, Michael
Alogon.
Baudelaire Series (excerpt).
Changes around the Bay.
The Classical Style.
The Comet.

Dearest Reader.
Documentation.
Notes for Echo Lake 5.
Notes for Echo Lake 11.
On the Way to Language.
Song of the Round Man.
Symmetrical Poem.
The Theory of the Flower.
The Classical Style.
View from an Apartment.
The Village of Reason.
Voice and Address.
Palmer, Miriam
Raccoon Poem.
"Vierge Ouvrante."
What If Jealousy...
Palmer, Nettie
The Mother.
Palmer, Ray
Faith.
I Give My Heart to Thee.
I Saw Thee.
Jesus, These Eyes Have Never
Seen.
Lord, My Weak Thought in
Vain Would Climb.
My Faith Looks Up to Thee.
O Jesus! Sweet the Tears I
Shed.
Palmer, Samuel
Shoreham: Twilight Time.
Palmer, Vance
The Farmer Remembers the
Somme.
The Snake.
Palmer, William
The Smack in School.
Palmer, Winthrop
Arlington Cemetery Looking
toward the Capitol.
Palquera, Shem-Tob
Adapt Thyself.
The Mouth and the Ears.
Paman, Clement
On Christmas Day.
Pan Chao
Needle and Thread.
Pan Chieh-yu
A Present from the Emperor's
New Concubine.
Panatattu
True Knowledge.
The Unity of God.
Pankey, Eric
Renaming the Evening.
Panormitanus
Rome.
Pape, Greg
For Rosa Yen, Who Lived
Here.
In the City of Bogota.
La Llorona.
Mercado.
My Happiness.
October.
The Porpoise.
Sharks, Caloosahatchee River.
Papenhausen, Carol
Album.
**Paradise, Caroline Wilder
(Fellowes)**
Little Theocritus.
Paramore., Edward E., Jr.
The Ballad of Yukon Jake.
Paraone, Tiwai
Chant to Io.
Paraske, Larin
My Little Love Lies on the
Ground.
Sad Is the Seagull.
A Woman Grows Soon Old.

Paravicino y Arteaga, Hortensio Felis
The Divine Passion.
Parham, Robert
Sunday in South Carolina.
Parini, Jay
Amores.
The Missionary Visits Our Church in Scranton.
Snake Hill.
Tanya.
To His Dear Friend, Bones.
Parish, Michell
Star Dust.
Parisi, Philip
Niagara Falls.
Park, Roswell
Jesus Spreads His Banner O'er Us.
Parke, Walter
His Mother-in-Law.
Limerick: "There was a princess of Bengal."
Limerick: "There was a young man who was bitten."
Limerick: "There was an old stupid who wrote."
Parker, Dorothy
Ballade of a Talked-Off Ear.
Ballade of Big Plans.
Ballade of Unfortunate Mammals.
Bohemia.
A Certain Lady.
Chant for Dark Hours.
Coda.
Comment.
The Counselor.
The Crusader.
The Danger of Writing Defiant Verse.
The Dark Girl's Rhyme.
Dilemma.
The Evening Primrose.
Experience.
Fable.
Fair Weather.
Fighting Words.
The Flaw in Paganism.
From a Letter from Lesbia.
Frustration.
The Gentlest Lady.
George Sand.
Godmother.
Interior.
Inteview.
Inventory.
The Little Old Lady in Lavender Silk.
Love Song.
Men.
News Item.
Observation.
Of a Woman, Dead Young.
On Being a Woman.
One Perfect Rose.
Partial Comfort.
Philosophy.
Pictures in the Smoke.
De Produndis.
Prologue to a Saga.
Resume.
Sanctuary.
Social Note.
Song of Perfect Propriety.
Sonnet for the End of a Sequence.
Story.
Symptom Recital.
Theory.
They Part.
Threnody.

Tombstones in the Starlight.
Two-Volume Novel.
Unfortunate Coincidence.
Verse for a Certain Dog.
Walter Savage Landor.
Parker, Edwin Pond
Master, No Offering.
Parker, Julia Benson
The Perfect Gift.
Parker, Martin
A Description of a Strange (and Miraculous) Fish.
Keep a Good Tongue in Your Head...
The King Enjoys His Own Again.
The Maunding Soldier.
Saylors for My Money.
When the King Enjoys His Own Again.
The Wooing Maid.
Parker, Patricia
From the Cavities of Bones.
I Followed a Path.
There Is a Woman in This Town.
Parker, Sir Gilbert
Reunited.
The World in Making.
Parker, Stephen
Winter in Etienburgh.
Parker, Stewart
Chicago Allegory.
Health.
Three Fitts.
Parker, Theodore
The Higher Good.
Jesus.
The Way, the Truth, and the Life.
Parkes, Francis Ernest Kobina
Apocalypse.
Blind Steersmen.
Three Phases of Africa.
Parkes, Frank
African Heaven.
Parkes, Henry
Our Coming Countrymen.
Parkwood, Rose
The Garden.
Parlatore, Anselm
Accommodation.
Although in a Crystal.
Cancer Research.
Family Chronicle.
Lovely Girls with Flounder on a Starry Night.
Parmenter, Catherine
Christmas Eve.
Silent Testimony.
Parnell, Fanny
After Death.
Parnell, Thomas
An Elegy, to an Old Beauty.
The Hermit.
A Hymn to Contentment.
A Night-Piece on Death.
The Small Silver-Coloured Bookworm.
Song.
Song: "When thy Beauty appears."
Parnell, Thomas and Alexander Pope
On Riding to See Dean Swift in the Mist of the Morning.
Parone, Edward
The Morning Track.
Parra, Nicanor
Beggar.
I Move the Meeting Be Adjourned.

Seven.
We Let It Go That He Was a Perfect Man.
Young Poets.
Parrish, Elsie
Some Things That Easter Brings.
Parrish, John
The Democratic Barber; or, Country Gentleman's Surprise.
Parrish, Randall
Your Lad, and My Lad.
Parrot, Henry
Fatales Poetae.
In Obitum Promi.
On a Poet.
Parrott, E. O.
Ode on a Grecian Urn (parody).
Parry, David Fisher
The Bachelor's Ballade.
Miniver Cheevy, Jr. (parody).
Parry, Edward Abbott
I Would Like You for a Comrade.
The Jam Fish.
Pater's Bathe.
Parry, Joseph
New Friends and Old Friends.
Parry, Robert
Except I Love.
Song: "Fond affection, hence, and leave me!"
Parson, Tom
Meeting at the Local.
The Victory of the Battle of Wounded Knee.
Parsons, Clere
Difference.
Introduction.
Parsons, Kitty
My Valentine.
Parsons, Thomas William
Andrew.
Dirge.
Dirge: For One Who Fell in Battle.
Her Epitaph.
Into the Noiseless Country.
"Like as the Lark."
Mary Booth.
O Ye Sweet Heavens!
Obituary.
On a Bust of Dante.
Paradisi Gloria.
Saint Peray.
To a Lady: With a Head of Diana.
To a Young Girl Dying.
Parsons, William
Epigram on the Play-House at Amsterdam.
Epigram: The Man of Taste.
Ode to the Lake of Geneva.
On Descending the River Po.
To a Friend in Love during the Riots.
Partridge, Sybil F.
Just for To-day.
Partridge, William Ordway
Nathan Hale.
Parun, Vesna
Mother of Man.
A Return to the Tree of Time.
Parvin, Betty
Edwardian Hat.
Pascal, Paul
Tact.
Pasolini, Pier Paolo
To a Pope.

Tuesday, 4 March (Morning) 1963.
Pass, John
Junction.
Theresa.
Passerat, Jean
Love in May.
Song: "Shephard loveth thow me vell?"
Passy, Nancy
Listening.
Pastan, Linda
After Reading Nelly Sachs.
After X-Ray.
April.
At the Jewish Museum.
The City.
Death's Blue-Eyed Girl.
Dido's Farewell.
Elsewhere.
Ethics.
In the Old Guerilla War.
Jump Cabling.
Love Letter.
Marks.
Old Woman.
Pears.
Poet.
A Real Story.
Secrets.
September.
A Symposium: Apples.
Waiting for E. gularis.
Whom Do You Visualize as Your Reader?
Why Not?
Writing While My Father Dies.
Yom Kippur.
Pasternak, Boris
The Caucasus.
The Cocks.
Definition of the Soul.
Evil Days.
Fresh Paint.
"Garden of Gethsemane."
Hamlet in Russia, A Soliloquy.
Here the Trace.
Hops.
In the Breeze.
Magdalene.
May It Be.
Out of Superstition.
Poem: "So they begin."
September.
Sparrow Hills.
Spring.
Three Variations.
Waving a Bough.
The Wedding (1957).
Winter Night.
Paston, Linda
Grammar Lesson.
Pastorius, Francis Daniel
As Often as Some Where before My Feet.
Delight in Books from Evening.
Epigrams.
Extract the Quint-essence.
Great God, Preserver of All Things.
I Have a Pretty Little Flow'r.
If Any Be Pleased to Walk into My Poor Garden...
If Thou Wouldest Roses Scent.
Learn, Lads and Lasses.
Most Weeds, Whilst Young.
On His Garden Book.
Though My Thoughts.

Thy Garden, Orchard, Fields.
To God Alone, the Only
  Donour.
When I Solidly Do Ponder.
When One or Other Rambles.
Patchen, Kenneth
  All the Roary Night.
  And What with the
    Blunders...
  The Animal I Wanted.
  As We Are So Wonderfully
    Done with Each Other.
  At the New Year.
  Because Going Nowhere
    Takes a Long Time.
  Because He Liked to Be at
    Home.
  Because in This Sorrowing
    Statue of Flesh.
  Because Sometimes You Can't
    Always Be So.
  Because They Were Very Poor
    That Winter.
  Behold, One of Several Little
    Christs...
  Biography of Southern Rain.
  The Character of Love Seen
    as a Search for the Lost.
  The Constant Bridegrooms.
  The Deer and the Snake.
  Do the Dead Know What
    Time It Is?
  An Easy Decision.
  Elegy for the Silent Voices
    and the Joiners of
    Everything.
  Empty Dwelling Places.
  The Everlasting Contenders.
  Fog.
  The Fox.
  From My High Love.
  Gautama in the Deer Park at
    Benares.
  The Hunted City, V.
  I'd Want Her Eyes to Fill
    with Wonder.
  I Have Lighted the Candles,
    Mary.
  I Went to the City.
  In Judgment of the Leaf.
  In Memory of Kathleen.
  In Order To.
  In the Footsteps of the
    Walking Air.
  The Journal of Albion
    Moonlight (excerpt).
  The Known Soldier.
  Like a Mourningless Child.
  The Lions of Fire Shall Have
    Their Hunting.
  The Little Green Blackbird.
  The Magical Mouse.
  Midnight Special.
  The Naked Land.
  Nice Day for a Lynching.
  A Note on The Hunted City,
    1939-1967.
  O All Down within the Pretty
    Meadow.
  O My Love the Pretty Towns.
  O Now the Drenched Land
    Wakes.
  O Terrible Is the Highest
    Thing.
  The Orange Bears.
  The Origin of Baseball.
  Pastoral.
  The Reason for Skylarks.
  Saturday Night in the
    Parthenon.
  Street Corner College.
  A Temple.

There Is Nothing False in
  Thee.
A Trueblue Gentleman.
Twenty-third Street Runs into
  Heaven.
The Village Tudda.
We Go out Together.
What There Is.
Where?
Where Two O'Clock Came
  From.
Pater, Walter
  Mona Lisa.
Paterson, A. B.
  Old Man Platypus.
  Weary Will.
Paterson, Andrea
  Because I Could Not Dump
    (parody).
**Paterson, Andrew Barton
  ("Banjo")**
  A Bush Christening.
  A Bushman's Song.
  Clancy of the Overflow.
  Father Riley's Horse.
  The Man from Ironbark.
  The Man from Snowy River.
  Old Australian Ways.
  The Road to Hogan's Gap.
  Song of the Artesian Water.
  The Travelling Post Office.
Paterson, Evangeline
  And That Will Be Heaven.
  Armaments Race.
  Death on a Crossing.
  Parting from My Son.
Patey, Tom
  The Last of the Grand Old
    Masters.
  Macinnes's Mountain Patrol.
Patmore, Coventry
  Across the Sky the Daylight
    Crept.
  The Amaranth.
  The Angel in the House.
  Auras of Delight.
  The Azalea.
  The Barren Shore.
  The Child's Purchase.
  Courtesy.
  Dartmoor.
  Deliciae Sapientiae de Amore.
  Epigram: "Save by the Old
    Road none attain the new."
  Epigram: "Science, the agile
    ape, may well."
  Epitaph: "How fair a flower is
    sown."
  Faint Yet Pursuing.
  A Farewell.
  The First Spousal.
  The Flesh-Fly and the Bee.
  Going to Church.
  If I Were Dead.
  The Joyful Wisdom.
  King William's Dispatch to
    Queen Augusta...
  The Kiss.
  Legem Tuam Dilexi.
  A London Fete.
  Love at Large.
  Love in Action.
  Love Serviceable.
  Magna Est Veritas.
  Pain in All Love.
  Parting.
  Perspective.
  Preludes.
  Prophets Who Cannot Sing.
  The Rainbow.
  Regina Coeli.
  Remembered Grace.

The Rosy Bosom'd Hours.
Saint Valentine's Day.
Sensuality.
The Shadow of Night.
Shame.
The Storm.
Tamerton Church-Tower; or,
  First Love.
Too soon, too soon comes
  Death to show.
Truth.
'Twas When the Spousal Time
  of May.
The Two Deserts.
The Unknown Eros.
The Victories of Love.
A Warning.
Wind and Wave.
Woman.
Paton, Alan
  I Have Approached.
  The Prison House.
Patrick, Bishop
  An Invocation.
Patrick, Johnstone G.
  Closing Prayer.
  Grace.
  Prayer for Peace.
Patrick, Luther
  Sleepin' at the Foot O' the
    Bed.
Patrick, Saint
  The Deer's Cry.
  God's Blessing on Munster.
Patten, Brian
  After Frost.
  The Beast.
  Little Johnny's Confession.
  Ode on Celestial Music.
  Party Piece.
  Portrait of a Young Girl
    Raped at a Suburban Party.
  A Small Dragon.
  Through All Your Abstract
    Reasoning.
  Where Are You Now
    Superman?
Patten, Karl
  Mr. Secretary.
  Wreathmakertraining.
Patterson, Charles
  Listen.
Patterson, Lindsay
  At Long Last.
Patterson, Raymond Richard
  The Accident.
  At That Moment.
  Birmingham 1963.
  Black All Day.
  I've Got a Home in That
    Rock.
  In Time of Crisis.
  Letter in Winter.
  A Love Song.
  Night-Piece.
  Riot Rhymes U.S.A. (excerpt).
  When I Awoke.
  You Are the Brave.
Pattison, William
  Ad Coelum.
  The Unfortunate Reminder.
Patton, Charlie
  34 Blues.
  Bird Nest Bound.
  Hang It on the Wall.
  High Sheriff Blues.
  High Water Everywhere.
  Moon Going Down.
  Revenue Man Blues.
Patton, G. W.
  The Emigrant's Dying Child.

Patton, Margaret French
  Needle Travel.
Patton, Patti
  Birthday Party.
Pau-Llosa, Ricardo
  Links.
Pauker, Ted
  Garland for a Propagandist.
  A Grouchy Good Night to
    the Academic Year.
  Limeraiku: "There's a vile old
    man."
  A Trifle for Trafalgar Day.
Paul, Dorothy
  The Captive Ships at Manila.
  Figurehead.
Paul, James
  Everything.
  Feet, a Sermon.
  Honeysuckle.
  This Town.
  The Water Tower.
"Paul, John" *See* **Webb, Charles
  Henry**
Paul, Louis
  Cynical Portraits.
Paulding, James Kirke
  Ode to Jamestown.
  The Old Man's Carousal.
Paulin, Tom
  Anastasia McLaughlin.
  And Where Do You Stand on
    the National Question?
  Arthur.
  Ballywaire.
  The Book of Juniper.
  Cadaver Politic.
  Descendancy.
  Desertmartin.
  Evening Harbour.
  From.
  The Hyperboreans.
  Inishkeel Parish Church.
  Manichean Geography I.
  Newness.
  Of Difference Does It Make.
  Off the Back of a Lorry.
  The Other Voice.
  Personal Column.
  Politik.
  A Rum Cove, a Stout Cove.
  Settlers.
  Song for February.
  States.
  Still Century.
  Thinking of Iceland.
  Where Art Is a Midwife.
  A Written Answer.
Paulinus of Nola
  To Ausonius.
Paulus Silentiarius
  Epigram: "Kissing
    Hippomenes."
  No Matter.
  United.
Pavlich, Walter
  Revisiting the Field.
Pavlova, Karolina
  To Madame A. V. Pletneff.
Paxton, Jean Grigsby
  Preparedness.
Paxton, Tom
  I Can't Help but Wonder
    Where I'm Bound.
  My Ramblin' Boy.
  We Didn't Know.
Payn, James
  I never had a piece of toast.
Payne, Anne Blackwell
  Silver Sheep.
Payne, John
  Kyrielle.

A Merry Ballad of Vintners.
Of Three Damsels in a
Meadow.
Rococo.
Rondeau Redouble.
Payne, John Howard
Home, Sweet Home.
Payne, William Morton
El Blot Til Lyst.
Incipit Vita Nova.
Lohengrin.
Tannhauser.
Paz, Octavio
Landscape.
The Street.
Touch.
Peabody, Josephine Preston
After Music.
Caravans.
A Changeling Grateful.
Cradle Song.
A Far-Off Rose.
The House and the Road.
Hymn.
Isolation.
A Man's Bread.
Prelude.
Rubric.
The Singing Man.
Song of a Shepherd Boy at
Bethlehem.
Sonnet in a Garden.
Spinning in April.
To a Dog.
Wood-Song.
Peabody, William Bourne Oliver
Lament of Anastasius.
Peace, Angela
Indian Mounds.
Peach, Arthur Wallace
Cap'n.
The Mosaic Worker.
O Youth with Blossoms
Laden.
The Secret.
Peacham, Henry
Nuptial Hymn.
Peacock, Molly
Just About Asleep Together.
The Lull.
Now Look What Happened.
Old Roadside Resorts.
So, When I Swim to the
Shore.
Two Figures.
Peacock, Thomas Love
Andonis, My Daughter.
Beech and Oak.
Beneath the Cypress Shade.
A Border Ballad (parody).
Castles in the Air.
Chorus: "Hail to the
Headlong!"
Chorus: "If I drink water
while this doth last."
Crochet Castle.
Crotchet Castle.
Earth Song.
Epitaph.
The Fate of a Broom—An
Anticipation.
Fear.
For the Children.
The Friar.
Glee—The Ghosts.
The Grave of Love.
The Grey Friar.
In Respect of the Elderly.
In the Days of Old.
The Indignation of Taliesin.
A Letter from School.
Lines from Crotchet Castle.

Love and Age.
Margaret Love Peacock.
Merlin's Apple-Trees.
The Misfortunes of Elphin:
The War-Song of Dinas
Vawr.
A New Order of Chivalry.
Newark Abbey.
Nightmare Abbey: Three Men
of Gotham.
Not Drunk Is He.
The Priest and the Mulberry
Tree.
Rhododaphne.
Rich and Poor; or, Saint and
Sinner.
Seamen Three.
Six Eagles.
Song by Mr. Cypress.
Song: "For the tender beech
and the sapling oak."
Song: "In his last bin Sir
Peter lies."
Song: "It was a friar of orders
free."
Song of Gwythno.
The Song of the Four Winds.
The Sun-Dial.
The World.
Peake, Mervyn
My Uncle Paul of Pimlico.
Peale, Rembrandt
Don't Be Sorrowful, Darling.
Pearce, Ellen
The Orange Tree.
The Turtle's Belly.
Pearce, J.
Heaving the Lead.
Pearce, Norman V.
Blind.
Pearse, Mark Guy
Don't Trouble Trouble.
Facing the New Year.
Pearse, Padraic
The Fool.
Ideal.
Lullaby of the Woman of the
Mountain.
The Mother.
Renunciation.
The Rebel.
To Death.
The Wayfarer.
Peavy, Linda
Riders.
Wisdom.
Peck, Elisabeth
Between the Walls of the
Valley.
Walthena.
Peck, Harry Thurston
Heliotrope.
The Other One.
Wonderland.
Peck, John
Cider and Vesalius.
Colophon for Lan-t'ing Hsiu-
Hsi.
Here Is a Song.
In Front of a Japanese
Photograph.
A Quarrel.
The Ringers.
Rowing Early.
The Spring Festival on the
River.
The Watcher.
What If the Saint Must Die.
Peck, Kathryn Blackburn
The Carpenter's Son.
The Lord of Heaven to Earth
Came Down.

Rejoice! He Liveth!
Peck, Samuel Minturn
Autumn's Mirth.
The Captain's Feather.
A Kiss in the Rain.
My Little Girl.
Sassafras.
A Southern Girl.
Pedroso, Regino
Opinions of the New Student.
Peele, George
And Who Has Seen a Fair
Alluring Face.
Celanta at the Well of Life.
David and Bethsabe.
Fair and Fair.
A Farewell to Arms.
A Farewell to Sir John Norris
and Sir Francis Drake.
Hot Sunne, Coole Fire,
Temperd with Sweet Aire.
Not Iris in Her Pride.
O Gentle Love.
Oenone's Complaint.
The Old Knight.
The Old Wife's Tale.
Polyhymnia: His Golden
Lock.
The Shepherd's Dirge.
A Sonet: "His Golden lockes,
Time hath to Silver turn'd."
Song of Coridon and
Melampus.
Song of Oenone and Paris.
Strive No More.
What Thing Is Love.
Peerson, Martin
Madrigal: "Since just disdain."
Madrigal: "The spring of joy
is dry."
Madrigal: "Where shall I
sorrow great."
Peguy, Charles
Happy Are Those Who Have
Died.
The Mystery of the Innocent
Saints (excerpt).
Night (excerpts).
The Passion of Our Lady.
Peifer, Mrs. Roy L.
Crucifixion.
Pellew, George
Death.
On a Cast from an Antique.
Pellow, J. D. C.
The Temple of the Trees.
Peloubet, Maurice E.
The Eternal Kinship.
**Pembroke, Mary Herbert,
Countess of**
Of Death.
Psalm 62. Donne Deo.
Psalm CXXXIX.
Wondrous Love.
**Pembroke, William Herbert,
Earl of**
Disdain Me Still.
A Paradox.
Pence, Susan
Night Harvest.
Pendergast, James
Before the War.
Penfold, Gerda
The Lust for Murder.
La Pesadilla.
Penkethman, John
A Schoolmaster's Precepts.
Some Boys.
Pennant, Edmund
Hold My Hand.
Into & At.
Lost Explorer.

Pennecuik, Alexander
A Marriage Betwixt Scrape,
Monarch of the
Maunders...(excerpt).
Pennell, Henry Cholmondeley
See **Cholmondeley-Pennell,
Henry**
Pennington, Lee
Before the Breaking.
Penny, Rob
And We Conquered.
He Cool, Baby.
I Remember How She Sang.
The Real People Loves One
Another.
Penny, W. E.
The Town of Nogood.
Penrose, Roland
The Road Is Wider Than
Long (excerpt).
Penrose, Thomas
The Helmets, a Fragment.
Percival, James Gates
Apostrophe to the Island of
Cuba.
The Coral Grove.
Elegiac.
It Is Great for Our Country
to Die.
New England.
Seneca Lake.
Percy, Thomas
The Friar of Orders Gray.
O Nancy! Wilt Thou Go With
Me?
A Song.
Percy, William
Relent, My Deere, Yet
Unkind Coelia.
Sonnet: "It shall be said I
died for Coelia!"
Percy, William Alexander
Dirge.
Epilogue (excerpt).
Farmers.
Hymn to the Sun.
In an Autumn Wood.
A Little Page's Song.
The Little Shepherd's Song.
Overtones.
A Page's Road Song.
They Cast Their Nets in
Galilee.
To an Old Tune.
To Butterfly.
The Unloved to His Beloved.
A Volunteer's Grave.
Wonder and a Thousand
Springs.
Pereira, Francesca Yetunde
The Burden.
Mother Dark.
The Paradox.
Two Strange Worlds.
Peret, Benjamin
Little Song of the Maimed.
Making Feet and Hands.
The Staircase with a Hundred
Steps.
Peretz, Isaac L.
All through the Stranger's
Wood.
Believe Not.
Eternal Sabbath.
Hope and Faith.
In the Silent Night.
Little People.
The Three Seamstresses.
Perez-Diotima, Leigh
Lake Walk at New Year's.
Perkins, David
The Blue Gift.

Falling in Love.
How Long Hast Thou Been a
  Gravemaker?
Perkins, Emily Swan
  Thou Art, O God, the God of
    Might.
Perkins, James A.
  Black Holes.
Perkins, Louis Saunders
  Genius.
Perkins, Lucy Alice
  Laborers Together with God.
Perkins, Lucy Fitch
  Honey Bee.
Perkins, Michael
  The Carpenter.
Perkins, Silas H.
  The Common Road.
Perkoff, Stuart
  Feasts of Death, Feasts of
    Love.
Perkoff, Stuart Z.
  Aleph.
  Flowers for Luis Bunuel.
  Gimel.
  Hai.
  The Recluses.
Perlberg, Mark M.
  Hiroshige.
  When at Night.
Perlin, Terry M.
  The Clarity of Apples.
Perlman, Anne S.
  At Liberty.
  The Specialist.
  Viking 1 on Mars–July 20,
    1976.
Perlman, Jess
  Winterscape.
Perpetuo, Betty
  A Morning Prayer.
Perreault, Ellen
  Those Trees That Line the
    Northway.
Perreault, John
  Boomerang.
  Disguised.
  Forty Years Ago.
  Friends.
  High.
  The Metaphysical Paintings.
  No One in Particular.
  The Nude Republic.
  Readymade.
  Shoe.
  Talk.
Perronet, Edward
  All Hail the Power of Jesus'
    Name.
  Coronation.
Perry, Georgette
  Recognition.
Perry, Gordon
  Aids for Latin.
  The Great Lakes of Canada.
Perry, Grace
  Time of Turtles.
Perry, Julianne
  No Dawns.
  To L.
Perry, Lilla Cabot
  Art.
  Life and Death.
  Meeting After Long Absence.
Perry, Martha Eugenie
  The Lonely Shell.
  The Mainspring.
  The Water-Witch.
Perry, Nora
  Balboa.
  The Coming of Spring.
  Cressid.

In June.
The Love-Knot.
Next Year.
Riding Down.
Running the Blockade.
Some Day or Days.
Too Late.
Perry, Ronald
  Prologue for a Bestiary.
  The Shellpicker.
  Still-Life.
Perry, Thomas
  The Antarctic Muse.
Perry, Tod
  For Nicholas, Born in
    September.
Perse, Saint-John
  Anabasis, IV.
  Song: Under the Bronze
    Leaves.
**"Perse, St.-John" (Alexis Saint-
  Léger Léger)**
  Anabasis.
Persius See **Flaccus, Aulus
  Persius**
Peseroff, Joyce
  The Hardness Scale.
Peskett, William
  Photographs.
Pestel, Thomas
  On Tobacco.
  Psalm for Christmas Day.
  A Psalm for Sunday Night.
  The Relief on Easter Eve.
  Song: "Silly Boy, there is no
    cause."
Petaccia, Mario
  A Death in the Streets.
  How to Find Your Way
    Home.
  Leaving Raiford.
  Six Days.
  Walking on Water.
"Peter"
  Out of the Dark Wood.
Peters, Edmund W.
  Bicychiamity.
Peters, Lenrie
  After They Put Down Their
    Overalls.
Peters, Mary
  Jesus, How Much Thy Name
    Unfolds!
Peters, Patricia
  In Grandfather's Glasses.
Peters, Robert
  Allen Ginsberg Blesses a
    Bride and Groom: A
    Wedding Night Poem.
  The Beach.
  .Blessing a Bride and Groom:
    A Wedding Night Poem
    (parody).
  Buying a Record (parody).
  Claremont.
  Crazy Bill to the Bishop
    (parody).
  The Darkling Chicken
    (parody).
  Feathered Friends (parody).
  Final Soliloquy on a Randy
    Rooster (in a Key of Yellow)
    (parody).
  I, Lessimus, of Salt Lake City
    (parody).
  Meeting Mick Jagger
    (parody).
  Melon-Slaughterer; or, A Sick
    Man's Praise for a Well
    Woman (parody).
  Reflecting on the Aging-
    Process (parody).

A Study in Aesthetics
  (parody).
Petersen, Donald
  The Ballad of Dead Yankees.
  Narcissus.
  Sonnet in Autumn.
  True to a Dream.
  Walking Along the Hudson.
Petersen, M.
  A Kitchen Prayer.
Petersen, Nils
  Hazard.
Peterson, Arthur
  Kelpius's Hymn.
Peterson, Elizabeth
  The Lesson.
Peterson, Frederick
  The Bridge.
  Solitude.
  Wild Geese.
Peterson, Henry
  The Death of Lyon.
  Ode for Decoration Day.
  Ode for Decoration Day
    (excerpt).
  Rinaldo.
Peterson, Mattie J.
  I Kissed Pa Twice after His
    Death.
Peterson, Peter
  On First Looking into
    Chapman's Homer II
    (parody).
Peterson, Robert
  At Veronica's.
  Dear America.
  For the Minority.
  The Groom's Lament.
  Highway Patrol Stops Me,
    Going Too Slow.
  Robert's Rules of Order.
  To Myself, Late, in a Myrtle
    Grove.
  Untitled Poem. "A swim in
    Ohuira Bay."
  Untitled Poem. "Hands folded
    like napkins in my lap."
  Untitled Poem. "In the 2
    A.M. Club, a working man's
    bar."
  Wingwalking in Oregon.
  The Young Conquistador.
Peterson, Ruth Delong
  Midwest Town.
Petofi, Sandor
  In the Forest.
Petrakos, Chris
  Call Them Back.
Petrarch (Francesco Petrarca)
  Against the Court of Rome.
  The Amorous Worms' Meat.
  Blest Be the Day.
  Canzone: "Clear, fresh, sweet
    waters."
  A Complaint by Night of the
    Lover Not Beloved.
  Complaint of a Lover
    Rebuked.
  The Eyes That Drew from
    Me.
  Father in Heaven.
  The Flying Lesson.
  Go, Grieving Rimes of Mine.
  Great Is My Envy of You.
  He Wishes He Might Die and
    Follow Laura.
  Imitated from Rime CCLXIX:
    "The piller pearisht is
    whearto I Lent."
  Imitated from Sonetto in
    Morte 42.
  It Was the Morning.

The Jealous Enemy.
Laura Waits for Him in
  Heaven.
The Lover Compareth His
  State to a Ship in Perilous
  Storm...
Mine Old Dear Enemy, My
  Froward Master.
The Nightingale.
Ode to the Virgin.
Of England, and of Its
  Marvels.
Rime CXC: "Who so list to
  hounte I know where is an
  hynde."
Rime CXL: "Love that doth
  raine and live within my
  thought."
Rime CXL: "The longe love,
  that in my thought doeth
  harbar."
Rime CXXXIV: "I fynde no
  peace and all my warr is
  done."
Rime LVII: "Ever myn happe
  is slack and slo in
  commyng."
Rime XLIX: "Bicause I have
  the still kept fro lyes and
  blame."
She Used to Let Her Golden
  Hair Fly Free.
The Song of Troylus.
Sonnet.
Sonnets to Laura.
To the Virgin Mary.
Visions.
Whoso liest to hunt, I know
  where is an hind.
Petrie, Paul
  The Church of San Antonio
    de la Florida.
  The Dream.
  The Enigma Variations.
  From the Point.
  The Murderer.
  Not Seeing Is Believing.
  The Old Pro's Lament.
  The Phases of Darkness.
  Story from Another World.
Petroczi, Kata S.
  Swift Floods.
**Petronius Arbiter (Caius
  Petronius Arbiter)**
  Doing, a filthy pleasure is, and
    short.
  Encouragement to Exile.
  Foeda Est In Coitu.
  The Malady of Love Is
    Nerves.
  A Plea for Haste.
  A Plea for Postponement.
  The Snow-Ball.
  Three Lyrics.
  We Are Such Stuff As
    Dreams...
Petroski, Henry
  Chairs.
  Horse-Girl.
Petrosky, Anthony
  Jurgis Petraskas, the Workers'
    Angel, Organizes...
Petrova, Olga
  To a Child Who Inquires.
Petrykewycz, Susan
  Home Again.
  Remembering Home.
Pett, Stephen
  Trench.
Pettengill, Margaret Miller
  There Will Be Peace.

Petties, Arthur
Out on Santa-Fe–Blues.
Pettingell, Phoebe
Frog Prince.
Ode on Zero.
Pettit, Michael
A Cappella.
A Day in My Union Suit.
Fire and Ice.
Herdsman.
Poker Poem.
Sunday Stroll.
Pevear, Richard
Ovid.
Pfeiffer, Edward H.
The Soul Speaks.
Pfingston, Roger
About the Cows.
Entering the Room.
The Photographer.
State Fair Pigs.
Waiting for Nighthawks in
Illinois.
Pflum, Richard
Home in Indianapolis.
Phaedrus
Aesop at Play.
The Dog in the River.
The Man and the Weasel.
The Purpose of Fable-Writing.
Phair, George E.
The Old-Fashioned Pitcher.
Phelp, J. A.
The Duke of Buccleuch.
Phelps, Arthur L.
The Wall.
Phelps, Charles Henry
Henry Ward Beecher.
Rare Moments.
Yuma.
Phelps, Elizabeth Stuart
Eternal Christmas.
A Generous Creed.
A Message.
Phelps, Sylvanus D.
Saviour, Thy Dying Love.
Something for Jesus.
Philbrick, Stephen
Leaving Here.
Philemon
Onions.
Philip, John
Manly Ferry.
The Subject of the Bishop's
Miracle.
Philip of Thessaloni
Epigram: "You were a pretty
boy once."
Philipa, Princess
To Holy Jesus.
Philipott, Thomas
On the Death of a Prince: A
Meditation.
On the Nativity of Our
Saviour.
Philipps, Stephen
The Poet's Prayer.
Philipps, Thomas
I Love a Flower.
The Peace of the Roses.
Philips, Ambrose
Fragment of Sappho.
The Happy Swain.
Pastoral Landscape.
Song.
To Miss Charlotte Pulteney in
Her Mother's Arms.
To Miss Margaret Pulteney,
Daughter of Daniel Pulteney,
Esq.
To Signora Cuzzoni.
To the Earl of Dorset.

To the Memory of Lord
Halifax (excerpt).
To the Right Honourable
Robert Walpole, Esq.
Philips, Joan *See* "Ephelia"
Philips, John
Blenheim (excerpt).
Cyder, I: How to Catch
Wasps.
Pruning.
The Thirsty Poet.
Philips, Katherine ("Orinda")
Against Love.
An Answer to Another
Persuading a Lady to
Marriage.
Friendship's Mystery.
Lucasia, Rosania and Orinda
Parting at a Fountain, July
1663.
Orinda to Lucasia.
Orinda to Lucasia Parting,
October, 1661, at London.
Parting with Lucasia: A Song.
A Sea-Voyage from Tenby to
Bristol, Begun Sept. 5,
1652...
Song: "'Tis true our life is but
a long dis-ease."
To Antenor.
To Mr. Henry Lawes.
To My Excellent Lucasia, on
Our Friendship.
Upon Absence.
Upon the Double Murther of
King Charles I...
Phillimore, John Swinnerton
In a Meadow.
Phillip, John
Lullaby.
Phillips, Charles
Music.
Phillips, Cleve
Up against the Wall.
Phillips, David
Fighting Her.
The Lover to Himself.
Notes on a Long Evening.
Old Storm.
Orange Juice Song.
Things of Late.
The Wave.
Words.
Phillips, Frank Lamont
Daybreak.
A Special Moment.
Phillips, Harriett C.
We Bring No Glittering
Treasures.
Phillips, Homer
Handyman.
Phillips, J. A.
The Factory Girl.
Phillips, John
The Splendid Shilling
(parody).
Phillips, Louis
78 Miners in Mannington,
West Virginia.
Considering the Death of John
Wayne.
A Day at the Races.
Phillips, Marie Tello
Sorrow.
Phillips, Patrice
The Function Room.
Phillips, Robert
The Death of Janis Joplin.
Decks.
Haiku: "Pluck a daisy here–."
Haiku: "That early riser."
Haiku: "That silver balloon."

Haiku: "The cat spreads
herself."
Haiku: "To write too many."
Haiku: "Tow-head
dandelions."
Inside and Out.
A Letter to Auden.
Lump.
The Married Man.
Miss Crustacean.
The Persistence of Memory,
the Failure of Poetry.
Vital Message.
Phillips, Rodney
Out of You.
Phillips, Stephen
The Apparition.
Grief and God.
I in the Grayness Rose.
Phillips, Susan K.
The Rose of Eden.
Phillpotts, Eden
The Houses.
Man's Days.
Miniature.
The Puddle.
Philodemos of Gadara
Remonstrance.
Philpot, William
Maritae Suae.
Phocas, Nikos
The Diver.
Piatt, John James
The Dear President.
Farther.
Ireland.
Leaves at My Window.
The Lost Genius.
The Mower in Ohio.
October Morning.
Purpose.
Rose and Root.
Suggested Device of a New
Western State.
To a Lady.
To Abraham Lincoln.
To Guerdon.
Torch-Light in Autumn.
Piatt, Sarah
After Wings.
A Call on Sir Walter Raleigh.
Envoy.
In Clonmel Parish
Churchyard.
Into the World and Out.
An Irish Wild-Flower.
My Babes in the Wood.
The Term of Death.
Transfigured.
The Watch of a Swan.
The Witch in the Glass.
Picano, Felice
The Gilded Boys.
The Heart Has Its Reasons.
Picasso, Pablo
Poem: "Hasten on your
childhood to the hour."
Poem: "In secret."
Poem: "In the corner a violet
jug."
Piccolo, Lucio
Veneris Venefica Agrestis.
Piccone, Anthony
The Raquette River, Potsdam,
New York....
Pichaske, David R.
H. S. Beeney Auction Sales.
Reflections.
Pichette, Henri
Apoem I.
Pickard, Cynthia
Cinderella.

Pickard, Deanna Louise
An Old Polish Lesson.
The Voyeur.
Pickard, Tom
Rape.
Pickering, John
Song: "Farewell, adieu, that
court-like life!"
Pickthall, Marjorie
Bega.
The Bridegroom of Cana.
A Child's Song of Christmas.
Duna.
Ebb Tide.
I Sat among the Green
Leaves.
The Immortal.
The Lamp of Poor Souls.
The Little Sister of the
Prophet.
Little Songs.
The Lovers of Marchaid.
Mary Shepherdess.
Mary Tired.
A Mother in Egypt.
On Amaryllis A Tortoyse.
Pere Lalement.
Quiet.
Resurgam.
Swallow Song.
Two Souls.
Pico della Mirandola, Giovanni
Consider.
The Golden Sestina.
Picot, James
Do You Not Hear?
Finale.
The Lord in the Wind.
To the Rosella in the
Poinsettia Tree.
A Volume of Chopin.
Piddington, R. A.
Literary Zodiac.
Tudor Aspersions.
Pien Chih-lin
The Composition of Distances.
The History of
Communications and a
Running Account.
Pierce, Dorothy Mason
Good Night.
John Plans.
Sprinkling.
Pierce, Edith Lovejoy
Apocalypse.
Christmas Amnesty.
Great Powers Conference.
In the Wilderness.
Let Me Not Die.
O Christ, Thou Art within Me
Like a Sea.
On Christmas Eve.
Prayer.
Prayer for the Useless Days.
Remember Thy Covenant.
Song of the Wise Men.
Supplication.
The Third Day.
Pierce, Jason Noble
Which Sword?
Piercy, Marge
Apron Strings.
Attack of the Squash People.
Barbie Doll.
Beauty I Would Suffer for.
Burying Blues for Janis.
The Common Living Dirt.
Councils.
Crabs.
The Development.
For the Young Who Want
To.

The Friend.
Going In.
Gracious Goodness.
Hare in Winter.
Hello up There.
Hummingbird.
I Awoke with the Room Cold.
The Inside Chance.
Insomnia.
Kneeling Here, I Feel Good.
Learning Experience.
Let Us Gather at the River.
Looking at Quilts.
The Low Road.
The Market Economy.
Night Letter.
Noon of the Sunbather.
Nothing More Will Happen.
The Peaceable Kingdom.
A Proposal for Recycling
  Wastes.
The Quiet Fog.
Rape Poem.
The Root Canal.
Simple Song.
Snow, Snow.
Someplace Else.
Song of the Fucked Duck.
The Spring Offensive of the
  Snail.
To Be of Use.
To the Pay Toilet.
The Total Influence or
  Outcome of the Matter: THE
  SUN.
Unclench Yourself.
A Valley where I Don't
  Belong.
The Watch.
We Become New.
What's That Smell in the
  Kitchen?
Why the Soup Tastes Like the
  Daily News.
The Woman in the.
A Work of Artiface.

Pierpont, James S.
Jingle Bells.
We Conquer or Die.

Pierpont, John
The Ballot.
Centennial Hymn.
The Exile at Rest.
The Fourth of July.
The Fugitive Slave's
  Apostrophe to the North
  Star.
The Kidnapping of Sims.
My Child.
On Laying the Corner-Stone
  of the Bunker Hill
  Monument.
The Pilgrim Fathers.
The Sparkling Bowl.
Warren's Address at Bunker
  Hill.
Whittling.

Pierson, Philip
Technique.

Pieterse, Cosmo
Guerrilla.
Song (We Sing).
To White South Africa.

Pietri, Pedro Juan
The Night Has Twenty-Four
  Hours.
Silent Movies.
Underground Poetry.
You Jump First.

Piety, Chauncey R.
Come Back, Lincoln.
Gifts.

A New Patriotism.
The Soul of Lincoln.
Thanksliving.

Pigott, Mostyn T.
The Hundred Best Books.

Pike, Albert
Buena Vista.
Dixie.
Song of the Navajo.
To the Mocking-Bird.
The Widowed Heart.

Pikeryng, John
Haltersick's Song.

Pilibin, An
Retrospect.

Pilibosian, Helene
With the Bait of Bread.

Pilinszky, Janos
The Desert of Love.
Fable.

Pilkington, Francis
Madrigal: "Have I found her."
Madrigal: "Stay, nymph."
Madrigal: "Wake, sleepy
  Thyrsis."
O Softly Singing Lute.

Pilkington, Lawrence
What Called Me to the
  Heights?

Pillen, [(or Pillin)] William
Akriel's Consolation.
Farewell to Europe.
Night Poem in an Abandoned
  Music Room.
O, Beautiful They Move.
Ode on a Decision to Settle
  for Less.
A Poem for Anton Schmidt.
Poem: "To be sad in the
  morning."

Pilling, Christopher
The Adoration of the Magi.

Pilz, J. Michael
Renoir's Confidences.

Pimentel Coronel, Ramon
Jesus.

Pincas, Israel
Mediterranean.

Pinckney, Josephine
The Misses Poar Drive to
  Church.

Pindar
The First Olympionique to
  Hiero of Syracuse.
Goober Peas.
Life After Death.
Nemea 11 (excerpt).
Nemean Ode: VI.
Ode on Theoxenos.
The Power of Music (excerpt).

"Pindar, Peter" *See* **Wolcot,
  John**

Pinero, Miguel
There Is Nothing New in
  New York.

"Ping Hsin" (Hsieh Wang-ying)
Multitudinous Stars.
The Spring Waters.
The Stars.
Three Poems.

"Pink"
The Groaning Board.

Pinkerton, Helen
Degrees of Shade.
Deprivation.
Error Pursued.
Indecision.
The Prism.

Pinkham, Cora M.
God's Ideal Mother.
With Thee.

Pinkney, Dorothy Cowles
Dame Liberty Reports from
  Travel.

**Pinkney, Edward Coate [(or
  Coote)]**
A Health.
A Serenade.
Song: "We break the glass,
  whose sacred wine."
Votive Song.

Pinsker, Sanford
For Allen Ginsberg, Who Cut
  Off His Beard.
An Untitled Poem, about an
  Uncompleted Sonnet.

Pinsky, Robert
The Changes.
December Blues.
Discretions of Alcibiades.
Dying.
Essay on Psychiatrists.
Faeryland.
The Figured Wheel.
History of My Heart.
Icicles.
Local Politics.
Memorial.
The New Saddhus.
Poem about People.
The Questions.
Ralegh's Prizes.
Serpent Knowledge.
Song of Reasons.
The Street.

Pinto, Vivian de Sola
At Piccadilly Circus.

Piper, Edwin Ford
Bindlestiff.
The Church.
Gee-Up Dar, Mules.

Piper, Linda
Missionaries in the Jungle.
Sweet Ethel.

Pisan, Christine de
Alone am I, and alone I wish
  to be.
Christine to Her Son.
The Epistle of Othea to
  Hector (excerpt).
Fountain of Tears, River of
  Grief.
I am a widow, robed in black,
  alone.
I'll always dress in black and
  rave.
If Frequently to Mass.
Marriage Is a Lovely Thing.

Pise, Charles Constantine
The American Flag.
Let the Deep Organ Swell.

Pitcher, Oliver
The Pale Blue Casket.
Raison d'Etre.
Salute.

Pitchford, Kenneth
104 Boulevard Saint-Germain.
Aunt Cora.
The Blizzard Ape.
Death Swoops.
Good for Nothing Man.
Homosexual Sonnets.
Leviathan.
Lobotomy.
Off Viareggio.
The Queen.
Reflections on Water.

Pitkin, Anne
The Homes.

Pitt, Christopher
On the Masquerades.

Pitt, Marie E. J.
A Gallop of Fire.

Pitt, William
Sailor's Consolation.

Pitter, Ruth
The Bat.
The Beautiful Negress.
But for Lust.
Close, Mortal Eyes.
The Coffin-Worm.
Digdog.
Dun Colour.
The Estuary.
The Eternal Image.
The Fishers.
For Sleep, or Death.
Help, Good Shepherd.
Hen Under Bay-Tree.
The Lost Tribe.
The Military Harpist.
The Missal.
Morning Glory.
O Come Out of the Lily.
An Old Woman Speaks of the
  Moon.
Rainy Summer.
A Solemn Meditation.
The Sparrow's Skull.
The Stockdove.
Stormcock in Elder.
The Swan Bathing.
The Task.
Three Cheers for the Black,
  White and Blue.
The Tigress.
Time's Fool.
To J. S. Collis.
The Train Will Fight to the
  Pass.
The Unicorn.
Urania.
The Viper.

Pittis, William
The Battle Royal between Dr.
  Sherlock, Dr. South, and Dr.
  Burnet.

Pitts, William S.
Little Brown Church in the
  Vale.

Piuvkaq
It Is Hard to Catch Trout.
The Joy of a Singer.
Mocking Song against
  Qaqortingneq.

Pixner, Stef
A Day in the Life...

Pizarnik, Alejandra
Apart from Oneself.
Dawn.
Fear.
The Mask and the Poem.
Privilege.
The Tree of Diana.
Vertigos or Contemplation of
  Something That Is Over.
Who Will Stop His Hand
  from Giving Warmth.

**"Placido" (Gabriel de la
  Conception Valdes)**
Farewell to My Mother.
Prayer to God.

Planché, James Robinson
Ching a Ring.
A Literary Squabble.
Love, You've Been a Villain.
The Sea-Serpent.
To Mollidusta.

Plantenga, Bart
Fire. 10/78.

Plantier, Therese
Doors.
Ovedue Balance Sheet.

Planz, Allen
12 Oct.

Handlining Tockers &
  Gizmos.
Plarr, Vicor
Che Sara Sara.
Plarr, Victor
Epitaphium Citharistriae.
Of Change of Opinions.
Shadows.
Platen, August von
Sonnets to Karl Theodor
  German.
To Bulow–2.
To Liebig–6.
To Liebig–7.
To Rotenham–3.
To Schmidlein–2.
Plath, Sylvia
Aftermath.
All the Dead Dears.
Amnesiac.
Among the Narcissi.
The Applicant.
Ariel.
The Arrival of the Bee Box.
The Babysitters.
Balloons.
Barren Woman.
The Bee Meeting.
The Beekeeper's Daughter.
Black Rook in Rainy
  Weather.
Blackberrying.
Blue Moles.
Brasilia.
By Candlelight.
Candles.
Child.
Cinderella.
The Colossus.
The Couriers.
Crossing the Water.
Cut.
Daddy.
Death & Co.
The Death of Myth-Making.
The Disquieting Muses.
Edge.
Elm.
Event.
Fever 103.
Flute Notes from a Reedy
  Pond.
Frog Autumn.
Full Fathom Five.
The Ghost's Leavetaking.
The Goring.
Gulliver.
The Hanging Man.
Hardcastle Crags.
Kindness.
Lady Lazarus.
Last Words.
A Life.
Love Letter.
The Manor Garden.
Mary's Song.
Medallion.
Medusa.
Memoirs of a Spinach-Picker.
Metamorphosis.
Metaphors.
Mirror.
The Moon and the Yew Tree.
Morning Song.
The Munich Mannequins.
Mushrooms.
Mussel Hunter at Rock
  Harbor.
Mystic.
New Year on Dartmoor.
Nick and the Candlestick.
The Night Dances.

Paralytic.
Parliament Hill Fields.
Point Shirley.
Poppies in July.
Poppies in October.
The Rabbit Catcher.
Sheep in Fog.
Sleep in the Mojave Desert.
Snakecharmer.
Spinster.
Stars over the Dordogne.
Stings.
The Stones.
Suicide off Egg Rock.
Three Women.
Tulips.
Two Campers in Cloud
  Country.
Two Views of a Cadaver
  Room.
Water Color of Granchester
  Meadows.
Winter Trees.
Wintering.
Words.
You're.
Plato
The Apple.
Aster.
Country Music.
Dedication of a Mirror.
Epigram: "All I said was–
  Alexis is gorgeous."
Epigram: "For Hekabe."
Farewell.
Farmer and Sailor.
The Inner Man.
Kissing Helen.
Love Sleeping.
My Star.
On a Seal.
On Alexis.
On Archaeanassa.
On the Athenian Dead at
  Ecbatana.
Plato, Ann
The Natives of America.
Reflections, Written on
  Visiting the Grave of a
  Venerated Friend.
To the First of August.
Platov, Mariquita
Whispering Clouds.
Playford, John
The Jovial Marriner; or, The
  Sea-Man's Renown.
Plescoff, Jorge
The Ladder Has No Steps.
Ourobouros.
Tongues of Fire.
Violins in Repose.
Plimpton, Florus B.
Fort Duquesne.
Plomer, William
Archaic Apollo.
Atheling Grange: or, The
  Apotheosis of Lotte
  Nussbaum.
Bamboo.
Blind Samson.
The Caledonian Market.
The Death of a Snake.
The Devil-Dancers.
Europa.
Father and Son: 1939.
The Flying Bum: 1944.
French Lisette: A Ballad of
  Maida Vale.
Ganymede.
Headline History.
In the Snake Park.
A Levantine.

Mews Flat Mona.
Namaqualand After Rain.
The Playboy of the Demi-
  World: 1938.
Positive, A Coxcomb.
The Prisoner.
A Right-of-Way: 1865.
The Scorpion.
September Evening, 1938.
Seven Rainy Months.
A Shot in the Park.
Tattooed.
To the Moon and Back.
Ula Masondo's Dream.
A Walk in Wurzburg.
The Widow's Plot; or, She
  Got What Was Coming to
  Her.
Plowman, Max
Her Beauty.
Plumly, Stanley
After Grief.
American Ash.
Another November.
Blossom.
Early Meadow-Rue.
Fifth & 94th.
For Esther.
Fungo.
Giraffe.
Heron.
The Iron Lung.
My Mother's Feet.
Now That My Father Lies
  down Beside Me.
Out-of-the-Body Travel.
Peppergrass.
Posthumous Keats.
Tree Ferns.
Virginia Beach.
Waders and Swimmers.
Wildflower.
Plummer, Mary Wright
Irrevocable.
Plumpp, Sterling D.
Beyond the Nigger.
For Mattie & Eternity.
Half Black, Half Blacker.
I Told Jesus.
The Living Truth.
Plumptre, Annabella
Ode to Moderation (excerpt).
Plumptre, James
The Lakers: Prologue
  (excerpt).
Plunkett, Edward J. M. D.
Songs from an Evil Wood.
Plunkett, Joseph Mary
The Claim That Has the
  Canker on the Rose.
I See His Blood upon the
  Rose.
My Lady Has the Grace of
  Death.
O Sower of Sorrow.
Our Heritage.
See the Crocus' Golden Cup.
Sic Transit.
The Spark.
To G. K. Chesterton.
White Dove of the Wild Dark
  Eyes.
Plutzik, Hyam
The Airman Who Flew over
  Shakespeare's England.
The Begetting of Cain.
The Geese.
I Am Disquieted When I See
  Many Hills.
The Importance of Poetry; or,
  the Coming Forth from
  Eternity into Time.

Jim Desterland.
The King of Ai.
The Mythos of Samuel
  Huntsman.
Of Objects Considered as
  Fortresses in a Baleful Place.
On the Photograph of a Man
  I Never Saw.
To My Daughter.
Pluvkaq
I Wonder Why.
Po Chu-i
The Cranes.
Eating Bamboo-Shoots.
The Flower Market.
Good-bye to the People of
  Hang-Chow.
The Harper of Chao.
Having Climbed to the
  Topmost Peak of the
  Incense-Burner Mountain.
Hearing the Early Oriole.
In Early Summer Lodging in
  a Temple to Enjoy the
  Moonlight.
Invitation to Hsiao Ch'U-
  Shih.
Lao-Tzu.
Lazy Man's Song.
Lodging with the Old Man of
  the Stream.
Losing a Slave Girl.
An Old Charcoal Seller.
On Being Sixty.
Planting Flowers on the
  Eastern Embankment.
The Red Cockatoo.
Rejoicing at the Arrival of
  Ch'en Hsiung.
Remembering Golden Bells.
Sleeping on Horseback.
Starting Early from the Ch'U-
  Ch'eng Inn.
The Temple.
To Li Chien.
Pocock, Isaac
Song: "Oh! say not woman's
  love is bought."
Poe, Edgar Allan
Al Aaraaf.
Alone.
Annabel Lee.
The Bells.
The City in the Sea.
The Coliseum.
The Conqueror Worm.
The Doomed City.
Dream-Land.
A Dream Within a Dream.
Dreams.
Eldorado.
Eulalie. A Song.
Evening Star.
The Fall of the House of
  Usher: The Haunted Palace.
For Annie.
From Childhood's Hour.
The Happiest Day, the
  Happiest Hour.
Hymn.
Introduction.
Israfel.
The Lake.
Lenore.
The Raven.
Romance.
The Sleeper.
Sonnet–To Science.
Sonnet–To Silence.
Sonnet–To Zante.
Spirits of the Dead.
Stanzas.

Tamerlane.
To Helen.
To My Mother.
To One in Paradise.
Ulalume.
The Valley of Unrest.
Poitiers, Guillaume de See
  Guillaume de Poitiers
  Behold the Meads.
Polite, Allen
  Am Driven Mad.
  Stopped.
Polite, Frank
  Adman into Toad.
  Carmen Miranda.
  Empty at the Heart of Things.
  Imitations Based on the
    American (parody).
  The Japanese Consulate.
  Lantern.
  Mine.
Politzer, Heinz
  My Language.
Poliziano, Andrea
  Three Ballate.
  Unto the Breach.
Polk, Noel
  Wreck.
Pollack, Thomas B.
  Father, Into Thy Hands.
Pollak, Felix
  Dial Tone.
  Speaking: The Hero.
  Widow.
Pollard, A. A.
  The Secret Place.
Pollard, Josephine
  Price of a Drink.
Pollitt, Katha
  Archaeology.
  Ballet Blanc.
  Composition in Black and
    White.
  A Discussion of the
    Vicissitudes of History under
    a Pine Tree.
  In Memory.
  Night Blooming Flowers.
  Of the Scythians.
  Riverside Drive, November
    Fifth.
  Seal Rock.
  When We Drive at Night.
  Woman Asleep on a Banana
    Leaf.
Pollock, Edward
  Olivia.
Pollock, Walter Herries
  A Conquest.
Pollok, Robert
  Ocean.
Polonsky, Yakov
  The Cosmic Fabric.
Polson, Don
  Sons.
Polwhele, Richard
  The Influence of Local
    Attachment (excerpt).
Pombo, Rafael
  Our Madonna at Home.
Pomerantz, Berl
  End of Summer.
  Young Virgins Plucked
    Suddenly.
Pomerantz, Marsha
  Adam and Eve at the Garden
    Gate.
  How to Reach the Moon.
Pomeroy, Marnie
  April Fool's Day.
  Ground Hog Day.
  Halloween.

In Nakedness.
January 1.
Labor Day.
News.
Pomeroy, Ralph
  Between Here and Illinois.
  Confession.
  Corner.
  English Train, Summer.
  Gone.
  High Wind at the Battery.
  In Hotels Public and Private.
  In the Redwood Forest.
  Islands.
  The Leather Bar.
  Letter to Pasternak.
  Looking at the Empire State
    Building.
  Near Drowning.
  Patrol.
  Snow.
  A Tardy Epithalamium for E.
    and N.
  To Janet.
  To My Father.
  To Words.
  Trying to Sleep.
Pomfret, John
  The Choice.
Pommy-Vega, Janine
  Rites of the Eastern Star.
  The Voices.
Pompili, Vittoria
  Fear.
  Finally.
Ponchon, Raoul
  The Shepherd's Tale.
Ponciano, Angelo de See **De**
  Ponciano, Angelo
Pond, Margaret
  Sheep Country.
Ponge, Francis
  The Delights of the Door.
  The End of Fall.
  The Horse.
  The Oyster.
  Trees Lose Parts of
    Themselves inside a Circle of
    Fog.
Ponsot, Marie
  Communion of Saints: The
    Poor Bastard under the
    Bridge.
  Multipara: Gravida 5.
  Possession.
  Subject.
  To the Age's Insanities.
Ponting, Herbert George
  The Sleeping-Bag.
Poole, John
  Song: Hamlet. "When a man
    becomes tired of his life"
    (parody).
Poole, Tom
  I/ wonder why.
Poor Wolf
  Poor Wolf Speaks.
Pope, Alexander
  The Alley. An Imitation of
    Spenser.
  Ambition.
  Apologia pro Vita Sua.
  The Balance of Europe.
  Bufo.
  The Challenge.
  Characters of Women.
  The Court of Charles II.
  A Dialogue.
  The Domicile of John.
  The Duke of Buckingham.
  The Dunciad.

The Dying Christian to His
  Soul.
Elegy to the Memory of an
  Unfortunate Lady.
Eloisa to Abelard.
Epigram: "Cibber! write all
  thy verses upon glasses."
Epigram Engraved on the
  Collar of a Dog Given to His
  Royal Highness...
Epigram, in a Maid of
  Honour's Prayer-Book.
Epigram on One who Made
  Long Epitaphs.
Epigram on the Toasts of the
  Kit-Kat Club, Anno 1716.
Epigram: "Sir, I admit your
  gen'ral rule."
Epigram: "You beat your
  pate, and fancy wit will
  come."
Epilogue to the Satires.
An Epistle from Mr. Pope to
  Dr. Arbuthnot.
Epistle to a Lady: Of the
  Characters of Women.
Epistle to Augustus (excerpt).
Epistle to Miss Teresa Blount,
  on Her Leaving the Town...
Epistle to Richard Boyle, Earl
  of Burlington (excerpt).
The Epistle to Sir Richard
  Temple (excerpt).
Epitaph for One Who Would
  Not Be Buried in
  Westminster Abbey.
Epitaph: "Here lie two poor
  lovers, who had the mishap."
Epitaph Intended for Sir Isaac
  Newton, in Westminster
  Abbey.
Epitaph on Himself.
Epitaph on James Moore
  Smythe.
Epitaph: "See here, nice
  Death, to please his palate."
Epitaph V On Mrs. Corbet,
  Who Dyed of a Cancer in
  her Breast.
Epitaph XI On Mr. Gay. In
  Westminster Abbey, 1732.
An Essay on Criticism.
An Essay on Man.
Faith.
A Farewell to London In the
  Year 1715.
Field Sports.
The First Epistle of the First
  Book of Horace Imitated
  (excerpt).
The First Epistle of the
  Second Book of Horace.
First Satire of the Second
  Book of Horace.
The First Satire of the Second
  Book of Horace Imitated
  (excerpt).
The Gardens of Alcinous.
The Gem and the Flower.
The Happy Life of a Country
  Parson (parody).
Heaven's Last Best Work.
Hector and Andromache.
An Heroick Epistle from a
  Dog at Twickenham to a
  Dog at Court.
Honest Fame.
A Hymn Written in Windsor
  Forest.
I Am His Highness' Dog at
  Kew.
The Ideals of Satire.

Imitation of Chaucer (parody).
Inscriptio.
Lines by a Person of Quality.
Lines on Bounce.
Lines on Swift's Ancestors.
Lord Coningsby's Epitaph.
The Maimed Debauchee.
Messiah.
Moral Essays.
Most Souls, 'Tis True, but
  Peep Out Once an Age.
O Sons of Earth.
Ode for Music on St. Cecilia's
  Day.
Ode on Solitude.
Ode to Quinbus Flestrin.
Ombre at Hampton Court.
On a Certain Lady at Court.
On a Lady Who P-ssed at the
  Tragedy of Cato.
On Authors and Booksellers.
On Certain Ladies.
On Colley Cibber's
  Declaration That He Will
  Have the Last Word...
On Dennis.
On Poets.
On Queen Caroline's
  Deathbed.
On the Benefactions in the
  Late Frost, 1740.
On the Candidates for the
  Laurel.
On the Erection of
  Shakespeare's Statue in
  Westminster Abbey.
A Paraphrase on Thomas a
  Kempis.
Pastorals: Summer.
The Poet's Use.
Poetical Numbers.
Prayer of St. Francis Xavier.
Priam and Achilles.
Prologue to Mr. Addison's
  Tragedy of Cato.
The Pyre of Patroclus.
The Quiet Life.
The Rape of the Lock.
Rise, Crowned with Light.
Satire.
The Second Satire of the First
  Book of Horace (excerpt).
Sylvan Delights.
Three Epitaphs on John
  Hewet and Sarah Drew.
Timon's Villa.
To James Craggs, Esq;
  Secretary of State.
To Mr. C, St. James's Place,
  London, October 22nd.
To Mr. Gay...On Finishing
  His House.
To Mr. Jervas, with Fresnoy's
  Art of Painting, Translated
  by Dryden.
To Mrs. M. B. on Her Birth-
  day.
To Robert Earl of Oxford,
  and Earl Mortimer.
Tom Southerne's Birth-Day
  Dinner at Ld. Orrery's.
Two or Three: A Recipe to
  Make a Cuckold.
The Universal Prayer.
Upon a Girl of Seven Years
  Old.
Verbal Critics.
Verbatim from Boileau.
The Vestal.
Vice.

The Wife of Bath Her
Prologue, from Chaucer
(excerpt).
The Wild Garden.
Windsor-Forest To the Right
Honourable George Lord
Lansdown.
Woman's Ruling Passions.
Pope, Deborah
There Is Something.
Pope, J. R.
A Word of Encouragement.
Pope, Jenny
Doggin' Me around Blues.
Pope, Jessie
Our Visit to the Zoo.
Pope, Liston
Sea Turtle.
Pope, Walter
The Old Man's Wish.
Popham, Hugh
The Usual Exquisite Boredom
of Patrols.
Popham, Ivor
The Child.
Pordage, Samuel
Corydon's Complaint.
Porson, Richard
The Bathos.
The Devil's Thoughts
(excerpt).
Epigram on an Academic
Visit to the Continent.
The Mutual Congratulations
of the Poet's Anna Seward
and Hayley.
On a Doctor of Divinity.
On a Fellow of Trinity
College, Cambridge.
On the Latin Gerunds.
Porson on German
Scholarship.
Porson on His Majesty's
Government.
To Dr. Kipling.
Portal, Magda
Film Vermouth: Six O'Clock
Show.
Shores of Anguish.
W o m a n.
Porter, Adrian
The Perfect Child.
Porter, Alan
The Dean.
The Stallion.
Porter, Bruce
Limerick: "H was an indigent
Hen."
Porter, Cole
Always True to You in My
Fashion (excerpt).
Anything Goes.
Brush Up Your Shakespeare.
I Hate Men.
Let's Do It.
My Heart Belongs to Daddy.
Night and Day.
So in Love.
You're the Top.
Porter, Fairfield
The Island in the Evening.
Porter, Hal
Adam–The First Kiss.
Bi-focal.
Four Winds.
Hobart Town, Van Diemen's
Land.
In a Bed-Sitter.
Lalique.
Sheep.
Porter, Ina M.
Mumford.

Porter, Jenny Lind
In the Beginning.
Porter, Katherine Anne
Requiescat.
Porter, Kenneth
Beaver Sign.
Epitaph for a Man from
Virginia City.
Old Thad Stevens.
Street Scene–1946.
Thistle, Yarrow, Clover.
Porter, Mrs. David
Thou Hast Wounded the
Spirit That Loved Thee.
Porter, Peter
Annotations of Auschwitz.
The Cats of Campagnatico.
Christenings.
A Consumer's Report.
An Exequy.
Gertrude Stein at Snails Bay.
Made in Heaven.
May, 1945.
Metamorphosis.
Mort aux Chats.
Nine O'Clock Thoughts on
the 73 Bus.
Non Piangere, Liu.
On This Day I Complete My
Fortieth Year.
Phar Lap in the Melbourne
Museum.
The Smell on the Landing.
Soliloquy at Potsdam.
A St. Cecilia's Day Epigram.
Vienna.
What I Have Written I Have
Written.
Your Attention Please.
Porter, Samuel Judson
The Way; The Truth; The
Life.
Porter, William Sidney *See*
Henry, O.
Porumbacu, Veronica
Of Autumn.
Posey, Alexander L.
On the Capture and
Imprisonment of Crazy
Snake, January, 1900.
Posner, David
The Birds.
The Campus.
Mourningsong for Anne.
On a Recent Protest against
Social Conditions.
Post, Jonathon V.
Footnote to Feynman.
Post, L. F.
Gila Monster Route.
Poster, Carol
Finds Something in New
Jersey (parody).
Synthesizing Several Abstruse
Concepts with an Experience
(parody).
Potamkin, Harry Alan
Cargoes of the Radanites.
Poteat, Edwin McNeill
Eternal God Whose Searching
Eye Doth Scan.
Grace at Evening.
Prayer at Dawn.
Prayer for Contentment.
Pothinus, Saint
Epigram on Marcus the
Gnostic.
Pott and Wright
Epigram.
The Grammar of Love.
To Sextus.

Potter, Beatrix
The Old Woman.
Potter, Miriam Clark
Cake.
Present.
Potter, Reuben M.
Hymn of the Alamo.
Potts, Paul
For My Father.
Jean.
The Muse to an Unknown
Poet.
Poulin, Jr, A.
I Woke Up Revenge.
Poulsson, Emilie
Baby's Breakfast.
Bed-Time Song.
Books Are Keys.
The Breakfast Song.
The First Christmas.
The Lovable Child.
Nutting Time.
Santa Claus and the Mouse.
While Stars of Christmas
Shine.
Pound, Ezra
De Aegypto.
The Age Demanded.
Alba.
The Alchemist.
Ancient Music.
Ancient Wisdom, Rather
Cosmic.
And the Days Are Not Full
Enough.
And Thus in Nineveh.
Apparuit.
April.
L'Art, 1910.
Ballad for Gloom.
Ballad of the Goodly Fere.
A Ballad of the Mulberry
Road.
Ballatetta.
The Bathtub.
Cantico del Sole.
Canto sels.
Cino.
Clara.
Coda.
The Coming of War: Actaeon.
Commission.
Contemporania: Tenzone.
Dance Figure.
Doria.
A Draft of XXX Cantos, XII:
"Said Jim X..."
Epigram: "I dreamt that I was
God Himself."
Epilogue.
Fan-Piece, for Her Imperial
Lord.
The Faun.
The Flame.
For E. McC.
Fragmenti.
La Fraisne.
Further Instructions.
The Garden.
The Garret.
A Girl.
Greek Epigram.
Homage to Sextus Propertius.
L'Homme Moyhen Sensuel
(excerpt).
The House of Splendour.
Hugh Selwyn Mauberley, sels.
Image from d'Orleans.
An Immorality.
Impressions of Francois-Marie
Arouet (de Voltaire)
(excerpt).

In a Station of the Metro.
Ite.
Kore.
The Lake Isle.
Lustra, III: Further
Instructions.
Mauberley.
Me Happy, Night, Night Full
of Brightness.
Meditatio.
Monumentum Aere, Etc.
Mr. Housman's Message.
N.Y.
Near Perigord.
O Atthis.
Ortus.
A Pact.
Phyllidula.
Piere Vidal Old.
The Pisan Cantos (excerpt).
Portrait.
Portrait d'une Femme.
Provincia Deserta.
Reflection and Advice.
The Rest.
The Return.
Ritratto.
Salutation.
Salutation the Second.
The Seafarer.
Sestina: Altaforte.
Sextus Propertius: Turning
Aside from Battles.
Silet.
Soiree.
The Study in Aesthetics.
Tame Cat.
The Tea Shop.
The Temperaments.
To Kaaon.
To Whistler, American.
The Tomb at Akr Caar.
Translator to Translated.
The Tree.
Ts'ai Chi'h.
Vergier.
Villanelle: The Psychological
Hour.
A Virginal.
Well Pleaseth Me the Sweet
Time of Easter.
The White Stag.
Pounds, Jessie B.
Beautiful Isle of Somewhere.
Pounds, Leonard
"Rake" Windermere.
Poupo, Pierre
Prayers of a Christian
Bridegroom.
Powell, Anthony
Caledonia.
Powell, Charles
Jack and Jill (parody).
Powell, Frederick York
The Pretty Maid.
The Sailor and the Shark.
Power, John
Thy Name We Bless and
Magnify.
Power, Marguerite
A Friend.
Powers, Horatio Nelson
Chimney Swallows.
The New Year.
Our Sister.
The Year Ahead.
Powers, Jessica
And in Her Morning.
Cancer Patient.
The Cloud of Carmel.
Wanderer.

Powers, Star
Harvest Time.
Powys, John Cowper
In a Hotel Writing-Room.
Poyner, Ken
Therapy.
Pozzi, Antonia
To Trust.
Prada, Gonzalez
Who Translates a Poet Badly.
Praed, Winthrop Mackworth
Arrivals at a Watering-Place.
Charade.
The Chaunt of the Brazen
Head (excerpt).
The County Ball (excerpt).
The Covenanter's Lament for
Bothwell Brigg.
Epitaph on the Late King of
the Sandwich Isles.
Every-Day Characters.
Fairy Song.
Good-Night to the Season.
Latin Hymn.
A Letter of Advice.
Mater Desiderata.
The Newly-Wedded.
Ode to Popularity.
One More Quadrille.
Royal Education.
School and Schoolfellows.
Schoolfellows.
A Song of Impossibilities.
Song: "The pints and the
pistols, the pike-staves and
pottles."
Stanzas on Seeing the Speaker
Asleep...
The Talented Man.
Time's Song.
To —.
To Helen.
Prager, Marie-Francoise
I'll act out a weird dream.
Prather, W. H.
The Indian Ghost Dance and
War.
Prati, Giovanni
The Holy Viaticum Comes to
Me.
Pratt, Anna Maria
Early News.
A Mortifying Mistake.
Pratt, Edwin John
Brebeuf and His Brethren.
Burial at Sea.
The Cachalot.
Come away, Death.
Come Not the Seasons Here.
The Dying Eagle.
Erosion.
From Stone to Steel.
Frost.
The Ground-Swell.
The Ice-Floes.
Invisible Trumpets Blowing.
The Prize Cat.
The Ritual.
The Sea Cathedral.
Sea Gulls.
The Shark.
Silences.
The Titanic (excerpt).
Towards the Last Spike.
The Truant.
The Way of Cape Race.
Pratt, Lenore
Midwinter Thaw.
The Old Boat.
Pratt, William W.
Same Old Trick.

Praxilla
Fragments.
Girl of the Lovely Glance.
Loveliest of What I Leave
behind Is the Sunlight.
Most beutiful of things I leave
is sunlight.
You gaze at me teasingly
through the window.
Pray, Benjamin Sturgis
Motorcycle.
Preil, Gabriel
Arriving.
Autumn Music.
Biographical Note.
Fishermen.
From Jerusalem: A First
Poem.
Giving Up on the Shore.
A Late Manuscript at the
Schocken Institute.
A Lesson in Translation.
Letter Out of the Gray.
Like David.
Memory of Another Climate.
Parting.
Rains on the Island.
A Summing Up.
Words of Oblivion and Peace.
Prelutsky, Jack
The First Thanksgiving.
The Ghoul.
Harvey Always Wins.
It's Halloween.
The Pancake Collector.
Skeleton Parade.
Toucannery.
The Visitor.
Prentice, George Denison
Memories.
New England: For a
Celebration in Kentucky of
the Landing of ...
The Ocean.
Prentice, John A.
Washington.
Prentiss, Elizabeth Payson
Kitty.
More Love to Thee, O Christ.
Prescot, Kenrick
Balsham Bells.
Prescott, Mary Newmarch
In the Dark, in the Dew.
Press, John
African Christmas.
Farewell.
Narcissus.
Womanisers.
Preston, Keith
An Awful Responsibility.
Chicago Analogue.
The Complete Cynic.
The Durable Bon Mot.
Effervescence and
Evanescence.
The Humorist.
Lapsus Linguae.
An Original Cuss.
The Parental Critic.
Warm Babies.
Preston, Margaret Junkin
Acceptation.
Dirge for Ashby.
The First Proclamation of
Miles Standish.
The First Thanksgiving Day.
A Grave in Hollywood
Cemetery, Richmond.
The Hero of the Commune.
The Last Meeting of
Pocahontas and the Great
Captain.

The Mystery of Cro-A-Tan.
Under the Shade of the Trees.
Virginia Capta.
The Vision of the Snow.
Pretorius, S. J.
The Madman.
Prettyman, Quandra
The Birth of the Poet.
Blues.
Crawl into Bed.
Lullaby.
The Mood.
Photograph.
Still Life: Lady with Birds.
When Mahalia Sings.
Prevert, Jacques
Alicante.
La Belle Saison.
Late Rising.
The Message.
Price, Edith Ballinger
To Patricia on Her
Christening Day.
Price, Herbert
The Buffalo.
Price, Jonathan
A Considered Reply to a
Child.
Price, Laurence
Win at First and Lose at Last;
or, A New Game at Cards.
Price, Nancy
Harbor.
One-Night Fair.
Price, Nell Goodale
School Begins.
Price, Victor
Highland Region.
Prideaux, Tom
Skip-Scoop-Anellie.
Priest, Nancy Woodbury
Over the River.
Prince, Alison
One-Line Poems from a New
Statesman Competition.
Prince, Frank Templeton
At a Parade.
The Babiaantje.
In a Province.
The Old Age of Michelangelo.
The Question.
Soldiers Bathing.
To a Friend on His Marriage.
The Token.
The Wind in the Tree.
Prince, Thomas
Give Ear, O God, to My
Loud Cry.
O Lord, Bow Down Thine
Ear.
With Christ and All His
Shining Train.
Pringle, Thomas
Afar in the Desert.
The Caffer Commando
(excerpt).
The Desolate Valley.
The Hottentot.
The Lion-Hunt.
Prinzivalle, Doria
Canzone: Of His Love, with
the Figure of a Sudden
Storm.
Prior, Matthew
Adriani Morientis ad Animam
Suam.
Advice to the Painter.
Against Modesty in Love.
Alma: or, The Progress of the
Mind.
Another True Maid.

A Better Answer (to Cloe
Jealous).
Cause and Effect.
The Chameleon.
Chaste Florimel.
Cupid Mistaken.
Daphne and Apollo.
Democritus and Heraclitus.
The Divine Blacksmith.
Down Hall.
A Dutch Proverb.
Earning a Dinner.
An English Ballad, on the
Taking of Namur by the
King...
An English Padlock.
Epigram: "Thy nags (the
leanest things alive)."
Epigram: "To John I ow'd
great obligation."
Epigram: "Tom's sickness did
his morals mend."
Epigram: "When Bibo thought
fit from the world to
retreat."
Epigram: "When Pontius
wished an edict might be
passed."
Epigram: "Yes, every poet is a
fool."
An Epitaph: "Interr'd beneath
this marble stone."
Epitaph on Francis Atterbury,
Bishop of Rochester.
An Epitaph on True, Her
Majesty's Dog.
The Epitaph upon Gilbert
Glanvill...
Les Estreines.
A Fable.
Fatal Love.
The Female Phaeton.
For My Own Monument.
The Fortune-Teller To a
Young Lady in Search of
Her Destiny.
Great Bacchus: from the
Greek.
Helen Was Just Slipped into
Bed.
Human Life.
In Imitation of Anacreon.
The Insatiable Priest.
Jinny the Just.
The Lady Who Offers Her
Looking Glass.
A Letter to Lady Margaret
Cavendish Holles-Harley,
when a Child.
Love and Reason.
A Lover's Anger.
The New Year's Gift to
Phyllis.
Nonpareil.
An Ode: "The merchant, to
secure his treasure."
On a Pretty Madwoman.
On Beauty. A Riddle.
On Himself.
On My Birthday, July 21.
A Paraphrase from the
French.
Photogenes and Apelles.
Phyllis's Age.
Picture of Seneca Dying in a
Bath.
Power.
Prior's Epitaph.
The Question to Lisetta.
Quid Sit Futurum Cras Fuge
Quaerere.
A Reasonable Affliction.

The Remedy Worse Than the
Disease.
The Secretary Written at the
Hague, in the Year 1696.
A Simile.
Solomon on the Vanity of the
World.
A Song: "If Wine and Musick
have the Pow'r."
Song: "In vain you tell your
parting lover."
Song: "The merchant, to
secure his treasure."
They Never Taste Who
Always Drink.
To a Child of Quality.
To a Friend on His Nuptials.
To a Lady: She Refusing to
Continue a Dispute with
Me...
To a Young Gentleman in
Love: A Tale.
To the Honorable Charles
Montague, Esq.
The Town Mouse and the
Country Mouse (parody).
A True Maid.
The Turtle and the Sparrow
(excerpt).
Verses Written at The Hague.
Ano 1696.
When You with Hogh Dutch
Heeren Dine.
The Woman's Wish.
Written in an Ovid.
Written in the Beginning of
Mezeray's History of France.
Pritam, Amrita
The Annunciation.
Daily Wages.
Pritchard, N. H.
Metagnomy.
Pritchard, Sheila
Some Kind of Giant.
Pritchard II, Norman Henry
Aswelay.
Gyre's Galax.
Love.
Self.
Privett, Katharine
Watching My Daughter Sew.
Windmill in March.
Probst, Anita Endrezze
Canto Llano.
Eclipse.
Exodus.
In the Flight of the Blue
Heron: To Montezuma.
Learning the Spells: A
Diptych.
Manifest Destiny.
Notes from an Analyst's
Couch.
The Stripper.
The Truth about My Sister
and Me.
Probyn, May
The Bees of Middleton
Manor.
The Beloved.
A Christmas Carol.
Is It Nothing to You?
Procter, Adelaide Anne
Cleansing Fires.
A Doubting Heart.
Envy.
Fidelis.
Give Me Thy Heart.
A Legend.
A Lost Chord.
My Picture.
One by One.

Per Pacem ad Lucem.
The Present.
The Shadows of the Evening
Hours.
Thankfulness.
The Warrior to His Dead
Bride.
A Woman's Question.
Procter, Bryan Waller *See also*
"Cornwall, Barry"
For a Fountain.
Hermione.
The Poet's Song to His Wife.
Softly Woo Away Her Breath.
A Song for the Seasons.
A Vision (excerpt).
Proctor, Alan
At Night.
Proctor, Edna Dean
The Brooklyn Bridge.
The Captive's Hymn.
Columbia's Emblem.
Columbus Dying.
Forward.
The Glory of Toil.
Heaven, O Lord, I Cannot
Lose.
Heroes.
John Brown.
The Lost War-Sloop.
Sa-ca-ga-we-a.
Take Heart.
Proctor, Thomas
A Proper Sonnet, How Time
Consumeth All Earthly
Things.
Respice Finem.
Prokosch, Frederic
The Conspirators.
Eclogue.
Fable.
The Festival.
The Gothic Dusk.
Propertius, Sextus
Ah Woe Is Me.
Carmina, II, 28.
The Complaint of Tarpeia's
Door.
Cynthia, Cynthia.
Hylas.
Light, Light of My Eyes.
Revenge to Come.
The Watering Place.
"Prout, Father" *See* **Mahony,
Francis Sylvester**
Provost, Sarah
These Magicians.
Prowse, William Jeffery
The City of Prague.
**Prudentius (Aurelius Clemens
Prudentius)**
Before Sleep.
The Burial of the Dead.
Cathemerinon: O Noble
Virgin.
The Holy Innocents.
Laudate for Christmas.
Of the Father's Love
Begotten.
Prudhomme, Sully
The Struggle.
Prunty, Wyatt
Repetition.
The Wake.
Prutkov, Kozma
Junker Schmidt.
Prys, Thomas
A Poem to Show the Trouble
That Befell Him When He
Was at Sea.
Prys-Jones, A. G.
St. Govan.

Ptichford, Kenneth
Five Lyrics from "Good for
Nothing Man".
Pudjipangu
Aeroplane.
Pudney, John
After Bombardment.
For Johnny.
Map Reference T994724.
Missing.
On Seeing My Birthplace from
a Jet Aircraft.
Stiles.
To You Who Wait.
Pugliesi, Giacomino
Canzone: Of His Dead Lady.
Canzonetta: Of His Lady in
Absence.
Pukui, Mary Kawena
Behold.
Pulci, Luigi
Appeal for Illumination.
Prophecy.
Pullen, Elisabeth Cavazza
Alicia's Bonnet.
Derelict.
Her Shadow.
Love and Poverty.
The Sea-Weed.
Pullen, Eugene Henry
Children's Prayers.
Pulsifer, Harold Trowbridge
The Duel.
The Harvest of Time.
I Accept.
Of Little Faith.
Peace.
Thoughts upon a Walk with
Natalie, My Niece, at
Houghton Farm.
Purcell, Henry
Come Ye Sons of Art
(excerpt).
Purdom, George
Robens' Promised Land.
Purdy, A. W.
The Dead Seal.
Girl.
Purdy, Al
Alive or Not.
The Cariboo Horses.
The Country North of
Belleville.
The Dead Poet.
Lament for the Dorsets.
Love at Roblin Lake.
Night Song for a Woman.
Nine Bean-Rows on the
Moon.
Poem: "You are ill and so I
lead you away."
Remains of an Indian Village.
Spinning.
Trees at the Arctic Circle.
Purdy, Alfred W.
At Roblin Lake.
Landscape.
The Rattlesnake.
The Sculptors.
Wilderness Gothic.
Purohit Swami
I Know That I Am a Great
Sinner.
A Miracle Indeed.
Shall I Do This.
Pushkin, Aleksandr
Elegy.
Pushkin, Alexander
Autumn.
The Coach of Time.
The Crucifix.

I loved you; even now I may
confess.
Message to Siberia.
No, Never Think.
Phantoms of the Steppe.
The Prophet.
Sweet Boy, Gentle Boy.
To Madame A. P. Kern.
The Upas Tree.
Verses Written During a
Sleepless Night.
When in My Arms.
With Freedom's Seed.
Work.
**Putnam, Howard Phelps (Phelps
Putnam)**
About Women.
Ballad of a Strange Thing.
Hasbrouck and the Rose.
Romeo and Juliet.
To the Memory of Yale
College.
Puttenham, George
Cruel You Be.
Puziss, Marla
Following Van Gogh
(Avignon, 1982).
Pye, Henry James
Aerophorion (excerpt).
Pygge, Edward
Crow Resting (parody).
Notes for a Revised Sonnet
(parody).
Notes for a Sonnet (parody).
Occam's Razor Starts in
Massachusetts (parody).
Revised Notes for a Sonnet
(parody).
Shantih shantih shantih
(parody).
The Wasted Land (parody).
What about You? (parody).
Pyle, Katharine
August.
The Circus Parade.
Clever Peter and the Ogress.
The Sea Princess.
The Sweet Tooth.
The Toys Talk of the World.
The Visitor.
Waking.
The Wonder Clock.
Pyrlaeus, Johann C.
Jesu, Come on Board.

Q

"Q" *See* **Quiller-Couch Sir
Arthur Thomas**
Qarshe, Cabdullaahi
Colonialism.
Qorratu'l-Ayn
He the Beloved (excerpt).
Quagliano, Tony
The Edward Hopper
Retrospective.
Quarles, Francis
The Authour's Dreame.
Be Sad, My Heart.
Canticles II. XVI.
A Divine Rapture.
Emblems.
Epigram: "My soul, sit thou a
patient looker-on."
Epigram: "My soul, what's
lighter than a feather?
Wind."
False World, Thou Liest.

A Forme of Prayer.
A Good Night.
Hos Ego Versiculos.
Like as the Damask Rose.
My Glass Is Half Unspent.
O Whither Shall I Fly?
Of Common Devotion.
On Change of Weathers.
On Judas Iscariot.
On Off'rings.
On the Cuckoo.
On the Infancy of Our
  Saviour.
On the Needle of a Sun-Dial.
On the Plough-Man.
On the World.
On Those That Deserve It.
On Zacchaeus.
Why Dost Thou Shade Thy
  Lovely Face?
Quasimodo, Salvatore
The Gentle Hill.
Going Back.
The High Sailboat.
Man of My Time.
The Rain's Already With Us.
Quennell, Peter
The Divers.
The Flight into Egypt.
Hero Entombed I.
Leviathan.
Procne.
Small Birds.
The Sunflower.
While I Have Vision.
Queremel, Angel M.
Manifesto of the Soldier Who
  Went Back to War.
**Quevedo y Villegas, Francisco
  Gomez de**
Death Warnings.
The Fly.
Sonnet: Death Warnings.
Quick, Richard
The Reagan (parody).
Quick-To-See-Smith, Jaune
The Ronan Robe Series.
Quickenden, Beatrice
Hail, Oh Hail to the King.
Quigless, Helen
Concert.
**Quiller-Couch, Sir Arthur
  Thomas ("Q")**
Alma Mater.
Chant Royal of High Virtue.
The Famous Ballad of the
  Jubilee Cup.
Lady Jane.
A Letter.
The lion is a beast to fight.
The New Ballad of Sir Patrick
  Spens (parody).
Retrospection.
Sage Counsel.
The Splendid Spur.
De Tea Fabula.
Upon Eckington Bridge, River
  Avon.
Upon New Year's Eve.
Quillet, Claude
The Best Time for
  Conception.
How to Conceive Boys.
The Process of Conception.
Quillinan, Edward
The Hour Glass.
Quinn, John Robert
At Times I Feel Like a
  Quince Tree.
A Foxhole for the Night.
Row of Houses.
Whistling Boy.

Quinn, Roderic
The Camp Within the West.
The Fisher.
Quint, Beverly
A View.
Quintana, Leroy V.
Last Night There Was a
  Cricket in Our Closet.
Legacy II.
Nine Years after Viet Nam.
Quirk, Cathleen
Another Night on the Porch
  Swing.
Quirk, Charles J.
Quatrains.

R

Raab, Esther
Folk Tune.
A Serenade for Two Poplars.
Raab, Lawrence
The Assassin's Fatal Error.
Attack of the Crab Monsters.
Pastoral.
This Day.
Two Clouds.
Valediction.
Visiting the Oracle.
Voices Answering Back: The
  Vampires.
Rab
The Kingdom of God.
Raba, Gyorgy
Conversation.
Message.
Rabbit, Thomas
Casino Beach.
County Roads.
The Dancing Sunshine
  Lounge.
Gargoyle.
Rape.
The Weight Room.
Rabearivelo, Jean
Flute Players.
Here She Stands.
Rabelais, Francois
Shrovetide's Countenance.
Rabi'a, Daughter of Ka'b,
A Curse.
Rabi'a bint Isma'il
Sufi Quatrain.
Rabi'a of Balkh
My Wish for You.
Raboff, Paul
Jars.
Reb Hanina.
Rachel, Yank (James)
Lake Michigan Blues.
T-Bone Steak Blues.
Rachel Annand, Taylor
The End of the Duel.
"Rachel" (Rachel Blumstein)
Barren.
Dawn.
Jonathan.
My Dead.
My White Book of Poems.
Perhaps.
Rachel.
Revolt.
Rachow, George
Captured Bird.
Going Back.
Survival in a Stone Maze.
Textile Mills and Prison
  Reform.

Toward Tenses Two Moons.
Racine, Jean Baptiste
Athalie: Chorus (excerpt).
Phaedra: The Conquest of
  Love.
Radcliffe, Alexander
As Concerning Man.
Radford, Dollie
Soliloquy of a Maiden Aunt.
Radford, Ernest
Quiet.
Upon Julia (parody).
Radford, Mrs. Ernest
Plymouth Harbor.
Radishchev, Alexander
Sapphic Stanzas.
Radnoti, Miklos
Charm.
Forced March.
Fragment.
Hesitating Ode.
I Hid You.
In Your Arms.
Letter to My Wife.
Metaphors.
Picture Postcards.
The Ragged Robin Opens.
Rain Falls. It Dries...
Root.
Seventh Eclogue.
Song: "Whipped by sorrow
  now."
Rae, Hugh C.
Mountain Creed.
Raffel, Burton
Creation Myths.
Ecological Lecture.
On Watching the Construction
  of a Skyscraper.
Raffles
O Lord! My Hiding Place.
Rafi of Merv
The Roses of Thy Cheeks.
Raftery, Anthony
County Mayo.
I Am Raftery.
The Lass from Bally-Na-Lee.
Mary Hynes.
Raftery, Gerald
Apartment House.
Rago, Henry
The Coming of Dusk upon a
  Village in Haiti.
The Green Afternoon.
The Knowledge of Light.
Meeting of a Poetry Society.
The Monster.
Promise Your Hand.
A Sky of Late Summer
  (excerpt).
The Summer Countries.
Rahschulte, Mark
Untitled.
Raile, Arthur Lyon
The Waning of Love.
Raine, Craig
Birth.
A Martian Sends a Postcard
  Home.
The Onion, Memory.
Raine, Kathleen
Air.
The Ancient Speech.
Beinn Naomh, IV: The
  Summit.
By the River Eden.
The Crystal Skull.
Daisies of Florence.
Desire.
Easter Poem.
Envoi.
Eudaimon.

The Fall.
For Posterity.
Images.
In Time.
The Instrument.
Isis Wanderer.
Lachesis.
Last Things.
London Night.
Love Poem.
Message from Home.
My Mother's Birthday: "I
  used to watch you sleeping."
Natura Naturans.
Night in Martindale.
Nocturne.
Old Paintings on Italian
  Walls.
On Leaving Ullswater.
Oreads.
Parting.
Puer Aeternus.
The Pythoness.
Question and Answer.
Requiem.
Rock (excerpt).
Scala Coeli.
Seen in a Glass.
Seventh Day.
Shells.
Spell against Sorrow.
Spell of Creation.
Spell of Sleep.
Statues.
Still Life.
The Still Pool.
To My Mountain.
"Tu Non Se' In Terra, Si
  Come Tu Credi...".
Two Invocations of Death.
Water (excerpt).
The Wilderness.
The World.
Worry about Money.
Written in Exile.
Rainer, Dachine
Ashokan.
At Eighty-Seven.
Double Ritual.
Epithalamium for Cavorting
  Ghosts.
Night Musick for Therese.
Samis Idyll.
Upon Being Awakened at
  Night by My Four Year Old
  Daughter.
Rainey, Ma
Don't Fish in My Sea.
Southern Blues.
Rainsford, Christina
Shadbush.
Raisor, Philip
Demolition.
Rak, Jan
Illusion.
Rakosi, Carl
Americana.
The Avocado Pit.
Being Natural.
The China Policy.
The Experiment with a Rat.
Florida.
In a Warm Bath.
The Indomitable.
A Lamentation.
Meditation.
The Medium IV Sights.
The Memoirs.
No One Talks about This.
Poetry.
Tune.
The Vow.

Woman.
Young Couples Strolling By.
Ralegh, Sir Walter
The Advice.
Affection and Desire.
All the World's a Stage.
Another of the Same.
The Artist.
"As you came from the holy land of Walsingham."
Come to Me Soon.
The Conclusion.
A Description of Love.
Dulcina.
The Eleventh and Last Book of the Ocean to Cynthia.
Epitaph on the Earl of Leicester.
An Epitaph upon the Right Honorable Sir Philip Sidney...
Even Such Is Time.
The Excuse.
A Farewell to False Love.
Farewell to the Court.
Feed Still Thyself.
The Hermit.
His Petition to Queen Anne of Denmark (1618).
"If Cynthia be a Queen..."
In Commendation of George Gascoigne's Steel Glass (1576).
The Last Booke of the Ocean to Scinthia (excerpt).
The Lie.
Lines from Catullus.
Marius Victor.
My Body in the Walls Captived.
"My days' delight, my springtime joys fordone."
My Thoughts Are Winged with Hopes, My Hopes with Love.
Nature, That Washed Her Hands in Milk.
The Nimphs Reply to the Sheepheard.
Of Edmund Spenser's Fairy Queen...
On Dulcina.
On the Cards and Dice.
On the Snuff of a Candle.
Petition to the Queen.
The Pilgrimage.
A Poem Entreating of Sorrow.
A Poem of Sir Walter Rawleighs.
A Poem Put into My Lady Laiton's Pocket.
Reply.
The Shepherd's Praise of Diana.
The Silent Lover.
Sir Walter Ralegh to His Son.
Sir Walter Ralegh to the Queen.
"Sweet are the thoughts where hope persuadeth hap."
Sweet Unsure.
To His Love When He Had Obtained Her.
To the Translater of Lucan's Pharsalia (1614).
Virtue the Best Monument.
A Vision Upon This Conceipt of the Faerie Queene.
What Is Our Life?
"What tears, dear prince, can serve to water all."
Wishes of an Elderly Man.

The Wood, the Weed, the Wag.
Ralph, Nathan
When They Grow Old.
Ralston, W. R. S.
The Plaint of the Wife.
Ramage, Joyce
My Companion.
Ramanujan, A. K.
The Hindoo: He Doesn't Hurt a Fly or a Spider Either.
The Last of the Princes.
Small-Scale Reflections on a Great House.
Some Indian Uses of History on a Rainy Day.
Ramie, Marian
Will You, One Day.
Ramirez, Valentino
Fishin' Blues.
Ramke, Bin
The Green Horse.
The Magician.
The Monkish Mind of the Speculative Physicist.
The Obscure Pleasure of the Indistinct.
Sadness and Still Life.
Spring Poem.
Why I Am Afraid to Have Children.
Ramsaur, Hugh Wilgus
Epitaph, Found Somewhere in Space.
Ramsay, Allan
The Carle He Came O'er the Croft.
The Caterpillar and the Ant.
A Dainty Song.
Epigram: "Lasses, like nuts at bottom brown."
Give Me a Lass.
Katy's Answer.
The Lass o' Patie's Mill.
Lass with a Lump of Land.
Lochaber No More.
Look up to Pentland's Tow'ring Tap.
Peggy.
A Poet's Wish: An Ode.
Polwart on the Green.
Song: "At setting day and rising morn."
An Thou Were My Ain Thing (excerpt).
The Twa Books.
Up in the Air.
The Widow.
The Young Laird and Edinburgh Katy.
Ramsay, Andrew Michael
Friendship in Perfection.
Ramsey, Allen Beville
No teacher I of boys or smaller fry.
Ramsey, Jarold
Indian Painting, Probably Paiute, in a Cave near Madras, Oregon.
Lupine Dew.
Ontogeny.
The Tally Stick.
Ramsey, Paul
On the Porch of the Antique Dealer.
Ramsey, T. W.
Caught by Chance.
Power Station.
Ranaivo, Flavien
Love Song.
Song of a Common Lover.

Ranasinghe, Anne
Auschwitz from Colombo.
Holocaust 1944.
Ranchan, Som Parkash
Swan Song.
Rand, Kenneth
The Lonely Road.
Rand, Theodore Harding
The Dragonfly.
June.
The Loon.
Randall, Dudley
Abu.
After the Killing.
Analysands.
Ancestors.
Ballad of Birmingham.
Black Poet, White Critic.
Blackberry Sweet.
Booker T. and W. E. B.
A Different Image.
George.
Green Apples.
Hail, Dionysos.
I Loved You Once (From the Russian of Alexander Pushkin).
The Idiot.
The Intellectuals.
Langston Blues.
Legacy: My South.
The Melting Pot.
Memorial Wreath.
Old Witherington.
On Getting a Natural.
Pacific Epitaphs.
Perspectives.
Primitives.
The Profile on the Pillow.
The Rite.
Roses and Revolutions.
The Southern Road.
Souvenirs.
To the Mercy Killers.
Randall, James Ryder
After a Little While.
John Pelham.
Maryland, My Maryland.
My Maryland.
Why the Robin's Breast Was Red.
Randall, Julia
For a Homecoming.
To William Wordsworth from Virginia.
Randall, Virginia D.
October Winds.
Randall, Jr, James A.
Don't Ask Me Who I Am.
Execution.
Jew.
Untitled.
When Something Happens.
Who Shall Die?
Randall-Mills, Elizabeth
Crossing the County Line.
Randolph, Anson Davies Fitz
The Master's Invitation.
Randolph, Innes
The Rebel.
Randolph, Thomas
Come from Thy Palace.
A Devout Lover.
An Elegie.
A Gratulatory to Mr. Ben. Johnson for His Adopting of Him...
He Lives Long Who Lives Well.
Invocation.
A Maske for Lydia.

The Milkmaid's Epithalamium.
Now come, my boon companions.
Ode on Leaving the Great Town.
An Ode to Mr. Anthony Stafford to Hasten Him into the Country.
On a Maide of Honour Seene by a Schollar in Sommerset Garden.
On the Death of a Nightingale.
A Parley with His Empty Purse.
A Pastoral Courtship (excerpt).
Phyllis.
The Poet.
Poetry and Philosophy.
Song: "Music, thou queen of souls, get up and string."
This Definition Poetry Doth Fit.
To One Admiring Her Selfe in a Looking-Glasse.
Upon His Picture.
Upon Love Fondly Refus'd for Conscience Sake.
Upon the Losse of His Little Finger.
Rands, William Brighty ("Matthew Browne")
The Cat of Cats.
Clean Clara.
The Dream of a Boy Who Lived at Nine Elms.
The Dream of a Girl Who Lived at Sevenoaks.
The Drummer-Boy and the Shepherdess.
The First Tooth.
A Fishing Song.
The Flowers.
Godfrey Gordon Gustavus Gore.
Gypsy Jane.
I Saw a New World.
Lilliput Levee.
The Pedlar's Caravan.
Praise and Love.
A Shooting Song.
The Thought.
Topsyturvey-World.
Winifred Waters.
The Wonderful World.
Rangiaho
Song of Despair.
Rankin, Carroll Watson
Limerick: "Of inviting to dine, in Epirus."
Rankin, Jeremiah Eames
The Babie.
Fairest of Freedom's Daughters.
God Be with You Till We Meet Again.
Laboring and Heavy Laden.
The Word of God to Leyden Came.
Rankin, Paula
Being Refused Local Credit.
For My Mother, Feeling Useless.
Love in Magnolia Cemetery.
Middle Age.
Somewhere Else.
Tending.
Rankin, Ruth
The Woman Who Combed.

Rankins, William
Satire Septimus Contra
Sollistam.
Satyrus Peregrinana.
Ranko
The Fall of the Plum
Blossoms.
Ransford, R. W.
She Found Me Roots
(parody).
Ransom, John Crowe
Address to the Scholars of
New England.
Agitato Ma Non Troppo.
Amphibious Crocodile.
Antique Harvesters.
Armageddon.
Bells for John Whiteside's
Daughter.
Blackberry Winter.
Blue Girls.
Captain Carpenter.
Conrad in Twilight.
Dead Boy.
Dog.
Emily Hardcastle, Spinster.
The Equilibrists.
First Travels of Max.
Good Ships.
Her Eyes.
Here Lies a Lady.
Inland City.
Janet Waking.
Judith of Bethulia.
Lady Lost.
Little Boy Blue.
Man without Sense of
Direction.
Master's in the Garden Again.
Miriam Tazewell.
Miss Euphemia.
Old Man Pondered.
Old Mansion.
Our Two Worthies.
Painted Head.
Parting at Dawn.
Parting, without a Sequel.
Persistent Explorer.
Philomela.
Piazza Piece.
Prelude to an Evening.
Somewhere Is Such a
Kingdom.
Spectral Lovers.
Spiel of the Three
Mountebanks.
Survey of Literature.
The Swimmer.
Tom, Tom, the Piper's Son.
Triumph.
Two in August.
Vaunting Oak.
Vision by Sweetwater.
Winter Remembered.
Ransom, W. M.
Catechism, 1958.
Critter.
Grandpa's .45.
Indian Summer: Montana,
1956.
Message from Ohanapecosh
Glacier.
On the Morning of the Third
Night above Nisqually.
Statement on Our Higher
Education.
Ransome, Basil
Travellers Turning over
Borders (parody).
Rao, K. Raghavendra
The Journey to Golgotha.

Raphael, Lennox
Infants of Summer.
Mike 65.
Rapport, Solomon *See* "Ansky,
S."
Ras, Barbara
At the Beginnings of the
Andes.
Rascas, Bernard
The Love of God.
Rashidd, Amir
Eclipse.
Rashidd, Niema
Warriors Prancing, Women
Dancing...
Rashley, R. E.
Caterpillar.
Portrait of an Indian.
Voyageur.
Raskin, Selma
Tee-Vee Enigma.
Rasof, Henry
The Fourth Option.
Ratcliffe, Dorothy Una
Rake.
The Song of Nidderdale.
St. Bridget's Lullaby.
Ratcliffe, Stephen
Postscript, on a Name.
Ratner, Rochelle
Davening.
The Maiden.
The Poor Shammes of
Berditchev.
Ratosh, Yonathan
Lament.
Ratti, John
Division.
Inside, Outside, and Beyond.
Rauschenbusch, Walter
The Postern Gate (excerpt).
Rautenstrauch, Luis, Montoto y
See Montoto y
Our Poets' Breed.
Raven, John
Assailant.
An Inconvenience.
The Roach.
Ravenel, Beatrice
Intervals.
Ravenscroft, Thomas
By the Moon.
Hawking for the Partridge.
Madrigal: "My mistress is as
fair as fine."
Ravikovich, Dahlia
The Blue West.
A Dress of Fire.
The Everlasting Forests.
Hills of Salt.
On the Road at Night There
Stands the Man.
Poem of Explanations.
Requiem after Seventeen
Years.
Surely You Remember.
Ravitch, Melech
Conscience.
Let Us Learn.
A Poem–Good or Bad–A
Thing–With One Attribute–
Flat.
Twelve Lines About the
Burning Bush.
Twilight Thoughts in Israel.
Verses Written on Sand.
Rawes, Henry Augustus
The Last Hour.
Rawnsley, Hardwick Drummond
A Ballad of the Conemaugh
Flood.
The Old Parish Church,
Whitby.

Raworth, Tom
Collapsible.
The Empty Pain-Killer
Bottles.
Hot Day at the Races.
My Face Is My Own, I
Thought.
Rawson, Grindall
To the Learned and Reverend
Mr. Cotton Mather...
Upon the Death of His Much
Esteemed Friend Mr Jno
Saffin Junr....
Ray, David
At Grand Canyon's Edge.
The Card-Players.
The Carolinas.
Death-Lace.
Dragging the Main.
Extreme Unction in Pa.
Genitori.
Greens.
Hansel and Gretel Return.
The Jogger: Denver to Kansas
City.
Love Letter.
On a Fifteenth-Century
Flemish Angel.
On the Poet's Leer.
Orphans.
A Piece of Shrapnel.
The Problems of a Writing
Teacher.
Sonnet to Seabrook.
Stopping near Highway 80.
Throwing the Racetrack Cats
at Saratoga.
Ursula.
W. C. W.
X-Ray.
Ray, Henrietta Cordelia
Antigone and Oedipus.
The Dawn of Love.
Idyl: Sunrise.
Idyl: Sunset.
Milton.
Robert G. Shaw.
To My Father.
Ray, Judy
Rose Bay Willow Herb.
Ray, Louise Crenshaw
Philippine Madonna.
Rayaprol, Srinavas
On Growing Old.
Rayford, Julian Lee
Boom.
Junkyards.
Raymond, Harry
Hallelujah, I'm A-Travelin'.
Raymond, Rossiter Worthington
Concerning Them That Are
Asleep.
Raymund, Bernard
Wonder.
Rea, Susan Irene
Love Poem.
Poem for Dorothy Holt.
Rea, Tom
Rumors of War in Wyoming.
Read, Elfreida
Return to the Valley.
Read, John
Down by the Old Mill
Stream.
Read, Sir Herbert
Beata L'Alma.
Bombing Casualties: Spain.
Champ de Manoeuvres.
Childhood.
Cranach.
The Crucifix.
The End of a War.

Equation.
The Execution of Cornelius
Vane.
The Falcon and the Dove.
Garden Party.
Mutations of the Phoenix
(excerpt).
My Company.
A Northern Legion.
The Refugees.
The Retreat.
The Seven Sleepers.
Sic et Non.
A Song for the Spanish
Anarchists.
The Sorrow of Unicume.
Summer Rain.
To a Conscript of 1940.
Villages Demolis.
The Well of Life.
The White Isle of Leuce.
Woodlands.
A World within a War.
Read, Thomas Buchanan
The Attack.
Blennerhassett's Island.
The Brave at Home.
The Closing Scene.
Drifting.
The Eagle and Vulture.
The Flag of the Constellation.
Lines to a Blind Girl.
The Rising.
Sheridan's Ride.
Valley Forge.
The Windy Night.
Read, Vail
This New Day.
Realf, Richard
The Defence of Lawrence.
Indirection.
De Mortuis Nil Nisi Bonum.
An Old Man's Idyl.
The Word.
Reaney, James
The Alphabet.
The Baby.
The Chough.
Clouds.
The Gramophone.
Granny Crack.
The Great Lakes Suite.
The Horn.
June.
The Katzenjammer Kids.
Klaxon.
The Lost Child.
The Oracular Portcullis.
The Plum Tree.
The Red Heart.
The School Globe.
A Suit of Nettles.
The Upper Canadian.
Reape, Lisa
Leavetaking.
Reavey, George
The Bridge of Heraclitus.
Dismissing Progress and its
Progenitors.
How Many Fires.
Never.
Rebearivelo, Jean-J.
What Invisible Rat.
Rebelo, Jorge
Poem: "Come, brother, and
tell me your life."
Reccardi, Joe
Remembering Him.
Rechter, Judith
FayWray to the King.

Rector, Liam
My Grandfather Always
Promised Us.
Redding, Edward C.
When the Saints Come
Marching In.
Redfern, Roger A.
Night Expedition from Ben
Alder Cottage.
Redgrove, Peter
Against Death.
Bedtime Story for My Son.
Christiana.
Corposant.
The Curiosity-Shop.
Design.
Dismissal.
Dog Prospectus.
Early Morning Feed.
The Eggs.
For No Good Reason.
The Ghostly Father.
I Stroll.
The Idea of Entropy at
Maenporth Beach.
Intimate Supper.
The Million.
New Forms.
On Catching a Dog-Daisy in
the Mower.
Red Indian Corpse.
Required of You This Night.
The Secretary.
Serious Readers.
Shearing Grass.
Story from Russian Author.
To the Postmaster General.
The Visible Baby.
Redi, Francesco
Bacchus in Tuscany (excerpt).
Bacchus on Beverages.
The Creation of My Lady.
Redl-Hlus, Carolyn D.
Melissa.
Redmond, Eugene B.
Definition of Nature.
Gods in Vietnam.
Love Necessitates.
Main Man Blues.
Midway in the Night:
Blackman.
**Redner, Lewis H. and Philip
Brooks**
Oh, Little Town of
Bethlehem.
Redpath, Beatrice
But I Shall Weep.
The Star.
Redshaw, Thomas Dillon
Voice from Danang.
Redwing, A. K.
Agent of Love.
A Blue Jeaned Rock Queen in
Search of Happiness...
Chrome Babies Eating
Chocolate Snowmen in the
Moonlight.
Cosmic Eye.
The Hoofer.
A Lost Mohican Visits Hell's
Kitchen.
Sitting Bull's Will Versus the
Sioux Treaty of 1868 and
Monty Hall.
Tornado Soup.
Two Hookers.
The World's Last Unnamed
Poem.
Written in Unbridled
Repugnance near Sioux Falls,
Alabama...

Reed, Edward Bliss
Despair.
The Heritage.
Poplars.
Prayer.
September Is Here.
Reed, Henry
Chard Whitlow.
Chrysothemis.
The Door and the Window.
Lessons of the War.
Lives.
A Map of Verona.
Morning.
Naming of Parts.
Sailors' Harbour.
The Wall.
Reed, Ishmael
Al Capone in Alaska.
Badman of the Guest
Professor.
Beware : Do Not Read This
Poem.
Black Power Poem.
Dialog outside the Lakeside
Grocery.
The Feral Pioneers.
The Gangster's Death.
I Am a Cowboy in the Boat
of Ra.
Instructions to a Princess.
The Katskills Kiss Romance
Goodbye.
Rain Rain on the Splintered
Girl.
The Reactionary Poet.
Sermonette.
Skirt Dance.
Sky Diving.
Untitled I.
Reed, J. D.
Cripples.
The Gorilla at Twenty Nine
Years.
Lost Silvertip.
Organ Transplant.
Out from Lobster Cove.
The Reports Come In.
Stony Brook Tavern.
Strange Kind (II).
Reed, John
Fog.
Proud New York.
Reed, Joseph Samuel
A Soldier's Plea for the
Y.M.C.A.
Reed, Langford
Limerick: "A patriot, living at
Ewell."
Limerick: "All hail to the
town of Limerick."
Limerick: "Consider the
lowering Lynx."
Reed, Mary Davis
One Year to Live.
Reed, Nan Terrell
Life.
Vases.
Reed, Thomas
The Indian.
Reed, Jr, David
Love Me, and the World Is
Mine.
Reedy, Arnold
Lament for Apirana Ngata.
Reedy, Carlyle
Have You Noted the White
Areas.
Rees, Grover, III
Abelard at Cluny.
Reese, Doc
Ol' Hannah.

Reese, Florence
Which Side Are You On?
Reese, Lizette Woodworth
After.
Anne.
April Weather.
At Cockcrow.
Bible Stories.
A Book.
A Carol.
A Christmas Fold-Song.
Compensation.
Daffodils.
The Dust.
A Flower of Mullein.
Ghost Night.
A Girl's Mood.
The Good Joan.
His Mother in Her Hood of
Blue.
A Holiday.
Immortality.
In Harbor.
In Time of Grief.
Keats.
The Lark.
A Little Song of Life.
Love Came Back at Fall o'
Dew.
Lydia.
Lydia is Gone This Many a
Year.
Ownership.
The Portrait of a Florentine
Lady.
Possessions.
Prayer of an Unbeliever.
A Puritan Lady.
Reserve.
The Road of Remembrance.
Robert Louis Stevenson.
Spicewood.
Spring Ecstasy.
A Street Scene.
Taps.
Tears.
Tell Me Some Way.
Telling the Bees.
That Day You Came.
This Very Hour.
Thistledown.
To a Town Poet.
Trust.
Wild Cherry.
Wise.
Reese, S. Carolyn
Letter from a Wife.
Reeve, F. D.
Alcoholic.
Botany Lesson.
The Falls.
Hope.
We Settled by the Lake.
Reeve, James
Fireworks.
Reeve, Paul Eaton
Succumbing.
Reeves, Billy
Shew! Fly, Don't Bother Me.
Reeves, James
A Bagatelle.
Beech Leaves.
The Bogus-Boo.
Catullus to Lesbia.
The Ceremonial Band.
Cows.
Doctor Emmanuel.
The Double Autumn.
The Doze.
The Four Horses.
Giant Thunder.
The Grey Horse.

The Horn.
If Pigs Could Fly.
The Intruder.
The Little Brother.
Little Fan.
Mick.
Mr. Tom Narrow.
My Singing Aunt.
The Nonny.
Old Crabbed Men.
Old Moll.
The Old Wife and the Ghost.
A Pig Tale.
Queer Things.
The Snitterjipe.
Stocking and Shirt.
The Stone Gentleman.
Things to Come.
The Toadstool Wood.
The Travelers.
The Two Old Women of
Mumbling Hill.
W.
The Wooing Frog.
You'd Say It Was a Funeral.
You in Anger.
Zachary Zed.
Reeves, William Pember
The Albatross.
A Colonist in His Garden.
The Dutch Seamen and New
Holland.
Nox Benigna.
The Passing of the Forest.
Regelson, Abraham
Moses on Mount Nebo.
Regnier, Henri de
Autumn Twilight.
Je Ne Veux de Personne
aupres de ma Tristesse.
Night.
Regnier, Mathurin
Epitaph on Himself.
Regniers, Beatrice Schenk de
See De Regniers, Beatrice
Schenk
Reich, Heather Tosteson
Waltz.
Reich, Max Isaac
For Every Man.
The One Thing Needful.
Reich, Shlomo
The Golem.
A Tribe Searching.
The Vigil.
The Windmill of Evening.
Reid, Alastair
Calenture.
Casa d'Amunt.
Curiosity.
Daedalus.
The Figures on the Frieze.
For Her Sake.
A Game of Glass.
Geneva.
Ghosts.
Ghosts' Stories.
The Glass Town.
In Memory of My Uncle
Timothy.
An Instance.
A Lesson in Handwriting.
Me to You.
Outlook Uncertain.
Pigeons.
Small Sad Song.
The Tale the Hermit Told.
To Lighten My House.
Reid, Barrie
Nothing.
St. Kilda.

Reid, Christopher
Gladstone Gave His Name to the Gladstone Bag.
Letter to Myself (parody).
Reid, Dorothy E.
Coach into Pumpkin.
Reid, John, of Stobo
The Thre Prestis of Peblis: Prologue.
Reid, Monty
Her Story.
The Road Back and Forth to Ryley.
Rock Tumbler.
The Shorebirds.
Spring Ease.
Test Drive.
Tractor Hour.
Reid, III, Robert F.
Shadow Life.
Reiner, Lois
Father.
Reingold, Paula
And This Is Love.
Reinmar von Hagenau
As on the Heather.
A Childish Game.
Reinmar von Zweter
I Came A-Riding.
Reisen, Abraham
Burn out Burn Quick.
An Endless Chain.
The Family of Eight.
Girls from Home.
Healing.
Newcomers.
Two Songs, II.
The Watchman.
What Is the Case in Point?
Reiss, James
Approaching Washington Heights.
The Breathers.
Brothers (I).
The Green Tree.
Habla Usted Espanol?
The Macy's Poem.
On Hot Days.
A Slight Confusion.
Suenos.
Reissig, Julio Herrera
The Parish Church.
Reiter, Thomas
Bait Shop.
The First Day Out.
The First Lesson.
It's Not Bad Once the Water Goes Down.
The Other Side.
Reitz, Albert Simpson
The Cradle and the Cross.
Thy Will Be Done.
Relph, Josiah
Hay-Time; or The Constant Lovers. A Pastoral.
Remaly, Nancy
August Afternoon.
Rendall, Elizabeth
And of Laughter That Was a Changeling.
Needs.
The Wind.
Rendall, Robert
Angle of Vision.
The Planticru.
Shore Tullye.
Rendleman, Danny
Toward a Theory of Instruction.
Renfrow, Grace B.
My Choice.
That's Jesus.

Trusting Jesus.
Upheld by His Hand.
Renner-Tana, Patti
Hershey Kiss.
Renton, William
After Nightfall.
Crescent Moon.
The Foal.
The Fork of the Road.
Moon and Candle-Light.
The Shadow of Himself.
Replansky, Naomi
A Brick Not Used in Building.
Housing Shortage.
I Met My Solitude.
In the Sea of Tears.
An Inheritance.
The Mistress Addresses the Wife.
Two Women.
Repplier, Agnes
Le Repos en Egypte.
Resnikoff, Alexander
Bad and Good.
Retallack, Joan
Southern Liebeslieder.
Revard, Carter
Advice from Euterpe.
Another Sunday Morning.
But Still in Israel's Paths They Shine.
Coming of Age in the County Jail.
The Coyote.
Discovery of the New World.
Driving in Oklahoma.
ESP.
Getting Across.
Home Movies.
January 15 as a National Holiday.
North of Santa Monica.
Not Just Yet.
On the Bright Side.
Support Your Local Police Dog.
Revell, Donald
Belfast.
Central Park South.
In Lombardy.
Revere, Paul
Unhappy Boston.
Rewak, William J.
Quick Now, Here, Now, Always–.
The Visit.
Rewey, Marion Brimm
Love Song for a Tyrant.
Rexford, Eben E.
On Easter Morning.
A Trust-Song.
Rexroth, Kenneth
About the Cool Water.
Andree Rexroth.
Antipater of Thessalonica.
Autumn Rain.
The Bad Old Days.
A Bestiary.
The City of the Moon (excerpt).
Fact.
Fifty.
Fish Peddler and Cobbler.
For a Masseuse and Prostitute.
For Mary.
From the Persian.
Further Advantages of Learning.
The Great Canzon.
The Heart of Herakles.

Kings River Canyon.
A Letter to William Carlos Williams.
A Living Pearl.
Lute Music.
Lyell's Hypothesis Again.
Marcus Argentarius.
Maximian Elegy V.
Mother Goose Rhyme.
Observations in a Cornish Teashop.
On Flower Wreath Hill (excerpt).
On the Eve of the Plebiscite.
Only Years.
Our Canoe Idles in the Idling Current.
Parity.
Proust's Madeleine.
Quietly.
Rogation Days.
The Signature of All Things.
Song for a Dancer.
Strength through Joy.
A Sword in a Cloud of Light.
This Shall Be Sufficient.
Time Is the Mercy of Eternity.
Vitamins and Roughage.
The Wheel Revolves.
Reyes, Margarita Baldenegro
The Old Man Who Is Gone Now.
Reynolds, Barney
The Cranberry Song.
Reynolds, Blind Willie (Joe)
Married Man Blues.
Nehi Blues.
Reynolds, Elizabeth Gardner
The Little Black Dog.
Reynolds, George Nugent
Mary Le More.
Reynolds, John
Death's Vision (excerpt).
A Nosegay.
Reynolds, John Hamilton
Farewell to the Muses.
Gallantly within the Ring.
Peter Bell.
Sonnet: "Sweet poets of the gentle antique line."
Sonnet to–.
Reynolds, Lloyd J.
Weathergrams.
Reynolds, Lucile Hargrove
To the New Owner.
Reynolds, Malvina
Little Boxes.
What Have They Done to the Rain.
Reynolds, Tim
To a Bad Heart.
A Walk in March.
Rezmerski, John C.
Sonship.
Reznikoff, Charles
About an Excavation.
After I Had Worked All Day.
Autobiography: Hollywood.
The Body Is Like Roots Stretching.
Depression (excerpt).
Dew.
Domestic Scenes, 2.
The Hebrew of Your Poets, Zion.
The House-Wreckers Have Left the Door and a Staircase.
I Will Go into the Ghetto.
I Will Write Songs Against You.

Jacob.
Lament of the Jewish Women for Tammuz.
The Lamps Are Burning.
Let Other People Come as Streams.
The Letter.
Luzzato.
New Year's.
The Old Men.
On a Sunday.
Out of the Strong, Sweetness.
Puerto Ricans in New York.
Raisins and Nuts.
Te Deum.
These Days the Papers in the Street.
Two Girls...
Walk about the Subway Station.
Winter Sketches.
The Young Fellow Walks About.
Rhabanus Maurus
Sancte Confessor.
Rhianus
Epigram: "Most inexplicable the wiles of boys I deem."
Rhinow, Arthur B.
And Yet–.
Rhodes, Eugene Manlove
The Hired Man on Horseback.
Rhodes, Hugh
Rising in the Morning.
Rhodes, R.
Limerick: "That the Traylee's the best cigarette."
Rhys, Ernest
An Autobiography.
Dagonet's Canzonet.
Diana.
The Lament for Urien.
The Song of the Graves.
Words.
Rhys, Keidrych
The Good Shepherd.
Letter to My Wife.
Third and Fourth.
Tragic Guilt.
Ribback, Alan
Ar(chibald')s Poetica (parody).
Ribemont-Dessaignes George
Sliding Trombone.
Ribera Chevremont, Evaristo
The Boy and the Lantern (excerpt).
Rice, Albert
The Black Madonna.
Rice, Cale Young
Chanson of the Bells of Oseney.
Kinchinjunga.
A Litany for Latter-Day Mystics.
The Mystic.
New Dreams for Old.
Nights on the Indian Ocean.
On the Moor.
Providence.
Submarine Mountains.
To the Afternoon Moon, at Sea.
Rice, Grantland
Alumnus Football.
The First Division Marches.
Two Sides of War.
Rice, Harvey
Cuba.
Rice, Les
Banks of Marble.

Rice, Stan
  The 29th Month.
  America the Beautiful.
  The Bicycle.
  The Cry-Bird Journey.
  The Dogchain Gang.
  Flesh.
  History: Madness.
  Incanto.
  The Last Supper.
  Metaphysical Shock while
    Watching a TV Cartoon.
  Poem Following Discussion of
    Brain.
  Round Trip.
  Singing Death.
  The Skyjacker.
  Some Lamb.
Rice, Thomas D.
  Jump Jim Crow.
Rice, Wallace
  The Armstrong at Fayal.
  Battle-Song of the Oregon.
  Blood Is Thicker Than Water.
  The Brooklyn at Santiago.
  Defeat and Victory.
  The Destroyer of Destroyers.
  Dewey and His Men.
  The End.
  The First American Sailors.
  Firstfruits in 1812.
  Immortal Flowers.
  Jackson at New Orleans.
  The Minute-Men of North-
    Boro'.
  Spain's Last Armada.
  The Sudbury Fight.
  Tender, Slow.
  Under the Stars.
  Wheeler's Brigade at Santiago.
Rice, William
  Sweet Clover.
Rich, Adrienne
  5:30 A.M.
  After Dark.
  The Afterwake.
  Artificial Intelligence.
  At a Bach Concert.
  At Majority.
  Attention.
  August.
  Aunt Jennifer's Tigers.
  Autumn Sequence.
  Bears.
  Blood-Sister.
  Breakfast in a Bowling Alley
    in Utica, New York.
  The Burning of Paper Instead
    of Children.
  Burning Oneself In.
  The Celebration in the Plaza.
  Charleston in the 1860s.
  A Clock in the Square.
  Coast to Coast.
  The Corpse-Plant.
  The Demon Lover.
  Dialogue.
  Diving into the Wreck.
  Double Monologue.
  Epilogue for a Masque of
    Purcell.
  Face to Face.
  Focus.
  For the Conjunction of Two
    Planets.
  From a Survivor.
  From an Old House in
    America.
  From the Prison House.
  Gabriel.
  Grandmothers.
  Holiday.

  I Am in Danger–Sir–.
  I Dream I'm the Death of
    Orpheus.
  Ideal Landscape.
  Incipience.
  The Insomniacs.
  The Insusceptibles.
  The Knot.
  Leaflets.
  Like This Together.
  Living in Sin.
  Love in the Museum.
  Lucifer in the Train.
  Meditations for a Savage
    Child.
  Merced.
  The Middle-Aged.
  The Mirror in Which Two
    Are Seen as One.
  Mourning Picture.
  Moving in Winter.
  Necessities of Life.
  New Year's Eve in Troy.
  Nightbreak.
  The Ninth Symphony of
    Beethoven Understood at
    Last as a Sexual Message.
  Novella.
  November 1968.
  Orient Wheat.
  Origins and History of
    Consciousness.
  Orion.
  Peeling Onions.
  Phantasia for Elvira Shatayev.
  Planetarium.
  Power.
  A Primary Ground.
  Prospective Immigrants Please
    Note.
  Rape.
  The Raven.
  Re-Forming the Crystal.
  Readings of History.
  Recorders in Italy.
  A Revivalist in Boston.
  The Roofwalker.
  Shooting Script (excerpt).
  Sisters.
  Snapshots of a Daughter-in-
    law.
  Song: "You're wondering if
    I'm lonely."
  Storm Warnings.
  The Stranger.
  The Survivors.
  The Tourist and the Town.
  Toward the Solstice.
  Transit.
  Translations.
  The Trees.
  Trying to Talk with a Man.
  A Tryst in Brobdingnag.
  Twenty-One Love Poems.
  Two Songs.
  An Unsaid Word.
  Upper Broadway.
  A Valediction Forbidding
    Mourning.
  Versailles (Petit Trianon).
  Waking in the Dark.
  A Walk by the Charles.
  The Will to Change.
  A Woman Mourned by
    Daughters.
  Women.
Rich, Hiram
  Jerry an' Me.
  Morgan Stanwood.
  The Skipper-Hermit.
Rich, Richard
  Newes from Virginia.

Rich, Vera
  Lion Gate.
**Richard Coeur de Lion (Richard
  Lion-Heart)**
  Prison Song.
Richard of Caistre
  A Hymn to Jesus.
Richards, Edward Hersey
  A Wise Old Owl.
Richards, George
  Long as the Darkening Cloud
    Abode.
  Th' Almighty Spake, and
    Gabriel Sped.
Richards, I. A.
  Spendthrift.
Richards, Laura E.
  Alibazan.
  Antonio.
  At Easter Time.
  The Baby Goes to Boston.
  Bird Song.
  The Difference.
  Eletelephony.
  Gregory Griggs.
  The High Barbaree.
  In Foreign Parts.
  Jippy and Jimmy.
  Jumbo Jee.
  Kindness to Animals.
  The King of the
    Hobbledygoblins.
  A Legend of Lake
    Okeefinokee.
  The Mermaidens.
  Molly Pitcher.
  The Monkeys and the
    Crocodile.
  The Mouse.
  Mrs. Snipkin and Mrs.
    Wobblechin.
  My Uncle Jehoshaphat.
  A Nursery Song.
  The Owl and the Eel and the
    Warming-Pan.
  A Party.
  The Postman.
  Prince Tatters.
  Punkydoodle and Jollapin.
  Some Fishy Nonsense.
  Talents Differ.
  The Umbrella Brigade.
  A Valentine.
  Was She a Witch?
  Why Does It Snow?
Richards, Michael
  After Christmas.
Richardson, Charles Francis
  After Death.
  A Conjecture.
  The Perfect Life.
  Prayer.
Richardson, Dorothy Lee
  Modern Grimm.
Richardson, Dorothy M.
  Message.
Richardson, Dow
  The Cost-of-Living Mother
    Goose.
Richardson, George Lynde
  1886 A.D.
  Classical Criticism.
Richardson, James
  Dividing the House.
Richardson, Jonathan
  On My Late Dear Wife.
  Self-Consciousness Makes All
    Changes Happy.
Richardson, Justin
  Afterthought.
  Back Room Joys.
  La Carte.

  Garlic.
  High-Life Low-Down.
  The Oocuck.
  Red Wine.
  Rhyme for Remembering
    How Many Nights There
    Are in the Month.
  Rhyme for Remembering the
    Date of Easter.
  What'll Be the Title?
Richardson, Marion Muir
  The Gold Seekers.
Richardson, Robert
  Epitaph.
Richardson, Thomas
  Take Heed of Gazing
    Overmuch.
Richman, Norma Hope
  A Daughter's House.
  Poem to Help My Father.
Richstone, May
  Naming the Baby.
Richter, C. F.
  My Soul Before Thee
    Prostrate Lies.
Rickert, Wendy G.
  "Somedays now".
Rickword, Edgell
  The Cascade.
  The Contemporary Muse.
  Cosmogony.
  The Encounter.
  The Handmaid of Religion.
  Rimbaud in Africa.
  Trench Poets.
  Winter Warfare.
Riddell, Alan
  At the Hammersmith Palais...
Riddell, Elizabeth
  The Children March.
  Country Tune.
  Forebears.
  The Letter.
  News of a Baby.
  The Soldier in the Park.
  Suburban Song.
  Under the Casuarina.
  Wakeful in the Township.
Riddell, Henry Scott
  Scotland Yet.
Ridge, Lola
  Art and Life.
  Chicago.
  The Edge.
  The Legion of Iron.
  Reveille.
  Snow-Dance for the Dead.
  Wind in the Alleys.
Ridhiana
  Tricked Again.
Riding, Laura
  Auspice of Jewels.
  Because of Clothes.
  Dear Possible.
  The Flowering Urn.
  For-Ever Morning.
  The Forgiven Past.
  The Map of Places.
  Opening of Eyes.
  Respect for the Dead.
  Three Sermons to the Dead.
  The Wind Suffers.
  The Wind, the Clock, the We.
  With the Face.
Ridland, John
  Another Easter.
  Assassination Poems.
  The Light Year.
Ridler, Anne
  Bathing Song.
  Beads from Blackpool.
  Before Sleep.

Bring Back.
Bunhill's Fields.
Choosing a Name.
Christmas and Common
　Birth.
A Dream Observed.
Edlesborough.
For a Child Expected.
For a Christening.
A Letter.
Lumber of Spring.
Making Love, Killing Time.
A Matter of Life and Death.
A Mile from Eden.
News of the World.
Now as Then.
Now Philippa Is Gone.
O Love, Answer.
On a Picture by Michele da
　Verona, of Arion as a Boy
　Riding...
The Phoenix Answered.
Poem for a Christmas
　Broadcast.
River God's Song.
The Speech of the Dead.
The Spring Equinox.
Stone Angel.
Venetian Scene.
Zennor.

Ridley, George
Cushie Butterfield.
Ridlon, Marci
Fernando.
That Was Summer.
Riedemann, Myra von
Horses.
Last Will of the Drunk.
There Are Places.
Rieu, Emile Victor
Dirge for a Bad Boy.
The Flattered Flying Fish.
The Green Train.
The Lesser Lynx.
Meditations of a Tortoise
　Dozing under a Rosetree...
Night Thought of a Tortoise
　Suffering from Insomnia...
The Paint Box.
Solioquy of a Tortoise on
　Revisiting the Lettuce Beds...
Tony the Turtle.
Two People.
The Unicorn.
Rigby, Ralph
The Branding Iron Herd.
Riggs, Dionis Coffin
The Clamdigger.
Riggs, Katherine Dixon
Mockery.
Riggs, Lynn
Spring Morning–Santa Fe.
Rigsbee, David
Green Frogs.
Rihaku See also Li Po
Riley, C. L.
There Are Gods.
Riley, James Whitcomb
At Sea.
Away.
Back to Griggsby's Station.
A Barefoot Boy.
Bereaved.
Billy Could Ride.
A Boy's Mother.
Craqueodoom.
The Days Gone By.
The Diners in the Kitchen.
Dwainie.
The Elf Child.
Extremes.
Good-By er Howdy-Do.

Home Folks: The Name of
　Old Glory.
Honey Dripping from the
　Comb.
Ike Walton's Prayer.
An Impetuous Resolve.
Just Be Glad.
The Kentucky Thoroughbred.
Knee-Deep in June.
A Life-Lesson.
Lincoln.
The Little Hunchback.
Little Orphant Annie.
The Little Red Ribbon.
A Liz-Town Humorist.
Love's Prayer.
The Lugubrious Whing-
　Whang.
A Man by the Name of Bolus.
The Man in the Moon.
Maymie's Story of Red
　Riding-Hood.
The Nine Little Goblins.
The Old Man and Jim.
An Old Sweetheart of Mine.
The Old Swimmin'-Hole.
The Old Times Were the Best.
On the Death of Little
　Mahala Ashcraft.
Our Hired Girl.
Out of the Hitherwhere.
Out to Old Aunt Mary's.
A Parting Guest.
The Raggedy Man.
Rain.
A Rose in October.
A Sea-Song from the Shore.
A Sleeping Beauty.
The Spirk Troll-Derisive.
The Way the Baby Woke.
When She Comes Home.
When the Frost Is on the
　Punkin.
Riley, Michael D.
Macrame.
Rilke, Rainer Maria
Abishag.
Adam.
Annunciation.
Annunciation over the
　Shepherds (excerpt).
Archaic Torso of Apollo.
Autumn.
Autumn Day.
Birth of Christ.
The Book of Hours (excerpt).
The Book of Pilgrimage.
Bridge of the Carousel.
Childhood.
Christ's Descent into Hell.
Closing Piece.
Do You Know, I Would
　Quietly.
Duino Elegies.
Eve.
For, Lord, the Crowded Cities
　Be...
From a Childhood.
The Garden of Olives.
The Grief.
I Live My Life.
Initiation.
Joseph's Suspicion.
The Kings of the World...
The Knight.
Lament.
The Last Evening.
The Last Supper.
Leda.
Lovesong.
The Man Watching.
The Merry-Go-Round.

Moving Ahead.
On the Death of Mary.
Palm of the Hand.
The Panther.
Pieta.
Praise.
Prayer of the Maidens to
　Mary.
Presaging.
Silent Hour.
Solemn Hour.
The Solitary.
Solitude.
The Song of Love.
Sonnets to Orpheus.
To the Angel.
We Are All Workmen.
You, Neighbor God.
The Youth Dreams.
Rimbaud, Arthur
After the Flood.
Barbarian.
Charleville.
Childhood, IV.
Dawn.
The Drunken Boat.
Eighteen-Seventy.
Hunger.
The Lice-Finders.
The Louse-Catchers.
Memory.
My Mouth Is Often Joined
　against His Mouth.
The Poet at Seven.
Poets Seven Years Old.
The Poor in Church.
Royalty.
Sensation.
Shame.
Song of the Highest Tower.
Sonnet: "Dead men of 'ninety-
　two, also of 'ninety-three."
Sonnet: To the Asshole.
The Strolling Player.
The Tortured Heart.
Vowels.
Rimmer, Christine
How Night Falls in the
　Courtyard.
Rimon. I. Z
I Am a King.
Rimos, Moses
Elegy (For Himself).
Rinaldi, Nicholas
Black.
Teahouse.
Rinaldo d'Aquino
The Crusade.
Rinkart, Martin
Now Thank We All Our God.
Rioff, Suzanne Berger
Cycles, Cycles.
The Seduction.
Rios, Alberto
Belita.
Cinco de Mayo, 1862.
Cortes.
Incident at Imuris.
Juan Rulfo Moved Away.
Lost on September Trail,
　1967.
The Man She Called Honey,
　and Married.
The Man Who Named
　Children.
Mi Abuelo.
Morning.
Nani.
The Purpose of Altar Boys.
Saints, and Their Care.
Sundays Visiting.

Ripley, Elizabeth
Limerick: "There was a young
　hopeful named Sam."
Ripley, G.
Poem for Vladimir.
Risley, R. V.
Dewey in Manila Bay.
Ritchey, Belle MacDiarmid
I Shall Not Weep.
Rittenhouse, Jessie B.
Debts.
My Wage.
Seven Times the Moon Came.
Transformation.
Youth.
Ritter, Margaret Tod
Faith, I Wish I Were a
　Leprechaun.
Indictment.
Rive, Richard
Where the Rainbow Ends.
Rivera, Etnairis
I Pull out of the Depths of
　the Earth.
Rivera, Marina
The Man of O.
Rivera, Tomas
My Son Doesn't See a Thing.
Rivera-Aviles, Sotero
Good Memory.
Rainy Morning.
Rivero, Alina
In the Fall.
Rivers, Conrad Kent
The Death of a Negro Poet.
For All Things Black and
　Beautiful.
Four Sheets to the Wind and
　a One-Way Ticket to France.
If Blood Is Black Then Spirit
　Neglects My Unborn Son.
In Defense of Black Poets.
Malcolm, a Thousandth
　Poem.
A Mourning Letter from
　Paris.
On Passing Two Negroes on a
　Dark Country Road
　Somewhere in Georgia.
On the Death of William
　Edward Burghardt Du Bois...
Prelude.
The Still Voice of Harlem.
To Richard Wright.
The Train Runs Late to
　Harlem.
Watts.
Rivers, James W.
Tonsilectomy.
Rives, Amelie
My Laddie.
Rixson, Denis
Glen Pean.
The Ice Has Spoken.
Rlliot, George Tracy
Winter Twilight.
Roat, Charles E.
What a Friend We Have in
　Mother.
Robbins, Howard Chandler
And Have the Bright
　Immensities.
Put Forth, O God, Thy
　Spirit's Might.
The Sabbath Day Was By.
Saviour, Whose Love Is Like
　the Sun.
Spirit from Whom Our Lives
　Proceed.
Robbins, Martin
A Cantor's Dream before the
　High Holy Days.

On Seeing a Torn Out Coin
  Telephone.
Spring Is a Looping-Free
  Time.
Spring Rites.
Robbins, Richard
For My Grandfather.
Robbins, S. D.
The Master.
Robbins, Shellie Keir
Yielding.
Roberson, Ed
18,000 FEET.
Blue Horses.
Eclipse.
If the Black Frog Will Not
  Ring.
Mayday.
Othello Jones Dresses for
  Dinner.
Poll.
Seventh Son.
When Thy King Is a Boy
  (excerpt).
Robert II, King of France
Strength, Love, Light.
Veni, Sancte Spiritus.
Robert of Gloucester
Town against Gown at
  Oxford.
Roberts, Cecil
Charing Cross.
Prayer for a Pilot.
Springtime in Cookham Dean.
Roberts, Daniel C.
God of Our Fathers, Whose
  Almighty Hand.
Roberts, Dick
Duty to Death, LD.
Roberts, Dorothy
Cold.
Dazzle.
The Goose Girl.
Sisters.
Roberts, Elizabeth Madox
August Night.
Autumn.
Autumn Fields.
The Butterbean Tent.
A Child Asleep.
Christmas Morning.
Cinderella's Song.
The Circus.
The Cornfield.
Crescent Moon.
Dick and Will.
Evening Hymn.
Father's Story.
Firefly.
The Hens.
Horse.
In the Night.
Little Rain.
Milking Time.
Mr. Wells.
Mumps.
Orpheus.
The People.
The Rabbit.
Shells in Rock.
The Sky.
Strange Tree.
Stranger.
The Twins.
Uncle Mells and the Witches'
  Tree.
Water Noises.
The Woodpecker.
Roberts, George
Lament.

While Dissecting Frogs in
  Biology Class Scrut
  Discovers...
Roberts, Hortense Roberta
Farmers.
Roberts, Jean
I Never Saw the Train.
Roberts, Kevin
The Fish Come in Dancing.
July 1st, French Creek.
Roberts, LeVan
The Unemployed.
Roberts, Lloyd
Deep Dark River.
The Fruit Rancher.
One Morning When the Rain-
  Birds Call.
Roberts, Lynette
Low Tide.
Poem from Llanybri.
The Shadow Remains.
These Words I Write on
  Crinkled Tin.
Roberts, Mary M.
Little Pudding (parody).
Roberts, Michael
The Caves.
The Green Lake.
H.M.S. Hero.
Hymn to the Sea.
Hymn to the Sun.
In Our Time.
In the Flowering Season.
Midnight.
Les Planches-en-Montagnes.
St. Gervais.
St. Ursanne.
Roberts, Michele
Madwoman at Rodmell.
Magnificat.
Out of Chaos Out of Order
  Out.
The Sibyl's Song.
Roberts, Michelle
Inconsistencies.
Last Generation.
Moon Blast.
No One Is Asleep.
Purple Dry Buds.
The Spell.
Roberts, P. R.
Winter's Edge.
Roberts, Sheila
Poem for My Dead Husband.
Roberts, Sir Charles G. D.
Afoot.
The Aim.
An April Adoration.
At Tide Water.
Autochthon.
A Ballad of Manila Bay.
The Brook in February.
Brooklyn Bridge.
Canada.
Epitaph for a Sailor Buried
  Ashore.
The Flight of the Geese.
The Frosted Pane.
The Hawkbit.
The Herring Weir.
Ice.
The Iceberg.
In Apia Bay.
In the Night Watches.
In the Wide Awe and Wisdom
  of the Night.
Kinship.
The Logs.
Marsyas.
The Mowing.
O Earth, Sufficing All Our
  Needs.

O Solitary of the Austere Sky.
The Pea-Fields.
The Potato Harvest.
The Recessional.
The Salt Flats.
The Skater.
The Solitary Woodsman.
The Sower.
Tantramar Revisited.
The Unknown City.
When the Sleepy Man Comes.
Roberts, Theodore Goodridge
The Blue Heron.
Fiddler's Green.
Gluskap's Hound.
The Lost Shipmate.
The Maid.
The Reformed Pirate.
The Wrecker's Prayer.
Roberts, Walter Adolphe
On a Monument to Marti.
San Francisco.
Vieux Carre.
Villanelle of Washington
  Square.
Roberts, William H.
I Will Believe.
Robertson, Brian
The Party at the Contessa's
  House.
Robertson, Clyde
Mistress of the Matchless
  Mine.
The Woman in the Wagon.
The Yellow Witch of Caribou.
Robertson, Edith Anne
The Deean Tractorman, Clear.
The Deean Tractorman,
  Deleerit.
Robertson, Harrison
Kentucky Philosophy.
Two Triolets.
Robertson, James Logie
The Discovery of America.
A Schule Laddie's Lament on
  the Lateness o' the Season.
Spring on the Ochils.
Robertson, Kell
Between a Good Hat & Good
  Boots.
Crossing West Texas (1966).
Julio.
Landscape, New Mexico.
Robertson, Kirk
The Clorox Kid.
The Giant Squid of Tsurai.
Postcard to a Foetus.
Robertson, T. A. ("Vagaland")
Tuslag.
Robertson, W. Graham
Glad Day.
Robertson, Winifred
The Perfect Garden.
Robey, George
Limerick: "An eccentric old
  person of Slough."
Robins, Gurdon
There Is a Land Mine Eye
  Hath Seen.
When Thickly Beat the
  Storms of Life.
**Robinson, Agnes Mary Frances
(Mme Emile Duclaux)**
Ah Me, Do You Remember
  Still.
Aubade Triste.
A Ballad of Orleans.
Celia's Home-Coming.
Cockayne Country.
Dawn-Angels.
Etruscan Tombs.
Let Us Forget.

Neurasthenia.
An Orchard at Avignon.
Pallor.
Red May.
Retrospect.
Rispetto.
Le Roi Est Mort.
Rosa Rosarum.
Sometimes When I Sit Musing
  All Alone.
Temple Garlands.
Twilight.
Robinson, Anne
April and May.
Conversation.
The Drummer.
To Laddie.
Robinson, Annie Douglas See
  also "Douglas, Marian"
A Good Thanksgiving.
One Saturday.
Robinson, Barbara B.
Foreign Student.
Robinson, Charles
Had I but Strength Enough,
  and Time (parody).
Robinson, Corinne Roosevelt
Beloved, from the Hour That
  You Were Born.
Life, A Question.
Lincoln.
The Path That Leads
  Nowhere.
Sagamore.
Robinson, David
Awakening.
Robinson, Edwin Arlington
Aaron Stark.
As It Looked Then.
Ballade of Dead Friends.
Ben Jonson Entertains a Man
  from Stratford.
Bewick Finzer.
Calvary.
Calverly's.
Captain Craig (excerpt).
Cassandra.
Charles Carville's Eyes.
The Children of the Night.
A Christmas Sonnet.
Clavering.
The Clerks.
Cliff Klingenhagen.
The Companion.
Credo.
The Dark Hills.
Dear Friends.
Demos.
Doricha.
L'Envoi.
Eros Turannos.
Exit.
The Field of Glory.
Firelight.
Flammonde.
The Flying Dutchman.
For a Dead Lady.
For Arvia.
Fragment.
George Crabbe.
The Gift of God.
Glass Houses.
Hillcrest.
The House on the Hill.
How Annandale Went Out.
An Inscription by the Sea.
Isaac and Archibald.
James Wetherell.
John Evereldown.
John Gorham.
Karma.
The Klondike.

Lais to Aphrodite.
Leonora.
LLewellyn and the Tree.
The Long Race.
Lost Anchors.
Luke Havergal.
The Man Against the Sky.
Many Are Called.
The Master.
The Mill.
The Miller's Wife.
Miniver Cheevy.
Momus.
Mr. Flood's Party.
New England.
The New Tenants.
Nimmo.
Old King Cole.
An Old Story.
Pasa Thalassa Thalassa.
The Pity of the Leaves.
A Poem for Max Nordau.
The Poor Relation.
The Prodigal Son.
Reuben Bright.
Reunion.
Richard Cory.
The Sheaves.
Sonnet: "Oh for a poet–for a
  beacon bright."
Sonnet: "The master and the
  slave go hand in hand."
Souvenir.
Supremacy.
Tact.
Thomas Hood.
The Three Taverns: Out of
  Wisdom Has Come Love.
Too Much Coffee.
The Torrent.
Toussaint l'Ouverture.
The Tree in Pamela's Garden.
Twilight Song.
Two Men.
Uncle Ananias.
The Unforgiven.
Vain Gratuities.
Variations of Greek Themes.
Veteran Sirens.
Vickery's Mountain.
Walt Whitman.
The Wandering Jew.
Why He Was There.
Zola.
Robinson, Edwin Meade
The Annual Solution.
The David Jazz.
A Disagreeable Feature.
It Happens, Often.
Limerick: "A jug and a book
  and a dame."
Limerick: "Lucasta," said
  Terence O'Connor."
Limerick: "There once was a
  guy named Othello."
Limerick: "There was a young
  man named Achilles."
Ode to Eve.
Spoon River Anthology.
The Story of Ug.
Villanelle of a Villaness.
Robinson, Eloise
To-Day I Saw Bright Ships.
Robinson, Elsie
Beauty as a Shield.
Help Me Today.
Pain.
Robinson, Grant P.
I Fights Mit Sigel!
Robinson, Harriet H.
Oh! Isn't It a Pity.

Robinson, Henry Morton
Chantey of Notorious Bibbers.
Cock-Crow: Woodstock.
Earth-Canonized.
Novembeer Fugitive.
Second Wisdom.
Robinson, James Miller
The Coweta County
  Courthouse.
Robinson, John
More Truth and Light.
Robinson, Kenneth Allan
American Laughter.
Lines to Dr. Ditmars.
Robinson, Kit
Archangel.
In the Orpheum Building.
It's A.
Up Early.
Robinson, Lila Cayley
Glow Worm.
Robinson, Lucy
A Ballade of Islands.
The Fire i' the Flint.
Hic Me, Pater Optime,
  Fessam Deseris.
Robinson, Roland
Casuarina.
The Cradle.
The Creek.
The Dancers.
Deep Well.
I Breathed into the Ash.
The Lyre-Bird.
Rock-Lily.
The Tank.
The Wanderer (excerpt).
Waratah.
Robinson, Selma
Gentle Name.
Harvesting.
Pendulum Rhyme.
Robinson, Tom
Autumn Color.
Hard Lines.
Little Lady Wren.
My Dog.
Shoes.
Robinson, Tracy
Song of the Palm.
Robinson, Wey
Horse & Rider.
Robles, Al
Boy and the Wandering
  Recluse.
Manong Federico Delos Reyes
  and His Golden Banjo.
Manong Jacinto Santo Tomas.
A Mountain-Toilet Thief.
Sushi-Okashi and Green Tea
  with Mitsu Yashima.
Robson, J. P.
California.
Robson, Jeremy
The Departure.
Roche, James Jeffrey
Albemarle Cushing.
Andromeda.
The Constitution's Last Fight.
Don't.
The Fight of the Armstrong
  Privateer.
The Flag.
Gettysburg.
The Gospel of Peace.
If.
Jack Creamer.
The Kearsarge.
The Men of the Alamo.
My Comrade.
The Net of Law.
Panama.

Reuben James.
A Sailor's Yarn.
The Skeleton at the Feast.
The V-a-s-e.
Washington.
The Way of the World.
Roche, Paul
The Brick.
Courage for the
  Pusillanimous.
Rochester, John Wilmot, Earl of
Against Constancy.
All My Past Life.
An Allusion to Horace. The
  Tenth Satire of the First
  Book.
As Chloris Full of Harmless
  Thought.
The Bully.
The Chaste Arabian Bird.
Constancy: A Song.
A Dialogue between Strephon
  and Daphne.
The Disabled Debauchee.
The Disappointment.
An Epistolary Essay from
  M.G. to O.B. upon Their
  Mutual Poems.
Epitaph on Charles II.
Et Cetera.
The Fall.
Farewell to the Court
  (excerpt).
Grecian Kindness.
Homo Sapiens.
The Imperfect Enjoyment.
Insulting Beauty.
The King's Answer.
A Letter from Artemisa...
Love and Life.
A Lovely Lass to a Friar
  Came.
Lycias.
The Mistress: A Song.
The Mistress (excerpt).
On Poet Ninny.
On the Supposed Author of a
  Late Poem "In Defense of
  Satire."
A Panegyric on Nelly
  (excerpt).
A Pastoral Courtship.
The Platonic Lady.
Poet, Whoe'er Thou Art.
A Rodomontade on His Cruel
  Mistress.
A Satire against Reason and
  Mankind.
A Satire on Charles II.
Sodom; or, The Quintessence
  of Debauchery (excerpt).
Song: "Absent from thee, I
  languish still."
Song: "Give me leave to rail
  at you."
Song: "I promised Sylvia to be
  true."
Song: "Leave this gaudy
  gilded stage."
Song: "Love a woman? You're
  an ass!"
A Song: "My dear mistress
  has a heart."
A Song of a Young Lady to
  Her Ancient Lover.
Song: Phillis be Gentler.
A Song to Cloris.
Song: "Too late, alas! I must
  confess."
Spoken Extempore.
To Chuse a Friend, but Never
  Marry.

To His Mistress.
To My More Than
  Meritorious Wife.
Tunbridge Wells.
Upon Drinking in a Bowl.
Upon His Leaving His
  Mistress.
Upon Nothing.
A Very Heroical Epistle in
  Answer to Ephelia.
Were I, Who to My Cost
  Already Am.
While on Those Lovely Looks
  I Gaze.
Wretched Man.
Written in a Lady's Prayer
  Book.
Rock, Madeleine Caron
He is the Lonely Greatness.
Rockett, Winnie Lynch
A Mother before a Soldier's
  Monument.
Rockwell, Glen
Keys.
Rockwell, Levi
From a Connecticut
  Newspaper.
Rockwell, Margaret
Hiroshima.
Rodd, Rennell
A Song of Autumn.
Rodd, Sir James Rennell
A Roman Mirror.
Rodefer, Stephen
Codex.
Pretext.
Rodenbach, Georges
You Are My Sisters.
Roderick, John M.
Passage.
Rodger, Alex
Twilight at the Zoo.
Rodger, Alexander
Behave Yoursel' before Folk.
Rodgers, Carolyn M.
And When the Revolution
  Came.
And While We Are Waiting.
Breakthrough.
A Common Poem.
For H. W. Fuller.
For Muh' Dear.
For Sapphires.
How I Got Ovah.
"In This House, There Shall
  Be No Idols".
Jazz.
Jesus Was Crucified or: It
  Must Be Deep.
Look at My Face.
Mama's God.
Masquerade.
Me, in Kulu Se & Karma.
Missing Beat.
Now Ain't That Love?
One.
Phoenix.
Poem/Ditty-Bop.
Poem for Some Black Women.
Proclamation/From Sleep,
  Arise.
Rebolushinary x-mas/eastuh
  julie 4/ etc. etc. etc. etc.
Remember Times for Sandy.
Setting/Slow Drag.
Some Me of Beauty.
Somebody Call (For Help).
Testimony.
U Name This One.
Voodoo on the Un-Assing of
  Janis Joplin:Warning:To Ole
  Tom.

We Dance Like Ella Riffs.
What Color Is Lonely.
Yuh Lookin GOOD.
Rodgers, W. R.
  The Airman.
  Apollo and Daphne.
  Armagh.
  As Yet.
  Autumn.
  Awake!
  Beagles.
  Carol.
  Christ Walking on the Water.
  Directions to a Rebel.
  Express.
  Field Day.
  The Fountains.
  An Irish Lake.
  Lent.
  Life's Circumnavigators.
  The Lovers.
  Nativity.
  Neither Here Nor There.
  The Net.
  Paired Lives.
  Pan and Syrinx.
  The Party.
  The Raider.
  Resurrection–An Easter
    Sequence (excerpt).
  Scapegoat.
  Sing, Brothers, Sing!
  Snow.
  Song for Peace.
  Song for War.
  Spring.
  Stormy Day.
  Stormy Night.
  Summer Holidays.
  Summer Journey.
  The Swan.
  War-Time.
  Words.
Roditi, Edouard
  Aurora Borealis.
  A Beginning and an End.
  Habakkuk.
  Hand.
  Kashrut.
  The Paths of Prayer.
  Seance.
  Shekhina and the Kiddushim.
Rodman, Frances
  Lost Dog.
  Spring Cricket.
Rodman, Selden
  Consuelo at the Country Club.
  Daphne.
  Harpers Ferry.
  Lawrence: The Last Crusade
    (excerpt).
  Man, Not His Arms.
  Norris Dam.
  On a Picture by Pippin,
    Called "The Den."
  Time of Day.
  V-Letter to Karl Shapiro in
    Australia.
Rodman, Thomas P.
  The Battle of Bennington.
Rodriguez, Aleida
  Explorations Bronchitis: The
    Rosario Beach House.
Rodriguez, Judith
  At the Nature-Strip.
  Eskimo Occasion.
  The Handloom.
  How Come the Truck-Loads?
  A Lifetime Devoted to
    Literature.
  New York Sonnet.
  Rebeca in a Mirror.

Rodriguez Frese, Marcos
  Beginning.
  June 10.
  Leit.
  What Is Needed.
Rodriguez Nietzche, Vicente
  Mural (excerpt).
  Poem H.
Rodriguez de Padron
  Prayer to the Blessed Virgin.
Roe, Sir Thomas
  On Gustavus Adolphus, King
    of Sweden.
Roethke, Theodore
  Academic.
  All Morning.
  The Bat.
  The Beast.
  Big Wind.
  Bound.
  The Ceiling.
  The Centaur.
  Child on Top of a
    Greenhouse.
  The Chums.
  The Coming of the Cold.
  The Cow.
  Cuttings.
  Cuttings, later.
  The Decision.
  Dinky.
  Dolor.
  The Donkey.
  Double Feature.
  The Dream.
  Elegy.
  Elegy for Jane.
  Epidermal Macabre.
  The Exorcism.
  The Far Field.
  A Field of Light.
  The Flight.
  For an Amorous Lady.
  Forcing House.
  Four for Sir John Davies.
  Frau Bauman, Frau Schmidt,
    and Frau Schwartze.
  From the Notebooks.
  The Geranium.
  Give Way, Ye Gates.
  Heard in a Violent Ward.
  Her Longing.
  The Heron.
  Highway: Michigan.
  The Hippo.
  I Cry, Love! Love!
  I'm Here.
  In a Dark Time.
  In Evening Air.
  Infirmity.
  Interlude.
  The Kitty-Cat Bird.
  The Lady and the Bear.
  A Light Breather.
  Light Listened.
  The Lizard.
  Long Live the Weeds.
  The Long Waters.
  The Longing.
  The Lost Son.
  The Marrow.
  The Meadow Mouse.
  Meditation at Oyster River.
  Meditations of an Old
    Woman.
  Mid-Country Blow.
  The Minimal.
  Mips and Ma the Mooly Moo.
  The Moment.
  Moss-Gathering.
  My Dim-Wit Cousin.
  My Papa's Waltz.

  Night Crow.
  Night Journey.
  North American Sequence:
    Journey to the Interior.
  Old Florist.
  Open House.
  Orchids.
  Poem: "I knew a woman,
    lovely in her bones."
  Praise to the End!
  Prayer.
  Prayer before Study.
  The Premonition.
  The Reckoning.
  The Renewal.
  The Reply.
  The Return.
  Root Cellar.
  The Rose.
  A Rouse for Stevens.
  The Saginaw Song.
  Second Shadow.
  The Sensualists.
  The Sequel.
  The Serpent.
  The Shape of the Fire.
  She.
  The Shimmer of Evil.
  The Siskins.
  The Sloth.
  The Small.
  Snake.
  The Song.
  Song for the Squeeze-Box.
  Song: "From whence cometh
    song?–".
  Song: "Under a southern
    wind."
  Specialist.
  The Storm.
  The Swan.
  They Sing.
  The Thing.
  Three Epigrams.
  Vernal Sentiment.
  The Visitant.
  The Voice.
  The Waking.
  Weed Puller.
  What Can I Tell My Bones?
  Where Knock Is Open Wide.
  Wish for a Young Wife.
  Words for the Wind.
  The Young Girl.
Rogers, Alex
  The Rain Song.
  Why Adam Sinned.
Rogers, D.H.
  At Sea.
  Homeward Bound.
Rogers, Del Marie
  Sleep.
  War Requiem.
Rogers, George
  As Gentle Dews Distill.
Rogers, John
  Upon Mrs. Anne Bradstreet
    Her Poems, &c.
Rogers, Pattiann
  Achieving Perspective.
  Concepts and Their Bodies
    (The Boy in the Field
    Alone).
  For Stephen Drawing Birds.
  The Man Hidden behind the
    Drapes.
  This Evening, without
    Blinking.
Rogers, Robert Cameron
  The Dancing Faun.
  Doubt.
  A Health at the Ford.

  The Rosary.
  The Shadow Rose.
  A Sleeping Priestess of
    Aphrodite.
  Virgil's Tomb.
Rogers, Ron
  Bear Dance.
  Black Mesa.
  The Death of Old Joe Yazzie.
  Elf Night.
  Montana Remembered from
    Albuquerque; 1982.
Rogers, Samuel
  Another and the Same.
  Bologna, and Byron.
  Byron Recollected at Bologna.
  Captivity.
  An Epitaph on a Robin-
    Redbreast.
  Fond Youth.
  Ginevra.
  The Great St. Bernard.
  Inscription on a Grot.
  An Interview near Florence.
  Man's Going Hence.
  Naples.
  On a Tear.
  On J. W. Ward.
  The Sleeping Beauty.
  A Wish.
Rogers, Thomas
  The Spirit of Night.
Rogers, William Robert
  White Christmas.
Rokeah, David
  Beginning.
  I Am Like a Book.
  Zealots of Yearning.
Rokwaho
  Amber the Sky.
  Clickstone.
  Owl.
  (...Prelude).
  Twoborn.
Roland, Patrick
  Spring Burning.
Roland, Walter
  45 Pistol Blues.
Roland-Holst, H.
  Concerning the Awakening of
    My Soul.
  I Looked for a Sounding-
    Board.
  Mother of Fishermen.
  Small Paths.
  Throughout the Day We Are
    Able to Ban the Voices.
Rolfe, Edwin
  Definition.
  Elegy for Our Dead.
  No Man Knows War.
  A Poem to Delight My
    Friends Who Laugh at
    Science-Fiction.
  Song (2).
Rolfe, Frederick William
  Ballade of Boys Bathing.
Rolfe, Harvey E.
  Resolutions?–New and Old.
Rolland, John
  The Sevin Seages: Epilogue.
Rolle, Richard
  Ghostly Gladness.
  Love Is Life.
  My Trewest Tresowre.
  A Song of Love for Jesus.
  A Song of the Love of Jesus.
Rolle of Hampole, Richard
  A Song of the Passion.
Rolleston, Thomas William
  Clonmacnoise.
  Cois na Teineadh.

Night.
The Grave of Rulry.
Song of Maelduin.
Rollins, Alice Wellington
The Death of Azron.
Many Things Thou Hast
  Given Me, Dear Heart.
Vita Benefica.
Rolls, Eric
Bamboo.
Dog Fight.
Little Sticks.
Rain Forest.
Sheaf-Tosser.
Rolnik, Joseph
At God's Command.
I'm Not Rich.
In Disguise.
Thank God.
Romain, Jules
The Church.
Romaine, Harry
Ad Coelum.
Romains, Jules
Another Spirit Advances.
Roman Breviary
The Morning Purples All the
  Sky.
Romanelli, Samuele
From Battle Clamour.
Love.
Romanes, George J.
The Sloth.
Romanes, George John
Simple Nature.
Romano, Jennie
Old Houses.
Romano, Liboria E.
Lyric Barber.
Romilu, Myrtle
If to Die–.
Ronan, John
Fat Cat.
Ronksley, William
To Cheer Our Minds.
Ronsard, Pierre de
Corinna in Vendome.
Four Sonnets to Helen.
And Lightly, Like the
  Flowers.
Deadly Kisses.
Fragment of a Sonnet.
His Lady's Death.
His Lady's Tomb.
Of His Lady's Old Age.
On His Lady's Waking.
The Paradox of Time.
The Revenge.
The Rose.
Roses.
To His Young Mistress.
To the Moon.
Roses.
Rooney, John Jerome
A Beam of Light.
The Homing.
Joined the Blues.
Marquette on the Shores of
  the Mississippi.
McIlrath of Malate.
The Men behind the Guns.
The Rahat.
Root, E. Merrill
Carpenter of Eternity.
Chicago Idyll.
Prayer for Dreadful Morning.
Root, George Frederick
The Battle-Cry of Freedom.
Just before the Battle, Mother.
Rosalie, the Prairie Flower.
Tramp! Tramp! Tramp!

Root, Judith C.
The Gerbil Who Got Away.
Root, William Pitt
Answering Dance.
Circle of Struggle.
Exchanging Glances.
Fleshflower.
From the Other Shore.
The Jellyfish.
KRAA.
A Natural History of Dragons
  and Unicorns My Daughter
  and I Have Known.
Nightswim.
Sea-Grape Tree and the
  Miraculous.
Sometimes Heaven Is a Mean
  Machine.
Song of Returnings.
Under the Umbrella of Blood.
Wheel Turning on the Hub of
  the Sun.
White Horse of the Father,
  White Horse of the Son.
Rorie, David
The Pawky Duke.
Rorty, James
Gray Shore.
Rosales, Luis
That Which You Call "Love
  Me."
Roscoe, William Caldwell
The Butterfly's Ball.
Parting.
The Poetic Land.
Spiritual Love.
To Spring: On the Banks of
  the Cam.
**Roscommon, Wentworth Dillon,
Earl of**
An Essay on Translated Verse
  (excerpt).
On the Death of a Lady's
  Dog.
Song on a Young Lady Who
  Sung Finely.
Rose, Alexander Macgregor
Kaiser & Co.
Rose, Billy
Barney Google.
Does the Spearmint Lose Its
  Flavor on the Bedpost
  Overnight?
The Unknown Soldier.
Rose, Greta Leora
Spring Is at Work with
  Beginnings of Things.
Rose, Harriet
Mellisandra.
The Succubus.
The Wedding Coat.
Rose, Mary Catherine
The Clown.
A Parade.
Rose, Sir George
A Chancery Suit.
Rose, Wendy
America.
Builder Kachina: Home-
  Going.
Calling Home the Scientists.
Celebration for My Mother.
Chasing the Paper-Shamans.
Detective Work.
Entering the Desert: Big
  Circles Running.
Epilog (to Lost Copper).
Epitaph.
Evening Ceremony: Dream for
  G.V.
For Mabel: Pomo
  Basketmaster and Doctor.

For My People.
For Steph.
For Walter Lowenfels.
Grunion.
Halfbreed Chronicles: Isamu.
Hanabi-ko.
How I came to be a graduate
  student.
I Expected My Skin and My
  Blood to Ripen.
The Indian Women Are
  Listening: To the Nuke
  Devils.
Julia.
Learning to Understand
  Darkness.
Long Division: A Tribal
  History.
Loo-Wit.
The Man Who Dreamt He
  Was Turquoise.
Mount Saint Helens/Loowit:
  An Indian Woman's Song.
Naming Power.
Oh Father.
Oh My People I Remember.
The Parts of a Poet.
Poem to a Redskin.
The Poet Haunted.
Poet Woman's Mitosis:
  Dividing All the Cells Apart.
Protecting the Burial
  Grounds.
The Pueblo Women I
  Watched Get down in
  Brooklyn.
Punk Party.
Saint Patrick's Day, 1973.
Sarah: Cherokee Doctor.
Self Dirge.
They Sometimes Call Me.
Three Thousand Dollar Death
  Song.
To an Imaginary Father.
To Some Few Hopi Ancestors.
Walking on the Prayerstick.
The Well-intentioned question.
Roseliep, Raymond F.
Auden.
Campfire Extinguished.
Elegy for Ezra.
Lady of Letters.
Marianne Moore (1887-1972).
Symphony in Blue.
To Mary: At the Thirteenth
  Station.
When I Was Nine.
Where Do I Love You,
  Lovely Maid?
Rosemergy, Jim
Human Dilemma.
Rosen, Kenneth
Abstinence.
An Act.
Confab.
Girls.
Rosen, Michael
Christmas Dinner.
The Hidebehind.
Rosenbaum, Benjamin
O Pity Our Small Size.
Rosenbaum, Nathan
Pictures at an Exhibition.
Rosenberg, Betsy
Bird Song.
Unearthing.
Rosenberg, David
Maps to Nowhere.
Rain Has Fallen on the
  History Books.
Rosenberg, Dorothy
Bim Bam.

Rosenberg, Harold
Epos.
Rosenberg, Isaac
August 1914.
Beauty.
Break of Day in the Trenches.
The Burning of the Temple.
Chagrin.
Daughters of War.
The Dead Heroes.
Dead Man's Dump.
The Destruction of Jerusalem
  by the Babylonian Hordes.
Expression.
The Female God.
Girl to Soldier on Leave.
God.
Home-Thoughts from France.
I Am the Blood.
If You Are Fire.
The Immortals.
The Jew.
Louse Hunting.
Love and Lust.
Marching.
Midsummer Frost.
My Soul Is Robbed.
On Receiving News of the
  War.
The One Lost.
Returning, We Hear the
  Larks.
Saul.
Soldier: Twentieth Century.
Spiritual Isolation.
Spring.
Through These Pale Cold
  Days.
Wedded.
A Worm Fed on the Heart of
  Corinth.
Rosenberg, James Naumberg
Darkness.
Rosenberg, Joel
The First Wedding in the
  World.
The Violin Tree.
Rosenberg, L. M.
For Leningrad, and My
  Jewish Ancestors.
To My Mother.
Rosenberger, Francis Coleman
Are You Just Back for a Visit
  or Are You Going to Stay?
Poets Observed.
Rosenblatt, Joe
The Ant Trap.
Cat.
Fish.
Ichthycide.
It's in the Egg.
Of Dandelions & Tourists.
Rosenfeld, Marjorie Stamm
David Homindae.
Rosenfeld, Morris
Another While.
A Cry from the Ghetto.
Exile Song.
For Hire.
I Know Not Why.
The Jewish May.
My Camping Ground.
Simchas Torah.
So Long Ago.
Rosenfeld, Rita
Stacking Up.
Rosenfield, Loyd
Ode to a Vanished Operator
  in an Automatized Elevator.
You Take the Pilgrims, Just
  Give Me the Progress.

Rosenfield, Monroe F. *See also*
"Belasco, F."
Those Wedding Bells Shall
Not Ring Out.
Rosenhane, Gustav
Sonnets, I: "Deep in a vale
where rocks on every side."
Sonnets, II: "And then I sat
me down, and gave the rein."
Rosenius, Carl Olof
With God and His Mercy.
Rosenmann-Taub, D.
Elegy and Kaddish.
Moral Ode.
Prelude.
Reconciliation.
Sabbath.
To a Young Girl.
Rosensaft, Menachem Z.
The Second Generation.
Rosenthal, Abby
June Song.
Rosenthal, Bob
The Eighties Becoming.
Kissing Game.
Pretty Vomit.
Publishing 2001.
Rude Awakenings.
Slightly Old.
Rosenthal, John
Love's Fool.
Roskolenko, Harry
Come Unto Us Who
Are...Laden.
Nationalism.
Old World, New World.
Symbols.
Waiting for God.
Rosner, Martin C.
Listening-Post.
Rosner, Paul
Don't Say You Like
Tchaikowsky.
Ross, Abram Bunn
An Indignant Male.
Two in Bed.
Ross, Alan
Antwerp Musee des Beaux-
Arts.
At Only That Moment.
In Bloemfontein.
Koala.
Leave Train.
Mess Deck Casualty.
Off Brighton Pier.
Radar.
Stanley Matthews.
Ross, Alexander
Woo'd and Married and A'.
Wooed and Married and A'.
Ross, Allison
Game Out of Hand.
Ross, Cary
Sonnet on a Somewhat
Inferior Radio Outfit.
Ross, Charles Henry
Jack.
John, Tom, and James.
An Old Woman.
Ross, Charles Sarsfield
Dear Old Mothers.
Old Mothers.
Ross, D. M.
Bloody Bill.
Ross, David
Houses Should Have Homes
to Live in.
I Am Your Loaf, Lord.
Lament of Granite.
Limerick: "A Briton who shot
at his king."
News Reel.

On Apples.
Ross, Gertrude Robison
I Was Made of This and This.
Ross, Ronald
Lines Written after the
Discovery ... of the Germ of
Yellow Fever.
Ross, W. W. Eustace
The Creek.
The Diver.
Fish.
If Ice.
In the Ravine.
Pine Gum.
The Saws Were Shrieking.
The Snake Trying.
The Summons.
There's a Fire in the Forest.
The Walk.
Ross, William
Another Song.
Rosselson, Leon
Palaces of Gold.
Rossetti, Christina Georgina
Advent.
After Death.
All the Bells Were Ringing.
All Things Wait upon Thee.
Aloof.
Amor Mundi.
And Timid, Funny, Brisk
Little Bunny.
An Apple Gathering.
Ash Wednesday.
Autumn.
The Battle Within.
Before the Beginning.
Before the Paling of the Stars.
A Better Resurrection.
A Birthday.
Bitter for Sweet.
A blue-eyed phantom far
before.
The Bourne.
Bread and Milk.
Bride Song.
But Give Me Holly, Bold and
Jolly.
By the Sea.
Caterpillar.
Cherry Tree.
Child's Talk in April.
A Christmas Carol.
The City Mouse and the
Garden Mouse.
Clouds.
Color.
Comparisons.
Consider.
The Convent Threshold.
A Crown of Wildflowers.
December.
Did any bird come flying.
A Dirge.
Dream-Land.
Dream-Love.
An Easter Carol.
Easter Monday.
Echo.
Eight O'Clock.
An Emerald Is as Green as
Grass.
An End.
Endure Hardness.
Enrica, 1865.
Epigram: "I dug and dug
amongst the snow."
Epigram: "What are heavy?
sea-sand and sorrow."
Eve.
The Face of Jesus Christ.
Ferry Me across the Water.

The First Spring Day.
Flint.
Fly away, Fly away over the
Sea.
Freaks of Fashion.
A Frog's Fate.
From Sunset to Star Rise.
From the Antique.
Goblin Market.
Golden Silences.
Good Friday.
Good Friday Evening.
Growing in the Vale,.
Grown and Flown.
The Half Moon Shows a Face
of Plaintive Sweetness.
Heaven Is Heaven.
Heaven Is Not Far.
Heaven Overarches Earth and
Sea.
Herself a Rose Who Bore the
Rose.
Hold Thou Me Fast.
Holy Innocents.
Hope and Joy.
The Horses of the Sea.
The House of Cards.
How Many Seconds in a
Minute?
Hurt No Living Thing.
I Bore with Thee, Long,
Weary Days.
I Do Not Look for Love That
Is a Dream.
I Have a Room whereinto No
One Enters.
I Will Accept.
If I Were a Queen.
If Only.
Immalee.
In an Artist's Studio.
In Progress.
In the Bleak Mid-Winter.
Italia, Io Ti Saluto!
Judge Not According to the
Appearance.
Lady Moon.
The Lambs of Grasmere,
1860.
Last Rites.
Later Life, VII.
A Life's Parallels.
Long Barren.
Lord, Grant Us Calm.
Lord, Save Us, We Perish.
The Lowest Place.
Lullaby.
Luscious and Sorrowful.
Marvel of Marvels.
Maude Clare.
May.
Meeting.
Memory.
The Milking-Maid.
Minnie and Mattie.
Mirage.
Mix a Pancake.
Monna Innominata.
Mother Country.
Mother Shake the Cherry-
Tree.
My Dream.
My Gift.
Next of Kin.
No, Thank You, John.
Noble Sisters.
None Other Lamb, None
Other Name.
November.
O Sailor, Come Ashore.
O Wind, Why Do You Never
Rest.

Oh, Fair to See.
An Old-World Thicket.
On the Death of a Cat.
On the Wing.
The One Certainty.
One Sea-Side Grave.
Paradise.
Passing and Glassing.
Passing Away.
A Pause of Thought.
The Poor Ghost.
A Prayer.
The Prince's Progress: Bride
Song.
De Profundis.
Promises Like Pie-Crust.
Pussy Has a Whiskered Face.
The Rainbow.
Remember.
Rest.
Riddle: "First it was a pretty
flower."
Riddle: "There is one that has
a head without an eye."
A Royal Princess.
Seasons.
Send Me.
Shadows To-Day.
She listen'd like a cushat
dove.
The Shepherds Had an Angel.
Shut Out.
Sing-Song: Is the Moon Tired?
A Sketch.
Sleep at Sea.
Sleeping at Last.
Somewhere or Other.
A Song for the Least of All
Saints.
A Song of Flight.
Song: "Oh roses for the flush
of youth."
Song: "She sat and sang
alway."
Song: "When I am dead, my
dearest."
A Soul.
Spring.
Spring Quiet.
St. Peter.
Stay, June, Stay!
Summer.
The Summer Is Ended.
A Summer Wish.
Symbols.
There Is but One May in the
Year.
They Lie at Rest, Our Blessed
Dead.
The Three Enemies.
Three Seasons.
To My First Love, My
Mother.
A Triad.
Tune Me, O Lord, into One
Harmony.
Twice.
Twilight Calm.
Two doves upon the selfsame
branch.
Up-Hill.
A Valentine to My Mother.
Weary in Well-Doing.
Wednesday in Holy Week.
What Does the Bee Do?
What Is Pink?
What Would I Give?
When Fishes Set Umbrellas
Up.
Who Has Seen the Wind?
The Wind.

The Wind Has Such a Rainy
　Sound.
The Wind of January.
Winter: My Secret.
Winter Rain.
Wisdom.
The World.
Wrens and Robins in the
　Hedge.
Rossetti, Dante Gabriel
Antwerp and Bruges.
Aspecta Medusa.
At Her Step the Water-Hen.
Autumn Song.
Ave.
Beauty.
Beauty and the Bird.
Beauty's Pageant.
The Blessed Damozel.
The Bride's Prelude.
Broken Music.
The Burden of Nineveh.
The Card-Dealer.
Chimes.
Cloud and Wind.
The Cloud Confines.
Dante at Verona.
A Dark Day.
Dawn on the Night-Journey.
The Day-Dream.
A Day of Love.
Death's Songsters.
Eden Bower.
Equal Troth.
Even So.
Farewell to the Glen.
For a Venetian Pastoral by
　Giorgione.
For An Allegorical Dance of
　Women by Andrea
　Mantegna.
For Our Lady of the Rocks
　by Leonardo da Vinci.
For Ruggiero and Angelica by
　Ingres.
For the Holy Family by
　Michelangelo.
For the Wine of Circe.
From Dawn to Noon.
Gracious Moonlight.
A Half-Way Pause.
He and I.
The Heart of the Night.
Heart's Compass.
Hedro's Lamp.
Hoarded Joy.
The Honeysuckle.
Hope Overtaken.
The House of Life.
Jenny.
The Lamp's Shrine.
The Landmark.
A Last Confession.
Last Fire.
Life the Beloved.
Limerick: "There is a young
　artist named Whistler."
Limerick: "There is an old he-
　wolf named Gambart."
Limerick: "There's a
　combative Artist named
　Whistler."
Limerick: "There's a
　Portuguese person named
　Howell."
Limerick: "There was a
　painter named Scott."
Limerick: "There was a young
　Fir-tree of Bosnia."
A Little While.
Love and Hope.
The Love-Letter.

Love-Lily.
The Love-Moon.
Love's Baubles.
Love's Fatality.
Love's Lovers.
Love's Testament.
Mary Magdalene.
Mary's Girlhood.
A Match with the Moon.
Memorial Thresholds.
Memory.
Michelangelo's Kiss.
The Mirror.
The Monochord.
The Moonstar.
The Morrow's Message.
My Sister's Sleep.
Newborn Death.
Nuptial Sleep.
Old and New Art.
An Old Song Ended.
On Himself.
On Leaving Bruges.
On Refusal of Aid between
　Nations.
On Robert Buchanan, Who
　Attacked Him under the
　Pseudonym...
On the Painter Val Prinsep.
On the Poet O'Shaughnessy.
On the Same.
On the Site of a Mulberry-
　Tree.
On the "Vita Nuova" of
　Dante.
The Orchard-Pit.
Parted Love.
Passion and Worship.
The Passover in the Holy
　Family.
Penumbra.
The Portrait.
Retro me, Sathana!
Saint Luke the Painter.
The Sea-Limits.
A Sea-Spell.
Secret Parting.
Sestina (after Dante).
Sister Helen.
Smithereens.
The Song of the Bower.
The Song-Throe.
Sonnets for Pictures: Our
　Lady of the Rocks.
Soul-Light.
The Soul's Sphere.
The Staff and Scrip.
The Sun's Shame.
Sunset Wings.
Supreme Surrender.
Three Shadows.
To Art.
Tom Agnew, Bill Agnew.
Transfigured Life.
The Trees of the Garden.
A Trip to Paris and Belgium
　(excerpt).
Troy Town.
True Woman.
The Vase of Life.
Venus.
Venus Victrix.
The White Ship.
Winged Hours.
Winter.
Without Her.
The Woodspurge.
Words on the Windowpane.
World's Worth.
A Young Fir-Wood.
Youth's Spring-Tribute.

Rostand, Edmond
The Cathedral of Rheims.
Cyrano de Bergerac, III:
　"Love, I love beyond
　Breath."
Rosten, Norman
Aesthetic.
Black Boy.
Byron in Greece.
Face on the Daguerreotype.
From the Provinces.
Out of Our Shame.
This Child.
To Ariake Kambara.
Roston, Ruth
Salesman.
Two Windows by Magritte.
Rostrevor, George
Bodily Beauty.
The Cell.
Rotella, Guy
High Summer.
Somewhere Farm.
Roth, Hemda
The Song.
Treason of Sand.
A Young Deer/Dust.
Roth, Joseph
Ahasuerus.
Rothenberg, Jerome
48 Words for a Woman's
　Dance Song.
The Alphabet Came to Me.
The Beadle's Testimony.
A Bodhisattva Undoes Hell.
Cokboy, Part Two.
Esther K. Comes to America:
　1931.
A Letter to Paul Celan in
　Memory.
A Little Boy Lost.
The Others Hunters in the
　North The Cree.
A Poem in Yellow after
　Tristan Tzara.
Poland/1931.The Wedding.
Portrait of a Jew Old Country
　Style.
The Seven Hells of the Jigoku
　Zoshi (excerpt).
The Seventh Hell...
Sightings I.
Soap (II).
The Stationmaster's Lament.
The Structural Study of Myth.
Three Landscapes (excerpt).
Young Woman's Neo-Aramaic
　Jewish Persian Blues.
**Rothenstein, William and Max
Beerbohm**
Eli the Thatcher.
Rothfork, John
The Deep Calling.
Rottman, Larry
What Kind of War?
Rouget de Lisle, Claude Joseph
The Marseillaise.
Roughton, Roger
Building Society Blues.
Soluble Noughts and Crosses;
　or, California, Here I Come.
Roumain, Jacques
Guinea.
Roumer, Emile
A Black Girl Goes By.
The Peasant Declares His
　Love.
Rounds, Emma
Johnny.
Plane Geometry.

Rous, Francis
Help, Lord, Because the
　Godly Man.
I to the Hills Will Lift Mine
　Eyes.
The Lord's My Shepherd, I'll
　Not Want.
Routhier, Adolphe
O Canada!
Rowbotham, David
The Bus-Stop on the Somme.
The Cliff.
Little White Fox.
The Moment.
Mullabinda.
Nebuchadnezzar's Kingdom-
　Come.
Prey to Prey.
The Town.
Rowe, Henry
Moon.
Sun.
Rowe, James Wilton
Lake Chemo.
Rowe, Nicholas
Cato's Address to His Troops
　in Lybia.
Colin's Complaint.
Pompey and Cornelia.
Rowell, Charles H.
The Old Women Still Sing.
Rowland, J. R.
Canberra in April.
London.
A Traveller.
Rowlands, Samuel
The Melancholy Knight: Sir
　Eglamour.
The Melancholy Knight: The
　Poetaster.
Rowlandson, Thomas
Epitaph on a Willing Girl.
Rowles, Catharine Bryant
New Snow.
Rowley, William
The Chase.
**Rowley, William and Thomas
Middleton**
Song: "Trip it Gipsies, trip it
　fine."
Rowse, A. L.
The White Cat of Trenarren.
Rowswell, Albert K.
Should You Go First.
Royde-Smith, Naomi
The Horse.
Royden, Matthew
On Sir Philip Sidney.
Royle, Edwin Milton
Doan't You Be What You
　Ain't.
Rozewicz, Tadeusz
Poem of Pathos.
Posthumous Rehabilitation.
To the Heart.
Ruark, Gibbons
Finding the Pistol.
The Goods She Can Carry:
　Canticle of Her Basket Made
　of Reeds.
Lost Letter to James Wright,
　with Thanks for a Map of
　Fano.
Nightmare Inspection Tour
　for American Generals.
Soaping Down for Saint
　Francis of Assisi: The
　Canticle of Sister Soap.
Talking Myself to Sleep in the
　Mountains.
To the Swallows of Viterbo.

Watching You Sleep under
Monet's Water Lilies.
Working the Rain Shift at
Flanagan's.
Rubadiri, David
Begging A.I.D.
Thoughts after Work.
The Tide That from the West
Washes Africa to the Bone.
Yet Another Song.
Rubadiri, James D.
Stanley Meets Mutesa.
Rubenstein, Carol
Dayak Man Making Fishtrap.
Rubin, Ilya
Escape.
Handful of Ashes.
No Sense Grieving.
Poem from "The Revolution."
Slow Oxen.
Rubin, Larry
The Addict.
The Brother-in-Law.
The Exile.
The Lesson.
The Manual.
The Pact.
Registered at the Bordello
Hotel (Vienna).
The Son, Condemned.
Temporary Problems.
Ruby, Harry and Bert Kalmar
America, I Love You.
Rudaki
Came to me–/Who?
Ruddick, Bruce
Freighter.
Plaque.
Ruddock, Margot
Autumn, Crystal Eye.
The Child Compassion.
I Take Thee Life.
Love Song.
O Holy Water.
Spirit, Silken Thread.
Take away.
Rudel, Jaufre
Quan Lo Ruis De La
Fontana.
Rudman, Andrew
When Shall My Pilgrimage,
Jesus My Saviour, Be Ended?
Rudnik, Raphael
Amsterdam Street Scene,
1972.
The Lady in the Barbershop.
Penny Trumpet.
Rudnitsky, Leah
Birds Are Drowsing on the
Branches.
Rudolf, Anthony
Ancient of Days.
Ashkelon.
Dubrovnik Poem (Emilio
Tolentino).
Evening of the Rose.
Hands up.
Prayer for Kafka and
Ourselves.
Rudolph, Lee
Warming Up for the Real
Thing.
Rudyerd, Sir Benjamin
Why Do We Love.
Ruebner, Tuvia
Among Iron Fragments.
Document.
First Days.
I Left.
Rueckert, Friedrich
Barbarossa.
The Ride Round the Parapet.

Ruelfe, Mary
Written.
Ruffin, Paul
Cleaning the Well.
Grandma Chooses Her Plot at
the County Cemetery.
Grandpa's Picture.
Hotel Fire: New Orleans.
Rufinus Domesticus
Andante, Ma Non Assai.
Epigram: "Boy-mad no
longer."
Faint Heart.
The Lover's Posy.
Requirements.
To Melite.
Ruggles, Eugene
Deeper in the Tank–The Last
Middle East Crisis, 1972.
Rugo, Marieve
In the Season of Wolves and
Names.
Limbo.
Sundays.
Ruiz, Juan, Archpriest of Hita,
The Book of True Love
(excerpt).
Praise of Little Women.
Prayer to Santa Maria Del
Vade.
Rukeyser, Muriel
Ajanta.
Akiba.
Along History.
Are You Born?
Boy with His Hair Cut Short.
Boys of These Men Full
Speed.
Ceiling Unlimited.
Children's Elegy.
Children, the Sandbar, That
Summer.
Citation for Horace Gregory.
City of Monuments.
Crayon House.
Darkness Music.
Despisals.
Don Baty, the Draft Resister.
Double Ode.
Easter Eve 1945.
Effort at Speech between Two
People.
Endless.
Even during War.
Eyes of Night-Time.
Fields Where We Slept.
The Gates, VI: The Church of
Galilee.
Gauley Bridge.
George Robinson: Blues.
Gibbs (excerpt).
Holy Family.
Homage to Literature.
Islands.
Ives (excerpt).
Kathe Kollwitz.
A Leg in a Plaster Cast.
Letter to the Front.
Looking at Each Other.
Madboy's Song.
The Meeting.
Mendings.
More Clues.
More of a Corpse Than a
Woman.
The Motive of All of It.
Mrs. Walpurga.
Myth.
Night Feeding.
Night-Music: Time Exposures.
No One Ever Walking This
Our Only Earth.

Nuns in the Wind.
On the Death of Her Mother.
Painters.
The Place at Alert Bay.
Poem (I Lived in the First
Century).
Poem out of Childhood.
The Question.
Reading Time: 1 Minute 26
Seconds.
Resurrection of the Right
Side.
Rondel.
Rotten Lake Elegy.
Rune.
Song: "The world is full of
loss."
The Soul and Body of John
Brown.
The Speaking Tree.
The Speed of Darkness.
St. Roach.
Tenth Elegy. Elegy in Joy.
Then.
Then I Saw What the Calling
Was.
This Morning.
This Place in the Ways.
To Be a Jew in the Twentieth
Century.
The Trial.
Trinity Churchyard.
Waiting for Icarus.
The Watchers.
Rumaker, Michael
The Fairies Are Dancing All
over the World.
Rumens, Carol
An Easter Garland.
Geography Lesson.
Rumi, Jalal ed-Din or al-Din
Happy the Moment When We
Are Seated in the Palace,
Thou and I.
I Am Your Mother, Your
Mother's Mother.
I Saw the Winter Weaving.
Lo, for I to Myself Am
Unknown.
Love You Alone Have Been
with Us.
Not in India.
Resurgence.
Thou Art the Source.
Runeberg, Johan Ludvig
Trouble Not the Maiden's
Soul.
Rungren, Lawrence R.
Sunday.
Runkle, Bertha Brooks
The Song of the Sons of Esau.
Runyon, Alfred Damon
A Song of Panama.
Rushton, Edward
Human Debasement. A
Fragment.
Ruskin, John
Awake! Awake!
La Madonna dell' Acqua.
My Dog Dash.
The Needless Alarm.
Trust Thou Thy Love.
The Zodiac Song.
Russ, Lawrence
The Price of Paper.
The Wedding Poem (excerpt).
Russ, Lisa
Piano.
Russ, Virginia
The Shape of Autumn.
Russell, Charles E.
The Fleet at Santiago.

Russell, Ethel Green
Letter from the Vieux Carre.
**Russell, George William
("A.E.")**
Ancient.
Babylon.
By the Margin of the Great
Deep.
Carrowmore.
Chivalry.
The Cities.
The City.
Continuity.
Dark Rapture.
Desire.
Dust.
Epilogue.
Exiles.
A Farewell.
Frolic.
The Garden of God.
The Gates of Dreamland.
The Gay.
Germinal.
The Gift.
The Great Breath.
A Holy Hill.
Immortality.
It Might Have Been Worse.
A Leader.
The Lonely.
The Man to the Angel.
A Memory of Earth.
A Mountain Wind.
New York.
On Behalf of Some Irishmen
Not Followers of Tradition.
The Outcast.
Pain.
The Place of Rest.
Prisoner.
Promise.
Reconciliation.
Refuge.
Salutation.
The Secret.
The Secret Love.
Self-Discipline.
Terence MacSwiney.
Tragedy.
Truth.
Twilight of the Earth.
Unity.
The Unknown God.
The Vesture of the Soul.
When.
Winds of Eros.
Russell, Irwin
Blessing the Dance.
De Fust Banjo.
Nebuchadnezzar.
Russell, James I.
Where the River Shannon
Flows.
Russell, Matthew
A Thought from Cardinal
Newman.
Russell, Norman H.
Appearance.
The Cherokee Dean.
Indian School.
The Message of the Rain.
The Tornado.
The Tree Sleeps in the Winter.
Russell, Sanders
Poem: "I keep feeling all
space as my image."
Russell, Solveig Paulson
Mistletoe Sprites.
Russell, Sydney King
Death Was a Woman.
Dust.

For Vicki at Seven.
Midsummer.
Phyllis.
Russell, Thomas
The Maniac.
The New Testament.
The Old Testament.
Philoctetes.
Sonnet: "Could then the Babes from yon unshelter'd cot."
Sonnet Suppos'd to Be Written at Lemnos.
Sonnet to Oxford.
Sonnet to Valclusa.
Russo, Lola Ingres
Autumn Squall–Lake Erie.
Rustico di Filippo
Sonnet: Of the Making of Master Messerin.
Rutan, Catherine
Still Birth.
Ruth, Fern Pankratz
Guyana.
Rutilius
Roma.
Rutledge, Archibald
O Mariners!
Oblique.
Rutsala, Vern
Bijou.
Eagle Squadron.
Fame.
The Fat Man.
The Final Cut.
Less Is More...
Marriage Contract.
The New House.
Pursuit.
Sunday.
The War of the Worlds.
Washrags.
Words.
The World.
Ryan, Abram Joseph
Better Than Gold.
A Child's Wish.
The Conquered Banner.
The Rosary of My Tears.
Sentinel Songs.
Ryan, Anne
Music.
Ryan, Kathryn White
The Mother.
Ryan, Margaret
The Alexandrite Ring.
Ryan, Michael
After.
Barren Poem.
Consider a Move.
In Winter.
Letter from an Institution, III.
My Dream by Henry James.
Prothalamion.
Speaking.
This Is a Poem for the Dead.
When I Was Conceived.
Where I'll Be Good.
Ryan, Richard
Deafness.
El Dorado.
From My Lai the Thunder Went West.
Ireland.
Knockmany.
Kohoutek.
O, Saw Ye the Lass.
A Wet Night.
Wulf and Eadwacer.
Ryberg, Barbara C.
Step by Step.

Ryden, Ernest Edwin
The Twilight Shadows Round Me Fall.
Ryerson, Alice
The Death Watchers.
Ryman, James
Farewell Advent!
Mary and Her Son Alone.
Now the Most High Is Born.
Rymer, Thomas
To–.
Ryojin Hisho
May the man who gained my trust yet did not come.
Ryota
Haiku: "No one spoke."
The Moon in the Water.
Ryskind, Morrie
Horace the Wise.
To Natalie.
Ryuho
The Moon.
Ryvel (Raphael Levy)
The Pilgrimage to Testour.

S

"S, A.W."
The Life That Counts.
"S., C.N."
Thenot Protests.
"S., E."
Being Forsaken of His Friend He Complaineth.
"S.C, M'K."
Quiet from Fear of Evil.
Saarikoski, Pentti
The Guest.
Une Vie.
Saba, Umberto
The Goat.
Sleepless on a Summer Night.
Three Streets.
Woman.
Sabin, Edwin L.
Easter.
Sabina, Maria
Shaman.
Sabines, Jaime
Amen.
You Have What I Look For.
Sabir, Adib-i
Epitaph for a Tyrannous Governor Who Choked on Wine.
Saboly, Nicolas
Boots and Saddles.
Bring a Torch, Jeanette, Isabella.
The Shepherd Boys.
Sacchetti, Franco
Ballata: His Talk with Certain Peasant-Girls.
On a Wet Day.
Sachs, Elizabeth Newton
Celebration.
Sachs, Nelly
Above the Rocking Heads of the Mothers.
Awakening–.
Burning Sand of Sinai.
But Perhaps.
Chorus of the Rescued.
Chorus of the Unborn.
Hasidim Dance.
In flight in escape.
In the blue distance.
Landscape of Screams.

The last one.
Line Like.
O Night of the Crying Children.
O the Chimneys.
Oblivion!
One Chord.
The Sleepwalker.
To You Building the New House.
Vainly.
What Secret Desires of the Blood.
White Serpent.
Sackville, Charles, Earl of Dorset
The Advice.
The Dainty Young Heiress of Lincoln's Inn Fields.
Epigram: "Cloe's the wonder of her sex."
An Excellent New Ballad Giving a True Account of the Birth...
The Fire of Love.
A Madame, Madame B. Beaute Sexagenaire.
May the Ambitious Ever Find.
On Mr. Edward Howard, upon His British Princes.
On the Countess of Dorchester.
On the Young Statesmen.
Song: "Dorinda's sparkling wit, and eyes."
Song: "Methinks the poor town has been troubled too long."
Song: "Phillis, for shame let us improve."
Song: "To all you ladies now at land."
To Mr. Bays.
Sackville, Lady Margaret
The Apple.
An Epitaph.
Resurrection.
A Sermon.
To One Who Denies the Possibility of a Permanent Peace.
Sackville, Thomas, Earl of Dorset
Commendatory Sonnet to Hoby's Courtier.
The Complaint of Henrie Duke of Buckinghame.
The Induction to the Mirror for Magistrates.
The Shield of War.
Winter.
Sackville-West, Victoria Mary (Vita)
The Aquarium, San Francisco.
Bee-Master.
Black Tarn.
Craftsmen.
A Dream.
Full Moon.
The Greater Cats.
The Land.
On the Lake.
The Owl.
Sea-Sonnet.
Sometimes when Night...
Song: "If I had only loved your flesh."
Song: "My spirit like a shepherd boy."
To Any M.F.H.
Wood-cut.

Young Stock.
Sadeh, Pinhas
Elegy.
In the Forest.
In the Garden of the Turkish Consulate.
Raya Brenner.
Sa'di, Muslih-ud-Din
Adam's Race.
The Bustan.
Contentment.
A Factory Rainbow.
The Gulistan.
Hyacinths to Feed Thy Soul.
Ode.
On True Worth.
The Sieve.
Sadoff, Ira
A Concise History of the World.
The Fifties.
Hopper's "Nighthawks." (1942).
My Father's Leaving.
Poem after Apollinaire.
Seurat.
Saez Burgos, Juan
That Poem.
This Afternoon...
Saffarzadeh, Tahereh
Birthplace.
Saffin, John
An Acrostick on Mrs. Elizabeth Hull.
An Acrostick on Mrs. Winifret Griffin.
A Brief Elegie on My Dear Son John the Second of That Name of Mine.
Consideratus Considerandus.
An Elegie On the Deploreable Departure of ...John Hull.
A Lamentation on My Dear Son Simon Who Dyed of the Small Pox...
One Presenting a Rare Book to Madame Hull Senr: His Vallintine.
A Satyretericall Charracter of a Proud Upstart.
Sweetly (My Dearest) I Left Thee Asleep.
To His Excellency Joseph Dudley Eqr Gover: &c.
Saffold, Thomas
Saffold's Cures.
Safford, William Harrison
The Battle of Muskingum.
Safiya bint Musafir
At the Badr Trench.
Sagami, Lady
In the gathering dew.
Sage, Rufus B.
Night on the Prairie.
Summer on the Great American Desert.
The Wanderer's Grave.
"Sagittarius" (Olga Katzin)
Nerves.
Sagoff, Maurice
Preface ShrinkLit: Elements of Style William Strunk, Jr. & E. B. White.
Robinson Crusoe Daniel Defoe.
Saha, P. K.
The Child's Power of Wonder.
Sahl, Hans
Greeting from a Distance.
Memo.
Sa'ib of Isfahan
Cliques and Critics.

Saidy, Fred
For a Little Lady.
Saigyo Hoshi
Although I Do Not Know.
In My Boat That Goes.
Like Those Boats Which Are
Returning.
Mingling My Prayer.
Since I Am Convinced.
Startled.
Two Poems.
Sail, Lawrence
Christmas Night.
Sainsbury, Ian
Loveliest of Counties,
Shropshire Now (parody).
Saint-Gelais, Mellin de
The Sonnet of the Mountain.
St. Germain, Mark
Cannon Park.
St. John, David
Acadian Lane.
The Avenues.
Blue Waves.
Dolls.
Elegy.
For Lerida.
Guitar.
Hotel Sierra.
Hush.
Iris.
Poem: "Your face."
The Shore.
Slow Dance.
Two Sorrows.
Wavelength.
St. John, Peter
The Descent on Middlesex.
St. John, Primus
Benign Neglect/Mississippi,
1970.
Elephant Rock.
Lynching and Burning.
The Morning Star.
Tyson's Corner.
St John Damascene
Today in Bethlehem Hear I.
St. Leger, Warham
A False Gallop of Analogies.
To My Hairdresser.
Saint-Marthe, M.
Choosing a Wet-Nurse.
Cravings during Pregnancy.
Infant Diseases and Their
Treatment.
Labour.
St. Martin, Laura
As I Look Out.
The Ocean.
St. Virginia, Sister Mary
A Nun to Mary, Virgin.
Shrine in Nazareth.
Saiser, Marjorie
Morning.
Saito, Fumi
The palm of my hand.
Sakanoye, The Lady of See
Otomo of Sakanoe, Lady
Sala, G. A.
Epitaph for John Camden
Hotten.
Sala, Jerome
At the Treatment Center.
The Ballad of Helmut Franze.
Mother's Day.
The Party.
Salamah, Son of Jandal,
The Mufadaliyat: Gone Is
Youth.
Salamun, Tomaz
Air.
Eclipse.

Salcman, Michael
Open Heart.
Saldana, Diego de
Eyes So Tristful.
Saleh, Dennis
The Bed.
The Furniture of the Poem.
A Guide to Familiar
American Incest: Inventing a
Family.
Nesting.
The Return.
Story.
The Thumb.
Salinas, Luis Omar
Pedro.
Salinas, Pedro
Razon de Amor (excerpt).
Salis-Seewis, Johann Gaudenz
Song of the Silent Land.
Salisbury, Ralph
"Among the Savages..."
By Now.
A Halo.
A Second Molting.
This Is My Death-Dream.
Three Migrations.
Salkeld, Blanaid
Anchises.
Evasion.
Leave Us Religion.
Meditation.
Men Walked To and Fro.
No Uneasy Refuge.
Now Is Farewell.
Optimism.
Peggy.
Templeogue.
Terenure.
That Corner.
Youth.
Salkeld, Cecil Ffrench
Water-Front.
Salkey, Andrew
Postcard from London,
23.10.1972.
Salome, Brian S.
Hello There (parody).
Salomon, I. L.
Song for the Greenwood
Fawn.
Salomon, Louis B.
Univac to Univac.
Salsbury, Nate
Apex.
Take Nothing for Granite.
Salsich, Albert
Staying Up on Jack's Fork
Near Eminence, Missouri.
Salter, Mary Jo
England.
Saltillo, Don Jose de
Rio Bravo–A Mexican
Lament.
Saltman, Benjamin
The Fathers.
The Journey with Hands and
Arms.
Saltus, Francis Saltus
The Andalusian Sereno.
The Bayadere.
The Ideal.
Pastel.
The Sphinx Speaks.
Salusbury, Sir John
Buen Matina.
Salvadori, Giulio
The Presence of the Spirit.
Salverson, Laura Goodman
If a Maid Be Fair.
Premonition.

Salway, Owen C.
He Cares.
Salz, Helen
Late.
Salzburg, J.L.
Bill.
Sam, David A.
On the Pavement.
Samain, Albert
From Summer Hours.
Pannyra of the Golden Heel.
Sammis, J.H.
All Needs Met.
Sampley, Arthuir M.
The Defender.
Sampter, Jessie
Kadia the Young Mother
Speaks.
Sampter, Jessie E.
The Promised Land.
Summer Sabbath.
San Geminiano, Folgore da
On Knighthood.
Sonnet: Of Virtue.
Sonnets of the Months.
Sanborn, Franklin Benjamin
Ariana.
Samuel Hoar.
Sanchez, Carol Lee
Conversations with the
Nightmare.
Love Longs to Touch.
Open Dream Sequence.
Prologue.
(The Syl La Ble Speaks En
Erg y/Sound).
Tribal Chant.
The Way I Was...
Yesterday.
Sanchez, Luis Anibal
Brother Dog.
Sanchez, Ricardo
I Remember.
Sanchez, Sonia
–Answer to Yo/Question of
Am I Not Yo/Woman...
Black Magic.
A Chant for Young / Brothas
& Sistuhs.
Definition for Blk/Children.
Don't Wanna Be.
For Our Lady.
Homecoming.
Hospital/Poem.
Listenen to Big Black at S.F.
State.
Malcolm.
Memorial.
Nigger.
Now Poem. For Us.
Poem at Thirty.
Poem for Etheridge.
A Poem for My Father.
Poem: "Look at Me 8th
Grade."
Present.
Right On: White America.
Small Comment.
So This Is Our Revolution.
Summary.
Summer Words for a Sister
Addict.
To All Brothers.
To All Sisters.
Sandag
The "Word" of a Watch-Dog.
The "Word" of a Wolf
Encircled by the Hunt.
The "Word" of an Antelope
Caught in a Trap.
Sandall, Harold C.
Song.

Sandburg, Carl
Accomplished Facts.
Adelaide Crapsey.
Alice Corbin Is Gone.
All One People.
Aprons of Silence.
Arithmetic.
At a Window.
Baby Toes.
Balloon Faces.
Bas-Relief.
Being Born Is Important.
Blacklisted.
Blue Island Intersection.
Bones.
Bricklayer Love.
Broken-Face Gargoyles.
Broken Sky.
Bronzes.
Buffalo Dusk.
Bundles.
Caboose Thoughts.
Chicago.
Chicago Boy Baby.
Child.
Child of the Romans.
Circles.
Clinton South of Polk.
Clocks.
Cool Tombs.
Counting.
Crapshooters.
Death Snips Proud Men.
Doors.
Dream Girl.
Early Copper.
Early Lynching.
Early Moon.
An Electric Sign Goes Dark.
Elephants Are Different to
Different People.
Explanations of Love.
Falltime.
A Fence.
Fish Crier.
Flash Crimson.
Fog.
For You.
Four Preludes on Playthings
of the Wind.
Fourth of July Night.
Gargoyle.
Gone.
Good Morning America
(excerpt).
Grass.
Grassroots.
Graves.
The Great Hunt.
Handfuls.
Happiness.
The Harbor.
Hazardous Occupations.
Hits and Runs.
Home Thoughts.
Hope Is a Tattered Flag.
Horses and Men in the Rain.
I Am the People, the Mob.
Ice Handler.
Improved Farm Land.
In Tall Grass.
Jazz Fantasia.
Killers.
The Lawyers Know Too
Much.
Limited.
Little Candle.
Little Girl, Be Careful What
You Say.
Localities.
Losers.
Lost.

Love in Labrador.
Mammy Hums.
The Man in the Street Is Fed.
Manufactured Gods.
Mist Forms.
Moist Moon People.
Mr. Attila.
Muckers.
Mysterious Biography.
Nocturn Cabbage.
Nocturne in a Deserted
  Brickyard.
North Atlantic.
The Old Flagman.
Old Timers.
On a Flimmering Floom You
  Shall Ride.
One Modern Poet.
Ossawatomie.
Our Prayer of Thanks
  (excerpt).
The People, Yes.
Personality.
Plunger.
Pool.
Population Drifts.
Portrait of a Motorcar.
Potomac Town in February.
Prairie.
Prayer after World War.
Prayers of Steel.
Precious Moments.
Primer Lesson.
Psalm of Those Who Go
  Forth before Daylight.
Rat Riddles.
Repetitions.
River Roads.
Sandhill People.
The Sea Hold.
Sea-Wash.
The Shovel Man.
The Sins of Kalamazoo.
Sketch.
Skyscraper.
Sleep Is a Suspension.
Slippery.
Smoke and Steel (excerpt).
Soup.
Special Starlight.
Splinter.
Street Window.
Summer Stars.
Sunsets.
Swell People.
Ten Definitions of Poetry.
Theme in Yellow.
They All Want to Play
  Hamlet.
Three Spring Notations on
  Bipeds.
Threes.
To a Contemporary
  Bunkshooter.
To Beachey, 1912.
To the Ghost of John Milton.
Trinity Place.
Upstream.
Wall Shadows.
Washington Monument by
  Night.
When Death Came April
  Twelve 1945.
"Who can make a poem of
  the depths of weariness."
Who Shall Speak for the
  People?
Wilderness.
Wind Song.
Wingtip.
Work Gangs.
Working Girls.

Young Sea.
Sandburg, Helga
  Cantata for Two Lovers.
  The Importance of Mirrors.
Sandeen, Ernest
  Nearing Winter.
  Views of Our Sphere.
Sandell, Lina
  Security.
Sanders, Ed
  Elm Fuck Poem.
  The Five Feet.
  For Sergeant Fetta.
  The Pilgrimage.
  Sheep-Fuck Poem.
  Soft-Man 1.
  Soft-Man 3.
  Toe Queen Poems (excerpt).
  Yiddish Speaking Socialists of
  the Lower East Side.
Sanders, Edward
  The Fugs.
  Holy Was Demeter Walking
  th' Corn Furrow.
  Pindar's Revenge.
Sanders, Mark
  Gone Fishing.
  Happening In.
  Stockton Lake; Stockton,
  Missouri.
Sanders, Thomas E.
  Machine Out of the God.
Sanders, Velma
  Old House Place.
Sandford, James
  Of Love.
Sands, Robert Charles
  The Green Isle of Lovers.
Sandy, Stephen
  The Ballad of Mary Baldwin.
  Declension.
  The Destruction of Bulfinch's
  House.
  Et Quid Amabo Nisi Quod
  Aenigma Est.
  Getting On.
  Hiawatha.
  Hunter's Moon.
  The Woolworth Philodendron.
Sandys, Edwin
  In Pilgrim Life Our Rest.
Sandys, George
  The Bounty of Jehovah Praise.
  Deo Opt. Max.
  Judah in Exile Wanders.
  Lines Written at the Temple
  of the Holy Sepulchre.
  O Blest Estate, Blest from
  Above.
  Ovid's Metamorphosis: Sixth
  Book.
  Psalme CXXXVII.
Saner, Reg
  Anasazi at Mesa Verde.
  Clear Night, Small Fire, No
  Wind.
  The Day the Air Was on Fire.
  The Fifth Season.
  Flag.
  Homing.
  How the Laws of Physics
  Love Chocolate!
  Orchestra.
  Passing It On.
  The Space Eater Camps at
  Fifth Lake.
Sanfedele, Ann
  The Part of Fortune.
Sanfield, Steve
  Dynamic Tension.

Sanford, Christy Sheffield
  Dreams of Snakes, Chocolate
  and Men.
  The Romance of Citrus.
  The Romance of Imprinting.
  Scattered Fog.
  Traveling through Ports That
  Begin with "M".
Sanford, Frank Elwood
  The Outcast.
Sangster, Charles
  Evening.
  Pleasant Memories: The
  Meadow-Field.
  The Rapid.
  The Red Men.
  Sonnet: "Blest Spirit of Calm
  that dwellest in these
  woods!"
  Sonnets Written in the Orillia
  Woods, VII.
  The St. Lawrence and the
  Saguenay.
Sangster, Margaret
  Are the Children at Home?
  The Building of the Nest.
  The Work of Love.
Sangster, Margaret E.
  The Average Man.
  Awakening.
  A Bit of the Book.
  The Blind Man.
  Face to Face with Trouble
  (excerpt).
  Faith.
  Forgiven.
  If Christ Were Here To-
  Night.
  Midnight.
  A Mother's Prayer.
  Now and Then.
  Our Own.
  Patience With the Living.
  Peace.
  A Prayer for Faith.
  Security.
  Show Me Thyself.
  The Sin of Omission.
  A Song for Our Flag.
  Sunrise.
  Thanksgiving.
  They Never Quite Leave Us.
  A Thought.
  Whittier.
  Within the Veil.
Sannazaro, Jacopo
  Celestial Queen.
Sansom, Clive
  Butterflies.
  Ladybird.
  Matthew.
  Snowflakes.
  The Witnesses: The
  Innkeeper's Wife.
Sant' Angelo, Bartolomeo di
  Sonnet: He Jests Concerning
  His Poverty.
Sant'Ana, Gloria de
  African Day.
Santayana, George
  After Grey Vigils.
  As in the Midst of Battle
  There Is Room.
  Athletic Ode.
  Before a Statue of Achilles.
  Cape Cod.
  Deem Not.
  Faith.
  I Sought On Earth.
  I Would I Might Forget That
  I Am I.

  A Minuet on Reaching the
  Age of Fifty.
  O Martyred Spirit.
  O World.
  Ode: "My heart rebels against
  my generation."
  Odes.
  On a Piece of Tapestry.
  On the Death of a
  Metaphysician.
  Prosit Neujahr.
  The Rustic at the Play.
  Solipsism.
  Sorrow.
  We Needs Must Be Divided.
  What Riches Have You.
  With You a Part of Me.
Santeuil, Jean-Baptiste de
  Ascension Hymn.
Santic, Aleksa
  Dalmatian Nocturne.
Santos, Aires de A.
  When My Brothers Come
  Home.
Santos, Arnaldo
  Season of Blood.
Santos, Sherod
  The Breakdown.
  Childhood.
  Country Landscape.
  The Enormous Aquarium.
  Evening Refrain.
  Goodbye.
  Sirens in Bad Weather.
Sanuki, Lady
  Like a Great Rock, Far out at
  Sea.
Saphier, William
  Meeting.
Sappho
  ...About the Cool Water.
  Achtung.
  All the while, believe me, I
  prayed.
  Alone (fragment).
  Andromache's Wedding.
  Andromeda forgot.
  Arignota Remembers.
  Be Kind to Me.
  Bride's Lament.
  The Bridegroom Is So Tall.
  Caller Rain Frae Abune.
  Come, holy tortoise shell.
  Come Out of Crete.
  Come to Me from Crete to
  This Holy Temple.
  Congratulations: Two
  Versions.
  Deid Sall Ye Ligg, and Ne'er
  a Memorie.
  Don't Ask Me What to Wear.
  The Door-Keeper Has Big
  Feet.
  The Dust of Time (fragment).
  Evening Star.
  Farewell to Anactoria.
  Forever Dead.
  Full Moon (fragment).
  The glow and beauty of the
  stars.
  He Is More Than a Hero.
  Here are fine gifts, children.
  Hermes came to me in a
  dream.
  Hesperos, you bring home all
  the bright dawn disperses.
  Honestly I wish I were dead!
  I could not hope.
  I Have Had Not One Word
  from Her.
  I have no embroidered
  headband.

I Hear That Andromeda.
I Taught the Talented.
If my nipples were to drip
milk.
In gold sandals.
It Was You, Attis.
It would be wrong for us.
Leave Krete and come to this
holy temple.
Life the Very Gods in My
Sight Is He Who.
Like a mountain whirlwind.
Like a sweet apple reddening
on the high.
Lonely Night.
Love–bittersweet,
irrepressible–.
Love (fragment).
The Marriage of Hector and
Andromache.
Mother darling, I cannot work
the loom.
My Atthis, although our dear
Anaktoria.
My mother always said.
My Muse, What Ails This
Ardour?
Night Singers.
Note to Gongyla.
Now in my heart.
O dream from the blackness.
O Gongyla, my darling rose.
Ode: "Peer of gods he seemeth
to me."
Ode to Anactoria.
Ode to Aphrodite.
On My Sweet Mother.
On your dazzling throne,
Aphrodite.
One Girl.
Orchard Song.
The Parting.
Peer of the Gods Is That
Man.
People Do Gossip.
Round about Me (fragment).
Sappho, if you do not come
out.
Seizure.
The Silver Moon.
Some say cavalry and others
claim.
Some There Are Who Say
That the Fairest Thing Seen.
Someone, I tell you.
Then I said to the elegant
ladies.
There's a Man, I Really
Believe....
Timas.
To me he seems like a god.
Tonight I've Watched.
We Put the Urn Aboard Ship.
You came. And you did well
to come.
You Know the Place.
You lay in wait.
Sarah, Robyn
Broom at Twilight.
Cat's Cradle.
An Early Start in Mid-Winter.
An Inch of Air.
Maintenance.
Suckers for Truth.
Sarbiewski, Casimir
On the Victory of Poland and
Her Allies over the Sultan
Osman, 1621.
Sarett, Lew
Breakers of Broncos.
Feud.
Four Little Foxes.

God Is at the Anvil.
The Granite Mountain.
The Great Divide.
Let Me Flower as I Will.
Let Me Go down to Dust.
The Loon.
Refuge.
The Sheepherder.
Wind in the Pine.
Sargent, Daniel
The Ark and the Dove.
The Last Day.
Preference.
Sargent, E. N.
The Break.
Child.
Paradise.
A Sailor at Midnight.
Sargent, Epes
The Death of Warren.
Deeds of Kindness.
Evening in Gloucester Harbor.
The Heart's Summer.
A Life on the Ocean Wave.
A Summer Noon at Sea.
Sunrise at Sea.
Tropical Weather.
Sargent, John Osborne
Horace.
Sargent, N.B.
Building for Eternity.
Sargent, Nettie M.
A Hymn of Trust.
Sargent, Robert
The Concept of Force.
The Epistemologist, over a
Brandy, Opining.
Sargent, William D.
Wind-Wolves.
Sarmed the Yahud
Quatrain.
Saroyan, Aram
Car swerves,/injures 11; driver
held.
Crickets.
French Poets.
Sarton, May
After All These Years.
Bears and Waterfalls.
Boulder Dam.
Burial.
By Moonlight.
A Celebration.
The Clavichord.
Conversation in Black and
White.
Definition.
Dutch Interior.
Eine Kleine Snailmusik.
Fore Thought.
In Time Like Air.
A Last Word.
Leaves Before the Wind.
A Light Left On.
Nativity.
New Year Wishes.
A Nobleman's House
(excerpt).
Prayer before Work.
Prothalamium.
Qords on the Wind: Fruit of
Loneliness.
The Sacred Order.
Santos: New Mexico.
The Snow Light.
Song: "Now let us honor with
violin and flute."
Summer Music.
These Images Remain.
Three Things.
Transition.
A Village Tale.

The White-Haired Man.
The Work of Happiness.
Sassoon, Siegfried
Absolution.
Aftermath.
All-Souls' Day.
Alone.
Arbor Vitae.
Asking for It.
At Daybreak.
At Max Gate.
At the Grave of Henry
Vaughan.
Attack.
Babylon.
Base Details.
Before Day.
Blighters.
Brevities.
The Case for Miners.
Cleaning the Candelabrum.
Concert-Interpretations (Le
Sacre du Printemps).
A Concert Party.
Conclusion.
Counter-Attack.
Dead Musicians.
The Death-Bed.
December Stillness.
Does It Matter?
Dreamers.
The Dug-Out.
Early Chronology.
Elected Silence.
Everyman.
Everyone Sang.
Falling Asleep.
Fancy Dress.
Fantasia on a Wittelsbach
Atmosphere.
The Fathers.
The General.
Glory of Women.
Grandeur of Ghosts.
Haunted.
The Hero.
I Stood with the Dead.
The Imperfect Lover.
In Barracks.
In Me, Past, Present, Future
Meet.
In the National Gallery.
In the Pink.
The Investiture.
Invocation.
The Kiss.
Lamentations.
Limitations.
Litany of the Lost.
A Local Train of Thought.
Middle Ages.
A Midnight Interior.
Morning Express.
Morning Glory.
A Musical Critic Anticipates
Eternity.
My Past Has Gone to Bed.
A Mystic as Soldier.
The Need.
On Passing the New Menin
Gate.
On Scratchbury Camp.
The One-Legged Man.
One Who Watches.
Picture-Show.
A Post-Mortem.
The Power and the Glory.
A Prayer from 1936.
Prehistoric Burials.
Presences Perfected.
The Rear-guard.
The Redeemer.

Repression of War Experience.
The Road.
Sheldonian Soliloquy.
Slumber Song.
Sporting Acquaintances.
Stand-To: Good Friday
Morning.
Storm on Fifth Avenue.
Strangeness of Heart.
Suicide in Trenches.
They.
To a Very Wise Man.
To an Old Lady Dead.
To His Dead Body.
Together.
The Troops.
Two Old Ladies.
Vigils.
Vigils: Down the Glimmering
Staircase.
Villa d'Este Gardens.
The Wisdom of the World.
A Working Party.
Satoru Sato
Japan That Sank under the
Sea.
Satz, Mario
Coconut.
Fish.
Lemon.
Saucedo, Maria
About Women's Liberation.
Sa'udi, Mona
How Do I Enter the Silence
of Stones.
When the Loneliness of the
Tomb Went down into the
Marketplace.
Why Don't I Write in the
Language of Air?
Saul, George Brandon
By Winter Seas.
Elizabeth.
Spring Song.
Sauls, Roger
My Grandfather Burning
Cornfields.
Reconcilable Differences.
Saunders, Donald G.
Ascent.
On Foinaven.
Saunders, Lesley
Mothers of Sons.
Saunders, Mary Wight
Remembering Day.
Saunders, R. Crombie
The Empty Glen.
Ressaif My Saul.
Saunders, Ruby C.
Hush, Honey.
Saunders, Thomas
End of Steel.
Horizontal World.
Savage, Ann Marie
In a Night.
Savage, D. S.
Absent Creation.
Confession.
Fall of Leaves.
February.
Living.
Scenario.
Separation.
The Wild Swan.
Winter Offering.
Savage, Frances Higginson
Duck in Central Park.
Savage, Minot Judson
Decorating the Soldiers'
Graves.
Life's Common Duties.
My Birth.

Savage, Philip Henry
Infinity.
Morning.
Silkweed.
Solitude.
Savage, Richard
The Animalcule, A Tale.
The Authors of the Town
(excerpt).
The Bastard.
London and Bristol
Delineated.
The Progress of a Divine
(excerpt).
To a Young Lady.
Savant, John
In the Time of the Rose.
Savoie, Terry
The Far North.
Savonarola, Girolamo
O Star of Galilee.
Sawyer, C. P.
I Used to Love My Garden.
Sawyer, Frederick William
The Recognition (parody).
Sawyer, Mark
Kite Days.
Sawyer, Ruth
Christmas Morn.
The Feast o' Saint Stephen.
Words from an Old Spanish
Carol.
Saxe, John Godfrey
The Blind Men and the
Elephant.
The Briefless Barrister.
Darling, Tell Me Yes.
Do I Love Thee?
Early Rising.
Echo.
The Game of Life.
How Cyrus Laid the Cable.
Justine, You Love Me Not!
My Familiar.
The News.
The Puzzled Census Taker.
Pyramus and Thisbe.
Rhyme of the Rails.
Solomon and the Bees.
Sonnet to a Clam.
The Story of Life.
To Lesbia.
To My Love.
Too Candid by Half.
Woman's Will.
Wouldn't You Like to Know.
The Youth and the
Northwind.
Saxon, Alvin
Black Power.
A Poem for Integration.
Watts.
Saxon, Dan
Walking in the Rain.
Saxton, Andrew Bice
The First Step.
Sayers, A. M.
It Always Seems (parody).
Sayers, Dorothy L.
The Choice of the Cross.
The Just Vengeance (excerpt).
Sayers, Frances Clarke
Who Calls.
Sayles, James M.
Star of the Evening.
Saylor, Mark
Hello, Sister.
Sayres, Cortlandt W.
Bankrupt.
Scalapino, Leslie
Areas.
Hmmmm.

A Sequence.
The Woman Who Could Read
the Minds of Dogs.
Scannell, Vernon
Act of Love.
Any Complaints?
Autumn.
Dead Dog.
The Discriminator.
Five Domestic Interiors.
The Great War.
Incendiary.
Jailbird.
The Jealous Wife.
Moods of Rain.
The Moth.
The Old Books.
Poetry Reading.
Reformed Drunkard.
Schoolroom on a Wet
Afternoon.
Six Reasons for Drinking.
Spot-Check at Fifty.
Tightrope Walker.
Walking Wounded.
Words and Monsters.
Scantlebury, Elizabeth E.
Hymn of Dedication.
Scarborough, Dorothy
The Organ Cactus.
Scarborough, George L.
To the Men Who Lose.
Scarbrough, George
Birth by Anesthesia.
Tenantry.
Viewpoint.
Scarbrough, Jessica
Birthsong.
Lunar Eclipse.
Professional Prisoner.
There Is No Vacancy.
Today, Prison Won.
Scarfe, Francis
Cat's Eyes.
Cats.
The Clock.
The Grotto.
Kitchen Poem.
The Merry Window.
Ode in Honour.
Progression.
Tyne Dock.
The Window.
Scarron, Paul
Thus, When Soft Love
Subdues the Heart.
Schaaf, Richard
Sparkling Water.
Schacht, Marshall
The First Autumn.
Not to Forget Miss
Dickinson.
Schaechter-Gottesman
Meditation.
Schaefer, M. Cherubim
Rejoice, Let Alleluias Ring.
Schaefer, Ted
Anxiety Pastorale.
The Parents-Without-Partners
Picnic.
Schaeffer, Susan Fromberg
The First Test.
Housewife.
Truth.
Womb Song.
Yahrzeit.
Schauffler, Robert Haven
Nonsense.
Scum o' the Earth.
Schaukal, Richard
Images.

Schaumann, Ruth
Evensong.
Fourth Station.
Mary on Her Way to the
Temple.
Schechter, Ruth Lisa
Vision of 400 Sunrises.
Schedler, Gilbert
A Spring Day on Campus.
Scheele, Roy
August.
Dancer.
Fishing Blue Creek.
The Gap in the Cedar.
A Kitchen Memory.
Poppies.
Scheffauer, Ethel Talbot
A Reply from the Akond of
Swat.
Scheffler, Johannes *See "Angelus
Silesius"*
Scheinert, David
The Drunken Stones of
Prague.
The Stone and the Blade of
Grass in the Warsaw Ghetto.
Scherzo, I. O.
Threnody.
Scheuer, Marjorie Somers
The Fox.
Schevill, James
The Crow-Marble Whores of
Paris.
Death of a Cat.
Freud: Dying in London, He
Recalls the Smoke of His
Cigar...
Green Frog at Roadside,
Wisconsin.
Huck Finn at Ninety, Dying
in a Chicago Boarding House
Room.
A Lesson in Hammocks.
London Pavement Artist.
Looking at Wealth in
Newport.
Mixed Media.
The Necessity of Rejection.
The Old Peasant Woman at
the Monastery of Zagorsk.
A Screamer Discusses
Methods of Screaming.
Schierloh, Samuel
Bucko-Mate.
Schiff, Jeff
Winter Twilight.
Schiller, Friedrich von
Columbus.
The Maid of Orleans.
Ode to Joy.
Steer, Bold Mariner, On!
Thekla's Song.
To My Friends.
The Unrealities.
The Visit of the Gods.
Schimmel, Harold
Ancestors.
Schjeldahl, Peter
Bonner's Ferry.
Che Guevara Is Dead.
Citizen.
Fear.
Life Studies.
The Page of Illustrations.
Release.
Smiles.
To the National Arts Council.
White Country.
A Younger Poet.
Schlegel, Katharina von
Be Still, My Soul.

Schlesinger, John
South Shore Line.
Schlipf, Benjamin
Contentment.
Schloerb, Rolland W.
O Thou Eternal Source of
Life.
Thou Light of Ages.
Schlonsky, Avraham
A New Genesis.
Prayer.
The Stars on Shabbat.
Schloss, David
The Poem.
Schmid, C. M.
Synekdechestai.
Schmidt, Lorenza
Heading for Eugene.
Schmidt, Tom
Black and White.
Broccoli.
Butcherboy.
Butter.
Civilization.
The Creeper.
Drowning in Spanish.
In the Garden.
A Long Overdue Thankyou
Note to the Girl Who
Taught Me Loving.
Seven Mexican Children.
Waking Up.
Schmitz, Dennis
Adolescence.
Arbeit Macht Frei.
The California Phrasebook.
The Chalk Angel.
Chicago: Near West-Side
Renewal.
Coma.
Dressing Game.
Eclogues.
Gill Boy.
Goodwill, Inc.
If I Could Meet God.
Kindergarten.
A Letter to Ron Silliman on
the Back of a Map of the
Solar System.
Making a Door.
Making Chicago.
The Man Who Buys Hides.
Mile Hill.
The Mole.
The Name of Our Country.
News.
A Picture of Okinawa.
Planting Trout in the Chicago
River.
Poke-Pole Fishing.
Queen of Heaven Mausoleum.
Rabbits.
Skinning-the-Cat.
Star & Garter Theater.
String.
Virgil: Georgics, Book IV.
Schmolck, Benjamin
Heavier the Cross.
My Jesus, As Thou Wilt.
Schmuller, Aaron
Legend of His Lyre.
Schnackenberg, Gjertrud
Darwin in 1881.
How Did It Seem to Sylvia?
The Living Room.
The Paperweight.
Signs.
Schneckenburger, Max
The Watch on the Rhine.
Schneider, Isidor
The Ambience of Love.
Insects.

Joy of Knowledge.
Riding Song.
Sunday Morning.
The Wall.

Schneider, Pat
In a Maple Wood.

Schneour, Zalman
Besieged.
Cherries.
Forsaken.
The Last Words of Don
Henriquez.
Like Water Down a Slope.
The Road.
A Star There Fell.
War Comes.
Welcome, Queen Sabbath.

Schoeck, R. J.
Homage.

Scholasticus
To an Aging Charioteer.

Scholem, Gershom
The Trial.

Scholl, J. W.
The Poet's Prothalamion
(Excerpt).

Scholten, Martin
Soliloquy by the Shore.

Schomberg, Ralph
Ay or Nay?
A Courtier's a Riddle.
Like Birds of a Feather.

Schonborg, Virginia
Construction.

Schoolcraft, Luke
Shine On.

Schorb, E. M.
Hush, Hush, New House in
Charlotte.
No.

Schotz, Myra Glazer
The First Love Poem.
Santa Caterina.
Thespian in Jerusalem.

Schoultz, Solveig von
The Deaths.

Schramm, Donald G. H.
Voyage.

Schreiber, Laura
A Delicate Balance.
Willows.

Schroeder, Peter
All Human Things (parody).

Schubart, Christian
Song of the Cape of Good
Hope.

Schubert, William H.
Educational Music or Erosion.

Schuchat, Simon
Anti-Memoirs.
A Long & Happy Life.

Schuck, L. Pearl
Solar Signals.
To a Butterfly.

Schuler, Ruth Wildes
Funeral of Rufino Contreras.

Schull, Joseph
The Legend of Ghost Lagoon:
The Pirates' Fight.

Schulman, Grace
Burial of a Fisherman in
Hydra.
Burn Down the Icons.
Epithalamion.
The Law.

Schultz, Lulu Minerva
What Price.

Schultz, Philip
The Apartment-Hunter.
Balance.
The Hemingway House in
Key West.

Like Wings.
Mrs. Applebaum's Sunday
Dance Class.
My Guardian Angel Stein.

Schulz, Dale
His Presence.

Schuyler, James
An Almanac.
Buried at Springs.
Can I Tempt You to a Pond
Walk?
Crocus Night.
The Crystal Lithium.
December.
Dining out with Doug and
Frank.
"Earth's Holocaust."
The Elizabethans Called It
Dying.
Faberge.
February.
Freely Espousing.
Going.
Greenwich Avenue.
A Head.
Hudson Ferry.
Ilford Rose Book.
A Man in Blue.
The Master of the Golden
Glow.
Milk.
Poem.
Poem: "This beauty that I
see."
Quick, Henry, the Flit!
A Reunion.
Roof Garden.
Salute.
Sorting, Wrapping, Packing,
Stuffing.
Stun.
Today.
A White City.

Schuyler, Montgomery
Carlyle and Emerson.

Schuylr, James
Self-Pity Is a Kind of Lying,
Too.

**Schuylr-Lighthall, William
Douw**
The Battle of La Prairie.

Schwabsky, Barry
Fragment of a Pastoral.

Schwager, Elaine
Tracks.

Schwartz, Delmore
Abraham:.
All of Us Always Turning
away for Solace.
America, America!
Aria.
At a Solemn Musick.
The Ballad of the Children of
the Czar.
The Ballet of the Fifth Year.
Baudelaire.
The Beautiful American
Word, Sure.
The Dark and Falling
Summer.
The Deceptive Present, The
Phoenix Year.
Do They Whisper behind My
Back?
A Dog Named Ego, the
Snowflakes as Kisses.
Dogs are Shakespearean,
Children Are Strangers.
During December's Death.
Far Rockaway.
Father and Son.

For One Who Would Not
Take His Life in His Hands.
For Rhoda.
For the One Who Would
Take Man's Life in His
Hands.
The Heart Flies Up, Erratic as
a Kite.
Holderlin.
How Strange Love Is, in
Every State of Consciousness.
I Am a Book I Neither Wrote
Nor Read.
I Did Not Know the Truth of
Growing Trees.
I Wakened to a Calling.
In the Naked Bed, in Plato's
Cave.
Is It the Morning? Is It the
Little Morning?
The Kingdom of Poetry:
Swift.
A Little Morning Music.
Look, in the Labyrinth of
Memory.
Mentreche il Vento, Come Fa,
Si Tace.
The Mind Is an Ancient and
Famous Capital.
The Passionate Shepherd to
His Love.
Poem: "Old man in the
crystal morning after snow."
Prothalamion.
The Repetitive Heart.
Sarah.
The Self Unsatisfied Runs
Everywhere.
The Sequel.
Shenandoah: Let Us Consider
Where the Great Men Are.
Socrates' Ghost Must Haunt
Me Now.
The Starlight's Intuitions
Pierced the Twelve.
Time's Dedication.
Tired and Unhappy, You
Think of Houses.
Today Is Armistice, a
Holiday.
The True, the Good and the
Beautiful.
Vivaldi.
What Curious Dresses All
Men Wear.
The Winter Twilight, Glowing
Black and Gold.
You Are a Jew!

Schwartz, Hillel
Bedtime.

Schwartz, Howard
Abraham in Egypt.
Adam's Dream.
Blessing of the Firstborn.
The Eve.
Gathering the Sparks.
Iscah.
The New Year for Trees.
Our Angels.
The Prayers.
Psalm.
Shira.
A Song.
These Two.
Vessels.

Schwob, Marcel
Actions.
Moments.
Things Dead.

Scollard, Clinton
Ad Patriam.

As I Came down from
Lebanon.
At the Tomb of Washington.
Ballad of Lieutenant Miles.
The Ballad of Paco Town.
The Battle of Plattsburg Bay.
Be Ye in Love with April-
Tide?
A Bell.
The Boasting of Sir Peter
Parker.
Cricket.
The Daughter of the
Regiment.
Deeds of Valor at Santiago.
The Eve of Bunker Hill.
The First Thanksgiving.
The First Three.
If Only the Dreams Abide.
Khamsin.
The King of Dreams.
King Philip's Last Stand.
Kris Kringle.
A Man!
Memnon.
The Men of the Maine.
The Men of the Merrimac.
Montgomery at Quebec.
On a Bust of Lincoln.
On an American Soldier of
Fortune Slain in France.
A Prayer.
Private Blair of the Regulars.
The Quest.
Rain Riders.
The Ride of Tench Tilghman.
Riding with Kilpatrick.
Saint Leger.
Sea Shells.
Sidney Godolphin.
The Sleeper.
Song for Memorial Day.
Sunflowers.
There Is a Pool on Garda.
To William Sharp.
The Unreturning.
The Valor of Ben Milam.
Wayne at Stony Point.

Scott, Alexander
A Bequest of His Heart.
Calvinist Sang.
Coronach.
Haar in Princes Street.
A Lament: 1547.
Lament of the Master of
Erskine.
Letter to Robert Fergusson.
Of May.
Problems.
Quha Is Perfyte.
Recipe: To Mak a Ballant.
Return Thee, Hairt.
A Rondel of Love.
Scrievin.
To Luve Unluvit.
Up, Helsum Hairt.
Wha Is Perfyte.

Scott, Clement
Oh Promise Me.
Rus in Urbe.
The Story of a Stowaway.

Scott, Diana
Lucy Taking Birth.
Prayer for the Little Daughter
between Death and Burial.
Winter Solstice Poem.

Scott, Duncan Campbell
At Delos.
At Gull Lake: August, 1810.
At the Cedars.
Bells.
Compline.

Ecstasy.
En Route.
The Fallen.
The Forsaken.
The Half-Breed Girl.
In the Selkirks.
Night and the Pines.
Night Hymns on Lake
   Nipigon.
A Night in June.
O Turn Once More.
Off Riviere Du Loup.
On the Way to the Mission.
The Onondaga Madonna.
The Piper of Arll.
A Prairie Water Colour.
Prairie Wind.
Rapids at Night.
The Sailor's Sweetheart.
Song: "In the air there are no
   coral-reefs or ambergris."
Thoughts.
Watkwenies.
Scott, Elizabeth
Now Let Our Hearts Their
   Glory Wake.
See How the Rising Sun.
Scott, Evelyn
Autumn Night.
Scott, F. R.
Bangkok.
Bonne Entente.
Brebeuf and His Brethren.
Calamity.
The Canadian Authors Meet.
Caring.
Conflict.
Eclipse.
Examiner.
Full Valleys.
A Grain of Rice.
Lakeshore.
Laurentian Shield.
Night Club.
Old Song.
Recovery.
Saturday Sundae.
Someone Could Certainly Be
   Found.
Tourist Time.
Trans Canada.
W.L.M.K.
Will to Win.
Windfall.
Scott, Fred Newton
Romeo and Juliet.
Scott, Frederick George
Dawn.
Easter Island.
In the Woods.
Requiescant.
The Snowstorm.
The Sting of Death.
Te Judice.
The Unnamed Lake.
Van Elsen.
Scott, G. Forrester See
"Halsham, John"
Scott, Geoffrey
All Our Joy Is Enough.
Frutta Di Mare.
The Skaian Gate (excerpt).
What Was Solomon's Mind?
Scott, Herbert
Butcher's Wife.
Help Is on the Way.
Letter from a Working Girl.
Passing the Masonic Home for
   the Aged.
That Summer.
Scott, John
How to Fertilize Soil.

Ode: "I hate that drum's
   discordant sound."
Retort on the Foregoing.
Scott, Johnie
The American Dream.
Scott, Lady John
The Comin' o' the Spring.
Ettrick.
Loch Lomond.
Scott, Louise Binder
Birthday Candles.
Scott, Margaret
Portrait of a Married Couple.
Scott, Robert B. Y.
O Day of God, Draw Nigh.
Scott, Sharon
Between Me and Anyone Who
   Can Understand–.
Come on Home.
Discovering–.
For Both of Us at Fisk.
Just Taking Note–.
A Little More About the
   Brothers and Sisters.
Mama Knows.
Oh—Yeah!
Okay–.
On My Stand.
Our Lives.
Sharon Will Be No/Where on
   Nobody's Best-Selling List.
Untitled: "fisk is/a/negroid/
   institution..."
Untitled (Hi Ronda).
Scott, Sir Walter
The Abbess.
Allen-a-Dale.
Anna-Marie, Love, Up Is the
   Sun.
The Antiquary. Chapt. 10:
   Why Sit'st Thou by That
   Ruin'd Hall.
The Book of Books.
The Bride of Lammermoor
   (excerpt).
Christmas in the Olden Time.
Claud Halcro's Invocation.
County Guy.
Datur Hora Quieti.
Dies Irae.
Donald Caird.
The Doom of Devorgoil, II, ii:
   Bonny Dundee.
The Dreary Change.
Edmund's Song.
Epigram: Sound, sound the
   clarion, fill the fife!
The Eve of Saint John.
False Love.
The Fire.
Football Song.
The Fortunes of Nigel
   (excerpt).
Gellatley's Song to the
   Deerhounds.
Glee for King Charles.
Glenfinlas; or, Lord Ronald's
   Coronach.
Guy Mannering. Chapt. 4:
   Twist Ye, Twine Ye! Even
   So.
Guy Mannering. Chapt. 27:
   Wasted, Weary, Wherefore
   Stay.
Harlaw.
Harp of the North, Farewell.
Heap on More Wood.
The Heart of Midlothian.
Hellvellyn.
The Herring Loves the Merry
   Moonlight.
An Hour with Thee.

It's up Glenbarchan's Braes I
   Gaed.
Ivanhoe. Chapt. 39: Rebecca's
   Hymn.
Jock of Hazeldean.
The Lady of the Lake.
The Lay of the Last Minstrel.
The Legend of Montrose.
   Chapt. 6: Annot Lyle's Song:
   "Birds of Omen".
The Lord of the Isles
   (excerpt).
Lullaby of an Infant Chief.
MacGregor's Gathering.
Madge Wildfire's Death Song.
The Maid of Neidpath.
Man the Enemy of Man.
Marmion.
Melrose Abbey.
The Minstrel Responds to
   Flattery.
The Monastery: Border
   Ballad.
The Monks of Bangor's
   March.
The Nativity Chant.
O, Woman!
Old Mortality.
On a Day's Stint.
On Having Piles.
On Leaving Mrs. Brown's
   Lodgings.
Patriotism.
Perveril of the Peak (excerpt).
Pibroch of Donald Dhu.
The Pirate (excerpt).
Rob Roy.
Rosabelle.
Saint Cloud.
Sir Walter Scott's Tribute.
Sir William of Deloraine at
   the Wizard's Tomb.
Song: "A weary lot is thine,
   fair maid."
Song of the Mermaids and
   Mermen.
Song of the White Lady of
   Avenel.
Song: "Where shall the lover
   rest."
St. Swithin's Chair.
The Sun upon the Weirdlaw
   Hill.
'Tis Merry in Greenwood.
To a Lady.
To a Lock of Hair.
To an Oak Tree.
Verses in the Style of the
   Druids (excerpt).
The Violet.
A Weary Lot is Thine.
Where Shall the Lover Rest.
William and Helen.
Woman's Faith.
Young Lochinvar.
Youth! Thou Wear'st to
   Manhood Now.
Scott, Tom
Angels, Roll the Rock Away!
Auld Sanct-Aundrians–Brand
   the Builder.
The Real Muse.
Sea Dirge.
Scott, W. N.
Bundaberg Rum.
Scott, William
Glenkindie.
Scott, William Bell
Death.
Love's Calendar.
Music.
A Rhyme of the Sun-Dial.

The Robin.
The Witch's Ballad.
Scott, Winfield Townley
Annual Legend.
Another Return.
Bermuda Suite.
Biography for Traman
   (excerpt).
Blue Sleigh.
Brief Encounter.
Come Green Again.
Confidential.
The Difference.
The Double Tree.
The First Reader.
The Fish Sonata.
Five for the Grace.
The Game.
The House.
Into the Wind.
The Ivory Bed.
Landscape as Metal and
   Flowers.
Mr. Whittier.
Mrs. Severin.
Natural Causes.
O Lyric Love.
Sonnet: "I watched the sea for
   hours blind with sun."
Sonnet XIII.
Sonnet XV: "This is the way
   we say it in our time."
Swedish Angel.
Three American Women and
   a German Bayonet.
To L.B.S.
Two.
Two Lives and Others.
The U. S. Sailor with the
   Japanese Skull.
Uses of Poetry.
Watch Hill.
Wax.
We'll All Feel Gay.
Scott-Gatty, Alfred
Maria Jane.
Scott-Hopper, Queenie
Very Nearly.
Scott of Amwell, John See **Scott,
John**
Scovell, E. J.
After Midsummer.
Alone.
A Betrothal.
Bloody Cranesbill on the
   Dunes.
The Boy Fishing.
A Dark World.
An Elegy.
The First Year (excerpt).
In a Wood.
Love's Immaturity.
An Open Air Performance of
   "As You Like It."
Shadows of Chrysanthemums.
The Swan's Feet.
"Scrace, Richard"
At the Place of the Roman
   Baths.
The Gipsies.
Scriven, Joseph
The Unfailing Friend.
What a Friend We Have in
   Jesus.
Scriven, R. C.
The Marrog.
Scroggie, Syd
And Happy Am I.
Ante Mortem.
At Last.
Change and Immutability.
The Drunken Dee.

Loch Ossian.
Long Ago.
Poem, 1972.
Space and Time.
Scroope, Sir Carr
The Author's Reply.
In Defense of Satire.
Scruggs, Anderson M.
Christmas 1930.
Scudder, Eliza
The Quest.
Thou Grace Divine,
Encircling All.
Thou Long Disowned,
Reviled, Oppressed.
To a Young Child.
Scudder, Vida
Thy Kingdom, Lord, We
Long For.
Scully, James
Crew Practice on Lake Bled,
in Jugoslavia.
The Day of the Night.
Enough!
Esperanza.
A Fantasy of Little Waters.
The Glass Blower.
The Grandson.
Innocence.
A Late Spring.
Midsummer.
What Is Poetry.
Scupham, Peter
To His Coy Mistress (parody).
Twelfth Night.
Seager, Francis
A Prayer to Be Said When
Thou Goest to Bed.
Seager, Ralph W.
The Stump Is Not the
Tombstone.
The Taste of Prayer.
Seagrave, Artis
Let All Created Things.
Seal, Brajendranath
The Quest Eternal (excerpt).
Sealey, Macey P.
God's Unspeakable Gift.
Seaman, E. William
Higgledy-Piggledy.
Seaman, Sir Owen
A Ballad of a Bun.
A Birthday Ode to Mr. Alfred
Austin.
The Bubbul.
England Expects?
The Englishman on the
French Stage.
In Praise of Commonplace.
An Ode to Spring in the
Metropolis.
Of Baiting the Lion.
The Old Songs.
The Penalties of Baldness.
A Plea for Trigamy.
The Rhyme of the Kipperling.
The Schoolmaster Abroad.
The Seamy Side of Motley.
The Sitting Bard.
A Song of Renunciation.
Time's Revenges.
To a Boy-Poet of the
Decadence.
To Julia in Shooting Togs
(parody).
To Julia under Lock and Key
(parody).
The Uses of Ocean.
The Warrior's Lament.
Searing, Laura Redden
Disarmed.

Sears, Edmund Hamilton
The Angels' Song.
Calm, on the Listening Ear of
Night.
It Came Upon the Midnight
Clear.
Sears, Edmun Hamilton
The Birth Song of Christ.
Sears, Peter
Rain.
Seaver, Edwin
To My People.
"Sec."
The News.
Secundus, Johannes
The Insatiate.
Neaera's Kisses.
Poems from the Greek
Anthology (excerpt).
The Wedding Night.
Sedar-Senghor, L.
Night of Sine.
Paris in the Snow.
Songs for a Three-String
Guitar.
Sedgwick, Henry Dwight
Leo to His Mistress.
Sedley, Sir Charles
Advice to the Old Beaux.
Ah Cloris! That I Now Could
Sit.
A Ballad.
Child and Maiden.
Get You Gone.
The Happy Pair (excerpt).
The Indifference.
On a Cock at Rochester.
On Fruition.
On the Happy Corydon and
Phyllis.
Out of French.
Phyllis Knotting.
Song: "Hears not my Phillis
how the birds."
Song: "Love still has
something of the Sea."
Song: "Phillis is my only joy."
Song: "Phillis, let's shun the
common Fate."
Song: "Smooth was the Water,
calm the Air."
A Song to Celia.
To Cloris.
To Julius.
To Nysus.
To Scilla.
To Sergius.
To Sextus.
Upon the Author of the
"Satire against Wit."
Sedulius, Caelius
The Easter Song.
Hail, Maiden Root.
The Magi Visit Herod.
The Miracle.
Sedulius Scottus
Apologia Pro Vita Sua.
Death of a Ram.
The Defeat of the Norsemen
(excerpt).
I Read, or Write.
Nunc Viridant Segetes.
Request for Meat and Drink.
Seeger, Alan
I Have a Rendezvous with
Death.
Ode in Memory of the
American Volunteers Fallen
for France.
To...in Church.

Seeger, Pete
Where Have All the Flowers
Gone? (excerpt).
**Seeger, Peggy and Ewan
MacColl**
Ballad of Springhill.
Seelbinder, Emily
Spring Morning: Waking.
Seferis, George
Now When So Much Has
Passed.
Sefton, Eva Weaver
Living Bread.
Segal, Carolyn Foster
The Wharf, May 1978.
Segal, Jacob Isaac
Candle.
Rest.
Segal, Y. Y.
King Rufus.
Rhymes.
Segooa, Demetrius
Praises of the Train.
Seib, Kenneth
The Fate of Birds.
Seidel, Frederick
Dayley Island.
A Dimpled Cloud.
A Negro Judge.
The Sickness.
To Robert Lowell and Osip
Mandelstam.
Seidman, Hugh
Drop the Wires.
The Great Nebula in
Andromeda.
The Making of Color.
The Modes of Vallejo Street
San Diego, Los Angeles
(excerpt).
N.
Science as Art.
Tale of Genji.
Seifert, Jaroslav
Dance-Song.
Seiffert, Marjorie Allen
Ballad.
Cubist Portrait.
The Dream House.
An Italian Chest.
The Old Woman.
Seitz, Don C.
Night at Gettysburg.
Sekula, Irene
Mother Goose (circa 2054).
Seldon, Frank H.
To My Setter, Scout.
Selgas y Carrasco, Jose
The Empty Cradle.
Seligman, Ulma
Truth Has Perished.
Seljouk, Mehdi Ali
Like the Prime Mover.
Selkirk, J.B.
A Border Burn.
Selle, Len G.
Hickory Stick Hierarchy.
Sellers, Bettie M.
If Justice Moved.
The Morning of the Red-
Tailed Hawk.
Sellers, John L.
A Catch-22 Test.
Hep-Cat.
How One-Thumb Willie Got
His Name.
Mule-Train.
Tractor.
Seltzer, George R.
Come, All Ye People.
Selva, Salomon de la
Tropical Towns.

Selyns, Henricus
Epitaph for Peter Stuyvesant,
Late General of New
Netherland.
O Christmas Night.
Of Scolding Wives and the
Third Day Ague.
On Maids and Cats.
On Mercenary and Unjust
Bailiffs.
Reasons For and Against
Marrying Widows.
Upon the Bankruptcy of a
Physician.
Semah, David
Prostration.
Sempill, Francis
Maggie Lauder.
Sempill, Robert
The Life and Death of Habbie
Simson, the Piper of
Kilbarchan.
Sen, Pradip
And Then the Sun.
Seneca (Lucius Annaeus Seneca)
Hercules Furens, IV: Chorus.
Hercules Oetaetus, II: Chorus.
Medea.
The End of Being.
The Quiet Life.
Thyestes, III: Chorus.
Troas, II: Chorus (latter end).
Hay, John
Thy Will Be Done.
Senesh, Hannah
The Blessed Match.
One-Two-Three.
Seng-Ts'an
On Trust in the Heart.
Senghor, Leopold Sedar
Black Woman.
New York.
On the Appeal From the Race
of Sheba: II.
Prayer for Peace: II.
Return of the Prodigal Son.
To New York.
We Delighted, My Friend.
Sepamla, Sipho
Home.
Pimville Station.
Soweto.
Tell Me News.
The Will.
The Work Song.
Serafino
What Nedeth These Thretning
Wordes and Wasted Wynde?
Serchuk, Peter
Bent Tree.
What the Animals Said.
Sergeant, Howard
The Inundation.
Man Meeting Himself.
Soft Landings.
Seroke, Jaki
Era.
Serote, Mongane Wally
City Johannesburg.
During Thoughts after Ofay-
Watching.
Heat and Sweat.
Hell, Well, Heaven.
Ofay-Watcher Looks Back.
A Poem in Black and White.
Serraillier, Ian
After Ever Happily.
Andrew's Bedtime Story.
Death of the Cat.
Falling Asleep.
The Fox Rhyme.
The Hare and the Tortoise.

The Headless Gardener.
The Hen and the Carp.
The Old Sussex Road.
Piano Practice.
Suppose You Met a Witch
  (excerpt).
The Tickle Rhyme.
The Witch's Cat.
Service, Robert W.
The Call of the Wild.
Carry On!
The Cremation of Sam
  McGee.
Inspiration.
The Law of the Yukon.
Men of the High North.
The Men That Don't Fit In.
My Madonna.
Rhymes of a Rolling Stone.
The Scribe's Prayer.
The Shooting of Dan
  McGrew.
The Skeptic.
The Spell of the Yukon.
When the Iceworms Nest
  Again.
The Wonderer.
Sessler, Thomas
When the Day.
You Move Forward.
Sethna, K. D.
Tree of Time.
**"Setoun, Gabriel", (Thomas
Nicoll Hepburn)**
How the Flowers Grow.
Jack Frost.
The Wind's Song.
The World's Music.
Setterberg, Ruth
A Mirage.
Patterns.
Settle, Elkanah
A Congratulatory Poem to the
  Honoured Edmund Morris,
  Esq....
The Medal Reversed.
Sewall, Frank
Roll Out, O Song.
Sewall, Harriet W.
Why Thus Longing?
Sewall, Jonathan Mitchell
On Independence.
The Trip to Cambridge.
Sewall, Samuel
The Humble Springs of
  Stately Sandwich Beach.
Once More, Our God,
  Vouchsafe to Shine.
This Morning Tom Child, the
  Painter, Died.
To Be Engraven on a Dial.
To the Rev'd Mr. Jno.
  Sparhawk on the Birth of
  His Son...
Wednesday, January 1, 1701.
Seward, Anna
Colebrook Dale (excerpt).
Elegy Written at the Sea-Side,
  and Addressed to Miss
  Honoria Sneyd.
Eyam (excerpt).
A Favourite Cat's Dying
  Soliloquy.
Llangollen Vale (excerpt).
An Old Cat's Dying
  Soliloquy.
Sonnet: "Ingratitude, how
  deadly is the smart."
To the Departing Spirit of an
  Alienated Friend.
A True Cat.

Sewell, Elizabeth
Epiphany: For the Artist.
Forgiveness.
Sewell, George
The Dying Man in His
  Garden.
Sexton, Anne
The Abortion.
The Addict.
All My Pretty Ones.
The Black Art.
The Child Bearers.
Cinderella.
Consorting with Angels.
Crossing the Atlantic.
December 18th.
The Division of Parts.
The Farmer's Wife.
Flee on Your Donkey.
For God While Sleeping.
For My Lover, Returning to
  His Wife.
The Fortress.
The Frog Prince.
Funnel.
The Fury of Cocks.
The Fury of Flowers and
  Worms.
The Fury of Hating Eyes.
Gods.
Hansel and Gretel.
Her Kind.
Housewife.
In Celebration of My Uterus.
In the Beach House.
In the Deep Museum.
January 1st.
Kind Sir: These Woods.
The Kiss.
Lament.
Letter Written on a Ferry
  Crossing Long Island Sound.
Little Girl, My Stringbean,
  My Lovely Woman.
Little Red Riding Hood.
The Lost Ingredient.
Love Song.
Lullaby.
Man and Wife.
Moon Song, Woman Song.
The Moss of His Skin.
Mothers.
Pain for a Daughter.
Rapunzel.
Riding the Elevator into the
  Sky.
Ringing the Bells.
The Risk.
The Road Back.
The Room of My Life.
Rowing.
Rumpelstiltskin.
Self in 1958.
Snow White and the Seven
  Dwarfs.
Some Foreign Letters.
The Starry Night.
The Sun.
That Day.
Three Green Windows.
The Truth the Dead Know.
Unknown Girl in the
  Maternity Ward.
Us.
Wanting to Die.
Water.
The Wedding Night.
Welcome Morning.
With Mercy for the Greedy.
Woman with Girdle.
You, Doctor Martin.
Young.

Seymour, William Kean
Caesar Remembers.
The Foiled Reaper.
To Music.
Seymour-Smith, Martin
He Came to Visit Me.
What Schoolmasters Say.
Shabistari, Sa'd ud-din Mahmud
In the Secret Rose Garden.
Shackleford, Theodore Henry
The Big Bell in Zion.
Shadwell, Bertrand
Aguinaldo.
Cervera.
Shadwell, Thomas
The Expostulation.
Let Some Great Joys Pretend
  to Find.
Love and Wine.
The Medal of John Bayes.
Song: "The fringed vallance of
  your eyes advance."
Shady, Dennis
Cell.
Grandfathers.
Moose Lake State Hospital.
Someone Gave Him Some
  Plastic Flowers Once.
Stories Relate Life.
The Wind Carries Me Free.
Shairp, John Campbell
The Bush Aboon Traquair.
Shakely, Lauren
Definition.
Shakespeare, William
All's Well That Ends Well, I,
  iii: "For I the ballad will
  repeat."
Antony and Cleopatra.
As You Like It.
Coriolanus.
The Courser and the Jennet.
Cymbeline.
Hamlet.
Julius Caesar.
King Henry IV.
King Henry V.
King Henry VI.
King Henry VIII.
King John.
King Lear.
King Richard II.
Limerick: "And let the
  canakin clink."
Love's Labour's Lost.
A Lover's Complaint.
Macbeth.
Madrigal: "Crabbed age and
  youth."
The Marriage of True Minds.
Measure for Measure.
The Merchant of Venice.
The Merry Wives of Windsor.
Methought I Saw a Thousand
  Fearful Wrecks.
Midnight.
A Midsummer Night's
  Dream.
A Morning Song for Imogen.
Much Ado about Nothing.
No Longer Mourn for Me.
Not Marble.
Othello.
An Outcry upon Opportunity.
The Passionate Pilgrim.
The Pedlar's Song.
Pericles.
The Phoenix and the Turtle.
Poor Wat.
The Rape of Lucrece.
Richard II.
Richard III.

Romeo and Juliet.
Sessions of Sweet Silent
  Thought.
Since Brass, Nor Stone, Nor
  Earth.
Sonnets, I: "From fairest
  creatures we desire increase."
Sonnets, II: "When forty
  winters shall besiege thy
  brow."
Sonnets, III: "Look in thy
  glass, and tell the face thou
  viewest."
Sonnets, V: "Those hours,
  that with gentle work did
  frame."
Sonnets, VI: "Then let not
  winter's ragged hand deface."
Sonnets, VIII: "Music to hear,
  why hear'st thou music
  sadly?"
Sonnets, IX: "Is it for fear to
  wet a widow's eye."
Sonnets, X: "For shame! deny
  that thou bear'st love to
  any."
Sonnets, XII: "When I do
  count the clock that tells the
  time."
Sonnets, XIII: "O! that you
  were yourself; but, love, you/
  are."
Sonnets, XIV: "Not from the
  stars do I my judgement
  pluck."
Sonnets, XV: "When I
  consider every thing that
  grows."
Sonnets, XVI: "But wherefore
  do not you a mightier way."
Sonnets, XVII: "Who will
  believe my verse in time to
  come."
Sonnets, XVIII: "Shall I
  compare thee to a summer's
  day?"
Sonnets, XIX: "Devouring
  Time, blunt thou the lion's
  paws."
Sonnets, XX: "A woman's
  face with nature's own hand
  painted."
Sonnets, XXI: "So is it not
  with me as with that Muse."
Sonnets, XXII: "My glass
  shall not persuade me I am
  old."
Sonnets, XXIII: "As an
  unperfect actor on the
  stage."
Sonnets, XXIV: "Mine eye
  hath play'd the painter, and
  hath steel'd."
Sonnets, XXV: "No more be
  grieved at that which thou
  hast done."
Sonnets, XXVII: "Weary with
  toil, I haste me to my bed."
Sonnets, XXVIII: "How can I
  then return in happy plight."
Sonnets, XXIX: "When in
  disgrace with fortune and
  men's eyes."
Sonnets, XXX: "When to the
  sessions of sweet silent
  thought."
Sonnets, XXXI: "Thy bosom
  is endeared with all hearts."
Sonnets, XXXII: "If thou
  survive my well-contented
  day."

Sonnets, XXXIII: "Full many a glorious morning have I seen."

Sonnets, XXXIV: "Why didst thou promise such a beauteous day."

Sonnets, XXXV: "No more be grieved at that which thou hast done."

Sonnets, XXXVI: "Let me confess that we two must be twain."

Sonnets, XL: "Take all my loves my love, yea take them all."

Sonnets, XLI: "Those pretty wrongs that liberty commits."

Sonnets, XLII: "Thou that last her, it is not all my grief."

Sonnets, XLIII: "When most I wink, then do mine eyes best see."

Sonnets, XLIV: "If the dull substance of my flesh were thought."

Sonnets, XLVI: "Mine eye and heart are at a mortal war."

Sonnets, XLVII: "Betwixt mine eye and heart a league is took."

Sonnets, LII: "So am I as the rich, whose blessed key."

Sonnets, LIII: "What is your substance, whereof are you made."

Sonnets, LIV: "O, how much more doth beauty beauteous seem."

Sonnets, LV: "Not marble, nor the gilded monuments."

Sonnets, LVI: "Sweet love, renew thy force."

Sonnets, LVII: "Being your slave, what should I do but tend."

Sonnets, LIX: "If there be."

Sonnets, LX: "Like as the waves make towards the pebbled shore."

Sonnets, LXI: "Is it thy wil, thy Image should keepe open."

Sonnets, LXII: "Sinne of selfe-love possesseth al mine eie."

Sonnets, LXIII: "Against my Love shall be, as I am now."

Sonnets, LXIV: "When I have seen by Time's fell hand defaced."

Sonnets, LXV: "Since brass, nor stone, nor earth, nor boundless sea."

Sonnets, LXVI: "Tired with all these, for restful death I cry."

Sonnets, LXVII: "Ah wherefore with infection should he live."

Sonnets, LXVIII: "Thus is his cheek the map of days outworn."

Sonnets, LXXI: "No longer mourn for me when I am dead."

Sonnets, LXXII: "O, lest your true love may seem false in this."

Sonnets, LXXIII: "That time of year thou mayst in me behold."

Sonnets, LXXIV: "But be contented: when that fell arrest."

Sonnets, LXXVI: "Why is my verse so barren of new pride."

Sonnets, LXXXI: "Or I shall live your epitaph to make."

Sonnets, LXXXVI: "Was it the proud full sail of his great verse."

Sonnets, LXXXVII: "Farewell! thou art too dear for my possessing."

Sonnets, LXXXIX: "Say that thou didst forsake me for some fault."

Sonnets, XC: "Then hate me when thou wilt; if ever, now."

Sonnets, XCI: "Some glory in their birth, some in their skill."

Sonnets, XCIII: "So shall I live, supposing thou art true."

Sonnets, XCIV: "They that have power to hurt, and will do none."

Sonnets, XCV: "How sweet and lovely dost thou make the shame."

Sonnets, XCVII: "How like a winter hath my absence been."

Sonnets, XCVIII: "From you have I been absent in the spring."

Sonnets, XCIX: "The forward violet thus did I chide."

Sonnets, C: "Where art thou, Muse, that thou forget'st so long."

Sonnets, CII: "My love is strengthen'd."

Sonnets, CIV: "To me, fair friend, you never can be old."

Sonnets, CVI: "When in the chronicle of wasted time."

Sonnets, CVII: "Not mine own fears, nor the prophetic soul."

Sonnets, CIX: "O, never say that I was false of heart."

Sonnets, CX: "Alas! 'tis true I have gone here and there."

Sonnets, CXIII: "Since I left you, mine eye is in my mind."

Sonnets, CXVI: "Let me not to the marriage of true minds."

Sonnets, CXVIII: "Like as to make our appetites more keep."

Sonnets, CXIX: "What potions have I drunk of Siren tears."

Sonnets, CXX: "That you were once unkind befriends me now."

Sonnets, CXXI: "'Tis better to be vile than vile esteemed."

Sonnets, CXXIII: "No, Time, thou shalt not boast that I do change."

Sonnets, CXXVII: "In the old age black was nor counted fair."

Sonnets, CXXIX: "Th' expense of spirit in a waste of shame."

Sonnets, CXXX: "My mistress' eyes are nothing like the sun."

Sonnets, CXXXII: "Thine eyes I love, and they, as pitying me."

Sonnets, CXXXIII: "Beshrew that heart that makes my heart to groan."

Sonnets, CXXXIV: "So, now I have confessed that he is thine."

Sonnets, CXXXV: "Whoever hath her wish, thou hast thy Will."

Sonnets, CXXXVII: "Thou blind fool, Love, what dost thou to mine eyes."

Sonnets, CXXXVIII: "When my love swears that she is made of truth."

Sonnets, CXLI: "In faith, I do not love thee with mine eyes."

Sonnets, CXLIII: "Lo, as a careful housewife runs to catch."

Sonnets, CXLIV: "Two loves I have of comfort and despair."

Sonnets, CXLVI: "Poor soul, the centre of my sinful earth."

Sonnets, CXLVII: "My love is as a feaver longing still."

Sonnets, CXLVIII: "O me! what eyes hath Love put in my head."

Sonnets, CLI: "Love is too young to know what conscience is."

The Taming of the Shrew.

The Tempest.

Timon of Athens.

Troilus and Cressida.

Twelfth Night.

The Two Gentlemen of Verona.

Venus Abandoned.

When in the Chronicle.

A Winter's Tale.

Youth and Age.

Shakur, Assata
What Is Left?

Shalom, Shin
Splendor.

Shanahan, Eileen
The Desolate Lover.
Epiphany.
The Kilkenny Boy.
Shankill.
Three Children near Clonmel.

Shane, Elizabeth
The Mountainy Childer.
Sheskinbeg.
Wee Hughie.

Shange, Ntozake
Dark Phrases.
For Colored Girls Who Have Considered Suicide...(excerpt).
Frank Albert & Viola Benzena Owens.
Nappy Edges (A Cross Country Sojourn).
No More Love Poems #1.

Somebody Almost Walked Off Wid Alla My Stuff.

Shanks, Edward
Boats at Night.
Drilling in Russell Square.
For the Eightieth Birthday of a Great Singer.
The Glow-Worm.
Going in to Dinner.
High Germany.
Lady Godiva.
A Night Piece.
Sleeping Heroes.
The Storm.
To the Unknown Light.

Shanly, Charles Dawson
Civil War.
Kitty of Coleraine.
The Walker of the Snow.

Shannon, Monica
Could It Have Been a Shadow?
Country Trucks.
Cow Time.
The Four-Leaf Clover.
Gallop, Gallop to a Rhyme.
How to Tell Goblins from Elves.
The Ideal Age for a Man.
Only My Opinion.
Raking Walnuts in the Rain.

Shapcott, Thomas W.
Autumn.
The Bicycle Rider.
The Finches.
Flying Fox.
June Fugue.
The Litanies of Julia Pastrana.
Near the School for Handicapped Children.
Piano Pieces (excerpt).
Sestina with Refrain.
Three Kings Came.

Shapiro, Arnold L.
I Speak, I Say, I Talk.

Shapiro, David
About This Course.
The Bicycle Rider.
The Contribution.
Elegy to Sports.
Falling Upwards.
Five Songs.
For the Princess Hello.
Four Stories.
From Malay.
The Heavenly Humor.
The Idea of a University.
In Memory of Your Body.
Master Canterel at Locus Solus.
Memory of the Present.
New World of Will.
Poem from Deal.
Sonnet: "Ice over time."
Two Poems on the Emotions.
Us Tasting the Air.

Shapiro, Harvey
Blue Max.
Exodus.
Father and Sons.
Feast of the Ram's Horn.
For the Yiddish Singers in the Lakewood Hotels of My Childhood.
Glory.
Happiness of 6 A.M.
The Heart.
Incident.
A Jerusalem Notebook.
Like a Beach.
Lines for the Ancient Scribes.
Mountain, Fire, Thornbush.

Musical Shuttle.
National Cold Storage
  Company.
Past Time.
Provincetown, Mass.
Riding Westward.
The Six Hundred Thousand
  Letters.
Where I Am Now.
Shapiro, Karl
  The 151st Psalm.
  Adam and Eve.
  Adam and Eve: The
    Recognition of Eve.
  Adam and Eve: The Sickness
    of Adam.
  All Tropic Places Smell of
    Mold.
  The Alphabet.
  Americans Are Afraid of
    Lizards.
  Aubade.
  Auto Wreck.
  The Bed.
  The Bourgeois Poet–67.
  The Bourgeois Poet–7.
  Boy-Man.
  Buick.
  A Calder.
  California Winter (excerpt).
  Christmas Eve.
  The Confirmation.
  The Conscientious Objector.
  Construction.
  A Cut Flower.
  The Dirty Word.
  The Dome of Sunday.
  Drug Store.
  Elegy for a Dead Soldier.
  Elegy for Two Banjos.
  Elegy Written on a
    Frontporch.
  Essay on Rime (excerpt).
  The First Time.
  The Fly.
  Full Moon: New Guinea.
  Garage Sale.
  The Geographers.
  Girls Working in Banks.
  The Glutton.
  Going to School.
  Haircut.
  Hollywood.
  Homecoming.
  Hospital.
  In India.
  The Intellectual.
  Interlude.
  Jew.
  The Jew at Christmas Eve.
  The Leg.
  Love for a Hand.
  Lower the Standard: That's
    My Motto.
  Man on Wheels.
  Manhole Covers.
  Midnight Show.
  The Minute.
  Moving In.
  The Murder of Moses.
  My Grandmother.
  Necropolis.
  The New Ring.
  Nigger.
  Nostalgia.
  October 1.
  Paradox: The Birds.
  Party in Winter.
  The Phenomenon.
  Poet.
  The Poets of Hell.
  The Potomac.

The Progress of Faust.
The Puritan.
Quintana Lay in the Shallow
  Grave of Coral.
Recapitulations.
Scyros.
Six Religious Lyrics: I
  (excerpt).
The Southerner.
Sunday: New Guinea.
Terminal.
Travelogue for Exiles.
Troop Train.
The Twins.
University.
V-Letter.
The Voyage.
Waiting in Front of the
  Columnar High School.
Washington Cathedral.
Western Town.
White-Haired Lover (excerpt).
Shapiro, Mark Elliott
  Dying under a Fall of Stars.
Shargal, Zvi
  I Will Go Away.
Shargel, Zvi
  Let Us Laugh.
  Pictures on the Wall.
Sharman, Lyon
  Old Man Pot.
Sharp, Constance
  I Show the Daffodils to the
    Retarded Kids.
Sharp, Saundra
  Moon Poem.
Sharp, William *See also*
  "Macleod, Fiona"
  Australian Transcripts, IX:
    The Bell-Bird.
  Australian Transcripts, V:
    Mid-Noon in January.
  Australian Transcripts, X: The
    Wood-Swallows.
  An Autumnal Evening.
  Dawn Amid Scotch Firs.
  A Dead Calm and Mist.
  The Eagle.
  The Field Mouse.
  Fireflies.
  Loch Coruisk (Skye).
  The Mystic's Prayer.
  On a Nightingale in April.
  A Paris Nocturne.
  The Rookery at Sunrise.
  Shule, Agrah!
  Sonnet VII.
  The Swimmer of Nemi.
  The Wasp.
  The White Peace.
Sharpe, Peter
  Cold Front.
Sharpe, R. L.
  A Bag of Tools.
Sharpe, Richard Scrafton
  The Country Mouse and the
    City Mouse.
Sharpless, Stanley J.
  Betjeman at the Post Office
    (parody).
  Go to the Ant.
  Hamlet.
  In Praise of Cocoa, Cupid's
    Nightcap.
  The Lost History Plays: King
    Canute (parody).
  Low Church.
  The Summonee's Tale
    (parody).
  To His Coy Mistress (parody).
Shatford, Sarah Taylor
  Found.

Shauger, Carol
  Preface.
Shaul, Anwar
  Mother.
  Prayers to Liberty.
  To a Cactus Seller.
Shaver, Eva Gilbert
  Dear Old Dad.
Shaw, Charles
  Dissembler.
  The Search.
Shaw, Cuthbert
  Time's Balm.
Shaw, David T.
  The Red, White and Blue.
Shaw, Dunstan
  Retrospection.
Shaw, Frances
  The Last Guest.
  Little Pagan Rain Song.
  Rain.
  Who Loves the Rain.
Shaw, Isabel
  Christmas Chant.
Shaw, John
  Sleighing Song.
  Song: "Who has robbed the
    ocean cave."
Shaw, Knowles
  The Handwriting on the Wall.
Shaw, Luci
  Craftsman.
  ....For They Shall See God.
  Getting inside the Miracle.
  The Groundhog.
  Judas, Peter.
  Man Cannot Name Himself.
  May 20: Very Early Morning.
  Need Is Our Name.
  Small Song.
  Stars in Apple Cores.
  To a Christmas Two-Year-
    Old.
Shaw, Neufville
  Drowned Sailor.
Shaw, Robert B.
  Partial Draft.
Shaw, Winifred
  Fine Clay.
Shceck, Laurie
  The Deer.
Shea, John Augustus
  The Ocean.
Sheaks, Barclay
  A Friend's Passing.
Sheard, Virna
  Exile.
  The Yak.
Sheck, Laurie
  Sleeping Beauty.
Shectman, Robin
  Breakfast.
  Telephone.
Sheehan, Timothy
  At Camino.
  Eclipse.
Sheers, Sir Henry
  A Long Prologue to a Short
    Play...
Sheffield, John
  An Essay upon Satire.
**Sheffield, John, Duke of
  Buckingham**
  The Happy Night.
  Love's Slavery.
  The Nine.
  On Mr. Hobbs, and His
    Writings.
  On One Who Died
    Discovering Her Kindness.
  On Writing for the Stage.
  The Reconcilement.

Song: "Come, Celia, let's
  agree at last."
To a Coquet Beauty.
To His Mistress.
Written over a Gate.
Shehabuddin, Jenab
  Your Mouth.
Sheldon, Gilbert
  St. Anthony's Township.
Shelley, Percy Bysshe
  Adonais.
  Alastor.
  Arethusa.
  Autumn.
  Autumn: A Dirge.
  The Aziola.
  The Boat on the Serchio
    (excerpt).
  A Bridal Song.
  The Cenci.
  Circumstance.
  The Cloud: Orbed Maiden.
  A Conversation.
  Daybreak.
  Death.
  A Dirge.
  Dirge for the Year.
  Epipsychidion.
  Epipsychidion (excerpt).
  Epithalamium for Charlotte
    Corday and Francis
    Ravaillac.
  Evening.
  Evening: Ponte al Mare, Pisa.
  Ever as We Sailed.
  Feelings of a Republican on
    the Fall of Bonaparte.
  Final Chorus.
  The Flight of Love.
  Fragment: Rain.
  A Fragment: To Music.
  From the Arabic.
  Ginevra (excerpt).
  Good-Night.
  A Hate-Song.
  Hellas: Chorus.
  Hymn of Apollo.
  Hymn of Pan.
  Hymn to Intellectual Beauty.
  I Fear Thy Kisses, Gentle
    Maiden.
  I Love Snow and All the
    Forms.
  The Indian Serenade.
  The Isle.
  Julian and Maddalo (excerpt).
  A Lament.
  Lines: "The cold earth slept
    below."
  Lines to a Critic.
  Lines to a Reviewer.
  Lines to an Indian Air.
  Lines: "When the Lamp Is
    Shattered."
  Lines Written among the
    Euganean Hills.
  Lines Written in the Bay of
    Lerici.
  Lines Written on Hearing the
    News of the Death of
    Napoleon.
  Love's Philosophy.
  Lumen de Lumine.
  The Mask of Anarchy.
  Mont Blanc.
  The Moon.
  Music.
  Mutability.
  Night.
  O Thou Immortal Deity.
  Ode to a Skylark.
  Ode to Liberty.

Ode to Naples (excerpt).
Ode to the West Wind.
On a Painted Woman.
On a Poet's Lips I Slept.
On Fanny Godwin.
On Keats Who Desired That
  On His Tomb Should Be
  Inscribed–.
One Word Is Too Often
  Profaned.
Ozymandias.
Peter Bell the Third.
Political Greatness.
Prometheus Unbound.
Queen Mab.
The Question.
The Recollection.
The Revolt of Islam.
The Sensitive Plant.
Similes for Two Political
  Characters of 1819.
Song: "A widow bird sate
  mourning for her love."
Song: "Men of England,
  Wherefore Plough."
Song: "Rarely, rarely, comest
  thou."
Sonnet: England in 1819.
Sonnet: "Lift not the painted
  veil which those who live."
St. Irvyne (excerpt).
Stanzas–April, 1814.
Stanzas to Edward Williams.
Stanzas Written in Dejection,
  Near Naples.
Summer and Winter.
Time.
Time Long Past.
To—.
To a Skylark.
To Constantia Singing.
To Ianthe.
To Jane: The Invitation.
To Jane: The Keen Stars
  Were Twinkling.
To Jane: The Recollection.
To Maria Gisborne in
  England, from Italy.
To Mary.
To Night.
To Stella.
To the Lord Chancellor
  (excerpt).
To the Moon.
To the Night.
To the Nile.
To William Shelley.
To Wordsworth.
The Trackless Deeps.
Tribute to America.
True Love.
The Two Spirits.
A Vision of the Sea.
The Waning Moon.
When the Lamp Is Shattered.
Who Reigns?
The Witch of Atlas.
With a Guitar, to Jane.
The World's Great Age
  Begins Anew.
The World's Wanderers.
Worlds on Worlds Are
  Rolling Ever.
The Zucca (excerpt).
Shelton, Richard
Alone.
The Angel and the Anchorite.
Brother.
Certain Choices.
Children of Night.
Connais-Tu le Pays?
Disintegration.

Excerpts from the Notebook
  of the Poet of Santo Tomas.
How to Amuse a Stone.
Letter to a Dead Father.
Letting Go.
My Love.
On Lake Pend Oreille.
One More Time.
The Prophets.
Requiem for Sonora.
Softly Softly.
The Soldiers Returning.
The Stone Garden.
War.
Why I Never Went into
  Politics.
Wonders of the World.
Youth.
Shembe, Isaiah
Come In.
Dance Hymn.
I Am the Beginning.
Let Zulu Be Heard.
The Springtime of the Earth.
Shen Ch'uan
Therefore We Preserve Life.
Shenhar, Aliza
The Akedah.
The Drunkeness of Pain.
Expectation.
Resurrection of the Dead.
Sea-Games.
Song of the Closing Service.
Trembling.
Shenstone, William
Elegy XI.
Hint from Voiture.
Hope (excerpt).
Lines Written on a Window at
  the Leasowes at a Time of
  Very Deep Snow.
O Sweet Anne Page.
Ode to a Young Lady,
  Somewhat Too Sollicitous
  about Her Manner...
On the Clerk of a Country
  Parish.
Pastoral Ballad: Absence.
A Pastoral Ballad in Four
  Parts.
The Poet and the Dun.
The School-Mistress. In
  Imitation of Spenser.
The Shepherd's Home.
A Solemn Meditation.
Song: "How pleas'd within my
  native bowers."
Song II. The Landskip.
Written at an Inn at Henley.
Shepard, Elizabeth Alsop
White Fox.
Shepard, Odell
The Adventurer.
The Elm.
The Flock at Evening.
The Hidden Weaver.
Home Thoughts.
Housemates.
In the Dawn.
Vespers.
Vistas.
Shepherd, J. Barrie
In Passing.
Lent Tending.
Shepherd, Nan
The Hill Burns.
Sgoran Dhu.
Shepherd, Nathaniel Graham
Roll-Call.
Shepherd, Sir Fleetwood
Epitaph on the Duke of
  Grafton.

Shepherd, Thomas
Alas, My God.
For Communion with God
  (excerpt).
Shepherd, William
Ode on Lord Macartney's
  Embassy to China.
Sheppard, Patricia
The Enlightenment.
Sher, Steven
The Groundhog
  Foreshadowed.
Pilgrimage to Hennessey's.
Sherburne, Sir Edward
And She Washed His Feet
  with Her Tears,...
Christus Matthaeum et
  Discipulos Alloquitur.
Conscience.
The Dream.
Ice and Fire.
Love's Arithmetic.
Violets in Thaumantia's
  Bosome.
Sheridan, Helen Selina *See also*
Dufferin, Helen Selina, Lady
Lament of the Irish Emigrant.
Love Hath a Language.
Sheridan, Niall
Ad Lesbiam.
Poem: "As rock to sun or
  storm."
Sheridan, Richard Brinsley
By Coelia's Arbor.
Clio's Protest.
Dry Be That Tear.
The Duenna (excerpt).
The Geranium.
"I Would," Says Fox, "A Tax
  Devise."
Oh Yield, Fair Lids.
On Lady Anne Hamilton.
The Pleasing Constraint.
School for Scandal.
Song.
Song: "Give Isaac the nymph
  who no beauty can boast."
Song: "Had I a heart for
  falsehood fram'd."
Sherman, Francis
The Builder.
The House of Colour.
In Memorabilia Mortis.
Let Us Rise Up and Live.
Sherman, Frank Dempster
At Midnight.
Baseball.
Blossoms.
Dawn.
February.
A Hollyhock.
January.
The Library.
Mary and the Lamb.
Moonrise.
On a Greek Vase.
On Some Buttercups.
A Prayer.
A Quatrain.
A Real Santa Claus.
The Rose's Cup.
The Shadows.
The Snow-Bird.
To a Rose.
Wizard Frost.
Sherman, Joseph
Sarai.
Sherman, Kenneth
My Father Kept His Cats
  Well Fed.
Sherman, Susan
Three Moments.

Sherry, James
Disinterment.
Sherry, Ruth Forbes
Promises.
Sherwin, Judith Johnson
The Balance.
Ballade of the Grindstones.
Construction # 13.
Dr. Potatohead Talks to
  Mothers.
Eat 'Em Up Smith Tells All
  in South Africa.
The Fabulous Teamsters.
A Gentle Heart: Two.
Goddess.
Just.
The Light Woman's Song.
Rhyme for the Child as a Wet
  Dog.
The Spoilers and the Spoils.
What Maisie Know She Don't
  Want No/Anger Game at
  Shinkolobwe.
Sherwin, Richard
Jacob's Winning.
Sherwood, Grace Buchanan
After Laughter.
Sherwood, Kate Brownlee
Albert Sidney Johnson.
Molly Pitcher.
Thomas at Chickamauga.
Ulric Dahlgren.
Sherwood, Margaret
In Memorium–Leo: A Yellow
  Cat.
Sherwood, Robert E.
The Old Hokum Buncombe.
Sherwood, Rupe
Me and Prunes.
Shevin, David
Dawn.
Shechem.
Shields, Carol
Great-Grandma.
The New Mothers.
Shields, Ren
In the Good Old Summer
  Time.
Shigeyuki, Minamoto-No-
Winter Has At Last Come.
Shihab, Naomi
Driving North from
  Kingsville, Texas.
Jefferson, Texas.
My Father & the Figtree.
Night Shift.
Shiki
Haiku: "Sandy shore: and
  why."
Haiku: "Things long
  forgotten–".
Shikishi, Princess
Autumn.
The blossoms have fallen.
Spring.
Winter.
Shiko
Lilies.
Maple Leaves.
Shillito, Edward
A Prayer for a Preacher.
Prayer of a Modern Thomas.
Shimon, Louis C.
I Know Something Good
  About You.
Shinkichi, Takahashi
Fish.
Snail.
Sparrow in Winter.
Shinn, Millicent Washburn
Song and Science.
When Almonds Bloom.

Yosemite.
Shiplett, Paul D.
James Gerard.
Louie.
Rap Sheet.
State School.
Swimmers.
Wire Monkey.
Shipley, Joseph T.
Meditation.
Shipley, Sir Arthur
Ere You Were Queen of
Sheba.
Shipley, Vivian
First Holes Are Fresh.
Shipman, Thomas
An Epitaph on His
Grandfather.
The Resolute Courtier.
Shipp, E. Richard
Eighteen-Ninety.
Shipp, Horace
Everest.
Shippen, William
The Character of a Certain
Whig.
Pasquin to the Queen's Statue
at St. Paul's, during the
Procession...
Shippey, Joseph
Columbia College, 1796.
Shipton, Anna
The Unerring Guide.
Shiraishi Kazuko
Phallic Root.
Phallus.
Shire, Kent
Earth Changes.
Shirk, Ottis
Resolved.
Shirley, James
Ajax and Ulysses: The Glories
of Our Blood and State.
The Bard.
Bard's Chant.
The Commonwealth of Birds.
Cupid and Death: Victorious
Men of Earth.
Cupid Ungodded.
Cupids Call.
Death, the Conqueror.
Dirge.
Epitaph Inscribed on a Small
Piece of Marble.
Equality.
The Garden.
A Hymn.
The Last Conqueror.
The Looking Glass.
Love's Victories.
O Fly My Soul.
On Her Dancing.
On the Duke of Buckingham.
The Passing Bell.
Piping Peace.
Song to the Masquers.
To His Mistris Confined.
To the Excellent Pattern of
Beauty and Virtue, Lady
Elizabeth...
To the Painter Preparing to
Draw M. M. H.
The Triumph of Beautie Song
(excerpt).
Upon Scarlet and Blush-
Coloured Ribbands, Given
by Two Ladies.
Shivell, Paul
In God's Eternal Studios.
Shlonsky, Avraham
Dress Me, Dear Mother.
Pledge.

Shlonsky. Abraham, Abraham
Grape-Gathering.
Shneurson, Zelda
The Wicked Neighbor.
Shockley, Martin Staples
Crossedroads.
Shoku, Princess
I Would That Even Now.
Sholl, Betsy
Urgency.
Shorb, Michael
First Ice of Winter.
Shore, Jane
Anthony.
An Astronomer's Journal.
Sleeping Beauty.
Shoreham, William of
Hours of the Passion.
Shorey, George H.
Bubbles.
Short, Clarice
The Old One and the Wind.
Short, J. D. (Jelly Jaw)
Snake Doctor Blues.
Telephone Arguin' Blues.
Short, John
Carol.
Shorter, Dora Sigerson
April.
Ballad of the Little Black
Hound.
Beware.
A Bird from the West.
The Comforters.
The Gypsies' Road.
Ireland.
The Kine of My Father.
The Mother's Prayer.
A New Year.
Nora.
The Patchwork Quilt.
The Piper on the Hill.
A Rose Will Fade.
The Wind on the Hills.
Shostakovitch, Dmitri
Salute to Life.
Shove, Fredegond
A Dream in Early Spring.
The Farmer.
Infant Spring.
The New Ghost.
Song: "Spring lights her
candles everywhere."
Sops of Light.
Showell, Jr, Samuel
To the Borrower of This
Book.
Shriver, Peggy
The Spirit of 34th Street.
Shuford, Gene
Harvest.
Shuler, Chester E.
The Faithful Few.
Shulman, David
A Diary of the Sailors of the
North.
Shulman, Max
Honest Abe Lincoln.
Shuraikh
Distich.
Shurmantine, Brad Lee
Tracks.
Shurtleff, Ernest W.
Lead On, O King Eternal.
Shute, Evan V.
Luck.
Night Comes Apace.
Poor Fool.
Twenty Years After.
Shuttle, Penelope
Early Pregnancy.
Expectant Mother.

Gone Is the Sleepgiver.
Locale.
Maritimes.
Shuttleworth, P. N.
A Wykehamist's Address to
Learning.
Shuttleworth, Paul
Tornado Watch.
Sibley, Charles
The Plaidie.
Sickels, David Banks
It Cannot Be.
Siddal, Elizabeth
Dead Love.
A Silent Wood.
Sidgwick, Frank
The Cheerful Chilterns
(parody).
A Christmas Legend.
Vision.
Sidgwick, Henry
Goethe and Frederika.
Sidney, James A.
The Irish Schoolmaster.
Sidney, Sir Philip
Absence.
Advice to the Same.
Arcadia.
Astrophel and Stella.
A Country Song.
Dear, Why Make You More
of a Dog than Me?
Dispraise of a Courtly Life.
Dorus's Song.
The Eighth Sonnet.
Eleventh Song.
Epithalamium.
A Farewell.
Geron and Histor.
He That Loves.
His Being Was in Her Alone.
In Wonted Walks.
Lady My Treasure.
Like as the Dove.
Like Those Sick Folks.
A Litany.
Madrigal: "Why dost thou
haste away."
Nymph of the Garden where
All Beauties Be.
O Dear Life, When Shall It
Be?
Only Joy! Now Here You
Are.
Philomela.
Psalm (I-XLIII).
Ring Out Your Bells.
The Seven Wonders of
England.
Since Nature's Works Be
Good.
Sleep, Baby Mine, Desire.
Song: "No, no, no, no, I
cannot hate my foe."
Song: "O fair! O sweet! when
I do look on thee."
Song: "Who hath his fancy
pleased."
Sonnet: "Lock up, fair lids,
the treasure of my heart."
A Tale for Husbands.
Thou Blind Man's Mark.
To Sleep.
To Stella.
Truth Doth Truth Deserve.
Voices at the Window.
What, Have I Thus Betrayed
My Liberty?
When To My Deadlie
Pleasure.
When Two Suns Do Appear.
Why Fear to Die?

The Yoke of Tyranny.
Siebert, Charles
City Butterfly.
Siebert, Glenn
This and More.
Siegel, Danny
Binni the Meshuggener.
The Crippler.
Snow in the City.
Siegel, Eli
Alfred-Seeable Philadelphia
Sky.
All the Smoke.
Disclaimer of Prejudice.
Duke of Parma's Ear.
Siegel, Robert
The Center of America.
Ego.
An Explanation of the
GrassWalking the Fields.
Mr. Brunt.
The Revenant.
Siegrist, Mary
The League of Nations.
Sieller, William Vincent
Windmill on the Cape.
Sigerson, George
My Own Cailin Donn.
Smith's Song.
Sigerson, Hester
Mad Song.
Sigmund, Jay G.
Grubber's Day.
Sigourney, Lydia Huntley
Advertisement of a Lost Day.
Blessed Comforter Divine.
Jesus of Nazareth Passeth By.
Laborers of Christ! Arise.
The Mother's Sacrifice.
Sigourney, Lydia Huntley
The Alpine Flowers.
California.
Columbus.
God Save the Plough.
Indian Names.
The Indian's Welcome to the
Pilgrim Fathers.
Niagara.
On the Death of Mrs. Felicia
Hemans (excerpt).
Onward, Onward, Men of
Heaven.
Request of a Dying Child.
The Return of Napoleon
From St. Helena.
We Praise Thee, If One
Rescued Soul.
Sikelianos, Anghelos
Doric.
On Death (excerpt).
Sila
My husband is the same man.
Silabhattarika
He Who Stole My Virginity.
Silber, Irwin
I Just Wanna Stay Home.
Put My Name Down.
Silberger, Julius
A Reply to Nancy Hanks.
Silberschlag, Eisig
Abraham.
Proust on Noah.
Silbert, Layle
Grand Hotel, Calcutta.
Silen, Ivan
To Teresa.
Why I Can't Write a Poem
about Lares.
Silentiarius, Paulus
Tantalus.

Silesius, Angelus *See* "Angelus Silesius" (Johannes Scheffler)
Silesky, Barry
White Pines.
Silk, Dennis
Guide to Jerusalem.
Matronita.
Silkin, Jon
The Coldness.
Death of a Bird.
Death of a Son.
A Death to Us.
First It Was Singing.
Furnished Lives.
It Says.
Jerusalem.
Light.
Lilies of the Valley.
Reclaimed Area.
Respectabilities.
Resting Place.
The Return.
The Shirt.
A Space in the Air.
A Word about Freedom and Identity in Tel Aviv.
Silko, Leslie Marmon
Alaskan Mountain Poem #1.
Deer Song.
Four Mountain Wolves.
Hawk and Snake.
Horses at Valley Store.
How to Write a Poem about the Sky.
In Cold Storm Light.
Indian Song: Survival.
Love Poem.
Poem for Ben Barney.
Poem for Myself and Mei: Abortion.
Prayer to the Pacific.
Preparations.
Slim Man Canyon.
Story from Bear Country.
Sun Children.
The Time We Climbed Snake Mountain.
Toe'osh: A Laguna Coyote Story.
When Sun Came to Riverwoman.
Where Mountain Lion Lay down with Deer February 1973.
Sill, Edward Rowland
A Baker's Duzzen Uv Wize Sawz.
Before Sunrise in Winter.
The Coup de Grace.
Dare You?
The Dead President.
Eve's Daughter.
Evening.
Five Lives.
The Fool's Prayer.
For the Gifts of the Spirit.
Force.
The Future.
Home.
Life.
The Lover's Song.
Opportunity.
A Prayer.
A Prayer for Peace.
Solitude.
Tempted.
A Tropical Morning at Sea.
Sill, Louise Morgan
Faith.

Sille, Nicasius de *See* De Sille, Nicasius
Sillery, Charles Doyne
She Died in Beauty.
Sillitoe, Alan
Picture of Loot.
Silva, Jose Asuncion
Art.
First Communion.
Nocturne–III.
Silvera, Edward S.
Forgotten Dreams.
Jungle Taste.
On the Death of a Child.
South Street.
Silverman, Maxine
Hair.
Silvers, Frances (Frankie)
Frankie Silvers.
Silverstein, David I.
There Are in Such Moments.
Silverstein, Shel
Clarence.
The Dirtiest Man in the World.
The Flag.
For Sale.
Friendship.
George Washington.
Hector the Collector.
The Horse.
Hug o' War.
I Must Remember.
If I Had a Firecracker.
In That Dark Cave.
Jimmy Jet and His TV Set.
The Lazy People.
Magical Eraser.
My Invention.
Nothing to Do?
Oh Did You Hear?
On Halloween.
One Inch Tall.
Peace and Joy.
Please Tell Me Just the Fabuli.
Sarah Cynthia Sylvia Stout Would Not Take the Garbage Out.
The Slithergadee Has Crawled out of the Sea.
Some Day.
There You Sit.
Think of Eight Numbers.
Valentine.
The Van Gogh Influence.
Wanted.
The Worst.
Silverton, Michael
The Adorable Paratroopess.
A Chasm.
Column A.
The Food Drops Off a Fork.
I Am Yours & You Are Mine So.
The King of Sunshine.
Life in the Country.
Neckwear.
So Long as Time & Space Are the Stars.
A Woman Came to Me.
Simcox, George Augustus
Love's Votary.
Simic, Charles
Animal Acts.
The Animals.
Ax.
Ballad.
Begotten of the Spleen.
Bestiary for the Fingers of My Right Hand.
The Bird.

Breasts.
Brooms.
Butcher Shop.
Charon's Cosmology.
Classic Ballroom Dances.
The Cold.
Elementary Cosmogony.
Empire of Dreams.
Errata.
Euclid Avenue.
Evening.
Fear.
Fork.
The Garden of Earthly Delights.
Green Moth.
Harsh Climate.
Hearing Steps.
Hunger.
The Lesson.
Midpoint.
My Shoes.
Nothing.
Old Couple.
Old Mountain Road.
The Partial Explanation.
Pastoral.
Poem.
Poem without a Title.
Poverty.
Prodigy.
Progress Report.
Psalm.
Return to a Place Lit by a Glass of Milk.
Second Avenue Winter.
Shirt.
Sleep.
Solitude.
The Spoon.
Starry Sky.
Stone.
The Story.
Strictly for Posterity.
Tapestry.
Unintelligible Terms.
A Wall.
Watch Repair.
Watermelons.
Winter Night.
Simison, Greg
My Family's under Contract to Cancer.
Simmerman, Jim
Cartoon.
Simmias
To Prote.
Simmons, Herbert A.
Ascendancy.
Simmons, J. Edgar
A Father in Tennessee.
Troubador.
Simmons, J. W.
Sumter's Band.
Simmons, James
Art and Reality.
A Birthday Poem: for Rachel.
Cavalier Lyric.
Experience.
Fear Test: Integrity of Heroes.
The First Goodbye Letter.
For Delphine.
Goodbye, Sally.
John Donne.
Letter to a Jealous Friend.
A Reformer to His Father.
The Summing Up.
Simmons, Judy Dothard
Alabama.
Generations.
It's Comforting.
Survivor.

Simmons, Laura
At Christmastide.
Next Time.
Noel! Noel!
Simmons, Jr, Gerald L.
Take Tools Our Strength...
Simms, William Gilmore
The Battle of Eutaw.
The Decay of a People.
The Grape-Vine Swing.
The Lost Pleiad.
Night Storm.
Song in March.
The Swamp Fox.
Simoko, Patu
Africa Is Made of Clay.
Corruption.
Did We Laugh or Did We Cry?
Simon, John
Ameinias.
Simon, John Oliver
The Cities Are Washed into Time.
Dont Tell Bad Dreams Says Tita's Mother.
For Alan Blanchard.
Living in the Boneyard.
A Tryptych for Jan Bockelson.
The Woodchuck Who Lives on Top of Mt. Ritter.
Simon, Paul
Richard Cory (parody).
Simone, Nina
Four Women.
Simonides (of Ceos)
Cleobulus' Epitaph.
Danae.
Epitaph of a Thessalian Hound.
On the Lacedaemonian Dead at Plataea.
On the Spartan Dead at Thermopylae.
On Two Brothers.
Timocreon.
Simpson, A. B.
Abiding.
Believe the Bible.
Glory to the Name of Jesus!
It Is I, Be Not Afraid.
Jesus Only.
Thanksgiving.
Thy Kingdom Come.
Why Doubt God's Word?
Simpson, Earl
Learning.
Simpson, F. A.
Lincoln and Liberty.
Simpson, George S.
Simpson's Rest.
Simpson, Henry
In February.
Simpson, Louis
Aegean.
After Midnight.
Against the Age.
American Classic.
American Dreams.
American Poetry.
As birds are fitted to the boughs.
The Ash and the Oak.
Back in the States.
The Battle.
Before the Poetry Reading.
Big Dream, Little Dream.
Birch.
The Bird.
The Boarder.
Carentan O Carentan.

Chocolates.
The Climate of Paradise.
The Constant Lover.
The Country House.
The Custom of the World.
Doubting.
A Dream of Governors.
Dvonya.
Early in the Morning.
A Friend of the Family.
Frogs.
The Green Shepherd.
The Heroes.
Hot Night on Water Street.
The Hour of Feeling.
Hubert's Museum.
I Dreamed That in a City
 Dark as Paris.
In California.
In the Suburbs.
The Inner Part.
Isidor.
It Was the Last of the
 Parades.
John the Baptist.
The Laurel Tree.
The Legend of Success, the
 Salesman's Story.
Love and Poetry.
Love, My Machine.
Luminous Night.
The Man Who Married
 Magdalene.
Mashkin Hill.
Memories of a Lost War.
The Middleaged Man.
The Morning Light.
Music in Venice.
My Father in the Night
 Commanding No.
New Lines for Cuscuscaraway
 and Mirza Murad Ali Beg.
A Night in Odessa.
On the Lawn at the Villa.
Outward.
Physical Universe.
Quiet Desperation.
The Redwoods.
The Riders Held Back.
Rough Winds Do Shake.
Sacred Objects.
Sailors.
Sensibility.
The Silent Generation.
The Silent Piano.
Simplicity.
A Son of the Romanovs.
Song: "Let's sing a song
 together once."
Squeal (parody).
A Story about Chicken Soup.
Stumpfoot on 42nd Street.
The Subway Grating Fisher.
Summer Storm.
The Tailor's Wedding.
There Is.
Things.
To the Western World.
Tom Pringle.
Tonight the Famous
 Psychiatrist.
The Troika.
The True Weather for
 Women.
The Union Barge on Staten
 Island.
The Wall Test.
Walt Whitman at Bear
 Mountain.
Why Do You Write about
 Russia?

Simpson, Margaret Winefride
Villanelle.
Simpson, Mark
X, Oh X.
Simpson, Nancy
On Certain Days of the Year.
Water on the Highway.
Simpson, R. A.
All Friends Together.
Antarctica.
Diver.
Lake.
Night Out.
Simpson, Sam L.
The Wagon Train.
Simpson, Tobey A.
For Mariella, in Antrona.
Simpson, William Haskel
Homesick Song.
Navajo.
Pity Not.
Saddle.
Taos Drums.
Yucca Is Yellowing.
Sims, George R.
Billy's Rose.
Christmas Day in the
 Workhouse.
A Garden Song.
The Lifeboat.
'Ostler Joe.
Undertones.
Sims, Henry
Tell Me Man Blues.
Sinason, Valerie
In the Beginning.
The Renaming.
Will You Come Out Now?
Sinclair, Bennie Lee
Decoration Day.
The Evangelist.
Sinclair, F. D.
Zimbabwe.
Sinclair, John
Breakthrough.
Sinclair, Keith
The Ballad of Halfmoon Bay
 (excerpt).
The Chronicle of Meola
 Creek.
For a Parting.
Lord of All I Survey.
Moors, Angels, Civil Wars.
Mother.
A Night Full of Nothing.
Poem.
War with the Weeds.
Sinclair, May
Field Ambulance in Retreat.
Singer, Burns
Marcus Antoninus Cui
 Cognomen Erat Aurelius.
Nothing.
Peterhead in May.
Sonnets for a Dying Man.
Still and All.
Words Made of Water.
Singer, James Burns
Birdsong.
Epilogue.
Singer, John
Stepney Green.
Singer, Sarah
Family Plot.
Sinisgalli, Leonardo
Orphic Interior.
Sinks, P.W.
Just Like Me.
Sipe, Muriel
Good Morning.
Siringo, Charles A.
Way Out West.

Sissman, L. E.
The Critic on the Hearth.
A Day in the City.
December 27, 1966.
A Disappearance in West
 Cedar Street.
Dying: An Introduction.
Elegy: E. W.
Henley, July 4: 1914–1964.
In and Out.
In and Out: Severance of
 Connections, 1946.
Luchow's and After.
The New York Woman.
Nocturne, Central Park South.
On the Island.
Pepys Bar, West Forty-Eight
 Street, 8 a.m.
Safety at Forty; or, An
 Abecedarian Takes a Walk.
Sweeney to Mrs. Porter in the
 Spring.
Talking Union: 1964.
The West Forties: Morning,
 Noon, and Night.
Sisson, C. H.
Adam and Eve.
A and B.
At First.
Cato.
Cranmer.
Easter.
Family Fortunes.
Human Relations.
Ightham Woods.
Knole.
A Letter to John Donne.
Marcus Aurelius.
Money.
The Nature of Man.
Over the Wall: Berlin, May
 1975.
The Queen of Lydia.
The Temple.
The Usk.
Sister M. Therese
The Contemplative.
For Simone Weil.
Interrogative.
Testament.
Sitwell, Edith
Ass-Face.
Aubade.
The Bat.
Bells of Grey Crystal.
The Canticle of the Rose.
Clowns' Houses.
The Coat of Fire.
Colonel Fantock.
Country Dance.
Daphne.
Dark Song.
The Drum: the Narrative of
 the Drummer of Tedworth.
Elegy for Dylan Thomas.
Epithalamium.
Evening.
The Fan.
Four in the Morning.
Gardener Janus Catches a
 Naiad.
Gold Coast Customs
 (excerpt).
The Hambone and the Heart.
Harvest.
Heart and Mind.
Hornpipe.
How Many Heavens...
The Innocent Spring.
Interlude.
Invocation.

The King of China's
 Daughter.
The Lament of Edward
 Blastock.
Lullaby.
Madam Mouse Trots.
Mademoiselle Richarde.
Most Lovely Shade.
Neptune–Polka.
An Old Woman.
An Old Woman Laments in
 Spring-Time.
Panope.
Perpetuum Mobile.
The Poet Laments the Coming
 of Old Age.
Prothalamium.
Sailor, What of the Isles?
The Satyr in the Periwig.
Scotch Rhapsody.
The Shadow of Cain.
Sir Beelzebub.
The Sleeping Beauty.
Solo for Ear-Trumpet.
Song: "Now that Fate is dead
 and gone."
A Song of Morning.
Song:"Once my heart was a
 summer rose."
Spinning Song.
Spring.
Still Falls the Rain.
Street Song.
The Swans.
Switchback.
Tears.
Three Poems of the Atomic
 Age: Dirge for the New
 Sunrise.
Trio for Two Cats and a
 Trombone.
Two Kitchen Songs.
Variations on an Old Nursery
 Rhyme.
Waltz.
The Web of Eros.
When Sir Beelzebub.
You, the Young Rainbow.
The Youth with Red-Gold
 Hair.
Sitwell, Osbert
Aubade: Dick, the Donkey-
 Boy.
The Ballad of Sister Anne.
Elegy for Mr. Goodbeare.
England Reclaimed (excerpt).
English Beach Memory: Mr.
 Thuddock.
Fountains.
Giardino Pubblico.
How Shall We Rise to Greet
 the Dawn?
Lament for Richard Rolston.
Lousy Peter.
Maxixe.
Mrs. Busk.
Mrs. Crudeman.
Mrs. Southern's Enemy.
The Next War.
On the Coast of Coromandel.
Osmund Toulmin.
Therefore Is the Name of It
 Called Babel.
To Charlotte Corday.
Trippers.
What Was Your Dream,
 Doctor Murricombe?
Winter the Huntsman.
Sitwell, Sacheverell
Agamemnon's Tomb.
Battles of the Centaurs:
 Centaurs and Lapithae.

Cherry Tree.
Derbyshire Bluebells.
Fisherman.
Fountains.
Kingcups.
Landscape with the Giant
  Orion: Orion Seeks the
  Goddess Diana (excerpt.
The Lime Avenue.
Magnolia Tree in Summer.
Outside Dunsandle.
Psittachus Eois Imitatrix Ales
  Ab Indis.
The Red-Gold Rain.
The Rio Grande.
The River God.
Tulip Tree.
Variation on a Theme by John
  Lyly.
The Venus of Bolsover Castle.

Sivan, Arye
Children's Song.
Forty Years Peace.
In Jerusalem Are Women.
To Xanadu, Which Is Beth
  Shaul.

Sizemore, George
Drill Man Blues.

Sjolander, John P.
The Last Longhorn's
  Farewell.
The Pine of Whiting Wood.

Skeat, Walter William
A Clerk Ther was of
  Cauntebrigge Also (parody).
Villanelle.

Skeen, Anita
Instructions.
Letter to My Mother.
Modern Poetry.
Outside Every Window Is a
  Flowering Thing.
Sailing in Crosslight.

Skelley, Jack
To Marie Osmond.
TV Blooper Spotter.

Skelton, John
Against Garnesche (excerpt).
Amends to the Tailors and
  Soutars.
Anathema of Cats.
The Auncient Acquaintance,
  Madam, betwen Us Twayn.
A Ballade of the Scottyshe
  Kynge.
The Bowge of Courte.
Colin Clout.
The Commendations of
  Mistress Jane Scrope.
A Curse on the Cat.
Elinor Rumming (excerpt).
L'Envoy: To His Book.
The Funeral of Philip
  Sparrow.
The Gift of a Skull.
Gup, Scot!
How the Doughty Duke of
  Albany Like a Coward
  Knight...(excerpt).
Knowledge, Acquaintance.
Lullay, Lullay.
Mannerly Margery Milk and
  Ale.
Maystress Jane Scroupe.
My Darling Dear, My Daisy
  Flower.
The Parrot.
Phyllyp Sparrowe (excerpt).
Prayer to the Father in
  Heaven.
Skelton Laureate, Defender,
  against Lusty Garnesche....

The Sleeper Hood-Winked.
The Sparrow's Dirge.
Speak, Parrot.
Though Ye Suppose.
To His Wife.
To Maystres Jane Blenner-
  Haiset.
To Mistress Anne.
To Mistress Gertrude
  Statham.
To Mistress Isabel Pennell.
To Mistress Margaret Tilney.
To Mistress Margery
  Wentworth.
To My Lady Mirriel Howard.
The Tunning of Elinor
  Rumming.
Unfriendly Fortune.
Upon a Dead Man's Head.
Why Come Ye Not to Court
  (excerpt).
With Lullay, Lullay.
Woefully Arrayed.
Womanhood, Wanton, Ye
  Want.

Skelton, Philip
To God, Ye Choir above.

Skelton, Robin
Angel.
A Ballad of a Mine.
The Brigg.
Eagle.
Lakeside Incident.
Wart Hog.

Skene, Don
After Reading Twenty Years
  of Grantland Rice.

Skillman, Judith
Waiting.

Skinner, Constance Lindsay
Song of Basket-Weaving.
Song of Cradle-Making.
Song of the Full Catch.
Three Songs from the Haida,
  III: Queen Charlotte's Island,
  B.C.

Skinner, Cornelia Otis
To the Sistine Madonna.

Skinner, Jeffrey
His Side/Her Side.

Skinner, John
Tullochgorum.

Skinner, Knute
Blackheads.
The Brockton Murder: A
  Page out of William James.
The Cold Irish Earth.
Imagine Grass.
Location.
An Old Lady Watching TV.
Organ Solo.

Skinner, Thomas
The Suttee.

Skipsey, Joseph
Dewdrop, Wind and Sun.
Get Up!
A Golden Lot.
A Merry Bee.
Mother Wept.
Not as Wont.
The Time Hath Been.
The Violet and the Rose.
Willy to Jinny.

Skirrow, Desmond
Ode on a Grecian Urn
  Summarized.

Skirving, Adam
Johnnie Cope.

Skjaeraasen, Einar
The Word of God.

Sklar, Morty
Poem to the Sun.

Sklarew, Myra
Benediction.
The Goodbye.
Hieroglyphic.
In Bed.
Instructions for the Messiah.
Marriage.
The Origin of Species.
Poem of the Mother.
Red Riding Hood at the
  Acropolis.
What Is a Jewish Poem?

Skloot, Floyd
My Daughter Considers Her
  Body.

Skoloker, Anthony
Her Praises.

Skrzynecki, Peter
Cattle.
Feliks Skrzynecki.

Skythinos
Epigram: "Great woe, fire &
  woe."

**Sladen, Douglas Brook
  Wheelton**
A Summer Christmas in
  Australia.
Under the Wattle.

Slate, Ron
The Accomplice.

Slater, Eleanor
Petition.
Sight and Insight.

Slater, Francis Carey
Drought (excerpt).

Slater, Robert
Survival Kit.
The Survivors.

Slavitt, David R.
Another Letter to Lord
  Byron.
Broads (parody).
Dead Bird (parody).
Eczema.
The Griefs of Women
  (parody).
In Memory of W. H. Auden.
In the Seraglio.
That Everything Moves Its
  Bowels (parody).

Slemp, John Calvin
O Christ, Who Died.

Slender, Pauline
The Vagrant.

Slesinger, Warren
Sandpaper, Sandpiper,
  Sandpit.

Slessor, Kenneth
The Atlas.
Beach Burial.
A Bushranger.
Country Towns.
Crow Country.
Earth-Visitors.
Five Bells.
Five Visions of Captain Cook.
Gulliver.
Metempsychosis.
North Country.
Out of Time (excerpt).
Polarities.
Serenade.
Sleep.
South Country.
Stars.
William Street.

Sloan, Errol B.
And Yet–.

Sloan, Jocelyn Macy
Eliza Telefair.

Sloate, Daniel
Your Birds Build Sun-Castles
  with Song.

Sloman, Joel
In a Remote Cloister
  Bordering the Empyrean.
The Tree.

Slonimski, Antoni
All.
Conrad.
Conversation with a
  Countryman.
Elegy.
He Is My Countryman.
Jerusalem.
London Spring.
Morning and Evening.
Remembrance.

Slowinsky, Stephanie
It's True I'm No Miss
  America.

Slutsky, Boris
Burnt.
Dreams of Auschwitz.
God.
How They Killed My
  Grandmother.

Sly, Muriel
The Chimpanzee.

Small, Adam
There's Somethin'.

Small, Floyd B.
Root Hog or Die.

Smart, Christopher
All the Scenes of Nature
  Quicken.
The Author Apologizes to a
  Lady for His Being a Little
  Man.
The Citizen and the Red Lion
  of Brentford.
Epithalamium on a Late
  Happy Marriage.
The Hop Garden (excerpt).
How to Cure Hops and
  Prepare Them for Sale.
Hymn to the Supreme Being
  on Recovery (excerpt).
Hymns and Spiritual Songs.
Hymns for the Amusement of
  Children.
The Instruments.
Jubilate Agno.
A Lark's Nest.
The Man of Prayer.
A Morning Hymn.
A Morning-Piece; or, An
  Hymn for the Hay-Makers.
A Night-Piece; or, Modern
  Philosophy.
On a Bed of Guernsey Lilies.
On My Wife's Birth-Day.
Praise.
Pray Remember the Poor.
Psalms, CXLVII.
A Song to David.
Song: "Where shall Celia fly
  for shelter."
Spring.

Smedley, Jonathan
Fancy.

Smedley, Menella Bute
A North Pole Story.
Wind Me a Summer Crown.

Smiley, Joseph Bert
St. Peter at the Gate.

Smith, A. J. M.
The Archer.
Brigadier.
Business as Usual 1946.
The Comman Man.
The Dead.

Far West.
The Fountain.
Good Friday.
Like an Old Proud King in a
  Parable.
The Lonely Land.
My Death.
News of the Phoenix.
Ode: On the Death of William
  Butler Yeats.
On Knowing Nothing.
The Plot against Proteus.
Political Intelligence.
Prothalamium.
Resurrection of Arp.
The Sorcerer.
The Taste of Space.
To Henry Vaughan.
To Hold in a Poem.
What Is That Music High in
  the Air?
The Wisdom of Old Jelly
  Roll.
Smith, Ada
In City Streets.
Smith, Alexander
Barbara.
Glasgow.
A Life-Drama (excerpt).
Scorned.
Smith, Arabella Eugenia
If I Should Die Tonight.
Smith, Barbara
Next Door to Monica's Dance
  Studio.
Physical for My Son.
Smith, Bessie
Black Mountain Blues.
Empty Bed Blues.
Jailhouse Blues.
Rock Water Blues.
Smith, Bradford
Winter Is Icumen In.
Smith, Bruce
Pelvic Meditation.
Smith, C. Fox
In the Trades.
Pictures.
What the Old Man Said.
Smith, Caroline Sprague
Tarry with Me, O My
  Saviour.
Smith, Charlotte
Beachy Head (excerpt).
The First Swallow.
The Glow-Worm.
The Gossamer.
He May Be Envied, Who with
  Tranquil Breast.
Invitation to the Bee.
Montalbert (excerpt).
Mute Is Thy Wild Harp,
  Now, O Bard Sublime!
Press'd by the Moon, Mute
  Arbitress of Tides.
Sonnet Written at the Close of
  Spring.
Thirty-Eight.
To the Moon.
Smith, Claude Clayton
Charlie Johnson in
  Kettletown.
The Kiss.
Smith, Dave
The Ancestor.
An Antipastoral Memory of
  One Summer.
Blues for Benny Kid Paret.
Chopping Wood.
The Collector of the Sun.
Cumberland Station.
Desks.

Dome Poem.
Elk Ghosts: A Birth Memory.
First Star.
Gramercy Park Hotel.
Hard Times, But Carrying
  On.
Hawktree.
In the House of the Judge.
Leafless Trees, Chickahominy
  Swamp.
Looking for the Melungeon.
Mending Crab Pots.
Night Fishing for Blues.
Of Oystermen, Workboats.
The Old Whore Speaks to a
  Young Poet.
On a Field at Fredericksburg.
The Perspective and Limits of
  Snapshots.
Photographic Plate, Partly
  Spidered, Hampton Roads,
  Virginia...
Pine Cones.
The Purpose of the
  Chesapeake & Ohio Canal.
Rain Forest.
Reading the Books Our
  Children Have Written.
The Roundhouse Voices.
Running Back.
Sea Owl.
Smithfield Ham.
Tide Pools.
Under the Scub Oak, a Red
  Shoe.
Smith, Dexter
Our National Banner.
Smith, Dill Armor
Twenty Years Ago.
Smith, Douglas
The Balcony Poems.
Smith, Edgar
Heaven Will Protect the
  Working Girl.
Smith, Elizabeth Oakes
The Drowned Mariner.
From "The Sinless Child."
Smith, Eunice
Dear Brethren, Are Your
  Harps in Tune?
Dear Happy Souls.
Smith, Florence
Song.
Smith, Funny Paper
Fool's Blues.
Smith, George
The Country Lovers.
Smith, Harry Bache
The Armorer's Song.
Gipsy Love Song.
The Long Night.
My Angeline.
The Song of the Turnkey.
The Tattooed Man.
Smith, Helen Rogers
He Lifted from the Dust.
Smith, Hilda W.
The Carpenter of Galilee.
**Smith, Horace (or Horatio) and
James**
The Baby's Debut (Parody on
  Wordsworth).
Loyal Effusion.
Macbeth (parody).
Smith, Horace (or Horatio)
Address to a Mummy.
Evening: an Elegy (parody).
The Gouty Merchant and the
  Stranger.
On a Stupendous Leg of
  Granite, Discovered Standing
  by Itself...

A Tale of Drury Lane.
Smith, Iain Crichton
At the Firth of Lorne.
Culloden and After.
Deer at the Roadside.
End of the Season on a
  Stormy Day–Oban.
For Angus MacLeod.
For My Mother.
John Knox.
Luss Village.
Old Woman.
Schoolgirl on Speech-Day in
  the Open Air.
Two Girls Singing.
The Window.
A Young Highland Girl
  Studying Poetry.
Smith, Iva
Third Alley Blues.
Smith, J. Danson
We'll Meet Again.
Smith, James
On the American Rivers.
Smith, Janet M.
Corries.
Smith, Jared
Something.
Smith, Joan
Alley-Walker.
Smith, John
First, Goodbye.
In the Due Honor of the
  Author Master Robert
  Norton.
John Smith of His Friend
  Master John Taylor.
The Sea Marke.
A Solitary Canto to Chloris
  the Disdainful.
Smith, Kay
The Eye of Humility.
Footnote to the Lord's Prayer
  (excerpt).
What Then, Dancer?
When a Girl Looks Down.
Smith, Ken
Possessions.
Train.
Smith, Langdon
Evolution.
Smith, Lanta Wilson
This, Too, Shall Pass Away.
Smith, Laurence
Christmas Tree.
Smith, Lewis Worthington
News from Yorktown.
Smith, Lucy
Face of Poverty.
Smith, Margoret
Cataract.
Smith, Marion Couthouy
King of the Belgians.
The Star.
Smith, Mary Brainerd
Poor for Our Sakes.
Smith, Mary Carter
Clubwoman.
Jungle.
Smith, May Riley
Departure.
God's Plans.
If We Knew.
My Life Is a Bowl.
My Uninvited Guest.
Sometime.
Tired Mothers.
The Tree-Top Road.
Smith, Mbembe Milton
Did They Help Me at the
  State Hospital for the
  Criminally Insane?

Smith, Michael
At the Appointed Hour They
  Came.
Blond Hair at the Edge of the
  Pavement.
The Desolate Rhythm of
  Dying Recurs.
Here Is the Abattoir Where.
Smith, Mrs. Albert
Scatter Seeds of Kindness.
Smith, Ninna May
If Some Grim Tragedy.
Smith, Norma E.
Evangeline.
Smith, Oswald J.
Another Year.
God Is with Me.
God's Presence Makes My
  Heaven.
A Heart That Weeps.
I Turn to Jesus.
The Master's Call.
The Saviour Can Solve Every
  Problem.
Smith, Phoebe
Via Dolorosa.
Smith, R. T.
Aunt Melissa.
Beneath the Mound.
Checking the Firing.
The Long Joke.
Poem for David Janssen.
Red Anger.
Roosevelt Considers Catfish
  Stew.
Rural Route.
Saving the Fish.
Suppose a Man.
What Black Elk Said.
Widow to Her Son.
Yonosa House.
Smith, Ray
The Apple.
Smith, Robert
The Exhortation of a Father
  to His Children.
Smith, Robert B.
Cafes.
Jailhouse Lawyers.
My Uncle Joe.
Razor.
Seabirds.
Smith, Robert Paul
Fielding Error.
Small Quiet Song.
Tie Your Tongue, Sir?
Smith, Roger
Lochan.
Smith, Samuel Francis
America.
As Flows the Rapid River.
Daybreak.
Down to the Sacred Wave.
The Morning Light Is
  Breaking.
Softly Fades the Twilight Ray.
Tree-Planting.
Smith, Samuel J.
Arise, My Soul! With Rapture
  Rise!
**Smith, Seba ("Major Jack
Downing")**
The Mother in the Snow-
  Storm.
Young Charlottie.
Smith, Sidney Goodsir
Can I Forget?
Largo.
Sang: Recoll O Skaith.
Whan the Hert Is Laich.

Smith, Stephen E.
The Death of Carmen Miranda.
Getting by on Honesty.

Smith, Stevie
Admire Cranmer!
Advice to Young Children.
The After-Thought.
The Airy Christ.
Anger's Freeing Power.
Away, Melancholy.
Be off!
The Bereaved Swan.
Bye Baby Bother.
The Celtic Fringe.
The Celts.
Childe Rolandine.
Correspondence between Mr. Harrison in Newcastle and ...
Dear Female Heart.
The Death Sentence.
The Deserter.
Distractions and the Human Crowd.
Drugs Made Pauline Vague.
Edmonton, Thy Cemetery...
Egocentric.
Everything Is Swimming.
Exeat.
The Frog Prince.
The Galloping Cat.
Goodnight.
He Told His Life Story to Mrs. Courtly.
The Heavenly City.
Here Lies...
A House of Mercy.
I Love...
I Remember.
I Rode with My Darling...
In My Dreams.
Infelice.
The Jungle Husband.
The Lads of the Village.
Lady "Rogue" Singleton.
The Little Boy Lost.
Lord Barrenstock.
Louise.
Love Me!
Magna Est Veritas.
Major Macroo.
Man Is a Spirit.
Miss Snooks, Poetess.
Monsieur Pussy-Cat, Blackmailer.
Mother, among the Dustbins.
Mr. Over.
The Murderer.
My Cats.
My Hat.
No Categories!
Not Waving but Drowning.
The Occasional Yarrow.
One of Many.
Our Bog Is Dood.
Pad, Pad.
Papa Love Baby.
The Parklands.
The Persian.
Pretty.
Private Means is Dead.
Quand On N'a Pas Ce Que l'on Aime, Il Faut Aimer Ce Que l'on A–.
Reversionary.
The River God.
Satin-Clad.
Scorpion.
Seymour and Chantelle or Un Peu de Vice.
The Singing Cat.
The Small Lady.
Some Are Born.
Sunt Leones.
Tenuous and Precarious.
This Englishwoman.
Thoughts about the Person from Porlock.
Thoughts on the Christian Doctrine of Eternal Hell.
To Carry the Child.
To School!
To the Tune of the Coventry Carol.
Valuable.
Was He Married?
Was It Not Curious?
The Weak Monk.
Who Is This Who Howls and Mutters?
Who Killed Lawless Lean?

Smith, Sydney Goodsir
Bishop Blomfield's First Charge to His Clergy.
Cokkils.
The Deevil's Waltz.
Defeat O' the Hert.
Elegy XIII.
Epistle to John Guthrie.
For My Newborn Son.
Hamewith.
The Ineffable Dou.
Leander Stormbound.
Loch Leven.
The Mandrake Hert.
The Mither's Lament.
On Seeing Francis Jeffrey Riding on a Donkey.
Recipe for Salad.
Saagin.
Under the Eildon Tree.
Ye Mongers Aye Need Masks for Cheatrie.
Ye Spier Me.

Smith, Virginia E.
Daysleep.

Smith, Vivian
At an Exhibition of Historical Paintings, Hobart.
Bedlam Hills.
Early Arrival: Sydney.
Fishermen, Drowned beyond the West Coast.
The Last Summer.
Reflections.
Still Life.
Summer Band Concert.
Tasmania.

Smith, Walter Chalmers
Coruisk.
Glenaradale.

Smith, Welton
The Beast Section.
A Folding and Unfolding.
Interlude.
Malcolm.
The Nigga Section.
Strategies.

Smith, William
Collin My Deere and Most Entire Beloved.
Some in Their Harts Their Mistris Colours Bears.
Sonnet: "My Love, I cannot thy rare beauties place."

Smith, William Jay
3 for 25.
Abruptly All the Palm Trees.
American Primitive.
Antelope.
At the Tombs of the House of Savoy.
Autumn.
Butterfly.
Clerihew: "Edmund Clerihew Bentley."
Clerihew: "William Penn."
The Closing of the Rodeo.
Convoy.
Crocodile.
Cupidon.
Dachshunds.
Dead Snake.
Death of a Jazz Musician.
Dog.
Dream.
Elegy.
Epitaph of a Stripper.
The Floor and the Ceiling.
Galileo Galilei.
A Green Place.
Gull.
Hotel Continental.
Independence Day.
Jittery Jim.
Laughing Time.
Limerick: "A lady who lived in Uganda."
Limerick: "A lady whose name was Miss Hartley."
Limerick: "A matron well known in Montclair."
Limerick: "A mother in old Alabama."
Limerick: "There was a young man on a plain."
Limerick: "There was a young person named Crockett."
Limerick: "There was an Old Lady named Crockett."
Limerick: "There was an old man by Salt Lake."
Limerick: "There was an old man of Toulon."
Limerick: "There was an old person who said."
Lovebirds.
The Lovers.
The Massacre of the Innocents.
Monkey.
Morels.
Morning at Arnheim.
Mr. Smith.
Neo-Classical Poem.
Nightwood.
Opossum.
Over and Under.
The Park in Milan.
A Pavane for the Nursery.
Persian Miniature.
Plain Talk.
Processional.
Quail in Autumn.
The Queen of the Nile.
Random Generation of English Sentences; or, The Revenge of the Poets.
Rear Vision.
Rondeau.
A Room in the Villa.
Seal.
Song for a Country Wedding.
The Tall Poets.
The Tempest.
Things.
The Toaster.
Today I Have Touched the Earth.
Unicorn.
Vincent Van Gogh.
The Voyages of Captain Cock.
Winter Morning.
The Wooing Lady.
Yak.
Zebra.

Smith, II, W. Atmar
The Piano Tuner.

Smith, Jr, LeRoy
Salvation Prospect.
Sappho Rehung.
Spring Song.
What Sanguine Beast?

Smither, Elizabeth
The Beak.
Change of School.
The Feast of All Saints.
Fr Anselm Williams and Br Leander Neville Hanged by Lutheran...
Song about My Father.
Sugar Daddy.

Smithyman, Kendrick
Cousin Emily and the Night Visitor.
Defenceless Children, Your Great Enemy.
Dirge for Two Clavichords and Bowler Hat.
Elegy Against a Latter Day.
Evening Music.
Friday Night.
Icarus.
Incident at Matauri.
The Last Moriori.
The Moment.
Night Walkers.
An Ordinary Day beyond Kaitaia.
Personal Poem.
Resort.
This Blonde Girl.
Waiwera.
Walk Past Those Houses on a Sunday Morning.

Smithyman, Kenrick
Considerations of Norfolk Island (excerpt).
Could You Once Regain.

Smoky Babe
Hottest Brand Goin'.

Smollett, Tobias
Ode to Leven Water.
The Tears of Scotland Written in the Year MDCCXLVI.

Smollett, Tobias George
Independence.
The Tears of Scotland.
To Leven Water.

Smyth, Florida Watts
Eternal Contour.
Green Mountain Boy.
Unclaimed.

Smyth, John
Strephon.

Smythe, Albert E. S.
Anastasis.

Smythe, Daniel
Driftwood.
From My Thought.

Snaith, Stanley
Birds in the Flax.
Blue Ghosts.
The Hare.
Parachute.
The Stack.
To Some Builders of Cities.

Snapp, Thomas
The Actor.

Snelling, Lois
Know It Is Christmas.

Snider, P. M.
Communion.

Snodgrass, C. A.
A Poem for Christmas.

Snodgrass, W. D.
After Experience Taught Me...
April Inventory.

The Campus on the Hill.
A Cardinal.
Child of My Winter.
Dr. Joseph Goebbels.
The Examination.
A Flat One.
A Friend.
Heart's Needle.
A Lady.
Leaving Ithaca.
Leaving the Motel.
Lobsters in the Window.
The Lovers Go Fly a Kite.
Lying Awake.
The Magic Flute.
Manet: The Execution of
  Emperor Maximilian.
The Marsh.
Mementos.
The Men's Room in the
  College Chapel.
Monet: "Les Nympheas."
No Use.
Old Apple Trees.
The Operation.
Orpheus.
Owls.
Partial Eclipse.
Planting a Magnolia.
Powwow.
Returned to Frisco.
Song: "Sweet beast, I have
  gone prowling."
A Teen-Ager.
Ten Days Leave.
These Trees Stand...
A Visitation.
Vuillard: "The Mother and
  Sister of the Artist."
What We Said.

Snow, Eliza R.
Think Not When You Gather
  to Zion.

Snow, Karen
Dream Girl.
Gifts.

Snow, Laura A. Barter
God Is in Every Tomorrow.

Snow, Sophia P.
Annie and Willie's Prayer.

Snow, Wilbert
Aged Ninety Years.

Snyder, Gary
Above Pate Valley.
After Work.
All the Spirit Powers Went to
  Their Dancing Place.
All through the Rains.
As for Poets.
August on Sourdough, a Visit
  from Dick Brewer.
August Was Foggy.
The Bath.
Before the Stuff Comes down.
Burning.
Burning the Small Dead.
By Frazier Creek Falls.
The Dead by the Side of the
  Road.
Eight Sandbars on the Takano
  River.
The Elwha River.
For a Far-Out Friend.
For Don Allen.
For John Chappell.
For Nothing.
For the Children.
For the West.
Four Poems for Robin.
Foxtail Pine.
Hay for the Horses.
A Heifer Clambers Up.

Hitch Haiku.
Hop, Skip, and Jump.
Hunting.
I Went into the Maverick Bar.
It.
It Pleases.
Journeys.
Kyoto: March.
The Late Snow and Lumber
  Strike of the Summer of
  Fifty-Four.
LMFBR.
Logging (excerpt).
Long Hair.
Looking at Pictures to Be Put
  away.
The Manichaeans.
Marin-An.
The Market.
Meeting the Mountains.
Mid-August at Sourdough
  Mountain Lookout.
Milton by Firelight.
Mother Earth: Her Whales.
Myths and Texts.
Nansen.
Nature Green Shit.
Nooksack Valley.
Oil.
Once Only.
Out West.
Pine Tree Tops.
Piute Creek.
Praise for Sick Women.
Prayer for the Great Family.
Riprap.
The Sappa Creek.
Sixth-Month Song in the
  Foothills.
The Snow on Saddle
  Mountain.
Some Good Things to Be Said
  for the Iron Age.
Song of the Taste.
Things to Do around a
  Lookout.
Things to Do around a Ship
  at Sea.
Things to Do around Kyoto.
This Tokyo.
Through the Smoke Hole.
To Hell with Your Fertility
  Cult.
Toward Climax.
Trail Crew Camp at Bear
  Valley, 9000 Feet....
The Truth Like the Belly of a
  Woman Turning.
Two Fawns That Didn't See
  the Light This Spring.
Vapor Trails.
A Walk.
Water.
What Do They Say.
What Happened Here before.
What You Should Know to
  Be a Poet.
Why Log Truck Drivers Rise
  Earlier Than Students of
  Zen.
The Wild Mushroom.
Work to Do Toward Town.

Snyder, Richard
The Aging Poet, on a Reading
  Trip to Dayton...
Blue Sparks in Dark Closets.
Chicago, Summer Past.
Christmas at a Decade's End.
Homage to Marian Pyszko.
A Mongoloid Child Handling
  Shells on the Beach.
O Whose Are These Children.

Of Pardons, Presidents, and
  Whiskey Labels.
A Small Elegy.
Sparrow in an Airport.
Wintered Sunflowers.

Snyder, Thurmond
Beale Street, Memphis.
The Beast with Chrome
  Teeth.
Seeds.

Snyder, Zilpha Keatley
Silent Hill.

Sobel, Lester A.
Transplantitis.

Sobiloff, Hy
Airship.
The Child's Sight.
Hans Christian Andersen in
  Central Park.
My Mother's Table.
Painting of a Lobster by
  Picasso.
Pittsburgh.
Wisdom.

Sobin, A. G.
Greeting Descendants.

Sodergran, Edith
A Decision.
Hope.
I Saw a Tree That Was
  Greater Than All the Others.
The Land That Is Not.
The Moon.
Pain.
Violet Twilights.
We Women.

Sologub, Fyodor
The Amphora.
Austere the Music of My
  Songs.

Solomon, Marvin
Cages.
The Cat and the Bird.
The Garden.
The Giraffe.
Lemon Sherbet.
The Vole.

Solomon ben Aaron, Salaman
These Things I Do
  Remember.

Solomon ibn Gabirol
The Royal Crown.

Solomos, George P.
Wisdom of the Gazelle.

Solon
Boys and Sport.

Solt, Mary Ellen
Forsythia.
Marriage.
Moonshot Sonnet.
Rain Down.
Wild Crab.

Solway, Arthur
Answers to the Snails.

Solway, David
The Powers of the Pawn.

Somervile, William
An Address to His Elbow-
  Chair, New Cloath'd.
Advice to the Ladies.
The Bowling-Green (excerpt).
The Chase (excerpt).
Field Sports (excerpt).
Hare-Hunting.
On Presenting to a Lady a
  White Rose and a Red on
  the Tenth of June.
The Wounded Man and the
  Swarm of Flies.

Somerville, Jane
Denials 1.

Sondheim, Steven
Gee, Officer Krupke.

Soné
Blessed...

Song, Cathy
Beauty and Sadness.
Blue Lantern.
The Day You Are Born.
Girl Powdering Her Neck.
Losing Track.
Lucky.
Who Makes the Journey.
The Youngest Daughter.

Soniat, Katherine
Initial Response.
Resounding.

Sonnenschein, Hugo
In the Ghetto.
In the Open Fields.

Sophocles
Ajax.
Antigone.
King Oedipus.
Oedipus at Colonus.
Oedipus Rex: Chorus.
Old Age.
Women of Trachis: Choruses.

Sora
Up the Barley Rows.

Sorell, Waltler
All That Matters...

Sorley, Charles Hamilton
All the Hills and Vales Along.
Expectans Expectavi.
In Memoriam S.C.W., V.C.
Marlborough (excerpt).
Peer Gynt.
Rooks.
The Seekers.
The Song of the Ungirt
  Runners.
Two Sonnets.
To Germany.
When You See Millions of the
  Mouthless Dead.

Soroka, Pauline E.
Understanding.

Sorrells, Helen
The Amputation.
Town I Left.

Sorrentino, Gilbert
Anatomy.
A Classic Case.
Handbook of Versification.
The Zoo.

Sosei (Sosei Hoshi)
Two Poems.

Sossaman, Stephen
A Viet Cong Sapper Dies.

Sostrom, Anne
Status Symbols.

Sotades
A Banquet.

Sotheby, William
Netley Abbey. Midnight.

Soto, Gary
After Tonight.
Angel.
At the Cantina.
Black Hair.
Brown Like Us.
Cruel Boys.
The Elements of San Joaquin.
The Firstborn.
Getting Serious.
Heaven.
History.
In the Madness of Love.
Kearney Park.
Lantern.
The Map.
Mission Tire Factory, 1969.

The Morning They Shot Tony
Lopez, Barber and Pusher
Who Went Too Far.
The Point.
Remedies.
The Street.
The Widow Perez.
Soule, Jean Conder
Surprises.
Sousa, John Philip
The Feast of the Monkeys.
Have You Seen the Lady?
Sousa, Noemia da See **Da Sousa,
Noemia**
Souster, Raymond
All Animals Like Me.
A Bed without a Woman.
Bernard.
The Bottle of Chianti.
The Collector.
The Day before Christmas.
Dog in the Fountain.
Dog, Midwinter.
The Falling of the Snow.
Flight of the Roller Coaster.
The Hunter.
Lagoons, Hanlan's Point.
The Lift.
The Man Who Finds That
His Son Has Become a Thief.
Need of an Angel.
Not Wholly Lost.
Old Dog.
On the Range.
Reality.
Search.
The Six-Quart Basket.
Speakers, Columbus Circle.
Summer Afternoon.
Sunday Night Walk.
This Poem Will Never Be
Finished.
Ties.
When I See Old Men.
The Worm.
Young Girls.
Soutar, William
Among High Hills.
The Auld House.
Auld Sang.
Ballad.
The Gowk.
A Hint o' Snaw.
In the Mood of Blake.
The Makar.
On the Hill.
Owre the Hill.
Parable.
The Permanence of the Young
Men.
Poetry.
Revelation.
A Riddle.
The Room.
Scotland.
Signs.
The Singing Bush.
Song: "Whaur yon broken
brig hings owre."
The Star.
Supper.
The Thocht.
The Tryst.
Wait for the Hour.
A Whigmaleerie.
Souter, Charles H.
After Johnson's Dance.
Irish Lords.
Old John Bax.
What the Red-haired Bo'sun
Said.

Southey, Caroline Bowles
The Young Gray Head.
Southey, Robert
The Battle of Blenheim.
The Bower of Peace.
A Calm Sea.
The Cataract of Lodore.
The Curse of Kehama.
The Dancing Bear.
The Devil's Walk.
The Ebb Tide.
Epitaph.
The Filbert.
God's Judgment on a Wicked
Bishop.
The Holly Tree.
Homeward Bound.
The Inchcape Rock.
Inscription for a Tablet on the
Banks of a Stream.
Inscriptions for the
Caledonian Canal.
The Island.
Lord! Who Art Merciful as
Well as Just.
Love Indestructible.
The March to Moscow.
My Days among the Dead
Are Past.
Night.
O God! Have Mercy in This
Dreadful Hour.
Ode to a Pig While His Nose
Was Being Bored.
The Old Man's Comforts and
How He Gained Them.
The Old Woman of Berkeley.
On a Picture by J. M. Wright,
Esq.
On the Death of a Favourite
Old Spaniel.
Recollections of a Day's
Journey in Spain.
She Comes Majestic with Her
Swelling Sails.
The Soldier's Wife.
Thalaba and the Banquet.
Thalaba and the Magic
Thread.
To a Goose.
To a Spider.
A Vision of Judgement.
The Well of St. Keyne.
The Widow.
Winter Portrait.
The Witch.
Written on a Sunday
Morning.
Southgate, Margaret
One-Line Poems from a New
Statesman Competition.
Southwell, Robert
At Fotheringay.
At Home in Heaven.
The Burning Babe.
A Child My Choice.
Christs Sleeping Friends.
Come to your Heaven, You
Heavenly Choirs!
Content and Rich.
Elegy for Margaret Howard,
Lady Buckhurst.
Ensamples of Our Saviour.
Lewd Love is Loss.
Look Home.
Loss in Delay.
Love's Servile Lot.
Marie Magdalen's Complaint
at Christ's Death.
The Martyrdom of Mary,
Queen of Scots.
The Nativity of Christ.

New Heaven, New War.
New Prince, New Pomp.
Of the Blessed Sacrament of
the Altar.
Our Lady's Salutation.
Seek Flowers of Heaven.
Sinnes Heavie Loade.
Stanzas from Saint Peter's
Complaint.
Tymes Goe by Turnes.
Upon the Image of Death.
The Virgin Mary to Christ on
the Cross.
Wassailer's Song.
Where Wards Are Weak.
Southwick, Marcia
A Burial, Green.
Dusk.
The Marsh.
No Such Thing.
Owning a Dead Man.
Southwold, Stephen
Mother of Men.
Soyinka, Wole
Abiku.
Telephone Conversation.
Spacks, Barry
An Emblem of Two Foxes.
Finding a Yiddish Paper on
the Riverside Line.
Freshmen.
The Last Fish.
Malediction.
The Muse.
My Mother's Childhood.
October.
Teaching the Penguins to Fly.
Washing Windows.
Who Then Is Crazy?
Spalding, Helen
The Dream.
Spalding, John Lancaster
Believe and Take Heart.
Forepledged.
God and the Soul.
Silence.
The Starry Host.
Spalding, Susan Marr
Fate.
The Sea's Spell.
A Song's Worth.
Spargur, Jill
Tragedy.
Spark, Muriel
Canaan.
Faith and Works.
The She Wolf.
Sparshott, Francis
The Naming of the Beasts.
Reply to the Committed
Intellectual.
Three Seasons.
Spaziani, Maria Luisa
Journey in the Orient.
Winter Moon.
Spear, Charles
1894 in London.
Die Pelzaffen.
Karl.
The Watchers.
Spear, Roberta
The Anniversary.
August/Fresno 1973.
The Bat.
Boundaries.
Bringing Flowers.
A Sale of Smoke.
The White Dress.
Spears, Dorothea
Begetting.
Spears, Heather
My Love behind Walls.

Spears, Woodridge
Restoration.
Speckled Red
The Dirty Dozens.
Spector, Albert
Eastside Chick with Drive.
Spee, Frederick
Dialogue at the Cross.
Speed, Samuel
The Flower.
Peace.
Speer, Laurel
Mirror Images.
Spellman, A. B.
For My Unborn & Wretched
Children.
I Looked & Saw History
Caught.
In Orangeburg My Brothers
Did.
John Coltrane an Impartial
Review.
Tomorrow the Heroes.
When Black People Are.
Zapata & the Landlord.
Spence, Lewis
The Prows o' Reekie.
The Wee May o'Caledon.
Spence, Michael
DNA Lab.
The Fish Will Swim as
Before.
The Orchard.
Spence, Skip
Motorcycle Irene.
Spencer, Anne
At the Carnival.
Before the Feast of Shushan.
Creed.
Dunbar.
For Jim, Easter Eve.
I Have a Friend.
Innocence.
Lady, Lady.
Letter to My Sister.
Life-Long, Poor Browning...
Lines to a Nasturtium.
Neighbors.
Questing.
Substitution.
Translation.
The Wife-Woman.
Spencer, Bernard
Aegean Islands 1940-41.
Behaviour of Money.
Boat Poem.
A Cold Night.
The Empire Clock.
Greek Excavations.
A Hand.
Ill.
Letters.
On the "Sievering" Tram.
Part of Plenty.
Regent's Park Terrace.
The Rendezvous.
A Spring Wind.
A Thousand Killed.
Yachts on the Nile.
Spencer, C. Mordaunt
The Rose of Tralee.
Spencer, Caroline
Living Waters.
Spencer, Lilian White
Aut Caesar Aut Nullus.
The Red Ghosts Chant.
Spring Song of Aspens.
Spencer, Lillian White
Hopi Woman.
Spencer, Theodore
The Californians.
A Circle.

Contemporary Song.
The Critics.
Eden: Or One View of It.
Entropy.
Epitaph.
Escapist's Song.
The Inflatable Globe.
Invocation (excerpt).
The Phoenix.
Return.
Song.
Spring Song.

Spencer, Thomas E.
How McDougal Topped the
Score.

Spencer, William Robert
Beth Gelert.

Spender, Stephen
Acts Passed beyond the
Boundary of Mere Wishing.
After They Have Tired of the
Brilliance of Cities.
Almond Blossom in Wartime.
Auf Dem Wasser Zu Singen.
Awaking.
The Barn.
Beethoven's Death Mask.
Central Heating System.
A Childhood.
The Coward.
Daybreak.
Discovered in Mid-Ocean.
The Double Shame.
The Drowned.
An Elementary School Class
Room in a Slum.
The Empty House.
Epilogue.
Epilogue to a Human Drama.
The Express.
Farewell in a Dream.
From All These Events.
The Funeral.
The Generous Years.
Hoelderlin's Old Age.
How Strangely This Sun
Reminds Me of My Love.
An "I" Can Never Be a Great
Man.
I Think Continually of Those
Who Were Truly Great.
Icarus.
Ice.
The Immortal Spirit.
In Railway Halls.
Judas Iscariot.
The Labourer in the Vineyard.
The Landscape Near an
Aerodrome.
A Man-Made World.
The Marginal Field.
Marston.
Mask.
Memento.
Midsummer.
Missing My Daughter.
Moving Through the Silent
Crowd.
My Parents Kept Me from
Children Who Were Rough.
New Year.
Not Palaces.
O Night O Trembling Night.
Oh young men oh young
comrades.
On the Pilots Who Destroyed
Germany in the Spring of
1945.
On the Third Day.
One More New Botched
Beginning.
Perhaps.

Polar Exploration.
Port Bou.
The Prisoners.
The Pylons.
Rolled over on Europe.
The Room Above the Square.
Seascape.
A Separation.
The Shapes of Death.
Song.
Sonnet: You Were Born; Must
Die.
Statistics.
A Stopwatch and an
Ordanance Map.
The Swan.
Thoughts during an Air Raid.
To a Spanish Poet.
To My Daughter.
To Poets and Airmen.
To T.A.R.H.
The Trance.
Two Armies.
Ultima Ratio Regum.
The Vase of Tears.
The War God.
What I Expected.
A Whim of Time.
Winter and Summer.
Winter Landscape.
Without That Once Clear
Aim.
Word.
Your Body Is Stars.

Spenser, Edmund
All This World's Riches.
Amoretti.
The Art of Eyes.
August.
Balme.
Beauty.
Behold, O Man.
The Bower of Bliss.
The Butterfly.
Cease, Then, My Tongue!
Colin Clout at Court.
Colin Clout's Come Home
Again.
The Contempt of Poetry.
Daphnaida (excerpt).
A Ditty.
Elisa.
Epithalamion.
The Faerie Queene.
Four Anacreontic Poems, 1.
Four Anacreontic Poems, 2.
Four Anacreontic Poems, 3.
Four Anacreontic Poems, 4.
The House of Richesse.
An Hymn of Heavenly Beauty
(excerpt).
Iambicum Trimetrum.
January Eclogue.
Lament for Daphnaida.
Let Not One Sparke of Filthy
Lustfull Fyre.
Like as a Huntsman.
May.
Next unto Him Was Neptune
Pictured.
Now Strike Your Sailes Ye
Jolly Mariners!
The Oak and the Brere.
Of This World's Theater in
Which We Stay.
Old January.
Penelope, for Her Ulysses'
Sake.
Perigot and Willye.
Prayer to Venus.
Prothalamion.
A Roundelay.

The Shepheardes Calender.
So Oft As I Her Beauty Do
Behold.
Trust Not the Treason.
Was It a Dream.
What Guile Is This.
Whilst It Is Prime.
Winter.

**"Speranza" See Wilde, Lady
Jane Francesca**

Speyer, Leonora
Answer.
Duet.
The Heart Recalcitrant.
I'll Be Your Epitaph.
Kleptomaniac.
The Ladder.
Little Lover.
Mary Magdalene.
Measure Me, Sky.
A Note from the Pipes.
Oberammergau.
Pain.
Protest in Passing.
Star-Fear.
Suddenly.
Swans.
Tears for Sale.
X-Ray.

Spicer, Anne Higginson
Hail and Farewell.

Spicer, J.L.
Communion.

Spicer, Jack
Among the Coffee Cups and
Soup Toureens Walked
Beauty.
Billy the Kid.
The Book of Merlin.
A Book of Music.
The Book of Percival.
Central Park West.
Five Words for Joe Dunn on
His 22nd Birthday.
Four Poems for The St. Louis
Sporting News, 4.
Graphemics (excerpt).
The Holy Grail: The Book of
Gawain (excerpt).
Imaginary Elegies, I-IV.

Spingarn, Joel Elias
Beauty.
Helios.
Italian Poppies.
Spring Passion.

Spingarn, Lawrence P.
Museum Piece.
Philatelic Lessons: The
German Collection.
Vignette: 1922.

Spire, Andre
Abishag.
The Ancient Law.
Dust.
Hear, O Israel.
It Was Not You.
Lonely.
Now You're Content.
Nudities.
Poetics.
Pogroms.
Spring.

Spires, Elizabeth
Courtesan with Fan.
Skins.
Tequila.
Wake.
Widow's Walk.

Spitta, Karl J. P.
O Blessed House, That
Cheerfully Receiveth.
Unchanging Jesus.

Spitteler, Carl
Theme.

Spivack, Kathleen
But You, My Darling, Should
Have Married the Prince.
A Child's Visit to the Biology
Lab.
Dido: Swarming.
Drifting.
Dust.
Fugue.
The Judgment.
Love U.S.A.
The Meeting.
Mythmaking.
Private Pain in Time of
Trouble.
Shining.
Visions.

Spivak, Kathleen
As Animals.
March 1st.

Spivey, Victoria
Blood Hound Blues.

Spofford, Harriet Prescott
Ballad.
Can't.
Evanescence.
Every Day Thanksgiving Day.
The Fossil Raindrops.
Godspeed.
Hereafter.
How We Became a Nation.
The Hunt.
Music in the Night.
Only.
Phantoms All.
The Pines.
A Sigh.
A Snowdrop.
Voice.

Spooner, Lawrence
A Looking-Glass for Smokers
(excerpt).

Sprague, Charles
The Brothers.
Curiosity: Fiction.
Curiosity: The News.
The Family Meeting.
Indians.
The Winged Worshippers.

Spratt, Thomas
On His Mistress Drown'd.

**Sprigg, Christopher St. John See
"Caudwell, Christopher"**

Spriggs, Edward S.
For Brother Malcolm.
For the Truth.

Spring-Rice, Cecil Arthur
I Am the Dean of Christ
Church, Sir.
In Memoriam, A.C.M.L.
(excerpt).

Springer, Thomas Grant
Giving and Forgiving.
Harmony.

Sprod, G. N.
Request Numbers.

Sproull, Lyman H.
The Emigrant's Child.
The Stationed Scout.

Sprouse, Sarah Elizabeth
A Little Song of Work.

Spurrier, Linda Westfall
Lines for the Planned
Parenthood Clinic.

Squire, J. C.
Another Generation.
Approaching America.
Ballade of Soporific
Absorption.
The Birds.

Break, Break, Break (parody).
The Celtic Lyric (parody).
Country Wooing (parody)
  (excerpt).
A Dog's Death.
Doris and Philemon (parody)
  (excerpt).
Elegy in the Cemetery of
  Spoon River...(parody).
An Epitaph.
The Everlasting Mercy
  (parody).
The Exquisite Sonnet.
The Hands-Across-the-Sea
  Poem.
The Happy Night.
Honesty at a Fire.
It Did Not Last.
The Little Commodore
  (parody).
The March.
My Father's Cot (parody)
  (excerpt).
Numerous Celts (parody).
The Passing of Arthur
  (parody).
The Poor Old Man (parody).
She Dwelt aong the
  Untrodden Ways (parody).
The Ship.
Sonnet.
The Swallow (parody)
  (excerpt).
There Was an Indian.
The Three Hills.
To a Bull-Dog.
To a Roman.
To Miss L.F.... (parody).
Under.
A Vision of Truth.

Squire, Sir John Collings
Ballade of the Poetic Life.
The Discovery.
If Pope Had Written "Break,
  Break, Break".
Interior.
The Pipe.
The Stockyard.
Winter Nightfall.

Stack, Philip
Admonition.

Staff, Leopold
The Golden Elegy.

Stafford, Wendell Phillips
America Resurgent.
Invocation.
Washington and Lincoln.

Stafford, William
Accountability.
Across Kansas.
An Address to the
  Vacationers at Cape
  Lookout.
Adults Only.
After Plotinus.
Among Strangers.
The Animal That Drank Up
  Sound.
Any Time.
Around You, Your House.
Ask Me.
At Cove on the Crooked
  River.
At the Bomb Testing Site.
At the Edge of Town.
At the Grave of My Brother.
At the Klamath Berry
  Festival.
At the Playground.
At the Un-National
  Monument along the
  Canadian Border.

A Baby Ten Months Old
  Looks at the Public Domain.
Before the Big Storm.
Behind the Falls.
Berkeley, Madison, Ann
  Arbor, Kent...
Bess.
A Bird inside a Box.
Birthday.
Bring the North.
Broken Home.
Ceremony.
Chickens the Weasel Killed.
The Concealment: Ishi, the
  Last Wild Indian.
The Day You Are Reading
  This.
Drummer Boy.
Ducks down in the Meadow.
Earth Dweller.
The Epitaph Ending in And.
The Escape.
An Evening Walk.
Fall Journey.
Fall Wind.
A Family Turn.
The Farm on the Great
  Plains.
Father and Son.
Father's Voice.
Fifteen.
The Fish Counter at
  Bonneville.
For a Child Gone to Live in a
  Commune.
For a Daughter Gone Away.
For a Plaque on the Door of
  an Isolated House.
For the Grave of Daniel
  Boone.
Found in a Storm.
Friend Who Never Came.
Friends.
Help from History.
Holding the Sky.
Humanities Lecture.
In a Museum in the Capital.
In Dear Detail, by Ideal
  Light.
In Fur.
In the Deep Channel.
In the Morning All Over.
In the Oregon Country.
In Time of Need.
An Introduction to Some
  Poems.
Lake Chelan.
Late at Night.
Late, Passing Prairie Farm.
Letter from Oregon.
Listening.
Long Distance.
Look.
Looking West.
Magic Lantern.
Maybe Alone on My Bike.
Memorandum.
A Message from Space.
Moles.
The Moment.
Monday.
Montana Eclogue.
The Mountain That Got
  Little.
Mouse Night: One of Our
  Games.
My Father: October 1942.
Near.
Notice What This Poem Is
  Not Doing.
Now.
Observation Car and Cigar.

Old Dog.
On Being Invited to a
  Testmonial Dinner.
One Home.
An Oregon Message.
Our Kind.
Outside.
Parentage.
Passing Remark.
Peace Walk.
People of the South Wind.
People Who Went by in
  Winter.
Priest Lake.
Quiet Town.
Religion Back Home.
Remembering Althea.
Report from a Far Place.
Requiem.
The Rescued Year.
Returned to Say.
Right Now.
A Ritual to Read to Each
  Other.
Room 000.
Sayings from the Northern
  Ice.
School Days.
Shepherd.
So Long.
Some Night Again.
A Sound from the Earth.
The Stick in the Forest.
Stories from Kansas.
A Story.
A Story That Could Be True.
The Stranger Not Ourselves.
Strangers.
Strokes.
Surviving a Poetry Circuit.
The Swerve.
Testimony to an Inquisitor.
These Days.
These Leaves.
Things That Happen.
This Town: Winter Morning.
Together Again.
Tornado.
Touches.
Traveling through the Dark.
The Trip.
Trouble-Shooting.
Ultimate Problems.
Vacation.
Vacation Trip.
The View from Here.
Walking the Wilderness.
Walking with Your Eyes Shut.
Ways of Seeing.
The Well Rising.
West of Your City.
Whatever Comes.
When We Looked Back.
The Whole Story.
Winterward.
With Kit, Age 7, at the
  Beach.
With My Crowbar Key.

Stager, Carol
In Its Place.

Stagnelius, Erik Johann
Memory.

Stalker, Philip A.
Talk.

Stallworthy, Jon
Again.
The Almond Tree.
The Beginning of the End.
Camel.
First Blood.
Here and There.
A Letter from Berlin.

Letter to a Friend.
Miss Lavender.
A Poem about Poems about
  Vietnam.
A Question of Form and
  Content.
Sindhi Woman.
The Source.
This Morning.
A True Confession.
Walking against the Wind.
War Story.

Stam, Betty Scott
Christmas.
Open My Eyes.

Stamp, Catriona
Rebirth.

Stampa, Gaspara
At dawn of the day the
  Creator.
Deeply Repentant of My
  Sinful Ways.
Holy angels, in envy I cast no
  sigh.
Hunger.
I Am Now So Weary with
  Waiting.
If I Could Believe That
  Death.
Love Made Me Such That I
  Live in Fire.
Often I Compare My Lord to
  Heaven.
Often when alone I liken my
  lord.
The Stars Have Given Me a
  Hard Fate.
When before those eyes, my
  life and light.
Women, whoever wishes to
  know my lord.

Stanaback, Lucille
Discouraged.

Standing, Sue
Dead Neck.

Stanely, Thomas
To One That Pleaded Her
  Own Want of Merit.

Stanfield, Leontine
The Little Cat Angel.

Stanford, Ann
The Bear.
Before.
The Center of the Garden.
Ceremonies.
The Deserted Garden.
The Genie.
The Gift.
Going Away.
The Omens.
Robert Fulton.
The Umbrella.
The Voices Inescapable.
Weeds.

Stanford, Derek
Carol for His Darling on
  Christmas Day.
The Tomb of Honey Snaps Its
  Marble Chains.

Stanford, Frank
Death and the Arkansas
  River.

Stanford, W. B.
Angelus-Time near Dublin.
Before Salamis.
To a Greek Ship in the Port
  of Dublin.
Undertone.

Stange, Ken
Poem on the End of
  Sensation.

Stanhope, Philip *See*
  **Chesterfield, Philip Stanhope,
  Earl of**
Stanhope, Rosamund
  At Eighty.
Stanley, Mary
  Per Diem et per Noctem.
  Record Perpetual Loss.
  The Wife Speaks.
Stanley, Robert M.
  Not Blindly in the Dark.
Stanley, Thomas
  All Things Drink.
  Beauty.
  La Belle Confidente.
  La Belle Ennemie.
  The Bracelet.
  Celia Singing.
  Chang'd, Yet Constant.
  The Combat.
  A Deposition from Beauty.
  The Divorce.
  Epigram: "Would I were air
    that thou with heat opprest."
  The Exequies.
  Expectation.
  The Farewell.
  The Leaves Come Again.
  Loves Heretick.
  The Magnet.
  Old I Am.
  On a Violet in Her Breast.
  Pan Piping.
  The Picture.
  The Relapse.
  The Repulse.
  Roses.
  The Snow-Ball.
  Song: "Fool, take up thy shaft
    again."
  Song: "I prithee let my heart
    alone."
  Song: "When I lie burning in
    thine eye."
  Spring.
  The Swallow.
  To Celia Pleading Want of
    Merit.
  The Tombe.
  When I Loved Thee.
  The Wish.
  Youthful Age.
Stansbury, Joseph
  The Lords of the Main.
  A New Song: "Has the
    Marquis La Fayette."
  To Cordelia.
Stansbury, Mary A. P.
  How He Saved St. Michael's.
  The Surprise at Ticonderoga.
Stanton, Frank Lebby
  De Good Lawd Know My
    Name.
  The Graveyard Rabbit.
  Just a Wearyin' for You.
  Keep A-Goin'.
  A Little Way.
  Mighty Lak' a Rose.
  The Mocking-bird.
  The Old Hymns.
  One Country.
  Our Flag Forever.
  A Plantation Ditty.
  Sweetes' Li'l' Feller.
  "Tollable Well."
  Wearyin' fer You.
Stanton, Henry T.
  The Moneyless Man.
Stanton, Maura
  The All-Night Waitress.
  Biography.
  Childhood.

Extracts: from the Journal of
  Elisa Lynch.
Good People.
Judith Recalls Holofernes.
Letter to Kafka.
Little Ode for X.
Palinode.
Shoplifters.
The Wilderness.
Stanway, Phil
  Ten Sonnets for Today.
Stanyhurst, Richard
  Dido to Aeneas.
  Nature in Her Working.
  Of Tyndarus.
  A Prayer to the Trinity.
  Sometime Lively Gerald.
  To the Trinity.
Staples, Barbara H.
  Room for Jesus.
Stapylton, Sir Robert
  The Bard's Song.
Starbird, Kaye
  Minnie Morse.
  Whistling Willie.
Starbuck, George
  Albany Schmalbany.
  Aspects of Spring in Greater
    Boston.
  Bone Thoughts on a Dry Day.
  Chip.
  Clippety Cloppity.
  Cold Fire.
  Communication to the City
    Fathers of Boston.
  Cora Punctuated with
    Strawberries.
  Double Semi-Sestina.
  High Renaissance.
  Late Late.
  Magnificat in Transit from the
    Toledo Airport.
  Margaret Are You Drug.
  Monarch of the Sea.
  New Strain.
  Of Late.
  On First Looking in on
    Blodgett's Keats's
    "Chapman's Homer."
  One Man's Goose; or, Poetry
    Redefined.
  Out in the Cold.
  Pit Viper.
  Poems from a First Year in
    Boston.
  Said Agatha Christie.
  Said J. Alfred Prufrock.
  The Skin Divers.
  Sonnet with a Different Letter
    at the End of Every Line.
  The Spell Against Spelling.
  The Starry Night.
  Technologies.
  To His Chi Mistress.
  Translations from the English.
  The Universe Is Closed and
    Has REMs.
  Whaddaya Do for Action in
    This Place?
Starbuck, Victor
  Moon-Madness.
  Night for Adventures.
  The Seekers.
Starck, Mary
  The Reign of Peace.
Stark, Bradford
  Always Modern Times.
Starkey, James *See* **O'Sullivan,
  Seumas**
Starkweather, Pauline
  Two Mountains Men Have
    Climbed.

Statius Publius Papinius
  Ah, Now I Know What Day
    This Is.
  Epithalamium for Stella and
    Violentilla: Why Do You
    Dally So?
  Of the Night, Let the
    Bridegroom Sing.
  Sleep.
  Sylvae, II (excerpt).
  Wishes for a Bridal Couple
    and Their Unborn Child.
Staudt, David
  Circa 1814.
Stauffer, Donald A.
  The Bulldozer.
  The Lemmings.
  Time Zones for Forty-Four.
Staughton, William
  Tell Us, Ye Servants of the
    Lord.
Stead, C. K.
  A Small Registry of Births
    and Deaths: All Night It
    Bullied You.
  This May Be Your Captain
    Speaking.
  Twenty-One Sonnets.
  Walking Westward (excerpt).
  The Young Wife.
Stead, William Force
  How Infinite Are Thy Ways.
  I Closed My Eyes Today and
    Saw.
  Sweet Wild April.
  Uriel.
Stearns, L. D.
  Triumph.
**Stebbins, Mary Elizabeth
  (Dewitt)**
  Harold the Valiant.
  The Sunflower to the Sun.
Stedman, Edmund Clarence
  Aaron Burr's Wooing.
  Abraham Lincoln.
  The Ballad of Lager Bier.
  Corda Condordia: Quest.
  Cuba.
  Custer.
  The Discoverer.
  The Doorstep.
  Falstaff's Song.
  The Flight of the Birds.
  Gettysburg.
  Going A-Nutting.
  The Hand of Lincoln.
  Helen Keller.
  How Old Brown Took
    Harper's Ferry.
  Hymn of the West.
  Invocation.
  Israel Freyer's Bid for Gold.
  Kearny at Seven Pines.
  Liberty Enlightening the
    World.
  Morgan.
  A Mother's Picture.
  On a Great Man Whose Mind
    is Clouding.
  The Ordeal by Fire (excerpt).
  Pan in Wall Street.
  Peter Stuyvesant's New Year's
    Call.
  Provencal Lovers.
  Salem.
  Song from a Drama.
  Sumter.
  Toujours Amour.
  Treason's Last Device.
  Voice of the Western Wind.
  Wanted–A Man.
  The World Well Lost.

Steece, Arvel
  There Is Yet Time.
  World Planners.
Steegmuller, Francis
  Le Hibou et la Poussiquette.
Steel, Laura A.
  Limerick: "There was an
    exclusive old oyster."
Steele
  The Only Name Given Under
    Heaven.
Steele, Anne
  Compassion So Divine.
  The Great Redeemer Lives.
  O How Sweet Are Thy
    Words!
Steele, Frank
  Country Greeting.
  The Departure.
  Greener Grass.
  Markings.
  Moving.
  Rhymes.
  Shaggy Dog Story.
Steele, Peggy
  I Know a Man.
Steele, Peter
  Marking Time.
Steele, Silas S.
  Kiss Me Quick and Go.
  Walk, Jaw-Bone.
Steele, Sir Richard
  Song: "Me Cupid made a
    Happy Slave."
  Song: "Why, lovely charmer,
    tell me why."
  Trim's Song: The Fair
    Kitchen-Maid.
Steele, Timothy
  Here Lies Sir Tact.
  Murder Mystery.
  Sapphics Against Anger.
  Wait.
Steendam, Jacob
  The Complaint of New
    Amsterdam.
  Oh, Sing to God.
  The Praise of New
    Netherland.
  When I Admire the
    Greatness.
Steere, Richard
  Earth Felicities, Heavens
    Allowances. A Blank Poem.
  A Monumental Memorial of
    Marine Mercy &c.
  On a Sea-Storm Nigh the
    Coast.
  A Poem, upon the Caelestial
    Embassy Perform'd by
    Angels...
Steese, Edward
  Tenth Reunion.
Steiger, Anatoly
  An Ancient Custom.
  Words from the Window of a
    Railway Car.
Stein, Dona
  The Wing Factory.
Stein, Evaleen
  Budding-Time Too Brief.
  Flood-Time on the Marshes.
  In Mexico.
  In Youth.
  November Morning.
  Wild Beasts.
Stein, Gary
  Jogging.
Stein, Gertrude
  Accents in Alsace: Alsace or
    Alsatians.
  Afterwards (excerpt).

Before the Flowers of
Friendship Faded Faded,
XXI.
Cezanne.
Four Saints in Three Acts:
"Pigeons on the grass alas."
I Am Rose.
Ladies' Voices.
Land of Nations (excerpt).
The Mother of Us All: "We
cannot retrace our steps."
A Petticoat.
Prothalamium for Bobolink
and His Louisa A Poem.
Sacred Emily.
Sacred Family (excerpt).
Stanzas in Meditation.
Susie Asado.
Tender Buttons: Objects.
A Time to Eat.
A Waist.
The Watch on the Rhine.
Yet Dish.

Stein, Kurt M.
Mama's Advice.
Morning Song.
Reflection.
An Unserer Beach.
Vor a Gauguin Picture zu
Singen.

Steinbarg, Eliezer
The Bayonet and the Needle.
The Horse and the Whip.
Shatnes or Uncleanliness.
A Terrible Thought.
The Umbrella, the Cane, and
the Broom.
Where Is Justice?

Steinberg, David
Mason Jar.

Steinberg, Jakov
A Donkey Will Carry You.
The Heart.
With a Book at Twilight.
The World Is Not a Fenced-
Off Garden.

Steingart, Moishe
Generations.
The Last Fire.

Steingass, David
For a Friend.

Steinman, D. B.
Blueprint.

"Stella" *See* **Johnson, Ester**

Stellwagon, Russell
In Memory of Two Sons.

Stembridge, Jane
City.
Loving.
Mrs. Hamer.

Stencl, A. N.
Ezekiel.

Stenhouse, William
The Empty Jar.

Stennett Samuel
Majestic Sweetness.

Stepanchev, Stephen
Autumn Song.
Inner Brother.
No Furlough.
Strength to War.

Stephanou, Lydia
A "Case of Assault."

Stephany
In the Silence.
Let Me Be Held When the
Longing Comes.
My Love When This Is Past.
That We Head Towards.
Who Is Not a Stranger Still.

Stephen, A. M.
Bring Torches.

Capilano.

Stephen, James Kenneth
The Ballade of the
Incompetent Ballade-Monger.
The burning–at first–would be
probably worst.
Cynicus to W. Shakspere.
Drinking Song.
An Election Address.
England and America.
A Grievance (parody).
In the Backs.
The Last Ride Together
(From Her Point of View)
(parody).
The Old School List.
A Remonstrance.
Senex to Matt. Prior.
Sincere Flattery of R. B.
Sincere Flattery of W. W.
A Sonnet: "Two voices are
there."
The Splinter.
A Thought.
To R. K. (parody).

Stephens, Alan
Prologue: Moments in a
Glade.

Stephens, Brunton
The Dominion of Australia.
My Other Chinee Cook.

Stephens, James
April Showers.
Blue Blood.
Breakfast Time.
The Cage.
The Canal Bank.
The Centaurs.
Check.
Chill of the Eve.
Christmas in Freelands.
College of Surgeons.
The Crackling Twig.
Crest Jewel.
The Daisies.
Danny Murphy.
Dark Wings.
Deirdre.
The Devil's Bag.
Egan O Rahilly.
Evening.
An Evening Falls.
Fossils.
The Frozen Logger.
A Glass of Beer.
The Goat Paths.
Good and Bad.
Hate.
Hawks.
In the Night.
In the Orchard.
In Waste Places.
The Lake.
Little Things.
The Main-Deep.
Midnight.
O Bruadair.
Odell.
On a Lonely Spray.
The Outcast.
The Paps of Dana.
The Pit of Bliss.
Psychometrist.
The Red-Haired Man's Wife.
The Rivals.
The Road.
Sarasvati.
The Satyr.
The Secret.
Seumas Beg.
The Shell.
The Snare.

Sweet Apple.
Tanist.
Theme.
To the Four Courts, Please.
The Turn of the Road.
A Visit from Abroad.
The Voice of God.
Washed in Silver.
The Waste Places.
The Watcher.
Westland Row.
What the Devil Said.
What Thomas an Buile Said
in a Pub.
The Whisperer.
White Fields.
The White Window.
Why Tomas Cam Was
Grumpy.
Wind.
A Woman Is a Branchy Tree.

Stephens, James Brunton
The Gentle Anarchist.

Stephens, Michael
The Good Ship.
Mom's Homecooked Trees.

Stephens, William
The Eyes Have It.
Standard Forgings Plant.

Stepney, George
On the University of
Cambridge's Burning the
Duke of Monmouth's...

Sterling, Andrew B.
Coax Me.
Meet Me in St. Louis.
On a Sunday Afternoon.
Under the Anheuser Bush.
What You Goin' to Do When
the Rent Comes 'Round?

Sterling, George
The Abalone Song.
The Black Vulture.
The City by the Sea.
The Cool, Grey City of Love.
Father Coyote.
The Final Faith.
The Gardens of the Sea.
The Guerdon of the Sun.
In Extremis.
The Last Days.
The Master Mariner.
Music at Twilight.
Omnia Exeunt in Mysterium.
Pumas.
Sails.
Saul.
Sonnets on the Sea's Voice.
Three Sonnets on Oblivion.

Sterling, John
Alfred the Harper.
Louis XV.

Stern, Bert
Looking for a Home.

Stern, David E.
Old Man.

Stern, Gerald
96 Vandam.
At Bickford's.
Baja.
Days of 1978.
Hanging Scroll.
I Remember Galileo.
Immensity.
Modern Love.
One Foot in the River.
The Power of Maples.
Straus Park.
Your Animal.

Stern, Noah
Grave at Cassino.
His Mother's Love.

Sternberg, Jacob
Little Birds.

Sternhold, Thomas
I Lift My Heart to Thee.
The Lord Descended from
Above.
The Majesty of God.
My Shepherd Is the Living
Lord.

Sternlieb, Barry
Valley Blood.

Sterry, Joseph Ashby
Spring's Delights.

Stetler, Charles
Arf, Said Sandy.
Free Enterprise.
The Graduate.
Jeep.
A Man of Action.
Policy of the House.
To Ellen.
A Toast.
World's Fare.

Stetson, Charlotte Perkins *See*
**Gilman, Charlotte Perkins
Stetson**

Stevens, Alex
In Scorching Time.

Stevens, George Alexander
Bartleme Fair.
Maria.
A Pastoral.
Repentance.
A Simple Pastoral.

Stevens, George W.
The Organist.

Stevens, Maxine
How Can You?

Stevens, Wallace
Academic Discourse at
Havana.
Anatomy of Monotony.
Anecdote of the Jar.
Anecdote of the Prince of
Peacocks.
Angel Surrounded by Paysans.
Anglais Mort a Florence.
Annual Gaiety.
Another Weeping Woman.
Arrival at the Waldorf.
As You Leave the Room.
Asides on the Oboe.
The Auroras of Autumn.
Autumn Refrain.
Bantams in Pine-Woods.
The Beginning.
Bethou Me, Said Sparrow.
The Bird with the Coppery,
Keen Claws.
Bouquet of Belle Scavoir.
The Brave Man.
The Candle A Saint.
The Comedian as the Letter
C.
Connoisseur of Chaos.
Conquistador: The Argument.
Continual Conversation with a
Silent Man.
Contrary Theses (I).
Converstion with Three
Women of New England.
The Course of a Particular.
Credences of Summer.
Crude Foyer.
Cuisine Bourgeoise.
The Curtains in the House of
the Metaphysician.
Dance of the Macabre Mice.
The Death of a Soldier.
Depression before Spring.
Disillusionment of Ten
O'Clock.

Domination of Black.
Dry Loaf.
Earthy Anecdote.
The Emperor of Ice Cream.
Esthetique du Mal.
Evening without Angels.
Extracts from Addresses to the Academy of Fine Ideas (excerpt).
Final Soliloquy of the Interior Paramour.
Flyer's Fall.
Gallant Chateau.
Girl in a Nightgown.
The Glass of Water.
The Great Statue of the General Du Puy.
Gubbinal.
Hibiscus on the Sleeping Shores.
High Poetry and Low.
A High-Toned Old Christian Woman.
Holiday in Reality.
Homunculus et la Belle Etoile.
The House Was Quiet and the World Was Calm.
The Idea of Order at Key West.
Idiom of the Hero.
In the Carolinas.
The Indigo Glass in the Grass.
The Irish Cliffs of Moher.
It Feels Good as It Is Without the Giant.
It Is the Celestial Ennui of Apartments.
Large Red Man Reading.
Less and Less Human, O Savage Spirit.
Life Is Motion.
The Lion Roars at the Enraging Desert.
Lions in Sweden.
Lunar Paraphrase.
Man Carrying Thing.
The Man on the Dump.
The Man with the Blue Guitar.
Martial Cadenza.
The Mechanical Optimist.
Men Made out of Words.
Metamorphosis.
Metaphor as Degeneration.
Metaphors of a Magnifico.
Le Monocle de Mon Oncle.
The Motive for Metaphor.
Mozart, 1935.
Mrs. Alfred Uruguay.
No Possum, No Sop, No Taters.
Nomad Exquisite.
Not Ideas about the Thing but the Thing Itself.
Notes Toward a Supreme Fiction: The President Ordains the Bee to Be.
Nuances of a Theme by Williams.
Of Mere Being.
Of Modern Poetry.
Of the Surface of Things.
On an Old Horn.
On the Road Home.
The Ordinary Women.
The Owl in the Sarcophagus.
The Paltry Nude Starts on a Spring Voyage.
Parochial Theme.
Peter Quince at the Clavier.
The Place of the Solitaires.

The Plain Sense of Things.
The Planet on the Table.
The Pleasures of Merely Circulating.
The Plot against the Giant.
Ploughing on Sunday.
The Poem That Took the Place of a Mountain.
The Poems of Our Climate.
Poetry Is a Destructive Force.
A Postcard from the Volcano.
The Prejudice against the Past.
Presence of an External Master of Knowledge.
A Primitive Like an Orb.
Prologues to What Is Possible.
Puella Parvula.
A Quiet Normal Life.
A Rabbit as King of the Ghosts.
Re-Statement of Romance.
Reality Is an Activity of the Most August Imagination.
Repetitions of a Young Captain.
The River of Rivers in Connecticut.
The Rock.
A Room on a Garden.
Sad Strains of a Gay Waltz.
Sailing after Lunch.
Sea Surface Full of Clouds.
The Sense of the Sleight-of-Hand Man.
The Snow Man.
So-and-So Reclining on Her Couch.
Soldier, There Is a War between the Mind.
Song of Fixed Accord.
The Souls of Women at Night.
Statue against a Clear Sky.
Study of Two Pears.
Sunday Morning.
Sur Ma Guzzla Gracile.
Table Talk.
Tattoo.
These Locusts by Day.
Thirteen Ways of Looking at a Blackbird.
This Solitude of Cataracts.
To an Old Philosopher in Rome.
To the One of Fictive Music.
Two Figures in Dense Violet Light.
Two Illustrations That the World Is What You Make of It.
The Ultimate Poem is Abstract.
Vacancy in the Park.
We Reason of These Things.
The Well Dressed Man with a Beard.
What We See Is What We Think.
When Was It That the Particles Became.
Whistle Aloud, Too Weedy Wren.
The Woman in Sunshine.
Woman Looking at a Vase of Flowers.
The Woman That Had More Babies Than That.
The World as Meditation.
World without Peculiarity.
Stevenson, Alec Brock
Et Sa Pauvre Chair.

Stevenson, Anne
After Her Death.
By the Boat House, Oxford.
The Dear Ladies of Cincinnati.
The Demolition.
From an Asylum: Kathy Chattle to Her Mother, Ruth Arbeiter.
Giving Rabbit to My Cat Bonnie.
Himalayan Balsam.
Indian Summer: Vermont.
Love.
The Mudtower.
North Sea Off Carnoustie.
Sous-Entendu.
Stabilities.
The Suburb.
Suicide.
Utah.
Stevenson, Burton Egbert
Henry Hudson's Quest.
The Peace Message.
Stevenson, Candace Thurber
Public Library.
Signatures.
Stevenson, D. E.
Six and Thirty.
Stevenson, James
The Gallant Fighting "Joe."
Stevenson, Lionel
Gulls and Dreams.
In a Desert Town.
Summer Interlude.
Stevenson, Matthew
Song.
Stevenson, Patric
Anglo-Eire Vignette.
Autumnal Consummation.
Corn Canon.
Dogrose.
Stevenson, Robert Louis
Alcaics: to H. F. B.
As with Heaped Bees at Hiving Time.
At the Sea-Side.
Autumn Fires.
Away with Funeral Music.
Bed in Summer.
Block City.
Browning.
Camper's Night Song.
The Canoe Speaks (excerpt).
The Careful Angler.
The Celestial Surgeon.
Christmas at Sea.
A Christmas Prayer.
A Christmas Sermon: To Be Honest, To Be Kind.
The Cow.
The Day Returns.
Ditty to an Air from Bach.
The Dumb Soldier.
Escape at Bedtime.
Evensong.
Fair Isle at Sea.
Farewell to the Farm.
Foreign Children.
Foreign Lands.
From a Railway Carriage.
The Gardener.
Gather Ye Roses.
Go, Little Book.
Good and Bad Children.
A Good Play.
Happy Thought.
He Hears with Gladdened Heart the Thunder.
Heather Ale.
Henry James.
Home No More Home to Me.

The House Beautiful.
I Am a Hunchback.
I Have Trod the Upward and the Downward Slope.
I Saw Red Evening through the Rain.
I Will Make You Brooches.
Ille Terrarum.
In Autumn When the Woods Are Red.
In Memoriam F. A. S.
In the Highlands.
In the States.
It's an Owercome Sooth for Age an' Youth.
The Lamplighter.
The Land of Counterpane.
The Land of Story-Books.
Last Night We Had a Thunderstorm in Style.
The Little Land.
Looking Forward.
Man Sails the Deep a While.
Marching Song.
A Mile an' a Bittock.
The Morning Drum-Call on My Eager Ear.
My Bed Is a Boat.
My House, I Say. But Hark to the Sunny Doves.
My Shadow.
My Ship and I.
My Valentine.
My Wife.
Nest Eggs.
Not I.
O to Be Up and Doing.
Over the Sea to Skye.
Pirate Story.
A Portrait.
Prayer.
A Prayer for the Household.
Rain.
Requiem.
Romance.
Say Not of Me That Weakly I Declined.
The Sick Child.
Since Thou Hast Given Me This Good Hope, O God.
Singing.
Skerryvore.
So Live, So Love, So Use That Fragile Hour.
A Song of the Road.
Songs of Travel.
The Spaewife.
Stormy Nights.
Summer Sun.
The Swing.
System.
Thou Strainest through the Mountain Fern.
Though He That Ever Kind and True.
Ticonderoga: A Legend of the West Highlands.
Time to Rise.
To a Gardener.
To an Island Princess.
To K. de M.
To Mrs. Will H. Low.
To N. V. de. G. S.
To the Muse.
Travel.
Tropic Rain.
The Vagabond.
Verses Written In 1872.
A Visit from the Sea.
When I am grown to man's estate.
Where Go the Boats?

Whole Duty of Children.
The Wind.
Windy Nights.
Winter Time.
Stevenson, William Frederick
Gammer Gurton's Needle:
Back and Side, Go Bare.
Life and Impellance.
Of Jolly Good Ale and Old.
A Planet of Descendance.
Steward, Joseph
God from His Throne with
Piercing Eye.
My Soul Would Fain Indulge
a Hope.
Stewart, Arthur
Fossils.
Stewart, Douglas
At the Entrance.
The Birdsville Track.
Brindabella.
The Bunyip.
A Country Song.
The Dosser in Springtime.
The Fisherman.
The Garden of Ships.
Glencoe.
Green Lions.
Helmet Orchid.
Lady Feeding the Cats
(excerpt).
Leopard Skin.
Mahony's Mountain.
Mending the Bridge.
Nesting Time.
Old Iron.
Rock Carving.
The Silkworms.
The Snow-Gum.
The Sunflowers.
Terra Australis.
Two Englishmen.
Stewart, Frank
Another Color.
Stewart, George Craig
As I Went Down to David's
Town.
Stewart, Gervase
The Landscape Lies Within
My Head.
Poem: "I burn for England
with a living flame."
Poem: "I take four devils with
me when I ride."
Red Cross Nurses.
Stewart, Harold
Dialogue of the Way.
Lament in Autumn.
The Leaf-Makers.
The Sage in Unison.
Stewart, Pamela
Central Park, 1916.
Punk Pantoum.
Stewart, Phillips
Hope.
Stewart, Robert
Ballet under the Stars.
The Plumber Arrives at Three
Mile Island.
Stewart, W.
Aristocrats of Labor.
The True Aristocrat.
Stewart, William
Thir Lenterne Dayis ar Luvely
Lang.
Stewart of Baldynnis, John
Medoro's Inscription for a
Cave.
To His Darrest Freind.
Stickney, Helen Frith
Habitue.

Stickney, Trumbull
Age in Youth.
At Sainte-Marguerite.
An Athenian Garden.
Be Still. The Hanging
Gardens Were a Dream.
Dramatic Fragment.
Driftwood.
Fidelity.
He Said: "If in His Image I
Was Made."
I Hear a River.
If I Have Wronged You.
If You Should Lightly.
In Ampezzo.
In Summer.
In the Past.
Leave Him Now Quiet.
Like a Pearl Dropped.
Live Blindly.
Love, I Marvel What You
Are.
The Melancholy Year.
Mnemosyne.
Near Helikon.
Not That, If You Had
Known.
Now in the Palace Gardens.
On Some Shells Found Inland.
The Passions That We Fought
With.
Six O'Clock.
Sonnets from Greece: Mount
Lykaion.
The Soul of Time.
This Is the Violin.
With Long Black Wings.
Stidger, William L.
The Cross and the Tree.
A Day.
I Saw God Wash the World.
Lest Thou Forget.
Motherhood.
The Waste of War.
We Are the Burden-Bearers
(excerpt).
Stiles, Nina
Thank You, God.
Still, James
Clabe Mott.
Dance on Pushback.
Rain on the Cumberlands.
Spring.
The Trees in the Road.
Uncle Ambrose.
With Hands Like Leaves.
Stillingfleet, Benjamin
Sonnet: True Ambition.
Stillman, Albert
Ballad of the Faithful Clerk.
The Truth about B. F.
When I Am Dead.
Stillman, Annie R.
Birth.
Stilwell, Joseph W.
Lyric to Spring.
Stineford, Raymond
Breathe on the Glass.
Stinson, Sam S.
Limerick: "Two ladies with
high social aims."
**Stirling, William Alexander,
Earl of**
Aurora.
Stirling-Maxwell, William
To Anne.
Stitch, Wilhelmina
Blessed Are They.
Little Roads to Happiness.
Stites, Edgar P.
I've Reached the Land of
Corn and Wine.

Stockard, Henry Jerome
As Some Mysterious
Wanderer of the Skies.
The Mocking-bird.
Over Their Graves.
Stocking, Jay T.
O Master Workman of the
Race.
Stockton, John H.
Come, Every Soul.
Stockwell, Brenda S.
Academic Affair.
Chances.
Easter Flood.
Stodart, M. A.
One Thing at a Time.
Stodart-Walker, Archibald
Counsel to Girls.
Early Bacon.
I Had a Duck.
Inflictis.
Stoddard, Charles Warren
Albatross.
Ave-Maria Bells.
The Bells of San Gabriel.
The Cocoa-Tree.
A Rhyme of Life.
The Royal Mummy to
Bohemia.
Stigmata.
The Toast.
Wind and Wave.
Stoddard, Elizabeth
In the Still, Star-Lit Night.
Last Days.
Mercedes.
November.
On the Campagna.
The Poet's Secret.
A Summer Night.
Unreturning.
Stoddard, Lavinia
The Soul's Defiance.
Stoddard, Richard Henry
Abraham Lincoln.
Adsum.
Arab Song.
At Last.
Birds.
A Catch.
Colonel Ellsworth.
The Divan.
The Dying Lover.
The Falcon.
The Flight of the Arrow.
The Flight of Youth.
A Gazelle.
A Hymn to the Sea.
The Jar.
The Little Drummer.
The Lover.
Men of the North and West.
Mors et Vita.
An Old Song Reversed.
The Sea.
The Shadow.
Songs.
Threescore and Ten.
Twilight on Sumter.
The Two Anchors.
Wine and Dew.
The Witch's Whelp.
Stoddart, Thomas Tod
Her, A Statue.
Mirthful Lunacy.
The Angler's Invitation.
Stokebury, Leon
Morning Song.
Stokes, Francis G.
Blue Moonshine.
Stokes, Frank
'Tain't Nobody's Business.

You Shall.
Stokes, Terry
All Morning.
The Blood Supply in New
York City Is Low.
Crimes of Passion.
The Farmer.
Giving the Moon a New
Chance.
A Man All Grown Up Is
Supposed To.
Travis, the Kid Was All
Heart.
Stokes, Whitley
The Viking.
Stokes, Will
Bugs.
Stokesbury, Leon
Beef.
Day Begins at Governor's
Square Mall.
East Texas.
A Funny Joke.
Gifts.
The Lover Remembereth Such
as He Sometimes Enjoyed...
To His Book.
To Laura Phelan: 1880-1906.
Unsent Message to My
Brother in His Pain.
Stoloff, Carolyn
Dinosaurs.
Stoltzenberg, Abo
The French Mood.
In Vistas of Stone.
What Am I?
Stone, Arlene
Germination.
Stone, John
Coming Home.
Double-Header.
Even Though.
An Example of How a Daily
Temporary Madness Can
Help a Man...
Explaining about the
Dachshund.
How I'd Have It.
Stone, Ruth
Advice.
Bargain.
Beginning to Live.
Codicil.
Dark Conclusions.
Denouement.
Green Apples.
Hunger.
I Have Three Daughters.
In an Iridescent Time.
In the Interstices.
Liberation.
The Magnet.
On the Mountain.
Orchard.
Periphery.
Private Pantomime.
Repetition of Words and
Weather.
Room.
Salt.
Snow.
The Talking Fish.
Vernal Equinox.
The Watcher.
Whose Scene?
Winter.
Years Later.
Stone, Samuel John
The Church's One
Foundation.
Stone, Walter
Compelled to Love.

Couple.
Nature.
On the Welsh Marches.
Stoner, Winifred Sackville
The History of the U.S.
Stopple, Libby
Calvary.
Storer, Thomas
Rivers.
Storey, Violet Alleyn
Dawn Song–St. Patrick's Day.
Neighborly.
A Prayer after Illness.
Prayer for a Very New Angel.
A Prayer for Broken Little
Families.
A Prayer for the New Year.
Prayer in Affliction.
A Prayer in Late Autumn.
Rainy Day Song.
Stork, Charles Wharton
A Bronze Statuette of Kwan-
Yin.
A Flemish Madonna.
God, You have Been Too
Good to Me.
A Painter in New England.
The Rose and God.
The Troubadour of God.
Storni, Alfonsina
Ancestral Weight.
Funeral Notices.
I Am Going to Sleep.
Lighthouse in the Night.
Men in the City.
My Sister.
Pain.
Sierra.
They've Come.
Words to My Mother.
Story, William Wetmore
Cleopatra.
The English Language.
Io Victis.
Snowdrop.
The Violet.
Stott, John G.
The Scottish Mountaineering
Club Song.
Stout, Liz
Waiting.
Stoutenburg, Adrien
Ants and Others.
Assembly Line.
Avalanche.
The Bear Who Came to
Dinner.
Brobdingnag.
Channel U.S.A.–Live.
Cicada.
Dogskin Rug.
Ivory Paper Weight.
Jack Rabbit.
Model T.
Rhinoceros.
Sky Diver.
Traveller's Guide to
Antarctica.
V.D. Clinic.
Stow, Randolph
As He Lay Dying.
Dust.
The Enemy.
The Ghost at Anlaby.
Mad Maid's Whim.
My Wish for My Land.
Ruins of the City of Hay.
The Singing Bones.
Strange Fruit.
Thailand Railway.
The Utopia of Lord Mayor
Howard.

Stowe, Harriet Beecher
Abide in Me, O Lord, and I
in Thee.
Hymn.
The Other World.
Still, Still with Thee.
When Winds Are Raging.
Stowman, Annette Burr
Fly, Ladybug.
Strabo, Wilafrid
To His Friend in Absence.
Strachan, Ian
The Silent Walls.
Silver in the Wind.
Strachey, Lytton
Cat.
Strachey, William
Aecclesiae et Reipub.
Strada, Famianus
The Nightingale.
Strahan, Bradley R.
Shabbat Morning.
Strahan, Speer
The Mad Lover.
The Poor.
Straley, John
Limerick: "There was a young
fellow from Boise."
Strand, Mark
The Babies.
Black Maps.
Breath.
The Coming of Light.
Coming to This.
Courtship.
The Dance.
The Dead.
The Door.
The Dreadful Has Already
Happened.
The Dress.
Eating Poetry.
Elegy for My Father.
For Her.
From a Litany.
The Garden.
Keeping Things Whole.
The Kite.
The Last Bus.
The Late Hour.
Letter.
The Man in Black.
The Man in the Mirror.
The Man in the Tree.
The Map.
The Marriage.
Moontan.
A Morning.
My Life by Somebody Else.
My Mother on an Evening in
Late Summer.
Night Piece.
Nights in Hackett's Cove.
The Prediction.
The Remains.
Shooting Whales.
Sleeping with One Eye Open.
Tomorrow.
The Tunnel.
Violent Storm.
When the Vacation Is Over
for Good.
Where Are the Waters of
Childhood?
You and It.
Strato
Epigram: "All through the
night."
Epigram: "At even, when the
hour drew nigh."
Epigram: "Boys' cocks,
Diodore."

Epigram: "Even if I try not to
ogle a boy in the street."
Epigram: "Gathering the
bloom of all the fairest boys
that be."
Epigram: "How shall I know
if my love lose his youth."
Epigram: "I am provoked."
Epigram: "I delight in the
prime of a boy of twelve."
Epigram: "I like them pale."
Epigram: "Like when the
burning sun doth rise."
Epigram: "Long hair, endless
curls."
Epigram: "Now art thou fair,
Diodorus."
Epigram: "Oh! Trouble not
Menedemos by guile."
Epigram: "Passing the flower-
stalls."
Epigram: "Perchance some
coming after."
Epigram: "Stolen kisses, wary
eyes."
Epigram: "There was this gym
teacher."
Epigram: "Those snooty boys
in all their purple drag."
Epigram: "Thy eyes are
sparks, Lycines."
Epigram: "When Graphicus
sat by the baths."
Epigram: "You recline that
magnificent pair of
buttocks."
Strauss, Avner
The Hollow Flute.
In the Discreet Splendor.
Lament for the European
Exile.
On the Path.
Portrait of a Widow.
Voice in the Dark.
Strawson, J. Adair
Limerick: "The bachelor
growls when his peace is."
"Streamer, Col. D." See
Graham, Harry
Strebeck, George
A Joyful Sound It Is.
Street, Alfred Billings
The Loon.
The Settler.
Streeter, Sebastian
A King Shall Reign in
Righteousness.
Lo, What Enraptured Songs
of Praise.
Stricklin, Robert
Hoot Owl Shift.
Stringer, Arthur
At the Comedy.
Memories.
Morning in the North-West.
Sappho's Tomb.
The Sod-Breaker.
There Is Strength in the Soil.
A Wanderer's Litany.
Stringer, R. E. C.
Sartorial Solecism.
Stripling, Kathryn
Lullabye.
Strobel, Marion
Another Song.
Captive.
Frightened Face.
Little Things.
Pastoral.
Stroblas, Laurie
Circumstance.

Strode, William
I'll tell you whence the Rose
did first grow red.
In Commendation of Music.
My Limbs I Will Fling.
My Love and I for Kisses
Play'd.
On a Gentlewoman Walking
in the Snowe.
On the Death of Mistress
Mary Prideaux.
On Westwell Downs.
Strodtmann, Adolf
O Spring, Come Prettily In.
Strong, George
The Epiphany.
Strong, George A.
The Modern Hiawatha
(parody).
Strong, Julia Hurd
The Huckster's Horse.
Son and Surf.
Strong, Leonard Alfred George
The Appointment.
The Brewer's Man.
Coroner's Jury.
Departure.
The Door.
Evening before Rain.
The Greek Anthology
(excerpt).
In Camus Fields.
In the Lane.
The Knowledgeable Child.
Lowery Cot.
The Mad Woman of Punnet's
Town.
Man's Way.
March Evening.
A Memory.
Mother of Ten.
The Mysteries.
Old Dan'l.
The Old Man at the Crossing.
An Old Woman, outside the
Abbey Theater.
The Return.
Rufus Prays.
Safe for Democracy.
Sheepstor.
Two Generations.
Zeke.
Strong, Nathan
Almighty Sovereign of the
Skies!
The Summer Harvest Spreads
the Fields.
Swell the Anthem, Raise the
Song.
Strong, Phillips Burrows
The Tongue.
Strongin, Josephine
Poem.
Strongin, Lynn
Emily Dickinson Postage
Stamp.
From: First Aspen.
Miniatures IV. Mute the
Hand Moves from the Heart.
Sayre.
Strongwolf, Chief Joseph
Indian Prayer.
Stroud, Dorothy Conant
The Bible.
He Lives! He Lives to Bless!
His Life Is Ours.
No Room.
Not One Is Turned away from
God.
You Will Find a Joy in
Service.

Stroud, Joseph
Above Machu Picchu, 129
Baker Street, San Francisco.
As for Me, I Delight in the
Everyday Way.
Below Mount T'ui K'oy,
Home of the Gods....
City.
Documentary.
Dragon.
Exile.
The Gold Country: Hotel
Leger, Mokelumne Hill,
Revisited.
Grandfather.
Lament.
Machupuchare. What the
Mountain Said. Shaking the
Dead Bones...
Memory.
Monte Alban.
Naming.
Poem on the Suicide of My
Teacher.
Poem to Han-Shan.
Poem to My Father.
Proportions.
The Room above the White
Rose.
Sibyl.
Signature.
To Christopher Smart.
Strunk, Jud
They're Tearing down a
Town.
Struther, Jan
Biography.
R. I. P.
Traveling America.
Struthers, Ann
Tea.
Watching the Out-Door
Movie Show.
Stryk, Lucien
Afternoon.
Awakening.
Away.
Downy Hair.
The Face.
Farmer.
Fishing with My Daughter in
Miller's Meadow.
Friendship.
The Liberator.
Stryker, Melancthon W.
Almighty Lord, with One
Accord.
God of Our Fathers.
Stuart, Alice V.
The Climbing Rope.
Lintie in a Cage.
Peewits on the Hills.
Stuart, Dabney
Begging on North Main.
Discovering My Daughter.
Exchange.
Fall Practice.
The Fisherman.
A Lesson in Oblivion.
The Refugee.
Rescue.
The River.
Separate Parties.
Ties.
Stuart, Floyd C.
Gravestones.
Settling In.
Stuart, Francis
Coogan's Wood.
Une Idole du Nord.
Ireland.
Southern Summer.

The Upper Lake.
Stuart, Henry Longan
Intempestiva.
Resurrexit.
Stuart, James
Morna's Hill: A Distant
Prospect of the the City of
Armagh.
Stuart, Jesse
By Sandy Waters.
Heart-Summoned.
I Sing America Now!
My Land Is Fair for Any
Eyes to See.
Our Heritage.
Speaks the Whispering Grass.
Up Silver Stairsteps.
Stuart, John
Come unto Me.
Stuart, Muriel
In the Orchard.
The Old Saint.
The Seed Shop.
Stuart, Ruth McEnery
The Endless Song.
Stubbs, Charles William
Conscience.
'Twas Jolly, Jolly Wat.
Stubbs, Jane
Sime Ines.
Stubbs, Marcia
In a Mirror.
Stubbs, William
A Hymn on Froude and
Kingsley.
**Studdert-Kennedy, G. Anketall
"Woodbine Willie"**
Awake, Awake to Love and
Work.
The Christian Soldier
(excerpt).
The Great Wager.
Indifference.
The Kiss of God.
The Lord of the World.
Patience.
Roses in December.
The Unutterable Beauty.
Stull, Richard
Dedication.
Stults, R. M.
The Sweetest Story Ever Told.
Stump, Roger
Fear.
Stupp, John
First Cold Night of Autumn.
Sturgeon, Lorena W.
Love's Tribute.
Sturm, Christoph Christian
Christ Is Risen!
Sturm, Frank Pearce
Still-Heart.
Style, Colin
100 Year Old Woman at
Christmas Dinner.
Su Tung-P'o
The End of the Year.
Moon, Flowers, Man.
On the Birth of His Son.
Spring Night.
The Terrace in the Snow.
To a Traveler.
Succorsa, Janice Appleby
My Garden.
Suckling, Sir John
Against Absence.
Against Fruition.
An Answer to Some Verses
Made in His Praise.
A Ballad upon a Wedding.
A Ballad upon a Wedding:
The Bride.

A Barley-Break.
A Candle.
The Careless Lover.
The Deformed Mistress.
Farewell to Love.
Love and Debt Alike
Troublesom.
Love's Clock.
Love's Offence.
Loves World.
Loving and Beloved.
Lutea Allison.
The Metamorphosis.
The Miracle.
My Dearest Rival.
On King Richard the Third,
Who Lies Buried under
Leicester Bridge.
On New-Years Day 1640 to
the King.
Orsames' Song.
A Pedlar of Small-Wares.
Proffered Love Rejected.
A Sessions of the Poets.
She's Pretty to Walk With.
Sir Toby Matthews.
A Soldier.
A Song: "Hast thou seen the
Down in the Air."
Song: "No, no, fair heretic."
Song: "Of thee, kind boy, I
ask no red and white."
Song: "Out upon it, I have
lov'd."
Song to a Lute.
Sonnet.
Sonnet: "Of thee (kind boy) I
ask no red and white."
Sonnet: "Oh! for some honest
Lovers ghost."
'Tis Now Since I Sate Down.
To a Lady That Forbad to
Love before Company.
To B. C.
To Master Davenant for
Absence.
To My Love.
Upon A. M.
Upon Christ His Birth.
Upon Christmas Eve.
Upon My Lady Carliles
Walking in Hampton-Court
Garden. Dialogue.
Upon My Lord Brohall's
Wedding.
Upon Sir John Lawrence's
Bringing Water over the
Hills...
Verses.
When, Dearest, I but Think of
Thee.
Why So Pale and Wan?
The Wits.
Woman's Constancy.
Suckow, Ruth
The Odd Ones.
Sudan, Nazzam Al
Al Fitnah Muhajir.
Sugar, Maurice
Soup Song.
Suhl, Yuri
And the Earth Rebelled.
The Permanent Delegate.
Sukenick, Lynn
Parting: A Game.
Suknaski, Andrew
Chinese Camp, Kamloops
(circa 1883).
The Snake.
Sullam, Elizabeth
Late Afternoon.

Sullam, Sarah Copia
My Inmost Hope.
Sullivan, A.M.
Destroyer.
The Flying Dutchman.
Late Autumn.
Monument.
Psalm to the Holy Spirit.
The Sextant.
The Whale and the Essex.
Sullivan, Alan
Suppliant.
The White Canoe.
Sullivan, James
As Sun, As Sea.
Sullivan, Jonny Kyoko
Sagimusume: The White
Heron Maiden.
Sullivan, Joseph J.
Where Did You Get That
Hat?
Sullivan, Nancy
Burial in the Sand.
The Death of the First Man.
Eclipses.
His Necessary Darkness.
The History of the World as
Pictures.
Telling It.
To My Body.
Sullivan, Timothy Daniel
God Save Ireland.
Sully-Prudhomme, Rene
The Naked World.
The Wheel.
Sulpicia
At last love has come.
Darling, I won't be your hot
love.
Do you have a sweet thought,
Cerinthus.
Drat My Hateful Birthday.
Have you heard? The troubles
of the road.
It's nice that though you are
casual about me.
My hated birthday is here,
and I must go.
Summers, Hal
Cerne Abbas.
My Old Cat.
On the Cliff.
A Valentine.
Wet Through.
The Yorkshire Moors.
Summers, Hollis
Concerning Unnatural Nature:
An Inverted Form.
Family Reunion.
Home.
The Lost Pictures.
Valentine.
Summers, Thomas O.
The Morning Bright, with
Rosy Light.
Summers, William C.
The Pastor.
Soft Job.
Sumner, Jezaniah
Ode on Science.
Sun-Ra
Nothing Is.
The Plane: Earth.
Primary Lesson: The Second
Class Citizens.
Sun Yun-feng
On the Road through Chang-
Te.
Starting at Dawn.
The Trail Up Wu Gorge.

Sund, Robert
Afternoon, with Just Enough
of a Breeze.
Bunch Grass #37.
A Fieldmouse.
Ladybug.
Sunny Boy
France Blues.
"Sunset Joe"
Lines on Mountain Villages.
Rivers of the West.
Supervielle, Jules
The Call.
Prophecy.
**"Surfaceman" See Anderson,
Alexander**
Surrey, Henry Howard, Earl of
Although I Had a Check.
Another Tribute to Wyatt.
As Oft as I Behold and See.
Bonum Est Mihi Quod
Humiliasti Me.
Brittle Beauty.
Complaint of the Absence of
Her Lover Being Upon the
Sea.
Complaint That His Ladie
after She Knew of His Love
Kept Her Face...
Consolation.
The Cornet.
Description and Praise of His
Love Geraldine.
Dido's Hunting.
Divers Thy Death.
Dyvers Thy Death Doo
Dyverslye Bemone.
Epitaph on Thomas Clere.
Exhortation to Learn by
Others' Trouble.
"The fancy, which that I have
served long."
From Certain Bokes of
Virgiles Aenaeis.
Geve Place, Ye Lovers, Here
Before.
"Girt in my guiltless gown..."
Give Place, Ye Lovers.
The Golden Gift That Nature
Did Thee Give.
The Golden Mean.
"The great Macedon, that out
of Persia chased."
How No Age Is Content.
"I never saw you, madam, lay
apart."
"If care do cause men cry..."
"If he that erst the form so
lively drew."
In Cipres Springes (Wheras
Dame Venus Dwelt).
In Praise of Wyatt's Psalms.
In the Rude Age.
In Windsor Castle.
"In winter's just return..."
The Lady Again Complains.
A Lady Complains of Her
Lover's Absence.
Laid in My Quiet Bed.
London, Hast Thou Accused
Me.
Love's Rebel.
Martial's Quiet Life.
"Martial, the things for to
attain."
The Means to Attain a Happy
Life.
O Happie Dames.
"O loathsome place..."
Of a Lady That Refused to
Dance with Him.

Prisoned in Windsor, He
Recounteth His Pleasure
There Passed.
Psalm LXXIII.
Psalm LXXXVIII.
The Restless Heart.
The Restless State of a Lover.
Sardanapalus.
A Satire on London.
The Seafarer.
Set Me whereas the Sun Doth
Parch the Green.
"Since fortune's wrath envieth
the wealth."
So Crewell Prison, Howe
Could Betyde, Alas.
"The soote season..."
Suche Waywarde Wais Hath
Love.
Thassyryans King, in Peas
with Fowle Desyre.
Though I Regarded Not.
"Too dearly had I bought my
green and youthful years."
Virgil's Aeneid, Book IV
(excerpt).
Vow to Love Faithfully,
Howsoever He Be Rewarded.
"When reckless youth in an
unquiet breast."
When Windsor Walles
Sustain'd My Wearied Arme.
When Youth Had Fled.
"Wrapt in my careless
cloak..."
Wyat Resteth Here, that
Quicke Coulde Never Rest.
Susskind, Harriet
Views.
Susskind, Von Trimberg
O Thought!
The Power of Thought.
The Virtuous Wife.
Why Should I Wander Sadly.
Sussman, M. L.
Poet's Prayer.
Return.
Sutheim, Susan
For Witches.
Sutherland, Efua (Morgue)
It Happened.
**Sutherland, Robert See
"Garioch, Robert"**
Sutphen, Van Tassel
Deep Waters.
Sutter, Barton
A Curse against the Owner.
Shoe Shop.
Static.
Swedish Lesson.
Warmth.
Sutton, Henry Septimus
The Inward Light.
Sutu, Sam Duby R.
Night.
Thaba Bosio.
Sutzkever, Abraham
The Banks of a River.
A Cartload of Shoes.
Here I Am.
How.
Landscape.
Like Groping Fingers.
On My Wandering Flute.
Poetry.
The Secret Town (excerpt).
Song for a Dance.
Song of Praise for an Ox.
Songs to a Lady Moonwalker.
To My Child.
Toys.
Under the Earth.

Yiddish.
Suwo, Lady
That spring night I spent.
Svetlov, Mikhail A.
Grenada.
Swaim, Alice Mackenzie
Chilled by Different Winds.
Swain, Charles
The Field-Path.
Home Is Where There Is One
to Love Us.
Smile and Never Heed Me.
Song: "A violet in her lovely
hair."
Take the World as It Is
(excerpt).
Tripping down the Field-Path.
Swain, John D.
Would I Be Shrived?
Swain, Leonard
My Soul, Weigh Not Thy
Life.
Swan, Emma
The Connecticut Elm.
Swan, Jon
Among Commuters.
Father Father Son and Son.
In Her Song She Is Alone.
The Kingdom.
March Weather.
Nebraska.
The Report.
Their Party, Our House.
Swanger, David
Probity.
Swann, Brian
Desert in the Sea.
Lines.
Masks.
Paradigms of Fire.
Quiet.
Year of the Bird.
Swann, Thomas Burnett
A Japanese Birthday Wish.
Swanton, John R.
Bear Song.
Swarberg, George W.
Mistakes.
Worry.
Sward, Robert
American Heritage.
Concert.
How Totally Unpredictable
We Are to One Another.
Kissing the Dancer.
Mothers-in-Law.
Movies, Left to Right.
Nightgown, Wife's Gown.
Pet Shop.
Proposal.
Terminal Theater.
There Is No Reason Why Not
to Look at Death.
Uncle Dog: The Poet at 9.
What It Was.
Swart, Edward Vincent
Casey Jones.
Tired of Eating Kisses.
Swarth, Helene
Candles.
Ecstasy.
Swartz, Roberta Teale
Our Father.
Prayer by Moonlight.
Sweeney, Barbara
For We Are All Madwomen.
Sweeney, Francis
Boy Playing an Organ.
**Sweeney, John R. and Edgar
Page**
Beulah Land.

Sweeney, Matthew
Alone with the Dawn.
Sweeney, Mildred McNeal
Chavez.
Sweet, Frank Herbert
Before It Is Too Late.
Sweetman, Elinor
The Orchard by the Shore: a
Pastoral.
Swenson, Karen
Come with Me into Winter's
Disheveled Grass.
Grave Clothes.
The Pro.
The Quarrel.
Woman, Gallup, N.M.
Swenson, May
Above the Arno.
After the Dentist.
All That Time.
Almanac.
At the Museum of Modern
Art.
August Night.
Beginning to Squall.
The Blindman.
Bronco Busting, Event #1.
Cafe Tableau.
Cardinal Ideograms.
Cat & the Weather.
The Centaur.
The Cloud-Mobile.
The Cross Spider.
Death Invited.
Evolution.
Fashion in the 70's.
Feel Like a Bird.
Feel Me.
Fire Island.
Five Horses.
A Fixture.
Frontispiece.
The Garden at St. John's.
Green Red Brown and White.
Hearing the Wind at Night.
How Everything Happens
(Based on a Study of the
Wave).
How to Be Old.
In a Museum Cabinet.
The James Bond Movie.
July 4th.
The Key to Everything.
Landing on the Moon.
Lion.
Living Tenderly.
Motherhood.
Naked in Borneo.
News from the Cabin.
Notes Made in the Piazza San
Marco.
On Addy Road.
Orbiter 5 Shows How Earth
Looks from the Moon.
Out of the Sea, Early.
A Pair.
The Poplar's Shadow.
The Promontory Moment.
Question.
Rain at Wildwood.
Riding the "A."
Scroppo's Dog.
The Secret in the Cat.
The Shape of Death.
Snow by Morning.
Snow in New York.
Some Small Shells from the
Windward Islands.
Southbound on the Freeway.
Sunday in the Country.
To the Shore.
To the Statue.

The Universe.
Waiting for IT.
Waking from a Nap on the
   Beach.
Was Worm.
The Watch.
Watching the Jets Lose to
   Buffalo at Shea.
Water Picture.
Women.
The Woods at Night.
Swett, Herbert B.
The Gathering.
Swett, John
In the Mines.
Swett, Susan Hartley
July.
Swickard, David
The Dragon of Red Lights.
Swift, Hildegarde Hoyt
I Came to the New World
   Empty-Handed.
My Name Was Legion.
Swift, Joan
The Line-Up.
Oxygen.
Vancouver Island.
Swift, Jonathan
Abroad and at Home.
Asparagus.
A Ballad to the Tune of "The
   Cut-Purse."
Baucis and Philemon.
The Beasts' Confession.
A Beautiful Young Nymph
   Going to Bed.
Cadenus and Vanessa
   (excerpt).
Cassinus and Peter.
The Cat and the Rain.
The Church and Clergy Here.
Clever Tom Clinch Going to
   be Hanged.
Critics.
Daphne.
The Day of Judgement.
A Description of a City
   Shower.
A Description of the Morning.
Dick, a Maggot.
Directions for Making a
   Birth-Day Song: "To form a
   just..."
An Epigram on Scolding.
Epigram on Seeing a Worthy
   Prelate Go out of Church...
Epigram: "With favour and
   fortune fastidiously blest."
An Excellent New Song,
   Being the Intended Speech of
   a Famous Orator...
An Excellent New Song on a
   Seditious Pamphlet.
An Excellent New Song upon
   His Grace...Lord Archbishop
   of Dublin.
The Fable of Midas.
Flattery.
The Furniture of a Woman's
   Mind.
A Gentle Echo on Woman.
Herrings.
Holyhead. Sept. 25, 1727.
Horace, Epistle VII, Book I,
   Imitated.
In Sickness.
Inscription for the Sign of
   "The Jolly Barber",...
Ireland.
The Lady's Dressing Room.
The Legion Club (excerpt).
A Libel on D.

The Life and Character of
   Dean Swift (excerpt).
Market Women's Cries.
Mary Gulliver to Captain
   Lemuel Gulliver.
Mary the Cook-Maid's Letter
   to Dr. Sheridan.
A Maypole.
Mrs. Frances Harris's
   Petition.
A New Song of Wood's
   Halfpence.
On a Window at the Four
   Crosses.
On an Ill-Managed House.
On an Upright Judge.
On Burning a Dull Poem.
On Censure.
On Dreams.
On Fleas.
On Gaulstown House.
On Himself.
On His Own Deafness.
On Mrs. Biddy Floyd Written
   in the Year 1707.
On Poetry, A Rhapsody.
On Stella's Birthday.
On the Astrologer and
   Almanac Maker, John
   Partridge.
On the Collar of Mrs.
   Dingley's Lap-Dog.
On the Death of Doctor Swift.
On the Irish Club.
On the World.
Oranges.
Oysters.
Phyllis; or, The Progress of
   Love.
The Place of the Damned.
The Power of Time.
The Progress of Beauty.
The Progress of Marriage.
The Progress of Poetry.
Prometheus.
A Quiet Life and a Good
   Name.
A Riddle: The Vowels.
A Satirical Elegy on the
   Death of a Late Famous
   General.
Shall I Repine?
A Soldier and a Scholar.
Stella at Wood-Park.
Stella's Birthday.
To Dr. Delany (excerpt).
To Stella.
To the Landlord.
A True and Faithful
   Inventory of the Goods
   Belonging to Dr Swift...
Vanbrug's House.
Verses Occasioned by the
   Sudden Drying up...(excerpt).
Verses Said to Be Written on
   the Union.
Verses Written upon
   Windows.
Verses Wrote in a Lady's
   Ivory Table-Book.
The Virtues of Sid Hamet, the
   Magician's Rod.
We Are God's Chosen Few.
Who Killed Kildare?
A Wicked Treasonable Libel.
Swift, Nicholas
Maxims of a Park Vagrant.
Swilky, Jody
Animation and Ego.
Nothing but Image.
Swinburne, Algernon Charles
After Death.

Anactoria (excerpt).
Apologia.
At a Month's End.
At Parting.
At the Piano.
Atalanta in Calydon.
August.
Ave Atque Vale.
A Ballad of Burdens.
The Ballad of Dead Men's
   Bay.
A Ballad of Death.
The Ballad of Dreamland.
A Ballad of Francois Villon.
A Ballad of Life.
Before Parting.
Before Sunset.
Before the Mirror.
Birth and Death.
By the North Sea.
A Channel Passage.
Child and Poet.
A Child's Future.
A Child's Laughter.
Child's Song.
Christmas Antiphones
   (excerpt).
A Christmas Carol.
Christopher Marlowe.
Cleopatra.
Come into the Orchard, Anne.
Cor Cordium.
A Dead King.
Death and Birth.
The Death of Meleager.
The Death of Richard
   Wagner.
Dedication: To Edward John
   Trelawny.
Delphic Hymn to Apollo.
A Dialogue.
Dolores.
Envoi.
Eros.
Erotion.
Etude Realiste.
Evening by the Sea.
Evening on the Broads.
Ex-Voto.
Faustine.
Felise.
A Forsaken Garden.
Fragoletta.
The Garden of Proserpine.
The Gardens of Cymodoce.
Grand Chorus of Birds.
Hawthorn Dyke.
Hendecasyllabics.
The Heptalogia.
Hermaphroditus.
Hertha.
Hesperia.
The Higher Pantheism in a
   Nutshell.
Hope and Fear.
Hymn of Man.
Hymn to Proserpine.
Ilicet.
In Guernsey.
In Harbour.
In Memory of "Barry
   Cornwall."
In Memory of Walter Savage
   Landor.
In the Orchard.
Insularum Ocelle.
An Interlude.
The Interpreters.
Itylus.
A Jacobite's Exile.
John Webster.
The Lake of Gaube.

The Laud of Saint Catherine.
Laus Veneris.
A Leave-taking.
The Leper.
Love and Sleep.
Love That Is First and Last.
A Lyric.
Madonna Mia.
Mary Beaton's Song.
The Masque of Queen Bersabe
   (excerpt).
A Match.
May Janet.
A Midsummer Holiday, VI:
   The Cliffside Path.
Nephelidia.
A Nympholept.
The Oblation.
On Arthur Hugh Clough.
On the Cliffs.
On the Death of Robert
   Browning.
On the Deaths of Thomas
   Carlyle and George Eliot.
Plus Ultra.
Poeta Loquitur.
Rococo.
Rondel: "Kissing her hair I
   sat against her feet."
Sapphics.
Sestina.
Seven Years Old.
Siena.
A Singing Lesson.
A Song in Time of Order
   1852.
A Song in Time of Revolution
   1860.
Song: "Love laid his sleepless
   head."
Songs Before Sunrise: Prelude.
Sonnet for a Picture (parody).
Sonnet: "This is the golden
   book of spirit and sense."
Stage Love.
The Sundew.
Sunrise at Sea.
Super Flumina Babylonis.
Thalassius.
To a Cat.
To a Seamew.
To Victor Hugo.
To Walt Whitman in
   America.
Tristram of Lyonesse.
The Triumph of Time.
Watchman, What of the
   Night?
When the Hounds of Spring.
Why Grudge Them Lotus-
   Leaf and Laurel.
William Shakespeare.
A Year's Burden.
Swingler, Randall
Letter I.
Letter VIII.
They Live.
Swiss, Thomas
Letter from Des Moines.
A Virtue of Shape.
Swope, Mary
Couple.
Sykes, Roosevelt
High Price Blues.
West Helena Blues.
Sykes, Velma West
Diptych.
Sylvester, Janet
Arrowhead Christian Center
   and No-Smoking
   Luncheonette.

Hard Strain in a Delicate
  Place.
The Late Show.
That Mulberry Wine.
Sylvester, Joshua
Autumnus.
Du Bartas: His Divine
  Weeks...Fifth Day of the
  First Week (excerpt).
A Contented Mind.
Fuimus Fumus.
The Garden.
Mundus Qualis.
Omnia Somnia.
Quatrain.
Rome, Conqueror, Conquered.
Sonnet: "They say that
  shadowes of deceased
  ghosts."
Sonnet: "Were I as base as is
  the lowly plain."
Sweet mouth, that send'st a
  musky-rosed breath.
Sylvester, William
Hookerlumps in the Love
  Canal.
Symmons, Robert
The Dam, Glen Garry.
Symonds, John Addington
The Camera Obscura.
Farewell.
Gaudeamus Igitur.
The Human Outlook.
In February.
An Invocation.
Ithocles, VI (excerpt).
Le Jeune Homme Caressant
  Sa Chimere.
Koina ta ton Philon.
Lauriger Horatius.
Love in Dreams.
Midnight at Baiae. A Dream
  Fragment of Imperial Rome.
Night.
On a Picture by Poussin
  Representing Shepherds in
  Arcadia.
A Poem of Privacy.
The Sonnet.
These Things Shall Be.
Venice.
Symons, Arthur
The Abandoned.
The Absinthe-Drinker.
Amends to Nature.
Amor Triumphans.
Amoris Exsul.
The Andante of Snakes.
April Midnight.
At Carbis Bay.
At Dawn.
At Dieppe: Green and Grey.
At the Cavour.
At Toledo.
The Barrel-Organ.
Bianca.
By Loe Pool.
By the Pool at the Third
  Rosses.
The Caged Bird.
City Nights, I: In the Train.
Clair de Lune.
Credo.
The Crying of Water.
The Dance of the Daughters
  of Herodias.
Dieppe, II: On the Beach.
The Dream.
Dreams.
During Music.
Ecstasy.
Emmy.

Envoi.
Escalade.
The Fairy Wood.
The Fisher's Widow.
The Gardener.
The Grey Wolf.
Hallucination: I.
Impression.
In Bohemia.
In Kensington Gardens.
In Winter.
Intermezzo: At Glan-Y-Wern.
Isolation.
Javanese Dancers.
The Last Memory.
Laus Virginitatis.
Leves Amores.
London Nights: In the Stalls.
The Loom of Dreams.
Magnificat.
Maquillage.
La Melinite: Moulin-Rouge.
Modern Beauty.
Nerves.
Night and Wind.
The Nun.
On an Air of Rameau.
Palm Sunday: Naples.
Paris.
Pastel: Masks and Faces.
The Prodigal Son.
Prologue.
Rain on the Down.
The Rat.
The Return.
A Roundel of Rest.
Scenes de la Vie de Boheme.
The Shadow.
Spain.
The Temptation of Saint
  Anthony.
A Tune.
Venice.
Violet.
Wanderer's Song.
White Heliotrope.
Symons, Julian
And the World's Face.
For My Wife.
For the Depressed.
Gladstone.
Hart Crane.
Homage to Our Leaders.
Hospital Observation.
Mr. Symons at Richmond,
  Mr. Pope at Twickenham.
Pub.
Reflections in Bed.
The Second Man.
Spring Poem.
Sunday, July 14th: A Fine
  Day at the Baths.
Synesius
Hymn.
Synge, John Millington
At Dawn.
Beg-Innish.
The Conviction.
The Curse.
Danny.
Dread.
Epigram: "I curse my bearing,
  childhood, youth."
Epigram: "I read about the
  Blaskets and Dunquin."
Epitaph after Reading
  Ronsard's Lines from
  Rabelais.
Epitaph: "If fruits are fed on
  any beast."
He Understands the Great
  Cruelty of Death.

I've Thirty Months.
In a Dream.
In Dream.
In Glencullen.
In Kerry.
In May.
In Rebellion.
Is It a Month.
The 'Mergency Man.
Notre Dames des Champs.
On a Birthday.
On an Anniversary after
  Reading the Dates in a Book
  of Lyrics.
On an Island.
The Passing of the Shee after
  Looking at One of A.E.'s
  Pictures.
Patch-Shaneen.
Prelude.
Queens.
A Question.
Rendez-vous Manque dans la
  Rue Racine.
To the Oaks of Glencree.
A Translation from Petrarch.
A Translation from Walter
  von der Vogelweide.
Two Translatons from Villon.
Winter.
A Wish.
"Syntax"
Soliloquy of the Returned
  Gold Adventurer.
Song for the Pike's Peaker.
Syquia, Luis
The New Manong.
Pan-Asian Holiday Tour.
Syrian, Ajan
The Syrian Lover in Exile
  Remembers Thee, Light of
  My Land.
Sze, Arthur
Black Lightning.
The Chance.
The Cloud Chamber.
Dazzled.
Magnetized.
Moenkopi.
The Moon Is a Diamond.
Szelki, Karl
The Chestnut Vendor.
Szumigalski, Anne
Angels.
In the Heat of the Morning.
A Midwife's Story: Two.
Visitors' Parking.
Want of Want of.
Szymborska, Wislawa
Homecoming.
I Am Too Near.
In Praise of a Guilty
  Conscience.
Starvation Camp near Jaslo.
The Women of Rubens.

T

"T, C."
Gastric.
Valentine.
"T, I."
When Stars Are Shrouded.
"T, J."
A Sea-Chaplain's Petition.
T-Bone Slim
The Popular Wobbly.

Ta' Abbata Sharra
Ever Watchful.
Tabb, John Banister
The Annunciation.

The Assumption.
At Lanier's Grave.
Becalmed.
Betrayal.
Bicycles! Tricycles!
Brother Ass and St. Francis.
The Bubble.
A Bunch of Roses.
The Child.
A Child's Prayer.
Childhood.
Christ and the Pagan.
Close Quarters.
Clover.
Communion.
The Departed.
The Druid.
Evolution.
Faith.
Fame.
Father Damien.
Foot Soldiers.
Fraternity.
God.
High and Low.
The Immaculate Conception.
Indian Summer.
Insomnia.
Inspiration.
Keats.
The Lake.
The Lamb-Child.
The Light of Bethlehem.
Limerick: "A boot and a shoe
  and a slipper."
Mater Dolorosa.
Missing.
Nekros.
The Old Pastor.
Out of Bounds.
Overflow.
The Precipice.
The Reaper.
A Rub.
Shakespeare's Mourners.
The Sisters.
The Tax-Gatherer.
The Test.
To a Photograph.
To a Rose.
To a Wood-Violet.
To Shelley.
To the Christ.
The Tryst.
The Water-Lily.
The White Jessamine.
The Wind.
Taber, Harry P.
Wihelmina Mergenthaler.
Tabrar, Joseph
Mary Ann.
Taft, Margo
I Have Been My Arm.
Tagami, Jeff
The Foreman's Wife.
The Horn Blow.
Now It Is Broccoli.
Stonehouse.
Without Names.
Taggard, Genevieve
American Farm, 1934.
Dilemma of the Elm.
Doomsday Morning.
The Enamel Girl.
First Miracle.
For Eager Lovers.
Galatea Again.

The Geraniums.
In the Tail of the Scorpion.
The Little Girl with Bands on
Her Teeth.
Millions of Strawberries.
A Poem to Explain
Everything about a Certain
Day in Vermont.
The Quiet Woman.
Sea-Change.
Solar Myth.
Song for Unbound Hair.
To the Veterans of the
Abraham Lincoln Brigade.
Try Tropic.
With Child.
Taggart, George
The Moth and the Flame.
Tagliabue, John
Archilochos:.
Assuming the Name of Any
Next Child.
The Bare Arms of Trees.
By a Rich Fast Moving
Stream.
Debussy and Proust.
December 1970.
Fast.
I Sought All over the World.
In the Palms of Ancient
Bodhisattvas.
Just a Few Scenes from an
Autobiography.
The Pinta, the Nina and the
Santa Maria.
The Riding Stable in Winter.
An Unseen Deer.
You.
Tagore, Rabindranath
Autumn.
The Bird.
Day after Day.
Epigrams (excerpt).
Fairyland.
For Strength.
Gitanjali.
The Home.
I Have Got My Leave.
If It Is Not My Portion.
In the Dusky Path of a
Dream.
The Journey nears the Road-
End.
Krishnakali.
Let This Be My Parting
Word.
My Song.
On the Slope of the Desolate
River.
A Song-Offering.
Thou Art the Sky.
The Yellow Bird Sings.
Yours.
Tahureau, Jacques
Moonlight.
Shadows of His Lady.
Taira no Kanemori
In spite of my efforts.
Tait, William J.
Gallow Hill.
Takvan, Marie
The Deepest Bow.
Talbot, Carlton
The Day Closes.
A Royal Pickle.
The Sisters Kastemaloff.
Talbot, Ethel
Crab-Apple.
Give Love To-Day.

Talbot, Norman
Ballad of Old Women & of
How They Are Constrained
to Stimulate...
Talbott, Carlton
Ballyhoo for a Mendicant.
Talfourd, Sir Thomas Noon
A Friend.
Taliesin
A Song to the Wind.
Tall, Grace Cornell
The Needle.
Tallante, Mossen Juan
Prayer to the Crucifix.
Tallet, Jose Z.
Rumba.
Tallmountain, Mary
Crazy Dogholkoda.
Good Grease.
Indian Blood.
The Ivory Dog of My Sister.
The Last Wolf.
Matmiya.
Once the Striped Quagga.
There Is No Word for
Goodbye.
Ts'eekkaayah.
The Women in Old Parkas.
Talmud
God to Man.
The Good Man.
Why?
Talpalar, Morris
True Happiness.
Tamekane, Kyogoku
On Love.
Tampa Red
You Got to Love Her with a
Feeling.
Tam'si, Tchicaya U
Debout (excerpt).
The Scorner.
Tan Pai, Joshua
The Life of Hard Times.
My Soul Hovers Over Me.
Trees Once Walked and
Stood.
Tan Ying
Drinking the Wind.
Tanaka, Ronald P.
The big trimmer.
Snacks.
Tanaquil, Paul
History.
T'ang Wan
To the Tune "The Phoenix
Hairpin."
T'ang Yin
Words for a Picture of
Newlyweds.
Tangikuku, Hine
A Song of Sickness.
Tankervil, George
Evensong.
Tannahill, Robert
The Braes o' Gleniffer.
By Yon Burn Side.
Jessie, the Flower o' Dunbane.
Loudoun's Bonnie Woods and
Braes.
The Midges Dance Aboon the
Burn.
O! Are Ye Sleepin, Maggie?
T'ao Chi'en
I Built My Hut.
A Long Time Ago.
Once More Fields and
Gardens.
Returning to the Fields.
Shady, Shady.
Tao Te Ching
He Walks at Peace.

Tao Yuan-Ming
Two Drinking Songs.
Tapahonso, Luci
The belly of the land.
The Dust Will Settle.
Hills Brothers Coffee.
It was a Special Treat.
Sheepherder blues.
Tapp, Gary
The Insect Shuffle Method.
Tappan, William B.
Gethsemane.
The Hour of Peaceful Rest.
The Ransomed Spirit to Her
Home.
Song of the Three Hundred
Thousand
Drunkards...(excerpt).
There Is an Hour of Peaceful
Rest.
'Tis Midnight and on Olive's
Brow.
Wake, Isles of the South.
Tapscott, Stephen
Parable: November.
Tarn, Nathaniel
Where Babylon Ends.
Tassin, Algernon
Attainment.
Tassis, Juan de
To a Cloistress.
Tasso, Torquato
Armida, the Sorceress.
Aminta: Chorus I.
The Crusaders Behold
Jerusalem.
Gerusalemme Liberata
(excerpt).
Godfrey of Bulloigne:
Armida...Sets out to undo
the Crusaders.
Jerusalem Delivered (excerpt).
Love.
To His Mistress in Absence.
To the Father of the Bride.
Tatana, Hannah
Seaweed, Seaweed.
Tate, Allen
Aeneas at Washington.
The Buried Lake.
The Cross.
Death of Little Boys.
Emblems.
The Eye.
Horatian Epode to the
Duchess of Malfi.
Idiot.
Jubilo.
Last Days of Alice.
The Mediterranean.
More Sonnets at Christmas.
Mother and Son.
Mr. Pope.
The Oath.
Ode: "Once more the country
calls."
Ode to the Confederate Dead.
The Paradigm.
Pastoral.
A Pauper.
The Rooftree.
Seasons of the Soul.
Shadow and Shade.
Sonnets at Christmas.
The Subway.
The Swimmers.
The Traveller.
Winter Mask.
The Wolves.
Tate, James
The Blue Booby.
The Book of Lies.

A Box for Tom.
Coda.
Conjuring Roethke.
Constant Defender.
Consumed.
Deaf Girl Playing.
Dear Reader.
The Distant Orgasm.
If It Would All Please Hurry.
It's Not the Heat So Much as
the Humidity.
Land of Little Sticks, 1945.
Little Yellow Leaf.
The Lost Pilot.
Love Making.
Miss Cho Composes in the
Cafeteria.
The Motorcyclists.
My Great Great etc. Uncle
Patrick Henry.
The Pet Deer.
Pity Ascending with the Fog.
The President Slumming.
The Professor Waking.
Riven Doggeries.
Same Tits.
Sloops in the Bay.
The Soup of Venus.
The Square at Dawn.
Stray Animals.
Tall Trees by Still Waters.
Teaching the Ape to Write
Poems.
The Wheelchair Butterfly.
Who Can Tell When He Is
Awake.
Tate, Nahum
The Blessed Virgin's
Expostulation.
The Choice.
Old England.
The Penance.
While Shepherds Watched
Their Flocks by Night.
Tatersal, Robert
The Bricklayer's Labours.
Tatham, John
The Letter.
Reason.
Tatnall, Frances Dorr
Art Thou the Same.
Tauhindauli
I Am Stone of Many Colors.
Tawney, Cyril
The Grey Funnel Line.
On a Monday Morning.
Reunion.
Sally Free and Easy.
Taylor, Allan
Ballad for the Unknown
Soldier.
Still He Sings.
Time.
Taylor, Andrew
Developing a Wife.
The Invention of Fire.
Taylor, Ann
The Baby.
The Baby's Dance.
Jane and Eliza.
Meddlesome Matty.
My Mother.
The Notorious Glutton.
The Pin.
The Plum-Cake.
The Tumble.
Washing and Dressing.
Taylor, Ann and Jane
The Cow.
The Sheep.
Taylor, Bayard
All or Nothing (parody).

America.
Angelo Orders His Dinner
  (parody).
Ariel in the Cloven Pine.
The Ballad of Hiram Hover.
Bedouin Love Song.
Camerados (parody).
Cimabuella (parody).
The Demon of the Mirror.
The Deserter.
The Fight of Paso del Mar!
Gwendoline (parody).
Kilimandjaro.
Lincoln at Gettysburg.
The National Ode.
Nauvoo.
A Night with a Wolf.
Nubia.
Ode on a Jar of Pickles
  (parody).
Palabras Grandiosas.
The Poet's Journal (excerpt).
The Promissory Note
  (parody).
The Quaker Widow.
Sir Eggnogg (parody).
The Song of the Camp.
Storm Song.
A Story for a Child.
The Sunshine of the Gods
  (excerpt).
The Three Songs.
Through Baltimore.
To M.T.
Taylor, Benjamin Franklin
The Isle of the Long Ago.
Taylor, Bert Leston
Aprilly.
Ataraxia.
The Bards We Quote.
Bygones (parody).
Canopus.
The Dinosaur.
Doxology.
Hence These Rimes.
The Lazy Writer.
Old Stuff.
The Passionate Professor.
Post-Impressionism.
The Road to Anywhere.
Those Flapjacks of Brown's.
Upon Julia's Arctics.
Taylor, Caleb J.
O Jesus, My Saviour, I Know
  Thou Art Mine.
Taylor, Charles Edward
For Sale, a Horse.
Taylor, Charles S.
A Scandal Among the
  Flowers.
Taylor, Deems
Concerning Mme. Robert.
Haec Olim Meminise Iuvabait.
Hors d'Oeuvre.
Proof Positive.
The Saddled Ass.
Turn to the Left.
Taylor, Edward
The Accusation of the Inward
  Man.
An Address to the Soul
  Occasioned by a Rain.
The Angels Sung a Carol.
The Ebb and Flow.
An Elegy upon the Death of
  That Holy Man...(excerpt).
The Experience.
The Frowardness of the Elect
  in the Work of Conversion.
God's Determinations.
Gods Determinations.
Huswifery.

I Kenning Through
  Astronomy.
In Heaven Soaring Up.
The Joy of Church Fellowship
  Rightly Attended.
Meditations.
Meditations.
Our Insufficiency to Praise
  God Suitably for His Mercy.
The Outward Man Accused.
Prologue.
The Reflection.
Thou Art the Tree of Life.
Upon a Spider Catching a
  Fly.
Upon a Wasp Chilled with
  Cold.
Upon Wedlock, and Death of
  Children.
When Let By Rain.
Taylor, Eleanor Ross
In the Churchyard.
Taylor, Emily
Mother.
Taylor, Frances Beatrice
The Husbandman.
A Wedgwood Bowl.
Taylor, Geoffrey
Admonition to the Muse.
Bluebell.
Boat-Haven, Co. Mayo.
Country Walk.
Cruel Clever Cat.
English Liberal.
Epitaph: "Nor practising
  virtue nor committing
  crime."
From an Irish-Latin
  Macaronic.
Gentlemen.
Song: "Rousing to rein his
  pad's head back."
Taylor, Helen
Bless This House.
Taylor, Henry
Artichoke.
Breakings.
Campaign Promise.
The Country Curate.
Depressed by the Death of the
  Horse... (parody).
The Flying Change.
Gets Hung up on a Dirty, of
  All Things, Joke (parody).
Getting at the Root of the
  Matter (parody).
The Horse Show at Midnight.
In Orbit (parody).
Landscape with Tractor.
Miss Creighton.
Riding a One-Eyed Horse.
Riding Lesson.
Says Something, Too (parody).
Shapes, Vanishings.
Sonnet in the Mail Coach.
Speech.
Taking to the Woods.
To Hear My Head Roar.
The View from a Cab.
Taylor, Jane
Contented John.
Dirty Jim.
The Disappointment.
The Gleaner.
Good-Night.
Greedy Richard.
Hymns for Infant Minds
  (excerpt).
I Like Little Pussy.
I Love Little Pussy.
Morning.
My Mother.

The Philosopher's Scales.
The Pigs.
Recreation.
The Star.
The Violet.
Taylor, Jane and Ann
The Little Fish That Would
  Not Do as It Was Bid.
Taylor, Jeffreys
The Lion and the Mouse.
Taylor, Jeremy
Christ's Coming in Triumph.
My Soul Doth Pant towards
  Thee.
The Penitent.
Taylor, John
The Egg of Nothing.
End of the Line.
The Mill.
Of Seals and Arms.
Roses Gone Wild.
Sonnet: Mockado, Fustian,
  and Motley.
Taylor's Travels from London
  to Prague (excerpt).
The Trumpet of Liberty.
Taylor, John W.
Chipeta's Ride.
Taylor, Joseph Russell
Blow Softly, Thrush.
Breath on the Oat.
Dove's Nest.
The Flute.
Taylor, Katherine Kelley
Flying Fish.
Taylor, Laurie
Business Trips.
Lake Harriet: Wind.
Taylor, Louis E.
Hang to Your Grit!
Taylor, Lucy
Leac A'Chlarsair.
Taylor, Morgan
Limerick: "A lieutenant who
  went out to shoot."
Taylor, Rachel Annand
Ecstasy.
The Joys of Art.
The Knights to Chrysola.
May-Music.
The Princess of Scotland.
The Question.
Taylor, Rod
Dakota: October, 1822.
  Hunkpapa Warrior.
The Death of Lester Brown,
  House Painter.
Taylor, Sarah Wingate
With Metaphor.
Taylor, Sir Henry
Elena's Song.
Song: "The bee to the
  heather."
Women Singing.
Taylor, Tom
Abraham Lincoln.
Taylor, Viola
Babylon.
Taylor, William
The Vision.
Taylor, William Edward
The Resurrection.
Tchernichovsky, Saul
Before the Statue of Apollo.
Credo.
The Dance of Saul with the
  Prophets.
The Death of Tammuz.
The Grave.
A Grave in Ukraine.
I Believe.
Man Is Nothing But.

Saul's Song of Love.
This Be Our Revenge.
To Ashtaroth and Bel.
Te-whaka-io-roa
Give Me My Infant Now.
Teasdale, Sara
All That Was Mortal.
The Answer.
Appraisal.
April.
August Night.
Barter.
Blue Squills.
Calm Morning at Sea.
Child, Child.
The Coin.
The Crystal Gazer.
A December Day.
Epitaph.
The Falling Star.
February Twilight.
The Flight.
Four Winds.
From the Sea.
Full Moon: Santa Barbara.
Grace Before Sleep.
I Am Not Yours.
I Shall Not Care.
Immortal.
In the Carpenter's Shop.
The Inn of Earth.
A June Day.
The Kiss.
The Lamp.
Late October.
Leaves.
Like Barley Bending.
The Long Hill.
The Look.
Mastery.
May Day.
Moon's Ending.
Moonlight.
Morning Song.
The Mystery.
The New Moon.
Night.
Night Song at Amalfi.
On the South Downs.
The Philosopher.
A Prayer.
September Midnight.
"Since There Is No Escape".
The Solitary.
Song: "Let it be forgotten, as
  a flower is forgotten."
Song Making.
Spring in War-Time.
Spring Night.
Stars.
There Will Come Soft Rains.
Those Who Love.
To Dick, on His Sixth
  Birthday.
To Rose.
Water-Lilies.
What Do I Care.
When I Am Not With You.
Winter Noon.
Wisdom.
Tegner, Esaias
The Eternal.
Frithiof's Farewell.
Teitoku
Both My Child.
Tejada, Juan Manuel Garcia
To Jesus on the Cross.
Tekahionwake
The Cattle Thief.
Tekeyan, Vahan
The Future.

Telemaque, Harold Milton
Adina.
Telesilla
O Artemis and your virgin
girls.
Teller. J. L
Lines to a Tree.
Minor Key.
To the Divine Neighbor.
Temkin, Mordecai
Foul Water.
Hidden Bow.
Seal of Fire.
Your Presence.
Templeton, J. D.
The New Year.
Tenchi, Emperor
Through the thatched roof.
Tennant, Edward Wyndham
Home Thoughts in Laventie.
Tennant, Robert
Wee Davie Daylicht.
Tennant, William
On the Road to Anster Fair.
Tennyson, Alfred, Lord
The Ancient Sage.
As Thro' the Land at Eve We
Went.
As When a Man.
Ask Me No More.
Audley Court.
Aylmer's Field.
A Ballad of the Fleet.
The Balloon.
The Beggar Maid.
Black Bull of Aldgate.
The Blackbird.
Break, Break, Break.
The Brook.
By an Evolutionist.
Calm Is the Morn without a
Sound.
The Captain.
The Charge of the Light
Brigade.
The City Child.
Claribel.
Columbus (excerpt).
Come into the Garden, Maud.
Come Not When I Am Dead.
The Coming of Arthur:
Merlin's Riddling.
Crossing the Bar.
The Daisy.
The Death of the Old Year.
The Deep Dark Night.
The Defense of Lucknow.
Demeter and Persephone.
Despair.
A Dream of Fair Women.
Duet.
The Dying Swan.
The Eagle.
Early Spring.
Edward Gray.
England and America in 1782.
Enoch Arden.
The Epic.
Epigram: "I ran upon life
unknowing, without or
science or art."
Epigram: "Somebody being a
nobody."
Epitaph: "In my youth the
growls!"
A Farewell.
Fatima.
The Flower.
Flower in the Crannied Wall.
Follow the Gleam.
"Frater Ave Atque Vale".

From Sorrow Sorrow Yet Is
Born.
Go By.
Go Not, Happy Day.
Godiva.
He Hears the Bugle at
Killarney.
Hendecasyllabics.
The Hesperides.
The Higher Pantheism.
The Human Cry.
I Stood on a Tower in the
Wet.
I Wage Not Any Feud with
Death.
Idylls of the King.
Ilion, Ilion.
In Memoriam A.H.H.
In the Children's Hospital.
In the Garden at Swainston.
In the Spring.
In the Valley of Cauteretz.
June Bracken and Heather.
The Kraken.
Lady Clara Vere De Vere.
The Lady of Shalott.
The Last Tournament.
The Letters.
Lilian.
Lines on Cambridge of 1830.
Locksley Hall.
Locksley Hall Sixty Years
After.
The Lotos-Eaters.
Lucretius.
Mariana.
Mariana in the South.
Marriage Morning.
The Marriage of Geraint:
Enid's Song.
Maud.
Mechanophilus (excerpt).
Merlin and the Gleam.
The Mermaid.
The Merman.
Midnight.
The Miller's Daughter.
Milton.
Minnie and Winnie.
Morte D'Arthur.
The Mystic.
The Northern Cobbler.
Northern Farmer, New Style.
Now Sleeps the Crimson
Petal.
O You Chorus of Indolent
Reviewers.
The Oak.
Ode on the Death of the
Duke of Wellington.
Ode Sung at the Opening of
the International Exhibition.
Ode to Memory.
Oenone.
Of Old Sat Freedom on the
Heights.
On His Publisher.
On Supporters of the
Baconian Theory.
On the Jubilee of Queen
Victoria (excerpt).
Over the Dark World Flies
the Wind.
Over! The Sweet Summer
Closes.
The Palace of Art.
The Pallid Thunderstricken
Sigh for Gain.
The Passing of Arthur.
Pelleas and Ettarre (excerpt).
The Poet.
The Poet's Song.

Poets and Their
Bibliographies.
Politics.
Popular.
The Princess.
Prologue to General Hamley.
Recollections of the Arabian
Nights.
The Reconciliation.
The "Revenge."
Ring Out, Wild Bells.
Rise, Happy Morn.
Rizpah.
The Roses on the Terrace.
Sadness.
The Sailor Boy.
Second Song–To the Same.
She Took the Dappled
Partridge Fleckt with Blood.
Sir Galahad: The Pure Heart.
Sir Launcelot and Queen
Guinevere (excerpt).
The Sisters.
The Sleeping House.
Song: A Spirit Haunts the
Year's Last Hours.
The Song of Love and Death.
Song of the Milkmaid.
Song: The Owl.
Song: "Who can say."
St. Agnes' Eve.
St. Simeon Stylites.
Strong Son of God.
Supposed Confessions of a
Second-Rate Sensitive Mind.
The Talking Oak: Olivia.
There Is Sweet Music Here.
The Throstle.
Tiresias.
Tithonus.
To–.
To Christopher North.
To E.L., on His Travels in
Greece.
To Edward Fitzgerald.
To Poesy.
To the Rev. F. D. Maurice.
To Vergil.
The Two Voices.
Ulysses.
Vastness.
The Vision of Sin.
The Voyage of Maeldune.
Wages.
Walking to the Mail.
What Does Little Birdie Say?
When Cats Run Home.
Will Waterproof's Lyrical
Monologue.
The Window (excerpt).
You Ask Me, Why, Tho' Ill
at Ease.
Tennyson, Frederick
The Glory of Nature.
Harvest Home.
The Holy Tide.
An Incident.
Iona.
Old Age.
The Skylark.
Tennyson, Charles Turner *See*
Turner, Charles Tennyson
Tepfer, Karen G.
The Nets on the Andrea
Doria.
Tepperman, Jean
Going through Changes.
Witch.
Teran, Jose Y., Jr.
The Field's Retention.
Javier.
Rapist.

Tugs.
Volleyball Teacher Ends the
Game.
Terral, Rufus
Chant Royal From a
Copydesk.
Terrazas, Francisco de
To a Beautiful but Heartless
Coquette.
Terrell, Myra Burnham
Theodosia Burr.
Terrill, Richard
From.
Terris, Virginia R.
Drinking.
Terry, Ellen
No Funeral Gloom.
Terry, Lucy
Bars Fight, August 28, 1746.
Terry, Reba
Lineage.
Terry, Uriah
The Wyoming Massacre.
Teschemacher, Edward
Because.
**Tessimond, Arthur Seymour
John**
The British.
Cats.
The Children Look at the
Parents.
Daydream.
Epitaph on Any Man.
Jamaican Bus Ride.
The Man in the Bowler Hat.
A Man of Culture.
Middle-Aged Conversation.
One Almost Might.
Postscript to a Pettiness.
Radio.
Where?
Thacker, Mary Afton
I Found God.
Thackeray, William Makepeace
Ad Ministram.
The Age of Wisdom.
At the Church Gate.
At the Zoo.
The Ballad of Bouillabaisse.
The Cane-Bottom'd Chair.
The Chronicle of the Drum
(excerpt).
Commanders of the Faithful.
A Credo.
The Crystal Palace.
Damages, Two Hundred
Pounds.
Dr. Birch and His Young
Friends: The End of the
Play.
The Due of the Dead.
The Garrett.
George I,–Star of Brunswick.
George II.
George III.
George IV.
Jeames of Buckley Square.
Jolly Jack.
The King of Brentford.
The King on the Tower.
Larry O'Toole (Parody on
Lever).
Little Billee.
The Mahogany Tree.
Mr. Molony's Account of the
Ball.
Old Fashioned Fun.
Peg of Limavaddy.
Pocahontas.
Ronsard to His Mistress.
Sorrows of Werther.
The Speculators.

A Tragic Story.
When Moonlike Ore the
  Hazure Seas.
Who Misses or Who Wins.
The Willow-Tree.
Thalman, Mark
The Burial.
Summit Lake.
Thatcher, Charles R.
Dick Briggs from Australia.
Look Out Below!
Moggy's Wedding.
Taking the Census.
Thatcher, Thomas
A Love Letter to Elizabeth
  Thatcher.
Thaxter, Celia
As Happy Dwellers by the
  Seaside Hear.
August.
Compensation.
The Cruise of the Mystery.
Flowers for the Brave.
Jack Frost.
Little Gustava.
May Morning.
Nikolina.
On Easter Day.
The Sandpiper.
Seaward.
Song.
Thayer, Ernest Lawrence
Casey at the Bat.
Thayer, Louis Edwin
The Little Child's Faith.
Thayer, Mary Dixon
Bird-Song.
Finding You.
A Prayer.
To Our Lady.
Treasures.
A Woman.
Thayer, Stephen Henry
Europa.
Poet of Earth.
The Waiting Chords.
Thayer, William Roscoe
The Last Hunt.
Man in Nature.
The Violin's Complaint.
Thelwall, John
Lines Written at Bridgwater,
  27 July 1797 (excerpt).
Sonnet. The Cell.
Theocritus
A Countryman's Wooing.
The Death of Adonis.
Epigrams.
Epithalamium for Helen: Song
  of the Sleepy Bridegroom.
Idylls.
Theodore of Studium, Saint
The Canon for Apocreos.
Theognis
Advice to Kyrnos.
Enjoyment.
Hope.
Immortality Conferred in
  Vain.
Poverty.
To Kurnos.
Theresa of Avila, Saint
En Las Internas Entranas.
If Lord Thy Love For Me Is
  Strong.
Let Mine Eyes See Thee.
The Life above, the Life on
  High.
Nothing Move Thee.
Shepherd, Shepherd, Hark.
St. Teresa's Book Mark.
To-Day a Shepherd.

Therese, Saint, of Lisieux
My Song of Today.
The Unpetalled Rose.
Thesen, Sharon
The Argument Begins with A.
Discourse.
The End.
Hello Goodbye.
Kirk Lonegren's Home Movie
  Taking Place Just North of
  Prince George...
Lecture Noir.
Loose Woman Poem.
Mean Drunk Poem.
Praxis.
Usage.
Thewlis, John
The Song of a Happy Rising.
Thibaudeau, Colleen
Balloon.
The Brown Family.
The Clock Tower.
The Green Family.
Poem: "I do not want only."
Thich Nhat Hanh
Condemnation.
Thiele, Colin
Aircraft, Landing.
Bert Schultz.
Radiation Victim.
Tom Farley.
Thom, William
The Blind Boy's Pranks.
The Mitherless Bairn.
They Speak o' Wiles.
Thomas, Beatrice Llewellyn
To Puck.
Thomas, Charles Edward
To a Moth Crushed Within
  the Leaves of an Iliad.
Thomas, Claire Richcreek
Flesh Will Heal and Pain Will
  Fade.
Heart Wounds.
Treasures.
Thomas, Cordia
The Lollypops.
Thomas, D. M.
Eden.
Smile.
Thomas, Donald
Tangier: Hotel Rif.
Thomas, Dylan
After the Funeral.
Altarwise by Owl-Light.
Among Those Killed in the
  Dawn Raid Was a Man
  Aged One Hundred.
And Death Shall Have No
  Dominion.
Ballad of the Long-Legged
  Bait.
Before I Knocked and Flesh
  Let Enter.
Ceremony after a Fire Raid.
A Conversation.
The Conversation of Prayer.
The Countryman's Return.
Do Not Go Gentle Into That
  Good Night.
Ears in the Turrets Hear.
Especially When the October
  Wind.
Fern Hill.
The Force That through the
  Green Fuse Drives the
  Flower.
Ghost Story.
A Grief Ago.
The Hand That Signed the
  Paper.

Hold Hard, These Ancient
  Minutes.
Holy Spring.
The Hunchback in the Park.
I, in My Intricate Image.
I See the Boys of Summer.
If I Were Tickled by the Rub
  of Love.
If My Head Hurt a Hair's
  Foot.
In a Shuttered Room I Roast.
In Country Sleep.
In My Craft or Sullen Art.
In the Beginning.
In the White Giant's Thigh.
It Is the Sinners' Dust-
  Tongued Bell Claps Me to
  Churches.
January 1939.
Lament.
Light Breaks Where No Sun
  Shines.
The Marriage of a Virgin.
Not from This Anger.
O Make Me a Mask.
October.
On No Work of Words.
On the Marriage of a Virgin.
Out of a War of Wits.
Over Sir John's Hill.
Poem in October.
Poem on His Birthday.
A Process in the Weather of
  the Heart.
A Refusal to Mourn the
  Death, by Fire, of a Child in
  London.
The Song of the Mischievous
  Dog.
The Spire Cranes.
This Bread I Break Was Once
  the Oat.
The Tombstone Told When
  She Died.
Twenty-Four Years.
Under Milk Wood (excerpt).
Vision and Prayer.
We Lying by Seasand.
When All My Five and
  Country Senses See.
When, Like a Running Grave.
Why East Wind Chills.
A Winter's Tale.
Thomas, Edith Matilda
Autumn Fashions.
Babushka.
The Betrayal of the Rose.
Breath of Hampstead Heath.
A Christopher of the
  Shenandoah.
The Cricket Kept the House.
Evoe!
A Far Cry to Heaven.
The Fir-Tree.
Frost.
In the Lilac-Rain.
Insomnia.
The Inverted Torch.
A Little Boy's Vain Regret.
Moly.
Mother England.
Mrs. Kriss Kringle.
The Muses.
Music.
Patmos.
Ponce de Leon.
The Quiet Pilgrim.
The Reply of Socrates.
The Soul in the Body.
Talking in Their Sleep.
The Tears of the Poplars.
Thefts of the Morning.

To Imagination.
To Spain–A Last Word.
The Triumph of Forgotten
  Things.
Winter Sleep.
**Thomas, Edward ("Edward
Eastaway")**
Adlestrop.
After Rain.
And You, Helen.
As the Team's Head-Brass.
Aspens.
The Barn.
Birds' Nests.
Bright Clouds.
The Brook.
By the Ford.
A Cat.
Celandine.
The Chalk-Pit.
The Cherry Trees.
The Clouds That Are So
  Light.
Cock-Crow.
The Combe.
The Cuckoo.
Digging.
Early One Morning.
February Afternoon.
Fifty Faggots.
The Gallows.
The Glory.
Good-Night.
The Green Roads.
The Gypsy.
Haymaking.
Head and Bottle.
Health.
If I Should Ever By Chance.
In Memoriam (Easter, 1915).
It Rains.
Liberty.
Lights Out.
Like the Touch of Rain.
Lob.
The Long Small Room.
Man and Dog.
The Manor Farm.
March the 3rd.
Melancholy.
The New House.
No One Cares Less Than I.
No One So Much As You.
October.
Old Man.
Out in the Dark.
The Owl.
The Path.
The Penny Whistle.
A Private.
Rain.
Sedge-Warblers.
The Sheiling.
The Sign-Post.
Snow.
Some Eyes Condemn.
Sowing.
The Sun Used to Shine.
Swedes.
Tall Nettles.
Tears.
Thaw.
There's Nothing Like the Sun.
There Was a Time.
To-Night.
The Trumpet.
Two Houses.
Two Pewits.
Under the Woods.
The Unknown.
The Unknown Bird.
What Shall I Give?

When First.
Will You Come?
Wind and Mist.
Women He Liked.
Thomas, Elvie
Motherless Child Blues.
Thomas, Evan
To the Noble Woman of
Llanarth Hall.
Thomas, Frederick William
Song: "'Tis said that absence
conquers love!"
Thomas, Gilbert
Across the Fens.
A Christmas Carol.
The Cup of Happiness.
Invocation.
The Ploughman.
Red Sky at Morning.
The Unseen Bridge.
Thomas, H. S.
The Hill Farmer Speaks.
Thomas, Henry
Bob McKinney.
Fishing Blues.
Thomas, J.R. and C. W. Elliot
Bonny Eloise.
Thomas, Jim
Dream Fishing.
Getting Loaded.
Spring Hawks.
Sunday Crappies.
Thomas, John
The Last Frontier.
Thomas, Joyce Carol
Church Poem.
I Know a Lady.
The MJQ.
Poem for Otis Redding.
Where Is the Black
Community?
Thomas, Laurence W.
Etudes.
Thomas, Lorenzo
Canzone.
Faith.
Guilt.
Historiography.
The Leopard.
MMDCCXIII 1/2.
Onion Bucket.
Otis.
Shake Hands with Your Bets,
Friend.
The Subway Witnesses.
Wonders.
Thomas, Louisa Carroll
What Is Charm?
Thomas, R. S.
Affinity.
After Jericho.
Alpine.
Aside.
At It.
A Blackbird Singing.
Bread.
Chapel Deacon.
Children's Song.
The Country Clergy.
Cynddylan on a Tractor in
Spring.
A Day in Autumn.
Enigma.
Farm Child.
The Hand.
Here.
In a Country Church.
Invasion on the Farm.
Ire.
January.
Lore.

Madrigal: "Your love is dead,
lady, your love is dead."
The Maker.
On a Line in Sandburg.
On the Farm.
The One Furrow.
Over.
A Person from Porlock.
Petition.
Pisces.
Poetry for Supper.
The Porch.
Postscript.
Selah.
Self-Portrait.
The Son.
Strangers.
The Survivor.
They.
Too Late.
The View from the Window.
The Village.
Welcome.
Welsh Landscape.
A Welshman to Any Tourist.
The Woman.
Thomas, Ramblin' (Willard)
Back Gnawing Blues.
No Job Blues.
Poor Boy Blues.
Thomas, Richard
Just Making It.
The Worker.
Thomas, Richard W.
Amen.
Life after Death.
Martyrdom.
Riots and Rituals.
To the New Annex to the
Detroit County Jail.
Thomas, Rosemary
Between Two Worlds.
East River (New York).
Thomas, Rudy
The One to Grieve.
Thomas a Kempis
The Joys of Heaven.
The Royal Way of the Holy
Cross.
Thomas Aquinas, Saint
Adoro Te Devote.
Hymn: "Sing, my tongue, the
Saviour's glory."
Thomas of Hales
A Love-Song.
Thomas of Celano
Dies Irae.
Thomas of Erceldoune
Sir Tristrem: Tristrem and the
Hunters.
Thomas of Hales
Where Is Paris and Helene?
Thompson, A. R.
Looking down a Hill.
Thompson, Alexander R.
Wayfarers in the Wilderness.
Thompson, Clara Ann
His Answer.
Mrs. Johnson Objects.
Thompson, D'Arcy Wentworth
Crazy Arithmetic.
Poor Dear Grandpapa.
That Little Black Cat.
Two Magpies Sat on a Garden
Rail.
A Very Odd Fish.
Thompson, Donald
On the Relative Merit of
Friend and Foe, Being Dead.
Thompson, Dorothy Brown
Arbor Day.
Autosonic Door.

The Boy Washington.
The City and the Trucks.
Continental Crossing.
Getting Back.
I Do Like Ogres–.
I Like House Cleaning.
Lemonade Stand.
Maps.
Our House.
Plans.
The Pony Express.
Round and Round.
This Is Halloween.
Thompson, Dunstan
Articles of War.
In All the Argosy of Your
Bright Hair.
A Knight of Ghosts and
Shadows.
Largo.
The Lay of the Battle of
Tombland.
The Moment of the Rose.
Nor Mars His Sword.
Ovid on the Dacian Coast.
This Loneliness for You Is
Like the Wound.
Thompson, Earle
The Corral.
Mythology.
Song: "Woman sits on her
porch."
Winter Count of Sean Spotted
Wolf.
Woman Made of Stars.
Thompson, Edith Osborne
The Monkeys.
Thompson, Edward
An Humble Wish (excerpt).
The Indian Maid.
Seven Sister Blues.
To Emma. Extempore.
Hyaena, off Gambia, June 4,
1779.
Thompson, Evarard V.
Diversity.
Thompson, Francis
The After Woman.
All Flesh.
All's Vast.
Any Saint (excerpt).
Arab Love-Song.
Assumpta Maria.
At Lord's.
Carmen Genesis.
A Child's Prayer.
Contemplation.
A Counsel of Moderation.
Daisy.
Dedication.
Dream-Tryst.
The End of It.
Envoy.
Ex Ore Infantium.
A Fallen Yew.
From the Night of Forebeing.
Grace of the Way (excerpt).
The Heart.
Heaven and Hell.
The Hound of Heaven.
A Judgment in Heaven.
The Kingdom of God.
Lilium Regis.
Lines for a Drawing of Our
Lady of the Night.
A May Burden.
Messages.
The Mistress of Vision.
O sweet is love, and sweet is
lack!
Ode to the Setting Sun: The
Sun.

Orient Ode.
The Poppy.
Sister Songs (excerpt).
To a Snowflake.
To Daisies.
To My Friend.
To Olivia.
The Veteran of Heaven.
We Poets Speak.
Thompson, Frederic
Heaven and Earth.
Thompson, H. S.
Lilly Dale.
Thompson, James W.
A Constant Labor.
The Greek Room.
The Plight.
The Spawn of Slums.
Work.
You Are Alms.
Thompson, Joanna
Funeral.
Gone.
Thompson, John
Adultery at the Plaza.
The Adventurers.
The Bread Hot from the
Oven.
Homecoming.
Letter to a Friend.
"Now you have burned..."
The Onion.
Thompson, John Randolph
Lee to the Rear.
Obsequies of Stuart.
Thompson, John Reuben
The Burial of Latane.
Music in Camp.
On to Richmond.
Thompson, Larry
Black is Best.
Thompson, Leslie
There Are So Many Ways of
Going Places.
Thompson, Lewis
Black Angel.
Rose.
Thompson, Lulu E.
In Hardin County, 1809.
Thompson, Maurice
The Ballad of Chickamauga.
A Creole Slave-Song.
An Early Bluebird.
A Flight Shot.
The Lion's Cub.
A Prelude.
A Prophecy.
Wild Honey.
Written on a Fly-Leaf of
Theocritus.
Thompson, Paul
The Golden Stallion.
Thompson, Phyllis
A Fairy Tale.
The Wind of the Cliff Ka
Hea.
Thompson, Raymond
Death May Leap on a Sunny
Day.
I Go to Whiskey Bars.
Journey.
North Clark Street.
Who Needs Charlie Manson?
Thompson, Samuel
April.
To a Hedgehog.
Thompson, Vance
Linen Bands.
Symbols.
Thompson, Will Henry
Come Love or Death.
The High Tide at Gettysburg.

Thompson, William
The Happy Life (excerpt).
Thompson, Jr, John
Birthday Poem, November 4th.
A Love for Patsy.
Thomson, Claire Aven
Tranquil Sea.
Thomson, Edward William
Aspiration.
The Canadian Rossignol.
Thomson, James (1700-48)
Approach of Winter.
Autumn.
The Autumnal Moon.
Birds in Spring.
Britannia's Empire.
British Commerce.
The Castle of Indolence.
Finis.
For Ever, Fortune, Wilt Thou Prove.
Frost at Night.
Happy Britannia.
Hymn on Solitude.
A Hymn on the Seasons.
Indifference to Fortune.
The Land of Indolence.
Lavinia.
Love of Nature.
Moonlight in Autumn.
Ode: "Tell me, thou soul of her I love."
A Poem Sacred to the Memory of Sir Isaac Newton.
The Praise of Industry.
Rule Britannia.
Sea-Birds.
The Seasons.
Song: "One day the god of fond desire."
The Sons of Indolence.
Spring.
Spring Flowers.
Summer.
Summer Evening and Night.
Summer Morning.
To Amanda.
To Fortune.
To the Memory of Sir Isaac Newton (excerpt).
To the Reverend Mr. Murdoch.
Winter.
A Winter Night.
The Witching Song.
A Wondrous Show.
Thomson, James (1834-82)
Art.
The Bridge.
The City of Dreadful Night.
E. B. B.
In the Room.
Midsummer Courtship.
A Requiem.
Song: "Let my voice ring out and over the earth."
Song: "Like violets pale i' the spring o' the year."
Song: "My love is the flaming Sword."
Sunday at Hampstead, X.
Sunday up the River.
To Our Ladies of Death.
Vanity.
The Vine.
William Blake.
Thomson, Mary A.
O King of Saints, We Give Thee Praise and Glory.

O Sion, Haste, Thy Mission High Fulfilling.
Thoreau, Henry David
All Things Are Current Found.
Among the Worst of Men.
At Midnight's Hour.
The Atlantides.
Between the Traveller and the Setting Sun.
Conscience.
Each More Melodious Note I Hear.
Epitaph on an Engraver.
Epitaph on the World.
The Fall of the Leaf.
The Fisher's Boy.
For Though the Caves Were Rabbited.
Forever in My Dream and in My Morning Thought.
The Great Adventure.
Great Friend.
Haze.
I Am a Parcel of Vain Strivings Tied.
I Am the Little Irish Boy.
I'm Thankful That My Life Doth Not Deceive.
I Saw a Delicate Flower Had Grown up 2 Feet High.
I Was Born upon Thy Bank, River.
I Was Made Erect and Lone.
Indeed Indeed, I Cannot Tell.
Independence.
Inspiration.
The Inward Morning.
It Is No Dream of Mine.
Lately, Alas, I Knew a Gentle Boy.
Love.
Love Equals Swift and Slow.
Low-Anchored Cloud.
March 8, 1840.
Men Say They Know Many Things.
Mist.
The Moon Now Rises to Her Absolute Rule.
My Boots.
"My Life Has Been the Poem..."
My Prayer.
Nature.
The Old Marlborough Road.
On the Sun Coming out in the Afternoon.
Pray to What Earth Does This Sweet Cold Belong.
Prayer.
The Railroad.
The River Swelleth More and More.
Sic Vita.
Smoke.
Smoke in Winter.
Stanzas.
Summer Rain.
Tall Ambrosia.
They Made Me Erect and Lone.
This Is My Carnac, Whose Unmeasured Dome.
Though All the Fates Should Prove Unkind.
To a Marsh Hawk in Spring.
To the Maiden in the East.
To the Mountains.
Walden.
We Need the Tonic of Wildness.

What's the Railroad.
When Winter Fringes Every Bough.
Who Sleeps by Day and Walks by Night.
Winter Memories.
Woof of the Sun, Ethereal Gauze.
Thorley, Wilfrid
Buttercups.
Chant for Reapers.
The Grocer and the Gold-Fish.
Hansom Cabbies.
The Happy Sheep.
The Harvest Elves.
Norse Sailor's Joy.
Of a Spider.
The Old Inn-Sign.
Roger Francis.
Thornbury, George Walter
The Cavalier's Escape.
The Court Historian.
The Jester's Sermon.
The Pompadour.
The Three Troopers.
La Tricoteuse.
Thornbury, William
The Sally from Coventry.
Thornton, James
She May Have Seen Better Days.
The Streets of Cairo.
Thornton, James and George Cooper
When You Were Sweet Sixteen.
Thornton, Lalia Mitchell
Forgive.
Thornton, M. B.
Limerick: "All young men should take note of the case."
Limerick: "There once was a popular crooner."
Thorold Rogers, J. E.
Another.
An Epitaph: "Here X. lies dead."
On a Distinguished Politician.
On the Historians Freeman and Stubbs.
A Suggestion Made by the Posters of the "Globe."
A Vulgar Error.
Thorp, N. Howard
Billy the Kid.
Little Joe the Wrangler.
Thorpe, Dwayne
The Gathering.
Rooftop Winter.
Thorpe, Rose Hartwick
Curfew Must Not Ring To-Night.
Thorsteinsson, Steingrimur
Swansong on the Moorlands.
Thrale Piozzio, Hester
The Three Warnings.
Thring, Godfrey
Jesus Comes on Clouds Triumphant.
Throne, Marilyn
What She Wished.
Thurber, James
Morals.
Thurlow, Edward, Lord See **Howell-Thurlow, Edward**
Thurman, Judith
Mare.
Thurston, Harry
March Sound.

Thwaite, Anthony
Ali Ben Shufti.
Arabic Script.
At Birth.
At Dunwich.
Child Crying.
Looking On.
Manhood End.
Mr. Cooper.
The Pond.
Rites for a Demagogue.
Sunday Afternoons.
Switzerland.
Thwaites, Michael
Easter Hymn.
Thermopylae.
To J. S. Bach.
Thynne, Francis
Ingratitude.
Tibble, Anne
Trials of a Tourist.
Tibullus, Albius
Dicamus Bona Verba.
No Harm to Lovers.
Odes (excerpt).
A Pastoral Elegy.
The Recantation.
Sulpicia's Rival.
Tichborne [(or Tichbourne)], Chidiock
Retrospect.
Tichnor, Francis Orrery
Our Left.
Tichy, Susan
The Hours.
Identity Card.
In an Arab Town.
Irrigation.
Tick, Edward
Kandinsky: "Improvision No. 27."
To My Wife Asleep.
Tickell, Thomas
Colin and Lucy.
Fairies.
An Ode: "Thou Dome, where Edward first enroll'd."
To the Earl of Warwick.
Ticknor, Francis Orrery [(or Orray)]
Albert Sidney Johnston.
A Battle Ballad.
Little Giffen.
A Song For the Asking.
The Virginians of the Valley.
Tieck, Johann Ludwig
Autumn Song.
Love.
Tiemer-Wille, Gertrude
Repast.
Tiempo, Cesar
Harangue on the Death of Hayyim Nahman Bialik.
I Tell of Another Young Death.
The Jewish Cemetery.
Weeping and Singing.
Tierney, Joseph Paul
Donne Redone.
Tietjens, Eunice
April.
The Bacchante to Her Babe.
Completion.
The Drug Clerk.
The Great Man.
Imprisoned.
The Most-Sacred Mountain.
Moving.
My Mother's House.
Old Maps.
On the Height.
Parting after a Quarrel.

The Pioneer Woman–in the North Country.
Psalm to My Beloved.
Thaw.
To My Friend, Grown Famous.

Tietz, Stephen
The Pinball Queen of South Illinois St.

Tikhonov, Nikolay
Fire, the Rope...

Tilden, Stephen
Braddock's Fate, with an Incitement to Revenge.
The British Lyon Roused.
O Heaven Indulge.

Tilghman, Zoe A.
Alibi.
Wind Song.

Tillam, Thomas
Hail, Holy Land.
Uppon the First Sight of New-England June 29, 1638.

Tiller, Terence
Bathers.
Egyptian Dancer.
The End of the Story.
Image in a Lilac Tree.
Killed in Action.
No Time.
Prothalamion.
Reading a Medal.
Street Performers, 1851.
The Vase.

Tillett, Wilbur Fisk
Incarnate Love.
My Father Knows.

Tillinghast, David
Women Hoping for Rain.

Tillinghast, Richard
Hearing of the End of the War.
The Knife.
Our Flag Was Still There.
Return.
September: Last Day at the Beach.
Shooting Ducks in South Louisiana.
Summer Rain.

Tillman, Charlie D.
Lost after All.

Tilney, Charles
The Cobblers' Song.

Tilton, Theodore
Coeur de Lion to Berengaria.
The Flight from the Convent.
God Save the Nation.
The Great Bell Roland.
The King's Ring.
Sir Marmaduke's Musings.

Timrod, Henry
Carolina.
Charleston.
Christmas.
The Cotton Boll.
A Cry to Arms.
Dreams.
Ethnogenesis.
Faint Falls the Gentle Voice.
I Know Not Why, but All This Weary Day.
Ode: "Sleep sweetly in your humble graves."
Ode to the Confederate Dead in Magnolia Cemetery.
Quatorzain.
Serenade.
Sonnet: "Most men know love but as a part of life."
Spring.
A Trifle.

The Unknown Dead.

Tindley, C.A.
Nothing Between.

Ting, Walasse
Pepsi Generation.

Tio, Elsa
I am furious with myself.

Tiplady, Thomas
Above the Hills of Time.
A Grace.

Tippett, James S.
Autumn Woods.
Building a Skyscraper.
Busy Carpenters.
Counting the Days.
Do Not Open Until Christmas.
Ducks at Dawn.
The Elevated Train.
Engine.
Familiar Friends.
Ferry-Boats.
Freight Boats.
George Washington.
Hang out the Flags.
I Like Christmas.
Old Log House.
The Park.
"Sh."
Sleet Storm.
Sunning.
Trains.
Up in the Air.

Tipple, E. H.
Hot Weather in the Plains– India.

Tisdale, Charles P.R.
My Childhood's Bedroom.
The Origins of Escape.

Titheradge, Peter
New Improved Sonnet XVIII (parody).
Teatime Variations.

Titherington, Richard Handfield
Faithful unto Death.

Tobin, James Edward
Madonna of the Exiles.

Todachine, Mike
Poem: "you can look into my face."

Todd, Barbara Euphan
Fairy Story.
Jeremy's Secrets.

Todd, Ruthven
Joan Miro.
The Lonely Month.
A Mantelpiece of Shells.
Paul Klee.
Personal History: For My Son.
Poem: "I walk at dawn across the hollow hills."
Six Winters.
To a Very Beautiful Lady.
Upon This Rock.
Various Ends.
Watching You Walk.

Todhunter, John
Aghadoe.
The Banshee.
The Black Knight.
Maureen.
Song: "Bring from the craggy haunts of birch and pine."
An Utter Passion Uttered Utterly (parody).

Toerien, Barend
Absent Daughter.
Campi Flegrei.
The Firmament Displays on High.
Quatrain.

Youth.

Toffler, Alvin
The League of Selves.

Tofte, Robert
Laura.
Love's Labour Lost.

Tohe, Laura
At Mexican Springs.
Cat or Stomp.
Female Rain.
Male Rain.
The Shooting.
To Shima sani.

Tohee, Mah-do-ge
Agnes.
Indian america.
Untitled.

Toleson, M. B.
John Henry in Harlem.

Tolkien, J. R. R.
The Dragon's Hoard.
The Hobbit (excerpt).
The Mewlips.
The Old Walking Song.
Oliphaunt.
Roads Go Ever Ever On.
Shadow-Bride.
The Stone Troll.

Tollefsen, Astrid
Toulouse Lautrec.
Workday Morning.

Toller, Ernst
The Book I Held Grew Cold.
Corpses in the Wood.
O Heavy Step of Slow Monotony.
O Master Masons.
O My Swallows.
The One Who Struggles.
To the Mothers.

Tollerud, Jim
Bird of Power.
Buzz.
Earth.
Elementary.
Eye of God.
Rainier.
Sunrise.
Thirsty Island.
Week-Seek.

Tollet, Elizabeth
Hypatia (excerpt).
Winter Song.

Tolnay, Thomas
The Basement Watch.

Tolson, Melvin B.
African China.
The Birth of John Henry.
Dark Symphony.
Freemon Hawthorne.
Harlem Gallery (excerpt).
A Legend of Versailles.
On the Founding of Liberia.
Peg Leg Snelson.
PSI.
Satchmo.
The Sea-Turtle and the Shark.
Sootie Joe.

Tomioka Taeko
Life Story.
Living Together.
Please Say Something.

Tomkis, Thomas
The Gordian Knot.

Tomlinson, Charles
At Barstow.
At Delft.
The Cavern.
The Chances of Rhyme.
Charlotte Corday.
The Chestnut Avenue at Alton House.

Civilities of Lamplight.
The Crane.
A Death in the Desert.
The Death of Will.
Descartes and the Stove.
Distinctions.
The Door.
A Dream.
Farewell to Van Gogh.
Fiascherino.
The Hand at Callow Hill Farm.
How Still the Hawk.
Icos.
In Arden.
In Defense of Metaphysics.
The Jam Trap.
Las Trampas U.S.A.
MacDuff.
A Meditation on John Constable.
More Foreign Cities.
Mr. Brodsky.
Le Musee Imaginaire.
Observation of Facts.
Ode to Arnold Schoenberg.
On the Hall at Stowey.
Oxen: Ploughing at Fiesole.
Paring the Apple.
The Picture of J. T. in a Prospect of Stone.
Poem.
Return to Hinton.
The Ruin.
Swimming Chenango Lake.
Through Binoculars.
Tramontana at Lerici.
Two Views of Two Ghost Towns.
Winter Encounters.
A Word in Edgeways.

Tompson, Benjamin
Chelmsfords Fate.
Edmund Davie....
Marlburyes Fate.
New-Englands Crisis: The Prologue.
On a Fortification at Boston Begun By Women.
Seaconk or Rehoboths Fate.
Seaconk Plain Engagement.
A Supplement.
To My Honoured Patron Humphrey Davie...
The Town Called Providence Its Fate.

Tomson, Graham R.
To My Cat.

Tonks, Rosemary
Farewell to Kurdistan.
Story of a Hotel Room.

Tonna, Charlotte Elizabeth
The Maiden City.

Tooker, Lewis Frank
He Bringeth Them Unto Their Desired Haven.
His Quest.
Homeward Bound.
The Last Fight.
The Old Conservative.
The Sea-King.
Sleep.

Toomer, Jean
At Sea.
Banking Coal.
Beehive.
The Blue Meridian.
Brown River, Smile.
Cotton Song.
Evening Song.
Face.
Five Vignettes.

Georgia Dusk.
Harvest Song.
Her Lips Are Copper Wire.
The Lost Dancer.
November Cotton Flower.
Portrait in Georgia.
Reapers.
Song of the Son.
Toplady, Augustus Montague
Ah! Give Me, LORD, the
  Single Eye.
Compared with Christ.
Deathless Principle, Arise.
Happiness Found.
Lord! It Is Not Life to Live.
Rejoicing in Hope.
Rock of Ages.
Torain, Joseph
Tracks.
Torberg, Friedrich
Amalek.
Seder, 1944.
Torel, Ali Sedat Hilmi
My Indian Girl.
Nirvana.
Torgerson, Eric
One Year Later.
Torlino
Therefore I Must Tell the
  Truth.
Torna
Lament for Corc and Niall of
  the Nine Hostages.
Tornai, Jozsef
Mr. T. S. Eliot Cooking Pasta.
Torrence, Ridgely
Adam's Dying.
Adam's Song of the Visible
  World.
The Bird and the Tree.
Ceremony for Birth and
  Naming.
Evensong.
Eye-Witness.
The House of a Hundred
  Lights.
Legend.
Santa Barbara Beach.
The Singers in a Cloud.
The Son.
Toshiyuki, Fujiwara-No-
Although It Is Not Plainly
  Visible to the Eye.
Toth, Judit
Dead Embryos.
Remembering.
The Southeast Ramparts of
  the Seine.
To the Newborn.
Wildfire.
"Totius" [(J. D. Du Toit)]
Forgive and Forget.
Toulet, Paul-Jean
Simple Things.
Toure, Askia Muhammad
Floodtide.
JuJu.
Tauhid.
Tourneur, Cyril
The Atheist's Tragedy.
The Revenger's Tragedy
  (excerpt).
The Transformed
  Metamorphosis: Awake, Oh
  Heaven.
Towle, Tony
After Dinner We Take a
  Drive into the Night.
The Allegorical Figure of
  Brooklyn.
The City in the Throes of
  Despair.

Collaboration.
Daybreak.
Elegy.
From the Spanish.
George Towle.
Music.
New York.
Poem.
Towne, Anthony
Dead of Winter.
Towne, Charles Hanson
Around the Corner.
At Nightfall.
The Best Road of All.
City Roofs.
An Easter Canticle.
In Summer.
The Messed Damozel
  (parody).
Messengers.
Of One Self-Slain.
A Prayer for the Old
  Courage.
Silence.
A Song at Easter.
Song: "I saw the day's white
  rapture."
The Time-Clock.
Townsend, Aurelian
Come Not To Me For Scarfs.
The Constant Lover.
A Dialogue betwixt Time and
  a Pilgrim.
An Elegie Made by Mr.
  Aurelian Townshend in
  Remembrance of the Ladie..
Let Not Thy Beauty.
A Paradox.
Pure Simple Love.
To the Countesse of Salisbury.
To the Lady May.
Upon Kinde and True Love.
Youth and Beauty.
Townsend, Charles
On the Lake Poets.
Townsend, Emily
Fish.
Townsend, F. H.
To the Cuckoo.
Townsend, George Alfred
In Rama.
My Correspondent's Last
  Ride.
Townsend, Henry
Poor Man Blues.
Townsend, Joanne
With Due Deference to
  Thomas Wolfe.
Townsend, Mary Ashley
At Set of Sun.
Creed.
The Dead Singer.
Down the Bayou.
Embryo.
A Georgia Volunteer.
Her Horoscope.
Reserve.
Virtuosa.
Townson, Hazel
Dirge.
Not Late Enough.
Tracy, Neil
I Doubt a Lovely Thing Is
  Dead.
Traherne, Thomas
Amendment.
The Apostasy.
The Approach.
The Bible.
Childhood.
Christendom.
Christian Ethics.

Consummation.
Desire.
Eden.
Hosanna.
An Infant's Eye.
Innocence.
Insatibleness.
Love.
My Spirit.
News.
On Christmas-Day.
On Leaping over the Moon.
Poverty.
The Preparative.
The Rapture.
Right Apprehension.
The Salutation.
A Serious and a Curious
  Night-Meditation.
Shadows in the Water.
Solitude.
Thanksgiving for the Body.
Thanksgivings for the Beauty
  of His Providence.
The Third Century.
To the Same Purpose.
The Vision.
Walking.
Wonder.
Traill, Henry Duff
After Dilettante Concetti
  (parody).
A Drawing-Room Ballad.
The Puss and the Boots
  (parody) (excerpt).
Vers de Societe (parody).
Trakl, Georg
In Hellbrunn.
On the Way.
The Rats.
Rest and Silence.
Transtromer, Tomas
Allegro.
An Extra Joyful Chorus for
  Those Who Have Read This
  Far.
The Man Awakened by a
  Song Above His Roof.
Open and Closed Space.
Schubertiana.
Track.
Tranter, John
Crying in Early Infancy:
  Sonnet.
The Death Circus.
Trapnell, Edna Valentine
The Fiddler.
Trapp, Joseph
Epigram.
Trask, Katrina
Aidenn.
At Last.
Love.
Sorrow.
Traubel, Horace L.
Epicedium.
How Are You, Dear World,
  This Morning?
I Served in a Great Cause.
If All the Voices of Men.
Trawick, Leonard
Feeling for Fish.
Traxler, Patricia
Waking in Nice.
Treasone, Grace
Life.
Tree, Iris
To My Father.
You Preach to Me of Laws.
Treece, Henry
Ballad.
Birdwatcher.

Conquerors.
The Crimson Cherry Tree.
Death Walks through the
  Mind's Dark Woods.
The Dyke-Builder.
The Haunted Garden.
The Heart's Wild Geese.
Horror.
In the Beginning Was the
  Bird.
In the Dark Caverns of the
  Night.
In the Third Year of War.
The Magic Wood.
Prayer in Time of War.
That Summer.
Through the Dark Aisles of
  the Wood.
The Waiting Watchers.
Walking at Night.
Trefethen, Florence
Slipping out of Intensive Care.
Tregonning, Charley
Cousin Jack Song.
Treinin, Avner
Deserted Shrine.
Salmon Cycle.
**Treinin, Avner and E. A.
  Levenston**
The Cage.
Treitel, Margot
The Trouble with Truck
  Drivers.
Tremayne, Sydney
Discomfort in High Places.
The Galloway Shore.
Moses.
North of Berwick.
Tremblay, Bill
The Court We Live On.
Tremblay, Gail
Crow Voices.
Trench, Herbert
A Charge.
Come Let Us Make Love
  Deathless.
I Heard a Soldier.
I Seek Thee in the Heart
  Alone.
Jean Richepin's Song.
She Comes Not When Noon
  Is on the Roses.
What Bids Me Leave.
Trench, Richard Chenevix
A Century of Couplets
  (excerpt).
Elegy.
Gibraltar.
God Our Refuge.
The Kingdom of God.
A Legend of Alhambra.
Lord, Many Times.
Prayer.
Recollections of Burgos.
Retirement.
Some Murmur When Their
  Sky Is Clear.
Sonnet: "I stood beside a pool,
  from whence ascended."
Sonnet: "A sound of many
  waters!–now I know."
Sonnet: "An open wound
  which has been healed
  anew."
Trent, Lucia
Architects of Dream.
Armistice Day.
Bread of Brotherhood.
The Dreamers Cry Their
  Dream.
From Beyond.
It Is Not Too Late.

Mary's Son.
Song for Tomorrow.
These Are My People.
Trevathan, Charles E.
The Bully Song.
Trevisa, John
Prologue to a Translation.
Trias, Arturo
Act of Faith.
Ars Poetica.
This Shirt.
Triem, Eve
Bordello, Revisited.
Gardens Are All My Heart.
Gerda, My Husband's Wife.
Misdemeanor.
Trifilio, Jim
Hokkaido.
Trifonov, Gennady
For Three Swift Days.
Triggs, Jeffery Alan
Man on Move Despite
  Failures.
Trimpi, Alison A.
The Skull in the Desert.
Trimpi, Wesley
Lines for a Wedding Gift.
Oedipus to the Oracle.
On a Bas-Relief.
To Giotto.
Trinidad, David
Meet the Supremes.
Monday, Monday.
Tripp, John
On My Fortieth Birthday.
Tropp, Stephen
My Wife Is My Shirt.
Trott, Harlan
Out from Gloucester.
Trott, Norman L.
No Time For God.
Trott, Perient
Negro Spiritual.
Trotter, Bernard Freeman
The Poplars.
"Troubadour"
The Law of Averages.
The Reversible Metaphor.
Troubetzkoy, Amelie
Before the Rain.
A Mood.
A Sonnet.
Troubetzkoy, Ulrich
Christmas Lullaby.
Out of the Wilderness.
Troupe, Quincy
The Day Duke Raised; May
  24th, 1974.
Dirge.
For Malcolm Who Walks in
  the Eyes of Our Children.
In Texas Grass.
The Old People Speak of
  Death.
Poem for Friends.
A Sense of Coolness.
South African Bloodstone.
These Crossings, These
  Words.
Transformation.
White Weekend.
Trowbridge, John Townsend
At Sea.
Columbus at the Convent.
The Cup.
Darius Green and his Flying-
  Machine.
Evening at the Farm.
Filling an Order.
Lincoln.
Midsummer.
Midwinter.

The Pewee.
Recollections of "Lalla
  Rookh."
The Vagabonds.
Widow Brown's Christmas.
Troy, Grace E.
I Would Not Ask.
Trials.
Truax, Hawley
Half.
Morning, Noon, and...
Trudell, Dennis
Hotel in Paris.
The Jump Shooter.
Trueba, Antonio de
Nightfall.
Truesdale, C. W.
Amanda, Playing.
Little Roach Poem.
Trumbell, Annie Eliot
To O.S.C.
Trumbull, John
The Country Clown.
M'Fingal.
The Progress of Dulness.
Prospect of the Future Glory
  of America.
Truth, Sojourner
Ain't I a Woman?
Trypanis, C. A.
Four Lovely Sisters.
To Theon from His Son
  Theon.
Ts'ai Yen
Eighteen Verses Sung to a
  Tatar Reed Whistle.
Tsaloumas, Dimitris
A Rhapsody of Old Men, VII.
Ts'ao Sung
A Protest in the Sixth Year of
  Ch'ien Fu.
The War Year.
Tschaikovsky
A Legend.
Ts'en Ts'an
A Song of White Snow.
Tso Ssu
The Scholar in the Narrow
  Street.
Tsuda, Kiyoko
To be a mistress.
Tsuda, Margaret
Commitment in a City.
Hard Questions.
Ts'uei T'u
On New Year's Eve.
Tsui, Kitty
Chinatown Talking Story.
It's in the Name.
Tsurayuki
The Time I Went to See My
  Sister.
Two Poems.
Tsuru
Willows in the Snow.
Tsvetayeva, Marina
Andre Chenier.
Ars.
An Attempt at Jealousy.
The Daughter of Jairus.
"...I'd like to live with you."
Insomnia (excerpt).
The Poem of the End
  (excerpt).
We Are Keeping an Eye on
  the Girls.
We Shall Not Escape Hell.
Tu Fu
Clear After Rain.
The Emperor.
The Excursion.
Jade Flower Palace.

Moon Festival.
The Newlyweds' Separation.
Night in the House by the
  River.
Night Thoughts While
  Travelling.
A Night Vigil in the Left
  Court of the Palace.
On Meeting Li Kuei-Nien
  Down the River.
The Return.
The Road to Pengya.
Snow Storm.
A Song of Dagger-Dancing
  (excerpt).
To My Retired Friend Wei.
The Willow.
Written on the Wall at
  Chang's Hermitage.
Tu-kehu and Wetea
O Beautiful Calm.
Oh, How My Love with a
  Whirling Power.
Tuck, Clyde Edwin
The Good Shepherd.
Tucker, Bessie
Frying Pan Skillet Blues.
Tucker, F. Bland
All Praise to Thee.
Our Father, by Whose Name.
Tucker, Paul
A Heavenly Friend.
Tucker, Robert
Security.
Tucker, St. George
The Cynic.
Days of My Youth.
The Discontented Student.
The Judge with the Sore
  Rump.
Tuckerman, Frederick Goddard
And So the Day Drops By.
"As Eponina Brought, to
  Move the King."
The Cricket.
Elegy in Six Sonnets.
Hast Thou Seen Reversed the
  Prophet's Miracle.
Here, where the Red Man
  Swept the Leaves away.
November.
Put Off Thy Bark from Shore,
  Though Near the Night.
The Question.
Refrigerium.
Roll On, Sad World!
Sometimes I Walk where the
  Deep Water Dips.
Sonnet XIV.
Sonnet XV.
Sonnets, sels.
Tall Stately Plants with Spikes
  and Forks of Gold.
Thin Little Leaves of Wood
  Fern, Ribbed and Toothed.
Under the Locust Blossoms.
An Upper Chamber in a
  Darkened House.
Yet Vain, Perhaps, the Fruits.
Tuckerman, Henry Theodore
Washington's Statue.
Tueni, Nadia
More Distant Than the Dead
  Sea.
Nothing but a man.
Would you come back if I
  said the earth.
Tuft, Ellen
Nuclear Land.
Tullar, Grant Colfax
As Thy Days.

Tulloch, Bill
Beinn a' Ghlo.
NN 616410.
Tunstall, Virginia Lyne
Evening on the Harbor.
Spinster Song.
Tupper, Helen Isabella
For Everything Give Thanks.
Tupper, Kathryn Munro
Fallen Leaves.
Tupper, Martin Farquhar
The African Desert (excerpt).
The Anglo-Saxon Race.
England's Heart.
Mercy to Animals.
Proverbial Philosophy.
The Train of Religion
  (excerpt).
Tuquan, Fadwa
After Twenty Years.
From behind the Bars.
Turberville, George
An Epitaph of Maister Win
  Drowned in the Sea.
The Lover Abused
  Renounceth Love.
The Lover Exhorteth His
  Lady to Take Time, While
  Time Is.
The Lover to His Lady.
The Lover to the Thames of
  London.
Of a Rich Miser.
Of Drunkenness.
Of One That Had a Great
  Nose.
Of the Clock and the Cock.
The Pine to the Mariner.
That All Things Are as They
  Are Used.
That He Findeth Others as
  Fair, But Not So Faithful as
  His Friend.
That No Man Should Write
  But Such as Do Excel.
To an Olde Gentlewoman,
  That Painted Hir Face.
To His Friend, Promising
  That Though Her Beauty
  Fade...
To His Love That Sent Him a
  Ring.
To His Ring, Given to His
  Lady.
To One That Had Little Wit.
To Parker.
To Spencer.
To the Roving Pirate.
Unable by Long and Hard
  Travel to Banish Love,
  Returns Her Friend.
Turbyfill, Mark
Benediction.
Turco, Lewis
Bell Weather.
Bordello.
The Depot.
Failed Fathers.
House and Shutter.
Nightpiece.
An Ordinary Evening in
  Cleveland.
The Wind Carol.
Turei, Mohi
Ruaumoko–The Earthquake
  God.
Turner, Alberta
Choosing a Death.
Learning to Count.
Turner, Charles Tennyson
A Brilliant Day.
The Artist on Penmaenmawr.

The Bee-Wisp.
The Buoy-Bell.
Calvus to a Fly.
A Country Dance.
Cader Idris at Sunset.
Cowper's Three Hares.
From Harvest to January.
Gout and Wings.
The Hydraulic Ram.
Julius Caesar and the Honey-
  Bee.
The Lattice at Sunrise.
Letty's Globe.
The Lion's Skeleton.
Maggie's Star.
Mary Queen of Scots.
Minnie and Her Dove.
The Needles' Lighthouse from
  Keyhaven, Hampshire.
On a Vase of Gold-Fish.
On Finding a Small Fly
  Crushed in a Book.
On Seeing a Little Child Spin
  a Coin of Alexander the
  Great.
On Shooting a Swallow in
  Early Youth.
On Some Humming-Birds in a
  Glass Case.
On Startling Some Pigeons.
On the Eclipse of the Moon of
  October 1865.
The Quiet Tide near
  Ardrossan.
The Steam Threshing-
  Machine.
A Summer Night in the
  Beehive.
A Summer Twilight.
To a Tenting Boy.
The Vacant Cage.
The White Horse of
  Westbury.
Turner, Darwin T.
Death.
Guest Lecturer.
Love.
Night Slivers.
The Sit-In.
Sonnet Sequence.
To Vanity.
Turner, Doris
Reckoning A. M. Thursday
  after an Encounter....
Turner, Doug
The Spirit.
Turner, Elizabeth
The Bird's Nest.
The Canary.
How to Write a Letter.
Politeness.
Rebecca's After-Thought.
The Two Little Miss Lloyds.
Turner, Godfrey
The Journal of Society.
Tattle.
Turner, Gordon
I Want to One Morning.
Turner, Nancy Byrd
Autumn!
The Bagpipe Man.
Black and Gold.
The Buccaneer.
Click o' the Latch.
Contrary Mary.
Dark-Eyed Lad Columbus.
Death Is a Door.
Down a Sunny Easter
  Meadow.
Easter Joy.
The Extraordinary Dog.
February Birthday.

The Fellowship of Prayer.
First Christmas Night of All.
The First Thanksgiving.
First Thanksgiving of All.
Going up to London.
I Wish.
Immigrants.
Legacy.
Let Us Have Peace.
Lincoln.
The Little Road.
More Than Flowers We Have
  Brought.
Old Quin Queeribus.
The Ordinary Dog.
Planting a Tree.
Prayer on Fourth of July.
The Rivers Remember.
The Sampler.
Ships.
Spring Wind.
A Sure Sign.
They Will Look for a Few
  Words.
Twenty Foolish Fairies.
Washington.
The Weather Factory.
When Young Melissa Sweeps.
Whenever I Say "America."
Wings and Wheels.
A Word About Woodpiles.
Turner, Samuel S.
November.
Turner, Steve
Christmas Is Really for the
  Children.
How to Hide Jesus.
Turner, Walter James
The Dancer.
Ecstasy.
Epithalamium.
Giraffe and Tree.
The Hunter.
Hymn to Her Unknown.
In the Caves of Auvergne.
In Time Like Glass.
India.
Life and Death.
The Lion.
A Love-Song.
Marriage.
Men Fade Like Rocks.
The Music of a Tree.
The Navigators.
Poetry and Science.
The Princess.
Reflection.
The Robber.
Romance.
The Seven Days of the Sun
  (excerpt).
Silence.
Song: "Lovely hill-torrents
  are."
The Sun.
Talking with Soldiers.
Tragic Love.
The Word Made Flesh?
Turner, William Price
Alien.
Coronary Thrombosis.
Turners Dish of Lentten
  Stuffe.
University Curriculum.
Tusiani, Joseph
Anticipation.
Rest O Sun I Cannot.
Tusser, Thomas
A Digression from
  Husbandrie: To a Poynt or
  Two of Huswifrie.

A Hundreth Good Poyntes of
  Husbandry.
Upon the Author's First
  Seven Years' Service.
The Winds.
Tussman, Malka
At the Well.
I Say.
Love the Ruins.
Mount Gilboa.
Songs of the Priestess.
Thou Shalt Not.
Water Without Sound.
Tuttle, Stella Weston
The Quickening.
Tuwhare, Hone
A Burnt Offering to Your
  Greenstone Eyes, Tangaroa.
Ron Mason.
Snowfall.
Tuwim, Julian
Epos.
The Gypsy Bible.
Jewboy.
Lodgers.
Mother.
A Prayer.
Pursuit.
Request for a Song.
There Is No Country.
**"Twain, Mark" (Samuel
Langhorne Clemens)**
The Aged Pilot Man.
Don't Copy Cat.
Emmeline Grangerford's "Ode
  to Stephen Dowling Bots,
  Dec'd."
Epitaph Placed on His
  Daughter's Tomb.
He Done His Level Best.
Imitation of Julia A. Moore.
Limerick: "A man hired by
  John Smith and Co."
The Miner's Lament.
A Missouri Maiden's Farewell
  to Alabama.
Twala, James
Biltong.
Tweedy, Henry Hallam
Christmas at Babbitt's.
Eternal God, Whose Power
  Upholds.
O Gracious Father of
  Mankind.
Twichell, Chase
Abandoned House in Late
  Light.
Blurry Cow.
Cedar Needles.
Watercress & Ice.
Twig, John
A Ballade of the Nurserie.
Twist, Horace
Our Parodies Are Ended.
Two Poor Boys
Two White Horses in a Line.
Tyack, Jim
25 Spontaneous Lines
  Greeting the World.
Tylee, Edward Sydney
Outward Bound.
Tyler, Inez M.
A Call to Pentecost.
Tyler, Parker
For the Noun C. BL.
Nijinsky.
To a Photograph.
Tyler, Royall
Anacreontic to Flip.
Gambling.
Hail to the Joyous Day.
Independence Day.

A Love Song.
Original Epitaph on a
  Drunkard.
The Widower.
Tymnes
The Dog from Malta.
Tymnes.
Tynan, Katharine *See also*
Hinkson, Katherine Tynan
Chanticleer.
The Childless Woman in
  Heaven.
The Doves.
Farewell.
I was born under a kind star.
The Making of Birds.
A Memory.
Tyrrell, Henry
The Masterful Man.
Tyrrell, Robert Yelverton
Johnny, I Hardly Knew Ye:
  Swinburnese (parody).
Tyrtaeus
How Can Man Die Better.
Tyutchev, Fyodor
As Ocean's Stream.
At Vshchizh.
Last Love.
Night Wind.
Nightfall.
Silentium.
Spring: a Formal Ode.
Tzara, Tristan
Evening.
Mothers.
Tzu Yeh
The Bare Branches Tremble.
I Had Not Fastened My Sash
  over My Gown.
It Is Night Again.

U

Uba, George
Firefly.
Gary Gotow.
How Do You Spell
  "Missile"?: Preliminary
  Instructions...
Old Photo, 1942.
Uceda, Julia
Time Reminded Me.
**Ucker, Henry and Charles C.
Sawyer**
Weeping Sad and Lonely.
Uda, Emperor
Like a wave crest.
Udall, Nicholas
I Mun Be Married a Sunday.
A Minion Wife.
Ufford, Edward Smith
Throw out the Lifeline.
Ugaas, Raage
Poet's Lament on the Death
  of His Wife.
Ugga Byan
Her Absent Lord (excerpt).
Uhland, Ludwig
The Castle by the Sea.
Durand of Blonden.
The Hostess' Daughter.
Ichabod! The Glory Has
  Departed.
In a Lovely Garden Walking.
A Leaf.
Spirits Everywhere.
Ukihashi
Haiku: "Whether I sit or lie."

Ulinover, Miriam
  Havdolah Wine.
  In the Courtyard.
Ullman, Leslie
  Last Night They Heard the
    Woman Upstairs.
  Proof.
**Ulrich von Liechtenstein [(or
  Lichten Stein)]**
  Love, Whose Month Was
    Ever May.
Unamuno, Miguel de
  The Atheist's Prayer.
  Castile.
  Domestic Scenes.
Underhill, Evelyn
  The Holy Spirit.
  Introversion.
  Supersensual.
  Theophany.
Underwood, Wilbur
  The Cattle of His Hand.
  To the Brave Soul.
Ungaretti, Giuseppe
  The Island.
  Quiet.
  Without More Weight.
Unger, Barbara
  Breasts.
  Geological Faults.
Unik, Pierre
  The Manless Society.
Unknown
  The Giver of Life.
Untermeyer, Jean Starr
  The Altar.
  Autumn.
  Clay Hills.
  Country of No Lack.
  Dew on a Dusty Heart.
  False Enchantment.
  From the Day-Book of a
    Forgotten Prince.
  Gothic.
  High-Tide.
  Lake-Song.
  Last Plea.
  Little Dirge.
  The Passionate Sword.
  Sinfonia Domestica.
  Sung on a Sunny Morning.
  Thaw.
Untermeyer, Louis See also
  "Lewis, Michael"
  Appeal to the Phoenix.
  At the Bottom of the Well.
  Burning Bush.
  Caliban in the Coal Mines.
  Catalogue.
  Cell-Mates.
  The Dance of Dust (parody).
  The Dark Chamber.
  Der Brief, Den Du
    Geshrieben.
  The Dream and the Blood.
  End of the Comedy.
  Equals.
  Feuerzauber.
  Folk-Song.
  Food and Drink (excerpt).
  Frustrate.
  Furchte Nichts, Geliebte
    Seele.
  Glad Day.
  Goliath and David.
  Hair-Dressing.
  Hands.
  Infidelity.
  Irony.
  Koheleth.
  Landscapes.
  Last Words before Winter.

  Lessons.
  Long Feud.
  Love.
  Mother Goose Up-to-Date.
  On Hearing Prokofieff's
    Grotesque for Two
    Bassoons...(parody).
  Only of Thee and Me.
  Owen Seaman.
  Portrait of a Child.
  Portrait of a Machine.
  Prayer.
  Prayer for a New House.
  Rapunzel.
  Relativities (parody).
  Repentance.
  Reveille.
  The Sagging Bough (parody).
  The Sleepers.
  Song Tournament: New Style.
  Spring Song of a Super-Blake
    (parody).
  Summer Storm.
  Supplication.
  Swimmers (excerpt).
  To a Vine-Clad Telegraph
    Pole.
  Victory in the Cabarets.
  Wallflower to a Moonbeam
    (parody).
  Waters of Babylon.
  Wind Gardens (parody).
  The Wise Woman.
Updike, John
  The Amish.
  August.
  Bendix.
  Commencement, Pingree
    School.
  Deities and Beasts.
  Die Neuen Heiligen (excerpt).
  Dog's Death.
  Ex-Basketball Player.
  From a Cheerful Alphabet.
  Golfers.
  The Great Scarf of Birds.
  The Grief of Cafeterias.
  Humanities Course.
  I Like to Sing Also.
  I Missed His Book, but I
    Read His Name.
  Insomnia the Gem of the
    Ocean.
  May.
  Mosquito.
  The Newlyweds.
  Note to the Previous Tenants.
  An Ode.
  Ohio.
  Party Knee.
  Philological.
  Player Piano.
  Recital.
  Scenic.
  Seagulls.
  Seven Stanzas at Easter.
  Some Frenchmen.
  Sonic Boom.
  Sunday Rain.
  Sunflower.
  Superman.
  Tao in the Yankee Stadium
    Bleachers.
  Taste.
  Telephone Poles.
  Time's Fool.
  Upon Shaving Off One's
    Beard.
  V. B. Nimble, V. B. Quick.
  Vow.
  Winter Ocean.
  Youth's Progress.

Upham, Thomas Cogswell
  Fear Not, Poor Weary One.
  Song of the Pilgrims.
Upson, Arthur
  Ex Libris.
  Failures.
  The Incurables.
  Old Gardens.
  Song: "Flame at the core of
    the world."
  Vers La Vie.
Upton, James
  The Lass of Richmond Hill.
Upton, Minnie Leona
  Limerick: "A schoolma'am of
    much reputation."
Urdang, Constance
  Because the Three Moirai
    Have Become the Three
    Maries...
  Birth.
  Birth of Venus.
  Bread.
  Change of Life.
  The Children.
  The Day the House Sank.
  Exercise for the Left Hand.
  His Sleep.
  The Invention of Zero.
  Leaving Mexico One More
    Time.
  The Madman.
  The Old Maid Factory.
  The One-Eyed Bridegroom.
  The Roots of Revolution in
    the Vegetable Kingdom.
  Safe Places.
Uribe, Armando
  I Love You and the
    Rosebush.
Urmy, Clarence
  The Arrow.
  As I Came Down Mount
    Tamalpais.
  At the Edge of the Day.
  Blondel.
  I Lay My Lute beside Thy
    Door.
  The Old Year.
  A Woodland Revel.
Urquhart, Sir Thomas
  Inscription above the Entrance
    to the Abbey of Theleme.
Usborne, Richard
  Casanova.
  Epitaph on a Party Girl.
Uschold, Maud E.
  Casual Gold.
  March Wind.
  November Rain.
Usher, John
  The Pipe of Tobacco.
Usher, Leila
  I Am the Cat.
Utahania
  Accusation.
Uvavnuk
  Song of Joy.
  A Woman Shaman's Song.
Uvlunuaq
  I Should Be Ashamed.

V

Vakalo, Eleni
  But There Was Once a Time
    When the Bones.
  Genealogy.

  My Father's Eye.
  Song of the Hanged.
Vala, Katri
  On the Meadow.
  Winter Is Here.
Valaitis, Laura
  A Field Poem.
Valdes, Gabriel de la Conception
  See "Placido"
Valdivielso, Jose de
  Seguidilla.
Valencia, Guillermo
  Sursum.
Valentine, Edward A.U.
  Helen.
  The Spirit of the Wheat.
Valentine, G.D.
  Night up There.
Valentine, Jean
  3 a.m. in New York.
  After Elegies.
  Anaesthesia.
  April.
  A Bride's Hours.
  December 21st.
  Dream Barker.
  Fidelities.
  The Field.
  The Forgiveness Dream: Man
    from the Warsaw Ghetto.
  He Said.
  The Knife.
  The Messenger.
  Moon Man.
  Orpheus and Eurydice.
  Pilgrims.
  Sasha and the Poet.
  The Second Dream.
  Sex.
  Silences: A Dream of
    Governments.
Valery, Paul
  Caesar.
  The Cemetery by the Sea.
  The Footsteps.
  Helen, the Sad Queen.
  The Kirkyaird by the Sea
    (excerpt).
  Narcissus.
  Pomegranates.
Valian, Maxine Kent
  Blessing at Kellenberger
    Road.
Valis, Noel Maureen
  Black Horse Running.
Vallana
  After he stripped off my
    clothes.
Valle, Carmen
  Glenn Miller's Music Is a
    Trunk.
  I'm Going to Break Out.
  What Is Lived.
Valle, Isabel
  A Very Minor Poet Speaks.
Valle, Victor M.
  Food.
Vallejo, Cesar
  And Don't Bother Telling Me
    Anything.
  The Anger That Breaks a
    Man Down into Boys.
  I Have a Terrible Fear of
    Being an Animal.
  Poem to Be Read and Sung.
Valli, Maria
  The Crows.
Vallis, Val
  Fishing Season.
  For This, the Tide.
Vanada, Lillian Schulz
  Fuzzy Wuzzy, Creepy Crawly.

Vanbrugh, Sir John
In the Sprightly Month of
May.
Van Brunt, H. L.
Cerberus.
In the Distance.
Lumiere.
Motels, Hotels, Other People's
Houses.
On the Death of Neruda.
Walking.
Vance, Thomas H.
The Frozen Hero.
Van Den Heever, C. M.
The Fallen Zulu Commander.
Vander Molen, Robert
In the Bar.
Sunny.
Vanderlip, Brian
Encounter with Hunger.
Van der Schelling, Bart
Viva la Quince Brigada.
Vandersee, Charles
The Exact Same Places.
Van de Water, Frederic F.
The Last Tourney.
Van Doren, Mark
The Ancient Couple on Lu
Mountain.
And Did the Animals?
And Then It Rained.
Apple Hell.
April, 1942.
Autonomous.
Axle Song.
Bitten.
Burial.
The Child at Winter Sunset.
City Songs.
Civil War.
The Close Clan.
Comedy.
Defeated Farmer.
The Distant Runners.
Donkey.
Down Dip the Branches.
Dunce Song 6.
The End.
Envy the Old.
Epitaphs: For a Fickle Man.
The Escape.
Eternity's Low Voice.
Exaggerator.
Family Prime.
The First Snow of the Year.
Foreclosure.
Former Barn Lot.
Ghost Boy.
The God of Galaxies.
Good Appetite.
Good Morning.
He's Coming.
His Trees.
History Lesson.
I Had to Be Secret.
If They Spoke.
Immortal.
Inconsistent.
It Should Be Easy.
Jonathan Gentry, III: Tom's
Sleeping Song.
King Wind.
Laly, Laly.
Let There Be Law.
Marriage.
Merry-Go-Round.
The Moments He Remembers.
Morning Worship.
Music God.
Needles and Pins.
No Faith.
Old Ben Golliday.

Old Hundred.
Only for Me.
Our Lady Peace.
Praise Doubt.
Praise Him Who Makes Us
Happy.
Private Worship.
Proper Clay.
The Pulse.
Return to Ritual.
The Runaways.
The Sad Child's Song.
The Seven Sleepers.
Slowly, Slowly Wisdom
Gathers.
The Story-Teller.
Tall Tale God.
That Day.
This Amber Sunstream.
To a Child with Eyes.
Tourist.
The Tower.
Tragedy.
Undersong.
Wait Till Then.
When the World Ends.
Where Did He Run To?
The Whisperer.
Why, Lord?
Will You, Won't You?
Wind in the Grass.
Winter Tryst.
Young Woman at a Window.
Van Dusen, Ruth B.
Prayer in a Country Church.
Van Duyn, Mona
The Ballad of Blossom.
Billings and Cooings from
"The Berkeley Barb."
Birthday Card for a
Psychiatrist.
Causes.
Economics.
The Fear of Flying.
Footnotes to "The
Autobiography of Bertrand
Russell."
The Gardener to His God.
The Gentle Snorer.
Leda.
Leda Reconsidered.
Letters from a Father.
Open Letter from a Constant
Reader.
The Pieta, Rhenish, 14th C.,
the Cloisters.
Relationships.
The Talker.
The Twins.
What the Motorcycle Said.
The Wish to Be Believed.
Van Dyke, Henry
America for Me.
America's Prosperity.
The Angler's Reveille.
An Angler's Wish.
The Builders (excerpt).
The Burning Bush.
The Child in the Garden.
Foundations.
Four Things.
The Gospel of Labor.
The Great River.
Home.
Hymn of Joy.
If All the Skies.
Jesus Return.
Jesus, Thou Divine
Companion.
Let Me Live but from Year to
Year.
The Lily of Torrow.

A Lost Word of Jesus.
A Lover's Envy.
Mare Liberum.
The Maryland Yellow-Throat.
A Mile with Me.
A Mother's Birthday.
My April Lady.
One in Christ.
Peace Hymn of the Republic.
Reliance.
Roslin and Hawthornden.
Tennyson.
These Are the Gifts I Ask.
They Who Tread the Path of
Labor.
The Things I Prize.
To the Child Jesus.
The Valley of Vain Verses.
The Veery.
Victoria.
Voyagers.
The Way.
Work.
The Zest of Life.
Van Fossan, Josephine
Mourning.
Van Geel, Christian J.
View.
Van Noppen, Leonard Charles
A Man of Men.
Van Plettenhaus, Louisa
Love to My Lord.
Van Rensselaer, James
A Note on Lizards' Feet.
**Van Rensselaer, Mariana
Griswold**
At Bedtime.
Love's Prisoner.
Manners.
Van Rensselaer, Peyton
At Twilight.
Van Slyke, Beren
The Shepherds.
Van Spanckeren, Kathryn
Muse Poem.
Van Stockum, Hilda
The Hut.
Van Toorn, Peter
Mountain Study.
Shake'nbake Ballad.
Van Voorhis, Linda Lyon
Ad Matrem in Coelis.
That Which Hath Wings Shall
Tell.
To a Humble Bug.
Van Vorst, Marie
Sing Again.
Van Walleghen, Michael
Driving into Enid.
Van Winckel, Nance
When You Are Gone.
Van Wyk Louw, N. P.
Armed Vision.
At Dawn the Light Will
Come.
Ballad of the Drinker in His
Pub.
From the Ballad of Evil.
The Gods Are Mighty.
The Little Chisel.
Oh the Inconstant.
Van Wynen, Peter
May God Give Strength.
Vanzetti, Bartolomeo
Last Speech to the Court.
Van Zyl, Tania
The Horses of Marini.
The House.
The Man with the Hollow
Breast.
The Rope.
She Waited.

Two Women.
Vardhill, Anna Jane
To a Skeleton.
Varela, Blanca
Before the Pacific.
The Captain.
Nobody will open the door for
you.
The Things I Say Are True.
Vas, Istvan
Catacombs.
Just This.
Tambour.
What Is Left?
Vasalis, M.
The Sea Dike.
Vasquez, Ricardo
The Maestro's Barber Shop.
Vaughan, Frances Downing
The New Calf.
Vaughan, Henry
After the Storm.
Ascension-Day.
Ascension-Hymn.
The Bird.
The Book.
The Burial of an Infant.
Buriall.
Childhood.
Christ's Nativity.
Cock-Crowing.
Come, Come, What Doe I
Here?
The Constellation.
Corruption.
The Dawning.
Dear, Beazuteous Death!
Death.
Distraction.
The Dwelling-Place.
Easter Hymn.
The Eclipse.
The Evening-Watch.
Fragment.
Friends in Paradise.
The Garland.
God's Saints.
H.Scriptures.
Idle Verse.
The Incarnation and Passion.
The Jews.
Joy of My Life!
Juvenal's Tenth Satire
Translated (excerpt).
The Knot.
Looking Back (excerpt).
Love and Discipline.
Man.
Midnight.
The Morning Watch.
The Nativity.
Of Life and Death (excerpt).
Palm-Sunday.
The Pursuite.
The Queer.
Quickness.
Regeneration.
Religion.
The Retreat.
The Revival.
A Rhapsody (excerpt).
Rules and Lessons.
The Search.
The Seed Growing Secretly.
Shall These Early Fragrant
Hours.
The Shepherds.
Silence and Stealth of Dayes!
Silex Scintillans.
Son-Dayes.
A Song to Amoret.
Sure, There's a Tie of Bodies!

They Are All Gone into the World of Light.
The Timber.
To a Bird after a Storm.
To Amoret Gone from Him.
To Etesia Looking from Her Casement at the Full Moon.
To His Books.
To His Friend–.
To His Retired Friend, an Invitation to Brecknock (excerpt).
To the Best and Most Accomplished Couple–.
To the River Isca (the Usk).
The True Christmas.
Unfold! Unfold!
Unprofitablenes.
Upon the Priory Grove, His Usual Retirement.
A Vision.
The Waterfall.
The World.

Vaughan, Thomas
So Have I Spent on the Banks of Ysca Many a Serious Hour.
The Stone.

Vaughan-Thomas, Wynford
Farewell to New Zealand.
Hiraeth in N.W.3.
To His Not-So-Coy Mistress.

Vaughn, F. E.
The Ballad of Chicken Bill.

Vaughn, James P.
Four Questions Addressed to His Excellency, the Prime Minister.
Movie Queen.
So?
Three Kings.
Two Ladies Bidding Us "Good Morning."

Vauquelin de la Fres, Jean
Religion.

Vautor, Thomas
Madrigal: "Dainty sweet bird."
Madrigal: "Sweet Suffolk owl."

Vaux, Thomas, Lord
The Aged Lover Renounceth Love.
Bethinking Hymself of His Ende.
Death in Life.
He Renounceth All the Effects of Love.
The Image of Death.
No Pleasure Without Some Pain.
Of a Contented Mind.
On the Instability of Youth.
The Sins of Youth.

Vazakas, Byron
All the Farewells.
The Enigmatic Traveler.
Midsummer Night's Dream.
The Pavilion on the Pier.
The Progress of Photography.
West Fifty-Seventh Street.

Veale, Peter
Bold Troubleshooters.
Johnsonian Poem in Progress: "I put my hat upon my head." (parody).

Vega, Jose Luis
Brotherhood.
Conditions.
Erotic Suite (excerpt).

Veitch, Tom
Candy Bar.

Cats Climb Trees.
Clipping.
Cowboy Song.
Fifteen Years Past.
The Final Toast.
A Fine Thing.
The Finest Thing.
Improved 4-Way.
It Is a Distinct Pleasure.
The Last Time.
Naval Engagement.
Ordinary People on Sunday.
Poison Meat.
Principally.
Something to Eat.

Velarde, Ramon Lopez
The Malefic Return.
My Cousin Agueda.

Velema
Tip-of-the-Single-Feather.

Veley, Margaret
Japanese Fan.

Venable, William Henry
Battle Cry.
El Emplazado.
The Founders of Ohio.
John Filson.
Johnny Appleseed.
My Catbird.
National Song.
The School Girl.
The Teacher's Dream.

Venantius Fortunatus, Saint
Hail, Day of Days! In Peals of Praise.
Hymn to the Holy Cross.
O Glory of Virgins.
Vexilla Regis.
Written on an Island off the Breton Coast.

Venmanipputi
What She Said to Her Girl-Friend.

Verdaguer, Jacinto
Five Roses.

Vere, Aubrey *See* **De Vere, Aubrey**

Vere, Earl of Oxford, Edward de *See* **De Vere, Edward, Earl of Oxford**

Verhaeren, Emile
The Cathedral of Rheims.
I Bring to You as Offering Tonight.
The Old Masters.
The Poor.
She of the Garden.

Verlaine, Paul
The Art of Poetry.
Auburn.
Autumn Song.
A Bad Sleeper.
Le Chevalier Malheur.
A Clymene.
A Confession.
Cortege.
A Crucifix.
Cythera.
Dans l'Allee.
En Bateau.
Fantoches.
Femme et Chatte.
God Has Spoken.
Green.
I Hate to See You Clad.
Il Pleut Doucement sur la Ville.
The Indolent.
A La Promenade.
Lassitude.
Lines in Order to Be Slandered.

Love Fallen to Earth.
Mandoline.
Moonlight.
My God, You Have Wounded Me with Love.
Ode: To My Lovers.
Pantomime.
Parsifal.
A Pastel.
Pensionnaires.
The Piano.
Retinue.
Sagesse.
Sentimental Conversation.
Sonnet: "And I have seen again the marvellous child."
Spleen.
Spring.
Tears in My Heart That Weeps.
Thousands and Three.
You would have understood me, had you waited.

Vernon, William J.
Catching Soft Craws.

Verplanck, Gulian
Prophecy.

Verry, Isabel Williams
Alcestis.

Verstegan, Richard
Our Lady's Lullaby.
A Vision of the World's Instability.

Verwey, Albert
The Bridge.

Very, Jones
Abdolonymus the Sidonian.
The April Snow.
Autumn Flowers.
The Barberry-Bush.
The Broken Bowl.
The Call.
The Clouded Morning.
The Columbine.
The Coming of the Lord.
The Cottage.
The Created.
The Day of Denial.
The Dead.
The Eagles.
The Earth.
Enoch.
The Fair Morning.
The Fugitive Slaves.
The Garden.
The Gifts of God.
The Grave-Yard.
The Hand and Foot.
Health of Body Dependent on Soul.
I Was Sick and in Prison.
The Idler.
In Him We Live.
The Lament of the Flowers.
The Latter Rain.
Life.
The Light from Within.
The Lost.
Love.
Man in Harmony with Nature.
Morning.
Nature.
The New Birth.
The New Man.
The New World.
October.
The Old Road.
On Finding the Truth.
On the Completion of the Pacific Telegraph.

On Visiting the Graves of Hawthorne and Thoreau.
The Prayer.
The Presence.
Psyche.
The Robin.
The Silent.
The Slave.
The Song.
Soul-Sickness.
The Spirit-Land.
The Strangers.
The Sumach Leaves.
Thy Beauty Fades.
Thy Brother's Blood.
To the Canary Bird.
Today.
The Tree.
The Trees of Life.
Wilt Thou Not Visit Me?
The Wind-Flower.
Yourself.

"Vesey, Paul" *See* **Allen, Samuel**

Vestal, Stanley
Fandango.
Kit Carson's Last Smoke.
Oliver Wiggins.

Viau, Theophile de
Sleep.

Vicente, Gil
The Angelic Vilancete.
Cantiga.
Hymn of the Angels and Sibyls.
Song: "Grace and beauty has the maid."
Song: "If thou art sleeping."
Song of the Three Angels.

Vickers, V. C.
The Moon Bird.
The Swank.

Victor, Florence
Contest.

Vida, Marco Girolamo
The Silkworm.

Vidal, Peire
Song of Breath.

Vidya
Friends, you are lucky you can talk.
Hiding in the Cucumber Garden.
Please keep an eye on my house for a few moments.
Substantiations (excerpt).
The Sun (excerpt).
The Wanton (excerpt).

Vieira, Luandino
Song for Luanda.

Viele, Herman Knickerbocker
The Good Inn.

Viereck, George Sylvester
After the Battle (1930).
The Haunted House.

Viereck, Peter
1912-1952, Full Cycle.
Affirmations: I, II, III.
Big Crash out West.
Blindman's Buff.
Counter-Serenade: She Invokes the Autumn Instant.
Crass Times Redeemed by Dignity of Souls.
The Day's No Rounder Than Its Angles Are.
Ennui.
For Two Girls Setting out in Life.
From Ancient Fangs.
Graves Are Made to Waltz On.
Homecoming.

Kilroy.
Love Song to Eohippus.
The Lyricism of the Weak.
Now Kindness.
Poet.
The Slacker Apologizes.
Small Perfect Manhattan.
Some Lines in Three Parts.
Some Refrains at the Charles
River.
Space-Wanderer's
Homecoming.
To Be Sung.
Vale from Carthage.
A Walk on Snow.
You All Are Static; I Alone
Am Moving.

Vigee, Claude
Destiny of the Poet.
Every Land Is Exile.
House of the Living.
Light of Judea.
The Phoenix of Mozart.
Poetry.
Song of Occident.
The Struggle with the Angel.
The Tree of Death.
The Wanderer.

Vigneault, Gilles
Lullaby.

Vigny, Alfred de
Nature.
The Shepherd's House.
The Sound of the Horn.

Vilakazi, B. W.
Because.
I Heard the Old Song.
In the Gold Mines.
Then I'll Believe.

Vildrac, Charles
After Midnight.

Villa, Jose Garcia
Be Beautiful.
Between God's Eyelashes.
Divine Poems.
God, Is, Like, Scissors.
God Said, "I Made a Man".
The Manner of a Poet's
Germination.
My, Fellowship, With, God.
My Most. My Most. O My
Lost.
My Mouth Is Very Quiet.
Now, If You Will Look in My
Brain.
Saw God Dead but Laughing.
The Way My Ideas Think Me.

Villanueva, Alma
I Was Always Fascinated.

Villanueva, Salvador
Maybe You Cannot
Comprehend.
O.

Villanueva, Tino
Aquellos Vatos.
Pachuco Remembered.

Villiers, George
Prayer.

Villon, Francois
Arbor Amoris.
Ballad against the Enemies of
France.
The Ballad of Dead Ladies.
Ballad of Ladies' Love,
Number Two.
Ballad of the Lords of Old
Time.
Ballad of the Women of Paris.
Ballad Written for a
Bridegroom.
Ballade of the Fair Helm-
Maker.

Ballade of the Hanged Men.
Ballade of Villon and Fat
Margot.
Ballade to His Mistress.
Ballat O the Hingit.
Ballat O the Leddies O
Langsyne.
The Complaint of the Fair
Armoress.
The Dispute of the Heart and
Body of Francois Villon.
A Double Ballad of Good
Counsel.
Epistle in Form of a Ballad to
His Friends.
The Epitaph in Form of a
Ballad.
The Epitaph, or Ballade of the
Hanged.
Fragment of Death.
His Mother's Service to Our
Lady.
No, I Am Not as Others Are.
The Old Lady's Lament for
Her Youth.
Rondel: "Good-by, the tears
are in my eyes."
To Death, of His Lady.

Vinal, Harold
The Enduring Music.
Hymnal.
Lesbia Sewing.
Miser.
The Nights Remembered.
The Quest.
Sea Born.

Vinaver, Stanislav
A Cathedral.
The European Night.
An Inscription.

Vincent, Stephen
Basketball.
Coming Up & Falling Down.
Elevator Landscapes.
Jealousy.
Mother.
The Relationship.
Requiem.
The Song of This House.

Vines, Eda H.
Ballade of the Old-Time
Engine.

Vinner, Shlomo
In the Cabinet.
Jerusalem.
Lullaby.
Midnight and Ten Minutes.
The Need to Love.
Parting.
Training on the Shore.

Vinograd, Julia
Investigation.

Vinz, Mark
Angler.
Business as Usual.
The Children.
In the Heartland.
Mac.
Morning After.
November Song.
Old Doc.
Postcards.
Primer Lesson.
Quilt Song.
Return.
Variations on a Theme.
Wild West.

Violante Do Ceo, Sister
The Night of Marvels.
While to Bethlehem We Are
Going.

Violi, Paul
At the Corner of Muck and
Myer.
Concordance.
Outside Baby Moon's.
Whalefeathers.

Viorst, Judith
Mother Doesn't Want a Dog.

Virgil (Publius Vergilius Maro)
The Aeneid.
Eclogues.
The Georgics.
The Odyssey, VII.
The Second Pastoral, or,
Alexis: The Argument.

Vittorelli, Jacopo
On a Nun.
Sonnet: Addressed by a
Father Mourning...

Vivante, Arturo
To a Victim of Radiation.

Vivien, Renee
The Pillory.
Toward Lesbos.
Words to My Friend.

Vizenor, Gerald
Anishinabe Grandmothers.
Auras on the Interstates.
Family Photograph.
February Park.
Haiku.
Holiday Inn at Bemidji.
Indians at the Guthrie.
Minnesota Camp Grounds.
North to Milwaukee.
Raising the Flag.
Seven Woodland Crows.
Thumbing Old Magazines.
Tropisms on John Berryman.
Tyranny of Moths.
Unhappy Diary Days.
White Earth Reservation
1980.

Vliet, R. G.
Games, Hard Press and Bruise
of the Flesh.
Girls on Saddleless Horses.
Love's Own Form Is Sufficient
Unto.

Vogel, David
Black Flags Are Fluttering.
Days Were Great as Lakes.
How Can I See You, Love.
In Fine, Transparent Words.
Now I Have Forgotten All.
Our Childhood Spilled into
Our Hearts.
Plain, Humble Letters.
When I Was Growing Up.

Vogelsang, Arthur
Americans in an Orange
Grove.
The Clouds.
Drive Imagining.
Feeling That Way Too.

Vogelweide, Walther von der See
Walther von der Vogelweide

Vogt, Anton
For a Child's Drawing.
For England, in Grateful
Appreciation (excerpt).

Voigt, Ellen Bryant
The Bat.
Blue Ridge.
Daughter.
Exile.
For My Husband.
January.
Jug Brook.
The Lotus Flowers.
Pastoral.
Rescue.

The Spring.
Tropics.
The Victim.
Why She Says No.
The Wife Takes a Child.

Volborth, Judith Mountain Leaf
Corn-Woman Remembered.
Dusk Chant.
Goat-Woman Dares.
How Came She to Such
Poppy-Breath?
Iron-Door-Woman.
Self-Portrait.
Three Songs to Mark the
Night.
A Time of Turquoise.
Vihio Images.

Volk, Joyce M.
Places I Have Been.

Vollmoeller, Karl Gustave
Nocturne in G Minor.

**Voltaire (Francois Marie
Arouet)**
Inscription for a Statue of
Love.
On Bell-Ringers.
On the Phrase, "To Kill
Time."

Volwerk, Leen
Bog.
Staoineag.

Vondel, Joost van den
Adam's Hymn in Paradise.
The Hymn of Adam.

von Ende, Frederick See **Ende,
Frederick von**

Von Hartmann, Max
The Seed of Reality.

von Hofmannsthal, Hugo See
Hofmannsthal, Hugo von

Von Schlichten, Henry J.
Lost, But Won.
Prayer of a Patriot.

**Von Tilzer, Harry and Dillon.
Will**
I Want a Girl.

Voorhees, Dayton
Limerick: "There was a young
man so benighted."
Limerick: "There was an old
man of Nantucket."

Vories, William M.
Let There Be Light.

Voronca, Ilarie
The Quick and the Dead.
The Seven-League Boots.

Vorpahl, Robert L.
Perspective.

Voss, Charles Hannibal
Yet Love Was Born.

Voss, J. H.
Who Does Not Love Wine,
Women and Song.

Voznesensky, Andrei
Darkmotherscream.
Dead Still.
I Am Goya.
New York Bird.
Soccer.

Vrepont, Brian
The Apple-Tree.
The Bomber.
The Net-Menders.

Vriesland, Victor van
Ars Poetica.
Evening.

Vroman, Leo
Old Miniatures.
The River.

W

"W, A."
Desire's Government.
Give Me Leave.
Hopeless Desire Soon Withers and Dies.
In Praise of the Sun.
Ladies' Eyes Serve Cupid Both for Darts and Fire.
A Song in Praise of a Beggar's Life.
To Time.
Upon Visiting His Lady by Moonlight.
Where His Lady Keeps His Heart.

"W, C.A."
Shakespearean Soliloquy in Progress: "To have it out or not?" (parody).

"W, J.J."
Brotherhood.

W.A., G.
The Yielded Life.

Wabnitz, William S.
The Hinds of Kerry.

Wachtel, Chuck
The Answer.
A Horror Story Written for the Cover of a Matchbook.
A Paragraph Made Up of Seven Sentences Which Have Entered My Memory...
A Sirventes against the Management of the Mammoth Supermarket.

Waddell, Helen
The Day of Wrath.

Waddell, Jean Percival
Half-Light.
Rhythm.

Wadding, Luke
Christmas Day Is Come.
For Innocents Day.
On the Circumsision: New Years Day.

Waddington, Miriam
Advice to the Young.
Cadenza.
Catalpa Tree.
Desert Stone.
The Field of Night.
Green World Two.
Icons.
Investigator.
Laughter.
Lullaby.
Old Women of Toronto.
Restricted.
The Season's Lovers.
The Survivors.
Ten Years and More.
Thou Didst Say Me.
Three Prison Portraits: The Drug Addict.
The Women's Jail.

Waddington, Samuel
The Inn of Care.
Morning.
Mors et Vita.
Soul and Body.

Wade, Blanche Elizabeth
The Song of the Christmas Tree.

Wade, James Palmer
A Hymn to No One Body.

Wade, John Stevens
May.

Wade, Thomas
The Coming of Night.
The Face.
The True Martyr.
The Winter Shore.

Wadsworth, Oliver A.
Over in the Meadow.

Wager, W.
The White Dove Sat on the Castle Wall.

Wagner, Charles A.
Three City Cantos.
The Unknown Soldier.
When I Loved You.

Wagner, Charles L. H.
Let's Forget.

Wagner, Linda
Love Poem.

Wagner, Mary Boyd
The Lethal Thought.

Wagoner, David
After the Speech to the Librarians.
Being Herded Past the Prison's Honor Farm.
The Calculation.
Canticle for Xmas Eve.
Clancy.
Closing Time.
The Death of the Moon.
Diary.
Elegy for a Woman Who Remembered Everything.
Elegy for Yards, Pounds, and Gallons.
Elegy while Pruning Roses.
The Emergency Maker.
Falling Asleep in a Garden.
The Feast.
The Fruit of the Tree.
Gift of a Mirror to a Lady.
House-Hunting.
In Distress.
In the Badlands.
The Labors of Thor.
Lament for the Non-Swimmer.
The Land behind the Wind.
Leaving Something Behind.
Looking for Mountain Beavers.
Lost.
Making up for a Soul.
The Man from the Top of the Mind.
Marsh Leaf.
Meeting a Bear.
Muse.
My Father's Ghost.
My Physics Teacher.
The Nesting Ground.
News from the Court.
Nine Charms against the Hunter.
Ode to the Muse on Behalf of a Young Poet.
The Poets Agree to Be Quiet by the Swamp.
Relics.
The Shooting of John Dillinger Outside the Biograph Theater...
Snake Hunt.
Songs My Mother Taught Me.
Staying Alive.
Sudden Frost.
Tan Ta Ra, Cries Mars...
To the Fly in My Drink.
The Trail Horse.
Travelling Light.
Tumbleweed.
Under the Sign of the Moth.

A Valedictory to Standard Oil of Indiana.
The Visiting Hour.
Walking in a Swamp.
A Warning to My Love.
The Water Lily.
The Words.
Working against Time.

Wagoner, Glenn E.
I Never Knew.

Wagstaff, Blanche Shoemaker
All Paths Lead to You.
Earth Trembles Waiting.
Quiet Waters.
Wildness.

Wah, Fred
Breathe dust...

Wahl, Jean
Decayed Time.
Evening in the Walls.
A Lean Day in a Convict's Suit.
Prayer of Little Hope.

Wain, John
Anecdote of 2 A.M.
Anniversary.
Apology for Understatement.
Arrival.
Au Jardin des Plantes.
A Boisterous Poem about Poetry (excerpt).
Brooklyn Heights.
The New Sun.
Pedagogue Arraigned.
Poem: "Like a deaf man meshed in his endless silence."
Poem without a Main Verb.
Reason for Not Writing Orthodox Nature Poetry.
Short History of Twentieth-Century Scholarship.
A Song about Major Eatherly.
This above All Is Precious and Remarkable.
Wildtrack: "Lie easy in your secret cradle."

Waite, Arthur Edward
At the End of Things.

Wakarpa
The Golden Sea-Otter.

Wakefield, Samuel
The Music of His Steps.

Wakeford, Amelia
Thou Alone Canst Save.

Wakeman, John
Love in Brooklyn.

Wakoski, Diane
Aging.
Anticipation of Sharks.
An Apology.
Apparitions Are Not Singular Occurrences.
Belly Dancer.
Coins and Coffins under My Bed.
The Empress.
The Father of My Country.
Fire Island Poem.
For a Man Who Learned to Swim When He Was Sixty.
For Whitman.
Greed, Part 4. The Turtle.
Having Replaced Love with Food and Drink.
The Ice Eagle.
Inside Out.
Italian Woman.
Journey.
Justice Is Reason Enough.
Love Letter Postmarked Van Beethoven.

The Mechanic.
The Night a Sailor Came to Me in a Dream.
No More Soft Talk.
Ode to a Lebanese Crock of Olives.
Patriotic Poem.
The Photos.
Placing a $2 Bet for a Man Who Will Never Go to the Horse Races ...
Poem to the Man on My Fire Escape.
A Poet Recognizing the Echo of the Voice.
The Ring.
Ringless.
Sestina from the Home Gardener.
Sestina to the Common Glass of Beer: I Do Not Drink Beer.
Six of Cups.
Smudging.
Summer.
Thank You for the Valentine.
Uneasy Rider.
Walking Past Paul Blackburn's Apt. on 7th St.
Wind Secrets.
You, Letting the Trees Stand as My Betrayer.

Walcott, Derek
Alba.
The Bridge.
The Chelsea.
Codicil.
A Country Club Romance.
Crusoe's Island.
Europa.
A Far Cry from Africa.
The Fist.
For the Altarpiece of the Roseau Valley Church, Saint Lucia.
Force.
The Gulf.
A Letter from Brooklyn.
Man O'War Bird.
Moon.
Nearing La Guaira.
New World.
Nights in the Gardens of Port of Spain.
Piano Practice.
Pocomania.
Ruins of a Great House.
Sea Canes.
A Sea-Chantey (excerpt).
The Season of Phantasmal Peace.
Spring Street in '58.
Tales of the Islands.
The Virgins.
Volcano.
The Whale, His Bulwark.

Waldeck, Heinrich Suso
Cleansing.

Waldheim, Franklin
Help Wanted.

Waldman, Anne
After Li Ch'ing-Chao.
Berthe Morisot.
Canzone.
Complaynt.
Goddess of Wisdom Whose Substance Is Desire.
July 4th.
Lady Tactics.
Number Song.
On Walt Whitman's Birthday.
Pressure.

Song: Time Drawes Neere.

Waldo, Rose
Welcome.

Waldrop, Keith
Around the Block.
Introducing a Madman.
On Measure.
Signals.
Song: Paper.

Waldrop, Rosemarie
The Ambition of Ghosts.
Confession to Settle a Curse.
Morning Has No House.

Waley, Arthur
Censorship.
The Little Cart.

Walford, William W.
Sweet Hour of Prayer.

Walker, Alice
Black Mail.
Burial.
Chic Freedom's Reflection.
Early Losses: A Requiem.
Expect Nothing.
In These Dissenting Times.
Light Baggage.
Love (excerpt).
Medicine.
On Stripping Bark from
Myself.
Once.
Revolutionary Petunias.
So We've Come at Last to
Freud.
Suicide.
Threatened.

Walker, Annie L.
Work, for the Night Is
Coming.

Walker, Brad
Instructions for a Park.

Walker, David
Catching Up.
Passages.

Walker, Dee
Et Cetera.

Walker, E. M.
Anno Domini.
Human Needs.
To America, on Her First
Sons Fallen in the Great
War.

Walker, J.
The Love Song of J. Alfred
Prufrock (parody).

Walker, James
Safe.

Walker, James J.
Will You Love Me in
December as You Do in
May?

Walker, Jeanne Murray
Deliver Me, O Lord, from My
Daily Bread.
Tracking the Sled, Christmas
1951.

Walker, Kath
Dawn Wail for the Dead.
Then and Now.
We Are Going.

Walker, Margaret
Ballad of the Hoppy-Toad.
Birmingham.
Childhood.
For Andy Goodman–Michael
Schwerner–and James
Chaney.
For Malcolm X.
For Mary McLeod Bethune.
For My People.
Girl Held without Bail.
Harriet Tubman.

Jackson, Mississippi.
Kissie Lee.
Lineage.
Molly Means.
October Journey.
Prophets for a New Day.
Street Demonstration.
Today.

Walker, Ted
Breakwaters.
By the Bridge.
By the Saltings.
The Emigres.
Estuary.
Heron.
Homing Pigeons.
Lemons.
Mules.
On Scafell Pike.
Skimmers.

Walker, William
High O'er the Hills.

Walker, William Sidney
Too Solemn for Day, Too
Sweet for Night.

Wallace, Bronwen
Generation Gap.
Profile.

Wallace, Edgar
War.

Wallace, Edna Kingsley
Growing Up.

Wallace, James Cowden
God the Omniscient.

Wallace, John A.
Prayer Moves the Hand That
Moves the World.

Wallace, Jon
The Linebacker at Forty.
Puberty.

Wallace, Lew
Ben Hur: Song.

Wallace, Robert
After the Swimmer.
Among the Finger Lakes.
Aubade: N.Y.C.
Ballad of the Mouse.
The Double Play.
Driving By.
Fly in December.
Girl in Front of the Bank.
The Girl Writing Her English
Paper.
The Gold Nest.
In a Spring Still Not Written
Of.
In One Place.
In the Field Forever.
In Winter.
On the College Archery
Range.
Out of the Past.
A Snapshot for Miss Bricka
Who Lost in the Semifinal
Round...
The Star-Nosed Mole.
The Storm.
Swimmer in the Rain.
Tulip.
The Two Old Gentlemen.

Wallace, Ronald
Art Work.
At the St. Louis Institute of
Music.
The Belly Dancer in the
Nursing Home.
Bird Watcher.
Father and Son.
Grandmother Grace.
Prayer for Fish.
The Real Thing.
Spring Again.

Tunes for Bears to Dance To.

Wallace, Wesley
Number 29.

Wallace, William Ross
The Hand That Rocks the
Cradle Is the Hand That
Rules the World.

Wallace-Crabbe, Chris
Ancient Historian.
Citizen.
The Dirigible.
Love Poem.
The Rebel General.
The Secular.
The Shape-Changer.
Sporting the Plaid.

Wallach, Yona
Cradle Song.
Death; She Was Always Here.
When the Angels Are
Exhausted.

Wallada
Angry at Zaidun's Interest in
Her Maid...
A Reply to Zaidun's
Complaint...
To Ibn Zaidun.
Wait Till the Darkness is
Deep.

Wallbank, Susan
Why So Many of Them Die.

Waller, Edmund
An Apologie for Having
Loved Before.
At Penshurst.
The Battel of the Summer-
Islands.
Chloris and Hilas. Made to a
Saraban.
The Dancer.
Instructions to a Painter.
Of a Fair Lady Playing with a
Snake.
Of English Verse.
Of His Majesties Receiving
the News of the Duke of
Buckingham's Death.
Of Loving at First Sight.
Of My Lady Isabella Playing
on the Lute.
Of the Last Verses in the
Book.
On a Girdle.
On Her Coming to London.
On St. James's Park, as Lately
Improved by His Majesty.
On the Friendship betwixt
Two Ladies.
A Panegyrick to My Lord
Protector.
Panegyrick upon O.
Cromwell.
A Plea for Promiscuity.
Poets Lose Half the Praise.
Puerperium.
Say, Lovely Dream.
The Selfe-Banished.
Song: "Go, lovely rose!"
Song: "Say, lovely dream!
where couldst thou find."
Song: "Stay Phoebus, stay."
The Story of Phoebus and
Daphne Applied...
To a Lady in a Garden.
To a Very Young Lady.
To Amoret.
To Chloris, upon a Favour
Received.
To Flavia.
To Mr. Henry Lawes.
To My Young Lady, Lucy
Sidney.

To One Married to an Old
Man.
To Phillis.
To the King on His Navy.
To the Mutable Fair.
To the Younger Lady Lucy
Sydney.
Under a Lady's Picture.
Upon Ben. Johnson.
Written in My Lady Speke's
Singing-Book.

Waller, Janet
Aviemore.

Waller, John
The Enemy.
Goldenhair.
Legend.
Limb and Mind.
When Sadness Fills a Journey.

Waller, John Francis
Kitty Neil.
The Spinning Wheel.

Wallis, Eleanor Glenn
The Deathless Ones.
The Hunter.
In a City Square.
Iulus.

Wallis, George B.
The Lovely Rivers and Lakes
of Maine.

Wallis, John
When a Twister, A-Twisting,
Will Twist Him a Twist.

Wally, Darryl
Tablerock.

Walpole, Henry
Martyrdom of Father
Campion.
The Song of Mary the Mother
of Christ.

Walpole, Horace
Ann Grenville, Countess
Temple, Appointed Poet
Laureate...
Epigram: "All praise your
face, your verses none
abuse."
Epitaphium Vivi Auctoris
1792.
Epitaphs on Two Piping-
Bullfinches of Lady Ossory's.
On the Translation of
Anacreon.
To Lady, When about Five
Years Old, with a Present of
Shells.
To the Gardener at Nuneham.

Walsh, Chad
Invocation.
My God, My God, Look
upon Me.
Ode on a Plastic Stapes.
Ode to the Finnish Dead.
Port Authority Terminal: 9
A.M. Monday.
A Quintina of Crosses.
There Is None to Help.
Why Hast Thou Forsaken
Me?

Walsh, Christina
Prayer to Isis.
A Woman to Her Lover.

Walsh, Edward
The Fairy Nurse.
Kitty Bhan.
Lament.

Walsh, Ernest
Doctor Bill Williams.
I Played on the Grass with
Mary.
Old Fellow.
A Serious Poem.

Sonnet: "My Duchess was the werst she laffed she bitte."

Walsh, Marnie
Thomas Iron-Eyes Born Circa 1840. Died 1919, Rosebud Agency, S.D.

Walsh, Ruth M.
Inadequate Aqua Extremis.
Rift Tide.

Walsh, Thomas
The Feast of Padre Chala.
La Preciosa.
A Russian Spring Song with Minaiev.
Tears against the Moon.

Walsh, William
Abigail's Lamentation for the Loss of Mr. Harley...
Against Marriage to His Mistress.
The Despairing Lover.
Epigram: "An epigram should be–if right."
Letter: The Japanese, to Her Husband at War.
Love and Jealousy.
Lyce.
Phillis's Resolution.
Rivals.
Sonnet on Death.
To His Book.

Walter, Beatrice
The Photograph the Cat Licks.

Walter, Howard Arnold
My Creed.

Walter, Nehemiah
An Elegiack Verse On the Death of the Pious and Profound...

Walter, Nina Willis
Candle and Book.

Walters, Anna
Hartico.
I Am of the Earth.
I Have Bowed before the Sun.
My Brothers...
Simplicity Aims Circularly.
A Teacher Taught Me.

Walters, Dorothy
Cinema Verite.
Flannery O'Connor.
Two Roads, Etc.

Walters, L. D'O.
Seville.

Walters, Lila V.
He Shall Speak Peace Unto the Nations.

Walther von der Vogelweide
Awake!
Maria Bright.
Song: "Under the lime-tree, on the daisied ground."
There Is a Lady.
Uncourtly Love.
Under the Lindens.
With a Rod No Man Alive.

Waltner, Thomas
A Bell in the Orthodox Steeple.
March 23, 1982 Tuesday Night.
Raven at Lemon Creek Jail.
Young Girl.

Walton, Alfred Grant
First Impressions.
Recipe for Living.
The Sincere Man.
The World We Make.

Walton, Eda Lou
How Our Forefather Got His Wife.

Indian Death.
Leda, the Lost.
Love Medicine.
The Marriage Dance.
A Necessary Miracle.

Walton, Izaak
The Angler's Song.
The Angler's Wish.

Walton, John
God, the Port of Peace.

Walworth, Clarence A.
Holy God, We Praise Thy Name.

Wanek, Connie
Bucket in the Well.

Wang Chi
Tell Me Now.

Wang Chien
Hearing That His Friend Was Coming Back from the War.
The Newlyweds' Cuisine.
The South.
Weaving at the Window.

Wang Ch'ing-hui
Now the lotuses in the imperial lake.

Wang Chung-ju
Complaint of a Young Girl.

Wang I
The Lychee.

Wang Tsan
War in Chang-An City.

Wang Wei
A Green Stream.
My Lodge at Wang-Ch'uan after a Long Rain.
A Parting.
Seeking a Mooring.

Wangara, Malaika Ayo
From a Bus.

Waniek, Marilyn
Dinosaur Spring.
Herbs in the Attic.
Light under the Door.
Old Bibles.
Other Women's Children.
Women's Locker Room.

Wanley, Nathaniel
Humaine Cares.
The Resurrection.
Royal Presents.
The Sigh.

Warburton, R. E. Egerton
Past and Present.

Ward, Artemus
Uncle Simon and Uncle Jim.

Ward, Edward
A Ballad on the Taxes.
Dialogue between a Squeamish Cotting Mechanic and his Sluttish Wife...
The Extravagant Drunkard's Wish.
A Journey to Hell.

Ward, Elizabeth Stuart Phelps
Afterward.
Conemaugh.
Gloucester Harbor.
The Lost Colors.
The Room's Width.

Ward, Jean
Autumn Healing.

Ward, John
Madrigal: "Come, sable night."

Ward, Kenneth
Investor's Solioquy.

Ward, Leo
Four Friends.
The Last Communion.

Ward, Lydia Avery Coonley
Christmas Song.

Flag Song.
Heredity.
To-Day.

Ward, May Williams
Wet Summer.

Ward, Nathaniel
Epigram: The World Is Full of Care.
Mercury Shew'd Apollo, Bartas Book.
Mr. Ward of Anagrams Thus.
Poetry's a Gift Wherein but Few Excell.
The World's a Well Strung Fidle, Mans Tongue the Quill.

Ward, Robert
Tenant Farmer.

Ward, Samuel
A Proem.

Ward, Terence
Kevin Barry.

Ward, William Hayes
The New Castalia.
To John Greenleaf Whittier.

Warden, Marine Robert
Ode to a Homemade Coffee Cup.

Ware, Eugene Fitch
The Aztec City.
A Ballad in "G"
He and She.
Manila.
Whist.
Zephyr.

Ware, Henry, Jr.
Great God, the Followers of Thy Son.
Lift Your Glad Voices in Triumph on High.

Warfield, Catherine Ann
Beauregard.
Manassas.

Waring, H. C.
Quite the Cheese (parody).

Warman, Cy
Creede.
Doing Railroads for the "Rocky Mountain News."
Old Red Hoss Mountain.
The Rise and Fall of Creede.
Sweet Marie.

Warne, Candice
Blackbird Sestina.

Warner, Anna B.
Jesus Loves Me, This I Know.
One More Day's Work for Jesus.

Warner, Charles Dudley
Bookra.

Warner, Eva
Irony of God.

Warner, J.
Down in Alabam'.

Warner, Rex
Palm Trees.
Sonnet: "The understanding of a medical man."

Warner, Sylvia Townsend
The Absence.
After He Had Gone.
The Alarum.
Benicasim.
Building in Stone.
Country Thought.
Elizabeth.
Four Epitaphs.
Gloriana Dying.
The Green Valley.
Killing No Murder.
King Duffus.
Modo and Alciphron.

Nelly Trim.
Now in This Long-Deferred Spring.
The Rival.
Sad Green.
The Sailor.
Song from the Bride of Smithfield.
Song: "She has left me, my pretty."
Triumph of Sensibility.
Tudor Church Music.

Warner, William
The Fate of Narcissus.
My Mistress.

Warr, Bertram
The Deviator.
The Heart to Carry On.
On a Child with a Wooden Leg.
Poets in Time of War.
There Are Children in the Dusk.
Trees, Who Are Distant.
Working Class.

Warren, Eugene
Chirstographia 35.

Warren, Hamilton
Requiem.

Warren, John Byrne Leicester
Circe.

Warren, Joseph
Free America.

Warren, Mrs. Mercy
Massachusetts Song of Liberty.

Warren, Robert Penn
American Portrait: Old Style.
Aubade for Hope.
The Ballad of Billie Potts.
Bearded Oaks.
Birth of Love.
Boy's Will, Joyful Labor without Pay, and Harvest Home (excerpt).
Boy Wandering in Simms' Valley.
Commuter's Entry in a Connecticut Diary.
Country Burying (1919).
Crime.
Croesus in Autumn.
Debate: Question, Quarry, Dream.
Dragon Country: To Jacob Boehme.
Dream, Dump-Heap, and Civilization.
End of Season.
Fairy Story.
Fall Comes in Back-Country Vermont.
The Flower.
Grandfather Gabriel.
He Was Formidable.
History.
Homage to Theodore Dreiser on the Centennial of His Birth (excerpt).
Internal Injuries.
Kentucky Mountain Farm.
Lessons in History.
Letter from a Coward to a Hero.
Letter of a Mother.
Letter to a Friend.
The Limited.
Man in the Street.
Mexico Is a Foreign Country, IV: The Mango on the Mango Tree.
Mortmain.

Myth on Mediterranean
Beach: Aphrodite as Logos.
Natural History.
Nightmare of Mouse.
Notes on a Life to Be Lived.
October Poems: The Garden.
Original Sin: A Short Story.
The Owl.
Patriotic Tour and Postulate
of Joy.
Penological Study: Southern
Exposure, 3. Wet Hair...
Pondy Woods.
Pro Sua Vita.
Promises, VIII. Founding
Fathers....
Pursuit.
A Real Question Calling for
Solution.
Recollection Long Ago: Sad
Music.
Remarks of Soul to Body.
Revelation.
Sila.
Skiers.
Swimming in the Pacific.
Terror.
There's a Grandfather's Clock
in the Hall.
To a Little Girl, One Year
Old, in a Ruined Fortress
(excerpt).
Treasure Hunt.
Two Pieces after Suetonius.
Watershed.
What Voice at Moth-Hour.
Where the Slow Fig's Purple
Sloth.
The Wrestling Match.

Warren, Rosanna
Alps.
Daylights.
Lily.
Omalos.
Virgin Pictured in Profile.

Warren, Thomas Herbert
Lines for a Sundial.
May-day on Magdalen Tower.

Warren, Valerie S.
I Was the Child.

Warren, William F.
I Worship Thee, O Holy
Ghost.

Warren, Jr., James E.
Schoolroom: 158–.
Seizure.

Warsh, Lewis
Love's Will.
March Wind.
Precious Mettle.

Warshawsky, Mark
Oyfn Pripetshuk.

Warton, Joseph
The Charms of Nature.
The Dying Indian.
The Enthusiast: or, The Lover
of Nature.
Ode I. To Fancy.
Ode to Evening.
Ode: To the Nightingale.
The Revenge of America.
Verses Written at Montauban
in France, 1750.

Warton, Jr., Thomas
The Grave of King Arthur.
Inscription in a Hermitage.
Ode: Solitude, at an Inn.
Ode Written at Vale-Royal
Abbey in Cheshire.
Ode X: The First of April
(excerpt).

On Leander's Swimming over
the Hellespont to Hero.
The Pleasures of Melancholy.
The Solemn Noon of Night.
Sonnet: "Deem not, devoid of
elegance, the sage."
Sonnet, to the River Loddon.
Sonnet Written after Seeing
Wilton-House.
Sonnet: Written at
Stonehenge.
Sonnet Written in a Blank
Leaf of Dugdale's
Monasticon.
Verses on Sir Joshua
Reynold's Painted Window
at New College, Oxford.

Warton, Sr., Thomas
An American Love-Ode.
Retirement, an Ode (excerpt).
A Runic Ode.

Washboard Sam
Big Woman.
I Been Treated Wrong.

Washbourne, Thomas
Casting All Your Care upon
God, for He Careth for You.
The Circulation.
Prayer.
Upon a Great Shower of
Snow That Fell on May-Day,
1654.
Upon a Passing Bell.

Washburn, E. A.
Still Thy Sorrow, Magdalena!

Washburn, Henry Stevenson
Almighty God, Thy Constant
Care.
Song of the Harvest.
The Vacant Chair.

Washington, George
Letter to the Governors, June
8, 1783.
Washington's Prayer for the
Nation.

Wason, Harriet L.
The Slide at the Empire Mine.

Wassall, Irma
Singing in the Dark.
Stone from the Gods.

Wasson, David Atwood
Joy-Month.

Wastell, Simon
Man's Mortality.

Wat, Aleksander
There Is No Place.
Willows in Alma-Ata.

Waterbury, Jared B.
I Have Fought the Good
Fight.
Sinner, Is Thy Heart at Rest?

Waterhouse, Gilbert
This Is the Last.

Waterman, Cary
Death on the Farm.
Pig Poem.

Waterman, Charles
Neighbor.
The New Cows.

Waterman, Nixon
Cheer for the Consumer.
Far from the Madding Crowd.
If We Didn't Have to Eat.
Johnny's Hist'ry Lesson.
Making a Man.
Recompense.
A Rose to the Living.
To Know All Is to Forgive
All.
What Have We Done Today?
Whistling Boy.

Watermeyer, G. A.
Harvest Time.

Waters, Michael
American Bandstand.
Among Blackberries.
Apples.
The Catfish.
Frank Sinatra.
The Mystery of the Caves.
Mythology.
Night Fishing.
Preserves.
Since Nothing Is Impossible.
Singles.
The Stories in the Light.

Waterston, Robert Cassie
Jesus Is Near.

Watkins, Edward
Acrobat.
Adam, Eve and the Big
Apple.
Figures of Authority.
What Is a Sonnet?

Watkins, Grace V.
The Greater Country.

Watkins, Lucian B.
Star of Ethiopia.
To Our Friends.
Two Points of View.

Watkins, Vernon
Ballad of the Three Coins.
Ballad of the Trial of Sodom.
Ballad of the Two Tapsters.
The Beaver's Story.
The Cave-Drawing.
The Collier.
The Compost Heap.
Cwmrhydyceirw Elegiacs.
The Dead Words.
Demands of the Muse.
Discoveries.
Earth and Fire.
The Feather.
Fingernail Sunrise.
The Fire in the Snow.
First Joy.
Foal.
For a Christening.
For a Wine Festival.
The Furnace of Colors.
Gravestones.
The Healing of the Leper.
The Heron.
Hurdy-Gurdy Man in Winter.
Indolence.
Infant Noah.
The Lady with the Unicorn.
A Lover's Words.
The Mother and Child.
The Mummy.
Music of Colours: the
Blossom Scattered.
Music of Colours–White
Blossom.
Napkin and Stone.
Old Triton Time.
Ophelia.
Peace in the Welsh Hills.
Poet and Goldsmith.
A Prayer.
Returning from Harvest.
She That Is Memory's
Daughter.
The Shooting of Werfel.
The Snow Curlew.
The Song of the Good
Samaritan.
The Spoils of War.
The Sunbather.
Swedenborg's Skull.
A True Picture Restored.
The Turning of the Leaves.

Two Decisions.
Waterfalls.
Yeats in Dublin (excerpt).
Yeats' Tower.
The Yew-Tree.

Watkyns, Rowland
Antipathy.
Bad Company.
Strange Monsters.
Upon Saul Seeking His
Father's Asses.
The Wish.
Worldly Wealth.

Watson, Albert Durrant
Breeze and Billow.
A Hymn for Canada.
Priest and Pagan.
Soul Lifted.

Watson, Barbara Bellow
Late Light.

Watson, Clyde
Dilly Dilly Piccalilli.
Do the Baby Cake-Walk.
Phoebe in a Rosebush.
Rock, Rock, Sleep, My Baby.

Watson, Edward Willard
Absolution.

Watson, Elaine
Museum Piece No. 16228.

Watson, Evelyn M.
A Sleeping Beauty.

Watson, J. Y.
The Soldier (parody).

Watson, James Wreford
The Gatineaus.
Our Love Shall Be the
Brightness.
Sic Transit Gloria Mundi.
Stay, Time.
We Shall Have Far to Go.

Watson, John Whittaker
The Beautiful Snow.

Watson, Minor
Constancy.

Watson, Robert
The Blue Whale.
Do You Love Me?
The Glass Door.
A Good Life.
Is There Life across the
Street?
Times Square Parade.

Watson, Rosamund Marriott
Ave Atque Vale.
The Farm on the Links.
The Last Fairy.
Omnia Somnia.
Requiescat.
A South Coast Idyll.

Watson, Sara Ruth
Bouncing Ball.

Watson, Sir Henry
It Is Finished.

Watson, Thomas
The Authour Still Pursuing
His Invention.
Come, Gentle Death!
The Ditty of the Six Virgins.
Here Lieth Love.
Love's Grave.
The Marigold So Likes the
Lovely Sun.
My Love Is Past.
Sonnet: "I saw the object of
my pining thought."
This Passion Is All Framed in
Manner of a Dialogue.
Time.
With Fragrant Flowers We
Strew the Way.

Watson, W. F. N.
The Hicche-Hykeres Tale
(parody).
Watson, Wilfred
Canticle of Darkness.
A Contempt for Dylan
Thomas.
Emily Carr.
In the Cemetery of the Sun.
The Juniper Tree.
Lines: I Praise God's
Mankind in an Old Woman.
O My Poor Darling.
The Windy Bishop.
Watson, William
Autumn.
The Church Today.
Dawn on the Headland.
Domine Quo Vadis?
Epigram: "'Tis human
fortune's happiest height."
An Epitaph.
God-Seeking.
The Great Misgiving.
The Hope of the World.
Hymn to the Sea.
Invention.
The Key-Board.
Lacrimae Musarum.
Leavetaking.
Love.
Ode in May.
The Poet.
Shakespeare.
Song: "April, April."
Song: "O, like a queen's her
happy tread."
Sonnets to Miranda.
The Sovereign Poet.
The Things That Are More
Excellent.
The Unknown God.
Vita Nuova.
The Woman with the
Serpent's Tongue.
Wordsworth's Grave.
Watt, Frederick B.
The Inspection.
Watt, Lauchlan MacLean
I Bind My Heart.
The Reapers.
A Wind from the West.
Watt, T. S.
From My Rural Pen.
Watt, W. W.
So This Is Autumn.
Summer Song.
Watterman, Catharine H.
Come unto Me, When
Shadows Darkly Gather.
Wattles, Willard
The Builder.
Comrades of the Cross.
Creeds.
The Family of Nations.
From the Parthenon I Learn.
Gabriel.
I Thought Joy Went by Me.
Jericho.
Pisgah.
Watts, Alaric Alexander
An Austrian Army.
The Siege of Belgrade.
Watts, Isaac
Accept Our Tribute.
The Adventurous Muse.
Against Quarrelling and
Fighting.
Broad Is the Road.
The Church the Garden of
Christ.

The Comparison and
Complaint.
A Cradle Hymn.
Crucifixion to the World by
the Cross of Christ.
The Day of Judgement.
Felicity.
Few Happy Matches.
For the Lord's Day Evening.
From All That Dwell below
the Skies.
God's Dominion and Decrees.
The Hazard of Loving the
Creatures.
The Heavens Declare Thy
Glory, Lord!
Horace Paraphrased.
Hosanna to Christ.
How Doth the Little Busy
Bee.
The Hurry of the Spirits, in a
Fever and Nervous
Disorders.
I Sing the Mighty Power of
God.
The Incomprehensible.
Innocent Play.
Jesus Shall Reign.
Joy to the World.
King Triumphant.
Look on Him Whom They
Pierced, and Mourn.
Love between Brothers and
Sisters.
Man Frail, and God Eternal.
Miracles at the Birth of
Christ.
O God Our Help in Ages
Past.
O How I Love Thy Law.
Our Saviour's Golden Rule.
The Passion and Exaltation of
Christ.
Praise for Mercies Spiritual
and Temporal.
A Prospect of Heaven Makes
Death Easy.
Quarrelling, or Let Dogs
Delight.
The Shortness and Misery of
Life.
Sincere Praise.
The Sluggard.
Spare Us, O Lord, Aloud We
Pray.
Submission to Afflictive
Providences.
Sweet Muse.
There Is a Land.
True Riches.
Where-e'er My Flatt'ring
Passions Rove.
Where Nothing Dwelt But
Beasts of Prey.
Why Do We Mourn
Departing Friends?
Watts, Marjorie Seymour
New Shoes.
The Policeman.
Watts-Dunton, Theodore
Coleridge.
The First Kiss.
Mother Carey's Chicken.
The Sonnet's Voice.
Waugh, Edwin
The Dule's i' This Bonnet o'
Mine.
Wayland, John Elton
An Epilogue at Wallack's.
Wayman, Tom
Another Poem about the
Madness of Women.

The Chilean Elegies: 5. The
Interior.
Picketing Supermarkets.
Poem Composed in Rogue
River Park...
Wayman in Love.
What Good Poems Are For.
Wayne, Jane O.
Looking Both Ways.
Wazyk, Adam
Ars Poetica.
Hotel.
Nike.
Weare, Mesech
The Blasted Herb.
Weatherly, Frederic Edward
A Carol.
The Cats' Tea-Party.
The Dustman.
The Holy City.
Limerick: "My name's Mister
Benjamin Bunny."
The Tale of a Tart.
When the Christ Child Came.
Weatherly, Tom
Arroyo.
Canto 4.
Canto 5.
Canto 7.
First Monday Scottsboro
Alabama.
Imperial Thumbprint.
Weaver, Edith
Lost Cinderella.
Weaver, John V. A.
Drug Store.
Ghost.
Legend.
Nocturne.
Two Ways.
Weaver, Robert
The Orb Weaver.
Weaver, Roger
December 24, 1979.
To J.F.K. 14 Years after.
Weaving, Willoughby
The Star.
Webb, Charles David
And Dust to Dust.
Jardin des Fleurs.
Monasteries.
Orestes Pursued.
Threshold.
**Webb, Charles Henry ("John
Paul")**
At the Ball!
Autumn Leaves.
Dictum Sapienti.
Dum Vivimus Vigilemus.
Gil, the Toreador.
March.
With a Nantucket Shell.
Webb, Francis
Airliner.
A Drum for Ben Boyd.
End of the Picnic.
Five Days Old.
For My Grandfather.
The Gunner.
Idyll.
Laid Off.
Leichhardt in Theatre: The
Room.
Morgan's Country.
The Sea.
This Runner.
A View of Montreal (excerpt).
Ward Two.
Webb, Frederick G.
The Dash for the Colors.
Webb, Mary
Green Rain.

Market Day.
The Water-Ousel.
Webb, Phyllis
The Days of the Unicorns.
Imperfect Sestina.
The Kropotkin Poems
(excerpt).
Making.
Marvell's Garden.
Poetics against the Angel of
Death.
Rilke.
Spots of Blood.
A Tall Tale; or, A Moral
Song.
To Friends Who Have Also
Considered Suicide.
Webb, Tessa Sweazy
Bright Abandon.
Webb, Thomas H. B.
An Ancient Prayer.
Webbe, Charles
Against Indifference.
Webber, Mary A.
Limerick: "I know a young
girl who can speak."
Weber, Helen
Lessons.
Weber, Nancy
Tidying Up.
Weber, Richard
Borderline Ballad.
Envying the Pelican.
In Memoriam.
The Lion and O'Reilly.
O'Reilly's Reply.
Observation.
On an Italian Hillside.
The Poet's Day.
A Primer for Schoolchildren.
A Visit to Bridge House.
Weber, Tom
I'm 92, Joe Said.
Webster, A. W.
Limerick: "A Conservative,
out on his motor."
Webster, Augusta
A Castaway (excerpt).
Medea in Athens (excerpt).
The Pine.
Seeds.
The Violet and the Rose.
Webster, Daniel
On the Death of My Son
Charles.
Webster, Diane
Memory Movie.
Webster, H. D. L.
Lorena.
Webster, John
The Duchess of Malfi.
An Execration against
Whores.
The Madman's Song.
Oh, Let Us Howl Some Heavy
Note.
Survey Our Progress from
Our Birth.
Vanitas Vanitatum.
The White Devil, V, iv: "Call
for the Robin Redbreast."
Webster, M. M.
The Marriage of Pocahontas.
Webster, Mary Morison
Grass.
I Set Aside.
Illi Morituri.
The Ox.
The Quiet of the Dead.
The Secret.
Webster, W. J.
To His Coy Mistress (parody).

Wedde, Ian
Cardrona Valley.
Dark Wood.
Earthly.
Hardon ("get one today").
Losing the Straight Way.
Wedderburn, James, John, Robert
Balulalow.
Wedgefarth, W. Dayton
Bum.
Mother's Hands.
Weeden, Craig
Calvin in the Attic Cleans.
A Pizza Joint in Cranston (parody).
Yachting in Arkansas.
Weeden, Howard
The Banjo of the Past.
The Borrowed Child.
Weeden, Lula Lowe
Dance.
The Little Dandelion.
Me Alone.
Robin Red Breast.
The Stream.
Weekes, Charles
In Brittany.
Poppies.
Solstice.
Think.
Weeks, James Eyre
On the Great Fog in London, December 1762.
Weeks, Ramona
The Indian Graveyard.
Weeks, Robert Kelley
Man and Nature.
Medusa.
A Song for Lexington.
Weeks, Robert Lewis
Appalachian Front.
Weelkes, Thomas
Fara Diddle Dyno.
Madrigal: "Ay me, alas, heigh ho, heigh ho!"
Madrigal: "Ha ha! ha ha! This world doth pass."
Madrigal: "The gods have heard my vows."
Weever, John
De Se.
Weever, Robert
In an Arbour Green.
Weigl, Bruce
Burning Shit at An Khe.
The Harp.
Homage to Elvis, Homage to the Fathers.
The Limits of Departure.
Snowy Egret.
Song of Napalm.
Weil, James L.
At a Loss.
A Coney Island Life.
Weiman, Andrew
Andy-Diana DNA Letter.
Wein, Jules Alan
Genesis.
Weingarten, Roger
Blue Bog Children.
Ethan Boldt.
Her Apron through the Trees.
Memoir.
These Obituaries of Rattlesnakes Being Eaten by the Hogs.
Weiser, Conrad
Jehovah, Lord and Majesty.
Weismiller, Edward
To the Woman in Bond Street Station.

The Trail.
World, Defined.
Weiss, Michael
Resurrection Hymn.
Weiss, Neil
The Aging Athlete.
The Hike.
The Word.
Weiss, Theodore
Art in America.
As You Like It.
Barracks Apt. 14.
Clothes Make the Man.
A Dab of Color.
The Dance Called David.
The Death of Fathers.
An Egyptian Passage.
The Fire at Alexandria.
The Greater Music.
House of Fire.
In the Round.
The Last Day and the First.
A Letter from the Pygmies.
The Life of....
The Moral.
Off to Patagonia.
Out of Your Hands.
Preface.
The Reapings.
The Sow's Ear.
This Narrow Stage.
To Forget Me.
The Ultimate Antientropy.
Ways of Loving.
The Web.
Yes, But...
Weissbort, Daniel
Anniversary.
Murder of a Community.
Walking Home at Night.
Weisslitz, E. F.
Baldpate Pond.
Weist, Carl S.
A Cross on a Hill.
Welburn, Ron
Avoidances.
Cecil County.
Eulogy for Populations.
Percussions.
Regenesis.
Welby, Amelia C.
Twilight at Sea.
Welch, Don
The Armless.
Bark.
Blue Heron.
Carved by Obadiah Verity.
The Dutchman.
Fishing, at Coot Shallows.
Funeral at Ansley.
Poet in Residence at a Country School.
The River.
The Small.
Spade Scharnweber.
We Used to Play.
Welch, James
Across to the Peloponnese.
Arizona Highways.
Blue Like Death.
Christmas Comes to Moccasin Flat.
Directions to the Nomad.
Going to Remake This World.
Harlem, Montana: Just Off the Reservation.
In My First Hard Springtime.
In My Lifetime.
Lady in a Distant Face.
Magic Fox.
The Man from Washington.
The Only Bar in Dixon.

Plea to Those Who Matter.
Please Forward.
The Renegade Wants Words.
Snow Country Weavers.
Surviving.
Thanksgiving at Snake Butte.
Verifying the Dead.
Visit.
Why I Didn't Go to Delphi.
D-Y Bar.
Welch, Lew
Chicago Poem.
Song of the Turkey Buzzard.
Taxi Suite: After Anacreon.
Wobbly Rock.
Welch, Livingston
Bang Street.
Welch, Marie de L.
Lord of Eden.
Mus Ridiculus Non.
Prelude to Commencement.
St. Francis and the Cloud.
Welch, Myra Brooks
The Touch of the Master's Hand.
Welch, Noel
Anne and the Peacock.
Welhaven, Johan Sebastian C.
Like an April Day.
Welish, Marjorie
Careers.
Picture Collection.
The Servant in Literature.
Welles, Winifred
Behind the Waterfall.
A Child's Song to Her Mother.
Climb.
Cobweb.
Cruciform.
Curious Something.
Dogs and Weather.
Gesture.
God's First Creature Was Light.
Green Grass and White Milk.
Indian Pipes.
Love Song from New England.
Old Ellen Sullivan.
River Skater.
Silence.
Skipping along Alone.
Starfish.
Stocking Fairy.
White Fear.
Winter Apples.
Wellesley, Dorothy
As Lambs into the Pen.
Asian Desert.
The Buried Child.
Camels in Persia.
Fire.
First Flight.
Fishing.
Horses.
Lenin (excerpt).
Matrix (excerpt).
The Morning After.
Wellesley, Henry
Demophilus.
Wells, Amos R.
The Ambitious Ant.
The Considerate Crocodile.
The Glorious Name.
The Inn That Missed Its Chance.
Mothers–and Others.
Pray!
Read the Bible Through.
Wells, Anna Maria
The Cow-Boy's Song.

The Little Maid.
Wells, Carolyn
Alone.
A Baker's Dozen of Wild Beasts.
Diversions of the Re-Echo Club.
A Dresscessional.
The Grandiloquent Goat.
How to Tell the Wild Animals.
Limerick: "A canner, exceedingly canny."
Limerick: "A dragon, who was a great wag."
Limerick: "A tutor who tooted a flute."
Limerick: "B was a beggarly bear."
Limerick: "Miss Minnie McFinney of Butte."
Limerick: "O was an ossified oyster."
Limerick: "T was a tidy young tapir."
Limerick: "The girl with the theater hat."
Limerick: "There once was a happy hyena."
Limerick: "There once was a man who said, 'Oh'."
Limerick: "There was a young fellow named Tait."
Limerick: "There was an old lady of Dover."
Limerick: "There was once a dear little gnome."
Limerick: "W was a wild worm."
A Marvel.
One Week.
Our Polite Parents.
An Overworked Elocutionist.
Oyster-Crabs (parody).
A Possibility.
The Poster Girl.
Puzzled.
The Swift Bullets.
To a Baked Fish.
A Travelogue: Clovelly.
The Tutor.
The Universal Favorite.
Wells, Faith
More Than We Ask.
Wells, James
The Golden Rule.
Wells, Marcus Morris
Holy Spirit, Faithful Guide.
Wells, Rollin J.
As We Grow Older.
Growing Old.
Wells, Will
The Fisherman.
Welsh, Anne
Between Seasons.
Many Birds.
Sharpeville Inquiry.
That Way.
Waterfall.
Welsh, Robert Gilbert
Azrael.
Welsh, William
8:00 a.m. Monday Morning.
Wasp.
Welshimer, Helen
Dusk.
Welsted, Leonard
Epigram.
The Invitation.
Welte, Lou Ann
Those Last, Late Hours of Christmas Eve.

Welty, Eudora
A Flock of Guinea Hens Seen from a Car.
Wen I-to
The Dead Water.
Early Summer Night.
Wenceslas, King of Bohemia
The Proffered Rose.
Wendt, Ingrid
The Newest Banana Plant Leaf.
Personal Poem.
Wenger, Rene
After Chagall.
Wentworth, William Charles
Australasia (excerpt).
Weores, Sandor
The Lost Parasol (excerpt).
Werfel, Franz
Exaltation.
For I Have Done a Good and Kindly Deed.
Litany of the Rooms of the Dead.
Loneliness.
A Song of Life.
Strangers Are We All upon the Earth.
Teach Us to Mark This, God.
To a Lark in War-Time.
Ye Sorrowers.
Wergeland, Henrik
The Flower.
Wergeland, Henrik and Arnold Thaulov
The Wall-Flower.
Werner, Alice
A Song of Fleet Street.
Werner, Martina
Monogram 4.
Monogram 23.
Monogram 29.
Wertheimer, Paul
Souls.
Wescott, Glenway
The Poet at Night-Fall.
The Summer Ending.
Wesley, Cecil Cobb
As Night Comes On.
Wesley, Charles
Ah! Lovely Appearance of Death!
Bid Me Sin No More.
Break My Heart of Stone.
A Charge to Keep I Have.
Christ, the Good Physician.
Christ the Lord Is Risen Today.
Claiming the Promise.
Come, Lord Jesus.
Come, Thou Almighty King.
The Conquering Love of Jesus.
The Covenant of His Grace.
The Cup of Blessing.
Draw Me, Saviour, After Thee.
Draw Near, O Son of God.
During His Courtship.
Dying That I Might Live.
Easter Hymn.
The Ever-Living Church.
Father, How Wide Thy Glories Shine.
Fly to Jesus.
For Christmas-Day.
For His Wife, on Her Birthday.
For Perfect Peace.
For the Peace of Jerusalem.
Free Grace.
Gentle Jesus.

Graven on the Palms of His Hands.
Great Shepherd of the Sheep.
Hark! The Herald Angels Sing.
The Horrible Decree (excerpt).
Hymn: "O Thou who camest from above."
I Know That My Redeemer Lives.
The Incarnation.
Inextinguishable Blaze.
Jesus, Lover of My Soul.
Jesus, the Name Most High.
Jesus, the Soul of Our Joys.
Jesus, Thou Art the King.
The Light Yoke and Easy Burden.
The Loadstone of His Love.
Love Divine, All Loves Excelling.
Morning Hymn.
My Companion.
The Nativity.
Now Is the Accepted Time.
O Thou Eternal Victim Slain.
On Sympathisers with the American Revolution.
On the Death of His Son.
Only Jesus Will I Know.
Speak the Word.
Still, O LORD, for Thee I Tarry.
Thy Conquering Name.
Thy Glorious Face Above.
Times without Number Have I Pray'd.
Triumph of His Grace.
Walking with Him in White.
Wash Me Whiter Than Snow.
The Well of Living Water.
The Whole Armour of God.
Wrestling Jacob.
Wesley, John
Hope Springing Up.
Hymn: "Thou hidden love of God, whose height."
I Believe Thy Precious Blood.
John Wesley's Rule.
Wesley, Samuel
Anacreontic, On Parting with a little Child.
Epigram on Miltonicks.
An Epitaph.
From a Hint in the Minor Poets.
Hymn to God the Father.
The Monument.
On the Setting Up of Mr. Butler's Monument in Westminster Abbey.
A Pindaric on the Grunting of a Hog.
The Saviour.
Wesley-Smith, Peter
The Ugstabuggle.
Weslowski, Dieter
Zoe and the Ghosts.
West, Annette Arkeketa
Blackbird Winter.
Calumet Early Evening.
Child Poem.
Coyote Brother Song.
Glenpool.
Naming the Rain.
Poem for My Father.
Salt Man.
West, Arthur Graeme
God, How I Hate You.
West, Don
My South.

West, Gilbert
The Island of the Blest.
West, John
Fair Hebe.
West, John Foster
Hill Hunger.
West, Kenyon
Thou Shouldst Be Living at This Hour!
West, Michael
Parts Man.
West, Paul
The Cumberbunce.
West, Robert A.
Come, Let Us Tune Our Loftiest Song.
Westcott, Joseph L.
The Legend of Grand Lake.
Westendorf, Thomas P.
I'll Take You Home Again, Kathleen.
Westerfield, Nancy G.
Carolers.
Where I Walk in Nebraska.
Westmoreland, Mildmay Fane, Earl of
In Obitum Ben. Jons.
In Praise of Fidelia.
My Happy Life.
Occasioned by Seeing a Walk of Bay Trees.
Weston, Mildred
Bleat of Protest.
Central Park Tourney.
Cider Song.
Echo.
Episode of the Cherry Tree.
Father.
Hat Bar.
Query.
To a Lady Holding the Floor.
To a Man in a Picture Window Watching Television.
Westrup, J. M.
Flying.
Westwood, Thomas
Little Bell.
Mine Host of "The Golden Apple."
Night of Spring.
Under My Window.
Wetherald, Ethelwyn
The House of the Trees.
In April.
Woodland Worship.
Wetherill, Hilda Faunce
Little Puppy.
Wevill, David
The Birth of a Shark.
Irish Hotel.
Monsoon.
The Poets.
Wexionius, Olof
On the Death of a Pious Lady.
Weyburn, Ruby T.
The True Apostolate.
Whalen, Philip
10:X:57, 45 Years Since the Fall of the Ch'ing Dynasty.
Denunciation; or, Unfrock'd Again.
For C.
For Kai Snyder.
Forty-Five Years Since the Fall of the Ch'ing Dynasty.
Further Notice.
How Was Your Trip to L.A.?
Life in the City. In Memoriam Edward Gibbon.

Literary Life in the Golden West.
Martyrdom of Two Pagans.
Plus Ca Change...
The Same Old Jazz.
Sourdough Mountain Lookout.
Take I, 4: II: 58.
Technicalities for Jack Spicer.
To the Muse.
Two Variations: All about Love.
Where or When.
Whalley, George
Night Flight.
We Who Are Left.
Wharton, Anne
How Hardly I Conceal'd My Tears.
Spite of Thy Godhead, Powerful Love.
Wharton, Edith
Experience.
Wharton, Thomas, Marquess of
Come, Gentle Sleep, Death's Image Though Thou Art.
Lilliburlero (A New Song).
Wharton, William H.
Ben Milam.
Whately, Richard
A Serio-Comic Elegy.
There Is a Place in Distant Seas.
Wheatcroft, John
Pisanello's Studies of Men Hanging on Gallows.
Wheatley, Phillis
Goliath of Gath.
An Hymn to the Morning.
Liberty and Peace.
On Being Brought from Africa to America.
On Imagination.
On Virtue.
To a Gentleman and Lady on the Death of the Lady's Brother and Sister.
To a Lady on the Death of Her Husband.
To His Excellency, General Washington.
To S. M. a Young African Painter, on Seeing His Work.
To the King's Most Excellent Majesty.
To the Right Honourable William, Earl of Dartmouth.
To the University of Cambridge, in New-England.
Wheatstraw, Peetie
More Good Whiskey Blues.
Wheeler, Charles Enoch
Adjuration.
Tumult.
Wheeler, Edward J.
Night's Mardi Gras.
Wheeler, Kathleen
A New Leaf.
Wheeler, Ruth Winant
Prayer for Shut-Ins.
Wheeler, Sylvia
Lost Contact.
Wheelock, John Hall
Afternoon: Amagansett Beach.
Amagansett Beach Revisited.
Autumn Along the Beaches.
Beethoven.
The Black Panther.
Bonac.
The Dark Memory.
Dawn on Mid-Ocean.
Dear Men and Women.

Dialectics of Flight.
The Divine Insect.
Earth.
Elegy.
Ernest Dowson.
Exile from God.
The Far Land.
The Fish-Hawk.
For Them All.
The Gardener.
Golgotha.
Hippopotamothalamion.
The Holy Earth: In the
   Immense Cathedral.
The House in the Green Well.
I Do Not Love to See Your
   Beauty Fire.
It Is Finished.
Legend.
The Letter.
The Lion-House.
Love and Liberation.
Mozart Perhaps.
New York.
Night Thoughts in Age.
Nirvana.
Prayer.
Random Reflections on a
   Cloudless Sunday.
Random Reflections on a
   Summer Evening.
Reconciliation.
Sea-Voyage.
Silence.
Slow Summer Twilight.
Solitudes.
The Sound of the Sea.
The Sun Men Call It.
Sunday Evening in the
   Common.
Symphony: First Movement.
Thanks from Earth to
   Heaven.
This Quiet Dust.
To the Modern Man.
Triumph of Love.
The Two Societies.
Unison.
The Unknown Beloved.
Valediction.
Vaudeville Dancer.
Wood-Thrush.
The Years.

Wheelock, Lucy
The Song of the Lilies.

Wheelwright, John
Apocryphal Apocalypse.
Ave Eva.
Canal Street.
Father.
Fish Food.
Gestures to the Dead
   (excerpt).
The Huntsman.
Paul and Virginia.
There Is No Opera Like
   "Lohengrin."
Train Ride.
Why Must You Know?

Wheelwright, John Brooks
Forty Days (excerpt).

Whetstone, George
Give Me My Work.

Whicher, George F.
Myrtle for Two.

Whicher, George Meason
Bacchylides.
To the Frivolous Muse.

Whinery, Verna
This Day Is Thine.

Whipple, George
Three Cezannes.

Whisenand, Emma Boge
Open Your Eyes.

Whisler, Robert F.
The Collector.
Pigeons.

Whistler, James
Limerick: "There is a creator
   named God."

Whistler, Laurence
A Form of Epitaph.
No Answer.
A Portrait in the Guards.
The Shape of a Bird.

Whitaker, Alexander
Leaving the Dance.

Whitaker, Robert
Easter.
My Country Is the World.
O Mothers of the Human
   Race.
Out-of-Doors.
The Starred Mother.
Worship.

Whitbread, Thomas
The CCC.
Civilities.
A Pool.
To My Fellow-Mariners,
   March, '53.

White, Booker
Aberdeen, Mississippi Blues.
Fixing to Die.
The Panama Limited.
Parchman Farm Blues.
Sic 'Em Dogs On.
Sleepy Man Blues.

White, Christine
Secret of Song.

White, Christy
Running under Street Lights.

White, Claire Nicholas
The Roses of Queens.

White, Cool
Lubly Fan.

White, E. B.
Affidavit in Platitudes.
Apostrophe to a Pram Rider.
Apostrophic Notes from the
   New-World Physics.
The Circus.
A Classic Waits for Me.
Commuter.
Critic.
Dog around the Block.
Fashions in Dogs.
A Father Does His Best.
I Paint What I See.
A Listener's Guide to the
   Birds.
Marble-Top.
The Red Cow Is Dead.
Song of the Queen Bee.
To a Lady across the Way.
Window Ledge in the Atom
   Age.

White, Edward Lucas
Genius.
The Last Bowstrings.

White, Eugene Richard
Of the Lost Ship.

White, Gail
Happy Endings.
The Housecleaner.
Return to Astolat.

White, George
I Came to Jesus.

White, Gilbert
The Naturalist's Summer-
   Evening Walk.
On the Dark, Still, Dry,
   Warm Weather ...

White, Gleason
A Primrose Dame.

White, Harriet R.
Uffia.

White, Henry Kirke
Clifton Grove (excerpt).
Description of a Summer's
   Eve.
Man's Littleness in Presence
   of the Stars.
On the Death of Dermody,
   the Poet.
Song from Fragment of an
   Eccentric Drama.
To an Early Primrose.

White, Hervey
I Saw the Clouds.

White, James Terry
Not by Bread Alone.

White, John
Limerick: "There once was a
   man, named Power."

White, Jon Manchip
The Captain.
Count Orlo in England.
Orlo's Valediction.
The Rout of San Romano.

White, Joseph Blanco
Black Is a Soul.
Mysterious Night.
To Night.

White, Julie Herrick
Like Children of the
   Summertime Playing at
   Cards.

White, Lillian Zellhoefer
Hangman's Tree.

White, Mary Jane
Lindeman.
Of All Plants, the Tree.

White, Ned
Apache Kid.
Bones in the Desert.

White, Patrick
Lyre.

White, Richard Edward
Discovery of San Francisco
   Bay.

White, T. H.
To Myself, after Forty Years.
The Witch's Work Song.

White, Vera
You Are on U.S. 40 Headed
   West.

White, William Allen
An Intermezzo for the Fourth
   Act.
A Rhyme of the Dream-
   Maker Man.

Whitebird, Joanie
Star.

Whitecotton, Moses
Fuller and Warren.

Whitehead, Charles
The Lamp.
A Summer Storm.

Whitehead, James
About a Year after He Got
   Married He Would Sit
   Alone...
Delta Farmer in a Wet
   Summer.
The Flood Viewed by the
   Tourist from Iowa.
He Records a Little Song for
   a Smoking Girl.
A Local Man Remembers
   Betty Fuller.
The Narrative Hooper and
   L.D.O. Sestina with a Long
   Last Line.
Poem Called Poem.

White, Gleason

Visionary Oklahoma Sunday
   Beer.

Whitehead, Paul
The Gymnasiad, or Boxing
   Match (excerpt).
A Hunting Song.

Whitehead, William
A Charge to the Poets
   (excerpt).
The Enthusiast: an Ode.
The Je Ne Scay Quoi: A
   Song.
New Night Thoughts on
   Death. A Parody.
On Friendship.
The Sweepers.

Whiteman, Roberta Hill
Beginning the Year at
   Rosebud, S.D.
Dream of Rebirth.
In the Longhouse, Oneida
   Museum.
The Long Parenthesis.
Midnight on Front Street.
Midwinter Stars.
Notes for Albuquerque.
Woman Seed Player.

Whiteside, Mary Brent
The Carpenter.
Who Has Known Heights.

Whitfield, Frederick
I Need Thee.
There Is a Name I Love to
   Hear.

Whitfield, James M.
America (excerpt).

Whiting, Charles Goodrich
Blue Hills Beneath the Haze.
The Eagle's Fall.
The Way to Heaven.

Whiting, Lilian
The Mystery.

Whiting, Nathaniel
The Office of Poetry.

Whiting, Seymour W.
Alamance.

Whiting, William
Hymn: "Eternal Father,
   strong to save."

Whitman, Cedric
Dissonance.

Whitman, Oscar
Variations on a Theme.

Whitman, Ruth
Almost Ninety.
Bubba Esther, 1888.
Castoff Skin.
Cutting the Jewish Bride's
   Hair.
Dan, the Dust of Masada Is
   Still in My Nostrils.
Dead Center.
Flight.
Human Geography.
Listening to Grownups
   Quarreling.
The Marriage Wig.
Mediterranean.
Sister Pharaoh.
Spring.
Translating.
Watching the Sun Rise over
   Mount Zion.
Yom Kippur: Fasting.

Whitman, Sarah Helen
Sonnet to Edgar Allan Poe.
Sonnets.

Whitman, Walt
Aboard at a Ship's Helm.
Afoot and Light-Hearted, I
   Take to the Open Road.
After an Interval.

After the Dazzle of Day.
After the Sea-Ship.
After the Supper and Talk.
Ages and Ages Returning at
   Intervals.
Ah, Poverties, Wincings, and
   Sulky Retreats.
All the Past We Leave
   Behind.
Are You the New Person
   Drawn toward Me?
An Army Corps on the
   March.
As Adam Early in the
   Morning.
As Consequent, etc.
As I Ebb'd with the Ocean of
   Life.
As I Lay with My Head in
   Your Lap Camerado.
As I Pondered in Silence.
As If a Phantom Caress'd Me.
As Toilsome I Wander'd
   Virginia's Woods.
The Base of All Metaphysics.
Battle of the Bonhomme
   Richard and the Serapis.
The Beautiful Swimmer.
Beauty.
The Beauty of the Ship.
Beginners.
Beginning My Studies.
Belief in Plan of Thee.
The Bodies of Men and
   Women Engirth Me.
A Boston Ballad.
Broadway.
A Broadway Pageant.
By Blue Ontario's Shore
   (excerpt).
Calamus.
The Centenarian's Story.
Chanting the Square Deific.
Children of Adam.
The City Dead-House.
City of Orgies.
A Clear Midnight.
Come, Said My Soul.
Come Up from the Fields
   Father.
The Commonplace.
Crossing Brooklyn Ferry.
Crowds of Men and Women.
The Dalliance of Eagles.
Darest Thou Now O Soul.
Dirge for Two Veterans.
The Dismantled Ship.
Drum-Taps.
Earth, My Likeness.
Eidolons.
Faces.
Facing West from California's
   Shores.
A Farm Picture.
The First Dandelion.
For You, O Democracy.
Give Me the Splendid Silent
   Sun.
A Glimpse.
Gods.
Had I the Choice.
Halcyon Days.
A Hand-Mirror.
Hast Never Come to Thee an
   Hour.
Here the Frailest Leaves of
   Me.
A Hub for the Universe.
Hush'd Be the Camps To-
   Day.
I Am He That Aches with
   Love.

I Believe a Leaf of Grass...
I Dote Upon Myself.
I Dream'd in a Dream.
I Have Not So Much
   Emulated the Birds that
   Musically Sing.
I Hear America Singing.
I Hear and See Not Strips of
   Cloth Alone.
I Hear It Was Charged
   against Me.
I Heard You Solemn-Sweet
   Pipes of the Organ.
I Saw in Louisiana a Live-Oak
   Growing.
I Saw the Vision of Armies.
I Sing the Body Electric.
I Stand as on Some Mighty
   Eagle's Beak.
In Cabin'd Ships at Sea.
In the Swamp in Secluded
   Recesses.
Infinity.
Italian Music in Dakota.
Joy, Shipmate, Joy!
The Last Invocation.
Leaves of Grass.
Long I Thought That
   Knowledge Alone Would
   Suffice.
Long, Too Long America.
Look down Fair Moon.
Mannahatta.
A March in the Ranks Hard-
   Prest, and the Road
   Unknown.
Marches Now the War Is
   Over (excerpt).
Me Imperturbe.
Memories.
Miracles.
My 71st Year.
Native Moments.
Night on the Prairies.
No Labor-Saving Machine.
Not Heat Flames Up and
   Consumes.
Not Heaving from My Ribb'd
   Breast Only.
Now Lift Me Close.
O Hymen! O Hymenee!
O Living Always, Always
   Dying.
O Magnet-South.
O Tan-Faced Prairie-Boy.
Of the Terrible Doubt of
   Appearances.
Oh Captain! My Captain!
An Old Man's Thought of
   School.
Old War-Dreams.
On the Beach at Night Alone.
Once I Pass'd Through a
   Populous City.
One Hour of Madness and
   Joy.
One's-Self I Sing.
Others May Praise What They
   Like.
Out of the Cradle Endlessly
   Rocking.
Out of the Rolling Ocean the
   Crowd.
The Ox-Tamer.
Passage to India.
Patroling Barnegat.
Pent-Up Aching Rivers
   (excerpt).
Pioneers! O Pioneers!
The Poet.
Poets to Come.
Prayer of Columbus.

Reconciliation.
Recorders Ages Hence.
Respondez!
Roots and Leaves Themselves
   Alone.
The Runner.
Salut Au Monde!
Shut Not Your Doors.
The Singer in the Prison.
The Sleepers.
So Long!
Sometimes With One I Love.
Song for All Seas, All Ships.
Song of Myself.
Song of the Answerer
   (excerpt).
Song of the Broad-Ax
   (excerpt).
Song of the Exposition
   (excerpt).
Song of the Open Road.
Song of the Redwood-Tree.
Song of the Universal.
The Soul, Reaching, Throwing
   Out for Love.
Sparkles from the Wheel.
Spontaneous Me.
Stallion.
Starting from Paumanok.
Still Though the One I Sing.
The Sum of All Known
   Reverence.
Tears.
Thanks in Old Age.
There Was a Child Went
   Forth.
This Compost.
This Moment Yearning and
   Thoughtful.
Thou Mother with Thy Equal
   Brood.
Thou Mother with Thy Equal
   Brood (excerpt).
To a Common Prostitute.
To a Stranger.
To-Day and Thee.
To Him That Was Crucified.
To One Shortly to Die.
To Rich Givers.
To the Man-of-War Bird.
To the Pending Year.
To the States.
!To Think of Time.
To You.
Trickle Drops.
Turn O Libertad.
Two Veterans.
The Unexpress'd.
The Untold Want.
Vigil Strange I Kept on the
   Field One Night.
Washington's Monument,
   February, 1885.
We Two Boys together
   Clinging.
Western Lines.
When I Heard at the Close of
   the Day.
When I Heard the Learn'd
   Astronomer.
When I Peruse the Conquer'd
   Fame.
Whispers of Heavenly Death.
Whoever You Are Holding
   Me Now in Hand.
A Woman Waits for Me.
"The world below the brine".
Years of the Modern.
Yonnondio.
You Felons on Trial in
   Courts.

You Lingering Sparse Leaves
   of Me.
You, Whoever You Are.
Youth, Day, Old Age, and
   Night.
Whitney, Adeline D. T.
Equinoctial.
February.
Humpty Dumpty.
Peace.
Whitney, Anna Temple
The Kneeling Camel.
Whitney, Ernest
Ute Pass.
Whitney, F. B.
God Knows the Answer.
Whitney, Geffrey
Content.
Whitney, Hattie
A Little Dutch Garden.
Whitney, Helen Hay
Song: "We only ask for
   sunshine."
To Diane.
Whitney, Joseph Ernest
A Drop of Ink.
Whittaker, Frederick
Custer's Last Charge.
Whittemore, Elizabeth
My Friends Are Little Lamps
   to Me.
Whittemore, Reed
Abbreviated Interviews with a
   Few Disgruntled Literary
   Celebrities.
After Some Day of Decision.
Alfred Lord Tennyson.
An American Takes a Walk.
A Campus in Summer.
Clamming.
A Day with the Foreign
   Legion.
The Departure.
The Fall of the House of
   Usher.
A Floridian Museum of Art.
The High School Band.
The Learning Soul.
The Line of an American
   Poet.
Lines on Being Refused a
   Guggenheim Fellowship.
Love Song.
Notes on a Certain Terribly
   Critical Piece.
Ode to New York.
On the Suicide of a Friend.
Only the Dead.
Out of My Study Window.
The Party.
A Projection.
The Radio under the Bed.
Recall.
Reflections upon a Recurrent
   Suggestion by Civil Defense.
Science Fiction.
The Self and the Weather.
The Seven Days, III: On First
   Knowing God.
Shakespeare, Possibly, in
   California.
Still Life.
A Storm from the East.
Summer Concert.
The Tarantula.
A Teacher.
Thinking of Tents.
A Treasure.
The Walk Home.
A Week of Doodle.
A Winter Scene.

Whittier, John Greenleaf
Abraham Davenport.
Adjustment.
All's Well.
Among the Hills: Prelude.
Amy Wentworth.
Andrew Rykman's Prayer
 (excerpt).
The Angel of Patience.
The Angels of Buena Vista.
Astraea.
Astraea at the Capitol.
At Last.
At Port Royal: Song of the
 Negro Boatman.
An Autograph.
Barbara Frietchie.
The Barefoot Boy.
The Bartholdi Statue.
The Battle Autumn of 1862.
Bayard Taylor.
The Book Our Mothers Read.
The Brewing of Soma.
Brown of Ossawatomie.
Burial of Barber.
Burning Drift-Wood.
The Cable Hymn.
The Call of the Christian.
Cassandra Southwick.
Centennial Hymn.
Chicago.
Clerical Oppressors.
Conductor Bradley.
The Corn-Song.
The Crisis.
The Dead Feast of the Kol-
 Folk.
The Dead Ship of Harpswell.
Disarmament (excerpt).
Divine Compassion.
The Double-Headed Snake of
 Newbury.
Drop Thy Still Dews.
The Emancipation Group
 (excerpt).
Epitaph for Bathsheba.
The Eternal Goodness.
Faith.
The Farewell.
First-Day Thoughts.
The Fishermen.
For a Little Girl Mourning
 Her Favorite Cat.
For an Autumn Festival
 (excerpt).
For Righteousness' Sake.
Forgiveness.
The Frost Spirit.
Harvest Hymn.
The Haschish.
Haverhill, 1640-1890.
The Healer (excerpt).
The Henchman.
The Hunters of Men.
Hymn from the French of
 Lamartine (excerpt).
I Call the Old Time Back.
Ichabod.
Immortal Love, Forever Full.
In Earthen Vessels.
In Memory of James T.
 Fields.
In School-Days.
In the "Old South."
John Underhill.
The Joy of Giving.
July.
Kallundborg Church.
The Kansas Emigrants.
The King's Missive.
Laus Deo.
Lexington.

Life and Love.
The Lost Occasion.
Le Marais du Cygne.
Massachusetts to Virginia.
Maud Muller.
The Moral Warfare.
Mulford.
My Playmate.
My Triumph.
My Trust.
Norembega.
The Norsemen.
O Thou! Whose Presence
 Went Before.
The Old Burying-Ground.
On the Big Horn.
The Over-Heart.
The Pageant.
The Palatine.
Palestine.
Pentucket.
The Pipes at Lucknow.
The Poor Voter on Election
 Day.
Prelude.
The Pressed Gentian.
The Proclamation.
Proem.
The Prophecy of Samuel
 Sewall.
The Pumpkin.
The Quaker of the Olden
 Time.
The Riddle of the World.
The Shadow and the Light
 (excerpt).
The Ship-Builders.
The Shoemakers.
The Sisters.
Skipper Ireson's Ride.
Snow-Bound.
Song of Slaves in the Desert.
Songs of Labor: Dedication.
St. John.
The Swan Song of Parson
 Avery.
Telling the Bees.
Texas.
Thou, Our Elder Brother.
The Three Bells.
To John C. Fremont.
To My Old Schoolmaster.
To Pius IX.
To Ronge.
To the Thirty-Ninth Congress.
To William Lloyd Garrison.
The Trailing Arbutus.
Trinitas.
The Two Angels.
The Two Rabbins.
The Vanishers.
Vesta.
The Vow of Washington.
The Waiting.
What the Birds Said.
Worship.
Whittingham, William
Now Israel May Say, and
 That Truly.
Whittle, Daniel W.
Moment by Moment.
Whur, Cornelius
The Female Friend.
Whythorne, Thomas
Now That the Truth Is Tried.
Wickham, Anna
The Affinity.
After Annunciation.
The Cherry-Blossom Wand.
The Conscience.
The Contemplative Quarry.
Creatrix.

Dedication of the Cook.
Divorce.
Envoi.
The Fired Pot.
The Fresh Start.
Friend Cato.
Gift to a Jade.
The Last Round.
Meditation at Kew.
Nervous Prostration.
Sehnsucht.
Self-Analysis.
Ship near Shoals.
The Singer.
Song: "I was so chill, and
 overworn, and sad."
The Song-Maker.
Soul's Liberty.
The Tired Man.
The Tired Woman.
To a Crucifix.
To Men.
Vanity.
Weapons.
Widdemer, Margaret
As I Lay Quiet.
The Awakened War God.
Barter.
Certainties.
Comfort.
A Cyprian Woman.
The Dark Cavalier.
The Factories.
God and the Strong Ones.
If You Should Tire of Loving
 Me.
The Little Carved Bowl.
Mary, Helper of Heartbreak.
The Masters.
The Modern Woman to Her
 Lover.
Mother-Prayer.
The New Victory.
Not unto the Forest.
Oiseaurie (parody).
The Old Road to Paradise.
Prescience.
The Procession.
Rainuv: A Romantic Ballad
 from the Early Basque
 (parody).
Rambuncto (parody).
Search.
Song: "Going down the old
 way."
Teresina's Face.
The Watcher.
The Willow Cats.
Widerberg, Siv
At Annika's Place.
Best?
Divorce.
Once.
Wiebe, Dallas E.
L'Elisir d'Amore.
Epilogue.
Wieber, Wendy
One, the Other, And.
Wieners, John
The Acts of Youth.
An Anniversary of Death.
Le Chariot.
For Jan.
In the Half Light of Holding
 and Giving.
The Meadow.
Moon Poems.
A Poem for Museum Goers.
A Poem for Painters.
A Poem for the Insane.
A Poem for the Old Man.
A Poem for Trapped Things.

A Series 5.8.
Two Years Later.
The Waning of the Harvest
 Moon.
What Happened?
Where Fled.
The Windows of Waltham.
Wier, Dara
Fear.
Keno.
Late Afternoon on a Good
 Lake.
This Cold Nothing Else.
Wigglesworth, Michael
The Day of Doom.
For Just Men Light Is Sown.
God's Controversy with New-
 England.
A Prayer unto Christ the
 Judge of the World.
A Song of Emptiness to Fill
 up the Empty Pages
 Following.
Welcome, Sweet Rest.
Wightman, Richard
The Pilgrim.
The Servants.
Wigson, John
On the Death of Squire
 Christopher, a Remarkably
 Fat Sportsman.
Wilber, Bill
My Babe My Babe.
Wilberforce, Robert
Peace Is the Tranquillity of
 Order.
Wilberforce, Samuel
If I were a Cassowary.
Wilbur, Richard
Advice to a Prophet.
After the Last Bulletins.
All These Birds.
Altitudes.
Apology.
April 5, 1974.
The Aspen and the Stream.
At Year's End.
A Baroque Wall-Fountain in
 the Villa Sciarra.
Beasts.
The Beautiful Changes.
Bell Speech.
Beowulf.
A Black November Turkey.
Boy at the Window.
Ceremony.
A Christmas Hymn.
Cigales.
Cottage Street, 1953.
The Death of a Toad.
Digging for China.
A Dubious Night.
Epistemology.
Exeunt.
The Eye.
Fall in Corrales.
A Fire-Truck.
First Snow in Alsace.
Folk Tune.
For K.R. on Her Sixtieth
 Birthday.
For the New Railway Station
 in Rome.
For the Student Strikers.
Francis Jammes: A Prayer to
 Go to Paradise with the
 Donkeys.
Grace.
Grasse: The Olive Trees.
A Grasshopper.
He Was.
A Hole in the Floor.

In a Churchyard.
In the Elegy Season.
In the Field.
In the Smoking Car.
John Chapman.
Juggler.
Junk.
Lamarck Elaborated.
A Late Aubade.
Looking into History.
Love Calls Us to the Things
 of This World.
Loves of the Puppets.
Lying.
Marginalia.
Merlin Enthralled.
The Mill.
A Miltonic Sonnet for Mr.
 Johnson...
Mind.
Museum Piece.
My Father Paints the
 Summer.
O.
Objects.
October Maples, Portland.
On the Marginal Way.
Pangloss's Song.
Parable.
The Pardon.
Part of a Letter.
Piazza di Spagna, Early
 Morning.
Piccola Commedia.
Place Pigalle.
Playboy.
Potato.
Praise in Summer.
The Prisoner of Zenda.
The Proof.
Rillons, Rillettes.
La Rose des Vents.
Running.
Seed Leaves.
A Shallot.
Shame.
She.
A Simile for Her Smile.
A Simplification.
Sleepless at Crown Point.
Some Opposites.
Sonnet: "The winter
 deepening, the hay all in."
Speech for the Repeal of the
 McCarran Act.
The Star System.
Statues.
Still, Citizen Sparrow.
Stop.
A Storm in April.
A Summer Morning.
The Terrace.
Then when the Ample Season.
Thyme Flowering among
 Rocks.
To an American Poet Just
 Dead.
To the Etruscan Poets.
Transit.
Two Voices in a Meadow.
Tywater.
The Undead.
A Voice from under the
 Table.
Walking to Sleep.
What Is the Opposite of a
 Prince?
What's Good for the Soul Is
 Good for Sales.
A World without Objects Is a
 Sensible Emptiness.
The Writer.

Year's End.
Wilbye, John
Love Not Me for Comely
 Grace.
Risposta.
**Wilchilsea, Anne Finch,
Countess of**
Essay on Marriage.
A Nocturnal Reverie.
A Sigh.
To Death.
To Silvia.
To the Nightingale.
Wilcox, Carlos
Sights and Sounds of the
 Night.
Wilcox, Ella Wheeler
Accept My Full Heart's
 Thanks.
Ad Finem.
Attainment.
Attraction.
Better, Wiser and Happier.
The Christian's New-Year
 Prayer (excerpt).
Communism.
Faith.
The Farewell of Clarimonde
 (excerpt).
Friendship.
Growing Old.
I Love You.
Illusion.
An Inspiration.
Interlude.
Life.
Life's Lesson.
Life's Scars.
Lifting and Leaning.
Love much. Earth has enough
 of bitter in it.
Midsummer.
Mistakes.
A Morning Prayer.
My Ships.
One of Us Two.
Optimism.
The Price He Paid.
Progress.
The Queen's Last Ride.
Recrimination.
Solitude.
Talk Not of Strength, Till
 Your Heart Has Know.
They Say.
Those We Love the Best.
To know thy bent and then
 pursue.
True Brotherhood.
The True Knight.
The Two Glasses.
Two Kinds of People.
Unanswered Prayers.
Uselessness.
Was, Is, and Yet-To-Be.
Whatever Is–Is Best.
Will.
The Winds of Fate.
With Every Rising of the Sun.
Worth While.
You Never Can Tell.
Wilczek, Frank
Virtual Particles.
Wild, Peter
Air Raid.
Dog Hospital.
For the El Paso Weather
 Bureau.
Gooseberries.
Ice Cream.
Riding Double.
Snakes.

Thomas and Charlie.
Variation.
Washing Windows.
Wild, Robert
A Copy of the Last Verses
 Made by Dr. Wild...
 (excerpt).
Epitaph for a Godly Man's
 Tomb.
Iter Boreale.
A Poem upon the
 Imprisonment of Mr. Calamy
 in Newgate.
Wilde, Heather
Sister Bernardo.
Wilde, J.
Verses to Miss —.
**Wilde, Lady Jane Francesca
("Speranza")**
The Famine Year.
Wilde, Oscar
Athanasia.
Ave Imperatrix!
Ave Maria Gratia Plena.
The Ballad of Reading Gaol.
Les Ballons.
La Bella Donna Della Mia
 Mente.
E Tenebris.
Endymion.
Fabien Dei Franchi.
For Our Sakes.
The Grave of Shelley.
The Harlot's House.
Helas!
Impression de Paris.
Impression du Matin.
Impression Japonais.
Impressions.
In the Forest.
In the Gold Room.
Le Jardin.
Magdalen Walks.
My Voice.
On the Sale By Auction of
 Keats' Love Letters.
Portia.
Requiescat.
Serenade.
Les Silhouettes.
Sonnet: "Nay, Lord, not
 thus!"
The Sphinx (excerpt).
Symphony in Yellow.
Taedium Vitae.
Theocritus.
Theoretikos.
To Milton.
Wilde, Richard Henry
A Farewell to America.
My Life Is Like the Summer
 Rose.
Stanzas.
To the Mocking-Bird.
Wilder, Amos N.
If I Have Lifted up Mine Eyes
 to Admire.
Prayer.
De Profundis.
Wilder, John Nichols
Stand by the Flag.
Wiley, Geechie
Eagles on a Half.
Wilhelm, Prince of Sweden,
The Madonna's Lamp.
Wiljer, Robert
Moose.
Wilk, Melvin
Blessing.
Learning to Speak.

Wilkes
Epitaph on the Lap-Dog of
 Lady Frail.
Wilkins, Alice
The Ducks.
The Elephant's Trunk.
New Shoes.
Snow.
Wilkins, Eithne
Anabasis.
And Only Our Shadow Walks
 with Us.
Barbed Wire.
Cockcrow.
The Dreamers and the Sea.
The Eye.
Failure.
A High Place.
Passage of an August.
Shark's Fin.
Spoken through Glass.
Variations on a Theme by
 Sidney Keyes.
Wilkins, Mary Eleanor
Now Is the Cherry in
 Blossom.
Wilkins, Robert
I'll Go with Her Blues.
Nashville Stonewall Blues.
That's No Way to Get Along.
Wilkins, Terri Meyette
Celebration 1982.
Childs Memory.
Prison Walls–Red Brick
 Crevices.
Wilkins, William
The Engine Driver's Story.
The Magazine Fort, Phoenix
 Park, Dublin.
Wilkinson, Anne
Carol.
A Cautionary Tale.
Daily the Drum.
Falconry.
In June and Gentle Oven.
Lens.
Nature Be Damned.
Once Upon a Great Holiday.
Summer Acres.
Wilkinson, Florence
At the Salon.
Students.
Wilkinson, H. E.
Topsy-Turvy Land.
Wilkinson, Marguerite
Before Dawn in the Woods.
A Chant out of Doors.
Christ and the Common Day.
The End.
Guilty.
Pawnbrokers.
A Proud Song.
A Psalm to the Son.
Scatheless.
A Song of Two Wanderers.
Time.
To the Lighted Lady Window.
Wilkinson, William Cleaver
Webster: An Ode (excerpt).
Will, Frederic
A Fire a Simple Fire.
Long Lonely Lover of the
 Highway.
Will, James
Mountain Sculpture.
Willard, Emma Hart
Rock'd in the Cradle of the
 Deep.
Willard, Nancy
Angels in Winter.
Blake Leads a Walk on the
 Milky Way.

Bone Poem.
The Flea Circus at Tivoli.
Foxfire.
How the Hen Sold Her Eggs
  to the Stingy Priest.
In the Hospital of the Holy
  Physician.
The Insects.
The King of Cats Sends a
  Postcard to His Wife.
Lightness Remembered.
Moss.
Night Light.
No-Kings and the Calling of
  Spirits.
Original Strawberry.
Questions My Son Asked Me,
  Answers I Never Gave Him.
Saint Pumpkin.
Saints Lose Back.
A Way of Keeping.
When There Were Trees.
Willett, Florence White
Crowded Out.
Willette, Florence Hynes
For a Girl in Love.
William, of Shoreham
Hymn to the Virgin.
A Song to Mary.
Williams, B. Y.
The Friend Who Just Stands
  By.
Trus' an' Smile.
Washington.
Williams, Beryle
Afterbirth.
A Message to the
  Photographer Whose Prints I
  Purchased.
Williams, Big Joe
President Roosevelt.
Someday Baby.
Stepfather Blues.
Williams, C. K.
Blades.
A Day for Anne Frank.
Downwards.
Floor.
From My Window.
The Rampage.
Spit.
Tar.
The World's Greatest Tricycle
  Rider.
Williams, Charles
At the "Ye that do truly."
A Dream.
Kings Came Riding.
Mount Badon.
Night Song for a Child!
Taliessin's Return to Logres.
Taliessin's Song of the
  Unicorn.
Williams, Charles Hanbury
Come, Chloe, and Give Me
  Sweet Kisses.
Williams, Clarence
Ugly Chile.
Williams, Francis Howard
Electra.
Song.
Walt Whitman.
Williams, George *See* **Awoonor,
Kofi**
Williams, Harry H.
In the Shade of the Old Apple
  Tree.
Williams, Helen Maria
To Hope.
Williams, Hugo
Aborigine.
The Butcher.

The Couple Upstairs.
Some Kisses from the Kama
  Sutra.
Williams, J. Rutherford
Hebrew Letters in the Trees.
Williams, John
The Dead.
For My Students, Returning
  to College.
A History.
The Leaf.
Matrimony.
The Meaning of Violence.
On Reading Aloud My Early
  Poems.
The Skaters.
Some Contemplations of the
  Poor, and Desolate State of
  the Church...
Williams, John A.
Safari West.
Williams, John Lloyd
Naming of Private Parts
  (parody).
Williams, Jonathan
The Adhesive Autopsy of
  Walt Whitman.
The Anthropophagites See a
  Sign on NC Highway 177...
The Bitch-Kitty.
The Distances to the Friend.
Fast Ball.
The Hermit Cackleberry
  Brown, on Human Vanity:.
The Honey Lamb.
In England's Green &.
In Lucas, Kansas.
A Little Tumescence.
Mahler (excerpt).
Mrs. Sadie Grindstaff, Weaver
  and Factotum, Explains...
Ovid, Meet a
  Metamorphodite.
Strung out with Elgar on a
  Hill (excerpt).
The Switch Blade (or, John's
  Other Wife.).
Those Troublesome Disguises.
Three Sayings from
  Highlands, North Carolina.
Uncle IV Surveys His Domain
  from His Rocker....
A Vulnerary.
Williams, Kim
Requiem for a River.
Williams, L. C.
You Never Miss the Water.
Williams, Mance
For Lover Man, and All the
  Other Young Men Who
  Failed to Return...
A Year without Seasons.
Williams, Max
The Empty House.
Williams, Miller
Alcide Pavageau.
For Victor Jara.
Getting Experience.
Love Poem.
The Neighbor.
Of Human Bondage.
On the Last Page of the Last
  Yellow Pad in Rome before
  Taking Off...
On the Symbolic
  Consideration of Hands and
  the Significance of Death.
Plain.
Rubaiyat for Sue Ella Tucker.
Sale.

Why God Permits Evil: For
  Answers to This Question of
  Interest...
Words.
Williams, Oscar
By Fiat of Adoration.
Chant.
Dwarf of Disintegration.
Edgar Guest.
The Elements.
The Golden Fleece.
I Sing an Old Song.
In Postures That Call.
Jeremiad.
The Last Supper.
The Leg in the Subway.
Little Steamboat.
The Man Coming Toward
  You.
The Man in That Airplane.
Milk at the Bottom of the
  Sea.
The Mirage.
On Meeting a Stranger in a
  Bookshop.
On the Couch.
One Morning the World
  Woke Up.
The Praying Mantis Visits a
  Penthouse.
The Road from Election to
  Christmas.
The Seesaw.
Shopping for Meat in Winter.
Spring.
Variations on a Theme.
Williams, Randall
Laying By.
Williams, Richard D'Alton
The Dying Girl.
Extermination.
Williams, Robert Pete
I Got So Old.
Williams, Roger
Adulteries, Murthers,
  Robberies, Thefts.
Boast Not Proud English, of
  Thy Birth and Blood.
Course Bread and Water's
  Most Their Fare.
The Courteous Pagan Shall
  Condemne.
God Gives Them Sleep on
  Ground, on Straw.
God Makes a Path.
How Busie Are the Sonnes of
  Men?
I Have Heard Ingenuous
  Indians Say.
If Birds That Neither Sow
  Nor Reap.
The Indians Count of Men as
  Dogs.
The Indians Prize Not English
  Gold.
Mans Restlesse Soule Hath
  Restlesse Eyes and Ears.
One Step Twix't Me and
  Death.
Our English Gamesters Scorne
  to Stake.
The Pagans Wild Confesse the
  Bonds.
They See Gods Wonders That
  Are Call'd.
Truth Is a Native, Naked
  Beauty.
What Habacuck Once Spake,
  Mine Eyes.
When Indians Heare That
  Some There Are.
When Sun Doth Rise.

Williams, Ruth M.
The Conqueror.
God Incarnate.
Living Water.
Williams, Sarah
Deep Sea Soundings.
Is It True?
The Old Astronomer to His
  Pupil.
Youth and Maidenhood.
Williams, Sherley Anne
Driving Wheel.
The Empress Brand Trim:
  Ruby Reminisces.
The House of Desire.
Say Hello to John.
Williams, Shirley
If He Let Us Go Now.
The Killing of the Birds.
Williams, Sir Charles Hanbury
An Epigram of Martial,
  Imitated.
Isabella: or, the Morning
  (excerpt).
An Ode on Miss Harriet
  Hanbury.
The Old General.
Williams, Susan Adger
Pockets.
Williams, Tennessee
Carrousel Tune.
Crepe de Chine.
Gold Tooth Blues.
Heavenly Grass.
Kitchen Door Blues.
Life Story.
The Paper Lantern.
Sugar in the Cane.
Williams, Theodore Chickering
Hast Thou Heard It, O My
  Brother.
My Country, to Thy Shore.
When Thy Heart with Joy
  O'erflowing.
Williams, Thomas Lanier
My Love Was Light.
Williams, Trevor
The Girl I Took to the
  Cocktail Party.
Williams, Ursula Vaughan
Memorial Service.
Williams, William
The Christian Pilgrim's
  Hymn.
The Divine Hand.
Williams, William Carlos
4th of July.
The Act.
The Aftermath.
All That Is Perfection in
  Woman.
Apology.
Approach to a City.
Apres le Bain.
The Artist.
Asphodel, That Greeny
  Flower.
At Kenneth Burke's Place.
At the Ball Game.
Ballad of Faith.
Between Walls.
The Botticellian Trees.
The Bull.
Burning the Christmas
  Greens.
Calypso.
The Catholic Bells.
The Children.
Classic Scene.
The Clouds.
Coda.
A Cold Front.

Complaint.
Daisy.
The Dance.
Danse Russe.
Dawn.
Death.
The Deceptrices.
The Descent of Winter
  (Section 10/30).
The Desert Music (excerpt).
Drink.
El Hombre.
An Elegy for D. H. Lawrence.
The End of the Parade.
The Eyeglasses.
Fine Work with Pitch and
  Copper.
First Praise.
Fish.
Flight to the City.
Flowers By the Sea.
A Folded Skyscraper
  (excerpt).
For Eleanor and Bill
  Monahan.
The Forgotten City.
The Gift.
A Goodnight.
The Graceful Bastion.
The Great Figure.
Gulls.
The Hard Listener.
The High Bridge above the
  Tagus River at Toledo.
A History of Love.
The Horse Show.
The Hounded Lovers.
The House.
Illegitimate Things.
The Injury.
The Intelligent Sheep-Man
  and the New Cars.
Iris.
The Ivy Crown.
January.
January Morning.
The Jungle.
Lament.
Landscape with the Fall of
  Icarus.
The Last Turn.
The Last Words of My
  English Grandmother.
Lear.
Lighthearted William.
The Locust Tree in Flower.
The Lonely Street.
Love Song.
The Manoeuvre.
March.
Marriage.
Le Medecin Malgre Lui.
The Mental Hospital Garden.
Metric Figure.
The Monstrous Marriage.
Nantucket.
Ol' Bunk's Band.
On Gay Wallpaper.
The Orchestra.
Pastoral.
Paterson.
Peace on Earth.
Philomena Andronico.
Pictures from Brueghel.
The Pink Locust.
A Place (Any Place) to
  Transcend All Places.
Poem: "As the cat."
Poem: "By the road to the
  contagious hospital."
Poem: "On getting a card."
Poem: "The rose fades."

The Poor.
Porous.
Portrait of a Lady.
Postlude.
The Pot of Flowers.
The Predicter of Famine.
Proletarian Portrait.
Puerto Rico Song.
Queen-Ann's-Lace.
Rain.
Raleigh Was Right.
The Raper from Passenack.
The Red Wheelbarrow.
The Red-Wing Blackbird.
The Return to Work.
The Revelation.
The Right of Way.
Rigmarole.
The Ritualists.
River Rhyme.
The Rose.
Russia.
Sappho, Be Comforted.
The Savage Beast.
The Sea-Elephant.
The Semblables.
Signs Everywhere of Birds
  Nesting, While.
Slow Movement.
Smell.
A Sort of a Song.
The Sparrow.
Sparrows among Dry Leaves.
Spring and All.
St. Francis Einstein of the
  Daffodils.
The Storm.
Sunday in the Park.
The Term.
These.
These Purists.
The Thinker.
This Is Just to Say.
This Is Pioneer Weather.
To.
To a Dead Journalist.
To a Dog Injured in the
  Street.
To a Friend Concerning
  Several Ladies.
To a Poor Old Woman.
To a Solitary Disciple.
To an Elder Poet.
To Be Recited to Flossie on
  Her Birthday.
To Daphne and Virginia.
To Elsie.
To Flossie.
To Ford Madox Ford in
  Heaven.
To Greet a Letter-Carrier.
To Mark Anthony in Heaven.
To Waken an Old Lady.
Tract.
Trala Trala Trala La-Le-La.
A Unison.
View by Color Photography
  on a Commercial Calendar.
The Wanderer.
When Structure Fails Rhyme
  Attempts to Come to the
  Rescue.
The Widow's Lament in
  Springtime.
Willow Poem.
The Winds.
Winter.
The Words, the Words, the
  Words.
The World Narrowed to a
  Point.
The Yachts.

The Yellow Flower.
The Yellow Season.
The Young Housewife.
Young Sycamore.

Williamson, Bruce
  Afternoon in Anglo-Ireland.
  For M–.
  Homage of War.
  A Thought for My Love.
Williamson, Sonny Boy
  Bad Luck Blues.
  Big Apple Blues.
  Moonshine.
  Welfare Store.
**"Willie, Woodbine" See
  Studdert-Kennedy, G. Anketall**
Willis, Gary
  Assignment: Descriptive
    Essay.
Willis, John
  Verses to Be Repeated by an
    Attorney...
Willis, Love Maria
  Father, Hear the Prayer We
    Offer.
Willis, Nathaniel Parker
  Ambition.
  Andre's Request to
    Washington.
  Chamber Scene.
  The Death of Harrison.
  The Declaration.
  The Lady Jane: A Humorous
    Novel in Rhyme (excerpt).
  The Leper.
  Love in a Cottage.
  On the Picture of a "Child
    Tired of Play."
  Parrhasius.
  To Giulia Grisi.
  To Helen in a Huff.
  To Laura W–, Two Years
    Old.
  To the Lady in the Chemisette
    with Black Buttons.
  The Torn Hat.
  Two Women.
  Unseen Spirits.
Willoby, Henry
  To Avisa.
Willson, Dixie
  The Mist and All.
  Tip-Toe Tail.
Willson, Forceythe
  Boy Brittan.
  In State (excerpt).
  The Old Sergeant.
Willson, Robert
  The Last Resort.
Wilmot, Alex
  The Landing of the British
    Settlers of 1820 (excerpt).
**Wilmot, John See Rochester,
  John Wilmont, Earl of**
Wilson, Alexander
  The Blue-Bird.
  The Fisherman's Hymn.
Wilson, August
  Theme One: The Variations.
Wilson, Dedie Huffman
  Speak to the Sun.
Wilson, Edmund
  Drafts for a Quatrain.
  A House of the Eighties.
  The Lido.
  Not Here.
  The Omelet of A. MacLeish.
  On Editing Scott Fitzgerald's
    Papers.
  Peterhof.
  Riverton.

Something for My Russian
    Friends.
  The Voice.
  When All the Young Were
    Dying.
  The White Sand.
Wilson, Edwin H.
  Where Is Our Holy Church?
Wilson, Elizabeth A.
  Snow Crystals on Meall Glas.
Wilson, Florence M.
  The Green Hunters.
Wilson, Gavin
  From the Caledonian
    Mercury.
Wilson, Grace
  Seaway.
Wilson, J. F.
  Limerick: "A coloratura
    named Luna."
  Limerick: "A mathematician
    named Bath."
  Limerick: "A woodchuck
    who'd chucked lots of
    wood."
  Limerick: "There was a young
    fellow named Hall."
Wilson, James
  Casey's Revenge.
Wilson, James Edward
  When I Am Dead.
Wilson, John
  The Armada, 1588.
  Calm as the Cloudless
    Heaven.
  Claudius Gilbert Anagram.
  Tis Braul I Cudgel.
  Come Forth, Come Forth!
  Confess We All, Before the
    Lord.
  A Copy of Verses.
  The Evening Cloud.
  For Lo! My Jonah How He
    Slumped.
  The Rose and the Gauntlet.
  Sacred Poetry.
  Whoso Would See This Song
    of Heavenly Choice.
  Written on the Banks of
    Wastwater during a Calm.
Wilson, Keith
  The Arrival of My Mother.
  The Celt in Me.
  The Idiot.
  The Lake above Santos.
  The Lamb.
  Old Women beside a Church.
  On Drinking & a New Moon
    through the Window.
  One Rose of Stone.
  A Prayer for Rivers.
  The Rancher.
  Twin Aces.
Wilson, Margaret Adelaide
  The Road to Babylon.
Wilson, McLandburgh
  Optimist and Pessimist.
Wilson, Meredith
  Seventy Six Trombones.
Wilson, Pat
  Anchorage.
  Childhood Church.
  Cuvier Light.
  Farewell.
  The Precious Pearl.
  Tree.
Wilson, R. N. D.
  Elegy in a Presbyterian
    Burying-Ground.
  Saint Apollinare in Classe.
  Woodcut.

Wilson, Ramona
Bags Packed and We
Expected This.
Eveningsong 1.
Eveningsong 2.
Keeping Hair.
Late in Fall.
The Meeting.
Overnight Guest.
Reading Indian Poetry.
Spring at Fort Okanogan.
Spring in Virginia.
Summer.
Wilson, Raymond
Epigram: "The arctic raven
tracks the caribou."
Wilson, Robert
New Brooms.
Simplicity's Song.
Wilson, Robert Burns
Ballad of the Faded Field.
Battle Song.
Cut the Cables.
The Dead Player.
It Is in the Winter That We
Dream of Spring.
The Passing of March.
Such Is the Death the Soldier
Dies.
The Sunrise to the Poor.
To a Crow.
Wilson, T. P. Cameron
Dulce et Decorum.
London.
Magpies in Picardy.
Wilson, V. B.
Ticonderoga.
Wilson, Jr, Ernest J.
Mae's Rent Party.
Paternal.
Wilson, Jr, Robley
Bridesmaid.
Porcupines.
Yankee Poet.
Wilton, Richard
Hymn to the Holy Spirit.
Winans, A. D.
My Woman.
Winant, Fran
Christopher Street Liberation
Day, June 28, 1970.
A Sacred Grove.
To Begin.
Winch, Terence
The Bells Are Ringing for Me
and Chagall.
Comfortable Strangers.
Iron Eyes.
Mysteries.
Success Story.
The Them Decade.
Winchester, Caleb T.
The Lord Our God Alone Is
Strong.
Winchester, Elhanan
Behold with Joy.
**Winchilsea, Anne Finch,
Countess of**
The Appology.
Clarinda's Indifference at
Parting with Her Beauty.
The Greater Trial.
The Introduction.
Jealousie is the Rage of a
Man.
A Letter to Dafnis April: 2d
1685.
On Myselfe.
The Petition for an Absolute
Retreat.
The Portrait.

A Song: "If for a woman I
would die."
A Song on the South Sea.
A Song: "The nymph in vain
bestows her pains."
To the Rt. Hon. the Lady C.
Tufton.
Trail All Your Pikes.
The Tree.
Winder, Barbara
Catching a Horse.
Cuban Refugees on Key
Biscayne.
February.
The Limits of Equitation.
On the Farm.
The Problem of Wild Horses.
Windom, W. H.
The Fatal Wedding.
Wine, Maria
Love Me.
Woman, You Are Afraid of
the Forest.
Wingate, Mary
Washington.
When Shall We See Thy Like
Again?
Wingate, Philip
I Don't Want to Play in Your
Yard.
Wingfield, Sheila
Lines for the Margin of an
Old Gospel.
Odysseus Dying.
Winter.
Young Argonauts.
Winkler, Manfred
I Love What Is Not.
If My Hands Were Mute.
One Goes with Me along the
Shore.
She.
Somewhere You Exist.
Winkworth, Catherine
I Am the Rose of Sharon.
Winn, Howard
Supreme Fiction.
Winner, Joseph E.
Little Brown Jug.
Winner, Robert
The Banjo.
Miss Alderman.
Winner, Septimus
Abraham's Daughter.
The Coolie Chinee.
Der Deitcher's Dog.
Lilliputian's Beer Song.
Ten Little Injuns.
Winslow, Anne Goodwin
The Beaten Path.
Winslow, Helen Maria
August.
Winslow, Pete
The Dream Motorcycle.
The Geriatric Whore.
The Mad Rapist of Calaveras
County.
Winsor, Frederick
The Space Child's Mother
Goose.
Winstanley, Gerrard
The Diggers' Song.
Winstanley, John
An Epigram on Florio.
Epigram on the First of April.
Fanny's Removal in 1714.
An Inventory of the Furniture
of a Collegian's Chamber.
A Last Will and Testament.
Miss Betty's Singing-Bird.
On a Certain Effeminate Peer.
On a Stingy Beau.

To the Revd. Mr.— on His
Drinking Sea Water.
Wintchevsky, Morris
The Child-King.
If I Felt Less.
Winter, Mary
Blessing the Hounds.
Lower Forms of Life.
Winter, William
Adelaide Neilson.
Age.
Arthur.
Asleep.
The Heart's Anchor.
I.H.B.
My Queen.
The Night Watch.
On the Verge.
The Passing Bell at Stratford.
Refuge.
The Rubicon.
Unwritten Poems.
Winters, Bayla
Finisterra.
Janis Joplin and the Folding
Company.
Winters, Yvor
April.
The Aspen's Song.
At the San Francisco Airport.
Before Disaster.
By the Road to the Air-Base.
The Castle of Thorns.
Dedication for a Book of
Criticism.
An Elegy.
A Fragment.
The Grave.
Hawk's Eyes.
Heracles.
Hymn to Dispel Hatred at
Midnight.
John Sutter.
The Journey.
The Manzanita.
The Marriage.
Night of Battle.
A Nocturne for October 31st.
An Ode on the Despoilers of
Learning in an American
University (1947).
On a View of Pasadena from
the Hills.
On Teaching the Young.
Orpheus.
A Prayer for My Son.
The Precision.
Quod Tegit Omnia.
The Rows of Cold Trees.
The Shadow's Song.
Sir Gawaine and the Green
Knight.
Sleep.
The Slow Pacific Swell.
A Song in Passing.
Song: "Where I walk out."
A Spring Serpent.
Static Autumn.
A Summer Commentary.
Summer Noon: 1941.
Theseus: A Trilogy.
Time and the Garden.
To a Military Rifle.
To My Infant Daughter (II).
To the Holy Spirit.
To the Moon.
A Vision.
Winthrop, Theodore
But Once.
Wintle, Walter D.
Thinking.

Winwar, Frances
Autumn.
Winward, Stephen F.
Day by Day.
"Wiolar"
Resolution.
Wipo
Victimae Paschali Laudes.
Wisdome, Robert
A Religious Use of Taking
Tobacco.
Wise, Isaac M.
In Mercy, Lord, Incline Thine
Ear.
Wise, Joseph
Glory.
Wise, William
Grownups.
Little Miss Pitt.
Telegram.
What to Do.
When I Grow Up.
Wiseman, Christopher
Delaying Tactics.
Wissinger, Kay
In the Lake Country.
Wister, Owen
The Pinto.
Said Aristotle Unto Plato.
Sheep Ranching.
The Smugglers.
Ten Thousand Cattle.
Wiswall, Ichabod
A Judicious Observation of
That Dreadful Comet.
Witheford, Hubert
Alone.
At the Discharge of Cannon
Rise the Drowned.
Elegy in the Orongorongo
Valley.
Invasion.
The Magnolia Tree.
Wither, George
Ah Me! Am I the Swaine.
Amaryllis I did woo.
Brittan's Remembrancer
(excerpt).
The Choice.
A Christmas Carroll.
A Collection of Emblemes,
Ancient and Moderne
(excerpt).
The Divided Heart.
Faire Virtue, the Mistresse of
Phil'arete: Shall I, Wasting
in Dispair.
Fidelia: Shall I, Wasting in
Despair.
For a Musician.
For Scholars and Pupils.
Haleluiah; or, Britain's Second
Remembrancer: Hymne I.
Hence, Away, You Sirens!
I Loved a Lass.
Lord, Many Times Thou
Pleased Art.
A Love Sonnet.
The Lover's Resolution.
The Marigold.
Our Joyful Feast.
Philarete Praises Poetry.
Philarete to His Mistress
(excerpt).
The Shepheards Hunting:.
Sleep, Baby, Sleep.
A Stolen Kiss.
The Tired Petitioner (excerpt).
A Widow's Hymn.
Witherby, Diana
Casualty.

Withers, Carl
Charlie Chaplin Went to
France.
Witherup, William
Crows.
Withington, Leonard
O Saviour of a World
Undone.
Witt, Harold
Aerosol.
Conservative.
Dog Alive.
Dream.
Dreamscape in Kummel.
First Photos of Flu Virus.
Her Birthday.
Into the Future.
More Nudes for Florence.
Mrs. Asquith Tries to Save
the Jacarandas.
Notre Dame Perfected by
Reflection.
Nude.
Rushmore.
Soaps.
Superbull.
Surprise.
Walking Milwaukee.
Witt, Sandra
Fish.
Witt, Shirley Hill
Punto Final.
Seboyeta Chapel.
Wittenberg, Ernest
The Sub-Average Time
Reader.
Wittlin, Jozef
A Hymn About a Spoonful of
Soup.
On the Jewish Day of
Judgment in the Year 1942.
St. Francis of Assisi and the
Miserable Jews.
To the Jews in Poland.
Woddis, Roger
Ethics for Everyman.
Final Curtain (parody).
The Hero (parody).
Nothing Sacred.
Wodehouse, E. A.
Afforestation.
Wodehouse, P. G.
The Gourmet's Love-Song.
Printer's Error.
Song about Whiskers.
Time Like an Ever-rolling
Stream.
To William (Whom We Have
Missed).
Woessner, Warren
Airwaves.
Chippewa Lake Park.
Driving Carl's '56 Chevy.
Driving to Sauk City.
Looking at Power.
Low Tide.
Woestijne, Karel van de
Elegy: "Child, your white face
is chanting memories."
Woiwode, Larry
A Deserted Barn.
Wojahn, David
Another Coast.
Cold Glow: Icehouses.
Floating Houses.
The Man Who Knew Too
Much.
Weldon Kees in Mexico, 1965.
Wolcot, John
Apple Dumplings and a King.
Ballade: To a Fish of the
Brooke.

Epigram: "Midas, they say,
possessed the art of old."
Instructions to a Celebrated
Laureat (excerpt).
Ode: "That I have often been
in love, deep love."
Ode to a Country Hoyden.
On a Stone Thrown at a Very
Great Man, but Which
Missed Him.
The Razor-Seller.
Resignation: an Ode to the
Journeymen Shoemakers
(excerpt).
The Sorrows of Sunday: An
Elegy (excerpt).
Spring Waters (excerpt).
To a Fly, Taken out of a
Bowl of Punch.
To a Kiss.
Wolcott, Roger
The Heart Is Deep.
Matthew X. 28.
Wolcott, Samuel
Christ for the World! We
Sing.
Father! I Own Thy Voice.
Wolf, Leonard
The Peasant.
Sonnet.
Wolf, Phyllis
Akawense.
Lac Courte Orielles: 1936.
Manomin.
Midewiwan.
Rolling Thunder.
Wolf, Robert Leopold
Eve.
A Pagan Reinvokes the
Twenty-Third Psalm.
Wolfe, Aaron R.
Complete in Thee, No Work
of Mine.
A Parting Hymn We Sing.
Wolfe, Charles
The Burial of Sir John Moore
after Corunna.
Go, Forget Me.
To Mary.
Wolfe, Edgar
Sparrows in College Ivy.
Wolfe, ffrida
Choosing Shoes.
Four and Eight.
What the Toys Are Thinking.
Wolfe, Humbert
Autumn.
The Blackbird.
The British Journalist.
The Celestial City (Excerpt).
The Dead Fiddle.
Dean Inge.
Denmark.
Epigram: "You cannot hope."
G. K. Chesterton.
The Gray Squirrel.
Green Candles.
D. H. Lawrence and James
Joyce.
Hilaire Belloc.
Iliad.
Journey's End.
The Lilac.
Love Is a Keeper of Swans.
Man.
The Saint.
Things Lovelier.
This Is Not Death.
Tulip.
The Uncelestial City (excerpt).
Untitled.
Wardour Street.

The Waters of Life.
When Lads Have Done
(parody).
The Zoo.
Wolfe, James
How Stands the Glass
Around?
Wolfe, Robert L.
The Man in the Dress Suit.
Wolfe, Thomas
Ben.
Burning in the Night.
Magic.
Observe the Whole of It.
October.
That Sharp Knife.
Thomas Wolfe's Tombstone
(excerpt).
You Can't Go Home Again
(excerpt).
Wolfenstein, Alfred
Exodus 1940.
Wolfert, Adrienne
Golda.
Wolff, Bill
What A Grand and Glorious
Feeling.
Wolff, Daniel
Heaven in Ordinarie.
Wolff, David
While We Slept.
Wolfram von Eschenbach, Sir
Fealty.
His Own True Wife.
Hope for Miracles.
Wolfskehl, Karl
And Yet We Are Here!
From Mount Nebo.
Shekhinah.
To Be Said at the Seder.
We Go.
Wolker, Jiri
Epitaph.
Love Poem.
On This My Sick-Bed Beats
the World.
The Pillar-Box.
Wolny, P.
Before Good-Bye.
From a Birch.
Harmonica Man.
Lightning Rides.
Separation.
Words, Like Spiders.
Wolstenholme-Elmy, Elizabeth
Woman Free (excerpt).
Wong, Nellie
Funeral Song for Mamie
Eisenhower.
How a Girl Got Her Chinese
Name.
New Romance.
Song of Farewell.
Under Our Own Wings.
Wong, Shawn
An Island.
Lapis.
Periods of Adjustment.
Woo, Merle
Poem for the Creative Writing
Class, Spring 1982.
The Subversive.
Yellow Woman Speaks.
Wood, A. J.
Rolling John (excerpt).
Wood, Alfred E.
The Fight at Dajo.
Wood, Charles Erskine Scott
The Desert.
Goats.
Sagebrush.
The Water-Hole.

Wood, Clement
Eagle Sonnets.
De Glory Road.
I Pass a Lighted Window.
A Prayer in Time of
Blindness.
Voyager's Song.
Wood, John A.
Morning from My Office
Window.
Wood, Marnie and Harnie
Limerick: "A cold had a
corpulent pig."
Wood, Mary
Flying Changes.
Wood, Peggy
My Aunt.
Wood, Robert Williams
The Elk. The Whelk.
The Parrot and the Carrot We
May Easily Confound.
The Pecan. The Toucan.
The Pen-Guin. The Sword-
Fish.
Wood, Stanley
Homes of the Cliff Dwellers.
Wood, Susan
Learning to Live without You.
Wood, William
A Deux.
The Kind of Waters, the Sea
Shouldering Whale.
Kinds of Shel-Fish.
The Kingly Lyon, and the
Strong Arm'd Beare.
The Princely Eagle, and the
Soaring Hawke.
Trees Both in Hills and
Plaines, in Plenty Be.
Wood-Thompson, Susan
Territory.
Woodberry, George Edward
Agathon: Song of Eros.
America to England.
At Gibraltar.
Comrades.
Edith Cavell.
Essex Regiment March.
The Islands of the Sea.
A Life.
Love's Rosary.
My Country (excerpt).
O Land Beloved.
The Old House.
On a Portrait of Columbus.
Our First Century.
Song of Eros.
Sonnets.
Sonnets Written in the Fall of
1914.
To Those Who Reproved the
Author for Too Sanguine
Patriotism.
Wild Eden.
Woodbourne, Harry
The Flute of May.
Woodbridge, Benjamin
Upon the Author; by a
Known Friend.
Upon the Tomb of the Most
Reverend Mr. John Cotton...
Woodcock, George
Green Grass and Sea.
Imagine the South.
The Island.
Merthymawr.
Pacifists.
Paper Anarchist Addresses the
Shade of Nancy Ling Perry.
Poem for Garcia Lorca.
Poem from London, 1941.

Sonnet: "Looking into the windows that doom has broken."
Sunday on Hampstead Heath.
Tree Felling.
White.
Woodford, Bruce P.
Going through.
Woodgate, M.V.
Fire.
Woodhouse, James
The Life and Lucubrations of Crispinus Scriblerus (excerpt).
Woodley, F. S.
The Beautiful.
Woodrow, Constance Davies
To a Vagabond.
Woodrum, Lon
The King of Kings.
Woods, John
The Deaths at Paragon, Indiana.
The Five Dreams.
The Girl Who Had Borne Too Much.
Guns.
Lie Closed, My Lately Loved.
Looking Both Ways before Crossing.
Lying Down with Men and Women.
Outburst from a Little Face.
Playwright.
Poem at Thirty.
Traveling North.
What Do You Do when It's Spring?
When Senses Fled.
Woods Gets Religion.
Woods, Margaret Louisa
Genius Loci.
March Thoughts from England.
The Mariners.
The Prayer of Beaten Men.
The Return (excerpt).
Young Windebank.
Woodward, Charles
The Midnight Ramble.
Woodworth, Samuel
The Hunters of Kentucky.
Loves She Like Me?
The Needle.
The Old Oaken Bucket.
Woody, Elizabeth
Black Fear.
Custer Must Have Learned to Dance.
Eagles.
In Impressions of Hawk Feathers Willow Leaves Shadow.
Night Crackles.
Woolagoodjah, Sam
Lalai (Dreamtime).
Wooley, Celia Parker
Refracted Lights.
Woolf, Virginia
Let Us God, Then, Exploring.
Woolner, Thomas
My Beautiful Lady.
Woolsey, Sarah Chauncey *See* "Coolidge, Susan"
Woolsey, Theodore Dwight
The Eclipse of Faith.
Woolson, Constance Fenimore
Kentucky Belle.
Wild March.
Yellow Jessamine.

"Worcester"
A Pastoral. In the Modern Style.
Wordsworth, C. W. V.
Song in Praise of Paella.
Wordsworth, Christopher
All Saints' Day, Nov. 1.
O Day of Rest and Gladness.
The Ship in the Midst of the Sea.
Wordsworth, Dorothy
Address to a Child during a Boistrous Winter Evening.
The Cottager to Her Infant.
He Said He Had Been a Soldier.
I Gathered Mosses in Easedale.
Loving and Liking.
We Saw Three Boys.
Wordsworth, Elizabeth
Good and Clever.
Wordsworth, William
Address to My Infant Daughter.
Admonition to a Traveller.
The Affliction of Margaret.
After-Thought.
Airey-Force Valley.
Alice Fell; or, Poverty.
Among All Lovely Things My Love Had Been.
Anecdote for Fathers.
Animal Tranquillity and Decay.
Apology.
At Florence.
At the Grave of Burns.
Between Namur and Liege.
Bleak Season Was It, Turbulent and Wild.
Blest Statesman He, Whose Mind's Unselfish Will.
By the Sea.
Calais, August 15, 1802.
Cave of Staffa, I.
Character of the Happy Warrior.
Characteristics of a Child Three Years Old.
The Childless Father.
A Complaint.
Composed at Neidpath Castle, the Property of Lord Queensberry, 1803.
Composed near Calais, on the Road Leading to Ardres, August 7, 1802.
Composed on the Eve of the Marriage of a Friend ...
Composed Upon an Evening of Extraordinary Splendour and Beauty.
The Contrast: The Parrot and the Wren.
Daffodils.
Decay of Piety.
Desideria.
Devotional Incitements.
Elegiac Stanzas Suggested by a Picture of Peele Castle...
Ellen Irwin; or, The Braes of Kirtle.
England, 1802.
Evening on Calais Beach.
An Evening Walk (excerpt).
The Excursion.
Expostulation and Reply.
Extempore Effusion upon the Death of James Hogg.
Faith and Freedom.
The Farmer of Tilsbury Vale.

Fidelity.
Fishing.
The Fountain.
The French Revolution.
The Gladness of May.
Glen-Almain, the Narrow Glen.
Goody Blake and Harry Gill (excerpt).
The Green Linnet.
Guilt and Sorrow.
Hart-Leap Well.
Her Eyes Are Wild.
Here Pause: The Poet Claims at Least This Praise.
I Grieved for Buonaparte.
I Wandered Lonely as a Cloud.
The Idiot Boy.
If Thou Indeed Derive Thy Light from Heaven.
In a Child's Album.
In These Fair Vales.
Incident at Bruges.
Incident Characteristic of a Favourite Dog.
Influence of Natural Objects.
The Inner Vision.
Inscribed upon a Rock.
Inside of King's College Chapel, Cambridge.
Intimations of Immortality from Recollections of Early Childhood.
It Was an April Morning.
The Kitten and the Falling Leaves.
Laodamia.
The Leaves That Rustled on This Oak-Crowned Hill.
A Lesson.
Liberty (excerpt).
Lines Composed a Few Miles above Tintern Abbey.
Lines Left upon a Seat in a Yew-Tree...
Lines Written in Early Spring.
Lines Written near Richmond, upon the Thames, at Evening.
Louisa.
Lucy.
Lucy Gray.
Lyre! Though Such Power Do in Thy Magic Live.
The Matron of Jedborough and Her Husband (excerpt).
Methought I Saw the Footsteps of a Throne.
Michael.
The Most Alluring Clouds That Mount the Sky.
Mutability.
My Heart Leaps Up.
Near Dover, September, 1802.
A Night-Piece.
November, 1806.
Nutting.
O Nightingale! Thou Surely Art.
October 1803.
Ode to Duty.
Oh There Is Blessing in This Gentle Breeze.
The Old Cumberland Beggar.
An Old Man.
Old Man Travelling.
On the Beach at Calais.
On the Departure of Sir Walter Scott from Abbotsford, for Naples.

On the Extinction of the Venetian Republic.
On the Frozen Lake.
On the Power of Sound.
On the Projected Kendal and Windermere Railway.
Our Birth Is but a Sleep and a Forgetting.
The Pass of Kirkstone.
Personal Talk.
The Pet Lamb.
The Pilgrim Fathers.
A Place of Burial in the South of Scotland.
Poems Chiefly of Early and Late Years: Prelude.
A Poet!–He Hath Put His Heart to School.
A Poet's Epitaph.
The Quantocks.
The Reaper.
The Recluse.
The Redbreast (excerpt).
Residence in France: The Prelude.
Resolution and Independence.
The Reverie of Poor Susan.
Ruth; or, the Influences of Nature.
The Sailor's Mother (excerpt).
She Was a Phantom of Delight.
Simon Lee the Old Huntsman.
The Simplon Pass.
A Slumber Did My Spirt Seal.
The Small Celandine.
So Fair, So Sweet, Withal So Sensitive.
The Solitary Reaper.
Song at the Feast of Brougham Castle.
Song for the Spinning Wheel.
Song for the Wandering Jew.
Sonnet: Composed after a Journey across the Hamilton Hill, Yorkshire.
Sonnet: Composed by the Side of Grasmere Lake.
Sonnet Composed upon Westminster Bridge, September 3, 1802.
Sonnet: Composed While the Author Was Engaged in Writing a Tract...
Sonnet: "England! the time is come when thou shouldst wean."
Sonnet: "It is a beauteous evening, calm and free."
Sonnet: "Nuns fret not at their convent's narrow room."
Sonnet: "Scorn not the sonnet."
Sonnet: September 1, 1802.
Sonnet: September, 1815.
Sonnet: "Surprised by joy– impatient as the Wind."
Sonnet: The French and the Spanish Guerillas.
Sonnet: The Wild Duck's Nest.
Sonnet: "The world is too much with us."
Sonnet: There Is a Bondage Worse.
Sonnet: To–.
Sonnet: To the Lady Beaumont.
Sonnet to the Virgin.
Sonnet: Where Lies the Land.

Sonnets upon the Punishment of Death (excerpt).
The Sparrow's Nest.
Stanzas Written in My Pocket Copy of Thomson's "Castle of Indolence."
Steamboats, Viaducts, and Railways.
Stepping Westward.
Strange Fits of Passion Have I Known.
The Stuffed Owl.
Suggested by a Picture of the Bird of Paradise.
The Sun Has Long Been Set.
Swans.
The Swiss Peasant.
The Tables Turned.
There Was a Boy.
There Was a Roaring in the Wind All Night.
This Prayer I Make.
The Thorn.
Thought of a Briton on the Subjugation of Switzerland.
The Three Cottage Girls.
Tintern Abbey.
'Tis Said That Some Have Died for Love.
To a Butterfly.
To a Child.
To a Highland Girl.
To a Skylark.
To a Young Lady.
To Hartley Coleridge.
To Lady Eleanor Butler and the Honourable Miss Ponsonby...
To M.H.
To My Sister.
To Sleep.
To the Cuckoo.
To the Daisy.
To the Men of Kent.
To the Same Flower.
To the Skylark.
To the Small Celandine.
To Toussaint L'Ouverture.
Tribute to the Memory of the Same Dog.
The Trosachs.
The Two April Mornings.
The Unremitting Voice of Nightly Streams.
Vaudracour and Julia (excerpt).
The Voice of the Derwent.
The Wanderer Recalls the Past.
Water Fowl.
We Are Seven.
Weak Is the Will of Man, His Judgment Blind.
Where Lies the Truth? Has Man, in Wisdom's Creed.
Why Art Thou Silent!
With How Sad Steps, O Moon, Thou Climb'st the Sky.
With Ships the Sea Was Sprinkled.
Written after the Death of Charles Lamb (excerpt).
Written in March.
Written in Very Early Youth.
Yarrow Revisited.
Yarrow Unvisited.
Yarrow Visited.
Yes, It Was the Mountain Echo.
Yew-Trees.

Work, Henry Clay
Father, Dear Father, Come Home with Me Now.
Grandfather's Clock.
Kingdom Coming.
Marching through Georgia.
The Ship That Never Returned.
Wake Nicodemus.
Worley, James
Mark Van Doren.
Touchstone.
Worley, Jeff
Whitley at Three O'Clock.
Worley, Mrs. J. B.
The Mighty Hunter.
Wormser, Baron
By-Products.
For My Brother Who Died before I Was Born.
The Mowing Crew.
Piano Lessons.
Poem to the Memory of H. L. Mencken.
Private.
Sunday Review Section.
Worrell, Edna Randolph
Christmas Legend.
Worsley, Alice F.
Has Been.
Worth, Douglas
Ghetto Summer School.
War Bride.
Worth, Kathryn
Circus Elephant.
Smells.
Worth, Valerie
Body.
Chairs.
Christmas Lights.
Christmas Ornaments.
Daisies.
Dinosaurs.
Duck.
Fireworks.
Haunted House.
Zinnias.
Worthington, Kim
I Held a Lamb.
Wortley, Mary See **Montagn, Mary Wortley**
Wortman, Denis
God of the Prophets! Bless the Prophets' Sons.
Today Beneath Benignant Skies.
Wotton, Sir Henry
The Character of a Happy Life.
A Dialogue betwixt GOD and the Soul.
Eternall Mover (excerpt).
The Happy Life.
A Hymn to My God in a Night of My Late Sicknesse.
A May Day.
De Morte.
D. O. M.
On a Banck as I Sate a Fishing.
On His Mistress, the Queen of Bohemia.
A Poem Written by Sir Henry Wotton, in His Youth.
Tears at the Grave of Sir Albertus Morton.
Upon the Death of Sir Albertus Morton's Wife.
Upon the Sudden Restraint of the Earle of Somerset.
Wotton, Sir John
In Praise of His Daphnis.

Woty, William
Lines Written in the Dog-Days.
A Mock Invocation to Genius (excerpt).
White Conduit House.
Wrafter, Denis
Braggart!
The Old Man to His Scythe.
On Hearing a Broadcast of Ceremonies in Connection with....
Sabbath Reflection.
Wratislaw, Theodore
Crimson Nor Yellow Roses.
Orchids.
To a Sicilian Boy.
Wreford, Heyman
Christ Is Coming.
Wreford, John R.
Lord, while for All Mankind.
Wright, Bruce McM.
The African Affair.
Journey to a Parallel.
Wright, Carolyne
Early Fall: The Adirondacks.
The Trestle Bridge.
Wright, Catharine Morris
Hillside Pause.
Wright, Celeste Turner
Daguerreotype of a Grandmother.
Kineo Mountain.
Murgatroyd.
Noblesse Oblige.
Thumbprint.
The View from Father's Porch.
Yugoslav Cemetery.
Wright, Charles
Blackwater Mountain.
Chinoiserie.
Clear Night.
Cloud River.
The Daughters of Blum.
Dead Color.
Death.
Delta Traveller.
Dog Creek Mainline.
Dog Day Vespers.
Dog Yoga.
Edvard Munch.
The Fever Toy.
Firstborn (excerpt).
Hawaii Dantesca.
Holy Thursday.
Homage to Paul Cezanne (excerpt).
Invisible Landscape.
Laguna Blues.
Mount Caribou at Night.
Negatives.
The New Poem.
Nightdream.
Nightletter.
Northhanger Ridge.
Photographs.
Portrait of the Artist with Hart Crane.
Self-Portrait in 2035.
Sitting at Night on the Front Porch.
Skins (excerpt).
Smoke.
Snow.
Spider Crystal Ascension.
Stone Canyon Nocturne.
Tattoos.
Two Stories.
Virgo Descending.
Yellow.

Wright, Charles David
Shaving.
Some Semblance of Order.
Wright, David
A Funeral Oration.
Grasmere Sonnets.
An Invocation to the Goddess.
Kleomedes.
Monologue of a Deaf Man.
Moral Story II.
On the Death of an Emperor Penguin in Regent's Park, London.
On the Margin: "An anniversary approaches of the birth of God."
Pastoral.
Rousecastle.
Seven South African Poems.
Walking to Dedham.
Wright, David McKee
Arlington.
Danny's Wooing.
Dark Rosaleen, IX.
The Duff.
In the Moonlight.
In Town.
Shearing.
While the Billy Boils.
Wright, Ernest Vincent
When Father Carves the Duck.
Wright, Franz
View from an Institution.
Wright, Frederick A.
Letter to the City Clerk.
Limerick: "An amateur, driving too fast."
Wright, George T.
Aquarium.
Wright, Helen M.
Golden Grain.
Wright, Hetty
To an Infant Expiring the Second Day of its Birth.
Wedlock. A Satire.
Wright, Ivan Leonard
The Want of You.
Wright, James
The Accusation.
Against Surrealism.
American Twilights, 1957.
Apollo.
Arrangements with Earth for Three Dead Friends.
As I Step over a Puddle at the End of Winter.
The Assignation.
At the Executed Murderer's Grave.
At the Slackening of the Tide.
At Thomas Hardy's Birthplace, 1953.
Autumn Begins in Martins Ferry, Ohio.
Before the Cashier's Window in a Department Store.
The Blessing.
A Breath of Air.
By a Lake in Minnesota.
The Cold Divinities.
Complaint.
Confession to J. Edgar Hoover.
Depressed by a Book of Bad Poetry, I Walk toward an Unused Pasture...
Discoveries in America.
A Dream of Burial.
Eisenhower's Visit to Franco, 1959.

Evening.
For the Marsh's Birthday.
A Gesture by a Lady with an Assumed Name.
A Girl in a Window.
Goodbye to the Poetry of Calcium.
Having Lost my Sons, I Confront One Wreckage of the Moon:...
"I Am a Sioux Brave," He Said in Minneapolis.
In Memory of Leopardi.
In Ohio.
In Response to a Rumor That the Oldest Whorehouse...
In Shame and Humiliation.
In Terror of Hospital Bills.
Inscription for the Tank.
The Jewel.
Late November in a Field.
The Life.
Lifting Illegal Nets by Flashlight.
The Lights in the Hallway.
A Little Girl on Her Way to School.
Little Marble Boy.
Living by the Red River.
Love in a Warm Room in Winter.
Lying in a Hammock at William Duffy's Farm in Pine Island, Minnesota.
A Mad Fight Song for William S. Carpenter, 1966.
Mantova.
A Message Hidden in an Empty Wine Bottle That I Threw into a Gulley ...
Micromutations.
Milkweed.
Miners.
The Minneapolis Poem.
A Moral Poem Freely Accepted from Sappho.
The Morality of Poetry.
Mutterings over the Crib of a Deaf Child.
Names in Monterchi: To Rachel.
Northern Pike.
A Note Left in Jimmy Leonard's Shack.
Ohio Valley Swains.
Ohioan Pastoral.
Old Age Compensation.
The Old Dog in the Ruins of the Graves at Arles.
On Minding One's Own Business.
On the Skeleton of a Hound.
Outside Fargo, North Dakota.
Paul.
A Poem about Breasts.
A Poem of Towers.
Poems to a Brown Cricket.
A Prayer to Escape from the Market Place.
A Prayer to the Lord Ramakrishna.
A Presentation of Two Birds to My Son.
The Private Meeting Place.
The Quest.
Rain.
Redwings.
Rip.
Saint Judas.
Saying Dante Aloud.
Sheep in the Rain.
Simon and the Tarantula.

Small Frogs Killed on the Highway.
Snowfall: A Poem about Spring.
A Song for the Middle of the Night.
Speak.
Stages on a Journey Westward.
Three Sentences for a Dead Swan.
To a Blossoming Pear Tree.
To a Defeated Saviour.
To a Salesgirl, Weary of Artificial Holiday Trees.
To Flood Stage Again.
To the Evening Star: Central Minnesota.
To the Ghost of a Kite.
To the Muse.
Trouble.
Twilights.
Two Hangovers.
Two Poems About President Harding.
Two Postures Beside a Fire.
The Ungathered Apples.
Vain Advice at the Year's End.
Venice.
Verona.
The Vestal in the Forum.
A Way to Make a Living.
What the Earth Asked Me.
Willy Lyons.
A Winter Daybreak above Vence.
With a Sliver of Marble from Carrara.
With the Shell of a Hermit Crab.
Written in a Copy of Swift's Poems, for Wayne Burns.
Your Name in Arezzo.
Youth.
Wright, Jay
Altars and Sacrifice.
The Charge.
The Dead.
Death As History.
The Homecoming Singer.
An Invitation to Madison County.
This Morning.
Wednesday Night Prayer Meeting.
Wright, Jeff
Flesh Coupon.
Higher Love.
Industrial Size.
Sermon on the Mount.
Stay Beautiful.
Wright, John
The Poor Man's Province.
Wright, Judith
The Ancestors.
...And Mr. Ferritt.
At Cooloolah.
Australia 1970.
The Blind Man (excerpt).
Brother and Sisters.
The Builders.
The Bull.
Bullocky.
The Company of Lovers.
The Cup.
Egrets.
Eli, Eli.
Extinct Birds.
Fire at Murdering Hut.
Habitat (excerpt).
The Hawthorn Hedge.

Legend.
Lyrebirds.
Nigger's Leap, New England.
Night and the Child.
The Old Prison.
Portrait.
Request to a Year.
South of My Days.
Sports Field.
Storm.
Tableau.
Train Journey.
Turning Fifty.
The Twins.
The Two Fires.
Wings.
Woman's Song.
Woman to Child.
Woman to Man.
Wonga Vine.
Wright, Kit
Dad and the Cat and the Tree.
I Don't Like You.
A New World Symphony.
Wright, Richard
Between the World and Me.
Four Haiku.
Haiku: "A balmy spring wind..."
Haiku: "An empty sickbed..."
Haiku: "Coming from the woods..."
Haiku: "I would like a bell..."
Haiku: "Just enough of rain..."
Haiku: "The crow flew so fast..."
Haiku: "The dog's violent sneeze..."
Haiku: "Why is the hail so wild..."
Haiku: "Winter rain at night..."
Hokku: In the Falling Snow.
Hokku Poems.
I Have Seen Black Hands.
Wright, Sarah E.
To Some Millions Who Survive Joseph E. Mander, Senior.
Until They Have Stopped.
Urgency.
Wright, Willard Huntington
Song against Women.
Wright, William Bull
The Brook (excerpt).
Wright, Jr., Fred W.
The Couch.
Wrighton, W. T.
The Dearest Spot on Earth.
Wrigley, Robert
Binding Arbitration.
Pain.
The Rattlesnake.
Wu Ti, Emperor
The Autumn Wind.
Liu Ch'e.
People Hide Their Love.
Wu Tsao
Bitter rain in my courtyard.
For the Courtesan Ch'ing Lin.
In the Home of the Scholar Wu Su-chiang from Hsin-an...
Wurdemann, Audrey
For Eros II.
Little Black Man with a Rose in His Hat.
Text.
Wyatt, Edith
On the Great Plateau.

Wyatt, Jiri
Us.
Wyatt, Sir Thomas
A! My Herte, A! What Aileth
Absence absenting causeth me to complain.
Accused though I be without desert.
After great storms the calm returns.
Alas! madam, for stealing of a kiss.
Alas, Poor Man, What Hap Have I.
Alas the grief and deadly woeful smart!
All heavy minds.
And if an eye may save or slay.
The Answer that Ye Made to Me, My Dear.
An Appeal.
As power and wit will me assist.
At last withdraw your cruelty.
At most mischief.
Behold, Love, Thy Power How She Despiseth!
Betrayal.
Blame Not My Lute, for He Must Sound.
Caesar, when that the traitor of Egypt.
Comfort thyself, my woeful heart.
Comparison of Love to a Streame Falling from the Alpes.
The Courtier's Life.
Deme As Ye List uppon Goode Cause.
Desire, alas, my master and my foe.
Disdain Me Not without Desert.
Domine Exaudi.
Domine ne in Furore.
Driven by desire I did this deed.
Dyvers Dothe Use as I Have Hard and Kno.
Eche Man Me Telleth I Chaunge Moost My Devise.
Epigram: "A face that should content me wonders well."
Epigram: "Sighs are my food, drink are my tears."
Epigram: "The enemy of life, decayer of all kind."
Epigram: "Who hath heard of such cruelty before?"
An Epitaph of Sir Thomas Gravener, Knight.
Epitaph: "The fruit of all the service that I serve."
Farewell all my welfare.
Farewell the reign of cruelty!
The flaming sighs that boil within my breast.
For shamefast harm of great and hateful need.
For to love her for her looks lovely.
For Want I Will in Woe I Plain.
Forget Not Yet.
From these high hills...
Full well it may be seen.
The furious gun in his raging ire.
Give place all ye that doth rejoice.

Hate Whom Ye List.
He is not dead that sometime hath a fall.
The heart and service to you proffered.
Heart Oppress'd with Desperate Thought.
Heaven and earth and all that hear me plain.
Helpe Me to Seke.
The Hind.
How oft have I, my dear and cruel foe.
I Am As I Am.
I Fynde No Peace.
I Have Sought Long with Steadfastness.
I Love, Loved, and So Doth She.
I see that chance hath chosen me.
If amour's faith...
If Chance Assign'd.
If ever man might him avant.
If fancy would favor.
If in the World There Be More Woe.
If it be so...
If Thou Wilt Mighty Be.
If Waker Care, If Sodayne Pale Coulor.
If with Complaint the Pain Might Be Express'd.
In eternum I was once determed.
In faith I wot not well what to say.
In Spain.
It May Be Good.
It Was My Choice.
The Joy So Short Alas, the Pain So Near.
The knot which first my heart did strain.
Lament my loss...
Liberty.
Like as the bird in the cage enclosed.
Like as the swan towards her death.
Like to These Unmeasurable Mountains.
The lively sparks that issue from those eyes.
Lo! how I seek and sue to have.
Lo, what it is to love!
Longer to muse.
Love and fortune and my mind...
Love doth again.
Love's Snare.
The Lover Beseecheth His Mistress Not to Forget...
The Lover Complaineth the Unkindness of His Love.
The Lover Forsaken.
The Lover, Having Dreamed of Enjoying His Love....
The Lover Rejoiceth the Enjoying of His Love.
The Lover's Appeal.
The Lover Sendeth Sighs to Move His Suit.
The Lover Sheweth How He Is Forsaken of Such as He Sometime Enjoyed.
Luckes, my fair falcon, and your fellows all.
The Lute Obeys.
Lyve Thowe Gladly, Yff So Thowe May.

Madam, withouten many words.
Marvel No More Although.
May Time.
Me List No More to Sing.
Mine old dear enemy...
Miserere mei, Domine.
Mistrustful Minds Be Moved.
My Galley.
My heart I gave thee...
My hope, alas, hath me abused.
My love is like unto th' eternal fire.
My Lute and I.
My Mothers Maydes when They Did Sowe and Spynne.
Mye Love Toke Skorne My Servise to Retaine.
Nature, that gave the bee so feat a grace.
No! Indeed.
Now all of change.
Now Must I Learn to Live at Rest.
O goodly hand.
O Miserable Sorrow, withouten Cure.
Of His Returne from Spaine.
Of Love.
Of purpose love chose first for to be blind.
Ons as Me Thought Fortune Me Kyst.
Pass forth, my wonted cries.
Patience, for I have wrong.
Patience for My Device.
Patience of all my smart.
Patience Though I Have Not.
Penitential Psalms: Introduction.
Perdy, I said it not.
The Pillar Perished Is.
Process of time worketh such wonder.
De Profundis.
A Promise.
Psalm VI.
Psalm XXXII.
Quondam Was I in My Lady's Grace.
A Renouncing of Love.
Resignation.
Resound My Voyse, Ye Wodes That Here Me Plain.
The restful place, reviver of my smart.
A Revocation.
Right true it is...
A Robyn Joly Robyn.
Satires.
She sat and sewed...
Since Love Is Such That as Ye Wot.
Since Love Will Needs That I Shall Love.
Since so ye please to hear me plain.
Since Ye Delight to Know.
Since you will needs that I shall sing.
So unwarely was never no man caught.
Some fowls there be...
Some Tyme I Fled the Fyre That Me Brent.
Sometime I sigh, sometime I sing.
Sonnet: "To rail or jest, ye know I use it not."
Sonnets, VI: "I abide and abide and better abide."

Speak Thou and Speed.
A Spending Hand That Alway Powreth Owte.
Spite hath no power to make me sad.
Steadfastness.
Stond Who So List upon the Slipper Toppe.
Such Hap as I Am Happed in.
Such is the course that nature's kind hath wrought.
Such vain thought as wonted to mislead me.
Suffering in sorrow in hope to attain.
Sufficed not, madam, tht you did tear.
Tagus, Fare Well, that Westward with Thy Stremes.
Take heed betime lest ye be spied.
Tanglid I Was Yn Loves Snare.
That Time That Mirth Did Steer My Ship.
There was Never Nothing More Me Pained.
They Fle from Me.
Tho' I Can Not Your Cruelty Constrain.
Though this the port and I thy servant true.
Throughout the World.
To a Lady To Answer Directly with Yea or Nay.
To cause accord or to agree.
To His Heart.
To His Pen.
To make an end of all this strife.
To seek each where, where man doth live.
To Sir Francis Brian.
To wet your eye withouten tear.
To wish and want and not obtain.
Treizaine.
V. Innocentia Veritas Viat Fides Circumdederunt Me Inimici Mei.
Varium et Mutabile.
Venomous thorns that are so sharp and keen.
Vixi Puellis Nuper Idoneus...
Vulcan begat me...
The Wandering Gadling.
What death is worse than this.
What Does This Mean.
What Once I Was.
What rage Is this?
What Vaileth Trouth?
What Wourde Is That That Chaungeth Not.
When First Mine Eyes Did View and Mark.
When that I call unto my mind.
Where shall I have at mine own will.
Who lyst his welthe and eas retayne.
Will ye see what wonders love hath wrought?
With Serving Still.
Within My Breast.
Ye know my heart...
Ye Old Mule.
Your Looks So Often Cast.
Ys Yt Possyble.

Wycherley, William
A Drinking-Song...
The Envious Critick.
A Song: In the Name of a Lover, to His Mistress...
A Spouse I Do Hate.
To a Fine Young Woman.
To a Good Physician.
To a Witty Man of Wealth and Quality...
Upon the Most Useful Knowledge, Craft or Cunning...
Wygodski, Stanislaw
Going to the North.
Those Betrayed at Dawn.
Voyage.
Winter Journey.
Wylie, Elinor
Address to My Soul.
Atavism.
August.
Beauty.
Birthday Sonnet.
Castilian.
Cold-Blooded Creatures.
Confession of Faith.
Desolation Is a Delicate Thing.
Doomsday.
The Eagle and the Mole.
Epitaph.
Escape.
Fair Annet's Song.
The Falcon.
Farewell, Sweet Dust.
Full Moon.
Golden Bough.
House Sonnet.
Hughie at the Inn.
Hymn to Earth.
Innocent Landscape.
The Knight Fallen on Evil Days.
Lament for Glasgerion.
Lavish Kindness.
Let No Charitable Hope.
Little Eclogue.
Little Elegy.
A Lodging for the Night.
Love Song.
Madman's Song.
Malediction upon Myself.
Nebuchadnezzar.
O Virtuous Light.
Parting Gift.
The Pebble.
Pegasus Lost.
Peregrine.
Peregrine's Sunday Song.
Peter and John.
Pretty Words.
Prophecy.
A Proud Lady.
The Puritan's Ballad.
Sanctuary.
Sea Lullaby.
Shepherd's Holiday.
Simon Gerty.
Sleeping Beauty.
Sonnet from "One Person".
Spring Pastoral.
This Corruptible.
To a Book.
The Tortoise in Eternity.
True Vine.
Velvet Shoes.
Wild Peaches.
Winter Sleep.
Wynard, Derk
Observation.

Wyndham, Charles
The Fair Thief.
Wyndham, Harald
An Anarchist's Letter.
Wynne, Annette
Columbus.
Excuse Us, Animals in the Zoo.
Harebells in June.
Hearts Were Made to Give Away.
I Keep Three Wishes Ready.
Indian Children.
The Leaves Do Not Mind At All.
A Letter Is a Gypsy Elf.
Memorial Day.
Once When You Were Walking.
Outside the Door.
People Buy a Lot of Things.
The Pilgrims Came.
Ring around the World.
Thanksgiving Day.
The Tree Stands Very Straight and Still.
Wynne, John Huddlestone
The Horse and the Mule.
Time.

Y

Yakamochi
By Way of Pretext.
Three Poems.
When Evening Comes.
Yako, St. J. Page
The Year's Ending.
Yamada, Mitsuye
Camp Notes.
Yamamoto, Traise
Biting Through.
Diving for Pearls.
In the Van Gogh Room.
Prelude.
Yamanaka, Tiroux
The Flesh.
Yamanoue Okura
An Elegy on the Death of Furuhi.
Yancey, Ma (and Jimmy)
Make Me a Pallet on Your Floor.
Yannai
And It Came to Pass at Midnight.
Yates, David C.
The Observer.
Yates, Edmund
All Saints'.
Yates, J. Michael
The Great Bear Lake Meditations (excerpt).
Yates, Lynda
The Disordering.
Yates, Peter
Smelling the End of Green July.
Star of Eternal Possibles and Joy.
Thought and the Poet.
Yau, John
Instant Coffee.
January 18, 1979.
The Kiss.
Shimmering Pediment.
Ybarra, Thomas Russell
Lay of Ancient Rome.

Limerick: "Mussolini's pet Marshal, Graziani."
Limerick: "There was a young fellow from Fife."
Ode to Work in Springtime.
Yearsley, Ann
To Mr. ****, an Unlettered Poet, on Genius Unimproved.
Yeatman, Jennette
Exile.
Yeatman, Robert J. and Walter Carruthers Sellar
How I Brought the Good News from Aix to Ghent or Vice Versa (parody).
Yeats, William Butler
An Acre of Grass.
Adam's Curse.
Aedh Hears the Cry of the Sedge.
After Long Silence.
Against Unworthy Praise.
All Souls' Night.
All Things Can Tempt Me.
Among School Children.
Apologia Addressed to Ireland in the Coming Days.
The Apparitions.
An Appointment.
The Arrow.
At Galway Races.
The Ballad of Father Gilligan.
The Ballad of the Foxhunter.
The Balloon of the Mind.
Before the World Was Made.
Beggar to Beggar Cried.
The Black Tower.
Blood and the Moon.
A Bronze Head.
Brown Penny.
Byzantium.
The Cap and Bells.
The Cat and the Moon.
Certain Artists Bring Her Dolls and Drawings.
The Chambermaid's Second Song.
The Choice.
Chosen.
Church and State.
The Circus Animals' Desertion.
A Coat.
The Cold Heaven.
The Collar-Bone of a Hare.
The Coming of Wisdom with Time.
Consolation.
Coole and Ballylee, 1931.
Coole Park, 1929.
A Cradle Song.
A Crazed Girl.
The Crazed Moon.
Crazy Jane and Jack the Journeyman.
Crazy Jane on the Mountain.
Cuchulain Comforted.
Cuchulains's Fight with the Sea.
The Curse of Cromwell.
The Dancer at Cruachan and Cro-Patrick.
The Dawn.
Death.
The Death of Cuchulain.
The Dedication to a Book of Stories Selected from the Irish Novelists.
A Deep-Sworn Vow.
Deirdre (excerpt).
A Dialogue of Self and Soul.

The Dolls.
Down by the Salley Gardens.
A Dream of Death.
A Drinking Song.
Easter, 1916.
Ego Dominus Tuus.
The End of Day.
Ephemera.
The Everlasting Voices.
A Faery Song.
Fairy Song.
Fallen Majesty.
The Falling of the Leaves.
The Fascination of What's Difficult.
Fergus and the Druid.
The Fiddler of Dooney.
The Fisherman.
The Folly of Being Comforted.
The Fool by the Roadside.
For Anne Gregory.
The Four Ages of Man.
Fragments.
Friends.
The Great Day.
The Gyres.
The Hawk.
He Gives His Beloved Certain Rhymes.
He Hears the Cry of the Sedge.
He Remembers Forgotten Beauty.
He Thinks of His Past Greatness...
He Thinks of Those Who Have Spoken Evil of His Beloved.
He Wishes for the Cloths of Heaven.
The Heart of the Woman.
Her Courage.
Her Courtesy.
Her Race.
The Host of the Air.
The Hosting of the Sidhe.
Hound Voice.
I Am of Ireland.
In Memory of Eva Gore-Booth and Con Markiewicz.
In Memory of Major Robert Gregory.
In the Seven Woods.
An Indian Song.
The Indian to His Love.
The Indian upon God.
Into the Twilight.
Introductory Lines (excerpt).
An Irish Airman Foresees His Death.
John Kinsella's Lament for Mrs. Mary Moore.
The Lady's Third Song.
The Lake Isle of Innisfree.
The Lamentation of the Old Pensioner.
Lapis Lazuli.
A Last Confession.
The Leaders of the Crowd.
Leda And The Swan.
Lines Written in Dejection.
Long-Legged Fly.
The Lover Mourns for the Loss of Love.
The Lover Tells of the Rose in His Heart.
Lullaby.
The Magi.
The Man Who Dreamed of Faeryland.

A Man Young and Old: The Friends of his Youth.
Meditations in Time of Civil War.
Memory.
Men Improve with the Years.
Meru.
Michael Robartes and the Dancer.
Michael Robartes Bids His Beloved Be at Peace.
A Model for the Laureate.
Mohini Chatterjee.
Mongan Laments the Change That Has Come upon Him and His Beloved.
The Moods.
The Mother of God.
The Municipal Gallery Revisited.
Never Give All the Heart.
The New Faces.
News for the Delphic Oracle.
Nineteen Hundred and Nineteen.
The Nineteenth Century and After.
No Second Troy.
Now Dreary Dawns the Eastern Light.
Oedipus at Colonus.
The Old Men Admiring Themselves in the Water.
The Old Pensioner.
On a Picture of a Black Centaur by Edmund Dulac.
On a Political Prisoner.
On Being Asked for a War Poem.
On Hearing That the Students of Our New University Have Joined...
On Those That Hated "The Playboy of the Western World", 1907.
On Woman.
The Only Jealousy of Emer (excerpt).
Pardon, Old Fathers.
Parnell.
Parting.
Paudeen.
The People.
The Pity of Love.
The Players Ask for a Blessing on the Psalteries and Themselves.
A Poet to His Beloved.
Politics.
A Prayer for My Daughter.
A Prayer for My Son.
The Priest of Coloony.
Purgatory.
The Ragged Wood.
Red Hanrahan's Song about Ireland.
The Renowned Generations.
Reprisals.
Responsibilities: Prologue.
Ribh Considers Christian Love Insufficient.
The Rose of Peace.
The Rose of the World.
The Rose Tree.
Running to Paradise.
The Sad Shepherd.
Sailing to Byzantium.
The Scholars.
The Second Coming.
September, 1913.
The Seven Sages.

She Turns the Dolls' Faces to the Wall.
Sixteen Dead Men.
Solomon and the Witch.
Solomon to Sheba.
A Song: I Thought No More Was Needed.
The Song of the Happy Shepherd.
The Song of the Old Mother.
The Song of Wandering Aengus.
The Sorrow of Love.
Spilt Milk.
The Spur.
The Statesman's Holiday.
The Statues.
The Stolen Child.
Swift's Epitaph.
Symbols.
That the Night Come.
Those Images.
A Thought from Porpertius.
The Three Bushes.
The Three Hermits.
Three Movements.
To a Friend Whose Work Has Come to Nothing.
To a Poet, Who Would Have Me Praise Certain Bad Poets...
To a Shade.
To a Squirrel at Kyle-Na-No.
To a Young Beauty.
To a Young Girl.
To an Isle in the Water.
To Be Carved on a Stone at Thoor Ballylee.
To Ireland in the Coming Times.
To the Rose upon the Rood of Time.
Tom O'Roughley.
Tom the Lunatic.
The Tower.
The Travail of Passion.
Two Songs from a Play.
Two Songs of a Fool.
The Two Trees.
Under Ben Bulben.
Under the Moon.
Upon a Dying Lady.
Upon a House Shaken by the Land Agitation.
Vacillation.
The Wanderings of Oisin.
What Then?
The Wheel.
When Helen Lived.
When You Are Old.
Whence Had They Come?
Where My Books Go.
The White Birds.
Who Goes with Fergus?
The Wicked Hawthorn Tree.
Wild Old Wicked Man.
The Wild Swans at Coole.
Wisdom.
The Witch.
Words for Music Perhaps.
Youth and Age.

Yehoash
At the Tomb of Rachel.
The Harp of David.
Hunting.
Jephthah's Daughter.
Mystery.
An Old Song.
A Prayer.
The Prophet.
Psalm.
Shadows.

A Song: "A song of grass."
A Song as Yet Unsung.
The Strongest.
Terror.
Thanksgiving.
That Is All I Heard.
The Tool of Fate.
The Wanderer.
A Withered Rose.
Yang-Se-Fu.

Yellen, Samuel
The Cloisters.
Discourse on the Real.
Grisaille with a Spot of Red.
Personal.
Prognostic.
A Time of Light, a Time of Shadow.
The Wood of the Self-Destroyers.
The Wooden Tiger.

Yen, Hsiao
A Spring Song of Tzu-Yeh.

Yerby, Frank
Calm After Storm.
The Fishes and the Poet's Hands.
Weltschmerz.
Wisdom.
You Are a Part of Me.

Yeshurun, Avot
The Poem on Our Mother, Our Mother Rachel.
The Poem on the Guilt.
The Poem on the Jews.

Yevtushenko, Yevgeny
Against Borders.
Birthday.
Colors.
People.
Waiting.

Yi-tuo, Wen
The Confession.

Yitzhok, Levi
Kaddish.

Yonathan, Nathan
And the Silver Turns into Night.
Another Poem on Absalom.
South Wind.

York, Eva Rose
I Shall Not Pass This Way Again.

York, Sarah E.
I Am Weary of Straying.

Yosano Akiko
As I Am Unhappy.
A Bird Comes.
I Can Give Myself to Her.
Spring is short.
Three Tanka, 1.
Three Tanka, 2.
Three Tanka, 3.
A Wave of Coldness.
You never touch.

Yoshihara, Sachiko
Madness.

Yots, Michael
On a Friend's Suicide.

Young, Al
Birthday Poem.
The Blues Don't Change.
Boogie with O. O. Gabugah.
A Dance for Ma Rainey.
A Dance for Militant Dilettantes.
Dance of the Infidels.
The Dancer.
Dear Old Stockholm.
For Poets.
Ho.
Identities.

In a Mist.
Intimacy.
Kiss.
Lemons, Lemons.
Lester Leaps In.
Loneliness.
Lonesome in the Country.
Moon Watching by Lake Chapala.
The Move Continuing.
Myself When I Am Real.
Not Her, She Aint No Gypsy.
The Old O. O. Blues.
One West Coast.
Pachuta, Mississippi / A Memoir.
A Poem for Players.
Ponce de Leon: A Morning Walk.
The Song Turning Back into Itself 3.
Visiting Day.
W. H. Auden & Mantan Moreland.
Yes, the Secret Mind Whispers.

Young, Andrew
At Arley.
Ba Cottage.
Beauty and Love.
The Beech.
The Black Rock of Kiltearn.
Christmas Day.
Climbing in Glencoe.
Culbin Sands.
Daisies.
The Dead Bird.
The Dead Crab.
A Dead Mole.
The Dead Sheep.
Dundonnel Mountains.
The Eagle.
The Echoing Cliff.
The Elm Beetle.
The Fallen Tree.
The Falls of Glomach.
Field-Glasses.
The Flesh-Scraper.
The Flood.
Hard Frost.
The Haystack.
Hymn.
In December.
In Teesdale.
The Lane.
Last Snow.
Late Autumn.
Loch Luichart.
Man and Cows.
March Hares.
Mist.
Nightfall on Sedgemoor.
The Old Tree.
On Middleton Edge.
On the Ridgeway.
The Paps of Jura.
Passing the Graveyard.
A Prehistoric Camp.
Prospect of a Mountain.
A Prospect of Death.
Reflections on the River.
The Round Barrow.
The Scarecrow.
The Shepherd's Hut.
Snow Harvest.
Song for Autumn.
Stay, Spring.
The Stockdoves.
Suilven.
Walking in Beech Leaves.
Wiltshire Downs.
Wood and Hill.

The Young Martins.

Young, Augustus
The Advice of an Efficiency Expert.
After Five Years.
Elegy for a School-Friend.
Heritage.
The Last Refuge.
She's My Love.
Woman, Don't Be Troublesome.

Young, Barbara
Being Gypsy.
I Hear It Said.
Road Fellows.
Sophisticate.

Young, Bartholomew
Song: "Shepherd, who can pass such wrong."

Young, David
August at the Lake.
The Boxcar Poem.
The Death of the Novel.
"It's a Whole World, the Body. A Whole World!"
Mandelstam.
Occupational Hazards.
Thoughts of Chairman Mao.

Young, Doctor Edward
Procrastination.

Young, Douglas
The Ballant o' the Laird's Bath.
For a Wife in Jizzen.
Ice-Flumes Owregie Their Lades.
Last Lauch.
Winter Homily on the Calton Hill.

Young, Edith Lillian
Disappointment.
Disappointment–His Appointment.

Young, Edward Hilton
The Art of Happiness.
A Bird in the Bush.
Characters of Women.
The Complaint, or Night Thoughts on Life, Death and Immortality.
The Criminality of War.
The Day of Judgement.
Epigram on Voltaire.
Epistles to Mr. Pope (excerpt).
The Instalment (excerpt).
The Lament of the Damned in Hell.
Love of Fame, The Universal Passion.
Night.
One to Destroy, Is Murder by the Law.
Procrastination.
Satire.
Under the Violets.

Young, Edwin
Have I Done My Best for Jesus?

Young, Ella
Greeting.
The Unicorn.

Young, Francis Brett
Atlantic Charter: 1942.
Bete Humaine.
The Dhows.
February.
Five Degrees South.
Prothalamion.
Seascape.
Song at Santa Cruz.
Song of the Dark Ages.

Young, Gary
The Doctor Rebuilds a Hand.
Equinox.
To an Estranged Wife.
Tornado Watch, Bloomington, Indiana.
Under the Catalpa Trees.
Young, Geoffrey
Rocks and Deals.
Young, George W.
Lips That Touch Liquor.
Young, Ian
At Rochdale.
Double Exposure.
Elephants from the Sea.
Honi Soit Qui Mal y Pense.
It's No Good.
The Skull.
A Sugar-Candy Bird.
Young, Jackman
Arkansas.
Young, Marguerite
Death by Rarity.
Noah's Ark.
Speculative Evening.
The White Rat.
Winter Scene.
Young, Ree
Blue Springs, Georgia.
Young, Roland
The Ape.
The Flea.
The Goat.
The Miscegenous Zebra.
Young, Sir John
On Ben Jonson, in Westminster Abbey.
Young, Virginia Brady
Taught to Be Polite.
The Teacher.
Young, William
The Bridal Pair.
Judith.
Philomel to Corydon.
The Victor.
Wishmakers' Town.
Young Bear, Ray A.
Another Face.
Before the Actual Cold.
Black Dog.
Celebration.
Coming Back Home.
The Cook.
The Crow-Children Walk My Circles in the Snow.
Differences.
Grandmother.
In Dream: The Privacy of Sequence.
In Missing.
In the first place of my life.
The last dream.
One chip of human bone.
The Place of O.
The Place of V.
A Poem for Diane Wakoski.
Poem for viet nam.
A Remembrance of a Color inside a Forest.
Rushing.
Star Blanket.
These Horses Came.
This House.
Trains Made of Stone.
Waiting to Be Fed.
War Walking Near.
The Way the Bird Sat.
What We Can.
Youngblood, Sarah
At the Western Shore.
Walking the Beach.

Youngs, Mary Fanny
The Edge of the World.
Yozei, Emperor
Falling from the ridge.
Yu Ch'ien
The Honeymooners.
Yu Hsuan-chi
Advice to a Neighbour Girl.
Answering Li Ying Who Showed Me His Poems about Summer Fishing.
At the End of Spring.
Boudoir Lament.
Composed on the Theme "Willows by the Riverside."
Elegy for the Wife of a Friend.
For a Neighbor Girl.
For Hidden Mist Pavilion.
For Kuo Hsiang.
Letting My Feelings Out.
On a Visit to Ch'ung Chen Taoist Temple...
Regretful Thoughts.
Rhyming a Friend's Poem.
Rhyming with a Friend.
Selling Ruined Peonies.
Sent to Wen T'ing-Yun on a Winter Night.
Spring Thoughts Sent to Tzu-an.
Staying in the Mountains in Summer.
Telling My Feelings.
To the Minister Liu.
Yuan Chen
Civilization.
An Elegy.
The Pitcher.
Song of the Weaving Woman.
Yuan Mei
In an Old Library.
Yud, Nachum
Like the Eyes of Wolves.
Yuhara, Prince
What Am I to Do With My Sister?
Yuke, Prince
With a rocking.
Yungman
Encounter in Safed.
Melons.
The Messiah.
Yungman, Moshe
Don't Say.
The Sacrifice.
Yvonne
Deborah Lee.
Emma.
Where She Was Not Born.

Z

"Z, X.Y."
Limerick: "There was a frank lady of Dedham."
Zabel, Morton Dauwen
Journal to Stella.
Zach, Natan
Against Parting.
As Sand.
A Foreign Country.
In This Deep Darkness.
Listening to Her.
No.
A Peaceful Song.
Perhaps It's Only Music.
The Quiet Light of Flies.

A Short Winter Tale.
To Be a Master in Your House.
When God First Said.
When the Last Riders.
Zaid, Gabriel
Late Again.
Zangwill, Israel
The Angels Came A-Mustering.
At the Worst.
At the Zoo.
Death's Transfiguration.
Despair and Hope.
Dreams.
Evolution.
In the City.
In the Morgue.
Inexhaustible.
Israel.
Jehovah.
Might Is Right.
Moses and Jesus.
Seder-Night.
Sundered.
A Tabernacle Thought.
Theodor Herzl.
To a Pretty Girl.
Vanitas Vanitatum.
Vision.
Why Do We Live?
Yom Kippur.
Zaranka, William
Conceit upon the Feet (parody).
The Cropdusting (parody).
The Cry of the Child (parody).
Here Begins the Continuation of the Cook's Tale (parody).
A High-Toned Old Fascist Gentleman (parody).
In the Ladies' Room at the Bus Terminal (parody).
Junk.
Lovers' Debouchment (parody).
Memories of Aunt Maria-Martha (parody).
Ode:"Mistah Berrybones, you daid?" (parody).
Parachuting Thoor Ballylee (parody).
Peruke of Poets (parody).
Quicksands (parody).
Ragout (parody).
Robert Frost's Left-Leaning TRESPASSERS WILL BE SHOT Sign (parody).
Zarco, Cyn
Emergency Poem 1973.
Flipochinos.
Lolo Died Yesterday.
Nights.
Poem in Nueva York.
Saxophonetyx.
Teaching Poetry.
What the Rooster Does before Mounting.
Zaturenska, Marya
Bird and the Muse.
The Daisy.
The False Summer.
Girl's Song.
The Girl Takes Her Place among the Mothers.
Head of Medusa.
Hymn to Artemis, the Destroyer.
The Intruder.
The Lovers.
The Lunar Tides.

Once in an Ancient Book.
Ophelia's Song.
Song: "Life with her weary eyes."
Song of a Factory Girl.
Spinners at Willowsleigh.
The Tempest.
Variations on a Theme by George Herbert.
The White Dress.
Woman at the Piano.
Zavatsky, Bill
Bald.
Being Adult.
The Ex-Poet.
Testament.
Zawadiwsky, Christine
As Long as the Heart Beats.
Riddles and Lies.
Zeb-un-Nissa, Princess
Lament: "Within my bosom stirs once more tonight."
Though I am Laila of the Persian romance.
Zeidner, Lisa
Still.
Zeiger, L. L.
The Snack (parody).
Zeitlin, Aaron
A Dream about an Aged Humorist.
The Empty Apartment.
Ode to Freedom.
Text.
Zelda
I Stood in Jerusalem.
In the Dry Riverbed.
Light a Candle.
The Moon Is Teaching Bible.
With My Grandfather.
Zeldis, Chayyim
The Holy Ones, the Young Ones.
Zelvin, Elizabeth
Insomnia.
Zerbe, Evelyn Arcad
In Memory of My Arab Grandmother.
Zerea Jacob, Emperor of Abyssinia
Salutation.
Zieroth, Dale
Baptism.
Beautiful Woman.
The Hunters of the Deer.
Zimmer, Paul
Apple Blight.
Driving North from Savannah on My Birthday.
Julian Barely Misses Zimmer's Brains.
Lester Tells of Wanda and the Big Snow.
Lord Fluting Dreams of America on the Eve of His Departure...
Missing the Children.
One for the Ladies at the Troy Laundry Who Cooled Themselves...
Phineas within and without.
Poem Ending with an Old Cliche.
Rollo's Miracle.
Suzie's Enzyme Poem.
Train Blues.
A Visit from Alphonse.
What Zimmer Would Be.
Zimmer and His Turtle Sink the House.

Zimmer Drunk and Alone,
  Dreaming of Old Football
  Games.
Zimmer Envying Elephants.
Zimmer in Fall.
Zimmer in Grade School.
Zimmer's Hard Dream.
Zimmer's Head Thudding
  against the Blackboard.
Zimmer's Last Gig.
A Zimmershire Lad.

Zimroth, Evan
Lilly's Song.

Zimunya, Musaemura Bonus
Climbers.
Fighter.
The Mountain.
Revolution.
To a Detainee.

Zinnes, Harriet
Wallace Stevens Gives a
  Reading.

Zinzendorf, Nicolaus
For Us No Night Can Be
  Happier.
Jesu, to Thee My Heart I
  Bow.
Lowly Bethlehem.

On Earth There Is a Lamb So
  Small.
Slain Lamb of God.

Zisquit, Linda
The Circumcision.
Rachel's Lament.
Sabbatical.

Zmuda, Bob
Love Song.

Zolotow, Charlotte
A Dog.
A Riddle.

Zolynas, Al
The Incubation.
Living with Others.
Two Childhood Memories.
The Zen of Housework.

Zorilla, Jose
Toledo.

Zoroaster
Divine Songs to Ahura
  Mazda.
Zoroaster Devoutly Questions
  Ormazd.

Zu-Bolton, Ahmos
Beachhead Preachment.

Zuckmayer, Carl
My Death.

Zukofsky, Louis
Ask of the Sun.
Cars Once Steel and Green,
  Now Old.
Catullus viii.
Chloride of Lime and
  Charcoal.
A (excerpt).
Expounding the Torah.
For You I Have Emptied the
  Meaning.
From the Head.
The Green Leaf.
The Guests.
I Walk in the Old Street.
In Arizona.
It's Hard to See but Think of
  a Sea.
Light, 4.
The Lines of This New Song
  Are Nothing.
Mantis.
Non Ti Fidar.
Of Dying Beauty.
Peri Poietikes.
Poem Beginning "The."
Reading and Talking.
So That Even a Lover.

Tall and Singularly Dark You
  Pass among the Breakers.
This Is after All Vacation.
You Who Were Made for
  This Music.

Zupan, Vitomil
A Fairy Tale.

Zussman, Ezra
At Dante's Grave.
The Last.

Zweig, Paul
Uptown.

Zweig, Stefan
Chosen of God.
Flowering without End.

Zwicky, Fay
The Chosen–Kalgoorlie, 1894.
Reckoning.
Summer Pogrom.

Zychlinska, Rayzel
The Clothes.
My Mother's Shoes.
Remembering Lutsky.

Zydek, Fredrick
Dark Room.
Pond.

KEYWORD INDEX

A

A.B.C.
Wil the Merry Weaver, and
Charity the Chamber-Maid.
Anonymous.

A-hunting
We'll All Go A-Hunting
Today. *Anonymous.*

A-roving
The Banks of the Nile.
Anonymous.
In Foreign Parts. Richards.
We'll Go No More A-Roving.
Henley.

Aaron
Three Helpers in Battle.
Coleridge.

Aaron Burr
Colonel B. Carrier.

Abandon (ed) (s)
Ah Me, Do You Remember
Still. Robinson.
Banana. Bell.
A'Chuilionn. Hutchison.
Conversations in Courtship
(excerpt). *Anonymous.*
The Empty Apartment.
Zeitlin.
The Garden of Olives. Rilke.
The Horse. Coppard.
The Jam Trap. Tomlinson.
The Married Man. Phillips.
A Natural History of
Southwestern Ontario, III.
Dewdney.
The New Calf. Hearst.

Abbess
The Abbess. Scott.

Abbey
With Death Doomed to
Grapple. Byron.

Abdicate
Of the French Kings Nativity,
&c. Harris.
To a Captious Critic.
Dunbar.
Translation. Fuller.

Abdomen
Calamiterror, VI. Barker.
Extempore Verses upon a
Trial of Skill.... Byrom.

Abe Lincoln
The Hill. Masters.
Lincoln Monument:
Washington. Hughes.

Abel
Brothers. Pagis.
The Discovery. Gibbon.
Midrash on Hamlet. Landy.

Aberdeen
Deep Sea Tug. *Anonymous.*
Epitaph from Aberdeen.
Anonymous.

Abhorrence
D. H. Lawrence and James
Joyce. Wolfe.

Abide (s)
Abide in Me, O Lord, and I
in Thee. Stowe.
Abide with Us. Bonar.

Come, Sleep. Beaumont.
Concerning Them That Are
Asleep. Raymond.
Depart from Me. Coleridge.
Faith and Sight. King.
A Film. Goldbarth.
Hymn. Browning.
Hymn of Unity. *Anonymous.*
I've Tasted My Blood.
Acorn.
In Her Praise. Graves.
Lullaby. Fletcher.
Margaret to Dolcino.
Kingsley.
Moment by Moment.
Whittle.
Morning Swim. Kumin.
My Bible and I. *Anonymous.*
Nostalgias. Mahon.
Rome. Du Bellay.
Samuel Allen. *Anonymous.*
She Rose to His
Requirement–Dropt.
Dickinson.
Signature. Livesay.
There Came A Wind Like A
Bugle. Dickinson.
There Is a Place. Hoellein.
Three Wise Kings. Brooks.
What Splendid Rays.
Gregor.
Within and Without.
Macdonald.

Able
Whole Duty of Children.
Stevenson.
Wit's-End Corner.
Anonymous.

Abode (s)
America A Prophecy. Blake.
Forgotten Island. Hall.
Love's Immortality. Barker.
Lumen de Lumine. Shelley.
My House, I Say. But Hark
to the Sunny Doves.
Stevenson.
On the Needle of a Sun-Dial.
Quarles.
Self-Acquaintance. Cowper.
The Staff and Scrip.
Rossetti.
Though the Great Waters
Sleep. Dickinson.
To the Right Honourable
William, Earl of
Dartmouth. Wheatley.

Abomination
If, on Account of the Political
Situation. Auden.

Abortion
Greasy Spoon Blues.
Gasparini.
In Memoriam: Martin Luther
King, Jr. Jordan.

Abortive song
An Hymn to the Morning.
Wheatley.

Above
The Boys of Sanpete County.
Anonymous.
Come Holy Spirit, Dove
Divine. Judson.
Contemplations. Bradstreet.

En Route. Mayo.
The Fear of Flying. Van
Duyn.
Fiction: A Message. Ewart.
Glow Worm. Robinson.
A Grain of Moonlight. Asya
(Asya Gray).
Here, Lord, Retired, I Bow in
Prayer. Bolles.
It Is Not Beauty I Demand.
Darley.
The Landlord's Wife. Chin.
Leaves. Teasdale.
Nuclear Land. Tuft.
Our Sister. Powers.
A Parental Ode to My Son.
Hood.
Prayer. Mousley.
Reflection from Sea and Sky.
Landor.
Sonnet to William
Wilberforce, Esq. Cowper.
Suburban Lovers. Dawe.
The Trees in the Road. Still.
The Watcher. Hale.

Abraham
Epitaph: "Mary Ann has gone
to rest." *Anonymous.*
The Mother's Sacrifice.
Sigourney.

Abroad
Runes for an Old Believer.
Humphries.
Three Children. *Anonymous.*

Absalom
Another Poem on Absalom.
Yonathan.
David's Lamentation.
Billings.

Absence (s)
Absences. Larkin.
Astrophel and Stella, CV.
Sidney.
A Bridal Song. Shelley.
Dispatch Number Sixteen.
Fetherling.
Epigram: "Dear, my familiar
hand in love's own gesture."
Cunningham.
Hello, Hello. Matthews.
Hush. St. John.
I Have Come Far to Have
Found Nothing. Corman.
A Journal from France:
Seamstress at St. Leon.
Clarke.
Last Meeting. Harwood.
Lines on Leaving a Scene in
Bavaria. Campbell.
Mediterranean. Whitman.
The Mistress (excerpt).
Rochester.
North of Berwick.
Tremayne.
The Odyssey. Homer.
Okay–. Scott.
One Way Down. Craig.
Sleeping Alone. Fickert.
Southeast Arkanasia.
Angelou.
The Way Down: They Return.
Macpherson.

Absent
A Letter from Li Po (excerpt).
Aiken.
Progress? Auden.
Sonnets, IV: "Two stars there
are in one faire firmament."
Barnfield.

Absolute
The Altars in the Street.
Levertov.
Assuming the Name of Any
Next Child. Tagliabue.
Beads from Blackpool.
Ridler.
Classroom in October.
Lieberman.
Revelation. Keesing.
Seven. Parra.

Absolution
Rest. Blind.
A Sermon on Swift. Clarke.

Absolve
The Great Magicians. Day
Lewis.
The Masque of the Inner-
Temple and Gray's Inne.
Beaumont.

Absorbed
August 13, 1966. Hine.

Abstinence
Boys in October. Layton.

Abstract (ion)
Fruit and Government.
Kurka.
New English Canaan, the
Authors Prologue.
Morton.
Nothing in Heaven Functions
As It Ought. Kennedy.
Rapist. Teran.
The Room. Day-Lewis.

Absurd (ities)
Dear Female Heart. Smith.
The Labyrinth. Auden.
Little Miss and Her Parrot.
Marchant.
Nino, the Wonder Dog.
Fuller.
The Redshanks. Bell.

Abundance
The Black Art. Sexton.
Brittan's Remembrancer
(excerpt). Wither.
For to love her for her looks
lovely. Wyatt.
O God, in Restless Living.
Fosdick.
Oxygen. Swift.
The Triads of Ireland
(excerpt). *Anonymous.*

Abuse (ed) (es) (ing)
At the St. Louis Institute of
Music. Wallace.
The Great Swamp Fight.
Hazard.
Limerick: "There was a young
poet of Thusis."
Anonymous.
The Rape of Lucrece.
Shakespeare.
Tenth Reunion. Steese.
Though Your Strangenesse
Frets My Hart. Campion.

Abuse

Where Are All Thy Beauties
Now, All Hearts
Enchaining? Campion.
Women's Longing. Fletcher.

Abysm

If This Be Love. Eberhart.

Abysmal

Limerick: "The babe, with a
cry brief and dismal."
Gorey.

Abyss (es)

"All Things Must Have an
End; the World Itself."
Longfellow.
Almighty God, Whose Justice
Like a Sun. Belloc.
Censorship. Waley.
The City of Dreadful Night.
Thomson.
Essay on Memory.
Fitzgerald.
Gulliver. Plath.
Hadad: The Demon-Lover.
Hillhouse.
Haunted Houses.
Longfellow.
In Nine Sleep Valley
(excerpt). Merrill.
In Space-Time Aware–.
Evans.
Look, in the Labyrinth of
Memory. Schwartz.
The Mares of the Camargue.
Mistral.
Prayer. Coignard.
The Prisoner. Plomer.
De Profundis.
""MacDiarmid.
PSI. Tolson.
The Splendid Shilling
(parody). Phillips.
Suburban Lullaby. Manifold.
Tall and Singularly Dark You
Pass among the Breakers.
Zukofsky.
They Sing. Roethke.
Thou Shalt Not. Tussman.

Academies

It Feels Good as It Is
Without the Giant.
Stevens.
Love Necessitates.
Redmond.

Acadians

The Emigration of the Fairies.
Hunter-Duvar.

Accent (ed) (s)

Evangeline. Longfellow.
Limerick: "There was a frank
lady of Dedham." "Z.
The Metre Columbian
(parody). Anonymous.
Old Country Talk. Farkas.
Some Trees. Ashbery.
We Whom the Dead Have
Not Forgiven. Field.

Accentuate

Epitaph for Liberal Poets.
MacNeice.

Accept (able) (ance) (ed) (s)

Ballata of Love's Power.
Cavalcanti.
The Birthday Bus.
Hoberman.
Children Waking: Indian Hill
Station. Currey.
Essay on Deity. Olson.
The God in Whom We Trust.
Anonymous.
King Henry V. Shakespeare.
Life. Anonymous.

Access

Song of the Open Road
(excerpt). Whitman.
A Thanksgiving to God for
His House. Herrick.
What Is There. Bell.
When Israel. Scott.
The Winter Twilight, Glowing
Black and Gold.
Schwartz.

A Vision Upon This Conceipt
of the Faerie Queene.
Ralegh.

Accessory

Sonnets, XXXV: "No more be
grieved at that which thou
hast done." Shakespeare.

Accident (s)

Beside a Fall. Garrigue.
December. Francis.
The Dolls. Yeats.
Good People. Stanton.
Grammar Commences with a
5-line Curse. Palladas.
Much Ado about Nothing.
Shakespeare.
No White Bird Sings.
Ciardi.
Spring 1940. Auden.
Yeats in Dublin (excerpt).
Watkins.

Acclaim

Farmer Goes Berserk. Elder.
In Memoriam A.H.H.,
LXXV. Tennyson.

Accomplice (s)

Interior. Squire.
Theme and Variations.
Millay.
Two Hookers. Redwing.

Accomplishment (s)

The Abnormal Is Not
Courage. Gilbert.
The Drowning Poet. Merrill.
Pure Death. Graves.
Reindeer Report. Fanthorpe.
View by Color Photography
on a Commercial Calendar.
Williams.
Yes, But... Weiss.

Accord (ance)

Homeric Hymns: Hymn to
Mercury. Anonymous.
Throughout the World.
Wyatt.

Account (ing)

Cole's Island. Olson.

Accounting

Forgiving My Father.
Clifton.
How to Keep Accounts.
Anonymous.
Mews Flat Mona. Plomer.

Accumulate

Financial Wisdom.
Anonymous.

Accurst

Apparent Failure. Browning.
Lucasta's Fan, with a
Looking-Glass in It.
Lovelace.
What Sugred Termes, What
All-Perswading Arte.
Lynche.

Accusation (s)

The Bloodhound. Anthony.
Clinton South of Polk.
Sandburg.
The Dirty Little Accuser.
Cameron.

Heart Oppress'd with
Desperate Thought.
Wyatt.
King Henry IV.
Shakespeare.
The Line-Up. Swift.
To Stella. Swift.

Ache (s)

Attica Is. Brisby.
Carmina. Catullus.
The Cruel Sister.
Anonymous.
Give Me My Infant Now.
Te-whaka-io-roa.
An Introduction. Das.
Lobsters in the Window.
Snodgrass.
Measure for Measure.
Shakespeare.
The Other One. Peck.
Seven Poems. Niedecker.
Sonnet. Berryman.
Sonnet in the Mail Coach.
Taylor.
A thousand years, you said.
Heguri.
Three Women. Dempster.
Water Music. Lewis.

Acheron

Hermes came to me in a
dream. Sappho.
Villanelle of Acheron.
Dowson.

Achievement (ing) (s)

Colorado. Dillenback.
Essay on Marriage.
Wilchilsea.
In a Shoreham Garden.
Lerner.
The Messiah. Frishman.

Achilles

Ballad of Hector in Hades.
Muir.
The Shield of Achilles.
Auden.
Thinking of Tents.
Whittemore.

Aching (s)

I Would I Might Forget That
I Am I. Santayana.
The North Country.
Lawrence.
A Simple Story. Harwood.
Sing On, Blithe Bird!
Motherwell.
Sundered. Barford.
Versions of Love. Fuller.
Virgilia (excerpt). Markham.

Acid

Prescription of Painful Ends.
Jeffers.
Reclaimed Area. Silkin.
Street Song. Gunn.

Acknowledge

Evasion. Salkeld.
For His Wife, on Her
Birthday. Wesley.
Prisoner Aboard the S.S.
Beagle. Murry.

Acorn (s)

Better, Wiser and Happier.
Wilcox.
The Moral. Mandeville.
Satires. Horace.
Sonnet in Autumn. Petersen.

Acquaintance

Galway Races. Anonymous.

Acquiescent

Discourse Heard One Day.
Babcock.

Acre (s)

Crickets. McCord.

The Mushroom Gatherers.
Davie.
Riders. Peavy.
When the Cows Come down
to Drink. Hoey.

Acropolis

Professor Kelleher and the
Charles River. O'Grady.

Across

The Blackbird by Belfast
Lough. Anonymous.
For Simone Weil. Sister M.
Therese.
Traffic Lights. Kasdaglis.

Act (ed)

After Shakespeare. Comfort.
By Rail through Istria.
Conquest.
Caledonia. McElroy.
The Constructed Space.
Graham.
Emblems. Quarles.
Epigram: "Above all gifts we
most should prize."
Landor.
Epigram: "My soul, sit thou a
patient looker-on."
Quarles.
Hazardous Occupations.
Sandburg.
How Do You Live?
Anonymous.
Jack the Giant Queller. An
Antique History. Brooke.
Last Verses. Chatterton.
Life's Testament.
Baylebridge.
Maud Muller Mutatur
(parody). Adams.
The Pond. Thwaite.
The Psalm of St. Priapus.
Broughton.
Satyr. Gullans.
The Strangers. Very.
Their Last Will and
Testament. MacNeice.
The Whip. Creeley.

Actia

Sonnets. Tuckerman.

Action (s)

Character. Emerson.
Cloud Country. Merrill.
A Cold Front. Williams.
Desert Warfare. Longley.
Europe. Dudek.
Gladstone. Symons.
Matins, or Morning Prayer.
Herrick.
My Creed. Kiser.
The Old Story. MacNeice.
Paul Jones. Anonymous.
Perhaps the Best Time.
Meredith.
The Praises. Olson.
A Satire Addressed to a
Friend (excerpt). Oldham.
The Seamen's Wives'
Vindication. Anonymous.
Sonnet LXX. Alabaster.
Unsolicited Letters to Five
Artists (parody). James.
Variations on a Line from
Shakespeare's Fifty-Sixth
Sonnet. Mayo.

Active

Contemplation. Thompson.
Limerick: "Wrote the clergy:
"Our Dear Madame
Prynne:". Fogle.

Actor (s)

Booth Killed Lincoln.
Anonymous.

The Roman Stage. Johnson.

Acts
The Aeneid. Virgil (Publius Vergilius Maro).
The Aim of Life: A Country Town. Bailey.
He Said the Facts. Moore.
Homer. Ehrenstein.
Locations. Fraser.
The Marriage of Heaven and Hell. Blake.
On Reading Gene Derwood's "The Innocent'. Maas.
The Siege of Belgrade. Watts.
To Christ Our Lord. Kinnell.

Actual (ity)
Granite and Steel. Moore.
Seal Rocks: San Francisco. Conquest.

Adam
Adam Driven from Eden. *Anonymous.*
Adam's Footprint. Miller.
Adam's Race. Sa'di.
An American Takes a Walk. Whittemore.
The Apple. Sackville.
At the Bottom of the Well. Untermeyer.
At the Firth of Lorne. Smith.
Brand Speaks. Ibsen.
Fuller and Warren. *Anonymous.*
I Thought I Saw Stars. Lister.
The Kropotkin Poems (excerpt). Webb.
Let Us Learn. Ravitch.
Orchard Snow. Goodenough.
Psalm LXXIII. Surrey.
A Reflection. Hood.
Sunday up the River. Thomson.
Swan. Lowbury.
To My Father. Baxter.
To "Philomela." Colman.
When Eve upon the First of Men. Moore.
Why Adam Sinned. Rogers.
Women's Degrees. Godley.
Wonders. Thomas.
Ye Sons of Columbia. *Anonymous.*

Adamant
A Reflection. Hood.
The Solemn Noon of Night. Warton, Jr..
A Song of Degrees. Ker.
'Twas Warm at First, Like Us. Dickinson.

Add (ed)
The Cost. Osgood.
On New-Years Day 1640 to the King. Suckling.
Wardance Soup. George.
Work. Cox.

Adder
An American Love-Ode. Warton, Sr..
Marriage. *Anonymous.*
Movements. MacCaig.
Paris. Kolmar.
World, Defined. Weismiller.

Addle
The Faeryes Farewell; or, God-A-Mercy Will. Corbett.
Farewell, Rewards and Fairies. Corbet.

Address (ed) (es)
The Aeneid. Virgil (Publius Vergilius Maro).
The Bandog. De la Mare.
Epilogue to the Satires. Pope.
The Final Cut. Rutsala.
The Headless Gardener. Serraillier.
If I Ride This Train. Johnson.
A New Ballad. *Anonymous.*
Requiem for and Abstract Artist. Kessler.
Satire. Pope.
Winter's Edge. Roberts.

Adieu (s)
Ah Me! Am I the Swaine. Wither.
Ann Grenville, Countess Temple, Appointed Poet Laureate... Walpole.
A Ballad. Sedley.
The Banks of Newfoundland (II). *Anonymous.*
Botany Bay. *Anonymous.*
An Epitaph of Maister Win Drowned in the Sea. Turberville.
Fourth Station. Schaumann.
The Irish Girl's Lament. *Anonymous.*
The Little Peach. Field.
Lover and Echo. O'Daly.
Madrigal: "Go, nightly Cares." Dowland.
My New Garden Field. *Anonymous.*
On Fame. Keats.
Ratcliffe Highway. *Anonymous.*
The Seamen's Wives' Vindication. *Anonymous.*
The Sense of Smell. MacNeice.
The Silk Weaver's Daughter. *Anonymous.*
Six Town Eclogues (excerpt). Montagu.
To Promise Is One Thing, To Perform Is Another. La Fontaine.
Vain World Adieu. *Anonymous.*
A Weary Lot is Thine. Scott.
Years. Landor.

Adjourned
I Move the Meeting Be Adjourned. Parra.

Adjust (ed)
I Don't Want to Get Adjusted. *Anonymous.*
The Submarine Bed. Bishop.

Admiral
Admiral Death. Newbolt.
The Death of Admiral Benbow. *Anonymous.*
Noah. Daniells.
Nothing but Death. Neruda.
Port Admiral. Marryat.
Statue against a Clear Sky. Stevens.

Admiration
Artificial Teeth. Brown.
A Letter to William Carlos Williams. Rexroth.
Milton. Blake.
The Mother Crab and Her Family. Manyase.
The Tide of Faith. Eliot.

Admire (d) (s) (ing)
An Answer to Some Verses Made in His Praise. Suckling.
The Borough. Crabbe.
In the Public Garden. Moore.
Lord Lovel. *Anonymous.*
Lord Thomas and Fair Ellinor. *Anonymous.*
Ode to Nea. Moore.
On a Female Rope-Dancer. *Anonymous.*
The Preparative. Traherne.
To Stella. Swift.
The Young Acacia. Bialik.

Admit (ted)
Because Going Nowhere Takes a Long Time. Patchen.
Farewell to Kurdistan. Tonks.
Louie. Shiplett.
Shadows in the Water. Traherne.

Adolescent eyes
First Day of Teaching. Overstreet.

Adonais
On Keats Who Desired That On His Tomb Should Be Inscribed–. Shelley.

Adonis
The Beggar's Opera. Gay.
Epigram: "Glad youth had come thy sixteenth year to crown." Ausonius.
The Faerie Queene. Spenser.
Lament for Adonis. Bion.

Adonoi
The Three Towns. Nemerov.

Adopted
First Love. Hemschemeyer.

Ador'd
The Bonhomme Richard and Serapis. Freneau.

Adoration
An April Adoration. Roberts.
Do We Not Hear Thy Footfall? Carmichael.
Old Fortunatus. Dekker.
Period Piece. Berlind.
Thy Rising Is Beautiful. Akhnaton (Amenhotep IV).
Veni Crator Spiritus, Translated in Paraphrase. Dryden.

Adore (d) (s)
Adeste Fideles. Bonaventure.
All Praise to Thee. Tucker.
Be Thou Then by Beauty Named. Campion.
The Conjuror. Lucas.
A Daughter of Admetus. Moore.
Eclogue. Drayton.
Emaricdulfe. "C.
FayWray to the King. Rechter.
God to Be First Served. Herrick.
The Highlands' Swelling Blue. Byron.
Hymn to Darkness. Norris.
I Took Leave of My Beloved One Evening. At Taliq.
I Turn to Jesus. Smith.
The Irish Language. Mangan.
Isabella: or, the Morning (excerpt). Williams.

Jesus First and Jesus Last. MacKellar.
The Jolly Plowboy. *Anonymous.*
On the Infancy of Our Saviour. Quarles.
Pan and the Cherries. Fort.
The Plain Golden Band. *Anonymous.*
Retirement, an Ode (excerpt). Warton, Sr..
The Sabbath Day Was By. Robbins.
Shopping for Midnight. Murray.
Sincere Praise. Watts.
So Far, So Near. Cranch.
Strive Not, Vain Lover, to Be Fine. Lovelace.
The Three Woes. De Vere.
To England. Moore.
To the Memory of Sir Isaac Newton (excerpt). Thomson.
Toledo. Zorilla.
Water and Worship: An Open-Air Service on the Gatineau River. Avison.
Wreck of the Deutschland. Hopkins.

Adoring
To...in Church. Seeger.

Adorn (ing)
At the Drapers. Hardy.
The Oyster. Ponge.
The Stars. "Ping Hsin" (Hsieh Wang-ying).

Adult
To a Small Boy Standing on My Shoes While I Am Wearing Them. Nash.
An Underdeveloped Country. Enright.

Adultery
On Bassa. Martial (Marcus Valerius Martialis).
To His Book. Herrick.
Upon Scobble. Epigram. Herrick.

Advance (s)
After Johnson's Dance. Souter.
At Midnight's Hour. Thoreau.
Autumnal Ode. De Vere.
The Battle of Bull Run. *Anonymous.*
Dark Symphony. Tolson.
Just an Old Sweet Song. MacDonagh.
The Knight in the Wood. De Tabley.
Seismograph. Auerbach.
The Starry Host. Spalding.
"Sweet are the thoughts where hope persuadeth hap." Ralegh.
Twenty-Four Years. Thomas.
Urania. Pitter.
Years of the Modern. Whitman.

Advantage (s)
Jim Haggerty's Story. *Anonymous.*
Sharks in Shallow Water. Levinson.
Song of the Forest Trees. *Anonymous.*

Advent
Charmides (excerpt). Mackie.

Adventure
Auspice of Jewels. Riding.
The Gospel of Mr. Pepys. Morley.
The India Guide.... Dallas.
A Trifle for Trafalgar Day. Pauker.

Adversary
The Mystery of the Innocent Saints (excerpt). Peguy.

Adverse winds
Contemplations. Bradstreet.

Adversity
Drowning is Not so Pitiful. Dickinson.
Meditations in Time of Civil War. Yeats.
Not Ours the Vows. Barton.
A Prayer. Ham.
That Room. Montague.

Advertise
Advertisement. Anonymous.
Wanted, a Minister's Wife. Anonymous.

Advertising
The Double Standard. Adams.
Quite Apart from the Holy Ghost. Mitchell.

Advice
From the Provinces. Rosten.
A Garland of Precepts. McGinley.
The Hen and the Oriole. Marquis.
I Have a Big Favor to Ask You, Brothers. Landau.
Idyllis. Theocritus.
A Manifesto for the Faint-Hearted. Oles.
Of Late. Starbuck.
Paradise Lost. Milton.
A Plea for Promiscuity. Waller.
Song of Thyrsis. Freneau.
To Phillis. Waller.

Advocate
Our Lady of Mercy. Bertrand.

Aegean
Greece. Haygarth.

Aeschylus
The Eumenides at Home (parody). Agate.

Aesthetic
A Snowfall. Eberhart.

Affair
Fourth Act. Jeffers.
In Peterborough Churchyard. Anonymous.
Julian and Maddalo (excerpt). Shelley.
"Out, Out–". Frost.
A Sparrow's Feather. Barker.
Waldeinsamkeit. Emerson.
The Wreck of the Rambler. Anonymous.

Affection (s)
Arcadia. Sidney.
Crime at Its Best. King.
A Fair Nymph Scorning a Black Boy Courting Her. Cleveland.
A Friend. De Carrion.
Jane and Eliza. Taylor.
Land of Nations (excerpt). Stein.
My Mother. Taylor.
Regeneration. Landor.
Serve Her Right. Barford.

Tell Me, O Love. Hammond.
The Tomb of Lt. John Learmonth, A.I.F. Manifold.
Woman (excerpt). McLachlan.

Affirmation
Deprivation. Pinkerton.
Meditation of a Mariner. Auchterlonie.

Afflict (ed) (tion) (tions)
The High Priest. Anonymous.
The Sherman Cyclone. Anonymous.
Though Mine Eye Sleep Not. Anonymous.
The Tree of Love. Lull.

Afford (s)
Maples (parody). Appleman.
Memo. Lynch.
Tree-Topped Hill. Anonymous.

Affright (s)
The Aeneid. Virgil (Publius Vergilius Maro).
The Marionettes. De La Mare.

Affront
The Stone Gentleman. Reeves.

Aflame
The Cry of the Age. Garland.
The Goldfish. Brown.

Afloat
The Hayeswater Boat (excerpt). Arnold.
On a Honey Bee. Freneau.
On the Great Fog in London, December 1762. Weeks.
To Meet, or Otherwise. Hardy.

Afraid
Aaron Nicholas, Almost Ten. Hale.
Advice to the Young. Waddington.
As Adam Early in the Morning. Whitman.
Body of the Queen. Evans.
The Bonfire. Frost.
The Book of Nightmares. Kinnell.
Branches Back Into. Belford.
Brother and Sisters. Wright.
By-Products. Wormser.
Color Blind. Paine.
Conversion. Angermayer.
The Crucifixion. Meynell.
The Derelict. Kipling.
The Dreame. Jonson.
Einstein's Father. Klauck.
Empire of Dreams. Simic.
The Entertainment of War. Fisher.
Epigrams. Martial (Marcus Valerius Martialis).
Faint Heart. Linton.
The Fear of Bo-talee. Momaday.
The Female Smuggler. Anonymous.
The Garden. Pound.
Haiku: "Deep in a windless." Buson (Taniguchi Buso).
The Hero. Jackson.
The House Dog's Grave. Jeffers.
A Huguenot. Coleridge.
I Am Afraid. Anonymous.

I Shall Not Be Afraid. Kilmer.
In Love with the Bears. Kuzma.
Instans Tyrannus. Browning.
Kunai-Mai-Pa Mo. Anderson.
The Letter. Auden.
Memories of Verdun. Dugan.
Modern Love, XXVII. Meredith.
Moving In. Engle.
Mule-Train. Sellers.
The Mysteries. Strong.
Nelly Trim. Warner.
The Oft-Repeated Dream. Frost.
The Pearl. Andersen.
Progress. Wilcox.
A Question. Anonymous.
Rabbi Ben Ezra. Browning.
Return to Dachau. Niditch.
The Succubus. Rose.
There Are No Wolves in England Now. Fyleman.
These Horses Came. Young Bear.
This One Heart-Shaken. Maris Stella.
To End Her Fear. Freeman.
To Turn Back. Haines.
What Music. Harjo.
White Bear. Griffin.
Woman. Saba.
Woman and Nature. Griffin.
Woman to Man. Wright.
Woman, You Are Afraid of the Forest. Wine.

Africa (n)
The African Trader's Complaint. Osadebay.
At Gibraltar. Woodberry.
A Bestiary. Rexroth.
Black Tambourine. Crane.
Black Trumpeter. Dumas.
The Caffer Commando (excerpt). Pringle.
Disinterment. Sherry.
Duns Scotus. Merton.
El Camino Verde. Blackburn.
Florida. Rakosi.
The Flying Cloud (II). Anonymous.
Goodbye David Tamunoemi West. Danner.
Heritage: What Is Africa to Me? Cullen.
Home-Thoughts, from the Sea. Browning.
I Am a Negro. Al-Fituri.
Mamparra M'gaiza. Craveirinha.
My Africa. Dei-Anang.
Neither This Nor That. Palés Matos.
Ode on Lord Macartney's Embassy to China. Shepherd.
Sadie's Playhouse. Danner.
This Narrow Stage. Weiss.
The Tide That from the West Washes Africa to the Bone. Rubadiri.
To a Brown Girl. Davis.

After
Heron Weather. Crase.
In Memoriam A.H.H., LXXXI. Tennyson.
The Indians on Alcatraz. Muldoon.

A Little While. Marquis.
Love at Roblin Lake. Purdy.
Melissa. Redl-Hlus.
November Snow. Carson.
Two Are Together. Grigson.

After-life
My Own Hereafter. Lee-Hamilton.
O Christmas Night. Selyns.
The Other Side. Fuller.
The World Well Lost. Stedman.

Aftermath
Limerick: "A mathematician named Bath." Wilson.

Afternoon
Amores. Parini.
Anniversary. Lattimore.
Backwater Pond: The Canoeists. Merwin.
Components. McDonald.
Death and the Maiden. Gallup.
The Double. Feldman.
An Elegy. Scovell.
I Am a Victim of Telephone. Ginsberg.
In the Fall. Rivero.
Lament for Ignacio Sanchez Mejias. Garcia Lorca.
The Love Bit. Oppenheimer.
Meditation for a Pickle Suite. Dillard.
A Meeting of Cultures. Davie.
On the Lawn at the Villa. Simpson.
A Poem for the Insane. Wieners.
Poem: "Hasten on your childhood to the hour." Picasso.
Rear Porches of an Apartment Building. Bodenheim.
Rest. Segal.
Ronsard. DeFord.
Sally Go Round the Sunshine. Anonymous.
Small-Scale Reflections on a Great House. Ramanujan.
The Tale the Hermit Told. Reid.
Woodpigeons at Raheny. Davie.

Aftertaste
Kissing Natalia. Grier.

Afterward (s)
"If care do cause men cry..." Surrey.
Prelude. Rosenmann-Taub.
You Don't Know What Love Is (parody). Carver.

Afton
Flow Gently, Sweet Afton. Burns.
Sweet Afton. Burns.

Again
Eve. Hodgson.
How Stands the Glass Around? Wolfe.
Limerick: "There was a young man on a plain." Smith.
Loving. Stembridge.
No Man's Land. Bogle.
A Poem about Breasts. Wright.
Riddle: "There was a king met a king." Anonymous.
Tell Me Again. Hanim.
Two Jazz Poems. Hines, Jr.
The Unknown Soldier. Rose.

The Wheel Revolves. Rexroth.

Against
Poem: "It doesn't look like a finger..." Davies.
The Second Thanksgiving, or The Reprisal. Herbert.

Agate
Analogue of Unity in Multeity. Eberhart.
I Change. Bynner.
Llanberis Summer. Loyd.

Age (d)
112 at Presidio. Long.
12 Gates to the City. Giovanni.
Above Salerno. Murray.
Almighty Sovereign of the Skies! Strong.
And Through the Caribbean Sea. Danner.
Athletic Ode. Santayana.
The Autumn Wind. Wu Ti.
Ballade of Youth and Age. Henley.
Bargain. Driscoll.
The Best Memory Course. Anonymous.
Birthdays. Driver.
A Boy. Ashbery.
The Broken Girth. Graves.
Caelica, XXVIII. Greville.
Chickory. Gal'ed.
Childhood. Tabb.
Come, All Ye People. Seltzer.
A Copy of Verses on Jefferys the Seaman. Anonymous.
County Mayo. Raftery,
Cupids Call. Shirley.
Dear, Do Not Your Fair Beauty Wrong. May.
The Discriminator. Scannell.
Epigram: "Sound, sound the clarion, fill the fife! Scott.
Epithalamium for the Dedication of a Church. Anonymous.
Farewell to the World of Richard Bishop. Anonymous.
Five Things White. May.
The Gentleman. Lonzano.
Good and Bad Children. Stevenson.
Great Friend. Thoreau.
Hans Christian Andersen in Central Park. Sobiloff.
High Fidelity. Gunn.
The Hind and the Panther. Dryden.
His Own Epitaph. Herrick.
The Holly Tree. Southey.
Honour with Age. Kennedy.
Hypocrite Auteur. MacLeish.
I thought that Love had been a boy. Anonymous.
The Ideal Age for a Man. Shannon.
Impression. Gosse.
In Memory of General Grant. Abbey.
The Insatiate. Secundus.
Jack the Giant Queller. An Antique History. Brooke.
Killarney. Larminie.
King Henry VIII. Shakespeare.
Let Us Declare! (excerpt). Morgan.

Letters to Live Poets. Beaver.
Limerick: "A canary, its woe to assuage." Herford.
The Lockless Door. Frost.
The Loyal General: Prologue. Dryden.
The Lucky Chance: Song. Behn.
Madrigal: "Sweet Cupid, ripen her desire." Corkine.
Measure for Measure. Shakespeare.
Memory. Browne.
Mother's Party. Fisher.
The Mountain Over Aberdare. Lewis.
Ode on a Distant Prospect of Clapham Academy. Hood.
The Offering of the Heart. Humphries.
The Old Couple, III, i: Love's Prime. May.
Old Women. Deutsch.
The Olden Days. Hall.
On Dennis. Pope.
On the Instability of Youth. Vaux.
On Youth, the Warden & Solitary! Baker.
Once for Candy Cook Had Stolen. Auden.
Paul Veronese. Ferguson.
Picasso's Women. Cabral.
Polyhymnia: His Golden Lock. Peele.
Ponce de Leon. Thomas.
The Praise of Age. Henryson.
Pretending. Livingston.
Prospero on the Mountain Gathering Wood. Gilbert.
Proverbial Advice on Marriage. Anonymous.
Rabbi Ben Ezra. Browning.
Rendezvous. Hillyer.
The Rock. Eliot.
Sacramentum Supremum. Newbolt.
Scotch Te Deum. Kethe.
The Seed-Picture. McGuckian.
The Shepherd's Song. Bunyan.
Since Youth Is All for Gladness. Dresbach.
Slow Summer Twilight. Wheelock.
Solitude. Grainger.
A Sonet: "His Golden lockes, Time hath to Silver turn'd." Peele.
Song: "Had I a heart for falsehood fram'd." Sheridan.
Sonnets, LXII: "Sinne of selfe-love possesseth al mine eie." Shakespeare.
The Spirit's Light. Cowper.
Spring. Feirstein.
Spring Burning. Roland.
Time. Graves.
To Age. Landor.
To His Excellency Joseph Dudley Eqr Gover: &c. Saffin.
To Pikes Peak. Hills.
To the Rainbow. Campbell.
To the Rose. Davies.
To the World the Perfection of Love. Habington.

To Theon from His Son Theon. Trypanis.
Today. Morgan.
Tom's Garland. Hopkins.
The Trees of the Garden. Rossetti.
Tyrannic Love. Dryden
Underneath a Cypress Shade, The Queen of Love Sat Mourning. Anonymous.
Views of the Oxford Colleges. Leary.
Virgidemiarum. Hall.
Whom the Gods Love. Bruner.
Wrestling Angels. Bottoms.
Youth's Agitations. Arnold.

Ageless
The Dead. Williams.
Edinburgh. Noyes.
O Child of Lowly Manger Birth. Blanchard.

Agent (s)
Annie and Willie's Prayer. Snow.
Poem: "the country". Levinson.
The Poet's Prothalamion (Excerpt). Scholl.

Ages
Abraham Lincoln. Cole.
The Bride. Hodgson.
Burial. Joachim.
Conscripts of the Dream (excerpt). Markham.
Conversation. More.
Crown of Days. Anonymous.
If I Were a Voice. Mackay.
Jesus Only. Nason.
Laudate for Christmas. Prudentius (Aurelius Clemens Prudentius).
Little Big Horn. McGaffey.
London Bridge. Anonymous.
Mine–By the Right of the White Election! Dickinson.
MMDCCXIII 1/2. Thomas.
The Mystery of Cro-A-Tan. Preston.
Now the Day Is over. Baring-Gould.
O Love, That Dost with Goodness Crown. Chadwick.
Of the Father's Love Begotten. Prudentius (Aurelius Clemens Prudentius).
The Present Age. Coxe.
Pyramus and Thisbe. Dakin.
A Sigh. Spofford.
Two Rivers. Emerson.
Untitled. Crowne.

Aggravate
To —. Shelley.

Aggrieved
Anatomy of Monotony. Stevens.

Agincourt
On a Boy's First Reading of "King Henry V". Mitchell.

Aging
Down the Nile. Lowell.
Make Way. Lavoie.
Nocturne in the Women's Prison. Beneyto.
The Sleeping Saint. La Follette.
A Walk by the Charles. Rich.

Agnes
The Persian. Smith.
Tear. Kinsella.

Agony
The Chrysanthemum Show. Day-Lewis.
The Common Lot. Coats.
The Destiny of Nations. Coleridge.
Don Juan. Byron.
Doors of the Temple. Huxley.
The Factory Hands. Chimedza.
Golgotha. Wheelock.
Hut Near Desolated Pines. Campbell.
It Is Finished. Bonar.
Last Speech to the Court. Vanzetti.
The Malice of Innocence. Levertov.
Nor Will These Tears Be the Last. Goethe.
The Old Ghost. Beddoes.
On the Struma Massacre. Gustafson.
Open House. Roethke.
Open Letter. Dodson.
Poem by the Charles River. Blaser.
The Sea-Mew. Browning.
Song: "Dark was de night an' col' was de groun'." Anonymous.
Suspense. Lawrence.
The Tunnel. Crane.
A Vision. Dearmer.

Agree (able) (d) (ment)
Booker T. and W. E. B. Randall.
Bucolic. Merwin.
Carry Her over the Water. Auden.
Dreaming in the Shanghai Restaurant. Enright.
The Husband's Message. Anonymous.
Life. Kreymborg.
Maine Sea Gulls. Hoban.
On Giles and Joan. Jonson
The Peace of the Roses. Philipps.
Reason. Tatham.
Roses. Anonymous.
Sleet Storm on the Merritt Parkway. Bly.
To couple is a custom. Anonymous.
To Cypassis, Corinna's Maid. Ovid (Publius Ovidius Naso).

Ahab
Memories of Aunt Maria-Martha (parody). Zaranka.

Ahead
After Working. Bly.
Charioteer. Bynner.
The Message. Meleager.
Something for Supper. Arnett.

Aid
Angels We Have Heard on High. Anonymous.
Dedication of the Chronicles of England and France. Fabyan.
The Heavenly Pilot. Cormac Mac Cuilenan.
Idea. Drayton.

Lines Written on a Window-
Shutter at Weston.
Cowper.
Psalm XLIII. Sidney.
The Song of the Four Winds.
Peacock.
Testing, Testing. Dillon.
That There Are Powers above
Us I Admit. Clough.
To a Lady Holding the Floor.
Weston.
Womankind. Massey.

Ail (eth) (ment) (s)
The Ghaists: A Kirk-Yard
Eclogue. Fergusson.
The Matron of Jedborough
and Her Husband (excerpt).
Wordsworth.
A! My Herte, A! What Aileth
The. Wyatt.
No Road. Larkin.

Aim (s)
And Yet. Molodovsky.
The Guard at the Binh Thuy
Bridge. Balaban.
On Teaching David to Shoot.
McDonald.
The Past Is Dark with Sin
and Shame. Higginson.
Plot Improbable, Character
Unsympathetic. Olson.
Seed Leaves. Wilbur.
Upon the Snail. Bunyan.

Aimless
The Night Moths.
Markham.

Air
Actual Vision of Morning's
Extrusion. Dugan.
The Aftermath. Williams.
Air. Denby.
All That Was Mortal.
Teasdale.
America for Me. Van Dyke.
The Amputee Soldier.
Dacey.
Angel Eye of Memory.
Brinnin.
The Angels for the Nativity of
Our Lord. Drummond.
Ants. Aal.
Ants. Hyde.
Apollo 113. Finne.
April. Belleau.
"...As When Emotion Too Far
Exceeds its Cause"–
Elizabeth Bishop. Oden.
At the Un-National
Monument along the
Canadian Border. Stafford.
The Autumn Leaves.
Anonymous.
The Autumnal Moon.
Thomson.
The Bat. Pitter.
The Battle of Aughrim:
Rapparees. Murphy.
The Beak. Smither.
The Begetting of Cain.
Plutzik.
Beginning by Example.
Gilbert.
The Biglow Papers. Lowell.
Blue Flag. Donnelly.
"Blue Is the Hero...
Berkson.
Blue Juniata: The Streets of
Air. Cowley.
Breathless. Noyce.
The Burial. Davis.
Butterfly. Lawrence.
Caelica, LVII. Greville.

Canto XXIX. Pound.
Castles in the Air.
Ballantine.
Celandine. Thomas.
Cerne Abbas. Summers.
Chez Jane. O'Hara.
A Child. Gilder.
Chronicle. Dorn.
The Clavichord. Sarton.
Clonfeacle. Muldoon.
The Coming of Night.
Wade.
Conservancies. Miles.
The Constant One. Dillon.
The Contented Bachelor.
Kendall.
Cut It Down. Coleridge.
Dark Romance. Corpi.
Death of King George V.
Betjeman.
Desert in the Sea. Swann.
The Deserted House.
Coleridge.
Diana. Constable.
Discomfort in High Places.
Tremayne.
Doctrinal Point. Empson.
Epitaph on the Fart in the
Parliament House.
Hoskyns.
Epitaph: "Sanquhar, whom
this earth could scarce
contain." Drummond.
Epitaphs of the War.
Kipling.
Even There. Lifshin.
The Excursion. Wordsworth.
Ezek'l Saw de Wheel
(excerpt). *Anonymous.*
Father's Voice. Stafford.
A Fete. Eigner.
Field Sports. Pope.
Fields Where We Slept.
Rukeyser.
Fisherman. Sitwell.
Flute Notes from a Reedy
Pond. Plath.
For Adolf Eichmann. Levi.
Fr Anselm Williams and Br
Leander Neville Hanged by
Lutheran... Smither.
From a Letter. Keats.
From Summer Hours.
Samain.
A Front. Jarrell.
Geography. Dransfield.
The Ghost of the Cargo Boat.
Neruda.
The Goldfish Wife.
Hochman.
Goodbye to Serpents.
Dickey.
The Great Scarf of Birds.
Updike.
Green Frog at Roadside,
Wisconsin. Schevill.
The Hermit. Halpern.
Hiawatha. Sandy.
High Island. Murphy.
High Windows. Larkin.
Homing. Bowman.
I Hear America Griping.
Bishop.
I'm Glad the Sky Is Painted
Blue. *Anonymous.*
I Think Continually of Those
Who Were Truly Great.
Spender.
I Want to Tell You.
Hochman.
I Will Go into the Ghetto.
Reznikoff.

Ibycus. Heath-Stubbs.
Idiom of the Hero. Stevens.
In the Backs. Cornford.
In the Twilight (excerpt).
O'Donnell.
Independence Day. Berry.
The Indian Queen: Song of
Aerial Spirits. Dryden.
Instructions for a Park.
Walker.
Jacob Tonson, His Publisher.
Dryden.
John Coil. *Anonymous.*
The Kitchen Chimney.
Frost.
Korf's Enchantment.
Morgenstern.
The Ladder. Baro.
Lady Lazarus. Plath.
Lamentations. Gluck.
Late. Bogan.
A Leg in a Plaster Cast.
Rukeyser.
Letter from Germany.
Grosholz.
Letters from Kazuko (Kyoto,
Japan–Summer 1980).
Lau.
Life Is Motion. Stevens.
Listen. Hagedorn.
A Litany in Time of Plague.
Nashe [(or Nash)] Thomas.
Loneliness. Young.
Love's Justification.
Michelangelo.
Lyric. Hewitt.
The Man of Kerioth (excerpt).
Norwood.
Mediterranean. Whitman.
Melodic Trains. Ashbery.
Mid-August at Sourdough
Mountain Lookout.
Snyder.
A Modern Ballad. Emerson.
Monologue of a Deaf Man.
Wright.
Morels. Smith.
Mother. Heaney.
My Olson Elegy. Feldman.
N. Seidman.
The Native. Merwin.
The Never Again.
Dobzynski.
New Strain. Starbuck.
No One Ever Walking This
Our Only Earth.
Rukeyser.
The Ocotillo in Bloom.
Guild.
Oenone. Tennyson.
The Old Lady under the
Freeway. O Hehir.
On a Morning Full of Sun.
Appleman.
On My Own. Levine.
On the Inconstancy of
Women: From the Latin of
Catullus. Lamb.
One A. M. Kennedy.
Only One Life. Bowman.
Orion. Horne.
The Oxford Girl (Expert
Town). *Anonymous.*
Paradise Lost. Milton.
The Party. Avison.
The Patient Is Rallying.
Kees.
Paul Veronese. Ferguson.
Pigeons. Kell.
The Pike. Bruce.
The Plea of the Midsummer
Fairies. Hood.

Poem. Towle.
Poem ("Woke This A.M.").
Brodey.
Praise of God. *Anonymous.*
The Praise of Industry.
Thomson.
The Precision. Winters.
Professional Amnesia.
Moure.
Proud Songsters. Hardy.
Ramble of the Gods through
Birmingham (excerpt).
Bisset.
Reality Is an Activity of the
Most August Imagination.
Stevens.
The Revolt of Islam.
Shelley.
The Rio Grande. Sitwell.
Roman Fountain. Bogan.
Rose. Thompson.
Sea Burial from the Cruiser
"Reve." Eberhart.
The Seasons. Thomson.
Shepherd and the Hawk.
Hart-Smith.
Signature. Livesay.
Signpost. Jeffers.
Signs. Schnackenberg.
The Small Towns of Ireland.
Betjeman.
The Snail. Lovelace.
Song for Ireland. Colclough.
Song My. Griffin.
The Song of a Heathen.
Gilder.
Song: "She sat and sang
alway." Rossetti.
Sonnet: "There is no God, as
I was taught in youth."
Masefield.
Sonnets, XX: "Now stands
our love on that still verge
of day." Agee.
South Country. Slessor.
Spring Cleaning. George.
Spring (excerpt). Gisborne.
Sweets That Die. Mitchell.
There Pipes the Wood-Lark.
Gray.
They Say the Butterfly Is the
Hardest Stroke. Durcan.
Thirteen, Full of Life.
Everett.
The Tourist and the Town.
Rich.
Tramp! Tramp! Tramp!
Root.
Transit. Wilbur.
Two Scenes. Ashbery.
Unclench Yourself. Piercy.
Veni Coronaberis. Hill.
Venice. Longfellow.
The Voyage. Shapiro.
The Voyage of Life.
Bernstein.
Vuillard: "The Mother and
Sister of the Artist."
Snodgrass.
Water and Air. Browning.
We Manage Most When We
Manage Small. Gregg.
What a Proud Dreamhorse.
Cummings.
What Is't to Us? Churchill.
What's in There?
Anonymous.
Where the Dropwort Springs
up Lithe and Tall.
Donaghy.
White Attic. Elmslie.

A Wondrous Show.
Thomson.
Written in a Copy of Swift's
Poems, for Wayne Burns.
Wright.
Air Canada
Love. Berrigan.
Air condition
The Dazzling Day.
MacAdams.
I Hear America Griping.
Bishop.
That the Neighborhood Might
Be Covered. Eigner.
Airfield
A Dimpled Cloud. Seidel.
Airman
Clocks. Sandburg.
Soldier Brave, Sailor True.
Anonymous.
Airplane (s)
The Last Warmth of Arnold.
Corso.
Threnody. Farrar.
Airy
Coming Awake. Lawrence.
Gentle Name. Robinson.
The Little Red Sled. Bush.
Alabama
The Alabama. *Anonymous.*
First Monday Scottsboro
Alabama. Weatherly.
A Missouri Maiden's Farewell
to Alabama. "Twain.
Oh, Susanna. *Anonymous.*
Roll, Alabama, Roll.
Anonymous.
The Titanic (B vers.).
Anonymous.
Uncle Ambrose. Still.
Walky-Talky Jenny (with
music). *Anonymous.*
With All Deliberate Speed.
Lee.
Alabastar
Snow. *Anonymous.*
Aladdin
Dance of the Abakweta.
Danner.
Hawthorne. Longfellow.
Alamo
Lament for the Alamo.
Guiterman.
The Men of the Alamo.
Roche.
Alarm-clock
Impressions, Number III.
Cummings.
On Certain Mornings
Everything Is Sensual.
Jauss.
Alarm (s)
In Conjunction. Madge.
Poem: "As rock to sun or
storm." Sheridan.
Squirrel in Sunshine.
Cowper.
Stormy Weather, Boys.
Anonymous.
When Will He Come?
Anonymous.
Albert Hall
The Dream. *Anonymous.*
A Poem about Poems about
Vietnam. Stallworthy.
Albion
A Little Boy Lost. Blake.
The Progress of Poesy.
Gray.
The Third Eclogue.
Drayton.

Visions of the Daughters of
Albion. Blake.
Alcohol
Lord Alcohol. Beddoes.
Alcove (s)
Love in a Life. Browning.
The Women of Rubens.
Szymborska.
Ale
Ad Ministram. Thackeray.
The Birth of the Squire.
Gay.
Bring Us in Good Ale.
Anonymous.
Epigram: "O mortal man, that
lives by bread." Ibbetson.
Epistle to John Guthrie.
Smith.
Gammer Gurton's Needle:
Back and Side, Go Bare.
Stevenson.
Hakluyt Unpurchased.
McDuffee.
I Am Forsaken. *Anonymous.*
In Praise of Ale. Bonham.
King Lot's Envoys. Allison.
Lustily, Lustily. *Anonymous.*
Mannerly Margery Milk and
Ale. Skelton.
The Merry Hoastess.
Anonymous.
The Muse. Davies.
O Thou That Sleep'st.
Davenant.
On a Quaker's Tankard.
Landor.
On Looking at Stubbs's
Anatomy of the Horse.
Lucie-Smith.
The Sea-Captain.
Anonymous.
Under Milk Wood (excerpt).
Thomas.
A Zimmershire Lad.
Zimmer.
Alexander
Forgiven. Milne.
The Knightly Code.
Deschamps.
Letter to Robert Fergusson.
Scott.
Alexandria
The Lost, Dancing. Field.
One of the Jews. Cavafy.
To Theon from His Son
Theon. Trypanis.
Alexis
Hexametra Alexis in Laudem
Rosamundi. Greene.
On Her Loving Two Equally.
Behn.
Alfonso
Don Juan. Byron.
In Honor of St. Alphonsus
Rodriguez. Hopkins.
Algiers
A Dutch Picture.
Longfellow.
Alibi
Small Dark Song. Dacey.
Alice
Buckingham Palace. Milne.
In an Iridescent Time.
Stone.
Shameful Death. Morris.
This Alice. Morris.
Tom Dixon. *Anonymous.*
Wild Thyme. Farjeon.
Alien
Abraham. Mitchell.
At the Battery Sea-Wall.
Laube.

Columbus (excerpt).
Tennyson.
Cradle-Song at Twilight.
Meynell.
Departure. Green.
Don Giovanni on His Way to
Hell. Gilbert.
Durer: Innsbruck, 1495.
Malley.
Encouragement to Exile.
Petronius.
Epigrams. Theocritus.
The Gardens of Proserpine.
Cassity.
Goldfish. Nemerov.
How. Sutzkever.
Lifelines. Ewart.
Long Roads. Matusovsky.
Naming. Stroud.
November Sun. Daryush.
Revelation. Soutar.
Rome Remember. Keyes.
Sonnet: "The crumbled rock
of London is dripping
under." Fuller.
To a Roman. Squire.
Winter Juniper. Langland.
Alienated
Abraham:. Schwartz.
Alike
Betwixt and Between.
Lofting.
Divina Commedia. Dante
Alighieri.
The Good-Morrow. Donne.
Limerick: "In the wax works
of Nature they strike."
Euwer.
To Chloe, Who Wished
Herself Young Enough For
Me. Cartwright.
The Unity of God.
Panatattu.
Alive
Apollo. Wright.
April Showers. Stephens.
Art McCooey. Kavanagh.
Ask No Return. Gregory.
An Autumn Walk. Bynner.
The Aztec City. Ware.
Benediction. Kaufman.
Campaign Promise. Taylor.
Carol: "Mary laid her Child
among." Nicholson.
Chevaliers de la Table Ronde.
Anonymous.
Cockles and Mussels.
Anonymous.
The Day the T.V. Broke.
Jonas.
Days in White. Bachmann.
The Dead. Williams.
Dead Girl. Hajnal.
The Delight Song of Tsoai-
Talee. Momaday.
Drowning with Others.
Dickey.
Ennui. Viereck.
Epigram on Prince Frederick.
Anonymous.
An Epitaph upon Mr. Ashton
a Conformable Citizen.
Crashaw.
Erotica. Farkas.
Final Curtain (parody).
Woddis.
Fishing for Sticklebacks, with
Rod and Line. Burnand.
For Great Grandmother and
Her Settlement House.
Darr.

From a Printed Bill, Fixed in
the Beak of One in a
Group... *Anonymous.*
From Scars Where Kestrels
Hover. Auden.
Great Things Have Happened.
Nowlan.
Hai. Perkoff.
Homage to John Millington
Synge. O Direain.
Homage to Mistress
Bradstreet. Berryman.
The Hotel. Monroe.
Household Remedies.
Anonymous.
I See My Plaint. Harington.
If Everything Happens That
Can't Be Done.
Cummings.
The Invitation. Buchan.
Jesse James. *Anonymous.*
Jig Tune: Not for Love.
McGrath.
Julian Barely Misses Zimmer's
Brains. Zimmer.
Letter. Bergman.
Letter to a Teacher of
English. Hillyer.
Life is Struggle. Clough.
Loveliness. Conkling.
Madrigal: "In nets of golden
wire." Morley.
Magic Word. Jackson.
Melancholia. Bly.
The Men of the Alamo.
Roche.
Missing. Auden.
Molly Malone. *Anonymous.*
No, I Am Not as Others Are.
Villon.
Noni Daylight Remembers the
Future. Harjo.
North Clark Street.
Thompson.
November. Cary.
Old Apple Trees. Snodgrass.
Poem for My Family: Hazel
Griffin and Victor
Hernandez Cruz. Jordan.
A Poor Relation. McGaffin.
Prelude to Memorial Song.
George.
Prescience. Hayes.
The Search Party.
Matthews.
Semen. Barks.
The Signature of All Things.
Rexroth.
Silence Concerning an Ancient
Stone. Castellános.
Song: "In mine own
monument I lie."
Lovelace.
Song of the Round Man.
Palmer.
Stella's Birthday. Swift.
The Task. Pitter.
The Tempest. Shakespeare.
Thank God for Life.
Anonymous.
To a Portrait of Lermontov.
Aliger.
To wish and want and not
obtain. Wyatt.
Today. Morgan.
The Turning. Levine.
Upon Master Edmund
Spenser, the Famous Poet.
Beaumont.
A Vagrant. Karlfeldt.
Vastness. Tennyson.
War Bride. Worth.

Workmen. Morris.

All
After All. Hayes.
All. Slonimski.
All of Her. Albert.
Another Grace for a Child.
    Herrick.
As for Poets. Snyder.
The Bear Went over the
    Mountain. *Anonymous.*
The Best for Us. Burnett.
Blue Black. Modisane.
The Building of the Ship.
    Longfellow.
C Is for Charms. Farjeon.
The Character of a Happy
    Life. Wotton.
Christ Alone. Monod.
Companions, a Tale of a
    Grandfather... Calverley.
The Counsels of O'Riordan,
    the Rann Maker.
    O'Bolger.
Cradle Song. MacNeice.
Crimes of Passion. Stokes.
Death. Jeffrey.
Dedication. Chamberlayne.
Discovery of This Time.
    MacLeish.
Double-Header. Stone.
Dr. Joseph Goebbels.
    Snodgrass.
Epigram: "Boys' cocks,
    Diodore." Strato.
An Epitaph of Maister Win
    Drowned in the Sea.
    Turberville.
An Essay on Criticism.
    Pope.
For All That Ever Has Been
    Ours. Landau.
Good Morning. Van Doren.
Happy He. *Anonymous.*
The Hazard of Loving the
    Creatures. Watts.
How Stands the Glass
    Around? Wolfe.
A Hymn to My God in a
    Night of My Late Sicknesse.
    Wotton.
I Tell of Another Young
    Death. Tiempo.
Illumination and Ecstasy.
    Baba Kuhi of Shiraz.
The Invitation. Herbert.
Jesus, My Saviour, Look on
    Me! MacDuff.
The Jewish Woman.
    Kolmar.
Kept for Jesus. Cherry.
The Last Years. Davies.
The Leaf. Williams.
Letter. Strand.
The Little Gentleman.
    Anonymous.
Little Musgrave and Lady
    Barnard (B version).
    Anonymous.
The Lookers-On. Heywood.
Love's Votary. Simcox.
Love Who Will, for I'll Love
    None. Browne.
Lying in the Grass. Gosse.
Manners. Nemerov.
Marlborough (excerpt).
    Sorley.
The Mother. Brooks.
Mother Goose Up-to-Date.
    Untermeyer.
My Faith. Acharya.
My Master Was So Very
    Poor. Lee.

The Naming of the Beasts.
    Sparshott.
No Love, to Love of Man and
    Wife. Eedes.
Nocturne. Murphy.
O Jesus! When I Think of
    Thee. Bethune.
O Ship of State. Longfellow.
Of Man and Wife. Eedes.
The Old Woman Who Bought
    a Pig. *Anonymous.*
Oxford Commination. Leary.
Platform Goodbye.
    Mallalieu.
Poem: "What's the balm."
    Dugan.
The Poet Questions Peace.
    Chapman.
The Popish Plot. Dryden.
Preaching Blues. Johnson.
The Quidditie. Herbert.
Rejoice. Miller.
Robert Lowell Is Dead.
    Gray.
A Robin. De la Mare.
Sh-Ta-Ra-Dah-Dey (Irish
    Lullaby). (with music).
    Anonymous.
Song of the Universal.
    Whitman.
Song Under Shadow. Benet.
Sonnets, XXXI: "Thy bosom
    is endeared with all hearts."
    Shakespeare.
Sonnets, CIX: "O, never say
    that I was false of heart."
    Shakespeare.
Stanky. Berkson.
Take Your Accusation Back!
    Kittaararter.
Thanksgiving. Sangster.
That's Jesus. Renfrow.
Those Who Come What Will
    They Say of Us. Knoepfle.
Thou Long Disowned,
    Reviled, Oppressed.
    Scudder.
The Thunderer. McGinley.
To Henry Vaughan. Smith.
Under the Old Elm. Lowell.
W. C. W. Ray.
Went up a year this evening!
    Dickinson.
Where Lies the Land?
    Clough.
Which Is the Bow?
    Anonymous.

All Saints'
All Saints'. Yates.
Poet's Wish. Larbaud.

Allah
Hush, Honey. Saunders.
Love Charm. *Anonymous.*
Theme One: The Variations.
    Wilson.

Allegiance
The Lovers Go Fly a Kite.
    Snodgrass.
Wapentake. Longfellow

Allegory
Autobiographies. Mahon.
Doves. Neugroschel.

Allelulia
The Akathistos Hymn.
    Anonymous.
As with Gladness Men of Old.
    Dix.
Praise Now Your God.
    Brucker.
Rejoice, Let Alleluias Ring.
    Schaefer.

Alley
The Ballad of Sally in our
    Alley. Carey.
For Sammy Younge. Cobb.
Sally in Our Alley. Carey.

Allies
The Fairies Are Dancing All
    over the World. Rumaker.
Is It Nothing to You?
    Kindig.
On Mrs. W–. Bentley.
On your dazzling throne,
    Aphrodite. Sappho.

Alligator
To a Fly, Taken out of a
    Bowl of Punch. Wolcot.

Allow (ed) (s)
The Death Sentence. Smith.
Love and Life. Rochester.
Play. Ammons.

Allures
Asian Desert. Wellesley.
Husbands and Wives.
    Anonymous.

Almighty
Athalie: Chorus (excerpt).
    Racine.
A Song in Passing. Winters.

Almond (s)
Angels. Burns.
Edward Lear in February.
    Middleton.
When Almonds Bloom.
    Shinn.

Alms
The Beggar to Mab, the Fairie
    Queen. Herrick.

Alone
Adare (excerpt). O'Donnell.
Advice to a Blue-Bird.
    Bodenheim.
After the Hunt. Liliencron.
After the Plague.
    Anonymous.
The Aged Lover Discourses in
    the Flat Style.
    Cunningham.
Alexandria. Durrell.
All Alone in My Little Cell.
    Anonymous.
All Saint's Day (excerpt).
    Guidacci.
Alone. Farrar.
Alone. Manger.
Alone. Scovell.
Alone (fragment). Sappho.
Alone up Here on the
    Mountain. *Anonymous.*
Anecdote of 2 A.M. Wain.
Anguish. Mallarme.
Answering a Letter from a
    Younger Poet. Ghiselin.
Anticipation of Sharks.
    Wakoski.
An Artist. Jeffers.
The Ash Grove. *Anonymous.*
At a Country Dance in
    Provence. Monro.
At a Solemn Musick.
    Schwartz.
The Attic. Coulette.
A Ballad for Katharine of
    Aragon. Causley.
Ballad of the Mouse.
    Wallace.
The Beast. Roethke.
The Beautiful Toilet.
    Anonymous.
Behaviour of Fish in an
    Egyptian Tea Garden.
    Douglas.
Beside the Sea. Johnston.

Bird Riddle: "One day I went
    down in the golden harvest
    field." *Anonymous.*
The Blackbird by Belfast
    Lough. *Anonymous.*
Boastful Husbandman.
    Anonymous.
The Burial of the Bachelor
    (parody). *Anonymous.*
By Moonlight. *Anonymous.*
The Call. Supervielle.
A Call to Action. Callinus.
Captive. Hirshbein.
Carol of the Numbers.
    Anonymous.
Cats. Chute.
The Cell of Himself.
    Freeman.
The Changing Wind. Orde.
Come Forth, Come Forth!
    Wilson.
Come Laugh with Me.
    Anonymous.
Come, Let Us Sing.
    Anonymous.
Constant Defender. Tate.
The Cowboy's Lament; or,
    The Streets of Laredo (A
    vers.). *Anonymous.*
Cupid's Revenge: Lovers,
    Rejoice! Fletcher.
The Dark Memory.
    Wheelock.
Darling, I won't be your hot
    love. Sulpicia.
Day after Day. Tagore.
Declaration at Forty. Crews.
Departed–to the Judgment.
    Dickinson.
Dick & Jane. Kroll.
The Dilly Song. *Anonymous.*
Dirge: "If thou wilt ease thy
    heart." Beddoes.
Dirge of the Lone Woman.
    Colum.
Dispatch Number Sixteen.
    Fetherling.
Don't Sing Love Songs.
    Anonymous.
East Bronx. Ignatow.
Edgar's Story. Kennedy.
Elegy Written on a
    Frontporch. Shapiro.
L'Envoi. Cather.
Epitaph for a Negro Woman.
    Dodson.
Epitaph on a Party Girl.
    Usborne.
Epitaph on Erotion. Hunt.
Epitaph on Himself.
    Coleridge.
Epitaph: Snake River.
    Henson.
Epitaphs of the War,
    1914-1918. Kipling.
The Eternal. Tegner.
The Evening Darkens Over.
    Bridges.
An Evening Walk. Stafford.
Exile in Nigeria. Mphahlele.
The Family of Eight. Reisen.
A Farewell. De Vere.
The Feast of the Snow.
    Chesterton.
Finger Dance. *Anonymous.*
The Food Drops Off a Fork.
    Silverton.
For Them All. Wheelock.
Fortune's Wheel. De Tabley.
The Fountains. Rodgers.
La Fraisne. Pound.
From a Letter. Keats.

The Funeral of Time. Hirst
Gabriel John. *Anonymous.*
The Game of Life. Saxe.
Glenpool. West.
God Set Us Here. de Sille.
Gorbo and Batte. Drayton.
The Gramophone. Reaney.
Growing Old. Wilcox.
Hannah Bantry. *Anonymous.*
Heart of Light. Campbell.
Here Am I, Little Jumping
  Joan. Mother Goose.
Home, Sweet Home.
  Bunner.
Hopi Woman. Spencer.
Horses Graze. Brooks.
A House by the Tracks.
  Etter.
I am a widow, robed in black,
  alone. Pisan.
I Can Fly. Holman.
I Hear an Army. Joyce.
I Saw as a Child. Mandela.
I Set Aside. Webster.
Idylls. Theocritus.
Il Piccolo Rifiuto.
  MacNeice.
The Immortal Part.
  Housman.
In and Out. Sissman.
In the Gloaming. Calverley.
In the Heat of the Morning.
  Szumigalski.
Indian Rock, Bainbridge
  Island, Washington.
  Niatum.
Inspiration. Thoreau.
Interlude. Wilcox.
It's a Gay Old World.
  Anonymous.
Jesus Reassures His Mother.
  Anonymous.
John's Song. Aiken.
Jumping Joan. *Anonymous.*
Kimono. Graham.
Kissing. Herbert of
  Cherbury
Knapweed. Benson.
Langaig. Hugo.
The Lay of the Last Minstrel.
  Scott.
The Lay of the Vigilantes.
  Anonymous.
The Libertine. MacNeice.
Life. Reed.
Little Black Man with a Rose
  in His Hat. Wurdemann.
The Little Lost Child.
  Marks.
Little Mary Cassidy. Fahy.
The Living God. Gilman.
Lonely Night. Sappho.
Long Are the Hours the Sun
  Is Above. Bridges.
Love. Jammes.
Love Comes Quietly.
  Creeley.
Love Redeemed.
  Baylebridge.
A Lover's Lament.
  Anonymous.
Lullaby. Sitwell.
LXXII A Sonnet for Dick
  Gallup. Berrigan.
Marvel of Marvels. Rossetti.
Mary and Gabriel. Brooke.
The Mask and the Poem.
  Pizarnik.
Me Alone. Weeden.
Mercedes, Her Aloneness.
  Inez.

The Mill-stream, Now that
  Noises Cease. Housman.
Mimma Bella. Lee-
  Hamilton.
Mist. Young.
Modern Love, XXVIII.
  Meredith.
Monna Innominata.
  Rossetti.
The Moon. Creeley.
A Morning. Strand.
My Love When This Is Past.
  Stephany.
My Prayer. Bonar.
The Need of the Hour.
  Markham.
New Jail. *Anonymous*
A Night in Lesbos. Horton
The Night Journey. Brooke.
The Night Wind. Bronte.
Ninety. Fullerton.
Not a Sou Had He Got
  (parody). Barham.
November Garden. Driscoll.
O Heaven Indulge. Tilden.
The Old Cove. Brownell.
Old Ego Song. Minczeski.
The Old Pastor. Tabb.
On a Ledge. Bell.
On a Sunday. Reznikoff.
On Meeting Li Kuei-Nien
  Down the River. Tu Fu.
Our Father. Swartz.
Overtones. Percy.
Owls. Snodgrass.
A Panegyric on Nelly
  (excerpt). Rochester.
Paradigm. Deutsch.
The Pass. Logan.
Peregrine Prykke's Pilgrimage
  (parody). James.
The Pines and the Sea.
  Cranch
Plain. Williams.
Poem: "This life like no
  other." Orr.
The Poet at Seven.
  Rimbaud.
The Poet's Secret. Stoddard
Political Greatness. Shelley.
Portrait of the Poet as
  Landscape. Klein.
The Postures of Love.
  Comfort.
The Prairies. Bryant.
A Prayer for Faith.
  Sangster.
Prince Sumiya. *Anonymous.*
Protestation. Bertrand.
Puer Ex Jersey. *Anonymous.*
The Quiet Flower. Johnson.
Reality. De Vere.
The Reason for Poetry.
  Morejo.
Reasons to Go Home.
  Forker.
The Reconciliation.
  MacLeish.
Red Jack. Durack.
Remonstrance. Lanier.
Riddle: "As I was walking in
  a field of wheat."
  Anonymous.
Romeo and Juliet.
  Shakespeare.
The Room. Nabokov.
Sabbath. De Haan.
Saul. Heavysege.
School Days. Stafford.
Sea Bells. Eberhart.
The Sea-Captain.
  Anonymous.

Seaward Bound. Brown.
The Secret Song. Brown.
Separation. Dickinson.
Sex without Love. Olds.
Shadow and Shade. Tate.
The Shooting. Tohe.
Silence. Hageman.
The Silver Moon. Sappho.
Six-Forty-Two Farm
  Commune Struggle Poem.
  Leifer.
Six Winter Privacy Poems.
  Bly.
Sohrab and Rustum. Arnold.
Solitary. Olds.
Solitary Travel. MacNeice.
Song: "She spoke to me gently
  with words of sweet
  meaning." MacDonogh.
Song: "There is no joy in
  water apart from the sun."
  Currey.
Sonnet: "Because my grief
  seems quiet and apart."
  Nathan.
Sonnets. Hillyer.
Sorrow. Chu Shu-chen.
Speeches at the Barriers
  (excerpt). Howe.
The Sphinx Speaks. Saltus.
Spring Offensive, 1941.
  Biggs.
Star Journey. Madgett.
Success. Brooke.
The Suire. Irwin.
Sunday Evenings. Hollander.
Sweet William's Ghost.
  Anonymous.
Taking a Walk with You.
  Koch.
Talking Designs. Bahe.
The Terror of Death. Keats.
Testament. Clifton.
Thalatta. Allen.
There Was a Brisk Girle.
  Anonymous.
They Closed Her Eyes.
  Becquer.
Things of Late. Phillips.
Thoughts in the Gulf Stream.
  Morley.
The Three Hills. Squire.
Thyrsis, Sleep'st Thou?
  Anonymous.
To a Waterfowl. Bryant.
To Be Sung. Viereck.
To His Mistress. Sheffield.
To Mary: It Is the Evening
  Hour. Clare.
To Time. "W.
Tonight I've Watched.
  Sappho.
Toro. Merwin.
Triolet against Sisters.
  McGinley.
True Riches. Watts.
Two Prayers. Adawiyya.
  Rabi'a al-.
Two Presentations. Duncan.
Ulster. Kipling.
Undersea Fever. Cole.
Valediction. Raab.
The Vision. Traherne.
Waking Alone. *Anonymous.*
Walking at Night. Hare.
The Warm of Heart Shall
  Never Lack a Fire.
  Coatsworth.
Washington's Prayer for the
  Nation. Washington.
Watching. Judson

What Grandma Knew.
  Field.
Wheel Turning on the Hub of
  the Sun. Root.
When I Was Lost. Aldis.
Where His Lady Keeps His
  Heart. "W.
Whose Voice. Bush.
Wide Open Are Thy Hands.
  Bernard of Clairvaux.
The Wife. Dinnies
The Willows by the Water
  Side. *Anonymous.*
The Winners. Kipling.
Winter-Solitude. Lampman.
Wisdom. Rossetti.
The Wolves. Tate.
X-Ray. Speyer.
You Are the Brave.
  Patterson.
You Will Know When You
  Get There. Curnow.
Youth. Rittenhouse.

Aloof
And What Is Love?
  Misunderstanding, Pain.
  Cunningham.
Iceland First Seen. Morris.
Letter. Empson.
The Old Angler. De La
  Mare.
Venice. Symons.

Alphabet
Holy Order. Boothroyd.
Lucky. Song.
Page. McPherson.
Poet. Pastan.
Reservation Special.
  Blockcolski.
Signatures. Stevenson.
Student. Miles.

Alps
Alexandria. Durrell.
But Can See Better There,
  and Laughing There.
  Brooks.
Connoisseur of Chaos.
  Stevens.
An Essay on Criticism.
  Pope.
De Gustibus. Hankin.
Nocturne of the Self-Evident
  Presence. MacGreevy.
On the Fly-Leaf of Pound's
  Cantos. Bunting.
Perhaps. Spender.

Altar (s)
The Altar. Herbert.
Ex Nihilo. Gascoyne.
Faith Healer Come to Rabun
  County. Bottoms.
The Fall of Hyperion.
  Keats.
Four Things. *Anonymous.*
Lines for the Ancient Scribes.
  Shapiro.
Lost in Yucatan. McKeown.
New Hampshire Farm
  Woman. Graham.
New Year's Eve. Housman.
Nubia. Taylor.
O Martyred Spirit.
  Santayana.
Palestine. Whittier.
The Poem Unwritten.
  Levertov.
Roslin and Hawthornden.
  Van Dyke.
Rufus Mitchell's Confession.
  Anonymous.
The Sacrifice to Apollo.
  Drayton.

The Sea Cathedral. Pratt.
Shechem. Shevin.
The Song of the Pilgrims.
  Brooke.
Thy Name We Bless and
  Magnify. Power.
A Year of Sorrow. De Vere.
Alter
Ad Finem. Wilcox.
The Ass. Allan.
The Careless Good Fellow
  Written March 9, 1680.
  Oldham.
Children's Song. Ford.
Flos Lunae. Dowson.
The Room. Jennings.
Alter ego
A Child's Visit to the Biology
  Lab. Spivack.
Alternative
Autumn Sequel, IV.
  MacNeice.
Altitude
Alpine View. Cane.
Kite. Jensen.
Purgatorio. Crane.
Aluminum
The Alchemist. Church.
In Galleries. Jarrell.
Always
The Creditor. MacNeice.
Eche Man Me Telleth I
  Chaunge Moost My Devise.
  Wyatt.
Emeritus, n. Coulette.
The Evangelist. Sinclair.
The First Goodbye Letter.
  Simmons.
New Jail. *Anonymous*
No Laws. Allwood.
Point Grey. Hine.
Southward Sidonian Hanno.
  Allen.
We Long to See Jesus.
  Hamilton.
Amateurs
The Old Trouper. Marquis.
Amaze (d)
The Beating. Hummer.
Burning Bush. Feinstein.
Clear Night, Small Fire, No
  Wind. Saner.
Come from Thy Palace.
  Randolph.
I Don't Care. Lenox.
The Invention of Zero.
  Urdang.
Modern Love, XXXVI.
  Meredith.
On This Day. Goffstein.
An Orchard at Avignon.
  Robinson.
Summer Days. Daniells.
The Wind. Davies.
Amazon (s)
The Faerie Queene. Spenser.
Leda and Her Swan.
  Broumas.
Young Girl. Huch.
Amber
Correspondences.
  Baudelaire.
Discovery. Flanner.
The Dying Garden.
  Nemerov.
Fickle in the Arms of Spring.
  Fry.
Glass World. Donnelly.
I know a place where summer
  strives. Dickinson.
Lie on the Sand. Campbell.

An Ode on the Birth of Our
  Saviour. Herrick.
Upon Julia's Voice. Herrick.
Ambiguity
And the Bitter Storm
  Augments; the Wild Winds
  Wage. Josselyn.
Construction # 13.
  Sherwin.
Ambition
Achitophel: the Earl of
  Shaftesbury. Dryden.
Epitaphium Vivi Auctoris
  1792. Walpole.
Fable IV: The Eagle, and the
  Assembly of Animals.
  Gay.
Fight with a Water-Spirit.
  Cameron.
A Letter to John Donne.
  Sisson.
Moved by Her Music.
  Gillman.
Regressing. Douskey.
Ambrosia
The Ambrosia of Dionysus
  and Semele. Graves.
Amoretti, XXXIX. Spenser.
Ambulance
A Fence or an Ambulance.
  Malins.
Ambush
Badman of the Guest
  Professor. Reed.
Invocation from a Lawn
  Chair. Irion.
Marcus Antoninus Cui
  Cognomen Erat Aurelius.
  Singer.
The Odyssey. Homer.
Amelia Earhart
25 Spontaneous Lines
  Greeting the World.
  Tyack.
Amen
Carol: "Now is the world
  withdrawn all in silence and
  night." Nemerov.
The Grasshopper's Song.
  Bialik.
He Is Coming, Adzed-Head.
  Anonymous.
Malcolm, a Thousandth
  Poem. Rivers.
Mass of Love. *Anonymous.*
A Solemn Meditation. Pitter.
The Spotted Flycatcher. De
  la Mare.
Amend (ed) (s)
A Consolatory Poem.
  Noyes.
Here Have I Been These One
  and Twenty Years.
  Clough.
A Hundreth Good Poyntes of
  Husbandry. Tusser.
A Midsummer Night's
  Dream. Shakespeare.
New York * December *
  1931. Deutsch.
A Supplement. Tompson.
These Women All. Heath.
A Warning. *Anonymous.*
When Two Suns Do Appear.
  Sidney.
Amenities
Pimville Station. Sepamla.
America (n) (s)
America First! Oldham.
Arson and Cold Lace (or
  How I Yearn to Burn Baby
  Burn). Long.

As Consequent, etc.
  Whitman.
The Battle of Baltimore.
  Anonymous.
The Battle of Manila.
  Hovey.
Black Soul of the Land.
  Jeffers.
Black Trumpeter. Dumas.
Bread Loaf to Omaha,
  Twenty-Eight Hours.
  Gray.
Brown River, Smile.
  Toomer.
Buffalo. Dumas.
Christopher Columbus.
  Adams.
The Cities Are Washed into
  Time. Simon.
Critical Observations.
  MacLeish.
The Cruise of the Fair
  American. *Anonymous.*
Daniel Boone, 1735-1820.
  Benét.
Detroit. Hall.
Down in a Coal Mine.
  Anonymous.
Dykes in the Garden. Barba.
Eisenhower's Visit to Franco,
  1959. Wright.
For My Father. Potts.
Gertrude Stein at Snails Bay.
  Porter.
God Bless America. Berlin.
God Bless America. Fuller.
Going to School in France or
  America. Clark.
I Am an American.
  Lieberman.
Immigrants. Turner.
In a Dream, the Automobile.
  Marcus.
In Goya's Greatest Scenes.
  Ferlinghetti.
Instruction from Bly.
  Macdonald.
Kearsarge and Alabama.
  Anonymous.
Lady. Berrigan.
Let America Be America
  Again. Hughes.
Lincoln. Cheney.
Lincoln. Lowell.
Major Andre. *Anonymous.*
A Man! Scollard.
Memorial Day. Garrison.
The Metamorphosis of Aunt
  Jemima. Childress.
Near Barbizon. Kinnell.
Ode on Science. Sumner.
Ode to Venice. Byron.
The Poem I Am Writing.
  Gold.
Poem: "Look at Me 8th
  Grade." Sanchez.
Poem to a Nigger Cop.
  Hamilton.
The Poet. Whitman.
Prophecy. Verplanck.
Public Journal. McGinley.
R-and-R Centre: An Incident
  from the Vietnam War.
  Enright.
Rhapsody. O'Hara.
Silent in America. Levine.
Snapshots of the Cotton
  South. Davis.
Song of the Truck. Frankel.
Those Rebel Flags. Jewett.
Tribute to America. Shelley.

The Trip to Cambridge.
  Sewall.
The True Knight. Wilcox.
Under Our Own Wings.
  Wong.
Washington. Turner.
When Something Happens.
  Randall, Jr.
Whenever I Say "America."
  Turner.
Amethyst
An Apology for the Revival of
  Christian
  Architecture...(excerpt).
  Hill.
A Dead Calm and Mist.
  Sharp.
I held a jewel in my fingers.
  Dickinson.
Amiss
Are the Sick in Their Beds as
  They Should Be?
  McIntosh.
The Bat. Roethke.
The Profane. Horace.
When All This All Doth Pass
  from Age to Age.
  Greville.
Amity
Les Belles Roses sans Mercie.
  Cripps.
The Men of the Maine.
  Scollard.
Ammunition
Praise the Lord and Pass the
  Ammunition! Loesser.
The School Children. Gluck.
Amnesia
A Right-of-Way: 1865.
  Plomer.
Amnesty
Return to the Valley. Read.
Amor (ous)
He Thinks of His Past
  Greatness... Yeats.
Madam Eglantine. Chaucer.
Mass of Love. *Anonymous.*
On an Engraved Gem of
  Leander. Keats.
Party at Bannon Brook.
  Nowlan.
The Souls of Women at
  Night. Stevens.
Three Epitaphs: For a Virgin
  Lady. Cullen.
When Aurelia First I Courted.
  Anonymous.
A Worm Fed on the Heart of
  Corinth. Rosenberg.
Amplitude
The Coming of Night.
  Wade.
Doubt. Gregh.
Leaves of Grass. Whitman
Amputate
Cutting the Jewish Bride's
  Hair. Whitman.
The One-Legged Man.
  Sassoon.
Amsterdam
A Late Manuscript at the
  Schocken Institute. Preil.
Amulet (s)
Lilith. Fainlight.
The Robin's Egg. Dalton.
Sarah: Cherokee Doctor.
  Rose.
The Warning. Creeley.
Amuse (ment)
Investigation. Vinograd.
The Task. Cowper.

Amusing
Ballade of Middle Age. Lang.
Anacreon
On Tom Moore's Translation of Anacreon. Erskine.
Anagram
Mr. Ward of Anagrams Thus. Ward.
Analogy (ies)
The Chinese Banyan. Meredith.
A Sparrow's Feather. Barker.
Analyst
A Right-of-Way: 1865. Plomer.
Analytics
The Marriage of Heaven and Hell. Blake.
Anarchy
Beyond the Presidency. Gibson.
Columbia. Anonymous.
Prayer. Moss.
The Value of Dentistry. Brown.
Anatomie (s)
Love's Exchange. Donne.
Mary's Ghost. Hood.
Ancestor (s)
The Mountain Sat upon the Plain. Dickinson.
My Aunt. Holmes.
The Poet Imagines His Grandfather's Thoughts on the Day He Died. Lum.
The Prophylactic. Edson.
Silence Concerning an Ancient Stone. Castellanos.
Those Were the Days. Anonymous.
Twilight of the Earth. Russell.
Anchor (age) (ed)
An Airline Breakfast. Matthews.
Arrival and Departure. Eglington.
The Captain. Brainard.
The Captain's Daughter. Fields.
Coming Homeward Out of Spain. Googe.
A Few Lines to Fill up a Vacant Page. Danforth.
Greyport Legend. Harte.
John Winter. Binyon.
The Leaving of Liverpool. Anonymous.
My Soul's Been Anchored in de Lord. Anonymous.
Reclining Figure. Hall.
The Ship. Mifflin.
Snowy Night. Haines.
To Her in Absence. Carew.
A Trip to the Grand Banks. Hanson.
Anchorite
The Muses Elizium. Drayton.
Ancient
Ajax. Sophocles.
August, 1914. Masefield.
Auschwitz from Colombo. Ranasinghe.
The Bard. Blake.
Baseball. Sherman.
Between Rivers and Seas. Henson.
Celestial Evening, October 1967. Olson.

Columbus and the Mayflower. Milnes.
Conversation. More.
Epigram: "Save by the Old Road none attain the new." Patmore.
Epitaph on Pegasus, a Limping Gay. Beccadelli.
Fishermen at Dawn. Meissner.
Flock. Henson.
A Hand of Snapshots (excerpt). MacNeice.
Hebrew Lesson. Brod.
The House Next Door. Dunn.
The House of Colour. Sherman.
I Am Not the Constant Reader. Brownstein.
Language of Ancients. Lenski.
The Last of the Fire Kings. Mahon.
Lords of the Wilderness. Leyden.
My Cousin Agueda. Velarde.
My Father Dreams of Baseball. Lieberman.
Now It Can Be Told. Levine.
Olive Trees. Colum.
On an Air of Rameau. Symons.
One Winter Night in August. Kennedy.
Paphos. Durrell.
Passing Out. Levine.
The Peacock Room. Hayden.
Preludes. Eliot.
The Rose of May. Howitt.
Sir Walter Scott at the Tomb of the Stuarts in St. Peter's. Milnes.
Slowly, Slowly Wisdom Gathers. Van Doren.
A Song of a Young Lady to Her Ancient Lover. Rochester.
The Song of Ancient Ways. Oandasan.
The Song of the Ancient People. Hay.
Sonnet VIII: "I live, I die, I burn myself and drown." Labe.
Sonnet: "Oh! Death will find me, long before I tire." Brooke.
Tea. Struthers.
Toward Climax. Snyder.
Vala; or, The Four Zoas. Blake.
The Web of Eros. Sitwell.
Whose Scene? Stone.
Zeyde. Metz.
Andrew Jackson
The Battle of New Orleans. English.
Jackson at New Orleans. Rice.
Andromeda
Ibant Obscurae. Brown.
Love—bittersweet, irrepressible—. Sappho.
Parallax. Anderson.
Anemone (s)
Christmas Eve. Davidson.
In the Breeze. Pasternak.
Tammuz. Heppenstall.

Angel Gabriel
The Honour of Bristol. Anonymous.
Angel (s)
12 Photographs of Yellowstone. Koertge.
Adam and Eve: The Sickness of Adam. Shapiro.
Adolph Hitler Meditates on the Jewish Problem. Hahn.
The Akedah. Shenhar.
Alexander's Feast or, the Power of Music. Dryden.
Although I put away his life. Dickinson.
And on My Return. Guri.
The Angel. Hayes.
The Angel's Whisper. Lover.
An Angel Unawares. Anonymous.
The Angels for the Nativity of Our Lord. Drummond.
De Angels in Heab'n Gwineter Write My Name. Anonymous.
The Angels of Buena Vista. Whittier.
The Angels' Song. Sears
Annunciation. Maura.
Annunciation Night. Hemenway.
Apocrypha. Moss.
Are They Not All Ministering Spirits? Hawker.
Art. Melville.
The Aspiration. Norris.
Astrophel and Stella, LXI. Sidney.
Autumn Journal. MacNeice.
Back to the Angels. De Bolt.
The Battle of Charleston Harbor. Hayne.
The Blind Man's Regret. Anonymous.
A Box for Tom. Tate.
Bride Song. Rossetti.
Caelica, XLVII. Greville.
Cease, Then, My Tongue! Spenser.
A Child's Christmas Song. Daly.
Christmas Morning. Behn.
A Clever Woman. Coleridge.
Composition in Late Spring. Layton.
Cynthia. Dyer.
The Dead Ship of Harpswell. Whittier.
The Death of General Uncebunke: A Biography in Little. Durrell.
Divina Commedia. Dante Alighieri.
Don Juan. Byron.
Dulnesse. Herbert.
Elizabethan Tragedy: A Footnote. Moss.
Epigram: "I dreamt that I was God Himself." Pound.
An Epitaph upon the Celebrated Claudy Philips, Musician... Johnson.
Epithalamium. Housman.
The Eternal Image. Pitter.
Evening Prayer. Hagedorn.
An Evening Thought. Hammon.
An Evil Spirit, Your Beauty Haunts Me Still. Drayton.
Excelsior. Emerson.

The Explosion of Thimbles. Di Cicco.
Fairest Lord Jesus. Anonymous.
Fall of the Year. Ellison.
Farewell to Earth. Doten.
Five Roses. Verdaguer.
"Flash:" The Fireman's Story. Carleton.
For a Musician. Wither.
For Perfect Peace. Wesley.
The Gardener. Keyes.
Gethsemane. Droste-Hulshoff.
The Glory of Nature. Tennyson.
God Is Here Again. Angoff.
God Knows the Answer. Whitney.
God Save the King, That King That Sav'd the Land. Harris.
The Good Great Man. Coleridge.
A Gratulatory to Mr. Ben. Johnson for His Adopting of Him... Randolph.
The Grave's Cherub. Clouts.
Hamlet. Shakespeare.
Hippies. Dempster.
Hymn for Christmas Day. Byrom.
I Know That My Redeemer Liveth. Boyle.
I Was Made of This and This. Ross.
Idle Words. Landor.
In a Cafe. Dobson.
In Praise of Music in Time of Pestilence. Hine.
In Tesla's Laboratory. Johnson.
In the Carpenter's Shop. Teasdale.
It Came Upon the Midnight Clear. Sears.
The Kidnapping of Sims. Pierpont.
The Knight Fallen on Evil Days. Wylie.
Lamentations. Gluck.
Let Me Go Where Saints Are Going. Hartsough.
A Libel on D. Swift.
Limerick: "There was a young Fir-tree of Bosnia." Rossetti.
Lines. Ada Sister Mary.
The Little Hunchback. Riley.
Love of Nature. Thomson.
Ludwig's Death Mask. Hughes.
The Maid of Honour. Massinger.
Marmion. Scott.
Mary's Assumption. Barrett.
Meet We No Angels, Pansie? Ashe.
Merlin. Emerson.
A Mother's Picture. Stedman.
The Mouse's Petition. Barbauld.
My Bird. Judson.
My Way's Cloudy. Anonymous.
A New Poet. Canton.
Night. Heavysege.
Night and Love. Lytton.
Nuptial Hymn. Peacham.

O Soul, With Storms Beset.
Ibn Gabirol.
O Terrible Is the Highest
Thing. Patchen.
Obligatory Love Poem.
Jacobs.
The Old Hundredth. Kethe.
Old Ladies. Dromgoole.
On Being Brought from
Africa to America.
Wheatley.
On Clarastella Singing.
Heath.
On Exodus, III, 14, I Am
That I Am. Prior.
On Oliver Goldsmith.
Garrick.
On the Path. Strauss.
Once More, O Lord. Doane.
The Opening Year.
Anonymous.
The Penalties of Baldness.
Seaman.
The Prophet. Gibran.
The Psalter of Avram
Haktani. Klein.
Queen Sabbath. Bialik.
Reconciliation. Doten.
Rejoicing in Hope. Toplady.
Rilke Speaks of Angels.
Donnelly.
Rip the Apple Seller Awakes;
or, after 50 Years, the
Great Depression.
Ackerson.
Row Gently Here. Moore.
Saint. Merilaas.
Satires. Boileau-Despréaux.
Selective Service. Forche.
Serenade of Angels. Lasnier.
The Shadow Remains.
Roberts.
She Was a Phantom of
Delight. Wordsworth.
Silex Scintillans. Vaughan.
Since to Be Loved Endures.
Bridges.
Slow Me Down. *Anonymous.*
Song: "O faire sweet face, O
eyes celestiall bright."
Beaumont.
Song, to the Gods, is Sweetest
Sacrifice. Fields.
Song: "When thy Beauty
appears." Parnell.
Springfield Mountain (A
vers.). *Anonymous.*
The Stampede. Coburn.
The Streams of Lovely Nancy.
Anonymous.
Sun Filters through My
Window. Gold.
Three Epitaphs. Davison.
'Tis Sorrow Builds the Shining
Ladder Up. Lowell.
To–. Tennyson.
To a Child. O'Conor.
To a New-Born Child.
Monkhouse.
To a New York Shop-Girl
Dressed for Sunday.
Branch.
To a Nightingale.
Drummond.
To a Writer of the Day.
Mitchell.
To Jesus on His Birthday.
Millay.
To Lucasta: Her Reserved
Looks. Lovelace.
To the Soul. Collop.
To Theodora. *Anonymous.*

Tobias and the Angel. Gray.
The Trouble with Angels.
Norris.
A Truth... Mitchell.
Two Fishermen. Moss.
Two Little Children.
Anonymous.
Upon the Heavenly Scarp.
Klein.
Venetian Air. Moore.
Verses Written during the
War 1756–1763.
Mordaunt.
Warm Tea. MacAdams.
Wedding-Hymn. Lanier.
White Azaleas. Kimball.
William Shakespeare.
Swinburne.
Woman. O'Hagan.
Women Pleased. Fletcher.
The Word. Kahn.
The Young Priest to His
Hands. Garesche.
Angelus
At Set of Sun. Townsend.
Battledore. Gray.
Fuchsia Hedges in Connacht.
Colum.
On a Ledge. Bell.
Poem: "To be sad in the
morning." Pillen.
Anger (ed) (s)
Achilles. Corwin.
The Bad Old Days. Rexroth.
The Book of Mysteries.
Barnett.
Bubba Esther, 1888.
Whitman.
Diary. Black Bear's Moon.
De Clue.
Dirge. Aragon.
The Fan. Gay.
First Star. Smith.
Girl in White. Dobyns.
High Country Weather.
Baxter.
In Time of Crisis. Patterson.
Jezebel. Middleton.
The Last Trial. *Anonymous.*
Look You, My Simple Friend.
Clough.
The Lovers. Rodgers.
Of Impatience Which Brings
All Our Gains to Nothing.
Jacopone da Todi.
Phoenix. Oliver.
The Seafarer. *Anonymous.*
Squirrel in Sunshine.
Cowper.
A Storm in Summer. Blunt.
The Stricken South to the
North. Hayne.
Tabernacles. Lansing.
To a Teacher of French.
Davie.
To the Colorado Desert.
Morris.
The Whisperer. Stephens.
You in Anger. Reeves.
Angle (s)
The Beekeeper's Dream.
Lorr.
Burial. Walker.
International Motherhood
Assoc. Hester.
Midsummer Jingle. Levy.
Of Time and the Line.
Bernstein.
Rousecastle. Wright.
Sonnets. Tuckerman.
Touch of zygosis. Fitzgerald.

Anglo-Saxon
Birth Report. Kennedy.
Angry
Country Pastor. Inoue.
The Dream. Behn.
Epistles. Horace.
Hercules Furens, IV: Chorus.
Seneca (Lucius Annaeus
Seneca).
A History of Lesbianism.
Grahn.
O Terry. Herschberger.
Questions ¼. Hall.
Teasing. Mack.
Titus and Berenice. Heath-
Stubbs.
To a Mosquito. Bryant.
The Vacuum. Nemerov.
Anguish
Amor Mysticus. Marcela de
Carpio.
The Awakening. Marquis.
Bitter Question. Macdougall.
Epigram: "Drink, unhappy
lover." Meleager.
Faith. Cambridge.
Four Anacreontic Poems, 4.
Spenser.
Friend and Lover.
"Madeline."
From Creature to Ghost.
Hanson.
I Like a Look of Agony.
Dickinson.
Lamentation. Otey.
Mourn Not the Dead.
Chaplin.
O, Woman! Scott.
Oh, My Liver and My Lungs.
Anonymous.
The Old Anguish. Chu Shu-
chen.
On Diverse Deviations.
Angelou.
A Small Thought Speaks for
the Flesh. Drewry.
So proud she was to die.
Dickinson.
'Twas Like a Maelstrom, with
a Notch. Dickinson.
We Who Are Left. Whalley.
When Two Are Parted.
Heine.
The Words of Jesus. Benet.
Animal (s)
Animal Crackers. Morley.
Animal Song. McHugh.
As Animals. Spivak.
The Barnyard. Burnham.
Bozzy and Piozzi (excerpt).
"Pindar.
Cortege. Verlaine.
Customs. Gelman.
Dromedary. Dodat.
Excuse Us, Animals in the
Zoo. Wynne.
Four Stories. Shapiro.
Hamlet. Shakespeare.
Horse. Gluck.
I Have Felt It as They've
Said. Eigner.
If You. Creeley.
Jack and His Pony, Tom.
Belloc.
The Leaf. Fagg.
Lion Hunts. Beer.
Me Imperturbe. Whitman.
Minstrel's Song. Hughes.
Parable. Pack.
Paradise. Bloch.
Part of the Darkness.
Gardner.

Poem: "After your death."
Knott.
Retinue. Verlaine.
Salute to the Elephant.
Apolebieji.
The Seduction. Rioff.
Seventh Georgic. Economou.
Since Then. Enright.
Skinning-the-Cat. Schmitz.
Song of Reasons. Pinsky.
Sudden Things. Hall.
Sun of the Center. Kelly.
The Temple of the Animals.
Duncan.
Tiger. *Anonymous.*
A Trial. Dugan.
Twenty-One Love Poems.
Rich.
Underwood. Moss.
Up out of the African.
Joans.
The Week-End Indian.
Endrezze-Probst.
The Welcome. Laughton.
When Senses Fled. Woods.
The Zoo. Logan.
Animalcules
Paterson. Williams.
Animation
The Nursery. Howe.
Quand On N'a Pas Ce Que
l'on Aime, Il Faut Aimer
Ce Que l'on A–. Smith.
Ankle (s)
Christmas Card. Hughes.
I Hear That Andromeda.
Sappho.
Jarcha: "I will make love."
Anonymous.
There Were Some Summers.
Lux.
A Winter Madrigal. Bishop.
Anna
Anna. Burns.
An Electric Sign Goes Dark.
Sandburg.
The Fairy Thorn. Ferguson.
The Gowden Locks of Anna.
Burns.
Old Sam's Wife. *Anonymous.*
Oleanna. *Anonymous.*
Anne
Across the Fields to Anne.
Burton.
Lydia Is Gone This Many a
Year. Reese.
My Dearling. Allen.
O Sweet Anne Page.
Shenstone.
On Lady Anne Hamilton.
Sheridan.
The Swan Swims So Bonny.
Anonymous.
Three Sisters. De la Mare.
Annie
Andrew Lammie.
Anonymous.
Corn Rigs Are Bonnie.
Burns.
For Annie. Poe.
A Merry Bee. Skipsey.
Annihilation
Epipsychidion. Shelley.
Ode to the Hayden
Planetarium. Guiterman.
On a Stupendous Leg of
Granite, Discovered
Standing by Itself... Smith.
Twentyseven Bums.
Cummings.
Anniversaries
Holidays. Longfellow.

Annoy (ance) (ed)
Amoretti, LXII. Spenser.
Astrophel and Stella, CVIII. Sidney.
A Farewell. Sidney.
Felicia Ropps. Burgess.
If amour's faith... Wyatt.
On Lady Poltagrue, a Public Peril. Belloc.
Our Polite Parents. Wells.

Anoint (ed) (ing)
At a March against the Vietnam War. Bly.
Extreme Unction. Dowson.
Psalm XVIII. Sidney.
Second Avenue Winter. Simic.
The Song of Hannah. Drayton.
Sunday Afternoon in Italy. Lawrence.
To Abraham Lincoln. Piatt.

Anonymous
Fame. Rutsala.
Mossbawn: Two Poems in Dedication. Heaney.
Our Hunting Fathers. Auden.
A Small Registry of Births and Deaths: All Night It Bullied You. Stead.
Song for Healing. Hill.

Another
Another and the Same. Rogers.
An Attempt at Jealousy. Tsvetayeva.
A Ballad of the Gold Country. Jackson.
The Beggar Woman. King.
A Bestiary. Rexroth.
The Death Bed. Hood.
Fighting Words. Parker.
The Gambler. Anonymous.
The Golden Rule. Wells.
He and She. Ware.
Inconstancy's the Greatest of Sins. Herbert of Cherbury.
A Letter from School. Peacock.
Love Serviceable. Patmore.
Meditation. Pain.
Moonlight. Harjo.
Mrs. Malone. Farjeon.
No Second Troy. Yeats.
On a Certain Engagement South of Seoul. Carruth.
A Picnic. Fisher.
Sonnets, X: "For shame! deny that thou bear'st love to any." Shakespeare.
Spring Song. Heppenstall.
Telemachus and the Bow. Colaizzi.
The Three Kings. Longfellow.
To Etesia Looking from Her Casement at the Full Moon. Vaughan.
The White Horse. Lawrence.
White Notes. Justice.

Answer (ed) (ing) (s)
Advertisement of a Lost Day. Sigourney.
Among His Effects We Found a Photograph. Ochester.
At the Mid Hour of Night. Moore.
Attainment. Wilcox.
The Bear. Stanford.
Benedicite. Brackett.

The Book of God's Madness. Chubb.
Carolina. Timrod.
Catechism Elegy. Gibson.
Chiffons! Johnson.
Childe Harold's Pilgrimage: Canto III. Byron.
Christmas Mass for a Little Atheist Jesus. Maillard.
Coming Up & Falling Down. Vincent.
Commanding a Telephone to Ring. Anderson.
Comrade in Arms. Moore.
Could You Spare Some Time for Jesus? Knickman.
The Death of the Hired Man. Frost.
Death Rites II. Anonymous.
The Dirty Little Accuser. Cameron.
Disappointment. Anonymous.
Do I Love Thee? Saxe.
Dog. Ferlinghetti.
An Early Illinois Winter. Kuo.
Epicedium. Miller.
Epigram: "I delight in the prime of a boy of twelve." Strato.
Epigrams. Theocritus.
Epithalamion. Spenser.
Errors of Ecstasie. Darley.
Etudes. Thomas.
The Fever. Dobson.
The Flash. Dickey.
The Fool. Pearse.
For One Who Died Young. Hays.
Four Legs, Two Legs, Three Legs. Empson.
The Future. Oppenheim.
The Gaelic. Kelly.
Goat-Woman Dares. Volborth.
Grandmothers. Rich.
The Gulistan. Sa'di.
The Hens. Roberts.
His Sovereignty. Ben Moses.
The History of the World as Pictures. Sullivan.
The House of Life. Rossetti.
I Wish. Turner.
If He Let Us Go Now. Williams.
In Answer to Your Query. Lazard.
In Memory of Bryan Lathrop. Masters.
Judaism. Newman.
Juniper. Duggan.
Letter VI. Graham.
Limerick: "There was once a dear little gnome." Wells.
Lousy Peter. Sitwell.
The Maid that Sold Her Barley. Anonymous.
Man and Wife. Goodman.
Mary and the Bramble. Abercrombie.
The Millman's Song. Anonymous.
Mother, I Am. Clifton.
Mythology. Waters.
New Wine, Old Bottles. Newbury.
Niagara. Sigourney.
Nothing but No and I, and I and No. Drayton.
O Divine Star of Heaven. Fletcher.

O God, Send Men. Burrowes.
O Lord, Save We Beseech Thee. Anonymous.
Once in Love with Amy. Loesser.
Opportunity. Ingalls.
Orion. Engle.
Orphan Boy, Fishing. Goldbarth.
Pan and Syrinx. Rodgers.
Personal. Hughes.
Prayer. Hickok.
The Quip. Herbert.
Reading the Books Our Children Have Written. Smith.
Red Wing Hawk. Applewhite.
Reveille. Untermeyer.
Riddle: "There is one that has a head without an eye." Rossetti.
The Ring. Mariani.
The Rose. Herbert.
Satyr. Gullans.
The Shade-Seller. Jacobsen.
The Shades of Night Were Falling Fast (parody). Housman.
Silences. O'Shaughnessy.
Somebody's Knockin' at Yo' Do'. Anonymous.
Sonnets from the Portuguese, I. Browning.
St. Irvyne (excerpt). Shelley.
Story. Saleh.
A Sweet Little Bell. Anonymous.
Taking a Walk with You. Koch.
The Temple. Dyment.
The Temple. Sisson.
Thomas at Chickamauga. Sherwood.
To a Portrait of Lermontov. Aliger.
To a Talkative Hairdresser. McGinley.
To Henrietta, on Her Departure for Calais. Hood.
To Lydia Languish. Dobson.
The Two Societies. Wheelock.
Walk-Up. Merwin.
We Read of a People. Anonymous.
What Riddle Asked the Sphinx. MacLeish.
When Did the World Begin. Clairmont.

Ant (heap) (hill)
Portrait of the Autist as a New World Driver. Murray.
To a Dead Elephant. Livingstone.

Ant (s)
The Baying Hounds. Gilmore.
Having Climbed to the Topmost Peak of the Incense-Burner Mountain. Po Chu-i.
Immanent. De la Mare.
Limerick: "Once a grasshoper (food being scant)." Herford.
Limerick: "There was a young curate of Hants." Knox.

A Mad Negro Soldier Confined at Munich. Lowell.
A Skilful Spearman! Anonymous.
Snow. Wright.
View from the Planetarium. Barker.

Antarctica
Antonio. Richards.
The Fortitude of the North. Melville.
Ramon. Lacey.

Antelope
Motorcycle. Pray.
Sand Creek. Ballard.

Antenna (e) (s)
After Tempest. MacKaye.
Communication on His Thirtieth Birthday. Bell.
"Let us suppose the mind." Moraff.
Row of Houses. Quinn.

Anthem (s)
A Gratulatory to Mr. Ben. Johnson for His Adopting of Him... Randolph.
Harmony. Springer.
The Lord in the Wind. Picot.
Mater Amabilis. De Vere.
Prayer of Columbus. Whitman.
What If the Saint Must Die. Peck.
When Shall My Pilgrimage, Jesus My Saviour, Be Ended? Rudman.

Anthony
The Temptations of Saint Anthony. McGinley.

Antichrist
Upon the Weathercock. Bunyan.

Antidote
Jesus, I Love Thy Charming Name. Doddridge.
Time! Where Dist Thou Those Years Inter. Habington.
To Meet, or Otherwise. Hardy.

Antietam
The Battle of Antietam Creek. Anonymous.
The Victor of Antietam. Melville.

Antipathy
If Thou Wouldest Roses Scent. Pastorius.
On Dr. Evans Cutting down a Row of Trees at St. John's College... Anonymous.

Antipodes
Altarwise by Owl-Light. Thomas.
The Bothie of Tober-na-Vuolich. Clough.

Antiquity
At Majority. Rich.
Attention. Rich.
Pink, Small and Punctual (Arbutus). Dickinson.

Antony
Cleopatra. Swinburne.
Cleopatra Dying. Collier.
Italian Poppies. Spingarn.
Queen Cleopatra. Aiken.

Anvil (s)
Chinese Camp, Kamloops (circa 1883). Suknaski.
The Village Blacksmith. Longfellow.

A Wanderer's Litany.
Stringer.

Anyone
Central. Kooser.
The Child. Keithley.
I Want to Know.
Drinkwater.
A Man in Our Village. Norris.
One Thing to Take, Another
to Keep. Del Monte.

Anything
Air. Jones.
Eve in My Legend. Devlin.
Fidelities. Valentine.
First Prelude. Dream in Ohio:
The Father. Logan.
Freaks of Fashion. Rossetti.
Golly, How Truth Will Out!
Nash.
Homosexual Sonnets.
Pitchford.
I, Too, Know What I Am
Not. Kaufman.
The Pit of Bliss. Stephens.
Poor Man Blues. Townsend.
The Road to Bologna.
MacNab.
The Rum Tum Tugger.
Eliot.
Sleep in the Heat. Jensen.
Sleepy Man Blues. White.
A Song with a Discord.
Colton.
When I Was Conceived.
Ryan.

Anywhere
Aran Islands. Layton.
The Keys of Canterbury.
Anonymous.
The Road to Anywhere.
Taylor.

Apache (s)
Geronimo. McGaffey.
Indian america. Tohee.

Apart
Adonis. Doolittle.
Coroner's Jury. Strong.
The Ecclesiast. Ashbery.
An Elegy Is Preparing Itself.
Justice.
Exodus 1940. Wolfenstein.
The Hands of God.
Lawrence.
Lily. Warren.
Rift Tide. Walsh.
Seaward Bound. Brown.
September: Last Day at the
Beach. Tillinghast.
The Shannon and the
Chesapeake. Bouve.
The Songs I Sing. Blanden.
Summer Solstice. Bowering.
The Tuft of Flowers. Frost.

Apartheid
Where? When? Which?
Hughes.

Ape (s)
Australia. Hope.
A Celebration of Charis.
Jonson.
The Great Poet. King.
Green Coconuts: Rio.
Durrell.
Lullaby. Sitwell.
Note. Lima.
Singing Aloud. Kizer.

Aphrodite
Hellenics: Blue Sleep.
Bryher.
In Memory of Sigmund
Freud. Auden.

Ode to Aphrodite. Sappho.
To the Fair Clarinda, Who
Made Love to Me, Imagin'd
More than Woman. Behn.
The Young Glass-Stainer.
Hardy.

Apocalypse
Bendix. Updike.
The Chronicle of Meola
Creek. Sinclair.
Come away, Death. Pratt.
The Great Hunger.
Kavanagh.
New Englanders Are Maples.
Coffin.
On the Death of Mr. Pope.
Anonymous.
The Soul's Expression.
Browning.

Apocryphal
The Whale, His Bulwark.
Walcott.

Apollo
The Birds. Aristophanes.
The Flowers of Apollo.
Flanner.
Gratiana Dauncing and
Singing. Lovelace.
The Lord of All. Markham.
On a Sunbeam. Heyrick.
The Sitting Bard. Seaman.

Apologies
I Am 25. Corso.
A Wartime Exchange: Letter
to an American Visitor.
Comfort.

Apostles
The Poor Parson. Chaucer.

Apparel
The Fear of God. Frost.

Apparition (s)
The European Night.
Vinaver.
Eyam (excerpt). Seward.

Appeal
Beyond Memory. De Boully.
Chickens the Weasel Killed.
Stafford.
Had I Been Mindful of My
High Descent. Hadewijch.
Poor Ellen Smith. Degraph.
The Rainbow Stands Red...A
Tiring Song. *Anonymous.*
To the Body. Meynell.

Appear
Ah Sweet Content, where Is
Thy Mylde Abode?
Barnes.
Evening Hymn (excerpt).
Macdonald.

Appearances
Magnetized. Sze.

Appenine (s)
Santa Maria del Fiore.
Clarke.

Appetite (s)
As in the Land of Darkness.
Miklitsch.
The Hermit. Moss.
In the Garden. Eberhart.
Metamorphoses. Ovid
(Publius Ovidius Naso).
October Poems: The Garden.
Warren.
The Odyssey. Homer.
The Recognition (parody).
Sawyer.
Sparrows among Dry Leaves.
Williams.
That it will never come again.
Dickinson.

A Very Odd Fish.
Thompson.
The Wounded Man and the
Swarm of Flies. Somervile.

Applaud (ed)
The Appology. Winchilsea.
Growing Old. Arnold.
Love. Ostroff.
The Voice of God. Barnard.

Applause
At the Front. Erskine.
Coup de Grace. Hope.
The Death of Wolfe.
Anonymous.
The Downfall of Piracy.
Franklin.
Equestrienne. Colby.
Fame Makes Us Forward.
Herrick.
Goodbye, Sally. Simmons.
The Gymnasiad, or Boxing
Match (excerpt).
Whitehead.
Johann Joachim Quantz's Five
Lessons. Graham.
Letters Found near a Suicide.
Horne.
The Practice of Magical
Evocation. Di Prima.
St. Simon and St. Jude's Day.
Alexander.
Sunset. Evans.
To Nobodaddy. Blake.

Apple blossom (s)
An Apple Orchard in the
Spring. Martin.
Swineherd. Chuilleanain.

Apple pie
Bonne Entente. Scott.
Ride a Cock-Horse.
Anonymous.

Apple (s)
An Adult Lullaby.
Anonymous.
Apology. Wilbur.
The Apple. Guernsey.
Apple Offering. *Anonymous.*
Apples. Kaufman.
Apples in New Hampshire.
Gilchrist.
At the Altar-Rail. Hardy.
August. Thaxter.
Birkett's Eagle. Howard.
Blossom. Plumly.
Catch Him, Crow! Carry Him,
Kite! *Anonymous.*
A Common Light. Orlen.
Eve. Wolf.
Evesong. Duffy.
The Foreman's Wife.
Tagami.
Fragments. Praxilla.
Getting a Poem in the Rain.
Lourie.
The Hero (parody). Woddis.
Hillside Pause. Wright.
Inspiration. Fullerton.
King Alfred Answers the
Danes. Chesterton.
The Kiss. Pack.
Larch Tree. Lee.
Life Cycle of Common Man.
Nemerov.
Little Friend. *Anonymous.*
Madrigal de Verano. Garcia
Lorca.
Moonlit Apples. Drinkwater.
Most betuiful of things I leave
is sunlight. Praxilla.
No Return. Miller.
Ode to Eve. Robinson.

Parable: November.
Tapscott.
Peace. Longley.
Poem of Explanations.
Ravikovich.
A Primer of the Daily Round.
Nemerov.
Riddle: "There was a man
who had no eyes."
Anonymous.
Ring the Bell. *Anonymous.*
Sharing Eve's Apple. Keats.
The Song of Wandering
Aengus. Yeats.
Song: "Three Moorish girls I
loved." *Anonymous.*
Sweet Apple. Stephens.
The Third Continent.
Erulkar.
Through the Whole Long
Night. Leivick.
Tropics. Voigt.
Ursula. Ray.
When It Rains. Maxson.
Yaddo. Herschberger.

Apple tree (s)
The Apple Tree. Baxter.
The Author to the Reader.
Jarrell.
Enigma. Murphy.
Family. MacCaig.
Garden Party. Read.
In the Shade of the Old Apple
Tree. Williams.
Johnny Appleseed. Benet.
Merlin's Apple-Trees.
Peacock.
Mine Host of "The Golden
Apple." Westwood.
Miss Jennian Jones.
Anonymous.
Mr. Johnson's Policy of
Reconstruction. Halpine.
My Orcha'd in Linden Lea.
Barnes.
The Planting of the Apple-
Tree. Bryant.
Portrait of a Lady. Williams.
When Both My Fathers Die.
Gillespie.

Appomattox
John Brown's Body. Benét.

Apprehend
Her Eyes. Ransom.

Apprehension (s)
Seagulls. Updike.
The Spirit of the Cairngorms.
Firsoff.
Varitalk. Holbrook.

Approach (able)
I Am the Way. Meynell.
Modern Midnight
Conversation: Between a
Contractor and His Wife.
Anonymous.
Le Musee Imaginaire.
Tomlinson.
Sonnet: "They say that
shadowes of deceased
ghosts." Sylvester.
Squid. Blumenthal.

Approval
In a Motion. Chester.
To My Father. Ray.
Troilus and Cressida. De
Vere.

Apricot (s)
Detach, Invading. Padgett.
Ode on His Majesty's
Proclamation, Commanding
the Gentry... Fanshawe.

April
After Reading Twenty Years
  of Grantland Rice. Skene.
Allie. Graves.
Ann's House. Lourie.
Any April. Beard.
April Midnight. Symons.
April Rain. Blind.
At April. Grimke.
Blue-Butterfly Day. Frost.
The Concert. McGinley.
Easter. Sabin.
For City Spring. Benét.
Forsythia Is the Color I
  Remember. Cherwinski.
Her Fairness, Wedded to a
  Star. O'Brien.
IV. Bruchac.
A Letter to Charles Townsend
  Copeland (excerpt).
  Hillyer.
March. Loveman.
Miss Packard and Miss Giles.
  Dodson.
The Morning After.
  Wellesley.
Nature Study, after Dufy.
  Bevington.
Poem for Good Friday.
  Jones.
Quest. Madgett.
Sanctuary. Guiney.
Santa Maria del Fiore.
  Clarke.
Schoolyard in April. Koch.
She Sews Fine Linen. Davis.
Sleeping Beauty. De La
  Mare.
Song: "O lovely April, rich
  and bright." Kahn.
Sonnet XV. Alabaster.
Sonnets. Lee.
Spring and All. Bauer.
Spring Cricket. Rodman.
Threnody for a Poet.
  Carman.
The Veterans. MacDonagh.
Weather Vanes. Frost.
The Worm. Souster.
The Yellow Violet. Bryant.
Apron (s)
Aprons of Silence. Sandburg.
A Great Favourite Song,
  Entitled The Sailor's
  Hornpipe. Anonymous.
Aqueduct
Quantum. Johnston.
Arab
The Gofongo. Milligan.
A Hand of Solo. Kinsella.
Horatio Alger Uses Scag.
  Jones.
O Hark to the Herald. Ben
  Kalir.
Toledo. Zorilla.
Arabesque
Nina. Dienstag.
Watching Gymnasts.
  Francis.
Arabia (n)
Autobiography. Dube.
The Fan. Sitwell.
Stony Limits.
  ""MacDiarmid.
Thalaba and the Banquet.
  Southey.
Two Nocturnes. Mansfield.
Arabic
On Dr. Samuel Ogden.
  Arden.

Araby
The Romance of the Rose:
  Love vs. Marriage.
  Meung.
Aragon
El Gusano. Layton.
Ararat
Ballad of the Flood. Muir.
The Great Wave: Hokusai.
  Finkel.
The Imbecile. Finkel.
Lakeshore. Scott.
Arc
Achieving Perspective.
  Rogers.
Horses Graze. Brooks.
A Moon Rainbow.
  Browning.
Ship Bottom. Lattimore.
The World. Rutsala.
Arcad (ia) (y)
Arcades: O'er the Smooth
  Enamelled Green. Milton.
Battles of the Centaurs:
  Centaurs and Lapithae.
  Sitwell.
The Carnival of Animals
  (excerpt). Nash.
Arcad (id) (y)
Arcady Revisited. Funge.
Awake! Awake! Ruskin.
The Haunts of the Halcyon.
  Luders.
Merits of Laughter and Lust.
  Mandel.
The Way to Arcady.
  Bunner.
Arch (es) (ing)
The Bridge. Verwey.
Choral Symphony Conductor.
  Coates.
Colosseum. Norse.
Eire. Drennan.
Eppur Si Muove? Hillyer.
Gabriel. Wattles.
Gathering the Bones Together.
  Orr.
In State (excerpt). Willson.
Archaic
Party. Carrier.
Wrath to Sadness. Grenier.
Archangel
Death of an Aircraft.
  Causley.
The Drowned. MacCaig.
Archbishop
The Song of Roland, XCVIII.
  Anonymous.
Archer (s)
Archers of the King. Mary
  Genoveva.
Dust to Dust. De La Mare.
Ganga. Blackburn.
The Hanging of Sam Archer.
  Anonymous.
Little John a Begging (B
  version). Anonymous.
What Her Girl-Friend Said to
  Her. Okkur Macatti.
Archetype
Greek Architecture.
  Melville.
Archipelago
Poem: "O gentle queen of the
  afternoon." Graham.
Architect (ure)
Cave of Staffa, I.
  Wordsworth.
How to Raise a Son. Martial
  (Marcus Valerius Martialis).
Now I Have Come to Reason.
  Day-Lewis.

Petition. Auden.
The Snake. Campbell.
Arctic
Annunciation. Jones.
Enueg. Beckett.
Lady Franklin's Lament (II).
  Anonymous.
Three Songs. Jackson.
Ardor
An Autumn Song. Dowden.
The Beauty of My Land Peers
  Warily. Brutus.
Deliciae Sapientiae de Amore.
  Patmore.
The Unknown Soldier.
  Aiken.
Argument (s)
Amoretti, LXXXII. Spenser.
Canal Bank Walk.
  Kavanagh.
Oxford & Cambridge.
  Browne.
The Pleasures of Love.
  Blunt.
Argus eyes
The Faerie Queene. Spenser.
Argyle
The Day of Inverlochy.
  Lom.
Ariel
Cutty Sark. Crane.
Arise (n)
Birds. Llywelyn.
The Combat of Ferdiad and
  Cuchulain. Anonymous.
Cymbeline. Shakespeare.
An Easter Hymn. Le
  Gallienne.
God's Promises. Anonymous.
Grief. Browning.
Harvest. Sitwell.
I Said Sometimes with Tears.
  Crossman.
Mary and Her Son Alone.
  Ryman.
Ode to Peace. Anonymous.
A Phoenix at Fifty.
  Ferlinghetti.
The Second Iron Age
  (1939-1945). Harrington.
Son of Erebus and Night.
  Browne.
Sonnets, LV: "Not marble,
  nor the gilded monuments."
  Shakespeare.
The Sunrise Call.
  Anonymous.
Thy Kingdom Come.
  Bernard of Clairvaux.
The Trumpet. Thomas.
Aristocracy
On Lake Pend Oreille.
  Shelton.
The Pedigree of Honey.
  Dickinson.
Sitting Pretty. Fishback.
Aristotle
Don Juan. Byron.
Arithmetic
The Anniverse: An Elegy.
  King.
Arithmetic. Sandburg.
Dialogue. Agathias.
Fragment of a Greek Tragedy.
  Housman.
Arizona
Modern Romance. Harris.
Rag Time Cowboy Joe.
  Muir.
Rimrock, Where It Is.
  Carruth.

Ark
Charles the Fifth and the
  Peasant. Lowell.
Chenille. Dickey.
The Eagle Swift. Adam of
  St. Victor.
The Fall Again. Nemerov.
Genesis (excerpt).
  Anonymous.
The Imbecile. Finkel.
Ireland. Stuart.
The Late Passenger. Lewis.
Limerick: "A chap has a
  shark up in Sparkill."
  Bishop.
Noah. Hagedorn.
O That I Had Wings Like a
  Dove. Anonymous.
The Old Ark's A-Moverin'.
  Anonymous.
The Store in Havana. Kozer.
To My People. Seaver.
Arkansas (Arkansaw)
Great-Great Grandma, Don't
  Sleep in Your Treehouse
  Tonight. Kennedy.
The Old Section Boss.
  Anonymous.
Variations for Two Pianos.
  Justice.
Arles
Midnight. "Mistral.
Arm-chair
Old Arm-Chair. Cook.
Arm (ed) (s)
After Making Love We Hear
  Footsteps. Kinnell.
Age. Mannes.
The Age of Reason.
  Graham.
Aged Ninety Years. Snow.
All Last Night...
  Abercrombie.
An Allegory. Boake.
Alone in the House. Bogin.
Among Iron Fragments.
  Ruebner.
Appeal. Da.
Ark Articulate. Macpherson.
Armed Vision. Van Wyk
  Louw.
At Least–To Pray–Is Left–Is
  Left. Dickinson.
An Austrian Army. Watts.
An Autumn Road.
  Dresbach.
Bad Dream. MacNeice.
Ballad of the Epiphany.
  Dalmon.
The Battel of the Summer-
  Islands. Waller.
Beyond the Presidency.
  Gibson.
The Boat. Gilman.
Boldness in Love. Carew.
Braggart! Wrafter.
Brussels in Winter. Auden.
Burn Down the Icons.
  Schulman.
Calculating Female. Hellyer.
Can I Say. Bird.
The Castle. Muir.
Chairs. Worth.
Childhood. O'Gorman.
Chimney Swallows. Powers.
Chiqui and Terra Nova.
  Hagedorn.
Choral Symphony Conductor.
  Coates.
The Christian Soldier
  (excerpt). Studdert-
  Kennedy.

A Christmas Dawn at Sea. Morgan.
Christmas Shopping. MacNeice.
Churchyard. Hass.
Compensation. Reese.
Confession to Settle a Curse. Waldrop.
Cruciform. Welles.
A Dance for Ma Rainey. Young.
Dawn. *Anonymous.*
Daybreak. Spender.
Diver. Simpson.
Division. Ratti.
Doe-Face. Moure.
Doors. Clark.
Drowning with Others. Dickey.
Duermete, Nino Lindo. *Anonymous.*
Dykes in the Garden. Barba.
The Electric Telegraph. Baker.
Ethan Boldt. Weingarten.
Exile. Beecham.
Exits and Entrances. Madgett.
The Fair Thief. Wyndham.
The Foggy Dew. *Anonymous.*
The Font in the Forest. Adams.
For a New Home. Marinoni.
The Free Woman. Garrison.
The Garland and the Girdle. Michelangelo.
Generalities. Conquest.
Gesture. Welles.
Give Way. Finkel.
The Glory of Nature. Tennyson.
Grieve Not, Ladies. Branch.
Halieutica. Oppian.
Happiness Amidst Troubles. Di Roma.
He Charges Her to Lay Aside Her Weapons. Ferriter.
Health. Parker.
Hear, O Israel. Spire.
Helen, the Sad Queen. Valery.
Hero and Leander. Chapman.
Hero and Leander. Marlowe.
His Shield. Moore.
The Homing Heart. Henderson.
How Will You Call Me, Brother? Evans.
I Am a Hunchback. Stevenson.
I could not hope. Sappho.
I Dreamed My Love. *Anonymous.*
Immolated. Melville.
In Space-Time Aware–. Evans.
In the Basement of the Goodwill Store. Kooser.
In the Operating Room. Nowlan.
In Your Arms. Radnoti.
Inside Out. Wakoski.
Invocation to the Social Muse. MacLeish.
Jackson. *Anonymous.*
Jackson (with music). *Anonymous.*
Jesus, Shepherd of Thy Sheep. Bethune.

Jimmy Bruder on Quincey Street. Montgomery.
A Lady to a Lover. Noel.
Last Night in Calcutta. Ginsberg.
Lay Your Arms Aside. Ferriter.
Letter to R. Maas.
Letters from Vicksburg, XII. Gildner.
The Lonely Isle. Claudian (Claudius Claudianus).
Looking On. Thwaite.
The Lord. Gabriel y Galan.
Lord Thomas and Fair Ellender. *Anonymous.*
Love in the Valley. Meredith.
Love's night & a lamp. Meleager.
Man Alone. Bogan.
The Man of Calvary. *Anonymous.*
A Map of Verona. Reed.
A Marriage Charm. Hopper.
May the Ambitious Ever Find. Sackville.
Moonlight. Harjo.
Moonlight (with music). *Anonymous.*
The Muddy Rat. Daigaku.
My Soul Doth Pant towards Thee. Taylor.
Mythological Sonnet XVI. Fuller.
New Love. Martial (Marcus Valerius Martialis).
News of the World. Barker.
Nina. Dienstag.
Nod. Bennett.
Notes for Echo Lake 5. Palmer.
Now. Browning.
Now Behold the Saviour Pleading. Leland.
Nuclear Wind, When Wilt Thou Blow. Dehn.
O That I Had Wings Like a Dove. *Anonymous.*
O Western Wind. *Anonymous.*
Odes (excerpt). Tibullus.
The Odyssey. Homer.
On a Gloomy Easter. Palmer.
On the Brink of Death. Michelangelo.
Other men are thorn. Mahadevi (Mahadeviyakka).
Pandosto: In Praise of his Loving and Best-Beloved Fawnia. Greene.
Paradise. Sargent.
Paradise Lost. Milton.
Passage to India. Whitman.
Peace. Pulsifer.
Pere Lalement. Pickthall.
The Persian Version. Graves.
Phallus. Shiraishi Kazuko.
A Philosopher. Foss.
A Poem of Privacy. Symonds.
Poland/1931.The Wedding. Rothenberg.
Politics. Yeats.
Prayer to Venus. Chaucer.
Recorders Ages Hence. Whitman.
Recrimination. Wilcox.
Response to Rimbaud's Latter Manner. Moore.

The Runner. Whitman.
Saint Judas. Wright.
The Scythe. Kanabus.
The Sea-Captain. Gould.
Seasons. Dempster.
Security. Sangster.
September Evening, 1938. Plomer.
Seven Poems. Niedecker.
The Shadow House of Lugh. "Carbery.
The Siege of Belgrade. Watts.
Sleep. Imbs.
Sleeping with Someone Who Came in Secret. Ise.
The Smiling Mouth and Laughing Eyen Grey. Orleans.
Solitude. Deutsch.
Sorrow seldom killeth any. Davison.
The Springfield Calibre Fifty. Hanson.
The Surrender of Cornwallis. *Anonymous.*
Sweet William. *Anonymous.*
Tarantula. O Hehir.
To Chloris. Drummond.
To His Maistres. Montgomerie.
To My Friend G. N. from Wrest. Carew.
To the Virgin Mary. Petrarch.
Tonight. Moulton.
The Truth. Jarrell.
Twenty-One Love Poems. Rich.
Two Sorrows. St. John.
Uncle Bull-Boy. Jordan.
Upon a Ribband. Carew.
The Visit. Mezey.
Waiting Inside. Ignatow.
Walking Wounded. Scannell.
The Wars of the Roses. Anonymous.
What a Friend We Have in Jesus. Scriven.
When I Heard at the Close of the Day. Whitman.
Where Love Is. Burr.
The White Skirt. Dobyns.
The Windmill. Longfellow.
A Woman Grows Soon Old. Paraske.
Your Snow-White Shoulder. Heine.

Arm-full
Evadne. Doolittle.

Armaggeddon
Nuclear Racial Lockdowns. Aguila.

Armament
Voyage to the Moon. Dickey.

Armenian
With the Bait of Bread. Pilibosian.

Armistice
The Conscientious Objector. Shapiro.
That Day. Van Doren.

Armor (ed)
Bronzeville Man with a Belt in the Back. Brooks.
Chinatown Talking Story. Tsui.
In That Dark Cave. Silverstein.
Jezebel. Middleton.
The Middle Ages. Haines.

A Perigord pres del Muralh. Bertrand.
Saul. Sterling.

Armour
Before I Knocked and Flesh Let Enter. Thomas.
Song: "Ladies, though to your Conqu'ring eyes." Etherege.

Armpit (s)
All Tropic Places Smell of Mold. Shapiro.
One for the Ladies at the Troy Laundry Who Cooled Themselves... Zimmer.

Arms (ed) (s)
Passages. Eigner.

Army (ies)
Autumn Journal. MacNeice.
The Battle of Lake Champlain. Freneau.
Better, Wiser and Happier. Wilcox.
Broken Sky. Sandburg.
Captain Jinks. *Anonymous.*
Captain Jinks. Lingard.
The Challenge. Longfellow.
Cold Is the Winter. *Anonymous.*
Dover Beach. Arnold.
Dying! To be afraid of thee. Dickinson.
Farewell to Winnipeg. Daniells.
The Forefather. Burton.
The French Revolution. Blake.
Gettysburg. Stedman.
Great Nature Is an Army Gay. Gilder.
I'm a Soldier in the Army of the Lord. *Anonymous.*
I Saw the Vision of Armies. Whitman.
In the Sea of Tears. Replansky.
In the Trenches. Aldington.
Limerick: "There was a young curate of Hants." Knox.
Love Song. Ewart.
Lyon. Melville.
Molly Pitcher. Sherwood.
Mr. Johnson's Policy of Reconstruction. Halpine.
Pslam XXIV. Sidney.
Shout for Joy. *Anonymous.*
Sitting Bull's Will Versus the Sioux Treaty of 1868 and Monty Hall. Redwing.
The Soldier. Aiken.
Thanks Just the Same. *Anonymous.*
Waters of the Sea. Goldbeck.
You're in the Army Now. *Anonymous.*

Aroma
Shoe. Perreault.

Arouse (d) (s)
Erotica. Farkas.
The Maximus Poems. Olson.
Sonnet, X: "When I catch sight of your fair head." Labé.
The Wind and the Bird. *Anonymous.*

Arrival
Keraunograph. Carruth.
Overland to the Islands. Levertov.
Sphere (excerpt). Ammons.

Arrive (d)
And Yet. Molodovsky.
Days Ago. Hai-Jew.
The Djanggawul Cycle, 27.
  Anonymous.
The Great Bear Lake
  Meditations (excerpt).
  Yates.
My Life by Somebody Else.
  Strand.
Oblique. Rutledge.
The Pleasure of Ruins.
  McClatchy.
The Rescue. Creeley.
The Tourist from Syracuse.
  Justice.

Arriving
Blue Horses. Roberson.
The Climbers. Jennings.

Arrogance
A Clock Stopped.
  Dickinson.
Dead Ponies. Chamberlain.
Iona: The Graves of the
  Kings. Jeffers.
Ode to the German Drama.
  Anonymous.

Arrow (s)
The Arrow of Desire.
  Anonymous.
Arrows. Heyen.
Astrophel and Stella, LXV.
  Sidney.
At the Door. Merriam.
Atalanta's Race. Morris.
Athlete. Maynard.
Brave Old World. Lambert.
Choosing a Mast. Campbell.
Cupid in a Bed of Roses.
  Anonymous.
Elsewhere. Pastan.
Envoy. Johnson.
The Faun Tells of the Rout of
  the Amazons. Moore.
Gisli, the Chieftain: The Song
  of the Arrow. Crawford.
Goddwyn: Ode to Liberty.
  Chatterton.
Hebrew Script. Loewenthal.
Image. Dumas.
The Insular Celts. Carson.
Let the Dead Depart in Peace.
  Anonymous.
Love in a Cottage. Willis.
Love's Franciscan.
  Constable.
An Other. Carew.
Praise. *Anonymous.*
Robin, Wren, Martin,
  Swallow. *Anonymous.*
The Song of Crede.
  Anonymous.
Sonnets: A Sequence on
  Profane Love. Boker.
The Summons. Dickey.
They Tell Me I Am Lost.
  Kenny.
The Two Brothers.
  Anonymous.
The Zen Archer. Kirkup.

Arrowroot
Changed. Calverley.

Arse (s)
The Description of an Irish
  Feast, or O'Rourk's Frolic.
  MacGowran.
Epigram: "Cibber! write all
  thy verses upon glasses."
  Pope.
Exhaustive Experimentation.
  Anonymous.

High Wonders (parody).
  Marks.
The Legion Club (excerpt).
  Swift.
On a Window at an Inn.
  Anonymous.

Arsehole
The Bastard from the Bush.
  Anonymous.

Art (s)
Against Borders.
  Yevtushenko.
Alogon. Palmer.
Answer to–'s Professions of
  Affection. Byron.
An Answer to Some Verses
  Made in His Praise.
  Suckling.
Art. *Anonymous.*
Art. Melville.
Art above Nature, to Julia.
  Herrick.
At the Lavender Lantern.
  Divine.
Bad Dreams. Browning.
Before a Saint's Picture.
  Landor.
Caelica, CI. Greville.
A Century Piece for Poor
  Heine. Logan.
Characters of Women.
  Young.
Ciampino. Denby.
Collages and Compositions.
  Lattimore.
The Criminality of War.
  Young.
The Dance of Love. Davies.
The Dog of Art. Levertov.
Easter. Herbert.
Fables for the Female Sex, V:
  The Poet and His Patron.
  Moore.
First Reunion in New
  Orleans: The Father as
  King of Revels. Logan.
Gaspar Becerra. Longfellow.
Grace. Herbert.
The Handmaid of Religion.
  Rickword.
I Would Not Paint a Picture.
  Dickinson.
The Ideals of Satire. Pope.
If, Jerusalem, I Ever Should
  Forget Thee. Heine.
In Memoriam A.H.H.,
  CXXVIII. Tennyson.
In the Person of Woman
  Kind. Jonson.
IT. Lattimore.
Jerusalem, the Golden.
  Bernard of Cluny.
Journey to Iceland. Auden.
The Joys of Art. Taylor.
Let Them Alone. Jeffers.
Light Showers of Light.
  Lindskoog.
Love-Charms. Campion.
Madrono. Harte.
The Makers. Galler.
Man's Medley. Herbert.
The martyr poets–did not tell–
  . Dickinson.
The Mistress. D'Avenant.
More Reformation. Defoe.
Mouth to mouth recitation.
  Fitzgerald.
The Needle. Woodworth.
A New Poet Arrives. Ewart.
No Harm to Lovers.
  Tibullus.

No Money in Art.
  Gustafson.
On Don Surly. Jonson.
On How the Cobler.
  Anonymous.
On My Lord Bacon.
  Danforth.
On the Life-Mask of Abraham
  Lincoln. Gilder.
One of the Jews. Cavafy.
An Open Air Performance of
  "As You Like It." Scovell.
Opposition. Lanier.
Pictures at an Exhibition.
  Rosenbaum.
A Poet's Progress.
  Hamburger.
The Point. Jones.
The Presence. Very.
Rain. Alling.
Robin Hood. Burr.
The Room. Jennings.
Shadow of Night: Hymnus in
  Noctem. Chapman.
Sonnet XXI: "What grandeurs
  make a man seem
  venerable?" Labe.
Thrice Toss These Oaken
  Ashes in the Air.
  Campion.
To a Blue Hippopotamus.
  Kay.
To a Lark in War-Time.
  Werfel.
To Benjamin West. Allston.
To Miss–. Johnson.
To the Muse. Stevenson.
To the Royal Society.
  Cowley.
Translator to Translated.
  Pound.
The Unremarkable Year.
  Fuller.
Verses on Sir Joshua
  Reynold's Painted Window
  at New College, Oxford.
  Warton, Jr..
Visit of Hope to Sydney Cove,
  near Botany-Bay. Darwin.
Wapentake. Longfellow
When the Light Falls.
  Kunitz.
The Wind at Penistone.
  Davie.
The Young Conquistador.
  Peterson.

Artery (ies)
America the Beautiful. Rice.
Mithridates. Emerson.
The Trumpet: Grass on the
  Cliff. Jeffers.

Artichokes
Elevator Landscapes, Floor:
  Five. Vincent.

Articulation
The City's Crown. Foulke.
Malcolm, a Thousandth
  Poem. Rivers.
The Poet. Keats.

Artillery (ee)
Macrocosm. Child.
Old King Cole. Anonymous.

Artisan (s)
Eclogue. Davidson.
It sifts from leaden sieves.
  Dickinson.
Lord Finchley. Belloc.

Artist (s)
Another Mother and Child.
  McLaughlin.
August 2. Jordan.

The Chauffeur of Lilacs.
  Hitchcock.
A Conversation. Howes.
Eclogue. Davidson.
Gallery Shepherds. Beer.
Never Marry an Artist.
  Filip.
Pan Cogito's Thoughts on
  Hell. Herbert.
Wigs and Beards. Graves.
The Worst Horror.
  Euripides.

Artium/Magistra
Ad Chloen, M.A. Collins.

Artless
The Last Turn. Williams.

Artois
The Bohemians. Gurney.

Ascend (ancy) (ing)
The Common Street. Cone.
Expansion to Aveline's.
  Brodey.
A Lark's Nest. Smart.
Lines Written in a Country
  Parson's Orchard. Daiken.
Paradise Lost. Milton.
A Part-Sequence for Change.
  Duncan.
Sorrow's Ladder. Callaghan.
Three Presidents: John F.
  Kennedy. Bly.

Ascension
Christ 2. Cynewulf.

Asceticism
This Be Our Revenge.
  Tchernichovsky.

Ascot
A Bestiary. Rexroth.

Ash (es)
After Mardi Gras. Mary
  Honora.
After Reading Twenty Years
  of Grantland Rice. Skene.
Amoretti, XXXII. Spenser.
And All the While the Sky Is
  Falling... Dunetz.
Ash. MacBeth.
The Ash and the Oak.
  Simpson.
Ashes. Heine.
Ashes of Roses. Eastman.
Asleep in Jesus. MacKay.
At Lulworth Cove a Century
  Back. Hardy.
Aubade for Hope. Warren.
The Auld Matrons.
  Anonymous.
Behind the Stove. Hearst.
Brazen Tongue. Benet.
But Then and There the Sun
  Bore Down. Momaday.
Caelica, CVIII. Greville.
Chelmsfords Fate. Tompson.
Coach into Pumpkin. Reid.
Come Michaelmas. Choyce.
Cremation. Jeffers.
The Curse: A Song. Herrick.
Discord in Childhood.
  Lawrence.
Doubt. Rogers.
Earth Buried. Mackenzie.
Elegy. Broumas.
Eternity of Love Protested.
  Carew.
The Eve of St. Agnes.
  Keats.
Evolution. Tabb.
Fires of Driftwood.
  MacKay.
Fleeting Restlessness.
  Ibarbourou.
Flower Song. Keating.

Ash

For St. Bartholomew's Eve.
Cowley.
La Fraisne. Pound.
The Garlic. Meyers.
Go Round. Chester.
Goodbye to the Poetry of
Calcium. Wright.
Grandmother. Young Bear.
The Great Blue Heron.
Kizer.
Hope's Okay. Ammons.
In a Surrealist Year.
Ferlinghetti.
Insomnia (excerpt).
Tsvetayeva.
Lines for the Ancient Scribes.
Shapiro.
The Little Milliner.
Buchanan.
Living. Savage.
Madrigal: "The gods have
heard my vows." Weelkes.
Mag Uidhir's Winter
Campaign. O Heoghusa.
Memento Vivendi. Brudne.
No Moon, No Chance to
Meet. Ono no Komachi.
O Brother Man. Whittier.
The Oak and the Ash.
Anonymous.
Old Bibles. Waniek.
On Neal's Ashes. Ginsberg.
Poetry. Rakosi.
Reveille. Hughes.
Sag', Wo Ist Dein Schones
Liebchen. Heine.
A Shropshire Lad.
Housman.
Simchas Torah. Rosenfeld.
Something Has Fallen.
Levine.
Soweto. Sepamla.
St. John. Whittier.
The Storm. Wallace.
Sutter's Fort, Sacramento.
Foote.
To a Recalcitrant Virgin.
Asclepiades.
To Be in Love. Brooks.
To My Fellow-Mariners,
March, '53. Whitbread.
To One of Little Faith.
Flanner.
Upon Love. Herrick.
The Vase of Life. Rossetti.
Vengeance. Kunene.
Virtue. De la Mare.
What Was a Cure for Love?
Godfrey.
When the Day. Sessler.
Wishful Thinking.
Blumenthal.
Women. Cartwright.

Ashamed

Ashamed of Jesus. Grigg.
Avoiding News by the River.
Merwin.
Even in my dreams. Ise.
Lament to Nana of Erech.
Anonymous.
My Brothers... Walters.
The Seamen's Wives'
Vindication. *Anonymous.*
Two Poems About President
Harding, I. Wright.
When I Think of the Hungry
People. O-Shi-O.

Asia

Epiphany. Duggan.
Hebrews. Oppenheim.
The Way a Ghost Dissolves.
Hugo.

Asia Minor

Afternoon. Stryk.

Asian rocks

In Memory of Leopardi.
Wright.

Ask (ed) (ing) (s)

Absalom. Gilead.
After Chagall. Wenger.
After the Rain. Collier.
The Agonizing Memory.
Louys.
All Needs Met. Sammis.
Andre's Request to
Washington. Willis.
Conscious. Owen.
Crimes of Passion. Stokes.
Diogenes. Eastman.
Epitaph for the Unknown
Soldier. Auden.
Epitaphs: For a Fickle Man.
Van Doren.
Explanations of Love.
Sandburg.
Fish Food. Wheelwright.
The Flower of Flame
(excerpt). Nichols.
Furnished Lives. Silkin.
A Harrow Grave in Flanders.
Ashburton.
He Runs into an Old
Acquaintance. Nowlan.
Hermione. Procter.
Hope Is the Thing with
Feathers. Dickinson.
Hours of Idleness. Byron.
I Ask, Who Will Buy a
Poem? O Hifearnain.
The Ignorance of Man.
Merrick.
The Indian Ghost Dance and
War. Prather.
John Garner's Trail Herd.
Anonymous.
Land of the Free. MacLeish.
A Long Overdue Thankyou
Note to the Girl Who
Taught Me Loving.
Schmidt.
Looking for a Rest Area.
Dunn.
The Man in the Street Is Fed.
Sandburg.
Maples (parody). Appleman.
My Legacy. Jackson.
Navajo. Simpson.
Never Ask Me Why.
Margolis.
O Thou Whose Image.
Clough.
Ode Recited at the Harvard
Commemoration. Lowell.
An Ode to the Framers of the
Frame Bill. Byron.
On Change of Weathers.
Quarles.
On Walking Back to the Bus.
Gardner.
The Organ-Grinder.
Garthwaite.
Praise of Mary. *Anonymous.*
Prime. Auden.
A Primer for Schoolchildren.
Weber.
Resolution in Four Sonnets.
Cotton.
Revolutionary Letter #19.
Di Prima.
Riddle #14: A Horn.
Anonymous.
Sing Song. Creeley.
Small Game. Levine.

Song: "When the birds sang."
Anonymous.
Spring Again. Wallace.
Surrender. Grimke.
Taisigh Agat Fein Do Phog.
Anonymous.
Tango. Jordana.
There Was a Time. Thomas.
To a Witty Man of Wealth
and Quality... Wycherley.
A Translation from Walter
von der Vogelweide.
Synge.
Who Will Buy a Poem?
O'Heffernan.
Why Do We Live? Zangwill.

Asleep

Adventure. Benet.
Analysands. Randall.
Asleep. Winter.
Asleep at the. *Anonymous.*
Asleep at the Switch. Hoey.
The Ballad of Father Gilligan.
Yeats.
The Ballad of Hampstead
Heath. Flecker.
Ballad of the Epiphany.
Dalmon.
Buckaroo Sandman.
Anonymous.
Counting Sheep. Edson.
Crossing Kansas by Train.
Justice.
Dead Still. Voznesensky.
The Declaration. Willis.
The Djanggawul Cycle, 174.
Anonymous.
Dolly's Lesson. *Anonymous.*
Everyone in the World.
Dailey.
Falling Asleep. Serraillier.
For Lo! My Jonah How He
Slumped. Wilson.
A Fragment: To Music.
Shelley.
Grecian Kindness.
Rochester.
The Grey Cock (A vers.).
Anonymous.
He. Ashbery.
Her Hair. Chester.
I'd Want Her Eyes to Fill
with Wonder. Patchen.
Indian Summer. Draper.
Insomnia. Thomas.
King Henry VIII.
Shakespeare.
Lady Bates. Jarrell.
Like Weary Trees. Glatstein.
Limerick: "There was a young
fellow named West."
Anonymous.
Lines on the Death of
Bismarck. Chapman.
The Little Drummer.
Stoddard.
London Rain. MacNeice.
Love. Kagawa.
Lullaby. Barnes.
The Macy's Poem. Reiss.
A Man's Need. *Anonymous.*
Mazeppa. Byron.
A Memory. Brooke.
Morning After. Vinz.
Muse and Poet. Bridges.
Music. Shelley.
My Father in the Night
Commanding No.
Simpson.
My Mother. McKay.
The New River Head, a
Fragment. Dower.

No One Is Asleep. Roberts.
Nocturne. Burr.
The Porch. Gildner.
Redwings. Wright.
The River Boats. Hicky.
Rough Winds Do Shake.
Simpson.
Rubric. Peabody.
Seduced Girl. Hedylos.
Semi-Private Room.
Nowlan.
Shadow-Love. Heine.
Sheep. Kraut.
Silhouette in Sepia. Carr.
Sir Hugh; or The Jew's
Daughter (D vers.).
Anonymous.
Six Questions (B vers.).
Anonymous.
The Sleeping Beauty:
Variation of the Prince.
Jarrell.
The Sleepy Song. Bacon.
Song of the Rain. McCrae.
Sweet William. *Anonymous.*
The Sweetest Thing.
Anonymous.
Tecumseh. Mair.
Tennyson. Huxley.
This Place in the Ways.
Rukeyser.
This Quiet Dust. Wheelock.
Three Kings Came.
Shapcott.
To a Child. O'Conor.
To a Lady Who Sent Me a
Copy of Verses at My
Going to Bed. King.
Two Sorrows. St. John.
The Visitor. Davies.
What the Thrush Said.
Keats.
A Woman's Last Word.
Browning.
The Wonder Clock. Pyle.

Asparagus

The Accident. Gasparini.
To the Statue. Swenson.
Turning away from Lies.
Bly.

Aspen

The Aspen and the Stream.
Wilbur.
Spring Song of Aspens.
Spencer.

Asphalt

Detroit City. Boyer.
The Rock. Eliot.
A Serenade for Two Poplars.
Raab.
Under Your Voice, among
Legends. Beauvais.

Aspire

Caelica, CVIII. Greville.
Mother Earth. Margolin.
Orchestra. Davies.
A Simile. Prior.
Sonnet: Of Why He Would Be
a Scullion. Angiolieri.
To a Musician. Austin.
Two Voices in a Meadow.
Wilbur.

Aspirin

Party Knee. Updike.

Ass (es)

Adapt Thyself. Palquera.
The Ass in the Lion's Skin.
Aesop.
The Blind Sheep. Jarrell.
Brother Ass and St. Francis.
Tabb.
The Burro. Gibbons.

The Carnal and the Crane.
Anonymous.
A Cause for Wonder.
Anonymous.
Charles II. *Anonymous.*
The Conquerors. Kemp.
Eighteen-Seventy. Rimbaud.
Epigrams. Pastorius.
The Fable of Midas. Swift.
The Gentleman. Lonzano.
Glory. Shapiro.
A Gulling Sonnet. Davies.
Hunting. Snyder.
Hygiene Sonnet. Gallup.
I Came A-Riding. Reinmar
von Zweter.
Limerick: "A well-buggered
boy named Delpasse."
Anonymous.
The Lion and the Cub. Gay.
Memorial. Sanchez.
Metamorphoses. Ovid
(Publius Ovidius Naso).
The Metamorphosis.
Suckling.
Midsummer Night's Dream.
Vazakas.
On the Murder of Sir
Edmund Berry Godfrey.
Anonymous.
On the Supposed Author of a
Late Poem "In Defense of
Satire." Rochester.
The Rubaiyat: A book of
verses underneath the
bough. Omar Khayyam.
This Island. Archilochus.
Unto the Breach. Poliziano.
Valentine. Hemingway.
Assault
Epigram. *Anonymous.*
High Summer. Kessler.
Of Scolding Wives and the
Third Day Ague. Selyns.
Assent (ion)
Belief and Unbelief.
Freneau.
The People in the Park.
Adams.
To Dianeme. Herrick.
Assign (ment)
Dromedary. Dodat.
On His 86th Birthday.
Hardy.
Assist (ance) (ant)
A Ballad to the Tune of "The
Cut-Purse." Swift.
Eleven Addresses to the Lord.
Berryman.
Epistle II: To a Socialist in
London. Bridges.
I Love My Jesus Quite Alone.
Kelpius.
Newes from Virginia. Rich.
Poems in Praise of Practically
Nothing. Hoffenstein.
Associates
In His Mental Illness, William
Cowper Finds He Is Not
Alone. Cowper.
Assuage (ed)
Limerick: "There was an old
man whose despair." Lear.
The Princess Casamassima.
Hoffman.
Assume
We Assume: On the Death of
Our Son, Reuben Masai
Harper. Harper.

Assumption
The Ascension and the
Assumption. Lopez
Velarde.
Assurance
The City of Dreadful Night.
Thomson.
A Country Life: To His
Brother, M. Tho: Herrick.
Herrick.
Astonish (ed) (ment)
The Adoration of the Magi.
Pilling.
The Burglar of Babylon.
Bishop.
Nosce Teipsum: An
Acclamation. Davies.
Pastoral. Dubie.
Pastoral. Williams.
Song of Myself. Whitman.
The Way We Wonder. Pack.
Words. Rodgers.
Astray
Epigram: "Truth I pursued, as
Fancy sketch'd the way."
Coleridge.
The Faerie Queene. Spenser.
Fair Florella (B vers.).
Anonymous.
The Golden Sequence.
Innocent III.
In Defense of Satire.
Scroope.
The Jealous Lover (B vers.).
Anonymous.
The Lion's Nature.
Anonymous.
The Moon. Bhasa.
There Were an Old and
Wealthy Man.
Anonymous.
Windows. Husid.
Written in an Ovid. Prior.
Astronaut
Astronaut's Choice. Darcy.
Astronomy
Song Set by John Dowland:
"What poor astronomers
are they." *Anonymous.*
Thomas More to Them That
Seek Fortune. More.
Asylum (s)
Asylum. Freeman.
The Gothic Dusk. Prokosch.
Historiography. Thomas.
At home
Arrivals at a Watering-Place.
Praed.
Plans for Altering the River.
Hugo.
Three Children. *Anonymous.*
Various Wakings. Buckley.
Ate
Bread. Dickey.
Breakfast. Gibson.
I Must Remember.
Silverstein.
No Country You Remember.
Mezey.
On a Certain Alderman.
Cunningham.
A Party. Richards.
St. Martin and the Beggar.
Gunn.
Trench Poets. Rickword.
The Wedding. Aiken.
Atheist (s)
Perfection. Carlin.
A Rapture. Carew.
Untitled. Randall, Jr.

Athens
Song: "The little Black Rose
shall be red at last!" De
Vere.
The Wayzgoose. Campbell.
Winter Homily on the Calton
Hill. Young.
Atlanta
We Don't Get No Justice
Here in Atlanta.
Anonymous.
Atlantic
Bahamas. Oppen.
Canadian Boat Song.
Anonymous.
Kennedy. Heffernan.
Man and Wife. Lowell.
Sundered. Zangwill.
Tangier: Hotel Rif. Thomas.
Atlantis
12 Gates to the City.
Giovanni.
Sailor and Inland Flower.
Maclaren.
Western Ways. Lattimore.
Atlas
The Neurotic. Day.
Street Song. Sitwell.
Atmosphere
The Autumn Leaves.
Anonymous.
The Ghost of the Cargo Boat.
Neruda.
The Imperfect Lover.
Sassoon.
Israel Freyer's Bid for Gold.
Stedman.
A Lovely Love. Brooks.
The Recollection. Shelley.
Atom (ic) (s)
All That Is, and Can Delight.
Farren.
A Backwards Journey. Page.
The Brick. Roche.
Calling Myself Home.
Hogan.
Choice. Dickinson.
Directions for Making a
Birth-Day Song: "To form a
just..." Swift.
Footnote to Feynman. Post.
For the Fly-Leaf of a School-
Book. Cameron.
The Hand and Foot. Very.
Improvisation on an Old
Theme. Livesay.
Joy of Knowledge.
Schneider.
The Life of Particles.
Benedikt.
Mary's Ghost. Hood.
Norris Dam. Rodman.
O Solitary of the Austere Sky.
Roberts.
The Poet's Day. Weber.
The Progress of Faust.
Shapiro.
Prudence. Emerson.
Signatures. Stevenson.
Trail Breakers. Daugherty.
Villanelle. Skeat.
We Who Are About to Die.
Fey.
When I Have Gone Weird
Ways. Neihardt.
Atone (ment)
Chant Royal From a
Copydesk. Terral.
Heart of Light. Campbell.
I Believe Thy Precious Blood.
Wesley.
In Tribute. House.

Sonnets: A Sequence on
Profane Love. Boker.
To Philip Levine, on the Day
of Atonement. Mezey.
Attack (s)
Five. Kees.
The Indians on Alcatraz.
Muldoon.
It Is Not Enough.
Henderson.
Sonnet III: "O interminable
desires, O futile hope."
Labe.
Waldere 2. *Anonymous.*
Wanderings: Champs
d'Honneur. Hemingway.
Attain (ed) (ments)
Columbus. Schiller.
Plea for Hope. Carlin.
Poem Read at Joan Mitchell's.
O'Hara.
Attempt (ing) (s)
The Bat. Nash.
The Self-Deceaver.
Montalvan.
Attend (ed)
A Ballad from the Seven Dials
Press... *Anonymous.*
The Grief of Cafeterias.
Updike.
I Am the Duke of Norfolk.
Anonymous.
Oxford Commination. Leary.
The South Carolina.
Anonymous.
Attention (s)
The Art of Love: Happy the
Man Who Has Two Breasts
to Crush. Koch.
I Am Yours & You Are Mine
So. Silverton.
Limerick: "There was a young
Fellow of Caius."
Anonymous.
Locations. Fraser.
The Moths. O Riordain.
The Soul Selects Her Own
Society. Dickinson.
Spring Day. Ashbery.
Where Are You Now
Superman? Patten.
Attic (s)
Absences. Larkin.
Deceptions. Larkin.
Goosey Goosey Gander.
French.
Attila
Dirge of Alaric the Visigoth.
Everett.
Audience (s)
Concert-Interpretations (Le
Sacre du Printemps).
Sassoon.
Departed–to the Judgment.
Dickinson.
Doctors' Row. Aiken.
Evening Ebb. Jeffers.
Gaiety: Queer's Song.
Howard.
Ode to Terminus. Auden.
Regent's Park Terrace.
Spencer.
Strangers. Thomas.
Audubon
Up from the Egg: The
Confessions of a Nuthatch
Avoider. Nash.
Augury
Acme and Septimius.
Catullus.

August
The Announcement. Ellenbogen.
August. Winslow.
La Belle Saison. Prevert.
Cuckoo Song. Hinkson.
Emblems. Tate.
The Fifth Season. Saner.
In lands I never saw, they say. Dickinson.
In the Wide Awe and Wisdom of the Night. Roberts.
Insomniac Poem. Loewinsohn.
Katydids. Lowell.
Las Trampas U.S.A. Tomlinson.
The Month of Falling Stars. Higginson.
The Oyster. Nash.
Remembering Althea. Stafford.
To the Cuckoo. *Anonymous.*

Augustine
Ladies' Voices. Stein.

Auld Lang Syne
The Relief of Lucknow. Lowell.

Aunt (s)
The Bath. Graham.
Call the Horse, Marrow. *Anonymous.*
Death. Jones.
I Am the Monarch of the Sea. Gilbert.
Impermanence. Lal Ded.
Insight. Goose.
Matilda. Belloc.
My Aunt. Hughes.
My Aunt. Wood.
Ode to a Lebanese Crock of Olives. Wakoski.
The Old Girl. Lenhart.
Out to Old Aunt Mary's. Riley.
A Poor Relation. McGaffin.
Riddle: "There were three sisters in a hall." *Anonymous.*
Song for the Old Ones. Angelou.
Thumb. Dacey.

Austere
Pussycat Sits on a Chair. Horn.
To a Beautiful but Heartless Coquette. Terrazas.

Austerity
This Land. Mudie.

Australia (n)
Cape Cod Girls. *Anonymous.*
Dick Briggs from Australia. Thatcher.
Five Visions of Captain Cook. Slessor.
Madrid, Iowa. Ikan.
One Day. Mathew.
The Settler's Lament. *Anonymous.*
Slide, Kelly, Slide. Kelly.
They'll Tell You About Me. Mudie.

Author (s)
Epitaph. Franklin.
Hamlet's Soliloquy Imitated (parody). Jago.
A Little While to Love and Rave. Hoffenstein.
A New-Yeares-Gift Sung to King Charles, 1635. Jonson.
Shakespearean Soliloquy in Progress: "To print, or not to..." (parody). Jago.
Sonnet: "The world's a stage." Belloc.
To Sir Edward Herbert at Julyers. Donne.

Authority
Household. Jensen.
Nausicaa with Some Attendants. Lowenstein.
The Negativess Person. Levine.
The Purpose of Altar Boys. Rios.

Auto-da-fe
El Emplazado. Venable.

Auto (mobile)
Grisaille with a Spot of Red. Yellen.
The Sidewalk Racer. Morrison.

Autographs
Femina. Marlatt.

Automation
Black Students. Fields.

Autumn
An Abortion. O'Hara.
Adam and Eve. Shapiro.
After the Persian. Bogan.
At 85. Ardinger.
At Night. Akhmadulina.
Autumn. *Anonymous.*
Autumn. Clare.
An Autumn Day. MacLean.
Autumn Flowers. Very.
Autumn Leaves. Webb.
Autumn's Mirth. Peck.
Autumn Squall–Lake Erie. Russo.
The Autumn Wind. Clare.
The Beech. Young.
A Bird Comes. Yosano Akiko.
Camel. Akhyaliyya.
The City of Falling Leaves. Lowell.
The Closing Scene. Read.
The Dustbowl. Elmslie.
Elegy. Fitzgerald.
The Excursion. Tu Fu.
First Love. Dorcey.
The Fisherman. Stewart.
Folk Song. *Anonymous.*
Gold Leaves. Chesterton.
Haiku: "On this road." Basho (Matsuo Basho).
The Hound. Deutsch.
The Humble Petition of Bruar Water to the Noble Duke of Athole. Burns.
I Wish I Could Lend a Coat. Akahito (Yamabe no Akahito).
In Autumn When the Woods Are Red. Stevenson.
In the gathering dew. Sagami.
In the Tail of the Scorpion. Taggard.
The Jewel Stairs' Grievance. Li Po.
The King of Ulster. *Anonymous.*
Late Autumn. Young.
Let Him Return. Hill.
Manyoshu: When, Loosened from the Winter's Bonds. Nukada. Princess
On the Road Home. Stevens.
Parting. Vinner.
Poem: "The tiny new emotions." Clark.
Proberbially Useful Dates for Weathermen. *Anonymous.*
Proud Riders. Davis.
The Ragged Robin Opens. Radnoti.
Rest and Silence. Trakl.
September. Pastan.
The Sequel. Roethke.
The Settlers. Hemschemeyer.
Skykomish River Running. Hugo.
So This Is Autumn. Watt.
Soliloquy in an Air-Raid. Fuller.
Song at the Beginning of Autumn. Jennings.
Summer 1970. Mabuza.
This Fall. Aliesan.
Three Tanka, 3. Yosano Akiko.
Troubled Woman. Hughes.
Turn Blind. Celan.
Two Poems. *Anonymous.*
The Very Old. Galloway.
Weather Vanes. Frost.
What Shall I Give My Children? Brooks.
The Widow. Davenport.
Winter is Another Country. MacLeish.
Winter Sign. Eiseley.
The Womanhood. Brooks.
The Yankee Man-of-War or The Stately Southerner. *Anonymous.*

Avalanche
Another Island Groupage. Elmslie
In a Museum in the Capital. Stafford.
Strength through Joy. Rexroth.

Avarice
Although I put away his life. Dickinson.
Hamatreya. Emerson.
On the Lord Gen. Fairfax at the Siege of Colchester. Milton.

Avenge (d) (r) (s)
The Battle of the Frogs and Mice. Homer
Don Juan. Byron.
He Biddeth Osiris to Arise from the Dead. Book of the Dead.
The Lady and the Dwarf-King. *Anonymous.*
La Promessa Sposa. Landor.
Yussouf. Lowell.

Avenging
On the Defeat at Ticonderoga or Carilong. *Anonymous*

Avenue
Food. Chute.
Leave Cancelled. Berkson.
Old Man. Thomas.
The Shore of Life. Fitzgerald.

Average man
The Average Man. Sangster.
My House. McKay.

Aversion
Lord Barrenstock. Smith.

Aviary
Aviary. McGuckian.
Limerick: "A vice most obscene and unsavoury." *Anonymous.*

Avoid
The Results of Stealing a Pin. *Anonymous.*

Avow (al)
A Circular Cry. Jabes.
The Holy Nunnery. *Anonymous.*

Await (ing)
The Bottle. De la Mare.
Easter Morn. Fletcher.
February 11, 1977. Morgan.
Glory Be to God for Dappled Things. Keating.
No Dawns. Perry.
Peter Emberley (I). *Anonymous.*

Awake (s)
The 20th Century. Gray.
Asleep. Owen.
Before Dawn. Chipp.
Book of the Dead, Prayer 14. Berssenbrugge.
The Burial. Davis.
The Canadian Rossignol. Thomson.
A Child's Evening Prayer. Coleridge.
A Christmas Carol. Herrick.
A Christmas Wish. Field.
Cradle Song. MacNeice.
Cradle Song. Peabody.
Creation of the Child. Litwack.
The Damsel. Omar B. Abi Rabi'a.
Dedication. Stull.
Delfica. Nerval.
The Desolate Valley. Pringle.
The Discovery. Gibbon.
Dreams. Cooper.
Epitaph. Teasdale.
First Dream (Excerpt). Juana Ines de la Cruz.
Fragment Thirty-Six. Doolittle.
The Great Bear Lake Meditations (excerpt). Yates.
Her Sweet Voice. Carew.
In Praise of Wyatt's Psalms. Surrey.
In Shadow. Hazard.
In Sorrow. Hastings.
Life Is a Platform. Levi.
Morning Prayer. Nash.
The Moss Supplicateth for the Poet. Dana.
Mother Earth. Margolin.
Muse and Poet. Bridges.
Night after Night. Bloede.
O Gracious Jesus, Blessed Lord! Fowler.
O Son of God, Afflicted. *Anonymous.*
On Death. Keats.
The Passing of a Dream. Clare.
Prothalamion (excerpt). Hillyer.
R.M.S. Titanic. Cronin.
Rino's Song. Lawner.
Rough Winds Do Shake. Simpson.
The Sailor. Warner.
Sea Monster. Merwin.
Shira. Schwartz.
A Shropshire Lad. Housman.
Song: "Awake thee, my Bessy, the morning is fair." Callanan.

The Song of the Tortured
Girl. Berryman.
Tarry with Me, O My
Saviour. Smith.
To His Valentine. Drayton.
To Sleep. Fialkowski.
Tom Thomson. Bourinot.
The Tree Sleeps in the Winter.
Russell.
The Twilight Shadows Round
Me Fall. Ryden.
View from an Apartment.
Palmer.
The Vindictive Staircase or
The Reward of Industry.
Gibson.
What the Thrush Said.
Keats.
Willie the Weeper.
Anonymous.
Wishmakers' Town. Young.
The Younger Van Eyck.
Bentley.

Awaken (ed) (ing) (ings) (s)
Awakening. Bly.
Clearing for the Plough.
Moll.
Dawns I Have Seen.
Gurney.
December 18, 1975. Hogan.
Falling in Love. Anderson.
Falling in Love. Perkins.
For Arvia. Robinson.
If the Owl Calls Again.
Haines.
In a Train. Bly.
Into the Glacier. Haines.
Loneliness. Young.
March Wind. Warsh.
Message. Richardson.
The Skunk (parody). Dow.
Spring and All. Williams.
With God Conversing.
Derwood.
The Wooing Lady. Smith.

Awards
The Death Sentence. Smith.

Aware
The Future. Benedikt.
Gift of Sight. Graves.
Infant Innocence. Housman.
The Odyssey. Homer.
The red road. NorthSun.
The Silken Tent. Frost.

Away
The Absence. Warner.
All Day and All October.
Lerner.
Amours de Voyage. Clough.
Antelope. Smith.
An Appeal to Cats in the
Business of Love.
Flatman.
Arthur. Paulin.
Away. Riley.
Ballade of the Heresiarchs.
Belloc.
Bell Horses, Bell Horses,
What Time of Day?
Mother Goose.
Bones. De La Mare.
Buckee Bene. Anonymous
By the Road. Grigson.
Cavalier Tunes. Browning.
A Certain Lady. Parker.
Chanson de Rosemonde.
Hovey.
Chicken. Etter.
City Streets and Country
Roads. Farjeon.
Cows. Reeves.

A Documentary on Airplane
Glue. Henderson.
Drifting away. Kingsley.
Fatness. Ansen.
Four Anacreontic Poems, 1.
Spenser.
The Hobbit (excerpt).
Tolkien.
The Hosting of the Sidhe.
Yeats.
I Had Been Hungry, All the
Years. Dickinson.
I'm Just a Stranger Here,
Heaven Is My Home.
Clemmons.
A Little Boy Lost. Blake.
Lully, Lulley. Anonymous.
Lulu. Anonymous.
Meeting Point. MacNeice.
The Old Lady of London.
Anonymous.
On Leaving Mrs. Brown's
Lodgings. Scott.
On the Quay. Bell.
The Sack of Deerfield.
English.
She sweeps with many-colored
brooms. Dickinson.
Shoe the Colt, Shoe the Colt.
Anonymous.
The Soul's Defiance.
Stoddard.
Success. Empson.
Swinburne at Tea. Pain.
We're All Bound to Go.
Anonymous.
The Whale. Anonymous.
When I Grow Up. Holland.
When My Love Was Away.
Bridges.

Awe (s)
The Angel in the House.
Patmore.
A Dream, or the Type of the
Rising Sun. Adams.
Hamlet. Shakespeare.
The Heretic. Carman.
The Law. Ibn Ezra.
Preludes. Patmore.
La Vita Nuova. Dante
Alighieri.

Awful
Drugged. De la Mare.
A Great Tempest on the Plain
of Ler. Anonymous.
He Loves and He Rides
Away. Dobell.
Songs of Cheng. Confucius.
Surprise. Witt.
Winter Evening. Lampman.

Awning
A Gone. Eigner.

Awoke
Dawn. Rimbaud.
Dream. Smith.
Dream of a Father.
Cochrane.
The Inverted Torch.
Thomas.
This Night. Mandelstam.
Van Dieman's Land.
Anonymous.
Waking Alone. Anonymous.
Yom Kippur. Zangwill.

Axe (s)
The Axe of the Pioneer.
Crawford.
The Double Axe.
Hazlewood-Brady.
Dream Songs. Berryman.
Man Arrested in Hacking
Death Tells Police He

Mistook Mother-in-Law...
Ludvigson.
The Martyrdom of Mary,
Queen of Scots. Southwell.
Ned Braddock. Palmer.
Sir Gawain and the Green
Knight. Anonymous.
The Sorcerer: Mr. Wells.
Gilbert.
Tables. Clark.
When he sailed into the
harbor. Korinna.
Woodman, Spare That Tree.
Morris.

Axiom (s)
The Balcony Poems. Smith.
From a Cheerful Alphabet.
Updike.

Azalea
Proportion. Lowell.

Azure
After the Fire. Holmes.
Childe Harold's Pilgrimage:
Canto IV, XXVII. Byron.
La Fontaine de Vaucluse.
Hacker.
She Dwelt aong the
Untrodden Ways (parody).
Squire.
The Sun Spirit. Chubb.
Sursum. Valencia.
Theophila: Cynthia.
Benlowes.

B

Baal
On Certain Wits. Nemerov.
Baal Shem Tov
The Strange Guest. Manger.
Babbling (s)
Epigram: "Why all the
racket." Anonymous.
Talking with Soldiers.
Turner.
To W.B.Yeats Who Says That
His Castle of Ballylee Is His
Monument. Gogarty.
Under the Casuarina.
Riddell.
Babe (s)
The Babes in the Wood.
Anonymous.
Bonnie James Campbell.
Anonymous.
Fare Thee Well, Babe.
Anonymous.
Farewell to the Old Year!
Farjeon.
For Us No Night Can Be
Happier. Zinzendorf.
Jamie Douglas (A vers.).
Anonymous.
Loss in Delay. Southwell.
My Dear, Do You Know.
Anonymous.
No Sweeter Thing. Love.
One Word More. Browning.
The Poor Children. Hugo.
Remembrance. Boner.
Revolutionary Letters. Di
Prima.
The Shepherd Left Behind.
Merryman.
The Storm-Wind. Barnes.
Theseus and Ariadne.
Mifflin.
Two Hoboes. Anonymous.

Babel
The Sedge-Warbler.
Hodgson.
Therefore Is the Name of It
Called Babel. Sitwell.
Baboon
The Ape, the Monkey and
Baboon Did Meet.
Anonymous.
Lord Lovel (parody).
Anonymous.
Baby grand
How About. Nelms.
Baby (ies)
The 29th Month. Rice.
Advent 1955. Betjeman.
After the Quarrel. Gibson.
Alice. Bashford.
All the Pretty Little Horses.
Anonymous.
Anne Hutchinson's Exile.
Hale.
Another Night on the Porch
Swing. Quirk.
Antony and Cleopatra.
Shakespeare.
As I Went A-Walking One
Fine Summer's Evening.
Anonymous.
Babies of the Pioneers.
Luckey.
The Baby. Reaney.
Baby Sleeps. Hinds.
Ballad of the Epiphany.
Dalmon.
Bed-Time. Erskine.
A Bestiary. Rexroth.
Bye, Baby Bunting. Mother
Goose.
Catch Him, Crow! Carry Him,
Kite! Anonymous.
The Cherry Tree. Gunn.
Chuck Will's Widow Song.
Anonymous.
Cigarettes Will Spoil Yer Life
(with music). Anonymous.
Communion. Giltinan.
Crooked Carol. Farber.
Dance a Baby Diddy.
Anonymous.
The Drunken Fool.
Anonymous.
Etude Realiste. Swinburne.
Eve of Easter. Mayer.
Faces. Anderson.
Family Chronicle. Parlatore.
Five Vignettes. Toomer.
Flashback. Ginsberg.
Flemish Primitive. Fraser.
Frightened. Ferlinghetti.
Go to Sleepy. Anonymous.
Good-Night. Taylor.
The Gosport Tragedy (A
vers.). Anonymous.
Here Are the Lady's Knives
and Forks. Anonymous.
Hush-a-Bye, Baby.
Anonymous.
Hush Thee, My Babby.
Anonymous.
Hymn to Mercury. Homer.
I Found God. Thacker.
I'll Go with Her Blues.
Wilkins.
In Spring in Warm Weather.
Aldis.
It's Cold in China Blues.
Nettles.
John of Tours. Anonymous.
Korf's Joke. Morgenstern.
The Lamb-Child. Tabb.

Baby

Limerick: "You remember that pastoral frolic." "B.
Little Boy Blue. Lockwood.
Little Feet. Akers.
Lorraine Loree. Kingsley.
The Lost Baby. *Anonymous.*
Lullaby. *Anonymous.*
Lullaby. Chipp.
Lullaby of the Iroquois. Johnson.
Marthy Virginia's Hand. Lathrop.
Mary and the Baby, Sweet Lamb. *Anonymous.*
Mimma Bella. Lee-Hamilton.
The Mocking Bird. *Anonymous.*
Mojo Hiding Woman. Fuller.
The Moon. Follen.
The Mouse's Lullaby. Cox.
My Face Is My Own, I Thought. Raworth.
The Night Was Smooth. Bertolino.
No Baby in the House. Dolliver.
On the Edge. Dwyer.
One Morning in May. *Anonymous.*
Only. Spofford.
Our Goodman (B vers.). *Anonymous.*
Our Polite Parents. Wells.
Poem from Deal. Shapiro.
Rain Rain on the Splintered Girl. Reed.
Regina Coeli. Patmore.
Rock-a-Bye Baby. Canning.
Rock-a-Bye Baby. Mother Goose.
Rosemary Lane. *Anonymous.*
Run Little Dogies. *Anonymous.*
Savannah Mama. McTell.
Soldier, Soldier, Won't You Marry Me? *Anonymous.*
Soldier, Won't You Marry Me? *Anonymous.*
Strictly Germ-Proof. Guiterman.
Take a Walk around the Corner. Carr.
Telephone Arguin' Blues. Short.
That Crawling Baby Blues. Jefferson.
That Lonesome Train Took My Baby Away. McCoy.
Those Trees That Line the Northway. Perreault.
To a Friend's Child. Barnstone.
A Tonversaton with Baby. Bishop.
Tucking the Baby In. May.
Under Milk Wood (excerpt). Thomas.
Waiting for Breakfast, While She Brushed Her Hair. Larkin.
The Way the Baby Woke. Riley.
We Women. Sodergran.
Wedding. Lipska.
What'll We Do with the Baby-O? *Anonymous.*
What the Donkey Saw. Fanthorpe.
Y M & V Blues. Hunter.

Babylon (ian)

Babylon. Taylor.
A Ballad of London. Le Gallienne.
The Burglar of Babylon. Bishop.
A Duet. Moore.
Echoes. Henley.
Harps Hung Up in Babylon. Colton.
The Heart. Thompson.
The Impious Feast. Landor.
London, Hast Thou Accused Me. Surrey.
On Alexander and Aristotle, on a Black-on-Red Greek Plate. Dugan.
Sheep. Francis.
Sonnets of the Months. San Geminiano.
Storm on Fifth Avenue. Sassoon.
Super Flumina Babylonis. Swinburne.
Tamburlaine the Great. Marlowe.

Bacchus

A Blackbird. Argentarius.
Epigram. Moore.

Bach

All Those Hymnings Up to God. Evans.
Beginnings. Biton.
The Climbing Rope. Stuart.
Dream. Moore.
I Know a Man. Steele.

Bachelor (s)

The Ballad of the Dark Ladie. Coleridge.
If Ever I Marry, I'll Marry a Maid. *Anonymous.*
Madrigal: "O I do love, then kiss me." Jones.
The Two Old Bachelors. Lear.
When Boys Go A-Courting. *Anonymous.*

Bachelor's button

I Used to Love My Garden. Sawyer.

Back door

Bullfrog Blues. Harris.
Slow Mama Slow. Collins.
Staying Ahead. Glass.
A Word About Woodpiles. Turner.

Back (ed) (s)

Adam in Love. Mitchell.
Adam Smith. Bentley.
Awakening. Robinson.
Bangkok. Scott.
The Beaten Path. Winslow.
The Beggar. Doak.
The Bewick and the Graeme. *Anonymous.*
A Big Ship Sailing. *Anonymous.*
The Brothers. Holloway.
Calico Pie. Lear.
Careless Love. *Anonymous.*
Children. Edson.
Coast to Coast. Rich.
The Couple. Blandiana.
The Distances. Merwin.
Don Juan in Hell. Baudelaire.
Donald. Abbey.
Drive Away Blues. McTell.
Duet. Speyer.
Easy Rider Blues. Jefferson.
Elephant. McFadden.
Epigrams. Theocritus.

Feeding the Lions. Jordan.
A Field Poem. Valaitis.
A Fieldmouse. Sund.
Fighter. Zimunya.
For Freckle-Faced Gerald. Knight.
For My Son, Born during an Ice Storm. *Anonymous.*
Forest. Blackwell.
Getting Older Here. Hauk.
Gift. Cohen.
The Green Briar Shore. *Anonymous.*
Griesly Wife. Manifold.
Hardcastle Crags. Plath.
He Maketh Himself One with the Only God, Whose Limbs Are the Many God. Book of the Dead.
Heavy-Hipted Woman. *Anonymous.*
I Am Raftery. Mahon.
If He Let Us Go Now. Williams.
The Invitation. MacDonagh.
Ireland Lake. Hershon.
Jerusalem Sonnets. Baxter.
Johnny. Rounds.
July in Washington. Lowell.
Lackey Bill. *Anonymous.*
Legacy II. Quintana.
Lend a Hand. Hale.
Limerick: "There was once a fastidious yak." Herford.
Little Black Man with a Rose in His Hat. Wurdemann.
Mademoiselle from Armentieres. *Anonymous.*
Mama and Daughter. Hughes.
Morning. Rios.
Not to Keep. Frost.
Olga Poems. Levertov.
On the Hill below the Lighthouse. Dickey.
The Oregon Trail. *Anonymous.*
Orpheus. Herrick.
Owed to America. Durrell.
The Pessimist. King.
The Photographer Whose Shutter Died. Meissner.
Polly Williams. *Anonymous.*
Psalm VI. Sidney.
Raging Canawl. *Anonymous.*
Rooftop. Barnstone.
A Room in the Past. Kooser.
Samadhi. Aiken.
Small Fountains. Abercrombie.
A Street Scene. Reese.
The Subversive. Woo.
Swans. Wordsworth.
To Be in Love While in Prison. Minarik.
The Tortoise in Eternity. Wylie.
Unwelcome. Coleridge.
A Vision That Appeared to Me. MacConglinne.
Wake-Up Niggers. Lee.
The Wedding of Alcmane and Mya. Chapman.
Woodstock. Mitchell.
Yesterday. Chesterman.

Backbone

Back Gnawing Blues. Thomas.
This Island. Archilochus.

Background

Nox Ignatiana. Daly.

A Person, a Mexican. Martinez.
Russia. Williams.

Backward (s)

The Bald Spot. McNair.
Courtship. O Hehir.
The Ethnic Life. Halpern.
Hate and Debate Rome through the World Hath Spread. Harington.
Ichabod. Whittier.
Migrants. Anderson.
On a Vulgar Error. Lewis.
The Plowman. Knister.
The Prophet. Gibran.
The Rock. Eliot.
The Subverted Flower. Frost.
Tell Me, O Love. Hammond.

Backyard

Come Back Blues. Harper.
The Difference. Chaffee.
Original Sin: A Short Story. Warren.
Returned to Frisco. Snodgrass.

Bacteria

World of Bacteria. Hagiwara.

Bacteria (l)

Come Unto These Yellow Sands (parody). Dehn.

Bad

A Box for Tom. Tate.
Chain Gang Trouble. Lincoln (Hicks).
Choosing a Wet-Nurse. Saint-Marthe.
Dakota: October, 1822. Hunkpapa Warrior. Taylor.
The Dog. Herford.
Emma. Yvonne.
Epitaph on Dr. Keene's Wife. Gray.
An Epitaph on His Grandfather. Shipman.
Fantasia on a Wittelsbach Atmosphere. Sassoon.
Five Lyrics from "Good for Nothing Man". Pitchford.
Four Children. *Anonymous.*
Fraulein Reads Instructive Rhymes. Kumin.
Free Little Bird. *Anonymous.*
From the Triads of Ireland. *Anonymous.*
Good News Bad News. Abbott.
I Been a Bad, Bad Girl. *Anonymous.*
I Came to This Country in 1865. *Anonymous.*
I'll Never Use Tobacco. *Anonymous.*
In Order To. Patchen.
It Might Have Been Worse. Russell.
Juan Rulfo Moved Away. Rios.
King Borborigmi. Aiken.
The Last Democrat. Enright.
Look Back. Arnett.
Macbeth. Shakespeare.
My Father, My Son. Brinnin.
Ode to Freedom. Zeitlin.
On Not Being Milton. Harrison.
Plane Geometer. McCord.

The Prophet. Gibran.
The Rime of the Auncient
Waggonere (parody).
Maginn.
The Robin and the Redbreast.
Anonymous.
Sayings from the Northern
Ice. Stafford.
Sonnets, LXVII: "Ah
wherefore with infection
should he live."
Shakespeare.
Sonnets, CXXI: "'Tis better to
be vile than vile esteemed."
Shakespeare.
Sonnets, CXLIV: "Two loves
I have of comfort and
despair." Shakespeare.
There Was a Little Girl.
Longfellow.
Up & out. NorthSun.
Where Are the War Poets?
Day-Lewis.
A Wild Rattling Cowboy.
Anonymous.

Badge
Calamity Jane Greets Her
Dreams. Lignell.
Chic Freedom's Reflection.
Walker.
The Last Chapter. De la
Mare.

Baffle (d) (s)
Muse in Late November.
Brooks.
Ode to a Lady Whose Lover
Was Killed by a Ball...
Byron.

Bag
Of Change of Opinions.
Plarr.

Bag (s)
The Bag of the Bee. Herrick.
The Common Cormorant.
Isherwood.
An Egyptian Passage. Weiss.
Evening. Sitwell.
Hard Times, But Carrying
On. Smith.
Shoplifters. Stanton.

Bagpipe (s)
The Bagpipe Man. Turner.
My Hobby Horse.
Anonymous.
The Pipes o' Gordon's Men.
Glasgow.

Bail (ing)
Roll in My Sweet Baby's
Arms. *Anonymous.*
Sartorial Solecism. Stringer.

Bairn (ies) (s)
The Battle of Harlaw (A
version). *Anonymous.*
Cuddle Doon. Anderson.
Dingle Dingle Doosey.
Anonymous.
Duriesdyke. *Anonymous.*
Lord Ingram and Chiel Wyet
(C version). *Anonymous.*
My Wife's a Wanton Wee
Thing. *Anonymous.*
The Purification. Cosmas.
The Schoolmaster.
Anonymous.
A Scottish Proverb.
Anonymous.

Bait (ed)
Bobber. Carver.
Certain Maxims of Archy.
Marquis.
Columbus. Hutchison.
The Fisherman. Stuart.

The Foreboding. Graves.
Jersey Bait Shack. Balakian.
The Moral Bully. Holmes.
To a Little Boy Learning to
Fish. Hoeft.
To Alexander Neville.
Googe.

Bake (d) (r) (s)
The Apple Dumplings and a
King. Wolcot.
Bendix. Updike.
Ode to Miss Hoyland
(parody). Chatterton.
The Tale of a Tart.
Weatherly.
To the Bat. *Anonymous.*
White People. Henderson.

Baking
The Duke of Athole's Nurse
(B version). *Anonymous.*

Balance (d) (s)
The Blind Man. Lewisohn.
Father-in-Law. Mahon.
Justice Is Reason Enough.
Wakoski.
Love Calls Us to the Things
of This World. Wilbur.
Mississippi Sawyer.
Anonymous.
The Organist in Heaven.
Brown.
To a Millionaire. Lampman.
Wesley in Heaven. Brown.
When Satan Fell. Lawrence.

Balcony (ies)
Paul Veronese. Ferguson.
The Right of Way.
Williams.
Saturday Night in the
Parthenon. Patchen.
Tales of the Islands, II.
Walcott.

Bald
The Desperado. *Anonymous.*
The Double Looking Glass.
Hope.
Fork. Simic.
In Memoriam A.H.H., VII.
Tennyson.
The Little Dandelion.
Weeden.
The Olympic Girl.
Betjeman.
Wart Hog. Skelton.

Bale (s)
The Battle of Glentilt (1847).
Maclagan.
Beauty's Queen. Kisa'i of
Merv.
I Have Set My Heart So
High. *Anonymous.*
Pick a Bale of Cotton.
Anonymous.
The Scholar-Gipsy. Arnold.

Baleful air!
Sesostris. Mifflin.

Balk
The Blood Horse.
"Cornwall.
On Censure. Swift.

Ball game
Take Me Out to the Ball
Game. Norworth.

Ball (s)
8-Ball at the Twilite. Baker.
All of Us Always Turning
away for Solace.
Schwartz.
At the Ball! Webb.
Autumn's Fete. McGeorge.
Baseball. Clark.

Because Sometimes You Can't
Always Be So. Patchen.
By Candlelight. Plath.
Casey's Revenge. Wilson.
Catalogue. Domin.
Cherry Tree. Rossetti.
Cinderella Grass. Fisher.
Don't Grow Weary, Boys.
Anonymous.
Epigrams in Distich, I: The
Fine Lady Reform'd.
Anonymous.
The Fight at Nevadaville.
Anonymous.
High and Low. Tabb.
How the Death of a City Is
Never More Than the Sum
of the Deaths... Coleman.
I felt a cleavage in my mind.
Dickinson.
Ladies' Voices. Stein.
Lanigan's Ball. *Anonymous.*
A Man Saw a Ball of Gold.
Padgett.
An Opium Fantasy. Lowell.
Out of Bounds. Tabb.
Percy Shelley. Bishop.
The Pinball Queen of South
Illinois St. Tietz.
A Snail's Derby. Lee-
Hamilton.
West Helena Blues. Sykes.

Ballad (s)
And Jesus Don't Have Much
Use for His Old Suitcase
Anymore. Kryss.
Down-Hall. Prior.
A faded boy in sallow clothes.
Dickinson.
Robin Hood's Birth, Breeding,
Valor, and Marriage.
Anonymous.

Ballerina
Fear. Schjeldahl.

Ballet
Turners Dish of Lentten
Stuffe. Turner.

Balloon (s)
The Cyclone. Brisby.
The Day They Busted the
Grateful Dead. Brautigan.
Flying. Westrup.
For My Mother. Jordan.
Moving. Matthews.
Pop. McFadden.
Public Holiday: Paris.
Horner.
Teacher. Dorman.
Ten Week Wife. Donovan.
What's the News?
Anonymous.

Ballot box
Fair and Free Elections.
Anonymous.
Security. Glover.

Ballroom
Rhymed Dance Calls.
Anonymous.

Balm (s)
Balm in Gilead. *Anonymous.*
Come Slowly–Eden.
Dickinson.
The Fall of Hyperion.
Keats.
Go Ahead; Goodbye; Good
Luck; and Watch Out.
Bronk.
In the Woods. Scott.
Netley Abbey. Midnight.
Sotheby.
The Night Serene. Leon.
A Prayer. Dunbar.

To Music. Herrick.
The world feels dusty.
Dickinson.

Balsam (ic)
Flowers. Mallarme.
Himalayan Balsam.
Stevenson.
The Penitent. Taylor.

Baltimore
The City of Baltimore.
Anonymous.
Learning. Simpson.
The Sack of Baltimore.
Davis.
Streets of Baltimore.
Anonymous.
Through Baltimore. Taylor.

Bamboo (s)
Boy and the Wandering
Recluse. Robles.
Eating Bamboo-Shoots. Po
Chu-i.
Elephants from the Sea.
Young.
Flute Player. *Anonymous.*
Under the Bamboo Tree.
Cole.

Bananas
The Market. Snyder.
My First Love. Graham.

Band of brothers
Every Christian Born of God.
Anonymous.
Hail! Columbia. Hopkinson.

Band (s)
The Drum. Farrar.
Holy-Cross Day. Browning.
If I were a Cassowary.
Wilberforce.
An Ode in Time of Hesitation:
Robert Gould Shaw.
Moody.
Prince Heathen (A version).
Anonymous.
Prince Heathen (B version).
Anonymous.
Query. Ebon.
Risen with Healing in His
Wings. John of Damascus.
The Spanish Gypsy (excerpt).
Eliot.
The Sprinters. Murchison.
Titanic Blues. Brown.
William Wallace. Adams.

Bandage
Age? Hays.
Carl Hamblin. Masters.
The Children of the Poor.
Brooks.
Fresh Paint. Pasternak.

Bandana
The Sound of Rain. Evans.
Traditional Funeral Songs.
Anonymous.

Bandits
Hangman's Tree. White.
Second Epistle to Robert
Graham. Burns.

Bandwagons
Epigram: "IN)/all those who
got". Cummings.

Bane (s)
Faur Wid I Dee? Milne.
Trust Not the Treason.
Spenser.
The Twa Corbies.
Anonymous.
Unsleeping City. Garcia
Lorca.

Bang
The History of the Flood.
Heath-Stubbs.

The Hollow Men. Eliot.
Last Words. Hollander.
Mother's Nerves. Kennedy.
The Party. Rodgers.
Poem to Help My Father.
Richman.

Bangkok
Growltiger's Last Stand.
Eliot.

Bangle (s)
The Power of Silence.
Davies.
Zalinka. MacInnes.

Bangor
Hiraeth in N.W.3. Vaughan-
Thomas.
The Old Orange Flute.
Anonymous.

Banish (ed)
The Cultural Presuppostion.
Auden.
Exodus from a Renaissance
Gallery. Acton.
Faint Heart. Rufinus
Domesticus.
Good and Bad. Stephens.
In Windsor Castle. Surrey.
Lenten Is Come.
Anonymous.
Preludes. Patmore.
Sonnet: "Sweet, when I think
how summer's smallest
bird." McLeod.
Truth's Complaint over
England. Lodge.
A View of the Town
(excerpt). Gilbert.

Banjo
Echoes of Childhood.
Corbin.
Git Along Down to Town.
Anonymous.
Goin' 'Cross the Mountain.
Anonymous.
LI. Berrigan.
Massa's in de Cold, Cold
Ground. Foster.
Oh, Susanna. *Anonymous.*
Rufus Mitchell's Confession.
Anonymous.

Bank (ing) (s)
Allan Water. Lewis.
Antelope. Smith.
Autumn. Carpenter.
The Banks of Dundee.
Anonymous.
The Banks of Newfoundland
(I). *Anonymous.*
The Banks of Sacramento
(with music). *Anonymous.*
The Banks of Sweet Dundee.
Anonymous.
Bendemeer. Moore.
Bonnie Annie (B version).
Anonymous.
California (with music).
Anonymous.
An Epitaph upon Doctor
Brook. Crashaw.
The Gloomy Night Is
Gath'ring Fast. Burns.
The Green Mossy Banks of
the Lee. *Anonymous.*
Inniskeen Road: July Evening.
Kavanagh.
An Interview near Florence.
Rogers.
Juniper. Lee.
Lines Composed a Few Miles
above Tintern Abbey.
Wordsworth.

The Man Who Broke the
Bank at Monte Carlo.
Gilbert.
The Overlander. *Anonymous.*
Sacramento. *Anonymous.*
A Song-Offering. Tagore.
Song: "There stands a lonely
pine-tree." Heine.
Twas Night. *Anonymous.*
The Virgins. Walcott.
A Wild Romantic Dell.
Mickle.

Banner (s)
Battle Cry. Venable.
Columbia the Gem of the
Ocean. Becket.
Contact. Livesay.
The Day is Coming. Morris.
The Half of Life. Hoelderlin.
His Banner over Me.
Massey.
How Goes the Night?
Anonymous.
Hymn of the Moravian Nuns
of Bethlehem. Longfellow.
In Prison. Morris.
Shall I Go Bound and You
Go Free? Colum.
Sherman's in Savannah.
Holmes.
Sherman's March to the Sea.
Byers.
The Shoemakers. Whittier.
Song: "Farewell, adieu, that
court-like life!" Pickering.
Song: "My love is the flaming
Sword." Thomson.
Song of Texas. Hosmer.
Sonnet: "Oh for a poet–for a
beacon bright." Robinson.
The Sun. Sexton.
Tulips from Their Blood.
Brooks.

Banquet
Marble-Top. White.
Sea Voyage. Empson.
The Voice of the Lobster.
"Carroll.

Baptist
Epigram: "Why should
scribblers discompose."
Landor.
The Scribblers. Landor.

Baptized
Dithyramb in Retrospect.
Hopegood.
Homeless Blues. Jackson.

Bar (s)
Any Father to Any Son.
Money-Coutts.
The Ballad of the Boat.
Garnett.
A Bar at Night. Hagiwara.
Bar Not the Door. Campion.
Bill. Kocan.
Blooming Sally. *Anonymous.*
Bushed. Birney.
Christmas Eve. *Anonymous.*
Crossing the Bar. Tennyson.
Dialog outside the Lakeside
Grocery. Reed.
Epigram: "If you see someone
beautiful." Adaios.
Fall. Francis.
Famous Poet. Hughes.
The Fury of Hating Eyes.
Sexton.
Get Up and Bar the Door (B
version). *Anonymous.*
Glints of the Year–from a
Window. Irwin.

The Heart of a Woman.
Johnson.
I never hear the word
"escape'. Dickinson.
Indian america. Tohee.
Jerry an' Me. Rich.
Johnie Blunt. *Anonymous.*
Lady, of Anonymous Flesh
and Face. Cunningham.
Leaving Raiford. Petaccia.
Limerick: "There was an old
person of Bar." Lear.
A May Sunday. Irwin.
Neither Out Far Nor In Deep.
Frost.
An Ode on the Despoilers of
Learning in an American
University (1947).
Winters.
Third Avenue in Sunlight.
Hecht.
The Three Fishers. Kingsley.
To a Foreign Friend.
Nathan.
A triumph may be of several
kinds. Dickinson.
The Usual Exquisite Boredom
of Patrols. Popham.
Wesley in Heaven. Brown.

Barbara
Abstinence. Rosen.
Exit Lines. Jonas.
The Private Dining Room.
Nash.

Barbarian (s)
Mother. Camerino.
October. Hahn.
The Queen of Lydia. Sisson.
The Scythians. Blok.
Translation. Fuller.

Barbed
The Old Battalion.
Anonymous.
What about You? (parody).
Pygge.

Barcelona
Poem: "In secret." Picasso.

Bard (s)
Ballad. Treece.
Bold Phelim Brady, the Bard
of Armagh. *Anonymous.*
Epistle to Augustus (excerpt).
Pope.
Gas and Hot Air. Bishop.
The Lay of the Last Minstrel.
Scott.
Lyric Barber. Romano.
The Ocean-Fight.
Anonymous.
That Did in Luve So Lively
Write. Adams.
That Idiot, Wordsworth.
Byron.
Throw away the Flowers.
Daryush.
To learn the transport by the
pain. Dickinson.
To the Canary Bird. Very.
To the Immortal Memory of
the Halibut on Which I
Dined This Day. Cowper.
The World Is a Mighty Ogre.
Johnson.

Bardic (s)
The War Ship of Peace.
Lover.

Bare
Biting Through. Yamamoto.
Brow of Nephin.
Anonymous.
Dirge of the Munster Forest
1581. Lawless.

Epigram: April. Nemerov.
Epigram: "The scentless laurel
a broad leaf displays."
Landor.
Fog. Binyon.
For My Mother. Smith.
The House in the Green Well.
Wheelock.
Hymn. Synesius.
Ice Dragons. Ackerman.
The Independent. McGinley.
The Martyr. Melville.
May. Bird.
Near the Ocean. Lowell.
The Newly Born.
Anonymous.
Of the Theme of Love.
Newcastle.
On Aesthetics, More or Less.
Dufault.
Prayer in Time of War.
Treece.
The Quest. Wright.
Saturday Shopping.
Edelman.
Sea Dirge. Scott.
Shoe a Little Horse.
Anonymous.
The Song of Roland: The Last
Battle. *Anonymous.*
The Stallion. Porter.
To One Who Quotes and
Detracts. Landor.
The Twa Corbies.
Anonymous.
Wave. Guest.

Barefoot
The Creek-Road. Cawein.
On Growing Old in San
Francisco. Gilbert.
Spring. Chute.

Bargain (ed) (s)
Age. Landor.
The Autocrat of the
Breakfast-Table. Holmes
The Better Bargain.
Congreve.
A Boston Ballad. Whitman.
A Curse against the Owner.
Sutter.
For the Marriage of Faustus
and Helen. Crane.
The Judge. Kopp.
Proverbial Advice on the
Conduct of Business.
Anonymous.
Soaping Down for Saint
Francis of Assisi: The
Canticle of Sister Soap.
Ruark.

Barge (s)
The Barge. Fyleman.
The Barge Horse. Jennett.
The Canterbury Tales:
General Prologue.
Chaucer.
The Dance of Death.
Lydgate.
Hospital Barge at Cerisy.
Owen.
In Spite of All This Much
Needed Thunder. Gilbert.
Limerick: "There was an old
man in a Barge." Lear.

Bark
The Ivy-Wife. Hardy.

Bark (s)
Autonomous. Van Doren.
The Campanero.
Anonymous.
Central Heating System.
Spender.

The Dog. Davies.
The Dog. Herford.
Dog Hospital. Wild.
The Hero. Jackson.
John Brown. Koopman.
Lily, Lois & Flaubert: The
  Site of Loss. Fraser.
A Little Dog-Angel.
  Holland.
Love without Love. Llorens
  Torres.
A Maltese Dog. *Anonymous.*
Motto for a Dog House.
  Guiterman.
My Brigantine. Cooper.
Of an Ancient Spaniel in Her
  Fifteenth Year. Morley.
On a Puppy. Feng Chih.
A Poet's Hope. Channing
Silly Dog. Livingston.
Sonnet, XX: "A seer foretold
  that I would love one day."
  Labé.
Sonnet: Where Lies the Land.
  Wordsworth.
A Virginal. Pound.
The Woodman's Dog.
  Cowper.

Barkentine
Corbitt's Barkentine.
  Anonymous.

Barley
Come Ride and Ride to the
  Garden. Gregory Lady.
He Singeth a Hymn to Osiris,
  the Lord of Eternity.
  Book of the Dead.
The Maid that Sold Her
  Barley. *Anonymous.*
The Ripe and Bearded Barley.
  Anonymous.
To Trust. Pozzi.
The Walking of the Moon-
  Women. Neilson.

Barleycorn
John Barleycorn.
  Anonymous.

Barn door
This Pig Got in the Barn.
  Anonymous.

Barn (s)
Barn Fire. Lux.
Bonnie James Campbell.
  Anonymous.
Catching a Horse. Winder.
Chew Mail Pouch. Klauck.
Elegy for the Monastery Barn.
  Merton.
The Farmer's Head. Padgett.
February. Winder.
The Harrington Barn Dance.
  Anonymous.
Land of Little Sticks, 1945.
  Tate.
Lodging with the Old Man of
  the Stream. Po Chu-i.
The Man in the Street Is Fed.
  Sandburg.
Miss Creighton. Taylor.
The Neighbor. Williams.
On the Hall at Stowey.
  Tomlinson.
Parable. Wilbur.
Three Presidents: Andrew
  Jackson. Bly.
Wherelings Whenlings.
  Cummings.

Barnacle (s)
Beggar to Beggar Cried.
  Yeats.
The Critics. Spencer.

Barnyard (s)
Barnyards of Delgaty.
  Anonymous.
The Clocking Hen.
  Anonymous.
Deranged. Fiacc.
The Parish Church. Reissig.

Barometers
How to Measure a Cat.
  Johnson.

Barrack (s)
For Decoration Day:
  1861-1865. Hughes.
A Soldier and a Scholar.
  Swift.

Barrel
Hiatus. Avison.
Song: "There's a barrel of
  porter at Tammany Hall."
  Halleck.
A Teen-Ager. Snodgrass.

Barren
The Barren Shore. Patmore.
Brow of Nephin.
  Anonymous.
The Complaint of the
  Morpethshire Farmer.
  Bunting.
The Dreary Change. Scott.
The Fault. Lucie-Smith.
An Indian at the Burial-Place
  of His Fathers. Bryant.
Italy and Britain. Addison.
On the Reed of Our Lord's
  Passion. Alabaster.
Sonnet Written in a Blank
  Leaf of Dugdale's
  Monasticon. Warton, Jr..
The Sun upon the Weirdlaw
  Hill. Scott.
Watts. Saxon.

Barrier
The Barrier. Lavater.
Come Not Near. Osborn.
Lisa. Carrier.
To His Dear Friend, Bones.
  Parini.

Barrow
Limerick: "There was an old
  person of Harrow." Lear.
Mr. Tom Narrow. Reeves.
Nostalgie d'Automne.
  Daiken.
Who Kill'd John Keats?
  Byron.

Base
Arcades Ambo (parody).
  Calverley.
Arcadia. Sidney.
Base Words Are Uttered.
  Auden.
Britannia's Empire.
  Thomson.
The Cottager's Complaint.
  Anonymous.
The Fire i' the Flint.
  Robinson.
The Human Races. Lister.
The Indian Ghost Dance and
  War. Prather.
Moment Musical in Assynt.
  MacCaig.
Near the Base Line. Albert.
On True Worth. Sa'di.
Sonnet: He Will Praise His
  Lady. Guinicelli.
The Story of Pyramid
  Thothmes. *Anonymous.*
Uncle Robert. Morgan.

Baseball
Double-Header. Stone.

Happy Lifetime to You.
  Adams.
May. Updike.
The Origin of Baseball.
  Patchen.
The Umpire. Gibson.

Bashful (ness)
So Look the Mornings.
  Herrick.
The Task. Cowper.

Bask (ing) (s)
How Night Falls in the
  Courtyard. Rimmer.
In the Grass. Garland.
A long, long sleep.
  Dickinson.
The March Bee. Blunden.
The Old Sailor. Milne.
The Prince of Peace.
  Bickersteth.
Seeds. De la Mare.
When I Would Image.
  Meredith.

Basket (s)
Being Called For. Dobson.
The Goods She Can Carry:
  Canticle of Her Basket
  Made of Reeds. Ruark.
The Laundress. Kinsella.
Owl and Rooster. Cardiff.
The Peasant Declares His
  Love. Roumer.
The Roof of the World.
  Browne.
Song for the Sun That
  Disappeared Behind the
  Rainclouds. *Anonymous.*
Song of a Sick Child.
  Anonymous.
A Wicker Basket. Creeley.

Basketball
Sunday Afternoon. Levertov.

Bass
After Tennyson: "Spoonmeat
  at Bill Porter's in the Hall."
  Lear.
After the Surprising
  Conversions. Lowell.
The Big One. Cabalquinto.
In All These Acts. Everson.
A Rise. McGaffey.

Bastard (s)
Bugger Burns. *Anonymous.*
Death News. Ginsberg.
A Freshet. Antiphilus of
  Byzantium.
Love's Grave. Watson.
The Midnight Court.
  Merriman.
Ode to Jamestown.
  Paulding.
Oedipus at San Francisco.
  Finkel.
One Is a Sign of Mischief.
  Anonymous.
Unhappy Bella. *Anonymous.*
A Wicked Treasonable Libel.
  Swift.
You, Whose Mother's Lover
  Was Grass. Corso.

Bastion (s)
The Great House. Muir.
I Have Approached. Paton.
Rant Block. McClure.
Silentium Altum. Kelly.

Batchelor
O I Do Love, Then Kiss Me.
  Anonymous.

Bat (s)
The Abominable Baseball Bat.
  Kennedy.

The Bat and the Scientist.
  Bigelow.
The Boy Actor. Coward.
Easy as a Bat. *Anonymous.*
From Government Buildings.
  Devlin.
I Went to the Toad That Lies
  under the Wall.
  Anonymous.
The King's Disguise (excerpt).
  Cleveland.
Song of the Elfin Steers -
  Man. Hill.
To a Baseball. *Anonymous.*

Bath (s)
The Abbey Church at Bath.
  Harington.
Bats. Macbeth.
The Brut. Layamon.
The Four Zoas. Blake.
Marriage. Corso.
News Report. Ignatow.
The Ring. Mathews.
The Ruin. *Anonymous.*
The Slough of Despond.
  Lowell.
St. Kevin. Lover.
Streets. Goldring.
Up the Country. Lawson.

Bathe (d) (s)
In a Warm Bath. Rakosi.
Letter. Dow.
Old Inn on the Eastern Shore.
  Matchett.
The Pomegranate. Dudek.
Thesis. Dorn.

Bathing
The Artist on Penmaenmawr.
  Turner.
Nursery Rhymes for the
  Tender-Hearted. Morley.

Bathroom
Miss Twye. Ewart.
Style. Bukowski.

Battalion (s)
Comrades. Door.
Freedom. Daniel. Peter
The Sailors' Wives.
  Anonymous.
When a People Reach the Top
  of a Hill. Crane.

Battel (d) (s)
The Faerie Queene. Spenser.

Batter (ed)
Coast to Coast. Rich.
The Equinox. Heyward.
How Singular. Hood.
On Laying up Treasure.
  Hiers.
The Pancake Collector.
  Prelutsky.
Pitcher. Francis.

Battery (ies)
Calligram, 15 May 1915.
  Apollinaire.
Camera. Kooser.
Mortal Love. Dowling.

Battle (d) (s)
Allatoona. *Anonymous.*
Amours de Voyage. Clough.
Armistice. Jewett.
At the Top of My Voice
  (excerpt). Mayakovsky.
The Ballad of Chickamauga.
  Thompson.
Battery Moving Up to a New
  Position from Rest Camp:
  Dawn. Nichols.
The Battle of Morris' Island.
  Anonymous.
Betsy's Battle-Flag. Irving.
Central Park West. Moss.

Battle

The Challenge. *Anonymous.*
Colloquy of the Ancients (excerpt). *Anonymous.*
Comrades. Housman.
Cullen. Page.
A Dead Soldier. Montgomery.
Don Juan. Byron.
The Dumb World. Davies.
Elene. Cynewulf.
Epitaphs of the War, 1914-18. Kipling.
The Faerie Queene. Spenser.
Fantasy. Carducci.
Fighting South of the Ramparts. *Anonymous.*
The Flag of the Constellation. Read.
Funeral of Napoleon I. Hagarty.
The General Elliott. Graves.
Gheluvelt. Bridges.
Gladioli for My Mother. Bernstein.
Green Frogs. Rigsbee.
The Guns in the Grass. Frost.
Hold the Fort. *Anonymous.*
The Hunted City, V. Patchen.
Idylls of the King. Tennyson.
The Iliad. Homer.
Immortality. Arnold.
Juanita. Miller.
King Philip's Last Stand. Scollard.
Lee to the Rear. Thompson.
Life's Testament. Baylebridge.
Looking Out. Chasin.
Manassas. Warfield.
Maud. Tennyson.
My Portrait. Halpern.
Nightingales Are Not Singing. Dor.
The Only Way to Win. *Anonymous.*
Perry's Victory–A Song. *Anonymous.*
Quebec. Grier.
The Recruiting Serjeant (excerpt). Bickerstaffe.
Reflections of a Trout Fisherman. Demon.
The Retort Discourteous. Benét.
A Russian Cradle Song. Nomberg.
Sailors on Leave. Dodson.
Savannah. Burroughs.
Some There Are Who Say That the Fairest Thing Seen. Sappho.
The Song of Roland, XCVII. *Anonymous.*
A Song of the Seamen and Land Soldiers. *Anonymous.*
The Song of the Valkyries. *Anonymous.*
Sonnet: "The master and the slave go hand in hand." Robinson.
Stir the Wallaby Stew. *Anonymous.*
Tan Ta Ra, Cries Mars... Wagoner.
There She Blows! *Anonymous.*

They Went Forth to Battle, but They Always Fell. O'Sheel.
A Thought on Human Life. *Anonymous.*
To a Hedgehog. Thompson.
Uccello on the Heath. Grigson.
War Song. Davidson.
Wild Eden. Woodberry.
With Corse at Allatoona. Byers.
Women Singing. Taylor.

Battle-ships

The Ballad of the White Horse. Chesterton.

Battlefield

Locus. Hayden.
You Stand and Hold the Post of My Small House. Auvaiyar.

Baudelaire

Hallucination: I. Symons.

Bawd (s)

Captain Barton's Distress on Board the Lichfield. *Anonymous.*
John Kinsella's Lament for Mrs. Mary Moore. Yeats.
To a Loudmouth Pontificator. Mizer.

Bawl (ing)

Excelsior (parody). *Anonymous.*
Ireland 1977. Durcan.
Mamma Sings. Hoffenstein.
A Prayer. Laird.

Bay (s)

Amoretti, XXIX. Spenser.
L'Art poetique. Boileau-Despreaux.
The Ballad of the Boat. Garnett.
The Blackbird by Belfast Lough. *Anonymous.*
Boats at Night. Shanks.
Bum's Rush. Dransfield.
Camptown Races. Foster.
Contentment. Estes.
Cut the Cables. Wilson.
Detail. Bethell.
Discovery of San Francisco Bay. White.
An Epitaph on William Whitehead... *Anonymous.*
A Few Lines to Fill up a Vacant Page. Danforth.
The First Satire of the Second Book of Horace Imitated (excerpt). Pope.
Hiawatha's Sailing. Longfellow.
In Imitation of Anacreon. Prior.
The Life of Service. Davie.
Limerick: "A hippo decided one day." *Anonymous.*
Mannahatta. Whitman
Nancy Hanks. Monroe.
Night Trip across the Chesapeake and After. Lea.
On the Death of Francis Thompson. Noyes.
Only Years. Rexroth.
The Schooner Fred Dunbar. Hanson.
September Butterfly. Boring.
This Day, under My Hand. Malouf.
Visit by Water. McLaren.

We'll to the Woods No More. Housman.

Bay State

John Underhill. Whittier.
Massachusetts to Virginia. Whittier.

Bayonet (s)

The Connaught Rangers. Letts.
Crispus Attucks. Hayden.
My country need not change her gown. Dickinson.

Bazaar (s)

14th St./new york. Jones.
Before Passover. Mayne.

Be

All That I Am. Arvey.
American Rhapsody. Fearing.
Ars Poetica. MacLeish.
The Clown. Rose.
A Clymene. Verlaine.
Friends. Brown.
The Purple Cow. Burgess.
To the Age's Insanities. Ponsot.
Young Woman's Neo-Aramaic Jewish Persian Blues. Rothenberg.

Beach (ed) (es)

Adam. Booth.
Bathing with Father. Fetherling.
The Culprit Fay. Drake.
Don Leon (excerpt). *Anonymous.*
The Enviable Isles. Melville
Helen in Egypt. Doolittle.
High Plains Harvest. Morton.
Home Again. Petrykewycz.
How Much Longer? Mezey.
In Memoriam A.H.H., LXXI. Tennyson.
Morning Song. Blakely.
Myself when Young (parody). Donnelly.
Nocturne. Frost.
The Same Side of the Canoe. Espirito Santo.
Sandhill People. Sandburg.
Sant'Angelo D'Ischia. Denby.
The Scholar-Gipsy. Arnold.
Storm Tide on Mejit. *Anonymous.*
Tales of the Islands, I. Walcott.
Two Poems. Abrams.
Voyage to the Moon. MacLeish.

Beacon (s)

The Battle of Bunker Hill. *Anonymous.*
Beacon Light. Clark.
The Cross. Pace.
The Face against the Pane. Aldrich.
The Needles' Lighthouse from Keyhaven, Hampshire. Turner.
Psalm. Yehoash.

Bead (s)

After X-Ray. Pastan.
Autumnal Consummation. Stevenson.
The Ballad of Adam's First. Davis.
A Farewell to Arms. Peele.
The House of Love: Pride of Youth. Rossetti.
The Indian. Reed.

Ode to the Cameleopard. Hood.
On the Symbolic Consideration of Hands and the Significance of Death. Williams.
Pastorale. Davis.
Polyhymnia: His Golden Lock. Peele.
The Rosary. Rogers.
A Sonet: "His Golden lockes, Time hath to Silver turn'd." Peele.
Tight Rope. Jones.

Beak (s)

The Beaks of Eagles. Jeffers.
The Bird. Greacen.
Captain Carpenter. Ransom.
The Changes. Pinsky.
The Earth Asks and Receives Rain. Haring.
Hot Day at the Races. Raworth.
I Move to Random Consolations. Heyen.
Poem of the Conscripted Warrior. Nogar.
The Progress of Poesy. Gray.
Return of the Goddess Artemis. Graves.
A Talisman. Moore.
The Vacant Cage. Turner.

Beam (ed) (ing) (s)

Alastor. Shelley.
An Answer to Another Persuading a Lady to Marriage. Philips.
Astrophel and Stella, XXXVI. Sidney.
Astrophel and Stella, XLI. Sidney.
Astrophel and Stella, LXXVI. Sidney.
Christmas. Herbert.
The Conversion of the Magdalene. Malon de Chaide.
The Holy Star. Bryant.
How Easily Men's Cheeks Are Hot. Heidenstam.
Hymn for the Feast of the Annunciation. De Vere.
Joy of My Life! Vaughan.
The Kings of the East. Bates.
Lament. Rilke.
A Looking-Glass. Carew.
Next unto Him Was Neptune Pictured. Spenser.
On a Frightful Dream. Bampfylde.
Overheard. Levertov.
Paradise Lost. Milton.
The Puppet Play. Colum.
That Wind. Bronte.
To His Lady. Davies.
To Master Denham, on His Prospective Poem. Herrick.
The Tree. Very.
Upon Julia's Recovery. Herrick.
Upon Some Alterations in My Mistress, after My Departure into France. Carew.
The Vision. Taylor.
Vita Nuova. Kunitz.
Where Now Are the Hebrew Children? *Anonymous.*

Bean (s)
Elf Night. Rogers.
Me List No More to Sing.
  Wyatt.
Merciless Beauty. Chaucer.
Song: "Rose and grape, pear
  and bean." *Anonymous.*

Bear (s)
After Wings. Piatt.
The Bosky Steer. Knibbs.
Cock-Throwing! Lluellyn.
The Dancing Bear. Field.
Dark Song. Sitwell.
Darwin on Species.
  Anonymous.
Death Chant. Blue Cloud.
The End. Thesen.
Envoi. Raine.
Florida. Abse.
For Little Boys Destined for
  Big Business. Hoffenstein.
Four for Sir John Davies.
  Roethke.
The Gardener. Housman.
Giving. *Anonymous.*
Grizzly Bear. *Anonymous.*
The Grizzly Bear is huge and
  wild. Housman.
House Sonnet. Wylie.
Hunting. Snyder.
If ever man might him avant.
  Wyatt.
In Fine, Transparent Words.
  Vogel.
Infant Innocence. Housman.
The Inward Morning.
  Thoreau.
Lent Tending. Shepherd.
Life's Joy. *Anonymous.*
Limerick: "There was an Old
  Person of Ware." Lear.
The Lion Roars at the
  Enraging Desert. Stevens.
The little tigers are at rest.
  Hood.
The Man That Hails You
  Tom or Jack. Cowper.
A Midsummer Night's
  Dream. Shakespeare.
Mothers. Giovanni.
My Cheap Lifestyle. Myles.
Night Sweat. Lowell.
Obatala, the Creator.
  Anonymous.
On Reading Gene Derwood's
  "The Innocent'. Maas.
On the Death of Doctor Swift.
  Swift.
Otto. Brooks.
Parentage. Meynell.
Percy/68. Myles.
Prayer under the Pressure of
  Violent Anguish. Burns.
The Prophecy of Dante.
  Byron.
Remembered Grace.
  Patmore.
A Scottish Proverb.
  Anonymous.
The Shakespearean Bear.
  Guiterman.
Songs of Seven. Ingelow.
Statement on Our Higher
  Education. Ransom.
The Three Wise Couples.
  Corbett.
To My Tortoise. Lee-
  Hamilton.
The Tortoise in Eternity.
  Wylie.
Two Monopolists. Byrom.
Uncle Henry. Auden.

D-Y Bar. Welch.
A Young Wife. Lawrence.
Zone. Bogan.

Beard (s)
Abishag. Spire.
Advice to a Forest.
  Bodenheim.
The Court of Neptune.
  Hughes.
The Double Looking Glass.
  Hope.
For Malcolm X. Alba.
The House of God. Hope.
A Lady's Prayer to Cupid.
  Carew.
The Last Cup of Canary.
  Cone.
Limerick: "A beautiful lady
  named Psyche."
  Anonymous.
The Man from Ironbark.
  Paterson.
The Numbers. Oppenheimer.
Old Beard A-Shakin'.
  Anonymous.
On the Cards and Dice.
  Ralegh.
Riding down from Bangor.
  Osborne.
Right true it is... Wyatt.
Schoolfellows. Praed.
Song: "Give Isaac the nymph
  who no beauty can boast."
  Sheridan.
Tapestry. Simic.
The Three Jovial Welshmen.
  Anonymous.
To Noel. "Mistral.
To the Young Man Jesus.
  Dalton.

Bearing
For Beauty, We Thank Thee.
  Oxenham.
The Golden Legend: This Is
  Indeed the Blessed Mary's
  Land. Longfellow.
In Parenthesis. Jones.
Julie-Jane. Hardy.
Nature's Travail.
  Anonymous.

Beast (s)
Affection and Desire.
  Ralegh.
Against Romanticism. Amis.
The Ageing Hunter. Avane.
Amoretti, LVI. Spenser.
Ariel. Campbell.
At Christmas. Duncan.
The Battle of Brunanburh
  (excerpt). *Anonymous.*
Buffalo. Brodsky.
Caelica, CVII. Greville.
Epitaph for a Horseman.
  Hamburger.
Eternity's Low Voice. Van
  Doren.
Evolution. Swenson.
The Fisher Cat. Eberhart.
Force. Walcott.
The Giraffe. Gumilev.
Golden Bough. Hoyt.
Hymn to the Air Spirit.
  Anonymous.
The Library. Logan.
Limerick: "A chap has a
  shark up in Sparkill."
  Bishop.
Limerick: "There was a
  sightseer named Sue."
  Anonymous.
Man Is but a Castaway.
  Day.

Matisse. Hirsch.
The Mutilated Soldier.
  Fisher.
The Nativity of Christ.
  Southwell.
Paradise Regained. Milton.
Piers the Ploughman.
  Langland.
The Rape of Lucrece.
  Shakespeare.
Riddle: "Itum Paradisum all
  clothed in green."
  Anonymous.
The Second Coming. Yeats.
Senzangakhona. *Anonymous.*
Sleep. Simic.
The Sleeping Beauty. Cohen.
Small Comment. Sanchez.
Somewhere Is Such a
  Kingdom. Ransom.
The Sower's Song. Carlyle.
Three Ghostesses.
  Anonymous.
The Tigress. Pitter.
Vancouver Lights. Birney.
Volto Sciolto e Pensieri
  Stretti. Mangan.
We Were Permitted to Meet
  Together in Prison to
  Prepare for Trial.
  Berrigan.
When Indians Heare That
  Some There Are.
  Williams.

Beastly
The Faerie Queene. Spenser.
The Malcontent. Marston.
The Times. Churchill.

Beat (s)
Advice to Julia. Luttrell.
Amoretti, XXIV. Spenser.
And Then No More.
  Mangan.
Boomerang. Hart-Smith.
Buckinghamshire.
  Anonymous.
Carmina. Catullus.
Crossing a Creek. Johnson.
Folk Tune. Wilbur.
The Forge. Heaney.
From a Brother Dreaming in
  the Rye. Cunningham.
Hush-a-Bye a Baa Lamb.
  Anonymous.
Jack. Ross.
The Judgement of God.
  Morris.
The King's Own Regulars.
  Anonymous.
Letter from Oregon.
  Stafford.
Lines. Martin.
Loudon Hill, or, Drumclog.
  Anonymous.
The Low-Backed Car.
  Lover.
A Masique Presented at
  Ludlow Castle (Comus).
  Milton.
The Mystic Drum. Okara.
Poems in Praise of Practically
  Nothing. Hoffenstein.
The Progress of Sir Jack Brag.
  Anonymous.
Proverbial Advice to
  Gentlemen. *Anonymous.*
Quoits. Newsome.
A Satire against Wit.
  Blackmore.
The Sea Serpant. Irwin.
Southern Blues. Rainey.
The Swank. Vickers.

The Talking Drums. Kyei.
The Tattooed Man. Smith.
There Is In Human Closeness
  a Sacred Boundary.
  Akhmatova.
To His Wife, for Striking Her
  Dog. Harington.
Words to a Song. Nagy.

Beating
Al Aaraaf. Poe.
The Arrival of My Mother.
  Wilson.
At a Country Dance in
  Provence. Monro.
Atameros. Beevers.
Blight. Bontemps.
Boy with His Hair Cut Short.
  Rukeyser.
Epilogue. Spender.
The Hands. Merwin.
I Think the New Teacher's a
  Queer. Brass.
Lines to a Nasturtium.
  Spencer.
The Loon. Sarett.
No Irish Need Apply.
  Anonymous.
Pole Vault. Murano.
Sources of Good Counsel.
  Idley.
Success. Cameron.
Young Master's Account of a
  Puppet Show. Marchant.

Beatitude (s)
Abide Not in the Realm of
  Dreams. Burleigh.
Deo Optimo Maximo.
  Guiney.
Of Wonder. Gilmore.
The Old Adam. Benet.

Beau (x)
A Description of the Spring in
  London. *Anonymous.*
The Life of a Beau. Miller.
More Reformation. Defoe.
Old Rosin the Beau.
  Anonymous.
On a Judge from Scotland.
  Erskine.
The Sun Shines over the
  Mountain. *Anonymous.*
When a Beau Goes In.
  Ewart.
White Conduit House.
  Woty.

Beauty
Above Salerno. Murray.
Abstinence Sows Sand All
  Over. Blake.
Adam and Eve: The
  Recognition of Eve.
  Shapiro.
After Storm. Morton.
Afterword. *Anonymous.*
Against Fulfillment of Desire.
  Anonymous.
The Age of a Dream.
  Johnson.
Alabama. Fields.
Alien. MacLeish.
All Day It Has Rained.
  Lewis.
An American to France.
  Miller.
Among the Coffee Cups and
  Soup Toureens Walked
  Beauty. Spicer.
Amsterdam Letter.
  Garrigue.
An Apologie for Having
  Loved Before. Waller.
The Apple. Plato.

Appreciation. Aldrich.
The Arraignment of a Lover.
  Gascoigne.
The Arrow. Yeats.
As imperceptibly as grief.
  Dickinson.
As When the Blowfish
  Perishing. Gregg.
As You Like It.
  Shakespeare.
Astrophel and Stella, CII.
  Sidney.
Baja–Outside Mexicali.
  McClure.
The Ballad of Adam's First.
  Davis.
Ballad of the Faded Field.
  Wilson.
The Bare Branches Tremble.
  Tzu Yeh.
The Bathers. Crane.
The Beautiful. Dorgan.
The Beautiful World.
  Childress.
Beauty. *Anonymous.*
Beauty Eternal: To-Day I Saw
  a Butterfly. Hooley.
Beauty Is Ever to the Lonely
  Mind. Nathan.
The Beauty of the Ship.
  Whitman.
Before the Ikon of the Mother
  of God. Constantine of
  Rhodes.
Being Her Friend. Masefield.
La Belle Ennemie. Stanley.
Birch Trees. Moreland.
The Birds. *Anonymous.*
Birds and Fishes. Jeffers.
Black Sister. Cumbo.
Blackmwore Maidens.
  Barnes.
Bonus. Ammons.
Breaking Silence. Mirikitani.
The Bride of Abydos.
  Byron.
By Fiat of Adoration.
  Williams.
Caelica, XIV. Greville.
Celia Singing. Carew.
The Celts. Smith.
Child and Maiden. Sedley.
Christian Ethics. Traherne.
Citation for Horace Gregory.
  Rukeyser.
The Cloud of Carmel.
  Powers.
A Coast View (excerpt).
  Harpur.
Come, Love, Let's Walk.
  Anonymous.
The Coming K–.
  Anonymous.
Companion of Her Lord Till
  Death. *Anonymous.*
Compensation. Jeffers.
The Confirmation. Muir.
The Constant Lover.
  Simpson.
Cormac Mac Airt Presiding at
  Tara. *Anonymous.*
The Cosmic Fabric.
  Polonsky.
The Craftsman. Christian.
Credo. Jeffers.
The Cruel Mother (P version).
  Anonymous.
Cynthia in the Snow.
  Brooks.
Dawn. Dudek.
The Dead. Morton.
Death. Clare.

Death and the Maiden
  (excerpt). Oliver.
The Death of the Flowers.
  Bryant.
Death Was a Woman.
  Russell.
A Deposition from Love.
  Carew.
Design for a Stream-Lined
  Sunrise. Mary Madeleva.
Diana. Constable.
Dirge: "Wail! wail ye o'er the
  dead!" Darley.
The Distant Orgasm. Tate.
Do You Not Hear? Picot.
Don Juan. Byron.
The Door. Strong.
Doron's Description of
  Samela. Greene.
The Double Transformation.
  Goldsmith.
A Dream of Death. Yeats.
Dream Tryst. Le Gallienne.
Drop Me the Seed.
  Masefield.
Dublinesque. Larkin.
E'en as the Flowers Do
  Wither. *Anonymous.*
Easter Parade. Chute.
Epigram: "Listen, you who
  know the pains of love."
  Meleager.
Epigram: "Love brought me
  quietly." Meleager.
Epitaph. Rose.
Epitaph for the Poet V.
  Ficke.
The Equilibrists. Ransom.
An Esthetic of Imitation.
  Finkel.
The Falcon. Wylie.
Fandango. Vestal.
Farewell, Peace. *Anonymous.*
Fashion in the 70's.
  Swenson.
The Field-Path. Swain.
Fields at Evening. Morton.
The Fired Pot. Wickham.
The Flattered Flying Fish.
  Rieu.
Flooer o the Gean. Hay.
For Beauty Being the Best of
  All We Know. Bridges.
For Real. Cortez.
For the Opening of the
  Hunting Season. Bishop.
Forgotten Island. Hall.
Four Anacreontic Poems, 3.
  Spenser.
Fragment of a Sonnet.
  Ronsard.
Frederick Douglass. Hayden.
From My Mother's Home.
  Goldberg.
Glimpses. Helton.
The Great Breath. Russell.
A Greeting. Davies.
Grieve Not for Beauty.
  Bynner.
Haiku: "Spring rain." Kaga
  no Chiyo.
Haiku: "The first night."
  Anonymous.
The Hairdresser. Hopes.
The Hairy Dog. Asquith.
Hamlet. Jarrett.
Hands. Finkel.
The Happy Husbandman; or,
  Country Innocence.
  Anonymous.
Hawk Nailed to a Barn Door.
  Blue Cloud.

Hawk's Way. Olson.
He Cometh Forth into the
  Day. Book of the Dead.
Heaven Is Here. Adams.
Here are fine gifts, children.
  Sappho.
Heroides: Oenone to Paris
  (excerpt). Ovid (Publius
  Ovidius Naso).
Hope. Mezquida.
Hymn of the Angels and
  Sibyls. Vicente.
I Call the Old Time Back.
  Whittier.
I Do Not Love to See Your
  Beauty Fire. Wheelock.
I'll Twine White Violets.
  Meleager.
I Must Complain, Yet Doe
  Enjoy My Love. Campion.
I'r hen Iaith A'i Chanedon
  (To the Old Tongue and its
  Songs). Dowding.
I Saw My Lady Weep.
  Anonymous.
I Think of Your Generation.
  Brasch.
The Immaculate Conception.
  Tabb.
In Louisiana. Paine.
In Memoriam A.H.H.,
  LXXIV. Tennyson.
In Memoriam A.H.H., XCI.
  Tennyson.
In the Backs. Stephen.
In the Distance. Van Brunt.
In Tyme the Strong and
  Statlie Turrets Fall.
  Fletcher.
Inanna Exalted (excerpt).
  Enheduanna.
Incident at Bruges.
  Wordsworth.
Indian Summer. Moodie.
Infidelity. Untermeyer.
The Inner Man. Plato.
The Islands of the Ever
  Living. *Anonymous.*
The Isles of Greece.
  Capetanakis.
John Darrow. Davidson.
Johnny German.
  Anonymous.
Johnson on Pope. Ferry.
June Twilight. Masefield.
Jungle Taste. Silvera.
Justice Is Reason Enough.
  Wakoski.
Kindly Vision. Bierbaum.
King Arthur. Dryden.
Lamentations. Gluck.
Landscapes. Untermeyer.
The Last Quarter Moon of the
  Dying Year. Brooks.
Late Comer. Hastings.
Laura Sleeping. Moulton.
Laus Virginitatis. Symons.
Lavinia. Thomson.
Lay of the Deserted
  Influenzaed.
  Cholmondeley-Pennell.
Leaves. Asch.
Lesbia Sewing. Vinal.
Lichen. Fullerton.
Licia (excerpt). Fletcher.
Life Is More True.
  Cummings.
Lily Adair. Chivers.
Look, How Beautiful.
  Jeffers.
Love Is a Secret Feeding Fire.
  Anonymous.

Love's Emblem. Clare.
Love You Alone Have Been
  with Us. Rumi.
Loves Heretick. Stanley.
Lyke Memnons Rocke
  Toucht, with the Rising
  Sunne. Fletcher.
Mabel Kelly. O'Carolan.
Maire My Girl. Casey.
Manhole Covers. Shapiro.
Mary Hynes. Fallon.
Masquerade. Rodgers.
The Massacre of the
  Innocents. Smith.
Maystress Jane Scroupe.
  Skelton.
McDonogh Day in New
  Orleans. Christian.
Metamorphosis. Mandel.
Methought I Saw the
  Footsteps of a Throne.
  Wordsworth.
Milton. Blake.
The Mirror in the Front Hall.
  Cavafy.
Molly of the North Country.
  Anonymous.
Month of January.
  Armstrong.
Morning and Myself.
  Francisco.
The Mosaic Worker. Peach.
Mr. Kurtz. McGovern.
My Fault's Small, About the
  Size of a Pin Prick.
  Miller.
My Garden. Succorsa.
My Heart Is in the East.
  Halevi.
My Mother's House (excerpt).
  Goldberg.
My Sons. Loewinsohn.
The Naked World. Sully-
  Prudhomme.
Narcissus in a Cocktail Glass.
  Howard.
Nature and the Poets.
  Beattie.
The Needle. Woodworth.
Needs Must I Leave, and Yet
  Needs Must I Love.
  Constable.
Nell Gwynne's Looking-Glass.
  Blanchard.
New Legends. Graves.
New Year. Spender.
Night. Southey.
No Single Thing Abides.
  Lucretius (Titus Lucretius
  Carus).
Nocturnal Visitor. Miller.
Nocturne. Church.
Notre Dame. Mandelstam.
November. Stoddard
O Love, Thy Hair! Kamal
  ud-Din of Isfahan.
O Ye Sweet Heavens!
  Parsons
October XXIX, 1795.
  Braithwaite.
Ode on a Grecian Urn
  (parody). Parrott.
Ode to a Nightingale
  (parody). Kelly.
Ode: "Without the evening
  dew and showers."
  Cotton.
Odes. Santayana.
Of His Mistress. Greene.
Of Wounds. Mary
  Madeleva.
Old Crabbed Men. Reeves.

On a Dead Poet. Osgood
On a Lonely Spray.
  Stephens.
On Getting a Natural.
  Randall.
On His Late Espoused Saint.
  Digby.
On the Tercentenary of
  Milton's Death. Ewart.
On the Vanity of Man's Life.
  Anonymous.
On the Wide Stairs.
  Amichai.
Ophra. Halevi.
Orara. Kendall.
The Origin of Didactic Poetry.
  Lowell.
Our Angels. Schwartz.
Our Love Shall Be the
  Brightness. Watson.
Pamela in Town. Cortissoz.
The Passing of the Forest.
  Reeves.
The Path of the Padres.
  Osborne.
Peeping Tom. Hope.
Pennsylvania Winter Indian
  1974. Littlebird.
Petition. Drinkwater.
Petition. Thomas.
Philomela. Ransom.
Piazza di Spagna, Early
  Morning. Wilbur.
Piazza Piece. Ransom.
Pied Beauty. Hopkins.
Poem: "As rock to sun or
  storm." Sheridan.
A Poem for Ed "Whitey"
  Ford. Holden.
Poem for People Who Are
  Understandably Too Busy
  to Read Poetry. Dunn.
Poem: "Is to love, this–to
  nurse a name." Coghill.
Poem Proud Papa. Farkas.
Poet's Bread. Mary Philip.
Poetry. Soutar.
Poetry, a Natural Thing.
  Duncan.
The Portrait. Winchilsea.
A Prayer of the Night Chant.
  Anonymous.
The Princess. Turner.
Question in a Field. Bogan.
The Rainbow. Patmore.
The Rape of the Lock.
  Pope.
Ravished by all that to the
  eyes is fair. Michelangelo.
The Rejected Lover.
  Anonymous.
Remember. Cory.
Rendezvous. Fitzgerald.
Reproach. Firdausi.
Revenge to Come.
  Propertius.
The Rhododendron Plant.
  Katzman.
Riddle of Night. Langer.
Roses are Beauty, but I Never
  See. Masefield.
The Royal Love Scene.
  Dowson.
The Saginaw Song. Roethke.
Saint Thomas Aquinas.
  Jones.
Samela. Greene.
Sarai. Sherman.
Sea-Change. Taggard.
Self-Portrait. Cassian.
September Afternoon.
  Carpenter.

Shadows. Plarr.
She Was a Beauty. Bunner.
Sheltered Garden. Doolittle.
Shine Out, Fair Sun.
  Anonymous.
The Singing Cat. Smith.
Skiers. Warren.
The Sleeping Beauty.
  Layzer.
The Sleeping Beauty. Mayo.
Sleeping on Her Couch.
  Leigh.
A Snapshot for Miss Bricka
  Who Lost in the Semifinal
  Round... Wallace.
Snowy Egret. Weigl.
Some Folks in Looks Take So
  Much Pride. *Anonymous.*
Some Me of Beauty.
  Rodgers.
A Song for My Mother–Her
  Hands. Branch.
Song: "Grace and beauty has
  the maid." Vicente.
Song: "I have loved flowers
  that fade." Bridges.
Song: "If you love God, take
  your mirror between your
  hands and look."
  Djellaladin Pasha.
Song: "In the air there are no
  coral-reefs or ambergris."
  Scott.
Song: "O faire sweet face, O
  eyes celestiall bright."
  Beaumont.
Song Set by Thomas Ford:
  "Unto the temple of thy
  Beauty." *Anonymous.*
Song: Wit and Beauty.
  Gould.
Sonnet: "Like Memnon's rock,
  touched with the rising
  sun." Fletcher.
Sonnet: "O shady vales, O fair
  enriched meads." Lodge.
Sonnets. Hillyer.
Sonnets, X: "For shame! deny
  that thou bear'st love to
  any." Shakespeare.
Sonnets, XIV: "Not from the
  stars do I my judgement
  pluck." Shakespeare.
Sonnets, XLI: "Those pretty
  wrongs that liberty
  commits." Shakespeare.
Sonnets, LXIII: "Against my
  Love shall be, as I am
  now." Shakespeare.
Sonnets, LXVIII: "Thus is his
  cheek the map of days
  outworn." Shakespeare.
Sonnets, XCIII: "So shall I
  live, supposing thou art
  true." Shakespeare.
Sonnets, CIV: "To me, fair
  friend, you never can be
  old." Shakespeare.
Sonnets, CXXVII: "In the ole
  age black was nor counted
  fair." Shakespeare.
The Sound of Rain. Evans.
Spray. Lawrence.
Spring-Joy Praising God.
  Praise of the Sun.
  Greiffenberg.
The Star. Conkling.
Star & Garter Theater.
  Schmitz.
Summer Afternoon. Souster.
Summer Morning. Clare.
Susan to Diana. Cornford.

Susanna and the Elders.
  Crapsey.
Sylvia. Croxall.
Take Tools Our Strength...
  Simmons, Jr.
Tears. Thomas.
The Testament of Beauty.
  Bridges.
Thaddeus Stevens. Cary.
Thank God for Life.
  Anonymous.
There Is No Balm in
  Birmingham. Deacon.
Third Sunday in Lent.
  Keble.
Three Epitaphs. Davison.
Thus Lovely Sleep. Leigh.
Time. Fletcher.
To --. Praed.
To a Gentleman and Lady on
  the Death of the Lady's
  Brother and Sister.
  Wheatley.
To a Lady. Scott.
To a Poet. Arensberg.
To a Wind-Flower. Cawein.
To Amanda. Thomson.
To Flossie. Williams.
To His Friend, Promising
  That Though Her Beauty
  Fade... Turberville.
To His Mistress. Cowley.
To My Lady Mirriel Howard.
  Skelton.
To My Mother. Ginsberg.
To My Mother. Rosenberg.
To Rotenham–3. Platen.
To the Rt. Hon. the Lady C.
  Tufton. Winchilsea.
To the Younger Lady Lucy
  Sydney. Waller.
The Train of Religion
  (excerpt). Tupper.
Trees at Night. Johnson.
Tripping down the Field-Path.
  Swain.
Ulysses and the Siren.
  Daniel.
Under the Moon. Yeats.
The Unknown God. Lyte.
The Unpredicted. Heath-
  Stubbs.
Unto the Upright Praise:
  Chorus. Luzzatto.
Vaudeville Dancer.
  Wheelock.
Verses under a Peacock
  Portrayed in Her Left
  Hand. Greene.
Virgins. Carlin.
Visions. Petrarch.
The Vocation of St. Francis.
  Eleanore.
The Voice That Beautifies the
  Land. *Anonymous.*
Voices at the Window.
  Sidney.
Waking in New York.
  Ginsberg.
The Wall. Phelps.
What Is the World? Dryden.
When before those eyes, my
  life and light. Stampa.
Whippet. Andrew.
The White Eagle.
  McDonald.
Who Are You, Little I.
  Cummings.
Who Pilots Ships. Hicky.
Who Walks with Beauty.
  Morton.

Why Did I Laugh To-night?
  Keats.
Winter. Sackville.
A Winter Madrigal. Bishop.
Wishes. Harjo.
Wishes for Her. Devlin.
With How Sad Steps, O
  Moon, Thou Climb'st the
  Sky. Wordsworth.
Women. Rich.
The Women in Vietnam.
  Paley.
Women Pleased. Fletcher.
The World As Wave and
  Idea. Coxe.
Yucca Is Yellowing.
  Simpson.

Beaver
The Hunting of the Snark.
  "Carroll.
Johnnie, Cock up Your
  Beaver. Burns.

Beckon (ed) (ing)
At Last. Whittier.
Dublin Bay. Milne.
Farm Child. Thomas.
The Hamlet of A. MacLeish
  (excerpt). MacLeish.
The Keys of Morning. De la
  Mare.
Parliament Hill. Bashford.
Rescue. Dargan.
Snow-Bound. Whittier

Becoming
Back in the States. Simpson.
The Gift Outright. Frost.
The Marsh, New Year's Day.
  Everwine.
Poems for the New. Fraser.
A Way of Speaking. Ehrlich.

Bed (s)
10:X:57, 45 Years Since the
  Fall of the Ch'ing Dynasty.
  Whalen.
After Shakespeare. Comfort.
The Age of the Butcher.
  Friebert.
The Alphabet. Greenaway.
The Anatomy of Angels.
  Nowlan.
Anemones for Miss Austen.
  Bergonzi.
The Apron. Friebert.
Arriving. Halpern.
As in the Old Days: Passages
  8. Duncan.
Asleep at the. *Anonymous.*
Autumn Even. Andriello.
Awake, My Lute. Lewis.
The Ballad of Mary Baldwin.
  Sandy.
The Ballad of Sally in our
  Alley. Carey.
The Bards. Graves.
Beautiful Woman. Zieroth.
A Beautiful Young Nymph
  Going to Bed. Swift.
The Bed. Merrill.
Bed in Summer. Stevenson.
Bed Time. Davison.
The Bird of Paradise.
  Davies.
Birthdays. Chute.
Bridal Couch. Lloyd.
Bubbles. Berkson.
Busy Old Fool (parody).
  Kelso.
Captain Wedderburn's
  Courtship (A version).
  Anonymous.
The Castle of Indolence.
  Thomson.

Changed. Calverley.
Christmas Card. Hughes.
A Christmas Prayer.
Stevenson.
Clerk Saunders. *Anonymous.*
Clothes Make the Man.
Weiss.
A Collection of Hymns...of
the Moravian Brethren
(excerpt). *Anonymous.*
Complaint of the Fisherman's
Wife. Nickerson.
A Constant Labor.
Thompson.
Corpus Christi (B vers.).
Anonymous.
Count Orlo in England.
White.
Courtyards in Delft. Mahon.
Crab-Apple. Talbot.
Cradle Hymn. Watts.
The Croodin Doo.
Anonymous.
Datur Hora Quieti. Hawker.
The Dead Pig. *Anonymous.*
Decoy. Ashbery.
Demeanour. *Anonymous.*
Description of a Summer's
Eve. White.
Does the Spearmint Lose Its
Flavor on the Bedpost
Overnight? Rose.
Dog. Monro.
Dream Songs. Berryman.
Drink To-day. Fletcher.
Dum Vivimus Vigilemus.
Webb.
The Earth Will Stay the
Same. Hill.
Eclogues. Virgil (Publius
Vergilius Maro).
End of The Affair. Grigson.
Epigram. Butler.
Epitaph: "How fair a flower is
sown." Patmore.
Epitaph on a Great Sleeper.
Cokayne.
Epitaph on a Party Girl.
Usborne.
An Epitaph upon a Sober
Matron. Herrick.
The Eremites. Graves.
Evening Star. Barker.
The Execution of King
Charles. Marvell.
A Family Man. Kumin.
Fare Thee Well Blues.
Calicott.
Fatal Love. Prior.
A Fiction of Edvard Munch.
di Michele.
Fourth Song the Night Nurse
Sang. Duncan.
Fox. Campbell.
Fragments. Cotton.
Frost Warning. McFarland.
Garcia Lorca. Dudek.
The Ghost of an Education.
Michie.
Go to Bed First.
Anonymous.
God Sour the Milk of the
Knacking Wench.
Nowlan.
The Gold Country: Hotel
Leger, Mokelumne Hill,
Revisited. Stroud.
The Golden Sea-Otter.
Wakarpa.
Good Fortune. Heine.
Good Night, God Bless You.
Anonymous.

Good Night, Sweet Repose.
Anonymous.
Green Grows the Rashes.
Anonymous.
Grizzel Grimme.
Anonymous.
The Hay Hotel. *Anonymous.*
"He Didn't Oughter..."
Herbert.
Hero and Leander.
Newman.
Hind Horn (A vers.).
Anonymous.
Hippity Hop to Bed.
Jackson.
A History of Peace. Graves.
Hon. Mr. Sucklethumbkin's
Story. Barham.
The Honey Lamb. Williams.
Horace Paraphrased. Watts.
How the Leaves Came Down.
"Coolidge.
The Hunt Is Up.
Anonymous.
I'm Ridin' Tonight round the
Dam Bed-Ground.
Anonymous.
The Iliad. Homer.
In Kansas. *Anonymous.*
In October.... Hamburger.
In the Holy Nativity of Our
Lord: Shepherds' Hymn.
Crashaw.
It's nice that though you are
casual about me. Sulpicia.
The Journey. Ignatow.
Keep a Poem in Your Pocket.
De Regniers.
Keep Smiling. *Anonymous.*
Knoxville, Tennessee.
Giovanni.
The Lady's Song in Leap
Year. *Anonymous.*
Lady, the Silly Flea.
Anonymous.
Letter from Slough Pond.
Gardner.
Limerick: "There was a young
soldier called Edser."
Milligan.
The Little Land. Stevenson.
Little Miss Pitt. Wise.
Lord Randal (C vers.).
Anonymous.
Love's Torment. *Anonymous.*
The Lucky Marriage.
Blackburn.
LV. Berrigan.
The Malcontent. Marston.
Many a Mickle. De La
Mare.
Marriage. Lowell.
The Milkman. Krows.
The Minyan. Myers.
Moon, So Round and Yellow.
Barr.
The Morning After. Heine.
Mr. Eliot's Day. Francis.
Mrs. Jaypher on Lemons.
Lear.
My Black Gal Blues. Estes.
My Papa's Waltz. Roethke.
My Son and I. Levine.
Nantucket. Williams.
Nebraska. Swan.
New York Bird.
Voznesensky.
Next of Kin. Rossetti.
Niagara Falls Nocturne.
Gasparini.
Nicholas Ned. *Anonymous.*

Night for Adventures.
Starbuck.
No Shop Does the Bird Use.
Coatsworth.
The Nurse Believed the Sick
Man Slept. Bronte.
O Western Wind.
Anonymous.
Observation. Herrick.
The Odyssey. Homer.
Old Moon My Eyes Are New
Moon. Ginsberg.
An Old Picture. Nemerov.
The Old Woman. Seiffert.
The Old Woman in a Shoe.
Anonymous.
On Honour. Mandeville.
On the Death of Dermody,
the Poet. White.
On the Deputy of Ireland's
Child. Davies.
On the Night. Gurney.
On the Staircase. Farjeon.
One-Night Expensive Hotel.
Everson.
A Palace Poem. Hsueh
Feng.
Passing the Graveyard.
Young.
Personal Column. Paulin.
Philander. Hall.
The Pilot in the Jungle.
Ciardi.
A Plea for Haste. Petronius
Arbiter (Caius Petronius
Arbiter).
Points of View. Lowell.
Pornography, Nebraska.
McPherson.
Prairie Lullaby. *Anonymous.*
Preludes for Memnon.
Aiken.
The Queen of Fairies.
Anonymous.
Radical Coherency. Antin.
The restful place, reviver of
my smart. Wyatt.
The Retired Boxer. Lucilius
[(or Lucillius)].
Returning. Harding.
The Road. Sassoon.
The Rokeby Venus.
Conquest.
Rollicking Bill the Sailor.
Anonymous.
The Rose. Lovelace.
Roses. Campion.
Sailing to an Island.
Murphy.
Sailing upon the River.
Crabbe.
The Scorpion. Belloc.
Screw Spring. Hoffman.
A Serious Poem. Walsh.
Shadrach. *Anonymous.*
Shame. Patmore.
Shitty. Amis.
The Silk Weaver's Daughter.
Anonymous.
Sing a Song of Moonlight.
Eastwick.
Six Questions (A vers.).
Anonymous.
The Sleep-Song of Grainne
Over Dermuid.
Anonymous.
Some Frenchmen. Updike.
A Song of Twilight.
Anonymous.
Song: "Softly, O midnight
Hours!" De Vere.

Song: "Westron wynde when
wyll thou blow."
Anonymous.
Songs of Cheng. Confucius.
Sonnet: The French and the
Spanish Guerillas.
Wordsworth.
Sonnet: "Women have loved
before as I love now."
Millay.
Sonnets of the Months. San
Geminiano.
The Sounds in the Morning.
Farjeon.
Spring. Verlaine.
Street Preacher. MacCaig.
Sweet William's Ghost (F
version). *Anonymous.*
Tenants. Gibson.
Things. Smith.
Three Women. Dempster.
To a Lady That Forbad to
Love before Company.
Suckling.
To Any Member of My
Generation. Barker.
To L.B.S. Scott.
To Turn from Love. Fabio.
Tobacco. Freneau.
Tone de Bell Easy.
Anonymous.
Tonight I've Watched.
Sappho.
Trains at Night. Frost.
Translation of Lines by
Benerade. Johnson.
The Traveller Has Regrets.
Fraser.
Troilus and Cressida.
Shakespeare.
Tumbling. *Anonymous.*
Twice a Week the Winter
Through. Housman.
The Two Friends. Leland.
Two Sonnets: "Altarwise by
owl-light." Thomas.
Ulysses. Graves.
Up-Hill. Rossetti.
Vala; or, The Four Zoas.
Blake.
Village before Sunset.
Cornford.
Virgil's Aeneid, Book IV
(excerpt). Surrey.
The Virgin Mother (excerpt).
Lawrence.
Waiting for the Doctor.
Inez.
Wake All the Dead.
Davenant.
We Dressed Each Other.
Eifuku.
Wedding. Brown.
Welcome to Prince of Ossory.
Mangan.
A Well-Wishing to a Place of
Pleasure. *Anonymous.*
What Shame Forbids to
Speak. Herrick.
Where. De La Mare.
The Whisperer. Van Doren.
Why Do We Lie. Johnson.
William I–1066. Farjeon.
The Wolves. Kinnell.
Words and Monsters.
Scannell.
Words for Hart Crane.
Lowell.

Bedlam
Canticle for Xmas Eve.
Wagoner.

The First Epistle of the
Second Book of Horace.
Pope.
Visits to St. Elizabeths.
Bishop.

Bedouin
A Cyclone at Sea. Hayne.
She Scorns Her Husband the
Caliph. Maisun.

Bedroom
Dividing the Field. Aberg.
She Told Me. Kilgore.
Speaking of Poetry. Bishop.
Submission. *Anonymous.*

Bee (s)
April. Valentine.
The Bee. Fandel.
The Beekeeper's Daughter.
Plath.
The Bees. Gibbon.
Black Hair. Muhammadji.
A Black Patch on Lucasta's
Face. Lovelace.
By the Road to the Air-Base.
Winters.
Dartmoor. Patmore.
Delphic Hymn to Apollo.
Swinburne.
Don Juan's Address to the
Sunset. Nichols.
Entering the Desert: Big
Circles Running. Rose.
The Garden. Grimald.
Hist, oh hist. Beddoes.
I would Like to be–A Bee.
Baruch.
Identity Card. Tichy.
If It's Ever Spring Again.
Hardy.
In an Old Nursery.
Chalmers.
In Tall Grass. Sandburg.
Inscription for a Fountain on
a Heath. Coleridge.
Invasion Weather. Newton.
June Song of a Man Who
Looks Two Ways. Daiken.
Lie on the Sand. Campbell.
Luss Village. Smith.
The March Bee. Blunden.
A Merry Bee. Skipsey.
Mr. and Mrs. Spikky Sparrow.
Lear.
Notes Toward a Supreme
Fiction: The President
Ordains the Bee to Be.
Stevens.
On a Piece of Music.
Hopkins.
On Watching the Construction
of a Skyscraper. Raffel.
One More Time. Aubert.
Opportunity. Graham.
The Parsons. Brown.
Precious to me–she still shall
be. Dickinson.
Quarries in Syracuse.
Goldberg.
Solomon and the Bees. Saxe.
Telling the Bees. Reese.
That Day You Came. Reese.
The Thousand and One
Nights: Haroun's Favorite
Song. *Anonymous.*
Under the Cliff. Grigson.
Where. De La Mare.
Wood-Song. Lee-Hamilton.

Beech
Beech and Oak. Peacock.
Song: "For the tender beech
and the sapling oak."
Peacock.

Beef
Git Along Little Dogies.
Anonymous.
A Laird, a Lord.
Anonymous.
Timocreon. Simonides (of
Ceos).

Beelzebub
When Sir Beelzebub. Sitwell.

Beer
Alabama Bound. Lipscomb.
Between a Good Hat & Good
Boots. Robertson.
The Biter Bit. Ayton [(or
Aytoun)] Sir Robert.
Chicago Analogue. Preston.
Christmas Comes but Once a
Year. *Anonymous.*
December 24 and George
McBride is Dead. Hugo.
Election Time (parody).
Anonymous.
Fate With Devoted... Ficke.
Hans Breitmann's Party.
Leland.
Inscription for the Sign of
"The Jolly Barber',...
Swift.
Lady, of Anonymous Flesh
and Face. Cunningham.
Lustily, Lustily. *Anonymous.*
Meeting My Best Friend from
the Eighth Grade.
Gildner.
Newport Street, E. Goldring.
A Poet's Epitaph. Amis.
Prohibition. Marquis.
The Ramble-eer.
Anonymous.
The Sea-Captain.
Anonymous.
Sestina to the Common Glass
of Beer: I Do Not Drink
Beer. Wakoski.
She's Gone Blues. Hicks.
Timocreon. Simonides (of
Ceos).
To the Memory of Yale
College. Putnam.
Triads. *Anonymous.*
Up the Country. Lawson.
A Way of Life. Nemerov.

Beetle (s)
Epigram: "'Reincarnating
Pythagoras, say."
Ausonius.
The Field Mouse. Sharp.
The Golden Shower.
Campbell.
On the Twenty-Fifth of July.
DeJong.

Befriend (ed)
The Faithful Shepherdess.
Fletcher.
Idiom of the Hero. Stevens.
The Judgement of Tiresias.
Jacob.
Rhymes. Segal.

Beg (ging)
Arrangements with Earth for
Three Dead Friends.
Wright.
The Canonization. Donne.
Hind Horn (In Scotland
Town). *Anonymous.*
Oh Cruel Was the Press-
Gang. *Anonymous.*
The Scholar. Cornford.
Silly Dog. Livingston.
To L.B.S. Scott.
Upon a Black Twist,
Rounding the Arm of the

Countess of Carlisle.
Herrick.
La Vita Nuova. Dante
Alighieri.
The Volunteer. *Anonymous.*
The West-Country Lover.
Brown.

Beg (ning)
The Price of Begging.
Frances.

Beggar (s)
Anachronism. Gogarty.
Aureng-Zebe. Dryden.
Aware. Lawrence.
Birds. Miller.
The Bristol Channel. Brown.
Craigbilly Fair. *Anonymous.*
Cupid. *Anonymous.*
Death's Jest Book. Beddoes.
Depression (excerpt).
Reznikoff.
Fairy Tales. Manger.
A Forme of Prayer. Quarles.
The Great Depression.
Goedicke.
A Grey Eye Weeping.
O'Rahilly.
Hagiograph. Heppenstall.
Hallowe'en. Hecht.
He Meditates on the Life of a
Rich Man. Gregory.
The Jolly Beggar.
Anonymous.
The Kiss. Teasdale.
Mandelstam. Burns.
The Map of Mock-Begger
Hall. *Anonymous.*
Of a Rich Miser.
Turberville.
A Plea for Mercy. Brew.
Portrait Philippines.
Duckett.
Rescue. Dargan.
The Return of Eve.
Chesterton.
Rhymes to Be Traded for
Bread: Prologue. Lindsay.
Running to Paradise. Yeats.
The Seven Sages. Yeats.
Small Country. Alegria.
The Spaewife. Stevenson.
The Speculators. Thackeray.
Summer and Winter.
Shelley.
Supper. Soutar.
The Suppliant. Johnson.
Ursula. Johnson.
With Lilacs in My Eye.
Coleman.

Beggared
At the Ascension. Leon.

Begin (ning)
About My Poems. Justice.
Against Still Life. Atwood.
Arcadia. Sidney.
Ballad of the Hidden Dragon.
Anonymous.
Barnabooth Enters Russia.
Hoover.
Beyond the End. Levertov.
A Brave-Hearted Maid.
Anonymous.
The Canterbury Tales:
Prologue to the Pardoner's
Tale. Chaucer.
Canticle for Xmas Eve.
Wagoner.
Church Poem. Thomas.
Corda Condoria: Quest.
Stedman.
The Cultivation of Christmas
Trees. Eliot.

Da Capo. Bunner.
Dawn. Logan, Jr.
Desiderium. Fletcher.
Digging It Out. Hollander.
The Discovery. MacEwen.
Doing, a filthy pleasure is, and
short. 02] ...never/Can this.
Petronius Arbiter (Caius
Petronius Arbiter).
East Coker. Eliot.
Epigram. *Anonymous.*
Epitaph upon Himself.
Belloc.
Explanations of Love.
Sandburg.
Father and Child. Harwood.
Foeda Est In Coitu.
Petronius Arbiter (Caius
Petronius Arbiter).
Forthfaring. Howells.
The Greenland Voyage.
Anonymous.
Hail to Thee, Blithe Owl.
Lardner.
A Hand-Mirror. Whitman.
The Hind and the Panther.
Dryden.
History. Soto.
Homecoming–Massachusetts.
Ciardi.
The Horses. Muir.
How Totally Unpredictable
We Are to One Another.
Sward.
I Am the One. Hardy.
In an Alien Place. Neidus.
In the Beginning. Fishman.
In the first place of my life.
Young Bear.
It would have starved a gnat.
Dickinson.
Jerusalem. Kanalenstein.
Johnny Appleseed's Hymn to
the Sun. Lindsay.
The Lamp. Vaughan.
Last Words, 1968. Henson.
Limerick: "There was an old
fellow of Lynn."
Anonymous.
Loss. Kuo.
Love. Thoreau.
Marginal Music. Meiners.
A Meditation: What is a
Stocking in Eternity?
MacAdams.
Moonless Darkness Stands
Between. Hopkins.
Morning. Davenant.
The Move Continuing.
Young.
No Armistice in Love's War.
Cheyney.
Open Your Hand. Fulton.
Paradise. Herbert.
The "Portland" Going Out.
Merwin.
Prayer of a Beginning
Teacher. Dunnam.
Rebels from Fairy Tales.
Hill.
Ronas Hill. Brown.
Saint Paul. Myers.
Shoreline. Barnard.
Silex Scintillans. Vaughan.
So It Begins. Agee.
A Soul's Soliloquy. Abbott.
Sphinxes Inclined to Be.
Orozco.
Starting over. Kaufman.
A Still Life. Kessler.
Their Beginning. Cavafy.
Time. Curnow.

Time and Eternity. Bunyan.
To Begin. Winant.
To Spring. Moore.
Unsubdued. Kiser.
A Valediction Forbidding
  Mourning. Donne.
We Continue. Merwin.
Where I Am. Dos Santos.

Beguil (ed) (es) (ing)
Angry at Zaidun's Interest in
  Her Maid... Wallada.
Apprehension. Ainslie.
The Book of Day-Dreams.
  Moore.
I Laid Me Down upon a
  Bank. Blake.
My Darling Dear, My Daisy
  Flower. Skelton.
Nature. Stone.
Nievie Nievie Nick Nack.
  Anonymous.
No and Yes. Ashe.
Once I Thought to Die for
  Love. Anonymous.
Though I get home how late,
  how late! Dickinson.

Behavior
Complaint. Hamilton.
The Man Who Married
  Magdalene. Simpson.
May Garden. Drinkwater.
Rules and Regulations.
  "Carroll.
A Translation from Walter
  von der Vogelweide.
  Synge.

Behead (ed) (ing)
For the Sin–. Anonymous.
Henry VIII. Anonymous.
The World's Way. Aldrich.

Behold (en) (ing)
Amoretti, VIII. Spenser.
Caelica, LVI. Greville.
Drinking Song. Hecht.
The Lover to His Lady.
  Turberville.
Meditation. Pain.
Remember Dear Mary.
  Clare.
Unseen. Crosby.
Venice. Symons.

Being
2nd Light Poem: For Diane
  Wakoski. MacLow.
Agnosco Veteris Vestigia
  Flammae. Cunningham.
At Least. Mattera.
Before Sleep. Ridler.
By Canoe through the Fir
  Forest. Dickey.
Demonstration. Finefrock.
Gate. McAleavey.
Here. Bell.
A House of Mercy. Smith.
Human Life: On the Denial of
  Immortality. Coleridge.
The Light of Stars. Furness.
The Livid Lightnings Flashed
  in the Clouds. Crane.
The Lost Dancer. Toomer.
Manet: The Execution of
  Emperor Maximilian.
  Snodgrass.
Moral Essays. Pope.
Ortus. Pound.
Pax. Lawrence.
The Poplar Field. Cowper.
Princess Elizabeth of
  Bohemia, as Perdita.
  O'Hara.
Song of Myself. Whitman.
Soweto. Sepamla.

They. Thomas.
To My Friends. De Vries.
The Tourists. Day-Lewis.
The Vicar. Crabbe.
A Vision. Winters.
What Form or Shape to
  Describe? Kabir.
Wild Ass. Colum.
Words for the Wind.
  Roethke.

Belch (ed) (ing)
The Giant Squid of Tsurai.
  Robertson.
The Miller That Made His
  Will. Anonymous.
Othello. Shakespeare.
Richard III. Shakespeare.
To a Publisher...cut-out.
  Jones.
Writing on Napkins at the
  Sunshine Club Macon,
  Georgia 1971. Bottoms.

Belfry
The Belfry of Bruges.
  Longfellow.
For Wilma. Johnson.
When Cats Run Home.
  Tennyson.

Belief
An Absolutely Ordinary
  Rainbow. Murray.
Alien. MacLeish.
Always Battling. O'Brien.
America Was Promises.
  MacLeish.
Amours de Voyage. Clough.
The Author's Apology.
  Carmi.
Authority. Huntington.
Autumn. Winwar.
Ballet. Kaplan.
Because My Faltering Feet.
  Belloc.
Beginning. Rodriguez Frese.
Birds and Bees. Anonymous.
The Breaking of the Day.
  Davison.
Burial. Sarton.
Celebration for My Mother.
  Rose.
Christian Ethics. Traherne.
Cockies of Bungaree.
  Anonymous. 7
Confessio Fidei. Dryden.
The Creation: According to
  Coyote. Ortiz.
A Creed. McLeod.
A Dedication to G****
  H******* Esq. Burns.
Detail from an Annunciation
  by Crivelli. Dobson.
The Dispensary. Garth.
Flowers for the Altar.
  Dolben.
Fly. Merwin.
Flyer's Fall. Stevens.
Food for Fire, Food for
  Thought. Duncan.
From the Epigrams of
  Martial. Michie.
The Ghostly Crew.
  Anonymous.
Growing Gray. Dobson.
Halloween. Livingston.
Hard to Bear. Jenks.
Heaven. Levine.
Her face was in a bed of hair.
  Dickinson.
Her Faith. Belloc.
The Hind and the Panther.
  Dryden.

The Horse Show at Midnight.
  Taylor.
I Cannot Believe That I Am
  of Wind. Greenberg.
I Will Believe. Roberts.
If We Believed in God.
  Gibbs.
Imaginary Elegies, I-IV.
  Spicer.
In Mysterious Ways.
  Kicknosway.
A Letter from Brooklyn.
  Walcott.
Lost Companions. Bryant.
Machine Out of the God.
  Sanders.
The Mailman. Contoski.
The Mechanic. Creeley.
A Mustacheless Bard.
  Coogler.
My heart I gave thee...
  Wyatt.
Nor Mars His Sword.
  Thompson.
Notes on a Life to Be Lived.
  Warren.
Nuts and Bolts Poem for Mr.
  MacAdams, Sr. Fraser.
O Spacred Head! Now
  Wounded. Gerhardt.
Of the Holy Eucharist.
  Anonymous.
Oh--Yeah! Scott.
Ourselves we do inter with
  sweet derision. Dickinson.
The Owl King. Dickey.
Paper Mill. Kalar.
Pastoral. Williams.
Pearl Bryan. Anonymous.
The Poets. Middleton.
Postlude: for Goya. Guthrie.
The Quilt. Levis.
The Rape of the Lock.
  Pope.
Religio Laici. Dryden.
The Sacrament. Donne.
Scene from a Play, Acted at
  Oxford, Called
  "Matriculation." Moore.
Sighed a Dear Little
  Shipboard Divinity.
  Aiken.
The Singer's House. Heaney.
Sisyphus. Miles.
Sonnet: To Dante Alighieri
  (He Reports in a Feigned
  Vision). Cavalcanti.
Sonnets to Aurelia. Nichols.
Tell Me, Dearest. Fletcher.
The Terrace. Wilbur.
The Third Day. Pierce.
This world is amazingly flat.
  Gorbanyevskaya.
A Thorn Forever in the
  Breast. Cullen.
Threnody. Parker.
To an Acquaintance.
  Anonymous.
The Triangular Field.
  Dobyns.
Upon the Swallow. Bunyan.
Waiting for Nighthawks in
  Illinois. Pfingston.
We Shall Overcome.
  Anonymous.
The Weasel. Pack.
When I Heard Dat White
  Man Say. Gilbert.
When Serpents Bargain for
  the Right to Squirm.
  Cummings.
The Witch of Atlas. Shelley.

You Are Lying, O Missionary.
  Kunene.
You Say You Love Me.
  Heath.

Bell (s)
The Anthill. Babcock.
At the New Year. Patchen.
At Year's End. Wilbur.
The Battle Autumn of 1862.
  Whittier.
Before the Anaesthetic; or, A
  Real Fright. Betjeman.
Bell Too Heavy to Ring.
  Kryss.
The Bellman's Song.
  Anonymous.
The Bells. Poe
The Bells of London.
  Anonymous.
Birds and Roses Are Birds
  and Roses. Heyen.
Country Nun. Page.
The Cruel Mother (B vers.).
  Anonymous.
Devotions. Donne.
Dialogue, between Crab and
  Gillian. D'Urfey.
Dingle Dingle Doosey.
  Anonymous.
Durer's Piece of Turf.
  Krapf.
Earliest Spring. Levertov.
The Evans Country. Amis.
Fairy Music. Ledwidge.
A Farewell. Flanner.
Five Bells. Slessor.
Flying Crow. King.
Fog. Reed.
Fuchsia Hedges in Connacht.
  Colum.
Giotto's Campanile. Butler.
Gone on the Wind. Mangan.
Great Tom. Corbet.
Here We Come A-Piping.
  Anonymous.
His Request. O'Sullivan.
Holes in the Sky (excerpt).
  MacNeice.
Humble Yo'self de Bell Done
  Ring. Anonymous.
I Heard You Solemn-Sweet
  Pipes of the Organ.
  Whitman.
Idolatry. Bontemps.
In Respectful Memory of Mr.
  Yarker. Close.
An Irishman in Coventry.
  Hewitt.
The Jester's Plea. Locker-
  Lampson.
John L. Sullivan Enters
  Heaven (parody). Frost.
Johnny Armstrong.
  Anonymous.
The King of China's
  Daughter. Sitwell.
Leave Train. Ross.
Leaves. Hughes.
Limerick: "A matron well
  known in Montclair."
  Smith.
Little Birds. "Carroll.
Little Dunkeld. Anonymous.
Love. Mangan.
Madrigal: "The nightingale,
  the organ of delight."
  Anonymous.
Mary an' Martha Jes' Gone
  'Long. Anonymous.
Mary Winslow. Lowell.
The Maximus Poems. Olson.
Memory. Stroud.

The Merchant of Venice.
Shakespeare.
A Mermaiden. Hennell.
Modern Love, III. Meredith.
More Nudes for Florence.
Witt.
The Morning Drum-Call on
My Eager Ear. Stevenson.
My Love. Cummings.
The Nets on the Andrea
Doria. Tepfer.
News from Norwood.
Middleton.
O City, Cities! (excerpt),.
Larsson.
The Old Gospel Ship.
Anonymous.
The Old Room. Merwin.
On the Clerk of a Country
Parish. Shenstone.
On Westwell Downs. Strode.
Oxford Bells. Hopkins.
The Parrots. Gibson.
The Passing Bell. Heywood.
Peg-Leg's Fiddle. Adams.
Peter, Go Ring Dem Bells.
Anonymous.
The Philosopher and Her
Father. Brooks.
Plain Dealing's Downfall.
Anonymous.
Poem: "A frail sound of a
tunic trailing." Machado.
Poems. Machado.
The Relish of the Muse.
Beaumont.
Restless as a Wolf. Halpern.
A Rhyme of the Sun-Dial.
Scott.
Riddle: "Down by the
waterside stand a house and
a plat." Anonymous.
Saint Erkenwald.
Anonymous.
School-Bell. Farjeon.
The Search. Herbert.
Secret Parting. Rossetti.
Sestina in Time of Winter.
Anderson.
Sleighing Song. Shaw.
Sonnet on a Still Night.
Cunningham.
The Sound of Morning in
New Mexico. Kelley.
Spring Snow and Tui.
Bethell.
Strike the Bell. Anonymous.
The Summer Countries.
Rago.
Sweet Silence after Bells!
Brennan.
Tacking Ship Off Shore.
Mitchell.
A Testament. Anonymous.
Those Wedding Bells Shall
Not Ring Out. Rosenfield.
Thoughts. Scott.
Three Poems about Children.
Clarke.
The Uninfected. Mayo.
Upon a Passing Bell.
Washbourne.
Upon a Ring of Bells.
Bunyan.
Upon the King's Return from
Flanders. Hall.
Virgil's Tomb. Rogers.
When I Was Well into Being
Savored. Kyger.
While the Bells Ring.
Dunetz.
Wonga Vine. Wright.

Belles
A Description of the Spring in
London. Anonymous.
The Pastime of Pleasure.
Hawes.
White Conduit House.
Woty.
The Yellow Rose of Texas.
Anonymous.
Bellow (s)
The Bellows Maker of Oxford.
Hoskyns.
The Forge. Heaney.
I breathed enough to take the
trick. Dickinson.
Winter. Clare.
Belly (ies)
A Ballad of Andrew and
Maudlin. Anonymous.
The Balloon of the Mind.
Yeats.
The belly of the land.
Tapahonso.
Elephants in the Circus.
Lawrence.
Epigram: "Poverty? wealth?
seek neither." Kassia.
Fetching Cows. MacCaig.
Flying Noises. Lux.
Green Grows the Rashes.
Anonymous.
The Gulistan. Sa'di.
Jacob Godbey. Masters.
John Hielandman.
Anonymous.
My Dim-Wit Cousin.
Roethke.
New Year's Eve in Troy.
Rich.
The Odyssey. Homer.
Of Jolly Good Ale and Old.
Stevenson.
Pregnant Image of
"Exaggerating the Village."
Dauenhauer.
Regent's Park Terrace.
Spencer.
Someone Talking. Harjo.
The Starry Night. Sexton.
Survey of Literature.
Ransom.
Trout. Hindley.
When to My Serene Body.
Laughton.
Woman. Chambers.
Belong (ing)
Do You Just Belong?
Anonymous.
Eleanor Rigby. Beatles.
For the Minority. Peterson.
In the Last Flicker of the
Sinking Sun. Markish.
The Marriage Dance.
Walton.
Mountain Creed. Nutter.
An Ode: "Not with slow,
funereal sound." Aldrich.
Parted Lovers. Halevi.
Take Your Fingers off It.
Anonymous.
They All Belong to Me.
Cook.
To God Alone, the Only
Donour. Pastorius.
The Working Man.
Donovan.
Beloved
Amours de Voyage. Clough.
The Bird Catcher.
Anonymous.
Broken Music. Rossetti.
The Bustan. Sa'di.

Deirdre's Farewell to
Scotland. Anonymous.
Dirge Sung at Death.
Anonymous.
Elegy to the Memory of an
Unfortunate Lady. Pope.
Epilogue. Heine.
The Face of Love. Jonker.
Gentian. Crane.
He Hears the Cry of the
Sedge. Yeats.
He Is Declared True of Word.
Book of the Dead.
Hexametra Alexis in Laudem
Rosamundi. Greene.
Hymn to Varuna, God of Fire
and Light. Anonymous.
The Illiterate. Meredith.
In the Egyptian Museum.
Lewis.
Jobson's Amen. Kipling.
The Lover and the Beloved.
Lull.
Nihon Shoki: Dawn Song.
Anonymous.
Odes, III. Hafiz.
A Prayer for Peace. Sill.
The Prophet. Gibran.
Sins Loathed, and Yet Loved.
Herrick.
Sonnets, X: "Thus was my
love, thus was my
Ganymed." Barnfield.
Three Things to Remember.
Blake.
To a Vagabond. Woodrow.
Vainly. Sachs.
A Valediction. Browning.
The White Birds. Yeats.
With Him. Martin.
Year after year I have
watched. Li Ch'ing-chao.
Belshazzar
The Bearer of Evil Tidings.
Frost.
Belt (s)
Chicago Allegory. Parker.
Considering the Bleakness.
Halpern.
The Monstrous Marriage.
Williams.
The New Saddhus. Pinsky.
Toast to a Departing Duchess.
Marot.
What If Jealousy... Palmer.
Ben Jonson
On Ben Jonson. Godolphin.
On Ben Jonson, in
Westminster Abbey.
Young.
Bend (ing)
Ballad of the Two Tapsters.
Watkins.
The City. Ignatow.
Great Friend. Thoreau.
Heron's Bay. Galvin.
Hope. Mezquida.
Indian Rock, Bainbridge
Island, Washington.
Niatum.
Lying Here, Everything In
Me. Atwood.
Meeting My Best Friend from
the Eighth Grade.
Gildner.
The Moon Ground. Dickey.
No Complaints. Hollo.
Ode on Celestial Music.
Patten.
Reply to Mr. Wordsworth
(excerpt). MacLeish.

The Ruin of Bobtail Bend.
Adams.
These Days. Jones.
To Mackinnon of Strath.
Lom.
The Undiscovered Planet.
Nicholson.
Vashti. Harper.
Young Lincoln. Markham.
Benediction (s)
Benediction. Sklarew.
Cinema Verite. Walters.
Eternal God, How They're
Increased. Mather.
The Hounded Lovers.
Williams.
Benefit (s)
Canberra in April. Rowland.
Pain Paint. Minck.
Poems Chiefly of Early and
Late Years: Prelude.
Wordsworth.
The Sloth. Romanes.
Thanksgiving. Herrick.
Benevolence
Songs for the Cisco Kid or
Singing Song #2. Lyle.
Benjamin Franklin
The Truth about B. F.
Stillman.
Bennington
Bennington. Babcock.
New England: For a
Celebration in Kentucky of
the Landing of ...
Prentice.
Bent
Baking Day. Joseph.
Clerk Colvill (A version).
Anonymous.
Drifting. Spivack.
The Library. Logan.
Moral Essays. Pope.
On Drinking & a New Moon
through the Window.
Wilson.
The Sagging Bough (parody).
Untermeyer.
Stray Dog. Mish.
Summer Is Ended. Rossetti.
Thou Who Taught the
Thronging People. Minde.
Tolerance. Hardy.
The Useful Plow.
Anonymous.
When Windsor Walles
Sustain'd My Wearied
Arme. Surrey.
Bequeath
Canto XLV. Pound.
"If care do cause men cry..."
Surrey.
A Last Will and Testament.
Anonymous.
Like as the swan towards her
death. Wyatt.
Sonnet IX. Drummond.
Bereavement
After the Last Breath.
Hardy.
A Broken Gull. Moore.
Indifference to Fortune.
Thomson.
Berries
The Barberry-Bush. Very.
Berrying. Emerson.
Count Filippo. Heavysege.
Difficult Times. Brecht.
Great Grief Came over Me.
Aleqaajik.
The Holly. De la Mare.
Pastoral. Voigt.

The Wry Rowan.
Anonymous.

Berserk
Hitchhiker.   Marshall.

Beseech (ing)
A Prayer for the Household.
Stevenson.
Sonnets, CXXXV: "Whoever
hath her wish, thou hast
thy Will."   Shakespeare.

Bess (ie) (y)
Bill Venero.   *Anonymous.*
Blues for Bessie.   O'Higgins.
Chicken.   De la Mare.
My Bonny Black Bess.
Anonymous.
Richard, Richard: American
Fuel.   Dixon.
Song: "Awake thee, my Bessy,
the morning is fair."
Callanan.
When This Old Hat Was
New.   *Anonymous.*

Best
Adam's Dying.   Torrence.
After Grey Vigils.
Santayana.
And Already the Minutes.
Aiken.
The Answered Prayer.   Flint.
The Anxious Farmer.
Johnson.
Aunt Beulah's Wisdom.
Box.
Autumn's Fete.   McGeorge.
Away Out West.   Hall.
The Battle of Bennington.
Rodman.
Be the Best of Whatever You
Are.   Malloch.
Best?   Widerberg.
The Best Choice.
Anonymous.
The Best for Me.
Anonymous.
The Best for Us.   Burnett.
The Best Game the Fairies
Play.   Fyleman.
Best of All.   *Anonymous.*
The Best Road of All.
Towne.
Caelica, XLI.   Greville.
Call to Conflict.   *Anonymous.*
A Catch-22 Test.   Sellers.
Change Thy Mind Since She
Doth Change.   Essex.
Child's Song in Spring.
Nesbit.
A Cigarette.   *Anonymous.*
The Clown.   Rose.
The Common Tasks.
Crowell.
Crosses.   Herrick.
The Cuckoo and the
Nightingale.   Clanvowe.
David's Song.   Browning.
The Death of Queen Jane.
Anonymous.
Dialogue: Lover and Lady.
Ciullo d'Alcamo.
Discouraged.   Stanaback.
Edgar Guest.   Williams.
Edge.   Montague.
Envy.   Procter.
Epigram: "Various the roads
of life."   Landor.
Fisbo (excerpt).   Nichols.
Five Short-Shorts.   Carruth.
A Fixture.   Swenson.
Foggy Mountain Top.
Anonymous.
Four Stories.   Shapiro.

Get Into the Boosting
Business.   *Anonymous.*
God's Key.   *Anonymous.*
Gregory Griggs.   Richards.
Half Past Four, October.
Hajnal.
He Done His Level Best.
"Twain.
A Heathen Hymn (excerpt).
Morris.
His Best.   *Anonymous.*
Home Song.   Longfellow.
How to Eat Alone.   Halpern.
I Would Not Ask.   Troy.
Ilicet.   Garrison.
In the Gloaming.   Orred.
Judgment.   *Anonymous.*
The Last o' the Tinkler.
Jacob.
Life's Mirror.   "Madeline.
Limerick: "There was an old
man with a ribbon."   Lear.
Look Home.   Southwell.
Love.   Oxenham.
Love Among the Ruins.
Browning.
Love's Alchemy.   Donne.
Magnets.   Binyon.
Man White, Brown Girl and
All That Jazz.   Oden.
Master and Man.   Newbolt.
May.   *Anonymous.*
The Muses.   Thomas.
Ode to Pornography.
Anderson.
Off to Patagonia.   Weiss.
Old Books Are Best.   Chew.
The Olden Days.   Hall.
The Omelet of A. MacLeish.
Wilson.
Part for the Whole.   Francis.
The Passionate Pilgrim.
Shakespeare.
Pep.   Bostwick.
Peter Cooper.   Miller.
A Poem Put into My Lady
Laiton's Pocket.   Ralegh.
Poem Read at Joan Mitchell's.
O'Hara.
A Poet's Wish: An Ode.
Ramsay.
Poetry's a Gift Wherein but
Few Excell.   Ward.
Proverbial Weather Rhymes.
Anonymous.
Rejoice.   Miller.
Reminiscence.   Irwin.
Resolutions?–New and Old.
Rolfe.
Revertere.   *Anonymous.*
The Robin Is the One.
Dickinson.
Salvos for Randolph Bourne.
Gregory.
The Shepherd's Song.
Bunyan.
The Ship of Earth.   Lanier.
Sometime.   Smith.
Song: "Can love be controll'd
by advice?"   Gay.
Song: "Indeed, my Caelia, 'tis
in vain."   Moore.
The Song of the Arrow.
Crawford.
The Song of the Robin.
Bergquist.
Sonnet: To His Lady Joan, of
Florence.   Cavalcanti.
Sonnets, CX: "Alas! 'tis true I
have gone here and there."
Shakespeare.
The Southerner.   Shapiro.

The Sparrow.   Williams.
Speaking of Cowboy's Home.
Anonymous.
St. Anthony and His Pig. A
Cantata.   Forrest.
The Summonee's Tale
(parody).   Sharpless.
Suppose.   Cary.
Take the World as It Is
(excerpt).   Swain.
Thanksliving.   Piety.
That Ever I Saw.
Anonymous.
That Little Black Cat.
Thompson.
That No Man Should Write
But Such as Do Excel.
Turberville.
They're Tearing down a
Town.   Strunk.
Thought for a New Year.
Burket.
Three Men.   Moore.
Threescore and Ten.
Stoddard.
To England.   Moore.
The Tramp.   Hill.
Up.   Kushner.
Up the Hill, Down the Hill.
Farjeon.
A Waist.   Stein.
Washington's Prayer for the
Nation.   Washington.
The Waves Gleam in the
Sunshine.   Heine.
Welcome, Fortune.
Anonymous.
West Sussex Drinking Song.
Belloc.
What Shall We Render.
Anonymous.
Whatever Is–Is Best.
Wilcox.
When One or Other Rambles.
Pastorius.
When Smoke Stood Up from
Ludlow.   Housman.
When the Wind Is in the
East.   *Anonymous.*
When Your Cheap Divorce Is
Granted.   Newell.
Which Loved Best?
"Allison.
Willie Macintosh (B version).
Anonymous.
Young Benjie.   *Anonymous.*

Bestow (al)
Nimphidia, the Court of
Fayrie.   Drayton.
Oh the Inconstant.   Van
Wyk Louw.
Thanksgiving.   Herrick.

Bet
Camptown Races.   Foster.
The Great Wager.   Studdert-
Kennedy.
I Bet God Understands about
Givin up Five.   Jamal.
Limerick: "A hearty old cook
of Lithonia."   Blount Roy.
The Rich Man.   Adams.
Taboo to Boot.   Nash.
Translations from the English.
Starbuck.

Bethlehem
Angel of Peace, Thou Hast
Wandered Too Long.
Holmes.
The Bethlehem Star Shines
On!   Mortenson.
A Carol.   Reese.
The Cherub-Folk.   Dinnis.

Children, Go Where I Send
Thee.   *Anonymous.*
Ex Maria Virgine.   Engels.
Five Carols for Christmastide.
Guiney.
The Forgotten Star.   Clark.
How Far to Bethlehem.
Miller.
Invitation.   Ibn Gabirol.
It Was Not Strange.   Hagg.
Jesus Borned in Bethlea.
Anonymous.
Let Christian Hearts Rejoice
Today.   de Brebeuf.
The Light of Bethlehem.
Tabb.
The Litany of the Dark
People.   Cullen.
Lowly Bethlehem.
Zinzendorf.
Mary of Bethlehem.   King.
The Mother's Tale.   Farjeon.
Noel.   Burket.
O Years Unborn.   Moreland.
Portico.   Dario.
The Second Coming.   Yeats.
The Shepherd Left Behind.
Merryman.
St. Bridget's Lullaby.
Ratcliffe.
Star of the East.   Field.
We Have Seen His Star in the
East.   Haley.

Betray (al) (ed)
Advice to a Painter.
Anonymous.
Barney's Invitation.   Freneau.
Caelica, LXXXIV.   Greville.
Dream Songs.   Berryman.
An Elegy on a Lap Dog.
Gay.
Evening Prayer.   Fitger.
Exhortation.   Bogan.
The Eye of Love.   Horton.
Eyes So Tristful.   Saldana.
The False Favorite's
Downfall.   *Anonymous.*
Fond Affection.   *Anonymous.*
Forsaken (He Once Did Love
with Fond Affection).
Anonymous.
Hengest Cyning.   Borges.
Idea.   Drayton.
Irish Hymn to Mary.
Anonymous.
The Liberator.   Stryk.
The Life of St. Cellach: Hail,
Fair Morning.
Anonymous.
Maine.   Nauen.
Modern Love: XLIII.
Meredith.
My Bird-Wrung Youth.
Anderson.
The New Calf.   Hearst.
Night, Death, Mississippi.
Hayden.
On His Dog.   Gay.
On the Death of the
Evansville University
Basketball Team...
Hamblin.
The People (excerpt).   Hyde.
The Shattering of Love.
Anonymous.
Song: "O, do not wanton with
those eyes."   Jonson.
Song: "When the heart's
feeling."   Moore.
This White and Slender Body.
Heine.
Timers.   Arnstein.

The Transfiguration. Muir.
A True Confession.
  Stallworthy.
Village-Born Beauty.
  Anonymous.
Voyeur. Hardy.
The War Horse. Boland.
Youth. Salkeld.

Betroth
The Inspiration.
  Montgomery.
To Our Blessed Lord upon
  the Choice of His
  Sepulchre. Crashaw.

Better
Any Wife or Husband.
  Haynes.
Arithmetic. Sandburg.
As Concerning Man.
  Radcliffe.
As We Grow Older. Wells.
Ataraxia. Taylor.
Back to the Angels. De Bolt.
Beachy Head (excerpt).
  Smith.
Bee! I'm Expecting You!
  Dickinson.
A Bestiary. Rexroth.
Betsey and I Are Out.
  Carleton.
The Bhagavad-Gita:
  Considerations of Murder.
  Anonymous.
The Birds of the Air.
  Freeman.
Broom, Green Broom.
  Anonymous.
Can the Circle Be Unbroken?
  Anonymous.
Carrier's Address.
  Anonymous.
The Collier Lad's Lament.
  Anonymous.
Confession. MacKenzie.
Contentment; or, The Happy
  Workman's Song. Byrom.
Convalescence. McAuley.
Crew Practice on Lake Bled,
  in Jugoslavia. Scully.
The Critic. Farrar.
The Death of an Angel.
  Edson.
The Evans Country. Amis.
Fame and Friendship.
  Dobson.
Flowers. Longfellow.
A Friend or Two. Nesbit.
Further Advantages of
  Learning. Rexroth.
Gormley's Laments (excerpt).
  Gormley.
The Grey Cock. *Anonymous.*
The Griefs of Women
  (parody). Slavitt.
Gunga Din. Kipling.
Harvey Always Wins.
  Prelutsky.
He Meditates on the Life of a
  Rich Man. Gregory.
He That Marries a Merry
  Lass. *Anonymous.*
Hooked on the Magic Muscle.
  King.
Hope Evermore and Believe.
  Clough.
In Postures That Call.
  Williams.
Ladies' Eyes Serve Cupid
  Both for Darts and Fire.
  "W.
Left Behind. Akers.

Limerick: "A young man on a
  journey had met her."
  Anonymous.
A Little Boy's Vain Regret.
  Thomas.
Mary Jane, the Milkmaid.
  Anonymous.
A Message. Phelps.
A Morning Prayer. Wilcox.
Mothers and Children.
  Johns.
Mr. Bleaney. Larkin.
Mule Skinner Blues.
  Anonymous.
My Money! O, My Money!
  Mavimbela.
My Wishes. Healy.
Neglectful Edward. Graves.
The Newly Pressed Suit.
  McGough.
Nimmo. Robinson.
Now or Never. Astra.
Ode to the Medieval Poets.
  Auden.
Of True Liberty. Beaumont.
Old Apple Trees. Snodgrass.
On Gaulstown House. Swift.
On the Death of Doctor Swift.
  Swift.
Once on a Time. Benson.
Out of Tune. Henley.
The Panchatantra: Poverty.
  Anonymous.
Peace. Cary.
Prayer to the Blessed Virgin.
  Rodriguez de Padron.
Proverbial Advice to
  Gentlemen. *Anonymous.*
A Question. *Anonymous.*
Rebecca's After-Thought.
  Turner.
Resolved. Shirk.
Rising in the Morning.
  Rhodes.
The Road. Stephens.
Say Well and Do Well.
  Anonymous.
She May Have Seen Better
  Days. Thornton.
Sonnets. Tuckerman.
The Soul of Dante.
  Michelangelo.
Spring Rain. Chute.
Surnames to Be Avoided in
  Marriage. *Anonymous.*
Teaching Poetry. Zarco.
To Yvor Winters, 1955.
  Gunn.
Waiting for Icarus.
  Rukeyser.
What Zimmer Would Be.
  Zimmer.
Whilst in This World I Stay.
  Pain.
You Are a Jew! Schwartz.
The Zoo. Sorrentino.

Betty
Black Betty. *Anonymous.*
The Rape of the Lock.
  Pope.

Beware
Asleep in the Deep. Lamb.
In Oxford City. *Anonymous.*
The Sympathizers. Miles.
Upon a Passing Bell.
  Washbourne.
Van Dieman's Land (A vers.).
  Anonymous.

Bewilderment
Learning by Doing.
  Nemerov.
A Nisei Picnic. Mura.

Bewitch
You're Not Alone. Drayton.
Bible
African Day. Sant'Ana.
Darky Sunday School.
  Anonymous.
From a London Bookshop.
  Anonymous.
Grandfather in the Old Men's
  Home. Merwin.
His Wish to God. Herrick.
Jesus Loves Me, This I Know.
  Warner.
The Jewish Lady.
  Anonymous.
A New England Church.
  Barrett.
Quatrina. Bennett.
Read the Bible Through.
  Wells.
Room Service. Moser.
The Sluggard. Watts.
To the Portrait of "A
  Gentleman." Holmes.
Viking 1 on Mars–July 20,
  1976. Perlman.

Bicker
The Rebel General. Wallace-
  Crabbe.

Bicycle (s)
17. IV. 71. Blackburn.
Daisy Bell (A Bicycle Built
  for Two). Dacre.
A Dawn of Jaffa Pigeons.
  Bachar.
Snapshot of Hue. Halpern.
Why Not? Pastan.

Bid (ding)
The Artisan. Brown.
At Casterbridge Fair.
  Hardy.
Capriccio. Deutsch.
Cover Her Face. Kinsella.
Song: "Oh, bid my tongue be
  still." Dixon.

Bide
The Houses of Corr an Chait
  Are Cold. Mac Cuarta.
I Saw Your Hinee.
  Anonymous.
A Man's Sliding Mood.
  Fullerton.
The Midnight Court.
  Merriman.

Bier
Atonement. Bruner.
Between the Porch and the
  Altar. Lowell.
God Made a Trance.
  Anonymous.
Helen Hunt Jackson.
  Coolbrith.
Indian Summer. Moodie.
On an Old Toper Buried in
  Durham Churchyard,
  England. *Anonymous.*
Song: "I have loved flowers
  that fade." Bridges.
Sonnet: Oft o'er My Brain.
  Coleridge.
The Ways and the Peoples.
  Jarrell.
When I Am Dead. Johnson.

Big (ger)
Adolphus Elfinstone.
  Burgess.
The Awakening. Morgan.
The Bigger Day. Bishop.
Chicago Boy Baby.
  Sandburg.
Chicken. Etter.

Cleaning Up, Clearing Out.
  Bronson.
Dance. Weeden.
Disaster (parody). Calverley.
Dives and Laz'us.
  Anonymous.
Elegy to the Sioux. Dubie.
Ephraim the Grizzly.
  Guiterman.
Epigram: "A head pure,
  sinless quite of brain or
  soul." Burns.
Fall Practice. Stuart.
Father. Lipkin.
The Forester. *Anonymous.*
Gift for the Queen.
  Anonymous.
Great Farm. Booth.
Growing Up. *Anonymous.*
Inconsistencies. Roberts.
Levee Camp Moan.
  Alexander.
Limerick: "There was a young
  critic of Kings." Hilton.
Little Brown Dog.
  Anonymous.
The Little Elf. Bangs.
Measuring a Man.
  Anonymous.
A Morning to Remember; or,
  E. Pluribus Unum. Dorn.
My Lord, What a Morning.
  Cuney.
The Neighbor. Williams.
Oil Painting of the Artist As
  the Artist. MacLeish.
Old Dan Tucker (Down Rent
  Verses). *Anonymous.*
On How the Cobler.
  Anonymous.
Phone Number. Collom.
The Price of Paper. Russ.
Red Indian Corpse.
  Redgrove.
Sagesse. Doolittle.
Skin Diving in the Virgins.
  Brinnin.
Sonnet: Of Becchina in a
  Rage. Angiolieri.
Sonnet to the Sea Serpent.
  Brainard.
Stone Age. Nolan.
Taunt. *Anonymous.*
Then. Aldis.
TV Blooper Spotter. Skelley.
The Voice of America 1961.
  Liddy.
When I Held You to My
  Chest, You Fit. Myers.

Bile
For George Santayana.
  Lowell.
In the Sky, Clearest Blue.
  Castro.
The Panther. *Anonymous.*

Bill
Artists Shouldn't Have
  Offspring. Marquis.
Bill the Whaler. Lawson.
Bloody Bill. Ross.
Dis Mornin', Dis Evenin', So
  Soon (with music).
  Anonymous.
Ducks. Harvey.
Farewell Frost, or Welcome
  the Spring. Herrick.
The Hart Loves the High
  Wood. *Anonymous.*
Little Billee. Thackeray.
On His Mistris that Lov'd
  Hunting. *Anonymous.*

The Rambling Soldier.
  Anonymous.
Spiv Song. Ellis.
The Turkey and the Ant.
  Gay.
Upon the King's Voyage to
  Chatham.... Anonymous.
Weary Will. Paterson.
When Oats Were Reaped.
  Hardy.
White Swan. Glanz-Leyeles.
  A.

Billboards
Animation and Ego. Swilky.

Billiards
My Object All Sublime.
  Gilbert.
Space Being(Don't Forget to
  Remember)Curved.
  Cummings.
The Temperance Billiards
  Rooms. Kavanagh.

Billow (s)
Beauty of This Earth. Opitz.
The Deserted Village.
  Goldsmith.
The Downfall of the Gael.
  O'Gnive.
Ending. Anonymous.
The Enviable Isles. Melville
Greenwich. Anonymous.
The India Guide.... Dallas.
Little Air. Mallarme.
Night Shore. Higgs.
Oh, Sing to God. Steendam.
Our Canoe Idles in the Idling
  Current. Rexroth.
Piyyut for Rosh Hashana.
  Guri.
Sunrise at Sea. Sargent.
The World's Wanderers.
  Shelley.

Bills
Christmas Bills. Hatton.
On the World. Quarles.
The Town Mouse and the
  Country Mouse (parody).
  Prior.
When I Went Off to Prospect.
  Anonymous.

Billy
The Ballad of Billy Rose.
  Norris.
The Ballad of Billy the Kid.
  Knibbs.
De Black Girl. Anonymous.
A Boy's Song. Hogg.
Pizen Pete's Mistake.
  Honey.
Some Ruthless Rhymes.
  Graham.
The Three Ravens (C vers.).
  Anonymous.
When Billy the Kid Rides
  Again. Barker.
Young Billy Crane.
  Anonymous.

Bind (ing) (s)
The Dying Girl. Williams.
The Eternal Kinship.
  Peloubet.
Eve-Song. Gilmore.
Foul Water. Temkin.
He is not dead that sometime
  hath a fall. Wyatt.
The Hydra of Birds.
  Engonopoulos.
The Jungle. Di Prima.
The Lay of the Last Minstrel.
  Scott.
Lucy Locket and Kitty Fisher.
  Anonymous.

On the Fly-Leaf of a Book of
  Old Plays. Learned.
That Room. Montague.
They Are Ours. Magil.
When Stars Are Shrouded.
  "T.

Binoculars
Horizon without Landscape.
  Lowenstein.
The Improved Binoculars.
  Layton.

Biography
But now the dentist cannot
  die. Lang.

Birch
Glanmore Sonnets. Heaney.
Hiking. Bruchac.
I Saw God Wash the World.
  Stidger.
Linota Rufescens. Donaghy.
My Fixed Abode Is Glen
  Bolcain. Geilt.
Seven Poems. Niedecker.

Bird (s)
12 Oct. Planz.
Abel. Lasker-Schüler.
About the Cool Water.
  Rexroth.
Absent Lover. Anonymous.
Adlestrop. Thomas.
Alison and Willie.
  Anonymous.
All That Was Mortal.
  Teasdale.
All the Bells Were Ringing.
  Rossetti.
Alone. Jammes.
Anabasis. "Perse.
And Grow. Hay.
Anti-Love Poems. Brewster.
An Ape, Lion, Fox and Ass.
  Anonymous.
The Apple-Tree. Campbell.
The Appointment. Strong.
Arbeit Macht Frei. Schmitz.
As I Went Singing over the
  Earth. Coleridge.
Australian Transcripts, X: The
  Wood-Swallows. Sharp.
Autumn Birds. Clare.
Autumn Scene. Dowling.
Aviary. McGuckian.
The Barnyard. Anonymous.
Beauty Imposes. Neilson.
The Bee, the Ant, and the
  Sparrow. Cotton.
Before I Stumbled. Carlin.
Before the sun goes down.
  Andersen.
The Begetting of Cain.
  Plutzik.
The Beggar's Opera. Gay.
La Belle Dame Sans Merci.
  Keats.
The Bird at Dawn. Monro.
A Bird in a Gilded Cage.
  Lamb.
The Bird of Paradise.
  Davies.
The Bird on Nellie's Hat.
  Lamb.
The Bird's Nest.
  Drinkwater.
Bird Watcher. Wallace.
Birds. Lawrence.
Birds. O'Sullivan.
Birds All Singing. MacCaig.
The Blackbird. Anonymous.
A Blackbird Suddenly.
  Auslander.
The Blinded Bird. Hardy.
Blizzard. Garfinkel.

The Book of Kells.
  Nemerov.
Bound. Roethke.
The Boyhood of Christ.
  Anonymous.
Bread. Burnshaw.
Britannia's Pastorals.
  Browne.
The Broken One. Holmes.
The Brook in February.
  Roberts.
The Builders. Wright.
But How It Came from Earth.
  Aiken.
Buttercups. Ginsberg.
The Cardinal Bird.
  Gallagher
The Case. Hays.
The Cat and the Bird.
  Solomon.
The Chaff. Merwin.
Chez-Nous. Austin.
Child with Six Fingers.
  Muske.
Cock-Crow: Woodstock.
  Robinson.
A Colloquy of Silences.
  Heffernan.
Compensation. Thaxter.
Composed near Calais, on the
  Road Leading to Ardres,
  August 7, 1802.
  Wordsworth.
The Conclusive Voyage.
  Jimenez.
Conditions. Vega.
Consuelo at the Country Club.
  Rodman.
The Continent That Lies
  Within Us. Nicol.
Copernicus. FitzGerald.
Coppersmith. Murphy.
Count Gismond. Browning.
The Courtship, Merry
  Marriage, and Picnic
  Dinner of Cock Robin...
  Anonymous.
Crash at Leithfield. Curnow.
The Crossing. Blackburn.
Cuchulain Comforted. Yeats.
Cuckoo. Lister.
Cypresses. Francis.
Dawn Has Yet to Ripple in.
  Cane.
The Dead Bird. Young.
Deirdre and the Poets.
  Milne.
The Deserted House.
  Coleridge.
Different Winter. Nicholl.
Ditty to an Air from Bach.
  Stevenson.
Earl Mar's Daughter.
  Anonymous.
Easter Week. Kingsley.
Ego Tripping. Giovanni.
The Elements. Davies.
Epilogue. De Vere.
Eshu, the God of Fate.
  Anonymous.
Especially When the October
  Wind. Thomas.
Eternity's Low Voice. Van
  Doren.
Even during War. Rukeyser.
Every Land Is Exile. Vigee.
Everything in the Air Is a
  Bird. Guest.
The Execution of Cornelius
  Vane. Read.
Exit Molloy. Mahon.
Fair Janet. Anonymous.

A Fallen Yew. Thompson.
Fast. Tagliabue.
Father and I in the Woods.
  McCord.
Father and Son. Higgins.
A Fiddler. De La Mare.
The First of May. Guest.
The Flamingo. Clark.
Flying Fish. Fenollosa.
The Flying Fish. Gray.
Footpaths Cross in the Rice
  Field. Lin Ling.
Fragments on the Poet and
  the Poetic Gift. Emerson.
From a Letter from Lesbia.
  Parker.
From Romany to Rome.
  Irwin.
Garden Lore. Ewing.
The Geese. Plutzik.
God's World. Millay.
Gone Is the Sleepgiver.
  Shuttle.
Grandma Fire. Ballard.
Graveside. Domanski.
Haiku: "Moor:". Basho
  (Matsuo Basho).
Hats. Dillard.
A Hint to the Wise. Barret.
Historiography. Thomas.
A History of Love.
  Williams.
Hunger. Stone.
The Hydra of Birds.
  Engonopoulos.
I Went Down into the Desert
  to Meet Elijah. Lindsay.
If Birds That Neither Sow
  Nor Reap. Williams.
If the Birds Knew. Ashbery.
Interlude. Duggan.
Interview. Lieberman.
The Island. Woodcock.
It May Not Always Be So.
  Cummings.
Juggling Jerry. Meredith.
The Kabbalist. Eibel.
King James and Brown.
  Anonymous.
Kopis'taya. Allen.
The Laborer. Dehmel.
The Labyrinth. Auden.
Lamenting Tauaba.
  Akhyaliyya.
Landeys. Anonymous.
The Last Summer. Smith.
Lauds. Auden.
Learning by Doing.
  Nemerov.
Leave the Top Plums.
  Chandler.
The Leg in the Subway.
  Williams.
Legacy: My South. Randall.
Let Us God, Then, Exploring.
  Woolf.
A Letter from a Friend.
  Maisel.
Limerick: "There once was a
  guy named Othello."
  Robinson.
Lines for Those to Whom
  Tragedy Is Denied. Oates.
Listening to Beethoven on the
  Oregon Coast. Carlile.
The Little Beach-Bird.
  Dana.
The Little Bird. De La
  Mare.
Little Bird, Go through My
  Window. Anonymous.
Little Birds. Sternberg.

Little Britain. *Anonymous.*
Little Miss and Her Parrot. Marchant.
The Little Shepherd's Song. Percy.
Local Politics. Pinsky.
The Long Joke. Smith.
Loves of the Puppets. Wilbur.
Madrigal: "Surcharged with discontent." *Anonymous.*
Madrigal: "The nightingale, the organ of delight." *Anonymous.*
Madrigal: "Well fare the nightingale." *Anonymous.*
Man Is but a Castaway. Day.
The Maryland Yellow-Throat. Van Dyke.
The Meaning of Africa. Nicol.
The Meeting. Rukeyser.
Mellowness & Flight. Barlow.
Milton. Blake.
Mirrorment. Ammons.
The Mocking-bird. Stanton.
Monster Alphabet. Fisher.
The Moon Pond. McGuckian.
The Morning Porches. Hall.
Murdered Little Bird. *Anonymous.*
Music. *Anonymous.*
My Grandfather Burning Cornfields. Sauls.
Mystic River. Ciardi.
Myths and Texts. Snyder.
Nativity. Rodgers.
Nested. Lulham.
The Nightingale. Barnfield.
No Question. Dillon.
Notes: II. Heap.
Now the Earth, the Skies, the Air. *Anonymous.*
Of A' the Airts the Wind Can Blaw. Burns.
L'Oiseau Bleu. Bottomley.
The Old Love. Hinkson.
On Another. Belloc.
One-Eyed Gunner. *Anonymous.*
One Last Word. Glassco.
The Other Journey. Chapin.
Over Sir John's Hill. Thomas.
Overtones. Percy.
The Owl. Bjornvig.
Owl against Robin. Lanier.
Owls. Fuller.
Pack, Clouds, away, and Welcome, Day! Heywood.
A Pastoral. Marzials.
Pheasant. Keyes.
Phil. Kooser.
Philomel. Barnfield.
The Philosopher and the Birds. Murphy.
The Phoenix and the Turtle. Shakespeare.
Piers the Ploughman. Langland.
The Play of the Weather: The English Schoolboy. Heywood.
Poem for Easter. Lee.
Poem for My Mother. Jaeger.
Poem: "To be sad in the morning." Pillen.

The Poor Can Feed the Birds. Neilson.
The Praise of Philip Sparrow. Gascoigne.
Prayer at Dawn. O'Shea.
Prayer for a Pilot. Roberts.
The Preachers. Nicholson.
Pretty Molly. *Anonymous.*
Pretty Polly. *Anonymous.*
The Priory of St Saviour, Glendalough. Davie.
Punkin Pie. Mills.
The Quarry. Miller.
Rabbit Cry. Lucie-Smith.
Reaching. Fagg.
The Recall. Lowell.
Recruiting Drive. Causley.
Red Bird. *Anonymous.*
The Redshanks. Bell.
The Retarded Children Find a World Built Just for Them. O Hehir.
Reveille. Ridge.
Rhyme for the Child as a Wet Dog. Sherwin.
Roads. Dallas.
Roma Aeterna. Crapsey.
Rural Legend. Osborn.
Sailor. Hughes.
Saint Francis. Bishop.
Saying Dante Aloud. Wright.
The Sea Bird. Douglas.
Sea-Change. Masefield.
Self-Protection. Lawrence.
The Self Unsatisfied Runs Everywhere. Schwartz.
Serenade. Darley.
The Seven-League Boots. Voronca.
Shooting Ducks in South Louisiana. Tillinghast.
The Sick Child. Stevenson.
Sleep upon the World. Alcman.
Snow. Thomas.
Sometimes I Walk where the Deep Water Dips. Tuckerman.
Somewhere Is Such a Kingdom. Ransom.
Song: "A rowan like a lipsticked girl." Heaney.
The Song of the Militant Romance. Lewis.
Song of the Navajo. Pike.
The Song of the Trout Fisher. Ikinilik.
Song of the Turkey Buzzard. Welch.
Songs to a Lady Moonwalker. Sutzkever.
Sonnets. Tuckerman.
Sophia Nichols. Blaser.
Sound. Harrison.
The Sounding. Aiken.
The Sparrow and Diamond. Green.
Spectral Lovers. Ransom.
Splendid and Terrible. O'Sullivan.
Spring. Williams.
Stanzas to Augusta. Byron.
Startled. Saigyo Hoshi.
Sukkot. Lachman.
Suspended Moment. Davenport.
The Temple. Dyment.
That Bright Chimeric Beast. Cullen.
That Which Hath Wings Shall Tell. Van Voorhis.

There Are Things to Be Said. Corman.
Thistle-Down. Bates.
Thomas of Erceldoune. *Anonymous.*
The Three Hermits. Yeats.
Three Maids a-Milking Would Go. *Anonymous.*
Thunderstorms. Davies.
To a Child Before Birth. Nicholson.
To a Daughter with Artistic Talent. Meinke.
To a Poet. Mary Angelita.
To an Oriole. Fawcett.
To J. S. Collis. Pitter.
To Miguel de Cervantes Saavadra. Munkittrick.
The Tomtit. De la Mare.
The Trail of the Bird. Courthope.
Transmigration. Cudjoe.
The Two Swans. Hood.
The Unknown Bird. Thomas.
Unregenerate. Embry.
Untitled. Naone.
Vietnam #4. Major.
Villanelle. Nist.
The Wakers. Freeman.
The Watch of a Swan. Piatt.
When in the Crowd I Suddenly Behold. Nathan.
When Oats Were Reaped. Hardy.
Where's Mary? Eastwick.
The White Birds. Yeats.
White Guardians of the Universe of Sleep. Cummings.
"The wind took up the northern things". Dickinson.
Windmill in March. Privett.
Wings and Wheels. Turner.
Wingtip. Sandburg.
Winter Landscape. Berryman.
A Wise Old Owl. Richards.
A Wise Old Owl Sat in an Oak. *Anonymous.*
Words to My Mother. Storni.
The Wounded Hawk. Palmer.
Yaddo. Herschberger.
Yom Kippur. Day.
You That Sing in the Blackthorn. Noyes.
Youth. Cloud.

Birds
In May. Davies.

Birth
After Annunciation. Wickham.
The Ages of Man. Ibn Ezra.
Ane Ballat of Our Lady. Dunbar.
Animula. Eliot.
The Annunciation. Tabb.
At Dead Low Water. Curnow.
At Fredericksburg. O'Reilly.
Autumn Healing. Ward.
An Autumn Song. Dowden.
Betweens. MacCaig.
Birth and Death. Swinburne.
Black Woman. Johnson.
Blue Hills Beneath the Haze. Whiting.
Calliope in the Labour Ward. Feinstein.

Christmas and Common Birth. Ridler.
Christmas Day. Fuller.
The Coming Child. Crashaw.
Credo. Symons.
Death and Birth. Swinburne.
Dialogue with a Door. Catullus.
The Disconnections. Engels.
Elegy. Loney.
Epigram: "I curse my bearing, childhood, youth." Synge.
Faith's Difficulty. Maynard.
Holy Night. Benson.
In Memory of David Archer (excerpt). Barker.
A Letter from Li Po (excerpt). Aiken.
Lincoln. Lowell.
Love's Immortality. Barker.
My Name Is Afrika. Kgositsile.
The Narrows of Birth. Everson.
Nobility. Cary.
North Labrador. Crane.
Ode: "We are the music-makers." O'Shaughnessy.
The Old Men. Kipling.
Out of Question & Mind... Mitchell.
Pieta. Rilke.
The Rape of the Lock. Pope.
The Rose That Bore Jesu. *Anonymous.*
Semele Recycled. Kizer.
The Shepherd's Tale. Ponchon.
Silent Night. Mohr.
Silex Scintillans. Vaughan.
Silver Lamps. Dix.
The Sinner-Saint. Blunt.
Sleep. Slessor.
Some Lines in Three Parts. Viereck.
Song (We Sing). Pieterse.
The Songs of Bilitis. Louys.
Special Starlight. Sandburg.
The Starfish. Coffin.
Tales of the Islands, IV. Walcott.
Time. Bhartrihari.
To a Book. Wylie.
True Love. Shelley.
Two Lives. Leonard.
An Unfinished Work (Excerpt). Kennedy.
Weir Bridge. Fallon.
What's Living? Hogan.

Birthday (s)
Another Birthday. Jonson.
The Birthday of the Lord. Carr.
A Child's Christmas Song. Daly.
Dandelions. Chute.
Dubrovnik Poem (Emilio Tolentino). Rudolf.
I'm Glad My Birthday Comes in May! Eastwick.
If You Saw a Negro Lady. Jordan.
My Mother's Table. Sobiloff.
Richer. Fisher.
Round and Round. Thompson.
Tree Birthdays. Davies.
The Waits. Nightingale.
The Wit. Bishop.

Written on the Raod.
Dodge.
Your Birthday Comes to Tell
Me This. Cummings.
Bisexual
Limerick: "A hermaphrodite
fairy of Kew."
Anonymous.
Limerick: "Said a gabby old
queer in Saint-Lo."
Anonymous.
Bishop (s)
Colenso Rhymes for Orthodox
Children. Harte.
A Familiar Epistle to J.B.
Esq.. Lloyd.
The Good Bishop.
Anonymous.
Hughie Grame (C version).
Anonymous.
Hyssop. De La Mare.
In Freiburg Station. Brooke.
Limerick: "And those two
young ladies of
Birmingham." *Anonymous.*
Limerick: "There were three
young women of
Birmingham."
Monkhouse.
Request for Meat and Drink.
Sedulius Scottus.
Robin Hood and the Bishop
of Hereford. *Anonymous.*
San Miguel De La Tumba.
Berceo.
Symon's Lesson of Wisdom
for All Manner of
Children... *Anonymous.*
They. Sassoon.
Upon the King's Voyage to
Chatham.... *Anonymous.*
The Vicar. Crabbe.
The Windy Bishop. Watson.
Bit
The Bald Cavalier.
Anonymous.
Carravagio. Hamill.
A Fragment. Bancks.
Ice Handler. Sandburg.
My Hands Are Withered.
Anonymous.
On When McCarthy Was a
Wolf among a Nation of
Queer-Queers. Dugan.
Our Bow's Bended.
Anonymous.
Bitch (es)
Behold, One of Several Little
Christs... Patchen.
The City Mouse and the
Garden Mouse. Rossetti.
Dowager. Montague.
An Epigram on Scolding.
Swift.
Grizzel Grimme.
Anonymous.
Hero's Portion. Montague.
Oil and Blood. Kizer.
Renewal. Kowit.
They Flee from Me That
Sometime Did Me Seek.
Ewart.
Unto the Breach. Poliziano.
Bite (s)
The Ambiguous Dog.
Guiterman.
Aunt Elsie's Night Music.
Oliver.
The Bat and the Scientist.
Bigelow.
Clouds. Levine.

Country Wooing (parody)
(excerpt). Squire.
The Devil-Dancers. Plomer.
The First Tooth. Rands.
The Glory. Thomas.
His Lunch Bucket. Cockrell.
I write to make you suffer.
Kegels.
If Thou Wilt Mighty Be.
Wyatt.
D Is for Dog. Davies.
Isolation Cell Poem. Green.
Jeans. Brummels.
Kisses. *Anonymous.*
Lady, the Silly Flea.
Anonymous.
Limerick: "There was an old
man of Blackheath."
Anonymous.
The Midnight Court.
Merriman.
Mir Traumte Wieder Der Alte
Traum. Heine.
My Father Kept a Horse.
Anonymous.
Nymph of the Garden where
All Beauties Be. Sidney.
O briar-scents, on yon wet
wing. Meredith.
On Fell. Lessing.
A Patching Together: The
Cell Lay inside Her Body.
Edmond.
Reclaimed Area. Silkin.
The Silken Snake. Herrick.
Springfield Mountain (C
vers.). *Anonymous.*
The Swank. Vickers.
Timid Hortense. Newell.
To His Book. Herrick.
A Wasp Bite Nobi on Her
Conch-Eye. *Anonymous.*
The Wounded Man and the
Swarm of Flies. Somervile.
Bitter (ness)
Almost Persuaded. Bliss.
America. Babcock.
Anna Playing in a Graveyard.
Gilman.
A Bewilderment at the
Entrance of the Fat Boy
into Eden. Hine.
Black and White. Duff.
A Black Man Talks of
Reaping. Bontemps.
Childe Harold's Pilgrimage:
Canto III. Byron.
Childhood. Walker.
The City of Slaughter.
Bialik.
The Crab Tree. Gogarty.
Fragment of a Love Lament.
Anonymous.
Frozen Fire. McLaren.
Grown and Flown. Rossetti.
Haiku: "Hardly Spring, with
ice." Chiyo.
He Has Fallen from the
Height of His Love.
Blunt.
His Saviour's Words, Going to
the Cross. Herrick.
I.M.H. Baring.
Life in the Castle. Hebert.
Lines: "The cold earth slept
below." Shelley.
Love-Songs, At Once Tender
and Informative.
Hoffenstein.
Love Which Frees. Fuertes.
Mother of Man. Parun.
Nearing La Guaira. Walcott.

Of Pardons, Presidents, and
Whiskey Labels. Snyder.
The Pillar-Box. Wolker.
A Sonnet. Lear.
The Sound of Afroamerican
History Chapt II.
Anderson.
A Thought. Lermontov.
A Tough Cuss from Bitter
Creek. Adams.
Troopship in the Tropics.
Lewis.
Una Bhan. Mac
Coisdealbhaigh.
Under Your Voice, among
Legends. Beauvais.
Vicarious Atonement.
Aldington.
A Wartime Exchange: As One
Non-Combatant to Another.
Comfort.
Winter Love Song.
Anonymous.
The Wooden Chamber.
Hebert.
Bittern (ness)
The Amphora. Sologub.
Beauty's Hands Are Cool.
Baker.
Breakfast in a Bowling Alley
in Utica, New York. Rich.
The Dedication to a Book of
Stories Selected from the
Irish Novelists. Yeats.
John Brown's Body. Benét.
Lord, Listen. Lasker-
Schuler.
Meditations in Time of Civil
War. Yeats.
Plowmen. Frost.
Prayer for Strength. Bruner.
Sonnet: Addressed by a
Father Mourning...
Vittorelli.
Sonnets for Pictures: Our
Lady of the Rocks.
Rossetti.
Timocreon. Simonides (of
Ceos).
Transformation. Alexander.
Winter Love Song.
Anonymous.
Black
11 Rue Daguerre.
Montague.
Adelaide Neilson. Winter.
Adulthood. Giovanni.
America. Hamilton.
The Animals Sick of the
Plague. Moore.
The Archer. Smith.
As I Went over the Water.
Anonymous.
As Proper Mode of
Quenching Legal Lust.
Massey.
At Night. Boimwall.
At the Nature-Strip.
Rodriguez.
Awareness. Lee.
Beautiful Black Men.
Giovanni.
Beowulf. *Anonymous.*
Berlin Interior with Jews,
1939. Emanuel.
Beware of Figs. Nicophon.
Black and Gold. Turner.
Black Blues. Modisane.
Black Bourgeoisie. Jones.
Black Cat. Dunetz.
De Black Girl. *Anonymous.*
Black Hair. Muhammadji.

Black Horse Running. Valis.
Black Is a Soul. White.
Black Lightning. Sze.
Black Majesty. Cullen.
Black Maps. Strand.
Black Narcissus. Barrax.
The Black Narrator.
Alhamisi.
Black Sketches, 7. Lee.
Black Snake. Hooker.
The Black Swan. Jarrell.
Blues. Mungin.
Bonnie Black Bess.
Anonymous.
Boys. Black. Brooks.
But He Was Cool. Lee.
Butterflies. Davidson.
Caelica, LVIII. Greville.
Canto Cantare Cantavi
Cantatum. Brown.
Captivity. Rogers.
Captured Bird. Rachow.
Casement's Funeral.
Murphy.
The Castle. Alexander.
The Change. Chimsoro.
Clerihew. Bentley.
Coplas. *Anonymous.*
Cottonwood Leaves. Clark.
Country Tune. Riddell.
A Cow and a Calf.
Anonymous.
The Crimson Cherry Tree.
Treece.
Cross. Hughes.
Darkened in the Soul. Napa.
A Dawn of Jaffa Pigeons.
Bachar.
The Dead in Melanesia.
Jarrell.
Dexter. Grayston.
Dick Turpin and Black Bess.
Anonymous.
Dream Songs. Berryman.
Dream Variation. Hughes.
The Dreary Black Hills.
Anonymous.
Drinking Time. O'Sullivan.
Durer: Innsbruck, 1495.
Malley.
The Edge of Town.
Clamurro.
Education. Lee.
An Elegie Made by Mr.
Aurelian Townshend in
Remembrance of the Ladie..
Townsend.
The Empty House. De la
Mare.
Eve. Gascoyne.
The Everlasting Gospel.
Blake.
Fairies. Conkling.
Feigned Courage. Lamb.
Find. Miles.
Fish. Rosenblatt.
For a Young South Dakota
Man. Manfred.
For Michael. Mitchell.
Fourth of July Night.
Sandburg.
From a Bus. Wangara.
Going. Everwine.
A Good Resolution.
Campbell.
Goodbye. Knott.
Gretel in Darkness. Gluck.
The Halt. Miles.
Harlem. Brierre.
Heaven in Ordinarie. Wolff.
The Hedgehog. Clare.
Her Longing. Roethke.

Here Is the Abattoir Where. Smith.

Hero and Leander. Chapman.

The Herring Weir. Roberts.

Higgledy, Piggledy, My Black Hen. Mother Goose.

The Highwayman. Noyes.

His Living Monument. Irving.

His Necessary Darkness. Sullivan.

How the Invalids Make Love. Feldman.

Human Geography. Whitman.

I am a widow, robed in black, alone. Pisan.

I Drift in the Wind. Jonker.

I Give You Thanks My God. Dadie.

I'll always dress in black and rave. Pisan.

I Only Am Escaped Alone to Tell Thee. Nemerov.

If the Black Frog Will Not Ring. Roberson.

In Bondage. McKay.

In May. Synge.

In the Twilight (excerpt). O'Donnell.

In Winter. Bretherton.

The Inner Part. Simpson.

Into Blackness Softly. Evans.

Is It Because I Am Black? Cotter.

Jefferson Valley. Hollander.

Jungle Taste. Silvera.

The King o' Spain's Daughter. Foster.

Kneeling Here, I Feel Good. Piercy.

The Last Evening. Rilke.

The Leader. Livesay.

The Letter Edged in Black. Anonymous.

Limerick: "There once was a guy named Othello." Robinson.

Limerick: "There was a young lady called Starky." Anonymous.

Limerick: "There was a young lady whose dream." Jordan.

Lines from a Misplaced Person. Hill.

The Little Black Train. Anonymous.

Love Songs. Anonymous.

Mandelstam. Young.

March. Williams.

Mary Arnold the Female Monster. Anonymous.

McDonogh Day in New Orleans. Christian.

Merry-Go-Round. Hughes.

Microcosmos. Heseltine.

Miss Grant. Downie.

Missionaries in the Jungle. Piper.

Modern Architecture. Nathan.

Mohammed Ibrahim Speaks. Beidler.

Monologue of Two Moons, Nudes with Crests. 1938. Dubie.

Montalbert (excerpt). Smith.

The Moon and the Yew Tree. Plath.

"More Light! More Light!" Hecht.

Mors, Morituri Te Salutamus. Money-Coutts.

Mortmain. Warren.

Mr. Cooper. Thwaite.

Music of Colours–White Blossom. Watkins.

My Black Hen. Anonymous.

My Lord, What a Morning. Cuney.

My Old Black Billy. Harrington.

Neurasthenia. Robinson.

The New Integrationist. Lee.

Night and the Child. Wright.

Night Fishing. Lewandowski.

Night Musick for Therese. Rainer.

Now in This Long-Deferred Spring. Warner.

Nunc Scio, Quid Sit Amor. Mackay.

Ode: Salute to the French Negro Poets. O'Hara.

Oh Ease Oh Body-Strain Oh Love Oh Ease Me Not! Wound-Bore. McClure.

Old Black Men Say. Emanuel.

On an Old Woman. Lucilius [(or Lucillius)].

On Getting a Natural. Randall.

On the Baptized Aethiopian. Crashaw.

One Home. Stafford.

One Way Down. Craig.

Open Letter. Dodson.

Overheard over S.E. Asia. Levertov.

Paddy's Metamorphosis. Moore.

Painlessly out of Ourselves. Page.

Part Winter. Bowering.

Penguin on the Beach. Miller.

Phaedra. Mandelstam.

The Phases of Darkness. Petrie.

Pigs o' Pelton. Anonymous.

Les Planches-en-Montagnes. Roberts.

Planning the Perfect Evening. Dove.

A Poem about Beauty, Blackness, Poetry. Bragg.

Poem No. 21. Long.

Poem: "The walls of the maelstrom are painted with trees." Madge.

Prisoners. Harvey.

Rainy Mountain Cemetery. Momaday.

Ransi-Tansi-Tay. Anonymous.

Red Sky at Morning. Thomas.

Remembrance of Things Past. Coleman.

Reservation Special. Blockcolski.

Return of the Prodigal Son. Senghor.

The Riddle. Johnson.

Rising High Water Blues. Jefferson.

Rondeau: "By two black eyes my heart was won." Anonymous.

Ruins at Sunset. Allingham.

Say Hello to John. Williams.

Scenery. Joans.

The Sister: Epilogue. Goldsmith.

A Small Bird's Nest Made of White Reed Fiber. Bly.

Solar Myth. Taggard.

Song Be Delicate. Neilson.

Song: "Dorinda's sparkling wit, and eyes." Sackville.

Song for Ishtar. Levertov.

The Song of the Smoke. Du Bois.

Songs for a Three-String Guitar. Sedar-Senghor.

Sonnet XIV: "Although I cry and though my eyes still shed." Labe.

Sonnets, LXIII: "Against my Love shall be, as I am now." Shakespeare.

Sonnets, LXV: "Since brass, nor stone, nor earth, nor boundless sea." Shakespeare.

Sonnets, CXLVII: "My love is as a feaver longing still." Shakespeare.

Sootie Joe. Tolson.

Spleen. Baudelaire.

Spontaneous Requiem for the American Indian. Corso.

St. John. Whittier.

The Starry Night. Starbuck.

Strings/Himo. Kageyama.

Suffer, Poor Negro. Diop.

Suffering. Ehrenstein.

Sun Set. Aridjis.

Taxis. Field.

A Technical Supplement. Kinsella.

Tenebris. Grimke.

There. Mezey.

Thomas Hardy and A. E. Housman. Beerbohm.

Thoughts of Chairman Mao. Young.

Tirocinium; or, A Review of Schools. Cowper.

To Strike for Night. Bethune.

Too Many Miles of Sunlight between Us. Myers.

Trivial, Vulgar, and Exalted: 19. Cunningham.

Trout Fishing: A Sign. Behm.

The True Import of Present Dialogue: Black vs. Negro. Giovanni.

The Undertakers' Club. Anonymous.

Walk about the Subway Station. Reznikoff.

War and Silence. Bly.

The Wedding of Alcmane and Mya. Chapman.

What Is Black? O'Neill.

When You Write Again. Jonker.

The White Man Pressed the Locks. Kilgore.

Will he always love me? Horikawa.

Will the Weaver. Anonymous.

The Wooden Chamber. Hebert.

The Word. Weiss.

The Work of the Weavers. Anonymous.

You Who Dog My Footsteps. Kwitko.

Blackberries

The Blackberry. Nicholson.

Hitch Haiku. Snyder.

Meditation at Lagunitas. Hass.

Mickleham Way. Eastwick.

The Railroad. Thoreau.

What's the Railroad. Thoreau.

With Tendrils of Poems. McClure.

Blackbird (s)

Belfast Lough. Anonymous.

Blackbird Sestina. Warne.

The Naughty Blackbird. Greenaway.

On Dwelling. Graves.

Sing a Song of Sixpence. Anonymous.

Sing a Song of Sixpence. Mother Goose.

Blackboard

The Unteaching. Oles.

Blackouts

Chronique Scandaleuse. Chima.

Blade (s)

Apopemptic Hymn. Auchterlonie.

Art and Civilization. Conquest.

At Last We Killed the Roaches. Clifton.

Chopping Wood. Smith.

Counter-Serenade: She Invokes the Autumn Instant. Viereck.

Decks Awash. Archilochus.

Foreign Aid. Kearns.

I Give My Soldier Boy a Blade. Anonymous.

John Knox. Smith.

Progress. Martin.

Schoolroom on a Wet Afternoon. Scannell.

That Summer. Hemschemeyer.

Those Makheta Nights. Chipasula.

Threnody for a Poet. Carman.

To Be Sung on the Water. Bogan.

Valentine Browne. O Rathaille.

Walking in Bush. Dowling.

Blame (d)

The Boy and the Wolf. Frere.

Caelica, XXXII. Greville.

Dear March, come in! Dickinson.

The Durham Lock-Out. Anonymous.

Epilogue to the Satires. Pope.

"Everybody Works but Father" as W. S. Gilbert Would Have Written It. Burgoyne.

The Family Fool. Gilbert.

Her Eyes. Ransom.

Invalid. McGaffin.

The Lamentation of Chloris. Anonymous.

Limerick: "A Conservative, out on his motor." Webster.
The Man from Changi. Hetherington.
Now I Am a Man. Marano.
A Quiet Life and a Good Name. Swift.
The Rising Village. Goldsmith.
Shapes, Vanishings. Taylor.
Six Jolly Wee Miners. *Anonymous.*
Sleep in the Heat. Jensen.
Some Who Do Not Go to Church. *Anonymous.*
A Storm of Love. Corke.
There Are Roughly Zones. Frost.
What Kin' O Pants Does the Gambler Wear (with music). *Anonymous.*
Your Last Drive. Hardy.

Blank
The Better Way. Leaf.
Handbook of Versification. Sorrentino.
Ignorance of Death. Empson.
The Lust of Gold. Montgomery.
View from an Institution. Wright.
A Week of Doodle. Whittemore.
When the Storms Come. Mphande.
Yonnondio. Whitman.

Blanket (s)
Animal Songs: Springbok. *Anonymous.*
The Appointment. Kumin.
Big Fun. Burns.
Chicken. Etter.
Extensions of Linear Mobility. Hathaway.
Indian Summer. Draper.
Meeting the British. Muldoon.
Moon-Come-Out. Farjeon.
Poem for a Suicide. Economou.

Blarney
Barney O'Hea. Lover.
An Irish Wind. Dennis.

Blast
Address to Plenty. Clare.
The Anniversary. Ai.
California. Robson.
Intention to Escape from Him. Millay.
Let Zeus Record. Doolittle.
A Moment of War. Lee.
Moon Blast. Roberts.
The Revolt of Islam. Shelley.
Song of the Sea. MacColmain.
Sonnet Found in a Deserted Mad-House. *Anonymous.*
Storm at Sea. *Anonymous*
When Each Bright Star Is Clouded. Callanan.

Blaze
How Many Fires. Reavey.
I Found the Phrase. Dickinson.
Interval with Fire. Livesay.
The Lay of the Last Minstrel. Scott.
The lively sparks that issue from those eyes. Wyatt.

Vapor Trail Reflected in the Frog Pond. Kinnell.
We Are Living, We Are Dwelling. Coxe.
Winter. Clare.

Blazing
Ballad of the Morning Streets. Jones.
Epigram: "The boys of Tyre are beautiful." Meleager.
For Mao Tse-Tung: A Meditation on Flies and Kings. Layton.
For That He Looked Not Upon Her. Gascoigne.
Joshua Hight. *Anonymous.*
A Little Morning Music. Schwartz.
The Magi. Gluck.
Marriage on a Mountain Ridge. Conn.
To Mrs. Will H. Low. Stevenson.
Whoso Draws Nigh to God. *Anonymous.*

Bleak
Evening Walk. Akesson.
Italy and Britain. Addison.
Snow Train. Erdrich.
Where the Lilies Used to Spring. Gray.

Bleat
Daisy's Song. Keats.
On the Wing. Rossetti.
The Prophecy of Famine. Churchill.
The Witnesses. Kennedy.

Bleed (ing)
The Allegory of the Wolf Boy. Gunn.
Astrophel and Stella, VII. Sidney.
Comrade Jesus. Cheyney.
The Corpus Christi Carol (from Scotland). *Anonymous.*
Cry from the Battlefield. Menth.
Daw's Dinner. Kilmer.
The Departure. King.
Domestic Scenes, 2. Reznikoff.
In the Dark, in the Dew. Prescott.
Lighthouse in the Night. Storni.
The Loss of the Birkenhead. Doyle.
Love and Sacrifice. O'Dowd.
Lunar Eclipse. Scarbrough.
The Marrow. Roethke.
O Holy Water. Ruddock.
On the Departure of the British from Charleston. Freneau.
A Poem. Mphahlele.
Song from the Bride of Smithfield. Warner.
Spring Song. Saul.
Supreme Fortune Falls Soonest. Herrick.
Survival in a Stone Maze. Rachow.
Sweet Muse. Watts.
Tannhauser. Payne.
Text. Wurdemann.
Unfrocked Priest. Campbell.
The Woman. Thomas.

Blemish
Cormac Mac Airt Presiding at Tara. *Anonymous.*
Sadness. Guest.

Blend (ing)
Anticipation. Tusiani.
Four Fawns. Howes.
The Heavenly Aeroplane. *Anonymous.*
My Last Afternoon with Uncle Devereux Winslow. Lowell.
Two Things. Babcock.

Bless (ed) (ing)
527 Cathedral Parkway. Lesser.
The Absent. Muir.
After. Grayson.
Against Marriage. *Anonymous.*
The Aim. Roberts.
Altar Prayers. *Anonymous.*
Amoretti, LXXVI. Spenser.
The Anglo-Saxon Race. Tupper.
Another Year. Smith.
April Rise. Lee.
Are We Thankful? *Anonymous.*
At the Museum. Brinnin.
The Bat. Pitter.
The Beggar. Moss.
Blessed Are They. Stitch.
Blessed Is God. *Anonymous.*
A Blessing on the Cows. O'Sullivan.
Bright Be the Place of Thy Soul! Byron.
Building in Stone. Warner.
Canticle of the Sun. Francis of Assisi.
Cassamen and Dowsabell. Drayton.
Childe Harold's Pilgrimage: Canto IV, XXVII. Byron.
Christmas Morning. Behn.
Clifton Grove (excerpt). White.
The Collector of the Sun. Smith.
Crusoe's Island. Walcott.
The Damsel. Omar B. Abi Rabi'a.
Day of God! Thou Blessed Day. Gould.
Decoration Day. Howe.
Devotional Incitements. Wordsworth.
A Dialogue of Self and Soul. Yeats.
A. E. Bronte.
Ending. Jordan.
England. Newman.
L'Envoi: The Return of the Sire de Nesle A.D. 16–. Melville.
Epitaphium Meum. Bradford.
Eternal. Macdonald.
The Excursion. Wordsworth.
The Farewell of Clarimonde (excerpt). Wilcox.
The Feast of Saint Brigid of Kildare. Brigid.
For Ever, Fortune, Wilt Thou Prove. Thomson.
Founder's Day. Bridges.
France. Goldsmith.
From Heaven High I Come to You. Luther.
From Potomac to Merrimac. Hale.
Future Blues. Brown.
The Gospel of Labor. Van Dyke.

Grace after Meals. *Anonymous.*
A Happy Man. Carphyllides
He Said, Lying There. Alta.
Henry K. Sawyer. *Anonymous.*
Hierarchie of the Blessed Angels (excerpt). Heywood.
High O'er the Hills. Walker.
Holocaust 1944. Ranasinghe.
Hunger in New York City. Ortiz.
The Husbandman and Serving-Man. *Anonymous.*
Hymns for the Amusement of Children. Smart.
I've seen a dying eye. Dickinson.
The Iliad. Homer.
In a Maple Wood. Schneider.
In Conjunction. Madge.
In India. Shapiro.
In Memoriam A.H.H., XXXII. Tennyson.
In Sorrow. Hastings.
Invocation. Horace.
An Invocation. Patrick.
It Is Too late to Call Thee Now. Bronte.
Jesus Shall Reign. Watts.
John Brown's Body. Benét.
Jubilate Agno. Smart.
King Henry VIII. Shakespeare.
King Triumphant. Watts.
King William's Dispatch to Queen Augusta... Patmore.
The Kingdom of God. Trench.
Knight Olaf. Heine.
Lalla Rookh. Moore.
Last Leave of the Hills. MacIntyre.
The Law. Ibn Ezra.
Let the Light Enter. Harper.
A Little Morning Music. Schwartz.
The Lost Pleiad. Simms
Lovely Mary Donnelly. Allingham.
Loyal Sins. Glatstein.
Lucky Lion! *Anonymous.*
Lullay My Liking. *Anonymous.*
The Medal Reversed. Settle.
The Mistress: A Song. Rochester.
Moving In. Shapiro.
The Music of His Steps. Wakefield.
My Happy Life. Westmoreland.
My Old Bible. *Anonymous.*
My Sort o' Man. Dunbar.
My Soul in the Bundle of Life. *Anonymous.*
Nativity Ode. Cosmas.
Natural Architecture. Hay.
New England's Annoyances. *Anonymous.*
Night. Sidney.
No. Zach.
No Cold Approach. Burns.
Nocturne. Raine.
O Day of Rest and Gladness. Wordsworth.
O God of Stars and Distant Space. Franzen.

O God, the Rock of Ages. Bickersteth.
Ode on a Decision to Settle for Less. Pillen.
The Old Oak Tree. *Anonymous.*
An Old Woman. Sitwell.
The Old Woman Remembers. Gregory, Augusta Gregory.
On a Sunday. Reznikoff.
On My Dear Grand-Child Simon Bradstreet... Bradstreet.
One Foot in Eden. Muir.
The Only One. Gardner.
The Phoenix Answered. Ridler.
Phyllidula. Pound.
The Players Ask for a Blessing on the Psalteries and Themselves. Yeats.
A Poem on England's Happiness. *Anonymous.*
The Poet's Journal (excerpt). Taylor.
A Praefatory Poem to the Little Book, Entituled, Christianus per Ignem. Noyes.
Prayer on Fourth of July. Turner.
Priest and Pagan. Watson.
Promenades and Interiors. Coppee.
Psalm II. Sidney.
Psalm III. Sidney.
Psalm XLI. Sidney.
Qui Laborat, Orat. Clough.
Real Happiness. Goldsmith.
The Repulse. Stanley.
Sardis. *Anonymous.*
Seabirds. Smith.
The Seasons. Kalidasa.
Shalom Aleichem. *Anonymous.*
Sir Launfal. Chestre.
Snow Fell with a Will. Gillman.
Song: "O memory! thou fond deceiver." Goldsmith.
Song of the Open Road (excerpt). Whitman.
Song of the Wind and the Rain. Ibn Gabirol.
Sonnet: Of His Lady's Face. Jacopo da Lentino.
Sonnet: "Time and the mortal will stand never fast." Camoens.
Sonnet to William Wilberforce, Esq. Cowper.
A Spider Danced a Cosy Jig. Layton.
Success. *Anonymous.*
Summer. Clare.
The Swiss Peasant. Wordsworth.
Table Graces, or Prayers for Adults: Morning Meal. *Anonymous.*
Temporary Problems. Rubin.
Their Last Will and Testament. MacNeice.
There Is a Love. Cleveland.
This Prayer I Make. Wordsworth.
Thomas Shadwell the Poet. Dryden.
Three Songs. Beaumont.
Thy Kingdom, Lord, We Long For. Scudder.

To a Lady: With a Head of Diana. Parsons
To Fortune. More.
To His Sacred Majesty, a Panegyrick... Dryden.
To Leven Water. Smollett.
To the Lord Chancellor (excerpt). Shelley.
To the Sister of Elia. Landor.
The Truth the Dead Know. Sexton.
Twelfth Night. Booth.
Verses Written at The Hague. Ano 1696. Prior.
We Thank Thee. Clark.
Wedding Song. Goethe.
Weldon Kees in Mexico, 1965. Wojahn.
The Whale. *Anonymous.*
What For. Hongo.
A Wish for the New Year. Brooks.
A Woman from the Book of Genesis. Knut.
Written on the Banks of Wastwater during a Calm. Wilson.
You came. And you did well to come. Sappho.
You Will Find a Joy in Service. Stroud.

Blight
Funeral Toast. Mallarme.
Laodamia. Wordsworth.
The White Witch. Johnson.

Blind
Above Ben Loyal. Ball.
Against Women. *Anonymous.*
Amoretti, XXCVIII. Spenser.
Any Father to Any Son. Money-Coutts.
Apopemptic Hymn. Auchterlonie.
The Aspen and the Stream. Wilbur.
The Beggar. *Anonymous.*
Black Mail. Walker.
Blind. Bangs.
The Blind. Baudelaire.
Blind. Kemp.
The Blind Beggar. *Anonymous.*
The Blind Fiddler. *Anonymous.*
The Book of Wisdom. Crane.
Breton Afternoon. Dowson.
Bruton Town. *Anonymous.*
Butterfly in the Fields. Campbell.
Caelica, XIII. Greville.
Caelica, LXIII. Greville.
The Chambermaid's Second Song. Yeats.
A Coronet for His Mistress Philosophy. Chapman.
The Cross-Eyed Lover. Finkel.
The Curse: A Song. Herrick.
The Day. Bynner.
Dedication. Allison.
Directions to a Rebel. Rodgers.
Elegy on Herakleitos. Callimachus.
Eros Turannos. Robinson.
Exquisite Lady. Osborn.
Extreme Unction in Pa. Ray.

Father and Son. Higgins.
For Dan Berrigan. Knight.
Fork. Simic.
From Beyond. Trent.
George III. Thackeray.
The Greater Cats. Sackville-West.
Helen Keller. Stedman.
Ignotum per Ignotius, or a Furious Hodge-Podge of Nonsense. *Anonymous.*
In Innocence. Cunningham.
In Perspective. Graves.
Japanese Hokku. Alexander.
Little Gray Songs from St. Joseph's, XLVII. Norton.
Lord, I Know Thy Grace Is Nigh Me. Ganse.
Love Songs. *Anonymous.*
The Lover's Song. Sill.
Loving She Stood Apart. Lane.
The Meat Epitaph. Benedikt.
Merry Christmas! Olson.
Mistral. Howes.
My Love. Shelton.
My Love Is Playing... *Anonymous.*
Mythics. Chasin.
Noon. "Field.
Not Changed, But Glorified. *Anonymous.*
Observation at Dawn. Kovner.
Old Dog, New Dog. Lea.
Old Joyce. Jennett.
On First Hearing Beethoven. Barker.
On the Death of Old Bennet the News-Crier. *Anonymous.*
An Ordinary Evening in Cleveland. Turco.
Out of Whack. Edson.
Peeping Tom. Hope.
A Prayer. Watkins.
The Princess. Tennyson.
Rachel. Gilbert.
Rooming House. Kooser.
Seven Rainy Months. Plomer.
The Shut-In. De Hearn.
Sight. Moton.
Silex Scintillans. Vaughan.
Six Poets in Search of a Lawyer. Hall.
A Sketch. Rossetti.
Snowfall in the Afternoon. Bly.
A Song of Honor. Hodgson.
Sonnet. Berryman.
Sonnets to Miranda. Watson.
Spirit, Silken Thread. Ruddock.
Sunday: Outskirts of Knoxville, Tennessee. Agee.
Tell All the Truth but Tell It Slant. Dickinson.
Three Blind Mice. *Anonymous.*
To B. C. Suckling.
To Fanny. Keats.
To Mr. Cyriack Skinner Upon His Blindness. Milton.
To White South Africa. Pieterse.
Tooten Out Blues. Bell.
Tourist. Van Doren.
The Travellers. Howe.
Tricks. Moure.

The Virgin Mary. Bowers.
The Waggoner. *Anonymous.*
World of Darkness. Chatain.
The Ziz. Hollander.

Blind man's room
Adam's Song of the Visible World. Torrence.
Among These Turf-Stacks. MacNeice.
The Barn. Heaney.
Bog and Candle. Fitzgerald.
Climbing. Epstein.
Coming Suddenly to the Sea. Dudek.
The Feather. Watkins.
Germination. Stone.
Hyperion. Keats.
In the Gorge. Merwin.
A Lover's Words. Watkins.
Monkshood XXIX. Gunnars.
O Terrible Is the Highest Thing. Patchen.
Partial Resemblance. Levertov.
Remarks of Soul to Body. Warren.
Rhymes for a Modern Nursery: Two Blind Mice. Dehn.
The Sakiyeh. Blind.
The Scales of the Eyes. Nemerov.
Sight. Gibson.
Spinning. Jackson.
To Ariake Kambara. Rosten.
Two Refugees. Marcus.
The Wind Is Blind. Meynell.
Womankind. Massey.

Blink
A Christmas Package: No. 7 (excerpt). McCord.
Famous Poet. Hughes.
I Would Be a Painter Most of All. Chandler.
Neuteronomy. Merriam.
Saw You My Father. *Anonymous.*

Bliss (ful)
Abstemia. Burgess.
Admonition to the Muse. Taylor.
Almighty God, Thy Constant Care. Washburn.
Amoretti, LXIII. Spenser.
Amoretti, LXXII. Spenser.
Amoretti, LXXXIX. Spenser.
Anthologistics. Guiterman.
Beauty's Queen. Kisa'i of Merv.
Bird on Briar. *Anonymous.*
Birthday Poem. Young.
Blue Moonshine. Stokes.
The Brome Abraham and Isaac. *Anonymous.*
The Bustan. Sa'di.
Caelica, XCIV. Greville.
Calm Was the Even. Dryden.
Cant. Davies.
The Canterbury Tales: The Nun's Priest's Tale. Chaucer.
Charlotte Nicholls. Clemo.
The Child's Sight. Sobiloff.
Compared with Christ. Toplady.
Content. Campion.
Content. Gale.
The Day Returns. Burns.

An Elegiack Verse On the Death of the Pious and Profound... Walter.
The Fox and the Wolf. *Anonymous.*
Guy Mannering. Chapt. 4: Twist Ye, Twine Ye! Even So. Scott.
Hap. Hardy.
Happiness Found. Toplady.
The Heart. Steinberg.
His Petition to Queen Anne of Denmark (1618). Ralegh.
Hymn. Doddridge.
I Die; But When the Grave Shall Press. Bronte.
I Know That My Redeemer Lives. Wesley.
Incident at Bruges. Wordsworth.
Jesus Contrasts Man and Himself. *Anonymous.*
Keep on Praying. Lyon.
Lines. Brooke.
Logan Braes. Mayne.
Long Since Last. Miller.
Look on Me with Thy Sweet Eyes. *Anonymous.*
Love Is All. Catullus.
Love's Longing. *Anonymous.*
Madrigal: "Sweet Cupid, ripen her desire." Corkine.
Madrigal: "The sound of thy sweet name, my dearest treasure." Davison.
Margaret to Dolcino. Kingsley.
Meditations. Taylor.
Miracle Play. *Anonymous.*
My Song of Today. Therese.
A New Year Wish. *Anonymous.*
Niplets. *Anonymous.*
Not Yet. Kyger.
Ode on a Distant Prospect of Eton College. Gray.
On His Mistress Going from Home. *Anonymous.*
On Leaping over the Moon. Traherne.
On New-Years Day 1640 to the King. Suckling.
Paradise Lost. Milton.
Petition to the Queen. Ralegh.
The Phoenix. *Anonymous.*
The Phoenix (excerpt). *Anonymous.*
Praxis. Thesen.
The Purple Island. Fletcher.
The Queer. Vaughan.
Quia Amore Langueo. *Anonymous.*
Rejoicing in Hope. Toplady.
Robin Hood and the Monk. *Anonymous.*
The Seasons. Kalidasa.
Serenade. Donnelly.
Sextains. Baylebridge.
Shall I Complain? Moulton.
Since Nature's Works Be Good. Sidney.
The Singer. Dowden.
Sir Gawain and the Green Knight. *Anonymous.*
Spring. Thomson.
The Temptation of Sir Gawain. *Anonymous.*
The Thief. Cowley.
Three Love Poems. Halevi.
To a Fine Young Woman. Wycherley.

To the Reverend Mr. Murdoch. Thomson.
Translation of Lines by Benerade. Johnson.
Two Married. Frazee-Bower.
Unshrinking Faith. Balhurst.
Upon the Death of Sir Antony Denny. *Anonymous.*
Veni, Sancte Spiritus. Robert II.
Western Emigration. Humphreys.
The Whale. *Anonymous.*
Whales Weep Not! Lawrence.
When the Turf Is Thy Tower. *Anonymous.*
The White Anemone. Meredith."
The World, the Devil, and Tom Paine. *Anonymous.*

Blithe
I Saw My Life as Whitest Flame. Brennan.
Ianthe. Landor.
Marriage and the Care O't. Lochore.
Moon Landing. Auden.
Verse. Gogarty.
A Week of Birthdays. Mother Goose.

Blizzard
Desert Gulls. Gillespie.
In the Shelter. Day Lewis.
Limerick: "There once was a wonderful wizard." Aiken.
Old Storm. Phillips.

Block
Boy Trash Picker. Howard.
Cawsand Bay. *Anonymous.*
The Last Word. Davison.
Living in the World. Lau.
Revisiting the Field. Pavlich.
Sometimes on My Way Back Down to the Block. Cruz.
To Sit in Solemn Silence. Gilbert.
The World's Greatest Tricycle Rider. Williams.

Block Island
The Phantom Ship. De Forest.

Blockade
Running the Blockade. Perry.

Blockhead
The Man of Taste. Bramston.

Blocks
Edmund Burke. Goldsmith.
The Fisherman's Wife. Mitchell.
A New Simile in the Manner of Swift. Goldsmith.

Blond (es)
A Country Club Romance. Walcott.
Fag-End. O'Connor.
I Sing of Olaf Glad and Big. Cummings.
A Letter from the Hotel. Barnstone.
Not Just Yet. Revard.
What's Wrong, Little Blonde. *Anonymous.*
Young Blondes. Ewart.

Blood
Absence. McKay.
Accepting. Miller.
Agent Orange. Kiefer.
The Apple. Guernsey.

The Art of War (excerpt). Fawcett.
At the Round Earth's Imagin'd Corners, Blow. Donne.
L'Aurore Grelottante. Levi.
The Battel of the Summer-Islands. Waller.
The Battle of Aughrim. Murphy.
Beachcomber. Oliver.
The Beast with Chrome Teeth. Snyder.
Before Breakup on the Chena outside Fairbanks. McElroy.
Bethlehem Town. Field.
Betty Zane. English.
Black Mesa. Rogers.
Blok Let Me Learn the Poem. Boyajian.
Blood. Bremser.
The Blood. Cassian.
Blood on the Sails. Colclough.
Blues for Bessie. O'Higgins.
Body of Jesus. Coxe.
Boomerang. Hart-Smith.
Bound. Roethke.
Boundaries. Fleming.
Braddock's Defeat. *Anonymous.*
Breaking Off from Waiting. Nicoidski.
The Bridal Bed. Mastoraki.
Buried at Springs. Schuyler.
Burying Blues for Janis. Piercy.
Caelica, XCV. Greville.
Calliope (with music). *Anonymous.*
A Calvinist in Love. Clemo.
Celia Bleeding, to the Surgeon. Carew.
Ceremony. Stafford.
Chicago. Ridge.
Children of Light. Lowell.
Church Lock and Key. Herbert.
The Civil Wars between the Two Houses of Lancaster and York. Daniel.
The Clothing's New Emperor. Finkel.
Cloud and Flame. Berryman.
The Courtship, Merry Marriage, and Picnic Dinner of Cock Robin... *Anonymous.*
Crucifying. Donne.
The Crusaders knew the Holy Places. Mastoraki.
A Dark Hand. Manger.
Debridement: Operation Harvest Moon: On Repose. Harper.
Discord in Childhood. Lawrence.
Dispossessions. Cooper.
Distances (excerpt). Okigbo.
Don Juan. Byron.
Dublin Made Me. MacDonagh.
The Duel. Pulsifer.
Eagle Valor, Chicken Mind. Jeffers.
The Editor's Wooing. Newell.
Elder Tree. Aiken.
Epitaph on the Earl of Strafford. Cleveland.

Factories. Hirsch.
Family Poem. Holloway.
The Festal Board. *Anonymous.*
The First Nowell. *Anonymous.*
The Five-Minute Orlando Macbeth. Macbeth.
The Flying Tailor (parody). Hogg.
Foliage of Vision. Merrill.
Food Strike. Hogan.
Forgiveness. Lyte.
Fowls in the Frith. *Anonymous.*
The fruits you give me are more savory than others. Burnat-Provins.
The Fugitive. Meynell.
The Fury of Cocks. Sexton.
The Gate's Open. Blight.
The Gathering on the Plains. Butler.
Glory. Lawrence.
Goat Dance. Loewinsohn.
God Save the Flag. Holmes.
The Gods Are Mighty. Van Wyk Louw.
Gothic Landscape. Layton.
Haitian Suite. Orr.
Hare in Winter. Piercy.
The Hawk in the Rain. Hughes.
Helicon. Hollander.
I Love What Is Not. Winkler.
I Saw One Hanging. *Anonymous.*
I Think Sometimes... Hartnett.
I've Tasted My Blood. Acorn.
Ice River. Baker.
If I Go Not, Pray Not, Give Not. *Anonymous.*
In the Gold Room. Wilde.
In the Subway. Jimenez.
Interval with Fire. Livesay.
Ireland Weeping. Livingston.
Isaac. Gilboa.
Jerusalem the Dismembered. Greenberg.
The Jewels. Baudelaire.
The Journey and Observations of a Countryman (excerpt). Hawthorn.
The Knot. Rich.
Lament for Azazel. Landy.
Lament for the Alamo. Guiterman.
Lament for the European Exile. Strauss.
Landfall in Unknown Seas. Curnow.
The Last Post. Graves.
The Last Supper. Williams.
Leave Train. Ross.
A Legend. Tschaikovsky.
Like Gulliver. Cassian.
Little Phoebe. *Anonymous.*
Loot. Gunn.
Losing the Straight Way. Wedde.
Love Songs. Loy.
Maritimes. Shuttle.
Marrakesh Women. Lifshin.
The Masterful Man. Tyrrell.
Monkeys. Colum.
Morning Dialogue. Aiken.
Morning Light the Dew-Drier. Newsome.

The Morning They Shot Tony Lopez, Barber and Pusher Who Went Too Far. Soto.
The Mothers of the West. Gallagher.
Motive for Mercy. Milburn.
Movie Actors Scribbling Letters Very Fast in Crucial Scenes. Garrigue.
The Murder of the Tsarevich Dimitri by Boris Godunov. *Anonymous.*
My America. La Grone.
My Brother Was Silent. Gilboa.
My Creed. Cary.
My Father Died This Spring. Kyger.
My Lady Has the Grace of Death. Plunkett.
My Love-Song. Lasker-Schüler.
My Mother Would Be a Falconress. Duncan.
My True Sailor Boy. *Anonymous.*
New Spring. Jimenez.
New Year's Day. Lowell.
Night. Bogan.
Night Cries, Wakari Hospital. Brasch.
A Night in Odessa. Simpson.
Night of Battle. Winters.
Nilotic Elegy. Fraser.
The Nineteenth of April. Larcom.
No-Man's Land. Knight-Adkin.
North Country. Slessor.
The Northern Cobbler. Tennyson.
Not to sigh and to be tender. Behn.
Now Evening Puts Amen to Day. Horgan.
A Nuptial Verse to Mistress Elizabeth Lee Now Lady Tracy. Herrick.
O. Villanueva.
O Saviour of a World Undone. Withington.
The Odyssey. Homer.
On a Fifteenth-Century Flemish Angel. Ray.
On a Line in Sandburg. Thomas.
On Our Crucified Lord, Naked and Bloody. Crashaw.
On the Death of Doctor Swift. Swift.
On the Marriage of a Virgin. Thomas.
Oracle at Delphi. Bagg.
Organ Transplant. Reed.
Orishas. Neal.
Ossawatomie. Sandburg.
Pardon, Old Fathers. Yeats.
Parnell. Kettle.
The Passing of the Poets. O Gnimh.
The Passion. Knevet.
The Past. Hodgson.
Peachstone. Abse.
Poem Proud Papa. Farkas.
Poem to Lou. Apollinaire.
Portrait of a Motorcar. Sandburg.
Portrait of the Autist as a New World Driver. Murray.

The Precious Blood. *Anonymous.*
Proverbial Advice on Marriage. *Anonymous.*
Put Down. Damas.
A Quintina of Crosses. Walsh.
Razor. Smith.
The Resolute Courtier. Shipman.
Responsibilities: Prologue. Yeats.
The Ribbon-Fish. Adamson.
Ribh Considers Christian Love Insufficient. Yeats.
The Rite. Randall.
The Rose Tree. Yeats.
The Rout of San Romano. White.
Sabbatical. Zisquit.
The School Globe. Reaney.
A Scientific Expedition in Siberia, 1913. Cherry.
The Shark. Pratt.
Siegfried. Jarrell.
Six O'Clock. Stickney.
Sleep, Holy Babe. Caswall.
Smoke and Steel (excerpt). Sandburg.
The Soldier Walks under the Trees of the University. Jarrell.
Someplace Else. Piercy.
Song for the Passing of a Beautiful Woman. *Anonymous.*
The Song of Ancient Ways. Oandasan.
Sonnet LXXI. Alabaster.
Sonnet: "Flesh, I have knocked at many a dusty door." Masefield.
Sonnets, II: "When forty winters shall besiege thy brow." Shakespeare.
Special Delivery. Montague.
Spleen. Baudelaire.
The Stars Go By. Lyon.
"The storms are past, these clouds are overblown." Surrey.
The Subway Witnesses. Thomas.
Talking to the Townsfolk in Ideal, Georgia. Black.
Tamburlaine the Great. Marlowe.
A Temple. Patchen.
A Terre. Owen.
There's an Unknown River in Soweto. Mandela.
They Who Possess the Sea. Adams.
The Third Century, The Recovery. Traherne.
This Is My Beloved (excerpt). Benton.
Thou Great God. *Anonymous.*
Three Prison Portraits: The Drug Addict. Waddington.
The Three Songs. Taylor.
Thy Brother's Blood. Very.
The Tide That from the West Washes Africa to the Bone. Rubadiri.
To a Child Before Birth. Nicholson.
To a Young Girl. Yeats.
To the Faithful. Ana.

To the Woman in Bond Street Station. Weismiller.
Trail End. *Anonymous.*
The Train Dogs. Johnson.
The Tree-Toad. Johns.
The Triple Dream. Lermontov.
Triumph of His Grace. Wesley.
Twilight in California. Dow.
Two Monopolists. Byrom.
Uneasy Rider. Wakoski.
Unfinished History. MacLeish.
Upon the Ensignes of Christes Crucifyinge. Alabaster.
The Venus of Bolsover Castle. Sitwell.
Verigin 3. Newlove.
Wait for the Hour. Soutar.
The Watch. Piercy.
Wednesday in Holy Week. Rossetti.
The Weight Room. Rabbit.
Whales Weep Not! Lawrence.
The Wheel. Yeats.
Where Fled. Wieners.
The White Ships and the Red. Kilmer.
A wounded deer leaps highest. Dickinson.
Your Pain. Guebuza.
Zippora Returns to Moses at Rephidim. Drachler.

Bloodhound (s)
The City Mouse and the Garden Mouse. Rossetti.
Design for Mediaeval Tapestry. Klein.

Bloom (ing) (s)
Above Salerno. Murray.
Almond Blossom. Arnold.
Almswomen. Blunden.
The Annunciation. Tabb.
Apologia. Swinburne.
The April Snow. Very.
Banana. Bell.
Beauty of This Earth. Opitz.
But We Shall Bloom. Guri.
Cadenus and Vanessa (excerpt). Swift.
Catalpa Tree. Colum.
Citizen. Wallace-Crabbe.
Double Gift. *Anonymous.*
The Dowie Houms o' Yarrow. *Anonymous.*
Duchess. Lyon.
Estuary. Walker.
An Evening Blessing. Edmeston.
Far from Africa. Danner.
Fear. Mitchell.
Full Moon (fragment). Sappho.
Gold-of-Ophir Roses. Dennen.
He Defendeth His Heart against the Destroyer. Book of the Dead.
I Am. Kushner.
I Saw Thee, Child, One Summer's Day. Bronte.
Identity Card. Tichy.
Immortal Flowers. Rice.
In the Old Guerilla War. Pastan.
Inniskeen Road: July Evening. Kavanagh.
Joys of Childhood. Clare.
A Late Spring: Eastport. Booth.

Like a sweet apple reddening on the high. Sappho.
The Mariposa Lily. Coolbrith.
Miss Nancy's Gown. Cocke.
My Wild Irish Rose. Olcott.
An Old Man's Son. Edson.
On the Slain Collegians. Melville.
A Pastoral. Hillyer.
Piping Peace. Shirley.
Poets Love Nature. Clare.
Prose for Des Esseintes. Mallarme.
The Ritual. Gwillim.
Solution. Emerson.
Spring-Joy Praising God. Praise of the Sun. Greiffenberg.
Spring Landscape. Ficke.
There She Stands a Lovely Creature. *Anonymous.*
Thy Beauty Fades. Very.
Tides. Blackwell.
To One of Little Faith. Flanner.
To the Marchesana of Pescara. Michelangelo.
The Trailing Arbutus. Whittier.
When I have gone away. Michizane.
With a First Reader. Hughes.
The Woman in the. Piercy.

Blossom (s)
Alternatives. Cooley.
The Birds. Blake.
The Blessing. Wright.
The Brook in February. Roberts.
Canticle. Berry.
Canticle. McClure.
The Celebration. Mezey.
Children of a Future Age. Blake.
City of Monuments. Rukeyser.
The Crowns. Freeman.
A Cure for the Spleen. Green.
Cycle. Hughes.
Down in the Forest. *Anonymous.*
A Drifting Petal. Fenollosa.
The Drynaun Dhun. *Anonymous.*
Earthly. Wedde.
Equality. Shirley.
Evening Prayer. *Anonymous.*
Fear. Mitchell.
The First of All My Dreams. Cummings.
The First Spring Day. Rossetti.
Flowers. Mallarme.
For a Girl in Love. Willette.
From My Arm-Chair. Longfellow.
From the Rain Down. Espaillat.
The Furnace of Colors. Watkins.
Ghosts. Munkittrick.
Go, Ploughman, Plough. Campbell.
Haiku: "After a long winter, giving." Chiyo.
Haiku: "These branches..." Joso.

He Bringeth Them Unto Their Desired Haven. Tooker.
He Is Like the Lotus. Book of the Dead.
Hendecasyllabics. Swinburne.
In Impressions of Hawk Feathers Willow Leaves Shadow. Woody.
In Memoriam A.H.H., CXV. Tennyson.
In the Dark. Bushnell.
Landscape with the Giant Orion: Orion Seeks the Goddess Diana (excerpt. Sitwell.
The Last Day and the First. Weiss.
Let Me Be Held When the Longing Comes. Stephany.
Love's Pains. Clare.
Moss. Willard.
Mother Dear, O! Pray for Me. *Anonymous.*
Nikolina. Thaxter.
O Love, That Wilt Not Let Me Go. Matheson.
Old Ellen Sullivan. Welles.
On Growing Old. Masefield.
One Girl. Sappho.
The Picture of Little T. C. in a Prospect of Flowers. Marvell.
Pipings. Paget-Fredericks.
Poem: "In the early evening, as now, a man is bending." Gluck.
Prayer for Good Dreams. *Anonymous.*
Prelude. Brentano.
Red Geranium and Godly Mignonette. Lawrence.
Reflections in a Slum. ""MacDiarmid.
Ringneck Parrots. *Anonymous.*
Rite of Spring. Kennedy.
Roadside Flowers. Carman.
Roof Garden. Filip.
The Rose. Browne.
Ryokan. Heyen.
Sequence. Barker.
Silex Scintillans. Vaughan.
Simon and Susan. *Anonymous.*
A Song. Schwartz.
Song: "Heron is harsh with despair." Chamberlain.
Substantiations (excerpt). Vidya.
Suspiria. Longfellow.
Symbol. Morton.
Take Heart. Proctor.
Three Ballate. Poliziano.
To Your Question. Niatum.
The Trumpet-Vine Arbour. Lowell.
Two Sonnets. Sorley.
Under the Boughs. Baro.
Visions. Browne.
When Both My Fathers Die. Gillespie.
Where You Passed. Burr.
The White Jessamine. Tabb.
Who Bids Us Sing? Carpenter.
Why Ye Blossome Cometh before Ye Leafe. Herford.
Wind-Song. *Anonymous.*

Blot
A Drop of Ink. Whitney.

The Ideals of Satire. Pope.
Lines Written in the Front of a Well-Read Copy of Burns's Songs. *Anonymous.*
Poets Lose Half the Praise. Waller.

Blow (ing) (s)
After Aughrim. Geoghegan.
Against Women Unconstant. Chaucer.
An April Morning. Carman.
The Arrogant Frog and the Superior Bull. Carryl.
As I out Rode. *Anonymous.*
The Beating. Hummer.
A Birthday Candle. Justice.
Birthday Candles. Scott.
The Black Ball Line. *Anonymous.*
Blow the Candle Out. *Anonymous.*
Blow the Candle Out (The Jolly Boatsman). *Anonymous.*
Blow the Man Down. *Anonymous.*
A Breath. De Vere.
Cake. Potter.
The Coast of Peru. *Anonymous.*
Directions for Making a Birth-Day Song: "To form a just..." Swift.
Discretion. *Anonymous.*
Epitaph: "A glassblower lies here at rest." Morton.
Epitaphs: For a Fickle Man. Van Doren.
God's Word. Clifford.
The Harvesting of the Roses. Ben Jacob.
Hol' de Win' Don't Let It Blow. *Anonymous.*
How Violets Came Blue. Herrick.
I Know a Flower So Fair and Fine. Grundtvig.
In Brunton Town. *Anonymous.*
In Memoriam A.H.H., XCVI. Tennyson.
In Memory of Eva Gore-Booth and Con Markiewicz. Yeats.
In Winter in the Woods Alone. Frost.
A Kite. *Anonymous.*
Last Snow. Young.
Limerick: "Young Frederick the great was a beaut." *Anonymous.*
The Mitherless Bairn. Thom.
My Johnny. *Anonymous.*
My Mouth Is Very Quiet. Villa.
A Myth. Kingsley.
Nanny's Sailor Lad. Allingham.
The Odyssey. Homer.
Off Riviere Du Loup. Scott.
Painting of my Father. Fallon.
The Rose and the Wind. Marston.
A Rub. Tabb.
The She Wolf. Spark.
Sleep, Holy Babe. Caswall.
Sonnets. Masefield.
The South Wind Brings Wet Weather. *Anonymous.*
Strike the Blow. *Anonymous.*

Thoughts on the Christian Doctrine of Eternal Hell. Smith.
Trade Winds. Masefield.
Translations from the Chinese. Morley.
The True Lovers Bold. *Anonymous.*
Tumor. Day.
Waiting for the Bus. Enright.
Whate'er You Dream with Doubt Possest. Clough.
The Wind. Graddon.
Written at the End of a Book. Mitchell.

Blue
Abracadabra. Livesay.
Accomplishments. MacDonald.
Advice to a Blue-Bird. Bodenheim.
After Twenty Years. Tuquan.
Alone. Poe.
Anima. O Hehir.
Arizona. *Anonymous.*
As Proper Mode of Quenching Legal Lust. Massey.
Aves. Morison.
Baby Toes. Sandburg.
The Barber's. De la Mare.
Beautiful Brown Eyes. *Anonymous.*
Bell Weather. Turco.
Blue Flag. Donnelly.
Blue Fly. De Assis.
Blue Horses: West Winds. Endrezze-Danielson.
The Blue Light. Dent.
Blue Moonshine. Stokes.
A Blue Valentine. Kilmer.
Bombardment. Aldington.
Bonnets So Blue. *Anonymous.*
The Bonnie Blue Flag. Macarthy.
Bread the Holy. Coatsworth.
The Captive Ships at Manila. Paul.
Carrier Letter. Crane.
Change. Coleridge.
Children's Song. Thomas.
Christabel. Coleridge.
The Clothes. Zychlinska.
Columbia the Gem of the Ocean. Becket.
The Convict. Frisch.
Construction. Schonborg.
Corn. Lanier.
The Coromandel Fishers. Naidu.
Country Tune. Riddell.
Cowboy Jack. *Anonymous.*
A Cradle Song. Colum.
Crockery. Budenz.
Daniel Webster. Holmes.
The Dark Girl Dressed in Blue. *Anonymous.*
Dayley Island. Seidel.
The Dead Cities Speak to the Living Cities. Fleg.
The Dean's Lady. Crabbe.
Did You Not See. Kuo.
A Discussion of the Vicissitudes of History under a Pine Tree. Pollitt.
Dream of Winter. Brown.
The Dress. Middleton.
Driving By. Wallace.

The Eagle of the Blue. Melville
Eighteen-Seventy. Rimbaud.
Energy. Cruz.
Enfidaville. Douglas.
Epigrams. Theocritus.
Evening: Ponte al Mare, Pisa. Shelley.
Exaltation. Werfel.
Exile. Voigt.
Figure for an Apocalypse. Merton.
Finding a Friend Home. Hamm.
Flag Song. Ward.
Fly around My Blue-Eyed Gal. *Anonymous.*
Fr Anselm Williams and Br Leander Neville Hanged by Lutheran... Smither.
Friend Who Never Came. Stafford.
From Four Lakes' Days. Eberhart.
The Gleaner. Taylor.
Green Grow the Lilacs. *Anonymous.*
The Green Horse. Ramke.
Gypsy Davey. *Anonymous.*
H.M.S. Glory at Sydney. Causley.
High Windows. Larkin.
The Hollow Land. Morris.
The House of a Hundred Lights. Torrence.
How the Laws of Physics Love Chocolate! Saner.
How Violets Came Blue. Herrick.
In Spain. Lawless.
Interruption. Graves.
The Invaders. Haines.
It troubled me as once I was. Dickinson.
Jacket So Blue. *Anonymous.*
A June Day. Teasdale.
The King o' Spain's Daughter. Foster.
Lakeside Incident. Skelton.
Leaping Falls. Kinnell.
Let Me Speak of Pure Things. Ho Chih-Fang.
Let Us Gather at the River. Piercy.
Little Blue Ben. *Anonymous.*
Little Roach Poem. Truesdale.
A Lost Illusion. Du Maurier.
Love. Dent.
The Lover's Lament for Her Sailor. *Anonymous.*
Lullaby, O Lullaby. Bennett.
The Man with the Blue Guitar. Stevens.
Mandrake's Song. Beddoes.
Marlow and Nancy. McPherson.
The Monastery: Border Ballad. Scott.
Monet Refused the Operation. Mueller.
The moon was but a chin of gold. Dickinson.
Mozart. Heath-Stubbs.
My "Patch of Blue." Carson.
My Valentine. Stevenson.
November Blue. Meynell.
October Maples, Portland. Wilbur.
Old Cat Care. Hughes.

On First Looking into Michael Grant's Cities of Vesuvius. Ewart.
On the Trail to Idaho. *Anonymous.*
Original Sin. Laing.
Others. *Anonymous.*
Out West. Snyder.
The Party. Sala.
Penny Whistle Blues. Island.
Pleasures. Levertov.
Poem: "To be sad in the morning." Pillen.
Poems, XCIII: "Mother, I cannot mind my wheel." Landor.
The Professionals. Grigson.
The Red, White and Blue. Shaw.
Regretful Thoughts, I. Yu Hsuan-chi.
Resurrection of the Right Side. Rukeyser.
The Retarded Class at F.A.O. Schwarz's Celebrates Christmas. Fisher.
The Return. Bishop.
Riddle: "Down by the waterside stand a house and a plat." *Anonymous.*
The Ring. Mathews.
RIP. Balderston.
A Rune for C. Howes.
Saint Harmony My Patroness. Goodman.
Sea-Distances. Noyes.
Sea Surface Full of Clouds. Stevens.
Seascape. Young.
Sentimental Lines to a Young Man Who Favors Pink Wallpaper... Fishback.
A Sentinel's Song. Kerehoma.
She Died in Beauty. Sillery.
Ships with Your Silver Nets. Oliver.
Snow. Rodgers.
So, When I Swim to the Shore. Peacock.
Soeur Marie Emilie. Houselander.
Song: "Christ keep the Hollow Land." Morris.
Song: "Like violets pale i' the spring o' the year." Thomson.
Statue against a Clear Sky. Stevens.
Strawberries in Mexico. Padgett.
The Stripper. Probst.
Sugar in the Cane. Williams.
Symphony in Blue. Roseliep.
The Thing. Roethke.
Thoughts of Chairman Mao. Young.
To Bring Spring. Keithley.
To Noel. "Mistral.
A Toast to the Flag. Daly.
Tree-Sleeping. Coffin.
The Trumpet-Vine Arbour. Lowell.
Truth. Nemerov.
Two Tile Beaks. Fonte Boa.
Two Years Later. Wieners.
Uncle. Levine.
Up in the Air. Tippett.
Vaquero. Dorn.
The Virgin Sturgeon. *Anonymous.*
Waiting. Yevtushenko.

Was Worm. Swenson.
We like March–his shoes are purple. Dickinson.
The Wedding (1957). Pasternak.
White People. Henderson.
When Sun Came to Riverwoman. Silko.
Who among You Knows the Essence of Garlic? Hongo.
A Winter's Tale. Dana.
Winter Scene. Ammons.
Winter with the Gulf Stream. Hopkins.
With a Bottle of Blue Nun to All My Friends. De Frees.
Woefully Arrayed. Skelton.
Words. Rhys.
The Work of the Weavers. *Anonymous.*
Your Flag and My Flag. Nesbit.
Bluebell (s)
Derbyshire Bluebells. Sitwell.
Dewdrops. Clare.
The Sphere of Glass. Lehmann.
Bluebird
The Big Rock Candy Mountain. *Anonymous.*
The Monkey's Glue. Goldsmith.
A Prayer after Illness. Storey.
Song to Promote Growth. *Anonymous.*
Blueprint
Saturday Night. Kefala.
Where I Hang My Hat. Gallup.
Blues
The Backlash Blues. Hughes.
Big Fat Woman. *Anonymous.*
Black Horse Blues. Jefferson.
Black Mountain Blues. Smith.
Blues. Prettyman.
De Blues Ain' Nothin'. *Anonymous.*
Canto 4. Weatherly.
Canto 7. Weatherly.
Coal Loadin' Blues. *Anonymous.*
Corinna. *Anonymous.*
Do Nothing till You Hear from Me. Henderson.
The Empress Brand Trim: Ruby Reminisces. Williams.
Empty Bed Blues. Smith.
Good Mornin', Blues. *Anonymous.*
Got the Blues, Can't Be Satisfied. Hurt.
The Habeas Corpus Blues. Aiken.
Lead. Cortez.
Lowdown Rounder's Blues. Howell.
Motherless Child Blues. Thomas.
My Black Gal Blues. Estes.
One Way Gal. Moore.
A Poem. Mphahlele.
Poor Man Blues. *Anonymous.*
Song: "I've put some/ASHES in my sweet papa's bed." *Anonymous.*

The Sound of Afroamerican History Chapt I. Anderson.
Weave Room Blues. *Anonymous.*
Winnsboro Cotton Mill Blues. *Anonymous.*
Woman Blue. *Anonymous.*
Blunder
George the Third. Bentley.
Love-Songs, At Once Tender and Informative. Hoffenstein.
Waiting. Henley.
Blunt
Ad Tusserum. *Anonymous.*
Sunday Morning. Fitzgerald.
The Thrifty Elephant. Holmes.
Blush
Astrophel and Stella, LXVI. Sidney.
At First Sight. Graves.
Blame Not My Lute, for He Must Sound. Wyatt.
Dawn. Dunbar.
The Dawning. Vaughan.
The Distaff. Erinna.
Envoy. Piatt.
Epitaph for One Who Would Not Be Buried in Westminster Abbey. Pope.
Fond Youth. Rogers.
Four Anacreontic Poems, 3. Spenser.
Good Counsel to a Young Maid. Carew.
Lady Geraldine's Courtship. Browning.
The Lass and the Friar. Burns.
A Lovely Lass to a Friar Came. Rochester.
The Meddow Verse or Aniversary to Mistris Bridget Lowman. Herrick.
Riding. Amoss.
Riding Down. Coan.
The Shoe-Tying. Herrick.
Songs of the Pixies. Coleridge.
A Sunset. Loveman.
Upon Scarlet and Blush-Coloured Ribbands, Given by Two Ladies. Shirley.
Washington. Byron.
White World. Doolittle.
The Wooyeo Ball. *Anonymous.*
Written to a Young Lady. Callanan.
Board
Cadaver Politic. Paulin.
A Carol for Twelfth Day. *Anonymous.*
Eclogues. Virgil (Publius Vergilius Maro).
The Gospel Train. *Anonymous.*
The Hay Hotel. *Anonymous.*
The League of Nations. Siegrist.
The Lion and O'Reilly. Weber.
A Question. Synge.
Union Train. Lampell.
Words for Hart Crane. Lowell.
Boarders
The Barn. Spender.
The City. Creeley.
Crepes Flambeau. Gallagher.

A Dream of Death. Yeats.
Duffy's Hotel. *Anonymous.*
Letters to Live Poets. Beaver.
A Lifetime Devoted to Literature. Rodriguez.
Prodigy. Simic.
Stirling's Hotel. *Anonymous.*
Boast (ing) (s)
The Battle of Baltimore. *Anonymous.*
The Battle of the Kegs. Hopkinson.
Betty Zane. English.
British Valor Displayed. Hopkinson.
A Card of Invitation to Mr. Gibbon, at Brighthelmstone. Hayley.
Ephraim the Grizzly. Guiterman.
Eternity. More.
Rufus's Mare. *Anonymous.*
Saint Leger. Scollard.
The Unseaworthy Ship. *Anonymous.*
You Can't Fool God. Kleiser.
Boat (s)
Abbreviated Interviews with a Few Disgruntled Literary Celebrities. Whittemore.
Antwerp Musee des Beaux-Arts. Ross.
The Ballad of the Boat. Garnett.
The Boat. Fyleman.
The Boat. Gilman.
The Boatie Rows. *Anonymous.*
Boats. Bennett.
Bryan O'Lynn. *Anonymous.*
Captain Cook. *Anonymous.*
A Coconut for Katerina. McPherson.
Dance to Your Daddie. *Anonymous.*
Dance to Your Daddie. Mother Goose.
Death of a Jazz Musician. Smith.
A Defeat. Levertov.
Dream Songs. Berryman.
Driving toward the Lac Qui Parle River. Bly.
Endymion, I. Keats.
Ever as We Sailed. Shelley.
Fish. Williams.
The Fisher's Widow. Symons.
The Fisherman's Wife. Lowell.
Fourth of July Night. Sandburg.
Golden Wings. Morris.
The Hayeswater Boat (excerpt). Arnold.
He Embarketh in the Boat of Ra. Book of the Dead.
The Honeymooners. Yu Ch'ien.
In Spite of All This Much Needed Thunder. Gilbert.
In the Past. Stickney.
Inland City. Ransom.
July 4th. Waldman.
Letter to Derek Mahon. Longley.
LXXII A Sonnet for Dick Gallup. Berrigan.
LXXIV. Berrigan.

Memorial Day: A Collaboration. Berrigan.
Michael, Row the Boat Ashore. *Anonymous.*
Ol' Hag, You See Mammy? *Anonymous.*
Our Lady of Good Voyage. Adee.
Pa, Pa, Build Me a Boat. *Anonymous.*
A Racing Eight. Cuthbertson.
Requiem 1935-1940. Akhmatova.
Return, Starting Out. Halpern.
Sky links cloud waves. Li Ch'ing-chao.
Sleeping Pill. O Hehir.
A Supermarket in California. Ginsberg.
Thaw in the City. Lipsitz.
To the Islands. Moss.
Turn the Glasses Over. *Anonymous.*
Two Sonnets. Ashbery.
The View from Father's Porch. Wright.
Visit by Water. McLaren.
Voyagers. Van Dyke.
Written on the Wall at Chang's Hermitage. Tu Fu.

Bod (ies) (y)
Accommodation. Parlatore.
De Aegypto. Pound.
After Li Ch'ing-Chao. Waldman.
After Peckinpah. Dempster.
After Your Death. James.
Ain't No Grave Can Hold My Body Down. *Anonymous.*
Amoretti, L. Spenser.
Ancestry. Brodsky.
And If I Turn. Bowering.
And in That Drowning Instant. Klein.
The Appeasement of Demeter. Meredith.
The Apple Tree. Baxter.
An Artist Draws a Peach. Hampl.
As Adam Early in the Morning. Whitman.
Astrophel and Stella, LII. Sidney.
At Castle Wood. Bronte.
At the Center of Everything Which Is Dying. Goedicke.
At the Funeral of Great-Aunt Mary. Bly.
Aunt Jane. Nowlan.
Autumn Begins in Martins Ferry, Ohio. Wright.
Autumn Journal. MacNeice.
The Baffled Knight. *Anonymous*
The Battle of Shiloh. *Anonymous.*
Beauty. Spenser.
Before a Statue of Achilles. Santayana.
The Better Bargain. Congreve.
Bill Peters, the Stage Driver. *Anonymous.*
The Blessing. Wright.
The Blood Supply in New York City Is Low. Stokes.
The Blossom. Donne.
Blue Lantern. Song.

The Blues Don't Change. Young.
Body of Jesus. Coxe.
Braemar. Kinnell.
The Brahms. Morris.
Caelica, LXXII. Greville.
Caelica, LXXXV. Greville.
Caelica, XC. Greville.
The Case. Norris.
The Cat. Baudelaire.
The Cat. Davies.
The Chalk Angel. Schmitz.
A Child Ill. Betjeman.
The Children. Heyen.
Chinese Camp, Kamloops (circa 1883). Suknaski.
Chinoiserie. Wright.
Closing Prayer. Patrick.
The Coal Miner's Child. *Anonymous.*
Colloquy at Peniel. Merwin.
The color of the flowers. Ono no Komachi.
Come Back Blues. Harper.
Come, Said My Soul. Whitman.
Counting Small-Boned Bodies. Bly.
Cruciform. Welles.
The Cubistic Lovers. Eaton.
The Cup of Blessing. Wesley.
Daisies. Nowlan.
Dear Body. Canan.
The Delicate, Plummeting Bodies. Dobyns.
Discerning the Lord's Body. Montgomery.
The Disconnections. Engels.
Dream Songs. Berryman.
A Drunkard. *Anonymous.*
The Duel. Cowley.
Early Morning. Dow.
The Ecstasy. Donne.
Edward Gray. Tennyson.
Elegy. Loney.
An Elegy for Bob Marley. Matthews.
Epigram: "Three things must epigrams." *Anonymous.*
Eton Boating Song. Cory.
Experience. Simmons.
The Faerie Queene. Spenser.
The Faithful Wife. Greenberg.
A Far Cry after a Close Call. Howard.
Feet, a Sermon. Paul.
Fifth & 94th. Plumly.
The First Kiss. Watts-Dunton.
A Football-Player. Lefroy.
For Decoration Day: 1861-1865. Hughes.
For Esther. Plumly.
Forgetfulness. Bodenheim.
Friend, on This Scaffold Thomas More Lies Dead. Cunningham.
Genius. Perkins.
Geordie (Georgie). *Anonymous.*
Ghost Poem Five. Korte.
The God of the Living. Ellerton.
Gudveig. Berry.
A Hanging. Chipasula.
He Said, Lying There. Alta.
Health. Thomas.
Her True Body. Metz.
Hialmar. Campbell.
Hills of Salt. Ravikovich.

Homage to Chagall. Niatum.
The Hospital–Retrospections. Mackenzie.
Howl, I. Ginsberg.
A Hundreth Good Poyntes of Husbandry. Tusser.
I Am He That Aches with Love. Whitman.
I'm Gonna Move to the Outskirts of Town. Broonzy.
I Want to Tell You. Hochman.
In a Country Church. Thomas.
In Spain. Wyatt.
In the Old City. Amichai.
In the Silks. Ackerman.
In Trouble and Shame. Lawrence.
Instead of Features. Moore.
Intimate Associations. Baudelaire.
James Whaland (with music). *Anonymous.*
The Journey to Golgotha. Rao.
July in Washington. Lowell.
June Morning. McCrae.
Kindergarten. Schmitz.
King Henry VI. Shakespeare.
Kiss. Young.
Lamia. Keats.
Last Rites. Citino.
Lay Dis Body Down. *Anonymous.*
The Lay of the Last Minstrel. Scott.
Like Any Other Man. Orr.
Locations. Fraser.
Looking into a Face. Bly.
Loss. Aldington.
The Lost Dancer. Toomer.
Love Is the Peace, whereto All Thoughts Doe Strive. Greville.
Love-Lily. Rossetti.
Love Poem. Rea.
Lullaby. Vinner.
Magnificat. Symons.
The Maladjusted: A Tragedy (excerpt). Bishop.
Manhattan. Hays.
Mater Dei. Fallon.
Medieval Norman Songs. *Anonymous.*
Menses. Millay.
Mira's Will. Leapor.
The Miracle. Dowling.
Mishka. Gray.
Moment. Creeley.
Mountain Bride. Morgan.
The Murder of Goins. *Anonymous.*
My Old Dutch: A Cockney Song. Chevalier.
The Necessity of Rejection. Schevill.
The New Ring. Shapiro.
The New Saddhus. Pinsky.
News from the House. Browne.
The Norfolk Rebellion: The Slaughter of the Rebels. *Anonymous.*
Not in India. Rumi.
Nothing. Burgos.
On the Death of His Child. Faydi.
On the Death of Ho Chi Minh. Mandel.

On Writing for the Stage. Sheffield.
The One Girl at the Boys Party. Olds.
The Orator's Epitaph. Brougham.
Out of Body. Moore.
Parted Love. Rossetti.
The Phoenix (excerpt). *Anonymous.*
Planetarium. Rich.
Plea to Eros. *Anonymous.*
Poem for Etheridge. Sanchez.
The Practice of Absence. Friend.
A Prayer for Charity. Kennedy.
Prelude. Rosenmann-Taub.
The Red Dog. Jensen.
Red o'er the Forest. Keble.
Reply to a Marriage Proposal. Irihapeti Rangi te Apakura.
Riddle: "Around the rick, around the rick." *Anonymous.*
Rip. Wright.
Roses. Ronsard.
The Sailor and His Bride. *Anonymous.*
Sanctimony. *Anonymous.*
Sent Ahead. Hay.
Somebody Call (For Help). Rodgers.
Somebody's Gone. Ford.
Song: "I know moon-rise. I know star-rise." *Anonymous.*
Song of the Forest Trees. *Anonymous.*
Sonnet XVII: "I flee the city, temples, and each place." Labe.
Sonnets, XVII: "Cherry-Lipt Adonis in his snowie shape." Barnfield.
The Soul. Cowley.
The Soul and the Body. Davies.
Star Journey. Madgett.
Step father. Fitzgerald.
The Suicides of the Rich. Contoski.
Summer. Asch.
T. B. Blues. Leadbelly.
Tabernacles. Lansing.
Take Up the Pen... *Anonymous.*
Tales of Shatz. Abse.
Taught to Be Polite. Young.
To a Lady on Her Marriage. Bell.
To a Woman Who Wants Darkness and Time. Barrax.
To L.H.B. Mansfield.
To My Father. Graham.
To My Mistress in Absence. Carew.
Together. Kumin.
Tombstone Epitaphs. *Anonymous.*
Touch. Paz.
The Tough Ones. Miller.
Transit. Wilbur.
The Traveler. Bottoms.
The Twelve Properties or Conditions of a Lover. More.
Unkindness Has Killed Me. *Anonymous.*

Upon the Curtain of Lucasta's
Picture It Was Thus
Wrought. Lovelace.
A Vegetarian Sings. Conard.
Vox Populi, Vox Dei
(excerpt). *Anonymous.*
War. Ish-Kishor.
The Weight Room. Rabbit.
What Do You Say When a
Man Tells You, You Have
the Softest Skin. Mackey.
What Is an Epigram?
Coleridge.
What Shines in Winter Burns.
Hummer.
Why May Not I Love
Johnny? *Anonymous.*
The Window of the Tobacco
Shop. Cavafy.
The Winter Storm at Sea.
Crabbe.
A Witch Going Down to
Egypt. Chalfi.
With the Most Susceptible
Element, the Mind, Already
Turned... Benton.
The Woman at the Washtub.
Daley.
Womanwork. Allen.
Words Spoken Alone. Abse.
Written Forty Miles South of
a Spreading City. Bly.
Year after year I have
watched. Li Ch'ing-chao.
You Rise Up. Eluard.
Young Edmondale.
Anonymous.
Young Edwin in the Lowlands
Low (B vers.).
Anonymous.
The Young Girl. Roethke.
Young Hunting. *Anonymous.*

Bog (s)
Although in a Crystal.
Parlatore.
The Field. Valentine.
I'm nobody! Who are you?
Dickinson.
Ireland. Ryan.
Little Black Rose.
Anonymous.
The One. Kavanagh.
Peat Bog Soldiers.
Anonymous.
Wester Ross. Mitchison.

Boil (ed) (s)
From the Joke Shop. Fuller.
In the Case of Lobsters.
Morstein.
Salad. Collins.
Soup on a Cold Day. Hill.

Boiled (ed) (s)
Clouds. Levine.
Early Discoveries. Malouf.
The Fox and the Hare.
Anonymous.
That Day. Leax.

Bold
The Laborer. Dehmel.
The Pontoon Bridge Miracle.
Lindsay.
The White Goddess. Graves.
The Young Ones. Jennings.

Bolivia
In Praise of Llamas.
Guiterman.
Limerick: "O's Operatic
Olivia." Bellows.

Bolt (s)
The Bull Moses. Hughes.
Carol for Advent. Heath-
Stubbs.

Defensive Position.
Manifold.
The Fascination of What's
Difficult. Yeats.
I Would Not Paint a Picture.
Dickinson.
Relics. Gegna.

Bomb (s)
An Anarchist's Letter.
Wyndham.
Apollo 8. Berryman.
Dear Mister Congressman.
Dylan.
His Wisdom. Breton.
If Any Be Pleased to Walk
into My Poor Garden...
Pastorius.
The Italian Soldier Shook My
Hand. Orwell.
The Killer Too. Gibson.
Letter to My Wife. Rhys.
Lo! As the Potter Mouldeth.
Anonymous.
More (parody). Appleman.
On a Monument in France...
Anonymous.
Portia. Wilde.
Quiet Town. Stafford.
You Know, Joe. Durem.

Bombay
The End of a Day in the
Provinces. Laforgue.
Limerick: "As a little fat man
of Bombay." *Anonymous.*

Bombers
2nd Air Force. Jarrell.
Eisenhower's Visit to Franco,
1959. Wright.
Native Working on the
Aerodrome. Fuller.

Bond (s)
Ascent to the Sierras. Jeffers.
Lord, Deliver, Thou Canst
Save. Follen.
Prayer before Meat. Harsen.
These Things Shall Be.
Symonds.
To Jesus on the Cross.
Tejada.
The Vedic Hymns: Varuna.
Anonymous.

Bondage
Behold with Joy.
Winchester.
A Diamond. Loveman.
Earth's Answer. Blake.
The Factory Girl. Phillips.
Like as the Dove. Sidney.
Moreton Bay. *Anonymous.*
The Silken Tent. Frost.
The Springs. Berry.

Bone (s)
Abel's Bride. Levertov.
Africa. Clifton.
Afterbirth. Williams.
Anath. Guri.
And of Columbus. Gregory.
Anthologistics. Guiterman.
Ark to Noah. Macpherson.
Artificial Death, II. James.
At the Keyhole. De La
Mare.
The Atoll in the Mind.
Comfort.
Autumn. Shapcott.
Bait Shop. Reiter.
The Ballad of Ballymote.
Gallagher.
The Banks of Sacramento
(with music). *Anonymous.*
Before I Knocked and Flesh
Let Enter. Thomas.

Beware the Months of Fire
They Are Twelve and
Contain a Year. Lane.
The Birds. Posner.
The Black Tower. Yeats.
Body of John. Mason.
Body's Freedom. Neville.
Boundaries. Fleming.
The Brut. Layamon.
The Caged Skylark.
Hopkins.
Carnival. Hervey.
Carol: "Mary laid her Child
among." Nicholson.
Child with Shell. Everson.
Childlessness. Merrill.
Cold Front. Sharpe.
The Cold Irish Earth.
Skinner.
The Collar-Bone of a Hare.
Yeats.
Covenant. Auster.
The Dark Birds. Meyers.
Dawn Hippo. Clouts.
Death's Jest Book. Beddoes.
The Defeated. Merwin.
Dese Bones Gwine to Rise
Again. *Anonymous.*
The Desolate Valley.
Pringle.
Discoveries of Bones and
Stone. Grigson.
The Drowned. Spender.
The Eagle and the Mole.
Wylie.
Eat with Care. *Anonymous.*
Elegy for a Diver. Booth.
English Beach Memory: Mr.
Thuddock. Sitwell.
Eumares. Asclepiades.
Evil Is No Black Thing.
Fabio.
The Faerie Queene. Spenser.
Fall in Corrales. Wilbur.
Fantastic World's End.
Moure.
Fe, Fi, Fo, Fum. Mother
Goose.
For Nicholas, Born in
September. Perry.
The Forging of the Anchor.
Ferguson.
Fowls in the Frith.
Anonymous.
The Fox and the Goose.
Anonymous.
A Fox Jumped up One
Winter's Night.
Anonymous.
Fragment 113. Doolittle.
From Colony to Nation.
Layton.
Genesis. Hill.
Girl's Song. *Anonymous.*
Girls. Rosen.
Gravestones. Stuart.
Gray Weather. Jeffers.
Green Haven Halls.
Culhane.
The Grinders, or the Saddle
on the Right Horse.
Anonymous.
Growing Up. Wallace.
Hazardous Occupations.
Sandburg.
Hero's Portion. Montague.
High Dive. Empson.
The Hill Above the Mine.
Cowley.
The Home Place. Currie.
The Homer Mitchell Place.
Engels.

The Horn. Adams.
The Horse. Levine.
Hot Weather in the Plains–
India. Tipple.
How to Fly by Standing Still
(excerpt). Baxter.
Hungry Grass. MacDonagh.
Hymn to the Sun. Roberts.
I Am a Jew. Martin.
I Lie on the Chilled Stones of
the Great Wall. Liu.
I Move to Random
Consolations. Heyen.
I Substitute for the Dead
Lecturer. Jones.
I Wanted to Die in the
Desert. *Anonymous.*
The Immortal Part.
Housman.
In a Ghetto. Glatstein.
In Come de Animuls Two by
Two. *Anonymous.*
In the Round. Weiss.
In the Van Gogh Room.
Yamamoto.
Internal. Auslander.
Jerry Jones. *Anonymous.*
Knowledge of Age. Avison.
Kohoutek. Ryan.
The Lady's-Maid's Song.
Hollander.
Lament. Chamberlain.
Landscapes. Eliot.
The Last Day. Sargent.
Letter to Statues. Brinnin.
Leukothea. Douglas.
The Lion over the Tomb of
Leonidas. *Anonymous.*
Love Poem–1940.
Hershenson.
Lower Forms of Life.
Winter.
Luzzato. Reznikoff.
The Man Who Married
Magdalene. Simpson.
The Marrow. Roethke.
Meditation on a Bone.
Hope.
My Hands Are Withered.
Anonymous.
My People. Lasker-Schüler.
My Song. Bialik.
National Winter Garden.
Crane.
November Song. Vinz.
Ode: "Why will they never
sleep." Bishop.
Oh, Bury Me Not on The
Lone Prairie (with music).
Anonymous.
Old Bangum. *Anonymous.*
The Old Peasant Woman at
the Monastery of Zagorsk.
Schevill.
The Old People Speak of
Death. Troupe.
The Old Whim Horse.
Dyson.
On Learning That Certain
Peat Bogs Contain Perfectly
Preserved Bodies.
Ludvigson.
On Playwright. Jonson.
One-Night Expensive Hotel.
Everson.
The Orchard. Spence.
Overheard over S.E. Asia.
Levertov.
Patience. Cattafi.
The Pheasant Hunter and the
Arrowhead. Gitzen.

Place Me in the Breach.
Karni.
Pocahontas to her English
husband, John Rolfe.
Allen.
Poem: "Form is the woods."
Harrison.
Poet's Lament on the Death
of His Wife. Ugaas.
Pond. Zydek.
Preparations. Silko.
The Progress of Poesy.
Arnold.
Radio. Tessimond.
Rain. Wright.
The Recognition. Levertov.
Rites of the Eastern Star.
Pommy-Vega.
Savage Portraits. Marquis.
Seal at Stinson Beach. Hill.
Shells. Mahony.
Sixteen Dead Men. Yeats.
The Skeleton of the Future.
""MacDiarmid.
Skin the Goat's Curse on
Carey. Anonymous.
Small Bones Ache. Dor.
Snatches: "Two wimen in one
house." Anonymous.
Soft Answers. Bagg.
Some Last Questions.
Merwin.
Song for the Heroes.
Comfort.
A Song in Time of Revolution
1860. Swinburne.
Songs in Flight (excerpt).
Bachmann.
A Sparrow in the Dust.
Domino.
The Spring Returns. Moore.
The Spring Waters. "Ping
Hsin" (Hsieh Wang-ying).
Standard Forgings Plant.
Stephens.
The Stone Troll. Tolkien.
Talking to the Townsfolk in
Ideal, Georgia. Black.
There Are Oceans. Harjo.
There is a pain–so utter.
Dickinson.
There Is No Balm in
Birmingham. Deacon.
Three. Kitchell.
The Thrifty Elephant.
Holmes.
To–. Tennyson.
To a Lady Friend. Davies.
To a Seaman Dead on Land.
Boyle.
To a Spanish Poet. Spender.
To T. S. Eliot. Litvinoff.
Trouble. Wright.
Twice a Week the Winter
Through. Housman.
Under the Shawl. Drachler.
Untitled: "Fivesucked the
features of my girl by
glory." Moore.
The Village. Crabbe.
Where I'll Be Good. Ryan.
Winter Day. Fried.
Winter Morning. Smith.
With Child. Taggard.
Words for a Resurrection.
Kennedy.
Wyat Resteth Here, that
Quicke Coulde Never Rest.
Surrey.
The Year of Winter.
LaPena.

Your Chase Had a Beast in
View. Bishop.
Bonfire
The Gunpowder Plot.
Anonymous.
Lady Maisry (A version).
Anonymous.
Patience of a People. Bryant,
Jr.,
Bonn (ie) (y)
Annan Water. Anonymous
Baby Lon; or, The Bonnie
Banks o' Fordie.
Anonymous.
Bonnie Annie (A version).
Anonymous.
The Broom of Cowdenknows
(A version). Anonymous.
The Broom of Cowdenknows
(B version). Anonymous.
The Doom of Devorgoil, II, ii:
Bonny Dundee. Scott.
The Douglas Tragedy.
Anonymous
The False Lover.
Anonymous.
Faur Wid I Dee? Milne.
Goodbye, Little Bonnie,
Goodbye. Anonymous.
I'll Aye Ca' in By Yon Town.
Burns.
The Jolly Plowboy.
Anonymous.
Jottings of New York.
McGonagall.
The Kirk of the Birds, Beasts
and Fishes. Anonymous.
The Laird o' Ochiltree Wa's.
Anonymous.
Lord Ingram and Chiel Wyet
(B version). Anonymous.
Monday's child is fair of face.
Mother Goose.
My Bonnie Lies over the
Ocean. Anonymous.
The Newport Railway.
McGonagall.
The One-Horned Ewe.
Anonymous.
Owre the Muir amang the
Heather. Glover.
The Robber. Anonymous.
The Trumpeter of Fyvie.
Anonymous.
Waillie. Anonymous.
Bonnet (s)
The Doom of Devorgoil, II, ii:
Bonny Dundee. Scott.
The Dule's i' This Bonnet o'
Mine. Waugh.
The Lady of the Lake. Scott.
Limerick: "There was a young
lady whose bonnet." Lear.
Lines in Ridicule of Certain
Poems Published in 1777.
Johnson.
The Love-Knot. Coan.
Railroad to Hell.
Anonymous.
Sunflower. Updike.
Wee Willie Gray. Burns.
Book (s)
The ABC Bunny. Gag.
Adventures. Kramer.
Alogon. Palmer.
The Art of Eyes. Spenser.
Ashes. Heine.
The Bicycle Rider. Shapiro.
A Bit of the Book. Sangster.
The Book Our Mothers Read.
Whittier.
Books Fall Open. McCord.

The Bookworm. De la Mare.
Charlotte, Her Book.
Bartlett.
The Complete Introductory
Lectures on Poetry.
Mayer.
The Dark Scent of Prayer.
Drachler.
Davening. Ratner.
Dedication for a Book of
Criticism. Winters.
The Discontented Student.
Tucker.
Doctor Faustus (excerpt).
Marlowe.
Dory Miller. Cornish.
Double Duty. Farbstein.
End of August. Orr.
England, 1802. Wordsworth.
The Flight. Teasdale.
A Fountain, a Bottle, a
Donkey's Ears and Some
Books. Frost.
Free Fantasia on Japanese
Themes. Lowell.
Gloriana Dying. Warner.
The Gold Country: Hotel
Leger, Mokelumne Hill,
Revisited. Stroud.
The Gypsy Bible. Tuwim.
H.Scriptures. Vaughan.
Here Do I Put My Name for
to Betraye. Anonymous.
His Wish to God. Herrick.
Homing. Saner.
I Dote Upon Myself.
Whitman.
I've Got a New Book from
My Grandfather Hyde.
Jackson.
If Someone Asks You.
Donian.
Impressions of My Father/I.
Country Ways. Masters.
In My Mind. MacCaig.
In My Own Album. Lamb.
Joined the Blues. Rooney.
Just One Book. Anonymous.
Knowledge. Anonymous.
Langston Hughes.
Blockcolski.
Lao-Tzu. Po Chu-i.
The Legend of Good Women.
Chaucer.
Limerick: "If you don't know
the meaning of snook."
Livingston.
Limerick: "If you're apt to be
ravenous, look."
Livingston.
The lips of the one I love are
my perpetual pleasure.
Hafiz.
Literary Gruk. Hein.
Madrigal to a Streetcar
Token. Alberti.
The Manner of a Poet's
Germination. Villa.
Neither Blemish This Book,
Nor the Leaves Double
Down. Anonymous.
The Never Again.
Dobzynski.
An Ode. Updike.
Of All Things for You to Go
Away Mad. Kyger.
The Old Books. Scannell.
Old Books Are Best. Chew.
Old Testament Contents.
Anonymous.
On Ben Jonson. Godolphin.
On His Books. Belloc.

On Opening a New Book.
Brown.
On When McCarthy Was a
Wolf among a Nation of
Queer-Queers. Dugan.
Opportunity. Graham.
The Oracle. Ficke.
Poems to a Brown Cricket.
Wright.
Rambling Gambler.
Anonymous.
Responsibilities: Prologue.
Yeats.
Reward of Virtue.
Guiterman.
Rhoda Pitkin. Masters.
The Romance of the Rose.
Guillaume de Lorris
Sag', Wo Ist Dein Schones
Liebchen. Heine.
Scholar I. Deane.
Seascape with Bookends.
Eaton.
Seven Times One Are Seven.
Hillyer.
Sleeping Beauty: August.
Knight.
Snatches: "This book is one."
Anonymous.
The Sofa. McGuckian.
Song of the Open Road.
Whitman.
Sonnet to Be Written from
Prison. Adamson.
Tarquin and Tullia.
Mainwaring.
There Is a Box. Greenberg.
There's Money in Mother and
Father. Bishop.
To a Certain Most Certainly
Certain Critic. McCord.
To Doctor Bale. Googe.
To Helen. Praed.
To His Noble Friend, Mr.
Richard Lovelace, upon His
Poems. Marvell.
To My Sister. Wordsworth.
To Shakespeare. Day.
To the Reader. Jonson.
Upon the Author of a Play
Called Sodom. Oldham.
View from an Institution.
Wright.
The Visible Baby. Redgrove.
Voyage. Wygodski.
Who Hath a Book. Nesbit.
A Winter Wish. Messinger.
Writing. Allingham.
Boom
Sally Go Round the Sunshine.
Anonymous.
The Seals in Penobscot Bay.
Hoffman.
Tarantella. Belloc.
View of the Capitol from the
Library of Congress.
Bishop.
Boon
Compensation. Dunbar.
The Country Inn: Song:
"Though richer swains thy
love pursue." Baillie.
One Gift I Ask. Harrison.
So Fair, So Sweet, Withal So
Sensitive. Wordsworth.
To His Wife. Ausonius.
Boot (s)
2 Poems for Black Relocation
Centers. Knight.
Braggin' Bill's Fortytude.
Hallock.

Buachaille Etive Mor and Buachaille Etive Beag. Mitchison.
The Cat and the Boot. *Anonymous.*
Cock-Crow. Thomas.
Conestoga. Murphy, Jr.
Conscience. Ravitch.
The Dancing Cabman. Morton.
Darwin in 1881. Schnackenberg.
A Drum for Ben Boyd. Webb.
The Emergency Maker. Wagoner.
Godolphin Horne. Belloc.
I Don't Like You. Wright.
Marry the Lass? Greig.
Monody on a Century. Birney.
My Head on My Shoulders. Ingalls.
Oregon Winter. McGahey
Our Photographs. Locker-Lampson.
Paddy Doyle. *Anonymous.*
The Return. Roethke.
The Right Heart in the Wrong Place. Joyce.
To Julia in Shooting Togs (parody). Seaman.

Booze
I Scream You Scream. McKay.
On a Portrait by Copley. Freeman.
Road Hazard. Green.
Villon's Straight Tip to All Cross Coves. Henley.

Border (s)
Farewell to Tobacco. Lamb.
Jock of Hazeldean. Scott.
Limerick: "There was an Old Man on the Border." Lear.
The Monastery: Border Ballad. Scott.
On Zion and on Lebanon. Onderdonk.
Put Your Word to My Lips. Korn.
To the River Isca (the Usk). Vaughan.
Toyland. MacDonough.

Bore (d)
Apocryphal Apocalypse. Wheelwright.
Archetypes. Bowers.
Autobiographical Fragment. Amis.
The Chance. Holmes.
The Design. Major.
The Fortunes of Nigel (excerpt). Scott.
Great Man. Johnson.
I Just Walk around, around, around. Kulbak.
I Wish That My Room Had a Floor. Burgess.
A Legend of the Northland. Cary.
Limerick: "Quoth the bookworm, "I don't care one bit." Herford.
Love, You've Been a Villain. Planché.
Mr. Strugnell (parody). Cope.
The Odyssey. Homer.
A Summing Up. Preil.
T. S. Eliot. Lowell.

To a Boy-Poet of the Decadence. Seaman.
To the Shore. Swenson.
The Travelers. Reeves.
Vacationer. Gibson.
Villeggiature. Nesbit.
The Whummil Bore. *Anonymous.*
With What Conviction the Young Man Spoke. Auden.
You never touch. Yosano Akiko.

Born
After Midnight. Vildrac.
Afterthoughts of Donna Elvira. Kizer.
American Rhapsody. Fearing.
Amoretti, VIII. Spenser.
Another Fan Belonging to Mademoiselle Mallarme. Mallarme.
Auguries of Innocence. Blake.
The Beautiful. Davies.
Bedtime. Schwartz.
The Birth of Venus. *Anonymous.*
By the Babe Unborn. Chesterton.
By the Sea. Rossetti.
Bye Baby Bother. Smith.
Casino. Auden.
Children, Go Where I Send Thee. *Anonymous.*
Christmas Song. Carman.
Cold Water. Hall.
The Day You Are Born. Song.
DNA Lab. Spence.
Dog in the Fountain. Souster.
Down in the Forest. *Anonymous.*
An Eclogue for Christmas. MacNeice.
Endless. Rukeyser.
An Epitaph on His Grandfather. Shipman.
Epitaph on Will Smith. *Anonymous.*
Eros. Swinburne.
Family Reunion. Summers.
The Feast o' Saint Stephen. Sawyer.
From Generation to Generation. Howells.
Getting Through. Kumin.
A Glimpse. Cornford.
Great Spaces. Moss.
He Is Like the Serpent Saka. Book of the Dead.
Hell and Heaven. *Anonymous.*
Ho Ho Ho Caribou. Ceravolo.
I've Tasted My Blood. Acorn.
I was born under a kind star. Tynan.
In Memoriam A.H.H., CXX. Tennyson.
In the Garden There Strayed. *Anonymous.*
In the Holy Nativity of Our Lord: Shepherds' Hymn. Crashaw.
In the Root Cellar. Kumin.
Jack Was Every Inch a Sailor. Anonymous.
Labor. Day.

The Language. Hollo.
Lester Leaps In. Young.
The Life of Man. Bacon.
Limerick: "A king, on assuming his reign." *Anonymous.*
Lo, for I to Myself Am Unknown. Rumi.
Look, Edwin! Millay.
Love-Songs, At Once Tender and Informative. Hoffenstein.
Man I Thought You Was Talking Another Language That Day. Cruz.
The Mediterranean. Tate.
Milford. *Anonymous.*
Mnemosyne Lay in Dust. Clarke.
Morning. Taylor.
Nesting. Saleh.
New Life. Kariuki.
Night and the Child. Wright.
Not Lost in the Stars. Bliven.
Old Tityrus to Eugenia. Cotton.
On Burning a Dull Poem. Swift.
On My Birthday, July 21. Prior.
On My Wife's Birth-Day. Smart.
One Wept Whose Only Child Was Dead. Meynell.
Our Movement. Eluard.
Out of Our Shame. Rosten.
A Pair. Gjellerup.
Po' Boy Blues. Hughes.
The Poem Circling Hamtramck, Michigan All Night in Search of You. Levine.
Poem on Hampstead Heath. Adeane.
A Poem, upon the Caelestial Embassy Perform'd by Angels... Steere.
Propriety. Moore.
The Rear Guard. Brown.
The Ring Of. Olson.
The Roof of the World. Browne.
Seascape. Young.
Signpost. Jeffers.
Song of the Last Jewish Child. Jabes.
Song: "She was lyin face down in her face." Knott.
The Soul of Dante. Michelangelo.
Spring. Rossetti.
St. Augustine's Pear Tree. Bowering.
The Stone and the Blade of Grass in the Warsaw Ghetto. Scheinert.
Stonewall Jackson's Way. Palmer.
Stratton Water. *Anonymous.*
Strip Me Naked, or Royal Gin for Ever. *Anonymous.*
To Fine Lady Would-Be. Jonson.
To His Retired Friend, an Invitation to Brecknock (excerpt). Vaughan.
Traditions. Heaney.
The Travel Bureau. Mitchell.

Turkey in the Straw. *Anonymous.*
The Two Coyotes. Marietta.
Ultimate Exile IV. Currey.
Valley Forge. Read.
Waked by the Gospel's Powerful Sound. Occom.
Weekend Stroll. Cornford.
What Do You Do when It's Spring? Woods.
When a Girl Looks Down. Smith.
Wonder. Traherne.
Years Later. Lerner.

Borrow (ed) (s)
The Addict. Sexton.
Epitaph for Jean Maillard. *Anonymous.*
Invocation. Randolph.
Judgment Day. Oxenham.
The Light and Glory of the World. Cowper.
Mortal, Sneer Not at the Devil. Heine.
My Dream. *Anonymous.*
On Laying up Treasure. Hiers.
Scroll-Section. Finch.
Shopping for Midnight. Murray.
The Spirit's Light. Cowper.
Three Score and Ten. *Anonymous.*
Uncle Jack. Kherdian.
The West-Country Lover. Brown.

Bosom
Amoretti, LXXIII. Spenser.
Anne Rutledge. Masters.
Aut Caesar Aut Nullus. Spencer.
Bonnie Wee Thing. Burns.
Bye Bye Baby Blues. Fuller.
Characteristics of a Child Three Years Old. Wordsworth.
Childe Harold's Pilgrimage: Canto III. Byron.
Christ's Bondservant. Matheson.
The Day Is Past and Gone. Leland.
Depreciating Her Beauty. Blunt.
The Desert. Wood.
Elegy Written in a Country Churchyard. Gray.
Epitaph on a Free but Tame Redbreast. Cowper.
Epitaphs of the War, 1914-18. Kipling.
Evening Shade. *Anonymous.*
The Fleece. Dyer.
A Flight of Wild Ducks. Harpur.
Jesus, Shepherd of Thy Sheep. Bethune.
The Kingfisher. Davies.
Love in Moonlight. Bhartrihari.
My Hope, My Love. *Anonymous.*
My Only Star. Davison.
Now Sleeps the Crimson Petal. Tennyson.
Off from Boston. *Anonymous.*
Pardon. Howe.
Quaerit Jesum suum Maria. Crashaw.
The River in the Meadows. Adams.

Bosom

Song: "When lovely woman stoops to folly." Goldsmith.
The Stars Have Not Dealt Me the Worst They Could Do. Housman.
Susan Van Dusan. *Anonymous.*
There Is Strength in the Soil. Stringer.
To Lydia, with a Coloured Egg, on Easter Monday. Jones.
To the World: a Farewell for a Gentlewoman, Virtuous and Noble. Jonson.
The Torso: Passages 18. Duncan.
Tryste Noel. Guiney.
A Zong. Barnes.

Bosom (s)

Epitaph XI On Mr. Gay. In Westminster Abbey, 1732. Pope.
A Fragment. Byron.
Solvitur Acris Hiems. Mahony.

Bosphorus

Poem on Azure. Noailles.
The Three Khalandeers. Mangan.

Boss

Black Cry. Craveirinha.
Evening at the Farm. Trowbridge.
Rain. Davis.
Sisyphus. "Garioch.
To G. K. Chesterton. Plunkett.

Boston

Communication to the City Fathers of Boston. Starbuck.
Flight 539. Brinnin.
The Thanksgiving in Boston Harbor. Butterworth.
Woolworth's. Hall.

Bottle (s)

The Archaeological Picnic. Betjeman.
Beth Appleyard's Verses. DeVries.
The Bold Pedlar and Robin Hood. *Anonymous.*
Charlie Cherry. Jackson.
Daley's Dorg Wattle. Goodge.
Derelict. Allison.
Edvard Munch. Wright.
Getting Under. Lightman.
Gluggity Glug. Coleman the Younger.
The Goat Paths. Stephens.
Heaving the Lead Line. *Anonymous.*
The Hole in the Sea. Bell.
The Hosts. Merwin.
I'll Have a Collier for My Sweetheart. Oliver.
I've Got a Dog as Thin as a Rail. *Anonymous.*
I've Rambled This Country Both Earlye and Late. *Anonymous.*
In Iceland. McCord.
Is 5. Cummings.
Kissing Game. Rosenthal.
Last Things. Manhire.
Limerick: "I saw Nelson at the Battle of the Nile." *Anonymous.*

The Man Whom the Sea Kept Awake. Bly.
Meditations Seven. Taylor.
Namkwin Pul. Gutteridge.
No Bargains Today. Kenner.
O Friendship! Friendship! the Shell of Aphrodite. Landor.
Roll, Alabama, Roll. *Anonymous.*
Said Aristotle Unto Plato. Wister.
Saint Peray. Parsons.
Sandy Lan'. *Anonymous.*
Some Ruthless Rhymes. Graham.
Sounding. Jauss.
The Storm (excerpt). O'Rahilly.
A Suit of Nettles. Reaney.
Tommy O'Linn. *Anonymous.*
Top Hand. *Anonymous.*
Trout. Hindley.
Uncle Claude. Evans.
Unto Jehovah Sing Will I. Ainsworth.
The Well of St. Keyne. Southey.
Wizard Oil (with music). *Anonymous.*
You're the Top. Porter.
Zimmer Drunk and Alone, Dreaming of Old Football Games. Zimmer.

Bottom (s)

Charlie Cherry. Jackson.
Getting Under. Lightman.
The Goat Paths. Stephens.
Heaving the Lead Line. *Anonymous.*
I'll Have a Collier for My Sweetheart. Oliver.
I've Got a Dog as Thin as a Rail. *Anonymous.*
Last Things. Manhire.
Limerick: "I saw Nelson at the Battle of the Nile." *Anonymous.*
The Man Whom the Sea Kept Awake. Bly.
O Friendship! Friendship! the Shell of Aphrodite. Landor.
Roll, Alabama, Roll. *Anonymous.*
Sandy Lan'. *Anonymous.*
Some Ruthless Rhymes. Graham.
Sounding. Jauss.
The Storm (excerpt). O'Rahilly.
Tommy O'Linn. *Anonymous.*
Top Hand. *Anonymous.*
Trout. Hindley.
Uncle Claude. Evans.
Words. Plath.
You're the Top. Porter.

Bough (s)

At Eighty. Stanhope.
The Bats. Hillyer.
Black Poplar-Boughs. Freeman.
Blight. Bontemps.
Chagrin. Rosenberg.
The Dance. Crane.
Do Not Expect Again a Phoenix Hour. Day-Lewis.
A Fallen Yew. Thompson.
For My Sister's Sake. Hitomaro.
In a Station of the Metro. Pound.

The Knot. Kunitz.
The Last Leaf. Holmes.
Love (fragment). Sappho.
Luriana, Lurilee. Elton.
Marble Statuette Harpist. Allen.
Misericordia. Mead.
The Oak. Tennyson.
Overheard. Levertov.
Revenge! Horace.
Rustic Childhood. Barnes.
Soldier (T. P.). Jarrell.
Spring. Stanley.
That Which Hath Wings Shall Tell. Van Voorhis.
'Tis Midnight. *Anonymous.*
To a Maple Seed. Mifflin.
The Tree. Bjornson.
The Trees of the Garden. Rossetti.
The Two April Mornings. Wordsworth.
The Ungathered Apples. Wright.
Walking-Sticks and Paperweights and Watermarks. Moore.
The Watcher. Peck.

Boulder (s)

Big Thompson Canon. Gower.
Bucyrus. Holmes.
Burial. Francis.
The Double Axe. Hazlewood-Brady.
Patience on a Monument. di Michele.
Tired of Eating Kisses. Swart.

Boulevard

Encounter. Devlin.
The Old Conservative. Tooker.
Sh-Ta-Ra-Dah-Dey (Irish Lullaby). (with music). *Anonymous.*

Bound

Ars Poetica. Vriesland.
Blow Ye Winds Westerly. *Anonymous.*
Christ Crucified. Crashaw.
The Codfish Shanty. *Anonymous.*
Epitaph: "Sanquhar, whom this earth could scarce contain." Drummond.
Eyes. De la Mare.
Frank James, the Roving Gambler. *Anonymous.*
Freedom. *Anonymous.*
The Grey Cock. *Anonymous.*
I Can't Help but Wonder Where I'm Bound. Paxton.
I Come from Salem City. *Anonymous.*
Ibant Obscurae. Brown.
If by Dull Rhymes Our English Must Be Chained. Keats.
The Journey with Hands and Arms. Saltman.
Leichhardt in Theatre: The Room. Webb.
My Heart Leaps Up. Wordsworth.
On a Pair of Garters. Davies.
On the Sonnet. Keats.
Sea-Voyage. Wheelock.
To Crown It. Herrick.
Unfulfilment. Bushnell.

The Wide Mizzoura (with music). *Anonymous.*
Woe Is Me, My Soul Says, How Bitter Is My Fate. Morpurgo.

Boundar (ies) (y)

Celebrating the Mass of Christian Burial. Mathis.
The Doomed Man. Alexander.
Philatelic Lessons: The German Collection. Spingarn.
The spider holds a silver ball. Dickinson.

Bount (ies) (y)

The Alphabet. *Anonymous.*
Elegiac. Mimnermus.
The Morning Hours. *Anonymous.*
Prologue to Hugh Kelly's "A Word to the Wise'. Johnson.
A Singing Lesson. Swinburne.
Table Graces, or Prayers for Adults: Noon Meal. *Anonymous.*
To Mr. George Herbert, with One of My Seals, of the Anchor and Christ. Donne.

Bouquet (s)

Autumn Fashions. Thomas.
First Photos of Flu Virus. Witt.
Plans. Brooks.
A Scandal Among the Flowers. Taylor.
Unseen Fire. Currey.

Bourbon

Dream Songs. Berryman.
Lady, of Anonymous Flesh and Face. Cunningham.
Lilies for Neal. Minor.

Bow

Regret. *Anonymous.*

Bow (ed) (s)

Arabesque. Johnson.
At Only That Moment. Ross.
Atalanta's Race. Morris.
Athlete. Maynard.
Away. Stryk.
The Birds' Courting Song. *Anonymous.*
Brave Old World. Lambert.
Clerk Colvill (A version). *Anonymous.*
The Clipper. Day.
The Clown. Hall.
Death's Blue-Eyed Girl. Pastan.
The Deepest Bow. Takvan.
The Deserted Kingdom. Dunsany.
The Elephant II. *Anonymous.*
Epigram: "Exhausted now her sighs, and dry her tears." Landor.
The Expostulation. Shadwell.
First Death. Justice.
Ganga. Blackburn.
Gnostology. Hamill.
The God-maker, Man. Marquis.
The Great Offence. Abu Nuwas.
Guide to the Symphony. Kees.

Hark, My Soul. Austin.
Hidden Bow. Temkin.
Homage. Hoyt.
An Humble Wish (excerpt).
  Thompson.
I Know a Lady. Thomas.
In the Oregon Country.
  Stafford.
It Was the Morning.
  Petrarch (Francesco
  Petrarca).
Jenny's Ribbons. Barnes.
Like Gulliver. Cassian.
Limerick:: "The cautious
  collapsible cow."
  Anonymous.
Limerick: "There was an old
  person of Bow." Lear.
Look-a How Dey Done My
  Lord. *Anonymous.*
My Purse. *Anonymous.*
On Fame. Keats.
On the Capture and
  Imprisonment of Crazy
  Snake, January, 1900.
  Posey.
One Year Ago. Landor.
Oraga Haru. Issa.
Pibroch. Hughes.
Praise. *Anonymous.*
The Rainbow. De la Mare.
Robin-a-Bobbin. *Anonymous.*
Robin, Wren, Martin,
  Swallow. *Anonymous.*
Rufus Mitchell's Confession.
  Anonymous.
She Used to Let Her Golden
  Hair Fly Free. Petrarch
  (Francesco Petrarca).
Signum Cui Contradicetur.
  Mary Angelita.
The Sister: Epilogue.
  Goldsmith.
Sur le Pont d'Avignon.
  Anonymous.
Suspended Moment.
  Davenport.
Thanksgiving. Osborne.
They Tell Me I Am Lost.
  Kenny.
A Translation from....
  Levinson.
The Tropics in New York.
  McKay.
The Two Brothers.
  Anonymous.
The Unicorn. Rieu.
The Visitor. Prelutsky.
The Wandering Lunatic Mind.
  Carpenter.
"Whole gulfs of red and fleets
  of red". Dickinson.
The Young Housewife.
  Williams.

Bow-wow
A Farmyard Song. Hastings.
For a Good Dog.
  Guiterman.
Hush-a-Bye a Baa Lamb.
  Anonymous.
Joan Brown, about Her
  Painting. Fraser.

Bowel (s)
The Cowboy's Lament (III).
  Anonymous.
On Queen Caroline's
  Deathbed. Pope.
Season of Blood. Santos.
Solo for Bent Spoon. Finkel.
Sunset Horn. O'Higgins.
Survey of Literature.
  Ransom.

To a Spider. Southey.

Bower (s)
Bendemeer. Moore.
Bessy Bell and Mary Gray.
  Anonymous.
Clerk Saunders. *Anonymous.*
Eden Bower. Rossetti.
Epithalamion. Hopkins.
The Faerie Queene. Spenser.
The Fairy King. Allingham.
God's Mother. Housman.
Her Sacred Bower.
  Campion.
I Have Been a Forester.
  Anonymous.
Jamie Douglas (B vers.).
  Anonymous.
Rain Forest. Rolls.
Song: "Where is the nymph,
  whose azure eye." Moore.
Stanzas (excerpt). Newton.
Summer Images. Clare.
Thanks, Gentle Moon, for
  Thy Obscured Light.
  Anonymous.
We'll to the Woods No More.
  Housman.
Winter Will Follow. Dixon.

Bowl (s)
The Boy Actor. Coward.
Fill the Bowl, Butler!
  Anonymous.
A Good Thing. Mathew.
It's Already Autumn.
  Pagliarani.
Little Lad. *Anonymous.*
Nature Morte. MacNeice.
An Opium Fantasy. Lowell.
Pigmeat. Leadbelly.
Riddle: "A hill full, a hole
  full." Mother Goose.
Soup Song. Sugar.
The Swashbuckler's Song.
  Montgomery.
Three wise men of Gotham.
  Mother Goose.
Trip It Gipsies, Trip It Fine.
  Middleton.
Wassailer's Song. Southwell.
Wine Bowl. Doolittle.
A Word to Peter Olds.
  Brasch.

Bowle (s)
Song: "Trip it Gipsies, trip it
  fine." Rowley.

Bowling alley
After Dinner We Take a
  Drive into the Night.
  Towle.

Box (es)
An Additional Poem.
  Ashbery.
All Things Have Savour.
  Anonymous.
The Answer. Wachtel.
The Dark House.
  Anonymous.
Heart Burial. Grigson.
Ice Cold. O Riordain.
Limerick: "There was an Old
  Man on some rocks."
  Lear.
Memory of a Porch. Justice.
Mid-Term Break. Heaney.
Plane Geometer. McCord.
Street Performers, 1851.
  Tiller.
Sunday Night in Santa Rosa.
  Gioia.
Things. De la Mare.
The Toilette. A Town
  Eclogue. Gay.

Wedding Party. Hall.

Boy friend
For Your Inferiority Complex.
  O'Rourke.
If You Don't Like My
  Apples. *Anonymous.*

Boy (s)
Adolescence. Schmitz.
Alabama Bus. Hairston.
Ballad of Human Life.
  Beddoes.
Ballade of Boys Bathing.
  Rolfe.
Bind-Weed. "Coolidge.
Bold Rangers. *Anonymous.*
The Boss Machine-Tender
  after Losing a Son.
  Corrigan.
A Boy's Prayer. Beeching.
A Boy's Summer Song.
  Dunbar.
The Boy We Want.
  Anonymous.
Boys and Sport. Solon.
Cages. Solomon.
Careless Love. Kunitz.
Carpenter. Brown.
Carry Me Back. Holmes.
The Cherry Boy (excerpt).
  Ellis.
Chiquita. Harte.
Christmas Day. Fuller.
Come to your Heaven, You
  Heavenly Choirs!
  Southwell.
The Confirmation. Shapiro.
Conversation between Mr. and
  Mrs. Santa Claus.
  Bennett.
Custer's Last Fierce Charge.
  Anonymous.
The Derby Ram, II.
  Anonymous.
The Drummer-Boy and the
  Shepherdess. Rands.
The Duel. Lovelace.
The Earth and Man.
  Brooke.
The End. Van Doren.
Epigram: "Cease your labours,
  lovers of boys."
  Anonymous.
Epigram: "Gathering the
  bloom of all the fairest boys
  that be." Strato.
Epigram: "I dined with
  Demetrios." Automedon.
Epigram: "Listen, you who
  know the pains of love."
  Meleager.
Epigram: "Passing the flower-
  stalls." Strato.
Evening Music. Smithyman.
The Fable of the Piece of
  Glass and the Piece of Ice.
  Frere.
Falling Upwards. Shapiro.
The Family of Nations.
  Wattles.
Fern House at Kew. Dehn.
The Fiftieth Birthday of
  Agassiz. Longfellow.
The Final Trawl.
  Anonymous.
The Fish. Gustafson.
Fool Song. Lengyel.
For a Neighbor Girl. Yu
  Hsuan-chi.
Freighter. Ruddick.
The Funeral. Spender.
Godolphin Horne. Belloc.

The Golden Voyage.
  Anonymous.
Great-Granddad.
  Anonymous.
Green Broom. *Anonymous.*
Habla Usted Espanol? Reiss.
The Haunted Garden.
  Treece.
Hold on, Abraham.
  Anonymous.
Holly and Mistletoe.
  Farjeon.
How's My Boy? Dobell.
How to Raise a Son. Martial
  (Marcus Valerius Martialis).
If I Had But Two Little
  Wings. Hood.
In Dream: The Privacy of
  Sequence. Young Bear.
Incident of the French Camp.
  Browning.
Interlude. Duggan.
Itiskit, Itaskit. *Anonymous.*
James McCosh. Bridges.
The Janitor's Boy. Crane.
Kree. Gordon.
Lang Johnny More.
  Anonymous.
A Leap for Life. Colton.
Letter to a Substitute Teacher.
  Gildner.
Life Story. Tomioka Taeko.
The Little Boy Found.
  Blake.
Love and Folly. La
  Fontaine.
The Lyre Player. George.
Manhattan Lullaby. Field.
Manly Ferry. Philip.
The Martin Cat Long Shaged
  of Courage Good. Clare.
Meditations in Time of Civil
  War. Yeats.
The Milking Shed. Clare.
Mother and Child. Eastwick.
My Love, She Passed Me By.
  Anonymous.
My Pretty Little Pink (with
  music). *Anonymous.*
Night Storm. Simms.
Old Age. Tennyson.
The Old Man Dreams.
  Holmes.
One Bright Morning...
  Anonymous.
One, Two, Three! Bunner.
Over the fence. Dickinson.
Pastoral Landscape. Philips.
Pearl Bryan. *Anonymous.*
Pedagogical Principles.
  Amoss.
Poor Boy Blues. Thomas.
Rory of the Hill. Kickham.
School and Schoolfellows.
  Praed.
The Silk Merchant's Daughter
  (I). *Anonymous.*
The Sixth Pastoral. Philips.
Snowstorm. Clare.
So Handy. *Anonymous.*
Some Litanies. Benedikt.
The Song. Very.
A Song: "Come, cheer up, my
  lads, like a true British
  band." *Anonymous.*
The South Country. Belloc.
Special Pleading. Bernstein.
A Spool of Thread.
  Eastman.
Stamp Blues. Hollins.
The Summer Rentals.
  Halpern.

The Taming of the Shrew.
Shakespeare.
The Teacher Sees a Boy.
Morningstar.
A Thousand Killed. Spencer.
To Corydon. Beccadelli.
Tom Dooley. *Anonymous.*
Tony Get the Boys.
Graham.
Treasures. Thomas.
Tsa'lagi Council Tree.
Cardiff.
The Twelve Oxen.
Anonymous
The Two Foscari: Swimming.
Byron.
Versions of Love. Fuller.
We Were Boys Together.
Morris.
Where Did He Run To?
Van Doren.
Where Is My Wandering Boy
Tonight? Lowry.
Where Is Your Boy Tonight?
Anonymous.
Whistling Boy. Waterman.
With Rue My Heart Is Laden
(parody). Hoffenstein.
The Yankee Doodle Boy.
Cohan.
A Young David: Birmingham.
Brooks.

Boyhood
The Old Home. Cawein.
An Old Man's Thought of
School. Whitman.
The Port o' Heart's Desire.
McGroarty.
The Song the Oriole Sings.
Howells.
The Swimmer. Layton.
Vanished. Eng.

Bracelets
For Her. Strand.
Moon Mattress. Di Prima.

Brag (s)
The Battle of the Kegs.
Hopkinson.
British Valor Displayed.
Hopkinson.
Games, Hard Press and Bruise
of the Flesh. Vliet.
Out and Fight. Leland.
The Roundup Cook. Carr.
With All Deliberate Speed.
Lee.

Braille
The Fish in the Stone. Dove.
Limerick: "The breasts of a
barmaid of Crale."
Anonymous.
Look for Me on England.
Mallalieu.

Brain (s)
The All-Night Waitress.
Stanton.
The Angel in the House.
Patmore.
Art's Variety. McFadden.
Autumn Poem. Cronin.
The Battle of the Cowpens.
English.
The Big One. Cabalquinto.
The Cock. Lipska.
Death. More.
Departure. Green.
The Desert Music (excerpt).
Williams.
Don't Hope to Gain by What
Has Preceded. Kyger.
Dream Songs. Berryman.

English Bards and Scotch
Reviewers. Byron.
The Fishes and the Poet's
Hands. Yerby.
The Foreign Gate (excerpt).
Keyes.
Galileo Galilei. Smith.
Heredity. Aldrich.
Instruction sore long time I
bore. Kingsley.
It. Snyder.
Judge Kroll. Greenberg.
King Lear. Shakespeare.
Kohoutek. Ryan.
Lamorna Cove. Davies.
Listening to a Broadcast.
Manifold.
The Mad Woman of Punnet's
Town. Strong.
Millom Old Quarry.
Nicholson.
Night Crow. Roethke.
On a Prohibitionist Poem.
Chesterton.
On Playwright. Jonson.
Orchestra. Davies.
The Photographer Whose
Shutter Died. Meissner.
Redo, 1-5. Hejinian.
Rontgen Photograph.
Eybers.
Shapes and Signs. Mangan.
Sheet Lightning. Blunden.
Silence. Orr.
Standard Forgings Plant.
Stephens.
Summer Song. Watt.
There Is a Pool on Garda.
Scollard.
The Thorn. Wordsworth.
Three Car Poems, III. Jones.
The Threshing Machine.
Meynell.
Titus and Berenice. Heath-
Stubbs.
Tray. Browning.
Wait for the Hour. Soutar.
The Washers of the Shroud.
Lowell.
We Heart. Chester.

Braine (s)
Black Thing. *Anonymous.*
The C. S. A. Commissioners.
Anonymous.
A Curse on the Cat.
Skelton.
The Flying Tailor (parody).
Hogg.
I Like Them Fluffy.
Herbert.
The Lake Isle. Pound.
The Murder of Saint Thomas
of Kent. *Anonymous.*
My Uncle Paul of Pimlico.
Peake.
A Perigord pres del Muralh.
Bertrand.
Portrait. Cummings.
The Quarrelsome Trio. G.
A Satire against Wit.
Blackmore.
Shack Poem. Bly.
Southbound on the Freeway.
Swenson.
The Steele Glas. Gascoigne.
To a Spider. Southey.
To the Memory of Yale
College. Putnam.
The Vision. Defoe.

Brakes
Limerick: "Said a girl from
beyond Pompton Lakes."
Bishop.
A Satire against Mankind.
Rochester.
Untitled. Nibbelink.

Branch (es)
The Barrier. Lavater.
Birch. Simpson.
The Blood-Letting. Harjo.
The Bull. Laughton.
The Childhood of an
Equestrian. Edson.
A Christmas Cradlesong.
Lope de Vega Carpio.
The City. Creeley.
Composition in Black and
White. Pollitt.
Dark Corner. Hough.
Elm Fuck Poem. Sanders.
Flaming Creatures. Elmslie.
Four Glosses. *Anonymous.*
From My Arm-Chair.
Longfellow.
How Many Nights. Kinnell.
Indolence. Watkins.
A Journey through the
Moonlight. Edson.
The Jungle (excerpt).
Fleming.
Lamenting Tauaba.
Akhyaliyya.
A Little Carol of the Virgin.
Lope de Vega Carpio.
Lord Lovel (A vers.).
Anonymous.
Love Poem. Miranda.
Love Song. Williams.
The Lullaby. Lope de Vega
Carpio.
The Mango Tree. Chock.
The Moon. Hall.
The Mysteries Remain.
Doolittle.
An Old Woman Laments in
Spring-Time. Sitwell.
Palm-Sunday. Vaughan.
The Park. Blaser.
Peking Man, Raining. Lorr.
Procne. Quennell.
The Progress of Learning:
Preface. Denham.
Salt. Gibbon.
The Sloth. Gardner.
Song: "Virtue's branches
wither, virtue pines."
Dekker.
The Sons of Levi.
Anonymous.
Spring's on the Curb.
Flanner.
Sunrise Sequence.
Anonymous.
Sweet Blooming Lavender.
Anonymous.
This Is What the Watchbird
Sings, Who Perches in the
Lovetree. Boyd.
Three in Transition.
Ignatow.
Trees. Merwin.
Two Hangovers. Wright.
Waiting. Corke.
Why She Says No. Voigt.

Brand (s)
A Cowboy Dance Song.
Anonymous.
My Own Brand. Cuelho.
Whose Old Cow?
Anonymous.

The Wrangler Kid.
Anonymous.

Brandy
Jackson. *Anonymous.*
Jackson (with music).
Anonymous.
Lines Declining a
Transatlantic Dinner
Invitation. Hacker.
The Man in the Moon.
Anonymous.
Punkydoodle and Jollapin.
Richards.
The Sea-Captain.
Anonymous.
Summer, 1970. Halpern.
Sweeney Erect. Eliot.

Brass
The Battel of the Summer-
Islands. Waller.
Epitaph for the Race of Man.
Millay.
My Father Dreams of
Baseball. Lieberman.
Our March. Mayakovsky.
The Spruce and Limber
Yellow-Hammer.
Coleridge.
The Story of the Pot and the
Kettle. Montagu.
True Knowledge. Panatattu.

Brave (ry)
The Alabama. Bell.
Albemarle Cushing. Roche.
Alexander's Feast or, the
Power of Music. Dryden.
As I Pondered in Silence.
Whitman.
The Banner of the Jew.
Lazarus.
A Battle Ballad. Ticknor.
The Battle of Baltimore.
Anonymous.
The Battle of Bennington.
Rodman.
The Battle of the Baltic.
Campbell.
A Christmas Prayer. Haley.
Crispus Attucks. O'Reilly.
Decoration. Higginson.
Dirge of Rory O'More. De
Vere.
Easter. Davies.
Epitaph. Wylie.
Epitaphs of the War, 1914-18.
Kipling.
An Evening's Love. Dryden.
The Field Hospital.
Muldoon.
Fort McHenry. *Anonymous.*
Four Poems for April.
Adeane.
Franciscan Aspiration.
Lindsay.
God Save the Flag. Holmes.
Heaven in Ordinarie. Wolff.
Henry Martyn. *Anonymous.*
How Cyrus Laid the Cable.
Saxe.
How the Little Kite Learned
to Fly. *Anonymous.*
I Sing of Olaf Glad and Big.
Cummings.
In Memoriam, A. H. 1916.
Baring.
In Vinculis: The Deeds That
Might Have Been. Blunt.
Interim. Delany.
John Underhill. Whittier.
Juan Belmonte, Torero.
Finkel.

Kearsarge and Alabama. *Anonymous.*
Lancer. Housman.
Legend. Waller.
Litany of the Heroes. Lindsay.
The Loss of the Cedar Grove. *Anonymous.*
Margaret Fuller. Alcott.
Memorial Day. Wynne.
Montcalm and Wolfe. *Anonymous.*
Nathan Hale. *Anonymous.*
Ned Christie. Conley.
A New Song: "As near beauteous Boston lying." *Anonymous.*
A Night in a Village. Nikitin.
Not Every Day Fit for Verse. Herrick.
Our Left. Tichnor.
Out of the Earth. Davies.
The Pike. Bruce.
Power Failure. Browne.
Python. *Anonymous.*
The Rigveda: Indra, the Supreme God. *Anonymous.*
Roll, Alabama, Roll. *Anonymous.*
Running the Batteries. Melville.
Song of the Brave. Altgood.
Song: "The primrose in the green forest." Deloney.
The Star-Spangled Banner. Key.
Strong Men, Riding Horses. Brooks.
Ten Little Indian Boys. Hutchinson.
To an Anti-poetical Priest. MacNamee.
To England. Moore.
The Tomb of the Brave. Hutton.
The Waterfall. Vaughan.
What You Need. Fraser.
When I Was a Brave Cowboy. *Anonymous.*

Bread
The Anathemata. Jones.
The Appeasement of Demeter. Meredith.
Au Tombeau de Mon Pere. McCuaig.
The Avenging Daughters. *Anonymous.*
The Birthday-Cake Glockenspiel. Henley.
Bread. Thomas.
Bread of Brotherhood. Trent.
Carrier's Address. *Anonymous.*
Cherry Tree. Sitwell.
Christmas. Betjeman.
Christmas 1970. Milligan.
Compensation. Kammeyer.
La Condition Botanique. Hecht.
The Crust of Bread. *Anonymous.*
The Cup of Blessing. Wesley.
Cycle. Miller.
Death Is a Second Cousin Dining with Us Tonight. Kudaka.
Deliver Me, O Lord, from My Daily Bread. Walker.

Domestic Scene. Hartnett.
The Dream of a Boy Who Lived at Nine Elms. Rands.
The Dream of a Girl Who Lived at Sevenoaks. Rands.
Drink, Friends. Ibn Ezra.
Encounter in Safed. Yungman.
Epigram. *Anonymous.*
Epitaph in Christ Church, Bristol, on Thomas Turner. Jeffrey.
Exchange. Mary Dorothy Ann.
Fe, Fi, Fo, Fum. Mother Goose.
For England, in Grateful Appreciation (excerpt). Vogt.
For Jeanette Piccard Ordained at 79. Golden.
The Fugitive. Meynell.
Gastric. "T.
The Geraniums. Taggard.
The Good Day. Bashford.
The Great St. Bernard. Rogers.
Harvest and Consecration. Jennings.
He Fishes with His Father's Ghost. Nordan.
Here's a Health to Them That's Awa'. Burns.
In Salem. Clifton.
In the Night Field. Merwin.
July Wakes. *Anonymous.*
Kibbutz Sabbath. Levi ben Amittai.
The King's Breakfast. Milne.
Landscape near a Steel Mill. Horn.
Lessons. Weber.
Lilith. Finkel.
Litany to Our Lady. Houselander.
Lyric Barber. Romano.
Mass at Dawn. Campbell.
Mister Frog Went A-Courting (with music). *Anonymous.*
My Spectre around Me Night & Day. Blake.
Nineteen Sections from a Twenty Acre Poem (excerpt). Martinson.
No Bread for the Poor (with music). *Anonymous.*
The Old Gray Goose. *Anonymous.*
On Barclay's Apology for the Quakers. Green.
On This Island. Auden.
Ordination. Mary Immaculate.
The Orphan Girl. *Anonymous.*
Poem for Marc Chagall. Cohen.
Rainpoem. Dransfield.
Raw Honey. MacAdams.
Robin Redbreast. Allingham.
A Scottish Cat. *Anonymous.*
Seven Wealthy Towns. *Anonymous.*
Short Eulogy. Gurevitch.
Soldier, There Is a War between the Mind. Stevens.
Sorrows of Werther. Thackeray.

St. Ciaran and the Birds. Carson.
The Story of Abraham and Hagar. Aphek.
The Tailor. "Ansky.
Tashkent Breaks into Blossom. Akhmatova.
This Bread I Break Was Once the Oat. Thomas.
To Make a Pastoral: A Receipt. *Anonymous.*
To the Snail. *Anonymous.*
The Two Witches. Graves.
The Watercress Seller. Miller.
Who Walks with Beauty. Morton.

Breadth
Divided. Ingelow.
Horizontal World. Saunders.
The Marshes of Glynn. Lanier.
O Mind of God, Broad as the Sky. Huckel.
Plenty. Jones.
Scientific Proof. Foley.

Break (ing) (s)
The Annunciation. Muir.
Aviemore. Waller.
Bagpipe Music. MacNeice.
The Bards We Quote. Taylor.
The Bastard from the Bush. *Anonymous.*
Because I Live. Ames.
Beetle Bemused. Lister.
Between God's Eyelashes. Villa.
The Blessing. Wright.
The Bonny Moorhen. *Anonymous.*
The Broken Heart. Beedome.
The Butterfly. Palmer.
Careless Love (with music). *Anonymous.*
Characters of Women. Pope.
Chivalry at a Discount. Fitzgerald.
Comfort. Doney.
Comfort thyself, my woeful heart. Wyatt.
Constancy: A Song. Rochester.
The Contrite Heart. Cowper.
Corinna. Campion.
Cupid and Death: Victorious Men of Earth. Shirley.
Cupid Ungodded. Shirley.
The Dawning. Vaughan.
The Dragonfly. Rand.
Drake. Noyes.
The Enchanted Knight. Muir.
Epistle to a Lady: Of the Character of Women. Pope.
Family. *Anonymous.*
The Fat Man in the Mirror. Lowell.
The Flowers of Apollo. Flanner.
Foolish Proverb. *Anonymous.*
"The furious gun in his raging ire." Wyatt.
The Gate of the Year. Haskins.
The Grandmother. Berry.
Hangman (with music). *Anonymous.*

The Harp That Once through Tara's Halls. Moore.
The Heart of a Woman. Johnson.
His Plan for Me. Nicholson.
The Hobbit (excerpt). Tolkien.
A Hot-Weather Song. Marquis.
Hymn to Comus. Jonson.
I Am New York City. Cortez.
I Lately Vowed. Oldmixon.
Idylls of the King. Tennyson.
If. Roche.
In Camus Fields. Strong.
In Summer. Towne.
The Indian Serenade. Shelley
It troubled me as once I was. Dickinson.
The Judge. McClane.
Knights Errant. Madeleva.
Land-Fall. Brady.
The Last Conqueror. Shirley.
Lines to an Indian Air. Shelley.
Love-Charms. Campion.
Love Poem. Nims.
Love's Rosary. Noyes.
Love's Stricken "Why." Dickinson.
The Lowest Trees Have Tops. Dyer.
The Magnolia's Shadow. Montale.
Maintenance. Sarah.
The Mariner. Cunningham.
Mother. Nagase Kiyoko.
My Heart Is a Lute. Barnard.
My Heart, Thinking. Otomo of Sakanoe.
Mystic River. Ciardi.
Next, Please. Larkin.
Of Corinna's Singing. Campion.
On the Name of Jesus. Crashaw.
Parable. Soutar.
Prayer. Washbourne.
Prince Robert. *Anonymous.*
The Reed. Carpenter.
Regina Confessorum. *Anonymous.*
Rencontre. Fauset.
Reply to Mr. Wordsworth (excerpt). MacLeish.
Ruins under the Stars. Kinnell.
Sally Simpkin's Lament. Hood.
Sappho. Carman.
The Sermon. Hughes.
So Fast Entangled. *Anonymous.*
Sonnet to Negro Soldiers. Cotter, Jr.
Sonnets. Tuckerman.
Sparkling and Bright. Hoffman
A Sparrow in the Dust. Domino.
Stalin. Lowell.
Surcease. Lane.
The Swallow. Stanley.
Tell Me Some Way. Reese.
Tennyson. Ansen.
That Summer. Treece.
Their Cone-Like Cabins. Ballard.

Then. Gildner.
There. Mezey.
There Were Some Summers. Lux.
Three Songs. Beaumont.
Thrice Toss These Oaken Ashes in the Air. Campion.
Thy Heart. *Anonymous.*
To a Lady on Her Passion for Old China. Gay.
To His Child. Bullokar.
To Mary. Cowper.
Treat the Woman Tenderly, Tenderly. *Anonymous.*
Tree Ferns. Plumly.
Turner's Camp on the Chippewa. *Anonymous.*
The Turning of the Leaves. Watkins.
Two Hangovers. Wright.
Two Solitudes. Ames.
Untitled: "Words do not grow on the landscape." Malley.
Visionary Oklahoma Sunday Beer. Whitehead.
Whist. Ware.
Who Walks with Beauty. Morton.
The Window. Creeley.
Woman Guard. Aguila.
Words for Love. Berrigan.
The Wyoming Massacre. Terry.

Breakfast
Adversaries. Johnson.
Anemones for Miss Austen. Bergonzi.
The Avenues. St. John.
The Battle of Muskingum. Safford.
Breakfast. Gibson.
The Chickens. *Anonymous.*
City without Walls. Auden.
The Fastidious Serpent. Johnstone.
Goodnight. Ciardi.
Hello, Girls (with music). *Anonymous.*
Invitation. Behn.
Little Gustava. Thaxter.
Little Lad. *Anonymous.*
Niagara Falls Nocturne. Gasparini.
Peter Stuyvesant's New Year's Call. Stedman.
The Reading Lesson. Murphy.
The Turkey and the Ant. Gay.
The Wounded Breakfast. Edson.

Breast (s)
Above the Arno. Swenson.
All-Knowing Lamp. *Anonymous.*
Alternatives. Amis.
Amoretti, XXVIII. Spenser.
The Amphora. Sologub.
The Art of Love: Life Is Full of Horrors and Hormones. Koch.
A Ballad of Andrew and Maudlin. *Anonymous.*
Boys and Sport. Solon.
Breakers over the Sea. *Anonymous.*
Calamity Jane Greets Her Dreams. Lignell.
Calm as the Cloudless Heaven. Wilson.
Canada. Roberts.

Chilled by the Blasts of Adverse Fate. Duche.
Christ and the Soul. John of the Cross.
Colonial Nomenclature. Lang.
The Colours of Love. Devlin.
Confession. Hayes.
Conversion. Hewitt.
Crimson Nor Yellow Roses. Wratislaw.
The Cross of Gold. Gray.
Dark Was the Night. *Anonymous.*
The Dead Horse. Meireles.
Dream Songs. Berryman.
The Dreamers. Garrison.
The Dying Ranger. *Anonymous.*
Easter Song. Leslie.
Eliza. Darwin.
Elm Fuck Poem. Sanders.
Epigram: "Would I were air that thou with heat opprest." Stanley.
Epitaph of a Stripper. Smith.
The Falls. Reeve.
Fawnia. Greene.
The Flight in the Desert. Everson.
For Chicle & Justina. Bickston.
Fracture of Light: Song in the Cold Season. Morse.
The Gardener. Housman.
Gates and Doors. Kilmer.
Gita Govinda. Jayadeva.
God's Grandeur. Hopkins.
God's Will. Howells.
The Guest. Saarikoski.
Halflives. Hoffman.
He Hears the Cry of the Sedge. Yeats.
The House of Colour. Sherman.
Hymn to the Sun. Percy.
I Am Long Weaned. Antoninus.
I Flung Me Round Him. Noel.
I Once Lov'd a Boy. *Anonymous.*
If my nipples were to drip milk. Sappho.
In the Night of the Full Moon. Busse.
Inanna and the Divine Essences. Enheduanna.
The Injured Moon. Baudelaire.
The Invitation (abridged). Owen.
The Kingfisher. Kelly.
Larch Tree. Lee.
Laura. Tofte.
Living in Sin. Clarke.
London City (B vers. with music). *Anonymous.*
Love Laughs at Winter. *Anonymous.*
Love Song. *Anonymous.*
Mad Marjory. McCrae.
Malcolm's Katie. Crawford.
Marriage. Moore.
A Miner Coming Home One Night. *Anonymous.*
The Miracle. Dowling.
The Mistress (excerpt). Rochester.
The Moon and the Night and the Men. Berryman.

Morality. Arnold.
My Mother. McKay.
Mythological Sonnet XVI. Fuller.
Nature. Vigny.
Nocturne. Burr.
Nothing More Will Happen. Piercy.
The Numbers. Oppenheimer.
On His Lady's Waking. Ronsard.
On the Death of a New Born Child. Mei Yao Ch'en.
The Orange Bough. Hemans.
Our March. Mayakovsky.
Pandosto: In Praise of his Loving and Best-Beloved Fawnia. Greene.
Peace. Calverley.
Peace. Longley.
Pears. Pastan.
Place Me under Your Wing. Bialik.
Please keep an eye on my house for a few moments. Vidya.
Le Repos en Egypte. Repplier.
Rhodanthe. Agathias.
Sadness. Guest.
Saint Ita's Fosterling. Ita.
San Francisco. Roberts.
The Sea Danceth. Davies.
Sequence for a Young Widow Passing. Munro.
Sibyl of the Waters. Fainlight.
A Sigh. Spofford.
Sister. "Mistral.
Sister Pharaoh. Whitman.
The Sleeper. Hume.
Smile at Me. Farhi.
A Song About Singing. Aldrich.
Song: "If you love God, take your mirror between your hands and look. Djellaladin Pasha.
Songs of the Sea-Children. Carman.
Sonnet: "My God, where is that ancient heat towards thee." Herbert.
The Splendid Lover. Moreland.
Spring is short. Yosano Akiko.
The Storm. Herbert.
Summoned. O Hehir.
Sunrise at Sea. Swinburne.
Therefore I Must Tell the Truth. Torlino.
The Thousand and One Nights: Inscription at the City of Brass. *Anonymous.*
Three Seasons. Sparshott.
To Hope. Williams.
To the Moon. Goethe.
The Tombe. Stanley.
Upon the Nipples of Julia's Breast. Herrick.
Ward Two. Webb.
When My Beloved Sleeping Lies. McLeod.
When to My Serene Body. Laughton.
The Whummil Bore. *Anonymous.*
The Windmill. Longfellow.
The Wisconsin Soldier Boy. *Anonymous.*

Woman. Layton.
Year of the Bird. Swann.
The Zulu Girl. Campbell.

Breath (e) (s) (ing)
The Abandoned. Symons.
And with March a Decade in Bolinas. Kyger.
Annales: "Like a shower of rain." Ennius.
The Annunciation. Merwin.
April Moment. Ficke.
As Life What Is So Sweet? Anonymous.
Autumn Song. Tieck.
Barter. Teasdale.
Becoming a Frog. Jones.
The Bellows Maker of Oxford. Hoskyns.
The Belly Dancer in the Nursing Home. Wallace.
A Birthday Poem: for Rachel. Simmons.
Blue Hills Beneath the Haze. Whiting.
Blue Moles. Plath.
Branch of the Sweet and Early Rose. Drennan.
Brand Fire New Whaling Song Right from the Pacific Ocean. *Anonymous.*
A Breath. De Vere.
Breath. Strand.
Breath of Hampstead Heath. Thomas.
Bright Star (Original version). Keats.
Burial. Francis.
But Two There Are... Day-Lewis.
Caelica, LXXXVII. Greville.
Chanting the Square Deific. Whitman.
Child. MacIntyre.
The Children of Stare. De la Mare.
Chinese Baby Asleep. Donnelly.
Collapsible. Raworth.
Come Holy Spirit, Dove Divine. Judson.
Contact. Livesay.
Curtains for a Spinster. Kerr.
Davening. Ratner.
A Day in My Union Suit. Pettit.
The Day Lady Died. O'Hara.
The Death of Marilyn Monroe. Olds.
Death of the Day. Landor.
Death Was a Woman. Russell.
Definition. Sarton.
Definitions of the Word Gout. Koyama.
Dialogue 4 1 Voice Only. Fetherling.
Dream Songs. Berryman.
Dryad Song. Fuller.
Eating Bamboo-Shoots. Po Chu-i.
Elegy. Layzer.
The End of the Parade. Williams.
Epigram: "Would I were air that thou with heat opprest." Stanley.
Epitaphs of the War. Kipling.
Europe. Ashbery.
Faith. Wilcox.

False Enchantment.
Untermeyer.
Fame Makes Us Forward.
Herrick.
The Farewell. *Anonymous.*
Fill a Glass with Golden
Wine. Henley.
Finis. Thomson.
Fire. Harjo.
The Fishermen. Whittier.
Flowers and Men.
Lawrence.
A Football-Player. Lefroy.
For My Daughter. Ochester.
Frau Bauman, Frau Schmidt,
and Frau Schwartze.
Roethke.
From the Dust. Dallman.
Full Fathom Five. Plath.
Gasco; or, The Toad. Grass.
The Golden Age.
Anonymous.
The Good Hour. Driscoll.
Grandpa's .45. Ransom.
Great God, How Frail a
Thing Is Man. Byles.
Growing Together. Oates.
Had I the Choice. Whitman.
Haiku: "That silver balloon."
Phillips.
The Hand. Feldman.
Hare-Hunting. Somervile.
The Harvest. Aberg.
The Heart of the Woman.
Yeats.
Her Dead Brother. Lowell.
Heron Weather. Crase.
Herons. Blaser.
Hogyn. *Anonymous.*
How My Father Died.
Ezekiel.
The Hurrier. Monro.
Hush, Hush. Leib.
In a Corner of Eden... Levi.
In Impressions of Hawk
Feathers Willow Leaves
Shadow. Woody.
In Our Boat. Craik.
In Praise of a Gentlewoman.
Gascoigne.
In the Dark. Bushnell.
In the House of the Judge.
Smith.
Insomnia. Piercy.
The Invitation in It. Boyle.
Ireland Weeping. Livingston.
Kentucky Moonshiner.
Anonymous.
The King's Highway.
McGroarty.
Kol Nidra. Leiser.
Lapidary. Alexander.
The Last Bus (parody).
Knox ("Evoe").
Life and Death. Perry.
Like as the swan towards her
death. Wyatt.
The Lilies. Berry.
Love. Tieck.
Love's Caution. Davies.
Love's Justification.
Michelangelo.
A Lover's Lament.
Anonymous.
Maker of Songs. Hall.
The Makers. Nemerov.
Man's Anxious, but
Ineffectual Guard Against
Death. Beddoes.
The Man under the Bed.
Jong.
Manong Benny. Cerenio.

Martha Blake at Fifty-One.
Clarke.
Maryland, My Maryland.
Randall.
A Matter of Life and Death.
Aldridge.
Meditation. Rakosi.
Memorandum / The
Accountant's Notebook.
Norris.
Memory Air. Dobzynski.
A Mock Charon. Lovelace.
A Moment of War. Lee.
Monna Innominata.
Rossetti.
Morning. Savage.
Morning Star. Ferril.
My Grandfather Dying.
Kooser.
The Mysterious Music of
Ocean. *Anonymous.*
Next Year, in Jerusalem.
Kaufman.
Night Trip across the
Chesapeake and After.
Lea.
Ode: "An idea of justice may
be precious." O'Hara.
On a Little Boy's
Endeavouring to Catch a
Snake. Foxton.
On a Valetudinarian. Ibn al-
Rumi.
On My Wife's Birth-Day.
Smart.
On the Edge of the Copper
Pit. Henson.
On the Meatwheel. Gallup.
One More Time. Goedicke.
Palace Dancer, Dancing at
Last. Green.
Parson Gray. Goldsmith.
The Party. Avison.
Passage. Roderick.
Physical Universe. Simpson.
The Pier-Glass. Graves.
Plunger. Sandburg.
Pocahontas. Morris.
Pontoosuce. Melville.
The Quarry. Miller.
The Ram. Coffin.
Reflection: After Visiting Old
Friends. Allison.
Remember Me! Haweis.
Remorse. Betjeman.
A Riddle: The Letter H.
Fanshawe.
The Rock. Merwin.
Root Cellar. Roethke.
Scarabs for the Living.
Blackmur.
Schoolgirls Hastening.
Neilson.
The Schooner Blizzard.
Anonymous.
Silex Scintillans. Vaughan.
Sleeping at the Beach. Burt.
Snowflakes. Behrend.
The Solitary. Rilke.
A Song in Time of Revolution
1860. Swinburne.
Song: "Is it dirty." O'Hara.
Song of the Three Angels.
Vicente.
Song Set by Robert Jones:
"Life is a poet's fable."
Anonymous.
Song to Death. Escriva.
Sonnet in a Garden.
Peabody.
Sonnet of Departure.
Hervey.

Sonnet: "There is no God, as
I was taught in youth."
Masefield.
Spring at Fort Okanogan.
Wilson.
The Stadium. Heyen.
The Struggle with the Angel.
Vigee.
Summer Rain. Read.
Swimming Pool. Horta.
Taking to the Woods.
Taylor.
Tapwater. Jensen.
Tasmania. Smith.
Testament. Hughes.
That First Gulp of Air We
All Took When First Born.
Paddock.
The Third Dimension.
Levertov.
Thistledown. Merrill.
To France. Chaplin.
To W.J.M. G.
The Tourist and the Town.
Rich.
Tramp! Tramp! Tramp!
Root.
Trembling. Shenhar.
The Triumphs of Owen.
Gray.
Tune Thou My Harp.
Carmichael.
Two Fusiliers. Graves.
A Typical 6:00 P.M. in the
Fun House. Berrigan.
Under the Locust Blossoms.
Tuckerman.
The Unquiet Grave.
Anonymous.
The Vacant Chair. Root.
George F.
Valentine. Summers.
Van Elsen. Scott.
Variation on a Theme by John
Lyly. Sitwell.
Veni Creator. Carman.
Waterfalls. Watkins.
We Are Leaning Away.
Harvey.
What the Bones Know.
Kizer.
When I went into my garden.
Bertken.
The Wind Blows.
MacDonagh.
The Wind, the Clock, the We.
Riding.
Winter Night. Coxe.
Woman in an Abandoned
House. Bily-Hurd.
Yeats in Dublin (excerpt).
Watkins.
Breathless
The Lady of the Lake. Scott.
The Old Adam. Benet.
Breathless million
The Race of the Oregon.
Meehan.
Breeches
Comedian. Johnson.
Don Juan. Byron.
Epitaph: "Hic jacet Tom
Shorthose." *Anonymous.*
Going into Breeches. Lamb.
The Miner's Lament.
"Twain.
The September Gale (excerpt).
Holmes.
Socrates Snooks. Ludlow.
To Mrs. Leigh Upon Her
Wedding Day. Canning.
Well I Never. *Anonymous.*

Breed (s) (ing)
49th & 5th, December 13.
Jacobsen.
America Remembers
(excerpt). Engle.
Bridge of the Carousel.
Rilke.
Carved by Obadiah Verity.
Welch.
A Christening. Davie.
Deep Down the Blackman's
Mind. Armattoe.
The English Race. Defoe.
An Excellent New Ballad
Called the Prince of
Darkness. *Anonymous.*
Farm Child. Thomas.
The Fisherman. Stuart.
Island Dogs. Bell.
Life Story. Kates.
Next, Please. Larkin.
On a Cat, Ageing. Gray.
A Pastoral. Breton.
Song: To the Masquers
Representing Stars.
Campion.
Sonnets, II: "Our doom is in
our being." Agee.
Sonnets, XII: "When I do
count the clock that tells
the time." Shakespeare.
The Supper after the Last.
Kinnell.
Tales of the Islands, VII.
Walcott.
Termites. Bell.
Breeze (s)
Adina. Telemaque.
Blow, Bugles, Blow.
McGroarty.
Breeze and Billow. Watson.
Cow. McFatter.
Diagnosis. Canan.
A flower of waves. Ise.
The gentian weaves her
fringes. Dickinson.
Glanmore Sonnets. Heaney.
Nanny's Sailor Lad.
Allingham.
The Nude Republic.
Perreault.
Stars Which See, Stars Which
Do Not See. Bell.
That's June. Butts.
Winter Life and Scenery.
Irwin.
Breign
Limerick: "A king, on
assuming his reign."
Anonymous.
Brest (s)
Amoretti, LXXVII. Spenser.
Ovid's Banquet of Sense.
Chapman.
A Song of the Passion. Rolle
of Hampole.
Upon the Death of the Lord
Hastings. Dryden.
Brethren
Robin Hood and the Beggar.
Anonymous.
To Him That Was Crucified.
Whitman.
Where Shall I Be when de
Firs' Trumpet Soun'?
Anonymous.
Brevity
Ad Leuconoen. Horace.
Paradox. Bennett.
What Is an Epigram?
Coleridge.

Brew (ing) (s)
  Beth Appleyard's Verses.
    DeVries.
  Dugall Quin (B version).
    Anonymous.
  Elementary. Tollerud.
  In Coventry. Daly.
  News! News! Farjeon.
Briar (s)
  Barbara Allen. *Anonymous.*
  Earl Brand (B vers.).
    Anonymous.
  If We Knew. Smith.
  Poem for L. C. Klappert.
Bribe (d)
  Another on the Same.
    Belloc.
  On a Replica of the
    Parthenon. Davidson.
  On the Death of the Lord
    Treasurer. Anonymous.
  Unhappy Boston. Revere.
Brick (s)
  Anniversary. Wain.
  Black Warrior. Jordan.
  Dublin. MacNeice.
  Medallion. Plath.
  Mrs. Mason's Basin.
    Anonymous.
  Symbolum. Goethe.
Brid (al) (es)
  Child Waters. *Anonymous.*
  The Courtship of Miles
    Standish. Longfellow.
  Evening Star. Sappho.
  Flowering Currant.
    MacDonogh.
Bridal song
  Bavarian Gentians.
    Lawrence.
  Bonny Baby Livingston (A
    version). *Anonymous.*
  The Bride. Hodgson.
  The Cage. Treinin.
  The Church's One
    Foundation. Stone.
  A Cinque Port. Davidson.
  Clarel. Melville.
  Come, O Friend, to Greet the
    Bride. Alkabez.
  The D Minor. Mayo.
  The Dirge of Kildare. De
    Vere.
  Dream Songs. Berryman.
  Dublin Bay. *Anonymous.*
  Earl Mar's Daughter.
    Anonymous.
  The First Olympionique to
    Hiero of Syracuse. Pindar.
  The Fleggit Bride.
    ""MacDiarmid.
  For the Queen Mother.
    Betjeman.
  Forepledged. Spalding.
  Geron and Histor. Sidney.
  Haiku: "For some time."
    Anonymous.
  Hero and Leander.
    Chapman.
  Hind Horn (B vers.).
    Anonymous.
  The Horse in the Drugstore.
    Gallagher.
  Hynd Horn. Anonymous.
  Hypatia (excerpt). Tollet.
  I Remember. Smith.
  Jackie Tar. *Anonymous.*
  Juanita. Norton.
  Katharine Jaffray (C version).
    Anonymous.
  Keen. Millay.

Kiss in the Ring.
  Anonymous.
A Lady Comes to an Inn.
  Coatsworth.
Leaves of Grass. Whitman
Leezie Lindsay. *Anonymous.*
The Lion's Bride. Harwood.
Malediction upon Myself.
  Wylie.
A Mammon-Marriage.
  Macdonald.
The Mariner's Bride.
  Mangan.
.Mary of the Wild Moor.
  Anonymous.
Medelwold and Sidselille.
  Anonymous.
Mr. and Mrs. Vite's Journey.
  Anonymous.
The Nobleman's Wedding.
  Allingham.
Our Lady with Two Angels.
  Childe.
The Phoenix. Nemerov.
Pleasant and Delightful.
  Anonymous.
Rabbi, Where Dwellest Thou?
  Come and See.
  Anonymous.
The Rival. Warner.
A Shropshire Lad.
  Housman.
Siena. Swinburne.
The Sleeping Beauty.
  Layzer.
Spring. Rodgers.
St. Agnes' Eve. Tennyson.
A Strappado for the Devil: Of
  Maids' Inconstancy.
  Brathwaite.
The Sun-Witch to the Sun.
  Howe.
'Tis the White Plum Tree.
  Neilson.
To Melite. Rufinus
  Domesticus.
The Turkish Lady.
  Anonymous.
The Waggon-Maker.
  Masefield.
Who? Who? *Anonymous.*
William and Mary.
  Anonymous.
Women Singing. Taylor.
The World. Vaughan.
Written in an Ovid. Prior.
Bride
  Love. Coleridge.
Bride's
  The Quakeress Bride.
    Kinney
Bridegroom
  At the Indian Killer's Grave.
    Lowell.
  The D Minor. Mayo.
  Her–"last Poems"–.
    Dickinson.
  Hind Horn (B vers.).
    Anonymous.
  Hurdy-Gurdy Man in Winter.
    Watkins.
  If They Honoured Me, Giving
    Me Their Gifts. "Field.
  Judas Iscariot. Buchanan.
  Leaves of Grass. Whitman
  A Mammon-Marriage.
    Macdonald.
  Of the Night, Let the
    Bridegroom Sing. Statius
    Publius Papinius.
  Roses. Campion.

The Sun-Witch to the Sun.
  Howe.
Whiteness. Hume.
The World. Vaughan.
Zippora Returns to Moses at
  Rephidim. Drachler.
Bridge (s)
  An Advancement of Learning.
    Heaney.
  The Airman Who Flew over
    Shakespeare's England.
    Plutzik.
  Annan Water. *Anonymous*
  The Bridge Builder.
    Dromgoole.
  A Builder's Lesson.
    O'Reilly.
  The Classical Style. Palmer.
  Don Juan. Byron.
  First Monday Scottsboro
    Alabama. Weatherly.
  Foreboding. Haines.
  Gathering the Bones Together.
    Orr.
  Grandfather. Coleman.
  Hay's Wharf. Church.
  How to Find Your Way
    Home. Petaccia.
  Interracial. Johnson.
  Lives. Reed.
  The Moment of Vision.
    Eberhart.
  Of London Bridge, and the
    Stupendous Sight, and
    Structure Thereof. Howell.
  Over the Bridge. Li Kwang-
    T'ien.
  The Poem of the End
    (excerpt). Tsvetayeva.
  Simply. Chester.
  Song of a Common Lover.
    Ranaivo.
  Three Presidents: Andrew
    Jackson. Bly.
  The Unutterable Beauty.
    Studdert-Kennedy.
  Water Picture. Swenson.
  Weldon Kees in Mexico, 1965.
    Wojahn.
Bridget
  A Ballad upon a Wedding.
    Suckling.
  The Bulge. Johnston.
  The Giveaway. McGinley.
Brief
  Anglosaxon Street. Birney.
  Brother and Sister. Eliot.
  Butterflies. Long.
  Coming across. Mehri.
  The Feast of Stephen.
    Hecht.
  Long Tom. Gibson.
  Nothing but a man. Tueni.
  Sonnets. Hillyer.
  Turn Me to My Yellow
    Leaves. Braithwaite.
  Twice Times Then Is Now.
    Ibn Hazm Al-Andalusi.
  Watch Long Enough, and
    You Will See. Aiken.
Briefcase (s)
  The Citizen. Howard.
  Man Lying on a Wall.
    Longley.
Brier
  Fair Janet. *Anonymous.*
  Topsyturvey-World. Rands.
Brigand
  He Said That He Was Not
    Our Brother. Banim.
Bright (er) (est)
  Acquaintance. Morton.

After Rain. Thomas.
An Answer to Another
  Persuading a Lady to
  Marriage. Philips.
Apology. Wordsworth.
April. Pound.
As Often as Some Where
  before My Feet. Pastorius.
Ballad of the Drinker in His
  Pub. Van Wyk Louw.
The Battle of Lovell's Pond.
  Longfellow.
Beauty and Terror. Harford.
Breath. Dickey.
The Bright Hillside. Coghill.
The Brightest of the Bright.
  O'Rahilly.
Cease, Then, My Tongue!
  Spenser.
A Conjecture. Richardson.
Coon Hunt, Sixth Month
  (1955). Lea.
Dirge. Hemans.
The Dying Child's Request.
  Gould.
Earthy Anecdote. Stevens.
Ecstasy. *Anonymous.*
The End of a War. Read.
Envying a Little Bird.
  Gregoria Francisca.
The Fair-Haired Girl.
  Anonymous.
Fairest Lord Jesus.
  Anonymous.
Farewell, Sweet Dust. Wylie.
Fits of Candor. Gallup.
The Flight of the War-Eagle.
  Auringer.
Flowers. Longfellow.
Glen Rosa. Jeffrey.
The Glow-Worm. Smith.
Gratitude. Gluck.
Hail, Mother of the Savior.
  Adam of St. Victor.
Hollywood. Blanding.
Home Thoughts From
  Abroad. Browning.
The Horses. Muir.
The House of Peers. Gilbert.
A Hundred Years to Come.
  Brown.
A Hymn Written in Windsor
  Forest. Pope.
I Shall Not Die for Thee.
  Hyde.
Jeanie with the Light Brown
  Hair. Foster.
The Joy of a Singer.
  Piuvkaq.
July the First. Currie.
Last Plea. Untermeyer.
Limerick: "An ostrich who
  lived at the zoo."
  Anonymous.
Limerick: "I'm bored to
  extinction with Harrison."
  Anonymous.
March. Bryant.
May. *Anonymous.*
Mock On, Mock On, Voltaire,
  Rousseau. Blake.
My Cheap Lifestyle. Myles.
My Thought Was on a Maid
  So Bright. *Anonymous.*
Nightfall in Inishtrahull.
  O'Sullivan.
North Philadelphia, Trenton,
  and New York. Lattimore.
North Wind in October.
  Bridges.
Of His Majesties Receiving
  the News of the Duke of

Buckingham's Death.
Waller.
On the Fifth Anniversary of
Bluma Sach's Death.
D'Ambrosio.
Peace. De la Mare.
Peachstone. Abse.
The Sea Birds. Brock.
Shadows of Chrysanthemums.
Scovell.
She Was a Phantom of
Delight. Wordsworth.
Sonnet XIV: "Although I cry
and though my eyes still
shed." Labe.
Sonnet Written after Seeing
Wilton-House. Warton,
Jr..
Sonnets, CXLVII: "My love is
as a feaver longing still."
Shakespeare.
Starlight. Meredith.
Summer. Wilson.
Three Poems for the Indian
Steelworkers in a Bar...
Bruchac.
Time Lags Abed. Cresswell.
Unless. Glynes.
Voluspo. *Anonymous.*
Voyage to the Moon.
MacLeish.
The Warrior to His Dead
Bride. Procter.
The Water-Drinker.
Johnson.
The Waterfall. Vaughan.
The Way of Pain. Berry.
A Wet August. Hardy.
When Last Seen. Flexner.
The World's Great Age
Begins Anew. Shelley.
Ye Golden Lamps of Heaven.
Doddridge.

Brightness
Amoretti, LXXXVIII.
Spenser.
Cinderella. Pickard.
The Class. Jacobsen.
A Coast View (excerpt).
Harpur.
The Dome of Sunday.
Shapiro.
Invocation before the Rice
Harvest. *Anonymous.*
On a Puppy. Feng Chih.
Patterns. Setterberg.
Reflection. Turner.
Requiem. Fearing.
Snow. Malouf.
Tour 5. Hayden.
Twelfth Night. Scupham.
Vigil. Knoll.
With the Face. Riding.

Brilliance
Autumn Change. Clare.
Cottage Street, 1953.
Wilbur.
Election Time (parody).
Anonymous.
Exodus. Oppen.
How many wise men and
heroes. Ch'iu Chin.
Lake Chemo. Rowe.
Little Light. Brodey.
The Moon. Bhasa.
Pathedy of Manners. Kay.
To the Muse. Whalen.
The Weather of the World.
Nemerov.

Brimstone
Contempt for the World, III.
Bernard de Morlas.

My Uncle Jehoshaphat.
Richards.
Brine
Columbus Goes West. Hart-
Smith.
The Court of Neptune.
Hughes.
Indifference. *Anonymous.*
On the Croun o Bidean.
Annand.
A Shadow Boat. Bates.
Sonnets, VIII: "The apples
ripen under yellowing
leaves. Irwin.
Voyage. Miles.
Where Avalanches Wail.
Anonymous.
Bring (ing) (s)
Abstinence. Rosen.
Ah Me, If I Grew Sweet to
Man. "Field.
Berkeley, Madison, Ann
Arbor, Kent... Stafford.
Bringing in the Sheaves.
Anonymous.
Childe Harold's Pilgrimage:
Canto III. Byron.
The Dissenters' Thanksgiving
for the Late Declaration.
Anonymous.
Do Not Think. Freeman.
Donald. Abbey.
The Donibristle Moss Moran
Disaster. *Anonymous.*
The Egg. Bowering.
Elegy Written in a Country
Coal-Bin. Morley.
Fain Would I Wed a Fair
Young Man. Campion.
The Farm-Woman's Winter.
Hardy.
First Flight. Hoffman.
A Friend. Johnson.
Goll Mac Morna Parts from
his Wife. *Anonymous.*
The Guerrilla. Frelimo.
The Invitation. Herrick.
Large Bad Picture. Bishop.
Lent. Rodgers.
The Line-Gang. Frost.
The Little Road. Turner.
Manos Karastefanis. Merrill.
Moon Song. Nweke.
The Mufaddaliyat: His Camel.
Alqamah.
Music and Memory. Albee.
The Mystery. Whiting.
On the Tombs in Westminster
Abbey. Beaumont.
Orchard. Doolittle.
Peasant. Merwin.
Pilgrim at Rome.
Anonymous.
Selah. Thomas.
Shepheards Sirena: Song to
Sirena. Drayton.
Ships at Sea. Gray.
Song: "If once I could gather
in song." Gibson.
Star of the East. Field.
Sun Song. Hughes.
There Were Ninety and Nine.
Clephane.
Thinking of "The Autumn
Fields." Bly.
To Be Quicker... Lee.
Vox Humana. Gunn.
Women of My Land.
Armstrong.
Brink
Piano Recital. Deutsch.
The Precipice. Tabb.

Bristle
Cupid's Darts. Herbert.
Britain
.The Alliterative Morte
Arthur. *Anonymous.*
The Anchorsmiths. Dibdin.
Andrew Rose. *Anonymous.*
The Art of Making Puddings.
King.
Australasia (excerpt).
Wentworth.
The Bold Dragoon.
Anonymous.
The Book of Merlin. Spicer.
Britannia's Baby. Lawrence.
The British Grenadier.
Anonymous.
Chesapeake and Shannon.
Anonymous.
Cornwallis's Surrender.
Anonymous.
Epigram: "With favour and
fortune fastidiously blest."
Swift.
The Four Dears. Elliott.
From the Caledonian
Mercury. Wilson.
The Great Brown Owl.
Browne (Aunt Effie).
The Horse and His Rider.
Baillie.
The House of Peers. Gilbert.
Instructions to a Painter.
Waller.
Intercessors. Clarke.
Jacob's Well. *Anonymous.*
Limerick: "There was a young
man who was bitten."
Parke.
The Little Boats of Britain.
Carsley.
Louisburg. *Anonymous.*
M'Fingal. Trumbull.
Macaulay at Tea. Pain.
The Neutral British
Gentleman. Newell.
Observing a Vulgar Name on
the Plinth of an Ancient
Statue. Landor.
Ode I. To Fancy. Warton.
Ode to Pity. Collins.
Odes. Horace.
The Old Chartist. Meredith.
Pennsylvania Song.
Anonymous.
Poems, II. O'Connor.
The Poets at Tea. Pain.
Political Intelligence. Smith.
Salem. Lowell.
Second of August.
Anonymous.
Slaves Cannot Breathe in
England. Cowper.
A Song About Charleston.
Anonymous.
Song of the Factory Girls.
Anonymous.
Take It from Me. Hanson.
To Signora Cuzzoni. Philips.
Wanting Out. Ewart.
Brittle
Decoration Day. Sinclair.
Homework for Annabelle.
McGinley.
Power. Prior.
Solomon on the Vanity of the
World. Prior.
Brittle bone
Cycle. Jennett.
Broad
In Memoriam Rev. J. J.
Lyons. Lazarus.

A Note on Master Crow.
Garrigue.
Romance. Stevenson.
To John Donne. Jonson.
Broadcast
Sonnet on a Somewhat
Inferior Radio Outfit.
Ross.
Broadcloth
In Good Old Colony Times.
Anonymous.
Broadway
Forty-Five Minutes from
Broadway. Cohan.
Give My Regards to
Broadway. Cohan.
In the Gazebo (parody).
Appleman.
Brogue (s)
I Stroll. Redgrove.
Nora. Shorter.
Broke (n)
Advice to Julia. Luttrell.
Afterglow. Borges.
Alabama Earth. Hughes.
The Angel and the Anchorite.
Shelton.
Antony and Cleopatra.
Coulette.
Aurelia. Nichols.
Broken Bodies. Golding.
Calumny. Osgood
Castles in the Air.
Ballantine.
The Cause of This I Know
Not. Long.
Children's Runes and Omens.
Anonymous.
Christus Triumphans.
Pallen.
The City of Satisfaction.
Hoffman.
Complaint of a Young Girl.
Wang Chung-ju.
The Condemned. Jabes.
The Contrite Heart. Cowper.
Conversations between Here
and Home. Harjo.
The Couple. Blandiana.
Dark Thoughts Are My
Companions.
Cunningham.
Dear Old Girl. Buck.
Dearest, Do Not You Delay
Me. Fletcher.
The Edge. Bowen.
Epitaph for G. B. Shaw.
Beerbohm.
Fair Ines. Hood.
For a Winnebago Brave.
Bruchac.
The Forced Bridal.
Anonymous.
The Fowler. Gibson.
Fragment of a Pastoral.
Schwabsky.
Garcia Lorca. Dudek.
Hart Crane. Creeley.
Hearing Russian Spoken.
Davie.
The House with Nobody in It.
Kilmer.
How Did It Seem to Sylvia?
Schnackenberg.
Hunger. Davies.
I Dreamed Last Night of My
True Love (with music).
Anonymous.
I Have Come to the
Conclusion. Fertig.
Icicles. Pinsky.

In the Face of Grief. Juana Ines de la Cruz.
A Jacobite's Epitaph. Macaulay.
Johnny. Rounds.
King Harald's Trance. Meredith.
Land-Fall. Brady.
Letter from the Street. Brush.
Limerick: "I must eat an apple," said Link." Blair.
Limerick: "There was a young man at St. Kitts." *Anonymous.*
Lincoln, Come Back. Clark.
Little Sparrow (Come All You Young and Handsome Ladies). *Anonymous.*
Love-Songs, At Once Tender and Informative. Hoffenstein.
The Lyre. Darley.
The Maid of Neidpath. Scott.
The Midnight Court. Merriman.
More Than. Fitzpatrick.
The Muscovy Drake. Lesoro.
My Dark Fathers. Kennelly.
My Love Is Playing... *Anonymous.*
No Cold Approach. Burns.
Nocturne of the Wharves. Bontemps.
On Off'rings. Quarles.
On the Margins of a Poem. Langer.
One by One. Procter.
Passage. Crane.
Penelope, for Her Ulysses' Sake. Spenser.
Piccadilly. Burke.
Playing Catch. Moul.
Poet's Lament on the Death of His Wife. Ugaas.
Poor Dear Grandpapa. Thompson.
Praise. Daley.
Prayer for Song. Noble.
Prince Heathen (B version). *Anonymous.*
The Princess and the Gypsies. Cornford.
R. I. P. Struther.
A Raccoon. Fox.
Radio. Tessimond.
Refuge. Lampman.
Restricted. Waddington.
Sitalkas. Doolittle.
Skyhook. Kizer.
The Slave's Dream. Longfellow.
Slievenamon. *Anonymous.*
Song: "I placed my dream in a boat." Meireles.
A Song of Autumn. Rodd.
The Song of the Ghost. Graves.
Spring Offensive, 1941. Biggs.
The Statue. Fuller.
Stone. Chayat.
Sunday on Hampstead Heath. Woodcock.
Sympathy. Bronte.
Text. Wurdemann.
There's No Place to Sleep in This Bed, Tanguy. Ford.
Threnody. Hayes.

The Thrush in February. Meredith.
'Tis but a Little Faded Flower. Howarth.
Tolerance. Hardy.
Two Figures. Peacock.
Two Horses. Harjo.
Upon Ford's Two Tragedies... Crashaw.
Van Dieman's Land. *Anonymous.*
Vases. Reed.
War in Chang-An City. Wang Tsan.

Bronco
Blood on the Saddle. *Anonymous.*
Bucking Bronco. *Anonymous.*
The Crooked Trail to Holbrook. *Anonymous.*
The Journey. Johnson.
Killer. *Anonymous.*

Bronze
The Alchemist. Church.
Dance of the Macabre Mice. Stevens.
A Different Image. Randall.
Fishnet. Lowell.
Further Instructions. O'Sullivan.
Hans Christian Andersen in Central Park. Sobiloff.
My Father Dreams of Baseball. Lieberman.
The Sense of the Sleight-of-Hand Man. Stevens.
The Skaian Gate (excerpt). Scott.

Brood (es) (ing) (s)
Autumn, Dark Wanderer. Daryush.
The City of Dreadful Night. Thomson.
Continuum. Levertov.
Endymion. Keats.
The Epicure Sung by One in the Habit of a Town Gallant. Jordan.
Georgics. Virgil (Publius Vergilius Maro).
In Memoriam A.H.H., XXI. Tennyson.
Lament, with Flesh and Blood. McPherson.
A Man's Sliding Mood. Fullerton.
May, 1840. Coleridge.
My Arkansas. Angelou.
Nicholas Nye. De La Mare.
Ode to Naples (excerpt). Shelley.
Peace. Hopkins.
The Pity of It. Hardy.
Poor Me. *Anonymous.*
Snow Storm. Tu Fu.
The Swan. Rodgers.
Tom on the Beach. Bruce.
Verses Occasioned by the Sudden Drying up...(excerpt). Swift.

Brook (s)
And of Laughter That Was a Changeling. Rendall.
The Biglow Papers. Lowell.
Cape Breton. Bishop.
Cinderella. Pickard.
Echoes from the Sabine Farm. Field.
Father and I in the Woods. McCord.
Fishing. Wordsworth.

From the Flats. Lanier.
Grandser. Brown.
Hope (excerpt). Shenstone.
Louisa. Wordsworth.
March 8, 1840. Thoreau.
Multitudinous Stars. "Ping Hsin" (Hsieh Wang-ying).
None Other Fame Mine Unambitious Muse. Daniel.
The Ocean. Moschus.
The Parting. Sappho.
Retrospect. Robinson.
Sleeping Beauty. Wylie.
Spring in Hiding. Frost.
Summer Rain. Coleridge.
To the Fountain of Bandusia. Horace.
Whither? Muller.

Brooklyn
East Hampton: The Structure of Sound. Appleman.
The Hour of Feeling. Simpson.
Invitation to Miss Marianne Moore. Bishop.
Limerick: "There was a young fellow from Boise." Straley.
The Toad. Locklin.

Broom (s)
Ballad with an Ancient Refrain. *Anonymous.*
Broom, Green Broom. *Anonymous.*
The Chimney Sweeper. *Anonymous.*
The Floor Is Dirty. Field.
Green Broom. *Anonymous.*
Halloween Witches. Holman.
The Lady of the Lake. Scott.
The Limited. Warren.
Minnie and Mrs. Hoyne. Fearing.
Reincarnation. Jackson.
The Widow's Old Broom. *Anonymous.*
Witchwood. Justus.

Broomstick (s)
The Air Vision. Hoddis.
Five Visions of Captain Cook. Slessor.

Brother (s)
Abel. Capetanakis.
Absolution. Sassoon.
And What Shall You Say? Cotter.
Archie O Cawfield (A vers.). *Anonymous.*
As He Lay Dying. Stow.
A Ballad of Francois Villon. Swinburne.
Behold the Sea. Kurtz.
Billy's Rose. Sims.
Boston in Distress. *Anonymous.*
Brotherhood. "W.
Brotherhood (excerpt). Morris.
The Brothers. Muir.
Bugger Burns. *Anonymous.*
Care Is Heavy. O'Riordan.
A Catch by the Hearth. *Anonymous.*
Challenge. Clark.
The Child's First Grief. Hemans.
Christopher Street Liberation Day, June 28, 1970. Winant.
Cole Younger. *Anonymous.*

Cuckoo, Cherry Tree. *Anonymous.*
Dark Testament. Murray.
Death of a Ram. Sedulius Scottus.
Drum-Taps. Whitman.
Dunlavin Green. *Anonymous.*
The Early Morning. Belloc.
Family Fortunes. Sisson.
Festal Song. Merrill.
Five for the Grace. Scott.
For a' That and a' That. Burns.
For You, My Son. Gregory.
Four Children. *Anonymous.*
Give Me Five. Harris.
The God-maker, Man. Marquis.
Grass. Webster.
He Is My Countryman. Slonimski.
A Helping Hand. Adams.
The House of Life. Rossetti.
Hymn for Nations. *Anonymous.*
Hymn of the Alamo. Potter.
I Stood in Jerusalem. Zelda.
I Stood Upon a High Place. Crane.
I Wonder What Became of Rand, McNally... Levy.
In the Mood of Blake. Soutar.
The Incarnation. Wesley.
Incense. Lindsay.
Inner Brother. Stepanchev.
Into the Dark. Monette.
Ireland 1972. Durcan.
A Joyful Noise. Finkel.
The Lament for Urien. Rhys.
The Merchant of Venice. Shakespeare.
Mother of Man. Parun.
A Mountain Wind. Russell.
My Brother. Frelimo.
The New Jewish Hospital at Hamburg. Heine.
The Odyssey. Homer.
On a Contentious Companion. Hoskyns.
On the Apparition of Oneself. Burford.
The Orphan. *Anonymous.*
Our Lives. Scott.
Over Their Graves. Stockard.
A Paragraph. Carruth.
A Parody on A Psalm of Life. Holmes.
Psalm of Those Who Go Forth before Daylight. Sandburg.
Random Generation of English Sentences; or, The Revenge of the Poets. Smith.
The Rooftree. Tate.
The Search. Crosby.
The Second Angel. Levine.
Serve Her Right. Barford.
Shechem. Shevin.
Song: "Had I a heart for falsehood fram'd." Sheridan.
The Soul of Man. Goodale.
The Sphere of Glass. Lehmann.
St. Francis of Assisi and the Miserable Jews. Wittlin.

Tales of a Wayside Inn.
Longfellow.
Talmudist. Burnshaw.
Tenebris Interlucentem.
Flecker.
This Holy Night. Farjeon.
Those Rebel Flags. Jewett.
To a Blossoming Pear Tree.
Wright.
To the Lighted Lady Window.
Wilkinson.
To the Reader. Baudelaire.
Tracking Rabbits: Night.
Barnes.
Venom. Dickey.
The Vow. Hecht.
The Way, the Truth, and the
Life. Parker.
When Thy Heart with Joy
O'erflowing. Williams.

Brotherhood
America the Beautiful.
Bates.
The Bells of Peace. Fisher.
Bread of Brotherhood.
Trent.
Brotherhood. Markham.
Day Dawn of the Heart.
Anonymous.
In the City. Zangwill.
Man, Not His Arms.
Rodman.
The New Trinity. Markham.
Not Alone for Mighty
Empire. Merrill.
On a World War Battlefield.
Clark.
Resurgence. Everett.
There Is So Much of
Loneliness. *Anonymous.*
True Brotherhood. Wilcox.
Your Glory, Lincoln.
Goodman.

Brow (s)
Anacreon to the Sophist.
"H.
Canada. Roberts.
Eternal. Macdonald.
The Islands of the Ever
Living. *Anonymous.*
Now, If You Will Look in My
Brain. Villa.
Pain in All Love. Patmore.
Questing. Spencer.
Sandy Star. Braithwaite.
Shakespeare. Arnold.
She Wore a Wreath of Roses.
Bayly.
Testament. Sister M.
Therese.
To Mackinnon of Strath.
Lom.
To Memory. Coleridge.
Two Songs in Praise of
Steingerd, 1.
Ogmundarson.
Uprising See the Fitful Lark.
Anonymous.
The Welcome to Sack.
Herrick.
Why the Robin's Breast Was
Red. Randall.
With Long Black Wings.
Stickney.
Words for a Resurrection.
Kennedy.

Brown
All Jolly Fellows That Follow
the Plow. *Anonymous.*
Baby Seed Song. Nesbit.
Barbecue Blues. Hicks.
A Black Pierrot. Hughes.

Brown-Eyed Lee.
Anonymous.
The Cat. Baudelaire.
Chock House Blues.
Jefferson.
Civilization. Schmidt.
College Formal: Renaissance
Casino. Hughes.
Coming Events. Montague.
Drifting. O'Donnell.
Drilling in Russell Square.
Shanks.
The Dying Cowboy of Rim
Rock Ranch. *Anonymous.*
Ego's Dream. Kreymborg.
Epitaph. Nathan.
Fair Ellender. *Anonymous.*
The Folly of Brown. Gilbert.
Harlem Sweeties. Hughes.
Idyll. Webb.
In These Dissenting Times.
Walker.
January. Dutton.
January. Hass.
John Watts. *Anonymous.*
Kansas Boys. *Anonymous.*
Lamia. Keats.
Landscape as a Nude.
MacLeish.
Leaving. Hogan.
Little Brown Baby. Dunbar.
Lord Thomas and Fair
Ellender. *Anonymous.*
March. Webb.
My Country. Mackellar.
Nature. Vigny.
Nature Morte. MacNeice.
Old Fence Post. Hanes.
Omnia Vincit. Cochrane.
On a Lute Found in a
Sarcophagus. Gosse.
Poems, VI. O'Connor.
Queen Anne. *Anonymous.*
Reply to the Provinces.
Kinnell.
Separation. Arnold.
Sonnet: "Say what you will."
Millay.
Spinners at Willowsleigh.
Zaturenska.
Visionary Oklahoma Sunday
Beer. Whitehead.
When I Loved You.
Wagner.
Winter Feast. Frost.
A Winter Twilight. Grimke.

Browse
A Dream of Burial. Wright.
Evening before Rain. Strong.
Somnambulistic Ballad.
Garcia Lorca.

Bruise (ed) (s)
The Bird in the Room.
Lehmann.
Black Fear. Woody.
The Cruel Falcon. Jeffers.
The Dandy Horse.
Anonymous.
Epilogue. Levertov.
The Horse in the Drugstore.
Gallagher.
Kingfisher Flat. Empson.
Monsoon. Wevill.
One Man's Goose; or, Poetry
Redefined. Starbuck.
Prisoner of War. Lutz.
Pussycat Sits on a Chair.
Horn.
Recollection. Donnelly.
The Reed. Carpenter.
Simon the Cyrenian Speaks.
Cullen.

Sorrow's Ladder. Callaghan.
The Tough Ones. Miller.
Under the Edge of February.
Cortez.

Brunette
Writing on Napkins at the
Sunshine Club Macon,
Georgia 1971. Bottoms.

Brush (ed)
Before the Ikon of the Mother
of God. Constantine of
Rhodes.
Birdwatcher. Treece.
A Charge to the Poets
(excerpt). Whitehead.
A Flemish Madonna. Stork.
Grandpa's .45. Ransom.
Hippocrene. Lowell.
Mama and Daughter.
Hughes.
Poem. Dickinson.
Sailing Homeward. Chan
Fang-sheng.
Thaw. Broughton.
You on the Tower. Hardy.

Brute (s)
Callypso Speaks. Doolittle.
The Caulker. Lewis.
The Cunning Cobbler Done
Over. Anonymous.
Dream Songs. Berryman.
Eden's Courtesy. Lewis.
El Ropero. Montoro.
Epitaph on Dr. Johnson.
Jenyns.
The Monarch. Cowper.
The Naming of the Beasts.
Sparshott.
The Painter in the Lion Cage.
Alver.
Preludes. Patmore.
The Scorpion. Belloc.
Words and Monsters.
Scannell.

Bubble (s)
The Atlas. Slessor.
Epigram: "My soul, what's
lighter than a feather?
Wind." Quarles.
Ezra Shank. *Anonymous.*
The Glass Bubbles.
Greenberg.
Lake Superior. Goodrich.
Look. Stafford.
Poem at Equinox. Corke.
Shoes Are Made to Fit the
Feet... *Anonymous.*

Buccaneer
The Last Buccaneer.
Macaulay.
Paul Jones. *Anonymous.*
The Tarry Buccaneer.
Masefield.

Bucket
Among Blackberries.
Waters.
Bucket in the Well. Wanek.
Fairy Tales. Flanders.
In the Orpheum Building.
Robinson.
The Old Oaken Bucket.
Woodworth.

Buckles
Chicago Allegory. Parker.
The Old Men. Corman.

Bud (s)
The Beast That Rode the
Unicorn. Meyer.
A Child's Thought of Harvest.
"Coolidge.
Do Not Ask. Lavant.
The Dynasts. Hardy.

The Express. Spender.
I Know a Flower So Fair and
Fine. Grundtvig.
Imitation of Spenser. Keats.
Love Is a Law. *Anonymous.*
Love's Pains. Clare.
Mimma Bella. Lee-
Hamilton.
Out There Somewhere.
Knibbs.
Purple Dry Buds. Roberts.
A Rose. Fanshawe.
A Scandal Among the
Flowers. Taylor.
Seeds. Snyder.
Sequence. Barker.
A Song. Schwartz.
Spring (excerpt). Miller.
Spring in Hiding. Frost.
A Spring Memorandum.
Duncan.

Buddha
Portrait of an Artist. Howes.
Proofs of Buddha's Existence.
Anonymous.
Satori. Jones.
A Short History of British
India. Hill.
Technicalities for Jack Spicer.
Whalen.
Translations from the Chinese:
Secret Thoughts. Morley.

Buffalo
Ballad of the Erie Canal.
Anonymous.
The Ballad of William
Sycamore. Benét.
Bigerlow (with music).
Anonymous.
The Bigler. *Anonymous.*
Buffalo Skinners.
Anonymous.
Caller of the Buffalo. Austin.
Containing Communism.
Cobb.
The E-RI-E. *Anonymous.*
Erie Canal. *Anonymous.*
Fort Wayne, Indiana 1964.
Lewis.
Funeral at Ansley. Welch.
Hunt the Buffalo.
Anonymous.
The Old Cowboy.
Anonymous.
Pioneers. Garland.
Shoot the Buffalo.
Anonymous.
Weep Not for a Warrior.
Mtshali.
Wilderness Sacred Wilderness.
Lamantia.
Would a circling surface
vulture. Mahadevi
(Mahadeviyakka).

Bug (s)
Ballet under the Stars.
Stewart.
Bugs. Stokes.
Money (with music).
Anonymous.
The Taming of the Shrew.
Shakespeare.
There Ain't No Bugs on Me.
Anonymous.
You All Are Static; I Alone
Am Moving. Viereck.

Buggered
Exhaustive Experimentation.
Anonymous.
To Phoebus. Martial
(Marcus Valerius Martialis).

Bugle (r) (s)
Armistice Day. Causley.
The Call of the Bugles. Hovey.
Carmina Amico. James.
Drum-Taps. Whitman.
The Lady of the Lake. Scott.
Limerick: "A bugler named Douglas MacDougal." Nash.
The Lonely Bugle Grieves. Mellen.
A New Year Carol. *Anonymous.*
On the Hill. Soutar.
The Singer of One Song. Beers.
Spring Snow and Tui. Bethell.
The Storm-Child. Byron.
Valley of the Shadow. Galsworthy.
Winter. Douglas.

Build (s)
The Axe of the Pioneer. Crawford.
The Baby. Reaney.
Before/and After... Amini.
Bonnie James Campbell. *Anonymous.*
The Builder. Giltinan.
Builder Kachina: Home-Going. Rose.
Builders. Deitz.
Easter Week. Kingsley.
Emblems of Conduct. Greenberg.
Evening Hymn in the Hovels. Adams.
The Faith Came First. Carter.
For an Age of Plastics. Plymouth. Davie.
For the Rebuilding of a House. Berry.
Forever Ambrosia. Morley.
Limerick: "There was an old lady of Harrow." *Anonymous.*
Man-Making. Markham.
The Master City. Orente.
Meditations in Time of Civil War. Yeats.
My Name Was Legion. Swift.
O God, Above the Drifting Years. Buckham.
Outside the Holy City. Gilkey.
Prayer for Kafka and Ourselves. Rudolf.
Russia. Williams.
Song: "Why do the houses stand." Macdonald.
Timber (with music). *Anonymous.*
We Shall Overcome. *Anonymous.*
Westward Ho. *Anonymous.*
Working Class. Warr.

Building (s)
Ballad of the Common Man. Kreymborg.
Beneath the Shadow of the Freeway. Cervantes.
A Brick Not Used in Building. Replansky.
The Brigade Must Not Know, Sir! *Anonymous.*
Canzone: Of His Love, with the Figure of a Sudden Storm. Prinzivalle.

The Color. Haines.
Dance with Banderillas. Duerden.
Dream Sequence, Part 9. Madgett.
The Elevated Train. Tippett.
Godiva. Tennyson.
The Great House. Muir.
Homage to the British Museum. Empson.
I Once Lov'd a Boy. *Anonymous.*
If I Had My Way. Johnson.
An Indian Summer Day on the Prairie. Lindsay.
Mr. Frost Goes South to Boston (parody). Houghton.
The Neighbor. Williams.
Quantum. Johnston.
Scaffolding. Heaney.
Service Supreme. *Anonymous.*
To Penshurst. Jonson.
Untitled Poem. "Hands folded like napkins in my lap." Peterson.
What I Saw in October. Carrier.
Winter Sketches. Reznikoff.

Bulbs
Central Park West. Spicer.
A Prayer for the New Year. Storey.
Visions. Spivack.

Bull (ies) (y)
Blow, Bullies, Blow. *Anonymous.*
Bob McKinney. Thomas.
The Bully. Rochester.
The Bully Song. Trevathan.
Lookin' for the Bully of the Town. *Anonymous.*
Mamma, Mamma. *Anonymous.*
Secret Idiom: Sanctuary. Dyment.

Bull (s)
The Bull. Wright.
Cock-Throwing! Lluellyn.
A Countryman's Wooing. Theocritus.
The Dissembler. Cowley.
The Duke of Buccleuch. Phelp.
Evening before Rain. Strong.
The First Birth. Jones.
For Little Boys Destined for Big Business. Hoffenstein.
Limerick: "There was a young lady of Hull." Lear.
Minotaur Poems. Mandel.
The Road to Hogan's Gap. Paterson.
The Search. Shaw.
Sonnet: To Dante Alighieri (He Writes to Dante...). Angiolieri.
The Spanish Girls. Arguelles.
Valley Blood. Sternlieb.
Written in Flight from His Royal Patron. Al Mutanabbi.

Bulldozer
The Bulldozer. Francis.
Bulldozers. Dec.
Dangerous Condition: Sign on Inner-City House. Atkins.

Bullet (s)
All Day It Has Rained. Lewis.

Aunt Elsie's Night Music. Oliver.
A Ballad Called the Haymarket Hectors. *Anonymous.*
The City of Beggars. Hayes.
The Devil's Dictionary: Lead. Bierce.
The Dissolution. Donne.
From My High Love. Patchen.
Inside Out. Wakoski.
A Moment of War. Lee.
A Pastoral Ballad. By John Bull. Moore.
Poem: "Come, brother, and tell me your life." Rebelo.
The Prophet's Warning; or, Shoot to Kill. Ebon.
Richard Cory. Robinson.
The Spring Waters. "Ping Hsin" (Hsieh Wang-ying).
Talking to the Townsfolk in Ideal, Georgia. Black.
The Tryst. Knox.

Bum (s)
All in June. Davies.
Decline and Fall of a Roman Umpire. Nash.
Erie Canal Ballad. *Anonymous.*
The Peasant Declares His Love. Roumer.
Shovelling Iron Ore. *Anonymous.*
The Splendid Village. Elliott.

Bumble Bee
A drunkard cannot meet a cork. Dickinson.
Meditation. Salkeld.

Bump
A Cornish Litany (excerpt). *Anonymous.*
From Ghoulies and Ghosties. *Anonymous.*
Litany for Halloween. *Anonymous.*

Bumper
Bold Adventures of Captain Ross. *Anonymous.*
My Sweetheart's the Mule in the Mines. *Anonymous.*
The Women All Tell Me. *Anonymous.*

Bundle (s)
Desert in the Sea. Swann.
Near Perigord. Pound.
Railroad to Hell. *Anonymous.*
That the Night Come. Yeats.

Bunker Hill
The Eve of Bunker Hill. Scollard.
New England: For a Celebration in Kentucky of the Landing of ... Prentice.

Burden (ed) (s)
Ad Coelum. Pattison.
As Thy Days So Shall Thy Strength Be. Holmes.
Be Still. Ayer.
The Beautiful Train. Empson.
The Burden of Everyday. Bose.
The Cry of Generations. Husid.
Dante's Angels: Gabriel. Dante Alighieri.
Footsteps. Hall.

Gravelly Run. Ammons.
The Hills of Sewanee. McClellan.
His Parting from Her. Donne.
Holy Cross. *Anonymous.*
How Gentle God's Commands. Doddridge.
In This World's Raging Sea. Drummond.
Levavi Oculos. Campbell.
Longjaunes His Periplus (excerpt). McCord.
Love Me Little, Love Me Long. *Anonymous.*
My Grace Is Sufficient for Thee. *Anonymous.*
Our Burden Bearer. Brooks.
Rhotus on Arcadia. Chalkhill.
Robin Hood. Keats.
The Rowers. Benet.
Silkweed. Savage.
Spring Mountain Climb. Eberhart.
Street Song. Sitwell.
Thought for a New Year. Burket.
To M. E. W. Chesterton.

Buri (al) (ed)
After Visiting a Home for Disturbed Children. Lipsitz.
Alison and Willie. *Anonymous.*
Always the Following Wind. Auden.
"As Eponina Brought, to Move the King." Tuckerman.
Astronomy. Housman.
At Last. Scroggie.
The Battle of Otterburn (B version). *Anonymous.*
Blue Bog Children. Weingarten.
Bonnie Annie (A version). *Anonymous.*
Bonnie Annie (B version). *Anonymous.*
Bonnie Barbara Allen (C vers.). *Anonymous.*
Bucyrus. Holmes.
Burial. Francis.
The Burial of the Dane. Brownell
Bury Me In a Free Land. Harper.
Bury Me in America. Karlen.
Canto XVI. Pound.
The Case. Norris.
Cleobulus' Epitaph. Simonides (of Ceos).
The Coble o Cargill. *Anonymous.*
Communion. Ignatow.
Cornfield Holler. *Anonymous.*
Coyote's Daylight Trip. Allen.
The Dead Man Dragged from the Sea. Gardner.
Death. Williams.
The Death of Friends. Levi.
Death Songs. *Anonymous.*
Death Valley Blues. Crudup.
Despair. Merwin.
Divination by a Daffadil. Herrick.
The Drawer. MacBeth.
A Dream. Bronte.

Elegy (excerpt). Bidart.
The Entailed Farm. Glassco.
Epigram. Butler.
An Epistle from Mr. Pope to Dr. Arbuthnot. Pope.
Epitaph for a Horseman. Hamburger.
Epitaph for the Tomb of Adolfo Baez Bone. Cardenal.
Epitaph of a Sailor. Leonidas of Tarentum
Esperanza. Scully.
Faithless Nellie Gray. Hood.
The Ferry. Boker.
Field. Griffin.
For Black Poets Who Think of Suicide. Knight.
The Fountain at the Tomb. Nicias.
Fragment. Clare.
A Gentleman of Fifty Soliloquizes. Marquis.
Georgics. Virgil (Publius Vergilius Maro).
Glen-Almain, the Narrow Glen. Wordsworth.
The Heavenly Tree Grows Downward. Lansing.
Hopi Lament. Beghtol.
The Housewife's Lament. Anonymous.
If I Felt Less. Wintchevsky.
The Iliad. Homer.
In a Staffordshire Churchyard. Anonymous.
In Missing. Young Bear.
In the Fall o' Year. Jones, Jr.
In the Garden There Strayed. Anonymous.
James Alley. Brown.
Johnny Stiles; or, The Wild Mustard River. Anonymous.
Julius Caesar. Shakespeare.
Letter to Seamus Heaney. Longley.
Limerick: "Yes, theirs was a love that was tidal." Kieffer.
Love Me and Never Leave Me. McCuaig.
A Machine Hand. Ashe.
The Martyred Earth. Milne.
Maud. Tennyson.
Medelwold and Sidselille. Anonymous.
Mosby at Hamilton. Cawein.
My Grave. Davis.
Neanderthal. Jackson.
The Ocean Burial. Anonymous.
Of Myself. Goldberg.
The Old Pines. Corman.
On Marcus the Physician. Nicarchos [(or Nicarchus)].
On Meeting a Stranger in a Bookshop. Williams.
Pat Cloherty's Version of the Maisie. Murphy.
Peggy-o. Anonymous.
A Poem for a Poet. Lorde.
Poet and Critic. Daniel.
Professor Noctutus. Macdonald.
Prospect of a Mountain. Young.
Prostration. Semah.
Rain to the Tribe. Al-Khansa.

Rehabilitative Report: We Can Still Laugh. Berrigan.
Robin Hood's Death. Anonymous.
Robin Hood's Progress to Nottingham. Anonymous.
The Secret. Stephens.
Silence Concerning an Ancient Stone. Castellânos.
Sir Hugh; or, The Jew's Daughter (A vers.). Anonymous.
The Songs of Maximus, 2. Olson.
Sonnet: "Looking into the windows that doom has broken." Woodcock.
Stopped. Polite.
Three Places Most Loved I Have Left. Cille.
To a Persistent Phantom. Horne.
To Be a Pilgrim. Conquest.
The Tombe. Stanley.
Tornado. Stafford.
The Tryst. Knox.
The Twins. Leigh.
Two Bits. Hall.
The Underground Gardens. Mezey.
The Unknown Dead. Timrod.
The Untended Field. Hillyer.
Upon the Holy Sepulchre. Crashaw.
Washington Heights, 1959. Blumenthal.
Way Over in the New Buryin' Groun' (with music). Anonymous
What the Animals Said. Serchuk.
When I Am Dead. Anonymous.

Burn (ed) (ing) (s)
Absence. Sidney.
After Emerson. Anonymous.
The Aleph Bet. Lipshitz.
Another Birthday. Jonson.
Ardor. Bradford.
Astrophel and Stella, XXII. Sidney.
Astrophel and Stella, XXV. Sidney.
At One Glance. Mihri Hatun.
August for the People. Auden.
The Auld Matrons. Anonymous.
Baucis and Philemon. Swift.
Behold This Dreamer. Bartlett.
The Break. Sargent.
Burning in the Night. Wolfe.
The Burning of Books. Brecht.
Burns and His Highland Mary. Anonymous.
Bus Stop. Justice.
Caelica, XV. Greville.
Caelica, XXXIV. Greville.
Caelica, LXXXIX. Greville.
Canto Cantare Cantavi Cantatum. Brown.
Carmina. Catullus.
Casabianca. Bishop.
Cecil County. Welburn.
Children of Light. Lowell.
Christmas Rede. Barlow.
The Cicada. Green.
Claim to Love. Guarini.

Clerihews. Bentley.
The Closed World. Levertov.
Cold. Roberts.
Coming Home, Detroit, 1968. Levine.
The Cruel Mother. Anonymous.
The Crystal Skull. Raine.
Daniel Boone, 1735-1820. Benét.
The Dead Shall Be Raised Incorruptible. Kinnell.
Dear John Wayne. Erdrich.
Decay. Herbert.
Desideravi. Maynard.
Desire. Raine.
Dido. Campion.
Dirge. Johnson.
Doctor Faustus (excerpt). Marlowe.
The Draft Riot. De Kay.
A Dress of Fire. Ravikovich.
Dunedin Revisited. Glover.
E Questo Il Nido in Che la Mia Fenice? Hope.
The Eclipse of Faith. Woolsey.
Elegy for My Mother. Katrovas.
The Employee. Holzapfel.
The Ending. Engle.
Epigram: Absent-Minded Professor. Nemerov.
Epigram: "Lo! Beauty flashed forth sweetly." Meleager.
Eternity of Love Protested. Carew.
The Evening Wind. Bryant.
Evensong. Moffett.
Fable. Prokosch.
Faithless. Anonymous.
Fallen Majesty. Yeats.
The Finches. Murray.
Fire. Harjo.
The Fire of Drift-Wood. Longfellow.
The Fishes and the Poet's Hands. Yerby.
For the Sin–. Anonymous.
Four Dates. Anonymous.
A Fragment. Bancks.
The Galliass. De la Mare.
Ghazals. Harrison.
Giles Corey of the Salem Farms: Prologue. Longfellow.
God's World. Millay.
Happiness. Gluck.
Harvest Poem. Fisher.
Have You Got a Brook. Dickinson.
He Comes among. Barker.
He Renounceth All the Effects of Love. Vaux.
He Speaks of His Condition through Love. Folcachieri.
Headsong. Bennett.
Here Lies a Lady. Ransom.
The Hibakusha's Letter (1955). Mura.
The Highway. Merwin.
Homeric Unity. Lang.
How Much Longer? Mezey.
If I Consider. Ise.
Irish History. Allingham.
It Started. Baca.
Ivy and Holly. Meyerstein.
January. Heath-Stubbs.
Keep Your Lamp Trimmed and Burning. Anonymous.

Lament for a Cricket Eleven. Allott.
Lancashire Winter. Connor.
The Lass of Roch Royal (C vers.). Anonymous.
Leadbelly Gives an Autograph. Jones.
Leaving. Hogan.
Life Story. Williams.
Like This Together. Rich.
Like to the seely fly. Davison.
Limerick: "Said Nero to one of his train." Anonymous.
The Lion-House. Wheelock.
Little Sticks. Rolls.
The Little Things. Isler.
Lives of Great Men. Anonymous.
Love Made Me Such That I Live in Fire. Stampa.
Love Song. Halevi.
Marian Drury. Carman.
Maryland, My Maryland. Randall.
Matilda. Belloc.
Memorial Couplets for the Dying Ego. Barker.
The Miracle. Suckling.
Misfortunes Never Come Singly. Graham.
Mothy Monologue. Gustafson.
Mr. East's Feast. Anonymous.
Night Flight. Johnson.
No Change in Me. Anonymous.
Not from This Anger. Thomas.
O King of Saints, We Give Thee Praise and Glory. Thomson.
O Martyred Spirit. Santayana.
Ode to a Nightingale (parody). Kelly.
Of Astraea. Davies.
Of My Lady Isabella Playing on the Lute. Waller.
Of Your Father's Indiscretions and the Train to California. Emanuel.
On File. Bangs.
On No Work of Words. Thomas.
On the Death-Bed. Hardy.
On the Lord Mayor and Court of Aldermen... Marvell.
A Picture. Cuthbertson.
The Portrait. Kunitz.
Prescription of Painful Ends. Jeffers.
Progress of Unbelief. Newman.
Purity. Lenski.
R. W. Gold.
Redondillas. Juana Ines de la Cruz.
Report from a Far Place. Stafford.
Rock, Be My Dream. Black.
The Rowan County Crew (Tolliver-Martin Feud Song). Anonymous.
Saint Stephen in San Francisco. La Follette.
Sanctuary. Parker.
Scrap Iron. Durgnat.
The Seasons. Kalidasa.
She-Devil. Goldring.

Burn

Six Birthday Candles Shining.
Carr.
Some Eyes Condemn.
Thomas.
Song of the Trees of the Black
Forest. Jabes.
Song: "You're wondering if
I'm lonely." Rich.
Songs for a Three-String
Guitar. Sedar-Senghor.
The Songs of Bilitis. Louys.
Sonnet I: "Not Ulysses, no,
nor any other man."
Labe.
Spring in the Old World.
Levine.
The Story of the Wild
Huntsman. Hoffmann.
The Sword. Abu Bakr.
This Town: Winter Morning.
Stafford.
To Mary. Shelley.
To My Mistris, I Burning in
Love. Carew.
To Stella. Swift.
To Terraughty, on His Birth-
Day. Burns.
To the Boston Women.
Anonymous.
The Tower. Pagis.
Twelfth Night. Booth.
Upon His Majesty's Being
Made Free of the City.
Marvell.
Upon Love. Herrick.
Uriel. Stead.
The Venus of Bolsover Castle.
Sitwell.
Victory. Johnson.
Watching Your Gray Eyes.
Marcus.
We Passed by Green Closes.
Clare.
White People. Henderson.
Win at First and Lose at Last;
or, A New Game at Cards.
Price.
A Winter Talent. Davie.
Within Us, Too. Grenville.
The Wood-Pile. Frost.
Written in Juice of Lemmon.
Cowley.
Yahrzeit Candle. Nordhaus.

Burrow

A Drumlin Woodchuck.
Frost.
Elf Owl. Austin.
The Jerboa. Moore.
The Plodder Seam.
Anonymous.
Staying Alive. Wagoner.

Burst

As I was going by Charing
Cross. Anonymous.
The Boys of Wexford.
Anonymous.
Funeral Poem. Jones.
The Holy Ones, the Young
Ones. Zeldis.
In Gaetam. Bastard.
Maiden Lane. Lee.
Marriage Is a Lovely Thing.
Pisan.
Melancholia. Anonymous.
Mir Traumte Von Einem
Konigskind. Heine.
The Odyssey. Homer.
Richard III. Shakespeare.
Salmon Cycle. Treinin.

Bus (es)

Balance. Schultz.
Bus Ride. Kandel.

Good Green Bus. Field.
If Not (parody). Evans.
In a Remote Cloister
Bordering the Empyrean.
Sloman.
Limerick:"There once was a
man who said: "Damn!"
Hare.
Some Indian Uses of History
on a Rainy Day.
Ramanujan.
Three Portraits. Hitchcock.
The Underground. Boas.
Uptown. Zweig.
Waiting for the Bus.
Enright.
You Know. Garrigue.

Bush (es)

The Affectionate Shepherd
(excerpt). Barnfield.
Australia. Langley.
Autumn Color. Robinson.
Birds and Roses Are Birds
and Roses. Heyen.
Buckinghamshire.
Anonymous.
Definition of Nature.
Redmond.
The Double Looking Glass.
Hope.
Draw a Pail of Water.
Anonymous.
The Golden Bird. Ingamells.
Good-bye. Emerson.
The Green Linnet.
Wordsworth.
Hares on the Mountain.
Anonymous.
I Sing an Old Song.
Williams.
A Man of Thessaly.
Anonymous.
March Hares. Young.
A Midsummer Night's
Dream. Shakespeare.
Mollesse. Jacobsen.
On the Mountain. Neidhart
von
Pictures from Brueghel.
Williams.
The Roaring Days. Lawson.
Snow Harvest. Young.
Veneris Venefica Agrestis.
Piccolo.
Yom Kippur. Chaet.

Business

An Act. Rosen.
The Aeneid. Virgil (Publius
Vergilius Maro).
Age. More.
And Dust to Dust. Webb.
As to Being Alone.
Oppenheim.
Beyond the Profit of Today.
Anonymous.
Birdie McReynolds.
Hoffenstein.
The Cavalier's Song.
Motherwell.
Christ i wudint know normal
if i saw it when. Bissett.
The Devil. Anonymous.
Don't Steal! Bierce.
An Epitaph. Ellis.
Epitaph at Upton-on-Severn.
Anonymous.
A Looking-Glass for Smokers
(excerpt). Spooner.
Lord Finchley. Belloc.
On to Richmond.
Thompson.
The Orange Tree. Pearce.

Out of Luck. Ibn Ezra.
Parity. Rexroth.
Patriotic Ode on
the...Persecution of Charlie
Chaplin. Kaufman.
Pedagogical Principles.
Amoss.
Poetry and the Poet.
Bunner.
Portrait of the Artist with
Hart Crane. Wright.
Salem, Massachusetts. Muir.
She Told Me. Kilgore.
Song: "When I was a
greenhorn and young."
Kingsley.
Suite from Catullus.
McHugh.
'Tain't Nobody's Business.
Stokes.

Bust

My Days of Love Are Over.
Byron.
On a Statue of Sir Arthur
Sullivan. Hamilton.
Poor Old Man. Anonymous.

Bustle

The Empty Woman. Brooks.
Moon-Come-Out. Farjeon.
De Rerum Natura.
Lucretius (Titus Lucretitus
Carus).

Busy

Flood. Feldman.
The Other Fellow's Job.
Gillilan.
When the Saints Come
Marching In. Lorde.

Butcher (s)

Bags of Meat. Hardy.
A Bestiary. Rexroth.
Butcherboy. Schmidt.
Didn't He Ramble. Handy.
Elegy. Roethke.
The Ram of Darby.
Anonymous.
A Street in Kaufman-Ville: or
a Note Thrown to
Carolyn... Cunningham.
Testimonies. Kees.
The Three Butchers.
Anonymous.

Butler (s)

The Feckless Dinner Party.
De la Mare.
Hair. Silverman.
Wassailer's Song. Southwell.

Butter

Betty Botter Bought Some
Butter. Anonymous.
The Birthday-Cake
Glockenspiel. Henley.
Butter's Etymological Spelling
Book, &c. Coleridge.
Churning. Anonymous.
E, the Feasting Florentines.
Hoffman.
The Eggs. Redgrove.
Father William. Anonymous.
Jack Sprat's Cat.
Anonymous.
The King's Breakfast. Milne.
Luxury. Justice.
Nantucket / Mussels /
October. Lewandowski.
On This Island. Auden.
A Present of Butter.
O'Huiginn.
Sorrows of Werther.
Thackeray.
Wheatlet Son of Milklet.
MacConglinne.

Buttercup (s)

The Bird. Hoffenstein.
Pastoral. Loewinsohn.
Sleepyhead. De la Mare.
Somersault. Aldis.
A Song the Grass Sings.
Blanden.
Than(By Yon Sunset's Wintry
Glow. Cummings.
The Words, the Words, the
Words. Williams.

Butterflies

After the War. Naggid.
After Wings. Piatt.
Amber the Sky. Rokwaho.
Auguries of Innocence.
Blake.
The Beautiful Woman Who
Sings. Allen.
Butterflies. Davidson.
The Butterfly. Friedmann.
Coin in the Fist. Brownell.
Eutopia. Palgrave.
The fallen flowers seemed.
Moritake.
A fuzzy fellow, without feet.
Dickinson.
The Genesis of Butterflies.
Hugo.
Gorgio Lad. Burr.
Haiku: "The falling flower."
Moritake.
I'd Be a Butterfly. Bayly.
Jackie. Kuka.
Lame Angel. Finkel.
Lilac. Flint.
Love-Song. Lasker-Schüler.
Lupine Dew. Ramsey.
LXXIV. Berrigan.
The Manless Society. Unik.
O My Love the Pretty Towns.
Patchen.
On Discovering a Butterfly.
Nabokov.
A science–so the savans say.
Dickinson.
The Second Dream.
Valentine.
Second Poem. Orlovsky.
Shankill. Shanahan.
Song of the Fallen Deer.
Anonymous.
Spring Scene. Buson
(Taniguchi Buso).
Suburb Hilltop. Moore.
Suburban Dusk. Meyers.
The Term of Death. Piatt.
The Vixen. Clare.
Wake Up! Wake Up! Basho
(Matsuo Basho).
When You Write Again.
Jonker.

Buttocks

Hitler, Frothy-Mouth.
Anonymous.
Mythological Sonnet XVI.
Fuller.

Button (s)

Christmas Morning I.
Freeman.
Dandelions. Frost.
Dilly Dilly Piccalilli.
Watson.
Dresses. Fraser.
Literary Life in the Golden
West. Whalen.
Old Ben Golliday. Van
Doren.
On the New Road. Lifshin.
Sic a Wife as Willie Had.
Burns.

Buy (s)
Aunt Eliza. Graham.
The Bargain. Neidhart von
Choosing Shoes. Wolfe.
The Coconut. Milne.
Consider. Pico della
  Mirandola.
Consider Well. More.
Construction. Shapiro.
Cripple Dick upon a Stick.
  Anonymous.
Dingle Dingle Doosey.
  Anonymous.
Fish Riddle: "Although it's
  cold no clothes I wear."
  Anonymous.
Footnote to Enright's
  "Apocalypse." Bell.
The Gifts of God. Very
Hattage. Herbert.
Husband and Heathen. Foss.
Hush, Little Baby, Don't Say
  a Word. *Anonymous.*
I paints and paints. Brooks.
Labor. *Anonymous.*
Last of the Poet's Car.
  Connor.
Levant. Durrell.
The Market. Snyder.
The Moone-Calfe. Drayton.
No Buyers. Hardy.
An Open-Letter-Poem-Note to
  Vincent Van G.
  Bernadine.
The Paper Cutter. Ignatow.
Poem by a Perfectly Furious
  Academician. Brooks.
Precious Mettle. Warsh.
Retrospection. Shaw.
Richard Dick upon a Stick.
  Anonymous.
Scrimshaw. Hogan.
The Sculptors. Purdy.
Selling Ruined Peonies. Yu
  Hsuan-chi.
Shop O' Meat-Weare.
  Barnes.
Such a Parcel of Rogues in a
  Nation. Burns.
Tommy Trot. *Anonymous.*
When I Came to London.
  Castelete.
White Sand and Grey Sand.
  Anonymous.
Buzzards
The Bear. Momaday.
I Wanted to Die in the
  Desert. *Anonymous.*
Bygone
After Sunset. Allingham.
The Husband's Message.
  Anonymous.

C

Cab
Knight, with Umbrella.
  Olson.
Prosser. Carver.
Taxi Suite: After Anacreon.
  Welch.
This Year. Hutchison.
Cabbage (s)
The Ballad of Imitation.
  Dobson.
Band Music. Fuller.
Bile Them Cabbage Down.
  Anonymous.

The End of My Sister's
  Guggenheim. Brinnin.
The Fields. Merwin.
The Four Nights' Drunk.
  Anonymous.
Gourds. Nicander.
Hangover Cure. Amphis.
Nocturn at the Institute.
  McElroy.
Three Nights Drunk.
  Anonymous.
The Victoria Markets
  Recollected in Tranquillity.
  Maurice.
Cabin
The Arkansas Traveler.
  Anonymous.
An Awful Responsibility.
  Preston.
A Grain of Salt. Irwin.
The Handsome Cabin Boy.
  Anonymous.
The Old Cabin. Dunbar.
Cabinets
An Apology for the Revival of
  Christian
  Architecture...(excerpt).
  Hill.
Of Taste; An Essay.
  Cawthorn.
Cable
How Cyrus Laid the Cable.
  Saxe.
Cactus
Black Mesa. Rogers.
Gunslinger. Dorn.
Cadence (s)
From the Righteous Man
  Even the Wild Beasts Run
  away. Bromwich.
Glanmore Sonnets. Heaney.
A Quarrel. Peck.
The Spirit of Poetry.
  Longfellow.
Caesar
Human Greatness. Barclay.
Julius Caesar. Shakespeare.
Non Dolet. Gogarty.
Ovid. Pevear.
Pompey and Cornelia.
  Rowe.
Cafe (s)
California #2. Cruz.
Epitaph: Jacob Epstein.
  Anonymous.
For My Father: Two Poems.
  Kherdian.
A Musician Returning from a
  Cafe Audition. Minard.
On Heaven. Ford.
Poem: "In secret." Picasso.
Cage (d) (s)
110 Year Old House.
  Ochester.
Backgammon. Broumas.
A Bird in Search of a Cage.
  Pack.
Cafes. Smith.
Captive. Hirshbein.
The False-Hearted Knight.
  Anonymous.
The Finches. Murray.
Imagery. Chattopadhyaya.
The Keeper of the Midnight
  Gate. Brown.
Lady Isabel and the Elf
  Knight. *Anonymous.*
Love Songs. *Anonymous.*
The Magic Flute. Snodgrass.
Mineral Point. Dana.
Nested. Lulham.
The Parrot. Campbell.

People Buy a Lot of Things.
  Wynne.
Poem for the Creative Writing
  Class, Spring 1982. Woo.
The Poem of Joao. De
  Sousa.
Pretty Polly (with music).
  Anonymous.
The Red Cockatoo. Po Chu-
  i.
The Row between the Cages.
  Armstrong.
Sudden Things. Hall.
Sympathy. Dunbar.
The Tale of Custard the
  Dragon. Nash.
Thaw. Broughton.
To a Foreign Friend.
  Nathan.
We Live in a Cage. Harris.
Cain
Children of Light. Lowell.
For Mack C. Parker.
  Murray.
Have Faith. Carpenter.
Invocation. Sitwell.
On the Jewish Day of
  Judgment in the Year 1942.
  Wittlin.
Cairn
A Girl's Song. Hinkson.
Long Ago. Scroggie.
Prospect of a Mountain.
  Young.
Telephone Ghosts. Frazier.
Cake (s)
At Shakespeare's Grave.
  Browne.
The Birthday Cake. Chase.
Birthday Cake. Eastwick.
Catherine. Kuskin.
Child Beater. Anthony
  ("Ai").
Clap Hands, Daddy Comes.
  Anonymous.
For K.R. on Her Sixtieth
  Birthday. Wilbur.
The Great Lakes Suite.
  Reaney.
Miss Fogerty's Cake.
  Anonymous.
Moving In. Miles.
The Peace: Midst the Free
  Green Fields.
  Aristophanes.
There Should Have Been.
  Lea.
To the Bat. *Anonymous.*
Unaccompanied. Andrews.
Walking for That Cake.
  Harrigan.
Why? Chima.
Calendars
If(Touched by Love's Own
  Secret)We,Like Homing.
  Cummings.
Three Brown Girls Singing.
  Holman.
Calf
Birth of Rainbow. Hughes.
A Charm for Love and
  Lasting Affection.
  Anonymous.
Evening. Tzara.
Johnny Armstrong.
  Anonymous.
Limerick: "The ankle's chief
  end is exposiery." Euwer.
The Naming. Hummer.
The New Baby Calf. Chase.
Retirement, an Ode (excerpt).
  Warton, Sr..

Testimonies. Kees.
The Wail of the Waiter.
  Clarke.
California
Cape Cod Girls. *Anonymous.*
Far West. Smith.
Just California. McGroarty.
O California. Murguia.
Reno, 2 a.m. Hamill.
Terminal Version. O Hehir.
Call (ed) (ing) (s)
Above the Wall. Malarkey.
Appeal to the Moongod
  Nanna-Suen to Throw Out
  Lugalanne... Enheduanna.
Arignota Remembers.
  Sappho.
Armistice Day. Causley.
The Atlantides. Thoreau.
Autobiographical Fragment.
  Amis.
A Ballad of the Captains.
  Brady.
The Birds of Tin. Madge.
Birmingham. MacNeice.
The Call. Mew.
A Cemetery in New Mexico.
  Alvarez.
The Collar. Herbert.
Cross Patch. Mother Goose.
Dear Brethren, Are Your
  Harps in Tune? Smith.
Death Rites II. *Anonymous.*
Doomsday Morning.
  Taggard.
Dream of a Decent Death.
  Borgese.
An Elegie On the Deploreable
  Departure of ...John Hull.
  Saffin.
The Elms Dispatch. Padgett.
Farmers. Lux.
Father and Son. Wallace.
Fire Burial. McInnis.
For All Sorts and Conditions.
  Nicholson.
Found. Muske.
Four Women. Simone.
A Friendly Game of Football.
  Dyson.
Glass. Merwin.
God's Call. *Anonymous.*
The Hermit's Song.
  Anonymous.
Hold Back Thy Hours.
  Fletcher.
Homecoming Blues. Miller.
Horologium: The Mother of
  God. *Anonymous.*
Hot Line. Dunann.
The House of Life. Rossetti.
Ibycus. Heath-Stubbs.
The Island of the Scots
  (excerpt). Ayton [(or
  Aytoun)] Sir Robert.
The Lighthouse. Anson.
Little Bessie. *Anonymous.*
Little Mousgrove and the
  Lady Barnet. *Anonymous.*
Lost Dog. Rodman.
The Lost Lagoon. Johnson.
Love's Guerdons. Nesbit.
The Lover's Song. Austin.
Mary Magdalene. Rossetti.
Mary's Lamb. Hale.
Message from Home. Raine.
'Morning, Morning.
  Mathew.
New Construction: Bath Iron
  Works. Koehler.
Noonday Sun. Jackson.

Now Behold the Saviour Pleading. Leland.
O Lord, Save We Beseech Thee. *Anonymous.*
The Old Home. Cawein.
The Old Room. Merwin.
On the Death of Echo. Coleridge.
Operation–Souls. *Anonymous.*
Our Father, Our King. *Anonymous.*
Photograph. Prettyman.
Picking Apples. Lindsay.
The Poet on the Island. Murphy.
Regina Angelorum. Chesterton.
Rizpah. Tennyson.
The Round-Up. Howard.
Running Back. Smith.
Sea Flower. Dorcey.
She Is My Dear. *Anonymous.*
The Shooting of the Cup. Neihardt.
Sing, My Soul. *Anonymous.*
Sir Hugh; or, The Jew's Daughter (B vers.). *Anonymous.*
The Skin Divers. Starbuck.
The Sonne. Herbert.
The Sunrise to the Poor. Wilson.
Tableau Vivant. Gallagher.
Thailand Railway. Stow.
Theology. Hughes.
To My Sister. Berggolts.
To the Infant Martyrs. Crashaw.
A Translation from Petrarch. Synge.
Traveling on My Knees. Goodwin.
True to a Dream. Petersen.
Two Bums Walk out of Eden. Francis.
The Umpire. Bracker.
Unwanted. Field.
A Vagabond Song. Carman.
A Visit to the Asylum. Millay.
What Bright Pushbutton? Allen.
What We Listened for in Music. Burr.
Will Beauty Come. Nathan.
Woman from the West Coast. Crozier.
Woman Work. Angelou.
The World's So Big. Fisher.
Yesterday. Chesterman.
Yom Kippur. Day.
You That Have Been Often Invited. *Anonymous.*
You Understand the Requirements. Lifshin.
Calm (ness) (s)
After. Ryan.
The Ant. Nash.
Aristotle to Phyllis. Hollander.
At Delft. Tomlinson.
At the Shelter-Stone. Macrow.
Body Fished from the Seine. Corso.
The Brewing of Soma. Whittier.
By the North Sea. Swinburne.

Calm Is the Morn without a Sound. Tennyson.
Christmas. Chute.
Cradle Song. Wallach.
The Creation of Man. *Anonymous.*
Death Is a Second Cousin Dining with Us Tonight. Kudaka.
Death of Little Boys. Tate.
The Diary of Amanda McFadden. Hogan.
Do you have a sweet thought, Cerinthus. Sulpicia.
Eastern Tempest. Blunden.
Epigram: "No charm can stay, no medicine can assuage." Landor.
Evening Fantasy. Hoelderlin.
Extras. Burton.
Farmer. Bailey.
Fields Where We Slept. Rukeyser.
Frascati's. Huxley.
Goodbye Nkrumah. Di Prima.
La Grande Jatte: Sunday Afternoon. Cole.
Green River. Bryant.
The Hand at Callow Hill Farm. Tomlinson.
Happiness. Gluck.
Hills of the Middle Distance. Mitchell.
I Love to Steal Awhile Away. Brown.
The Ice Skin. Dickey.
In Memory of Robin Hyde, 1906-39. Brasch.
In Time of Need. Stafford.
The Journey to the Insane Asylum. Lichtenstein.
The Lost Ingredient. Sexton.
Love Is Enough. Morris.
New York. Gunn.
Night. Rolleston.
Night Walkers. Smithyman.
On a Similar Occasion for the Year 1792. Cowper.
On Falling. Greig.
On Looking up by Chance at the Constellations. Frost.
On the Beach. Cornford.
Prometheus Unbound. Shelley.
Remember or Forget. Aïdé.
Saint Brendan's Prophecy. *Anonymous.*
A Sea-Chantey (excerpt). Walcott.
The Sea–in Calm. "Cornwall.
Snowdrops. MacBeth.
A Song of Dagger-Dancing (excerpt). Tu Fu.
Sonnet: "An open wound which has been healed anew." Trench.
Sonnet: Composed While the Author Was Engaged in Writing a Tract... Wordsworth.
The Sorrow of Unicume. Read.
A Stormy Day. *Anonymous.*
Tall Windows. Hass.
Terror. O'Brien.
That's All? Hajnal.
A Thought of the Nile. Hunt.
To Jane: The Recollection. Shelley.

Voyagers' Prayer. *Anonymous.*
The Wind Is Wild Tonight. *Anonymous.*
The Winds of Fate. Wilcox.
Calvary
A Christmas Carol. Cogswell.
Cold Iron. Kipling.
Come, Precious Soul. *Anonymous.*
Consecration. Kirby.
The Cross and the Tree. Stidger.
An Etching. Imelda.
Father in Heaven. Petrarch (Francesco Petrarca).
From Bethlehem to Calvary. Nicholson.
I Heard Christ Sing. "MacDiarmid.
Lincoln. Robinson.
The Litany of the Dark People. Cullen.
A Little Parable. Aldrich.
Mary's Baby. O'Sheel.
The Misfit-1939-1945. Day Lewis.
The Question. Taylor.
Santa Claus. Nemerov.
The Second Coming. Gale.
Soldier, What Did You See? Blanding.
This blessed Christ of Calvary. *Anonymous.*
The Unpetalled Rose. Therese.
A Virile Christ. Boundy.
Came
A Ballad upon a Wedding: The Bride. Suckling.
The Cat Came Back. Bonnell.
The First. Mannes.
Florine. Campbell.
I threw a penny in the air. *Anonymous.*
I Went into the Maverick Bar. Snyder.
A Leave-Taking. Holz.
Love's Coming. Neilson.
The Meeting. Hollis.
Roger and Dolly. *Anonymous.*
She Came and Went. Lowell
Slow Death. Martinez.
Snowbanks North of the House. Bly.
The Telephone. Frost.
To Keep the Memory of Charlotte Forten Grimke. Grimke.
The Two Rats. *Anonymous.*
Variation. Wild.
What Became of Them? *Anonymous.*
When I Set out for Lyonnesse. Hardy.
The World: a Ghazel. Mangan.
Camel (s)
Internal Firesides. Blind.
The Sexual Life of the Camel. *Anonymous.*
The Thirty-One Camels. Korn.
The White, Orphaned Camel Kid... *Anonymous.*
Camellia (s)
Memorial Day. Miles.
A Prospect of Swans. Donnelly.

The United States Prepare for the Permanent Revolution. Hitchcock.
Camelot
Mount Badon. Williams.
Sonnets of the Months. San Geminiano.
Camera
3 for 25. Smith.
Body Fished from the Seine. Corso.
Family Portrait. Hood-Adams.
Limerick: "A pretty young actress, a stammerer." Norwood.
Photographing the Facade–San Miguel de Allende. Colquitt.
Roll Call: A Land of Old Folk and Children. Black.
Camp (s)
The Camp Within the West. Quinn.
The Centenarian's Story. Whitman.
Fame and Fortune. Drayton.
If So the Man You Are. Lewis.
The Legend of Grand Lake. Westcott.
Lines. Mary Ada, Sister.
My Camping Ground. Rosenfeld.
New Minglewood Blues. Lewis's.
Open Range. Jackson.
Prospecting. Ammons.
Silver Jack's Religion. Jones.
The Town. Rowbotham.
We're Tenting To-Night. Kittredge.
When We Looked Back. Stafford.
Canaan
Didn't My Lord Deliver Daniel. *Anonymous.*
Farewell to Tobacco. Lamb.
The Lonesome Dove. *Anonymous.*
The Old Hymns. Stanton.
On Death. Killigrew.
Parting Friends. *Anonymous.*
Canada
Canada-I-O. *Anonymous.*
The Emigration of the Fairies. Hunter-Duvar.
Indian Night Tableau. Edelstein.
The Might Buck, the Immigrant Fuck, and Melting Pot Luck. Filip.
Night Wind in Fall. Moses.
Riverdale Lion. Colombo.
You Are More Than I Need. Kaplan.
Cancel (ed)
Dividends. Creekmore.
A Fugue. Church.
What Winter Floods, What Showers of Spring. Bronte.
Work. Lawrence.
Cancer
Altarwise by Owl-Light. Thomas.
Cinco de Mayo, 1862. Rios.
Sunny Prestatyn. Larkin.
Two Sonnets: "Altarwise by owl-light." Thomas.
Candle (s)
At the Party. Laughton.

A Birthday. Field.
Un-Birthday Cake. Fisher.
Blow the Candle Out.
  Anonymous.
Blow the Candle Out (The
  Jolly Boatsman).
  Anonymous.
Bog and Candle. Fitzgerald.
Catch What You Can.
  Garrigue.
Cherry Blossoms. "Lewis.
Chick! My Naggie.
  Anonymous.
Chrismas Carol. *Anonymous.*
The Christmas Tree.
  Cornelius.
A Circus Garland. Field.
Clerk Saunders. *Anonymous.*
The Death of Digenes Akritas.
  Heath-Stubbs.
Death of My Aunt.
  Anonymous.
The Dedicated. Larkin.
Every Earthly Creature.
  Brinnin.
The First of My Lovers.
  Carter.
For Three Swift Days.
  Trifonov.
The Frolicksome Farmer.
  Anonymous.
Give Place, Ye Lovers.
  Surrey.
How Beautiful You Are: 3.
  Edelman.
How Many Miles to Babylon?
  Goose.
The Interrogations. Knoll.
The Invitation in It. Boyle.
Jack Be Nimble. Mother
  Goose.
Little Candle. Sandburg.
A Lyke-Wake Dirge.
  Anonymous.
Make Way! Comfort.
The Merry Wives of Windsor.
  Shakespeare.
Moon and Candle-Light.
  Renton.
My Estate. Drinkwater.
My Father Died.
  Anonymous.
Myrtle. Kooser.
Night Expedition from Ben
  Alder Cottage. Redfern.
No Shop Does the Bird Use.
  Coatsworth.
Ode on a Decision to Settle
  for Less. Pillen.
Old Age Compensation.
  Wright.
On the Lake. Sackville-West.
On the Nativity of Christ Our
  Lord. Bennett.
Poem. Lima.
A Poem for Integration.
  Saxon.
Points of View. Lowell.
Prophecy. Wylie.
Queen Anne's Musicians.
  Hennell.
A Quiet Normal Life.
  Stevens.
Red Hanrahan's Song about
  Ireland. Yeats.
Riddle: What Am I? Aldis.
Shadbush. Rainsford.
She Comes Not When Noon
  Is on the Roses. Trench.
So? Vaughn.
The Stranger in the Pumpkin.
  Ciardi.

Strokes. Stafford.
The Telephone Operator.
  Francis of Assisi.
To Delmore Schwartz.
  Lowell.
Tonight in Chicago...
  Anonymous
Twilight. Hall.
Walthena. Peck.
Wild Old Wicked Man.
  Yeats.

Candor
Fall in Corrales. Wilbur.
Forcing a Way. *Anonymous.*

Candy
Bluebird, Bluebird, Fly
  Through My Window.
  Anonymous.
The Cambridge Ladies.
  Cummings.
Candy Man Blues. Hurt.
The Guest. Saarikoski.
Homecoming Blues. Miller.
I'd like a little. *Anonymous.*
The Oakey Street Evictions.
  Anonymous.
On the Edge. Dwyer.
Sunday Service (parody).
  Heffernan.
These Trees Are. Deal.
Weevily Wheat. *Anonymous.*

Cane (s)
A Creole Slave-Song.
  Thompson.
The Devil's Walk. Southey.

Cannibals
As in Their Time.
  MacNeice.
The Savages. Miles.

Canning
The Joy of Cooking:
  Conserves. Mus.
The Royal Line. Hunt.
Willis Beggs. Masters.

Cannon (s)
Amours de Voyage. Clough.
A Ballad Called the
  Haymarket Hectors.
  Anonymous.
Childe Harold's Pilgrimage:
  Canto III, XXII. Byron.
Clepsydra. Cotton.
The Invaders. Haines.
Peace Delegate. Livingstone.
The Soldier's Song. Kearney.
Sumter. Brownell.
To the Roving Pirate.
  Turberville.

Canoe
The Big One. Morin.
Dear America. Peterson.
The Djanggawul Cycle, 1.
  Anonymous
The Lake of the Dismal
  Swamp. Moore.
Memory. Rimbaud.
A Message to the
  Photographer Whose Prints
  I Purchased. Williams.
Paddle Your Own Canoe.
  Bolton.
The Same Side of the Canoe.
  Espirito Santo.

Canon (s)
Orange March. Murphy.
The Smoke-Blue Plains.
  Clark.
Winter in the Sierras.
  Austin.

Canopy
The Excursion. Wordsworth.
In State (excerpt). Willson.

Canto (s)
Clarel. Melville.
The Faerie Queene. Spenser.
Published Correspondence:
  Epistle to the Rapalloan.
  MacLeish.

Canvas
The After-Comers. Lowell.
Against Botticelli. Hass.
All Hands Unmoor!
  Falconer.
  Anonymous. Tabb.
Ballade of Boys Bathing.
  Rolfe.
A Fiction of Edvard Munch.
  di Michele.
Listens, Too (parody).
  Berry.
The Poet at Seven.
  Rimbaud.
To Licinius. Horace.

Canyon (s)
I Walk on the River at Dawn.
  Hart.
In Mutual Time. Lavoie.
The Trail to Lillooet.
  Johnson.
The Train Stops at Healy
  Fork. Haines.
Without Benefit of Tape.
  Livesay.

Cap (s)
Don't Sleep. Jonker.
Dream Songs. Berryman.
Fall. Hass.
Glasgow Schoolboys, Running
  Backwards. Dunn.
Homage to Max Jacob.
  Padgett.
I Came A-Riding. Reinmar
  von Zweter.
Joseph's Suspicion. Rilke.
The King of China's
  Daughter. Sitwell.
Lines on a Purple Cap
  Received as a Present from
  My Brother. Alsop.
On Seeing My Birthplace from
  a Jet Aircraft. Pudney.
There Is No. Kicknosway.

Cape Horn
Around Cape Horn.
  Anonymous.
The Girls around Cape Horn.
  Anonymous.
Limerick: "There was an old
  man of Cape Horn." Lear.
Paddy, Get Back.
  Anonymous.
Paddy West. *Anonymous.*
Rounding the Horn.
  Anonymous.
The Sailor's Way.
  Anonymous.

Cape (s)
At Midnight. Kooser.
The City of Beggars. Hayes.
The Day the Tide. Booth.
A Singer Asleep. Hardy.
Still Pond, No More Moving.
  Moss.

Capricorn
Altarwise by Owl-Light.
  Thomas.
Two Sonnets: "Altarwise by
  owl-light." Thomas.

Captain
The Aeneid. Virgil (Publius
  Vergilius Maro).
Ain't No More Cane on This
  Brazos. *Anonymous.*
The Anathemata. Jones.

The Armstrong at Fayal.
  Rice.
Army Bugle Calls: Reveille.
  Anonymous.
The Captain. White.
Captain Jinks. Lingard.
A Challenge. Kenyon.
David and Bethsabe. Peele.
Drive It On. *Anonymous.*
Frankie's Trade. Kipling.
I Am the captain of the
  Pinafore. Gilbert.
If Something Should Happen.
  Clifton.
The Lady's Diary. Dibdin.
Lament for Captain Paton.
  Lockhart.
The Last Meeting of
  Pocahontas and the Great
  Captain. Preston.
Light in the Darkness.
  Fisher.
Little Billee. Thackeray.
The Loss of the Cedar Grove.
  Anonymous.
My Captain. Day.
Pantomime Diseases. Abse.
Pendant Watch. Defrees.
Poems, VIII. O'Connor.
Ralegh's Prizes. Pinsky.
Sailing, Sailing. Burr.
The Shipwreck. Palmer.
A Song on the Duke's Late
  Glorious Success over the
  Dutch. *Anonymous.*
Terra Australis. Stewart.
William Taylor. *Anonymous.*
Yonder Comes the High
  Sheriff (with music).
  Anonymous.

Captive (s)
Alle Vogel Sind Schon Da.
  Chesterton.
Black Muslim Boy in a
  Hospital. Emanuel.
The Bracelet. Stanley.
The Cloisters. Yellen.
Compassion So Divine.
  Steele.
Crossing the Plains. Miller.
A Dispute over Suicide.
  Anonymous.
The Dray. Binyon.
Far from Our Friends.
  Belknap.
Field Sports (excerpt).
  Somervile.
A Green Refrain. Huss.
The Iliad. Homer.
The Lake. Tabb.
The Muses Elizium.
  Drayton.
On a Piece of Tapestry.
  Santayana.
Once the Striped Quagga.
  Tallmountain.
Parricide. Howe.
The Petty Officers' Mess.
  Fuller.
Sonnets to Miranda.
  Watson.
The Swan. Baudelaire.
Tambour. Vas.
Time Stands Still, with Gazing
  on Her Face! *Anonymous.*
To Tommaso de' Cavalieri.
  Michelangelo.
The Wasp. Davidson.
What Can You Expect.
  Maryam bint Abi.
The Wild Colonial Boy.
  Anonymous.

The Wild Montana Boy.
  Anonymous.
You Are Gorgeous and I'm
  Coming. O'Hara.
Car (s)
As Animals. Spivak.
Bad Day on the Boulder.
  Davis.
Bird Nest Bound. Patton.
Blue Island Intersection.
  Sandburg.
The Cage. Montague.
A Choctaw Chief Helps Plan
  a Festival... Barnes.
Do It Yrself. Eigner.
Early June. Dickey.
For the Bicentenary of Isaac
  Watts. Nicholson.
Hottest Brand Goin'. Smoky
  Babe.
Idylls. Theocritus.
The Iliad. Homer.
In Columbus, Ohio.
  Matthias.
Javier. Teran.
Last of the Poet's Car.
  Connor.
Married Three Months.
  Nelms.
Mary Ackerman, 1938,
  Eugene Buechel Photograph
  Museum of Modern Art...
  Glancy.
Miners. Wright.
Moving between Beloit and
  Monroe. Noll.
Portrait. Fox.
The Railroad Cars Are
  Coming (with music).
  Anonymous.
Remembering the Automobile.
  Baldwin.
Rides. Derwood.
Salem, Massachusetts. Muir.
See That One? Bagg.
Tank Town. Atherton.
To Elsie. Williams.
To the Soul. Broome.
Uptown. Zweig.
Violence on Television.
  Jenkins.
Who's in Charge Here? Bell.
Working at a Service Station,
  I Think of Shinkichi
  Takahashi. Finnell.
Caravan
"Garden of Gethsemane."
  Pasternak.
Happy Christmases (excerpt).
  O'Donnell.
The Mountaineer. Nathan.
Portico. Dario.
Time, You Old Gipsy Man.
  Hodgson.
Carbon
Nude Reclining at Word
  Processor, in Pastel.
  Conover.
Stars. Moss.
Carcass (es)
Around Cape Horn.
  Anonymous.
Between the Traveller and the
  Setting Sun. Thoreau.
Black Tambourine. Crane.
Herman Moon's Hourbook.
  Middleton.
Love's Exchange. Donne.
Sistern and Brethren.
  Anonymous.
Card (s)
Animal Acts. Simic.

Le Chariot. Wieners.
Dream 1971. Contoski.
Epitaph for a Man from
  Virginia City. Porter.
Family Photograph. Vizenor.
Jack o' Diamonds.
  Anonymous.
A Maiden's Denial.
  Anonymous.
Newton's Third. Hubbard.
The Second Advice to a
  Painter. Marvell.
Three-Handed Fugue.
  Gotlieb.
Win at First and Lose at Last;
  or, A New Game at Cards.
  Price.
Care (s)
After the Pleasure Party.
  Melville.
After Tschaikowsky. Gould.
Agamemnon's Tomb.
  Sitwell.
All Night ! Baker.
All Our Griefs to Tell.
  Newton.
Alone in an Inn at
  Southampton, April the
  25th, 1737. Hill.
Among His Books. Nesbit.
Answer to Master Wither's
  Song, "Shall I, Wasting in
  Despair?" Jonson.
Aucassin and Nicolete.
  Bourdillon.
A Baker's Dozen of Wild
  Beasts. Wells.
Beeny Cliff. Hardy.
Beforehand. Bynner.
Beware, Oh, Take Care.
  Anonymous.
A Burlesque Ode, on the
  Author's Clearing a New
  House...(excerpt). Keate.
The Butterfly. James.
Caesar, when that the traitor
  of Egypt. Wyatt.
The Carelesse Nurse Mayd.
  Hood.
Caring. Scott.
Casting All Your Care upon
  God, for He Careth for
  You. Washbourne.
Cerberus. Van Brunt.
The Choyce. Beedome.
The Coffin. Heine.
Consolation (parody).
  Guiterman.
Courage. Gerhardt.
Dies Irae. Thomas of
  Celano.
Dirge. Townson.
The Distant Fury of Battle.
  Hill.
A Ditty. Jacobs.
Diversity of Doctors.
  Anonymous.
The Divided Heart. Wither.
Echo. De la Mare.
Egocentric. Smith.
Epigram: The World Is Full
  of Care." Ward.
Epitaph. Teasdale.
Eternal Goodness. Whittier.
The Father Knows. "H..
The Faun. Long.
Feathered Faith.
  Anonymous.
Fidelia: Shall I, Wasting in
  Despair. Wither.
Fill the Bumper Fair.
  Moore.

The First Division Marches.
  Rice.
The First Year (excerpt).
  Scovell.
The Fleece. Dyer.
For Jane. Bukowski.
For My Own Monument.
  Prior.
A Fragment: To Music.
  Shelley.
Friend of Souls. *Anonymous.*
The Future. Sill.
God Cares. Casterline.
God Lyaeus. Fletcher.
God's Eye Is on the Sparrow.
  Meyer.
God's Goodness. Martin.
The Happy Night. Sheffield.
A Helping Hand. Adams.
His Grange, or Private
  Wealth. Herrick.
The Home Front. Bell.
How Can I Smile?
  Hodgdon.
How to Conceive Boys.
  Quillet.
I Hae a Wife O' My Ain.
  Burns.
I Love Somebody (I Love
  Little Willie). *Anonymous.*
I Thank Thee, Lord.
  Anonymous.
If Some Grim Tragedy.
  Smith.
Imitated from Sonetto in
  Morte 42. Petrarch
  (Francesco Petrarca).
The Inn of Care.
  Waddington.
Jack the Guinea Pig.
  Anonymous.
John Hielandman.
  Anonymous.
A Juju of My Own. Behune.
Kind Miss (with music).
  Anonymous.
King Henry VI.
  Shakespeare.
King Henry VIII.
  Shakespeare.
The Kiss-Fest. Edman.
Lament my loss... Wyatt.
Leave It with Him.
  Anonymous.
Letter from Smyrna to His
  Sisters at Crux-Easton,
  1733. Lisle.
Life. Crabbe.
Life's Little Things.
  Anonymous.
Lifting and Leaning. Wilcox.
The Lover's Resolution.
  Wither.
The Martyrdom of Mary,
  Queen of Scots. Southwell.
My Old Bible. *Anonymous.*
My Soul Thirsts for God.
  Cowper.
The Net and the Sword.
  LePan.
New England. Robinson.
Nobody. Burns.
The North. McKinnon.
Northern Boulevard. Denby.
A Northern Suburb.
  Davidson.
O Bruadair. Stephens.
On a Fair Morning.
  Anonymous.
On Sir John Guise.
  Anonymous.
Otto. Brooks.

Ou Phrontis. Causley.
Overheard in an Orchard.
  Cheney.
Peter Bell, the Third.
  Shelley.
Photographs. Peskett.
A Poem against Rats.
  Levinson.
A Poem Put into My Lady
  Laiton's Pocket. Ralegh.
A Prayer. Gifford.
The Recessional. Roberts.
Remembrance. Bruner.
The Rising Village.
  Goldsmith.
The Saucy Sailor.
  Anonymous.
Shakespeare, Possibly, in
  California. Whittemore.
Sleep and Poetry. Keats.
A Slum Dwelling. Crabbe.
Sometimes. Flint.
Song. Stevenson.
Songs for Fragoletta. Le
  Gallienne.
Sonnet: September, 1815.
  Wordsworth.
"The soote season..." Surrey.
Stella's Birthday. Swift.
Still Here. Hughes.
Strange, Is It Not. Kennedy.
The Suet Dumpling (parody).
  Anonymous.
Summoned. O Hehir.
Survivor. Simmons.
Thanksgiving. Yehoash.
They Have Taken It from Me.
  Corsellis.
To Clio. From Rome. Dyer.
To Scott. Letts.
To Winter. Blake.
The Trosachs. Wordsworth.
Truth. Patmore.
The Turn of the Road. Coe.
Two Kinds of People.
  Wilcox.
The Ty Cobb Story. Clark.
Upon Drinking in a Bowl.
  Rochester.
Vain Gratuities. Robinson.
The Victories of Love, II
  (excerpt). Patmore.
Waiting for Her. Nowlan.
The Well Rising. Stafford.
What Do I Care for Morning.
  Johnson.
Where Have You Been, My
  Good Old Man?
  Anonymous.
A Wind Rose in the Night.
  Kilmer.
A Woman Is a Worthy Thing.
  Anonymous.
Career
Charles Gustavus Anderson
  (II). *Anonymous.*
Elegy in the Cemetery of
  Spoon River...(parody).
  Squire.
Sketch of Lord Byron's Life.
  Moore.
The Way Through.
  Levertov.
Careful
Aunt Helen. Eliot.
Crossing West Texas (1966).
  Robertson.
Drowned Sailor. Shaw.
Gramercy Park Hotel.
  Smith.
Jane, Do Be Careful. Page.

Limerick: "A ghoulish old fellow in Kent." Bishop.
The Measuring. Carter.
Whisperin' Bill. Bacheller.

Careless
Bird Song. Hay.
Birds. Llywelyn.
The Kerry Lads. Garrison.
Of an Old Song. Lecky.
Prometheus. Goethe.
Vain and Careless. Graves.

Caress (ed) (es)
Agbor Dancer. Clark.
Caring. Scott.
Curriculum Vitae. Bachmann.
In Memorium–Leo: A Yellow Cat. Sherwood.
A Lady Stood. Dietmar von Aist.
Nightgown, Wife's Gown. Sward.
Riddle: "Clothed in yellow, red, and green." Anonymous.
Sappho, Be Comforted. Williams.
Scotland. Gray.
A Sweet Disorder in the Dress. Hooton.
Tattooed. Plomer.
To the Sun. Gezelle.
Ulysses Returns. Montgomery.
The Vacant Chair. Root. George F.
When to My Serene Body. Laughton.

Cargo
Big Wind. Roethke.
A Caravan from China Comes. Le Gallienne.
Coming Around the Horn. Anonymous.
Ode to a Lost Cargo in a Ship Called Save. Craveirinha.
Sailors' Harbour. Reed.

Carlisle
The Armada: A Fragment. Macaulay.
Bewick and Graham. Anonymous.
The Captive's Hymn. Proctor.

Carnage
April. Pound.
A High-Toned Old Fascist Gentleman (parody). Zaranka.

Carnal
Chastity. Milton.
The Virgin Mary. Bowers.

Carnation (s)
Micheal Mac Liammoir. Durcan.
To the Gardener at Nuneham. Walpole.

Carnival
Death and the Fairies. MacGill.
That There Should Be Laughter. Banda.

Carol
December. Rossetti.
Dove. Farber.
Giovinette, Che Fate All'Amore. Da Ponte.
In the Far Years. MacDonald.
Now Is Yule Come. Anonymous.
The Yule Days. Anonymous.

Caroline
Lady Isabel and the Elf-Knight (B vers.). Anonymous.
A Lilliputian Ode on Their Majesties' Accession. Carey.
On Queen Caroline's Deathbed. Pope.
Sweet Caroline. Anonymous.
To C.F.H. on Her Christening-Day. Hardy.

Carpentry
The Carpenter. Perkins.
Epigram: To English Connoisseurs. Blake.
Nature: The Artist. Knowles.
Softening to Heaven. Filip.

Carpet
The Figure in the Carpet. Camp.
Harriet. Lowell.
Naming the Rain. West.
Out of the Sea, Early. Swenson.
When Mary Goes Walking. Chalmers.

Carr (ied) (y)
Ad Patriam (excerpt). Foulke.
As I Was Going up the Hill. Anonymous.
Beauty and Sadness. Song.
Because He Is Young. Okura.
Birdwatcher. Treece.
The Coal-Owner and the Pitman's Wife. Anonymous.
Courtesy. Dodge.
The Cowboy's Lament (II). Anonymous.
Elegy for My Father. Strand.
Freight Boats. Tippett.
How Beautiful You Are: 3. Edelman.
How to Reach the Moon. Pomerantz.
The Old Lady of London. Anonymous.
On John Adams, of Southwell. Byron.
The Oregon Trail. Anonymous.
Over the River. Priest.
A Spool of Thread. Eastman.
Teatime Variations. Titheradge.
Trees. Merwin.
We Are the Burden-Bearers (excerpt). Stidger.
The Wind. Corbin.
You Are Growing into My Life... Harris.

Carriage (s)
O, the Marriage! Davis.
On the Road through Chang-Te. Sun Yun-feng.
Rock away, passenger. Anonymous.
Wedding. Lipska.

Carrion
Don Juan. Byron.
The Glutton. Graves.
Horror. Baum.
Jesus. Adams.
Julius Caesar. Shakespeare.
On the Site of a Mulberry-Tree. Rossetti.

Sunstrike. Livingstone.

Carrot (s)
Denunciation; or, Unfrock'd Again. Whalen.
Five Horses. Swenson.
The Flitting. McGuckian.
The Parrot and the Carrot We May Easily Confound. Wood.
Tema con Variazioni. "Carroll.

Cart (s)
A Carriage from Sweden. Moore.
On Dreams. Swift.
Ox Cart Man. Hall.
The Prejudice against the Past. Stevens.
The Refugees. Read.
The Shell. Stephens.
Signature. Stroud.
Waiting for the Doctor. Inez.

Carthage
San Francisco Arising. Markham.
Storm on Fifth Avenue. Sassoon.

Carve (d)
During Wind and Rain. Hardy.
Etruscan Notebook. Clementelli.
I Know a Man. Steele.
Needle and Thread. Pan Chao.
Opifex. Brown.
Orpheus to Woods. Lovelace.
Ox-Bone Madonna. Galvin.
Soliloquy II. Aldington.
To Luigi del Riccio, after the Death of Cecchino Bracci. Michelangelo.
To the Statue. Swenson.
The Toy-Maker. Colum.
Trilby. Brown.
When Father Carves the Duck. Wright.
Will Waterproof's Lyrical Monologue. Tennyson.

Case
Ballad of the Trial of Sodom. Watkins.
Elinda's Glove. Lovelace.
The Fly. Googe.
The Glove. Lovelace.
January Eclogue. Spenser.
Nothing in Heaven Functions As It Ought. Kennedy.
Old Poulter's Mare. Anonymous.
Once Musing as I Sat. Googe.
A Primary Ground. Rich.
The Sculptors. Purdy.
Sonnet to a Clam. Saxe.
Womb Song. Schaeffer.

Casement
The Contented Bachelor. Kendall.
Ode to Psyche. Keats.
A Pitcher of Mignonette. Bunner.

Casey
Casey Jones (D vers.). Anonymous.
Mama Have You Heard the News?(B vers. with music). Anonymous.

Cash
For the ERA Crusaders. Kennedy.
On the Publication of Diaries and Memoirs. Hood.
To an Artful Theatre Manager. Da Ponte.
Wiser Than the Children of Light. Gibbon.

Casket (s)
A Basket of Summer Fruit. Harpur.
The City of Satisfaction. Hoffman.
The Middle of a War. Fuller.
The Pale Blue Casket. Pitcher.
Play Ball! Francis.

Cast (s)
Act of Love. Scannell.
The Ant. Lovelace.
A Deposition from Love. Carew.
Diana. Constable.
Fair Weather. Parker.
A Farewell, a Welcome. Mueller.
For My Funeral. Housman.
The Gambler's Repentance. Gerald.
No Idle Boast. Lynskey.
The Odyssey. Homer.
One-Two-Three. Senesh.
Psalm XXXVI. Sidney.
Rock and Hawk. Jeffers.
Sancta Silvarum. Johnson.
Song of the Moderns. Fletcher.
Two Shapes. Gregor.
The Widow's Mites. Crashaw.

Castaway (s)
Passivity. Fullerton.
Youth's Spring-Tribute. Rossetti.

Caste
Blackpool Breezes. Anonymous.
Further Instructions. Pound.
O Brothers, Why Do You Talk. Mahadevi (Mahadeviyakka).

Castle (s)
Aladdin. Lowell.
The Candidate. Ezell.
Castles. Glanz-Leyeles. A.
Castles in the Air. Ballantine.
Depressed by a Book of Bad Poetry, I Walk toward an Unused Pasture... Wright.
Emily Hardcastle, Spinster. Ransom.
The Flitting. Clare.
King Richard II. Shakespeare.
The Kitchen Chimney. Frost.
The Norman Baron (excerpt). Longfellow.
Party in Winter. Shapiro.
The Princess Who Fled to the Castle. Landy.
Richard II. Shakespeare.
Rondel: "Strengthen, my Love, this castle of my heart." d'Orleans.
What Is't to Us? Churchill.
Youth. Clark.

Cat (s)
The Ad-dressing of Cats. Eliot.
The Appointment. Strong.
Bast. Benet.
Bird-Witted. Moore.
Can-Opener. McAleavey.
Cat and Mouse. Hughes.
The Cat and the Rain. Swift.
Cat Morgan Introduces Himself. Eliot.
The Cat-o-Nine-Tails. Blight.
Catch. Anonymous.
The Celtic Fringe. Smith.
Choosing Their Names. Hood.
Cinderella's Song. Roberts.
Coptic Poem. Durrell.
Dame Trot. Anonymous.
Dear Girl. Corso.
Death of the Cat. Serraillier.
Diamond Cut Diamond. Milne.
Dob and Mob. Anonymous.
Dog Body and Cat Mind. Joseph.
Early Spring. Keyes.
Epigram on the Toasts of the Kit-Kat Club, Anno 1716. Pope.
Epitaph for a Cat. Bruner.
Fiddle-I-Fee. Anonymous.
The Galloping Cat. Smith.
Genius Loci of the Morning. Fetherling.
Getting Up. Dobyns.
The Gift. Ochester.
Gunner. Jarrell.
Hip Shakin' Strut. Georgia Tom.
How a Good Greyhound Is Shaped. Anonymous.
I Am the Cat. Usher.
In Honour of Taffy Topaz. Morley.
The Intoxicated Rat. Anonymous.
Late Lights in Minnesota. Kooser.
The Lazy Pussy. Cox.
Limerick: "N is for naughty young Nat." Bellows.
The Little Man and the Little Maid. Anonymous.
May Colven. Anonymous.
Midnight. Middleton.
Mort aux Chats. Porter.
Mountain Town–Mexico. Grier.
Moving. Jarrell.
My cat and I. McGough.
My Old Cat. Summers.
The Mysterious Cat. Lindsay.
Nature Green Shit. Snyder.
New England. Robinson.
The Old Wife and the Ghost. Reeves.
On Reading Poems to a Senior Class at South High. Berry.
On Sitting up Late, Watching Kittens. Paff.
Partly to My Cat. Bass.
The Passionate Professor. Taylor.
The People, Yes. Sandburg.
The Philosopher and the Birds. Murphy.
The Photograph the Cat Licks. Walter.

Phyllis; or, The Progress of Love. Swift.
Pretences. Ibn Rashiq.
Reconcilable Differences. Sauls.
Riddle: "It has a head like a cat, feet like a cat." Anonymous.
Robin Redbreast. Anonymous.
The Rose Is Red, the Grass Is Green. Anonymous.
Scottsboro. Anonymous.
Skimbleshanks: the Railway Cat. Eliot.
Snow in the Suburbs. Hardy.
The Square at Dawn. Tate.
Supplication of the Black Aberdeen. Kipling.
Suzie's New Dog. Ciardi.
That Little Black Cat. Thompson.
Thoughts on Capital Punishment. McKuen.
Tiger-Cat Tim. Chase.
To Henrietta, on Her Departure for Calais. Hood.
The Tortoiseshell Cat. Chalmers.
Two and One Are a Problem. Nash.
Wanted. Silverstein.
We Were Permitted to Meet Together in Prison to Prepare for Trial. Berrigan.
What Could It Be? Cole.
The White Cat of Trenarren. Rowse.
"Who Are You?" Asked the Cat of the Bear. Coatsworth.
The Willow Cats. Widdemer.
Witch Cat. Bennett.
Woman Par Excellence. Owens.

Catalogue
A Ballade-Catalogue of Lovely Things. Le Gallienne.
Tutankhamen. Dickey.

Catastrophe
John Sutter. Winters.
Precarious Ground. Drake.
Theme and Variations. Millay.

Catch (es)
3:16 and One Half... Bukowski.
Captive. Strobel.
The Contemplative. Sister M. Therese.
The Contemplative Quarry. Wickham.
The Crocus. Crane.
The Crow and the Fox. La Fontaine.
Delicate the Toad. Francis.
Down from the Country. Blight.
Enigmas. Neruda.
Farm Gate. Krige.
The Feast of Stephen. Hecht.
For a Little Girl Mourning Her Favorite Cat. Whittier.
A Gnarled Riverina Gum-Tree. Moll.
The Golden Fish. Arnold.
Harbor. Price.

I Do Not Love to See Your Beauty Fire. Wheelock.
In a Railway Compartment. Fuller.
Jack Was Every Inch a Sailor. Anonymous.
Joses, the Brother of Jesus. Kemp.
Limerick: "There once were some learned MD's." Herford.
Little Sticks. Rolls.
The Little Turtle. Lindsay.
Living with You. Langfield.
Mariushka's Wedding Song. Anonymous.
Marriage and Midsummer's Night. Gregg.
The Methodist. Lloyd.
Mihailovich. McFadden.
Moonbeam. Conkling.
Nocturne: Georgia Coast. Hicky.
NW5 & N6. Betjeman.
O Girl, You Torment Me... Anonymous.
Of Certain Irish Fairies. Guiterman.
Phallus. Shiraishi Kazuko.
Poems, LVIII: "Twenty years hence my eyes may grow." Landor.
Pursuit. Rutsala.
The Quaker's Wooing. Anonymous.
The Raising of the Dead. Dobson.
Riddle: "A hill full, a hole full." Mother Goose.
Riddle: "House full, yard full." Anonymous.
Ring-A-Ring. Greenaway.
Robin Redbreast. Kunitz.
The Seasons. Holcroft.
Sisters. Roberts.
Sorrow seldom killeth any. Davison.
Think Small. Equi.
Timid Hortense. Newell.
To a Young Lady Swinging Upside Down on a Birch Limb... Koch.
Tommy Tittlemouse. Anonymous.
The Turning. Murray.
The Undertaker's Horse. Kipling.
Untitled. Rahschulte.
Ursa Major. Kirkup.
The Vixen. Clare.
Wili Woyi, Shaman, also known as Billy Pigeon. Conley.

Caterpillar (s)
The Butterfly and the Caterpillar. Lauren.
Fable XXIV: The Butterfly and the Snail. Gay.
On Court-Worme. Jonson.
Perdita. MacNeice.

Catfish
The Catfish. Waters.
Fools. Hardin.
Ol' Hag, You See Mammy? Anonymous.
Roosevelt Considers Catfish Stew. Smith.

Cathedral (s)
The Cathedral of Rheims. Verhaeren.
Pastorale. Davis.
Peter at Fourteen. Carrier.

The Puritan. Shapiro.
There Is. Simpson.

Catholic (s)
The Avenue Bearing the Initial of Christ into the New World. Kinnell.
Grandfather. Bowering.
Maternal Lady with the Virgin Grace. Lamb.
Night Thoughts. Coulette.
Poem against Catholics. Fuller. John

Cattle
Campi Flegrei. Toerien.
The Canadian Herd-Boy. Moodie.
Diamond Joe. Anonymous.
Donought Would Have Everything. Elliott.
Evangeline. Longfellow.
Growing Wild. Miller.
Highland Cattle. Mulock.
Jonah. Jarrell.
The Last Longhorn. Hall.
Limerick: "The heavyweight champ of Seattle." Anonymous.
Mamparra M'gaiza. Craveirinha.
O White Mistress. Johnson.
Picture Framing. Meyers.
Prairie Fires. Garland.
The Shearer's Wife. Esson.
Shechem. Shevin.
Song: "Grace and beauty has the maid." Vicente.
The Texas Song. Anonymous.
Two Poems after A. E. Housman. Kingsmill.
Wedding Wind. Larkin.
Wells. Hall.

Catullus
The Scholars. Yeats.
Veranius, My Dear Friend. Catullus.

Cauldron
Ariel. Plath.
Now He Is Dead. Campbell.
Winter. Anonymous.

Cause (s)
All for the Cause. Morris.
All Our Griefs to Tell. Newton.
At Epidaurus. Durrell.
Bacon's Epitaph, Made by His Man. Anonymous.
The Beginning of the End. Hopkins.
Cast Down, but Not Destroyed. Anonymous.
A Choice of Weapons. Kunitz.
A Christmas Ghost-Story. Hardy.
The Death of Lincoln. Bryant.
For Myself. Hines.
From the Epigrams of Martial. Michie.
A Full and True Account of a Horrid and Barbarous Robbery. Byrom.
I Am the Lord. Mack.
If You're the Man You Ought to Be. Isenhour.
Irradiations. Fletcher.
King Lear. Shakespeare.
My Lodging It Is on the Cold Ground. D'Avenant.
Opportunity. Sill.

Orinda to Lucasia Parting, October, 1661, at London. Philips.

The Procession: A New Protestant Ballad. *Anonymous.*

She Is More to be Pitied than Censured. Gray.

St. James Infirmary. *Anonymous.*

To Critics. Herrick.

When I Thy Parts Run O'er. Herrick.

The Wyoming Massacre. Terry.

The Young American. Everett.

Caution (s)

The Antiplatonick. Cleveland.

Rain. Fry.

Cautiou (s)

Einstein's Father. Klauck.

The Nurse Believed the Sick Man Slept. Bronte.

Cave (s)

Aeolian Harp. Allingham.

The Cage. Treinin.

The Dosser in Springtime. Stewart.

Homecoming. Baxter.

The Horses of Marini. Van Zyl.

The Hosts. Merwin.

The Leaves That Rustled on This Oak-Crowned Hill. Wordsworth.

The Little Girl Lost. Blake.

Lot Later. Nemerov.

Love Poem Investigation for A.T. Frate.

The Mermaids. De la Mare.

Mind. Wilbur.

Night Watch. Magid.

Nishikigi: The Love-Cave. Motokiyo.

Sirventes. Blackburn.

Sleep. Knott.

This Child. Rosten.

Yew-Trees. Wordsworth.

Cavern (s)

Canoe. Anderson.

The Sea-Deeps. Miller.

Song: "Christ keep the Hollow Land." Morris.

A Sunset. Coleridge.

This Is the Last Night. Borson.

Caw (s)

The Day Concludes Burning. O'Grady.

Hokku Poems. Wright.

Kaddish. Ginsberg.

Cease (s)

Battle of Somerset. Cullen.

Chez Madame. Harrison.

The Coward. Spender.

The Dispute of the Heart and Body of Francois Villon. Villon.

Hark, All Ye Lovely Saints. *Anonymous.*

I Said to Love. Hardy.

I Want to Die while You Love Me. Johnson.

Israel's Duration. Halevi.

It May Be So with Us. Masefield.

Landscapeople. Ashbery.

Praise of God. *Anonymous.*

Return of Autumn. Neruda.

Silverthorn Bush. Finch.

Summer Is A-Coming In. *Anonymous.*

To Wordsworth. Shelley.

Tolerance. Morris.

The War God. Spender.

While Shepherds Watched Their Flocks by Night. Tate.

Your Presence. Temkin.

Ceaseless

Essential oils–are wrung. Dickinson.

A Heart That Weeps. Smith.

Cedar (s)

Desert Song. Dresbach.

Drum-Taps. Whitman.

Imperfect Sestina. Webb.

The One Who Is Within. Francisco.

The Poet's Final Instructions. Berryman.

Sitting in the Woods: A Contemplation. Moses.

Venus Abandoned. Shakespeare.

The Violin Tree. Rosenberg.

We Are a People. Henson.

Ceiling (s)

The Boarder. Simpson.

The Floor and the Ceiling. Smith.

Homage to the Carracci. Disch.

Limerick: "There once was a spinster of Ealing." *Anonymous.*

Love, Love! What Nonsense It Is. Gorbanyevskaya.

Tuesday. Landau.

Celebrat (e) (ing) (ion)

40 Acres and a Mule. Gallup.

Dream Songs. Berryman.

Forsythia Is the Color I Remember. Cherwinski.

Growltiger's Last Stand. Eliot.

High Summer. Rotella.

Looking for Buddha. Jacinto.

Mother. Helburn.

Ovid in the Third Reich. Hill.

Psalm for Christmas Day. Pestel.

Rebolushinary x-mas/eastuh julie 4/ etc. etc. etc. etc. Rodgers.

Rite of Passage. Olds.

Rondel. Rukeyser.

Who of Those Coming After. Gottlieb.

Wreathmakertraining. Patten.

Celestial

Animal. Eastman.

The Bible. Traherne.

Epitaph on John Dove. Burns.

Eugenio Pacelli. Neilson.

For a Lady I Know. Cullen.

The Future Verdict. Cambridge.

His Body. McPherson.

Lost. Fisher.

My Mouth Is Often Joined against His Mouth. Rimbaud.

Of Edmund Spenser's Fairy Queen... Ralegh.

The Old Miner's Refrain. *Anonymous.*

The Ransomed Spirit to Her Home. Tappan.

Sonnet: True Ambition. Stillingfleet.

Tell Us, Ye Servants of the Lord. Staughton.

To His Friend–. Vaughan.

Welcome to the Sun. Douglas.

Celia

Boldness in Love. Carew.

Cassinus and Peter. Swift.

The Declaimer. Baker.

Hint from Voiture. Shenstone.

Lips and Eyes. Carew.

Lips and Eyes. Marino.

Sonnet on Death. Walsh.

Cell (s)

Adieu to the Stone Walls. *Anonymous.*

The Ant Village. Grider.

The Grave. Jones.

Hymn. Orban.

The Philosopher's Scales. Taylor.

Prison Cell Blues. Jefferson.

St. Govan. Prys-Jones.

Your Voice on the Telephone. Hall.

Cellar (s)

Christmas Comes but Once a Year. *Anonymous.*

Fate With Devoted... Ficke.

Haunted House. Worth.

Ring the Bell. *Anonymous.*

Scottsboro. *Anonymous.*

The Ungathered Apples. Wright.

Celluloid

Halo. Currey.

To the Film Industry in Crisis. O'Hara.

Cemetery

Charles Donnelly. MacDonagh.

Poem on Azure. Noailles.

Stagolee (A vers.). *Anonymous.*

Stagolee (B vers.). *Anonymous.*

Toads Revisited. Larkin.

Cenotaph

I Am the Blood. Rosenberg.

On a Bust of Lincoln. Scollard.

Poe's Cottage at Fordham. Boner.

Censors

On Hearing It Has Been Ordered in the Chapterhouses of Ireland... Haicead.

Censure (s)

A Letter to Dafnis April: 2d 1685. Winchilsea.

Lines on Being Refused a Guggenheim Fellowship. Whittemore.

To the Nightingale. Wilchilsea.

Cent (s)

The Hardship of Accounting. Frost.

Let Us Smile. Nesbit.

Price of a Drink. Pollard.

Centaur

A Thought from Porpertius. Yeats.

Tiresias (excerpt). Clarke.

Center (s)

Above It All. Levine.

Breasts. Unger.

Butcher's Wife. Scott.

Certified Copy. Deacon.

Dark Conclusions. Stone.

Errantry. Fitzgerald.

Eve's Song in the Garden. Gottlieb.

An Excuse of Absence. Carew.

Force. Walcott.

Four Heads & How to Do Them. Forbes.

Ghazals. Harrison.

Hitchhiker. Marshall.

Home. Summers.

Home Revisited: Midnight. Ciardi.

The Last Booke of the Ocean to Scinthia (excerpt). Ralegh.

Legacy II. Quintana.

Once Only. Snyder.

Prairie Graveyard. Marriott.

Prothalamium. Sarton.

Saints, and Their Care. Rios.

Summer Farm. MacCaig.

There Is a Place. Hoellein.

They Made Me Erect and Lone. Thoreau.

True Enough: To the Physicist (1820). Goethe.

What Is Love? Clare.

When I Cut My Hair. Green.

Centrifuge

Richard Hunt's Arachne. Hayden.

Centur (ies) (y)

Au Bout du Temps. Codrescu.

The Australian. Adams.

Baudelaire Series (excerpt). Palmer.

By Rail through the Earthly Paradise, Perhaps Bedfordshire. Levertov.

C Stands for Civilization. Fearing.

Children Not Kept at Home. Oates.

Christmas Eve. Day Lewis.

The Clouds. Mira Bai [(or Mirabai(].

The Dinner. Orr.

The Divine Narcissus. Juana Ines de la Cruz.

Fate. Cooper, Jr..

Follow Me. Longfellow.

"Garden of Gethsemane." Pasternak.

Him Evermore I Behold. Longfellow.

Just Lost, When I Was Saved! Dickinson.

A long, long sleep. Dickinson.

The Man with the Hoe. Markham.

The Newest Banana Plant Leaf. Wendt.

On the Coast near Sausalito. Hass.

Only in This Way. Burroughs.

Paiute Ponies. Barnes.

Snakebite. James.

So Beautiful Is the Tree of Night. Hanson.

Sun-Up in March. Evans.

The Voice of Christmas. Kemp.

The Waggoner. Blunden.

We Bear the Strain of Earthly
Care. Davis.
Wild Honey. Thompson.
Ceremony
Ceremony. Miller.
Little Epithalamium.
Kallman.
Long Live Our Dear and
Noble Queen. Foot.
Night Song for an Old Lover.
Glickman.
Ceres
Molly Moor. Farewell.
Certain (ly) (ty)
The Burning of the Leaves.
Binyon.
By Moonlight. *Anonymous.*
Certainty Enough. Burr.
Dying! To be afraid of thee.
Dickinson.
An English Wood. Graves.
Flux. Eberhart.
Girod Street Cemetery: New
Orleans. Morris.
Here Lies Fierce Strephon.
Hecht.
If I Could Meet God.
Schmitz.
Leaf. Hewitt.
Our True Beginnings.
Gardiner.
The Robin Is the One.
Dickinson.
Sarasvati. Stephens.
Sonnet: "Because my grief
seems quiet and apart."
Nathan.
The Story of Rimini. Hunt.
Two Married. Frazee-Bower.
The Way Sun Keeps Falling
Away from Every Window.
Lifshin.
The Western Approaches.
Nemerov.
Chaff (e)
Emblems. Quarles.
A Gentle Wind. Fu Hsuan.
The Harvest of Time.
Pulsifer.
The Harvest Waits. Mifflin.
The Name. Hay.
Not I. Stevenson.
Recollection. Aldrich.
Sifting. Beck.
Chain (s)
Alabama Earth. Hughes.
Andromeda. Roche.
Ballad of the Drover.
Lawson.
Bold Jack Donahue.
Anonymous.
The Boys of Wexford.
Anonymous.
Cerberus. Van Brunt.
The Convict. *Anonymous.*
The Courtier's Life. Wyatt.
Elegy on Mistress Boulstred.
Donne.
Fern Hill. Thomas.
The Firstborn. Goodchild.
From the Turkish. Byron.
The Fugitive Slaves. Very.
Give Peace, O God, the
Nations Cry. Norris.
Instructions to a Celebrated
Laureat (excerpt). Wolcot.
Jim Jones. *Anonymous.*
Julian M. and A.G. Rochelle.
Bronte.
A Lament for the Princes of
Tyrone and Tyrconnel.
Anonymous.

The Loon. Street.
Love's Slavery. Sheffield.
Mathematics of Love.
Hamburger.
Much madness is divinest
sense. Dickinson.
No More Will I Endure
Love's Pleasing Pain.
Anonymous.
Ode: "That I have often been
in love, deep love."
Wolcot.
Odes. Horace.
One by One. Procter.
The Power of Thought.
Susskind.
The Prison House. Paton.
A Prisoner's Song of
Jerusalem. *Anonymous.*
The Rusted Chain. Ben
Yeshaq.
Shore. O Hehir.
Silex Scintillans. Vaughan.
The Silk Weaver's Daughter.
Anonymous.
The Sirens. Finkel.
Sonnets: A Sequence on
Profane Love. Boker.
Suave Mari Magno.
Lucretius (Titus Lucretitus
Carus).
The Thousand and One
Nights: The Beautiful Boy.
Anonymous.
To One Who Quotes and
Detracts. Landor.
To Song. Berggolts.
To the Memory of J. Horace
Kimball. Ada Sister Mary.
Translation of Horace, Odes,
IV, VII. Horace.
Upon a Black Twist,
Rounding the Arm of the
Countess of Carlisle.
Herrick.
View from the Window.
McCoy.
The Vintage to the Dungeon.
Lovelace.
Virginia Capta. Preston.
The Will to Change. Rich.
Women of My Land.
Armstrong.
Chair (s)
Analysands. Randall.
Buchlyvie. *Anonymous.*
Carol for Advent. Heath-
Stubbs.
Chairs. Petroski.
Chairs to Mend. *Anonymous.*
The Chameleon. Prior.
The Cloak. Anderson.
The Domestic Stones. Arp.
Evening Musicale.
McGinley.
Five Visions of Captain Cook.
Slessor.
The Guests. Zukofsky.
Jack Rose. Bodenheim.
My Limbs I Will Fling.
Strode.
Ode on a Sermon against
Glory. Akenside.
Old Grandpaw Yet.
Anonymous.
The Pilgrimage. Herbert.
Spicewood. Reese.
Chaise
Distant as the Duchess of
Savoy. *Anonymous.*
The Lady's Diary. Dibdin.

Chalk
Elegy. Towle.
The End of Man Is Death.
Ibn Ezra.
The Factory. Cabral.
Paterson. Williams.
Train Window. Finch.
The Wench in the Street.
Anonymous.
Challenge
The Author Apologizes to a
Lady for His Being a Little
Man. Smart.
Interracial. Johnson.
Look Not to Me for Wisdom.
Divine.
Lourenco Marques.
Eglington.
November Garden. Driscoll.
Rainier. Tollerud.
Second Woman's Lament.
Chamberlain.
Snow-Bound. Whittier
Chamber pot
Approach of Winter.
Thomson.
Egnatius, Because His Teeth
Are White. Catullus.
House Blessing. Guiterman.
Shickered as He Could Be.
Anonymous
Verses Occasioned by the
Sudden Drying
up...(excerpt). Swift.
Chamber (s)
Admonition to the Muse.
Taylor.
All Hail, Thou Noble Guest.
Luther.
Arrows. Heyen.
Hero and Leander.
Chapman.
Lament to Nana of Erech.
Anonymous.
Lord Saltoun and
Auchanachie. *Anonymous.*
Moonlight. Moxon.
The Road at My Door.
Yeats.
An Upper Chamber.
Bannerman.
The Witch. Yeats.
Chameleon
Les Etiquettes Jaunes.
O'Hara.
How to Tell the Wild
Animals. Wells.
Champagne
Adam, Eve and the Big
Apple. Watkins.
Champagne. McGuckian.
Finnair Fragment.
Hoffmann.
Lalique. Porter.
A Rhemish Carol. Finch.
Champion (s)
The Earl of Westmoreland.
Anonymous.
A Flight Shot. Thompson.
The Great Adventure.
Thoreau.
Life. Brown.
Chance' (s)
Accident in Art. Hovey.
The Albion Battleship
Calamity. McGonagall.
Back Gnawing Blues.
Thomas.
Baseball's Sad Lexicon.
Adams.
Born Without a Chance.
Cooke.

Boys in October. Layton.
The Broken-Down Squatter.
Anonymous.
The Clarity of Apples.
Perlin.
Coastline. Feinstein.
Crab. Blight.
Delta Farmer in a Wet
Summer. Whitehead.
Despite and Still. Graves.
Down the Mississippi.
Fletcher.
Elementary Cosmogony.
Simic.
Epigram. Du Guillet.
Failures. Upson.
Flodden Field. *Anonymous.*
Green Frog at Roadside,
Wisconsin. Schevill.
A Hint from Herrick.
Aldrich.
Jess's Dilemma. *Anonymous.*
Knowledge. Grutzmacher.
Ladybug. Sund.
Laundry & School Epigrams.
Mayer.
Malice Domestic. Nash.
Mathematics of Love.
Hamburger.
Mexico City Blues: 229th
Chorus. Kerouac.
The People vs. the People.
Fearing.
The Possibility That Has Been
Overlooked Is the Future.
Hartnett.
A Prayer for Thanksgiving.
Auslander.
Rags. Cook.
Resignation. Arnold.
Roger and Me. Le Dressay.
Sigismundo. Gregg.
The Song of the Unsuccessful.
Burton.
Sonnets of the Months. San
Geminiano.
The Speculators. Thackeray.
Street Demonstration.
Walker.
The Task That Is Given to
You. Markham.
The Tay Bridge Disaster.
McGonagall.
Thais. Levy.
That Little Lump of Coal.
Anonymous.
The Time I've Lost in
Wooing. Moore.
To the Earl of Warwick.
Tickell.
To Whistler, American.
Pound.
Unintelligible Terms. Simic.
Vow to Love Faithfully,
Howsoever He Be
Rewarded. Surrey.
The white chrysanthemum.
Mitsune (Oshikochi no
Mitsune).
Chancellor
The Lord Chancellours
Villainies Discovered.
Anonymous.
The Susceptible Chancellor.
Gilbert.
Chandelier (s)
Glass World. Donnelly.
The Man in Black. Strand.
Salome. *Anonymous.*
Change (d) (s)
Ad Finem. Wilcox.

An Air by Sammartini. Dudek.
Ancestral Faces. Brew.
And the Same Words. Ignatow.
Anishinabe Grandmothers. Vizenor.
The Anti-Politician. Brome.
Apology for Youth. Madeleva.
Appreciation. Meredith.
Archaic Torso of Apollo. Rilke.
As You Leave the Room. Stevens.
As You Like It. Shakespeare.
The Beaks of Eagles. Jeffers.
Blest Statesman He, Whose Mind's Unselfish Will. Wordsworth.
Blossom Time. Larremore.
Blue Funk. Oppenheimer.
But Still in Israel's Paths They Shine. Revard.
By the North Sea. Swinburne.
Caelica, VII. Greville.
Caelica, XXX. Greville.
Caelica, XXXII. Greville.
Caelica, XLVIII. Greville.
Caelica, LXXVI. Greville.
Camels of the Kings. Norris.
Casino Beach. Rabbit.
Change. Greville.
Cheyenne Mountain. Jackson.
City Songs. Van Doren.
The Cold Divinities. Wright.
The Constancy of a Lover. Gascoigne.
The Coyote. Revard.
Did We Laugh or Did We Cry? Simoko.
Disguises. Jennings.
Don Juan. Byron.
Don't Want No Hungry Woman. Council.
The Doubt of Future Foes. Elizabeth I.
A Dream. Kinney
The Dust Will Settle. Tapahonso.
Earth and Sky. Euripides.
Elegies. Chenier.
The Emancipators. Jarrell.
Epigram: "First in his pride the orient sun's display." Belloc.
Even There. Lifshin.
Evening. Matheson.
The Faerie Queene. Spenser.
Farmers. Roberts.
The Feather. Lyon.
The Flying Change. Taylor.
Flying Changes. Wood.
Footwear. Justus.
For My Father. Field.
For Want I Will in Woe I Plain. Wyatt.
Fore Thought. Sarton.
Four Folk-Songs in Hokku Form, 3. *Anonymous.*
Frog Prince. Pettingell.
From One Who Stays. Lowell.
Gardener Janus Catches a Naiad. Sitwell.
The Geographers. Shapiro.
Green Grow the Lilacs. *Anonymous.*
Hesitating Ode. Radnoti.

The Hind and the Panther. Dryden.
His Mother in Her Hood of Blue. Reese.
Hopper's "Nighthawks." (1942). Sadoff.
The Horses. Muir.
How Our Forefather Got His Wife. Walton.
I Rode Southern, I Rode L. & N. *Anonymous.*
In Orknay. Fowler.
Interim. Ormsby.
Johnny, I Hardly Knew Ye: Swinburnese (parody). Tyrrell.
The Kid Has Gone to the Colors. Herschell.
Last Visit. Finch.
The Layers. Kunitz.
Leicester Chambermaid. *Anonymous.*
Life the Very Gods in My Sight Is He Who. Sappho.
Like a Whisper. Ayer.
Lines on the Author's Death. Burns.
The Lodger. Longley.
Love Not. Norton.
Love Poem. Kageyama.
Love's Change. Aldrich.
Lovers Relentlessly. Kunitz.
Luscious and Sorrowful. Rossetti.
Lycoris darling, once I burned for you. Martial (Marcus Valerius Martialis).
The Marchen. Jarrell.
Meditation. Pain.
Mimosa. Mathis.
Mirage. Rossetti.
Moonshine. Williamson.
Mountaineering Bus. McOwan.
My Mother's Love. *Anonymous.*
My Playmate. Whittier.
Napoleon and the British Sailor. Campbell.
Nature, that gave the bee so feat a grace. Wyatt.
Need. Deutsch.
North Haven. Bishop.
Not Wholly Lost. Souster.
On a Great Man Whose Mind is Clouding. Stedman.
On City Streets. Bruner.
One Year to Life on the Grand Central Shuttle. Lorde.
Ontogeny. Ramsey.
An Ordinary Day beyond Kaitaia. Smithyman.
Outside Every Window Is a Flowering Thing. Skeen.
Paradise Lost. Milton.
Pied Beauty. Hopkins.
A Primitive Like an Orb. Stevens.
Renewal. "Field.
Repetition of Words and Weather. Stone.
Riding Song. Schneider.
Riprap. Snyder.
A Rope for Harry Fat. Baxter.
The Sculptor. *Anonymous.*
Seminary. Carrier.
Sestina. Justice.
Snow. Avison.
Song of Oenone and Paris. Peele.

Sonnet: "To rail or jest, ye know I use it not." Wyatt.
Status Symbols. Sostrom.
Summary. Sanchez.
Sunflower Moccasins. George.
Sweet Peril. Macdonald.
Things I Used to Do (with music). *Anonymous.*
This Earthen Body. *Anonymous.*
Three Moves. Logan.
Time Will Not Grant. Keyes.
To —. Shelley.
To a Seamew. Swinburne.
To Lucia at Birth. Graves.
To My First Love, My Mother. Rossetti.
Too Late. Marston.
The Train Is off the Track. *Anonymous.*
Trash. Box.
Under the Catalpa Trees. Young.
Upon His Picture. Randolph.
We Settled by the Lake. Reeve.
Wednesday Night Prayer Meeting. Wright.
What Is Terrible. Fuller.
Who Would Have Thought. Howell.
The Woman at the Washington Zoo. Jarrell.

Changeless,
Ambarvalia. Clough.
The Capitals Are Rocked. Nekrasov.
The Constant Lover. Simpson.
The Cross of Snow. Longfellow.
For Elizabeth Madox Roberts. Lewis.
Gestures to the Dead (excerpt). Wheelwright.

Channel (s)
Addict. Montgomery.
Clevedon Church. Lang.
Long Person. Cardiff.
Sea Sonnet. Lay.
Silex Scintillans. Vaughan.

Chant (ed) (ing) (s)
The First Hunt. Anderson.
Hymn. Larcom.
I Heard the Bells on Christmas Day. Longfellow.
The Jews. Jastrun.
Landor. Albee.
Ode in May. Watson.
Piano at Evening. Palea.
Revolutionary Letters. Di Prima.
The Song-Maker. Fairbridge.
Three White Birds of Angus. Cox.
Tradition. Guiterman.
Yonosa House. Smith.

Chaos
Dawn on the Night-Journey. Rossetti.
The Diver. Howard.
Dutch Interior. Sarton.
From the Head. Zukofsky.
The Great House. Muir.
Hero Song. Duncan.
Night Wind. Tyutchev.

Ode Written at Vale-Royal Abbey in Cheshire. Warton, Jr..
Our Love Was a Grim Citadel. Mason.
Paradise Lost. Milton.
Port of Call: Brazil. Lewis.
September Sun: 1947. Gascoyne.
Serene Immediate Silliest and Whose. Cummings.
Song for These Days. Kirby.
The Three Kings. Dario.
The Titans. Alver.

Chapel
Amours de Voyage. Clough.
By a Chapel. *Anonymous.*
The Grotto. Fraser.
In a Boat. Belloc.

Chaplain
Manila Bay. Hale.
Mrs. Frances Harris's Petition. Swift.
A Sea-Chaplain's Petition. "T.

Chapter
A Ballad of Queensland (Sam Holt). Gibson ("Ironbark").
In Memory of Your Body. Shapiro.
A Receipt for Stewing Veal. Gay.

Character (s)
Ciampino. Denby.
Essay on Rime (excerpt). Shapiro.
The Jolly Beggars. Burns.
New England Is New England Is New England. Green.
Sleep Will Come Singly. Oliver.
To Be Carved on a Stone at Thoor Ballylee. Yeats.
You. Guest.

Charge (d) (s)
The Annuity. Outram.
Death As History. Wright.
Dies Irae. *Anonymous.*
The Dog Parade. Guiterman.
Don Quixote. Dobson.
The Famous Light Brigade. *Anonymous.*
The Five Best Doctors. Hoffman.
A Hundreth Good Poyntes of Husbandry. Tusser.
Master Charge Blues. Giovanni.
The Monkey's Wedding (with music). *Anonymous.*
On the Departure of Sir Walter Scott from Abbotsford, for Naples. Wordsworth.
Sappho. Carman.
Wayne at Stony Point. Scollard.

Chariot (s)
An Angel Describes Truth. Jonson.
The Female Parricide. *Anonymous.*
The Female Phaeton. Prior.
Georgics. Virgil (Publius Vergilius Maro).
The Iliad. Homer.
Low down Chariot. *Anonymous.*
Oh, My Good Lord, Show Me de Way. *Anonymous.*

Chariot

A Prayer. Hamilton.
Queen Mab. Shelley.
Roll de Ol' Chariot Along.
  Anonymous.
Rye Bread. Braithwaite.
Sing, Brothers, Sing!
  Rodgers.
Sleep and Poetry. Keats.
Some say cavalry and others
  claim. Sappho.
Song: "One day the god of
  fond desire." Thomson.
Written in Butler's Sermons.
  Arnold.

Charit (ies) (y)

At the Sea's Edge.
  Harwood.
Birds. Miller.
Bowery. Ignatow.
Classic Ballroom Dances.
  Simic.
The Divorce. Stanley.
Everyman. *Anonymous.*
Golden Wedding (excerpt).
  Mulgan.
Guard Thy Tongue. Barr.
Homage to William Cowper.
  Davie.
In Memoriam A.H.H., CXIV.
  Tennyson.
Modern Love, XX.
  Meredith.
On the Death of a Favourite
  Old Spaniel. Southey.
Opposition. Lanier.
Our Lady in the Middle Ages.
  Faber.
Perpetual Christmas. Field.
Perpetuum Immobile. Dawe.
The Pilgrim Fathers.
  Wordsworth.
Rest O Sun I Cannot.
  Tusiani.
Rosa Mystica. Hopkins.
Signs. Soutar.
Wreck of the Deutschland.
  Hopkins.

Charl (ey) (ie)

Charley Barley. *Anonymous.*
Desert Holy Man. Beecher.
Eulogy for a Tough Guy.
  Klauck.
For Charlie's Sake. Palmer.
Little Charlie Chipmunk.
  LeCron.
My Pretty Little Miss.
  Anonymous.
A New Song, Call'd The Red
  Wig. *Anonymous.*
O'er the Water to Charlie.
  Burns.
On the Charlie So Long.
  Anonymous.
Over the Water to Charlie.
  Anonymous.
Who Needs Charlie Manson?
  Thompson.

Charlemagne

Paradise Lost. Milton.
Whence Had They Come?
  Yeats.

Charles

George the Third's Soliloquy.
  Freneau.
The Obscured Prince; or, the
  Black Box Boxed.
  Anonymous.
Sketch of his Own Character.
  Gray.
The Tune to the Devonshire
  Cant. Ayloffe.

A Walk by the Charles.
  Rich.
When They Found Giotto.
  Laing.

Charm (ed) (ing) (s)

Autumn. Curran.
Brigham Young.
  Anonymous.
Charming. Matthews.
Christmas 1930. Scruggs.
The Death of Morgan.
  Anonymous.
The Deserted Village.
  Goldsmith.
Don Juan. Byron.
The Dumb Maid.
  Anonymous.
The Enemy. Waller.
Enraptured I Gaze.
  Hopkinson.
The Fair-Haired Girl.
  Anonymous.
Fair Hebe. West.
A Farewel to Worldly Joyes.
  Killigrew.
The Firstling. Davison.
The Foggy Dew.
  Anonymous.
For Kuo Hsiang. Yu Hsuan-
  chi.
Happiness Amidst Troubles.
  Di Roma.
The Hesperides. Tennyson.
Ill. Spencer.
The Je Ne Scay Quoi: A
  Song. Whitehead.
Lines Written in the Dog-
  Days. Woty.
London Is a Fine Town.
  Anonymous.
London Snow. Bridges.
Love-Charms. Campion.
The Love of Hell. Burstein.
Madrono. Harte.
Mars and Venus. Greene.
The Maryland Yellow-Throat.
  Van Dyke.
The Minstrel. Beattie.
An Ode on Miss Harriet
  Hanbury. Williams.
On a Vase of Gold-Fish.
  Tennyson.
A Petticoat. Stein.
Picturesque; a Fragment.
  Aiken.
Poem. Schuyler.
A Poem of Privacy.
  Symonds.
Prince Charming. Miller.
The Schoolmaster Abroad
  with His Son. Calverley.
Sea Eclogue. Diaper.
Song: "Do I venture away too
  far." Douglas.
Song: "Love in her Eyes sits
  playing." Gay.
Terence McDiddler.
  Anonymous.
To Music: A Song. Herrick.
Trust Not the Treason.
  Spenser.
Uncle Bull-Boy. Jordan.
When Sadness Fills a Journey.
  Waller.
Wild Oats. Larkin.

Charon

At the Ferry. Fanthorpe.
Pericles and Aspasia.
  Landor.

Chart

Dispatch Number Sixty.
  Fetherling.

The Flag. Roche.
I never saw a moor.
  Dickinson.
The Tempest. Smith.

Chase (d) (s)

Against Hope. Cowley.
The Childless Father.
  Wordsworth.
The European Night.
  Vinaver.
For Hope. Crashaw.
The Fox. Clare.
The Kilruddery Hunt.
  Mozeen.
Let Us Drink. Alcaeus.
Limerick: "There was an old
  man of Toulon. Smith.
The Lollypops. Thomas.
Lone Huntsman. Jeffries.
Love–bittersweet,
  irrepressible–. Sappho.
Making Feet and Hands.
  Peret.
Musselburgh Field.
  Anonymous.
O Say, My Brown Drimin.
  Anonymous.
A Pause of Thought.
  Rossetti.
Round About There Sat a
  Little Hare. *Anonymous.*
Two Men. Robinson.

Chasm (s)

Epithalamium. McFadden.
The Hambone and the Heart.
  Sitwell.
The Isle. Shelley.

Chaste

Anti-Platonicke. Daniel.
Crowds. Baudelaire.
The Downright Country-Man;
  or, The Faithful Dairy
  Maid. *Anonymous.*
Epitaph: "Here lie two poor
  lovers, who had the
  mishap." Pope.
A Fable for Critics. Lowell.
Five Things White. May.
The Fresh Start. Wickham.
Gaze Not on Youth.
  Anonymous.
His Muse Speakes to Him.
  Habington.
I Laid Me Down upon a
  Bank. Blake.
I Must Complain, Yet Doe
  Enjoy My Love. Campion.
Letter. Dow.
The Love Feast. Auden.
Love-Songs, At Once Tender
  and Informative.
  Hoffenstein.
Madrigal: "The sound of thy
  sweet name, my dearest
  treasure." Davison.
Mistress, Since You So Much
  Desire. Campion.
A Nymph and a Swain.
  Congreve.
The Pillar of Fame. Herrick.
Ragged Island. Millay.
A Roundelay. Drayton.
Some Boys. Penkethman.
Sonnets: A Sequence on
  Profane Love. Boker.
Sylvia. Drayton.
The Tempest. Cotton.
Three Epitaphs on John
  Hewet and Sarah Drew.
  Pope.
To the Learned Critic.
  Jonson.

Chastity

Come, Love, Let's Walk.
  Anonymous.
Epigram: "I am provoked."
  Strato.
Epigram: "The Hebrew
  Nation did not write it."
  Blake.
Whiteness, or Chastity.
  Beaumont.

Chatter (s)

Goody Blake and Harry Gill
  (excerpt). Wordsworth.
The Poet at Fifty. Lerner.
Song of Seyd Nimetollah of
  Kuhistan. Emerson.
Sounds. Creeley.
To My Hairdresser. St.
  Leger.
West of Alice. Harney.

Cheap

Arithmetic on the Frontier.
  Kipling.
From a London Bookshop.
  Anonymous.
Goosey Goosey Gander.
  French.
I'm Beginning to Lose
  Patience. Auden.

Cheat (ed) (s)

And on My Eyes Dark Sleep
  by Night. "Field.
Don't Steal! Bierce.
Harvey Always Wins.
  Prelutsky.
Kiss Me Quick and Go.
  Steele.
A Little Cheat! *Anonymous.*
Maze. Eberhart.
A New Song: "As near
  beauteous Boston lying."
  Anonymous.
The Pink Frock. Hardy.
Reprisals. Yeats.
Sally Sweetbread. Carey.
Up in the Air. Ramsay.
The War of the Secret Agents.
  Coulette.
Were I to Choose. Okara.

Cheek (s)

At First Sight. Graves.
The Childless Father.
  Wordsworth.
December. Schuyler.
The Divan. Stoddard.
Epigrams. Martial (Marcus
  Valerius Martialis).
The Fair Damsel from
  London (The Brown Girl–
  Pretty Sarah). *Anonymous.*
Go Not, Happy Day.
  Tennyson.
Growing Old. Henderson.
Inclusions. Browning.
Legend of His Lyre.
  Schmuller.
Lessons from the Gorse.
  Browning.
A Letter. Mu'tamid.
A Letter to Her Father.
  Inib-sarri.
Limerick: "There was an old
  cat named Macduff."
  Francis.
Love Letters, Unmailed.
  Merriam.
Love's Labour's Lost.
  Shakespeare.
The Maid Freed from the
  Gallows (D vers.).
  Anonymous.
March Sound. Thurston.

Masks. Aldrich.
The Meddow Verse or
Aniversary to Mistris
Bridget Lowman. Herrick.
My Sins in Their
Completeness. O
Brolchain.
Now. Browning.
On the Death of His Child.
Faydi.
Paris in the Snow. Sedar-
Senghor.
The Portrait. Kunitz.
Prothalamium. Sitwell.
Romeo and Juliet.
Shakespeare.
The Rosarie. Herrick.
Route. Ceravolo.
Song: "Choose now among
this fairest number."
Browne.
A Song for My Mother–Her
Hands. Branch.
Swimming by Night. Merrill.
The Thrush in February.
Meredith.
To Daphne. Besant.
To Lucasta: The Rose.
Lovelace.
Twilight. Longfellow.
The Unfading Beauty.
Carew.
Victorian Song. Farrar.
Within a Greenwood Sweet of
Myrtle Savour.
Anonymous.

Cheer (ed) (ful) (s)
Amoretti, XL. Spenser.
Apology. Wordsworth.
A Ballad of Hell. Davidson.
A Ballad of the Boston Tea-
Party, December 16, 1773.
Holmes.
The Battle Autumn of 1862.
Whittier.
The Birthday-Cake
Glockenspiel. Henley.
A Busy Man Speaks. Bly.
Christmas in the Olden Time.
Scott.
The Crossing at
Fredericksburg. Boker.
The Dance of Despair.
Bialik.
The Daughter of the
Regiment. Scollard.
Easter Song. Alishan.
Epigram: "O death, thy
certainty is such."
Luttrell.
From All That Dwell below
the Skies. Watts.
The Holly Tree. Southey.
"Hullo!" Foss.
I Never Knew a Night So
Black. Bangs.
Julian Grenfell. Baring.
My Picture. Procter.
My Son. Hughes.
November. Cleaveland.
Now Christmas Is Come.
Anonymous.
A Prophecy. Thompson.
The Rape of Lucrece.
Shakespeare.
The Red, White and Blue.
Shaw.
September Days Are Here.
Jackson.
A Song: "If for a woman I
would die." Winchilsea.

Sonnets, XCVII: "How like a
winter hath my absence
been." Shakespeare.
The Stampede. Caldwell.
This Is Your Hour.
Kaufman.
This Runner. Webb.
Thysia. Luce.
The Walls of Jericho.
Dickinson.
Water. Hughes.
What Kind of War?
Rottman.
Woods in Winter.
Longfellow.
Yarrow Visited.
Wordsworth.
Cheerless
Hadrian's Address to His Soul
When Dying. Hadrian.
Song: "Again rejoicing Nature
sees." Burns.
Cheese cake
Un-Birthday Cake. Fisher.
Burglar Bill. Guthrie.
On the Mountains. Alcman.
Cheese (s)
All-Nite Donuts. Goldbarth.
The Dream of a Boy Who
Lived at Nine Elms.
Rands.
Mister Frog Went A-Courting
(with music). *Anonymous.*
Quite the Cheese (parody).
Waring.
Rhinoceros. Hart-Smith.
To Make a Pastoral: A
Receipt. *Anonymous.*
Twirling. *Anonymous.*
What a Friend We have in
Cheeses! Cole.
Will You Be My Little Wife.
Greenaway.
Cherish (ed)
Amoretti, II. Spenser.
Autumn. *Anonymous.*
Casual Meeting. Bruner.
Dreaming of Cities Dead.
Cox.
Flora's Lamentable Passion.
Anonymous.
For a Good Dog.
Guiterman.
I Am Christmas.
Anonymous.
A Mery Gest How a
Sergeaunt Wolde Lerne to
Be a Frere. More.
Sea Gods. Doolittle.
Cherr (ies) (y)
11 Rue Daguerre.
Montague.
Adjectives. Nadir.
A Catch for Singing.
Gibson.
Cherries. Schneour.
Cherry-Ripe. Herrick.
Cherry Tree. Sitwell.
Chop-Cherry. Herrick.
Evening. Sitwell.
How to Choose a Wife.
Anonymous.
Jarcha: "If you really care for
me." *Anonymous.*
A Legend of Cherries.
Dalmon.
Loveliest of Trees.
Housman.
Nevertheless. Moore.
Ode on His Majesty's
Proclamation, Commanding
the Gentry... Fanshawe.

Of a Spider. Thorley.
One, Two, Three, Four.
Anonymous.
Picnic Day. Field.
Pit, Pat. *Anonymous.*
To Cherry-Blossomes.
Herrick.
Young Master's Account of a
Puppet Show. Marchant.
Cherub (im) (s)
For a Lady I Know. Cullen.
Jubilate Agno. Smart.
The Merchant of Venice.
Shakespeare.
On Virtue. Wheatley.
Poor Jack. Dibdin.
Shall I Take Thee, the Poet
Said. Dickinson.
Solomon on the Vanity of the
World. Prior.
Sonnet: "A plaintive Sonnet
flow'd from MILTON's
pen." Mason.
To Finde God. Herrick.
Transcendentalism: A Poem in
Twelve Books. Browning.
Chess
The Chess-Board. Lytton.
Good Times & No Bread.
Lockett.
The Hosts of Faery.
Anonymous.
Old Montague. Joseph.
Romance of the Cigarette. di
Michele.
Chest
The Aeneid. Virgil (Publius
Vergilius Maro).
Draft of a Reparations
Agreement. Pagis.
Driving through Minnesota
during the Hanoi Bombings.
Bly.
How to Murder Your Best
Friend. O Hehir.
An Italian Chest. Seiffert.
Lac Courte Orielles: 1936.
Wolf.
Late Autumn. Young.
Limerick: "There was a young
fellow named West."
Anonymous.
Motherhood. Swenson.
Nine Charms against the
Hunter. Wagoner.
Prostration. Semah.
Simple Song. Piercy.
A Visit from Alphonse.
Zimmer.
Chestnut (s)
Alcestis in Ely. Moore.
The Book of Juniper. Paulin.
The Graduate. Stetler.
The Little Milliner.
Buchanan.
The Ventriloquist. Huff.
Chew (ed) (ing) (s)
Alone. Holden.
Biltong. Twala.
Clinic: Examination.
Conard.
Driving the Mule.
Anonymous.
Fine Work with Pitch and
Copper. Williams.
Food. Chute.
Life in the Country.
Silverton.
My Sweetheart's the Mule in
the Mines. *Anonymous.*
New Jersey White-Tailed
Deer. Oates.

Says the Miner to the
Mucker. *Anonymous.*
Chicken (s)
Accountability. Dunbar.
Alimentary. Fadiman.
The Ascension: 1925.
Brinnin.
Asparagus. Swift.
A-Begging Buttermilk I Will
Go. *Anonymous.*
A Call to the Wild.
Dunsany.
Eggomania. Lamport.
An Event. Field.
Evidently Chicken Town.
Clarke.
The Gangster's Death. Reed.
Gracie. Kicknosway.
The Laird O' Cockpen.
Nairne.
Laundry & School Epigrams.
Mayer.
The Red Wheelbarrow.
Williams.
Shatnes or Uncleanliness.
Steinbarg.
She'll Be Coming 'Round the
Mountain. *Anonymous.*
Shopping. Nitzche.
The Shrimp. Browne.
The Smell of Coal Smoke.
Murray.
Some Modern Good Turns.
Dibben.
Treason. Dunetz.
Two Poems on the Emotions.
Shapiro.
Walking through a Cornfield
in the Middle of Winter...
(parody). Harr.
Wanderers. Calverley.
Chief (s)
Arcadia. Sidney.
The Brooklyn at Santiago.
Rice.
Dinnshenchas: The Story of
Macha. *Anonymous.*
Child (ren)
About Children. McGinley.
Accents in Alsace: Alsace or
Alsatians. Stein.
Adam's Footprint. Miller.
Advent Meditation. Meynell.
African China. Tolson.
After the Death of Her
Daughter in Childbirth...
Izumi Shikibu.
After the Speech to the
Librarians. Wagoner.
Against Quarrelling and
Fighting. Watts.
Against Unworthy Praise.
Yeats.
Ago. Jennings.
The Ailing Parent. Dunetz
All That Summer. Dunetz.
Along the Banks. Barlow.
American Child. Engle.
Among the Narcissi. Plath.
Amor Dei. *Anonymous.*
And We Conquered. Penny.
An Arbor Day Tree.
Anonymous.
Are All the Children In?
Anonymous.
As I Went A-Walking One
Fine Summer's Evening.
Anonymous.
As With My Hat. Johnson.
At Dawn the Light Will
Come. Van Wyk Louw.
At God's Command. Rolnik.

At High Mass. Benson.
Athanasia. Wilde.
Attitudes of a New Zealand
  Poet. Curnow.
Australia. Langley.
Autumn. Hulme.
Ballad of the Little Black
  Hound. Shorter.
Ballade of Illegal Ornaments.
  Belloc.
Bear in Mind, O Ye
  Recording Angels.
  Cameron.
The Beautiful. Davies.
The Beautiful Woman Who
  Sings. Allen.
Beauty. Wylie.
Before Salamis. Stanford.
Beginning the Year at
  Rosebud, S.D. Whiteman.
Belita. Rios.
Bereaved. Riley.
Between Rivers and Seas.
  Henson.
The Big Swing-Tree Is Green
  Again. Carr.
The Biplane. Orlen.
The Bird. Simpson.
Birth. Stillman.
The Birthday Child.
  Fyleman.
A Birthday Memorial to
  Seventh Street. Lorde.
A Birthday Prayer. Finley.
The Blessed Virgin compared
  to the Air we Breathe.
  Hopkins.
The Blessed Virgin's
  Expostulation. Tate.
Blue Bog Children.
  Weingarten.
The Book of Job and a Draft
  of a Poem to Praise the
  Paths... Oppen.
The Breasts of Mnasidice.
  Louys.
The Brick. Roche.
A Bridal Song. Shelley.
The Bridge. Peterson.
Brother Jonathan, Brother
  Kafka (excerpt).
  O'Sullivan.
The Brut. Layamon.
Caelica, XXV. Greville.
Caelica, XXVI. Greville.
Caelica, XLIII. Greville.
Captain Car, or, Edom o
  Gordon (A version).
  Anonymous.
A Case to the Civilians.
  Anonymous.
Catastrophe. Brock.
The Caughnawaga Beadwork
  Seller. Lighthall.
Chance Meeting. Griffin.
Channel Water. Miner.
Charm: "Bring the holy crust
  of Bread." Herrick.
Child and Poet. Swinburne.
The Child Bearers. Sexton.
The Child in the Garden.
  Van Dyke.
Child of God. Anonymous.
A Child of Hers. Marietta.
Child of Loneliness. Gale.
The Child of Peace.
  Lagerlof.
Child of the World. Baker.
A Child's Christmas without
  Jean Cocteau. Fisher.
A Child's Prayer.
  Anonymous.

A Child's Song of Christmas.
  Pickthall.
Childhood. Bradstreet.
Childhood. MacDonagh.
Children. McPherson.
The Children. Urdang.
Children of Auschwitz.
  Korzhavin.
Children of Night. Shelton.
Children, the Sandbar, That
  Summer. Rukeyser.
The Chivalrous Shark.
  Anonymous.
Christ's Prayer in
  Gethsemane. Anonymous.
Christendom. Traherne.
A Christmas Carol. Probyn.
Christmas Eve Legend.
  Frost.
Christmas Eve under Hooker's
  Statue. Lowell.
Christmas Legend. Worrell.
Christmas Lullaby for a New-
  Born Child. Gregory.
Christmas Morn. Sawyer.
Christmas Song. Ward.
Christmas Tree. Cook.
The Circus. Kaplan.
City Songs. Van Doren.
Cois na Teineadh. Rolleston.
The Collar. Herbert.
Confession to Settle a Curse.
  Waldrop.
Containing Communism.
  Cobb.
Conversation with
  Washington. Livingston.
The Cottager. Clare.
Cross Ties. Kennedy.
The Cry of the Child
  (parody). Zaranka.
Cycle. Jennett.
A Day of Notes. Green.
Death Killed the Rich.
  Anonymous.
Death May Be Very Gentle.
  Gogarty.
The Death Room. Graves.
Deeds of Kindness. Sargent.
Deliverance. Dawson.
Desks. Smith.
Dexter. Grayston.
Dicamus Bona Verba.
  Tibullus.
Distortions. Hutchinson.
Diving for Pearls.
  Yamamoto.
Dogget Gap. Anonymous.
Doris: A Pastoral. Munby.
Down with the Lambs.
  Anonymous.
Dragging in Winter.
  McElroy.
Dusk. Welshimer.
The Earthquake.
  Anonymous.
Ecstasy. Swarth.
Ecstasy. Symons.
The Eighties Becoming.
  Rosenthal.
Elijah Speaking. Fetherling.
Emblems. Tate.
Encounter with Hunger.
  Vanderlip.
Endless. Rukeyser.
England's Prayer. Blundell
  of Crosby.
Envoi. Mandel.
The Epicurean. Doyle.
Epigram: An Old Story.
  Nemerov.

Epitaph for an American
  Bomber. Bertram.
Ethics. Pastan.
An Evening Falls. Stephens.
The Explosion of Thimbles.
  Di Cicco.
Extremely Naughty Children.
  Godley.
Extremes. Riley.
The Eyes, the Blood.
  Meltzer.
Face of Poverty. Smith.
Faith Healing. Larkin.
Family Reunion. Summers.
The Famine Road. Boland.
The Far Land. Wheelock.
The Feast of the Snow.
  Chesterton.
February 12, 1809. Burket.
The Field. Valentine.
Finding You. Thayer.
First Surf. DiPasquale.
The Fisherman. Leonidas.
A Flower Given to My
  Daughter. Joyce.
The Follies. Epstein.
For Every Day. Havergal.
For Hettie. Jones.
For Johnny. Pudney.
For My Mother, Feeling
  Useless. Rankin.
For the Time Being. Auden.
The Four Zoas. Blake.
A Foxhole for the Night.
  Quinn.
Freedom. Green.
From a Venetian Sequence.
  Naude.
From the Cavities of Bones.
  Parker.
From "The Sinless Child."
  Smith
The Garden. Parkwood.
The Gardener. Symons.
Generations. Clark.
Getting Out. Maloney.
Getting Through. Merrill.
Ghetto Twilight. Brody.
The Gingerbread House.
  Ower.
The Gipsy's Warning.
  Anonymous.
A Glimpse. Cornford.
Gnawing the Breast.
  McPherson.
Go Throw Them Out.
  Halpern.
God Is There. Isenhour.
God's A-Gwineter Trouble de
  Water. Anonymous.
God, Who Hath Made the
  Daisies. Hood.
Good Master and Mistress...
  Anonymous.
Good Times. Clifton.
A Goodly Child.
  Anonymous.
Grand Abacus. Ashbery.
Grandmother's Story of
  Bunker-Hill Battle.
  Holmes.
The Gray Swan. Cary.
The Green Valley. Warner.
The Grinders, or the Saddle
  on the Right Horse.
  Anonymous.
"Guilty or Not Guilty?"
  Anonymous.
Gypsies. Nowlan.
Haircut. Packard.
The Handloom. Rodriguez.
The Happy Child. Davies.

The Happy Night. Sheffield.
Hast Thou Heard It, O My
  Brother. Williams.
The Hasty Pudding. Barlow.
Hatteras Calling. Aiken.
He Thinks of Those Who
  Have Spoken Evil of His
  Beloved. Yeats.
Heart for All Her Children.
  Hebert, Jr.
Henry C. Calhoun. Masters.
Henry King. Belloc.
Hesperos, you bring home all
  the bright dawn disperses.
  Sappho.
Hickory Stick Hierarchy.
  Selle.
The Holy Innocents. Lowell.
Home-Coming. Ehrenstein.
Home Leave. Howes.
Homecoming. Margolin.
The House in the Wood.
  Jarrell.
The House of Life. Rossetti.
How the Great Guest Came.
  Markham.
How Will You Call Me,
  Brother? Evans.
A Hunt in the Black Forest.
  Jarrell.
Hymn for Atonement Day.
  Halevi.
Hymns and Spiritual Songs.
  Smart.
I'd Love to Be a Fairy's
  Child. Graves.
I Found Her Out There.
  Hardy.
The Ice. Gibson.
If I Were Dead. Patmore.
In Dark Hour. MacManus.
In the Children's Hospital.
  Tennyson.
In the Forest. Sadeh.
In the Season of Wolves and
  Names. Rugo.
Independence. McFadden.
An Indian Mother about to
  Destroy Her Child.
  Montgomery.
Indians. Sprague.
Indifference. Graham.
Infant Innocence. Housman.
Innocence. Traherne.
Invocation before the Rice
  Harvest. Anonymous.
Iowa. Browne.
Irish Grandmother.
  Edelman.
Jane Smith (parody).
  Kipling.
Jessie. Harte.
Jesus Never Fails. Isenhour.
John Webster. Swinburne.
Kennedy Airport. Kramer.
Kindness. Plath.
The Kings of the East.
  Bates.
The Knowledgeable Child.
  Strong.
Kyoto: March. Snyder.
The Lady of the Lake. Scott.
The Lamplighter. Stevenson.
The Landfall. Dickey.
Langston Hughes.
  Blockcolski.
The Lass of Lynn's New Joy,
  for Finding a Father for
  Her Child. Anonymous.
Last Look at La Plata,
  Missouri. Barnes.
Latin Hymn. Praed.

Leaves at My Window. Piatt.
Let There Be Light. Vories.
Let Us Keep Christmas. Crowell.
Letters from a Father. Van Duyn.
The Lifeguard. Dickey.
Lilith's Child. Francisco.
Limerick: "That famous old pederast, Wilde." Anonymous.
Litany For Dictatorships. Benét.
A Little Carol of the Virgin. Lope de Vega Carpio.
Long, Too Long America. Whitman.
The Lord of Lorn and the False Steward. Anonymous.
Los Mineros. Dorn.
Love. Very.
Love Constraining to Obedience. Cowper.
Love Poem. Williams.
A Lovely Rose Is Sprung. Anonymous.
The Lowly Peasant. Anonymous.
The Mad Woman of Punnet's Town. Strong.
The Made Lake. Nicholl.
Madonna of the Empty Arms. Egan.
The Magus. Dickey.
Marquette on the Shores of the Mississippi. Rooney.
Masar. Landor.
May Morning. Thaxter.
Meditation on the Nativity. Jennings.
The Memorial Pillar. Hemans.
Men of the Rocks. MacLeod.
Middle-Aged Child. Hogan.
Milkmaid. Lee.
The Millman's Song. Anonymous.
The Mirror. Morris.
Missing the Children. Zimmer.
Mississippi Born. Lomax.
The Monaro. Campbell.
Monday's child is fair of face. Mother Goose.
Moses. Gilboa.
The Mother. Anonymous.
Mother Dark. Pereira.
Mother's Song. Anonymous.
Multipara: Gravida 5. Ponsot.
Music. Shelley.
Must Be the Season of the Witch. Alurista.
My Child. Griffin.
My Father in the Night Commanding No. Simpson.
My Grandfather's Days. Anonymous.
My Grandmother. Shapiro.
My Song to the Jewish People. Olitski.
My Trundle Bed. Baker.
Mythics. Chasin.
The Names. Edmond.
A Nativity. Kipling.
A Natural History of Southwestern Ontario, III. Dewdney.

Nechama. Kaufman.
Nerves. Symons.
Never Again, Orpheus. Antipater of Sidon.
New Leaves. Jimenez.
New Maths. Lehrer.
New Testament: Revised Edition. Mary Catherine.
The New Wife. Anonymous.
The New-Yeeres Gift, Sung to the King in the Presence at White Hall. Herrick.
The Next War. Sitwell.
Night. Benet.
Nobody's Child. Case.
Nosegay. Coatsworth.
Nursery Rhyme of Innocence and Experience. Causley.
The Nymphs (excerpt). Hunt.
Obatala, the Creator. Anonymous.
The Ocean Said to Me Once. Crane.
The Old Man and Young Wife. Anonymous.
The Old Mother. Anonymous.
On a Birth. Grigson.
On His Royal Blindness Paramount Chief Kwangala. Mapanje.
On the Deaths of Thomas Carlyle and George Eliot. Swinburne.
On the Mountain. Joseph.
On This Day. Goffstein.
Once in a Lifetime, Snow. Murray.
Once in Royal David's City. Alexander.
One of Many. Smith.
The One Thousandth Psalm. Hale.
Organ Transplant. Reed.
Our Lady of France. Johnson.
Our Polite Parents. Wells.
Page. McPherson.
Paper Anarchist Addresses the Shade of Nancy Ling Perry. Woodcock.
The Parade. Greene.
Parenthood. Farrar.
Parents. Meredith.
Parsifal. Verlaine.
Parvuli Ejus. De Vere.
Pearl Bryan. Anonymous.
Peasant. Merwin.
Penitential Psalm to the Goddess Anunit, IV. Anonymous.
Pent-Up Aching Rivers (excerpt). Whitman.
The People, Yes. Sandburg.
The Perfect Life. Carrera Andrade.
The Perfect Mother. Griffin.
Pharao's Daughter. Moran.
Piano. Lawrence.
Picking Apples. Lindsay.
Pipe Dreams. Bickston.
The Place of Rest. Russell.
Playing the Bones. Brewster.
Plus Ca Change... Whalen.
Poem for Friends. Troupe.
The Poem on the Guilt. Yeshurun.
Poem: "the country". Levinson.
Poem Touching the Gestapo. Heyen.

Poems, IV. O'Connor.
The Poet and the Child. Howells.
The Poor Man's Pig. Blunden.
Poor Old Horse. Holbrook.
Praise of a Child. Anonymous.
A Prayer. Macdonald.
The Princess. Tennyson.
Promises, VIII. Founding Fathers.... Warren.
Psalm XXII. Sidney.
The Question. Kuskin.
Questioning Faces. Frost.
Radiator Lions. Aldis.
Rain Magic Song. Anonymous.
Rain Riders. Scollard.
Raising the Flag. Vizenor.
Reconciliation. Russell.
The Red Herring. MacBeth.
Remembering the Automobile. Baldwin.
Repose. Lichtenstein.
Reproof. Anonymous.
Responsibilities: Prologue. Yeats.
Return. Vinz.
The Revolt of Islam. Shelley.
The Rhyme of the Chivalrous Shark. Irwin.
The Riddle. Auden.
The Riddle. Johnson.
The Riding of the Kings. Farjeon.
The Riding Stable in Winter. Tagliabue.
Ring around the World. Wynne.
A Ruined House. Aldington.
Sailor, What of the Isles? Sitwell.
Sakhara. Ford.
The Sale of the Pet Lamb. Howitt.
Sarah Cynthia Sylvia Stout Would Not Take the Garbage Out. Silverstein.
The Satyrs and the Moon. Gorman.
The Scourge. Kunitz.
The Sea. Davies.
Seasong. George.
Security. Hamburger.
Sent from Egypt with a Fair Robe of Tissue to a Sicilian Vinedresser. Moore.
Sestina. Bishop.
Shango. Anonymous.
She's Free! Harper.
The Shepherd's Hut. Young.
The Shepherd Speaks. Erskine.
The Shoofly. Anonymous.
Silent Hill. Snyder.
Six of Cups. Wakoski.
Sleep Watch. Henson.
The Smoked Herring. Cros.
Snow. Thomas.
Snow-Girl. Mortiz.
So Touch Our Hearts with Loveliness. Burket.
The Soldier's Wife. Southey.
The Soldiers Returning. Shelton.
Some Boys. Penkethman.
Some San Francisco Poems. Oppen.
Sometimes I Think of Maryland... Braxton.

Song. Noyes.
Song: "Life with her weary eyes." Zaturenska.
Song: "Love, by that loosened hair." Carman.
Song of the Rain. McCrae.
Sonnet: "This infant world has taken long to make." Macdonald.
Sonnet to a Friend... Coleridge.
Sonnet: To the River Otter. Coleridge.
Sonnet: "We will not whisper, we have found the place." Belloc.
Sonnets, XVII: "Who will believe my verse in time to come." Shakespeare.
Sonnets from a Sequence. Barker.
The Sounding. Aiken.
South Street. Silvera.
Souvenir. Robinson.
Spilled Milk. Haines.
Spirit-Like before Light. Gregor.
Star. Whitebird.
Stopping by Home. Huddle.
Story from Bear Country. Silko.
Sun Children. Silko.
Sunday: Outskirts of Knoxville, Tennessee. Agee.
Swedish Angel. Scott.
Tax Return. Anonymous.
Teacher. Dorman.
The Teacher. Hill.
That Day. Van Doren.
That There Should Be Laughter. Banda.
Theme in Yellow. Sandburg.
There Are Children in the Dusk. Warr.
These Horses Came. Young Bear.
Thesis. Dorn.
Things to Do around a Ship at Sea. Snyder.
The Thousand Things. Middleton.
Three Christmas Carols: I. Anonymous.
Three Poems about Children. Clarke.
Thrown. Hodgson.
The Tithe: To the Bride. Herrick.
To—. Rymer.
To a Friend. Arnold.
To an Insect. Holmes.
To David, about His Education. Nemerov.
To England. Boker.
To Her Lover's Complaint. Barker.
To His Book. Stokesbury.
To Laura W—, Two Years Old. Willis.
To My Daughter the Junkie on a Train. Lorde.
To My Father. Tree.
To My Little Son. Davis.
To Shelley. Landor.
To the Wind at Morn. Davies.
Toys. Sutzkever.
Trebetherick. Betjeman.
Two Children. Guillen.
Two Families. Bell.
Two Pictures. Anonymous.

The Two Sisters. *Anonymous.*
Two Temples. Hall.
Uncle Ananias. Robinson.
Unicorn. Smith.
Unintelligible Terms. Simic.
Unknown Girl in the Maternity Ward. Sexton.
Untitled. Blue Cloud.
Venus and Cupide. More.
The Vestal Lady on Brattle. Corso.
A Viet Cong Sapper Dies. Sossaman.
The View from an Attic Window. Nemerov.
Virgin and Unicorn. Heath-Stubbs.
War. Hall.
War. Shelton.
The Wassail Song. *Anonymous.*
The Watch of a Swan. Piatt.
Watchers. Merwin.
Watching Salmon Jump. Ortiz.
Water under the Earth. Bly.
We Sit Solitary. *Anonymous.*
We Who Are Left. Whalley.
Wealth. Emerson.
The Welcome. Laughton.
When Brothers Forget. Boyer.
When I Was Small. Chenier.
White Azaleas. Kimball.
White Fields. Stephens.
The Whole Year Christmas. Morgan.
Why Thus Longing? Sewall.
Willie's Lyke-Wake. *Anonymous.*
The Wind Bloweth Where It Listeth. Mitchell.
Winter News. Haines.
Winter Portrait. Southey.
Winter Rune. Coatsworth.
With a Posthumous Medal. Brinnin.
With a rocking. Yuke.
A Woman of Words. Hall.
The Woman Who Combed. Rankin.
The Woman with Child. Laughton.
The Wood, the Weed, the Wag. Ralegh.
Wordspinning. Kirsch.
Working Man Blues. Estes.
World's Centre. Dallas.

Childbirth
The Blowflies Buzz. Djalbarmiwi.
Djalbarmiwi's Song. *Anonymous.*

Childhood (s)
Airliner. Webb.
All That Summer. Dunetz.
Apricot Tree. Isanos.
A Bagatelle. Reeves.
The Builder of Houses. Cooper.
Danebury. *Anonymous.*
Desmet, Idaho, March 1969. Hale.
Divorce. Noll.
Eight Aspects of Melissa. Durrell.
Elegy. Big Eagle.
Epitaphs of the War, 1914-18. Kipling.
Eros out of the Sea. Laing.
Evening Song. Matthias.

Glenn Miller's Music Is a Trunk. Valle.
His Trees. Van Doren.
I Think of Oblivion. Amichai.
In a City Square. Wallis.
In All the Days of My Childhood. Edson.
Issues of the Fall. Lea.
Little Brown Church in the Vale. Pitts.
A Little Te Deum of the Commonplace (excerpt). Oxenham.
Mythology. Thompson.
Peace. Kavanagh.
The Quarry Pool. Levertov.
The Quiet Fog. Piercy.
Rockingchair. Morgan.
Softened by time's consummate plush. Dickinson.
Time. Graves.

Chill (ed) (y)
At Eighty-Seven. Rainer.
Cape Breton. Bishop.
Country of No Lack. Untermeyer.
Cremona. Doyle.
Hamatreya. Emerson.
Hands Clenched under My Shawl... Akhmatova.
Here Lies a Lady. Ransom.
The Horn. Adams.
The Lamplighter. O'Sullivan.
A Storm in April. Wilbur.
Thermometer Wine. Morgan.
A Toccata of Galuppi's. Browning.
A Winter Talent. Davie.

Chime (s)
At Delft. Tomlinson.
Australian Transcripts, IX: The Bell-Bird. Sharp.
The Colder the Air. Bishop.
Dartmoor. Patmore.
Denial. Herbert.
The Fountain. Wordsworth.
I Heard the Bells on Christmas Day. Longfellow.
John L. Sullivan Enters Heaven (parody). Frost.
Men Fade Like Rocks. Turner.
Sonnet on a Still Night. Cunningham.

Chimney (s)
Down the Mississippi. Fletcher.
Fragment: "–you see." Allingham.
Jesse James. (Version B). *Anonymous.*
Late Gothic. Gotlieb.
The Relationship. Vincent.
Sally Go Round the Sun. *Anonymous.*
Snow-Bound. Whittier
Sorrow. Lawrence.
The Storm. Williams.
To Lar. Herrick.
Tobacco. *Anonymous.*

Chin
Boy at a Certain Age. Francis.
Dresses. Fraser.
The Edge. Chandonnet.
Haven. Hayes.
In the Attic. Justice.

A Lady's Prayer to Cupid. Carew.
The Love-Knot. Coan.
Mantis. McCord.
Midnight. Shakespeare.
A Part of an Ode. Jonson.
To the Immortal Memory and Friendship of That Noble Pair... Jonson.

China
African China. Tolson.
The Alligator Bride. Hall.
Bells of Grey Crystal. Sitwell.
Birds in Their Little Nests Agree. Belloc.
Caroline Pink. *Anonymous.*
The Child's Power of Wonder. Saha.
Chronicle. Berssenbrugge.
Digging for China. Wilbur.
Domestic Didactics by an Old Servant: The Broken Dish. Hood.
Dreaming in the Shanghai Restaurant. Enright.
Ibadan. Clark.
Little Ah Sid (with music). *Anonymous.*
Lo, for I to Myself Am Unknown. Rumi.
Nine Nectarines and Other Porcelain. Moore.
Prayer to the Pacific. Silko.
The Pruned Tree. Moss.
Street Performers, 1851. Tiller.
Tea Poems: Smugglers. Brown.
Translations from the Chinese. Morley.
When Sun Came to Riverwoman. Silko.
The Wind Blow East. *Anonymous.*

Chinook
The Fish Counter at Bonneville. Stafford.
Weather Words. McCord.

Chips
The Cachalot. Pratt.
Cawsand Bay. *Anonymous.*
The Signature of All Things. Rexroth.

Chisel
For an Age of Plastics. Plymouth. Davie.
Limerick: "A mother in old Alabama." Smith.
Wine Bowl. Doolittle.

Chloe
Epigram on the First of April. Winstanley.
A Lamentable Case. Hanbury-Williams.
The Question to Lisetta. Prior.
The Temple of Venus. Jenyns.

Chocolate
Cairo Jag. Douglas.
The Chocolate Soldiers. Forbes.
A Girtonian Funeral. *Anonymous.*
Harlem Sweeties. Hughes.
Supermarket. Holman.

Choice (s)
5 Poems. Gray.
Affection and Desire. Ralegh.

Against the Evidence. Ignatow.
All on a Summer's Day. *Anonymous.*
The Best Choice. *Anonymous.*
Boogie with O. O. Gabugah. Young.
But Choose. Holmes.
The Centipede. Adams.
Certain Choices. Shelton.
A Channel Passage. Brooke.
The Choice. Corke.
Choose You a Seat 'n' Set Down. *Anonymous.*
Components. McDonald.
Conquistador. MacLeish.
Coon Song. Ammons.
Departing Words to a Son. Pack.
Dialogue between Mary and Gabriel. Auden.
The Documentary on Brazil. Corn.
An Elder's Reproof to His Wife. Muuse.
Elektra on Third Avenue. Hacker.
An Evasion. Livingstone.
The Fakir. Cambridge.
Flight. Johnson.
For My Husband. Voigt.
Ghosts. Jennings.
Good People. Stanton.
Here's a Poor Widow. *Anonymous.*
Hilaire Belloc. Wolfe.
How Odd. Ewer.
Ickle Ockle, Blue Bockle. *Anonymous.*
In My First Hard Springtime. Welch.
Is It Nothing to You? Kindig.
The King and the Clown. *Anonymous.*
The Lass of Richmond Hill. Upton.
Learning to Live without You. Wood.
Lines on Hearing the Organ. Calverley.
Love and Folly. La Fontaine.
Love Constraining to Obedience. Cowper.
A Lover's New Year's Gift. Lydgate.
Lyric. Hewitt.
Minus One. Ciardi.
Moses. Tremayne.
Obit. Lowell.
October Maples, Portland. Wilbur.
Of Disdainful Daphne. Nowell.
On the Death of Mr. Purcell. Dryden.
The Origin of the Praise of God. Bly.
Phillis and Corydon. Colton.
Sappho, Be Comforted. Williams.
The Secret. Clare.
Self-Portrait. Jackson.
Spring. Hopkins.
The Star-Song: A Carol to the King; Sung at White-Hall. Herrick.
The Summer Harvest Spreads the Fields. Strong.

Sunflower Sonnet Number
  One. Jordan.
Three Sunrises from Amtrak.
  Dolgorukov.
To a Lady on Her Passion for
  Old China. Gay.
To Julia under Lock and Key
  (parody). Seaman.
To the Cuckoo. Townsend.
War Poet. Fuller.
We Who Are About to Die.
  Fey.
Whore. King.
The Witnesses. Kennedy.
The Yellow Flower.
  Williams.

Choir (s)
The Adventurous Muse.
  Watts.
Coal Miner's Grace. Divine.
Deirdre and the Poets.
  Milne.
Elegy. Bell.
The Friar. Peacock.
Jesus, the Soul of Our Joys.
  Wesley.
June. MacDonald.
Nightingales. Bridges.
Now That the Winter's Gone.
  Carew.
The Old-Fashioned Garden.
  Hayes.
To Death, of His Lady.
  Villon.
Trouble in the "Amen
  Corner." Harbaugh.
Wolfhound. Murphy.

Choke (d) (s)
Family Album. Kaneko.
In the Cellars. Gold.
Limerick: "When Arthur was
  homeless and broke."
  Anonymous.
Morning. McCrae.
My Birthday. Crabbe.
Of Pick-Pockets. Gay.
On Tobacco. Pestel.
The Pressures. Jones.
Six Sunday. Bibbs.
There Are Three Who Await
  My Death. *Anonymous.*
The Voyage. Shapiro.

Chop
Awful Fix. Hawkins.
Ballad of Culinary
  Frustration. McGinley.
Beginnings (excerpt).
  Hayden.
I Had a Wife. *Anonymous.*

Chord (s)
L'Envoi. Robinson.
Fugue. Carrier.
Publishing 2001. Rosenthal.
Riding with the Fireworks.
  Darr.
Sincere Flattery of W. W.
  Stephen.
The Song of the Woman-
  Drawer. Gilmore.
Sonnets on the Sea's Voice.
  Sterling.
To a Traveler. Su Tung-P'o.

Chorus
Antigone. Sophocles.
Battle Hymn. Adolphus.
Carmen Saeculare. Horace.
Ceremonies. Stanford.
Cossimbazar. Leigh.
A Hot Time in the Old Town.
  Hayden.
John Marr (excerpt).
  Melville.

The Misfortunes of Elphin:
  The War-Song of Dinas
  Vawr. Peacock.
The People, Yes. Sandburg.
Victory in the Cabarets.
  Untermeyer.
West Sussex Drinking Song.
  Belloc.
Winter Coming On. Bell.

Chose (n)
The Anglers Song. Basse.
The Blue-Eyed Precinct
  Worker. Coulette.
The Crippler. Siegel.
God of Visions. Bronte.
IBM Hired Her. Gordon.
Jansenist Journey. Devlin.
Julie-Jane. Hardy.
Manichean Geography I.
  Paulin.
Moses. Tremayne.
So What (parody).
  Appleman.
Song of Liberty (excerpt).
  Garnett.
Summer Lightning. Moore.
The Time Will Surely Come.
  Daniel.
To His Kinsman, Master
  Thomas Herrick, Who
  Desired to Be in His Book.
  Herrick.
To Thee, O God, the
  Shepherd Kings. Brainard.

Christ
Adeste Fideles. Bonaventure.
African Christmas. Press.
The Ageless Christ. Byer.
Apologia Pro Vita Sua.
  Sedulius Scottus.
Apology. Cronin.
Approaches. Macdonald.
As I Sat on a Sunny Bank.
  Anonymous.
Ashamed of Jesus. Grigg.
Aspiration. Thomson.
Assurance. Munson.
At Easter Time. Richards.
Before Sleep. Prudentius
  (Aurelius Clemens
  Prudentius).
Before Sleeping. *Anonymous.*
Betrayal. Cholmondeley.
The Blessed Name. Bethune.
A Boat Song. Columcille.
Caelica, LXXXIX. Greville.
Caelica, XCVII. Greville.
Calvary. Robinson.
Caoilte. *Anonymous.*
Captain of the Years.
  Macdougall.
A Carol for Christmas Day.
  Kinwelmersh.
Carpenter Christ. Field.
Cause of Our Joy. Maris
  Stella.
Child. Sandburg.
The Christ. Oxenham.
Christ for the World! We
  Sing. Wolcott.
Christ in Alabama. Hughes.
The Christmas Candle.
  Brown.
A Christmas Carol. Rossetti.
Christmas Eve under Hooker's
  Statue. Lowell.
Christmas Still Lives.
  Hawkes.
The Conquerors. Kemp.
Consecration. Kirby.
Consorting with Angels.
  Sexton.

A Copy of Verses. Wilson.
Corpus Christi (B vers.).
  Anonymous.
The Crystal. Lanier.
The Debate of the Body and
  the Soul. *Anonymous.*
The Deer and the Snake.
  Patchen.
Discipleship. Bales.
Don'ts. Lawrence.
The Earliest Christian Hymn.
  Clement of Alexandria
  (Titus Flavius Clemens).
Easter, Day of Christ Eternal.
  Moore.
An Eclogue for Christmas.
  MacNeice.
Epigram: To English
  Connoisseurs. Blake.
Epiphany. Shanahan.
Epitaphium Meum.
  Bradford.
Eternal God, Whose Power
  Upholds. Tweedy.
Exhortation. Hastings.
Facts. Davies.
For His Sake. Denman.
For Just Men Light Is Sown.
  Wigglesworth.
For Soldiers. Gifford.
Georgia Dusk. Toomer.
The Girl Who Had Borne
  Too Much. Woods.
Glencoe. Chesterton.
Gloria in Excelsis.
  Anonymous.
Go Tell Them That Jesus Is
  Living. *Anonymous.*
Gothic Landscape. Layton.
The Great Wager. Studdert-
  Kennedy.
The Gude and Godlie Ballatis:
  Till Christ. *Anonymous.*
Harvest. Sitwell.
Have We Not Seen Thy
  Shining Garment's Hem.
  Carmichael.
He Lifted from the Dust.
  Smith.
Here Is a Song. Peck.
Hills of God, Break Forth in
  Singing. Buckham.
Himself (excerpt). Ellis.
Hymn to the Virgin Mary.
  O'Riordan.
I Saw Three Ships.
  Anonymous.
If Thou Wilt Hear. Grave.
In Dream. Synge.
In Portugal, 1912. Meynell.
In the Snack-Bar. Morgan.
The Informing Spirit.
  Emerson.
The Invitation (abridged).
  Owen.
It Isn't Far to Bethlehem.
  Macdougall.
It's G-L-O-R-Y to Know I'm
  S-A-V-E-D. *Anonymous.*
Jesus. Adams.
Jesus Christ. Guthrie.
Joseph, Jesus and Mary.
  Anonymous.
A King Shall Reign in
  Righteousness. Streeter.
Last Lines. O'Rahilly.
A Letter to John Donne.
  Sisson.
Lincoln. *Anonymous.*
Living Bread. Sefton.
Look, You Have Cast Out
  Love! Kipling.

The Loss of the Birkenhead.
  Doyle.
A Lyke-Wake Dirge.
  Anonymous.
Mangers. Davies.
Miss Marnell. Clarke.
More Sonnets at Christmas.
  Tate.
Motherhood. Stidger.
Mr. Eliot, Pastor of the
  Church of Christ at
  Roxbury... Johnson.
My Companion. Ramage.
My Legacy. Jackson.
My Need. *Anonymous.*
The New Testament.
  Russell.
No Help I'll Call Till I'm Put
  in the Narrow Coffin. O
  Rathaille.
Noah's Carpenters.
  Anonymous.
Noel! Noel! Simmons.
Not I. *Anonymous.*
Not Only in the Christmas-
  Tide. Dodge.
Now Every Child. Farjeon.
O Black and Unknown Bards.
  Johnson.
Ode on the Death of the
  Duke of Wellington.
  Tennyson.
Old Robin of Portingale.
  Anonymous.
On Easter Morning.
  Rexford.
On the Origin of Evil.
  Byrom.
On the Swag. Mason.
On Top of Troubled Waters.
  Langford.
Once More, Our God,
  Vouchsafe to Shine.
  Sewall.
One Step Twix't Me and
  Death. Williams.
The Open Door.
  Anonymous.
Our Tense and Wintry Minds.
  Carruth.
Outside the Holy City.
  Gilkey.
Peace Is the Tranquillity of
  Order. Wilberforce.
The Pilgrim. Embury.
A Poem, upon the Caelestial
  Embassy Perform'd by
  Angels... Steere.
The Poet Loosed a Winged
  Song. Campbell.
Prayer for Rich and Poor.
  Langland.
A Prayer for the New Year.
  Storey.
Profit and Loss: An Elegy
  upon the Decease of Mrs.
  Mary Gerrish... Danforth.
The Question. Auden.
R. B. Gorton.
The Reign of Peace. Starck.
Religion and Doctrine. Hay.
Resurrection. John of
  Damascus.
The Reverend Mr.
  Higginson... Johnson.
The Rune of Hospitality.
  Anonymous.
The Ship in the Midst of the
  Sea. Wordsworth.
Shop. Browning.
The Soldier. Hopkins.

Soldier, What Did You See?
Blanding.
Soldiers Bathing. Prince.
The Stick. O'Rourke.
Substitution. Browning.
Sweetness. *Anonymous.*
A Thanksgiving to God for
His House. Herrick.
This blessed Christ of Calvary.
Anonymous.
The Three Kings. Field.
To Pass the Place where
Pleasure Is. *Anonymous.*
A Tribute. *Anonymous.*
Triumph. Stearns.
Two Women. Willis.
Views of the Oxford Colleges.
Leary.
Waked by the Gospel's
Powerful Sound. Occom.
The Way of the World.
Roche.
Wayfarers in the Wilderness.
Thompson.
Wednesday, January 1, 1701.
Sewall.
While Shepherds Watched.
Deland.
The Whole Armour of God.
Wesley.

Christen (ed) (ing) (s)
As Joseph Was A-Walking.
Anonymous.
Camp Notes. Yamada.
Candles. Plath.
The First Test. Schaeffer.
Hind Etin. *Anonymous.*
Miss Kilmansegg and Her
Precious Leg. Hood.

Christian (s)
As Gentle Dews Distill.
Rogers.
Being a Christian.
Anonymous.
The Candidate. Gray.
The Church of England's
Glory. *Anonymous.*
The Croppy Boy.
Anonymous.
The Daughter of Jairus.
Tsvetayeva.
The Death of Don Pedro.
Anonymous.
Epigram: "The only Man that
e'er I knew." Blake.
Has no one seen my heart of
you? Beddoes.
Jesus Lives, and So Shall I.
Gellert.
Light and Love, Hope and
Faith. Gray.
Lord, I Want to Be a
Christian. *Anonymous.*
Onward Christian Soldiers!
Davis.
Pig Poem. Waterman.
Pray, Christian, Pray!
Anonymous.
A Satire upon the French
King. Brown.
The Savages. Miles.
Songe betwene the Quenes
Majestie and Englande.
Anonymous.
Sonnets of the Months. San
Geminiano.
The Soul's Tendency Towards
Its True Centre. Byrom.
The Two Friends. Leland.
With a Nantucket Shell.
Webb.

Christmas
African Christmas. Press.
After-Christmas Poem.
Long.
An Alphabet of Christmas.
Anonymous.
Annar-Mariar's Christmas
Shopping. Farjeon.
The Annual Solution.
Robinson.
The Annunciation.
Anonymous.
As I Sat on a Sunny Bank.
Anonymous.
As I Went Down to David's
Town. Stewart.
Ashes of the Christmas Tree.
Gillespie.
At Christmastide. Simmons.
The Birth Song of Christ.
Sears.
Calm, on the Listening Ear of
Night. Sears.
A Carol for Children. Nash.
Carol for the Last Christmas
Eve. Nicholson.
A Carol for Twelfth Day.
Anonymous.
Cause of Our Joy. Maris
Stella.
Christmas 1914. Harding.
Christmas Letter Home.
Fraser.
Christmas Song. Long.
Christmas Still Lives.
Hawkes.
A Christmas Wish. Field.
Come Christmas. McCord.
Counting the Days. Tippett.
The Daventry Wonder.
Agricola.
Dear Father Christmas
(parody). Davies.
December. Fisher.
December. Heath-Stubbs.
Eighth Street West. Field.
Festum Nativitatis. De Vere.
The First Christmas.
Poulsson.
First Christmas Night of All.
Turner.
First Cold Night of Autumn.
Stupp.
For Christmas. Field.
The Golden Carol.
Anonymous.
Golden Cobwebs. Bennett.
Hagar. Adams.
How Grand and How Bright.
Anonymous.
How to Paint a Perfect
Christmas. Holub.
I Wash My Face in a Golden
Vase. Anonymous.
In Lord Carpenter's Country.
Higgs.
In the Week When Christmas
Comes. Farjeon.
It's Almost Day.
Anonymous.
It Seems That God Bestowed
Somehow. Hall.
January Brings the Snow.
Mother Goose.
Jest 'Fore Christmas. Field.
Jesu, Joy of Man's Desiring.
Fitzgerald.
Lordings, Listen to Our Lay.
Anonymous.
Making It Simple December
8, 1969. McElroy.

Moonless Darkness Stands
Between. Hopkins.
Morte d'Arthur. Tennyson.
The New Nutcracker Suite
(excerpt). Nash.
A New-Year's Gift Sent to Sir
Simeon Steward. Herrick.
Nor House Nor Heart.
Lennen.
Now Is the Time of
Christmas. *Anonymous.*
A Nun Speaks to Mary.
Mary Madeleva.
Oh Come, Little Children.
McGinley.
Old Winter. Noel.
One Night. Chute.
Pipe Dreams. Bickston.
The Road from Election to
Christmas. Williams.
Santa Claus. *Anonymous.*
Shepherds' Carol. Nicholson.
Signs of Christmas. Lees.
Sing We Yule. *Anonymous.*
Song of the Wise Men.
Pierce.
Stay, Christmas! Eastwick.
Strange, All-Absorbing Love.
Dolben.
The Sun Came Out in April.
Day-Lewis.
Tenant Farmer. Ward.
Those Last, Late Hours of
Christmas Eve. Welte.
To a Young Wretch. Frost.
To See the Cross at
Christmas. Cooper.
Triolet on a Dark Day.
Fishback.
The True Christmas.
Vaughan.
Under the Snow. Collyer.
Winter Portrait. Southey.
Yet Love Was Born. Voss.

Christopher
By the Dominical Letter, to
Find on What Day of the
Week... *Anonymous.*
In My End Is My Beginning.
Dobson.
To Christopher North.
Tennyson.

Chromium
Causeway. Block.
The Leg in the Subway.
Williams.

Chrysalis
The Butterfly. Palmer.
A Conservative. Gilman.

Chrysanthemum (s)
Girl Powdering Her Neck.
Song.
Haiku: "No one spoke."
Ryota.
Poem to the Tune of "Tsui
Hua Yin." Li Ching-chao.

Church (es)
At Church Next Sunday.
Anonymous.
At Dunwich. Thwaite.
Attending Church.
Anonymous.
Bard's Chant. Shirley.
Black Power Poem. Reed.
The Bohemian Hymn.
Emerson.
Both Less and More. Dixon.
Brebeuf and His Brethren.
Pratt.
Casanova. Usborne.
The Character of a Trimmer.
Anonymous.

Childhood Church. Wilson.
The Church. Piper.
The Clarion-Call.
Anonymous.
Conversion. Hewitt.
Coridon's Song. Lodge.
The Cottager's Complaint.
Freeth.
A Dollar I Gave.
Anonymous.
Down-Hall. Prior.
The End. De La Mare.
The End of Clonmacnois.
O'Connor.
Enfidaville. Douglas.
Eternal God Whose Searching
Eye Doth Scan. Poteat.
Exit. MacDonald.
The False Favorite's
Downfall. *Anonymous.*
The Hippopotamus. Eliot.
Horror. Baum.
How Paddy Stole the Rope.
Anonymous.
How We Built a Church at
Ashcroft. Leahy.
I Never See the Red Rose
Crown the Year.
Masefield.
If You're the Man You Ought
to Be. Isenhour.
In Clonmel Parish
Churchyard. Piatt.
In These Dissenting Times.
Walker.
It Isn't the Church–It's You.
Anonymous.
It's You. McDonald.
Just Like Me. Sinks.
King Arthur's Death.
Anonymous.
The Kingdom. MacNeice.
The Landscape Near an
Aerodrome. Spender.
Letter Across Doubt and
Distance. Holman.
Letters from Birmingham.
Bond.
Limerick: "Said a fellow from
North Philadelphia."
Braley.
Limerick: "There was an old
lady of Harrow."
Anonymous.
Little Brown Church in the
Vale. Pitts.
Little John a Begging (A
version). *Anonymous.*
Lord, At This Closing Hour.
Fitch.
A Maypole. Swift.
Morte d'Arthur. Tennyson.
My Madonna. Service.
O for the Happy Hour.
Bethune.
On Dr. Chard. *Anonymous.*
The Onset. Frost.
The Paradox. *Anonymous.*
A Parting Hymn We Sing.
Wolfe.
The Poet's Lot. Holmes.
A Prognostication on Will
Laud, Late Archbishop of
Canterbury. *Anonymous.*
Romeo and Juliet.
Shakespeare.
Shaving. Wright.
Sketch of his Own Character.
Gray.
Some Who Do Not Go to
Church. *Anonymous.*

A Song of the Seasons.
Monkhouse.
That Radio Religion.
Ludlum.
Theme and Variation. De
Vries.
The Triumph of Infidelity.
Dwight.
Trouble in the "Amen
Corner." Harbaugh.
The Twelve Properties or
Conditions of a Lover.
More.
We Hurry On, Nor Passing
Note. Dolben.
The Well of St. Keyne.
Southey.
What Are They Thinking...
Guinness.
Where Nothing Dwelt But
Beasts of Prey. Watts.

Cicada (s)
The Cicada. Ou-yang Hsiu.
Haiku: "Once my parents
were older." Chiyo.
The Quest of Silence: Fire in
the Heavens, and Fire
Along the Hills. Brennan.

Cider
Limerick: "There was a young
lady of Ryde."
Anonymous.
The Man in the Moon.
Anonymous.
Sucking Cider Through a
Straw. *Anonymous.*
These Obituaries of
Rattlesnakes Being Eaten by
the Hogs. Weingarten.

Cigar (s)
Academic Affair. Stockwell.
Dear Wordsworth.
Hathaway.
A Lesson in Hammocks.
Schevill.
Revelation. Meltzer.
Song of the Round Man.
Palmer.
Thirteen, Full of Life.
Everett.
Waiting for Nighthawks in
Illinois. Pfingston.

Cigarette (s)
Baggot Street Deserta.
Kinsella.
Burning the Root. Gibson.
The Cowboy Up to Date.
Anonymous.
The Death of Professor
Backwards. Kennedy.
He Records a Little Song for
a Smoking Girl.
Whitehead.
"...I'd like to live with you."
Tsvetayeva.
Is 5. Cummings.
No Man Knows War. Rolfe.
The Parents-Without-Partners
Picnic. Schaefer.
The Tale of Lord Lovell.
Anonymous.
The Young Fellow Walks
About. Reznikoff.

Cinder (s)
Another Tribute to Wyatt.
Surrey.
Disappointment. O'Reilly.
End of the Seers' Convention.
Fearing.
The Lost History Plays:
Savanarola (parody).
Beerbohm.

Prisoners. Harvey.
Psalm of Those Who Go
Forth before Daylight.
Sandburg.
The Reckoning. Friman.
September Sun: 1947.
Gascoyne.

Cinnamon
After. Hodgson.
The Cinnamon Peeler.
Ondaatje.
Heritage: What Is Africa to
Me? Cullen.
I Took a Bow and Arrow.
Ciardi.
Lovemusic. Kizer.

Circe (s)
Barine, the Incorrigible.
Horace.
The Odyssey. Homer.
What Ulysses Said to Circe on
the Beach of Aeaea.
Layton.

Circle (s)
The Angels Came A-
Mustering. Zangwill.
Angler. Vinz.
The Bible. Levi.
Blessing of the Firstborn.
Schwartz.
Celebration. Sachs.
A Circle, a Square, a Triangle
and a Ripple of Water.
Cooper.
Communion. Tabb.
Cordoba. Mendelssohn.
First Ice of Winter. Shorb.
Glycerin. Lima.
De Guiana, Carmen Epicum.
Chapman.
How Still the Hawk.
Tomlinson.
I's the B'y. *Anonymous.*
Lament. Amichai.
The Linebacker at Forty.
Wallace.
Minor Elegy. Lisboa.
Morgain Le Fay. Crozier.
Outwitted. Markham.
Park Pigeons. Cane.
The Pilgrim Fathers.
Wordsworth.
Poet Wondering What He Is
Up To. Enright.
Red Rock Ceremonies.
Endrezze-Probst.
Scholar II. Deane.
The Shape of the Heart.
Nicholl.
Sound Advice. *Anonymous.*
Switchback. Sitwell.
These Two. Schwartz.
The Trinity. Osborne.
The True Heaven. Hayes.
A Valediction Forbidding
Mourning. Donne.
Women and Roses.
Browning.

Circuit (s)
Christopher at Birth.
Longley.
A Summer Twilight. Turner.
Sunrise. Sangster.

Circumference
At half-past three.
Dickinson.
I saw no way—the heavens
were stitched. Dickinson.
The Poets Light but Lamps.
Dickinson.

Circumstance (s)
Circumstance. Shelley.

The Departure. King.
New Students. Bell.
Othello. Shakespeare.
Rambuncto (parody).
Widdemer.
These Past Years: Passages 10.
Duncan.

Circus
C Is for the Circus.
McGinley.
The Death Circus. Tranter.
The Three Wise Couples.
Corbett.
What Happens. Jordan.
When I Went to the Circus.
Lawrence.
Winter Circus. Fisher.

Cistern
Driving to Sauk City.
Woessner.
Place-Names of China.
Bennett.

Cit (ies) (y)
Aftermath. McCulloch.
America, America!
Schwartz.
The Ancient One. Culhane.
Armistice Day. Causley.
Ballad of the Spanish Civil
Guard. Garcia Lorca.
Barriers Burned. Field.
The Base of All Metaphysics.
Whitman.
The Bed. Saleh.
Behind the Closed Eye.
Ledwidge.
Beyond. Johnson.
The Blackstone Rangers.
Brooks.
Boosting the Booster.
Anonymous.
The Breed of Athletes.
Euripides.
A Brook in the City. Frost.
Brussels in Winter. Auden.
Building for Eternity.
Sargent.
Canal Street, Chicago.
Fixmer.
Changes. Heaney.
The Changes. Pinsky.
Chestnut Stands. Field.
Chez Madame. Harrison.
City. Bruchac.
The City. North.
The City of God. Johnson.
The City's Crown. Foulke.
City Trees. Dargan.
Cold Water Flat. Booth.
Coming Home, Detroit, 1968.
Levine.
Commuter's Entry in a
Connecticut Diary.
Warren.
Comrade Jesus. Cheyney.
Conversation. Giovanni.
The Cool, Grey City of Love.
Sterling.
Crimes of Lugalanne.
Enheduanna.
A Curse on Uruk.
Enheduanna.
Dan, the Dust of Masada Is
Still in My Nostrils.
Whitman.
A Day in the City. Sissman.
Departure. Forche.
Disclaimer of Prejudice.
Siegel.
A Dream. Arnold.
Encounter in Jerusalem.
Lipshitz.

The Departure. King.
English Thornton. Masters.
Entry. Miles.
Epithalamium. Fairburn.
Evening Walk. Akesson.
Family Photograph. Vizenor.
Fifty Years Spent. Burt.
The Fisherman. Brown.
The Fisherman. Stewart.
The Fishvendor. Meredith.
The Flood. Mak.
Fragments. Corinna.
From a Marriage Broker's
Card, 1776. *Anonymous.*
Gare du Midi. Auden.
Grand Rapids. Moore.
The Grass, Alas. Emmons.
The Grief. Rilke.
Hail! The Glorious Golden
City. Adler.
Harlem Riot, 1943. Murray.
He Knoweth the Souls of the
East. Book of the Dead.
Heart-Hurt. *Anonymous.*
How Pleasant Is This Flowery
Plain. *Anonymous.*
How Was Your Trip to L.A.?
Whalen.
Hymn of the City. Bryant.
A Hymn to No One Body.
Wade.
I'm Gonna Run to the City of
Refuge. Johnson.
I Will Write. Graves.
The Ice Has Spoken.
Rixson.
Inanna and Ebih.
Enheduanna.
Indigo. Crozier.
The Inundation. Sergeant.
Jenny. Rossetti.
The Jewish Woman.
Kolmar.
Korea. Buckley.
The Lame One. Anderson.
Landscape of the Vomiting
Multitudes. Garcia Lorca.
Leap in the Smoke. Buchan.
The Light of Asia (excerpt).
Arnold.
Limerick: "Said Nero to one
of his train." *Anonymous.*
A Lion Named Passion.
Hollander.
The Lost Child. Reaney.
Madrigal: "Some there are as
fair to see to." Davison.
Magaica. De Sousa.
Mandelstam. Burns.
Manhattan. Beer.
Mary Speaks to Jesus.
Dempster.
Metamorphoses. Ovid
(Publius Ovidius Naso).
Metroliner. Du Vall.
Milking Before Dawn.
Dallas.
The Milky Way. Anderson.
Morgana. D'Annunzio.
Move On, Yiddish Poet.
Glatstein.
Naples. Rogers.
Night Piece. Strand.
The Noodle-Vendor's Flute.
Enright.
Norembega. Whittier.
The Novelty Shop. Niatum.
The Old City. Manning-
Sanders.
Open Roads. Donnell.
Outside the Holy City.
Gilkey.
A Pasture. Knowles.

Peace in the Welsh Hills.
Watkins.
Pedra. Burgon.
Perspective He Would Mutter
Going to Bed. Gilbert.
The Pilgrim and the Herdboy.
Buchanan.
The Poor. Williams.
The Prophecy Sublime.
Hosmer.
Prophets for a New Day.
Walker.
The Proposition. Blackburn.
Psychedelic Firemen.
Henderson.
Revolutionary Letters. Di
Prima.
The Rock. Eliot.
Rugby Chapel–November,
1857. Arnold.
The Sailor Cut down in His
Prime. *Anonymous.*
Seeds of Lead. Gilboa.
The Seekers. Masefield.
Sexual Privacy of Women on
Welfare. Lane.
Snow. Chiang.
South End. Aiken.
A State of Nature.
Hollander.
Suburban Dusk. Meyers.
The Sunset City. Cornwell.
The Thirteenth Song.
Drayton.
The Tired Worker. McKay.
Toledo. Campbell.
Trippers. Sitwell.
Troynovant. Dekker.
Twenty-One Love Poems.
Rich.
Up at a Villa–Down in the
City. Browning.
Veneta. Coleridge.
Volubilis, North Africa.
Currey.
Western Town. Shapiro.
Where Cross the Crowded
Ways of Life. North.
The Wish. Cowley.
Citizen (s)
Confession Overheard in a
Subway. Fearing.
Every Earthly Creature.
Brinnin.
Exile. Bloch.
A Fable for Critics. Lowell.
In Nakedness. Pomeroy.
Lines for a Dead Poet.
Ferry.
The New Roof. Hopkinson.
Poem of the Future Citizen.
Craveirinha.
The Purple, White and Green.
Morgan-Browne.
The Town I Was Born In.
Amichai.
Turtle Lake. Hugo.
Civilization
At the Cenotaph.
""MacDiarmid.
Australia. Hope.
Black People: This Is Our
Destiny. Jones.
Certain Maxims of Archy.
Marquis.
Dream, Dump-Heap, and
Civilization. Warren.
New Mexican Mountain.
Jeffers.
An Ode to Mr. Anthony
Stafford to Hasten Him into
the Country. Randolph.

Printed Words. Bahe.
Put Down. Damas.
Tired. Johnson.
Clack
Captain Carpenter. Ransom.
O, Beautiful They Move.
Pillen.
On His Own Deafness.
Swift.
Claim (ed) (ing) (s)
Bottom's Dream. Dow.
The Builder. Sherman.
The Dreamers Cry Their
Dream. Trent.
The Fisherman Writes a
Letter to the Mermaid.
Aiken.
Magnetism. Lazarus.
My Style. Bukowski.
One dignity delays for all.
Dickinson.
The Parsnip. Nash.
The Secret Irish. Hoey.
Shadow River. Johnson.
Sleepin' at the Foot O' the
Bed. Patrick.
The Swimmers. Tate.
The Wave. Phillips.
The Woman at the Washtub.
Daley.
The Woman Hanging from
the 13th Floor Window.
Harjo.
Clam (s)
Acres of Clams. *Anonymous.*
The Old Settler's Song.
Henry.
Clamour
An Argument–Of the Passion
of Christ. Merton.
Beggar to Beggar Cried.
Yeats.
Dirge. De Vere.
Pelvic Meditation. Smith.
Prayer for the Royal
Marriage. Masefield.
Clan (s)
For "Mr. Dudley," a Black
Spy. Emanuel.
In Hotels Public and Private.
Pomeroy.
Clap (ping) (s)
The Bellman's Song.
Anonymous.
Concert-Interpretations (Le
Sacre du Printemps).
Sassoon.
The Dutch. Canning.
Epitaph: "Here lie two poor
lovers, who had the
mishap." Pope.
A Farewell. Gascoigne.
The Freaks at Spurgin Road
Field. Hugo.
Gascoigne. Sackville.
Goosepimples. Barks.
Green Grass. *Anonymous.*
The Invention of Fire.
Taylor.
Mother of the Groom.
Heaney.
On the Erection of
Shakespeare's Statue in
Westminster Abbey. Pope.
The Plea of the Midsummer
Fairies. Hood.
Rain Forest. Smith.
A Raree Show. College.
Three Epitaphs on John
Hewet and Sarah Drew.
Pope.

Clarinet
Anabasis. Nelson.
At the Symphony. Nathan.
The Clouds. Aristophanes.
Clarity
About Women. Putnam.
An Aftermath. Blackburn.
Days of 1978. Stern.
The High Hills. Gurney.
An Inscription. Vinaver.
On Philosophy. Goldstein.
Spirits Unchained.
Kgositsile.
Clasp
A Barefoot Boy. Riley.
The Grape-Vine Swing.
Simms.
Half. Truax.
Haunted. Sassoon.
The Hillman Looks Back.
McOwan.
The Longing. Goodreau.
Madonna of the Empty Arms.
Egan.
That Which Hath Wings Shall
Tell. Van Voorhis.
Class (es)
Change of School. Smither.
Cousin Jack Song.
Tregonning.
February Morning. Kuka.
From a Lavatory Wall.
Anonymous.
The Hedge Schoolmasters.
MacManus.
The Hind and the Panther.
Dryden.
Clatter
Going in to Dinner. Shanks.
Half of Life. Holderlin.
Homing Pigeons. Walker.
The Teacher. Fisher.
Claw (s)
Allen Ginsberg Blesses a
Bride and Groom: A
Wedding Night Poem.
Peters.
.Blessing a Bride and Groom:
A Wedding Night Poem
(parody). Peters.
Cats Is Wheels.
Kicknosway.
Colloquy with a King-Crab.
Bishop.
Dusk. Lopez-Penha.
Jis' Knowin'. Nickens.
Local Politics. Pinsky.
Message from a Cross.
Harris.
My Claw Is Tired of Scribing!
Cille.
Nervous Miracles.
Gustafson.
The Owl. Warren.
Santa Claus. Moraes.
Turtle. Lowell.
Vicissitudes of the Creator.
MacLeish.
Your Woods. Holley.
Clay
Africa Is Made of Clay.
Simoko.
Child. MacIntyre.
Choice. Dickinson.
Clap Hands, Daddy's Coming.
Anonymous.
Clouds and Clay. Gillies.
Death is a dialogue.
Dickinson.
Epilogue (excerpt). Percy.
The Everlasting Gospel.
Blake.

Feathers and Moss. Ingelow.
Fine Clay. Shaw.
For John Chappell. Snyder.
God and the Soul: At the
Ninth Hour. Spalding.
The Great Hunger.
Kavanagh.
If You Were Here. Marston.
The Image of Death. Vaux.
Keramos. Longfellow.
The Lacking Sense. Hardy.
The Lament for Art O
Laoghaire (excerpt).
O'Connell.
Lord Thomas Stuart.
Anonymous.
The Man from Strathbogie.
FitzGerald.
My Sorrow, Donncha. O
Heigeartaigh.
A Mystic as Soldier.
Sassoon.
Old Michael. Brady.
On an American Soldier of
Fortune Slain in France.
Scollard.
On the Safe Side. Dunsany.
Pantoum. Ashbery.
Peter Emberley (II).
Anonymous.
A Poem To Be Said on
Hearing The Birds Sing.
Anonymous.
The Poet. Long.
The Poet and His Book.
Millay.
Prelude. Rivers.
The Princess. Tennyson.
The Rath in Front of the Oak
Wood. *Anonymous.*
The Reed. Carpenter.
The Revenant. De la Mare.
Ritual of Departure.
Kinsella.
The Road. Stephens.
Romance. Lang.
Rumination. Eberhart.
The Soldier's Grave. Muir.
The Song of the Heads.
Anonymous.
The Story of the Pot and the
Kettle. Montagu.
Three Proverbs. Mangan.
To Our Lady, the Ark of the
Covenants. Larsson.
The Tower. Pagis.
Turtle Mountain Reservation.
Erdrich.
Upon Christ His Birth.
Suckling.
View Me, Lord, a Work of
Thine. Campion.
Wherein Consists the High
Estate. Dayton.
Whoopee Blues. Hill.
Clean (ing)
All heavy minds. Wyatt.
Bait Shop. Reiter.
Baldy Bane. Graham.
Clay Hills. Untermeyer.
Dirty Jim. Taylor.
The Diseases of Bath
(excerpt). *Anonymous.*
Family Outing–A Celebration.
Jackowska.
For You. Sandburg.
Housework. Matthews.
Hudson Ferry. Schuyler.
I Saw God Wash the World.
Stidger.
Intercession in Late October.
Graves.

Keep It Clean. Jordan.
The Leper Cleansed. Collop.
Limerick: "A limerick packs
  laughs anatomical."
  Anonymous.
The Right Heart in the
  Wrong Place. Joyce.
The Seed Growing Secretly.
  Vaughan.
Soeur Marie Emilie.
  Houselander.
The Storm. Shanks.
Tableau at Twilight. Nash.
That Old Sauna High.
  Hollo.
Three Poems for Women, 2.
  Griffin.
To Make an Amblongus Pie.
  Lear.
The Translated Way.
  Adams.
Tree Ferns. Plumly.
The Washer-Woman.
  Bohanan.
Welcome to the New Year.
  Farjeon.
What Would I Give?
  Rossetti.

Clear (er) (ness)
After Working. Bly.
Air Raid. Wild.
At the Telephone Club.
  Coulette.
Ballade of Sayings. Merwin.
Becoming a Nun. Jong.
The Captain's Daughter.
  Fields.
Christ in You. *Anonymous.*
A Coast View (excerpt).
  Harpur.
Courage. Arnold.
Day on Kind Continent.
  Cohen.
Each to Each. Cane.
Folded Power. Cromwell.
Home in Indianapolis.
  Pflum.
Hope (excerpt). Shenstone.
An Hymn on the
  Omnipresence. Byrom.
In Praise of a Guilty
  Conscience. Szymborska.
A Letter from Rome.
  Clough.
Like Water Down a Slope.
  Schneour.
Limerick: "There was a young
  fellow named Shear."
  Ciardi.
Lines on a Young Lady's
  Photograph Album.
  Larkin.
Mary Queen of Scots.
  Turner.
The Monk and His Pet Cat.
  Anonymous.
Night of the Immaculate
  Conception. Maragall.
Old-Testament Gospel.
  Cowper.
On the Ineffable Inspiration of
  the Holy Spirit.
  Greiffenberg.
Pity Ascending with the Fog.
  Tate.
Psalm XXXII. Sidney.
Religio Laici. Dryden.
The River. Stuart.
The River of Heaven.
  Anonymous.
The Road from Election to
  Christmas. Williams.

Seeds of Lead. Gilboa.
Setting/Slow Drag. Rodgers.
The Shirt. Morley.
Soul's Liberty. Wickham.
Sun of the Sleepless. Byron.
To Brander Matthews.
  Dobson.
To the Ghost of a Kite.
  Wright.
The Tournament of Man.
  Crosby.
Trouble Not the Maiden's
  Soul. Runeberg.
Under Glass. Kreymborg.
Upon Visiting His Lady by
  Moonlight. "W."
Walking to Sleep. Wilbur.
Water Ouzel. Matchett.
The Wilderness. Raine.
Your Looks So Often Cast.
  Wyatt.

Cleave
The Creation. *Anonymous.*
The Enigma. Eberhart.
The Lovers. Cary.
They Who Tread the Path of
  Labor. Van Dyke.
To the Polyandrous Lydia.
  Adams.

Cleft
A Fine, a Private Place.
  Ackerman.
Matlock Bath. Betjeman.

Cleopatra
Italian Poppies. Spingarn.

Clerk
Acton Beauchamp,
  Herefordshire.
  Anonymous.
Missouri Town. Palen.
A Recent Dialogue. Moore.
Sunken Evening. Lee.

Clever
Albatross. Lele-io-Hoku.
Crow Voices. Tremblay.
Fate in Incognito. Benedikt.
From Greenland to Iceland.
  Anonymous.
Good and Clever.
  Wordsworth.
The Life and Lucubrations of
  Crispinus Scriblerus
  (excerpt). Woodhouse.
The Omelet of A. MacLeish.
  Wilson.
On Falling Asleep to
  Birdsong. Meredith.
Pease Porridge Hot, Pease
  Porridge Cold. *Anonymous*
The Sampler. Turner.
Soiree. Pound.
The Turtle. Nash.
Winter in Etienburgh.
  Parker.

Click (ing)
The Boar. Kelly.
The Delights of the Door.
  Ponge.
I Am a Dangerous Woman.
  Harjo.
Nothing in Heaven Functions
  As It Ought. Kennedy.
Parting after a Quarrel.
  Tietjens.

Client
Country Pleasures. Martial
  (Marcus Valerius Martialis).
The Courser and the Jennet.
  Shakespeare.
Epistles. Horace.

Cliff (s)
All Quiet. Ignatow.

The Beacons. Milman.
Darkened Windows.
  Bottrall.
The Dead Seal near McClure's
  Beach. Bly.
Dream. Smith.
Haitian Suite. Orr.
Kineo Mountain. Wright.
Night Airs. Landor.
Sibyl. Stroud.
The Sick Image of My Father
  Fades. Horder.
Slim Man Canyon. Silko.
Swallow Song. Pickthall.
The Wind of the Cliff Ka
  Hea. Thompson.
You. Tagliabue.

Climate
The Climate. Denby.
Early Pregnancy. Shuttle.
"I've been going around
  everywhere without any
  skin." Miles.
West Wind. Koch.

Climax
Conversational. *Anonymous.*
Toward Climax. Snyder.

Climb (ing) (s)
After the Swimmer. Wallace.
At Luca Signorelli's
  Resurrection of the Body.
  Graham.
August 12, 1952. Fishman.
The Bean-Stalk. Millay.
Bell-Bottomed Trousers.
  Anonymous.
Bicycling Song. Beeching.
Birthday. Kavanagh.
Circumambulation of Mt.
  Tamalpais. Hoyem.
Climbers. Zimunya.
Count Filippo. Heavysege.
Doing the Dubhs.
  Anonymous.
Ecce Homo. Bynner.
The Emergency Maker.
  Wagoner.
Father. Weston.
The Flood. Mak.
Hills. Guiterman.
The Hours. Tichy.
I Hear You've Let Go.
  Ferre.
Kineo Mountain. Wright.
Last Night They Heard the
  Woman Upstairs. Ullman.
Lewesdon Hill. Crowe.
Lines for a Feast of Our
  Lady. Maris Stella.
Looking down a Hill.
  Thompson.
The Mountaineers. Abse.
The New House.
  McDougall.
Nocturne. Aldrich.
Notes from a Journey. Hunt.
O Aa the Manly Sports.
  Annand.
Old Santa Is An Active Man.
  Lenski.
On Looking at an Old
  Climbing Photograph.
  Fraser.
Over the fence. Dickinson.
The Paps of Jura. Young.
Per Ardua ad Astra.
  Oxenham.
A Renouncing of Love.
  Wyatt.
Rock Leader. Bathgate.
The Schreckhorn. Hardy.

This Poem Will Never Be
  Finished. Souster.
To the Soul. Broome.
Turris Eburnea. *Anonymous.*
Variations on a Theme.
  Williams.
The Victim. Mphande.
A Waist. Stein.

Clime
All Things Are Current
  Found. Thoreau.
The Doomed City. Poe.
The Hind and the Panther.
  Dryden.
In Memory of General Grant.
  Abbey.

Cling (ing)
Among the Orchards.
  Lampman.
From the Crag. Leib.
Hast Thou Not Seen an Aged
  Rifted Tower. Coleridge.
Hope Overtaken. Rossetti.
The Languages We Are.
  Bryant.
The Last Leaf. Holmes.
Limerick: "The young things
  who frequent picture-
  palaces." *Anonymous.*
Many Are Called. Robinson.
My Mother Once Told Me.
  Amichai.
The Old Rugged Cross.
  Bennard.
The Sleeper. Hay.
Thysia. Luce.
Who Is Not a Stranger Still.
  Stephany.

Cloak
Blessed Are Those Who Sow
  and Do Not Reap. Ben-
  Yitzhak.
Caesar, when that the traitor
  of Egypt. Wyatt.
Der Heilige Mantel Von
  Aachen. Musser.
Epitaph: "Hic jacet Tom
  Shorthose." *Anonymous.*
Hymn of the Moravian Nuns
  of Bethlehem. Longfellow.
Of the Surface of Things.
  Stevens.
On Hedylus. Martial
  (Marcus Valerius Martialis).
On Lady Anne Hamilton.
  Sheridan.
Recreation. Taylor.
Summer Oracle. Lorde.
Tak' Your Auld Cloak about
  Ye. *Anonymous.*

Clock (s)
Another Year Come.
  Merwin.
At Lincoln. Adams.
Big Night Blues. Jefferson.
A Bright Day. Montague.
Cancer Research. Parlatore.
Carnival. Hervey.
Cinderella. Plath.
The Clock. Holman.
A Clock in the Square.
  Rich.
The Clod. Curran.
The Colder the Air. Bishop.
The Dog beneath the Skin.
  Auden.
Eight O'Clock. Housman.
The Empty House. Hoban.
Four. Gibbs.
Fracture of Light: Song in the
  Cold Season. Morse.
Halt and Parley. Clarke.

Holding the Mirror up to Nature. Nemerov.
If(Touched by Love's Own Secret)We,Like Homing. Cummings.
Kaddish. Ginsberg.
A Love Affair. Bennett.
Les Luths. O'Hara.
Methinks the Measure. Hutchison.
Moist Moon People. Sandburg.
Moriturus. "Marie.
Nahant. Emerson.
November Poppies. Corke.
Of One That Had a Great Nose. Turberville.
Of the Clock and the Cock. Turberville.
On Riots. Leslie.
The Pit of Bliss. Stephens.
The River God. Sitwell.
Song: "Silly Boy, there is no cause." Pestel.
States. Paulin.
Striking. Calverley.
Thank You for the Valentine. Wakoski.
The Time-Clock. Towne.
Time Passes. Lister.
A Timepiece. Merrill.
To Turn from Love. Fabio.
Too Soon the Lightest Feet. Hall.
The Unknown God. Watson.
Valediction to My Contemporaries. Gregory.
What Secret Desires of the Blood. Sachs.

Cloe
Characters of Women. Pope.
Cloe. Granville.
Epistle to a Lady: Of the Character of Women. Pope.
To Cloe. Jacob.

Cloister (ed)
The Fall of Maubila. English.
The Friar and the Nun. Anonymous.
Ghost-Flowers. Higginson.

Close (ness) (d) (ing)
Agamemnon. Aeschylus.
Archery. De la Mare.
The Best Old Feller in the World. Anonymous.
The Bird. Tagore.
Bus Stop. O'Sullivan.
Coloring Margarine. Hathaway.
The Columbine. Very.
Coots. Bruchac.
The Death Room. Graves.
The Djanggawul Cycle, 12. Anonymous.
Dull Is My Verse. Landor.
The Dying Girl. Williams.
Each to Each. Cane.
Epithalamium. Crashaw.
The Ex-Queen among the Astronomers. Adcock.
Finding You. Thayer.
Fish Story. Jacobs.
A Grief Ago. Thomas.
I Love My Love in the Morning. Griffin.
In a Garret. Allen.
In a Museum. Deutsch.
In Memory of Your Body. Shapiro.
Iowa Land. Bell.

The Kings of the World... Rilke.
Laura's Song. Brown.
Like a Mourningless Child. Patchen.
Lines to an Indian Air. Shelley.
The Little Boy to the Locomotive. Low.
Looking at Power. Woessner.
The Lover's Farewell. Mangan.
Magma. Dutton.
Man's Going Hence. Rogers.
A Minuet on Reaching the Age of Fifty. Santayana.
Mysterious Britain. Clampitt.
Nocturnal Sounds. Cumbo.
Noel! Noel! Simmons.
Once I Pass'd Through a Populous City. Whitman.
The Open Door. Anonymous.
The Open Sea. Meredith.
The Page of Illustrations. Schjeldahl.
Pocket Poem. Kooser.
Remembering Home. Petrykewycz.
Reprisals. Yeats.
Resurgam. Burt.
A Seeker in the Night. Coates.
Sinkholes. McFatter.
The Skein. Kizer.
So Close Should Be Our Love. Anonymous.
Softly Fades the Twilight Ray. Smith.
Sonnet: "So shoots a star as doth my mistress glide." Davies.
Spring Air. Derwood.
Stocking Fairy. Welles.
The Surrender at Appomattox. Melville.
Teeth. Holub.
There Is a Love. Cleveland.
This Morning. Wright.
Tiresias. Tennyson.
Verses Written during the War 1756–1763. Mordaunt.

Close (ness) (d) (s)
Advice to a Painter. Anonymous.
Bachelor Farmer. McDonald.
The Banks of Sweet Dundee. Anonymous.
Blue Homespun. Call.
The Bridge. Verwey.
The Bull Moses. Hughes.
The Campus. Posner.
The Contented Bachelor. Kendall.
The Departure from Hydra. Koch.
Epithalamium. Gosse.
First Death. Justice.
The Flight from the Convent. Tilton.
Funeral. Meyer.
Horses. Riedemann.
I Pass a Lighted Window. Wood.
The Jealous Lover. Anonymous.
A Magus. Ciardi.

Memorial Day: A Collaboration. Berrigan.
Okay "Negroes." Jordan.
The Paisley Officer. Anonymous.
Parachutes, My Love, Could Carry Us Higher. Guest.
Parting after a Quarrel. Tietjens.
Poem: "I believe the yellow flowers think with me." Notley.
A Poem of a Maid Forsaken. Anonymous.
The Preacher's Vacation. Anonymous.
The Savage Beast. Williams.
Sketch of Lord Byron's Life. Moore.
The Stockyard. Squire.
The Symposium (excerpt). Goldberg.
To a Republican Friend. Arnold.
True Love. Anonymous.
Vitae Summa Brevis Spem Nos Vetat Incohare Longam. Dowson.
When the Last Riders. Zach.
Workday Morning. Tollefsen.

Closet (s)
Adulescentia. Fitzgerald.
The European Shoe. Benedikt.
Last Night There Was a Cricket in Our Closet. Quintana.
Love in a Life. Browning.
The Rubaiyat of Omar Khayyam. Omar Khayyam.
Walking through the Upper East Side. Jong.
When You Are Gone. Van Winckel.

Closing
Bonner's Ferry Beggar. Clark.
A Dancer's Life. Justice.
Dreaming about Freedom. Baca.
God That Doest Wondrously. Ibn Ezra.
Nothing More Will Happen. Piercy.
Reconcilable Differences. Sauls.
The Relish of the Muse. Beaumont.
The Return. Saleh.
The Rhythm. Creeley.
Summer Storm. Untermeyer.
The Thermal Stair. Graham.
To His Not-So-Coy Mistress. Vaughan-Thomas.

Cloth
Balgu Song. Anonymous.
The Curtain Poem. Brock.

Clothe (d) (s)
Across the Western Ocean. Anonymous.
Adults Only. Stafford.
Astrophel and Stella, CI. Sidney.
August. Updike.
The Ballad of the Harp-Weaver. Millay.
The Boarder. Feirstein.
Bum. Wedgefarth.
By Frazier Creek Falls. Snyder.

Captain Cook. Anonymous.
The Children of the Poor. Hugo.
The Custom of the World. Simpson.
A Death in the Streets. Petaccia.
The Disordering. Yates.
Dry Your Tears, Africa! Dadie.
Dusk. Belford.
Embarrassed Judge. Anonymous.
The Gentleman. Lonzano.
Good Night, Sweet Repose. Anonymous.
Hanging Out the Linen Clothes (with music). Anonymous.
Hold up Your Head. Anonymous.
If I had as much money as I could/spend. Mother Goose.
In the Cafe. Borson.
Letters. Spencer.
Limerick: "'Tis strange how the newspapers honor." Field.
Lord High-Bo. Belloc.
The One Who Is Within. Francisco.
The Ploughman. Anonymous.
Rondel. Kennedy.
The Sailor's Mother (excerpt). Wordsworth.
Shadows. Anonymous.
The Soul's Garment. Newcastre.
Time of Waiting. Dutton.
Warmth. Sutter.
Weaving at the Window. Wang Chien.
When the Dawn Comes. Anonymous.

Cloud (s) (y)
Advice to My Best Brother, Colonel Francis Lovelace. Lovelace.
All Souls' Eve. Mannix.
Alone. Poe.
Amoretti, XL. Spenser.
And There Will I Be Buried. Davidson.
The Angel in the House. Patmore.
Another. Lovelace.
April 1885. Bridges.
April Rain. Blind.
Arizona Highways. Welch.
Ascension-Day. Vaughan.
Astraea at the Capitol. Whittier.
Autumn. Hood.
Because They Were Very Poor That Winter. Patchen.
Bologna, and Byron. Rogers.
Bombardment. Aldington.
Bone Yard. Barnes.
Bread the Holy. Coatsworth.
The Broken. Merwin.
The Burial. Thalman.
Castleconnell. De Vere.
Chimes. Meynell.
The Climate of Thought. Graves.
The Cloud Factory. Haines.
The Cloud Parade. Jensen.
Cloud Spots. Lavoie.
The Clouds. Croswell.
The Colder the Air. Bishop.

The Cowboy's Life. Adams.
The Cowboy's Life. *Anonymous.*
The Dark-Eyed Sailor. *Anonymous.*
The Dark Swimmers. Eigner.
Darkness. Byron.
The Departed. Tabb.
Diana Enamorada: Ring Forth, Fair Nymphs, Your Joyful Songs. Gil Polo.
Don't Break It. Ceravolo.
Edinburgh after Flodden (excerpt). Ayton [(or Aytoun)] Sir Robert.
England. Salter.
Environ S. Eigner.
A Fable for Critics. Lowell.
False Nancy. *Anonymous.*
The Farmer's Clothes Are Soaked Through and Never Dried. Ise Tayu.
The Final Painting. Harwood.
Flight of the Roller Coaster. Souster.
From the Spanish. Towle.
The Graceful Bastion. Williams.
Heart-Summoned. Stuart.
Heraclitus in the West. Bell.
Home on the Range. *Anonymous.*
The Hunter. O'Hara.
Idiom of the Hero. Stevens.
Imitation of Spenser. Keats.
In Grandfather's Glasses. Peters.
In Hellbrunn. Trakl.
In Memory of Marie A. Brecht.
In the Madness of Love. Soto.
In the Woods. Scott.
Intimations of Immortality from Recollections of Early Childhood. Wordsworth.
The Isle. Shelley.
Leaving Troy. Irwin.
Life. Crabbe.
Life's Evil. Montale.
The limb of forests rises up. Caroutch.
A Little Song of Spring. Austin.
Love in Action. Patmore.
Love Letter. Pastan.
Love's Witness. Behn.
Lying on a Bridge. Brock.
The Marriage of Heaven and Hell. Blake.
Medusa's Hair Was Snakes. Was Thought, Split Inward. Fraser.
The Mind's Liberty. Davies.
More Than People. Fulton.
The Motto. Cowley.
The Mountain Afterglow. Laughlin.
Night's Ancient Cloud. Keohler.
O Lord, My Best Desire Fulfil. Cowper.
O Word of God Incarnate. How.
Ode on Indolence. Keats.
Ode on Melancholy. Keats.
Old Man Mountain. Noyes.
Our Youth. Ashbery.
The Pit of Bliss. Stephens.

Poem, to Jane Wilson on Television. Broley.
The Pylons. Spender.
Question. Swenson.
Rain Chant. Mertins.
Remember Thy Covenant. Pierce.
A Reply to Zaidun's Complaint... Wallada.
The Revenge of Hamish. Lanier.
The River. Welch.
Rolling Thunder. Wolf.
Rules and Lessons. Vaughan.
The Search. Vaughan.
The Ship. Hendry.
Silex Scintillans. Vaughan.
Smoke in Winter. Thoreau.
Sonnets. Hillyer.
Sonnets, I: "The rough green wealth of wheaten fields that sway." Irwin.
Sparrow Hills. Pasternak.
Spring. Behn.
Spring. Hovey.
The Stampede. Brininstool.
The Stampede. Coburn.
A Story from the Bushmen. Ceravolo.
The Stranger. Baudelaire.
Summer Sky. Gordon.
The Sun God. De Vere.
Surfaces. Meinke.
The Tale of Genji (excerpt). Murasaki Shibiku.
Thanksgiving. Koch.
Third Madrigal. Derwood.
Three Poems, III. Castellânos.
To Modigliani to Prove to Him That I Am a Poet. Jacob.
To Rosemary. Benét.
To the Choice Bridegroom. Halevi
Tropic Rain. Stevenson.
The Two Gentlemen of Verona. Shakespeare.
Under Restless Clouds. Michaelis.
Under the Pot. Graves.
The Unknown God. Watson.
Utah. Stevenson.
Venice. Longfellow.
Vertigo. Henderson.
Weeding in January. Brodsky.
The Wheelbarrow. Edson.
When Silence Divests Me. Birnbaum.
When Yon Full Moon. Davies.
Where Fled. Wieners.
Wings in the Dark. Gray.
Without Her. Rossetti.
Written in Butler's Sermons. Arnold.
The Yorkshire Moors. Summers.
Cloudburst
Tennis Pro. Dessner.
Clover (s)
Consolations of Philosophy. Mahon.
A faded boy in sallow clothes. Dickinson.
The Flitting. McGuckian.
Forefathers. Blunden.
Honey Bee. Perkins.
In the Field Forever. Wallace.

The Night before Larry Was Stretched. *Anonymous.*
Portrait by a Neighbor. Millay.
Pride and Hesitation. Farallon.
The Question. Tuckerman.
Scythe Song. Lang.
Shop of Dreams. Carr.
Sleeping at Last. Rossetti.
A Song off Clover. Holm.
Spring Song. Smith, Jr.
Third Limick. Nash.
A Trot, and a Canter, a Gallop, and Over. *Anonymous.*
Clown (s)
Content Thyself with Thy Estate. *Anonymous.*
A Defence of Poetry. Macconmidhe.
Good Morning America (excerpt). Sandburg.
Hope. Anderson.
The Life and Lucubrations of Crispinus Scriblerus (excerpt). Woodhouse.
Little Clown Puppet. Haywood.
Loving. Stembridge.
On the Road to Anster Fair. Tennant.
Sitting Bull's Will Versus the Sioux Treaty of 1868 and Monty Hall. Redwing.
Club (s)
The Ball and the Club. Lindsay.
Central Park. Lowell.
The Evening Out. Nash.
Love between Brothers and Sisters. Watts.
On Himself. Swift.
Orion. Engle.
Saul. Lasker-Schüler.
What Thou Lovest Well, Remains American. Hugo.
Clues
Macrame. Riley.
More Clues. Rukeyser.
Whole and Without Blessing. Gregg.
Cluster (s)
The Assignation. Imr el Kais.
At the Scenic Drive-In. McAleavey.
The Businessman of Alicante. Levine.
The Double Vision. Day.
Seurat. Sadoff.
View of Louisiana. Mathis.
Clutch
After Li Ch'ing-Chao. Waldman.
Animal Pictures. Locke.
The Beauty of Dawn. Mnthali.
Christ 1: Advent Lyrics, VIII. *Anonymous.*
In flight in escape. Sachs.
Pine Boat a-Shift. *Anonymous.*
Clutter
The Master of the Golden Glow. Schuyler.
Out of Chaos Out of Order Out. Roberts.
Coach (es)
The Bee. Dickey.
Black Bart, P08. Bierce.

He That Ne'er Learns His ABC. *Anonymous.*
The Journey. Hansbrough.
The Joy of Church Fellowship Rightly Attended. Taylor.
Modern Midnight Conversation: Between a Contractor and His Wife. *Anonymous.*
Old John Bax. Souter.
Profiles of My Father. McMaster.
Shih Ching. *Anonymous.*
Tom Southerne's Birth-Day Dinner at Ld. Orrery's. Pope.
Coachman
Astrophel and Stella, CV. Sidney.
Epigram. *Anonymous.*
Lady M. M—'s Farewel to Bath. Montagu.
The Mistaken Resolve. Martial (Marcus Valerius Martialis).
To Julius. Sedley.
Coal
After Elegies. Valentine.
Alone by the Hearth. Arnold.
At the Jewish Museum. Pastan.
Bad Man Ballad. *Anonymous.*
Banking Coal. Toomer.
Black Cry. Craveirinha.
Clerk Saunders. *Anonymous.*
The Cloud of Unknowing. Murray.
Cold Fire. Starbuck.
The Counselor. Parker.
Didyma. *Anonymous.*
Disappointment. O'Reilly.
Down in a Coal Mine. *Anonymous.*
Looking Down on West Virginia. Dickson.
McAndrew's Hymn. Kipling.
Meditations. Taylor.
The Miner's Doom. *Anonymous.*
Night-Music. Larkin
Ol' John Brown. *Anonymous.*
The Old Miner. *Anonymous.*
The Opportune Overthrow of Humpty Dumpty. Carryl.
The Panama Limited. White.
Proem. Gibson.
Raven. Niatum.
Sam Bass. *Anonymous.*
Scientific Proof. Foley.
Southern Season. Claudel.
That Little Lump of Coal. *Anonymous.*
Three against One. *Anonymous.*
Two Hundred Men and Eighteen Killed. Henry.
An Unseen Fire. Cooke.
Virtue. Herbert.
Walls. Allen.
We Passed by Green Closes. Clare.
Coarse
The Vision. Herrick.
Coast
Afternoons with Baedeker. Lancaster.
Canterbury. Dowling.

Chester. Billings.
The High Barbaree. *Anonymous.*
The High Barbaree. Richards.
Hydrographic Report. Frost.
I love and fear him. Kasa.
The Progress of Poesy. Gray.
Seashore. Emerson.
The Shrine. Doolittle.
Up Silver Stairsteps. Stuart.

Coat (s)
Abram Brown. Anonymous.
The Apparitions. Yeats.
The Battle of Harlaw (B version). *Anonymous.*
The Beaches (excerpt). Hyde.
Candlemas. Brown.
Cleaning Up, Clearing Out. Bronson.
The Coolun. O'Dugan.
The Cure's Progress. Dobson.
Dandelions. Frost.
Dorcas. Macdonald.
The Dying Hobo. *Anonymous.*
An Egyptian Passage. Weiss.
I Gathered Mosses in Easedale. Wordsworth.
I'll Tell. *Anonymous.*
I Spoke to the Violet. Neilson.
Lenox Avenue. Alexander.
The Monkey's Raincoat. Basho (Matsuo Basho).
A Proud Song. Wilkinson.
Real Old Mountain Dew. *Anonymous.*
A Shepherd's Coat. Lyon.
Taffy. *Anonymous.*
Taffy Was a Welshman. *Anonymous.*
Uncertain Sonnets. Johnston.
Variety: Why Do We Grumble? *Anonymous.*
Walking through the Upper East Side. Jong.
When First to This Country a Stranger I Came. *Anonymous.*
When the spent day begins to frail. Cummings.
White Apples. Hall.
The Woodman's Dog. Cowper.
The Work of the Weavers. *Anonymous.*

Cobbler
Beth Appleyard's Verses. DeVries.
Limerick: "An amateur, driving too fast." Wright.

Cobra (s)
The Bayadere. Saltus.
Dreams of Snakes, Chocolate and Men. Sanford.
Long Distance. Naone.
My Cobra Girl. *Anonymous.*
The Paisley Ceiling. Arnold.

Cobweb (s)
Beloved, Let Us Once More Praise the Rain. Aiken.
In Grandfather's Glasses. Peters.
September Butterfly. Boring.
To the Lady-Bird. *Anonymous.*
Trip: San Francisco. Hughes.

Cocaine
Lacrimas; or, There Is a Need to Scream. Lyle.
My Street Baby's Lament. Franklin.

Cock (s)
And the Cock Begins to Crow. Avery.
The Axe-Helve. Frost.
The Barn in Winter. MacIntosh.
Blue Calf. *Anonymous.*
The Clocking Hen. *Anonymous.*
The Cock of the Game. *Anonymous.*
Eerily Sweet. Coatsworth.
Fetching the Wounded. Binyon.
The Grave. Blair.
The Hag and the Slavies. La Fontaine.
How the Death of a City Is Never More Than the Sum of the Deaths... Coleman.
In an Arab Town. Tichy.
Madrigal: "The white hen she cackles." *Anonymous.*
Melon-Slaughterer; or, A Sick Man's Praise for a Well Woman (parody). Peters.
Nineteen Hundred and Nineteen. Yeats.
Of the Clock and the Cock. Turberville.
The Torn Nightgown. Oppenheimer.
Upon Prudence Baldwin Her Sickness. Herrick.
The Vineyard. Merwin.

Cockatoo
For the Marsh's Birthday. Wright.
The Stringybark Cockatoo. *Anonymous.*
To Eliza, Duchess of Dorset. Bennett.
What the Lord High Chamberlain Said. Cloud.

Cockle (s)
Cockles and Mussels. *Anonymous.*
Molly Malone. *Anonymous.*
The Town of Passage. *Anonymous.*

Cockroach (es)
Birds in the Night. Cernuda.
Certain Maxims of Archy. Marquis.
Psalm III. Ginsberg.

Coconuts
A Bestiary. Rexroth.
Green Coconuts: Rio. Durrell.

Cod
Escapade. Leslie.
High Overhead My Little Daughter. Brown.
I Caught a Fish. Murray.
Mrs. Busk. Sitwell.

Code (s)
Christ's Life Our Code. Copeland.
Consequences. Meredith.
Snails. Blodgett.
The Sonnets. Berrigan.

Coffee
40 Acres and a Mule. Gallup.
96 Vandam. Stern.
A Blessing. McBride.

The Child Reads an Almanac. Jammes.
Elegy Written in a Country Coal-Bin. Morley.
Good Morning Love! Blackburn.
The Morning After. Clark.
Prayerwheel/2. Meltzer.
Six Winter Privacy Poems. Bly.
Trail Crew Camp at Bear Valley, 9000 Feet.... Snyder.
Truck Drivers. Haag.

Coffin (s)
And Don't Bother Telling Me Anything. Vallejo.
Bonnie Annie (A version). *Anonymous.*
Bonnie Annie (B version). *Anonymous.*
Daredevil. Congdon.
Fin De Siecle. Cook.
The Grandmother. Berry.
Harvest of the Sea. Mhac an tSaoi.
How Old Brown Took Harper's Ferry. Stedman.
In After Days. Cameron.
It Isn't the Cough. *Anonymous.*
Lady Margaret. *Anonymous.*
New Year's. Reznikoff.
Ohioan Pastoral. Wright.
Orpheus to Woods. Lovelace.
Reconciliation. Whitman.
Those Gambler's Blues (with music). *Anonymous.*
When I Am Dead. *Anonymous.*
Wild Bill Jones. *Anonymous.*

Coil (ed) (s)
Diary. Wagoner.
The Golden Fleece. Williams.
Hawk and Snake. Silko.
Interview with Doctor Drink. Cunningham.
Nemesis. Emerson.
Passive Resistance. Bruchac.
Threnos. Hervey.

Coin (s)
The Apple Dumplings and a King. Wolcot.
Beggar. Parra.
Being Called For. Dobson.
The Bounty of Our Age. Farley.
Desert Flowers. Douglas.
Dorothy. Kreymborg.
Elegy for a Diver. Booth.
Fat Tuesday. Di Piero.
Herman Moon's Hourbook. Middleton.
Limbo. Rugo.
Looking for Maimonides: Tiberias. Kaufman.
Maple Leaves. Aldrich.
Mercian Hymns (excerpt). Hill.
Napoleon and the British Sailor. Campbell.
Napoli Again. Hugo.
Nude Kneeling in Sand. Logan.
Satires. Wyatt.
The Tapestry Weaver. Chester.
This Very Hour. Reese.
To T. H., a Lady Resembling My Mistress. Carew.

Under the Umbrella of Blood. Root.

Cold
Absence. Mangan.
Adieu to Old England. *Anonymous.*
Advent. Rossetti.
The Aeneid. Virgil (Publius Vergilius Maro).
After Death. Rossetti.
Alas! 'Tis Very Sad to Hear. Landor.
Almeria. Neruda.
Alone. Shelton.
America. Babcock.
Apopemptic Hymn. Auchterlonie.
At a Potato Digging. Heaney.
At the Dark Hour. Dehn.
At the Telephone Club. Coulette.
L'Aurore Grelottante. Levi.
The Battle of Muskingum. Safford.
Becoming a Nun. Jong.
Biafra. Mack.
Biting Through. Yamamoto.
Blackbird Winter. West.
Blame Not My Cheeks. Campion.
Bread and Milk. Rossetti.
Burning Mountain. Merwin.
Canine Amenities. *Anonymous.*
Cape Horn Gospel-I. Masefield.
Carol. Short.
The Castle of Thorns. Winters.
Cats and Egypt. Hughes.
Cerberus. Van Brunt.
A Christmas Fold-Song. Reese.
Christmas Tree. Smith.
Come, Gentle Death! Watson.
Come, Happy Children. *Anonymous.*
Common Sense and Genius. Moore.
The Convict of Clonmala. *Anonymous.*
Cottonwood Leaves. Clark.
Courtyard in Winter. Montague.
Da Leetla Boy. Daly.
Darwinity. Merivale.
Dauber. Masefield.
Death. Bodenheim.
The Death of Ailill. Ledwidge.
Depot in Rapid City. Hill.
Doubt. Rogers.
Down in the Meadows. *Anonymous.*
Dreams. Daley.
The Early Days. Dowling.
Early in the Morning. Simpson.
The Eggplants Have Pins and Needles. Matveyeva.
The End. De La Mare.
Epitaph on a Free but Tame Redbreast. Cowper.
Fable. Prokosch.
Farewell to the Old Year! Farjeon.
The Fault. Lucie-Smith.
The Fear. Gibson.
The Feast o' Saint Stephen. Sawyer.

The Feast of the Snow.
Chesterton.
Feathered Friends (parody).
Peters.
The First Day of the Hunting
Moon. Low.
Five Serpents. Burgess.
Flos Lunae. Dowson.
Forms of the Earth at
Abiquiu. Momaday.
Fortune's Wheel. De Tabley.
From Garvey's Farm: Seneca,
Wisconsin. Hoeppner.
The Gardener. *Anonymous.*
The Generous Years.
Spender.
Gift to a Jade. Wickham.
The Goldfish. Brown.
A Grace. Tiplady.
Growing Old. Learned.
Gwendoline (parody).
Taylor.
Haifa. Knut.
The Hard Listener.
Williams.
Harsh Climate. Simic.
Have You Any Work for a
Tinker, Mistris.
Anonymous.
He Said He Had Been a
Soldier. Wordsworth.
Health and Fitness. Morton.
Helen. Lamb.
Hoelderlin's Old Age.
Spender.
The Hounded Lovers.
Williams.
House Is an Enigma. Jensen.
How Was Your Trip to L.A.?
Whalen.
I thought that Love had been
a boy. *Anonymous.*
I Walk on the River at Dawn.
Hart.
Ice River. Baker.
Impromptu Lines on Being
Asked by Sir Thomas
Robinson... Chesterfield.
In Memoriam Paul Celan.
Hollander.
In the Case of Lobsters.
Morstein.
Inscription for a Wayside
Spring. Cornford.
Ipswich Bar. Bates.
Jadis. Dowson.
The Jazz of This Hotel.
Lindsay.
Jeny Kiss'd Me When We
Met. Dehn.
Jesu, Swete Sone Dere.
Anonymous.
Jimmy's Enlisted; or, The
Recruited Collier.
Anonymous.
Joe. McCord.
Joy and Pleasure. Davies.
June. Feinstein.
Kane. O'Brien.
A Last World. Ashbery.
Leaving Mexico One More
Time. Urdang.
A Life. Plath.
The Little Lady Lairdie.
Anonymous.
The Lonesome Dove.
Anonymous.
Lost Light. Akers.
Love. Butler.
Love's Victories. Shirley.
Love Song. Leon.

The Lover: A Ballad.
Montagu.
A Man Adrift on a Slim Spar.
Crane.
Man Carrying Thing.
Stevens.
The Man in the Moon.
Anonymous.
The Manichaeans. Snyder.
Mary and Gabriel. Brooke.
May. Rossetti.
Memory. Deutsch.
The Merchant of Venice.
Shakespeare.
The Mermaid. *Anonymous.*
Midwinter Thaw. Pratt.
A Moment. Brooke.
Monsieur Qui Passe. Mew.
Montalbert (excerpt). Smith.
The More It Snows. Milne.
Mourning and Melancholia.
Alvarez.
My Comrade. Roche.
The New Moon. Kobayashi
Issa.
New Year's Song. Hughes.
Night opens like an almond.
Caroutch.
North. Booth.
November. Tuckerman.
Now from the East.
Masahongva.
The Old Story. MacNeice.
On the Closing of Millom
Ironworks. Nicholson.
On the Rising Generation.
Dietz.
Once. Ives.
The One Certainty. Rossetti.
One Flesh. Jennings.
Paddy West. *Anonymous.*
The palm of my hand. Saito.
Parting, without a Sequel.
Ransom.
The Passing of Lydia.
Horace.
Passing Out. Levine.
Le Pere Severe. *Anonymous.*
Piccola Commedia. Wilbur.
A Poet's Progress.
Hamburger.
Precaution. Heine.
The Precision. Winters.
Ravenna. MacNeice.
Reflections. Pichaske.
Remembrances. Clare.
Return to Prinsengracht.
Blue-Swartz.
Robin Redbreast. Kunitz.
Romance. Lang.
Rooftop Winter. Thorpe.
The Ruined Motel. Gibbons.
Search for Love. Johnson.
Self-Portrait in a Convex
Mirror. Ashbery.
Sepulchre. Herbert.
The Shark. Pratt.
Shore Scene. Logan.
The Signature of All Things.
Rexroth.
Singular Indeed. McCord.
The Sleeping-Bag. Ponting.
Snow Queen's Portrait.
Berman.
Some Hot, Some Cold.
Campion.
The Song of the Heads.
Anonymous.
The Song of the Old Mother.
Yeats.
A Song of the Seasons.
Monkhouse.

The Song of Troylus.
Petrarch.
Song of Winter. *Anonymous.*
Song on a Young Lady Who
Sung Finely. Roscommon.
Song: "Stop! Don't touch me."
Anonymous.
A Song: "The nymph in vain
bestows her pains."
Winchilsea.
Sonnet XVI: "After an age
when thunderbolts and
hail." Labe.
Sonnets, II: "When forty
winters shall besiege thy
brow." Shakespeare.
Stanzas. Brainard.
Stanzas Concerning Love.
George.
Sugar in the Cane. Williams.
Sun of the Sleepless. Byron.
Sunset after Rain. Merwin.
A Testimony. Lyon.
There Were Some Summers.
Lux.
This Air That Blows in from
the Sea. Coatsworth.
Thought. Emerson.
To an Old Poet. Landor.
To Death. Wilchilsea.
To Keep the Cold Wind
away. *Anonymous.*
To the Pines. *Anonymous.*
Tramontana at Lerici.
Tomlinson.
Trout. Heaney.
The Unknown Eros.
Patmore.
The Virgin's Song.
Anonymous.
The Vision of Sir Launfal.
Lowell.
Waillie, Waillie! (with music).
Anonymous.
The Warning. Crapsey.
Water. Lowell.
Watercress & Ice. Twichell.
Watkwenies. Scott.
What the Bullet Sang.
Harte.
Where the Lilies Used to
Spring. Gray.
White Fear. Welles.
The Widow. Davenport.
The Wilderness. Raine.
Wildflower. Plumly.
Winter. Mair.
Winter Feast. Frost.
Winter is Another Country.
MacLeish.
The Winter Lightning for
Paul. Nemerov.
Within the Dream You Said.
Larkin.

Colin
The Old Woman's Three
Cows. *Anonymous.*
Collapse
Elegy. Towle.
To Modigliani to Prove to
Him That I Am a Poet.
Jacob.
Collar
The Clothing's New Emperor.
Finkel.
The Pitcher. Yuan Chen.
Collect (ion) (s)
The Collector. Souster.
Eclogue between the
Motherless. MacNeice.
In the National Gallery.
Sassoon.

Nude Descending a Staircase.
Kennedy.
On the Ruins of a Country
Inn. Freneau.
Quite Shy Actually but
Obsessed. Miller.
Stanzas Occasioned by the
Ruins of a Country Inn.
Freneau.
Colleen
The Faery Reaper.
Buchanan.
Where the River Shannon
Flows. Russell.
College
The Beginning of a Long
Poem on Why I Burned the
City. Benford.
Eastside Chick with Drive.
Spector.
His Own Epitaph, When He
Was Sick, Being Fellow in
New College... Hoskyns.
Snapdragon. Newman.
Cologne
The Good Bishop.
Anonymous.
On My Joyful Departure from
the City of Cologne.
Coleridge.
Color (s)
Above Salerno. Murray.
Anglais Mort a Florence.
Stevens.
Anniversary Poem for the
Cheyennes Who Fell at
Sand Creek. Henson.
Autumn Color. Robinson.
A Child. Gilder.
Cleaning Up. Dyson.
The Coal Mine Disaster's Last
Trapped Man Contemplates
Salvation. Meissner.
Coming and Going.
Johnson.
Concert Scene. Logan.
Country Villa. Garrigue.
Crumbs or the Loaf. Jeffers.
A Dab of Color. Weiss.
The Digger's Song. Boake.
Division. Ratti.
The Drawing out of Colour.
Dewdney.
Early Influences. Akenside.
Eclipse. Salamun.
For My Grandfather.
Robbins.
The Glens. Hewitt.
The Green and the Black.
Bailey.
Half-Way, for One
Commandment Broken.
Housman.
I used to wrap my white doll
up in. Jackson.
In Carrowdore Churchyard.
Mahon.
The Investment. Frost.
Johnny, I Hardly Knew Ye:
Swinburnese (parody).
Tyrrell.
Lullaby for Ann-Lucian.
Forbes.
Maggie Mac. *Anonymous.*
The Map. Bishop.
The Maximus Poems. Olson.
My Last Afternoon with
Uncle Devereux Winslow.
Lowell.
No More Love Poems #1.
Shange.

No, Thou Hast Never Griev'd but I Griev'd Too. Landor.
Nocturne. Lane.
Notes on a Child's Coloring Book. Dana.
Old Photo, 1942. Uba.
Our Country's Emblem. *Anonymous.*
Powwow 79, Durango. Allen.
The Princess Who Fled to the Castle. Landy.
Race Riot, Tulsa, 1921. Olds.
Rainbow Writing. Merriam.
Salt Man. West.
Separation. Merwin.
Song for the Dead, III. *Anonymous.*
Song: "Though I am dark." *Anonymous.*
Sonnets, XCIX: "The forward violet thus did I chide." Shakespeare.
Sonnets from the Portuguese, XLIV. Browning.
The Spirit of the Cairngorms. Firsoff.
Still He Sings. Taylor.
Thou Art the Sky. Tagore.
Twilight. Longfellow.
Variety: Why Do We Grumble? *Anonymous.*
The Vision of Piers Plowman. Langland.
Walking through the Door. Henderson.
What Color Is Lonely. Rodgers.
When the Fairies. Dorn.
When the Storms Come. Mphande.
When You Leave. Hahn.
Why I Am Afraid to Have Children. Ramke.
You Know, Joe. Durem.

Colt
The Council of Horses. Gay.
Unclaimed. Smyth.

Columbine (s)
And Can the Physician Make Sick Men Well. *Anonymous.*
In Ampezzo. Stickney.
Land Where the Columbines Grow. Fynn.
Lily, Germander, and Sops-in-Wine. *Anonymous.*

Columbus
The Discovery of America. Robertson.
The Sea-Weed. Pullen.

Comb (ed) (ing)
Evening Refrain. Santos.
Fantasia. Livesay.
I Love My Love. Adam.
If you go away. *Anonymous.*
Last Poems. Housman.
Madrigal: "The white hen she cackles." *Anonymous.*
O Night of the Crying Children. Sachs.
The Poems Come Easier. Mathew.
Sacred Objects. Simpson.

Combine (d)
The Art of Love. Grossman.
Verses Found in Thomas Dudley's Pocket after His Death. Dudley.

View of the Cathedral. Henri.
What If the Saint Must Die. Peck.

Come (s)
A 14-Year-Old Convalescent Cat in the Winter. Ewart.
The Absence. Levertov.
Absence. Mew.
Advice to a Neighbour Girl. Yu Hsuan-chi.
After Work. Oxenham.
Almost Ninety. Whitman.
The Anathemata. Jones.
At Daybreak. Hoyt.
Aunt Selina. Haynes.
The Avengers. Markham.
Baby-Sitting. Clarke.
Ballad. Spofford.
Be Kind to Me. Sappho.
Beyond the Smiling and the Weeping. Bonar.
Bird in a Cage (with music). *Anonymous.*
The Boys of the Island. *Anonymous.*
Break, Break, Break. Tennyson.
Breath. Dickey.
Bringing in the Sheaves. *Anonymous.*
The Brook. Tennyson.
Buy Me an Ounce and I'll Sell You a Pound. Cummings.
By the Pool at the Third Rosses. Symons.
Cairngorm, November 1971. Berry.
The Cambric Shirt. *Anonymous.*
Certainty. Hardy.
Changeless Shore. Ash.
The Changeling. Mew.
Children's Elegy. Rukeyser.
Cinderella. Jarrell.
Clara. Pound.
Come Forth, Come Forth! Wilson.
Come to Me Soon. Ralegh.
Coming Back. Gregg.
Complaint of the Absence of Her Lover Being Upon the Sea. Surrey.
Content and Rich. Southwell.
Coridon's Song. Chalkhill.
Cuckoo, noisy among the Shenbaka flowers. Andal.
Deer in the Bush. Bloch.
Died of Love. *Anonymous.*
Discouraged. Stanaback.
Do You Know, I Would Quietly. Rilke.
The Dove Apologizes to His God for Being Caught by a Cat. Eaton.
Driftwood. Stickney.
Dust Bowl. Hughes.
Eclogues. Virgil (Publius Vergilius Maro).
Epitaph on the Monument of Sir William Dyer at Colmworth, 1641. Dyer.
Errore. Di Cicco.
Farmer. Bailey.
Fatal Interview. Millay.
The Flight of Youth. Stoddard.
Garland Sunday. Colum.
He Never Will Forget. "H..
He Said That He Was Not Our Brother. Banim.

The Hero. Nicoll.
Hills of God, Break Forth in Singing. Buckham.
The Humble Springs of Stately Sandwich Beach. Sewall.
I'm Leery of Firms with Easy Terms. Jennison.
I Wish, I Wish. *Anonymous.*
If She but Knew? O'Shaughnessy.
In a Motion. Chester.
In This Dark House. Davison.
Intimations of Immortality from Recollections of Early Childhood. Wordsworth.
The Invisible Bride. Markham.
Invitation Standing. Blackburn.
Julius Caesar. Shakespeare.
Just As I Am. Elliott.
The Last Bus. Strand.
The Last Instructions to a Painter. Marvell.
Life's Mirror. "Madeline.
The Little Ghosts. Jones, Jr.
Little Maid, Pretty Maid. *Anonymous.*
London Poets. Levy.
Longing. Korn.
Love among the Manichees. Dickey.
The Man. Creeley.
Maryland, My Maryland. Randall.
Me to You. Reid.
The Moon. Best.
More Good Whiskey Blues. Wheatstraw.
The Mouse. Richards.
My Lord. Nicholson.
My Mother Said. *Anonymous.*
Nat Turner. Allen.
The Naughty Preposition. Bishop.
The Night before the Battle of Waterloo. Byron.
O Boy Cutting Grass. Hitomaro.
Ode on a Distant Prospect of Clapham Academy. Hood.
Old Father Annum. Jackson.
On a Bookseller. Goldsmith.
On the Esplanade des Invalides. Fisher.
On the Morning of the Third Night above Nisqually. Ransom.
One, Two, Whatever You Do. *Anonymous.*
Orphan Boy, Fishing. Goldbarth.
The Peace: Midst the Free Green Fields. Aristophanes.
The Pessimist. King.
Peter Grimes. Crabbe.
Picnic. Mathew.
Please to Ring the Belle. Hood.
A Poem on Inter-Uterine Device. Ghazi.
Priest Lake. Stafford.
Putting on Nightgown. *Anonymous.*
Rains for the Harvest. *Anonymous.*
A Red Red Rose. Burns.

Refusals. Anderson.
Rendezvous. Hillyer.
Robin Hood. *Anonymous.*
The Runaway. Frost.
Safely Home. *Anonymous.*
Sailing to Byzantium. Yeats.
Santo Domingo Corn Dance. Dickey.
Saturday Morning. Howard.
She'll Be Comin' Round the Mountain. *Anonymous.*
A Shropshire Lad. Housman.
Skins (excerpt). Wright.
Song of Loneliness. Halevi.
Song of the Blue-Corn Dance. *Anonymous.*
Song of the Highest Tower. Rimbaud.
Sonnets. Lee.
Spirits, Dancing. Gregor.
The Strange Visitor. *Anonymous.*
Summer. Aiken.
Summer Sunshine. Lathbury.
Susannah Prout. De la Mare.
The Sycamore Tree. *Anonymous.*
Timothy Boon. Eastwick.
To Our Ladies of Death. Thomson.
To the Muse. Wright.
Translation into the Original. Gilbert.
'Twas Just This Time, Last Year, I Died. Dickinson.
Two Invocations of Death, II. Raine.
Two Letters from Chang-Kan. Li Po.
Two Trinities. Mackenzie.
Ulysses Returns. Montgomery.
Unwanted. Field.
The Voice. De la Mare.
Wake Up, Jacob. *Anonymous.*
The Wanderer. Dobson.
Water-Boy. *Anonymous.*
When. "Coolidge.
When the Clouds Are upon the Hills. *Anonymous.*
The Wife A-Lost. Barnes.
Will He No Come Back Again? *Anonymous.*
The Woman. Thomas.
You Begin. Atwood.
A Young Deer/Dust. Roth.
Young Men You Are So Beautiful up There. Goedicke.

Comedy
The Donkey and the Lapdog. La Fontaine.
Pity Ascending with the Fog. Tate.

Comet (s)
Death & Empedocles 444 B.C. Gregory.
A Ship Burning and a Comet All in One Day. Eberhart.
Why East Wind Chills. Thomas.

Comfort (s) (ed) (ing)
Adjuration. Wheeler.
Analyst. Fisher.
The Anatomy of Humor. Bishop.
Arcadia. Sidney.
At the Dark Hour. Dehn.
Auf Wiedersehen. Hayes.

Bluebells. Markham.
Daddy. Clifton.
The Dark Road. Clifford.
Do What You Will. Hobson.
Dunce Song 6. Van Doren.
Erie Canal Ballad.
  Anonymous.
The False Lover Won Back
  (B version). *Anonymous.*
The Folly of Being
  Comforted. Yeats.
For Jim, Easter Eve.
  Spencer.
For Mary McLeod Bethune.
  Walker.
For the Rain It Raineth Every
  Day. Graves.
Four Legs, Two Legs, Three
  Legs. Empson.
Francis Beaumont's Letter
  from the Country to
  Jonson. Jonson.
Going Away Blues.
  Kimbrough.
Home, Sweet Home.
  Bunner.
Hyperion. Keats.
I have neither plums nor
  cherries. Breton.
I Know My Soul. McKay.
I Think That God Is Proud.
  Crowell.
Insomnia. Tabb.
The Lady and the Dwarf-
  King. *Anonymous.*
The Last Moriori.
  Smithyman.
The Life of Lincoln West.
  Brooks.
Litany to the Holy Spirit
  (excerpt). Herrick.
A Little Dog-Angel.
  Holland.
The Man Who Dreamed of
  Faeryland. Yeats.
Man without Sense of
  Direction. Ransom.
Mother Poem. Oppenheimer.
My God. Ibn Gabirol.
My Mother's Birthday: "I
  used to watch you
  sleeping." Raine.
O Powers Celestial, with
  What Sophistry. Barnes.
The Ocean Wood. De
  Tabley.
Pere Lalement. Pickthall.
A Poem Put into My Lady
  Laiton's Pocket. Ralegh.
The Prince. Bowers.
Psalm XLIII. Sidney.
The Sacrament of Sleep.
  Oxenham.
Scene from a Dream. Hale.
The Seafarer (excerpt).
  Anonymous.
Set Me whereas the Sun Doth
  Parch the Green. Surrey.
Silex Scintillans. Vaughan.
The Single Woman.
  Cornford.
The Song of Hungarrda.
  Ngunaitponi.
Spell of Sleep. Raine.
Submission to Afflictive
  Providences. Watts.
Suburban Sonnet. Harwood.
Suicid/ing Indian Women.
  Allen.
Summer Rain. Coleridge.

The Tree of the Cross.
  "Angelus Selesius"
  (Johannes Scheffler).
Unawares. Lent.
Upon Boys Diverting
  Themselves in the River.
  Foxton.
Valuable. Smith.
Washington. Goodman.
When I Am Not With You.
  Teasdale.
When Your Eyes.
  Anonymous.
Your Catullus Is Depressed.
  Catullus.
Comfortable
Monument to Pushkin.
  Brodsky.
She Remembers. Aldis.
Windy Trees. Ammons.
Comforter
Aaron Hatfield. Masters.
Immortality. Reese.
Returning to the World.
  Chester.
Comfortless
The False Lover Won Back
  (B version). *Anonymous.*
La Madonna dell' Acqua.
  Ruskin.
My hope, alas, hath me
  abused. Wyatt.
Songs of Ch'en. Confucius.
Treizaine. Wyatt.
Triptych. Heaney.
Comical
Limerick: "A limerick packs
  laughs anatomical."
  Anonymous.
Limerick: "Sir Bedivere Bors
  was a chivalrous knight."
  Opper.
Coming
Advent: A Carol. Dickinson.
After Hours. Mezey.
The Approach of the Storm.
  Anonymous.
At the Airport. Brinnin.
Baby Mine. Mackey.
Back to the Ghetto.
  Glatstein.
Buying the Dog. Ondaatje.
The Coming of His Feet.
  Allen.
The Door. Tomlinson.
Eleven Addresses to the Lord.
  Berryman.
The Empty Glen. Saunders.
The Fine Old English
  Gentleman New Version.
  Dickens.
Funeral Song. *Anonymous.*
Grandma Chooses Her Plot at
  the County Cemetery.
  Ruffin.
Growing Up. Milne.
He Is Coming. Gearhart.
Homosexual Sonnets.
  Pitchford.
The Horses. Muir.
How You Get Born. Jong.
Isabelle (parody). Hogg.
Mr. Wells. Roberts.
The Mugger. Pack.
The New Mothers. Shields.
Our Smoke Has Gone Four
  Ways. Henson.
A Prayer for the New Year.
  Anonymous.
A Raccoon. Fox.
Rejoice, O Bridegroom!
  Anonymous.

Revelation. Gregory.
The Roving Gambler.
  Anonymous.
Saturday Afternoon, when
  Chores Are Done. Mullen.
Something Is There. Moore.
Things. Simpson.
Three Hundred Thousand
  More. Gibbons.
To a Bull-Dog. Squire.
Topsy-Turvy Land.
  Wilkinson.
Violence on Television.
  Jenkins.
W's for Windows.
  McGinley.
Waiting for Winter.
  Keithley.
The Wind Is Blowing West.
  Ceravolo.
Command (s)
The Body Is Like Roots
  Stretching. Reznikoff.
Every Day. Bachmann.
Holy Sonnets, XVI. Donne.
The Idler. Very.
An Infant's Eye. Traherne.
The Islands of the Sea.
  Woodberry.
The Knight and Shepherd's
  Daughter (A version).
  Anonymous.
Lens. Wilkinson.
A Little Kingdom I Possess.
  Alcott.
The Master Spirit.
  Chapman.
The Negativess Person.
  Levine.
On a Picture by Michele da
  Verona, of Arion as a Boy
  Riding... Ridler.
Paul Jones. *Anonymous.*
The Reply. Levine.
To Anthea, Who May
  Command Him Anything.
  Herrick.
Valediction. Heaney.
Waiting. Davidson.
Walk. Horne.
Commence
The Golden Age.
  Anonymous.
The Wagoner's Lad.
  Anonymous.
Commend
A Funeral Elogy... Norton
  II.
O! Mistress Mine.
  Anonymous.
Song: To the Masquers
  Representing Stars.
  Campion.
To Scott. Letts.
Commerce
A Descriptive Poem,
  Addressed to Two Ladies....
  Dalton.
Large Bad Picture. Bishop.
A Pact. Pound.
Prince Alfrid's Itinerary
  (excerpt). *Anonymous.*
Common
Against Surrealism. Wright.
The Blind Boy's Pranks.
  Thom.
Caelica, LI. Greville.
Cloe. Granville.
Cloud Spots. Lavoie.
The Common Road.
  Perkins.

The Common Sailor.
  Anonymous.
Crochet Castle. Peacock.
Dance with Banderillas.
  Duerden.
The Days of the Unicorns.
  Webb.
Do They Whisper behind My
  Back? Schwartz.
Epigram: On Inclosures.
  Anonymous.
The Epiphany. Strong.
The Fate of the Oak.
  "Cornwall.
First Sight of Her and After.
  Hardy.
A Flower of Mullein. Reese.
Forgiveness. Whittier.
The Hands. Levertov.
His Sleep. Urdang.
I Entrust My All to You,
  Aurelius." Catullus.
Lily, Lois & Flaubert: The
  Site of Loss. Fraser.
The Lincoln Statue. Collins.
Many Indeed Must Perish in
  the Keel. Hofmannsthal.
The Merchant and the Fidler's
  Wife. *Anonymous.*
Miriam: Chorus. Carew.
More Lovely Grows the
  Earth. Coleman.
The News. "Sec."
Ode to the Lake of Geneva.
  Parsons.
On Mr. Pitt's Hair-Powder
  Tax. Burns.
Our Birth Is but a Sleep and a
  Forgetting. Wordsworth.
The Pessimist. King.
The Purple, White and Green.
  Morgan-Browne.
San Francisco from the Sea.
  Harte.
Sentiment. Chatterton.
The Six Badgers. Graves.
Te Deum. Reznikoff.
Tellers of Tales. Kallman.
Tragedy. Moss.
A Valediction Forbidding
  Mourning. Rich.
The Virgin Martyr.
  Cambridge.
Commonplace
I Have Found Such Joy.
  Crowell.
Next Day. Jarrell.
Piano Practice. Moss.
Vision. Devaney.
Commonwealth
Bad Bishop Jegon.
  Anonymous.
Epitaph on the Fart in the
  Parliament House.
  Hoskyns.
The Fairies' Farewell.
  Corbet.
Farewell to the Fairies.
  Corbet.
Technologies. Starbuck.
Commotion
Ars Amoris. Cunningham.
The Broken Heart. Ford.
News That Stays News.
  Mariani.
Tides. Blackwell.
Communication
1,000 Illustrations & a
  Complete Concordance.
  André.
The Auroras of Autumn.
  Stevens.

Readings, Forecasts, Personal Guidance. Fearing.

Tourist Time. Scott.

Communion

Another Spirit Advances. Romains.

Black Church on Sunday. Mosley.

Epigram on the Play-House at Amsterdam. Parsons.

Ludwig's Death Mask. Hughes.

On the Death of William Edward Burghardt Du Bois... Rivers.

The Pear Tree. Millay.

Psalm–People Power at the Die-In. Levertov.

Youth's Thankfulness. Kramer.

Communist

The Ballad of Helmut Franze. Sala.

H–y P–tt. *Anonymous.*

My Father, Who's Still Alive. Kozer.

Strawberries Mit Cream. Owens.

Community

Epistle II: To a Socialist in London. Bridges.

The Old O. O. Blues. Young.

Companion (s)

Childhood. Tabb.

The Full Heart. Nichols.

Image-Nation (the Poésis). Blaser.

The Ladder of St. Augustine: The Heights. Longfellow.

Letter to Statues. Brinnin.

Man in Harmony with Nature. Very.

Meditation. Schaechter-Gottesman

Memphis Minnie-Jitis Blues. Minnie.

On a Painting by Patient B of the Independence State Hospital... Justice.

Prospect Beach. Lipsitz.

Sometimes when Night... Sackville-West.

To the Noble Sir Francis Drake. Beedome.

Company

Alcibiades to a Jealous Girl. Ficke.

Arcadia. Sidney.

Asleep in the Bosom of Youth. Halevi.

Battle Problem. Meredith.

Benediction. Kunitz.

The Blake Mistake. Castle.

The Boston Burglar. *Anonymous.*

A Cigarette. *Anonymous.*

An Essay on Man. Pope.

Fifine at the Fair, XCIII (excerpt). Browning.

For Love. Creeley.

Good Company. *Anonymous.*

Heartbreak Road. Cone.

Hellhound on My Trail. Johnson.

Labor and Capital: Impression. Howells.

The Lay of Prince Marvan. *Anonymous.*

Marcus Argentarius. Rexroth.

The Marriage of the Frog and the Mouse. *Anonymous.*

Nanak and the Sikhs (excerpt). *Anonymous.*

Of All the Sounds Despatched Abroad. Dickinson.

The Pilgrim. Palfrey.

Sonnets. Tuckerman.

Thoughts. Ignatow.

Valentine to a Little Girl. Newman.

La Vita Nuova. Dante Alighieri.

Watching for Dolphins. Constantine.

Without My Friends the Day Is Dark. Ibn Ezra.

Compare

Conceit upon the Feet (parody). Zaranka.

Mother Love. Alford.

Sonnets, CXXX: "My mistress' eyes are nothing like the sun." Shakespeare.

They are rebuilding. Ise.

Tune: Magnolia Blossom. Li Ching-chao.

Compass

Ann Grenville, Countess Temple, Appointed Poet Laureate... Walpole.

How Looks the Night? Hopkins.

Lady Ralegh's Lament. Lowell.

Lilith. Goll.

Plane Geometer. McCord.

Prayer. Pierce.

Tecumseh. Mair.

Traveling North. Woods.

The Waning of Love. Raile.

We Shall Have Far to Go. Watson.

Wind of the Prairie. Howes.

Compassion

Caelica, IV. Greville.

Complaint. Williams.

A Correct Compassion. Kirkup.

Crumbs or the Loaf. Jeffers.

Dies Irae. Thomas of Celano.

Editorial Poem on an Incident of Effects Far-Reaching. Atkins.

An Epitaph: "Here X. lies dead." Thorold Rogers.

The Fancy Frigate. *Anonymous.*

How Can You? Stevens.

Loved of My Soul. Najara.

Oh, Who Regards. *Anonymous.*

The Sea! O the Sea! *Anonymous.*

The Silent Lover. Ralegh.

Sir Walter Ralegh to the Queen. Ralegh.

Small Country. Alegria.

Treason of Sand. Roth.

Upon the Ensignes of Christes Crucifyinge. Alabaster.

Waiting. Cooper.

You Little Stars That Live in Skies. Greville.

Competition

For Your Inferiority Complex. O'Rourke.

The Latest Decalogue. Clough.

The Origin of Species. Sklarew.

Complain (t) (s)

Amoretti, XII. Spenser.

Any Complaints? Scannell.

Blues #8. *Anonymous.*

Caelica, LXVIII. Greville.

Farewell all my welfare. Wyatt.

Go, Sad Complaint. Orleans.

The Jovial Tinker; or, The Willing Couple. *Anonymous.*

The Lover Sendeth Sighs to Move His Suit. Wyatt.

Metamorphoses. Ovid (Publius Ovidius Naso).

A New Song Composed on the Death of Lord Nelson. *Anonymous.*

On Being Sixty. Po Chu-i.

Proverbial Advice on the Conduct of Business. *Anonymous.*

Shall I Complain? Moulton.

Silent, You Say, I'm Grown of Late. Landor.

Solitude. Grainger.

Symphony: First Movement. Wheelock.

To Sleep Easy All Night. *Anonymous.*

Wingwalking in Oregon. Peterson.

Complete (d) (ly) (ness)

Away out Yonder in Arizony. *Anonymous.*

Baedeker for Metaphysicians. Higgins.

Brief Farewell. Delius.

The Bubble. Tabb.

Celebration. Sachs.

The Christmas Trees. Butts.

The Dog Yelped. Eigner.

Ezekiel. Binyon.

My Father's Close. *Anonymous.*

The Newest Banana Plant Leaf. Wendt.

O Mally's Meek, Mally's Sweet. Burns.

The Offensive. Douglas.

Revelation. Keesing.

The Stone Fleet. Melville.

To Know If It Be Leap Year. *Anonymous.*

What Must I Do to Be Saved? *Anonymous*

Completion

Autumn: An Ode. Gullans.

The Second Violinist's Son. Greger.

The Spring. Voigt.

Complexion

At a Reading. Aldrich.

Government Injunction. Miles.

Compliment (s)

Atomic Courtesy. Jacobson.

Epigram: To Hunt. Blake.

To a Poetic Lover. Hay.

Composition

Pat Young. Mackenzie.

Shakespeare, an Epistle to David Garrick, Esq.. Lloyd.

Comprehend (s)

Caelica, LXXXVIII. Greville.

Crucifix. Olson.

The Rabbit-Hunter. Frost.

'Tis Hard to Find God. Herrick.

To Giotto. Trimpi.

The Track into the Swamp. Morse.

Twelve Lines About the Burning Bush. Ravitch.

Compromise

Couple. Stone.

Directions to a Rebel. Rodgers.

There are two mays. Dickinson.

Compulsion

Classic Encounter. "Caudwell.

A Lover of Peace..... Gorton.

Comrade (s)

Absolution. Sassoon.

Armistice. Lehmer.

As Toilsome I Wander'd Virginia's Woods. Whitman.

The Autumn Day Its Course Has Run. Bronte.

Bright Abandon. Webb.

Calamus. Whitman.

The Christ of the Andes (excerpt). Markham.

The Dying Hobo. *Anonymous.*

I Hear It Was Charged against Me. Whitman.

I Stood Upon a High Place. Crane.

An Invocation. Patrick.

Leavetaking. Watson.

Mary's Son. Trent.

No Labor-Saving Machine. Whitman.

O Mary Pierced with Sorrow. Kipling.

Odes. Horace.

Paper Anarchist Addresses the Shade of Nancy Ling Perry. Woodcock.

The Stampede. Caldwell.

The Two Captains. Cory.

Wanderers. Clark.

Conceal (ed)

Darling, I won't be your hot love. Sulpicia.

Deaf School. Hughes.

The Goose and the Swans (excerpt). Moore.

Merlin. Emerson.

People, male and female. Mahadevi (Mahadeviyakka).

Seal of Fire. Temkin.

Shadows. Milnes.

Sonnets, XIX: "Those former loves wherein our lives have run." Agee.

Strange Meetings. Monro.

Concern (s)

The Inventory. Burns.

Jinny the Just. Prior.

Notation in Haste. Lieberman.

Concert

The Dream. *Anonymous.*

Welcome Every Guest. *Anonymous.*

Conclude (d) (s)

A Drink with Something in It. Nash.

In Praise of His Daphnis. Wotton.

Limerick: "There was an old person of Cromer." Lear.

Love-Songs, At Once Tender
and Informative.
Hoffenstein.
Now or Never. Moffett.
Roy Bean. *Anonymous.*

Conclusion (s)
Answers. Jennings.
The Chances of Rhyme.
Tomlinson.
The Deceptrices. Williams.
A Green Refrain. Huss.
Poem on the End of
Sensation. Stange.
The Wasps' Nest. Macbeth.

Concord
An April Adoration.
Roberts.
The Flood of Years. Bryant.

Concrete
For Brother Malcolm.
Spriggs.
For the Poet Who Said Poets
Are Struck by Lightning
Only... Klappert.
Holiday Inn at Bemidji.
Vizenor.

Condemn (ed) (s)
The Bible Is an Antique
Volume. Dickinson.
The Bible Is an Antique
Volume. Dickinson.
The Law. Butler.
The Living Truth. Plumpp.
Packing a Photograph from
Firenze. Matchett.
La Promessa Sposa. Landor.
Thus Speaketh Christ Our
Lord. *Anonymous.*
What My Child Learns of the
Sea. Lorde.

Condition (ed) (s)
The Angel in the House.
Patmore.
Enterprise and Boxer.
Anonymous.
Fable XX: The Old Hen and
the Cock. Gay.
Handsome Friend, Charming
and Kind. Beatrice de
Dia.
I'm Here. Ignatow.
The Kind of Poetry I Want
(excerpt). ""MacDiarmid.
The Olive Tree. Baring-
Gould.
Two Masks Unearthed in
Bulgaria. Meredith.
Washing Windows. Spacks.

Conduct
Credo. Johnson.
The Instalment (excerpt).
Young.

Conductor
Polly Perkins. *Anonymous.*
Tubes. Mollin.
We Settled by the Lake.
Reeve.

Cone (s)
Confrontions of March.
Dillow.
In Memory of Jane Fraser.
Hill.
Legal Fiction. Empson.

Confess (ed) (ion)
Art above Nature, to Julia.
Herrick.
Ave Maris Stella.
Anonymous.
Carmina. Catullus.
Confession of a Stolen Kiss.
Orleans.
The Deer's Cry. Patrick.

For Real. Cortez.
Her Voice Could Not Be
Softer. Clarke.
Meditatio. Pound.
My Ghostly Father.
Anonymous.
De Ponto. Ovid (Publius
Ovidius Naso).
A Self Accuser. Donne.
To Archinus. Callimachus.
To the Most Virtuous
Mistress Pot, Who Many
Times Entertained Him.
Herrick.
What I'm Doing Here.
Cohen.
When He Spoke to Me of
Love. Mokhomo.

Confidence
Annunciation. Jones.
A Dubious Night. Wilbur.
A Hymn of Trust. Sargent.
Metaphysical Poem.
Bodenheim.
The Old Peasant in the
Billiard Saloon. Menai.
De Profundis. Wyatt.
Trust in Women.
Anonymous.
Whan netilles in wynter bere
rosis rede. *Anonymous.*
Ye Shall Live Also. Coxe.

Confident
Advice to Julia. Luttrell.
And This of All My Hopes.
Dickinson.
Carmel Point. Jeffers.
Daddy. Clifton.
The Good-Natur'd Man:
Prologue. Johnson.

Confirm (ing)
Extraordinary Will. Jackett.
Limerick: "And those two
young ladies of
Birmingham." *Anonymous.*
Limerick: "There were three
young women of
Birmingham."
Monkhouse.
To the Frivolous Muse.
Whicher.

Conflagration (s)
The Clouds. Williams.
The Devil's Thoughts.
Coleridge.
The Lilacs and the Roses.
Aragon.
Self-Consciousness Makes All
Changes Happy.
Richardson.
Too Bright a Day. MacCaig.
Wreck. Polk.

Confound (ed)
Absolute and Abitofhell.
Knox.
Barracks Apt. 14. Weiss.
Te Deum Laudamus.
Anonymous.

Confuse (d)
Astrophel and Stella, XXXIV.
Sidney.
By Hallucination Visited.
Horan.
On the Masquerades. Pitt.
St. Valentine,. Moore.
Visitations. Durrell.

Confusion (s)
Aaron Burr. Benét.
Directive. Frost.
In Broken Images. Graves.
Japanese Beetles. Kennedy.

Old Amusement Park.
Moore.
The Poet Questions Peace.
Chapman.
Rare News. Breton.
Signatures. Hoffman.
To Haydn. Holcroft.
A Tryst in Brobdingnag.
Rich.

Congo
Summer, 1960, Minnesota.
Bly.

Congratulate
On the Reverend Jonathan
Doe. *Anonymous.*
To One Shortly to Die.
Whitman.

Congregation
Acton Beauchamp,
Herefordshire.
Anonymous.
The City of Dreadful Night.
Thomson.
In Church. Hardy.

Conjures
Duchess. Lyon.
London Tom-Cat.
Hamburger.

Connect (ed) (ion) (ions)
Christmas Is Really for the
Children. Turner.
Crow, Straight Flier, but
Dark. Firestone.
The Late Show. Sylvester.
Memories of West Street and
Lepke. Lowell.
Route 29. Brosman.

Connoisseur
A drunkard cannot meet a
cork. Dickinson.
Friend Cato. Wickham.

Conquer (ed) (s) (ing)
The Rejected "National
Hymns". Newell.

Conquer (s) (ed) (ing)
Bar Kochba. Lazarus.
The Battle of Boyne.
Anonymous.
Battle of the King's Mill.
English.
A Captive of Love. Ovid
(Publius Ovidius Naso).
Characters of Women.
Young.
The Condor. Hogan.
Fling Out the Banner!
Doane.
Fort Bowyer. Jones.
The Gordian Knot. Tomkis.
Jesus, Thou Art the King.
Wesley.
John Henry in Harlem.
Toleson.
Kitchen Window. Ebberts.
Last Letter to the Western
Civilization. Ogilvie.
The Love Song. Gurney.
Mirror for the Barnyard.
Myers.
The Mockery of Life. Blunt.
Of the Nativity of the Lady
Rich's Daughter.
Constable.
Oh! for a Steed. Davis.
The Peacemaker. Kilmer.
Preparing for the Wedding.
Claudian.
Relent, My Deere, Yet
Unkind Coelia. Percy.
Robin Hood and the Ranger.
Anonymous.
Room for Jesus. Staples.

The Spirit of the "Bluenose."
MacIntosh.
Time Stands Still, with Gazing
on Her Face! *Anonymous.*
Towards the Last Spike.
Pratt.
Truxton's Victory.
Anonymous.
The United States and
Macedonian. *Anonymous.*
Van Elsen. Scott.
We Conquer or Die.
Pierpont.
Welcome over the Door of an
Old Inn. *Anonymous.*
What Is to Come. Henley.
Will to Win. Scott.
William of Orange.
Anonymous.
Wind Song. Tilghman.

Conqueror (s)
A Captive of Love. Ovid
(Publius Ovidius Naso).
The Dawn on the Lievre.
Lampman.
Hymn to Night. *Anonymous.*
On a Very Young, Very Dead
Soldier. Gillman.
To His Lady, Who Had
Vowed Virginity. Davison.
To the Eternal Feminine.
Corbiere.
Truck Drivers. Haag.

Conquest
Boston. O'Reilly.
The Bracelet. Stanley.
Caravaggio Dying, Porto
Ercole, July 1610, Aged 36.
Lucie-Smith.
Conquistador: The Argument.
Stevens.
The Faerie Queene. Spenser.
Idea. Drayton.
Lead On, O King Eternal.
Shurtleff.
A Song of Dalliance.
Cartwright.
Thou Joy'st, Fond Boy.
Campion.
To a Greek Ship in the Port
of Dublin. Stanford.
To the King, Upon His
Comming with His Army
into the West. Herrick.
Windmill on the Cape.
Sieller.

Conscience
The Candle Indoors.
Hopkins.
Conscience. Stubbs.
The Conscientious Objector.
Shapiro.
A Contented Mind.
Sylvester.
Do. Tolson.
Far Rockaway. Schwartz.
From One of Case's Pill-
Boxes. Case.
Give Our Conscience Light.
Carter.
Hudibras. Butler.
Hymns and Spiritual Songs.
Smart.
In Answer to a Question.
Blunt.
Key West. Crane.
Myself. Guest.
Simplicity's Song. Wilson.
Sleeplessness of Our Time.
Ford.
Sonnets, CLI: "Love is too
young to know what

conscience is."
Shakespeare.
Stanzas from Saint Peter's
Complaint. Southwell.
Summer Song. Watt.
Tell Me News. Sepamla.
To His Importunate Mistress.
De Vries.
To the Lord General
Cromwell. Milton.
The Traveller. Goldsmith.
The Village Blacksmith.
Anonymous.
Wealth. Emerson.
The Windows. Herbert.

Consciousness
Fishing Drunk. Mondy.
I never hear that one is dead.
Dickinson.
I Wakened to a Calling.
Schwartz.
Lest any doubt that we are
glad that they were born
Today. Dickinson.
The Nets on the Andrea
Doria. Tepfer.
No Rack Can Torture Me.
Dickinson.
Over Bright Summer Seas.
Hillyer.
The Sleeping Beauty. De
Ford.
The Sleeping Beauty. Owen.
Those Not Live Yet.
Dickinson.
The United States of America
We. Abrams.

Consecrat (ed)
George Crabbe. Robinson.
Land of the Free. Hosking.
Lincoln at Gettysburg.
Taylor.
O Thou Whose Gracious
Presence Blest. Benson.
Odes. Horace.
Rose Aylmer. Landor.

Consent (ed) (ing)
Colloquy with a King-Crab.
Bishop.
A Curt Addendum.
Anonymous.
For Tinkers Who Travel on
Foot. Avison.
Proposal. Sward.
Requirements. Rufinus
Domesticus.
Sonnet: "Is there a great green
commonwealth of
Thought." Masefield.
To Whom Else? Graves.

Consequence
An Act. Rosen.
Peripatetic. Lima.
Reflection by a Mailbox.
Kunitz.

Consider
Debate: Question, Quarry,
Dream. Warren.
Way-Out Morgan. Brooks.

Consolation (s)
Aaron Hatfield. Masters.
Absence. Mangan.
Angelus. Blumgarten
(Yehoash)
Letter to My Wife. Fuller.
Lullaby for My Dead Child.
Jallais.
No More Than Five.
Levinson.
Our Lady of the Passion.
Mauropus.

Peace and Joy in Jesus Christ.
Franck
Too Late. Perry.
Two Vast Enjoyments
Commemorated.
Danforth.
Urania. Pitter.
The Visit. Rewak.
Words from the Window of a
Railway Car. Steiger.
Yoke Soft and Dear. Kunze.

Consonants
Remains of an Indian Village.
Purdy.
Survey of Literature.
Ransom.

Consort
Alonzo the Brave and Fair
Imogine. Lewis.
An Appeal to My
Countrywomen. Harper.
A Poem upon the Triumphant
Translation of a Mother in
Our Israel. Danforth.
Queen Mother to New Queen.
Graves.

Constancy
B. Eigner.
Caelica, LIII. Greville.
Caelica, LXI. Greville.
Colonel Sharp. *Anonymous.*
Constancies. *Anonymous.*
The Constant. Ammons.
The Constant Swain and
Virtuous Maid.
Anonymous.
The Flight of the Goddess.
Aldrich.
Love-Letter One.
Anonymous.
On the Smooth Brow and
Clustering Hair. Landor.
Robin Redbreast. Doane.
Shall We Forget. Mitchell.
Sonnet: "It shall be said I
died for Coelia!" Percy.
Telephone Poles. Updike.
To a Young Brother.
Jewsbury.
To Barba. May.

Constellation (s)
At the Scenic Drive-In.
McAleavey.
Can the Mole Take. Day-
Lewis.
The Desert. Wood.
Drummer Hodge. Hardy.
Gemini Jones. Espy.
It Is the Stars That Govern
Us. Magee.
A Little Girl. Angoff.
Losing Track. Song.
Odes. Santayana.
Original Strawberry.
Willard.
Refugees. MacNeice.
She Wept, She Railed.
Kunitz.
Thorn Leaves in March.
Merwin.
To the Angel. Rilke.

Constitution
The Change. Chimsoro.
The Federal Constitution.
Milns.
The Fight at Sumter.
Anonymous.
Van Amburgh's Menagerie.
Anonymous.

Consul
For Under the Volcano.
Lowry.

Still This, Still That I Would!
Lithgow.

Consume (d) (r) (s)
Cheer for the Consumer.
Waterman.
Egg. MacPherson.
Five Birds Rise. Hayward.
Hope Is a Subtle Glutton–.
Dickinson.
Love Is a Shark.
Anonymous.
To a Baked Fish. Wells.
Who Doth Not See the
Measure of the Moon?
Davies.

Consummation (s)
Kinship. Roberts.
The Light of Asia. Arnold.
The New Vintage. Le Pan.
Sleep. Berssenbrugge.

Consumption
Limerick: "A certain young
man of great gumption."
Anonymous.
Milkcow Blues. Estes.
The Texas Cowboy.
Anonymous.

Contact
Naturally the Foundation Will
Bear Your Expenses.
Larkin.
Presbyterian Church
Government. Butler.

Contain (s)
Love's Labour's Lost.
Shakespeare.
Psalm. Mendes.
Sonnets, LXXIV: "But be
contented: when that fell
arrest." Shakespeare.
Transcendence. Hovey.

Contemplate (d)
The Grave. Winters.
High Diver. Francis.
In the Time of the Rose.
Savant.
This Is after All Vacation.
Zukofsky.

Contemplation
Large Bad Picture. Bishop.
The Lark. *Anonymous.*
Thanksgiving for the Body.
Traherne.

Contempt
Caelica, XVIII. Greville.
An Epitaph. Watson.
The Grace-Note. Levertov.
On Himself. Churchill.
Sonnet: "This virgin, beautiful
and lively day." Mallarme.

Content (ed) (ly) (ment)
Les Amours. Cotton.
Ancient Wisdom, Rather
Cosmic. Pound.
An Answer to Some Verses
Made in His Praise.
Suckling.
The Anxious Dead. McCrae.
Careless Content. Byrom.
Christian Ethics. Traherne.
A'Chuilionn. Hutchison.
Compensation. Brainard.
Comrade in Arms. Moore.
The Consolation of
Philosophy. Boethius.
Content. Crane.
A Contented Mind.
Sylvester.
Contention between Four
Maids... Davies.
The Cottager's Complaint.
Freeth.

Day-Dreams. Canton.
Dogskin Rug. Stoutenburg.
Eating Lechon, with my
Brothers and Sisters.
Cabalquinto.
Eleven Addresses to the Lord.
Berryman.
Epitaph. *Anonymous.*
Epitaph on Any Man.
Tessimond.
Fane Wald I Luve. Clerk.
The Female Sailor.
Anonymous.
Flooer o the Gean. Hay.
Friends. Goose.
A Glimpse. Whitman.
The Grasses Green of Sweet
Content. Clough.
Growing Old. Fraser.
The Grumbling Hive: or,
Knaves turn'd Honest.
Mandeville.
Hail South Australia.
Anonymous.
The Happy Wanderer.
Addleshaw.
The Heather. Munro.
The House Beautiful.
Anonymous.
How Pleasant Is This Flowery
Plain. *Anonymous.*
I'm Here. Ignatow.
I Never Asked for More Than
Thou Hast Given.
Dickinson.
I Went to Heaven.
Dickinson.
If ever man might him avant.
Wyatt.
If Thou Indeed Derive Thy
Light from Heaven.
Wordsworth.
In Memoriam A.H.H.,
LXXXIV. Tennyson.
The Insatiable Priest. Prior.
Leaf After Leaf..... Landor.
Little Lute. Corbet.
The Lookers-On. Heywood.
Love's Prayer. Riley.
The Lover Rejoiceth the
Enjoying of His Love.
Wyatt.
The Miscegenous Zebra.
Young.
Mock Orange. Gluck.
The Morning-Glory. Coates.
Morning in the North-West.
Stringer.
My Glass Is Half Unspent.
Quarles.
A New Hunting Song.
Anonymous.
No and Yes. Ashe.
Of Fortune. More.
Oh, Baby, Baby, Baby Dear.
Nesbit.
The Old King. Heath-
Stubbs.
The Old Ox. Hamilton.
Olney Hymns. Cowper.
On a Shrew. *Anonymous.*
On a Whore. Hoskyns.
Passiontide Communion.
Hinkson.
The Phoenix. Benson.
The Pines. Spofford.
Platonick Love. Herbert of
Cherbury.
The Pleasing Constraint.
Sheridan.

The Poet Loves a Mistress,
But Not to Marry.
Herrick.
Prayer for Contentment.
Poteat.
The Quaker Widow. Taylor.
A Question of Form and
Content. Stallworthy.
Ranch at Twilight.
Anonymous.
A Reply to an Imitation of
the Second Ode....of
Horace. Bentley.
Requiem for a Young Soldier.
Coates.
Risposta. Wilbye.
Second of August.
Anonymous.
Sonnet: To–. Wordsworth.
Sonnet: To Guido Cavalcanti.
Dante Alighieri.
Speech. Taylor.
The Suet Dumpling (parody).
Anonymous.
A Tale for Husbands.
Sidney.
Tamerton Church-Tower; or,
First Love. Patmore.
There Was a Man with a
Tongue of Wood. Crane.
They Say the Butterfly Is the
Hardest Stroke. Durcan.
Three Girls on a Buttress.
Nisbet.
To a Friend on His Marriage.
Prince.
To His Books. Vaughan.
Two Songs, II. Reisen.
The Unquiet Grave.
Anonymous.
Valediction to Life. Ignoto.
The Variety. Dancer.
Virgidemiarum: "A Gentle
Squire would gladly
entertain." Hall.
Vow to Love Faithfully,
Howsoever He Be
Rewarded. Surrey.
What Shall I Give? Thomas.
A Youth in Apparel That
Glittered. Cranc.

Conterfeit
American Change. Ginsberg.

Contest
Why Should Vain Mortals
Tremble. Niles.

Continent (s)
Apples. Waters.
Cheshire Cat. Allott.
From Le Havre. Bell.
The Geographers. Shapiro.
Human Geography. Fuertes.
O'er Continent and Ocean.
Holmes.
The River. Lorentz.
Rout. Booth.
Welcome to the Nations.
Holmes.
Ye Sons of Columbia.
Fessenden.

Continue
Beauty. Ashley.
Family History. Bishop.
The Farewell. *Anonymous.*
Old Furniture. Hardy.
Once and Future. Chang.
To Stella. Swift.

Contract
He Done His Level Best.
"Twain.
Occupation: Housewife.
McGinley.

Contraction
From a Connecticut
Newspaper. Rockwell.
An Hymeneall Dialogue.
Carew.
String. Schmitz.

Contradict (ion)
Human Life: On the Denial of
Immortality. Coleridge.
Husbandry. Hammond.
Inconsistent. Van Doren.
To a Young Lady. Savage.

Contrast
Proverbial Philosophy.
Tupper.
The Tour of Dr. Syntax: In
Search of the Picturesque.
Combe.

Contrition
Lord! Who Art Merciful as
Well as Just. Southey.
My triumph lasted till the
drums. Dickinson.

Control
The Book of Day-Dreams.
Moore.
The Dream of Flying Comes
of Age. Nemerov.
Fifty Faggots. Thomas.
For My People. Walker.
Idyl: Sunset. Ray.
July in Washington. Lowell.
The Moon in September.
Ghose.
O Solitary of the Austere Sky.
Roberts.
Singing Aloud. Kizer.
A Snowfall. Eberhart.
The Sound of the Sea.
Longfellow.
Take I, 4: II: 58. Whalen.
Twenty-One Love Poems.
Rich.

Conundrum
Epitaph for the Poet.
Barker.
The Poultries. Nash.
The Woodlot. Clampitt.

Convention (s)
La Cucaracha (with music).
Anonymous.
Holidays. Mylonas.
Hypnopompic Poem. Cole.
Time Poem. Hill.

Conversation
Carious Exposure. Cardiff.
Carmina. Catullus.
The Doctor Who Sits at the
Bedside of a Rat. Miles.
Frogs. Simpson.
Grand Conversation on Brave
Nelson. *Anonymous.*
He Told His Life Story to
Mrs. Courtly. Smith.
I, being born a woman and
distressed. Millay.
Je Suis une Table. Hall.
The Marriage of Heaven and
Hell. Blake.
On Paunch, A Parasite.
Belloc.
The Partial Explanation.
Simic.
Prelude. Synge.
Sestina. Hall.
Sixteen Dead Men. Yeats.
Sonnet to Oxford. Russell.
Under the Rose. *Anonymous.*
Warning to a Guest.
Holloway.
A Word in Edgeways.
Tomlinson.

You'd Say It Was a Funeral.
Reeves.

Convict (s)
For God While Sleeping.
Sexton.
The New Warden. Baca.
The Singer in the Prison.
Whitman.
Starry Sky. Simic.

Conviction (s)
Autobiography. Fuertes.
Fraudulent Days. Benedikt.

Convince (d)
The Bat. Nash.
A Guerrilla Handbook.
Jones.
Nightmare. Field.

Convulsion (s)
Drinking Song for Present-
Day Gatherings. Bishop.
A Green Refrain. Huss.

Cook (ed) (s)
Atheling Grange: or, The
Apotheosis of Lotte
Nussbaum. Plomer.
Critics. Martial (Marcus
Valerius Martialis).
Epigram. *Anonymous.*
Five Visions of Captain Cook.
Slessor.
Gasco; or, The Toad. Grass.
I Don't Like Beetles.
Fyleman.
Men May Talk of Country-
Christmasses. Massinger.
Mercury Bay Eclogue.
Joseph.
The Mistaken Resolve.
Martial (Marcus Valerius
Martialis).
New Romance. Wong.
On the Planet of Flies.
Morgenstern.
The Paradox. *Anonymous.*
The Partial Explanation.
Simic.
The Ship's Cook, a Captive
Sings. Hofmannsthal.
Thanksgiving Magic.
Barrett.
Three Cooks. *Anonymous.*
To Julius. Sedley.
A Trip on the Erie.
Anonymous.

Cookie
Naming the Baby.
Richstone.
Psychological Prediction.
Brasier.

Cool (ed) (ing) (ness)
Afterwards, They Shall
Dance. Kaufman.
Bacchanal. Layton.
Collusion between a Alegaiter
and a Water-Snaik.
Morris.
Contemporania: Tenzone.
Pound.
The Fountain. Liasides.
Hesitating Ode. Radnoti.
His Wife. Kaufman.
Hunger in New York City.
Ortiz.
In the Heat of the Morning.
Szumigalski.
Intimate Supper. Redgrove.
Joy o' Living. Hall.
King's College Chapel.
Causley.
Landscape. Mason.
Las Trampas U.S.A.
Tomlinson.

Letter from Des Moines.
Swiss.
Lines Written in the Dog-
Days. Woty.
Links. Pau-Llosa.
Manifesto. Leary.
Minnows. Keats.
Mountain Vigil. Fraser.
New Every Morning.
Anonymous.
An Old Woman's Song.
Akjartoq.
On Heaven. Ford.
One Night Stand. Jones.
Pleasures. Levertov.
Rainy Summer. Pitter.
The River. Stuart.
Sadie's Playhouse. Danner.
Starlings. Jensen.
A Summer Wish. Rossetti.
The Sun and Wind.
Felltham.
Ternissa! You Are Fled.
Landor.
Those Troublesome Disguises.
Williams.
The Wake. Prunty.
With Long Black Wings.
Stickney.
Wreck. Polk.

Copper
Chrysalides. Kinsella.
Dance-Song of the Lightning.
Anonymous.
Early Copper. Sandburg.
Fine Work with Pitch and
Copper. Williams.
The Fox and the Hare.
Anonymous.
La Gialletta Gallante.
Herbert of Cherbury.
Idyll. Webb.
Parents. Buckley.

Cops
The Cabdriver's Smile.
Levertov.
Driving While under the
Influence. Casey.
A Gesture by a Lady with an
Assumed Name. Wright.
No Great Matter. Lawson.
State School. Shiplett.

Copy (ing)
Astrophel and Stella, III.
Sidney.
Construction. Shapiro.
The Cult of the Celtic.
Deane.
Jolly Jack. Thackeray.
Limerick: "Said a lady who
wore a swell cape."
Herford.

Coral
After X-Ray. Pastan.
The Coral Grove. Percival.
Coralville, in Iowa. Bell.
Dead Marine. Coxe.
The Epistemological Rag.
Burr.
An Indian Song. Yeats.
Leviathan. Pitchford.
Mary, Mother of Christ.
Cullen.
Of the Pythagorean
Philosophy. Dryden.
Up There. Auden.

Cord (s)
Bunker's Hill; or, the Soldier's
Lamentation. Freeth.
I Bind My Heart. Watt.
I Hear You've Let Go.
Ferre.

Power. Prior.
A Prayer. Rossetti.
Prayer. Washbourne.
Solomon on the Vanity of the World. Prior.
Song: Lift Boy. Graves.
Wild Eden. Woodberry.

Core
Adam and Eve at the Garden Gate. Pomerantz.
Almond Blossom. Lawrence.
Archery. De la Mare.
Black and White. Duff.
Epilogue. Levertov.
For M. S. Singing Fruhlingsglaube in 1945. Cornford.
The Glory. Thomas.
How Many Heavens... Sitwell.
Lord, Listen. Lasker-Schuler.
Pedantic Literalist. Moore.

Corinna
Amores. Ovid (Publius Ovidius Naso).
The Eye. Herrick.
Fragments. Corinna.

Cork (s)
Irish-American Dignitary. Clarke.
Jottings of New York. McGonagall.

Cormorant
The Devil's Thoughts (excerpt). Porson.
Paradise Lost. Milton.

Corn
"Among the Savages..." Salisbury.
August. Thaxter.
The Beauty of My Land Peers Warily. Brutus.
Breakfast with Gerard Manley Hopkins. Brode.
Butterfly Maidens. Lahpu.
Columbia's Emblem. Proctor.
Corn-Grinding Song. *Anonymous.*
Cornfield. Cox.
Country Summer. Adams.
A Deserted Home. Lysaght.
Dublin Bay. Milne.
Edom. *Anonymous.*
Emblems. Quarles.
An Epithalamy to Sir Thomas Southwell and His Lady. Herrick.
An Essay on Criticism. Pope.
Five Kernels of Corn. Butterworth.
Flying Blossoms. Davies.
The Four Winds. Leslie.
Full Moon in Malta. Asphodel.
The Gaol Song. *Anonymous.*
Give Me Three Grains of Corn, Mother. Edwards.
Green Corn. *Anonymous.*
Greer County. *Anonymous.*
Hymn to the Winds. Du Bellay.
I Wonder How My Home Is. *Anonymous.*
If I Could Go On Kissing Your Honeyed Eyes. Catullus.
Jim Crack Corn. *Anonymous.*
The Land War. O'Sullivan.

Limerick: "A lady who lived at Bordeaux." *Anonymous.*
Molasses River. Munkittrick.
My Maid Mary. *Anonymous.*
Real Property. Monro.
Reapers. Blind.
Sally Goodin. *Anonymous.*
Seed. Bosman.
The Seed-Eaters. Francis.
Starving to Death on a Government Claim. *Anonymous.*
The Villain. Davies.
The Waving of the Corn. Lanier.
Willie O Winsbury. *Anonymous.*
The Wreck of the Great Northern. Hedin.
The Year 1812. Mickiewicz.
Young Man Who Wouldn't Hoe Corn. *Anonymous.*

Corner (s)
Around the Corner. *Anonymous.*
Around the Corner. Towne.
Collapsible. Raworth.
Corner Boys. MacMahon.
Ecclesiastes. Mahon.
Epigram: "Give me a boy whose tender skin." Martial (Marcus Valerius Martialis).
Fairyland. Tagore.
Father Mat. Kavanagh.
Four Choctaw Songs. Barnes.
Frisco Whistle Blues. Bell.
A God Once Commanded Us. Goldberg.
The Great Hunger. Kavanagh.
Hero's Portion. Montague.
Houston and Bowery, 1981. Burns.
The Married Man. Phillips.
Mother and Sister of the Artist. Cabral.
Ol' Mother Hare. *Anonymous.*
Parting. Massey.
Penetration and Trust. Meredith.
The Poor. Williams.
Riddle: "Black within and red without." *Anonymous.*
Song for a Cracked Voice. Irwin.
Statesboro Blues. McTell.
Travel. Stevenson.
Two Views of a Cadaver Room. Plath.
The Wife. Garrison.

Cornerstone
The People's King. Allen.
Prayer for Kafka and Ourselves. Rudolf.
Today Beneath Benignant Skies. Wortman.

Cornucopia
Flight to the City. Williams.
Indian Summer. Howes.

Coronet
Caelica, XCII. Greville.
Ulric Dahlgren. Sherwood.

Corps
Black Sketches, 3. Lee.
Invective against Ibis (excerpt). Ovid (Publius Ovidius Naso).

Corpse (s)
Ballad of Hector in Hades. Muir.
The Beautiful Swimmer. Whitman.
Blighters. Sassoon.
Chaplin's Sad Speech. Alberti.
The Dead Liebknecht. ""MacDiarmid.
The Dead Shall Be Raised Incorruptible. Kinnell.
Death. Bronte.
The Dispossessed. Kinsella.
The Earl of Aboyne. *Anonymous.*
Foreign Woman. Castellânos.
The Fury of Flowers and Worms. Sexton.
Gorg, a Detective Story. Nichol.
Heiress and Architect. Hardy.
Horsey Gap. *Anonymous.*
A Journey through the Moonlight. Edson.
The Largess. Eberhart.
The Mu'allaqat: Ode. Imr el Kais.
Mystic. Lawrence.
Now Is Farewell. Salkeld.
Of Death. Harding.
Selective Service. Forche.
She Attempts to Refute the Praises That Truth... Juana Ines de la Cruz.
Spirit of Plato. *Anonymous.*
Spleen. Baudelaire.
Tell Me News. Sepamla.
This Coloured Counterfeit That Thou Beholdest. Juana Ines de la Cruz.
To Her Portrait. Juana Ines de la Cruz.
The War Year. Ts'ao Sung.
The Worms of History. Graves.

Corral (s)
Buckaroo Sandman. *Anonymous.*
The Cowboy. *Anonymous.*
Empty Saddles. *Anonymous.*
Mules. Walker.

Correct (ed) (ion)
The Country Clergy. Thomas.
Epigram: Absent-Minded Professor. Nemerov.
Epitaph. Franklin.
For the Book of Love. Laforgue.
Fragment of a Greek Tragedy. Housman.
Hot Afternoons Have Been in West 15th Street. Blackburn.
Idea. Drayton.
Marching. *Anonymous.*
Mater Dei. Fallon.
Mind. Wilbur.
Two Roads, Etc. Walters.

Corruption (s)
12 O'Clock News. Bishop.
George I,–Star of Brunswick. Thackeray.
A Girl of Pompeii. Martin.
Honi Soit Qui Mal y Pense. Young.
The Mount of the Muses. Herrick.

Sodom; or, The Quintessence of Debauchery (excerpt). Rochester.
Upon Thought Castara May Die. Habington.

Cosmos
The. Underwood.
December Eclipse. Lockwood.
Landscape of Screams. Sachs.

Cost (s)
Arm, Arm, Arm, Arm! Fletcher.
At Cheyenne. Field.
Beauty. *Anonymous.*
The Contemporary Muse. Rickword.
Invocation. Drewry.
Invocation for the New Year. Armstrong.
Let Us Smile. Nesbit.
Music and Memory. Albee.
On the Same. Belloc.
The Plumber Arrives at Three Mile Island. Stewart.
To the Borrower of This Book. Showell, Jr.
Twilight of Freedom. Mandelstam.

Cot
The Dean's Lady. Crabbe.
The Eolian Harp. Coleridge.
The German Legion. Dobell.
Skerryvore. Stevenson.
Westward Ho. *Anonymous.*

Cottage (s)
Aimee McPherson. *Anonymous.*
Christmas Everywhere. Brooks.
A Cottage in the Wood. Edson.
The Despairing Lover. Walsh.
Ground for the Floor. *Anonymous.*
Marmion. Scott.
Snow White. Ochester.
To Hugh MacDiarmid. Morgan.
To Make a Pastoral: A Receipt. *Anonymous.*
What Is Charm? Thomas.

Cotton
Cotton-Mill Colic. *Anonymous.*
Down the Mississippi. Fletcher.
First Love. Calverley.
Go back to the Country. Jazz Gillum.
I Have Lived This Way for Years and Do Not Wish to Change. Blumenthal.
I'll Wear Me a Cotton Dress. *Anonymous.*
Izaac Walton, Cotton, and William Oldways. Landor.
Mamana Saquina. Craveirinha.
On Tom Holland and Nell Cotton. *Anonymous.*
Roll the Cotton down. *Anonymous.*
Share-Croppers. Hughes.
Starlight. Downie.
Trot, Trot! Butts.

Couch (es)
The Day of Denial. Very.
Epigram: "All through the night." Strato.

Epigram: "No charm can stay, no medicine can assuage." Landor.
For Hidden Mist Pavilion. Yu Hsuan-chi.
Interlude. Bodenheim.
The Mystery. Hyde.
Othello. Shakespeare.
Piccante. Di Michele.
Thanatopsis. Bryant.

Cough (ing) (s)
Explorations Bronchitis: The Rosario Beach House. Rodriguez.
Love Letter. Ray.
Mine. Hudgins.
Night on the Shore. Heine.
A Reply to Lines by Thomas Moore. Landor.
Soft-Man 1. Sanders.

Counsel (ing) (s)
Edward, Edward. *Anonymous.*
Modern Love, XXXVIII. Meredith.
The Newspaper. Crabbe.
The Nine. Sheffield.

Count (ed) (ing)
Counting Sheep. Edson.
The Hours. Dubie.
Love Letter Postmarked Van Beethoven. Wakoski.
Mountain Talk. Ammons.
You, Doctor Martin. Sexton.

Count (ed) (ing) (s)
At Woodward's Gardens. Frost.
Chesapeake. Kennedy.
Downtown-Boy Uptown. Henderson.
I Am Too Near. Szymborska.
Invocation for the New Year. Armstrong.
The Isles of Greece. Capetanakis.
January Snow. Fisher.
Lessons. Untermeyer.
The Life That Counts. "S.
A Lincolnshire Shepherd. *Anonymous.*
Mahler (excerpt). Williams.
A Negro Cemetery Next to a White One. Nemerov.
Riddle: "Purple, yellow, red, and green." *Anonymous.*
Ruth. McElroy.
Satin-Clad. Smith.
To a Foreign Friend. Nathan.
You Jump First. Pietri.
Zurich, zum Storchen. Celan.

Countenance
Atlantis. Auden.
Besse Bunting. *Anonymous.*
Blessing of the Priests. *Anonymous.*
Faust. Goethe.
The House of Life. Rossetti.
King Henry V. Shakespeare.
Orpheus and Eurydice. Hill.
The Pastime of Pleasure. Hawes.
Sonnets, LXXXVI: "Was it the proud full sail of his great verse." Shakespeare.
To an Elderly Virgin. O Brolchain.

Counterpart
Mine Eyes Beheld the Blessed Pity. Dante Alighieri.

Thee, God, I Come from, to Thee Go. Hopkins.

Country
Advice to a Painter. *Anonymous.*
After Shiki. Eigner.
Against Love. Denham.
Another. Lovelace.
Anxiety about Dying. Ostriker.
The Atlas. Slessor.
The Battle of King's Mountain. *Anonymous.*
The Battle of Murfreesboro. Cornwallis.
Battle of the King's Mill. English.
A Bushman's Song. Paterson.
Camoes and the Debt. Andresen.
City Streets and Country Roads. Farjeon.
Come, Ye Lads, Who Wish to Shine. *Anonymous.*
Coming Homeward Out of Spain. Googe.
The Cool, Cool Country. Neilson.
Coridon's Song. Chalkhill.
The Country Store. *Anonymous.*
Crying in Early Infancy: Sonnet. Tranter.
The Day. Brady.
The Death of King Edward VII. *Anonymous.*
The Death of Warren. Sargent.
Dirge. Fearing.
The Djanggawul Cycle, 24. *Anonymous.*
Dolls. St. John.
The Dolphin's Return. *Anonymous.*
Duncan Spoke of a Process. Jones.
Farm Implements and Rutabagas in a Landscape. Ashbery.
Gloriana Dying. Warner.
The Helmets, a Fragment. Penrose.
Heritage. Young.
"I've been going around everywhere without any skin." Miles.
Inadequate Aqua Extremis. Walsh.
Into the Salient. Blunden.
Jack Tar. *Anonymous.*
John Henry (F vers.). *Anonymous.*
A July Dawn (excerpt). O'Donnell.
The Landscape Lies Within My Head. Stewart.
The League of Nations. Siegrist.
A Letter for Allhallows. Dufault.
A Letter to Three Irish Poets. Longley.
Lines for a Dead Poet. Ferry.
Little Political Poem. Hirsch.
The Long Voyaage. Cowley.
Love Rejected. Clifton.
Lullaby. O'Sullivan.
Madrigal: "My love is neither young nor old." Jones.

May 30, 1893. Bangs.
Metamorphoses. Ovid (Publius Ovidius Naso).
Mnemosyne. Stickney.
The Monaro. Campbell.
Moral Essays. Pope.
Morgan's Country. Webb.
Mother Goose Up-to-Date. Untermeyer.
My Ain Countree. Demarest.
A Nation Once Again. Davis.
O'Donnell Aboo. McCann.
The Oak and the Ash. *Anonymous.*
Oh! Weep for Those. Byron.
On the Departure of the British from Charleston. Freneau.
On Walt Whitman's Birthday. Waldman.
The One Thing That Can Save America. Ashbery.
Our Flag Forever. Stanton.
Part of the 9th Ode of the 4th Book of Horace... Horace.
Paul Jones's Victory. *Anonymous.*
Persistent Explorer. Ransom.
Plain Dealing. Brome.
Poem for the Young White Man Who Asked Me How I, an Intelligent... Cervantes.
A Prayer. Gale.
Prayer. Moss.
Raleigh Was Right. Williams.
A Reformer to His Father. Simmons.
The Rejected "National Hymns". Newell.
Remember That Country. Garrigue.
Rendezvous. Hillyer.
Report from a Planet. Lattimore.
The Return. Silkin.
Robert's Farm. *Anonymous.*
The Scales. Empson.
She's Gone Blues. Hicks.
The Shepherd's Star. Jimenez.
Song: "How happy were my days, till now." Bickerstaffe.
Sonnet on Passing the Bridge of Alcantra, Near Lisbon. Mickle.
South of My Days. Wright.
The Streets of Cairo. Thornton.
The Sun Rises Bright in France. Cunningham.
To a Gardener. Stevenson.
To Friend and Foe. *Anonymous.*
To Hugh MacDiarmid. Morgan.
To the Little House. Morley.
To the Nightingale. Davies.
The Town Clerk's Views. Betjeman.
The Town Mouse and the Country Mouse (parody). Prior.
Trumpet Voluntary. Hoover.
Upon the Death of the Earl of Dundee. Dryden.
Verifying the Dead. Welch.
The Vigil. Reich.

Walking Past Paul Blackburn's Apt. on 7th St. Wakoski.
War Song. *Anonymous.*
Washington. Williams.
Where Love Is. Burr.
Yale Boola March. Loomis.

County
Chain Gang Blues. *Anonymous.*
Reincarnation (I). Dickey.
Spawning in Northern Minnesota. McElroy.
Stud Groom. Glassco.

Couple (s)
The Children Grown. Jackson.
Drugs Made Pauline Vague. Smith.
Earl Brand. *Anonymous.*
Hell's Bells. Fishback.
Jack Monroe (Jackie's Gone A-Sailing). *Anonymous.*
Lewis Carroll. Farjeon.
The London Prentice. *Anonymous.*
The Merry-ma-Tanzie. *Anonymous.*
On Giles and Joan. Jonson.
Some San Francisco Poems. Oppen.
There Should Have Been. Lea.
The Villanelle. Harington.
A Waist. Stein.
William Hall. *Anonymous.*

Courage
The Assistance. Blackburn.
The Battle of Murfreesboro. Cornwallis.
Courage to Live. Crowell.
England. Montgomery.
Everest. Shipp.
The Exercise of Affection. Ayton [(or Aytoun)] Sir Robert.
The Expedition to Wessagusset. Longfellow.
Fear. Peacock.
The Glorious Victory of Navarino! *Anonymous.*
Have Courage, My Boy, to Say, No. M. Hilton.
The Husband with No Courage in Him. *Anonymous.*
Hymn to the Sun. Percy.
The Impossible Dream. Darion.
In White Tie. Huddle.
Invocation. Byron.
It Was Your Song. Kowit.
Let Me Live but from Year to Year. Van Dyke.
Limerick: "He died in attempting to swallow." Campbell.
The Little Farm; or, The Weary Ploughman. *Anonymous.*
Masar. Landor.
Never Admit the Pain. Gilmore.
No! Cook.
O Desolate Eves. Brennan.
Prayer. Trench.
Prayer for Shut-Ins. Wheeler.
Remember or Forget. Aïdé.
The Same Continued. Blunt.
Shadows. Milnes.

Spring Landscape. La
Follette.
There Is Something I Want to
Say. Kuo.
They Live. Swingler.
To a Living Author.
Anonymous.
Word over All. Day Lewis.
Course (s)
An Astrologer's Song.
Kipling.
At Best. O'Reilly.
The Call of the River Nun.
Okara.
Concert at Sea. Creekmore.
Endymion. Keats.
The Faerie Queene. Spenser.
The Greater Music. Weiss.
Hawk's Eyes. Winters.
Her Window. Leigh.
Horses on the Camargue.
Campbell.
Julius Caesar. Shakespeare.
King Henry V. Shakespeare.
The Lady of the Lake. Scott.
Limerick: "I have often been
told," said the horse."
Herford.
Lucy. Wordsworth.
Oh There Is Blessing in This
Gentle Breeze.
Wordsworth.
On a Tear. Rogers.
Riddle. Storm: "At times I am
fast confined by my
Master." *Anonymous.*
The Royal Palace of the
Highest Heaven.
Montgomerie.
Sea-Chill. Guiterman.
Ways of Pronouncing "Ough'.
Anonymous.
The Willis. Duffield.
Court (s)
The Banks of the Roses.
Anonymous.
Carol. *Anonymous.*
A Court Lady. Browning.
The Court of Charles II.
Pope.
The Death Sentence. Smith.
Eclogues. Virgil (Publius
Vergilius Maro).
Fame and Fortune. Drayton.
Fine! Barker.
The Frog and the Golden
Ball. Graves.
The Harlequin of Dreams.
Lanier.
The Iliad. Homer.
In High Places. Monroe.
The Last Instructions to a
Painter. Marvell.
Madrigal: "Some there are as
fair to see to." Davison.
The Merry Jovial Beggar.
Casey.
On Some Trees Needlessly
Slain. Coblentz.
Othello. Shakespeare.
Out of Your Sleep Arise and
Wake. *Anonymous.*
Parliament Hill Fields.
Betjeman.
The Passionate Shepherd.
Breton.
Phoebe on Latmus. Drayton.
A Preface to the Memoirs.
Merrill.
A Radical Song of 1786.
Honeywood.

The Rambling Sailor.
Anonymous.
The Resolve. Chudleigh.
Rose in the Garden.
Anonymous.
The Ship Is All Laden.
Anonymous.
To Friend and Foe.
Anonymous.
Unguarded. Murray.
Way down the Ohio.
Anonymous.
When Your Eyes.
Anonymous.
Courtesy
As When the Blowfish
Perishing. Gregg.
The Queen of Courtesy.
Anonymous.
Yung Wind. Confucius.
Courtship
A Brisk Young Widow.
Anonymous.
A Devout Lover. Randolph.
The King-Fisher Song.
"Carroll.
Larrie O'Dee. Fink.
Cousin
Andrea Del Sarto.
Browning.
The Boston Evening
Transcript. Eliot.
The Cry of the Lovelorn.
Martin.
The Dirty Dozens. Speckled
Red.
Great Tom. Corbet.
Polonius. De La Mare.
Wheels. Donnelly.
Cove
Exercise in a Meadow.
Elliot.
What Must (iii). MacLeish.
Covenant (s)
Astrophel and Stella, LXIX.
Sidney.
Noah's Prayer. Gastold.
Poem: "To be sad in the
morning." Pillen.
Cover (ed) (ing) (s)
After Love. Aleixandre.
Auspex. Lowell.
Behold the Manly
Mesomorph. Auden.
A Box for Tom. Tate.
Bums, on Waking. Dickey.
Burning Shit at An Khe.
Weigl.
Chinoiseries. Lowell.
Day Flight. Davis.
Epitaph: "Insured for every
accident." Armour.
Epitaph on a Virgin.
Herrick.
An Epitaph upon a Virgin.
Herrick.
First Pregnancy. Alta.
Going to Bed. Donne.
Green Red Brown and White.
Swenson.
Happy Death. Freeman.
I Am Yours & You Are Mine
So. Silverton.
The Iron Gate (excerpt).
Holmes
Kalaloch. Forche.
Limerick: "These places
abound in the old."
Libaire.
Monday. Stafford.
My Black Gal Blues. Estes.
Ogres and Pygmies. Graves.

Pavane for the Passing of a
Child. Chester.
People, male and female.
Mahadevi (Mahadeviyakka).
The Quilt. Newsome.
Room Poems. Bachar.
The Runner. Chadwick.
Says Something, Too (parody).
Taylor.
Sonnets, XI: "Sighing, and
sadly sitting by my Love."
Barnfield.
St. Ciaran and the Birds.
Carson.
St. Francis Einstein of the
Daffodils. Williams.
Three Around the Old
Gentleman. Berryman.
Two Folk Songs, 2.
Anonymous.
Upon a Child That Died.
Herrick.
The Waistcoat. Fallon.
The Wakeupworld. Cullen.
Without Regret. Lorraine.
The Ziz. Hollander.
Covet (ed)
Amoretti, XXXVII. Spenser.
The Blasted Herb. Weare.
The Converts. Bloch.
The Latest Decalogue.
Clough.
Selling Ruined Peonies. Yu
Hsuan-chi.
Cow (s)
And When They Fall.
Montague.
Black and White. Schmidt.
A Blessing on the Cows.
O'Sullivan.
Boy in the Lamont Poetry
Room, Harvard. Jones.
Charley Warlie. *Anonymous.*
A Charm for Love and
Lasting Affection.
Anonymous.
Charm to Quell a Rival.
Anonymous.
The Cow-Boy's Song. Wells.
A Cow Camp on the Range.
Anonymous.
Cow Time. Shannon.
The Cowboy's Fate. Coburn.
Dead Cow Farm. Graves.
Dear Country Cousin.
Burrows.
Ecological Lecture. Raffel.
Fetching Cows. MacCaig.
The Flowing Summer.
Bruce.
The Good Moolly Cow.
Follen.
The Harmonious Heedlessness
of Little Boy Blue. Carryl.
The Haystack. Young.
Horace, Book V, Ode III.
Graves.
An Insult. *Anonymous.*
Limerick: "There was an Old
Man who said: "How."
Lear.
The Milk Jug. Herford.
The Milkman. O'Sullivan.
Oh! Weary Mother. Pain.
The Old Cow Died.
Anonymous.
Our Little Calf. Aldis.
Pastourelle. *Anonymous.*
Rossetti at Tea. Pain.
Same Old Trick. Pratt.
Sassafras. Peck.
Showing Off. *Anonymous.*

Song for Past Midnight.
Lehmann.
Spring. Still.
Third Limick. Nash.
Thunder. De la Mare.
'Tis Midnight. *Anonymous.*
Tracks. Schwager.
Trail to Mexico. *Anonymous.*
Trees and Cattle. Dickey.
Triads. *Anonymous.*
The Triads of Ireland
(excerpt). *Anonymous.*
Two Tongue-Pointing
(Satirical) Songs.
Anonymous.
The U-S-U Range. Barr.
The Way to Hump a Cow.
Cummings.
What Is Veal? *Anonymous.*
Whistle, Daughter, Whistle.
Anonymous.
Wild Roses. Newsome.
Coward (s)
Cogitabo Pro Peccato Meo.
Habington.
An Evening's Love. Dryden.
Fighting McGuire. French.
Jesus Christ. Guthrie.
The Moving Finger. Omar
Khayyam.
Pennsylvania Song.
Anonymous.
Six Sunday. Bibbs.
Speaking: The Hero. Pollak.
Valiant Love. Lovelace.
Cowboy (s)
Code of the Cow Country.
Barker.
The Cowboy's Dance Song.
Anonymous.
The Cowboy's Lament.
Anonymous.
The Cowboy's Lament; or,
The Streets of Laredo (A
vers.). *Anonymous.*
The Cowboy's Return.
Anonymous.
The Drifter. *Anonymous.*
Far West. Smith.
The High-Loping Cowboy.
Fletcher.
Hot Ir'n! Barker.
A Kansas Cowboy.
Anonymous.
The Old Cowboy.
Anonymous.
The Pinto. Wister.
Rag Time Cowboy Joe.
Muir.
The Texas Cowboys.
Anonymous.
Vaquero. Dorn.
When I Was a Brave Cowboy.
Anonymous.
Cower
Conscience. Ravitch.
The Thunder Mutters Louder
and More Loud. Clare.
Coxcomb
And Angling, Too. Byron.
The Man of Taste.
Bramston.
Words for Music Perhaps.
Yeats.
Coy
Colonel B. Carrier.
Limerick: "A young person of
precious precocity."
Livingston.
O You among Women.
Higgins.
Odes. Horace.

Coyote (s)
Coyote and the Star.
Guiterman.
Dead on the Desert.
Conrard.
For Don Allen. Snyder.
Long Division: A Tribal
History. Rose.
The Structural Study of Myth.
Rothenberg.
There Are Places.
Riedemann.
The Toll of the Desert.
Monroe.
Turning on Daytime TV.
Kuo.

Crabs
Crustaceans. Fuller.
The Newcomer's Wife.
Hardy.
The Old Quartermaster.
Grant.

Crack (ed) (ing) (s)
Andrew's Bedtime Story.
Serraillier.
The Atlas. Slessor.
Behaviour of Money.
Spencer.
Blemishes. Hart.
DOA in Dulse. Burns.
Favour. Fitzgerald.
Funeral. Thompson.
Jim Crack Corn.
Anonymous.
The Little Black Dog Ran
Round the House.
Anonymous.
The Merry Hay-Makers.
Anonymous.
The Mountain and the
Squirrel. Emerson.
The Mountainy Childer.
Shane.
Of the Lost Ship. White.
Over and Under. Smith.
Prophecy. Wylie.
Re-Forming the Crystal.
Rich.
Terra Cotta. Lyle.
Tick Picking in the Quetico.
Johnson.
To My Quick Ear.
Dickinson.
Tugs. Teran.
You Lovely People. Cerenio.

Crackle (s)
Static. Sutter.

Cradle (s)
Brennan on the Moor.
Anonymous.
Bright Sparkles in de
Churchyard. Anonymous.
Carpenter. Brown.
Cradle Hymn. Luther.
Desire. Arnold.
Fair Mary of Wallington.
Anonymous.
February 12, 1809. Burket.
Gates and Doors. Kilmer.
I Sing America Now! Stuart.
In the Fishing Village.
Nickerson.
Jemmy Dawson. Anonymous.
Negroes. Bodenheim.
Night. "Mistral.
An Ocean Lullaby. Keeler.
The Pieta, Rhenish, 14th C.,
the Cloisters. Van Duyn.
Rock-a-Bye Baby. Mother
Goose.
Rock'd in the Cradle of the
Deep. Willard.

The Storm-Wind. Barnes.
This Night. Mandelstam.
Under the Willow-Shades.
Davenant.
Watching the Jets Lose to
Buffalo at Shea. Swenson.
The Wild Rippling Water.
Anonymous.
Youth and Beauty.
Townsend.

Craft
Arizona. Hall.
The Makers. Galler.
November Day at McClure's.
Bly.
Now all of change. Wyatt.
Robin Hood. Burr.
The Vacant Cage. Turner.

Crag (s)
America. Melville.
Blue Moonshine. Stokes.
From the Crag. Leib.

Cram (med)
"For Whom the Bell Tolls".
Ewart.
Hang up the Baby's Stocking!
Anonymous.
We Are God's Chosen Few.
Swift.

Cramped
Apartment House. Raftery.
May 10th. Kumin.

Cranes
The Cranes. Po Chu-i.
Mother's Song. Anonymous.
This Night. Alterman.
The Youngest Daughter.
Song.

Crape
Craqueodoom. Riley.
The Spirk Troll-Derisive.
Riley.

Crash (ed) (ing)
The Clouds. Aristophanes.
The Heavenly Humor.
Shapiro.
Last Words. Hollander.
Long Plighted. Hardy.
Truth. North.
Unhappy Diary Days.
Vizenor.
The Work-Out. Movius.

Crater (s)
Now Is the High-Tide of the
Year. Lowell.
The Raider. Rodgers.
Ye Spier Me. Smith.

Crave
The Faithful Shepherdess.
Fletcher.
Give Me Not Tears.
Lathrop.
Love's Will. Warsh.
De Profundis. Wyatt.
To the One of Fictive Music.
Stevens.

Crawfish
Sweet Thing. Anonymous.
To a Young Lady, with Some
Lampreys. Gay.

Crawl (ed) (ing) (s)
Ants. Hyde.
The Eighties Becoming.
Rosenthal.
Exeunt. Wilbur.
I Know That He Exists.
Dickinson.
Jane Retreat. Honig.
The Name of Our Country.
Schmitz.
A Sight. Creeley.

The String of My Ancestors.
Nyhart.
These Damned Trees Crouch.
Barnes.
These Days. Stafford.
Tick Picking in the Quetico.
Johnson.
The Tickle Rhyme.
Serraillier.
Verses Occasioned by the
Sudden Drying
up...(excerpt). Swift.
The Victim. Voigt.
We Need the Tonic of
Wildness. Thoreau.

Crazy
At the St. Louis Institute of
Music. Wallace.
The Elephant and the Flea.
Anonymous.
Fly around My Blue-Eyed
Gal. Anonymous.
I Thought Joy Went by Me.
Wattles.
Julio. Robertson.
Kirk Lonegren's Home Movie
Taking Place Just North of
Prince George... Thesen.
Letter from an Institution, III.
Ryan.
The Love Bit. Oppenheimer.
One Winter Afternoon.
Cummings.
The Parents of Psychotic
Children. Bell.
The Parents-Without-Partners
Picnic. Schaefer.
The Poem. Kinnell.
The Poet. Davies.
Snake Eyes. Jones.
A Son of the Romanovs.
Simpson.
This Darknight Speed.
Healy.

Creak (ing) (s)
The Howling of Wolves.
Hughes.
The Last Word. Davison.
Song of Occident. Vigee.
Still Life. Whittemore.
To Cynthia, Not to Let Him
Read the Ladies'
Magazines. Hubbard.
Visit. Welch.

Cream
Book Review. Davies.
A Favourite Cat's Dying
Soliloquy. Seward.
Fresh Cheese and Cream.
Herrick.
The Hermit Picks Berries.
Kumin.
Lord Tennyson and Lord
Melchett. Lawrence.
Mares of Night. Long.
Next unto Him Was Neptune
Pictured. Spenser.
Old Age in His Ailing.
Melville.
Song: "Smooth was the Water,
calm the Air." Sedley.
Sonnets of the Months. San
Geminiano.
Vacation. Stafford.

Creases
The James Bond Movie.
Swenson.
Limerick: "The bachelor
growls when his peace is."
Strawson.

Create (d) (s)
The Craftsman. Christian.

Fate. Emerson.
How Shall We Rise to Greet
the Dawn? Sitwell.
Prayer. Goll.
Shells. Raine.
Sunday. Miles.
What I Expected. Spender.

Creation
By the Deep Sea. Byron.
The Call across the Valley of
Not Knowing. Kinnell.
Deer's Cry. Anonymous.
The Deer's Cry. Patrick.
The Dream of the Rood.
Anonymous.
Hallelujah! Praise the Lord.
Hatfield.
Lakeshore. Scott.
The Light of the World.
Alquit.
A Little Girl. Angoff.
O, Beautiful They Move.
Pillen.
Our Lady. Bridges.
The Pond. Thwaite.
The Progress of Man.
Canning.
Prologue. Eichenrand.
Rest from Loving and Be
Living. Day-Lewis.
Space Fiction. MacCaig.
The Time of Creation Has
Come. Anonymous.
Wake the Song of Jubilee.
Bacon.

Creator (s)
Deer's Cry. Anonymous.
The Deer's Cry. Patrick.
Epitaph for Himself. Herbert
of Cherbury.
The Factories. Widdemer.
The Fascinating Chill That
Music Leaves. Dickinson.
Graffiti in a University
Restroom... Mitsui.
The Immortal Spirit.
Spender.
A Sinner's Lament. Herbert
of Cherbury.

Creature (s)
Amendment. Traherne.
Another Full Moon.
Fainlight.
Ark to Noah. Macpherson.
Be Present at Our Table,
Lord. Cennick.
The Beast. Patten.
Before I got my eye put out.
Dickinson.
The Blind Beggar of Bednall
(Bethnal) Green.
Anonymous.
Cantico del Sole. Francis of
Assisi.
The Choice. Wither.
Christmas Eve Legend.
Frost.
The Complaint of Troilus.
Chaucer.
Crab. Blight.
The Day Thou Gavest.
Ellerton.
Epigram. Del Medigo.
The Faerie Queene. Spenser.
The Giraffes. Fuller.
The Granite Mountain.
Sarett.
Guard. Martin.
Hail, Day of Days! In Peals of
Praise. Venantius
Fortunatus.
The Heart. Shapiro.

Hosanna. Traherne.
The Hunting of the Hare. Newcastle.
The Huntress. Johnston.
The Image. Fuller.
The Intruder. Reeves.
Lament for Chaucer and Gower. Hoccleve.
The Last of the Fire Kings. Mahon.
Laura Sleeping. Cotton.
Limerick: "There was an old miser at Reading." Anonymous.
Little Things. Stephens.
O Maister Deere and Fader Reverent! Hoccleve.
Prayer. Schlonsky.
Proper Pride. Lawrence.
Psalm to the Holy Spirit. Sullivan.
The Riddle. Auden.
The Setting Sun. Horton.
Song (2). Rolfe.
Tarantula. O Hehir.
Two Invocations of the Virgin. Chaucer.
The Vision of Piers Plowman. Langland.
Walking the Beach. Youngblood.

Credit
Deus Ex Machina. Armour.
Distrust. Herrick.
The Evangelist. Davie.
Limerick: "There is a creator named God." Whistler.
A New Song of Wood's Halfpence. Swift.
On the Painter Val Prinsep. Rossetti.

Creed (s)
At Fredericksburg. O'Reilly.
The Beginnings of Faith. Morris.
Christ's Life Our Code. Copeland.
His Creed. Herrick.
The Hypocrite. Ben Kalonymos.
Negro Hero. Brooks.
The New Dial. Anonymous.
A New England Church. Barrett.
The Rise and Fall of Creede. Warman.
Le Roi Est Mort. Robinson.
To the Laggards. Bovshover.
Washington. Goodman.

Creek (s)
Bell-Birds. Kendall.
Silex Scintillans. Vaughan.
Treaties. Ammons.

Creep (ing) (s) (y)
1916 Seen from 1921. Blunden.
Before Sleep. Ridler.
Blue Symphony. Fletcher.
The Caterpillar and the Ant. Ramsay.
The Country Justice. Langhorne.
Description of a Summer's Eve. White.
A Gesture by a Lady with an Assumed Name. Wright.
The Grey Cock (A vers.). Anonymous.
I Can't Think What He Sees in Her. Herbert.
Ladybird, Ladybird. Mother Goose.

The Marshes of Glynn. Lanier.
Night. Coleridge.
The Nightingale and Glow-Worm. Cowper.
Old Shellover. De La Mare.
The Silent Slain. MacLeish.
Supervising Examinations. Lucy.
To Cynthia, Not to Let Him Read the Ladies' Magazines. Hubbard.
Two Houses. Thomas.
The Voice of the Grass. Boyle
Youth in Arms: IV. Carrion. Monro.

Cremated
The Author's Epitaph. Anonymous.
Shelly. McIntyre.
Shipment to Maidanek. Fogel.
Some Folks I Know. Hoffenstein.

Crest (s)
Aunt Zillah Speaks. Palmer.
Ducks down in the Meadow. Stafford.
Gordon Childe. Martin.
Lines for My Father. Gray.
May-Day at Sea. Finerty.
A Midsummer Night's Dream. Shakespeare.
Proud Resignation. Marcus.
Schiehallion. Cruickshank.
Sonnets, CVII: "Not mine own fears, nor the prophetic soul." Shakespeare.
Woods and Kestrel. Bell.

Crete
Ithocles, VI (excerpt). Symonds.
Limerick: "There was a young person of Crete." Lear.

Crevice (s)
Coda. Williams.
A Drumlin Woodchuck. Frost.
Priapus and the Pool. Aiken.
Tick Picking in the Quetico. Johnson.
Twilit Revelation. Adams.

Crew
The Arethusa. Hoare.
The Ballad of the Ivanhoe. Adams.
The Chauffeur of Lilacs. Hitchcock.
Clarel. Melville.
Close Quarters. Tabb.
A Crew Poem. Blount.
Grace Darling. Anonymous.
The Lifeboat. Sims.
On the Ruins of a Country Inn. Freneau.
A Satire on the O'Haras. O Huiginn.
Son. Emanuel.
Sonnet: Written on the Day that Mr. Leigh Hunt Left Prison. Keats.
The Yarn of the "Nancy Bell'. Gilbert.

Cricket
Autumn Song. Long.
The Cricket and the Star. Newsome.
Depressed by a Book of Bad Poetry, I Walk toward an Unused Pasture... Wright.

Goat-Woman Dares. Volborth.
Heart's Needle. Snodgrass.
How McDougal Topped the Score. Spencer.
Last Night There Was a Cricket in Our Closet. Quintana.
Limerick: "An angry young husband called Bicket." Galsworthy.
Limerick: "There was an old man of Bengal." Guthrie.
On the Death of Little Mahala Ashcraft. Riley.
Pelvic Meditation. Smith.
A Prayer in Darkness. Chesterton.
Sleep in the Mojave Desert. Plath.
Symphony in Gray Major. Dario.
Written in July, 1824. Mitford.

Crie (d) (s)
The Adepts. Durrell.
Aubade: Dick, the Donkey-Boy. Sitwell.
The Avondale Mine Disaster. Anonymous.
De Blin' Man Stood on de Road an' Cried. Anonymous.
Blind Man. Anonymous.
Caelica, LXVIII. Greville.
The Cherry-Tree Carol, III. Anonymous.
Child Crying. Thwaite.
The Coweta County Courthouse. Robinson.
The Crows. Valli.
Cuban Refugees on Key Biscayne. Winder.
Dead. Johnson.
The Demolition. Stevenson.
The Djanggawul Cycle, 11. Anonymous.
Domine ne in Furore. Wyatt.
The Dutch Seamen and New Holland. Reeves.
The Dwelling. Dor.
The Eagle. Daly.
Ego Dominus Tuus. Yeats.
Epitaph on a Tyrant. Auden.
Faint Falls the Gentle Voice. Timrod.
Father. Kooser.
The Fish. Brooke.
Five Vignettes. Toomer.
Fog-Horn. Merwin.
For Colored Girls Who Have Considered Suicide...(excerpt). Shange.
Gods. Sexton.
Gulls. Muir.
The Half-Breed Girl. Scott.
The Hill. Brooke.
How Many Nights. Kinnell.
I Dreamed That I Was Old. Kunitz.
The Iliad. Homer.
Into the World and Out. Piatt.
Ireland. Hewitt.
Jerusalem. Blake.
Kilroy. Viereck.
Listening to Beethoven on the Oregon Coast. Carlile.
Love Is a Sickness. Daniel.

The Ludlow Massacre. Guthrie.
The Mask. Harjo.
The Morning. Gay.
My Father, My Son. Brinnin.
O Grief! Anonymous.
O. T.'s Blues. Cuney.
Of Commerce and Society. Hill.
Old Emily. Hill.
Only for Me. Van Doren.
Only the Beards Are Different. Dawe.
The Parish Church. Reissig.
Po' Boy (with music). Anonymous.
Prayer. Flecker.
The Satyrs and the Moon. Gorman.
Sea and Land Victories. Anonymous.
Singing on the Moon. Hughes.
The Snow. Keyes.
Tales of the Islands, VIII. Walcott.
The Tempest. Shakespeare.
Ten Thousand Miles Away from Home (with music). Anonymous.
There's Wisdom in Women. Brooke.
To Children. McGaugh.
To Rosemary. Benét.
Trooper and Maid, II. Anonymous.
The Truth. Jarrell.
The Voice of God. Stephens.
When I See Old Men. Souster.
When My Dog Died. Littledale.
The White Bird. McFadden.

Crime (s)
An Appeal to My Countrywomen. Harper.
The Artist. Ralegh.
Basia, VIII. Johannes Secundus.
Be Always in Time. Anonymous.
The Borough. Crabbe.
The Broken One. Holmes.
Come, My Celia. Jonson.
Consolation. Yeats.
Crucifixion. Isbell.
Elegy. Baruch of Worms.
Epigram. Butler.
The Faerie Queene. Spenser.
Feast on Wine or Fast on Water. Chesterton.
For an Autograph (excerpt). Lowell.
Forest. Garrigue.
Four Quartz Crystal Clocks. Moore.
Go Down, You Little Red Rising Sun. Anonymous.
If I Have Wronged You. Stickney.
Jerusalem. Blake.
The Little Green Blackbird. Patchen.
On Passing the New Menin Gate. Sassoon.
The Parliament of Bees. Day.
Pater Filio. Bridges.
Pearl Bryan. Anonymous.
Pearl Bryant. Anonymous.

The Poor Working Girl (with music). *Anonymous.*
Screaming Tarn. Bridges.
Song To Celia. Jonson.
The Time Is Ripe and I Repent. Ceile De.
To Archinus. Callimachus.
Two-Cent Coal. *Anonymous.*

Criminal (s)
Apology of Genius. Loy.
Pedagogy. Locklin.
The Third Satire of Juvenal. Dryden.

Crimson
Ave Imperatrix! Wilde.
Ballad. Baring.
Flash Crimson. Sandburg.
The Garden. Wilde.
I Wear a Crimson Cloak To-Night. Montross.
Impressions. Wilde.
In Memoriam A.H.H., XCVIII. Tennyson.
In Memoriam A.H.H., CIII. Tennyson.
The Nativity of Christ. Gongora y Argote.
No Return. Miller.
Red May. Robinson.
The Rose and God. Stork.
Strawberries in November. Neilson.
Vigil. Dehmel.

Cripple (s)
Event. Plath.
O For Doors to Be Open. Auden.
Three Crooked Cripples Went through Cripplegate. *Anonymous.*
Transit. Rich.

Crisis
Nerves. "Sagittarius" (Olga Katzin).
Tell Jesus. *Anonymous.*

Critic (ism) (s)
Don Juan. Byron.
English Bards and Scotch Reviewers. Byron.
Every Critic in the Town. Murray.
Friend Cato. Wickham.
Goodbye, Sally. Simmons.
An Ode: Secundum Artem. Cowper.
The Summer Ending. Wescott.
Ultra-Germano-Criticasterism. Hunt.
A Written Answer. Paulin.

Croak (ing)
Hard to Bear. Jenks.
The Man Sentenced to Death. Genet.
Mothers. Tzara.
The Poets Agree to Be Quiet by the Swamp. Wagoner.
Who Was It Came. Hoffman.

Crocodile
The Crocodile. *Anonymous.*
Idea. Drayton.
If You Should Meet a Crocodile... *Anonymous.*
Limerick: "Oh, there once was a merry crocodile." Heath.

Crocus (es)
C Is for the Circus. McGinley.
Crocus Night. Schuyler.
For City Spring. Benét.

The Thrush in February. Meredith.
Winter in the Fens. Clare.

Cromwell
An Essay on Man. Pope.
To Milton. Wilde.

Crook (ed) (s)
About to Die. *Anonymous.*
Awake, My Soul. Ibn Ezra.
A Book. Reese.
For Deep Deer-Copse Beneath Mount Han. *Anonymous.*
God Our Help. *Anonymous.*
The Horn Blow. Tagami.
In Space-Time Aware–. Evans.
Journal, Part IV. Jones.
Knightsbridge of Libya. MacLean.
Othello Jones Dresses for Dinner. Roberson.
Portrait. Landor.
Savage Portraits. Marquis.
Teasing Song. Magogo.
Winter Moon. Hughes.

Croon (ed) (ing)
Mater Amabilis. Lazarus.
A Photo of Miners. Galvin.
Static. Humphries.
Tae Titly. *Anonymous.*
Trade Winds. Masefield.
Week-End Sonnet No. 1. Monro.

Crop (s)
The Apology. Emerson.
Apology of Genius. Loy.
The Dysynni Valley (Wales). Holmes.
The Farm Hands. Laing.
Hell. *Anonymous.*
James Rigg (parody). Hogg.
A Musician Returning from a Cafe Audition. Minard.
Praying. Kavanagh.
The Rape of Lucrece. Shakespeare.
The Task. Cowper.
The Wind of Our Enemy (excerpt). Marriott.
A Woman Waits for Me. Whitman.

Cross (ed) (es) (ing)
An A.B.C. of Devotion. *Anonymous.*
Abroad As I Was Walking. *Anonymous.*
An Advancement of Learning. Heaney.
Affliction. Herbert.
After Two Thousand Years. ""MacDiarmid.
Amazing Grace. Newton.
Animal Songs: Zebra. *Anonymous.*
Apology. Cronin.
Arise, Arise. *Anonymous.*
The Ballad of the Cross. Garrison.
Barthram's Dirge. *Anonymous.*
Beer. Arnold.
Behold, My Cross Was Gone! Mortenson.
The Bishop's Harp. Mannyng.
The Bonnie Blue Flag. Ketchum.
A Child's Christmas Day. *Anonymous.*
The Choice of the Cross. Sayers.

Christ and His Mother at the Cross. Jacopone da Todi.
A Christ-Cross Rhyme. Hawker.
Cincophrenicpoet. Kaufman.
Columbus. Jackson.
Comrades of the Cross. Wattles.
Conscience. Herbert.
Consecration. Kirby.
Consolation. *Anonymous.*
Cross and Throne. Bonar.
The Cross of Gold. Gray.
A Cross on a Hill. Weist.
The Crossed Swords. Frothingham.
Crowds of Men and Women. Whitman.
Crucifixion. "Marie.
Death-Bed Reflections of Michel-Angelo. Coleridge.
The Demon of the Mirror. Taylor.
Depression. Cope.
Distribution of Honours for Literature. Landor.
Divided. Ingelow.
The Dream of the Cross. *Anonymous.*
Dying. Holt.
The Edge of the World. Youngs.
Everyman. *Anonymous.*
Flight. Hall.
For a Nativity. Mueller.
For His Sake. Denman.
For Jean Vincent d'Abbadie, Baron St.-Castin. Nowlan.
Funeral Notices. Storni.
Gesture. Welles.
The Good Shepherd. Lope de Vega Carpio.
Green Plumes of Royal Palms. Brant.
Heavier the Cross. Schmolck.
The Horrible Decree (excerpt). Wesley.
House-Hunting. Wagoner.
Hymn to Tammuz. *Anonymous.*
A Hymne to God the Father. Jonson.
I See His Blood upon the Rose. Plunkett.
I See the Boys of Summer. Thomas.
Idylls of the King. Tennyson.
If Love Were Jester at the Court of Death. Knowles.
In the Time of Revolution. Lester.
Jacob's Ladder. *Anonymous*
Jefferson, Texas. Shihab.
Jesu, to Thee My Heart I Bow. Zinzendorf.
A Jewish Child Prays to Jesus. Blumenthal-Weiss.
The Landing of the British Settlers of 1820 (excerpt). Wilmot.
Late Corner. Hughes.
Lincoln. Robinson.
The Little Black Dog. Reynolds.
A Little Parable. Aldrich.
Lives. Reed.
Love Is Where the Glory Falls. Hafiz.
Love's Consolation. Dixon.
Marriage: To K. Hall.

The Martyr. Flohr.
Metamorphoses. Nemerov.
More Than We Ask. Wells.
The Mountain. Finch.
An Old Maid Early. Blake.
On a Nomination to the Legion of Honour. *Anonymous.*
On a Sculptured Head of the Christ. Fisher.
On the Brink of Death. Michelangelo.
On the Crucifix. Michelangelo.
One More River to Cross. *Anonymous.*
Onward, Christian Soldiers. Baring-Gould.
Pat Cloherty's Version of the Maisie. Murphy.
The Peacemaker. Kilmer.
Pennies. Kilmer.
Petition. McCurdy.
Pieta. McAuley.
Power Station. Ramsey.
Prayer in Affliction. Storey.
Premonition. Salverson.
Prince Henry the Navigator. Clouts.
Pro Libra Mea. Clarke.
A Quintina of Crosses. Walsh.
Requiescat. Porter.
The Ribbon-Fish. Adamson.
The Rising in the North. *Anonymous.*
The Romance of Imprinting. Sanford.
The Room's Width. Ward.
The Rosary. Rogers.
The School of Sorrow. Hamilton.
Sharing His Cross. Fero.
Sir William of Deloraine at the Wizard's Tomb. Scott.
Soliloquy on a Southern Strand. Montague.
A Song of Four Priests who Suffered Death at Lancaster. *Anonymous.*
Songs for the Four Parts of the Night. Owl Woman.
Sonnet. Petrarch.
The Stick. O'Rourke.
The Story of Fidgety Philip. Hoffmann.
Swearing. Fitzsimon.
There Is a Man on the Cross. Cheney.
There Is Never a Day So Dreary. Alexander.
There Was No Room on the Cross. *Anonymous.*
Thermopylae. Hillyer.
A Thought. Sangster.
The Tide That from the West Washes Africa to the Bone. Rubadiri.
To See the Cross at Christmas. Cooper.
The Tree of the Cross. "Angelus Selesius" (Johannes Scheffler).
The Trestle Bridge. Wright.
The Turtle. *Anonymous.*
Twickenham Ferry. Marzials.
Two Poems on the Catholic Bavarians. Bowers.
Unlucky Boat. Brown.
Untitled. Hine.
Via Dolorosa. Smith.

A Virile Christ. Boundy.
Wake-Up Niggers. Lee.
Water on the Highway.
 Simpson.
The Way of the Cross.
 Clarke.
We Am Clim'in' Jacob's
 Ladder. *Anonymous.*
We Have Seen His Star in the
 East. Haley.
When I Was Nine. Roseliep.
Who's in Charge Here? Bell.
The Wide Mizzoura (with
 music). *Anonymous.*
The Windmill. Longfellow.
Work. Kennedy

Crossroads
Lament. Ratosh.
To the Thoughtful Reader.
 Meredith.

Crotch
Dream Songs. Berryman.
Kafka's Other Metamorphosis.
 Gasparini.

Crouch (es) (ing)
The Awakened War God.
 Widdemer.
Central Park West. Spicer.
Dante. Duncan.
The Giant Puffball. Blunden.
Quatrain: "Better to live as a
 rogue and a bum."
 Mahsati.
Where Is Justice? Steinbarg.

Crow (ed) (ing)
The Chickens Are A-Crowing.
 Anonymous.
Cock before Dawn.
 MacCaig.
The Grave. Blair.
The Little Black Dog Ran
 Round the House.
 Anonymous.
The Parish Church. Reissig.

Crow (ed) (ing) (s)
All of a Row. *Anonymous.*
And the Cock Begins to
 Crow. Avery.
Bee Wassail. *Anonymous.*
Brainstorm. Nemerov.
The Bush Speaks. Moll.
Cock. Amir.
The Crow. Canton.
The Crow. Page.
Epigram: "I ran upon life
 unknowing, without or
 science or art." Tennyson.
Epigram: "Those snooty boys
 in all their purple drag."
 Strato.
Examination at the Womb-
 Door. Hughes.
The Eye. Tate.
Fallow Land. Clark.
A Foreigner Comes to Earth
 on Boston Common.
 Gregory.
The French, 1870-1871.
 Anonymous.
Gingilee. Halpern.
A Good Resolution.
 Campbell.
Hobart Town, Van Diemen's
 Land. Porter.
How to Choose a Horse.
 Anonymous.
In Air. Clarke.
The Kangarooster. Cox.
Kansas Boy. Lechlitner.
Let me see you. Mira Bai
 [(or Mirabai)].
Let us not Pretend. Mathew.

My Sister Jane. Hughes.
My Wish for My Land.
 Stow.
A New Poem (for Jack
 Spicer). Duncan.
A Parody on A Psalm of Life.
 Holmes.
The Passing of the Shee after
 Looking at One of A.E.'s
 Pictures. Synge.
Pocomania. Walcott.
Poor Wolf Speaks. Poor
 Wolf.
Preachment for Preachers.
 Barclay.
Prometheus. Swift.
Reading Indian Poetry.
 Wilson.
Riverside Drive, November
 Fifth. Pollitt.
The Ship of Fools. Barclay.
Showing Off. *Anonymous.*
Sunday in the Country.
 Swenson.
Sweating It Out on Winding
 Stair Mountain. Barnes.
The Tolerance of Crows.
 Donnelly.
What I Did Last Summer.
 Ikan.

Crowd (ed) (s)
14 July 1956. Lerner.
About the Cows. Pfingston.
The American Book of the
 Dead: Six Selections.
 Giorno.
The Blue Horses. McAuley.
Chinatown. Mezquida.
Civil Elegies (excerpt). Lee.
Critics. Swift.
Don't Talk about It.
 Anonymous.
The Duke Is the Lad.
 Moore.
El Blot Til Lyst. Payne.
For Those Who Died. Clark.
I Am the People, the Mob.
 Sandburg.
King John's Castle. Kinsella.
The Man from the Crowd.
 Foss.
Merry-Go-Round. McAuley.
The Mountain Whippoorwill.
 Benét.
The Mountebanks. Luders.
One Night away from Day.
 Digby.
Party. Justice.
Praising the Poets of That
 Country. Nemerov.
The Red Heart. Reaney.
Return of a Popular
 Statesman. Buckley.
Santa Claus. Nemerov.
Shadow of the Old City.
 Amichai.
Travelling Backward. Baro.
When You Are Old. Yeats.

Crown (ed) (s)
Afraid? Of whom am I afraid?
 Dickinson.
L'Art poetique. Boileau-
 Despreaux.
As a Bell in a Chime.
 Johnson.
Athletic Ode. Santayana.
Autumnal Consummation.
 Stevenson.
Beer. Arnold.
The Birthday Crown.
 Alexander.
The Blackbird. *Anonymous.*

Blessings on Doneraile.
 O'Kelly.
The Brome Abraham and
 Isaac. *Anonymous.*
Circumstance. Aldrich.
Congal: The Land Is Ours.
 Ferguson.
Content Thyself with Thy
 Estate. *Anonymous.*
A Copy of the Last Verses
 Made by Dr. Wild...
 (excerpt). Wild.
Coronation. Perronet.
The Coronet. Marvell.
Cradle and Throne.
 Anonymous.
Crown of Happiness.
 Hebert.
A Crown of Wildflowers.
 Rossetti.
Delayed till she had ceased to
 know. Dickinson.
Dream Songs. Berryman.
Epitaph. *Anonymous.*
Europe. Dudek.
The Expensive Wife. Ibn
 Sabbatai.
A Fable. Prior.
Fairy Tales. Manger.
For C. K. Kelleher.
For Little Boys Destined for
 Big Business. Hoffenstein.
For Tu Fu. Feng Chih.
Fourth Station. Claudel.
Fragments. Yeats.
Free Grace. Wesley.
The Gallery. Marvell.
Girl to Woman. Handy.
God Incarnate. Williams.
The Guerdon of the Sun.
 Sterling.
He Wore a Crown of Thorns.
 Mortenson.
Heavier the Cross.
 Schmolck.
Hind Etin (A version).
 Anonymous.
The Holly and the Ivy.
 Anonymous.
Hoot Owl Shift. Stricklin.
I'm ceded–I've stopped being
 theirs. Dickinson.
I Wish Sometimes, Although
 a Worthlesse Thing.
 Fletcher.
If I Forget Thee. Litvinoff.
John Adkins' Farewell.
 Anonymous.
Jumbo Jee. Richards.
Life. Sill.
Marmion. Scott.
Metamorphoses. Ovid
 (Publius Ovidius Naso).
Mistress, Since You So Much
 Desire. Campion.
Mount Vernon, the Home of
 Washington. Day.
Mr. Eliot, Pastor of the
 Church of Christ at
 Roxbury... Johnson.
My Sweetest Lesbia.
 Campion.
Never Admit the Pain.
 Gilmore.
November Blue. Meynell.
O Children, Would You
 Cherish? Dock.
O Thou, Who Didst Ordain
 the Word. Chapin.
The Obscured Prince; or, the
 Black Box Boxed.
 Anonymous.

An Ode for the New Year.
 Gay.
Ode Sung at the Opening of
 the International Exhibition.
 Tennyson.
Oh King of Saints, How
 Great's Thy Work, Say We.
 Johnson.
Old Christmas. Howitt.
The Old Rugged Cross.
 Bennard.
On Board the '76. Lowell.
On the Birth of His Son. Su
 Tung-p'o.
Our Country. Howe.
Ourselves were wed one
 summer–dear. Dickinson.
Peter. Benet.
The Poet. Davies.
Power Station. Ramsey.
A Prophecy. Lee.
Queen of the World.
 Anonymous.
The Queens. Fitzgerald.
The Race Question.
 Madgett.
The Retirement. *Anonymous.*
Samson Agonistes. Milton.
The School of Sorrow.
 Hamilton.
The Scratch. Dickey.
Sea Born. Vinal.
September. Hughes.
Sharing His Cross. Fero.
Sir Gawain and the Green
 Knight. *Anonymous.*
Slaves of Thy Shining Eyes.
 Hafiz.
A Song of Renunciation.
 Seaman.
Songs of the Squatters, I.
 Lowe.
Stanzas. Poe.
Steamboats, Viaducts, and
 Railways. Wordsworth.
Stonewall Jackson. Flash.
Suicide. MacNeice.
Tamburlaine the Great.
 Marlowe.
The Tapestry Weaver.
 Chester.
They Pray the Best Who Pray
 and Watch. Hopper.
Tit, Tat, Toe. *Anonymous.*
To a Young Leader of the
 First World War. George.
To Guerdon. Piatt.
To Mistress Katherine
 Bradshaw, the Lovely, That
 Crowned Him... Herrick.
To the New Year. Carew.
Truth. North.
Under the Stars. Rice.
Upon the Double Murther of
 King Charles I... Philips.
Upon the Hill before
 Centreville. Boker.
The Variety. Dancer.
Virgil's Farewell to Dante.
 Binyon.
The Western Rebel.
 Anonymous.
When Mary Goes Walking.
 Chalmers.
While I Am Young. Ballou.
Wisdom. Fallon.
The Wits. Suckling.
The Wreath. Graves.
A Wreath. Herbert.
Yee Shall Not Misse of a Few
 Lines in Remembrance of
 Thomas Hooker. Johnson.

Crucible
Young and Radiant, He Is
  Standing. Cross.
Young Girl. Huch.

Crucible
The Crucible of Life (excerpt).
  Guest.
Fulfilment. Barker.

Crucified
Caelica, XCVII. Greville.
A Christmas Sonnet.
  Robinson.
Compulsive Qualifications
  (excerpt). Howard.
The Crucifix. Lamartine.
The Eagle. Young.
Faith's Difficulty. Maynard.
The Funeral. J. M.
The Mantle of Mary.
  O'Connor.
One Crucifixion is Recorded
  Only. Dickinson.
Poem. Mason.
A Prayer for Charity.
  Kennedy.
The Prince of Life.
  Oxenham.
Le Repos en Egypte.
  Repplier.
Sequel to Finality. Kirby.
The Temptation of Saint
  Anthony. Symons.
Walking in London.
  Gardiner.

Crucifix
The Ballad of Fisher's
  Boardinghouse. Kipling.
Letter from the Vieux Carre.
  Russell.
Old Maid. Nicolson.
A Proem. Ward
The Rooftree. Tate.
Thoughts in Separation.
  Meynell.
Written on a Girl's Table-
  Napkin at Wiesbaden.
  Duncan.
The Young Neophyte.
  Meynell.

Cruel (ty)
Amoretti, XXXI. Spenser.
Amoretti, XLII. Spenser.
And on My Eyes Dark Sleep
  by Night. "Field.
The Angler. Bhartrihari.
Ante Mortem. Jeffers.
Birthday Party. Patton.
Bottom's Dream. Dow.
Comfort. Widdemer.
Dialogue at the Cross. Spee.
Ellora. Nathan.
Four Winds. Teasdale.
Gill Boy. Schmitz.
A Jew Walks in Westminster
  Abbey. Hodes.
Kissing Helen. Plato.
Lady of Miracles. Cassian.
Last Words to Miriam.
  Lawrence.
Lauda. Beneveni.
Limerick: "A patriot, living at
  Ewell." Reed.
Look to the Back of the
  Hand. Minty.
The Magnet. Stanley.
The Maid I Left Behind.
  Anonymous.
Mother and Sister of the
  Artist. Cabral.
My Gang. Kerouac.
Notre Dame. Mandelstam.
Now, My Usefulness Over.
  Honig.

Ode to Fortune. Drake.
Of Rosalind. Lodge.
On Being Head of the English
  Department. Lane.
Over to God. Harrigan.
Quatrain. Blanden.
The Relapse. Stanley.
Remon. Anonymous.
Search for Love. Johnson.
The Secret of Poetry.
  Anderson.
Since Ye Delight to Know.
  Wyatt.
A Song from the Italian.
  Dryden.
Song: "Ye happy swains,
  whose hearts are free."
  Etherege.
Sonnet VII: "We see each
  living thing finally die."
  Labe.
Sonnet: "My Love, I cannot
  thy rare beauties place."
  Smith.
Sonnets, LX: "Like as the
  waves make towards the
  pebbled shore."
  Shakespeare.
To a Beautiful but Heartless
  Coquette. Terrazas.
A Valediction: of Weeping.
  Donne.
The Way of the Cross.
  Clarke.
What rage Is this? Wyatt.
Wild Horse Jerry's Story.
  Howard.
The Woods at Night.
  Swenson.
Ye know my heart... Wyatt.

Cruise
The Cruise of the Monitor.
  Boker.
Goldfish. Nemerov.

Crumb (s)
As You Like It. Weiss.
Bread and Milk. Rossetti.
The Common Cormorant.
  Isherwood.
Famine Song. Anonymous.
February. Berkson.
History. Graham.
Hope Is the Thing with
  Feathers. Dickinson.
I Saw Eternity. Bogan.
Metropolitan Nightmare.
  Benét.
Miniature. Phillpotts.
Psalm III. Ginsberg.
Putting in the Seed. Frost.
Return Thee, Hairt. Scott.
Unaccompanied. Andrews.
The Wind of January.
  Rossetti.

Crumble (d) (s)
Beleaguered Cities. Lucas.
Could Mortal Lip Divine.
  Dickinson.
Delfica. Nerval.
I Am Like a Book. Rokeah.
On a View of Pasadena from
  the Hills. Winters.
On the Fly-Leaf of Pound's
  Cantos. Bunting.
Sunny. Vander Molen.
Woman in an Abandoned
  House. Bily-Hurd.

Crunch
Edwin A. Nelms. Nelms.
The Jug of Punch.
  Anonymous.

Crush (ed)
The Annunciation. Kriel.
Another Reply to In Flanders
  Fields. Armstrong.
Archys Autobiography.
  Marquis.
Beetle on the Shasta Daylight.
  Kaufman.
Beowulf: The Fire-Dragon and
  the Treasure. Anonymous.
From Mythology. Herbert.
An Indian at the Burial-Place
  of His Fathers. Bryant.
Instructions of King Cormac.
  Cormac Mac Cuilenan.
Lost Moments. Davis.
Midnight Dancer. Hughes.
Nostalgia. Lawrence.
Poem to the Man on My Fire
  Escape. Wakoski.
Smithereens. Rossetti.

Crust (s)
At a Potato Digging.
  Heaney.
Greek Excavations. Spencer.
The Gulistan. Sa'di.
Larch Hill. Daiken.
Miniature. Phillpotts.
Sandwich Man. Johnson.
The Soldier That Has Seen
  Service. Anonymous.
The Soul Speaks. Pfeiffer.
Wilful Waste Brings Woeful
  Want. Anonymous.

Crutch (es)
Cripples. Cassian.
Of Change of Opinions.
  Plarr.
The Volunteer. Anonymous.
The Widow's Mite. Locker-
  Lampson.

Cry (ing)
After Reading Sylvia Plath:.
  Alta.
Alcestis on the Poetry Circuit.
  Jong.
Alternatives. Cooley.
Andy-Diana DNA Letter.
  Weiman.
The Animal I Wanted.
  Patchen.
Ash-Wednesday. Eliot.
At Birth. Thwaite.
Awake. Coleridge.
The Aziola. Shelley.
The Barrel-Organ. Symons.
Beach Talk. MacCaig.
The Beagle's Cry.
  Anonymous.
Before the Flowers of
  Friendship Faded Faded,
  XXI. Stein.
The Beggar's Opera. Gay.
The Best Old Fellow in the
  World. Anonymous.
The Bird. Simpson.
Birds Are Drowsing on the
  Branches. Rudnitsky.
The Black Plateau. Merwin.
The Black Swan. Merrill.
A Boat Song. Columcille.
Bow Down Your Head and
  Cry. Anonymous.
Brothers. Hopkins.
By the Pool at the Third
  Rosses. Symons.
By the River Eden. Raine.
Caelica, XXIII. Greville.
Caelica, XXXV. Greville.
Caelica, XLIII. Greville.
Calvary's Cry. Cunningham.

Carmina Burana (excerpt).
  Anonymous.
Carroll's Sword. MacMore.
The Cats. Kees.
The Cell of Himself.
  Freeman.
Chairs to Mend. Anonymous.
Chanson un Peu Naive.
  Bogan.
Chez Madame. Harrison.
Childhood. O'Gorman.
Christmas Landscape. Lee.
Circe. Hope.
A Circular Cry. Jabes.
Color. Hughes.
A Considered Reply to a
  Child. Price.
The Course of a Particular.
  Stevens.
The Cry of Generations.
  Husid.
The Cry of the Child
  (parody). Zaranka.
The Cry of the Peoples.
  Brody.
The Crying of Water.
  Symons.
Dana Point. Ghiselin.
The Day. Fuller.
Daybreak. Cornford.
The Deer and the Snake.
  Patchen.
The Deer Which Lives.
  Onakatomi Yoshinobu.
Democritus and Heraclitus.
  Prior.
Departure. Lim.
Diana. Constable.
Diana's Hunting-Song.
  Dryden.
The Djanggawul Cycle, 67.
  Anonymous.
Do the Dead Know What
  Time It Is? Patchen.
Don Juan. Byron.
Don' Let Yo' Watch Run
  Down (with music).
  Anonymous.
Dragon. Stroud.
The Duel. Lovelace.
Each Day Is Anxious.
  Akhmatova.
Edinburgh Spring. MacCaig.
The Effect of Example.
  Keble.
Encounter. Hammond.
Ephemera. Yeats.
Epistle to Be Left in the
  Earth. MacLeish.
Epitaph on the Earl of
  Strafford. Cleveland.
Faberge. Schuyler.
The Family Cat. Fuller.
A Far Cry to Heaven.
  Thomas.
The Feast. Hass.
For Anne, Who Doesn't
  Know. Fox.
For Malcolm X. Walker.
For Sale. Silverstein.
The Form and Function of
  the Novel. Goldbarth.
Foul Water. Temkin.
Fragment. Fauset.
Free Little Bird. Anonymous.
Friendless Blues. Gilbert.
Gemwood. Bell.
Girl in White. Dobyns.
God of the Nations. Bowie.
Good-By. Litchfield.
Half-heard. Koch.
Helios. Spingarn.

His Hand Shall Cover Us.
Ben Samuel.
Home Thoughts. Shepard.
The House of Desire.
Williams.
Hurrying away from the
Earth. Bly.
I Am the Wind. Akins.
I Came from Salem City.
Anonymous.
I Have Felt It as They've
Said. Eigner.
I Will Give My Love an
Apple. *Anonymous.*
The Idiot. Naude.
If I had as much money as I
could/spend. Mother
Goose.
If You Want to Know Me.
De Sousa.
Immortal Autumn.
MacLeish.
Imprisoned. Tietjens.
In an Autumn Wood. Percy.
In March. Martin.
An Inconclusive Evening.
Bellerby.
Inebriety (parody). Crabbe.
The Jews. Herbert.
Johnie Cam to Our Toun.
Anonymous.
King John's Castle. Kinsella.
The King's Son. Boyd.
Kyran's Christening.
Nowlan.
Lassitude. Verlaine.
Late Last Night. Hughes.
The Lay of the Levite.
Aytoun.
The Lice-Finders. Rimbaud.
A Life-Lesson. Riley.
The Life of Man. Bacon.
Lindedi Singing. Banda.
Little Boy Blue. Mother
Goose.
Little Feet. Akers.
Long Lonesome Road.
Anonymous.
A Loon Call. Eberhart.
The Lord of the Isle.
George.
The Man in the Onion Bed.
Ciardi.
Memnon. Scollard.
Midnight. Lampman.
Molly Brannigan.
Anonymous.
Montgomery. Hall.
Mother England. Thomas.
The Murder Trial. Adams.
My Atthis, although our dear
Anaktoria. Sappho.
Neila. Goll.
News from Yorktown.
Smith.
Night Visitors. Molodovsky.
Notes on a Life to Be Lived.
Warren.
Ode: The Spirit Wooed.
Dixon.
The Offended. Hebert.
Oh Yes. Matthews.
An Old Inmate. Mackenzie.
Open House. Roethke.
Orient Ode. Thompson.
Other Women's Children.
Waniek.
Paddling Song. *Anonymous.*
Paudeen. Yeats.
A Poem about Love. Fraser.
Poem for Lorry. Hausman.
The Poet. Morgan.

Poor Boy. *Anonymous.*
The Rain's Already With Us.
Quasimodo.
Recognition. Chadwick.
Remember Me! Haweis.
The Riddle Song.
Anonymous.
The Road. Johnson.
The Roundhouse Voices.
Smith.
A Rum Cove, a Stout Cove.
Paulin.
Running the River Lines.
Baker.
Sales Talk for Annie.
Bishop.
Scottsboro, Too, Is Worth Its
Song. Cullen.
Sea-Birds. Thomson.
The Search. John of the
Cross.
Seneca. Merton.
Shoo over! *Anonymous.*
Sila. Warren.
Six Questions (B vers.).
Anonymous.
Sketch for a Job Application
Blank. Harrison.
The Snow Curlew. Watkins.
Song: "He found me sitting
among flowers." De Vere.
The Songs. *Anonymous.*
Sonnets, CXLIII: "Lo, as a
careful housewife runs to
catch." Shakespeare.
The Sorrow of Love. Yeats.
South of the Border.
Nicholas.
Spring. Rodgers.
The Starry Night. Sexton.
Startled. Saigyo Hoshi.
Straus Park. Stern.
The Strong Bond.
Ibarbourou.
Swans at Night. Gilmore.
Sweet Voice of the Garb.
Geilt.
Symbols. Moreland.
Then Came I to the Shoreless
Shore of Silence. Aiken.
This Hour. La Grone.
This Is the Violin. Stickney.
This Particular Christian.
Johnson.
Thou Who Createdst
Everything. *Anonymous.*
The Thousand and One
Nights: Pearls Seen through
Amber. *Anonymous.*
Three Floors. Kunitz.
The Thresher's Labour.
Duck.
The Time I Went to See My
Sister. Tsurayuki.
To-ta Ti-om. Blue Cloud.
To Thee, Then, Let All
Beings Bend. Evans.
The Toy Lamb Seller.
Anonymous.
Tree in December. Cane.
The Triumph of Time.
Swinburne.
Trouble, Trouble.
Anonymous.
True Freedom. Mackay.
Turning away from Lies.
Bly.
The Two Burdens. Marston.
Two Married. Frazee-Bower.
Unintelligible Terms. Simic.
Wedlock. Noll.
Wee Hughie. Shane.

Western Star (excerpt).
Benét.
What's worse than this past
century? Akhmatova.
When Lovely Woman. Cary.
When My Uncle Willie Saw.
Freeman.
The Whisperer. Van Doren.
The Widower. Tyler.
Wild Swans. Millay.
Without Benefit of
Declaration. Hughes.

Crystal (s)
After the Persian. Bogan.
An Apology for the Revival of
Christian
Architecture...(excerpt).
Hill.
Autumn. Campbell.
La Beaute. Baudelaire.
Behind the Waterfall.
Welles.
The Enduring Music. Vinal.
Evening on the Moselle.
Ausonius.
The Fossil. Donaghy.
Full Moon: Santa Barbara.
Teasdale.
Good Weather. Belli.
Haiku: "Sprayed with strong
poison." Goodman.
Here and Now. Cater.
The Italian Soldier Shook My
Hand. Orwell.
Larch Hill. Daiken.
Mother to Son. Hughes.
On Keats Who Desired That
On His Tomb Should Be
Inscribed–. Shelley.
On the Annunciation of Fra
Angelico. Machado.
Psittachus Eois Imitatrix Ales
Ab Indis. Sitwell.
A Quilled Quilt, a Needle
Bed. Leithauser.
Song: "Distil not poison in
mine ears." Hall.
The Spring Festival on the
River. Peck.
To Rosemary. Benét.
Vermont. Cleghorn.

Cub (s)
The Destiny of Nations.
Coleridge.
A Gaggle of Geese, A Pride
of Lions. Moore.
Julia. Rose.
Limerick: "Teacher Bruin
said, "Cub, bear in mind."
Fenderson.
The Lion's Cub. Thompson.

Cuba
The Gathering. Swett.
The Store in Havana. Kozer.
'Way Down in Cuba.
Anonymous.

Cuckold (ing) (s)
Dialogue between a Squeamish
Cotting Mechanic and his
Sluttish Wife. Ward.
The Dream. Bendo.
The Merry Cuckold.
Anonymous.
A New Song, Called the
Frolicsome Sea Captain, or
Tit for Tat. *Anonymous.*
The Old Farmer and His
Young Wife. *Anonymous.*
The Temperaments. Pound.
Two or Three: A Recipe to
Make a Cuckold. Pope.

Cuckoo (s)
Amoretti, XIX. Spenser.
April. Thompson.
Bow-Wow, Says the Dog.
Anonymous.
The Cuckoo. *Anonymous.*
The Fresh Air. Monro.
The Gowk. Soutar.
Larches. Gurney.
Madrigal: "Well fare the
nightingale." *Anonymous.*
Of the Cuckoo. Bunyan.
Our Clock. Eakman.
Pot and Kettle. Graves.
Santa Claus in a Department
Store. Hassall.
The Trail Up Wu Gorge.
Sun Yun-feng.

Cucumber (s)
The Confession. Barham.
Day of These Days. Lee.
Fragments. Praxilla.
Loveliest of What I Leave
behind Is the Sunlight.
Praxilla.
Most beutiful of things I leave
is sunlight. Praxilla.
What's Your Name?
Anonymous.

Cue
I Am Raftery. Mahon.
My Object All Sublime.
Gilbert.

Culprit
Dies Irae. *Anonymous.*
Surgeons Must Be Very
Careful. Dickinson.

Cunning
Apparuit. Pound.
The Last Conqueror.
Shirley.
The Puss and the Boots
(parody) (excerpt). Traill.
The Royal Palace of the
Highest Heaven.
Montgomerie.
The Song of Hiawatha.
Longfellow.

Cunt
Epigram: "My better half,
why turn a peevish scold."
Martial (Marcus Valerius
Martialis).
Epigram: "No more of your
titled acquaintants boast."
Burns.
Mr. Muscle-On.
Kicknosway.

Cup (s)
Autumn. Campbell.
Burdens. Dowden.
The Crocus. Crane.
The Cup of Happiness.
Thomas.
The Damsel. Omar B. Abi
Rabi'a.
December. Padgett.
Don Juan. Byron.
The Edge. Ridge.
Elektra on Third Avenue.
Hacker.
Fairy Godmothers. Lee-
Hamilton.
Fall Days. Conger.
Fill the Bowl, Butler!
Anonymous.
Gift Hour. Banus.
Hebe. Lowell.
Hey-ho Knave: A Catch.
Anonymous.
I Peeped through the
Window. *Anonymous.*

In the Old City. Fichman.
Japanese Girl with Red Table.
  Dobyns.
Keep Hidden from Me.
  Korn.
A Lesson in Detachment.
  Miller.
The Living Chalice.
  Mitchell.
November Song. Vinz.
Prayer. Fowler.
The Rosy Days Are
  Numbered. Ibn Ezra.
Rufus Prays. Strong.
Scotland Yet. Riddell.
Smithfield Ham. Smith.
Spicewood. Reese.
The Stirrup Cup. Kilmer.
There Was a Maid Went to
  the Mill. Anonymous.
The Well-Aimed Stare.
  Margenat.
The Woodspurge. Rossetti.

Cupboard (s)
Great A, Little a.
  Anonymous.
In the Hospital. Jensen.
Saturday Shopping.
  Edelman.
To an Estranged Wife.
  Young.

Cupid (s)
Beauty, Since You So Much
  Desire. Campion.
Caelica, XLIX. Greville.
Caelica, LXXXIV. Greville.
Four Anacreontic Poems, 2.
  Spenser.
Four Anacreontic Poems, 3.
  Spenser.
He That Hath No Mistress.
  Anonymous.
Hero and Leander. Marlowe.
Hob upon a Holiday.
  Anonymous.
Inst., Ult., and Prox.: Answer.
  Herbert.
Love and Honour. Greville.
Love-Songs, At Once Tender
  and Informative.
  Hoffenstein.
The Muses. Anonymous.
Polifemo y Galatea: The Love
  Song of Polyphemus.
  Gongora y Argote.
Song: "Dorinda's sparkling
  wit, and eyes." Sackville.
Song of the Stygian Naiades.
  Beddoes.

Cupidity
Boat-Haven, Co. Mayo.
  Taylor.
Recessional for the Class of
  1959... Cowen.

Curb
Cantica: Our Lord Christ.
  Francis of Assisi.
The Dog Parade.
  Guiterman.
Jerked Heartstrings in Town.
  Jones.
Wait for the Hour. Soutar.

Cure (d) (s)
Adventures of Isabel. Nash.
...And Mr. Ferritt. Wright.
But Art Thou Come, Dear
  Saviour? Anonymous.
Concerning the Nature of
  Love. Lucretius (Titus
  Lucretitus Carus).
Diversity of Doctors.
  Anonymous.

An Epigram: "Great Charles,
  among the holy gifts of
  grace." Jonson.
The Expostulation.
  Shadwell.
A Familiar Letter. Holmes.
His Ejaculation to God.
  Herrick.
How Stands the Glass
  Around? Wolfe.
In the Hospital of the Holy
  Physician. Willard.
The Indifference. Sedley.
Lydia Pinkham (with music).
  Anonymous.
Mad Song. Levertov.
Misery. Holmes.
Piscatorie Eclogues.
  Fletcher.
Red Ants. Anonymous.
Shelby County, Ohio.
  November 1974. Murray.
Silex Scintillans. Vaughan.
Snail. Eybers.
Song for a Lost Art. Brasier.
Sonnet: "O Time! who
  know'st a lenient hand to
  lay." Bowles.
Visitor. Anonymous.
Who's That Ringing At My
  Door Bell? Anonymous.
A Wish. Arnold.

Curiosity
The Curiosity-Shop.
  Redgrove.
My Father Died This Spring.
  Kyger.
Post Mortem. Harden.

Curious
Curious Something. Welles.
Fleche... Eigner.
King Henry VI.
  Shakespeare.
Limerick. Anonymous.
Limerick: "There was a young
  girl of Asturias."
  Anonymous.
Meeting Together of Poles &
  Latitudes: in Prospect.
  Avison.
The Quantocks.
  Wordsworth.
Was It Not Curious? Smith.

Curl (ed) (s) (y)
Arms and the Boy. Owen.
A Cottage in the Wood.
  Edson.
Down the Mississippi.
  Fletcher.
Hunkie Tunkie. Jordan.
I Am Fur from My
  Sweetheart. Anonymous.
Murder in the Cathedral.
  Eliot.
A New Song Called The
  Curling of the Hair.
  Anonymous.
Paddy's Metamorphosis.
  Moore.
Saga of Leif the Lucky
  (excerpt). Allen.
Sanctuary. Parker.
The Shellpicker. Perry.
The Statue. Finch.
To a Wild Rose Found in
  October. Hayes.
The Toad-Eater. Burns.
We Put the Urn Aboard Ship.
  Sappho.

Currants
Ed and Sid and Bernard.
  MacDuff.

The fruits you give me are
  more savory than others.
  Burnat-Provins.

Current (s)
The Boats Are Afloat. Chu
  Hsi.
Church Lock and Key.
  Herbert.
The Circulation of the Blood.
  Blackmore.
The Excursion. Wordsworth.
The Fall. Raine.
Feeling the Quiet Strike.
  Minor.
The Ghost of an Education.
  Michie.
Hamlet. Shakespeare.
In Praise of Water-Gruel.
  Green.
Jonathan. "Rachel" (Rachel
  Blumstein).
The Mountain Heart's-Ease.
  Harte.
No More the Slow Stream.
  McLaren.
Presence of Snow. Cane.
Sunset. Evans.
There Are Oceans. Harjo.
Trout. Heaney.
Winter Holding Off the Coast
  of North America.
  Momaday.

Curse (d) (s)
Ajax. Sophocles.
Art of Love (excerpt). Ovid.
Astrophel and Stella, LX.
  Sidney.
Astrophel and Stella, CV.
  Sidney.
Catullus to Lesbia. Reeves.
A Curse for a Nation.
  Browning.
The Curse of Kehama.
  Southey.
The Dead in Europe.
  Lowell.
Dinnshenchas: The Story of
  Macha. Anonymous.
Don Juan. Byron.
The Donkey. Kaikini.
Envy. Procter.
Epigram. Anonymous.
Epigram: "I curse my bearing,
  childhood, youth." Synge.
Fields Where We Slept.
  Rukeyser.
Fragment. Radnoti.
The Future. Sill.
Have I, This Moment, Led
  Thee from the Beach.
  Landor.
The Heart Is Deep. Wolcott.
John Barley-Corn, My Foe.
  Adams.
Madam Gabrina, or the Ill-
  Favour'd Choice. King.
Modern Love, VII.
  Meredith.
Motets, II. Anonymous.
Noble Sisters. Rossetti.
On Judas Iscariot. Quarles.
Operatic Note. Cane.
Parable. Soutar.
Paradise Lost. Milton.
Prairie Wolves. Carr.
A Protest from a Bushman
  (Masarwa). Malikongwa.
The Royal Adventurer.
  Freneau.
The Sack of Baltimore.
  Davis.

Satyrs upon the Jesuits:
  Prologue. Oldham.
Seabirds. Smith.
Shelly Beach. Koch.
Slaves to London. Motteux.
Three Songs. Beaumont.
To My Ingenious and Worthy
  Friend William Lowndes,
  Esq. Gay.
To the Lord Chancellor
  (excerpt). Shelley.
Two Women. Willis.
Unseen Flight. Georgeou.
Vagabonds. "Marie.
The Violet. Story.
Woman. Anonymous.

Curtain (s)
The Boy Actor. Coward.
Carmen. Levy.
The Dying Girl. Williams.
Essay on Man. Anonymous.
Failure. Brooke.
The Fire Place. Mandel.
He Abjures Love. Hardy.
Homage to Vaslav Nijinsky.
  Kirkup.
The Lace Curtains.
  MacAdams.
Morning. Davenant.
Muse Poem. Van
  Spanckeren.
Nun Snow. Kreymborg.
Ode on the Poetical
  Character. Collins.
The Offensive. Douglas.
Robespierre and Mozart as
  Stage. Lowell.
Summons. Ficke.
The Sun Drops Red. Miller.
The Sunset City. Cornwell.

Curve (d) (s)
Ars. Tsvetayeva.
Bombardment. Lawrence.
Buffalo Dance. Corbin.
Driving Home. London.
July Dawn. Bogan.
Let Him Return. Hill.
Mantle. Heyen.
O Make Me a Mask.
  Thomas.
Overnight Guest. Wilson.
Poem: "Is to love, this–to
  nurse a name." Coghill.
The Sphinx (excerpt). Wilde.

Custom (er) (ers)
Catalogue Army. Nye.
Fable XIII: The Tame Stag.
  Gay.
Letter Containing a Panegyric
  on Bath. Anstey.
Lilliput Levee. Rands.
May Evening. Brennan.
Park. Ignatow.
Waiwera. Smithyman.

Cut (s) (ing)
Altarwise by Owl-Light.
  Thomas.
Broom, Green Broom.
  Anonymous.
Charlie Johnson in
  Kettletown. Smith.
David and Goliath. Crouch.
Earliness at the Cape.
  Deutsch.
Strawberry Moon. Oliver.

Cut (s) (ting)
Alma Mater, Forget Me.
  Cole.
And Three Hundred and
  Sixty-Six in Leap Year.
  Nash.
The Answer. Wachtel.

A Baker's Dozen of Wild Beasts. Wells.
The Bermondsey Tragedy. *Anonymous.*
Charity Overcoming Envy. Moore.
A Creole Slave-Song. Thompson.
A Curse on Mine-Owners. *Anonymous.*
Epitaph at Great Torrington, Devon. *Anonymous.*
The Flash Colonial Barman. Coxon.
Friend, on This Scaffold Thomas More Lies Dead. Cunningham.
The Grave. Tchernichovsky.
Hey Betty Martin. *Anonymous.*
L'Homme Moyhen Sensuel (excerpt). Pound.
Hornpout. Evarts.
The Horse Wrangler. O'Malley.
How the Helpmate of Blue-Beard Made Free with a Door. Carryl.
I Hear You've Let Go. Ferre.
The Knight in Disguise. Lindsay.
Limerick: "A railway official at Crewe." *Anonymous.*
The Lodging-House Fuschsias. Hardy.
Lord Lovel (A vers.). *Anonymous.*
My Father Was a Frenchman. *Anonymous.*
No Mean City. MacDonogh.
The Obscured Prince; or, the Black Box Boxed. *Anonymous.*
On Reading–. Aldrich.
The Parcae, or Three Dainty Destinies: The Armillet. Herrick.
The Peasant. Wolf.
The Pueblo Women I Watched Get down in Brooklyn. Rose.
Purple Dry Buds. Roberts.
Relent, My Deere, Yet Unkind Coelia. Percy.
Rhymes. Steele.
She and I. Cameron.
Signature. Orlock.
Since I've Felt This Pain. Ono no Komachi.
Song: Lift Boy. Graves.
Thou, Lord, Hast Been Our Sure Defense. Hopkins.
To the Boston Women. *Anonymous.*
Words. Phillips.

Cute
A Boston Ballad. Whitman.
Canine Amenities. *Anonymous.*
Honey Moon. Baker.

Cycle (s)
Bicycles! Tricycles! Tabb.
Centennial Hymn. Whittier
Converstion with Three Women of New England. Stevens.
Just Lost, When I Was Saved! Dickinson.
Papa above. Dickinson.

Cyclone (s)
Come Unto These Yellow Sands (parody). Dehn.
Cyclone Blues. *Anonymous.*
The Man in the Street Is Fed. Sandburg.
Physical Geography. Nicholl.

Cynthia
Caelica, XLVIII. Greville.
The Forest's Queen. Massinger.
My Thoughts Are Winged with Hopes. Clifford.
To Cynthia. Clifford.

Cypress (es)
Beneath the Cypress Shade. Peacock.
The Cats of Campagnatico. Porter.
Program Note on Sibelius. Babcock.

D

Dachau
Golda. Wolfert.
Safari West. Williams.
Sonnets from China (excerpt). Auden.

Dad (dy)
Automobile Mechanics. Baruch.
Bell-Bottomed Trousers. *Anonymous.*
Big Night Blues. Jefferson.
A Child to His Sick Grandfather. Baillie.
Commencement, Pingree School. Updike.
Dad's Greatest Job. *Anonymous.*
Dance to Your Daddy. *Anonymous.*
Dear Old Dad. Shaver.
Domestic Science. *Anonymous.*
Eagles on a Half. Wiley.
Epitaph on a Pessimist. Hardy.
The Fat Budgie. Lennon.
For Sapphires. Rodgers.
The Fox Walked Out, A vers. *Anonymous.*
France Blues. Sunny Boy.
Got Dem Blues (with music). *Anonymous.*
I'll Buy You a Tartan Bonnet. *Anonymous.*
I Want a Girl. Von Tilzer.
Island. Hughes.
John Brown's Body. Benét.
The Killing of the Birds. Williams.
The Moss of His Skin. Sexton.
New Approach Needed. Amis.
Newspaper. Fisher.
Old Emily. Hill.
The Origins of Escape. Tisdale.
Otto. Brooks.
Poems, IX. O'Connor.
The Rantin Dog the Daddie O't. Burns.
Rock, Rock, Sleep, My Baby. Watson.

Shabby Old Dad. Campbell.
Six and Thirty. Stevenson.
The Snack (parody). Zeiger.
Two Hopper. Ikan.
Visitors. Behn.
When Slavery Seems Sweet. Bullins.
While Cecil Snores: Mom Drinks Cold Milk. Cunningham.

Daffodil (s)
An April Morning. Carman.
Daffodils. Harding.
Daffodils. Wordsworth.
Hello! Garnett.
Holiday. Lowry.
A Hymn to Bacchus. Herrick.
The Lent Lily. Housman.
The Lilies of the Field. Mackenzie.
Old Michael. Brady.
To Butterfly. Percy.

Daily
Bar-Room Matins. MacNeice.
In the City. Zangwill.
Sacrifice. Issaia.
Unanswered Prayers. Wilcox.

Dainty
The Faerie Queene. Spenser.
Flowers. Hood.
Madrigal: "Ladies, you see time flieth." Morley.
Pigeons. Moore.

Dais (ies) (y)
Consolations of Philosophy. Mahon.
Duckle, Duckle, Daisy. Jackson.
For a Lamb. Eberhart.
Free Enterprise. Stetler.
The Gypsy Laddie (C vers.). *Anonymous.*
Hippies. Dempster.
How many times these low feet staggered. Dickinson.
Madrigal: "My mistress is as fair as fine." Ravenscroft.
De Mortuis Nil Nisi Bonum. Realf.
A Nosegay. Reynolds.
Of bronze and blaze. Dickinson.
One Winter Afternoon. Cummings.
Play Song. Clarke.
Sad Green. Warner.
Sailor. Page.
The Serf's Secret. Moody.
Went up a year this evening! Dickinson.
The Wisdom of Merlyn. Blunt.

Dally
In Between the Curve. Bacon.
Poussin. MacNeice.

Dam (s)
And the Gas Chamber Drones in the Distance. Forker.
Boulder Dam. Sarton.
Requiem for a River. Williams.
Six-Year-Old Marjory Fleming Pens a Poem. Fleming.
The Wedding. Hood.

Damage
The Damage You Have Done. Komey.
The Hero. Graves.

Santa Claus in a Department Store. Hassall.

Dame (s)
An Ancient Castle. Morris.
Come up, My Horse, to Budleigh Fair. *Anonymous.*
Epigram on a Dog. Johnson.
Father Short. *Anonymous.*
From a Marriage Broker's Card, 1776. *Anonymous.*
Remon. *Anonymous.*
Spin Dame. *Anonymous*
There Is Nothin' Like a Dame. Hammerstein.

Damn (ed)
Ariel in the Cloven Pine. Taylor.
At Ease. De La Mare.
Caries. Brown.
Der Blinde Junge. Loy.
Eighteen-Ninety. Shipp.
Epitaph on a Tuft-Hunter. Moore.
Epitaph on James Grieve, Laird of Boghead. Burns.
Frisco's Defi. Hooper.
The Gresford Disaster. *Anonymous.*
Impasse. Hughes.
Limerick: "A half-baked potato, named Sue." Libaire.
No More. Clark.
Observation. Parker.
On the World. Swift.
Poem in Time of Winter. Mathew.
Sisyphus. Miles.
The Suicide. Lang.
Swearing. Fitzsimon.
To a Fine Young Woman. Wycherley.
To Mr. Murray. Byron.
Tom Tiler; or, The Nurse. *Anonymous.*
Unregenerate. Embry.
The Vicar. Crabbe.

Damon
Ipecacuanha. Canning.
On Her Loving Two Equally. Behn.
To Sir William, of Hawthornden Alexander. Drummond.

Damp
A Folding and Unfolding. Smith.
The Influence of Local Attachment (excerpt). Polwhele.
The Mad Gardener's Song. "Carroll.
Poems. Machado.
Sorrow. *Anonymous.*

Damsel (s)
Amanda's Complaint. Freneau.
The Minstrel's Song. Chatterton.

Dance (d) (r) (s)
Aisling. Clarke.
All Sung. Le Gallienne.
Alone by the Road's Edge. O Hehir.
Among School Children. Yeats.
Andy-Diana DNA Letter. Weiman.
Angel Spirits of Sleep. Bridges.

Anthropology in Fort Morgan, Colorado. Hamod.

At dawn of the day the Creator. Stampa.

Autumn Journal. MacNeice.

Ballad: "My lady was found mutilated." Cohen.

Ballad of the Ten Casino Dancers. Meireles.

Bear Dance. Rogers.

The Beauty of Dawn. Mnthali.

Behaviour of Money. Spencer.

Belly Dancer. Wakoski.

The Belly Dancer in the Nursing Home. Wallace.

The Blind Man (excerpt). Wright.

The Blue Flag (parody). Miller.

A Brown Girl Dead. Cullen.

Buffalo Gals. *Anonymous.*

The Bunyip. Stewart.

Burning. Snyder.

Can't They Dance the Polka! *Anonymous.*

Cat or Stomp. Tohe.

The Cave of Night. Montague.

Chanuke, O Chanuke. *Anonymous.*

Coming Back. Bruchac.

A Country Dance. Tennyson.

The Cowboy's Dance Song. *Anonymous.*

Coyote and the Star. Guiterman.

The Dance. Gustafson.

Dance of Death. Flaccus.

The Dance of the Rain. Marais.

The De'il's awa' wi' the Exciseman. Burns.

The Deathless. Hayes.

Demonstration. Finefrock.

A Deserted Home. Lysaght.

Discretions of Alcibiades. Pinsky.

Dream Songs. Berryman.

A Drunk Man Looks at the Thistle (excerpt). ""MacDiarmid.

Epilogue for a Masque of Purcell. Rich.

An Epistle. Hope.

Epitaph. Spencer.

The Eve. Schwartz.

The Fairies Are Dancing All over the World. Rumaker.

The Fairies' Farewell. Corbet.

Fatigues. Aldington.

Finger Dance. *Anonymous.*

Firebowl. Clouts.

The First Snow of the Year. Van Doren.

Gay Boys. Kirkup.

The Gilded Boys. Picano.

Giovinette, Che Fate All'Amore. Da Ponte.

A Goblinade. Jaques.

The Gods Must Not Know Us. Gregg.

Golden Oldie. Mariani.

Grotesque. Lowell.

Hasidic Jew from Sadagora. Auslander.

How and When and Where and Why. Gotlieb.

I Am a Cowboy in the Boat of Ra. Reed.

I Bet God Understands about Givin up Five. Jamal.

I Enter by the Darkened Door (parody). King.

I Expected My Skin and My Blood to Ripen. Rose.

I Wandered Lonely as a Cloud. Wordsworth.

I Want to Tell You. Hochman.

Iceland First Seen. Morris.

In Answer of an Elegiacall Letter upon the Death of the King of Sweden. Carew.

In France. Cornford.

In Like a Lion. Hewitt.

In the Dome Car of the "Canadian'. Marty.

Independence Day. Tyler.

Into & At. Pennant.

Irish Dancer. *Anonymous.*

Kopis'taya. Allen.

The Laboratory. Browning.

Lachlan Gorach's Rhyme. *Anonymous.*

Lady Sara Bunbury Sacrificing to the Graces, by Reynolds. Hine.

Late Winter. Hall.

Leaving the Dance. Whitaker.

The Liberator. Coleman.

Little tree. Cummings.

Lord of the Dance. Carter.

Louisiana Girls. *Anonymous.*

The Lynching. McKay.

MacPherson's Farewell. Anonymous.

The Masque of Christmas. Jonson.

Matisse. Hirsch.

The Mer-Man and Marstig's Daughter. *Anonymous.*

The Merry Bagpipes. *Anonymous.*

Midsummer Night. Edey.

Mohini Chatterjee. Yeats.

Moon, Moon. *Anonymous.*

A Morning-Piece; or, An Hymn for the Hay-Makers. Smart.

The Morning Prayers of the Hasid, Rabbi Levi Yitzhok. Gotlieb.

Music. Farjeon.

The Music Crept by Us. Cohen.

My Country. Lermontov.

My Dancing Day. *Anonymous.*

Nancy, You Dance. Johnson.

Nationalism. Roskolenko.

The New Cows. Waterman.

The New Platform Dances. Mapanje.

The Newborn Colt. Kennedy.

Next Door to Monica's Dance Studio. Smith.

Nowhere, Not among the Warriors at Their Festival. Atimantiyar.

Obon by the Hudson. Oyama.

October. Pape.

The Odyssey. Homer.

Of Dancing. Brownjohn.

Off the Ground. De la Mare.

An Old Cracked Tune. Kunitz.

On a Female Rope-Dancer. *Anonymous.*

On the Desert. Crane.

On the Way to the Island. Ferry.

The Others. O'Sullivan.

The Owl and the Pussy-Cat. Lear.

The Poet Loves from Afar. O'Grady.

Praise Doubt. Van Doren.

Prison Graveyard. Knight.

The Prophet. Gibran.

The Psalter of Avram Haktani. Klein.

The Ration Card. Bahe.

The Redeemer. Muchemwa.

Remember. Harjo.

Robin Hood and the Bishop of Hereford. *Anonymous.*

The Serpent. Langland.

Shadow-Bride. Tolkien.

She Plans Her Funeral. Bowman.

The She Wolf. Spark.

Shekhina and the Kiddushim. Roditi.

Shulamit in Her Dreams. Falk.

Sightseers in a Courtyard. Guillen.

The Silk Merchant's Daughter (I). *Anonymous.*

Sings a Bird. Nist.

Slow Dance. St. John.

Song of Farewell. Wong.

The Spirit of the Birch. Ketchum.

Tambour. Vas.

There Was a Dance, Sweetheart. Harjo.

There Were Fierce Animals in Africa. Aubert.

Tiger People. Hobson.

The Time Hath Been. Skipsey.

To a Midge. Nisbet.

To-Morrow Shall Be My Dancing Day. *Anonymous.*

To Potapovitch. Crane.

Tom O'Roughley. Yeats.

A Tribe Searching. Reich.

A Triviality. Cuney.

Tullochgorum. Skinner.

Unalterables. Gregor.

The Waltzer in the House. Kunitz.

Washing Day. *Anonymous.*

When de Saints Go Ma'chin' Home. Brown.

When Diamonds, Nibbling in my Ears. Davies.

Winter in Another Country. Anthony ("Ai").

The Witch's Ballad. Scott.

Woman Painter of Mithila. Mumford.

You Shall Above All Things Be Glad and Young. Cummings.

Dancing

All the Spirit Powers Went to Their Dancing Place. Snyder.

Are They Dancing. Dorn.

The Bear on the Delhi Road. Birney.

The Bridge. Thomson.

The Broncho That Would Not Be Broken. Lindsay.

The Cat in the Box. Jonas.

The Cats. Kees.

Christmas Song. Carman.

Come Out of Crete. Sappho.

The Daisies. Carman.

The Dance. Halpern.

The Dance of the Daughters of Herodias. Symons.

Dancing at Whitsun. Marshall.

The Dancing Bear. Paine.

Dark Girl. Bontemps.

Daughters Will You Marry? *Anonymous.*

Eternal Sabbath. Peretz.

The Faerie Queene. Spenser.

The First Tooth. Lamb.

For a Nativity. Mueller.

Four for Sir John Davies. Roethke.

Gnat-Psalm. Hughes.

A Hollyhock. Sherman.

Imogen. Newbolt.

In the Time of the Rose. Savant.

Johnny Faa, the Gypsy Laddie. *Anonymous.*

Late October. Carleton.

Letter. Empson.

May Mornings. Eastwick.

Milton. Blake.

Modern Love, XXXIX. Meredith.

Not Just Yet. Revard.

On a Morning Full of Sun. Appleman.

On Flower Wreath Hill (excerpt). Rexroth.

Orchestra. Davies.

Pearly Beads. *Anonymous.*

The Poet. Clifton.

The Rich Lady from Dublin. *Anonymous.*

The Sea Danceth. Davies.

The Sense of Responsibility. Mathews.

Sleigh Bells at Night. Coatsworth.

Sonship. Rezmerski.

Spring Song. Spencer.

To the Fountain of Bandusia. Horace.

The Waters of Life. Wolfe.

A Wedgwood Bowl. Taylor.

When Faces Called Flowers. Cummings.

The Window. Dobyns.

Wolf. Blue Cloud.

The Women Are Grieving. Hogan.

Dandelion (s)

Beer Drops. Boyd.

Fear of the Earth. Comfort.

The First Dandelion. Whitman.

Goldfinches. Keats.

Little Dandelion. Bostwick.

The Medium IV Sights. Rakosi.

The Park. Tippett.

Parliament Hill Fields. Betjeman.

War with the Weeds. Sinclair.

Dandy

Chesapeake and Shannon. *Anonymous.*

The Constitution and Guerriere. *Anonymous.*

Peeler and the Goat. *Anonymous.*

Shaemus. Aiken.

Dane (s)
Beowulf: The Lay of Finn.
Anonymous.
Qua Song. Inez.
Scyros. Shapiro.
Danger Court
Whim Alley. Allen.
Danger (ous) (s)
City. Biasotti.
Confess We All, Before the
Lord. Wilson.
Conversation. Berryman.
The Destruction of Troy:
Aeneid II. Denham.
The Eyes of Children at the
Brink of the Sea's Grasp.
Jacobsen.
The Four Deer. Jones.
The Golden Voyage.
Anonymous.
He. Ashbery.
Hector and Andromache.
Pope.
Hymn Against Pestilence.
Colman.
I Am With Thee. Allen.
I Think of Him as One Who
Fights. Branch.
Julius Caesar. Shakespeare.
Lady Isabel and the Elf
Knight (B version).
Anonymous.
Learning to Type. O Hehir.
The Love-Knot. Coan.
A Maid's Complaint.
Campion.
Much madness is divinest
sense. Dickinson.
The Name of Jesus. Flint.
Of Crossing the Street. Gay.
The ordinary valour only
works. Anstey.
Prayer by Moonlight.
Swartz.
A Prayer for My Son. Yeats.
Some San Francisco Poems.
Oppen.
Three Roundels of Love
Unreturned. Chaucer.
To Pyrrha. Browne.
Triolet. McPherson.
Twickenham Ferry.
Marzials.
Useful for Avoiding Collisions
at Sea. *Anonymous.*
The Watershed. Auden.
What You Should Know to
Be a Poet. Snyder.
Dangle (s)
Hera, Hung from the Sky.
Kizer.
The Natives. Mura.
On a Friend's Suicide. Yots.
The spider holds a silver ball.
Dickinson.
Dante
Don Juan. Byron.
On a Bust of Dante. Parsons
Sonnet: To Dante Alighieri
(He Writes to Dante...).
Angiolieri.
To an Imperilled Traveller.
Dole.
Walking Milwaukee. Witt.
Dare (d) (s)
Astrophel and Stella, LIV.
Sidney.
By Blue Ontario's Shore
(excerpt). Whitman.
Byron: In Men Whom Men
Condemn as Ill. Miller.
Closing Piece. Rilke.

Creed. Spencer.
The Fall of Hyperion.
Keats.
Fragment. Berlind.
The Gray Hills Taught Me
Patience. Cross.
Interim. Delany.
John Baynham's Epitaph.
Dermody.
The Little Boy to the
Locomotive. Low.
Mother England. Thomas.
The Motive of All of It.
Rukeyser.
New Storefront. Atkins.
Night Watchmen.
Garthwaite.
Ode Recited at the Harvard
Commemoration. Lowell.
On Some-Thing, That Walkes
Some-Where. Jonson.
Tetelestai. Aiken.
To the Veterans of the
Abraham Lincoln Brigade.
Taggard.
Under the Mistletoe. Cullen.
The Unicorn. Young.
Young Africa's Resolve.
Osadebay.
Daring
The Numerella Shore.
"Cockatoo Jack".
On Fort Sumter.
Anonymous.
The Song of the Camp.
Taylor.
Dark (en) (er)
Across Kansas. Stafford.
Adam's Footprint. Miller.
Adultery at the Plaza.
Thompson.
After Rain. Thomas.
After They Put Down Their
Overalls. Peters.
After Work. Snyder.
Against Seasons. Mezey.
The Ancient Couple on Lu
Mountain. Van Doren.
The Animals. Berg.
The Annihilation of Nothing.
Gunn.
Ark Anatomical.
Macpherson.
As an Old Mercer. Fisher.
Ascension. Devlin.
Astrophel and Stella, XCIX.
Sidney.
The Atoll in the Mind.
Comfort.
August. Pyle.
Auras on the Interstates.
Vizenor.
Autonomous. Van Doren.
A Balcony with Birds. Moss.
The Ballad of the White
Horse. Chesterton.
The Barrier. McKay.
The Bear Who Came to
Dinner. Stoutenburg.
Beowulf. *Anonymous.*
The Besom-Man. Campbell.
Bird at Night. Hamilton.
The Blind Man. Sangster.
Bone Thoughts on a Dry Day.
Starbuck.
Bordello. Turco.
Braque. Joseph.
Bridges. Bacmeister.
Bring Torches. Stephen.
The Businessman of Alicante.
Levine.

By a Lake in Minnesota.
Wright.
By Canoe through the Fir
Forest. Dickey.
Candles. *Anonymous*
Canticle. McClure.
Cardrona Valley. Wedde.
Cat. Baruch.
Child. Plath.
Chilly Winds. *Anonymous.*
The Clouds That Are So
Light. Thomas.
The Collector of the Sun.
Smith.
Come Turn to Mee, Thou
Pretty Little One.
Anonymous.
Conservative. Witt.
Consider the Lilies.
Donnelly.
The Country Bedroom.
Cornford.
Country Drive-In. Jacobsen.
Court and Country Love.
Anonymous.
Crazy Movie. Barrios.
Dark Wood. Wedde.
The Dash for the Colors.
Webb.
Dawn and Dark. Gale.
The Day of Denial. Very.
The Day's No Rounder Than
Its Angles Are. Viereck.
Daybreak. Phillips.
Days and Nights. Moore.
The Dead Sheep. Young.
Death and the Bridge.
Lowell.
The Death of Chiron.
McAuley.
Der Blinde Junge. Loy.
A Difficult Adjustment.
Edmond.
Dismissal. Redgrove.
Dive. Hughes.
Doe. Dow.
Domus Caedet Arborem.
Mew.
The Don. Howes.
Don Giovanni on His Way to
Hell. Gilbert.
Down with the Lambs.
Anonymous.
The Dream and the Blood.
Untermeyer.
Drinking. Terris.
Dylan, Who Is Dead. Allen.
Earth's Night. Allingham.
Eclipse. Scott.
An Elegy. Gascoyne.
Elegy for a Diver. Booth.
An Elegy Is Preparing Itself.
Justice.
Eternal Moment. "Hale.
Eve in Old Age. Holland.
The Faerie Queene. Spenser.
A Family Album. Brody.
Farewell. Chao Li-hua.
The Farmer Remembers the
Somme. Palmer.
The Feast o' Saint Stephen.
Sawyer.
Feeding the Lions. Jordan.
First Blood. Stallworthy.
The Fish. Brooke.
The Fisherman. Fawcett.
For a College Yearbook.
Cunningham.
For Adolf Eichmann. Levi.
For Fran. Levine.
For the Rebuilding of a
House. Berry.

For We Are All Madwomen.
Sweeney.
Full Moon. Hayden.
George Washington Goes to a
Girlie Movie. Boyajian.
Girl with Long Dark Hair.
Gray.
Girls in Their Seasons.
Mahon.
Glory Be to God for Dappled
Things. Keating.
Gods Determinations.
Taylor.
Goldfish on the Writing Desk.
Brod.
The Gouty Merchant and the
Stranger. Smith.
The Great Figure. Williams.
Halloween. Pomeroy.
A Halo. Salisbury.
The Heretic's Tragedy.
Browning.
Hiding in the Cucumber
Garden. Vidya.
His Immortality. Hardy.
A History. Williams.
Hold-Up. MacNeice.
Horizon Thong. Abbe.
Hotel de l'Univers et Portugal.
Merrill.
The Hours. Bishop.
The Hunchback in the Park.
Thomas.
The Hymn of Adam.
Vondel.
I'll Be Your Epitaph.
Speyer.
If I Were Old. Ogilvie.
The Ikons. Baxter.
Images. Schaukal.
In a Remote Cloister
Bordering the Empyrean.
Sloman.
In Memorium. Alcott.
In Memory of W. H. Auden.
Slavitt.
In the Dark. Bushnell.
In the New Sun. Levine.
In the Street. Neilson.
In the Vaulted Way. Hardy.
In This Dark House.
Davison.
Incantation for Rain.
Anonymous.
Innocence. MacCaig.
Interlude. Lowell.
The Introduction.
Winchilsea.
The Ivory Dog of My Sister.
Tallmountain.
June Fugue. Shapcott.
Keep It Dark. *Anonymous.*
The Kiss. Moore.
The Lake. Coxe.
The Landscape of Love.
Cole.
A Last Address to My
Ghosts. Orr.
Late at Night during a Visit
of Friends. Bly.
Leaves Compared with
Flowers. Frost.
Legend. Wheelock.
Light. Silkin.
The lightning is a yellow fork.
Dickinson.
The Little Boy Lost. Smith.
The Little Dark Rose.
MacWard.
A Little Dog-Angel.
Holland.
The Long River. Hall.

Lost Light. Akers.
Love. Dent.
Love at Roblin Lake. Purdy.
Made Shine. Miles.
A Man-Made World.
 Spender.
A Man's Love. Ditlevsen.
The Martyr. Flohr.
Masks. Swann.
Master's in the Garden Again.
 Ransom.
The Medusa. Davenport.
Merchandise. Jennett.
Midnight. Lampman.
Midweek. Miles.
Morning Hymn of Adam and
 Eve. Milton.
Murder in the Cathedral.
 Eliot.
Nelly Trim. Warner.
Night. Sutu.
Night along the Mackinac
 Bridge. Hill.
Night Out, Tom Cat.
 deGravelles.
Nightswim. Root.
No Difference in the Dark.
 Herrick.
Nostalgia. De La Mare.
November. Turner.
Now That My Father Lies
 down Beside Me. Plumly.
The Nurse's Lament.
 Coleridge.
Old Devil. Carter.
On a Noisy Polemic. Burns.
On a Soldier Fallen in the
 Philippines. Moody.
On the Death of a Child.
 Silvera.
On the Night Express to
 Madrid. Dunetz.
On the Way to the Island.
 Ferry.
The One-Eyed Bridegroom.
 Urdang.
The Owl. De la Mare.
Parallel Texts. Kelly.
The Parents-Without-Partners
 Picnic. Schaefer.
Parting. Yeats.
The Passionate Professor.
 Taylor.
Paterson. Williams.
Pete at the Zoo. Brooks.
Phoebus with Admetus.
 Meredith.
The Pilot. Edson.
Places of Nestling Green.
 Hunt.
Poll. Roberson.
The Portrait of a Florentine
 Lady. Reese.
Power Failure. Browne.
The Practice of Absence.
 Friend.
Program Note on Sibelius.
 Babcock.
The Queen. Pitchford.
Queen Mab. Hood.
Race Riot, Tulsa, 1921.
 Olds.
The Rainy Day. Longfellow.
Rearmament. Jeffers.
Repentance. Chapman.
Rest Only in the Grave.
 Mangan.
The Retreat. Read.
Revolution. Housman.
Rhyme for Night. Aiken.
The Rhythm. Creeley.

The Riders Held Back.
 Simpson.
The Ring and the Book.
 Browning.
Rondel: Autumn. Field.
The Rooftop. Gunn.
Running Back. Smith.
The Same Continued. Blunt.
The Scholar and the Cat.
 Anonymous.
The Sea of Death. Hood.
The Seals in Penobscot Bay.
 Hoffman.
The Second Night. Hester,
 Jr.
Sestina in Time of Winter.
 Anderson.
Seventh Son. Roberson.
Shalom. Levertov.
Sheep in Fog. Plath.
The Shepherds. Vaughan.
The Sick Rose. Blake.
Sigh Not for Love. Hay.
Silex Scintillans. Vaughan.
A Sky Pair. Frost.
Sky Patterns. Maino.
The Sleeping. Emanuel.
Somewhere. Creeley.
Somewhere Else. Rankin.
Somewhere Farm. Rotella.
The Song. Roth.
Sonnet of Black Beauty.
 Herbert of Cherbury.
Sonnet: "There, on the
 darkened deathbed, dies the
 brain." Masefield.
Southern Summer. Stuart.
Spring Floods. Orr.
States. Paulin.
Stop. Wilbur.
Storm. Nagy.
The Sun. Turner.
Sunday Evenings. Hollander.
The Sundowner. Neilson.
The Survivor. Graves.
Swedish Angel. Scott.
Talking to the Moon #002.
 Harjo.
The Temptation of Sir
 Gawain. Anonymous.
Then the Ermine. Moore.
This Evening, without
 Blinking. Rogers.
This Is the Violin. Stickney.
Those Makheta Nights.
 Chipasula.
Three Poems for Your Eyes.
 McAlpine.
Threshold. Webb.
Thunder in the Garden.
 Morris.
Ties. Stuart.
To Flood Stage Again.
 Wright.
To Know the Dark. Berry.
To Laddie. Robinson.
Too Dark. McCloskey.
Trippers. Sitwell.
Tulip. Wallace.
The Turkish Bakery.
 Anonymous.
The Turtle-Doves' Nest.
 Anonymous.
Una Bhan. Mac
 Coisdealbhaigh.
The Unknown Eros.
 Patmore.
Vegetables. Field.
Verses Written During a
 Sleepless Night. Pushkin.
Violent Storm. Strand.
Voronezh. Akhmatova.

Wandsworth Common.
 Bromwich.
When My Love Becomes.
 Ono no Komachi.
When the Last Riders. Zach.
The White Skirt. Dobyns.
Why I Like Movies. Jones.
William Blake Sees God.
 McFadden.
Willy to Jinny. Skipsey.
Winter Watch. Marion.
Wisdom. Middleton.
With every note.
 Anonymous.
A Woman. Johnson.
Woman's Song. Wright.
The Woolworth Philodendron.
 Sandy.
Words and Monsters.
 Scannell.
The World Outside.
 Levertov.
Written on an Island off the
 Breton Coast. Venantius
 Fortunatus.
Years Later. Lerner.
The Young Man Who Loved
 the Girl Who Took Care of
 Her Aging Father.
 Kuzma.

Darkest
Arcadia. Sidney.
Dwell with Me, Lovely
 Images. Maynard.
Sonnet: "Lock up, fair lids,
 the treasure of my heart.
 Sidney.
A Walk in March.
 Reynolds.

Darkness
After the Publication of
 Under the Volcano.
 Lowry.
Ah! Give Me, LORD, the
 Single Eye. Toplady.
Alastor. Shelley.
Anactoria (excerpt).
 Swinburne.
Anarchist. Dugdale.
At the Appointed Hour They
 Came. Smith.
At the Sign-Painter's.
 Carter.
Autumn 1940. Auden.
The Bad Kittens.
 Coatsworth.
The Bad Mother. Griffin.
Bavarian Gentians.
 Lawrence.
A Beautifull Mistress.
 Carew.
The Blind Man at the Fair.
 Campbell.
Blue Symphony. Fletcher.
The Burning of the Law.
 Meir of Rothenburg.
By the Sea. Hollander.
Canto XV. Pound.
Carrion Comfort. Hopkins.
Cat on the Porch at Dusk.
 Harriman.
The Cemetery Is. McGaffin.
The Chance. Sze.
Chickens. Hewitt.
Circle of Struggle. Root.
Contemporania: Tenzone.
 Pound.
A Coronet for His Mistress
 Philosophy. Chapman.
Dark Room. Zydek.
Darkness. Byron.
The Day of Denial. Very.

Deaf-and-Dumb School.
 Delius.
The Death of the Moon.
 Wagoner.
Degrees of Shade. Pinkerton.
DNA Lab. Spence.
Downstream. Kinsella.
The Dunciad. Pope.
The Dwelling. Dor.
Dying under a Fall of Stars.
 Shapiro.
Edge. Fitzgerald.
An Etching. Imelda.
Evening Song. Matthias.
The Expanding Universe.
 Nicholson.
Fantasy in Purple. Hughes.
The First Epistle of the First
 Book of Horace Imitated
 (excerpt). Pope.
First Song. Kinnell.
Fish. Satz.
Flying Letters. Gilead.
For All Sorts and Conditions.
 Nicholson.
For Euse, Ayi Kwei & Gwen
 Brooks. Kgositsile.
The Gipsy Girl. Hodgson.
Give Our Conscience Light.
 Carter.
Good Friday: The Madman's
 Song. Masefield.
The Hamlet of A. MacLeish
 (excerpt). MacLeish.
Hero and Leander.
 Chapman.
Hero and Leander. Marlowe.
His Necessary Darkness.
 Sullivan.
How Shall I Build. Blunt.
Hyena. Anonymous
An Hymn on the
 Omnipresence. Byrom.
I am a little church (no great
 cathedral). Cummings.
The Idea of Entropy at
 Maenporth Beach.
 Redgrove.
In Dispraise of the Moon.
 Coleridge.
In Memoriam A.H.H.,
 XXXIV. Tennyson.
In Memoriam A.H.H.,
 LXXIV. Tennyson.
In Praise of Antonioni.
 Holden.
In the Distress upon Me.
 Ainsworth.
In This Deep Darkness.
 Zach.
Isaac and Esau. Drachler.
Isolation. Symons.
Kennedy. Heffernan.
Kind Hearts. Anonymous.
The Lamp. Teasdale.
The Landscape of Love.
 Cole.
Lantern. Polite.
Last Rites. Citino.
Late Moon. Levine.
Life's Lesson. Wilcox.
Lines Written near Richmond,
 upon the Thames, at
 Evening. Wordsworth.
The List. McClure.
A Little Morning Music.
 Schwartz.
The Lord of the East. Chu
 Yuan.
Mahler (excerpt). Williams.
Marching. Rosenberg.
The Mediator. Browning.

Moonrise. Sherman.
Move On, Yiddish Poet. Glatstein.
Multitudes Turn in Darkness. Aiken.
Music of Colours: the Blossom Scattered. Watkins.
My Grandfather Burning Cornfields. Sauls.
My Grandmother. Adams.
My Song. Hall.
Night, Death, Mississippi. Hayden.
Nightfall. Olson.
November Morning. Stein.
O Word of God Incarnate. How.
Oedipus to the Oracle. Trimpi.
Oh, Thou! Who Dry'st the Mourner's Tear. Moore.
Ojisan after the Stroke: Three Notes to Himself. Koyama.
The Old-Marrieds. Brooks.
On Minding One's Own Business. Wright.
On the Threshold. Kraus.
Our Lady's Labor. Duffy.
Out of the Darkness. Armstrong.
Pangur Ban. *Anonymous.*
Paul. Oxenham.
Pirates. Noyes.
Poem for Jacqueline Hill. *Anonymous.*
Political Meeting. Klein.
Pray! Arnold.
A Prayer for Peace. Sill.
Preludes. Aiken.
Presentiment. Dickinson.
Pro Sua Vita. Warren.
Psalm CXXXIX. Pembroke.
Rainy Season Love Song. Hayford.
The Rats. Trakl.
Remember Sabbath Days. Eigner.
Revolt. "Rachel" (Rachel Blumstein).
Riddle #14: A Horn. *Anonymous.*
Rimrock, Where It Is. Carruth.
The River. Leitch.
Riverside Drive, November Fifth. Pollitt.
The Room. Aiken.
Sand Paintings. Corbin.
The Second Life. Morgan.
Shadow of Darkness. Laluah.
Shadows To-Day. Rossetti.
Ships That Pass in the Night. Longfellow.
Singing in the Dark. Wassall.
Sister Zahava. Bruck.
Sligo and Mayo. MacNeice.
Slump. Miller.
Song: "Mother Mother shave me." *Anonymous.*
Sonnet of Black Beauty. Herbert of Cherbury.
Sonnets from the Portuguese, XXII. Browning.
The Stand-To. Day-Lewis.
Stood-Up. Byfield.
Summer Band Concert. Smith.
Sunday Morning. Stevens.

Surfaces. Mayhall.
The Sweet. Ai.
Tablerock. Wally.
Then Came I to the Shoreless Shore of Silence. Aiken.
Three Landscapes (excerpt). Rothenberg.
To an Old Lady. Empson.
To His Father on Praising the Honest Life of the Peasant. E'tesami.
To My Father. Pomeroy.
To S. T. C. on His 179th Birthday, October 12th, 1951. Carpenter.
To the Ivy. Clare.
To the Reverend W.L. Bowles. Coleridge.
The Tundra. Haines.
Twilight. Heine.
Two Songs from a Play. Yeats.
Upon a Black Twist, Rounding the Arm of the Countess of Carlisle. Herrick.
The Valley of the Shadow of Death. Cowper.
Verses at Night. Abse.
Verses Written on Sand. Ravitch.
Vision. Augustini.
Visions. Blake.
The Visit. Mezey.
Voice in the Dark. Strauss.
Wart Hog. Skelton.
What of the Darkness? Le Gallienne.
When Howitzers Began. Carruth.
Why Hast Thou Forsaken Me? Walsh.
Wind and Impulse. Big Eagle.
Winter Rains: Cataluna. Levine.
Without Her. Rossetti.
The Woods. Mahon.
You Tell Me to Sit Quiet. Jordan.
You, the Young Rainbow. Sitwell.
Youth, Day, Old Age, and Night. Whitman.
Zermatt. Hardy.

Darling (s)
At Bedtime. Van Rensselaer.
A Bathing Girl. Jensen.
The Bride. Mitchell.
Callahan. *Anonymous.*
Epigrams. Theocritus.
Epitaph on the Lady Mary Villers. Carew.
Epitaph on the Lady Mary Villiers. Carew.
Granny Crack. Reaney.
I'll Strike You with a Feather. Lloyd.
I Saw a Maiden. *Anonymous.*
Jesu Dulcis. Bernard of Clairvaux
Knightsbridge of Libya. MacLean.
The Leaving of Liverpool. *Anonymous.*
Leezie Lindsay. *Anonymous.*
The Letter. Wheelock.
Moonlight (with music). *Anonymous.*

O My Poor Darling. Watson.
An Old Man's Idyl. Realf.
Old Woman All Skin and Bone. *Anonymous.*
Paradise Lost. Milton.
Patrick Sarsfield, Lord Lucan. *Anonymous.*
Salangadou. *Anonymous.*
Skip to My Lou. *Anonymous.*
The Sporting Cowboy. *Anonymous.*
Thou Hast Diamonds. Heine.
To—. Keats.
What Then Is Love But Mourning. Campion.

Dart (s)
After the fiercest pangs of hot desire. Duke.
Australian Transcripts, X: The Wood-Swallows. Sharp.
Confess We All, Before the Lord. Wilson.
Good Christians. Herrick.
Haskell. Bynner.
The Horn. Reaney.
I Am No Subject unto Fate. *Anonymous.*
Il Pastor Fido. Guarini.
Madrigal: "When in her face mine eyes I fix." Stirling.
Plea to Eros. *Anonymous.*
The Rising Village. Goldsmith.
Saint's Parade. Layzer.
Strephon. Smyth.
To Cupid. Davison.

Dash (ed) (es)
The Answer of Mr. Waller's Painter to His Many New Advisers. *Anonymous.*
The Battle of Stonington on the Seaboard of Connecticut. Freneau.
Heron. Booth.
Love and fortune and my mind... Wyatt.

Date
Easter. Herbert.
Fame. Browning.
It struck me every day. Dickinson.
Lest any doubt that we are glad that they were born Today. Dickinson.
Letter from Pretoria Central Prison. Nortje.
The Lovers. Aiken.
Permission to Speak. Orlen.
The Poplar Field. Cowper.
Sonnets, XIV: "Not from the stars do I my judgement pluck." Shakespeare.

Daughter (s)
Ad Persephonen. Adams.
Addendum to the Ten Commandments. *Anonymous.*
All You Others, Eat. Djurberaui.
Answering Dance. Root.
Avalon. McGaffin.
Award. Durem.
Birthday: Tara Regina. Mosby.
The Blind Beggar of Bednall (Bethnal) Green. *Anonymous.*
Casey's Daughter at the Bat. Graham.

Child Beater. Anthony ("Ai").
The Children March. Riddell.
The Crafty Farmer. *Anonymous.*
The Daughter of Mendoza. Lamar.
The Devil and the Angel. Dobson.
Don Juan. Byron.
Eighteen. Mary Honora.
Epigram: "Do you not wish to renounce the Devil?" Lanusse.
Epigram: The Mother's Choice. *Anonymous.*
Farewell. Clare.
The Farewell. Whittier
Father Poem. Oppenheimer.
For My Daughter. Kees.
For My Father. Field.
For Refugio Talamante. Ochester.
The Ghyrlond of the Blessed Virgin Marie. Jonson.
Gray Goose and Gander. *Anonymous.*
Guided Missiles Experimental Range. Conquest.
Home on the Range, February 1962. Dorn.
In the White Giant's Thigh. Thomas.
In Time of War. Auden.
Is This Africa? Dempster.
Johnie Scot. *Anonymous.*
The Jolly Beggar. *Anonymous.*
Kafoozalum. *Anonymous.*
Laus Veneris. Moulton.
Lineage. Terry.
Little Willie. *Anonymous.*
Marina. Eliot.
Miscarriage. Longley.
The New Arrival. Cable.
Notes for a History of Poetry. Daiches.
The Odyssey. Homer.
An Old Song Resung. Graves.
The Only Daughter. *Anonymous.*
Parable. Bennett.
Paradise Lost. Milton.
The Place of O. Young Bear.
Pocahontas. Thackeray.
Polly Oliver's Rambles. *Anonymous.*
Prayer for the Little Daughter between Death and Burial. Scott.
Queen Guennivar's Round. Hawker.
Restricted. Merriam.
Rhymes for a Modern Nursery: Jack and Jill. Dehn.
The River Don. *Anonymous.*
Rosy Apple, Lemon, or Pear. *Anonymous.*
Scene from a Dream. Hale.
Separate Parties. Stuart.
Snapshots of a Daughter-in-law. Rich.
Song. Sheridan.
Song for Naomi. Layton.
Song to Be Sung by the Father of Infant Female Children. Nash.

Song: Under the Bronze Leaves. Perse.
Sunglasses. Clark.
Three Brethren from Spain. *Anonymous.*
To England. Boker.
Troilus and Cressida. Shakespeare.
Under Which Heading Does All This Information Go? Kurka.
The Vase of Tears. Spender.
Villanelle of a Villaness. Robinson.
The Warrior Maid. Branch.
Wasn't your mother a woman? Honnamma.
What Does It Mean to Be American? Montgomery.
Young Allan. *Anonymous.*

David
By the Dominical Letter, to Find on What Day of the Week... *Anonymous.*
Dead Fly. Chuilleanain.
Domestic Asides; or, Truth in Parentheses. Hood.
Don Juan. Byron.
Killing. Greenberg.
King John and the Bishop. *Anonymous.*
A Model Sermon. *Anonymous.*
Negro Spirituals. Benét.
Paradise Regained. Milton.
Psalm XVIII. Sidney.
Saul. Alterman.
The Sons of Levi. *Anonymous.*
Tears. Reese.
To a Flea in a Glass of Water. Greig.
To Manon. Blunt.
Ut, Re, Mi, Fa, Mi, Re, Ut. *Anonymous.*
"When reckless youth in an unquiet breast." Surrey.

Dawn (ed) (ing) (s)
Abdication of Fergus Mac Roy. Ferguson.
Above the Arno. Swenson.
Adoration of the Disk by King Akhn-Aten and Princess Nefer Neferiu.. Book of the Dead.
Alba. Pound.
Alba Innominata. *Anonymous.*
Apollo and Daphne. Rodgers.
Apology for Bad Dreams. Jeffers.
April. Shorter.
At Dawn. Symons.
Aubade. MacNeice.
Aus Einer Kindheit. Koch.
Aux Carmelites. Hinkson.
The Beauty of the Stars. Ibn Ezra.
A Bed without a Woman. Souster.
Bugle Song of Peace. Clarke.
Cain Shall Not Slay Abel Today on Our Good Ground. Lowry.
The Californian. Hutchinson.
The Catch. Ghiselin.
The Cricket Kept the House. Thomas.
The Culprit Fay. Drake.

The Dark Lord of Savaiki. Campbell.
Dawn. *Anonymous.*
Dawn. Dunbar.
Dawn. Ortmayer.
The Dawn. Yeats.
Dawn and Dark. Gale.
Dawning. Dixon.
The Dawning of the Day. *Anonymous.*
The Day is Coming. Morris.
Daybreak. Phillips.
Diary of a Raccoon. Bennett.
Down the Mississippi. Fletcher.
Dress Me, Dear Mother. Shlonsky.
Ducks down in the Meadow. Stafford.
The Dykes. Kipling.
Early News. Pratt.
East Hampton: The Structure of Sound. Appleman.
Ego Dominus Tuus. Yeats.
Epitaphs of the War, 1914-18. Kipling.
Evensong. Lewis.
The Everlastings. Dubie.
Fainne Gael An Lae. Milligan.
A Farewell. Russell.
Father. Ficke.
The Fiddler. Trapnell.
Fiddler's Green. Roberts.
The First Swallow. Smith.
The Fisherman. Yeats.
The Flock at Evening. Shepard.
For Thomas Hardy. Cooper.
From Burton the Anatomist. Craig.
From My Window. Williams.
The Garibaldi Hymn. Mercantini.
A Gateway to the Sea–St. Andrews. Bruce.
Gethsemane, Illinois. Allwood.
Ghazals. Harrison.
Goodmorning with Light. Ciardi.
The Grotto. Scarfe.
Horses. Wellesley.
The Hour of Peaceful Rest. Tappan.
Hymn to Colour. Meredith.
I Am a Negro. Al-Fituri.
I Am a Victim of Telephone. Ginsberg.
I Dreamed I Saw the Crescent Moon. *Anonymous.*
The Iliad. Homer.
Immortality. Mitchell.
In Memoriam A.H.H., XLIII. Tennyson.
In the Beginning. Fishman.
In the Web. Mayo.
In the Year of Two Thousand. Katz.
Ireland. Ryan.
The Island of Rhum. Ferguson.
Jesus Comes on Clouds Triumphant. Thring.
Joy o' Living. Hall.
The Lady of the Lake. Scott.
Laila Boasting. Akhyaliyya.
The Land of Dreams. Hoyt.
The Leader. Belloc.

Light Breaks Where No Sun Shines. Thomas.
The lips of the one I love are my perpetual pleasure. Hafiz.
Little Songs. Pickthall.
Magpie Song. *Anonymous.*
Man to Man. McClure.
Massada. Lamdan.
The Message of the Bells. Clark.
Metaphysician. Fitzgerald.
The moon upon her fluent route. Dickinson.
Moonlight on Lake Sydenham. MacDonald.
Morning. Davenant.
Morning Prayer. Aua.
Mountain Evenings. Holme.
The Mountain Sat upon the Plain. Dickinson.
My Delight and Thy Delight. Bridges.
A Myth. Kingsley.
Need of an Angel. Souster.
The Neighbors. Garrison.
New Every Morning. *Anonymous.*
Night. Jones.
Night Dive. Johnson.
Night up There. Valentine.
Nightingale Weather. Lang.
Nightingales. Bridges.
Nihon Shoki: Dawn Song. *Anonymous.*
Nimbus. Le Pan.
Nocturne: Lake Huron. Kelly.
Not in Narrow Seas. Curnow.
Now She Is Like the White Tree-Rose. Day-Lewis.
La Nuit Blanche. Kipling.
O Christ, Thou Art within Me Like a Sea. Pierce.
Pinay. Cerenio.
Pioneers. Clark.
Poem for Easter. Lee.
Poem for Jacqueline Hill. *Anonymous.*
A Prayer for Peace. Sill.
R-E-M-O-R-S-E. Ade.
Remnant Ghosts at Dawn. La Grone.
Resurgam. Burt.
The Roc. Eberhart.
The Room above the White Rose. Stroud.
Saturday Night. Hughes.
The Schreckhorn. Hardy.
Second Best. Brooke.
Semantic. Conquest.
Shadow-Bride. Tolkien.
Shadows of Sails. Anderson.
Shepherd, Shepherd, Hark. Theresa of Avila.
Sing-Song: Is the Moon Tired? Rossetti.
Snake Hill. Parini.
Song: "Come at dawn, good friend." *Anonymous.*
Sonnet XXIII: "What good is it to me if long ago." Labe.
Sonnet to Negro Soldiers. Cotter, Jr.
Sonnets. Tuckerman.
Spirit of Life, in This New Dawn. Marlatt.
The Stampede. Brininstool.
Star Song. Johnson.
The Stars Are Lit. Bialik.

Sunrise Trumpets. Auslander.
The Testament of John Davidson: The Last Journey. Davidson.
There is a morn by men unseen. Dickinson.
Those Betrayed at Dawn. Wygodski.
To an Ambitious Friend. Horace.
To the Bridegroom. Halevi.
To the (Supposed) Patron. Hill.
The Trick Is Consciousness. Allen.
Troubadour Alba. *Anonymous.*
Twinkling Gown. Johnson.
Two Campers in Cloud Country. Plath.
Two Poems Based on Fact. Lepkowski.
Vanguardia. Esteves.
Walking the Wilderness. Stafford.
The Wars of the Roses. Anonymous.
We Dressed Each Other. Eifuku.
We Woke Together. Brennan.
What Do I Care for Morning. Johnson.
When All Is Done. Dunbar.
When Dawn Comes to the City: New York. McKay.
Woman at the Piano. Zaturenska.
Work. Pushkin.
Worship. Jones, Jr.
You Also, Gaius Valerius Catullus. MacLeish.
You Tell Me to Sit Quiet. Jordan.

Day (s)
Absence. Knies.
Adios. Babcock.
Admonition to a Traveller. Wordsworth.
Africa Speaks. Dei-Anang.
After a Journey. Hardy.
After Sunset. Allingham.
Alas, My God. Shepherd.
America Prays. Field.
Anarchist. Dugdale.
Ancestor. Baca.
The Angel in the House. Patmore.
Another Stone Poem. Dacey.
The Answer. Jeffers.
Apple Hell. Van Doren.
An April Day. Cotter.
April Showers. Stephens.
Arachne. Cooke.
Archangel. Robinson.
Armistice. Daryush.
As Thy Days. Tullar.
At last, to be identified! Dickinson.
At Parting. Swinburne.
At Set of Sun. Eliot.
The Avenue Bearing the Initial of Christ into the New World. Kinnell.
Back through the Looking Glass to This Side. Ciardi.
A Ballad of a Mine. Skelton.
De Band o' Gideon. *Anonymous.*
The Battle of Trenton. *Anonymous.*

Be Careful. *Anonymous.*
A Beautifull Mistress.
   Carew.
Bed in Summer. Stevenson.
Begin the Day with God.
   Anonymous.
The Belfry. Binyon.
Between Life and Death.
   Gottlieb.
The Bindweed. De la Mare.
Birthday. Kavanagh.
Birthday. Lawrence.
A Bit of the Book. Sangster.
Bits of Straw. Clare.
Blasting from Heaven.
   Levine.
Blurry Cow. Twichell.
Bombardment. Lawrence.
A Bon Mot. *Anonymous.*
The Boomerang. Nichols.
The Boyne Walk. Higgins.
Boys and Sport. Solon.
The Braes o' Gleniffer.
   Tannahill.
Bread. "Mistral.
Break, Break, Break.
   Tennyson.
Brow of Nephin.
   Anonymous.
Burial of a Fisherman in
   Hydra. Schulman.
But Give Me Holly, Bold and
   Jolly. Rossetti.
By Night. Francis.
Bye Baby Bother. Smith.
The Cachalot. Pratt.
The Californian.
   Hutchinson.
Camel. Akhyaliyya.
Canzone: He Beseeches Death
   for the Life of Beatrice.
   Dante Alighieri.
The Castle of Indolence.
   Thomson.
The Celestial Passion.
   Gilder.
The Celtic Cross. McGee.
A Certain Peace. Giovanni.
Chamber Music. Joyce.
Chapter Heading.
   Hemingway.
A Child. Gilder.
Child of Blue. Hogan.
Childhood. More.
Chill of the Eve. Stephens.
Christmas Eve. Day Lewis.
The Cicada. Green.
Claustrophobia. O Riordain.
Clock-a-clay. Clare.
Columbia's Agony. Newell.
Columbus. Lowell.
Comets and Princes.
   Johnson.
The Coming of Spring.
   Perry.
The Coracle Fishers.
   Bloomfield.
A Corn-Song. Dunbar.
The Cottager to Her Infant.
   Wordsworth.
Counsel. Davis.
The Creditor. MacNeice.
The Cry of a Dreamer.
   O'Reilly.
Daniel Defoe. Landor.
Daughters of War.
   Rosenberg.
Dawn-Angels. Robinson.
Dawn in Inishtrahull.
   O'Sullivan.
Dawn Patrol: Chicago.
   Durham.

The Dawning. Vaughan.
The Dawning of the Day.
   Anonymous.
Day and Night. Alexander.
The Day is Coming. Morris.
The Day You Are Born.
   Song.
Days of the Leaders, 1925:
   The Deaf. Lamprey.
Deirdre's Song at Sunrise.
   Maura.
Dejection. Bridges.
Derry. Deane.
A Description of an Author's
   Bedchamber. Goldsmith.
Dieppe, II: On the Beach.
   Symons.
The Dowie Dens of Yarrow.
   Anonymous.
Dream Girl. Sandburg.
The Dream of Gerontius.
   Newman.
Dull Is My Verse. Landor.
Dust of Snow. Frost.
The Edge of the World.
   Youngs.
Effie. Brown.
Elegies. Ovid (Publius
   Ovidius Naso).
Elegy. St. John.
Elegy Written on a
   Frontporch. Shapiro.
The End which Comes.
   Arnold.
Epigram: "This is my curse,
   Pompous, I pray."
   Cunningham.
Epistle to Richard Boyle, Earl
   of Burlington (excerpt).
   Pope.
An Epitaph on His
   Grandfather. Shipman.
An Escape. Abu Nuwas.
Eternity. Herrick.
Expectant Mother. Shuttle.
The Face of the Waters.
   Fitzgerald.
The Fairest of Her Days.
   Anonymous.
The Faithful Shepherdess.
   Fletcher.
Fall, Leaves, Fall. Bronte.
False Nancy. *Anonymous.*
Farewell. Symonds.
Farm Implements and
   Rutabagas in a Landscape.
   Ashbery.
Fat Tuesday. Di Piero.
Father Grumble.
   Anonymous.
Father in Heaven. Petrarch
   (Francesco Petrarca).
The Fathers. Muir.
February. Schuyler.
The Female Phaeton. Prior.
Fire, the Rope... Tikhonov.
The First and the Last.
   Bonar.
First Light. Kinsella.
The First Olympionique to
   Hiero of Syracuse. Pindar.
The Florist Rose. Graves.
For Sleep, or Death. Pitter.
For the Earth God.
   Anonymous.
The Forsaken Girl. Jarrell.
The Fossils. Kinnell.
The Fountain. Smith.
Four O'Clock Flower Blues.
   Anonymous.
Four Seasons of the Year:
   Spring. Bradstreet.

Fragment of an Ode to Maia.
   Keats.
Friends. Johnson.
From Soil Somehow the
   Poet's Word. Leslie.
From the House of Yemanja.
   Lorde.
The Fundamental Project of
   Technology. Kinnell.
The Garden. Parkwood.
The Garret. Thackeray.
Gascoigne's Good Morrow.
   Gascoigne.
Getting Up Ahead of
   Someone (Sun). O'Hara.
Glad Day. Robertson.
Glad Day. Untermeyer.
The Glory. Thomas.
God Incarnate. Williams.
God of Abraham, of Isaac,
   and of Jacob. *Anonymous.*
God's Language. Fainlight.
A Good Start. Moffi.
Grace at Evening. Guest.
The Grandson. Scully.
Grief. Berry.
Guy Mannering. Chapt. 27:
   Wasted, Weary, Wherefore
   Stay. Scott.
Haiku: "That early riser."
   Phillips.
Harvest. Cortissoz.
Hast Thou Heard It, O My
   Brother. Williams.
Having No Ear. Davie.
Hawk's Eyes. Winters.
Health Food. *Anonymous.*
Hear the Voice of the Bard!
   Blake.
The Heart. Ignatow.
Heart of Light. Campbell.
The Hemorrhage. Kunitz.
His Parting from Her.
   Donne.
Honey-Mead. *Anonymous.*
Hope. O'Connor.
Hope Overtaken. Rossetti.
The House Beautiful.
   Stevenson.
Hymn. Holmes.
Hymn. Peabody.
I Am Christmas.
   Anonymous.
I don't have the energy...
   Gold.
I Lived in a Town.
   Anonymous.
Ice Cold. O Riordain.
The Idle Life I Lead.
   Bridges.
If Bees Stay at Home.
   Anonymous.
If fancy would favor. Wyatt.
If You Had Known. Hardy.
If You Were Here. Marston.
The Iliad. Homer.
Immortal Israel. Halevi.
The Importance of Poetry; or,
   the Coming Forth from
   Eternity into Time.
   Plutzik.
In His Utter Wretchedness.
   Audelay.
In Memoriam A.H.H., XCV.
   Tennyson.
In Old Tucson. Conrard.
In Scorching Time. Stevens.
In the Orchard. Swinburne.
The Insomniac Sleeps Well for
   Once and. Carruth.
Interim. Delany.

Irish-American Dignitary.
   Clarke.
The Island and the Cattle.
   Moore.
The Isle of Portland.
   Housman.
Israel's Duration. Halevi.
The Ivory Bed. Scott.
Jamaican Bus Ride.
   Tessimond.
Jesus Comes on Clouds
   Triumphant. Thring.
Judith of Minnewaulken:
   Judith Remembers.
   Anderson.
A June Day. Teasdale.
Katie May. Hopkins.
Kennedy. Heffernan.
The Kilkenny Boy.
   Shanahan.
Kind Are Her Answers.
   Campion.
The Kingdom of God. Rab.
The Kumulipo: The Dawn of
   Day. *Anonymous.*
Lancelot. Bontemps.
Landscape as Metal and
   Flowers. Scott.
Landscape with Leaves and
   Figure. Broumas.
The Last Moriori.
   Smithyman.
Less Lonely. Kreymborg.
Let me see you. Mira Bai
   [(or Mirabai)].
The Life of.... Weiss.
"Like as the Lark." Parsons
LMFBR. Snyder.
Longing. Arnold.
The Look. Teasdale.
Lord, I Know Thy Grace Is
   Nigh Me. Ganse.
The Lordly and Isolate Satyrs.
   Olson.
Love in Particular. Brinnin.
Love Is Enough. Morris.
Love on the Mountain.
   Boyd.
Love's Rosary. Noyes.
Love Song. Be'er.
Love Unknown. Crossman.
Lucasia, Rosania and Orinda
   Parting at a Fountain, July
   1663. Philips.
The Luck of Edenhall.
   Longfellow.
Lullaby of an Infant Chief.
   Scott.
The Magnet. Stone.
Making It Simple December
   8, 1969. McElroy.
The Man of Kerioth (excerpt).
   Norwood.
Many Things Thou Hast
   Given Me, Dear Heart.
   Rollins.
Le Marais du Cygne.
   Whittier.
Marmion. Scott.
The Marrowbone Itch.
   Anonymous.
May. Wade.
May the Ambitious Ever
   Find. Sackville.
Measure of Success.
   Anonymous.
Medieval Mirth. *Anonymous.*
Medieval Norman Songs.
   Anonymous.
Meditations for August 1,
   1666. Pain.

Meditations for July 19, 1666. Pain.
Melons. Dodge.
Memorial Day: A Collaboration. Berrigan.
Milton by Firelight. Snyder.
Mister Charlie. Hopkins.
Morituri Salutamus. Longfellow.
Morning Hymn. Wesley.
Morning in Camp. Bashford.
Mother of Men. Southwold.
The Mountain Sat upon the Plain. Dickinson.
Mrs. Macintosh. Hall.
Musgrove. *Anonymous.*
My Delight and Thy Delight. Bridges.
My Heart Leaps Up. Wordsworth.
My Horses. Jaszi.
My New World. Browne.
My Sins in Their Completeness. O Brolchain.
My Song Is Love Unknown. Crossman.
My Sons. Loewinsohn.
Nature, That Washed Her Hands in Milk. Ralegh.
New World. Ghiselin.
The Newest Banana Plant Leaf. Wendt.
The News Stand. Berrigan.
A Nickle Bet. Knight.
Night. Lovelace.
Night and Day. Porter.
A Night-Piece on Death. Parnell.
Nightingales. Bridges.
No Furlough. Stepanchev.
Nocturnal Heart. Kegels.
Nocturnal Thoughts. Huss.
Northfield. *Anonymous.*
Note from an Intimate Diary. Litvinoff.
Notes on a Life to Be Lived. Warren.
Nuptial Song. De Tabley.
Nuts and Bolts Poem for Mr. MacAdams, Sr. Fraser.
O Lord, Save We Beseech Thee. *Anonymous.*
O Merry Hae I Been Teethin' a Heckle. Burns.
O Tender under Her Right Breast. Barker.
Odes. Horace.
The Odyssey. Homer.
Oft, in the Stilly Night. Moore.
Old and New Art. Rossetti.
Old Man in the Wood. *Anonymous.*
The Old Man Who Lived in the Woods. Anonymous.
Old Ships. Ginsberg.
On an Engraving by Casserius. Hope.
On Seeing a Poet of the First World War on the Station at Abbeville. Causley.
On Virtue. Wheatley.
One Day More. *Anonymous.*
Orlo's Valediction. White.
Our share of night to bear. Dickinson.
Out of the Rolling Ocean the Crowd. Whitman.
Oxford Nights. Johnson.
Pangur Ban. *Anonymous.*
Paradise Lost. Milton.

Paradisi Gloria. Parsons
Parting at Dawn. *Anonymous.*
The Passionate Reader to His Poet. Le Gallienne.
A Patch of Old Snow. Frost.
Personal Talk. Wordsworth.
Poem. Dickinson.
Poem: "Entombed in my heart." Dodson.
A Poem, upon the Caelestial Embassy Perform'd by Angels... Steere.
Poems. Drummond.
The Poet's Voice. Blake.
Prayer at Dawn. Poteat.
Prime. Auden.
The Princess. Tennyson.
Private Devotion. Brown.
Privilege. Pizarnik.
Prospecting. Ammons.
Psalm CXXXIX. Pembroke.
The Rain's Already With Us. Quasimodo.
The Rainy Day. Longfellow.
Raking Leaves. Pack.
Recognition. Perry.
A Refusal. Googe.
Remember Thy Creator Now. Long.
Residence in France: The Prelude. Wordsworth.
Resurrection. Donne.
Retro me, Sathana! Rossetti.
A Rich Old Miser. *Anonymous.*
Rising in the Morning. Rhodes.
Riverton. Wilson.
Roisin Dubh. MacWard.
The Rookery at Sunrise. Sharp.
Rooks. Sorley.
The Room. Soutar.
Roses on the Breakfast Table. Lawrence.
A Sabbath of Rest. Luria.
Sad Story. Day.
Saint Stephen and King Herod. *Anonymous.*
Samson Agonistes. Milton.
Saw You My True Love John? *Anonymous.*
The Sea Marke. Smith.
Seascape. Young.
See a Pin and Pick It Up. *Anonymous.*
Self-Pity Is a Kind of Lying, Too. Schuylr.
Sent from the Capital to Her Elder Daughter. Otomo of Sakanone [(or Sakanoe)].
A Serenade. Pinkney.
Sextus Propertius: Turning Aside from Battles. Pound.
The Shepherd's Pipe: Dawn of Day. Browne.
The Shepherds. Vaughan.
A Silent Wood. Siddal.
Silex Scintillans. Vaughan.
Sinner Man. *Anonymous.*
The Sleepers. Whitman.
So Fly by Night. Osborne.
Some Are Born. Smith.
Somewhere. Arnold.
A Song: "If Wine and Musick have the Pow'r." Prior.
Song: "Love laid his sleepless head." Swinburne.
Song of a Prison Guard. Mphande.

Song of the Dew. *Anonymous.*
Song of the Highest Tower. Rimbaud.
Song of the Leadville Mine Boss. Cameron.
Song of the Little Villages. Dollard.
Song: "When, dearest, I but think of". Felltham.
Songs of Seven. Ingelow.
Sonnet, XIII: "As long as I continue weeping." Labé.
Sonnet XIV. Tuckerman.
Sonnet XXXVII. Alabaster.
Sonnet: England in 1819. Shelley.
Sonnets, XLIII: "When most I wink, then do mine eyes best see." Shakespeare.
Sonnets, CVI: "When in the chronicle of wasted time." Shakespeare.
Sonnets after the Italian. Gilder.
Sonnets of the Months. San Geminiano.
The Sound of Night. Kumin.
The Specter. Hardt.
Spirit from Whom Our Lives Proceed. Robbins.
Spring Flowers from Ireland. McCarthy.
Spring Song. Heppenstall.
The Story of Rimini. Hunt.
The Stranded Whales. Dutton.
Suburban Lovers. Dawe.
Summer. Rossetti.
A Summer Night in the Beehive. Turner.
The Sun's Golden Bowl. Mimnermus.
Sunday. Miles.
Sunset Song. *Anonymous.*
Swan Song. Ranchan.
Take down the Fiddle, Karl! Neilson.
The Teacher's Dream. Venable.
That Corner. Salkeld.
That Did in Luve So Lively Write. Adams.
There Is a Love. Cleveland.
Things That Happen. Stafford.
This above All Is Precious and Remarkable. Wain.
Thou Art the Sky. Tagore.
Thou Bounteous Giver of the Light. Hilary of Arles.
Thysia. Luce.
Time Lags Abed. Cresswell.
Time of Day. Rodman.
To a Butterfly. Wordsworth.
To A Child. Morley.
To a Negro Boy Graduating. Maleska.
To an Ambitious Friend. Horace.
To Arms. Benjamin.
To His Coy Mistress (parody). Bird.
To My Sister. Wordsworth.
To the Muse. Whalen.
Today Is Armistice, a Holiday. Schwartz.
Tomorrow. Coates.
Trifling Women. *Anonymous.*

The True Lover's Farewell. *Anonymous.*
Turn on Your Side and Bear the Day to Me. Barker.
The Turtle-Dove. *Anonymous.*
The Twa Dogs. Burns.
Twelfth Night. Shakespeare.
Twilight. Lawrence.
Two at a Fireside. Markham.
Two Married. Frazee-Bower.
The Two Spirits. Shelley.
An Unborn Child. Mahon.
The Unsung Heroes. Dunbar.
Up at a Villa–Down in the City. Browning.
Upon Visiting His Lady by Moonlight. "W."
The Useful Plow. *Anonymous.*
The Valley of Men. Greenberg.
Venetian Air. Moore.
Vergier. Pound.
Vesperal. Dowson.
The Vestal. Pope.
Vigil. Henley.
Villanelle of the Poet's Road. Dowson.
Vision. Merwin.
Vive la Canadienne. *Anonymous.*
Voice of the Western Wind. Stedman.
Voices from Things Growing in a Churchyard. Hardy.
The Wakening. *Anonymous.*
Waking from Sleep. Bly.
The Wandering Knight's Song. Lockhart.
War in Chang-An City. Wang Tsan.
The Wayside Station. Muir.
We Are Such Stuff As Dreams... Petronius.
We Would See Jesus. *Anonymous.*
The Wearin' o' the Green. *Anonymous.*
A Week of Doodle. Whittemore.
Weep Not To-Day. Bridges.
West-Running Brook. Frost.
What Profit? Di Roma.
When None Shall Rail. Lewis.
Where I Am. Dos Santos.
While the Days Are Going By. Cooper.
Who Be Kind To. Ginsberg.
Wilderness Theme. Mudie.
Winter Garden. Gascoyne.
Winter Wakens All My Care. *Anonymous.*
Winter with the Gulf Stream. Hopkins.
The Witch-Bride. Allingham.
With every note. *Anonymous.*
Woman's Song. Wright.
The Wonderful Old Man. *Anonymous.*
Wood-Song. Lee-Hamilton.
The Yucca Moth. Ammons.
Zip Coon. *Anonymous.*

Daybreak
The Bells of San Blas. Longfellow.
Cockcrow. Wilkins.

Daybreak

Daybreak. Kinnell.
Daybreak in Alabama.
  Hughes.
Noon Glare. Brennan.
O Rose, O Rainbow. Moore.

Daylight

As I Lay Quiet. Widdemer.
Bending the Bow. Duncan.
The Chickens Are A-Crowing.
  Anonymous.
Compline. Greger.
Dark Rosaleen, IX. Wright.
The Death of a Toad.
  Wilbur.
Greenland Whale Fishery.
  Anonymous.
In Distress. Wagoner.
Nights in the Gardens of Port
  of Spain. Walcott.
Paradise. Bloch.
A Singer Asleep. Hardy.
The Sonnet. Symonds.
Waking, the Love Poem Sighs.
  Hall.
The Wanderer. Vigee.
World of Darkness. Chatain.

Daytime

Star & Garter Theater.
  Schmitz.
Working Man Blues. Estes.

Daze

Dancing-Girl's Song.
  Kshetrayya.
I Don't Care. Lenox.

Dazzle (d)

Dazzle. Roberts.
Leaving Barra. MacNeice.
Sun Set. Aridjis.
Tell All the Truth but Tell It
  Slant. Dickinson.
To Rupert Brooke. Gibson.

Dead

25 Spontaneous Lines
  Greeting the World.
  Tyack.
Abraham. Bogin.
Act of Faith. Trias.
Advice. Stone.
After Some Day of Decision.
  Whittemore.
Agamemnon's Tomb.
  Sitwell.
Ahmad. Bensel.
Aideen's Grave. Ferguson.
Ajax. Sophocles.
Alba. Beckett.
"All in green went my love
  riding". Cummings.
All Sung. Le Gallienne.
All the Hills and Vales Along.
  Sorley.
"All Things Must Have an
  End; the World Itself."
  Longfellow.
Altarwise by Owl-Light.
  Thomas.
Anchises. Salkeld.
And. Creeley.
And the Winner Is. Forker.
And There shall Be No More
  Death (excerpt). Gilbert.
The Angel in the House.
  Patmore.
Another Song. Ross.
Anticipation. De Tabley.
Apple Hell. Van Doren.
Approaching Washington
  Heights. Reiss.
Arbor Vitae. Patmore.
The Archaeology of Love.
  Murphy.
Archetypes. Bowers.

Armistice Day.
  Montgomery.
"As you came from the holy
  land of Walsingham."
  Ralegh.
Aspiration. Drennan.
The Astronomers of Mont
  Blanc. Bowers.
At Ease. De La Mare.
At Twilight. Van Rensselaer.
An Autumn Day. MacLean.
Autumn Day. Rilke.
Autumn Song. Verlaine.
Awakening. Bly.
Away. Riley.
Bachelor Hall. Field.
Baja. Stern.
Balance. Schultz.
A Ballad. Sedley.
The Ballad of the Foxhunter.
  Yeats.
Ballade of the Old-Time
  Engine. Vines.
Ballata: He Reveals, in a
  Dialogue, His Increasing
  Love for Mandetta.
  Cavalcanti.
The Baron's Last Banquet.
  Greene.
Bath. Kirstein.
Batson. *Anonymous.*
Battle: Hit. Gibson.
Becalmed. Blight.
The Bees of Middleton
  Manor. Probyn.
The Beggar. Mitchell.
Beyond Memory. De Boully.
Birds in Snow. Doolittle.
Black Bart, P08. Bierce.
The Blue Closet. Morris.
Bobby Campbell.
  Anonymous.
The Bodies of Men and
  Women Engirth Me.
  Whitman.
La Boheme. Gallup.
The Botanist's Vision.
  Dobell.
Boulder Dam. Sarton.
Bracken Hills in Autumn.
  ""MacDiarmid.
Break, Break, Break.
  Tennyson.
The Bride. Lawrence.
Bumi. Jones.
The Burial of the Dane.
  Brownell.
The Burning of the Birds.
  Kaufman.
Caelica, LVII. Greville.
Caesar. Merwin.
Canned Heat Blues.
  Johnson.
Canopic Jar. Lesser.
Canzone: His Lament for
  Selvaggia. Cino da Pistoia.
The Carillon. Castro de
  Murguia.
Carol: "Mary laid her Child
  among." Nicholson.
Casey Jones (G vers.).
  Anonymous.
Cave. Pacheco.
Cedar Mountain. Fields.
The Celestial Surgeon.
  Stevenson.
Celia Singing. Stanley.
The Centenarian's Story.
  Whitman.
The Centipede. Herbert.
Chair, Dog, and Clock.
  Corke.

The Challenge. Longfellow.
Charlemagne. Longfellow.
Children's Crusade, 1939.
  Brecht.
Chopping Wood. Smith.
Christina. MacNeice.
Christmas Eve Service at
  Midnight at St. Michael's.
  Bly.
Christmas Rede. Barlow.
The Church Today. Watson.
The City Dead-House.
  Whitman.
Cleitagoras. Leonidas.
Clementine. *Anonymous.*
Cold Water. Hall.
Come on Home. Scott.
The Coming. Delius.
Complaint on the Oblivion of
  the Dead. Laforgue.
The Computation. Donne.
Comrades. Woodberry.
The Container. Corman.
Contemporary. Flexner.
Convoy. Smith.
The Corn Husker. Johnson.
Coyote's Daylight Trip.
  Allen.
The Cranes of Ibycus.
  Lazarus.
Crash at Leithfield. Curnow.
Crawl into Bed. Prettyman.
Crazed Man in Concentration
  Camp. Gergely.
Crazy Jane and Jack the
  Journeyman. Yeats.
The Cross. Tate.
Crossing the Atlantic.
  Sexton.
The Crucifix. Lamartine.
The Cuckoo. Thomas.
The Cup. Wright.
Curiosity. Reid.
Custer's Last Fierce Charge.
  Anonymous.
Cwmrhydyceirw Elegiacs.
  Watkins.
The Cyclamen. Bates.
Dance of Death. Flaccus.
The Dancing Faun. Rogers.
Dancing Partners. Child.
Dark Girl. Bontemps.
Dark Thoughts Are My
  Companions.
  Cunningham.
Darling Cora. *Anonymous.*
Dawn on the East Coast.
  Lewis.
Daybreak. Cornford.
The Dead. Morton.
The Dead Butterfly.
  Levertov.
The Dead Child. Barlow.
Dead Dog. Scannell.
The Dead Feast of the Kol-
  Folk. Whittier.
The Dead Horse. Meireles.
The Dead Man Dragged from
  the Sea. Gardner.
Dead Man's Dump.
  Rosenberg.
Dead Musicians. Sassoon.
The Dead Pan. Browning.
The Dead Poet. Douglas.
The Dead Solomon. Dorgan.
Death. Byatt.
Death-Doomed. Carleton.
Death of a Friend. Murray.
The Death of Ailill.
  Ledwidge.
The Death of Ben Hall.
  Ogilvie.

The Death of Friends. Levi.
Death of the Cat. Serraillier.
Death's Jest Book. Beddoes.
Deborah as Scion. Dickey.
December among the
  Vanished. Merwin.
Delivering Children.
  Holbrook.
Demolition. Raisor.
Depression. "Field.
The Devil's Dictionary: Lead.
  Bierce.
Diana. Constable.
Diffugere Nives, 1917.
  Baring.
Ding Dong Dollar.
  Henderson.
Dirge for Ashby. Preston.
Dirge for Small Wilddeath.
  Moffett.
Dirge of the Munster Forest
  1581. Lawless.
The Distant Runners. Van
  Doren.
Divina Commedia. Dante
  Alighieri.
The Diviner. Heaney.
Divinities. Merwin.
Do It Now. Braley.
Dog and Tiger. Greenberg.
The Doll. Orr.
The Dream. Bishop.
Dream Songs. Berryman.
The Dug-Out. Sassoon.
Dumb Dick. Fiedler.
A Dying Tiger—Moaned for
  Drink. Dickinson.
Earl Brand (A vers.).
  Anonymous.
The Earth Asks and Receives
  Rain. Haring.
The Edge. Bowen.
Edmonton, Thy Cemetery...
  Smith.
The Elder Edda: The First
  Lay of Gudrun.
  Anonymous.
An Electric Sign Goes Dark.
  Sandburg.
Elegy for Helen Trent.
  Leary.
Elegy on the Eve. Barker.
Elegy while Pruning Roses.
  Wagoner.
Elephants May Parade Before
  Your House. *Anonymous.*
Emblems. Quarles.
The Epic of Gilgamesh
  (excerpt). *Anonymous.*
Epigram on Prince Frederick.
  Anonymous.
Epigram: "Our youth was
  happy: why repine."
  Landor.
Epigrams in Distich, I: The
  Fine Lady Reform'd.
  Anonymous.
Epitaph. Abercrombie.
Epitaph. Comfort.
Epitaph. Herbert of
  Cherbury.
Epitaph. Southey.
Epitaph: "Beneath this smooth
  stone by the bone of his
  bone." *Anonymous.*
Epitaph. Caecil. Boulstr.
  Herbert of Cherbury.
Epitaph: "Here lies my poor
  wife, without bed or
  blanket." *Anonymous.*

Epitaph: "Here lies the body of Andrew Gear." *Anonymous.*
An Epitaph on Doctor Donne, Deane of Pauls. Corbett.
Epitaph on Francis Atterbury, Bishop of Rochester. Prior.
Epitaph: "Two sweeter babes you nare did see." *Anonymous.*
An Epitaph Upon–. Marvell.
Epithalamium. Sitwell.
Erected to the Memory of Mr. Jonathan Gill, Esq. *Anonymous.*
Eurydice. Doolittle.
Evangeline. Longfellow.
An Evening. Allingham.
Evening of the Rose. Rudolf.
Evil Days. Pasternak.
Exile. Beecham.
Exile of the Sons of Uisliu (excerpt). *Anonymous.*
Experience. O'Reilly.
The Expiration. Donne.
Eyes of Men Running, Falling, Screaming. *Anonymous.*
The Face Upon the Floor. D'Arcy.
The Fair Beauty Bride. *Anonymous.*
The Fallen Tree. Maybin.
The Fallen Tree. Young.
The Farewell. *Anonymous.*
A Farewell to English (excerpt). Hartnett.
Farewell Voyaging World! Aiken.
The Fate of Narcissus. Warner.
Father. Wheelwright.
The Fear. Gibson.
The Female Parricide. *Anonymous.*
Festubert: The Old German Line. Blunden.
Finnegan's Wake. *Anonymous.*
Flannan Isle. Gibson.
Flight. Cawein.
A Flower. Nangolo.
Foal. Watkins.
For a War Memorial. Chesterton.
For the Candle Light. Grimke.
For the Eating of Swine. Jones.
Forecasting the Economy. Morin.
Forever Dead. Sappho.
A Forsaken Garden. Swinburne.
The Fortune Teller. Holmes.
The Four. Grigson.
From Generation to Generation. Newbolt.
Gangrene. Levine.
The Garden of God. Russell.
Gaspara Stampa. Benet.
The Gauls Sacrifice. Doughty.
Ghazals. Harrison.
The Glory of the Day Was in Her Face. Johnson.
Good People. Stanton.
Goodbye to Regal. Huws.
Grandmother Poems. Chin.
The Grave. Jones.

Graves in Queens. Hugo.
Gravestones. Watkins.
The Gray Swan. Cary.
The Guardians. Hill.
A Guerrilla Handbook. Jones.
Guild's Signal. Harte.
The Gulf. Walcott.
Hansel and Gretel Return. Ray.
Hard Frost. Young.
Harvest. Sitwell.
Has Been. Worsley.
Hasbrouck and the Rose. Putnam.
Hayseed (with music). *Anonymous.*
He and She. Arnold.
He Did Not Know. Kemp.
The Head-Stone. Barnes.
The Heart to Carry On. Warr.
The Heavenly Tree Grows Downward. Lansing.
Helen. "Coolidge.
Hens. Nowlan.
Here Is a Song. Peck.
His Lady's Tomb. Ronsard.
Ho, Brother Teig. *Anonymous.*
Hopi Woman. Spencer.
Hot Afternoons Have Been in West 15th Street. Blackburn.
The Hour-Glass. Herrick.
House-Mates. Gellert.
The House of Dust: Portrait of One Dead. Aiken.
The House of Night (excerpt). Freneau.
How Did You Die? Cooke.
Hugh Selwyn Mauberley, IV. Pound.
Hurrying away from the Earth. Bly.
The Hyaenas. Kipling.
A Hymn to the Sea. Stoddard.
I don't sleep. Mira Bai [(or Mirabai)].
I Doubt a Lovely Thing Is Dead. Tracy.
I Know Not Why, but All This Weary Day. Timrod.
I Who Had Been Afraid. Maris Stella.
I Will Write. Graves.
The Ice-Floes. Pratt.
The Imaginative Life. Hill.
The Immortality of Verse. Horace.
In a Cafe. Brautigan.
In a Churchyard. Wilbur.
In After Days. Cameron.
In health and ease am I. Davison.
In India. Shapiro.
In Jerusalem Are Women. Sivan.
In Memory of a Friend. Barker.
In Memory of "Barry Cornwall." Swinburne.
In Memory of Basil, Marquess of Dufferin and Ava. Betjeman.
In Memory of My Uncle Timothy. Reid.
In the Land Where We Were Dreaming. Lucas.
In the Morgue. Zangwill.

In the Mountain Tent. Dickey.
In Time of Need. Hinkson.
Incident of the French Camp. Browning.
Incompatibility. De Vere.
Investigation. Vinograd.
The Invisible King. Goethe.
An Irish Lamentation. Goethe.
The Iron Lung. Plumly.
The Island. Jennett.
An Italian Chest. Seiffert.
Jarama Valley. *Anonymous.*
The Jester in the Trench. Gellert.
The Jews. Jastrun.
Jews at Haifa. Jarrell.
John Endicott: Prologue. Longfellow.
John Kinsella's Lament for Mrs. Mary Moore. Yeats.
Johnny Armstrong. *Anonymous.*
Journal. Ciardi.
Judgment. Benet.
"The killers that run...'. Cohen.
Kindness during Life. *Anonymous.*
Knowledge of Age. Avison.
Lament. Livesay.
The Land. Burt.
Last Antiphon: To Mary. Donohue.
Last Child. Kennedy.
The Last Fierce Charge. *Anonymous.*
Last Snow. Young.
Late Wisdom. Crabbe.
Leafless Trees, Chickahominy Swamp. Smith.
The Leaves Come Again. Stanley.
Leaving Buffalo. Martin.
Let the Dead Depart in Peace. *Anonymous.*
The Liar. *Anonymous.*
The Liar. Hayden.
Like Loving Chekhov. Levertov.
Limerick: "A pointless old miser named Quince." Ciardi.
Limerick: "There was a young soldier called Edser." Milligan.
Limerick: "There was an Archdeacon who said." *Anonymous.*
The Linen Workers. Longley.
Lines for an Interment. MacLeish.
Lines Written after a Battle. *Anonymous.*
Lines Written on Hearing the News of the Death of Napoleon. Shelley.
Litany of the Rooms of the Dead. Werfel.
Little Big Horn. McGaffey.
Little Boys of Texas. Coffin.
Little General Monk. *Anonymous.*
The Living Dog and the Dead Lion. Moore.
The Lizard. Murray.
The Lost Shipmate. Roberts.
Love. *Anonymous.*
Love Poem. Logan.
A Lover's Plea. Campion.

Lullaby. Harris.
Lullaby for My Dead Child. Jallais.
Macrame. Riley.
MACV Advisor. Gray.
Madonna of the Hills. Allen.
Majuba Hill. MacNab.
A Man of Rain. Barbeitos.
A Man of Words. *Anonymous.*
Map Reference T994724. Pudney.
The March. Squire.
Mariana. Tennyson.
Market Women's Cries. Swift.
Marsh Leaf. Wagoner.
Mary at the Cross. McGee.
Mary Wyatt and Henry Green. Anonymous.
Maud. Tennyson.
Melancholia. Bridges.
A Memento for Mortality. Basse.
Memorial Poem. Fuller.
The Message. Prevert.
Methought I Saw a Thousand Fearful Wrecks. Shakespeare.
Mid-Ocean in War-Time. Kilmer.
Mimma Bella. Lee-Hamilton.
Moon Shadows. Crapsey.
Moral Essays. Pope.
Mounds of Human Heads Are Wandering into the Distance. Mandelstam.
Mr. Cooper. Thwaite.
Mr. Over. Smith.
Mugford's Victory. Chadwick.
Music's Duel. Crashaw.
My Babes in the Wood. Piatt.
My Body in the Walls Captived. Ralegh.
My City. Johnson.
My Gal Sal. Dresser.
My God, My God, Look upon Me. Walsh.
My Love Was Light. Williams.
My Soul Before Thee Prostrate Lies. Richter.
My triumph lasted till the drums. Dickinson.
Naples. Rogers.
New Year's Eve. Housman.
New Years and Old. Jackson.
The News Stand. Berrigan.
Night. Jami.
The Night a Sailor Came to Me in a Dream. Wakoski.
The Nine Little Goblins. Riley.
No Coward's Song. Flecker.
No Swan So Fine. Moore.
Not Any Sunny Tone. Dickinson.
November. Fisher.
November Eves. Flecker.
O Earth! Art Thou Not Weary? Dorr.
Obituary. Brode.
The Objects of the Summer Scene. Irwin.
Ode for Decoration Day. Peterson.
An Ode: "Not with slow, funereal sound." Aldrich.

The Odor of Blood. McGrath.
Officers' Mess. Monro.
Oh! Susanna. Foster.
Old Age. Tennyson.
Old Christmas. Helton.
The Old Gray Goose. *Anonymous.*
Old Mother Hubbard. *Anonymous.*
An Old Waterford Woman. O'Neill.
On an Insignificant Fellow. Curzon.
On Himselfe. Herrick.
On Kingston Bridge. Cortissoz.
On Learning to Adjust to Things. Ciardi.
On Supporters of the Baconian Theory. Tennyson.
On the Dates of Poets. Johnson.
On the Death of Her Mother. Rukeyser.
On the Death of Robert Lowell. Myles.
On the Eve of the Feast of the Immaculate Conception: 1942. Lowell.
On the Suicide of a Friend. Whittemore.
On the Tombs in Westminster Abbey. Beaumont.
One Bright Morning... *Anonymous.*
One Down. Armour.
The Only Son. Newbolt.
Oreads. Raine.
"Out, Out–". Frost.
Oystering. Howard.
Pallor. Robinson.
The Panchatantra: Poverty. *Anonymous.*
Paracelsus. Browning.
The Paradox. Donne.
The Pardon. Wilbur.
Parole Denial. Green.
Per Amica Silentia Lunae. Carvalho.
The Pessimist. *Anonymous.*
Pete's Error. Chapman.
The Pheasant. Coffin.
Picking Lilies. *Anonymous.*
The Pillory. Vivien.
A Pine-Tree Buoy. Morris.
Planting Trees. Friedlaender.
Plot Improbable, Character Unsympathetic. Olson.
(Poem) (Chicago) (The Were-Age). Knott.
Poem for Vladimir. Ripley.
A Poem of the Forty-Eight States. Koch.
Poetry Perpetuates the Poet. Herrick.
Poisoned Lands. Montague.
The Pond. Davies.
Prayer. Lewis.
Prescience. Hayes.
The Priest Rediscovers His Psalm-Book. *Anonymous.*
The Princess. Tennyson.
Promise of Peace. Jeffers.
The Prophet. Yehoash.
Purgatory. Yeats.
Quoniam Ego in Flagella Paratus Sum. Habington.
Rain. Moss.
The Raising of Lazarus. Clifton.

Readen Ov a Head-Stwone. Barnes.
A Rebel. Fletcher.
Reflection. Turner.
Remember Me. Douglas.
Requiem for the Plantagenet Kings. Hill.
Rescue the Dead. Ignatow.
Reserve. Aldington.
Resurrection. Sackville.
The Return. Fields.
The River. Arnold.
The River. Vroman.
The Road of Birds. Humes.
The Road to Bologna. MacNab.
The Road to Zoagli. Beerbohm.
Robin Hood's Death. *Anonymous.*
Rocks and Deals. Young.
Le Roi Est Mort. Robinson.
A Rose to the Living. Waterman.
Rotten Lake Elegy. Rukeyser.
A Rule for Shooting. *Anonymous.*
The Rustler. *Anonymous.*
S.S.R., Lost at Sea–The Times. Gustafson.
Le Sacre-Coeur. Mew.
Saint. Graves.
Sam Hall. *Anonymous.*
Saon of Acanthus. Callimachus.
Says Robin to Jenny, "If you will be mine.'. *Anonymous.*
Scene-Shifter Death. O'Neill.
Seven Woodland Crows. Vizenor.
Shadow to Shadow. Allen.
Shall I Come, Sweet Love, to Thee. Campion.
Shall I Compare Thee to a Summer's Day? Moss.
She. Gippius.
She and He. Arnold.
She Warns Him. Cornford.
Shekhina and the Kiddushim. Roditi.
Silex Scintillans. Vaughan.
A Simplification. Wilbur.
Simplify Me When I'm Dead. Douglas.
Sir Hugh; or, The Jew's Daughter (B vers.). *Anonymous.*
Sir Hugh, or, The Jew's Daughter (C version). *Anonymous.*
Sir Olaf. Herder.
The Sisters. Whittier.
The Skin-and-Bone Lady. *Anonymous.*
The Sleeper. Poe
The Snoring Bedmate. *Anonymous.*
So Long! Whitman.
Sometime during Eternity. Ferlinghetti.
Song for War. Rodgers.
Song from the Waters. Beddoes.
A Song in Time of Revolution 1860. Swinburne.
Song: "Make this night loveable." Auden.
The Song of the Demented Priest. Berryman.

Sonnet: "Oh! Death will find me, long before I tire." Brooke.
Sonnet to a Tyrant. Ellis.
Sonnet: Written on the Day that Mr. Leigh Hunt Left Prison. Keats.
Sonnets of a Portrait Painter. Ficke
Spare Us, O Lord, Aloud We Pray. Watts.
The Speech of the Dead. Ridler.
Spinners at Willowsleigh. Zaturenska.
The Spirit of Night. Rogers.
Spring Bereaved. Drummond.
Spring Death. Marano.
The Spring Will Come. Lowry.
Squall. Moss.
The Square at Dawn. Tate.
The Stab. Harney.
Star. Derwood.
Stoic. Durrell.
A Story About the Body. Hass.
Strange Meetings. Monro.
The Stranger. De la Mare.
Strangers. Thomas.
Suburban. Ciardi.
Summons for the Undead. Keating.
Sunday Review Section. Wormser.
Suppose in Perfect Reason. Griffin.
Supremacy. Robinson.
Supreme Death. Dunn.
Sweet William's Ghost (B vers.). *Anonymous.*
Synekdechestai. Schmid.
The Tailor. Leftwich.
Tales of the Islands, IX. Walcott.
A Talisman. Moore.
Talk with a Poet. Bevington.
Tapestry Trees. Morris.
The Task. Pitter.
Tell Me Some Way. Reese.
Telling the Bees. Whittier.
Ten Thousand God-Damn Cattle. *Anonymous.*
Terminal. Shapiro.
The Terrible Dead. Davies.
There Is No Death. McCreery.
There's Nothing Like the Sun. Thomas.
There Was an Old Woman. *Anonymous.*
These Things to Come. Butler.
They Closed Her Eyes. Becquer.
Things Dead. Schwob.
The Things That Matter. Nesbit.
This Way Only. Harford.
This Wind. Kryss.
Those Were the Days. *Anonymous.*
Three Epitaphs. Davison.
The Three Ravens. *Anonymous.*
Three Sentences for a Dead Swan. Wright.
Threnody. Kreymborg.
Through These Pale Cold Days. Rosenberg.
Thysia. Luce.

Time and the Garden. Winters.
Tired Mothers. Smith.
To a Maple Seed. Mifflin.
To a Portrait of Lermontov. Aliger.
To a Vine-Clad Telegraph Pole. Untermeyer.
To Heliodora, Dead. Meleager.
To Philip Levine, on the Day of Atonement. Mezey.
To Stella. Shelley.
To the Dead of '98. Johnson.
To the Laggards. Bovshover.
To the Muse. Kennedy.
To the Pay Toilet. Piercy.
Tom Ball's Barn. Kooser.
A Tragedy. Marzials.
The Travellers. Howe.
Trench Blues. *Anonymous.*
Triad. Crapsey.
Truth. Cowper.
Twenty-One Sonnets. Stead.
Two Figures. Peacock.
Two Fusiliers. Graves.
Two Little Boys. *Anonymous.*
Two Loves. Eberhart.
Two Sonnets. Sorley.
The Two Stars. Davies.
Under the Ruins of Poland. Manger.
The United Fruit Co. Neruda.
Upon Absence. Philips.
Upon the Death of a Gentleman. Crashaw.
Valediction. MacNeice.
The Varuna. Boker.
La Vie C'est La Vie. Fauset.
The Violin Calls. Livesay.
Virgin Pictured in Profile. Warren.
Virtue the Best Monument. Ralegh.
A Vision of the World's Instability. Verstegan.
A Volunteer's Grave. Percy.
Wake. Hughes.
Waking on a Greyhound. Henry.
Wang Peng's Recommendation for Improving the People. Eldridge.
The Warnings. Furlong.
Washington Heights, 1959. Blumenthal.
Waterfront. Jenkins.
We Who Are Dead. Benjamin.
The Weary Blues. Hughes.
Weather. Bethell.
Webster: An Ode (excerpt). Wilkinson.
Welcome, Thou Safe Retreat! Habington.
Were Not the Gael Fallen. O'Mulconry.
What Bids Me Leave. Trench.
When I Am Dead. Stillman.
When the Dead Men Die. O'Neill.
Where the Dead Men Lie. Boake.
Where the Fight Was. Corbin.
Willie the Weeper. *Anonymous.*

A Wind from the West.
  Watt.
Winter Sketch. Bourinot.
Wisdom. Ford.
Wise. Reese.
Words. Eberhart.
Words for Music Perhaps.
  Yeats.
Written. Ruelfe.
The Yellow Bittern. Mac
  Giolla Ghunna.
Yes, the Agency Can Handle
  That. Fearing.
The Yew-Tree. Watkins.
You Are Alms. Thompson.
You Who Dog My Footsteps.
  Kwitko.

Deadly
Don't Go. Eigner.
The Female of the Species.
  Kipling.
For the Time Being. Auden.
How oft have I, my dear and
  cruel foe. Wyatt.
The Lover, Having Dreamed
  of Enjoying His Love....
  Wyatt.
November Walk. Doyle.
Over to God. Harrigan.
Sonnet XI: "O eyes clear with
  beauty, O tender gaze."
  Labe.
The Worst Horror.
  Euripides.
Young Benjie. *Anonymous.*

Deaf (en)
Abraham and Sarah.
  Manger.
Directions to a Rebel.
  Rodgers.
The Eccho. Leigh.
Grand Street & the Bowery.
  Ghitelman.
Helen Keller. Stedman.
In Memory of Basil, Marquess
  of Dufferin and Ava.
  Betjeman.
Leaving Raiford. Petaccia.
Listen. Patterson.
New Year. Harada.
The Osprey Suicides.
  Lieberman.
Prayer of Little Hope. Wahl.
Six Poets in Search of a
  Lawyer. Hall.
Song (October 1969). Fraser.
Were I to Mount beyond the
  Field. Keyes.
White Pines. Silesky.

Deal (er) (s)
Cash In. Hall.
Coosaponakeesa (Mary
  Mathews Musgrove
  Bosomsworth)... Green.
Down and Out. Hay.
The Eel. De La Mare.
It Was a Funky Deal.
  Knight.
Landscapes. Hugo.
The Mythos of Samuel
  Huntsman. Plutzik.
A Question. Cole.
The Ticket Agent. Leamy.

Dean
Lucretius Versus the Lake
  Poets. Frost.
A Receipt for Stewing Veal.
  Gay.
A Wykehamist's Address to
  Learning. Shuttleworth.

Dear (er) (est) (ie) (ly) (s)
Absence. *Anonymous.*

Amaturus. Johnson-Cory.
Apprehension. Ainslie.
Arithmetic on the Frontier.
  Kipling.
Ay Waukin O. Burns.
Beauty, Sleeping. Freeman.
Ca' the Yowes. Burns.
Ca' the Yowes to the Knowes.
  Pagan.
Cam' Ye By. *Anonymous.*
The Child's Wish Granted.
  Lathrop.
The Chinese Banyan.
  Meredith.
Conflict. Clive.
Constancy. Watson.
Contented at Forty.
  Cleghorn.
Cressida. Baxter.
Dear March, come in!
  Dickinson.
A Delicate Balance.
  Schreiber.
Delphic Hymn to Apollo.
  Swinburne.
Dirge. Crapsey.
Duality. Hobson.
Farther. Piatt.
First or Last. Hardy.
The Giveaway. McGinley.
I Saw a Maiden.
  Anonymous.
I Send Thee Here of Ribbon a
  Whole Yard. *Anonymous.*
In Praise of Three Young
  Men. O Dalaigh.
Invocation. Stedman.
Jack Sprat's Cat.
  Anonymous.
Jean. Burns.
Kindness. *Anonymous.*
Lackey Bill. *Anonymous.*
A Leaf. Uhland.
Life's Common Things.
  Allen.
The Midges Dance Aboon the
  Burn. Tannahill.
Mir Traumte Von Einem
  Konigskind. Heine.
My Prayer. *Anonymous.*
On the High Cost of Dairy
  Products. McIntyre.
Post-Meridian. Garrison.
The Praise of Derry.
  Columcille.
Satisfied. Cole.
Shut Out. Rossetti.
Song: "There's a barrel of
  porter at Tammany Hall."
  Halleck.
Spring. Guarini.
Sunday Evening in the
  Common. Wheelock.
System. Stevenson.
To My Mother. Poe.
The Tombstone Told When
  She Died. Thomas.
Under All Change. Johnson.
When My Beloved Sleeping
  Lies. McLeod.
When the Sleepy Man Comes.
  Roberts.
Your Lad, and My Lad.
  Parrish.

Dearth
The Exiles. Auden.
In Time of Need. Hinkson.
A Prayer in Late Autumn.
  Storey.

Death (s)
Abraham:. Schwartz.
Abstrosophy. Burgess.

Achilles. Myers.
Address to the Crown.
  O'Donnell.
Admonition for Spring.
  Mackay.
The Adventurers. Byron.
Age in Prospect. Jeffers.
The Age of a Dream.
  Johnson.
Alarum. Koziol.
Algernon Sidney's Farewell.
  Anonymous.
All Day It Has Rained.
  Lewis.
Alone up Here on the
  Mountain. *Anonymous.*
Although Tormented. Ben
  Judah.
Amor Mysticus. Marcela de
  Carpio.
Amoretti, VII. Spenser.
Amoretti, XXXVI. Spenser.
Ancient Murderess Night.
  Margolin.
And Death Shall Have No
  Dominion. Thomas.
And I Am Old to Know.
  Hanson.
And If at Last. Labe.
And There shall Be No More
  Death (excerpt). Gilbert.
And What with the
  Blunders... Patchen.
Annual Legend. Scott.
Another on the Same.
  Belloc.
Another Poem for Me.
  Knight.
Another Weeping Woman.
  Stevens.
The Ant Trap. Rosenblatt.
Antony and Cleopatra.
  Shakespeare.
April-And Dying. Aldrich.
April Moment. Ficke.
April Mortality. Adams.
Arcadia. Sidney.
As a Great Prince. Honig.
As Lambs into the Pen.
  Wellesley.
As with Heaped Bees at
  Hiving Time. Stevenson.
The Assault on the Fortress.
  Dwight.
The Astrologer Argues Your
  Death. deGravelles.
Astrophel and Stella, VII.
  Sidney.
Astrophel and Stella, XXI.
  Sidney.
Asylum. Freeman.
At an Inn. Hardy.
At Dead Low Water.
  Curnow.
At Shagger's Funeral. Dawe.
At the Top of the Road.
  Going.
Atavism. Wylie.
Athletes. Gibson.
Atropos. O'Hara.
An Autobiography. Rhys.
Autumn: An Ode. Gullans.
Autumn Night. Scott.
Autumn Song. Stepanchev.
Ayohu Kanogisdi Death Song.
  Arnett.
A Ballad of Past Meridian.
  Meredith.
Balme. Spenser.
Barbara. Smith.
Barbecue Blues. Hicks.
A Beautiful Night. Beddoes.

Before Passover. Mayne.
Before Sunset. Swinburne.
Begging A.I.D. Rubadiri.
The Beirut-Hell Express.
  Adnan.
Bell Speech. Wilbur.
Ben Milam. Wharton.
Benicasim. Warner.
A Bestiary. Rexroth.
The Betrayal. Furlong.
Beyond the Grave. Bruner.
Bird at Night. Hamilton.
Birth and Death. Swinburne.
The Black Vulture. Sterling.
Blood. Bremser.
Blue Ey'd Mary.
  Anonymous.
Blueprint. Steinman.
The Bonny Earl of Livingston.
  Anonymous.
The Broken-Hearted
  Gardener. *Anonymous.*
The Brut. Layamon.
The Bubble. Tabb.
The Bungalows. Ashbery.
Burial. Walker.
The Burial of an Infant.
  Vaughan.
By Day and by Night.
  Merwin.
By the Wood. Nichols.
Caelica, LXXXVII. Greville.
Caelica, XCIX. Greville.
Captain Death. *Anonymous.*
The Card-Dealer. Rossetti.
Carentan O Carentan.
  Simpson.
Carol: "Mary laid her Child
  among." Nicholson.
Carpe Diem. Lodge.
Casa de Pollos. Fraser.
Cavalier. Bruce.
Celebrating the Mass of
  Christian Burial. Mathis.
Celestial Love.
  Michelangelo.
Certain Artists Bring Her
  Dolls and Drawings.
  Yeats.
Cesar Franck. Auslander.
Chamonix. Hookham.
Charitas Nimia, or the Deare
  Bargain. Crashaw.
Charles Gustavus Anderson
  (II). *Anonymous.*
The Child Dying. Muir.
A Child's Question. Nason.
The Children. Dyment.
The Children's Ghosts.
  Letts.
A Christopher of the
  Shenandoah. Thomas.
Churchyard of St. Mary
  Magdalene, Old Milton.
  Heath-Stubbs.
The Cid: Two Lovers in the
  Toils of Honor. Corneille.
City Johannesburg. Serote.
Clandestine Work. Goll.
A Clear Midnight.
  Whitman.
A Clear Shell. Bellerby.
Climbing. Fuertes.
The Closing Scene. Read.
De Coenatione Micae.
  Martial (Marcus Valerius
  Martialis).
The Cold Divinities. Wright.
Cold Feet in Columbus.
  Heath.
Colonel Fantock. Sitwell.

Come, Gentle Sleep, Death's Image Though Thou Art. Wharton.
Come Out, Come Out, Ye Souls That Serve. Brennan.
Come with Me into Winter's Disheveled Grass. Swenson.
A Comparison of the Life of Man. Barnfield.
Compensation. Collier.
Compensation. Dunbar.
Complaint of a Lover Rebuked. Surrey.
Confession of Faith. Wylie.
Consolation in War. Mumford.
Constancy. Watson.
A Contemplation upon Flowers. King.
Contentment. Felltham.
The Conviction. Synge.
The Coral Reef. Blight.
Corporal Pym. De la Mare.
The Corpse-Plant. Rich.
Counter-Attack. Sassoon.
The Cowboy. *Anonymous.*
The Creation. *Anonymous.*
Credo. Symons.
A Creed. *Anonymous.*
Crispus Attucks. O'Reilly.
Crossing the Tropics. Melville
Cruel Clever Cat. Taylor.
The Curtains Now Are Drawn. Hardy.
Dain Eile (excerpt). MacLean.
Damon the Mower. Marvell.
The Dance of Death. Dobson.
Dancing the Shout to the True Gospel. Brown.
Dangerous Condition: Sign on Inner-City House. Atkins.
Death. Pellew.
Death. Yeats.
Death and Birth. Swinburne.
Death and Doctor Hornbook. Burns.
Death and the Fairies. MacGill.
Death in Life. Vaux.
A Death in the Desert. Tomlinson.
Death Invited. Swenson.
The Death of Dermid. Ferguson.
The Death of the Bird. Hope.
Death's Songsters. Rossetti.
Death Seed. Huch.
Death Sting Me Blues. Martin.
Death, Thou Hast Seized Me. Luzzatto.
A Death to Us. Silkin.
Death Warnings. Quevedo y Villegas.
December. Francis.
Deep Sea Soundings. Williams.
Deep Spring. *Anonymous.*
Defeated Farmer. Van Doren.
Deus Noster Ignis Consumens. Housman.
The Devil's Dictionary: Prospect. Bierce.
Devoide of Reason, Thrale to Foolish Irc. Lodge.

A Dialogue. Swinburne.
The Dirge of Kildare. De Vere.
Disquisition on Death (excerpt). Fairburn.
Divine Poems. Villa.
Dollar Bill. Nims.
Don Juan. Byron.
A Donkey Will Carry You. Steinberg.
The Doom of Beauty. Michelangelo.
Down the Field. Humphries.
Down the Little Big Horn. Brooks.
Dr. Donne. Alling.
Dream and Image. Heinrich von Morungen.
The Dream of Aengus Og. Cox.
A Dreamed Realization. Corso.
The Drunkard. Levine.
The Duel. Maynard.
The Dying Gaul. O'Grady.
The Dying Reservist. Baring.
A Dying Viper. "Field.
Early Morning Feed. Redgrove.
Easter Thought. Cox.
Egypt. Doolittle.
The Elected Knight. *Anonymous.*
Elegie. Habington.
Elegies for the Hot Season. McPherson.
Elegy. Nemerov.
Elegy. Sadeh.
Elegy. Wheelock.
Elegy and Flame. Gregory.
An Elegy Upon My Best Friend. King.
Elegy Wrote in the Tower, 1554. Harington.
Empedocles. Jones, Jr.
Empedocles on Etna. Mallalieu.
End of the Flower-World (A.D. 2300). Burnshaw.
The Entertainment, or Porch-Verse, at the Marriage.... Herrick.
Envy. Procter.
Epigram. *Anonymous.*
Epigram: Fatum Supremum. *Anonymous.*
Epigrams. Martial (Marcus Valerius Martialis).
An Epistle to a Lady. Leapor.
Epitaph. *Anonymous.*
Epitaph: "Daniel and Abigail." Barrios.
Epitaph for a Bigot. Johnson.
Epitaph for a Tyrannous Governor Who Choked on Wine. Sabir.
Epitaph for Elizabeth Ranquet. Corneille.
Epitaph: "If fruits are fed on any beast." Synge.
Epitaph: "In my youth the growls!" Tennyson.
Epitaph on a Child Killed by Procured Abortion. *Anonymous.*
Epitaph on a Vagabond. Gray.
Epitaph on Himself. Regnier.

An Epitaph upon My Dear Brother, Francis Beaumont. Beaumont.
Epitaphs of the War, 1914-18. Kipling.
Equality, Father! Bruck.
The Escapade. Ignatow.
Eve's Song in the Garden. Gottlieb.
Exchange. Stuart.
The Execution of Montrose. Aytoun.
Exile from God. Wheelock.
Exile Song. Rosenfeld.
The Exiles. Auden.
Experience. Wharton.
Fable. Pilinszky.
Faces in the Street. Lawson.
Fading-Leaf and Fallen-Leaf. Garnett.
The Faerie Queene. Spenser.
Faith of Our Fathers. Faber.
The Far Land. Wheelock.
The Farewell. *Anonymous.*
Farewell for a While. Daryush.
Farewell to the World of Richard Bishop. *Anonymous.*
The Farmer. Shove.
Father and Son. Higgins.
Father to the Man. Knight.
Fear. Pizarnik.
The Fear of Dying. Holmes.
The Feast. Wagoner.
Feed Still Thyself. Ralegh.
A Fiction of Edvard Munch. di Michele.
Figures of Authority. Watkins.
Fill a Glass with Golden Wine. Henley.
Fillmore. *Anonymous.*
The Firing Squad. Mathews.
First It Was Singing. Silkin.
Fish in River. *Anonymous.*
Flesh. Rice.
The Flying Cloud. *Anonymous.*
The Foiled Reaper. Seymour.
For a Pessimist. Cullen.
For Adolf Eichmann. Levi.
For Any Beachhead. Joseph.
For My Grandfather. Webb.
For Now. Merwin.
For Tony, Dougal, Mick, Bugs, Nick et al. Bathgate.
The Force of Love. Jones.
Forever. O'Reilly.
The Fox. Patchen.
Frankenstein. Field.
Fredericksburg. Aldrich.
From Malay. Shapiro.
From the Parthenon I Learn. Wattles.
From Thy Fair Face I Learn. Michelangelo.
Funeral Oration for a Mouse. Dugan.
Gamecock. Dickey.
The Garden. Very.
Gascoygnes Good Night. Gascoigne.
The Geranium. Sheridan.
Getting Across. Revard.
Gift from Kenya. Miller.
Girls. Neruda.
God Save Elizabeth! Palgrave.

Gold Coast Customs (excerpt). Sitwell.
A Good-By. Hayes.
The Good Man in Hell. Muir.
Goodby Betty, Don't Remember Me. Cummings.
Grace to Be Said at the Supermarket. Nemerov.
Grandfather. Stroud.
Guerrilla. Pieterse.
Guerrilla Promise. Nangolo.
Guyana. Ruth.
The Half-Breed Girl. Scott.
The Happy Night. Squire.
The Harvesting of the Roses. Ben Jacob.
The Hatters. McDonald.
Haunted. Sassoon.
He Has Fallen from the Height of His Love. Blunt.
He Is More Than a Hero. Sappho.
He Walks at Peace. Tao Te Ching.
Headsong. Bennett.
Hear Us, in This Thy House. Doddridge.
The Heart of the Night. Rossetti.
Helen in Egypt: Thetis Is the Moon-Goddess. Doolittle.
Helicon. Hollander.
Her Courage. Yeats.
Her Music. Dickinson.
Heraclitus. Cory.
Here Followeth the Songe of the Death of Mr. Thewlis. *Anonymous.*
Here Lies... Smith.
Here Lieth Love. Watson.
The Hermit Marban. *Anonymous.*
Hero and Leander. Hood.
Hidesong. Higo.
His Lady's Death. Ronsard.
His Life Is Ours. Stroud.
His Mother's Joy. Chadwick.
Hobart Town, Van Diemen's Land. Porter.
Homecoming Blues. Miller.
Horror Movie. Moss.
The House of Life. Rossetti.
How Much Longer Will I Be Able to Inhabit the Divine Sepulcher... Ashbery.
How to Kill. Douglas.
Hummingbird. Piercy.
Hunger Strike. Franklin.
Hungry China. Cha Liang-cheng.
Hunting for Blueberries. James.
Hymmnn. Ginsberg.
Hymn to Proserpine. Swinburne.
Hymn to the Holy Cross. Venantius Fortunatus.
A Hymn to the Name and Honour of the Admirable Saint Teresa. Crashaw.
Hymns and Spiritual Songs. Smart.
I Am Like a Slip of Comet. Hopkins.
I Could Not Sleep for Thinking of the Sky. Masefield.

I Danced Before I Had Two Feet. Dunn.
I Have a Rendezvous with Life. Cullen.
I Met My Solitude. Replansky.
I Spoke to the Violet. Neilson.
I Was Always Fascinated. Villanueva.
I Will Make You Brooches. Stevenson.
Icarus. Koopman.
Idea. Drayton.
Ideal. Pearse.
The Ideal. Saltus.
If God Exists. Lipska.
If Thou Wilt Mighty Be. Wyatt.
If to Die–. Romilu.
Imitated from Rime CCLXIX: "The piller pearisht is whearto I Lent. Petrarch (Francesco Petrarca).
Immortality. Russell.
Immustabilis. Bunner.
In a Museum. Deutsch.
In Death. Bradley.
In Defense of Metaphysics. Tomlinson.
In Memoriam A.H.H., XLV. Tennyson.
In Memoriam A.H.H., LXXIV. Tennyson.
In Memory of Major Robert Gregory. Yeats.
In Mortem Venerabilis Andreae Prout Carmen. Mahony.
In No Way. Ignatow.
In Pace In Idipsum Dormiam Et Requiescam. O'Connor.
In Praise of His Lady. Grove.
In the Highlands. Stevenson.
In the Summer of Sixty. Anonymous.
In the Thirtieth. Cunningham.
In Your Arms. Radnoti.
In Youth. Stein.
Incanto. Rice.
The Incarnation and Passion. Vaughan.
Incompatibility. De Vere.
Indecision. Pinkerton.
Indian Mounds. Peace.
Inevitable. Betjeman.
The Inner Part. Simpson.
The Inscription. Barker.
Inscription in a Book. Douglas.
Ione. De Vere.
An Irish Airman Foresees His Death. Yeats.
The Irish Wife. McGee.
Isolation. Symons.
Janet Waking. Ransom.
January. Kees.
Jesus, I Love Thy Charming Name. Doddridge.
Jesus, My Saviour, Look on Me! MacDuff.
John Donne's Defiance. Hervey.
Johnny Germany. Anonymous.
Journey of the Magi. Eliot.
Joy o' Living. Hall.
Joy's Treachery. Blunt.
Joyce Kilmer. Burr.
Julius Caesar. Shakespeare.

Kaddish. Ginsberg.
Katydids. Lowell.
Keats. Longfellow.
The Key. Oxenham.
A la Bourbon. Lovelace.
The Lady's Complaint. Heath-Stubbs.
Lady Sara Bunbury Sacrificing to the Graces, by Reynolds. Hine.
The Laird of Wariston (B vers.). Anonymous.
The Lake. Hughes.
Lake Leman. Byron.
Lament. Thomas.
Lan Nguyen: The Uniform of Death 1971. Mura.
The Last Evening. Rilke.
The Last Fight. Tooker.
The Last Quarter Moon of the Dying Year. Brooks.
Last Refuge. Michelangelo.
Late Reflections. Deutsch.
Laurels and Immortelles. Anonymous.
The Lemmings. Masefield.
Ler to Loven as I Love Thee. Anonymous.
Let Mine Eyes See Thee. Theresa of Avila.
Let's Go to the Wood, Says This Pig. Anonymous.
Letter from a Coward to a Hero. Warren.
A Letter from Brooklyn. Walcott.
Letter to a Librarian. Layton.
Letter VIII. Swingler.
Lettice. Craik.
Lewd Love is Loss. Southwell.
Life. Brown.
Life Flows to Death as Rivers to the Sea. Cunningham.
Life or Death. Dresbach.
Life Story. Williams.
Life the Very Gods in My Sight Is He Who. Sappho.
Like an Ideal Tenant. Daigon.
Like to the seely fly. Davison.
The Lily of the Valley. Beddoes.
Lines to Accompany Flowers for Eve. Kizer.
Lines Written after the Discovery ... of the Germ of Yellow Fever. Ross.
Lines Written beneath a Picture. Byron.
A Litany for Old Age. Harsen.
Little Elegy. Kennedy.
Live Not, Poor Bloom, but Perish. Anonymous.
Living Marble. O'Shaughnessy.
Lochiel's Warning. Campbell.
Lollingdon Downs. Masefield.
Love and Death. Catullus.
Love and Death. Deland.
Love and Death. Mulholland.
Love between Brothers and Sisters. Watts.
Love in Exile. Blind.
Love Is Strong. Burton.

Love on the Farm. Lawrence.
Love's Assize. Cavalcanti.
Love's Grave. Watson.
Love, Time and Death. Locker-Lampson.
Lovers Relentlessly. Kunitz.
Luscious and Sorrowful. Rossetti.
Lying. Wilbur.
The Lying Muslims. Anonymous.
Madboy's Song. Rukeyser.
Madonna Mia. Swinburne.
Madrigal: The Beautie, and the Life. Drummond.
A Maid Me Loved. Hannay.
The Maiden of the Smile. Austin.
Making a Man. Waterman.
Man's Mortality. Wastell.
The Man with Three Friends. Greenwell.
The Man Without Faith. Church.
Mancheser by Night. Blind.
The March of Humanity. Miller.
Marcus Curtius. Gogarty.
Marriage. Lowell.
The Marseillaise. Rouget de Lisle.
Martyrdom. Thomas.
The "Mary Gloster." Kipling.
Mary Hamilton. Anonymous.
The Master of Time. Nijlen.
Maybe Love. Ginsberg.
The Means to Attain a Happy Life. Surrey.
Measure for Measure. Shakespeare.
Meditations for August 1, 1666. Pain.
Memorial Poem. Glatstein.
Memories of Verdun. Dugan.
Messages. Thompson.
Mezzo Cammin. Longfellow.
Michelangelo's Kiss. Rossetti.
Mid-August. Driscoll.
Middle Passage. Hayden.
Mirror. De Vries.
La Misere (parody). Appleman.
The Mocking Bird. Lanier.
The Modern Fine Lady. Jenyns.
Modern Love, XI. Meredith.
Modern Midnight Conversation: Between an Unemployed Artist... Anonymous.
Modern Romance. Harris.
Moments. Schwob.
Monna Innominata. Rossetti.
Morning. Savage.
The Morning Track. Parone.
Mors et Vita. Stoddard.
Mors et Vita. Waddington.
Mors, Morituri Te Salutamus. Money-Coutts.
Mortal Love. Dowling.
De Morte. Anonymous.
De Morte. Wotton.
Mortem, Quae Violat Suavia, Pellit Amor. Cory.
Mortification. Herbert.
Les Morts Vont Vite. Bunner.

The Mother. Ryan.
Mountain Creed. Rae.
The Mountain Lake. Church.
Mr. Roger Harlackenden. Johnson.
Mr. Secretary. Patten.
The Mu'allaqat: Pour Us Wine. Ibn Kolthum.
Music (after Sully Prudhomme). Du Maurier.
The Music of His Steps. Wakefield.
My Baptismal Birthday. Coleridge.
My Enemy. Brotherton.
My Father's Country. Lee.
My Head on My Shoulders. Ingalls.
My love is like unto th' eternal fire. Wyatt.
My Naked Aunt. MacLeish.
My Name Is Afrika. Kgositsile.
Mystery. Browning.
The Name of Jesus. Newton.
Nature's Questioning. Hardy.
The Nesting Ground. Wagoner.
Never Again, Orpheus. Antipater of Sidon.
The New Birth. Very.
Newborn Death. Rossetti.
News Reel. Ross.
The Next War. Owen.
A Nice Part of Town. Hayes.
Night. Jeffers.
Night. Montgomery.
Night. Rolleston.
The Night Is Falling. Mangan.
Night on the Prairies. Whitman.
The Night-Walker. Gregory.
Night Walkers. Smithyman.
Nightpiece. Turco.
Nights on the Indian Ocean. Rice.
Nightsong. Booth.
No Pleasure Without Some Pain. Vaux.
Nobody will open the door for you. Varela.
Noise Grimaced. Eigner.
Nor Mars His Sword. Thompson.
North Labrador. Crane.
Not in the Guide-Books. Jennings.
Not Wholly Lost. Souster.
Nothing Better. Anonymous.
Nothing but Death. Neruda.
November. Fisher.
Now. Dodge.
O Could I Find from Day to Day. Cleavland.
O.D. Gilbert.
O Friends! Who Have Accompanied Thus Far. Landor.
O Thou Eternal Source of Life. Schloerb.
Obligations. Cooper.
Ode: "Peer of gods he seemeth to me." Sappho.
Ode to Chloris. Cotton.
Ode to the Muse on Behalf of a Young Poet. Wagoner.
Odes. Horace.

Of Change of Opinions. Plarr.
Of Fortune. Kyd.
Of His Death. Meleager.
Ogier the Dane: Song. Morris.
Oh, Let Us Howl Some Heavy Note. Webster.
Okefenokee Swamp. Hicky.
The Old Beauty. McGinley.
The Old Man Who Is Gone Now. Reyes.
The Old Men. Kipling.
On Clarastella Singing. Heath.
On Disbanding the Army. Humphreys.
On Finding a Small Fly Crushed in a Book. Turner.
On the Death of Robert Browning. Swinburne.
On the Death of Squire Christopher, a Remarkably Fat Sportsman. Wigson.
On the Moor. Rice.
On the Universality and Other Attributes of the God of Nature. Freneau.
On the Vanity of Man's Life. Anonymous.
On Time. Milton.
On Top of Troubled Waters. Langford.
On Waking. Campbell.
One Last Word. Glassco.
One Token. Davies.
One Way Down. Craig.
Onward, Onward, Men of Heaven. Sigourney.
Ordinary People on Sunday. Veitch.
The Others Hunters in the North The Cree. Rothenberg.
The Oviparous Tailor. Beddoes.
Pacific Sonnets. Barker.
Pain. Sodergran.
Pain for a Daughter. Sexton.
Pale Is Death. Du Bellay.
Palermo, Mother's Day, 1943. Belvin.
The Panchatantra: True Friendship. Anonymous.
The People Has No Obituary. Clark.
People Who Died. Berrigan.
Perfect Rhyme. Nims.
Pesach Has Come to the Ghetto Again. Heller.
Phil. Kooser.
The Philosophic Flight. Bruno.
Pictures on the Wall. Shargel.
The Pigs. Lehmann.
The Pilgrimage. Herbert.
The Pillar Perished Is. Wyatt.
The Place of O. Young Bear.
Plain Song Talk. Eberhart.
Poem by the Charles River. Blaser.
Poem for Jacqueline Hill. Anonymous.
Poem: "The haven and last refuge of my pain." Machiavelli.
Poems from the Coalfields, 1: Air Shaft. Healy.

The Poet. Leitch.
The Poet. Mathews
Poet of Earth. Thayer.
Pontoosuce. Melville.
A Poor Christian Looks at the Ghetto. Milosz.
Power. Collier.
Praising the Poets of That Country. Nemerov.
Prayer Against Indifference. Davidman.
Prayer for Boom. Grenier.
Prayer for Living and Dying. La Farge.
A Prayer for Purification. Michelangelo.
Prayer in Mid-Passage. MacNeice.
The Precious Name. Newton.
Prelude. George.
Preludes to Definition: Time in the Rock (excerpt). Aiken.
The Presence. Graves.
The Princess. Tennyson.
Prison. Ashley.
A Prisoner Freed. Dutton.
Prometheus. Byron.
A Psalm for Sunday Night. Pestel.
Pshytik. Bomze.
The Purification. Cosmas.
Purification of the Blessed Virgin. Beaumont.
The Quakeress Bride. Kinney
Quand On N'a Pas Ce Que l'on Aime, Il Faut Aimer Ce Que l'on A–. Smith.
The Queen's Marie. Anonymous.
The Quest. Vinal.
Rabbi Ben Ezra. Browning.
Ragged Island. Millay.
Raziel. Goll.
Record Perpetual Loss. Stanley.
Reflections in Bed. Symons.
Regeneration. Vaughan.
Religion. Vauquelin de la Fres
Remember Thou Me. Anonymous.
Renunciation. Pearse.
Requiem. Raine.
Requiem for Sonora. Shelton.
Requiescat. Arnold.
Respondez! Whitman.
The Resurrection. Wanley.
Resurrection–An Easter Sequence (excerpt). Rodgers.
Resurrection of the Dead. Shenhar.
Resurrexit. Stuart.
Return. Vinz.
The Rise and Fall of Creede. Warman.
Rissem. Gilbert.
Ritual Three. Ignatow.
The River of Stars. Noyes.
Roisin Dubh. De Vere.
Roisin Dubh. MacWard.
Romance of the Cigarette. di Michele.
A Rose. Fanshawe.
The Rose of Life. Gongora y Argote.
Roses. Ronsard.

Ruaumoko–The Earthquake God. Turei.
A Runic Ode. Warton, Sr..
A Russian Spring Song with Minaiev. Walsh.
Sacco-Vanzetti. Halpern.
The Sacred Children. Hays.
The Sailor Boy. Tennyson.
Saint Coyote. Hogan.
Saint Germain-en-Laye. Dowson.
Salmon Draught at Inveraray. Nunley.
Salutations to Mary, Virgin. Anonymous
Samuel Hoar. Sanborn.
Sarah Lorton. Finnin.
Satisfied. Mason.
Say, Lovely Dream. Waller.
The Seasons. Humphries.
The Secular. Wallace-Crabbe.
Seek the Lord. Campion.
Sehnsucht. Wickham.
The Self-Deceaver. Montalvan.
Sense and Spirit. Meredith.
The Sense of Death. Hoyt.
A Serious and a Curious Night-Meditation. Traherne.
Seventh Eclogue. Radnoti.
Shakespeare's Mourners. Tabb.
The Shanty-Man's Life (with music). Anonymous.
The Shapes of Death. Spender.
The Sharp Ridge. Graves.
She Tasted Death. Giorno.
She Took the Dappled Partridge Fleckt with Blood. Tennyson.
The Ship. MacKay.
The Shock. Eigner.
Shores of Anguish. Portal.
Signals. Waldrop.
Silex Scintillans. Vaughan.
Simple Things. Toulet.
"Since There Is No Escape". Teasdale.
The Singers in the Snow. Anonymous.
Sir Eggnogg (parody). Taylor.
The Skaian Gate (excerpt). Scott.
Sleep Brings No Joy. Bronte.
The Sleeping House. Tennyson.
The Slide at the Empire Mine. Wason.
The Slip. Berry.
Slow Drivers. Barrax.
Slow Rain. "Mistral.
The Small Square. Andresen.
The Smell of Death Is So Powerful. Marguerite de Navarre.
The Smiles of the Bathers. Kees.
A Snail's Derby. Lee-Hamilton.
The Snake. Berry.
The Snake. MacKenzie.
Snap-Dragon. Lawrence.
Some Lamb. Rice.
Somehow, Somewhere, Sometime. Letts.
A Song for the Least of All Saints. Rossetti.

Song: "If love were but a little thing." Coates.
The Song of Chess. Ibn Ezra.
A Song of the Wave. Lodge.
Song: "Old Farmer Oats and his son Ned." Chapman.
Song, on Reading That the Cyclotron has Produced Cosmic Rays... Hoffenstein.
Song on the Water. Beddoes.
Song: "Say, lovely dream! where couldst thou find." Waller.
Song: "Sweet are the Charms of her I love." Booth.
Song: "There is no joy in water apart from the sun." Currey.
Songs from an Evil Wood. Plunkett.
Songs in Flight (excerpt). Bachmann.
Sonnet IX. Drummond.
Sonnet, XIII: "As long as I continue weeping." Labé.
Sonnet XIV: "Although I cry and though my eyes still shed." Labe.
Sonnet: "A passing glance, a lightning long the skies." Drummond.
Sonnet–Age. Garnett.
Sonnet: To a Friend Who Does Not Pity His Love. Cavalcanti.
Sonnet: You Were Born; Must Die. Spender.
Sonnets, VI: "Then let not winter's ragged hand deface." Shakespeare.
Sonnets, CXLVI: "Poor soul, the centre of my sinful earth." Shakespeare.
Sonnets for a Dying Man. Singer.
Sonnets from the Portuguese, I. Browning.
Sonnets from the Portuguese, XXII. Browning.
Sonnets to Miranda. Watson.
The Soul. Cawein.
Sounds. Ashley.
Southern Mansion. Bontemps.
Souvenir. Musset.
The Spoilers and the Spoils. Sherwin.
Spring in War-Time. Teasdale.
Spring Snow and Tui. Bethell.
St. Stephen's Day. Keble.
The Stationmaster's Lament. Rothenberg.
The Story of a Stowaway. Scott.
Strangeness of Heart. Sassoon.
The Streets of Laredo. MacNeice.
Strong as Death. Bunner.
The Stupid Old Body. Carpenter.
Such Is the Death the Soldier Dies. Wilson.
Summer Afternoon. Harrod.
A Summer Evening. Lampman.
Summer Magic. Hill.

Summer Rain. Read.
The Sunrise to the Poor.
　Wilson.
Surrender. Harding.
Survey of Cornwall. Carew.
The Suttee. Skinner.
The Sweater. Orr.
The Sword of Tethra.
　Larminie.
Sylvoe: A Song. Dryden.
Tallahassee (excerpt).
　Merkel.
Tam Samson's Elegy. Burns.
Tan Ta Ra Ran Tan Tant:
　Cries Mars on Bloody
　Rapier. *Anonymous.*
The Task. Campbell.
The Team. Maurice.
Tecumseh. Mair.
Tennis in San Juan. Denney.
That after horror that was Us.
　Dickinson.
Then. Muir.
There Is a Land. Watts.
There Was a Man of Double
　Deed. *Anonymous.*
There Was a Time. Thomas.
These Men. Booth.
Things. Dow.
Things That Are Worse Than
　Death. Olds.
This Is Not Death. Wolfe.
This Was My Brother.
　Gould.
Those Wedding Bells Shall
　Not Ring Out. Rosenfield.
Thou Didst Say Me.
　Waddington.
Thou Grace Divine,
　Encircling All. Scudder.
A Thought for My Love.
　Williamson.
Three Dreams. Michie.
Three Memorial Sonnets.
　Barker.
Three Star Final. Aiken.
Threnody. Cuney.
Thy Beauty Fades. Very.
Time. Bhartrihari.
Time; or, How the Line
　About Chagall's Lovers
　Disappears. Miller.
The Tip. Goldbarth.
'Tis Sorrow Builds the Shining
　Ladder Up. Lowell.
The Titans. Alver.
To a Magnolia Flower in the
　Garden of the Armenian
　Convent in Venice.
　Mitchell.
To a Military Rifle. Winters.
To a Very Wise Man.
　Sassoon.
To America, on Her First
　Sons Fallen in the Great
　War. Walker.
To an Old San Francisco
　Poet. Abbott.
To Any Member of My
　Generation. Barker.
To Charlotte Corday.
　Sitwell.
To Clarastella on St.
　Valentines Day Morning.
　Heath.
To Death, of His Lady.
　Villon.
To My First Love, My
　Mother. Rossetti.
To Naples. Mallalieu.
To Night. Beddoes.
To O.S.C. Trumbell.

To Robert Louis Stevenson.
　Henley.
To the Modern Man.
　Wheelock.
To the Polyandrous Lydia.
　Adams.
To Vittoria Colonna.
　Michelangelo.
The Tobacconist of Eighth
　Street. Eberhart.
Tomorrow. Coates.
Too soon, too soon comes
　Death to show. Patmore.
The Tornado. Russell.
Toward Tenses Two Moons.
　Rachow.
The Town-Rakes. Motteux.
The Tragedy of Pete. Cotter.
Tree in December. Cane.
The Tree of the Cross.
　"Angelus Selesius"
　(Johannes Scheffler).
The Trick. Davies.
The Triumphs of Owen.
　Gray.
The True Weather for
　Women. Simpson.
Truth. Lloyd.
The Turtle Thus with
　Plaintive Crying. Gay.
Two Garden Scenes.
　Burgess.
The Two Mysteries. Dodge.
The Two Spirits. Kenyon.
The Two Wives. Howells.
Ultima Ratio Regum.
　Spender.
An Unbeliever. Branch.
Unchanging Jesus. Spitta.
Under the Stars. Rice.
The Undersong. Emerson
The Unknown Child.
　Jennings.
Unseen Flight. Georgeou.
The Upas Tree. Pushkin.
Upon a Wife that Dyed Mad
　with Jealousie. Herrick.
Upon His Spaniell Tracie.
　Herrick.
A Valediction: of Weeping.
　Donne.
Van Elsen. Scott.
Vanity (I). Herbert.
The Vase. Tiller.
Vegetable Destiny. Cassian.
Verses Written during the
　War 1756-1763.
　Mordaunt.
Viable. Ammons.
Vigilantius. Mather.
Visions. Petrarch.
La Vita Nuova. Dante
　Alighieri.
The Voice of the Void.
　Lathrop.
Vox Oppressi to the Lady
　Phipps. Henchman.
Vulture. Jeffers.
Waiting in Front of the
　Columnar High School.
　Shapiro.
The Wall. Reed.
The Wall-Flower.
　Wergeland.
Walt Whitman. Morris.
The Wandering Lunatic Mind.
　Carpenter.
We Who Are About to Die.
　Fey.
The West's Asleep. Davis.
The Whale. *Anonymous.*

What Am I Who Dare.
　Habington.
What is Life? Coleridge.
What Is Winter? Blunden.
What Profit? Di Roma.
What's Living? Hogan.
What Secret Desires of the
　Blood. Sachs.
What Was a Cure for Love?
　Godfrey.
What You Should Know to
　Be a Poet. Snyder.
When I See the Earth Ornate
　and Lovely. Gambara.
When the Most Is Said. De
　Vere.
When They Grow Old.
　Ralph.
White as Snow. *Anonymous.*
The White Rainbow.
　Nelson.
Who Taught Thee First to
　Sigh? De Vere.
Why Did I Laugh To-night?
　Keats.
Why I Didn't Go to Delphi.
　Welch.
Why the Resurrection Was
　Revealed to Women.
　Greiffenberg.
A Widow's Hymn. Wither.
The Wife Speaks. Stanley.
Wild Peaches. Wylie.
Wine. Lebensohn.
Winter Anemones. Brasch.
The Winter Lakes.
　Campbell.
Wisdom. Fallon.
Wishmakers' Town. Young.
With a Posthumous Medal.
　Brinnin.
With Thee to Soar to the
　Skies. *Anonymous.*
Woman of This Earth
　(excerpt). Frost.
Wood-Pigeons. Masefield.
Wrapped Hair Bundles.
　LaPena.
The Wreck of the Hesperus.
　Longfellow.
Wynyard Sailor. Mathew.
You'll Love Me Yet!
　Browning.
A Young Highland Girl
　Studying Poetry. Smith.
Young Windebank. Woods.
Zagonyi. Boker.

Deathless
Ave Atque Vale. Jones, Jr.
The Bivouac of the Dead.
　O'Hara.
Blondel. Urmy.
Change. Howells.
The Coplas on the Death of
　His Father, the
　Grandmaster of Santiago.
　Manrique.
Epigram. Garnett.
Friendship's Mystery.
　Philips.
An Inconclusive Evening.
　Bellerby.
Long as the Darkening Cloud
　Abode. Richards.
Mohini Chatterjee. Yeats.
Noone and a Star Stand, Am
　to Am. Cummings.
The Rattlesnake. Carr.
When Young Hearts Break.
　Heine.

Debate
Invective against Ibis
　(excerpt). Ovid (Publius
　Ovidius Naso).
Paradise Lost. Milton.
Said death to passion.
　Dickinson.
Sonnets, LXXXIX: "Say that
　thou didst forsake me for
　some fault." Shakespeare.
To the Marquis of Graham on
　His Marriage. *Anonymous.*
The Velvet Hand. McGinley.
Deborah
Sonnets, First Series.
　Tuckerman.
Through a Glass Eye, Lightly.
　Kizer.
Debris
The Dump. Kuzma.
Moving. Steele.
Poem for My Thirty-Second
　Birthday. Ciardi.
The Room. Jennings.
Debt (or) (s)
The Baby. Taylor.
Behold the Man!
　Anonymous.
Byrontown. *Anonymous.*
The Carpet-Weaver's Lament.
　Anonymous.
Clarimonde. Gautier.
Claude Allen. *Anonymous.*
Dr. Donne. Alling.
Fear. Hajnal.
From a Connecticut
　Newspaper. Rockwell.
The Garden. Very.
Harpers Ferry. Rodman.
His Gift and Mine. Gurley.
How Happy the Soldier.
　Anonymous.
Human Frailty. Freneau.
Lament for the Alamo.
　Guiterman.
Lollocks. Graves.
Long Time a Child.
　Coleridge.
Next of Kin. Mallalieu.
On the Death of Doctor Swift.
　Swift.
Poets' Corner. Graves.
A Promise Made.
　Anonymous.
A Secret Love or Two I Must
　Confess. Campion.
Shall We Forget. Mitchell.
Song Making. Teasdale.
Tales of a Wayside Inn.
　Longfellow.
To Spain—A Last Word.
　Thomas.
To the Most Virtuous
　Mistress Pot, Who Many
　Times Entertained Him.
　Herrick.
Upon the Dramatick Poems of
　Mr. John Fletcher.
　Cartwright.
Decay (ed) (s)
Ballad of the Drinker in His
　Pub. Van Wyk Louw.
The Dead Sparrow.
　Catullus.
The Deserted Village.
　Goldsmith.
Doing, a filthy pleasure is, and
　short. 02] ...never/Can this.
　Petronius Arbiter (Caius
　Petronius Arbiter).
The Drowned Mariner.
　Smith

The Faerie Queene. Spenser.
Foeda Est In Coitu.
　Petronius Arbiter (Caius
　Petronius Arbiter).
Gold Is the Son of Zeus:
　Neither Moth Nor Worm
　May Gnaw It. "Field.
The Hammers. Hodgson.
Hymns for Infant Minds
　(excerpt). Taylor.
I Was a Bustle-Maker Once,
　Girls. Barrington.
If Crossed with All Mishaps.
　Drummond.
Invitation to Youth.
　Anonymous.
Love. Kinsella.
The Maunding Soldier.
　Parker.
The Midnight Court.
　Merriman.
Of Dying Beauty. Zukofsky.
On a Portrait of a Deaf Man.
　Betjeman.
Remembrances. Clare.
Rest and Silence. Trakl.
Semele Recycled. Kizer.
Sonnet: "I have not spent the
　April of my time." Griffin.
The Thirsty Poet. Philips.
Three Brown Girls Singing.
　Holman.
To His Book. Walsh.
To His Muse. Breton.
To the World the Perfection
　of Love. Habington.
Virgidemiarum. Hall.
When Youth and Beauty Meet
　Together. Anonymous.
The Wood-Pile. Frost.

Decease
Cardinal Bembo's Epitaph on
　Raphael. Hardy.
Here Lies My Wife.
　Cunningham.
Uncollected Poems and
　Epigrams, 2. Cunningham.

Deceit (ful)
The Blacksmith. Anonymous.
Memorial Lines on the
　Gender of Latin
　Substantives. Kennedy.
Mr. Symons at Richmond,
　Mr. Pope at Twickenham.
　Symons.
Riddle: "Every lady in the
　land." Anonymous.

Deceive (d) (r) (s)
Birds and Bees. Anonymous.
Caelica, XLVIII. Greville.
Caelica, XCI. Greville.
A Christmas Message.
　Ewart.
The Cock and the Fox. La
　Fontaine.
Farewell for a While.
　Daryush.
How Hardly I Conceal'd My
　Tears. Wharton.
I Thought You Loved Me.
　Anonymous.
John Riley. Anonymous.
Juan's Song. Bogan.
King James II. Dryden.
Little Ponds. Guiterman.
Prologue. Auden.
The Revenger's Tragedy
　(excerpt). Tourneur.
Revolution. Zimunya.
Sonnets to Aurelia. Nichols.
The Things. Aiken.

Upon Mrs. Eliz. Wheeler,
　under the Name of
　Amarillis. Herrick.
The Witch. Douglas.
A Woman's Love. Hay.

December
Flame-Heart. McKay.
Fool Song. Lengyel.
Frozen Hands. Bruchac.
The Haunted House.
　Graves.
Ice. Spender.
The Naughty Lord & the Gay
　Young Lady. Anonymous.
The Stallion. Porter.
Will You Love Me in
　December as You Do in
　May? Walker.

Decent
Dirty Jim. Taylor.
Epigram, in a Maid of
　Honour's Prayer-Book.
　Pope.
Of Commerce and Society.
　Hill.
On Thomas Moore's Poems.
　Anonymous.
Reaping. Lowell.

Deception (s)
Air (parody). Dow.
Four Sonnets to Helen, 3.
　Ronsard.
No One in Particular.
　Perreault.

Decipher
Caelica, LXXXIII. Greville.
Cattle. Skrzynecki.

Decision
The Federal Convention.
　Anonymous.
Water-Images. Osborn.
The Watershed. Auden.

Deck (s)
The City of Baltimore.
　Anonymous.
Continental Crossing.
　Thompson.
Evening Hymn in the Hovels.
　Adams.
The Iliad. Homer.
A Leap for Life. Colton.
Making Land. Day.
The Old Ships. Flecker.
One Year After. Kizer.
Population. Oppen.
A Question. Anonymous.
The Valiant Sailor.
　Anonymous.

Declare
Earth. Wheelock.
Robin Hood and the Ranger.
　Anonymous.

Decline
On the Duke of Buckingham,
　Slain by Felton...
　Felltham.
Sonnet: There Is a Bondage
　Worse. Wordsworth.

Decorum
Dulce et Decorum Est.
　Owen.
Funeral Song for Mamie
　Eisenhower. Wong.
The Jolly Beggars. Burns.

Decrease
The Praise of Waterford
　(excerpt). Anonymous.
Were I to Mount beyond the
　Field. Keyes.

Decree
A Gulling Sonnet. Davies.

How Happy Is the Little
　Stone. Dickinson.
The Timid Gazelle.
　Kasmuneh.

Dede
Bruce Meets Three Men with
　a Wethe. Barbour.
Lyarde Is an Old Horse.
　Anonymous.
Prayer to St. Helena.
　Anonymous.
Snatches: "Wela! qwa sal thir
　hornes blau." Anonymous.

Dee
The Higher Pantheism in a
　Nutshell. Swinburne.
Limerick: "There was an Old
　Man of the Dee." Lear.
Mary Hamilton. Anonymous.
The Miller of Dee.
　Anonymous.
The Sands of Dee. Kingsley.

Deed (s)
Abraham Lincoln. Stedman.
After Reading St. John the
　Divine. Derwood.
Ahab Mohammed. Legare.
Behold the Deeds! Bunner.
A Border Burn. Selkirk.
The Challenge. Kleiser.
The Charge at Santiago.
　Hayne.
Dear Master, in Whose Life I
　See. Hunter.
Decoration Day. Barbour.
Dedication to Hunger.
　Gluck.
Dedication to the Generation
　Knocking at the Door.
　Davidson.
The Democratic Barber; or,
　Country Gentleman's
　Surprise. Parrish.
Despair and Hope. Zangwill.
En Las Internas Entranas.
　Theresa of Avila.
Extraordinary Will. Jackett.
Fort McHenry. Anonymous.
From the Domain of
　Arnheim. Morgan.
The Green Mountain Boys.
　Bryant.
House and Home. Hugo.
How Shall We Honor Them?
　Markham.
Hymn to Evil. Ginsberg.
Johnny Appleseed. Venable.
The Land War. O'Sullivan.
The Leg in the Subway.
　Williams.
The Lion-Hunt. Pringle.
A Little Cabin. Johnson.
Meditation of a Mariner.
　Auchterlonie.
Mi Y'Malel. Anonymous.
Mistakes. Swarberg.
Odes. Horace.
Our Fathers Fought for
　Liberty. Lowell.
Peasantry. Duggan.
The Portrait of Henry VIII.
　Howard.
The Prince of Life.
　Oxenham.
Renunciation. Pearse.
Revolutionary Letters. Di
　Prima.
Salutation to Jesus Christ.
　Calvin.
Service. Browning.
Song of Coridon and
　Melampus. Peele.

Sonnets: A Sequence on
　Profane Love. Boker.
The Stump Is Not the
　Tombstone. Seager.
Temper. Anonymous.
To a Cactus Seller. Shaul.
To Geron. Jacob.
To Hold in a Poem. Smith.
To Mother Nature.
　Knowles.
Troilus and Cressida. De
　Vere.
The Village Blacksmith.
　Longfellow.

Deep (er) (est) (s)
Alastor. Shelley.
The Ancient Couple on Lu
　Mountain. Van Doren.
Angler. Vinz.
At the Playground. Stafford.
Atavism. Lake.
The Brigg. Skelton.
By the Statue of King Charles
　at Charing Cross.
　Johnson.
Calm Is the Morn without a
　Sound. Tennyson.
Charon's Cosmology. Simic.
The Cruel Mother.
　Anonymous.
Daniel Webster. Holmes.
The Dead and the Living One.
　Hardy.
The Deep. Brainard.
Deep Water. Anonymous.
The Dream House. Seiffert.
Duality. Hobson.
Duet. Tennyson.
England and America in 1782.
　Tennyson.
Evening on the Broads.
　Swinburne.
Feeling for Fish. Trawick.
A Film. Goldbarth.
Frutta Di Mare. Scott.
The Great Voices. Brooks.
The Gunner. Webb.
Home. Nicholson.
Horoscope. Cunningham.
Hyperion. Keats.
I Feel an Apparition. Le
　Roy.
I Know Not Why.
　Rosenfeld.
I Never Will Marry.
　Anonymous.
In Memoriam A.H.H., CIII.
　Tennyson.
In Our Boat. Craik.
Insomnia. Bishop.
Intimations of Immortality
　from Recollections of Early
　Childhood. Wordsworth.
The Inverted Torch.
　Thomas.
It Is at Moments after I Have
　Dreamed. Cummings.
It Is No Dream of Mine.
　Thoreau.
Jack Was Every Inch a Sailor.
　Anonymous.
Jacklight. Erdrich.
The Last Instructions to a
　Painter. Marvell.
Legend. Torrence.
Limerick: "The Thames runs,
　bones rattle, rats creep."
　Cope.
The Lookout. Collins.
Love Is Not Solace. Maris
　Stella.

Love-Songs, At Once Tender and Informative. Hoffenstein.
March Light. Mills, Jr.
The Marriage of Heaven and Hell. Blake.
Maud. Tennyson.
My Father Is the Nightingale. *Anonymous.*
The Nature of Man. Sisson.
Naughty Boy. Creeley.
Nearing La Guaira. Walcott.
The Night Moths. Markham.
Not for That City. Mew.
Ode to England. Lord
An Old Malediction. Hecht.
On an Engraving by Casserius. Hope.
On Knowing Nothing. Smith.
On the Death of Karl Barth. Clemo.
The Owl. Warren.
A Plea for Postponement. Petronius Arbiter (Caius Petronius Arbiter).
The Plow. Horne.
Poets Observed. Rosenberger.
A Presentation of Two Birds to My Son. Wright.
Quien Sabe? Morris.
Rain. Sears.
The Reader Writes. Crane.
Resurgam. *Anonymous.*
Returning to the World. Chester.
A Ritual to Read to Each Other. Stafford.
Rock'd in the Cradle of the Deep. Willard.
Rolling Thunder. Wolf.
The Sea-Deeps. Miller.
She lay as if at play. Dickinson.
Signature for Tempo. MacLeish.
Sky Diver. Stoutenburg.
Song Be Delicate. Neilson.
Song for a Transformation (excerpt). Arrivi.
Songs of Kabir. Kabir.
Stonefish and Starfish. Blight.
A Story. Stafford.
Summer. Thomson.
Summer Pogrom. Zwicky.
T. B. Blues. Leadbelly.
Taos Drums. Simpson.
To a School-Girl. Neilson.
To the Reverend W.L. Bowles. Coleridge.
Twice Shy. Heaney.
Variations on a Theme. Whitman.
Villanelle with a Line by Yeats. Bennett.
Waratah. Robinson.
Waterchew! Corso.
While O'er the Deep Thy Servants Sail. Burgess.
Winter Sleep. Wylie.
Yves Tanguy. Gascoyne.

Deer
The Age of Animals. *Anonymous.*
Beinn a' Ghlo. Tulloch.
Epigram: "Boy-mad no longer." Rufinus Domesticus.
Geordie. *Anonymous.*

Hunting-Song. *Anonymous.*
In the gathering dew. Sagami.
Indian Song: Survival. Silko.
Myths and Texts. Snyder.
Nones. Auden.
O Spirit of Venus Whom I Adore. *Anonymous.*
The Pet Deer. Tate.
Pine Tree Tops. Snyder.
Riddle: "On yonder hill there is a red deer." *Anonymous.*
Springer Mountain. Dickey.
When in the Woods I Wander All Alone. Hovell-Thurlow.
Woodlore. Kurt.

Defeat (ed)
As He Is. Auden.
As I Lay with My Head in Your Lap Camerado. Whitman.
At the Executed Murderer's Grave. Wright.
Caught by Chance. Ramsey.
Charlie Johnson in Kettletown. Smith.
Defeat. Bynner.
For the Depressed. Symons.
The French, 1870-1871. *Anonymous.*
God to Thee We Humbly Bow. Boker.
A Hero. Coates.
A Hymn to No One Body. Wade.
The Man Watching. Rilke.
The Mountain Cemetery. Bowers.
The Pro. Swenson.
The Romantic. Ellis.
Song: "O'er the waste of waters cruising." Freneau.
Three Sermons to the Dead. Riding.
To His Chi Mistress. Starbuck.
To the Unknown Warrior. Chesterton.
Two Generations. Strong.
The Vanquished. Eglington.
The "Wanderer." Masefield.
William Yeats in Limbo. Keyes.

Defect (s)
Easter. Herbert.
The New World. Jones.
To Varus. Catullus.

Defence
The Battle of Lake Champlain. Freneau.
The Bee-Wisp. Turner.
Liberty Tree. Paine.
Samson Agonistes. Milton.
Some Trees. Ashbery.
Sometimes. Flint.

Defend (ed) (er) (ing) (s)
Cushla Ma Chree. Curran.
The Defender. Sampley.
Epitaph on an Army of Mercenaries. Housman.
Farewell to England. *Anonymous.*
A Full and True Account of a Horrid and Barbarous Robbery. Byrom.
"Girt in my guiltless gown..." Surrey.
The Graveyard Rabbit. Stanton.

Massachusetts Song of Liberty. Warren.
The Name of Jesus. Flint.
Part of the 9th Ode of the 4th Book of Horace... Horace.
This Feast of the Law. *Anonymous.*

Defer
Master's in the Garden Again. Ransom.
Petition. Thomas.

Defiance
Idea. Drayton.
Marmion. Scott.
Oh, Ye Censurers. Ibn Adiya.
On Dr. Samuel Ogden. Arden.
The Spirit. Turner.

Defile (d)
God to Man. Talmud.
The Hyaenas. Kipling.
King James and Brown. *Anonymous.*
Terly Terlow. *Anonymous.*

Defy
America. Coxe.
The Author Apologizes to a Lady for His Being a Little Man. Smart.
Beyond the End. Levertov.
Diptych. Sykes.
Paradise Lost. Milton.

Degree (s)
The End of April. Murray.
A Fable for Critics. Lowell.
The "Gloria Patri." Heywood.
Safari West. Williams.
Sea Voyage. Empson.

Deity
The Approach. Traherne.
Graffiti. Bold.
On the Miracle of Loaves. Crashaw.
Poverty. Traherne.
Thought. Emerson.
Truth is as old as god. Dickinson.
We. Kirillov.

Delaware
Across the Delaware. Carleton.
New Jersey Turnpike. Cumbie.

Delay (s)
Buffalo. Daniells.
Choose. Bishop.
Chorale. Hope.
Death Invoked. Massinger.
Delay. Bates.
The Dell. Ewart.
The Geese. Graham.
Now. Ken.
Paradise Lost. Milton.
Sonnet: "To rail or jest, ye know I use it not." Wyatt.

Delicate
37th Dance–Banding–22 March 1964. MacLow.
Champagne. Dove.
Conversation. Berryman.
The Ice Castle. Harris.
The Map. Bishop.
Pisces. Thomas.
Some Kind of Giant. Pritchard.
Susanna and the Elders. Crapsey.
Two Views of a Cadaver Room. Plath.

Delicious
The Birthday Child. Fyleman.
Gislebertus' Eve. Berryman.
Goober Peas. Pindar.
Invitation to the Bee. Smith.
Sneezing. Hunt.
Solioquy of a Tortoise on Revisiting the Lettuce Beds... Rieu.
Squid. Blumenthal.
When I Loved You. Moore.

Delight (ed) (ful) (s)
The Aeneid. Virgil (Publius Vergilius Maro).
All That Is, and Can Delight. Farren.
All Things Wait upon Thee. Rossetti.
Un-American Investigators. Hughes.
Artificial Teeth. Brown.
Astrophel and Stella, XLIX. Sidney.
Ave-Maria Bells. Stoddard.
Ballata of Love's Power. Cavalcanti.
Caelica, LXXII. Greville.
Casey Jones. Swart.
Cathleen Sweeping. Johnston.
Chorus. Daniel.
Chorus of Satyrs, Driving Their Goats. Euripides.
Christ 3: The Last Judgement. *Anonymous.*
Columcille's Greeting to Ireland. Columcille.
Come to Me. *Anonymous.*
Dismissal. Campion.
Electra. Williams.
The Faerie Queene. Spenser.
Fair Is the Rose. *Anonymous.*
Follow Your Saint. Campion.
The Frailty of Beauty. "C.
The Friar. Peacock.
God's Controversy with New-England. Wigglesworth.
Gracious Saviour, We Adore Thee. Cutting.
The Handball Players at Brighton Beach. Feldman.
The Happy Pair (excerpt). Sedley.
Healing the Wound. Heine.
The Hippopotamus. Nash.
Hymn. Doddridge.
I'm Seventeen Come Sunday. *Anonymous.*
Insatiableness. Traherne.
The Instruments. Smart.
Lady, the Silly Flea. *Anonymous.*
Lamorna Cove. Davies.
Limerick: "W's a well-informed wight." Herford.
The Lincolnshire Poacher. *Anonymous.*
Lines Where Beauty Lingers. Adams.
The Lion-House. Wheelock.
Little Son. Johnson.
Madrigal: "My dearest mistress." Corkine.
The Marriage of Heaven and Hell. Blake.
Melancholia. Bridges.
Memory. Deutsch.
A Mile from Eden. Ridler.
Moment Musicale. Carman.

My Pretty Rose Tree. Blake.
Norse Sailor's Joy. Thorley.
Notre Dames des Champs.
  Synge.
Ode to Pity. Collins.
Ode to the Lake of Geneva.
  Parsons.
Poem: "on getting a card."
  Williams.
The Poet to the Sleeping Saki.
  Goethe.
The Quartette. De La Mare.
Radiant Is the World Soul.
  Kook.
Reunion. Merwin.
Riddle: "Close in a cage a
  bird I'll keep."
  Anonymous.
Rowland's Rhyme. Drayton.
Rupert Brooke. Gibson.
Sacred Emily. Stein.
Saviour, Whose Love Is Like
  the Sun. Robbins.
Sestina. Swinburne.
Shadow. Delius.
She Was All That You Loved.
  Laxness.
The Shepherdess. Meynell.
A Shining Night; or, Dick
  Daring, the Poacher.
  Anonymous.
A Solitary Life. Drummond.
Song in the Wood. Fletcher.
Song: "Love laid his sleepless
  head." Swinburne.
Sonnet: "Madam, 'tis true,
  your beauties move."
  Godolphin.
Spring Landscape. Ficke.
The Stream's Song.
  Abercrombie.
Thrice Happy He.
  Drummond.
To a Lady Who Did Sing
  Excellently. Herbert of
  Cherbury.
To a River in the South.
  Newbolt.
To Amanda. Thomson.
To Colman Returning.
  Colman.
To Night. Anonymous.
The Tour of Dr. Syntax: In
  Search of the Picturesque.
  Combe.
A Very Phoenix. Lodge.
Delirium
Owed to New York.
  Newton.
The Poem of the End
  (excerpt). Tsvetayeva.
The Power Station. Merrill.
The Praise of Ben Dorain.
  MacIntyre.
Deliver (ed)
A Cornish Litany (excerpt).
  Anonymous.
The Cropdusting (parody).
  Zaranka.
Distressed Men of War.
  Anonymous.
The Doctor Rebuilds a Hand.
  Young.
From Ghoulies and Ghosties.
  Anonymous.
In Passing. Shepherd.
Litany for Halloween.
  Anonymous.
A Litany for Old Age.
  Harsen.
Moving Day. Horne.
Psalm XXV. Sidney.

Threnos. Hervey.
Dell (s)
Ode: "To orisons, the
  midnight bell." Beckford.
The Redingote and the
  Vamoose. Munkittrick.
There is a morn by men
  unseen. Dickinson.
Deluge
Charles the Fifth and the
  Peasant. Lowell.
Eugenia: Presage of Storme.
  Chapman.
Exodus 1940. Wolfenstein.
An Inhabited Emptiness.
  Gold.
Meditation. Pain.
Delusion (s)
The Broken Girth. Graves.
The Indian Burying Ground.
  Freneau.
Lines Written Immediately
  after Parting from a Lady.
  Brydges.
Delve
The Battle of Aughrim:
  Rapparees. Murphy.
Miracle Play: The Lament of
  Eve. Anonymous.
Over in the Meadow.
  Wadsworth.
Demand (s)
Ashokan. Rainer.
Cudworth's Undergraduate
  Ode to a Bare Behind.
  Ower.
Death's Apology. Mello.
The Poet's Request.
  Anonymous.
Resolution in Four Sonnets.
  Cotton.
Transplantitis. Sobel.
Democracy
The Black Draftee from Dixie.
  Clifford.
The Black Man Speaks.
  Hughes.
Bonfire of Kings. Evans.
The Prairie Dog. Guiterman.
To Milton. Wilde.
Demon (s)
Alone. Poe.
The Ashland Tragedy, II.
  Anonymous.
The Envious Critick.
  Wycherley.
The Forest Fire. Monroe.
From Childhood's Hour.
  Poe.
How the Bulls Were Begotten:
  The Two Bulls.
  Anonymous.
Modern Love, XXVII.
  Meredith.
Quebec Farmhouse. Glassco.
Simfunny of Thee Hold
  Whorl. Lynch.
The Snowstorm. Crouch.
Visiting Father. Lim.
The Waste Places. Stephens.
Den
Address to the Deil. Burns.
The Gipsy Girl. Hodgson.
A Hazel Stick for Catherine
  Ann. Heaney.
Old Bangum. Anonymous.
Over in the Meadow.
  Anonymous.
Denial
104 Boulevard Saint-Germain.
  Pitchford.

Against Modesty in Love.
  Prior.
Amores. Ovid (Publius
  Ovidius Naso).
The Author to His Booke.
  Heywood.
Christ at the Door.
  Anonymous.
Contentment; or, The Happy
  Workman's Song. Byrom.
Error Pursued. Pinkerton.
Giant Decorative Dahlia.
  Holden.
If We Break Faith–.
  Auslander.
The Ignorance of Man.
  Merrick.
Inanna and the Anunna.
  Enheduanna.
The Lady's Resolve.
  Montagu.
The Last Trial. Anonymous.
The New Calf. Hearst.
A New Song of Wood's
  Halfpence. Swift.
O What Pleasure 'Tis to Find.
  Behn.
The Pink Locust. Williams.
Providence. Filicaja.
Resolution in Four Sonnets.
  Cotton.
The Scientist. Burroway.
Song: "So large a morning, so
  itself, to lean." Auden.
Sonnets for a Dying Man.
  Singer.
Sweet Meat Has Sour Sauce.
  Cowper.
Tetelestai. Aiken.
Three Epigrams.
  Cunningham.
To Little or No Purpose.
  Etherege.
Two Decisions. Watkins.
The Two Fires. Wright.
The Voice of Christmas.
  Kemp.
You Felons on Trial in
  Courts. Whitman.
Dentist
Archy at the Zoo. Marquis.
Shakespearean Soliloquy in
  Progress: "To have it out or
  not?" (parody). "W.
Depart (ed) (ing)
Another Song. Ross.
Aware. Lawrence.
Be Not Silent. Anonymous.
Beauty Imposes. Neilson.
The Celestial Pilot. Dante
  Alighieri.
Dark Song. Ammons.
Dear Body. Canan.
The Devil and the Angel.
  Dobson.
Distances. Kingston.
Florine. Campbell.
The Glorious Gift of God.
  Beddome.
God Be in My Head.
  Anonymous.
The Gulistan. Sa'di.
In These Fair Vales.
  Wordsworth.
Lament of a Man for His Son.
  Austin.
Last Verses. Motherwell.
Little Thomas. Evans.
London after the Great Fire,
  1666. Dryden.
Lord Thomas and Fair Annet
  (B vers.). Anonymous.

The Moon. Best.
Out of Sight, Out of Mind.
  Googe.
The Passing Bell. Heywood.
A Reproach to Morvyth.
  Dafydd ap Gwilym.
Seaweed. Longfellow.
Taking Leave of a Friend.
  Li Po.
The Time Is Swiftly Rolling
  On. Hicks.
To the First of August.
  Plato.
Tommies in the Train.
  Lawrence.
Translations from the Chinese:
  Secret Thoughts. Morley.
The Way to the Sea. Lerner.
Whispering Ghosts of the
  West. Anonymous
Whoever You Are Holding
  Me Now in Hand.
  Whitman.
The Year That's Awa'.
  Dunlop.
Departure (s)
After the Hunt. Liliencron.
Departure in the Dark. Day
  Lewis.
The Elephant. Hochman.
Keraunograph. Carruth.
Mari Magno. Clough.
More Distant Than the Dead
  Sea. Tueni.
Parting. Halevi.
Things That Are Worse Than
  Death. Olds.
Upon the Losse of His
  Mistresses. Herrick.
Deprive
Elegy. Maclaurin.
The Envious Critick.
  Wycherley.
Depth (s)
The Bothie of Tober-na-
  Vuolich. Clough.
Consummation. Anonymous.
The Creek. Ross.
Death Sonnet I. "Mistral.
Deborah as Scion. Dickey.
Deep Waters. Sutphen.
Divided. Ingelow.
A Grave. Moreland.
Hand. Roditi.
Inside and Out. Phillips.
Limerick: "The babe, with a
  cry brief and dismal."
  Gorey.
Love has seven names.
  Hadewijch.
The Movement of Fish.
  Dickey.
Oh Lovely Fishermaiden.
  Heine.
On the Welsh Marches.
  Stone.
Painting. Jacobs.
Prayer. Mak.
A Prayer. Tuwim.
Rescue. Stuart.
Review from Staten Island.
  Oden.
Schubertiana. Transtromer.
Throughout the Day We Are
  Able to Ban the Voices.
  Roland-Holst.
The Trees of Life. Very.
Derision
Eyes That Last I Saw in
  Tears. Eliot.

On the Portrait of a Woman
  About to be Hanged.
  Hardy.
To Fortune. Herrick.
Twilight on Sumter.
  Stoddard.

Derry
Lament for the Poets: 1916.
  Ledwidge.
Novelettes III: The Gardener.
  MacNeice.

Descartes
Theological. Fadiman.
Unpredictable but
  Providential. Auden.

Descend (ing) (s)
Ambition. Davies.
Caelica, X. Greville.
A Christmas Hymn. Wilbur.
Colonialism. Qarshe.
The Homeward Journey.
  Aaronson.
Invitation to a Spirit.
  Anonymous.
On the Pole. Greenberg.
Our Lady's Salutation.
  Southwell.
Poor Angels. Hirsch.
Pride of Ancestry. Frost.
The Queen. Pitchford.
Scala Coeli. Raine.
Shaman. Sabina.
T-Bar. Page.

Description
I Keep to Myself Such
  Measures. Creeley.
Memo. Sahl.
On Meeting the Clergy of the
  Holy Catholic Church in
  Osaka. Kogawa.
The Operation. Creeley.
Verse. Lattimore.

Desert (s)
Absence. Barnes.
Air. Merwin.
Allah's Tent. Colton.
And So Should You.
  Anonymous.
At Barstow. Tomlinson.
At Gibraltar. Woodberry.
A Ballad of London. Le
  Gallienne.
The Blood Horse.
  "Cornwall.
The Boar and the Dromedar.
  Beissel.
Bones in the Desert. White.
Caelica, LXXIII. Greville.
Caravans. Peabody.
Cat-Goddesses. Graves.
Comrades. Woodberry.
A Day with the Foreign
  Legion. Whittemore.
The Dead of the Wilderness.
  Bialik.
A Denunciation. Hassan.
Desert Places. Frost.
Drifting. Bushby.
Epitaphs of the War, 1914-18.
  Kipling.
Golden Calf. MacCaig.
Hawktree. Smith.
Hitch Haiku. Snyder.
Honey from the Lion.
  Drake.
I Walked in a Desert.
  Crane.
Jars. Raboff.
The Kasidah. Burton.
Khamsin. Scollard.
Life and Death. Turner.

The Life of St. Cellach: He
  Who Forsakes the Clerkly
  Life. Anonymous.
Lines: I Praise God's
  Mankind in an Old Woman.
  Watson.
London Adulterations.
  Anonymous.
Midsummer. Kinsella.
Morning Song. Blakely.
The Mountain. Lermontov.
Nepenthe. Darley.
New Mexican Desert.
  Bynner.
No, Thou Hast Never Griev'd
  but I Griev'd Too.
  Landor.
Now and Then. Sangster.
Oh, You Wholly Rectangular.
  Cole.
The Orchard and the Heath.
  Meredith.
The Phoenix. Darley.
Poet and Critic. Daniel.
Praise. Grenville.
Prayer. Ewart.
Rebuff. Albert.
The Retarded Children Find a
  World Built Just for Them.
  O Hehir.
The Rock of Cashel. De
  Vere.
Sakhara. Ford.
Salt Lake City. Carruth.
The Skylark. Hogg.
Song for Dov Shamir. Abse.
Spring in the Desert.
  Merrill.
Stanzas from the Grande
  Chartreuse. Arnold.
Symphony: First Movement.
  Wheelock.
To My Son. Byron.
A View of the Town
  (excerpt). Gilbert.
The Water-Hole. Wood.
Western Ways. Lattimore.
Winding down the War.
  Appleman.

Deserted
Blind Steersmen. Parkes.
The Deserted Garden.
  Stanford.
The House Carpenter's Wife.
  Anonymous.
In the Land of Magic.
  Michaux.
Jubilate Agno. Smart.
Loveliest of Counties,
  Shropshire Now (parody).
  Sainsbury.

Deserve (d)
Fragment. Berlind.
The Lover Exhorteth His
  Lady to Be Constant.
  Anonymous.
The Lover Sheweth How He
  Is Forsaken of Such as He
  Sometime Enjoyed. Wyatt.
May Song. Berry.
To a Bad Heart. Reynolds.

Design (s) (ed)
Americans Are Afraid of
  Lizards. Shapiro.
Bears and Waterfalls.
  Sarton.
The Child's Power of Wonder.
  Saha.
Design. Frost.
A Hint from Herrick.
  Aldrich.

The Martyr and the Army.
  Henderson.
On His Mistress, the Queen of
  Bohemia. Wotton.
The Orchestra. Williams.
Prayer. Thoreau.
Relics. Gegna.
To My Excellent Lucasia, on
  Our Friendship. Philips.
Vapor Trails. Snyder.

Desire (d) (s)
Agathon: Song of Eros.
  Woodberry.
Ageless. Anonymous.
All Fellows (excerpt).
  Housman.
The Angel in the House.
  Patmore.
At a Hasty Wedding.
  Hardy.
Athletic Ode. Santayana.
A Ballad of Burdens.
  Swinburne.
Ballata: He Will Gaze upon
  Beatrice. Dante Alighieri.
Beauty, a Silver Dew.
  Anonymous.
Before the Feast of Shushan.
  Spencer.
Benedictio Domini. Dowson.
Black Marble.
  O'Shaughnessy.
Caelica, XVII. Greville.
Caelica, XL. Greville.
Caelica, LIV. Greville.
Caelica, LXVII. Greville.
Caelica, LXXVI. Greville.
Cafe Tableau. Swenson.
Clay Hills. Untermeyer.
Corn-Woman Remembered.
  Volborth.
Crimson Nor Yellow Roses.
  Wratislaw.
Desire. Traherne.
Desire's Government. "W.
Destiny. Arnold.
Drunken Americans.
  Ashbery.
The Excesses of God.
  Jeffers.
Feed Still Thyself. Ralegh.
For My Daughter. Kees.
Frustration. Daryush.
Gitanjali. Tagore.
Godfrey of Bulloigne:
  Armida...Sets out to undo
  the Crusaders. Tasso.
The Gulf Stream.
  Bellamann.
He That Loves. Sidney.
The Heavenly Humor.
  Shapiro.
Here are fine gifts, children.
  Sappho.
The Higher Empiricism.
  Golffing.
Hopeless Desire Soon Withers
  and Dies. "W.
House of Fire. Weiss.
Hypocrite Swift. Bogan.
I turn you out of doors.
  Chartier.
I Would in Rich and Golden
  Coloured Raine. Lodge.
Image. Noailles.
In Memoriam A.H.H., CX.
  Tennyson.
Jonathan Houghton.
  Masters.
Keats to Fanny Brawne.
  Masters.

The Lark. Bernard de
  Ventadour
The Life above, the Life on
  High. Theresa of Avila.
Life's Circumnavigators.
  Rodgers.
The Locust Hunt. Murray.
The Love-Making: His and
  Hers. Merriam.
Love's Ending. Anonymous.
A Lover's Envy. Van Dyke.
Make Way. Lavoie.
The Marriage of Heaven and
  Hell. Blake.
Moral Story II. Wright.
Morning Glory. Sassoon.
My Father's Heart. Friebert.
Natura Naturans. Clough.
Night. Rolleston.
Non Que Je Veuille Oter La
  Liberte. Guillet.
November Sunday Morning.
  Feinman.
Nuptial Hymn. Peacham.
The Nurse-Life Wheat.
  Greville.
O Gongyla, my darling rose.
  Sappho.
Odes, VIII. Hafiz.
Oh the Inconstant. Van
  Wyk Louw.
On Sitting Down to Read
  "King Lear" Once Again.
  Keats.
On Some Buttercups.
  Sherman.
The Orotava Road. Bunting.
The Painter. Fitzgerald.
Parted Lovers. Halevi.
Patron of Flawless Serpent
  Beauty. Mayrocker.
Pauca Mea: I Said, This
  Misery Must End.
  Brennan.
The Pentecost Castle
  (excerpt). Hill.
The Pet Deer. Tate.
Postlude. Williams.
The Progress of Poesy.
  Gray.
Les Realites. Guest.
Redo, 1-5. Hejinian.
Returning to Roots of First
  Feeling. Duncan.
Rich Mine of Knowledge.
  Chapman.
Richie Story (A version).
  Anonymous.
The Road. Stephens.
The Royal Crown. Solomon
  ibn Gabirol.
The Secrets of the Earth.
  Blake.
The Sequel. Roethke.
Sestina on Her Portrait.
  Nemerov.
The Snake-Charmer. Naidu.
Sonet XXV. Stirling.
The Song. Dorn.
Song: "Fire, fire." Bold.
Song of Eros. Woodberry.
Sonnet I: "Not Ulysses, no,
  nor any other man."
  Labe.
Sonnet: "The winter
  deepening, the hay all in."
  Wilbur.
The Spectacle of Truth.
  Hewitt.
Though I Regarded Not.
  Surrey.
Threatened. Walker.

Desire
The Tiger of Desire.
  MacInnes.
To the Blessed Sacrament.
  Constable.
Visions. Blake.
Watching You Sleep under
  Monet's Water Lilies.
  Ruark.
The Ways of Trains.
  Coatsworth.
A White Rose. O'Reilly.
The Wish. Watkyns.
The Woman. Thomas.
Work. Codrescu.
Youth and Maturity.
  Greville.

Desk (s)
Arriving. Halpern.
Complicity. Gallagher.
Don Juan. Byron.
Ghosts. Reid.
I Wonder How Many People
  in This City. Cohen.
Ivory Paper Weight.
  Stoutenburg.
The Small Silver-Coloured
  Bookworm. Parnell.
This Book Is Mine.
  Anonymous.

Desolate
Autumn Refrain. Stevens.
The Burial in Flanders.
  Nichols.
Cling to Me. Brereton.
The Dead of the Wilderness.
  Bialik.
The Death of Cleopatra.
  Horace.
The Horse. Eguren.
Il Pleut Doucement sur la
  Ville. Verlaine.
The Lonesome Grove.
  Anonymous.
Of Boston in New England.
  Bradford.
The Prodigal Son. Symons.
A Small Faculty Stag for the
  Visiting Poet. Birney.
Somebody's Gone. Ford.
Sorrow of Mydath.
  Masefield.
The Well. Brown.
Written on Seeing the
  Flowers, and Remembering
  My Daughter. Ch'i.
You Are Desolate, Fort of
  Kings. *Anonymous.*

Desolation
Boston. O'Reilly.
Hundred-Gated Thebes.
  Darley.
Indian Summer: Vermont.
  Stevenson.
Letter to R. Maas.
Occupation: Housewife.
  McGinley.
On My Wandering Flute.
  Sutzkever.
Still the Mind Smiles.
  Jeffers.
Welcome the Wrath. Kunitz.
Winter Westerlies. Devaney.

Despair (ing) (s)
Ad Coelum. Pattison.
Always Before Your Voice
  My Soul. Cummings.
Amboyna. Dryden.
The Angel in the House.
  Patmore.
The Answer. Jeffers.
The auctioneer of parting.
  Dickinson.

Autumn. Hood.
The Bag. Herbert.
Caelica, VIII. Greville.
Caelica, XXVII. Greville.
The City of Dreadful Night.
  Thomson.
The Combat. Muir.
Composed near Calais, on the
  Road Leading to Ardres,
  August 7, 1802.
  Wordsworth.
Engine Failure. Corsellis.
Epilogue Spoken by Mrs.
  Boutell. Dryden.
Far from Africa. Danner.
Footsteps. Hall.
Footsteps of Spring. Bialik.
Frenzy. Crabbe.
From the Hymn of
  Empedocles. Arnold.
Hate! Antokolsy.
Hear Me Yet. *Anonymous.*
Hollandaise. Bryan.
Hope's Okay. Ammons.
Hyperion. Keats.
I Cannot Live With You.
  Dickinson.
I Know Not How It Falls on
  Me. Bronte.
Idea. Drayton.
Koskiusko. Coleridge.
Leaves Before the Wind.
  Sarton.
Like a Pearl Dropped.
  Stickney.
Limerick: "There was an old
  man whose despair." Lear.
The Lover Compareth His
  State to a Ship... Wyatt.
The Milkman. Gardner.
Montalbert (excerpt). Smith.
The Moral. Weiss.
Moses and Jesus. Zangwill.
My Angel. Brooks.
My Galley. Wyatt.
On When McCarthy Was a
  Wolf among a Nation of
  Queer-Queers. Dugan.
Only the Heart. Campbell.
Paradise Lost. Milton.
Pasquin to the Queen's Statue
  at St. Paul's, during the
  Procession... Shippen.
Recalling War. Graves.
Repression. Corsellis.
The Rescue. Logan.
Song: "Ye happy swains,
  whose hearts are free."
  Etherege.
Songs of the People. Bialik.
Southeast Arkanasia.
  Angelou.
Speak This Kindly to Her.
  Bagg.
Strangers. Thomas.
The Studio. Mahon.
This Last Pain. Empson.
Threnody. Scherzo.
To a Woman. Glover.
Trivial, Vulgar, and Exalted:
  19. Cunningham.
The Unseen Bridge.
  Thomas.
Wet Summer: Botanic
  Gardens. McDonald.

Desperate
Poem: "Like a deaf man
  meshed in his endless
  silence." Wain.

Despise (d) (s)
At One O'Clock in the
  Morning. Baudelaire.

Autumn. *Anonymous.*
Egloge V (excerpt). Barclay.
A Hue and Cry after Fair
  Amoret. Congreve.
Leave Them Alone.
  Kavanagh.
The Lion and the Mouse.
  Taylor.
Lord, Hear My Prayer.
  Clare.
My Mother. Taylor.
On Seeing the Royal Palace at
  Stirling in Ruins. Burns.
Only the Polished Skeleton.
  Cullen.
A Pastoral Elegy. Tibullus.
Praise of Homer. Chapman.
To Nature. Coleridge.
Years and Years I Have
  Loved You. Gillett.

Destination
Among Commuters. Swan.
Bury Our Faces. Millard.
For Sale. Lowell.
The Kiss. Yau.
Nostalgia for 70. Miller.
You Drive in a Circle.
  Hughes.

Destiny
Albert Sidney Johnson.
  Sherwood.
The Answer of Mr. Waller's
  Painter to His Many New
  Advisers. *Anonymous.*
Anticipaton. Bronte.
Black Woman. Senghor.
The Broom. Leopardi.
Calais, August 15, 1802.
  Wordsworth.
Corydon's Complaint.
  Pordage.
The Evening Cloud. Wilson.
The Farewell. Stanley.
The Feast of Stephen.
  Nichols.
For a Child's Drawing.
  Vogt.
Fulfilment. Barker.
Girl Walking. Bell.
Guardianship. Johnson.
The Messiah. Frishman.
The New Negro. McCall.
Parvuli Ejus. De Vere.
The Photos. Wakoski.
A Prayer Brings Rain.
  Fairfax.
The proverb reporteth, no
  man can deny...
  Anonymous.
Remember, Sinful Youth.
  Anonymous.
Sestina d'Inverno. Hecht.
Those Various Scalpels.
  Moore.
To an Infant Expiring the
  Second Day of its Birth.
  Wright.
The Way of Life. Danquah.
Whatever You Say Say
  Nothing. Heaney.
You Masks of the
  Masquerade. Kahn.

Destitute
Epitaph. Chiabrera.
Lord, Hear My Prayer.
  Clare.

Destroy (ed) (es) (ing) (s)
Amoretti, LVI. Spenser.
Astrophel and Stella, XL.
  Sidney.
Before an Old Painting of the
  Crucifixion. Momaday.

Caelica, X. Greville.
Charleston. Gilder.
Destroyer Life. *Anonymous.*
Esthetique du Mal. Stevens.
In Evil Long I Took Delight.
  Newton.
The Mouldering Vine.
  Anonymous.
Mustapha. Greville.
New Construction: Bath Iron
  Works. Koehler.
No Coward Soul Is Mine.
  Bronte.
Oya. Lorde.
Prayer to the Trinity.
  Edmeston.
Prospero without His Magic.
  Gilbert.
The Sick Rose. Blake.
The Sleeper. Hay.
Song: "Ye happy swains,
  whose hearts are free."
  Etherege.
Time Eating. Douglas.
To an Enemy. Bodenheim.
Too Late. Thomas.
The Unbeliever. Bishop.
Upon Boys Diverting
  Themselves in the River.
  Foxton.
Us. Lester.
A Walk in Wurzburg.
  Plomer.
Water. Emerson.
With the Most Susceptible
  Element, the Mind, Already
  Turned... Benton.

Destruction
The Dead City. Calkins.
A Dead Weasel. Helwig.
Paradise Lost. Milton.
People. Yevtushenko.
Permanently. Koch.
World War. Eberhart.

Detest
Astrophel and Stella, XCVI.
  Sidney.
Don Juan. Byron.

Detroit
Abandoning Your Car in a
  Snowstorm: Rosslyn,
  Virginia. Blumenthal.
Andrew Jackson's Speech.
  Bly.

Deuce
Inertia. McGaffin.
The Protest of the Illiterate.
  Burgess.

Devastation
An Interlude. Bishop.
Song: "Whilst landmen
  wander, though controlled."
  Anonymous.

Devil (s)
The Abbot of Derry.
  Bennett.
The Apostasy of One and But
  One Lady. Lovelace.
Arizona Boys and Girls.
  Anonymous.
Begetting. Spears.
Copy of an Intercepted
  Despatch. Moore.
The Cow Ate the Piper.
  Anonymous.
The Cowboy at Church.
  Anonymous.
Cowboy's Salvation Song.
  Carr.
The Dance of Despair.
  Bialik.
Death's Jest Book. Beddoes.

Dives and Lazarus. *Anonymous.*
Drinking Song. *Anonymous.*
Epigram. *Anonymous.*
Epitaph for a Tyrannous Governor Who Choked on Wine. Sabir.
Epitaph on a Great Sleeper. Cokayne.
An Evening's Love. Dryden.
An Evil Spirit, Your Beauty Haunts Me Still. Drayton.
The Farmer's Curst Wife (B vers.). *Anonymous.*
Father Riley's Horse. Paterson.
Finger Nails. *Anonymous.*
The Ghost. Churchill.
Hilaire Belloc. Wolfe.
How the Fire Queen Crossed the Swamp. Ogilvie.
I Am the Poet Davies, William. Davies.
I Have Labored Sore. *Anonymous.*
The Imperfect Lover. Sassoon.
In Spain. Lawless.
Johnny McCardner. *Anonymous.*
The Lay of the Vigilantes. *Anonymous.*
The Lexington Murder. *Anonymous.*
The Litany. Cotton.
Lord Coningsby's Epitaph. Pope.
Macbeth (parody). Smith.
The Marriage of the Frog and the Mouse. *Anonymous.*
Marthy Had a Baby. *Anonymous.*
Men May Talk of Country-Christmasses. Massinger.
Miss Kilmansegg's Honeymoon. Hood.
Mog the Brunette. *Anonymous.*
O do not grieve, Dear Heart, nor shed a tear. Newcastle.
Old Sam's Wife. *Anonymous.*
On the Path. Strauss.
On the Reverend Jonathan Doe. *Anonymous.*
Our Saviour's Love. *Anonymous.*
Passivity. Fullerton.
The Peeler's Lament. *Anonymous.*
Prison Graveyard. Knight.
The Procession: A New Protestant Ballad. *Anonymous.*
Promises of Freedom. *Anonymous.*
Prospero without His Magic. Gilbert.
Reformation of Manners. Defoe.
Said the Whisky Flask. *Anonymous.*
Sally Goodin. *Anonymous.*
De Se. Weever.
She Proves the Inconsistency of the Desires and Criticism of Men... Juana Ines de la Cruz.
Sin. Herbert.
The Singing-Woman from the Wood's Edge. Millay.
Sonnet C. Greville.

The Sorrows of Sunday: An Elegy (excerpt). Wolcot.
Tee Roo. *Anonymous.*
The Temptations of Saint Anthony. McGinley.
They Can't Do That. *Anonymous.*
To God. Blake.
To Lucasta: Her Reserved Looks. Lovelace.
Tomah Stream. *Anonymous.*
Tyin' a Knot in the Devil's Tail. Gardner.
The Tyrant Apple Is Eaten. MacCaig.
The Utah Iron Horse. *Anonymous.*
When This Carnival Finally Closes. Mapanje.
Where Are You Going, My Good Old Man? *Anonymous.*
Devotion
The Adoration of the Wise Men. Alexander.
The Adventurous Muse. Watts.
The Bounty of Our Age. Farley.
Colin Clout. Skelton.
The Cradle and the Cross. Reitz.
Katy's Answer. Ramsay.
Love. *Anonymous.*
Misunderstanding. Layton.
Of a Zealous Lady. Harington.
On the Use of Jayshus. Gogarty.
Sequaire. Godeschalk.
Spiritual Love. Roscoe.
To a Louse. Burns.
To the Virgin. Lydgate.
The Voice of Ardent Zeal Speaks from the Lollard's Tower of St. Paul's. Farley.
Womankind. Massey.
Devour (ed) (s)
The Earth Asks and Receives Rain. Haring.
Grandmother's Apple Pies. Munro.
If night takes the form of a whale. Fraire.
In Goya's Greatest Scenes. Ferlinghetti.
The Man in the Ocelot Suit. Brookhouse.
A Memory of the Players in a Mirror at Midnight. Joyce.
The Poor of London. Forster.
Schedules. Dean.
To Stew a Rump-Steak. *Anonymous.*
The True Encounter. Millay.
Dew (s)
Another Sunday Morning. Revard.
The Blossom of the Soul. Johnson.
Dabbling in the Dew. *Anonymous.*
The Dance. Duncan.
Envoy. Piatt.
An Expanded Want Ad. Leithauser.
The Flock at Evening. Shepard.

The Foggy Dew. *Anonymous.*
For My Sister's Sake. Hitomaro.
The Good-Night or Blessing. Herrick.
Good Ol' Mountain Dew. *Anonymous.*
In April. Wetherald.
In Fields of Summer. Kinnell.
In the Dark, in the Dew. Prescott.
The Inner Vision. Wordsworth.
Into the Twilight. Yeats.
Koina ta ton Philon. Symonds.
Late Air. Bishop.
Lessons from the Gorse. Browning.
The Lord in the Wind. Picot.
Love Song. Al-Harizi.
The Milkmaid. *Anonymous.*
Morning Light the Dew-Drier. Newsome.
Morning Song. Stokebury.
New Every Morning. *Anonymous.*
Noon. Clare.
On Addy Road. Swenson.
On Parting with Moses Ibn Ezra. Halevi.
The Paint Box. Rieu.
Paris in the Snow. Sedar-Senghor.
Pebbles. Melville.
Play about, Do. Basho (Matsuo Basho).
Prince Lucifer: Mother-Song. Austin.
Rain at Wildwood. Swenson.
Resurgam. Burt.
The Riddles of Change. Mnthali.
The Rose's Cup. Sherman.
Shaman. Sabina.
The Skylark. Tennyson.
Sleepyhead. De la Mare.
Song of the Dew. *Anonymous.*
Song of the Invisible Corpse in the Field. Orr.
A Song of the Moon. McKay.
A Summer Wish. Rossetti.
Sympathy. Gyles.
There Are Sweet Flowers. Landor.
Thinking of a Master. Church.
Three Fragments. Allingham.
To an Irish Blackbird. MacAlpine.
Two Poems. Hitomaro.
Voices. De la Mare.
When the Angels Are Exhausted. Wallach.
Wind on the Lyre. Meredith.
Wine and Dew. Stoddard.
Yahrzeit. Jaffe.
Diadem (s)
Address to the Crown. O'Donnell.
Advice to Julia. Luttrell.
Exiles. Russell.
Gentilesse. Chaucer.
My Soul, Weigh Not Thy Life. Swain.

The Rosary. Maura.
The sky is low, the clouds are mean. Dickinson.
Dial
A Clock Stopped. Dickinson.
The Fifteen Days of Judgement. Evans.
Notes on a Track Meet. McCord.
The Secret in the Cat. Swenson.
Dialogue
Debora Sleeping. Logan.
The Man Who Knew Too Much. Wojahn.
Diamond (s)
The Bonnie Ship the Diamond. *Anonymous.*
Cotton Eye Joe. *Anonymous.*
Farewell and Good. Devlin.
For My Son, Born during an Ice Storm. Jauss.
Full Consciousness. Jimenez.
Gift for the Queen. *Anonymous.*
God's Determinations. Taylor.
Gods Determinations. Taylor.
The Greek Room. Thompson.
Jew. Morhange.
The Moon Is a Diamond. Sze.
On Reading–. Aldrich.
A Remonstrance. Gerrard.
Sonnets. Tuckerman.
Tears. Sitwell.
Treasures. Thayer.
The Unbeliever. Bishop.
Upon the Death of My Ever Desired Friend Doctor Donne Dean of Pauls. King.
Vitality. Fonte Boa.
When Diamonds, Nibbling in my Ears. Davies.
You All Are Static; I Alone Am Moving. Viereck.
Diana
Dianae Sumus in Fide. Catullus.
Fly, Love, That Art So Sprightly. *Anonymous.*
Miss James. Milne.
Villkins and His Dinah. *Anonymous.*
Dice
Constancies. *Anonymous.*
The Dice Were Loaded. Gilmore.
The Gold-Seekers. Garland.
Hughie at the Inn. Wylie.
Late Light. Watson.
Machupuchare. What the Mountain Said. Shaking the Dead Bones... Stroud.
My Love. Shelton.
Dick
Praise-God Barebones. Cortissoz.
Privy-Love for my Landlady. Farewell.
A Quiet Life and a Good Name. Swift.
Die (d) (s)
13 Ways of Eradicating Blackbirds (parody). DeFoe.
Abraham Lincoln. Brownell.

After Death in Arabia.
Arnold.
After Music. Peabody.
After the fiercest pangs of hot
desire. Duke.
Alcestis on the Poetry Circuit.
Jong.
Alien. Turner.
All for the Cause. Morris.
All in Due Time.
Cunningham.
All Things Decay and Die.
Herrick.
All Up and Down the Lines.
Cooperman.
An Allegory. Boake.
Allegory in Black. Clark.
Among Strangers. Stafford.
Amoretti, II. Spenser.
Amoretti, XLVII. Spenser.
And Three Hundred and
Sixty-Six in Leap Year.
Nash.
Andy-Diana DNA Letter.
Weiman.
Anguish. Mallarme.
Annie of Lochroyan.
Anonymous.
Another Death. Borrell.
Another Dying Chieftain.
Green.
Antigone and Oedipus. Ray.
The Apologist's Evening
Prayer. Lewis.
An Apology for the Foregoing
Hymn.... Crashaw.
Art. Noyes.
As I Came O'er Cairney
Mount. Anonymous.
As You Like It.
Shakespeare.
At Dieppe: Green and Grey.
Symons.
At Last. Trask.
At the Natural History
Museum. Meredith.
The Atheist's Tragedy.
Tourneur.
Attainment. Tassin.
Author Unknown.
Montgomerie.
Autumnal. Dowson.
Away! Frost.
La Bagarede. Kinnell.
Ballad. Baring.
Ballade to Our Lady of
Czestochowa. Belloc.
Barbara Allen. Anonymous.
The Battle-Flag of Sigurd.
Greenwell.
The Battle of Boyne.
Anonymous.
Battle Won Is Lost. George.
Beauty. Wylie.
Before Action. Hodgson.
Before Disaster. Winters.
Before Sleeping. Anonymous.
The Beggar's Opera. Gay.
Behaviour of Money.
Spencer.
Behold the Manly
Mesomorph. Auden.
Bereaved. Riley.
Bim Bam. Rosenberg.
A Birthday Memorial to
Seventh Street. Lorde.
The Blue Bells of Scotland.
Jordan.
Bragging Song. Anonymous.
Brave Wolfe. Anonymous.
Brebeuf and His Brethren.
Pratt.

Brennan on the Moor.
Anonymous.
Bronc Peeler's Song.
Anonymous.
The Butcher Boy.
Anonymous.
By the Sea. Rossetti.
By the Waters of Minnetonka.
Cavanass.
Bye Baby Bother. Smith.
Caelica, XXVIII. Greville.
The California Stage
Company. Anonymous.
Call Out My Number.
Burgos.
Calvary. Anonymous.
Camping Out. Empson.
Un Canadien Errant.
Anonymous.
Canzone: He Perceives His
Rashness in Love, but Has
No Choice. Guinicelli.
Canzonetta: He Will Neither
Boast Nor Lament to His
Lady. Jacopo da Lentino.
Cap'n, I Believe (with music).
Anonymous.
Captain Kid's Farewell to the
Seas. Anonymous.
Care. Murphy.
The Careless Lover.
Suckling.
Catechisms: Talking with a
Four-Year-Old. Lyon.
The Cavalier's Song.
Motherwell.
Celebration 1982. Wilkins.
A Celebration of Charis.
Jonson.
The Changes to Corinna.
Herrick.
Characters of Women. Pope.
A Charge to Keep I Have.
Wesley.
Chaucer's Complaint to His
Empty Purse (modern
version). Chaucer.
Cherry Blossoms. "Lewis.
Chicago Poem. Welch.
A Child Ill. Betjeman.
A Child My Choice.
Southwell.
The Children Band. De
Vere.
The Choice. Norris.
Christenings. Porter.
Christmas Eve (excerpt).
Browning.
A Christmas Ghost-Story.
Hardy.
Chronique Scandaleuse.
Chima.
The Colour of God's Face.
Livesay.
Come, Gentle Sleep, Death's
Image Though Thou Art.
Wharton.
Come to the Stone. Jarrell.
Commemoration Ode.
Monroe.
Conemaugh. Ward.
Construction. Shapiro.
Content. Crane.
The Contrast. Cone.
Conversion. Angermayer.
The Cool Web. Graves.
Corydon to His Phyllis.
Dyer.
The Couple Overhead.
Meredith.
Courtship. Brome.
The Crazy World. Gay.

Credo. O'Sullivan.
The Cross. Calderon de la
Barca.
A Crown of Wildflowers.
Rossetti.
Crusoe in England. Bishop.
The Cry of a Dreamer.
O'Reilly.
The Cuckoo. Anonymous.
A Curse on Uruk.
Enheduanna.
A Cut Flower. Shapiro.
Cut Thistles in May.
Anonymous.
Cynical Portraits. Paul.
Dandelions. Albee.
The Dark Stag. Crawford.
Death by Drowning.
Brewster.
Death Killed the Rich.
Anonymous.
Death of a Son. Silkin.
The Death of Jefferson.
Butterworth.
The Death of the Ball Turret
Gunner. Jarrell.
The Death of Warren.
Sargent.
Deeply Repentant of My
Sinful Ways. Stampa.
Deer Song. Silko.
A Dialogue. Ignatow.
A Dialogue betwixt GOD and
the Soul. Wotton.
Didymus. MacNeice.
Died of Love. Anonymous.
Dig My Grave. Anonymous.
The Dirt Doctor. Brown.
Don Juan. Byron.
The Donibristle Moss Moran
Disaster. Anonymous.
The Doomed City. Mayo.
Dorcas. Macdonald.
Dream. Dixon.
The Dream. Donne.
The Dream of the Cross.
Anonymous.
The Drummer Boy of Shiloh.
Anonymous.
The Duchess of Malfi.
Webster.
Dulce et Decorum. Wilson.
The Dying Child. Clare.
Early in the Spring.
Anonymous.
The Earthly Paradise.
Morris.
Ecce Quomodo Moritur
Justus. Diogenes Laertius.
El Alamein Revisited.
MacNab.
Elegy for a Dead Soldier.
Shapiro.
Elegy on the Death of a Mad
Dog. Goldsmith.
Emergency Haying. Carruth.
The End of the Duel.
Rachel Annand.
End of the World. Lasker-
Schüler.
Endymion. Keats.
Epigram. Anonymous.
Epigram: "Paddy, I have but
stol'n your living." Elliott.
Epigram: "The world laid low,
and the wind blew like a
dust." Anonymous.
Epigram: "Tom's sickness did
his morals mend." Prior.
Epigrams. Martial (Marcus
Valerius Martialis).
Epipsychidion. Shelley.

Epitaph. Claudian (Claudius
Claudianus).
Epitaph. Corbiere.
An Epitaph. Heywood.
Epitaph. Wolker.
Epitaph from a Yorkshire
Churchyard. Anonymous.
Epitaph: "Here lie two poor
lovers, who had the
mishap." Pope.
Epitaph (Inscription from
Anticyra). Anonymous.
An Epitaph: "Interr'd beneath
this marble stone." Prior.
Epitaph on Elizabeth, L. H.
Jonson.
Epitaph on Washington.
Anonymous.
Epitaph: "Sanquhar, whom
this earth could scarce
contain." Drummond.
Epitaph to Thomas Thetcher.
Anonymous.
Epitaph: "We mourn the
loss." Bierce.
Epitaphs of the War.
Kipling.
Escalade. Symons.
Eternal Values. Crowell.
Evening Dance of the Grey
Flies. Page.
Every Earthly Creature.
Brinnin.
Execution. Randall, Jr.
The Faerie Queene. Spenser.
Fair Helen. Anonymous.
Fair Margaret and Sweet
William. Anonymous.
Faith. Daley.
Faith's Vista. Abbey.
Fame is a fickle food.
Dickinson.
Fare Thee Well! Byron.
A Fear. Ledwidge.
The Fear of Death. Dryden.
February 14, 22 B. C.
Adams.
Felise. Swinburne.
The Female Warrior.
Anonymous.
A Field Flower.
Montgomery.
Figurehead. Paul.
Fin De Siecle. Cook.
Five Songs. Shapiro.
The Flaming Heart.
Crashaw.
Fleche... Eigner.
Flee on Your Donkey.
Sexton.
The Flight of the Arrow.
Stoddard.
The Fly. Blake.
The Flying Cloud.
Anonymous.
Foetus. Haring.
Follow Your Saint.
Campion.
For a Picture Where a Queen
Laments over the Tomb of
a Slain Knight. Carew.
For a Winnebago Brave.
Bruchac.
For All We Have and Are.
Kipling.
For Cal. Cunningham.
For-Ever Morning. Riding.
For the Last Wolverine.
Dickey.
For the Time Being. Auden.
Ford Madox Ford. Lowell.
The Four Calls. Hadley.

Four Sheets to the Wind and a One-Way Ticket to France. Rivers.
Four Sonnets to Helen, 2. Ronsard.
Four Ways of Dying. Chimombo.
Fourth Poem. Andrade.
Frederick Douglass: 1817-1895. Hughes.
Friendship's Mystery. Philips.
From Creature to Ghost. Hanson.
From Generation to Generation. Howells.
Fulfillment. Johnson.
The Funeral of Youth: Threnody. Brooke.
The Gambler. Anonymous.
The Garden. Shirley.
The Gardener at Thirty. Kessler.
The Gardener to His God. Van Duyn.
The General Elliott. Graves.
Ghosts. Munkittrick.
Give Me Leave. "W.
Glaucopis. Hughes.
The Glory of Nature. Tennyson.
Go, Rose. Gay.
The Goal and the Way. Oxenham.
Golden Falcon. Coffin.
Good Creatures, Do You Love Your Lives. Housman.
Good Friday. Anonymous.
The Good Hour. Driscoll.
The Good-Morrow. Donne.
Good News Bad News. Abbott.
The Good Shepherd. Gwynne.
Goodbye. Bloch.
Goodbye 'Liza Jane. Anonymous.
The Gosport Tragedy. Anonymous.
Grandfather Gabriel. Warren.
The Grapevine. Ashbery.
The Greater Trial. Winchilsea.
The Greek Anthology (excerpt). Anonymous.
Green and Yellow. Anonymous.
The Gully. Maurice.
Hail and Farewell. Spicer.
Hare-Hunting. Somervile.
He Is Like the Serpent Saka. Book of the Dead.
The Heart Asks Pleasure First. Dickinson.
Heiress and Architect. Hardy.
Helen of Kirconnell. Anonymous.
Hellas: Chorus. Shelley.
Help, Good Shepherd. Pitter.
Henry Green. Anonymous.
Henry VIII. Anonymous.
Her Apron through the Trees. Weingarten.
Her Strong Enchantments Failing. Housman.
Hiding Place. Armour.

Hippodromania; or Whiffs from the Pipe (excerpt). Gordon.
A Hit at the Times. McGrew.
Ho Ho Ho Caribou. Ceravolo.
Hoc Cygno Vinces. Hawkins.
Hope. Sodergran.
Horse Chestnut. Miranda.
The Housewife's Lament. Anonymous.
How Oft Has the Banshee Cried. Moore.
"I Am a Sioux Brave," He Said in Minneapolis. Wright.
I Am a Wild Young Irish Boy. Anonymous.
I Did Not Lose My Heart in Summer's Even. Housman.
I Have Fought the Good Fight. Waterbury.
I Have Heard Ingenuous Indians Say. Williams.
I Kenning Through Astronomy. Taylor.
I.M.H. Baring.
I'm Sad. Farrokzad.
I Met This Guy Who Died. Corso.
I Serve a Mistress. Munday.
I Shall Not Die for Thee. Hyde.
I Want to Die Easy when I Die. Anonymous.
I Will Not Die for You. Anonymous.
I Would in Rich and Golden Coloured Raine. Lodge.
Idea. Drayton.
Identity. Aldrich.
Idylls. Theocritus.
Idylls of the King. Tennyson.
The Iliad. Homer.
The Immigration Act of 1924. Mar.
The Immortal Mind. Byron.
In Arcadia. Durrell.
In Immemoriam. "Bede.
In Manchester Square. Meynell.
In Memoriam. "Adeler.
In Memoriam A.H.H., VIII. Tennyson.
In Nunhead Cemetery. Mew.
In Orangeburg My Brothers Did. Spellman.
In Our Time. Roberts.
In Postures That Call. Williams.
In the Thirtieth. Cunningham.
Independence Bell–July 4, 1776. Anonymous.
India the Magic. Jules-Bois.
The Indian's Grave. Mountain.
Innocence. Kavanagh.
The Innocent. Derwood.
Instructions to the Double. Gallagher.
Iowa Land. Bell.
Irony. Untermeyer.
Is. Kavanagh.
Is It Really Worth the While? Anonymous.
Is It True? Williams.

It Is When the Tribe Is Gone. Bigger.
It's Such a Little Thing to Weep. Dickinson.
The Jailhouse Blues. Collins.
James Honeyman. Auden.
The Jealous Lover. Anonymous.
Jeremiah. Bynner.
Jesus Tender Shepherd. Duncan.
The Jewish Conscript. Frank.
Jim Bludso of the Prairie Belle. Hay.
Joe Hill. Hayes.
John Henry (C vers.). Anonymous.
Julie-Jane. Hardy.
The King. Coleridge.
The King and the Clown. Anonymous.
The Kiss. Jonson.
Knole. Sisson.
Ku Klux. Cawein.
The Lads in Their Hundreds. Housman.
Lament for the Death of Eoghan Ruadh O'Neill. Davis.
Laurana's Song. Hovey.
The Lay of the Last Minstrel. Scott.
The League of Selves. Toffler.
The Leg. Shapiro.
Letter II. Graham.
Levee Camp Blues. Anonymous.
Lewd Love is Loss. Southwell.
Lexington. Lanier.
The Life above, the Life on High. Theresa of Avila.
The Life and Character of Dean Swift (excerpt). Swift.
The Life of Man. Bacon.
The Life of Man. Barnes.
Lift Your Glad Voices in Triumph on High. Ware.
Like to the Thundering Tone. Corbet.
Limerick: "There once was a young man named Hall." Anonymous.
Limerick: "There was a young man who was bitten." Parke.
Lines on a Bill of Mortality, 1790. Cowper.
Lines Written in Kensington Gardens. Arnold.
The Lion and the Wave. Allingham.
Lion Hunts. Beer.
Lis'en to de Lam's. Anonymous.
The Little Fish That Would Not Do as It Was Bid. Taylor.
A Little Litany to St. Francis. Murray.
Little Mathiue Grove. Anonymous.
Little Musgrave and Lady Barnard (Little Matthy Groves). Anonymous.
Little Papoose. Chapman.
Living with Children. Miller.
Liza Jane. Anonymous.

London City (B vers. with music). Anonymous.
London Despair. Cornford.
London Night. Raine.
Looking On. Thwaite.
Lord Saltoun and Auchanachie. Anonymous.
Losses. Jarrell.
Love for a Hare. La Follette.
Love, I Marvel What You Are. Stickney.
Love-In-Idleness. Beddoes.
Love Is Teasing. Anonymous.
Love Me Little, Love Me Long. Herrick.
Love Not. Norton.
Love on the Farm. Lawrence.
Love Poem. Logan.
Love Restored (excerpt). Jonson.
Love's Despair. Lynch.
Love's Emblems. Fletcher.
Love's Entreaty. Michelangelo.
Love's Horoscope. Crashaw.
Love Song. Zmuda.
Lower the Standard: That's My Motto. Shapiro.
Lucy Lake (parody). Mackintosh.
Madrigal: "Dainty sweet bird." Vautor.
Madrigal: "Penelope, that longed for the sight." Byrd.
Madrigal: "When in her face mine eyes I fix." Stirling.
Madrigal: "Where shall I sorrow great." Peerson.
The Maid Freed from the Gallows ("Hangman, Slack on the Line"). Anonymous.
The Man of Calvary (Easter Day Service). Anonymous.
Many Die Here. Jones.
Many without Elegy. Graham.
Maple and Sumach. Day-Lewis.
The Mapmaker on His Art. Nemerov.
The Marchen. Jarrell.
Mary at the Cross. McGee.
The Masked Shrew. Gardner.
May, 1945. Porter.
Meg Merrilies. Keats.
Memory. Browne.
Meridian. Ghiselin.
The Merry Jovial Beggar. Casey.
Metamorphoses. Ovid (Publius Ovidius Naso).
The Miller and His Sons. Anonymous.
The Miller That Made His Will. Anonymous.
Mimnermus in Church. Cory.
The Minstrel's Song. Chatterton.
Miss Lavender. Stallworthy.
Miss Millay Says Something Too. Hoffenstein.
Modern Beauty. Symons.
The Mole. Schmitz.
The Monk of Great Renown. Anonymous.

Montgomery. *Anonymous.*

Moonlight (with music). *Anonymous.*

Moonset, Gloucester, December 1, 1957, 1:58 AM. Olson.

More Than We Ask. Wells.

The Moss Supplicateth for the Poet. Dana.

Mother Goose's Garland. MacLeish.

Mountain Top. *Anonymous.*

Mountains Are Steadfast but the Mountain Streams. Hwang Chin-i.

The Mulch. Kunitz.

Muskrat. *Anonymous.*

My Glass Is Half Unspent. Quarles.

My Lady Has the Grace of Death. Plunkett.

My Life had stood–a Loaded Gun. Dickinson.

My Love Is Young. Birney.

My Mother's Bible. Morris.

My Old Cat. Summers.

My portion is defeat–today. Dickinson.

My Son, My Executioner. Hall.

The Mystic Magi. Hawker.

Myths and Texts. Snyder.

Nappy Head Blues. Grant.

Nature in Couplets. Ogburn.

Near the Lake. Morris.

The Negatives. Levine.

Never Said a Mumbalin' Word. *Anonymous.*

The New House. McDougall.

A New Song Composed on the Death of Lord Nelson. *Anonymous.*

News. Lima.

The Night Wind. Bronte.

No More Words! To the Field, to Arms! Franco.

Nova. Jeffers.

Now I Lay Me Down to Sleep. *Anonymous.*

Now When So Much Has Passed. Seferis.

Nydia's Song. Lytton.

O Brazil, the Isle of the Blest. Griffin.

O Christ, Who Died. Slemp.

O Death, Rock Me Asleep. Boleyn.

O Softly Singing Lute. Pilkington.

O Spaced Head! Now Wounded. Gerhardt.

O Virgin. *Anonymous.*

Oblivion. Komey.

Ode: "Good night, my Love, may gentle rest." Cotton.

Ode in Memory of the American Volunteers Fallen for France. Seeger.

Ode to a Beautiful Woman. Clark.

Ode to a Pig While His Nose Was Being Bored. Southey.

Ode to Anactoria. Sappho.

Odes. Horace.

Of Misery. Howell.

Of the Loss of Time. Hoskyns.

Oh, Give Me the Hills. *Anonymous.*

The Old Cumberland Beggar. Wordsworth.

The Old Ladies. Ellis.

The Old Lady Who Swallowed a Fly. *Anonymous.*

Old Maid's Song. *Anonymous.*

Old Soldiers Never Die. *Anonymous.*

An Old Story. Robinson.

On a Certain Alderman. Cunningham.

On a Honey Bee. Freneau.

On Burning a Dull Poem. Swift.

On Christmas Day. Paman.

On Fell. Lessing.

On His Exile to Iona. Columcille.

On Mr. Hobbs, and His Writings. Sheffield.

On One That Lived Ingloriously. Hoskyns.

On Seeing a Fine Frigate at Anchor in a Bay off Mount Edgecumbe. Carrington.

On Seeing a Torn Out Coin Telephone. Robbins.

On the Pilgrim's Way in Kent, as It Leads to the Coldrum Stones. Asphodel.

One dignity delays for all. Dickinson.

One Eyed Black Man in Nebraska. Cornish.

One-Eyed Gunner. *Anonymous.*

One of Many. Smith.

Onward Christian Soldiers! Davis.

Our Blackness Did Not Come to Us Whole. Bragg.

Our Rock. Key.

Out of Luck. Ibn Ezra.

Out of Tune. Henley.

The Owl in the Sarcophagus. Stevens.

Oxford Canal. Flecker.

Panic. Davis.

Paradise Lost. Milton.

Paranoia. Browne.

The Parrot. Campbell.

Passengers. Johnson.

Patriotic Tour and Postulate of Joy. Warren.

Pax Paganica. Guiney.

Pelleas and Ettarre (excerpt). Tennyson.

Peter Grimes. Crabbe.

Pheasant. Ghose.

Phineas Pratt. MacArthur.

Phineas within and without. Zimmer.

The Phoenix. Darley.

Phyllis. Lodge.

The Piano. Verlaine.

A Piazza Tragedy. Field.

The Pilgrimage. Albrecht von Johannsdorf.

The Pitch Piles Up in Part. O'Grady.

Planting a Magnolia. Snodgrass.

The Pluralist and Old Soldier. Collier.

Poem for a Singer. Acorn.

Poem of Pathos. Rozewicz.

Poem of the Son. "Mistral.

Poem: "Old man in the crystal morning after snow." Schwartz.

Poem on His Birthday. Thomas.

The Poem on the Guilt. Yeshurun.

Poggio. Durrell.

Poor Is the Life That Misses. *Anonymous.*

Poor Old Horse. *Anonymous.*

Poor Old Lady. *Anonymous.*

The Poplar Field. Cowper.

Possessions. Gurney.

The Powers of the Pawn. Solway.

A Prayer. Hinkson.

Prey to Prey. Rowbotham.

The Price of Begging. Frances.

The Properties of the Shires of England. *Anonymous.*

Prospecting Dream. *Anonymous.*

Protocols. Jarrell.

Quatrains. Jahin.

The Queen's Marie. *Anonymous.*

Questions for the Candidate. Holmes.

The Raven. Nicarchos [(or Nicarchus)].

Re-Birth. *Anonymous.*

Ready. Cary.

The Reaper. Duncan.

The Reason Why. Beddoes.

A Recollection. Cornford.

Red Whiskey. *Anonymous.*

The Red, White and Red. *Anonymous.*

Regeneration. Vaughan.

Religio Laici. Dryden.

The Remedy Worse Than the Disease. Prior.

De Rerum Natura. Lucretius (Titus Lucretitus Carus).

Rescue. Dargan.

Reveille. Godfrey.

The Revel. Dowling.

A Riddle: The Letter H. Fanshawe.

Riding Adown the Country Lanes. Bridges.

Rinaldo. Peterson

Rise, O My Soul! *Anonymous.*

Robin Hood and the Ranger. *Anonymous.*

Rock Leader. Bathgate.

Rock Painting. Cope.

The Rocky Island. *Anonymous.*

Roddy M'Corley. *Anonymous.*

Roll, Jordan, Roll. *Anonymous.*

A Romance. Kallman.

Romeo and Juliet. Shakespeare.

Root Hog or Die. Small.

The Rosciad. Churchill.

Rosh Pina. Knut.

A Row of Thick Pillars. Crane.

Rural Sports. Gay.

A Russian Fantasy. Dole.

Rye Whisky. *Anonymous.*

Sacrifice. Emerson.

Sailors on Leave. Dodson.

Salt. Stone.

Samis Idyll. Rainer.

Saul. Heavysege.

Scarred. *Anonymous.*

Scots Wha Hae. Burns.

A Sea-Spell. Rossetti.

Seferis. Durrell.

The Sequel. Schwartz.

A Sergeant's Prayer. Brodie.

Sestina of the Tramp-Royal. Kipling.

Seven Long Years in State Prison (with music). *Anonymous.*

The Seven Virgins. *Anonymous.*

Sex Play in Four Acts. Fetherling.

Shadow and Shade. Tate.

Shango I. *Anonymous.*

She dealt her pretty words like blades. Dickinson.

She Remembers. Aldis.

Shouting Song. *Anonymous.*

Signum Cui Contradicetur. Mary Angelita.

Silvia. Etherege.

Simon the Cyrenean. Lyttleton.

The Sit-In. Turner.

The Sleepers. Davies.

Small Woman on Swallow Street. Merwin.

The Smooth Divine. Dwight.

The Snake It Was That Died. Demodocus.

So Tir'd Are All My Thoughts. Campion.

The Soldier in the Park. Riddell.

Solemn Hour. Rilke.

A Soliloquy of One of the Spies Left in the Wilderness. Hopkins.

Somewhere I Chanced to Read. Davidson.

A Song about Great Men. Hamburger.

Song: "He found me sitting among flowers." De Vere.

Song: "How can that tree but withered be." *Anonymous.*

Song: "Man's a poor deluded bubble." Dodsley.

Song: "Methinks the poor town has been troubled too long." Sackville.

Song of a Man about to Die in a Strange Land. *Anonymous.*

Song of a Woman Abandoned by the Tribe... Austin.

Song of Agony. De Lemos.

Song of Hannibal: Rome. Christian.

A Song of Living. Burr.

The Song of Love and Death. Tennyson.

Song of Myself. Whitman.

Song of the Negro on the Ferry. Craveirinha.

Song Set by Robert Jones: "Life is a poet's fable." *Anonymous.*

Song: "When lovely woman stoops to folly." Goldsmith.

Sonnet 21. Goodman.

Sonnet for My Father. Justice.

Sonnets, XXXII: "If thou survive my well-contented day." Shakespeare.

Sonnets, LXVI: "Tired with all these, for restful death I cry." Shakespeare.
Sonnets for a Dying Man. Singer.
Sonnets Written in the Orillia Woods, VII. Sangster.
The Soul Speaks. Pfeiffer.
The Southern Cross. Hawker.
Souvenir. Robinson.
The Sow Took the Measles. *Anonymous.*
Spanish Folk Songs. *Anonymous.*
The Sparrow's Dirge. Skelton.
The Spoils of War. Watkins.
Spring. Rossetti.
Stack Arms! Alston.
The Starling. Buchanan.
Stepney Green. Singer.
The Stranded Whales. Dutton.
A Strange Passion of a Lover. Gascoigne.
Strangers Are We All upon the Earth. Werfel.
Stratton Water. *Anonymous.*
The Streams of Bunclody. *Anonymous.*
Sugar Babe. *Anonymous.*
The Sugar Cane. Grainger.
A Survey of the Amphitheatre. Browne.
The Swan. Gosse.
Sweet Evelina. *Anonymous.*
Tailor of Bicester. *Anonymous.*
Take Me Back to Old Montana. *Anonymous.*
Tall Trees by Still Waters. Tate.
Tantalus. Silentiarius.
The Teasers. Empson.
The Technique of Laughter. Kessler.
Tenants. Gibson.
Terminal. Shapiro.
The Testament of Beauty. Bridges.
That Summer. Hemschemeyer.
There She Blows! *Anonymous.*
There Was an Old Woman. *Anonymous.*
Thermopylae. Thwaites.
The Thief's Niece. Keithley.
Things. Kilmer.
This House. Young Bear.
Though My Wanderings Are Many. Geilt.
Though You Are Young. Campion.
Three Car Poems, III. Jones.
Three Lyrics. Petronius Arbiter (Caius Petronius Arbiter).
Time. Wynne.
Time of Turtles. Perry.
Time To Die. Dandridge.
To a Lady on Reading Sherlock upon Death. Chesterfield.
To a Withered Rose. Bangs.
To a Young Poet. Millay.
To Anthea, Who May Command Him Anything. Herrick.

To Clarastella on St. Valentines Day Morning. Heath.
To Death. Herrick.
To Delia. Daniel.
To Graecinus, on Loving Two Women at Once. Ovid (Publius Ovidius Naso).
To Mr. Hobbes. Cowley.
To See God's Bleeding Lam'. *Anonymous.*
To Song. Jones, Jr.
To the State of Love. Cleveland.
To Thee, Dear Henry Morison. Moryson.
Toll the Bell for Damon. Anderson.
Tom Dooley. *Anonymous.*
Too Busy. *Anonymous.*
The Tourist. Keizer.
Tragic Verses. *Anonymous.*
The Tree. Ehrenburg.
Troy. Muir.
True Happiness. Talpalar.
The True Lover's Farewell. *Anonymous.*
Trust. Reese.
Truth Never Dies. *Anonymous.*
Truxton's Victory. *Anonymous.*
Twilight's Last Gleaming. Monks.
The Twins. Leigh.
The Two Friends. Leland.
Two Heroes. Monroe.
Two Lives. Leonard.
Two Poems About President Harding, I. Wright.
Uncourtly Love. Walther von der Vogelweide.
Under the Sign of the Moth. Wagoner.
The United States and Macedonian. *Anonymous.*
The Unreturning. Scollard.
Upon a Cock-Horse to Market I'll Trot. *Anonymous.*
Upon Batt. Herrick.
Upon One of the Maids of Honour to Queen Elizabeth. Hoskyns.
Upon the Death of Sir Albert Morton's Wife. Wootton.
Upon the Image of Death. Southwell.
Upon the Losse of His Mistresses. Herrick.
Ursa Major. Kirkup.
The Valiant Sailor. *Anonymous.*
Vertigos or Contemplation of Something That Is Over. Pizarnik.
The Vicar of Wakefield. Goldsmith.
The Violet and the Rose. Webster.
The Vision of Judgment. Byron.
Visions. Browne.
Vita Brevis. *Anonymous.*
The Volunteer. Cutler.
W. H. Eheu! Coleridge.
Wages. Tennyson.
Walking Along the Hudson. Petersen.
Walking for That Cake. Harrigan.
War. McLean.

We Conquer or Die. Pierpont.
Welcome, Fortune. *Anonymous.*
Western Civilization. Neto.
What a Court Hath Old England. *Anonymous.*
What If a Much of a Which of a Wind. Cummings.
What Is Liquid. Newcastle.
What Is Our Life? Ralegh.
"What tears, dear prince, can serve to water all." Ralegh.
What the King Has. Fuller.
What Was Your Dream, Doctor Murricombe? Sitwell.
When He Thought Himself Contemned. Howell.
Where It Is Winter. O'Neil.
While on Those Lovely Looks I Gaze. Rochester.
Whilst Alexis Lay Prest. Dryden.
Whilst in This World I Stay. Pain.
The White Women. Coleridge.
Who's That at My Bedroom Window? *Anonymous.*
Who Will Stop His Hand from Giving Warmth. Pizarnik.
Why Do We Love. Rudyerd.
The Wicked Hawthorn Tree. Yeats.
The Wife. Creeley.
William of Orange. *Anonymous.*
William Was a Royal Lover. *Anonymous*
Windle-Straws. Dowden.
The Window. Scarfe.
Winter: East Anglia. Blunden.
Winter Will Follow. Dixon.
A Woman's Sorrow (excerpt). Ho Nansorhon.
The Wooing Maid. Parker.
Work. Lowell.
The Workbox. Hardy.
Working the Rain Shift at Flanagan's. Ruark.
Working the Skeet House. Eastman.
World's Bliss. Notley.
The World, the Devil, and Tom Paine. *Anonymous.*
Yahrzeit. Schaeffer.
The Young Dead Soldiers. MacLeish.
Young Waters. *Anonymous.*
Youth in Arms: IV. Carrion. Monro.

Diet
Idea. Drayton.
Parisian Nectar. Burgess.
A Sparrow-Hawk Proud. *Anonymous.*

Differ (ence) (ent)
Another Mother and Child. McLaughlin.
Arf, Said Sandy. Stetler.
An Aspect of Love, Alive in the Ice and Fire. Brooks.
At the Trough. Gregor.
Chilled by Different Winds. Swaim.
Classical Criticism. Richardson.
Climbing. Clark.

Codicil. Walcott.
A Dab of Color. Weiss.
The Difference between a Lie and the Truth. Dessus.
Epigram on Handel and Bononcini. Byrom.
Father Mat. Kavanagh.
The Ivory Dog of My Sister. Tallmountain.
Jacob. Cary.
Love for Instance. Gerber.
Lucy. Wordsworth.
Lucy Lake (parody). Mackintosh.
Michael Robartes and the Dancer. Yeats.
Mirror for the Barnyard. Myers.
The Nature of an Action. Gunn.
Night Light. Willard.
Of the Principal and Vice-Principal of the Ladies' College, Cheltenham. *Anonymous.*
Ol' Hannah. Reese.
Our Coming Countrymen. Parkes.
The Revolution. Gilbert.
The Road Not Taken. Frost.
Seder, 1944. Torberg.
Song of Myself. Whitman.
Spring. Catullus.
The Star-Splitter. Frost.
The Survivors. Gardons.
Tennesse Crickets. Outlaw.
To a Republican Friend. Arnold.
Toro. Merwin.
The Traveller: The First, Best Country. Goldsmith.
The Unhistoric Story. Curnow.
Visitors' Parking. Szumigalski.
The Wives of Mafiosi. Jong.

Difficult (ies) (y)
Another Epitaph on an Army of Mercenaries. ""MacDiarmid.
Beauty, Sleeping. Freeman.
Bozzy and Piozzi (excerpt). "Pindar.
A Child's Thought. Moore.
I Come Home Wanting to Touch Everyone. Dunn.
The Monk and His Pet Cat. *Anonymous.*
Practical People. Jeffers.
Some Opposites. Wilbur.
The Song. Dorn.
To a Friend Whose Work Has Come to Nothing. Yeats.

Dig
Father. Pack.
In Nunhead Cemetery. Mew.
Last Lines. Kennedy.
Over in the Meadow. Wadsworth.
Short History of Twentieth-Century Scholarship. Wain.
The Song of the Graves. Rhys.
Thistledown. Monro.

Digest
As I Grow Older and Fatten on Myself. Carson.
The Confession. Barham.
Epitaph on Dr. Keene. Gray.

Dignity
The Business Life. Ignatow.
Congal: The Land Is Ours.
Ferguson.
Few Things Can More
Inflame. Day-Lewis.
Memorial to the Great Big
Beautiful Self-Sacrificing
Advertisers. Ebright.
Niagara Falls. Dugan.
Samela. Greene.

Dim (ness)
Beauty's Hands Are Cool.
Baker.
I Want to Die while You
Love Me. Johnson.
If She Sang. Barrax.
Iphione. Irwin.
Lohengrin. Payne.
My Mother's House.
Tietjens.
No Room. Stroud.
Not Blindly in the Dark.
Stanley.
O Martyred Spirit.
Santayana.
An Old Song Ended.
Rossetti.
Raya Brenner. Sadeh.
The Shepherds. Vaughan.
Silex Scintillans. Vaughan.
A Soldier's Prayer. Freeman.
Song Be Delicate. Neilson.
Too Solemn for Day, Too
Sweet for Night. Walker.
Urania. De Vere.
La Vita Nuova. Dante
Alighieri.
Where Shall Wisdom Be
Found. Euripides.

Dime (s)
Alabama Bound. Lipscomb.
The Autocrat of the
Breakfast-Table. Holmes
Black Sketches, 2. Lee.
Brother, Can You Spare a
Dime? Harburg.
Capital. McHugh.
Dynamic Tension. Sanfield.
Element. Page.
In These Dissenting Times.
Walker.
Karma. Robinson.
Mulberry Street.
Herschberger.
Shout, Little Lulu.
Anonymous.
Wheat Metropolis.
Hamilton.

Diminished
Equanimity. Murray.
Old Maps. Tietjens.
Riding a One-Eyed Horse.
Taylor.

Dine (d)
Banbury Fair. Anonymous.
Beer. Calverley.
Bishop Blomfield's First
Charge to His Clergy.
Smith.
The Bold Pedlar and Robin
Hood. Anonymous.
Colonel Fazackerley.
Causley.
The Cow. Taylor.
Epigram on Fasting.
Anonymous.
Gastrology (excerpt).
Archestratus.
Gude Wallace (A version).
Anonymous.

Horse Guards Parade.
Brown.
Lord Walter's Wife.
Browning.
My Name Is George
Nathaniel Curzon.
Anonymous.
Philosopher, Whom Dost
Thou Most Affect."
Garnett.
To a Young Beauty. Yeats.
Vision. Howells.

Dinner
The Burial of Linnet. Ewing.
Daily Paradox. Hay.
Days through Starch and
Bluing. Fulton.
Earning a Dinner. Prior.
The Fastidious Serpent.
Johnstone.
Frank O'Hara. Berrigan.
Get Up, Get Up.
Anonymous.
Going in to Dinner. Shanks.
Hey Ding a Ding.
Anonymous.
In the Field. Janik.
The Landrail. Clare.
Melodies. "Carroll.
Mexico City Blues. Kerouac.
My Dad's Dinner Pail.
Harrigan.
Revelation. Meltzer.
A Roxbury Garden. Lowell.
Sapphics. Lewis.
Satisfaction. Ammons.
The Ship's Cook, a Captive
Sings. Hofmannsthal.
The Story of Fidgety Philip.
Hoffmann.
The Sycophantic Fox and the
Gullible Raven. Carryl.
Tinker's Wife. Kavanagh.

Dionysus
Hail, Dionysos. Randall.
King Midas. Moss.
Rye Bread. Braithwaite.
The Vine and the Goat.
Aesop.

Dip
In Memoriam A.H.H.,
XLVIII. Tennyson.
Johnie Cock (K version).
Anonymous.
Landscapes. Eliot.
Little Phoebe. Anonymous.
Old Mansion. Ransom.
Pater's Bathe. Parry.
The Rhyme of the Three
Captains. Kipling.
The Uses of Ocean. Seaman.

Direction (s)
Arcadia. Sidney.
Assassination. Lee.
A Baby Ten Months Old
Looks at the Public
Domain. Stafford.
The Death of a Soldier.
Stevens.
The Far Side of Introspection.
Lee.
God and Man. Hazo.
The Little Star. Anonymous.
Mowing the Lawn. Bensko.
Not Heat Flames Up and
Consumes. Whitman.
Notes from a Slave Ship.
Field.
The Resolve. Levertov.

Dirge (s)
Communication to the City
Fathers of Boston.
Starbuck.
The Dead Sparrow.
Cartwright.
Dirge of Rory O'More. De
Vere.
Epitaph on Achilles.
Anonymous.
The Fallen Star. Darley.
The Grave of King ARthur.
Warton, Jr..
Hey, Boys! Up Go We!
Anonymous.
Inanna and Ishkur.
Enheduanna.
Lament over the Ruins of the
Abbey of Teach Molaga.
Mangan.
The Last Hunt. Thayer.
Meditations of a Hindu
Prince. Lyall.
On the Death of M. D'Ossoli
and His Wife, Margaret
Fuller. Landor.
Rosabelle. Scott.

Dirt (y)
The Beggar. Doak.
Blake Leads a Walk on the
Milky Way. Willard.
California Winter (excerpt).
Shapiro.
The Dirt Doctor. Brown.
The Dirtiest Man in the
World. Silverstein.
Elegy. Loney.
Epitaph for My Cat.
Garrigue.
Epitaph for the Poet.
Barker.
An Event. Field.
The Fable of Midas. Swift.
Father's Whiskers.
Anonymous.
The First Epistle of the First
Book of Horace Imitated
(excerpt). Pope.
Gabriel's Blues. Forbes.
Grassroots. Sandburg.
Hoosen Johnny.
Anonymous.
The Houses of Corr an Chait
Are Cold. Mac Cuarta.
The Housewife's Lament.
Anonymous.
I Cannot Wash My Eye
without an Eyecup.
Anonymous.
I Saw God Wash the World.
Stidger.
The Immortals. Rosenberg.
A Late Spring. Scully.
New York City. Bodenheim.
Of Only a Single Poem.
Dutton.
On an Ill-Managed House.
Swift.
A Pastoral. Stevens.
Poems in Praise of Practically
Nothing. Hoffenstein.
Pretty Molly. Anonymous.
Ransi-Tansi-Tay.
Anonymous.
Root Cellar. Roethke.
A Satire against Reason and
Mankind. Rochester.
A Satirical Elegy on the
Death of a Late Famous
General. Swift.

Disappear (ed) (s)
April Fourth. Mezey.

Black Warrior. Jordan.
Blossoms. Sherman.
The Crackling Twig.
Stephens.
Davideis. Cowley.
Dreaming America. Oates.
End-of-Summer Poem.
Bennett.
Evensong. Drewry.
A Farewell to the Moon.
Ochester.
First Dark. Oates.
The Garden. Strand.
How Was Your Trip to L.A.?
Whalen.
The Leaf. Williams.
Lullaby. Nohomaiterangi.
The Man in the Mirror.
Strand.
Merce Cunningham and the
Birds. Mueller.
Mimosa. Mathis.
Ol' Dynamite. Le Noir.
On a Sunbeam. Heyrick.
Poem for Hemingway & W.
C. Williams. Carver.
Poem to Han-Shan. Stroud.
The Quarry. Moody.
Requiem for My Mother.
Kgositsile.
The Road Back and Forth to
Ryley. Reid.
The Sequel. Schwartz.
Song of the Old Woman.
Anonymous.
Tonsilectomy. Rivers.
Translations. Lum.
A Trip to Four or Five
Towns. Logan.
We Were in the 8th Grade.
Berryman.
"Whole gulfs of red and fleets
of red". Dickinson.

Disappoint (ed)
Elegy. Loney.
Encouraged. Dunbar.
Martha Blake at Fifty-One.
Clarke.
Rain. Thomas.

Disappointment (s)
Backing into the Fan Mail
(Unreceived). Gallup.
Love's Memories Haunt My
Footsteps Still. Clare.
Love-Songs, At Once Tender
and Informative.
Hoffenstein.
These Lacustrine Cities.
Ashbery.
Watching for Dolphins.
Constantine.
Wood Butcher. Hindley.

Disaster (s)
Alphabet. Lear.
As Camels Who Have Become
Thirsty...The Poet's
Lament. Bowndheri.
The Brief Journey West.
Nemerov.
The Crafty Miss of London;
or, The Fryar Well Fitted.
Anonymous.
Dark Aspect and Prospect.
Anonymous.
Early Morning Feed.
Redgrove.
Hookerlumps in the Love
Canal. Sylvester.
One Art. Bishop.
The Phantom Ship. De
Forest.
Self-Portrait, 1969. Bidart.

The Snowbound City.
Haines.
Sound of Breaking. Aiken.
The Upas Tree. Pushkin.
The Window. Muir.
Disc
Crescent Moon. Renton.
Down the Mississippi.
Fletcher.
Song of Occident. Vigee.
Discharge
Alone in an Inn at
Southampton, April the
25th, 1737. Hill.
Boots. Kipling.
Odes. Horace.
Disciple (s)
One of the Jews. Cavafy.
The River Swelleth More and
More. Thoreau.
Though I am Laila of the
Persian romance. Zeb-un-
Nissa.
Discipline (s)
Get the Gasworks. Ignatow.
The Lady in the Barbershop.
Rudnik.
Not for Its Own Sake...
Littlefield.
Religio Novissima. De Vere.
Woodtown Manor.
Montague.
Disclose
Dirge of the Moolla of Kotal.
Lanigan.
The First One Drew Me.
Kook.
Discontent
The Aim. Roberts.
The Barricades. Levertov.
Epitaph on Any Man.
Tessimond.
The Passionate Pilgrim.
Shakespeare.
Youth's Agitations. Arnold.
Discourse
Lily, Lois & Flaubert: The
Site of Loss. Fraser.
The Morning Hours.
Anonymous.
Discover (ed) (s) (y)
The Benefactors. Hay.
The Fountain of Youth.
Butterworth.
I drag a boat over the ocean.
Lal Ded.
Illusion. Rak.
Le Jazz Hot. Hollo.
My Days Are Gliding Swiftly
By. Nelson.
Of Reason and Discovery.
Mattera.
One-Way Song. Lewis.
The Primrose. Herrick.
Return to Prinsengracht.
Blue-Swartz.
Solomon: To Truth.
Anonymous.
Towards a City That Sings.
Jordan.
Disdain (s)
Against Indifference. Webbe.
Arab Song. Stoddard.
Astrophel and Stella, XII.
Sidney.
By the Boat House, Oxford.
Stevenson.
Caelia: Sonnet. Murray.
Caelica, IX. Greville.
Celia Singing. Carew.
The Complaint of New
Amsterdam. Steendam.

A Deposition from Beauty.
Stanley.
Dogs and Weather. Welles.
Great Is My Envy of You.
Petrarch (Francesco
Petrarca).
Harpalus' Complaint.
Anonymous.
Mediocrity in Love Rejected.
Carew.
Ode on Science. Sumner.
The Range Riders.
Anonymous.
Song: "Fool, take up thy shaft
again." Stanley.
Song: "In vain you tell your
parting lover." Prior.
Urania. Arnold.
What rage Is this? Wyatt.
When I Loved Thee.
Stanley.
Disease
Arcadia. Sidney.
Believe and Take Heart.
Spalding.
Epitaph. Chiabrera.
It Is Not Sweet Content, Be
Sure. Clough.
Prayer against Love.
Catullus.
Sodom; or, The Quintessence
of Debauchery (excerpt).
Rochester.
Sonnet against the Too-Facile
Mystic. Harrod.
To Doctor Empirick.
Jonson.
To Luve Unluvit. Scott.
Disgrace (d) (s)
The Cathedral of Rheims.
Verhaeren.
Confession of a Glutton.
Marquis.
The Cottager's Complaint.
Anonymous.
Dear Companion.
Anonymous.
The Hypocrite. Ben
Kalonymos.
Los Cuatro Generales.
Anonymous.
My Angel. Brooks.
The Notorious Glutton.
Taylor.
Prelude to Space. Lewis.
Psyche to Cupid: Her Ditty.
Broughton.
Publication Is the Auction.
Dickinson.
Shameful Impotence: Book
III, Elegia VII. Ovid.
Sir Toby Matthews.
Suckling.
Sonnet: "If chaste and pure
devotion of my youth."
Drayton.
A Waist. Stein.
Disguise (d)
I Am Partly Moon...
Huidobro.
An Image of Leda. O'Hara.
The Marriage Wig.
Whitman.
The Missing Person. Justice.
Opportunity. Cawein.
Portrait of a Marriage.
Abse.
Sundays. Rugo.
Upon the Weathercock.
Bunyan.

Disgust (ed) (ing)
For an Egyptian Boy, Died c.
700 B.C. Baron.
Get the Gasworks. Ignatow.
The Glow-Worm. Smith.
Lowdown Rounder's Blues.
Howell.
Tardiness. Burgess.
To God. Maurice.
Vaquero. Miller.
What She Wanted. Koertge.
Dish (es)
The Angel in the House.
Patmore.
Aubade after the Party.
O'Grady.
The Ballad of Mary Baldwin.
Sandy.
A Collection of Hymns...of
the Moravian Brethern
(excerpt). *Anonymous.*
A Curious Discourse That
Passed between the Twenty-
Five Letters... *Anonymous.*
Das Liebesleben. Gunn.
Epitaph on Sir Walter Pye,
Attorney of the Wards...
Hoskyns.
From Mythology. Herbert.
Home Life. Nolan.
How Sweet Thy Precious Gift
of Rest. Ben Makhir.
Hunting Season. Auden.
Intruder. Feldman.
Mary and the Lamb.
Sherman.
My Plan. Chute.
Of Death. Harding.
Trim's Song: The Fair
Kitchen-Maid. Steele.
Two Graces. Herrick.
Word. Spender.
The Zodiac Song. Ruskin.
Dislike (d) (s)
I Don't Care. Lenox.
Limerick: "There was a faith-
healer of Deal."
Anonymous.
Sins Loathed, and Yet Loved.
Herrick.
Thoughts on One's Head.
Meredith.
Dismay
Dolor. Miles.
Frenzy. Crabbe.
A House All Pictures.
George.
The Monochord. Rossetti.
Under the Moon. Yeats.
Disorder (ed) (s)
At the Sign-Painter's.
Carter.
The Compound Eye.
Davison.
The Dark-Red Shadow-Spots.
Kanbara.
Davideis. Cowley.
Heaps on Heaps. Concanen.
Will he always love me?
Horikawa.
Dissolution
The Colours of Love.
Devlin.
The Estate: "Waking by
Night'. Brasch.
The Microbe's Serenade.
Ade.
One of the Boys. Dacey.
To Giotto. Trimpi.
True and Joyful News.
Anonymous.

Dissolve (d) (s)
The Final Painting.
Harwood.
The Gypsy Bible. Tuwim.
I Seek Thee in the Heart
Alone. Trench.
Ightham Woods. Sisson.
Letter of a Mother. Warren.
Man's Mortality. Wastell.
Religio Laici. Dryden.
September 2. Berry.
Summer Interlude.
Stevenson.
Distance (s)
Ambulances. Larkin.
At the Entrance. Stewart.
Border Line. Hughes.
The D.L. and W.'s Phoebe
Snow. *Anonymous.*
Dreams Are the Royal Road
to the Unconscious.
Goodman.
Escape. Jones.
First Star. Smith.
Going to Norway.
Anderson.
Horses at Valley Store.
Silko.
Lessons of the War. Reed.
Lion Gate. Rich.
Man and Wife. Sexton.
The Map. Strand.
The Men of Old. Milnes.
Mission Bay. Koethe.
Moved Towards a Future.
Chester.
My Aim. Banks.
The Mystic Borderland.
Fischer.
No Possum, No Sop, No
Taters. Stevens.
The Octopussycat. Cox.
Out of Sight, Out of Mind.
Googe.
Rex Mundi. Gascoyne.
The Runner. Chadwick.
Skunks (excerpt). Jeffers.
Sleeping with Foxes. Hill.
Sylvia. Leopardi.
Undue significance.
Dickinson.
Washing between the
Buildings. Eigner.
A Wave of Coldness.
Yosano Akiko.
Wessex Heights. Hardy.
Distant
Above Machu Picchu, 129
Baker Street, San Francisco.
Stroud.
Advent 1955. Betjeman.
Afar in the Desert. Pringle.
Bathing with Father.
Fetherling.
The Book of How. Moore.
The Ex-Queen among the
Astronomers. Adcock.
For a College Yearbook.
Cunningham.
From All These Events.
Spender.
Middle Age. Lehmann.
Night along the Mackinac
Bridge. Hill.
Old Man. Henry.
Seashore. Emerson.
Sun of the Sleepless. Byron.
A Vision. Konopnicka.
Distress (ed)
Crepe de Chine. Williams.
The Fear. Abercrombie.
The Hard Lovers. Dillon.

Distress (continued)

Henry K. Sawyer.
Anonymous.
Limerick: "There was an old
lady of Chertsey." Lear.
Limerick: "There was an old
person of Brussels." Lear.
Much Distressed.
Anonymous.
None Is Happy. Hartmann
von Aue.
Rural Life. Crabbe.
A Slum Dwelling. Crabbe.
Small Paths. Roland-Holst.
Some Day, Some Day.
Castillejo.
To the Queen of Dolors.
Maura.
To the Right Noble,
Valourous, and Learned
Prince Henry... Davies.
Truth in Poetry. Crabbe.
Whilst Eccho Cryes, What
Shall Become of Mee.
Constable.

Distribution
Canto XIV. Pound.
The Coral Reef. Lieberman.
Unequal Distribution.
Hoffenstein.

Disturb (ance) (ed) (s)
At My Father's Grave.
Ciardi.
Autumn. Shikishi.
The Contagiousness of
Dreams. Middlebrook.
In Tenebris. Hardy.
Of a Lady That Refused to
Dance with Him. Surrey.
Sonnets to Orpheus. Rilke.
The Wheel. Yeats.

Ditch (es)
Army Bugle Calls: Fatigue
Call. Anonymous.
Avarice. Herbert.
Canadians. Gurney.
Easy as a Bat. Anonymous.
Ground Hog Day. Pomeroy.
Sonnet: Of Why He Is
Unhanged. Angiolieri.
Tommy Tittlemouse.
Anonymous.

Ditty
Psalm XIII. Sidney.
Ravings (parody). Hood.
St Patrick of Ireland, My
Dear! Maginn.

Dive (d)
Before the Dive. Kempf.
Falconry. Wilkinson.
In Quest to Have Not.
Honig.
Kinds of Shel-Fish. Wood.

Divide (d) (s)
Birch. Simpson.
Comfort. Doney.
Epitaph. Claudian (Claudius
Claudianus).
Evening in Paradise. Milton.
If I Could Shut the Gate
against My Thoughts.
Daniel.
Over the Dark World Flies
the Wind. Tennyson.
The Slate at the Empire Mine.
Wason.
Song Set by Michael
Cavendish: "Faustina hath
the fairer face."
Anonymous.
To the Earl of Warwick.
Tickell.

We Never Said Farewell.
Coleridge.
The Weed. Bishop.
The Will. Sepamla.
Year's End. Benson.

Divine
The Acts of Youth. Wieners.
At the Mermaid Inn.
Hildreth.
The Blinded Bird. Hardy.
A Carrion. Baudelaire.
Christ. Holmes.
The Cloud of Carmel.
Powers.
Cortege for Colette.
Garrigue.
The Curtains Now Are
Drawn. Hardy.
Death. Pellew.
Drum-Taps. Whitman.
Egoisme a Deux. Bevington.
Faith. Santayana.
Flora's Flower. Anonymous.
The Hawkbit. Roberts.
Indirection. Realf.
Iphione. Irwin.
The Line of Beauty.
O'Shaughnessy.
Love. Jonson.
Man and Cows. Young.
Night on the Shore. Heine.
No Thanks. Cummings.
O Thou Whose Gracious
Presence Shone. Ham.
On the Death of Karl Barth.
Clemo.
On the Death of Mr.
Crashaw. Cowley.
Plain Song. Cocteau.
Preludes. Patmore.
Prometheus Unbound.
Shelley.
Sarah Threeneedles. Bates.
Sonnet: "Could then the Babes
from yon unshelter'd cot."
Russell.
Sonnets: A Sequence on
Profane Love. Boker.
Theologians. De La Mare.
The Third Century, The
Recovery. Traherne.
This Compost. Whitman.
To My Dog Blanco.
Holland.
Vowel Movements. Hine.
The Water Lady. Hood.

Diving
The Buried Stream. Baxter.
For Mariella, in Antrona.
Simpson.
Nurse Sharks. Matthews.
Sailing upon the River.
Crabbe.

Divinity
Bellerophon: There Are No
Gods. Euripides.
Brother... Amini.
Christmas Eve. Ammons.
The Cold Divinities. Wright.
The Dark Angel. Johnson.
The Immaculate Conception.
Tabb.
A Musical Critic Anticipates
Eternity. Sassoon.
My Sun-Killed Tree. Harris.
Of His Majesties Receiving
the News of the Duke of
Buckingham's Death.
Waller.
On a Doctor of Divinity.
Porson.
Shasta. Bynner.

Sonnet: "Sweet secrecy, what
tongue can tell thy worth?"
Drayton.
St. Isaac's Chruch, Petrograd.
McKay.
There Was a Young Man
from Trinity. Anonymous.
Three Persons. Nicholl.
Whom Jesus Loved.
Barford.
The Wind Bloweth Where It
Listeth. Mitchell.

Divorce (d)
As Proper Mode of
Quenching Legal Lust.
Massey.
Don Juan. Byron.
Henry VIII. Anonymous.
Malvolio (parody). Landor.
Medea. Seneca.

Dixie
Dixie. Pike
Down South on the Rio
Grande. Anonymous.
Notes for a Southern Road
Map. McGinley.
War Song. Anonymous.
Wheeler's Brigade at Santiago.
Rice.

Do
Abnegation. Martial
(Marcus Valerius Martialis).
Adventures. Kramer.
Ain't No Tellin. Hurt.
All I Do, De Church Keep A-
Grumblin'. Anonymous.
American Rhapsody.
Fearing.
Assassination Poems.
Ridland.
By the Fire-Side. Browning.
Casting All Your Care upon
God, for He Careth for
You. Washbourne.
The Change. O'Bruadair.
A Christening. Davie.
Consolation in War.
Mumford.
Crazy Song to the Air of
"Dixie." (with music).
Anonymous.
The Deserter. Manifold.
The Duenna (excerpt).
Sheridan.
Eggs and Marrowbone.
Anonymous.
Epitaph. Anonymous.
Faults, Male and Female.
Anonymous.
Friendship. Silverstein.
From St. Luke's Hospital.
L'Engle.
General Store. Field.
Gloucester Moors. Moody.
The Golden Rule. Wells.
The Isle of Man.
Anonymous.
It Is March. Merwin.
It's No Use Raising a Shout.
Auden.
J.B. (excerpt). MacLeish.
James Wetherell. Robinson.
John Kinsella's Lament for
Mrs. Mary Moore. Yeats.
Letter to Manlius Torquatus.
Catullus.
Limerick: "There was a
princess of Bengal."
Parke.
Lines on Hearing That Lady
Byron Was Ill. Byron.
Magnets. Binyon.

Making. Webb.
Making Miso. Inada.
The Morning Duke Ellington
Praised the Lord...
Dodson.
My Creed. Gilder.
Night Shift. Shihab.
Nine Times a Night.
Anonymous.
Our Traveller.
Cholmondeley-Pennell
Philosophy. Parker.
Riots and Rituals. Thomas.
The Scars Remaining.
Coleridge.
Scots Wha Hae. Burns.
Sleepy Man Blues. White.
Sonnets from the Portuguese,
XXXII. Browning.
Sonnets to Aurelia. Nichols.
The Star of Calvary.
Hawthorne
That's What We'd Do.
Dodge.
To a New-Born Child.
Monkhouse.
To Cloe. Moore.
To Labor. Gilman.
A Valediction Forbidding
Mourning. Rich.
What Do You Do when It's
Spring? Woods.
What'll We Do with the
Baby-O? Anonymous.
Young Africa's Resolve.
Osadebay.

Dobbin
The Brisk Girl. Anonymous.
An Elegy on the Death of
Dobbin, the Butterwoman's
Horse.
Indecsion Means Flexibility.
Abhau.

Doctor (s)
Adventures of Isabel. Nash.
Aubade. Larkin.
The Country Doctor.
Carleton.
The Doctor Who Sits at the
Bedside of a Rat. Miles.
Greenwich Avenue.
Schuyler.
The Happy Life of a Country
Parson (parody). Pope.
Hardly a Man Is Now Alive.
Lardner.
Health Food. Anonymous.
Lost. Fisher.
Mother Tabbyskins. Hart.
O Doctor Dear My Love.
Halley.
To a Young Poet. Meacham.
Upon the Author of the
"Satire against Wit."
Sedley.
Variations on a Theme by
William Carlos Williams.
Koch.
The Vet. Boas.

Doctrine
Cleon. Browning.
Letter Containing a Panegyric
on Bath. Anstey.
Rillons, Rillettes. Wilbur.

Documents
The Book-Burning Pit. Lo
Yin.
Squatter's Children. Bishop.

Doe
La Bella Bona-Roba.
Lovelace.

The Broomfield Hill. *Anonymous.*
The Buck in the Snow. Millay.
Free Martin. Hopegood.
Dog days
Alphabetical Song on the Corn Law Bill. *Anonymous.*
A Dog Day. Field.
Under Sirius. Auden.
Dog (s)
1867: Last Sounds. O'Egan.
The Accident. Patterson.
Accident at Three Mile Island. Barnes.
Actaeon. Heppenstall.
Arf, Said Sandy. Stetler.
The Assignation. Ibarbourou.
At the Fishing Settlement. Campbell.
Bad Company. Watkyns.
Bang Street. Welch.
Bingo Has an Enemy. Fyleman.
The Birthplace. Heaney.
Bow, Wow, Wow! Mother Goose.
Brave Rover. Beerbohm.
Brother Dog. Sanchez.
The Bull. Wright.
Bullocky Bill. *Anonymous.*
Caelica, XX. Greville.
Climbing. Maiden.
Cominus, You Reprobate Old Goat. Catullus.
Couple. Swope.
The Creek-Road. Cawein.
Der Deitcher's Dog. Winner.
Didactic Sonnet. La Follette.
Dilemma. Bhartrihari.
Dob and Mob. *Anonymous.*
The Dog. *Anonymous.*
The Dog. Nash.
Dog, Dog in My Manger. Barker.
A Dog in San Francisco. Ondaatje.
Dog (parody). Berry.
A Dog's Vigil. Bruner.
The Durable Bon Mot. Preston.
The Ear. MacNeice.
Elegy V. Barker.
Elegy on the Death of a Mad Dog. Goldsmith.
En Garde, Messieurs. Lindsey.
The End of Exploring. Campbell.
An Epigram on Scolding. Swift.
An Epitaph. Byron.
Epitaph of Nearchos. Ammianus.
Exodus for Oregon. Miller.
Fear. Wier.
The Friar. Peacock.
George Ridler's Oven. *Anonymous.*
The Haunted Garden. Treece.
A Heterodoxy. Dunsany.
Hometown. Cabalquinto.
I Am His Highness' Dog at Kew. Pope.
I Think I Know No Finer Things Than Dogs. Brent.
Instructions to a Celebrated Laureat (excerpt). Wolcot.
Investigator. Waddington.

Invocation. Randolph.
The Irish Wolf-Hound. McCarthy.
Jubilate Canis. Jong.
Koheleth. Untermeyer.
The Lady's-Maid's Song. Hollander.
Last Lines. Kennedy.
Last Look at La Plata, Missouri. Barnes.
Limerick: "There once was a man of Bengal." *Anonymous.*
The Little Dog under the Wagon. *Anonymous.*
Manly Ferry. Philip.
The Martin Cat Long Shaged of Courage Good. Clare.
Mathematics. Oppenheimer.
Me and My Dog. *Anonymous.*
The Midnight Court. Merriman.
Money Is King. *Anonymous.*
Mort aux Chats. Porter.
Mother Tabbyskins. Hart.
My Airedale Dog. Mason.
My Estate. Drinkwater.
My Little Maid. *Anonymous.*
Mycenae. Fisher.
Nude in a Fountain. MacCaig.
Old Blue. *Anonymous.*
The Old Pack. *Anonymous.*
Phyllis; or, The Progress of Love. Swift.
Porcupines. Wilson, Jr.
The Power of the Dog. Kipling.
Precedent. Dunbar.
Prophets Who Cannot Sing. Patmore.
Radiator Lions. Aldis.
The Rain. *Anonymous.*
The Rantin Dog the Daddie O't. Burns.
The Renowned Generations. Yeats.
The Rose Is Red, the Grass Is Green. *Anonymous.*
Ruins of the City of Hay. Stow.
Saturday Blues. Bracey.
The Savage Beast. Williams.
Says Something Too (parody). Hoffenstein.
Scroppo's Dog. Swenson.
Song of Hannibal: Rome. Christian.
Spit, Cat, Spit. Mother Goose.
Stop Kicking My Dog around. *Anonymous.*
Sunday in the Park. Williams.
The Taxis. MacNeice.
A Terrible Thought. Steinbarg.
Tim, an Irish Terrier. Letts.
To a Poet, Who Would Have Me Praise Certain Bad Poets... Yeats.
To the Ingleezee Khafir, Calling Himself Djann Bool Djenkinzun. Mangan.
Tom Tinker's Dog. *Anonymous.*
The Victor Dog. Merrill.
Winter Rune. Coatsworth.
Dogies
The Cowboy's Dream. Finger.

Cowboy's Salvation Song. Carr.
Doney Gal. *Anonymous.*
Doing (s)
And Ut Pictura Poesis Is Her Name. Ashbery.
The Art of Love. Grossman.
George Washington Goes to a Girlie Movie. Boyajian.
Land. Arnett.
Letter to N. Y. Bishop.
Lines Left at Mr. Theodore Hook's House in June, 1834. Barham.
A Little More About the Brothers and Sisters. Scott.
The Omelet of A. MacLeish. Wilson.
On Fruition. Sedley.
Passing and Glassing. Rossetti.
Tess's Lament. Hardy.
The Weaver. *Anonymous.*
Doll (s)
Dominic Has a Doll. Cummings.
Epitaph for an American Bomber. Bertram.
Guys and Dolls. Loesser.
How to Be Old. Swenson.
Letter to My Daughter at the End of Her Second Year. Finkel.
The Lost Doll. Kingsley.
A Mortifying Mistake. Pratt.
Organ Transplant. Reed.
A Pretty a Day. Cummings.
She Turns the Dolls' Faces to the Wall. Yeats.
Snapshot. Fuller.
Toys. Sutzkever.
Dollar (s)
Ding Dong Dollar. Henderson.
Don't Let Your Deal Go Down. *Anonymous.*
Epigram: "Me Polytimus vexes and provokes." Martial (Marcus Valerius Martialis).
Last of the Poet's Car. Connor.
Song of the Leadville Mine Boss. Cameron.
The Story of Zeros. Cruz.
Walking Blues. Johnson.
Dolphin (s)
The Dark Lord of Savaiki. Campbell.
Nantucket's Widows. Foerster.
On a Horse Carved in Wood. Hall.
Dome
Aeneid. McAllister.
Parsifal. Verlaine.
The Progress of Faust. Shapiro.
The Sea Marke. Smith.
Sermon. Mayer.
Snow. Rodgers.
To K. H. Brown.
Dominion (s)
And Death Shall Have No Dominion. Thomas.
Breadth. Circle. Desert. Monarch. Month. Wisdom. Hollander.
The Inscription. Barker.
Leaving Seoul: 1953. Lew.
Listening-Post. Rosner.

A Prayer. Channing.
Shoreline. Barnard.
Done
Admonition to Montgomerie. James I,
Advice. Bierce.
An Air by Sammartini. Dudek.
An Artichoke for Montesquieu. Graham.
The Bees of Middleton Manor. Probyn.
Between Birthdays. Nash.
Certain True Woords Spoken Concerning One Benet Corbett. Corbett.
Cherry Tree Carol. *Anonymous.*
Childhood. Bradstreet.
The City of the Dead. Burton.
A Corn-Song. Dunbar.
The Corner Stone. De la Mare.
Creation. Gurr.
The Curse upon Edward. Gray.
Damon and Cupid. Gay.
Dayak Man Making Fishtrap. Rubenstein.
Destroying Angel. Corke.
The Djanggawul Cycle, 174. *Anonymous.*
The Don. Howes.
Doom. O'Shaughnessy.
The Engagement. Clough.
Evening Primrose. Clare.
The Execution of Montrose. Aytoun.
Focus. Norris.
For Hollis Sigler. Equi.
For one who says he feels. Morstein.
For the Goddess Too Well Known. Gidlow.
Forgive. Thornton.
The Forsaken Girl. Jarrell.
Frankie and Johnny, I (with music). *Anonymous.*
Harvest Song. Campbell.
Hay for the Horses. Snyder.
His Best. *Anonymous.*
A Hymn to God the Father. Donne.
I Set Forth Hopeful. Lalleswari.
The Icosasphere. Moore.
In the End. Everwine.
Incantation to Oedipus. Dryden.
Irrevocable. Plummer.
It Can Be Done. *Anonymous.*
The Last Wolf. Tallmountain.
Lilac Time. Hein.
Limerick: "A father once said to his son." *Anonymous.*
Limerick: "There was a young man of Ostend." *Anonymous.*
Lines on Hearing That Lady Byron Was Ill. Byron.
The Lover Complaineth the Unkindness of His Love. Wyatt.
A Man's Bread. Peabody.
Martin Luther King Jr. Brooks.
A Message from Reverend Fat Back Made Possible by... Brown.

Metaphor for My Son.
Holmes.
The Muses. Thomas.
My Heart Is a Lute.
Barnard.
Mystery Story. Nemerov.
Nightmare of a Cook.
Kallman.
A Nocturne. Blunt.
Now That Can Never Be
Done. Maris Stella.
Nymphidia. Drayton.
The Old Mother.
Anonymous.
Old Rowley the King.
Anonymous.
On a Night of Snow.
Coatsworth.
On the Suicide of a Friend.
Whittemore.
One Step at a Time.
Anonymous.
Out from Lobster Cove.
Reed.
The Parcae, or Three Dainty
Destinies: The Armillet.
Herrick.
Passing and Glassing.
Rossetti.
Preparations. Silko.
Regret and Refusal.
Anonymous.
Retrospect. Tichborne [(or
Tichbourne)].
Rondeau. Smith.
Shakespearean Soliloquy in
Progress: "To shave, or not
to..." (parody). Croker.
Silhouette in Sepia. Carr.
A Song to David. Smart.
Song: "Would you know
what's soft?" Carew.
Stanzas in Meditation. Stein.
Take down the Fiddle, Karl!
Neilson.
This I Can Do. Lefevre.
Thoughts on the Christian
Doctrine of Eternal Hell.
Smith.
The Time Is Today. Farrar.
To Master Henrye Cobham,
of the Most Blessed State of
Lyfe. Googe.
The Toaster. Smith.
The Turtle-Dove.
Anonymous.
Unprofitablenes. Vaughan.
A Voice from the Roses.
Kumin.
The Waiting. Whittier.
The Walk in the Garden.
Aiken.
Wash-Day Wonder.
Faubion.
Watchman, What of the
Night? Swinburne.
What Have They Done to the
Rain. Reynolds.
What Have We Done Today?
Waterman.
When All Is Done. Dunbar.
Winter with the Gulf Stream.
Hopkins.
Wizard Frost. Sherman.

Donegal
It's a Far, Far, Cry. Macgill.
A Road of Ireland.
O'Donnell.

Donkey
An Arab and His Donkey.
Anonymous.
Donkey Riding. *Anonymous.*

In Life's Stable.
Molodovsky.
Kindness. *Anonymous.*
The Legends of Evil.
Kipling.
The Test. Friend.

Donne
Homage to Literature.
Rukeyser.
To a Young Beauty. Yeats.

Doom (ed)
Admiral Byng. *Anonymous.*
Astrophel and Stella,
LXXXVI. Sidney.
The Boatswain's Call.
Anonymous.
Caelica, XLI. Greville.
Caelica, CIX. Greville.
Change. Greville.
Conclusion. Sassoon.
The Cottager's Complaint.
Freeth.
Cyder, I: How to Catch
Wasps. Philips.
Damned Women.
Baudelaire.
Elegy for the Monastery Barn.
Merton.
England and America in 1782.
Tennyson.
Epilogue to a Human Drama.
Spender.
Epitaph. Chiabrera.
Epitaph for the Race of Man.
Millay.
Germinal. Russell.
He Would Have His Lady
Sing. Dolben.
Immortal Flowers. Rice.
In the Cemetery of the Sun.
Watson.
In the Twilight (excerpt).
O'Donnell.
"In winter's just return..."
Surrey.
Matlock Bath. Betjeman.
The Mothers' Lament at the
Slaughter of the Innocents.
Anonymous.
My Company. Read.
Ode: "How are thy Servants
blest, O Lord!" Addison.
On Death. Keats.
The Philosophic Flight.
Bruno.
A Prayer. Laird.
Press'd by the Moon, Mute
Arbitress of Tides. Smith.
Rooming-House Melancholy.
Kastner.
Sally Simpkin's Lament.
Hood.
Sequence. Barker.
Tales from a Family Album.
Justice.
Tarantella. Belloc.
To a Mountain Daisy.
Burns.
To the Departing Spirit of an
Alienated Friend. Seward.
The Weaver. Burleigh.
The Wife's Lament.
Anonymous.
The Woman at the Washtub.
Daley.
Young People Who Delight in
Sin. *Anonymous.*

Doomsday
Caelica, LXXII. Greville.
The Debate of the Body and
the Soul (excerpt).
Anonymous.

The Question. Gibson.
The Sleepers. Harvey.
The Stranger. Everson.

Door (s)
Abandoned House in Late
Light. Twichell.
Abdelfatteh. Lacey.
Absence. Meinke.
Allah's Tent. Colton.
Alma Mater. Osborn.
Alone in the House. Bogin.
Annie of Lochroyan.
Anonymous.
Another Day. Brown.
At the Grave of Henry
Vaughan. Sassoon.
Au Clair de la Lune. Lully.
The Author to Her Book.
Bradstreet.
Ballad of Mistress Death.
Devlin.
The Banjo. Winner.
Bar Not the Door. Campion.
The Beverley Maid and the
Tinker. *Anonymous.*
Bless This House. Taylor.
Blue Homespun. Call.
The Bull Moses. Hughes.
The Campus. Posner.
Careless Love. *Anonymous.*
Cat into Lady. La Fontaine.
The Cats' Tea-Party.
Weatherly.
The Cautious Struggle.
Anonymous.
Christ at the Door.
Anonymous.
Christmas Eve. *Anonymous.*
Christmas Singing.
Chandler.
The Coming Forth by Day of
Osiris Jones: The Nursery.
Aiken.
Cromwell. Francis.
The Dark. Heyen.
Daybreak. Meyers.
Death Is a Door. Turner.
The Death of the Old Year.
Tennyson.
Decision. *Anonymous.*
The Departure from Hydra.
Koch.
Diagnosis. Canan.
Don't Ask Me Who I Am.
Randall, Jr.
A Door. Merwin.
Doors. Clark.
Doors. Hagedorn.
El Greco. Mayo.
Elysium is as far as to.
Dickinson.
An Epigram on Florio.
Winstanley.
Every Night When the Sun
Goes In. *Anonymous.*
Fame. *Anonymous.*
Feathers or Lead?
Broughton.
The Five Dreams. Woods.
Five Were Foolish. Hodge.
For the New Railway Station
in Rome. Wilbur.
From the Day-Book of a
Forgotten Prince.
Untermeyer.
Get Up and Bar the Door.
Anonymous.
Get Up and Bar the Door (B
version). *Anonymous.*
Gods. Sexton.
Going Home. Kenny.
Good Tradition. *Anonymous.*

Grey Woman. Cardiff.
Hard Time Killin' Floor
Blues. James.
Health Counsel. Harington.
Hiroshima Exit. Kogawa.
How Gray the Rain.
Coatsworth.
Humpty Dumpty's Recitation.
"Carroll.
I Have Trod the Upward and
the Downward Slope.
Stevenson.
I know some lonely houses off
the road. Dickinson.
I Lay My Lute beside Thy
Door. Urmy.
I Taught Myself to Live
Simply and Wisely.
Akhmatova.
If So the Man You Are.
Lewis.
The Ilex Tree. Lee.
In a Garret. Allen.
In Honor of St. Alphonsus
Rodriguez. Hopkins.
In the Old House. Hall.
The Inn of Earth. Teasdale.
Jittery Jim. Smith.
Johnie Blunt. *Anonymous.*
The Keyhole in the Door.
Anonymous.
The Knife. Valentine.
The Knitters. Colum.
The Light That Came.
Clifton.
Limerick: "There was a young
genius of Queens." Hilton.
Little Dirge. Untermeyer.
Lonely House. Dickinson.
The Longing. Goodreau.
Looking Both Ways. Wayne.
A Lovely Young Moor.
Anonymous.
Man Is in Pain. Lamantia.
May Morn. McClure.
Midnight Lamentation.
Monro.
Morning. Kavanagh.
Mother Shake the Cherry-
Tree. Rossetti.
Mushrooms. Plath.
My Dog. Bangs.
My Uninvited Guest. Smith.
My Way Is in the Sand
Flowing. Beckett.
Obituary. Kees.
Objets d'Art. MacDonald.
Old Essex Door. Hickey.
On a Night of Snow.
Coatsworth.
On the Day of Atonement.
Amichai.
On This Day I Complete My
Fortieth Year. Porter.
The Open Door.
Anonymous.
Open the Door. *Anonymous.*
The Outlandish Knight.
Anonymous.
Parting after a Quarrel.
Tietjens.
The Party. Rodgers.
Piyyut for Rosh Hashana.
Guri.
Poem: "I heard of a man."
Cohen.
Pretty Polly (with music).
Anonymous.
Prospective Immigrants Please
Note. Rich.
The Rain Comes Sobbing to
the Door. Kendall.

The Raven Visits Rawhide. *Anonymous.*
Rebecca, Who Slammed Doors for Fun and Perished Miserably. Belloc.
Riddle: "A long white barn." *Anonymous.*
Riding the Elevator into the Sky. Sexton.
Scintilla. Braithwaite.
Sermon. Mayer.
Six Week Old Blues. Barbee.
Song: "She spoke to me gently with words of sweet meaning." MacDonogh.
Starry Sky. *Anonymous.*
Sun Gonna Shine in My Door Some Day. *Anonymous.*
Sunday Afternoon in Italy. Lawrence.
Suppose This Moment Some Stupendous Question. Nowlan.
These Men. Gellert.
They Came to the Wedding. Deutsch.
Through an Embrace. Eluard.
To America, on Her First Sons Fallen in the Great War. Walker.
To Silvestre Revueltas of Mexico, in His Death. Neruda.
To the Thawing Wind. Frost.
To Ultima Thule. Dangerfield.
The Trooper's Horse. *Anonymous.*
Two Poems on the Emotions. Shapiro.
Understanding. Soroka.
The Unreturning. Owen.
The Waiting Watchers. Treece.
Wandering. Flexner.
We Are Leaning Away. Harvey.
The Weaver. Mueller.
When the Ambulance Came. Morgan.
When You've Been Here Long Enough. Joseph.
Who Is This Who Howls and Mutters? Smith.
Why God Permits Evil: For Answers to This Question of Interest... Williams.
Wisdom. Hicky.
With the Door Open. Ignatow.
The Wizard's Funeral. Dixon.
Wood-Thrush. Wheelock.
Written. Ruelfe.
You Have What I Look For. Sabines.
Your Body Is Stars. Spender.

Doorstep
Alison. Gold.
Mother Doorstep. Daley.

Doorway (s)
The Devil and the Angel. Dobson.
Dirge for Two Clavichords and Bowler Hat. Smithyman.
Galileo Galilei. Smith.
My Father's Ghost. Wagoner.

A Northern Spring. Baro.
Pleasant the House. *Anonymous.*
Revelation. Soutar.
Seven Dreams. Bayliss.
Song of Cradle-Making. Skinner.

Dots
The Changes. Pinsky.
Safe in Their Alabaster Chambers. Dickinson.
Seurat. Sadoff.
Up Early. Robinson.
What Hath Man Wrought Exclamation Point. Bishop.

Double (s)
Diana's Hunting-Song. Dryden.
Don Juan. Byron.
The Epistemological Rag. Burr.
Epitaph. Cowper.
The Ferry. Boker.
Gone Are the Days. MacCaig.
Letters to Walt Whitman. Johnson.
Love-Song of the Water Carriers. *Anonymous.*
Man's Medley. Herbert.
My Neighbor's Reply. *Anonymous.*
Porson on His Majesty's Government. Porson.
The Sergeant, He Is the Worst of All (with music). *Anonymous.*
Shield. *Anonymous.*
The Spelling of Elliot. *Anonymous.*
To Man Who Goes Seeking Immortality, Bidding Him Look Nearer Home. Crapsey.
To the Same Man's Life. Hammond.

Doubt (ing) (s)
Audiences. Hollander.
Auguries of Innocence. Blake.
The Baker's Boy. Newsome.
Benevolence. Akenside.
Cathleen Sweeping. Johnston.
Childe Harold's Pilgrimage: Canto III. Byron.
The Church. Muir.
Crematorium. Betjeman.
The Deeper Seas. Bellamann.
Dialogue. Rich.
The Doppelganger. Hine.
Faith. Wilcox.
The Feast of Padre Chala. Walsh.
The Grand Inquisitor's Song. Gilbert.
Holy Sonnets, XVII. Donne.
Jews at Haifa. Jarrell.
June Song. Rosenthal.
The Labyrinth. Auden.
Last Letter to the Western Civilization. Ogilvie.
A Letter to John Dryden (excerpt). McAuley.
Michelangelo: "The Creation of Adam." Djanikian.
No Doubt. Adams.
Ourselves we do inter with sweet derision. Dickinson.
Pete's Error. Chapman.

Philonous' Paradox. Gilbert.
Prayer for Kafka and Ourselves. Rudolf.
The Primrose. Carew.
Retired This Hour from Wondering Crowds. Landor.
Retractions. Cabell.
Sir Walter Scott's Tribute. Scott.
Some Refrains at the Charles River. Viereck.
Song: "Thyrsis, when we parted, swore." Gray.
Soul and Body. Waddington.
The Tempest. Shakespeare.
A Thorn Forever in the Breast. Cullen.
To a Reviewer Who Admired My Book. Ciardi.
To L-. Cresswell.
The Traveller. Dennis.
Upon the Infant Martyrs. Crashaw.
Upon the Swallow. Bunyan.
Voice of the Crocus. Hoyer.
Walken Hwome at Night. Barnes.
The Wall. Reed.
Watching. Judson
When All the Young Were Dying. Wilson.
Why Art Thou Silent! Wordsworth.
The Women All Tell Me. *Anonymous.*

Doubtful
For My Wife. Symons.
Time Lags Abed. Cresswell.
The White-Tailed Hornet. Frost.

Dough
The Apple Dumplings and a King. Wolcot.
Epitaph in Christ Church, Bristol, on Thomas Turner. Jeffrey.
Money Isn't Everything! Hammerstein.
On Maids and Cats. Selyns.
Reason I Stay on Job So Long. *Anonymous.*
Situation. Hughes.

Dove (s)
The Animals. Jacobsen.
Ave Maria Gratia Plena. Wilde.
Bear, Cat and Dove. Greenberg.
The Beauty of the Stars. Ibn Ezra.
The Chaste Arabian Bird. Rochester.
A Child Screening a Dove from a Hawk. Landon.
Connubii Flores, or the Well-Wishes at Weddings. Herrick.
Desert Gulls. Gillespie.
Did any bird come flying. Rossetti.
Die Rose, Die Lilie, Die Taube. Heine.
Dove. Farber.
Doves. Neugroschel.
Epigrams. Theocritus.
The Feast of All Saints. Smither.
Few Happy Matches. Watts.
The Friendly Beast. *Anonymous.*
Girl with Doves. Gray.

Philonous' Paradox. Gilbert.

The International Brigade Arrives at Madrid. Neruda.
Lamenting Tauaba. Akhyaliyya.
Late. Salz.
Letter to Alex Comfort. Abse.
Love's Resume. Heine.
Lying. Wilbur.
Memento. Spender.
Minnie and Her Dove. Turner.
Mother's Nerves. Kennedy.
No One So Much As You. Thomas.
Noah's Song. Jones.
O Lord, I Come Pleading. Lawson.
Old Smoky. *Anonymous.*
The Pigeon-Feeders in Battery Park. Altrocchi.
Poem by the Clock Tower, Summer. Baxter.
Prayer for Messiah. Cohen.
The Sea Shroud. Kerouac.
Sonnets from the Portuguese, XXXV. Browning.
Three Seasons. Rossetti.
Uncle an' Aunt. Barnes.
The Usk. Sisson.
The Welcome. Cowley.
Wife of Kohelet. Cohen.
Winter. Leib.
Woodpigeons at Raheny. Davie.

Dover
Abroad Thoughts. Blishen.
As I Was Going up the Hill. *Anonymous.*
Because. Fitzgerald.
The Eel. De La Mare.
Limerick: "There was an old person of Dover." Lear.

Down
Advice to Country Girls. *Anonymous.*
All through the Rains. Snyder.
Arizona Boys and Girls. *Anonymous.*
The Black Ball Line. *Anonymous.*
Blow the Man Down. *Anonymous.*
Budmouth Dears. Hardy.
C.C. Rider (with music). *Anonymous.*
Carmen. Levy.
Cleaning Up. Dyson.
Crow on the Fence. *Anonymous.*
The Crucifixion. Meynell.
The Curtains in the House of the Metaphysician. Stevens.
Dark Angel. Bartlett.
Death. Herbert.
Down, Down, Down. *Anonymous.*
Down-Hall. Prior.
Farmer. Fallon.
Farmers. Lux.
First Flight. Hoffman.
Go to Old Ireland. *Anonymous.*
Grand Finale. Layton.
The Grand Old Duke of York. Mother Goose.
Grandfather's Heaven. Nye.
Here in Katmandu. Justice.

The King of France.
Anonymous.
The Kingfisher. Clampitt.
Lament. Sexton.
Let Me Not Die. Pierce.
Liberty (excerpt).
Wordsworth.
Limerick: "A housewife called
out with a frown."
Anonymous.
Little Red Riding Hood.
Sexton.
Looking Up at Down.
Broonzy.
The Maiden's Complaint.
Anonymous.
The Mermaid. Tennyson.
Metaphysic of Snow. Finkel.
The Noble Duke of York.
Anonymous.
Ode to a Vanished Operator
in an Automatized Elevator.
Rosenfield.
Old Black Men. Johnson.
A Part of an Ode. Jonson.
Peter. Benet.
The Poet's Request.
Anonymous.
Post-Rail Song (with music).
Anonymous.
Red Iron Ore. Anonymous.
Rise Me up from down below.
Anonymous.
Roan Stallion. Jeffers.
Somewhere Down below Me
Is a Street. Maloney.
Song: Lift Boy. Graves.
Songs about Life and Brighter
Things Yet. Hoffenstein.
Spike Driver Blues. Hurt.
The Stolen Fifer. Fiacc.
The Swan. Spender.
Things to Do around a
Lookout. Snyder.
The Titanic. Anonymous.
To the Immortal Memory and
Friendship of That Noble
Pair... Jonson.
Tom Wedgwood Tells.
Aldiss.
Words. Williams.
You Got to Go Down.
Davis.

Downfall
The Agnostic's Creed.
Malone.
She Is More to be Pitied than
Censured. Gray.
Ye Sons of Columbia.
Anonymous.

Dowry
Nana Kru. Anonymous.
The Streets of Laredo.
MacNeice.

Doze (d)
Bats. Newsome.
The Doze. Reeves.
Limerick: "There was an Old
Man who supposed."
Lear.
Mother. Libera.
Shrovetide's Countenance.
Rabelais.
Slow Waker. Gunn.
To My Friend, behind Walls.
Kizer.

Dozen (s)
I Am the Monarch of the Sea.
Gilbert.
Kentucky Blues. Jones.

The Mad Farmer Stands Up
in Kentucky for What He
Thinks Is Right. Hall.
Sir Toby Matthews.
Suckling.

Dr (ied) (y)
Andrew Bardeen.
Anonymous.
The Author Loving These
Homely Meats... Davies.
Ba Cottage. Young.
Bob Stanford. Anonymous.
A Bought Embrace. Fraser.
City Johannesburg. Serote.
The Day It Was Night.
Desnos.
Dialogue. Nemerov.
Dry Be That Tear. Sheridan.
Duo-tang. Elmslie.
An Epitaph upon Doctor
Brook. Crashaw.
Exeunt. Wilbur.
Face to Face. Rich.
Fairy Wings. Howard.
Fare Ye Well, My Darlin'.
Anonymous.
Farewell. Wilson.
For the Candle Light.
Grimke.
Gerontion. Eliot.
Have You Got a Brook.
Dickinson.
Heaven and Hell.
Anonymous.
Herbs in the Attic. Waniek.
The Hut. Van Stockum.
In a Double Rainbow.
Littlebird.
Invasion North. Hugo.
Landscape of Screams.
Sachs.
The Last Utterance of the
Delphic Oracle.
Anonymous.
Like a Great Rock, Far out at
Sea. Sanuki.
Little Light. Brodey.
Mackerel Sky. Anonymous.
My Creed. Cary.
Nunc Viridant Segetes.
Sedulius Scottus.
The Ocean Spills.
Hoffenstein.
Ode of Odium on Aquariums.
Guiterman.
Ode to Popularity. Praed.
Oh, Sing to God. Steendam.
On the Thirteenth Day of
Christmas. Causley.
Overture to Strangers.
Haring.
The Palmer. Langland.
Peer of the Gods Is That
Man. Sappho.
Pisces Child. McPherson.
The Ploughman.
Anonymous.
The Rattlesnake. Wrigley.
The Republic 1939. Liddy.
The Rick of Green Wood.
Dorn.
The Servant of Rosemary
Lane. Anonymous.
Sir Andrew Barton (Andrew
Batann). Anonymous.
Song of the Argonauts.
Morris.
Sweet Violets. Anonymous.
Town I Left. Sorrells.
Two Views of Two Ghost
Towns. Tomlinson.
Vanity. Graves.

The Vision of Piers Plowman.
Langland.
Words for Music Perhaps.
Yeats.

Draft (s)
Around You, Your House.
Stafford.
The Origins of Life. Carus.
Staff-Nurse: New Style.
Henley.

Drag (s)
Aka. Eckman.
Another While. Rosenfeld.
Around Cape Horn.
Anonymous.
Ballade to His Mistress.
Villon.
The Balloon of the Mind.
Yeats.
Graves Are Made to Waltz
On. Viereck.
Hey Dorolot. Anonymous.
Limerick: "A dragon, who
was a great wag." Wells.
O-Bar Cowboy. Anonymous.
River Sound Remembered.
Merwin.
Roll the Chariot (with music).
Anonymous.
Song: "One day the god of
fond desire." Thomson.
To a Fly, Taken out of a
Bowl of Punch. Wolcot.

Dragon (s)
Awake! Awake! Ruskin.
The Dragon of the Seas.
Page.
The Frozen Hero. Vance.
In Memory of David Archer
(excerpt). Barker.
A Mock Song. Lovelace.
A Seamark. Carman.
The Song of the Seeress.
Anonymous.
Sospetto d'Herode. Crashaw.

Drain (ed)
Escape and Return.
Jennings.
Here the Trace. Pasternak.
In the Cemetery. Hardy.
On a Fifteenth-Century
Flemish Angel. Ray.

Drake (s)
Hares on the Mountain.
Anonymous.
The Manlet (parody).
"Carroll.
Nell Flaherty's Drake.
Anonymous.
Sam, the Sportsman.
Anonymous.

Drama
Alfonso Churchill. Masters.
Amphimachos the Dandy.
McHugh.
God's Work. Cushman.
She Was All That You Loved.
Laxness.

Drank
A Decanter of Madeira, Aged
86, to George Bancroft,
Aged 86. Mitchell.
Dream Songs. Berryman.
Envoy. Carman.
Gethsemane. Kipling.
The Greater Music. Weiss.
Next to of Course God
America I. Cummings.
On a Certain Alderman.
Cunningham.
On a Young Man and an Old
Man. May.

The Vision of Piers Plowman.
Langland.

Paddy Murphy. Anonymous.
Robin Hood's Delight.
Anonymous.
Snatches: "Here I was and
here I drank."
Anonymous.
The Springs. Berry.
Two Married. Frazee-Bower.
Urania. Andrews.
Zion's Sons and Daughters.
Anonymous.

Drapery
Autumn Melancholy.
Hamill.
Clothes Do But Cheat and
Cozen Us. Herrick.
Thanatopsis. Bryant.

Draught
An Apologie for the Precedent
Hymns on Teresa.
Crashaw.
The Kiss and the Cup.
Anonymous.
Thomas Hardy and A. E.
Housman. Beerbohm.
The Wine Cup. Meleager.

Draw (ing) (n)
After a Parting. Meynell.
Alba: March. Hacker.
Crayon House. Rukeyser.
L'Envoi. Kipling.
I Saw a Tree That Was
Greater Than All the
Others. Sodergran.
The Lesson. Bentley.
Like Children of the
Summertime Playing at
Cards. White.
Mezzo Cammin. Moffett.
The Miracle of Dawn.
Cawein.
One Writing against His
Prick. Anonymous.
Sonnets, XXIV: "Mine eye
hath play'd the painter, and
hath steel'd. Shakespeare.
Stand, Stately Tavie.
Anonymous.
Sudan. Jackson.
Sun and Cloud. Cane.
The Sunset City. Cornwell.
Too Much Coffee. Robinson.
Tyranny of Moths. Vizenor.
We Have Been Happy.
Eastman.
The Weather. Crozier.

Drawer (s)
Diagnosis. Canan.
Eclipse. Salamun.
Human Relations. Sisson.
I wanted to see you.
Miccolis.
The Manual. Rubin.
When You Are Gone. Van
Winckel.

Dread (ed) (ful) (s)
The Abduction. Kunitz.
Alone up Here on the
Mountain. Anonymous.
Aria. Schwartz.
The Candles Draw Well after
All. Jensen.
Christ 1: Advent Lyrics, I.
Anonymous.
The Cloth of Gold (excerpt).
Krishnamurti.
Cradle Song. Blake.
The Dark. Fuller.
Death. Coleridge.
The Dreaded Task. Bruner.
The Faerie Queene. Spenser.
The Fear. Gibson.

Garryowen. *Anonymous.*
Hate! Antokolsy.
Head of Medusa.
  Zaturenska.
I Was Washing outside in the
  Darkness. Mandelstam.
In the Seraglio. Slavitt.
It May Be Good. Wyatt.
A Judgment in Heaven.
  Thompson.
Landlady. Page.
The Last Landlord. Allen.
The Legend of Heinz Von
  Stein. Leland.
The Love Song of J. Alfred
  Prufrock (parody).
  Walker.
The Masters. Widdemer.
Matlock Bath. Betjeman.
Midweek. Miles.
My Comrade. Markham.
Of Fortune. Kyd.
Of History More Like Myth.
  Garrigue.
Satyrs upon the Jesuits:
  Prologue. Oldham.
The Seraph and the Snob.
  Kendall.
The Service. Johnson.
Sir Eustace Grey. Crabbe.
The Skeleton at the Feast.
  Roche.
The Soldier's Wooing.
  Anonymous.
Tenebrae. Clarke.
The Terrible Dead. Davies.
The Unreturning. Owen.
Vaunting Oak. Ransom.
The Wild Geese. Morse.
Wood-Pigeons. Masefield.
Dream (ed) (ing) (s)
1939 Mercury. Drake.
2 Little Whos. Cummings.
Abishag Writes a Letter
  Home. Manger.
Absolution. Watson.
Across Kansas. Stafford.
African Dream. Kaufman.
After Some Day of Decision.
  Whittemore.
After Summer. Marston.
After the Death of an Elder
  Klallam. Niatum.
Afterglow. Borges.
All Animals Like Me.
  Souster.
Alma to Her Sister. Gregg.
Along South Inlet. Kuzma.
The Alpine Flowers.
  Sigourney.
Among These Turf-Stacks.
  MacNeice.
The Ancestors. Wright.
Ancient Lullaby. Griffin.
And Did the Animals? Van
  Doren.
And on My Return. Guri.
And to the Young Man.
  Moore.
Anecdote of 2 A.M. Wain.
The Angel in the House.
  Patmore.
Another Cross. Gardner.
Another Way. Bierce.
Application for a Grant.
  Hecht.
Ark Parting. Macpherson.
The Armorer's Daughter.
  Greger.
Army Bugle Calls: Taps.
  Anonymous.
Art. Gautier.

Artificial Intelligence. Rich.
As I Grew Older. Hughes.
Aswelay. Pritchard II.
At the Saturday Club.
  Holmes.
Awake, My Fair. Halevi.
Babylon. Taylor.
A Balcony with Birds. Moss.
Ballad of the Icondic.
  Ciardi.
Barcarolle. O'Shaughnessy.
Battery Park, High Noon.
  Belitt.
Batyushkov. Mandelstam.
Beale Street. Hughes.
Becoming Real. Goldensohn.
Beethoven's Death Mask.
  Spender.
Beggars. Carpenter.
Belief in Plan of Thee.
  Whitman.
Birth of a Country. Gergely.
The Blue Ridge. Monroe.
The Blue Room. Hart.
The Bomber. Vrepont.
The Book of the Duchess.
  Chaucer.
The Boxer Turned Bartender.
  Kizer.
Breasts. Gallagher.
The Brickster. *Anonymous.*
The Bride. Bierce.
Bring a Torch, Jeanette,
  Isabella. Saboly.
Brooklyn Bridge at Dawn.
  Le Gallienne.
The Burning of the Birds.
  Kaufman.
But How It Came from Earth.
  Aiken.
By the Beautiful Ohio.
  LaBombard.
By the North Sea.
  Swinburne.
California Joe. *Anonymous.*
The Call to a Scot. Harding.
Capilano. Stephen.
The Carnation. Hannigan.
Carried Away. Elder.
Catherine. Kuskin.
Chanticleer. Irvin.
The Chauffeur of Lilacs.
  Hitchcock.
The Childless Woman in
  Heaven. Tynan.
Childs Memory. Wilkins.
Christmas Eve. Parmenter.
Circus Nerves and Worries.
  Elmslie.
Clair de Lune. Symons.
The Climbers. Jennings.
The Collector. Behm.
A Comparison. Farrar.
Composed on the Theme
  "Willows by the Riverside."
  Yu Hsuan-chi.
Confession of Faith. Wylie.
A Convict's Tour to Hell.
  MacNamara.
The Coup de Grace. Sill.
Cradle Song. Naidu.
The Crane Is My Neighbour.
  Neilson.
Cressida. Baxter.
Crest Jewel. Stephens.
The Dance of Dust (parody).
  Untermeyer.
Dawn of Womanhood.
  Monro.
The Day-Dream. Rossetti.
Day Dreams, or Ten Years
  Old. Johnson.

Daybreak. Spender.
A Dead Calm and Mist.
  Sharp.
Dead in Bloody Snow. Le
  Sueur.
The Dean. Porter.
Dear Friends. Robinson.
Dear Master, in Whose Life I
  See. Hunter.
The Dearest Poets. Hunt.
Death. Coates.
Deep Dark River. Roberts.
Deep Sea Tug. *Anonymous.*
The Departure. Pack.
Dervish. McElhaney.
Desert Song. Dresbach.
Dew on a Dusty Heart.
  Untermeyer.
Dirge. Parsons.
Dirge: For One Who Fell in
  Battle. Parsons
Doom-Devoted. Golding.
Drake. Noyes.
The Dream. Bishop.
The Dream. Donne.
The Dream. Sherburne.
The Dream. Symons.
The Dream Called Life.
  Calderon de la Barca.
Dream Fishing. Thomas.
A Dream in Early Spring.
  Shove.
The Dream of a Boy Who
  Lived at Nine Elms.
  Rands.
The Dream of a Girl Who
  Lived at Sevenoaks.
  Rands.
Dream of the Black Mother.
  Dos Santos.
Dream Song. Middleton.
Dream Songs. Berryman.
The Dream-Teller. Gregory.
A Dream within a Dream.
  Poe.
The Dreamer. Nunan.
Dreamer of Dreams.
  Carruth.
Dreams. Herrick.
Dreams. Hughes.
Dreams of Snakes, Chocolate
  and Men. Sanford.
Drugged. De la Mare.
The Drunkard. Levine.
Dry-Point. Larkin.
Dry Your Tears, Africa!
  Dadie.
Dust Bowl. Davis.
The Dynasts. Hardy.
Early Morn. Davies.
Ebb and Flow. Curtis.
Elegy. Hillyer.
Elegy for Drowned Children.
  Dawe.
En Bateau. Verlaine.
The Enchanted Heart.
  Davison.
(End) of Summer (1966).
  Knott.
The End which Comes.
  Arnold.
Epigram: "Love brought me
  quietly." Meleager.
Epipsychidion. Shelley.
Eve's Advice to the Children
  of Israel. Neugroschel.
Everyone in the World.
  Dailey.
Exodus. Probst.
Expostulation and Reply.
  Wordsworth.
The Faerie's Child. Irwin.

The Far North. Savoie.
A Farewell. Russell.
Farewell. Symonds.
Farmyard. Dallas.
Finding Them Lost. Moss.
First Light. Kinsella.
The First Reader. Scott.
The First Thanksgiving.
  Turner.
The Fisherman. Wells.
Flora. Fraser.
Folk Tune. Raab.
For a Moment. *Anonymous.*
For a Poet. Cullen.
The Forbidden Lure. Davis.
Frederick Douglass. Hayden.
The Fringilla Melodia. Hirst
From Jerusalem: A First
  Poem. Preil.
From the Hymn of
  Empedocles. Arnold.
Fruitionless. Coolbrith.
The Gardener. Keyes.
The Gardener at Thirty.
  Kessler.
The Gardener's Cat.
  Chalmers.
Georgia Dusk. Toomer.
The Ghost's Leavetaking.
  Plath.
The Grave. Jones.
The Great Bear Lake
  Meditations (excerpt).
  Yates.
Greeting. Young.
A Grey Day. Moody.
Habakkuk. Roditi.
The Haunts of the Halcyon.
  Luders.
He Wishes for the Cloths of
  Heaven. Yeats.
The Heart. Steinberg.
Heliodore. Logan.
Her Answer. Bennett.
Her Hair. Baudelaire.
The Herald Crane. Garland.
High Summer on the
  Mountains. Davies.
Hold Fast Your Dreams.
  Driscoll.
Homosexual Sonnets.
  Pitchford.
Hope. Hughes.
Hope. Stewart.
Horatian Variation. Bacon.
Horse. Benson.
Hotel de l'Univers et Portugal.
  Merrill.
Housing Shortage.
  Replansky.
How Well for the Birds.
  Anonymous.
Howard Lamson. Masters.
The Hunter. Turner.
I Am Glad Daylong.
  Braithwaite.
I am so lost. Narihira
  (Ariwara no Narihira).
I Asked the Little Boy Who
  Cannot See. *Anonymous.*
I Dream a World. Hughes.
I Dreamed My Love.
  Anonymous.
I Dreamed That in a City
  Dark as Paris. Simpson.
I Gazed Within. Bronte.
I go to this window.
  Cummings.
I Have Exhausted the
  Delighted Range...
  Hartnett.

I Reckon When I Count at All. Dickinson.
I Shall Never Go. Hovde.
The Ice Castle. Harris.
Idylls. Theocritus.
If It Is Not My Portion. Tagore.
If Only the Dreams Abide. Scollard.
If You Can't Eat You Got To. Cummings.
If You Were Here. Marston.
Immortality. Russell.
In a Rose Garden. Bennett.
In an Artist's Studio. Rossetti.
In Nature There Is Neither Right nor Left nor Wrong. Jarrell.
In Prague. Celan.
In the Gloaming. Calverley.
In the Grass. Droste-Hulshoff.
In the Land Where We Were Dreaming. Lucas.
In Your Arms. Radnoti.
Indian Summer. Howes.
Infidelity. Berggolts.
The Inner Silence. Monroe.
Insomnia. MacCarthy.
The Insult. Layzer.
Interlude. Bodenheim.
Intimations of Immortality from Recollections of Early Childhood. Wordsworth.
Introduction. Poems, 1831]. Poe.
Irish Hotel. Wevill.
It Comes during Sleep. Dow.
It Is Finished. Bush.
It Is in the Winter That We Dream of Spring. Wilson.
It May Be. Jacob.
It's a Long Way. Braithwaite.
It's Comforting. Simmons.
Jack Frost. "Setoun. Gabriel"
Jeanie Morrison. Motherwell.
The Jungle. Dudek.
Kaire. Eberhart.
The King of Dreams. Scollard.
Kinnereth. Bluwstein.
The Knights to Chrysola. Taylor.
Lachesis. Daley.
Lake-Song. Untermeyer.
The Lamp of Poor Souls. Pickthall.
The last dream. Young Bear.
The Last of His Tribe. Kendall.
The Last Violet. Herford.
The Last Word. Knowles.
The Late, Last Rook. Hodgson.
Latin Lullaby. Anonymous.
The Laud of Saint Catherine. Swinburne.
Learning to Count. Turner.
A Life. Bloch.
Like Rousseau. Jones.
Lines to Fanny (excerpt). Keats.
Lines Written near Linton, on Exmoor (parody). Hoffman.
Little Big Horn. McGaffey.

The little tigers are at rest. Hood.
Living among the Dead. Matthews.
Living in the Present. Lott.
Logic. Murry.
London Voluntaries. Henley.
Love Is Loathing & Why. Ford.
Love Song. Ranaivo.
Love Sonnets, VIII. Harpur.
The Lover, Having Dreamed of Enjoying His Love.... Wyatt.
The Lover Tells of the Rose in His Heart. Yeats.
The Lunar Probe. Kumin.
Mab the Mistress-Fairy. Jonson.
MacKenna's Dream. Anonymous.
Magic Fox. Welch.
Magnets. Binyon.
The Man. Browne.
A Man Called Dante, I Have Heard. King.
The Man in the Ocelot Suit. Brookhouse.
The Man in the Recreation Room. Harkness.
Many a Mickle. De La Mare.
Mater Desiderata. Praed.
Mayday. Roberson.
Meditation on a Memoir. Cunningham.
Meditations in Time of Civil War. Yeats.
Memories. Prentice.
Mercian Hymns (excerpt). Hill.
The Messiah. Yungman.
The Midnight Court. Merriman.
The Milker. Duggan.
Miners. Owen.
Miss Jennian Jones. Anonymous.
The Misty Island. Anonymous.
Moon Watching by Lake Chapala. Young.
Moschatel. O'Sullivan.
Moth-Terror. De Casseres.
Mother. Ehrmann.
Mother's Habits. Giovanni.
Mourning Picture. Rich.
Mousemeal. Nemerov.
Multitudes Turn in Darkness. Aiken.
Music. Lowell.
Music (after Sully Prudhomme). Du Maurier.
My House. McKay.
My Mother. Burr.
Nails. Gildner.
The Names. Edmond.
Near the Border of Insanities. Abse.
Nerves. Symons.
A Net to Snare the Moonlight. Lindsay.
New Dreams for Old. Rice.
Night and Love. Lytton.
Night for Adventures. Starbuck.
Night Interpreted. Hoagland.
Night Landscape. Aiken.
The Night Nurse Goes Her Round. Gray.

Night Song for an Old Lover. Glickman.
Night the Ninth Being the Last Judgment. Blake.
Night Thoughts in Age. Wheelock.
Nightmares. Fox.
Nights on the Indian Ocean. Rice.
No One Is Asleep. Roberts.
Nocturnal. Marron.
North and South. McKay.
Not for That City. Mew.
November. Binyon.
November. Bridges.
Now the Leaves Are Falling Fast. Auden.
A Nympholept. Swinburne.
Ode: "Tell me, thou soul of her I love." Thomson.
Ode: "We are the music-makers." O'Shaughnessy.
Off to the Fishing Ground. Montgomery.
The Oft-Repeated Dream. Frost.
Old Ego Song. Minczeski.
Old Man. Booth.
Old Ships. Ginsberg.
Old War-Dreams. Whitman.
Omnia Somnia. Sylvester.
On a Friend's Suicide. Yots.
On the Road There Stands a Tree. Manger.
The Other World. Stowe.
The Painter Dreaming in the Scholar's House. Nemerov.
Paiute Ponies. Barnes.
Palace Dancer, Dancing at Last. Green.
Pallor. Robinson.
Palo Alto: The Marshes. Hass.
Paradise Lost. Milton.
Parks and Ponds. Emerson.
Parting from My Son. Paterson.
Pax Nobiscum. Marlatt.
Pax Paganica. Guiney.
Perhaps. "Rachel" (Rachel Blumstein).
The Pet Deer. Tate.
Peyote Vision. Blockcolski.
Phantasia for Elvira Shatayev. Rich.
Phantom or Fact. Coleridge.
Philosophy. Bangs.
The Place of O. Young Bear.
Playing Catch. Moul.
Poem about People. Pinsky.
Poem Following Discussion of Brain. Rice.
Poem for My Twentieth Birthday. Koch.
Poem: "We are such stuff as dreams are made of." Hofmannsthal.
Poems about Playmates. Davis.
Poet and Lark. De Vere.
Poetry and Science. Turner.
Poor for Our Sakes. Smith.
The Poppy. Thompson.
The Porch. Gildner.
Port of Embarkation. Jarrell.
A Prayer for the Old Courage. Towne.
Presumption. Duggan.
Pretending Not to Sleep. Hamilton.

Pretty Saro. Anonymous.
Public School 168. Brisby.
Pulling Weeds. Chock.
Pumas. Sterling.
Quiet. Radford.
The Rainy Pleiads Wester. Housman.
The Rat. Symons.
Reality. Dickinson.
The Recantation. Tibullus.
The Red-Breast of Aquitania. Mahony.
The Reed-Player. MacLeish.
Remembering Apple Times. Hitchner.
Reno, 2 a.m. Hamill.
Requiescat. Watson.
Le Reve. Bowers.
Revving Up La Reve. Dailey.
Reynard the Fox (excerpt). Masefield.
A Rhyme of the Dream-Maker Man. White.
The Road at My Door. Yeats.
Rock, Be My Dream. Black.
Romeo and Juliet. Shakespeare.
Row, Row, Row Your Boat. Anonymous.
Rubric. Peabody.
Rumors of War in Wyoming. Rea.
Rural Lines after Breughel. Krapf.
Sad Memories. Calverley.
San Francisco Falling. Markham.
Santa Barbara Beach. Torrence.
Santa Caterina. Schotz.
Scene-Shifter Death. O'Neill.
Scholars. De la Mare.
The Schoolboy Reads His Iliad. Morton.
The Scratch. Dickey.
Sea-Fever. Masefield.
The Seasons. Kalidasa.
Serenade. Lockhart.
Shabbat Morning. Strahan.
The Shadow on the Stone. Hardy.
Shadow River. Johnson.
Shulamit in Her Dreams. Falk.
The Sick Child. Stevenson.
Sightings I. Rothenberg.
The Silkworms. Stewart.
Since I Am Convinced. Saigyo Hoshi.
The Sinew of Our Dreams. Jackson.
Sioux Indians. Anonymous.
Sir Humphrey Gilbert. Longfellow.
The Sixth Day. Adcock.
The Skilful Listener. Cheney.
The Skinny Girl. Hebert.
The Skylark. Tennyson.
The Sleep of Spring. Clare.
Snow. Lampman.
Snow. Pomeroy.
Snow-Bound. Whittier.
The Soldier's Dream. Campbell.
Solipsism. Santayana.
Some Dreams They Forgot. Bishop.

Song: "Don't Tell Me What You Dreamt Last Night." Adams.

Songs for a Colored Singer. Bishop.

Songs of the Sea-Children. Carman.

Songs to a Lady Moonwalker. Sutzkever.

The Sonnet. Symonds.

Sonnet: "It is as true as strange, else trial feigns." Davies.

Sonnet of Fishes. Barker.

Sonnet: The French and the Spanish Guerillas. Wordsworth.

Sonnet–To Science. Poe.

The Sonnets. Berrigan.

Sonnets. Hillyer.

Sonnets, VI: "Awakened, I behold through dewy leaves." Irwin.

Sonnets, VI: "Sweet Corrall lips, where Nature's treasure lies." Barnfield.

Sonnets, XLIII: "When most I wink, then do mine eyes best see." Shakespeare.

Sonnets: A Sequence on Profane Love. Boker.

Sonnets from the Portuguese, XXVI. Browning.

Sonnets to Karl Theodor German. Platen.

Soul-Sickness. Very.

Space and Dread and the Dark. Henley.

The Spanish Needle. McKay.

Speaks the Whispering Grass. Stuart.

Sphere (excerpt). Ammons.

Spring Night. Mukerji.

The Spring Will Come. Lowry.

Still Century. Paulin.

A Summer's Dream. Bishop.

Summer Storm. Untermeyer.

Sunset. Cummings.

Supper. De La Mare.

The Swallow. Stanley.

The Swallows. Agathias.

Swedes. Thomas.

Sweet Genevieve. Cooper.

Swimming in the Pacific. Warren.

Tables. Clark.

The Task. Cowper.

Teatime Variations. Titheradge.

The Tempest. Shakespeare.

The Terror by Night. Leopardi.

Thanatopsis. Bryant.

Thanksgiving. Coates.

That Which We Call a Rose. Dransfield.

Theme. Stephens.

There Is a Woman in This Town. Parker.

There's Been Some Sort of Mistake. Gilfillan.

Things Lovelier. Wolfe.

Thoughts upon a Walk with Natalie, My Niece, at Houghton Farm. Pulsifer.

Three Songs to Mark the Night. Volborth.

Three Tanka, 1. Yosano Akiko.

Thus Spoke My Love. Hooft.

The Ticket Agent. Leamy.

Tidying Up. Weber.

To a Candle. De La Mare.

To a Child. O'Conor.

To a Defeated Saviour. Wright.

To a Vine-Clad Telegraph Pole. Untermeyer.

To an Obscure Poet Who Lives on My Hearth. Hildreth.

To My Daughter Riding in the Circus Parade. Labombard.

To Nature. Hoelderlin.

To Sleep. MacKaye.

To the New Owner. Reynolds.

To the Newborn. Toth.

The Town without a Market. Flecker.

Training for the Apocalypse. Frym.

The Travail of Passion. Yeats.

Treetops. Bell.

Trifle. Johnson.

Turn the Key Deftly. Brock.

Turvey Top. Anonymous.

The Twelve Weapons of Spiritual Battle. More.

Twenty Golden Years Ago. Mangan.

Two Sonnets for a Lost Love. DeWitt.

Under the Moon. Yeats.

Unguarded. Murray.

The Urban Experience. Blockcolski.

Vagabond House. Blanding.

The Vengeance of Finn: The Awakening of Dermuid. Clarke.

A Vision. Winters.

Visions. Leamy.

Vitae Summa Brevis Spem Nos Vetat Incohare Longam. Dowson.

Voices. De la Mare.

Waking, the Love Poem Sighs. Hall.

A Walk. Lachmann.

Water. McPheron.

We Are a People. Henson.

We dream–it is good we are dreaming. Dickinson.

The Wedding (1957). Pasternak.

Week-End Sonnet No. 1. Monro.

What Bids Me Leave. Trench.

What the Prince of I Dreamt. Cholmondeley-Pennell.

What Was My Dream? O'Connor.

When Evening Comes. Yakamochi.

When Structure Fails Rhyme Attempts to Come to the Rescue. Williams.

When This Tide Ebbs. Harden.

William Brown. Miller.

Willie the Weeper. Anonymous.

The Winter Lightning for Paul. Nemerov.

Wishful Thinking. Blumenthal.

With Kathy at Wisdom. Hugo.

Wooden Ships. Morton.

Woodland Worship. Wetherald.

Word Poem. Giovanni.

The World Is Full of Remarkable Things. Jones.

Wormwood. Kinsella.

Yiddish Poet. Jacobs.

You Tell Me Your Dream, I'll Tell You Mine. Brown. Albert H.

The Young Woman of Beare. Clarke.

Youth. Clark.

Ypres. Binyon.

Dreamer (s)

Dream the Great Dream. Coates.

The Dreamers Cry Their Dream. Trent.

Fisherman. Booth.

Gold and Black. Ondaatje.

A New Song: "As near beauteous Boston lying." Anonymous.

Nightmare. Gardner.

Old Counsel of the Young Master of a Wrecked California Clipper. Melville.

Sonnet on Life. Boothby.

Spring Passion. Spingarn.

The Thinker. Braley.

Troopship for France, War II. Bogin.

Dreamfish

Uncertain Sonnets. Johnston.

Dreamland

Ballade of the Dreamland Rose. Hooker.

The Dancers. Gibson.

Indoor Games near Newbury. Betjeman.

On the Frozen Lake. Wordsworth.

Waking. Pyle.

Young Woman at a Window. Van Doren.

Dreamless

The Dancers. Gibson.

On the Frozen Lake. Wordsworth.

Young Woman at a Window. Van Doren.

Dreamlight

She Comes Not When Noon Is on the Roses. Trench.

Dregs

And What Sordello Would See There. Browning.

Epistles to Mr. Pope (excerpt). Young.

The Mufaddaliyat: His Camel. Alqamah.

Drench (ed)

Chorus: "If I drink water while this doth last." Peacock.

Song: "Misty and dim, a bush in the wilds of Kapa'a." Kaiama.

Through the thatched roof. Tenchi.

Dress (ed) (es)

Art Gallery. Dickson.

The Boat. Pack.

The Burial of an Infant. Vaughan.

The Butterfly and the Bee. Bowles.

Cherry Blossoms. "Lewis.

Chinoiseries. Lowell.

Clothes Make the Man. Weiss.

The Compound Eye. Davison.

The Cruel Mother (C vers.). Anonymous.

Dancer. Scheele.

The Dawning. Vaughan.

Dresses. Fraser.

Epitaph on a Young Child. Gurney.

The Everlasting Mercy. Masefield.

The Five-Day Rain. Levertov.

Franklin Hyde. Belloc.

Frederick Douglass. Cornish.

Free Little Bird. Anonymous.

French Cookery. Moore.

I'll always dress in black and rave. Pisan.

Lucasta's Fan, with a Looking-Glass in It. Lovelace.

Miss Alderman. Winner.

Of Your Father's Indiscretions and the Train to California. Emanuel.

Open Poetry Reading. Melendez.

The Outward Man Accused. Taylor.

The Pitcher. Yuan Chen.

Railroad to Hell. Anonymous.

The Resurrection. Wanley.

The Sluggard. Davies.

The Standing. McGuckian.

Strawberries. Hemschemeyer.

Sunday Afternoon. Levertov.

Sweeney in Articulo (parody). Buttle.

Tlanusi'yi, the Leech Place. Cardiff.

To the Royal Society. Cowley.

Vanity. Wickham.

Washing Day. Anonymous.

Woman through the Window. Falk.

Drew

Alexander's Feast or, the Power of Music. Dryden.

Country School. Curnow.

The Frosted Pane. Roberts.

Hippies. Dempster.

The Murmur of a Bee. Dickinson.

Nepenthe. Darley.

Drift (ed) (ing) (s)

After Drinking All Night with a Friend... Bly.

As I Ebb'd with the Ocean of Life. Whitman.

Bucyrus. Holmes.

A Concert Party. Sassoon.

The Discovery. Brasch.

Drift. Glover.

Early Dutch. Palen.

Eternal Goodness. Whittier.

The Great Blue Heron. Kizer.

The Great Divide. Sarett.

The Great Garret; or, 100 Wheels. McMichael.

A Home without a Bible (excerpt). Meigs.

In the Shelter. Day Lewis.

In the Winter of My Thirty-Eighth Year. Merwin.
Journey. Harrison.
Mappemounde. Birney.
Medusa. Bogan.
Metonymy as an Approach to a Real World. Bronk.
Modern Love, XXXI. Meredith.
Monkey. Smith.
Night. Hayes.
Quiet Waters. Wagstaff.
Remembering Apple Times. Hitchner.
Report from California. Moyles.
Rolling Log Blues. Kimbrough.
Sea Wrack. O'Neill.
Such Stuff as Dreams Are Made Of. Higginson.
Sunday at the End of Summer. Nemerov.
The Teeth Mother Naked at Last. Bly.
Three Elements. Benét.
Three Songs. Jackson.
Twelfth Night. Coatsworth.
The Union Barge on Staten Island. Simpson.
The Vision of Sir Launfal. Lowell.
Watertower. Bellg.
The Wheelbarrow. Edson.

Drink (ing) (s)
Africland. La Grone.
After the Persian. Bogan.
All Things Drink. Stanley.
Amber Beads. Brown.
Among the Finger Lakes. Wallace.
And Then What? Kelly.
The Angler's Invitation. Stoddart.
Another Little Drink. *Anonymous.*
At the Tavern. *Anonymous.*
Ballade of Liquid Refreshment. Bentley.
A Better Resurrection. Rossetti.
Birlinn Chlann-Raghnaill. MacDonald.
A Boat, a Boat. *Anonymous.*
Bone China. Lister.
Bridegroom Dick (excerpt). Melville.
The Canterbury Tales: The Words of the Host to the Phisicien... Chaucer.
Captain Car, or, Edom o Gordon (H version). *Anonymous.*
Changed. Calverley.
Chevaliers de la Table Ronde. *Anonymous.*
Childhood Is the Kingdom Where Nobody Dies. Millay.
Click Go the Shears. Anonymous.
Cod Liver Ile. *Anonymous.*
The Corrupt Man in the French Pub. Higgins.
The Damsel. Omar B. Abi Rabi'a.
Darling Corey. *Anonymous.*
Desert Holy Man. Beecher.
Drinking Song. Brome.
Drinking Song. Harrison.
Drunk Last Night. *Anonymous.*

The Dumb World. Davies.
Dumpy Ducky. Larcom.
Epigram. Field.
An Epitaph. Ellis.
Epitaph in a Churchyard at Thetford, in Norfolk. *Anonymous.*
Epitaph on the Secretary to the Muses. Barker.
Evening in the Suburbs. Barnett.
Fishing Drunk. Mondy.
Forty Pounds of Blackberries Equals Thirteen Gallons of Wine. Hoeft.
Four Prayers, II. *Anonymous.*
A Frolic. Herrick.
George Towle. Towle.
The Girl I Love. Callanan.
Graffiti. Bold.
Grotesques (excerpt). Marquis.
The Heavenly Banquet. Brigid.
Herman Moon's Hourbook. Middleton.
Horace Paraphrased. Watts.
Horatian Variation. Bacon.
How, Butler, How! *Anonymous.*
How We Logged Katahdin Stream. Hoffman.
Human Life. Prior.
Hunting Song. Fielding.
I Am Forsaken. *Anonymous.*
If all the world were apple-pie. Mother Goose.
Independence Day. Tyler.
The Inefficacious Egg. Bishop.
Ivesiana. Berkson.
The King of Thule. Goethe.
The Knight of the Burning Pestle. Fletcher.
Last Will of the Drunk. Riedemann.
Late Afternoon on a Good Lake. Wier.
Lauriger Horatius. Symonds.
Letter to a Friend. Thompson.
A Letter to Ben Jonson. Beaumont.
The Man in the Moon. Anonymous.
The Man-Moth. Bishop.
Marvels. *Anonymous.*
Memories of Aunt Maria-Martha (parody). Zaranka.
Miniver Cheevy. Robinson.
Monangamba. Jacinto.
Montgomery. *Anonymous.*
Morning in the North-West. Stringer.
The Mower in Ohio. Piatt.
My Sins in Their Completeness. O Brolchain.
No Continuing City. Longley.
Not Drunk Is He. Peacock.
Nothing. Burgos.
Now the Leaves Are Falling Fast. Auden.
The Nut-Brown Ale. Marston.
Old I Am. Stanley.
Omnes Gentes Plaudite! *Anonymous.*
On Imitation. Coleridge.

On the Candidates for the Laurel. Pope.
On the Lakes of Ponchartrain. *Anonymous.*
The Overlander. *Anonymous.*
Pass around Your Bottle. *Anonymous.*
A Pastoral. Stevens.
A Pipe of Tobacco. Browne.
Portrait of a Lady. Eliot.
Price of a Drink. Pollard.
Pride of Ancestry. Frost.
A Radical War Song. Macaulay.
Raftery's Dialogue with the Whiskey. Fallon.
Rain for Ka-waik. Allen.
A Religious Use of Taking Tobacco. Wisdome.
The River. Stuart.
The Roving Shanty Boy. *Anonymous.*
The Rowan County Crew (Tolliver-Martin Feud Song). *Anonymous.*
Sally's Garden. *Anonymous.*
The Same Forever. Bonar.
Satire upon the Licentious Age of Charles II. Butler.
Scotland Yet. Riddell.
The Sea-Captain. *Anonymous.*
The Sea Fight in '92. *Anonymous.*
She's Gone Blues. Hicks.
Sir John Barleycorn. *Anonymous.*
Sloe Gin. Heaney.
Smithfield Ham. Smith.
Song of Poverty. *Anonymous.*
A Song of Sack. *Anonymous.*
A Song of the Moon. McKay.
Sonnet XXXII. Alabaster.
The Sonnets. Berrigan.
The South Country. Belloc.
The Spanish Friar. Dryden.
The Sparkling Bowl. Pierpont.
The Stirrup-Cup. Lanier.
The Stormy Scenes of Winter. *Anonymous.*
The Sugar Cane. Grainger.
Take a Drink on Me. *Anonymous.*
Technique. Pierson.
Therefore Is the Name of It Called Babel. Sitwell.
These Obituaries of Rattlesnakes Being Eaten by the Hogs. Weingarten.
Thirst. Farhi.
This Stone. *Anonymous.*
Thou Art Not Lovelier Than Lilacs. Millay.
The Thousand and One Nights: To Lighten My Darkness. *Anonymous.*
Tim. Montague.
Tirade on Tea. McGinley.
To--. Hood.
To His Friend J. H. Brome.
To Ladies' Eyes. Moore.
Tom Dooley. *Anonymous.*
Troilus and Criseyde. Chaucer.
Two Comical Folk. *Anonymous.*
Up in the Air. Ramsay.
Vernal Showers. O'Neil.
Verses on a Cat. Daubeny.

A Vision of Truth. Squire.
Wasp Sex Myth (Two). Hollo.
A Way of Life. Nemerov.
We'll Have Another Drink before the Boat Shoves Off. *Anonymous.*
Wells. Hall.
When as I Do Record. *Anonymous.*
When I Was Young I Tried to Sing. Finkel.
Whitsuntide an' Club Walken. Barnes.
Willie's and Nellie's Wish. Moore.
Wine and Dew. Stoddard.
Workmen. Morris.
Yes Please Gentlemen. Fairburn.
You Serve the Best Wines Always, My Dear Sir. Martial (Marcus Valerius Martialis).
Zion's Sons and Daughters. *Anonymous.*

Drive (n) (s)
At Cove on the Crooked River. Stafford.
The Bad Mother. Griffin.
The Ballad of Longwood Glen. Nabokov.
The Birth of My Father. Dempster.
Busy Carpenters. Tippett.
Cat into Lady. La Fontaine.
The Coachman. *Anonymous.*
A Denunciation. Hassan.
Dreaming America. Oates.
Driving; Driven. McAleavey.
Emergency Haying. Carruth.
For Fear. Creeley.
The House on Buder Street. Gildner.
The Iliad. Homer.
In Columbus, Ohio. Matthias.
The Lumber Camp Song ("The Shanty Boy's Song"). *Anonymous.*
Midnight. Lampman.
Mike. *Anonymous.*
Mothers, Daughter. Kaufman.
The Odd Woman. De Frees.
Odes. Horace.
On Tom Onslow, Earl of Onslow. *Anonymous.*
On Vacation. Creeley.
Picture Framing. Meyers.
Prophets for a New Day. Walker.
The Rainbow. McCord.
The Rancher. Wilson.
The Seasons. Thomson.
Sonnets. Hillyer.
Sorrow. *Anonymous.*
Taxi Suite: After Anacreon. Welch.
Test Drive. Reid.
Thistledown. Reese.
The Tired Woman. Wickham.
To Elsie. Williams.
Ulster. Kipling.
Unsolicited Letters to Five Artists (parody). James.
Wood Butcher. Hindley.

Driver (s)
At Port Royal: Song of the Negro Boatman. Whittier.

Highway: Michigan.
Roethke.
Jay Gould's Daughter.
Anonymous.
Raging Canawl. *Anonymous.*

Driving
Amsterdam Street Scene, 1972. Rudnik.
From a Very Little Sphinx. Millay.
The Jolly Driver.
Anonymous.
The Queen's Last Ride. Wilcox.
Stopping by Home. Huddle.
The U.S. Coast and Geodetic Survey Ship Pioneer. Hershon.

Drone (s)
The Ear. MacNeice.
Fleadh. Longley.
King Henry V. Shakespeare.
The Parsons. Brown.
Song of the Queen Bee. White.
The Sundial. Cooper.
The Terrace in the Snow. Su Tung-P'o.
To a Talkative Hairdresser. McGinley.

Drop out
A Garden Lyric. Locker-Lampson.
Last Things, Black Pines at 4 a.m. Lowell.

Drop (s) (ped) (ping)
Art. Silva.
At a Child's Baptism. Miller.
The Beggar on the Beach. Gregory.
A Blue Jeaned Rock Queen in Search of Happiness... Redwing.
The Boss's Wife.
Anonymous.
Chrysalides. Kinsella.
Died. Browning.
Dirge in the Woods. Meredith.
An Essay on Man. Pope.
Excelsior. Emerson.
Fill the Bumper Fair. Moore.
For a Dewdrop. Farjeon.
For to Admire. Kipling.
Girl at the Seaside. Murphy.
Going for Water. Frost.
Goosey Goosey Gander. French.
Harvest. Maino.
Hate! Antokolsy.
Heraclitus in the West. Bell.
How Gentle God's Commands. Doddridge.
If. Howells.
If the Stars Should Fall. Allen.
Immortality. Reese.
Incantation for Rain.
Anonymous.
Journey. Wakoski.
The King of Thule. Goethe.
The Letter. Beer.
Love Song. Al-Harizi.
Morning. Ditlevsen.
Mother. Dempster.
Mother. Fyleman.
On a Wet Summer. Bampfylde.
Paiute Ponies. Barnes.

The Poetess's Bouts-Rimes.
Anonymous.
Poor Fool. Shute.
Powwow Remnants. Blockcolski.
Relativity. Millay.
Rural Sports. Gay.
Satellites. Lenhart.
A Savage. O'Reilly.
The Second Brother. Beddoes.
A Shantyman's Life (I).
Anonymous.
The Sick Image of My Father Fades. Horder.
Sonic Boom. Updike.
The Stockdoves. Young.
Summit Lake. Thalman.
There is a pain–so utter. Dickinson.
Tim Turpin. Hood.
To Giulia Grisi. Willis.
Trickle Drops. Whitman.
A Vision of Truth. Squire.
Walking through a Cornfield in the Middle of Winter... (parody). Harr.
Why Must You Know? Wheelwright.
Women Transport Corps.
Anonymous.
The Yellow Bittern. Mac Giolla Ghunna.

Dross
How Firm a Foundation. Keith.
The Indians Prize Not English Gold. Williams.
T. S. Eliot. Lowell.
Upon Faireford Windowes. Corbett.
Windham. *Anonymous.*

Drought
Drought (excerpt). Slater.
The Farmer. Herbert.
The Green Inn. Garrison.
Many Years Ago. Barbeitos.
O Heart, Small Urn. Doolithe.

Drove
The Defeat of the Norsemen (excerpt). Sedulius Scottus.
Hell Hath No Fury... Bukowski.
Hymn to the Air Spirit.
Anonymous.
The One Horse Chay.
Anonymous.
The Stringybark Cockatoo.
Anonymous.
The Train to Glasgow. Horsburgh.

Drown (ed) (ing) (s)
The Abandoned. Symons.
The Air in Spring. Dowling.
Alec Yeaton's Son. Aldrich.
The Answer. Jeffers.
Autumnall. Bennett.
The Bramble Briar.
Anonymous.
By the Exeter River. Hall.
Camp Notes. Yamada.
Convalescence. McAuley.
Conventicle. Lansing.
Deep Blue Sea. *Anonymous.*
Der Mond Ist Aufgegangen. Heine.
Dreamscape in Kummel. Witt.
Eternity. Herrick.

The False Knight and the Wee Boy. *Anonymous.*
Fisherman. Sitwell.
A Fly about a Glass of Burnt Claret. Lovelace.
Flying Fish. Fenollosa.
Giles Corey of the Salem Farms: Prologue. Longfellow.
The Great Freight. Bachmann.
Green Grass and Sea. Woodcock.
Hera, Hung from the Sky. Kizer.
Hibernia. Howard-Jones.
The Hock-Cart, or Harvest Home. Herrick.
I Looked Up from My Writing. Hardy.
I Wonder What It Feels Like to Be Drowned? Graves.
Idea. Drayton.
In Defense of Superficiality. Olson.
In the Interstices. Stone.
Interview with a Tourist. Atwood.
The Jewels. Baudelaire.
John Brown's Body. Benét.
The Jungle. Dudek.
Lakeshore. Scott.
A Legend of Lake Okeefinokee. Richards.
The Little White Cat.
Anonymous.
The Love Song of J. Alfred Prufrock. Eliot.
The Low-Down, Lonesome Low. *Anonymous.*
The Lowlands o' Holland.
Anonymous.
The Man Against the Sky. Robinson.
Marginalia. Wilbur.
Midwestern Man. Giandi.
Moonlight Night on the Port. Keyes.
Morning on the Shore. Campbell.
A Muse of Water. Kizer.
Nessa. Durcan.
Night's Fall. Graham.
Noah. Daniells.
Nod. Bennett.
Paul Klee. Haines.
Peg. *Anonymous.*
A Personality Sketch: Bill. Davis.
A Poem of Towers. Wright.
Pretty Molly. *Anonymous.*
Rare Willie Drowned in Yarrow, or, The Water o Gamrie (A version).
Anonymous.
Reasons For and Against Marrying Widows. Selyns.
The Sad Shepherd. Jonson.
Salmon Drowns Eagle. Lowry.
Satire. Donne.
Shelly. McIntyre.
A Short Song of Congratulation. Johnson.
Sigismundo. Gregg.
Silly Willy. "B.
Skycoast. Hazo.
The Small Man Orders His Wedding. Lewis.
Some San Francisco Poems. Oppen.
A Song-Offering. Tagore.

Sonnet XVI: "After an age when thunderbolts and hail." Labe.
Stillness. Flecker.
Subjectivity at Sestos. Hubbard.
Swimmer. Francis.
Theodosia Burr. Terrell.
The Titanic (A vers.).
Anonymous.
To a Defeated Saviour. Wright.
To My Daughter. Michie.
The Two Sisters.
Anonymous.
Upon Some Alterations in My Mistress, after My Departure into France. Carew.
Visions. Petrarch.
Weepe O Mine Eyes.
Anonymous.
The Whale. *Anonymous.*
The Woman's Dream. Horovitz.
Written After Swimming From Sestos to Abydos. Byron.

Drowsy
Breasts. Simic.
The Mowing Crew. Wormser.
Plum Blossoms. Chu Shuchen.
The Silent Ranges. Bird.

Drudge
Atheling Grange: or, The Apotheosis of Lotte Nussbaum. Plomer.
Caelica, LXI. Greville.
Fair and Softly. Ayres.

Drug (s)
Marking Time. Steele.
Romeo and Juliet. Shakespeare.
A Satire against Wit. Blackmore.
Soft Wood. Lowell.
Sonnet: "When I was marked for suffering, love forswore." Cervantes Saarvedra.
The United States of America We. Abrams.

Druid (s)
Green Ice. Finch.
The Loss of the Druid.
Anonymous.
The Pleasures of Melancholy. Warton, Jr..
Stormy Weather, Boys.
Anonymous.

Drum (s)
Avoidances. Welburn.
Bird of Power. Tollerud.
Blenheim (excerpt). Philips.
The Charge by the Ford. English.
La Chute. Olson.
Coming Back. Bruchac.
Comrades. Door.
The Cuckoo. *Anonymous.*
The Destroyers (excerpt). Fleming.
Drum-Taps. Whitman.
The Drum: the Narrative of the Drummer of Tedworth. Sitwell.
The Drummer Boy of Waterloo. *Anonymous.*
Dry Loaf. Stevens.

The Eagle-Feather Fan.
Momaday.
Egyptian Dancer. Tiller.
Farewell. Bahe.
For Drum Hadley.
Littlebird.
How Happy the Soldier.
Anonymous.
I dreaded that first Robin, so.
Dickinson.
The Ice-Floes. Pratt.
The Inheritors. Livesay.
Jungle. Haring.
King William Was King
George's Son. *Anonymous.*
The Mill. Taylor.
My Hobby Horse.
Anonymous.
On the Danger of War.
Meredith.
Panic. MacLeish.
A Portrait of Rudy.
Cunningham.
Rain on a Cottage Roof.
Laughton.
Reilly's Daughter.
Anonymous.
Secret-Love. Dryden.
Some we see no more,
tenements of wonder.
Dickinson.
The Sound of the Drum.
Anonymous.
A Starling's Spring Rondel.
Cousins.
Toward a True Peace.
Cheyney.
Valediction. MacNeice.
A White-Throat Sings.
Eaton.

Drummer (s)
The Drummer. Robinson.
He Came to Visit Me.
Seymour-Smith.
Hush-A-Byes. *Anonymous.*
The Little Drummer.
Stoddard.
Switzerland. Thwaite.

Drumming
The Fence. McHugh.
X-Ray. Ray.

Drunk (en)
16. ix. 65. Merrill.
After the Industrial
Revolution, All Things
Happen at Once. Bly.
And Don't Bother Telling Me
Anything. Vallejo.
Ariosto. Mandelstam.
Ballade of Soporific
Absorption. Squire.
Battle Song. Macuilxochitl.
The Bee and the Petunia.
Hoskins.
Bowery. Ignatow.
Canso Strait. *Anonymous.*
Corn-Planter. Kenny.
Dead Drunk Blues. Miller.
Drinking. Terris.
Drug Store. Shapiro.
Epigram: "When Bibo thought
fit from the world to
retreat." Prior.
Epitaph. Durrell.
The Fisherman. Harrison.
Frying Trout While Drunk.
Emanuel.
Grand Hotel, Calcutta.
Silbert.
Grecian Kindness.
Rochester.

Haroun al-Rachid for Heart's-
Life. *Anonymous.*
Hasbrouck and the Rose.
Putnam.
I'll Never Get Drunk Any
More. *Anonymous.*
Jerusalem Sonnets. Baxter.
John Adkins' Farewell.
Anonymous.
Keep My Skillet Good and
Greasy. *Anonymous.*
The Last Instructions to a
Painter. Marvell.
Let Minions Marshal Every
Hair. *Anonymous.*
Let Us All Be Unhappy on
Sunday. Neaves.
Letting My Feelings Out.
Yu Hsuan-chi.
Lord Alcohol. Beddoes.
Lust. Matthews.
Memory Gardens. Ginsberg.
Moggy's Wedding. Thatcher.
Monangamba. Jacinto.
My Country. Lermontov.
New York. Garcia Lorca.
October. Hahn.
October. Pape.
The Odyssey. Homer.
On Alexander and Aristotle,
on a Black-on-Red Greek
Plate. Dugan.
On Delia. Jacob.
On the Way. Trakl.
(One!). Cummings.
Orange Juice Song. Phillips.
Packin' Trunk Blues.
Leadbelly.
Pete Orman. *Anonymous.*
Poem for viet nam. Young
Bear.
The Potter. *Anonymous.*
The Quest of the Sangraal:
The Coming of the
Sangraal. Hawker.
Rank. Kirstein.
Somewhere West. Jones.
Song for "Buvez les Vins du
Postillon"–Advt.
Garrigue.
Song of the Hesitations.
Blackburn.
Song of the Vivandiere.
Heine.
Sonnet and Limerick.
Bishop.
Sporting Acquaintances.
Sassoon.
The Stone. Blackburn.
Swans. Durrell.
A Thought from Porpertius.
Yeats.
Tomorrow Is My Birthday:
"The thing is sex, Ben."
Masters.
Tree of Time. Sethna.
Venezuela. *Anonymous.*
The Vestal Lady on Brattle.
Corso.
The Wild Flower Man. Lu
Yu.
You Got to Go Down.
Davis.

Drying
Coming Back. Gregg.
The Djanggawul Cycle, 33.
Anonymous.
To the Old Masters. Lum.

Dublin
Inscription for a Headstone.
Clarke.
Is It a Month. Synge.

Working the Rain Shift at
Flanagan's. Ruark.

Duck (s)
Back. McCabe.
The Bat. Sitwell.
Charley Barley. *Anonymous.*
Gets Hung up on a Dirty, of
All Things, Joke (parody).
Taylor.
The Honeymooners. Yu
Ch'ien.
The Hunter. Nash.
The Keepsake Corporation.
Fisher.
The Lout. Clare.
Poem in Time of Winter.
Mathew.
Regent's Park. Fyleman.
When Father Carves the
Duck. Wright.

Due regard
Due (s)
Equipment. Dunbar.
The Eye. Wilbur.
His Saviour's Words, Going to
the Cross. Herrick.
How They Brought the Good
News From Ghent to Aix.
Browning.
The Sailor's Lamentation.
Anonymous.
Why I Sing the Blues. King.
Zoo You Too! Joans.

Duke (s)
The Common Sailor.
Anonymous.
The Duke Is the Lad.
Moore.
Elegy for the Duke of
Marmalade. Palés Matos.
Epitaph on a Tuft-Hunter.
Moore.
For the Queen Mother.
Betjeman.
The Knight's Ghost.
Anonymous.
Ozymandias Revisited.
Bishop.
Tirocinium; or, A Review of
Schools. Cowper.
The Waltz: Hail, Spirit-
Stirring Waltz. Byron.

Dull (er) (ness)
An Author's Epitaph. Written
by Himself. Evans.
Ballade Tragique a Double
Refrain. Beerbohm.
Beginning to Squall.
Swenson.
Come, Holy Babe! Bangham.
A Contempt for Dylan
Thomas. Watson.
Day's End. Harford.
Down from the Country.
Blight.
Epitaphium Citharistriae.
Plarr.
I Know Not Whether I Am
Proud. Landor.
Inertia. McGaffin.
Inscriptio. Pope.
The Life and Character of
Dean Swift (excerpt).
Swift.
My Dog Tray. Byrom.
Now It Can Be Told.
Levine.
On Dennis. Pope.
A Song: "Hark! 'tis Freedom
that calls, come, patriots,
awake!" *Anonymous.*

Sonnets, XCVII: "How like a
winter hath my absence
been." Shakespeare.
Sonnets, CII: "My love is
strengthen'd."
Shakespeare.
The Testament of Beauty.
Bridges.
Thomas Shadwell the Poet.
Dryden.
To a Sicilian Boy.
Wratislaw.
To a Talkative Hairdresser.
McGinley.
The Trip. Stafford.
Upon Absence. Philips.
Whence and Whither.
Bialik.
Wreathe the Bowl. Moore.

Dumb
Addressed to Haydon.
Keats.
Afternoon at Cannes. Davis.
The Angel in the House.
Patmore.
Blond Hair at the Edge of the
Pavement. Smith.
Blues for Benny Kid Paret.
Smith.
A Choctaw Chief Helps Plan
a Festival... Barnes.
Diana. Constable.
Driving through Coal Country
in Pennsylvania. Holden.
The Dumb World. Davies.
Evelyn. Johnson.
Field. Griffin.
The Graveyard. Bialik.
Helen Keller. Stedman.
Humane Thought. McCann.
In Bohemia. Symons.
Invocation of Silence.
Flecknoe.
Joy and Pleasure. Davies.
Loneliness. Essex.
Much Ado about Nothing.
Shakespeare.
Newcomers. Reisen.
On First Hearing Beethoven.
Barker.
Origins and History of
Consciousness. Rich.
Out of a War of Wits.
Thomas.
The Peepers in Our Meadow.
MacLeish.
Poets. Kilmer.
Prayer of Little Hope. Wahl.
Quien Sabe? Morris.
Shall I Charge Like a Bull.
Auvaiyar.
Silence Invoked. Flecknoe.
Six Movements on a Theme.
Ignatow.
Six Poets in Search of a
Lawyer. Hall.
Song: "Love took my life and
thrill'd it." Morris.
Songs. Deutsch.
Stormy Day. Rodgers.
The United Fruit Co.
Neruda.
The Upper Lake. Stuart.
What Was Solomon's Mind?
Scott.
When the Dumb Speak. Bly.
The Witches' Charm.
Jonson.

Dump
Blues for Benny Kid Paret.
Smith.

Driving through Coal Country in Pennsylvania. Holden.
Shall I Charge Like a Bull. Auvaiyar.
The United Fruit Co. Neruda.

Dunce
First Lessons in Musical Time. *Anonymous.*
The Progress of Error. Cowper.
Riddle: "Take of letters the first." *Anonymous.*
The Task. Cowper.

Dundee
An Address to the New Tay Bridge. McGonagall.
Limerick: "There was an Old Man of Dundee." Lear.
Pretty Mary. *Anonymous.*

Dune (s)
Evening. Vriesland.
The Man in the Mune Is Making Shune. *Anonymous.*
A Paris Nocturne. Sharp.
The Sea. Gorter.
Surrealism in the Middle Ages. Lamantia.

Dung
Epigram: "I ran upon life unknowing, without or science or art." Tennyson.
The Lady's Dressing Room. Swift.
A Shrewish, Barren, Bony, Nosy Servant. O Bruadair.
Signature. Stroud.
Voyage to Cythera. Baudelaire.

Dungeon (s)
The Complaints of Poetry (excerpt). James.
A Family Photograph 1939. Baxter.
In a Lovely Garden Walking. Uhland.
Palm House, Botanic Gardens. Hetherington.
Samson Agonistes. Milton.
Under Sorrow's Sign. O'Dalaigh.

Dusk
And of Laughter That Was a Changeling. Rendall.
At the Funeral of Great-Aunt Mary. Bly.
The Camp of Souls. Crawford.
Comatas. Mathews.
The Dark and Falling Summer. Schwartz.
Daydreamers. Davis.
The Death of an Elephant. Pagnucci.
Dreams. Daley.
The Dynasts. Hardy.
The Final Word. Moraes.
Formerly a Slave. Melville.
French Peasants. Gibbon.
The Homing Heart. Henderson.
I Will Write Songs Against You. Reznikoff.
L'Ile du Levant: The Nudist Colony. Howes.
The Incentive. Cleghorn.
Injured Maple. Everson.
Love on the Mountain. Boyd.
My Language. Politzer.
Nature's Key-Notes. Irwin.

Our Mr. Toad. McCord.
Over Three Nipple-Stones. Celan.
Sabbath. Rosenmann-Taub.
Sandhill People. Sandburg.
Saskatchewan Dusk. Buckaway.
September. Kyger.
Serenade. De Vere.
Sketch. Farnsworth.
Song for September. Fitzgerald.
Sonnet: "I stood beside a pool, from whence ascended." Trench.
Spring. Behn.
Tableau at Twilight. Nash.
The Testament of John Davidson: The Last Journey. Davidson.
There Are Children in the Dusk. Warr.
Transfigured Bird. Merrill.
A Traveller. *Anonymous.*
W's for Windows. McGinley.
The Wanderer. Brennan.
Whitsuntide an' Club Walken. Barnes.
Winter Anemones. Brasch.
A Woodland Revel. Urmy.

Dust (y)
The Abbey Church at Bath. Harington.
Advice to a Raven in Russia December 1812. Barlow.
The Aged Lover Renounceth Love. Vaux.
Akriel's Consolation. Pillen.
Amanda Barker. Masters.
Anne Rutledge. Masters.
An Apology for the Foregoing Hymn.... Crashaw.
Ash Wednesday. Burke.
L'Avenir. Dobell.
Awake, My Soul! Doddridge.
The Backward Look. Nemerov.
Ballade of Dead Actors. Henley.
Banishment from Ur. Enheduanna.
Barnfire during Church. Bly.
Because we suspected. Ise.
Beleaguered Cities. Lucas.
Birthday Sonnet. Wylie.
Blemishes. Hart.
Blood River Day. Brutus.
Blue Ghosts. Snaith.
Bronco Busting, Event #1. Swenson.
Burning Sand of Sinai. Sachs.
The Cariboo Horses. Purdy.
The Centuries Are His. Ebeling.
Childhood. Traherne.
The Children's Hour. Longfellow.
Chorus of the Rescued. Sachs.
The Circulation. Washbourne.
A City Flower. Dobson.
A Colorado Sand Storm. Field.
The Complaints of Poetry (excerpt). James.
Confusion. Cruz.
Cool Tombs. Sandburg.
Curtain. Henson.

Cwmrhydyceirw Elegiacs. Watkins.
A Daughter's House. Richman.
A Dead Warrior. Housman.
Death. Herbert.
Death and Resurrection. Croly.
Deja Vu. Kaufman.
A Denunciation. Hassan.
The Departure. Robson.
Dilemma. Parker.
Driving through Coal Country in Pennsylvania. Holden.
Duel with Verses over a Great Man. *Anonymous.*
Eagle Sonnets. Wood.
Elegy for a School-Friend. Young.
Elegy for Dylan Thomas. Sitwell.
Elliott Hawkins. Masters.
Ember Grease. Gallup.
The End of Desire. McCrae.
Envoy. Carman.
Epitaph. Davenant.
Epitaph. Marzan.
Epitaph. Peacock.
Epitaph: "Here lies the great. False marble, where?" *Anonymous.*
Epitaph: Iohannis Sande. Bastard.
Epitaph on the Monument of Sir William Dyer at Colmworth, 1641. Dyer.
Epitaph on William Hogarth. Johnson.
Epithalamium. Ditsky.
Equality. Shirley.
Esperanza. Scully.
Eumares. Asclepiades.
The Everlasting Gospel. Blake.
Family. *Anonymous.*
The Feast of Stephen. Nichols.
First Communion. Silva.
The Flowing Summer. Bruce.
Frederick Douglass. Cornish.
From the Dust. Dallman.
Gascoygnes Good Night. Gascoigne.
Ghosts. MacCarthy.
Gold Coast Customs (excerpt). Sitwell.
The Great Depression. Goedicke.
Greek Archipelagoes. Leigh-Fermor.
Green Things Growing. Craik.
Hamewith. Smith.
Hammerstoke. Domanski.
The Harper of Chao. Po Chu-i.
Heaven and Hell. *Anonymous.*
Her Way. Benet.
Hero Entombed I. Quennell.
The Hide of My Mother. Dorn.
High Wheat Country. Jacobs.
His Own Epitaph, When He Was Sick, Being Fellow in New College... Hoskyns.
Homeward Bound. Brodey.
House Poem. Cooper.
The Housecleaner. White.

Human Greatness. Barclay.
Humanity. Dixon.
The Hunt. Spofford.
Hymn. Browning.
Hymn Written after Jeremiah Preached to Me in a Dream. Dodson.
I Saw God Wash the World. Stidger.
The Image of Death. Vaux.
In a City Square. Wallis.
In a Night. Savage.
In Distrust of Merits. Moore.
Indian Names. Sigourney.
The Inscription on the Tombe of the Lady Mary Wentworth. Carew.
Intaglio. Coulette.
Jacob's Winning. Sherwin.
John Brown's Body. Benét.
July in Indiana. Fitzgerald.
Keramos. Longfellow.
The Laboratory. Browning.
A Lady. Lowell.
A Last Word. Dowson.
Life's Testament. Baylebridge.
Lines to a Blind Girl. Read.
Liverpool. *Anonymous.*
Longing. Herbert.
Lorena. *Anonymous.*
Love and fortune and my mind... Wyatt.
The Magical Mouse. Patchen.
Maintenance. Sarah.
Marianne Moore (1887-1972). Roseliep.
Marigold. Haines.
Marmion. Scott.
The Martyred Earth. Milne.
The Miner's Helmet. Macbeth.
Monument. Sullivan.
Moon-Witches. Hughes.
Morality. Garrigue.
Mount Vernon. *Anonymous.*
Mrs. Southern's Enemy. Sitwell.
Must. Lewis.
My Creed. Cary.
My Days among the Dead Are Past. Southey.
My Days of Love Are Over. Byron.
Nature. Herbert.
Nevertheless. Davidson.
Nightdream. Wright.
Note to Wang Wei. Berryman.
Nox Benigna. Reeves.
"O loathsome place..." Surrey.
D. O. M. Wotton.
O the Little Rusty Dusty Miller. *Anonymous.*
The Old Man to His Scythe. Wrafter.
Old Men Pitching Horseshoes. Kennedy.
On Reading–. Aldrich.
On Some Shells Found Inland. Stickney.
On the Tombs in Westminster Abbey. Beaumont.
Our People. Anderson.
Out of Superstition. Pasternak.
The Parental Critic. Preston.
The Parrot. Skelton.
Pastures of Plenty. Guthrie.

Poem in Three Parts. Bly.
The Poet. Grannis.
The Poet and His Book. Millay.
Prairie. Sandburg.
The Praise of Dust. Chesterton.
Prelude. Aldington.
Prelude. Rivers.
Protest in Passing. Speyer.
A Psalm for Sunday Night. Pestel.
Quatrain. *Anonymous.*
The Rape of the Lock. Pope.
The Rat. Symons.
The Rattlesnake Band. Conley.
Receiving Communion. Miller.
Reflections, Written on Visiting the Grave of a Venerated Friend. Plato.
A Remembrance of My Friend Mr. Thomas Morley. Davies.
Reprisals. Yeats.
Requiem. Maynard.
Requiescat. Watson.
Return of a Reaper. Creighton.
Return to Ritual. Van Doren.
The Reward of Innocent Love. Habington.
The River. Emerson.
Roof Garden. Filip.
Room Poems. Bachar.
Samos. Merrill.
The Sea and the Skylark. Hopkins.
Senex. Betjeman.
Sermon in a Churchyard. Macaulay.
Sextains. Baylebridge.
She Attempts to Refute the Praises That Truth... Juana Ines de la Cruz.
The Shooting of Werfel. Watkins.
Silex Scintillans. Vaughan.
Since "The Pillow Knows All." Ise.
Sister Pharaoh. Whitman.
A Soldier: His Prayer. Kersh.
Song: "O lady, when the tipped cup of the moon blessed you." Hughes.
Sonnets. Masefield.
Sonnets, XI: "Ye two fair trees that I so long have known." Irwin.
The Sovereigns. Mifflin.
Spanish Blue. Morris.
Star Quilt. Hill.
Stumptown Attends the Picture Show. Bottoms.
The Sun Drops Red. Miller.
Suspiria. Longfellow.
Tan Ta Ra, Cries Mars... Wagoner.
Tears at the Grave of Sir Albertus Morton. Wotton.
The Teeth Mother Naked at Last. Bly.
This Coloured Counterfeit That Thou Beholdest. Juana Ines de la Cruz.
This Mad Carnival of Loving. Heine.

Thomas Dudley Ah! Old Must Dye. *Anonymous.*
To a Recalcitrant Virgin. Asclepiades.
To God. Maurice.
To Her Portrait. Juana Ines de la Cruz.
To Lizard Head. Laube.
To Our Lady, the Ark of the Covenants. Larsson.
To Redoute. Ashbery.
Toward Tenses Two Moons. Rachow.
The Trail Horse. Wagoner.
Troilus and Cressida. Shakespeare.
The Troops. Sassoon.
Two Somewhat Different Epigrams. Hughes.
Unseen Flight. Georgeou.
The Valley of Vain Verses. Van Dyke.
View Me, Lord, a Work of Thine. Campion.
The Way, the Truth, and the Life. Parker.
What Far Kingdom. Bourinot.
The White Dust. Gibson.
Woman Seed Player. Whiteman.
The Wraith-Friend. Barker.
The Young Dove. Ibn Ezra.
Yours. Tagore.

Dutch
The Dutch. Canning.
Love-Songs, At Once Tender and Informative. Hoffenstein.
Men May Talk of Country-Christmasses. Massinger.
My Old Dutch: A Cockney Song. Chevalier.

Duty
Abraham Davenport. Whittier.
Amours de Voyage. Clough.
An Armoury. Alcaeus.
Captain Reece. Gilbert.
The Chimney Sweeper. Blake.
Christ and the Little Ones. Gill.
Confession Overheard in a Subway. Fearing.
The Double Transformation. Goldsmith.
Duty. Markham.
The Elfin Wife. Falstaff.
Forbidden Fruit. Dickinson.
The Forbidden Lure. Davis.
Great Churches. *Anonymous.*
Let Us Have Faith That Right Makes Might. Lincoln.
Love Constraining to Obedience. Cowper.
Lucretius. Tennyson.
The Night Express. Monkhouse.
The Nightingale and Glow-Worm. Cowper.
The Odyssey. Homer.
A Petition from the Chain Gang at Newcastle to Captain Furlong... MacNamara.
A Reminiscence of 1820. Dugmore.
Sherman. Gilder.
The Smile of the Goat. Herford.

Song for a Little House. Morley.
Sphinxes Inclined to Be. Orozco.
Titian's "Bacchanal" in the Prado at Madrid (excerpt). Moore.
A Truth... Mitchell.
The Warrior's Lament. Seaman.
Zoroaster Devoutly Questions Ormazd. Zoroaster.

Dwarf (s)
The Bear. Stanford.
The Dwarf of the Hill Caves. Mphande.
The Faerie Queene. Spenser.
The Georgiad. Campbell.
Lines. Ewart.
Maxixe. Sitwell.
The Words of the All-Wise (excerpt). *Anonymous.*

Dwell (s)
The Angora. Gerard.
Arcadia. Sidney.
Christ Inviting Sinners to His Grace (excerpt). Alline.
The Church's One Foundation. Stone.
The Deserter. Cotter.
The Educational Administration Professor's Prayer. Bobango.
Fiammetta. Boccaccio.
The Gale of August, '27. *Anonymous.*
His Sailing from Julia. Herrick.
Hope. Johnson.
How Sleep the Brave! Collins.
Jesus Tender Shepherd. Duncan.
The Mower against Gardens. Marvell.
The Needles' Lighthouse from Keyhaven, Hampshire. Turner.
Psalm IV. Sidney.
Song: "In the air there are no coral-reefs or ambergris." Scott.
Sonnets, LV: "Not marble, nor the gilded monuments." Shakespeare.
Sunday Bells. Allingham.
Sweet Violets. *Anonymous.*
To My Setter, Scout. Seldon.
To Penshurst. Jonson.
Unguarded. Murray.
Vert-Vert, the Parrot. Gresset.
Waked by the Gospel's Powerful Sound. Occom.
When God Descends with Men to Dwell. Ballou I.

Dwelling (s)
Black Tarn. Sackville-West.
The Companion. Robinson.
Fates of the Apostles. Cynewulf.
I Sought On Earth. Santayana.
In Him. Flint.
Mexico City Blues. Kerouac.
A Motet. Amner.
Musk Oxen. Igjugarjuk.
My Shepherd Is the Living Lord. Sternhold.
On Blenheim House. Evans.
Our Father, by Whose Name. Tucker.

Prayer for the Home (excerpt). Guest.
Simplicity's Song. Wilson.
The Spirit's Grace. Heyward.
Through Unknown Paths. Hosmer.
The Tomb of Diogenes. *Anonymous.*
Verses on Blenheim. Martial (Marcus Valerius Martialis).

Dye (d) (s)
Come, Chearfull Day, Part of My Life, to Mee. Campion.
Distraction. Vaughan.
Epitaph on Elizabeth, L. H. Jonson.
Epitaph: On Sir Walter Rawleigh at His Execution. *Anonymous.*
Fables: The Sick Man and the Angel. Gay.
The Fly. Quevedo y Villegas.
Fly from the World. *Anonymous.*
How I wish I had known. *Anonymous.*
In Memory of the Vertuous and Learned Lady Madre de Teresa. Crashaw.
The Latter Part of the Third Book of Lucretius... Dryden.
Longing. Herbert.
Love Is Life. Rolle.
Murdering Beauty. Carew.
Mynstrelles Songe. Chatterton.
On Court-Worme. Jonson.
A Paradox. Townsend.
Stond Who So List upon the Slipper Toppe. Wyatt.
Thomas Dudley Ah! Old Must Dye. *Anonymous.*
To My Mistris, I Burning in Love. Carew.
To the Nightingale. Ayres.
When I Read Shakespeare–. Lawrence.

Dying
1944–On the Invasion Coast. Beeching.
Advent. Coffey.
Agatha. Austin.
Amoretti, XIV. Spenser.
An Anatomy of the World. The First Anniversary. Donne.
An Ancient Virgin. Crabbe.
And What with the Blunders... Patchen.
Bachelor Hall. Field.
The Ballad of Sue Ellen Westerfield. Hayden.
Because in This Sorrowing Statue of Flesh. Patchen.
Birthday on Deathrow. Otey.
Blanid's Song. Bottomley.
Blues for Bessie. O'Higgins.
By the Waters of Babylon. Heine.
Cardinal Bembo's Epitaph on Raphael. Hardy.
Careless Love. Johnson.
The Comrade. Dodd.
Comrades of the Cross. Wattles.
Coplas about the Soul Which Suffers with

Impatience...(excerpt). Cruz.
The Cowboy's Lament; or, The Streets of Laredo (A vers.). *Anonymous.*
The Dandy O. *Anonymous.*
The Dark Girl's Rhyme. Parker.
The Dead Feast of the Kol-Folk. Whittier.
The Death of Wolfe. *Anonymous.*
A Dirge. Rossetti.
Do Not Go Gentle Into That Good Night. Thomas.
Es Fallt Ein Stern Herunter. Heine.
Evening Landscape. Mont.
Eyes of Men Running, Falling, Screaming. *Anonymous.*
Fatima. Tennyson.
Favonius. Church.
Fidelity. Stickney.
Fin de Siecle. Mackintosh.
Finally. Pompili.
Finis. Thomson.
Flower Herding on Mount Monadnock. Kinnell.
For My Grandmother. Cullen.
A Grammarian's Funeral. Browning.
Harmonica Man. Wolny.
Have I Done My Best for Jesus? Young.
Hellvellyn. Scott.
The Hermit's Song. *Anonymous.*
Hunting Season. Auden.
Hymn to the Virgin Mary. O'Riordan.
I'd Be a Butterfly. Bayly.
I Held a Shelley Manuscript. Corso.
In Barracks. Sassoon.
In Memoriam A.H.H., VIII. Tennyson.
In Praise of Country Life. Chamberlain.
The Islands. Jarrell.
Jesus, I Love Thy Charming Name. Doddridge.
John Henry (F vers.). *Anonymous.*
A Lady to a Lover. Noel.
Last Lines (excerpt). Meredith.
The Life above, the Life on High. Theresa of Avila.
Lobotomy. Pitchford.
Love Breathing Thanks and Praise (excerpt). Baxter.
Madrigal: "Shall I look." Jones.
Memorandum. Graham.
Miserere, My Maker. *Anonymous.*
Monet: "Les Nympheas." Snodgrass.
Moon's Ending. Teasdale.
Mortification. Herbert.
Museums. MacNeice.
Mustapha. Greville.
My Stars. Ibn Ezra.
No Furlough. Stepanchev.
No, No, Poor Suffering Heart. Dryden.
The Obsequies of the Lord Harrington. Donne.
Ode: "Once more the country calls." Tate.

Ode to Joy. O'Hara.
Oh Oh Blues. Mays.
Old Soldiers Home at Marshalltown, Iowa. Barnes.
On a Memory of Beauty. Fraser.
Pearl Perch. Blight.
Peer of the Gods Is That Man. Sappho.
Percolating Highway. Castro.
Prayer A: "Lord, make me an instrument of Thy peace." Francis.
Prayer of St. Francis of Assisi for Peace. Francis.
Pro Patria Mori. Moore.
Psalme CXXXVII. Sandys.
Ragged and Dirty. *Anonymous.*
Rain Forest. Rolls.
The Ram. Coffin.
Razon de Amor (excerpt). Salinas.
Richard Hunt's Arachne. Hayden.
Solstice. George.
A Song: "Fair, sweet and young, receive a prize." Dryden.
Song: "In vain you tell your parting lover." Prior.
Sonnets for a Dying Man. Singer.
Southern Cop. Brown.
The Springboard. MacNeice.
The Starfish. Coffin.
Strength to War. Stepanchev.
Swan Song. Ranchan.
Then. Muir.
A Thorn Forever in the Breast. Cullen.
To Doctor Bale. Googe.
Town I Left. Sorrells.
A Valediction: Of My Name in the Window. Donne.
Waiting, the Hallways under Her Skin Thick with Dreamchildren. Lifshin.
Walking Parker Home. Kaufman.
The Waradgery Tribe. Gilmore.
The Watch. Piercy.
Way Over in the New Buryin' Groun' (with music). *Anonymous*
The Ways and the Peoples. Jarrell.
When the Light Falls. Kunitz.
When the Vacation Is Over for Good. Strand.
A Widow in Wintertime. Kizer.
A Wind from the West. Watt.
The Wind Suffers. Riding.
Witness. Miles.

E

Eager
Autumn Dawn. Machado.
The Poet. Morgan.

Thou Beautiful Sabbath. *Anonymous.*
Eagle (s)
1 September 1939. Berryman.
The Age of Animals. *Anonymous.*
America. Dumas.
The Beaks of Eagles. Jeffers.
A Bestiary. Rexroth.
Carolers. Westerfield.
Christ in the Hospital. Campbell.
The Dance. Crane.
Dawn. Scott.
Eagles and Isles. Gibson.
Fire on the Hills. Jeffers.
The Fugitive Slave's Apostrophe to the North Star. Pierpont.
The Garden. Brady.
Gisli, the Chieftain: The Song of the Arrow. Crawford.
A Happy View. Day-Lewis.
Horace. Sargent.
Hyperion. Keats.
The Ice Eagle. Wakoski.
The Islands of the Sea. Woodberry.
The King's Disguise (excerpt). Cleveland.
Loch Coruisk (Skye). Sharp.
Malcolm. Clifton.
The Messenger. Horovitz.
One to Nothing. Kizer.
A Poem for the Meeting of the American Medical Association. Holmes.
The Red Ghosts Chant. Spencer.
The Renegade Wants Words. Welch.
Rumba of the Three Lost Souls. Madge.
The Stars Are Thundering. *Anonymous.*
Timber Line Trees. Holme.
Twoborn. Rokwaho.
Ear (s)
The Ancient Law. Spire.
Astrophel and Stella, LV. Sidney.
At the Party. Auden.
The Bat and the Scientist. Bigelow.
Boldness in Love. Carew.
The Boy. Field.
The Business Life. Ignatow.
A Canticle to Apollo. Herrick.
Cernunnos. Maxton.
A Christmas Carol. Herrick.
A Cloud in Trousers: Prologue. Mayakovsky.
Dedication: To Edward John Trelawny. Swinburne.
A Delicate Impasse. Atchity.
Delphic Hymn to Apollo. Swinburne.
A Deposition by John Wilmot. McHugh.
Dislike of Tasks. Lattimore.
The Drummer. Robinson.
Duke of Parma's Ear. Siegel.
The Ear-Maker and the Mould-Mender. La Fontaine.
Ears. Akesson.
The End. Ginsberg.
An Epigram upon a Young Gentleman Refusing to

Walk with the Author... Garrick.
Epistemology. Wilbur.
An Epitaph upon My Dear Brother, Francis Beaumont. Beaumont.
Fatal Interview. Millay.
Father William. *Anonymous.*
Fossils. Stewart.
The Fury of Flowers and Worms. Sexton.
Gary Gotow. Uba.
The Great Nebula in Andromeda. Seidman.
Habits. Merwin.
Hope. Fanshawe.
I Know Not Whether I Am Proud. Landor.
I Show the Daffodils to the Retarded Kids. Sharp.
I Years Had Been from Home. Dickinson.
If I Could Meet God. Schmitz.
In Arizona. Zukofsky.
In Memoriam A.H.H., XXXVIII. Tennyson.
In the Sprightly Month of May. Vanbrugh.
John Coltrane an Impartial Review. Spellman.
Lament over the Ruins of the Abbey of Teach Molaga. Mangan.
Limerick: "H was an indigent Hen." Porter.
Limerick: "In a high-fashion journal for queers." *Anonymous.*
Limerick: "There was a young fellow from Fife." Ybarra.
Lord of Life, All Praise Excelling. Moore.
Lyric. Gregor.
The Magic Words. Koertge.
Mid-Country Blow. Roethke.
The Middleaged Man. Simpson.
The Mouth and the Ears. Palquera.
My Laddie. Rives.
My Picture Left in Scotland. Jonson.
Noah. Bloch.
Nocturnal Sounds. Cumbo.
Non Ti Fidar. Zukofsky.
A Northern Hoard. Heaney.
Ode to Walt Whitman. Garcia Lorca.
The Old Flagman. Sandburg.
On the Danger of War. Meredith.
Over Three Nipple-Stones. Celan.
Paradox. Miller.
The Perfect Life. Carrera Andrade.
Pericles. Shakespeare.
A Play of Opposites. Burr.
A Poem for Diane Wakoski. Young Bear.
Psalm of the Singing Grave. Janta.
Radio. O'Hara.
The Rattlesnake. Wrigley.
Reprisals. Yeats.
Rhyme for the Child as a Wet Dog. Sherwin.
Room. Stone.
Running Blind. Jones.

Rural Legend. Osborn.
Sappho. Catullus.
The Seafarer. *Anonymous.*
The Storm-Child. Byron.
Survivor. MacLeish.
Tapestry. Simic.
Taylor's Travels from London
 to Prague (excerpt).
 Taylor.
To Music: A Song. Herrick.
To My Soul. Fletcher.
Transplantitis. Sobel.
The Virgin's Slumber Song.
 Carlin.
Watch Repair. Simic.
The Windows. Herbert.
You Read Us Your Verse.
 Martial (Marcus Valerius
 Martialis).
Zimmer's Last Gig. Zimmer.

Earl (s)
And Thou, Dalhousie, the
 Great God of War.
 Anonymous.
Beowulf. *Anonymous.*
The Bonnie Earl of Moray.
 Anonymous.
The Bonny Earl of Murray (A
 vers.). *Anonymous.*
Did the Harebell. Dickinson.
Johnny Faa, the Lord of Little
 Egypt. *Anonymous.*
Johny Faa. *Anonymous.*
Lament for the O'Neills.
 Montague.
My Lord Tomnoddy.
 Brough.
On the Earl of Leicester.
 Anonymous.
Robin Hood and the Curtal
 Friar. *Anonymous.*
The Sisters. Tennyson.
The Squirrel. Nash.
The Vision of Sir Launfal.
 Lowell.

Early
The Dirty Word. Shapiro.
The Drunken Sailor (Early in
 the Morning). *Anonymous.*
Fall Colors. Mazzaro.
Father and Child. Harwood.
Fifth Sunday after Easter.
 Kinsella.
The Gombeen. Campbell.
Homecoming. Dawe.
I Had a Wife. *Anonymous.*
It Is Too late to Call Thee
 Now. Bronte.
Japan That Sank under the
 Sea. Satoru Sato.
The Masked Shrew.
 Gardner.
Mississippi Mornings. Dent.
A Morning Letter. Duncan.
Spring Morning: Waking.
 Seelbinder.
There Let Thy Bleeding
 Branch Atone. Bronte.

Earn (ed)
Jesse James. Benét.
Royal Education. Praed.
The Seed Growing Secretly.
 Vaughan.
The Watercress Seller.
 Miller.
What's In It For Me?
 Guest.

Earnest
The Canterbury Tales:
 Prologue to the Miller's
 Tale. Chaucer.
The Faerie Queene. Spenser.

What Is Our Life? Ralegh.
Earth (ly)
Adam and Eve: The Sickness
 of Adam. Shapiro.
Adams and Liberty. Paine.
Afterthought. Jennings.
Against Gravity. Cutting.
Agbor Dancer. Clark.
Aged Ninety Years. Snow.
Ah Sweet Content, where Is
 Thy Mylde Abode?
 Barnes.
Alpine Spirit's Song.
 Beddoes.
Always. Neruda.
Amber Beads. Brown.
Among the Hills: Prelude.
 Whittier.
Amoretti, LXXII. Spenser.
The Ancient Briton: The
 Dance of the Sword.
 Anonymous.
The Ancient Doctrine.
 Browning.
The Anniversary. Spear.
Another Epitaph on an Army
 of Mercenaries.
 ""MacDiarmid.
April. Belleau.
An April Adoration.
 Roberts.
April Rain. Blind.
Aridity. Lewis.
Arizona. *Anonymous.*
Assembly Line. Stoutenburg.
At the Edge of the Jungle.
 Lane.
At the Funeral of Great-Aunt
 Mary. Bly.
At the President's Grave.
 Gilder.
August. Spenser.
Axle Song. Van Doren.
Ballad of Springhill. Seeger.
 Peggy
Barbara. Smith.
The Battle of Aughrim:
 Rapparees. Murphy.
Beachy Head (excerpt).
 Smith.
Before the Actual Cold.
 Young Bear.
Benediction. Turbyfill.
The Birth of Venus.
 Anonymous.
Blood River Day. Brutus.
Blurry Cow. Twichell.
The Body Is the Victory and
 the Defeat of Dreams.
 Anghelaki-Rooke.
Bound. Roethke.
The Broken Tower. Crane.
The Butterfly. James.
By Frazier Creek Falls.
 Snyder.
Caelica, LXII. Greville.
Caelica, LXXI. Greville.
CANDU Can't Do. Filip.
Canzone: He Beseeches Death
 for the Life of Beatrice.
 Dante Alighieri.
Cassandra. Bogan.
A Cathedral. Vinaver.
Causes. Van Duyn.
Challengers. Dorn.
Chant to Io. Paraone.
The Chanting Cherubs - A
 Group by Greenough.
 Dana.
Childbirth. Hughes.
Christ in the Hospital.
 Campbell.

Christ, the Conqueror.
 Burder.
Christmas 1898 (excerpt).
 Morris.
A Christmas Carol.
 Coleridge.
Christmas Carol. Newell.
Christmas Songs. Kennedy.
The Cliff Rose. Fewster.
Clouds. Brooke.
The Cocks. Pasternak.
Come All Ye Mourning
 Pilgrims. Granade.
The Coming Child.
 Crashaw.
A Common Poem. Rodgers.
A Communion Hymn.
 Palmer.
Concert. Arvey.
Contemplations. Bradstreet.
Daisies. Worth.
The Dancers. Robinson.
Dante. Michelangelo.
Dark Song. Sitwell.
The Dark Stag. Crawford.
Daybreak on a Pennsylvania
 Highway. Daunt.
The Dead. Very
Dead Love. Siddal.
The Dead President. Sill.
The Deceptive Present, The
 Phoenix Year. Schwartz.
Dies Irae. Scott.
Dirge. Percy.
A Ditty. Jacobs.
The Diver. Nathan.
Do Something. *Anonymous.*
Don Juan. Byron.
Dust. Cuney.
E'en as the Flowers Do
 Wither. *Anonymous.*
Eagles. Woody.
Earth's Bondman. Dabney.
Earth Took of Earth.
 Anonymous.
Easter. Kilmer.
Ego's Dream. Kreymborg.
Elected Silence. Sassoon.
The Elements. Newman.
The Employee. Holzapfel.
En Route. Mayo.
The English Succession.
 Anonymous.
Envoy. Hovey.
Epigram: "First in his pride
 the orient sun's display."
 Belloc.
The Epistemological Rag.
 Burr.
Epitaph. Chiabrera.
Epitaph of Pyramus and
 Thisbe. Cowley.
Epitaph on a Well-Known
 Poet. Moore.
Epithalamion. Schulman.
Eudaimon. Raine.
The Everlasting Mercy.
 Masefield.
Except the Lord, That He for
 Us Had Been. Ainsworth.
The Excursion. Wordsworth.
The Eye. Jeffers.
Fable XIII: Plutus, Cupid,
 and Time. Gay.
The Faithful Shepherdess.
 Fletcher.
Falling Upwards. Shapiro.
Father's Voice. Stafford.
Faust. Goethe.
Feet, a Sermon. Paul.
Fleeting Restlessness.
 Ibarbourou.

Florence Vane. Cooke.
The Flower and the Leaf.
 Anonymous.
Footnote to Feynman. Post.
For John Berryman I.
 Lowell.
A Forest Meditation. Legg.
Freedom. Barlow.
Friends. Moore.
From a Litany. Strand.
From the Brothers Grimm to
 Sister Sexton to Mother
 Goose (parody).
 Cummings.
Funeral. Meyer.
The Gate's Open. Blight.
Genesis. Hill.
The Gettysburg Address.
 Lincoln.
The Gift. Anonymous.
Go Fly a Saucer. McCord.
God Is There. Isenhour.
God Is Working His Purpose
 Out. Ainger.
Going to the Water.
 Hobson.
Good Friday: The Madman's
 Song. Masefield.
Goodbye Nkrumah. Di
 Prima.
The Gospel of Labor. Van
 Dyke.
Grandmother. Minarik.
A Green Place. Smith.
The Grey-Eyed King.
 Akhmatova.
The H. Communion.
 Herbert.
Hail, Day of Days! In Peals of
 Praise. Venantius
 Fortunatus.
Hail, Oh Hail to the King.
 Quickenden.
Hallowed Ground.
 Campbell.
Hamlet. Shakespeare.
Hark the Herald Angels Sing.
 Beecham.
The Heart of Herakles.
 Rexroth.
Heaven Is Heaven. Rossetti.
Henceforth, from the Mind.
 Bogan.
Hiking up Hieizan with Alam
 Lau/Buddha's Birthday
 1974. Hongo.
His Body. McPherson.
Hold Thou Me Fast.
 Rossetti.
The Holy Longing. Goethe.
Home. Chalmers.
The House of Pain. Coates.
The Howling of Wolves.
 Hughes.
Hymn: "Now we must praise
 heaven-kingdom's
 Guardian." Caedmon.
Hymnal. Vinal.
Hyperion. Keats.
I Am Alone. Bhanot.
I Am the Beginning.
 Shembe.
I Have Cared for You, Moon.
 Conkling.
I'll Build My House. Hall.
I Shall Not Want: In Deserts
 Wild. Deems.
I Was Sick and in Prison.
 Very.
Idea. Drayton.
If It Offend Thee... Gregory.
The Iliad. Homer.

In Defiance to the Dutch. *Anonymous.*
In the Isle of Dogs. Davidson.
In the Twilight (excerpt). O'Donnell.
Inisgallun. Figgis.
Insomnia. Oates.
The Interpreters. Swinburne.
Ireland. Hewitt.
Iron Heaven. Alver.
It Happened. Sutherland.
Jehovah. Zangwill.
The Jewish Woman. Kolmar.
Johnson's Cabinet Watched by Ants. Bly.
Just an Old Sweet Song. MacDonagh.
Justice Denied in Massachusetts. Millay.
Kissing Natalia. Grier.
Lakshmi. Fallon.
The Lament of Saint Ann. *Anonymous.*
A Lamentation. Rakosi.
Lamentations. Gluck.
Landfall. *Anonymous.*
The Last Camp-Fire. Hall.
Last Lines. Kennedy.
Last Songs. Kinnell.
A Last Word. Dowson.
The Laughing Faces of Pigs. Lape.
Leaves. Teasdale.
Let Me Go down to Dust. Sarett.
Like This Together. Rich.
Lines. Ada Sister Mary.
Lines Written among the Euganean Hills. Shelley.
Little Things. Carney.
London Nightfall. Fletcher.
Long Summer. Lee.
Looking Down on Mesopotamia. Bethell.
Lord God of Hosts. Knapp.
Lord, Grant Us Calm. Rossetti.
Love Is Not Solace. Maris Stella.
Love's Justification. Michelangelo.
Lucasta's World. Lovelace.
Luzzato. Reznikoff.
Madonna di Campagna. Kreymborg.
A Man's Woman. Davies.
The Man Who Invented Las Vegas. Costanzo.
Mankind. *Anonymous.*
The Marriage of Earth and Heaven. Macpherson.
Mary Booth. Parsons
Mater Dei. Fallon.
May Carols. De Vere.
Meditation under Stars. Meredith.
The Meeting. Hollis.
Meeting at the Local. Parson.
Memento Homo quod Cinis Es Et in Cinerem Reverteris. *Anonymous.*
Miles Keogh's Horse. Hay.
The Minyan. Myers.
Mission Bay. Koethe.
A Modern Dragon. Bennett.
Montcalm and Wolfe. *Anonymous.*
Morning. Very.

Morning Hymn. Gregory the Great.
A Morning Hymn. Smart.
The Morning Purples All the Sky. Roman Breviary.
The Muted Screen of Graham Greene. McGinley.
My Love Is a Tower. Day.
My Olson Elegy. Feldman.
My Prayer. *Anonymous.*
The Native. Merwin.
The Nativity. Wesley.
Nearing Winter. Sandeen.
Ngoni Burial Song. *Anonymous.*
Night Thoughts While Travelling. Tu Fu.
Night-Wind. Lloyd.
The Noise That Time Makes. Moore.
Norembega. Whittier.
Nostalgia. MacNeice.
Nothing but a man. Tueni.
Nox Nocti Indicat Scientiam. Habington.
O Earth! Art Thou Not Weary? Dorr.
O Master Masons. Toller.
Ode for Soft Voice. McClure.
Ode on a Grecian Urn. Keats.
Odes, X. Hafiz.
Oedipus. Muir.
Oenone. Tennyson.
Of Dandelions & Tourists. Rosenblatt.
Old Creation Chant. *Anonymous.*
The Old Men. Feldman.
Old Moon My Eyes Are New Moon. Ginsberg.
Old Photo, 1942. Uba.
An Old Waterford Woman. O'Neill.
Om. *Anonymous.*
On a Fine Morning. Hardy.
On a Tear. Rogers.
On Refusal of Aid between Nations. Rossetti.
On the Ineffable Inspiration of the Holy Spirit. Greiffenberg.
On True Worth. Sa'di.
Once I Played and Danced in My Parents' Kingdom. *Anonymous.*
The Ossianic Cycle: The Song of Finn. *Anonymous.*
The Others. O'Sullivan.
Our Ever-Present Guide. *Anonymous.*
Our Love Shall Be the Brightness. Watson.
Over All the Face of Earth Main Ocean Flowed. Milton.
The Oxford Girl (Expert Town). *Anonymous.*
The Paisley Officer. *Anonymous.*
Palinode. Gogarty.
Parachute. Snaith.
The Passion Drinker. Endrezze-Probst.
Peace on Earth. Longfellow.
Pennsylvania Station. Hughes.
Perseus. MacNeice.
Pictor Ignotus. Browning.

The Plot to Assassinate the Chase Manhattan Bank. Larsen.
Poem. Simic.
Poem: "Hasten on your childhood to the hour." Picasso.
Poem to My Father. Stroud.
Poem to the Man on My Fire Escape. Wakoski.
The Poet's Day. Weber.
Polyolbion. Drayton.
Portrait of a Very Old Man. Carsley.
A Prayer. Yehoash.
Prayer for Dew. Ben Kalir.
Prelude. Whittier.
Progress. *Anonymous.*
The Prophet. Gibran.
Psalm XXXIX. Sidney.
Psychology Today. Jerome.
The Quest. Vinal.
Quien Sabe? Morris.
The Rahat. Rooney.
Rain. Alling.
Rebirth. Bruner.
Relationships. Di Cicco.
Release. Lawrence.
Reparation. Hoyt.
Requiem. Maynard.
Requiescat. Wilde.
Return. Kunjufu.
The Return of Astraea. Jonson.
Revelation. Keesing.
Rhododaphne. Peacock.
Rite of Spring. Kennedy.
The Roots of Revolution in the Vegetable Kingdom. Urdang.
Salt of the Earth. Lawrence.
Scalp Dance Song. *Anonymous.*
Sea Burial from the Cruiser "Reve." Eberhart.
Sea Flower. Dorcey.
The Sea-Limits. Rossetti.
The Season of Phantasmal Peace. Walcott.
The Seasons. Thomson.
She Hears the Storm. Hardy.
Shine, Perishing Republic. Jeffers.
Silence. Morse.
Silence. Orr.
Silence and Stealth of Dayes! Vaughan.
Silver Lamps. Dix.
Sing, Sing for Christmas. Egar.
Sinnes Heavie Loade. Southwell.
Six Feet of Earth. *Anonymous.*
Sky Diver. Stoutenburg.
Sleeping Beauty. Wylie.
Smoke. McGuckian.
Snow in the City. Siegel.
So It Begins. Agee.
Solomon on the Vanity of the World. Prior.
Something. Smith.
Song: "All phantoms of the day." Mezey.
The Song of a Heathen. Gilder.
Song of Maelduin. Rolleston.
The Song of the Body Dreamed in the Spirit's Mad Behest. Antoninus.

Song of the Sky Loom. *Anonymous.*
Song: "Stay Phoebus, stay." Waller.
Sonnet VII: "That learned Graecian (who did so exell)." Drummond.
Sonnet: September 1, 1802. Wordsworth.
Sonnet: There Is a Bondage Worse. Wordsworth.
Sonnet to Chatterton. Keats.
Sonnet to William Wilberforce, Esq. Cowper.
Sonnets, XX: "Now stands our love on that still verge of day." Agee.
Speaks the Whispering Grass. Stuart.
The Spectre Is on the Move. Allana.
Spring Is at Work with Beginnings of Things. Rose.
Spring Whistles. Larcom.
The Stolen Fifer. Fiacc.
Stolen Pleasure. Drummond.
Stories Relate Life. Shady.
Stratfield. *Anonymous.*
Substance and Shadow. Newman.
Suggested by a Picture of the Bird of Paradise. Wordsworth.
A Suggestion Made by the Posters of the "Globe." Thorold Rogers.
Summer's Farewell. Nashe [(or Nash[) Thomas.
Sunday. Herbert.
Sunlight. Bruchac.
Tales of a Wayside Inn. Longfellow.
Tamburlaine the Great. Marlowe.
Thamuris Marching. Browning.
There Is a City. *Anonymous.*
There Was No Place Found. Coleridge.
These Are My People. Trent.
They May Rail at This Life. Moore.
They Will Look for a Few Words. Turner.
Things Known: Under the Hill. Eberhart.
This Earth. Minthorn.
This Poem Is for Nadine. Janeczko.
Thou Art Coming! Havergal.
Three Epitaphs. Davison.
Three Hours. Lindsay.
Time in the Sun. Nicholl.
A Time to Dance: The Flight. Day-Lewis.
Tiresias. Tennyson.
The Titans. Alver.
To Christ Our Lord. Kinnell.
To-Day. Ward.
To Drift Down. Chandler.
To Lady Eleanor Butler and the Honourable Miss Ponsonby... Wordsworth.
To Silvestre Revueltas of Mexico, in His Death. Neruda.
To the Excellent Pattern of Beauty and Virtue, Lady Elizabeth... Shirley.

To the Film Industry in Crisis. O'Hara.
To Thomas Lord Chancellor. Jonson.
Toroi Bandi. *Anonymous.*
The Tortoise in Eternity. Wylie.
The Trailing Arbutus. Whittier.
Trance and Transformation. Goethe.
The Traveller. Auden.
The Tree of the Cross. "Angelus Selesius" (Johannes Scheffler).
The True Story of Snow White. Bennett.
Turris Eburnea. *Anonymous.*
Turtle Mountain Reservation. Erdrich.
Twilight. Custance.
The Twilight of Disquietude: The Years That Go to Make Me Man. Brennan.
Twilight of Freedom. Mandelstam.
Two Folk Songs, 2. *Anonymous.*
Two Look at Two. Frost.
Two Pewits. Thomas.
The Two Stars. Davies.
Ultimatum. Church.
Under Sorrow's Sign. O'Dalaigh.
Unkept Good Fridays. Hardy.
Unto Our God Most High We Sing. Cheney.
Upon a Child That Died. Herrick.
Upon a Funeral. Beaumont.
Upon the Heavenly Scarp. Klein.
Urn Burial. Hughes.
Vapor Trail Reflected in the Frog Pond. Kinnell.
A Virgin Declares Her Beauties. Barberino.
Visions. Petrarch.
The Voiceless. Holmes
Waking in the Dark. Rich.
A Walk on Snow. Viereck.
The Walking Road. Hughes.
Walt Whitman. Morris.
The Wanderer (excerpt). Robinson.
War. Apollinaire.
Washington. Roche.
We Did It. Amichai.
We Must Not Part. *Anonymous.*
We Needs Must Be Divided. Santayana.
Weir Bridge. Fallon.
A Welcome to Dr. Benjamin Apthorp Gould. Holmes.
What A Grand and Glorious Feeling. Wolff.
What Guardian Counsels? March.
What We Listened for in Music. Burr.
When I Am Dead. Wilson.
White Violets. Low.
Who. Honig.
Wild Eden. Woodberry.
Winter Sunset. Laforgue.
Wisdom. Hughes.
A Wish. Lerner.
Woman Guard. Aguila.
Words and Music (excerpt). Beckett.

The World's Great Age Begins Anew. Shelley.
Would you come back if I said the earth. Tueni.
Written in a Lady's Prayer Book. Rochester.
Written in a Thunder Storm July 15th 1841. Clare.
You Laughed and Laughed and Laughed. Okara.
You, the Young Rainbow. Sitwell.
A Young Fir-Wood. Rossetti.
Your cheeks flat on the sand. Khoury-Gata.
Zermatt. Hardy.
Earthquake
Arcadia. Sidney.
Childe Harold's Pilgrimage: Canto III. Byron.
Reflections on the River. Young.
Volcanic Venus. Lawrence.
Ease (d)
At Carmel Highlands. Lewis.
The City of the Dead. Burton.
Come, Break with Time. Bogan.
Depression. Burwell.
Eclogue. Diaper.
The Fairies' Farewell. Corbet.
A free woman. At last free! *Anonymous.*
Jack and His Father. Heywood.
Letter from Smyrna to His Sisters at Crux-Easton, 1733. Lisle.
Like Those Sick Folks. Sidney.
Limerick: "There once were some learned MD's." Herford.
Look, You Have Cast Out Love! Kipling.
Memory. Rossetti.
Miniatures IV. Mute the Hand Moves from the Heart. Strongin.
Passivity. Fullerton.
The Quiet Tide near Ardrossan. Turner.
Rondelay. Dryden.
Satire. Young.
Sonnet: Death Is Not without but within Him. Cino da Pistoia.
The Task. Cowper.
Th Unifying Principle. Ammons.
To a Lady. Gay.
To the Learned and Reverend Mr. Cotton Mather... Rawson.
Two Songs on the Economy of Abundance. Agee.
Upon a House Shaken by the Land Agitation. Yeats.
Useful for Avoiding Collisions at Sea. *Anonymous.*
We Two Boys together Clinging. Whitman.
Wedlock. A Satire. Wright.
What Was a Cure for Love? Godfrey.
Your World. Johnson.
East
At a Ruined Croft. Manson.

Celan. Asya (Asya Gray).
Celebration. Young Bear.
Corn-Grinding Song. *Anonymous.*
Dawn-Angels. Robinson.
Exhortation: Summer, 1919. McKay.
First World War. Alling.
The Gate of the Year. Haskins.
The Haschish. Whittier.
The Horseman on the Skyline. Lawson.
Hymn to the Sun. Doughty.
I Am. Kushner.
I Remember How She Sang. Penny.
I think of him. *Anonymous.*
If All the Voices of Men. Traubel.
A Jerusalem Notebook. Shapiro.
Little Sally Sand. *Anonymous.*
The Lord of the East. Chu Yuan.
Love on the Mountain. Boyd.
The Moon. Shelley.
Moonlight...Scattered Clouds. Bloomfield.
My Africa. Dei-Anang.
New Hymns for Solitude. Dowden.
New Year's Water. *Anonymous.*
Of Her Breath. Herrick.
Ohio. Updike.
Prayers to Liberty. Shaul.
The Protagonist. Hopegood.
Resignation. Chatterton.
Rudel to the Lady of Tripoli. Browning.
Spring. Irwin.
Surprised by Me. Darring.
To San Francisco. Alexander.
The Triumph. Lanier.
Unwelcome. Coleridge.
What Needeth All This Travail. *Anonymous.*
Window to the East. Evans.
The young bloods come round less often now. Horace.
Easter
Bonnie Barbara Allen (C vers.). *Anonymous.*
Early, Early Easter Day. Fisher.
Glanmore Sonnets. Heaney.
Good Friday: The Third Nocturn. Abelard.
If Easter Be Not True. Barstow.
The Legend of the Easter Eggs. O'Brien.
Rhyme for Remembering the Date of Easter. Richardson.
The Shawls. Gibbon.
To Find Easter Day. *Anonymous.*
What Does Easter Mean to You? Conrad.
Easy
Amor Mundi. Rossetti.
Clio's Protest. Sheridan.
The Collies. Anthony.
The Deer. Shceck.
Driving through the Pima Indian Reservation. Cook.

Epigram: "There was this gym teacher." Strato.
From Another Room. Corso.
Guadalupe, W.I. Guillen.
Hourly I Die. Dryden.
In Judgment of the Leaf. Patchen.
In Rain. Berry.
A Letter for Marian. McGrath.
The Libertine. MacNeice.
A Midsummer Night's Dream. Shakespeare.
Night Fishing. Kuzma.
Poem of Angela Yvonne Davis. Giovanni.
The Sun Used to Shine. Thomas.
Eat (ing) (s)
Academic Curse: An Epitaph. Court.
Against the Grain. Brownstein.
Angelo Orders His Dinner (parody). Taylor.
Annotations of Auschwitz. Porter.
Another Tribute to Wyatt. Surrey.
Be Careful. *Anonymous.*
The Beak. Smither.
The Bread of Our Affliction. Grossman.
Butter's Etymological Spelling Book, &c. Coleridge.
Canadians. Gurney.
Chief Leschi of the Nisqually. Niatum.
Childlessness. Merrill.
The Circus. Roberts.
The Cit's Country Box. Lloyd.
Claremont. Peters.
The Derby Ram. *Anonymous.*
Didactic Sonnet. La Follette.
Directions. Matthews.
Disillusion. *Anonymous.*
Early Discoveries. Malouf.
Eat and Walk. Hall.
Edmund Burke. Goldsmith.
The Egg Boiler. Brooks.
Epitaph on Dr. Keene. Gray.
Eve's Song in the Garden. Gottlieb.
Evensong. Stevenson.
Fame is a fickle food. Dickinson.
The Fat Man. Rutsala.
Fifteen Years Past. Veitch.
For Dr. and Mrs. Dresser. Avison.
For Mary. Rexroth.
Four Prayers, II. *Anonymous.*
Giving Rabbit to My Cat Bonnie. Stevenson.
Goodbye. Bloch.
Grace. *Anonymous.*
The Grizzly Bear is huge and wild. Housman.
Ground Hog. Anonymous.
The Helmet. Levine.
Here's a Health to Them That's Awa'. Burns.
Hero Song. Duncan.
Houses, Past and Present. Bachar.
Human Life. Prior.

Humorous Verse: "The caliph shot a gazelle." Abu Dolama.
I Saw a Little Squirrel. Anonymous.
If We Didn't Have to Eat. Waterman.
Improvisations on Aesop. Hecht.
In the Park. Harwood.
The Indian Convert. Freneau.
The Inefficacious Egg. Bishop.
Infant Innocence. Housman.
Jerry Hall. Anonymous.
The Knight of the Burning Pestle. Fletcher.
Lady Lazarus. Plath.
Lament for Taramoana. Makere.
The Last Families in the Cabins. Brand.
The Last Rite. Frost.
Leaf-Eater. Kinsella.
A Letter to Ron Silliman on the Back of a Map of the Solar System. Schmitz.
Life Cycle of Common Man. Nemerov.
Limerick: "A hearty old cook of Lithonia." Blount Roy.
Limerick: "There was a princess of Bengal." Parke.
Little Fishes in a Brook. Anonymous.
Little Pudding (parody). Roberts.
Love. Herbert.
Loving and Liking. Wordsworth.
Madrigal de Verano. Garcia Lorca.
Making Miso. Inada.
Maria Jane. Scott-Gatty.
Minutes. Johnson.
Miss T. De La Mare.
Mouse and Mouser. Anonymous.
New York. Towle.
Night. Everwine.
No Continuing City. Longley.
On the Eve of the Feast of the Immaculate Conception: 1942. Lowell.
The Peaches. Oppenheimer.
Penguin on the Beach. Miller.
Pie in the Sky. Anonymous.
Poem: "In the stump of the old tree." Davies.
Potato. Wilbur.
The Power of Maples. Stern.
The Preacher and the Slave (with music). Anonymous.
Proof. Ullman.
Pussy Cat. Anonymous.
Raspberries. Lerner.
Red Dust. Levine.
Riddle: "First I am frosted." Austin.
Riddle: "Runs all day and never walks." Mother Goose.
Rumpty-Iddity, Row, Row, Row. Anonymous.
A Scottish Cat. Anonymous.
Setting the Table. Aldis.

Eaves
Shakespearean Soliloquy in Progress: "To starve, or not to..."(parody). Ireland.
Soliloquy at Potsdam. Porter.
A Sometimes Love Poem. Leong.
Song for the Squeeze-Box. Roethke.
Sonnets, I: "From fairest creatures we desire increase." Shakespeare.
The Specter. Hardt.
Spider. Lattimore.
The Spider and the Ghost of the Fly. Lindsay.
Stepping Westward. Levertov.
Style. Nemerov.
The Swank. Vickers.
That Moment. Hughes.
Things of Late. Phillips.
Three Fields. Heyduk.
The Three Hills. Squire.
To a Swallow. Euenos.
To L.H.B. Mansfield.
The Tomboy. Burford.
Tortoise. De Longchamps.
Translations from the English. Starbuck.
The Two Boys. Lamb.
Under All This Slate. Hayford.
Upon a Snail. Bunyan.
The Walrus and the Carpenter. "Carroll.
Watermelons. Simic.
When in Rome. Evans.
When You Send Out Invitations, Don't Ask Me. Palladas.
You. Clark.

Ebb tide (s)
Ebb Tide. Pickthall.
Love. Kinsella.
The 'Mergency Man. Synge.
Youth and Age on Beaulieu River, Hants. Betjeman.

Ebbing
The Slow Pacific Swell. Winters.
The Sonnet's Voice. Watts-Dunton.
Tie Your Tongue, Sir? Smith.

Ebony
The Blindman. Swenson.
My Cousin Agueda. Velarde.

Echo (es)
The Angel Michael. Bental.
The Ascension. Beaumont.
Awake, Mine Eyes! Anonymous.
Capital Square. Anderson.
Countee Cullen. Maleska.
The Country Clown. Trumbull.
Country Gods. Cometas.
Doris and Philemon (parody) (excerpt). Squire.
Earth Psalm. Levertov.
Echo. Saxe.
Echoes. Lazarus.
Epithalamion. Spenser.

Fear. Pizarnik.
Heaven. Herbert.
Henceforth, from the Mind. Bogan.
In My Dreams I Searched for You. Anonymous.
Mad Blake. Benet.
Morning. Reed.
Mother Goose Up-to-Date. Untermeyer.
The Mountain Lake. Church.
Narcissus. Campbell.
Odes, VIII. Hafiz.
On the Death of Echo. Coleridge.
Passenger Pigeons. Morgan.
Peace. Bhartrihari.
Richard, Richard: American Fuel. Dixon.
A San Diego Poem: January–February 1973. Ortiz.
The Silent Ranges. Bird.
Slow Dancer That No One Hears but You. Niatum.
The Snow. Creeley.
Solitude. Grainger.
Song of Longing. Anonymous.
The Walls of Jericho. Dickinson.
The Weaving of the Wing. Hodgson.
Why Would I Have Survived? Bruck.
With Due Deference to Thomas Wolfe. Townsend.
Without Benefit of Tape. Livesay.
The Woods Are Still. "Field.

Eclipse
Debt. Anonymous.
Is Love Not Everlasting? McCuaig.
On His Mistress, the Queen of Bohemia. Wotton.
Sarah. Hyde.
Two Ladies Bidding Us "Good Morning." Vaughn.

Ecstasy
Barter. Teasdale.
Boys, By Girls Held in Their Thighs. Bishop.
A Christmas Eve Choral. Carman.
Father Mat. Kavanagh.
The Fire. Bell.
Harvest and Consecration. Jennings.
Her careful distinct sex whose sharp lips comb. Cummings.
Mandoline. Verlaine.
The Moth. De la Mare.
Mythics. Chasin.
On Fruition. Sedley.
Paterson: Unnamed. Williams.
The Poet. Lowell.
Psychometrist. Stephens.
Rapture: An Ode. Dixon.
Renaissance/A Triptych. Minczeski.
Saint Francis and the Birds. McFadden.
The Songs of Bilitis. Louys.
The Star. Redpath.
Surrender. Harding.
Young Shepherd Bathing His Feet. Clarke.

Your Chase Had a Beast in View. Bishop.

Eden (s)
An American Takes a Walk. Whittemore.
Baby. Eastman.
Bears and Waterfalls. Sarton.
By the Weir. Gibson.
Did the Harebell. Dickinson.
The Faerie Queene. Spenser.
Forest Leaves in Autumn (excerpt). Keble.
In a Garden. Jennings.
Independence. Mason.
Limerick: "There was a dear lady of Eden." Anonymous.
Marian. Meredith.
A Midrash (excerpt). Meltzer.
My Epitaph. Gray.
Pallor. Robinson.
Paradise Lost. Milton.
The Quiet Glades of Eden. Graves.
Rondeau: "Of Eden lost." Ellis.
Unearth. Barrett.
Westering. Kane.
What Is–"Paradise". Dickinson.
A World for Love. Clare.

Edge (s)
Art and Civilization. Conquest.
Bay Poem. Henson.
Black Holes. Perkins.
Deer Hunt, Salt Lake Valley. Handley.
Edge. Montague.
The Escape. Stafford.
Falling. Kaufman.
Here. Creeley.
The Horizon Is Definitely Speaking. Chang.
In Between the Curve. Bacon.
Moonlight Night: Carmel. Hughes.
An Old Cracked Tune. Kunitz.
On the Edge of a Safe Sleep. Cader.
Perpetuum Immobile. Dawe.
Poem about a Seashell. Crosby.
Six Variations. Levertov.
Slender Maid. Eliyia.
Song of the Intruder. Jacobs.
Sonnets, XCV: "How sweet and lovely dost thou make the shame." Shakespeare.
Tractatus. Mahon.

Eel (s)
The Conger Eel. MacGill.
The Eel. Nash.
Marriage. Anonymous.
Samuel Hearne in Wintertime. Newlove.
Song of Hate for Eels. Guiterman.
To Miss * * * * * on the Death of her Goldfish. Meredyth.

Effect (s)
Astrophel and Stella, XXV. Sidney.
Hence These Rimes. Taylor.
Oppian's Halieuticks (parody). Diaper.
Pernicious Weed. Cowper.

To Critics. Herrick.

Effort (s)
Call to Conflict. *Anonymous.*
Celestial Queen. Sannazaro.
Disillusionment. Alegria.
Gemini and Virgo.
  Calverley.
It Is True. Garcia Lorca.
On Queen Caroline.
  Anonymous.
Too Anxious for Rivers.
  Frost.

Egg (s)
Cousin Emily and the Night
  Visitor. Smithyman.
Divorce. Jong.
The Djanggawul Cycle, 8.
  Anonymous.
Easter Snowfall. Behn.
Eggs. Asquith.
Epigram. Butler.
The Farmer's Wife and the
  Raven. Gay.
French Cookery. Moore.
Hello There (parody).
  Salome.
The Hen. Herford.
Hen and Cock. *Anonymous.*
An Importer. Frost.
In Some Seer's Cloud Car.
  Middleton.
In the Courtyard. Ulinover.
It's in the Egg. Rosenblatt.
The Lark's Nest. Clare.
The Little Birds.
  Anonymous.
Malison of the Stone-chat.
  Anonymous.
Mallee in October. Hudson.
Mating Answer. Bottrall.
The Missel-Thrush's Nest.
  Clare.
Motherhood. Calverley.
Of the Cuckoo. Bunyan.
Parodies of Cole Porter's
  "Night and Day".
  Lardner.
The Risk. Sexton.
The Robin and the Redbreast.
  Anonymous.
Rollo's Miracle. Zimmer.
Salad. Collins.
The Sergeant. Johnson.
Soft-Boiled Egg. Hoban.
To Lydia, with a Coloured
  Egg, on Easter Monday.
  Jones.
A War. Jarrell.
When I Vexed You.
  Browning.
When I Was a Lad.
  Anonymous.
Why Then (Quod I) Old
  Proverbs Never Fail.
  Gascoigne.
A Woman's Song. McElroy.
The Wounded Breakfast.
  Edson.

Egypt
Abraham in Egypt.
  Schwartz.
All for Love. Dryden.
The Avenue Bearing the
  Initial of Christ into the
  New World. Kinnell.
Birds in Snow. Doolittle.
The Bread of Our Affliction.
  Grossman.
The Cow. O'Dowd.
Kilimandjaro. Taylor.
Man and Cows. Young.
Mark Anthony. Cleveland.

The Monadnock. Fletcher.
The Old Saint. Stuart.
Passover Dachau. Niditch.
Politik. Paulin.
Travel. Stevenson.
Whenas the Nightingale.
  Cleveland.

Eight
The Age of the Butcher.
  Friebert.
Be Just (Domestick
  Monarchs) unto Them.
  Alsop.
Limerick: "A salmon
  remarked to his mate."
  Jaffray.
The Prison Guard. Maloney.
A Racing Eight.
  Cuthbertson.
Riddle: "Purple, yellow, red,
  and green." *Anonymous.*
Something Very Elegant.
  Fisher.
A Teacher. Whittemore.
Twenty-Two Minutes.
  Martinez.

Eighteen
Chipeta's Ride. Taylor.
Eighteen. Banus.
Mother Shipton's Prophecies.
  Hindley.
My Dream. *Anonymous.*
Sonnet for My Son. Barber.
Words from Hell. Helwig.

Elders
.The Alliterative Morte
  Arthur. *Anonymous.*
Childhood. Bradstreet.
Give Ear, O Heavens, to That
  Which I Declare.
  Ainsworth.
Susannah and the Elders.
  Anonymous.
The Woyi. Blockcolski.

Election
Election Songs. *Anonymous.*
Fair and Free Elections.
  Anonymous.
Late Lunch, San Antonio.
  O'Sullivan.
Old Brown's Daughter.
  Anonymous.

Electric
Always We Watch Them.
  Mariah.
Men Working. Millay.
My Crime. Bill.
Saying One Thing. Long.
This Shall Be Sufficient.
  Rexroth.

Elegance
Mrs. Alfred Uruguay.
  Stevens.
The Old Athens of the West
  Is Now a Blue Grass Tour.
  Hall.

Elegy
An Aged Writer.
  McFadden.
Corydon's Farewell, on Sailing
  in the Late Expedition
  Fleet. *Anonymous.*
Elegy. Johnson.
Lines in Ridicule of Certain
  Poems Published in 1777.
  Johnson.
Poem from Llanybri.
  Roberts.
Soon at Last My Sighs and
  Moans. Ginsberg.

To the Memory of Gavin
  Wilson (Boot, Leg and Arm
  Maker). Galloway.
To the Reader. Oakes.
Yehuda Amichai. Mayne.

Element (s)
Alas, Kind Element. Adams.
Boats in a Fog. Jeffers.
Britannia's Pastorals.
  Browne.
The Elements. Williams.
Fire. Carpenter.
For All Things Black and
  Beautiful. Rivers.
Fulfilment. Barker.
In Me, Past, Present, Future
  Meet. Sassoon.
The Jam Trap. Tomlinson.
Lumber of Spring. Ridler.
Man Is God's Nature.
  Eberhart.
Melancthon. Moore.
On Portents. Graves.
Pause. Bethell.
Poem: "I keep feeling all
  space as my image."
  Russell.
The Ring Of. Olson.
Sonnets, XLIV: "If the dull
  substance of my flesh were
  thought." Shakespeare.
The Way up Is the Way
  down. Brasch.

Elephant (s)
At the Zoo. Milne.
Ballade of Unfortunate
  Mammals. Parker.
The Blind Men and the
  Elephant. Saxe.
Champagne. McGuckian.
The Dance of the Elephants.
  Harper.
A Difference of Zoos. Corso.
For Christmas. Aldis.
The Ganges. Dubie.
Hip Shakin' Strut. Georgia
  Tom.
Lady "Rogue" Singleton.
  Smith.
Look at All Those Monkeys.
  Milligan.
On Alexander and Aristotle,
  on a Black-on-Red Greek
  Plate. Dugan.
The Rat and the Elephant.
  La Fontaine.
Tit for Tat: A Tale. Aikin.
To Speak of Woe That Is in
  Marriage. Lowell.
What Could Be Lovelier Than
  to Hear. Coatsworth.

Eleven
He That Would Thrive.
  Anonymous.
The Ladybird. *Anonymous.*
Pendulum Rhyme.
  Robinson.
Rain before Seven.
  Anonymous.
Riddle: "Twelve pears hanging
  high." *Anonymous.*
To Find Easter Limit, or the
  Day of the Paschal Full
  Moon... *Anonymous.*

Elf
The Redbreast (excerpt).
  Wordsworth.
To A Child. Morley.

Elizabeth (s)
Amoretti, LXXIV. Spenser.
For Elizabeth Madox Roberts.
  Lewis.

God Save Elizabeth!
  Palgrave.
Kings and Queens: "First
  William the Norman."
  Anonymous.
Life-Long, Poor Browning...
  Spencer.
Of a Certain Green-Eyed
  Monster. Duff.
The Voice. Gale.
Written with a Diamond on
  Her Window at Woodstock.
  Elizabeth I.

Elm (s)
The Book of Juniper. Paulin.
A Circus Garland. Field.
Falling Moon. Hill.
Guess Who. Chappell.
Midnight on Front Street.
  Whiteman.
On the Marriage. Beaumont.
Poem: "About the size of an
  old-style dollar bill."
  Bishop.
A Rune for C. Howes.
Sleep and Poetry. Keats.
To the Memory of Yale
  College. Putnam.

Eloquence
Land's End. Coblentz.
The Pinta, the Nina and the
  Santa Maria. Tagliabue.
A Simplification. Wilbur.
To a Phoebe-Bird. Bynner.

Elysian
Epipsychidion. Shelley.
The Mushroom Gatherers.
  Davie.
True Love. Shelley.

Embers
Cottonwood Leaves. Clark.
The Jewish May. Rosenfeld.
The Last Guest. Shaw.
What Trinkets? Ferril.
Wolfhound. Murphy.

Emblem (s)
From a Litany. Strand.
Immortality. Jefferson.
Lexington. Holmes.
A Marching Litany to Our
  Martyrs. Mapanje.
More Than People. Fulton.
A Panegyric upon Oates.
  Duke.
The Road the Crows Own.
  Astor.
'Tis Said the Gods Lower
  Down That Chain Above.
  Alsop.
The Train Will Fight to the
  Pass. Pitter.
Unrest. Dixon.
When This Cruel War Is
  Over. *Anonymous.*
Wind, Gentle Evergreen.
  Anonymous.

Embrace (d) (s)
The Accusation of the Inward
  Man. Taylor.
An Acrostick on Mrs.
  Elizabeth Hull. Saffin.
Anthropology: Cricket at
  Kano. Brown.
Arcadia. Sidney.
Attraction. Wilcox.
The Beloved. Probyn.
Birth. Gilboa.
Britannia's Pastorals.
  Browne.
Chicago. Kinnell.
The Crow-Marble Whores of
  Paris. Schevill.

The Discovery of the Pacific.
Gunn.
Doric. Sikelianos.
Egyptian Hieroglyphics.
Anonymous.
Eros. Bridges.
Faith. Pope.
Fatima. Tennyson.
The Fever Toy. Wright.
For Angela. Gilbert.
Girl Sitting Alone at Party.
Justice.
Goodbye. Kinnell.
Grandmother. Minarik.
The Holly Bough. Mackay.
I Am of the Earth. Walters.
In the Nuptial Chamber.
Hardy.
Inscription for the Entrance to
a Wood. Bryant.
Jew. Morhange.
Juniper. Lee.
Limerick: "All young men
should take note of the
case." Thornton.
Love's Matrimony.
Newcastle.
Packet of Letters. Bogan.
Phallic Root. Shiraishi
Kazuko.
Poems from a First Year in
Boston. Starbuck.
A Runic Ode. Warton, Sr..
The Sacrament of Sleep.
Oxenham.
Swans. Wordsworth.
To a Child Running with
Outstretched Arms in
Canyon de Chelly.
Momaday.
To Ruin. Burns.
The Villanelle. Harington.
The Voice. Wilson.
When She Comes Home.
Riley.

Embryo (S)
Epigram: "Hail, blissfulest
maiden." *Anonymous.*
Father. Pack.
Marvellous Martin. Harpur.
The Progress of a Divine
(excerpt). Savage.
Written on a Paper Napkin.
Gasparini.

Emerald (s)
Amasis. Binyon.
The City Tree. Crawford.
Fall Again. Coursen.
In Memoriam A.H.H.,
XCVIII. Tennyson.
Love That Is First and Last.
Swinburne.
The Magazine Fort, Phoenix
Park, Dublin. Wilkins.
Marmion. Scott.
The Mistress of Vision.
Thompson.
Prologue for a Bestiary.
Perry.
Travelin' Blues. McTell.
What the Sonnet Is.
Hamilton.

Emerge (d) (s)
A Love Poem for My
Country. Chipasula.
O Never Star Was Lost.
Browning.
On Christmas Eve. Di Piero.
The Rubaiyat of Omar
Khayyam. Omar
Khayyam.

Vitae Summa Brevis Spem
Nos Vetat Incohare
Longam. Dowson.

Emotion (s)
Epilogue. Pound.
Nightmares: Part Three.
Moskowitz.

Emperor (s)
At Hans Christian Andersen's
Birthplace, Odense,
Denmark. Lindsay.
The Emperor of Ice Cream.
Stevens.
The Kingship of the Hills.
Ogilvie.
Marcus Aurelius. Sisson.
The Memory. Dunsany.
A Psalm of Onan for Harp,
Flue and Tambourine.
Nowlan.

Empire (s)
America. Newlove.
The Dying Eagle. Pratt.
The Electric Cop. Cruz.
De Guiana, Carmen Epicum.
Chapman.
Hero Song. Duncan.
Immanent. De la Mare.
Leaving Me, and Then Loving
Many. Cowley.
Lewis and Clark. Benét.
One Race, One Flag.
Fairburn.
Paradise Lost. Milton.
Paradise Regained. Milton.
Peace with Honor.
Appleman.
Russia. Williams.
Star of Columbia. Dwight.
To God. Maurice.
Unsatisfied. Holmes.
Verses Copied From the
Window of an Obscure
Lodging-House.
Anonymous.
Waterloo. De Vere.

Emptiness
Apology for E. H.
Hathaway.
Brother of My Heart.
Kinnell.
Cubist Portrait. Seiffert.
The Farm. Miller.
John Nobody. Moraes.
Moving Through the Silent
Crowd. Spender.
NN 616410. Tulloch.
On the Danger of War.
Meredith.
Poems of Night. Kinnell.
Portrait. Gluck.
Some Knots. Honig.
The Starry Night. Starbuck.
A Vision. Konopnicka.
Writing. Allingham.

Empty
1867: Last Sounds. O'Egan.
An Abandoned, Overgrown
Cemetery in the Pasture
near Our House. Orr.
And Jesus Don't Have Much
Use for His Old Suitcase
Anymore. Kryss.
An Apology. Morris.
Art in America. Weiss.
The Ballad of Reading Gaol.
Wilde.
Bedtime Story for My Son.
Redgrove.
Brain. Barks.
The Californians. Spencer.
Canoe. Anderson.

Childless. MacConmidhe.
The Church and Clergy Here.
Swift.
The Coffin-Worm. Pitter.
Columbus in Chains.
Freneau.
Comcomly's Skull. Barnes.
Constantly Risking Absurdity.
Ferlinghetti.
The Cry of the Peoples.
Brody.
Disappointment. Collier.
Doubt. Chipp.
Dream Songs. Berryman.
The Earthly Paradise.
Morris.
Empty Bed Blues. Smith.
A Fable for Critics. Cooper.
Family Outing–A Celebration.
Jackowska.
Father to Son. Jennings.
Finding the Pistol. Ruark.
Flight. Johnson.
For a Child Gone to Live in a
Commune. Stafford.
The Friar. Casal.
Fungo. Plumly.
Glass. Merwin.
Hard Strain in a Delicate
Place. Sylvester.
Hawk's Way. Olson.
Hie to the Market, Jenny
Come Trot. *Anonymous.*
The House-Wreckers Have
Left the Door and a
Staircase. Reznikoff.
Hubert Horatio Humphrey
(1911-1978). Galvin.
I, Pluto. Daswani.
Image. Noailles.
Ingmar Bergman's Seventh
Seal. Duncan.
Joseph Mary Plunkett.
Meynell.
The Lamp. Greene.
Let Some Great Joys Pretend
to Find. Shadwell.
Letters to Live Poets.
Beaver.
Lillian's Chair. Cabral.
Lost Moment. Fuller.
Luck. Shute.
The Map of Mock-Begger
Hall. *Anonymous.*
Mothers. Sexton.
My Fault's Small, About the
Size of a Pin Prick.
Miller.
New World. Ghiselin.
An Ordinary Evening in
Cleveland. Turco.
Our Lady. Coleridge.
Our Lucy. Goodman.
Paradise Lost. Milton.
Parting: A Game. Sukenick.
Party. Justice.
Political Activist Living
Alone. Arrowsmith.
The Remains. Strand.
Remembering Lutsky.
Zychlinska.
The Return. Ostenso.
Rhapsodies. Dabydeen.
The Rubaiyat of Omar
Khayyam. Omar
Khayyam.
Seasons of the Soul. Tate.
The Sepulcher. Flint.
The Shadow. De la Mare.
Sopolis. Callimachus.
Stanes. Glen.

Storm Over Rockefeller
Center. Holden.
Summer 1970. Mabuza.
Summer in a Small Town.
Gregg.
Terror. Warren.
Thinking of Love. Jennings.
The Thousand and One
Nights: Abu Nuwas for the
Barmacides. *Anonymous.*
Through a Glass Eye, Lightly.
Kizer.
The Track. Christopher.
Trinidad, 1958. Mondy.
The Vase of Life. Rossetti.
A Venetian Night.
Hofmannsthal.
You Who Occupy Our Land.
Margarido.
The Young Gray Head.
Southey.

Emulation
The Nightingale. Strada.
Troilus and Cressida.
Shakespeare.

Enchantment
Accordance. Kanabus.
Such Stuff as Dreams Are
Made Of. Higginson.
Winds of Eros. Russell.

Enchantress
The Rousing Canoe Song.
Fraser.

Encounter (s)
Cole's Island. Olson.
Explanation. Barber.
The Shark's Parlor. Dickey.
This Beast That Rends Me.
Millay.

End (ed) (ing) (s)
10th Dance–Coming on As a
Horn–20 February 1964.
MacLow.
12th Dance–Getting Leather
by Language–21 February
1964. MacLow.
Advent. Coffey.
Advice to a Lady in Autumn.
Chesterfield.
Along Walking. *Anonymous.*
Amoretti, XI. Spenser.
Anger. Creeley.
Arcadia. Sidney.
At the Roadside. Knoepfle.
Audrey. Dienstag.
Autumn Journal. MacNeice.
Bags Packed and We
Expected This. Wilson.
A Ballad of Burdens.
Swinburne.
The Ballad of East and West.
Kipling.
A Ballad of Queensland (Sam
Holt). Gibson
("Ironbark").
Ballad of the Hidden Dragon.
Anonymous.
Ballad Written for a
Bridegroom. Villon.
Barnabooth Enters Russia.
Hoover.
The Battle of Charlestown.
Brownell.
Beowulf. *Anonymous.*
Bethou Me, Said Sparrow.
Stevens.
Between Two Prisoners.
Dickey.
A Bit of the Book. Sangster.
Caelica, LXXXVIII.
Greville.

Canticle for Xmas Eve. Wagoner.

Chevy Chase. *Anonymous.*

Childhood, IV. Rimbaud.

Christ Walks in This Infernal District Too. Lowry.

Christmas Eve. Kooser.

Church Poem. Thomas.

A Cinque Port. Davidson.

Clonmel Jail. *Anonymous.*

Cocoon. McCord.

The Consolation of Philosophy. Boethius.

Corda Condordia: Quest. Stedman.

The Cottage at Chigasaki. Blunden.

The Cow. Nash.

Daily Growing. *Anonymous.*

The Day of Resurrection. John of Damascus.

Desiderium. Fletcher.

Diary (excerpt). Fuller.

Dies Irae. *Anonymous.*

Dies Irae. Thomas of Celano.

Digging It Out. Hollander.

Disquisition on Death (excerpt). Fairburn.

Dockery and Son. Larkin.

Down on My Luck. Fairburn.

Dreaming in the Trenches. McCabe.

Eagle Sonnets. Wood.

East Coker. Eliot.

The Elder Edda: The Short Lay of Sigurd (excerpt). *Anonymous.*

The Electric Cop. Cruz.

Elegy in the Cemetery of Spoon River...(parody). Squire.

Elegy, Montreal Morgue. MacDonald.

Emergency Poem 1973. Zarco.

The End Is Near the Beginning. Gascoyne.

The End of the Way. Cole.

England's Triumph. *Anonymous.*

Envoy. Henley.

Epigram: "An epigram should be–if right." Walsh.

Epitaph. Spencer.

Epitaph upon Himself. Belloc.

Epitaphs of the War, 1914-18. Kipling.

Evensong. Torrence.

The Everlasting Love. Flint.

Explanations of Love. Sandburg.

Explorations. MacNeice.

The Faerie Queene. Spenser.

Families. Blackburn.

Faust. Goethe.

The Feeling. Bronk.

The Finding of the Tain. Farren.

First Love. *Anonymous.*

Flight to the City. Williams.

The Flowing Summer. Bruce.

For the Fallen. Binyon.

Four Quartets. Eliot.

A Friend. Power.

From the Santa-Fe Trail. Lindsay.

A Funeral Elogy... Norton II.

The Gate at the End of Things. *Anonymous.*

The Glass of Pure Water (excerpt). ""MacDiarmid.

God Be in My Head. *Anonymous.*

The Gods of the Earth Beneath. Blunden.

The Golden Heart. Bynner.

Good Night! Good Night! Holmes.

The Great Statue of the General Du Puy. Stevens.

The Great War. Scannell.

The Gulistan. Sa'di.

The Gypsies' Road. Shorter.

The Hammer. Coolidge.

Hangover Cure. Alexis.

He Lifted from the Dust. Smith.

Here Followeth the Songe of the Death of Mr. Thewlis. *Anonymous.*

Hippodromania; or Whiffs from the Pipe (excerpt). Gordon.

His Wish to God. Herrick.

Homecoming–Massachusetts. Ciardi.

Hugging the Jukebox. Nye.

Hymn to Amen Ra, the Sun God. *Anonymous.*

I Am the One. Hardy.

I Know. Group.

I Promessi Sposi. Corman.

Identity. Mary Helen.

If Mr. H.W. Longfellow Had Written Miss Millay's. Adams.

Ilicet. Swinburne.

In an Alien Place. Neidus.

In Memoriam A.H.H., LXV. Tennyson.

In Pilgrim Life Our Rest. Sandys.

In Tyme the Strong and Statlie Turrets Fall. Fletcher.

The Ineffable Dou. Smith.

Infirmity. Roethke.

Instead of Features. Moore.

Johnny Appleseed's Hymn to the Sun. Lindsay.

The Judgement of Tiresias. Jacob.

A June Day. Teasdale.

The K.K.K. Disco... Mitchell.

Kirk Lonegren's Home Movie Taking Place Just North of Prince George... Thesen.

Kyrielle. Payne.

The Lamp. Vaughan.

Landscape, New Mexico. Robertson.

Last Poem. Berrigan.

Let There Be New Flowering. Clifton.

Let This Be My Parting Word. Tagore.

Let Us Have Faith That Right Makes Might. Lincoln.

Letter VIII. Swingler.

The Light of Asia. Arnold.

Light Shining Out of Darkness. Borthwick.

Like a Whisper. Ayer.

A Lilliputian Ode on Their Majesties' Accession. Carey.

The Little Girl with Bands on Her Teeth. Taggard.

A Little While. Rossetti.

LMFBR. Snyder.

Lochan. Smith.

Lord Galloway. Burns.

Love. Traherne.

Lutea Allison. Suckling.

"A Lutel Soth Sermun': Going to Hell. *Anonymous.*

MacKenna's Dream. *Anonymous.*

A Man-Made World. Spender.

Market Day. Webb.

Martyrdom of Father Campion. Walpole.

Matins, or Morning Prayer. Herrick.

Merlin in the Cave: He Speculates without a Book. Gunn.

The Midnight Court. Merriman.

Mismatch. Lindner.

The Moment. Roethke.

The Monkey's Wedding (with music). *Anonymous.*

Mother Shipton's Prophecies. Hindley.

Mr. and Mrs. Discobbolos. Lear.

My Aunt. Hughes.

My Picture. Procter.

A Nameless Epitaph. Arnold.

Night. Bialik.

No Armistice in Love's War. Cheyney.

No Complaints. Hollo.

November. Bridges.

Now Is Yule Come. *Anonymous.*

Nunc Gaudet Maria. *Anonymous.*

O Little Well. *Anonymous.*

Oberon's Feast. Herrick.

The Obsession. Liggett.

Ode to Work in Springtime. Ybarra.

Old Age. Al-Aswad.

Old Man. Thomas.

The Old One and the Wind. Short.

One Flight Up. Holman.

Our History. Coblentz.

Outlook Uncertain. Reid.

Palladium. Arnold.

Paradise. Herbert.

Paradise Lost. Milton.

The Passionate Pilgrim. Shakespeare.

Pastoral: The Tenth Eclogue. Drayton.

The Path. Thomas.

Peace. Markham.

Pedlar. *Anonymous.*

A Perfect Day. Bond.

Personal Talk. Wordsworth.

Pilgrim's Song. Ingemann.

Poem. Blaser.

The Poem of the End (excerpt). Tsvetayeva.

A Poor Man's Work Is Never Done. *Anonymous.*

A Portrait. Stevenson.

Postlude: for Goya. Guthrie.

Psalm. Simic.

Psalm XLI. Sidney.

Queen of Heaven. *Anonymous.*

Removal: Last Part. Arnett.

Resurgam. Pickthall.

Revenge to Come. Propertius.

Rhymes. Segal.

Rilloby-Rill. Newbolt.

The River. Vroman.

The Road. Chalmers.

The Road of Life. Morris.

Ronas Hill. Brown.

The Rubaiyat of Omar Khayyam. Omar Khayyam.

The Rubinstein Staccato Etude. Dett.

Rumors. Arkell.

The Rural Lass. Jemmat.

Sailor Man. Bailey.

Saint Paul. Myers.

Saturday Afternoon, when Chores Are Done. Mullen.

The Seesaw. Williams.

Self-Deception. Arnold.

Shoreline. Barnard.

The Short Lay of Sigurd. *Anonymous.*

Silex Scintillans. Vaughan.

The Simplon Pass. Wordsworth.

The Smile. Blake.

The Smugglers. Wister.

Soliloquy on a Southern Strand. Montague.

The Song of Mehitabel. Marquis.

A Song of the Wave. Lodge.

Song of Welcome. Fraser.

Sonnet: Death Warnings. Quevedo y Villegas.

Sonnets, XIV: "Not from the stars do I my judgement pluck." Shakespeare.

Sorrow. De Vere.

Source of News. *Anonymous.*

The Space Childs' Mother Goose. Winsor.

Sphinxes Inclined to Be. Orozco.

The Spirit. Turner.

The Stirrup Cup. Kilmer.

Stormpetrel. Murphy.

The Strong Swimmer. Benet.

A Study in Aesthetics (parody). Peters.

The Suburbs Is a Fine Place. *Anonymous.*

The Tale of Jorkyns and Gertie; or, Vice Rewarded. Lister.

The Testament of Cathaeir Mor. *Anonymous.*

Thanksgiving. Morris.

Things. Smith.

Thinking of Tents. Whittemore.

This Year, Before It Ends. Langley.

Thou Art Coming! Havergal.

Thoughts about the Person from Porlock. Smith.

Time. Curnow.

Time. Fletcher.

Time and Eternity. Bunyan.

To a Republican. Freneau.

To Aunt Rose. Ginsberg.

To His Muse. Breton.

"To make an end of all this strife." Wyatt.

To Master Edward Cobham. Googe.

To My Infant Daughter (II). Winters.

To the Translation of Palingenius. Googe.

Tortoise Gallantry. Lawrence.
Training for the Apocalypse. Frym.
Trala Trala Trala La-Le-La. Williams.
The Travelers. Reeves.
The Traveller. Berryman.
The Traveller. Tate.
The Triumph of Time. Swinburne.
Upon a Funeral. Beaumont.
Upon Nothing. Rochester.
A Valediction Forbidding Mourning. Donne.
The Valley of Men. Greenberg.
Values in Use. Moore.
Various Ends. Todd.
La Vita Nuova. Dante Alighieri.
Water Music. Lewis.
We Who Are Dead. Benjamin.
Wei Wind. Confucius.
Welcome, Thou Safe Retreat! Habington.
When All the Young Were Dying. Wilson.
When the Storms Come. Mphande.
Where I Am. Dos Santos.
The Whole Story. Stafford.
The World's End. Empson.
Would I Were Chang'd into That Golden Shower. Gorges.
Young Forbest. *Anonymous.*
The Zealless Xylographer. Dodge.

Endless
Ascension Hymn. Santeuil.
Auguries of Innocence. Blake.
The Capitals Are Rocked. Nekrasov.
Christ's Resurrection and Ascension. Doddridge.
Civil War. Van Doren.
Contemplations. Bradstreet.
Death Comes for the Old Cowboy. Clark.
Descend, Fair Sun! Chapman.
Epithalamion. Spenser.
The Excursion. Wordsworth.
Father. Carroll.
Hallelujah! Praise the Lord. Hatfield.
High Windows. Larkin.
I Am a Book I Neither Wrote Nor Read. Schwartz.
If My Head Hurt a Hair's Foot. Thomas.
Lament. Amichai.
Living Marble. O'Shaughnessy.
A Morning Hymn. Smart.
My Father's Country. Lee.
The Retirement. *Anonymous.*
A Shropshire Lad. Housman.
Spring Mountain Climb. Eberhart.
To Stella. Chapone.
Tristium. Ovid (Publius Ovidius Naso).
William Jones. Masters.

Endurance
In the Half Light of Holding and· Giving. Wieners.

Nightmares: Part Three. Moskowitz.
Ostia Antica. Hecht.
Poem for John My Brother. Aberg.

Endure (d) (s)
About the Phoenix. Merrill.
All Is Vanity, Saith the Preacher. Byron.
The Angel in the House. Patmore.
The Angel of Patience. Whittier.
As the Mist Leaves No Scar. Cohen.
Behold the Meads. Poitiers.
Black Bart, P08. Bierce.
Cities and Thrones and Powers. Kipling.
Despair and Hope. Zangwill.
Epigram. Butler.
Epitaphs of the War, 1914-18. Kipling.
Eternal Reward, Eternal Pain. More.
He Thinks of His Past Greatness... Yeats.
The Hem of His Garment. Hamilton.
I Shall Not Want: In Deserts Wild. Deems.
If These Endure. Lorraine.
Lines Written in Dejection. Yeats.
Lo! how I seek and sue to have. Wyatt.
Love's Slavery. Sheffield.
Madrigal: "My dearest mistress." Corkine.
The Man That Lives. *Anonymous.*
Morning Vigil. George.
Mutability. Shelley.
Narcissus. Gullans.
The Necessity of Rejection. Schevill.
The Nightingale. Petrarch (Francesco Petrarca).
Off Viareggio. Pitchford.
The Old Men. Kipling.
Out of the Sea. Bynner.
Scotch Te Deum. Kethe.
Seravezza. Fuller.
Shore Birds. Gale.
Sierra Kid. Levine.
Sleeping Beauty. Drummond.
The Snake. Suknaski.
Sonnets from the Portuguese, XLI. Browning.
The Sounding. Aiken.
The Summons. Laughlin.
There's a Man, I Really Believe.... Sappho.
The Three Woes. De Vere.
Threescore and Ten. Stoddard.
Twelfth Night. Shakespeare.
Winter is Another Country. MacLeish.

Endymion
Madrigal: "Stay, nymph." Pilkington.
The Poet. Benton.

Enem (ies) (y)
The Advice. *Anonymous.*
Again. Halas.
The Battle of Philiphaugh. *Anonymous.*
Battle Songs of the King Tshaka. Anonymous.
Best of All. *Anonymous.*

Blue Calf. *Anonymous.*
The Brut. Layamon.
The Castle. Muir.
Change of Venue. Clockadale.
The Children Look at the Parents. Tessimond.
Conversation. Berryman.
Drunken Gunner. Joseph.
The Duel. Lovelace.
Elegy. Keyes.
Expect No Thanks. Catullus.
Fable. Craig.
The Fear of Bo-talee. Momaday.
Five for the Grace. Scott.
For a Man Who Learned to Swim When He Was Sixty. Wakoski.
Hans Beimler. Busch.
I have no embroidered headband. Sappho.
The Inundation. Sergeant.
Jeanne d'Arc. Gluck.
King Henry VIII. Shakespeare.
Love Making. Tate.
Love Songs. *Anonymous.*
The Lovesleep. Ewart.
Make Friends. Ali Ben Abu Taleb.
Male Rain. Tohe.
Nelson's Death and Victory. *Anonymous.*
The New Mistress. Housman.
No Season for Our Season. Maas.
No Uneasy Refuge. Salkeld.
The Owslebury Lads. *Anonymous.*
Paper Anarchist Addresses the Shade of Nancy Ling Perry. Woodcock.
The Pike. Bruce.
Roosters. Bishop.
Songs of the People. Bialik.
Talking to the Mule. Jensen.
Theoretikos. Wilde.
To a President. Bynner.
Vulcan begat me... Wyatt.
The Youth and the Northwind. Saxe.

Energy
Album. Miles.
His Plans for Old Age. Meredith.
Moonshot. Kelly.
My Sad Captains. Gunn.
New Students. Bell.
The Place at Alert Bay. Rukeyser.
Psalm–People Power at the Die-In. Levertov.
Snowdrops. MacBeth.
Song of Myself. Whitman.
To the Postmaster General. Redgrove.

Engine (s)
Clear Night. Wright.
Georgie Allen. *Anonymous.*
Guild's Signal. Harte.
Last Came, and Last Did Go. Milton.
Man Has No Smokestack. *Anonymous.*
Ol' John Brown. *Anonymous.*
Re-Forming the Crystal. Rich.
A Satire against Reason and Mankind. Rochester.

A Song of Panama. Runyon.

Engineer
Casey Jones (G vers.). *Anonymous.*
Twenty-One Sonnets. Stead.
The Whore That Rides in Us Abides. *Anonymous.*

England
Agincourt. Drayton.
The Ambassadors. Lawson.
Amours de Voyage. Clough.
Balaclava. *Anonymous.*
The Banished Duke of Grantham. *Anonymous.*
The Bastard King of England. *Anonymous.*
The Battle of Manila. Hovey.
Blenheim. Addison.
A Chant of Hate against England. Lissauer.
The Coastwise Lights. Kipling.
Darien. Arnold.
The Death of Queen Jane. *Anonymous.*
The Defense of Lucknow. Tennyson.
A Description of a Strange (and Miraculous) Fish. Parker.
The Dying Sergeant. *Anonymous.*
The Fair Flower of Northumberland. *Anonymous.*
The Fighting Temeraire. Newbolt.
For All We Have and Are. Kipling.
For England, in Grateful Appreciation (excerpt). Vogt.
The General Elliott. Graves.
Green Fields of England. Clough.
Greenland Whale Fishery. *Anonymous.*
How Beastly the Bourgeois Is–. Lawrence.
In Springtime. Kipling.
In the States. Stevenson.
Jane Was a Neighbor. *Anonymous.*
Jump-to-Glory Jane. Meredith.
King Estmere. *Anonymous.*
The Last Instructions to a Painter. Marvell.
Lines on Swift's Ancestors. Pope.
The Manor Farm. Thomas.
The Miller of Dee. *Anonymous.*
Mole Catcher. Blunden.
Nerves. "Sagittarius" (Olga Katzin).
On Sir John Fenwick. Hall.
On Squire Neale's Projects. *Anonymous.*
Painting of my Father. Fallon.
Riddle: "As I was going o'er London Bridge." *Anonymous.*
Rodney's Glory. O'Sullivan.
The Romance of Imprinting. Sanford.
Saint George of England. Fox-Smith.
The Sea Martyrs. *Anonymous.*

Sir Walter Rauleigh His
Lamentation. *Anonymous.*
Snatches: "The Cat, the Rat,
and Lovel our dog."
Anonymous.
A Song in Praise of Old
English Roast Beef.
Leveridge.
The Stately Homes of England
(parody). Coward.
To–. Hood.
To the Nightingale. Davies.
Ulster. Kipling.
Villanelle: The Psychological
Hour. Pound.
The White Cliffs. Miller.
Writing in England Now.
O'Connor.

English
The Ancient Mansion.
Crabbe.
Another of the Same.
Ralegh.
The Beginnings (1914-1918).
Kipling.
The Change. O'Bruadair.
Civil Irish and Wild Irish.
Bhaird
The Crowns. Freeman.
Don Juan. Byron.
The Dream of the Cabal.
Anonymous.
The Emigres. Walker.
England's Heart. Tupper.
The English Race. Defoe.
The Englishman on the
French Stage. Seaman.
An Epigram on Scolding.
Swift.
Epigram: "The world laid low,
and the wind blew like a
dust." *Anonymous.*
The Everlasting Gospel.
Blake.
An Excellent New Ballad
Giving a True Account of
the Birth... Sackville.
A Fable for Critics. Lowell.
The German Legion. Dobell.
De Gustibus. Hankin.
Henry Wadsworth Longfellow.
Dobson.
The Holiday. Bignold.
Hope. O'Connor.
In the National Gallery.
Sassoon.
Incident at Bruges.
Wordsworth.
The Instruments. Smart.
An Invocation. Cory.
It Always Seems (parody).
Sayers.
Limerick: "I know a young
girl who can speak."
Webber.
Little Songs. Pickthall.
Lusty Juventus. Madge.
Mad Dogs and Englishmen.
Coward.
Mans Restlesse Soule Hath
Restlesse Eyes and Ears.
Williams.
Mr. Gunman. Garbutt.
The Native Irishman.
Anonymous.
Oak and Olive. Flecker.
Omnipresence. Hale.
Once Alien Here. Hewitt.
Pocahontas. Thackeray.
Robert the Bruce. Muir.
The Sea Fight in '92.
Anonymous.

A Ship Sails up to Bideford.
Asquith.
Song for My Father.
Hagedorn.
Spring in England. Going.
Such a Parcel of Rogues in a
Nation. Burns.
Tara Is Grass. *Anonymous.*
To Bert Campaneris. Clark.
To the Greek Anthologists.
Hamilton.
Washing the Coins. Dunn.
Where a Roman Villa Stood,
above Freiburg. Coleridge.
Why English Is So Hard.
Anonymous.
Ypres. Binyon.

Enjoy (s)
All Night Long. Cassian.
Astrophel and Stella, XCVII.
Sidney.
From Solitude to Solitude
towards Life. Eluard.
Gallery of My Heart. Kuka.
Gifts. Harris.
The Golden Glove.
Anonymous.
Guide to Jerusalem. Silk.
Limerick: "There is little in
afternoon tea." Burgess.
Loving and Liking.
Wordsworth.
Ode to Leven Water.
Smollett.
The Suet Dumpling (parody).
Anonymous.
The Swiss Peasant.
Wordsworth.
This Is My Carnac, Whose
Unmeasured Dome.
Thoreau.
The Ultimate Poem is
Abstract. Stevens.
Upon A. M. Suckling.

Enlist (ed)
The Biglow Papers. Lowell.
Some we see no more,
tenements of wonder.
Dickinson.
When the War Is Over.
Merwin.

Ennui
Don Juan. Byron.
Handling Synne. De Brunne.
Inquests Extraordinary, III:
On the Same. *Anonymous.*

Enough
At the Nursing Home. Cain.
August, at an Upstairs
Window. McCurdy.
Baldpate Pond. Weisslitz.
The Bells Are Ringing for Me
and Chagall. Winch.
Birdie McReynolds.
Hoffenstein.
Cuba, 1962. Anthony
("Ai").
The Difference. Richards.
Enough! Scully.
Enough Not One. Franklin.
February. Moffi.
Femina Contra Mundum.
Chesterton.
For a Mouthy Woman.
Cullen.
Gascoigne's Memories.
Gascoigne.
Graffiti for Lovers. Hall.
How Come the Truck-Loads?
Rodriguez.
It Is Enough (parody).
Appleman.

Kissing. Herbert of
Cherbury
The Manchester Ship Canal.
Anonymous.
Minutes. Johnson.
News of the palace. Ise.
Nothing Is Enough. Binyon.
Ode: "They journeyed." Ibn
al-Arabi.
On His Mistress. Donne.
Parole Board. Butler.
Rural Lines after Breughel.
Krapf.
A Scottish Proverb.
Anonymous.
She Found Me Roots
(parody). Ransford.
Si Hubbard (with music).
Anonymous.
Song: "Chloris, forbear a
while." Bold.
What We Can. Young Bear.
What Would I Do White?
Jordan.
You want the summer
lightning, throw the knives.
Bachmann.

Enter (ed) (ing) (s)
Another Year Come.
Merwin.
Christ Alone. Helsley.
Christmas Eve. *Anonymous.*
The Closed Door. Garrison.
Egyptian Hieroglyphics.
Anonymous.
Farewell to Narcissus.
Horan.
The Frontier. Hewitt.
High Diver. Francis.
How Gray the Rain.
Coatsworth.
Jehovah, God, Who Dwelt of
Old. Amis.
Lying Here, Everything In
Me. Atwood.
Mary's Song. Causley.
Multitudes Turn in Darkness.
Aiken.
Ngoni Burial Song.
Anonymous.
Notes for the Chart in 306.
Nash.
The Old Pastor. Tabb.
Prayer. Bynner.
Reply to Mr. Wordsworth
(excerpt). MacLeish.
Since Nothing Is Impossible.
Waters.
Two Songs, II. Kabir.
World of Darkness. Chatain.

Enterprise
Captain Craig (excerpt).
Robinson.
A Coat. Yeats.
Temporary Problems. Rubin.

Entertain (ed) (ing) (ment)
Home Cooking Cafe. Field.
Lines Written at the Temple
of the Holy Sepulchre.
Sandys.
Martial. Heyrick.
On Taine. Ainger.
What Did I Dream? Graves.

Enthroned
When I Admire the
Greatness. Steendam.

Entomb (ed)
Epitaph on Mr. Robert Port.
Cotton.
Fatal Interview. Millay.

For Mao Tse-Tung: A
Meditation on Flies and
Kings. Layton.
Rigor Viris. Avison.
To Saint Catherine.
Constable.

Entrails
Dead Ponies. Chamberlain.
Distances (excerpt). Okigbo.
Tales of the Islands, IX.
Walcott.
Three Poems, III.
Castellânos.

Entrance
The Coastguard House.
Montale.
Proceedings of the Wars.
Moure.
Rite of Spring. Heaney.
To Rich Givers. Whitman.

Entreat (ies) (s)
Amoretti, XXIV. Spenser.
The Birds of Tin. Madge.
Caelica, LIII. Greville.
Of the Going Down of the
Sun. Bunyan.

Env (ied) (y)
The Bishop Orders His Tomb
at Saint Praxed's Church.
Browning.
Harry Carey's General
Reply... Carey.
His Shield. Moore.
On Leaving Prison. Leon.

Envelope
A Letter. Korn.
A Letter from Home.
Oliver.
No Holes Marred. Douglass.
Oblivion. Fauset.

Envious
Amoretti, LXXXV. Spenser.
Animal Tranquillity and
Decay. Wordsworth.
Another Tribute to Wyatt.
Surrey.
Around the Child. Landor.
Birth of the Foal. Juhasz.
Caelica, LI. Greville.
Counting Kisses. Catullus.
The Dispensary. Garth.
Earth. Bryant.
Epigram: "Heat goes deep as
cold." *Anonymous.*
The Eugenist. Graves.
Fable XLV: The Poet and the
Rose. Gay.
The Faerie Queene. Spenser.
First Love. Campion.
Go, Rose. Gay.
Lament while Descending a
Shaft. *Anonymous.*
The Lass That Died of Love.
Middleton.
Love Is All. Catullus.
Martial in London. Collins.
Midnight. Dryden.
Music in Venice. Simpson.
My Marriage with Mrs.
Johnson. Gilbert.
O, the Marriage! Davis.
Off to the Fishing Ground.
Montgomery.
An Old Man. Wordsworth.
On a Visit to Ch'ung Chen
Taoist Temple... Yu
Hsuan-chi.
On Leaving Prison. Leon.
On Snow-Flakes Melting on
His Lady's Breast.
Johnson.

A Pastoral Ballad in Four Parts. Shenstone.
Pier delle Vigne. Dante Alighieri.
Poems. Drummond.
Press'd by the Moon, Mute Arbitress of Tides. Smith.
A Reed. Mandelstam.
Songs of the People. Bialik.
Sonnetto XXXV: "My Lady's face it is they worship there." Cavalcanti.
To Poets. Landor.
To the Same. Jonson.
A Tribute to Dante. Boccaccio.
Trivial, Vulgar, and Exalted: 19. Cunningham.
Upon the Same. Herrick.
When I Peruse the Conquer'd Fame. Whitman.
Written in Prison. Clare.

Epilogue (s)
An Epilogue at Wallack's. Wayland.
De Morte. *Anonymous.*
De Morte. Wotton.
The Village of Reason. Palmer.

Epitaph
At His Father's Grave. Ormond.
The First Solitude. Gongora y Argote.
His Metrical Vow. Graham.
Like to the Thundering Tone. Corbet.
Lines on the Execution of King Charles I. Graham.
Nonsense. Corbett.
On the British King's Speech. Freneau.
Song for a Proud Relation. MacDonogh.
Upon a Maid That Died the Day She Was Married. Meleager.
Verses Found in Thomas Dudley's Pocket after His Death. Dudley.

Equal
Admonition. Stack.
All Things Being Equal. Humphrey.
The Animalcule, A Tale. Savage.
Ascension Hymn. Santeuil.
Bonfire of Kings. Evans.
Dr. Joseph Goebbels. Snodgrass.
Hertha. Swinburne.
His Petition to Queen Anne of Denmark (1618). Ralegh.
I Kissed You. *Anonymous.*
I Saw My Father. Mayo.
May, 1945. Porter.
The Mouse's Petition. Barbauld.
A Negro Cemetery Next to a White One. Nemerov.
A Panegyric on Nelly (excerpt). Rochester.
A Pastoral Ballad in Four Parts. Shenstone.
Petition to the Queen. Ralegh.
The Point. Montague.
The Snow-Ball. Petronius Arbiter (Caius Petronius Arbiter).
A Song of Pleasure. Massinger.

The Soul of Dante. Michelangelo.
That Room. Montague.
A Was an Apple Pie, B Bit It, C Cut It. *Anonymous.*

Equation
I reason, earth is short. Dickinson.
Mathematics of Encounter. Gardner.

Erased
Anthony. Shore.
In Death's Field. Al-Khansa.
Instant Coffee. Yau.
Magical Eraser. Silverstein.
To the Divine Neighbor. Teller. J. L.

Erection
What Ulysses Said to Circe on the Beach of Aeaea. Layton.
A Yankee View. *Anonymous.*

Erin
A Day in Ireland. *Anonymous.*
God Save Ireland. Sullivan.
How Oft Has the Banshee Cried. Moore.
Irish History. Allingham.
Oh! Where's the Slave So Lowly. Moore.
The Orange Lily O. *Anonymous.*
Rodney's Glory. O'Sullivan.
The Song of O'Ruark, Prince of Breffni. Moore.
To * * * * *. Callanan.
The War Ship of Peace. Lover.
The West's Asleep. Davis.

Ermine
On the Relinquishment of a Title. Grigson.
Poem for Mother's Day. Fishback.
The Queens. Fitzgerald.
Wihelmina Mergenthaler. Taber.

Eros
In Memory of Sigmund Freud. Auden.
Love. Watson.

Err ('d) (ed)
Byron Recollected at Bologna. Rogers.
Courtesy. Patmore.
Four Anacreontic Poems, 3. Spenser.
Invitation. *Anonymous.*
Quantum Est Quod Desit. Moore.
Would You Like to Sin. *Anonymous.*

Error (s)
Astrophel and Stella, LXVII. Sidney.
Be Still. The Hanging Gardens Were a Dream. Stickney.
Carmina. Catullus.
English Bards and Scotch Reviewers. Byron.
Hymn. Holmes.
Knowledge. Cassian.
Let Others Sing of Knights and Palladines. Daniel.
Lunch with Girl Scouts. Bryan.
Mind. Wilbur.
The Music. Baudelaire.

O Wearisome Condition. Brooke.
On a Recent Protest against Social Conditions. Posner.
Pete's Error. Chapman.
The Pisan Cantos (excerpt). Pound.
Simple Faith. Cowper.
Song: "Man's a poor deluded bubble." Dodsley.
A Theory of Wind. Goldbarth.
Tightrope Walker. Scannell.
Upon Mrs. Anne Bradstreet Her Poems, &c. Rogers.
When Stars Are Shrouded. "T.

Escape (d) (s)
The Abyss. Baudelaire.
As imperceptibly as grief. Dickinson.
Autobiography of a Lungworm. Fuller.
The Cage. Stephens.
Cicada. Libero.
The Dam, Glen Garry. Symmons.
The Dark Cat. Brown.
Elegy for a Woman Who Remembered Everything. Wagoner.
Epitaphs of the War, 1914-18. Kipling.
The Farm Hands. Laing.
Father. Reiner.
The Gulistan. Sa'di.
Highway: Michigan. Roethke.
Houses. Justice.
The Hunt of Sliabh Truim (excerpt). *Anonymous.*
The Individualist Speaks. MacNeice.
Letters for the New England Dead. Baron.
Limerick: "A surgeon once owned a big ape." *Anonymous.*
Making Love, Killing Time. Ridler.
Morning in the Park. Ciardi.
Mother and Sister of the Artist. Cabral.
A Motorbike. Hughes.
O Artemis and your virgin girls. Telesilla.
On a Stone Thrown at a Very Great Man, but Which Missed Him. Wolcot.
Our Youth. Ashbery.
Poem: "Time and the weather wear away." Justice.
Pressure. Waldman.
Return to Lane's Island. Matchett.
The River. Welch.
To Children. McGaugh.
To flee from memory. Dickinson.
To Julia, the Flaminica Dialis, or Queen-Priest. Herrick.
Where the Cedars. Glatstein.

Essence (s)
Autumn Orchard. Jacobs.
Ax. Simic.
A Carrion. Baudelaire.
In Time Like Air. Sarton.
Inanna and the Divine Essences. Enheduanna.
Indirection. Realf.
Let Heroes Account to Love. Dugan.

"Now you have burned..." Thompson.
On Not Saying Everything. Day-Lewis.
The Photographer. Pfingston.
Synthesizing Several Abstruse Concepts with an Experience (parody). Poster.

Estate (s)
The Beggar's Opera. Gay.
No Pains Comparable to His Attempt. *Anonymous.*
The Patricians. Dunn.
The Pitt-Rivers Museum, Oxford. Fenton.
The Tourists. Day-Lewis.

Esteem
Carmina. Catullus.
Satire. Donne.
To His Book. Walsh.

Eternal
Agamemnon. Aeschylus.
April Moment. Ficke.
Babylon. Russell.
A Bather in a Painting. Greene.
Bhagavad-Gita: Debate Between Arjuna and Sri Krishna. *Anonymous.*
Britannia's Empire. Thomson.
Burial of an Irish President. Clarke.
By the Sea. Wordsworth.
Celan. Asya (Asya Gray).
A Child's Evening Prayer. Coleridge.
The Day Is Dying in the West. Lathbury.
The Day of Doom. Wigglesworth.
Death with a Coda. Belli.
Destiny. Arnold.
Ephemera. Yeats.
Eternal Light. Binney.
The Ever-Living Church. Wesley.
Finds Something in New Jersey (parody). Poster.
The Garden of Proserpine. Swinburne.
Give Peace, O God, the Nations Cry. Norris.
The Glory of Lincoln. Clark.
He That Never Read a Line. *Anonymous.*
Homage to the Philosopher. Deutsch.
Hymn. Orban.
Hymn: "My God, I love thee, not because." Francis.
I Am Stone of Many Colors. Tauhindauli.
I Consider the Tree. Buber.
I Will Praise the Lord at All Times. Cowper.
Immortality. Arnold.
In Consort to Wednesday, Jan. 1st. 1701... Henchman.
In Extremis. Sterling.
In Memory of My Mother. Kavanagh.
Jade Flower Palace. Tu Fu.
June Night. Hall.
The Largess. Eberhart.
A Lark's Nest. Smart.
The Lizard. Markham.
Love's Vision. Carpenter.

Lumen de Lumine. Shelley.
Man Frail, and God Eternal. Watts.
The Marriage of Heaven and Hell. Blake.
Miracles at the Birth of Christ. Watts.
Myths. Butler.
A New Year's Wish. J. H..
The Noise That Time Makes. Moore.
Nox Ignatiana. Daly.
O God Our Help in Ages Past. Watts.
O Solitary of the Austere Sky. Roberts.
Ode: "My heart rebels against my generation." Santayana.
Ode to Moderation (excerpt). Plumptre.
On Our Thirty-Ninth Wedding Day. Odell.
On the Baptized Aethiopian. Crashaw.
On the Cliffs. Swinburne.
Paradise Lost. Milton.
A Pastoral of Tasso. Daniel.
Poem in the Matukituki Valley. Baxter.
The Poet of Gardens. Henderson.
Prayer A: "Lord, make me an instrument of Thy peace." Francis.
Prayer of St. Francis of Assisi for Peace. Francis.
Rabbi Yom-Tob of Mayence Petitions His God. Klein.
Raphael's San Sisto Madonna. Miles.
Rapture. George.
The Rejected "National Hymns". Newell.
Rose-Cheeked Laura. Campion.
Silex Scintillans. Vaughan.
The Snake-Charmer. Hake.
Sonnet: "Could then the Babes from yon unshelter'd cot." Russell.
The Soul and the Body. Davies.
Stowaway. Adams.
The Sun-Dial. Peacock.
Sweet Is the Budding Spring of Love. Hippisley.
Tarry with Me, O My Saviour. Smith.
The Testament of Beauty. Bridges.
To Laurels. Herrick.
To the Queen. Blake.
Two Prayers. Adawiyya. Rabi'a al-.
Upanishads: Third Adhyaya. Anonymous.
Veni Crator Spiritus, Translated in Paraphrase. Dryden.
Washington and Lincoln. Stafford.
Ways of War. Johnson.
Welcome, Sweet Rest. Wigglesworth.

Eternity
After Tempest. MacKaye.
Aging. Jarrell.
An Anodyne. Ken.
As Happy Dwellers by the Seaside Hear. Thaxter.
Athanasia. Wilde.

The Atlas. Slessor.
Aurora Leigh. Browning.
Autumn. Clare.
Autumn Mushrooms. Mackenzie.
Ballad: "He passed by with another." Mistral.
Beacon Light. Clark.
Bearded Oaks. Warren.
La Beaute. Baudelaire.
Blest Be the Tie That Binds. Fawcett.
The Bustle in a House. Dickinson.
Caelica, XXCII. Greville.
Caelica, LXXXII. Greville.
Caelica, LXXXV. Greville.
The Cannibal Hymn. Anonymous.
Ceremonial Ode Intended for a University. Abercrombie.
Choice. Morgan.
Dead Embryos. Toth.
The Dead Musician. O'Donnell.
Death. Bronte.
Death with a Coda. Belli.
The Divine Lover. Wesley.
Easter. Whitaker.
Egyptian Hieroglyphics. Anonymous.
Epilogue to the Satires. Pope.
Epipsychidion. Shelley.
Epitaph for Any New Yorker. Morley.
Eternal Life. More.
Eternity. Blake.
The Eternity of Nature. Clare.
Etruscan Notebook. Clementelli.
Ex Nihilo. Gascoyne.
The Extasie. Cowley.
Fly to Jesus. Wesley.
Four Mountain Wolves. Silko.
The Garden of Earthly Delights. Simic.
George Jones. Anonymous.
Glimmers. Marshall.
God Is in Every Tomorrow. Snow.
God of the Strong, God of the Weak. Gilder.
Great God, Preserver of All Things. Pastorius.
The Hidden Weaver. Shepard.
Home. Nicholson.
Hymn. Holmes.
I Am of the Earth. Walters.
I Am Still Rich. Clark.
I Cannot Sing the Old Songs. Anonymous.
If I Could Tell How Glad I Was. Dickinson.
Impiety (excerpt). Margaret.
In These Dissenting Times. Walker.
Is Love, Then, So Simple. McLeod.
It Was for Me. Gray.
It Was the Worm. Broughton.
Jesus, My God and My All. Faber.
Letter to Lord Byron. Auden.
Life's Testament. Baylebridge.

Little Things. Fletcher.
Live Christ. Oxenham.
Lives of the Saints. Anderson.
Looking Down on Mesopotamia. Bethell.
Love Is the Peace, whereto All Thoughts Doe Strive. Greville.
Love What It Is. Herrick.
A Man about the Kitchen. Hobson.
Men Told Me, Lord! Jordan.
Musgrove. Anonymous.
My Diet. Cowley.
The Mystery of Emily Dickinson. Bell.
The New Birth. Very.
Night. Young.
O Day of Light and Gladness. Hosmer.
O Land Beloved. Woodberry.
Obit. Lowell.
On John Donne's Book of Poems. Marriot.
On the Defeat of Henry Clay. Lord.
On this wondrous sea. Dickinson.
On Time with God. Nutter.
The Perfect Life. Richardson.
Pocomania. Walcott.
Prairie. Bates.
Praise. Herbert.
Praise Ye the Lord, O Celebrate His Fame. Folger.
A Prayer for Pentecost. Brown.
A Prayer for the New Year. Storey.
Prayer in April. Hay.
Prelude. Brentano.
Reality. Havergal.
Rebirth. Stamp.
The Reply. Levine.
The Retreat. Vaughan.
Roots. Ginsberg.
The Rose. Williams.
Saviour, Thy Dying Love. Phelps.
See How the Rising Sun. Scott.
The Seven Blessings of Mary. Anonymous.
Shall These Early Fragrant Hours. Vaughan.
Silentium Altum. Kelly.
Since Cleopatra Died. Higginson.
Something for Jesus. Phelps.
Sometimes When I Sit Musing All Alone. Robinson.
Song: "Because the rose must fade." Gilder.
Song for a Day (excerpt). Arrivi.
Song's Eternity. Clare.
Sonnet for My Son. Barber.
Sonnet: "Whilst thus my pen strives to eternise thee." Drayton.
The Sovereign Poet. Watson.
Speak Gently. Langford.
Sunday Morning, King's Cambridge. Betjeman.
The Taste of Prayer. Seager.
Thanks to God. Hultman.
These Men. Gellert.
The Tip. Goldbarth.

To a Friend. Coleridge.
To Alan. Fraser.
To Ausonius. Paulinus of Nola.
To Colman Returning. Colman.
To His Watch, When He Could Not Sleep. Herbert of Cherbury.
To know just how he suffered would be dear. Dickinson.
To Man Who Goes Seeking Immortality, Bidding Him Look Nearer Home. Crapsey.
To Monsieur de la Mothe le Vayer. Moliere.
To Thee, Then, Let All Beings Bend. Evans.
Twelve Lines About the Burning Bush. Ravitch.
Variations on a Time Theme. Muir.
Verbum Supernum. Ambrose of Milan.
Walnut. Andrade.
Washington. Prentice.
Weighing the Baby. Beers.
The Well. Palés Matos.
Wondrous Love. Means.
Written in Butler's Sermons. Arnold.
Yes, I Have Been to Calvary. Christiansen.

Eunuchs
Woman. Anonymous.
Written in Flight from His Royal Patron. Al Mutanabbi.

Europa
At a Summer Hotel. Gardner.
Cupid a Plowman. Moschus.

Europe
And Forgetful of Europe. Grigson.
Black Sketches, 3. Lee.
The Coldness. Silkin.
Epiphany. Duggan.
La Fayette. Madison.
Letty's Globe. Turner.
To T. S. Eliot. Litvinoff.
Written on the Sense of Isolation in Contemporary Ireland. Greacen.

Eurydice
The Great Frost. Gay.
Orpheus. Herrick.
Thus Sung Orpheus to His Strings. Anonymous.

Eve
An Adult Lullaby. Anonymous.
At the Firth of Lorne. Smith.
A Circle. Spencer.
The Creek. Robinson.
Devotional Incitements. Wordsworth.
Don Juan. Byron.
Eve. Herford.
Fuller and Warren. Anonymous.
I Look into My Glass. Hardy.
I Thought I Saw Stars. Lister.
In the Orchard. Friend.
The Indian to His Love. Yeats.
Korea. Buckley.

Lollay, Lollay, Little Child!
  Anonymous.
The Lover and the Syringa
  Bush. Melville.
The Marriage of Pocahontas.
  Webster.
Orchard Snow. Goodenough.
Sonnets, XCIII: "So shall I
  live, supposing thou art
  true." Shakespeare.
Sunday up the River.
  Thomson.
Ye Sons of Columbia.
  Anonymous.

Evening
After Midnight. Vildrac.
Almswomen. Blunden.
Among the Finger Lakes.
  Wallace.
Arcadia. Sidney.
At Gibraltar. Woodberry.
At Grass. Larkin.
At the Appointed Hour They
  Came. Smith.
August at the Lake. Young.
A Bit of the Book. Sangster.
The Blue-Hole. Bell.
Changeless Shore. Ash.
Chateau Papineau. Harrison.
A Cold Spring. Bishop.
The Curfew Breakers.
  Chimsoro.
Elegy. Big Eagle.
Encounter. Devlin.
The End of the Street.
  Haines.
Evening. Shelley.
Evening: Ponte al Mare, Pisa.
  Shelley.
The Evening Star.
  Carmichael.
Fairy Music. Ledwidge.
Flowers and Men.
  Lawrence.
For Daphne at Lone Lake.
  Haines.
Four Stories. Shapiro.
He Maketh Himself One with
  the God Ra. Book of the
  Dead.
In the Forest. Edson.
Inspiration. Thoreau.
Intimate Supper. Redgrove.
The Island in the Evening.
  Porter.
It Is Not Likely Now.
  Bellerby.
Jogging at Dusk.
  Grossbardt.
The Land of the Evening
  Mirage. *Anonymous.*
Letters from a Father. Van
  Duyn.
Man to Man. McClure.
Mediterranean. Pincas.
The Mountain Over Aberdare.
  Lewis.
O God of Stars and Distant
  Space. Franzen.
O Love That Lights the
  Eastern Sky. Benson.
Ode to a Dressmaker's
  Dummy. Justice.
The Odyssey. Homer.
Of Swimming in Lakes and
  Rivers. Brecht.
The Old Anguish. Chu Shu-
  chen.
The Old House. Woodberry.
Paradise Lost. Milton.
The Park at Evening.
  Norris.

Planting Flowers on the
  Eastern Embankment. Po
  Chu-i.
Psalm. Ben-Yitzhak.
Runes for an Old Believer.
  Humphries.
The Sea Wind. Martinson.
The Seasons. Kalidasa.
Seneca Lake. Percival.
Sketch. O'Sullivan.
Spring. Irwin.
Sunday Afternoon Service in
  St. Enodoc Church,
  Cornwall. Betjeman.
Sunset. Montague.
Tell Old Bill. *Anonymous.*
Then and Now. Murray.
Thou Shalt Surely Die...: No
  Ghost Is True. Fiedler.
Thoughts from Abroad.
  Maybin.
Thyrsis. Arnold.
To Cordelia. Stansbury.
True Love. Lowell.
Trying to Believe. Gregg.
Voices. De la Mare.
Watertower. Bellg.
What the Birds Said.
  Whittier.
When I Was Growing Up.
  Vogel.
The White Knight's Song.
  "Carroll.
You Came as a Thought.
  Laughlin.
Zoroaster Devoutly Questions
  Ormazd. Zoroaster.

Evening's
A Prayer. Ehrmann.
Stanzas (excerpt). Newton.

Evening star
Evening. Shelley.
Evening: Ponte al Mare, Pisa.
  Shelley.
The Evening Star.
  Carmichael.
O Love That Lights the
  Eastern Sky. Benson.
Sketch. O'Sullivan.
Thyrsis. Arnold.
True Love. Lowell.
You Came as a Thought.
  Laughlin.

Event (s)
Artemis Prologizes.
  Browning.
Autumn Burial: A Meditation.
  Gullans.
A Different Speech. Nicholl.
The Dispensary. Garth.
For Tinkers Who Travel on
  Foot. Avison.
The Hound. Francis.
The Old Folk. Ditlevsen.
Parentage. Stafford.
St. Alphonsus Rodriguez.
  Hopkins.

Everlasting
Basketball. Lewisohn.
Coedmon's Hymn.
  Anonymous.
Hymn for the Feast of the
  Annunciation. De Vere.
A Hymn to Christ at the
  Author's Last Going into
  Germany. Donne.
Ice. Ai.
In Distrust of Merits.
  Moore.
The Jesus Infection. Kumin.
The Joys of Paradise.
  Augustine.

Little Marble Boy. Wright.
Meditation. Pain.
Our Captain Cried All Hands.
  Anonymous.
Pennies. Kilmer.
Request of a Dying Child.
  Sigourney.
Turn Again. *Anonymous.*
Victory. *Anonymous.*
Waiting for the Morning.
  Anonymous.
Wherever Beauty Has Been
  Quick in Clay. Masefield.

Evermore
The Flight of the Earls, 1607
  (excerpt). MacWard.
If Thou Wouldst Know.
  Bialik.
In Memoriam A.H.H., XLI.
  Tennyson.
Of the Father's Love
  Begotten. Prudentius
  (Aurelius Clemens
  Prudentius).
Philological. Updike.
Ships at Sea. Gray.
Softly Woo Away Her Breath.
  Procter.
Song: ""A weary lot is thine,
  fair maid." Scott.
The Sting of Death. Scott.

Everything
Against Still Life. Atwood.
As You Like It.
  Shakespeare.
Ballade of the Back Road.
  Block.
The Bear. Hughes.
Being Aware. Cooper.
Chops Are Flyin. Crouch.
City. Stroud.
Estat ai en greu cossirier.
  Dia.
Everything. Levine.
Everything. Paul.
Exercise. Merwin.
Farewell to the Farm.
  Stevenson.
February. Moffi.
Freaks of Fashion. Rossetti.
I Blow My Pipes. McCrae.
Madness. Yoshihara.
My Sister. Storni.
Not-Knowing. Hinshaw.
An Ode in the Praise of Sack.
  Anonymous.
Old Hannah. *Anonymous.*
Old Man Travelling.
  Wordsworth.
On Not Saying Everything.
  Day-Lewis.
The Other Side of This
  World. Forbes.
The Pit of Bliss. Stephens.
Potomac Town in February.
  Sandburg.
A Practical Program for
  Monks. Merton.
Revolutionary Letter #19.
  Di Prima.
Sonnet XI. Greeff.
Spleen. Gray.
Spleen. Verlaine.
Take I, 4: II: 58. Whalen.
Today's News. Berrigan.
What We Can. Young Bear.
When Spring Came.
  Anonymous.

Everywhere
Beagles. Rodgers.
Camerados (parody). Taylor.
Cedar Needles. Twichell.

Common Dawn. Butler.
The Fools' Adventure: The
  Seeker. Abercrombie.
Funiculi, Funicula. Denza.
Gout and Wings. Tennyson.
Hallowed Places. Palmer.
Letter to the Revolution.
  Griffin.
Lying Awake. Hardy.
The Mirrors of Jerusalem.
  Lefcowitz.
My Feet They Haul Me
  'Round the House.
  Burgess.
Our Movement. Eluard.
The Renewal. Roethke.
The Wind Is Ill. Brinnin.

Evidence
Against the Evidence.
  Ignatow.
Belief and Unbelief.
  Freneau.
Ego. MacCaig.
Faith. Tabb.
Morning Has No House.
  Waldrop.
News from a Pacified Area.
  Baxter.
Notes on a Life to Be Lived.
  Warren.

Evil (s)
Astrophel and Stella,
  LXXVIII. Sidney.
Ballad against the Enemies of
  France. Villon.
The Beggar. Mitchell.
Bellerophon: There Are No
  Gods. Euripides.
Botany Bay. *Anonymous.*
Brothers. Pagis.
The Brut. Layamon.
Burd Isabel and Earl Patrick.
  Anonymous.
Byron. Coogler.
Caelica, C. Greville.
The Church Universal.
  Longfellow.
Cleanness (excerpt).
  Anonymous.
The Cuckoo and the
  Nightingale. Clanvowe.
Dance of the Macabre Mice.
  Stevens.
Deor's Lament. *Anonymous.*
The Dog beneath the Skin.
  Auden.
An Epigram: "Great Charles,
  among the holy gifts of
  grace." Jonson.
An Essay on Man. Pope.
Evil-Hearted Man.
  Anonymous.
Fish Food. Wheelwright.
Four Prayers, III.
  Anonymous.
Hillside. Craig.
Hudibras. Butler.
Hymn to Marduk.
  Anonymous.
Jezebel: Her Progress
  (excerpt). Hanscombe.
Kevin Barry. Ward.
Last Days of Alice. Tate.
The Lord's Prayer in Verse.
  Hill.
The Marriage of Heaven and
  Hell. Blake.
May, 1945. Porter.
Me and the Devil Blues.
  Johnson.
A Monument. Madge.
A Mood Apart. Frost.

Night. Jeffers.
October 1942. Fuller.
The Phoenix (excerpt).
  Anonymous.
Rev. Homer Wilbur's "Festina
  Lente." Lowell.
The Rock. Eliot.
Security. Tucker.
Six Week Old Blues. Barbee.
Sonnets from China (excerpt).
  Auden.
The Spell. Herrick.
Sunflower. Jacobsen.
Thou Who Taught the
  Thronging People. Minde.
The Ungrateful Garden.
  Kizer.
Vesperal. Dowson.
Vinegaroon. Bynner.
Works and Days. Hesiod.

Example
After the Pleasure Party.
  Melville.
A Celebration of Charis.
  Jonson.
Elegy Against a Latter Day.
  Smithyman.
Her Race. Yeats.
In Time of War. Auden.
The Song of Roland, LXXIX.
  Anonymous.

Excellence
The Abnormal Is Not
  Courage. Gilbert.
Caelica, X. Greville.
The Deceased. Douglas.
Dream Songs. Berryman.
In a Season of
  Unemployment. Avison.
Love's Labour's Lost.
  Shakespeare.
Mistress Hale of Beverly.
  Larcom.
One of the Regiment. Le
  Pan.
The Passionate Pilgrim.
  Shakespeare.
The Things That Are More
  Excellent. Watson.
To Yvor Winters, 1955.
  Gunn.
When Land Is Gone and
  Money Spent. *Anonymous.*

Excess
Dante's Angels: The Angels of
  Protection. Dante
  Alighieri.
Equal Troth. Rossetti.
Isabel. Dobell.
Promises Like Pie-Crust.
  Rossetti.

Exchange (d)
The Exchange. Coleridge.
The Hag and the Slavies. La
  Fontaine.
In These Dissenting Times.
  Walker.

Excuse (s)
Bete Humaine. Young.
Conceits. Bates.
Confessions of the Life Artist.
  Gunn.
The Dell. Ewart.
Hit or Miss. "Carroll.
The Journey and Observations
  of a Countryman (excerpt).
  Hawthorn.
Pure Simple Love.
  Townsend.
The Schooner Blizzard.
  Anonymous.
Walking Around. Galler.

Why Do We Lie. Johnson.
Excusing
Though Your Strangenesse
  Frets My Hart. Campion.
Execution (s)
Reflections. Gardner.
Upon Love. Herrick.
Warden's Day. Baxter.
Executioner
To a Good Physician.
  Wycherley.
To Dianeme. Herrick.
You Move Forward. Sessler.
Exercise (d)
August, at an Upstairs
  Window. McCurdy.
Grieve Not, Dear Love.
  Bristol.
Henry's Secret. Kilner.
The Image of Irelande
  (excerpt). Derricke.
In Passing. Helton.
Orchestra. Davies.
Stately Verse. *Anonymous.*
Exhaust (ed) (ion)
Crepe de Chine. Williams.
Eclogue. Bergman.
Gas and Hot Air. Bishop.
La Maquina a Houston.
  Dorn.
Welcome, Ye Hopeful Heirs
  of Heaven. Brown.
Exile (s)
Canadian Boat Song. Galt.
Exile from God. Wheelock.
Hamewith. Smith.
I have no embroidered
  headband. Sappho.
Instead of an Interview.
  Adcock.
Jewish Arabic Liturgies.
  Anonymous.
My Grief on Fal's Proud
  Plain. Keating.
A Night in the Red Sea.
  Lyall.
The Rest. Pound.
Sonnet XVII: "I flee the city,
  temples, and each place."
  Labe.
The Syrian Lover in Exile
  Remembers Thee, Light of
  My Land. Syrian.
Yet Another Song. Rubadiri.
Exist (ed) (ence) (ing) (s)
The Atheist's Prayer.
  Unamuno.
The Blind Singer.
  Hoelderlin.
A Coney Island of the Mind.
  Ferlinghetti.
Constantly Risking Absurdity.
  Ferlinghetti.
Dance-Song. Seifert.
Drought. Oumar Ba.
Hominization. Holub.
In the Half Light of Holding
  and Giving. Wieners.
Listening. Michaelis.
My Mother's House.
  Tietjens.
Not Heaving from My Ribb'd
  Breast Only. Whitman.
Quatrain. Sarmed the
  Yahud.
September 1, 1965. Leary.
These Trees Are No Forest of
  Mourners. Jones.
This little bride & groom are.
  Cummings.
Tree. Otey.
The Turtle's Belly. Pearce.

The Unknown. Thomas.
While we were fearing it.
  Dickinson.
Exit (s)
Gorg, a Detective Story.
  Nichol.
The Great Lakes Suite.
  Reaney.
How I'd Have It. Stone.
Idyll. Webb.
In England's Green &.
  Williams.
Looking Both Ways. Wayne.
Expect (ed)
The Election. Pack.
Essay on Marriage.
  Wilchilsea.
A Poem Intended to Incite
  the Utmost Depression.
  Hoffenstein.
The thirty eighth year.
  Clifton.
Untitled Requiem for
  Tomorrow. Conyus.
Winter Solstice–For Frank.
  Asphodel.
Expectation (s)
Christmas Eve. Day Lewis.
Habitations. Belloc.
Improvisations: Light and
  Snow (excerpt). Aiken.
Expedition
Climbing You. Jong.
Voyage to the Moon.
  Dickey.
Experience
Catacombs. Vas.
The Constant. Ammons.
Dream Songs. Berryman.
The Lads of the Village.
  Smith.
My Definition of Poetry.
  Blazek.
New York. Moore.
On an Invitation to the
  United States. Hardy.
Sonnets to Orpheus. Rilke.
Thoughts of Thomas Hardy.
  Blunden.
Various Ends. Todd.
We Separate the Days.
  Nordbrandt.
When the Ripe Fruit Falls.
  Lawrence.
The Winter of '73.
  Anonymous.
Expire (d) (s)
Epipsychidion. Shelley.
Filling Station. Morin.
The Galley Slave (excerpt).
  Anonymous.
The Lament of the Damned in
  Hell. Young.
Life's Last Scene. Johnson.
Raya Brenner. Sadeh.
The Rubaiyat of Omar
  Khayyam. Omar
  Khayyam.
The Sacrifice to Apollo.
  Drayton.
Song of the Evil Spirit of the
  Woods. Moore.
The Wanderer's Grave.
  Sage.
Explain (ed)
A Counterpoint. Creeley.
Dreamscape. Booth.
The First One Drew Me.
  Kook.
Gets Hung up on a Dirty, of
  All Things, Joke (parody).
  Taylor.

Good Friday. De Bevoise.
Green Grass Growing.
  Evans.
Hunger. Simic.
Irreconcilables. Gregor.
Life Studies. Schjeldahl.
Limerick: "There was a young
  lady of station." "Carroll.
Magic Worlds. Nalungiaq.
New Hampshire, February.
  Eberhart.
Odes, XI. Hafiz.
Of Commerce and Society.
  Hill.
To R. B. Hopkins.
The Track into the Swamp.
  Morse.
Untitled Poem. "In the 2
  A.M. Club, a working
  man's bar." Peterson.
Explode (d) (s)
Ballad of an Empty Table.
  Kryss.
Lenox Avenue Mural.
  Hughes.
The Nonny. Reeves.
The Nuclear Family. Brown.
One Morning We Brought
  Them Order. Lee.
The Raspberry in the
  Pudding. O'Connor.
Tennis Pro. Dessner.
When I'm Going Well.
  Everson.
The Woman in the. Piercy.
Explore (d)
The Birds. Squire.
Elegy for a Diver. Booth.
Nursery Rhymes for the
  Tender-Hearted. Morley.
The Recovery. Blunden.
The Supremacy of Bacteria.
  Frazier.
Explosion (s)
The Cave of Night.
  Montague.
A Nice Part of Town.
  Hayes.
Sailing from the United States.
  Moss.
Space Fiction. MacCaig.
The Trimdon Grange
  Explosion. *Anonymous.*
Vengeance. Kunéne.
The Wild Swan. Savage.
Express (ed)
Aegean Islands 1940-41.
  Spencer.
The Engine Driver's Story.
  Wilkins.
For Under the Volcano.
  Lowry.
I Built My Hut. T'ao
  Chi'en.
In Thankfull Remembrance
  for My Dear Husband's
  Safe Arrivall.... Bradstreet.
Silence. Spalding.
To Cloris. Sedley.
Extinct (ion)
The Beach. Peters.
The Critic on the Hearth.
  Sissman.
The Dodo. Lucie-Smith.
Extinct Birds. Wright.
The Great Auk's Ghost.
  Hodgson.
Memo from the Desk of X.
  Justice.
Nights Passed on Ward's
  Island, Toronto Harbour.
  Fetherling.

On a Piece of Unwrought Pipeclay. Bryant.
Wyvern. Connell.

Extinguish (ed) (ing)
Deeper in the Tank–The Last Middle East Crisis, 1972. Ruggles.
The Invitation in It. Boyle.
A Prayer to the Wind. Carew.
Rain in the Desert. Fletcher.
Small Bones Ache. Dor.
To a Victim of Radiation. Vivante.

Extremity
Circe. Gibson.
Hope Is the Thing with Feathers. Dickinson.
The Lay of the Last Minstrel. Scott.
The Peninsula. Heaney.

Eye (s)
1948 Plymouth Abandoned on the Ice. Meissner.
3 a.m. in New York. Valentine.
Above It All. Levine.
Abraham's Knife. Garrett.
After Visiting a Home for Disturbed Children. Lipsitz.
Agamemnon. Aeschylus.
All Thumbs. Giber.
Allah. Mahlmann.
Amboyna. Dryden.
Amoretti, XXCVIII. Spenser.
Amoretti, XXI. Spenser.
Ancestors' Graves in Kurakawa. Kogawa.
Ancient and Modern Rome (excerpt). Keate.
Ancient Songs of the Women of Fez. Anonymous.
And if an eye may save or slay. Wyatt.
Another for the Briar Rose. Morris.
The Appointment. Kumin.
Approaching Washington Heights. Reiss.
Arcadia. Sidney.
L'Art, 1910. Pound.
Art above Nature, to Julia. Herrick.
The Art of Eyes. Spenser.
The Art of Love: Life Is Full of Horrors and Hormones. Koch.
Artemis. Nerval.
As by the dead we love to sit. Dickinson.
As in a Dusky and Tempestuous Night. Drummond.
As on the Heather. Reinmar von Hagenau.
As You Like It. Shakespeare.
At Wonder Donut. Mar.
Aubade. Laing.
Awakening–. Sachs.
The Bacchante to Her Babe. Tietjens.
Bacchus. Empson.
The Bag of the Bee. Herrick.
Ballad. Seiffert.
Ballad of Sam Hall. Anonymous.
Ballade of Illegal Ornaments. Belloc.

The Banks of Sweet Dundee. Anonymous.
Baroque Comment. Bogan.
Baseball Pitcher. Kuykendall.
Beale Street, Memphis. Snyder.
Beauty, Alas, Where Wast Thou Born. Greene, Robert.
Beauty's Queen. Kisa'i of Merv.
Beets. Nowlan.
Before I got my eye put out. Dickinson.
The Best Old Fellow in the World. Anonymous.
Bestiary for the Fingers of My Right Hand. Simic.
Betsy Jane's Sixth Birthday. Noyes.
Big Sheep Knocks You About. Bryan.
Birthplace. Big Eagle.
Black Dog. Young Bear.
Black-Out. Jeffers.
The Blackberry. Nicholson.
Blackpool Breezes. Anonymous.
The Blue Booby. Tate.
Blue Ey'd Mary. Anonymous.
Body and Spirit. Davies.
Bridegroom Dick (excerpt). Melville.
Bright Winter Morning. Klein.
Brother Ass. Irvin.
Bruton Town. Anonymous.
The Bubble: A Song. Herrick.
But We by a Love, So Much Refined. Donne.
Caelica, VII. Greville.
Caelica, XXVIII. Greville.
Caelica, XLVIII. Greville.
Caelica, LVI. Greville.
Caelica, LXIII. Greville.
The Caged Bird. Symons.
Calais Sands. Arnold.
Canticle. Berry.
Castilian. Wylie.
The Cat and the Moon. Yeats.
Cats. Scarfe.
Celebration. Young Bear.
Change. Greville.
The Children. Vinz.
The Children of the Poor. Brooks.
The Chough. Reaney.
The Choyce. Beedome.
Christ's Sympathy. Lytton.
A Christmas Carol. Herrick.
Christmas Lullaby for a New-Born Child. Gregory.
Clerimont's Song. Jonson.
The Coffin-Worm. Pitter.
Coleridge Crossing the Plain of Jars: 1833. Dubie.
Collapsible. Raworth.
The Columbine. Very.
Come Let Us Make Love Deathless. Trench.
Complaint. Williams.
Comrades. Johnson.
Conquest. Desportes.
Cordoba. Mendelssohn.
The Corral. Thompson.
The Counterpart. Jennings.
Cradle-Song at Twilight. Meynell.

Credit. Anonymous.
The Curse. Hollander.
Dans l'Allee. Verlaine.
Darkness. Rosenberg.
A Day in My Union Suit. Pettit.
The Day of Judgment. Buchanan.
Death of a Son. Silkin.
The Death Room. Graves.
December: Of Aphrodite. Merwin.
December Storm. Hay.
A Dedication. Coleridge.
Deer in Aspens. Hall.
Deirdre (excerpt). Yeats.
Desire. De Botton.
Deuteronomy. Bringhurst.
Diana. Constable.
Diehard. Moffett.
Divine Compassion. Whittier.
The Discoverer. Stedman.
Disillusionment. Graham.
The Dog of Art. Levertov.
Dolphin. Lowell.
Don Juan. Byron.
Don't You Hurry Worry with Me. Anonymous.
Down Dip the Branches. Van Doren.
The Dragonfly. Chisoku.
Dream-Tryst. Thompson.
Drifting Sands and a Caravan. Langworthy.
Droving Man. Astley.
Due North. Low.
During Music. Symons.
Dust. Russell.
The Dutchess of Monmouth's Lamentation for the Loss of her Duke. Anonymous.
The Dying Girl. Williams.
Early Copper. Sandburg.
Easter in the Woods. Frost.
Eclipse. Probst.
Ecstasy. Turner.
Edgar's Story. Kennedy.
The Eel. Morgan.
The Election. Pack.
An Elegy. Yuan Chen.
Elegy in Six Sonnets. Tuckerman.
The Elusive Maid. Ibn Chasdai.
Encounter. Livesay.
End of Season. Warren.
Epigram: "One boy alone." Meleager.
Epigram: "Thy eyes are sparks, Lycines." Strato.
An Epitaph. Watson.
An Essay on Criticism. Pope.
Esther's Tomcat. Hughes.
Eternal Masculine. Benet.
Evening Music. Smithyman.
Evening Prayer. Hagedorn.
Exhortation: Summer, 1919. McKay.
The Expanding Universe. Nicholson.
Expression. Gunn.
The Eye. Herrick.
The Eye. Wilbur.
The Eyes Have It. Stephens.
The Eyes of Children at the Brink of the Sea's Grasp. Jacobsen.
A Face. Browning.
Faded Pictures. Moody.
A Fairy Song. Lyly.

The Fall of Hyperion. Keats.
The Fathers. Morris.
The Faun Tells of the Rout of the Amazons. Moore.
Faustus. Hope.
The Fawn in the Snow. Benet.
The Fear of Bo-talee. Momaday.
Feeling That Way Too. Vogelsang.
Felicia's Cafe. McGuckian.
Field Trip. Miranda.
Fighting Her. Phillips.
The Finches. Murray.
The Fire. Creeley.
The first day's night had come. Dickinson.
First Death. Justice.
Five Lyrics from "Good for Nothing Man". Pitchford.
Five Visions of Captain Cook. Slessor.
Flooded Mind. MacCaig.
The Fool on the Hill. Beatles.
For a Child's Drawing. Vogt.
For Annie. Poe.
For Brother Malcolm. Spriggs.
For Delphine. Simmons.
For Prodigal Read Generous. Cummings.
For Stephen Drawing Birds. Rogers.
For the Field. Chock.
Fortitude. Anonymous.
Fox. Campbell.
Freedom of Love. Breton.
From Garvey's Farm: Seneca, Wisconsin. Hoeppner.
From the Window of the Beverly Wilshire Hotel. McClure.
Funeral Lament from Epiros. Anonymous.
Further Instructions. O'Sullivan.
A Garden Lyric. Locker-Lampson.
The Gipsy Girl. Hodgson.
Give Me the Splendid Silent Sun. Whitman.
The Giver of Life. Unknown.
The Glass Bubbles. Greenberg.
Goethe's Death Mask. Gregg.
Going to Mass Last Sunday. MacDonagh.
Going to Moscow. Edmond.
Goodbye to the Poetry of Calcium. Wright.
Grace at Evening. Poteat.
The Grace of Cynthia's Maidenhood. D'Ambrosio.
Gray Glove. Borson.
A Grey Eye Weeping. O'Rahilly.
The Half Door. O'Sullivan.
Hamasah: His Children. Hittan of Tayyi.
The Hands. Moses.
Hangman. Anthony ("Ai").
Hard Daddy. Hughes.
A Hazel Stick for Catherine Ann. Heaney.
He is the Lonely Greatness. Rock.

He Kindleth a Fire.   Book of the Dead.
He That Loves a Rosy Cheek. Carew.
The Heart of Herakles. Rexroth.
Henry Miller: A Writer. Lem.
Her Application to Elysium. Norris.
Here and There: Nocturnal Landscape.   Cowley.
Hero and Leander.   Marlowe.
Highland Region.   Price.
Homage to Chagall.   Niatum.
The Homecoming Singer. Wright.
Homeward Bound.   Tooker.
Horse in a Field.   De La Mare.
Hot Day at the Races. Raworth.
The House of Life.   Rossetti.
Household.   Jensen.
How I Got Ovah.   Rodgers.
Humanities Lecture. Stafford.
Hunting for Blueberries. James.
Hymn of Weeping.   Ben Shefatiah.
I Close Her Eyes.   Heine.
I Don't Want to Be a Gambler (with music). Anonymous.
I Drift in the Wind.   Jonker.
I let the incense grow cold. Li Ch'ing-chao.
I Met by Chance.   Heine.
I saw her crop a rose.   Clare.
I Thank You God for Most This Amazing.   Cummings.
Idiot.   Tate.
If When I Die.   Fowler.
Imagining How It Would Be to Be Dead.   Eberhart.
In Days of New.   Bartlett.
In Judgment of the Leaf. Patchen.
In Love with the Bears. Kuzma.
In Memoriam.   Longley.
In Memoriam A.H.H., LXII. Tennyson.
In Memory.   Pollitt.
In Memory of V. R. Lang. Hammond.
In Phaeacia.   Flecker.
In Progress.   Rossetti.
In Quest to Have Not. Honig.
In the Breeze.   Pasternak.
In the Forest of Your Eyes. Barbeitos.
The Initiate.   Merwin.
Initiation.   Rilke.
The Inn of Earth.   Teasdale.
Into the World and Out. Piatt.
Intrusion.   Levertov.
Investigator.   Waddington.
Iron-Door-Woman. Volborth.
Is 5.   Cummings.
It's a Different Story When You're Going Into the Wind.   McFadden.
It's Over Now; I've Known It All.   Bronte.
The Jealous Lover. Anonymous.
The Jealous Lovers.   Hall.

Jealousy.   DeVries.
Jinny Git Around. Anonymous.
John Otto.   Merwin.
Joy.   Jeffers.
Justice.   Hughes.
Kathe Kollwitz.   Rukeyser.
Keep Your Eyes on the Prize. Anonymous.
The Kid: The Awakening (excerpt).   Aiken.
The Knot.   Rich.
Krishnakali.   Tagore.
The Lady with the Unicorn. Watkins.
Lament.   Williams.
Lament of a Last Letter. Harrison.
The Languages We Are. Bryant.
Lapis Lazuli.   Yeats.
The Lark's Song.   Blake.
The Last Boats.   Ady.
The Last Journey.   Leonidas.
The Late Show.   Sylvester.
Laura's Song.   Brown.
Lesbia.   Congreve.
Let Me Enjoy.   Hardy.
Let Me Look At Me. Martin.
The Life of....   Weiss.
Limerick: "There once was a spinster of Ealing." Anonymous.
Lines I Told Myself I Wouldn't Write.   Mariani.
Lines Written at Bridgwater, 27 July 1797 (excerpt). Thelwall.
Little Boy Blue.   Ransom.
The Little Dancers.   Binyon.
The Litttle Black-Eyed Rebel. Carleton.
The Living Book.   Bates.
Longing.   Halevi.
Look Not to Me for Wisdom. Divine.
Lost.   Sandburg.
A Lost Soul.   Macpherson.
Love-Charms.   Campion.
Love Has Eyes.   Forster.
Love Is Enough.   Morris.
Love's Language. MacDonagh.
Love's Prisoner.   Van Rensselaer.
Love, the Light-Giver. Michelangelo.
The Lover to His Lady. Turberville.
The Lovers.   Zaturenska.
Lucasta's Fan, with a Looking-Glass in It. Lovelace.
Lullaby.   Harris.
The Lunar Games.   Manner.
Mac Diarmod's Daughter. Carlin.
Made to See.   Nist.
Malest Cornifici Tuo Catullo. Ginsberg.
Man.   Greenberg.
Man O'War Bird.   Walcott.
The Man Who Buys Hides. Schmitz.
The Market Town.   Carlin.
Mask of Stone.   Johnson.
Matin Song.   Field.
May the Ambitious Ever Find.   Sackville.
Maze.   Eberhart.

Medieval Christ Speaks on a Spanish Sculpture of Himself.   Owens.
Meeting-House Hill.   Lowell.
Michelangelo: "The Creation of Adam."   Djanikian.
The Middleaged Man. Simpson.
The Midnight Court. Merriman.
A Miner's Life.   Anonymous.
Miners' Wives.   Corrie.
A Minuet on Reaching the Age of Fifty.   Santayana.
The Mistress Addresses the Wife.   Replansky.
Mohammed Ibrahim Speaks. Beidler.
A Mood Apart.   Frost.
The Moon Is Distant from the Sea.   Dickinson.
Moon-Witches.   Hughes.
"More Light! More Light!" Hecht.
Multitudes Turn in Darkness. Aiken.
My Darling Dear, My Daisy Flower.   Skelton.
My Grandmother and the Voice of Tolstoy.   Orlen.
My Love Is Playing... Anonymous.
My Love, Oh, She Is My Love.   Anonymous.
My Picture Left in Scotland. Jonson.
My Star.   Plato.
My Sweet Gazelle!   Di Roma.
My sweet old etcetera. Cummings.
Narcissus.   Press.
A Natural History of Dragons and Unicorns My Daughter and I Have Known.   Root.
The New House.   Rutsala.
Night Flight.   Johnson.
A Nisei Picnic.   Mura.
No One Talks about This. Rakosi.
Not from This Anger. Thomas.
Nothing to Save.   Lawrence.
Now.   Browning.
Now Is Farewell.   Salkeld.
Nystagmus.   Matuzak.
O Night Flower.   Barbeitos.
O Sweet Delight.   Campion.
Ode–Imitated from the Psalms.   Gilbert.
Of Pick-Pockets.   Gay.
Old Crabbed Men.   Reeves.
The Old Cumberland Beggar. Wordsworth.
The Old Flagman. Sandburg.
The Old Men.   Javitz.
An Old Song Ended. Rossetti.
On a Piece of Unwrought Pipeclay.   Bryant.
On a Portrait by Copley. Freeman.
On a Squinting Poetess. Moore.
On a Vase of Gold-Fish. Tennyson.
On Falling.   Greig.
On Mites, To a Lady.   Duck.
On the Thirteenth Day of Christmas.   Causley.
On the Threshold.   Kraus.

One Eyed Black Man in Nebraska.   Cornish.
One Man Down.   Anthony ("Ai").
Orinda to Lucasia.   Philips.
Orpheus to Beasts.   Lovelace.
Orphic Interior.   Sinisgalli.
Our Lady of Mercy. Bertrand.
Out of Catullus.   Crashaw.
The Outer from the Inner. Dickinson.
The Painter Dreaming in the Scholar's House. Nemerov.
A Pair of Fireflies.   Liu.
The Paisley Officer. Anonymous.
Parade's End.   Guest.
Paradise Lost.   Milton.
Paradox.   Miller.
Passing It On.   Saner.
Past Love.   Keiter.
Patience of a People.   Bryant, Jr.,
The Patient: Rockland County Sanitarium.   Hernton.
The Pear-Tree.   Gilmore.
Pearl Perch.   Blight.
Pearly Beads.   Anonymous.
The Perfect Garden. Robertson.
Peripatetic.   Lima.
Petition.   Drinkwater.
Phantasus.   Holz.
A Philosopher.   Foss.
Pigeon.   Fuller.
The Pilots.   Levertov.
The Pitcher.   Yuan Chen.
...Plashes the Fountain. Celan.
Poem: "As rock to sun or storm."   Sheridan.
Poem for Epiphany. Nicholson.
Poem for My Father.   West.
The Poem in the Park. Davison.
Poem: "you can look into my face."   Todachine.
Poems, XCIII: "Mother, I cannot mind my wheel." Landor.
A Poet at Twenty.   Hall.
The Point.   Soto.
Polyolbion.   Drayton.
Pondy Woods.   Warren.
The Portrait.   Lytton.
Potatoes.   Donnell.
The Power of Interval.   De Tabley.
A Prayer.   Douglas.
Prayer.   Marr.
The Predicter of Famine. Williams.
The Presence.   Naone.
Pretty Mary.   Anonymous.
Prince Lucifer: Mother-Song. Austin.
Princess Elizabeth of Bohemia, as Perdita. O'Hara.
The Progress of Poesy. Gray.
Prophecy on Lethe.   Kunitz.
Psalm.   Yehoash.
A Psalm to the Son. Wilkinson.
Punch and Judy. Anonymous.
Quarrelling, or Let Dogs Delight.   Watts.

The Quartette. De La Mare.
Rapture. Carlson.
Ravenna. MacNeice.
Ravished by all that to the
  eyes is fair. Michelangelo.
The Recovery. Blunden.
The Reflection. Taylor.
Reflections on the Death of a
  Parrot. Jacinto.
Religion. Heine.
The Reminder. Adams.
Remnant Ghosts at Dawn.
  La Grone.
Renewal. Kowit.
Reproach. Firdausi.
Resignation–To Faustus.
  Clough.
A Responsory, 1948.
  Merton.
The Return. Aiken.
The Revelation. Williams.
Rio Grande de Loiza.
  Burgos.
Rise, Lady Mistress, Rise!
  Field.
The Road along the Thumb
  and Forefinger. Hickey.
Round. Boimwall.
Running Blind. Jones.
Saints, and Their Care. Rios.
Samson to His Delilah.
  Crashaw.
The Sanctuary. Hueffer.
Santa Claus. Moraes.
Sappho. Catullus.
Sea Town. Frost.
The Seasons. Thomson.
Secretary. Hughes.
Seeing Oloalok. Bowering.
Seen from the Train. Day
  Lewis.
Self-Portrait. Pack.
Self-Portrait. Thomas.
September 30. Lourie.
September Midnight.
  Teasdale.
The Serenity in Stones.
  Ortiz.
The Serving Girl. Hayford.
The Seventh Hell...
  Rothenberg.
A Shadow Boat. Bates.
Shadow-Love. Heine.
The Shadowgraphs.
  Lattimore.
The Shadows. Sherman.
She Is Not for Me.
  Anonymous.
Ship from Thames.
  Ingamells.
The Silent Woman:
  Clerimont's Song. Jonson.
Sleep. Imbs.
Sleeping Beauty. Sheck.
Snake Hunt. Wagoner.
A Snapshot for Miss Bricka
  Who Lost in the Semifinal
  Round... Wallace.
Soft White. Harwood.
Some Refrains at the Charles
  River. Viereck.
Song: "Delicious beauty, that
  doth lie." Marston.
Song for a Cracked Voice.
  Irwin.
Song for Tomorrow. Trent.
Song: "Going down the old
  way." Widdemer.
Song: "How do I love you?"
  McLeod.
Song: "I placed my dream in
  a boat." Meireles.

Song in the Same Play, by the
  Wavering Nymph. Behn.
Song: "Like violets pale i' the
  spring o' the year."
  Thomson.
A Song of Honor. Hodgson.
Song: "Singer within the little
  streets." Gibbon.
Song: To the Masquers
  Representing Stars.
  Campion.
Song: "Where did you borrow
  that last sigh." Berkeley.
Sonnet. Duncan.
Sonnet XI: "O eyes clear with
  beauty, O tender gaze."
  Labe.
Sonnet, XXIV: "Don't scold
  me, Ladies, if I have loved."
  Labé.
Sonnet LXXI. Alabaster.
Sonnet: "How that vast
  heaven intitled First is
  rolled." Drummond.
Sonnet: "Lock up, fair lids,
  the treasure of my heart."
  Sidney.
Sonnet: "So shoots a star as
  doth my mistress glide."
  Davies.
Sonnet: "Sweet poets of the
  gentle antique line."
  Reynolds.
Sonnet: To Dante Alighieri
  (He Reports in a Feigned
  Vision). Cavalcanti.
Sonnets, XVIII: "Shall I
  compare thee to a summer's
  day?" Shakespeare.
Sonnets, XXIII: "As an
  unperfect actor on the
  stage." Shakespeare.
Sonnets, XLVII: "Betwixt
  mine eye and heart a league
  is took." Shakespeare.
Sonnets, CVI: "When in the
  chronicle of wasted time."
  Shakespeare.
Sonnets, CXIII: "Since I left
  you, mine eye is in my
  mind." Shakespeare.
Sonnets for a Dying Man.
  Singer.
Sonnets from the Portuguese,
  XLIV. Browning.
Sonnets to Philomel. Davies.
The Southern Cross.
  Hawker.
Sparrow in an Airport.
  Snyder.
Speak to the Sun. Wilson.
The Speaker. Ballard.
Spinning in April. Peabody.
The Spoils of War. Watkins.
The Spring. Carew.
The Star Watcher. Davison.
Stella. Crandall.
A Story in the Snow.
  Crouch.
The Stranger. Rich.
The Strangers. Very.
Struck Was I, Nor Yet by
  Lightning. Dickinson.
Stylite. MacNeice.
Submission. Herbert.
Such Soft Ideas All My Pains
  Beguile. Montagu.
A Suite of Six Pieces for
  Siskind. Logan.
Suite to Fathers. Harrison.
Summer Storm. Untermeyer.
Supplication. Untermeyer.

Talking in Their Sleep.
  Thomas.
Tarry Ye. *Anonymous.*
Teresina's Face. Widdemer.
That Day. Leax.
They Go By, Go By, Love,
  the Days and the Hours.
  Jesus.
This Child. Rosten.
Thisbe. Cone.
Thoughts on the
  Commandments. Baker.
The Thousand and One
  Nights: Drinking Song.
  Anonymous.
The Three Ravens.
  Anonymous.
Thrice Toss These Oaken
  Ashes in the Air.
  Campion.
Through a Shop Window.
  Farjeon.
Thus Saith My Chloris Bright.
  Guarini.
Time Reminded Me. Uceda.
To–. Morse.
To a Very Young Lady.
  Etherege.
To a Young Girl. Yeats.
To Adhiambo. Okara.
To Beauty. Baudelaire.
To Flood Stage Again.
  Wright.
To His Wife. Skelton.
To K.M. De La Mare.
To Morfydd. Johnson.
To My Daughter. Spender.
To My Mother. Rosenberg.
To My Soul. Fletcher.
To Night. *Anonymous.*
To the Man Who Sidled Up
  to Me and Asked: "How
  Long You in fer, Buddy?"
  Knight.
The Tombe. Stanley.
Transience. Naidu.
A Translation from Petrarch.
  Synge.
A Trucker. Gunn.
The Truth the Dead Know.
  Sexton.
The Turning of the Leaves.
  Watkins.
Two Variations. Levertov.
Twoborn. Rokwaho.
Under the Blue. Browne.
The Unfading Beauty.
  Carew.
The Unknown God. Russell.
The Unknown Soldier.
  Lewis.
Up Rising. Duncan.
The Vacant Cage. Turner.
Vagabonds. "Marie.
Vanitas Vanitatum.
  Zangwill.
Verse Written in the Album
  of Mademoiselle–.
  Dalcour.
Vision. Sidgwick.
Visions. Petrarch.
Vowels. Rimbaud.
The Wandering Jew.
  Robinson.
The War of the Secret Agents.
  Coulette.
We All Have a Bench in the
  Park to Reach. Jonas.
We Become New. Piercy.
Weekend Sonnets. McQueen.
Weeping Willow. Aldridge.
Wet or Fine. Hare.

When I Set out for Lyonnesse.
  Hardy.
Where Do the Gipsies Come
  From? Bashford.
Where the Picnic Was.
  Hardy.
While Someone Telephones.
  Bishop.
Who Are My People?
  Marinoni.
Who Loves the Rain. Shaw.
Why? De La Mare.
Wife of Kohelet. Cohen.
A Wife Talks to Herself.
  Berg.
The Wind Like an Ocean.
  Eigner.
The Window. Creeley.
Window to the East. Evans.
Winter Song. Macdonald.
Winter Swan. Bogan.
The Witches' Wood.
  Coleridge.
With Lilacs in My Eye.
  Coleman.
Witnesses. Merwin.
Woman. *Anonymous.*
A Woman's Pride. Hay.
Written at Mr. Pope's House
  at Twickenham. Lyttelton.
Yes. Blackmore.
The Yoke of Tyranny.
  Sidney.
You're a Grand Old Flag.
  Cohan.
You Refuse to Own.
  Atwood.
The Young Woman of Beare.
  Clarke.
Your Eyes. Chantikian.
Your Eyes Have Their
  Silence. Barrax.
Zone of Death. Everson.
A Zong. Barnes.

Eyebrows
Helen Was Just Slipped into
  Bed. Prior.
Ibby Damsel. *Anonymous.*
Our Polite Parents. Wells.
Poem to the Tune of "Yi
  Chian Mei." Li Ching-
  chao.
The Toilette. Chu Ching-Yu.

Eyelash
I don't have the energy...
  Gold.
Preludes to Definition: Time
  in the Rock (excerpt).
  Aiken.

Eyelid (s)
Alone. Akhmatova.
Autumn. Levine.
Country Music. Plato.
The Death of the Moon.
  Wagoner.
Hats. Dillard.
Love and Sleep. Swinburne.
Metamorphoses. Ovid
  (Publius Ovidius Naso).
Mona Lisa. Pater.
Ode to the Moon. Hood.
On a Blind Girl. Baha Ad-
  din Zuhayr.
The Sibyl. LaBombard.
Sierra. Storni.
Singing in the Dark.
  Wassall.
Southwest Passage. Fitts.
To a Linnet in a Cage.
  Ledwidge.

Eyesight
The Chameleon. Merrick.

The Heavenly Foreigner.
Devlin.
Lost Objects.　O Hehir.

F

Fable (s)
Another Easter.　Ridland.
Elegy.　Hillyer.
Eyes.　Davies.
Fable.　Mills.
Fabulary Satire, IV.　Hine.
Paradise Lost.　Milton.
When I Came from Colchis.
Merwin.
Winter Tryst.　Van Doren.
Fabric
The Descent of Odin.　Gray.
Life and the Weaver.　Dewar.
That Day.　Kherdian.
Fabulous
Blind Man.　Hamburger.
For the Nightly Ascent of the
Hunter Orion over a Forest
Clearing.　Dickey.
Facade
Allegory in Black.　Clark.
This Year, Before It Ends.
Langley.
Face (s)
The Accusation.　Wright.
Addressed to a Young Lady.
Cowper.
After.　Browning.
After Elegies.　Valentine.
After Lorca.　Hughes.
Afternoon 3.　Kuroda.
Against the Court of Rome.
Petrarch (Francesco
Petrarca).
Against Women.　Juvenal
(Decimas Junius Juvenalis).
Ago.　Jennings.
All Nature Has a Voice to
Tell.　Lawson.
Amend Me.　Anonymous.
The Anatomy of Happiness.
Nash.
And in Her Morning.
Powers.
And the Seventh Dream in
the Dream of Isis.
Gascoyne.
Anecdote of the Sparrow.
Pack.
Animal Songs: Baboon 2.
Anonymous.
The Animals in That Country.
Atwood.
Another November.　Plumly.
Approaching Washington
Heights.　Reiss.
The Assumption.　Brunini.
At Daybreak.　Sassoon.
At Eighty.　Stanhope.
At Grandfather's.　Bates.
At Quebec.　Blewett.
Autochthon.　Roberts.
Autumn.　Hulme.
Autumn Evening.　Anthony.
Baboon.　Anonymous.
Back Road.　Guernsey.
The Ballad of East and West.
Kipling.
Banishment from Ur.
Enheduanna.
Begging on North Main.
Stuart.

Being Her Friend.　Masefield.
Between the World and Me.
Wright.
Black People!　Jones.
The Black Virgin.
Chesterton.
Blest Be the Wondrous Grace.
Cheever.
Blind Louise.　Dewet.
Breaking.　Allan.
Breath of Hampstead Heath.
Thomas.
Breathe on the Glass.
Stineford.
Brothers Together in Winter.
Elliott.
Bushed.　Lillard.
Calamity Jane Greets Her
Dreams.　Lignell.
Cape Coast Castle Revisited.
Hall-Evans.
Cease, Then, My Tongue!
Spenser.
The Cello.　Gilder.
Challenge.　Hazo.
Chameleon.　LeClaire.
A Charm for Love and
Lasting Affection.
Anonymous.
The Chorus Speaks Her
Words as She Dances.
Gregg.
Christ and the Pagan.　Tabb.
Christ the Carpenter.
Haskin.
City Jail.　Maloney.
A Clear Shell.　Bellerby.
The Cloud.　Muir.
Cloud River.　Wright.
The Cobbler.　Chaffee.
Cold Glow: Icehouses.
Wojahn.
Colors.　Yevtushenko.
Common Sense.　Fields
Comrades.　Housman.
Conceits.　Bates.
A Conjecture.　Richardson.
Conrad in Twilight.
Ransom.
Conversation.　Berryman.
Cotton-eyed Joe.
Anonymous.
The Crack.　Goldman.
Cradle Song.　Durrell.
Crazy Arithmetic.
Thompson.
The Cross-Eyed Lover.
Finkel.
A Dark Hand.　Manger.
Day after Day.　Tagore.
A Dead March.　Monkhouse.
Dear Female Heart.　Smith.
Death.　Williams.
The Death of the Old Year.
Tennyson.
Death Was a Woman.
Russell.
A Deep-Sworn Vow.　Yeats.
A Disagreeable Feature.
Robinson.
A Divine Image.　Blake.
Do They Whisper behind My
Back?　Schwartz.
Dogs.　Griffin.
Dolor.　Roethke.
Don Juan.　Byron.
Dragging the Main.　Ray.
The Dragonfly.　Chisoku.
Dream.　Dixon.
The Dream of Aengus Og.
Cox.

Dreams in War Time
(excerpt).　Lowell.
A Drum for Ben Boyd.
Webb.
Earth Changes.　Shire.
Elegy: "Child, your white face
is chanting memories."
Woestijne.
The Elusive Maid.　Ibn
Chasdai.
Epigram: "All praise your
face, your verses none
abuse."　Walpole.
Eros.　Bridges.
Esperanza.　Scully.
Essay on Rime (excerpt).
Shapiro.
Evasion.　Salkeld.
Every Night When the Sun
Goes In.　Anonymous.
Everything Passes and
Vanishes.　Allingham.
Evidence at the Witch Trials.
Baxter.
Exits and Entrances.
Madgett.
Fable.　Opperman.
Faces.　Ciardi.
The Faded Face.　Hardy.
A Fancy.　Anonymous.
Fate.　Block.
Father and Son.　Higgins.
Father and Son.　Kunitz.
Father and Sons.　Shapiro.
The Fathers.　Saltman.
Felicity.　Watts.
Femina.　Marlatt.
Feri's Dream.　Cornford.
Finally.　Pompili.
The Fired Pot.　Wickham.
Fish Crier.　Sandburg.
For a Friend.　Lifshin.
For a Pessimist.　Cullen.
For Allen Ginsberg, Who Cut
Off His Beard.　Pinsker.
For Communion with God
(excerpt).　Shepherd.
For Doreen.　Davie.
Fortune.　Madge.
Fragments.　Praxilla.
Freshmen.　Spacks.
Fury's Field.　Bodker.
The Future.　Tekeyan.
The Gauls Sacrifice.
Doughty.
The General's Death.
O'Connor.
Getting down to Get over.
Jordan.
Gipsy Queen.　Chapman.
Girl of the Lovely Glance.
Praxilla.
Give Me the Splendid Silent
Sun.　Whitman
Glanmore Sonnets.　Heaney.
Good Friday, 1613. Riding
Westward.　Donne.
Good Friday: The Madman's
Song.　Masefield.
He Knows the Way.
Anonymous.
He Would Have His Lady
Sing.　Dolben.
Heaven.　Dolben.
Her Courage.　Yeats.
Hero and Leander.　Marlowe.
High Flight.　Magee, Jr.
His Are the Thousand
Sparkling Rills.
Alexander.
Homage.　Kahn.
Horrible Things.　Fuller.

Houses Burning: Quebec.
Anderson.
A Hunt in the Black Forest.
Jarrell.
Hunting for Blueberries.
James.
The Hydra of Birds.
Engonopoulos.
The Hymn of Saint Thomas
in Adoration of the Blessed
Sacrament.　Crashaw.
I Shall Be Satisfied.　Behemb.
I Sit and Wait for Beauty.
Cowdery.
If Fathers Knew But How to
Leave.　Anonymous.
If It Be True.　Johnson.
Ike Walton's Prayer.　Riley.
The Iliad.　Homer.
Impenitentia Ultima.
Dowson.
In Front of the Seine,
Recalling the Rio De La
Plata.　Ocampo.
In Memoriam, A.C.M.L.
(excerpt).　Spring-Rice.
In Memory.　Pollitt.
In the Night.　Roberts.
In the Restaurant.　Hardy.
In the Rude Age.　Surrey.
In Time.　Raine.
Inconsistencies.　Roberts.
The Invention of New Jersey.
Anderson.
Invocation.　Walsh.
It May Not Always Be So.
Cummings.
It's in Your Face.
Anonymous.
Jacob and the Angel.
Brother Antoninus.
Japanese Girl with Red Table.
Dobyns.
A Japanese Love-Song.
Noyes.
Johnny, I Hardly Knew Ye:
Swinburnese (parody).
Tyrrell.
A Joyful Noise.　Finkel.
Judgment Day.　Howells.
Juliana.　Cynewulf.
Katherine's Dream.　Lowell.
The King in His Beauty.
Deck.
Kivers.　Cobb.
The Lamb.　Wilson.
The Lamentation of the Old
Pensioner.　Yeats.
The Last Chrysanthemum.
Hardy.
The Last Good-By.
Moulton.
Last Meeting.　Harwood.
The Last of His Tribe.
Kendall.
Late at Night during a Visit
of Friends.　Bly.
Laura.　Tofte.
Leave Train.　Ross.
Leaving Forever.　Levertov.
A Legend of Alhambra.
Trench.
Lesson for Dreamers.
Janeczko.
Letter from the Vieux Carre.
Russell.
Letter to Frances.　Kistler.
Like a Pearl Dropped.
Stickney.
Limerick: "No matter how
grouchy you're feeling."
Euwer.

Limerick: "There was a young lady of Riga." *Anonymous.*
The Little Angels. Jacopone da Todi.
Little Cosmic Dust Poem. Haines.
Little Gray Songs from St. Joseph's, XXX. Norton.
Look for Me on England. Mallalieu.
Look, I Have Thrown All Right. MacKay.
The Looking Glass. Shirley.
The Lost Tribe. Finch.
Love's Change. Aldrich.
Love's Matrimony. Newcastle.
The Lover. Duncan.
Lying on a Bridge. Brock.
The Madonna's Lamp. Wilhelm.
Madrigal: "Lais now old." Gibbons.
A Maiden and Her Hair. Davies.
Mammy Hums. Sandburg.
The Man in That Airplane. Williams.
A Marriage Prospect. Mallock.
Martha Graham. Lifshin.
Martyr. Fullerton.
A Message. Phelps.
The Messenger. Gunn.
Minotaur Poems. Mandel.
Moon Compasses. Frost.
Moon Mattress. Di Prima.
Moonlight Night on the Port. Keyes.
The Morning Bright, with Rosy Light. Summers.
Morning on the Shore. Campbell.
Mother Wept. Skipsey.
The Mountain Heart's-Ease. Harte.
My Garden. Davies.
My Mirror. Kilmer.
The Mystery. Hodgson.
Nancy Hanks, Mother of Abraham Lincoln. Lindsay.
The Natural History of Pliny. McHugh.
Negro Servant. Hughes.
The Negro Singer. Corrothers.
Nell Gwynne's Looking-Glass. Blanchard.
New Day. Madgett.
The Newcomer's Wife. Hardy.
The News Stand. Berrigan.
Night Catch. McHugh.
The Night Sits in This Chair. Notley.
Not One Is Turned away from God. Stroud.
Notes on a Girl. Dufault.
Now, before Shaving. Kramer.
Nursery Rules from Nannies. *Anonymous.*
O God, I Cried, No Dark Disguise. Millay.
O Gracious Jesus, Blessed Lord! Fowler.
The Obscene Caller. Fein.
The Old Biograph Girl. Benbow.

The Old Familiar Faces. Lamb.
Old Houses. D'Lettuso.
Old Iron. Stewart.
The Old Jockey. Higgins.
The Old Pensioner. Yeats.
On a Painted Woman. Shelley.
On a Portrait by Copley. Freeman.
On a Puritan. Belloc.
On Forelands High in Heaven. Housman.
On His Mistress Looking in a Glass. Carew.
On the House of a Friend. Logan.
On the Photograph of a Man I Never Saw. Plutzik.
On the Thirteenth Day of Christmas. Causley.
One-Night Expensive Hotel. Everson.
One Year Later. Torgerson.
Our Presidents. *Anonymous.*
Outside. Lorde.
Overheard in the Louvre. Kennedy.
Parting is Hard. *Anonymous.*
Passing the Masonic Home for the Aged. Scott.
Pastel: Masks and Faces. Symons.
Peace by Night. Mary Madeleva.
The Photographer's Wife. Beeler.
Photographic Plate, Partly Spidered, Hampton Roads, Virginia... Smith.
Piano. Russ.
Pictures at an Exhibition. Rosenbaum.
The Pilgrim from the East. Kahn.
The Pillory. Vivien.
Pleasures. Goldbarth.
Poem: "High on a ridge of tiles." Craig.
Poem: "The walls of the maelstrom are painted with trees." Madge.
Poems from a First Year in Boston. Starbuck.
The Pond. Davies.
The Poor. Strahan.
The Praise of Dust. Chesterton.
Pray On! *Anonymous.*
Prayer to the Father in Heaven. Skelton.
The Premonition. Roethke.
The Presence. Everson.
Press Onward. *Anonymous.*
The Priest Rediscovers His Psalm-Book. *Anonymous.*
Psalm LXXXVIII. Surrey.
Pyramus and Thisbe. Dakin.
Rabbits. Baruch.
Rain, Rain, Go to Spain. *Anonymous.*
Raphael's San Sisto Madonna. Miles.
A Reason. Creeley.
Recrimination. Wilcox.
Resuscitation Team. Fanthorpe.
The Return. Tu Fu.
Ring around the World. Wynne.
The River of Heaven. *Anonymous.*

The Road. Aiken.
La Rue de la Montagne Sainte-Genevieve. Dudley.
Sacred Family (excerpt). Stein.
The Sacred Order. Sarton.
Saddle and Cell. Marias.
Saint Thomas Aquinas. Jones.
Salmon. Graham.
The Sanctuary. Hueffer.
Sandhill People. Sandburg.
Sargent's Portrait of Edwin Booth at "The Players". Aldrich.
Saturday Afternoon at the Movies. Logan.
Say Not That Beauty. Flower.
Seal of Fire. Temkin.
A Second Birthday. Kayper-Mensah.
Self-Portrait. Volborth.
Seventh Eclogue. Radnoti.
Shadows. *Anonymous.*
The Shedpherd's Week. Gay.
Skiers. Warren.
The Snowbound City. Haines.
So Runs Our Song. Kitchel.
So Well I Love Thee, as Without Thee I. Drayton.
Soldiers. Bodenheim.
Song: "Dorinda's sparkling wit, and eyes." Sackville.
Song for a New Generation. Lutz.
A Song in the Front Yard. Brooks.
Sonnets. Hillyer.
Sonnets to Aurelia. Nichols.
A Soul. Rossetti.
Spain, 1809. Lucas.
Speak. Wright.
The Spectre Is on the Move. Allana.
The Spoils of War. Watkins.
St. John the Baptist. O'Shaughnessy.
Standardization. Hope.
Statues. Yeats.
The Statute of Liberty. Field.
Stoic. Durrell.
The Story of the Baby Squirrel. Aldis.
The Strand. MacNeice.
Strange Hells. Gurney.
Sulky Sue. *Anonymous.*
Sunday Night in Santa Rosa. Gioia.
Sure You Can Ask Me a Personal Question. Burns.
Susan. Magowan.
Symbols. Thompson.
The Tennis Court Oath. Ashbery.
Theme Brown Girl. Hill-Abu Ishak.
They Are Killing All the Young Men. Henderson.
They dropped like flakes. Dickinson.
They Say, in Other Days. Gray.
They Say She Is Veiled. Grahn.
Third Enemy Speaks. Day Lewis.
The Third Light. Longley.
Those Who Love. Teasdale.

Through the Blowing Leaves. Dresbach.
Thy Glorious Face Above. Wesley.
Tim, the Fairy. Livesay.
To--. Nichols.
To a Republican Friend. Arnold.
To a Young Lady. Cowper.
To an Artist. Burns.
To Imagination. Thomas.
To Jessie's Dancing Feet. Ellwanger.
To My Brothers. Keats.
To My Daughter. Plutzik.
To My Father Norman Alone in the Blue Mountains. Lindsay.
To My Little Son. Davis.
To the Choice Bridegroom. Halevi
To the Portrait of "A Gentleman." Holmes.
To--, with an Ivory Hand-Glass. Douglas.
The Toadstool Wood. Reeves.
Tonight the City. Cook.
Too Young for Love. Horace.
Toward Myself. Goldberg.
Travelling Song. McGrath.
The Trumpet: Grass on the Cliff. Jeffers.
Try Smiling. *Anonymous.*
The Tumble. Taylor.
The Two Little Miss Lloyds. Turner.
Two X "16 heures l'Etoile." Cummings.
Ultimatum. Church.
Unseen. Crosby.
Unusual. Eigner.
A Valentine for a Lady. Lucilius [(or Lucillius)].
Verses Made the Night before He Died. Drayton.
View from Heights. Ficke.
A Vision. Dearmer.
The Vision of St. Bernard. Hess.
Walking with Lulu in the Wood. Lazard.
Wanting a Child. Graham.
A Warning to Conquerors. MacDonagh.
Was a Man. Booth.
The Watch. Swenson.
The Way a Ghost Dissolves. Hugo.
We Reason of These Things. Stevens.
When the Green Lies over the Earth. Grimke.
When Two Suns Do Appear. Sidney.
When You Are Old. Yeats.
A Wife--at Daybreak I Shall Be. Dickinson.
Wildflower. Plumly.
William Wordsworth. Keyes.
The Wind at Your Door. FitzGerald.
Windfall. Arsenault.
Wondrous Son of God. Goertz.
The World's Miser. Maynard.
The Years. Wheelock.
Yellow Dusk: Messenger Fails to Appear. *Anonymous.*
You're. Plath.

Zealot Without a Face.
Dobzynski.

Fact (s)
3 for 25. Smith.
Because in This Sorrowing
Statue of Flesh. Patchen.
A Dying Tiger—Moaned for
Drink. Dickinson.
The Floating Candles. Lea.
For an Old Friend. Krapf.
Gemwood. Bell.
History: Madness. Rice.
The Invisible Man.
Matthews.
The Kiwi Bird in the Kiwi
Tree. Bernstein.
Not to Forget Miss
Dickinson. Schacht.
The Only Way to Have a
Friend. *Anonymous.*
The Past. Emerson.
Saturday Afternoon at the
Movies. Logan.
Sonnet XI. Greeff.

Factor (ies) (y)
1937 Ford Convertible.
McKeown.
The Chilean Elegies: 5. The
Interior. Wayman.
City Life. Lawrence.
The Eyes Have It. Stephens.
The Factory Hands.
Chimedza.
Thaw in the City. Lipsitz.
The Weather Factory.
Turner.
Why the Soup Tastes Like the
Daily News. Piercy.
Women Called Bossy
Cowboys. Jankola.

Fade away
December. Clare.
The Fancy. Benet.
Grandfather. Barnstone.
The Homecoming of Emma
Lazarus. Kinnell.
Hos Ego Versiculos.
Quarles.
Noon's Dream-Song. Lee-
Hamilton.
The Nutcrackers and the
Sugar-Tongs. Lear.
Old Soldiers Never Die.
Anonymous.
Sob, Heavy World. Auden.
Sonnet: "There, on the
darkened deathbed, dies the
brain." Masefield.
The Spirit of the Wheat.
Valentine.
Waillie, Waillie! (with music).
Anonymous.

Fade (d) (s)
After the Winter. McKay.
And on This Shore.
Holman.
Clair de Lune. Symons.
Do Come Back Again.
Anonymous.
Elena's Song. Taylor.
Fable XLV: The Poet and the
Rose. Gay.
Fading Beauty. *Anonymous.*
Fleur de Lys. Heppenstall.
Gabriel. Wattles.
Glenkindie. Scott.
Hand. Roditi.
Hymn of Unity. *Anonymous.*
Inscription on the Flyleaf of a
Bible. Abse.
The Life of Man. Barnes.
The Long Night. Smith.

Longing for the Emperor.
Iwa no Hime.
Looking Back (excerpt).
Vaughan.
Midsummer. Wilcox.
Molly of the North Country.
Anonymous.
Month of January.
Armstrong.
Movie-Going. Hollander.
The Night Journey. Brooke.
The Rejected Lover.
Anonymous.
A Rose Will Fade. Shorter.
Shot? So Quick, So Clean an
Ending? Housman.
Sonnets, LIV: "O, how much
more doth beauty beauteous
seem." Shakespeare.
To A. L. Carew.
Upon a Gloomy Night.
Campbell.
With Rue My Heart Is Laden.
Housman.
With Rue My Heart Is Laden
(parody). Hoffenstein.

Fading
The Dark Hills. Robinson.
Dreams. Daley.
Falling Asleep. Sassoon.
Homage of War.
Williamson.
Most Quietly at Times.
Flaischlen.
Requiem. Matheus.
Without Me You Won't Be
Able to See Yourself.
Grade.

Faggot (s)
Evidence at the Witch Trials.
Baxter.
A Poem for Black Hearts.
Jones.
The Woman. Lima.

Fail (ed) (ing) (s)
Alexander. Morgan.
All the Way from There to
Here. Gilbert.
The Balcony Poems. Smith.
The Ballad of the White
Horse. Chesterton.
Bos'n Hill. Albee.
Deception. Corn.
Dingman's Marsh. Moore.
Disarmament (excerpt).
Whittier.
Dugall Quin (B version).
Anonymous.
Enamored Architect of Airy
Rhyme. Aldrich.
An Epitaph. Ellis.
Essex Regiment March.
Woodberry.
For Sheridan. Lowell.
Forms of the Earth at
Abiquiu. Momaday.
G.M.B. Davie.
He Leads Us Still.
Guiterman.
The Hills. Braley.
I Have a Rendezvous with
Death. Seeger.
I never hear the word
"escape'. Dickinson.
The Imperfect Artist.
Hamilton.
In Spain. Wyatt.
Infinity. Savage.
Invocation for the New Year.
Armstrong.
It's up Glenbarchan's Braes I
Gaed. Scott.

Journal. Ciardi.
Lilies of the Valley.
Gardner.
Madrigal: "Come, sable
night." Ward.
Momus. Robinson.
Most Like an Arch This
Marriage. Ciardi.
The Open Door. Coolidge.
The Penance. Tate.
Postscript to a Pettiness.
Tessimond.
Prayer. Richardson.
Quiet Work. Arnold.
A Seaman's Confession of
Faith. Kemp.
The Silly Fool. Auden.
Tell Him So. *Anonymous.*
To a Lady Troubled by
Insomnia. Adams.
V-Letter. Shapiro.
What Five Books Would You
Pick To Be Marooned
with... Leary.
The Wind Blows.
MacDonagh.

Failure (s)
Because He Lives. Lathrop.
Epigram: Invocation.
Nemerov.
For an Autograph (excerpt).
Lowell.
How We Built a Church at
Ashcroft. Leahy.
I Substitute for the Dead
Lecturer. Jones.
Letter to Reed from Lolo.
Hugo.
The Moral. Weiss.
On Don Juan del Norte, Not
Don Juan Tenorio del Sur.
Dugan.
Rock and Hawk. Jeffers.
A Violinist. Bourdillon.

Faint (ed) (ing) (s)
After he stripped off my
clothes. Vallana.
The Consolation of
Philosophy. Boethius.
Evening Primrose. Clare.
Fragment of Sappho.
Philips.
Infinity. Savage.
A Leap for Life. Colton.
Madrigal: "Come, sable
night." Ward.
Night up There. Valentine.
O Earnest Be. *Anonymous.*
Ode to Memory. Tennyson.
On the Rising Generation.
Dietz.
Prayer. Flecker.
The Primrose. Herrick.
Slow Movement. Williams.
A Soliloquy of One of the
Spies Left in the
Wilderness. Hopkins.
A Song of Arno. Channing-
Stetson.
Times Gettin' Hard, Boys
(with music). *Anonymous.*
Two Poems on the Catholic
Bavarians. Bowers.
What Rider Spurs Him from
the Darkening East?
Millay.

Fair (er) (est)
Advice to My Best Brother,
Colonel Francis Lovelace.
Lovelace.
Agnes. Lyte.
Air an' Light. Barnes.

Alexander's Feast or, the
Power of Music. Dryden.
Amanda's Complaint.
Freneau.
Amoretti, XV. Spenser.
Amoretti, XLI. Spenser.
Amoretti, LXXXIV.
Spenser.
The Assumption. Brunini.
Astrophel and Stella, XXI.
Sidney.
Astrophel and Stella, XXXIII.
Sidney.
Astrophel and Stella, XLI.
Sidney.
August 1914. Rosenberg.
Ballade of My Lady's Beauty.
Kilmer.
The Barrier. McKay.
Be Not Proud of Your Sweet
Body. *Anonymous.*
The Beauty of Job's
Daughters. Macpherson.
The Bishop Orders His Tomb
at Saint Praxed's Church.
Browning.
Du Bist Wie Eine Blume.
Heine.
Blind-Man's Buff. Blake.
Caelica, VIII. Greville.
Caelica, XLII. Greville.
The Canterbury Tales: The
Knight's Tale. Chaucer.
Carmina. Catullus.
Celestial Love.
Michelangelo.
Chanson of the Bells of
Oseney. Rice.
The Comparison. Carew.
Complaint That His Ladie
after She Knew of His Love
Kept Her Face... Surrey.
A Compliment to the Ladies
(parody). Blake.
Consequences. Meredith.
The Country Justice.
Langhorne.
Dagonet's Canzonet. Rhys.
Dear If I with Guile.
Campion.
A Deposition from Beauty.
Stanley.
The Downright Country-Man;
or, The Faithful Dairy
Maid. *Anonymous.*
A Dream. Keats.
Dreaming of Cities Dead.
Cox.
Earl Brand (Sweet William).
Anonymous. 03] The
Cornet.
Epigram: "Most inexplicable
the wiles of boys I deem."
Rhianus.
Fair and Unfair. Francis.
The Fair Maid by the Shore.
Anonymous.
The Fairest Flower.
Audelay.
False Linfinn. *Anonymous.*
The Frolicsome Parson
Outwitted. *Anonymous.*
Gee up, Neddy, to the Fair.
Anonymous.
Give Beauty All Her Right.
Campion.
Go, ill-sped book. Berryman.
The Hairdresser's Art.
Claudian.
Hark, All Ye Lovely Saints.
Anonymous.

Hexametra Alexis in Laudem
  Rosamundi. Greene.
Hope and Despair.
  Abercrombie.
I'd Be a Butterfly. Bayly.
"I never saw you, madam, lay
  apart." Surrey.
Icarus. *Anonymous.*
The Incomprehensible.
  Watts.
The Incurables. Upson.
The Individualist Speaks.
  MacNeice.
Jill Came from the Fair.
  Farjeon.
Labor. *Anonymous.*
Lady Diamond. *Anonymous.*
The Lay of the Last Minstrel.
  Scott.
Let Not One Sparke of Filthy
  Lustfull Fyre. Spenser.
The Looking Glass. Shirley.
Lord Banner. *Anonymous.*
Love. Stevenson.
Love Is a Secret Feeding Fire.
  Anonymous.
The Lover's Choice.
  Bedingfield.
Madrigal: "Some there are as
  fair to see to." Davison.
March Hares. De la Mare.
Mary's a Grand Old Name.
  Cohan.
May Poems. *Anonymous.*
Medieval Norman Songs.
  Anonymous.
Meet Me in St. Louis.
  Sterling.
Mezzo Cammin. Moffett.
The Milkmaid. *Anonymous.*
Moments of Vision. Hardy.
Morning Compliments.
  Dayre.
Morning in the Hills.
  Carman.
Mount Zion. *Anonymous.*
Much Has Been Said...
  Anonymous.
The Mule-Skinners.
  Caldwell.
Musings. Barnes.
My Twelve Oxen.
  Anonymous.
Nelson Street. O'Sullivan.
Night of the Immaculate
  Conception. Maragall.
Nonpareil. Prior.
O Nancy! Wilt Thou Go With
  Me? Percy.
O World, Be Not So Fair.
  Norton.
An Ode. Herbert of
  Cherbury.
Of England, and of Its
  Marvels. Petrarch.
Oh, Fair to See. Rossetti.
Old Age. Keary.
On the Picture of the Three
  Fates in the Palazzo Pitti,
  at Florence. Hallam.
Once. Batterham.
One Good Turn Deserves
  Another. *Anonymous.*
The Ovibos. Hale.
A Painted Whore, the Mask
  of Deadly Sin. Lithgow.
The Pass of Kirkstone.
  Wordsworth.
A Pastoral. Byrom.
Pearl of the White Breast.
  Anonymous.

Per Diem et per Noctem.
  Stanley
A Poet's Grace. Burns.
Polly Vaughn (Molly Brawn).
  Anonymous.
Quantity and Quality. Letts.
Queen Anne. *Anonymous.*
The Quiet Hour. Bowman.
The Rainbow. *Anonymous.*
Revelation. Dickinson.
The Rhyme of the Three
  Captains. Kipling.
Roses. Ronsard.
A Roundelay. Drayton.
San Francisco. Miller.
The Second Pastoral, or,
  Alexis: The Argument.
  Virgil (Publius Vergilius
  Maro).
She Is Not Fair to Outward
  View. Coleridge.
The Sign. Bhartrihari.
Similes. Moxon.
The Sisters. Tennyson.
Snowfall. "I. V. S. W."
A Song. Percy.
Song. Stevenson.
Song: "I make my shroud but
  no one knows." Crapsey.
Song: "Me Cupid made a
  Happy Slave." Steele.
Song: "O, strew the way with
  rosy flowers." Mangan.
The Song of Bekotsidi.
  Anonymous.
A Song of Praise. Cullen.
Song: "Song is so old."
  Hagedorn.
Sonnet to Chatterton. Keats.
Sonnets. Hillyer.
Sonnets. Tuckerman.
Sonnets, XII: "Some talke of
  Ganymede th' Idalian Boy."
  Barnfield.
Sonnets, CXLVII: "My love is
  as a feaver longing still."
  Shakespeare.
Sonnets to Miranda.
  Watson.
State Fair Pigs. Pfingston.
Sunday up the River.
  Thomson.
Sylvia. Drayton.
That Ever I Saw.
  Anonymous.
That He Findeth Others as
  Fair, But Not So Faithful
  as His Friend. Turberville.
There Is None, O None But
  You. Campion.
The Thought Eternal.
  Goethe.
The Three Sisters. Ficke.
To His Mistress. Cowley.
To His Unconstant Friend.
  King.
To His Young Mistress.
  Ronsard.
To Hope. Williams.
To Lucasta. Lovelace.
To S. M. a Young African
  Painter, on Seeing His
  Work. Wheatley.
To the Noblest and Best of
  Ladies, the Countess of
  Denbigh. Crashaw.
To Thee, O God, the
  Shepherd Kings. Brainard.
The Trees of Life. Very.
Triumph of Bacchus and
  Ariadne. Medici.
Troia Fuit. Kauffman.

Tropical Weather. Sargent.
Verazzano. Butterworth.
Weep No More. Fletcher.
Well, World, You Have Kept
  Faith with Me. Hardy.
What of the Darkness? Le
  Gallienne.
When I Loved Thee.
  Stanley.
When You and I Were
  Young, Maggie.
  Butterfield.
The Willows. Eaton.
The Wreck. De la Mare.

Fairy
Amoretti, LXXX. Spenser.
The Ants. Clare.
Bubbles. Shorey.
The Building of the Nest.
  Sangster.
Chopin Prelude. Norton.
Christmas Island. Bates.
The Culprit Fay. Drake.
The Dance. Lehmann.
The Dawn of Love. Ray.
Death and the Fairies.
  MacGill.
Dreams. Alexander.
Emilia. Cleghorn.
Epithalamion. Hopkins.
The Faerie Queene. Blaser.
The Faerie Queene. Spenser.
The Fairy Book. Brown.
The Fairy Folk. Bird.
A Fairy Tale. Zupan.
The Four-Leaf Clover.
  Shannon.
The Green Fiddler. Field.
Holly Fairies. Fisher.
I Keep Three Wishes Ready.
  Wynne.
The Leprahaun. Joyce.
Limerick: "Some Harvard
  men, stalwart and hairy."
  Gorey.
The Little Red Sled. Bush.
Modern Love, X. Meredith.
Mother. Fyleman.
Ode to a Nightingale: The
  Nightingale. Keats.
Of a Spider. Thorley.
Oh! Where Do Fairies Hide
  Their Heads? Bayly.
Opportunity. Cawein.
Outward Bound. Aldrich.
The Salesman. Mezey.
Sometimes. Fyleman.
Song: "A lake and a fairy
  boat." Hood.
Song: "Morning opened."
  Justice.
Sonnets, IX: "An isle of trees
  full foliaged in a meadow."
  Irwin.
Trapping Fairies in West
  Virginia. Burgess.
The Vagrant. Slender.
The Violin Calls. Livesay.
The Vision of Sir Launfal.
  Lowell.
Western Magic. Austin.

Fairyland (s)
The Broken Girth. Graves.
Conversation with an April
  Fool. Bennett.
Dedication on the Gift of a
  Book to a Child. Belloc.
A Fairy Voyage.
  Anonymous.

Faith
The Adoration of the Wise
  Men. Alexander.

Adventure. Mason.
Alone. Sassoon.
Among High Hills. Soutar.
The Ancient Speech. Raine.
Astraea at the Capitol.
  Whittier.
The Awakening. Morgan.
The Battle of Charleston
  Harbor. Hayne.
Boys. Black. Brooks.
Caelica, LXIII. Greville.
Caelica, LXXV. Greville.
Charite Esperance et Foi.
  Birney.
Charleston. Timrod.
Columbus the World-Giver.
  Egan.
A Conversation. Shelley.
The Country Faith. Gale.
Day by Day the Manna Fell.
  Conder.
Deare, If You Change.
  Anonymous.
Deathless Principle, Arise.
  Toplady.
The Deserter. Cotter.
Doron's Jigge. Greene.
Dream Farmer. Boyer.
The Dreams Ahead. Litsey.
The Eclipse of Faith.
  Woolsey.
Erin. Digby.
Facts. Davies.
Faith. Tabb.
Fall of the Year. Ellison.
Feelings of a Republican on
  the Fall of Bonaparte.
  Shelley.
The Forgotten Star. Clark.
Getting inside the Miracle.
  Shaw.
Girl in a White Coat.
  Brinnin.
God Wants a Man.
  Anonymous.
Have You Lost Faith?
  Anonymous.
Her sweet weight on my heart
  a night. Dickinson.
His Mother's Service to Our
  Lady. Villon.
Hotel Fire: New Orleans.
  Ruffin.
Hymn to the Creator. Clare.
Hymnal. Vinal.
If it be so... Wyatt.
In Country Sleep. Thomas.
In Green Old Gardens.
  "Fane.
In the Carpenter's Shop.
  Teasdale.
International Conference.
  Ellis.
Irish Astronomy. Halpine.
Ishmael. Palmer.
Lambeth Lyric. Johnson.
Lament for Chaucer and
  Gower. Hoccleve.
The Land Called Scotia.
  Donatus.
Lemon. Satz.
The Lilies of the Field.
  Mackenzie.
Look Up. Nicholson.
The Lord Our God Alone Is
  Strong. Winchester.
A Lost World. Graves.
Love's Limit. *Anonymous.*
The Lover Beseecheth His
  Mistress Not to Forget...
  Wyatt.

The Lover Proved False.
Anonymous.
Madrigal: "Dear, if you
change." Dowland.
Matrimony. Williams.
Media Vita. Notker
Balbulus.
Melchior Vulpius. Moore.
Memorandum / The
Accountant's Notebook.
Norris.
My God, I Thank Thee.
Norton.
The New Year. Templeton.
New Year's Day. Crashaw.
No Marvel Is It. Bernard de
Ventadour.
Not Ours the Vows. Barton.
Now World. Anonymous.
O Ship of State. Longfellow.
Ode to a Butterfly.
Higginson.
The Old Year's Prayer.
Irving.
On Exodus, III, 14, I Am
That I Am. Prior.
The Orotava Road. Bunting.
Our Country. Howe.
Our Lady of the Refugees.
Maura.
Our Nation Forever. Bruce.
Pamela in Town. Cortissoz.
Phyllis. Lodge.
The Pilgrimage to Testour.
Ryvel (Raphael Levy).
The Pilot. Anonymous.
The Pinta, the Nina and the
Santa Maria. Tagliabue.
Pioneers. Clark.
Poems Chiefly of Early and
Late Years: Prelude.
Wordsworth.
The Poet. Leitch.
Poet's Prayer. Love.
The Power and the Glory.
Sassoon.
Prayer. Anonymous.
A Prayer for Faith.
Michelangelo.
Report on Experience.
Blunden.
Retractions. Cabell.
The Road to Dieppe. Finley.
Robert the Bruce. Muir.
The Sacred Order. Sarton.
A Seaman's Confession of
Faith. Kemp.
Shadows of Sails. Anderson.
Song. Meredith.
Song of the Answerer
(excerpt). Whitman.
The Song of the Strange
Ascetic. Chesterton.
Song with Words. Agee.
Swearing. Fitzsimon.
A Thanksgiving. Newman.
That's Faith. Leitner.
There Is No Unbelief. Case.
The Three Taverns: Out of
Wisdom Has Come Love.
Robinson.
To D'Annunzio: Lines from
the Sea. Nichols.
Tom the Lunatic. Yeats.
The Traveller. Goldsmith.
Trust the Form of Airy
Things. Harington.
Truth. Jonson.
Twilight. Hall.
The Two Prayers. Gillies.
The Watchers. Bates.

What Though the Dark!
Edwards.
When I Had Need of Him.
Kiser.
The Widow's Mite. Locker-
Lampson.
Worry. Swarberg.
Zeal and Love. Newman.
Faithful (ly) (ness)
Amantium Irae. Edwards.
Come unto Me. Stuart.
The Crocuses. Harper.
An Essay on Man. Pope.
Gun Teams. Frankau.
Hymn. Nicholl.
Hymn to Priapus. Lawrence.
Lee in the Mountains.
Davidson.
Let Us with a Gladsome
Mind. Milton.
The Lover Abused
Renounceth Love.
Turberville.
The Mother. Pearse.
The Nameless Saints. Hale.
Old-Testament Gospel.
Cowper.
Old Witherington. Randall.
Praise the Lord. Milton.
A Ribbon Two Yards Wide.
Kreymborg.
Sinful to Flirt (Willie down by
the Pond). Anonymous.
Soldier, There Is a War
between the Mind.
Stevens.
Song. Clare.
Song: "Beloved, it is morn!"
Hickey.
Song: "I came to the door of
the House of Love."
Noyes.
The Star of Sangamon.
Allen.
Tabernacles. Lansing.
The Ten Commandments.
Anonymous.
To a Lady on Her Passion for
Old China. Gay.
To a Young Brother.
Jewsbury.
Two Chorale-Preludes. Hill.
Faithless (ness)
At a Potato Digging.
Heaney.
Cancer Patient. Powers.
Hymn to Priapus. Lawrence.
Oh, Think Not I Am Faithful
to a Vow! Millay.
On Why I Would Betray You.
Graham.
A Pastoral Ballad in Four
Parts. Shenstone.
To His Mistress. Herrick.
Falcon (ry) (s)
Affirmations: I, II, III.
Viereck.
The Airman Who Flew over
Shakespeare's England.
Plutzik.
The Case. Norris.
The Falcon and the Dove.
Read.
I Live My Life. Rilke.
Mariushka's Wedding Song.
Anonymous.
Sonnet: A Lady Laments for
Her Lost Lover...
Anonymous.
Fall (en) (ing)
The Autumn Leaves.
Anonymous.

A Ballad of the Captains.
Brady.
Ben Bolt. Anonymous.
Boxcars. Keating.
The Bushfeller. Duggan.
Canto XIII. Pound.
Crispus Attucks. Hayden.
December 27, 1966.
Sissman.
Delta Traveller. Wright.
An Early Christian. Brough.
Epithalamium. Sitwell.
Falling Upwards. Shapiro.
For My Grandmother, Bridget
Halpin. Hartnett.
Forsaken. Schneour.
Havdolah. Litwack.
Helen Grown Old. Lewis.
I Am Too Near.
Szymborska.
The Indigestion of the
Vampire. Merwin.
An Irish Wild-Flower. Piatt.
It Is Becoming Now to
Declare My Allegiance.
Day-Lewis.
Iulus. Wallis.
John Brown's Body. Benét.
Listen. Put on Morning.
Graham.
Lost Cinderella. Weaver.
Love-Songs, At Once Tender
and Informative.
Hoffenstein.
Lyrics. Agee.
Midnight. "Mistral.
Murder of a Community.
Weissbort.
The Nativity of Christ.
Gongora y Argote.
O King of the World.
Anonymous.
On a Gentlewoman Walking
in the Snowe. Strode.
On Meeting Li Kuei-Nien
Down the River. Tu Fu.
Paradise Regained. Milton.
A Parisian Idyl (excerpt).
Moore.
The Prodigal Son. Symons.
Rain. Guri.
Rain. Williams.
Rorschach. Fargas.
The Rubaiyat of Omar
Khayyam. Omar
Khayyam.
A Serenade. Hood.
The Shepherd's Calendar.
Clare.
Slaves to the World.
Anonymous.
The Snow. Hall.
Soldier's Dove. Forsyth.
Songs in the Turtle Dance at
Santa Clara. Anonymous.
Sonnet: "Ingratitude, how
deadly is the smart."
Seward.
St. Augustine's Pear Tree.
Bowering.
The Stampede. Caldwell.
The Suicides of the Rich.
Contoski.
Survey. Lawson.
Tall and Singularly Dark You
Pass among the Breakers.
Zukofsky.
To a Dog. Peabody.
To Be Sung. Viereck.
Two Poems. Hitomaro.
Vision. Augustini.
Watering the Horse. Bly.

Ways of Seeing. Stafford.
The Weight. Aberg.
When Banners Are Waving.
Anonymous.
When These Old Barns Lost
Their Inhabitants....
Kherdian.
Where He Hangs His Hat.
Lee.
Wild Bees. Baxter.
Written on a Leaf.
Anonymous.
Fall (s)
After the Night Hunt.
Dickey.
All Things Decay and Die.
Herrick.
Although I Remember the
Sound. Huff.
Ambition. Davies.
Anarchist. Cronin.
Arlington. Wright.
Auden. Roseliep.
The Author, of His Own
Fortune. Harington.
Autumn. Rilke.
Autumn Orchard. Jacobs.
The Benjamins' Lamentation
for Their Sad Loss at Sea,
by Storms... Anonymous.
Blackbird Sestina. Warne.
Bridal Couch. Lloyd.
Castles. Glanz-Leyeles. A.
Ch'in Chia's Wife's Reply.
Anonymous.
Chant for Skippers.
Gallagher.
Chestnut Stands. Field.
Church-Monuments.
Herbert.
A Circus Dancer. Dropkin.
The City of Falling Leaves.
Lowell.
The Colder the Air. Bishop.
Colloquy at Peniel. Merwin.
The Commonwealth of Birds.
Shirley.
Counter-Serenade: She
Invokes the Autumn
Instant. Viereck.
A Cry from the Ghetto.
Rosenfeld.
Death. Coleridge.
Deities and Beasts. Updike.
The Devil's Dictionary:
Corporal. Bierce.
Dissonance. Whitman.
Don Juan. Byron.
The Dragonfly. Bogan.
Dreams Old and Nascent.
Lawrence.
Drinking Song. Brome.
Dunciad Minor. Hope.
The Eagle. Tennyson.
An Elegye. Campion.
Emblem. Quarles.
End of The Affair. Grigson.
English Bards and Scotch
Reviewers. Byron.
An Epistle to a Friend, to
Persuade Him to the Wars.
Jonson.
Epistle to Augustus (excerpt).
Pope.
Fading-Leaf and Fallen-Leaf.
Garnett.
Fallen Rain. Dixon.
Famine. Heym.
The Far Country. Greacen.
The Farmer's Clothes Are
Soaked Through and Never
Dried. Ise Tayu.

Farmers. Lux.
The Fathers. Muir.
Field Sports. Pope.
Fragment. Lowell.
From Emily Dickinson in Southern California. Kennedy.
The Fundament Is Shifted. Evans.
The Game. Gibson.
Genesis. Higgins.
Geneva. Reid.
Geography. Dransfield.
The Gift of God. Robinson.
God Hasn't Made Room. Mririda n'Ait Attik.
God Save Ireland. Sullivan.
Grape Daiquiri. Koyama.
Green Rain. Webb.
The Green-Sickness Beauty. Herbert of Cherbury.
Hang It on the Wall. Patton.
The House of Love: Pride of Youth. Rossetti.
How the Sky Begins to Fall. Colby.
I Have Fought the Good Fight. Waterbury.
I Will Bow and Be Simple. *Anonymous.*
The Immortal. Blake.
In Clementina's Artless Mien. Landor.
In Solitary Confinement, Sea Point Police Cells. Driver.
Inconsistencies. Roberts.
The Ivy-Wife. Hardy.
The Last Ascent. Lehmann.
Last Fall of the Alamo. Henry.
The Lazy Writer. Taylor.
The Leaves Do Not Mind At All. Wynne.
Limerick: "There once was a young man named Hall." *Anonymous.*
Limerick: "There was a young fellow named Hall." Wilson.
Lord of the Winds. Coleridge.
The Lord's Prayer in Verse. Hill.
Love. *Anonymous.*
Love Continual. Heywood.
The Lover Exhorteth His Lady to Take Time, While Time Is. Turberville.
A Lover's Curse. Meleager.
The Maid of Tottenham. *Anonymous.*
Mark Van Doren. Worley.
McKinley Brook. *Anonymous.*
Media Vita. Notker Balbulus.
Mimma Bella. Lee-Hamilton.
Mimnermus Incert. Landor.
The Mist and All. Willson.
Mountain Top. *Anonymous.*
My Lord, What a Mourning. *Anonymous.*
The Net and the Sword. LePan.
The Nigga Section. Smith.
The Nightingale. Moxon.
No Fault in Women. Herrick.
No Sky At All. Hashin.

O, Rocks Don't Fall on Me. *Anonymous.*
Occasioned by Seeing a Walk of Bay Trees. Westmoreland.
Oh! for a Steed. Davis.
Old Gardens. Upson.
On the Meetings of the Scotch Covenanters. *Anonymous.*
The Orchard. Ehrlich.
Packing a Photograph from Firenze. Matchett.
Parable. Soutar.
Per Amica Silentia Lunae. Carvalho.
The Pines. Lippmann.
A Portrait in the Guards. Whistler.
Privation. Carruth.
A Prognostication on Will Laud, Late Archbishop of Canterbury. *Anonymous.*
Pub. Symons.
The Purple Island. Fletcher.
Quatrains. Bennett.
Queen of Cheese. McIntyre.
The Quest of the Orchis. Frost.
Rare News. Breton.
Recapitulations. Shapiro.
The Red-Gold Rain. Sitwell.
Ring-a-Ring o' Roses. *Anonymous.*
Ring-Around-a-Rosy. Mother Goose.
Rispetti: On the Death of a Child. Heyse.
The River God. Sitwell.
Rome. Du Bellay.
Rondeau. Orleans.
Satin-Clad. Smith.
The Scare-Fire. Herrick.
September. Fallis.
Should the Wide World Roll Away. Crane.
The Sign. Blackburn.
A Simple Pastoral. Stevens.
Sky Diving. Reed.
The Snowdrop. Bary.
Snowflakes. Nemerov.
A Soldier: His Prayer. Kersh.
Sonnet On a Family Picture. Edwards.
Sonnet: The Army Surgeon. Dobell.
The Spirit of the Fall. Dandridge.
Spoken through Glass. Wilkins.
Squash in Blossom. Francis.
The Sumach Leaves. Very.
Table Talk. Stevens.
Taking Long Views. Kendall.
The Terror by Night. Leopardi.
That's Our Lot. Halpern.
The Theory of the Flower. Palmer.
Those Troublesome Disguises. Williams.
Timber Line Trees. Holme.
Time Will Not Grant. Keyes.
To a Fine Young Woman. Wycherley.
To an Irish Blackbird. MacAlpine.
To D--, Dead by Her Own Hand. Nemerov.
To His Book. Herrick.

Tragedy. Moss.
Training on the Shore. Vinner.
Triolet. Chesterton.
Two Pieces after Suetonius. Warren.
Ulster. Kipling.
Upon the Death of the Earl of Dundee. Dryden.
Upon the Death of the Viscount of Dundee. Dryden.
Upon the Troublesome Times. Herrick.
A Valediction. Cartwright.
The View. Nemerov.
Waiting. Skillman.
The Wall. Reed.
A War Song. Blake.
Waterfalls. Watkins.
What's the Life of a Man? *Anonymous.*
When the Work's All Done This Fall. *Anonymous.*
When You Speak to Me. Gallagher.
Wild Bees. Baxter.
Wilderness Gothic. Purdy.
Willow Poem. Williams.
With Whom Is No Variableness, Neither Shadow of Turning. Clough.
Within the Veil. Sangster.

Fallow
Epigram: "Milo's from home; and, Milo being gone." Martial (Marcus Valerius Martialis).
Memoirs of a Turcoman Diplomat. Devlin.
The Ploughman. Baker.
A Poem for Max Nordau. Robinson.

False
Alonzo the Brave and Fair Imogine. Lewis.
American Muse. Benét.
And Fall Shall Sit in Judgment. Lorde.
A Ballad upon the Popish Plot. Gadbury.
Broad Is the Road. Watts.
The Conquest of Granada. Dryden.
Deare, If You Change. *Anonymous.*
The Death of Parcy Reed (A vers.). *Anonymous.*
The Duellist. Churchill.
Early, Early in the Spring. *Anonymous.*
Earlye, Earlye, in the Spring. *Anonymous.*
English Bards and Scotch Reviewers. Byron.
False World, Thou Liest. Quarles.
Green Willow, Green Willow. *Anonymous.*
Hamlet. Shakespeare.
The House of a Hundred Lights. Torrence.
In Memoriam A.H.H., XVI. Tennyson.
The Indifferent. Donne.
Lady, Weeping at the Crossroads. Auden.
Lambkin. *Anonymous.*
The Lass of Roch Royal (C vers.). *Anonymous.*

Madrigal: "Dear, if you change." Dowland.
Manchouli. Empson.
The Message. Donne.
Modern Love: XLIII. Meredith.
My Horses Ain't Hungry. *Anonymous.*
Newark Abbey. Peacock.
Oenone's Complaint. Peele.
The "Pater Noster". *Anonymous.*
Poet in Winter. Lucie-Smith.
Private Pain in Time of Trouble. Spivack.
Ring Out, Wild Bells. Tennyson.
Saint Pumpkin. Willard.
Seth Compton. Masters.
Snatches: "Wel were him that wiste." *Anonymous.*
A Song: "Hast thou seen the Down in the Air." Suckling.
Song to a Lute. Suckling.
Sonnet: "A warm rain whispers, but the earth knows best." Leslie.
Sonnet for the End of a Sequence. Parker.
Sonnet: Guido Cavalcanti to Dante. Cavalcanti.
Sonnets, XLI: "Those pretty wrongs that liberty commits." Shakespeare.
Sonnets, LXVIII: "Thus is his cheek the map of days outworn." Shakespeare.
Sonnets, CXXXVII: "Thou blind fool, Love, what dost thou to mine eyes. Shakespeare.
The Storms Are on the Ocean. *Anonymous.*
Temperance and Virginity. Milton.
To My Inconstant Mistress. Carew.
To Those Who Reproved the Author for Too Sanguine Patriotism. Woodberry.
Trail All Your Pikes. Winchilsea.
True and False. Crawford.
Valentine Promise. *Anonymous.*
We Are Acrobats. Gerez.
Youth! Thou Wear'st to Manhood Now. Scott.

Falsehood
In the Forest. Petofi.
Song: "Ye happy swains, whose hearts are free." Etherege.
Sound from Leopardi. Berkson.
Thyme Flowering among Rocks. Wilbur.
Truth. Jonson.

Falter (ed) (s)
Alma. Lehrer.
Canto LXXXI. Pound.
The Drunkeness of Pain. Shenhar.
Father Father Son and Son. Swan.
The Goal and the Way. Oxenham.
I Should Be Ashamed. Uvlunuaq.
The Pisan Cantos (excerpt). Pound.

Right Is Right. Faber.
The Stormy Petrel.
  "Cornwall.
Sweet Marie. Warman.
Fame (d) (s)
1886 A.D. Richardson.
Ad Matrem. Fane.
The Aeneid. Virgil (Publius
  Vergilius Maro).
Amoretti, LXXXV. Spenser.
Beowulf. *Anonymous.*
Caelica, XCIII. Greville.
Caelica, CIV. Greville.
A Call for a Song.
  Anonymous.
Caries. Brown.
The Centennial Ode: Dear
  Land of All My Love.
  Lanier.
Chaucer. Brawley.
Childe Harold's Pilgrimage:
  Canto III, XXVI. Byron.
Died. Browning.
The Duke of Buckingham.
  Pope.
England's Darling.
  Anonymous.
Epitaph. Cowper.
Epitaph of Pyramus and
  Thisbe. Cowley.
An Essay on Man. Pope.
Fame Makes Us Forward.
  Herrick.
The Fleet at Santiago.
  Russell.
For My Own Monument.
  Prior.
The Great Adventure.
  Thoreau.
Harriet Beecher Stowe.
  Dunbar.
He Bringeth Them Unto
  Their Desired Haven.
  Tooker.
Hector and Andromache.
  Pope.
The Hind and the Panther.
  Dryden.
Honest Fame. Pope.
Hurrah for Greer County.
  Anonymous.
In Praise of Seafaring Men, in
  Hopes of Good Fortune.
  Grenville.
J.B. Bunner.
Johnny, I Hardly Knew Ye:
  Miltonese (parody).
  Gogarty.
Lochiel's Warning.
  Campbell.
Malvern Waters.
  Anonymous.
Mary Queen of Scots.
  Turner.
Medea. Seneca.
Modern Critics. Coleridge.
My Epitaph. Daniel.
On My Lord Bacon.
  Danforth.
One to Destroy, Is Murder by
  the Law. Young.
The Parliament of Bees.
  Day.
The Petition of Tom
  Dermondy to the Three
  Fates in Council Sitting.
  Dermody.
Poe's Cottage at Fordham.
  Boner.
De Ponto. Ovid (Publius
  Ovidius Naso).
Praise of Homer. Chapman.

The Prophet. Cowley.
Rome. Hardy.
The Sea-Watcher. De Vere.
Second Epistle to Robert
  Graham. Burns.
Since. Auden.
Sleepin' at the Foot O' the
  Bed. Patrick.
Sonnet: Written on the Day
  that Mr. Leigh Hunt Left
  Prison. Keats.
Sonnets, C: "Where art thou,
  Muse, that thou forget'st so
  long." Shakespeare.
Stairs. Herford.
The Suspition upon His Over-
  Much Familiarity with a
  Gentlewoman. Herrick.
Tarquin and Tullia.
  Mainwaring.
The Terror of Death. Keats.
These Plaintive Verse, the
  Postes of My Desire.
  Daniel.
To an Aging Charioteer.
  Scholasticus.
To an Olde Gentlewoman,
  That Painted Hir Face.
  Turberville.
To Delia. Daniel.
To George Sand: A Desire.
  Browning.
To Petronius Arbiter.
  Gogarty.
To the Lady Lucy, Countess
  of Bedford. Daniel.
To the Right Worthy Knight
  Sir Fulke Greville. Daniel.
Tristium. Ovid (Publius
  Ovidius Naso).
The True Aristocrat.
  Stewart.
The True-Born Englishman.
  Defoe.
Washington's Monument.
  Anonymous.
White Conduit House.
  Woty.
Why Did I Laugh To-night?
  Keats.
Willie Riley. *Anonymous.*
The Writer to His Book.
  Campion.
Familiar
Cloud Spots. Lavoie.
The Convent Threshold.
  Rossetti.
The Forgotten City.
  Williams.
The Largest Life. Lampman.
Our Lady of the Refugees.
  Maura.
Return of the Native. Jones.
The Seasons. Thomson.
Spicewood. Reese.
Tapwater. Jensen.
To My Daughter. Plutzik.
Family
The 1st. Clifton.
Accents in Alsace: Alsace or
  Alsatians. Stein.
All. Gom.
All Quiet. Ignatow.
Annette Myers; or, A Murder
  in St. James's Park.
  Anonymous.
Bind-Weed. "Coolidge.
Cloisters. Barnett.
The Disgrace. di Michele.
The Doll House. Kitzman.
Family. *Anonymous.*

From My Mother's Home.
  Goldberg.
Further Instructions. Pound.
Garlic. Bell.
Grandmother. Carlile.
The Grumble Family.
  Anonymous.
Heritage. Hogan.
Homeward Bound. Brodey.
Improved Farm Land.
  Sandburg.
The Israeli Navy. Bell.
The Lion. Lindsay.
The Movies. Gilbert.
My Guardian Angel Stein.
  Schultz.
The Nobleman and
  Thresherman. *Anonymous.*
On a Female Snob, Surprised.
  Dickinson.
Proposition. Guillen.
The Pulkovo Meridian:
  Leningrad: 1943. Inber.
Responsibilities. Hall.
Rusia en 1931. Hass.
Saturday Night. Oppenheim.
Such a Pleasant Familee.
  Irwin.
Tongues. Martin.
The True-Born Englishman.
  Defoe.
War on the Periphery.
  Johnston.
Weathers. Hardy.
Wedding Celebration. Kono.
Famine (d)
A Famished End to My Tale
  This Night. O Domhnaill.
Hungry Grass. MacDonagh.
Idylls. Theocritus.
On Seeing an Officer's Widow
  Distracted. Barber.
Famous
Cole Younger. *Anonymous.*
Folds of a White Dress/Shaft
  of Light. Keenan.
The Forgotten City.
  Williams.
Fan (s)
A Circus Garland. Field.
The Cornfield. Roberts.
Etruscan Notebook.
  Clementelli.
Flags. Brooks.
Full Moon. Sackville-West.
Hymn to the Winds. Du
  Bellay.
A Kitchen Memory. Scheele.
Limeraiku: "There's a vile old
  man." Pauker.
The Painted Lady. Danner.
Portrait of a Cree. "Hale.
Soldier's Dove. Forsyth.
Song:"Where shall Celia fly
  for shelter." Smart.
Story of Isaac. Cohen.
The Teacher. Bevington.
Youth Sings a Song of
  Rosebuds. Cullen.
Fancies
The Hour Glass. Quillinan.
The Seasons. Kalidasa.
Fancy
Beauty. Cowley.
Bedtime Story for My Son.
  Redgrove.
Castles in the Air. Peacock.
The Daisy. Tennyson.
A Day Dream. Bronte.
Disillusion. Burge.
Disillusioned. "Carroll.
Drum-Taps. Whitman.

The Epistemological Rag.
  Burr.
Fancy, Farewell. Dyer.
The Green Knight's Farewell
  to Fancy. Gascoigne.
Hallo My Fancy. Cleland.
Hymn to Proust. Ewart.
In the Spring. Tennyson.
Indifference to Fortune.
  Thomson.
Julie-Jane. Hardy.
The Lark Ascending.
  Meredith.
Laurence Bloomfield in
  Ireland. Allingham.
Lowshot Light. Barnes.
A Midsummer Night's
  Dream. Shakespeare.
Not Every Day Fit for Verse.
  Herrick.
On the Poet O'Shaughnessy.
  Rossetti.
Prologue to The Tempest.
  Dryden.
Salad. Collins.
Stay, Shade of My Shy
  Treasure! Juana Ines de la
  Cruz.
The Succubus. Graves.
The Triads of Ireland
  (excerpt). *Anonymous.*
Twelfth Night. Shakespeare.
A Valediction (Liverpool
  Docks). Masefield.
Whistle an' I'll Come to Ye,
  My Lad. Burns.
Widow's Walk. Spires.
Fanny
Delay Has Danger. Crabbe.
Limerick: "Mussolini's pet
  Marshal, Graziani."
  Ybarra.
Mr. Molony's Account of the
  Ball. Thackeray.
The Sad Lover. Crabbe.
Fantasies
Desires of Men and Women.
  Berryman.
Suicid/ing Indian Women.
  Allen.
Fantastic
The Indolent. Verlaine.
Fantasy
Along History. Rukeyser.
Frightened. Ferlinghetti.
Receiving Communion.
  Miller.
Transcendentalism.
  Anonymous.
The Turncoat. Jones.
The Wharf of Dreams.
  Markham.
The World an Illusion.
  Anonymous.
Far
Above the Dock. Hulme.
Ariana. Sanborn.
As the Mist Leaves No Scar.
  Cohen.
At the Fountain.
  Marcabrun.
At Times I Feel Like a
  Quince Tree. Quinn.
Bacchylides. Whicher.
Because We Do Not See.
  Anonymous.
The Blackleg Miners.
  Anonymous.
The Boyne Walk. Higgins.
Childhood. Stanton.
Cockayne Country.
  Robinson.

The Cold. Simic.
A Comrade Rides Ahead.
 Malloch.
Counting. Sandburg.
The Cricket and the Star.
 Newsome.
Dulcimer Maker. Forche.
Elysee. Eigner.
Facts. "Carroll.
The Far Land. Wheelock.
A Farewell Hymn to the
 Valley of Irwan.
 Langhorne.
A Farm Picture. Whitman.
For the Noun C. BL. Tyler.
Going. Kelly.
He That Is Near Me Is Near
 the Fire. Origen.
A Hillside Farmer. Farrar.
The Horse and the Mule.
 Wynne.
Idol. Driscoll.
In Memoriam A.H.H.,
 LXXXII. Tennyson.
Invocation. MacNeice.
Jackie Frazier. *Anonymous.*
John-John. Macdonagh.
The Judgment of the May.
 Dixon.
The Key to Everything.
 Swenson.
Lament for the Great Music
 (excerpt). ""MacDiarmid.
The Lass of Roch Royal (B
 vers.). *Anonymous.*
Liberty Tree. Paine.
Lines on Brueghel's Icarus.
 Hamburger.
The Little Rose Is Dust, My
 Dear. Conkling.
Missing the Children.
 Zimmer.
My Child Came Home.
 George.
My Old Kentucky Home.
 Foster.
Night. Teasdale.
O Brazil, the Isle of the Blest.
 Griffin.
Origins. Harjo.
The Poem as Striptease.
 Dacey.
Poem: "To go, to leave the
 classics and the buildings."
 Ewart.
A Primer of the Daily Round.
 Nemerov.
Rain. Sears.
Rocky Acres. Graves.
Round Her Neck She Wore a
 Yellow Ribbon.
 Anonymous.
Separation. Dickinson.
Shop. Browning.
The Sky. Roberts.
Sleeping in a Cave. Nye.
Song: "Ah hate to see de
 evenin' sun go down."
 Anonymous.
Song: "Were I laid on
 Greenland's coast." Gay.
Sonnet: "Since I keep only
 what I give away."
 Hetherington.
The Sporting Cowboy.
 Anonymous.
Spring Quiet. Rossetti.
Suburban Wife's Song.
 Hutchinson.
Uncle Claude. Evans.
The Unquiet Grave.
 Anonymous.

Verifying the Dead. Welch.
The Visitor. Davies.
La Vita Nuova. Dante
 Alighieri.
We Never Said Farewell.
 Coleridge.
With the Shell of a Hermit
 Crab. Wright.
Farce
Catherine Ogg. Masters.
David Garrick, the Actor, to
 Sir John Hill, a Physician...
 Garrick.
Journal of a Tour through the
 Courts of Germany
 (excerpt). Boswell.
The Loyal General: Prologue.
 Dryden.
Fare (d) (s)
The Agricultural Show,
 Flemington, Victoria.
 Maurice.
Beauty Is Most at Twilight's
 Close. Lagerkvist.
The Cabdriver's Smile.
 Levertov.
The Gray Mare (Young
 Johnny the Miller).
 Anonymous.
My Heart and I. Browning.
The Old Miner. *Anonymous.*
A Perilous Life. *Anonymous.*
Sir Orfeo. *Anonymous.*
Still Growing. *Anonymous.*
Three Sorrowful Things.
 Anonymous.
To a Covetous Churl. May.
The Trip. Jarrett.
Viaticum. MacCarthy.
The Wagoner's Lad.
 Anonymous.
With Pipe and Flute.
 Dobson.
Farewell
Adieu to the Stone Walls.
 Anonymous.
Angel Eye of Memory.
 Brinnin.
Antony and Cleopatra.
 Lytle.
Before the Birth of One of
 Her Children. Bradstreet.
Black Jack Davie.
 Anonymous.
The Blackbird. *Anonymous.*
Bonnie Black Bess.
 Anonymous.
Casey Jones. *Anonymous.*
Cherry Blossoms. "Lewis.
The Conservative Shepherd to
 His Love. D'Arcy.
Councell Given to Master
 Bartholmew Withipoll...
 Gascoigne.
The Days of Our Youth.
 Anonymous.
The Departure. King.
The Dying Californian.
 Anonymous.
The Dying Indian. Warton.
Epistle to a Desponding Sea-
 Man. Freneau.
Epitaph on Elizabeth, L. H.
 Jonson.
Fancy, Farewell. Dyer.
Farewell to My Mother.
 "Placido" (Gabriel de la
 Conception Valdes).
Farewell to Summer.
 Arnold.
Farewell to the Muses.
 Reynolds.

Farewell, Unkind! Farewell! to
 Me, No More a Father!
 Anonymous.
The Ghost's Leavetaking.
 Plath.
The Goodbye. Sklarew.
The Hambone and the Heart.
 Sitwell.
Harvest Home. Guiterman.
Heaven and earth and all that
 hear me plain. Wyatt.
His Further Resolution.
 Anonymous.
His Sailing from Julia.
 Herrick.
In Memory of "Barry
 Cornwall." Swinburne.
In Summer. Towne.
King Richard II.
 Shakespeare.
Kings of France. Lincoln.
Last Days. Stoddard
The Little House in Lithuania.
 Marshak.
Love Me Little, Love Me
 Long. *Anonymous.*
The Lovesick Cowboy.
 Anonymous.
Meeting. Saphier.
A Mile with Me. Van Dyke.
The Mist over Pukehina.
 Anonymous.
Morning Express. Sassoon.
The Muses Elizium.
 Drayton.
Ode to Evening. Warton.
Ode to the End of Summer.
 McGinley.
Old. *Anonymous.*
The Olden Days. Hall.
On the Burial of His Brother.
 Catullus.
On the Threshold.
 Anonymous.
Out from Gloucester. Trott.
The Parting Hour. Custance.
Pericles. Shakespeare.
The Retreat. King.
Richard II. Shakespeare.
De Roberval. Hunter-Duvar.
The Romish Lady.
 Anonymous.
Rouge Bouquet. Kilmer.
Sir Walter Rauleigh His
 Lamentation. *Anonymous.*
A Song of Dust. De Tabley
Sonnet: Where Lies the Land.
 Wordsworth.
Sonnets of a Portrait Painter.
 Ficke
The Sparrow. Williams.
Stanzas in Memory of the
 Author of "Obermann'.
 Arnold.
There Is a Nook Among the
 Alders. Frost.
To His Book. Herrick.
To Parker. Turberville.
To the Archdeacon.
 Farewell.
Toil Away. Chapman.
Upon Ben Johnson. Herrick.
Wedding Procession.
 Emanuel.
World without End.
 Catullus.
Written at the White Sulphur
 Springs. Key.
Farm (s)
Aurora Leigh. Browning.
Ballad of the Bushman.
 Duggan.

Beehive. Toomer.
Cock-Crow. Thomas.
The Contempt of Poetry.
 Spenser.
The Cradle. Robinson.
The Death of Myth-Making.
 Plath.
Dialogue–2 Dollmakers.
 Corso.
The Early Purges. Heaney.
Follow the Leader. Behn.
From the Epigrams of
 Martial. Michie.
The Garden. Brady.
Getting Loaded. Thomas.
Hitch Haiku. Snyder.
Lost Picture. Fraser.
Summer Farm. MacCaig.
Times Are Getting Hard.
 Anonymous.
Women Called Bossy
 Cowboys. Jankola.
Farmer (s)
A Farmer's Boy.
 Anonymous.
The Farmer (with music).
 Anonymous.
The Harmonious Heedlessness
 of Little Boy Blue. Carryl.
Harvest. Shuford.
A House of Readers. Miller.
The Jolly Farmer.
 Anonymous.
The Mare. Asquith.
Pity Poor Labourers.
 Anonymous.
Po' Farmer. *Anonymous.*
The Rewards of Farming.
 Anonymous.
Seed. Bosman.
This Is the Way the Ladies
 Ride. Mother Goose.
Tractor. Sellers.
The Wars of Santa Fe.
 Anonymous.
Fart (s)
Epigrams in Distich, II: To a
 Flatterer. *Anonymous.*
Epitaph for G. B. Shaw.
 Beerbohm.
Family Life. *Anonymous.*
No Names. *Anonymous.*
Quicksands (parody).
 Zaranka.
Rebolushinary x-mas/eastuh
 julie 4/ etc. etc. etc. etc.
 Rodgers.
Upon Jack and Jill. Epigram.
 Herrick.
Farthing
Death of My Aunt.
 Anonymous.
A Farthing. *Anonymous.*
Reply to a Creditor.
 Harding.
Fashion
How Shall We Rise to Greet
 the Dawn? Sitwell.
In Praise of Clothes. Jong.
Neckwear. Silverton.
The Prophecy of Famine.
 Churchill.
Some Who Do Not Go to
 Church. *Anonymous.*
Sonnet: He Will Not Be Too
 Deeply in Love.
 Angiolieri.
Sonnet: "Into these loves who
 but for passion looks."
 Drayton.
Summer. Rossetti.

The Testament of Beauty.
Bridges.
To a Young Ass.   Coleridge.
Whitman in Black.   Berrigan.
Fast (er) (est)
The Day Is Gone.   Keats.
The Djanggawul Cycle, 12.
Anonymous.
The Fall of Rome.   Auden.
For Your Inferiority Complex.
O'Rourke.
Freedom.   *Anonymous.*
Give Us Sober Men.
Isenhour.
The Green Inn.   Garrison.
A Hundreth Good Poyntes of
Husbandry.   Tusser.
Jackrabbits.   Barker.
Mantle.   Heyen.
Merry It Is.   *Anonymous*
Morning Rush.   Clark.
Neurasthenia.   Robinson.
O Doctor Dear My Love.
Halley.
Pornography, Nebraska.
McPherson.
Proust's Madeleine.   Rexroth.
Retirement.   Trench.
The Sea of Silence Exhales
Secrets.   Bialik.
A Seeker in the Night.
Coates.
Song: "I am weaving a song
of waters."   Bennett.
Spot-Check at Fifty.
Scannell.
A Story from the Bushmen.
Ceravolo.
Those Hours When Happy
Hours Were My Estate.
Millay.
Twilit Revelation.   Adams.
The Twins.   Roberts.
Warblers.   Hartley.
Weakness of Nature.
Froude.
When I Saw You Last, Rose.
Dobson.
Women in Love.   Justice.
Fastidious
Limerick: "There once was a
sculptor called Phidias."
Herford.
Shine on Me, Secret Splendor.
Markham.
Fat
Be off!   Smith.
A Cat.   Herrick.
The Country Mouse and the
City Mouse.   Sharpe.
December 24 and George
McBride is Dead.   Hugo.
The Edge.   Bowen.
Epistle to Augustus (excerpt).
Pope.
The Fat Man in the Mirror.
Lowell.
Food of the North.
Lawrence.
Husbandry.   Hammond.
Last night thin rain, gusty
wind.   Li Ch'ing-chao.
Limerick: "As a little fat man
of Bombay."   *Anonymous.*
Limerick: "There was an Old
Man of Kamschatka."
Lear.
Neutrality.   MacNeice.
The Nine.   Sheffield.
Oil.   Hogan.
On a Spring-Board.   Lefroy.

One, Two, Buckle My Shoe.
Mother Goose.
The Orange Bears.   Patchen.
The Perils of Obesity.
Graham.
Poem: "Some who are
uncertain compel me."
Lange.
Protecting the Burial
Grounds.   Rose.
Reflecting on the Aging-
Process (parody).   Peters.
River Rhyme.   Williams.
Rocky Acres.   Graves.
Some Pieces.   Forbes.
Summer Journey.   Rodgers.
Tea.   Embry.
To a Noisy Politician.
Freneau.
Uncle.   Levine.
Waking from a Nap on the
Beach.   Swenson.
The Wives of Spittal.
Anonymous.
Words Made of Water.
Singer.
Fatal
Caelica, XCVI.   Greville.
Charles Guiteau, I.
Anonymous.
The Farmer's Boy.
Bloomfield.
In Orangeburg My Brothers
Did.   Spellman.
Life of the Mannings.
Anonymous.
Love and Honour.   Greville.
Love-Songs, At Once Tender
and Informative.
Hoffenstein.
Mamano.   Craveirinha.
Poem in Time of War.
Abrahams.
Solomon on the Vanity of the
World.   Prior.
Fate (s)
After the Festival.   George.
Against Constancy.
Rochester.
Almond Blossom in Wartime.
Spender.
Apology for E. H.
Hathaway.
The Babes in the Wood.
Anonymous.
A Ballad of Queensland (Sam
Holt).   Gibson
("Ironbark").
Baudelaire in Brussels.
Cronin.
The Blue Horses.   McAuley.
Caelica, VII.   Greville.
Cartography.   Bogan.
A Challenge.   Kenyon.
Christian Ethics.   Traherne.
The City of Golf.   Murray.
Come, All Ye Youths.
Otway.
Come Up, Methuselah.   Day-
Lewis.
Conjectured to Be upon the
Death of Sir Walter Ralegh.
King.
Contentment.   Felltham.
Culture.   Emerson.
A Curse on a Closed Gate.
Cousins.
The Dead.   Day-Lewis.
Dear Possible.   Riding.
Death of a Fair Girl.   Butler.
Death Warnings.   Quevedo y
Villegas.

The Druid.   Tabb.
Dupree (B vers.).
Anonymous.
Elegy on the Death of Mme.
Anna Pavlova (excerpt).
Meyerstein.
Empedocles on Etna.
Arnold.
Epistles.   Horace.
An Epitaph.   Watson.
Eric.   Barford.
The Exequies.   Stanley.
The Fate of John Burgoyne.
Anonymous.
Father Coyote.   Sterling.
Feel Like a Bird.   Swenson.
From Generation to
Generation.   Howells.
Full Moon: New Guinea.
Shapiro.
Give Love To-Day.   Talbot.
Haar in Princes Street.
Scott.
Helpmate.   Chapin.
Hero and Leander.   Marlowe.
Holiday.   Davidson.
House Guest.   Bishop.
How Great My Grief.
Hardy.
The Hunter.   Souster.
In Memory of My Dear
Grandchild Elizabeth
Bradstreet.   Bradstreet.
Indecsion Means Flexibility.
Abhau.
The Inevitable.   Bolton.
The Jam at Gerry's Rock.
Anonymous.
Like an Adventurous Sea-
Farer Am I.   Drayton.
Lines by a Person of Quality.
Pope.
Loyal Sins.   Glatstein.
Madrigal: "Where shall I
sorrow great."   Peerson.
Mathematics of Love.
Hamburger.
Mercedes.   Stoddard
The Mockery of Life.   Blunt.
Montalbert (excerpt).   Smith.
The Motives of Rhythm.
Conquest.
Mutual Love.   Hammond.
My Epitaph.   Daniel.
My Sister.   Storni.
Naboth's Vineyard.   Caryll.
Notes on My Father.
Anghelaki-Rooke.
October in Tennessee.
Malone.
On a Pair of Shoes Presented
to Him (excerpt).
O'Rahilly.
On a Replica of the
Parthenon.   Davidson.
On the Tombs in Westminster
Abbey.   Beaumont.
Panic.   MacLeish.
Poem to Lou.   Apollinaire.
Prairie Wolves.   Carr.
A Prayer of the Peoples.
MacKaye.
Prosit Neujahr.   Santayana.
The Rape of the Lock.
Pope.
The Resolve.   Chudleigh.
Retractions.   Cabell.
Runner.   Auden.
Shadows.   Milnes.
The Shepherd's Week:.   Gay.

A Song: "Boast no more fond
Love, thy Power."
D'Urfey.
Sonnet. I.   Suckling.
Sonnets.   Tuckerman.
St. Valentine,.   Moore.
The Texas Cowboys.
Anonymous.
There Was a Brisk Girle.
Anonymous.
Thoughts of Thomas Hardy.
Blunden.
The Three Warnings.   Thrale
Piozzio.
Time Was.   Hill.
To A Dark Girl.   Bennett.
To a Young Wretch.   Frost.
To Mars.   Chapman.
To the Memory of Mr.
Oldham.   Dryden.
The Tool of Fate.   Yehoash.
Traveller's Ditty.   DeFord.
Under a Lady's Picture.
Waller.
Upon the Death of the
Viscount of Dundee.
Dryden.
Uptown.   Ginsberg.
Villanelle.   Feld.
The Wandering Knight's
Song.   Lockhart.
When I See the Earth Ornate
and Lovely.   Gambara.
Whether There Is Sorrow in
the Demons.   Berryman.
The Wife's Lament.
Anonymous.
A Wry Smile.   Fuller.
Father (S)
Above in Inverkirkaig.
MacCaig.
The Addict.   Rubin.
After Grief.   Plumly.
Anabasis, IV.   Perse.
Are You There?   Gillilan.
At Last.   Stoddard.
At Night.   Eberhart.
The Ballad of the Children of
the Czar.   Schwartz.
Bar Mitzvah.   Goldemberg.
Battle Pledge.   *Anonymous.*
Before the Breaking.
Pennington.
The Bird.   De.
Blow Gabriel.   Davis.
Building for Eternity.
Sargent.
Burlesque Translation of Lines
from Lope de Vega's
"Arcadia'.   Butler.
A Busy Man Speaks.   Bly.
Caelica, XXIII.   Greville.
The Call of the Christian.
Whittier.
The Canon for Apocreos.
Theodore of Studium.
The Canterbury Tales: A
Squire.   Chaucer.
The Canterbury Tales:
Prologue. A Squire.
Chaucer.
The Cataract at Lodore
(parody).   Bevington.
Charm for Burns.
Anonymous.
The Child's Heritage.
Neihardt.
The Child's Wish Granted.
Lathrop.
Christmas Day.   Young.
The City.   Betjeman.

Clap Hands, Clap Hands. *Anonymous.*
Classic Encounter. "Caudwell.
Come Down. Macdonald.
Consider. Rossetti.
Consolation in July. Heppenstall.
Conversation with Washington. Livingston.
Creation. Gurr.
The Crooked Footpath. Holmes.
The Crow and the Nighthawk. Kirkconnell.
Crow, Crow, Get out of My Sight. *Anonymous.*
Crow Jane. Jones.
Deacon Morgan. Madgett.
Dear Mother. Jarrett.
Dentyne. Lurie.
The Desk. Bottoms.
The Discontented Student. Tucker.
Double Take at Relais de l'Espadon. Davis.
Drop the Wires. Seidman.
The Drowsy Sleeper (A vers.). *Anonymous.*
Elegy for Jane. Roethke.
Elegy Written in a Country Churchyard. Gray.
The Entailed Farm. Glassco.
Epitaph. Ignatow.
Epitaph from a Yorkshire Churchyard. *Anonymous.*
Epitaphs of the War. Kipling.
Epos. Tuwim.
Failed Fathers. Turco.
Faith. Sangster.
Faith. Sill.
Father's Whiskers. *Anonymous.*
Father Son and Holy Ghost. Lorde.
Flying. Carlile.
Football Song. Scott.
For a Father. Cronin.
The Four Maries. *Anonymous.*
Funeral Hymn. Howe.
A Funny Joke. Stokesbury.
The Garden of Olives. Rilke.
The Gardener. Wheelock.
The Gay Goshawk (E version). *Anonymous.*
Ghazal. Dow.
Gil Brenton. *Anonymous.*
Girl in White. Dobyns.
God Supreme! To Thee We Pray. Moise.
Going Home. Kenny.
Grandfathers. Castro.
The Groundhog Foreshadowed. Sher.
Habla Usted Espanol? Reiss.
He Maketh Himself One with the God Ra. Book of the Dead.
He Who Has Lost All. Diop.
Hind Etin (A version). *Anonymous.*
Home. Cornish.
House of Fire. Weiss.
Hull's Surrender. *Anonymous.*
Hunter's Prayer. *Anonymous.*
Hunting Civil War Relics at Nimblewill Creek. Dickey.

Hunting with My Father. Absher.
Hymn for Atonement Day. Halevi.
Hymn of Dedication. Scantlebury.
Hymn to Mary. Zerea Jacob.
I'r hen Iaith A'i Chanedon (To the Old Tongue and its Songs). Dowding.
I Sit with My Dolls. *Anonymous.*
In Memoriam, Private D. Sutherland. Mackintosh.
In the Time of Trouble. Clark.
In the Valley of the Elwy. Hopkins.
In Time of War. Auden.
An Inheritance. Replansky.
Inside History. McCabe.
Interceding. Gibbs.
The Invisible King. Goethe.
Isaac. Jacobs.
Jim. Howes.
John Plans. Pierce.
The Journey into France. *Anonymous.*
The Joys of Mary. *Anonymous.*
Kitchen Tables. Huddle.
The Lady of the Lake. Scott.
The Lass of Lynn's New Joy, for Finding a Father for Her Child. *Anonymous.*
Last Lines. O'Rahilly.
Let There Be Law. Van Doren.
The Letters of the Book. Drachler.
Light of the Soul. Caswall.
Limerick: "There was a young monk of Siberia." *Anonymous.*
Lines for a Worthy Person Who Has Drifted by Accident... Herbert.
Linnets. Levis.
Lizzie Borden. *Anonymous.*
Lord Ingram and Chiel Wyet (C version). *Anonymous.*
The Love of the Father. *Anonymous.*
The Man in That Airplane. Williams.
The Messenger. Valentine.
Mignon. Goethe.
The Miner's Doom. *Anonymous.*
Morning Hymn. Ken.
Mother Shake the Cherry-Tree. Rossetti.
Motherless Children. *Anonymous.*
Music. Phillips.
Mustapha. Greville.
My Death. Zuckmayer.
My Father's Ghost. Wagoner.
My Father's Heart. Friebert.
My Father's Voice in Prayer. Nottage.
My Father's Watch. Ciardi.
My Father, Who's Still Alive. Kozer.
My Fatherland. Lawton.
My Ghostly Father. *Anonymous.*
My Mother's Table. Sobiloff.
Nelly Trim. Warner.

New Garden Fields. *Anonymous.*
Night Fishing. Waters.
Noble Sisters. Rossetti.
November, 1941. Fuller.
Ode to the Spirit of Earth in Autumn. Meredith.
Oh Father. Rose.
The Old Man and Young Wife. *Anonymous.*
On the Death of My Son Charles. Webster.
Our Father, Our King. *Anonymous.*
Our Father's Hand. Flint.
The Outlandish Knight. *Anonymous.*
Parable. Bennett.
Paterson. Williams.
The Phoenix. Nemerov.
Pied Beauty. Hopkins.
The Pitt-Rivers Museum, Oxford. Fenton.
A Post Card out of Panama. Barney.
Prayer for the Journey. *Anonymous.*
Prayer of St. Francis Xavier. Pope.
A Presentation of Two Birds to My Son. Wright.
Pretty Polly. *Anonymous.*
Prodigals. O'Donnell.
Rainbow. Huff.
Reflections. Coleridge.
Regina Coeli. *Anonymous.*
Remember the Ladies. Lifshin.
Requiem. Vincent.
Rhyme of the Fishermen's Children. *Anonymous.*
Rigadoon, Rigadoon, Now Let Him Fly. *Anonymous.*
The Ring and the Book. Browning.
Rise, Happy Morn. Tennyson.
A Road of Ireland. O'Donnell.
A Rouse for Stevens. Roethke.
The Sacrifice. Bloch.
Sailor, What of the Isles? Sitwell.
Sir Hugh; or, The Jew's Daughter (B vers.). *Anonymous.*
Sleep and Poetry. Keats.
Someone Knocks. Everwine.
The Somerset Dam for Supper. Holmes.
Song: "Hang sorrow, cast away care." *Anonymous.*
Song of the Sky Loom. *Anonymous.*
A Song to the Wind. Taliesin.
Sonnets, XIII: "O! that you were yourself; but, love, you/are." Shakespeare.
Spring Death. Marano.
The Spring Is Late. Moulton.
Still Wrestling. Boiarski.
Stonecarver. Oles.
The Store in Havana. Kozer.
Sunday Funnies. Keiter.
The Theology of Jonathan Edwards. McGinley.
Therefore, We Thank Thee, God. Grossman.

This Is a Poem for the Dead. Ryan.
Three Hundred Thousand More. Gibbons.
Through the Night of Doubt and Sorrow. Baring-Gould.
A Thunder-Storm. Dickinson.
To a Visiting Poet in a College Dormitiory. Kizer.
To Henry Wright of Mobberley, Esq. on Buying the Picture... Byrom.
To Mistress Anne Cecil. Burleigh.
To My God in His Sickness. Levine.
True Son of God, Eternal Light. Cormican.
The Unveiling. Bernhardt.
The Urn. Crane.
The Violin Tree. Rosenberg.
The Visible Baby. Redgrove.
Visit. Coccimiglio.
Vox Populi. Dryden.
The Wanderer's Grave. Sage.
Washrags. Rutsala.
We Shall Walk through the Valley. *Anonymous.*
Wednesbury Cocking. *Anonymous.*
Welcome O Great Mary. O'Gallagher.
Whalen's Fate (George Whalen). *Anonymous.*
Why? Talmud.
The Wind's Song. "Setoun. Gabriel"
Within and Without. Macdonald.
A Wonderful Man. Fisher.
You and I Will Go to Finegall. *Anonymous.*

Fatherland
The Fatherland. Lowell.
The Greater Country. Watkins.
The Postern Gate (excerpt). Rauschenbusch.
To Gabriel of the Annunciation. Abelard.

Fatherless
Another Kind of Burning. Fox.
Jubilate Agno. Smart.
Sheep in Fog. Plath.

Fatigue (d) (s)
Consider This and in Our Time. Auden.
Original Child Bomb (excerpt). Merton.
Thoughts on Pausing at a Cottage near the Paukataug River. Knight.
Tightrope Walker. Scannell.
The Wall. Jones.
Yehuda Amichai. Mayne.

Fault (s)
An Allusion to Horace. The Tenth Satire of the First Book. Rochester.
Amoretti, XXIV. Spenser.
Be Careful What You Say. Kronthal.
Charity. *Anonymous.*
A Child My Choice. Southwell.
Dido's Hunting. Surrey.

The Disappointed Sailor. *Anonymous.*
Dream Land. Kemble.
Early Thoughts of Marriage. Cotton.
Elm. Plath.
The Elm Speaks. Plath.
Epigram. *Anonymous.*
An Essay on Criticism. Pope.
Fame and Friendship. Dobson.
Fan. Lew.
The Four Seasons of the Year. Bradstreet.
The Great Magicians. Day Lewis.
Here Lieth Love. Watson.
If amour's faith... Wyatt.
Judgement. Herbert.
No Fault in Women. Herrick.
Prologue to Antonio's Revenge. Marston.
Sea Canes. Walcott.
The Teasing Lovers. Horace.
To Mrs. Ann Flaxman. Blake.
Two Sons. Mac An Bhaird.
Tyrannic Love. Dryden
Upon a Great Shower of Snow That Fell on May-Day, 1654. Washbourne.
The Waltz: Hail, Spirit-Stirring Waltz. Byron.
"When reckless youth in an unquiet breast." Surrey.
The Wind at Your Door. FitzGerald.

Faultless
Hard Strain in a Delicate Place. Sylvester.
A Hot Day in Sydney. *Anonymous.*

Fauns
Canto II. Pound.
The Golden Age: Hymn to Diana. Heywood.
Moonlight. Verlaine.

Favor (ed) (s)
Autumn. Scannell.
Aweary Am I. Abu-l-Ala al-Maarri.
Cinderella. Broumas.
Epigram: "And now I, Meleager..." Meleager.
Epigram: "Exhausted now her sighs, and dry her tears." Landor.
Epitaphs of the War, 1914-18. Kipling.
An Excellent New Ballad, Called The Brawn Bishop's Complaint. Mainwaring.
Gascoigne's Praise of His Mistress. Gascoigne.
Hello, Sister. Saylor.
Not Yet Dead, Not Yet Alone. Mandelstam.
The Outlaw Murray. *Anonymous.*
Prologue to Antonio's Revenge. Marston.
Regina Confessorum. *Anonymous.*
Second Night, or What You Will. Humphries.
When Sadness Fills a Journey. Waller.
The World's Illusion. Ibn Ezra.

Favourite
Dream Songs. Berryman.
How We Beat the Favourite. Gordon.

Fawn (ed) (ing)
Caenlochan. Cruickshank.
An Elegy on a Lap Dog. Gay.
In Cool, Green Haunts. Fisher.
Old Man Pondered. Ransom.
On His Dog. Gay.
Smoke. McGuckian.

Fear (ed) (ful) (s)
Abraham Davenport. Whittier.
And if an eye may save or slay. Wyatt.
And When I Am Entombed. Emerson.
The Apparition. Melville.
At Cooloolah. Wright.
At Port Royal: Song of the Negro Boatman. Whittier.
At the Grave of Burns. Wordsworth.
Attainment. Cawein.
Autumn. Hood.
Autumn Testament (excerpt). Baxter.
Bagpipe Music. ""MacDiarmid.
The Barge Horse. Jennett.
The Battle of Monmouth. *Anonymous.*
The Bird. Hollander.
Black Power. Saxon.
The Blessed Virgin's Expostulation. Tate.
The Blue Horse. La Follette.
Bold Princess Royal. *Anonymous.*
The Bold Soldier. *Anonymous.*
Boy at the Window. Wilbur.
Caelica, XV. Greville.
Caelica, XXVII. Greville.
Caelica, LIV. Greville.
Caelica, LXV. Greville.
Caelica, XCV. Greville.
Caelica, CI. Greville.
The Camelopard. Belloc.
Chameleon. Engle.
Chimney Swallows. Powers.
Chopping Fire-Wood. Pack.
Christmas Eve–Another Ceremony. Herrick.
City. Mocarski.
The City Rat and the Country Rat. La Fontaine.
Colin and Lucy. Tickell.
Confidence. *Anonymous.*
Contentment. Felltham.
Corporal Pym. De la Mare.
Dance Hymn. Shembe.
Death Songs. Mack.
Death the Great. Lasynys.
Deep Sea Soundings. Williams.
Derry. Deane.
Document. Ruebner.
A Doe at Evening. Lawrence.
Double Ode. Rukeyser.
The Downfall of Charing Cross. *Anonymous.*
Dream Songs. Berryman.
Drive Imagining. Vogelsang.
The Dutch Seamen and New Holland. Reeves.
Ecclesiastes. Langland.

Effectively coming through slaughter. Fitzgerald.
Epigram. *Anonymous.*
Epigram. Butler.
Epigrams. Martial (Marcus Valerius Martialis).
Epitaphs of the War. Kipling.
Epitaphs of the War, 1914-18. Kipling.
An Exequy. Porter.
Expectation. Stanley.
The Fable of Acis, Polyphemus, and Galatea. Dryden.
Fable XIII: The Tame Stag. Gay.
Fear. Pizarnik.
Fear. Stump.
The Fear of Bo-talee. Momaday.
The Female Transport. *Anonymous.*
Fire. 10/78. Plantenga.
The Firetail's Nest. Clare.
For Miriam. Macgoye.
Friends. Brown.
The Fringilla Melodia. Hirst
From a Hint in the Minor Poets. Wesley.
Give to the Winds Thy Fears. Gehardt.
The Gnat. Beaumont.
God Lyaeus. Fletcher.
Going the Rounds: A Sort of Love Poem. Hecht.
Grandmother and Child. Dallas.
Grief of a Girl's Heart. Gregory.
Harden Now Thy Tired Heart. Campion.
Hares at Play. Clare.
The Heap of Rags. Davies.
Her Face Her Tongue Her Wit. Gorges.
Hopi Prayer. Beghtol.
Horatian Ode. Beach.
The Horses. Muir.
How Still the Hawk. Tomlinson.
Hush, Hush, New House in Charlotte. Schorb.
A Hymn to God the Father. Donne.
Hymn to Intellectual Beauty. Shelley.
I Have Approached. Paton.
I Played on the Grass with Mary. Walsh.
I Think the New Teacher's a Queer. Brass.
I Who Had Been Afraid. Maris Stella.
In Teesdale. Young.
In the Dry Riverbed. Zelda.
In the Season of Wolves and Names. Rugo.
The Invaders. Haines.
Invented a Person. Marshall.
Islands: A Song. Brinnin.
The Jealous Wife. Scannell.
Judge Not According to the Appearance. Rossetti.
June Night. Hall.
The Jungle. Dudek.
Knowledge. Cassian.
Kora for March 5th. MacAdams.
The Lake of Gaube. Swinburne.

The Lament for O'Sullivan Beare. *Anonymous.*
A Letter Catches Up with Me. Chaet.
Limerick: "There was a good Canon of Durham." Inge.
Lines for an Eminent Poet and Critic. Dickinson.
A Litany for Old Age. Harsen.
The Location of Things. Guest.
Lord of the World. *Anonymous.*
The Lover Disceived by His Love Repenteth Him of the True Love ... *Anonymous.*
Lucasia, Rosania and Orinda Parting at a Fountain, July 1663. Philips.
Magnolia Tree in Summer. Sitwell.
The Marionettes. De La Mare.
Medieval Norman Songs. *Anonymous.*
A Meditation upon the Toothache. Lerner.
Midnight. Nortje.
The Minute. Shapiro.
Money in the Bank. Ehrhart.
Muster Out the Rangers. *Anonymous.*
The Name of Jesus. Flint.
Nathan Hale. *Anonymous.*
Need. Deutsch.
Never Love. Campion.
The New Year. Homer-Dixon.
Night Cries, Wakari Hospital. Brasch.
No Dawns. Perry.
Nova. Jeffers.
A Nymph's Passion. Jonson.
O Jesus, My Saviour, I Know Thou Art Mine. Taylor.
O Mad Spring, One Waits. Moore.
O Ship of State. Longfellow.
Ode to Fear. Collins.
Oh, Ye Censurers. Ibn Adiya.
The Old Astronomer to His Pupil. Williams.
The Old Woman of Berkeley. Southey.
Older Grown. Greenaway.
On a Recent Protest against Social Conditions. Posner.
On a Return from Egypt. Douglas.
On Death. Landor.
On His Mistris that Lov'd Hunting. *Anonymous.*
On the Death of Neruda. Van Brunt.
Out of Body. Moore.
Packing in with a Man. McCombs.
Parachute Descent. Bourne.
Paradise Lost. Milton.
Phantoms of the Steppe. Pushkin.
The Planets Line Up for a Demonstration. Kearns.
Poem: "This room is very old and very wise." Harrison.
Political Greatness. Shelley.
The Pony Express. Thompson.
The Pool. Mayo.

Port Bou. Spender.
The Primrose. Carew.
Prison Letter. Knoll.
Psalm X. Sidney.
Resurrexit. Stuart.
Roast Swan Song.
  Anonymous.
The Scarlet Woman.
  ""MacDiarmid.
The Seasons. Thomson.
Security. Tucker.
Self. Pritchard II.
The Shape of Death.
  Swenson.
She Employed the Familiar
  "Tu" Form. Fetherling.
The Soldier's Wooing.
  Anonymous.
Song: "Down the dimpled
  green-sward dancing."
  Darley.
Song for a Birth or a Death.
  Jennings.
A Song in Passing. Winters.
Song, on Reading That the
  Cyclotron has Produced
  Cosmic Rays...
  Hoffenstein.
Sonnet I. Alabaster.
Sonnet: "Shall I be fearful
  thus to speak my mind."
  McLeod.
A Sonnet: "Weeping,
  murmuring, complaining."
  Goldsmith.
Sonnets, LXIV: "When I have
  seen by Time's fell hand
  defaced." Shakespeare.
Sonnets, First Series.
  Tuckerman.
Sonnets to Karl Theodor
  German. Platen.
Spirits and Men (excerpt).
  Elliott.
Stanzas. Corneille.
Stoklewath; or, The Cymbrian
  Village. Blamire.
Stone Walls. Lippmann.
Storm on the Island.
  Heaney.
Stormy Weather, Boys.
  Anonymous.
Sufi Quatrain. Rabi'a bint
  Isma'il.
Surgical Ward: Men.
  Graves.
The Taming of the Shrew.
  Shakespeare.
The Task. Cowper.
Thiepval Wood. Blunden.
Thou Grace Divine,
  Encircling All. Scudder.
Threatened. Walker.
Three Gates. Day.
The Tiger. Creeley.
To a Field Mouse. Burns.
To a Poetic Lover. Hay.
To D--, Dead by Her Own
  Hand. Nemerov.
To My Mother at 73.
  Jennings.
To Olivia. Thompson.
The Two Stars. Davies.
Upon Love. Herrick.
Upon This Rock. Todd.
A Version of a Song of
  Failure. Eigner.
The Viking Terror.
  Anonymous.
The Vikings. *Anonymous.*
Vilanelle. Kerr.
Voice in the Crowd. Joans.

The Wail of Prometheus
  Bound. Aeschylus.
Warning to Travailers Seeking
  Accomodations at Mr.
  Devills Inn. Knight.
Waterchew! Corso.
When They Grow Old.
  Ralph.
Whistle an' I'll Come to Ye,
  My Lad. Burns.
Whitsunday. Keble.
The Whore That Rides in Us
  Abides. *Anonymous.*
The Wind Has Wings.
  Anonymous.
The Witch. Southey.
With a Book at Twilight.
  Steinberg.
Without More Weight.
  Ungaretti.
Wonders. *Anonymous.*
The Worm. Barnstone.
Wprroes/. *Anonymous.*
Feast (s)
L'Art, 1910. Pound.
The Art of War (excerpt).
  Fawcett.
Be Present at Our Table,
  Lord. Cennick.
Cana Revisited. Heaney.
Cancer Patient. Powers.
Colophon for Lan-t'ing Hsiu-
  Hsi. Peck.
The Country Mouse and the
  City Mouse. Sharpe.
Dream Songs. Berryman.
The Fairy Temple; or,
  Oberon's Chapel....
  Herrick.
The Feast-Time of the Year.
  Anonymous.
Flying Fox. Shapcott.
For Christmas Day. Farjeon.
From Another Room.
  Corso.
Gascoigne's Memories.
  Gascoigne.
The Grasshopper. Cowley.
The Grasshopper's Song.
  Bialik.
Horsey Gap. *Anonymous.*
Lord Jesus Christ, We
  Humbly Pray. Jacobs.
Mighty Mary, Hear Me. O
  Dalaigh.
Mill Valley. Livingston.
Morels. Smith.
Music of Colours: the
  Blossom Scattered.
  Watkins.
Nymphidia. Drayton.
Ode: To My Lovers.
  Verlaine.
The Odyssey. Homer.
A Pastoral Courtship.
  Rochester.
Silex Scintillans. Vaughan.
Son-Dayes. Vaughan.
Spirit Song. *Anonymous.*
Table Graces, or Prayers for
  Adults: Noon Meal.
  Anonymous.
To Sally. Horace.
A View of the Burning.
  Merrill.
Feather bed
Arizona. *Anonymous.*
The Blackbird of Derrycairn.
  Anonymous.
The Book of Nightmares.
  Kinnell.
Childs Memory. Wilkins.

Crow's Way. Niatum.
Digging Out the Roots.
  Niatum.
The Djanggawul Cycle, 33.
  Anonymous.
The False Fox Came into Our
  Croft. *Anonymous.*
The Fog Dream. Gilbert.
If I Were a Pilgrim Child.
  Bennett.
In My Heart's Depth.
  Akazome Emon.
Juvenal's Sixth Satire.
  Dryden.
Kopis'taya. Allen.
Mating Answer. Bottrall.
Meditations. Taylor.
Nursing the Hide. Dunne.
Of Mere Being. Stevens.
Owls. Fuller.
The Pheasant. Coffin.
Pleasant Sounds. Clare.
Poem: "Form is the woods."
  Harrison.
The Raven. Rich.
A Shropshire Lad.
  Housman.
Snow. Stone.
So Many Feathers. Cortez.
Some Feathers. Gallup.
The Squirrel. *Anonymous.*
The Swan. Spender.
Swans Mating. Longley.
Three Women Blues.
  McTell.
Visions of Mexico While at a
  Writing Symposium in Port
  Townsend... Cervantes.
Yourself and Myself.
  Anonymous.
Feather (s)
Black Humor. MacLeish.
Don't Sleep. Jonker.
A Good Resolution.
  Campbell.
Henley, July 4: 1914–1964.
  Sissman.
John Burns of Gettysburg.
  Harte.
Jubilate Agno. Smart.
Loss of an Oil Tanker.
  Causley.
The Old Boat. Pratt.
Poem to Ease Birth.
  Anonymous.
The Power of Silence.
  Davies.
Too happy time dissolves
  itself. Dickinson.
The Translation of Verver.
  Berssenbrugge.
A Utilitarian View of the
  Monitor's Fight. Melville.
The Wing Factory. Stein.
Feature (s)
As Kingfishers Catch Fire,
  Dragonflies Draw Flame.
  Hopkins.
At the Savoy Chapel.
  Graves.
Canto VII. Pound.
The Groves of Blarney.
  Millikin.
The Midnight Court.
  Merryman.
On Learning That Certain
  Peat Bogs Contain Perfectly
  Preserved Bodies.
  Ludvigson.
Poem: "He watched with all
  his organs of concern."
  Auden.

The Statue of Shadow.
  Bishop.
Visions. Petrarch.
Winter Term. Brinnin.
Fed
At the Center of Everything
  Which Is Dying.
  Goedicke.
The Beggar. Bruner.
Canadians. Gurney.
Chance Meeting. Griffin.
Course Bread and Water's
  Most Their Fare.
  Williams.
For Johnny. Pudney.
The Gazelles. Moore.
The Happy Family. Ciardi.
Morning Swim. Kumin.
Observations in a Cornish
  Teashop. Rexroth.
Sehnsucht. Wickham.
The Sower's Song. Carlyle.
To the Swallow. *Anonymous.*
To the Young Man Jesus.
  Dalton.
Trinity Place. McGinley.
Fee
A Benedictine Garden.
  Brown.
Interview with Doctor Drink.
  Cunningham.
King Henry Fifth's Conquest
  of France (B vers.).
  Anonymous.
The Romance of the Rose:
  Love vs. Marriage.
  Meung.
Sonnet Sonnet. Engle, Jr.
Sonnet: "When, from the
  tower whence I derive love's
  heaven." *Anonymous.*
Sonnets, CXX: "That you
  were once unkind befriends
  me now." Shakespeare.
Thoughts from a Bottle.
  Clark.
Feeble
Easter Communion.
  Hopkins.
Express. Allingham.
Instructions of King Cormac.
  Cormac Mac Cuilenan.
Operatic Note. Cane.
The Song of the Old Mother.
  Yeats.
Thailand Railway. Stow.
Wino. Hughes.
Feed (ing) (s)
After the Centennial.
  Cranch.
America, I Love You. Ruby.
And on This Shore.
  Holman.
The Animal Howl. J. M.
The Banded Cobra.
  Leipoldt.
The Biglow Papers. Lowell.
A Black Man Talks of
  Reaping. Bontemps.
Britannia's Pastorals.
  Browne.
Cannibalism. Chang.
The Centipede. Adams.
Certain Dead. Haines.
Chicago Poem. Welch.
The Christmas Hymn.
  Ephrem.
Contempt for the World, III.
  Bernard de Morlas.
Enough. Gregor.
The Farmer Is the Man.
  Anonymous.

The Farmer (with music).
Anonymous.
The Flight in the Desert.
Everson.
The Foal. Renton.
The Grey Wolf. Symons.
His Picture. Donne.
How to Choose a Horse.
Anonymous.
Hunger and Thirst. Bishop.
The Irish Council Bill, 1907.
Anonymous.
Julius Caesar. Shakespeare.
Kyoto: March. Snyder.
Limerick: "Of inviting to dine,
in Epirus." Rankin.
The Living Dog and the Dead
Lion. Moore.
The Maiden's Complaint.
Anonymous.
The Meaning of Violence.
Williams.
The Modern World. Ellis.
More Sonnets at Christmas.
Tate.
Mystic. Lawrence.
On the Cuckoo. Quarles.
The Poor Can Feed the Birds.
Neilson.
Prayer before Meat. Harsen.
Prelude. Benson.
Proem. Gibson.
The Puzzled Game Birds.
Hardy.
To the Immortal Memory of
the Halibut on Which I
Dined This Day. Cowper.
Two Old Ladies. Sassoon.
Upon Jack and Jill. Epigram.
Herrick.
With the Most Susceptible
Element, the Mind, Already
Turned... Benton.

Feel (s) (felt)
Abbreviated Rumination.
Jacobs.
Absent Creation. Savage.
The Aim of Life: A Country
Town. Bailey.
American Rhapsody.
Fearing.
Bright Star (Original version).
Keats.
Calling Lucasta from Her
Retirement. Lovelace.
Carmina. Catullus.
Courthouse Square. Merrill.
Credo. Gale.
Divine Compassion.
Whittier.
Don Quixote. Betts.
The Doorstep. Stedman.
Dusk. "Mistral.
The Eel. Nash.
The Eighteenth Song.
Hadewijch.
Eloisa to Abelard. Pope.
Epigrams. Martial (Marcus
Valerius Martialis).
Far from Africa. Danner.
Farewell! If Ever Fondest
Prayer. Byron.
Fencing School. Manifold.
Four Poems for The St. Louis
Sporting News, 4. Spicer.
A Friend. Talfourd.
Friends. Brown.
Good Company.
Anonymous.
Her Praises. Skoloker.
Housewife. Schaeffer.

How My Father Died.
Ezekiel.
I Wonder What It Feels Like
to Be Drowned? Graves.
In the Night of the Full
Moon. Busse.
In Time of War. Auden.
Liddell and Scott. Hardy.
Limerick: "A lady who signs
herself "Vexed."". Gorey.
Limerick: "There was a faith-
healer of Deal."
Anonymous.
The Londoner in the Country.
Church.
Marlborough (excerpt).
Sorley.
Mosby at Hamilton. Cawein.
My Life, the Quality of
Which. Knight.
Natural Magic. Browning.
Nature. Clare.
The Night-Blooming Cactus.
Bensko.
The Night Is Falling.
Mangan.
O Thou Whose Image.
Clough.
An Old Man. Wordsworth.
Out of Mourning. Abbott.
Pain. Storni.
Passage. Eberhart.
Pearl Harbor Day 1970.
Lourie.
Pick a Fern, Pick a Fern,
Ferns Are High.
Anonymous.
Poem: "Hate is only one of
many responses." O'Hara.
Poems. Gildner.
Rain Journal: London: June
65. Harwood.
Retrospection. Quiller-
Couch.
The Sacrament of Sleep.
Oxenham.
Samuel Hall. Anonymous.
She sat and sewed... Wyatt.
The Shirt. Morley.
So Late Removed from Him
She Swore. Landor.
Song of Myself. Whitman.
Sunflakes. Asch.
This Book Is One Thing.
Anonymous.
To a Republican Friend.
Arnold.
To a Single Shadow without
Pity. Cornish.
To Be Black, To Be Lost.
Kahn.
Tropical Weather. Sargent.
Water under the Earth. Bly.
Where the Dropwort Springs
up Lithe and Tall.
Donaghy.
White as a Paper A-Sail in the
Air. Anonymous.
The Whole Duty of a Poem.
Guiterman.
The Wind of January.
Rossetti.
The Woman Poet. Kolmar.
Zeppelin. Glaze.

Feeling (s)
The Dutchman. Welch.
Failing the Examination.
Meng Chiao.
The Field of the Grounded
Arms. Halleck.
Fox. Dyment.

The Garden of Earthly
Delights. Simic.
The Illiterate. Meredith.
Large Red Man Reading.
Stevens.
Letter to My Kinder.
Gaskin.
Monday, Monday. Trinidad.
Moving Ahead. Rilke.
My Past. Cooper.
The People at the Party.
Mueller.
Song. O'Reilly.
Sonnets to Orpheus. Rilke.
Stanzas. Bronte.
Stanzas. Poe.
The Student. Moore.
To His Wife. Ch'in Chia.
To Jane: The Keen Stars
Were Twinkling. Shelley.
The Vowels of Another
Language. Disch.
When Lovely Woman. Cary.
Winter Dawn. Lawrence.
You Got to Love Her with a
Feeling. Tampa Red.

Feet
The 49 Stomp. Blockcolski.
Ad Infinitum. Aronsten.
After Chagall. Wenger.
After Reading Homer.
Dolben.
Aircraft, Landing. Thiele.
An Appeal to Cats in the
Business of Love.
Flatman.
As I Ebb'd with the Ocean of
Life. Whitman.
At last, to be identified!
Dickinson.
Autobiography. Akesson.
The Ballad of Sir Patrick
Spens. Anonymous.
The Beautiful Train.
Empson.
Benediction. Hayes.
Blanket Street. Hogan.
Both My Child. Teitoku.
The Boy. Field.
Boy's Day. Henderson.
Calling in the Cat.
Coatsworth.
Cave Sedem! MacManus.
Cernunnos. Maxton.
The Chough. Reaney.
Circumstance. Aldrich.
A City Song. Mitchell.
The Cliff-Top. Bridges.
The Clothes Pit. Dunn.
The Comforters. Shorter.
The Coming of His Feet.
Allen.
The Coronet. Marvell.
Dance Figure. Pound.
Dante at Verona. Rossetti.
Dawn. Masefield.
The Deathless. Hayes.
Desires. Bensley.
Doll's Boy's Asleep.
Cummings.
Dust. Russell.
Eau-Forte. Flint.
Elegy on the Death of Mme.
Anna Pavlova (excerpt).
Meyerstein.
England Expects. Nash.
Envoi. Lewis.
Epigrams. Theocritus.
Epitaph for a Timid Lady.
Cornford.
Evil Days. Pasternak.

Faith–is the Pierless Bridge.
Dickinson.
Father. Weston.
Feet. Aldis.
Fleet Street. Leslie.
Flowers in the Ward.
Neilson.
Foots It (parody). Berry.
For the Magdalene.
Drummond.
Fragoletta. Swinburne.
The Garden of the Holy
Souls. King.
Genius Loci of the Morning.
Fetherling.
Green Song. Booth.
De Guiana, Carmen Epicum.
Chapman.
Haitian Suite. Orr.
Hands. Aldis.
The Happy Sheep. Thorley.
He Gives His Beloved Certain
Rhymes. Yeats.
He Has Fallen from the
Height of His Love.
Blunt.
History Lesson for My Son.
Kooser.
The House of Life. Rossetti.
How Gentle God's
Commands. Doddridge.
Ice River. Baker.
If I Were a Voice. Mackay.
Invitation. Contoski.
Jobson's Amen. Kipling.
John Brown's Body. Benét.
Kitty Neil. Waller.
The Lady of Life. Kettle.
Lalla Rookh. Moore.
The Land behind the Wind.
Wagoner.
Late Winter. Hall.
Leaps over the Aisle of
Syllogism (parody). Berry.
Limerick: "T was a tidy
young tapir." Wells.
The Lion's Skeleton. Turner.
The Little Girl. Moore.
The Little Knight in Green.
Bates.
A Little Pig Asleep.
Jackson.
The Little Shoes That Died.
Gilmore.
Lord of the Winds.
Coleridge.
Lord Thomas and Fair
Ellender. Anonymous.
A Love Symphony.
O'Shaughnessy.
The Maximus Poems. Olson.
Mea Culpa. "Carbery.
Montgomery. Cornish.
Mother of Men. Southwold.
My Childhood's Bedroom.
Tisdale.
My Queen. Winter.
The Myall in Prison.
Gilmore.
Nest Eggs. Stevenson.
Newness. Paulin.
No Single Thing Abides.
Lucretius (Titus Lucretius
Carus).
On Mary Magdalen.
Drummond.
The Open Door.
Coatsworth.
The Passing of March.
Wilson.
Poem for My Dead Husband.
Roberts.

Poor Brother. *Anonymous.*
Port Authority Terminal: 9
  A.M. Monday. Walsh.
Presentiment. Bierce.
Procne. Quennell.
Psalm XI. Sidney.
Pudgy. Lima.
Rachel. "Rachel" (Rachel
  Blumstein).
The Rat. Symons.
Resurrection. Kemp.
The Return. Fauset.
The River of Stars. Noyes.
The Road of Life. Morris.
The Rose of the World.
  Yeats.
The Ruin. Hughes.
Saint Mary Magdalene.
  Crashaw.
Saturn Fallen. Keats.
Senior Members. Lucy.
Seven Mexican Children.
  Schmidt.
She Bewitched Me.
  Burbidge.
The Shed. O'Donnell.
Silhouette. M'Baye.
Somewhere Down below Me
  Is a Street. Maloney.
Song: "A violet in her lovely
  hair." Swain.
Song from the Story of
  Acontius and Cydippe.
  Morris.
The Song of the Four Winds.
  Peacock.
Spikenard. Housman.
The Stargazer. *Anonymous.*
Stockton Lake; Stockton,
  Missouri. Sanders.
The Strand. MacNeice.
Sweet Marie. Warman.
Teeth. Griffin.
There Are So Many Ways of
  Going Places. Thompson.
They Came This Evening.
  Damas.
Three White Birds of Angus.
  Cox.
Thy Heart. *Anonymous.*
Time. Collier.
Tir-Nan-Og. Hendry.
To an Indian Skull (excerpt).
  McLachlan.
To Be in Love While in
  Prison. Minarik.
To Jessie's Dancing Feet.
  Ellwanger.
To St. Mary Magdalen. Hill.
To the Brave Soul.
  Underwood.
To William Stanley
  Braithwaite. Johnson.
The Tragedy of Pete. Cotter.
The Train of Religion
  (excerpt). Tupper.
Tresco. Grigson.
Tristan da Cunha. Campbell.
True Love. Cary.
Two Songs, II. Reisen.
An Unsuspected Fact.
  Cannon.
Upon Master Walter
  Montagu's Return from
  Travel. Carew.
Victoria Market. Brabazon.
A View. Quint.
The Vision. O Rathaille.
War. Langland.
The Well Rising. Stafford.
White Goat, White Ram.
  Merwin.

The Wide Land. Ammons.
Windle-Straws. Dowden.
Winter. Donaghy.
Witches. Hughes.
Woman Me. Angelou.
The World. Rossetti.
The Yielded Life. W.A..
Yves Tanguy. Gascoyne.

Feign
Accused though I be without
  desert. Wyatt.

Felicity
Christian Ethics. Traherne.
The Familiar Colloquies:
  Sweet Temper and Mutual
  Affection. Erasmus.
A Lost World. Graves.
The Minute before Meeting.
  Hardy.
Mrs. Crudeman. Sitwell.
Mustapha. Greville.
The Preparative. Traherne.
Ressaif My Saul. Saunders.

Fell
The Abandoned. Symons.
L'Aura Amara. Daniel.
Betty at the Party.
  Anonymous.
The Case. Hays.
The Chums. Roethke.
Coda. Bunting.
Divina Commedia. Dante
  Alighieri.
Dream Songs. Berryman.
The Faerie Queene. Spenser.
Five Vignettes. Toomer.
Gus: the Theatre Cat. Eliot.
I Should Be Ashamed.
  Uvlunuaq.
Icarus. *Anonymous.*
In the Sprightly Month of
  May. Vanbrugh.
The Ivy-Wife. Hardy.
Limerick: "There was a young
  lady of Lynn."
  Anonymous.
Mamma! Horne.
Minotaur Poems. Mandel.
A Mood. Howells.
Mules. Muldoon.
My Correspondent's Last
  Ride. Townsend.
Nursery Rhyme. Burke.
Old Bandy Legs.
  Anonymous.
On Eleanor Freeman.
  Anonymous.
The Philosopher's Scales.
  Taylor.
The Poet's Prayer. Philipps.
R. I. P. Struther.
Sainclaire's Defeat.
  Anonymous.
A Scottish Shoe.
  Anonymous.
Spontaneous Requiem for the
  American Indian. Corso.
Spring Rain. Chute.
The Squirrel. *Anonymous.*
They Went Forth to Battle,
  but They Always Fell.
  O'Sheel.
Through the Whole Long
  Night. Leivick.
The Underground Stream.
  Dickey.
Vigil Strange I Kept on the
  Field One Night.
  Whitman.
What My Lover Said.
  Greene.

Fellow (s)
The Bird. Hoffenstein.
Brent: A Poem to Thomas
  Palmer, Esq. Diaper.
Captain Death. *Anonymous.*
The Deserter. Smith.
Dobbin Dead. Barnes.
Extract from Memoirs.
  Nemerov.
If I Only Was the Fellow.
  Adkin.
Incident Characteristic of a
  Favourite Dog.
  Wordsworth.
Limerick: "A young engine-
  driver called Hunt." Gray.
The Little Chap Who Follows
  Me. *Anonymous.*
Measuring a Man.
  Anonymous.
The Merry Minuet. Harnick.
Mexico City Blues. Kerouac.
O Dirty Bird Yr Gizzard's
  Too Big & Full of Sand.
  Koller.
On the Death of Mrs. Bowes.
  Montagu.
Shemuel. Bowen.
Sherman. Gilder.
Sonnet: Of Moderation and
  Tolerance. Guinicelli.
Spider. Colum.
Steam (excerpt). Elliott.
To Midnight Nan at Leroy's.
  Hughes.
The Trucker. Dyson.
The Wind at Penistone.
  Davie.

Fellowship
Dartmouth Winter-Song.
  Hovey.
The Fellowship of Prayer.
  Turner.
Housemates. Shepard.
A Little Song of Work.
  Sprouse.
The mountains grow
  unnoticed. Dickinson.

Female (s)
As Like the Woman as You
  Can. Henley.
The Female of the Species.
  Kipling.
Hmmmm, 22. Scalapino.
The Lass in the Female
  Factory. *Anonymous.*
Laundry & School Epigrams.
  Mayer.
Palais des Arts. Gluck.
Samson Agonistes. Milton.
A Song on the South Sea.
  Winchilsea.
Take Heed of Gazing
  Overmuch. Richardson.
To Nobodaddy. Blake.

Fence (s)
Caelica, XXXVIII. Greville.
Comfort. Doney.
Extempore Verses upon a
  Trial of Skill.... Byrom.
The Fence. McHugh.
The Firstborn. Soto.
Fishing on a Lake at Night.
  Bly.
Milking Time. Roberts.
Old Fence Post. Hanes.
Postcards. Vinz.
Retirement. Trench.
Road. Merwin.
Sin. Herbert.
Sonnets. Tuckerman.
The Survivors. Slater.

Way Out West. Siringo.

Fens
Poly-Olbion. Drayton.
Prelude. Synge.

Fern (s)
After the Funeral. Thomas.
Amber the Sky. Rokwaho.
Autumn Rain. Rexroth.
Calling in the Cat.
  Coatsworth.
Living by the Red River.
  Wright.
March. Coatsworth.
Noon. "Field.
The Open Door.
  Coatsworth.
Poem: "I walk at dawn across
  the hollow hills." Todd.
The Sphere of Glass.
  Lehmann.
Views of the Oxford Colleges.
  Howes.

Ferry
Being Called For. Dobson.
Brown's Ferry Blues.
  Anonymous.
Ferry Me across the Water.
  Rossetti.
Horsey Gap. *Anonymous.*
Lost. Auden.
Lost Letter to James Wright,
  with Thanks for a Map of
  Fano. Ruark.
The Sailor's Complaint.
  Anonymous.
San Francisco. Austin.

Fertility
The Bitch-Kitty. Williams.
The Impious Feast. Landor.
The Invention of Zero.
  Urdang.
Rain on the Cumberlands.
  Still.
The Turtle. Nash.

Fester
Avoidances. Welburn.
On Dr. Keene, Bishop of
  Chester. Gray.
Sonnets, XCIV: "They that
  have power to hurt, and
  will do none."
  Shakespeare.

Festival
The Morning Prayers of the
  Hasid, Rabbi Levi Yitzhok.
  Gotlieb.
Prodigals. O'Donnell.

Fetch
The Melancholy Knight: Sir
  Eglamour. Rowlands.
The Song of the Galley.
  Anonymous.

Fetter (s)
Amoretti, XXXVII. Spenser.
Certain Maxims of Hafiz.
  Kipling.
The Flitch of Dunmow.
  Carnegie.
His Wife. Blaustein.
Love to Faults Is Always
  Blind. Blake.
Magellan. Curnow.
Massachusetts to Virginia.
  Whittier.
Owen of Carron. Langhorne.
A Prisoner's Song of
  Jerusalem. *Anonymous.*
Song: "I went to her who
  loveth me no more."
  O'Shaughnessy.
A Summer Noon at Sea.
  Sargent.

What Guile Is This. Spenser.

Fever
Canzonetta: A Bitter Song to His Lady. Moronelli da Fiorenza
Epitaphs of the War, 1914-18. Kipling.
Epithalamium. Miller.
Farewell to Malta. Byron.
Garlic. Bell.
Heat. Anacreon.
The Ideal. Baudelaire.
The Invitation. Herrick.
The Island. Ungaretti.
Out-of-the-Body Travel. Plumly.
A Satire on Samuel Butler (excerpt). Oldham.
Self-Dependence. Arnold.
To Master Davenant for Absence. Suckling.
Troilus and Cressida. Shakespeare.
You Cannot Go down to the Spring. Neilson.

Few (er)
After Sunset. Allingham.
Alps. Warren.
Apples in New Hampshire. Gilchrist.
The Battle of New Orleans. Anonymous.
The Betrothal. Millay.
Code of the Cow Country. Barker.
Come, Chloe, and Give Me Sweet Kisses. Williams.
The Cuckoo. Anonymous.
Distrust. Herrick.
Eulogy for Alvin Frost. Lorde.
Fashions in Dogs. White.
Freedom, New Hampshire. Kinnell.
Good and Clever. Wordsworth.
The Great House. Muir.
The Jolly Thresherman. Anonymous.
Lovers, and a Reflection. Calverley.
Many without Elegy. Graham.
The Mask of Anarchy. Shelley.
My Birthday. Crabbe.
The Nightingale. Petrarch (Francesco Petrarca).
Poem after Apollinaire. Sadoff.
Riddle 9 (Cuckoo). Anonymous.
The Roses of Thy Cheeks. Rafi of Merv.
Seasons and Times. Barnes.
The Strangers. Very.
Success. Guest.
A Virgin Declares Her Beauties. Barberino.
What Frenzy Has of Late Possess'd the Brain! Garth.
Whenever I Go There. Merwin.

Fickle
April Fantasie. Cortissoz.
He Came Too Late. Bogart.
I'm Ashamed of My Thoughts. Anonymous.
On the Flightiness of Thought. Anonymous.

A Song: "Hast thou seen the Down in the Air." Suckling.
Song to a Lute. Suckling.

Fiction (s)
Discourse on the Real. Yellen.
The Minstrel's Last Lay. Barth.
Pantomime Diseases. Abse.
The Purpose of Fable-Writing. Phaedrus.
Wishes to His Supposed Mistress. Crashaw.

Fiddle (s)
Adieu to Bon County. Anonymous.
The Ceremonial Band. Reeves.
The Dark Man. Hopper.
The Dead Fiddle. Wolfe.
Echoes of Childhood. Corbin.
Elinda's Glove. Lovelace.
Epilogue. Heine.
I Wish I Were. Anonymous.
Jacky, Come Give Me Thy Fiddle. Anonymous.
Jonathan Swift Somers. Masters.
Liddell and Scott. Hardy.
Rock, Ball, Fiddle. Anonymous.
She's Hoy'd Me Out o' Lauderdale. Anonymous.

Fiddler (s)
Old King Cole Was a Merry Old Soul. Mother Goose.
The Unicorn. Rieu.

Field (s)
Across the Fields to Anne. Burton.
Alamance. Whiting.
And the Days Are Not Full Enough. Pound.
The Apple Trees. Gluck.
Aside. Thomas.
Ask of the Sun. Zukofsky.
August 1914. Rosenberg.
Aylmer's Field. Tennyson.
Bacchanalia (excerpt). Arnold.
Be Swift O Sun. Mason.
A Beam of Light. Rooney.
The Bird Catcher. Anonymous.
Birds Are Drowsing on the Branches. Rudnitsky.
The Black Regiment. Boker.
Bread and Wine, Part 7. Holderlin.
Bridal Song. Brentano.
Busby, Whose Verse No Piercing Beams, No Rays. Moore.
Bystanders. Matthews.
Caelica, XXXVIII. Greville.
Charles Donnelly. MacDonagh.
Childe Harold's Pilgrimage: Canto III, XXIII. Byron.
Clerk Saunders. Anonymous.
Country Wooing (parody) (excerpt). Squire.
The Crow Sat on the Willow. Clare.
Days. Larkin.
Deaf Girl Playing. Tate.
Death as a Lotus Flower. Anonymous.
Death of Saint Guthlac. Cynewulf.

Demeter and Persephone. Tennyson.
The Dysynni Valley (Wales). Holmes.
Eisenhower's Visit to Franco, 1959. Wright.
The Elm Beetle. Young.
Emergency Haying. Carruth.
Epochs. Lazarus.
Evangeline. Smith.
An Expanded Want Ad. Leithauser.
The Fatal Sisters. Gray.
Father Mat. Kavanagh.
Field Day. Rodgers.
The Fields. Merwin.
The Frightened Ploughman. Clare.
Fury's Field. Bodker.
God, How I Hate You. West.
Haiku: "The crow flew so fast..." Wright.
He Is Like the Lotus. Book of the Dead.
Henry James at Newport. Kees.
Hokku Poems. Wright.
I Fear No Power a Woman Wields. McGaffey.
I Wonder How My Home Is. Anonymous.
The Iliad. Homer.
In a Country Museum. Beer.
In France. Cornford.
In Memoriam A.H.H., XL. Tennyson.
In the Fields. Mew.
In the Old Guerilla War. Pastan.
In Your Arrogance. Lawner.
Ireland. Ryan.
Journey. Harrison.
The Land War. O'Sullivan.
Landscape with Tractor. Taylor.
Leaflight. Donnelly.
Lifelines. Ewart.
Like a Field Waiting. Chalfi.
Lines on the Mermaid Tavern. Keats.
Love Song. Sexton.
Marriage. Williams.
May 20: Very Early Morning. Shaw.
Midwest. Nims.
Mist. Thoreau.
Mount Badon. Williams.
The Mower. Anonymous.
My Grandfather Always Promised Us. Rector.
The Nativity of Christ. Southwell.
Natural Causes. Scott.
The New Man. Very.
Odes. Horace.
Of the Child with the Bird at the Bush. Bunyan.
The Old City. Manning-Sanders.
Old I Am. Bosman.
Old King Cole. Anonymous.
On Not Hearing the Birds Sing in Ireland. Colum.
On Seeing the Field Being Singed. Ise.
Out in the Fields. Anonymous.
The Ploughman. Baker.
Poem for Hemingway & W. C. Williams. Carver.
The Ponies. Gibson.

Praise of Ceres. Heywood.
A Prayer in Late Autumn. Storey.
Pyrography. Ashbery.
The Recruit. Housman.
Return of a Reaper. Creighton.
Riddle: The Swan: "Silent my robe, when I rest on earth." Anonymous.
Romeo and Juliet. Shakespeare.
Rural Lines after Breughel. Krapf.
Salute. Schuyler.
Sea Hunger. Mitchell.
Selective Service. Forche.
September. Pastan.
The Shepherd Speaks. Erskine.
Six Epigrams (excerpt). Hopkins.
Snow-Flakes. Longfellow.
A Song from Sylvan. Guiney.
Song: "Love, that looks still on your eyes." Browne.
Specialist. Roethke.
Sports Field. Wright.
Spring Ease. Reid.
Summer Rain. Coleridge.
Sunday Morning. Schneider.
That's Our Lot. Halpern.
There Is a Charm in Solitude That Cheers. Clare.
To Flavia. Waller.
To the Field Mice. Eberhart.
The Track. Christopher.
Tractor. Sellers.
Two Voices in a Meadow. Wilbur.
Vacation Song. Millay.
Windsor-Forest To the Right Honourable George Lord Lansdown. Pope.
A Winter Twilight. Grimke.
Winter Verse for His Sister. Meredith.
With Rue My Heart Is Laden. Housman.
Your Burnt-Out Body. Markish.

Fiend (s)
The Ceremonies for Candlemas Day. Herrick.
The Frost Spirit. Whittier.
The Great Hunger. Kavanagh.
Gus: the Theatre Cat. Eliot.
Im Traum Sah Ich Ein Mannchen Klein Und Putzig. Heine.
The Last Cup of Canary. Cone.
Memorial Poem. Fuller.
On Reading Mr. Ytche Bashes' Stories in Yiddish. Ehrlichman.
On Ryneveld, an Unpopular Dutch Judge at the Cape of Good Hope. Anonymous.
The "Pater Noster". Anonymous.

Fierce
America A Prophecy. Blake.
Beautiful. Anonymous.
A Bright Day. Montague.
Jessie. Field.
Lilies of the Valley. Silkin.
March. Williams.
Mother Cat. Montague.

Our Lady Peace. Van
Doren.
A Poet's Household. Kizer.
The Sibyl's Song. Roberts.
Sun and Moon. Macpherson.
To the Girls of My
Graduating Class. Layton.
The Warrior Maid. Branch.
What Habacuck Once Spake,
Mine Eyes. Williams.

Fiery
Chinese Winter. Higgins.
The Cross. Tate.
Dust on Spring Street.
Grudin.
Radiant Ranks of Seraphim.
Bryusov.
Song: "All phantoms of the
day." Mezey.

Fife
Auld Reikie. Fergusson.
I'm Seventeen Come Sunday.
Anonymous.
King William Was King
George's Son. *Anonymous.*

Fifteen
Bird in a Cage. *Anonymous.*
Blank Verse for a Fat
Demanding Wife. Lindsey.
To His Very Friend, Master
Richard Martin. Davies.

Fifth
Higgledy-Piggledy. Seaman.
Imperial Thumbprint.
Weatherly.
De Morte. *Anonymous.*
Paradise Lost. Milton.
The Story of Augustus Who
Would Not Have Any
Soup. Hoffmann.

Fifty
Ali Ben Shufti. Thwaite.
The Chaunt of the Brazen
Head (excerpt). Praed.
I Had but Fifty Cents.
Anonymous.
It Is Enough (parody).
Appleman.
Lord Derwentwater (A
version). *Anonymous.*
Lovewell's Fight.
Anonymous.
A New Song Called the
Gaspee. *Anonymous.*
On the Same. Belloc.
Praise. Cooper.
The Winchester Wedding.
D'Urfey.

Fig
The Englishman in Italy.
Browning.
The Lady of the Lake. Scott.
No Fig. Booker.
A Soldier and a Scholar.
Swift.

Fight (ing) (s)
Abraham's Daughter.
Winner.
Achilles and the King.
Logan.
America. Dobell.
Annus Mirabilis. Dryden.
The Approaches. Merwin.
Asolando. Browning.
At the Cenotaph.
""MacDiarmid.
The Ballad of Billy Rose.
Norris.
The Battle of Maldon.
Anonymous.
The Battle of Plattsburg.
Anonymous.

Battle of Somerset. Cullen.
The Battle of Tippecanoe.
Anonymous.
Be Strong. Babcock.
The Bloody Injians.
Anonymous.
Bold General Wolfe.
Anonymous.
Bury Them. Brownell.
The Captain Stood on the
Carronade. Marryat.
The Castle. Muir.
The Cavalier's Song.
Motherwell.
Chesapeake and Shannon.
Anonymous.
Childe Harold's Pilgrimage:
Canto III, XXIII. Byron.
A Chip on His Shoulder.
Anonymous.
Christ's Love. *Anonymous.*
Claudius Gilbert Anagram.
Tis Braul I Cudgel.
Wilson.
Conquest. Johnson.
Conquistador. MacLeish.
The Constitution and
Guerriere. *Anonymous.*
The Cowboy. *Anonymous.*
A Cry from the Ghetto.
Rosenfeld.
Dandelion. Conkling.
David and Bethsabe. Peele.
Dewey in Manila Bay.
Risley.
A Drum for Ben Boyd.
Webb.
Epitaphs of the War, 1914-18.
Kipling.
The Female Warrior.
Anonymous.
Fight. *Anonymous.*
The Fighting Failure.
Appleton.
Gallantly within the Ring.
Reynolds.
General Howe's Letter.
Anonymous.
Hare. Holden.
I Fights Mit Sigel!
Robinson.
If You Ask Me Who I Am.
Guebuza.
Jeannette and Jeannot.
Jeffries.
Jeannot's Answer. Jeffries.
Johnny Armstrong.
Anonymous.
Just One Signal. *Anonymous.*
Keep a Stiff Upper Lip.
Cary.
The King's Own Regulars.
Anonymous.
The Last Round. Wickham.
Lines for My Father. Gray.
Little Things. *Anonymous.*
Locks and Bolts.
Anonymous.
A London Fete. Patmore.
The Lonely Bugle Grieves.
Mellen.
A Long Prologue to a Short
Play... Sheers.
Mulata–to Skinny. Lima.
Mustang Gray. *Anonymous.*
My Brother. Frelimo.
Nigerian Unity/or little
niggers killing little niggers.
Lee.
Ode: Salute to the French
Negro Poets. O'Hara.
Ode to Aphrodite. Sappho.

Oh! for a Steed. Davis.
The Old Whore Speaks to a
Young Poet. Smith.
On the Late Successful
Expedition against
Louisbourg. Hopkinson.
Peace. Kavanagh.
The Poetaster. Jonson.
Prayer for Pain. Neihardt.
The Purple, White and Green.
Morgan-Browne.
The Rebel Girl. Hill.
Reid at Fayal. Palmer.
Revolutionary Letters. Di
Prima.
A Ripping Trip. *Anonymous.*
Robin Hood and the
Scotchman. *Anonymous.*
The Rush of the Oregon.
Guiterman.
Santiago. Janvier.
Smudging. Wakoski.
Sometimes on My Way Back
Down to the Block. Cruz.
St. Valentine. Aguila.
Street Fight. Monro.
A Survey of the
Amphitheatre. Browne.
Thomas at Chickamauga.
Sherwood.
To Arms. Benjamin.
To Nearly Everybody in
Europe To-Day.
""MacDiarmid.
Truxton's Victory.
Anonymous.
Two Little Kittens.
Anonymous.
The Virginia Song.
Anonymous.
The Vixen. Clare.
War. Joseph.
You Fight On (with music).
Anonymous.

Fighter (s)
The Bad Man from the
Brazos. *Anonymous.*
The Proclamation.
Longfellow.

Figure (s)
The Allegorical Figure of
Brooklyn. Towle.
The Bear. Frost.
Epilogue. Lowell.
Homage to David Smith.
Haines.
Home Leave. Howes.
Landscape with Figures.
Douglas.
Limerick: "A lady there was
of Antigua." Monkhouse.
Neckwear. Silverton.
The Pill. Clarke.
Plucking out a Rhythm.
Inada.
Poem for L. C. Klappert.
River Skater. Welles.
Sleep. Naone.
Telephone Lineman. Kroll.
To Emily. Gregor.

File (d)
An Art Master. O'Reilly.
In Answer to Your Query.
Lazard.
Limerick: "There was an old
man of the Nile." Lear.
On File. Bangs.
Solitude. Wilcox.

Fill (ed) (s)
An Abandoned, Overgrown
Cemetery in the Pasture
near Our House. Orr.

The Annunciation. Duffy.
Batches of New Leaves.
London.
Bucket in the Well. Wanek.
Caelica, LXIV. Greville.
Comfort of the Fields.
Lampman.
Daphnaida (excerpt).
Spenser.
Earth Took of Earth.
Anonymous.
The Finches. Murray.
The Flesh and the Spirit.
Bradstreet.
Flood-Time on the Marshes.
Stein.
For Avi Killed in Lebanon.
Osaki.
Giant Thunder. Reeves.
Going through Changes.
Tepperman.
Happy Myrtillo. Carey.
Landfill. Harper.
The Minstrel's Last Lay.
Barth.
Monogamania. Merriam.
Mouths. Dudek.
My Sons. Loewinsohn.
On Dr. Chard. *Anonymous.*
Poem to the Memory of H. L.
Mencken. Wormser.
Poetry and Science. Turner.
The Power and the Glory.
Sassoon.
The Retrieval System.
Kumin.
The Rock. Eliot.
The Rooftop. Gunn.
The Shell's Song. Keats.
Shine Just Where You Are.
Anonymous.
A Simple Pastoral. Stevens.
Sled Burial, Dream Ceremony.
Dickey.
To My Grandmother.
McGuckian.
Towards the Last Spike.
Pratt.
Urban History. Kallman.
Wedding Party. Hall.

Film
The Cloud Chamber. Sze.
Eskimoes Again. Gallup.
Touch of zygosis. Fitzgerald.

Filter
Aunt Eliza. Graham.
Sister Nell. *Anonymous.*

Filth
Hay Scuttle. Morgan.
Ode to a Ditch. *Anonymous.*
Remarks of Soul to Body.
Warren.

Fin (s)
Aubade. Shapiro.
Basking Shark. MacCaig.
A Fish Answers. Hunt.
The Lesson. Lucie-Smith.
Skins. Spires.
The Wanderings of Oisin.
Yeats.

Final
Alceste in the Wilderness.
Hecht.
And the Dead. Jennett.
Arthur Ridgewood, M.D.
Davis.
Boosting the Booster.
Anonymous.
Cattle. Skrzynecki.
Child of Our Time. Boland.
Construction # 13.
Sherwin.

The Death of Friends. Levi.
Dream Songs. Berryman.
Eagle. Skelton.
The Ending. Engle.
The Final Green. Drake.
Georges Bank. Older.
I Can Change Myself.
  Atwood.
In Defense of Superficiality.
  Olson.
Love Poem. Aubert.
Mips and Ma the Mooly Moo.
  Roethke.
Murder in the Cathedral.
  Eliot.
Night Song for a Child!
  Williams.
On the Pole. Greenberg.
The Passing of Arthur
  (parody). Squire.
Pause en Route. Kinsella.
Thus Spake the Saviour.
  Belknap.
Time's Times Again.
  Ammons.
To Alan. Fraser.
What Can I Tell My Bones?
  Roethke.
Find (ing) (s)
40 Acres and a Mule.
  Gallup.
Alien. Frazee-Bower.
American History. Harper.
The Ancient Sage.
  Tennyson.
Astrophel and Stella, CI.
  Sidney.
Ben Plays Hide & Seek in the
  Deep Woods. Hewitt.
The Birds of Arles. Fisher.
Builder Kachina: Home-
  Going. Rose.
The Ceiling. Roethke.
Charity. *Anonymous.*
Chorus: "If I drink water
  while this doth last."
  Peacock.
Clerihews. Bentley.
Columbus. Lowell.
The Crack. Hall.
Doubting. Simpson.
Dream. Ignatow.
The Edward Hopper
  Retrospective. Quagliano.
Epitaph on the Lady Mary
  Villiers. Carew.
Evening in a Lab. Holub.
The Fascination of What's
  Difficult. Yeats.
Find. Miles.
Folk Wisdom. Kinsella.
For My People. Rose.
For Witches. Sutheim.
Forty Years Ago. Perreault.
The Fountain of Tears.
  O'Shaughnessy.
Foxfire. Willard.
The Frog and the Mouse.
  Anonymous.
"From sex, this sea...'.
  Jones.
Getting Older Here. Hauk.
Getting to Rome.
  Anonymous.
Goose Pond. Kunitz.
Harps Hung Up in Babylon.
  Colton.
Hearing That His Friend Was
  Coming Back from the
  War. Wang Chien.
How Came She to Such
  Poppy-Breath? Volborth.

How Far? Miller.
Hymn. Ammons.
Hymn from the French of
  Lamartine (excerpt).
  Whittier.
I Believe I'll Dust My Broom.
  Johnson.
I Cannot Believe That I Am
  of Wind. Greenberg.
I Have Cut an Eagle.
  Koller.
In Praise of Wisdom. Ibn
  Gabirol.
In the Third Year of War.
  Treece.
Jack. Ross.
Kiph. De la Mare.
A Kitchen Prayer. Petersen.
Last Night There Was a
  Cricket in Our Closet.
  Quintana.
Little Blue Ben. *Anonymous.*
Little Friend. *Anonymous.*
Lochan. Smith.
Loose Woman. Kennedy.
Lord, I Know Thy Grace Is
  Nigh Me. Ganse.
Love Play. Newcastle.
Love's Entreaty.
  Michelangelo.
Love Song. *Anonymous.*
The Mad Maid's Song.
  Herrick.
A March Calf. Hughes.
A Mare. Barnes.
The Message of the Rain.
  Russell.
Mixed Media. Schevill.
A Morning Prayer.
  Perpetuo.
New England's Annoyances.
  Anonymous.
Novelettes III: The Gardener.
  MacNeice.
Of a Mouse and Men.
  Hovde.
Old Walt. Hughes.
On a Return from Egypt.
  Douglas.
Our True Beginnings.
  Gardiner.
Pearl Bryan. *Anonymous.*
Pilgrim at Rome.
  Anonymous.
Poem for Easter. Kelly.
A Postcard to Send to Sumer.
  Bronk.
The Questionings. Hedge.
Renewal. Kowit.
Rev Owl. Klein.
The Rose Is a Royal Lady.
  Blanden.
Santa Claus. *Anonymous.*
The Secret in the Cat.
  Swenson.
She died–this was the way she
  died. Dickinson.
Sheltered Garden. Doolittle.
The Sleeper. Field.
Sonnet: "But love whilst that
  thou may'st be loved
  again." Daniel.
Sopolis. Callimachus.
The Sparrow's Skull. Pitter.
St. Augustine Contemplating
  the Bust of Einstein.
  Ackerman.
The Stick. Bennett.
A Store-House. Dudek.
Success. *Anonymous.*
Such Love Is Like a Smoky
  Fire. Chapman.

Sunflower. Updike.
The Swarthmore Phi Beta
  Kappa Poem. Lattimore.
Thinking Happiness. Farley.
Three Wise Old Women.
  Corbett.
Tommy O'Linn. *Anonymous.*
Two Sonnets for a Lost Love.
  DeWitt.
Under the Sign of the Moth.
  Wagoner.
The Untold Want. Whitman.
An Upper Chamber.
  Bannerman.
Variation on a Theme by John
  Lyly. Sitwell.
Violets in Thaumantia's
  Bosome. Sherburne.
The Wakeupworld. Cullen.
The Wavering Planet.
  Anonymous.
We Cared for Each Other.
  Heine.
We Let It Go That He Was a
  Perfect Man. Parra.
When Things Go Wrong.
  Anonymous.
The white chrysanthemum.
  Mitsune (Oshikochi no
  Mitsune).
Whitman. Levis.
The Wind at Penistone.
  Davie.
Worth While. Wilcox.
Fine
Ain't It Fine Today!
  Malloch.
Armstrong Spring Creek.
  Davis.
Chock House Blues.
  Jefferson.
The Faerie Queene. Spenser.
For the Cultural Campaign.
  Jigmed.
The Hunt. De La Mare.
It's Fine Today. Malloch.
Its a Good Thing to Join a
  Union. *Anonymous.*
Life is Fine. Hughes.
Limerick: "There once was a
  warden of Wadham."
  Anonymous.
Love Unlike Love.
  Anonymous.
The Market Economy.
  Piercy.
A Memory. Tynan.
My Crime. Bill.
Not Saying Much. Gregg.
Pleasent Delusion of a
  Sumpteous Citty. Knight.
The Revolution. Gilbert.
Running the River Lines.
  Baker.
The Sickness of Friends.
  Coulette.
Song: "I make my shroud but
  no one knows." Crapsey.
Stowaway. Adams.
Summer. Manhire.
Tales of the Islands, III.
  Walcott.
The Translated Way.
  Adams.
When You and I Must Part.
  Anonymous.
When You Send Out
  Invitations, Don't Ask Me.
  Palladas.
Finger (s)
Advice. Di Pasquale.
After Lorca. Hughes.

Amasis. Binyon.
Annie Breen. *Anonymous.*
Autumn. Campbell.
Balboa, the Entertainer.
  Jones.
Bird Watcher. Wallace.
Carol for His Darling on
  Christmas Day. Stanford.
Case. Janowitz.
Casino Beach. Rabbit.
Coach into Pumpkin. Reid.
Counting Small-Boned Bodies.
  Bly.
Crocodiles. Kurka.
Death on a Live Wire.
  Baldwin.
A Dragonfly. Farjeon.
Dream Songs. Berryman.
Driving into Enid. Van
  Walleghen.
The Dyke-Builder. Treece.
Elegy on Herakleitos.
  Callimachus.
Energy for a New Thang.
  Mkalimoto.
The Fall of Hyperion.
  Keats.
Fall of Leaves. Savage.
For a Friend. Steingass.
For My Torturer, Lieutenant
  D–. Djabali.
Fragment of a Character.
  Moore.
Frightened Face. Strobel.
A Glance. *Anonymous.*
Gold Is the Son of Zeus:
  Neither Moth Nor Worm
  May Gnaw It. "Field.
Grassroots. Sandburg.
A Happy View. Day-Lewis.
I'll Build My House. Hall.
If You Want to Go A-
  Courting. *Anonymous.*
In One Battle. Jones.
In Passing. Helton.
In the Cathedral. Beer.
In the Small Boats of Their
  Hands. Kircher.
Indian Love Song.
  Blockcolski.
Jealousy. *Anonymous.*
The Key-Board. Watson.
Labour of the Brain, Ballad of
  the Body. Forman.
The Lake in the Sky.
  Haines.
Learning to Type. O Hehir.
The Lesson. Mariani.
A Letter to Her Father.
  Inib-sarri.
Letters to My Daughters.
  Minty.
Localities. Sandburg.
Map Reference T994724.
  Pudney.
The Moods. Davis.
Moral Ode. Rosenmann-
  Taub.
Morvin. Fuller.
Observation at Dawn.
  Kovner.
On a Field at Fredericksburg.
  Smith.
Once. Walker.
One, Two, Three, Four, Five.
  Anonymous.
Pain. Henry.
Palaces of Gold. Rosselson.
Poetry. Sutzkever.
Policemen Laughing. Fraser.
Pomegranate. Harada.

The Poor in Church.
Rimbaud.
Preexistence. Cornford.
Sea Lullaby. Wylie.
Short Short Story. Jacobsen.
The Smell of Fish. Meissner.
Spinning Song. *Anonymous.*
Spring Pastoral. Wylie.
Suppose... Horne.
Surf. Morrison.
The Temple by the Sea.
Dutton.
Through All Your Abstract
Reasoning. Patten.
Uncle Robert. Morgan.
Welt. Johnson.
Would you come back if I
said the earth. Tueni.
Yellow. Wright.

Finish (ed)
An Accommodating Lion.
Jenks.
After Ever Happily.
Serraillier.
America Bleeds. Lewis.
Ares. Ehrenstein.
At a Private Showing in 1982.
Kumin.
Bereaved of All, I Went
Abroad. Dickinson.
The Body Is the Victory and
the Defeat of Dreams.
Anghelaki-Rooke.
The Country of a Thousand
Years of Peace. Merrill.
Falltime. Sandburg.
The Half Moon Shows a Face
of Plaintive Sweetness.
Rossetti.
I felt a Funeral, in my Brain.
Dickinson.
It Is Not Likely Now.
Bellerby.
Letter from a Working Girl.
Scott.
The Old-Fashioned Pitcher.
Phair.
Once There Were Three
Fishermen. *Anonymous.*
Phases of the Moon.
Browning.
The Sea Dike. Vasalis.
The View from the Window.
Thomas.

Fins (s)
On Reading Poems to a
Senior Class at South High.
Berry.
Rural Sports. Gay.
The Sharks. Levertov.

Fionn
Generosity. *Anonymous.*
Oisin. *Anonymous.*
The Praise of Fionn.
Anonymous.
The Wry Rowan.
Anonymous.

Fir (s)
The Ballad of Blossom. Van
Duyn.
Blocks. O'Hara.
Have Sky. MacAdams.
Logging (excerpt). Snyder.
The Lost Lagoon. Johnson.
Moonrise in the Rockies.
Higginson.
Oread. Doolittle.
Tree. Wilson.

Fire (s)
Address to Certain Gold
Fishes. Coleridge.

Advice to Bachelors.
Anonymous.
After the Centennial.
Cranch.
An Age. Jensen.
The Alchemist. Church.
All in the Downs. Hood.
The Anger That Breaks a
Man Down into Boys.
Vallejo.
Another to the Maids.
Herrick.
Anthem for St. Cecilia's Day.
Auden.
Arcadia. Sidney.
Art. Thomson.
As Ocean's Stream.
Tyutchev.
The Assault on the Fortress.
Dwight.
Astrology. Marshall.
The Auroras of Autumn.
Stevens.
Beauty. Hille.
Beauty. Stanley.
Before Chilembwe Tree.
Mapanje.
Beginning to Live. Stone.
Birthday Gifts. Asquith.
The Bonfire. Frost.
Broken Sky. Sandburg.
The Buck's Elegy.
Anonymous.
Burncombe Hollow. Barnes.
The Burning Bush.
Nicholson.
Burning the Christmas
Greens. Williams.
Caelica, XXXIV. Greville.
Candle-Lighting Song.
Ketchum.
The Card-Players. Larkin.
Careers. Welish.
Carol: "Fire is what's precious
now..." Boodson.
Carolina Spring Song. Allen.
A Casual Song. Noel.
A Century of Couplets
(excerpt). Trench.
Checking the Firing. Smith.
A Child's Winter Evening.
John.
Christine. Hay.
Christmas Carol. del
Castillo.
Christmas Comes to Moccasin
Flat. Welch.
Christmas Tree. Smith.
Colloquy in Black Rock.
Lowell.
Come, Gentle Death!
Watson.
Come Holy Spirit, Dove
Divine. Judson.
The Conflict. Day Lewis.
The Contented Bachelor.
Kendall.
Continent's End. Jeffers.
The County Ball (excerpt).
Praed.
Cranmer. Sisson.
The Cubical Domes.
Gascoyne.
The Cup. Trowbridge.
The Dark Birds. Meyers.
Darling, I won't be your hot
love. Sulpicia.
Dawn. Pizarnik.
The Dead Words. Watkins.
Death of a Cat. Schevill.
Desire. Traherne.

Desire Is a Witch. Day-
Lewis.
A Devonshire Rhyme.
Anonymous.
Dies Irae. Hagerup.
Dirge for Small Wilddeath.
Moffett.
Don Juan. Byron.
Doors of the Temple.
Huxley.
Doubt. Rogers.
The Dove. Eliot.
Dream Songs. Berryman.
A Dressed Man and a Naked
Man. Orwell.
Driftwood. Bynner.
Easter Eve 1945. Rukeyser.
The Ebb and Flow. Taylor.
Elegy for 41 Whales Beached
in Florence, Ore., June,
1979. Bierds.
Emily Sparks. Masters.
The Energy of Light. Hay.
Epigram: "Thy eyes are
sparks, Lycines." Strato.
Epistle for Spring. Larsson.
Epitaph of a Courtesan.
Asclepiades.
An Evening Walk (excerpt).
Wordsworth.
Exit, Pursued by a Bear.
Nash.
The Extasie. Cowley.
Feed Still Thyself. Ralegh.
The Female Parricide.
Anonymous.
The Female Phaeton. Prior.
Fire Island Poem. Wakoski.
The Fire of Drift-Wood.
Longfellow.
A Fire-Truck. Wilbur.
Firebowl. Clouts.
Firefly. Uba.
The First Olympionique to
Hiero of Syracuse. Pindar.
Flute Player. *Anonymous.*
The Flying Cloud.
Anonymous.
For Them. Brownstein.
From "The River-Fight."
Brownell
Frost. Pratt.
A Full and True Account of a
Horrid and Barbarous
Robbery. Byrom.
Funeral in Hungary. Boyle.
Gallow Hill. Tait.
Girl's Song. *Anonymous.*
Go Down, Ol' Hannah.
Anonymous.
God from His Throne with
Piercing Eye. Steward.
Godfrey of Bulloigne:
Armida...Sets out to undo
the Crusaders. Tasso.
Grandmother. Young Bear.
Gretel in Darkness. Gluck.
Habitation. Atwood.
He Renounceth All the Effects
of Love. Vaux.
He Sits down on the Floor of
a School for the Retarded.
Nowlan.
Heart and Mind. Sitwell.
Hearthstone. Monro.
Hebrew Script. Loewenthal.
Hera, Hung from the Sky.
Kizer.
Hermetic Bird. Lamantia.
The Highwaymen. Gay.
Hokkaido. Trifilio.
The Hounds. Dickinson.

House of the Living. Vigee.
The House Remembers.
Francis.
A Hymn to Night.
Michelson.
I Enter by the Darkened Door
(parody). King.
I Heard the Old Song.
Vilakazi.
I Know a Name!
Anonymous.
I Served in a Great Cause.
Traubel.
I Shall Weep. Hirshbein.
I sighed and owned my love.
Anonymous.
Ice and Fire. Sherburne.
Idea. Drayton.
The Impetuous Lover.
Fairburn.
In Apia Bay. Roberts.
In Days of New. Bartlett.
In Praise of Music in Time of
Pestilence. Hine.
Innocent Play. Watts.
The Invention of Fire.
Taylor.
Inventory–to 100th Street.
Lima.
The Invitation. Herrick.
The Iron Gate (excerpt).
Holmes
January. Voigt.
The Jew at Christmas Eve.
Shapiro.
The Killing. MacBeth.
The Kiss. Sexton.
The Lament of the Damned in
Hell. Young.
Laus Veneris. Moulton.
The Light'ood Fire. Boner.
The Lilly in a Christal.
Herrick.
Lines Concerning the
Unknown Soldier: "Arteries
juicy with blood."
Mandelstam.
Little Girl, My Stringbean,
My Lovely Woman.
Sexton.
The Little Johnny Mine.
Detrick.
Lollingdon Downs.
Masefield.
Loneliness. Young.
Loss. Aldington.
The Lover Sendeth Sighs to
Move His Suit. Wyatt.
Madrigal: "Wake, sleepy
Thyrsis." Pilkington.
Magma. Dutton.
Memorial Couplets for the
Dying Ego. Barker.
Metamorphosis. Porter.
The Milwaukee Fire.
Anonymous.
The Miramichi Fire.
Anonymous.
The Mirrors. Andresen.
Moonrise in the Rockies.
Higginson.
A Mother Is a Sun. Bennett.
My Little Wife. *Anonymous.*
My Muse and I, Ere Youth
and Spirits Fled. Colman.
Native Origin. Brant.
The Night Loves Us.
Adeane.
The Nimble Stag. Knox.
No Moon, No Chance to
Meet. Ono no Komachi.
Noon. Jeffers.

The North Sea Undertaker's Complaint. Lowell.
Nude with Green Chair. Oldknow.
Nunc Scio, Quid Sit Amor. Mackay.
A Nuptial Song, or Epithalamie, on Sir Clipseby Crew and His Lady. Herrick.
October in Tennessee. Malone.
October Morning. Piatt.
Ode for Soft Voice. McClure.
Ode Written in 1966. Borges.
Oenone. Tennyson.
The Offended. Hebert.
Old Country Talk. Farkas.
The Old Tree. Young.
Old Winter. Noel.
On Teaching David to Shoot. McDonald.
One Flesh. Jennings.
One Poet Visits Another. Davies.
The Palm Willow. Bridges.
Paradox: That Fruition Destroys Love (excerpt). King.
The Patriarch. Burns.
Peat-Cutters. Johnson.
The Phoenix of Mozart. Vigee.
The Pilgrim's Progress. Bunyan.
The Power and the Glory. Sassoon.
The Princess Casamassima. Hoffman.
Proem. Gibson.
Prometheus. Mastoraki.
Prometheus Unbound. Hope.
Prophecy in Flame. Howard.
Prose Poem. Jennings.
The Public Garden. Lowell.
Pyramus and Thisbe. Ovid (Publius Ovidius Naso).
Raven. Niatum.
Reb Hanina. Raboff.
The Red Room. Berke.
De Rerum Natura. Lucretius (Titus Lucretitus Carus).
Revelation. Bright.
Right true it is... Wyatt.
The Rock. Eliot.
Rotten Lake Elegy. Rukeyser.
Rumination. Eberhart.
Ruth. Murray.
Sacco-Vanzetti. Halpern.
The Sacred Hearth. Gascoyne.
A Sale of Smoke. Spear.
Sea Burial from the Cruiser "Reve." Eberhart.
The Sea Cathedral. Pratt.
The Shadow. Symons.
Sin, Despair, and Lucifer. Fletcher.
Six Movements on a Theme. Ignatow.
The Snow-Ball. Stanley.
The Snow Curlew. Watkins.
Solvitur Acris Hiems. Mahony.
Sonet XXV. Stirling.
Song. Anonymous.
Song: "When I lie burning in thine eye." Stanley.

Sonnet XVI: "After an age when thunderbolts and hail." Labe.
The Sonnet of the Mountain. Saint-Gelais.
Sonnets: A Sequence on Profane Love. Boker.
A Spring Wind. Spencer.
Still Though the One I Sing. Whitman
Style. Nemerov.
Such Love Is Like a Smoky Fire. Chapman.
Taffy Was a Welshman. Anonymous.
Talk Not of Strength, Till Your Heart Has Know. Wilcox.
Tears, Flow No More. Herbert of Cherbury.
The Teeth Mother Naked at Last. Bly.
Territory. Wood-Thompson.
Theresienstadt Poem. Mezey.
This Night of No Moon. Ono no Komachi.
The Tired Man. Wickham.
Tissue. Griffin.
To Be Said at the Seder. Wolfskehl.
To Her Againe, She Burning in a Feaver. Carew.
To His Lady. Davies.
To His Lady, Who Had Vowed Virginity. Davison.
To L. C. Hawkins.
To Ping-Ku, Asleep. Durrell.
To the Lord Love. "Field.
Tongues of Fire. Plescoff.
The Town Called Providence Its Fate. Tompson.
Trials of a Tourist. Tibble.
Trust in Me. Anonymous.
Turning Point. Holshouser.
Two at a Fireside. Markham.
Two Drinking Songs. Alcaeus.
Two Long Vacations: Grasmere. Butler.
Unable by Long and Hard Travel to Banish Love, Returns Her Friend. Turberville.
The Unknown. Davidson.
Upon His Timorous Silence in Her Presence. Davison.
Upon the Author; by a Known Friend. Woodbridge.
Venus. Rossetti.
The Very Pretty Maid of This Town... Anonymous.
The View of Rangitoto. Brasch.
Watching the Sun Rise over Mount Zion. Whitman.
Waterspout. Camoens.
Weathercock. Jennings.
The Wild Knight. Chesterton.
The Wilderness. Keyes.
The Wind of January. Rossetti.
The Wing Factory. Stein.
Winter. Anonymous.
The Winter House. Cameron.
Winter Is Here. Vala.
Winter to Spring. Horace.

A Winter Wish. Messinger.
With the Sun's Fire. Ignatow.
Wolf Hunting near Nashoba. Barnes.
Women. Cartwright.
Yogi, don't go away. Mira Bai [(or Mirabai)].
Yom Kippur. Chaet.
You Northern Girl. Ballard.
Youth Sings a Song of Rosebuds. Cullen.
Zarathustra. Jones, Jr.

Fired
Canning Time. Morgan.
The New Song. Field.
The Virgin Sturgeon. Anonymous.
A Visit from Abroad. Stephens.

Fireflies
The Begetting of Cain. Plutzik.
Blue Ridge. Voigt.
Going Back. Quasimodo.
I Will Write Songs Against You. Reznikoff.
Nocturne: Georgia Coast. Hicky.
Peasant and Geisha Songs. Anonymous.

Firelight
The Adventurer. Shepard.
The Beatific Vision. Chesterton.
The Colors of Night. Momaday.
New Year's Eve. Lawrence.
Safe. Walker.
What the Orderly Dog Saw. Ford.

Fireside
To a Cricket. Bennett.

Firm
Baby Running Barefoot. Lawrence.
The Beautiful Train. Empson.
A bright moon illumines the night-prospect. Anonymous.
Mankind. Anonymous.
The New Roof. Hopkinson.
Om. Anonymous.
The Sudbury Fight. Rice.

Firmament
His Muse Speakes to Him. Habington.
Joy Enough. Eastman.
The New Moon. Blunden.

First
All Service Ranks the Same with God. Browning.
Barley-Break; or, Last in Hell. Herrick.
Before the Storm. Dehmel.
Believe It. Logan.
A Birthday. Muir.
Black People: This Is Our Destiny. Jones.
Breakfast. Shectman.
Bridesmaid. Wilson, Jr.
Brown Like Us. Soto.
Caelica, LXXXVIII. Greville.
Camp Notes. Yamada.
Cartography. Oppenheimer.
Chelmsfords Fate. Tompson.
Crocus. Murray.
The Cultivation of Christmas Trees. Eliot.
Degas. Monette.

Distich. Hay.
A Dream of Death. Yeats.
An Elegy upon the Death of the Dean of St. Paul's, Dr. John Donne. Carew.
Epigram: "When Pontius wished an edict might be passed." Prior.
Epistle to Augusta. Byron.
Epitaph (Inscription from Anticyra). Anonymous.
An Epitaph on Master Vincent Corbett. Jonson.
Epitaph on the Late King of the Sandwich Isles. Praed.
The Evening-Watch. Vaughan.
Family Cups. Orlen.
February. Winder.
Finding a Poem. Merriam.
The First Day of Creation. Milton.
First Departure. Frost.
First in the Pentathlon. Lucilius [(or Lucillius)].
The First Kiss of Love. Byron.
First Light. Kinsella.
First Reader. Leary.
The First Song. Burton.
Five Epigrams. Hall.
The Flight. Teasdale.
For a Marriage. Jong.
Freely, from a Song Sung by Jewish Women of Yemen. Levy.
From the Night of Forebeing. Thompson.
Gascoigne's Memories. Gascoigne.
Get Up and Bar the Door. Anonymous.
God's First Creature Was Light. Welles.
God to Be First Served. Herrick.
Heliodore. Logan.
Hero and Leander. Marlowe.
Hide, O Hide Those Hills of Snow. Fletcher.
Holy Thursday. Wright.
Homecoming. George.
Homosexual Sonnets. Pitchford.
How Great My Grief. Hardy.
Hymn to the Supreme Being on Recovery (excerpt). Smart.
I Would Like My Love to Die. Beckett.
Imperial Adam. Hope.
In Nature There Is Neither Right nor Left nor Wrong. Jarrell.
In Passing. Helton.
In the Beginning. Monroe.
Introversion. Underhill.
Isis Wanderer. Raine.
Legend. Waller.
The Lily of Torrow. Van Dyke.
Limbo. Rugo.
Living in the Boneyard. Simon.
Memories. Aldrich.
A Midsummer Night's Dream. Shakespeare.
Mrs. Seymour Fentolin. Herford.
My Master and I. Anonymous.

No Accident.   MacCaig.
Old Man Travelling.
   Wordsworth.
Paradise Lost.   Milton.
The Penitent Nun.
   Lockman.
The Pinto.   Wister.
Poem for Roslyn.   Lewisohn.
A Portrait in the Guards.
   Whistler.
The Pro.   Swenson.
The Pulkovo Meridian:
   Leningrad: 1943.   Inber.
The Queen of Seasons.
   Newman.
Rain in the Night.   Burr.
Ready, Ay, Ready.   Merivale.
Rebeca in a Mirror.
   Rodriguez.
Repentance.   Untermeyer.
Retractions.   Cabell.
Rhyme for Remembering the
   Date of Easter.
   Richardson.
Rhyme of Rain.   Holmes.
De Roberval.   Hunter-Duvar.
The Simplon Pass.
   Wordsworth.
Solomon and Morolph, Their
   Last Encounter.   Levertin.
St. Peter at the Gate.
   Smiley.
St. Stephen's Day.
   Dickinson.
The Temple of Infamy
   (excerpt).   Harpur.
That First Gulp of Air We
   All Took When First Born.
   Paddock.
Tho' You May Boast You're
   Fairer.   *Anonymous.*
Time, Real and Imaginary.
   Coleridge.
To a Child.   Herrick.
To Zion.   Halevi.
Transfiguration.   Barnes.
The Triumph of Time.
   Swinburne.
Unter der Linde.
   Ellenbogen.
We Give Thee but Thine
   Own.   How.
Were the Bright Day No
   More to Visit Us.
   Anonymous.
The Windows of Waltham.
   Wieners.
Woman's Ruling Passions.
   Pope.
Yussouf.   Lowell.
The Zulu Girl.   Campbell.
Fish (ed) (es) (ing)
12 Oct.   Planz.
Accordance.   Kanabus.
All Things Can Tempt Me.
   Yeats.
Amergin's Songs.
   Anonymous.
The Aquarium, San Francisco.
   Sackville-West.
At the Water Zoo.   Knox.
Baits for Various Fish.
   Barker.
Blackbirds and Thrushes.
   Anonymous.
The Bulldog on the Bank.
   Anonymous.
By Loe Pool.   Symons.
Caelica, LVII.   Greville.
Canadice Lake.   Mondy.
Catch.   Hughes.
Circe.   Warren.

City Life.   Lawrence.
Cleaning the Fish.   Pack.
Cleopatra to the Asp.
   Hughes.
Codes.   Chang.
The Considerate Crocodile.
   Wells.
Darkness.   Kuzma.
Detroit.   Hall.
The Djanggawul Cycle, 7.
   Anonymous.
Dream Fishing.   Thomas.
Drinking Song.   Harrison.
Drunk as drunk on
   turpentine.   Neruda.
Emblems.   Dunn.
Enigmas.   Neruda.
Evolution.   Smith.
Father Fisheye.   Balakian.
Festoons of Fishes.
   Kreymborg.
The Final Trawl.
   Anonymous.
The Fish.   Bishop.
Fish Crier.   Sandburg.
A Fish Story.   Fishman.
The Fish Upstairs.   Dickey.
The Fisherman.   Fawcett.
The Fisherman's Wife.
   Mitchell.
A Fishing Song.   Rands.
The Flying Fish.   Cope.
The Flying Fish.   Gray.
Goldfish.   Monro.
A Green Stream.   Wang Wei.
Heaven.   Brooke.
Hippopotamus.   Cole.
Historical Incidents.   Day.
Hope (excerpt).   Shenstone.
The House I Go to in My
   Dream.   Barker.
How Doth the Little
   Crocodile.   "Carroll.
Hunting Season.   Auden.
Into Fish.   Nelms.
An Invitation to the
   Zoological Gardens.
   Anonymous.
Jerusalem Sonnets.   Baxter.
Jig.   Day-Lewis.
Katharine Jaffray (C version).
   Anonymous.
Katherine Johnstone.
   Anonymous.
The Lady and the Bear.
   Roethke.
Lament for a Sailor.   Dehn.
A Lesson from Van Gogh.
   Moss.
Liard Hot Springs.
   Massman.
Limbo.   Heaney.
Limerick: "When a jolly
   young fisher named Fisher."
   Anonymous.
Loss of an Oil Tanker.
   Causley.
Love Dirge.   *Anonymous.*
Low Tide.   Woessner.
The Lure.   O'Reilly.
Magic Fox.   Welch.
The Magnolia's Shadow.
   Montale.
Manong Jacinto Santo Tomas.
   Robles.
Materia Nupcial.   Neruda.
Mirror.   Plath.
The Moorhen Pond.   Earley.
Mountain Study.   Van
   Toorn.
Moving Ahead.   Rilke.
Nature Morte.   MacNeice.

Nature's Lineaments.
   Graves.
The Net of Law.   Roche.
Off to the Fishing Ground.
   Montgomery.
On Becoming Man.   Lister.
On His Queerness.
   Isherwood.
On the Dangers Attending
   Altruism on the High Seas.
   Chesterton.
An Ordinary Evening in
   Cleveland.   Turco.
The P'eng That Was a K'un.
   Lao Tse [or Lao Tzu].
Penguin on the Beach.
   Miller.
Pepsi Generation.   Ting.
Photograph of My Father in
   His Twenty-Second Year.
   Carver.
Poly-Olbion.   Drayton.
The Praise of New
   Netherland.   Steendam.
Psychoanalysis.   Ewart.
The Raquette River, Potsdam,
   New York....   Piccone.
Return to Hinton.
   Tomlinson.
Rock Tumbler.   Reid.
Round the Bay of Mexico.
   Anonymous.
Seeking a Mooring.   Wang
   Wei.
The Signs of the Zodiac.
   Brewer.
The Silver Question.
   Herford.
Sir Launfal.   Moultrie.
The Small.   Welch.
The Smell of Fish.   Meissner.
Sonnet: "My Duchess was the
   werst she laffed she bitte."
   Walsh.
Summer.   Wakoski.
Surf-Casting.   Merwin.
Terence McDiddler.
   Anonymous.
To Calliope.   Graves.
To the (Supposed) Patron.
   Hill.
Tommy Tittlemouse.
   Anonymous.
Two Old Ladies.   Sassoon.
Unclench Yourself.   Piercy.
Useless Day.   Castellános.
Wash.   Chuilleanain.
Wasp.   Welsh.
We Manage Most When We
   Manage Small.   Gregg.
What Do You Say When a
   Man Tells You, You Have
   the Softest Skin.   Mackey.
The Wounded Hawk.
   Palmer.
Fisherman
Angling, a Day.   Kinnell.
Blood on the Sails.
   Colclough.
The Bold Fisherman.
   Anonymous.
Did I Ever Think.   Ono no
   Takamura.
The Dirigible.   Wallace-
   Crabbe.
The Fisherman"s Song.
   D'Urfey.
Fishermen.   Emanuel.
Seaman, 1941.   Holden.
Fissure (s)
The Ice Has Spoken.
   Rixson.

Limerick: "When a jolly
   young fisher named Fisher."
   Anonymous.
You Will Know When You
   Get There.   Curnow.
Fist (s)
The Armadillo.   Bishop.
Autumn.   Roberts.
The Bad-Tempered Wife.
   Anonymous.
Building Bridges.   Mahaka.
Cancer's a Funny Thing.
   Haldane.
Christmas at Vail: On Staying
   Indoors.   Monaghan.
Church-Monuments.
   Herbert.
The City of Satisfaction.
   Hoffman.
Cousin Ella Goes to Town.
   Lyon.
Coyote Brother Song.   West.
Death of a Hind.   MacLean.
The Distant Drum.   Hernton.
The Drunk Man.
   Anonymous.
Entering the Body: The
   Survivor.   Berg.
The Faerie Queene.   Spenser.
For My Daughter.   Ochester.
Goddwyn: Ode to Liberty.
   Chatterton.
Greatness.   *Anonymous.*
Green Lions.   Stewart.
A Grief Ago.   Thomas.
I Have Seen Black Hands.
   Wright.
Iron Landscapes (and the
   Statue of Liberty).   Gunn.
Limerick: "There was a gay
   damsel of Lynn."
   Anonymous.
Lines.   Swann.
A Magus.   Ciardi.
Man with One Small Hand.
   Page.
Matthew V: 29-30.   Mahon.
The Melmac Year.   Hilton.
Midsummer.   Spender.
Militant.   Hughes.
The Mill-stream, Now that
   Noises Cease.   Housman.
Modern Midnight
   Conversation: Between a
   Contractor and His Wife.
   Anonymous.
Monks.   Newman.
The Person from Porlock.
   Graves.
The Piano.   Davey.
Praxis.   Thesen.
The Runner.   Whitman.
Sonnet against the Too-Facile
   Mystic.   Harrod.
Sorting, Wrapping, Packing,
   Stuffing.   Schuyler.
Vittoria Colonna.   Marz.
Fit (s)
The Bad-Tempered Wife.
   Anonymous.
Cancer's a Funny Thing.
   Haldane.
Church-Monuments.
   Herbert.
The City of Satisfaction.
   Hoffman.
Cousin Ella Goes to Town.
   Lyon.
The Faerie Queene.   Spenser.
Greatness.   *Anonymous.*

Limerick: "There was a gay damsel of Lynn." *Anonymous.*
Lines. Swann.
Man with One Small Hand. Page.
Matthew V: 29-30. Mahon.
The Melmac Year. Hilton.
Modern Midnight Conversation: Between a Contractor and His Wife. *Anonymous.*
Monks. Newman.
Sonnet against the Too-Facile Mystic. Harrod.
Sorting, Wrapping, Packing, Stuffin. Schuyler.

Five
The Banished Gods. Mahon.
Berthe Morisot. Waldman.
Bicycalamity. Peters.
Birthday Poem from Venice. Beer.
The Choice of the Cross. Sayers.
The Cinque Ports. *Anonymous.*
The Composition of Distances. Pien Chih-lin.
Dives and Lazarus. *Anonymous.*
Epitaph on a Madman's Grave. Gilbert.
The Famous Fight at Malago. *Anonymous.*
First in the Pentathlon. Lucilius [(or Lucillius)].
For Maria at Four. Becker.
The God of War. Brecht.
Hints on Pronunciation for Foreigners. *Anonymous.*
Image in a Lilac Tree. Tiller.
In Dives' Dive. Frost.
Lament for Ignacio Sanchez Mejias. Garcia Lorca.
Letters from an Irishman to a Rat. Logue.
Solitude. Lampman.
Something Has Fallen. Levine.
A Song of the GPO. Hamill.
The Test. Emerson.
Those Images. Yeats.
Tomorrows. Merrill.
Two Souls. Pickthall.
The Winchester Wedding. D'Urfey.
Wine from the Cape. Cassity.

Fix (ed)
All Saint's Day (excerpt). Guidacci.
Ballade of Boys Bathing. Rolfe.
The Clock. Holman.
Fire. Carpenter.
Handyman. Phillips.
Here and There: Nocturnal Landscape. Cowley.
The Misery of Mechanics. Booth.
Perfect. ""MacDiarmid.
Romance of the Range. Carr.
Sestina. Kroll.
Since I Heard. Mitsune (Oshikochi no Mitsune).
Sonnet: "Could then the Babes from yon unshelter'd cot." Russell.
The Taj. Keene.

The Turtle. Nash.
Words. Plath.
The Yellowhammer. Clare.

Fl (ies) (y)
Absence. Sidney.
The Aleph Bet. Lipshitz.
All God's Children Got Shoes. *Anonymous.*
America. Dumas.
Amoretti, LXXXVI. Spenser.
Arrows. Heyen.
As Long as the Heart Beats. Zawadiwsky.
The Aspiration. Norris.
The Bad Man from the Brazos. *Anonymous.*
Becoming Is Perfection. Johnson.
Bee! I'm Expecting You! Dickinson.
Bird Song. Hay.
The Birdcatcher. Hodgson.
Black Tambourine. Crane.
Bring me the sunset in a cup. Dickinson.
A Bull. Deutsch.
Calendar. Bodker.
Carmina. Catullus.
A Caution to Everybody. Nash.
Chimes. Meynell.
Choosing a Mast. Campbell.
Christiana. Redgrove.
Combinations. Hoberman.
Consider the Auk. Nash.
Country Burying (1919). Warren.
The Cuckoo. *Anonymous.*
The Cuckoo Comes in April. *Anonymous.*
Curiosity: The News. Sprague.
Dear, Do Not Your Fair Beauty Wrong. May.
Death. Coleridge.
A Death to Us. Silkin.
A Difference. Clark.
Drinking the Wind. Tan Ying.
Driving in Oklahoma. Revard.
The Duel. Cowley.
Ego Tripping. Giovanni.
The End of Summer. Minty.
Envoi. Swinburne.
The Epitaph Ending in And. Stafford.
Fall Letter. Kelly.
The Final Word. Moraes.
First Death. Justice.
Fly-Fishing. Gay.
Gaiety of Descendants. Newton.
The Gay. Russell.
The Gentle Anarchist. Stephens.
Geo-Politics. Cardona-Hine.
Giving Potatoes. Mitchell.
The Gnu. Belloc.
Harriet. Lowell.
The Hindoo: He Doesn't Hurt a Fly or a Spider Either. Ramanujan.
Horse. Blasing.
Hymn. Peabody.
If Pigs Could Fly. Reeves.
The Immortal. Blake.
Invitation. Behn.
It Is Time. Joans.
Jailbird. Scannell.
The Knot. Kunitz.

Ladybird! Ladybird! Bronte.
The Lion at Noon. Hugo.
The Lonely Scarecrow. Kirkup.
Look to the Leaf. *Anonymous.*
Love. Baker.
A Love-Song by a Lunatic. *Anonymous.*
Loving Henry. *Anonymous.*
The Magician Suspends the Children. Oles.
The Maiden Hind. *Anonymous.*
The Man in That Airplane. Williams.
The Man of Calvary. *Anonymous.*
May No Man Sleep in Your Hall. *Anonymous.*
Mike 65. Raphael.
Modern Love, XIX. Meredith.
Moonlight (with music). *Anonymous.*
My Catbird. Venable.
My Country. Mackellar.
My Friend the Wind. Kuka.
The News & the Weather. Lesser.
The Nightingale and Glow-Worm. Cowper.
Now Sleeps the Gorge. Campbell.
O All You Little Blackey-Tops. *Anonymous.*
Ode: "Without the evening dew and showers." Cotton.
Of Oystermen, Workboats. Smith.
Of Three Damsels in a Meadow. Payne.
On His Royal Blindness Paramount Chief Kwangala. Mapanje.
On the Lawn at Ira's. Orr.
The Pets. Farren.
Pigeons. Whisler.
Pine Boat a-Shift. *Anonymous.*
Portrait of a Widow. Strauss.
Quarrel. *Anonymous.*
Questions My Son Asked Me, Answers I Never Gave Him. Willard.
The Range in the Desert. Jarrell.
A Riddle: The Vowels. Swift.
The Road to Pengya. Tu Fu.
The Robin. Scott.
Savage Portraits. Marquis.
Seven Long Years in State Prison (with music). *Anonymous.*
Song for December Thirty-First. Frost.
Song of Man Chipping an Arrowhead. Merwin.
To a Butterfly. Schuck.
To a Dead Elephant. Livingstone.
To His Book. Stokesbury.
To Mary at Christmas. Brunini.
Too happy time dissolves itself. Dickinson.
The Trail of the Bird. Courthope.

Triumph of Bacchus and Ariadne. Medici.
Truth. Nemerov.
Under the Williamsburg Bridge. Kinnell.
View from a Window. Grier.
The Virtuous Fox and the Self-Righteous Cat. Cunningham.
What Does Little Birdie Say? Tennyson.
Winter Feast. Frost.
You're Not Alone. Drayton.
Young Hunting. *Anonymous.*
Young Hunting (Loving Henry). *Anonymous.*

Flag (s)
Albert Sidney Johnson. Sherwood.
America for Me. Van Dyke.
Arabic Script. Thwaite.
The Battle of Boyne. *Anonymous.*
A Bestiary. Rexroth.
Bijou. Rutsala.
The Bonnie Blue Flag. Ketchum.
A Boy. Ashbery.
Celebrating the Freak. Macdonald.
Commentaries on the Song of Songs. Herzberg.
Crow Blacker Than Ever. Hughes.
Death of a Young Son by Drowning. Atwood.
A drop fell on the apple tree. Dickinson.
Drum-Taps. Whitman.
Epithalamion. Longley.
The Flag Speaks. Balch.
The Flag We Fly. Fisher.
For a Very Old Man, on the Death of His Wife. Cooper.
Fourth of July Song. Lenski.
Garfield's Ride at Chickamauga. Butterworth.
Grand Opening of the People's Theatre. Goldrick.
A Hymn. Nekrasov.
In a Moonlit Hermit's Cabin. Ginsberg.
It's Wonderful. Isenhour.
John Wasson. Masters.
The Kearsarge. Roche.
The Kid Has Gone to the Colors. Herschell.
The Last Buccaneer. Macaulay.
The Lights Go On. McCloskey.
Memorial Day. Ching.
My Love for Thee. Gilder.
The Next War. Owen.
Our Country's Emblem. *Anonymous.*
Our Flag Forever. Stanton.
The Pageant of Seaman. Byron.
Raison d'Etre. Pitcher.
The Rhyme of the Three Captains. Kipling.
A Song for Our Flag. Sangster.
The Spectre Ship. Collier.
To an Olde Gentlewoman, That Painted Hir Face. Turberville.

William of Orange.
Anonymous.
You're a Grand Old Flag.
Cohan.

Flake (s)
Breakfast with Gerard Manley
Hopkins. Brode.
From Harvest to January.
Tennyson.
In Memoriam A.H.H.,
XCVIII. Tennyson.
Kriss Kringle. Aldrich.
The Lost Carnival. Chappell.
Montana Eclogue. Stafford.
My Land Is Fair for Any
Eyes to See. Stuart.
News. Schmitz.
Presence of Snow. Cane.
The Snowing of the Pines.
Higginson.
Street Scene. Mezey.
A Time of Light, a Time of
Shadow. Yellen.
Watering the Horse. Bly.

Flame (s)
Admire Cranmer! Smith.
Against Platonick Love.
Anonymous.
The Amorist. *Anonymous.*
Annus Mirabilis. Dryden.
Another Old Song. Bush.
The April Earth. Eastman.
At the Salon. Wilkinson.
Beauty. Rosenberg.
A Beauty That All Night
Long. Julal ed-Din Rumi.
The Candlelight Fisherman.
Anonymous.
Catch What You Can.
Garrigue.
A Cathedral. Vinaver.
Charade. Praed.
Colonial Nomenclature.
Lang.
Commemoration. McKay.
Creative Force. Hadden.
Daffodils. Harding.
The Death of Adonis.
Theocritus.
The Decress of God. Chao
Ying-Tou.
Dedication: To Edward John
Trelawny. Swinburne.
The Descent of Odin. Gray.
A Description of Maidenhead.
Anonymous.
The Divers. Quennell.
Dorothy. Kreymborg.
Down the Mississippi.
Fletcher.
Drum-Taps. Whitman.
Earliest Spring. Levertov.
Elegy. Sadeh.
Epigram: "At 12 o'clock in
the afternoon." Meleager.
Epilogue. Russell.
Epitaph on a Free but Tame
Redbreast. Cowper.
Epitaphs of the War.
Kipling.
Father Malloy. Masters.
Faustus Triumphant. Gunn.
Fiorentina. Myers.
The Fire of Love. Sackville.
Friend. Brooks.
The Gean Trees. Jacob.
George Crabbe. Robinson.
The Gully. Maurice.
Helen. Valentine.
I Saw from the Beach.
Moore.

I sighed and owned my love.
Anonymous.
Impression du Matin. Wilde.
The Invitation in It. Boyle.
Invites His Nymph to His
Cottage. Ayres.
Janie Swecker and Me and
Gone with the Wind.
Huddle.
A Last Word. Ashbery.
Last Words to Miriam.
Lawrence.
Leaves. Manning.
Letters to Walt Whitman.
Johnson.
Light-Winged Smoke, Icarian
Bird. Thoreau.
Looking at New-Fallen Snow
from a Train. Bly.
Lost. Brand.
Love. LeClaire.
The Lovers' Death.
Baudelaire.
Lucasta's World. Lovelace.
May It Be. Pasternak.
A Method of Preserving Hay
from Being Mow-Burnt, or
Taking Fire. Dodsley.
The Million. Redgrove.
The Moth and the Flame.
Taggart.
No More Destructive Flame.
Connolly.
Nomad Exquisite. Stevens.
Norman Morrison. Mitchell.
October's Song. Farjeon.
On Archaeanassa. Plato.
On Burning a Dull Poem.
Swift.
The Pageant of Seaman.
Byron.
Paradise. Barnstone.
Paradise Lost. Milton.
Pastorals: Summer. Pope.
Perry's Victory—A Song.
Anonymous.
A Pilot from the Carrier.
Jarrell.
A Poem for Museum Goers.
Wieners.
The Poetic Land. Roscoe.
The Progress of Poesy.
Gray.
Riddles Wisely Expounded.
Anonymous.
Rondeau: "By two black eyes
my heart was won."
Anonymous.
The Sacrifice to Apollo.
Drayton.
The Second Life of Lazarus.
Harwood.
Self-Analysis. Wickham.
September 1, 1939. Auden.
Sin and Death. Milton.
Smoke. Thoreau.
Sonnet XV. Tuckerman.
Sonnet XLVI. Alabaster.
Sonnet LXXXVI. Greville.
Spider. Cole.
Sunrise on Mansfield
Mountain. Brown.
Terra Australis. McAuley.
Those Makheta Nights.
Chipasula.
To a Wanton. Habington.
To Celia Pleading Want of
Merit. Stanley.
To Shelley. Tabb.
To the Blessed Sacrament.
Constable.
To the Statue. Swenson.

The True Martyr. Wade.
Violets in Thaumantia's
Bosome. Sherburne.
Watts. Saxon.
When Aurelia First I Courted.
Anonymous.
When Youth Had Fled.
Surrey.
You Drop a Pearl...
Anonymous.
Young People Who Delight in
Sin. *Anonymous.*

Flaming
Arachne. Kazantzis.
Dearest Friend, Thou Art in
Love. Heine.
The Grey Ones. MacNeice.
Wellfleet Harbor. Goodman.

Flamingos
Animal Pictures. Locke.
Boy in the Roman Zoo.
MacLeish.

Flanders
America's Answer. Lilliard.
Another Reply to In Flanders
Fields. Armstrong.
In Flanders Fields. McCrae.
The Old Houses of Flanders.
Ford.
Reply to In Flanders Fields.
Mitchell.
Songs from an Evil Wood.
Plunkett.

Flank (s)
A January Morning.
Lampman.
The Lido. Wilson.
Three Rounded Flanks I
Loved. *Anonymous.*

Flare (s)
The Bird with the Coppery,
Keen Claws. Stevens.
Elegy. Bell.
The Firstborn Land.
Bachmann.
On the Mountain. Stone.
Women of Trachis: Choruses.
Sophocles.

Flash (es)
Begging on North Main.
Stuart.
A Casual Song. Noel.
Flash Crimson. Sandburg.
The Fundamental Project of
Technology. Kinnell.
Godiva (parody). Berry.
Like the Eyes of Wolves.
Yud.
The Look. Daryush.
Pannyra of the Golden Heel.
Samain.
Poem on Canada: Cold
Colloquy. Anderson.
A Quarrel. Peck.
The Radiance of Extinct Stars.
Horvitz.
Ratcliffe Highway.
Anonymous.
The Springtime It Brings on
the Shearing. Overbury.
Uncertain Sonnets. Johnston.
The Wandering Jew.
Robinson.

Flashing (s)
The Fire at Alexandria.
Weiss.
Recovery. Scott.
White Dove of the Wild Dark
Eyes. Plunkett.

Flashlight (s)
After I Have Voted. Jensen.

Elegies for the Hot Season.
McPherson.
Looking for Mountain
Beavers. Wagoner.
Nights Primarily III.
Lipman.

Flat
12 October. Livingston.
Although in a Crystal.
Parlatore.
Fragment of a Song on the
Beautiful Wife of Dr. John
Overall... *Anonymous.*
I Stand Corrected. Fishback.
Low Fields and Light.
Merwin.
One Way Down. Craig.
A Poem—Good or Bad—A
Thing—With One Attribute—
Flat. Ravitch.
Renascence. Millay.
A Roundabout Turn.
Charles.
Sonnets. Tuckerman.
The Wife Takes a Child.
Voigt.

Flatter (y)
Epigram: "One boy alone."
Meleager.
Fable XLV: The Poet and the
Rose. Gay.
Slain. Crosland.
Sonnets, XLII: "Thou that
last her, it is not all my
grief." Shakespeare.
Young and Simple Though I
Am. Campion.

Flavor
Candy Bar. Veitch.
Does the Spearmint Lose Its
Flavor on the Bedpost
Overnight? Rose.
The Girl in the Foreign
Movie. Goedicke.
Nightmare Number Three.
Benét.
Ode to Salt. Neruda.
Persimmons and Plums.
Hodges.

Flaw (ed) (less)
Elegy: Three. Deane.
Limerick: "A flea and a fly in
a flue." *Anonymous.*
Northern Water Thrush.
Jones.
Proof. Ullman.
The Sonnet. Symonds.
Unless. Glynes.

Flax
Flax. Bunin.
Keats. Longfellow.
A Non Sequitor. Corbett.
Oberon's Palace. Herrick.
Whipping Cheare.
Anonymous.

Flea (s)
Bad Company. Watkyns.
The Book of Nightmares.
Kinnell.
Brow, Brow, Brenty.
Anonymous.
Chez-Nous. Austin.
Darwinism in the Kitchen.
Anonymous.
Dover to Munich. Calverley.
The Flea. Donne.
Jackrabbits. Barker.
Lady, the Silly Flea.
Anonymous.
Lines for an Eminent Poet
and Critic. Dickinson.

My Father Kept a Horse.
  Anonymous.
To a Poet, Who Would Have
  Me Praise Certain Bad
  Poets... Yeats.
Fled
Aeolian Harp. Allingham.
Astrophel and Stella, LXVI.
  Sidney.
The Burgesses of Calais.
  Minot.
The Deserted Village.
  Goldsmith.
Divina Commedia. Dante
  Alighieri.
Fish Story. Armour.
The Hare. De la Mare.
Heavy-Hearted. Al-Harizi.
I Years Had Been from
  Home. Dickinson.
"In winter's just return..."
  Surrey.
It Was Not You. Spire.
Limerick: "A greedy small
  lassie once said."
  Anonymous.
Limerick: "There was a young
  lady of Limerick." Lang.
Little Miss Muffet (parody).
  Anonymous.
Long May. Castro.
Lost Ships. Ferril.
A Love Symphony.
  O'Shaughnessy.
Marriage. Cotton.
Odes, IX. Hafiz.
Opportunity. Machiavelli.
Paradise Lost. Milton.
A Pastorall Dialogue.
  Carew.
The Skater. Roberts.
Slow Dancer That No One
  Hears but You. Niatum.
Then I'll Believe. Vilakazi.
To Thomas Lord Chancellor.
  Jonson.
Truth's Complaint over
  England. Lodge.
The Vision of Piers Plowman.
  Langland.
Fledgling
The Assumption. Tabb.
The Sandpiper. Bynner.
Flee
Because He Was Tempted.
  Anonymous.
Combinations. Hoberman.
I Would I Were a Careless
  Child. Byron.
In Spain. Wyatt.
Jackrabbits. Barker.
The Last Flight of the Great
  Wallenda. Hyett.
The March 2. Lowell.
On the Defeat of Ragnall by
  Murrough King of Leinster
  A.D. 994. *Anonymous.*
Repeated Pilgrimage.
  Brunini.
Stand Fast, O My Heart.
  Anonymous
Tacita. Kenyon.
To J. S. Collis. Pitter.
Ubi Sunt Qui Ante Nos
  Fuerunt? *Anonymous.*
Wee Willie Gray. Burns.
You Tell Me to Sit Quiet.
  Jordan.
Fleece
Harald, the Agnostic Ale-
  Loving Old Shepherd...
  Brown.

I Love My Love. Adam.
Locale. Shuttle.
Nursing the Hide. Dunne.
Paphnutius (excerpt).
  Hroswitha von
  Grandersheim.
To Noel. "Mistral.
Fleet (ness) (s) (ing)
The Death of Nelson.
  Anonymous.
The Derby Ram.
  Anonymous.
Epitaph. Chiabrera.
The First Olympionique to
  Hiero of Syracuse. Pindar.
The Half Moon Shows a Face
  of Plaintive Sweetness.
  Rossetti.
John Smith of His Friend
  Master John Taylor.
  Smith.
Leaving Troy. Irwin.
Love can do all but raise the
  dead. Dickinson.
A Lyke-Wake Dirge.
  Anonymous.
Many Birds. Welsh.
Panegyrick upon O.
  Cromwell. Waller.
Prose Poem. Jennings.
The St. Lawrence and the
  Saguenay. Sangster.
The Stone Fleet. Melville.
A Tryst in Brobdingnag.
  Rich.
We Love the Venerable
  House. Emerson.
When as a Lad. Mackay.
Flesh
Advent 1966. Levertov.
Afterbirth. Williams.
Agbor Dancer. Clark.
Ah! Lovely Appearance of
  Death! Wesley.
At Luca Signorelli's
  Resurrection of the Body.
  Graham.
At the Executed Murderer's
  Grave. Wright.
Autumnall. Bennett.
Ave-Maria Bells. Stoddard.
Awakening. Haines.
Before I Knocked and Flesh
  Let Enter. Thomas.
Bitter rain in my courtyard.
  Wu Tsao.
The Body. Herrick.
Bordello. Turco.
The Bull. Hodgson.
Caelica, XCI. Greville.
Caelica, XCIV. Greville.
Child Owlet. *Anonymous.*
Chopping Wood. Smith.
Christmas Eve. Ammons.
A Clash with Cliches.
  Miller.
Clothes Do But Cheat and
  Cozen Us. Herrick.
Color Blind. Paine.
Could You Once Regain.
  Smithyman
Coyote Brother Song. West.
Creatures. Kumin.
Cruelty. Hummer.
Definition. Shakely.
Effectively coming through
  slaughter. Fitzgerald.
Encounter. Miller.
Epigram: "Dear, my familiar
  hand in love's own gesture."
  Cunningham.

Epitaph on a Young Child.
  Gurney.
An Epitaph: On Elizabeth
  Chute. Jonson.
Fear Has Cast Out Love.
  Blunt.
Fish. Townsend.
Five Arabic Verses in Praise
  of Wine. *Anonymous.*
Five Lyrics from "Good for
  Nothing Man". Ptichford.
Flesh. Rice.
The Flitting. McGuckian.
For Miriam. Macgoye.
....For They Shall See God.
  Shaw.
Heriot's Ford. Kipling.
Hunger and Thirst. Bishop.
Hymn. Browning.
I Bring to You as Offering
  Tonight. Verhaeren.
Incarnation Poem. Leax.
Island Dogs. Bell.
Judges, Judges. Baro.
Julian M. and A.G. Rochelle.
  Bronte.
Korea. Buckley.
Landscape and Figure.
  Kinsella.
The Last Word. Davison.
Lector Aere Perennior.
  Cunningham.
Letter to Statues. Brinnin.
Life Is Motion. Stevens.
Little Light. Brodey.
Liverpool. *Anonymous.*
Love. ""MacDiarmid.
Love Redeemed.
  Baylebridge.
The Lull. Peacock.
Lyell's Hypothesis Again.
  Rexroth.
Madonna of the Dons.
  MacGillvray.
Marriage. Lowell.
Metamorphoses. Ovid
  (Publius Ovidius Naso).
Mexico. Lowell.
Neutrality. MacNeice.
Night Out, Tom Cat.
  deGravelles.
Not to sigh and to be tender.
  Behn.
Now in the Time of This
  Mortal Life. Nicholson.
O Could I Find from Day to
  Day. Cleavland.
On a Fifteenth-Century
  Flemish Angel. Ray.
On Hearing the First Cuckoo.
  Church.
On the Apparition of Oneself.
  Burford.
On the Cards and Dice.
  Ralegh.
On the Death of Doctor Swift.
  Swift.
Our Vegetable Love Shall
  Grow. Feinstein.
Paths to God. Farhi.
Patience. Cattafi.
The Penitent Palmer's Ode.
  Greene.
Poem. Sinclair.
Poem for J. Berry.
Poems for My Daughter.
  Gregory.
Poly-Olbion. Drayton.
The Pomegranate. Dudek.
A Prisoner's Song of
  Jerusalem. *Anonymous.*
The Project. Orr.

Receiving Communion.
  Miller.
Refugees. Grade.
Rhotus on Arcadia.
  Chalkhill.
A Rondeau of Remorse.
  Johnson.
The Same Gesture.
  Montague.
The Secrets of the Earth.
  Blake.
She lay wrapped... Fox.
The Snapper. Heyen.
Sonnet: "Flesh, I have
  knocked at many a dusty
  door." Masefield.
Sonnets. Tuckerman.
The Soul's Expression.
  Browning.
Such Comfort as the Night
  Can Bring to Us. Cooley.
Sunday Afternoon. Levine.
Thinking of Love. Jennings.
Those Not Elect. Adams.
Turtle. Lowell.
Two Monopolists. Byrom.
Two Things. Babcock.
Villanelle. Laing.
A Vision That Appeared to
  Me. MacConglinne.
When I Went to the Circus.
  Lawrence.
Winter and Red Berries.
  Moore.
Woman of This Earth
  (excerpt). Frost.
Womanisers. Press.
The Women of Rubens.
  Szymborska.
Yehuda Amichai. Mayne.
Flew
African Sunday. Owen.
The Angel in the House.
  Patmore.
Bird. Nagy.
Catch a Little Rhyme.
  Merriam.
The Empty Cradle. Selgas y
  Carrasco.
Epitaph. *Anonymous.*
Horace. Sargent.
I, Icarus. Nowlan.
Images. Schaukal.
Limerick: "A flea and a fly in
  a flue." *Anonymous.*
A Little Cock Sparrow Sat on
  a Green Tree. *Anonymous.*
My Angel. Brooks.
L'Oiseau Bleu. Coleridge.
Paradise Lost. Milton.
A Pity. We Were Such a
  Good Invention. Amichai.
Poems, VII. O'Connor.
Song of the Murdered Child
  Whose Bones Grew into a
  Milk-white Dove.
  Anonymous.
Tall Tale God. Van Doren.
Upon Time. Herrick.
What's in the Cupboard.
  Anonymous.
You on the Tower. Hardy.
Flick (ing) (s)
The Late Show. Heyen.
Naked Poetry. Cooley.
Flicker (ing) (s)
Cold Fire. Starbuck.
George Crabbe. Robinson.
The Gothic Dusk. Prokosch.
Lake Harriet: Wind. Taylor.
Rapture. Carlson.
S. S. City of Benares. Fraser.

What Will Remain after Me?
Naigreshel.
Flight (s)
The Acrobat from Xanadu
Disdained All Nets.
Georgakas.
All That Was Mortal.
Teasdale.
Arctic Tern in a Museum.
Newsome.
The Battle Royal between Dr.
Sherlock, Dr. South, and
Dr. Burnet. Pittis.
The Bear. Momaday.
Becoming Is Perfection.
Johnson.
The Beekeeper's Dream.
Lorr.
Bring Me the Cup. Ibn
Ezra.
The Chanting Cherubs - A
Group by Greenough.
Dana.
Come away, Come Sweet
Love. Anonymous.
Corn-Woman Remembered.
Volborth.
Dawn. Scott.
The Dawning of the Day.
Anonymous.
Dialectics of Flight.
Wheelock.
Dolphin Seen Alone.
Lattimore.
Dreams of Auschwitz.
Slutsky.
Ear Is Not Deaf. Dayton.
Easter Wings. Herbert.
The Educated Love Bird.
Newell.
The Egg of Nothing. Taylor.
The Eyes of God. Hagedorn.
The Fir-Tree. Thomas.
Fledglings. Meredith.
From Far away. Agustini.
Grania. Anonymous.
The Granite Mountain.
Sarett.
Les Halles d'Ypres.
Blunden.
Hawk Nailed to a Barn Door.
Blue Cloud.
Heavenly Jerusalem,
Jerusalem of the Earth.
Goldberg.
Horn. Anonymous.
Hunting Song. Burns.
If Blood Is Black Then Spirit
Neglects My Unborn Son.
Rivers.
Imagery. Chattopadhyaya.
Imaginary Elegies, I-IV.
Spicer.
Lament: "Within my bosom
stirs once more tonight."
Zeb-un-Nissa.
Let's Talk, Mother. Bruck.
Love's Language.
MacDonagh.
Love Songs. Loy.
The Loves Who Many Years
Held All My Mind.
Landor.
Marriage and Midsummer's
Night. Gregg.
Measure Me, Sky. Speyer.
Mystic River. Ciardi.
The Noosing of the Sun-God.
MacKay.
Ode to Joy. McClure.
On the Edge of a Safe Sleep.
Cader.

One Last Word. Glassco.
The Owl. Davison.
The Paper Kite (excerpt).
Bowden.
Poets. Akenside.
Promise Your Hand. Rago.
The Raven Visits Rawhide.
Anonymous.
Reid at Fayal. Palmer.
Rejoice, O Youth, in the
Lovely Hind. Ibn Ezra.
A Requiem for Soldiers Lost
in Ocean Transport.
Melville.
Saint Patrick's Day, 1973.
Rose.
Saying Dante Aloud.
Wright.
September 2. Berry.
Simile. Momaday.
Spring (excerpt). Gisborne.
Survivors. Hogan.
Switzerland. Thwaite.
To Music, to Becalm His
Fever. Herrick.
To Night. Shelley.
To the Mutable Fair. Waller
To Youth. Landor.
A Translation of the Cywdd
to Morvydd....
Anonymous.
Trees and Cattle. Dickey.
The Turncoat. Jones.
Unsent Message to My
Brother in His Pain.
Stokesbury.
Vernon Castle. Monroe.
We Will Watch the Northern
Lights. Anonymous.
The Wind Was There. Imbs.
Flinch
Clever Tom Clinch Going to
be Hanged. Swift.
Departure. Lim.
The Wandering Jew.
Robinson.
The Wasp. Oates.
Fling (s)
Dream Songs. Berryman.
Innocent Play. Watts.
Wild Eden. Woodberry.
Flint
Amoretti, XVIII. Spenser.
Art. Gautier.
Bushed. Birney.
Bussy d'Ambois. Chapman.
Dark. Healy.
An Emerald Is as Green as
Grass. Rossetti.
Silex Scintillans. Vaughan.
A Technical Supplement.
Kinsella.
Flip
The Bad Man from the
Brazos. Anonymous.
Titus, Son of Rembrandt:
1665. Lyons.
Flit (ted) (ting)
New Heaven, New War.
Southwell.
The Ordinary Women.
Stevens.
Rome. Du Bellay.
Ruines of Rome. Du Bellay.
Float (ed) (ing) (s)
After the Anonymous
Swedish. Harrison.
The Cumberland and the
Merrimac. Anonymous.
A Dark World. Scovell.
The Event. Moore.

The Genesis of Butterflies.
Hugo.
The Great River. Van Dyke.
Hymns of the Marshes:
Sunrise. Lanier.
I, who cut off my sorrows.
Akazome Emon.
An Inhabited Emptiness.
Gold.
A Journey through the
Moonlight. Edson.
Like a ravaged sea. Ise.
Loss. Ammons.
Lotuses. Bynner.
Mother. Vincent.
Nocturnal Heart. Kegels.
Oh There Is Blessing in This
Gentle Breeze.
Wordsworth.
Orchids. Minty.
A Penguin. Herford.
Poem in Which My Legs Are
Accepted. Fraser.
Return, Starting Out.
Halpern.
Sea-Ward, White Gleaming
through the Busy Scud.
Coleridge.
She Speaks the Morning's
Filigree. Lamantia.
Sorrow. Lawrence.
The Tailor. Garfinkel.
Tin-Ore. Anonymous.
To Be in Love While in
Prison. Minarik.
To His Book. Stokesbury.
The waters chased him as he
fled. Dickinson.
Way out West. Jones.
The White Horse of
Westbury. Turner.
Flock (s)
About the Heavenly Life.
Leon.
The Cemetery by the Sea.
Valery.
The Children of Greenock.
Graham.
Colin Clout. Skelton.
Colin Clout's Come Home
Again. Spenser.
Deer. Drinkwater.
Glory, Glory to the Sun.
Alford.
Hymn to Sunrise.
Anonymous.
I'll Tell You How the Sun
Rose. Dickinson.
The Life of the Blessed.
Leon.
Like the Honeycomb
Dropping Honey.
Hildegard von Bingen.
Midsummer Pause. Lape.
Moonlight...Scattered Clouds.
Bloomfield.
My Grandfather Burning
Cornfields. Sauls.
October Winds. Randall.
On the Death of a
Nightingale. Randolph.
Paradise Lost. Milton.
Pastoral Landscape. Philips.
Poly-Olbion. Drayton.
The Queen of the Angels.
Boccaccio.
Shepherd and Shepherdess.
Hennell.
The Sixth Pastoral. Philips.
Song for the Spinning Wheel.
Wordsworth.

Song: "Though I am dark."
Anonymous.
Summer Morning. Thomson.
Flood (s)
Archangel. Robinson.
The Banded Cobra.
Leipoldt.
The Clovers. Garrigue.
Coole and Ballylee, 1931.
Yeats.
The Desire of Water.
Jarman.
Dissatisfaction with
Metaphysics. Empson.
The Dying Swan. Tennyson.
An Early Bluebird.
Thompson.
Easter. O'Hara.
The Elephant Is Slow to
Mate. Lawrence.
The Fall Again. Nemerov.
Flood. Feldman.
For Sergeant Fetta. Sanders.
The Garden Party. Belloc.
Gideon at the Well. Hill.
Goats. Wood.
Her Mood around Me.
Ghiselin.
In a Double Rainbow.
Littlebird.
In the Heart of the Hills...
Anonymous.
Jehovah. Zangwill.
Jehu. MacNeice.
Lines on Seeing a Lock of
Milton's Hair. Keats.
Look Out There.
Anonymous.
Lord Maxwell's Last
Goodnight. Anonymous.
The Loves of the Plants.
Darwin.
Midstream. Enright.
Night Walkers. Smithyman.
Noah and the Waters: Chorus.
Day Lewis.
On the Great Fog in London,
December 1762. Weeks.
On the Third Day. Spender.
Paradise Lost. Milton.
Pluviose. Bell.
The Red-Gold Rain. Sitwell.
The Return. Strong.
Riddle: The Swan: "Silent my
robe, when I rest on earth."
Anonymous.
The Sea. Anonymous.
The Second Brother.
Beddoes.
A Song-Offering. Tagore.
Songs of Joy. Davies.
Sonnet: Addressed by a
Father Mourning...
Vittorelli.
Tenant at Number 9. Blight.
To Forget Me. Weiss.
To the Mocking-Bird. Pike
The Tombstone Told When
She Died. Thomas.
The Triad of Things Not
Decreed. Furlong.
Two Animals, One Flood.
Glancy.
Upon Some Alterations in My
Mistress, after My
Departure into France.
Carew.
What's My Thought Like?
Moore.
Floor (s)
Analysands. Randall.
The Barn. Spender.

The Barren Moors.
Channing
Coming Home from Camp.
Kaneko.
Departure. Hitchcock.
Divorce. Jennings.
Dr. Coppelius. Gardiner.
The Great Aunts of My
Childhood. Fulton.
The Heavenly Humor.
Shapiro.
A Hollyhock. Sherman.
How the Joy of It Was Used
Up Long Ago. Gregg.
The Hurricane. Crane.
Limerick: "There was a young
girl of Lahore."
Monkhouse.
London Interior. Monro.
Make Me a Pallet on Your
Floor. Yancey.
Mist. Man.
Moon Man. Valentine.
Moving. Steele.
A New Song on the Birth of
the Prince of Wales.
Anonymous.
Not Blindly in the Dark.
Stanley.
Note to the Previous Tenants.
Updike.
Ode on Celestial Music.
Patten.
The Poem on the Guilt.
Yeshurun.
Resolution. Merwin.
The Sonnet. Gilder.
Standard Forgings Plant.
Stephens.
Step father. Fitzgerald.
Three Poems for Women, 2.
Griffin.
Vertigo. Henderson.

Florence
Hollywood. Shapiro.
Merry Old Souls (excerpt).
Bishop.
More Nudes for Florence.
Witt.

Flour
Al Nist by the Rose.
Anonymous.
Elf Night. Rogers.
May Poems. *Anonymous.*
Worry about Money. Raine.

Flourish (ed) (ing)
Benediction for the Tent.
Anonymous.
Childhood. Traherne.
Gaudeamus Igitur.
Anonymous.
Grace for Children. Herrick.
I'll tell you whence the Rose
did first grow red. Strode.
The Iliad. Homer.
In Stone Settlements When
the Moon Is Stone. Levi.
Jane Was a Neighbor.
Anonymous.
The Life of Man. Barnes.
Looking On. Thwaite.
The Sunshade. Hardy.
Sylvan Delights. Pope.
To Mrs. Ann Flaxman.
Blake.
To the Spring. Davies.

Flout (s)
Early Thoughts of Marriage.
Cotton.
The Loon. Rand.

Flow (ed) (ing) (s)
Animal Kingdom. Clouts.

At Arley. Young.
At the Fishhouses. Bishop.
Chamber Music. Joyce.
During Thoughts after Ofay-
Watching. Serote.
The Excesses of God.
Jeffers.
Fragmenti. Pound.
The Great Lakes Suite.
Reaney.
Hymn, to Light. Cowley.
In the Fall. Rivero.
An Invocation. Cory.
The Jugs. Celan.
Memory of the Present.
Shapiro.
Morning Glory Pool.
McPherson.
My Honeyed Languor.
"Bagritsky.
Nanny's Sailor Lad.
Allingham.
October's Song. Farjeon.
On Death. Killigrew.
Poem of the Intimate Agony.
Burgos.
Poem: "This beauty that I
see." Schuyler.
The River Glideth in a Secret
Tongue. Ostroff.
Song of the Artesian Water.
Paterson.
Song: "When, dearest, I but
think of". Felltham.
The Sun-Dial. Peacock.
Thought. Cranch.
Tyrannic Love. Dryden
Tzu Yeh Songs. *Anonymous.*
Up Early. Robinson.
The Village. Crabbe.

Flower (s)
The African Tramp.
Haresnape.
After a Journey. Hardy.
After Passing the
Examination. Meng
Chiao.
All Night by the Rose.
Anonymous.
Alleys. McPherson.
Amber the Sky. Rokwaho.
And Lightly, Like the
Flowers. Ronsard.
The Angel in the House.
Patmore.
Anklet Song. *Anonymous.*
Annunciation. Jones.
April Puddle. Bennett.
Arise and Pick a Posy.
Anonymous.
At Midnight. Sherman.
At the Jewish Cemetery in
Prague. Levertin.
Aucassin and Nicolete.
Bourdillon.
Baby Running Barefoot.
Lawrence.
Ballad of the Londoner.
Flecker.
Beauty and Love. Young.
The Bee. Fandel.
Bella Ciao. *Anonymous.*
La Bella Donna Della Mia
Mente. Wilde.
Benediction for the Tent.
Anonymous.
Bill and Parson Sim.
Anonymous.
Bloom. Kreymborg.
Bloom is result. Dickinson.

Bombardment. Lawrence.
The Book of Kells.
Nemerov.
The Buildings. Berry.
Burial of the Young Love.
Cuney.
Butterfly. Armstrong.
Caresses. Barker.
Carol. Guiney.
The Clote. Barnes.
The Columbine. Very.
Coming and Going.
Goodman.
Counting on Flowers.
Ciardi.
The Cow. Stevenson.
Crack in the Wall Holds
Flowers. Miller.
Credo (excerpt). Gilder.
The Cuckoo. *Anonymous.*
Cyclops. Euripides.
Daisies. Nowlan.
Dandelion. Annan.
Dandelions. Chute.
Daphnis Came on a Summer's
Day. *Anonymous.*
A Dead March. Monkhouse.
A Death. Jennings.
The Death of the Flowers.
Bryant.
A Description of Beauty,
Translated out of Marino.
Daniel.
Desire. De Botton.
The Diary of the Waning
Moon (excerpt). Abutsu.
Directions. Onitsura.
Dirge. *Anonymous.*
Dirge for the Year. Shelley.
Disguised. Perreault.
Distortions. Hutchinson.
Don Juan. Byron.
Don't Ask Me What to Wear.
Sappho.
Dont Worry Yr Hair.
Bissett.
A Dream of Flowers. Coan.
A Dream of November.
Gosse.
The Drunken Stones of
Prague. Scheinert.
Easily onward, thorough
flowers and weed... Keats.
An Elegy for D. H. Lawrence.
Williams.
Elena's Song. Taylor.
Elevation. Baudelaire.
Elizabeth. Saul.
Elsdon. Downie.
Emily Dickinson. Longley.
Endymion. Keats.
Epigram: "Gathering the
bloom of all the fairest boys
that be." Strato.
Epitaph. Driscoll.
Essex Regiment March.
Woodberry.
Evening. Sill.
The Evening Primrose.
Langhorne.
The Example. Davies.
The Fable Merchant.
Dobzynski.
The Faerie Queene. Spenser.
Family Reunion. Miller.
The Fancy. Benet.
Fanny. Aldrich.
The Fear of Flowers. Clare.
The First Fathers. Hawker.
First Joy. Watkins.
Five Little Sisters Walking in
a Row. Greenaway.

The Flower. Holmes.
The Flower. Wergeland.
Flower Herding on Mount
Monadnock. Kinnell.
The Flower Market. Po
Chu-i.
Flowers in the Valley.
Anonymous.
The Flowers of Apollo.
Flanner.
Flowers of Darkness. Davis.
The Flowers of the Forest.
Cockburn.
The Flowers That Bloom in
the Spring. Gilbert.
For James Dean. O'Hara.
For Maria. Mathis.
For No Clear Reason.
Creeley.
For the Children. Snyder.
For the Master's Use.
Anonymous.
A Fragment: To Music.
Shelley.
Friend Sparrow. Basho
(Matsuo Basho).
From a Churchyard in Wales.
Anonymous.
From an Irish-Latin
Macaronic. Taylor.
From the Notebooks.
Roethke.
The Furnace of Colors.
Watkins.
The Gallery. Marvell.
The Garden. Grimald.
Garden. Marvell.
A Garland for Heliodora.
Meleager.
The Gem and the Flower.
Pope.
The Gift. Stanford.
Give Them the Flowers Now.
Anonymous.
Go, Happy Rose. Martial
(Marcus Valerius Martialis).
Golden Bough. Hoyt.
Graves of Infants. Clare.
The Great South Land
(excerpt). Ingamells.
Hast Thou Seen Reversed the
Prophet's Miracle.
Tuckerman.
The Haunted House.
Graves.
Hawthorn Dyke. Swinburne.
He Defendeth His Heart
against the Destroyer.
Book of the Dead.
Hendecasyllabics.
Swinburne.
Hermontimus. Ayton [(or
Aytoun)] Sir Robert.
The Hibakusha's Letter
(1955). Mura.
The Holy Spirit. Underhill.
Houseplant. Napier.
How Strange Love Is, in
Every State of
Consciousness. Schwartz.
I Am. Kushner.
I Believe. Tchernichovsky.
I Closed My Eyes Today and
Saw. Stead.
I Need No Sky. Bynner.
I Saw Thee, Child, One
Summer's Day. Bronte.
In Back of the Real.
Ginsberg.
In Panelled Rooms.
Herschberger.

In the Grave No Flower. Millay.

In the Half-Point Time of Night. Menebroker.

In the land of dwarfs. Farrokhzad.

In the Old Guerilla War. Pastan.

Intempestiva. Stuart.

Intermezzo: At Glan-Y-Wern. Symons.

Intimations of Immortality from Recollections of Early Childhood. Wordsworth.

Invocation to the Wind. Kalar.

A Japanese Love-Song. Noyes.

Jessie, the Flower o' Dunbane. Tannahill.

Jo Jo, My Child. Anonymous.

Johnny German. Anonymous.

Junglegrave. Anderson.

Kaddish. Ginsberg.

King Henry Fifth's Conquest of France (B vers.). Anonymous.

Lambs Frolicking Home. Lape.

Last night I saw your corpse. Mansour.

The Leader. Livesay.

Let Me Flower as I Will. Sarett.

Lie Closed, My Lately Loved. Woods.

Life's Common Duties. Savage.

Lilith. Gregg.

Live Blindly. Stickney.

Love and Age. Peacock.

The Lovers. Byron.

Luxury. Justice.

The Maid's Thought. Jeffers.

Maiden in the Mor. Anonymous.

Make Way! Negri.

May. Cornwell.

The May Day Garland. Blunden.

Medea's Magic. Gower.

Meditation under Stars. Meredith.

Memorial Day. Gilder.

Memorial Day. Lent.

Memory. Rossetti.

Mick. Reeves.

Mid-August. Driscoll.

A Midnight Interior. Sassoon.

Minor Elegy. Lisboa.

A Mirage. Setterberg.

Moly. Gunn.

The Moon. Sodergran.

Mourning Pablo Neruda. Bly.

Music. Shelley.

My Epitaph. Gray.

The Nativity of Christ. Gongora y Argote.

New Age. Kgositsile.

A Night at the Napi in Browning. Hugo.

No! Hood.

Noel. Gilder.

Nonpareil. Prior.

Noon. "Field.

Not Iris in Her Pride. Peele.

November Poppies. Corke.

Ode on Celestial Music. Patten.

Ode Sung at the Opening of the International Exhibition. Tennyson.

An Old Maid Early. Blake.

On Eleanor Freeman. Anonymous.

On Himselfe. Herrick.

On the Death of Keats. Logan.

On Thomas Carew. Anonymous.

Open Poetry Reading. Melendez.

The Orange Lily O. Anonymous.

The Ossianic Cycle: The Song of Finn. Anonymous.

Others. Behn.

Pansy. Newsome.

The Pansy and the Prayer-Book. Edwards.

The Path. Bryant.

Patty, 1949-1961. Libera.

Pennsylvania Academy of Fine Arts. Kroll.

People Hide Their Love. Wu-Ti.

Piano Pieces (excerpt). Shapcott.

The Plight. Thompson.

Poem: "In the earnest path of duty." Forten.

Poem: "What's the balm." Dugan.

Poems. Drummond.

Portrait of a Marriage. Abse.

Prayer for This Day. Flanner.

Prehistoric Burials. Sassoon.

Puna's Fragrant Glades. Lili, u-o-ka-lani.

The Reaper and the Flowers. Longfellow.

Recollections of "Lalla Rookh." Trowbridge.

Resurrection of the Right Side. Rukeyser.

The Rhyme. Creeley.

Roof Garden. Schuyler.

Roots and Leaves Themselves Alone. Whitman.

The Rose. Howell.

Rose Pogonias. Frost.

The Rosemary Spray. Gongora y Argote.

The Runaway. Hicky.

Sarah Lorton. Finnin.

Seek Flowers of Heaven. Southwell.

The Sentry. Lewis.

A Separation. Cory.

Shadows of Chrysanthemums. Scovell.

A Shallot. Wilbur.

The Shape of the Fire. Roethke.

Sic Vita. Thoreau.

Sightings I. Rothenberg.

Sing, Woods and Rivers All. Claudian.

Six of Cups. Wakoski.

Sniff. Frost.

The Solitary. Teasdale.

Someone Gave Him Some Plastic Flowers Once. Shady.

A Song at Easter. Towne.

A Song: "Hark! 'tis Freedom that calls, come, patriots, awake!" Anonymous.

Song: "Hither haste, and gently strew." Beddoes.

A Song of Autumn. Ceravolo.

Song of the Closing Service. Shenhar.

Song Set by Nicholas Yonge. Anonymous.

Song: "There in the flower garden." Anonymous.

Songs of Kabir. Kabir.

Sonnet XIV. Tuckerman.

Sonnet: "But love whilst that thou may'st be loved again." Daniel.

Sonnet to Edgar Allan Poe. Whitman.

Sonnet Written in a Blank Leaf of Dugdale's Monasticon. Warton, Jr..

Sonnets. Tuckerman.

Sonnets, XCIX: "The forward violet thus did I chide." Shakespeare.

A Sort of a Song. Williams.

The Southerner. Shapiro.

Spell of Creation. Raine.

Spirit Flowers. Burt.

Spring Poem. Symons.

Spring Song. Conkling.

Star Song of the Bushman Women. Anonymous.

Stinging Nettle. Head.

A Summer Santuary. Ingham.

The Swimmer of Nemi. Sharp.

Talking in Their Sleep. Thomas.

Thanksgiving. Driscoll.

There Is but One May in the Year. Rossetti.

This Is after All Vacation. Zukofsky.

Those Gambler's Blues (with music). Anonymous.

The Thousand and One Nights: Death. Anonymous.

Three Barrows Down. Brooke.

Three Moments. Sherman.

Through Storm and Wind. Anonymous.

Thunderstorms. Davies.

Time. Graves.

'Tis but a Little Faded Flower. Howarth.

To a Blue Flower. Neilson.

To a Pet Cobra. Campbell.

To Favonius. Bolton.

To God, on His Sickness. Herrick.

To Guerdon. Piatt.

To His Tomb-Maker. Herrick.

To My Friend, Grown Famous. Tietjens.

To My Sister, from the Twenty-Seventh Floor. Knoll.

To O.E.A. McKay.

To the Maiden in the East. Thoreau.

To the Marchesana of Pescara. Michelangelo.

To the Western Wind. Herrick.

To Two Bereaved. Ashe.

.Train Journey. Wright.

Tuberose. Block.

Tulips and Addresses. Field.

Two Dedications, I: The Chicago Picasso. Brooks.

Under the Leaves. Laighton.

The Unknown Soldier. Wagner.

Upon a Snail. Bunyan.

Variations on a Line from Shakespeare's Fifty-Sixth Sonnet. Mayo.

A Very Old Woman. Eshleman.

Violets for Mother. Kaneko.

Virgil: Georgics, Book IV. Schmitz.

A Vow to Heavenly Venus. Du Bellay.

Walking down Jalan Thamrin. Brissenden.

The Walls Do Not Fall. Doolittle.

Waratah. Robinson.

Wash Day. Mollin.

The Watered Lilies. Anonymous.

What Is Poetry. Ashbery.

When a Warlock Dies. Gardner.

Where Wards Are Weak. Southwell.

Wherever Beauty Has Been Quick in Clay. Masefield.

The White Jessamine. Tabb.

Who knows if the moon's. Cummings.

Wild Flowers. Newell.

The Wild Honey Suckle. Freneau.

Wildwood Flower. Anonymous.

The Winter's Tale. Shakespeare.

Woman (excerpt). McLachlan.

Wonga Vine. Wright.

Words for a Picture of Newlyweds. T'ang Yin.

The Yellow Violet. Bryant.

Yesterday Evening I Saw Your Corpse. Mansour.

Flowering

And the Silver Turns into Night. Yonathan.

Before Invasion, 1940. Betjeman.

Bermuda Suite. Scott.

Calenture. Reid.

The Gardener to His God. Van Duyn.

The Lyre-Bird. Robinson.

Tree Planting. Farkas.

Flown

At the Fishhouses. Bishop.

Here's a String o' Wild Geese. Anonymous.

The Lass of Roch Royal (D version). Anonymous.

To My Lady. Boker.

Voice of the Western Wind. Stedman.

The Wild Swans at Coole. Yeats.

Fluent

Epitaph: "Here lies a poet, briefly known as Hecht." Hecht.

The Sense of the Sleight-of-Hand Man. Stevens.

Flush
  Blind Panorama of New York.
    Garcia Lorca.
  The North Wind Came Up
    Yesternight. Bridges.
Flute (s)
  At the Symphony. Nathan.
  Autumn. Shapcott.
  Campi Flegrei. Toerien.
  The Ceremonial Band.
    Reeves.
  The Coyote and the Locust.
    Anonymous.
  Delicate the Toad. Francis.
  Dusk in Winter. Merwin.
  Elderberry Flute Song. Blue
    Cloud.
  Elegy on the Death of Mme.
    Anna Pavlova (excerpt).
    Meyerstein.
  Epilogue. Heine.
  The Flute of May.
    Woodbourne.
  Flute Player. *Anonymous.*
  Flute Players. Rabearivelo.
  The Hollow Flute. Strauss.
  A Junkie with a Flute in the
    Rain. Fisher.
  Khristna and His Flute.
    Hope.
  Limerick: "Young Frederick
    the great was a beaut."
    Anonymous.
  Love and Music.
    Anonymous.
  Multitudinous Stars. "Ping
    Hsin" (Hsieh Wang-ying).
  My Master Hath a Garden.
    Anonymous.
  The Old Orange Flute.
    Anonymous.
  The Old Prison. Wright.
  On Hearing a Flute at Night
    from the Wall of Shou-
    Hsiang. Li Yi.
  The Opium Den.
    Anonymous.
  The Ould Orange Flute.
    Anonymous.
  Prophet and Fool. Golding.
  Snatches: "Levere is the
    wrenne." *Anonymous.*
  Soliloquy at Potsdam.
    Porter.
  Song: "My spirit like a
    shepherd boy." Sackville-
    West.
  Song: "The gross sun squats
    above." Moraes.
  Songs in Flight (excerpt).
    Bachmann.
  The Summer Is Coming.
    Guinness.
  Tree to Flute. Hajnal.
  With Pipe and Flute.
    Dobson.
  Woman Painter of Mithila.
    Mumford.
Flutter (s)
  The Fate of Birds. Seib.
  Long-Billed Gannets.
    Emery.
  The Ocotillo in Bloom.
    Guild.
  Oh, Lovely Appearance of
    Death. *Anonymous.*
  Rain Falls. It Dries...
    Radnoti.
  Summer. Crase.
Flying
  Colonialism. Qarshe.
  Death. Knott.

The Djanggawul Cycle, 22.
  Anonymous.
Dynamic Tension. Sanfield.
The High Jump.
  Anonymous.
Late. Salz.
Letter to a Friend in an
  Unknown Place. Barrows.
The Pelican. Kuzma.
The Poor Relation.
  Robinson.
Secret-Love. Dryden.
Sermon. Mayer.
The Silkworms. Stewart.
Some Painful Butterflies Pass
  Through. Gallagher.
They've Come. Storni.
This Is My Death-Dream.
  Salisbury.
We Become New. Piercy.
What's worse than this past
  century? Akhmatova.
White Dove of the Wild Dark
  Eyes. Plunkett.
Witch. Tepperman.
Foam (ing)
  The Ark and the Dove.
    Sargent.
  Atalanta in Calydon.
    Swinburne.
  Before an Old Painting of the
    Crucifixion. Momaday.
  The Chase (excerpt).
    Somervile.
  Choosing a Mast. Campbell.
  Condemned Women.
    Baudelaire.
  Death of a Cat. Schevill.
  The Djanggawul Cycle, 18.
    Anonymous.
  The Djanggawul Cycle, 6.
    Anonymous.
  Epilogue. Russell.
  Greek Transfiguration. Friar.
  House of the Living. Vigee.
  Laus Veneris. Moulton.
  Like a ravaged sea. Ise.
  News for the Delphic Oracle.
    Yeats.
  Ode to a Nightingale: The
    Nightingale. Keats.
  One Chord. Sachs.
  A Passer By. Bridges.
  Phraseology. Cortez.
  The Pilgrim Fathers.
    Pierpont.
  A Plum. Leib.
  Sailor. Page.
  Sleepless. Al-Khansa.
  Solomon on the Vanity of the
    World. Prior.
  Song of Gwythno. Peacock.
  A Sound from the Earth.
    Stafford.
  The Sun God. De Vere.
  There Was a Young Lady of
    Rome. Nash.
  To a Courtesan a Thousand
    Years Dead. Eldridge.
  To the South. Ghiselin.
  Venus of the Salty Shell.
    Devlin.
Focus
  The Butterfly. Burr.
  Stopping by Shadows.
    Fulton.
Fodder
  The Nativity of Christ.
    Southwell.
  When the Frost Is on the
    Punkin. Riley.

Foe (s)
  Admiral Benbow.
    Anonymous.
  Alfred the Harper. Sterling.
  Another Reply to In Flanders
    Fields. Armstrong.
  A Ballad of the Boston Tea-
    Party, December 16, 1773.
    Holmes.
  The Battle of Bridgewater.
    Anonymous.
  Battle Song. Elliott.
  The Brooding of Sigurd.
    Morris.
  The Call to the Colors.
    Guiterman.
  Capture of Little York.
    Anonymous.
  A Chant of Hate against
    England. Lissauer.
  Childe Harold's Pilgrimage:
    Canto III, XXV. Byron.
  Christ 1: Advent Lyrics, VIII.
    Anonymous.
  Cologne. Bate.
  Come, Follow Me. Campion.
  Driven by desire I did this
    deed. Wyatt.
  The Duel. Maynard.
  An Essay on Criticism.
    Pope.
  The Fate of John Burgoyne.
    Anonymous.
  From all the jails the boys
    and girls. Dickinson.
  The Good Samaritan.
    Newman.
  Gulf Stream. "Coolidge.
  Haidee. Byron.
  The Hare. De la Mare.
  The House of Night.
    Freneau.
  In After Days. Cameron.
  Italy. Filicaja.
  John Brown's Body. Benét.
  The Jungle. Lewis.
  Let Not the Sluggish Sleep.
    Anonymous.
  Men of the North. Neal.
  The Mourning Conquest.
    Anonymous.
  Mundus Qualis. Sylvester.
  The Nature of the Turtle
    Dove. *Anonymous.*
  New Heaven, New War.
    Southwell.
  The Night before the Battle of
    Waterloo. Byron.
  Obsequies of Stuart.
    Thompson.
  Ode: "As it fell upon a day."
    Barnfield.
  On Scaring Some Waterfowl
    in Loch Turit... Burns.
  On Tobacco. Pestel.
  One Country. Stanton.
  Prayer for Light. Coblentz.
  Pretty Maids Beware!!!
    Anonymous.
  Reflections in an Iron Works.
    ""MacDiarmid.
  Room for Jesus. Staples.
  Sarah Hazard's Love Letter.
    Ellis.
  Song: "O memory! thou fond
    deceiver." Goldsmith.
  The Song of the Lower
    Classes. Jones.
  Sonnets, XL: "Take all my
    loves my love, yea take
    them all." Shakespeare.

The Story of Cruel Psamtek.
  Anonymous.
To D'Annunzio: Lines from
  the Sea. Nichols.
Unkindness. Herbert.
Welcome over the Door of an
  Old Inn. *Anonymous.*
Written on a Wall at
  Woodstock. Elizabeth I.
Foemen
  Ever Watchful. Ta' Abbata
    Sharra.
  The Last Bowstrings. White.
  The Victory Wreck.
    Carleton.
Fog
  Autumn Poem. Cronin.
  First Rainfall. Lightman.
  Fog 9/76. Dey.
  From a Birch. Wolny.
  Mocking Song against
    Qaqortingneq. Piuvkaq.
  Not That Far. Miller.
  Unprofitablenes. Vaughan.
  Yankee Cradle. Coffin.
Foghorn
  By Achmelvich Bridge.
    MacCaig.
  A Day in France. Holbrook.
  No Fear. Curran.
Foil (ed)
  The Character of a Good
    Person. Dryden.
  New Heaven, New War.
    Southwell.
  Old Grey. Lape.
  The Valley of the Shadow of
    Death. Cowper.
  The Vole. Solomon.
Fold (ed) (ing) (s)
  As Day Begins to Wane.
    Coleman.
  Azrael. Welsh.
  Dear Saviour, If These Lambs
    Should Stray. Hyde.
  Die My Shriek. Kushniroff.
  Dirge. Percy.
  Epitaph: "Here he lies
    moulding." Mellichamp.
  Fragment from "Clemo Uti—
    The Water Lilies."
    Lardner.
  The Good Shepherd. Tuck.
  The Gully. Maurice.
  A Hiroshima Lullaby.
    Langland.
  The Holy Eclogue. del
    Castillo.
  The Horn. Reeves.
  Hunchbacked and Corrected.
    Belford.
  An Island. Wong.
  The James Bond Movie.
    Swenson.
  Love Is Life. Rolle.
  Magnificat. Roberts.
  New Horizons. Lysaght.
  Night. Blake.
  Nike. Wazyk.
  Of the Surface of Things.
    Stevens.
  Pity Not. Simpson.
  The Possibility of New Poetry.
    Bly.
  Prayer for Neighborhood
    Evangelism. Jansen.
  Refuge. Lampman.
  The Return. Silkin.
  A Rich Tuft of Ivy. Geilt.
  Summer Morning. Thomson.
  Thinking Twice in the
    Laundromat. Elliott.

Tick Picking in the Quetico.
Johnson.
Two Poems after A. E.
Housman. Kingsmill.

Folk (s)
Advice to Julia. Luttrell.
Ay, 'Tis Thus. *Anonymous.*
Behave Yoursel' before Folk.
Rodger.
Christmas at Sea. Stevenson.
Died of Love. *Anonymous.*
Evening Prayer. *Anonymous.*
Fin de Siecle. Mackintosh.
Folks and Me. Crites.
Frog Autumn. Plath.
From the Day-Book of a
Forgotten Prince.
Untermeyer.
In Thine Arms. Holmes.
Kissin'. *Anonymous.*
Life's Scars. Wilcox.
Limerick: "There was an Old
Man on the Border."
Lear.
Me. Mearns.
Night of Battle. Winters.
Old Folks at Home. Foster.
Sonnet: Of All He Would Do.
Angiolieri.
Suppose You Met a Witch
(excerpt). Serraillier.
To an Ungentle Critic.
Graves.
The Untutored Giraffe.
Herford.
A Wedgwood Bowl. Taylor.
Working Man Blues. Estes.

Foll (ies) (y)
Abraham Lincoln Walks at
Midnight. Lindsay.
Carmina. Catullus.
The Fault Is Not Mine.
Landor.
For Though the Caves Were
Rabbited. Thoreau.
French Lisette: A Ballad of
Maida Vale. Plomer.
Impatient with Desire.
Granville.
Invitation to the Dance.
Anonymous
The Irish Lady. *Anonymous.*
Johnson on Pope. Ferry.
Love and Folly. La
Fontaine.
Mother, among the Dustbins.
Smith.
Nerves. Symons.
The News. Saxe.
Ode on a Distant Prospect of
Eton College. Gray.
Oh Light Was My Head.
Day Lewis.
On the Road. Jenks.
Our Love Was a Grim
Citadel. Mason.
Prayer to the Virgin of
Chartres. Adams.
Preludes. Patmore.
Song. Clare.
The Tree. Pound.
A Voyage to Tintern Abbey.
Davies.
Ward Two. Webb.
When One or Other Rambles.
Pastorius.
A Word to the Wise. Duer.
Youth! Thou Wear'st to
Manhood Now. Scott.

Follow (ed) (ing) (s)
Alcyone. Mace.

All or Nothing (parody).
Taylor.
The Anglers Song. Basse.
Arabian Proverb.
Anonymous.
Archie O Cawfield (B vers.).
Anonymous.
At the Edge of Town.
Stafford.
Atalanta in Calydon.
Swinburne.
August. Ledwidge.
Award. Durem.
Aware. Lawrence.
Beacon Light. Clark.
Bless, Dear Saviour, This
Child. Beck.
Braving the Wilds All
Unexplored. Freeman.
Carol. Rodgers.
A Carrouse to the Emperor,
the Royal Pole...
Anonymous.
Children of Adam.
Whitman.
Children of the Heavenly
King. Cennick.
Christ. Burdette.
Come Up from the Fields
Father. Whitman.
A Curt Addendum.
Anonymous.
Discipleship. Bales.
Doctor Freud. Lazar.
Elegie. Habington.
Epitaph. *Anonymous.*
The Exequy. Dobbs.
Fallen Leaves. *Anonymous.*
The Fiddler. Trapnell.
Follower. Arvey.
For John Berryman I.
Lowell.
For My Mother: Genevieve
Jules Creeley. Creeley.
The Gallant Fighting "Joe."
Stevenson.
God Leads the Way.
Cleanthes.
God's Funeral. Hardy.
Gracious Saviour, We Adore
Thee. Cutting.
Grandfather. Henson.
Hares on the Mountain.
Anonymous.
He Who Knows.
Anonymous.
The High Tide on the Coast
of Lincolnshire. Ingelow.
Hind Horn (In Scotland
Town). *Anonymous.*
Hither We Come, Our
Dearest Lord. Freeman.
Home Burial. Frost.
How They Came from the
Blue Snows. Kenseth.
The Hunchback in the Park.
Thomas.
I watched the moon around
the house. Dickinson.
Ideal Beauty. Herrera.
Impressions of Francois-Marie
Arouet (de Voltaire)
(excerpt). Pound.
Incident. Kopp.
Indian Painting, Probably
Paiute, in a Cave near
Madras, Oregon. Ramsey.
The Inner Silence. Monroe.
Joy. Bantock.
Judas, Joyous Little Son.
Farber.
Judith. Young.

Kicking the Leaves. Hall.
The Last Meeting of
Pocahontas and the Great
Captain. Preston.
Late Tutorial. Buckley.
The Lights Go On.
McCloskey.
Limerick: "A ghoulish old
fellow in Kent." Bishop.
The Little Dog under the
Wagon. *Anonymous.*
The Living Book. Bates.
Love on the Mountain.
Boyd.
Love Wears Roses' Elegance.
Bertken.
The Malady of Love Is
Nerves. Petronius.
The Man with the Hoe: A
Reply. Cheney.
La Maquina a Houston.
Dorn.
The Marigold. Wither.
Mary's Lamb. Hale.
The Master's Invitation.
Randolph.
Matthew. Sansom.
May-Music. Taylor.
Melancholetta. "Carroll.
Men's Loving Is a False
Affection. *Anonymous.*
A Mormon Immigrant Song.
Anonymous.
My Bangalorey Man.
Anonymous.
A Northern Legion. Read.
Now the lotuses in the
imperial lake. Wang
Ch'ing-hui.
O Gather Me the Rose.
Henley.
The O'Lincon Family.
Flagg.
Observation Car and Cigar.
Stafford.
Oisin. *Anonymous.*
The Old Pope is Comforted
by the Thought of the
Young Pompilia.
Browning.
Old Pudding-Pie Woman.
Anonymous.
On Fame. Keats.
On Time with God. Nutter.
The Poor Parson. Chaucer.
Prelude. George.
The Princess. Tennyson.
Prowling the Ridge. Minty.
The Queen of Hearts.
Anonymous.
A Question. *Anonymous.*
Quid Non Speremus,
Amantes? Dowson.
The Rigveda: Pushan, God of
Pasture. *Anonymous.*
Rise Up, Shepherd, and
Follow. *Anonymous.*
The Royal Mummy to
Bohemia. Stoddard.
The Run from Manassas
Junction. *Anonymous.*
Saturday Night in the Village.
Leopardi.
Sea School. Howes.
Service Supreme.
Anonymous.
Sexual Privacy of Women on
Welfare. Lane.
She That Holds Me Under the
Laws of Love. Gorges.
The Silence. MacLeish.
Skimmers. Walker.

So lonely am I. Ono no
Komachi.
The Song of Love and Death.
Tennyson.
Song Set by Robert Jones: "In
Sherwood lived stout Robin
Hood." *Anonymous.*
Strong as Death. Bunner.
Temptation in Harvest.
Kavanagh.
The Texas Cowboy.
Anonymous.
Titty Cum Tawtay.
Anonymous.
To a Butterfly. Schuck.
To a Negro Boy Graduating.
Maleska.
To Venus. Horace.
The True Apostolate.
Weyburn.
Ulysses. Tennyson.
Verses Placed Over the Door
at the Entrance into the
Apollo Room... Jonson.
Victoria. Van Dyke.
Virginiana. Johnson.
The Volunteer. Cutler.
Who Follows in His Train?
Heber.
Wild Eden. Woodberry.
The Wind's Way. Conkling.
The Woman Who
Disapproved of Music at
the Bar. Gregory.
The Women's Marseillaise.
Macaulay.
Woolworth's. Hall.

Fond (ness)
Cradle-Song at Twilight.
Meynell.
A Day Dream. Bronte.
Erotion. Swinburne.
A Fishing Song. Rands.
Good Appetite. Van Doren.
In the Valley of the Elwy.
Hopkins.
Love. Munday.
Odes (excerpt). Tibullus.
Passage to India. Whitman.
She Smiled Like a Holiday.
Anonymous.
Song. Clare.
Spiritual Passion. Barlow.
To Silence. Moore.

Food
Amanda. *Anonymous.*
The Ant and the Cricket.
Anonymous.
Artichoke. Taylor.
Bad and Good. Resnikoff.
The Bird's Nest. Turner.
Birlinn Chlann-Raghnaill.
MacDonald.
Bread. Dickey.
Burke and Wills. Barratt.
Case. Janowitz.
The Church the Garden of
Christ. Watts.
The Cypress Curtain of the
Night. Campion.
The Gulistan. Sa'di.
The H. Communion.
Herbert.
He Who Has Never Known
Hunger. Coatsworth.
Human Needs. Walker.
Kneeling Here, I Feel Good.
Piercy.
Lament for a Husband.
Anonymous.
Landfall. *Anonymous.*
Lilith. Gregg.

The Lovely Youth. Aneirin.
Metamorphoses. Ovid
(Publius Ovidius Naso).
A Method of Preserving Hay
from Being Mow-Burnt, or
Taking Fire. Dodsley.
The Moth. Scannell.
The Nature of the Eagle.
Anonymous.
Peat-Cutters. Johnson.
Picketing Supermarkets.
Wayman.
The Prophecy of Famine.
Churchill.
The Question. Duncan.
The Retirement. *Anonymous.*
Russians Breathing.
Hammial.
Sarah Threeneedles. Bates.
Satires. Horace.
Some Bird. *Anonymous.*
Spleen. Baudelaire.
Sunrise. Tollerud.
Table Talk. Mattam.
To a Chameleon. Moore.
The Truth. Davies.
The Two Sisters.
Anonymous.
Wasp Sex Myth (Two).
Hollo.
The Wild Mushroom.
Snyder.
With the Sun's Fire.
Ignatow.
Written in Dejection near
Rome. Bly.

Fool (s)
Against Garnesche (excerpt).
Skelton.
All Night Long Fooling Me.
Anonymous.
The Amish. Updike.
Angels. Hall.
Another Full Moon.
Fainlight.
Arcadia. Sidney.
L'Art poetique. Boileau-
Despreaux.
Atheist. Harburg.
Aureng-Zebe. Dryden.
Ballad. Treece.
Being to Timelessness as It's
to Time. Cummings.
Boxer Shorts Named
Champion. Brown.
Bringing Him Up. Dunsany.
Callypso Speaks. Doolittle.
Christians at War. Kendrick.
A Cold Rendering (parody).
Anonymous.
Colophon. Gogarty.
A Credo. Thackeray.
Death. More.
Dialogue between a Squeamish
Cotting Mechanic and his
Sluttish Wife... Ward.
Dragging the Main. Ray.
Dream Songs. Berryman.
The Dunciad. Pope.
Early Morning at Bargis.
Hagedorn.
Elegies. Chenier.
Embarrassed Judge.
Anonymous.
The Emulation. Egerton.
Epigram: "Yes, every poet is a
fool." Prior.
An Epitaph of the Death of
Nicholas Grimald. Googe.
Escape. Jones.
An Essay on Man. Pope.

Fables for the Female Sex, V:
The Poet and His Patron.
Moore.
The Farmer's Boy.
Bloomfield.
Flee on Your Donkey.
Sexton.
The Folly of Brown. Gilbert.
The Fool of Love.
Anonymous.
Fool's Blues. Smith.
Four Poems for Robin.
Snyder.
The Fox and the Crow. La
Fontaine.
A Free Parliament Litany.
Anonymous.
From a Letter from Lesbia.
Parker.
The Future Verdict.
Cambridge.
Generalization. Capp.
He Meditates on the Life of a
Rich Man. Gregory.
He's a Fool. Anonymous.
Homage to Texas. Graves.
Honey-Mead. *Anonymous.*
The House of a Hundred
Lights. Torrence.
I Hardly Ever Ope My Lips.
Garnett.
If Women Could Be Fair.
De Vere.
Insights. Davis.
January. Voigt.
A Jewish Poet Counsels a
King. De Carrion.
Joe Tinker. Hall.
Juniper. Duggan.
The Kingdom of Poetry:
Swift. Schwartz.
Lack Wit. *Anonymous.*
Landscape near a Steel Mill.
Horn.
The Last Instructions to a
Painter. Marvell.
Laughing Backwards. Hall.
Let Them Alone. Jeffers.
Love's Fool. Rosenthal.
Love's Labour's Lost.
Shakespeare.
Love-Songs, At Once Tender
and Informative.
Hoffenstein.
The Loves of the Birds.
Anonymous.
Madrigal: "The silver swan."
Gibbons.
The Maiden's Choice.
Anonymous.
The Man of Taste.
Bramston.
The Man Who Frets at
Worldly Strife. Drake.
Married Man Blues.
Reynolds.
Martin Said to His Man.
Anonymous.
The Merchant of Venice.
Shakespeare.
Mountain Liars. Hafen.
The Newer Vainglory.
Meynell.
The Nightmare. MacLean.
An Ode for the New Year.
Gay.
On Don Surly. Jonson.
On the Irish Club. Swift.
On the New Laureate.
Anonymous.
On the World. Swift.

Once Did My Thoughts.
Anonymous.
The Optimist. *Anonymous.*
Paradise: A Hindoo Legend.
Birdseye.
Parrhasius. Willis
Peace. Kavanagh.
Piney Woods Money Mama.
Jefferson.
The Prophecy of Famine.
Churchill.
Punchinello. Burgh.
Rabbit Foot Blues. Jefferson.
Reflection. Stein.
Reflections in an Iron Works.
""MacDiarmid.
Retort. Dunbar.
The Search. Brew.
Sir Fopling Flutter. Dryden.
The Sleeping House.
Tennyson.
Song in the Same Play, by the
Wavering Nymph. Behn.
Song: "It is all one in Venus'
wanton school." Lyly.
Sonnets, LVII: "Being your
slave, what should I do but
tend." Shakespeare.
Sundays Visiting. Rios.
The Suppliant. Johnson.
Symbols. Yeats.
A Tale of Drury Lane.
Smith.
Theme in Yellow. Sandburg.
Thou Didst Say Me.
Waddington.
Though a Fool. Francis.
Though You Are Young.
Campion.
A Thousand Martyrs I Have
Made. Behn.
'Tis Now Since I Sate Down.
Suckling.
To His Books. Vaughan.
To Nysus. Sedley.
To the Respective Judges.
Anonymous.
Tommy. Kipling.
The Touch-Stone. Bishop.
The Triple Fool. Donne.
The Trucker. Dyson.
Upon a Fool. Hoskyns.
Upon the Downs. Etherege.
Victory. Axford.
Vox Populi. Dryden.
Waterchew! Corso.
We Are Acrobats. Gerez.
Who Does Not Love Wine,
Women and Song. Voss.
The Wife of Kelso (The Wily
Auld Carle). *Anonymous.*
You Can't Fool God.
Kleiser.

Foolish (ness)
Advice to Colonel Valentine.
Graves.
Allergy. Gibson.
Astrophel and Stella, XXXIII.
Sidney.
Ballad of the Mouse.
Wallace.
Because of Clothes. Riding.
The Bell of the Hermitage.
Anonymous.
The Cat. Herford.
Challenge. Brown.
Church Bell in the Night.
Anonymous.
Down by the Salley Gardens.
Yeats.
Gun Teams. Frankau.
Gypsy-Heart. Bates.

If Fathers Knew But How to
Leave. *Anonymous.*
If Frequently to Mass.
Pisan.
In a Country Cemetery in
Iowa. Kooser.
In Memoriam A.H.H.,
LXVIII. Tennyson.
Lady Clara Vere De Vere.
Tennyson.
Landlord Fill the Flowing
Bowl. *Anonymous.*
Little Willie's My Darlin'.
Anonymous.
The Maiden. Hille.
Variations on Sappho.
"Field.
The War of the Worlds.
Rutsala.

Foot
74th Street. Livingston.
Aeglamour's Lament.
Jonson.
All Those Hymnings Up to
God. Evans.
Bad and Good. Resnikoff.
Breech Birth. Dauenhauer.
The Burden of Decision.
Everwine.
Chicken. Kelly.
Chorus of Spirits. Darley.
Clams. Moss.
Domine, Quo Vadis?
Anonymous.
A Drunkard. *Anonymous.*
Epigrams (excerpt). Tagore.
The Five Feet. Sanders.
Hymn to Her Unknown.
Turner.
I Know That I Must Die
Soon. Lasker-Schüler.
If Fathers Knew But How to
Leave. *Anonymous.*
Invocation. Miller.
Let Other People Come as
Streams. Reznikoff.
The Little Cradle Rocks
Tonight in Glory.
Anonymous.
Mid-Term Break. Heaney.
Movie Queen. Vaughn.
Mushrooms. Plath.
My Physics Teacher.
Wagoner.
One and One. Dodge.
One Foot in the River.
Stern.
Poetry and Philosophy.
Randolph.
Ruines of Rome. Du Bellay.
Silly Sweetheart.
Anonymous.
Spider. Cole.
Spring Song. Finkel.
Sun in the East. *Anonymous.*
Thoughts. Benedikt.
To a Cat. Swinburne.
When You and I Must Part.
Anonymous.

Football
The City. Betjeman.
Football and Rowing–An
Eclogue. Godley.

Footfall (s)
An Ancient Castle. Morris.
Ball's Bluff. Melville.
The Footsteps. Valery.
An Indian Song. Yeats.
The Indian to His Love.
Yeats.
Look Up. Nicholson.
The Secret Muse. Campbell.

The Skilful Listener.
Cheney.
Trees. Hughes.

Footprint (s)
Afternoon: Amagansett Beach.
Wheelock.
Akawense. Wolf.
Cat in the Snow. Fisher.
The Caves. Roberts.
Eskimo Chant. *Anonymous.*
Footprints. Brown.
Heart-of-the-Daybreak.
Marais.
Hieroglyphic. Sklarew.
Hospital Evening. Harwood.
The Plains. Dixon.
The Progress of Poetry.
"Caudwell.
Pursuit of an Ideal.
Kavanagh.
Snowfall. Merwin.
Tales of a Wayside Inn.
Longfellow.
This Version of Love.
Hewett.

Footstep (s)
An Appeal to My
Countrywomen. Harper.
The Changing Road. Bates.
Christ's Coming in Triumph.
Taylor.
Convention. Lee.
Everything Passes and
Vanishes. Allingham.
Fairies. Tickell.
The Four Cardinal Times of
Day. Daumal.
High Field–First Day of
Winter. Eddy.
In Front of the Landscape.
Hardy.
March. Coatsworth.
Men's Loving Is a False
Affection. *Anonymous.*
On the Way. Husid.
The Passing Bell at Stratford.
Winter.
Persephone. Longley.
Seasons and Times. Barnes.
Skylights. Gallagher.
Stanzas Cancelled from the
Elegy. Gray.
This Wind. Kryss.

Forbidden
I Have a Blue Piano.
Lasker-Schüler.
Quebec Farmhouse. Glassco.
The Scholar's Wife. Mernit.

Force (d) (s)
Before the Storm. Hanson.
Burial in the Sand. Sullivan.
The Cabin Creek Flood.
Anonymous.
Courage. Arnold.
Death by Drowning.
Brewster.
The Eternal Kinship.
Peloubet.
The Fair Singer. Marvell.
Forbearance. Leitner.
The Hidden Truth. Jami.
Hiroshima. Rockwell.
Hurlygush. Lindsay.
If Wishing for the Mystic Joys
of Love. Chatterton.
In Impressions of Hawk
Feathers Willow Leaves
Shadow. Woody.
Life Cycle of Common Man.
Nemerov.
Love's Labour Lost. Tofte.
Manhood. More.

Money Gets the Mastery.
Herrick.
The Mower. *Anonymous.*
My hated birthday is here,
and I must go. Sulpicia.
Oh Cruel Was the Press-
Gang. *Anonymous.*
Oxford & Cambridge.
Browne.
Pine Boat a-Shift.
Anonymous.
The Rape of the Lock.
Pope.
A Riddle. Cowper.
The Seasons. Thomson.
Sonnets to Orpheus. Rilke.
A Spring Memorandum.
Duncan.
Switzerland. Arnold.
Three Poems, III.
Castellânos.
The Tide of Faith. Eliot.
To a Lady, with a Compass.
Napier.
To England. Boker.
To the Winds. A Song.
Ayres.
To You Who Wait. Pudney.
Tree-Topped Hill.
Anonymous.
A Voice from the Roses.
Kumin.
Whiplash. Matthews.

Ford (s)
The Island of the Scots
(excerpt). Ayton [(or
Aytoun)] Sir Robert.
Jurgis Petraskas, the Workers'
Angel, Organizes...
Petrosky.
Pass to thy Rendezvous of
Light. Dickinson.
Rock and Roll. James.

Forefathers
Destinie. Cowley.
Southern Cross. Melville.
Weep Not for a Warrior.
Mtshali.

Forehead
Barren Woman. Plath.
The Bicycle Rider. Shapcott.
Birdwatchers of America.
Hecht.
The Cage. Montague.
David. Mandel.
Grotesque. Lowell.
Hills picking up the
moonlight. Cassian.
I Like a Look of Agony.
Dickinson.
In the First Cave. Mayne.
The Lady of the Lake. Scott.
Out-of-the-Body Travel.
Plumly.
A Refusal. Hardy.
Song for a Day (excerpt).
Arrivi.
Sonnets, I: "Sporting at fancie,
setting light by love."
Barnfield.
South Carolina to the States
of the North. Hayne.
Spring Floods. Orr.
What She Said.
Centamputan.
Your Air of My Air.
Margenat.

Foreign
Bar Mitzvah. Orlen.
Blessed and Resting Uncle.
Elliott.
Cedar Needles. Twichell.

Chorus for Survival (excerpt).
Gregory.
Come away, Death. Pratt.
The Emigrant. McLachlan.
Homage to John Millington
Synge. O Direain.
John Knox. Smith.
Lord Beichan and Susie Pye.
Anonymous.
On the Death of a Prince: A
Meditation. Philipott.
The Turn of the Road.
Stephens.
The Wind's Song. "Setoun.
Gabriel"
Young Heroes. Horne.

Foreman
The Jam at Gerry's Rock.
Anonymous.
Poems in Praise of Practically
Nothing. Hoffenstein.
Saturday Night. Oppenheim.
Young Monroe at Gerry's
Rock. *Anonymous.*

Forest (s)
"America, My Country..."
Emerson.
Among the Beautiful Pictures.
Cary.
Amy. Legare.
Autumn. *Anonymous.*
Before Rereading
Shakespeare's Sonnets.
Moore.
Brother Juniper. Kelly.
The Brownies' Celebration.
Cox.
Captain Jones' Invitation.
Freneau.
The Childhood of an
Equestrian. Edson.
Colonial Set. Bailey.
A Day in the City. Sissman.
Evangeline. Longfellow.
Extinct Birds. Wright.
The Flowers of the Forest.
Cockburn.
The Forest Fire. Monroe.
The Forest's Queen.
Massinger.
Geography. Dransfield.
Hair. Gourmont.
He Fumbles at Your Soul.
Dickinson.
History. Graham.
If Ice. Ross.
In Phaeacia. Flecker.
In the Caves of Auvergne.
Turner.
In the Forest. Edson.
In the Forest of Your Eyes.
Barbeitos.
The Indian Student.
Freneau.
Into the Noiseless Country.
Parsons
A Japanese Birthday Wish.
Swann.
The King of Sunshine.
Silverton.
The Krankenhaus of
Leutkirch. Lattimore.
Limerick: "There was a
professor of Beaulieu."
Joad.
London Tom-Cat.
Hamburger.
Meeting a Bear. Wagoner.
The Mocking-Bird. Hayes.
My Father's Wedding 1924.
Bly.

My Heart Burns for Him.
Anonymous.
My Sweetheart in the
Rippling Hills of Sand.
Likelike.
My Valentine. Stevenson.
Need of an Angel. Souster.
Nones. Auden.
Not unto the Forest.
Widdemer.
November. Fisher.
November: Epping Forest.
Davidson.
O Spirit of Venus Whom I
Adore. *Anonymous.*
October in Tennessee.
Malone.
On an American Soldier of
Fortune Slain in France.
Scollard.
Peking Man, Raining. Lorr.
Prefatory Sonnet. Kendall.
The Seed Shop. Stuart.
Solitude. Savage.
The Song of the Pilgrims.
Brooke.
Song of the Trees of the Black
Forest. Jabes.
Southern Summer. Stuart.
The Speaker. Ballard.
St. Malachy. Merton.
They. Leib.
Toward Climax. Snyder.
Two Folk Songs, 1.
Anonymous.
Two Sorrows. St. John.
Veneris Venefica Agrestis.
Piccolo.
Vihio Images. Volborth.
The Waste Places. Stephens.
A Way of Keeping. Willard.
When from the Calyx-Canopy
of Night. Laughton.
When Winter Fringes Every
Bough. Thoreau.
Wildness. Wagstaff.
Winter Night. Fairburn.
A Winter Piece. Bryant.
You, Letting the Trees Stand
as My Betrayer. Wakoski.

Foretold
Christmas Carol. Helmore.
Praise. Cooper.
A Song: I Thought No More
Was Needed. Yeats.

Forever
The Ailing Parent. Dunetz.
Armor. Dickey.
Ballade of Sayings. Merwin.
Bride's Lament. Sappho.
Companionship. Babcock.
Curtain Speech. Braude.
Derry. Deane.
Dianae Sumus in Fide.
Catullus.
Forever and a Day. Aldrich.
From the Journals of the Frog
Prince. Mitchell.
Fulfilment. Ledoux.
God of Our Fathers, Bless
This Our Land. Hopkins,
Jr.
The Grief of Cafeterias.
Updike.
The Hardness Scale.
Peseroff.
The Hostess' Daughter.
Uhland.
Hotels. Donnell.
I Am a Victim of Telephone.
Ginsberg.

I Lift My Eyes Up to the
  Hills.　Mather.
I Love Old Women.
  Kloefkorn.
I Saw Eternity.　Bogan.
The Importance of Poetry; or,
  the Coming Forth from
  Eternity into Time.
  Plutzik.
Lines by a Fond Lover.
  Anonymous.
The Little Lady.　Edson.
The Long Road West.
  Knibbs.
Mutations: Midsummer.
  Fitzgerald.
My Dead.　"Rachel" (Rachel
  Blumstein).
Night Poem.　Dodd.
Paraphrase of Luther's Hymn.
  Hedge
The Path of the Stars.　Jones,
  Jr.
Pigeons.　Reid.
Poem in Three Parts.　Bly.
Poetry Paper.　Codrescu.
Portraits.　Fagg.
Recollections of "Lalla
  Rookh."　Trowbridge.
Saints in Glory, We Together.
  Adams.
September: Last Day at the
  Beach.　Tillinghast.
Sonnet: "I watched the sea for
  hours blind with sun."
  Scott.
The Story of the Rose.
  "Alice".
Strictly for Posterity.　Simic.
This Is Our Music.　Leong.
Threnos.　Hervey.
To Hold in a Poem.　Smith.
Under the Blue.　Browne.
Vivaldi.　Schwartz.
Waking Early Sunday
  Morning.　Lowell.
The Whole Universe Is Full of
  God.　Emre.
The Wrestling Match.
  Warren.

Forfeit (s)
Garland for a Storyteller.
  Farnham.
Paranoia in Crete.　Corso.
The Wits.　Suckling.

Forge (d)
Dare You See a Soul at the
  White Heat?　Dickinson.
Lauds.　Berryman.
On Donne's Poetry.
  Coleridge.
The Rock.　Eliot.
To Earth.　Applewhite.

Forget (ting) (s)
A 14-Year-Old Convalescent
  Cat in the Winter.　Ewart.
Act of Love.　Moore.
After the Quarrel.　Gordon.
Aftermath.　Sassoon.
All One.　Brand.
Ancient Quatrain.
  Anonymous.
Arac's Song.　Gilbert.
Artificial Intelligence.　Rich.
Astrophel and Stella, CV.
  Sidney.
At Casterbridge Fair.
  Hardy.
Autumn Healing.　Ward.
Awee'.　Francisco.
The Baby.　Taylor.

The Ballad of Camden Town.
  Flecker.
Ballade of Unfortunate
  Mammals.　Parker.
Ballata: Of His Lady among
  Other Ladies.　Cavalcanti.
Bay Violets.　Maris Stella.
Belle.　*Anonymous.*
Birthday on Deathrow.
  Otey.
The Blue Hill Is My Desire.
  Hwang Chin-i.
Both My Grandmothers.
  Field.
Bottle Should Be Plainly
  Labeled Poison.　Hay.
Carol.　McClure.
The Case.　Norris.
Cat of Many Years.　Lutz.
A Childhood.　Spender.
Corn Rigs Are Bonnie.
  Burns.
The Crowing of the Red
  Cock.　Lazarus.
A Curse.　Feldman.
Death Songs.　Mack.
Dialogue on the Headland.
  Graves.
Do They Whisper behind My
  Back?　Schwartz.
Doors.　Sandburg.
Dream Songs.　Berryman.
Dreams.　Symons.
Easter, 1923.　Neihardt.
El Alamein Revisited.
  MacNab.
Evening Song of Senlin.
  Aiken.
Exercise.　Nolan.
Eyes of Summer.　Merwin.
The Fancy Frigate.
  Anonymous.
The Fault Is Not Mine.
  Landor.
The Flag.　Silverstein.
Football Field: Evening.
  McKellar.
For E.J.P.　Cohen.
Forget about It.　Currie.
Forget It.　*Anonymous.*
Forgetting God.　Harvey.
The Fountain in the Park.
  Haley.
The Fragment.　Belloc.
From the Prison House.
  Rich.
Games.　McPherson.
The Gate.　Jamal.
Good-Bye for a Long Time.
  Fuller.
Good-Bye to the
  Mezzogiorno.　Auden.
Graves.　Sandburg.
Growing Smiles.　*Anonymous.*
Having a Wonderful Time.
  Lewis.
Hedgehog.　Muldoon.
The Hopes.　Fringell.
How Can the Heart Forget
  Her.　Davison.
How to Go and Forget.
  Markham.
A Hymne on the Nativitie of
  My Saviour.　Jonson.
Icons.　Waddington.
The Immortal Mind.　Byron.
In Memory of Two Sons.
  Stellwagon.
Instructions for Crossing the
  Border.　Pagis.
It Was You, Attis.　Sappho.

Jeames of Buckley Square.
  Thackeray.
John Brown's Body.　Benét.
Journal of the Storm.
  Kuzma.
The Keeper.　Carpenter.
The Lambs on the Green
  Hills Stood Gazing on Me.
  Anonymous.
Lament.　Millay.
A Letter to Ron Silliman on
  the Back of a Map of the
  Solar System.　Schmitz.
Lines.　De Vere.
Lines for a Drawing of Our
  Lady of the Night.
  Thompson.
Lines for a Friend Who Left.
  Logan.
Little Pagan Rain Song.
  Shaw.
A Little While.　Rossetti.
Longer to muse.　Wyatt.
Love's Kiss.　Hay.
Love's Last Suit.　Davidson.
The Lover Beseecheth His
  Mistress Not to Forget...
  Wyatt.
The Lucky Sailor.
  Anonymous.
Man Lying on a Wall.
  Longley.
Marry the Lass?　Greig.
Memorabilia.　Browning.
Memory of a Scholar.
  Lattimore.
The Men of the Merrimac.
  Scollard.
The Mexico Trail.
  Anonymous.
Monangamba.　Jacinto.
A Mourning Letter from
  Paris.　Rivers.
Music and Words.　Jennings.
New York in the Spring.
  Budbill.
No One Talks about This.
  Rakosi.
Nursery Rules from Nannies.
  Anonymous.
Obit.　Lowell.
The Obscure Night of the
  Soul.　John of Damascus.
Ode to the Evening Star.
  Akenside.
Oh, No! We Never Mention
  Her.　Bayly.
The Old Age of Michelangelo.
  Prince.
On a Thrush Singing in
  Autumn.　Morris.
On Mr. Hearne, the Great
  Antiquary.　*Anonymous.*
The One before the Last.
  Brooke.
Parable.　Auden.
Pericles and Aspasia.
  Landor.
The Rainbow.　Colby.
Remember.　Rossetti.
Remember or Forget.　Aïdé.
Rispetto.　Robinson.
Rococo.　Swinburne.
Running Vines in a Field.
  Brown.
Russians.　Douglas.
Sappho, if you do not come
  out.　Sappho.
September Midnight.
  Teasdale.
Sitting Alone in Tulsa Three
  A.M.　Henson.

Sleep Brings No Joy.　Bronte.
Song.　Miller.
Song for My Father.
  Hagedorn.
The Song of the Flags.
  Mitchell.
Song: "Only the wanderer."
  Gurney.
The Sporting Cowboy.
  Anonymous.
This Way Out.　Fishback.
Thompson Street.　McCoy.
To a Common Prostitute.
  Whitman.
To Each His Own.　Garvin.
To His Love.　Gurney.
To the Canary Bird.　Very.
To the Noble Sir Francis
  Drake.　Beedome.
The Tsigane's Canzonet.
  King.
Tubal Cain.　Mackay.
Twelve Lines About the
  Burning Bush.　Ravitch.
Two Poems.　Tsurayuki.
The Unknown.　Laughlin.
A Valentine.　Gillespy.
The Verb "To Think'.
  Enright.
Warning.　Frost.
Washington Monument by
  Night.　Sandburg.
What Profit?　Di Roma.
When I Am Dead.　Neihardt.
When I have gone away.
  Michizane.
The Whole World Now Is but
  the Minister.　Bridges.
Why Would I Have Survived?
  Bruck.
Willows in Alma-Ata.　Wat.
Without Names.　Tagami.
Without Regret.　Lorraine.
The World as Meditation.
  Stevens.
Young Companions.
  Anonymous.

Forgetful (ness)
At Toledo.　Symons.
Pain.　Storni.
Pindar.　Antipater of Sidon.
This Stone.　*Anonymous.*

Forgive (s)
Aaron Burr's Wooing.
  Stedman.
Alonso to Ferdinand.
  Auden.
Armistice Day.　Trent.
Attend, Young Friends, While
  I Relate.　*Anonymous.*
An Autograph.　Whittier
Babi Yar.　Ozerov.
The Ballad of Camden Town.
  Flecker.
Blooming Nelly.　Burns.
A Christmas Prayer.
  Stevenson.
Confession to J. Edgar
  Hoover.　Wright.
Danae.　Simonides (of Ceos).
The Death of Goody Nurse.
  Clarke.
Delia Very Angry.
  Anonymous.
Diminutivus Ululans.
  MacNamara.
Disarmed.　Searing.
The Doll.　Friend.
Ecce Puer.　Joyce.
Epigram: "To forgive enemies
  Hayley does pretend."
  Blake.

The Epitaph in Form of a Ballad. Villon.
The Epitaph, or Ballade of the Hanged. Villon.
Father to Son. Jennings.
Forgive Me When I Whine. *Anonymous.*
Forgive, O Lord, My Little Jokes on Thee. Frost.
Forgiveness. Whittier.
A Fugue. Church.
Giving and Forgiving. Springer.
The Heart Has Its Reasons. Picano.
Inscription above the Entrance to the Abbey of Theleme. Urquhart.
Jill. Laing.
The Judgement. Goodale.
Landscape with Next of Kin. Broumas.
Last Verses. Chatterton.
The Law. Schulman.
Lessons. Untermeyer.
The Lily of the West. *Anonymous.*
Lines. De Vere.
The Masquerader. Kilmer.
My Parents Kept Me from Children Who Were Rough. Spender.
Nearing Winter. Sandeen.
Old Clothes. Hey.
On Frozen Fields. Kinnell.
Pardon. Howe.
Pater Filio. Bridges.
Rebecca's After-Thought. Turner.
Saturninus. Conway.
Song. Spencer.
Sonnet: "O little self, within whose smallness lies." Masefield.
The Soviet Union. Berryman.
Ten Years and More. Waddington.
Their Last Will and Testament. MacNeice.
The Thrush. Corsellis.
To a Dog. Peabody.
To His Verse. Landor.
To My Mother. Brock.
When I Cut My Hair. Green.
The Witch. Hinkson.
Would I Be Called a Christian? Moser.

Forgiven (ess)
The Appology. Winchilsea.
As Difference Blends into Identity. Miles.
Ay, 'Tis Thus. *Anonymous.*
Ballade d'une Grande Dame. Chesterton.
A Child's Christmas without Jean Cocteau. Fisher.
The Composer. Auden.
Crisis. Auden.
Cwmrhydyceirw Elegiacs. Watkins.
Cycle. Lonergan.
Eternal Lord! Eased of a Cumbrous Load. Michelangelo.
Forgiveness. Sewell.
G.M.B. Davie.
Hesperus. Clare.
His Sovereignty. Ben Moses.
Isolation Cell Poem. Green.

Nor Mars His Sword. Thompson.
On the Benefactions in the Late Frost, 1740. Pope.
A Prayer. Scollard.
The Rubaiyat of Omar Khayyam. Omar Khayyam.
Visit. Coccimiglio.
William and Helen. Scott.

Forgot (ten)
Alison. *Anonymous.*
The Angel in the House. Patmore.
The Book. Fagg.
By the Pool at the Third Rosses. Symons.
A Caution to Everybody. Nash.
Country Landscape. Santos.
Crusader's Song. *Anonymous.*
The Cumberland's Crew. *Anonymous.*
Custer Lives in Humboldt County. Hale.
The Day-Dream. Rossetti.
A Day of Love. Rossetti.
Death Songs. Mack.
Do You Love Me. *Anonymous.*
Dum and Dee. *Anonymous.*
The Earthly Paradise. Morris.
Elegy to the Memory of an Unfortunate Lady. Pope.
Eli the Thatcher. Rothenstein.
Eliot's Oak. Longfellow.
Epigram: "When Bibo thought fit from the world to retreat." Prior.
The Farmer Is the Man. *Anonymous.*
The Fatal Dream; or, The Unhappy Favourite. Collins.
Forget Thee? Moultrie.
A Georgia Volunteer. Townsend.
Hearing Steps. Simic.
Her Horoscope. Townsend.
In North Great George's Street. O'Sullivan.
An Interlude. Swinburne.
J'Accuse. Klappert.
John Smith Is My Name. *Anonymous.*
Johnie Cam to Our Toun. *Anonymous.*
The Lay of the Last Minstrel. Scott.
Love and Age. Landor.
A Lover's Anger. Prior.
The Mailman. Contoski.
Mariana in the South. Tennyson.
Martyr's Memorial. Guiney.
The Mathmid. Bialik.
May 30, 1893. Bangs.
Mear. *Anonymous.*
Meditation by Mascoma Lake. Babcock.
The Merry Window. Scarfe.
The Messenger. Noyes.
The Midnight Court. Merriman.
The moon upon her fluent route. Dickinson.
Night Mail. Auden.
Nocturnal Heart. Kegels.
Nocturnal Thoughts. Huss.

Odes, IX. Hafiz.
Of Common Devotion. Quarles.
Oh My People I Remember. Rose.
On the Fly-Leaf of a Book of Old Plays. Learned.
On the Proposal to Erect a Monument in England to Lord Byron. Lazarus.
An Outdoor Litany. Guiney.
A Patch of Old Snow. Frost.
The Path of the Padres. Osborne.
Pro Sua Vita. Warren.
Reading Today's Newspaper. Abbott.
Reflection in a Green Arena. Corso.
Rye Whisky. *Anonymous.*
San Francisco from the Sea. Harte.
Shadow Life. Reid, III.
The Sick Image of My Father Fades. Horder.
The Sirens. Manifold.
Sleep: and between the Closed Eyelids of Sleep. Aiken.
Sometime It May Be. Colton.
Song: "Bring from the craggy haunts of birch and pine." Todhunter.
Song: "'Tis said that absence conquers love!" Thomas.
Sonnet: "Sweet Spring, thou turn'st with all thy goodly train." Drummond.
Souvenirs. Randall.
A Sparrow's Feather. Barker.
Tales of Shatz. Abse.
Tears. Thomas.
Teatime Variations. Titheradge.
That's Our Lot. Halpern.
There Let Thy Bleeding Branch Atone. Bronte.
To a Lady on Her Marriage. Bell.
To Faustine. Colton.
To the Colorado Desert. Morris.
Tweedle-Dum and Tweedle-Dee. *Anonymous.*
Upon Shaving Off One's Beard. Updike.
The Want of You. Wright.
What Is Being Forgotten. Healy.
When You Have Forgotten Sunday: The Love Story. Brooks.
The White Dress. Spear.
Words. Brooks.
The Young Author. Johnson.
Your Hands. Grimke.

Fork
The Constant Cannibal Maiden. Irwin.
Eve. Rossetti.
For the Eating of Swine. Jones.
The Gourmand (parody). Graham.
Irish-American Dignitary. Clarke.
Letters to My Daughters. Minty.

Forlorn
Columbus. Sigourney.

The Death of Cleopatra. Horace.
Forever Dead. Sappho.
Hadrian's Address to His Soul When Dying. Hadrian.
Mariana in the South. Tennyson.
The Old Angler. De La Mare.
The Old Summerhouse. De la Mare.
A Prayer for Purification. Michelangelo.
The Singers in the Snow. *Anonymous.*
The Sound of the Horn. Vigny.
Stanzas. Ibn Gabirol.
Trees. De la Mare.
Tulip Tree. Sitwell.
The Youth with Red-Gold Hair. Sitwell.

Form (s)
The Abyss. Baudelaire.
The Angel in the House, VIII. Patmore.
Are You Born? Rukeyser.
Beauty. Spenser.
Blind, I Speak to the Cigarette. De Longchamps.
Caelica, X. Greville.
Catacombs. Vas.
The Comet at Yalbury or Yell'ham. Hardy.
Conscience. Churchill.
Dandelions. Albee.
Death of the Day. Landor.
Double Ode. Rukeyser.
A Dream. Keats.
The Dying Child's Request. Gould.
England. Day.
Farewell to Winnipeg. Daniells.
A Finger Points to the Moon. Laing.
The First Olympionique to Hiero. Pindar.
Girl Athletes. Long.
The Green Linnet. Wordsworth.
The House of Hospitalities. Hardy.
I Was a Brook. Coleridge.
In Memoriam A.H.H., XCI. Tennyson.
Insomnia. Zelvin.
Leaves Like Fish. Cardiff.
Lions in Sweden. Stevens.
Listen to the Bird. Firestone.
The Living Temple. Holmes
Masque of Hymen: Glad Time Is at His Point Arrived. Jonson.
Metaphysical Poem. Bodenheim.
Mimma Bella. Lee-Hamilton.
The Naked Land. Patchen.
The Naked World. Sully-Prudhomme.
The Odyssey. Homer.
Of His Mistress. Greene.
Paradise Regained. Milton.
The Past Is the Present. Moore.
Prayer before Work. Sarton.
A Question of Form and Content. Stallworthy.
Seagulls. Francis.

Form

The Song of Bekotsidi. *Anonymous.*
The Strayed Reveller. Arnold.
Thou Art the Sky. Tagore.
Threnody. Beddoes.
To Mr. Jervas, with Fresnoy's Art of Painting, Translated by Dryden. Pope.
To My Daughter. Plutzik.
To My Friends. Schiller.
What Form the World Has. Bronk.
Where Is She Now? *Anonymous.*

Former

Bone China. Lister.
The Finished Course. Joseph of the Studium.
Jerusalem. Vinner.
The Lonely Man. Jarrell.
Metamorphoses. Ovid (Publius Ovidius Naso).
The Miner's Progress. Delano.

Formless

The Camera Obscura. Symonds.
A Finger Points to the Moon. Laing.
The Kearsarge. Roche.

Forsake (n)

Awake, Arise, You Drowsy Sleeper. *Anonymous.*
Calvary. Howells.
The Cuckoo (A vers.). *Anonymous.*
The Drowsy Sleeper (A vers.). *Anonymous.*
False Gods. De La Mare.
The Flirt. Davies.
How Firm a Foundation. *Anonymous.*
The Queen of Hearts. *Anonymous.*
The restful place, reviver of my smart. Wyatt.
The Swallow (parody) (excerpt). Squire.
To a Musician. Austin.

Fort (s)

A Ballad of Orleans. Robinson.
Boy with a Hammer. Hoban.
Contemplations. Bradstreet.
Crow's Last Stand. Hughes.
Roman History in Rhyme (excerpt). Goodwin.
Three Elements. Benét.
To the Noblest and Best of Ladies, the Countess of Denbigh. Crashaw.
You Are Desolate, Fort of Kings. *Anonymous.*

Forth

The Faerie Queene. Spenser.
Lord, Grant Us Calm. Rossetti.
Salmon Cycle. Treinin.

Fortitude

A Christmas Sermon: To Be Honest, To Be Kind. Stevenson.
Johnny, I Hardly Knew Ye: Miltonese (parody). Gogarty.
Knapweed. Benson.
Nantucket Whalers. Henderson.

Fortress

The Heavenly Foreigner. Devlin.
King John's Castle. Kinsella.
The Paper Nautilus. Moore.

Fortune (s)

Advice to the Same. Sidney.
Ah Cloris! That I Now Could Sit. Sedley.
Arise, Arise. *Anonymous.*
Aweary Am I. Abu-l-Ala al-Maarri.
Ballade of England. MacNeice.
A Bird's Nest. Biton.
The Burial of Latane. Thompson.
Crowds. Baudelaire.
The Duke of Buckingham. Pope.
An Epitaph of the Death of Nicholas Grimald. Googe.
Farewell to the Court. Ralegh.
Gascoigne's Praise of His Mistress. Gascoigne.
The Golden Mean. Cowper.
Great Churches. *Anonymous.*
Hylas. Propertius.
A Hymne to Our Saviour on the Cross. Chapman.
Idea. Drayton.
Jack Tar. *Anonymous.*
The Lover Consults with Reason. Carew.
Nobility. Cary.
The Noble Balm. Jonson.
Of Fortune. More.
Of Three Damsels in a Meadow. Payne.
On Her Coming to London. Waller.
On the Grave of a Young Cavalry Officer Killed in the Valley... Melville.
A Prayer Brings Rain. Fairfax.
Remember That Night. *Anonymous.*
Sleepin' at the Foot O' the Bed. Patrick.
Things We Dreamt We Died For. Bell.
This Was a Poet. Dickinson.
The Undersong. Emerson
Visions. Petrarch.
Western Wagons. Benét.
When I Think of the Hungry People. O-Shi-O.

Forty

Ad Xanthiam Phoceum. Horace.
The Age of Wisdom. Thackeray.
Anne. Reese.
Birthday Card for a Psychiatrist. Van Duyn.
The Birthday Dream. Dickey.
The Borrowed Child. Weeden.
Drivin' Steel (with music). *Anonymous.*
Forty Years Ago. *Anonymous.*
Go back to the Country. Jazz Gillum.
Marvelous. Kaplan.
Phineas Pratt. MacArthur.
The Pioneer Woman–in the North Country. Tietjens.

Proffered Love Rejected. Suckling.
Riddle: "A wide mouth, no ears nor eyes." *Anonymous.*
The Starry Frost Descends. Geilt.

Forty-nine

The Days of 'Forty-Nine. *Anonymous.*
My Rival. Kipling.
To Find Easter Limit, or the Day of the Paschal Full Moon... *Anonymous.*

Forward

Day Begins at Governor's Square Mall. Stokesbury.
The Faerie Queene. Spenser.
Finistere. Kinsella.
I Saw Red Evening through the Rain. Stevenson.
Kearny at Seven Pines. Stedman.
Laughing Backwards. Hall.
Love Poem: The Dispossessed. Hummer.
Signs Everywhere of Birds Nesting, While. Williams.
To a Field Mouse. Burns.
A Way of Speaking. Ehrlich.
The Work-Out. Movius.
Young Africa's Resolve. Osadebay.

Fossil (s)

The Fossils. Kinnell.
Imitation of Julia A. Moore. "Twain.
The Law. Haynes.
The Poem Unwritten. Levertov.
Wind Flowers. Lockwood.

Fought

Balaclava. *Anonymous.*
The Bravest Battle. Miller.
The City of Baltimore. *Anonymous.*
The Feast of All Saints. Smither.
Happy Death. Freeman.
The Honour of Bristol. *Anonymous.*
Hornpout. Evarts.
If These Endure. Lorraine.
Inevitable. Betjeman.
Macdonald's Raid. Hayne.
May 30, 1893. Bangs.
The Mother. Pearse.
Old Fort Meigs. *Anonymous.*
Peschiera. Clough.
Plain-Chant for America. Chapin.
Remembrances. Clare.
The Reprisall. Herbert.
The Second Thanksgiving, or The Reprisal. Herbert.
Through Fire in Mobile Bay. Anonymous.
Two Heroes. Monroe.
Zapata & the Landlord. Spellman.

Foul

Caelica, XLII. Greville.
Chevy-Chace. *Anonymous.*
Freshmen. Spacks.
The Incurables. Upson.
Julius Caesar. Shakespeare.
Kath'rine Jaffrey. *Anonymous.*
Katharine Jaffray (A vers.). *Anonymous.*
The Living Dog and the Dead Lion. Moore.

Moments of Vision. Hardy.
Omnia Vanitas. Buchanan.
A Painted Whore, the Mask of Deadly Sin. Lithgow.
Suilven. Young.
To God Alone, the Only Donour. Pastorius.
A View of the Town (excerpt). Gilbert.
Wash Well the Fresh Fish. *Anonymous.*

Found

An Air by Sammartini. Dudek.
Alas How Long. *Anonymous.*
Arson and Cold Lace (or How I Yearn to Burn Baby Burn). Long.
At White River. Haines.
The Bridal Pair. Young.
Bury Them. Brownell.
Cow. McFatter.
The Diggers. Merwin.
The Dispossessed. Kinsella.
The Dreamer. Gould.
The Event. Moore.
Exchanges. Dowson.
Ferdinando and Elvira. Gilbert.
For Jane. Bukowski.
He Was. Wilbur.
Hen's Nest. Clare.
High Water Everywhere. Patton.
Horace, Epistle VII, Book I, Imitated. Swift.
I Have Always Found It So. Bell.
In the Wilderness. Pierce.
The Jews. Vaughan.
The Marriage of Heaven and Earth. Nemerov.
Message to the Bard. Livingston.
The Mountaineer. Nathan.
My Sister, My Self. Filip.
Napkin and Stone. Watkins.
Navajo. Simpson.
On Going Home. Agnew.
The Quiet Kingdom. Busse.
A Rhyme of Life. Stoddard.
The Search. Crosby.
Search. Marriott.
A Slight Confusion. Reiss.
Sonnets from a Sequence. Barker.
The Source. Stallworthy.
Th Unifying Principle. Ammons.
Under Stars. Gallagher.
Unfulfilment. Bushnell.
The Vanishers. Whittier
Wanderer. Powers.
Wedlock. Grahame.
Where the Blessed Feet Have Trod. "Field.
Wino. Hughes.

Foundation (s)

Autumn. Carpenter.
Canning Time. Morgan.
Good Creatures, Do You Love Your Lives. Housman.
The Lay of St. Cuthbert (excerpt). Barham.
Lord, Who's the Happy Man. Brady.
My Country (excerpt). Woodberry.
The New World. Very.
The Pillar of Fame. Herrick.

Fount
The Cow. Herford.
A Dream. Kinney
Fairy Song. Hemans.
Fountain (s)
The Ancient Sage.
Tennyson.
Beautiful Things. Allerton.
Continent's End. Jeffers.
Dearest Reader. Palmer.
Elegy. Fitzgerald.
Evangeline. Longfellow.
The Fountain in the Park.
Haley.
Fountain of Tears, River of
Grief. Pisan.
The Fountain of Youth.
Butterworth.
Fragment. Robinson.
The Green and the Black.
Bailey.
How Strange Love Is, in
Every State of
Consciousness. Schwartz.
I am Hermes. Anyte.
Middle-Age. Jones.
Napoli Again. Hugo.
Nichols Fountain. Miner.
The Old Age Home.
Holmes.
On the Road to California.
Anonymous.
Our Captain Cried All Hands.
Anonymous.
Pigeons. Kell.
Retirement. Trench.
Shooting at the Moon. Kim
Yo-sop.
A Short History of the
Teaching Profession.
Maura.
This Child Is the Mother.
Oden.
This Is the Garden.
Cummings.
This Life Is All Chequer'd
with Pleasures and Woes.
Moore.
A Trucker. Gunn.
Vanity. Graves.
Whale at Twilight.
Coatsworth.
While Strolling through the
Park. Haley.
The Wilderness. Raine.
Four
Alexander Jannai. Cavafy.
The Allegory of the Wolf Boy.
Gunn.
Be Just (Domestick
Monarchs) unto Them.
Alsop.
Bill. Salzburg.
Brown Adam (A version).
Anonymous.
Burial. Sarton.
Canto XVI. Pound.
Columbia College, 1796.
Shippey.
Duality. Abse.
Epigrams. Martial (Marcus
Valerius Martialis).
The Four-Legg'd Elder.
Birkenhead.
The Four of Them. Karni.
Ho! Ye Sun, Moon, Stars.
Anonymous.
I Am the Little Irish Boy.
Thoreau.
Idaho. French.
Joan's Door. Farjeon.
Joseph Mica. *Anonymous.*

On Thomas, Second Earl of
Onslow. *Anonymous.*
The Place of V. Young
Bear.
A Quatrain. Sherman.
Recorders in Italy. Rich.
Requiem. Vincent.
A Roman Thank-You Letter.
Martial (Marcus Valerius
Martialis).
Sophisticate. Young.
Spring Song of a Super-Blake
(parody). Untermeyer.
Syrinx. Merrill.
To the Landlord. Swift.
Tuscaloosa Sam. Newell.
Wine from the Cape.
Cassity.
Fourth of July
I Asked My Mother for
Fifteen Cents. Mother
Goose.
Listen to the People:
Independence Day, 1941
(excerpt). Benét.
Fowl
The Animals in the Ark.
Anonymous.
The Monarch. Cowper.
The Overthrow of Lucifer.
Fletcher.
Fox (es)
A Call to the Wild.
Dunsany.
Cursor Mundi: The Flight
into Egypt. *Anonymous.*
Gerda, My Husband's Wife.
Triem.
Hiding in the Cucumber
Garden. Vidya.
I Light Your Streets. Le
Sueur.
In the Library. Brewster.
John Peel. Graves.
Night of Wind. Frost.
Now the Holy Lamp of Love.
MacDonogh.
On Addy Road. Swenson.
On Imitation. Coleridge.
Paracelsus. Browning.
The Pastoral on the King's
Death. Written in 1648.
Brome.
Snatches: "Winter alle etes."
Anonymous.
The Stars Go By. Lyon.
To Any M.F.H. Sackville-
West.
The White-footed Deer.
Bryant.
The Year of the Foxes.
Malouf.
Fragile
Absence. Landor.
Anthropology: Cricket at
Kano. Brown.
Dingman's Marsh. Moore.
The Hawkbit. Roberts.
Little Things. Strobel.
Love Poem. Edmond.
Wiser Than the Children of
Light. Gibbon.
Fragment (s)
Bhagavadgita: The One.
Anonymous.
The Cambridge Ladies.
Cummings.
Fragment from the
Elizabethans. Bridges-
Adams.
Hallelujah! Housman.
Maker of Songs. Hall.

More Distant Than the Dead
Sea. Tueni.
My Book of Life.
Humphrey.
On a Ruined House in a
Romantic Country.
Coleridge.
The Rape of the Lock.
Pope.
Two Graces. Herrick.
Two Illustrations That the
World Is What You Make
of It. Stevens.
Fragrance
Alabaster Boxes.
Anonymous.
Apple Blossoms. Larcom.
As in a Rose-Jar. Jones, Jr.
Ask Me No More. Carew.
Back Lane. Murphy.
Blessed Nearness. Bullock.
The Burial of the Dead.
Prudentius (Aurelius
Clemens Prudentius).
Buster Keaton & the Cops.
Keithley.
Doubts. Brooke.
The Dusk of Horses.
Dickey.
Epigram: "Gathering the
bloom of all the fairest boys
that be." Strato.
Her Dwelling-Place. Murray.
I Know a Flower So Fair and
Fine. Grundtvig.
I Know a Man. Steele.
Ill Luck. Baudelaire.
John Smith's Approach to
Jamestown. Hope.
Lilies of the Valley.
Gardner.
Love Song. Williams.
Mild the Mist upon the Hill.
Bronte.
My Hope, My Love.
Anonymous.
My Mother's Garden. Allen.
The Question, Is It? Bailey.
Raccoon on the Road.
Brennan.
The Rose-Bud To a Young
Lady. Broome.
Sea Rose. Doolittle.
A Serenade for Two Poplars.
Raab.
The Shepherd's Star.
Jimenez.
Spring in England. Going.
To a Mayflower. Marshall.
Frail
August Night, 1953. Harrod.
Epitaph. Chiabrera.
The Great Wave off Kanagwa.
Egemo.
Light mist, then dense fog.
Li Ch'ing-chao.
On Hearing the First Cuckoo.
Church.
Poem to the Tune of "Tsui
Hua Yin." Li Ching-chao.
The Protection of Plants.
Darwin.
Solomon on the Vanity of the
World. Prior.
The Song of the Pen. Al-
Harizi.
Frame (d)
After War. Gurney.
Baptism. McKay.
Caelica, LXXXV. Greville.
The Clock. Ducic.
Crepes Flambeau. Gallagher.

Documentation. Palmer.
Eros. Swinburne.
An Essay on Man. Pope.
I Look into My Glass.
Hardy.
Intaglio. Coulette.
Love Is the Peace, whereto
All Thoughts Doe Strive.
Greville.
The Ship. Hendry.
To the Lady Margaret,
Countess of Cumberland.
Daniel.
Watt's Improvements to the
Steam Engine. Baker.
West Wind. Koch.
Ye Realms Below the Skies.
Ballou II.
France
Amours de Voyage. Clough.
Ballad against the Enemies of
France. Villon.
Be Swift O Sun. Mason.
Clocks. Sandburg.
Duns Scotus's Oxford.
Hopkins.
George Sand. Parker.
Going to School in France or
America. Clark.
Great Tom. Corbet.
The Hero of the Commune.
Preston.
Herve Riel. Browning.
In France. Cornford.
Inscription for the Door of
the Cell in Newgate...
Canning.
King Henry to Rosamond.
Drayton.
Ode in Memory of the
American Volunteers Fallen
for France. Seeger.
One for Sorrow, Two for
Mirth. *Anonymous.*
The Pisan Cantos (excerpt).
Pound.
Poly-Olbion. Drayton.
A Private. Thomas.
Song of the Dark Ages.
Young.
St. Aubin d'Aubigne. Dehn.
The Testament of Beauty.
Bridges.
They Who Wait. Going.
The Truth about B. F.
Stillman.
Who Has Not Walked Upon
the Shore. Bridges.
Worsening Situation.
Ashbery.
Yorktown Centennial Lyric.
Hayne.
Your Lad, and My Lad.
Parrish.
Francis
Amsterdam. Jammes.
Brother Dog. Sanchez.
A Messe of Nonsense.
Anonymous.
Saint Francis. Bishop.
Saint Francis Borgia or a
Refutation for Heredity.
McGinley.
Trimming the Sails. Miller.
Frank
An American Girl.
Matthews.
Crime at Its Best. King.
Frank James, the Roving
Gambler. *Anonymous.*
Hye Nonny Nonny Noe.
Anonymous.

Frank

The Rantin Laddie.
Anonymous.

Frankincense

Avarice. Hecht.
A Christmas Carol. Thomas.
The Fossils. Kinnell.
The Springfield of the Far
Future. Lindsay.

Fraternal

Architects of Dream. Trent.
Housemates. Shepard.
Lines Written at Bridgwater,
27 July 1797 (excerpt).
Thelwall.
The Revolt of Islam.
Shelley.

Fraud

Alps. Warren.
Borges. Barnstone.
To England. Boker.
Ulysses. Graves.

Freak

Limerick: "Of inviting to dine,
in Epirus." Rankin.
Whippet. Andrew.

Free

Advice to Young Ladies.
Hope.
Against Women Either Good
or Bad. Norton.
Alec Yeaton's Son. Aldrich.
The Animal Runs, It Passes,
It Dies. Anonymous.
The Answer that Ye Made to
Me, My Dear. Wyatt.
Ariel in the Cloven Pine.
Taylor.
As Tranquil Streams. Ham.
At the Long Island Jewish
Geriatric Home. Graham.
Ballade of Good Counsel
(modern version).
Chaucer.
The Battle Within. Rossetti.
The Beach Homos.
Anderson.
A Beam of Light. Rooney.
Birth. Lyon.
Caelica, XXXIX. Greville.
Caelica, XLII. Greville.
A Cause for Wonder.
Anonymous.
A Child's Future.
Swinburne.
The Children's Crusade.
Levine.
The Choice. Corke.
Christ Crucified. Crashaw.
Christmas Dawn. Adcock.
A Clever Woman. Coleridge.
Close Season for Marriage.
Anonymous.
Conscience. Sherburne.
Creation's Lord, We Give
Thee Thanks. Hyde.
The Crisis. Whittier.
Degli Sposi. Lesser.
A Drifting Petal. Fenollosa.
A Drinking-Song...
Wycherley.
E. B. B. Thomson.
Emblems. Quarles.
The English Rider. Hyde.
Eudaimon. Raine.
Everything Is Possible. Pack.
Express Train. Kraus.
Faith. Sangster.
Far from Our Friends.
Belknap.
The Flitch of Dunmow.
Carnegie.
Fourth of July Song. Lenski.

Freedom. Anonymous.
Freedom Is a Constant
Struggle. Anonymous.
The Fruits of War (excerpt).
Gascoigne.
The Gathering. Swett.
Georgie Wedlock.
Anonymous.
The Golden Fish. Arnold.
The Graveyard. Cooper.
Haiku: "That silver balloon."
Phillips.
The Hand of Lincoln.
Stedman.
Hang out the Flags. Tippett.
He Is Our Peace. Haley.
He Made Us Free. Egan.
Hide, O Hide Those Hills of
Snow. Fletcher.
His Wisdom. Breton.
Holy Spirit, Truth Divine.
Longfellow.
Homage. Schoeck.
Homecoming Celebration.
Catacalos.
Hope of Our Hearts. Denny.
The House Was Still–The
Room Was Still. Bronte.
How a Girl Was Too Reckless
of Grammar. Carryl.
I Heard Immanuel Singing.
Lindsay.
I Lost the Love of Heaven.
Clare.
If by Dull Rhymes Our
English Must Be Chained.
Keats.
If We Believed in God.
Gibbs.
Independence. Faleti.
Initials. Glaser.
An Interview. Brasfield.
Irish Hymn to Mary.
Anonymous.
Jack Is Every Inch a Sailor.
Anonymous.
Jack the Guinea Pig.
Anonymous.
Jailhouse Lawyers. Smith.
Judith. Young.
The Kansas Emigrants.
Whittier.
Lament my loss... Wyatt.
Letter. Empson.
Letter to Pearse Hutchinson.
Chuilleanain.
The Liberty Song.
Dickinson.
The Lines. Jarrell.
Love in the Valley.
Meredith.
Love Restored (excerpt).
Jonson.
Love That's Pure, Itself
Disdaining. Gruber.
Lovers. Fullerton.
The Man of Kerioth (excerpt).
Norwood.
Margaret Fuller. Alcott.
The Martin Cat Long Shaged
of Courage Good. Clare.
The Merchant and the Fidler's
Wife. Anonymous.
Merciless Beauty. Chaucer.
A Mood. Troubetzkoy.
Morning Song. Teasdale.
My Garden, My Daylight.
Graham.
My Great-Grandfather's
Slaves. Berry.
My Name Was Legion.
Swift.

Mythology. Durrell.
A Name for All. Crane.
Near Dover, September, 1802.
Wordsworth.
The New Roof. Hopkinson.
A New Wind A-Blowin'.
Hughes.
New Words to the Tune of
"O'Donnel Abu." Connell.
O say, dear life, when shall
these twinborn berries.
Anonymous.
Ode to Chloris. Cotton.
Oedipus to the Oracle.
Trimpi.
Oh Freedom. Anonymous.
Old Age. Keary.
Old Marse John.
Anonymous.
The Old Song. Chesterton.
On a Pair of Garters.
Davies.
On the Prorogation.
Anonymous.
On the Wide Heath. Millay.
One Way of Looking at It.
Munby.
Our Fathers Fought for
Liberty. Lowell.
Oya. Lorde.
The Peace of Wild Things.
Berry.
Plain Language from Truthful
James. Harte.
The Poet Loosed a Winged
Song. Campbell.
Poets Love Nature. Clare.
Praise the Lord and Pass the
Ammunition! Loesser.
Praising the Poets of That
Country. Nemerov.
A Prayer for a Sleeping Child.
Davies.
Prayer of a Patriot. Von
Schlichten.
Prayer of Thanksgiving.
Baker.
The Preparative. Traherne.
President Lincoln's Grave.
Mason.
A Pride of Ladies. Halley.
The Princess in the Ivory
Tower. Davidman.
Pro Femina. Kizer.
Protea. Mattera.
Prothalamion. Schwartz.
The Rantin Laddie.
Anonymous.
Razor. Smith.
Remembrance. Bruner.
Rescue the Dead. Ignatow.
Reverdure. Berry.
Rivers Unknown to Song.
Meynell.
The Road to Anywhere.
Taylor.
Rodney's Ride. Anonymous.
Roger and Me. Le Dressay.
Runagate Runagate.
Hayden.
A Satire Addressed to a
Friend (excerpt). Oldham.
Sea Gulls. Pratt.
A Sea Song. Anonymous.
The Shadow People.
Ledwidge.
The Ship Canal from the
Atlantic to the Pacific.
Lieber.
Silent Is the Night. Glick.
Sing Me a New Song.
Clarke.

Slave Story. Carter.
Smoking Drugs with
Strangers. Bowering.
Song for an Allegorical Play.
Ciardi.
Song. Love Arm'd. Behn.
Sonnet: "Not wrongly moved
by this dismaying scene."
Empson.
Sonnet Sonnet. Engle, Jr.
Sonnet: To Guido Cavalcanti.
Dante Alighieri.
Sonnet to the Prince Regent.
Byron.
Sonnets, CXXXIV: "So, now
I have confessed that he is
thine." Shakespeare.
Sonnets to Orpheus. Rilke.
Sound the Loud Timbrel.
Moore.
The Star-Spangled Banner.
Key.
The Storm Cone. Kipling.
Suicide. Stevenson.
Summer Solstice. Keating.
A Summer Wooing.
Moulton.
Sung on a Sunny Morning.
Untermeyer.
The Surrender of Spain.
Hay.
The Suspition upon His Over-
Much Familiarity with a
Gentlewoman. Herrick.
This Is America. Clark.
Thysia. Luce.
'Tis Sorrow Builds the Shining
Ladder Up. Lowell.
To Geron. Jacob.
To Mary: It Is the Evening
Hour. Clare.
To the Evening. Bampfylde.
To the Memory of J. Horace
Kimball. Ada Sister Mary.
To Women. Hugo.
Tramp! Tramp! Tramp!
Root.
Tristram of Lyonesse: The
Death of Urgan.
Swinburne.
The Turkish Lady.
Anonymous.
Turn All Thy Thoughts.
Campion.
Upon a Diamond Cut in
Forme of a Heart... Ayton
[(or Aytoun)] Sir Robert.
The Usurpers. Muir.
The Viking. Stokes.
A Vision. Clare.
A Vision of Judgement.
Southey.
The Vocation of St. Francis.
Eleanore.
The Wasp. Davidson.
Watts. Rivers.
What Guile Is This. Spenser.
When de Good Lord Sets You
Free. Anonymous.
When This Cruel War Is
Over. Anonymous.
Whirlwinds of Danger.
Anonymous.
The White Steed of the
Prairies. Barber.
Why Should I Care for the
Men of Thames? Blake.
Wildness. Wagstaff.
A Wish. Lerner.
The Worm. Barnstone.
Written in a Time of Crisis.
Benét.

The Yacht. Catullus.
You Are a Part of Me. Yerby.
You Are Always New. Akhmatova.
You Shall. Stokes.

Freed
The Bore. Horace.
Christ Speaks. Hopkins.
The Conquest of Granada. Dryden.
His Living Monument. Irving.
The Lucky Coin. Clarke.
On the Death of a Prince: A Meditation. Philipott.
On the Lord Mayor and Court of Aldermen... Marvell.
Robin Hood and the Three Squires. *Anonymous.*
The Rooftree. Tate.
Spring. Thomson.
The Thirteenth Song. Drayton.
Visiting the Dead. Carson.

Freedom
Ain't Gonna Let Nobody Turn Me Round. *Anonymous.*
Alamance. Whiting.
American Independence. Hopkinson.
Apology to My Lady. Falco.
Authority. Huntington.
Ballad of Ho Chi Minh. MacColl.
Barbara Frietchie. Whittier.
The Battle Autumn of 1862. Whittier.
The Battle-Cry of Freedom. Root.
The Bird, Let Loose in Eastern Skies. Moore.
Boston. Emerson.
The Brave at Home. Read.
Burial of Barber. Whittier.
By Day and by Night. Merwin.
The Call. Clark.
Chee Lai! (Arise!). *Anonymous.*
Concerning One Responsible Negro with Too Much Power. Giovanni.
Elegy Wrote in the Tower, 1554. Harington.
Erin Go Braugh! *Anonymous.*
The Finder Found. Muir.
The Flood Viewed by the Tourist from Iowa. Whitehead.
For Zorro. Bickston.
Freedom of the Hills. Fraser.
From Mistra: A Prospect. Higgs.
The Gathering. Swett.
The General Armstrong. *Anonymous.*
The Guerrilla. Frelimo.
Hallelujah, I'm A-Travelin'. Raymond.
Harriet Beecher Stowe. Dunbar.
I Have Not So Much Emulated the Birds that Musically Sing. Whitman.
In What Manner the Body Is United with the Soule. Graham.

The Indifferent. Beaumont.
John Brown. Proctor.
Just To Be Needed. Eversley.
Karl Heinrich Marx. Enzensberger.
The King's Missive. Whittier.
Korea Bound, 1952. Childress.
Land of the Wilful Gospel. Lanier.
Liberty and Peace. Wheatley.
Living Together. Tomioka Taeko.
Married and Single Life. *Anonymous.*
The Maryland Battalion. Palmer.
Midnight–September 19, 1881. O'Reilly.
Mr. Whittier. Scott.
My Country, Right! Clark.
My Political Faith. Cameron.
The Night Loves Us. Adeane.
Night-Thoughts. Ibn Gabirol.
No More Beneath the Oppressive Hand. *Anonymous.*
O! Come to the Greenwood Shade. McLachlan.
O God, in Whom the Flow of Days. Babcock.
O Thou! Whose Presence Went Before. Whittier.
Ode Sung in the Town Hall. Emerson.
On the Completion of the Pacific Telegraph. Very.
Our Orders. Lowe
Parnell. Yeats.
Parted Souls. Herbert of Cherbury.
Prison. Ashley.
The Prisoner of Chillon. Byron.
The Proclamation. Whittier.
A Prophecy. Thompson.
Prospect of the Future Glory of America. Trumbull.
The Rebel Girl. Hill.
Returning to the Fields. T'ao Ch'ien.
The Revolt of Islam. Shelley.
Runner. Auden.
Security. Glover.
Self-Portrait. Jackson.
The Settler. Street.
The Shepherd's Calendar. Clare.
Shine, Republic. Jeffers.
Songs of Education. Chesterton.
Spirit of Freedom, Thou Dost Love the Sea. Dodge.
Star of Columbia. Dwight.
The Surrender of Cornwallis. *Anonymous.*
To Pyrrha. Browne.
To Ronge. Whittier.
To Walt Whitman in America. Swinburne.
Tom Dunstan, or, The Politician. Buchanan.
Transmigration. Cudjoe.
The Virginia Song. *Anonymous.*

The Vole. Solomon.
Warriors Prancing, Women Dancing... Rashidd.
Washington's Monument, February, 1885. Whitman.
Wednesday Night Prayer Meeting. Wright.
Why I Am a Liberal. Browning.
The Will to Change. Rich.
Woke Up This Morning with My Mind on Freedom. *Anonymous.*

Freez (e) (ing)
The Arctic Ox. Moore.
Blizzard. Garfinkel.
Brave Old World. Lambert.
Caelica, XV. Greville.
Chilled by Different Winds. Swaim.
Cold Is the Winter. *Anonymous.*
The Comedian. Layton.
A Fear. Francis.
I Wish I Were by That Dim Lake. Moore.
Iambes VIII. Chenier.
Lines for the Margin of an Old Gospel. Wingfield.
Love at Large. Patmore.
A Lover's Plea. Campion.
No Change in Me. *Anonymous.*
The Pilgrim Fathers. Pierpont.
To the Poet T. J. Mathias. Landor.
Up from the Wheelbarrow. Nash.
Upon His Timorous Silence in Her Presence. Davison.
Wonders. *Anonymous.*

Freight
Chicago. Sandburg.
Chicago. Sandburg.
Landscape as Metal and Flowers. Scott.
Plaque. Ruddick.
The Truth about Horace. Field.

French
Amours de Voyage. Clough.
Ballet. Hillman.
Can. Hist. Birney.
For Janice and Kenneth to Voyage. O'Hara.
La Grande Jatte: Sunday Afternoon. Cole.
John Knox. Smith.
King Henry Fifth's Conquest of France (B vers.). *Anonymous.*
Paul Jones. *Anonymous.*
The Shoemaker's Holiday. Dekker.
Sonnet Ending with a Film Subtitle. Hacker.
Widow's Walk. Spires.

Frenzy
Above These Cares. Millay.
Attis. Catullus.
A Garden of Situations. Anderson.
I, being born a woman and distressed. Millay.
Regenesis. Welburn.

Fresh
The Adirondacs. Emerson.
A Blackbird Singing. Thomas.
The Bush Aboon Traquair. Shairp.

Capture of Little York. *Anonymous.*
Conversation. Raba.
Divina Commedia. Dante Alighieri.
Eleven Addresses to the Lord. Berryman.
The End of the Story. Tiller.
The Faerie Queene. Spenser.
Foliage. Hemans.
Garden at Heidelberg. Landor.
In the Study. Hardy.
Learn, Lads and Lasses. Pastorius.
Lycidas. Milton.
New Moon. Lawrence.
Old Ellen Sullivan. Welles.
Proportions. Stroud.
The Show. Owen.
Song of Nature. Emerson.
Sonnets, IV: "Remote from smoky cities, aged and grey." Irwin.

Fret
Are You There? Gillilan.
The Old Pensioner. Yeats.
Robin Hood, Robin Hood. *Anonymous.*
A Room on a Garden. Stevens.
Written on the Sense of Isolation in Contemporary Ireland. Greacen.

Freud
Doctor Freud. Lazar.
Song: "Don't Tell Me What You Dreamt Last Night." Adams.

Friar
Coyote. Harte.
The Friar and the Fair Maid. *Anonymous.*

Friday
Blackbirds and Thrushes. *Anonymous.*
Lines Written by a Bear of Very Little Brain. Milne.
Music in the Air. McCuaig.
Robinson Crusoe Daniel Defoe. Sagoff.

Fried
Butcher's Wife. Scott.
The Cultured Girl Again. King.
King Arthur. *Anonymous.*
A Trueblue Gentleman. Patchen.
White People. Henderson.

Friend (s)
108 Tales of a Po'Buckra, No. 106. Inman.
Accused though I be without desert. Wyatt.
Achilles. Myers.
Aetate XIX. Merivale.
The Affliction of Margaret. Wordsworth.
Against Love. Denham.
All Morning. Stokes.
Among the Anthropophagi. Nash.
The Angel and the Anchorite. Shelton.
Anna Playing in a Graveyard. Gilman.
Any Wife or Husband. Haynes.
Anything God, but Hate. *Anonymous.*
The Arrow and the Song. Longfellow

Articles of War. Thompson.
As You Like It. Shakespeare.
The Ball and the Club. Lindsay.
A Ballad. Sedley.
Ballade of Dead Friends. Robinson.
Battle of Somerset. Cullen.
Beckon Me, Ye Cuillins. Hendrie.
The Best Treasure. Moment.
Beware : Do Not Read This Poem. Reed.
Beyond the Grave. Bruner.
The Blinded Soldier to His Love. Noyes.
The Blossom. Donne.
Books Are Keys. Poulsson.
Borges. Barnstone.
The Bridge Builder. Dromgoole.
The Bridge: Indiana. Crane.
Bright Abandon. Webb.
Britannia's Pastorals. Browne.
The Brooklyn Theater Fire. Anonymous.
Bum. Wedgefarth.
The Bustan. Sa'di.
By Memory Inspired. Anonymous.
Call from the Afterworld. Gerez.
The Canary. Turner.
The Cats. Exler.
Celestial Love. Michelangelo.
Certain Choices. Shelton.
Chamber Music. Joyce.
Chloris, 'Tis Not in Your Power. Etherege.
Cincinnati. Corman.
Come, Follow Me. Campion.
Commonwealth. Bierce.
Communion. Ignatow.
The Complaint. Akenside.
The Composition of Distances. Pien Chih-lin.
Confide in a Friend. Anonymous.
Constant. Dickinson.
Contemporary. Flexner.
The Corridor. Gunn.
The Cottage. Very.
The Counsel. Brome.
Counsels of Sigrdrifa. Anonymous.
Dagger. Lermontov.
Dan Taylor. Anonymous.
The Dancing Sunshine Lounge. Rabbit.
The Day Glo Question of Identity. Miller.
A Death in Hospital. Lehmann.
Dedicatory Ode: They Say That in the Unchanging Place. Belloc.
Deirdre. Stephens.
Delia Holmes. Anonymous.
The Diggins-Oh. Anonymous.
The Dog. Faber.
Don't. Anonymous.
A Dream. Akhmadulina.
A Dream. Connell.
The Dream. Petrie.
The Dream of Gerontius. Newman.
Dream Songs. Berryman.
The Duel. Maynard.

Duffy's Hotel. Anonymous.
The Duke of Buckingham. Pope.
Earth Dweller. Stafford.
Echoes from Theocritus. Lefroy.
Eclogues. Virgil (Publius Vergilius Maro).
The Egg. Day.
Elegy. Ignatow.
An Elegy, or Friend's Passion, for His Astrophel (excerpt). Anonymous.
Epigram. Anonymous.
Epigram: "How often, when life's summer day." Landor.
Epigram: "There are two miseries in human life." Landor.
Epigram: "To forgive enemies Hayley does pretend." Blake.
Epigrams. Theocritus.
Epistle in Form of a Ballad to His Friends. Villon.
An Epitaph. Beattie.
Epitaph: "I was buried near this dyke." Blake.
Epitaphs of the War, 1914-18. Kipling.
Ernest Dowson. Wheelock.
Escape to Love. MacDonogh.
An Essay on Criticism. Pope.
Face in a Mirror. Anderson.
Fair England. Cone.
The Faithful Friend. Cowper.
The Fathers. Sassoon.
Fernando. Ridlon.
Finnair Fragment. Hoffmann.
The Fish Sonata. Scott.
For John Berryman I. Lowell.
For Them. Brownstein.
For Victor Jara. Williams.
Forbearance. Emerson
Four Things Make Us Happy Here. Herrick.
A Friend. Power.
A Friend. Talfourd.
Friend and Lover. "Madeline.
A Friend or Two. Nesbit.
A Friend's Greeting. Guest.
The Friend Who Just Stands By. Williams.
Friends. Clark.
Friends. Stafford.
The Fruit Plucker. Coleridge.
Funebrial Reflections. Nash.
Gates of Damascus. Flecker.
The Ghost at Anlaby. Stow.
Go Get the Axe. Anonymous.
Go, Then. Bruck.
Gonna Lay My Head down on Some Railroad Line. Anonymous.
The Good Inn. Viele.
Guide to the Perplexed. Malouf.
He Was a Friend of Mine. Anonymous.
Hearth Song. Johnson.
Hearthstone. Monro.
Hellvellyn. Scott.

Herman Moon's Hourbook. Middleton.
The High Jump. Anonymous.
His Parting from Her. Donne.
The House by the Side of the Road. Foss.
A Hue and Cry after Blood and Murder. Anonymous.
The Hunting of the Snark. "Carroll.
I Have a Friend. Spencer.
I Never Knew. Wagoner.
I Wait My Lord. Anonymous.
I Wake, My Friend, I. Kicknosway.
Imitation of Julia A. Moore. "Twain.
In Me, Past, Present, Future Meet. Sassoon.
In Memoriam A.H.H., LXIV. Tennyson.
In My Dreams. Smith.
In the Doorway. Browning.
In Time of War. Auden.
In Tyme the Strong and Statlie Turrets Fall. Fletcher.
The Invitation. Welsted.
Invocation. Eastman.
The Island Cemetery. Auden.
It's an Owercome Sooth for Age an' Youth. Stevenson.
Italy. Filicaja.
The Jungle. Lewis.
Just Folks. Guest.
The Kindly Neighbor. Guest.
The Lantern out of Doors. Hopkins.
Last Poem. Berrigan.
Letter to Levertov from Butte. Hugo.
Life. Very.
The Liner She's a Lady. Kipling.
Lines to My Father. Daiken.
Lines Written on a Window at the Leasowes at a Time of Very Deep Snow. Shenstone.
Lines Written on a Window-Shutter at Weston. Cowper.
Little Libbie. Moore.
A Local Train of Thought. Sassoon.
Logan Braes. Mayne.
The Lonely Dog. Bruner.
Longing for the Persimmon Tree. Brand.
Lord, while for All Mankind. Wreford.
Love. Croft.
Love. Traherne.
Love-Songs, At Once Tender and Informative. Hoffenstein.
Loyalty. Braley.
Luckes, my fair falcon, and your fellows all. Wyatt.
Ma Lord. Hughes.
Macinnes's Mountain Patrol. Patey.
The Mailman. Contoski.
The Man and the Weasel. Phaedrus.
Man Unto His Fellow Man. Corwin.

The March of the Women. Hamilton.
Me. Mearns.
Medea: Chorus. Euripides.
A Medieval Poem of the Nativity. Anonymous.
Meditatio. Pound.
Meditation. Shipley.
Memorial Service. Williams.
The Miner's Lament. Anonymous.
Minutes of Gold. Anonymous.
The Mistaken Resolve. Martial (Marcus Valerius Martialis).
The Modes of the Court. Gay.
Mount Vernon. Anonymous.
Mr. Flood's Party. Robinson.
The Municipal Gallery Revisited. Yeats.
My Airedale Dog. Mason.
My Buried Friends. Anonymous.
My Friend. Allen.
My friend must be a Bird. Dickinson.
My Friends Are Little Lamps to Me. Whittemore.
Mysterious East. Cole.
New Friends and Old Friends. Parry.
A New Song to Sing about Jonathan Bing. Brown.
Night. Montgomery.
The Nightingale. Coleridge.
No Mean City. MacDonogh.
No More Than Five. Levinson.
No Woman No Nickel. Bumble Bee Slim.
Nonsense. Anonymous.
North Haven. Bishop.
Ode: "As it fell upon a day." Barnfield.
Ode–Imitated from the Psalms. Gilbert.
An Ode on the Popular Superstitions of the Highlands of Scotland... Collins.
Ode to the German Drama. Anonymous.
The Odyssey. Homer.
Old Dog. Stafford.
The Old Story. Argentarius.
On a Young Man and an Old Man. May.
On Forelands High in Heaven. Housman.
On Himself. Oldys.
On Poet Ninny. Rochester.
On the Death of Phillips. Anonymous.
One Fish Ball. Anonymous.
One Thousand Feet of Shadow. Craig.
The Onion, Memory. Raine.
Our House. Thompson.
The Outcast. Russell.
Paperweight Escape. Booker.
Part of the 9th Ode of the 4th Book of Horace... Horace.
A Parting. Wang Wei.
People Who Died. Berrigan.
A Perfect Day. Bond.
The Persian. Smith.
Plea to Those Who Matter. Welch.

Poem: "I loved my friend." Hughes.
Poem in Time of War. Abrahams.
Poetry Reading. Myles.
A Postcard. Denby.
A Prayer. Sherman.
Prayer. Villiers.
Prayer of an Unemployed Man. Ackerly.
Prepare. Bynner.
The Promise of a Constant Lover. *Anonymous.*
Qords on the Wind: Fruit of Loneliness. Sarton.
Quaere. Farewell.
Quo Vadis? Connolly.
Readings, Forecasts, Personal Guidance. Fearing.
Real Property. Monro.
Recorders Ages Hence. Whitman.
Requiem. Gurney.
Rest of the Weary. *Anonymous.*
Return to Life. Evans.
The Revolving Door. Levy.
The Rime of the Ancient Feminist (excerpt). Markman.
Robin Hood's Delight. *Anonymous.*
Rolling Home. *Anonymous.*
Roosters. Bishop.
Roundel of Passion-Tide. *Anonymous.*
The Seasons. Kalidasa.
Sensitive Sydney. Irwin.
A Serious Danger. Davenport.
Sestina to the Common Glass of Beer: I Do Not Drink Beer. Wakoski.
Shine on Me, Secret Splendor. Markham.
The Ships. Maynard.
The Shooting of the Cup. Neihardt.
A Shot at Random. Lewis.
The Sincere Man. Walton.
Sir Menenius Agrippa, the Friend of the People. Brough.
Sir Thomas Armstrong's Last Farewell to the World. *Anonymous.*
Soft Landings. Sergeant.
Softly Softly. Shelton.
Song. Dinis.
Song: "Had I a heart for falsehood fram'd." Sheridan.
Sonnet XIV. Tuckerman.
Sonnet XVIII: "Kiss me again, rekiss me, kiss me more." Labe.
Sonnet to Oxford. Russell.
Source of News. *Anonymous.*
Spirits. Cruz.
The Stalin Epigram. Mandelstam.
Success. Guest.
Suicide. Stevenson.
The Sunbeam. *Anonymous.*
Supreme Death. Dunn.
Sweetly (My Dearest) I Left Thee Asleep. Saffin.
A Teacher Taught Me. Walters.
The Telephone. Field.
Thanksgiving. Sangster.

They Say, and I am Glad They Say. Belloc.
Things to Do in New York (City). Berrigan.
Time. Fletcher.
To a Faithless Friend. Arrabey.
To a Friend, Inviting Him to a Meeting upon Promise. Habington.
To a President. Bynner.
To Julius. Sedley.
To L–. Cresswell.
To My Friend. Thompson.
To My Most Dearely-loved Friend Henery Reynolds Esquire. Drayton.
To My Worthy Friend, Mr. James Bayley... Noyes.
To Our Friends. Watkins.
To Silence. Moore.
To Sir Edward Herbert at Julyers. Donne.
To the Archdeacon. Farewell.
To the Reader. Oakes.
To the Spirit Great and Good. Hunt.
To the Yew and Cypress to Grace His Funeral. Herrick.
To William Simpson, Ochiltree. Burns.
Trees. Clark.
Triads. *Anonymous.*
The Triumph. Lanier.
The Troubled Soldier. *Anonymous.*
True to theBest. Keech.
Us Tasting the Air. Shapiro.
The Wanderer from the Fold. Bronte.
The Wanderer's Grave. Sage.
Wanderers. Clark.
Wanting a Mummy. McPherson.
The Waves Gleam in the Sunshine. Heine.
A Widow's Hymn. Wither.
X Minus X. Fearing.
The Youth and the Northwind. Saxe.

Friendly
Be Friendly. Isenhour.
Epigram: "Lo! Beauty flashed forth sweetly." Meleager.
Fellowship. *Anonymous.*
May He Lose His Way on the Cold Sea. Archilochus.
A Time to Talk. Frost.

Friendship
Ajax. Sophocles.
Am I to Lose You? Bevington.
The Angler's Invitation. Stoddart.
Blest Be the Tie That Binds. Fawcett.
Controlling the Tongue. Chaucer.
Davideis. Cowley.
The Death of Custer. Crawford.
The Fault Is Not Mine. Landor.
A Friend. De Carrion.
He May Be Envied, Who with Tranquil Breast. Smith.
Hersilia. Johnson.
In Memoriam A.H.H., CXVI. Tennyson.

It Started. Baca.
Madrigal: "Since just disdain." Peerson.
May God Give Strength. Van Wynen.
Mr. Symons at Richmond, Mr. Pope at Twickenham. Symons.
No, Thank You, John. Rossetti.
Not Heat Flames Up and Consumes. Whitman.
Paysage Moralise. Hollander.
Rebeca in a Mirror. Rodriguez.
Sarah Hazard's Love Letter. Ellis.
She, to Him. Hardy.
Sir Helmer Blaa and His Bride's Brothers. *Anonymous.*
A Temple to Friendship. Moore.
To a Young Brother. Jewsbury.
To America. Austin.
To G.R. Cottam.
To the Memory of Yale College. Putnam.
Trelawny Lies by Shelley. O'Donnell.
Wisdom. Middleton.

Fright
Grieve Not, Dear Love. Bristol.
Havdolah Wine. Ulinover.
Jesse James. (Version B). *Anonymous.*
Poem in Karori. Johnson.
The Summer Ending. Wescott.
The Tiger Stalking in the Night. Horn.
Winter Will Follow. Dixon.
Within These Doors Assembled Now. Holden.

Frighten (ed) (ing)
The Emergency Room. Fisher.
The Fear of Trembling. Hollander.
Frightened Flower. Harris.
The Harlot's House. Wilde.
Invitation to Youth. *Anonymous.*
Limerick: "A skeleton once in Khartoum." *Anonymous.*
Prison Break. Hogan.
Rhymes for a Modern Nursery: Little Miss Muffet. Dehn.
Satyrs upon the Jesuits: Prologue. Oldham.
Survivor. Simmons.
Tweedle-Dum and Tweedle-Dee. *Anonymous.*
When night is almost done. Dickinson.
The Witches' Wood. Coleridge.

Frog (s)
Between Leaps. Leithauser.
A Big Turtle. *Anonymous.*
Canto II. Pound.
The Early Frogs. Mills.
A Fairy Tale. Thompson.
A Frog's Fate. Rossetti.
Haiku: "No need to cling." Joso.
The History of Insipids. Freke.

Katharine Jaffray (A vers.). *Anonymous.*
Katharine Jaffray (C version). *Anonymous.*
Katherine Johnstone. *Anonymous.*
A Lonely Pond in Age-Old Stillness Sleeps. Basho (Matsuo Basho).
Noblesse Oblige. Wright.
Notice. McCord.
The Old-Fashioned Garden. Hayes.
On Yes Tor. Gosse.
Poetry Today. Heath-Stubbs.
Praises of the King Dingana (Vesi). *Anonymous.*
Some Fishy Nonsense. Richards.
Song for Seven Parts of the Body, 3. Kumin.
Song: "The owl is abroad." *Anonymous.*

Frolic (s)
Blind, I Speak to the Cigarette. De Longchamps.
Butterfly Maidens. Lahpu.
Carnival. Hervey.
Lullaby Town. Diller.
Ode on the Spring. Gray.
The Thracian Filly. Anacreon.
Two Sonnets. Berenberg.

Front
Beach Burial. Slessor.
Children of Adam. Whitman.
Deaf School. Hughes.
Dentyne. Lurie.
A Door. Merwin.
Limerick: "A young engine-driver called Hunt." Gray.
My Face. Euwer.
A Room I Once Knew. Birnbaum.
War Blinded. Dunn.

Frontier (s)
Destiny. Morris.
The Gathering on the Plains. Butler.
Huck Finn at Ninety, Dying in a Chicago Boarding House Room. Schevill.
I am afraid to own a body. Dickinson.
Whispers of Heavenly Death. Whitman.

Frost (s)
Address Not Known. Heath-Stubbs.
An Apology for the Revival of Christian Architecture...(excerpt). Hill.
Death and Love. Jonson.
Dream Songs. Berryman.
The Earth-Spirit. Channing, II.
Eclogues. Schmitz.
The Frozen Heart. Herrick.
The Heart of Thomas Hardy. Betjeman.
Hendecasyllabics. Swinburne.
The Innocent Country-Maid's Delight. *Anonymous.*
Invitation to Youth. *Anonymous.*
It Is the Time of Rain and Snow. Izumi Shikibu.
Lobotomy. Pitchford.

Madrigal: "Vain Hope, adieu."
  Attey.
Minuet in a Minor Key.
  Janowitz.
My Grandfather Dying.
  Kooser.
October. Koeppel.
On a Grave in Christ-Church,
  Hants. Adams.
The Sad Shepherd. Jonson.
So Handy, Me Boys, So
  Handy. *Anonymous.*
Sons. Cope.
The Star-Tribes. *Anonymous.*
Summerhouse. La Follette.
To a Snowflake. Thompson.
Unable by Long and Hard
  Travel to Banish Love,
  Returns Her Friend.
  Turberville.
Upon a Delaying Lady.
  Herrick.
The Vision of Sir Launfal.
  Lowell.
When the Frost Is on the
  Punkin. Riley.
Winter in Durnover Field.
  Hardy.

Frown (ed) (s)
Canal Street, Chicago.
  Fixmer.
Chill of the Eve. Stephens.
The Conquest. Gogarty.
The Disquieting Muses.
  Plath.
First Miracle. Taggard.
From all the jails the boys
  and girls. Dickinson.
Grotesque. Graves.
How to Cure Hops and
  Prepare Them for Sale.
  Smart.
In Time of War. Auden.
A Lawn-Tennisonian Idyll
  (parody). *Anonymous.*
My Father's Watch. Ciardi.
My Springs. Lanier.
Our Lady Peace. Van
  Doren.
Phyllis Knotting. Sedley.
The Poets. Wevill.
She Is Not Fair to Outward
  View. Coleridge.
Song: "Hears not my Phillis
  how the birds." Sedley.
Sonnets, I: "Sporting at fancie,
  setting light by love."
  Barnfield.
To a Friend in Love during
  the Riots. Parsons.
To the Mountains. Thoreau.

Froze (n)
Autumn, Crystal Eye.
  Ruddock.
The Blackbird. Tennyson.
Boy in Ice. Lee.
Burying Blues for Janis.
  Piercy.
Cleavage. Nicholl.
Emmonsail's Heath in Winter.
  Clare.
The Hammam Name.
  Flecker.
If Love Were Jester at the
  Court of Death. Knowles.
Labor and Capital:
  Impression. Howells.
Lupercalia. Hughes.
Micromutations. Wright.
My Christmas: Mum's
  Christmas. Forsyth.

No Country You Remember.
  Mezey.
Now It Is Broccoli. Tagami.
The Refrigerator. Moss.
Results of a Scientific Survey.
  Cutler.
The Round. Booth.
The Runner. Gildner.
The Snow-Man. "Douglas.
Sonnet: "I saw magic on a
  green country road."
  Hartnett.
Star-Talk. Graves.

Fruit (s)
Abstinence Sows Sand All
  Over. Blake.
All for Love. Dryden.
The Argument. Moreland.
Autumnus. Sylvester.
Ave Maria. Charasson.
Blind Panorama of New York.
  Garcia Lorca.
The Book of Merlin. Spicer.
A Bridal Song. Shelley.
Cortes. Rios.
The Death of Carmen
  Miranda. Smith.
A December Frost.
  Krmpotic.
Dirge in the Woods.
  Meredith.
Do Not Expect Again a
  Phoenix Hour. Day-Lewis.
Epigram: "O King of the
  Friday." *Anonymous.*
The Faerie Queene. Spenser.
The Flowering Urn. Riding.
Flying Foxes and Others.
  Boyle.
The Garden. Grimald.
Goodbye. Bloch.
The Grass Is a Reasonable
  Colour. Newlove.
In a Country Church.
  Thomas.
Iscah. Schwartz.
Keepsake from Quinault.
  Alyea.
The Lament of Saint Ann.
  Anonymous.
Lancelot. Bontemps.
The Lancet. Devlin.
Live Christ. Oxenham.
Love for a Hand. Shapiro.
The Love Song of J. Alfred
  Prufrock (parody).
  Walker.
Love Speaks at Last.
  Herbert of Cherbury.
The Lychee. Wang I.
A Memory of the Players in a
  Mirror at Midnight.
  Joyce.
Metaphors of a Magnifico.
  Stevens.
Mid-August. Driscoll.
The Moon Now Rises to Her
  Absolute Rule. Thoreau.
The Musical Orchard.
  Dunn.
The New Year for Trees.
  Schwartz.
No! Hood.
Nonpareil. Prior.
O Taste and See. Levertov.
Ode Sung at the Opening of
  the International Exhibition.
  Tennyson.
Of Caution. Barberino.
Of Love. Wyatt.
An Old Folks Home. Lake.

The Old Santa Fe Trail.
  Burton.
A Part of an Ode. Jonson.
Pear Tree. Doolittle.
The Peasant Declares His
  Love. Roumer.
Rondeau: "Of Eden lost."
  Ellis.
Seek the Lord. Campion.
Shut Out That Moon.
  Hardy.
Sic Vita. Thoreau.
Song. *Anonymous.*
Song of Fairies Robbing an
  Orchard (excerpt). Hunt.
Spanish Folk Songs.
  Anonymous.
Spring. Whitman.
Stone Horse Shoals. Cowley.
Strange Fruit. Stow.
Swimming Pool. Horta.
Symbols. Rossetti.
The Thirsty Poet. Philips.
This Is What the Watchbird
  Sings, Who Perches in the
  Lovetree. Boyd.
Thou Art the Tree of Life.
  Taylor.
To the Immortal Memory and
  Friendship of That Noble
  Pair... Jonson.
To the South. Ghiselin.
The Tree. Auchterlonie.
Tree of Knowledge.
  Lowbury.
Two Young Maids.
  Anonymous.
Under the Boughs. Baro.
The United Fruit Co.
  Neruda.
When the Seed of Thy Word
  Is Cast. Mather.
Where Is the Fruit. Banda.
Woman to Child. Wright.
Words to a Song. Nagy.
The World's Illusion. Ibn
  Ezra.

Fruitful
By Rail through Istria.
  Conquest.
Deliverance from a Fit of
  Fainting. Bradstreet.
The Female Husband, Who
  Had Been Married to
  Another Female....
  Anonymous.
Guided Missiles Experimental
  Range. Conquest.
Oysters. Swift.
The Prophet. Gibran.
The Sower. Cowper.

Fruition
The Finished Course. Joseph
  of the Studium.
Not Alone for Mighty
  Empire. Merrill.
Tamburlaine the Great.
  Marlowe.
Tuberose. Block.

Fry
It's Not Bad Once the Water
  Goes Down. Reiter.
Love Laughs at Winter.
  Anonymous.

Frying-pan
Advice to Bachelors.
  Anonymous.
The Pilgrim's Progress.
  Bunyan.

Fuck (ed)
Dream Songs. Berryman.
For Nothing. Castro Rios.

Who Then Is Crazy? Spacks.
Fuel
Deliver Me. Carmichael.
Preludes. Eliot.
Song. *Anonymous.*
Sonnet: "My God, where is
  that ancient heat towards
  thee." Herbert.

Fugitive (s)
At War. Atkins.
A Fable for Critics. Lowell.
The Hidden Weaver.
  Shepard.
The Last Days. Sterling.
Lines on a Purple Cap
  Received as a Present from
  My Brother. Alsop.
Sonnet XVII: "I flee the city,
  temples, and each place."
  Labe.
Unwritten Poems. Winter.
When I Solidly Do Ponder.
  Pastorius.

Full
The Beggar Boy. Alexander.
Blessing of the Firstborn.
  Schwartz.
The Bush-Fiddle. Green.
Comcomly's Skull. Barnes.
Dream Songs. Berryman.
Edvard Munch. Wright.
Gift Hour. Banus.
Heart's Needle. Snodgrass.
Houses, Past and Present.
  Bachar.
I cannot dance upon my toes.
  Dickinson.
July Dawn. Bogan.
The Lost Orchard. Masters.
The Modern Fine Gentleman
  (excerpt). Jenyns.
Moon Blast. Roberts.
Mr. Ody met a body.
  Nesbit.
Ode to Food. Gray.
Othello. Shakespeare.
Photogenes and Apelles.
  Prior.
Poems, XCVIII: "In spring
  and summer winds may
  blow." Landor.
The Restless Heart. Surrey.
Rhyme for Remembering the
  Date of Easter.
  Richardson.
The Sailor's Complaint.
  Anonymous.
Starlight Scope Myopia.
  Komunyakaa.
Summer Journey. Rodgers.
Thus Spake the Saviour.
  Belknap.
Thyrsis. Arnold.
What Semiramis Said.
  Lindsay.

Fullness
Across the Fens. Thomas.
I Have Not So Much
  Emulated the Birds that
  Musically Sing. Whitman.
The Leaves. Loewinsohn.
Lines from an Orchard Once
  Surveyed by Thoreau.
  Booth.
Mary's Girlhood. Rossetti.
The Mathmid. Bialik.
O Day of Light and Gladness.
  Hosmer.
Pastourelle. Hayes.

Fume
On the Vanity of Man's Life.
  Anonymous.

Fun
An Awful Responsibility.
   Preston.
"Blue Is the Hero...
   Berkson.
Blues. Fuller.
Bundles. Farrar.
Cow Dance. Beaver.
Cripple Creek. *Anonymous.*
Family Court. Nash.
Finnegan's Wake.
   Anonymous.
Football. Mason.
Fun in a Garret. Dowd.
Grasshopper Green.
   Anonymous.
Grig's Pig. *Anonymous.*
Hardon ("get one today").
   Wedde.
Honest, Wouldn't You?
   Anonymous.
The House of Cards.
   Rossetti.
Human Needs. Walker.
In Honour of Taffy Topaz.
   Morley.
It's Fun to Go out and Buy
   New Shoes to Wear.
   Hoberman.
Jingle Bells. Pierpont.
The Lazy Roof. Burgess.
Letter to My Sister. Spencer.
Little Fish. Lawrence.
Little Joe Gould Has Lost His
   Teeth and Doesn't Know
   Where. Cummings.
Manly Diversion. Kopp.
Pass around Your Bottle.
   Anonymous.
Rubin. Cooper.
A Shot in the Park. Plomer.
The Song of the Strange
   Ascetic. Chesterton.
The Statue. Allott.
Very Lovely. Fyleman.
A Victory Dance. Noyes.
The Wind in a Frolic.
   Howitt.
Funeral (s)
A Boisterous Poem about
   Poetry (excerpt). Wain.
Caged Rats. Elliott.
Desire. Raine.
Enoch Arden. Tennyson.
Fame and Friendship.
   Dobson.
A Fly That Flew into My
   Mistress's Eye. Carew.
Jane Austen at the Window.
   Beer.
John Maynard. Alger.
Lean Gaius, Who Was
   Thinner Than a Straw.
   Lucilius [(or Lucillius)].
Let Us Now Praise Famous
   Men. Day-Lewis.
Looking at Wealth in
   Newport. Schevill.
The Lovely Youth. Aneirin.
Night Funeral in Harlem.
   Hughes.
The River. Emerson.
Ross's Poems. Lehmann.
The Tao Teh King (excerpt).
   Anonymous.
The Tears of the Poplars.
   Thomas.
Torch-Light in Autumn.
   Piatt.
War. Heym.
The Windy Night. Read.

Funny
The Anatomy of Humor.
   Bishop.
Ants. Kreymborg.
Cosher Bailey's Engine.
   Anonymous.
Daddy. Fyleman.
Epistle to the Reader.
   Gibson.
The Family Fool. Gilbert.
Funny Rigs of Good and
   Tender-Hearted Masters.
   Anonymous.
The Height of the Ridiculous.
   Holmes.
If Easter Eggs Would Hatch.
   Malloch.
Limerick: "My name's Mister
   Benjamin Bunny."
   Weatherly.
My Puppy. Fisher.
The Seamy Side of Motley.
   Seaman.
Some Ruthless Rhymes.
   Graham.
T.V. (2). Hollo.
Uncultivated Accent.
   Anonymous.
What the Prince of I Dreamt.
   Cholmondeley-Pennell.
Fur (ies) (y)
Achilles and the King.
   Logan.
Admiral Benbow.
   Anonymous.
After the Hurricane. Hazo.
Antiphonal Hymn in Praise of
   Inanna. Enheduanna.
Astrophel and Stella, L.
   Sidney.
The Curse: A Song. Herrick.
Devoide of Reason, Thrale to
   Foolish Ire. Lodge.
During a Bombardment by V-
   Weapons. Fuller.
Fox. Dyment.
Freud: Dying in London, He
   Recalls the Smoke of His
   Cigar... Schevill.
Fury's Field. Bodker.
Goose Pond. Kunitz.
Ice. Roberts.
Lines to a Nasturtium.
   Spencer.
The Old Peasant Woman at
   the Monastery of Zagorsk.
   Schevill.
The Sentry. Lewis.
Song: "Make this night
   loveable." Auden.
Spring Burning. Roland.
The Storm. Donne.
Such is the course that
   nature's kind hath wrought.
   Wyatt.
Sun-Up in March. Evans.
Then. Muir.
They. Leib.
Vivisection (excerpt).
   Fowler.
Fur (s)
Adolescence–II. Dove.
Ashcake. Page.
Corn-Woman Remembered.
   Volborth.
Dreams. Breton.
Furry Bear. Milne.
The Life of the Wolf.
   Gildner.
Marceline, to Her Husband.
   Libbey.
The Monkeys. Moore.

Night. McKay.
Nursing the Hide. Dunne.
Of Dandelions & Tourists.
   Rosenblatt.
Old Country Talk. Farkas.
One for the Ladies at the
   Troy Laundry Who Cooled
   Themselves... Zimmer.
Silences. Pratt.
To Mrs. Reynold's Cat.
   Keats.
Would You Like to Sin.
   Anonymous.
Furious
Adolphus Elfinstone.
   Burgess.
Ballad of the Mouse.
   Wallace.
The Ocean. St. Martin.
Things Kept. Dickey.
To the Woman in Bond Street
   Station. Weismiller.
Furnace (s)
Cleansing Fires. Procter.
Didn' My Lord Deliver
   Daniel? *Anonymous.*
A Divine Image. Blake.
The Eel. Montale.
The Furnace of Colors.
   Watkins.
Going In. Piercy.
The Heat in the Room.
   Kees.
In Deadly Fear. Blake.
None Is Happy. Hartmann
   von Aue.
Prairie Fires. Garland.
Prejudice. Johnson.
Sin and Death. Milton.
The Worthless Heart. Di
   Roma.
Furniture
Clubwoman. Smith.
God's Residence. Dickinson.
Melodic Trains. Ashbery.
The Studio. Mahon.
Furrow (s)
Behind the Plough. Cousins.
Civilities of Lamplight.
   Tomlinson.
Monogamania. Merriam.
The One Furrow. Thomas.
Process. O'Donnell.
Student. *Anonymous.*
To a Mountain Daisy.
   Burns.
Untrodden Ways. Machar.
Youth in Arms: IV. Carrion.
   Monro.
Fuss
After You, Madam.
   Comfort.
Ancient History. Guiterman.
The Birthday Bus.
   Hoberman.
John Donne. Simmons.
The Mountain in Labor.
   Aesop.
Futile
Auditors In. Kavanagh.
Bewick Finzer. Robinson.
Christus Triumphans.
   Pallen.
Home-Thoughts from France.
   Rosenberg.
The Zoo in the City. Allen.
Future
Agnosco Veteris Vestigia
   Flammae. Cunningham.
Ascent to the Sierras. Jeffers.
Ax. Simic.
Bologna, and Byron. Rogers.

Chorus of the Unborn.
   Sachs.
Danger. Paine.
The Dead President. Sill.
A Dresscessional. Wells.
Early Influences. Akenside.
The Elementary Scene.
   Jarrell.
Enigma. Murphy.
The Fable Merchant.
   Dobzynski.
The Faerie Queene. Spenser.
First and Last Man. McTell.
Fishnet. Lowell.
For Righteousness' Sake.
   Whittier.
Four Quartets. Eliot.
Freshmen. Spacks.
Frightened. Ferlinghetti.
A Garage in Co. Cork.
   Mahon.
Grandfather Yoneh.
   Borenstein.
A Hard Frost. Day Lewis.
Help from History. Stafford.
Here and Now. Cater.
I Had a Future. Kavanagh.
In Fur. Stafford.
Lancashire Winter. Connor.
Light of Judea. Vigee.
Limbo. Coleridge.
The Long Night Home.
   Gordon.
The Mercies of the Year,
   Commemorated.
   Danforth.
The Mirror. Bowers.
My Aim. Banks.
My People. Himel.
Now and Again. Borson.
Ode to the Sea. Baker.
Old and New Art. Rossetti.
Only in This Way.
   Burroughs.
Orpheus and Eurydice.
   Browning.
Party. Carrier.
The Poet's Simple Faith.
   Hugo.
The Present Crisis. Lowell.
Reveille. Hughes.
The Room and the Windows.
   Feng Chih.
A Russian Cradle Song.
   Nomberg.
Six Years Later. Brodsky.
Song of the Redwood-Tree.
   Whitman.
Spring-Gazing Song. Hsueh
   T'ao.
Tenth Symphony. Ashbery.
Tittery-Irie-Aye. *Anonymous.*
To George Pulling Buds.
   O'Keeffe.
To His Sacred Majesty, a
   Panegyrick... Dryden.
To Those Who Reproved the
   Author for Too Sanguine
   Patriotism. Woodberry.
Tragic Love. Turner.
The Twins. Wright.
Urn Burial. Hughes.
What Fifty Said. Frost.
Where I Hang My Hat.
   Gallup.
The Wise Men. Bowers.

G

Gabriel
The Bells of San Gabriel.
Stoddard.
Christmas Carol. Helmore.
The Crusader. Parker.
Dakota Land. *Anonymous.*
The Eyes of Texas.
Anonymous.
I envy seas, whereon he rides–
. Dickinson.
Sam Bass. *Anonymous.*

Gael (s)
The Return. Macgillivray.
To an Anti-poetical Priest.
MacNamee.

Gaelic
The Fair Hills of Eire, O!
Mangan.
Limerick: "There was an auld
birkie ca'ed Milton."
Lang.
The Little Clan. Higgins.
Miss Grant. Downie.

Gag
Advice. Di Pasquale.
Memorandum for Minos.
Kell.
Moose. Wiljer.

Gain (ed) (s)
Alice Ray. Hale.
The Ancient Doctrine.
Browning.
The Answer that Ye Made to
Me, My Dear. Wyatt.
Arcadia. Sidney.
The Blank Book Letter.
Greenberg.
The Blessings of Surrender.
Helphingtine.
Caelica, VI. Greville.
The Clerical Cabal.
Anonymous.
Cold's the Wind. Dekker.
Content and Rich.
Southwell.
The Fading Rose: Epitaph.
Freneau.
Faith. Pope.
Full well it may be seen.
Wyatt.
Harlem Riot, 1943. Murray.
Here Huntington's Ashes
Long Have Lain. Bierce.
The Hunters of Men.
Whittier.
Lessons of the Year.
Anonymous.
Listening to a Confucious.
Grynberg.
The Mystery of the Innocent
Saints (excerpt). Peguy.
Ode to Eve. Robinson.
An Old Song Reversed.
Stoddard.
Our Life Is Hid with Christ in
God. Herbert.
Peace. Cary.
Plea for Hope. Carlin.
De Rerum Natura.
Lucretius (Titus Lucretitus
Carus).
Riddle: "I have no wings, but
yet I fly." Austin.
Self-Deception. Arnold.
Sonnets, CXIX: "What
potions have I drunk of
Siren Tears." Shakespeare.

Sonnets: A Sequence on
Profane Love. Boker.
The Soul's Desire. Hull.
Stewball. *Anonymous.*
Upon Rook: Epigram.
Herrick.
Washington. Prentice.
The Way. Morse.

Gait
Do It Now! *Anonymous.*
The Game. Scott.
Nirvana. Torel.
Timon's Epitaph.
Callimachus.

Gal (s)
Buffalo Gals. *Anonymous.*
Hangtown Girls.
Anonymous.
Maggie Campbell Blues.
Johnson.
My Yallow Gal. *Anonymous.*
Number Twelve Train.
Anonymous.
Rosie. *Anonymous.*
Seven Sister Blues.
Thompson.
Sourwood Mountain.
Anonymous.

Galaxies
At the Scenic Drive-In.
McAleavey.
Coalface universe. Gunnars.
Maps to Nowhere.
Rosenberg.
The Swarm. Moore.
View from the Planetarium.
Barker.

Gale (s)
The Ballad of Halfmoon Bay
(excerpt). Sinclair.
Black Absence Hides upon the
Past. Clare.
Canso Strait. *Anonymous.*
Contentment. Cotton.
Inscription for a Fountain on
a Heath. Coleridge.
Juxta. Jacoby.
Love at the Door. Meleager.
Mihailovich. McFadden.
Old Ironsides. Holmes.
The Snowstorm. Crouch.
The Spectre Ship. Collier.
Stanzas. Clare.
Straws. Coatsworth.
The Swallow. Aiken.
To a Young Friend.
Coleridge.
Voyage. Donaghy.
Wild Iron. Curnow.

Galilee
Confession. Barker.
Despised and Rejected.
Bates.
Fishing. Wellesley.
The Gates, VI: The Church of
Galilee. Rukeyser.
If I Could Grasp a Wave
from the Great Sea.
Moreland.
In Galilee. Butts.
A Phantasy of Heaven.
Kemp.

Gall (ed)
Judah in Exile Wanders.
Sandys.
The Quarrelsome Trio. G.
Richard II. Shakespeare.
Upon Appleton House, to My
Lord Fairfax. Marvell.
The Windhover. Hopkins.

Gallant
Balboa. Perry.

Colin Clout at Court.
Spenser.
The Coquette. Behn.
The Cropper Lads.
Anonymous.
The Declining of a Gallant.
Anonymous.
The Demon Lover.
Anonymous.
To Patricia on Her
Christening Day. Price.
The White Steed of the
Prairies. Barber.
Young Lochinvar. Scott.

Gallop (ed) (ing) (s)
Auld Reikie. Fergusson.
Come, Ride with Me to
Toyland. Bennett.
The Hare and the Tortoise.
Serraillier.
Here Comes My Lady with
Her Little Baby.
Anonymous.
The Huntsmen. De La
Mare.
The King's Son. Boyd.
A Last Word. Ashbery.
A Last World. Ashbery.
Romeo and Juliet.
Shakespeare.
Windy Nights. Stevenson.

Gallows
The Cruel Brother.
Anonymous.
Death-Doomed. Carleton.
Depression. Burwell.
Escape. Rubin.
Execution of Five Pirates for
Murder. *Anonymous.*
The Lover Proved False.
Anonymous.
MacPherson's Farewell.
Anonymous.
The Maid Freed from the
Gallows (B vers.).
Anonymous.
Pirates. Coatsworth.
Rose Connoley. *Anonymous.*
Song: "Know then, my
brethren, heaven is clear."
Anonymous.

Galway
The Man for Galway. Lever.
Snow Storm. Mary
Madeleva.
Undertone. Stanford.

Gambl (ed) (er) (ing) (s)
As I Set down to Play Tin-
Can. *Anonymous.*
Behold, One of Several Little
Christs... Patchen.
The Gambler. *Anonymous.*
The Gambler's Blues (St.
James Infirmary Blues).
Anonymous.
In Place of a Curse. Ciardi.
Macaffie's Confession.
Anonymous.
Rambling, Gambling Man.
Anonymous.
The Roving Gambler.
Anonymous.
Santa Fe Trail. Guest.
Snow White and the Seven
Dwarfs. Dahl.
St. James Infirmary.
Anonymous.
What You Should Know to
Be a Poet. Snyder.
Wild Bill Jones. *Anonymous.*
YGreen Grows the Laurel.
Anonymous.

Yonder Comes My Pretty Girl
(B vers.). *Anonymous.*

Game (s)
Age. More.
Autumn Dawn. Machado.
Ballade of Big Plans. Parker.
Becket's Diadem.
Anonymous.
The Canterbury Tales:
Prologue to the Miller's
Tale. Chaucer.
A Childish Game. Reinmar
von Hagenau.
A Children's Don't.
Graham.
A Clerk Ther was of
Cauntebrigge Also (parody).
Skeat.
The Cock of the Game.
Anonymous.
A Coney Island Life. Weil.
Elinor Rumming (excerpt).
Skelton.
Epiderm. Dransfield.
Five for the Grace. Scott.
Five Visions of Captain Cook.
Slessor.
Four Things Choctaw.
Barnes.
Frisbee. Humphries.
Grubber's Day. Sigmund.
I Was Playing Golf That Day.
Anonymous.
Last Call. Hughes.
Laugh and Be Merry.
Masefield.
Limerick: "Should a plan we
suggest, just that minute."
Anonymous.
Line-Up for Yesterday.
Nash.
Lines on His Birthday.
Logan.
A Little Scraping. Jeffers.
Love Equals Swift and Slow.
Thoreau.
My Grandpa Died Today.
Fassler.
No More Words.
Lushington.
The Old-Fashioned Pitcher.
Phair.
On a Dead Child.
Middleton.
On Imitation. Coleridge.
The Picnic. Logan.
Pleasures, Beauty. Ford.
Poem for Black Boys.
Giovanni.
Portrait. Wright.
Prologue to a Translation.
Trevisa.
Shooting Gallery. Galvin.
A Song about Great Men.
Hamburger.
Sonnet: "We will not whisper,
we have found the place."
Belloc.
Stag-Hunt. *Anonymous.*
Step on His Head. Laughlin.
Symbols. Roskolenko.
Tennis. Nyhart.
The Thieves' Anthology
(excerpt) (parody).
Martin.
Three Christmas Carols: III.
Anonymous.
To a Pair of Egyptian
Slippers. Arnold.
Tomorrow. Masefield.
Troilus and Cressida.
Shakespeare.

Upon My Lord Brohall's
Wedding. Suckling.
Vitai Lampada. Newbolt.
Vitamins and Roughage.
Rexroth.
Worldly Wisdom. Omar
Khayyam.
Yonder Comes My Pretty Girl
(B vers.). *Anonymous.*

Gander
Epitaph: "Here lies Landor."
Landor.
Mother Goose. *Anonymous.*
Old Mother Goose.
Anonymous.
Sourwood Mountain.
Anonymous.

Gang (s)
Bathing the Aged. Monette.
The Kirkyaird by the Sea
(excerpt). Valery.
My Father Gave Me a Lump
of Gold. *Anonymous.*
School Begins. Price.

Ganymede
Epigram: "Glad youth had
come thy sixteenth year to
crown." Ausonius.
New Love. Martial (Marcus
Valerius Martialis).

Gap (d) (s)
Anxious Thought. Hoccleve.
Ark Apprehensive.
Macpherson.
Embarrassed Judge.
Anonymous.
Epitaph: "Here lies the body
of Andrew Gear."
Anonymous.
On Looking at Stubbs's
Anatomy of the Horse.
Lucie-Smith.

Garbage
Don't Hope to Gain by What
Has Preceded. Kyger.
In the Year of Many
Conversions and the Private
Soul. Ciardi.
Refugees. Grade.
Sarah Cynthia Sylvia Stout
Would Not Take the
Garbage Out. Silverstein.

Garden (s)
The. MacNeice.
13th Dance–Matching
Parcels–21 February 1964.
MacLow.
Adam–The First Kiss.
Porter.
After a Lecture on Keats.
Holmes.
All a Green Willow Is My
Garland. Heywood.
Altitudes. Wilbur.
An Autumn Garden.
Carman.
Bee-Master. Sackville-West.
The Beloved. Hinkson.
The Buccaneer. Turner.
Dear Old Mothers. Ross.
The Deserted Garden.
Stanford.
The Deserted Village.
Goldsmith.
The Dog beneath the Skin.
Auden.
Don Juan. Byron.
Dream Record: June 8, 1955.
Ginsberg.
Dream Songs. Berryman.
The Drunkards. *Anonymous.*

An Easter Garland.
Rumens.
Edmund's Song. Scott.
Eve. Herford.
Eve's Song in the Garden.
Gottlieb.
Evening. Sill.
The Faerie Queene. Spenser.
Fause Foodrage (B version).
Anonymous.
Fear of the Earth. Comfort.
For Doreen. Davie.
Four and Eight. Wolfe.
The Garden. Giltinan.
The Garden. Parkwood.
The Gardens of the Sea.
Sterling.
Gates of Damascus. Flecker.
The Glory of the Garden.
Kipling.
The Gorilla. Hathaway.
Hearts and Flowers. Brine.
Henry and Mary. Graves.
Her Dairy. Newell.
How a Poet's Soul Comes
Into Play. Browning.
I Met Her in the Garden
Where the Praties Grow
(with music). *Anonymous.*
I Planned to Have a Border of
Lavender. Goodman.
If by Dull Rhymes Our
English Must Be Chained.
Keats.
If There Are Any Heavens.
Cummings.
In Favor of One's Time.
O'Hara.
In the Breeze. Pasternak.
Intimate Supper. Redgrove.
Invisible, indivisible Spirit.
Doolittle.
Invitation to the Bee. Smith.
An Ivied Tree-Top.
Anonymous.
J. A. G. Howe.
Jason. Hecht.
The Job That's Crying to Be
Done. Kipling.
John Graydon. MacDonald.
The Keening of Mary.
Anonymous.
Last Month. Ashbery.
Lemon Sherbet. Solomon.
The Lord God Planted a
Garden. Gurney.
Love and Time. Lloyd.
A Map of the Western Part of
the County of Essex in
England. Levertov.
Mary, Mary (parody).
Deane.
Meditations. Ibn Gabirol.
The Mocking Fairy. De la
Mare.
Moonlight. Verlaine.
The Mulch. Kunitz.
My mother always said.
Sappho.
My Nightingale. Auslander.
O Come Out of the Lily.
Pitter.
October. Spacks.
Odes. Horace.
The Old Garden.
Eichendorff.
Old Mothers. Ross.
An Old Story. Lee.
On an Old Muff. Locker-
Lampson.
On the Sonnet. Keats.
The Path. Bryant.

The Perfect Garden.
Robertson.
Phyllida and Corydon.
Breton.
Pirate Story. Stevenson.
The Plea. Drinkwater.
Poems. Machado.
The Press. *Anonymous.*
Pumpkins. Cotton.
The Puritan. Shapiro.
Roadside Flowers. Carman.
The Rose. Browne.
The Rubaiyat of Omar
Khayyam. Omar
Khayyam.
Rupert Brooke. Gibson.
Seeds of Lead. Gilboa.
She Wore a Wreath of Roses.
Bayly.
Sloops in the Bay. Tate.
Spring Night. Su Tung-P'o.
The Stallion. Merrill, Jr.
Stanzas for My Daughter.
Gregory.
Suburb. Monro.
Sunflowers. Scollard.
The Tempest. Zaturenska.
Termites. Chock.
Thy Garden. Mu'tamid.
Tiger-Lilies. Aldrich.
Time. Bethell.
To the Fly in My Drink.
Wagoner.
To the Learned Critic.
Jonson.
To the New Year. Carew.
Unclench Yourself. Piercy.
Visions. Browne.
The Visitor. Browne.
Weather. Bethell.
Whale at Twilight.
Coatsworth.
What Are Outward Forms.
Bickerstaffe.
Where's Mary? Eastwick.
A White Iris. Barrington.
Winter. Shikishi.
Woodstock. Mitchell.
The World's Illusion. Ibn
Ezra.

Garland (s)
All a Green Willow Is My
Garland. Heywood.
Edmund's Song. Scott.
The End of the Story. Tiller.
The Faerie Queene. Spenser.
If by Dull Rhymes Our
English Must Be Chained.
Keats.
J. A. G. Howe.
Love Is Like the Wild Rose-
Briar. Bronte.
My mother always said.
Sappho.
Odes. Horace.
On the Sonnet. Keats.
Phyllida and Corydon.
Breton.
She Wore a Wreath of Roses.
Bayly.
Song: "O Brignall banks are
wild and fair." Scott.
Stanzas for My Daughter.
Gregory.
To the Learned Critic.
Jonson.
To the New Year. Carew.
Weather. Bethell.

Garlic
The Avenue Bearing the
Initial of Christ into the
New World. Kinnell.

When I Was Nine. Roseliep.
Garment (s)
The Cosmic Fabric.
Polonsky.
The Feast of Stephen.
Nichols.
His Garments. Hagg.
Invitation to the Dance.
Apollinaris.
Limerick: "A bright little
maid in St. Thomas."
Christgau.
On a Gentlewoman Walking
in the Snowe. Strode.
On Our Crucified Lord,
Naked and Bloody.
Crashaw.
A Prayer. Sill.
The Prison House. Paton.
Sous-Entendu. Stevenson.
Summer Night. Bialik.
The Swan. Macpherson.
To Bring the Dead to Life.
Graves.
Walk in the Precepts. Ibn
Ezra.
The Water-Lily. Tabb.
You lay in wait. Sappho.

Gas (es)
Archy at the Zoo. Marquis.
Clerihew. Bentley.
Crossing West Texas (1966).
Robertson.
The Death Balloon.
Goedicke.
Death in Leamington.
Betjeman.
Deeper in the Tank–The Last
Middle East Crisis, 1972.
Ruggles.
Gethsemane. Kipling.
Innate Helium. Frost.
"It Out-Herods Herod, Pray
You Avoid It." Hecht.
Limerick: "Said a girl from
beyond Pompton Lakes."
Bishop.
Tumbling Mustard. Cowley.

Gasoline
At Barstow. Tomlinson.
The Cariboo Horses. Purdy.
The Moose. Bishop.
Tiempo Muerto. Alonso.

Gasp (ing)
The Evening-Watch.
Vaughan.
Stormpetrel. Murphy.

Gate (s)
Abel. Capetanakis.
Ad Limina. Campbell.
The Alchemical Cupboard.
Benveniste.
Amours de Voyage. Clough.
A Ballad of Orleans.
Robinson.
Black Flags Are Fluttering.
Vogel.
Brown of Ossawatomie.
Whittier.
The Children's Ghosts.
Letts.
Credo. Symons.
Delfica. Nerval.
The Dog. Davies.
Dreamland (excerpt). Mair.
Eden: Or One View of It.
Spencer.
An Epistle to a Lady.
Leapor.
Farm Gate. Krige.

First Party at Ken Keseys with Hell's Angels. Ginsberg.
Fishing on a Lake at Night. Bly.
Fleshflower. Root.
Flower of Exile. Dunn.
Gate. McAleavey.
The Gate at the End of Things. *Anonymous.*
The Gates of the Year. Hull.
The Gift. *Anonymous.*
Goethe's Blues. Levertov.
Haiku: "I called to the wind." Kyorai.
Harlem Riot, 1943. Murray.
He Establisheth His Triumph. Book of the Dead.
A Heart That's Been Broken. Owen.
Hippolytus. Euripides.
Homage to Malcolm Lowry. Mahon.
Humbug Steamship Companies. *Anonymous.*
I Have a Blue Piano. Lasker-Schüler.
In Memoriam A.H.H., XCIV. Tennyson.
Invasion on the Farm. Thomas.
Iter Supremum. Hardy.
Jerusalem. Blake.
The Lover's Farewell. Mangan.
Man into a Churchyard. Gutteridge.
The Marriage of Geraint: Enid's Song. Tennyson.
Middle of the World. Lawrence.
The New Year. Powers.
No Season for Our Season. Maas.
Our Journey Had Advanced. Dickinson.
Panama. Roche.
Paradise Lost. Milton.
Poems in Praise of Practically Nothing. Hoffenstein.
The Poet. Leitch.
Presbyterian Knight and Independent Squire. Butler.
Returned to Frisco. Snodgrass.
A Rhyme of Life. Stoddard.
Sabbath. Fried.
Samson. Gilboa.
Scala Coeli. Raine.
Security. Tucker.
Song of Reasons. Pinsky.
Sonnets, XIII: "I walk of grey noons by the old canal." Irwin.
The Soul. Cawein.
The Spell. Hoyt.
The Spell. Roberts.
There Shall Always Be the Church. Eliot.
Those Hours When Happy Hours Were My Estate. Millay.
To His Friend in Elysium. Du Bellay.
To My Auld Dog Dash. Barr.
A Turkish Legend. Aldrich.
Two White Horses (with music). *Anonymous.*
Vision of Belshazzar. Byron.
The Walker. Giovannitti.

The White Knight's Song. "Carroll.
Words from Hell. Helwig.
Zebaoth. Lasker-Schüler.
Gather (ed) (ing) (s)
Above the Hills of Time. Tiplady.
Ah Were She Pitiful. Greene.
Alley Blues. Holmes.
Anath. Guri.
The Blood-Letting. Harjo.
Bucko-Mate. Schierloh.
Complicity. Gallagher.
Cutting Redbud: An Accidental Death. Cotterill.
Departure. Hitchcock.
Eden. Thomas.
Falling Moon. Hill.
The Fort of Ard Ruide. *Anonymous.*
The Green-Sickness Beauty. Herbert of Cherbury.
Hallelujah! Housman.
If recollecting were forgetting. Dickinson.
In an Old Library. Yuan Mei.
In Memoriam (Easter, 1915). Thomas.
Labor of Fields. Coatsworth.
A Little While. Marquis.
Missouri Town. Palen.
My Love for All Things Warm and Breathing. Kloefkorn.
Nothing Gold Can Stay. Farber.
O Love, how thou art. Newcastle.
The Old Sexton. Benjamin.
Power Failure. Jacobsen.
The Reckoning. Friman.
Riddle: "Banks fou, braes fou." *Anonymous.*
Snowfall: A Poem about Spring. Wright.
The Song of Cove Creek Dam. Anonymous.
The Two Sisters. *Anonymous.*
Upon the Infant Martyrs. Crashaw.
Visions of Mexico While at a Writing Symposium in Port Townsend... Cervantes.
The Wisdom of Merlyn. Blunt.
Gaunt
Don Juan. Canto XVII. Clason.
Northern Ireland: Two Comments. Deane.
The Settled Men. Brady.
War Swaggers. Litvinoff.
Gay
The Baffled Knight. *Anonymous*
Book-Lender's Lament. *Anonymous.*
By the Beautiful Sea. Cole.
The Convict of Clonmala. *Anonymous.*
Cycle. Hughes.
The Dance. Lehmann.
The Description of a Good Boy. Dixon.
The Double Transformation. Goldsmith.

Epitaph XI On Mr. Gay. In Westminster Abbey, 1732. Pope.
For the Lost Generation. Kinnell.
Gay Boys. Kirkup.
The Host of the Air. Yeats.
Joan Miro. Todd.
Lapis Lazuli. Yeats.
London Bridge. *Anonymous.*
Low Church. Sharpless.
Master's in the Garden Again. Ransom.
Medieval Norman Songs. *Anonymous.*
The Moon Is Up. *Anonymous.*
The Muse Reviving. Davies.
News of the World. Ridler.
On a Banck as I Sate a Fishing. Wotton.
The Operation. Snodgrass.
The Rape of the Lock. Pope.
Richie Story (B version). *Anonymous.*
Says Something Too (parody). Hoffenstein.
To His Mistress. Cowley.
A Week of Birthdays. Mother Goose.
Winds A-Blowing. Justus.
Gaze (d) (s)
All Goats. Coatsworth.
All Saint's Day (excerpt). Guidacci.
Alone by the Hearth. Arnold.
The Annunciation. Muir.
Ascendancy. Simmons.
Carcassonne. Nadaud.
Children of Darkness. Graves.
Dark Earth and Summer. Bowers.
Disturb Me Not. *Anonymous.*
Fireworks. Reeve.
Footnotes to "The Autobiography of Bertrand Russell." Van Duyn.
Galatea Again. Taggard.
Gone. Thompson.
Hope. Stewart.
The Human Outlook. Symonds.
Ichabod. Whittier.
Icos. Tomlinson.
Initial. Boyars.
Isabella: or, the Morning (excerpt). Williams.
It Is the Stars That Govern Us. Magee.
Judas Iscariot. Spender.
A Late Spring Day in My Life. Bly.
Love can do all but raise the dead. Dickinson.
Madonna's Lullaby. Alphonsus Liguori.
Mark Anderson. Gibson.
A Mask Presented at Ludlow Castle (Comus). Milton
The Master Mariner. Sterling.
The Mountains. Dudek.
My Former Hopes Are Fled. Cowper.
Olga Poems. Levertov.
On Being Asked for a Peace Poem. Nemerov.

Overlooking the River Stout. Hardy.
Poetic Thought. *Anonymous.*
Robben Island. Dederick.
Song of Egla. Brooks.
Sunrise in Summer. Clare.
This Day. Raab.
To a Cloistress. Tassis.
To My Cat. Tomson.
To My Nose. Forrester.
To William Shelley. Shelley.
Whispers. Hill.
Gazelle
A Ghazel of Absence. Lansing.
'Twas Ever Thus. Leigh.
Wisdom of the Gazelle. Solomos.
Gazette
Epilogue to the Satires. Pope.
Satire. Pope.
Gears
Clear Night. Wright.
The Crowd. Masefield.
Human Relations. Jarrett.
Gem (s)
Aspects of the Pines. Hayne.
Consideratus Considerandus. Saffin.
An Epistle to R. Dunkin.
The Gem and the Flower. Pope.
Haiku: "To write a blues song." Knight.
Helena Embarks for Palestine. Cynewulf.
Here Too the Spirit Shafts. Mechtild of Magdeburg.
Song: "The fringed vallance of your eyes advance." Shadwell.
South-Wind. Lathrop.
There Are in Such Moments. Silverstein.
To a Plagiarist. Ibn Ezra.
The Valley of Unrest. Poe.
General (s)
Achilles Deatheridge. Masters.
At the Gate of Heaven. Byron.
Booze Turns Men into Women. Mayer.
A Code of Morals. Kipling.
Come All You Bold Canadians. *Anonymous.*
The Crimean Heroes. Landor.
Design. Redgrove.
The Great Statue of the General Du Puy. Stevens.
Hot Springs. Birney.
Lady "Rogue" Singleton. Smith.
Little General Monk. *Anonymous.*
Malcom, Iowa. Itzin.
Upon a Great Shower of Snow That Fell on May-Day, 1654. Washbourne.
When Statesmen Gravely Say "We Must Be Realistic." Auden.
Generation (s)
After Five Years. Young.
Ceremony. Kunjufu.
Combing. Cardiff.
Day of the Parade. Lau.
The Drill. Brown.
Extensions of Linear Mobility. Hathaway.

For the Lost Generation.
Kinnell.
Give Ear, O God, to My
Loud Cry. Prince.
Grandfathers. Shady.
The Great-Grandmother.
Graves.
The House That Was.
Binyon.
Last Sheet. Fuller.
Lee in the Mountains.
Davidson.
Milton. Blake.
On the Building of Springfield.
Lindsay.
Out of the Dark Wood.
"Peter".
St. Patrick's Hymn before
Tara. Mangan.
An Upper Room. Kelleher.
Walking Westward (excerpt).
Stead.
Yiddish. Sutzkever.
Generous
George IV. Thackeray.
Mully of Mountown (excerpt).
King.
The Tragic Condition of the
Statue of Liberty. Mayer.
Genesis
Ceremony after a Fire Raid.
Thomas.
Grandmother. Carlile.
Song in Spring. Ginsberg.
Genius
2001: The Tennyson/Hardy
Poem. Ewart.
The Adirondacs. Emerson.
Bartol. Alcott.
Curse. Greaccn.
Danse Russe. Williams.
Divine Poems. Villa.
Epitaph on Laurence Sterne.
Garrick.
Fate. Emerson.
God Said, "I Made a Man".
Villa.
I Think of Your Generation.
Brasch.
The Kiss. Sexton.
The Last Turn. Williams.
The Mortified Genius.
Graeme.
Namby-Pamby. Carey.
No. Schorb.
Pride of Ancestry. Frost.
Tercets. Llywarch Hen.
Gentle (ness)
Amoretti, LXXI. Spenser.
Beowulf. *Anonymous.*
The Death of the Flowers.
Bryant.
Elegy for the Monastery Barn.
Merton.
A Flower Given to My
Daughter. Joyce.
The Hermaphrodite's Song.
Mitchell.
I Love Little Pussy. Taylor.
I Ponder on Life. Ehrmann.
In His Steps. Bates.
Letter from a State Hospital.
Mundorf.
Old Black Joe. Foster.
The Old Man's Wish. Pope.
The Ovibos. Hale.
Plaza Real with Palmtrees.
Blackburn.
Primroses. Austin.
The Rape of Lucrece.
Shakespeare.
Skye Summer. Donaldson.

Small Poem about the Hounds
and the Hares. Mueller.
St. Stephen's Day.
Dickinson.
The Statue and the Perturbed
Burghers. Devlin.
Stopping near Highway 80.
Ray.
To My Mother. Heine.
Travel Song. Hofmannsthal.
Gentleman (men)
Astrophel and Stella, XIII.
Sidney.
Away out Yonder in Arizony.
Anonymous.
A Bird Sings to Establish
Frontiers. Gilbert.
Cantata for Two Lovers.
Sandburg.
The Devil's Walk. Southey.
The Dove Says, Coo, Coo.
Anonymous.
A Friend's Passing. Sheaks.
The Gift to Be Simple.
Moss.
If I should die. Dickinson.
Into Their True Gentleness.
Hutchinson.
The Irishman and the Lady.
Maginn.
Lincoln. Boker.
Manners at Table When away
from Home. *Anonymous.*
A Modest Wit. Osborn.
Mourningsong for Anne.
Posner.
My Uncle Joe. Smith.
Old Grimes. Greene.
Pale Is Death. Du Bellay.
Pet Crane. *Anonymous.*
Peter Bell, the Third.
Shelley.
Prelude. Rosenmann-Taub.
Robin Redbreast. Doane.
The Roundup Cook. Carr.
Salutamus. Brown.
The Shires. *Anonymous.*
Two Sonnets: "Altarwise by
owl-light." Thomas.
When Adam Delved.
Anonymous.
Who Misses or Who Wins.
Thackeray.
George
Corbitt's Barkentine.
Anonymous.
The Faerie Queene. Spenser.
The Kings and Queens of
England. *Anonymous.*
A Lilliputian Ode on Their
Majesties' Accession.
Carey.
Lines on Succession of the
Kings of England.
Anonymous.
On Gaulstown House. Swift.
On the Queen's Visit to
London. Cowper.
Tardy George. *Anonymous.*
Which Washington.
Merriam.
You Were Wearing. Koch.
Germ (s)
Bonner's Ferry. Schjeldahl.
Jack and Jill. Morgridge.
Signatures. Stevenson.
German (y)
Belfast Linen. *Anonymous.*
The Cathedral of Rheims.
Rostand.
The Cranial Nerves.
Anonymous.

The Doves of Venice.
Hutton.
Edith Cavell. Woodberry.
The German Fatherland.
Arndt.
High Germany. Shanks.
The Labors of Hercules.
Moore.
Limerick: "An anal erotic
named Herman."
Anonymous.
Poly-Olbion. Drayton.
Porson on German
Scholarship. Porson.
A Snow in Jerusalem.
Naggid.
Gestapo
The Extermination of the
Jews. Bell.
Gesture (s)
Aleph. Perkoff.
Cabbage. Norman.
The Diver. Mayo.
The Explosion of Thimbles.
Di Cicco.
Feeding Ducks. MacCaig.
Flight. Hemschemeyer.
Hardy Perennial. Eberhart.
A House All Pictures.
George.
How to Change the U.S.A.
Edwards.
O Mothers of the Human
Race. Whitaker.
Poem of Holy Madness, IV.
Bremser.
Poem out of Childhood.
Rukeyser.
The Same Gesture.
Montague.
A Small Boy, Dreaming.
Herzing.
To Drink. "Mistral.
You're Nothing but a Spanish
Colored Kid. Luciano.
Get (s) (ting)
About Motion Pictures.
Darr.
Birthdays. Domin.
Caboose Thoughts.
Sandburg.
A Communication to Nancy
Cunard. Boyle.
Dream Songs. Berryman.
Epitaph. *Anonymous.*
The Fabulous Teamsters.
Sherwin.
For a Far-Out Friend.
Snyder.
Get Up and Bar the Door.
Anonymous.
Heaven. *Anonymous.*
Hesitation Blues.
Anonymous.
Horses. Armour.
I'm a Baby. Corman.
In the Library. Hearn.
Lazy Mary. *Anonymous.*
Let Us Keep Christmas.
Crowell.
Limerick: "That the Traylee's
the best cigarette."
Rhodes.
A Living. Lawrence.
Lowdown Dirty Blues.
Anonymous.
Oedipus at San Francisco.
Finkel.
The Omelet of A. MacLeish.
Wilson.
Phone Number. Collom.

Prelude to Commencement.
Welch.
The Prophecy of Famine.
Churchill.
School Dinners. *Anonymous.*
Some of Us Are Exiles from
No Land. O Hehir.
Something Is There. Moore.
Song of the Darkness.
Bricuth.
Strictly for Posterity. Simic.
Success. *Anonymous.*
Those Zionists. Del Monte.
To Paul Eluard. Graham.
Woodstock. Mitchell.
Your Back Is Rough.
Atwood.
Gethsemane
For Jim, Easter Eve.
Spencer.
Gethsemane. Kipling.
In Shadow. Hazard.
Unearth. Barrett.
Ghent
The End of My Sister's
Guggenheim. Brinnin.
How They Brought the Good
News From Ghent to Aix.
Browning.
Ghetto
The Butterfly. Friedmann.
The Golem. Reich.
In the Old Jewish Cemetery,
Prague, 1970. Lowbury.
Promised Land. Engel.
Ghost (ly) (s)
Almanac. Swenson.
The Andalusian Sereno.
Saltus.
Ballad of Ira Hayes. La
Farge.
The Beautiful Ruined
Orchard. Berrigan.
Beyond Kerguelen. Kendall.
The Bomber. Lowell.
Breath. McHugh.
By the Pacific Ocean. Miller.
Call Them Back. Petrakos.
Can. Lit. Birney.
Colin's Complaint. Rowe.
The Computation. Donne.
The Curate Thinks You Have
No Soul. Lucas.
Cycle. Lonergan.
The Dark House.
Anonymous.
Dibdin's Ghost. Field.
The Empty House. Howells.
English Thornton. Masters.
Epigram on Sir Roger
Phillimore and His Brother,
George Phillimore.
Anonymous.
Etude. Brodsky.
First Confession. Kennedy.
Flying Fish. Fenollosa.
The Fountain. Smith.
Fragment. Brooke.
Ghost. Weaver.
The Ghost in the Cellarage.
Heath-Stubbs.
Ghost Night. Reese.
Ghosts. Munkittrick.
God! How I Long for You...
Mackenzie.
Growing Old. Arnold.
Hallowe'en 1971. Browne.
The Hosts. Brady.
The Hunt. Spofford.
If in Beginning Twilight.
Cummings.

The Island of Yorrick. Bodecker.
The Japanese Lovers. *Anonymous.*
Judges, Judges. Baro.
A Letter for Allhallows. Dufault.
Letter to My Wife. Fuller.
The Looking-Glass. Kipling.
The Lost Genius. Piatt.
Love Poem on Theme by Whitman. Ginsberg.
Luss Village. Smith.
Man's Anxious, but Ineffectual Guard Against Death. Beddoes.
Meeting. Harrison.
Mess Deck Casualty. Ross.
Metrum Parhemiacum Tragicum. Eugenius III.
Miss Jennian Jones. *Anonymous.*
Molly Bond. *Anonymous.*
Molly Means. Walker.
More Than People. Fulton.
Moth-Song. Cortissoz.
The Mountains. De la Mare.
The New Ghost. Shove.
Nicholas Nye. De La Mare.
Nocturne. Davison.
Ode to a Dressmaker's Dummy. Justice.
The Odor of Blood. McGrath.
Oh young men oh young comrades. Spender.
Old Gramophone Records. Kirkup.
One Star Fell and Another. Aiken.
Optimism. Salkeld.
Orchids. Roethke.
Our Little Ghost. Alcott.
Panther Man. Emanuel.
Poem: "I take four devils with me when I ride." Stewart.
The Prodigal Son. Robinson.
Remember the Promise, Dakotah. Carr.
A Ribbon Two Yards Wide. Kreymborg.
Rome Remember. Keyes.
S. S. City of Benares. Fraser.
The Santa Fe Trail. Chapman.
Second Seeing. Golding.
The Shepherd's Hut. Young.
Snowy Night. Haines.
Song from the Waters. Beddoes.
The Spectre Ship. Collier.
Their Party, Our House. Swan.
To Delia. Daniel.
To Perilla. Herrick.
The Tragi-Comedy of Titus Oates. *Anonymous.*
Troilus and Cressida. Dryden.
Tudor Church Music. Warner.
Two Views of Two Ghost Towns. Tomlinson.
Voluntaries. Emerson.
What Then? Yeats.
Witch Hazel. Enslin.
Giant (s)
After Reading Homer. Dolben.
The Albatross. Baudelaire.

The Child Who Was Shot Dead by Soldiers at Nyanga. Jonker.
A Friendly Game of Football. Dyson.
I'd run about. *Anonymous.*
The Poem Unwritten. Levertov.
A Primitive Like an Orb. Stevens.
Soft Answers. Bagg.
Telephone Poles. Updike.
Gift (s)
The 90th Year. Levertov.
Absence. Landor.
The Ajax Samples. Jensen.
Alchemy. Love.
"Among the Savages..." Salisbury.
Ane Sang of the Birth of Christ, with the Tune of Baw Lula Low. *Anonymous.*
Angels' Song. Causley.
Arcadia. Sidney.
At Penshurst. Waller.
At the British War Cemetery, Bayeux. Causley.
A Ballad of Remembrance. Hayden.
The Bean Vield. Barnes.
A Birthday in Hospital. Jennings.
The Blossom of the Branches (excerpt). Gilbert.
Boomerang. Hart-Smith.
Christmas. Dodge.
A Christmas Prayer. Hines.
Decks. Phillips.
The Destruction of Troy: Aeneid II. Denham.
Developing a Wife. Taylor.
Dream Songs. Berryman.
Four Stories. Shapiro.
The Gift. Lourie.
The Gift. Ochester.
Giving and Taking. Kirkup.
God of Mercy. Molodovsky.
The Greater Gift. Bruner.
The Greeks. Clark.
Happiness of 6 A.M. Shapiro.
He Took My Place. Bonar.
Helena Embarks for Palestine. Cynewulf.
Hero and Leander. Marlowe.
Himself. Hoffman.
His Toy, His Dream, His Rest. Berryman.
Idleness. Mitchell.
The Iliad. Homer.
Immaculate Palm. Keith.
In Dispraise of Poetry. Gilbert.
Letters to Live Poets. Beaver.
The Life of St. Cellach: Hail, Fair Morning. *Anonymous.*
Love. Lane.
Love Letter. Plath.
Love Song. Be'er.
Luchow's and After. Sissman.
The Magi Visit Herod. Sedulius.
Maritae Suae. Philpot.
Moonlight. Longfellow.
Napoleon and the British Sailor. Campbell.
Near the Death of Ovid. Conquest.

Neither Shadow of Turning. Clemo.
A New-Years-Gift to Brian Lord Bishop of Sarum... Cartwright.
O Tan-Faced Prairie-Boy. Whitman.
The Odyssey. Homer.
On the Death of Her Mother. Rukeyser.
Paradox. Miller.
The Perfect Gift. Cooke.
Poem H. Rodriguez Nietzche.
Poverty. Simic.
A Present from the Emperor's New Concubine. Pan Chieh-yu.
Proem. Whittier.
Proposals for Building a Cottage. Clare.
Robin Hood and Queen Katherine (B version). *Anonymous.*
Saint Nicholas,. Moore.
Service Is No Heritage. *Anonymous.*
Silex Scintillans. Vaughan.
Sleep. Martin.
A Song for Beauty. Lal.
Sonnet: To–. Wordsworth.
Suppose That Christ Had Not Been Born. Nicholson.
Tennyson. Aldrich.
Thanks Be to God. Alford.
They Crucified My Lord. *Anonymous.*
To a Reviewer Who Admired My Book. Ciardi.
To Melody. Allen.
To Rich Givers. Whitman.
To S.A. Lawrence.
To the Pending Year. Whitman.
Truth. Cowper.
Understanding. *Anonymous.*
Waiting. Stout.
The Way We Wonder. Pack.
The Woman and the Aloe. Adams.
Wrapped Hair Bundles. LaPena.
The young bloods come round less often now. Horace.
Zeal and Love. Newman.
Giggle (s)
Epigram: "The breath of my life." Meleager.
I've Got the Giggles. Herbert.
Memorandum for Minos. Kell.
Only My Opinion. Shannon.
The Perturbations of Uranus. Fuller.
Philosophy. Dunbar.
Gild (ed)
A Bird in a Gilded Cage. Lamb.
The Builders (excerpt). Van Dyke.
Caelica, CVII. Greville.
Ideal Landscape. Rich.
The Philosophic Pill. Gilbert.
Sonnet: "Could then the Babes from yon unshelter'd cot." Russell.
Strive Not, Vain Lover, to Be Fine. Lovelace.
Why Do I Hate That Lone Green Dell? Bronte.

Why They Waged War. Bishop.
Gilt
It Is Becoming Now to Declare My Allegiance. Day-Lewis.
Troilus and Cressida. Shakespeare.
Gin
The Ballad of Reading Gaol. Wilde.
The Boar and the Dromedar. Beissel.
The Cooky-Nut Trees (A Tale of the Pilliwinks). Paine.
Epigram on the Play-House at Amsterdam. Parsons.
Eunice in the Evening. Brooks.
Gone Are the Days. MacCaig.
Huxley Hall. Betjeman.
Limerick: "From the bathing machine came a din." Gorey.
My Home. *Anonymous.*
Portrait. Cummings.
A Radical War Song. Macaulay.
Snow White. Ochester.
To Delmore Schwartz. Lowell.
To-Morrow's the Fair. *Anonymous.*
Werena My Heart Licht I Wad Dee. Baillie.
Where Didst Thou Find, Young Bard. Keats.
Ginger
The Boar and the Dromedar. Beissel.
The Cooky-Nut Trees (A Tale of the Pilliwinks). Paine.
Eunice in the Evening. Brooks.
Portrait. Cummings.
Snow White. Ochester.
To-Morrow's the Fair. *Anonymous.*
Girl (s)
Abroad As I Was Walking. *Anonymous.*
Adolescence. Schmitz.
After Visiting a Home for Disturbed Children. Lipsitz.
The Artist on Penmaenmawr. Turner.
As I Walked Out One Morning. *Anonymous.*
At the Lavender Lantern. Divine.
Ballad. Simic.
Ballad of Human Life. Beddoes.
Be off! Smith.
The Beverley Maid and the Tinker. *Anonymous.*
Bow Down Your Head and Cry. *Anonymous.*
Boys of These Men Full Speed. Rukeyser.
Brown-Eyed Lee. *Anonymous.*
Catch. Hughes.
A Circus Garland. Field.
The City Clerk. Ashe.
Clinic Day. Barnes.
Coal Diggin' Blues. *Anonymous.*
The Comedy of Billy and Betty. *Anonymous.*

Conversation between Mr. and Mrs. Santa Claus. Bennett.
Count Orlo in England. White.
Courtship. Strand.
Cuckoo Waltz (with music). *Anonymous.*
Cut. Plath.
A Dance Song. Burkhard von Hohenfels.
The Dark Girl Dressed in Blue. *Anonymous.*
Deaf Girl Playing. Tate.
Death and the Maiden. *Anonymous.*
Degrees of Gray in Philipsburg. Hugo.
Don't Anybody Move. Epstein.
Dragon Lesson. Hearst.
Dream Songs. Berryman.
Early in One Spring. *Anonymous.*
Early One Morning. *Anonymous.*
El Sueno de la Razon. Cooper.
Elizabeth Ann Peabody. Eastwick.
The End. Van Doren.
Epitaph on a Young Child. Gurney.
Evening Music. Smithyman.
Everything Is Round. "Mistral.
The Faun Tells of the Rout of the Amazons. Moore.
Fifty Years Spent. Burt.
The First of the Emigrants. *Anonymous.*
Foggy Mountain Top. *Anonymous.*
The Girl I Left behind Me. Davis.
The Girl I Left behind Me. Lover.
The Girls around Cape Horn. *Anonymous.*
Girls' Voices. Gill.
The Good Little Girl. Milne.
Gossip Grows Like Weeds. Hitomaro.
La Guerre. Cummings.
Habana. Bond.
The Heart of a Girl is a Wonderful Things. *Anonymous.*
Homeward Bound. Rogers.
Hush, Li'l' Baby. *Anonymous.*
I Don't Let the Girls Worry My Mind. *Anonymous.*
I Taught the Talented. Sappho.
I Want a Girl. Von Tilzer.
The Insomniac Sleeps Well for Once and. Carruth.
The Intelligent Sheep-Man and the New Cars. Williams.
Jackson. *Anonymous.*
Jackson (with music). *Anonymous.*
Just as the Tide Was A-Flowing. *Anonymous.*
Kearney Park. Soto.
King Lot's Envoys. Allison.
Kitty Kline. *Anonymous.*
Lauriger Horatius. Symonds.
Lifelines. Ewart.

Limerick: "A Lesbian born under Pisces." *Anonymous.*
Limerick: "There was a young girl of Majorca." Lear.
Lo-Yang. Ch'ien Wen-ti.
Lolly-Too-Dum. *Anonymous.*
The Lone Star Trail. *Anonymous.*
Longface Mahoney Discusses Heaven. Gregory.
Longshore Intellectual. Lucy.
The Lovable Child. Poulsson.
Love's Fool. Rosenthal.
The Love Song. Gurney.
The Love Token. *Anonymous.*
Lovely Girls with Flounder on a Starry Night. Parlatore.
Lyrics. Agee.
The Maid I Left Behind. *Anonymous.*
Maire My Girl. Casey.
The Man. Browne.
The Man on the Flying Trapeze. Leybourne.
A Man's Need. *Anonymous.*
Matter of Taste. *Anonymous.*
The Mexico Trail. *Anonymous.*
The Miner Boy, I. *Anonymous.*
Miss Betty's Singing-Bird. Winstanley.
Moon Man. Valentine.
Mrs. Vickers' Daughter. *Anonymous.*
Music in the Air. McCuaig.
My Love Is Playing... *Anonymous.*
My Pretty Little Pink (with music). *Anonymous.*
My Pretty Pink. *Anonymous.*
Natural Causes. Scott.
Near Helikon. Stickney.
The Norfolk Girls. *Anonymous.*
Note to Gongyla. Sappho.
Of Joan's Youth. Guiney.
Of Your Father's Indiscretions and the Train to California. Emanuel.
An Old Man's Thought of School. Whitman.
An Omar for Ladies. Bacon.
On Growing Old in San Francisco. Gilbert.
On Not Being Your Lover. McGuckian.
Pacific Epitaphs. Randall.
The Paradox. *Anonymous.*
A Pearl, a Girl. Browning.
Pedagogical Principles. Amoss.
Philander. Hall.
Picture of a Castle. Meredith.
The Pill. Clarke.
The Plain Golden Band. *Anonymous.*
The Pleiades. Barnard.
De Produndis. Parker.
Prologue to a Saga. Parker.
The Rattle Bag. Ap Gwillym.
Red Whiskey. *Anonymous.*
The Rejected Lover. *Anonymous.*
The Right of Way. Williams.

Rigoletto. Levy.
The River Walk. Fallon.
Romance. Howells.
The Sailor Cut down in His Prime. *Anonymous.*
The Sampler. Turner.
Sensibility. Simpson.
The Ship Rambolee. *Anonymous.*
Sight Unseen. Amis.
The Silk Merchant's Daughter (I). *Anonymous.*
Song: "He that will court a Wench that is coy." *Anonymous.*
Song: "I don't want to be a nun." *Anonymous.*
Special Pleading. Bernstein.
Stony Town. Neilson.
Suicide. Stevenson.
Summer Lightning. Moore.
Summum Bonum. Browning.
The Swans. Sitwell.
Sweet Robinette. *Anonymous.*
Tales of the Islands, VIII. Walcott.
They All Love Jack. *Anonymous.*
Things to Do around a Ship at Sea. Snyder.
This Town: Winter Morning. Stafford.
Time's Revenges. Seaman.
To a Young Girl Leaving the Hill Country. Bontemps.
To an Athlete Dying Young. Housman.
To Bring Spring. Keithley.
Turn the Glasses Over. *Anonymous.*
Variation on the Gothic Spiral. Merwin.
Vaunting Oak. Ransom.
Ward Two. Webb.
Weevily Wheat. *Anonymous.*
Western Star (excerpt). Benét.
Who's Gonna Shoe Your Pretty Little Foot? *Anonymous.*
A Wild Rattling Cowboy. *Anonymous.*
Winter to Spring. Horace.
With Rue My Heart Is Laden. Housman.
With Rue My Heart Is Laden (parody). Hoffenstein.
Yankee Doodle. Bangs.
The Yankeys' Return from Camp. *Anonymous.*
You Never Miss the Water. Williams.
Your Hands. Dowson.

Giv (er) (es) (ing) (s) (gave)
The Agonizing Memory. Louys.
Alice Ray. Hale.
All Jolly Fellows That Follow the Plow. *Anonymous.*
Alone Is the Hunter. Littlebird.
America. Coxe.
The Answered Prayer. Flint.
Arc. Clark.
At the British War Cemetery, Bayeux. Causley.
Away. Miles.
The Beggar Boy. Alexander.
Body. Worth.
The Buxom Young Dairy Maid. *Anonymous.*

Canzone. Hacker.
The Caulker. Lewis.
Christmas Brownie. Bennett.
Cobbler, Cobbler. *Anonymous.*
A Confession. Verlaine.
Courtship. Corbin.
Dare Quam Accipere. Blind.
Dedication. Thompson.
Defeat and Victory. Rice.
Direct Song. Merriam.
Don't Give Up. *Anonymous.*
England. Newman.
Epigram: "I know him." *Anonymous.*
Epitaphs of the War, 1914-18. Kipling.
The Event. Moore.
An Excellent New Song Called "Mat's Peace," or The Downfall of Trade. Mainwaring.
Faith. Pope.
The Fallow Field. Dorr.
Firm Belief. *Anonymous.*
For a Far-Out Friend. Snyder.
For the Stranger. Forche.
For Them. Farjeon.
The Framework-Knitters Petition. *Anonymous.*
A Friend. Johnson.
Generosity. *Anonymous.*
A Girl in a Window. Wright.
Giving and Forgiving. Springer.
A Good Thanksgiving. Robinson.
A Grave in Hollywood Cemetery, Richmond. Preston.
Hands. Cloud.
He Said He Had Been a Soldier. Wordsworth.
Hearts Were Made to Give Away. Wynne.
How Long Shall I Give? *Anonymous.*
I Rode Southern, I Rode L. & N. *Anonymous.*
If I Should Ever By Chance. Thomas.
In October.... Hamburger.
In Place of a Curse. Ciardi.
In Vain Was I Born. Nezalhualcoyotl.
Jesus and I. Crawford.
July. Johnson.
Keeping Christmas. Farjeon.
The Kind of Act of. Creeley.
Lessons. Untermeyer.
The Light and Glory of the World. Cowper.
Limerick: "A lady whose name was Miss Hartley." Smith.
Limerick: "A woodchuck who'd chucked lots of wood." Wilson.
Limerick: "That the Traylee's the best cigarette." Rhodes.
Lineage. Terry.
Love's Prerogative. Oxenham.
Love Song. Ruddock.
A Lover's Envy. Van Dyke.
Mary Middling. Fyleman.
Masters. Amis.
Meditation. Pain.
The Meeting. Louys.

Mother's Nerves. Kennedy.
My Father. Dalven.
My Gift. Rossetti.
My God, You Have Wounded
Me with Love. Verlaine.
My Master Was So Very
Poor. Lee.
A New Year's Promise.
Anonymous.
New Zealand. Baxter.
O the Little Rusty Dusty
Miller. *Anonymous.*
Ode of Anacreon. Moore.
Ode to Beauty. Emerson.
Old Dog. Stafford.
On Devenish Island.
Ormsby.
The Passionate Reader to His
Poet. Le Gallienne.
Personal. Hughes.
Peter Cooper. Miller.
Poem H. Rodriguez
Nietzche.
Poem in Prose. MacLeish.
A Poet's Proverbs.
Guiterman.
The Poet Speaks. Johnson.
Popular Songs of Tuscany.
Anonymous.
The Power of the Dog.
Kipling.
A Prayer for Faith. Norris.
The Prophet. Gibran.
Recuerdo. Millay.
Resolutions?—New and Old.
Rolfe.
Revolutionary. Friel.
Riddle: "As I went through a
garden gap." *Anonymous.*
Robin at My Window.
Melville.
Robin Hood and Queen
Katherine (B version).
Anonymous.
Someone Like No One Else.
Farrokhzad.
Song. Sandall.
The Song of the Lilies.
Wheelock.
Spring Day. Ashbery.
Success. *Anonymous.*
Surprised by Me. Darring.
Take Time to Live. Clark.
Tattoos. Wright.
That There Are Powers above
Us I Admit. Clough.
There Were an Old and
Wealthy Man.
Anonymous.
The Things of the North.
McOwan.
To Find the Dominical Letter.
Anonymous.
To His Wife. Ch'in Chia.
To the Snail. *Anonymous.*
Treasures. Thayer.
Turn of the Moon. Graves.
Upstairs Downstairs. Allen.
The Velvet Hand. McGinley.
A Vision. Clare.
Wash the Dishes, Wipe the
Dishes. Mother Goose.
Welcome to My Heart.
Anonymous.
What Is Poetry. Ashbery.
The Widow's Mites.
Crashaw.
Women's Tug of War at
Lough Arrow. Gallagher.
Yielding. Robbins.
Glad (ly) (ness)
The Absence. Levertov.

Adieu to Old England.
Anonymous.
Afreet. McCord.
The Ambitious Ant. Wells.
Are You Glad. *Anonymous.*
At Little Virgil's Window.
Markham.
Audley Court. Tennyson.
The Beggar Man. Aiken.
Birthday. Emans.
The Blossom. Donne.
Calm as the Cloudless
Heaven. Wilson.
Canzone: He Perceives His
Rashness in Love, but Has
No Choice. Guinicelli.
The Christian Soldier
(excerpt). Studdert-
Kennedy.
Christmas Eve. Drinkwater.
A Cigarette. *Anonymous.*
The Circus Ringmaster's
Apology to God. Dubie.
Come Forth, Come Forth!
Wilson.
The Crusaders Behold
Jerusalem. Tasso.
Daufuskie. Evans.
The Dawn in Britain.
Doughty.
Drum-Taps. Whitman.
Eadwacer. *Anonymous.*
A Father's Heart Is Touched.
Hoffenstein.
Fish Crier. Sandburg.
A Fishing Song. Rands.
The Flight of the Goddess.
Aldrich.
The Frogs Who Wanted a
King. Aesop.
The Gangster's Death. Reed.
George Washington. Benét.
Ghostly Gladness. Rolle.
A Greeting. Davies.
The Heavenly Stranger.
Blenkhorn.
Hey Nonny No. Merington.
The Home. Tagore.
The Hunter of the Prairies.
Bryant.
Hymn: "Eternal Father,
strong to save.". Whiting.
In My Dreams. Smith.
Innocence. Chappell.
Instead of a Journey.
Hamburger.
Journey of the Magi. Eliot.
The Joy of Giving. Whittier.
Kris Kringle. Scollard.
The Lament of the Flowers.
Very.
Laundromat. McCord.
Lines for an Old Man. Eliot.
The Lover Compareth Himself
to the Painful Falconer.
Anonymous.
May. Cornwell.
My Ain Countree.
Demarest.
Nature's Easter Music.
Larcom.
Now I Have Nothing.
Benson.
O Blisful Light: Troilus and
Criseide. Chaucer.
Ode. In Imitation of Pastor
Fido Written Abroad, in
1729. Lyttelton.
The Old Filthy Beer Pail.
Hall.
Open Your Eyes.
Whisenand.

The Pastime of Pleasure.
Hawes.
The Penitent. Millay.
Pine Trees and the Sky:
Evening. Brooke.
Pourquoi. *Anonymous.*
A Prayer. Garrison.
A Rhyme of One. Locker-
Lampson.
Romp. Etter.
Rose-Marie of the Angels.
Crapsey.
The Search Party.
Matthews.
Self-Portrait. Thomas.
The Silkworm. Vida.
Six Birthday Candles Shining.
Carr.
Sleep and Poetry. Keats.
Sonnets of the Months. San
Geminiano.
The Tennis Court Oath.
Ashbery.
To C.F.H. on Her
Christening-Day. Hardy.
To Chloris, upon a Favour
Received. Waller.
To the Daisy. Wordsworth.
To the Same Flower.
Wordsworth.
The Twelve Weapons of
Spiritual Battle. More.
A Vagrant. Karlfeldt.
Welcome to Prince of Ossory.
Mangan.
What Grandma Knew.
Field.
Wine. Lebensohn.
The Yielded Life. W.A..
Glade (s)
At Common Dawn. Ellis.
The Auroras of Autumn.
Stevens.
The Cascade. Rickword.
The Deathless. Hayes.
Giardino Pubblico. Sitwell.
It Always Happens. Horace.
The Quiet Glades of Eden.
Graves.
Sonnets Written in the Orillia
Woods, VII. Sangster.
Glance (d) (s)
At Tea. Hardy.
Coach. Farjeon.
Death in the Home. Moore.
The Destruction of
Sennacherib. Byron.
Epigram: "I like them pale."
Strato.
The Firstborn Land.
Bachmann.
George the Fourth in Ireland.
Byron.
Graves at Elkhorn. Hugo.
Hardy Perennial. Eberhart.
Hmmm, 15. Scalapino.
Lesbian Play on T.V.
Gilfillan.
Lot's Wife. Akhmatova.
Mamba the Bright-Eyed
(excerpt). McRae.
A March with All Drums
Muffled. Denney.
Metamorphoses. Ovid
(Publius Ovidius Naso).
A Moral in Sevres. Howells.
Omniscience. Kelly.
On the Photograph of a Man
I Never Saw. Plutzik.
Poetry Is in the Darkness.
Boyajian.

Prisoner Aboard the S.S.
Beagle. Murry.
Somewhere You Exist.
Winkler.
Song: "Delicious beauty, that
doth lie." Marston.
The Time I've Lost in
Wooing. Moore.
To a Wood-Violet. Tabb.
To T.A.R.H. Spender.
Glare (s)
At dawn of the day the
Creator. Stampa.
Cat. Strachey.
The Closed World.
Levertov.
Crab Orchard Sanctuary: Late
October. Kinsella.
For a Very Old Man, on the
Death of His Wife.
Cooper.
The Sow's Ear. Weiss.
Winding down the War.
Appleman.
Glass
African Day. Sant'Ana.
After Twenty Years.
Tuquan.
Allegro. Transtromer.
Alleys. McPherson.
Anecdote of the Sparrow.
Pack.
Aquarium. Wright.
At Eighty. Stanhope.
Bagpipe Music. MacNeice.
Blow Ye Winds. *Anonymous.*
Children's Song. Sivan.
Come Not Near. Osborn.
The Dead Ride Fast.
Blackmur.
Delirium in Vera Cruz.
Lowry.
Denials 1. Somerville.
England. Salter.
Family Matters. Grass.
Flight to the City. Williams.
For a Wine Festival.
Watkins.
From the Ballad of Evil.
Van Wyk Louw.
The Frosted Pane. Roberts.
Glass. Lento.
Harald, the Agnostic Ale-
Loving Old Shepherd...
Brown.
The House. Bowering.
How Did It Seem to Sylvia?
Schnackenberg.
Humanity. Dixon.
Hydrographic Report. Frost.
The Ice Skin. Dickey.
If You Will. Miles.
In Sleep. Meynell.
In Time Like Glass. Turner.
The Island. Ungaretti.
John Butler Yeats. Foster.
The Last Supper. Williams.
Lovers Conceits Are Like a
Flattring Glasse.
Anonymous.
Loyalty. Davies.
Mark Anderson. Gibson.
Midsummer. Hesse.
My Father's Watch. Ciardi.
New Year's Eve. Mallalieu.
Next to of Course God
America I. Cummings.
Notre Dame Perfected by
Reflection. Witt.
An Old Song Re-sung.
Masefield.

On the Way to the Island.
Ferry.
Orlando Furioso. Ariosto.
Out of the Deepness.
Jackson.
The Parting Glass. Freneau.
The Poppy. Corman.
Public School 168. Brisby.
The Resolve. Brome.
Sayre. Strongin.
The Shadow Dance.
Moulton.
Sunday Morning, King's
Cambridge. Betjeman.
Tears at the Grave of Sir
Albertus Morton. Wotton.
The Testament of Beauty.
Bridges.
They Are All Gone into the
World of Light. Vaughan.
Three Poems, II.
Castellânos.
Three Songs. Beaumont.
Traveling through Ports That
Begin with "M". Sanford.
True Night. Char.
The Two Trees. Yeats.
Unhappy Diary Days.
Vizenor.
Verses Made the Night before
He Died. Drayton.
Wasp. Nowlan.
Waves. Emerson
Wayfarers. Burnet.
The Ways and the Peoples.
Jarrell.
When Was It That the
Particles Became. Stevens.
Wine from the Cape.
Cassity.
Yet Dish. Stein.

Glasses
Beetle Bemused. Lister.
The Company of Scholars.
Bevington.
Eyeglasses. Clark.
Falling Asleep Over the
Aeneid. Lowell.
Hiatus. Avison.
A Simple Pastoral. Stevens.
That Night When Joy Began.
Auden.

Gleam (ing) (s)
Bring Torches. Stephen.
The Fiddler. Trapnell.
Follow the Gleam.
Tennyson.
I Light Your Streets. Le
Sueur.
Merlin and the Gleam.
Tennyson.
Mossbawn: Two Poems in
Dedication. Heaney.
Now It Can Be Told.
Levine.
The Raven Days. Lanier.
Sweet Innisfallen. Moore.
Thinking Twice in the
Laundromat. Elliott.
Time's Bright Sand. Finch.
To the Choice Bridegroom.
Halevi

Glee
For Them. Farjeon.
Ghostly Gladness. Rolle.
It's a Gay Old World.
Anonymous.
Moon Mission. Baxter.
O Mothers of the Human
Race. Whitaker.

Oh King of Saints, How
Great's Thy Work, Say We.
Johnson.
Pounds and Ounces.
Brownstein.
The Rising of the Session.
Fergusson.
Song's Eternity. Clare.

Glen (s)
Cadmus and Harmonia.
Arnold.
Empedocles on Etna.
Arnold.
Foxgloves and Snow. Angus.
Invocation. Iremonger.
Meet Me in the Primrose
Lane. Clare.
Moorburn in Spring.
Anonymous.
The Return. Macgillivray.
Son David. *Anonymous.*
Sweeney the Mad (excerpt).
Anonymous.

Glide (d) (s)
Choosing a Wet-Nurse.
Saint-Marthe.
The Clown: He Dances in the
Clearing by Night.
Guthrie.
The Ducks. Wilkins.
Into Fish. Nelms.
Paradox: The Birds. Shapiro.
The Power of Thought.
Susskind.
Program Note on Sibelius.
Babcock.
The Solitary-Hearted.
Coleridge.
Some Scribbles for a
Lumpfish. Johnson.
A Speck of Sand. Cclan.
To Blossoms. Herrick.
The Year's End. Cole.

Glimmer (ing) (s)
Dark Corner. Hough.
Dragon Country: To Jacob
Boehme. Warren.
Marriage. Turner.
Martyrdom. Learsi.
Pine Gum. Ross.

Glimpse
An Autumn Garden.
Carman.
The Raising of the Dead.
Dobson.
Right Now. Stafford.

Glitter (ed) (ing) (s)
All That Glitters Is Not Gold.
Anonymous.
The Alliance of Education
and Govenment. Gray.
Back to Base. Joseph.
I Am a Negro. Al-Fituri.
Internal Injuries. Warren.
Ship from Thames.
Ingamells.
The Sound of the Sea.
Wheelock.
There Was a Roaring in the
Wind All Night.
Wordsworth.
To a Young Girl. Yeats.
"Trade" Rat. Glenn.
Upon Julia's Clothes.
Herrick.

Globe (s)
For Elizabeth Bishop.
McPherson.
Landscape I. Madge.
The Night is Freezing Fast.
Housman.
Pearl Diver. Benet.

Spring Song. Saul.
Swimming by Night. Merrill.
Tears at the Grave of Sir
Albertus Morton. Wotton.
To Bring Spring. Keithley.
To Thee the Tuneful Anthem
Soars. Byles.

Gloom (s) (y)
The Aeneid. Virgil (Publius
Vergilius Maro).
Aftermath. Longfellow.
Ancient Lullaby. Griffin.
Andrew Magrath's Reply to
John O'Tuomy. Magrath.
Arthur's Seat (excerpt).
Mercer.
The Burning of the Law.
Meir of Rothenburg.
The Cloth of Gold (excerpt).
Krishnamurti.
The Clouded Morning. Very.
Composed on the Theme
"Willows by the Riverside."
Yu Hsuan-chi.
Dedication. Allison.
Derry Morning. Mahon.
Down the Bayou. Townsend.
The Fish. Brooke.
Geography. Koch.
Gracious Moonlight.
Rossetti.
I Dare Not Pray to Thee.
Baring.
In Memoriam A.H.H.,
XXXIX. Tennyson.
June Bracken and Heather.
Tennyson.
Kitty Bhan. Walsh.
Life's Lessons. *Anonymous.*
A Moth. Baildon.
Old Gardens. Upson.
The Oxen. Hardy.
A Person from Porlock.
Thomas.
Remembered Grace.
Patmore.
The Second Asgard. Arnold.
Song: "Again rejoicing Nature
sees." Burns.
Song: "He found me sitting
among flowers." De Vere.
To Mackinnon of Strath.
Lom.
Too Solemn for Day, Too
Sweet for Night. Walker.
The Train Stops at Healy
Fork. Haines.
Warp and Woof. Halbisch.
We Cannot Kindle. Arnold.
What Is Young Passion.
Coleridge.
The White Jessamine. Tabb.
A Winter Talent. Davie.
Written on a Sunday
Morning. Southey.

Glor (ies) (y)
An A B C for Grown
Gentlemen. Bouflers.
Address to My Infant
Daughter. Wordsworth.
Adoro Te Devote. Thomas
Aquinas.
After Death. Parnell.
Allatoona. *Anonymous.*
Alleluia! Alleluia! Let the
Holy Anthem Rise.
Anonymous.
America. Taylor.
L'Angelo. Irwin.
Annul Wars. Nahman of
Bratzlav.
The Annunciation. Nerses.

Annus Mirabilis. Dryden.
As I Look Out. St. Martin.
As When a Man. Tennyson.
The Assumption. Brunini.
At the End of the Day.
Hovey.
An Autumn Park.
Gascoyne.
The Ballad of O'Bruadir.
Higgins.
The Balloon. Tennyson.
Bartol. Alcott.
The Battle of Brunanburh.
Anonymous.
The Battle of the Baltic.
Campbell.
The Birde's Marriage-Cake.
Anonymous.
The Blade of Grass Sings to
the River. Goldberg.
The Blessings of Surrender.
Helphingtine.
Blind. Kemp.
Brasilia. Plath.
The Burial of the Bachelor
(parody). *Anonymous.*
Caelica, LXII. Greville.
Caelica, LXXXV. Greville.
Caelica, CI. Greville.
Christ 3: The Last Judgement.
Anonymous.
The Christ of God.
Kauffman.
Christmas. Stam.
The Church's Testimony.
Dryden.
The Claim That Has the
Canker on the Rose.
Plunkett.
The Coliseum. Poe.
The Court. *Anonymous.*
Crecy. Palgrave.
Credo. Robinson.
The Days Gone By. Riley.
The Dean's Lady. Crabbe.
Dionysus. Andresen.
A Dirge upon the Death of
the Right Valiant Lord,
Bernard Stuart. Herrick.
Dogwood Blossoms.
McClellan.
Down to the Sacred Wave.
Smith.
Dream Songs. Berryman.
Entering by His Door.
Baxter.
Epigram: "If true that notion,
which but few contest."
Anonymous.
Epilogue to Lessing's
Laocoon. Arnold.
Epitaph. Cowper.
Epitaph on Johnson.
Cowper.
Evangeline. Longfellow.
The Evening Sun. Bronte.
Everybody's Welcome.
Anonymous.
Face on the Daguerreotype.
Rosten.
The Fairest He. Bonar.
The Fancy. Benet.
A Farewell to Sir John Norris
and Sir Francis Drake.
Peele.
Father! I Own Thy Voice.
Wolcott.
For Every Day. Havergal.
Friends in Paradise.
Vaughan.
Garryowen. *Anonymous.*
Giardino Pubblico. Sitwell.

Giotto's Tower. Longfellow.
De Glory Road. Wood.
Go, Ploughman, Plough. Campbell.
God Is Working His Purpose Out. Ainger.
God of Our Fathers, Bless This Our Land. Hopkins, Jr.
God Send Easter. Clifton.
Hail, Mother of the Savior. Adam of St. Victor.
His Prayer for Absolution. Herrick.
Holy angels, in envy I cast no sigh. Stampa.
Hospital. Funk.
Housewifery. Taylor.
A Hymn: "A hymn of glory let us sing." Bede.
Hymn for the Lighting of the Lamps. Athenogenes.
I Am Weary of These Times and Their Dull Burden. Beebe.
I Am with You Alway. Nevin.
I Once May See when Yeares Shall Wreck My Wrong. Daniel.
I've Reached the Land of Corn and Wine. Stites.
The Idiot Boy. Wordsworth.
The Iliad. Homer.
In Cemeteries. Enright.
In Defiance to the Dutch. Anonymous.
In Heaven Soaring Up. Taylor.
In Honour of That High and Mighty Princess Queen Elizabeth... Bradstreet.
In the Due Honor of the Author Master Robert Norton. Smith.
The Interpreters. Swinburne.
Intimations of Immortality from Recollections of Early Childhood. Wordsworth.
Iter Boreale. Wild.
Jesu, to Thee My Heart I Bow. Zinzendorf.
The Job That's Crying to Be Done. Kipling.
Lachin Y Gair. Byron.
The Lads in Their Hundreds. Housman.
Leiroessa Kalyx. Baring.
Let Erin Remember the Days of Old. Moore.
Life After Death. Pindar.
Light of the Soul. Caswall.
Lines Written on Hearing the News of the Death of Napoleon. Shelley.
Lord, At This Closing Hour. Fitch.
Lord North's Recantation. Anonymous.
The Love of Hell. Burstein.
Many Birds. Welsh.
Mary, Queen of Scots. Bell.
Meditation of a Mariner. Auchterlonie.
Meditations. Taylor.
Meeting. Rossetti.
A Mile from Eden. Ridler.
Morning Hymn. Gregory the Great.
Mr. Davis's Experience. Anonymous.

"My days' delight, my springtime joys fordone." Ralegh.
A Name in the Sand. Gould.
New Students. Bell.
A New Year's Wish. J. H..
The Night Is Falling. Mangan.
No Room. Stroud.
Not a Sou Had He Got (parody). Barham.
O Mariners! Rutledge.
Ode in Memory of the American Volunteers Fallen for France. Seeger.
Of Little Faith. Pulsifer.
The Old Hundredth. Kethe.
Old Pictures in Florence. Browning.
On a Drop of Dew. Marvell.
On His Mistress, the Queen of Bohemia. Wotton.
On the "Sievering" Tram. Spencer.
Our Father, God. Judson.
Our Father in Heaven. Hale.
A Palinode. Bolton.
Panhandle Cob. Anonymous.
Pentecost. Bennett.
Poem for a Christmas Broadcast. Ridler.
The Precious Blood. Anonymous.
The Range Rider's Soliloquy. Brininstool.
Ravenna. MacNeice.
The Retirement. Anonymous.
A Revivalist in Boston. Rich.
Revive Us Again. Husband.
River Song. Brewster.
Rodney's Glory. O'Sullivan.
Rome. Menendez y Pelayo.
The Royal Way of the Holy Cross. Thomas à Kempis.
Saviour, Sprinkle Many Nations. Coxe.
Secret Prayer. Belle.
September. Arnold.
She Died in Beauty. Sillery.
The Shepherds Had an Angel. Rossetti.
The Shortness and Misery of Life. Watts.
Sic Transit Gloria Mundi. Watson.
Some There Are Who Say That the Fairest Thing Seen. Sappho.
Son-Dayes. Vaughan.
Song: "Too late, alas! I must confess." Rochester.
Songs Set by Thomas Morley, II. Anonymous.
Sonnet: "But love whilst that thou may'st be loved again." Daniel.
Sonnet: "The azured vault, the crystal circles bright." James I.
Sonnet: True Ambition. Stillingfleet.
Sonnet Written in Disgust of Vulgar Supersitition. Keats.
Sonnets. Tuckerman.
St. Peter. Rossetti.
Stand Up for Jesus. Duffield, Jr..
Stanzas Written on the Road between Florence and Pisa. Byron.

The Steam-Engine (parody) (excerpt). Baker.
Stone Angel. Ridler.
Sunrise. Tollerud.
Sweet Pity, Wake. Anonymous.
Te Deum. Le Fort.
Tetelestai. Aiken.
That Thou Art Nowhere to Be Found. Macdonald.
Thou Shouldst Be Living at This Hour! West.
Timber (with music). Anonymous.
To God the Son. Constable.
To Groves. Herrick.
To the Moon, 1969. Deutsch.
To the Muse. Whalen.
To Zion. Halevi.
The United States and Macedonian. Anonymous.
Unto Our God Most High We Sing. Cheney.
Upon Ben Johnson. Herrick.
Upon Wedlock, and Death of Children. Taylor.
Vanitas Vanitatum. Zangwill.
Very Fair My Lot. Kamzon.
Virginia Britannia. Moore.
The Vision of St. Bernard. Hess.
Were I to Mount beyond the Field. Keyes.
The White Rainbow. Nelson.
Widsith, the Minstrel. Anonymous.
The Woodcutter's Wife. Benet.
The World's Miser. Maynard.
Worship. Jones, Jr.
You. Masefield.
You Who Were Made for This Music. Zukofsky.
Zion's Sons and Daughters. Anonymous.
Zollicoffer. Flash.

Glorie (s)
A Collection of Emblemes, Ancient and Moderne (excerpt). Wither.
Loch Leven. Smith.
Love Is the Peace, whereto All Thoughts Doe Strive. Greville.
Shadow of Night: Hymnus in Noctem. Chapman.
To John Donne. Jonson.

Glorify
Albert Sidney Johnston. Ticknor.
Come to Calvary's Holy Mountain. Montgomery.
Hermann Ludwig Ferdinand von Helmholtz. Meinke.
Joshua's Face. Gilboa.
The Moonstar. Rossetti.
On Clarastella Singing. Heath.
Pennsylvania Station. Hughes.
Tomorrow's Men. Johnson.
The Trumpet. Ehrenburg.
The Virgin Mary. Bowers.
Where She Was Not Born. Yvonne.

Glorious
As Often as Some Where before My Feet. Pastorius.

Battle Won Is Lost. George.
Columbus. Sigourney.
The Dash for the Colors. Webb.
Entoptic Colours. Goethe.
Epistle from Mrs. Yonge to Her Husband. Montagu.
The Hour of Prayer. Hoy.
Jesus, These Eyes Have Never Seen. Palmer.
The Muses Elizium. Drayton.
Often when alone I liken my lord. Stampa.
Paradise Lost. Milton.
Paul. Oxenham.
Perhaps Today. Anonymous.
The Philosophic Flight. Bruno.
Psalm XXII. Sidney.
Sonnet on Passing the Bridge of Alcantra, Near Lisbon. Mickle.
Very Lovely. Fyleman.
When Our Earthly Sun Is Setting. Nevin.

Gloucester
The Destroyer of Destroyers. Rice.
From Gloucester Out. Dorn.
Gloucester Harbor. Ward.
Letter 27. Olson.

Glove (s)
The Aeneid. Virgil (Publius Vergilius Maro)
Butchery. McPherson.
The Evans Country. Amis.
Ice. Driscoll.
Love. Herbert.
The Misogynist. Morgan.
Outside Baby Moon's. Violi.
Private Pantomime. Stone.
Romeo and Juliet. Shakespeare.
A Skater's Valentine. Guiterman.
Sonnets, XIV: "Here, hold this glove." Barnfield.
The Spirit of 34th Street. Shriver.

Glow (ed) (ing) (s)
Adam in Love. Mitchell.
All Gold. Anonymous.
The Chandelier as Protagonist. Davis.
Chicago. Kinnell.
Childe Harold's Pilgrimage: Canto IV, XXVIII. Byron.
The Companions. Nemerov.
The Dead Prospector. Chapman.
Directions. Matthews.
Documentary. Stroud.
E Questo Il Nido in Che la Mia Fenice? Hope.
The Fairy Temple; or, Oberon's Chapel.... Herrick.
The Firefly. Nash.
The First Olympionique to Hiero. Pindar.
The Glow-Worm. Shanks.
If You Are Fire. Rosenberg.
Mary Immaculate. Donnelly.
Maud. Tennyson.
A Myth. Kingsley.
On the Death of Francis Thompson. Noyes.
Sermon on the Mount. Wright.

The Snowbound City. Haines.
Thought. Emerson.
To the Mercy Killers. Randall.
Two at a Fireside. Markham.
A Very Minor Poet Speaks. Valle.
Vessels. Schwartz.
Waterspout. Camoens.

Glum (ly)
The Climate. Denby.
The Fiddlehead. McFadden.
Sonnet: He Will Not Be Too Deeply in Love. Angiolieri.

Glutton (s) (y)
The Dustbowl. Elmslie.
The Notorious Glutton. Taylor.
On Gut. Jonson.
The Plum-Cake. Taylor.
The Song of Roland, CUV. Anonymous.
The Song of Roland, XCIII. Anonymous.
Song of the Three Hundred Thousand Drunkards...(excerpt). Tappan.
Tales of a Wayside Inn. Longfellow.

Gnaw (ing)
Back Gnawing Blues. Thomas.
If Justice Moved. Sellers.
The Mole. Schmitz.

Gnu
Limerick: "It was a refractory gnu." Anonymous.
Limerick: "There was a sightseer named Sue." Anonymous.

Go (es) (ing) (ne)
The Abandoned House. Hubbell.
The Abandoned House. Hubbell.
Absence. Barnes.
Aerosol. Witt.
After. Ryan.
After Snow. Clark.
After the Quarrel. Dunbar.
Almost Everybody Is Dying Here: Only a Few Actually Make It. Berrigan.
American History. Moses.
The Anathemata. Jones.
And Yet. Molodovsky.
Angel Surrounded by Paysans. Stevens.
Another Man Done Gone. Anonymous.
Another One for the Devil. Childers.
The Ant Village. Grider.
The Anvil of God's Word. Clifford.
Arizona Nature Myth. Michie.
As a Child Seeing a Cardinal. Gill.
As I was coming down the stair. Anonymous.
As the Day Breaks. McGaffey.
As the Mist Leaves No Scar. Cohen.
The Atlas. Slessor.
Aut Caesar Aut Nullus. Spencer.

Aves. Morison.
Away We Go. Fisher.
Baby, Please Don't Go. Anonymous.
Back to the Angels. De Bolt.
Bad Dream. MacNeice.
Ballade of the Session after Camarillo. Galler.
The Beach in August. Kees.
Becoming a Frog. Jones.
Behold, My Cross Was Gone! Mortenson.
A Bestiary of the Garden for Children Who Should Know Better. Gotlieb.
Birthdays. Domin.
Bivouac. Lewis.
The Blue Animals. Anderson.
Blue Smoke. Frost.
Bootie Black and the Seven Giants All Sipping Chili... Cook.
Bounce Buckram. Anonymous.
The Boys of the Island. Anonymous.
Brandy Leave Me Alone. Anonymous.
Bride's Lament. Sappho.
The Brook. Tennyson.
Brown Skin Girl. McClennan.
The Buried Life. Arnold.
Buttermilk Hill. Anonymous.
The Cage. Gascoyne.
Called Away. Le Gallienne.
Capriccio. Deutsch.
A Case. Anonymous.
Casey Jones. Swart.
Casey Jones (G vers.). Anonymous.
Catechism, 1958. Ransom.
Catullus Talks to Himself. Catullus.
Chant-Pagan. Kipling.
The Charge. Levertov.
The Child Bearers. Sexton.
Childe Harold's Pilgrimage: Canto IV, XXIX. Byron.
The Children. MacDonald.
Chinoiseries. Lowell.
Christmas 1942. Irvin.
Clementine. Montrose.
The Coast of Peru. Anonymous.
The Cobblers' Song. Tilney.
Cold and Heat. Anonymous.
Come with Me into Winter's Disheveled Grass. Swenson.
Comes Fall. Nathan.
Complaint on the Oblivion of the Dead. Laforgue.
The Comrade. Dodd.
Consolation (parody). Guiterman.
Contemplations. Bradstreet.
Content and Rich. Southwell.
The Continuance. Bronk.
The Cool Web. Graves.
Corinna. Anonymous.
Courtesan with Fan. Spires.
The Cruel War Is Raging. Anonymous.
A Cry from the Shore. Cortissoz.
The Curate's Kindness. Hardy.
The Day Will Soon Be Gone. Michinobu.

The Dead of the World. Finley.
Death in the Corn. Liliencron.
The Death of the Gods. An Ode. Ker.
Death's Blue-Eyed Girl. Pastan.
Deer Isle. Booth.
Deer Song. Silko.
A Dialogue. Ignatow.
Distance Spills Itself. Bat-Miriam.
Dream 2: Brian the Still-Hunter. Atwood.
Drinking Song. Anonymous.
Drive It On. Anonymous.
Ending. Ewart.
Enigma for Christmas Shoppers. McGinley.
Epigram: "Various the roads of life." Landor.
Epilogue. Singer.
An Epitaph. Benjacob.
An Ever-Fixed Mark. Amis.
Exeat. Smith.
Expanse Cannot Be Lost. Dickinson.
The Expiration. Donne.
Facing the New Year. Anonymous.
A Fairy Went A-Marketing. Fyleman.
The Falling Star. Teasdale.
Farewell. Press.
The Fastidious Serpent. Johnstone.
Fiammetta. Boccaccio.
Fickle in the Arms of Spring. Fry.
Fire in My Meditation Burned. Ainsworth.
Flight of the Heart. MacNeice.
The Flower Vendor. Cabalquinto.
Fragments on the Poet and the Poetic Gift. Emerson.
France Blues. Sunny Boy.
Free Will. Clark.
French Peasants. Gibbon.
The Frog and the Mouse. Anonymous.
A Frosty Night. Graves.
Full Moon. De La Mare.
Furniture. Bloch.
The Game. Scott.
The Garden by Moonlight. Lowell.
The Garden of Ships. Stewart.
Go By. Tennyson.
Going up to London. Turner.
Grandma Chooses Her Plot at the County Cemetery. Ruffin.
The Great Farewells. Hall.
Grief. Browning.
Hammers and Anvil. Clifford.
Here Is a Toast That I Want to Drink. Lathrop.
Hey! Now the Day Dawns. Montgomerie.
The High Sailboat. Quasimodo.
High Water Everywhere. Patton.
The Higher Catechism. Foss.
Home No More Home to Me. Stevenson.

The Horsemen. Baro.
The House and the Road. Peabody.
The Human Animal. Mayhall.
The Husband. Finkel.
Hymen: Never More Will the Wind. Doolittle.
I Know a Man. Creeley.
I Know the Reputation. Kii.
I Met a Man. Anonymous.
I Ride an Old Paint. Anonymous.
I to the Hills Will Lift Mine Eyes. Rous.
I Was the Child. Warren.
I Will Not Let Thee Go. Bridges.
I Wonder How Many People in This City. Cohen.
Idea. Drayton.
If You See My Mother. Maze.
In Memoriam A.H.H., XX. Tennyson.
In Passing. Jonas.
In Tenebris. Hardy.
Indian Camp. McFatter.
Indian Macho. Oliver.
Inspiration. Knox.
Intuition. Delius.
The Invitation. Buchan.
Is It True That You Live Where There Is Sorrow. Anonymous.
Jack Frenchman's Defeat. Congreve.
January. Coatsworth.
John Clare. Halperin.
Journey through the Night. Holloway.
Judy-One. Lee.
Keep Your Lamp Trimmed and Burning. Anonymous.
The Key to Everything. Swenson.
"The killers that run...'. Cohen.
The King-Fisher Song. "Carroll.
Kit Hath Lost Her Key. Anonymous.
The lamp burns sure, within. Dickinson.
The Last Coachload. De la Mare.
The Last Supper. Williams.
Let Me Go. Anonymous.
Let Us Laugh. Shargel.
Letter to N. Y. Bishop.
Light Lover. Kilmer.
Limerick: "On pianos and organs she lbs." Anonymous.
Limerick: "There was an old person of Twickenham." Lear.
The Listeners. De la Mare.
Little Bessie. Anonymous.
Little Birdie. Anonymous.
Little Fan. Reeves.
The Little Man Who Wasn't There. Mearns.
The Little Red Sled. Bush.
Locations. Fraser.
Lonesome Valley. Anonymous.
Long Gone. Anonymous.
The Lordly and Isolate Satyrs. Olson.
The Lost Mr. Blake. Gilbert.
Love Is a Babel. Anonymous.

Love, My Machine. Simpson.
Love Song. *Anonymous.*
Lover to Lover. Morton.
The Mad Rapist of Calaveras County. Winslow.
Madaket Beach. Barr.
The Maniac. Russell.
The Mantis Friend. McHugh.
Mary Had a Baby. *Anonymous.*
May Evening. Brennan.
May It Be. Pasternak.
A-Maying, A-Paying. Nashe [(or Nash() Thomas.
Mignon. Goethe.
Molly Bawn. *Anonymous.*
Moon Eclipse Exorcism. *Anonymous.*
Morgan. Harrington.
Morning. Saiser.
The Morning-Glory. Coates.
Mourning Pablo Neruda. Bly.
Moving: New York–New Haven Line. Corn.
My Familiar. Saxe.
My Language. Politzer.
My Man John. *Anonymous.*
My Muse and I, Ere Youth and Spirits Fled. Colman.
My Poem. Giovanni.
Nashville Stonewall Blues. Wilkins.
Never More Will the Wind. Doolittle.
The Nicht Is Neir Gane. Montgomerie.
The Night Is Darkening Round Me. Bronte.
The No-Night. Feldman.
O By the By. Cummings.
The Ocean. Prentice.
Ode on a Distant Prospect of Clapham Academy. Hood.
Off Brighton Pier. Ross.
Oh, oh, you will be sorry for that word! Millay.
The Old Familiar Faces. Lamb.
The Old Farmer and His Young Wife. *Anonymous.*
The Old Lady's Lament for Her Youth. Villon.
The Old Pensioner. Yeats.
Old River Road. Keysner.
Old Seawoman. LeClaire.
Old Smoky. *Anonymous.*
An Old Woman. *Anonymous.*
On an Engraved Gem of Leander. Keats.
On Music. Landor.
On Queen Caroline. *Anonymous.*
On Scratchbury Camp. Sassoon.
On the Way. Trakl.
One Day When We Went Walking. Hobbs.
One for Money. *Anonymous.*
Out on Santa-Fe–Blues. Petties.
Outside. Beauvais.
Pad, Pad. Smith.
The Paradox of Time. Ronsard.
Partial Eclipse. Snodgrass.
The Passing of the Buffalo. Garland.
Past. Galsworthy.

Pause. Hamilton.
Peggy Said Good Morning. Clare.
Pierrette in Memory. Griffith.
Pneumonia Blues. Jefferson.
Poem: "This beauty that I see." Schuyler.
The Poem You Asked For. Levis.
Poems, CXL: "The burden of an ancient rhyme." Landor.
The Poet. Grannis.
The Poet's Fate. Hood.
The Poet Tries to Turn in His Jock. Hilton.
The Policeman. Watts.
A Poor Wayfaring Stranger. *Anonymous.*
Possession. Ponsot.
The Postman. Richards.
Practicing. Gernes.
Prayer. Bynner.
A Queen Wasp. De La Mare.
A Raccoon. Fox.
A Racing Eight. Cuthbertson.
The Rahat. Rooney.
Reservation Special. Blockcolski.
Revolutionary Letters. Di Prima.
Riddle: "I have no wings, but yet I fly." Austin.
River. Locke.
Rizpah. Tennyson.
Road Runner. Hall.
The Roc. Lowbury.
Roger and Dolly. *Anonymous.*
Room. Kaufman.
Rudel to the Lady of Tripoli. Browning.
Sale. Williams.
Salute. Pitcher.
Sam. De La Mare.
San Francisco Falling. Markham.
Scorpion. Smith.
The Sea Bird to the Wave. Colum.
Sea Song. Holland.
The Self-Slaved. Kavanagh.
Sensation. Rimbaud.
Sentence. Bynner.
Separate Peace. Morris.
Serenade of Angels. Lasnier.
A Servant to Servants. Frost.
Seven Times the Moon Came. Rittenhouse.
Shall I Compare Thee to a Summer's Day? Moss.
She Didn't Even Wave. Ai.
A Ship Comes in. Jenkins.
Since You Seem Intent... Locklin.
Skins (excerpt). Wright.
Soliloquy in a Motel. Gibson.
Solvitur Acris Hiems. Mahony.
Some Keep the Sabbath Going to Church. Dickinson.
Song. Williams.
Song: Hamlet. "When a man becomes tired of his life" (parody). Poole.
Song of the Farmworker. Jahns.

Song of the Harper. *Anonymous.*
Song: "When I was a greenhorn and young." Kingsley.
Sonnet: "Because my grief seems quiet and apart." Nathan.
Sonnets, LXVI: "Tired with all these, for restful death I cry." Shakespeare.
Sonnets, LXXI: "No longer mourn for me when I am dead." Shakespeare.
The Sound of the Trees. Frost.
Spit. Williams.
Stanzas. Brainard.
Step It Up and Go. *Anonymous.*
Stock Exchange Wisdom. *Anonymous.*
Summer Is Gone. *Anonymous.*
Summer Sun. Stevenson.
Sunday in the Country. Swenson.
Sweeping the Sky. *Anonymous.*
Sweet Is Childhood. Ingelow.
Sweet Is the Swamp with Its Secrets. Dickinson.
Taking Off. *Anonymous.*
Tales from a Family Album. Justice.
Tarry Ye. *Anonymous.*
Telling the Bees. Whittier.
There Was a Child Went Forth. Whitman.
Thesis, Antithesis, and Nostalgia. Dugan.
Things. Simpson.
Things to Do in New York (City). Berrigan.
This Is a Poem for the Fathers and for Michael Ryan. Lux.
Through the Waters. Flint.
Thyrsis (excerpt). Arnold.
Tie-Shuffling Chant. *Anonymous.*
Tie the strings to my life, my Lord. Dickinson.
Time and Tide. Lamarre.
To a Departing Favorite. Horton.
To One. Munch-Petersen.
To Rupert Brooke. Gibson.
To the Etruscan Poets. Wilbur.
Tom Cat Blues. *Anonymous.*
The Tomb at Akr Caar. Pound.
Topsy-Turvy Land. Wilkinson.
Touching. Gilbert.
Toward Myself. Goldberg.
Trench Blues. *Anonymous.*
Twentieth-Century Blues. Fearing.
Twilight. Lawrence.
The Twins. Wright.
Two Clouds. Raab.
Two Ways. Weaver.
Uncle Jack. Kherdian.
Under a Hill. *Anonymous.*
Unloading Rails. *Anonymous.*
Up the Barley Rows. Sora.
Upon the Horse and Rider. Bunyan.

Uru-tu-sendo's Song. *Anonymous.*
The Utmost in Friendship. McCann.
The Vanished Night. MacMurray.
The Viper. Pitter.
A Visit. Anderson.
La Vita Nuova. Dante Alighieri.
Wake Up, You Drowsy Sleepers. *Anonymous.*
The Wakening. *Anonymous.*
The Waking. Roethke.
Water Noises. Roberts.
Water Whirligigs. Opperman.
We Go. Wolfskehl.
We'll Go No More A-Roving. Henley.
Welfare Store. Williamson.
What the Donkey Saw. Fanthorpe.
What Triumph Moves on the Billows So Blue? Lewis.
Whate'er You Dream with Doubt Possest. Clough.
Where shall I have at mine own will. Wyatt.
Whittier. Sangster.
Whittling. Pierpont.
Who's Gonna Shoe Your Pretty Little Foot? *Anonymous.*
Why Come Ye Not to Court (excerpt). Skelton.
Why He Was There. Robinson.
Will ye see what wonders love hath wrought? Wyatt.
The Wind Has Such a Rainy Sound. Rossetti.
The Wind Is Blowing West. Ceravolo.
Winter Song. Macdonald.
Wisdom. Teasdale.
Woman's Constancy. Suckling.
Words. Eberhart.
Words at Farewell. Derian.
Written in March. Wordsworth.
The Yellow Bittern. Mac Giolla Ghunna.
Yonnondio. Whitman.
You. Clark.
The Young Acacia. Bialik.
The Youth with Red-Gold Hair. Sitwell.

Goad (s)
The Aim. Roberts.
If You Were Coming in the Fall. Dickinson.
Sonnet: To Dante Alighieri (He Writes to Dante...). Angiolieri.

Goal (s)
Abraham. Mitchell.
The Ampler Circumscription. Baylebridge.
Balboa. Perry.
The Bridge of Heraclitus. Reavey.
City Girl. Bodenheim.
Columbus Never Knew. Burket.
The Comet. Makai.
Commemoration Ode. Monroe.
The Continuing City. Housman.

The Face of the Waters.
Fitzgerald.
In the Dawn. Shepard.
Inflictis. Stodart-Walker.
Land of Our Fathers.
Scollard.
The Landmark. Rossetti.
Proving. Johnson.
The Song of the Bower.
Rossetti.
Three Cezannes. Whipple.
Under the Goal Posts.
Guiterman.
Washington. Prentice.
Where Is Our Holy Church?
Wilson.
Written in Prison. Clare.
Goat (s)
Castaway. Nerber.
Coptic Poem. Durrell.
Don't You Like It?
Anonymous.
Epigram. Del Medigo.
Hesperos, you bring home all
the bright dawn disperses.
Sappho.
Lullaby. Sexton.
Mating the Goats.
Barnstone.
News Report. Ignatow.
Officer Brady. Chambers.
Omalos. Warren.
A Pastoral. In the Modern
Style. "Worcester".
The Teacher. Fisher.
'Tis Midnight. *Anonymous.*
A Veld Eclogue: The
Pioneers. Campbell.
The Wild Goat. McKay.
Words without Music.
Layton.
Written on a Fly-Leaf of
Theocritus. Thompson.
Goblin (s)
The Bad Kittens.
Coatsworth.
Ceremony upon Candlemas
Eve. Herrick.
How to Tell Goblins from
Elves. Shannon.
If You Were Coming in the
Fall. Dickinson.
God
The. Underwood.
The Abbey Walk. Henryson.
About an Allegory.
Arensberg.
Acceptance. Hughes.
Acceptation. Preston.
Accident in Art. Hovey.
An Account of the Cruelty of
the Papists... Harris.
Adam–The First Kiss.
Porter.
Addition to Kipling's "The
Dead King (Edward VII),
1910." Beerbohm.
An Address to Miss Phillis
Wheatley (excerpt).
Hammon.
Afar in the Desert. Pringle.
After Lorca. Hughes.
After Reading Certain Books.
Coleridge.
Against the Court of Rome.
Petrarch (Francesco
Petrarca).
The Agnostic's Creed.
Malone.
The Agony in the Garden.
Hemans.

Alba Innominata.
Anonymous.
All God's Children Got
Shoes. *Anonymous.*
All Is God's. De Haan.
All Things Bright and
Beautiful. Alexander.
America. Smith.
Anabasis. "Perse.
The Ancient Thought. Kerr.
Andromeda. Browning.
The Animals' Carol.
Causley.
Anticipation. Tusiani.
An Antipastoral Memory of
One Summer. Smith.
Antique Harvesters.
Ransom.
Any Complaints? Scannell.
Any Saint (excerpt).
Thompson.
The Apology Addressed to the
Critical Reviewers.
Churchill.
Apparent Failure. Browning.
Apparently with No Surprise.
Dickinson.
Approaches. Macdonald.
Arabs. Kreymborg.
Aristocrats of Labor.
Stewart.
Arlington Cemetery Looking
toward the Capitol.
Palmer.
The Artisan. Brown.
As Some Mysterious
Wanderer of the Skies.
Stockard.
Ascension Hymn. Santeuil.
The Ashland Tragedy, I.
Anonymous.
At Little Virgil's Window.
Markham.
At the Roman Baths, Bath.
Lucie-Smith.
Atheist. Harburg.
Author of Light, Revive My
Dying Spright. Campion.
Ave Maris Stella.
Anonymous.
Ballade of the Hanged Men.
Villon.
The Ballot. Pierpont.
The Battle of Boyne.
Anonymous.
Because. Teschemacher.
Beloved, It Is Morn. Hickey.
Bereft. Frost.
The Best of All. Crosby.
The Birds. Aristophanes.
Birds and Fishes. Jeffers.
The Birth of Moshesh.
Bereng.
Bishop Doane on His Dog.
Doane.
Black-Out. Jeffers.
Blacklisted. Sandburg.
The Blessed Virgin's
Expostulation. Tate.
Blind. Pearce.
Blood and the Moon. Yeats.
Bodily Beauty. Rostrevor.
Boggy Creek. *Anonymous.*
Bordello. Turco.
Bosworth Field: Richard III's
Speech. Beaumont.
The Breaking. Anderson.
The British Church.
Herbert.
The Bunch of Grapes.
Herbert.
The Burnt Bush. Clemo.

Byron: In Men Whom Men
Condemn as Ill. Miller.
Caelica, XXXIV. Greville.
Caelica, LXXXVIII.
Greville.
Camoens in the Hospital.
Melville.
Canada-I-O. *Anonymous.*
Captain Kelly Lets His
Daughter Go to Be a Nun.
Feeney.
Carol. *Anonymous.*
The Carpenter. Whiteside.
Carrion Comfort. Hopkins.
Cat and Mouse. Hughes.
Chanuke, O Chanuke.
Anonymous.
A Charm for Bees.
Anonymous.
The Child-Musician.
Dobson.
Child of God. *Anonymous.*
A Child's Thought. Moore.
Childlike Heart. Catlin.
Chorus: Sacerdotum.
Greville.
Chosen of God. Zweig.
Christ. Cynewulf.
Christ 3: The Last Judgement.
Anonymous.
Christ Is Arisen. Goethe.
Christmas. Stam.
The Chronicle. Cowley.
The Church. Romain.
Circumstance. Shelley.
The City. North.
City. Stroud.
The Clay Jug. *Anonymous.*
Cleopatra. Swinburne.
The Cliff Rose. Fewster.
Club 82: Lisa. Genser.
A Cocker of Snooks.
Gotlieb.
Coedmon's Hymn.
Anonymous.
Colorado. Dillenback.
Columbus. Hale.
Come, Lord Jesus. Wesley.
Come, Ye Disconsolate.
Moore.
Communion. Spicer.
Communion. Tabb.
Composed while Under
Arrest. Lermontov.
Compulsive Qualifications
(excerpt). Howard.
The Condemned. Howland.
Conscience. Thoreau.
A Contemplation on Night.
Gay.
The Convent. D'Orge.
Conversation in Avila.
McGinley.
Convinced by Sorrow.
Browning.
The Corn-Song. Whittier.
A Coronet for His Mistress
Philosophy. Chapman.
Courage. Brooke.
The Courtship of Miles
Standish. Longfellow.
The Cross. Calderon de la
Barca.
A Crowned Poet. Aldrich.
The Cruel Mother (B vers.).
Anonymous.
Crusader's Song.
Anonymous.
A Cry to Mary. Godric.
The Cuckoo and the
Nightingale. Clanvowe.

The Dancers of Colbek.
Mannyng.
Dancing Gal. Davis.
David's Song. Browning.
Dawn on Mid-Ocean.
Wheelock.
The Day before April.
Davies.
The Day of Judgement.
Young.
Days of My Youth. Tucker.
The Death of Meleager.
Swinburne.
Dedication to Hunger.
Gluck.
Deer at the Roadside.
Smith.
Deliver Me. Carmichael.
A Departed Friend. Moore.
The Desolate Valley.
Pringle.
Deus Immensa Trinitas.
Anonymous.
Did any bird come flying.
Rossetti.
Dies Irae. *Anonymous.*
Differences. Young Bear.
Dirge. Percy.
Dive for Dreams.
Cummings.
A Divine Image. Blake.
The Divine Passion.
Paravicino y Arteaga.
The Divine Presence. De
Vere.
Door-Mats. Davies.
A Dream of Surreal Science.
Ghose.
The Dream of the Rood.
Anonymous.
Dream Songs. Berryman.
A Dubious Night. Wilbur.
The Dying Swan. Moore.
Each in His Own Tongue.
Carruth.
Easter Communion.
Hopkins.
Easter Monday. McFee.
An Easy Poem. Kennedy.
Echo Canyon. *Anonymous.*
Eclogues. Virgil (Publius
Vergilius Maro).
Ecstasy. *Anonymous.*
Egocentric. Smith.
Elegy V. Barker.
Elegy (For Himself). Rimos.
Elegy Written in a Country
Churchyard. Gray.
The Elixir. Herbert.
Ellsworth. *Anonymous.*
Emblems. Quarles.
L'Envoi. Kipling.
Epigram on Seeing a Worthy
Prelate Go out of Church...
Swift.
Epitaph. *Anonymous.*
The Epitaph. Hinkson.
Epitaph on an Army of
Mercenaries. Housman.
Epitaph on Himself. Pope.
Epitaph on Peter Robinson.
Jeffrey.
Epitaphs of the War, 1914-18.
Kipling.
Errore. Di Cicco.
An Essay on Man. Pope.
Eternal Goodness. Whittier.
The Eternal Image. Pitter.
The Eternal Jew. Cohen.
Etude Realiste. Swinburne.
Eulogy for Hasdai Ibn
Shaprut. *Anonymous.*

An Evening Hymn. Ken.
Evening in Gloucester Harbor. Sargent.
Evening on the Broads. Swinburne.
Everest. Shipp.
Exile from God. Wheelock.
Face to Face with Trouble (excerpt). Sangster.
The Faerie Queene. Spenser.
Fair England. Cone.
Faith. Daley.
Faith. Sill.
A Faithless Shepherd. Clare.
Fare Ye Well, My Darlin'. Anonymous.
The Father's Business. Markham.
Feet. Davies.
Fidessa, More Chaste Than Kind, XXXVII. Griffin.
Fielding Error. Smith.
Fifteen Ships on George's Banks. Anonymous.
Finite Reason. Dryden.
The First Spousal. Patmore.
Flash Crimson. Sandburg.
The Fledgling Bard and the Poetry Society. Part I (excerpt). Margetson.
A Flemish Madonna. Stork.
Flower in the Crannied Wall. Tennyson.
Flowering without End. Zweig.
Flute Notes from a Reedy Pond. Plath.
Fool's Blues. Smith.
For Decoration Day: 1898-1899. Hughes.
For Hope. Crashaw.
For Love of Appin. MacKay.
For St. Bartholomew's Eve. Cowley.
For the Lord's Day Evening. Watts.
For Whom, Pyrrha? Horace.
Forgetting God. Harvey.
Formations. Freedman.
The Fortification of New Ross (excerpt). Anonymous.
Forward. Proctor.
Four Prayers, IV. Anonymous.
Four Things. Van Dyke.
The Friendly Blight. De Vere.
From Age to Age They Gather. Hosmer.
From the Depths. Fischer.
From the Garden of Heaven. Hafiz.
From Thy Fair Face I Learn. Michelangelo.
A Funeral Oration. Wright.
The Furniture of a Woman's Mind. Swift.
Ganga. Blackburn.
A Generous Creed. Phelps.
George Allen. Anonymous.
Give Way! Gilman.
God. Bradford.
God and the Strong Ones. Widdemer.
God Forward. G.
God Gives Them Sleep on Ground, on Straw. Williams.
God Is Nigh. Anonymous.
God Is There. Isenhour.

God Is Working His Purpose Out. Ainger.
God Know What He's About. Anonymous.
God Makes a Path. Williams.
The God of Comfort. Anonymous.
God of the Earth, the Sky, the Sea. Longfellow.
God Prays. Morgan.
God's Acre. Bynner.
God's Pay. Anonymous.
God's World. Keeling.
God, through All and in You All. Longfellow.
God to Be First Served. Herrick.
Gold Is the Son of Zeus: Neither Moth Nor Worm May Gnaw It. "Field.
Good-by and Keep Cold. Frost.
Good-bye. Emerson.
Good-Bye, Brother (with music). Anonymous.
Good Friday. Smith.
Grace at the Atlanta Fox. Cassity.
Granny Crack. Reaney.
"The great Macedon, that out of Persia chased." Surrey.
The Great Sad One. Greenberg.
Guns. Woods.
Hagar to Ishmael. Eibel.
Hammer and Anvil. Cole.
Hammerstoke. Domanski.
Hanukah. De Haan.
Hast Thou Heard It, O My Brother. Williams.
Haverhill, 1640-1890. Whittier.
He Leadeth Me. Gilmore.
He Said: "If in His Image I Was Made." Stickney.
He Walketh by Day. Book of the Dead.
He Whom a Dream Hath Possessed. O'Sheel.
Hear Us, in This Thy House. Doddridge.
Heaven and Hell. Thompson.
Heaven Is Here. Adams.
Hedgehog. Muldoon.
Henry K. Sawyer. Anonymous.
High Flight. Magee, Jr.
High Overhead My Little Daughter. Brown.
Hippies. Dempster.
History of Ideas. Cunningham.
Holy Sonnets, VIII. Donne.
Hope Springing Up. Wesley.
Hospital. Funk.
The Hours. Tichy.
The House of a Hundred Lights. Torrence.
How a Poet's Soul Comes Into Play. Browning.
How We Heard the Name. Dugan.
Hymn. Call.
Hymn. Synesius.
Hymn before Sunrise, in the Vale of Chamouni. Coleridge.
Hymn: "My God, I love thee, not because." Francis.

Hymn to Christ the Saviour. Clement of Alexandria (Titus Flavius Clemens).
Hymn to Proserpine. Swinburne.
Hymn to the Sea. Watson.
Hymn Written after Jeremiah Preached to Me in a Dream. Dodson.
Hymns and Spiritual Songs. Smart.
Hyperion. Keats.
I Bet God Understands about Givin up Five. Jamal.
I Come to Supplicate. Ben Abun.
I Crossed the Pynot. Anonymous.
I Didn't Know My Soul. Ben-Yitzhak.
I Give You Thanks My God. Dadie.
I Lie Down with God. Anonymous.
I Loved You Once (From the Russian of Alexander Pushkin). Randall.
I Minded God. Ainsworth.
I Saw the Winter Weaving. Rumi.
I Sing the Mighty Power of God. Watts.
Idyllis. Theocritus.
If I Ride This Train. Johnson.
If, on Account of the Political Situation. Auden.
If We Believed in God. Gibbs.
If You Had a Friend. Lewis.
The Immortal. Pickthall.
In a Closed Universe. Hayford.
In A Year. Browning.
In an Empty Window. Fraser.
In Galilee. MacKay.
In Rebellion. Synge.
In the Distress upon Me. Ainsworth.
In the Hospital. Guiterman.
In the Orchard. Swinburne.
In the Stable. Goudge.
In the Van Gogh Room. Yamamoto.
In the Yucca Land. Morris.
In Trust. Dodge.
Incarnate Love. Tillett.
Incarnatio Est Maximum Donum Dei. Alabaster.
The Incarnation. Wesley.
Independence. Anonymous.
Insatiableness. Traherne.
Inscription above the Entrance to the Abbey of Theleme. Urquhart.
The Invisible Bride. Markham.
Is It True? Williams.
It Is Too late to Call Thee Now. Bronte.
Jacob's Destiny. Beer-Hofmann.
Jay Gould's Daughter (with music). Anonymous.
Jeremiad. Williams.
Jerusalem. Vinner.
Jerusalem, Port City. Amichai.
Jesus. Adams.
Jesus, Master, O Discover. Anonymous.

Jezebel. Middleton.
John Charles Fremont. Lummis.
Johnny Appleseed's Hymn to the Sun. Lindsay.
Jonah. Anonymous.
A Joyful New Ballad. Deloney.
Jubilate. Arnold.
Jubilate Canis. Jong.
July 1914. Akhmatova.
Just the Same Today. Anonymous.
The King of Ulster. Anonymous.
The King's Highway. McGroarty.
King William's Dispatch to Queen Augusta... Patmore.
Lady Isabel and the Elf Knight (B version). Anonymous.
The Landing of the Pilgrim Fathers. Hemans.
Landscape of Screams. Sachs.
The Last Man. Campbell.
The Last Supper. Rice.
Laudate for Christmas. Prudentius (Aurelius Clemens Prudentius).
Laus Deo. Whittier.
Laus Veneris. Swinburne.
The Lay Preacher Ponders. Davies.
Lead On, O King Eternal. Shurtleff.
The Least of Carols. Jewett.
The Leper. Swinburne.
Let Us Learn. Ravitch.
"Let us suppose the mind." Moraff.
Letter V. Graham.
Letters from the Astronomers, II: Johannes Kepler (1571-1630). Fox.
Letters: With Happiness Stretchd Across the Hills. Blake.
Leviathan. Anonymous.
Life. Deland.
Life. Sill.
The Lights in the Hallway. Wright.
Like a Mourningless Child. Patchen.
Limerick: "There is a creator named God." Whistler.
Lines to the Blessed Sacrament. Callanan.
Lines Written on a Window-Shutter at Weston. Cowper.
Little Musgrave and Lady Barnard (B version). Anonymous.
A Little Rhyme and a Little Reason. Anstadt.
A Little Sequence (excerpt). Money-Coutts.
Little Things. Anonymous.
Living Waters. Spencer.
The Lookout. Collins.
Lord Coningsby's Epitaph. Pope.
The Lord God Planted a Garden. Gurney.
The Lord Our God Alone Is Strong. Winchester.
Lordings, Listen to Our Lay. Anonymous.

The Loss of the Due
Dispatch. *Anonymous.*
Love Is of God. Bonar.
Love of Nature. Thomson.
Love Song: "My boat sails
downstream." *Anonymous.*
The Lovesick Cowboy.
Anonymous.
The Lowest Place. Rossetti.
The Lust of Gold.
Montgomery.
Luzzato. Reznikoff.
M-Y T-E-M-P-E-R.
Anonymous.
La Madonna dell' Acqua.
Ruskin.
The Maid. Bregy.
The Maid I Left Behind.
Anonymous.
Maidenhood. Longfellow.
Manufactured Gods.
Sandburg.
Marquette on the Shores of
the Mississippi. Rooney.
The Marriage of Heaven and
Hell. Blake.
The Marrow. Roethke.
Mary, Queen of Heaven.
Anonymous.
Mashkin Hill. Simpson.
The Master's Touch. Bonar.
The Masterpiece. Arensberg.
The Masterpiece. Malone.
Mater Dei. Hinkson.
A May Day Carol.
Anonymous.
May God Give Strength.
Van Wynen.
The May Magnificat.
Hopkins.
Me Happy, Night, Night Full
of Brightness. Pound.
The Mecklenburg Declaration.
Elam.
Meditation on the Nativity.
Jennings.
Memorial Sonnet. Meeker.
Michigan I-O. *Anonymous.*
Minot's Ledge. O'Brien.
Mistrustful Minds Be Moved.
Wyatt.
The Mitherless Bairn. Thom.
Morality. Arnold.
More Love. *Anonymous.*
The Morning Purples All the
Sky. Roman Breviary.
Morte d'Arthur. Tennyson.
Moses and Joshua. Lasker-
Schüler.
The Moss Supplicateth for the
Poet. Dana.
Mother, among the Dustbins.
Smith.
Mother-Prayer. Widdemer.
The Mother's Lullaby.
Clare.
Mothers. *Anonymous.*
Mrs. Saunder's Experience.
Anonymous.
Music of the Dawn.
Harrison.
My Church. G.
My Dead. Hosmer.
My Dog Jock. Carruth.
My Doves. Browning.
My Garden. Succorsa.
The Mystic. Rice.
The Mythos of Samuel
Huntsman. Plutzik.
A Nameless Epitaph.
Arnold.
The Nativity. Wesley.

The Need of the Hour.
Markham.
New Hymns for Solitude.
Dowden.
The New World: The New
God. Bynner.
New Year's. Reznikoff.
New Years and Old.
Jackson.
New York City. Abbe.
News from Yorktown.
Smith.
Niagara. Sigourney.
A Night in June. Scott.
The Night of Marvels.
Violante Do Ceo.
The Nineteenth of April.
Larcom.
No Doubt. Adams.
Noon. Jeffers.
The Nut-Brown Maid.
Anonymous.
O God, I Cried, No Dark
Disguise. Millay.
O Land Beloved.
Woodberry.
O My Belly. *Anonymous.*
O Thou Whose Pow'r.
Boethius.
An Ode. Herbert of
Cherbury.
Ode to Apollo. Keats.
Ode to Joy. Schiller.
Ode to Solitude (excerpt).
Grainger.
An Ode Which was Prefixed
To a Prayer Booke.
Crashaw.
Of Common Devotion.
Quarles.
Of Gods Omnipotencie.
Hume.
Of the Day Estivall. Hume.
Of Wounds. Mary
Madeleva.
Oh, Stop Being Thankful All
Over the Place. Nash.
The Old Ark's A-Moverin'.
Anonymous.
The Old Road. Very
An Old Story. Lee.
The Old Woman Remembers.
Gregory, Augusta Gregory.
An Old Woman's Answer to a
Letter from Her Girlhood.
Emory.
On a Drawing by Flavio.
Levine.
On a Papyrus of
Oxyrhynchus. *Anonymous.*
On a Prayer Book Sent to
Mrs. M. R. (excerpt).
Crashaw.
On Listening to the Spirituals.
Jeffers.
On the Farm. Thomas.
On the Painter Val Prinsep.
Rossetti.
On the Plough-Man.
Quarles.
The One. Kavanagh.
One Country. Stanton.
One Gift I Ask. Harrison.
One Immortality. Engels.
One of Us Two. Wilcox.
Only of Thee and Me.
Untermeyer.
Open the Gates. *Anonymous.*
Our Journey Had Advanced.
Dickinson.
Our Nation Forever. Bruce.
Our Orders. Lowe

Out in the Fields.
Anonymous.
Out of the Vast. Bamberger.
The Pagans Wild Confesse the
Bonds. Williams.
Pain. Robinson.
The Pansy and the Prayer-
Book. Edwards.
Papa's Letter. *Anonymous.*
Paradise Lost. Milton.
Paradise Regained. Milton.
The Path of Wisdom.
Anonymous.
The Patriot. Browning.
The Peaks. Crane.
The People. Creeley.
Perfection. Carlin.
Personality. Sandburg.
Phantasy. *Anonymous.*
Philip, My King. Craik.
Pioneer Woman. Crawford.
Pisgah. Wattles.
The Place at Alert Bay.
Rukeyser.
Plaint. Elliot.
Plead for Me. Bronte.
Poem About Your Face.
Alterman.
Poem for Easter. Lee.
Poem: "Like a deaf man
meshed in his endless
silence." Wain.
A Poem with Capital Letters.
Cooper.
Poets. Kilmer.
Poets Love Nature. Clare.
The Poor Working Girl (with
music). *Anonymous.*
Porphyria's Lover.
Browning.
A Portrait. Stevenson.
A Postscript to Verses on the
History of France.
Anonymous.
A Prayer. Cotter.
Prayer. Villiers.
A Prayer for Purification.
Michelangelo.
The Precept of Silence.
Johnson.
Prelude. Aldington.
The Present Age. Coxe.
Prison. Ashley.
The Problem. Blackburn.
Proclaim the Lofty Praise.
Judson.
The Proclamation.
Longfellow.
Promises, VIII. Founding
Fathers.... Warren.
The Prophet Lost in the Hills
at Evening. Belloc.
Prospice. Browning.
Psalm XLIII. Sidney.
A Psalm of Montreal.
Butler.
The Psalm of St. Priapus.
Broughton.
Psalmodist. Leib.
The Queen's Speech.
Mainwaring.
Quickness. Vaughan.
A Quintina of Crosses.
Walsh.
Rabbi Ben Ezra. Browning.
The Rann of the Three.
Anonymous.
Recipe for Living. Walton.
The Reed. Houselander.
A Reflection on the Foregoing
Ode. Cowper.
Reinforcements. Lynch.

Relieving Guard. Harte.
Reply to Dipsychus. Clough.
Requiescant. Scott.
The Resident Worm.
Hayford.
Resignation. Chatterton.
Resurgam. Bitton.
The Ring and the Book.
Browning.
Rise Up, O Men of God.
Merrill.
The Robin and the Wren.
Anonymous.
Robin, Wren, Martin,
Swallow. *Anonymous.*
The Rock Crumbles. Lasker-
Schüler.
Romance VIII. John of
Damascus.
Rome. Menendez y Pelayo.
Rose-Marie of the Angels.
Crapsey.
A Royal Princess. Rossetti.
Rural Legend. Osborn.
Safed. Knut.
Satire. Donne.
Savonarola. Bentley.
The Scarlet Thread.
Henderson.
The Sea. Frankenberg.
Sea-Nurtured. Ingelow.
The Seafarer. *Anonymous.*
A Seaman's Confession of
Faith. Kemp.
The Second Iron Age
(1939-1945). Harrington.
Second Seeing. Golding.
The Secret of the Cross.
Clarkson.
Security. Glover.
Seder-Night. Zangwill.
Self-Consciousness Makes All
Changes Happy.
Richardson.
Self-Knowledge. Coleridge.
Send Forth, O God, Thy
Light and Truth. Adams.
The Serpent of God.
Farallon.
The Servants. Wightman.
The Sheep-Herder. Clark, Jr.
The Shepherd of King
Admetus. Lowell.
Siena. Swinburne.
Silence. Hageman.
Silence. Towne.
The Silent. Very.
A Silent Wood. Siddal.
Silex Scintillans. Vaughan.
Singe We Alle and Say We
Thus. *Anonymous.*
Sins' Round. Herbert.
Sister Rose. Martin.
The Skeptic. Service.
Slav'ry Chain (Joshua Fit de
Battle). *Anonymous.*
The Smuggler's Victory.
Anonymous.
The Snare. MacDonogh.
Snatches: "When ye see the
sunne amis." *Anonymous.*
The Soldier's Wife (parody).
Frere.
Sometime. Smith.
Song: "Beloved, it is morn!"
Hickey.
A Song from Sylvan. Guiney.
A Song of Thanks. Jones.
The Song of the Body
Dreamed in the Spirit's
Mad Behest. Antoninus.

Song: "Since I'm a girl." *Anonymous.*
Songs of Seven. Ingelow.
Sonnet LVI. Alabaster.
Sonnet: Of Why He Is Unhanged. Angiolieri.
Sonnet on a Somewhat Inferior Radio Outfit. Ross.
Sonnet on Chillon. Byron.
Sonnets. Whitman
Sonnets from the Portuguese, XXVI. Browning.
Sonnets of the Triple-Headed Manichee: II. Barker.
The Sorrows of Sunday: An Elegy (excerpt). Wolcot.
Soul's Liberty. Wickham.
Souvenir. Musset.
Spinster's Lullaby. Miller.
The Spring. Barnes.
Spring. Williams.
Spring is the Period. Dickinson.
Springfield Mountain. *Anonymous.*
St. Francis and the Cloud. Welch.
St. Valentine's Day. Blunt.
The Staff and Scrip. Rossetti.
The Star. Redpath.
The Struggle. Prudhomme.
Sub Specie Aeternitatis. Hayden.
Submission in Affliction. *Anonymous.*
The Sudbury Fight. Rice.
Sunrise. Sangster.
Suppose That Christ Had Not Been Born. Nicholson.
The Swan. Roethke.
Swans. Speyer.
The Task. Cowper.
Testament. Sister M. Therese.
Thailand Railway. Stow.
Thank You, God. Stiles.
Thanksgiving. Morgan.
Theology. Hughes.
The Theology of Bongwi, the Baboon. Campbell.
The Theology of Jonathan Edwards. McGinley.
Theoretikos. Wilde.
There. Coleridge.
There Is a High Place. Markham.
There Is a Land Mine Eye Hath Seen. Robins.
There Is a Place. Hoellein.
There Is No Country. Tuwim.
There Is None to Help. Walsh.
These Things Shall Be. Symonds.
They. Sassoon.
They Cast Their Nets in Galilee. Percy.
They dropped like flakes. Dickinson.
This World Fares as a Fantasy. *Anonymous.*
Thou Art of All Created Things. Calderon de la Barca.
Thou Art the Tree of Life. Taylor.
The Thousand and One Nights: The Wazir Dandan

for Prince Sharkan. *Anonymous.*
The Three Bells. Whittier.
The Three Woes. De Vere.
Threnody for a Poet. Carman.
Through All the World. *Anonymous.*
Through Unknown Paths. Hosmer.
Thy Will Be Done. *Anonymous.*
Thysia. Luce.
Tim, an Irish Terrier. Letts.
Time-Servers. Halevi.
The Tinkers. Campbell.
To a Lock of Hair. Scott.
To a Nun. Ormond.
To a Republican Friend. Arnold.
To Brooklyn Bridge. Crane.
To Clelia. Coppinger.
To Columbus. Dario.
To-Day a Shepherd. Theresa of Avila.
To Death. Herrick.
To God. Blake.
To His Dead Body. Sassoon.
To Ibn Zaidun. Wallada.
To Julia de Burgos. Burgos.
To Melite. Rufinus Domesticus.
To Men. Wickham.
To-Morrow Shall Be My Dancing Day. *Anonymous.*
To My Mother. Brock.
To Our Blessed Lady. Constable.
To Our Friends. Watkins.
To Pile Like Thunder to Its Close. Dickinson.
To Pyrrha. Horace.
To Search Our Souls. Lanning.
To St. Mary Magdalen. Hill.
To the Authoress of "Aurora Leigh". Dobell.
To the Body. Meynell.
To the Dandelion. Lowell.
To the Right Honourable William, Earl of Dartmouth. Wheatley.
To Trust. Pozzi.
To Walt Whitman in America. Swinburne.
To Whom Shall the World Henceforth Belong? Oxenham.
The Toiler (excerpt). Markham.
Tour de Force. Dufault.
Trees. Kilmer.
The Triumph of Doubt. Bishop.
A Trust-Song. Rexford.
A Turkish Legend. Aldrich.
The Turning. Levine.
Turris Eburnea. *Anonymous.*
Twelfth Night. Lee.
Twenty-One Sonnets. Stead.
Twice Fed. Bassett.
Two Carols to Our Lady. *Anonymous.*
Two Gifts. *Anonymous.*
Two Went up to the Temple to Pray. Crashaw.
Under Which Lyre. Auden.
Unitarian Easter. McPherson.
Unity. De Haan.
The Unknown God. Watson.
Unless. Glynes.

The Unquiet Grave. *Anonymous.*
The Unsung Heroes. Dunbar.
A Valediction. Browning.
The Virgin Unspotted. *Anonymous.*
The Vision of Sir Launfal. Lowell.
The Voice of God. Stephens.
The Waiting. Whittier.
Walking against the Wind. Stallworthy.
Walking in the Light. Barton.
Walking with Lulu in the Wood. Lazard.
A Wanderer's Litany. Stringer.
The Wants of Man. Adams.
Ward Two. Webb.
The Way. Van Dyke.
We Are Living, We Are Dwelling. Coxe.
The Weasel. Pack.
Wednesday Night Prayer Meeting. Wright.
What Called Me to the Heights? Pilkington.
What Makes a Nation Great. Blackburn.
What the Devil Said. Stephens.
When Any Mortal. Cummings.
When I Think of the Hungry People. O-Shi-O.
When the Great Gray Ships Come in. Carryl.
When This Carnival Finally Closes. Mapanje.
When Thy Heart with Joy O'erflowing. Williams.
Where Cross the Crowded Ways of Life. North.
Where Knock Is Open Wide. Roethke.
Where the Blessed Feet Have Trod. "Field.
Wherein Consists the High Estate. Dayton.
The White Ship. Rossetti.
Who Does Not Love True Poetry. Hall.
Why Linger Yet upon the Strand? Benson.
Wild Eden. Woodberry.
The Wild Ride. Guiney.
Wild Sports of the West. Montague.
The Wilderness. Stanton.
William Shakespeare. Swinburne.
The Winged Worshippers. Sprague.
The Witch. Douglas.
Witch Doctor. Hayden.
Witchcraft: New Style. Abercrombie.
A Woman's Thought. Gilder.
A Woman to Her Lover. Walsh.
Woman with Girdle. Sexton.
The Wonderer. Service.
A Word to New England. Bradford.
Words. *Anonymous.*
Wordspinning. Kirsch.
Work. Thompson.
Work: A Song of Triumph. Morgan.

World Enough. Hathaway.
World's Worth. Rossetti.
The Worm. Barnstone.
Worry. Swarberg.
Worship. Lord
Written on a Wall at Woodstock. Elizabeth I.
Yale Boola March. Loomis.
Ye Scattered Nations. Cradock.
Yes, It Was the Mountain Echo. Wordsworth.
You Can't Fool God. Kleiser.
Young Democracy (excerpt). O'Dowd.

Goddess
Arcadia. Sidney.
Birth of Venus. Urdang.
Calliope in the Labour Ward. Feinstein.
Diana. Constable.
Eclogues. Virgil (Publius Vergilius Maro).
Feuerzauber. Untermeyer.
Five Poems about Poetry (excerpt). Oppen.
The Flight of the Goddess. Aldrich.
Hollywood. Blanding.
Homeric Hymns: Hymn to Aphrodite (abridged). *Anonymous.*
Kinship. Heaney.
Love Song: "My loved one is unique, without a peer." *Anonymous.*
The Odyssey. Homer.
The Sun (excerpt). Vidya.
To Caelia. *Anonymous.*
Without Me You Won't Be Able to See Yourself. Grade.

Godiva
To a Lady across the Way. White.

Gods
Ad Coelum. Romaine.
Alcibiades to a Jealous Girl. Ficke.
Art. Noyes.
At the Museum. Brinnin.
Aubade. MacNeice.
The Beacon. Gregor.
Because that you are going. Dickinson.
A Bestiary. Rexroth.
The Birds. Aristophanes.
Caelica, XXVI. Greville.
Caelica, CV. Greville.
Celebration. Cohen.
Certain Maxims of Archy. Marquis.
Circe. Gibson.
The City. Russell.
Dionysus. Andresen.
Doctors' Row. Aiken.
Drowning of Conaing. *Anonymous.*
Empedocles on Etna. Arnold.
Epic. Kavanagh.
Epilogue. Aldington.
Epitaphs of the War, 1914-18. Kipling.
Evarra and His Gods. Kipling.
Exile. Yeatman.
The First Olympionique to Hiero of Syracuse. Pindar.
Four for Sir John Davies. Roethke.

Give All to Love.   Emerson.
Gods.   Whitman.
The Hero Leaves His Ship.
  Guest.
Hold My Hand.   Pennant.
Hush!   Emerson.
Investiture.   Henderson.
Irrigation.   Tichy.
King David.   Benét.
Light-Winged Smoke, Icarian
  Bird.   Thoreau.
Little Eclogue.   Wylie.
Madrigal: "Penelope, that
  longed for the sight."
  Byrd.
The Magnanimous.   Kay.
Man Alone.   Levertov.
Maurice de Guerin.   Egan.
Meditation at Kew.
  Wickham.
Methinks the Measure.
  Hutchison.
My Birth.   Savage.
The Nereids.   Kingsley.
No Harm to Lovers.
  Tibullus.
No More.   Clark.
The Novel.   Levertov.
Odes.   Horace.
Odes.   Santayana.
The Pleasure of Ruins.
  McClatchy.
The Plougher.   Colum.
A Roman Officer Writes.
  Doughty.
Saadi.   Emerson.
The Sea's Voice.   Foster.
Seagulls.   Updike.
The Second Advice to a
  Painter.   Marvell.
Smoke.   Thoreau.
Sonnet CV.   Greville.
Sonnets, III: "Regions of soft
  clear air, of cold green
  leaves."   Irwin.
Sonnets, First Series.
  Tuckerman.
Spring over the City.
  Hebert.
Stones: Avesbury.   Aldan.
These Green-Going-to-Yellow.
  Bell.
To One Elect.   Hayakawa.
The Twa Books.   Ramsay.
Uriel.   Emerson.
A Well-Wishing to a Place of
  Pleasure.   Anonymous.
Gold (en)
Admiral.   Allen.
African Easter.   Nicol.
Ahab Mohammed.   Legare.
All One People.   Sandburg.
All That Glitters Is Not Gold.
  Anonymous.
America A Prophecy.   Blake.
The American Eagle.
  Lawrence.
Amy Margaret.   Allingham.
And She Washed His Feet
  with Her Tears,...
  Sherburne.
And When They Fall.
  Montague.
The Angel in the House.
  Patmore.
Anxiety Pastorale.   Schaefer.
Aphrodite Pandemos.
  Anonymous.
The Apple Tree.   Brown.
The Art of Making Puddings.
  King.

As I Came over the Grey,
  Grey Hills.   Campbell.
Ass-Face.   Sitwell.
Avarice.   Hecht.
Awakening.   Sangster.
Baldy Green.   Anonymous.
The Ballad of the Ivanhoe.
  Adams.
Band Music.   Fuller.
The Banks of the Sacramento.
  Anonymous.
Beachcomber.   Brown.
Beachcomber.   Oliver.
The Beatific Vision.
  Chesterton.
Beauty and the Bird.
  Rossetti.
The Beggar's Opera.   Gay.
Better Than Gold.   Ryan.
Birth of the Foal.   Juhasz.
Black and Gold.   Turner.
Blind Date.   Aiken.
The Bookworms.   Burns.
Boys in October.   Layton.
British Commerce.
  Thomson.
Burragorang.   McDonald.
By the Klondike River.
  Coren.
California (with music).
  Anonymous.
Californy Stage.   Anonymous.
Canto I.   Pound.
Captain Kelly Lets His
  Daughter Go to Be a Nun.
  Feeney.
Caravatt's Junkyard.
  Morgan.
The Castle.   Muir.
The Caverns of the Grave I've
  Seen.   Blake.
Celanta at the Well of Life.
  Peele.
Chamber Music.   Joyce.
Changeful Beauty.   Lang.
Chanson d'Or.   Hamilton.
Chavez.   Sweeney.
Child.   Sargent.
Childhood.   Justice.
Columbus.   Hutchison.
The Commendations of
  Mistress Jane Scrope.
  Skelton.
The Corn-Song.   Whittier.
Could It Have Been a
  Shadow?   Shannon.
The Courtier's Life.   Wyatt.
The Cowboy.   Anonymous.
Croesus in Autumn.   Warren.
Cuckoo Waltz (with music).
  Anonymous.
Das Jahr Der Seele (excerpt).
  George.
Davis Matlock.   Masters.
Dawn.   "Rachel" (Rachel
  Blumstein).
Days.   Baker.
Death by Rarity.   Young.
Dragon Lesson.   Hearst.
The Dream of the Rood.
  Anonymous.
Drink.   Williams.
Ducks down in the Meadow.
  Stafford.
The Duke of Marlborough.
  Anonymous.
The Dying Girl.   Williams.
East Virginia.   Anonymous.
Eden-Gate.   Dobell.
Elegies.   Ovid (Publius
  Ovidius Naso).
Elegy.   Sadeh.

The Elements.   Williams.
Enamoured of the Miniscule.
  Hartnett.
Ere the Golden Bowl Is
  Broken.   Branch.
Escapist's Song.   Spencer.
Evening Songs.   Cheney.
The Fairy Maimoune.
  Moultrie.
Fairy Tales.   Manger.
The Fallow Field.   Dorr.
Farmers.   Roberts.
The Feast of the Snow.
  Chesterton.
Felicia's Cafe.   McGuckian.
For a Copy of Theocritus.
  Dobson.
For Arvia.   Robinson.
For shamefast harm of great
  and hateful need.   Wyatt.
For the Word is Flesh.
  Kunitz.
For the Yiddish Singers in the
  Lakewood Hotels of My
  Childhood.   Shapiro.
The Fossils.   Kinnell.
The Frowning Cliff.
  Asquith.
La Gialletta Gallante.
  Herbert of Cherbury.
Gifts.   Coleridge.
The Gifts of God.   Very
Go Take the World.
  Macpherson.
Go to Bed First.
  Anonymous.
God's Plans.   Smith.
Gold.   Jones.
The Gold-Seekers.   Garland.
Golden Gates.   Anonymous.
The Golden Mile-Stone.
  Longfellow.
Golden Stockings.   Gogarty.
The Graveyard Road.
  McKeown.
The Greater Music.   Weiss.
The Green Family.
  Thibaudeau.
The Greenland Men.
  Anonymous.
A Guard of the Sepulcher.
  Markham.
The Gypsy Countess.
  Anonymous.
The Harvest Dawn Is Near.
  Burgess.
Harvest Hymn.   Whittier.
He Has Observ'd the Golden
  Rule.   Blake.
He Whom a Dream Hath
  Possessed.   O'Sheel.
Hematite Lake.   Galvin.
Hero and Leander.   Marlowe.
The Highwaymen.   Gay.
The Hobbit (excerpt).
  Tolkien.
The Hog-Eye Man (with
  music).   Anonymous.
Holiday.   Lowry.
Holy Ghost.   Anonymous.
Homage to the Weather.
  Hamburger.
Hope (excerpt).   Shenstone.
Horses and Men in the Rain.
  Sandburg.
How Could We, Beforehand,
  Live in Quiet.   Gumilev.
How Firm a Foundation.
  Keith.
How Sweet I Roam'd.
  Blake.

How the Hen Sold Her Eggs
  to the Stingy Priest.
  Willard.
Hubert Horatio Humphrey
  (1911-1978).   Galvin.
Hymn to the Winds.   Du
  Bellay.
Hynd Horn.   Anonymous.
Hyperion.   Keats.
I Love My Love.   Adam.
Ibby Damsel.   Anonymous.
Idylls.   Theocritus.
Impression.   Symons.
In a Boat.   Belloc.
In Christ.   Oxenham.
In Spain.   Lawless.
The Investiture.   Sassoon.
Janette's Hair.   Halpine.
John Graydon.   MacDonald.
John Saw the Holy Number.
  Anonymous.
Judean Summer.   Lipshitz.
A Kansas Cowboy.
  Anonymous.
Key West.   Crane.
King Henry Fifth's Conquest
  of France (B vers.).
  Anonymous.
The King in May.   Browne.
The King of Ulster.
  Anonymous.
The Klondike.   Robinson.
Labor Day.   Pomeroy.
Lady Isabel and the Elf
  Knight.   Anonymous.
The Laureate (parody).
  Aytoun.
Lemon Pie.   Guest.
Lenore.   Poe.
The Letter.   Anonymous.
Letter to a Mute.   James.
Letter to Viscount Cobham.
  Congreve.
Letty's Globe.   Turner.
Like a Laverock in the Lift.
  Ingelow.
The List.   McClure.
Load.   Hewitt.
London Voluntaries.   Henley.
Looking at the Empire State
  Building.   Pomeroy.
The Lost Lagoon.   Johnson.
Lousy Miner.   Anonymous.
The Love of Older Men.
  Kirkup.
Lullaby.   O'Sullivan.
Madrigal: To His Lady
  Selvaggia Vergiolesi...
  Cino da Pistoia.
Magic.   Wolfe.
Magic Lariat.   Dresbach.
The Man from Strathbogie.
  FitzGerald.
Man of Constant Sorrow.
  Anonymous.
A Man Saw a Ball of Gold.
  Padgett.
Manufactured Gods.
  Sandburg.
May Morn.   McClure.
Midnight Show.   Shapiro.
Miser.   Vinal.
Morgana.   D'Annunzio.
Morte d'Arthur.   Tennyson.
Mother Dear, O! Pray for Me.
  Anonymous.
Mr. Coggs.   Lucas.
Museum Piece.   Spingarn.
Mythics.   Chasin.
The Name.   Hay.
The New Colossus.   Lazarus.

New Friends and Old Friends. Parry.
Nightingales Are Not Singing. Dor.
Nil Admirari. Congreve.
Nimbus. Le Pan.
Nonsense. Schauffler.
Not Three–But One. Duff.
Nothing Gold Can Stay. Farber.
Nothing Gold Can Stay. Frost.
Nunc Scio, Quid Sit Amor. Mackay.
O All Down within the Pretty Meadow. Patchen.
"O For a Booke." *Anonymous.*
Objets d'Art. MacDonald.
Oblation. Choyce.
Old Miniatures. Vroman.
The Old Wife's Tale. Peele.
On a Piece of Music. Hopkins.
On a Seal. Plato.
On Edward Seymour, Duke of Somerset. *Anonymous.*
On Lisa's Golden Hair. Campbell.
On Saturday Night Shall Be My Care. *Anonymous.*
On Seeing a Hair of Lucretia Borgia. Landor.
On the Fine Arts Garden, Cleveland. Atkins.
Ovid's Metamorphosis: Sixth Book. Sandys.
The Painter's Mistress. Flecker.
Palaces of Gold. Rosselson.
Patterns. Setterberg.
The Perfect Gift. Cooke.
Poems from the Greek Anthology (excerpt). Asclepiades.
The Poet. Morgan.
Poet and Goldsmith. Watkins.
The Poor Scholar. Ibn Chasdai.
A Postcard from the Volcano. Stevens.
A Prayer for a Marriage. Davies.
Pretty Polly (with music). *Anonymous.*
A Proem. Ward
The Proverbs of Alfred: Wealth and Wisdom. *Anonymous.*
Psyche. Very.
The Puddle. Phillpotts.
Quivira. Guiterman.
Rains on the Island. Preil.
Ravenna. MacNeice.
Recollection. Donnelly.
The Refiner's Fire. *Anonymous.*
Reminiscences of a Day: Wicklow. O'Donnell.
Respectabilities. Silkin.
Revelation. Bullis.
Rhapsody of the Deaf Man. Corbiere.
Robespierre and Mozart as Stage. Lowell.
Robin Hood and Queen Katherine (B version). *Anonymous.*
The Romance of the Rose: Love vs. Marriage. Meung.

Rosa Nascosa. Hewlett.
Rye Whiskey. *Anonymous.*
Sacramento. *Anonymous.*
Saint Germain-en-Laye. Dowson.
School Is Out. Frost.
Seboyeta Chapel. Witt.
Sexsmith the Dentist. Masters.
The Sextant. Sullivan.
Shall Then Another. Mackenzie.
She Walks. Keith.
The Sheaves. Robinson.
Shechem. Shevin.
The Shepherd and the Shepherdess. *Anonymous.*
The Ship. Mifflin.
The Ship. Squire.
Siasconset Song. Booth.
Six of Cups. Wakoski.
The Sleeping Beauty. Sitwell.
Small Fountains. Abercrombie.
The Sod-Breaker. Stringer.
The Solemn Noon of Night. Warton, Jr..
Song: "When de golden trumpets sound." *Anonymous.*
Sonnet: "High on the wall that holds Jerusalem." Chesterton.
Springfield Mountain (A vers.). *Anonymous.*
Sunken Gold. Lee-Hamilton.
Sunrise. Bennett.
A Sunset at Les Eboulements. Lampman.
The Sunshine of Thine Eyes. Lathrop.
The Tapestry Weaver. Chester.
Tell Her So. *Anonymous.*
This Shall Be Sufficient. Rexroth.
'Tis but a Little Faded Flower. Howarth.
To a Cherokee Rose. Hayne.
To Autumn. Blake.
To Delia. Daniel.
To Liebig–7. Platen.
To the Lady Margaret, Countess of Cumberland. Daniel.
The Tramp's Song. O'Neill.
Transition. Sarton.
Treasure Boat. Fujino.
Trumpet Player. Hughes.
The Turkish Lady. *Anonymous.*
Twink Drives Back, in a Bad Mood, from a Party in Massachusetts. Amabile.
Uccello. Corso.
Ulysses Returns. Montgomery.
Venice. Moss.
Venus Abandoned. Shakespeare.
Verses Wrote in a Lady's Ivory Table-Book. Swift.
The Villain. Davies.
Washing Up. *Anonymous.*
A Way Up on Clinch Mountain (A vers. with music). *Anonymous.*
Weathercock. Jennings.
What Guile Is This. Spenser.
What Semiramis Said. Lindsay.

When Men Shall Find. Daniel.
The Whisperer. Bullen.
Windham. *Anonymous.*
Wintered Sunflowers. Snyder.
The Woman in the. Piercy.
Worlds on Worlds Are Rolling Ever. Shelley.
The Wreck of Number Nine. *Anonymous.*
The Yellow Witch of Caribou. Robertson.
The Yellowhammer. Clare.
Yom Kippur. Bloch.
You Know the Place. Sappho.
Young Argonauts. Wingfield.
The Zen Archer. Kirkup.

Goldenrod
Caravth's Junkyard. Morgan.
Load. Hewitt.
The Woman in the. Piercy.

Golfer (s)
The City of Golf. Murray.
Golf Ball. Delaney.
One Down. Armour.

Goliath
Back Again from Yucca Flats. Kelley.
The Cave of Night. Montague.
I took my power in my hand. Dickinson.
Perhaps It's Only Music. Zach.
Stone Words for Robert Lowell. Eberhart.
Who Did Swallow Jonah? *Anonymous.*

Gong
Byzantium. Yeats.
A Conversation. Howes.
Limerick: "There was a composer named Bong." *Anonymous.*
Limerick: "There was an old man with a gong." Lear.
Rome Once Alone. Coolidge.

Good
Advice to the Ladies. Somervile.
After Reading Certain Books. Coleridge.
After Reading the Life of Mrs Catherine Stubbs... Hann.
Almighty God in Being Was. Ballou.
Ambitious. Gustafson.
America Is Great Because... de Tocqueville.
America the Beautiful. Bates.
Amoretti, XXXVIII. Spenser.
An Amorous Dialogue between John and His Mistress. *Anonymous.*
The Angler's Reveille. Van Dyke.
The Animals' Christmas. Dacey.
Another Academy. Bukowski.
The Answered Prayer. Flint.
Arawata Bill. Glover.
As You Like It. Shakespeare.

At the Gate of Heaven. Byron.
At the Grave of Henry James. Auden.
Bad Luck Blues. Williamson.
Bagpipes. *Anonymous.*
A Ballad of a Mine. Skelton.
Ballad of the Women of Paris. Villon.
Barbara Frietchie. Whittier.
Base Words Are Uttered. Auden.
Be with Me, Lord. Macdonald.
A Bell in the Orthodox Steeple. Waltner.
Bellerophon: There Are No Gods. Euripides.
Blind Adolphus. McCabe.
Blooming Nelly. Burns.
Bottom's Dream. Dow.
Buffalo Boy. *Anonymous.*
Butterfly. Smith.
Caelica, XIX. Greville.
The Camels Have Come. *Anonymous.*
The Canterbury Tales: The Merchant's Tale. Chaucer.
Canticle for Xmas Eve. Wagoner.
Car Wash. Livingston.
Carol. *Anonymous.*
Cell Song. Knight.
Chantey of Notorious Bibbers. Robinson.
Character of the Happy Warrior. Wordsworth.
Charlie Piecan. *Anonymous.*
Child Poem. West.
The Children. Dickinson.
The Christian's "Good-Night". Doudney.
Christmas. Mother Goose.
Christmas Carol. Newell.
Christmas Letter Home. Fraser.
Civilization. Yuan Chen.
Clancy. Wagoner.
Cockroach. Hoberman.
Cold's the Wind. Dekker.
Comanche. Clark.
The Comparison. Carew.
Compensation. Jeffers.
Congal: Simile. Ferguson.
Congratulations: Two Versions. Sappho.
Conversations from Childhood: The Victrola. Langland.
The Cowboy. *Anonymous.*
Credo (excerpt). Gilder.
The Cruel Mother (P version). *Anonymous.*
The Cuckoo and the Nightingale. Clanvowe.
The Daisies. Carman.
Daphne and Apollo. Prior.
Dawn. *Anonymous.*
The Day the Tide. Booth.
Dead Marine. Coxe.
Dead Snake. Smith.
Death. Vaughan.
Dedication of the Chronicles of England and France. Fabyan.
Dedicatory Sonnet to S. T. Coleridge. Coleridge.
Die Heimkehr (excerpt). Heine.
The Disabled Debauchee. Rochester.

Disintegration. Shelton.
The Divine Office of the Kitchen. Hallack.
Don Juan. Byron.
The Donkey. *Anonymous.*
The Door. Davies.
Dream Song. *Anonymous.*
Echo. Weston.
Elegy. Ignatow.
Elegy. Smith.
L'Envoy: To His Book. Skelton.
Epigram. Du Guillet.
Epigram: "A fool much bit by fleas put out the light." Lovelace.
Epigram: "He drank strong waters and his speech was coarse." Kipling.
Epistle to a Lady: Of the Characters of Women. Pope.
Epitaph. Chiabrera.
Epitaph on Mistress Mary Draper. Cotton.
An Essay on Man. Pope.
Eternal Goodness. Whittier.
The Eumenides at Home (parody). Agate.
An Excelente Balade of Charitie. Chatterton.
The Excursion. Wordsworth.
The Exequy. Dobbs.
Fables: The Shepherd and the Philosopher. Gay.
A Farewell. Russell.
The Father. O'Grady.
Fifteenth Raga/for Bela Lugosi. Meltzer.
The Fifties. Sadoff.
Fine Fish to Net. *Anonymous.*
The Fledgling Bard and the Poetry Society. Part I (excerpt). Margetson.
Flight. Howes.
For Just Men Light Is Sown. Wigglesworth.
For My Wife. Symons.
Fortitude. Eeinmar von Zweter.
Four Wise Men on Edward II's Reign. *Anonymous.*
The Fox at the Point of Death. Gay.
The Galloping Cat. Smith.
The General Public. Benét.
Getting Experience. Williams.
Gingilee. Halpern.
The Girl Who Learned to Sing in Crow. Mariani.
Give Me That Old Time Religion. *Anonymous.*
Glee–The Ghosts. Peacock.
Good and Clever. Wordsworth.
Good News Bad News. Abbott.
Good-Night. Benedict.
Good Night. Pierce.
Good-Night. Shelley.
Good-Night. Thomas.
A Good Thanksgiving. Robinson.
The Greek Athlete. Euripides.
The Grip. Kennelly.
A Grouchy Good Night to the Academic Year. Pauker.

Hazardous Occupations. Sandburg.
Hear, Hear, O Ye Nations. Hosmer.
Heaven. *Anonymous.*
Henry VIII. Farjeon.
Here Have I Dwelt. *Anonymous.*
Hillside. Craig.
His Presence. Schulz.
Hope Evermore and Believe. Clough.
How They Brought the Good News From Ghent to Aix. Browning.
How to Change the U.S.A. Edwards.
I Heard the Bells on Christmas Day. Longfellow.
I Know Something Good About You. Shimon.
I Saw a Jolly Hunter. Causley.
The Ides of March. Fuller.
Image in the Mirror. Kenner.
The Imagination of Necessity. Codrescu.
In Memoriam A.H.H., XX. Tennyson.
In Praise of Beverly. Orlen.
In the Coach: Conjergal Rights. Brown.
In the Orchard. Stuart.
Inscription for an Old Bed. Morris.
Interlude. Landor.
Jackson. *Anonymous.*
Jackson (with music). *Anonymous.*
The Joys of Heaven. Thomas a Kempis.
Jubilate. Arnold.
July. Johnson.
Kindness. *Anonymous.*
Last Song. Guthrie.
Life! I Know Not What Thou Art. Barbauld.
Like a Mourningless Child. Patchen.
Limerick: "There was a young fellow named Sydney." Marquis.
Little Bell. Westwood.
Little Jack Horner. Mother Goose.
The Lonely Man. Jarrell.
Long Summer. Lee.
Lord Barrenstock. Smith.
Lord Maxwell's Last Goodnight. *Anonymous.*
Love. Herbert.
Love and Debt Alike Troublesom. Suckling.
Love and Wine. Shadwell.
Love Song. Be'er.
Mama Knows. Scott.
Maratea Porto: Saying Goodbye to the Vitolos. Hugo.
A Match with the Moon. Rossetti.
May, 1945. Porter.
Me and My Chauffeur Blues. Minnie.
Me and Samantha. Johnson, Jr.
The Meaning of a Letter. *Anonymous.*
Mending Wall. Frost.

Metamorphoses. Ovid (Publius Ovidius Naso).
Midnight. Stephens.
The Miner's Lament. *Anonymous.*
Miss Betty's Singing-Bird. Winstanley.
A Monumental Memorial of Marine Mercy &c. Steere.
Morning Dialogue. Aiken.
Morning from My Office Window. Wood.
Morning Prayer. Ezekiel.
Mother. Fyleman.
Mrs. Barks. Fyleman.
My Aim. Banks.
My Mother's Childhood. Spacks.
Nature. Very.
New World. Walcott.
Nigger's Leap, New England. Wright.
No No Blues. Baker.
A Nonsense Carol. *Anonymous.*
Notes on the Post-Industrial Revolution. Morin.
Nymphidia. Drayton.
Of Jolly Good Ale and Old. Stevenson.
Of One Who Seemed to Have Failed. Mitchell.
Oh send to me an apple that hasn't any kernel. *Anonymous.*
An Old Cat's Confession. Cranch.
Old Christmas. Howitt.
Old Men and Old Women Going Home on the Street Car. Moore.
On a Calm Summer's Night. Nicholson.
On a Gentleman Marrying His Cook. Ellis.
On Clergymen Preaching Politics. Byrom.
On Dwelling. Graves.
On Earth. Farrokhzad.
On Our Crucified Lord, Naked and Bloody. Crashaw.
On the Train. McAlpine.
Oracle: Iwori Wotura. *Anonymous.*
An Oriental Apologue. Lowell.
Out of the Earth. Davies.
The Oyster. Ponge.
Palabras Carinosas. Aldrich.
Palm Sunday. *Anonymous.*
A Panegyric to Sir Lewis Pemberton. Herrick.
Parts. Landau.
The Pass of Kirkstone. Wordsworth.
A Pastoral Courtship (excerpt). Randolph.
Patience for My Device. Wyatt.
Perpetual Christmas. Field.
Picturesque; a Fragment. Aiken.
Pneumonia Blues. Jefferson.
Poem against the British. Bly.
Poem for Unwed Mothers. Giovanni.
Porson on His Majesty's Government. Porson.
A Prayer. Sill.

Prayer in a Country Church. Van Dusen.
Prologue to a Translation. Trevisa.
Prologue to Love Triumphant. Dryden.
The Prophet. Gibran.
Proverbial Advice on Marriage. *Anonymous.*
Queen Mab. Hood.
The Renegade Wants Words. Welch.
Request for Requiems. Hughes.
Rev. Homer Wilbur's "Festina Lente." Lowell.
Revenue Man Blues. Patton.
Riddle: "Promotion lately was bestow'd." *Anonymous.*
Riddle: "There were three sisters in a hall." *Anonymous.*
Robert Barnes, Fellow Fine. *Anonymous.*
Robin Hood. *Anonymous.*
Robin Hood and the Prince of Aragon. *Anonymous.*
The Rock. Eliot.
Rondeau after a Transatlantic Telephone Call. Hacker.
A Round Song. McMaster.
Rydal. Coleridge.
The Sadness of Things for Sappho's Sickness. Herrick.
Say Well and Do Well. *Anonymous.*
Scorned. Smith.
The Sea-Gull. *Anonymous.*
The Shepherd and the Shepherdess. *Anonymous.*
Sing, Sing for Christmas. Egar.
Sir Marmaduke's Musings. Tilton.
Sir Patrick Spens. *Anonymous.*
Sisters. Lowell.
Smothered Fires. Johnson.
Snatches: "Here I was and here I drank." *Anonymous.*
So We've Come at Last to Freud. Walker.
Song: Stop All the Clocks. Auden.
Song Under Shadow. Benet.
Sonnet: He Compares All Things with His Lady, and Finds Them Wanting. Cavalcanti.
Sonnet: "If chaste and pure devotion of my youth." Drayton.
Sonnet: Of Virtue. San Geminiano.
Sonnets, XXXVI: "Let me confess that we two must be twain." Shakespeare.
Souster. Fraser.
Sowing. Thomas.
St. Simon and St. Jude's Day. Alexander.
Starlings. Jensen.
Stocking Feet Blues. Jefferson.
The Stones. Plath.
Street. Oppen.
Streets. Goldring.
A Study in Aesthetics (parody). Peters.

The Sun Was Slumbering in the West. Hood.
The Swallow. Cowley.
"Sweet are the thoughts where hope persuadeth hap." Ralegh.
Talking Blues. *Anonymous.*
Temper. Fyleman.
Things That Endure. Olson.
Time's Dedication. Schwartz.
To Cupid. Drayton.
To His Friend, Promising That Though Her Beauty Fade... Turberville.
To Mistress Isabel Pennell. Skelton.
To The Magpie. *Anonymous.*
Together. Sassoon.
A Translation from Walter von der Vogelweide. Synge.
Trust and Obedience. *Anonymous.*
Trying. Nathan.
Up the Mountain to Pick Mawu. *Anonymous.*
Villon's Good-night. Henley.
The Visitor. Bogin.
The Wail of Archy (excerpt). Marquis.
Washing and Dressing. Taylor.
Washington Cathedral. Shapiro.
Waspish. Frost.
A Week of Birthdays. Mother Goose.
Were I in Trouble. Frost.
What I Live For. Banks.
What the Earth Asked Me. Wright.
When. Russell.
When Death Came April Twelve 1945. Sandburg.
When I was a good and quick little girl. *Anonymous.*
When Things Go Wrong. *Anonymous.*
Where I'll Be Good. Ryan.
The Winds. Tusser.
The Witch, V, i. Middleton.
With a Rod No Man Alive. Walther von der Vogelweide.
Witness to Death. Lattimore.
Wm. Brazier. Graves.
Women. *Anonymous.*
Wood-Song. Peabody.
Written after the Death of Charles Lamb (excerpt). Wordsworth.
Young. Sexton.

Good -by (e)
My Lulu (with music). *Anonymous.*
The Old Man and Jim. Riley.
The Three Fishers. Kingsley.
Whether or Not. Lawrence.

Goodbye
The Allegorical Figure of Brooklyn. Towle.
Angle of Vision. Bosworth.
At First I Was Given Centuries. Atwood.
Departing Words to a Son. Pack.
The Departure. Whittemore.
Der Brief, Den Du Geshrieben. Untermeyer.

Dirge Written for a Drama. Beddoes.
The Discovery of Tradition. Inada.
Elegy. Pushkin.
False Cadence. Berger.
First, Goodbye. Smith.
Fuller and Warren. Whitecotton.
The Ghost's Leavetaking. Plath.
Goodbye. De la Mare.
Goodbye. Santos.
I Resigned Myself to Being Here. Giorno.
In the Yellow Light of Brooklyn. Lee.
January. Coatsworth.
Jenny. Rossetti.
Last Impression of New York. Mason.
Leave Her, Johnny. *Anonymous.*
The Leaving of Liverpool. *Anonymous.*
Little Trotty Wagtail. Clare.
Look to the Leaf. *Anonymous.*
The Lost, Dancing. Field.
Mananitas (with music). *Anonymous.*
Morning from My Office Window. Wood.
Older Grown. Greenaway.
On Himself. Swift.
Poem: "Get your tongue." Kooser.
Random Generation of English Sentences; or, The Revenge of the Poets. Smith.
Seven Poems. Niedecker.
Snow. Coatsworth.
Some San Francisco Poems. Oppen.
Song for the New Year. Auden.
Song of Maelduin. Rolleston.
Stocking and Shirt. Reeves.
The Story We Know. Collins.
The Street. Soto.
Survivors. Marcus.
Sweet Is Childhood. Ingelow.
There Is No Word for Goodbye. Tallmountain.
Three Lyrics. Petronius Arbiter (Caius Petronius Arbiter).
The Universe Is Closed and Has REMs. Starbuck.
Untitled Poem. Dugan.
Vale. Ciardi.
Valentine. Summers.
Vision song (cheyenne). Henson.

Goodness
Birds and Fishes. Jeffers.
Caelica, LXXXVIII. Greville.
Incarnatio Est Maximum Donum Dei. Alabaster.
The Mole and the Eagle. Hale.
O Love, That Dost with Goodness Crown. Chadwick.
To Be Quicker... Lee.

Goose (Geese)
Barnacle Geese. Higham.

Bas-Relief. Sandburg.
The Boy and the Geese. Fiacc.
Clear After Rain. Tu Fu.
Elegy. Auslander.
Epigram: On Inclosures. *Anonymous.*
Epitaph on Dr. Keene. Gray.
The Fire. Scott.
The Goblin Goose (parody). *Anonymous.*
The Goose Girl. Roberts.
Intery, Mintery, Cutery Corn. Mother Goose.
Madrigal: "The silver swan." Gibbons.
My Pretty Little Miss. *Anonymous.*
A Panegyric on Geese. Mahony.
The Peacock "At Home'. Dorset.
Poem: "About the size of an old-style dollar bill." Bishop.
Precious Stones. Calverley.
Trooper and Maid, I. *Anonymous.*
The Upper Canadian. Reaney.
When Molly Smiles. *Anonymous.*
When the Rain Raineth. *Anonymous.*
Wild Geese. Hart-Smith.
The Wild Geese. Masefield.
Wild Strawberries. Graves.

Gospel
Cromwell, Our Chief of Men. Milton.
The Gospel According to You. *Anonymous.*
Living Bread. Sefton.
Sir Henry Clinton's Invitation to the Refugees. Freneau.
To Pledge or Not to Pledge. *Anonymous.*
To the Lord General Cromwell. Milton.
Your Own Version. Gilbert.

Government (s)
An Appointment. Yeats.
The Chilean Elegies: 5. The Interior. Wayman.
Colum-Cille's Farewell to Ireland. *Anonymous.*
Hurrah for Greer County. *Anonymous.*
The New Roof. Hopkinson.
A Poem Like a Grenade. Haines.
The Shoulder. Denby.
Ten Thousand Miles away. *Anonymous.*
Trinity Place. Sandburg.

Gown (s)
Autumn Morning at Cambridge. Cornford.
Blow away the Morning Dew. *Anonymous.*
The Child-Bride. Oates.
The Coolun. O'Dugan.
In Philistia. Carman.
Life. Reed.
The Masque of Balliol (excerpt). Beeching.
Mater Dei. Hinkson.
Toast to a Departing Duchess. Marot.
Tomorrow's Men. Johnson.

Grace
Abide, Good Men. *Anonymous.*
Admonition to Montgomerie. James I.
The Age of a Dream. Johnson.
Almighty! What Is Man? Ibn Gabirol.
American against Solitude. Dugan.
American Bandstand. Waters.
Amoretti, LVII. Spenser.
Angelic Guidance. Newman.
As Well as They Can. Hope.
Astrophel and Stella, LXXIII. Sidney.
The Attic Landscape. Melville.
Attraction. *Anonymous.*
Ballet. Hillman.
Basic Communication. Ferril.
Blessed Comforter Divine. Sigourney.
The Bog Lands. Byrne.
Break, Break, Break. Tennyson.
Britannia's Pastorals. Browne.
The British Church. Herbert.
Cape Ann: A View. Brinnin.
Casting All Your Care Upon Him. *Anonymous.*
Charlie Rutledge. *Anonymous.*
Christ 3: The Last Judgement. *Anonymous.*
Christian Ethics. Traherne.
The Cliff Rose. Fewster.
The Clock Tower. Thibaudeau.
A Cocker of Snooks. Gotlieb.
Compassion So Divine. Steele.
Complaint of the Common Weill of Scotland. Lyndsay.
Conductor Bradley. Whittier.
A Coney Island of the Mind. Ferlinghetti.
Confiteor. *Anonymous.*
Consecration. *Anonymous.*
Diana. Constable.
Do I Really Pray? Burton.
The Dreme: The Compleynt of the Comoun Weill of Scotland. Lindsay.
The Earl of Westmoreland. *Anonymous.*
Elegy Before Death. Millay.
England's Darling. *Anonymous.*
Enterprise. Ezekiel.
Epitaph. Di Rossi.
Epitaph on a Worthy Clergyman. Franklin.
Face to Face with Reality. Oxenham.
The Faerie Queene. Spenser.
Fair Maiden, Who Is This Bairn? *Anonymous.*
A Farewell to a Fondling. Churchyard.
Fillmore. *Anonymous.*
First Fight. Then Fiddle. Brooks.
For Hope. Crashaw.

Forcing a Way. *Anonymous.*
Fourth Sation. Colum.
The Gift of Gravity. Berry.
Good Frend. Doolittle.
Grace. Herbert.
The Happy Hen. Agee.
Harley Lyrics: Now fade the rose and lily-flower. *Anonymous.*
He Knows the Way. *Anonymous.*
He Praises His Wife When She Had Gone from Him. Flower.
The Heavens Declare Thy Glory, Lord! Watts.
Hitherto and Henceforth. Flint.
Hold the Fort. Bliss.
Homage. Kahn.
Hope of Our Hearts. Denny.
The House-Builders. Das.
Housewife's Letter: to Mary. Halley.
I Came to Jesus. White.
I Reckon When I Count at All. Dickinson.
I Shall Be Satisfied. Behemb.
Impenitentia Ultima. Dowson.
In a Desert Town. Stevenson.
In God's Eternity. Ballou I.
The Ineffable Dou. Smith.
Its Name Is Known. Kelleher.
January 1939. Thomas.
The Joyful Wisdom. Patmore.
Lais. Feinstein.
Last Days of Alice. Tate.
Less Nonsense. Herbert.
Little Mousgrove and the Lady Barnet. *Anonymous.*
Lord, I Am Thine. Davies.
Lord, Thou Hast Promised. Cox.
Love Is Life. Rolle.
Lucy Taking Birth. Scott.
Lullay, My Child. *Anonymous.*
LV. Berrigan.
M. Crashaws Answer for Hope. Crashaw.
Madrigal: "Is Love a boy?" Byrd.
Madrigal: "To be a whore, despite of grace." Cotton.
Meditations for July 25, 1666. Pain.
The Minute before Meeting. Hardy.
Montana Eclogue. Stafford.
Most Sovereign Lady. *Anonymous.*
Motherhood. Ludvigson.
My Creed. Gilder.
My Garden Is a Pleasant Place. Driscoll.
My Grace Is Sufficient for Thee. *Anonymous.*
Nantucket Whalers. Henderson.
The Nature of the Eagle. *Anonymous.*
The Need. Sassoon.
Never Admit the Pain. Gilmore.
A New Ballade of the Marigolde. *Anonymous.*
Night Clouds. McKeown.
No Accident. MacCaig.

Now Sleeps the Gorge. Campbell.
O Desolate Eves. Brennan.
O Jesus Christ, True Light of God. Ernst.
O Love, Thy Hair! Kamal ud-Din of Isfahan.
Of John Bunyans Life &c. James.
Of the Incomparable Treasure of the Scriptures. *Anonymous.*
Oh send to me an apple that hasn't any kernel. *Anonymous.*
Oh, Stop Being Thankful All Over the Place. Nash.
Olney Hymns. Cowper.
On Amaryllis A Tortoyse. Pickthall.
One Word More. Browning.
The Other Person's Place. Hover.
Our Times Are in His Hands. Freeze.
Passengers. Johnson.
Pastel: Masks and Faces. Symons.
The Peace of Wild Things. Berry.
The Peaceful Western Wind. Campion.
Per Ardua ad Astra. Oxenham.
Phyllis. Lodge.
Praise to Jesus! Ball.
Prayer. Guiterman.
A Prayer. Oxenham.
Prayer before Meat. Harsen.
Prayer for the Home (excerpt). Guest.
Pre-Existence. Hayne.
The Preacher's Wife. *Anonymous.*
Prevision. Murray.
The Pysidanthera. Bristol.
The Ride to the Lady. Cone.
Saint. Merilaas.
Satire. Marston.
Saviour, Who Thy Flock Art Feeding. Muhlenberg.
Shall I Be Silent? Herbert.
Shall Man, O God of Light. Dwight.
The Slave and the Iron Lace. Danner.
Slowly, Slowly Wisdom Gathers. Van Doren.
So Little and So Much. Oxenham.
Some Contemplations of the Poor, and Desolate State of the Church... Williams.
Song: "Love in her Eyes sits playing." Gay.
A Song of the Love of Jesus. Rolle.
Sonnet: "If ever Sorrow spoke from soul that loves." Constable.
Sonnets, XL: "Take all my loves my love, yea take them all." Shakespeare.
Sonnets to Miranda. Watson.
Spade Scharnweber. Welch.
St. Patrick's Hymn before Tara. Mangan.
Suite for Celery and Blind Date (parody). Dow.
Tamburlaine the Great. Marlowe.

Thou Art Coming to a King. Newton.
Thou Art, O God, the God of Might. Perkins.
To King James. Jonson.
To the Lord Love. "Field.
To the Mountains. Thoreau.
The Triumphs of Thy Conquering Power. Bathurst.
Upon Gryll. Herrick.
Upon the Image of Death. Southwell.
A Valediction. La Follette.
View Me, Lord, a Work of Thine. Campion.
The Vision. Burns.
The Vision of Piers Plowman. Langland.
Who Follows in His Train? Heber.
Willows. Langland.
A Wish. Garland.
Women Hoping for Rain. Tillinghast.
The World. Herbert.

Graces
Amoretti, LXXIV. Spenser.
Around the Child. Landor.
Caelica, XCIX. Greville.
The Good-Night or Blessing. Herrick.
Psalm XIII. Sidney.
Quick-Step. Creeley.
Verses on Sir Joshua Reynold's Painted Window at New College, Oxford. Warton, Jr..
Written in My Lady Speke's Singing-Book. Waller.

Gracious
Alcestis. Euripides.
Hamlet. Shakespeare.
The History of the Flood. Heath-Stubbs.
The Poplars. Garrison.
Prayer before Sleep. Lucas.
Troopship in the Tropics. Lewis.

Grail
The Five Feet. Sanders.
The Holy Grail: The Book of Gawain (excerpt). Spicer.

Grain (s)
The Beautiful Lawn Sprinkler. Nemerov.
Calypso. Kell.
Charm for Unfruitful Land. *Anonymous.*
Children of Light. Lowell.
Daily Wages. Pritam.
Dawn. "Rachel" (Rachel Blumstein).
The Farmer. Fullerton.
The Farmer. Herbert.
Georgiques Chretiennes (excerpt). Jammes.
Glanmore Sonnets. Heaney.
Happy Are Those Who Have Died. Peguy.
Hmmmm, 14. Scalapino.
A Hopi Prayer. Conrard.
Knowing. Coghill.
Mary, Queen of Scots. Bell.
Not Like a Cypress. Amichai.
Old Women beside a Church. Wilson.
Recollection. Aldrich.
Ripe Grain. Goodale.
The Talmud Student. Bialik.
The Untended Field. Hillyer.

The White and the Black. Khaketla.

Grammar
An Excellent New Ballad Giving a True Account of the Birth... Sackville.
Grammar Commences with a 5-line Curse. Palladas.
One Word More. Browning.
Perspective He Would Mutter Going to Bed. Gilbert.

Grand
Burial of the Spirit. Hughes.
The Climate of Thought. Graves.
Ho! Westward Ho!. Dodge.
Louisburg. *Anonymous.*
Mary's a Grand Old Name. Cohan.
Mise en Scene. Fitzgerald.
The Tragedy of Pompey the Great (excerpt). Masefield.

Grandchildren
Burning Mountain. Merwin.
The Caledonian Market. Plomer.
Future generation. NorthSun.
Kyoto: March. Snyder.
Parents. Meredith.
Scrapbooks. Giovanni.
Voice in the Blood. Bush.

Grandeur
Colorado. Fitzgerald.
Ezry. MacLeish.
Mount Vernon, the Home of Washington. Day.
Resignation: an Ode to the Journeymen Shoemakers (excerpt). Wolcot.
Samuel Hoar. Sanborn.
Sea-Hawk. Eberhart.
The Winter Shore. Wade.
You'd Take the Entire Universe to Bed with You. Baudelaire.

Grandfather
At Cooloolah. Wright.
Be a Monster. Fuller.
The Big Nasturtiums. Hale.
Bucolic Eclogues: Waking, Child, While You Slept. Anderson.
The Chosen–Kalgoorlie, 1894. Zwicky.
Freemon Hawthorne. Tolson.
Great-Granddad. *Anonymous.*
I've Got a New Book from My Grandfather Hyde. Jackson.
Legacy II. Quintana.
My Grandfather Was a Quantum Physicist. Big Eagle.
Once Again. Bahe.
Peekaboo, I Almost See You. Nash.
Poor Grandpa. O'Brien.
Statesboro Blues. McTell.
To My Grandmother. Locker-Lampson
Walls. Allen.
West Paddocks. Davies.

Grandmother
For Mattie & Eternity. Plumpp.
Grandmother's Story of Bunker-Hill Battle. Holmes.

The Great Lakes Suite.
Reaney.
An Importer. Frost.
Measles in the Ark.
"Coolidge.
Nancy Cock. *Anonymous.*
Old Dubuque. Etter.
One Foot in the Door.
Elder.
Sermon in a Stocking.
Jewett.
Shooting Crows. Huddle.
Statesboro Blues. McTell.
To the Anxious Mother.
Malangatana.
We'll All Feel Gay. Scott.

Granite
The Carousel. Oden.
English Beach Memory: Mr.
Thuddock. Sitwell.
Epilogue. Mallalieu.
Erosion. Pratt.
Horse Graveyard. Lape.
Lament of Granite. Ross.
Of Difference Does It Make.
Paulin.
Old Song. Scott.
Watershed. Warren.
Who Shapes a Balustrade?
Aiken.

Grant (s)
Advice to the Old Beaux.
Sedley.
Blocking the Pass. Madge.
Can't. Spofford.
Fair Maiden, Who Is This
Bairn? *Anonymous.*
Honest Fame. Pope.
Old-Testament Gospel.
Cowper.
Poem Composed in Rogue
River Park... Wayman.
Prayer. Lord.
Prayer to Venus. Spenser.
Providence. Filicaja.
Shame. Rimbaud.
The Song of Sherman's Army.
Halpine.
The Surrender at
Appomattox. Melville.

Grape (s)
A Blackbird. Argentarius.
Bullocky. Wright.
Ears in the Turrets Hear.
Thomas.
Epigram: "I am provoked."
Strato.
The Fugitive. Meynell.
Midnight Dancer. Hughes.
Monody. Melville.
New England's Growth.
Bradford.
October. Frost.
An Ode to Master Endymion
Porter, upon His Brother's
Death. Herrick.
On Laying up Treasure.
Hiers.
Picking Grapes in an
Abandoned Vineyard.
Levis.
Seven. Parra.
The Shovel Man. Sandburg.
Song: "Rose and grape, pear
and bean." *Anonymous.*
Sun Moon Kelp Flower or
Goat. Gregg.
Two Gardens. De Bevoise.
The Vine and the Goat.
Aesop.

Grasp (ed) (s)
Ashboughs. Hopkins.

Everything That Acts Is
Actual. Levertov.
The Hillman Looks Back.
McOwan.
Resurgam. Burt.
Sicelides: Woman's
Inconstancy. Fletcher.
Sisyphus Angers the Gods of
Condescension. Murry.
Some Kind of Giant.
Pritchard.
Stinging Nettle. Head.
Thysia. Luce.

Grass
Appleton House (excerpt).
Marvell
The Artist. Koch.
Assembly Line. Stoutenburg.
August, 1914. Masefield.
The Auld House. Nairne.
The Auroras of Autumn.
Stevens.
The Ballad of the White
Horse. Chesterton.
Beginning. Rokeah.
Benediction. Hayes.
Bert Kessler. Masters.
The Best Dance.
Anonymous.
The Blades of Grass. Crane.
Blues for Benny Kid Paret.
Smith.
Breaking Green. Ondaatje.
Can-Opener. McAleavey.
Cezanne. Stein.
A Circus Garland. Field.
Civil War. Van Doren.
Clearing for the Plough.
Moll.
Dandelion. Conkling.
The Death of Crazy Horse.
Neihardt.
Les Demoiselles de Sauve.
Gray.
Descent for the Lost. Child.
Distance. Delius.
Dont Tell Bad Dreams Says
Tita's Mother. Simon.
Down a Woodland Way.
Howells.
A Dragonfly. Farjeon.
A Dream of Burial. Wright.
The Drivers of Boston.
Gross.
E Uni Que A The Hi A Tho,
Father. Hill.
Edom. *Anonymous.*
The Elephant I. *Anonymous.*
Envoy. MacLean.
Epitaph. Spencer.
Eveningsong 1. Wilson.
Exeunt. Wilbur.
Exit. MacDonald.
The Fancy. Benet.
Fear Has Cast Out Love.
Blunt.
The Final Green. Drake.
First Love. Lee.
For Arthur Gregor. Field.
From. Paulin.
Full Moon (fragment).
Sappho.
The Garden. Wilde.
Girl with the Green Skirt.
Naone.
Grass. Corn.
Grass. Sandburg.
The Grass on the Mountain.
Austin.
The Great South Land
(excerpt). Ingamells.

Haiku: "Once upon a time".
Issa.
Haufi. *Anonymous.*
Here, as in a Painting, Noon
Burns Yellow.
Gorbanyevskaya.
The Hero. Nicoll.
Les Hiboux. Baudelaire.
Highway Construction.
Chapin.
Home, Boys, Home.
Anonymous.
The House of Life. Rossetti.
The House of the Mouse.
Mitchell.
Imagine Grass. Skinner.
Intimations of Immortality
from Recollections of Early
Childhood. Wordsworth.
Irradiations. Fletcher.
It Moves Across. Mayer.
Jealous Adam. Manger.
Lament for Richard Rolston.
Sitwell.
Lawn-Mower. Baruch.
Lenox Christmas Eve 68.
Cornish.
Let the Wind Blow High or
Low. *Anonymous.*
Life's Common Duties.
Savage.
Little Birches. Newsome.
Long Feud. Untermeyer.
Manly Ferry. Philip.
Meadowsweet. Allingham.
Meditation in Winter. Mann.
Memorial. Goodman.
Midsummer. Hesse.
Mishka. Gray.
Monumentum Aere, Etc.
Pound.
The Moon. Ryuho.
The Moths. Merwin.
A Mountain Wind. Russell.
The Mower. *Anonymous.*
The Mower's Song. Marvell.
Mrs. Smith. Locker-
Lampson.
My Kate. Browning.
Not Iris in Her Pride. Peele.
Nothing Strange. Kryss.
Of bronze and blaze.
Dickinson.
On Hearing a Broadcast of
Ceremonies in Connection
with.... Wrafter.
The Other Side. Heaney.
The Penitent Palmer's Ode.
Greene.
Poisoned Lands. Montague.
Polo Match. Ciardi.
Prairie Wind. Scott.
Prayer. Mousley.
Prayer for the Little Daughter
between Death and Burial.
Scott.
Presentiment. Dickinson.
The Rattlesnake. Purdy.
A Removal from Terry Street.
Dunn.
Respice Finem. Proctor.
Roads Go Ever Ever On.
Tolkien.
A Rondeau of Remorse.
Johnson.
Rose Pogonias. Frost.
Rustic Childhood. Barnes.
The Sandpiper. Bynner.
Scythe Song. Lang.
The Serf's Secret. Moody.
The Shadow-Child. Monroe.
Sheep. Hoffenstein.

Smells. Worth.
Song: "If thou art sleeping."
Vicente.
Song-Maker. Endrezze-
Danielson.
Song: "Softly, O midnight
Hours!" De Vere.
A Song the Grass Sings.
Blanden.
Song: "The night is an ancient
sorceress." Frug.
The Songs of Bilitis. Louys.
Sonnets, XIV: "Now, winter's
dolorous days are o'er."
Irwin.
Spring. Still.
The Stone and the Blade of
Grass in the Warsaw
Ghetto. Scheinert.
Storm. Nagy.
The Stranger's Grave.
Lawless.
A Suit of Nettles. Reaney.
Summer. Page.
Sun Children. Silko.
The Tall Toms. Honig.
Tasmania. Smith.
Telephone. Shectman.
That Summer.
Hemschemeyer.
These Days. Jones.
These Locusts by Day.
Stevens.
Though Ye Suppose.
Skelton.
Three Women. Plath.
Time Out. Montague.
To Dorothy. Bell.
Tortoise Family Connections.
Lawrence.
A True Picture Restored.
Watkins.
Two Clouds. Raab.
Two Illustrations That the
World Is What You Make
of It. Stevens.
Voyage. Donaghy.
Waking. MacDonogh.
A Walk in the Country.
Kinnell.
Where Children Live. Nye.
Where Wards Are Weak.
Southwell.
Wherever Beauty Has Been
Quick in Clay. Masefield.
Winter Burn. Hill.
Winter Solstice Poem. Scott.
With Eyes at the Back of Our
Heads. Levertov.
Yeats' Tower. Watkins.

Grasshopper (s)
Canto XVII. Pound.
In the Palms of Ancient
Bodhisattvas. Tagliabue.
Persian Miniature. Smith.
Thin Little Leaves of Wood
Fern, Ribbed and Toothed.
Tuckerman.
Thinking of a Master.
Church.

Grateful
Actaeon. Clough.
The Australian Dream.
Campbell.
The clear water of the
imperial pond. Ise Tayu.
Cleitagoras. Leonidas.
Daily Bread. *Anonymous.*
Dancing School. Holden.
Day by Day the Manna Fell.
Conder.
An Evening Hymn. Ken.

An Excellent New Ballad,
Called The Brawn Bishop's
Complaint. Mainwaring.
Homage of War.
Williamson.
The Hottentot. Pringle.
Humphrey Hardfeature's
Descriptions of Cast-Iron
Inventions. *Anonymous.*
Life Owes Me Nothing.
Anonymous.
Little White Fox.
Rowbotham.
My Soul Thirsts for God.
Cowper.
O, Thou Eternal One!
Derzhavin.
Simon Lee the Old Huntsman.
Wordsworth.
Song: "Come, Celia, let's
agree at last." Sheffield.
Sonnet for the End of a
Sequence. Parker.
Thanksgiving Day. Bangs.
Thanksliving. Piety.
The Wife's Tale. Heaney.

Grave (s)
The Abbey. Eguren.
The African Desert (excerpt).
Tupper.
After Death in Arabia.
Arnold.
Ah Dearest Love, for How
Long. Mechtild of
Magdeburg.
Ain't No Grave Can Hold My
Body Down. *Anonymous.*
Alastor. Shelley.
Algernon Sidney's Farewell.
Anonymous.
All's Well. Kimball.
All Souls. Lawrence.
Am I Failing? Meredith.
Ambition. Willis.
Amen. Thomas.
The Angels at Hamburg.
Jarrell.
The Angels Sung a Carol.
Taylor.
The Angler's Wish. Walton.
Anna Playing in a Graveyard.
Gilman.
The Archer. Smith.
As He Came Near Death.
Fisher.
At Delos. Scott.
At the Zoo. Zangwill.
Autumn. Shelley.
Ballad: "My lady was found
mutilated." Cohen.
Ballade de Marguerite.
Anonymous.
The Banks of Newfoundland
(I). *Anonymous.*
The Battle-Field. Bryant.
Battle Song. Elliott.
The Bay Fight. Brownell.
The Belle of the Balkans.
Levy.
Bethinking Hymself of His
Ende. Vaux.
Between Here and Illinois.
Pomeroy.
Beyond the Potomac.
Hayne.
The Blindness of Samson.
Milton.
Bluebeard's Wife. Hine.
C. L. M. Masefield.
Call All. *Anonymous.*
Cargoes of the Radanites.
Potamkin.

Cassandra. Bogan.
The Cemetery Is. McGaffin.
The Choice. Tate.
The Cold Irish Earth.
Skinner.
The Conspiracy of Charles,
Duke of Byron. Chapman.
Correspondent. Bynner.
Country Cemetery. Bunner.
Country Greeting. Steele.
A Courtier's a Riddle.
Schomberg.
The Covenanter's Lament for
Bothwell Brigg. Praed.
The Cowboy's Lament (II).
Anonymous.
Cowper's Grave. Browning.
Credo. Tchernichovsky.
Crossing Alone the Nighted
Ferry. Housman.
Cui Bono? Carlyle.
Culbin Sands. Young.
Cymbeline. Shakespeare.
Daily Trials. Holmes.
Darlin' Corey. *Anonymous.*
The Dawning. Herbert.
Death. Clare.
Death and Love. Jonson.
A Death in the Streets.
Petaccia.
The Death of Robin Hood.
Anonymous.
The Death of Yeats. Barker.
Death's Jest Book. Beddoes.
Death Songs. *Anonymous.*
Decoration. Higginson.
Demos. Robinson.
The Deserted Village.
Goldsmith.
Desire. Arnold.
The Drummer Boy of
Waterloo. *Anonymous.*
The Dying Cowboy.
Anonymous.
A Dying Wife to Her
Husband. Ibn Ezra.
E. B. B. Thomson.
Edmund Davie.... Tompson.
Elegy: E. W. Sissman.
Elegy on Coleman.
Anonymous.
The Elfin Wife. Falstaff.
Emblems. Tate.
The Entertainment, or Porch-
Verse, at the Marriage....
Herrick.
The Epicure. Cowley.
Epitaph. Morton.
Epitaph. Wylie.
Epitaph on an Infant.
Crinagoras.
Epitaph on the Proofreader of
the Encyclopedia
Britannica. Morley.
An Evil World. *Anonymous.*
Existentialism. Frankenberg.
The Fair Beauty Bride.
Anonymous.
Fame. Rutsala.
Family Reunion. Miller.
Final Curtain (parody).
Woddis.
The Finding of the Tain.
Farren.
First Joy. Watkins.
Fixing to Die. White.
For All Things Black and
Beautiful. Rivers.
Fourth Song the Night Nurse
Sang. Duncan.
From the Harbor Hill.
Kobbe.

Go Bring Me Back My Blue-
Eyed Boy (with music).
Anonymous.
Gold. Hall.
Good-By, Mother.
Anonymous.
Grave at Cassino. Stern.
A Grave in Hollywood
Cemetery, Richmond.
Preston.
Had Sorrow Ever Fitter Place.
Daniel.
Haiku: "To write a blues
song." Knight.
Haitian Suite. Orr.
Hamatreya. Emerson.
Hamlet. Shakespeare.
Hang Me, O Hang Me, and
I'll Be Dead and Gone.
Anonymous.
The Happy Wanderer.
Addleshaw.
He Loves and He Rides
Away. Dobell.
Here Lies a Prisoner. Mew.
Herndon. Mitchell.
The Hill Wife. Frost.
Hiroshige. Perlberg.
His Son. Callimachus.
The Horse Thief. Benet.
The House Carpenter's Wife.
Anonymous.
How I came to be a graduate
student. Rose.
Hurry Me Nymphs. Darley.
I Know That My Redeemer
Liveth. Boyle.
I Once Knew a Man.
Clifton.
I remember... Jackson.
I Saw the Clouds. White.
I Sing America Now! Stuart.
I Went Down to the Depot
(with music). *Anonymous.*
If to Die–. Romilu.
In a Churchyard. Wilbur.
In an Old Orchard. Dufault.
In Brunton Town.
Anonymous.
In Rainy-Gloomy Weather.
Davies.
Infidelity. Untermeyer.
It's an Owercome Sooth for
Age an' Youth. Stevenson.
A Jacobite's Exile.
Swinburne.
John Filson. Venable.
John Wasson. Masters.
King Christian. Evald.
The Lady of the Manor.
Crabbe.
Lament for Sean MacDermott.
O'Sullivan.
The Last Furrow. Markham.
Lawyer Clark Blues. Estes.
A Lay of the Famine.
Anonymous.
Life. Wilcox.
Life and Death. Henley.
Life's a Game. *Anonymous.*
Like Flowers We Spring.
Anonymous.
Lilly Dale. Thompson.
Lines: "I followed once a fleet
and mighty serpent."
Beddoes.
Lines Written after the
Discovery ... of the Germ of
Yellow Fever. Ross.
The Lion over the Tomb of
Leonidas. *Anonymous.*
Living. Howells.

Lord Lovel (A vers.).
Anonymous.
The Lord of the Isles
(excerpt). Scott.
Love's Kiss. Hay.
Lovelye William.
Anonymous.
A Lover's Lament.
Anonymous.
The Lovers of Marchaid.
Pickthall.
Lucy. Wordsworth.
Lumumba's Grave. Hughes.
Lyrics. Agee.
A Machine Hand. Ashe.
The Man Who Dreamed of
Faeryland. Yeats.
Maximian Elegy V. Rexroth.
The May Sun Sheds an
Amber Light. Bryant.
Memorial Day. Gilder.
Methought I Saw the
Footsteps of a Throne.
Wordsworth.
Modern Love, XXIX.
Meredith.
Mohammed and Seid.
Morris.
Monumentum Aere, Etc.
Pound.
The Mother and Child.
Watkins.
The Mother's Prayer.
Shorter.
Mourning Pablo Neruda.
Bly.
Mumford. Porter.
Music's Duel. Crashaw.
My Burial Place. Jeffers.
My Kate. Browning.
My Political Faith.
Cameron.
Natural History. Warren.
New Year's. Reznikoff.
Ode to the Confederate Dead.
Tate.
Oh! Weep for Those. Byron.
The Old Swimmin'-Hole.
Riley.
The Olive. Housman.
On a Fly-Leaf of Burn's
Songs. Knowles.
On a Similar Occasion for the
Year 1792. Cowper.
On Button the Grave-Maker.
Anonymous.
On Knowing Nothing.
Smith.
One Foot in the Door.
Elder.
One Rose of Stone. Wilson.
Out of the corpse-warm
vestibule of heaven steps the
sun. Bachmann.
Over Their Graves.
Stockard.
The Past. Bryant.
Pentecost. Anthony ("Ai").
Picasso's Women. Cabral.
A Piece of Shrapnel. Ray.
Poet and Critic. Daniel.
A Poet's Epitaph.
Wordsworth.
The Portents. Marlowe.
Praise of Women. Palladas.
Prayer. Roethke.
Procrastination. Young.
The Prodigal Son. Robinson.
Quatrain. Sylvester.
The Radio under the Bed.
Whittemore.
Re-Act for Action. Lee.

Grave

Rearrange a Wife's Affection? Dickinson.
Regina Angelorum. Chesterton.
A Requiem. Thomson.
Rest. Blind.
Resurrection. Lanier.
The Retrieval System. Kumin.
The Road to Nijmegen. Birney.
The Sad Shepherd. Jonson.
The Sagging Bough (parody). Untermeyer.
Saint. Graves.
Scenes from Carnac. Arnold.
The Sea. Stoddard.
A Sea Boy on the Giddy Mast. Clare.
Sestina on Her Portrait. Nemerov.
Seven Sister Blues. Thompson.
Sheridan at Cedar Creek. Melville.
Short History of Twentieth-Century Scholarship. Wain.
A Shropshire Lad. Housman.
The Shudder. Hall.
Sick Love. Graves.
Silex Scintillans. Vaughan.
The Silly Old Man. Anonymous.
A Solemn Meditation. Pitter.
Soliloquy. Ledwidge.
Solitude. Grainger.
Sometime It May Be. Colton.
Song from Fragment of an Eccentric Drama. White.
Song from the Waters. Beddoes.
The Songs of Maximus, 2. Olson.
Sorrow. Daniel.
The Spider. Gould.
Spring. Timrod.
The Story of Life. Saxe.
Struggle. Lanier.
Summer. Clare.
Summer Rain. Lee.
The Supper after the Last. Kinnell.
Tarpauling Jacket. Anonymous.
Thekla's Song. Schiller.
There is a shame of nobleness. Dickinson.
There Was a Boy. Wordsworth.
They're Moving Father's Grave. Anonymous.
They're Shifting Father's Grave. Anonymous.
This Crosse-Tree Here. Herrick.
Three Poems on Morris Graves' Paintings. Logan.
Thysia. Luce.
The Tin-Whistle Player. Colum.
To a Print of Queen Victoria. Baxter.
To a Young Girl. Rosenmann-Taub.
To a Young Lady. Wordsworth.
To Blossoms. Herrick.
To His Mistresse on Her Scorne. Beedome.

To the Earl of Warwick. Tickell.
To Two Bereaved. Ashe.
Tom O'Roughley. Yeats.
The Tornado. De Kay.
Tropical Towns. Selva.
Twelfth Night. Shakespeare.
Twins. Graves.
Two Days. Henley.
Two Little Boys. Anonymous.
The Unconstant Lover. Anonymous.
Under the Violets. Young.
United States. Keble.
Upon the Holy Sepulchre. Crashaw.
V.D. Clinic. Stoutenburg.
Variations on a Theme. Williams.
Verdancy. Anonymous.
Veteran Sirens. Robinson.
The Victories of Love. Patmore.
Villkins and His Dinah. Anonymous.
Wake All the Dead. Davenant.
Weed Puller. Roethke.
The Week-End Indian. Endrezze-Probst.
The West-Country Damosel's Complaint. Anonymous.
Westland Row. Stephens.
When I Die. Johnson.
When the Day. Sessler.
Why Did They Dig Ma's Grave So Deep? Cooper.
The World Is Not a Fenced-Off Garden. Steinberg.
The World Needs. Anonymous.
Wreck on the C. and O.(Or) Death of Jack Hinton. Anonymous.
Wrestling Angels. Bottoms.
Yes, the Agency Can Handle That. Fearing.

Gravel

In Rainy-Gloomy Weather. Davies.
Ringed Plover by a Water's Edge. MacCaig.
The Scolding Wives Vindication. Anonymous.

Gravity

Apartments on First Avenue. MacDonald.
Capsule Philosophy. Lamport.
The Gift of Gravity. Berry.
Lake Chelan. Stafford.
A Prisoner Freed. Dutton.
Science as Art. Seidman.
Waiting. Skillman.

Gray (grey)

Aeneid. McAllister.
The Aged Woman to Her Sons. Deutsch.
The Amorous Worms' Meat. Petrarch (Francesco Petrarca).
The Angel. Blake.
Aux Carmelites. Hinkson.
The "Black' Country. Enright.
The Blue and the Gray. Finch.
By the River Eden. Raine.
The Captain of St. Kitts. May.
The Cat's Song. Anonymous.

Ceremonies. Stanford.
Changeful Beauty. Lang.
Childe Harold's Pilgrimage: Canto IV, XXIX. Byron.
The Cloud Factory. Haines.
A Colloquy of Silences. Heffernan.
Corner Boys. MacMahon.
The Country Mouse and the City Mouse. Sharpe.
The Dance of Gray Raccoon. Guiterman.
Daylights. Warren.
The Days. Garrison.
December. Irwin.
A Discussion of the Vicissitudes of History under a Pine Tree. Pollitt.
The Djanggawul Cycle, 18. Anonymous.
Dolor. Roethke.
England Reclaimed (excerpt). Sitwell.
Epigram: "Most inexplicable the wiles of boys I deem." Rhianus.
A Fable for Critics. Lowell.
Fame. Browning.
Felix Randal. Hopkins.
From Sorrow Sorrow Yet Is Born. Tennyson.
Gravel. Mariah.
Gray Days. Lawlor.
Gray Thrums. Bates.
The Grey Linnet. McCarroll.
His Statement of the Case. Morse.
Ichabod. Whittier.
Lee to the Rear. Thompson.
Leg-acy of a Blue Capricorn. Cunningham.
Life-Hook. Ibarbourou.
Looking Down on West Virginia. Dickson.
Man in the Street. Warren.
Mary and Gabriel. Brooke.
Matin Song. Field.
May. Rossetti.
The Merry Man of Paris. Mead.
Morgan's Country. Webb.
Mouse. Conkling.
Not Three–But One. Duff.
November. Harvey.
November. Tuckerman.
Oblation. Choyce.
Old. Anonymous.
The Old. Mosby.
The Old Gray Mare. Anonymous.
The Old Grey Wall. Carman.
The Oul' Grey Mare. Anonymous.
Rat Riddles. Sandburg.
The Rear Guard. Brown.
Rise, Lady Mistress, Rise! Field.
Roll On, Sad World! Tuckerman.
The Sampler. Field.
The Secret Song. Brown.
Separation. Arnold.
Serenade. De Vere.
Snow-Bound. Whittier.
Soft White. Harwood.
Song for Healing. Hill.
Sonnets. Tuckerman.
Stranded in My Ontario. Everson.
The Street. Pinsky.

There Once Was a Time. Anonymous.
Unbeliever. Dow.
The Virgin Sturgeon. Anonymous.
La Vita Nuova. Kees.
Water Color. Mooney.
Were-Wolf. Hawthorne.
When the Great Gray Ships Come in. Carryl.
Working Girls. Sandburg.

Graze

Buffalo. Eglington.
Harvest Time. Watermeyer.
Psalm of the Fruitful Field. Klein.
Songs of the Squatters, I. Lowe.

Grease (d)

A Dish for a Poet. Anonymous.
For the Union Dead. Lowell.
Oh, No! Dodge.
Pourquoi. Anonymous.
Something Has Fallen. Levine.
Tat for Tit. De la Mare.

Great (er) (est) (ness)

The Accursed. Baudelaire.
Action. Oppenheim.
All Things Bright and Beautiful. Alexander.
Arcadia. Sidney.
Behold the Meads. Poitiers.
Bussy d'Ambois. Chapman.
By Deputy. Adcock.
Caelica, LXXXI. Greville.
Caelica, XCII. Greville.
Cato's Address to His Troops in Lybia. Rowe.
Changes around the Bay. Palmer.
A Child's Evening Prayer. Coleridge.
The Chronicle of the Drum (excerpt). Thackeray.
The Coming of Arthur: Merlin's Riddling. Tennyson.
The Complaint, or Night Thoughts on Life, Death and Immortality. Young.
The Cowboy's Fate. Coburn.
The Days of the Unicorns. Webb.
Death's Apology. Mello.
The Deathless Ones. Wallis.
The Demon Speaks. Calderon de la Barca.
Don Juan. Byron.
The Feast-Time of the Year. Anonymous.
February 12, 1809. Burket.
Fiction and the Reading Public. Larkin.
The Flowering of the Rod. Doolittle.
Forgive, O Lord, My Little Jokes on Thee. Frost.
From Far away. Morris.
From the Dust. Dallman.
Grace to Be Said at the Supermarket. Nemerov.
Grain Elevator. Klein.
Great Fleas. Anonymous.
The Great Hunt. Sandburg.
A Hawthorne Garland: Caution. Fogle.
Hearing of the End of the War. Tillinghast.
Hebrew Script. Loewenthal.

The Heroic Age. Gilder.
Himself. Hoffman.
His Petition to Queen Anne of
 Denmark (1618). Ralegh.
History. Lange.
History of a Literary
 Movement. Nemerov.
Hope for Miracles. Wolfram
 von.
Hotels. Donnell.
How Big Was Alexander?
 Jones.
How We Became a Nation.
 Spofford.
Hunting with My Father.
 Absher.
Hymn to the Sea. Watson.
Hymns for the Amusement of
 Children. Smart.
I Live My Life. Rilke.
The Icehouse in Summer.
 Nemerov.
Improvisations: Light and
 Snow (excerpt). Aiken.
In the Local Museum. De la
 Mare.
The Inevitable. Bolton.
Inscription on the Flyleaf of a
 Bible. Abse.
Irony. Untermeyer.
The Jewish Woman.
 Kolmar.
Johannes Milton, Senex.
 Bridges.
Julius Caesar. Shakespeare.
Let America Be America
 Again. Hughes.
Let's Forget. Wagner.
Lilith: Adam to Lilith.
 Brennan.
Lines. Brooke.
Love and Jealousy. Walsh.
Man and Bat. Lawrence.
The Man Watching. Rilke.
Mars and Venus. Greene.
A May Day Carol.
 Anonymous.
Meditations in Time of Civil
 War. Yeats.
Moonrise. Doolittle.
Mountain Song. Monroe.
Mountains Are Steadfast but
 the Mountain Streams.
 Hwang Chin-i.
Mouths. Dudek.
The Mufadaliyat: Gone Is
 Youth. Salamah.
Mwilu/ or Poem for the
 Living. Lee.
My Country, Right! Clark.
The National Ode. Taylor.
National Presage. Ingram.
Near Dover, September, 1802.
 Wordsworth.
Night Quarters. Brownell.
On a Picture of Lincoln.
 Cheney.
On Don Surly. Jonson.
On Fleas. De Morgan.
On the Extinction of the
 Venetian Republic.
 Wordsworth.
The Passionate Reader to His
 Poet. Le Gallienne.
The Pigs for Circe in May.
 Kyger.
Pleasure Reconciled to Vertue:
 A Masque. Jonson.
The Poet Laments the Coming
 of Old Age. Sitwell.
Polyolbion. Drayton.
Precious Stones. Calverley.

Riddle: "I never speak a
 word." Austin.
The Shanty-Man's Life (with
 music). Anonymous.
So Long as Time & Space Are
 the Stars. Silverton.
Spirit of Sadness. Le
 Gallienne.
St. Simon and St. Jude's Day.
 Alexander.
The Star System. Wilbur.
Starvation Peak Evening.
 O'Neil.
Summing Up in Italy.
 Browning.
The Teacher to Heloise (After
 Waddell). Burke.
Th Child's Purchase.
 Patmore.
Then Sings My Soul.
 Mariani.
The Thought Eternal.
 Goethe.
To a Bird after a Storm.
 Vaughan.
To My Native Land.
 Mangan.
To Spencer. Turberville.
To the Countesee of Bedford.
 Donne.
Today Is a Day of Great Joy.
 Cruz.
The Torrent. Robinson.
True Riches. Martin.
Trust the Great Artist.
 Clark.
A Turkish Legend. Aldrich.
The Unknown City. Roberts.
Unmanifest Destiny. Hovey.
Upon the Downs. Etherege.
Variations on Southern
 Themes. Justice.
Voyagers. Van Dyke.
West of Chicago. Dimoff.
Whiskey Bill,–A Fragment.
 Anonymous.
Who Are They? Anonymous.
The World Is a Bundle of
 Hay. Byron.
The World Is with Me Just
 Enough. Abrams.
You Can Get Despondent.
 Careme.

Gree (ce) (k) (ks)
An A B C for Grown
 Gentlemen. Bouflers.
Across to the Peloponnese.
 Welch.
Another Island Groupage.
 Elmslie
The Attic Landscape.
 Melville.
The Critic's Rules. Lloyd.
Cynisca. Anonymous.
A Dream of Judgement.
 Dunn.
A Fable for Critics. Lowell.
The Iliad. Homer.
An Invocation. Cory.
Keats. Reese.
Laocoon. Hall.
Ode I. To Fancy. Warton.
Of Ballad-Singers. Gay.
Sleet Storm on the Merritt
 Parkway. Bly.
Western Ways. Lattimore.

Greed (y)
The 1913 Massacre. Guthrie.
At the Lincoln Tomb.
 Bryant.
Come, Let's to Bed.
 Anonymous.

Confined Love. Donne.
Das Schloss. Kirstein.
Epigram: "Diodorus is nice..."
 Meleager.
Fashion. Cambridge.
It Is Not Too Late. Trent.
Lullaby for Ann-Lucian.
 Forbes.
Naseby: Late Autumn.
 Dowling.
Robin Redbreast's Testament.
 Anonymous.
The Sweet Tooth. Pyle.
To His Book. Herrick.
Variation on the Gothic
 Spiral. Merwin.
Wild Horse Jerry's Story.
 Howard.
Winter. Mair.

Green
100 Year Old Woman at
 Christmas Dinner. Style.
8-Ball at the Twilite. Baker.
About Marriage. Levertov.
After Aughrim. Geoghegan.
After kicking on the swing.
 Anonymous.
All a Green Willow Is My
 Garland. Heywood.
All, All A-lonely.
 Anonymous.
All Songs. Page.
Aloha. Griffith.
Animal Fair. Booth.
April. Pastan.
At Roblin Lake. Purdy.
Aubade: Lake Erie. Merton.
August Afternoon. Edey.
Awakening. Sangster.
Bare Almond-Trees.
 Lawrence.
Ben Alder 1963-1977.
 Hannigan.
Between Walls. Williams.
The Bitch-Kitty. Williams.
Brindabella. Stewart.
The Brothers. Muir.
Burning Off. Dutton.
The Bush Aboon Traquair.
 Shairp.
Bushes and Briars.
 Anonymous.
The Candle A Saint.
 Stevens.
Captivity. Rogers.
The Cauliflower. Haines.
Causeway. Block.
The Cell. Rostrevor.
The Churchyard. Buchanan.
Circa 1814. Staudt.
The Clavichord. Sarton.
Cloud Country. Merrill.
Colin's Complaint. Rowe.
Come Green Again. Scott.
The Connaught Rangers.
 Letts.
Corn. Lanier.
The Countryman's Return.
 Thomas.
Credo. Cohen.
The Creek. Ross.
Croesus in Autumn. Warren.
The Cruel Mother.
 Anonymous.
December Day, Hoy Sound.
 Brown.
Decoration Day. Sinclair.
Dollar Bill. Nims.
A Dream. Kinney
The Dustman. Weatherly.
Dying: An Introduction.
 Sissman.

Easter Thought. Cox.
The Echoing Green. Blake.
Elegy in Six Sonnets.
 Tuckerman.
Encounter in the Cage
 Country. Dickey.
England Reclaimed (excerpt).
 Sitwell.
Examiner. Scott.
The Exquisite Sonnet.
 Squire.
The Faerie Queene. Spenser.
Fair and Fair. Peele.
Farmers. Roberts.
The Fear of Dying. Holmes.
First Love. Gullans.
Fishing. Wordsworth.
The Five Voyages of Arnor.
 Brown.
Footnote. Delius.
Former Barn Lot. Van
 Doren.
The Forsaken Bride.
 Anonymous.
Freighting from Wilcox to
 Globe. Anonymous.
From an Irish-Latin
 Macaronic. Taylor.
From the Window of the
 Beverly Wilshire Hotel.
 McClure.
Girl with the Green Skirt.
 Naone.
Glenaradale. Smith.
Grass. Webster.
Grass, Grass. Bowering.
Green. Barnes.
The Green-Gown.
 Anonymous.
Green Grass and Sea.
 Woodcock.
The Green Grass Growing All
 Around. Anonymous.
Green Grow the Lilacs.
 Anonymous.
The Green Horse. Ramke.
The Green Leaves All Turn
 Yellow. Kenney.
The Green Little Shamrock of
 Ireland. Cherry.
Green Revolutions. Guest.
Green Things Growing.
 Craik.
The Green Tree. Reiss.
Green Valley. Johnson.
The Grey Linnet.
 McCarroll.
Growing in Grace. Clemo.
Halifax Station. Anonymous.
Hampstead: The Horse
 Chestnut Trees. Gunn.
The Harper of Chao. Po
 Chu-i.
Here and There.
 Stallworthy.
Here Is the Place Where
 Loveliness Keeps House.
 Cawein.
The History of the Human
 Body.... Nauen.
The Holly and the Ivy.
 Anonymous.
Home, Dearie, Home.
 Anonymous.
Hope. Carmichael.
Hypocrite Swift. Bogan.
I Am Like a Rose.
 Lawrence.
I Had a Duck. Stodart-
 Walker.
In Orbit (parody). Taylor.

In the Cool of the Evening.
  Noyes.
In Vinculis: The Deeds That
  Might Have Been. Blunt.
The Introduction. MacNeice.
Inventory–to 100th Street.
  Lima.
Ireland, Ireland. Newbolt.
Irrigation. Tichy.
Island of Mull. Anonymous.
The Ivy Green. Dickens.
Jake Hates All the Girls.
  Cummings.
Jason and Medea. Gower.
Jefferson Valley. Hollander.
John Donne's Statue.
  Bishop.
June Bracken and Heather.
  Tennyson.
The Keeper. Anonymous.
Killing the Rooster. Nelms.
Lady Isabel and the Elf
  Knight (Pretty Polly).
  Anonymous.
Last Night. Ignatow.
Learning Destiny. Bosman.
Leg-acy of a Blue Capricorn.
  Cunningham.
Let Us Gather at the River.
  Piercy.
Letter to a Substitute Teacher.
  Gildner.
Lightly Like Music Running.
  Garrigue.
The Little Green Orchard.
  De La Mare.
A little madness in the spring.
  Dickinson.
Locations. Harrison.
London. Rowland.
Love and Discipline.
  Vaughan.
Love, Meet Me in the Green
  Glen. Clare.
Lucy. Wordsworth.
Malvern Hill. Melville.
May. Spenser.
Memorial. Goodman.
Merry-Go-Round. Jenkins.
Mezzo Cammin. Moffett.
Michael. Wordsworth.
Mine Host of "The Golden
  Apple." Westwood.
The Moment. Rowbotham.
My Fair Lady. Anonymous.
My Friend (parody).
  Appleman.
My Land Is Fair for Any
  Eyes to See. Stuart.
My Valentine. Stevenson.
Natural History. Howard.
The Netherlands. Coleridge.
New Season. Levine.
Nightmare, with Angels.
  Benét.
October Journey. Walker.
Ode on the Departing Year.
  Coleridge.
Oh, Breathe Not His Name.
  Moore.
Oh! Where Do Fairies Hide
  Their Heads? Bayly.
Ohioan Pastoral. Wright.
On the Death of a Young and
  Favorite Slave. Martial
  (Marcus Valerius Martialis).
Orient Wheat. Rich.
The Pentland Hills.
  Anonymous.
Peter Rabbit. McPherson.
Poem for Thel–the Very Tops
  of Trees. Major.

Prayer. Moss.
The Pressures. Jones.
The Professionals. Grigson.
Quarry/Rock. Mariah.
The Rainbow. Hopkins.
Rat Riddles. Sandburg.
Regretful Thoughts, I. Yu
  Hsuan-chi.
Sadie's Playhouse. Danner.
The Sigh of Silence. Keats.
Silex Scintillans. Vaughan.
Sioux Indians. Anonymous.
The Skinny Girl. Hebert.
Smells. Worth.
Song: "Afternoon cooking in
  the fall sun." Hass.
Song from Fragment of an
  Eccentric Drama. White.
Sonnet–To Silence. Poe.
Sonnets, LXIII: "Against my
  Love shall be, as I am
  now." Shakespeare.
Speaking of Television: Robin
  Hood. McGinley.
Spring Oak. Kinnell.
Starlings. MacCaig.
Storm. Doolittle.
The Story of Two Gentlemen
  and the Gardener. Logue.
Summer. Page.
The Swimming Lesson.
  Hershon.
Tailor of Bicester.
  Anonymous.
Thaw. Untermeyer.
These Days. Jones.
The Thousand and One
  Nights: Love. Anonymous.
Three Ballate. Poliziano.
Three Women. Plath.
To "Philomela." Colman.
To the Lady Portrayed by
  Margaret Dumont.
  Hollander.
Translations from the Chinese.
  Morley.
The Tray. Cole.
Trees in the Garden.
  Lawrence.
Tune: Crimson Lips Adorned.
  Li Ching-chao.
The Unquiet Grave.
  Anonymous.
Upon Wedlock, and Death of
  Children. Taylor.
Walking on the Green Grass.
  Anonymous.
Was Worm. Swenson.
Washing Day. Anonymous.
The Wearin' o' the Green.
  Anonymous.
Weeds. Stanford.
The Whaleman's Song.
  Anonymous.
Whales. Bates.
What Is the Opposite of a
  Prince? Wilbur.
What's the Life of a Man?
  Anonymous.
When De Whale Get Strike.
  Anonymous.
When the Nightingale Sings.
  Anonymous.
Willows. Langland.
Winter Juniper. Langland.
With Me My Lover Makes.
  Day-Lewis.
Woodlands. Read.
Working against Time.
  Wagoner.
Working Girls. Sandburg.
Written in Prison. Clare.

Green-wood
The Birth of Robin Hood.
  Anonymous.
The Old Love. Hinkson.
The Rick of Green Wood.
  Dorn.
Robin Hood and Allen A
  Dale. Anonymous.
Robin Hood and the Curtal
  Friar. Anonymous.
Robin Hood and the Two
  Priests. Anonymous.
Robin Hood's Golden Prize.
  Anonymous.
Song for the Greenwood
  Fawn. Salomon.
Song Set by Robert Jones: "In
  Sherwood lived stout Robin
  Hood." Anonymous.
Three little children sitting in
  the sand. Anonymous.
Greenland
Cordial Advice. Anonymous.
Ghazals. Harrison.
Gudveig. Berry.
Greenwood
Beech and Oak. Peacock.
The Cambridge Songs
  (excerpt). Anonymous.
The Cruel Mother (C vers.).
  Anonymous.
The Death of Robin Hood.
  Field.
Erlinton (A version).
  Anonymous.
I walk in loneliness through
  the greenwood.
  Anonymous.
John Thomson and the Turk
  (A version). Anonymous.
Johnny Appleseed. Venable.
Robin and Gandelyn.
  Anonymous.
The Scribe. Anonymous.
Song for the Greenwood
  Fawn. Salomon.
Song: "For the tender beech
  and the sapling oak."
  Peacock.
Under the Greenwood Tree.
  Anonymous.
The Unquiet Grave.
  Anonymous.
The Wife from Fairyland.
  Le Gallienne.
William and Phyllis.
  Anonymous.
Greet (ed) (ing) (s)
Artificial Teeth. Brown.
The Bonnie Blue Flag.
  Ketchum.
The Cats. Kees.
The Chateau Hardware.
  Ashbery.
Cousins. Cullen.
The Cranes of Ibycus.
  Lazarus.
The Drunken Stones of
  Prague. Scheinert.
Endymion. Keats.
Fable. Opperman.
God's Pity. Driscoll.
A Good Start. Moffi.
Home-Coming. Hume.
The Idiot. Naude.
Last Words. Droste-
  Hulshoff.
Life Owes Me Nothing.
  Anonymous.
Of Tact. Guiterman.
Old People Working (Garden,
  Car). Brooks.

An Old Sweetheart of Mine.
  Riley.
Once More. Farrokhzad.
Pure Death. Graves.
Reconsecration. Gould.
Return. Deane.
The Serf's Secret. Moody.
The Stained Glass Man.
  Macdonald.
A Talisman. Moore.
Thou Beautiful Sabbath.
  Anonymous.
Through Fire in Mobile Bay.
  Anonymous.
To—. Nichols.
To My Child. Sutzkever.
To the Returning Brave.
  Johnson.
Tokyo West. Corn.
An Upper Room. Kelleher.
A Visit Home. Glazer.
When We Two Parted.
  Byron.
The White Dream. Doney.
The White-Haired Man.
  Sarton.

Grief (s) (grieve)
The Accountings.
  Goldbarth.
Adelaide Neilson. Winter.
The Aeneid. Virgil (Publius
  Vergilius Maro).
After Sunset. Conkling.
Ah Woe Is Me. Propertius.
Ain't Gonna Grieve My Lord
  No More. Anonymous.
Alarum. Koziol.
The Amish. Doreski.
L'Angelo. Irwin.
Animals That Stand in
  Dreams: The Panda.
  Elliott.
The Antiquary. Chapt. 10:
  Why Sit'st Thou by That
  Ruin'd Hall. Scott.
Ark Artefact. Macpherson.
As He Is. Auden.
At Dawn the Virgin Is Born...
  Lope de Vega Carpio.
Autumn's Mirth. Peck.
The Awful Mother. Griffin.
Baby's in Jail; the Animal
  Day Plays Alone. Ford.
Baby Sleeps. Hinds.
Bi-focal. Porter.
The Biggest Killing. Dorn.
Birds in the Wood.
  Anonymous.
The Birds of Paradise.
  Bishop.
The Blackbird Calls in Grief.
  Anonymous.
Blessed Art Thou, O Lord.
  Anonymous.
The Blessings of Surrender.
  Helphingtine.
Britannia's Pastorals.
  Browne.
Burr Oaks: The Attic.
  Eberhart.
By Night. Cleveland.
By the Potomac. Aldrich.
Caelica, LIV. Greville.
The Calling. Contardo.
Camouflage. Clampitt.
Charles Gustavus Anderson
  (I). Anonymous.
A Child in Prison. O
  Dalaigh.
Clear Eyes. De la Mare.
Cloak of Laughter. Cresson.

Come All Ye Fair and Tender Maidens. *Anonymous.*
Come from Thy Palace. Randolph.
Convicted (excerpt). Mills.
Corn-Woman Remembered. Volborth.
Cornfield. Cox.
Country of No Lack. Untermeyer.
The Crucifixion. Meyer.
The Curiosity-Shop. Redgrove.
The Dead Marten. Landor.
The Defence of Night. Michelangelo.
Dew. Maiden.
Electra. Williams.
Elegy Against a Latter Day. Smithman.
Elegy over a Tomb. Herbert of Cherbury.
Epitaphs of the War. Kipling.
Eve Am I, Great Adam's Wife. *Anonymous.*
Exit. MacDonald.
Exodus to Connacht. O Meallain.
The Family Cat. Fuller.
A Famished End to My Tale This Night. O Domhnaill.
Fare Ye Well, Lovely Nancy. *Anonymous.*
Fiddler's Green. Roberts.
Forza D'Agro. Denby.
A Funerall Song (Lamenting Syr Phillip Sidney). *Anonymous.*
Gluskap's Hound. Roberts.
Goll Mac Morna Parts from his Wife. *Anonymous.*
Great Grief Came over Me. Aleqaajik.
The Greenland Whale. *Anonymous.*
Grief. Berry.
Grief Plucked Me out of Sleep. King.
Holy Sonnets, VIII. Donne.
How I Was Her Kitchen-Boy. Grass.
How to Read Me. Landor.
Humaine Cares. Wanley.
The Huntress. Johnston.
If All the Skies. Van Dyke.
The Iliad. Homer.
In Guernsey. Swinburne.
In Harbour. Swinburne.
In Memory of Ernst Toller. Auden.
Invisible Landscape. Wright.
It Is the Sinners' Dust-Tongued Bell Claps Me to Churches. Thomas.
Jane, Jane. *Anonymous.*
Johnny Dyers. *Anonymous.*
Joy to the World. *Anonymous.*
King Henry VIII. Shakespeare.
The Ladybirds. Lucie-Smith.
Lenore. Poe.
Let Us Laugh. Shargel.
A Letter from Brooklyn. Walcott.
Like Those Sick Folks. Sidney.
Limerick: "There was an Old Man of the Dee." Lear.
The Linden Tree. Aist, Dietmar von.

Little Lover. Speyer.
Long Division: A Tribal History. Rose.
Love and Life. Lippmann.
Love in Exile (excerpt). Blind.
Maryland Resolves. *Anonymous.*
Mater Incognita. Benvenuta.
Memory. Browne.
Memory. Rossetti.
Menaphon. Greene.
Minnie and Her Dove. Turner.
Moan, Moan, Ye Dying Gales. Neele.
The Mother. Coleridge.
Mourning. Marvell.
Mully of Mountown (excerpt). King.
My White Book of Poems. "Rachel" (Rachel Blumstein).
Nine Bean-Rows on the Moon. Purdy.
The Ninth Symphony of Beethoven Understood at Last as a Sexual Message. Rich.
Nova. Jeffers.
Nuit Blanche. Hoskins.
Of Death. Pembroke.
Old Woman. Pastan.
On a Gentlewoman Walking in the Snowe. Strode.
On a Picture by J. M. Wright, Esq. Southey.
On a Pretty Madwoman. Prior.
On My Late Dear Wife. Richardson.
On One Who Died Discovering Her Kindness. Sheffield.
On the Death of Mr. William Hervey. Cowley.
On the Extinction of the Venetian Republic. Wordsworth.
Overflow. Tabb.
A Pastoral. Hill.
Prayer to the Crucifix. Tallante.
The Prisoners. Spender.
Protagonist. Henrich.
Quha Is Perfyte. Scott.
Renewal. Cromwell.
Riding Adown the Country Lanes. Bridges.
The Road to Nijmegen. Birney.
Rondeau for You. De Andrade.
Rontgen Photograph. Eybers.
Rosamond's Appeal. Daniel.
The Sacrifice. Herbert.
Sandpaper, Sandpiper, Sandpit. Slesinger.
Saturday Night in the Village. Leopardi.
The Seasons. Kalidasa.
Sephestia's Song to Her Child. Greene.
The Snow. Dyment.
Somebody. *Anonymous.*
The Son. Thomas.
Song of the Bowmen of Shu. *Anonymous.*
Song: "We only ask for sunshine." Whitney.

Sonnet: "Beauty, sweet Love, is like the morning dew." Daniel.
Sonnets. Tuckerman.
Sonnets, XXVIII: "How can I then return in happy plight." Shakespeare.
Sonnets from the Portuguese, XIII. Browning.
Spell against Sorrow. Raine.
Spring, and the Blind Children. Noyes.
Stark County Holidays. Oliver.
The Stars Stand Up in the Air. *Anonymous.*
Structure of Rime. Duncan.
The Sun Now Risen. Beissel.
Surgical Ward: Men. Graves.
Symptoms of Love. Graves.
These Trees Are No Forest of Mourners. Jones.
Thysia. Luce.
To a Crucifix. Wickham.
To Janet. Pomeroy.
To My Father. Tree.
To Primroses Fill'd with Morning-Dew. Herrick.
Translations. Rich.
Twenty-One Love Poems. Rich.
The Valley of the Shadow of Death. Cowper.
The Vase of Tears. Spender.
Vashti. Harper.
Vespers. Shepard.
The Victoria Markets Recollected in Tranquillity. Maurice.
A Vision of the World's Instability. Verstegan.
La Vita Nuova. Dante Alighieri.
Walking to Dedham. Wright.
Wha Is Perfyte. Scott.
When I Am Dead. Johnson.
When I was a good and quick little girl. *Anonymous.*
The Will to Live. McBride.
Works and Days. Hesiod.
The Wrecker's Prayer. Roberts.
The Yew-Tree. Watkins.
Young Charlottie. Carter.

Grim
The Christian Soldier (excerpt). Studdert-Kennedy.
Red Sky at Morning. Thomas.
Swing One, Swing All. Bradley.

Grin (ning)
Blind Samson. Plomer.
Brainwashing Dramatized. Johnson.
Comedian. Johnson.
Gerda, My Husband's Wife. Triem.
The Judgement of God. Morris.
The Menagerie. Moody.
Might and Right. Day.
The New Ancient of Days. Melville.
Planting Trout in the Chicago River. Schmitz.
The Puppet Player. Grimke.
Reaching. Fagg.

Spot-Check at Fifty. Scannell.
Teapots and Quails. Lear.
To George Barker. Derwood.
A View of the Burning. Merrill.

Grind (ing) (s)
The Carousel. Oden.
Conversations between Here and Home. Harjo.
Eye. Burr.
Fe, Fi, Fo, Fum. Mother Goose.
The Gaol Song. *Anonymous.*
The Grinders, or the Saddle on the Right Horse. *Anonymous.*
The Mills of the Gods. *Anonymous.*
The Mother's Song. Cloud.
Popular Songs of Tuscany. *Anonymous.*
Shore Leave Lorry. Fuller.
The Water Mill. Doudney.

Grip
Because Our Past Lives Every Day. Lipman.
The Breakdown. Santos.
Epitaph for a Bigot. Johnson.
Old Roads. Chuilleanain.

Grit
The Best Dance Hall in Iuka, Mississippi. Johnson.
Brooding Likeness. Gluck.
Saxon Grit. Collyer.

Groan (s)
Ae Fond Kiss. Burns.
All for Love. Dryden.
Blenheim (excerpt). Philips.
Celebration. Cohen.
Crew Cut. McCord.
The Flying Tailor (parody). Hogg.
From Generation to Generation. Newbolt.
Gentle River, Gentle River. *Anonymous.*
Guy Mannering. Chapt. 27: Wasted, Weary, Wherefore Stay. Scott.
Hymn: Crucifixus Pro Nobis. Carey.
The Lay of the Last Minstrel. Scott.
Lenore. Poe.
The Roman Earl. *Anonymous.*
The Seasons. Thomson.
St. Irvyne (excerpt). Shelley.
Thou Lingering Star. Burns.
The Villagers and Death. Graves.

Groat
And Now a Fig for the Lower House. Cary.
Our Parodies Are Ended. Twist.
Riddle: "As I went through a garden gap." *Anonymous.*
Riddle: "Riddle me, riddle me ree." *Anonymous.*

Groin
Billy the Kid. Spicer.
Epigrams on Priapus. *Anonymous.*
The Hemingway Syndrome. Louis.
Rome. Hardy.
Shore Scene. Logan.
Sonnet. Wolf.

Groom
At Newmarket. Bishop.
Bavarian Gentians.
　Lawrence.
The Rival. Warner.
Sepulchral Imprecation.
　Crinagoras.

Grope (s)
Ashboughs. Hopkins.
Christ and the Pagan. Tabb.
The Clouded Morning. Very.
Holy Was Demeter Walking
　th' Corn Furrow. Sanders.
Leaf-Eater. Kinsella.
The Message of the Bells.
　Clark.
Spring is short. Yosano
　Akiko.

Ground (ed) (s)
The Baffled Knight.
　Anonymous
La Banditaccia, 1979.
　Lesser.
Ben Bolt. *Anonymous.*
Black Is the Colour.
　Anonymous.
Bone Yard. Barnes.
The Castle of Indolence.
　Thomson.
A Catch. Stoddard.
Come, Ye Lads, Who Wish to
　Shine. *Anonymous.*
Dialogue of the Way.
　Stewart.
Dream. Ignatow.
Duty to Death, LD.
　Roberts.
The Earth Worm. Levertov.
The Fabulous Teamsters.
　Sherwin.
Fifty-Seventh Street and Fifth.
　Corn.
The First Love Poem.
　Schutz.
The Flower and the Leaf.
　Anonymous.
Folklore. Dabydeen.
For Alva Benson, and for All
　Those Who have Learned to
　Speak. Harjo.
Gifts of Rain. Heaney.
The Goat Paths. Stephens.
Going to School. Shapiro.
The Gypsy Laddie (C vers.).
　Anonymous.
The Hairdresser. Hopes.
He Bringeth Them Unto
　Their Desired Haven.
　Tooker.
The Holly. King.
How Can Man Die Better.
　Tyrtaeus.
If my bark sink. Dickinson.
In Heaven, I Suppose, Lie
　down Together. Day-
　Lewis.
Ireland Weeping. Livingston.
It Should Be Easy. Van
　Doren.
Mile Hill. Schmitz.
Mind. Graham.
Miners. Owen.
Mole in the Ground.
　Anonymous.
Monkey. Smith.
The Night before Larry Was
　Stretched. *Anonymous.*
A Nosegay Always Sweet, for
　Lovers to Send for Tokens
　of Love... Hunnis.
O Love, That Wilt Not Let
　Me Go. Matheson.

October Dusk. Finley.
The Old Oak Tree.
　Anonymous.
On Christmas Day. Paman.
On This Day I Complete My
　Thirty-sixth Year. Byron.
One Eyed Black Man in
　Nebraska. Cornish.
Paradise Lost. Milton.
The Peninsula. Heaney.
Plenary. *Anonymous.*
Rain after a Vaudeville Show.
　Benét.
Red Stockings, Blue
　Stockings. *Anonymous.*
Rehearsal. Dabydeen.
Return. Deane.
A Rhyme-beginning
　Fragment. *Anonymous.*
Schmaltzenor. Branch.
Seasons and Times. Barnes.
Song: "A violet in her lovely
　hair." Swain.
Song for the Heroes.
　Comfort.
Soweto. Sepamla.
The Springs. Berry.
The Squid-Jiggin' Ground.
　Anonymous.
Stranded in My Ontario.
　Everson.
Supervising Examinations.
　Lucy.
The Texas Cowboy.
　Anonymous.
That Mulberry Wine.
　Sylvester.
Through the Smoke Hole.
　Snyder.
To Live in Hell, and Heaven
　to Behold. Constable.
Tom Farley. Thiele.
Tommy O'Linn. *Anonymous.*
A Trial. Dugan.
Two White Horses in a Line.
　Two Poor Boys.
White Goat, White Ram.
　Merwin.
Willow Poem. Williams.
The X of the Unknown.
　Clark.

Group
The Byrnies. Gunn.
The Leather Bar. Pomeroy.
Skinning-the-Cat. Schmitz.

Grove (s)
Ascent. Berry
A Card of Invitation to Mr.
　Gibbon, at Brighthelmstone.
　Hayley.
Carol of the Three Kings.
　Merwin.
City Pigeons. Chasin.
Cypress Grove Blues. James.
The Divine Narcissus. Juana
　Ines de la Cruz.
Gardens Are All My Heart.
　Triem.
Grongar Hill. Dyer.
Honestly I wish I were dead!
　Sappho.
The Jew of Malta: The Song
　of Ithamore. Marlowe.
O Now the Drenched Land
　Wakes. Patchen.
The Progress of Poesy.
　Gray.
Snatches: "Thei thou the wulf
　hore hode to preste."
　Anonymous.
Sospetto d'Herode. Crashaw.
The Spinning Wheel. Waller.

The Third Advice to a
　Painter. Marvell.
Train Ride. Wheelwright.

Grow (ing) (n) (s)
Abraham Lincoln. Benét.
Adolphus Elfinstone.
　Burgess.
Advice to Colonel Valentine.
　Graves.
After Death. Richardson.
Baby. Oates.
The Blue-Flag in the Bog.
　Millay.
The Boy We Want.
　Anonymous.
Buxom Lass. *Anonymous.*
Changes. Heaney.
Children's Elegy. Rukeyser.
Comanche Ghost Dance.
　Henson.
A Cradle Song. Yeats.
Daily Growing. *Anonymous.*
Dilemma of the Elm.
　Taggard.
The Dressmaker's Dummy as
　Scarecrow. Howes.
Easy to Grow. Giorno.
Epitaph on a Young Poet
　Who Died before Having
　Achieved Success. Lowell.
Feeding the Fire. Finkel.
First Light. Kinsella.
First Sight. Larkin.
Firwood. Clare.
For My Grandmother.
　Cullen.
Gethsemane, Illinois.
　Allwood.
A Grain of Rice. Scott.
Growing Up. Wallace.
Her Dairy. Newell.
I Come and Stand at Every
　Door. Hikmet.
I Did Not Know the Truth of
　Growing Trees. Schwartz.
I Dreamed I Saw the Crescent
　Moon. *Anonymous.*
The Image of Irelande
　(excerpt). Derricke.
In a London Terminus.
　Lehmann.
In Our Time. Roberts.
An Irish Wild-Flower. Piatt.
It's Raining, It's Pouring.
　Anonymous.
Jesus, My God and My All.
　Faber.
Laodamia. Wordsworth.
Lesson. Behn.
The Life of Service. Davie.
Lines for a Feast of Our
　Lady. Maris Stella.
The Little Car. Apollinaire.
A Little Song of Life. Reese.
Man-Making. Markham.
The Man Watching. Rilke.
The Mountain. Merwin.
The Murdered Girl Is Found
　on a Bridge. Hayman.
The North Country Maid.
　Anonymous.
Nothing Strange. Kryss.
An Old Field Mowed.
　Meredith.
The Old Mother.
　Anonymous.
Old Quin Queeribus. Turner.
Old Woman's Song. Cole.
Orient Wheat. Rich.
Picketing Supermarkets.
　Wayman.
The Place of Backs. Merwin.

Poem/Ditty-Bop. Rodgers.
Poem of Circumstance.
　Cocteau.
Poplars. Grynberg.
Prayer. *Anonymous.*
Protective Colors. Logan.
Red, and White Roses.
　Carew.
Rhymes for a Modern
　Nursery: Two Blind Mice.
　Dehn.
Riddle: "Little Nancy
　Etticoat." Mother Goose.
The Routine. Blackburn.
Screw Spring. Hoffman.
Song of the Cauld Lad of
　Hylton. *Anonymous.*
Song To Celia. Jonson.
Song: "What binds the atom
　together." Dow.
Spring Song. McKuen.
Star of Eternal Possibles and
　Joy. Yates.
Sun and I. Mammone.
To Any Daddy. *Anonymous.*
To Rose. Teasdale.
Toward a Theory of
　Instruction. Rendleman.
The Trees So High.
　Anonymous.
Two Voices. Corbin.
The Undersong. Emerson
Upon a Delaying Lady.
　Herrick.
Waiting. Behn.
Warrior Nation Trilogy.
　Henson.
While April Rain Went By.
　O'Sheel.
The Woodcutter's Wife.
　Benet.
Words to the Wind. Di
　Cicco.

Grow (ing) (n) (s) (grew)
Ah Were She Pitiful.
　Greene.
Catch a Little Rhyme.
　Merriam.
A Dialogue between the Soul
　and Body. Marvell.
Memo to the 21st Century.
　Appleman.
On Approaching My
　Birthday. Miller.

Growl (ed)
Axle Song. Van Doren.
Biafra. Mack.
An Example of How a Daily
　Temporary Madness Can
　Help a Man... Stone.
Poor Old Man. *Anonymous.*

Grownup
Afterlives. Mahon.
Curiosity. Behn.
Grownups. Wise.
The Hump. Kipling.
The Hunter. Nash.
Reflections upon a Recurrent
　Suggestion by Civil Defense.
　Whittemore.

Guard (ed) (s)
Adon 'Olam. *Anonymous.*
The Air Sentry. Barrington.
Author of Light, Revive My
　Dying Spright. Campion.
Bega. Pickthall.
Begotten of the Spleen.
　Simic.
Christmas in Penang.
　Leyden.
The Cotter's Saturday Night.
　Burns.

Could It Have Been a Shadow? Shannon.
Death and the Maiden. *Anonymous.*
A Dialogue between King William and the Late King James... Blount.
Epigram: "Queen,/thou holdest in thine arms." *Anonymous.*
Four Walls. Dickinson.
A Gentle Echo on Woman. Swift.
God Save the King, That King That Sav'd the Land. Harris.
The Last Instructions to a Painter. Marvell.
Man Frail, and God Eternal. Watts.
The Marines' Hymn. *Anonymous.*
Mule-Train. Sellers.
Night. Blake.
Ode to Leven Water. Smollett.
The Pleasures of Imagination. Akenside.
Prisoner. George.
Rules for Daily Life. Anonymous.
Sonnet Sequence. Turner.
The Swiss Peasant. Wordsworth.
Touch Thou Mine eyes. Ham.
Visits. Klauck.

Guardian (s)
The Bog Lands. Byrne.
A Captive of Love. Ovid (Publius Ovidius Naso).
Central Park, 1916. Stewart.
God's Dark. Martin.
Here's to the Ranger! *Anonymous.*
In Memoriam A.H.H., XLIV. Tennyson.
Man As He Shall Be. Owens.
Old Ladies. Dromgoole.
Swedenborg's Skull. Watkins.
To My Son (excerpt). Barker.
Watch-Dog. Brasch.

Guess (ed) (es)
Amyntas Led Me to a Grove. Behn.
At the beginning of winter a cold spirit comes. *Anonymous.*
The Breakfast Song. Poulsson.
A Fable. Frere.
Give Me Five. Harris.
Guessing. *Anonymous.*
Pick a Quarrel, Go to War. Auden.
Religio Laici. Dryden.
Sarah Byng. Belloc.
She Dried Her Tears. Bronte.
Sonnets from the Portuguese, XX. Browning.
Ten Definitions of Poetry. Sandburg.
The Third Day. Pierce.
To a Field Mouse. Burns.
'Way Down in Cuba. *Anonymous.*
What'll Be the Title? Richardson.

The Willing Mistress. Behn.
Winter: My Secret. Rossetti.

Guest (s)
Amoretti, LXXVII. Spenser.
Book-Moth. *Anonymous.*
Building a House. Gallup.
Candles. Plath.
Chicago: Near West-Side Renewal. Schmitz.
The Cloisters. Yellen.
Critics. Martial (Marcus Valerius Martialis).
Death Songs. *Anonymous.*
Ecstasy. Symons.
Entreaty. Fitzgerald.
Epipsychidion. Shelley.
The Guest. Berry.
Guest. Enright.
The Guest. Kimball.
The Guests. Zukofsky.
The Holy Longing. Goethe.
Hospitality in Ancient Ireland. *Anonymous.*
Hymn for a Household. Henderson.
Leningrad. Mandelstam.
Of Only a Single Poem. Dutton.
The Parachutist. Anderson.
The Picture of Her Mind. Jonson.
A Question of Form and Content. Stallworthy.
Roasted Sucking Pig (parody). *Anonymous.*
To Night. Shelley.
Trance and Transformation. Goethe.
The Two Captains. Cory.
Was It a Dream. Spenser.
What Is Lived. Valle.

Guidance
Credo. Johnson.
Everest. Shipp.
On Australian Hills. Cambridge.
The Will. Sepamla.

Guide (d) (s)
Baby-Land. Cooper.
The Blind Man. Sangster.
A Call to Pentecost. Tyler.
A Christopher of the Shenandoah. Thomas.
The Consolation of Philosophy. Boethius.
The Fairy Temple; or, Oberon's Chapel.... Herrick.
A Fairy Voyage. *Anonymous.*
The Fishermen. Whittier.
Have Faith in God. Budzynski.
A Hundreth Good Poyntes of Husbandry. Tusser.
In Memoriam. De Brun.
It Cannot Be. Sickels.
Joy of My Life! Vaughan.
Land of the Free. Hosking.
Love and Folly. La Fontaine.
Love and Reason. Prior.
Madonna Natura. "Macleod.
A Mexican Scrapbook. Oliphant.
Nemean Ode: VI. Pindar.
O Night, O Jealous Night. *Anonymous.*
On a Tear. Rogers.
Our Father's Hand. Flint.
Pere Lalement. Pickthall.
The Pilot. Chapman.

The Ship of Fools. Barclay.
Sonnet at Dover Cliffs. Bowles.
Tarry Ye. *Anonymous.*
The Thirty-One Camels. Korn.
Thou, Our Elder Brother. Whittier.
To a Lady, with a Present of a Walking-Stick. Frere.
To Mr. Cyriack Skinner Upon His Blindness. Milton.
To the End. Bode.
The Unutterable Beauty. Studdert-Kennedy.
Wind of the Prairie. Howes.
Woak Hill. Barnes.

Guile
Andrew Magrath's Reply to John O'Tuomy. Magrath.
O Lady Full of Guile. Ceitinn.
The Prince. Bowers.
Remonstrance. Lanier.
True and False. Crawford.

Guilt (y)
The Art of Preserving Health (excerpt). Armstrong.
Astrophel and Stella, LXVI. Sidney.
Ballade to My Psychoanalyst. Lillington.
Being with Men. Gregg.
Bring the War Home. Matthews.
Dies Irae. Thomas of Celano.
The Dreame. Jonson.
The Dreamers and the Sea. Wilkins.
Echo Poem. Allan.
Father and Son. Schwartz.
The Impious Feast. Landor.
In the Jury Room. Carter.
Jacob's Destiny. Beer-Hofmann.
The Killing. MacBeth.
Lines on His Birthday. Logan.
The Music of the Spheres. Bell.
Naboth's Vineyard. Caryll.
The Net. Rodgers.
On the Pilots Who Destroyed Germany in the Spring of 1945. Spender.
The Palace of Art. Tennyson.
Photos of a Salt Mine. Page.
Scarred. *Anonymous.*
The Sins of Youth. Vaux.
Sir Eustace Grey. Crabbe.
Some Foreign Letters. Sexton.
The Song of O'Ruark, Prince of Breffni. Moore.
Spirits and Men (excerpt). Elliott.
The Triple Mirror. Oden.
A Village Tale. Sarton.
When Jesus Wept. Billings.
Who Never Ate with Tears His Bread. Goethe.
You Move Forward. Sessler.
Youth. Hope.

Guitar (s)
After I Have Voted. Jensen.
Guitar. St. John.
Make Music with Your Life. O'Meally.
The Man with the Blue Guitar. Stevens.

The Music. Hoagland.
The Road Is Wider Than Long (excerpt). Penrose.
Song of a Common Lover. Ranaivo.
The Tape. Livingston.

Gulf (s)
The Castaway. Cowper.
The Excursion. Wordsworth.
Hemlock Mountain. Cleghorn.
Icebergs. Foster.
Interracial. Johnson.
Lost Jimmie Whalen. *Anonymous.*
The Lost Shipmate. Roberts.
On the Ice Islands Seen Floating in the German Ocean. Cowper.
Prince Henry the Navigator. Clouts.
The River. Crane.
The River. Lorentz.
Sir Humphrey Gilbert. Longfellow.
Song of the Gulf Stream. Ford.
Veni Coronaberis. Hill.

Gull (s)
Among These Turf-Stacks. MacNeice.
The Artist on Penmaenmawr. Turner.
The Coast: Norfolk. Cornford.
Countersign. Ketchum.
Dialogue between a Squeamish Cotting Mechanic and his Sluttish Wife... Ward.
Eagle Sonnets. Wood.
Emblems. Tate.
Epitaphs of the War. Kipling.
The Glaucous-Gull's Death. O'Sullivan.
H.M.S. Hero. Roberts.
Halcyon. Doolittle.
Homage to Hart Crane. Balakian.
Kansas Boy. Lechlitner.
Night Thoughts While Travelling. Tu Fu.
Oedipus at Colonus. Sophocles.
Passages. Eigner.
Provincetown, Mass. Shapiro.
The Self Unsatisfied Runs Everywhere. Schwartz.

Gum (s)
The Alchemist, 1610. Jonson.
Father of the Victim. Ballard.
On His Royal Blindness Paramount Chief Kwangala. Mapanje.
Pine Gum. Ross.
Tea for Two. Nolan.

Gun (s)
45 Pistol Blues. Roland.
After Bombardment. Pudney.
August, 1914. Masefield.
The Battle of Charleston Harbor. Hayne.
Behold the Manly Mesomorph. Auden.
Bobby Campbell. *Anonymous.*
The Contours of Fixation. Kees.

Coogan's Wood. Stuart.
The Corbie and the Crow.
Anonymous.
The Cropper Lads.
Anonymous.
Cuba. Kearney.
The Desert. Knibbs.
Epitaph for a Man from
Virginia City. Porter.
Europe and America.
Ignatow.
Face to Face. Rich.
The Falling of the Snow.
Souster.
The Famous Outlaw Stops in
for a Drink. James.
Grace. Wilbur.
Her Story. Madgett.
Ho, Brother Teig.
Anonymous.
I Am a Dangerous Woman.
Harjo.
It Is Not Too Late. Trent.
James Gerard. Shiplett.
Johnny Get Your Gun.
"Belasco.
Killer. Anonymous.
The Last Lap. Kipling.
Limerick: "There was a young
man who said, "Run."
Anonymous.
Little Britain. Anonymous.
The Men behind the Guns.
Rooney.
A Mother Speaks: The Algiers
Motel Incident, Detroit.
Harper.
My Woodcock. Chalmers.
Old Emily. Hill.
Right On: White America.
Sanchez.
Schoolroom on a Wet
Afternoon. Scannell.
Scrap Iron. Durgnat.
Screw-Guns. Kipling.
The Seals in Penobscot Bay.
Hoffman.
The Sergeant, He Is the Worst
of All (with music).
Anonymous.
The Shooting. Pack.
Sis Joe. Anonymous.
South Dakota Refuge.
Crozier.
The Unconcerned. Flatman.
The Voices. Anonymous.
The Wagoner's Lad.
Anonymous.
War on the Periphery.
Johnston.
We Pity Our Bosses Five.
Anonymous.

Gunpowder
The Great Panjandrum.
Foote.
New Year. Harada.
Self-Portrait. Bodker.

Gust (s)
The Angel in the House.
Patmore.
The Bat. Spear.
The Happy Bird. Clare.
Love Pictures You as Black
and Long-Faced. Jeffers.
Pigeons. Kell.
To Fanny. Keats.

Gut (s)
Cominus, You Reprobate Old
Goat. Catullus.
Cycles, Cycles. Rioff.
The End of Clonmacnois.
Anonymous.

The End of Clonmacnois.
O'Connor.
Infant Diseases and Their
Treatment. Saint-Marthe.
Limerick: "There was a young
fellow named Nutz.
Anonymous.
Southbound on the Freeway.
Swenson.
The Stars Have Not Dealt Me
the Worst They Could Do.
Housman.
To-Morrow's the Fair.
Anonymous.
Uccello on the Heath.
Grigson.
Yaddo. Herschberger.

Guy (s)
Back through the Looking
Glass to This Side. Ciardi.
Consumer's Report.
Kennedy.
Grandfather Gabriel.
Warren.
Guys and Dolls. Loesser.
Louie. Montoya.
Mr. Vachel Lindsay Discovers
Radio (parody).
Hoffenstein.
No Empty Hands.
Brownstein.
Reflections in a Hospital.
Eisenberg.

Gyps (ies) (y)
And This Is My Father.
Grapes.
Ballad of the Spanish Civil
Guard. Garcia Lorca.
Dorothy. Kreymborg.
The Gipsy Laddie.
Anonymous.
Gorgio Lad. Burr.
Gypsies. Nowlan.
Hands up. Rudolf.
I Was Made of This and This.
Ross.
Johnny Faa, the Gypsy
Laddie. Anonymous.
The Kirk's Alarm. Burns.
Political Poem. Jones.
The Raggle Taggle Gypsies.
Anonymous.

H

Habit (s)
The Bards We Quote.
Taylor.
The Buried Stream. Baxter.
Canberra in April. Rowland.
Gather Ye Rosebuds (parody).
Fowler.
Love Calls Us to the Things
of This World. Wilbur.
The Mother. Gardons.
Mother of Fishermen.
Roland-Holst.
The Mountains in the Desert.
Creeley.
Once You Git the Habit.
Anonymous.
An Original Cuss. Preston.
The Victim. Voigt.
West End Blues. Hollander.

Hades
Ajax. Sophocles.
Anacreon to the Sophist.
"H.

Andromeda forgot. Sappho.
Gone on the Wind. Mangan.

Hail (ed)
Carroll's Sword. MacMore.
Cuckoo, Cherry Tree.
Anonymous.
La Donna E Mobile. "K..
Drum-Taps. Whitman.
La Fayette. Madison.
The Jealous Brothers.
Anonymous.
The Message of the Bells.
Clark.
The Mint Julep. Hoffman
Norway. Dubie.
On the Burial of His Brother.
Catullus.
The Staircase. Allen.
Tennyson. Van Dyke.

Hair (s) (y)
10th Dance–Coming on As a
Horn–20 February 1964.
MacLow.
After Love. Aleixandre.
The Aged Woman to Her
Sons. Deutsch.
Along the Strand. Mombert.
Am Driven Mad. Polite.
And She Washed His Feet
with Her Tears,...
Sherburne.
Another Late Edition
(excerpt). Cabral.
Ante-Natal Dream.
Kavanagh.
The Ape. Young.
As I Was Walkin' Down
Wexford Street (with
music). Anonymous.
Autumn. Levine.
Ballade of Muhammad Din
Tilai. Anonymous.
Because Sometimes You Can't
Always Be So. Patchen.
Ben. Wolfe.
The Berkeley Pier. Addiego.
Black Bear. Lepan.
Black Hair. Soto.
Black Is the Color.
Anonymous.
The Boy Who Dreamed the
Country Night. Koch.
Casement's Funeral.
Murphy.
Celanta at the Well of Life.
Peele.
A Chanted Calendar.
Dobell.
Children of a Future Age.
Blake.
Childs Memory. Wilkins.
Complaint. Williams.
Conquest. Desportes.
The Court of Neptune.
Hughes.
Cressid. Perry.
Crimson Nor Yellow Roses.
Wratislaw.
The Cure's Progress.
Dobson.
Daddy Shot a Bear.
Anonymous.
Daphne. Rodman.
Days. Baker.
Death. Bodenheim.
Delphine. Anderson.
Descending. Iremonger.
The Desert. Wood.
Dolor. Roethke.
Don't Ask Me What to Wear.
Sappho.
Donkey. Van Doren.

Doubts. Brooke.
Downy Hair. Stryk.
East Coast Journey. Baxter.
Exaltation. Werfel.
A Fable. Prior.
The Feast of Stephen.
Hecht.
The Fiend. Dickey.
Figures of Authority.
Watkins.
Following Van Gogh
(Avignon, 1982). Puziss.
For Emily (Dickinson).
Owen.
For My Torturer, Lieutenant
D–. Djabali.
For One Moment. Ignatow.
For the Magdalene.
Drummond.
The Fortunate Fall. Alvarez.
From Here to There.
Anonymous.
A Glance. Anonymous.
Going down the Mountain.
Iremonger.
The Golden-Robin's Nest.
Chadwick.
Hair. Gourmont.
Hair-Dressing. Untermeyer.
Hair Poem. Knott.
The Hairy Dog. Asquith.
Half-Way, for One
Commandment Broken.
Housman.
Heavy-Hearted. Al-Harizi.
Hey Betty Martin.
Anonymous.
Hickety, Pickety, I-Silicity.
Anonymous.
How Can One E'er Be Sure.
Horikawa.
The Hut. Van Stockum.
Hypocrite Women. Levertov.
I Love My Love. Adam.
Idyl. Mombert.
If You Want to Go A-
Courting. Anonymous.
The Impatient Poet.
Cresswell.
In a Wood Clearing.
MacDonald.
Indian. Jensen.
It's True I'm No Miss
America. Slowinsky.
Jack Rose. Bodenheim.
Joe Bowers. Anonymous.
Judas Iscariot. Buchanan.
Katharine. Heine.
Keeping Hair. Wilson.
Last Poems. Housman.
Laura. Tofte.
A Lean Day in a Convict's
Suit. Wahl.
Let Me Love Bright Things.
Choyce.
Letting My Feelings Out.
Yu Hsuan-chi.
Levee Moan (with music).
Anonymous.
The Licorice Fields at
Pontefract. Betjeman.
Lilith. Grossman.
Limerick: "A matron well
known in Montclair."
Smith.
Limerick: "C is for Curious
Charlie." Bellows.
Limerick: "I have heard," said
a maid of Montclair."
Bishop.
Lines for My Father. Gray.
Lining Track. Anonymous.

Little Rain. Roberts.
Long Hair. Snyder.
Love Me. Wine.
Lovelocks. De la Mare.
The Lyricism of the Weak.
  Viereck.
Madrigal: "Have I found her."
  Pilkington.
Martha Graham. Lifshin.
Meeting. Rossetti.
A Message to the
  Photographer Whose Prints
  I Purchased. Williams.
The Minotaur. Gibb.
The Mother of God. Yeats.
My Grandmother Had Bones.
  Hemschemeyer.
The Narrative Hooper and
  L.D.O. Sestina with a Long
  Last Line. Whitehead.
Negatives. Wright.
The Newborn Colt.
  Kennedy.
Night Song. Fairburn.
No Complaints. Hollo.
A Nonsense Song. Benét.
Not Three–But One. Duff.
O Night of the Crying
  Children. Sachs.
Of Nicolette. Cummings.
The Old Flagman.
  Sandburg.
Old Road Song Poem. Gold.
On Mary Magdalen.
  Drummond.
On Seeing a Hair of Lucretia
  Borgia. Landor.
On the Tower. Droste-
  Hulshoff.
Only My Opinion. Shannon.
Orpheus and Eurydice.
  Valentine.
Palinode. Stanton.
The Pear-Tree. Gilmore.
Perdita. Drennan.
Peruke of Poets (parody).
  Zaranka.
Perversity. Griffin.
Poem by the Bridge at Ten-
  Shin. Li Po.
Poem for My Mother. Fox.
Private Rooms. O Hehir.
Prize-Giving. Harwood.
Queen. Moraes.
Radiation Leak. Aliesan.
The Rape of the Lock.
  Pope.
Rapping along with Ronda
  Davis. Cunningham.
Rapunzel. Untermeyer.
Regretful Thoughts, II. Yu
  Hsuan-chi.
The Rejected Member's Wife.
  Hardy.
Sacred Objects. Simpson.
Sam's World. Cornish.
September 30. Lourie.
She Bewitched Me.
  Burbidge.
Site of Ambush: Narration.
  Chuilleanain.
Slips. McGuckian.
So Fast Entangled.
  Anonymous.
Soluble Noughts and Crosses;
  or, California, Here I Come.
  Roughton.
Song for Healing. Hill.
Song for September.
  Fitzgerald.
Song of Snow-White Heads.
  Cho Wen-chun.

Song of the Old Woman.
  Anonymous.
Song: "Rousing to rein his
  pad's head back." Taylor.
Spain. Symons.
The Squirrel. Anonymous.
A Star. MacBeth.
Stars. Brown.
Stony Town. Neilson.
The Swan. Spender.
Symbols. Thompson.
The Tales the Barbers Tell.
  Bishop.
Tamerlane. Poe.
Tapestry. Simic.
There Once Was a Time.
  Anonymous.
They Were Welcome to Their
  Belief. Frost.
'Tis but a Little Faded
  Flower. Howarth.
'Tis the White Plum Tree.
  Neilson.
To a Woman. Glover.
To Chloe. Anonymous.
To Delia. Daniel.
To K.M. De La Mare.
The Toll-Gate Man.
  MacDonald.
Tom Starr. Conley.
Tombstone Epitaphs.
  Anonymous.
The Tombstone Told When
  She Died. Thomas.
A Traveller. Rowland.
Two Scenes. Ashbery.
Unbridled Now. LeGear.
Vieux Carre. Roberts.
Waking Up. Schmidt.
The Walk. Clark.
The War of the Secret Agents.
  Coulette.
We Put the Urn Aboard Ship.
  Sappho.
The Web of Eros. Sitwell.
The Wedding Poem (excerpt).
  Russ.
Welt. Johnson.
What Can the Matter Be?
  Anonymous.
What Dim Arcadian Pastures.
  Corbin.
White Fear. Welles.
The Witch in the Glass.
  Piatt.
Would I Might Go Far Over
  Sea. Marie de France.
Wrapped Hair Bundles.
  LaPena.
Your Hand Full of Hours.
  Celan.
Half (halves)
At the Cavour. Symons.
Butterfly. Anonymous.
Christmas in the Olden Time.
  Scott.
Cobbler, Cobbler.
  Anonymous.
The Death of Admiral
  Benbow. Anonymous.
Death of My Aunt.
  Anonymous.
The Exequy. To His
  Matchlesse Never to Be
  Forgotten Freind. King.
Give All to Love. Emerson.
The Kerry Recruit.
  Anonymous.
The Minyan. Myers.
Not All There. Frost.
Now. Gilbert.

On the Supposed Author of a
  Late Poem "In Defense of
  Satire." Rochester.
Over the Hill to the Poor-
  House. Carleton.
A Piper. O'Sullivan.
Rabbi Ben Ezra. Browning.
Rumoresque Senum
  Severiorum. Argentarius.
A Semi-Revolution. Frost.
Sent with a Rose to a Young
  Lady. Deland.
Similes. Moxon.
Some Ruthless Rhymes.
  Graham.
These Days. Jones.
To Licinius. Horace.
To the Most Virtuous
  Mistress Pot, Who Many
  Times Entertained Him.
  Herrick.
Vital Message. Phillips.
W.L.M.K. Scott.
What Shall I Give My
  Children? Brooks.
You Simple Bostonians.
  Anonymous.
Hall
Beside My Grandmother.
  Lee.
Docker. Heaney.
The Don. Howes.
The Earthly Paradise.
  Morris.
Goosey Goosey Gander.
  French.
Nocturn at the Institute.
  McElroy.
The Obsession. Liggett.
Oh young men oh young
  comrades. Spender.
Psalm XXIII. Sidney.
Room 000. Stafford.
Winter Night. Coxe.
Hallelujah (s)
Courage. Brooke.
Let Tyrants Shake Their Iron
  Rod. Billings.
The Messiah-Blower.
  Goodman.
My Own Hallelujahs.
  Gilbert.
The People, Yes. Sandburg.
Resurrection Hymn. Weiss.
When Wild Confusion Wrecks
  the Air. Byles.
Halloween
Black and Gold. Turner.
Empire of Dreams. Simic.
Hey-How For Hallowe'en!
  Anonymous.
If You've Never. Fowler.
It's Halloween. Prelutsky.
Skeleton Parade. Prelutsky.
This Is Halloween.
  Thompson.
Halo
The Action of Electricity.
  Darwin.
Lady of Miracles. Cassian.
Limerick: "G is a grumbler
  gruff." Herford.
The Necromancers. Nims.
Poem. Towle.
The Poet. Keats.
The Return. Moreh.
A Serendipity of Love.
  Aldridge.
A Wartime Exchange: As One
  Non-Combatant to Another.
  Comfort.

Halt (s)
The Happy Wanderer.
  Addleshaw.
I Love a Hill. Hodgson.
Lofty Lane. Gerard.
On the March. Aldington.
The Riders. Friend.
Songs for a Colored Singer.
  Bishop.
Waltzing It. Moncrieff.
Halter
The Ass. Allan.
On a Rope Maker Hanged.
  Browne.
Wheatlet Son of Milklet.
  MacConglinne.
Ham
Don't Fish in My Sea.
  Rainey.
Sonnet to Vauxhall. Hood.
Tummy Ache. Fisher.
Hamlet
If So the Man You Are.
  Lewis.
They All Want to Play
  Hamlet. Sandburg.
Wanting Out. Ewart.
Your Burnt-Out Body.
  Markish.
Hammer (s)
The Anvil of God's Word.
  Clifford.
Apoem I. Pichette.
Drivin' Steel (with music).
  Anonymous.
Ever Since Uncle John Henry
  Been Dead (with music).
  Anonymous.
Hammer and Anvil. Cole.
The Hammers. Hodgson.
Hammers and Anvil.
  Clifford.
If I Die a Railroad Man (with
  music). Anonymous.
John Henry (A vers.).
  Anonymous.
John Henry (C vers.).
  Anonymous.
The Lay of Thrym.
  Anonymous.
Limerick: "A mother in old
  Alabama." Smith.
The Midnight Court.
  Merriman.
A Mock Invocation to Genius
  (excerpt). Woty.
The North Sea Undertaker's
  Complaint. Lowell.
An Old Man He Courted Me.
  Anonymous.
On Linden Street. Ehrlich.
Preparedness. Markham.
Ramble of the Gods through
  Birmingham (excerpt).
  Bisset.
The Shoemaker. Anonymous.
To a Snowflake. Thompson.
Hand (s)
3 More Things. Nauen.
About an Allegory.
  Arensberg.
About This Course. Shapiro.
Absent Star. Duval.
Acrobat. Watkins.
An Acrostick on Mrs.
  Elizabeth Hull. Saffin.
Adam in Love. Mitchell.
Adversaries. Johnson.
After They Put Down Their
  Overalls. Peters.
Afterbirth. Williams.
All That Matters... Sorell.

Alternatives. Amis.
Amaze. Crapsey.
America. Di Cicco.
America, I Love You. Ruby.
Amoretti, XVII. Spenser.
Anasazi at Mesa Verde.
　Saner.
The Ancestors. Barrows.
Anseo. Muldoon.
Anti-Memoirs. Schuchat.
Appomattox. Kantor.
Astrophel and Stella, XLIX.
　Sidney.
At Cambridge. McGaffin.
At His Father's Grave.
　Ormond.
At Last. Whittier.
At Last We Killed the
　Roaches. Clifton.
At the Place of the Sea.
　Flint.
August 1968. Auden.
August for the People.
　Auden.
Autobiography. Dube.
B's the Bus. McGinley.
Back from the Word
　Processing Course, I Say to
　My Old Typewriter.
　Blumenthal.
Ballad: "I put my hat upon
　my head." Johnson.
A Ballad of a Nun.
　Davidson.
The Ballad of Longwood
　Glen. Nabokov.
The Balloon Man. Aldis.
Baptism. Nowlan.
Bard. Black.
A Barren Soul. Ezobi.
Barren Woman. Plath.
Batches of New Leaves.
　London.
Because One Is Always
　Forgotten. Forche.
The Bee-Wisp. Turner.
Beneath the Shadow of the
　Freeway. Cervantes.
Bess. Stafford.
Better, Wiser and Happier.
　Wilcox.
The Birds. Dracontius.
Black Dog. Young Bear.
The Blind Man. Lewisohn.
Bloom Street. McCabe.
Border River. Bailey.
The Boy with a Cart
　(excerpt). Fry.
The Brandy Glass.
　MacNeice.
The Bread Hot from the
　Oven. Thompson.
A Bride's Hours. Valentine.
The Brown Family.
　Thibaudeau.
Caelica, XXVIII. Greville.
A Call to Action. Callinus.
Captured. MacLeish.
Carol of the Three Kings.
　Merwin.
Castilian. Wylie.
A Character. Bates.
Childe Harold's Pilgrimage:
　Canto IV. Byron.
The Choice. Wither.
The Choyce. Beedome.
Christ's Sympathy. Lytton.
Clap Hands, Daddy's Coming.
　Anonymous.
Clean & Clear. Brownstein.

Coasting toward Midnight at
　the Southeastern Fair.
　Bottoms.
Cold Glow: Icehouses.
　Wojahn.
Columbus Dying. Proctor.
The Comedian Said It.
　Bigger.
Conquest. Desportes.
Continental Crossing.
　Thompson.
The Corridor. Gunn.
Could Man Be Drunk for
　Ever. Housman.
The Coward. Merriam.
Craftsmen. Sackville-West.
Creatrix. Wickham.
Crimson Nor Yellow Roses.
　Wratislaw.
The Cry of an Aged One.
　Fraser.
The Curate Thinks You Have
　No Soul. Lucas.
The Daisies. Stephens.
The Daughters of Blum.
　Wright.
The Days. Garrison.
Death Sonnet I. "Mistral.
The Deceptive Grin of the
　Gravel Porters. Ewart.
Dirge for the Ninth of Ab.
　Anonymous.
A Dog. Zolotow.
Dog Day Vespers. Wright.
Dolphin. Lowell.
Don't Forget. Berg.
The Door. Strand.
A Dream as Reported.
　Earle.
The Dress. Middleton.
Drinking Song. Hecht.
The Drunken Stones of
　Prague. Scheinert.
The Dutchman. Welch.
E Tenebris. Wilde.
Earth Changes. Shire.
Ecclesiastes. Bishop.
Eclipse. Rashidd.
The Egoist Dead. Brewster.
The End. Rice.
Epigram on Seeing a Worthy
　Prelate Go out of Church...
　Swift.
An Epithalamium upon the
　Marriage of Captain
　William Bedloe. Duke.
The Equinox. Heyward.
Ernest Dowson. Wheelock.
Esau. Kwitko.
Eternal. Macdonald.
The Eternal Justice. Aldrich.
Evening Song. Lanier,
The Everlasting Mercy.
　Masefield.
Exile. Hall.
An Extra Joyful Chorus for
　Those Who Have Read
　This Far. Transtromer.
Faith Healer Come to Rabun
　County. Bottoms.
Fall Comes in Back-Country
　Vermont. Warren.
Far and Wide She Went.
　Caedmon.
A Farewell. Gascoigne.
Father. Livingston.
February Park. Vizenor.
Feet. Aldis.
Fellowship. Anonymous.
The Feral Pioneers. Reed.
Film Vermouth: Six O'Clock
　Show. Portal.

A Finished Gentleman.
　Dutton.
First Love. Gullans.
The First Tooth. Rands.
The Fishes' Lamentation.
　Anonymous.
Five Epigrams.
　Cunningham.
Flight. Whitman.
Folds of a White Dress/Shaft
　of Light. Keenan.
Football Song. Scott.
Footnote to History.
　Coatsworth.
For a Friend. Steingass.
For Brother Malcolm.
　Spriggs.
For Edward Hicks. Helwig.
Fourth Station. Schaumann.
A Fragment. Bancks.
The Friend. Piercy.
Friends. Stafford.
From All Peoples (excerpt).
　Alterman.
The Frozen Hero. Vance.
The Gallant Fighting "Joe."
　Stevenson.
Garcia Lorca. Dudek.
Gascoigne. Sackville.
Giovanni da Fiesole on the
　Sublime or Fra Angelico's
　"Last Judgment."
　Howard.
The Glove. Bond.
God's Will Is Best. Curtis.
Going. Larkin.
The Good Day. Bashford.
Government Injunction.
　Miles.
Grandpa's Picture. Ruffin.
Grass. Holmes.
The Great Society. Bly.
Grey October. "The
　Critics."
Guadalajara Hospital. Ai.
Gude Wallace (G version).
　Anonymous.
The Gulistan. Sa'di.
The Half Door. O'Sullivan.
The Hand. Fawcett.
The Hand. Jones.
A Hand. Spencer.
The Hand That Rocks the
　Cradle Is the Hand That
　Rules the World. Wallace.
Hands. Aldis.
The Handwriting on the Wall.
　Shaw.
Handy Dandy. Anonymous.
Hats. Dillard.
He's Got the Whole World in
　His Hands. Anonymous.
Heart's Needle. Snodgrass.
Here Be Dragons.
　Friedlander.
Heron. Plumly.
High Flight. Magee, Jr.
His Hands. Moreland.
Hold On. Anonymous.
Home-Coming. Adams.
Hope. Cowper.
The House of Love: Pride of
　Youth. Rossetti.
Hugh Spencer's Feats in
　France (B version).
　Anonymous.
Hushed by the Hands of
　Sleep. Grimke.
Hymn. Howard.
I Am Your Loaf, Lord.
　Ross.

I Dwell in Possibility.
　Dickinson.
I Have Been My Arm. Taft.
I Held a Lamb.
　Worthington.
I Keep to Myself Such
　Measures. Creeley.
I Know de Lord's Laid His
　Hands on Me.
　Anonymous.
I Sit and Wait for Beauty.
　Cowdery.
I Wasn't No Mary Ellen.
　King.
I Will Not Let Thee Go.
　Bridges.
Icarus. Spender.
The Idea of a University.
　Shapiro.
The Idler. Very.
If We Knew. Smith.
The Iliad. Homer.
Imagine the South.
　Woodcock.
Immortal is an ample word.
　Dickinson.
The Impulse of October.
　Moses.
In Dream: The Privacy of
　Sequence. Young Bear.
In Memoriam A.H.H.,
　LXXV. Tennyson.
In Memoriam A.H.H., CXIX.
　Tennyson.
In Memorium—Leo: A Yellow
　Cat. Sherwood.
In Memory. Johnson.
In Memory of My Dear
　Grandchild Elizabeth
　Bradstreet. Bradstreet.
In My Mind. MacCaig.
In the Baggage Room at
　Greyhound. Ginsberg.
In the Cabinet. Vinner.
In the Churchyard. Taylor.
In the Subway. Jimenez.
In the Van Gogh Room.
　Yamamoto.
Incident. MacCaig.
Inclusions. Browning.
Innocence. Scully.
Inspiration. Fullerton.
Invocation. Sitwell.
An Ironical Encomium.
　Anonymous.
Is Love, Then, So Simple.
　McLeod.
It's Already Autumn.
　Pagliarani.
It's Just the Same to Me.
　Hesse.
The Jackfruit. Ho Xuan
　Huong.
James Rigg (parody). Hogg.
Jay Gould's Daughter (with
　music). Anonymous.
Jehovah, God, Who Dwelt of
　Old. Amis.
Jerusalem. Blake.
Jew. Shapiro.
John Henry (C vers.).
　Anonymous.
John Nobody. Moraes.
The Journey nears the Road-
　End. Tagore.
Junction. Pass.
Kate Dalrymple.
　Anonymous.
Keeping Victory. Isenhour.
Kelp. Dauenhauer.
The Knot. Clark.
A Lady. Snodgrass.

Lament. Livesay.
Lament for Sean MacDermott.
  O'Sullivan.
The Lamp. Greene.
Lapis. Wong.
The Last Meeting of
  Pocahontas and the Great
  Captain. Preston.
The Leap. Dickey.
Leda Reconsidered. Van
  Duyn.
Lend a Hand. Hale.
The Lesbian Hell. Crowley.
The Letter. Blackburn.
The Life of Particles.
  Benedikt.
Life's Testament.
  Baylebridge.
Light a Candle. Zelda.
The Lightning Flash.
  Anonymous.
The Limits of Equitation.
  Winder.
Lines to a Tree. Teller. J. L.
Lispy Bails Out. Barker.
Little Bessie. *Anonymous.*
The Little General. Muir.
Little Steamboat. Williams.
The Living God. Ibn Ezra.
Loneliness and July Ninth.
  Alegria.
The Lonely Road. Rand.
Look to the Back of the
  Hand. Minty.
Look Up! Hale.
The Lookout. Collins.
Loot. Gunn.
Lord of Each Soul. Engle.
Love Poem–1940.
  Hershenson.
Love Song. *Anonymous.*
Love Song. Halevi.
The Loved One. Hansen.
A Lover, upon an Accident
  Necessitating His
  Departure.... Carew.
Madonna Natura. "Macleod.
Madrigal: "No, no, Nigella!"
  Morley.
Magnificat. Symons.
Mail Call. Bensko.
Making a Fist. Nye.
Making Port. McKay.
The Market Town. Carlin.
Marthy Virginia's Hand.
  Lathrop.
A Masique Presented at
  Ludlow Castle (Comus).
  Milton.
The Master Weaver.
  Anonymous.
The Maul. Nealy.
Michael's Room. Gibbons.
Milking Time. Roberts.
A Miner's Life. *Anonymous.*
Modern Love, XIX.
  Meredith.
Mona Lisa. Pater.
The Monks at Ards.
  Maybin.
Monte Alban. Stroud.
Moon Compasses. Frost.
The Mosaic Worker. Peach.
Mother's Hands.
  Wedgefarth.
Music of the Dawn.
  Harrison.
My Blessing Be on Waterford.
  Letts.
My Dog. Robinson.
My God, My God, Look
  upon Me. Walsh.

My Hand Has a Pain.
  Columcille.
My Love Is Sleeping. Leslie.
My Mistress's Boots.
  Locker-Lampson.
My Mother Once Told Me.
  Amichai.
Naso, You're All Men's Man.
  Catullus.
The New Negro. McCall.
New Zealand. Baxter.
The Newly-Wedded. Praed.
Nightsong. Coxe.
No Man, If Men Are Gods.
  Cummings.
Not in Narrow Seas.
  Curnow.
Notes for Echo Lake 5.
  Palmer.
November. Morris.
Now. Gilbert.
Nunc Scio, Quid Sit Amor.
  Mackay.
O Mad Spring, One Waits.
  Moore.
Odes. Horace.
Odes, II. Hafiz.
Of the Terrible Doubt of
  Appearances. Whitman.
Old Botany Bay. Gilmore.
Old Counsel of the Young
  Master of a Wrecked
  California Clipper.
  Melville.
Old Couple. Simic.
On a Picture by Pippin,
  Called "The Den."
  Rodman.
On Bell-Ringers. Voltaire
  (Francois Marie Arouet).
On Certain Mornings
  Everything Is Sensual.
  Jauss.
On Reading Poems to a
  Senior Class at South High.
  Berry.
One of the Principal Causes of
  War. ""MacDiarmid.
Opportunity. Machiavelli.
Organ Solo. Skinner.
Orpheus and Eurydice. Hill.
Our Hands in the Garden.
  Hebert.
Out of That Sea. Ferry.
Out-of-the-Body Travel.
  Plumly.
Out of the Old House, Nancy.
  Carleton.
Over Their Graves.
  Stockard.
The Paperweight.
  Schnackenberg.
Paradise Lost. Milton.
Paradox: That Fruition
  Destroys Love (excerpt).
  King.
Paris. Garnett.
Paris in the Snow. Sedar-
  Senghor.
Party at Hydra. Layton.
A Patching Together: The
  Cell Lay inside Her Body.
  Edmond.
Permit Me Voyage. Agee.
Personal Poem #8.
  Berrigan.
Peter Rabbit. McPherson.
The Petition of the Gray
  Horse, Auld Dunbar.
  Dunbar.
Photograph. Prettyman.
The Piano. Davey.

Piano Practice. Moss.
Piers Plowman (excerpt).
  Anonymous.
Plato, a Musician. Leontius.
The Players Ask for a
  Blessing on the Psalteries
  and Themselves. Yeats.
Plea to Those Who Matter.
  Welch.
Ploughman at the Plough.
  Golding.
The Plowman. Harris.
A Plum. Leib.
Poem: "Entombed in my
  heart." Dodson.
A Poem for the Old Man.
  Wieners.
Poem: "This life like no
  other." Orr.
Poem: "You are ill and so I
  lead you away." Purdy.
The Poet and the Child.
  Howells.
The Power of Interval. De
  Tabley.
Prayer. Bro.
Preface to a Twenty Volume
  Suicide Note. Jones.
Preludes. Eliot.
De Profundis. Rossetti.
Promises, VIII. Founding
  Fathers.... Warren.
Psalm. Ben-Yitzhak.
Psalm XVI. Sidney.
Psalm XXXII. Wyatt.
Put Down. Damas.
Quarrelling, or Let Dogs
  Delight. Watts.
Radiation Leak. Aliesan.
Rain. Wright.
Rain Forest. Smith.
The Rapture. Traherne.
Reality. Souster.
The Rebel. Belloc.
The Red Sea Place in Your
  Life. Flint.
The Rejected Member's Wife.
  Hardy.
Request to a Year. Wright.
Requiescat. Porter.
Return of Autumn. Neruda.
Reveille. Brown.
Revelation. Markham.
Riddle: "Stiff standing on the
  bed." *Anonymous.*
Riding. Grossman.
The Riflemen at Bennington.
  Anonymous.
Rock Painting. Arnett.
Rocks. Heide.
Romeo and Juliet.
  Shakespeare.
Sacco Writes to His Son.
  Lewis.
Sacrifice. Kinsella.
San Miguel De La Tumba.
  Berceo.
The Scribe's Prayer.
  Guiterman.
Scrievin. Scott.
Sea Love. Mew.
The Sea-Maiden. De Forest.
Seance. King.
Searching for Lambs.
  Anonymous.
The Secret Garden. Kinsella.
The Secret Heart. Coffin.
The Seed Shop. Stuart.
September 7. Bass.
The Serenity in Stones.
  Ortiz.
Seven Poems. Niedecker.

Seven Years at Sea.
  Anonymous.
The Shadowgraphs.
  Lattimore.
The Shamrock. Egan.
She Contrasts with Herself
  Hippolyta. Doolittle.
Shetland Pony. Lindsay.
Shoplifters. Stanton.
Sick unto Death of Love.
  Anonymous.
A Simpler Thing, a Chair.
  Mezey.
Sisyphus Angers the Gods of
  Condescension. Murry.
Six Winters. Todd.
A Skater's Valentine.
  Guiterman.
Sleeping Beauty. Johnson.
Snapshot. Garrett.
Somewhere I Have Never
  Travelled, Gladly Beyond.
  Cummings.
Son. Emanuel.
Song for September.
  Fitzgerald.
A Song from Armenia. Hill.
Song: "I placed my dream in
  a boat." Meireles.
Song: "O lady, when the
  tipped cup of the moon
  blessed you." Hughes.
A Song of Angiola in Heaven.
  Dobson.
Song of the Bride. Mernit.
Song: "Of thee, kind boy, I
  ask no red and white."
  Suckling.
Song: "Stop! Don't touch me."
  Anonymous.
Song to the Masquers.
  Shirley.
Sonnet XV: "This is the way
  we say it in our time."
  Scott.
Sonnet: "And I have seen
  again the marvellous child."
  Verlaine.
Sonnet: "Innumerable
  Beauties, thou white haire."
  Herbert of Cherbury.
Sonnet: "Of thee (kind boy) I
  ask no red and white."
  Suckling.
Sonnet to a Young Lady Who
  Sent Me a Laurel Crown.
  Keats.
Sonnet to the Prince Regent.
  Byron.
Sonnets. Tuckerman.
Sonnets to Laura. Petrarch.
Sooner or Later. Cornish.
The Sower. Cowper.
Sphinxes Inclined to Be.
  Orozco.
Spring Air. Derwood.
Spring Catch. Keeler.
Spring Floods. Orr.
Spring is short. Yosano
  Akiko.
Stand, Stately Tavie.
  Anonymous.
Steamboats, Viaducts, and
  Railways. Wordsworth.
Step by Step. Ryberg.
Stigmata. Lane.
Stillness. Flecker.
Stories Relate Life. Shady.
The Story of Lava. Evans.
The Story of Two Gentlemen
  and the Gardener. Logue.

The Stranger Not Ourselves. Stafford.
A Street in Kaufman-Ville: or a Note Thrown to Carolyn... Cunningham.
Submission. Herbert.
Subversive. Benet.
The Subway Witnesses. Thomas.
Such Hap as I Am Happed in. Wyatt.
Sunday. Herbert.
Surf-Casting. Merwin.
The Swimming Lady. Anonymous.
Taking Off My Clothes. Forche.
Tales of the Islands, III. Walcott.
Tall Stately Plants with Spikes and Forks of Gold. Tuckerman.
A Testimony. Lyon.
Text. Wurdemann.
There Is In Human Closeness a Sacred Boundary. Akhmatova.
There Is Something. Pope.
They Came This Evening. Damas.
Things That Happen. Stafford.
Think. Weekes.
This Place in the Ways. Rukeyser.
This Poem Is for Nadine. Janeczko.
Three Poems. Yakamochi.
Thy Brother's Blood. Very.
Time Passes. Lister.
Tir-Nan-Og. Hendry.
The Tired Woman. Wickham.
The Titans. Alver.
To a Cat. Swinburne.
To Charles Cowden Clarke. Keats.
To Delia. Daniel.
To God. Maurice.
To His Friend, on the Untunable Times. Herrick.
To His Sister, Mrs. S. the Rose. Hammond.
To Man Who Goes Seeking Immortality, Bidding Him Look Nearer Home. Crapsey.
To My Brother George. Keats.
To Ronge. Whittier.
To the Spring Sun. Laughton.
To the Thirty-Ninth Congress. Whittier.
To Thee, O God. Holmes.
The Toaster. Smith.
Tomorrow. Leitner.
Touch. Paz.
The Touch of Human Hands. Clark.
Toward the Solstice. Rich.
The Tragical Death of A, Apple Pie. Anonymous.
Treason of Sand. Roth.
Treasure. Long.
The Tree. Auchterlonie.
Tristram's End. Binyon.
The Tunnel. Crane.
Two Lovers Discoursing. Anonymous.
Two Poems on the Emotions. Shapiro.

Two Postures Beside a Fire. Wright.
The Unicorn. Rieu.
The Unloved to His Beloved. Percy.
Upheld by His Hand. Renfrow.
Upon Master Walter Montagu's Return from Travel. Carew.
Upon the King's Return from Flanders. Hall.
Upon the Losse of His Little Finger. Randolph.
An Utter Passion Uttered Utterly (parody). Todhunter.
The Valley. Moss.
Villanelle. Empson.
Walking Along the Sea of Galilee. Knut.
Walking Late. Montague.
Walking the Wilderness. Stafford.
Walking with God. Anonymous.
Wandering. Flexner.
Warm Hands. Anonymous.
Warning to Travailers Seeking Accomodations at Mr. Devills Inn. Knight.
Water. McPheron.
Watts. Kaufman.
Wedlock. Noll.
Week-End by the Sea. Masters.
The Western Rebel. Anonymous.
What Changes, My Love. Honig.
What Thomas an Buile Said in a Pub. Stephens.
When You Touch. Hart-Smith.
The White-Haired Man. Sarton.
Why I Am Offended By Miracles. Bergman.
Wicked Polly. Anonymous.
Widows. Masters.
The Window of the Tobacco Shop. Cavafy.
Winter. Jaszi.
Wishes for My Son. Macdonagh.
Woman Free (excerpt). Wolstenholme-Elmy.
Woman Me. Angelou.
The Wood of the Self-Destroyers. Yellen.
Yonosa House. Smith.
You Begin. Atwood.
The Young Priest to His Hands. Garesche.
Zalinka. MacInnes.

Handful
Blake Leads a Walk on the Milky Way. Willard.
Elms of the Eastern Gate. Anonymous.
The Horse Chestnut Tree. Eberhart.
Orpheus and Eurydice. Valentine.
Pastoral. Voigt.

Handkerchief (s)
Belita. Rios.
The Dawning. Herbert.
Eighteen-Seventy. Rimbaud.
I Had a Little Husband. Mother Goose.

The Laird of Wariston (B vers.). Anonymous.
Life. Gold.
The Magician. Ramke.
My Grandmother Sent Me a New-Fashioned Three-Cornered Cambric... Anonymous.
Stocking and Shirt. Reeves.
Train. Smith.
White Heliotrope. Symons.

Handle (s)
Arawata Bill. Glover.
Humpty Dumpty's Recitation. "Carroll.
The Last Galway Hooker. Murphy.
Plow. Anonymous.
Portrait of a Cree. "Hale.
Somebody Almost Walked Off Wid Alla My Stuff. Shange.
Subterranean Homesick Blues. Dylan.

Handmaid (en) (s)
A Faith on Trial (excerpt). Meredith.
The Housewife's Prayer. Kelly.
Swinburne at Tea. Pain.
To Kaaon. Pound.

Handshake
The Potato Eaters. Graziano.
The Summer Rentals. Halpern.

Handsome (ly)
Cock-a-Bandy. Anonymous.
Kind Miss (with music). Anonymous.
Rotten Row. Locker-Lampson.
Sayre. Strongin.
Work and Play. Martial (Marcus Valerius Martialis).

Handy
The Ebenezer. Anonymous.
Poem. Mason.
So Handy. Anonymous.
So Handy, Me Boys, So Handy. Anonymous.
Yankee Doodle. Bangs.
The Yankeys' Return from Camp. Anonymous.

Hang (ed) (ing) (s) (hung)
Ane Satire of the Three Estaitis (excerpt). Lyndsay.
Antiquary. Donne.
A Ballad of the Rising in the North. Anonymous.
A Ballade of Suicide. Chesterton.
Bird Riddle: "As I went out, so I came in." Anonymous.
Brown Robin (B version). Anonymous.
Contentment. Osaki.
The Cruel Brother. Anonymous.
The Deer and the Snake. Patchen.
Dobbin. Bowering.
Doll Thy Ale. Anonymous.
Dream of the Forgotten Lover. Fox.
Epigram on a Lawyer's Desiring One of the Tribe to Look.... Fergusson.

Epitaph: "Here lies Sir John Plumpudding of the Grange." Anonymous.
Epitaph on the Politician Himself. Belloc.
Epitaph on Will Smith. Anonymous.
Frigate Jones, the Pussyfooter. Burke.
The Gallows Pole. Anonymous.
Generations. Awad.
The Great Bear. Hollander.
Hanging Johnny. Anonymous.
Homing Pigeons. Walker.
How Annandale Went Out. Robinson.
How Robin Hood Rescued the Widow's Sons. Anonymous.
In a Boat. Belloc.
In Lieu. MacNeice.
In the Dusk the Path. Izumi Shikibu.
Jack and His Father. Heywood.
The Jinx Blues. House.
John Thomson and the Turk (A version). Anonymous.
The King of China's Daughter. Sitwell.
Lament for a Cricket Eleven. Allott.
Lesbia Railing. Catullus.
Limerick: "A Briton who shot at his king." Ross.
Lord Randall. Anonymous.
The Maid Freed from the Gallows (B vers.). Anonymous.
A Mermaiden. Hennell.
Moonrise. Sherman.
The Murder of Maria Marten. Corder.
Museum Piece. Wilbur.
Notes from an Analyst's Couch. Probst.
The Obscene Caller. Dacey.
Of All the Seas That's Coming. Anonymous.
The Old Battalion. Anonymous.
On a Bright and Summer's Morning. Anonymous.
On a Nomination to the Legion of Honour. Anonymous.
The Oxford Girl (Expert Town). Anonymous.
The Parliament Soldiers. Anonymous.
Pearl Bryan. Anonymous.
A Poem about Poems about Vietnam. Stallworthy.
Prospecting Dream. Anonymous.
The proverb reporteth, no man can deny... Anonymous.
Queen Eleanor's Confession (A version). Anonymous.
Robin Hood and the Widow's Three Sons. Anonymous.
A Short Song of Congratulation. Johnson.
A Shropshire Lad. Housman.
Signs. Murphy.
Sir Henry Clinton's Invitation to the Refugees. Freneau.

Snaps for Dinner, Snaps for Breakfast, and Snaps for Supper. Horton.
Song: "Fire, fire." Bold.
A Song: "I'll sing you a song." *Anonymous.*
Song of the Trees of the Black Forest. Jabes.
Spirits of the Dead. Poe.
Suburban. Coursen.
The Sycamore Tree. *Anonymous.*
The Thousand and One Nights: The Song of the Narcissus. *Anonymous.*
Three-Toed Sloth. Donnelly.
To One Who Quotes and Detracts. Landor.
We'll Roll the Golden Chariot Along. *Anonymous.*
We May Not Know. Alexander.
What's Good for the Soul Is Good for Sales. Wilbur.

Hangman
The Execution. Nowlan.
Gaiety: Queer's Song. Howard.
The Gallows Tree. Higgins.
Gulliver. Slessor.
The Maid Freed from the Gallows ("Hangman, Slack on the Line"). *Anonymous.*
So Help Me God. Catullus.

Happ (ier) (ily) (iness) (y)
Above the Bright Blue Sky. Midlane.
Acres of Clams. *Anonymous.*
After great storms the calm returns. Wyatt.
Air: "The Love of a Woman." Creeley.
Amoretti, LIX. Spenser.
Anacreontea: The Grasshopper. *Anonymous.*
April Showers. Stephens.
Arc. Clark.
Arrivals, Departures. Larkin.
At Torrey Pines State Park. Mazzaro.
An Athenian Garden. Stickney.
Awakening. Stryk.
Back to Griggsby's Station. Riley.
A Bad Sleeper. Verlaine.
The Bagel. Ignatow.
The Ballad of Private Chadd. Milne.
Barbie Doll. Piercy.
Be off! Smith.
The Beautiful. Woodley.
The Beckett Kit. Gregg.
The Beggar. Doak.
Biography. Struther.
Biography (excerpt). Masefield.
The Bird in the Room. Lehmann.
Birthday Poem from Venice. Beer.
Blue Bottle. *Anonymous.*
Born Yesterday. Larkin.
Buffalo Creek. Brereton.
Calm Winter Sleep. Corke.
Caroline and Her Young Sailor Bold. *Anonymous.*
Cast Our Caps and Cares Away. Fletcher.

Celestial Wisdom. Juvenal (Decimas Junius Juvenalis).
A Certain Peace. Giovanni.
Charlie Piecan. Anonymous.
Christmas Carol. *Anonymous.*
The Churches of Rome and of England. Dryden.
Civilizing the Child. Mueller.
Clarence. Silverstein.
Cliff Klingenhagen. Robinson.
Coming. Larkin.
The Cottager. Clare.
Cranston near the City Line. Berrigan.
Credences of Summer. Stevens.
The Creek of the Four Graves (excerpt). Harpur.
Crown of Happiness. Hebert.
Curtain! Dunbar.
Decline and Fall of a Roman Umpire. Nash.
The Deformed Mistress. Suckling.
The Deserted Garden. Browning.
Discovery of the New World. Revard.
Don Juan. Byron.
Don Juan's Address to the Sunset. Nichols.
The Dunce. De la Mare.
Eclogue. Lear.
Elegy on the Eve. Barker.
Elephant. Brownjohn.
The Enquiry. Dyer.
Epitaph: "If fruits are fed on any beast." Synge.
The Equinox. Heyward.
Europe. Dudek.
Evening. Behn.
Evening Hymn in the Hovels. Adams.
The Faerie Queene. Spenser.
The Fairy Maimoune. Moultrie.
Fairy Story. Warren.
The Flower-Boat. Frost.
For a Copy of Theocritus. Dobson.
For One Lately Bereft. Bruner.
For You, Falling Asleep after a Quarrel. Middlebrook.
A Fortune-Teller. Bynner.
The French Revolution. Wordsworth.
The Glorious Game. Burton.
Gnostics on Trial. Gregg.
God Has Pity on Kindergarten Children. Amichai.
The Gods Must Not Know Us. Gregg.
Good-Bye to the Mezzogiorno. Auden.
Graffiti. Bold.
Grieve Not for Beauty. Bynner.
Happiness. Isenhour.
Happy at 40. Meinke.
The Happy Night. Squire.
A Holiday. Reese.
How Pleasant Is This Flowery Plain. *Anonymous.*
Hymn to Marriage, for Manlius and Junia. Catullus.

If Life's a Lousy Picture, Why Not Leave before the End. McGough.
Important Statement. Kavanagh.
In a Train. Bly.
In Reference to Her Children, 23. June, 1656. Bradstreet.
The Indian Emperor. Dryden.
Janna. Kuka.
January. Lambdin.
Jolly Jack. Thackeray.
A Kitchen Prayer. Petersen.
Koala. Ross.
Lady Byron's Reply to Lord Byron's Fare Thee Well. *Anonymous.*
Lady Maria, in You Merit and Distinction. Bieiris de Romans.
Letter to the Governors, June 8, 1783. Washington.
Lied in Crete. Mutis.
Like a Beach. Shapiro.
Like as the Dove. Sidney.
Lines. McHugh.
Little Things. Carney.
Lonely Love. Blunden.
Long May. Castro.
Lord! It Is Not Life to Live. Toplady.
Lost. Auden.
Map of My Country. Holmes.
Maria Bright. Walther von der Vogelweide.
Matthew X. 28. Wolcott.
Mean Old Twister. Arnold.
Meditations of an Old Woman. Roethke.
Money (with music). *Anonymous.*
Mr. Over. Smith.
My Friend the Wind. Kuka.
New Time. *Anonymous.*
A New World Symphony. Wright.
New Year's Wishes. Havergal.
Night. Coleridge.
Night Song from Backbone Mountain. Epstein.
Nikki-Rosa. Giovanni.
No More Beneath the Oppressive Hand. *Anonymous.*
Northern Pike. Wright.
O Merry May the Maid Be. Clerk.
Oblivion. Fauset.
Of God We Ask One Favor. Dickinson.
Old Maids. *Anonymous.*
Old Men Working Concrete. Hey.
On a Shrew. *Anonymous.*
One, Two, Buckle My Shoe. Nash.
One Who Watches. Sassoon.
Our Ship She Lies in Harbour. *Anonymous.*
The Parliament Dissolved at Oxford. Ayloffe.
Personal Poem. O'Hara.
The Place of the Damned. Swift.
Poetry Reading. Myles.
The Quangle Wangle's Hat. Lear.
The Queen's Speech. Mainwaring.

The Rantin Laddie. *Anonymous.*
The Rapture. Baker.
Recessional for the Class of 1959... Cowen.
The Reconcilement. Sheffield.
The Rigs o' Barley. Burns.
Rowland's Rhyme. Drayton.
Running. Wilbur.
Sally. Durcan.
Savage Portraits. Marquis.
The Serenity in Stones. Ortiz.
Set Down, Servant. *Anonymous.*
The Shepherd's Dog. Norris.
The Shoe Factory. Harwood.
Sit Down, Sad Soul. "Cornwall.
Sittin' on the Porch. Guest.
Sleep and Poetry. Keats.
The Sleep of Spring. Clare.
Soft Falls the Sweet Evening. Clare.
Son of a Gun. *Anonymous.*
Song: "I could make you songs." Dow.
The Song of Hungarrda. Ngunaitponi.
The Sonnet-Ballad. Brooks.
Sonnet Written at the Close of Spring. Smith.
Still Century. Paulin.
Success Story. Winch.
The Sun. Drinkwater.
Tea for Two. Caesar.
The Technique of Love. Kessler.
The Thanksgiving for America. Butterworth.
Their Wedded Love. Milton.
Then and Now. Walker.
The Thieves of Love. Ford.
This Happy Day. Behn.
This Moment Yearning and Thoughtful. Whitman.
Time's Fool. Pitter.
The Times Have Altered. *Anonymous.*
'Tis Said That Some Have Died for Love. Wordsworth.
To an Indian Poet. Harjo.
To His Sacred Majesty, a Panegyrick... Dryden.
To Hope. Williams.
To Silvia. Wilchilsea.
To the Rev. F. D. Maurice. Tennyson.
Towser Shall Be Tied Tonight. *Anonymous.*
The Toy Horse. Iremonger.
Trebetherick. Betjeman.
The Trial. Auden.
The Truro Bear. Oliver.
Turkey in the Straw. *Anonymous.*
Twilight. Robinson.
Urban Ode. McPherson.
Vanity. Wickham.
The Vanity of Human Wishes. Johnson.
Various Wakings. Buckley.
Veranius, My Dear Friend. Catullus.
View from My Window. MacLean.
Virgidemiarum. Hall.
The Watch on the Rhine. Stein.

Weep Love's Losing. Imr el Kais.
When Adam Was First Created. *Anonymous.*
When Boys Go A-Courting. *Anonymous.*
When I Heard at the Close of the Day. Whitman.
The Willow Tree. *Anonymous.*
Winter. Thomson.
With the Door Open. Ignatow.
Woman Asleep on a Banana Leaf. Pollitt.
Youth and Age. Arnold.

Happen (ed) (ing) (ings) (s)
The Author's Apology. Carmi.
A Backward Spring. Hardy.
The Current. Merrill.
A Friend Advises Me to Stop Drinking. Mei Yao Ch'en.
The Head. Fallon.
The Hollow Thesaurus. McDonald.
How Everything Happens (Based on a Study of the Wave). Swenson.
I Write Poems. Fuertes.
Jeane Dixon's America. Costanzo.
The Little Bird. *Anonymous.*
The Maine Trail. McGiffert.
Ofay-Watcher Looks Back. Serote.
Sleeping with One Eye Open. Strand.
Waiting for IT. Swenson.

Happy New Year
Christmas Carol. *Anonymous.*
God Bless the Master of This House. *Anonymous.*
New Time. *Anonymous.*
New Year's Wishes. Havergal.

Harbor (s)
The Captain's Daughter. Fields.
Decks. Phillips.
Eagle Sonnets. Wood.
From the Harbor Hill. Kobbe.
A Horse Would Tire. Coatsworth.
I Many Times Thought Peace Had Come. Dickinson.
If Something Should Happen. Clifton.
In Foreign Parts. Richards.
In Harbor. Hayne.
The Incredible Yachts. Booth.
Like a wave crest. Uda.
Love at the Door. Meleager.
Not That Far. Miller.
Offshore Breeze. Acorn.
The Pilot. Anonymous.
Pirate Story. Stevenson.
Plymouth Harbor. Radford.
The Prophet Lost in the Hills at Evening. Belloc.
Reclining Figure. Hall.
A Ship Comes in. Jenkins.
Storm Song. Taylor.
To a Cloistress. Tassis.
The Two Gentlemen of Verona. Shakespeare.
The William P. Frye. Foster.

Hard (en) (er) (est)
Album. Miles.

Alone. Holden.
American Laughter. Robinson.
At a Welsh Waterfall. Hopkins.
The Ballad of Charity. Leland.
The Banjo. Winner.
Beauty. Wylie.
Big Man. Mason.
Bricking the Church. Morgan.
Broken Treaties: Teeth. Contoski.
The Bumper Sticker on His Pickup Said, "I'm a Lover, I'm a Fighter..." Fox.
Catalogue. Untermeyer.
The Cloud-Mobile. Swenson.
Coralville, in Iowa. Bell.
Cryderville Jail. *Anonymous.*
Dido: Swarming. Spivack.
Dislike of Tasks. Lattimore.
The Execution. Nowlan.
Finds Something in New Jersey (parody). Poster.
The First Time I Met You. Montgomery.
A Funeral Elogy... Norton II.
Fury against the Moslems at Uhud. Hind bint Utba.
Hard Times. *Anonymous.*
Hills. Munro.
Irish Hotel. Wevill.
It's Hard on We Po' Farmers. *Anonymous.*
It's Here In The. Atkins.
The Jazz of This Hotel. Lindsay.
Jim Bludso of the Prairie Belle. Hay.
Just. Sherwin.
Lesbian Play on T.V. Gilfillan.
The Life of Hard Times. Tan Pai.
Little Willie. *Anonymous.*
The Looking-Glass. Kipling.
The Miracle. Suckling.
A Mother's Prayer. Sangster.
Motherless Children. Johnson.
Nude Reclining at Word Processor, in Pastel. Conover.
Oh, Babe, It Ain't No Lie. Cotton.
The Old Flagman. Sandburg.
Once More A-Lumbering Go. *Anonymous.*
The Other Side of Jordan. *Anonymous.*
The palm of my hand. Saito.
Parrot, Fish, Tiger and Mule. Greenberg.
The Plea of the Midsummer Fairies. Hood.
Po" Boy. *Anonymous.*
The Protest of the Illiterate. Burgess.
Robert's Farm. *Anonymous.*
The Runaways. Van Doren.
Salad. Collins.
The Sleeping-Bag. Ponting.
Song: One Hard Look. Graves.
Sonnets. Lee.
The Struggle. Prudhomme.

That No Man Should Write But Such as Do Excel. Turberville.
There Was a Strife 'Twixt Man and Maid. Kipling.
Things About Comin' My Way. *Anonymous.*
Timon's Villa. Pope.
To My Ill Reader. Herrick.
Toads. Larkin.
Triolet. Bridges.
Troopship in the Tropics. Lewis.
An Unsaid Word. Rich.
Untitled Poem. Dugan.
The Wanton (excerpt). Vidya.
When Young Ladies Get Married. *Anonymous.*
Woman of This Earth (excerpt). Frost.
The Writer. Wilbur.
Youth and Age. Mimnermus.

Hardship
Day and Night Handball. Dunn.

Hare
Beagles. Rodgers.
The Collar-Bone of a Hare. Yeats.
Emblems. Tate.
The Horn. Adams.
The Hunting of the Gods. Anonymous.

Hark (en) (ing)
Call John the Boatman. *Anonymous.*
The Faerie Queene. Spenser.
The Lion's Nature. *Anonymous.*
My Wish for My Land. Stow.
The Passing Bell. Heywood.
A Pine-Tree Buoy. Morris.
Recollection. Carpenter.
Reynard the Fox. *Anonymous.*
Southerly Wind. *Anonymous.*

Harlem
Harlem Shadows. McKay.
Lenox Avenue Mural. Hughes.
To a Fighter Killed in the Ring. Lipsitz.

Harlot (s)
Africa. McKay.
In the Vices. Evans.
Morgan. Stedman.
Sabbath Reflection. Wrafter.
Silent, Silent Night. Blake.
Tirocinium; or, A Review of Schools. Cowper.

Harm (ed) (s)
Baby Sleeps. Hinds.
The Ballad of Fisher's Boardinghouse. Kipling.
The Blue Animals. Anderson.
The Burial of Latane. Thompson.
The Cardinal and the Dog. Browning.
Charm: "Let the superstitious wife." Herrick.
The Chimney Sweeper. Blake.
The Dove. MacColl.
Dream Songs. Berryman.
The Fieldmouse. Alexander.
The Graveyard Rabbit. Stanton.

The House of Fame: The Eagle Converses with Chaucer. Chaucer.
John Watts. *Anonymous.*
Lake Leman. Byron.
The Lament of the Flowers. Very.
On a Vase of Gold-Fish. Tennyson.
Ophelia's Song. Zaturenska.
Parleyings with Certain People of Importance in Their Day. Browning.
Passengers. Johnson.
A Prayer for a Sleeping Child. Davies.
Stanzas from Saint Peter's Complaint. Southwell.
To a Sleeping Friend. Cocteau.
To Chloris. Drummond.
Tom Jones's Plum Tree (The Juniper Tree). *Anonymous.*
Twilight Song. Hunter-Duvar.
A Volume of Chopin. Picot.
When All This All Doth Pass from Age to Age. Greville.
Witches. Hughes.

Harmless
On Being Photographed. Gass.
What Harvest Half So Sweet Is. Campion.

Harmon (ies) (y)
Against the Silences to Come. Loewinsohn.
Come, Let Us Sound with Melody, the Praises. Campion.
Das Jahr Der Seele (excerpt). George.
Duino Elegies. Rilke.
His Request. O'Sullivan.
Hunger. Stampa.
Ice Cream in Paradise. Hollander.
Immortality. Dana.
Man in Harmony with Nature. Very.
Milton. Blake.
An Old-Fashioned Poet. Murray.
Orpheus to Beasts. Lovelace.
Santa Lucia. *Anonymous.*
Shall the Dead Praise Thee? Macdonald.
Sonnet: "Oh, if thou knew'st how thou thyself dost harm." Stirling.
The Unremarkable Year. Fuller.
Virtue the Best Monument. Ralegh.
Wedding Celebration. Kono.
Wood Music. King.

Harness
Is. Kavanagh.
The Midnight Court. Merriman.
The Sailor's Grace. *Anonymous.*

Harp (s)
The Bishop's Harp. Mannyng.
Die Pelzaffen. Spear.
The Eyes That Drew from Me. Petrarch (Francesco Petrarca).
The Fairy Harpers. Dollard.

The Five Voyages of Arnor.
Brown.
Harp in the Rigging.
Maclaren.
The Harper of Chao. Po
Chu-i.
The Hobbit (excerpt).
Tolkien.
Inanna and Ishkur.
Enheduanna.
Limerick: "G is a grumbler
gruff." Herford.
Lit'le David Play on Yo'
Harp. Anonymous.
Love Me! Smith.
Music of the Dawn.
Harrison.
Of My Lady Isabella Playing
on the Lute. Waller.
Paradise Lost. Milton.
Passion and Worship.
Rossetti.
Persistency of Poetry.
Arnold.
Resurgence. Rumi.
Seascape. Spender.
Shopping for Meat in Winter.
Williams.
That Harp You Play So Well.
Moore.
There Is a Tavern in the
Town. Anonymous.
To * * * * *. Callanan.

Harpoon
Captain Bunker. Anonymous.
Hymn to the Air Spirit.
Anonymous.

Harpsichord
Albert Ayler: Eulogy for a
Decomposed Saxophone
Player. Crouch.
On an Air of Rameau.
Symons.

Harry
The Casual Man. Glover.
Epitaph on Prince Henry.
Holland.
Epitaph on Queen Elizabeth,
Wife of Henry VII.
Anonymous.
Highland Harry Back Again.
Burns.
The Hunt Is Up.
Anonymous.
I Remember. Glover.
John Wasson. Masters.
Lake, Mountain, Tree.
Glover.
Malisons, Malisons, More
Than Ten. Anonymous.
On a Boy's First Reading of
"King Henry V".
Mitchell.
Once the Days. Glover.
The Raisin. Hall.
A Rope for Harry Fat.
Baxter.
Songs. Glover.
Themes. Glover.

Harsh
The Art of Love. Ovid
(Publius Ovidius Naso).
November. Tuckerman.
To a Calvinist in Bali.
Millay.
To the Frivolous Muse.
Whicher.
The Tombstone Told When
She Died. Thomas.

Hart
Amoretti, III. Spenser.
Amoretti, L. Spenser.

Arcadia. Sidney.
Breake Now My Heart and
Dye! Campion.
My Heart Is Woe.
Anonymous.
O My Harte is Wo.
Anonymous.
Perigot and Willye. Spenser.
Sonnet XIX. Alabaster.
To Live in Hell, and Heaven
to Behold. Constable.

Harvard
Address to the Scholars of
New England. Ransom.
Experiential Religion. Du
Priest.
I Walked over the Grave of
Henry James. Eberhart.

Harvest (s)
Adonais. Harney.
The Bird and the Tree.
Torrence.
The Bonny Harvest Moon.
Barr.
Bread of Brotherhood.
Trent.
Calm. Camerino.
Child of My Winter.
Snodgrass.
Cooney Potter. Masters.
Dante. Bryant.
Diary of a Church Mouse.
Betjeman.
Epigram: "You were a pretty
boy once." Philip of
Thessaloni.
Gathering Leaves. Frost.
Harvest. Anonymous.
Harvest. Cortissoz.
Harvest. Nashe [(or Nash)]
Thomas.
Harvest Time. Powers.
He Liveth Long Who Liveth
Well. Bonar.
High Summer. Kessler.
I Will Go with My Father A-
Ploughing. Campbell.
If I Could Go On Kissing
Your Honeyed Eyes.
Catullus.
In Your Arrogance. Lawner.
The Mosquito. Jones.
Mothers. Tzara.
Nam Semen Est Verbum Dei.
Guiney.
Odes. Santayana.
On the Big Horn. Whittier.
Our Life Is Hid with Christ in
God. Herbert.
A Part of an Ode. Jonson.
Prayer to the Blessed Virgin.
Rodriquez de Padron.
The Reaper. Tabb.
Returning from Harvest.
Watkins.
The Roots of Revolution in
the Vegetable Kingdom.
Urdang.
Ruth. Hood.
The Scarecrow. De la Mare.
The Seasons. Holcroft.
Sonnet: "Nay, Lord, not
thus!" Wilde.
To the Immortal Memory and
Friendship of That Noble
Pair... Jonson.
Views from the High Camp.
Merwin.
A Vision of Judgement.
Southey.
The Waggon-Maker.
Masefield.

The Zulu Girl. Campbell.

Haste (n)
Anonymous. Cruz.
Bunker Hill. Calvert.
The Children's Ghosts.
Letts.
The Clarity of Apples.
Perlin.
Cultural Exchange. Hughes.
Don Juan. Byron.
Fables: The Sick Man and the
Angel. Gay.
Farewell to the Court.
Ralegh.
Gascoigne's Memories.
Gascoigne.
Il Janitoro. Ade.
Shining. Spivack.
Starting from Paumanok.
Whitman.
The Tortoise. Corman.
A Valentine. Betham-
Edwards.
Wake, Lady! Baillie.

Hat (s)
Ballad: "I put my hat upon
my head." Johnson.
The Beggar on the Beach.
Gregory.
Cardinal Fisher. Heywood.
Coplas. Anonymous.
Cupid's Darts. Herbert.
The Dying Hobo.
Anonymous.
Elegy in Six Sonnets.
Tuckerman.
An Exchange of Hats. Moss.
False Friends-Like. Barnes.
Fragment: The Furl of Fresh-
Leaved Dog-Rose Down.
Hopkins.
How the waters closed above
him. Dickinson.
In January, 1962. Kooser.
In the Ladies' Room at the
Bus Terminal (parody).
Zaranka.
Infirm. Martin.
An Intermezzo for the Fourth
Act. White.
Jerry Hall. Anonymous.
John Burns of Gettysburg.
Harte.
The Lady. Coatsworth.
Lee to the Rear. Thompson.
Liverpool Girls. Anonymous.
Look at All Those Monkeys.
Milligan.
The Moral Taxi Ride.
Kastner.
Mr. Vachel Lindsay Discovers
Radio (parody).
Hoffenstein.
My Infundibuliform Hat.
Adams.
My Old Straw Hat. Cook.
Notice. McCord.
Nottingham Fair.
Anonymous.
Old King Cabbage.
Munkittrick.
The Old Man at the Crossing.
Strong.
Railroad to Hell.
Anonymous.
Rhyme of Rain. Holmes.
A Second Stanza for Dr.
Johnson. Hall.
Shooting Ducks in South
Louisiana. Tillinghast.
Short Eulogy. Gurevitch.
Tin Cup Blues. Jefferson.

Hatched
A-Begging Buttermilk I Will
Go. Anonymous.
Easter Egg. Kieffaber.

Hatchet
The Cropper Lads.
Anonymous.
Dear Father, Look up.
Newell.
The Entailed Farm. Glassco.
The Last Refuge. Young.
A Love Dirge to the
Whitehouse (or It Soots
You Right). Fletcher.
My Darling Dear, My Daisy
Flower. Skelton.
That Little Hatchet. Butler-
Andrews.

Hate (d) (s) (ful)
The Alarm. Jacob.
Amalek. Torberg.
Apology to My Lady. Falco.
As If a Phantom Caress'd Me.
Whitman.
At a Calvary Near the Ancre.
Owen.
At Bickford's. Stern.
Ballymurphy. Anonymous.
The Beginnings (1914-1918).
Kipling.
The Bird. Greacen.
Birmingham. Walker.
Bona de Mortuis. Beddoes.
Brown of Ossawatomie.
Whittier.
Caelica, CII. Greville.
The Caged Bird. Symons.
Caledonia. McElroy.
Camouflage. Manifold.
The Complete Misanthropist.
Bishop.
The Crow. Creeley.
Cupid's Revenge: Lovers,
Rejoice! Fletcher.
The Dark Girl's Rhyme.
Parker.
Dear Reader. Tate.
A Degenerate Age. Ibn
Gabirol.
Desire, alas, my master and
my foe. Wyatt.
The Desolate Lover.
Shanahan.
Dialogue. Erskine.
Epigram: "Why do the Graces
now desert the Muse?"
Landor.
Epistles. Horace.
The External Element.
McFadden.
The Fear of Flying. Van
Duyn.
For One Who Would Not
Take His Life in His
Hands. Schwartz.
Fragment of a Song.
"Carroll.
The Glorious Twelfth.
Greacen.
The Good Man in Hell.
Muir.
Hagar. Eybers.
Hate and Debate Rome
through the World Hath
Spread. Harington.
Hatred. Bennett.
Her Love Poem. Clifton.
The Hindoo: He Doesn't Hurt
a Fly or a Spider Either.
Ramanujan.
I Hate Men. Porter.
I'm Black and Blue. Heine.

I Will Accept. Rossetti.
Impossibilities, to His Friend. Herrick.
Indeed Indeed, I Cannot Tell. Thoreau.
Ireland. Johnson.
Jew. Morhange.
The Judgement of God. Morris.
Kind Hearts. *Anonymous.*
King Lear. Shakespeare.
Lindeman. White.
Lines to a Critic. Shelley.
Lines to a Reviewer. Shelley.
Love and Hate. O'Connor.
Love Longs to Touch. Sanchez.
Merced. Rich.
Missa Papae Marcelli. McAuley.
The Mouse. Garrigue.
My Love I Gave for Hate. *Anonymous.*
O do not grieve, Dear Heart, nor shed a tear. Newcastle.
O Wearisome Condition. Brooke.
Of Drunkenness. Turberville.
Of Women No More Evil. *Anonymous.*
On Love. Tamekane.
On the Earl of Leicester. *Anonymous.*
Othello. Shakespeare.
Peer Gynt. Sorley.
The Photos. Wakoski.
The Pillar Perished Is. Wyatt.
Prayer for Peace: II. Senghor.
Prey to Prey. Rowbotham.
The Prohibition. Donne.
Rain Inters Maggiore. Kreymborg.
The Rattlesnake. Carr.
Reference to a Passage in Plutarch's Life of Sulla. Jeffers.
Respect for the Dead. Riding.
The Road to Dieppe. Finley.
The Rubicon. Winter.
Sonnet. Malon de Chaide.
Sonnet for the End of a Sequence. Parker.
Sonnets, XVII: "Cherry-Lipt Adonis in his snowie shape." Barnfield.
Sonnets, LXXXIX: "Say that thou didst forsake me for some fault." Shakespeare.
Sonnets to Karl Theodor German. Platen.
Space. Kennedy.
The Splendid Village. Elliott.
The Stone Orchard. Oates.
Such is the course that nature's kind hath wrought. Wyatt.
Surfaces. Meinke.
Tea for Two. Nolan.
There Will Be No Peace. Auden.
Timon of Athens. Shakespeare.
'Tis Now Since I Sate Down. Suckling.
To a Millionaire. Lampman.
To Everlasting Oblivion. Marston.
To Naples. Mallalieu.

The Triumph of Time. Swinburne.
Trivial, Vulgar, and Exalted: 19. Cunningham.
Under the Mountain. MacNeice.
The Visit. Emerson.
When He Thought Himself Contemned. Howell.
When I Loved You. Moore.
The White City. McKay.
The White House. McKay.
The Winter Lakes. Campbell.
The Witch. Hinkson.
The World State. Chesterton.
Written on a Paper Napkin. Gasparini.

Hatless
Death of King George V. Betjeman.
New King Arrives in His Capital by Air... Betjeman.

Haughty
Cacophonous Couplet on Cardinal Wolsey. *Anonymous.*
Gwendoline (parody). Taylor.
The Lover's Posy. Rufinus Domesticus.
The Splendid Spur. Quiller-Couch.

Haunt (ed) (s)
Almae Matres. Lang.
Bombers. Day-Lewis.
A Casual Song. Noel.
Donec Eris Felix Multos Numerabis Amicos. *Anonymous.*
The Empty House. Howells.
Fairies. Tickell.
The Family. Lydston.
Fresh Spring. Daryush.
The Ghost at Anlaby. Stow.
Ghosts. Jennings.
The Haunted House. Hood.
Hester Macdonagh. Edwards.
In a Dream. Synge.
Lough Bray. O'Grady.
Modern Love, XVI. Meredith.
Mr. Meant-To. *Anonymous.*
Never More, Sailor. De la Mare.
Solitude. Keats.
A Song. Schwartz.
There Is a Pool on Garda. Scollard.
Urban History. Kallman.

Haven (s)
Envoi. Swinburne.
Ever as We Sailed. Shelley.
Heaven-Haven. Hopkins.
Love at Large. Patmore.
New Horizons. Lysaght.
Rhodanthe. Agathias.
The Rosary of My Tears. Ryan.
To His Tutor. Hall.
The Wife to Her Husband. *Anonymous.*
Winter Heavens. Meredith.

Havoc
Lo, I Am Stricken Dumb. *Anonymous.*
On the Way. Husid.
Sir Dilberry Diddle, Captain of Militia. *Anonymous.*

Hawk (e) (s)
The Automobile. MacKaye.
The Beggar. Mitchell.
Blessed and Resting Uncle. Elliott.
Dead Ponies. Chamberlain.
Dingman's Marsh. Moore.
Discomfort in High Places. Tremayne.
Emblems. Tate.
Faintly and from Far away. Miller.
A Farewell to a Fondling. Churchyard.
Hawk's Way. Olson.
A High Place. Wilkins.
I Have Exhausted the Delighted Range... Hartnett.
The Life Not Given. Habercom.
Madrigal: "The greedy hawk with sudden sight of lure." *Anonymous.*
The Midshipman. Falconer.
Minotaur Poems. Mandel.
Minus One. Ciardi.
O. Wilbur.
On the Plains. Brooks.
Polly. Gay.
A Reflection of Night. Marietta.
Solitudes. Wheelock.
Song: "Whipped by sorrow now." Radnoti.
Spring Hawks. Thomas.
Summer Wish. Bogan.

Hawthorn
Faith, I Wish I Were a Leprechaun. Ritter.
May-Day at Sea. Finerty.
The Milk White Doe. *Anonymous.*
Song: "Heron is harsh with despair." Chamberlain.
Stranger to Europe. Butler.
Venus of the Salty Shell. Devlin.

Hay
Ametas and Thestylis Making Hay-Ropes. Marvell.
The Best Dance. *Anonymous.*
Childs Memory. Wilkins.
The City Clerk. Ashe.
Epigram: "Thy nags (the leanest things alive)." Prior.
Four Years. Craik.
From the Santa-Fe Trail. Lindsay.
The grass so little has to do. Dickinson.
Having Read Books. McHugh.
Horses Chawin' Hay. Garland.
How Our Forefather Got His Wife. Walton.
If It's Ever Spring Again. Hardy.
Ire. Thomas.
The King of Yellow Butterflies. Lindsay.
Labor of Fields. Coatsworth.
Marriage. Lowell.
Minnie Morse. Starbird.
Morning. George.
Mowing. Frost.
Rosies. Hanrahan.

Sonnets, XIII: "I walk of grey noons by the old canal." Irwin.
This Is the Hay That No Man Planted. Coatsworth.
The Thunder Mutters Louder and More Loud. Clare.
Waltz against the Mountains. Ferril.
Willy Boy. *Anonymous.*
Work Horses. Chase.

Hayseed
Ante-Natal Dream. Kavanagh.
The Hayseed. Kellog.
Hayseed (with music). *Anonymous.*

Haze
At Queensferry. Henley.
Memory. Hamburger.
The Men of Old. Milnes.
What Is Winter? Blunden.

Hazel
Bob Robin. *Anonymous.*
The Diviner. Heaney.
From the Hazel Bough. Birney.
Glenarm. Donaghy.
The Lapful of Nuts. Ferguson.
Localities. Sandburg.
The People of Blakeney. *Anonymous.*

Head (s)
527 Cathedral Parkway. Lesser.
Advice to Country Girls. *Anonymous.*
Aedh Hears the Cry of the Sedge. Yeats.
Amoretti, XXIX. Spenser.
Amours de Voyage. Clough.
Andrew's Bedtime Story. Serraillier.
The Angel. Blake.
L'Art poetique. Boileau-Despreaux.
The Aspen and the Stream. Wilbur.
At the Edge of the Jungle. Lane.
Aunt Rhody. *Anonymous.*
Aut Caesar Aut Nullus. Spencer.
Autumnal Consummation. Stevenson.
The Axe-Helve. Frost.
The Bad Season Makes the Poet Sad. Herrick.
Ballad. Treece.
The Battle of Bunker Hill. *Anonymous.*
Baudelaire Series (excerpt). Palmer.
The Belfry. Binyon.
The Birdcatcher. Hodgson.
The Bowling-Green (excerpt). Somervile.
Braggart! Wrafter.
Brainstorm. Nemerov.
Breaking. Allan.
The Briefless Barrister. Saxe.
Britannia's Pastorals. Browne.
Building Bridges. Mahaka.
Cairo Jag. Douglas.
The Calculation. Wagoner.
Cardinal Fisher. Heywood.
Castles in the Air. Ballantine.
Caution. *Anonymous.*

The Cooper & Bailey Great London Circus. Hershon.

The Coronet. Marvell.

Courtship. O Hehir.

The Creation of the Moon. *Anonymous.*

Dark Was the Night. *Anonymous.*

Darwinity. Merivale.

David and Goliath. Crouch.

A Dawn Horse. Harmon.

The Day's March. Nichols.

The Desolate Lover. Shanahan.

Dime Call. Goldbarth.

Discourse Heard One Day. Babcock.

The Djanggawul Cycle, 18. *Anonymous.*

Doctor Emmanuel. Reeves.

Don' Let Yo' Watch Run Down (with music). *Anonymous.*

Down in the Valley. *Anonymous.*

The Dream. Bogan.

The Dream. Spalding.

Dream Songs. Berryman.

A Drinking-Song... Wycherley.

The Driver in Italy. Christopher.

The Dying Fisherman's Song. *Anonymous.*

Edwardian Hat. Parvin.

Elegy for the Silent Voices and the Joiners of Everything. Patchen.

The Elephant's Trunk. Wilkins.

End of the Picnic. Webb.

Epigram. Butler.

An Epithalamium upon the Marriage of Captain William Bedloe. Duke.

Essay on Psychiatrists. Pinsky.

The Execution of King Charles. Marvell.

Exile of the Sons of Uisliu (excerpt). *Anonymous.*

Fantasia. Chesterton.

The Feral Pioneers. Reed.

The Finches. Murray.

First Death. Justice.

Fleance. Longley.

For Little Boys Destined for Big Business. Hoffenstein.

For My Husband. Voigt.

For Stephen Dixon. Gilbert.

The Forbidden. Haring.

Fork. Simic.

Frankenstein Gets His Man. Carr.

Friend, on This Scaffold Thomas More Lies Dead. Cunningham.

The Gardener. *Anonymous.*

Gold. Jones.

Good Susan, Be as Secret as You Can. *Anonymous.*

Grania. *Anonymous.*

The Great Society. Bly.

Guinea. Roumain.

Having Climbed to the Topmost Peak of the Incense-Burner Mountain. Po Chu-i.

Hazard. Petersen.

Horse in a Field. De La Mare.

How to Choose a Horse. *Anonymous.*

The Human Fold. Muir.

Hyperion. Keats.

I Had a Wife. *Anonymous.*

I Went Down into the Desert to Meet Elijah. Lindsay.

Ice Cream. Wild.

An Idler's Calendar: January. Blunt.

If I Forget Thee. Litvinoff.

Ingestion. McDonald.

Invocation. Johnson.

The Jackdaw. Cowper.

Jane Retreat. Honig.

January Eclogue. Spenser.

Jesus. Pimentel Coronel.

The Jewish Lady. *Anonymous.*

John Henry (A vers.). *Anonymous.*

The Junk Shop. Coulette.

Killing. Greenberg.

King Arthur and King Cornwall. Anonymous.

Last Night My Soul Departed. O Dalaigh.

The Last Post. Graves.

Lay Your Head on My Shoulder. Amichai.

Letters & Other Worlds. Ondaatje.

Limerick: "There was an old miser at Reading." *Anonymous.*

Little Cock Robin. *Anonymous.*

London Bells. *Anonymous.*

Long Lonesome Road. *Anonymous.*

Loony, 29: The Good Folks at the Camp Meeting. Kloefkorn.

Lord of Each Soul. Engle.

Love Letter. Pastan.

Love without Hope. Graves.

The Ludlow Massacre. Guthrie.

Making Contact. Manifold.

The Man. Browne.

The Man Hidden behind the Drapes. Rogers.

The Man Who Buys Hides. Schmitz.

Matty Groves. *Anonymous.*

Metamorphoses of M. Bishop.

A Midrash (excerpt). Meltzer.

A Moment Please. Allen.

Motive for Mercy. Milburn.

Movie Queen. Vaughn.

Mrs. Santa Claus' Christmas Present. Morris.

My Legs Are So Weary. Burgess.

Mysterious East. Cole.

Nativity. Rodgers.

Night Club. MacNeice.

Night Shore. Higgs.

"No Quarrel." Herbert.

Nottingham Fair. *Anonymous.*

O Have You Caught the Tiger. Housman.

Odes, X. Hafiz.

Of Drunkenness. Turberville.

The Old Girl. Lenhart.

On a Peacock. Heyrick.

On a Visit to Ch'ung Chen Taoist Temple... Yu Hsuan-chi.

On Being Invited to a Testmonial Dinner. Stafford.

On Leaping over the Moon. Traherne.

On Meeting a Stranger in a Bookshop. Williams.

On the Death of His Wife. O'Connor.

On the Death of His Wife. O Dalaigh.

On the Snake. *Anonymous.*

One A. M. Kennedy.

One and One. Dodge.

Oraga Haru. Issa.

P Is for Paleontology. Bracker.

Paper Matches. Jiles.

The Paperweight. Schnackenberg.

Paradise. Bloch.

Paris. Kolmar.

Peg. *Anonymous.*

The Pell Mell Celebrated. Gay.

People on Sunday. Denby.

Peyote Vision. Blockcolski.

The Pity of Love. Yeats.

Plato Told. Cummings.

Poor Brother. *Anonymous.*

Poor Old Man. *Anonymous.*

Portrait. Donaghy.

Power to the People. Nemerov.

Prelude to an Evening. Ransom.

Pro Femina. Kizer.

Puppy. Lape.

Radiation Leak. Aliesan.

"Rake" Windermere. Pounds.

Recollection. Mumford.

Relics. Wagoner.

Retort. Dunbar.

Revenge Fable. Hughes.

Richard Cory. Robinson.

Riddle: "King Charles the First walked and talked." *Anonymous.*

Riddle: "Long legs, crooked thighs." *Anonymous.*

Riddle: "See, see, what shall I see?" *Anonymous.*

The Road to the Bow. Corrothers.

Saint John. Coatsworth.

The Sea Horse. Graves.

A Second Stanza for Dr. Johnson. Hall.

The Serpent's Nature. *Anonymous.*

The Shadow and the Light (excerpt). Whittier.

The Shadow on the Stone. Hardy.

The Shawls. Gibbon.

She and I. Cameron.

Signum Cui Contradicetur. Mary Angelita.

Sir Lark and King Sun: A Parable. Macdonald.

Skating. Kipling.

Socrates Prays a Day and a Night. O'Neil.

"Somedays now". Rickert.

The Song Called "His Hide Is Covered with Hair.'. Belloc.

A Song of Renunciation. Seaman.

Song: "The moth's kiss, first!" Browning.

The Sower. Binyon.

Spate in Winter Midnight. Maccaig.

The Splendid Lover. Moreland.

Spring Song. Finkel.

Springtime. Kreymborg.

Static Autumn. Winters.

Strange Monsters. Watkyns.

Suburban Lovers. Dawe.

Suffering. Ehrenstein.

The Sunken Garden. De La Mare.

Takes All Kinds. Dickey.

A Tall Man Executes a Jig. Layton.

Theory. Parker.

Three Seasons. Sparshott.

To a Squirrel at Kyle-Na-No. Yeats.

To Amarantha. Lovelace.

To Sleep. Graves.

To Victor Hugo. Swinburne.

The Tombstone Told When She Died. Thomas.

Towering O'er the Wrecks of Time. Bowring.

The Tragedy of Pete. Cotter.

The Trooper's Horse. *Anonymous.*

The Tropics in New York. McKay.

Troubled Woman. Hughes.

The Twelve. Blok.

Two Dogs Have I. Nash.

The Two of Cups. Jarrett.

Unicorn. Smith.

The Untutored Giraffe. Herford.

Verses to Miss —. Wilde.

Waking in the Dark. Livesay.

When My Beloved Sleeping Lies. McLeod.

Wisdom of the Gazelle. Solomos.

Witches. Hughes.

Woman Free (excerpt). Wolstenholme-Elmy.

A Working Party. Sassoon.

"Wrapt in my careless cloak..." Surrey.

Wreck. Polk.

Yee Shall Not Misse of a Few Lines in Remembrance of Thomas Hooker. Johnson.

The Young Man. MacAdams.

The Ziz. Hollander.

Headache

Crepe de Chine. Williams.

Hangover Cure. Alexis.

Horace I. Field.

The Merry Month. *Anonymous.*

White Zombie. Fisher.

Headlines

Chant Royal From a Copydesk. Terral.

Finding a Yiddish Paper on the Riverside Line. Spacks.

The Mummies. Kumin.

Heal (ed) (er) (ing) (s)

Abraham Lincoln. Auslander.

Ah, necromancy sweet! Dickinson.

The Altar. Untermeyer.

Amoretti, L. Spenser.

Aucassin and Nicolette: Who Would List. *Anonymous.*

Balm in Gilead. *Anonymous.*
Bear's blood. Malancioni.
The Blackstone Rangers.
  Brooks.
Breathing the Strong Smell.
  Norse.
Bumi. Jones.
Caelica, II. Greville.
Come, Ye Disconsolate.
  Moore.
Complicity. Gallagher.
The Contrite Heart. Cowper.
Dakota Badlands.
  Landeweer.
The Dearest Poets. Hunt.
Elegy for Her Brother, Sakhr.
  Khansa.
Elegy on an Australian
  Schoolboy. Cross.
For Mabel: Pomo
  Basketmaster and Doctor.
  Rose.
Fourth Station. Donaghy.
Holy Sonnets, V. Donne.
In Railway Halls. Spender.
Janitor Working on
  Threshold. Avison.
The Jews. Vaughan.
Joy of Life. Ibn Ezra.
Knife and Sap. Leslie.
The Knot. Rich.
Longing. Herbert.
Looking into a Tide Pool.
  Bly.
The Minimal. Roethke.
The Moon in September.
  Ghose.
Morte d'Arthur. Tennyson.
Second Half. McCord.
The Shadow. Stoddard.
Shattered Sabbath.
  Goldstein.
Sin and Its Cure.
  Anonymous.
The Slip. Berry.
Small Prayer. Kees.
Songs from Cyprus.
  Doolittle.
Under the Red Cross.
  Hickox.
Waiting for God.
  Roskolenko.
The Wound. Gunn.

Health (y)
After great storms the calm
  returns. Wyatt.
Ayii, Ayii. I Walked on the
  Ice of the Sea.
  Anonymous.
Bold Reynard the Fox.
  Anonymous.
Cigarettes Will Spoil Yer Life
  (with music). *Anonymous.*
Citizenship. Chesterton.
The Cock Crows in the Morn.
  Anonymous.
The Cup of O'Hara.
  O'Carolan.
The Duke of Buckingham.
  Pope.
The Girl I Love. Callanan.
Glee for King Charles.
  Scott.
The Grave-Yard. Very.
A Health at the Ford.
  Rogers.
Holy Baptism. Herbert.
I'll Never Use Tobacco.
  Anonymous.
The Indian Lass.
  Anonymous.

The Joys of Heaven.
  Thomas a Kempis.
Knapweed. Benson.
Letter to Bell from Missoula.
  Hugo.
A Letter to Ben Jonson.
  Beaumont.
The New Doctor. "Mix.
The Norfolk Girls.
  Anonymous.
O Sons of Earth. Pope.
Ode I Allusion to Horace.
  Akenside.
On Learning to Adjust to
  Things. Ciardi.
On the Lakes of Ponchartrain.
  Anonymous.
The Overlander. *Anonymous.*
Paddy Murphy. *Anonymous.*
Perry's Victory. *Anonymous.*
Poor Henry. De La Mare.
Prayer against Love.
  Catullus.
De Profundis. Wilder.
Proverbial Advice on Keeping
  Healthy. *Anonymous.*
The Roaring Lad and the
  Ranting Lass. *Anonymous.*
Robert Frost. Lowell.
She Stoops to Conquer.
  Goldsmith.
The Sherman Cyclone.
  Anonymous.
The Song of Hungarrda.
  Ngunaitponi.
Spirit Song. *Anonymous.*
Submission in Affliction.
  Anonymous.
Tartar. Brown.
To Helen. Praed.
To Mistress Anne Cecil.
  Burleigh.
To Sleep. Wordsworth.
To Thomas Moore. Byron.

Heap (ed) (s)
The Art of Poetry. Dryden.
Axle Song. Van Doren.
The Battle of Bridgewater.
  Anonymous.
The Bobolinks. Cranch.
The Country Store.
  Anonymous.
The Dying Desperado.
  Anonymous.
Home. Guest.
Monogamania. Merriam.
Ode to a Ditch. *Anonymous.*
On Catching a Dog-Daisy in
  the Mower. Redgrove.
Only a Little Litter.
  Livingston.
A Place (Any Place) to
  Transcend All Places.
  Williams.
The Reaper. Tabb.

Hear (d) (ing) (s)
9 Verses of the Same Song.
  Berry.
The After-Thought. Smith.
Air: Cat Bird Singing.
  Creeley.
Airship. Sobiloff.
All Our Griefs to Tell.
  Newton.
Alphabet. Lear.
The Animal I Wanted.
  Patchen.
Astrophel and Stella, XCI.
  Sidney.
At Port Royal: Song of the
  Negro Boatman. Whittier.

A Ballad from the Seven Dials
  Press... *Anonymous.*
Bats. Macbeth.
The Battle Royal between Dr.
  Sherlock, Dr. South, and
  Dr. Burnet. Pittis.
Beauty and the Bird.
  Rossetti.
Between Birthdays. Nash.
Bird and the Muse.
  Zaturenska.
The Birthplace. Heaney.
Black Sheep. Burton.
Bouquets. Francis.
The Breathing. Levertov.
Bright Star (Original version).
  Keats.
The Brook in February.
  Roberts.
Bury Me beneath the Willow.
  Anonymous.
By Night. Francis.
By the Road to the Air-Base.
  Winters.
Caelica, LXVI. Greville.
Canonical Hours. Dickey.
Captain Spud and His First
  Mate, Spade. Ciardi.
A Celebration of Charis.
  Jonson.
The Celestial City. Fletcher.
Chamber Music. Joyce.
Chamonix. Hookham.
A Child to His Sick
  Grandfather. Baillie.
The Children's Bells.
  Farjeon.
Christchurch Bells.
  Anonymous.
Christmas Eve. Field.
A Christmas Eve Choral.
  Carman.
Christmas Trees. Hill.
Cinderella. Plath.
City Walk-Up, Winter 1969.
  Forche.
Coal Miner's Grace. Divine.
The Concert. McGinley.
Conrad. Slonimski.
The Cricket and the Star.
  Newsome.
Cries Out of Blindness.
  Corbiere.
Cuento. Cumpian.
The Dark Dialogues, II.
  Graham.
David. Davies.
The Deaf Woman's Courtship.
  Anonymous.
The Desert Music (excerpt).
  Williams.
Desnos Reading the Palms of
  Men on Their Way to the
  Gas Chambers. Berg.
Dirge. Crapsey.
Divine Songs to Ahura
  Mazda. Zoroaster.
Division. Ratti.
The Dog beneath the Skin.
  Auden.
Don Juan. Byron.
The Donner Party (excerpt).
  Keithley.
The Dove Apologizes to His
  God for Being Caught by a
  Cat. Eaton.
Dream of a Decent Death.
  Borgese.
Drop the Wires. Seidman.
Ellis Park. Hoyt.
Emigration. Barrows.

Emily Dickinson Postage
  Stamp. Strongin.
Every Christian Born of God.
  Anonymous.
Expounding the Torah.
  Zukofsky.
The Eyes, the Blood.
  Meltzer.
The Fabulists. Kipling.
The Faerie Queene. Spenser.
A Farewel to Worldly Joyes.
  Killigrew.
The Fifth Sense. Beer.
Florence MacCarthy's
  Farewell to Her English
  Lover. De Vere.
Footprints on the Glacier.
  Merwin.
The Forests of Lithuania.
  Davie.
Fragments of Ancient Poetry
  (excerpt). Macpherson.
Furniture. Bloch.
Gibberish. Coleridge.
Girl in White. Dobyns.
Give Me Jesus. *Anonymous.*
The Goat. Saba.
God's Call. *Anonymous.*
Good-Night. Benedict.
Gray Glove. Borson.
Growing Old. Arnold.
Hawthorn Dyke. Swinburne.
Her Husband. Hughes.
The Heritage. Reed.
The Higher Pantheism.
  Tennyson.
Homecoming. Viereck.
The Horse Show. Williams.
How My Father Died.
  Ezekiel.
Hurry On, My Weary Soul.
  Anonymous.
I Hear the Wave.
  Anonymous.
I Taught Myself to Live
  Simply and Wisely.
  Akhmatova.
I Will Go Away. Shargal.
I, Woman. McClaurin.
In Memoriam A.H.H.,
  LXXXII. Tennyson.
In Memoriam A.H.H., XCIV.
  Tennyson.
In Praise of Limestone.
  Auden.
In the House of the Judge.
  Smith.
In the Season of Wolves and
  Names. Rugo.
In Your Absence. Baxter.
An Incident in the Early Life
  of Ebenezer Jones, Poet,
  1828. Betjeman.
An Inconclusive Evening.
  Bellerby.
Jerry an' Me. Rich.
John Marr (excerpt).
  Melville.
Johnny Rich. Carleton.
A Journey to Hell. Ward.
Judgement Day. *Anonymous.*
June. Bryant.
King Henry V. Shakespeare.
The Lady of Life. Kettle.
Langley Lane. Buchanan.
Leaves of Grass. Whitman
The Leaves That Rustled on
  This Oak-Crowned Hill.
  Wordsworth.
Lenox Avenue Mural.
  Hughes.

Lenox Christmas Eve 68. Cornish.
Letter from Germany. Grosholz.
Letters. Emerson.
Life. Very.
Lines. Ada Sister Mary.
Listening. Fisher.
Listening to Foxhounds. Dickey.
The Livid Lightnings Flashed in the Clouds. Crane.
Longing. *Anonymous.*
Lord Heygate. Belloc.
The Lost Lagoon. Johnson.
Love for a Hare. La Follette.
Love Me! Smith.
Love's Fancy. Dryden.
The Lowest Trees Have Tops. Dyer.
Lullaby. Moraes.
The Lying Muslims. *Anonymous.*
Mad Song. Sigerson.
Madrigal: "Come, doleful owl, the messenger of woe." *Anonymous.*
Man and Woman. Lee.
The Man in the Street Is Fed. Sandburg.
The Man on the Dump. Stevens.
March Weather. Swan.
The Marching Song of Stark's Men. Hale.
Maybe Alone on My Bike. Stafford.
Memphis Minnie-Jitis Blues. Minnie.
A Midsummer Night's Dream. Shakespeare.
Miners. Wright.
The Mixer. MacNeice.
The Monster. Kuzma.
Moriturus. "Marie.
'Morning, Morning. Mathew.
Morning on the Lievre. Lampman.
Mr. Brunt. Siegel.
Mr. Molony's Account of the Ball. Thackeray.
Mririda. Mririda n'Ait Attik.
Mrs. Santa Claus' Christmas Present. Morris.
Music. *Anonymous.*
My Atthis, although our dear Anaktoria. Sappho.
My Body. Korn.
My Dim-Wit Cousin. Roethke.
My Garden Is a Pleasant Place. Driscoll.
My Sense of Sight. Herford.
My Woodcock. Chalmers.
Myths and Texts. Snyder.
Neural Folds. Day.
Next Year, in Jerusalem. Kaufman.
Night. Bialik.
Nightmare at Noon. Benét.
No One Cares Less Than I. Thomas.
Nobody Riding the Roads Today. Jordan.
Noel Tragique. Guthrie.
Oh, When Shall I See Jesus? *Anonymous.*
Old Black Joe. Foster.
Old Cat Care. Hughes.

An Old Woman. *Anonymous.*
Old Woman, Old Woman. *Anonymous.*
On a Celtic Mask by Henry Moore. Gregory.
On His Own Deafness. Swift.
Optimism. Wilcox.
Oracle. Mayo.
Orpheus to Beasts. Lovelace.
Paradox. Miller.
The Pariah's Prayer. Goethe.
A Pastoral. Breton.
Pick upon Pick... Comfort.
The Plum Tree. Reaney.
Poem: "I heard of a man." Cohen.
The Poet's Welcome to His Illegitimate Child. Burns.
Poetry Today. Heath-Stubbs.
The Poets at Tea. Pain.
Prayer. Reed.
The Preacher's Prayer. Macdonald.
Prologue to Mr. Addison's Tragedy of Cato. Pope.
Protect Me. Adler.
Prothalamium. MacDonagh.
Psalm XX. Sidney.
Reading Today's Newspaper. Abbott.
The Reason for Poetry. Morejo.
Regent's Park Terrace. Spencer.
Remains of an Indian Village. Purdy.
Requiem. Stafford.
The Retreat of Ita Cagney. Hartnett.
A Revivalist in Boston. Rich.
Rex Mundi. Gascoyne.
Rice and Rose Bowl Blues. Mark.
The River. MacNab.
River Sound Remembered. Merwin.
The Roman Earl. *Anonymous.*
The Sacrilege. Hardy.
Safed. Knut.
The Salesman. Mezey.
Sapphics. Swinburne.
Sea-Wind. Mallarme.
Seeds. Webster.
Serenade. Middleton.
She Is My Dear. *Anonymous.*
A Shropshire Lad. Housman.
The Sick Stockrider. Gordon.
Sight. Gibson.
Sing Song. Creeley.
The Singer's House. Heaney.
Smokey the Bear Sutra. *Anonymous.*
Solemn Rondeau. Bell.
The Solitary Reaper. Wordsworth.
Some Ruthless Rhymes. Graham.
Song: "Make this night loveable." Auden.
The Song of Samuel Sweet. Causley.
Song to Promote Growth. *Anonymous.*

Song: "Under the Winter, dear." Lee-Hamilton.
Sonnet. At Ostend, July 22, 1787. Bowles.
Sonnets, XXIII: "As an unperfect actor on the stage." Shakespeare.
Sonnets on the Sea's Voice. Sterling.
Sparrows in College Ivy. Wolfe.
Speech. Taylor.
Spider. Farber.
Spring 1940. Auden.
Stack o' Dollars. Estes.
The Storm. Hay.
Storm at Sea. Davenant.
The Storm-Wind. Barnes.
The Story of the Shepherd. *Anonymous.*
Strangeness of Heart. Sassoon.
Such Soft Ideas All My Pains Beguile. Montagu.
Supremacy. Robinson.
Survivor. MacLeish.
Sweet Voice of the Garb. Geilt.
The Swimmers. Tate.
Swinburne at Tea. Pain.
Take Thou Our Minds, Dear Lord. Foulkes.
Taking a Walk with You. Koch.
The Talking Drums. Kyei.
The Teacher. Fisher.
These. Williams.
Three Poems for Women, 1. Griffin.
To a God Unknown. Eller.
To Seem the Stranger Lies My Lot. Hopkins.
To the Lady with a Book. *Anonymous.*
Trees. Hughes.
The Triumph of Time. Swinburne.
Troll Chanting. Hollo.
The Two Societies. Wheelock.
The Unbidden Wedding Guest. Marti.
Unless We Guard Them Well. Merchant.
The Unremitting Voice of Nightly Streams. Wordsworth.
Upon Being Awakened at Night by My Four Year Old Daughter. Rainer.
Variations on a Theme. Vinz.
The Veery. Van Dyke.
La Vita Nuova. Dante Alighieri.
Voice. Moss.
Walk Slowly. Love.
Wesley in Heaven. Brown.
When the fifth month comes. Ise.
While I walked in the moonlight. Murasaki Shibiku.
The White Bird. Akhmatova.
Who Says. Farhi.
The Widow. Davenport.
Widow to Her Son. Smith.
Winter, New Hampshire. Kherdian.
Wolves. MacNeice.
Woman and Nature. Griffin.

The Woman Poet. Kolmar.
Woods Night. Hennen.
Wounds. Minty.
Ye Walls! Sole Witnesses of Happy Sighs. Landor.
Zechariah. Marlatt.

Hearse (s)
Alabama. Simmons.
Auguries of Innocence. Blake.
Dismissing Progress and its Progenitors. Reavey.
Exeunt. Wilbur.
Frontispiece. Swenson.
The Last Fruit off an Old Tree. Landor.
The Lawyers Know Too Much. Sandburg.
Mutual Love. Hammond.
The Welsh Marches. Housman.

Heart (s)
Abishag. Fichman.
Absent Yet Present. Lytton.
Acadia (excerpt). Howe.
Adam's Dying. Torrence.
The Advantages of Washing. Armstrong.
After a Parting. Meynell.
Afterbirth. Williams.
Ah Cupid, I mistook thee. Davison.
Al Aaraaf. Poe.
Albert Sidney Johnson. Sherwood.
The Alexandrite Ring. Ryan.
All Hail, Thou Noble Guest. Luther.
"All in green went my love riding". Cummings.
Always in the Parting Year. Lasker-Schüler.
America. Babcock.
America First! Oldham.
American Names. Benét.
Amoretti, XL. Spenser.
Amours de Voyage. Clough.
Anacreontea: Young Men Dancing. *Anonymous.*
And if an eye may save or slay. Wyatt.
Angels We Have Heard on High. *Anonymous.*
Anke von Tharau. *Anonymous.*
Annie Breen. *Anonymous.*
Annunciation Night. Conway.
Answer to–'s Professions of Affection. Byron.
Anticipation. Tusiani.
Approaches. Macdonald.
Arab Love-Song. Thompson.
Arcadia. Sidney.
Are They Shadows That We See? Daniel.
Ariel. Campbell.
Arizona. Hall.
Ark Anatomical. Macpherson.
The Arrow and the Song. Longfellow.
Art above Nature, to Julia. Herrick.
Art of Love (excerpt). Ovid.
As Gentle Dews Distill. Rogers.
"As I Was Going." *Anonymous.*
As I was going by Charing Cross. *Anonymous.*

As in a Rose-Jar. Jones, Jr.
As in Smooth Oil the Razor Best Is Whet. *Anonymous.*
Ashes of Roses. Eastman.
Aspects of Robinson. Kees.
Astrology. Marshall.
Astrophel and Stella, I. Sidney.
Astrophel and Stella, XX. Sidney.
Astrophel and Stella, XLVII. Sidney.
Astrophel and Stella, XCI. Sidney.
At a Bach Concert. Rich.
At a Country Dance in Provence. Monro.
At Lanier's Grave. Tabb.
At Saint Patrick's Purgatory. O'Dala.
At the Last. Marston.
At the Zoo. Zangwill.
Atameros. Beevers.
Auf Meiner Herzliebsten Augelein. Heine.
Aurelia. Nichols.
Awake. Coleridge.
Awake, My Soul. Ibn Ezra.
Azouou. Mririda n'Ait Attik.
Bab-Lock-Hythe. Binyon.
Backgammon. Broumas.
Bad Dreams. Browning.
Bahnhofstrasse. Joyce.
Ballad. Treece.
Ballata: He Reveals, in a Dialogue, His Increasing Love for Mandetta. Cavalcanti.
Ballykinlar: May 1940. Maybin.
Ballywaire. Paulin.
Barney's Invitation. Freneau.
The Barrel-Organ. Symons.
The Bastard. Savage.
The Battle of Otterburn (C version). *Anonymous.*
The Baying Hounds. Gilmore.
Be Sad, My Heart. Quarles.
Be Still, My Heart. *Anonymous.*
Beauty. Spingarn.
Before Day. Sassoon.
Begin the Day with God. *Anonymous.*
Beginning. Rodriguez Frese.
Behold the Meads. Poitiers.
The Beloved's Image. *Anonymous.*
Below Mount T'ui K'oy, Home of the Gods.... Stroud.
Between Rivers and Seas. Henson.
Between the Acts. Kunitz.
Beware the Cuckoo. Moll.
The Big Sunflower. Newcomb.
Biothanatos. Beaumont.
Black Angel. Thompson.
The Black Vulture. Sterling.
The Blackbird. Henley.
The Blackbird Calls in Grief. *Anonymous.*
Blessed Art Thou, O Lord. *Anonymous.*
The Blind Singer. Hoelderlin.
The Blood-Letting. Harjo.
Blossom Time. Larremore.

The Blue Bells of Scotland. Jordan.
Blue Funk. Oppenheimer.
Bombardment. Lawrence.
The Book of Day-Dreams. Moore.
Bouzouki. Hanson.
Break My Heart of Stone. Wesley.
Breakfast in a Bowling Alley in Utica, New York. Rich.
Broccoli. Schmidt.
Brown Boy to Brown Girl. Cullen.
Browning at Asolo. Johnson.
The Burial. Davis.
But Once. Winthrop.
Bwagamoyo. Bethune.
By-Low, My Babe. *Anonymous.*
Bye Bye Baby Blues. Fuller.
Caelica, III. Greville.
Caelica, LXVII. Greville.
The Cage. Treinin.
California. Sigourney.
Canberra in April. Rowland.
Careless Love. *Anonymous.*
Careless Love (with music). *Anonymous.*
The Carver. Aiken.
Casabianca. Hemans.
The Castle of Thorns. Winters.
The Celestial City (Excerpt). Wolfe.
The Cenci. Shelley.
Certainties. Widdemer.
Chang'd, Yet Constant. Stanley.
Chanson: "If they say my furred cloak." Du Guillet.
Chanson Mystique. *Anonymous.*
Characters of Women. Pope.
Charm. Radnoti.
Childe Harold's Pilgrimage: Canto IV. Byron.
The Choyce. Beedome.
Christ's Gift to Man. *Anonymous.*
Christine. Hay.
Christmas at Melrose. Hill.
Christmas Bells. Mortenson.
A Circle Begins. Littlebird.
The Circulation of the Blood. Blackmore.
A City Flower. Dobson.
Clerimont's Song. Jonson.
Click o' the Latch. Turner.
Cloistered. Brown.
Cock-Crow. Currey.
The Coffin-Worm. Pitter.
Columbus. Lowell.
Come, Lord Jesus. Wesley.
Come Not near My Songs. *Anonymous.*
Come to Me, Dearest. Brenan.
Come, Walk with Me. Bronte.
Comfort. Doney.
Comforted. Carmichael.
Coming Back. Gregg.
The Coming of Dusk upon a Village in Haiti. Rago.
Common Sense. Fields
Communion. Dowden.
Compel Them to Come In. Dodd.
A Complaint. Wordsworth.
Compline. Scott.

Considerations of Norfolk Island (excerpt). Smithyman.
Constancy: A Song. Rochester.
The Convict of Clonmala. *Anonymous.*
Corinna. Campion.
The Cottager's Complaint. *Anonymous.*
Could Man Be Drunk for Ever. Housman.
Count Filippo. Heavysege.
The Courser and the Jennet. Shakespeare.
The Cowboy's Life. *Anonymous.*
Cradle Song. Peabody.
Credo. Jeffers.
Crimes of Passion. Stokes.
Crowded Ways of Life. Gresham.
The Cruel Sister. *Anonymous.*
The Crusade. Rinaldo d'Aquino.
The Cry of the Age. Garland.
The Cubical Domes. Gascoyne.
Cupid and Death: Victorious Men of Earth. Shirley.
Cupid Drowned. Hunt.
Cupid Stung. Moore.
Cupid Ungodded. Shirley.
Cupids Call. Shirley.
Cynthia on Horseback. Ayres.
The Dainty Young Heiress of Lincoln's Inn Fields. Sackville.
Dance of the Infidels. Young.
The Dart. *Anonymous.*
David's Lament for Jonathan. Abelard.
Daw's Dinner. Kilmer.
Dawn. Masefield.
A Day in Autumn. Thomas.
The Day Returns. Burns.
Day's End. Binyon.
The Day the Winds. Miles.
Dead Love. Adams.
Dead Marine. Coxe.
Dearest, Do Not You Delay Me. Fletcher.
Dearest Man-in-the-Moon. Jong.
Death of a Hind. MacLean.
The Death of Richard Wagner. Swinburne.
Death of Rimbaud. Fisher.
Decoration Day. Barbour.
Defiance. Ibn Gabirol.
Deportation. Glanz-Leyeles.
The Deserted Home. Meyer.
Design for Peace. Bangs.
Desolation Is a Delicate Thing. Wylie.
A Dialogue betweene Araphill and Castara. Habington.
Diana. Constable.
Dido's Farewell. Pastan.
Die Blauen Veilchen Der Augelein. Heine.
A Digression from Husbandrie: To a Poynt or Two of Huswifrie. Tusser.
Dinna Ask Me. Dunlop.
Dirge for Two Veterans. Whitman.
Disappointment. O'Reilly.

Disarm the Hearts. Jordan.
Do you have a sweet thought, Cerinthus. Sulpicia.
Does the Pearl Know? Hay.
The Doll. Friend.
Doll's Boy's Asleep. Cummings.
Domine ne in Furore. Wyatt.
Don Quixote. Betts.
Donkey. Van Doren.
Dorothy. Lathrop.
The Dragonfly. Rand.
Draherin O Machree. *Anonymous.*
A Dream of Fair Women. Tennyson.
A Dream of Venus. Bion.
Dream Songs. Berryman.
The Dreamers. Garrison.
Dreams. Symons.
The Dreams of the Dreamer. Johnson.
Duino Elegies. Rilke.
The Earl of Surrey to Geraldine. Drayton.
The Early Days. Dowling.
Earth and Fire. Watkins.
Easter. Coatsworth.
Easter Song. Alishan.
Ebbtide at Sundown. "Field.
Ecclesiastes. Bishop.
The Edge. Ridge.
Edward Gray. Tennyson.
Egyptian Hieroglyphics. *Anonymous.*
Eighteen Verses Sung to a Tartar Reed Whistle. Ts'ai Yen.
The Eighteenth Song. Hadewijch.
Elegy. Trench.
Elegy for Lucy Lloyd. Goch.
Elegy for My Father. Louthan.
Ellen Bawn. Mangan.
Embryo. Townsend.
Emily Dickinson. Hagerup.
Emily Dickinson's Sestina for Molly Bloom. Lefcowitz.
The Enchanted Knight. Muir.
Enfant Perdu. Heine.
The Enigma Variations. Petrie.
Epigram: "Give me a boy whose tender skin." Martial (Marcus Valerius Martialis).
Epigram: "O Diodorus." *Anonymous.*
An Epigram on Woman. Ayres.
Epistle to a Lady: Of the Character of Women. Pope.
Epistle to Henry Wriothesley, Earl of Southhampton. Daniel.
Epitaph for the Race of Man. Millay.
Euch, Are You Having Your Period? Alta.
Ev'ry Time I Feel de Spirit. *Anonymous.*
Eve-Song. Gilmore.
The Evening of the Feast-Day. Leopardi.
Ever Watchful. Ta' Abbata Sharra.
The Exchange. Coleridge.

The Exequy. To His Matchlesse Never to Be Forgotten Freind. King.

Exile in Nigeria. Mphahlele.

Face to Face with Trouble (excerpt). Sangster.

Fair Weather. Parker.

Fairy Song. Yeats.

The Fairy Thrall. Byron.

Faith. *Anonymous.*

Fantasia. Chesterton.

Far Sweeter Than Honey. Ibn Ezra.

Farewell. Chao Li-hua.

The Farm. Miller.

Farm Gate. Krige.

The Fatal Spell. Byron.

The Fate of Birds. Seib.

Father Death Blues. Ginsberg.

Felixstowe, or The Last of Her Order. Betjeman.

Fine Knacks for Ladies. Dowland.

Fireflies. Fawcett.

The First Song. Burton.

First Song. Kinnell.

Fishing the Big Hole. Holbrook.

The Fist. Walcott.

Flower Song. Keating.

The Flute: A Pastoral. Heredia.

Flux. Eberhart.

Flying Fish. Miller.

The Folly of Being Comforted. Yeats.

Football Song. Scott.

For Christmas-Day. Wesley.

For Every Day. Havergal.

For Everything Give Thanks. Tupper.

For I Have Done a Good and Kindly Deed. Werfel.

For Paul Laurence Dunbar. Cullen.

For What As Easy. Auden.

Forsaken (He Once Did Love with Fond Affection). *Anonymous.*

Fossils. Stewart.

Four Sonnets to Helen, 2. Ronsard.

Friendship. Stryk.

Friendship's Mystery. Philips.

From Prologue, Each to the Other. La Farge.

From Sunset to Star Rise. Rossetti.

From the Turkish. Byron.

The Fruit of the Tree. Wagoner.

Funeral. Bennett.

"The furious gun in his raging ire." Wyatt.

The Gallant Fighting "Joe." Stevenson.

Gautama. Jones, Jr.

The Gay Goshawk (E version). *Anonymous.*

Generalities. Conquest.

Gentle Jesus. Wesley.

The Gentlest Lady. Parker.

Geraldine's Daughter. O'Rahilly.

Give My Heart a Song. Gilleland.

The Gladness of May. Wordsworth.

A Glance at the Album. Burr.

Glen Rosa. Jeffrey.

Gloucester Harbor. Ward.

God and the Soul: Nature and the Child. Spalding.

Going Back. Rachow.

Good and Bad. Stephens.

A Grace. Tiplady.

Grandma Shorba and the Pure in Heart. Manfred.

Greed, Part 4. The Turtle. Wakoski.

The Green Fiddler. Field.

Green Haven Halls. Culhane.

The Green Hunters. Wilson.

The Greenback Dollar. *Anonymous.*

Greeness. Grimke.

The Grey Wolf. Symons.

The Gypsy Rover. *Anonymous.*

Hangman (with music). *Anonymous.*

A Happy Christmas. Havergal.

Harlem. Brierre.

The Harp That Once through Tara's Halls. Moore.

The Harvest of the Sea. McCrae.

Haunted. Sassoon.

He Approacheth the Hall of Judgment. Book of the Dead.

He Biddeth Osiris to Arise from the Dead. Book of the Dead.

He Came Too Late. Bogart.

He Lives! He Lives to Bless! Stroud.

He Satisfies. Faber.

The Heart. Crane.

The Heart. Ignatow.

The Heart. Shapiro.

Heart and Mind. Sitwell.

A Heart Made Full of Thought. O Domhnaill.

The Heart of a Girl is a Wonderful Things. *Anonymous.*

Heart-of-the-Daybreak. Marais.

Heart's Compass. Rossetti.

The Heart's Friend. Austin.

The Heart's Summer. Sargent.

The Heart's Wild Geese. Treece.

A Heart to Praise Thee. Herbert.

Hearts and Flowers. Brine.

Henry to Rosamond. Drayton.

The Heptalogia. Swinburne.

Her Dead Brother. Lowell.

Her Hair. Chester.

Her Heart. Griffin.

The Hidden Line. Alexander.

Hide, O Hide Those Hills of Snow. Fletcher.

High Country Weather. Baxter.

High Resolve. *Anonymous.*

His Answer. Thompson.

His Heart Was True to Poll. Burnand.

His Quest. Tooker.

History. Warren.

Holidays. Longfellow.

Holy Father, Great Creator. Griswold.

Home. Kowit.

Home from Abroad. Lee.

Home-Thoughts from France. Rosenberg.

Homesick Song. Simpson.

Homeward Bound. Tooker.

How Can the Heart Forget Her. Davison.

How Many Heavens... Sitwell.

How Shall I Build. Blunt.

The Human Heart. Nelson.

Hungering Hearts. *Anonymous.*

Hunting. Yehoash.

Hymen: Never More Will the Wind. Doolittle.

Hymn. Howard

The Hypocrite. Caryll.

I Am Sitting Here. Amichai.

I Am What You Make Me. Lane.

I Do Not Love to See Your Beauty Fire. Wheelock.

I Expected My Skin and My Blood to Ripen. Rose.

I Fear Thy Kisses, Gentle Maiden. Shelley.

I Hear You've Let Go. Ferre.

I in the Grayness Rose. Phillips.

I Live Not Where I Love. *Anonymous.*

I Sat among the Green Leaves. Pickthall.

I Saw My Darling. Morgan.

I Saw the Clouds. White.

I Saw Thee. Palmer.

I Scattered My Sighs to the Wind. Bialik.

I Send Our Lady. Mary Therese.

I Served in a Great Cause. Traubel.

I Think That God Is Proud. Crowell.

I Walked with My Reason. MacLean.

I Wandered Angry as a Cloud (parody). Dehn.

I Wandered Lonely as a Cloud. Wordsworth.

I Was Made Erect and Lone. Thoreau.

I Work All Day Long for You. *Anonymous.*

Idea. Drayton.

The Idler. Very.

If. Roche.

If in the World There Be More Woe. Wyatt.

If Thou Wert by My Side, My Love. Heber.

If Thou Wilt Hear. Grave.

Il Pleut Doucement sur la Ville. Verlaine.

Image-Nation 13 (the Telephone). Blaser.

Impression du Matin. Wilde.

Imprisoned. Tietjens.

In a Cathedral City. Hardy.

In Camus Fields. Strong.

In Jail. Corretjer.

In Kensington Gardens. Symons.

In Me, Past, Present, Future Meet. Sassoon.

In Memoriam. Gingell.

In Memory of G. K. Chesterton. De la Mare.

In Memory of My Arab Grandmother. Zerbe.

In Service. Letts.

In the Bleak Mid-Winter. Rossetti.

In the Desert. Crane.

In the Moonlight. Wright.

In the Night. Stephens.

In the Park. Hoyt.

In the Tree House at Night. Dickey.

In Thine Own Heart. "Angelus Silesius"

In Vain Was I Born. Nezalhualcoyotl.

In Which She Satisfies a Fear with the Rhetoric of Tears. Juana Ines de la Cruz.

Incognita of Raphael. Butler.

Indian Guys at the Bar. Ortiz.

Infelice. Smith.

Innocence. Scully.

Inscape. Litwack.

Inspiration. Fullerton.

Intercession in Late October. Graves.

An Intercessor. *Anonymous.*

Interior. Parker.

The Inverted Torch. Thomas.

The Invitation in It. Boyle.

Irish. Celan.

An Irishman in Coventry. Hewitt.

D Is for Dog. Davies.

Is There No Balm in Christian Lands? *Anonymous.*

IT. Lattimore.

It's a Far, Far, Cry. Macgill.

It's Over Now; I've Known It All. Bronte.

Ivanhoe. Chapt. 39: Rebecca's Hymn. Scott.

Jack Is Every Inch a Sailor. *Anonymous.*

Jeanie Morrison. Motherwell.

Jeremiad. Williams.

Jerusalem. Blake.

Jew. Morhange.

John Brown's Body. Benét.

Johnny Dyers. *Anonymous.*

Jottings of New York. McGonagall.

The Journeyman. *Anonymous.*

Joy-Month. Wasson.

The Joy of Giving. Whittier.

A Judicious Observation of That Dreadful Comet. Wiswall.

July the First. Currie.

June Twilight. Masefield.

Kangaroo by Nightfall. Macainsh.

Kate Dalrymple. Anonymous.

Keep on Praying. Lyon.

Keeping Hair. Wilson.

Killing No Murder. Warner.

King Henry to Rosamond. Drayton.

The King of Kings. Woodrum.

Kingfisher Flat. Empson.

Kitty Bhan. Walsh.

Kitty Neil. Waller.

Knights Errant. Madeleva.

Know Ye the Land? Byron.

Ladybug's Christmas. Farber.
Laieikawai's Lament after Her Husband's Death. *Anonymous.*
A Lament. Gibson.
Lament. Roberts.
The Lament of the Border Widow. *Anonymous.*
The Lament of the Flowers. Very.
Lament: "Within my bosom stirs once more tonight." Zeb-un-Nissa.
Lamkin (K version). *Anonymous.*
The Lamp's Shrine. Rossetti.
Landfall. *Anonymous.*
Lasca. Desprez.
The Lass of Lochroyan. Anonymous
The Lass of Roch Royal (D version). *Anonymous.*
Lassitude. Blind.
The Last Conqueror. Shirley.
Last Fire. Rossetti.
Last Refuge. Michelangelo.
A Last Word. Dowson.
Laura. Tofte.
Laus Mortis. Knowles.
The Lay of the Last Minstrel. Scott.
Learn to Wait. *Anonymous.*
Leaving Me, and Then Loving Many. Cowley.
Let Me Live but from Year to Year. Van Dyke.
The Letter. Murphy.
Letter to Alex Comfort. Abse.
Letter to the Revolution. Griffin.
Levitation. Aubert.
Life. Deland.
Like a mountain whirlwind. Sappho.
Like Odysseus under the Ram. Archilochus.
Limerick: "There was an Old Man who said: "How." Lear.
Lines Left upon a Seat in a Yew-Tree... Wordsworth.
Lines on Cambridge of 1830. Tennyson.
Lines to a Nasturtium. Spencer.
The Lip and the Heart. Adams.
Little Lute. Corbet.
Little Sir Hugh. *Anonymous.*
Little Sticks. Rolls.
Little Words. Keech.
Littoral. Flax.
Living Waters. Spencer.
The Londoner in the Country. Church.
The Looks of a Lover Enamoured. Gascoigne.
Lord, I Want to Be a Christian. *Anonymous.*
Lord Livingston. *Anonymous.*
Lorena. *Anonymous.*
Lorena. Webster.
The Lost Shipmate. Roberts.
Love. LeClaire.
Love Came Back at Fall o' Dew. Reese.
Love doth again. Wyatt.
Love in Exile. Blind.

Love Is Not Solace. Maris Stella.
Love! Love! McMahon.
Love Poem. Raine.
Love's Apparition and Evanishment. Coleridge.
Love's Stricken "Why." Dickinson.
Love Song from New England. Welles.
Love-Song of the Water Carriers. *Anonymous.*
Love That's Pure, Itself Disdaining. Gruber.
Love Vagabonding. Drummond.
Love without Love. Llorens Torres.
The Lovely Lass o' Inverness. Burns.
A Lover's Envy. Van Dyke.
The Lover's Farewell. Mangan.
The Lover Tells of the Rose in His Heart. Yeats.
The Lover Thinks of His Lady in the North. O'Sheel.
The Lovers. Byron.
The Lovers. Zaturenska.
Loving the Rituals That Keep Men Close. Palladas.
Lullaby. O'Sullivan.
Lyttelton Harbor. Cresswell.
Mad Apples. Keating.
Madrigal to the City of Santiago. Garcia Lorca.
Madrigal: "Wake, sleepy Thyrsis." Pilkington.
Madrigal: "You black bright stars." Morley.
Magnets. Cullen.
The Maid of Neidpath. Scott.
Majestic Sweetness. Stennett Samuel.
The Maker. Thomas.
Malcolm. Smith.
Man and Wife. Sexton.
Mandala. Boland.
Margaret Fuller. Alcott.
The Mariner. Cunningham.
Maritae Suae. Philpot.
Marrakech. Eberhart.
Marriage. Lowell.
The Marseillaise. Rouget de Lisle.
Martin Buber in the Pub. Harris.
The Mask. McClaurin.
May 20: Very Early Morning. Shaw.
May-Day: April and May. Emerson.
The Mechanic. Wakoski.
Meditation. Rakosi.
Meeting After Long Absence. Perry.
Meeting of the Waters. Moore.
The Memorial Pillar. Hemans.
Memory. Rossetti.
A Memory of the Players in a Mirror at Midnight. Joyce.
Merchant Marine. Miles.
The Mighty Heart. Emerson
Mimma Bella. Lee-Hamilton.
Mine. Polite.
The Miracle. Dowling.

Mistakes. Swarberg.
The Mole. Schmitz.
The Moment of the Rose. Thompson.
Money. Contoski.
The Monks at Ards. Maybin.
The Moods. Davis.
The Moon. Best.
Moon Shadows. Crapsey.
The Morning Glory. *Anonymous.*
Morning in Camp. Bashford.
Morning Light Song. Lamantia.
The Most Acceptable Gift. Claudius.
Most Lovely Shade. Sitwell.
Motets: "My love, how could your heart consider." *Anonymous.*
Mother. Clark.
The Mothers' Lament at the Slaughter of the Innocents. *Anonymous.*
Motif for Mary's Dolors. Mary Madeleva.
The Music of a Tree. Turner.
My Angel. Levine.
My Creed. Cary.
My Father's Cot (parody) (excerpt). Squire.
My Gift. Rossetti.
My Heart and I. Browning.
My Heart, How Very Hard It's Grown! Mather.
My Heart Stood Still. Hart.
My Heart Was Wandering. Brennan.
My Lady Nature and Her Daughters. Newman.
My Life Is a Bowl. Smith.
My Little Dreams. Johnson.
My Mind Keeps out the Host of Sin. Elys.
My Morning Song. Macdonald.
My New Year Prayer. *Anonymous.*
My Old Counselor. Hall.
My Owen. Downing.
My Own Dark Head (My Own, My Own). Anonymous.
My Song. Hall.
My spouse, Chunaychunay. *Anonymous.*
My White Book of Poems. "Rachel" (Rachel Blumstein).
Nature, that gave the bee so feat a grace. Wyatt.
Needs Must I Leave, and Yet Needs Must I Love. Constable.
Neither Spirit Nor Bird. *Anonymous.*
Nelson's Death and Victory. *Anonymous.*
Never Could I Think. Izumi Shikibu.
The New Heart. *Anonymous.*
New Season. Levine.
A New Spring. Mackie.
The New Sun. Wain.
The New York Woman. Sissman.
Night. Bogan.
Night. Ibn Gabirol.
Night and Wind. Symons.

The Night Loves Us. Adeane.
Night of Rain. Kenyon.
Night Thoughts: Baby & Demon. Harwood.
The Nima. Isaacs.
No Cold Approach. Burns.
No Faith. Van Doren.
No Miracle. Corkery.
No More, O Maidens. Alcman.
No More Will I Endure Love's Pleasing Pain. *Anonymous.*
No Other Choice. *Anonymous.*
"No Quarrel." Herbert.
Nocturne II. Dario.
Noel. Burket.
Non Piangere, Liu. Porter.
Norfolk. Betjeman.
The North Sea Undertaker's Complaint. Lowell.
Not Being Wise. Elson.
Now Ain't That Love? Rodgers.
Now She Is Like the White Tree-Rose. Day-Lewis.
The Nun. Symons.
O God, Though Countless Worlds of Light. Knowles.
O Softly Singing Lute. Pilkington.
The Oblation. Swinburne.
Ode. Freneau.
Ode. In Imitation of Pastor Fido Written Abroad, in 1729. Lyttelton.
Ode to the Norther. Chittenden.
Of Corinna's Singing. Campion.
Of Cynthia. *Anonymous.*
Of the Nativity of the Lady Rich's Daughter. Constable.
Of Wonder. Gilmore.
The Offended. Hebert.
Oh! To Have A Birthday. Lenski.
Oh, Who Regards. *Anonymous.*
The Old Adam. Benet.
The Old Place. Baughan.
The Old Woman. Bunker.
Olney Hymns: The Happy Change. Cowper.
Omnia Somnia. Watson.
On a Ferry Boat. Burton.
On a Lady Who P-ssed at the Tragedy of Cato. Pope.
On a Picture by J. M. Wright, Esq. Southey.
On Amaryllis A Tortoyse. Pickthall.
On Death and Love. Hale.
On J. W. Ward. Rogers.
On Lydia Distracted. Ayres.
On the Cliffs. Swinburne.
On the Collar of Mrs. Dingley's Lap-Dog. Swift.
On the Life-Mask of Abraham Lincoln. Gilder.
On W. R-, Esq. Burns.
One, Two, Buckle My Shoe. Nash.
One Who Watches. Sassoon.
Only the Heart. Campbell.
Open Earth. Nicoidski.
Open Heart. Salcman.
Other Lives. Hooper.
The Other One. Peck.

The Outward Man Accused.
Taylor.
Over the Wintry Threshold.
Carman.
The Overturned Lake. Ford.
The Owl. Bjornvig.
Owl Woman's Death Song.
Anonymous.
Painting of a White Gate and
Sky. Erdrich.
Pallid Cuckoo. Campbell.
A Panegyric on Geese.
Mahony.
Pantisocracy. Coleridge.
Pantomime. Verlaine.
Parted Love. Rossetti.
The Parthenon. Heath-
Stubbs.
Parting after a Quarrel.
Tietjens.
Pastourelle. Hayes.
Patience on a Monument. di
Michele.
The Peak. Gibson.
Pear Tree. Doolittle.
The Pearl. Andersen.
Penitential Psalms:
Introduction. Wyatt.
The Pet Lamb. Wordsworth.
Petition. Drinkwater.
Piccadilly. Burke.
The Piper's Progress.
Mahony.
Plato, a Musician. Leontius.
The Plea of the Midsummer
Fairies. Hood.
Poem of the Intimate Agony.
Burgos.
Poem: "Pity, repulsion, love
and anger." Fuller.
Poem to the Tune of "Yi
Chian Mei." Li Ching-
chao.
Poema Morale. Gullans.
The Poetic Land. Roscoe.
Poetry. Foote.
Portrait. Gluck.
Pot and Kettle. Graves.
The Power of the Dog.
Kipling.
Pray-Give-Go. Flint.
A Prayer. McLeod.
Prayer. Reed.
A Prayer. Tuwim.
Prayer during Battle.
Hagedorn.
Prayer for Boom. Grenier.
Prayer for Strength. Bruner.
The Prejudice against the
Past. Stevens.
Presentiment. Bierce.
Priapus and the Pool. Aiken.
Pride and Hesitation.
Farallon.
Prince Heathen (A version).
Anonymous.
Prince Heathen (B version).
Anonymous.
Prince Robert. *Anonymous.*
The Princess and the Gypsies.
Cornford.
The Princess in the Ivory
Tower. Davidman.
Pro Libra Mea. Clarke.
Process. O'Donnell.
Prodigal. Gilbert.
Proem. Heine.
De Profundis. Rossetti.
The Prophet. Pushkin.
Proverbs. Ha-Nagid.
Proving. Johnson.
Psalm XXVII. Sidney.

Psalm XXXII. Sidney.
Psalmodist. Leib.
Pudgy. Lima.
Puna's Fragrant Glades.
Lili, u-o-ka-lani.
Purer in Heart. *Anonymous.*
Purity of Heart. Keble.
The Puss and the Boots
(parody) (excerpt). Traill.
Pussy Has a Whiskered Face.
Rossetti.
Quiet Days. Mey.
Quo Vadis? Connolly.
The Rainbow. Colby.
Rattler, Alert. Ghiselin.
Recollection. Big Eagle.
Red lotus incense fades on the
jewelled curtain. Li
Ch'ing-chao.
Regent's Park Terrace.
Spencer.
Rejoice, O Youth, in the
Lovely Hind. Ibn Ezra.
Reliance. Van Dyke.
Religion. Heine.
Remembering Home.
Petrykewycz.
Remembering Lincoln.
Mundorf.
A Remembrance. Clarke
Reminiscence. Aldrich.
Remorse. Lattimore.
Rencontre. Fauset.
Renouncement. Meynell.
Requests. Dolben.
Requiem. O'Connor.
Retirement. Trench.
Revolutionary Letters. Di
Prima.
The Rich Interior Life.
Eberhart.
Richie Story (A version).
Anonymous.
Riding Adown the Country
Lanes. Bridges.
Riding the Blue Sapphire
Mountains. Mahadevi
(Mahadeviyakka).
Rising High Water Blues.
Jefferson.
The Risk. Sexton.
The Rite. Randall.
The Road. Ogarev.
The Road of Remembrance.
Reese.
The Robber. Eastwick.
Robin Redbreast.
Allingham.
Romance. Lang.
A Rondel of Merciless Beauty.
Chaucer.
Rondel: "Strengthen, my
Love, this castle of my
heart." d'Orleans.
Rosalynde. Lodge.
The Rose and the Thorn.
Hayne.
The Rubaiyat of Omar
Khayyam. Omar
Khayyam.
The Runner. Grilikhes.
Running through Sleep.
Norris.
Rural Route. Smith.
Sacrifice. Kinsella.
Salt Man. West.
Sand Dunes and Sea.
Moreland.
The School of Night. Hope.
The Science of the Night.
Kunitz.

The Scottish Merchant's
Daughter. *Anonymous.*
The Sea Cathedral. Pratt.
The Sea Hath Its Pearls.
Heine.
The Sea-Maiden. De Forest.
The Sea of Silence Exhales
Secrets. Bialik.
The Seafarer. *Anonymous.*
The Seafarer (excerpt).
Anonymous.
Seasons. Dempster.
The Seasons. Thomson.
Second Best. Brooke.
The Secret. Peach.
The Secret Muse. Campbell.
Secret of Song. White.
The Seeds of Love.
Anonymous.
The Seesaw. Williams.
Seguidilla. Valdivielso.
Self-Consciousness Makes All
Changes Happy.
Richardson.
Sent to a Lady, with a Seal.
Lloyd.
Separation. Dickinson.
Separation. Savage.
The Serious Merriment of
Women. Goedicke.
The Sermon. Hughes.
Sextains. Baylebridge.
The Shanty-Man's Life (with
music). *Anonymous.*
Shao and the South.
Confucius.
She Walks in Beauty. Byron.
Shepherd's Song at Christmas.
Hughes.
The Ship-Builders. Whittier.
Ships at Sea. Gray.
Shop. Browning.
Siberia. Mangan.
Sidney Godolphin. Scollard.
Sight and Insight. Slater.
The Silence at Night.
Denby.
Silent Love. *Anonymous.*
The Silent Woman:
Clerimont's Song. Jonson.
Silex Scintillans. Vaughan.
Since First I Saw Your Face.
Anonymous.
Sir Roland; a Fragment.
Merry.
Sketch. Farnsworth.
Sleepless. Al-Khansa.
The Smell of Death Is So
Powerful. Marguerite de
Navarre.
Smithereens. Rossetti.
The Snapper. Heyen.
A Solemn Meditation.
Shenstone.
The Solitary Reaper.
Wordsworth.
Solitude. Mollineux.
Solstitium Saeculare.
Fitzgerald.
Some Ruthless Rhymes.
Graham.
Sometimes when Night...
Sackville-West.
A Song. Hawthorne.
Song. Osgood.
Song. Williams.
Song for a Jewess. Goll.
A Song for Beauty. Lal.
Song for the Last Act.
Bogan.
Song: "Going down the old
way." Widdemer.

A Song: I Thought No More
Was Needed. Yeats.
Song: "Join once again, my
Celia, join." Cotton.
Song: "Ladies, though to your
Conqu'ring eyes."
Etherege.
Song. Love Arm'd. Behn.
Song: "O spirit of the
Summertime!" Allingham.
A Song of a Young Lady to
Her Ancient Lover.
Rochester.
A Song of Arno. Channing-
Stetson.
A Song of Derivations.
Meynell.
Song of the Border. Norris.
The Song of the Bow.
Doyle.
Song of the Brave. Altgood.
The Song of the Ghost.
Graves.
Song of the Sabbath.
Molodovsky.
Song of the Stygian Naiades.
Beddoes.
Song: "Rarely, rarely, comest
thou." Shelley.
Song Set by Michael
Cavendish: "Faustina hath
the fairer face."
Anonymous.
Song: "There is many a love
in the land, my love."
Miller.
Song Under Shadow. Benet.
Song: "When the heart's
feeling." Moore.
Songs of Cheng. Confucius.
A Sonnet. Troubetzkoy.
Sonnet: "I must now grieve
my Love, whose eyes would
read." Daniel.
Sonnet: "I saw the object of
my pining thought."
Watson.
Sonnet XI: "O eyes clear with
beauty, O tender gaze."
Labe.
Sonnet: "Between my love and
me there runs a thread."
McLeod.
Sonnet: "Fair is my Love,
when her fair golden
heares." Spenser.
A Sonnet Made on Isabella
Markham. Harington.
Sonnet: "My simple heart,
bred in provincial
tenderness." Fraser.
Sonnet: "O Time! who
know'st a lenient hand to
lay." Bowles.
A Sonnet of the Moon. Best.
Sonnet. The Cell. Thelwall.
Sonnet: To a Friend Who
Does Not Pity His Love.
Cavalcanti.
Sonnet to Edgar Allan Poe.
Whitman.
Sonnet to the Prince Regent.
Byron.
Sonnet: "When, from the
tower whence I derive love's
heaven." *Anonymous.*
Sonnets. Lee.
Sonnets. Tuckerman.
Sonnets, XXII: "My glass
shall not persuade me I am
old." Shakespeare.

Sonnets, XXIV: "Mine eye hath play'd the painter, and hath steel'd. Shakespeare.
Sonnets, XLVI: "Mine eye and heart are at a mortal war." Shakespeare.
Sonnets, XLVII: "Betwixt mine eye and heart a league is took." Shakespeare.
Sonnets: A Sequence on Profane Love. Boker.
Sonnets from the Portuguese, XIII. Browning.
Sonnets of a Portrait Painter. Ficke
Sonnets of the Months. San Geminiano.
Sonnets to Philomel. Davies.
The Sorrow of Unicume. Read.
Sorrow Shatters My Heart. Ibn Ezra.
The Soul of the World. Crosby.
The Soul Winner's Prayer. Harrison.
The Souldier Going to the Field. Davenant.
Sovereign and Transforming Grace. Hedge.
The Speckled Horse... Anonymous.
Spell of Sleep. Raine.
The Spider and the Ghost of the Fly. Lindsay.
Spite of Thy Godhead, Powerful Love. Wharton.
Splendid and Terrible. O'Sullivan.
The Spring. Carew.
Spring. Feirstein.
Spring 1943. Fuller.
Spring Morning–Santa Fe. Riggs.
St. Louis Blues. Handy.
Stand Fast, O My Heart. Anonymous
Stanzas. Bronte.
Stanzas to the Po. Byron.
Star of the East. Field.
Star of the Morning. Johnstone.
The Stars Go By. Lyon.
A Step Away from Them. O'Hara.
Strains of Sight. Duncan.
Strip Mining Pit. Gillespie.
Such as in God the Lord Do Trust. Kethe.
Suddenly. Blaser.
Sulpicia's Rival. Tibullus.
Summer in a Small Town. Gregg.
Summer Song. Nesbit.
Summerhouse. La Follette.
Superballs. Clark.
The Survivor. Thomas.
Sweet Violets. Anonymous.
Swift Floods. Petroczi.
The Tables Turned. Wordsworth.
Tadoussac. Bancroft.
Talking to Myself. McHugh.
Tan Ta Ra Ran Tan Tant: Cries Mars on Bloody Rapier. Anonymous.
Tar. Williams.
Tell Me Some Way. Reese.
The Ten Commandments. Anonymous.
The Test. Landor.
A Thankful Heart. Herrick.

Thanksgiving. Oxenham.
Then. Cooke.
Then. Gildner.
Then I said to the elegant ladies. Sappho.
Theory of Poetry. MacLeish.
There Are Roughly Zones. Frost.
There Came a Gray Owl at Sunset. Anonymous.
There Is a High Place. Markham.
There Is Always a Place for You. Campbell.
There Is In Human Closeness a Sacred Boundary. Akhmatova.
Theresienstadt Poem. Mezey.
A thing which fades. Ono no Komachi.
This Day Is Thine. Whinery.
This Evening, My Love, Even as I Spoke Vainly. Juana Ines de la Cruz.
This Is My Beloved (excerpt). Benton.
This Is the Violin. Stickney.
This Night of No Moon. Ono no Komachi.
Thou Hast Made Us for Thyself. Augustine.
Though Here in Flesh I Be. Howard.
The Thousand and One Nights: Abu Nuwas for the Barmacides. Anonymous.
Three Poems of the Atomic Age: Dirge for the New Sunrise. Sitwell.
The Timid Gazelle. Kasmuneh.
To a Bad Heart. Reynolds.
To a Boy. Anonymous.
To a Carmelite Postulant. Earls.
To a Cherokee Rose. Hayne.
To a Golden-Haired Girl in a Louisiana Town. Lindsay.
To a Madonna. Baudelaire.
To a Young Lady, with Some Lampreys. Gay.
To Argos. Durrell.
To Ask for All Thy Love. Anonymous.
To Constantia Singing. Shelley.
To Cupid. Davison.
To Etesia Looking from Her Casement at the Full Moon. Vaughan.
To His Love That Sent Him a Ring. Turberville.
To His Ring, Given to His Lady. Turberville.
To Ireland in the Coming Times. Yeats.
To J. S. Bach. Thwaites.
To Love A Sonnet. Ayres.
To Marie. Anonymous.
To Mary. Cowper.
To Miss–. Johnson.
To Mr C.B. Donne.
To My Honoured Patron Humphrey Davie... Tompson.
To Myself, after Forty Years. White.
To seek each where, where man doth live. Wyatt.
To Sir Thomas Egerton. Daniel.

To Terraughty, on His Birth-Day. Burns.
To the Blessed Sacrament. Constable.
To the Countesse of Salisbury. Townsend.
To the Daisy. Wordsworth.
To the Evening. Bampfylde.
To the Same Flower. Wordsworth.
The Tortured Heart. Rimbaud.
Toward a True Peace. Cheyney.
Travelling Light. Wagoner.
The Tree of Hatred. Moreh.
The Triumph of Time. Swinburne.
Troll the Bowl! Dekker.
True Love. Anonymous.
Tulips. McGuckian.
Turn to the Left. Taylor.
The Turtle Dove. Hill.
Two Poems. Abrams.
Two Solitudes. Ames.
Two Songs, II. Kabir.
Two Veterans. Whitman.
Uncourtly Love. Walther von der Vogelweide.
An Unfinished Work (Excerpt). Kennedy.
Ungathered Love. Marston.
The Unknown Grave. Landon.
Unless. Glynes.
The Unremitting Voice of Nightly Streams. Wordsworth.
Upon a Ribband. Carew.
Upon Christ His Birth. Suckling.
Upon His Timorous Silence in Her Presence. Davison.
Valediction. Wheelock.
Valentine. Gasparini.
A Valentine. Richards.
Vanity. Graves.
Vapour and Blue. Campbell.
Venus of the Louvre. Lazarus.
Verses Copied From the Window of an Obscure Lodging-House. Anonymous.
Vicksburg. Hayne.
Victimae Paschali Laudes. Wipo.
Victory in Defeat. Markham.
Une Vie. Saarikoski.
Violet. Symons.
La Vita Nuova. Dante Alighieri.
Voice in Darkness. Dehmel.
Voyeur. Hardy.
Waikiki. Brooke.
Waiting for the Dawning. Anonymous.
The Wanderer. Brennan.
The Wandering Gadling. Wyatt.
War. Hall.
Warning and Reply. Bronte.
Warum Sind Denn Die Rosen So Blass. Heine.
Washington. Williams.
Washington. Wingate.
Water-Girl. Anonymous.
Water Music. Lewis.
A Way of Keeping. Willard.
Wayne at Stony Point. Scollard.

We Have Seen His Star in the East. Haley.
We Heart. Chester.
We Lying by Seasand. Thomas.
We Needs Must Be Divided. Santayana.
We Never Speak as We Pass By. Anonymous.
We Thank Thee. Clark.
We Thank Thee. Oxenham.
The Weed. Bishop.
The Western Rebel. Anonymous.
What Do I Care. Teasdale.
What Is Good. O'Reilly.
Whatsoever I Do. Hector.
When First Mine Eyes Did View and Mark. Wyatt.
When I Admire the Greatness. Steendam.
When Israel. Scott.
When She a Maiden Slim. Hewlett.
When Summer's End Is Nighing. Housman.
When They Have Lost. Day-Lewis.
When Thy Heart with Joy O'erflowing. Williams.
When We Are Parted. Aïdé.
When Wild Confusion Wrecks the Air. Byles.
When You Touch. Hart-Smith.
Where Avalanches Wail. Anonymous.
Where Love Is. Burr.
Where You Passed. Burr.
While the Days Are Going By. Cooper.
Whispering Hope. Hawthorne.
White Fear. Welles.
White Swan. Glanz-Leyeles. A.
Whither Shall I Go. Anonymous.
Widow Machree. Lover.
The Wife. Garrison.
The Wife's Lament. Anonymous.
Wild Ass. Colum.
The Wind's Way. Le Gallienne.
Winter's End. Moss.
The Wisdom of Folly. Fowler.
Wishes for My Son. Macdonagh.
Witchcraft by a Picture. Donne.
The Witnesses. Kennedy.
Woman (excerpt). McLachlan.
Woman Free (excerpt). Wolstenholme-Elmy.
A Woman's Pride. Hay.
A Woman's Question. Procter.
A Woman to Her Lover. Walsh.
Woman to Man. Ai.
Women Damned. Baudelaire.
Wonders. Anonymous.
The Wood of the Self-Destroyers. Yellen.
Words for Hart Crane. Lowell.
Words for Love. Berrigan.

Wreck of the Deutschland. Hopkins.
Written in My Lady Speke's Singing-Book. Waller.
X-Ray. Ray.
The Yoke of Tyranny. Sidney.
Yosemite. Shinn.
You Are Reading This Too Fast. Norris.
You, Letting the Trees Stand as My Betrayer. Wakoski.
You See the Worst of Love, but Not the Best. Landor.
You, the Young Rainbow. Sitwell.
The Young Rhymer Snubbed. Barnes.
Youth. Rittenhouse.
Youth and Maidenhood. Williams.
Youth's Spring-Tribute. Rossetti.
Zimbabwe. Sinclair.
Zola. Robinson.

Heartbeat (s)
Altarwise by Owl-Light. Thomas.
Blue Ruth: America. Harper.
Early Winter. Kees.
Need. Deutsch.
Of the New Prosody. Ghiselin.
Orange County Plague: Scenes. Lieberman.
Where the Dropwort Springs up Lithe and Tall. Donaghy.

Heartbreak
Mary, Helper of Heartbreak. Widdemer.
Rust. Davies.
Sound of Breaking. Aiken.

Hearth
Abel's Bride. Levertov.
The Beatific Vision. Chesterton.
Celia's Home-Coming. Robinson.
Corinne at the Capitol. Hemans.
Disappointment. Collier.
The Jewish May. Rosenfeld.
The Sea-Watcher. De Vere.
Tall Hat. Daley.
The Tree. Winchilsea.
Wayfarers. Burnet.
Work. Pushkin.

Heat
The Aeneid. Virgil (Publius Vergilius Maro).
Anti-Platonicke. Daniel.
April Fourth. Mezey.
The Arid Lands. Bashford.
Becoming a Nun. Jong.
Developing a Wife. Taylor.
Didyma. *Anonymous.*
A Dream of Fair Women. Tennyson.
The Dunciad. Pope.
Filling Station. Morin.
The Fire of Love. Sackville.
The Fleece. Dyer.
Food for Fire, Food for Thought. Duncan.
Forcing House. Roethke.
Gamesters All. Heyward.
The Glass Eaters. Jonas.
Glitter of Pebbles. Moraes.
Heat. Mackenzie.

The Heavens Do Declare. *Anonymous.*
I Once May See when Yeares Shall Wreck My Wrong. Daniel.
A Kitchen Memory. Scheele.
The Lion's Skeleton. Turner.
Macinnes's Mountain Patrol. Patey.
Manitou. Ikan.
The Observatory Ode. Nims.
On Mt. Iron. Brasch.
Pot of Tea. Griffin.
The Refiner's Fire. *Anonymous.*
She Rebukes Hippolyta. Doolittle.
Six Young Men. Hughes.
The Spirit of the Wheat. Valentine.
Summer. Clare.
Sun Moon Kelp Flower or Goat. Gregg.
To Age. Landor.
To His Coy Mistress (parody). Webster.
To My Mistris, I Burning in Love. Carew.
To Summer. Blake.

Heath
The Fairies' Farewell. Corbet.
The Gossamer. Smith.
Lord Fluting Dreams of America on the Eve of His Departure... Zimmer.
A Roundabout Turn. Charles.
The Sand Martin. Clare.

Heathen (s)
An Address to Miss Phillis Wheatley (excerpt). Hammon.
Awake Yee Westerne Nymphs, Arise and Sing. Danforth.
Epitaphs of the War, 1914-18. Kipling.
I Want to Be a Cowboy. *Anonymous.*
The Indian's Grave. Mountain.
Monkshood XXIII. Gunnars.
Of Thomas Traherne and the Pebble outside. Clouts.
Psalm IX. Sidney.
The Slaughter of Grendel by Beowulf. *Anonymous.*
With All My Heart, Jehovah, I'll Confess. Ainsworth.

Heather
Among the Heather. Allingham.
The Call of the Morning. Darley.
For Summer's Here. Barnett.
June Bracken and Heather. Tennyson.
Owre the Muir amang the Heather. Glover.
The Return. Macgillivray.
Scotland Small? ""MacDiarmid.

Heave
A Burnt Offering to Your Greenstone Eyes, Tangaroa. Tuwhare.
A Trip to the Grand Banks. Hanson.

Heaven (ly)
Acceptation. Preston.
Addition to Kipling's "The Dead King (Edward VII), 1910." Beerbohm.
Addressed to a Young Lady. Cowper.
Adieu to the Stone Walls. *Anonymous.*
The Advantage of the Outside. Eberhart.
Affliction. Herbert.
African Heaven. Parkes.
After Sunday Dinner We Uncles Snooze. Ciardi.
Afternoon: Amagansett Beach. Wheelock.
Ah Sweet Content, where Is Thy Mylde Abode? Barnes.
Aideen's Grave. Ferguson.
Almighty God, Thy Constant Care. Washburn.
The Alpine Flowers. Sigourney.
Altarwise by Owl-Light. Thomas.
Amazing Sight! The Saviour Stands. Alline.
Amend Me. *Anonymous.*
Among the Hills: Prelude. Whittier.
Among the Millet. Lampman.
Among the Worst of Men. Thoreau.
Amoretti, LV. Spenser.
Amoretti, LXI. Spenser.
The Antagonist. Ferry.
The Apple-Tree. Campbell.
The Argument of His Book. Herrick.
The Armorer's Daughter. Greger.
An Art Master. O'Reilly.
As Down a Valley. Dwight.
As We Dance Round. *Anonymous.*
Astraea. Whittier
At Penshurst. Waller.
At the Church Gate. Thackeray.
At the Edge of the Day. Urmy.
At the Fountain. Marcabrun.
At the Symphony. Nathan.
At Timber Line. Mayer.
Ave Atque Vale. *Anonymous.*
The Babie. Rankin.
The Bad-Tempered Wife. *Anonymous.*
The Ballad of the White Horse. Chesterton.
Ballata V: "Light do I see within my Lady's eyes." Cavalcanti.
The Battle of Otterburn (A vers.). *Anonymous.*
BC : AD. Fanthorpe.
Beachcomber. Brown.
The Beggar. Moss.
Beulah Land. Sweeney.
The Bible. Levi.
A Blason. Hope.
Blest Retirement. Goldsmith.
The Blind. Baudelaire.
Bonny Bee Hom. *Anonymous.*

Brahma, the World Idea. *Anonymous.*
Breasts. Gallagher.
Britannia's Pastorals. Browne.
Buffalo. Eglington.
The Builder. Wattles.
Builders. Deitz.
Caelica, XLVII. Greville.
A Canticle to Apollo. Herrick.
Canto Espiritual. Maragall.
Capability Brown. Cowper.
The Car Cemetery. Carson.
Catherine Kinrade. Brown.
The Celestial Passion. Gilder.
Chanson Mystique. *Anonymous.*
The Chaunt of the Brazen Head (excerpt). Praed.
Child, Child. Teasdale.
A Child's Song of Christmas. Pickthall.
Children's Song. Thomas.
Christmas. Stam.
A Christmas Eve Choral. Carman.
Church Music. Herbert.
Clock without Hands. Nims.
The Clod and the Pebble. Blake.
A Coal Miner's Goodbye. *Anonymous.*
Come, Lord Jesus. Wesley.
The Coming Child. Crashaw.
A Communion Hymn. Palmer.
Composed while Under Arrest. Lermontov.
Comrades. Blood.
Consecration. Hoppe.
Contemplations. Bradstreet.
Corn. Lanier.
The Cowboy. *Anonymous.*
The Cruel Mother (Down by the Greenwood Side). *Anonymous.*
Curse of the Cat Woman. Field.
Cushla Ma Chree. Curran.
The Damsel. Omar B. Abi Rabi'a.
The Dance. Strand.
Dante at Verona. Rossetti.
Day and Dark. Lodge.
Death, Always Cruel. Dante Alighieri.
Death's Jest Book. Beddoes.
Death's Songsters. Rossetti.
Death the Great. Lasynys.
Defend Us, Lord, from Every Ill. Hay.
The Deserted Pasture. Carman.
A Development of Idiotcy. Jones.
Dew on a Dusty Heart. Untermeyer.
Dies Irae. Scott.
Dig My Grave. *Anonymous.*
Dirge. Eastman
Dirge. Hemans.
The Dog. Davies.
The Donner Party (excerpt). Keithley.
Dry Be That Tear. Sheridan.
Duel with Verses over a Great Man. *Anonymous.*
Durand of Blonden. Uhland.

During His Courtship. Wesley.
Dusk. Lopez-Penha.
The Dying Child's Request. Gould.
The Dying Fisherman's Song. Anonymous.
Dying That I Might Live. Wesley.
A. E. Bronte.
Each a Part of All. Bamberger.
The Eagle Swift. Adam of St. Victor.
The Earl O' Quarterdeck. MacDonald.
Earth and Fire. Watkins.
Earth-Canonized. Robinson.
Earth Felicities, Heavens Allowances. A Blank Poem. Steere.
Easter Hymn. Housman.
Easter Island. Scott.
Elected Silence. Sassoon.
Elegiac. Percival.
An Elegie on the Lady Jane Pawlet, Marchion: of Winton. Jonson.
An Elegy on the Death of Furuhi. Yamanoue Okura.
Elisa, or an Elegy upon the Unripe Decease... Fletcher.
Endymion. Keats.
The English Succession. Anonymous.
The Enjoyment. Anonymous.
Epigram: "First in his pride the orient sun's display." Belloc.
Epigram: "Grown old in Love from Seven till seven times Seven." Blake.
Epipsychidion. Shelley.
An Epistle from Mr. Pope to Dr. Arbuthnot. Pope.
Epitaph. Claudian (Claudius Claudianus).
An Epitaph. Davies.
Epitaph at Upton-on-Severn. Anonymous.
Epitaph: "Beneath this stone, in hope of Zion." Anonymous.
An Epitaph for a Godly Man's Tomb. Wild.
Epitaph: "Sanquhar, whom this earth could scarce contain." Drummond.
Epithalamium on a Late Happy Marriage. Smart.
An Essay on Man. Pope.
Eugenia: Presage of Storme. Chapman.
An Evening Blessing. Edmeston.
Evening in Paradise. Milton.
An Evening Walk in Bengal. Heber.
The Expectation. Faber.
A Face. Browning.
Face to Face. Cochrane.
Fair Annie of Lochyran. Anonymous.
Fair Maiden, Who Is This Bairn? Anonymous.
Faith, Hope and Love. Anonymous.
The Fallen Star. Darley.
A Far Cry to Heaven. Thomas.
Farewell to Juliet. Blunt.

Fast. Tagliabue.
Faust. Goethe.
Feathered Faith. Anonymous.
The Fire-bringer. Moody.
The Fishermen. Whittier.
The Flesh and the Spirit. Bradstreet.
The Flight of the War-Eagle. Auringer.
Fog. Patchen.
For Soldiers. Gifford.
For the New Railway Station in Rome. Wilbur.
For Two Girls Setting out in Life. Viereck.
Four Things. Van Dyke.
Friend of Souls. Anonymous.
The Frog Prince. Smith.
From Heaven High I Come to You. Luther.
From William Tyndale to John Frith. Bowers.
Fronleichnam. Lawrence.
The Gaelic Litany to Our Lady. Anonymous.
The Gentle Check. Beaumont.
The Gift. Ciardi.
Girl of Constant Sorrow. Gunning.
Giving and Taking. Kirkup.
The Glance. Herbert.
God. Lamartine.
God Is There. Isenhour.
God of the World, Thy Glories Shine. Cutting.
God's Presence Makes My Heaven. Smith.
Gods Determinations Touching His Elect. Taylor.
A Gratulatory to Mr. Ben. Johnson for His Adopting of Him... Randolph.
Haiku: "The halo of the moon." Buson (Taniguchi Buso).
Hail, Day of Days! In Peals of Praise. Venantius Fortunatus.
Hamlet. Shakespeare.
The Hand. Jones.
The Happiest Heart. Cheney.
Happiness Found. Toplady.
The Hard-Working Miner. Anonymous.
He Lives! He Lives to Bless! Stroud.
He Who Hath Loved. Malone.
The Head That Once Was Crowned with Thorns. Kelly.
The Heart of God. Littlewood.
Heaven. Levine.
Heaven Is Heaven. Rossetti.
Heaven Is Here. Adams.
Heaven, O Lord, I Cannot Lose. Proctor.
Heaven Will Protect the Working Girl. Smith.
The Heavenly Aeroplane. Anonymous.
The Heavenly Banquet. Brigid.
Hell. Anonymous.
Henry Green. Anonymous.
Her Husband. Hughes.
Her Kisses. Beddoes.

Here Followeth the Songe of the Death of Mr. Thewlis. Anonymous.
A Heterodoxy. Dunsany.
Ho, Everyone That Thirsteth. Housman.
Hold Thou Me Fast. Rossetti.
The Holy Field. Milman.
Home. Beaumont.
The Hour of Peaceful Rest. Tappan.
How the Ploughman Learned His Paternoster. Anonymous.
How Things Fall. Finkel.
Hugh Stuart Boyd: His Blindness. Browning.
Human Frailty. Cowper.
The Human Plan. Crandall.
Hurry On, My Weary Soul. Anonymous.
The Husbandman and Serving-Man. Anonymous.
Hymns and Spiritual Songs. Smart.
I Am the Rose of Sharon. Winkworth.
I'm Not Rich. Rolnik.
I Need No Sky. Bynner.
I's Gonna Shine. Anonymous.
I Shall Not Want: In Deserts Wild. Deems.
I Stood Within the Heart of God. Moody.
I Walked with My Reason. MacLean.
Idea. Drayton.
Idea's Mirrour. Drayton.
Ideal Beauty. Herrera.
If I Got My Ticket, Can I Ride? Anonymous.
If I Have Sinn'd in Act. Coleridge.
Immortal is an ample word. Dickinson.
An Imprecation Against Foes and Sorcerers. Atharva Veda.
In Defiance to the Dutch. Anonymous.
In Memoriam. Milnes.
In Rama. Townsend.
In the Name of Jesus Christ. Cranston.
Indian Summer. Tabb.
The Interpreters. Swinburne.
The Isle of Man Shore (The Desolate Widow). Anonymous.
It troubled me as once I was. Dickinson.
Jesus, I Live to Thee. Harbaugh.
Jesus Tender Shepherd. Duncan.
John L. Sullivan Enters Heaven (parody). Frost.
Keep Thou My Way, O Lord. Crosby.
King Henry VIII. Shakespeare.
Lalla Rookh. Moore.
The Lass of Roch Royal (D version). Anonymous.
The Last Day. Sargent.
A Last Will and Testament. Anonymous.
The Lay of the Last Minstrel. Scott.

The Leaves of Life. Anonymous.
Legacy. Turner.
Leila. Hill.
Let Not Your Heart Be Troubled. Mortenson.
Letters from Birmingham. Bond.
Life's Chequer-Board. Oxenham.
"Like as the Lark." Parsons
Little Jim. Farmer.
Little Lyric (of Great Importance). Hughes.
Little Moses. Anonymous.
Little Things. Carney.
Lochiel's Warning. Campbell.
The Locomotive to the Little Boy. Low.
Lost in Heaven. Frost.
The Lost Leader. Browning.
Love. Oxenham.
Love and Life. Rochester.
Love Poem. Padgett.
A Love-Song. Thomas of.
Lover of the Lord. Anonymous.
Luck. Hughes.
Lust. Shakespeare.
Lux in Tenebris. Anonymous.
Macbeth. Shakespeare.
Mad Maid's Whim. Stow.
The Maimed Debauchee. Pope.
Malest Cornifici Tuo Catullo. Ginsberg.
The Marriage of Earth and Heaven. Macpherson.
The Marriage of Heaven and Hell. Blake.
Mary. Farren.
Mary's Assumption. Barrett.
A Mask Presented at Ludlow Castle (Comus). Milton.
The Master Singers. Carpenter.
A Mastic Presented at Ludlow Castle (Comus). Milton.
The Mermaid. Anonymous.
Metamorphoses. Ovid (Publius Ovidius Naso).
Miss You. Cory.
Morality. Arnold.
A Morning Hymn. Smart.
The Morning Purples All the Sky. Roman Breviary.
The Mother. Anonymous.
Mr. Eliot, Pastor of the Church of Christ at Roxbury... Johnson.
Mr. Frost Goes South to Boston (parody). Houghton.
My Child. Pierpont.
My Delight. Bradford.
My Lady Carenza of the lovely body. Anonymous.
My Mother's Prayer. O'Kane.
My Sister. Storni.
The Naked Seed. Lewis.
The Nativity. Anonymous.
Ne Plus Ultra. Coleridge.
Nerves. Symons.
Nevada. Gurney.
New England. Percival.
New Heaven, New War. Southwell.
A New Hunting Song. Anonymous.

New Prince, New Pomp.
  Southwell.
Newes from Virginia.   Rich.
Night.   Montgomery.
Night Thoughts While
  Travelling.   Tu Fu.
No, I Am Not as Others Are.
  Villon.
Norembega.   Whittier.
O God, Great Father, Lord,
  and King.   Hoss.
O Sing to Me of Heaven.
  Dana.
Ode to Apollo.   Keats.
Oedipus Rex: Chorus.
  Sophocles.
Of God We Ask One Favor.
  Dickinson.
The Old Burying-Ground.
  Whittier.
The Old-Time Cowboy.
  Anonymous.
On a Wednesday.   Aliesan.
On Heaven.   Ford.
On King Richard the Third,
  Who Lies Buried under
  Leicester Bridge.   Suckling.
On Listening to the Spirituals.
  Jeffers.
On the Blessed Virgin's
  Bashfulness.   Crashaw.
On the Death of a Pious
  Lady.   Wexionius.
On the Death of Catarina de
  Attayda.   Camoens.
On the Death of Southey.
  Landor.
On the Edge of the Copper
  Pit.   Henson.
On the Sicilian Strand a Hare
  Well Wrought.   Ausonius.
Once I Lived in Cottonwood.
  Anonymous.
One Way of Love.
  Browning.
Only.   Spofford.
Our Ever-Present Guide.
  Anonymous.
Out of the Vast.   Bamberger.
Overheard in an Orchard.
  Cheney.
Paean.   Brooks.
Pandora's Song.   Moody.
Paradise Lost.   Milton.
Peace.   Anonymous.
Pearl Bryan.   Anonymous.
Perhaps.   Dobell.
The Pet Name.   Browning.
Peter, Go Ring Dem Bells.
  Anonymous.
The Petition for an Absolute
  Retreat.   Winchilsea.
Petition of Youth before
  Battle.   Bunker.
The Poem.   Merwin.
Poetry and Philosophy.
  Randolph.
Portrait of a Very Old Man.
  Carsley.
A Prayer.   Chawner.
A Prayer for Faith.
  Michelangelo.
The Preacher's Vacation.
  Anonymous.
Prelude.   Whittier.
The Present Tense.   Oates.
Progress.   Anonymous.
The Progress of Learning:
  Preface.   Denham.
A Prospect of Death.
  Young.
Puppy.   Lape.

Quaerit Jesum suum Maria.
  Crashaw.
The Quest.   Vinal.
Rec Room in Paradise.
  Clark.
Red o'er the Forest.   Keble.
Red Whiskey.   Anonymous.
Refuge.   Winter.
Remembrance.   Lathrop.
Reparation.   Hoyt.
Reply.   Godolphin.
The Restoration of
  Enheduanna to Her Former
  Station.   Enheduanna.
The Return of Astraea.
  Jonson.
Rhododaphne.   Peacock.
Ripe Grain.   Goodale.
The Rising Village.
  Goldsmith.
Risposta.   Wilbye.
The Robin.   Very.
Roll, Jordan, Roll.
  Anonymous.
The Rose of Peace.   Yeats.
Royal Palm.   Crane.
Rufus's Mare.   Anonymous.
The Saint.   Wolfe.
Saint Ita's Fosterling.   Ita.
Sanctity.   Kavanagh.
Satire Septimus Contra
  Sollistam.   Rankins.
Saviour, Whose Love Is Like
  the Sun.   Robbins.
The Sea Hath Its Pearls.
  Heine.
Service Is No Heritage.
  Anonymous.
The Shepherds Had an Angel.
  Rossetti.
The Siege: Seal Up Her Eyes,
  O Sleep.   Cartwright.
Silence and Stealth of Dayes!
  Vaughan.
Silver Lamps.   Dix.
Sister Helen.   Rossetti.
The Snares.   Koutchak.
Snow in the City.   Siegel.
So Have I Spent on the Banks
  of Ysca Many a Serious
  Hour.   Vaughan.
So Oft As I Her Beauty Do
  Behold.   Spenser.
Solitude.   Clare.
Solitudes.   Wheelock.
Some Things You Cannot
  Will to Men.   Isenhour.
Sometimes I Wish That I
  Were Helen-Fair.   Harford.
The Son of Man.   Langford.
Song: "My love is the flaming
  Sword."   Thomson.
A Song of Arno.   Channing-
  Stetson.
Song of Nexahualcoyotl.
  Anonymous.
Song on a Young Lady Who
  Sung Finely.   Roscommon.
Song: "With my frailty don't
  upbraid me."   Congreve.
Sonnet LXXXVI.   Greville.
Sonnet to Edgar Allan Poe.
  Whitman.
Sonnets.   Whitman
Sonnets, XXXIII: "Full many
  a glorious morning have I
  seen."   Shakespeare.
Sonnets, CX: "Alas! 'tis true I
  have gone here and there."
  Shakespeare.

Sonnets, CXXIX: "Th'
  expense of spirit in a waste
  of shame."   Shakespeare.
Spain.   Livesay.
Speaks the Whispering Grass.
  Stuart.
The Spirit Craft.   Ballard.
The Spring of the Year.
  Cunningham.
Stanzas.   Bronte.
Stanzas to—.   Bronte.
Starlight.   Downie.
A Storm in Summer.   Blunt.
The Story of Samuel Jackson.
  Leland.
Substance and Shadow.
  Newman.
The Summer Harvest Spreads
  the Fields.   Strong.
A Sun-Day Hymn.   Holmes.
Sunday.   Herbert.
Sunlight and Sea.   Noyes.
Sweet Muse.   Watts.
Sweet Unsure.   Ralegh.
Swell the Anthem, Raise the
  Song.   Strong.
Table Graces, or Prayers for
  Adults: Evening Meal.
  Anonymous.
Teneriffe (excerpt).   Myers.
Terence MacSwiney.   Russell.
Thamuris Marching.
  Browning.
Thanksgiving for the Earth.
  Goudge.
There Is Good News.
  Jacobsen.
This Darknight Speed.
  Healy.
This World Is All a Fleeting
  Show.   Moore.
Though She Slumbers.
  Keith.
Three Hours.   Lindsay.
Three Poems about Children.
  Clarke.
The Thunderer.   McGinley.
'Tis so much joy!   Dickinson.
To a Calvinist in Bali.
  Millay.
To a Nun.   Anonymous.
To a Post-Office Inkwell.
  Morley.
To a Skylark.   Wordsworth.
To America, on Her First
  Sons Fallen in the Great
  War.   Walker.
To an Oriole.   Fawcett.
To Begin the Day.
  Anonymous.
To Betsey-Jane, on Her
  Desiring to Go
  Incontinently to Heaven.
  Eden.
To Celia, upon Love's
  Ubiquity.   Carew.
To-Day.   Ward.
To Duty.   Higginson.
To God.   Herrick.
To Julius.   Sedley.
To Lucasta, on Going Beyond
  the Seas.   Lovelace.
To Mark Anthony in Heaven.
  Williams.
To Music, to Becalm His
  Fever.   Herrick.
To My Most Gracious Dread
  Sovereign.   Davies.
To Prote.   Simmias.
To Queen Elizabeth.   Davies.

To the Best and Most
  Accomplished Couple—.
  Vaughan.
To the Excellent Pattern of
  Beauty and Virtue, Lady
  Elizabeth...   Shirley.
To the Moon.   Ronsard.
To the Skylark.
  Wordsworth.
To the Spring.   Davies.
To Theodora.   Anonymous.
To Thomas Lord Chancellor.
  Jonson.
The Transformed
  Metamorphosis: Awake, Oh
  Heaven.   Tourneur.
Trouble Not the Maiden's
  Soul.   Runeberg.
Turris Eburnea.   Anonymous.
'Twas When the Spousal Time
  of May.   Patmore.
Twelfth Night.   Lee.
Two Angels.   Milnes.
Two Sorrows.   St. John.
Two Tramps in Mud Time.
  Frost.
Two Voices in a Meadow.
  Wilbur.
Unequal Distribution.
  Hoffenstein.
The Unreturning.   Owen.
Up Silver Stairsteps.   Stuart.
Upon a Fool.   Hoskyns.
Upon My Lord Chief Justice's
  Election of My Lady Anne
  Wentworth...   Carew.
Upon the Infant Martyrs.
  Crashaw.
The Vagabond.   Stevenson.
Valediction to Life.   Ignoto.
Verses Copied From the
  Window of an Obscure
  Lodging-House.
  Anonymous.
Vision.   Sidgwick.
The Voiceless.   Holmes
The Vow of Washington.
  Whittier.
Walking on Water.   Dickey.
Walking on Water.   Petaccia.
Walking the Beach.
  Youngblood.
The Watcher.   Widdemer.
The Way I Read a Letter's—
  This.   Dickinson.
The Way-Side Well.   Cotter.
We Are God's Chosen Few.
  Swift.
We'll Never Know.
  Hoellein.
We Must Not Part.
  Anonymous.
Weakness of Nature.
  Froude.
The Weaver.   Forrester.
Wesley in Heaven.   Brown.
The West Palm Beach Storm.
  Anonymous.
Western Town.   Cannon, Jr..
What Tidings?   Audelay.
What You See Is Me.   Gibbs.
When Satan Fell.   Lawrence.
Where Lies the Truth? Has
  Man, in Wisdom's Creed.
  Wordsworth.
Where Now Are the Hebrew
  Children?   Anonymous.
Which Shall It Be?   Beers.
While Shepherds Watched
  Their Flocks by Night.
  Tate.

While to Bethlehem We Are
  Going. Violante Do Ceo.
White Magic: An Ode.
  Braithwaite.
Whitehall Stairs. Hill.
Why? Talmud.
Winter Twilight. Rlliot.
A Wish. Rogers.
With Wordsworth at Rydal.
  Fields
The World's Great Age
  Begins Anew. Shelley.
The Wren. *Anonymous.*
Year after year I have
  watched. Li Ch'ing-chao.
The Year's at the Spring.
  Browning.
You Are Gorgeous and I'm
  Coming. O'Hara.
Young Men You Are So
  Beautiful up There.
  Goedicke.
Yours. Tagore.

Heavens
Address to My Infant
  Daughter. Wordsworth.
Ancient Lights. Clarke.
As to Being Alone.
  Oppenheim.
Assumpta Maria.
  Thompson.
A Battle. Crawford.
Black Poplar-Boughs.
  Freeman.
Domestic Scenes. Unamuno.
The Dove. *Anonymous.*
Except the Lord, That He for
  Us Had Been. Ainsworth.
Fair Days; or, Dawns
  Deceitful. Herrick.
Fancy Dress. Sassoon.
A Farewell. Russell.
For Innocents Day.
  Wadding.
Hell, Well, Heaven. Serote.
I Buried the Year. Luff.
"In winter's just return..."
  Surrey.
John Rogers' Exhortation to
  His Children. *Anonymous.*
King Lear. Shakespeare.
The Lady's Third Song.
  Yeats.
On a Prayer Book Sent to
  Mrs. M. R. (excerpt).
  Crashaw.
The Parklands. Smith.
Patience. Horne.
Reflections on the River.
  Young.
Sic Transit. Plunkett.
Study Peace. Jones.
Summer's Farewell. Nashe
  [(or Nash[) Thomas.
The Swan. Rodgers.
To a Skylark. Meredith.
To William Stanley
  Braithwaite. Johnson.
Two Folk Songs, 1.
  Anonymous.
The White Kite. *Anonymous.*
Wyat Resteth Here, that
  Quicke Coulde Never Rest.
  Surrey.
Your cheeks flat on the sand.
  Khoury-Gata.

Heavy
Amid the Din of Earthly
  Strife. Hawkes.
Amoretti, LXII. Spenser.
Bell Too Heavy to Ring.
  Kryss.

Burning and Fathering:
  Accounts of My Country.
  Gilbert.
By an' By. *Anonymous.*
Chaucer's Complaint to His
  Empty Purse (modern
  version). Chaucer.
Cherry Tree Carol.
  Anonymous.
The Coffin. Heine.
The Complaint of Chaucer to
  His Empty Purse.
  Chaucer.
Four Things Choctaw.
  Barnes.
The Guarded Wound.
  Crapsey.
Hush'd Be the Camps To-
  Day. Whitman.
If I Went Away. O'Grady.
In Fine, Transparent Words.
  Vogel.
Jerusalem Sonnets. Baxter.
The Little Shroud. Landon.
Love Poem. Lewis.
The Masque of Christmas.
  Jonson.
A Missouri Traveller Writes
  Home: 1830. Bly.
My Honeyed Languor.
  "Bagritsky.
My Sister Laura. Milligan.
The Name of Our Country.
  Schmitz.
New Year's Carol.
  Anonymous.
Nocturne of Birth and Water.
  Domanski.
On Bertrand Russell's
  "Portraits from Memory'.
  Davie.
The Onondaga Madonna.
  Scott.
Pavane for the Passing of a
  Child. Chester.
The Peaceable Kingdom.
  Piercy.
A Row of Stalls: Nell.
  Knister.
Schoolfellows. Praed.
Self-Portrait. Mendelssohn.
Ship-Building Emperors
  Commanded... Levi.
Sisyphus. Miles.
Slow Death. Martinez.
Snowy Night. Haines.
Song. Williams.
Song from a Country Fair.
  Adams.
Though I've a Clever Head.
  Anonymous.
Three American Women and
  a German Bayonet. Scott.
Untitled I. Reed.
Yellow Light. Hongo.
Your Light. Lee.

Hebrew
Buying a Shop on Dizengoff.
  Biton.
Dew. Reznikoff.
Jealousie is the Rage of a
  Man. Winchilsea.

Hebrides
The Misty Island.
  Anonymous.
On the Memory of Mr.
  Edward King Drown'd in
  the Irish Seas. Cleveland.

Hedge (s)
The Corbie and the Crow.
  Anonymous.

The Hawthorn Hedge.
  Wright.
The Hedge Schoolmasters.
  MacManus.
June in Wiltshire. Grigson.
Lawrence: The Last Crusade
  (excerpt). Rodman.
A Little Girl on Her Way to
  School. Wright.
Penal Rock: Altamuskin.
  Montague.
A Serenade for Two Poplars.
  Raab.
To a Conscript of 1940.
  Read.

Heed (s)
The Beggar's Opera. Gay.
Crotalus Rex. Ghiselin.
Fountains. Sitwell.
Gratitude. Lermontov.
A Pastoral. Byrom.
Pearl Bryan. *Anonymous.*
Smile and Never Heed Me.
  Swain.
Take Thou Our Minds, Dear
  Lord. Foulkes.
There Was a Time. Thomas.

Heel (s)
Aside. Dugan.
Asphodel. Malouf.
Baby Taffy. *Anonymous.*
The Bull. Wright.
Empedocles. Meredith.
The Friar of Orders Grey.
  Anonymous.
A Frieze. Bishop.
From Mythology. Herbert.
The Glorious Game. Burton.
Hossolalia. Luton.
Master Skylark. Bennett.
Odes. Horace.
Old Bandy Legs.
  Anonymous.
Once upon a Nag.
  McMahon.
The Piercing Chill I Feel.
  Buson (Taniguchi Buso).
The Thief's Niece. Keithley.
Thrown. Hodgson.
Twenty Years After. Shute.
Two Stories. Wright.
Up in the Lift Go We.
  Anonymous.
Warning. Cook.

Height (s)
Among Friends. Kuzma.
At Parting. Swinburne.
At Sunrise. Marinoni.
Autumn, Dark Wanderer.
  Daryush.
The Bermondsey Tragedy.
  Anonymous.
By an Evolutionist.
  Tennyson.
Deep Waters. Sutphen.
The Down-Pullers. Isenhour.
The Dwarf of the Hill Caves.
  Mphande.
The Eve of Bunker Hill.
  Scollard.
Fair Iris and Her Swain.
  Dryden.
Falling Upwards. Shapiro.
Horizontal World. Saunders.
The Inverted Torch.
  Thomas.
Marriage on a Mountain
  Ridge. Conn.
Milton. Tennyson.
Modern Romance. Harris.
Mules. Muldoon.
Patience. Studdert-Kennedy.

Philotas: Chorus. Daniel.
The Poet's Prayer. Philipps.
Rapture: An Ode. Dixon.
The Shepherds Had an Angel.
  Rossetti.
Song: "Of thee, kind boy, I
  ask no red and white."
  Suckling.
The Spanish Gypsy (excerpt).
  Eliot.
Sunset. Bayldon.

Heir (s)
Brand Speaks. Ibsen.
Citation for Horace Gregory.
  Rukeyser.
Epigram. Welsted.
From the Epigrams of
  Martial. Michie.
In All the Argosy of Your
  Bright Hair. Thompson.
An Irish Lamentation.
  Goethe.
Johnny Scot. *Anonymous.*
The Lady Isabella's Tragedy.
  Anonymous.
Of a Rich Miser.
  Turberville.
On Our Thirty-Ninth
  Wedding Day. Odell.
A Song of Handicrafts.
  Matheson.
Soul-Drift. Blind.
Thysia. Luce.
The Widow's Curse.
  Anonymous.

Heirloom
Heirloom. Cohen.

Helen
Artificial Beauty. Lucian [or
  Lucianus].
As Helen Once. Lee.
Her Pedigree. Ficke.
The Lawn Roller. Layzer.
On the Bust of Helen by
  Canova. Byron.
To a History Professor.
  Anonymous
Triangular Legs. Herbert.
Troubadours. Ficke.
Troy. Flower.
Venus Victrix. Rossetti.
The White Isle of Leuce.
  Read.
Winter Love. Doolittle.

Hell
After Death. Swinburne.
Algernon Sidney's Farewell.
  Anonymous.
Alley-Walker. Smith.
Arcadia. Sidney.
The Argument of His Book.
  Herrick.
The Ashland Tragedy, II.
  Anonymous.
Astrophel and Stella, II.
  Sidney.
At the Gate of Heaven.
  Byron.
The Bad-Tempered Wife.
  Anonymous.
A Ballad of Abbreviations.
  Chesterton.
Barley-Break; or, Last in Hell.
  Herrick.
A Battle. Crawford.
Best Friends.
  Hemschemeyer.
Beyond the Chagres.
  Gilbert.
A Bodhisattva Undoes Hell.
  Rothenberg.
Bunhill's Fields. Ridler.

Canonicus and Roger
  Williams. *Anonymous.*
Cave Sedem! MacManus.
The Character of a Certain
  Whig. Shippen.
The Character of Holland.
  Marvell.
Childe Harold's Pilgrimage:
  Canto I. Byron.
Le Christianisme. Owen.
Click Go the Shears.
  Anonymous.
The Clod and the Pebble.
  Blake.
Comedian. Johnson.
The Comedian. Layton.
Cotton Field Song.
  Anonymous.
The Cruel Mother.
  Anonymous.
The Cruel Mother (B vers.).
  Anonymous.
The Cruel Mother (Down by
  the Greenwood Side).
  Anonymous.
The Curse of Doneraile.
  O'Kelly.
The Dalesman's Litany.
  Anonymous.
The Dance of the Seven
  Deadly Sins. Dunbar.
Dante at Verona. Rossetti.
Darky Sunday School.
  Anonymous.
The Day of Doom.
  Wigglesworth.
A Dead King. Swinburne.
Death the Great. Lasynys.
A Dream. Jones.
Dream Songs. Berryman.
Ellen Flannery. *Anonymous.*
Epigram: "Grown old in Love
  from Seven till seven times
  Seven." Blake.
Epigram on Lord Chesterfield
  and His Son. Anonymous.
Epipsychidion. Shelley.
Epitahlamium for Cavorting
  Ghosts. Rainer.
An Epitaph. Davies.
Eve Am I, Great Adam's
  Wife. *Anonymous.*
The Everlasting Mercy.
  Masefield.
Fair Summer Droops. Nashe
  [(or Nash)] Thomas.
Family Portrait. Feeney.
Farewell to Juliet. Blunt.
Farmer Jones's Wife.
  Anonymous.
The Farmer's Curst Wife (B
  vers.). *Anonymous.*
A Fear. Ledwidge.
Five Lyrics from "Good for
  Nothing Man". Ptichford.
For a Mouthy Woman.
  Cullen.
For All Blasphemers. Benét.
For the Word is Flesh.
  Kunitz.
For Two Girls Setting out in
  Life. Viereck.
Frustration. Parker.
The Gift. Russell.
A Great Tempest on the Plain
  of Ler. *Anonymous.*
The Gresford Disaster.
  Anonymous.
H–y P–tt. *Anonymous.*
The Hearse Song.
  Anonymous.
Hell in Texas. *Anonymous.*;

The Heptalogia. Swinburne.
Hermes came to me in a
  dream. Sappho.
The History of Arizona: How
  It Was Made and Who
  Made It. Brown.
The Holy Field. Milman.
The House of Life. Rossetti.
I Go to Whiskey Bars.
  Thompson.
I Knew a Boy with Hair Like
  Gold. La Follette.
I Walked with My Reason.
  MacLean.
I Want to Be a Cowboy.
  Anonymous.
If I Have Sinn'd in Act.
  Coleridge.
In a Dream. Ignatow.
In Cold Hell, In Thicket.
  Olson.
In Extremis. Fishback.
The Inner Light. Myers.
Ireland. Johnson.
Jack the Jolly Tar.
  Anonymous.
The Kent State Massacre.
  Dane.
Killyburn Brae. *Anonymous.*
Lewd Love is Loss.
  Southwell.
Lost Moment. Fuller.
Love Song. Allen.
Lust. Shakespeare.
Macbeth. Shakespeare.
The Marriage of Heaven and
  Hell. Blake.
Memory. Rossetti.
Menses. Millay.
The Mermaid. *Anonymous.*
Micromutations. Wright.
The Mormon Bishop's
  Lament. *Anonymous.*
Mother Goose Rhyme.
  Rexroth.
Mullabinda. Rowbotham.
My life closed twice before its
  close. Dickinson.
My love is like unto th'
  eternal fire. Wyatt.
The Nature of the Turtle
  Dove. *Anonymous.*
New National Anthem.
  Anonymous.
A New Song, Call'd The Red
  Wig. *Anonymous.*
Ode for Music on St. Cecilia's
  Day. Pope.
Old. *Anonymous.*
Old Nick in Sorel. O'Grady.
On a Puritan. Belloc.
On the Meetings of the Scotch
  Covenanters. *Anonymous.*
Our Saviour's Love.
  Anonymous.
Paradise Lost. Milton.
The Patrol. Knight-Adkin.
The Peeler's Lament.
  Anonymous.
A Perverse Custom.
  Anonymous.
The Power of Music. Lisle.
A Prayer from 1936.
  Sassoon.
The Present Tense. Oates.
Processional. Smith.
The Progress of Learning:
  Preface. Denham.
A Prospect of Death.
  Young.
The Queen of Elfan's Nourice.
  Anonymous.

Quite Shy Actually but
  Obsessed. Miller.
Rags. Cook.
The Rear-guard. Sassoon.
Remorse–is memory–awake.
  Dickinson.
Ride 'Im Cowboy.
  Freebairn.
Ridin'. Clark, Jr.
Rimbaud in Africa.
  Rickword.
Road's End. Jacobsen.
The Rose of Peace. Yeats.
The Rowan County Crew
  (Tolliver-Martin Feud
  Song). *Anonymous.*
Rufus's Mare. *Anonymous.*
The Salesman. Mezey.
Same Tits. Tate.
Sang: Recoll O Skaith.
  Smith.
Shame. Patmore.
The Sharp Ridge. Graves.
Shut Up, I Said. Bennett.
The Silent Room. Amis.
Sister Helen. Rossetti.
The Slaughter of Grendel by
  Beowulf. *Anonymous.*
The Slough of Despond.
  Lowell.
Song of a Rat. Hughes.
Song of the Sea.
  MacColmain.
Sonnet, XX: "A seer foretold
  that I would love one day."
  Labé.
Sonnet XLVI. Alabaster.
Sonnets, CXXIX: "Th'
  expense of spirit in a waste
  of shame." Shakespeare.
Sonnets, CXLVII: "My love is
  as a feaver longing still."
  Shakespeare.
St. Irvyne (excerpt). Shelley.
Stanzas. Bronte.
Storm at Sea. *Anonymous*
The Superfluous Saddle. La
  Fontaine.
Sweating It Out on Winding
  Stair Mountain. Barnes.
Sweet William's Ghost (B
  vers.). *Anonymous.*
That Hill. Dickinson.
There Was No Place Found.
  Coleridge.
They Went Forth to Battle,
  but They Always Fell.
  O'Sheel.
Three Poems about Children.
  Clarke.
To Dives. Belloc.
To the Brave Soul.
  Underwood.
To the Ghost of John Milton.
  Sandburg.
Up against the Wall.
  Phillips.
Upon a Fool. Hoskyns.
Village-Born Beauty.
  Anonymous.
Walking Milwaukee. Witt.
War with the Weeds.
  Sinclair.
Warning to Travailers Seeking
  Accomodations at Mr.
  Devills Inn. Knight.
We Are Four Bums (with
  music). *Anonymous.*
We Shall Not Escape Hell.
  Tsvetayeva.
We've Done Our Hitch in
  Hell. *Anonymous.*

Wedlock. A Satire. Wright.
The Whale's Nature.
  Anonymous.
When Orpheus Went Down.
  Lisle.
Where He Takes Tea with
  Cromwell. *Anonymous.*
Whitebeard on Videotape.
  Merrill.
The World. Rossetti.
You Are Always New.
  Akhmatova.

Hello
Americana. Rakosi.
California, This Is Minnesota
  Speaking. Dunn.
Goodby "Hello." Dow.
Say Hello to John. Williams.
The Universe Is Closed and
  Has REMs. Starbuck.
Visit the Sick. Metcalfe.

Helmet (s)
Hector. Iremonger.
The Iliad. Homer.
On the Sultan Mahmud.
  Firdausi.
Poem in Time of War.
  Abrahams.
St. Aubin d'Aubigne. Dehn.

Help (ed) (s)
The Angel in the House.
  Patmore.
Ballade to His Mistress.
  Villon.
Blind Man Lay Beside the
  Way (with music).
  Anonymous.
The Burgesses of Calais.
  Minot.
A Chosen Light. Montague.
Come, Precious Soul.
  Anonymous.
The Crow. Boumi-Pappas.
Diana. Constable.
Did They Help Me at the
  State Hospital for the
  Criminally Insane? Smith.
Don't Want No Hungry
  Woman. Council.
An Easy Poem. Kennedy.
Epigram. *Anonymous.*
Epitaph: "The fruit of all the
  service that I serve."
  Wyatt.
Eternal Lord! Eased of a
  Cumbrous Load.
  Michelangelo.
Explorers as Seen by the
  Natives. Fetherling.
Forever Ambrosia. Morley.
Frog Went A-Courtin.
  Anonymous.
Grandfathers. Castro.
The Guide. Gregor.
The Gulistan. Sa'di.
Help, Good Shepherd.
  Pitter.
Help Is on the Way. Scott.
A Helping Hand. Adams.
Hold Back Thy Hours.
  Fletcher.
The Housewife's Prayer.
  Kelly.
Hymn Against Pestilence.
  Colman.
I'm Troubled in Mind.
  Anonymous.
John Coltrane an Impartial
  Review. Spellman.
Johnny Rich. Carleton.
Leaders. *Anonymous.*

Help

Limerick: "There was a young lady at Bingham." *Anonymous.*
The Lovesick Cowboy. *Anonymous.*
Mister Frog Went A-Courting (with music). *Anonymous.*
My Cross. Cocke.
My Mother's Death. Hemschemeyer.
My Prayer. *Anonymous.*
The New Poem. Wright.
Night Letter. Piercy.
On a Dying Boy. Bell.
One-Way Song. Lewis.
Prayer for Rain. Jama.
A Prayer for the Household. Stevenson.
The Priest of Felton. *Anonymous.*
The Rapist's Villanelle. Disch.
Riddle: "Promotion lately was bestow'd." *Anonymous.*
She's Pretty to Walk With. Suckling.
A Shepherd's Complaint. Barnfield.
Slavery Chain Done Broke at Last. *Anonymous.*
Somebody Call (For Help). Rodgers.
Song for the Squeeze-Box. Roethke.
Song: "Since I'm a girl." *Anonymous.*
A Song to John, Christ's Friend. *Anonymous.*
Spain 1937. Auden.
Think It Over. *Anonymous.*
To Whom Shall They Go? *Anonymous.*
Troll the Bowl! Dekker.
Unanswered Prayers. Wilcox.
Variations on a Theme by Sidney Keyes. Wilkins.
Visiting the Dead. Carson.
Willy Boy. *Anonymous.*
The Wyoming Massacre. Terry.
Ye Simple Men. Blackie.

Helpless

Epitaph: "The fruit of all the service that I serve." Wyatt.
Fog. Binyon.
For Haroun al Raschid. Abu'l-Atahija.
Ghosts. Jennings.
The Horse Named Bill (with music). *Anonymous.*
Love Songs. *Anonymous.*
Poem without a Main Verb. Wain.
The Stampede. Caldwell.
Withstanders. Barnes.
Years Later. Lerner.

Helpmate

Australia. O'Dowd.
Monna Innominata. Rossetti.
When Adam Was First Created. *Anonymous.*

Hem

Apologia Addressed to Ireland in the Coming Days. Yeats.
Hem and Haw. Carman.
Needle Travel. Patton.

Hemispheres

The Convergence of the Twain. Hardy.
Reproduction of Life. Darwin.

Hemlock

Midwinter Thaw. Pratt.
Misgivings. Melville.
A Pastoral. Hillyer.

Hen (s)

Epigram. Butler.
Hens. Nowlan.
Limerick: "The Reverend Henry War Beecher." Holmes.
Limerick: "There was a young lady of Venice." *Anonymous.*
The Lout. Clare.
Motherhood. Calverley.
Random Reflections on a Summer Evening. Wheelock.
The Robin and the Wren. *Anonymous.*

Henry

Captain Stratton's Fancy. Masefield.
Dream Songs. Berryman.
Epitaph on the Duke of Grafton. Shepherd.
Henry VIII. Farjeon.
The Lochmaben Harper. *Anonymous.*

Her (s) (self)

All of Her. Albert.
All One. Brand.
Arcadia. Sidney.
Blest Be the Day. Petrarch (Francesco Petrarca).
Bones of a French Lady in a Museum. Gillman.
Calenture. Reid.
The Clue. Bates.
Constant. Dickinson.
The Dalliance of Eagles. Whitman.
Distress. Griffin.
The Diver. Nathan.
A Dream of Flowers. Coan.
The Dressmaker's Dummy as Scarecrow. Howes.
Fable. Parker.
The Faerie Queene. Spenser.
Family Romance. Levis.
The First Kiss. Watts-Dunton.
The Girl in the Willow Tree. Maisel.
The Golden Spurs. *Anonymous.*
De Guiana, Carmen Epicum. Chapman.
I Know a Lovely Lady Who Is Dead. Burt.
January 18, 1979. Yau.
Jephthah's Daughter. Yehoash.
A Joyful New Ballad. Deloney.
The Laud of Saint Catherine. Swinburne.
The Leader. Belloc.
Leaving Seoul: 1953. Lew.
Life Study. Orlen.
Lines Suggested By the Fourteenth of February. Calverley.
Master's in the Garden Again. Ransom.
Monna Lisa. Lowell.
The Musmee. Arnold.

My Mother. Burr.
The Night Court. Mitchell.
Offering. Macdonagh.
On Seeing Swift in Laracor. MacNamara.
Phantom. Coleridge.
Phyllis. Lodge.
Present. Sanchez.
Properzia Rossi. Hemans.
Rumors of War in Wyoming. Rea.
There She Is. Gregg.
To Cupid. Davison.
To Mr. I. L. Donne.
To Our Daughter. Armitage.
To the New Year. Carew.
The Ultimate Antientropy. Weiss.
Wait for Me. Creeley.
What Mystery Pervades a Well! Dickinson.
While Strolling through the Park. Haley.
Why So Pale and Wan? Suckling.
Winter Tryst. Van Doren.
With Serving Still. Wyatt.
The Woman of the House. Murphy.
The Yawn. Blackburn.
Zalka Peetruza. Dandridge.

Herald (s)

Cock-Crow: Woodstock. Robinson.
The Dirge of Kildare. De Vere.
The Fight over the Body of Keitt. *Anonymous.*
When Will He Come? *Anonymous.*

Herb (s)

Ah, necromancy sweet! Dickinson.
The Flowering of the Rod. Doolittle.
The Garden. Grimald.
Garden. Marvell.
Good Frend. Doolittle.
The Lingam and the Yoni. Hope.
Memory. Hamburger.
Mist. Thoreau.
Parks and Ponds. Emerson.
Rose Bay Willow Herb. Ray.
Silex Scintillans. Vaughan.
Snake Doctor Blues. Short.

Hercules

Let Heroes Account to Love. Dugan.
The Threshing Machine. Meynell.

Herd (s)

Being Herded Past the Prison's Honor Farm. Wagoner.
The Dysynni Valley (Wales). Holmes.
Epilogue. Baudelaire.
The Lowveld. Eglington.
The Mowing. Roberts.
Nature's Charms. Beattie.
On the Appeal From the Race of Sheba: II. Senghor.
Robene and Makyne. Henryson.
Sir Fopling Flutter. Dryden.
Song: "Softly, O midnight Hours!" De Vere.
The Stampede. Brininstool.
The Whistle. Murray.

Hereafter

Concepts and Their Bodies (The Boy in the Field Alone). Rogers.
The Ghosts. Longfellow.
On the Twenty-Third Psalm. *Anonymous.*
The Poetess Ko Ogimi. Chasin.
The Song of Hiawatha. Longfellow.

Heresy

On Behalf of Some Irishmen Not Followers of Tradition. Russell.
Saturday Sundae. Scott.
When Doctrines Meet with General Approbation. Garrick.

Heritage

By the Potomac. Aldrich.
Cigarette for the Bambino. Ewart.
Dirge. Troupe.
The Disinherited, IX. Gilmore.
Heir to Several Yesterdays. Kelley.
The Lay of Prince Marvan. *Anonymous.*
Poem from Llanybri. Roberts.
Poets in Time of War. Warr.
The Reports Come In. Reed.
A Sea Song. Cunningham.
Service Is No Heritage. *Anonymous.*
Sometimes I Think of Maryland... Braxton.
To Thee, O God, the Shepherd Kings. Brainard.
A Warning to Those Who Serve Lords. *Anonymous.*
A Wet Sheet. Cunningham.

Hermes

Canto LXXIX. Pound.
This Torch, Still Burning in My Hand. Crinagoras.
To the Fair Clarinda, Who Made Love to Me, Imagin'd More than Woman. Behn.

Hermit

The Ballad of Yukon Jake. Paramore.
Country Wooing (parody) (excerpt). Squire.
Sanctuary. Guiney.

Hero (es)

After the Broken Arm. Padgett.
B Stands for Bear. Belloc.
Caldwell of Springfield. Harte.
Clever Tom Clinch Going to be Hanged. Swift.
Crispus Attucks McCoy. Brown.
Dead Heroes. Karoniaktatie.
The Exiled Heart. Lindsay.
The Female Smuggler. *Anonymous.*
The Hero. Nicoll.
Hero and Leander. Hood.
John Maynard. Alger.
Lament for Mafukuzela. *Anonymous.*
Lindbergh. *Anonymous.*
The Lyre Player. George.
Mythics. Chasin.
Night. Ibn Gabirol.
Speaking: The Hero. Pollak.
Wild Horse. Olson.

Hero (es) (ic)
Admiral Byrd. Nash.
Bacchylides. Whicher.
The Bush on Mount Venus.
  Finkel.
Circus Maximus. Bowering.
The Eagle and Vulture.
  Read.
For a Man Who Learned to
  Swim When He Was Sixty.
  Wakoski.
The Geraldine's Daughter
  (excerpt). Mangan.
The Heroic Age. Gilder.
The Jervis Bay. *Anonymous.*
Kleomedes. Wright.
Lexington. Holmes.
Limerick: "There was a young
  man named Achilles."
  Robinson.
Man Alone. Levertov.
The Naturalist's Summer-
  Evening Walk. White.
O'Hussey's Ode to the
  Maguire. Mangan.
On the Discoveries of Captain
  Lewis. Barlow.
One to Destroy, Is Murder by
  the Law. Young.
Opportunity. Sill.
Our Heroes. Cary.
Pagan Prayer. Brown.
Scenes of Childhood.
  Merrill.
Sleeping Heroes. Shanks.
Tweedle-Dum and Tweedle-
  Dee. *Anonymous.*
The Unknown Soldier.
  Aiken.

Heron (s)
As I Was Going to Saint Ives.
  Hoffman.
The China Policy. Rakosi.
Chinoiseries. Lowell.
Days of 1956. Magowan.
For Daphne at Lone Lake.
  Haines.
Herons. *Anonymous.*
The Hill Above the Mine.
  Cowley.
How many evenings in the
  arbor by the river. Li
  Ch'ing-chao.
Michael. McPherson.

Hesperus
Masque of Cupid: Up, Youths
  and Virgins, Up, and Praise.
  Jonson.

Hew (ed) (s)
The Battle of Maldon.
  Anonymous.
Evening Hymn in the Hovels.
  Adams.
Proem. Gibson.
The Ridiculous Optimist.
  Anonymous.
Sir Hugh, or, The Jew's
  Daughter (C version).
  Anonymous.

Hiawatha
The Song of Hiawatha.
  Longfellow.

Hickory
Andrew Jackson. Benét.
Andrew Jackson. Keller.
O. Wilbur.
The One Who Is Within.
  Francisco.

Hid (den)
Back Room Joys.
  Richardson.

Becoming Is Perfection.
  Johnson.
Christ and the Pagan. Tabb.
City Sparrow. Mayhall.
A Connacht Caoine.
  Anonymous.
The Crack. Hall.
Editor Whedon. Masters.
For Every Day. Havergal.
Good Christians. Herrick.
The Great Canzon. Rexroth.
The Hairy Dog. Asquith.
House. O Hehir.
Instructions for the Messiah.
  Sklarew.
Keep Me Still, for I Do Not
  Want to Dream. Eigner.
Lost in Yucatan. McKeown.
A Lover's Words. Watkins.
The Mouse's Petition.
  Barbauld.
Prayer to the God Thot.
  Anonymous.
Red Cross Nurses. Stewart.
Renaming the Evening.
  Pankey.
A Silver Lantern. Baker.
Sonnets to Philomel. Davies.
To Cynthia, Not to Let Him
  Read the Ladies'
  Magazines. Hubbard.
To Her Body, Against Time.
  Kelly.
Variations on a Theme.
  Williams.
When She Comes Home.
  Riley.
You. Clark.
The Young Author.
  Johnson.

Hide (s) (hiding)
At the Polo-Ground.
  Ferguson.
Bird Shadows Mounting.
  Eigner.
Bo-Peep. *Anonymous.*
The Bowling-Green (excerpt).
  Somervile.
Breaking. Allan.
By the Conemaugh. Coates.
Caelica, LXV. Greville.
Cattle. Nance.
The Chimney-Sweeper's
  Complaint. Alcock.
Confidential. Scott.
The Conspiracy of Charles,
  Duke of Byron. Chapman.
Dark. Healy.
Death. Williams.
Disguises. Jennings.
Early January. Merwin.
Epitaph. *Anonymous.*
Essay on Rime (excerpt).
  Shapiro.
Fable of the Speckled Cow.
  Opperman.
Father's Whiskers.
  Anonymous.
For Paul Laurence Dunbar.
  Cullen.
Growing Up. Behn.
Haiku: "Did I see her."
  Anonymous.
The Hare. Snaith.
The Hawthorn Hedge.
  Wright.
The Hippopotamus. Belloc.
Hold Back Thy Hours.
  Fletcher.
I Have Cut an Eagle.
  Koller.

I Sit and Wait for Beauty.
  Cowdery.
If I Were Old. Ogilvie.
Jack and Dinah Want
  Freedom. *Anonymous.*
Lais. Feinstein.
Leavings (parody). Benson.
Little Cock Robin.
  Anonymous.
Location. Skinner.
Love Medicine. Walton.
News from a Pacified Area.
  Baxter.
No Matter. Paulus
  Silentiarius.
Of England, and of Its
  Marvels. Petrarch.
One Token. Davies.
Out of the Dark Wood.
  "Peter".
Pentimento. Fisher.
The Petrified Leaf. Branch.
Plain Song. Fondane.
Prodigal. Gilbert.
De Profundis Clamavi.
  Baudelaire.
Psalm LXXXVIII. Surrey.
Revelation. Frost.
Rock of Ages. Toplady.
The Rousing Canoe Song.
  Fraser.
Samuel Hall. *Anonymous.*
The Sequel. Schwartz.
The Ship. Hendry.
The Silent Lover. Ralegh.
Song of Longing.
  Anonymous.
Song of Man Chipping an
  Arrowhead. Merwin.
Speak. Wright.
Submission. *Anonymous.*
Summer. Clare.
Though All the Fates Should
  Prove Unkind. Thoreau.
To Chloris. Drummond.
Umbrellas. Bennett.
Vern. Brooks.
When I Held You to My
  Chest, You Fit. Myers.
The Winter's Walk.
  Johnson.
Winter Swan. Bogan.
The World As Wave and
  Idea. Coxe.
X-Ray. Ray.

High (er) (est)
Amoretti, LXXXII. Spenser.
Arcadia. Sidney.
Asleep in Jesus. MacKay.
At the Playground. Stafford.
Because You Care. Crane.
Behold the Meads. Poitiers.
Carol. Rodgers.
The Church's One
  Foundation. Stone.
The Circus. Kaplan.
Comrade in Arms. Moore.
Crow's Nest. Armknecht.
Epigram: "Glad youth had
  come thy sixteenth year to
  crown." Ausonius.
Epitaphium Vivi Auctoris
  1792. Walpole.
Farewell. Wilson.
The Gate of the Year.
  Haskins.
Get Up, Blues. Emanuel.
God's Goin' to Set This
  World On Fire (B vers.)
  (with music). *Anonymous.*
The Grand Canyon. Merrill.

The Hawthorn Hedge.
  Wright.
Heroique Stanzas, Consecrated
  to the Glorious Memory...
  Dryden.
High and Low. Cousins.
The High Barbaree.
  Richards.
I Die; But When the Grave
  Shall Press. Bronte.
An Immorality. Pound.
In Defiance to the Dutch.
  Anonymous.
Invocation. Johnson.
John Brown. Proctor.
The Jovial Tinker; or, The
  Willing Couple.
  Anonymous.
Kate o' Belashanny.
  Allingham.
Limerick: "A new servant
  maid named Maria."
  Anonymous.
Lullaby. Rossetti.
Miss Biddy Fudge to Miss
  Dorothy (excerpt). Moore.
The MJQ. Thomas.
Mountain Sculpture. Will.
My Dog Ponto. Masters.
Of Boston in New England.
  Bradford.
Old Botany Bay. Gilmore.
An Open-Letter-Poem-Note to
  Vincent Van G.
  Bernadine.
Paradise Lost. Milton.
The Passionate Sword.
  Untermeyer.
The Poet's Request.
  Anonymous.
Polifemo y Galatea: The Love
  Song of Polyphemus.
  Gongora y Argote.
A Prognostication on Will
  Laud, Late Archbishop of
  Canterbury. *Anonymous.*
Psalm VII. Sidney.
Rhyming Prophecy for a New
  Year. Cooper.
The Runaways. Van Doren.
Sea Things. MacEwen.
Slow Death. Martinez.
Small Woman on Swallow
  Street. Merwin.
Soul's Liberty. Wickham.
The Srawberry Roan.
  Anonymous.
The Strawberry Roan.
  Fletcher.
The Sun's over the Foreyard.
  Morley.
Tall Tale God. Van Doren.
That No Man Should Write
  But Such as Do Excel.
  Turberville.
To Postumus. Horace.
To the Reverend Mr.
  Murdoch. Thomson.
Two Sorrows. St. John.
Vistas. Shepard.
We Am Clim'in' Jacob's
  Ladder. *Anonymous.*
Young Democracy (excerpt).
  O'Dowd.

Highland (s)
As I Came O'er Cairney
  Mount. *Anonymous.*
Bonny John Seton.
  Anonymous.
Harlaw. Scott.
James Grant. *Anonymous.*

The Lady of Arngosk.
Anonymous.
My Heart's in the Highlands.
Burns.
The Rose Is a Royal Lady.
Blanden.

Highway (s)
Battle-Song of Failure. Burr.
Biography. Stanton.
Down, Down Derry Down
(with music). Anonymous.
Fear. Wier.
For a Friend. Kooser.
For My Son on the Highways
of His Mind. Kumin.
Heralds of Christ.
Copenhaver.
Incident. Kopp.
The King's Highway.
McGroarty.
The Maid Freed from the
Gallows (D vers.).
Anonymous.
My Bonny Black Bess.
Anonymous.
"The Straight Road.
Hooper.
To Desi as Joe as Smoky the
Lover of 115th Street.
Lorde.
White Pines. Silesky.
Who's in Charge Here? Bell.

Hill (s)
Abraham Lincoln Walks at
Midnight. Lindsay.
And Then the Sun. Sen.
Animal Songs: Baboon.
Anonymous.
Art and Life. Ridge.
At Arley. Young.
At St. Jerome. Harrison.
At the Shelter-Stone.
Macrow.
Auld Daddy Darkness.
Ferguson.
Autumn Journey. Levertov.
Bennachie. Murray.
The Blue Hill Is My Desire.
Hwang Chin-i.
Blue Sleigh. Scott.
The Boyne Walk. Higgins.
The Bride. Mitchell.
Burial. Francis.
Burma Hills. Gutteridge.
Canticle. Griffith.
Centennial Hymn. Pierpont.
A Child's Grave Marker.
Kooser.
Christmas Eve. Drinkwater.
Constancy. Daniel.
A Cross on a Hill. Weist.
A Cry from the Canadian
Hills. Leveridge.
Descending. Pack.
Don Juan. Byron.
Eclogues. Virgil (Publius
Vergilius Maro).
The Elfin Knight.
Anonymous
Emus. Fullerton.
An Essay on Criticism.
Pope.
An Even-Song. Dobell.
The Fair Hills of Ireland.
Ferguson.
Farewell to the Muses.
Reynolds.
The Flight of the War-Eagle.
Auringer.
Florence: Design for a City.
Jennings.

The Gate of the Year.
Haskins.
The Gatineaus. Watson.
The Giantess. Baudelaire.
Gibraltar. Blunt.
Gloaming. Brown.
Hamlet. Shakespeare.
The Hang-Glider's Daughter.
Hacker.
The Harlot. Brown.
He Fell Among Thieves.
Newbolt.
The Herons. Ledwidge.
High Up on Suilven.
MacCaig.
The Hill. Creeley.
Hills. Guiterman.
Hills. Munro.
The Hills of Tsa la gi.
Conley.
The Hollow Land. Morris.
I Am Now So Weary with
Waiting. Stampa.
I Heard Immanuel Singing.
Lindsay.
I Leave Tonight from Euston.
Anonymous.
I Love a Hill. Hodgson.
Ibadan. Clark.
Idylls. Theocritus.
If I Had Ridden Horses.
Maynard.
The Iliad. Homer.
Impressions of My Father/I.
Country Ways. Masters.
In the Cheviots. Lindsay.
In the Gold Mines. Vilakazi.
Iowa. Browne.
The Lane. Young.
The Lent Lily. Housman.
Levavi Oculos. Campbell.
Lonesome Water. Helton.
Lost Ships. Ferril.
Love in the Wind. Hovey.
A Lover's Words. Watkins.
Madrigal: "My love is neither
young nor old." Jones.
Men Loved Wholly Beyond
Wisdom. Bogan.
Men of the Rocks.
MacLeod.
The Messenger. Horovitz.
Mocking Song against
Qaqortingneq. Piuvkaq.
The Monster. Kuzma.
The Moon behind the Hill.
Anonymous.
Mountain Days. Fraser.
Mountaineering Bus.
McOwan.
My Doves. Browning.
The New Man. Very.
No Single Thing Abides.
Lucretius (Titus Lucretius
Carus).
Now the Noisy Winds Are
Still. Dodge.
Ol' Doc' Hyar. Campbell.
Older Now. Gingell.
On Calvary's Lonely Hill.
Johnson.
On Ellson Fell. Landles.
On the Grasshopper and the
Cricket. Keats.
Orchard. Stone.
Our Heritage. Stuart.
Over the Hills and Far Away.
Henley.
Paracelsus. Browning.
Part Winter. Bowering.
Parting. Corbin.

Pennsylvania Winter Indian
1974. Littlebird.
Play Song. Clarke.
The Poets. Wevill.
Prophets for a New Day.
Walker.
The Redingote and the
Vamoose. Munkittrick.
Requiem. Stevenson.
Roads. Brown.
The Sea and the Hills.
Kipling.
Second Poem. Orlovsky.
Senlin. Aiken.
Seventh Son. Roberson.
Singing the Reapers
Homeward Come.
Anonymous.
Sir Gawaine and the Green
Knight. Winters.
Sleet Storm. Tippett.
Somnambulistic Ballad.
Garcia Lorca.
The Song. Dorn.
Song: "Christ keep the Hollow
Land." Morris.
Song of the Hill. Lodge.
Song: "Were I laid on
Greenland's coast." Gay.
Songs of Seven. Ingelow.
A Spell before Winter.
Nemerov.
The Starling Lake.
O'Sullivan.
Storm Warning. Bardsley.
Summer. Thomson.
Summer Rain. Lee.
Thanksgiving. Booth.
These People. Corning.
They Are All Gone into the
World of Light. Vaughan.
This Town. Paul.
Three Green Trees. Morgan.
To a Friend. Coleridge.
To a Sparrow. Ledwidge.
To Atalanta. Dow.
To Autumn. Blake.
To Krishna Haunting the
Hills. Andal.
To Morning. Blake.
To the Western Wind.
Halevi.
The Toll-Gate Man.
MacDonald.
Tragedy. Moss.
A Travelogue: Clovelly.
Wells.
The Trooper and Maid.
Anonymous.
Vacation Song. Millay.
Venus Abandoned.
Shakespeare.
The Way Through.
Levertov.
We Lying by Seasand.
Thomas.
We Who Were Born. Lewis.
Weather. Conkling.
Weekend Sonnets. McQueen.
Why I Can't Write a Poem
about Lares. Silen.
Will Beauty Come. Nathan.
With Corse at Allatoona.
Byers.
With Hands Like Leaves.
Still.
Without Her. Rossetti.
Wood and Hill. Young.
The Word. Realf.

Hillside (s)
The Burden of Junk.
Glassco.

The First Three. Scollard.
Howard Lamson. Masters.
Rock Climbing. Cooper.
Sally Goodin. Anonymous.

Hilltop
Dawn-Song to Waken the
Lovers. Anonymous.
The Grey Horse. Reeves.
New Hampshire Farm
Woman. Graham.

Him (self)
Action Would Kill It/A
Gamble. Adamson.
All One. Brand.
Ars Poetica About Ultimates.
Combs.
At North Farm. Ashbery.
Attraction. Anonymous.
The Author of Christine.
Howard.
Beautiful Lily. Mortenson.
Blue and White. Coleridge.
The Bull Moses. Hughes.
Cantico del Sole. Francis of
Assisi.
Christ and the Common Day.
Wilkinson.
A Clock Stopped.
Dickinson.
Convicted (excerpt). Mills.
The Cost of Pretending.
Davison.
Don't Be Sorrowful, Darling.
Peale.
Gaily I Lived. Anonymous.
The Grasshopper. Lovelace.
Happy He. Anonymous.
The Husband. Finkel.
I Turn to Jesus. Smith.
Inscription on the Pyramid of
Unas. Anonymous.
Julius Caesar. Shakespeare.
A Lamentation. Campion.
Lincoln. Boker.
Lonesome Valley.
Anonymous.
Lord, I Know Thy Grace Is
Nigh Me. Ganse.
Love Serviceable. Patmore.
Love Song. Anonymous.
A March Calf. Hughes.
The Missing Person. Justice.
The Mouse. Garrigue.
The Mushroom Is the Elf of
Plants–. Dickinson.
My Name and I. Graves.
On Clinton Edward Dawkins,
Commoner of Balliol.
Mackail.
On Seeing Swift in Laracor.
MacNamara.
Out Fishing. Howes.
Overripe Fruit. Kasmuneh.
Pass It On. Burton.
Praise Doubt. Van Doren.
Rothko. Moore.
Sather Gate Illumination.
Ginsberg.
The Second Violinist's Son.
Greger.
A Serio-Comic Elegy.
Whately.
Sing, My Soul. Anonymous.
Tattoos. Wright.
The Three Movements. Hall.
To Antenor. Philips.
To the Tune of the Coventry
Carol. Smith.
Tomorrow. Leitner.
Undertakers. Bierce.
Van Elsen. Scott.

Vision song (cheyenne).
Henson.
Who Is That A-Walking in
the Corn? Johnson.

Hinder (s)
Another. Herrick.
Big Steamers. Kipling.
Four trees upon a solitary
acre. Dickinson.
Power to the People.
Nemerov.
Quaerit Jesum suum Maria.
Crashaw.
To His Book. Herrick.
Why Should a Foolish
Marriage Vow. Dryden.

Hinges
Figures in a Ruined Ballroom.
Hitchcock.
Piyyut for Rosh Hashana.
Guri.
To the Swallows of Viterbo.
Ruark.

Hint
Dauber. Masefield.
Pass it on grandson.
Palmanteer.
A Space in the Air. Silkin.

Hips
August 1968. Auden.
Back from the Word
Processing Course, I Say to
My Old Typewriter.
Blumenthal.
Notes Made in the Piazza San
Marco. Swenson.
Verifying the Dead. Welch.

Hireling
Datur Hora Quieti. Hawker.
The Muse to an Unknown
Poet. Potts.

His
Against Quarrelling and
Fighting. Watts.
A Birthday Prayer. Finley.
Christ, My Salvation. Gray.
A Christmas Prayer.
Macdonald.
The Dalliance of Eagles.
Whitman.
Elegy on the L.C. Donne.
Enoch Arden. Tennyson.
Epigram: "Broad and ample
he warms himself."
Anonymous.
Heartbreak Camp.
Campbell.
Paradise Regained. Milton.
Possession. Anonymous.
Whittling. Pierpont.
Your Place. Oxenham.

Hiss (ed) (es) (ing)
Ars. Tsvetayeva.
Civil War. Van Doren.
The Kiss-Fest. Edman.
Limerick: "One evening a
goose, for a treat."
Herford.
My True Memory. Asya
(Asya Gray).
Ohioan Pastoral. Wright.
Our Mother's Body Is the
Earth. McAnally.
To the Ladies. Kenseth.

Histor (ies) (y)
Abraham Lincoln. Stoddard.
Acceleration near the Point of
Impact. Oates.
Afternoons with Baedeker.
Lancaster.
Agnosco Veteris Vestigia
Flammae. Cunningham.

Arrowheads. Gom.
At Vshchizh. Tyutchev.
The Ballad of Banners.
Lehmann.
Blue Ruth: America.
Harper.
Bony. Ortiz.
Cannon Park. St. Germain.
The Captive Stone. Barnes.
Caravan. Longley.
Chantey of Notorious Bibbers.
Robinson.
China. Empson.
Claus Von Stauffenberg.
Gunn.
Considerations of Norfolk
Island (excerpt).
Smithyman.
Cordoba. Mendelssohn.
Getting down to Get over.
Jordan.
The Gift. Ciardi.
Gryll's State. Blount Roy.
H. S. Beeney Auction Sales.
Pichaske.
The Historical Judas.
Nemerov.
How the waters closed above
him. Dickinson.
In Humbleness. Hoffman.
In Random Fields of Impulse
and Repose. Hathaway.
In the Annals of Tacitus.
Murray.
In the Garden: Villa
Cleobolus. Durrell.
In the Naked Bed, in Plato's
Cave. Schwartz.
Ironic:LL.D. Braithwaite.
King's College Chapel.
Causley.
Like Snow. Graves.
MacDuff. Tomlinson.
The Marble-Streeted Town.
Hardy.
Melancholy. Thomas.
Mexico. Lowell.
The Mule-Skinners.
Caldwell.
Negro Dreams. Long.
Nigger's Leap, New England.
Wright.
Not Being Oedipus. Heath-
Stubbs.
October. Bayliss.
Poland, October. Brasch.
Poll. Roberson.
Relaxation. Gallup.
Robin Hood. Burr.
The Seven Houses. Brown.
The Silent Generation.
Simpson.
The Statue. Fuller.
Surabaja. Berkson.
Tragic Guilt. Rhys.
The Vandals. Mastoraki.
The Visit. Rewak.
The Wayside Station. Muir.
Wendell Phillips. Alcott.
Were I to Mount beyond the
Field. Keyes.
Winter. Stone.
The Young Fenians. Fallon.

Hit
Constant Defender. Tate.
Cupid. Anonymous.
Dogie Song. Anonymous.
Fury against the Moslems at
Uhud. Hind bint Utba.
Hunting. Snyder.
The Lion and O'Reilly.
Weber.

To Silvia. Wilchilsea.
Why We Bombed Haiphong.
Holden.
Willy Wet-Leg. Lawrence.

Hither
By the Turnstile. O'Donnell.
The Great Merchant, Dives
Pragmaticus, Cries His
Wares. Newbery.
Song of the Blue-Corn Dance.
Anonymous.

Hive
As on Serena's Panting Breast.
Anonymous.
The Aztec City. Ware.
The Bee. Hawkins.
Breasts. Simic.
Fog. Binyon.
On a Honey Bee. Freneau.

Ho Chi Minh
Ballad of Ho Chi Minh.
MacColl.

Hoard (ed) (es) (s)
Exeter Book: Maxims.
Anonymous.
Gifts of Rain. Heaney.
A More Ancient Mariner.
Carman.
The Silver Flask. Montague.
Song Set by Robert Jones: "O!
How my thoughts do beat
me. Anonymous.

Hobby
Ego Sum. Burgess.
I Know a Barber. Anthony.

Hockey
Osmund Toulmin. Sitwell.
Rink Keeper's Sestina.
Draper.

Hoe
Bridal Song. Brentano.
In a Garden. Babcock.
In the Pauper's Turnip-Field.
Melville.
Justice Denied in
Massachusetts. Millay.
Lament while Descending a
Shaft. Anonymous.
Monogamania. Merriam.
Young Man Who Wouldn't
Hoe Corn. Anonymous.

Hog (s)
Groun' Hog. Anonymous.
High on the Hog. Fields.
Snatches: "The Cat, the Rat,
and Lovel our dog."
Anonymous.

Hold (ing) (s) (held)
Appearance. Russell.
As I Step over a Puddle at the
End of Winter. Wright.
At a Vacation Exercise.
Milton.
Autumn. Rilke.
The Ballad of the Cross.
Garrison.
Be Still, My Heart.
Anonymous.
Before Your Waking. Greki.
Best Friends.
Hemschemeyer.
A Betrothal. Scovell.
Birth. Melinescu.
Black Bart. Anonymous.
Boys in October. Layton.
Brain Coral. Bassen.
A Call to Action. Ch'iu
Chin.
Companionship. Coleridge.
The Consolation of
Philosophy. Boethius.

A Copy of Verses Sent by
Cleone to Aspasia.
Landor.
Craftsmen. Sackville-West.
Degli Sposi. Lesser.
A Dollar I Gave.
Anonymous.
Everything That Acts Is
Actual. Levertov.
The Face. Stryk.
Father and Son. Stafford.
The Father's Gold.
Anonymous.
The Flagpole Sitter. Finkel.
For My Grandmother.
Cullen.
Foreign Soil. Hai-Jew.
Getting Out. Mathis.
The Gully. Maurice.
Hearing Men Shout at Night
on MacDougal Street. Bly.
Heart's Needle. Snodgrass.
His Hands. Moreland.
Holding Hands. Link.
Hugh Spencer's Feats in
France (B version).
Anonymous.
I Keep to Myself Such
Measures. Creeley.
I Years Had Been from
Home. Dickinson.
In a Railway Compartment.
Fuller.
The Lady Pitcher.
Macdonald.
Language Lesson, 1976.
McHugh.
The Last Invocation.
Whitman.
Limerick: "When our dean
took a pious young
spinster." Gray.
A Little Dutch Garden.
Whitney.
The Lost Children.
Eberhart.
Michelangelo's Kiss.
Rossetti.
Moving. Jarrell.
My Father's Ghost.
Wagoner.
Never Will You Hold Me.
Divine.
The New Year. Cotton.
No-Kings and the Calling of
Spirits. Willard.
Old Adam (with music).
Anonymous.
On a Drawing by Flavio.
Levine.
On the Fly-Leaf of Manon
Lescaut. Learned.
Phallic Root. Shiraishi
Kazuko.
Play. Asch.
The Prayer Rug. Kennedy.
Radiation Leak. Aliesan.
A Rain of Rites. Mahapatra.
Returning to the Town Where
We Used to Live.
Musgrave.
The Road along the Thumb
and Forefinger. Hickey.
The Road to the Bow.
Corrothers.
Rocks. Heide.
Rooftop Winter. Thorpe.
Runaway. Coghill.
Saint Judas. Wright.
Scene from a Dream. Hale.
A Seeker in the Night.
Coates.

The Shape of the Fire.
  Roethke.
The Shooting of John
  Dillinger Outside the
  Biograph Theater...
  Wagoner.
Since Nature's Works Be
  Good. Sidney.
Snake Hunt. Wagoner.
Sonnets, CII: "My love is
  strengthen'd."
  Shakespeare.
The Spoilers and the Spoils.
  Sherwin.
Suburban Lullaby. Manifold.
The Teak Forest: For This Is
  Wisdom. Hope.
Telling the Cousins. Murray.
Therefore I Must Tell the
  Truth. Torlino.
To a Lost Sweetheart.
  Marquis.
To Ben, at the Lake.
  McQueen.
True Love. Johnson.
True to a Dream. Petersen.
The Turning. Murray.
Twilight at Sea. Welby.
Upheld by His Hand.
  Renfrow.
Walking with God.
  Anonymous.
When My Beloved Sleeping
  Lies. McLeod.
Woman to Man. Wright.
Women's Tug of War at
  Lough Arrow. Gallagher.

Hole
The Anniversary. Ai.
August Rain. Bly.
Bim Bam. Rosenberg.
Birthday. Kavanagh.
Bob Stanford. *Anonymous.*
Crow Jane. Jones.
The Dead Lady Canonized.
  Jones.
Eclipse. Roberson.
Fleance. Longley.
From 2nd Chance Man: The
  Cigarette Poem.
  Kicknosway.
The Golfer's Rubaiyat
  (parody). Boynton.
I'd run about. *Anonymous.*
I'll Tell. *Anonymous.*
The Intoxicated Rat.
  Anonymous.
Johann Gaertner (1793-1887).
  Gildner.
The Making of the Cross.
  Everson.
A Memory. Bell.
The Moral Taxi Ride.
  Kastner.
Nechama. Kaufman.
On Hedylus. Martial
  (Marcus Valerius Martialis).
Optimist and Pessimist.
  Wilson.
Pockets. Nemerov.
Santa Claus and the Mouse.
  Poulsson.
A Story. Stafford.
The Virtues of Carnation
  Milk. *Anonymous.*
What Invisible Rat.
  Rebearivelo.
World's End. Chettur.

Hole (s)
The Ballet of the Boll Weevil
  (A vers.). *Anonymous.*
Crocodiles. Kurka.

Curse of a Fisherman's Wife.
  Chalpin.
Driving to Sauk City.
  Woessner.
Elegy for the Silent Voices
  and the Joiners of
  Everything. Patchen.
The Far North. Savoie.
Invitation. Contoski.
Looking for Mountain
  Beavers. Wagoner.
Santa Claus. Moraes.
Some Knots. Honig.
Song for Seven Parts of the
  Body, 7. Kumin.

Holiday (s)
End of the War in Merida.
  Ostroff.
Epitaphs of the War.
  Kipling.
Limerick: "Annoying Miss
  Tillie McLush." Newman.
The Little Factory Girl to a
  More Fortunate Playmate.
  Anonymous.
Oraga Haru. Issa.
A Servant-Girl's Holiday.
  Anonymous.
Shacked Up at the Ritz.
  Fetherling.
Sir Roderic's Song. Gilbert.
The Song in Making of the
  Arrows. Lily.
To Janet. Pomeroy.
The Unwilling Guest: An
  Urban Dialogue. Gregory.
The Zoo in the City. Allen.

Holland
The Leak in the Dike. Cary.
On Sir John Fenwick. Hall.
On Tom Holland and Nell
  Cotton. *Anonymous.*
The Suffolk Miracle (B vers.).
  Anonymous.

Hollow
Accountability. Stafford.
Adam's Curse. Yeats.
All in June. Davies.
Autumn Apples. Lee.
Clouds and Clay. Gillies.
Crazy Horse. Henson.
Depot Blues. Lincoln
  (Hicks).
Hope. Theognis.
I Saw Them Lynch.
  Freeman.
In Memoriam
  A.H.H.,LXXVI.
  Tennyson.
Liddell and Scott. Hardy.
The Mu'allaqat: Ode. Imr el
  Kais.
The Odyssey. Homer.
Psalm VI. Wyatt.
Rondeau Redouble. Payne.
Saturday Market. Mew.
Sexsmith the Dentist.
  Masters.
A Song for My Mother–Her
  Hands. Branch.
Three. Kitchell.
Youth! Thou Wear'st to
  Manhood Now. Scott.

Holly
Carol. Wilkinson.
Description of Elysium.
  Agee.
Green Grow'th the Holly.
  Anonymous.
Green Groweth the Holly.
  Henry VIII.
The Holly Bough. Mackay.

Nay, Ivy, Nay. *Anonymous.*
Rock Pilgrim. Palmer.
Young Hunting. *Anonymous.*

Holy
All through the Night.
  Boulton.
And Lo, the Star! Haley.
The Angelic Vilancete.
  Vicente.
Apocalypse. Pierce.
Approach to a City.
  Williams.
Artemis. Nerval.
At High Mass. Benson.
Base Chapel, Lejeune 4/79.
  Hobson.
Between Ourselves. Lorde.
Bless Him. *Anonymous.*
The Brave at Home. Read.
The Builders (excerpt). Van
  Dyke.
Chard Whitlow. Reed.
A Child's Wish. Ryan.
Christ 2. Cynewulf.
The Church Mouse. Bullett.
The Compost Heap.
  Watkins.
Dark Rapture. Russell.
Ditty. Chester.
Early Death. Coleridge.
An Election. Marcus.
Elegy for the Giant Tortoises.
  Atwood.
Elene. Cynewulf.
Far and Wide She Went.
  Caedmon.
Father Abraham.
  Anonymous.
First Confession. Kennedy.
Flower Ensnarer of Psalms.
  Ombres.
For a Christening. Watkins.
The Friar of Orders Gray.
  O'Keeffe.
Funeral Poem. Jones.
Gentlemen. Taylor.
Ghosts, Places, Stories,
  Questions. Buckley.
Glad Tidings from the King
  of Kings. Coffin.
God, Whom Shall I Compare
  to Thee? Halevi.
Hail, Holy Land. Tillam.
Homesick. Lasker-Schüler.
Housewifery. Taylor.
Hymn. Young.
Hymnal. Vinal.
Idylls of the King.
  Tennyson.
Immanence. Hovey.
In the Garden of the Lord.
  Keller.
In Time Like Air. Sarton.
The Inward Light. Sutton.
It Was Not Fate. Moore.
Jesus, Thou Joy of Loving
  Hearts. Bernard of
  Clairvaux.
John Saw the Holy Number.
  Anonymous.
King Henry VIII.
  Shakespeare.
The Kona Sea. *Anonymous.*
The Land of Cokaygne.
  Anonymous.
The Light. Holloway.
Longing for Jerusalem.
  Halevi.
The Marriage of Heaven and
  Hell. Blake.
Mayflower. Aiken.
Meeting. Harrison.

Midnight in Bonnie's Stall.
  Johnson.
More Lovely Grows the
  Earth. Coleman.
A Name for All. Crane.
New Territory. Boland.
O Christ of Bethlehem.
  Lanier.
O Paradise! O Paradise!
  Faber.
O Terrible Is the Highest
  Thing. Patchen.
O Thou Whose Gracious
  Presence Blest. Benson.
Oh, Hear Me Prayin'(Lord,
  Feed My Lam's).
  Anonymous.
Old Robin of Portingale.
  Anonymous.
An Old Woman. Sitwell.
The Old Women. Brown.
On Earth There Is a Lamb So
  Small. Zinzendorf.
Our Father! While Our Hearts
  Unlearn. Holmes.
The Poor in Church.
  Rimbaud.
The Portrait. Rossetti.
Psalm III. Ginsberg.
Psalm for Christmas Day.
  Pestel.
Puberty Rite Dance Song.
  Anonymous.
Radiant Ranks of Seraphim.
  Bryusov.
Reality. De Vere.
Red Hanrahan's Song about
  Ireland. Yeats.
Riddle. Bible: "A stern
  destroyer struck out my
  life." *Anonymous.*
Sabbath. Burden.
Saints. Garrett.
The Salt Pork. Casto.
Sapphics Against Anger.
  Steele.
The Scholar's Wife. Mernit.
The School of Night. Hope.
The Sinner. Bruner.
Sir Walter Scott at the Tomb
  of the Stuarts in St. Peter's.
  Milnes.
A Song of Liberty. Blake.
Sonnets, I: "Deep in a vale
  where rocks on every side."
  Rosenhane.
Spiritual Passion. Barlow.
A Sun-Day Hymn. Holmes.
The Theology of Jonathan
  Edwards. McGinley.
These Magicians. Provost.
Timid Lover. Cullen.
To Helen. Poe.
The Unerring Guide.
  Shipton.
The Vision. Traherne.
Ward Two. Webb.
What I Saw in October.
  Carrier.
White Goat, White Ram.
  Merwin.
Whitebeard on Videotape.
  Merrill.
With a Guitar, to Jane.
  Shelley.
Yet Love Was Born. Voss.

Holy Ghost
Ascension Hymn. Santeuil.
The Blasphemies. MacNeice.
Charm for Burns.
  Anonymous.
Christmas Day. Young.

The Earth. Mann.
Funeral Hymn. Howe.
Gloria in Excelsis.
   Anonymous.
The Joys of Mary.
   Anonymous.
Life's Testament.
   Baylebridge.
Light of the Soul. Caswall.
Morning Hymn. Ken.
Prayer for the Journey.
   Anonymous.
The Shadow and the Light
   (excerpt). Whittier.
Through Warmth and Light
   of Summer Skies. Faricy.
True Son of God, Eternal
   Light. Cormican.
Victoria. Van Dyke.
Holy Grail
Mentis Trist. Hillyer.
Homage
The Cradle and the Cross.
   Reitz.
Easter Morn. Fletcher.
House of Fire. Weiss.
In February. Simpson.
Inanna and the Anunna.
   Enheduanna.
King Henry V. Shakespeare.
Lord of the Worlds Below!
   Freeman.
A Love Story. Graves.
Modern Love, XXVIII.
   Meredith.
Passin Ben Dorain. Mackie.
Song in the Same Play, by the
   Wavering Nymph. Behn.
A World of Light. Jennings.
Home (s) (ward)
Above the Hills of Time.
   Tiplady.
Abroad and at Home. Swift.
Accepting. Miller.
Adultery at the Plaza.
   Thompson.
Adventure. Behn.
After. Levine.
After the Comanches.
   Anonymous.
Afterlives. Mahon.
Ah Dearest Love, for How
   Long. Mechtild of
   Magdeburg.
Airliner. Webb.
Airwaves. Woessner.
Albert Sidney Johnston.
   Ticknor.
The Alchemical Cupboard.
   Benveniste.
All Paths Lead to You.
   Wagstaff.
All through the Night.
   Anonymous.
Amnesiac. Plath.
Anacreon to the Sophist.
   "H.
The Angelus. Coates.
The Angora. Gerard.
Another of Seafarers,
   Describing Evil Fortune.
   Anonymous.
Apartment House. Raftery.
Are the Children at Home?
   Sangster.
As a Boy with a Richness of
   Needs I Wandered.
   Dyment.
The Ash Grove. *Anonymous.*
The Assumption. Tabb.
At Sea. Riley.
At the Ball! Webb.

The Augsburg Adoration.
   Jarrell.
Autumn. Untermeyer.
D'Avalos' Prayer. Masefield.
A Baby-Sermon. Macdonald.
Back through the Looking
   Glass to This Side. Ciardi.
Balearic Idyll. Packard.
The Ballad of Bunker Hill.
   Hale.
Ballad of the Boll Weevil.
   Anonymous.
De Ballet of De Boll Weevil
   (with music). *Anonymous.*
The Ballet of the Boll Weevil
   (B vers.). *Anonymous.*
Ballit of De Boll Weevil.
   Anonymous.
Banbury Fair. *Anonymous.*
Beach Fire. Frost.
Bear the News, Mary.
   Anonymous.
The Beast. Patten.
Beauty and Sadness. Song.
Beethoven. Wheelock.
Bend as the Bow Bends.
   Aiken.
Beowulf: The Lay of Finn.
   Anonymous.
A Bestiary. Rexroth.
Beulah Land. Sweeney.
Big Night Blues. Jefferson.
Bill Bailey. Cannon.
Bill Peters, the Stage Driver.
   Anonymous.
The Birds of Scotland
   (excerpt). Grahame.
Birth by Anesthesia.
   Scarbrough.
The Birth of John Henry.
   Tolson.
Bitter Sanctuary. Monro.
Black and White. Schmidt.
The Blake Mistake. Castle.
The Blessed Virgin compared
   to the Air we Breathe.
   Hopkins.
Blessing the Dance. Russell.
Blest Winter Nights.
   Armstrong.
The Blind Fiddler.
   Anonymous.
The Blue Bowl. Kuder.
Blue Like Death. Welch.
The Boll Weevil Song.
   Anonymous.
Bone Poem. Willard.
Bonnard: A Novel. Howard.
Braddock's Fate, with an
   Incitement to Revenge.
   Tilden.
Bring 'Em Home. Dane.
British Valor Displayed.
   Hopkinson.
Brown's Descent; or, The
   Willy-Nilly Slide. Frost.
Brumana. Flecker.
Bryan O'Lynn. *Anonymous.*
Bucko-Mate. Schierloh.
Burnet's Character.
   Anonymous.
Burning Bush. Baker.
Bury Me in America.
   Karlen.
Bus Ride. Kandel.
A Busy Yellow Bee.
   Anonymous.
Caelica, XCV. Greville.
The Call. *Anonymous.*
Calling Home the Scientists.
   Rose.

Calumet Early Evening.
   West.
Canso Strait. *Anonymous.*
The Cavern. Tomlinson.
Cherry Tree Carol.
   Anonymous.
Chippewa Lake Park.
   Woessner.
Christ and Satan:
   Lamentations of the Fallen
   Angels. *Anonymous.*
Christmas at Sea. Stevenson.
Christmas Night of '62.
   McCabe.
City Roofs. Towne.
Clothes Make the Man.
   Weiss.
Come Back. Herbert.
Come Home. *Anonymous.*
Come Home, Come Home!
   Clough.
Coming Home from Camp.
   Kaneko.
Confessio Amantis. Gower.
Conquerors. Treece.
The Conservative Shepherd to
   His Love. D'Arcy.
Contest. Victor.
Cotton Manuscript: Maxims.
   Anonymous.
A Country Boy in Winter.
   Jewett.
The Cowboy's Life Is a Very
   Dreary Life. *Anonymous.*
The Coy Shepherdess; or,
   Phillis and Amintas.
   Anonymous.
Crabbing. Levine.
The Cranes. Po Chu-i.
The Cricket's Story. Nason.
A Cry from the Canadian
   Hills. Leveridge.
Cymon and Iphigenia.
   Dryden.
Daffodil's Return. Carman.
The Daily Manna. Hay.
Damn the Filipinos.
   Anonymous.
Damnation of Vancouver:
   Speech of the Salish Chief.
   Birney.
Dance to Your Daddy.
   Anonymous.
Darlin'. *Anonymous.*
The Dead Feast of the Kol-
   Folk. Whittier.
The Dead Seal near McClure's
   Beach. Bly.
The Dead Sister. Gilman.
The Dearest Spot on Earth.
   Wrighton.
Death on a Crossing.
   Paterson.
Deceitful Brownskin Blues.
   Jefferson.
Defensive Position.
   Manifold.
Deja Vu. Kaufman.
The Dell. Ewart.
Derry Morning. Mahon.
The Desert. Knibbs.
Desert March. Norvig.
A Desolate Shore. Henley.
Despised and Rejected.
   Bates.
Die in de Fiel'. *Anonymous.*
The Difference. Scott.
Dis Mornin', Dis Evenin', So
   Soon (with music).
   Anonymous.

Do Don't Touch-A My
   Garment, Good Lord, I'm
   Gwine Home. *Anonymous.*
Do Not Think. Freeman.
Do They Think of Me at
   Home. Carpenter.
The Dockyard Gate.
   Anonymous.
Doggerel by a Senior Citizen.
   Auden.
The Doggies Went to the
   Mill. *Anonymous.*
Domestic Asides; or, Truth in
   Parentheses. Hood.
Domestic Science.
   Anonymous.
Down Home. Outlaw.
A Dream. Blake.
Dream-Land. Poe.
The Dream of Gerontius.
   Newman.
The Dream of the Rood.
   Cynewulf.
A Dream of Women.
   Maisel.
The Dreamers. Garrison.
The Dress That My Brother
   Has Put on Is Thin.
   Otomo of Sakanoe.
Driving Home. London.
Driving North from
   Kingsville, Texas. Shihab.
The Drowned Children.
   Gluck.
Drowning of Conaing.
   Anonymous.
The Drunken Man. Orlen.
The Drynaun Dhun.
   Anonymous.
Duck. Worth.
Dunkirk. Nathan.
Eagle Squadron. Rutsala.
The Earth. Mann.
Eclogue IV. The Poet
   (excerpt). Jenner.
Elegy. McFadden.
The Elements. Newman.
The Elm's Home. Heyen.
The Empty House. Howells.
An Encomium upon a
   Parliament. Defoe.
Epilogue: The Flower of Old
   Japan. Noyes.
An Epistle Written in the
   Country to.... Jenyns.
An Epistolary Essay from
   M.G. to O.B. upon Their
   Mutual Poems. Rochester.
An Essay on Man. Pope.
Eternal Spirit, Source of
   Light. Davies.
The Everlasting Mercy
   (parody). Squire.
Exile. Sheard.
The Factory Hands.
   Chimedza.
Fair Annie. *Anonymous.*
Fancy. Keats.
A Farewell. Flanner.
The Farm on the Links.
   Watson.
Fatal Love. Prior.
Father. Wheelwright.
Father, Into Thy Hands.
   Pollack.
The Female Sailor.
   Anonymous.
Fetching Cows. MacCaig.
Few Days. *Anonymous.*
First Philosopher's Song.
   Huxley.

First Travels of Max. Ransom.
Five Songs. Shapiro.
Flodden Field. *Anonymous.*
Fly, Ladybug. Stowman.
The Fog. Davies.
A Folded Skyscraper (excerpt). Williams.
For Drum Hadley. Littlebird.
For No Good Reason. Redgrove.
The Forgotten Rock. Eberhart.
Freighting from Wilcox to Globe. *Anonymous.*
Fresh Spring. Daryush.
Friends. Housman.
Frigid and sweet her parting face. Dickinson.
From Grenoble. Flecker.
Frost Heaves. Dorris.
Gaily the Troubadour. Bayley.
The Gangster's Death. Reed.
Garlic. Bell.
Gee, but I Want to Go Home. *Anonymous.*
Genitori. Ray.
George Washington. Silverstein.
Getting Lost in Nazi Germany. Bell.
The Ghost of a Ghost. Leithauser.
Git Along Little Dogies. *Anonymous.*
The Gnome. Behn.
Go Home. McFatter.
God Bless America. Berlin.
Going to Town. Lape.
The Golden Voyage. *Anonymous.*
Good-Bye, Fare You Well. *Anonymous.*
Grandfather. Stroud.
Grandfather Watts's Private Fourth. Bunner.
Graveyard by the Sea. Lux.
The Great House. Muir.
The Great Round-Up. *Anonymous.*
The Green Family. Thibaudeau.
The Green Isle of Lovers. Sands.
Green Slates. Hardy.
Guardian Angel. Newman.
Hal's Birthday. Larcom.
Half Sigh. *Anonymous.*
Hallo My Fancy. Cleland.
Handful of Ashes. Rubin.
He Raise a Poor Lazarus. *Anonymous.*
The Heart's Low Door. Mitchell.
The Heart's Wild Geese. Treece.
Heaven. *Anonymous.*
Here's to the Ranger! *Anonymous.*
Heritage. Hogan.
Hesperos, you bring home all the bright dawn disperses. Sappho.
High Water Everywhere. Patton.
Highway Patrol Stops Me, Going Too Slow. Peterson.
His Task–and Ours. Gould.

His Toy, His Dream, His Rest. Berryman.
History. Graham.
Holy Spirit, Faithful Guide. Wells.
Homage to William Cowper. Davie.
Homage to Wren. MacNeice.
Home. *Anonymous.*
Home. Chalmers.
Home. Guest.
Home. Hines.
Home. Kowit.
Home. Sepamla.
Home. Sill.
Home. Van Dyke.
Home in That Rock. *Anonymous.*
Home Song. Longfellow.
Home, Sweet Home. *Anonymous.*
Homecoming. Dawe.
The Homecoming Singer. Wright.
The Homing Heart. Henderson.
Hon. Mr. Sucklethumbkin's Story. Barham.
Honolulu and Back. Logan.
House and Land. Curnow.
The Housekeeper. Bourne.
Houses Should Have Homes to Live in. Ross.
How Far to Bethlehem. Miller.
How to Amuse a Stone. Shelton.
Hunting Pheasants in a Cornfield. Bly.
Hush, Hush, New House in Charlotte. Schorb.
I Am 25. Corso.
I Can't Feel at Home in This World Anymore. *Anonymous.*
I drag a boat over the ocean. Lal Ded.
I Got a Home in-a Dat Rock. *Anonymous.*
I Have Some Friends Before Me Gone. *Anonymous.*
I Just Wanna Stay Home. Silber.
I Know That I Must Die Soon. Lasker-Schüler.
I live where darkness. Mukta Bai.
I'll Take You Home Again, Kathleen. Westendorf.
I've Reached the Land of Corn and Wine. Stites.
An Idler's Calendar: January. Blunt.
Idylls. Theocritus.
Illumination for Victories in Mexico. Greenwood.
In Memoriam. De Brun.
In Misty Blue. Binyon.
In Random Fields of Impulse and Repose. Hathaway.
In Tall Grass. Sandburg.
In the Glorious Epiphanie of Our Lord God. Crashaw.
In the Inner City. Clifton.
In the Mines. Swett.
In the Snowfall. Mechain.
Indian Summer: Montana, 1956. Ransom.
Inspiration. Service.
Iris. St. John.

It was a Special Treat. Tapahonso.
Jazz Band in a Parisian Cabaret. Hughes.
Jehovah-Rophi. Cowper.
Johnny Carroll's Camp. *Anonymous.*
Johnny Fife and Johnny's Wife. Merryman.
The Jolly Shilling. *Anonymous.*
Josie (with music). *Anonymous.*
Joyfully, Joyfully Onward I Move. Hunter.
Jubilate. Arnold.
Jump–Jump–Jump. Greenaway.
Just Forget. Dryden.
Kearsarge and Alabama. *Anonymous.*
Keen. Millay.
King Estmere. *Anonymous.*
The Kingdom. Swan.
Laboring and Heavy Laden. Rankin.
Lady Franklin's Lament (I). Anonymous.
Lady Lost. Ransom.
The Lame Soldier. *Anonymous.*
Lament of Hsi-Chun. Hsi-chun.
The Last Days. Sterling.
The Last Fairy. Watson.
Last Journey. Davidson.
Leaving Town Blues. Bracey.
Leda and the Swan. Friman.
Let Me Be Held When the Longing Comes. Stephany.
Life in a Half-breed Shack. *Anonymous.*
The Lily-white Rose. *Anonymous.*
Limerick: "O was an ossified oyster." Wells.
The Limits of Departure. Weigl.
Lines to a World-Famous Poet... Nash.
The Little Lost Child. Marks.
The Little Road. Turner.
Little Roads to Happiness. Stitch.
The Long Voyaage. Cowley.
Looking Down on West Virginia. Dickson.
Lord Thomas and Lady Margaret. *Anonymous.*
The Lordly Hudson. Goodman.
Lost But Found. Bonar.
Lost Objects. O Hehir.
Love Restored (excerpt). Jonson.
Love's Caution. Davies.
Love-Songs, At Once Tender and Informative. Hoffenstein.
The Lucky Sailor. *Anonymous.*
The Mad Maid's Song. Herrick.
The Maid and the Palmer. *Anonymous.*
The Man Who Knew Too Much. Wojahn.
Marching Song. Stevenson.

Mardi Gras / Grandmothers Portrait in Red and Black Crayon. Nolan.
Mariale (excerpt). Bernard of Cluny.
The Martyrs of the Maine. Hughes.
Mary Winslow. Lowell.
The Maryland Battalion. Palmer.
The Master of Time. Nijlen.
A Memory. Tynan.
The Menu. Aldrich.
The Miner's Lament. *Anonymous.*
Missions. *Anonymous.*
A Misspelled Tail. Corbett.
Mister Charlie. Hopkins.
Moanish Lady! (with music). *Anonymous.*
Model. Ammons.
Moon-Like Is All Other Love. *Anonymous.*
The Moor. Hodgson.
The Mother. *Anonymous.*
Mother's Advice. *Anonymous.*
The Mower to the Glow-worms. Marvell.
The Muscovy Drake. Lesoro.
My brother has on a thin robe. Otomo of Sakanoe .
My Dame Hath a Lame Tame Crane. *Anonymous.*
My Hat. Smith.
My Son Doesn't See a Thing. Rivera.
The Mystery of the Caves. Waters.
Mystic and Cavalier. Johnson.
Nature Green Shit. Snyder.
The New Ahasuerus. Kiss.
New England. Percival.
New Mexico. Boyden.
New Skills. Nye.
News. Pomeroy.
News of the World. Barker.
No Continuing City. Longley.
A Nonsense Carol. *Anonymous.*
Not That Far. Miller.
Notes for Albuquerque. Whiteman.
November. Cleaveland.
Now all that sound of laughter, sound of singing. Castro.
O Strong to Bless. Daryush.
O Thou Whose Gracious Presence Blest. Benson.
The Oak and the Ash. *Anonymous.*
An Ocean Lullaby. Keeler.
The Ocean Wood. De Tabley.
Odysseus. Merwin.
The Odyssey. Homer.
Oh Freedom. *Anonymous.*
Oh, How My Love with a Whirling Power. Tu-kehu and Wetea.
L'Oiseau Bleu. Bottomley.
Okay–. Scott.
De Ol' Ark's A-Movering' an' I'm Goin' Home. *Anonymous.*
The Old Farmer and His Young Wife. *Anonymous.*
Old Folks at Home. Foster.

The Old Man of Verona. Claudian (Claudius Claudianus).

Old Wichet. *Anonymous.*

On the Death of Her Mother. Rukeyser.

On the Debt My Mother Owed to Sears Roebuck. Dorn.

On the Quay. Bell.

On Time with God. Nutter.

On Vacation. Creeley.

One Sweetly Solemn Thought. Cary.

The Open Door. Coolidge.

The Orphan Girl. *Anonymous.*

Our Jack's Come Home Today. *Anonymous.*

Our Modest Doughboys. Andrews.

Our Visit to the Zoo. Pope.

Over Jordan. *Anonymous.*

Ovid. Pevear.

Pa. Dangel.

Painted Passages. Harada.

Paper Words. Franklin.

Pater Vester Pascit Illa. Hawker.

Pet Shop. MacNeice.

The Pettichap's Nest. Clare.

The Phoenix. *Anonymous.*

Pigs. Cotton.

Pisgah. Wattles.

The Place of the Damned. Swift.

Po' Mourner's Got a Home at Las'. *Anonymous.*

Poem for Myself and Mei: Abortion. Silko.

Poem for the Conguero in D-yard. Fernandez.

Poem near midway truck stop. Henson.

The Poem That Took the Place of a Mountain. Stevens.

The Poetry Reading. Manhire.

Politics. Emerson.

Poor Boy Blues. Thomas.

Poor Lonesome Cowboy. *Anonymous.*

A Poor Wayfaring Stranger. *Anonymous.*

Postcards from Kodai. Crossley-Holland.

Praise of a Train. *Anonymous.*

A Prayer for a Little Home. Bone.

Primavera. Lima.

Prison Moan. *Anonymous.*

The Prodigal. Bishop.

The Progress of Error. Cowper.

The Queen of Fairies. *Anonymous.*

Questions of Travel. Bishop.

The Quip. Herbert.

Rabbit Foot Blues. Jefferson.

Raising the Flag. Vizenor.

The Rat. Davies.

The Rebel Soldier. *Anonymous.*

Recreation. Taylor.

Requests. Dolben.

Requiem. Stevenson.

Requiem for and Abstract Artist. Kessler.

Return of the Goddess Artemis. Graves.

The Return of the Native. Matthews.

Revolution. Harford.

Richard Cory. Robinson.

The Ride-by-Nights. De la Mare.

Ride On, Moses. *Anonymous.*

Rise, Glorious Conqueror! Rise. Bridges.

The River That Is East. Kinnell.

The Road to Babylon. Wilson.

Roads. Field.

Robin. A Pastoral Elegy. Dobson.

A Robin and a Robin's Son. *Anonymous.*

The Robin Is the One. Dickinson.

Rock, Rock, Sleep, My Baby. Watson.

Roger and Me. Le Dressay.

Rolled over on Europe. Spender.

Rolling Home. *Anonymous.*

Rondeau in Wartime. Bertram.

The Rose. Creeley.

The Royal Tour. "Pindar.

Ruth. Hood.

Sadie (with music). Anonymous.

Sage Counsel. Quiller-Couch.

Sail Peacefully Home. Frug.

The Sailor's Return. *Anonymous.*

Saint George of England. Fox-Smith.

Salmon Fly Hatch on Yankee Jim Canyon of the Yellowstone. Keeler.

The Scales of the Eyes. Nemerov.

The Seagull. Howitt.

Seascape. Hughes.

Second Carolina Said-Song. Ammons.

The Secret Town (excerpt). Sutzkever.

Serenade. Carnevali.

The Serving Maid. Munby.

The Sextant. Sullivan.

Shadows among the Ettrick Hills. Addison.

Shanty-Boy and the Farmer's Son. *Anonymous.*

A Shantyman's Life (II). *Anonymous.*

Shepherd. Stafford.

The Shepherd Boys. Saboly.

Ships. Turner.

A Shropshire Lad. Housman.

The Silk Merchant's Daughter. *Anonymous.*

Sing, My Soul. *Anonymous.*

Sir, So Suspicious. *Anonymous.*

Sirmio. Catullus.

Sleeping Pill. O Hehir.

The Small Lady. Smith.

Snow. Akers.

The Snow. Creeley.

Soft Landings. Sergeant.

The Soldier Is Home. Neilson.

Soldier, Soldier, Won't You Marry Me? *Anonymous.*

The Solitary. Nietzsche.

Sometimes I Feel Like a Motherless Child. *Anonymous.*

Song for Mother's Day. Matthews.

Song: "I wrastled wid Satan, I wrastled wid sin." *Anonymous.*

Song of Grief. Liu Hsi-Chun.

The Song of Shadows. de la Mare.

Song: "Oh! that we two were Maying." Kingsley.

Song: "Rarely, rarely, comest thou." Shelley.

Sounds. Creeley.

The Southeast Ramparts of the Seine. Toth.

Spencer the Rover. *Anonymous.*

Spirit-Like before Light. Gregor.

The Square at Dawn. Tate.

The St. Lawrence and the Saguenay: The Thousand Islands. Sangster.

The Stalin Epigram. Mandelstam.

Standin' on the Walls of Zion (with music). *Anonymous.*

Staoineag. Volwerk.

The Star-Spangled Banner. Key.

The Starlight Night. Hopkins.

Stars over the Dordogne. Plath.

Staying in the Mountains in Summer. Yu Hsuan-chi.

Stopped. Polite.

Stopping by Home. Huddle.

The Strand. MacNeice.

The Swallow. Aiken.

Swannanoa Tunnel. *Anonymous.*

A Sweetheart in the Army (B vers.). *Anonymous.*

Take My Hand, O Blessed Master. Calenberg.

Tall Hat. Daley.

The Testament of John Davidson: The Last Journey. Davidson.

Texas Rangers. *Anonymous.*

There Is a Land Mine Eye Hath Seen. Robins.

Things Not of This Union. Gregg.

Things to Do around Kyoto. Snyder.

This Easter Day. Nicholson.

This Landscape, These People. Ghose.

This Little Pig Went to Market. *Anonymous.*

This Morning I Wakened among Loud Cries of Seagulls. MacDonogh.

This One Is about the Others. Jaffe.

Thou Hast Wounded the Spirit That Loved Thee. Porter.

Three Women Blues. McTell.

Threnody. Harding.

Through Unknown Paths. Hosmer.

The Titanic (A vers.). *Anonymous.*

To a Skylark. Wordsworth.

To G. K. Chesterton. Plunkett.

To Maynard on the Long Road Home. Ehrhart.

To Mr. Newton on His Return from Ramsgate. Cowper.

To N. V. de. G. S. Stevenson.

To Silvestre Revueltas of Mexico, in His Death. Neruda.

To Some Few Hopi Ancestors. Rose.

To the Child Jesus. Van Dyke.

To the Cuckoo. Wordsworth.

To the Skylark. Wordsworth.

To the World: a Farewell for a Gentlewoman, Virtuous and Noble. Jonson.

To Thee, O God. Holmes.

The Tollund Man. Heaney.

Tom Long. *Anonymous.*

A Tonversaton with Baby. Bishop.

Tractor. Sellers.

Tragedy. Russell.

Tramp! Tramp! Tramp! Root.

The Traveler. *Anonymous.*

The Traveller. Dennis.

Travelogue for Exiles. Shapiro.

The Trip. Dennis.

Trot along Pony. Grider.

The Troubled Soldier. *Anonymous.*

Trouvaille. Murphy.

Truck Drivers. Haag.

The True Lovers Bold. *Anonymous.*

The Two Brothers. *Anonymous.*

Two Heavens. Hunt.

Two Lives and Others. Scott.

The Umbrella. Stanford.

Unable by Long and Hard Travel to Banish Love, Returns Her Friend. Turberville.

Unshrinking Faith. Balhurst.

Until I Reach-a Ma Home. *Anonymous.*

The Unwilling Gypsy. Johnson.

Upon New Year's Eve. Quiller-Couch.

The Urn. Cowley.

Vacation Time. Bennett.

Vaticide. O'Higgins.

Verigin 3. Newlove.

Vespers. Shepard.

Walking Home at Night. Weissbort.

The Wanderer. Field.

The Wanderer. Hall.

The Wars of Santa Fe. *Anonymous.*

Washington Heights, 1959. Blumenthal.

Wasp Sex Myth (One). Hollo.

The Wastrel. Kauffman.

The Watchers. Braithwaite.

Water. McPheron.

Watercress & Ice. Twichell.

We'll Go No More A-Roving. Henley.

We Manage Most When We
  Manage Small. Gregg.
We Men Are of Two Worlds.
  Colman.
We Won't Go Home Till
  Morning. *Anonymous.*
Weathers. Hardy.
Weeping Willow. Aldridge.
What Bright Pushbutton?
  Allen.
What She Wished. Throne.
What Voice at Moth-Hour.
  Warren.
When Brothers Forget.
  Boyer.
When I Grow Up. Holland.
When Johnny Comes
  Marching Home. Gilmore.
When the Ambulance Came.
  Morgan.
When Thy King Is a Boy
  (excerpt). Roberson.
Where Hudson's Wave.
  Morris.
Where Love Is. Burr.
While O'er the Deep Thy
  Servants Sail. Burgess.
White Center. Hugo.
Whiteness. Hume.
Who Drags the Fiery Artist
  Down? Day.
The Whole Armour of God.
  Wesley.
Widow's Lament.
  Anonymous.
A Wife's Song. Bennett.
Wild Eden. Woodberry.
Winds of Africa. Obi.
Winter News. Haines.
Wise Owl. Goedicke.
With All Deliberate Speed.
  Lee.
A Woodland Revel. Urmy.
A Word of Warning.
  Anonymous.
The World Narrowed to a
  Point. Williams.
World of Darkness. Chatain.
Yellow. Wright.
The Yellowhammer. Clare.
Young Man Cut Down in His
  Prime. *Anonymous.*
Zimmer's Hard Dream.
  Zimmer.
Zito the Magician. Holub.
Zlotchev, My Home.
  Halpern.

Homeland
Beggars. Carpenter.
The Homeland. Haweis.
Talmudist. Burnshaw.
To My Generation. Galai.

Homeless
How the Great Guest Came.
  Markham.
In This Deep Darkness.
  Zach.
New Testament: Revised
  Edition. Mary Catherine.
Summer and Winter.
  Shelley.
Under Restless Clouds.
  Michaelis.
You, Neighbor God. Rilke.

Homely
Accepting. Miller.
A Coast View (excerpt).
  Harpur.
Ranchers. Lesemann.
To My Friend, Grown
  Famous. Tietjens.

Homer
A Cure for Poetry.
  Anonymous.
Life and Fame. Cowley.
Of Edmund Spenser's Fairy
  Queen... Ralegh.
On First Looking into
  Chapman's Homer I
  (parody). Griffiths.
Petit, the Poet. Masters.
Seven Wealthy Towns.
  Anonymous.
Sickle Pears (For Glidden
  Parker). Dodson.
Tradition. Guiterman.

Homesick (ness)
The Decision. Dodson.
Dying. Alvarez.
Fringed Gentians. Lowell.
The Hill of Intrusion.
  Graham.
In the Ghetto.
  Sonnenschein.
The Inglorious Milton.
  Letters.
On Hearing a Flute at Night
  from the Wall of Shou-
  Hsiang. Li Yi.

Honest (y)
Amboyna; or, The Cruelties of
  the Dutch.... Dryden.
At Lucky Moments We Seem
  on the Brink. Auden.
Behind the Falls. Stafford.
The Burning of Jamestown.
  English.
Democritus and Heraclitus.
  Prior.
The Forgiven Past. Riding.
The Garment of Good Ladies.
  Henryson.
General Ludd's Triumph.
  Anonymous.
Gladstone. Symons.
The Grumbling Hive: or,
  Knaves turn'd Honest.
  Mandeville.
Herons. Blaser.
Horse Sense. *Anonymous.*
Loves World. Suckling.
The Moral. Mandeville.
Nell Gwynne's Looking-Glass.
  Blanchard.
Nobility. Cary.
On a Maide of Honour Seene
  by a Schollar in Sommerset
  Garden. Randolph.
Philomela's Ode in Her
  Arbour. Greene.
The Poet's Prayer.
  Anonymous.
Poor Crow! Dodge.
The Sea and the Tiger.
  Collinson.
Sitting by a River Side.
  Greene.
Squire and Milkmaid.
  Anonymous.
To a Rogue. Addison.
To Make Your Candles Last
  for Aye. *Anonymous.*
To My Booke. Jonson.
Untitled. Conley.
Upon Bunce: Epigram.
  Herrick.

Honey
16. ix. 65. Merrill.
Ah Me, If I Grew Sweet to
  Man. "Field.
Am I Failing? Meredith.
April (excerpt). McLeod.

As You Like It.
  Shakespeare.
Billy the Kid. Spicer.
The Brown Bear. Austin.
Burning and Fathering:
  Accounts of My Country.
  Gilbert.
The Buzzing Doubt. Hill.
The Captived Bee; or, The
  Little Filcher. Herrick.
Carrowmore. Russell.
The Death of the Bronx.
  Bloch.
Dink's Song. *Anonymous.*
Eclogue. Virgil (Publius
  Vergilius Maro).
Epigram: "Three things must
  epigrams." *Anonymous.*
The Five Little Fairies.
  Burnham.
Forefathers. Blunden.
The Harvester. Lawrence.
Harvey Logan. *Anonymous.*
He Who in His Pocket Hath
  No Money. *Anonymous.*
The Honest Whore, I, 1604.
  Dekker.
Hymns for the Amusement of
  Children. Smart.
I, Lessimus, of Salt Lake City
  (parody). Peters.
Jonathan. "Rachel" (Rachel
  Blumstein).
Ladies in the Dinin' Room.
  Anonymous.
Lost Silvertip. Reed.
Love Sleeping. Plato.
The Lovers. Byron.
Mary Was Watching.
  Anonymous.
Modern Love, XXIX.
  Meredith.
My Happiness. Pape.
My Honey, My Love.
  Harris.
Nebuchadnezzar. Wylie.
Old Lady Sitting in the
  Dining Room.
  Anonymous.
The Old Testament (excerpt).
  Anonymous.
The Old Vicarage,
  Grantchester. Brooke.
On the Pole. Greenberg.
The Plough-Hands' Song.
  Harris.
The Quaker's Wooing (with
  music). *Anonymous.*
The Quest. Scollard.
The Rainy Summer.
  Meynell.
Raw Honey. MacAdams.
The Rosemary Spray.
  Gongora y Argote.
Song: "The bee-keeper kissed
  me." *Anonymous.*
Sonnet: To the Asshole.
  Rimbaud.
A Summer Night in the
  Beehive. Turner.
Take a Drink on Me.
  Anonymous.
The Tragic Mary Queen of
  Scot. "Field.
True Vine. Wylie.
Untitled Poem. Dugan.
Upon a Mole in Celia's
  Bosom. Carew.
Virgil: Georgics, Book IV.
  Schmitz.
What Changes, My Love.
  Honig.

What Does the Bee Do?
  Rossetti.

Honeycomb (s)
A Busy Yellow Bee.
  Anonymous.
Cherry Tree. Sitwell.
In Tall Grass. Sandburg.
My Fathers Came from
  Kentucky. Lindsay.
No New Thing. Buckley.
On the Curve-Edge. Evans.
Sonnets, VIII: "Sometimes I
  wish that I his pillow
  were." Barnfield.
Willowware Cup. Merrill.
Winter Sketches. Reznikoff.

Honeymoon
A Bride's Hours. Valentine.
The Children Grown.
  Jackson.
Niagara Falls Nocturne.
  Gasparini.

Honor (ed) (s)
Ad Matrem. Fane.
Aesthetic. Rosten.
After You, Madam.
  Comfort.
Alcestis. Euripides.
Amoretti, VII. Spenser.
Annul Wars. Nahman of
  Bratzlav.
As I Went to Bonner.
  Anonymous.
Astrophel and Stella, VII.
  Sidney.
Astrophel and Stella, XXI.
  Sidney.
Ballata: He Will Gaze upon
  Beatrice. Dante Alighieri.
The Bath. Graham.
Black Bart. *Anonymous.*
Bruce Addresses His Army.
  Barbour.
Cacophonous Couplet on
  Cardinal Wolsey.
  Anonymous.
Caelica, III. Greville.
Cervera. Shadwell.
Chanson: "If they say my
  furred cloak." Du Guillet.
The Chronicler. Bergman.
Cleitagoras. Leonidas.
Do It Right. Buckner.
Elegy on Shakespeare. Basse.
Epitaph on Mr. Robert Port.
  Cotton.
A (excerpt). Zukofsky.
The Excrement Poem.
  Kumin.
A Farewell to Sir John Norris
  and Sir Francis Drake.
  Peele.
The Flea. Donne.
The Golden Gift That Nature
  Did Thee Give. Surrey.
Government Injunction.
  Miles.
The Heart's Anchor. Winter.
Hebe. Lowell.
Hen Under Bay-Tree. Pitter.
In Defiance to the Dutch.
  Anonymous.
In the Due Honor of the
  Author Master Robert
  Norton. Smith.
Knowest Thou Isaac Jogues?
  Grey.
Lee's Parole. Manville.
The Loss of the Cedar Grove.
  Anonymous.
Loving and Beloved.
  Suckling.

Madrigal: "Flow forth, abundant tears." Attey.
Meeting a Bear. Wagoner.
Men. MacLeish.
Metamorphoses. Ovid (Publius Ovidius Naso).
Miles Keogh's Horse. Hay.
Mourning Letter, March 29 1963. Dorn.
Movie-Going. Hollander.
An Ode to Myself. Dermody.
On a Little Boy's Endeavouring to Catch a Snake. Foxton.
On a Maide of Honour Seene by a Schollar in Sommerset Garden. Randolph.
On Certain Ladies. Pope.
On the Death of Captain Nicholas Biddle. Freneau.
The Parrot. Skelton.
Peace with Honor. Appleman.
Perry Zoll. Masters.
A Poem upon the Death of Oliver Cromwell (excerpt). Marvell.
A Prayer to Be Said When Thou Goest to Bed. Seager.
The Progress of a Divine (excerpt). Savage.
Protecting the Burial Grounds. Rose.
Queen Mab. Shelley.
Robert E. Lee. Howe.
A Satirical Elegy on the Death of a Late Famous General. Swift.
Song: "Thyrsis, when we parted, swore." Gray.
The Thieves. Graves.
This Crosse-Tree Here. Herrick.
To Spenser. Keats.
To the Right Worthy Knight Sir Fulke Greville. Daniel.
To the United States of America. Bridges.
Trail All Your Pikes. Winchilsea.
Under the Old Elm. Lowell.
White as Snow. *Anonymous.*
Willie Riley. *Anonymous.*
Young Windebank. Woods.
The Young Workman. Frear.
Zeppelin. Glaze.

Honorable
The Good Man. Talmud.
Mingling My Prayer. Saigyo Hoshi.

Hood (ed)
On Thomas Hood. Landor.
Pastorale. Davis.
Snatches: "Gret hunting by rivers and wood." *Anonymous.*
A Song: "Good neighbour, why do you look awry?" *Anonymous.*
Through All Your Abstract Reasoning. Patten.

Hoof (s) (hooves)
The Cattle of His Hand. Underwood.
Celebrant. Mitchell.
The Closing of the Rodeo. Smith.
A Dream of Horses. Hughes.

Earth and I Gave You Turquoise. Momaday.
Faun-Taken. O'Neill.
Horses. Wellesley.
The Law of the Jungle. Kipling.
The Listeners. De la Mare.
Metrical Feet. Coleridge.
The Mount. Adams.
My Father Dragged by Horses. Broughton.
The New Cows. Waterman.
The Origin of Centaurs. Hecht.
The Pony Express. Thompson.
The Strangers. Brown.
Touching the River. Kinsella.

Hook (s)
And Angling, Too. Byron.
Crawl Blues. McHugh.
Dial Tone. Pollak.
Distinguishing Ru from Chu. Hitchcock.
The Fisherman. Macpherson.
The Foreboding. Graves.
The Old Angler. De La Mare.
The Parthenon. Heath-Stubbs.
Sharks. Overton.
Summit Lake. Thalman.
To Alexander Neville. Googe.
Under the Boathouse. Bottoms.

Hoot (er) (s)
Limerick: "There was a young fellow of Ceuta." *Anonymous.*
An Owl Is an Only Bird of Poetry. Duncan.
Stone Trees. Freeman.
Winter, New Hampshire. Kherdian.

Hop
Boy Trash Picker. Howard.
Charley. *Anonymous.*
Handy Spandy. Mother Goose.
I've Got a Dog as Thin as a Rail. *Anonymous.*
Nature Note. Guiterman.
Song of Abuse. Anonymous.

Hope (d) (s)
Ad Patriam (excerpt). Foulke.
After great storms the calm returns. Wyatt.
Against Fruition. Suckling.
Albert Sidney Johnson. Sherwood.
Alien. Turner.
All Day We've Longed for Night. Fabio.
Aloof. Rossetti.
Amaryllis I did woo. Wither.
Antigone and Oedipus. Ray.
The Argument of His Book. Herrick.
Arrangements with Earth for Three Dead Friends. Wright.
The Assassination. Hillyer.
At the Mermaid Inn. Hildreth.
At the President's Grave. Gilder.

Aunt Elsie's Night Music. Oliver.
Autumn. De la Mare.
Bartol. Alcott.
Be Hopeful. Gillilan.
Beauty as a Shield. Robinson.
Because. McAuley.
Before a Fall. Grigson.
The Bestiary: The Whale. *Anonymous.*
Bethlehem of Judea. *Anonymous.*
A Bird in the Bush. Young.
Breakfast. Gunn.
The Buried Stream. Baxter.
Caelica, XXXVII. Greville.
Caelica, LIV. Greville.
Calais, August 15, 1802. Wordsworth.
Capability Brown. Cowper.
Charleston. Gilder.
Childe Harold's Pilgrimage: Canto III, XXVII. Byron.
Christ. *Anonymous.*
Christ and the Pagan. Tabb.
Christ for the World! We Sing. Wolcott.
Christmas Still Lives. Hawkes.
Claiming the Promise. Wesley.
The Conquered Banner. Ryan.
Daddy. Clifton.
Decayed Time. Wahl.
Dieppe, II: On the Beach. Symons.
The Divine Wooer. Fletcher.
Don't Tell Me. *Anonymous.*
Dream Girl. Sandburg.
Dreams. Poe.
Dry Your Tears, Africa! Dadie.
Earl Brand. *Anonymous.*
Elegy. Maclaurin.
An Elegy for Bob Marley. Matthews.
Elegy for Lucy Lloyd. Goch.
An Elegy in Memory of the Worshipful Major Thomas Leonard Esq.... Danforth II.
Elegy over a Tomb. Herbert of Cherbury.
The Emigrant. O'Grady.
Emigrant Song. "Ansky.
The End of May. Morris.
End of Season. Warren.
Epitaph. Chiabrera.
Epitaph. Morton.
Epitaph on the Politician Himself. Belloc.
Exceptional. Lewis.
Expectation. Stanley.
Faith for Tomorrow. Clark.
The Family Altar. Adams.
For My Father: Two Poems. Kherdian.
The Forgotten Star. Clark.
Form Rejection Letter. Dacey.
The Four Calls. Hadley.
Fragment. Hopkins.
Get a Transfer. *Anonymous.*
The Giant Puffball. Blunden.
The Goat. Young.
Godfrey of Bulloigne: Armida...Sets out to undo the Crusaders. Tasso.
Government Injunction. Miles.

The Great Despair of the London Whigs. *Anonymous.*
Happy Lifetime to You. Adams.
Hatikvah–A Song of Hope. Imber.
Have You Lost Faith? *Anonymous.*
He Lifted from the Dust. Smith.
Heat. Mackenzie.
A Heathen Hymn (excerpt). Morris.
Her Absent Lord (excerpt). Ugga Byan.
The Herald Crane. Garland.
His Poetry His Pillar. Herrick.
Ho, Everyone That Thirsteth. Housman.
Homage to a Government. Larkin.
Hope. Bowles.
Hope. Bradford.
Hope and Joy. Rossetti.
Hope's Song. Carlin.
Hopeless Desire Soon Withers and Dies. "W.
The Horrid Voice of Science. Lindsay.
Humpty Dumpty. Whitney.
Hymn (excerpt). Gilder.
If I Consider. Ise.
If Love's a Yoke. Berry.
If You Want to Know Me. De Sousa.
Impossibilities, to His Friend. Herrick.
In the Snowfall. Mechain.
The Incomparable Light. Eberhart.
Infants of Summer. Raphael.
Interlude. Roethke.
The International Brigade Arrives at Madrid. Neruda.
International Conference. Ellis.
Inventory. Parker.
The Jealous Enemy. Petrarch (Francesco Petrarca).
Jesus Only. Simpson.
John Darrow. Davidson.
The Lady of the Lake. Scott.
Lament. Gudmundsson.
Land of My Heart. Foulke.
Leaves Before the Wind. Sarton.
Letter to the Governors, June 8, 1783. Washington.
Life. Wilcox.
Lines Written beneath a Picture. Byron.
Lines Written on Hearing the News of the Death of Napoleon. Shelley.
The Lonely Road. Rand.
Love and Hope. Rossetti.
Love's Spite. De Vere.
Love Song. Ranaivo.
The Lover's Song. Sill.
Lucasia, Rosania and Orinda Parting at a Fountain, July 1663. Philips.
Madrigal: "Come, sable night." Ward.
Madrigal: To His Lady Selvaggia Vergiolesi... Cino da Pistoia.

Hope

Mae's Rent Party. Wilson, Jr.
Man Is a Weaver. Ibn Ezra.
Marriage. Clarke.
The Masters. Hope.
The Midnight Court. Merriman.
Mortality. Madgett.
Newark Abbey. Peacock.
A Nickle Bet. Knight.
Not Ours the Vows. Barton.
O Lord! My Hiding Place. Raffles.
Odes, IX. Hafiz.
An Old Song Resung. Graves.
The Old Year and the New. Flint.
On Her Loving Two Equally. Behn.
Orpheus. Davie.
The Overtakelessness of Those. Dickinson.
Parchman Farm Blues. White.
The Passing of the Poets. O Gnimh.
The Passionate Encyclopedia Britannica Reader to His Love. "Maggie".
Pastoral Ballad: Absence. Shenstone.
The Pearly Everlasting. Fewster.
The Pessimist. *Anonymous.*
The Phallic Symbol. Moore.
The Picture of Little T. C. in a Prospect of Flowers. Marvell.
The Pinta, the Nina and the Santa Maria. Tagliabue.
Plea for Hope. Carlin.
The Ploughman. Thomas.
Poem for Nana. Jordan.
Poem: "Love being what it is, full of betrayals." Herschberger.
A Poet's Wish: An Ode. Ramsay.
Political Greatness. Shelley.
Portrait of a Child. Untermeyer.
A Prayer. Gale.
A Prayer for Every Day. Davies.
De Profundis. Rossetti.
Puerperium. Waller.
The Quarry. Boscan.
Reality. Morgan.
Refracted Lights. Wooley.
Remembrance. Slonimski.
The Return of the Proconsul. Herbert.
Rise, Happy Morn. Tennyson.
The Rising Village. Goldsmith.
The River. Arnold.
The Roses of Queens. White.
The Rustler. *Anonymous.*
Samson Agonistes. Milton.
A Sea Boy on the Giddy Mast. Clare.
Shadows of Sails. Anderson.
She That Holds Me Under the Laws of Love. Gorges.
Shetland, Hill Dawn. Munro.
The Single Woman. Cornford.
Sit Down, Sad Soul. "Cornwall.

So Little Wanted. Corman.
Some Verses Upon the Burning of Our House, July 10th, l666. Bradstreet.
Song: Hamlet. "When a man becomes tired of his life" (parody). Poole.
The Song of the Mischievous Dog. Thomas.
Sonnet: "My simple heart, bred in provincial tenderness." Fraser.
Sonnets. Whitman.
Sonnets, II: "Our doom is in our being." Agee.
The Starling. Buchanan.
Steamboats, Viaducts, and Railways. Wordsworth.
The Steeple-Jack. Moore.
Stone Walls. Lippmann.
Sufi Quatrain. Rabi'a bint Isma'il.
The Supreme Sacrifice. Arkwright.
Swansea Town. *Anonymous.*
The Task. Cowper.
The Te Deum. *Anonymous.*
The Three Taverns: Out of Wisdom Has Come Love. Robinson.
Tired of Eating Kisses. Swart.
To —. Braithwaite.
To Cynthia. Clifford.
To God. Maurice.
To God, on His Sickness. Herrick.
To His Mistress in Absence. Tasso.
To Imagination. Bronte.
To Mrs. Diana Cecyll. Herbert of Cherbury.
To My Least Favorite Reviewer. Nemerov.
The Tourist from Syracuse. Justice.
The Travail of Passion. Yeats.
The Triumph of Beautie Song (excerpt). Shirley.
The Universe Is Closed and Has REMs. Starbuck.
Upon Bunce: Epigram. Herrick.
Upone Tabacco. Ayton [(or Aytoun)] Sir Robert.
Verse for Vestigials. Allen.
Vespers. Shepard.
Vicksburg. Hayne.
The Vigil. Reich.
La Vita Nuova. Dante Alighieri.
W. H. Eheu! Coleridge.
Waiting Rooms. Nemerov.
The Wall. Phelps.
Warp and Woof. Halbisch.
We See Jesus. Flint.
The Whale's Nature. *Anonymous.*
When We in Kind Embracements Had Agre'd. *Anonymous.*
The World's Bible. Flint.
Worry. Swarberg.
The Young Conquistador. Peterson.
Your Mouth. Shehabuddin.

Hopeless (ness)

Angelic Guidance. Newman.
At Darien Bridge. Dickey.
In Sepia. Anderson.

Lesbia loads me night & day with her curses. Catullus.
Remembering. Angelou.
This Beach Can Be Dangerous. Curnow.
A Weary Song to a Slow Sad Tune. Li Ch'ing-chao.

Horace

Epitaph for One Who Would Not Be Buried in Westminster Abbey. Pope.
To his Friend Ben. Johnson, of his Horace made English. Herbert of Cherbury.

Horizon (s)

Blackfish Poem. Acorn.
Buffalo Trace. Morgan.
City Girl. Bodenheim.
Ecstasy. Turner.
Flammonde. Robinson.
The Hawk. Knister.
Invitation of the Mirrors. McKeown.
Lent in a Year of War. Merton.
New Forms. Redgrove.
Steady Rain. Merrill.
The Thin Man. Justice.
This Particular Christian. Johnson.
To Julia de Burgos. Burgos.
Two Horses. Harjo.
Upon Leaving the Parole Board Hearing. Conyus.
What I Saw Passages 3. Duncan.

Horn (s)

Against Women's Fashions. Lydgate.
At Port Royal: Song of the Negro Boatman. Whittier.
The Ballad of Yukon Jake. Paramore.
The Balloon Man. Aldis.
Before the Carnival. Gunn.
Blue Peter. Lynch.
The Bull. Laughton.
The Bull Moose. Nowlan.
Caelica, XXXI. Greville.
Cattle. Nance.
The Composer's Winter Dream. Dubie.
The Deer. Asya (Asya Gray).
Discretion. *Anonymous.*
The Ear-Maker and the Mould-Mender. La Fontaine.
Evangeline. Longfellow.
The Executive's Death. Bly.
The Eyes of Texas. *Anonymous.*
The Field Mouse. Sharp.
Frankie's Trade. Kipling.
Good Susan, Be as Secret as You Can. *Anonymous.*
The Green Valley. Warner.
Haiku: "Coming from the woods..." Wright.
A History of Love. Williams.
Horn. Hayford.
I've Been Workin' on the Railroad. *Anonymous.*
In the Year of Many Conversions and the Private Soul. Ciardi.
Lament for Thomas MacDonagh. Ledwidge.
The Last Hunt. Thayer.
March. *Anonymous.*
Mercado. Pape.

On Seeing a Little Child Spin a Coin of Alexander the Great. Tennyson.
On Sir John Calf. *Anonymous.*
On the Cards and Dice. Ralegh.
A Parable. Kress.
Riddle: "Itum Paradisum all clothed in green." *Anonymous.*
Riddle: "Little Billy Breek." *Anonymous.*
Scala Coeli. Raine.
Sonnet: Mockado, Fustian, and Motley. Taylor.
Wedding Procession. Emanuel.
When the Days Grow Long. Bialik.
Wrath. Hollander.

Horrid

The Cenci. Shelley.
The Ghost. Churchill.
High O'er the Poop the Audacious Seas Aspire. Falconer.
A Low Trick. Burgess.
On the Staircase. Farjeon.
The Palace of Humbug. "Carroll.
There Was a Little Girl. Longfellow.

Horror (s)

Alive or Not. Purdy.
Alone up Here on the Mountain. *Anonymous.*
The Apparition. Melville.
"L'Apparition" of Gustave Moreau. Bottomley.
The Art of Preserving Health (excerpt). Armstrong.
Golfers. Updike.
Homage to William Cowper. Davie.
Ingmar Bergman's Seventh Seal. Duncan.
The Journey to the Insane Asylum. Lichtenstein.
The Laboratory. Browning.
Limerick: "A well-bred young girl of Gomorrah." *Anonymous.*
The Octopus. ""MacDiarmid.
Pacific Sonnets. Barker.
The Rising Village. Goldsmith.
To Paint a Water Lily. Hughes.
Upon the Double Murther of King Charles I... Philips.
Wisdom. Yeats.

Horse (back) (s)

Aids for Latin. Perry.
Another Charme for Stables. Herrick.
As I Was Standing in the Street. *Anonymous.*
The Bad Habit. Ford.
Bijou. Rutsala.
Birth. Dickey.
Cavalier Tunes. Browning.
Censorship. Waley.
Charioteer. Bynner.
The Chase. Davies.
Chiquita. Harte.
Clickety-Clack. Blackburn.
Country Wooing (parody) (excerpt). Squire.
Crepes Flambeau. Gallagher.

Cynthia on Horseback.
Ayres.
A Dance Chant. *Anonymous.*
The Dandy Horse.
Anonymous.
Daniel Webster's Horses.
Coatsworth.
The Dead Horse.
Anonymous.
A Dream of Horses.
Hughes.
An Elegy on the Death of
Dobbin, the Butterwoman's
Horse.
The English Language.
Story.
Epigram. *Anonymous.*
Father Riley's Horse.
Paterson.
The Flying Bum: 1944.
Plomer.
For Want of a Nail.
Anonymous.
Forgotten Objects on a Beach.
Excell.
A Fragment: "Not a drum
was heard." *Anonymous.*
The Funeral. Dubie.
The Gentleman. Lonzano.
Georgics. Virgil (Publius
Vergilius Maro).
The Gingerbread Man.
Anonymous.
Go to Sleepy. *Anonymous.*
Good-Bye Old Paint.
Anonymous.
Haiku: "Cherry-blossoms,
more." Onitsura.
The Haystack. Young.
The Heath. Boyd.
The Hippopotamus. Herford.
A horse and a flea and three
blind mice. *Anonymous.*
Horse Graveyard. Lape.
House of the Living. Vigee.
Ice Horses. Harjo.
In Teesdale. Young.
In the Bar. Vander Molen.
Kentucky Belle. Woolson.
The Kentucky Thoroughbred.
Riley.
The Last Campaign.
Lehmann.
Leaving Mendota, 1956.
Locke.
Letter from a Black Soldier.
Anderson.
Limerick: "Said a sporty
young person named
Groat." *Anonymous.*
Little Joe the Wrangler.
Thorp.
Loudon Hill, or, Drumclog.
Anonymous.
Love Poem. Comfort.
Mary Gulliver to Captain
Lemuel Gulliver. Swift.
Mathematics. Oppenheimer.
Merry-Go-Round. Hughes.
Mi Caballo Blanco.
Anonymous.
Monologue of the Rating
Morgan in Rutherford
County. MacIntyre.
Motorcycle. Pray.
My Bonny Black Bess.
Anonymous.
The Newmarket Song.
D'Urfey.
Nuances of a Theme by
Williams. Stevens.

Obsequies of Stuart.
Thompson.
Oedipus at Colonus.
Sophocles.
The Old Lady Who
Swallowed a Fly.
Anonymous.
Old Men Pitching Horseshoes.
Kennedy.
The Old Sussex Road.
Serraillier.
The Old Whim Horse.
Dyson.
Omens. Hamburger.
On a Horse and a Goat.
Lister.
On Frosty Days. Campbell.
On Scratchbury Camp.
Sassoon.
On Some South African
Novelists. Campbell.
One Poet Visits Another.
Davies.
Original Sin: A Short Story.
Warren.
Parable. Wilbur.
Pattonio, the Pride of the
Plain. *Anonymous.*
Poor Old Horse.
Anonymous.
Praying. Kavanagh.
Proud Riders. Davis.
Proust's Madeleine. Rexroth.
Richard Dick upon a Stick.
Anonymous.
The Rider Victory. Muir.
Riding. Grossman.
Robert Barnes, Fellow Fine.
Anonymous.
Sagebrush. Wood.
The Sailor's Grace.
Anonymous.
The Song of Samuel Sweet.
Causley.
Spring at Fort Okanogan.
Wilson.
St. Valentine's Day. Blunt.
Straws. Coatsworth.
Swift. Irwin.
Taking Leave of a Friend.
Li Po.
The Task. Cowper.
Tasmania. Smith.
Terenure. Salkeld.
Thank You. Koch.
Themes. Glover.
Theological. Fadiman.
To Fuscus Aristus. Horace.
To Women. Hugo.
Tonto. Koertge.
Tune. Rakosi.
Two at Showtime. Brabant.
Two Horses. Merwin.
Unseen Horses. Grayston.
Upon Appleton House, to My
Lord Fairfax. Marvell.
The War God's Horse Song.
Anonymous.
Watching the Out-Door
Movie Show. Struthers.
Watering the Horse. Bly.
White Horses. Howard.
The Wind Sprang up at Four
O'Clock. Eliot.
Woodcut. Wilson.
Your Air of My Air.
Margenat.
The Youth Dreams. Rilke.
Host (s)
The Book of Day-Dreams.
Moore.
A Child's Wish. Ryan.

The Deserted Pasture.
Carman.
Divina Commedia.
Longfellow.
Dream of the Lynx. Haines.
Etruscan Notebook.
Clementelli.
God of the World. Najara.
God, Whom Shall I Compare
to Thee? Halevi.
Immolation. Farren.
Lay of the Last Frontier.
Hersey.
News of a Baby. Riddell.
The Night-March. Melville
Penelope. Laederach.
Saint Apollinare in Classe.
Wilson.
Saint Germain-en-Laye.
Dowson.
The Task. Cowper.
Water. Hughes.
Hostess
Don't Say You Like
Tchaikowsky. Rosner.
Mrs. Brown and the Famous
Author. King.
Hostile
The New Calf. Vaughan.
Hostile bands
The Assault on the Fortress.
Dwight.
Cornwallis's Surrender.
Anonymous.
Public Library. Abse.
Hot
Against Death. Redgrove.
Alligator on the Escalator.
Merriam.
The Ambience of Love.
Schneider.
Astrophel and Stella, XLVI.
Sidney.
Blow, Wind, Blow! and Go,
Mill, Go. Mother Goose.
But He Was Cool. Lee.
The Cat of the House. Ford.
Changsha Shoe Factory.
Barnstone.
Come, Gentle Death!
Watson.
Custer (2). Baker.
Davy Dumpling.
Anonymous.
The Dead. Williams.
Early June. Dickey.
For Them. Brownstein.
Good Friday. *Anonymous.*
Good Friday. Nims.
The Hit. Drinkwater.
Hornpipe. Sitwell.
Hot Ir'n! Barker.
A Hot Time in the Old Town.
Hayden.
The Jazz of This Hotel.
Lindsay.
John Coil. *Anonymous.*
Joseph Mica. *Anonymous.*
Matrimony. Williams.
Ming the Merciless.
Hagedorn.
The Mowing Crew.
Wormser.
Oracle at Delphi. Bagg.
Piere Vidal Old. Pound.
Pleasures. Levertov.
Robert's Rules of Order.
Peterson.
Robin. Allen.
Rope and Drum. Currie.
Smells. Morley.

Some Hot, Some Cold.
Campion.
Song: "Now let us honor with
violin and flute." Sarton.
Song of the Seaweed. Cook.
A Stanza Completed.
Mansel.
"The Time Has Come," the
Walrus Said. "Carroll.
Weeksville Women. Loftin.
Zoo Dream. Barker.
Hot dog
Ingestion. McDonald.
The Mad Rapist of Calaveras
County. Winslow.
My father owns the butcher
shop. *Anonymous.*
Hotel (s)
Dispatch Number Sixteen.
Fetherling.
The Evans Country. Amis.
Following Van Gogh
(Avignon, 1982). Puziss.
Image of City. Henson.
In This Hotel. Carnevali.
Life Story. Williams.
Hound (s)
All Out and Down.
Leadbelly.
The Angry Poet. O'Connor.
Baby's Awake Now.
Berkson.
Blessing the Hounds.
Winter.
Blue Peter. Lynch.
Childhood. Read.
Cruel Boys. Soto.
Dirge for Two Clavichords
and Bowler Hat.
Smithyman.
An Evening Walk (excerpt).
Wordsworth.
The Foray of Con O'Donnell,
A.D. 1495. MacCarthy.
The Fox. Clare.
Gluskap's Hound. Roberts.
The Grip. Kennelly.
Hero's Portion. Montague.
Hold. Chalmers.
Hound Voice. Yeats.
In Hospital: Poona (II).
Lewis.
Love Me, Love My Dog.
Crawford.
Madman's Song. Wylie.
The Moments He Remembers.
Van Doren.
Moon Rock. Mally.
My Laddie's Hounds.
Easter.
My Last Terrier. "Halsham.
Polly. Gay.
Rural Lines after Breughel.
Krapf.
Shirley Temple Surrounded by
Lions. Elmslie.
Song for "The Jaquerie".
Lanier.
Two Songs of a Fool. Yeats.
The White Stag. Pound.
Hour (s)
About Women. Putnam.
Adultery at the Plaza.
Thompson.
Amanda Dreams She Has
Died and Gone to the
Elysian Fields. Kumin.
Amazing Grace. *Anonymous.*
Amoretti, LXXXVI.
Spenser.
Another Letter to Joseph
Bruchac. Anderson.

At Lincoln. Adams.
Auguries of Innocence. Blake.
Autumn Woods. Bryant.
B Stands for Bear. Belloc.
Bell Speech. Wilbur.
Beyond Labelling Me. Di Cicco.
The Body Is Like Roots Stretching. Reznikoff.
Caesar and Pompey. Chapman.
Clocks. Locker.
Compensation. Emerson.
Cows. Reeves.
Dawn on the Night-Journey. Rossetti.
Days and Nights. Moore.
The Days of Our Youth. Anonymous.
A Description of Beauty, Translated out of Marino. Daniel.
Dirge for the Year. Shelley.
Eden Bower. Rossetti.
End of the Picnic. Webb.
Epitaph. Driscoll.
An Epithalamion, or Marriage Song. Donne.
The Faerie Queene. Spenser.
Fainne Gael An Lae. Milligan.
The Farmer's Ingle. Fergusson.
The Fate of the Cabbage Rose. Irwin.
The First Solitude. Gongora y Argote.
For a Masseuse and Prostitute. Rexroth.
The Hands-Across-the-Sea Poem. Squire.
Happy the Man. Dryden.
He Abjures Love. Hardy.
A Hill. Hecht.
Hippopotamothalamion. Wheelock.
Hobart Town, Van Diemen's Land. Porter.
Homosexual Sonnets. Pitchford.
Hope. Johnson.
The Hour of Prayer. Hoy.
An Hour with Thee. Scott.
How to Get There. O'Hara.
Hymns for the Amusement of Children. Smart.
I Closed My Shutters Fast Last Night. Johnson.
In Memoriam A.H.H., XII. Tennyson.
Intimations of Immortality from Recollections of Early Childhood. Wordsworth.
Life Owes Me Nothing. Anonymous.
Limerick: "There once was a man, named Power." White.
Love Is a Law. Anonymous.
Love's Witchery. Lodge.
The Lovers. Aiken.
Low Tide. Roberts.
The Maine Trail. McGiffert.
Meditations for July 25, 1666. Pain.
Message. Richardson.
The Minute before Meeting. Hardy.
Moriturus. "Marie.
Nativity Song. Jacopone da Todi.

Night Feeding. Rukeyser.
Night-Music: Time Exposures. Rukeyser.
No! Cook.
Ode of Anacreon. Moore.
Old and New Art. Rossetti.
On Man. Landor.
The Other One Comes to Her. Aldis.
Out of French. Sedley.
An Outcry upon Opportunity. Shakespeare.
Paradise Lost. Milton.
Prayer. Moss.
The Pysidanthera. Bristol.
Renewal. Cromwell.
Rest Hour. Johnston.
Resurrection. Sackville.
Riddle: "King Charles the First walked and talked." Anonymous.
The Rose of Eden. Phillips.
Rudolph Is Tired of the City. Brooks.
San Francisco Falling. Markham.
Sent from the Capital to Her Elder Daughter. Otomo of Sakanone [(or Sakanoe)].
Shadows. Claudel.
Sheep in the Sheade. Barnes.
Shoplifters. Stanton.
Sir Peter's Leman. Anonymous.
Sleep. Imbs.
Some wretched creature, savior take. Dickinson.
The Stable. Hoffman.
Sweet Voice of the Garb. Geilt.
Tara Is Grass. Anonymous.
Tattoos. Wright.
They Found Him Sitting in a Chair. Gregory.
Thirty-Eight. Smith.
Those Last, Late Hours of Christmas Eve. Welte.
The Thoughts That Move the Heart of Man. Oakley.
To a Calvinist in Bali. Millay.
To a Very Young Lady. Waller.
To D'Annunzio: Lines from the Sea. Nichols.
To Music. Seymour.
To Pikes Peak. Hills.
Turkey in the Straw. Anonymous.
Warning. Hughes.
We Cannot Kindle. Arnold.
When night is almost done. Dickinson.
Whoroscope. Beckett.
Will. Wilcox.

House (s)
Absence. Barnes.
Address to a Child during a Boistrous Winter Evening. Wordsworth.
After Midnight. Vildrac.
The Albion Battleship Calamity. McGonagall.
Architect. Nicholl.
The Arrow of Desire. Anonymous.
Asmodai. Hill.
Aubade. Larkin.
August. Pyle.
Aunt Alice in April. Matchett.

Beached Whales Off Margate. Dunn.
La Bella Donna Della Mia Mente. Wilde.
Ben Jonson Entertains a Man from Stratford. Robinson.
Blueline. Belford.
Bombers. Day-Lewis.
Bouncing Ball. Watson.
Builders. Flexner.
Burning. Kinnell.
The Cambric Shirt. Anonymous.
Careers. Welish.
Childhood Is the Kingdom Where Nobody Dies. Millay.
The Chinese Banyan. Meredith.
Christmas Eve in Whitneyville, 1955. Hall.
The Church in the Heart. Beer.
The City Dead-House. Whitman.
The Confessor. Belli.
Daufuskie. Evans.
The Dazzling Day. MacAdams.
The Demon Lover. Anonymous.
Denunciation; or, Unfrock'd Again. Whalen.
Directive. Frost.
The Dispossessed. Berryman.
The Domicile of John. Pope.
Doors. Plantier.
Dream House. Newell.
The Dual Site. Hamburger.
Dufferin, Simcoe, Grey. Atwood.
The Dykes. Kipling.
Earth Tremor in Lugano. Kirkup.
Elegy for the Silent Voices and the Joiners of Everything. Patchen.
Emergency at 8. Hewitt.
England's Prayer. Blundell of Crosby.
Evening. Manger.
Evening Quatrains. Cotton.
The Eyes of Flesh. Hochman.
The Faerie Queene. Spenser.
The Fall of the House of Usher. Whittemore.
The Family. Lydston.
Far from the Heart of Culture. Auden.
For Though the Caves Were Rabbited. Thoreau.
From Scars Where Kestrels Hover. Auden.
A Gentleman of the Old School. Dobson.
The Goblin. Fyleman.
Going Away. Nemerov.
The Grandmother Came down to Visit Us. Bruchac.
The Gulistan. Sa'di.
Haiku: "For some time." Anonymous.
Happening. Honig.
Hen Under Bay-Tree. Pitter.
The Hermit. Halpern.
The Hill Wife. Frost.
Home. Guest.
The House. Bowering.
The House Beautiful. Anonymous.

The House Carpenter's Wife. Anonymous.
The House Carpenter (with music). Anonymous.
House Fear. Frost.
A House in Taos. Hughes.
A House of Mercy. Smith.
The House with Nobody in It. Kilmer.
Hut Window. Celan.
I Done Got So Thirsty That My Mouth Waters at the Thought of Rain. Jones.
I Love the Woods. Neidus.
In My Crib. Ceravolo.
In the House of the Judge. Smith.
In Time of War. Auden.
An Interview. Gransden.
Iowa, June. Browne.
Is It True That You Live Where There Is Sorrow. Anonymous.
Jehovah, God, Who Dwelt of Old. Amis.
Jubilate Herbis. Farber.
The Katskills Kiss Romance Goodbye. Reed.
Lady Day. Fallon.
Lament of the Mangaire Sugach. Magrath.
Lancaster County Tragedy. Kay.
Leady-Day, an' Ridden House. Barnes.
Letters from an Irishman to a Rat. Logue.
Life after Death. Thomas.
The Life and Death of Jason. Morris.
Lines to a World-Famous Poet... Nash.
Le Livre Est sur la Table. Ashbery.
Love That's Pure, Itself Disdaining. Gruber.
The Man of the House. Hinkson.
The Mariner's Wife. Mickle.
Master's in the Garden Again. Ransom.
Maybe You Cannot Comprehend. Villanueva.
The Meaning. Gustafson.
Meditations in Time of Civil War. Yeats.
Men at Forty. Justice.
Ming the Merciless. Hagedorn.
Missing. Auden.
Moon Eclipse Exorcism. Anonymous.
Morning After. Vinz.
Mr. Ibister. Anonymous.
My Shepherd Is the Living Lord. Sternhold.
My True Memory. Asya (Asya Gray).
The Nativity Chant. Scott.
The Neighbors Help Him Build His House. Anonymous.
Neoplatonic Soliloquy. Babcock.
No Continuing City. Longley.
Nocturne, Central Park South. Sissman.
The Noodle-Vendor's Flute. Enright.
Notes on a Life to Be Lived. Warren.

Nothing-At-All. *Anonymous.*
The Nurse's Lament. Coleridge.
Oh, How My Love with a Whirling Power. Tu-kehu and Wetea.
Ol' Doc' Hyar. Campbell.
Old Houses. D'Lettuso.
The Old Houses of Flanders. Ford.
Old Log House. Tippett.
On Blenheim House. Evans.
On the Hall at Stowey. Tomlinson.
On the Night in Question. Goedicke.
The Onset. Frost.
Out of the Old House, Nancy. Carleton.
Packing a Photograph from Firenze. Matchett.
The Paper Cutter. Ignatow.
Paradise Regained. Milton.
Paris: This April Sunset Completely Utters. Cummings.
Parliament Hill Fields. Plath.
A Poet's Epitaph. Wordsworth.
Quiet Desperation. Simpson.
The Rain. *Anonymous.*
Rain. Haines.
Rain on a Cottage Roof. Laughton.
Rain on the Green Grass. *Anonymous.*
Reflections on a Womb Which Is Called "Vacant." Hathaway.
Rest Only in the Grave. Mangan.
Resurrection. Kaschnitz.
Ringleted Youth of My Love. *Anonymous.*
Roan Stallion. Jeffers.
Rock Climbing. Cooper.
A Roman Roman. Del Monte.
A Room I Once Knew. Birnbaum.
Row of Houses. Quinn.
The Ruined Cabin. King.
Rushing. Young Bear.
Salem, Massachusetts. Muir.
Samuel Brown. Cary.
Saul. Sterling.
The Seven Houses. Brown.
Shango I. *Anonymous.*
The Shiny Little House. Hayes.
The Snail. Conkling.
Softly, White and Pure. Fulton.
Somerset Wassail. *Anonymous.*
Song: "I came to the door of the House of Love." Noyes.
The Song of the Forest Ranger. Bashford.
Songs of T'ang. Confucius.
The Stack. Snaith.
Strand on the Green. *Anonymous.*
Stray Animals. Tate.
Subversive. Benet.
Sudden Shower. Clare.
Summer in a Small Town. Gregg.
Tamar: Part III. Jeffers.
The Tenancy. Gilmore.

They. Thomas.
The Things. Aiken.
Things. Simpson.
Thinking of Love. Jennings.
Three-Handed Fugue. Gotlieb.
To His Father on Praising the Honest Life of the Peasant. E'tesami.
Tree. Wilson.
The Two Gretels. Morgan.
An Urban Convalescence. Merrill.
A Veld Eclogue: The Pioneers. Campbell.
Verses on Blenheim. Martial (Marcus Valerius Martialis).
Visits to St. Elizabeths. Bishop.
Wanted. Silverstein.
Ward Two. Webb.
Weapons. Wickham.
Wedlock. Noll.
Wellington. Manhire.
The West. Muir.
When My Grandmother Died. Cornish.
Where Knock Is Open Wide. Roethke.
Wide Walls. *Anonymous.*
The Windows. Loewinsohn.
Winter Fairyland in Vermont. Osgood.
A Winter without Snow. McClatchy.
A World within a War. Read.
Wraith. Millay.
Yellow Woman Speaks. Woo.
Young Benjie. *Anonymous.*
Your House. *Anonymous.*

Household
By Vows of Love Together Bound. Fitch.
Danse Russe. Williams.
Deacon Morgan. Madgett.
In Memoriam A.H.H., XCIV. Tennyson.
Mythics. Chasin.
New York. Gunn.
Saadi. Emerson.
Shutting the Curtains. Noll.
A Small Farm. Hartnett.

Housewife
Ghost. Morgenstern.
How many times these low feet staggered. Dickinson.
The spider holds a silver ball. Dickinson.

Howl (ed) (ing) (s)
African Moonrise. Campbell.
December Day, Hoy Sound. Brown.
The Drenching Night Drags On. O Rathaille.
Earthly. Wedde.
Homage to Mistress Bradstreet. Berryman.
In the Dock. De La Mare.
The Monster. Kuzma.
One-Line Poems from a New Statesman Competition. Prince.
Small Town. Joyce.
Tales of the Islands, IX. Walcott.
They Say, in Other Days. Gray.

Hudson
My Plan. Chute.
New York. Garcia Lorca.

Wild Dreams of a New Beginning. Ferlinghetti.

Hue (s)
Constancy to an Ideal Object. Coleridge.
If Pope Had Written 'Break, Break, Break'. Squire.
Paradise Lost. Milton.
A Summer Storm. Whitehead.
The Translation of Verver. Berssenbrugge.

Hug (s)
The Beauty of Dawn. Mnthali.
A Boy's Mother. Riley.
Edwin A. Nelms. Nelms.
The Ghost of Lucrece: To Vesta. Middleton.
The Lord's Chameleons. Klappert.
Negro Reel (with music). *Anonymous.*
The Rime of the Ancient Feminist (excerpt). Markman.
Rise You Up, My True Love. *Anonymous.*
She Didn't Even Wave. Ai.
Sonnets: A Sequence on Profane Love. Boker.
The Stalin Epigram. Mandelstam.
Whatever You Say Say Nothing. Heaney.

Huge
After the fiercest pangs of hot desire. Duke.
Early Arrival: Sydney. Smith.
The Faerie Queene. Spenser.
Family Life. Laing.
The Gate. Muir.
Metamorphosis. Porter.
Not Quite Spring. Lifshin.
On the Author of the Treatise of Human Nature. Beattie.
R.M.S. Titanic. Cronin.
A Sea-Change: For Harold. Langland.
The Word. Weiss.

Hulk (ing)
The Derelict. Foote.
Human Things. Nemerov.
The Legion of Iron. Ridge.
Planning the Perfect Evening. Dove.
The River Map and We're Done. Olson.

Hull
Curse of a Fisherman's Wife. Chalpin.
The Dalesman's Litany. *Anonymous.*
Maiden Lane. Lee.
The Way to Jerusalem (excerpt). *Anonymous.*

Hum (ming) (s)
Alicia's Bonnet. Pullen.
The Darkened Mind. Lowell.
False Prophet. O'Malley.
Homing. Saner.
I, Woman. McClaurin.
Inscription for a Fountain on a Heath. Coleridge.
Into the Book. Grossman.
Langaig. Hugo.
Luss Village. Smith.
A Mongoloid Child Handling Shells on the Beach. Snyder.

The Novices. Levertov.
Orpheus. Roberts.
The Railroad Cars Are Coming (with music). *Anonymous.*
The Rainy Summer. Meynell.
Remedies. Soto.
Schubertiana. Transtromer.

Human (ity) (kind) (s)
Against the False Magicians. McGrath.
Alma Mater. Osborn.
And When I Am Entombed. Emerson.
Andre Chenier. Tsvetayeva.
Art. Emerson.
Asking for It. Sassoon.
Assignment: Descriptive Essay. Willis.
At an Exhibition of Historical Paintings, Hobart. Smith.
The auctioneer of parting. Dickinson.
Avoiding News by the River. Merwin.
Bagpipe Music. ""MacDiarmid.
The Bat. Roethke.
Behold, One of Several Little Christs... Patchen.
Benediction for the Tent. *Anonymous.*
Benevolence. Akenside.
Beware. Shorter.
Black Mother. Da Cruz.
Breakthrough. Sinclair.
The Buddha at Kamakura. Kipling.
Burma Hills. Gutteridge.
By the Waters of Babylon. Fondane.
Cave of Staffa, I. Wordsworth.
Cheyenne Mountain. Jackson.
A Chinese Vase. Hirsch.
Christmas Still Lives. Hawkes.
Cleanliness. Lamb.
Coriolanus. Shakespeare.
The Courteous Pagan Shall Condemne. Williams.
The Dancing Bear. Southey.
Darkness. Clough.
Deathwatch. Harper.
The Devil's Advice to Story-Tellers. Graves.
The Diaspora. Auden.
Distractions and the Human Crowd. Smith.
A Divine Image. Blake.
The Dwarf. Locklin.
E Tenebris. Wilde.
Endymion. Keats.
The Entertainer. Beaver.
Epistle to Dr. Blacklock. Burns.
Epitaph. Chiabrera.
Eternal God, Whose Power Upholds. Tweedy.
Eternal God Whose Searching Eye Doth Scan. Poteat.
Ex Libris. Upson.
Fears in Solitude. Coleridge.
Five Lyrics from "Good for Nothing Man". Ptichford.
For Angus MacLeod. Smith.
For the One Who Would Take Man's Life in His Hands. Schwartz.
Geronimo. McGaffey.

The Goal of Intellectual Man. Eberhart.
God's-Acre. Longfellow.
Goldfish on the Writing Desk. Brod.
The Grave's Cherub. Clouts.
Handful of Ashes. Rubin.
He Is My Countryman. Slonimski.
Heard on the Mountain. Hugo.
Hmmmm, 14. Scalapino.
Homage to Theodore Dreiser on the Centennial of His Birth (excerpt). Warren.
Hospital. Shapiro.
How many wise men and heroes. Ch'iu Chin.
Hunger Strike. Franklin.
Hymn to Intellectual Beauty. Shelley.
I'm Here. Ignatow.
I Thirst... Bregy.
In Time Like Air. Sarton.
Incident. MacCaig.
The Internationale. Degeyter.
The Judas Goat. Musgrave.
Lady Clara Vere De Vere. Tennyson.
Lay Your Sleeping Head, My Love. Auden.
Legend of His Lyre. Schmuller.
A Letter to Auden. Phillips.
Letter to Wagoner from Port Townsend. Hugo.
Life Is So Short. Hall.
The Line of Beauty. O'Shaughnessy.
Lines on Carmen Sylva. Lazarus.
March, Upstate. Bronk.
The Marriage of Heaven and Hell. Blake.
Matthew V: 29-30. Mahon.
Mimma Bella. Lee-Hamilton.
The Minstrel. Beattie.
Montana Remembered from Albuquerque; 1982. Rogers.
Museum-Piece. Brown.
Myths. Klauck.
Nativity. Sarton.
Night Falls on China. Auden.
Night Song for a Woman. Purdy.
Nihil Humani Alienum. Coan.
Old Clothes. Hey.
Our Love Shall Be the Brightness. Watson.
Pan-Asian Holiday Tour. Syquia.
Parting. Raine.
A Prayer for My Son. Yeats.
Prayer in Affliction. Storey.
Prelude. Gibson.
The Priory of St Saviour, Glendalough. Davie.
Promises, VIII. Founding Fathers.... Warren.
Race Riot, Tulsa, 1921. Olds.
Reading in the Night. Fuller.
Recollection. Govan.
The Sea-Mew. Browning.
Self-Portrait. Cassian.

Silences: A Dream of Governments. Valentine.
Some Things You Cannot Will to Men. Isenhour.
A Son Lit. Johnson.
Songs to Survive the Summer. Hass.
Sonnet: The Wild Duck's Nest. Wordsworth.
Spring 1943. Fuller.
Stars Fade. Hirshbein.
Strawberries in November. Neilson.
The Suicide. Oates.
The Telephone. Field.
There Is So Much of Loneliness. Anonymous.
These Past Years: Passages 10. Duncan.
A Thought of the Nile. Hunt.
The Three Kingdoms of Nature. Lessing.
To a Lady That Desired Me I Would Bear My Part with Her in a Song. Lovelace.
To God. Maurice.
To the Mother of Christ, the Son of Man. Meynell.
To the Mothers. Toller.
The Tomb of Lt. John Learmonth, A.I.F. Manifold.
Tossed on a Sea of Trouble. Archilochus.
The Trackless Deeps. Shelley.
Two Girls... Reznikoff.
Volto Sciolto e Pensieri Stretti. Mangan.
Walking Parker Home. Kaufman.
When Was It That the Particles Became. Stevens.
The Wind-Flower. Very.
The Witnesses. Kennedy.
Words in the Mourning Time. Hayden.
World's Bliss. Notley.
Zimmer's Hard Dream. Zimmer.

Humble
Can't You Live Humble? Anonymous.
Cato's Address to His Troops in Lybia. Rowe.
Clams. Moss.
A Conceited Man. Anonymous.
Epitaphium Vivi Auctoris 1792. Walpole.
A Fancy. Anonymous.
The Gardener's Cat. Chalmers.
The God-maker, Man. Marquis.
Gun Teams. Frankau.
Hunger in New York City. Ortiz.
Jewish Arabic Liturgies. Anonymous.
Let the Deep Organ Swell. Pise.
The Names of the Humble. Murray.
No Sweeter Thing. Love.
Otoe County in Nebraska. Kloefkorn.
The Praise of Pindar in Imitation of Horace His Second Ode, Book 4. Cowley.

Proper Pride. Lawrence.
The Stars Have Given Me a Hard Fate. Stampa.
To Show How Humble. Anonymous.
When Israel. Scott.

Humiliation
The Desolate Rhythm of Dying Recurs. Smith.
The Hunter. O'Hara.
Paradise Lost. Milton.
Privation. Carruth.

Humility
A bee his burnished carriage. Dickinson.
Canticle of the Sun. Francis of Assisi.
Foetus. Haring.
The Lark's Song. Blake.
The Magnanimous. Kay.
Proper Pride. Lawrence.
Proud of my broken heart since thou didst break it. Dickinson.
Proud Resignation. Marcus.
Release. Schjeldahl.
To God the Son. Constable.
Trimming the Sails. Miller.

Hummingbird (s)
How Came She to Such Poppy-Breath? Volborth.
O Night Flower. Barbeitos.
Suspended Moment. Davenport.
Unless We Guard Them Well. Merchant.
Vision. Eberhart.
What the Light Was Like. Clampitt.

Humor
Epitaph on Laurence Sterne. Garrick.
Hadrian's Address to His Soul When Dying. Hadrian.
Marriage. Lowell.
A Suite of Six Pieces for Siskind. Logan.
Whimper of Awakening Passion. Jones.

Hump
The Minstrel's Last Lay. Barth.
On First Looking in on Blodgett's Keats's "Chapman's Homer." Starbuck.
The Sexual Life of the Camel. Anonymous.
The Way to Hump a Cow. Cummings.

Hundred
American Commencement. Boyajian.
The Animal Store. Field.
Barbarossa. Rueckert.
Cut the Cables. Wilson.
The Festival. Prokosch.
For Patrick, Aetat: LXX. Betjeman.
Holly Beareth Berries (excerpt). Anonymous.
Independence. Mason.
Little Hundred. Anonymous.
Love. Calverley.
On a Magazine Sonnet. Loines.
Out of Time (excerpt). Slessor.
The Pilot's Walk. Gerlach.
Poor Little Johnny. Anonymous.

The Portrait of a Florentine Lady. Reese.
The Revenge of Rain-In-The-Face. Longfellow.
Rye Whisky. Anonymous.
The Seven Ages of Elf-Hood. Field.
Sonnet XIX: "After having slain very many beasts." Labe.
Space and Time. Scroggie.
Whitman's Ride for Oregon. Butterworth.
Winter Twilight. Lipsitz.
Yung Wind. Confucius.

Hungary
Happiness. Sandburg.
An Immorality. Pound.
Music of Hungary. Aldrich.

Hunger (s) (hungry)
The Aeneid. Virgil (Publius Vergilius Maro).
Affinity. Thomas.
The Affinity. Wickham.
Animal. Eastman.
Answering Dance. Root.
Artichoke. Taylor.
Bagman O'Reilly's Curse. Murray.
Beyond Labelling Me. Di Cicco.
The Cabin Creek Flood. Anonymous.
The Cattle Thief. Tekahionwake.
Charter Boat. Hindley.
The Death Circus. Tranter.
Directions. Matthews.
A Divine Image. Blake.
Eating. Gibbons.
Eclogues. Virgil (Publius Vergilius Maro).
Esthetique du Mal. Stevens.
Feast. Millay.
The Feather. Watkins.
Fishermen at Dawn. Meissner.
The Great St. Bernard. Rogers.
Harvest Song. Toomer.
Holy Thursday. Blake.
Hungering Hearts. Anonymous.
In My First Hard Springtime. Welch.
Kane. O'Brien.
Kreutzer Sonata. Hughes.
The Last Fish. Spacks.
Late Rising. Prevert.
The Light Woman's Song. Sherwin.
The Makers. Kell.
The Masked Shrew. Gardner.
Mundus et Infans. Auden.
Museum of Cruel Days. Hugo.
The Name of Jesus. Newton.
Not Being Wise. Elson.
O Mad Spring, One Waits. Moore.
O Taste and See. Levertov.
Old Storm. Phillips.
Ordination. Mary Immaculate.
Our Hunting Fathers. Auden.
Pit Viper. Momaday.
Poet's Bread. Mary Philip.
Prelude to an Evening. Ransom.
Prevision. Murray.

The Rampage. Williams.
Reflection from Rochester.
  Empson.
The Return of Robinson
  Jeffers. Hass.
Rusia en 1931. Hass.
Sea Things. MacEwen.
Someone Could Certainly Be
  Found. Scott.
Stages. Macnab.
The Taste of Prayer. Seager.
The Thocht. Soutar.
Trinity Place. McGinley.
Trumpet and Flute.
  Hernaes.
Two Married. Frazee-Bower.
The Vacuum. Nemerov.

Hunt (ed) (ing) (s)
Against Hope. Cowley.
Aristocrats. Douglas.
The Bat. Pitter.
La Belle Sauvage. Duvar.
Broke and Hungry.
  Jefferson.
Burning Hills. Ondaatje.
Down in Lehigh Valley.
  Anonymous.
Groundhog. *Anonymous.*
A Hand. Spencer.
The Heptalogia. Swinburne.
The Hunt. De La Mare.
The Hunt. Spofford.
The Hunt Is Up.
  Anonymous.
The Hunters of Men.
  Whittier.
The Hunting of the Gods.
  Anonymous.
The Huntress. Johnston.
I Wonder Why. Pluvkaq.
In the Field. Janik.
India. Turner.
It Is Hard to Catch Trout.
  Piuvkaq.
The Keepsake Corporation.
  Fisher.
The Kingfishers. Olson.
A Little Scraping. Jeffers.
Lord Rendal. *Anonymous.*
The Maids of Simcoe.
  Anonymous.
Muckle-Mou'd Meg.
  Ballantine.
Nephelidia. Swinburne.
New England's Chevy Chase,
  April 19, 1775. Hale.
Progress. Lamport.
Rural Lines after Breughel.
  Krapf.
Sacrifice of a Red Squirrel.
  Langland.
Scatheless. Wilkinson.
Solon's Song. D"Urfey.
Springer Mountain. Dickey.
Sulpicia's Rival. Tibullus.
Three Jovial Gentlemen.
  Hoffman.
Valse Oubliee. Heath-Stubbs.
Viking Dublin: Trial Pieces.
  Heaney.
Walrus Hunting. Aua.

Hunter (s)
Amen. Mutis.
Autumn Dawn. Machado.
Blessing the Hounds.
  Winter.
Diana's Hunting-Song.
  Dryden.
Early Morning Feed.
  Redgrove.
Evangeline. Longfellow.
The Four Deer. Jones.

The Great South Land
  (excerpt). Ingamells.
Hidden Bow. Temkin.
The Hunt of the Poem.
  Behm.
The Hunter's Song.
  "Cornwall.
The Hunters of Kentucky.
  Woodworth.
The Hunters of the Deer.
  Zieroth.
In the Caves of Auvergne.
  Turner.
Indian Song. Johnson.
Kob Antelope. *Anonymous.*
Last Things, Black Pines at 4
  a.m. Lowell.
Lord Epsom. Belloc.
Man and Beast. Dyment.
The Moon Is Teaching Bible.
  Zelda.
My Father's Wedding 1924.
  Bly.
Requiem. Stevenson.
Sir Lionel. *Anonymous.*
To Morning. Blake.

Hurl
Black Warrior. Jordan.
Coasting toward Midnight at
  the Southeastern Fair.
  Bottoms.
Living. Howells.

Hurricane
An Antipastoral Memory of
  One Summer. Smith.
Jeronimo's House. Bishop.
Solar Signals. Schuck.

Hurry
The Casual Man. Glover.
A Classical Quatrain.
  Goodman.
Elegy on the Dust. Gunn.
Epitaph at Hadleigh, Suffolk.
  Anonymous.
I Got to Roll. *Anonymous.*
Indictment. Ritter.
Life. Hare.
Moon Song. Conkling.
O, Gambler, Git Up Off o'
  Yo' Knees. *Anonymous.*
Signs of Winter. Clare.
The Strath of Kildonan.
  Morris.
Treasure Hunt. Warren.
Van Winkle. Crane.

Hurt (ing) (s)
The Akathistos Hymn.
  Anonymous.
Al the Meryere. *Anonymous.*
Another Letter to Joseph
  Bruchac. Anderson.
Aurora Leigh. Browning.
By-Products. Wormser.
Charm for a Sudden Stitch.
  Anonymous.
A Contempt for Dylan
  Thomas. Watson.
Cynthia in the Snow.
  Brooks.
Driven by desire I did this
  deed. Wyatt.
Eclipse. Fagg.
An Emblem of Two Foxes.
  Spacks.
Everything: Eloy, Arizona,
  1956. Anthony ("AI").
A Father's Heart Is Touched.
  Hoffenstein.
The First. Mannes.
For Fear. Creeley.
The Gift. Ciardi.

Good-Bye for a Long Time.
  Fuller.
Helpe Me to Seke. Wyatt.
Here. Thomas.
I'll Never Use Tobacco.
  Anonymous.
I'm Through with You.
  Anonymous.
If Waker Care, If Sodayne
  Pale Coulor. Wyatt.
In Her Only Way. Graves.
Jean Richepin's Song.
  Trench.
Jesus to Those Who Pass By.
  Anonymous.
Jone o' Grinfield.
  Anonymous.
The Kingis Quhair: The
  Coming of Love. James I,
Leaves of Grass. Whitman
Lines to His Son on Reaching
  Adolescence. Logan.
Luveli Ter of Loveli Eyghe.
  Anonymous.
A Mistress without Compare.
  Orleans.
Moonlight. Teasdale.
The Mountain Woman.
  Heyward.
A! My Herte, A! What Aileth
  The. Wyatt.
Ode: "Who can support the
  anguish of love?" Ibn al-
  Arabi.
On Apis the Prizefighter.
  Lucilius [(or Lucillius)].
The One before the Last.
  Brooke.
A Prayer for a Sleeping Child.
  Davies.
Proletarian Portrait.
  Williams.
The Rasslers. Barney.
Rime XLIX: "Bicause I have
  the still kept fro lyes and
  blame." Petrarch
  (Francesco Petrarca).
Rosebud. Anderson.
San Miguel De La Tumba.
  Berceo.
Sea-Weed. Lawrence.
See! Here, My Heart.
  Anonymous.
The Snow. Creeley.
A Soldier. Suckling.
Sonnet: "Beckie, my luve!–
  What is't, ye twa-faced
  tod?-". Hay.
The Sun of Grace.
  Anonymous.
Take This Hammer.
  Anonymous.
Tamping Ties. *Anonymous.*
The Temple. Herbert.
Three Things to Remember.
  Blake.
To His Dying Brother, Master
  William Herrick. Herrick.
Tricked Again. Ridhiana.
Undo Your Heart.
  Anonymous.
Vergissmeinicht. Douglas.
Verses Found in Thomas
  Dudley's Pocket after His
  Death. Dudley.
When Things Go Wrong with
  You. *Anonymous.*
Wishing Africa. Bowering.
A wounded deer leaps highest.
  Dickinson.
Wreaths. Hill.
Ye Spier Me. Smith.

The Young Ones, Flip Side.
  Emanuel.
Husband (s)
Agatha. Major.
The Arid Husband. Mesens.
The Best Old Fellow in the
  World. *Anonymous.*
The Blowflies Buzz.
  Djalparmiwi.
Caelica, L. Greville.
Cassie O'Lang. *Anonymous.*
Daily Paradox. Hay.
Decoy. Ashbery.
Dis Alitr Visum; or, le Byron
  de nos Jours. Browning.
Farmer Jones's Wife.
  Anonymous.
Final Prayer. Enheduanna.
For My Mother, Feeling
  Useless. Rankin.
Home on the Range, February
  1962. Dorn.
A Hundreth Good Poyntes of
  Husbandry. Tusser.
In Her Boudoir, the Young
  Lady,–Unacquainted with
  Grief. *Anonymous.*
Jessie. Field.
Lady Isabel and the Elf-
  Knight (A vers.).
  Anonymous.
Laieikawai's Lament after Her
  Husband's Death.
  Anonymous.
Love Songs. *Anonymous.*
Lysistrata. Aristophanes.
The Mikveh. Greenberg.
A Net for a Night Raven.
  Anonymous.
The Nymphs (excerpt).
  Hunt.
O Dear O. *Anonymous.*
The Oyster. Nash.
Penal Servitude for Mrs.
  Maybrick. *Anonymous.*
Pro Femina. Kizer.
Red River Shore.
  Anonymous.
St. Kilda. Reid.
Tee Roo. *Anonymous.*
There Was an Old Woman,
  and What Do You Think?
  Mother Goose.
Urgency. Sholl.
When Lovely Woman. Cary.
The Winds. Williams.
A Woman Grows Soon Old.
  Paraske.
Hush (ed)
Archaic Apollo. Plomer.
At Carmel Highlands.
  Lewis.
Babyhood. Holland
Building in Stone. Warner.
The Darkened Mind.
  Lowell.
Fulfillment. Miller.
The Giantess. Baudelaire.
The Hills and the Sea.
  Campbell.
In Memorial. Coogler.
The Inner Source. Codrescu.
Late Winter. Hall.
The Lost Lagoon. Johnson.
Love. Watson.
The Seasons. Thomson.
Shiloh, A Requiem. Melville.
Song: "Let it be forgotten, as
  a flower is forgotten."
  Teasdale.
The Song of the Spanish
  Main. Bennett.

Taos Drums. Simpson.
To Mary: I Sleep with Thee,
and Wake with Thee.
Clare.
To Sleep. Keats.
Unintelligible Terms. Simic.
When There Is Music.
Morton.

Husk (s)
At the Natural History
Museum. Meredith.
The Blue Gift. Perkins.
Creed. Townsend.
Doubt. Jackson.
The Real Thing. Wallace.
The Wreck of the Great
Northern. Hedin.

Hut (s)
Environ S. Eigner.
The Old Bark Hut.
Anonymous.
To a Young Poet Who Fled.
Logan.
Tree. Wilson.

Hyacinth (s)
Admonition for Spring.
Mackay.
Hyacinths to Feed Thy Soul.
Sa'di.
A Pretty Ambition.
Freeman.
The Rubaiyat of Omar
Khayyam. Omar
Khayyam.

Hymen
As You Like It.
Shakespeare.
A Debate on Marriage versus
Virginity. Catullus.

Hymn (s)
The Bohemian Hymn.
Emerson.
Devotions of the Fowls.
Lydgate.
Discovering God Is Waking
One Morning. L'Heureux.
Divinities. Merwin.
The Heptalogia. Swinburne.
A Hymn of the Sea. Bryant.
If I were a Cassowary.
Wilberforce.
Landor. Albee.
The Last Hymn.
Farningham.
O'Duffy's Ironsides.
Anonymous.
O Martyred Spirit.
Santayana.
Ode to Evening. Collins.
Pig Song. Atwood.
The Rock. Stevens.
Sea-Nurtured. Ingelow.
The Shepherd Boy. O'Brien.
The Silent Town. Dehmel.
Testament. Sister M.
Therese.

Hynn (s)
Alastor. Shelley.
Arcadia. Sidney.
Assumpta est Maria.
Brophy.
Beginnings. Biton.
Holy Thursday. Wright.
Mrs. Macintosh. Hall.
Precious Child, So Sweetly
Sleeping. Hoppe.
Resurrection. John of
Damascus.
To the Small Celandine.
Wordsworth.

Hypocrisy
Fair Days; or, Dawns
Deceitful. Herrick.
The Lancashire Puritane.
Anonymous.
A Madame, Madame B.
Beaute Sexagenaire.
Sackville.
Modern Love, XLIV.
Meredith.
The Prairie Dog. Guiterman.
Quatrain: "Better to live as a
rogue and a bum."
Mahsati.
The Rebel. Pearse.

Hysteria
A Place by the River.
Keens.
Singular Singulars, Peculiar
Plurals. Espy.

I

Icarus
Bird, Bird. Derwood.
Icarus. Spender.
Landscape with the Fall of
Icarus. Williams.
Pictures from Brueghel.
Williams.

Ice
Achitophel: the Earl of
Shaftesbury. Dryden.
The Auroras of Autumn.
Stevens.
The Beggar Wind. Austin.
Bum's Rush. Dransfield.
Chicago. Ridge.
Chinese Winter. Higgins.
Christmas Carol. del
Castillo.
The Clink of the Ice. Field.
Cold Glow: Icehouses.
Wojahn.
Epigram: "Time was when
once upon a time."
Glaucus.
Golden Gates. *Anonymous.*
Grace Abounding. Ammons.
Haiku: "Under moon
shadows." Knight.
He Sits down on the Floor of
a School for the Retarded.
Nowlan.
The Hills of Cualann.
Campbell.
Ice. Driscoll.
Ice and Fire. Sherburne.
The Ice Castle. Harris.
Ice Cold. O Riordain.
Icicle. Huddle.
Idea. Drayton.
Late Afternoon on a Good
Lake. Wier.
A Looking-Glass. Carew.
Love Letter. Plath.
Lucasta's World. Lovelace.
The Miracle. Suckling.
Monody. Melville.
Nechama. Kaufman.
No Change in Me.
Anonymous.
November through a Giant
Copper Beech. Honig.
On a Child Beginning to Talk.
Bastard.
Prometheus Unbound.
Shelley.

Prose Poem. Jennings.
Returning from Harvest.
Watkins.
Singular Indeed. McCord.
The Skaters. Williams.
The Slushy Snow Splashes and
Sploshes. Hoberman.
The Smacksman.
Anonymous.
Sonnet I. Alabaster.
Summer Is Gone.
Anonymous.
To Mr C.B. Donne.
Toward the Splendid City.
Ochester.
The Uninvited. Livesay.
Winter Central. Dewdney.
Winter Saint. Ammons.
Young Virgins Plucked
Suddenly. Pomerantz.

Ice cream
Alaska. Miller.
Catherine. Kuskin.
Eastward to Eden.
Bogardus.
The Emperor of Ice Cream.
Stevens.
The Greater Friendship
Baptist Church. Gregory.
Ice Cream. Wild.
Pacified. Nickens.
The Patient Is Rallying.
Kees.
Puppy. Fisher.
R is for the Restaurant.
McGinley.
Star Motel. Berkson.
Warning of Winter. Bethell.
Washington Heights, 1959.
Blumenthal.
Willy. Moore.
You. Clark.

Icicle (s)
Leaping Falls. Kinnell.
A Meditation on Rhode
Island Coal. Bryant.
Mistakable Identity. Emans.
Parting, without a Sequel.
Ransom.

Idea
A Blue Jeaned Rock Queen in
Search of Happiness...
Redwing.
The Board Meeting. Gloag.
The Glass of Water. Stevens.
The Horse Chestnut Tree.
Eberhart.
It's No Good. Young.
Little Pudding (parody).
Roberts.
On Exodus, III, 14, I Am
That I Am. Prior.
Portrait of a Lady. Eliot.
Principally. Veitch.
Sacrifice of a Red Squirrel.
Langland.
Slow Death. Martinez.
Two Egrets. Ciardi.
A Wealthy Man. Allingham.

Ideal (s)
Among These Turf-Stacks.
MacNeice.
Die Neuen Heiligen (excerpt).
Updike.
The Englishman on the
French Stage. Seaman.
An Exchange of Hats. Moss.
God's Ideal Mother.
Pinkham.
The Great Idealist. Jami.
The Man Coming Toward
You. Williams.

The Mute Phenomena.
Mahon.
Proverbial Philosophy: Of
Reading. Calverley.
Sonnets Written in the Fall of
1914. Woodberry.
There Is No Opera Like
"Lohengrin."
Wheelwright.

Identify
Eleven Addresses to the Lord.
Berryman.
Some Tips on Watching Birds.
Hudson.
To Nature Seekers.
Chambers.

Idiocy
Sonnet: "Ingratitude, how
deadly is the smart."
Seward.

Idiot (s)
Abstrosophy. Burgess.
The Beating. Hummer.
A Father's Heart Is Touched.
Hoffenstein.
For Though the Caves Were
Rabbited. Thoreau.
Hypatia (excerpt). Tollet.
In the Last Few Moments
Came the Old German
Cleaning Woman. Cooper.
Processional. Smith.
The Subway. Tate.
You That Are Jealous and
Have a Wife. *Anonymous.*

Idle (ness)
Fara Diddle Dyno. Weelkes.
Force. Minsky.
How Busie Are the Sonnes of
Men? Williams.
I Shall Forget You Presently,
My Dear. Millay.
Loch Ossian. Scroggie.
Past. Howells.
The Rose. "Angelus
Selesius" (Johannes
Scheffler).
The Sluggard. Davies.
Soldier from the Wars
Returning. Housman.
The Temple. Po Chu-i.
To My Sister. Wordsworth.
Two Illustrations That the
World Is What You Make
of It. Stevens.

Idol (atry) (s)
Don Juan. Byron.
The Eagles. Very.
The Great Hunger.
Kavanagh.
If I Have Lifted up Mine Eyes
to Admire. Wilder.
An Invocation (excerpt).
Iqbal.
Metaphysician. Fitzgerald.
Now I knew I lost her.
Dickinson.
Once More, Our God,
Vouchsafe to Shine.
Sewall.
Progress of Unbelief.
Newman.
Quatrain. Sarmed the
Yahud.
To the Right Honourable the
Countesse of C.
Habington.

Ignorance
Einstein's Father. Klauck.
Eternal Light. Binney.
Goodbye to Regal. Huws.

The lightning is a yellow fork.
Dickinson.
Ode on a Distant Prospect of
Eton College. Gray.
Past Time. Shapiro.
Piazza di Spagna, Early
Morning. Wilbur.
The Unsettled Motorcyclist's
Vision of His Death.
Gunn.

Ignore (d) (s)
Dilemma of the Elm.
Taggard.
Half-heard. Koch.
Tramontana at Lerici.
Tomlinson.
What Matter? *Anonymous.*

Iliad (s)
Poor Devil That I Am, Being
So Attacked. Palladas.
The Sea and Ourselves at
Cape Ann. Ferlinghetti.
The Wind in the Pines.
Cawein.

Ill (ness) (s)
Against Blame of Woman.
Desmond.
Against Women Either Good
or Bad. Norton.
Army Bugle Calls: Sick Call.
Anonymous.
Be with Me, Lord.
Macdonald.
Breton Afternoon. Dowson.
Caelica, XCII. Greville.
The Cardinal and the Dog.
Browning.
Count William's Escapade.
Guillaume de Poitiers.
The Courteous Pagan Shall
Condemne. Williams.
Enough of Thought,
Philosopher. Bronte.
From Venice Was That
Afternoon. Garrigue.
Good and Bad. Stephens.
The Happy Nightingale.
Anonymous.
The Ignorance of Man.
Merrick.
Lament of Anastasius.
Peabody.
Macbeth. Shakespeare.
The Mad Gardener's Song.
"Carroll.
Notes on the Post-Industrial
Revolution. Morin.
Of One Who Seemed to Have
Failed. Mitchell.
Oh, England. Sick in Head
and Sick in Heart.
Anonymous.
On His Mistris that Lov'd
Hunting. *Anonymous.*
On the Duke of Buckingham,
Slain by Felton...
Felltham.
Once the Days. Glover.
Rough Winds Do Shake.
Simpson.
A Shropshire Lad.
Housman.
Song: "The merchant, to
secure his treasure." Prior.
Sonnet: He Will Not Be Too
Deeply in Love.
Angiolieri.
Sonnet: Of Virtue. San
Geminiano.
Sonnets, CXIX: "What
potions have I drunk of
Siren Tears." Shakespeare.

Stupidity. Fullerton.
The Sweetest Home.
Anonymous.
Thin Ice. McCord.
To a Little Boy, Who Had
Destroyed a Nest of Young
Birds. *Anonymous.*
To His Book. Herrick.
To His Muse. Herrick.
To Stand Up Straight.
Housman.
Tulips. McGuckian.
Virgidemiarum. Hall.
Virtue the Best Monument.
Ralegh.
Wedding Anniversary.
Bruner.
What Is the Use? (excerpt).
Ellsworth.
Whether Men Do Laugh or
Weep. Campion.
A Whigmaleerie. Soutar.
A Wish. Arnold.
The Witch, V, i. Middleton.

Illogical
Out of My Study Window.
Whittemore.

Illuminat (ed) (es) (ion)
2nd Light Poem: For Diane
Wakoski. MacLow.
Buddha. Holmes.
First Dream (Excerpt).
Juana Ines de la Cruz.
Flannery O'Connor. Walters.
The Friendship Game.
DiCicco.
Holy Night. Clifton.
Jerusalem. Silkin.
Style. Nemerov.

Illumine (d)
An Interview near Florence.
Rogers.
Sonnet: England in 1819.
Shelley.
To the Unknown Light.
Shanks.

Illusion (s)
Against Seasons. Mezey.
Alonso to Ferdinand.
Auden.
At the Bottom of the Well.
Untermeyer.
Camping at Thunder Bay.
Fedo.
Galente Garden. Jimenez.
N. Seidman.
Night Clouds. McKeown.
O White Mistress. Johnson.
Povre Ame Amoureuse.
Labe.
Solitude and the Lily.
Horne.
Vancouver Island. Swift.

Image (s)
Afternoon: Amagansett Beach.
Wheelock.
A Backwards Journey. Page.
Beautiful Lily. Mortenson.
Cannibalism. Chang.
Channel U.S.A.–Live.
Stoutenburg.
Characteristics of a Child
Three Years Old.
Wordsworth.
Childhood. Rilke.
Composition. Blue Cloud.
The Creek. Robinson.
Diana. Constable.
Enfidaville. Douglas.
Epigram: "At 12 o'clock in
the afternoon." Meleager.

Epigram: Invocation.
Nemerov.
The Famous Outlaw Stops in
for a Drink. James.
Five Epigrams. Hall.
The Four of Them. Karni.
Geraldine's Daughter.
O'Rahilly.
Going to School. Shapiro.
The Gypsy Girl. Alford.
Handbook of Versification.
Sorrentino.
Harmonie du Soir.
Baudelaire.
High Dive. Empson.
House Is an Enigma. Jensen.
Image in a Lilac Tree.
Tiller.
Image in a Mirror.
Goodman.
Images. Raine.
The Lines of This New Song
Are Nothing. Zukofsky.
Love. Traherne.
A Love-Song. Turner.
The Lover Tells of the Rose
in His Heart. Yeats.
The Master's Touch. Bonar.
Negative Passage. Newman.
Night. Coleridge.
No Images. Cuney.
L'Oiseau Bleu. Coleridge.
Olive Grove. Merrill.
On the Defeat of Henry Clay.
Lord.
Poem: "Pity, repulsion, love
and anger." Fuller.
Primer of Plato. Garrigue.
Reading in War Time. Muir.
The Real Muse. Scott.
Recital (excerpt). Nicholl.
Results of a Scientific Survey.
Cutler.
Rose in the Afternoon.
Joseph.
The Same Dream. Cohen.
The Shadow Dance.
Moulton.
Smoking Flax. Benson.
Sonnet IX. Drummond.
Sonnets, XXXI: "Thy bosom
is endeared with all hearts."
Shakespeare.
The Statue. Belloc.
Statues. Wilbur.
To an Enemy. Bodenheim.
Twelfth Night. Scupham.
Veracruz. Hayden.
A Way of Looking.
Jennings.
Wellington. Harpur.
Written in My Lady Speke's
Singing-Book. Waller.

Imagination (s)
Charleston in the 1860s.
Rich.
The Confession. Yi-tuo.
Einstein's Father. Klauck.
A Man of Sense. Eberhart.
Night. Oates.
Pegasus. Kavanagh.
The Rokeby Venus.
Conquest.
Triphammer Bridge.
Ammons.
The Usurpers. Muir.
With a China Chamberpot, to
the Countess of
Hillsborough. Holland.

Imagine (d) (s)
Deaf Girl Playing. Tate.

Double Mock Sonnet.
Hartman.
The Gourd Dancer.
Momaday.
Jehu. MacNeice.
A Knight of Ghosts and
Shadows. Thompson.
Mowing the Lawn. Bensko.
Nine Nectarines and Other
Porcelain. Moore.
The Ninth of July.
Hollander.
Spring. Hogan.
The Visiting Hour.
Wagoner.
The Wives of Mafiosi. Jong.

Imitation
Anacreontea: The
Grasshopper. *Anonymous.*
Euridice Saved. Gregg.
Five Epigrams. Hall.
In Memoriam A.H.H., CX.
Tennyson.
The Mother Crab and Her
Family. Manyase.

Immaculate
Christ 1: Advent Lyrics, IX.
Anonymous.
The Easter Song. Sedulius.
Helen in Egypt: Thetis Is the
Moon-Goddess. Doolittle.
Mulier Amicta Sole. Chavez.
The Quiet Flower. Johnson.

Immortal (ity)
Adam's Hymn in Paradise.
Vondel.
Apology. Miller.
Apology of Genius. Loy.
At the Wedding March.
Hopkins.
A Ballad of Redhead's Day.
Glaenzer.
Du Bartas: His Divine
Weeks...Fifth Day of the
First Week (excerpt).
Sylvester.
Birthday. Birney.
The Book of Day-Dreams.
Moore.
Brief History. Briggs.
Buthaina. Jamil.
The Cloud Chamber. Sze.
The Computation. Donne.
The Crib. Morley.
The Criminality of War.
Young.
Dean Inge. Wolfe.
The Death of Lyon.
Peterson.
The Deceptive Present, The
Phoenix Year. Schwartz.
Don Juan. Byron.
Edge-Hill. Jago.
Epipsychidion. Shelley.
Epitaph. Cowper.
Epitaph: "When you look on
my grave." *Anonymous.*
Epitaphs of the War, 1914-18.
Kipling.
The Exquisite Sonnet.
Squire.
The First Note, Simple; the
Second Note, Distinct.
Aiken.
The First Three. Scollard.
For a Venetian Pastoral by
Giorgione. Rossetti.
A Frieze. Bishop.
He Maketh Himself One with
the Only God, Whose
Limbs Are the Many God.
Book of the Dead.

Homeric Unity. Lang.
Hymn to the Holy Spirit.
Wilton.
I Live Only to Do Thy Will.
Ansari of Herat.
If my bark sink. Dickinson.
Immortality. Jefferson.
Immortality. Minsky.
Inscription at Mount Vernon.
Anonymous.
Inside of King's College
Chapel, Cambridge.
Wordsworth.
Kaire. Eberhart.
The Key-Board. Watson.
Laurels and Immortelles.
Anonymous.
Lest any doubt that we are
glad that they were born
Today. Dickinson.
Life's Chequer-Board.
Oxenham.
Lincoln's Birthday. Bangs.
Little Ode. Goodman.
Love Not. Norton.
Love's Lovers. Rossetti.
Malcolm's Katie. Crawford.
The Mice at the Door.
McHugh.
My Latest Sun Is Sinking
Fast. Haskell.
A New-Year's Sacrifice.
Carew.
Nicolas Gatineau. Bourinot.
Ode to England. Lord
On His Mistress Looking in a
Glass. Carew.
Poem: "In the earnest path of
duty." Forten.
Poet of Earth. Thayer.
The Rejected "National
Hymns". Newell.
Sappho's Death: Three
Pictures by Gustave Moreau
(excerpt). Moore.
Say Not That Beauty.
Flower.
Shadow. Mars.
Shaemus. Aiken.
She Took the Dappled
Partridge Fleckt with
Blood. Tennyson.
A Song of Derivations.
Meynell.
Sonnet Written in Disgust of
Vulgar Supersitition.
Keats.
Soul, Wherefore Fret Thee?
Bloede.
.Spirituality. Greenberg.
Stevenson's Birthday. Miller.
The Stone and the Blade of
Grass in the Warsaw
Ghetto. Scheinert.
Sweets That Die. Mitchell.
That Nature Is a Heraclitean
Fire... Hopkins.
That such have died enable
us. Dickinson.
There Is No Death.
Anonymous.
The Thousand and One
Nights: The Wazir Dandan
for Prince Sharkan.
Anonymous.
Thysia. Luce.
The Tiger. Blake.
Time and the Garden.
Winters.
To a Lady on the Death of
Her Husband. Wheatley.

To an Aging Charioteer.
Scholasticus.
To My Excellent Lucasia, on
Our Friendship. Philips.
To the Most Beautiful Lady,
the Lady Bridget Manners.
Barnes.
To This Hill Again.
Macmillan.
Vienna. Porter.
A Vision. Clare.
The Vision of Judgment.
Byron.
We thirst at first. Dickinson.
When Shall We All Meet
Again? *Anonymous.*
Winter in Another Country.
Anthony ("Ai").
Zollicoffer. Flash.
Impart
Consecration. *Anonymous.*
For Her Heart Only.
Anonymous.
Psalm XXVII. Sidney.
Impartiality
The Discriminator. Scannell.
Impatient
En Garde, Messieurs.
Lindsey.
Envying a Little Bird.
Gregoria Francisca.
For Peter. Gerlach.
Romeo and Juliet.
Shakespeare.
A Summer Noon at Sea.
Sargent.
The Task. Cowper.
To Celia. Cotton.
Imperfect
Blackheads. Skinner.
Eve's Version. Harrison.
Heracles. Winters.
My Son, My Executioner.
Hall.
Six Divine Circles. Ghai.
Imperial
Childe Harold's Pilgrimage:
Canto IV. Byron.
Christophe. Atkins.
Moral Essays. Pope.
The Roman Stage. Johnson.
The stimulus beyond the
grave. Dickinson.
Impiety
Epigram on Marcus the
Gnostic. Pothinus.
The High Mind. Daniel.
Memorial Lines on the
Gender of Latin
Substantives. Kennedy.
Importance
Blond Hair at the Edge of the
Pavement. Smith.
The Citizen. Howard.
Epic. Kavanagh.
Impossible
At My Father's Grave.
""MacDiarmid.
The Great Sad One.
Greenberg.
Keys. Rockwell.
Life and Thought. Arnold.
Love's Spite. De Vere.
Princess Elizabeth of
Bohemia, as Perdita.
O'Hara.
Th Child's Purchase.
Patmore.
To Be a Jew in the Twentieth
Century. Rukeyser.
To cause accord or to agree.
Wyatt.

Impotence
The Desertion of the Women
and Seals. Brown.
The Disappointment. Behn.
The Disappointment.
Rochester.
The Discriminator. Scannell.
The Fathers. Sassoon.
"Nature" Is What We See.
Dickinson.
On the Threshold. Levy.
Paradise Saved. Hope.
Speakers, Columbus Circle.
Souster.
What Is That in Thine Hand?
Gray.
Improper
Clerihew: "The Empress
Poppaea." *Anonymous.*
Limerick: "There was a young
lady from Joppa."
Anonymous.
Improvement
Brief Reflection on the Insect.
Holub.
A Meditation on John
Constable. Tomlinson.
Impulse
The Flowing Summer.
Bruce.
I Mix in Life. Coleridge.
Wind and Impulse. Big
Eagle.
Incandescent
Her Lips Are Copper Wire.
Toomer.
Incantation
Fire-Queen. Fainlight.
Incarnate
Hymns and Spiritual Songs.
Smart.
The Tapestry. George.
The White-Haired Man.
Sarton.
Incense
Great Lord of All, Whose
Work of Love. Duche.
The Hawthorn Hath a
Deathly Smell. De la
Mare.
My Love. Cummings.
Noble Love. Flecknoe.
Thinking of "The Autumn
Fields." Bly.
To Rosina Pico. Lord
To the Muse. Kennedy.
The Universal Prayer. Pope.
Inch (es)
Aunt Elsie's Night Music.
Oliver.
Bridges and Tunnels.
Bentley.
Cocoon. Ishigaki Rin.
Filling Station. Morin.
Gesture. Finkel.
Good Counsel. James I
King of Scotland.
Hound on the Church Porch.
Coffin.
I Cut in Two. Hwang Chin-
i.
An Inch of Air. Sarah.
Keep A-Inchin' along.
Anonymous.
So Long Solon. Myers.
A Wet Night. Ryan.
Incline (d)
I Know Not Whether I Am
Proud. Landor.
The Mystic. Bynner.
Sovereign and Transforming
Grace. Hedge.

Incompetent
From the Sustaining Air.
Eigner.
Incomplete
Absence. Landor.
Choosing the Devil. Gregg.
On a Child with a Wooden
Leg. Warr.
Scotland Small?
""MacDiarmid.
Inconstant
La Donna E Mobile. "K..
Love, Whose Month Was
Ever May. Ulrich von
Liechtenstein [(or Lichten
Stein)].
On the Flightiness of
Thought. *Anonymous.*
Incorrigible
Spring Omnipotent Goddess.
Cummings.
Increase
All This Sunday Long.
Johnson.
Amoretti, XLIV. Spenser.
Apology for Love.
Boccaccio.
Congal: The Land Is Ours.
Ferguson.
The Female Husband, Who
Had Been Married to
Another Female....
Anonymous.
A Hymn. Shirley.
Puerperium. Waller.
Silex Scintillans. Vaughan.
The Tombe. Stanley.
Independence
A Bestiary. Rexroth.
Death of the Lincoln
Despotism. *Anonymous.*
The Filbert. Southey.
Liberty and Independence.
Anonymous.
Index
Epitaph on the Proofreader of
the Encyclopedia
Britannica. Morley.
India
The Final Toast. Veitch.
Grand Hotel, Calcutta.
Silbert.
Troilus and Cressida.
Shakespeare.
Indian (s)
48 Words for a Woman's
Dance Song. Rothenberg.
The Auroras of Autumn.
Stevens.
Big Chief Blues. Lewis.
Boast Not Proud English, of
Thy Birth and Blood.
Williams.
California Dead. Murray.
Comanche. Clark.
Equinoctial. Whitney.
Florida. Bishop.
Hitch Haiku. Snyder.
Indian Dance. Niven.
Indian Night Tableau.
Edelstein.
The Longing. Roethke.
Lonnie Kramer. Hobson.
The Maestro's Barber Shop.
Vasquez.
Mans Restlesse Soule Hath
Restlesse Eyes and Ears.
Williams.
Memo to the 21st Century.
Appleman.
Mexico City Hand Game.
Green.

Mr. Brodsky. Tomlinson.
My Dog Jock. Carruth.
The Pinto. Wister.
Pioneers. Garland.
Rich Man. *Anonymous.*
Ten Little Injuns. Winner.
Wagon Full of Thunder.
    Oliver.
What If Jealousy... Palmer.
When Something Happens.
    Randall, Jr.
Where Have All the Indians
    Gone? Hale.
Wild Dreams of a New
    Beginning. Ferlinghetti.
You Northern Girl. Ballard.

Indifference
Apartment Cats. Gunn.
At Dieppe: Green and Grey.
    Symons.
The Berg. Melville.
The Chestnut Avenue at
    Alton House. Tomlinson.
Codicil. Walcott.
A Curfew: December 13,
    1981. Clampitt.
Elegy for N. N. Milosz.
Elegy: Ise Lamenting the
    Death of Empress Onshi.
    Ise.
Last Days. Hugo.
Leda And The Swan. Yeats.
Macquarie Place.
    FitzGerald.
Meadow Grass. Mott.
On the Eve of the Plebiscite.
    Rexroth.
Our Father. Swartz.
The River Again and Again.
    Gregg.
What Has Happened.
    Angoff.
Windows in Providence.
    Barnstone.
Women of Trachis: Choruses.
    Sophocles.
Your Last Drive. Hardy.

Indigence
None Can Experience Stint.
    Dickinson.

Indigestion
Love's Torment. *Anonymous.*

Indiscreet
Epigram: An Old Story.
    Nemerov.
The Garden. Pound.
Limerick: "Aging old queers
    are no treat." *Anonymous.*
On Why I Would Betray You.
    Graham.
Rather Too Good, Little
    Peggy! O'Keeffe.
Vaudracour and Julia
    (excerpt). Wordsworth.

Indispensable
The Children of the State.
    Lewisohn.

Indolence
But I am Growing Old and
    Indolent. Jeffers.
To Petronius Arbiter.
    Gogarty.

Indust (rious) (ry)
The Praise of Pindar in
    Imitation of Horace His
    Second Ode, Book 4.
    Cowley.

Infamy
The Faerie Queene. Spenser.
A Sketch. Byron.

Infan (cy) (t)
Another Kind of Burning.
    Fox.
Avarice. Hecht.
The Babe. Gibbon.
Chimney Swallows. Powers.
Dain Eile (excerpt).
    MacLean.
The Erl-King. Goethe.
The Isle of Man Shore (The
    Desolate Widow).
    Anonymous.
King Triumphant. Watts.
Living in Sin. Clarke.
Man with One Small Hand.
    Page.
Modern Love, XI. Meredith.
A Mother's Picture.
    Stedman.
Not in Narrow Seas.
    Curnow.
Now Sleep My Little Child So
    Dear. Kriebel.
On a Discovery Made Too
    Late. Coleridge.
On Hearing a Broadcast of
    Ceremonies in Connection
    with.... Wrafter.
Right Apprehension.
    Traherne.
Rockingchair. Morgan.
To Cara, after an Interval of
    Absence. Moore.
Wisdom. Yeats.

Infect (ed) (s)
An Essay on Criticism.
    Pope.
Gare du Midi. Auden.
A Poem for Diane Wakoski.
    Young Bear.
Resignation. Arnold.

Infinity
The Biggest Killing. Dorn.
The Cannibal Hymn.
    Anonymous.
Christian Ethics. Traherne.
The Circle. Coates.
Damned Women.
    Baudelaire.
Day and Night Handball.
    Dunn.
Dieppe, II: On the Beach.
    Symons.
Distance Spills Itself. Bat-
    Miriam.
The East Wind. Lodge.
Friends. Moore.
Highest Divinity.
    Anonymous.
Home. Sill.
I'm Happiest When Most
    Away. Bronte.
Insatiableness. Traherne.
Jerusalem. Molodovsky.
Midsummer. Spender.
The Nature of Love.
    Kirkup.
Numbers and Faces (excerpt).
    Auden.
Ode to Salt. Neruda.
Polyolbion. Drayton.
Prayer to the Virgin of
    Chartres. Adams.
A Se Stesso. Leopardi.
Song: "Flame at the core of
    the world." Upson.
Tell Me, Tell Me, Smiling
    Child. Bronte.
There are two mays.
    Dickinson.

Inflame (s)
Epigram: "I don't care for
    women." *Anonymous.*
"If he that erst the form so
    lively drew." Surrey.
The Iliad. Homer.

Influence
The Disappointment. Behn.
I Mix in Life. Coleridge.
Moon Watching by Lake
    Chapala. Young.
An Ode upon a Question
    Moved, Whether Love
    Should Continue For Ever?
    Herbert of Cherbury.
The Survivors. Slater.
To the Evening Star. Blake.
The Trinity. Osborne.

Ingratitude
The Dog. *Anonymous.*
The False Favorite's
    Downfall. *Anonymous.*
The Poet: A Rhapsody.
    Akenside.

Inherit (ed) (ance)
Bequest. Gilburt.
The Division of Parts.
    Sexton.
The Faerie Queene. Spenser.
Helas! Wilde.
The Inheritors. Geddes.
The Lay of the Captive
    Count. Goethe.
The Native. Merwin.
Nekros. Tabb.
New Year's. Reznikoff.
O Thou Most High Who
    Rulest All. Bradstreet.
Poems from a First Year in
    Boston. Starbuck.
Praise of a Child.
    Anonymous.
The Prophet. Gibran.
Requiescat. Arnold.
The Return (excerpt).
    Woods.
Salutation. Eliot.
Senior Members. Lucy.
The Song of the Trout Fisher.
    Ikinilik.
The Soul of Lincoln. Piety.
Voices Answering Back: The
    Vampires. Raab.
Welcome, Sweet Rest.
    Wigglesworth.
When Israel out of Egypt
    Came. Housman.

Inhumanity
Ah Me! The Mighty Love.
    Cameron.
Man's Inhumanity to Man.
    Burns.

Iniquity
The Image of Irelande
    (excerpt). Derricke.

Injure
A Magic Mist. O
    Suilleabhain.
Tom O' Bedlam's Song.
    Anonymous.

Ink
Astrophel and Stella, CII.
    Sidney.
Cacoethes Scribendi. Holmes
Edvard Munch. Wright.
Fragment. Clare.
The Jest. Clarke.
Limerick: "Teacher Bruin
    said, "Cub, bear in mind."
    Fenderson.

Movie Actors Scribbling
    Letters Very Fast in Crucial
    Scenes. Garrigue.
A Poet's Epitaph. Amis.
Said the monkey to the
    donkey. *Anonymous.*
Something Has Fallen.
    Levine.
The Thresher's Labour.
    Duck.
Upon the Ensignes of Christes
    Crucifyinge. Alabaster.
The Woman in My Notebook.
    Cervantes.

Inland
Far inland go my sad
    thoughts. *Anonymous.*
Song of the Rejected Woman.
    Kibkarjuk.

Inn
Beauty and the Bird.
    Rossetti.
Christmas Day Is Come.
    Wadding.
The Coach of Time.
    Pushkin.
The Faerie Queene. Spenser.
The Foreign Gate (excerpt).
    Keyes.
Here I Sit in My Infested
    Cubicle. Greenwood.
Idle Words. Landor.
The Lord of the Isles
    (excerpt). Scott.
The Man of Life Upright.
    Campion.
The Odyssey, VII. Virgil
    (Publius Vergilius Maro).
The Old Inn-Sign. Thorley.
Orgy. MacCaig.
Quits. Aldrich.
Roots and Branches.
    Duncan.
Soldier from the Wars
    Returning. Housman.
Stone. Simic.
Upon Christ His Birth.
    Suckling.
Written at an Inn at Henley.
    Shenstone.

Innocence
All the World Moved.
    Jordan.
Anecdote of the Prince of
    Peacocks. Stevens.
The Apparition. Donne.
Autumn Song. Brettell.
Cigarettes Will Spoil Yer Life
    (with music). *Anonymous.*
The Circuit Judge. Masters.
Confab. Rosen.
Deer in Aspens. Hall.
The Eyes of Children at the
    Brink of the Sea's Grasp.
    Jacobsen.
History. Lowell.
The Human Tragedy
    (excerpt). Austin.
I Pressed Her Rebel Lips.
    Anonymous.
In a London Schoolroom.
    Kirkup.
In Memory of G. K.
    Chesterton. De la Mare.
Inscription for a Tablet on the
    Banks of a Stream.
    Southey.
Isaac. Holtz.
Let's Talk, Mother. Bruck.
The Lonesome Dream.
    Mueller.

Lunch with Girl Scouts.
Bryan.
The Master. Merwin.
The Missal. Pitter.
October Poems: The Garden.
Warren.
The Oeconomy of Love
(excerpt). Armstrong.
On a Ledge. Bell.
Photos of a Salt Mine. Page.
A Prayer for St. Innocent's
Day. Eden.
Return. Montague.
Send Forth the High Falcon.
Adams.
She Walks in Beauty. Byron.
The Sleepy Giant. Carryl.
Small Colored Boy in the
Subway. Deutsch.
Summa Contra Gentiles.
Leary.
To His Son, Vincent.
Corbet.
To My Daughter. Plutzik.
To My Excellent Lucasia, on
Our Friendship. Philips.
To the Countesee of Bedford.
Donne.
To the Mother of Christ, the
Son of Man. Meynell.
Tuesday, 4 March (Morning)
1963. Pasolini.
Two Girls... Reznikoff.
A Walk by the Charles.
Rich.
Inquiry
Advertisement of a Lost Day.
Sigourney.
Letter #8. Brutus.
Inquisition
Dark Room. Zydek.
Inscription
Untitled: "Fivesucked the
features of my girl by
glory." Moore.
Wildfire. Toth.
Insect (s)
The Bee-Wisp. Turner.
Corn. Mayer.
The Corpse-Plant. Rich.
A Cottage in the Wood.
Edson.
The Cultural Presuppostion.
Auden.
Elegy. Gilbert.
The Hard Listener.
Williams.
I come to you with the
vertigoes of the source.
Caroutch.
Learning to Understand
Darkness. Rose.
Metropolitan Nightmare.
Benét.
The Mocking Bird. Lanier.
O Sailor, Come Ashore.
Rossetti.
Proud Hollyhock. Buller.
Ronsard. DeFord.
Titus and Berenice. Heath-
Stubbs.
The Toad-Eater. Burns.
Visit. Ammons.
Voices of the Air. Mansfield.
Inside
After the War. Dunn.
Bottled. Johnson.
Children among the Hills.
Gregg.
The Clay Jug. _Anonymous._
Conundrum. Clark.
Dream. Issaia.

February Park. Vizenor.
Hell in Texas. _Anonymous._;
Homage to Elvis, Homage to
the Fathers. Weigl.
Hustlers. Cooper.
Jack Was Every Inch a Sailor.
Anonymous.
A Land Not Mine.
Akhmatova.
Limerick: "There was a young
lady of Ryde."
Anonymous.
The Music of the Future.
Herford.
My love is in my house.
Mira Bai [(or Mirabai)].
Oil. Hogan.
The Old Nudists. Colby.
Out There. Berkson.
The Recluses. Perkoff.
Secrets. Fowler.
To a Young Poet. Bennett.
Insight
Composed on the Eve of the
Marriage of a Friend ...
Wordsworth.
Families. Blackburn.
The Tobacconist of Eighth
Street. Eberhart.
We Cannot Kindle. Arnold.
Insignificance
Adultery. Dugan.
The Significance of a
Veteran's Day. Ortiz.
Insolence
The New Tenants.
Robinson.
Sunday Morning. Jenkins.
Inspiration
Dreams. Giovanni.
For Myself. Hines.
The Inner Vision.
Wordsworth.
Usufruct. Clarke.
Instant
Fuimus Fumus. Sylvester.
The Gutter. Fortini.
On the Farm. Winder.
She That Is Memory's
Daughter. Watkins.
Six Young Men. Hughes.
Instinct (s)
Creative Force. Hadden.
Doubt. Jackson.
The Fishvendor. Meredith.
Hugh Selwyn Mauberley, XI.
Pound.
Marriage and Midsummer's
Night. Gregg.
A Prayer. Channing.
Instrument (s)
29th Dance–Having an
Instrument–22 March 1964.
MacLow.
Bard. Black.
Chamber Music. Joyce.
Endymion's Convoy.
Drayton.
Face on the Daguerreotype.
Rosten.
Ives (excerpt). Rukeyser.
Lines on the Death of
Bismarck. Chapman.
My New Year Prayer.
Anonymous.
Robert Fulton. Stanford.
Tamburlaine. Marlowe.
The Wagoner's Lad.
Anonymous.
The Web. Weiss.
A Younger Poet. Schjeldahl.

Insult
Crucifixion. Isbell.
The Eagle's Fall. Whiting.
My Mother Was a Lady.
Marks.
Insurance
I Promessi Sposi. Corman.
Untitled. Nibbelink.
Insurrection
Still Though the One I Sing.
Whitman
Integration
Harlem Gallery (excerpt).
Tolson.
Integrity
Camouflage. Manifold.
Sonnet: Guido Cavalcanti to
Dante. Cavalcanti.
Intellect (ual)
A Letter to David Campbell
on the Birthday of W. B.
Yeats, 1965. Hope.
Near Barbizon. Kinnell.
Recapitulations. Shapiro.
Sonnets to Laura. Petrarch.
Talking Nothin'.
Anonymous.
To the Much Honoured R. F.
Esq. Chamberlain.
Intelligence
The Falcon. Lovelace.
The Flight of Apollo.
Kunitz.
Life at War. Levertov.
The Painter Dreaming in the
Scholar's House.
Nemerov.
A Rapier of Treason.
Anonymous.
Intend (ed)
The Beholders. Dickey.
December. Francis.
Ex Libris. Upson.
For Sheridan. Lowell.
Lavish Kindness. Wylie.
Limerick: "There was a young
man of Ostend."
Anonymous.
Stark County Holidays.
Oliver.
Urceus Exit: Triolet.
Dobson.
Intention (s)
Barbarians. Fowles.
Certain Maxims of Archy.
Marquis.
The Gate of the Year.
Haskins.
I Can't Hold You and I Can't
Leave You. Juana Ines de
la Cruz.
War Walking Near. Young
Bear.
Intercourse (s)
Monologue of the Rating
Morgan in Rutherford
County. MacIntyre.
The Poet. Keats.
Interest
The Debt. Dunbar.
The Firm of Happiness,
Limited. Cameron.
The Lady's-Maid's Song.
Hollander.
Napoleon Hoped That All the
World Would Fall beneath
His Sway. _Anonymous._
The Spring Vacation.
Mahon.
To Think of Time.
Whitman.

Interfere
John Gilbert Was a
Bushranger. _Anonymous._
Memo. Ballard.
The Observer. Yates.
Town Ghost. Edmond.
Interior
A Plan to Live My Life
Again. O Hehir.
The Sleeping Saint. La
Follette.
Interpret (ed) (er) (s)
Awake, My Fair. Halevi.
Death's Lecture at the
Funeral of a Young
Gentleman. Crashaw.
An Eclogue for Christmas.
MacNeice.
Last Mathematician.
Edelstein.
Silence. Masters.
Sunday, July 14th: A Fine
Day at the Baths.
Symons.
The Word of Water. Mayo.
Interrupt (ing) (ed)
I Got So I Could Hear His
Name. Dickinson.
My Children's Book. Morris.
Intertwined
The Death of an Old Man.
Hamburger.
Head Couples. Matchett.
Interview
The Death of Will.
Tomlinson.
Spring is the Period.
Dickinson.
Introduce (d)
The Introduction. MacNeice.
My Woman. Winans.
Under the Anheuser Bush.
Sterling.
Introspective
An Astronomer's Journal.
Shore.
Intruder (s)
Apparition of Splendor.
Moore.
From a Rise of Land to the
Sea. Hoffmann.
Rumors of War in Wyoming.
Rea.
Intuitions
Color–Caste–Denomination.
Dickinson.
Rogue Pearunners. Everson.
Invaders
D-Dawn. McGarvey.
On Independence. Sewall.
Sea-Chronicles. Ingamells.
The War of the Worlds.
Rutsala.
Invalid
The Flash Frigate.
Anonymous.
Waiting for Breakfast, While
She Brushed Her Hair.
Larkin.
Invention (s)
Brave Old World. Lambert.
Broncho Versus Bicycle.
Crawford.
Leaflets. Rich.
Letter to an Imaginary
Friend. McGrath.
The Meeting. Jackowska.
Night Clouds. McKeown.
La Reproduction Interdite /
Not to Be Reproduced.
Fraser.

The Season's Lovers.
Waddington.
Seferis. Durrell.

Invincible
Mrs. Southern's Enemy.
Sitwell.

Invisible
Amphibious Crocodile.
Ransom.
Celestine. Fitzgerald.
Crazy Movie. Barrios.
A Dance Chant. *Anonymous.*
Daphne Stillorgan. Devlin.
Daybreak. Kinnell.
I in Thee, and Thou in Me.
Cranch.
The Lovers Go Fly a Kite.
Snodgrass.
Morituri Salutamus.
Longfellow.
A Natural History of Dragons
and Unicorns My Daughter
and I Have Known. Root.
The Rainbow. Patmore.
Silex Scintillans. Vaughan.
The Tower. Van Doren.
Under Glass. Kreymborg.

Invitation (s)
Believe It. Logan.
The Birds of Arles. Fisher.
The Challenge. Murry.
Christmas Eve. Berkson.
The Dream Motorcycle.
Winslow.
Happening In. Sanders.
The Instructions of King
Cormac (excerpt).
Anonymous.
Limerick: "There was a young
man so benighted."
Voorhees.
Mae's Rent Party. Wilson,
Jr.
A Pastoral Courtship.
Rochester.
Poem: "The eager note on my
door said 'Call me.'.
O'Hara.
Sonnet, XX: "A seer foretold
that I would love one day."
Labé.
Waiting Carefully. Kamm.

Invocation
Love Charm. *Anonymous.*
To an Obscure Poet Who
Lives on My Hearth.
Hildreth.

Inward
Advice against Travel.
Mangan.
Caelica, XVII. Greville.
Former Barn Lot. Van
Doren.
Satires. Wyatt.
See in the Midst of Fair
Leaves. Moore.
Song of Joy. Uvavnuk.
Sonnet C. Greville.
Sonnet. The Cell. Thelwall.
To Cynthia, Not to Let Him
Read the Ladies'
Magazines. Hubbard.
True Riches. Watts.

Iota
Indeed Indeed, I Cannot Tell.
Thoreau.
Limerick: "A Conservative,
out on his motor."
Webster.

Iowa
Amazing Grace. Hollo.

Double Semi-Sestina.
Starbuck.
Seeing Auden off. Booth.

Ireland (Irish)
The Agricultural Irish Girl.
Anonymous.
Andromeda. Roche.
Anglo-Eire Vignette.
Stevenson.
The Antiquary. Campbell.
A Ballad of Master McGrath.
Anonymous.
A Bird from the West.
Shorter.
The Call. Corkery.
Cois na Teineadh. Rolleston.
Dawn Song–St. Patrick's Day.
Storey.
The Dawning o' the Year.
Blake.
Earl Brand; or, The Douglas
Tragedy (B vers.) (excerpt).
Anonymous.
Easter Week. *Anonymous.*
Epigram: "Peace is made with
a warlike man–."
Anonymous.
The Fair Hills of Ireland.
Ferguson.
The Girl I Left behind Me.
Davis.
The Green Little Shamrock of
Ireland. Cherry.
I Am a Wild Young Irish
Boy. *Anonymous.*
I Am Ireland. Gregory.
I Am of Ireland. Yeats.
I'll Wear a Shamrock.
Davies.
If I Owned All of Alba.
Cille.
In Memory of Those
Murdered in the Dublin
Massacre, May 1974.
Durcan.
Invocation to Ireland.
Amergin.
Ireland Lake. Hershon.
Irish Astronomy. Halpine.
Irish Dancer. *Anonymous.*
The Irishman and the Lady.
Maginn.
Kevin Barry: Died for
Ireland,/1st November,
1920. *Anonymous.*
The Mail Boat, Leinster.
Anonymous.
A New Song on the Taxes.
Anonymous.
New Words to the Tune of
"O'Donnel Abu." Connell.
No Irish Need Apply.
Anonymous.
On a Dead Scholar.
Anonymous.
Once Alien Here. Hewitt.
The Ould Plaid Shawl.
Fahy.
Patrick Sarsfield, Lord Lucan.
Anonymous.
Pattern of Saint Brendan.
MacManus.
Poem to a Nigger Cop.
Hamilton.
The Potatoes' Dance.
Lindsay.
The Queen's Afterdinner
Speech (excerpt). French.
The Sonnet. Hoffman.
Spenser's Ireland. Moore.
A Strong Wind. Clarke.

The Tain: Before the Last
Battle. *Anonymous.*
The Testament of Cathaeir
Mor. *Anonymous.*
Tone's Grave. Davis.
Traditions. Heaney.
Two Songs in Praise of
Steingerd, 2.
Ogmundarson.
Uptown. Ginsberg.
The Viking Terror.
Anonymous.
The Violin Calls. Livesay.
Written on the Sense of
Isolation in Contemporary
Ireland. Greacen.

Iris (es)
The Cave-Drawing. Watkins.
In the Carolinas. Stevens.
Irises. Colum.
May All Earth Be Clothed in
Light. Hitchcock.

Iron
The Avengers. Markham.
The Birdsville Track.
Stewart.
Cargoes. Masefield.
Carmen Bellicosum.
McMaster.
Cleator Moor. Nicholson.
Coon Can (Poor Boy) (with
music). *Anonymous.*
Cupidon. Smith.
Dead in the Sierras. Miller.
The Dragon's Hoard.
Tolkien.
Famine. Heym.
The Forge. Heaney.
Jack Donahoe. *Anonymous.*
Love's Fatality. Rossetti.
The Martyr. Melville.
Mr. Cromek to Mr. Stothard.
Blake.
Nothing More Will Happen.
Piercy.
O Sweet Delight. Campion.
On the Road to Anster Fair.
Tennant.
The Servant Man (The Iron
Door). *Anonymous.*
Stanzas for My Daughter.
Gregory.
The Technique of Power.
Kessler.
Thou Didst Say Me.
Waddington.
Traditional Red. Huff.
Two Men in Armour.
Heath-Stubbs.
Washington Monument by
Night. Sandburg.
The Water-Wheel. Clemo.
The White Dress.
Zaturenska.
The Worker. Thomas.

Ironside
The Constitution's Last Fight.
Roche.
Three Poems about Children.
Clarke.

Irony
The Age of Sheen. Hughes.
Autumn Orchard. Jacobs.
Charlotte Corday.
Tomlinson.
Preliminary Poem. Heath-
Stubbs.

Isaac
A Letter to His Friend Isaac.
Halevi.
Rebecca. Eliyia.

Isabel
Adventures of Isabel. Nash.

Isabella
Orlando Furioso. Ariosto.

Isadore
The Widowed Heart. Pike

Iscariot
Motherhood. Lee.
The Sack of Baltimore.
Davis.
This Very Hour. Reese.

Ishmael
The Ballad of Ishmael Day.
Anonymous.
The Bedouins of the Skies.
Kenyon.
Hagar to Ishmael. Eibel.
Song for Unbound Hair.
Taggard.

Island (s)
At Pont-Aven, Gauguin's Last
Home in France.
Grossbardt.
A Ballad of John Silver.
Masefield.
A Ballade of Islands.
Robinson.
Barred Islands. Booth.
Biddy, Biddy. *Anonymous.*
Black Jess. Dufault.
Born Was the Island.
Anonymous.
Calypso's Song to Ulysses.
Mitchell.
Childe Harold's Pilgrimage:
Canto IV, XXVII. Byron.
Crossing the Straits. Brasch.
The Dancing Seal. Gibson.
Discovering My Daughter.
Stuart.
Do Not Embrace Your
Mind's New Negro Friend.
Meredith.
England. Channing-Stetson
Fishermen, Drowned beyond
the West Coast. Smith.
The Flying Dutchman.
Robinson.
Hershey Kiss. Renner-Tana.
The High Sailboat.
Quasimodo.
Hugging the Jukebox. Nye.
If Once You Have Slept on an
Island. Field.
Incident at Matauri.
Smithyman.
Instructions to a Painter.
Waller.
Invocation and Prelude.
George.
The Island. Southey.
The Island. Woodcock.
The Island in the Evening.
Porter.
The Island of Yorrick.
Bodecker.
Islands. Rukeyser.
Kindness. Moore.
Landfall in Unknown Seas.
Curnow.
Letter to Derek Mahon.
Longley.
Live Blindly. Stickney.
Marmion. Scott.
Nocturne. Raine.
On the Memory of Mr.
Edward King Drown'd in
the Irish Seas. Cleveland.
On the Wings of a Dove.
Miller.
A Poem. Mphahlele.
The Revolution. Gilbert.

Southward Sidonian Hanno.
  Allen.
Theme and Variations. Ker.
Thirsty Island. Tollerud.
Toward Lesbos. Vivien.
Triptych. Heaney.
War Song of O'Driscol.
  Griffin.
We Never Said Farewell.
  Coleridge.

Isle (s)
At Euston. Harbord.
The Ballad of the White
  Horse. Chesterton.
Beautiful Isle of Somewhere.
  Pounds.
Burning Drift-Wood.
  Whittier.
Cap'n. Peach.
Christmas Island. Bates.
Eagles and Isles. Gibson.
The Enchanted Island.
  Conolly.
Fair Isle at Sea. Stevenson.
Glasgow Peggie. *Anonymous.*
High Germany. *Anonymous.*
How Dear to Me the Hour.
  Moore.
Johnny Bull, My Jo, John.
  Anonymous.
The Last Buccaneer.
  Kingsley.
Manhattan. Hart.
Outward Bound. Aldrich.
A Passer By. Bridges.
Patmos. Thomas.
Sailor, What of the Isles?
  Sitwell.
The Story of Vinland.
  Lanier.
To an Isle in the Water.
  Yeats.
The Voyage of Maeldune.
  Tennyson.
Welcome to the Nations.
  Holmes.

Israel
Approaching Washington
  Heights. Reiss.
At the Pantomime. Holmes.
Blessed Is Everyone.
  Anonymous.
Evening Prayer. *Anonymous.*
Gehazi. Kipling.
Hatikvah–A Song of Hope.
  Imber.
If I Forget Thee. Litvinoff.
Marriage Song. Halevi.
Mockery. Blake.
O the Chimneys. Sachs.
Oh! Weep for Those. Byron.
Paradise Regained. Milton.
Pictures at an Exhibition.
  Rosenbaum.
Psalm XIV. Sidney.
Psalm XXV. Sidney.
A Sabbath of Rest. Luria.
Upon the Tomb of the Most
  Reverend Mr. John
  Cotton... Woodbridge.
The World's Justice.
  Lazarus.

Italy (Italian)
Ballad of the D-Day Dodgers.
  Anonymous.
The D-Day Dodgers.
  Henderson.
The Gauls Sacrifice.
  Doughty.
Her–"last Poems"–.
  Dickinson.

A Map of Montana in Italy.
  Hugo.
Maratea Porto: Saying
  Goodbye to the Vitolos.
  Hugo.
New York City–1935.
  Corso.
To Maria Gisborne in
  England, from Italy.
  Shelley.
Walt Whitman at Bear
  Mountain. Simpson.
The Watershed. Meynell.

Itch (ed)
The Canadian Prairies View of
  Literature. Donnell.
A Day with the Foreign
  Legion. Whittemore.
Heavenly Grass. Williams.
The Hermit Has a Visitor.
  Kumin.
Taboo to Boot. Nash.
Unto the Breach. Poliziano.

Ithaca
Ithaca. Cavafy.
Odysseus' Song to Calypso.
  Dufault.

Ivory
Champagne. McGuckian.
The Horseman. De la Mare.
Pretty Polly (with music).
  Anonymous.
The Princess of Dreams.
  Dowson.
A Proem. Ward
A Responsory, 1948.
  Merton.
Rotation. Bond.
Scala Coeli. Raine.

Ivy
The Buckle. De la Mare.
Epigram: "I celebrate
  Rhegion." *Anonymous.*
Epithalamium. Ditsky.
Holly against Ivy.
  Anonymous.
The Ivy Green. Dickens.
The Little Bird. De La
  Mare.
November. Coleridge.
The Oak and the Ash.
  Anonymous.
A Singular Metamorphosis.
  Nemerov.
Song: "Take, oh take those
  Lips away." Beaumont.
Spring Arithmetic.
  Anonymous.
The Vacant Farm House.
  De La Mare.

J

Jack
All Work and No Play Makes
  Jack a Dull Boy.
  Anonymous.
Ballad of a Strange Thing.
  Putnam.
The Bookworm. De la Mare.
The Domicile of John. Pope.
The Double Transformation.
  Goldsmith.
Ghost Story. Thomas.
Here Comes My Lady with
  Her Little Baby.
  Anonymous.

I Am an Ancient Mariner.
  Anonymous.
Jack Robinson. *Anonymous.*
The Kola Run. *Anonymous.*
Little Jack Frost.
  Anonymous.
Lob. Thomas.
Music in the Air. McCuaig.
My Mother Was a Lady.
  Marks.
Off to Sea Once More.
  Anonymous.
The Old Keg of Rum.
  Anonymous.
Poor Jack. Dibdin.
A Puzzling Example.
  Benjamin.
Red Jack. Durack.
Robin and Richard.
  Anonymous.
The Sad Story of a Little Boy
  That Cried. *Anonymous.*
Shot My Pistol in de Heart of
  Town. *Anonymous.*
The Story of Uriah. Kipling.
That Nature Is a Heraclitean
  Fire... Hopkins.
There Were Two Blackbirds
  Sitting on a Hill. Mother
  Goose.
They All Love Jack.
  Anonymous.
Thumb He. *Anonymous.*
The Wars of Santa Fe.
  Anonymous.

Jackass
On Seeing Francis Jeffrey
  Riding on a Donkey.
  Smith.
Top Hand. *Anonymous.*
Why Mira Can't Go Back to
  Her Old House. Mira Bai
  [(or Mirabai)].

Jacket
How the waters closed above
  him. Dickinson.
Jacket So Blue. *Anonymous.*
Ode to Popularity. Praed.
The Parental Critic. Preston.

Jackhammer (s)
On the Pavement. Sam.
Triplets. Brownstein.

Jackson
Andrew Jackson. Keller.
Casey Jones (F vers.).
  Anonymous.
Dirty Joke. Klauck.
The Loss of the Druid.
  Anonymous.

Jacob
Between the Sunken Sun and
  the New Moon. Hayne.
Building a Skyscraper.
  Tippett.
Nine Men out of a Minyan.
  Guri.

Jade
I Change. Bynner.
Proud Hollyhock. Buller.
To Li Chien. Po Chu-i.
Treasure Boat. Fujino.

Jail
The Carpet-Weaver's Lament.
  Anonymous.
The Funeral Parlor.
  Johnson.
Invasion Song. *Anonymous.*
The Lay of the Labourer.
  Hood.
Limerick: "A maiden caught
  stealing a dahlia."
  Anonymous.

Mae's Rent Party. Wilson,
  Jr.
Ned Bratts. Browning.
On a Travelling Speculator.
  Freneau.
Oppression. Hughes.
Ordinary People on Sunday.
  Veitch.
Stir the Wallaby Stew.
  Anonymous.
Street Demonstration.
  Walker.
The Third Satire of Juvenal.
  Dryden.
'Tis Sorrow Builds the Shining
  Ladder Up. Lowell.
To an Old San Francisco
  Poet. Abbott.
To Heliodora: A Fretful
  Monody. Meleager.

Jam
The Dream of a Girl Who
  Lived at Sevenoaks.
  Rands.
Il Piccolo Rifiuto.
  MacNeice.
Impetuous Samuel. Graham.
The Pond. Thwaite.
Sonnet: To the Asshole.
  Rimbaud.
This Little Pig Had a Rub-a-
  Dub. *Anonymous.*

James
Bringing Him Up. Dunsany.
Epitaph: "Here lie my
  husbands One Two Three."
  Anonymous.
The Four Friends. Milne.
Henry James. Stevenson.
Miss James. Milne.
Vers de Societe (parody).
  Traill.

Jane
Dulce Ridentem. Benét.
The Emigrant's Dying Child.
  Patton.
Fair Annie. *Anonymous.*
Jane and Eliza. Taylor.
Janes's Marriage. Kipling.
The Little Dove.
  Anonymous.
Mary Jane. *Anonymous.*
Newberry (Lonesome Dove).
  Anonymous.
Out of the Hurly-Burly.
  "Adeler.
The Penitent Nun.
  Lockman.
Repentance. Untermeyer.
Sweet Jane. *Anonymous.*
The Swift Bullets. Wells.
With a Guitar, to Jane.
  Shelley.

Janet
Herself. Holmes.
Sir Colin. Anonymous.

January
Advent. Kavanagh.
January. Sherman.
Perspective. Vorpahl.
Saint-Henri Spring. Acorn.

Janus
The Character of a Trimmer.
  Anonymous.

Japan (ese)
Away. Stryk.
From the Grove Press.
  Hecht.
On the Twenty-Fifth of July.
  DeJong.
The Verb "To Think'.
  Enright.

Jar (s)
The Convergence of the
Twain. Hardy.
The Empty Jar. Stenhouse.
The Jar. Stoddard.
My Face. Euwer.
Old Man Pot. Sharman.
The Pond. Thwaite.
Shark's Fin. Wilkins.

Jasmine
Like a Silkworm Weaving.
Mahadevi (Mahadeviyakka).
Like Treasure Hidden in the
Ground. Mahadevi
(Mahadeviyakka).
Malaga. Hutchinson.
On the Death of His Child.
Faydi.
Popular Songs of Tuscany.
Anonymous.
Till You've Earned.
Mahadevi (Mahadeviyakka).

Jason
Finding Is the First Act.
Dickinson.
Strange Kind (II). Reed.

Jaw (s)
Among Sharks. Lee.
How Doth the Little
Crocodile. "Carroll.
In Kerry. Synge.
In Memoriam A.H.H.,
XXXIV. Tennyson.
Prague Spring. Harrison.
Seasons of the Soul. Tate.
Suppositions. Faulkner.
Walk, Jaw-Bone. Steele.
The Wyoming Massacre.
Terry.

Jay
Jay A-Pass'd. Barnes.
The Man with the Blue
Guitar. Stevens.
Riley. Causley.

Jazz
Battle Report. Kaufman.
For Our Lady. Sanchez.
Four Glimpses of Night.
Davis.
Le Jazz Hot. Hollo.
Jazzonia. Hughes.
Lester Young. Joans.
Miles' Delight. Joans.
Reuben, Reuben. Harper.

Jazzmen
Jazz Fantasia. Sandburg.

Jealous (y)
Against Mosquitoes.
Meleager.
Animal Songs: Zebra Stallion.
Anonymous.
Epitaphs of the War, 1914-18.
Kipling.
In Oxford City. *Anonymous.*
Lilith. Fainlight.
Love and Jealousy. Greene.
Midsummer Jingle. Levy.
Once on a Time a Thousand
Different Men. Henry.
Patrico's Song. Jonson.
So proud she was to die.
Dickinson.
To Phyllis. Field.
Turn All Thy Thoughts.
Campion.
Unearthing. Rosenberg.
You, Whose Mother's Lover
Was Grass. Corso.

Jean
Glenlogie, or, Jean o Bethelnie
(A version). *Anonymous.*

Heresy for a Class-Room.
Humphries.
Of A' the Airts the Wind Can
Blaw. Burns.
Tam i' the Kirk. Jacob.

Jehovah
Bless Him. *Anonymous.*
Holy Father, Great Creator.
Griswold.
Springfield Mountain (A
vers.). *Anonymous.*
A triumph may be of several
kinds. Dickinson.

Jelly
Beth Appleyard's Verses.
DeVries.
The Birth in a Narrow Room.
Brooks.
Ghost Story. Thomas.
Hambone Blues. Bell.
Haunted House. Worth.
If It Looks Like Jelly, Shakes
Like Jelly, It Must Be Gel-
a-Tine. Lincoln (Hicks).
The Lizards of La Brea. De
Baca.
A Ternarie of Littles, Upon a
Pipkin of Jelly Sent to a
Lady. Herrick.
Triolet. Chesterton.
You'll Never Miss Your Jelly.
Johnson.

Jellyfish
I Have Lived This Way for
Years and Do Not Wish to
Change. Blumenthal.
Skip-Scoop-Anellie.
Prideaux.

Jenny
Fidget. *Anonymous.*
The Liner She's a Lady.
Kipling.
Walk, Jaw-Bone. Steele.
When as I Do Record.
Anonymous.
Whip Jamboree. *Anonymous.*
Words of Oblivion and Peace.
Preil.
Yule's Come, and Yule's
Gane. *Anonymous.*

Jersey
A Farmer's Boy.
Anonymous.
The Hour of Feeling.
Simpson.
Legend. Weaver.

Jerusalem
Anglo-Saxon. Mayo.
Answer. Goldberg.
The City of God. Palgrave.
Crusade. Belloc.
The Crusaders Behold
Jerusalem. Tasso.
Dan, the Dust of Masada Is
Still in My Nostrils.
Whitman.
Evening Prayer. *Anonymous.*
Evening Walk. Akesson.
A Fable for Critics. Lowell.
Gates. Mary Madeleva.
I Have Been through the
Gates. Mew.
Jerusalem. Blake.
The Last Abbot of Gloucester.
Childe.
Like a Young Levite.
Mandelstam.
No One Talks about This.
Rakosi.
A Prisoner's Song of
Jerusalem. *Anonymous.*
Run Come See. *Anonymous.*

Shine On. Schoolcraft.
Theodor Herzl. Zangwill.
To F. C. in Memoriam
Palestine. Chesterton.
The Traveler. *Anonymous.*
Walk in Jerusalem Jus' Like
John. *Anonymous.*
The Wandering Jew Comes to
the Wall. Fleg.
We Sit Solitary. *Anonymous.*
When I Came to Israel.
Meyers.
With My Grandfather.
Zelda.

Jest (er) (s)
As One Who Bears beneath
His Neighbor's Roof.
Hillyer.
The Defiance. Behn.
Departmental Ditties: Prelude.
Kipling.
The Dust of the Overland
Trail. Adams.
Epitaph: "A great philosopher
did choke." Butler.
Epitaphs of the War.
Kipling.
The Faerie Queene. Spenser.
For Paul Laurence Dunbar.
Cullen.
The Harlequin of Dreams.
Lanier.
Idea. Drayton.
The Kings of Europe A Jest.
Dodsley.
Lucasta Laughing. Lovelace.
Museum-Piece. Brown.
The Skeleton. Chesterton.
Thorns Arm the Rose.
Claudian.
To a Young Gentleman in
Love: A Tale. Prior.
What Is Our Life? Ralegh.
When Helen Lived. Yeats.

Jesus
All in the Morning.
Anonymous.
Anecdote from William IV
Street. Enright.
The Annunciation.
Anonymous.
At His Feet. Carpenter.
At Least–To Pray–Is Left–Is
Left. Dickinson.
Atomic Pantoum. Meinke.
Ave Maria. Charasson.
Ave Regina Coelorum.
Anonymous.
Awake Yee Westerne
Nymphs, Arise and Sing.
Danforth.
A Better Resurrection.
Rossetti.
Bible Stories. Reese.
The Bridegroom of Cana.
Pickthall.
Caelica, CIX. Greville.
A Carol. Weatherly.
Cecil County. Welburn.
Children of Love. Monro.
Christ Is All. Bonar.
Christ Is Risen! Sturm.
Christmas Bells. Mortenson.
Christmas, the Year One, A.
D. Hay.
Comrade Jesus. Cleghorn.
The Confession Stone.
Dodson.
The Cost. Osgood.
Down in the Forest.
Anonymous.

Draw Near, O Son of God.
Wesley.
Elephant Rock. St. John.
The Everlasting Gospel.
Blake.
The Face of Jesus Christ.
Rossetti.
Father, Teach Me. Lee.
Fish Shop Windows.
Dutton.
Forgiveness. Lyte.
A Foxhole for the Night.
Quinn.
A Gift of God. *Anonymous.*
Give Me Jesus. *Anonymous.*
Go Down Death. Johnson.
Go Tell. *Anonymous.*
Go Tell It on the Mountain.
Anonymous.
God Rest You Merry,
Gentlemen. Mulock Craik.
The Great Redeemer Lives.
Steele.
Harry Semen.
""MacDiarmid.
Help Thy Servant.
Broaddus.
Herself a Rose Who Bore the
Rose. Rossetti.
His Creed. Herrick.
The Holy Well. *Anonymous.*
Hospitality in Ancient Ireland.
Anonymous.
How of the Virgin Mother
Shall I Sing? Ennodius.
Hymn Against Pestilence.
Colman.
Hymns for the Amusement of
Children. Smart.
I am a young girl, gay.
Anonymous.
I Give My Heart to Thee.
Palmer.
I Got a Letter from Jesus
(with music). *Anonymous.*
I Love to Tell the Story.
Hankey.
I'm Only a Broken-Down
Miner. *Anonymous.*
I'm Troubled in Mind.
Anonymous.
I Saw Thee. Palmer.
If Jesus Came to Your House.
Anonymous.
In Lord Carpenter's Country.
Higgs.
Jacob's Well. *Anonymous.*
Jesus. Pimentel Coronel.
Jesus Christ. Guthrie.
Jesus, in Sickness and in Pain.
Gallaudet.
Jesus Is Near. Waterston.
Jesus Loves Me, This I Know.
Warner.
Jesus Was Crucified or: It
Must Be Deep. Rodgers.
Jesus, Won't You Come B'm-
By?(with music).
Anonymous.
Karma. Robinson.
Keep A-Inchin' along.
Anonymous.
Keep Me, Jesus, Keep Me.
Carmichael.
Last Antiphon: To Mary.
Donohue.
The Last Hymn.
Farningham.
A Lementable New Ballad
upon the Earle of Essex
Death. *Anonymous.*
The Leper. Willis.

Jesus (continued)

The Life of St. Cellach: Dear Was He. *Anonymous.*
Lift Your Glad Voices in Triumph on High. Ware.
The Light Now Shineth. *Anonymous*
A Little Talk wid Jesus Makes It Right. *Anonymous.*
Lord, At This Closing Hour. Fitch.
Love-Joy. Herbert.
Lowly Bethlehem. Zinzendorf.
The Man of Calvary. *Anonymous.*
The Man of Calvary (Easter Day Service). *Anonymous.*
Mangers. Davies.
Miracle Play. *Anonymous.*
My Choice. Renfrow.
My Daily Prayer. Gray.
Nigger. Shapiro.
No Room at the Inn. *Anonymous.*
Noel. Belloc.
Nothing to Wish or to Fear. Newton.
Notre Dame des Petits. Mercier.
Now I Have Found a Friend. Hope.
O Jesus, My Saviour, I Know Thou Art Mine. Taylor.
O Sion, Haste, Thy Mission High Fulfilling. Thomson.
O, That I Had Some Secret Place. *Anonymous.*
Oh, Give Us Back the Days of Old. Neale.
Old English Charm Song. *Anonymous.*
Olney Hymns: The Happy Change. Cowper.
On Christmas Eve. Pierce.
On Mary Magdalen. Drummond.
One More Day's Work for Jesus. Warner.
Only Jesus Will I Know. Wesley.
Only One Life. Bowman.
Onward, Christian Soldiers. Baring-Gould.
Our Rock. Key.
Peace, Perfect Peace. Bickersteth.
Perfect Love. *Anonymous.*
Plastic Jesus. *Anonymous.*
Pray! Wells.
A Prayer. Dolben.
Prayer for Neighborhood Evangelism. Jansen.
Prayer to the Virgin. *Anonymous.*
Psalms, CXLVII. Smart.
Remember the Day of Judgment. *Anonymous.*
Resolutions?–New and Old. Rolfe.
Saints in Glory, We Together. Adams.
The Salutation of the Blessed Virgin. Byrom.
Sinner, Is Thy Heart at Rest? Waterbury.
Soft Job. Summers.
Sonnet XXIV. Alabaster.
Sonnet LXXIV. Alabaster.
The Soul of Jesus Is Restless. Mitchell.

Speak Out for Jesus. *Anonymous.*
Streets of Glory. *Anonymous.*
The Survival of the Fittest. Cleghorn.
Take Time to Be Holy. Longstaff.
Tell Jesus. *Anonymous.*
The Teresian Contemplative. Benson.
Thankfulness. Procter.
That's Faith. Leitner.
That's Jesus. Renfrow.
There Is a Name I Love to Hear. Whitfield.
There Is Never a Day So Dreary. Alexander.
There Is No Name So Sweet on Earth. Bethune.
To a Contemporary Bunkshooter. Sandburg.
To Show How Humble. *Anonymous.*
To the Lighted Lady Window. Wilkinson.
Too Busy. *Anonymous.*
Troubled Jesus. Cuney.
Trust in Jesus. Conder.
Two Old Lenten Rhymes: II. *Anonymous.*
Until the Shadows Lengthen. Newman.
Victory. *Anonymous.*
Wake the Song of Jubilee. Bacon.
We Need a Whole Lot More of Jesus. *Anonymous.*
Weddase Maryam. *Anonymous.*
Weeping Sinner, Dry Your Tears. Holden.
What Christ Is to Us. *Anonymous.*
What Happiness Can Equal Mine. David.
What Shall We Render. *Anonymous.*
When Jesus Wept. Billings.
Whom Jesus Loved. Barford.
A Wish. *Anonymous.*

Jets
Miami. Epstein.
Seven Sharp Propeller Blades. Ciardi.
A Technical Supplement. Kinsella.

Jew (s)
Ancestors. Schimmel.
And the Earth Rebelled. Suhl.
Blessing. Wilk.
But Not So Odd. Browne.
Caelica, XCVII. Greville.
Childhood. Bruck.
Crossing. Barnett.
The Daughter of Jairus. Tsvetayeva.
Debate with the Rabbi. Nemerov.
Dew. Reznikoff.
Diaspora Jews. Boimwall.
Domestics. Cumbo.
Elegy. Baruch of Worms.
The Everlasting Gospel. Blake.
An Evil Man. Beer-Hofmann.
The First Time. Shapiro.
G. K. Chesterton. Wolfe.
Hilaire Belloc. Wolfe.

How Odd. Ewer.
The Hypocrite. Ben Kalonymos.
In the Old Jewish Cemetery, Prague, 1970. Lowbury.
Invisible Trumpets Blowing. Pratt.
Jewboy. Tuwim.
A Jewish Child Prays to Jesus. Blumenthal-Weiss.
Land of Nations (excerpt). Stein.
Morgan. Stedman.
Osip Mandelshtam. Layton.
Shakespeare. Emerson.
Riddle. Heyen.
To Russia. Miller.
Scraps. Kamenetz.
The Store in Havana. Kozer.
The Survivors. Waddington.
The Turning. Levine.
The Wall. Merriam.
What Is a Jewish Poem? Sklarew.
The World's Wonders. Jeffers.

Jewel (s)
Across clear drops of dew. Asayasu.
"L'Apparition" of Gustave Moreau. Bottomley.
At the Smithsonian. Haley.
Author Unknown. Montgomerie.
Bonnie Wee Thing. Burns.
A Brilliant Day. Tennyson.
California. Sigourney.
Coal. Lorde.
Folk Wisdom. Kinsella.
Friends. Ashbery.
Getting Lost in Nazi Germany. Bell.
Hansel and Gretel Return. Ray.
Her Praises. Skoloker.
In the Henry James Country. Abrahams.
A Marriage Betwixt Scrape, Monarch of the Maunders...(excerpt). Pennecuik.
On Dives. Crashaw.
On Reading Gene Derwood's "The Innocent'. Maas.
On the Beach. Calverley.
The Race Question. Madgett.
Sisters. McPherson.
Song: "The night is an ancient sorceress." Frug.
Sonnets of the Months. San Geminiano.
The Stars. Dodge.
A Tear. Dobson.
To His Mistresses. Herrick.
To K. de M. Stevenson.
To Mrs. Will H. Low. Stevenson.
Vigil of the Immaculate Conception. Egan.

Jig (s)
Could You Do That? Burns.
Jenny Wren. *Anonymous.*
Little Piggy. Hood.
Medley. *Anonymous.*
The Old Marquis and His Blooming Wife. *Anonymous.*
On Hearing Prokofieff's Grotesque for Two Bassoons...(parody). Untermeyer.

Jill
Art and Life. Ridge.
Five Eyes. De la Mare.
There Were Two Blackbirds Sitting on a Hill. Mother Goose.
The Yeoman of the Guard (excerpt). Gilbert.

Jim
I Have No Pain. *Anonymous.*
Little Jim. Farmer.
Modern Ode to the Modern School. Erskine.
The Old Man and Jim. Riley.
'Spacially Jim. Morgan.
Uncle Simon and Uncle Jim. Ward.

Jim Crow
Jim Jones. *Anonymous.*
Status Quo. Dismond.

Jingle
A Catch. Hood.
The Jester's Plea. Locker-Lampson.
Mister Tambourine Man. Dylan.
On the Oxford Book of Victorian Verse. ""MacDiarmid.

Jive
Charleston Blues. Hill.
Tales of the Islands, VI. Walcott.

Joan
Careless Talk. Hollis.
Court and Country Love. *Anonymous.*
Girls' Names. Farjeon.
The Good Joan. Reese.
Joan to Her Lady. *Anonymous.*
To His Coy Mistress (parody). Sharpless.
Will to Win. Scott.

Job
Dan Dunder. Ciardi.
The Daniel Jazz. Lindsay.
Elegy for Alfred Hubbard. Connor.
Elmer Ruiz. Oresick.
Girl Friday. Equi.
I Don't Want Your Millions, Mister. Garland.
In Order To. Patchen.
In This Hotel. Carnevali.
Muckers. Sandburg.
The Other Fellow's Job. Gillilan.
The Overlander. *Anonymous.*
A Practical Woman. Hardy.
Sad Story. Day.
Self-Employed. Ignatow.
Seventeen Warnings in Search of a Feminist Poem. Jong.
The Thinker. Braley.

Jock
Cloudburst and Soaring Moon. ""MacDiarmid.
Yule's Come, and Yule's Gane. *Anonymous.*

Joe
Bill and Joe. Holmes.
Joe. McCord.
Lenox Avenue Mural. Hughes.
Old Black Joe. Foster.
Old Joe. Anonymous.
Old Joe Clark. *Anonymous.*
Only a Miner. *Anonymous.*

John
The Baby's Name.　Jenks.
The Birthday-Cake
　Glockenspiel.　Henley.
Bored.　Brown.
Boys' Names.　Farjeon.
A Dead Letter.　Dobson.
The Death of Robin Hood.
　Anonymous.
Deedle, Deedle, Dumpling,
　My Son John.　Mother
　Goose.
Diddle, Diddle, Dumpling,
　My Son John.　*Anonymous.*
Didn' Ol' John Cross the
　Water on His Knees?
　Anonymous.
Happiness.　Milne.
The Indian Ghost Dance and
　War.　Prather.
Little John Nobody.
　Anonymous.
Long John.　Anonymous.
Lowlands.　*Anonymous.*
O No, John!　*Anonymous.*
Oh No John.　*Anonymous.*
Rolling John (excerpt).
　Wood.
Say Hello to John.　Williams.
Status Symbol.　Evans.
The Visitor.　Pyle.
Walk in Jerusalem Jus' Like
　John.　*Anonymous.*
The Wall.　Askenazy.
The Workbox.　Hardy.

John Brown
The Battle of Charlestown.
　Brownell.
October 16: The Raid.
　Hughes.

John Bull
A New Song to an Old Tune.
　Anonymous.
The World Is a Bundle of
　Hay.　Byron.

John Doe
Richard Roe and John Doe.
　Graves.

Johnny
The Alphabet.　*Anonymous.*
Benign Neglect/Mississippi,
　1970.　St. John.
But That Was Yesterday.
　Fisher.
Did Ya Hear?　Jamal.
Gently, Johnny, My Jingalo.
　Anonymous.
The Gray Mare (Young
　Johnny the Miller).
　Anonymous.
I Know Where I'm Going.
　Anonymous.
The Idiot Boy.　Wordsworth.
Kansas Boys.　Anonymous.
Lost Johnny.　Anonymous.
The Oakey Street Evictions.
　Anonymous.
On the Banks of the Little
　Eau Pleine.　*Anonymous.*
The Springtime It Brings on
　the Shearing.　Overbury.
Time's Changes.　Bramston.
When Johnny Comes
　Marching Home.　Gilmore.

Join (ed) (ing) (s)
The Ballad of Tonopah Bill.
　Anonymous.
A Bed without a Woman.
　Souster.
Birthday Card for a
　Psychiatrist.　Van Duyn.

Champagne Charlie.
　Leybourne.
Colin and Lucy.　Tickell.
DOA in Dulse.　Burns.
The Egg.　Day.
The Gofongo.　Milligan.
Jardin des Fleurs.　Webb.
The Light.　Holloway.
The Lightning Flash.
　Anonymous.
Metroliner.　Du Vall.
Moods.　Kwitko.
A New Dance.　Anderson.
No Help I'll Call Till I'm Put
　in the Narrow Coffin.　O
　Rathaille.
Oyster-Crabs (parody).
　Wells.
Paracelsus.　Browning.
A Parting Hymn We Sing.
　Wolfe.
Pit Viper.　Starbuck.
Searching for Lambs.
　Anonymous.
Shout for Joy.　Anonymous.
Sonnet.　Duncan.
To Ask for All Thy Love.
　Anonymous.
True Freedom.　Mackay.
Walking against the Wind.
　Stallworthy.
You Gotta Go Down (And
　Join the Union).
　Anonymous.

Joke (s)
Adam, Lilith, and Eve.
　Browning.
Autograph Book/Prophecy.
　Halley.
Blighters.　Sassoon.
Cain.　Layton.
Cowboy Song.　Veitch.
How Did It Seem to Sylvia?
　Schnackenberg.
How We Built a Church at
　Ashcroft.　Leahy.
Kate and the Cowhide.
　Anonymous.
Last Judgment.　Fletcher.
Misapprehension.　Dunbar.
Modern Love, VI.　Meredith.
More Sonnets at Christmas.
　Tate.
The Old Songs.　Seaman.
Periphery.　Stone.
Sensitive Sydney.　Irwin.
Sonnets of the Months.　San
　Geminiano.
Sphinx.　Hayden.
That Nature Is a Heraclitean
　Fire...　Hopkins.
Twenty Foolish Fairies.
　Turner.
Washyuma Motor Hotel.
　Ortiz.
Wasp.　Nowlan.

Jolly
Gloucestershire Wassail.
　Anonymous.
Heave Away.　Anonymous.
Jolly Jack.　Thackeray.
The Jolly Wagoner.
　Anonymous.
The King of Yvetot.
　Beranger.
The Man-of-War's Garland.
　Anonymous.
The Miner Boy, II.
　Anonymous.
Nose, Nose, Jolly Red Nose.
　Mother Goose.
Pirate Treasure.　Brown.

The Rolling Sailor.
　Anonymous.
The Schooner Kandahar.
　Anonymous.
Thames Head Wassailers'
　Song.　*Anonymous.*
Though a Fool.　Francis.
When Lovely Woman Stoops
　to Folly (parody).
　Demetriadis.

Jonquil
Lalique.　Porter.
Look Not in My Eyes, for
　Fear.　Housman.

Jordan
Ev'ry Time I Feel de Spirit.
　Anonymous.
John the Baptist.　Simpson.
Odes.　Horace.
The Other Side of Jordan.
　Anonymous.
Roll, Jordan, Roll.
　Anonymous.
Stan' Still Jordan.
　Anonymous
Zionist Marching Song.
　Imber.

Joseph
After the Death of an Elder
　Klallam.　Niatum.
Angels We Have Heard on
　High.　*Anonymous.*
Machupuchare. What the
　Mountain Said. Shaking the
　Dead Bones...　Stroud.
Mary Passed This Morning.
　Dodson.
O Child of Beauty Rare.
　Goethe.
A Panegyrick to My Lord
　Protector.　Waller.
The Wall.　Askenazy.

Joshua
Afternoon in the Garden.
　Anderson.
The Body Is Like Roots
　Stretching.　Reznikoff.

Journey (s)
Akiba.　Rukeyser.
All through the Night.
　Anonymous.
Anastasia McLaughlin.
　Paulin.
Baedeker for Metaphysicians.
　Higgins.
Bard.　Bantock.
The Brut.　Layamon.
Budding Spring.　Lindsay.
Buying a Shop on Dizengoff.
　Biton.
The Child Who Was Shot
　Dead by Soldiers at
　Nyanga.　Jonker.
Country Letter.　Clare.
Die in de Fiel'.　*Anonymous.*
Ecce Homo.　Gascoyne.
An Evening Revery.　Bryant.
Foreboding.　Haines.
God's Determinations.
　Taylor.
The Good Inn.　Viele.
Happy, Saviour, Would I Be.
　Nevin.
The Heart Recalcitrant.
　Speyer.
How Easily Men's Cheeks Are
　Hot.　Heidenstam.
I Have Got My Leave.
　Tagore.
Kings and Stars.　Erskine.
Love at Roblin Lake.　Purdy.
Marston.　Spender.

May 10th.　Kumin.
Near the Border of Insanities.
　Abse.
Night Train.　Fineran.
O.　Villanueva.
Open Your Hand.　Fulton.
The Pilgrimage.　Herbert.
Praise Ye the Lord, O
　Celebrate His Fame.
　Folger.
Precious Mettle.　Warsh.
The Saint's Delight.
　Anonymous.
Seed Journey.　Corso.
Seeing.　Donaghy.
The Sign-Post.　Thomas.
Sioux Indians.　*Anonymous.*
Sleep and Poetry.　Keats.
Song: "Distil not poison in
　mine ears."　Hall.
Song of Welcome.　Fraser.
Song: "Spring lights her
　candles everywhere."
　Shove.
Southern Ships and Settlers,
　1606-1732.　Benét.
Supplication.　Cotter.
Sympathy.　Bronte.
Things I Didn't Know I
　Loved.　Hikmet.
Tom O'Bedlam.　*Anonymous.*
Tonight Everyone in the
　World Is Dreaming the
　Same Dream.　Litwack.
The Trail Up Wu Gorge.
　Sun Yun-feng.
The Traveller.　Berryman.
The Trees of the Garden.
　Rossetti.
Trust in Me.　*Anonymous.*
Until I Reach-a Ma Home.
　Anonymous.
Variations on a Time Theme.
　Muir.
Welcome, Thou Safe Retreat!
　Habington.
With Ships the Sea Was
　Sprinkled.　Wordsworth.

Jove
Battle Hymn of the Spanish
　Rebellion.　Mackey.
Home-Thoughts, from the
　Sea.　Browning.
Love Perfumes All Parts.
　Herrick.
The Mint Julep.　Hoffman
Of His Majesties Receiving
　the News of the Duke of
　Buckingham's Death.
　Waller.
Of His Returne from Spaine.
　Wyatt.
Plato To Theon.　Freneau.
To a Friend on His Nuptials.
　Prior.
To the King, at His Entrance
　into Saxham.　Carew.
Troynovant.　Dekker.

Joy (ful) (ous) (s)
An Acrostick on Mrs.
　Winifret Griffin.　Saffin.
Adequacy.　Browning.
After a Journey.　Hardy.
The After-Glow.　Blind.
Amoretti, LI.　Spenser.
Amoretti, LXXXVII.
　Spenser.
Andante, Ma Non Assai.
　Rufinus Domesticus.
The Angel in the House.
　Patmore.
The Angler.　Chalkhill.

The Answer. Teasdale.
The Antiquary. Chapt. 10:
Why Sit'st Thou by That
Ruin'd Hall. Scott.
As I Sat on a Sunny Bank.
Anonymous.
As in the Land of Darkness.
Miklitsch.
The Ascetic. Daley.
Astrophel and Stella, XLIV.
Sidney.
Astrophel and Stella, CVIII.
Sidney.
Australian Transcripts, X: The
Wood-Swallows. Sharp.
Ayii, Ayii. The Great Sea Has
Set Me in Motion.
Anonymous.
Back to the Ghetto.
Glatstein.
Balloon Man. North.
The Barefoot Boy. Whittier.
The Barge. Fyleman.
Be Useful. Herbert.
Behind the Glass Wall.
Norse.
A Bell. Scollard.
The Best Friend. Davies.
Beyond Feith Buidhe.
Brown.
Bird Song. Richards.
Birth of Christ. Rilke.
The Blind Man's Regret.
Anonymous.
The Bustan. Sa'di.
Caelica. I. Greville.
Caelica, XCIV. Greville.
California. Harris
A Carol for Christmas Day.
Byrd.
Casey's Daughter at the Bat.
Graham.
A Choice of Weapons.
Kunitz.
Christmas Carol. del
Castillo.
Christmas Is Remembering.
Binns.
The Chrysanthemum Show.
Day-Lewis.
The Church-Porch. Herbert.
Cinderella. Broumas.
Clams. Moss.
Come into Animal Presence.
Levertov.
Come, Sleep. Beaumont.
The Comin' o' the Spring.
Scott.
The Common Lot. Coats.
The Commonwealth of Toil.
Chaplin.
Consolation. Surrey.
The Cool Gold Wines of
Paradise. Farren.
Corydon's Farewell, on Sailing
in the Late Expedition
Fleet. Anonymous.
Counting Kisses. Catullus.
The Courtier's Life. Wyatt.
The Crows. Engels.
Darest Thou Now O Soul.
Whitman
David and Bethsabe. Peele.
The Day of Resurrection.
John of Damascus.
Dear Happy Souls. Smith.
Debate: Question, Quarry,
Dream. Warren.
Dementia Praecox. Bishop.
The Deserted Village.
Goldsmith.

Dispatch Number Nine.
Fetherling.
The Doubt of Future Foes.
Elizabeth I.
Dragon Country: To Jacob
Boehme. Warren.
Dream-Land. Rossetti.
A Dream of Artemis.
Ledwidge.
Durham Old Women.
Anonymous.
Dusk of the Gods (excerpt).
Funaroff.
The Easter Song. Sedulius.
Eating Poetry. Strand.
Eighteen. Mary Honora.
The Eighteenth Song.
Hadewijch.
England's Triumph.
Anonymous.
Epitaph for Himself. Herbert
of Cherbury.
An Epitaph on a Robin-
Redbreast. Rogers.
Epithalamion. Auden.
Eternal Reward, Eternal Pain.
More.
Evening Schoolboys. Clare.
The Everlasting Mercy.
Masefield.
Faint Heart. Rufinus
Domesticus.
A Farewell. Sidney.
Farewell, Unkind! Farewell! to
Me, No More a Father!
Anonymous.
The Female Friend. Whur.
The Fiddlehead. McFadden.
Fill and Illumined. Ceravolo.
First Ice of Winter. Shorb.
First Song. Kinnell.
The Fleet at Santiago.
Russell.
For Every Day. Havergal.
For Perfect Peace. Wesley.
For the Time Being. Auden.
Forget. Anonymous.
Fragment. Hopkins.
Friendship. Blair.
From Heaven High I Come to
You. Luther.
Fulfilment. Nichols.
The Gash. Everson.
Glenara. Campbell.
The Glorious Twelfth.
Greacen.
Go not too near a house of
rose. Dickinson.
God of Might, God of Right.
Anonymous.
Harold at Two Years Old.
Myers.
Have You Seen the Lady?
Sousa.
The Head That Once Was
Crowned with Thorns.
Kelly.
Heap on More Wood. Scott.
Heart Oppress'd with
Desperate Thought.
Wyatt.
Her Courage. Yeats.
High and Low. Cousins.
The Higher Catechism. Foss.
Hippolytus. Euripides.
Homecoming in Storm.
Kenyon.
Hope and Joy. Rossetti.
How Shall a Man Fore-
Doomed. Coleridge.
How Happy the Lover.
Dryden.

How to Read Me. Landor.
Hymn to the Holy Spirit.
Wilton.
A Hymn to My God in a
Night of My Late Sicknesse.
Wotton.
Hymn to the Supreme Being
on Recovery (excerpt).
Smart.
I Never See the Red Rose
Crown the Year.
Masefield.
I Will Go with My Father A-
Ploughing. Campbell.
In Fine, Transparent Words.
Vogel.
In Harbour. Swinburne.
In Sweet Communion.
Newton.
In the Grass. Droste-
Hulshoff.
In the Marble Quarry.
Dickey.
Infant Joy. Blake.
The Influence of Local
Attachment (excerpt).
Polwhele.
Jesus, in Sickness and in Pain.
Gallaudet.
Jill Came from the Fair.
Farjeon.
The Jolly Shepherd Wat.
Anonymous.
Joy May Kill. Michelangelo.
Joy to the World.
Anonymous.
The Joys of Heaven.
Thomas a Kempis.
Juncture. Duncan.
The Keys of Canterbury.
Anonymous.
A Kitchen Prayer. Petersen.
Knee Deep. Joans.
Last Generation. Roberts.
Late Winter. McAuley(
The Law. Ibn Ezra.
Leave Krete and come to this
holy temple. Sappho.
Lenten Is Come.
Anonymous.
A Lesson in Detachment.
Miller.
Let Some Great Joys Pretend
to Find. Shadwell.
The Light in the Temple.
Benet.
Lines Descriptive of
Thomson's Island. Lynde.
The Lingam and the Yoni.
Hope.
A Little Bird I Am. Guyon.
Liverpool. Anonymous.
Lo! how I seek and sue to
have. Wyatt.
Lordings, Listen to Our Lay.
Anonymous.
Love Beleagured. Chapin.
The Love of Hell. Burstein.
Love's Fancy. Dryden.
Love Which Is Here a Care.
Drummond.
Lullaby: "Come sleep, and
with the sweet deceiving."
Fletcher.
Madrigal: "Oft thou hast with
greedy ear." Cooper.
A Maid Me Loved. Hannay.
The Making of Birds.
Tynan.
Martyrdom of Father
Campion. Walpole.
Matins. Levertov.

Medieval Norman Songs.
Anonymous.
Memories. Whitman.
The Midges Dance Aboon the
Burn. Tannahill.
Midnight Dancer. Hughes.
Misdemeanor. Triem.
The Moment. Roethke.
The Moon. Best.
Moon Song. Nweke.
The Morality of Poetry.
Wright.
Morna's Hill: A Distant
Prospect of the the City of
Armagh. Stuart.
The Mother. Palmer.
Mountain Medicine. Long.
A Mourning Letter from
Paris. Rivers.
Murdering Beauty. Carew.
Mustapha. Greville.
My Neighbor's Reply.
Anonymous.
My Prayer. Anonymous.
My Ramblin' Boy. Paxton.
The Mysterious Music of
Ocean. Anonymous.
New Guinea. McAuley.
New Heaven, New War.
Southwell.
The Newborn Colt.
Kennedy.
The Nightingale. Petrarch
(Francesco Petrarca).
No Pleasure Without Some
Pain. Vaux.
O Sons of Earth. Pope.
Ode on Advancing Age.
Dixon.
Ode to Joy. McClure.
Ode to Wisdom. Carter.
Ode to Zion. Halevi.
Odes. Horace.
Odes, IX. Hafiz.
The Odyssey. Homer.
An Old Cracked Tune.
Kunitz.
Oh, Give Us Back the Days
of Old. Neale.
On Ben Dorain. MacIntyre.
On a Forsaken Lark's Nest.
Blind.
On the Marriage of T. K. and
C. C. the Morning Stormy.
Carew.
Once Musing as I Sat.
Googe.
One Hour of Madness and
Joy. Whitman.
The Only Name Given Under
Heaven. Steele.
Out of Catullus. Crashaw.
The Outcast. Stephens.
Over the Great City.
Carpenter.
An Owl Is an Only Bird of
Poetry. Duncan.
A Palinode. Bolton.
Paradise Lost. Milton.
Parting at Morning. Dietmar
von Aist.
The Passing Strange.
Masefield.
The Pastime of Pleasure.
Hawes.
Peace. Sangster.
The Peasant Poet. Clare.
A Poem Containing Some
Remarks on the Present
War. Anonymous.
The Poet Describes His Love.
Nathan.

Poetry and Science. Turner.
Pomona. Morris.
The Porch. Pain.
Prayer. *Anonymous.*
Prayer. Hedges.
A Prayer for Every Day. Davies.
Progress. *Anonymous.*
Prometheus Unbound. Shelley.
Protagonist. Henrich.
Psalm XXVII. Sidney.
Puerperium. Waller.
Rain after a Vaudeville Show. Benét.
Reconciliation. Russell.
Reconsecration. Gould.
Relics. Cameron.
Return of the Native. Jones.
The River. Arnold.
The Robin. Very.
Robin Hood's Golden Prize. *Anonymous.*
The Rubaiyat of Omar Khayyam. Omar Khayyam.
Safely Home. *Anonymous.*
Saints. Garrett.
The Satisfying Portion. *Anonymous.*
The Scottish Mountaineering Club Song. Stott.
The Sea. Davies.
The Shepherd upon a Hill. *Anonymous.*
Silent, Silent Night. Blake.
Silent Testimony. Parmenter.
Silex Scintillans. Vaughan.
Sin, Despair, and Lucifer. Fletcher.
Somebody's Mother. Brine.
Song of Joy. Uvavnuk.
Song of the Horse. *Anonymous.*
Song of the Ill-Married. *Anonymous.*
Song of the Sirens. Browne.
The Song of the Tortured Girl. Berryman.
A Song-Offering. Tagore.
Song: Phillis be Gentler. Rochester.
Song to Death. Escriva.
Songs: "Now in golden glory goes." Johnson.
Sonnet XCIV. Greville.
Sonnet. At Ostend, July 22, 1787. Bowles.
A Sonnet, to the Noble Lady, the Lady Mary Worth. Jonson.
Sonnets, XLII: "Thou that last her, it is not all my grief." Shakespeare.
Sonnets to Orpheus. Rilke.
The Soul's Bitter Cry. *Anonymous.*
South-Wind. Lathrop.
The Sparrow's Nest. Wordsworth.
Speak Gently. Langford.
Spring: a Formal Ode. Tyutchev.
Stanzas Written in Dejection, Near Naples. Shelley.
Stolen Pleasure. Drummond.
The Sun and Moon So High and Bright. *Anonymous.*
The Sundial. Cooper.
Swallowing. Bond.
The Task. Cowper.

The Teacher Sees a Boy. Morningstar.
Tee-Vee Enigma. Raskin.
Thames Head Wassailers' Song. *Anonymous.*
Thanksgivings for the Beauty of His Providence. Traherne.
This Little Vigil. Bell.
This World. Evans.
Thou Art the Way. Doane.
Though Here in Flesh I Be. Howard.
Thomas Hood. Robinson.
The Times. Churchill.
To a Little Girl, One Year Old, in a Ruined Fortress (excerpt). Warren.
To a Tenting Boy. Turner.
To an Athlete Turned Poet. Meinke.
To an Unborn Pauper Child. Hardy.
To Dianeme. Herrick.
To His Friend in Absence. Strabo.
To My Son. Byron.
To Phillis. Waller.
To the Man-of-War Bird. Whitman.
To the Rev. Mr. Newton. Cowper.
To the Virgin. Lydgate.
To Usward. Bennett.
Today. Bangs.
Today in Bethlehem Hear I. St John Damascene.
Trees Once Walked and Stood. Tan Pai.
'Twas Jolly, Jolly Wat. Stubbs.
Two Springs. Li Ch'ing-chao.
Ubi Sunt Qui Ante Nos Fuerunt? *Anonymous.*
Undertakers. Bierce.
Upon a Spider Catching a Fly. Taylor.
Upon Mrs. Eliz. Wheeler, under the Name of Amarillis. Herrick.
Venice. Symons.
The Vesture of the Soul. Russell.
Victory in Defeat. Markham.
Visions of the Daughters of Albion. Blake.
La Vita Nuova. Dante Alighieri.
The Voice of Toil. Morris.
The Vow. Hecht.
The Wandering Maiden; or, True Love at Length United. *Anonymous.*
The Wassail Song. *Anonymous.*
We Have Lived and Loved Together. Jefferys.
Wedding Song. *Anonymous.*
The West-Country Lover. Brown.
When Diamonds, Nibbling in my Ears. Davies.
When Winds Are Raging. Stowe.
Where Beeth They Biforen Us Weren. *Anonymous.*
The White Island. Herrick.
Winter. Thomson.
With Christ and All His Shining Train. Prince.

With Fragrant Flowers We Strew the Way. Watson.
A Woman Shaman's Song. Uvavnuk.
Wonder. Traherne.
The Woodman's Dog. Cowper.
Written in a Lady's Prayer Book. Rochester.
Yoke Soft and Dear. Kunze.
Your Presence. Diop.

Jubilee
The Famous Ballad of the Jubilee Cup. Quiller-Couch.
On the Jubilee of Queen Victoria (excerpt). Tennyson.
Poke-Pole Fishing. Schmitz.

Judah
The Harp of David. Yehoash.
The Library. Mills.

Judas
Alexander Jannai. Cavafy.
Apparition. Bishop.
A Ballad of Christmas. De la Mare.
Betrayal. Cholmondeley.
The Feet of Judas. McClellan.
Jesus Christ. Guthrie.
The League of Nations. Siegrist.
The Morning After. Wellesley.

Judge (d) (s)
Ascension-Day. Vaughan.
At the Dog Show. Morley.
Believe Not. Peretz.
Bethinking Hymself of His Ende. Vaux.
Bucolic Eclogues: Waking, Child, While You Slept. Anderson.
Caelica, LXI. Greville.
Chain Gang Blues. *Anonymous.*
Earth. Bryant.
Fine! Barker.
Giovanni da Fiesole on the Sublime or Fra Angelico's "Last Judgment." Howard.
I'll Sail upon the Dog-star. Durfey.
If, Jerusalem, I Ever Should Forget Thee. Heine.
In the House of the Judge. Smith.
In the Lane. Strong.
The Judge is Fury: Epigraph. Cunningham.
The Judgement. Goodale.
King Henry V. Shakespeare.
Perhaps It's Only Music. Zach.
Saffold's Cures. Saffold.
Satires. Alamanni.
Satires. Wyatt.
Satyrus Peregrinana. Rankins.
Silex Scintillans. Vaughan.
Sonnet XIV: "When Faith and Love which parted from thee never." Milton.
Sonnet: Of Moderation and Tolerance. Guinicelli.
This Is My Letter to the World. Dickinson.
To a Wanton. Habington.
To Her–Unspoken. Burr.

A Treatie of Human Learning. Greville.
Unhappy Boston. Revere.
We. Kirillov.
The Weaver. *Anonymous.*
Who Is the Man? *Anonymous.*
Without More Weight. Ungaretti.

Judge (s)
Books. Crabbe.
Close-Ups of Summer. MacCaig.
Domaine Public. Hill.
Epilogue Spoken by Mrs. Boutell. Dryden.
First Satire of the Second Book of Horace. Pope.
The Parts of a Poet. Rose.
Tuesday, 4 March (Morning) 1963. Pasolini.

Judgment Day
The Bank Thief. Farrell.
Count My Time by Times That I Meet Thee. Gilder.
Endpiece. *Anonymous.*
The Framework-Knitters Petition. *Anonymous.*
Lady Franklin's Lament (II). *Anonymous.*
Latimer's Light. *Anonymous.*
Mutans Nomen Evae. Gill.
O Jesus! Sweet the Tears I Shed. Palmer.
On Some Trees Needlessly Slain. Coblentz.
The Poor Ghost. Rossetti.
Shady Grove. *Anonymous.*
Wait for the Wagon. *Anonymous.*
The Wants of Man. Adams.

Judgment (s)
An Allusion to Horace. The Tenth Satire of the First Book. Rochester.
Astraea at the Capitol. Whittier.
Believe Not. Peretz.
Conscience. Stubbs.
Echo Canyon. *Anonymous.*
Epistle to the President, Vice-President, and Members...(excerpt). Geddes.
"Garden of Gethsemane." Pasternak.
God's Judgment on a Wicked Bishop. Southey.
Joan to Her Lady. *Anonymous.*
The Lady's Complaint. Heath-Stubbs.
The Last Redoubt. Austin.
The Mediatix of Grace. Burke.
Night Song. Fairburn.
O Day of God, Draw Nigh. Scott.
O Lord, Almighty God. *Anonymous.*
On Entering a Forest. Lennen.
Ostrava. Bezruc.
The Philosophic Apology. Greenberg.
Poem, 1972. Scroggie.
Revenge of the Hunted. Ford.
The Sacrilege. Hardy.
The Sherman Cyclone. *Anonymous.*
The Shipmen. Hunnis.

Someone, I tell you. Sappho.
Sonnets, LV: "Not marble, nor the gilded monuments." Shakespeare.
Sonnets upon the Punishment of Death (excerpt). Wordsworth.
Supplication of the Black Aberdeen. Kipling.
Tenson. Carenza.
Thomas More to Them That Seek Fortune. More.
To His Noble Friend, Mr. Richard Lovelace, upon His Poems. Marvell.
Variations. Jarrell.
Yours Truly. Nathan.

Judy
The Ladies. Kipling.
Punch and Judy. Anonymous.
The Sabine Farmer's Serenade. Mahony.
When Ol' Sis' Judy Pray. Campbell.

Jug (s)
All Jolly Fellows That Follow the Plow. Anonymous.
Days Were Great as Lakes. Vogel.
Little Brown Jug. Winner.
The Minstrel's Last Lay. Barth.
Undying Thirst. Antipater of Sidon.

Juice (s)
Flipochinos. Zarco.
The Jackfruit. Ho Xuan Huong.
Knee Deep. Joans.
Pictures of the Rhine. Meredith.
Sonnets to Orpheus. Rilke.
You Take the Pilgrims, Just Give Me the Progress. Rosenfield.

Julep
Have You Seen the Lady? Sousa.
When the Mint Is in the Liquor. Ousley.

Julia
Discovering–. Scott.
Herrick's Julia (parody). Bevington.
Pentachromatic. Burgos.
The Rosarie. Herrick.
So Look the Mornings. Herrick.

July
Cut Thistles in May. Anonymous.
The Fisherman's Son. Bruce.
Midsummer Frost. Rosenberg.
Old Kimball. Anonymous.
The Oyster. Nash.
The Pink Frock. Hardy.
That's July. Butts.

Jump (ed) (ing) (s)
Chops. Dixon.
Come to Me. Anonymous.
Conrad. Slonimski.
The Crackling Twig. Stephens.
Crescent Moon. Roberts.
The Curate's Kindness. Hardy.
The Fire. Duncan.
The Fishes. Anonymous.
In Memoriam. "Adeler.

The Intoxicated Rat. Anonymous.
A Man of Thessaly. Anonymous.
Old Farmer Giles. Anonymous.
Patrick Ewing Takes a Foul Shot. Ackerman.
Preachin' the Blues. House.
Starfish. Welles.
Tales of the Islands, VI. Walcott.
To D––, Dead by Her Own Hand. Nemerov.
Zebra. Smith.

June
August. Winslow.
Contrary Mary. Turner.
The Cuckoo. Anonymous.
A Far-Off Rose. Peabody.
Four O'Clock Flower Blues. Anonymous.
Harebells in June. Wynne.
June Is Bustin' Out All Over. Hammerstein.
Midsummer. Allingham.
The Mowing. Roberts.
Nightfall on Sedgemoor. Young.
Ourselves were wed one summer–dear. Dickinson.
The Oyster. Nash.
Rhymes for a Modern Nursery: Hey Diddle Diddle. Dehn.
The Rose. Howell.
School after Christmas. Garthwaite.
She Died in Beauty. Sillery.
Six in June. Davies.
The Spring. Carew.
That's June. Butts.
Two Married. Frazee-Bower.

Jungle (s)
Dandelions for Chains. Kirsch.
Far from Africa. Danner.
India. Turner.
The Interrogations. Knoll.
Men in Green. Campbell.
The Nature of Jungles. Moses.
Piano and Drums. Okara.
Rare Moments. Phelps.
Song of Napalm. Weigl.
To Krishna Haunting the Hills. Andal.
The Wabash Cannonball. Anonymous.

Junk (s)
The Fishing Fleet. Colcord.
Hector the Collector. Silverstein.
Limerick: "Now the ears, so I always had thunk." Euwer.
On the Farm. Winder.
Sweet Patuni. James.
To My Daughter the Junkie on a Train. Lorde.

Junkie
Blues for Sister Sally. Kandel.

Juno
Going or Gone (parody). Lamb.
Love Perfumes All Parts. Herrick.
My Loves. Blackie.

Jury
Call It a Good Marriage. Graves.

The Judge is Fury: Epigraph. Cunningham.
Naomi Wise. Anonymous.

Just
The Ashland Tragedy, I. Anonymous.
A Bestiary. Rexroth.
Dear Mother. Jarrett.
Epilogue Spoken at Oxford by Mrs. Marshall. Dryden.
Epilogue Spoken by Mrs. Boutell. Dryden.
An Epitaph for a Godly Man's Tomb. Wild.
The Eternal Justice. Aldrich.
God's Key. Anonymous.
Greens (with music). Anonymous.
The Hand and Foot. Very.
His Metrical Prayer: Before Execution. Graham.
Hymn to Darkness. Norris.
In Mortem Venerabilis Andreae Prout Carmen. Mahony.
It Is Far from Just between Us. Anonymous.
King Lear. Shakespeare.
A Lady with a Falcon on Her Fist. Lovelace.
Limerick: "A canny old codger at Yalta." Anonymous.
Mercy and Love. Herrick.
A New Catch in Praise of the Reverend Bishops. Anonymous.
The New Mars. Coates.
The Newspaper. Crabbe.
O Thou! Whose Presence Went Before. Whittier.
Pass forth, my wonted cries. Wyatt.
Philoctetes. De Tabley.
Rapture. Carlson.
Sonnet to William Wilberforce, Esq. Cowper.
Thy Kingdom, Lord, We Long For. Scudder.
To Cupid. Davison.
The Victories of Love. Patmore.
Where Are All Thy Beauties Now, All Hearts Enchaining? Campion.
Why? Crane.

Justice (s)
Ahmad. Bensel.
Amoretti, XII. Spenser.
Another September. Kinsella.
Armistice Day Vow. Gould.
Behind the Falls. Stafford.
Bush Justice. Harpur.
The Call. Clark.
Children's Rhymes. Hughes.
Columbus. Coates.
The Dancing Bear. Southey.
The Death of Justice. Hawkins.
Decay. Herbert.
Dedication for a Book of Criticism. Winters.
The Deepest Sensuality. Lawrence.
The Draft Riot. De Kay.
Elegy (For Himself). Rimos.
The Excursion. Wordsworth.
The Fairies' Farewell. Corbet.
Farewell to the Fairies. Corbet.

God, Give Us Men! Holland.
God of the Nations, Near and Far. Holmes.
Half-Way, for One Commandment Broken. Housman.
The Heavens Declare Thy Glory, Lord! Watts.
The Historical Judas. Nemerov.
Jew. Morhange.
Judge Harsh Blues. Lewis.
Law in the Country of the Cats. Hughes.
The Murder of Moses. Shapiro.
Pledge of Allegiance. Anonymous.
Poor Ellen Smith. Degraph.
Sarah. Schwartz.
Submission to Afflictive Providences. Watts.
To Julia de Burgos. Burgos.
To Sir Thomas Egerton. Daniel.
We Don't Get No Justice Here in Atlanta. Anonymous.
When Wilt Thou Teach the People—? Lawrence.
Witch. Beer.

Justify
Consolation in War. Mumford.
Ill Met by Zenith. Nash.
Juvenal's Sixth Satire. Dryden.
My Mother's Sister. Day-Lewis.
A Nun to Mary, Virgin. St. Virginia.
Paradise Lost. Milton.
Paradise Saved. Hope.
The Vandals. Mastoraki.
When Any Mortal. Cummings.

K

Kane
O Kane, O Lono of the Blue Sea. Anonymous.
Old Creation Chant. Anonymous.
Prayer of the Fishing Net. Anonymous.

Kangaroo
The Duck and the Kangaroo. Lear.
An Explanation of the GrassWalking the Fields. Siegel.
An Explanaton of the Grasshopper. Lindsay.

Kansas
The Center of America. Siegel.
The Hide of My Mother. Dorn.
In Kansas. Anonymous.
Kneading. Crooker.

Karma
Me, in Kulu Se & Karma. Rodgers.
Mexico City Blues: 229th Chorus. Kerouac.

Kate
Garnyvillo. Lysaght.
The Gray Mare (Young
Johnny the Miller).
Anonymous.
An Irish Love-Song.
Johnson.
The Shoemaker. *Anonymous.*
The Tryst. Knox.
The Two Sisters.
Anonymous.
Katy
Katy Cline. *Anonymous.*
Little Katy. *Anonymous.*
Keats
Homage to Literature.
Rukeyser.
Moonlight Song of the
Mocking-bird. Hayne
On the Death of Keats.
Logan.
Keel (ed) (s)
Anabasis. "Perse.
The Dhows. Young.
Epitaphs of the War, 1914-18.
Kipling.
Fields Where We Slept.
Rukeyser.
The Keel Row. *Anonymous.*
Love's Labour's Lost.
Shakespeare.
Merry May the Keel Row.
Anonymous.
Misgivings. Melville.
The New Moon. Kobayashi
Issa.
The Nightfishing (excerpt).
Graham.
Keep (er) (ing) (s)
Achilles in Scyros (excerpt).
Bainbridge.
All to Myself. Nesbit.
The Ant. Herford.
Apple Offering. *Anonymous.*
As a Possible Lover. Jones.
Bacchanal. Layton.
The Ballad of Fisher's
Boardinghouse. Kipling.
Blind Date. Aiken.
Degli Sposi. Lesser.
The Dove Says, Coo, Coo.
Anonymous.
The Doves. Tynan.
Dragon Lesson. Hearst.
Duality. Hardy.
Duck. Worth.
Foxfire. Willard.
God Is with Me. Smith.
Gratitude. McGee.
Hawk Roosting. Hughes.
I Eat My Peas with Honey.
Anonymous.
I Was a Wandering Sheep.
Bonar.
In Thine Arms. Holmes.
Inflictis. Stodart-Walker.
Keeping Christmas. Farjeon.
Law Like Love. Auden.
Markings. Steele.
Mary and Martha. Flint.
The New Year. Templeton.
Night Fishing. Kuzma.
November Twenty-Sixth
Nineteen Hundred and
Sixty-Three. Berry.
Now the Laborer's Task Is
O'er. Ellerton.
On Devenish Island.
Ormsby.
Otters. Hart-Smith.
Paradise. Bloch.

Penal Servitude for Mrs.
Maybrick. *Anonymous.*
Plowman. Keyes.
Polly. Gay.
Preserves. Waters.
The Profile on the Pillow.
Randall.
The Prophecy of Famine.
Churchill.
Recipe for an Ocean in the
Absence of the Sea.
Howard.
Rules for Daily Life.
Anonymous.
The Sixth Day. Adcock.
Song. Sandall.
Song of a Second April.
Millay.
Song: "Rose and grape, pear
and bean." *Anonymous.*
The Songs I Sing. Blanden.
Tamer and Hawk. Gunn.
These Locusts by Day.
Stevens.
The Tongue. Strong.
With You a Part of Me.
Santayana.
Zohara. Hirschman.
Kelly (s)
The Bushrangers.
Harrington.
David Garrick. Goldsmith.
The Fighting Race. Clarke.
Slide, Kelly, Slide. Kelly.
Kennel
Dog. Jonker.
The Hunchback in the Park.
Thomas.
Nephelidia. Swinburne.
Kentucky
Crazy Song to the Air of
"Dixie." (with music).
Anonymous.
Darling Nellie Gray. Hanby.
The Hunters of Kentucky.
Woodworth.
My Old Kentucky Home.
Foster.
Pearl Bryant. *Anonymous.*
Kettle
Departure. Millay.
The Moon. Hall.
Morning. Calverley.
Personal Talk. Wordsworth.
Key (s)
An Almanac. Schuyler.
Autumn Refrain. Stevens.
Cuba. Rice.
Daybreak. Meyers.
The Elements. Newman.
Errant. Godfrey.
For Walter Lowenfels. Rose.
Foreign Summer. Merwin.
Gramercy Park Hotel.
Smith.
How About. Nelms.
I am alive–I guess.
Dickinson.
The Illumination. Kunitz.
In Obitum Promi. Parrot.
In the Cabinet. Vinner.
An Italian Chest. Seiffert.
Keys. Rockwell.
Like Any Other Man. Orr.
Lock the Dairy Door.
Anonymous.
Lost Objects. O Hehir.
My Uninvited Guest. Smith.
Panama. Roche.
Pennies. Kilmer.
The Poem. Merwin.
A Prayer. Channing.

The Present Crisis. Lowell.
Some Ruthless Rhymes.
Graham.
Sonatina in Yellow. Justice.
The Spell. Roberts.
The Students of Justice.
Merwin.
The Tale of Lord Lovell.
Anonymous.
Thank You for the Valentine.
Wakoski.
This Is the Key of the
Kingdom. *Anonymous.*
The Walker. Giovannitti.
The Way to Heaven.
Whiting.
Keyhole
Caravaggio Dying, Porto
Ercole, July 1610, Aged 36.
Lucie-Smith.
Daddy Shot a Bear.
Anonymous.
The Keyhole in the Door.
Anonymous.
Oh! Where Do Fairies Hide
Their Heads? Bayly.
Kick (ed) (ing) (s)
Assimilation. Feldman.
Captain Wattle and Miss Roe.
Dibdin.
The Description of an Irish
Feast, or O'Rourk's Frolic.
MacGowran.
Dinky Di. *Anonymous.*
An Expostulation.
Bickerstaffe.
Father William. "Carroll.
Fire. 10/78. Plantenga.
Gnawing the Breast.
McPherson.
Golden Pheasant. Hart-
Smith.
Horse Sense. *Anonymous.*
Hudibras. Butler.
Jubilate Agno. Smart.
Lantern. Polite.
Levee Camp Blues.
Anonymous.
Old Crumbly Crust.
Anonymous.
On Supporters of the
Baconian Theory.
Tennyson.
Rainuv: A Romantic Ballad
from the Early Basque
(parody). Widdemer.
Red-Herring. Lawrence.
Salome. *Anonymous.*
Stop Kicking My Dog around.
Anonymous.
Three Men. Moore.
The Vision. Taylor.
We Used to Play. Welch.
Kid (s)
Bogey. Berkson.
The Confession. Cooley.
The Contempt of Poetry.
Spenser.
The Election. Pack.
Exigencies. Gilbert.
Five Arabic Verses in Praise
of Wine. *Anonymous.*
The Grotto. Fraser.
Had Gadya–A Kid, a Kid.
Anonymous.
Hallowe'en Indignation
Meeting. Fishback.
Hammerin' Hank. Martin.
Hands up. Rudolf.
High-Life Low-Down.
Richardson.

If You Can't Eat You Got
To. Cummings.
Merry-Go-Round. Hughes.
Note in Lieu of a Suicide.
Finkel.
The Oregon Trail.
Anonymous.
Speak when you're spoken to.
Anonymous.
Three Men. Moore.
The Wrangler Kid.
Anonymous.
Kill (ed) (er) (ing) (s)
After the Killing. Randall.
The Albion Battleship
Calamity. McGonagall.
All of a Row. *Anonymous.*
Another Sin I Had Forgot.
Anonymous.
An Appeal to John Harralson.
Anonymous.
At Cambridge. McGaffin.
Australia 1970. Wright.
Bad Man Ballad.
Anonymous.
Beauty. Cowley.
A Bestiary. Rexroth.
Beyond the Alps. Lowell.
The Bhagavad-Gita:
Considerations of Murder.
Anonymous.
The Birth of Shaka. Mtshali.
The Blue Horse. La Follette.
Boast of Masopha.
Mangoaela.
Bugger Burns. *Anonymous.*
Camoes and the Debt.
Andresen.
Campaign Promise. Taylor.
Canned Heat Blues.
Johnson.
The Carpenter's Real
Anguish. Gardner.
Cassie O'Lang. *Anonymous.*
Central Heating System.
Spender.
Chain Gang Blues.
Anonymous.
Chanson d'Or. Hamilton.
Charles Guiteau, II.
Anonymous.
Chronicle. Dorn.
Cigarettes Will Spoil Yer Life
(with music). *Anonymous.*
Clap Your Hands for Herod.
Hanzlik.
Come Love or Death.
Thompson.
Connolly. MacGowan.
Crow, Crow, Get out of My
Sight. *Anonymous.*
The Cruel Maid. Herrick.
Darling Cora. *Anonymous.*
The Devil-Dancers. Plomer.
The Downfall of Piracy.
Franklin.
Drivin' Steel (with music).
Anonymous.
Early Lynching. Sandburg.
Ease It to Me Blues. Hicks.
Elm. Plath.
The Elm Speaks. Plath.
Envoi. Mandel.
Epistle to the Gentiles.
Hayes.
Epitaph for a Scientist.
Banning.
Ever Since Uncle John Henry
Been Dead (with music).
Anonymous.
The Face. Muir.

The Falling of the Snow.
   Souster.
The Fish Come in Dancing.
   Roberts.
A Flat One. Snodgrass.
For Masturbation. Dugan.
The Forgotten Rock.
   Eberhart.
The Friendship. Mezey.
Frightened Face. Strobel.
The Frozen Zone; or, Julia
   Disdainful. Herrick.
The Georgiad (excerpt).
   Campbell.
The Giraffe. Solomon.
Grey October. "The
   Critics."
I'm Sad and I'm Lonely.
   Anonymous.
If, Jerusalem, I Ever Should
   Forget Thee. Heine.
If So It Hap, This Of-Spring
   of My Care. Daniel.
In Evil Long I Took Delight.
   Newton.
The Indians Count of Men as
   Dogs. Williams.
Insulting Beauty. Rochester.
Jewish Ballad. Anonymous.
Jig Tune: Not for Love.
   McGrath.
John Standish, Artist.
   Fearing.
Killer Diller. Minnie.
Killers. Sandburg.
Latin. Anonymous.
Laurana's Song. Hovey.
Leopard. Anonymous.
Letter to the City Clerk.
   Wright.
The Lie. Ralegh.
Limerick: "There was an Old
   Man of Madras." Lear.
The Long Season. Haug.
Love in Exile. Blind.
Love Letter. Gregory.
Lying Down with Men and
   Women. Woods.
The Meaning of Violence.
   Williams.
Milkcow Blues. Estes.
Missing Dates. Empson.
Molly Bawn. Anonymous.
The Money Cry. Davison.
Moonshiner. Anonymous.
My Life had stood–a Loaded
   Gun. Dickinson.
Naomi Wise. Anonymous.
Nice Day for a Lynching.
   Patchen.
Not Marching away to Be
   Killed. Fuller.
Not Palaces. Spender.
O Hymen! O Hymenee!
   Whitman.
O-U-G-H. Loomis.
Observation of a Bee.
   Goldberg.
Ode: "Once more the country
   calls." Tate.
Ohio Valley Swains. Wright.
On a Grave in Christ-Church,
   Hants. Adams.
On the Birth of My Son,
   Malcolm Coltrane. Lester.
One Bright Morning...
   Anonymous.
One-Eyed Gunner.
   Anonymous.
One Morning We Brought
   Them Order. Lee.
Only a Miner. Anonymous.

Othello. Shakespeare.
Outlaw. Giorno.
The Park. Blaser.
Parsley. Dove.
Pentecost. Anthony ("Ai").
The People. Campanella.
Place Pigalle. Wilbur.
A Plague of Starlings.
   Hayden.
Poem: "These grasses, ancient
   enemies." Douglas.
Poetry Is a Destructive Force.
   Stevens.
The Progress of a Divine
   (excerpt). Savage.
Psyche. Coleridge.
The Quarry. Boscan.
The Rabbit. Davies.
The Rabbit Catcher. Plath.
Raise the Shade. Cummings.
The Rasslers. Barney.
Road Hazard. Green.
Safe for Democracy. Strong.
Schoolroom on a Wet
   Afternoon. Scannell.
She'll Be Comin' Round the
   Mountain. Anonymous.
Shooting of His Dear.
   Anonymous.
Siberia. Mangan.
The Sixth Day. Adcock.
Snail Hunters. Anonymous.
Song: "Methinks the poor
   town has been troubled too
   long." Sackville.
The Song of Hiawatha.
   Longfellow.
The Song of the Lower
   Classes. Jones.
Song: "There in the flower
   garden." Anonymous.
Sonnet: "Leave me, all sweet
   refrains my lip hath made."
   Camoens.
Sonnets, CXXXV: "Whoever
   hath her wish, thou hast
   thy Will." Shakespeare.
The Sounding. Aiken.
The Sparrow and Diamond.
   Green.
St. Valentine. Aguila.
The Tay Bridge Disaster.
   McGonagall.
The Technique of Power.
   Kessler.
Ther's Many a Man Killed on
   the Railroad (with music).
   Anonymous.
Therefore We Preserve Life.
   Shen Ch'uan.
The Three Butchers.
   Anonymous.
To Delmore Schwartz.
   Lowell.
To George Pulling Buds.
   O'Keeffe.
To Miss Margaret Pulteney,
   Daughter of Daniel
   Pulteney, Esq. Philips.
To Sextus. Sedley.
Try Tropic. Taggard.
Twicknam Garden. Donne.
Upon a Cock-Horse to Market
   I'll Trot. Anonymous.
Upon Love, by Way of
   Question and Answer.
   Herrick.
Visiting Day. Young.
Wang Peng's
   Recommendation for
   Improving the People.
   Eldridge.

Wire Monkey. Shiplett.
With the Most Susceptible
   Element, the Mind, Already
   Turned... Benton.
You Are Like the Snow Only.
   Cummings.

Kilts
Limerick: "There was a young
   lady of Wilts."
   Monkhouse.

Kin
Adam Smith. Bentley.
Beowulf: The Fire-Dragon and
   the Treasure. Anonymous.
Brevard Fault. Morgan.
Chicago. Harte.
Childlike Heart. Catlin.
Crucified to the World.
   Anonymous.
Family Plot. Singer.
The Forgiveness Dream: Man
   from the Warsaw Ghetto.
   Valentine.
Methinks the Measure.
   Hutchison.
Neutrality. MacNeice.
One Race, One Flag.
   Fairburn.
Poem for David Janssen.
   Smith.
The Song of the Graves.
   Rhys.
The Turkish Lady.
   Anonymous.
Unguarded. Murray.

Kind (ness)
Advice to a Lady in Autumn.
   Chesterfield.
Amanda. Anonymous.
Are Women Fair? Davison.
Auld Robin Gray. Barnard.
Baja. Stern.
Be Useful. Herbert.
A Bronze Statuette of Kwan-
   Yin. Stork.
Brothers. Hopkins.
But I Do Not Need Kindness.
   Corso.
Cliques and Critics. Sa'ib of
   Isfahan.
The Cruel Mother (A vers.).
   Anonymous.
A Deposition from Beauty.
   Stanley.
The Difference. Anonymous.
Do Not Weep, Maiden, for
   War Is Kind. Crane.
Drop a Pebble in the Water.
   Foley.
Epigram: "I know him."
   Anonymous.
Epilogue Spoken at Oxford by
   Mrs. Marshall. Dryden.
Epilogue Spoken by Mrs.
   Boutell. Dryden.
Epitaph. Jeffrey.
Exit. Robinson.
The Farewell. Stanley.
Footnote to "Howl."
   Ginsberg.
For My Son Noah, Ten Years
   Old. Bly.
Four Winds. Teasdale.
Getting Lost in Nazi
   Germany. Bell.
Heureux Qui, Comme Ulysse,
   A Fait Un Beau Voyage.
   Du Bellay.
Holy Poems. Barker.
How Stands the Glass
   Around? Wolfe.
Humane Thought. McCann.

I Lately Vowed. Oldmixon.
I'm a Decent Boy from
   Ireland. Anonymous.
I Yield Thee Praise.
   Cleveland.
Idylls. Moschus.
In Memoriam A.H.H., XX.
   Tennyson.
In Mind. Levertov.
Inhuman Henry or Cruelty to
   Fabulous Animals.
   Housman.
Invocation. Stedman.
John J. Curtis. Gallager.
The Jungle. Lewis.
Lewti. Coleridge.
Love. Thoreau.
Love and Death. Deland.
Love (excerpt). Walker.
Madrigal: "Some there are as
   fair to see to." Davison.
Many Wings. Conant.
March. Everson.
The March 2. Lowell.
Mary's Lamb. Hale.
Moguls and Monks.
   MacAdams.
O say, dear life, when shall
   these twinborn berries.
   Anonymous.
Obituary. Brode.
On a Picture of Lincoln.
   Cheney.
On His Mistress, the Queen of
   Bohemia. Wotton.
Open Your Eyes.
   Whisenand.
The Other Person's Place.
   Hover.
The Reconcilement.
   Sheffield.
Roses. Ronsard.
San Francisco Bay. Miller.
Satire on Old Rowley.
   Anonymous.
Seasons of the Soul. Tate.
Second Night, or What You
   Will. Humphries.
Since Thou Hast Given Me
   This Good Hope, O God.
   Stevenson.
Song. Manifold.
Song: "Come, Celia, let's
   agree at last." Sheffield.
Song: "I lately vow'd, but
   'twas in haste." Oldmixon.
Song: "Singer within the little
   streets." Gibbon.
Song: To the Masquers
   Representing Stars.
   Campion.
Spring and All. Bauer.
Talking in Bed. Larkin.
To a Golden-Haired Girl in a
   Louisiana Town. Lindsay.
To Delia. Daniel.
To His Mistress. Sheffield.
To His Young Mistress.
   Ronsard.
To My Mother at 73.
   Jennings.
To the Right Noble,
   Valourous, and Learned
   Prince Henry... Davies.
To William Blake. Dargan.
Treat the Woman Tenderly,
   Tenderly. Anonymous.
Two Girls Singing.
The Unfortunate Miller; or,
   The Country Lasses Witty
   Invention. Anonymous.

The Victories of Love.
  Patmore.
What Harvest Half So Sweet
  Is. Campion.
What Is Good. O'Reilly.
When Aurelia First I Courted.
  Anonymous.
When I Loved Thee.
  Stanley.
Would I Be Called a
  Christian? Moser.
You Naughty, Naughty Men.
  Kennick.
Young Strephon and Phillis.
  Anonymous.

King (s)
Abdication Street Song.
  Anonymous.
Abiding. Simpson.
About Savannah.
  Anonymous.
The Aeneid. Virgil (Publius
  Vergilius Maro).
Agincourt. Drayton.
All the World. Anonymous.
Ambition. Herrick.
Andrew Bardeen.
  Anonymous.
The Anti-Politician. Brome.
The Appeal to Harold.
  Bunner.
Archers of the King. Mary
  Genoveva.
Armagh. Rodgers.
As for Me, I Delight in the
  Everyday Way. Stroud.
As with Gladness Men of Old.
  Dix.
Asleep in the Bosom of
  Youth. Halevi.
Astrophel and Stella, LXIX.
  Sidney.
At Length There Dawns the
  Glorious Day. Davis.
The Ballad of the Harp-
  Weaver. Millay.
Ballade of the Old-Time
  Engine. Vines.
The Bastard King of England.
  Anonymous.
The Battle of Ivry.
  Macaulay.
Battle-Song of Failure. Burr.
Black Majesty. Cullen.
Bless the Blessed Morn.
  Bonar.
Bosworth Field: Richard III's
  Speech. Beaumont.
The Bounty of Jehovah Praise.
  Sandys.
Bryan, Bryan, Bryan, Bryan.
  Lindsay.
Caelica, XXXVI. Greville.
Caelica, XCV. Greville.
Caelica, CI. Greville.
Calais, August 15, 1802.
  Wordsworth.
Camel. Miller.
The Candidate. Ezell.
Cannily, Cannily.
  Anonymous.
A Carol. Weatherly.
The Chapter of Kings.
  Collins.
Charles the Fifth and the
  Peasant. Lowell.
The Chinese Book of Rites
  (excerpt). Anonymous.
Christ 3: The Last Judgement.
  Anonymous.
Christ's Victory and Triumph.
  Fletcher.

A Christmas Carol. Rossetti.
The Civil Wars between the
  Two Houses of Lancaster
  and York. Daniel.
Coda. Bunting.
The Complaint of Henrie
  Duke of Buckinghame.
  Sackville.
The Complaynt of Schir
  David Lindesay: The
  Childhood of James V.
  Lindsay.
Converstion with Three
  Women of New England.
  Stevens.
The Country Lovers.
  Anonymous.
The Courtier's Health; or,
  Merry Boys of the Times.
  Anonymous.
The Covenant of His Grace.
  Wesley.
The Cowboy's Life.
  Anonymous.
A Crowned Poet. Aldrich.
The Day Closes. Talbot.
The Dead Solomon. Dorgan.
A Dialogue between King
  William and the Late King
  James... Blount.
The Diggers' Song.
  Winstanley.
Diptych. Sykes.
The Diver. Herbin.
The Dolphin's Return.
  Anonymous.
The Dove of Dacca.
  Kipling.
The Downfall of Charing
  Cross. Anonymous.
Dreams of Snakes, Chocolate
  and Men. Sanford.
Durham Field. Anonymous.
Dynastic Tiff. Hellman.
Echoes. Henley.
Edwin Booth. Brown.
Effigy. McElhaney.
An Elegy. Winters.
Elegy on Albert Edward the
  Peacemaker. Anonymous.
England's Sovereigns in Verse.
  Anonymous.
The English Rider. Hyde.
An Epigram: "Great Charles,
  among the holy gifts of
  grace." Jonson.
Epigram: "Prepare to meet the
  King of Terrors." Elliott.
An Epigram to the Queen,
  Then Lying In. Jonson.
Esther. Chavez.
Ever On. Anonymous.
A Farewell. Russell.
The First Nowell.
  Anonymous.
Flora MacDonald and the
  King. Anonymous.
For the Lady Olivia Porter; a
  Present upon a New-years
  Day. Davenant.
A Forced Music. Graves.
The Forsaken Merman.
  Arnold.
The Fort of Rathangan.
  Meyer.
French Clock. Flexner.
The Furniture of a Woman's
  Mind. Swift.
The Gardens of Alcinous.
  Pope.
Gates and Doors. Kilmer.
A Glass of Beer. Stephens.

Glee for King Charles.
  Scott.
God Incarnate. Williams.
God Save the King. Carey.
God-Seeking. Watson.
Gone. De la Mare.
Good Morning America
  (excerpt). Sandburg.
The Goose Girl. Roberts.
The Grey-Eyed King.
  Akhmatova.
Hail Man! Morgan
Henry and Mary. Graves.
Henry Before Agincourt.
  Lydgate.
Henry Martyn (E version).
  Anonymous.
An Historical Poem.
  Anonymous.
Hokey, Pokey, Whisky,
  Thum. Anonymous.
The Holy Man. Anonymous.
A House and Grounds.
  Hunt.
How the Ploughman Learned
  His Paternoster.
  Anonymous.
The Huron Carol.
  Middleton.
Hymn for Christmas Day.
  Byrom.
I Know Not Where the Road
  Will Lead. Cummins.
If I Were King. McCarthy.
If I Were King. Milne.
The Impatient Poet.
  Cresswell.
In Disguise. Rolnik.
In Hoc Signo. Bradby.
Inniskeen Road: July Evening.
  Kavanagh.
An Invective Against the
  Wicked of the World.
  Breton.
Iolanthe. Gilbert.
It May Be. Jacob.
Ivry. Macaulay.
Jeannot's Answer. Jeffries.
The Journey into France.
  Anonymous.
The Junk Shop. Coulette.
King I Sit. Anonymous.
The King of Harlem. Garcia
  Lorca.
King of Ireland's Son.
  Hopper.
The King of Yvetot.
  Beranger.
King Orfeo. Anonymous.
The Kiss. Teasdale.
The Knight and Shepherd's
  Daughter (B vers.).
  Anonymous.
Labor Day. Pomeroy.
Lady Isabel and the Elf-
  Knight (A vers.).
  Anonymous.
The Land of Cokaigne.
  Anonymous.
Let War's Tempests Cease.
  Longfellow.
Letters for the New England
  Dead. Baron.
Leviathan. Anonymous.
The Liberty Pole.
  Anonymous.
Like an Old Proud King in a
  Parable. Smith.
Limerick: "There was a young
  critic of Kings." Hilton.

Limerick: "There was a young
  fellow called Green."
  Anonymous.
The Linen Weaver.
  Anonymous.
Lord of the Worlds Below!
  Freeman.
Love and Wine. Shadwell.
A Low Prayer, a High Prayer.
  Anonymous.
Loyalty Confin'd.
  L'Estrange.
Macdonald's Raid. Hayne.
Maerchen. De La Mare.
The Maid Freed from the
  Gallows (C vers.).
  Anonymous.
The Majesty of God.
  Sternhold.
Malcom, Iowa. Itzin.
March of the Three Kings.
  Anonymous.
The Mariner's Song. Davies.
A Match. Swinburne.
A Maypole. Swift.
Me Alone. Weeden.
A Morning Letter. Duncan.
My Lady Carenza of the
  lovely body. Anonymous.
Mythics. Chasin.
The Neighbors of Bethlehem.
  Anonymous.
Nephelidia. Swinburne.
A New Order of Chivalry.
  Peacock.
Night: an Epistle to Robert
  Lloyd. Churchill.
Night on the Prairie. Sage.
No Help I'll Call Till I'm Put
  in the Narrow Coffin. O
  Rathaille.
No Swan So Fine. Moore.
Notes after Blacking Out.
  Corso.
Now Thrice Welcome
  Christmas. Anonymous.
O Lord, How Lovely Is the
  Place. Hopkinson.
O Merry May the Maid Be.
  Clerk.
October in Tennessee.
  Malone.
An Ode: "Awake, faire Muse;
  for I intend." Browne.
Of Silk Is Her Fishing-Line.
  Anonymous.
On First Entering
  Westminster Abbey.
  Guiney.
On Squire Neale's Projects.
  Anonymous.
One Day. Brooke.
Out of Whack. Edson.
The Outlaw Murray.
  Anonymous.
The Panchatantra: Kings.
  Anonymous.
Paradise Regained. Milton.
Passing Out. Levine.
The Passionate Shepherd.
  Breton.
Perhaps the Best Time.
  Meredith.
Petition. Drinkwater.
Phillis's Resolution. Walsh.
Plain Dealing. Brome.
A Poem Sacred to the
  Memory of Sir Isaac
  Newton. Thomson.
Poems. Drummond.
Poet. Emerson.
The Pompadour. Thornbury.

Prayer of St. Francis Xavier. Pope.
The Pretzel Man. Field.
Prince of Wales' Marriage. Anonymous.
Proclaim the Lofty Praise. Judson.
Psalm XX. Sidney.
Pslam XXIV. Sidney.
Quebec Liquor Commission Store. Klein.
The Queen of Courtesy. Anonymous.
Quiet from Fear of Evil. S.C.
The Rath in Front of the Oak Wood. Anonymous.
The Reading Lesson. Murphy.
Reconciliation. Russell.
The Reign of Peace. Starck.
Rejoice! He Liveth! Peck.
Richard II. Shakespeare.
Riddle: "As round as an apple, as deep as a cup." Mother Goose.
Riddle: "Little Billy Breek." Anonymous.
Ride On, Moses. Anonymous.
Robin Hood and Queen Katherine (B version). Anonymous.
The Royal Angler. Anonymous.
Running to Paradise. Yeats.
The Sea Fight in '92. Anonymous.
The Sentiments. Anonymous.
The Shash. Anonymous.
Sincere Praise. Watts.
Sing a Song of Joy! Campion.
Sion. Herbert.
Sir Andrew Barton. Anonymous.
Sir Andrew Barton (Andrew Batann). Anonymous.
Sir Lark and King Sun: A Parable. Macdonald.
Sir Tristrem: Tristrem and the Hunters. Thomas of Erceldoune
The Sluggard. Davies.
The Smuggler's Victory. Anonymous.
So Young Ane King. Lindsay.
Soldier's Song. Hume.
Song from a Drama. Stedman.
Song of Apollo. Lyly.
The Song of the Demented Priest. Berryman.
The Song of the Turnkey. Smith.
Sonnets, XXIX: "When in disgrace with fortune and men's eyes." Shakespeare.
Sons of the Kings. Agnew.
The Sovereigns. Mifflin.
Spassky at Reykjavik. Fisher.
A Spiritual. Dunbar.
Star of the East. Field.
The Star-Song: A Carol to the King; Sung at White-Hall. Herrick.
Stir Me. Anonymous.
A Story That Could Be True. Stafford.
Strange Monsters. Watkyns.

Supersensual. Underhill.
The Terrible Sons. Ben Kalir.
There Is No Name So Sweet on Earth. Bethune.
The Third Century. Traherne.
The Tired Petitioner (excerpt). Wither.
To a Republican. Freneau.
To King James. Jonson.
To My Father. Tree.
To Our Lady. Henryson.
To Thee. Anonymous.
The Torso: Passages 18. Duncan.
The Tribes. Fuller.
Tudor Portrait. Lattimore.
The Variety. Dancer.
The Vicar of Bray. Anonymous.
The Vulture. Hoh.
Wake the Song of Jubilee. Bacon.
The Waltz: Hail, Spirit-Stirring Waltz. Byron.
War in Chang-An City. Wang Tsan.
We Need a King. Macdougall.
We Were Permitted to Meet Together in Prison to Prepare for Trial. Berrigan.
When the King Enjoys His Own Again. Parker.
Willie Brew'd a Peck o' Maut. Burns.
Wishes. Ault.
The Witnesses. Kennedy.
Wreck of the Deutschland. Hopkins.

Kingdom (s)
The Avenue Bearing the Initial of Christ into the New World. Kinnell.
BC : AD. Fanthorpe.
Carol: "Now is the world withdrawn all in silence and night." Nemerov.
The Centuries Are His. Ebeling.
Ceremony after a Fire Raid. Thomas.
An Essay on the Fleet Riding in the Downes. Anonymous.
Fern. Hughes.
The Fleece. Dyer.
For Edward Hicks. Helwig.
The Golden Age. Cheney.
A Happy Christmas. Havergal.
He That Is Near Me Is Near the Fire. Origen.
The Hills of Pomeroy. Milne.
How Pleasant Is This Flowery Plain. Anonymous.
I Don't Want to Be a Gambler (with music). Anonymous.
I Have Lighted the Candles, Mary. Patchen.
I Want to Tell You. Hochman.
I Wish Sometimes, Although a Worthlesse Thing. Fletcher.
Janet Waking. Ransom.
Kingdom Coming. Work.

Lafayette to Washington. Anderson.
Lord God of Hosts. Knapp.
The Man with the Hoe: A Reply. Cheney.
The Master. Robbins.
My House, I Say. But Hark to the Sunny Doves. Stevenson.
A New Hampshire Boy. Bishop.
A New Patriotism. Piety.
O God, Above the Drifting Years. Buckham.
O God of Youth. Burt.
On the Death of Doctor Swift. Swift.
On the "Vita Nuova" of Dante. Rossetti.
One Step from an Old Dance. Helwig.
Our Father, God. Judson.
Our Father Which in Heaven Art. Anonymous.
Paraphrase of Luther's Hymn. Hedge
The Postern Gate (excerpt). Rauschenbusch.
Reflections. Coleridge.
Sheep. Hoffenstein.
Statues. Wilbur.
This Is the Key of the Kingdom. Anonymous.
This Town. Paul.
Thy Kingdom Come. Simpson.
Thy Kingdom, Lord, We Long For. Scudder.
Tombstone Epitaphs. Anonymous.
Virgin Pictured in Profile. Warren.
The Wandering Lunatic Mind. Carpenter.
What Far Kingdom. Bourinot.
Ye Sorrowers. Werfel.

Kingfisher (s)
By the Ford. Thomas.
Colloquy in Black Rock. Lowell.

Kiss (ed) (es) (ing)
Across the Door. Colum.
Ad Lesbiam. Sheridan.
Adieu to His Mistress. Montgomerie.
After Chagall. Wenger.
Alone in April. Cabell.
Although I put away his life. Dickinson.
Ametas and Thestylis Making Hay-Ropes. Marvell.
Angelica and the Ork. Harington.
Animation and Ego. Swilky.
Another. Bissert.
Another Cynical Variation. "Helen".
Apocrypha. Deutsch.
Ask No Return. Gregory.
Astrophel and Stella, XXII. Sidney.
Astrophel and Stella, LXXIII. Sidney.
Astrophel and Stella, LXXXIV. Sidney.
At Baia. Doolittle.
At First I Was Given Centuries. Atwood.
Autobiography. Fuertes.
The Baby's Debut (Parody on Wordsworth). Smith.

The Balcony. Baudelaire.
Ballade of a Talked-Off Ear. Parker.
Before Parting. Swinburne.
Before the sun goes down. Andersen.
The Beggar's Opera. Gay.
The Best Friend. Davies.
The Betrayal. Furlong.
Betrayal. Tabb.
The Beverley Maid and the Tinker. Anonymous.
Black Hair. Muhammadji.
Born Again. Farrokhzad.
Boundaries. Spear.
The Breasts of Mnasidice. Louys.
A Bunch of Roses. Tabb.
By Mrs. Hopley, on Seeing Her Children Say Goodnight to Their Father. Hopkins.
Caelica, XXII. Greville.
Caelica, XLIX. Greville.
Calm Was the Even. Dryden.
Canoe. Douglas.
The Canterbury Tales: The Pardoner's Tale. Chaucer.
Canticle of Darkness. Watson.
Charleville. Rimbaud.
A Child's Thought of God. Browning.
The Children. Dickinson.
The Chimney Sweeper. Anonymous.
A Christmas Carol. Probyn.
Clarimonde. Gautier.
Clementine. Anonymous.
The Cliff Rose. Fewster.
The Collier's Wedding. Chicken.
The Comb. De la Mare.
Come, Landlord, Fill the Flowing Bowl. Anonymous.
Conception. Cuney.
Constancy. Watson.
A Copy of the Last Verses Made by Dr. Wild... (excerpt). Wild.
The Corner of the Field. Cornford.
The Corpse. Moore.
A Counterblast against Garlic. Field.
Counting. Sandburg.
Courtship. Brome.
Dakota Badlands. Landeweer.
The Damsel. Omar B. Abi Rabi'a.
Darien. Arnold.
Dark Rosaleen, IX. Wright.
The Dead City. Calkins.
The Dead Heroes. Rosenberg.
Deadly Kisses. Ronsard.
Dearest Man-in-the-Moon. Jong.
The Death of the Epileptic Poet Yesenin. Boyajian.
A Deux. Wood.
Developers at Crystal River. Merrill.
Dornroschen. Carruth.
A Dream. Keats.
Drum-Taps. Whitman.
Drunk as drunk on turpentine. Neruda.

A Drunkard to His Bottle.
Lefanu.
The Duke of Athole's Nurse.
Anonymous.
Dumbarton's Drums.
Anonymous.
Dunce Song 6. Van Doren.
The Dust. Hall.
Eight O'Clock Bells.
Anonymous.
En Monocle. Evans.
Endymion. Keats.
Endymion. Wilde.
Epigram: "He is my love."
Anonymous.
An Epigram of Martial,
Imitated. Williams.
Epitaph: "Lo worms enjoy the
seat of bliss." Burns.
Eternal Moment. "Hale.
Fair Margaret and Sweet
William. *Anonymous.*
The Fairy Lover. Fox.
The Faithful Shepherdess.
Fletcher.
The Falling of the Leaves.
Yeats.
False Enchantment.
Untermeyer.
Father. Weston.
Film Vermouth: Six O'Clock
Show. Portal.
A Fine Day. Drayton.
Fond Affection. *Anonymous.*
For Steph. Rose.
The Four Winds. Luders.
The Friendship Game.
DiCicco.
Frog Prince. Pettingell.
The Garden. Dolben.
A Garden by the Sea.
Morris.
The Garden of the Holy
Souls. King.
The Gardener. Wheelock.
The Gifts Return'd. Landor.
A Glimpse of Time. Binyon.
Glory. Shapiro.
Good Advice. Montagu.
Good Morning, Father
Francis. *Anonymous.*
The Gospel of Mr. Pepys.
Morley.
Grief and God. Phillips.
Growing. Frost.
The Gulistan. Sa'di.
The Gypsy Countess.
Anonymous.
The Hambone and the Heart.
Sitwell.
Hand-Clapping Rhyme.
Anonymous.
Hate. Stephens.
Healing the Wound. Heine.
Heart of My Heart.
Anonymous.
Her Mouth. Aldington.
Hmmmmm, 22. Scalapino.
Holly and Mistletoe.
Farjeon.
Home-Coming. Hume.
The Hummingbird. Kemp.
I Close Her Eyes. Heine.
I Did Not Lose My Heart in
Summer's Even.
Housman.
I Had a Black Man.
Anonymous.
I Have Always Heard of
These Old Men.
Anonymous.

I See the Boys of Summer.
Thomas.
I Sought with Eager Hand.
Dowling.
Ice Cold. O Riordain.
If I Could Go On Kissing
Your Honeyed Eyes.
Catullus.
If I Should Die before I
Wake. Mezey.
In May. Synge.
In Memory of Robin Hyde,
1906-39. Brasch.
In the Orchard. Stuart.
Incendiary. Scannell.
An Interlude. Swinburne.
Invitation to Dalliance.
Anonymous.
Is It Far to Go. Day.
It Really Happened. Henley.
It's True I'm No Miss
America. Slowinsky.
Jacob and the Angel.
Brother Antoninus.
Jenny. Rossetti.
Jenny Kiss'd Me. Hunt.
Jeny Kiss'd Me When We
Met. Dehn.
John of Hazelgreen (C vers.).
Anonymous.
Joined the Blues. Rooney.
Journal of a Tour through the
Courts of Germany
(excerpt). Boswell.
Jove for Europaes Love Tooke
Shape of Bull. Barnes.
Joy and Dream. Goethe.
Juggling Jerry. Meredith.
Juventius, My Honey.
Catullus.
Keep Your Kiss to Yourself.
Anonymous.
The Kicking Mule.
Anonymous.
A Kiss. *Anonymous.*
The Kiss. Jonson.
The Kiss. Landor.
The Kiss. Sassoon.
Kiss'd Yestreen. *Anonymous.*
A Kiss in the Rain. Peck.
Kiss Me Quick and Go.
Steele.
Kisses Desired. Drummond.
Kissing and Bussing.
Herrick.
Kit Logan and Lady Helen.
Graves.
The Lamentation for Celin.
Anonymous.
The Lass of Roch Royal.
Anonymous.
The Lass of Roch Royal (B
vers.). *Anonymous.*
The Last Conqueror.
Shirley.
Lauriger Horatius. Symonds.
Lesbian Play on T.V.
Gilfillan.
Lethe. Doolittle.
Little Bessie. *Anonymous.*
Little Boy Blue. Field.
The Little Knight in Green.
Bates.
The Little Lady Lairdie.
Anonymous.
A Little Way. Stanton.
London's Bridge Is A-Burning
Down. *Anonymous.*
Look to the Leaf.
Anonymous.
Love Is All. Catullus.
Love Poem. Padgett.

Love's Arithmetic.
Sherburne.
Love's Philosophy. Shelley.
The Lover to Himself.
Phillips.
Lullaby, O Lullaby. Bennett.
Maratea Porto: Saying
Goodbye to the Vitolos.
Hugo.
Marching 'Round the Levee.
Anonymous.
Marching to Quebec.
Anonymous.
Marriage. Turner.
Mary, Mother of Christ.
Cullen.
A Masque of Life and Death.
Bynner.
A Match with the Moon.
Rossetti.
The Merry-ma-Tanzie.
Anonymous.
A Message. Ives.
A Message. Phelps.
Mexico City Blues: 230th
Chorus. Kerouac.
Midas: Pan's Song. Lyly.
Mistletoe. De la Mare.
Modern Love, XIII.
Meredith.
Molly Asthore. Ferguson.
Morning. Waddington.
Music at Twilight. Sterling.
A Mustacheless Bard.
Coogler.
My Blessing Be on Waterford.
Letts.
My Enemy. Brotherton.
My Little Pretty Mopsy.
Anonymous.
My Love and I for Kisses
Play'd. Strode.
My Old True Love.
Anonymous.
A New England Bachelor.
Eberhart.
Nightfall. Kalidasa.
Nora. Shorter.
A Note from the Pipes.
Speyer.
Notice the Convulsed Orange
Inch of Moon. Cummings.
Now come, my boon
companions. Randolph.
Nymph of the Garden where
All Beauties Be. Sidney.
Obituary. Parsons
The Observatory Ode. Nims.
Of Tyndarus. Stanihurst.
Oh Beach Love Blossom.
Crews.
On a Dream (after Reading
Dante's Episode of Paolo
and Francesca). Keats.
On a Rainy Night (excerpt).
Mills.
On the Death of a
Nightingale. Randolph.
Once. Ives.
Open the Door, Who's There
Within? *Anonymous.*
The Other Voice. Paulin.
Out There Somewhere.
Knibbs.
Paradox. Grimke.
The Passing Flower. Kemp.
A Pastoral Courtship.
Rochester.
The Philanderer. Mendes.
A Pleasant New Court Song.
Anonymous.

The Pleasures of Love.
Blunt.
Poem: "Get your tongue."
Kooser.
Poem: "He lying spilt like
water from a bowl."
Boodson.
Polyolbion. Drayton.
Preludes for Memnon.
Aiken.
The Prodigy. Herbert.
Pygmalion to Galatea.
Graves.
Pyramus and Thisbe. Saxe.
The Quarrel. Aiken.
Quickness. Vaughan.
The Quiet Woman. Taggard.
Rapunzel. Broumas.
Recitative. McCuaig.
The Reconciliation.
Tennyson.
Remember Thy Covenant.
Pierce.
The Retirement. *Anonymous.*
Retractions. Cabell.
Returning, We Hear the
Larks. Rosenberg.
The Rich Widow.
Anonymous.
Riddles and Lies.
Zawadiwsky.
Rise You Up, My True Love.
Anonymous.
Romeo and Juliet.
Shakespeare.
The Rosary. Rogers.
A Rose. Bates.
Rubric. Peabody.
Rumplestiltskin Poems.
Hathaway.
The Rural Dance about the
Maypole. *Anonymous.*
The Sailor's Sweetheart.
Scott.
San Francisco Bay. Miller.
A Sapphic Dream. Moore.
A Sense of Humour.
Lindsay.
She That Denies Me.
Heywood.
Snow-Dance for the Dead.
Ridge.
Solitude. Deutsch.
A Song for New Orleans.
Keithley.
Song from the Story of
Acontius and Cydippe.
Morris.
Song: "O, it was out by
Donncarney." Joyce.
Song: "O, that joy so soon
should waste!". Jonson.
Song of the Milkmaid.
Tennyson.
Song: "Smooth was the Water,
calm the Air." Sedley.
Song: "Thy fingers make early
flowers." Cummings.
Song to the Masquers.
Shirley.
Song: "Trip it Gipsies, trip it
fine." Rowley.
The Songs of Bilitis. Louys.
Sonnet IX. Drummond.
Sonnet Found in a Deserted
Mad-House. *Anonymous.*
Sonnet: "Then whilst that
Latmos did contain her
bliss." Stirling.
Sonnets. Hillyer.
Sonnets: A Sequence on
Profane Love. Boker.

Sonnets of a Portrait Painter.
  Ficke
Sowing. Thomas.
Spring Offensive, 1941.
  Biggs.
The Statesman in Retirement.
  Cowper.
Stepfather: A Girl's Song.
  Komunyakaa.
A Storm in the Distance.
  Hayne.
Strange Lands. Alma-
  Tadema.
Suicide's Note. Hughes.
Summum Bonum. Browning.
Sylvia the Fair. Dryden.
Taedium Vitae. Wilde.
Tempted. Sill.
Thanks, Gentle Moon, for
  Thy Obscured Light.
  Anonymous.
That Beauty I Ador'd Before.
  Behn.
There Is a Lady. Walther
  von der Vogelweide.
There Was a Little Boy and a
  Little Girl. Anonymous.
There Was a Wyly Ladde.
  Anonymous.
Thou Art Not Fair.
  Campion.
Tide Turning. Nims.
Tired Mothers. Smith.
To a New York Shop-Girl
  Dressed for Sunday.
  Branch.
To a Sicilian Boy.
  Wratislaw.
To Death, Castara Being
  Sicke. Habington.
To Dindymus. Martial
  (Marcus Valerius Martialis).
To Electra. Herrick.
To George Sand: A Desire.
  Browning.
To Memory. Coleridge.
To My Brother George.
  Keats.
To the Eternal Feminine.
  Corbiere.
To the Water Nymphs,
  Drinking at the Fountain.
  Herrick.
Tom Jones's Plum Tree (The
  Juniper Tree). Anonymous.
Trip It Gipsies, Trip It Fine.
  Middleton.
True Woman. Rossetti.
Under the Scub Oak, a Red
  Shoe. Smith.
Upon the Priory Grove, His
  Usual Retirement.
  Vaughan.
Valerius on Women.
  Heywood.
Valse Jeune. Guiney.
Venus, with Young Adonis.
  Griffin.
Victorian Song. Farrar.
Westminster Drollery, 1671.
  Behn.
When I Was a Little Boy.
  Anonymous.
When I Was Small. Chenier.
Where Be You Going, You
  Devon Maid? Keats.
A White Rose. O'Reilly.
Who Will Shoe Your Pretty
  Little Foot? (with music).
  Anonymous.
Wildflower. Plumly.
Winter Song. Macdonald.

Wisdom. Hicky.
A Wish. Synge.
Wishing. Allingham.
Within a Greenwood Sweet of
  Myrtle Savour.
  Anonymous.
Woman. Rakosi.
The Word Made Flesh?
  Turner.
You Kissed Me. Hunt.
The Young Laird and
  Edinburgh Katy. Ramsay.

Kitchen
Alcoholic. Reeve.
Aubade: The Desert. Bock.
The Baron of Brackley (B
  version). Anonymous.
Bunny. Fahy.
Buttons. De La Mare.
Come On in My Kitchen.
  Johnson.
A Daughter's House.
  Richman.
December 24 and George
  McBride is Dead. Hugo.
Domestics. Cumbo.
Evening. Aldington.
Kitchen Door Blues.
  Williams.
Kitchen Poem. Scarfe.
March Sound. Thurston.
A New Song on the Birth of
  the Prince of Wales.
  Anonymous.
The Obscure Pleasure of the
  Indistinct. Ramke.
Riddle: "Hick-a-more, Hack-a-
  more." Anonymous.
A Song of Diligence. Frazee-
  Bower.
The Widow. Ludvigson.

Kite (s)
Captain Carpenter. Ransom.
Catch a Little Rhyme.
  Merriam.
A Farewell to a Fondling.
  Churchyard.
Holding On. Jackson.
The Lighthouse Invites the
  Storm. Lowry.
Minnie and Her Dove.
  Turner.
Narcissus and Some Tadpoles.
  Daley.
Shore. O Hehir.

Kitten (s)
Chaplinesque. Crane.
Geometry. Kreymborg.
The Little Cat Angel.
  Stanfield.
Mehitabel and Her Kittens.
  Marquis.
Mexico City Blues: 230th
  Chorus. Kerouac.
When a Man Turns
  Homeward. Hicky.

Knack
Mill Girl. Baxter.
A Pedlar of Small-Wares.
  Suckling.
The Yeoman of the Guard
  (excerpt). Gilbert.

Knapsack
The Wisconsin Soldier Boy.
  Anonymous.

Knave (s)
Barney's Invitation. Freneau.
Between the Acts. Kunitz.
Clerk Saunders. Anonymous.
Epigram: The Parson's Looks.
  Burns.

A Free Parliament Litany.
  Anonymous.
The Gulistan. Sa'di.
A Jewish Poet Counsels a
  King. De Carrion.
The Maiden's Choice.
  Anonymous.
Of Seals and Arms. Taylor.
On Lord Galloway. Burns.
On Squire Neale's Projects.
  Anonymous.
Plain Dealing's Downfall.
  Anonymous.
Robin and Gandelein.
  Anonymous.
Rub-a-Dub-Dub. Mother
  Goose.
To the Respective Judges.
  Anonymous.
The Touch-Stone. Bishop.
Victory. Axford.
Wretched Man. Rochester.

Knee (s)
America A Prophecy. Blake.
And When the Revolution
  Came. Rodgers.
Ballade des Belles
  Milatraisses. Jonas.
Because We Do Not See.
  Anonymous.
Canto Llano. Probst.
A Child of To-Day.
  Buckham.
Chloride of Lime and
  Charcoal. Zukofsky.
Distances (excerpt). Okigbo.
Diverus and Lazarus.
  Anonymous.
Dorothea. Cleghorn.
Early Bacon. Stodart-
  Walker.
Elektra on Third Avenue.
  Hacker.
Epigram: "Broad and ample
  he warms himself."
  Anonymous.
Eton Boating Song. Cory.
The Flirt. Davies.
The H. Scriptures. I.
  Herbert.
The Hanging of Sam Archer.
  Anonymous.
The Hero. Nicoll.
The Hog-Eye Man (with
  music). Anonymous.
Hossolalia. Luton.
I Come from Salem City.
  Anonymous.
Idea of a Swimmer. Bloch.
If You Are a Gentleman.
  Anonymous.
III. Berrigan.
In the Baggage Room at
  Greyhound. Ginsberg.
Is 5. Cummings.
The Jolly Waggoner.
  Anonymous.
The Knee on Its Own.
  Morgenstern.
The Labors of Thor.
  Wagoner.
The Land-Mine. MacBeth.
A Leaf-Treader. Frost.
The Limits of Equitation.
  Winder.
Little Maggie. Anonymous.
Lost on September Trail,
  1967. Rios.
Love. Herbert.
Mater Amabilis. Lazarus.
Mile Hill. Schmitz.
Miss Gee. Auden.

The Morning-Glory. Lowell
My sweet old etcetera.
  Cummings.
Naso, You're All Men's Man.
  Catullus.
Oh, Susanna. Anonymous.
Old Adam (with music).
  Anonymous.
Peter Rabbit. McPherson.
Prayer. Guiterman.
Preface to a Twenty Volume
  Suicide Note. Jones.
Puppy. Lape.
The Roundhouse Voices.
  Smith.
A Schoolmaster's Admonition.
  Anonymous.
Sepia Fashion Show.
  Angelou.
The Snowdrop. Bary.
The Song Called "His Hide Is
  Covered with Hair.".
  Belloc.
This dirty little heart.
  Dickinson.
Three Poems about Children.
  Clarke.
Tir-Nan-Og. Hendry.
To Sir Thomas Egerton.
  Daniel.
The Toast. Stoddard.
Traveling on My Knees.
  Goodwin.
Truth. McKay.
When a Man Has Married a
  Wife. Blake.
When Both My Fathers Die.
  Gillespie.
The Young Fenians. Fallon.

Kneel (ing) (s) (knelt)
Ah, Teneriffe! Dickinson.
The Berries. Heyen.
A Birthday Memorial to
  Seventh Street. Lorde.
The Black Virgin.
  Chesterton.
A Chinese Vase. Hirsch.
Christmas 1930. Scruggs.
Dumbarton's Drums.
  Anonymous.
End of Play. Graves.
An Epitaph for Sir Henry
  Lee... Anonymous.
Far Trumpets Blowing.
  Benson.
Five Days Old. Webb.
Gnostology. Hamill.
Hyperion. Keats.
Jurgis Petraskas, the Workers'
  Angel, Organizes...
  Petrosky.
On the Death of Mary.
  Rilke.
Pilgrimage. Clarke.
Prayer. Bro.
Senior Members. Lucy.
Sonnets. Hillyer.
To Shelley. Landor.
Words from an Old Spanish
  Carol. Sawyer.

Kneel (s) (knelt)
The Coweta County
  Courthouse. Robinson.
Deaf Girl Playing. Tate.
Sabbath Reflection. Wrafter.

Knell (ing)
Childe Harold's Pilgrimage:
  Canto III, XXI. Byron.
Cries Out of Blindness.
  Corbiere.
Decoration Day. Sinclair.

Dismissing Progress and its Progenitors. Reavey.
The Inchcape Rock. Southey.
Last Verses. Motherwell.
Macbeth. Shakespeare.
The Unremitting Voice of Nightly Streams. Wordsworth.

Knife (knives)
Arms and the Woman. Mackellar.
Autobiography of a Lungworm. Fuller.
The Betrayal. Johnson.
Black Marigolds. Bilhana.
Blackfish Poem. Acorn.
Casa de Pollos. Fraser.
Clarence Mangan. Kinsella.
The Constant Cannibal Maiden. Irwin.
Crematorium. Betjeman.
Cuchillo. Harjo.
Epistles. Horace.
Going Back Again. Lytton.
The Gourmand (parody). Graham.
Hieroglyph. Auster.
I Eat My Peas with Honey. Anonymous.
Irish-American Dignitary. Clarke.
Isaac. Guri.
Journey. Hall.
Judgment. Benet.
The Knife. Kaplan.
The Last Summer. Smith.
Leesome Brand (B version). Anonymous.
Marlowe. Bayldon.
Mother of Man. Parun.
My Head on My Shoulders. Ingalls.
The Necromancers. Nims.
Nine Charms against the Hunter. Wagoner.
On the Gift of a Knife. O Dalaigh.
Original Strawberry. Willard.
Our People. Burns.
Rabbi Yom-Tob of Mayence Petitions His God. Klein.
Rhapsody on a Windy Night. Eliot.
Sonnets, XCV: "How sweet and lovely dost thou make the shame." Shakespeare.
Sonnets, C: "Where art thou, Muse, that thou forget'st so long." Shakespeare.
The Sunflowers. Stewart.

Knight (ed) (hood) (s)
The Castle in the Fire. Carr.
The Duke of Athole's Nurse. Anonymous.
A Farewell to Arms. Peele.
Father of the Man. Bryan.
The First Satire of the Second Book of Horace Imitated (excerpt). Pope.
The Friar of Orders Gray. O'Keeffe.
Herndon. Mitchell.
The Holy Grail: The Book of Gawain (excerpt). Spicer.
Ipomadon: Ipomadon Plays the Fool at Court. Anonymous.
Kane. O'Brien.
The Knight's Ghost. Anonymous.

The Knightly Code. Deschamps.
Limerick: "There was a brave knight of Lorraine." Dodge.
Mounsier Mingo. Anonymous.
Polyhymnia: His Golden Lock. Peele.
Robin Hood and the Curtal Friar. Anonymous.
Sir Peter's Leman. Anonymous.
A Sonet: "His Golden lockes, Time hath to Silver turn'd." Peele.
Sonnet: "Women have loved before as I love now." Millay.
The Spanish Lions. McGinley.
St. Kevin. Lover.
Thomas o Yonderdale. Anonymous.
To His Friend Master R.L., in Praise of Music and Poetry. Barnfield.
The Uncouth Knight. McCrae.
Victoria. Van Dyke.

Knit (ter) (ting) (s)
Almost Human. Day-Lewis.
Amoretti, VI. Spenser.
Anno Domini. Walker.
Good Fortune. Heine.
A Grain of Salt. Irwin.
I Bind My Heart. Watt.
The Knitters. Colum.
Laila Boasting. Akhyaliyya.
The Lane. Young.
Man in the Street. Warren.
A Masique Presented at Ludlow Castle (Comus). Milton.
Mirror, Mirror. Graves.
Modern Kabbalist. Falk.
Mooncalf I. Keating.
Of All the Sounds Despatched Abroad. Dickinson.
The Old Woman Sits. Davis.
On a Professional Couple in a Side-Show. Dugan.
Psalmodist. Leib.
The Sound of Rain. Evans.
Wild Oats. MacCaig.

Knob
Clean & Clear. Brownstein.
The Comedian Said It. Bigger.
Meditations in an Emergency. O'Hara.

Knock (ed) (ing) (s)
After the Blitz, 1941. Ackerley.
Amor Triumphans. Symons.
The Cats' Tea-Party. Weatherly.
Chant Royal. Morgan.
The Children's Ghosts. Letts.
Doubt. Chipp.
Getting Through. Kumin.
Haiku: "I called to the wind." Kyorai.
Horse. Harrison.
I Taught Myself to Live Simply and Wisely. Akhmatova.
Jinny Git Around. Anonymous.
The Light That Came. Clifton.

Limerick: "There was an old man who screamed out." Lear.
Loss in Delay. Southwell.
The Man of Prayer. Smart.
Notes for the Chart in 306. Nash.
Quo Vadis? Connolly.
The Return. Symons.
Somebody's Knockin' at Yo' Do'. Anonymous.
Someone. De la Mare.
Sonnet: Addressed by a Father Mourning... Vittorelli.
Through the Ages. Hope.
Traveler's Rest. Nash.
The Trooper's Horse. Anonymous.

Knot (s)
Amoretti, VI. Spenser.
At a Welsh Waterfall. Hopkins.
Barbara Allen. Anonymous.
Charity Overcoming Envy. Moore.
For shamefast harm of great and hateful need. Wyatt.
Freedom and Love. Campbell.
Heir and Serf. Marquis.
Lord Lovel (B vers.). Anonymous.
To See Him Again. "Mistral.

Knot (ted) (s)
Phyllis Knotting. Sedley.
Shirt. Simic.
Song: "Hears not my Phillis how the birds." Sedley.
Song: "Where shall Celia fly for shelter." Smart.
Unseen Horses. Grayston.

Know (ing) (n) (s) (knew)
The Abduction. Kunitz.
Abraham. Bogin.
Ad Matrem in Coelis. Van Voorhis.
Advice. Bierce.
Affidavit in Platitudes. White.
After Death. Rossetti.
After the Rain. Crouch.
After the War. Le Gallienne.
Against Education. Churchill.
All Is Well. Clough.
All the Things You Are. Hammerstein.
All Things Confine. Hadewijch.
Amnesiac. Osaki.
Among School Children. Yeats.
Angel. Soto.
Another Poem about the Madness of Women. Wayman.
Another Song. Strobel.
The Answer. Herbert.
Antarctica. Simpson.
Anticipation. Tusiani.
Arioste. Mandelstam.
Ark Astonished. Macpherson.
Ars Poetica. Wazyk.
As Long as the Heart Beats. Zawadiwsky.
At Brill on the Hill. Anonymous.

At the beginning of winter a cold spirit comes. Anonymous.
At Woodward's Gardens. Frost.
Aubade. Lechlitner.
Autobiography: Last Chapter. Barnes.
The Avenue Bearing the Initial of Christ into the New World. Kinnell.
Baby's Breakfast. Poulsson.
Ballad for the Unknown Soldier. Taylor.
A Ballad in Blank Verse of the Making of a Poet. Davidson.
A Ballad of the Gold Country. Jackson.
Ballad of the Three Coins. Watkins.
The Barcarole of James Smith. Gorman.
Be Careful. Anonymous.
Bear Song. Swanton.
Beaucourt Revisited. Herbert.
Beforehand. Bynner.
A Beginning and an End. Roditi.
The Beginning of the End. Hopkins.
A Belated Violet. Herford.
The Bells of London. Anonymous.
Biography. Struther.
Birth of Love. Warren.
Birthday Poem. Young.
Bishop Butler of Kilcash. Anonymous.
Bloody Cranesbill on the Dunes. Scovell.
Blue Sparks in Dark Closets. Snyder.
The Boat on the Serchio (excerpt). Shelley.
Breaking Off from Waiting. Nicoidski.
Brief Encounter. Scott.
Broad Is the Road. Watts.
The Burden of Decision. Everwine.
The Buried Lake. Tate.
But You, My Darling, Should Have Married the Prince. Spivack.
Calling Lucasta from Her Retirement. Lovelace.
Camels of the Kings. Norris.
Cancion. Juan II of Castile.
Carmina. Catullus.
Carnal Knowledge. Gunn.
Carnal Knowledge. Harwood.
Cars Once Steel and Green, Now Old. Zukofsky.
Challenge. Murray.
The Cherry Tree. Gunn.
Children's Song. Ford.
The Christian's "Good-Night". Doudney.
City Trees. Millay.
The Cloud Confines. Rossetti.
The Coastguard House. Montale.
A Cock Crowing in a Poulterer's Shop. Ferguson.
Coda. MacNeice.
A Code of Morals. Kipling.

Come, my sweet, whiles every strain. Cartwright.

Come to Birth. Evans.

Comfort for the Sleepless. Bradby.

Commemoration Ode. Monroe.

The Complaint of Rosamond. Daniel.

The Complement. Carew.

Cottonmouth Country. Gluck.

Country Trucks. Shannon.

Crepuscular. Howard.

Crickets and Locusts, Cicadas. Castro.

Cullen. Page.

Dame Liberty Reports from Travel. Pinkney.

The Darkling Chicken (parody). Peters.

The Day after Sunday. McGinley.

Day and Dark. Lodge.

A Decanter of Madeira, Aged 86, to George Bancroft, Aged 86. Mitchell.

Deep Sea Soundings. Williams.

Degas. Monette.

A Degenerate Age. Ibn Gabirol.

Depressed by the Death of the Horse... (parody). Taylor.

Devotions. Donne.

Dialogue. Rich.

A Dialogue. Swinburne.

Dirge. Anonymous.

Dirge of the Moolla of Kotal. Lanigan.

Dornroschen. Carruth.

The Doubter. Gilder.

Doubting. Simpson.

Down in the Hollow. Fisher.

Driven by desire I did this deed. Wyatt.

Duality. Hardy.

The Duel. Field.

Early Love. Daniel.

Early Morning of Another World. McKeown.

Easter Eve. Cabell.

Edith Sitwell Assumes the Role of Luna. Francis.

Eight Lines for a Script Girl. Jonas.

Eighteen Verses Sing to a Tatar Reed Whistle. Ts'ai Yen.

Empty Dwelling Places. Patchen.

Epicedium. Miller.

Epigram: "Boys' cocks, Diodore." Strato.

Epilogue Spoken by Mrs. Boutell. Dryden.

Epitaph on the World. Thoreau.

Epitaph to a Dog. Byron.

Eternal Goodness. Whittier.

The Evans Country. Amis.

Eve in My Legend. Devlin.

Existential. Heyen.

Experience. Kilmer.

Faces. Ciardi.

The Faithful Wife. Greenberg.

Falling Asleep. Sassoon.

The Farm on the Great Plains. Stafford.

Field Day. Rodgers.

The First Division Marches. Rice.

The First Kiss. Watts-Dunton.

Fish. Williams.

The Fish in the Stone. Dove.

The Flight of the Arrow. Stoddard.

Flood. McGough.

For Don Allen. Snyder.

For Emily (Dickinson). Owen.

Foreign Streets. Crow.

Forever in My Dream and in My Morning Thought. Thoreau.

Four Choctaw Songs. Barnes.

The Four Zoas. Blake.

Freedom, New Hampshire. Kinnell.

A Friend Advises Me to Stop Drinking. Mei Yao Ch'en.

The Ghost. Corke.

Gil, the Toreador. Webb.

Girl with Long Dark Hair. Gray.

God's Eye Is on the Sparrow. Meyer.

The Gods. Lee.

The Gods Must Not Know Us. Gregg.

Good Friday, 1613. Riding Westward. Donne.

The Grapevine. Ashbery.

Gravel. Mariah.

The Greenback Dollar. Anonymous.

The Guest. Berry.

Gulls and Dreams. Stevenson.

The Gully. Maurice.

Haiku: "into a forest." Otsuji.

The Hand. Moss.

The Hands of God. Lawrence.

The Happiest Day, the Happiest Hour. Poe.

Happy He. Anonymous.

Haywood. Otey.

Hazard. Petersen.

He Runs into an Old Acquaintance. Nowlan.

He Who Knows. Anonymous.

Heartbreak Road. Cone.

A Heathen Hymn (excerpt). Morris.

Heaven Is Heaven. Rossetti.

The Helmsman. Doolittle.

Hermit. Baker.

His Content in the Country. Herrick.

Hold Thou Me Fast. Rossetti.

Homage to Vaslav Nijinsky. Kirkup.

Hotel Transylvanie. O'Hara.

The House of a Hundred Lights. Torrence.

The House of Dust: Portrait of One Dead. Aiken.

How a Girl Got Her Chinese Name. Wong.

How Great My Grief. Hardy.

How the Flowers Grow. "Setoun. Gabriel"

I Am He That Aches with Love. Whitman.

I Am the Great Professor Jowett. Anonymous.

I Come Again. Foeth.

I Did Not Know the Truth of Growing Trees. Schwartz.

I Do Not Ask Thee, Lord. Anonymous.

I felt a Funeral, in my Brain. Dickinson.

I Had Two Pigeons Bright and Gay. Anonymous.

I Have Heard Them Knock. Hartnett.

I Saw in Louisiana a Live-Oak Growing. Whitman.

I Sit with My Dolls. Anonymous.

I've Got to Know. Guthrie.

I Want to Know. Drinkwater.

The Icosasphere. Moore.

If I But Knew. Leigh.

If I Had Known. Davies.

If There Is a Perchance. McAfee.

If You Ask Me Who I Am. Guebuza.

If You're Ever Going to Love Me. Anonymous.

In Blanco County. Fowler.

In Memoriam. Fortini.

In Memoriam A.H.H., XLII. Tennyson.

In the Matter of Two Men. Carrothers.

In the Morgue. Zangwill.

In the Silent Midnight Watches. Coxe.

In the Vaulted Way. Hardy.

In These Dissenting Times. Walker.

Instructions for the Messiah. Sklarew.

The Invisible Woman. Morgan.

John Brown's Body. Benét.

Johnny, I Hardly Knew Ye. Anonymous.

Les Jours Gigantesques / The Titanic Days. Fraser.

June Rapture. Morgan.

Just Dropped In. Cole.

Just for the Ride. Anonymous.

King Midas Has Asses' Ears. Finkel.

Labor Not in Vain. Anonymous.

The Labyrinth. Muir.

The Lamed-Vow. Auslander.

The Lament of Edward Blastock. Sitwell.

Land of the Free. MacLeish.

The Last Wolf. Tallmountain.

The Laughing Hyena, by Hokusai. Enright.

Leaves of Grass. Whitman

Left Behind. Akers.

Lessons in History. Warren.

Letter to a Young Poet. Barker.

Letter to N. Y. Bishop.

Life Is a Jest, and All Things Show It. Gay.

Limerick: "O God, inasmuch as without Thee." Anonymous.

Limerick: "There was a young lady of Kent." Anonymous.

Limerick: "There was, in the village of Patton." Anonymous.

Lines. Brooke.

Lines Written at the Temple of the Holy Sepulchre. Sandys.

Little Eclogue. Wylie.

The Lizard. Lechlitner.

London Town. Johnson.

Loneliness. Jenkins.

A Long Overdue Thankyou Note to the Girl Who Taught Me Loving. Schmidt.

Love and a Question. Frost.

Love-Songs, At Once Tender and Informative. Hoffenstein.

Man Meeting Himself. Sergeant.

Manifesto of the Soldier Who Went Back to War. Queremel.

The Marrow. Roethke.

The Melmac Year. Hilton.

Men Say They Know Many Things. Thoreau.

The Milking Shed. Clare.

The Moon Is a Diamond. Sze.

Motels, Hotels, Other People's Houses. Van Brunt.

Mother and Son. Heyen.

The Mouse Whose Name Is Time. Francis.

Mules. Muldoon.

My Love. Ono-no-Yoshiki.

My Sister. Storni.

The Mysteries. Strong.

The Mystery. Teasdale.

Mythology. Waters.

De Naevo in Facie Faustinae. Bastard.

Nature. Longfellow.

New-Englands Crisis: The Prologue. Tompson.

New English Canaan, the Authors Prologue. Morton.

News from Detroit. Minty.

Night and Love. Lytton.

Night (excerpts). Peguy.

Night of Spring. Westwood.

No Room. Stroud.

Nobody Knows de Trouble I See. Anonymous.

Not I, But God. Flint.

Not Knowing. Brainard.

O Gracious Shepherd. Constable.

O, Where Were We before Time Was. Dunn.

Obituary in Bitcherel. Aiken.

Oblique. Rutledge.

Ode on a Grecian Urn. Keats.

Ode to Joy. Hoffman.

An Ode to Spring in the Metropolis. Seaman.

Odiham. Gray.

The Old Dog in the Ruins of the Graves at Arles. Wright.

The Old Nudists. Colby.

Old Voyager. Blackstock.

On a Doctor of Divinity. Porson.

On a Female Rope-Dancer. Anonymous.

On Change of Weathers.
Quarles.
On Death. Landor.
On Giles and Joan. Jonson.
On His Queerness.
Isherwood.
On Seeing the Royal Palace at
Stirling in Ruins. Burns.
On Sir John Guise.
Anonymous.
On the Last Page of the Last
Yellow Pad in Rome before
Taking Off... Williams.
On the Sale By Auction of
Keats' Love Letters.
Wilde.
Once When You Were
Walking. Wynne.
The Only Jealousy of Emer.
Anonymous.
Opportunity. Cawein.
Othello. Shakespeare.
The Other. Cooley.
Our Sister. Powers.
Our Strange and Lovable
Weather. Matthews.
Out Fishing. Howes.
Panegyric. Lenowitz.
Panic. Davis.
Paradise Lost. Milton.
A Parting Hymn We Sing.
Wolfe.
Patrol. Pomeroy.
The People Went to War.
Jacinto.
The People, Yes. Sandburg.
Peyote Poem. McClure.
The Phallic Symbol. Moore.
Pick a Fern, Pick a Fern,
Ferns Are High.
Anonymous.
Places I Have Been. Volk.
Pleasant Changes. Browne
(Aunt Effie).
Plymouth Harbor. Radford.
Po" Boy. Anonymous.
The Poet. Bynner.
Poet. Hayes.
Population Drifts. Sandburg.
Prayer. Hughes.
A Prayer for a Little Home.
Bone.
Prescience. Widdemer.
The Presence. Levertov.
The Prison Guard. Maloney.
The Promise. Kunjufu.
Puk-Wudjies. Chalmers.
Quatrain: "I knew like a song
your vows weren't strong."
Mahsati.
The Question. Gibson.
Rachel. Gilbert.
The Radical in the Alligator
Shirt. Lipsitz.
Rapunzel. Hay.
The Reason Why. Beddoes.
Recovery. Ikeda.
The Relics. Mathews.
Remembering Althea.
Stafford.
Retractions. Cabell.
Reunion. Herzberg.
The Rigveda: Hymn of
Creation. Anonymous.
Riley. Causley.
The River Again and Again.
Gregg.
The Robin. Scott.
Rock Painting. Cope.
A Roundel of Rest. Symons.
Sadness, Glass, Theory.
Fuller.

Scene with Figure. Deutsch.
The Sea Hold. Sandburg.
The Sea Shell. Lowell.
The Secret. Peach.
Seeds. Oxenham.
Self-Knowledge. Coleridge.
Senex to Matt. Prior.
Stephen.
Shake Hands with Your Bets,
Friend. Thomas.
The Ship of Fools. Barclay.
Signature. Stroud.
Silence, an Eloquent
Applause. Gregory.
Sister Bernardo. Wilde.
The Sloth. Roethke.
Small Song. Shaw.
The Snake. Corke.
Some Kind of Giant.
Pritchard.
The Somerset Dam for
Supper. Holmes.
Song. Spender.
The Song of the Ghost.
Graves.
South of the Great Sea.
Anonymous.
The Splendid Village. Elliott.
Springtime in Cookham Dean.
Roberts.
The Squirrels' Christmas.
Howard.
St. Roach. Rukeyser.
A Starling and a Willow-
Wren. Auden.
Statues. Raine.
Suenos. Reiss.
Superstition. Karibo.
Swahili Love Song.
Anonymous.
Sway. Johnson.
Sympathy. Dunbar.
Sympathy. Gyles.
Take Your Accusation Back!
Kittaararter.
Target Practice. Finkel.
Tell All the World. Kemp.
Testimony to an Inquisitor.
Stafford.
The Thanksgiving. Herbert.
Their Wedded Love. Milton.
Theory of Vision: The Green
Eye. Merrill.
There Is In Human Closeness
a Sacred Boundary.
Akhmatova.
These Stones. Menander.
The Things That Matter.
Nesbit.
Things to Come. Reeves.
The Third Day. Pierce.
This Moment. Flint.
Thoughts of Loved Ones.
Fishback.
Three Sorrowful Things.
Anonymous.
Three Wise Old Women.
Corbett.
Threnody. Cuney.
The Threshing Machine.
Meynell.
Time-Travel. Olds.
The Tinkers. Campbell.
Tirocinium; or, A Review of
Schools. Cowper.
To a Cat. Coleridge.
To a Friend Whose Work Has
Come to Nothing. Yeats.
To a Hurt Child. Litchfield.
To a Portrait of Whistler in
the Brooklyn Art Museum.
Cox.

To His Books. Vaughan.
To His Sacred Majesty, a
Panegyrick... Dryden.
To Know All Is to Forgive
All. Waterman.
To My Daughter. Plutzik.
To My Daughter Riding in
the Circus Parade.
Labombard.
To My Infant Daughter (II).
Winters.
To One Who Would Make a
Confession. Blunt.
To Stand Up Straight.
Housman.
To the Unknown God.
Nietzsche.
A Tragedy. Masson.
Trifling Women.
Anonymous.
The Triumph of Time.
Swinburne.
True Night. Char.
The Truth from Above.
Anonymous.
The Turtle's Belly. Pearce.
Two Lips. Hardy.
Two Poems. Sosei (Sosei
Hoshi).
Two Shapes. Gregor.
Two Sonnets. Sorley.
Two White Horses in a Line.
Two Poor Boys.
The U. S. Sailor with the
Japanese Skull. Scott.
Ulysses Returns.
Montgomery.
Under the Wattle. Sladen.
The Undiscovered Planet.
Nicholson.
Unmanifest Destiny. Hovey.
Until We Built a Cabin.
Fisher.
Upon My Lord Chief Justice's
Election of My Lady Anne
Wentworth... Carew.
Ursula. Johnson.
Utrillo's World. Glassco.
The Vedic Hymns: The Song
of Creation. Anonymous.
The Vestal Virgin. Llwyd.
Vickery's Mountain.
Robinson.
Waking from Sleep. Bly.
Walking with Your Eyes Shut.
Stafford.
Walter Jenks' Bath.
Meredith.
We Separate the Days.
Nordbrandt.
Went up a year this evening!
Dickinson.
What hundred books are best.
Bangs.
What Mystery Pervades a
Well! Dickinson.
What We Listened for in
Music. Burr.
Whate'er You Dream with
Doubt Possest. Clough.
When My Beloved Appears.
Ibn al-Arabi.
When the Saints Come
Marching In. Lorde.
While the Summer Trees
Were Crying. Iremonger.
Who Are My People?
Marinoni.
Wings and Wheels. Turner.
Wisdom. Ford.
The Wistful Days. Johnson.
Woman Poem. Giovanni.

A Woman's Sorrow (excerpt).
Ho Nansorhon.
Words Like Freedom.
Hughes.
Wouldn't You Like to Know.
Saxe.
The Year's Awakening.
Hardy.
Yomi, Yomi. Anonymous.
You told me: "I am not
worthy of you." Burnat-
Provins.
Zurich, zum Storchen.
Celan.
Knowledge
Aspects of Some Forsythia
Branches. Gustafson.
At the Fishhouses. Bishop.
Autobiography, Chapter
XVII. Barnes.
The Campus. Posner.
The Cat in the Box. Jonas.
Close-Ups of Summer.
MacCaig.
Comments. Kenner.
Ellas and the Statues. Akin.
An Essay on Man. Pope.
Faustus. Hope.
Going Towards Spain.
Googe.
Grenadier. Housman.
Harvest Song. Toomer.
The Homeward Journey.
Aaronson.
I Am the Great Professor
Jowett. Anonymous.
I Move to Random
Consolations. Heyen.
I Spread Out unto Thee My
Hand. Ainsworth.
Implicit Faith. De Vere.
Lines to a Tree. Teller. J. L.
Marriage: To K. Hall.
O Brother Tree. Michelson.
Old Paintings on Italian
Walls. Raine.
On the Death of Parents.
Barson.
The Only Jealousy of Emer.
Anonymous.
Paradise Regained. Milton.
The Rising Village.
Goldsmith.
Salomon. Morhange.
Sheridan at Cedar Creek.
Melville.
Sonnets, First Series.
Tuckerman.
Sunrise. Tollerud.
Sweet Stay-at-Home. Davies.
To One That Desired to
Know My Mistris. Carew.
To the Nile. Shelley.
A Treatie of Human Learning.
Greville.
A Twilight in Middle March.
Ledwidge.
Ulysses. Tennyson.
Womankind. Massey.
Word of God, Across the
Ages. Blanchard.
A Wry Smile. Fuller.
Knuckle (s)
720 Gabriel St. Outlaw.
The Flight in the Desert.
Everson.
Ford Pickup. Evans.
A Lesson in Detachment.
Miller.
Listens, Too (parody).
Berry.

The Man Hidden behind the
Drapes. Rogers.
On the Symbolic
Consideration of Hands and
the Significance of Death.
Williams.
The Sleeping Beauty.
Hutton.
The Truth the Dead Know.
Sexton.
Watts. Kaufman.

L

Labor (s)
Adam Driven from Eden.
Anonymous.
The Aeneid. Virgil (Publius
Vergilius Maro).
Among the Daffadillies.
Farnaby.
Amoretti, XXIII. Spenser.
Amoretti, LXIX. Spenser.
Annales: "Like a shower of
rain." Ennius.
Art Thou Poor, Yet Hast
Thou Golden Slumbers?
Dekker.
Awake, Awake! Campion.
The Blessings of Surrender.
Helphingtine.
A Digression from
Husbandrie: To a Poynt or
Two of Huswifrie. Tusser.
Epigram: "Give pensions to
the Learned Pig." Blake.
Epilogue to Lessing's
Laocoon. Arnold.
Epitaphium Meum.
Bradford.
Everyday Will Be Sunday.
Anonymous.
Express. Allingham.
Farmer Goes Berserk. Elder.
The Father and His Children.
Anonymous.
The Four Horses. Reeves.
The Guerdon of the Sun.
Sterling.
Hence, Away, You Sirens!
Wither.
Heroes. Creeley.
Jacob. Reznikoff.
Juggy's Christening.
Anonymous.
The Labouring Man.
Anonymous.
Lifting and Leaning. Wilcox.
Lord, Dear God! To Thy
Attending. Otto.
Madrid. Pai Wei.
The Mole. Clare.
New Words to the Tune of
"O'Donnel Abu." Connell.
On a Piece of Tapestry.
Santayana.
Praise. Smart.
A Prayer for Pentecost.
Brown.
A Prayer to the Trinity.
Stanyhurst.
Proceedings of the Wars.
Moure.
A Psalm of Life. Longfellow
The Rape of the Lock.
Pope.
A Reformer to His Father.
Simmons.

Samson Agonistes. Milton.
A Schoolmaster's Admonition.
Anonymous.
A Shropshire Lad.
Housman.
Snapshot. Garrett.
Some Tyme I Fled the Fyre
That Me Brent. Wyatt.
The Song of Bekotsidi.
Anonymous.
Songs of Labor: Dedication.
Whittier.
Sonnet: The Common Grave.
Dobell.
St. Columcille's Island
Hermitage. *Anonymous.*
Summer Beach. Cornford.
The Sunrise to the Poor.
Wilson.
Talking Union: 1964.
Sissman.
Teach Us to Serve Thee,
Lord. Ignatius Loyola.
There You Sit. Silverstein.
'Tis Hard to Find God.
Herrick.
To His Friend in Elysium.
Du Bellay.
Tomorrow's Men. Johnson.
Two Kinds of People.
Wilcox.
The Vineyard. *Anonymous.*
Visit of Hope to Sydney Cove,
near Botany-Bay. Darwin.
Which Are You?
Anonymous.
Wordsworth's Grave.
Watson.

Labyrinth (s)
Bridges and Tunnels.
Bentley.
Love's Triumph. Jonson.
On the Range. Souster.
De Rerum Natura.
Lucretius (Titus Lucretitus
Carus).
Some Small Shells from the
Windward Islands.
Swenson.

Lace (d)
Auras on the Interstates.
Vizenor.
Impressions. Wilde.
On the Wide Stairs.
Amichai.
Queen Anne's Lace.
Newton.
The Song in the Dell.
Carryl.
A Tawnymoor. *Anonymous.*
To a Conscript of 1940.
Read.
A Utilitarian View of the
Monitor's Fight. Melville.

Lack (s)
Blind, I Speak to the
Cigarette. De
Longchamps.
Can. Lit. Birney.
A Complaint by Night of the
Lover Not Beloved.
Petrarch.
Dinosaurs. Stoloff.
Fish Riddle: "Although it's
cold no clothes I wear."
Anonymous.
The Great Merchant, Dives
Pragmaticus, Cries His
Wares. Newbery.
Hymns for the Amusement of
Children. Smart.

The Raquette River, Potsdam,
New York.... Piccone.
Sunday in Glastonbury. Bly.
A Tabernacle Thought.
Zangwill.
The Things That Are More
Excellent. Watson.
To the Right Person. Frost.

Lackey
Beware Fair Maide.
Anonymous.
On a Distinguished Politician.
Thorold Rogers.

Lad (die) (s)
Ballad of Human Life.
Beddoes.
Because I Liked You Better.
Housman.
The Beggar-Laddie.
Anonymous.
The City Clerk. Ashe.
The Cock of the Game.
Anonymous.
Colleen Rue. *Anonymous.*
The Contrary Boy. Drake.
Dark-Eyed Lad Columbus.
Turner.
Down in a Coal Mine.
Anonymous.
Flora MacDonald and the
King. *Anonymous.*
The Flower. Dodd.
God Made Trees.
Anonymous.
The Housewife. Coblentz
I Hoed and Trenched and
Weeded. Housman.
The Jolly Waggoner.
Anonymous.
The Lads of Wamphray.
Anonymous.
Look Not in My Eyes, for
Fear. Housman.
The Maiden Hind.
Anonymous.
Miners. Owen.
Must I Go Bound?
Anonymous.
A New Song Called The
Curling of the Hair.
Anonymous.
The October Redbreast.
Meynell.
Oh Fair Enough Are Sky and
Plain. Housman.
The Omelet of A. MacLeish.
Wilson.
Our Ship She Lies in
Harbour. *Anonymous.*
The Pedlar's Song.
Shakespeare.
Post-Rail Song (with music).
Anonymous.
Recreation. Taylor.
The Reporters. Levy.
The Runaway. Hicky.
Shy Geordie. Cruickshank.
Some Say the Deil's Deid.
Anonymous.
Tears. Reese.
Teatime Variations: After
A.E. Housman (parody).
Titheradge.
There Is a Charming Land.
Oehlenschlager.
They Who Wait. Going.
Victory March. Joseph.
The Wastrel. Kauffman.

Ladder (s)
Bricklayer Love. Sandburg.
Crawl Blues. McHugh.
The Hours. Tichy.

Limerick: "While Titian was
grinding rose madder."
Anonymous.
My Mother's Table. Sobiloff.
The Steam Threshing-
Machine. Turner.
Stonehouse. Tagami.
Wood-cut. Sackville-West.

Lady (ies)
Ain't Gonna Rain (with
music). *Anonymous.*
Alcestis. Euripides.
Annunciation. Rilke.
Antiphonal Hymn in Praise of
Inanna. Enheduanna.
An Appeal to John Harralson.
Anonymous.
Away out Yonder in Arizony.
Anonymous.
Aztec Figurine. Beecher.
Balade Simple: "Fairest of
stars." Lydgate.
Ballade of My Lady's Beauty.
Kilmer.
Ballade of the Harrowing of
Hell. Lewis.
Ballata: Of a Continual Death
in Love. Cavalcanti.
The Bathtub. Pound.
Birthday Gifts. Asquith.
The Book of True Love
(excerpt). Ruiz.
The Buccaneer. Turner.
Canzo: "Can l'erba fresch'elh
folha par." Bernard de
Ventadour
The Challenge. Pope.
The Choir Boys. Heine.
Colts. *Anonymous.*
Companion of Her Lord Till
Death. *Anonymous.*
Court and Country Love.
Anonymous.
The Cruel Mother (P version).
Anonymous.
Cymbeline. Shakespeare.
Dancing at Whitsun.
Marshall.
Der Heilige Mantel Von
Aachen. Musser.
Dolores. Swinburne.
The Earl of Aboyne.
Anonymous.
An Epitaph. de la Mare.
Epitaph on a Warthog.
Morton.
Epitaph on the Lap-Dog of
Lady Frail. Wilkes.
Essential oils–are wrung.
Dickinson.
The Eve of Saint John.
Scott.
Evening Prayer. *Anonymous.*
Fair and Fair. Peele.
The Fair Flower of
Northumberland.
Anonymous.
First Praise. Williams.
For Sapphires. Rodgers.
The Frenchman's Ball.
Anonymous.
Georgie Wedlock.
Anonymous.
The Gipsy Laddie.
Anonymous.
Go Heart, Hurt with
Adversity. *Anonymous.*
The Gypsy Laddie (A vers.).
Anonymous.
The Gypsy Rover.
Anonymous.

I Asked a Thief to Steal Me a
Peach. Blake.
I Had a Little Pony.   Mother
Goose.
I Have a Gentle Cock.
Anonymous.
I'll Tell You What a Flapper
Is. Freeman.
In France. Cornford.
Introducing a Madman.
Waldrop.
It's Raining, It's Raining.
Anonymous.
The Jolly Beggar.
Anonymous.
King Orfeo. Anonymous.
The Ladies' Aid.
Anonymous.
Lady April. Le Gallienne.
A Lady Dying in Childbed.
Herrick.
Lady in a Distant Face.
Welch.
A Lady of High Degree.
Anonymous.
Lang Johnny More.
Anonymous.
The Lay of the Last Minstrel.
Scott.
Leadbelly Gives an
Autograph. Jones.
Leaving Ithaca. Snodgrass.
A Legend of Cherries.
Dalmon.
Lines to a Lady-Bird. De
Tabley.
Lord Derwentwater (The
King's Love-Letter).
Anonymous.
Love Me, Love My Dog.
Crawford.
Lucy McLockett. McGinley.
Magaica. De Sousa.
The Maid o' the West.
Clare.
Maisrie. MacKay.
Malisons, Malisons, More
Than Ten. *Anonymous.*
March Thoughts from
England. Woods.
The Martyred Democrat.
Dennis.
The Mechanical Optimist.
Stevens.
Mine Eyes Beheld the Blessed
Pity. Dante Alighieri.
Mother Goose Rhyme.
Rexroth.
The Motorcyclists. Tate.
Mrs. Green. Huddle.
The Mufadaliyat: Gone Is
Youth. Salamah.
My Dear Lady. *Anonymous.*
Names of Horses. Hall.
A New Courtly Sonnet of the
Lady Greensleeves.
Anonymous.
No Difference in the Dark.
Herrick.
Old-Time Service.
Churchyard.
On a Dog-Collar.
Anonymous.
On Being Told That One's
Ideas Are Victorian. Hay.
On Ladies' Accomplishments.
Anonymous.
On the Way to the Island.
Ferry.
Othello. Shakespeare.
Our Lady of the Skies.
Hayes.

Our Lady of the Snows.
Kipling.
Our Lady Peace. Van
Doren.
A Pastoral. Breton.
Phyllida and Corydon.
Breton.
Piazza Piece. Ransom.
The Play of the Four P.P.:
The Palmer. Heywood.
Politeness. Turner.
Praise of My Lady. Morris.
Prayer to Venus. Chaucer.
Prince Heathen (A version).
Anonymous.
The Puzzled Census Taker.
Saxe.
The Ranting Wanton's
Resolution; 1672.
Anonymous.
The Rover's Apology.
Gilbert.
Sad-Eyed Lady of the
Lowlands. Dylan.
Sheath and Knife .
Anonymous.
The Shellpicker. Perry.
The Shepherd's Wife's Song.
Greene.
The Shepherdess. Meynell.
The Siesta. *Anonymous.*
Sir John Butler. *Anonymous.*
Sonnet. Berryman.
Sonnet: Of His Lady in
Heaven. Jacopo da
Lentino.
Sonnet: Of the Eyes of a
Certain Mandetta, of
Toulouse... Cavalcanti.
Sonnet: On the 9th of June
1290. Dante Alighieri.
Squire and Milkmaid.
Anonymous.
Texas Rangers. *Anonymous.*
The Three Cherry Trees. de
la Mare.
To * * * * *. Callanan.
The Twa Knights.
Anonymous.
Two Carols to Our Lady.
Anonymous.
Unicorn. Smith.
Van Amburgh's Menagerie.
Anonymous.
A Virginal. Pound.
Washing Day. *Anonymous.*
The Waste Land. Eliot.
Wild Roses. Fawcett.
Willie O Douglas Dale.
Anonymous.
Winter Solstice Poem. Scott.
The Wooing of Etain.
Anonymous.
YGreen Grows the Laurel.
Anonymous.
Young Beichan and Susie Pye.
Anonymous.
Young John. *Anonymous.*
Ladybug
Down in the Hollow. Fisher.
Fall. Fisher.
Lair
A Call to the Wild.
Dunsany.
Hares at Play. Clare.
John Peel. Graves.
The little tigers are at rest.
Hood.
Nepenthe. Darley.
Unguarded Gates. Aldrich.

Laird (s)
Epitaph: "Lo worms enjoy the
seat of bliss." Burns.
The Knight's Ghost.
Anonymous.
Parcy Reed. *Anonymous.*
Lake (s)
Accordance. Kanabus.
The Agricultural Show,
Flemington, Victoria.
Maurice.
Among the Finger Lakes.
Wallace.
Angler. Vinz.
The Battle of Erie.
Anonymous.
The Beggar Wind. Austin.
Black Poplar-Boughs.
Freeman.
A Blessing. McBride.
The Case. Norris.
Crab Orchard Sanctuary: Late
October. Kinsella.
Derwent: An Ode. Carr.
Don Juan. Byron.
Down the Mississippi.
Fletcher.
For Daphne at Lone Lake.
Haines.
Guide to the Ruins.
Nemerov.
He Cometh Forth into the
Day. Book of the Dead.
How many evenings in the
arbor by the river. Li
Ch'ing-chao.
The Illustration–A Footnote.
Levertov.
In Hospital. Flecker.
In the Lake Country.
Wissinger.
The Lake. Poe.
The Lake of the Caogama.
Anonymous.
Lament, with Flesh and
Blood. McPherson.
Laziness and Silence. Bly.
The Legend of Grand Lake.
Westcott.
Limerick: "There was an old
man by Salt Lake." Smith.
The Loon. Street.
Lullaby. Waddington.
Many Years Ago. Barbeitos.
Maze. Eberhart.
Mexico City Blues: 127th
Chorus. Kerouac.
Minnesota Camp Grounds.
Vizenor.
Morning Swim. Kumin.
Mother. Vincent.
Night Wind in Fall. Moses.
An Old Song. Yehoash.
The Outer from the Inner.
Dickinson.
Perry's Victory. *Anonymous.*
Rob Roy. Scott
The Runner. Gildner.
Santa Fe Trail. Guest.
A Sermon. Sackville.
Seven Dreams. Bayliss.
The Sisters. Jackowska.
Skating. Asquith.
The Snow-Shower. Bryant.
Storm. Nagy.
Swallow the Lake. Major.
To the (Supposed) Patron.
Hill.
Twink Drives Back, in a Bad
Mood, from a Party in
Massachusetts. Amabile.
Upon the Lake. Lenski.

Walleye. Hoey.
Written on the Banks of
Wastwater during a Calm.
Wilson.
Lamb of God
It Was Not Strange. Hagg.
The Saviour. Wesley.
Lamb (s)
Accept Our Tribute. Watts.
The Blessed Virgin Mary
Compared to a Window.
Merton.
Brigham Young.
Anonymous.
Buckskin Joe. *Anonymous.*
Cursor Mundi: The Flight
into Egypt. *Anonymous.*
Everybody's Welcome.
Anonymous.
For a Lamb. Eberhart.
God's Dominion and Decrees.
Watts.
Hope of Our Hearts. Denny.
Hush, Honey. Saunders.
Hymn. Dunbar.
In Chagall's Village.
Auslander.
It Is Finished. Evans.
Jesus, Shepherd of Thy Sheep.
Bethune.
Jesus, the Name Most High.
Wesley.
A King Shall Reign in
Righteousness. Streeter.
Lamb. Browne.
The Lambs of Grasmere,
1860. Rossetti.
Loudoun's Bonnie Woods and
Braes. Tannahill.
Love Song for the Future.
Miller.
Lullaby. Dunbar.
Lullaby. Hoffenstein.
Mary's Lamb. Hale.
Money! Money! *Anonymous.*
A New Year. Shorter.
Not to March. Hackleman.
O Children, Would You
Cherish? Dock.
De Old Sheep Dey Know de
Road. *Anonymous.*
On Hearing a Broadcast of
Ceremonies in Connection
with.... Wrafter.
Paphnutius (excerpt).
Hroswitha von
Grandersheim.
Passover. Auslander.
Personal Talk. Wordsworth.
Ritual Not Religion. Indian.
The Sad Shepherd. Jonson.
Saviour, Sprinkle Many
Nations. Coxe.
Sheep and Lambs. Hinkson.
Some Lamb. Rice.
To Certain Critics. Cullen.
Walking with God. Cowper.
Lame
The Beggar. *Anonymous.*
Flowers in the Ward.
Neilson.
One fine day in the middle of
the night. *Anonymous.*
The Waste of War. Stidger.
You, Neighbor God. Rilke.
Lament (ation) (ed) (ing) (s)
The Ancient Law. Spire.
As Flows the Rapid River.
Smith.
Bitter-Sweet. Herbert.
The Goat. Saba.

A Graveyard in Queens. Montague.

The Groundhog. Eberhart.

The House of a Hundred Lights. Torrence.

Lines Written in Early Spring. Wordsworth.

Milton. Blake.

People. Yevtushenko.

Postscript. Thomas.

To Papilus. Martial (Marcus Valerius Martialis).

To the Departing Spirit of an Alienated Friend. Seward.

To the Sun. Bachmann.

When None Shall Rail. Lewis.

Wine and Grief. Ibn Gabirol.

The Zucca (excerpt). Shelley.

Lamp (s)

Cherry Blossoms. "Lewis.

Dance of the Abakweta. Danner.

Dances of Death. Blok.

Daybreak. Shelley.

Dusk. Welshimer.

Eternity of Love Protested. Carew.

Eveningsong 2. Wilson.

The Faerie Queene. Spenser.

The Firefly Lights His Lamp. Anonymous.

From Scars Where Kestrels Hover. Auden.

Guilt and Sorrow. Wordsworth.

Hero Entombed I. Quennell.

The Hill Wife. Frost.

His Fare-well to Sack. Herrick.

House Fear. Frost.

The House of Night. Freneau.

Ill. Spencer.

Impression de Nuit: London. Douglas.

In the Dusky Path of a Dream. Tagore.

Keep Your Lamp Trimmed and Burning. Anonymous.

The Lamp. Teasdale.

The Leaders of the Crowd. Yeats.

The Madonna's Lamp. Wilhelm.

A Midnight Interior. Sassoon.

Mingled Yarns. Kennedy.

Missing. Auden.

The Morning Watch. Vaughan.

My Friends Are Little Lamps to Me. Whittemore.

My Jack. O'Donnell.

The New Colossus. Lazarus.

Pastoral Dialogue Castara and Parthenia. Flatman.

Poems, VIII. O'Connor.

Preludes. Eliot.

Shag Rookery. Hart-Smith.

The Shore of Life. Fitzgerald.

Silex Scintillans. Vaughan.

Song of the Poor Man. Anonymous.

Song: "There's one great bunch of stars in heaven." Marzials.

The Sorceress! Lindsay.

The Starlighter. Guiterman.

Summer Evening and Night. Thomson.

To Her Lover's Complaint. Barker.

To the White Fiends. McKay.

Trees. De la Mare.

Uriel. Stead.

What Yo' Gwine to Do When Yo' Lamp Burn Down? Anonymous.

Winter Anemones. Brasch.

The Wolf. Davidson.

Lance (s)

Chivalry at a Discount. Fitzgerald.

Don Quixote. Dobson.

Regina Confessorum. Anonymous.

The Song of Roland, CCXL. Anonymous.

Lancelot

At Queensferry. Henley.

Land (s)

At Queensferry. Henley.

At the Top of the Road. Going.

Autumn Fields. Roberts.

The Base of All Metaphysics. Whitman.

The Battle of Brunanburh. Anonymous.

The Beauty of Job's Daughters. Macpherson.

The Beggar's Opera. Gay.

Blood Marksman and Kureldei the Marksman. Anonymous.

The Brazos River. Anonymous.

Buffalo Dance. Corbin.

By the Pacific. Bashford.

Cape Coast Castle Revisited. Hall-Evans.

The Christ of the Andes (excerpt). Markham.

Colum-Cille's Farewell to Ireland. Anonymous.

Come and Go with Me to That Land. Anonymous.

Communication. Jennings.

The Complaint of the Morpethshire Farmer. Bunting.

Crossing Alone the Nighted Ferry. Housman.

Curly Joe. Anonymous.

Dakota Badlands. Landeweer.

The Damage You Have Done. Komey.

The Dead Cities Speak to the Living Cities. Fleg.

Death; She Was Always Here. Wallach.

The Discovery. Brasch.

The Discovery of America. Robertson.

The Djanggawul Cycle, 12. Anonymous.

Dream Songs. Berryman.

E. B. B. Thomson.

Edward Lear. Auden.

Eight Miles South of Grand Haven. Kelly.

Empire Builders. MacLeish.

England Expects. Nash.

Evarra and His Gods. Kipling.

Exultation is the going. Dickinson.

The False Favorite's Downfall. Anonymous.

The Famine Year. Wilde.

Florence MacCarthy's Farewell to Her English Lover. De Vere.

Flowers. Longfellow.

From Potomac to Merrimac. Hale.

Generations. Clark.

Giles Corey of the Salem Farms: Prologue. Longfellow.

Glory, Glory to the Sun. Alford.

God, Give Us Men! Holland.

Grasmere Sonnets. Wright.

The Great Hunger. Kavanagh.

The Great Swamp Fight. Hazard.

The Hawk in the Rain. Hughes.

Heart for All Her Children. Hebert, Jr.

Heaven. Brooke.

The Heir of Linne. Anonymous.

Hiawatha's Wooing. Longfellow.

Holy-Cross Day. Browning.

Hope. Howells.

Hugh Spencer's Feats in France (A version). Anonymous.

A Hymn for Canada. Watson.

I Know a Name! Anonymous.

In a Wine Cellar. Daley.

In Louisiana. Paine.

In the Land Where We Were Dreaming. Lucas.

Indian Summer: Vermont. Stevenson.

Invocation. Stafford.

An Irish Blessing. Murray.

Is This Land Your Land? Anonymous.

The Island. Jennett.

The Islands of the Sea. Woodberry.

Jock the Leg and the Merry Merchant. Anonymous.

John Otto. Merwin.

A Joyful New Ballad. Deloney.

The Judge. Kopp.

July in Indiana. Fitzgerald.

The Land. Kipling.

The Land of Cockayne. Anonymous.

The Land of the Evening Mirage. Anonymous.

Laus Veneris. Swinburne.

The Leak in the Dike. Cary.

The Leper. Ka-ehu.

Listen to the Bird. Firestone.

Le Livre Est sur la Table. Ashbery.

Love's Land. Crawford.

Many Years Ago. Barbeitos.

Mary Hamilton. Anonymous.

The Master's Call. Smith.

Maud. Tennyson.

The Mediterranean. Tate.

Men. MacLeish.

The Men of the Maine. Scollard.

The Migrations of People. Leiser.

Monkey Difference. Howes.

My Africa. Dei-Anang.

"My days' delight, my springtime joys fordone." Ralegh.

My Land. Davis.

Napa, California. Castillo.

Nathan Hale. Partridge.

Native-Born. Langley.

Nelson Street. O'Sullivan.

The New Ezekial. Lazarus.

Night Journey. Roethke.

Novelettes III: The Gardener. MacNeice.

O Hear My Prayer, Lord. Craig.

Oisin in the Land of Youth. Comyn.

The Old Hymns. Stanton.

The Old Testament (excerpt). Anonymous.

On Independence. Sewall.

On the Death of His Son. Wesley.

On the Edge of the Pacific. Maynard.

One Friday Morn. Anonymous

One Home. Stafford.

Parachutes, My Love, Could Carry Us Higher. Guest.

Parted Lovers. Halevi.

Pegasus. Kavanagh.

A Poem on England's Happiness. Anonymous.

A Pretty Woman. Ortiz.

The Pride. Newlove.

Rain. Hollo.

The Rejected "National Hymns". Newell.

Rhymes of a Rolling Stone. Service.

Riddle 7 (Mute Swan). Anonymous.

The Road of Remembrance. Reese.

Rosebud. Anderson.

The Royal Adventurer. Freneau.

Salut Au Monde! Whitman.

Schizophrenic. Page.

The Sea-Gull. Anonymous.

Sea-Nurtured. Ingelow.

The Sea Serpent Chantey. Lindsay.

Secret Pleasures. Morgan.

The Seven against Thebes. Aeschylus.

Sing to the Lord Most High. Dwight.

Sioux Indians. Anonymous.

The Song-Maker. Wickham.

Song of a Train. Davidson.

A Song of Handicrafts. Matheson.

The Song of Hiawatha. Longfellow.

The Song of Nidderdale. Ratcliffe.

The Song of the Bow. Doyle.

The Song of the Ungirt Runners. Sorley.

Song: "The boat is chafing at our long delay." Davidson.

The Star-Spangled Banner. Key.

The Storm Is Over. Bridges.

The Summer Countries. Rago.

The Tempest. Shakespeare.

Text. Wurdemann.
Thar's More in the Man Than
  Thar Is in the Land.
  Lanier.
This Is America. Clark.
This Land. Mudie.
Three Poems for the Indian
  Steelworkers in a Bar...
  Bruchac.
To Arcady. Going.
To Chaucer. Occleve.
To the Memory of the Brave
  Americans. Freneau.
To the Returning Brave.
  Johnson.
To the River Isca (the Usk).
  Vaughan.
The Tomb of Crethon.
  Leonidas.
Tristram of Lyonesse: The
  Death of Urgan.
  Swinburne.
The Triumph. Lanier.
The Turkish Lady.
  Anonymous.
The Twelve-Elf.
  Morgenstern.
Two Sonnets. Sorley.
An Uninscribed Monument on
  One of the Battle-Fields of
  the Wilderness. Melville
The Usual Exquisite Boredom
  of Patrols. Popham.
Vacationer. Gibson.
Vampirella. Equi.
The Voice That Beautifies the
  Land. Anonymous.
The West Wind. Masefield.
What a Court Hath Old
  England. Anonymous.
What Will You Learn about
  the Brobinyak. Ciardi.
Where Is the Fruit. Banda.
The Wild Duck. Masefield.
Wild Roses. Fawcett.
Winter Rain. Rossetti.
Wishes. Ault.
Written in Ireland. Alcock.
The Young Dove. Ibn Ezra.
Zephyr. Ware.

Landed
Ambition. Bishop.
Limerick: "There once was a
  popular crooner."
  Thornton.
Northumberland Betrayd by
  Dowglas. Anonymous.
The Voyage of Maeldune.
  Tennyson.

Landing
Downstream. Kinsella.
Flies Love Me. Archer.
For Daphne at Lone Lake.
  Haines.
Some Boys. Ortleb.

Landlady
How Stands the Glass
  Around? Wolfe.

Landlord
False Linfinn. Anonymous.
Greed, Part 4. The Turtle.
  Wakoski.
The Swashbuckler's Song.
  Montgomery.
Vision. Howells.

Landlords
Inferno: A New Circle.
  Ormsby.

Landscape
The Action of Invisible Ink.
  Darwin.

A Bed of Campanula.
  "Crichton.
Bouzouki. Hanson.
The Emigrant. O'Grady.
Express Train. Kraus.
Homage to Literature.
  Rukeyser.
I need only fall asleep.
  Blandiana.
John Clare. Anderson.
The Lady Poverty. Meynell.
Memory of Another Climate.
  Preil.
More Distant Than the Dead
  Sea. Tueni.
The Mouth of the Hudson.
  Lowell.
Renewal by Her Element.
  Devlin.
Rivers and Mountains.
  Ashbery.
The Snowman. Page.
Sonnet: "You waken slowly.
  In your dream you're
  straying." Bell.
Street Musicians. Ashbery.
Woods and Kestrel. Bell.

Lane (s)
Beyond the Last Lamp.
  Hardy.
Dogs and Weather. Welles.
French Peasants. Gibbon.
Limerick: "There was an old
  man of El Hums." Lear.
Moments. Gurney.
Morning. Waddington.
Rosie Nell (with music).
  Anonymous.
Terra Australis. Stewart.
Up Early. Robinson.

Language (s)
All-Knowing God, 'Tis Thine
  to Know. Anonymous.
Arabic Script. Thwaite.
Bell Speech. Wilbur.
Breaking Silence. Mirikitani.
Caelica, LV. Greville.
Child Crying. Thwaite.
Etruscan Tombs. Robinson.
Father Land and Mother
  Tongue. Lover.
Finders Keepers. Finkel.
Hearing Steps. Simic.
In Allusion to the French
  Song, N'entendez Vous Pas
  ce Language. Lovelace.
January. Godin.
The Madwomen of the Plaza
  de Mayo. Mandel.
Man Meeting Himself.
  Sergeant.
Morning Dialogue. Aiken.
My Polish Grandma. Field.
A New Genesis. Schlonsky.
Newcomers. Reisen.
The Ninth of July.
  Hollander.
Page. McPherson.
Permanently. Koch.
The Poet's Day. Weber.
Remember. Harjo.
Required Course. Lankford.
Seal Rock. Pollitt.
Solo Native. Lux.
Suenos. Reiss.
Swedish Lesson. Sutter.
The Test. Friend.
Two Argosies. Bruce.
The Vows. Marvell.
The Wandering Jew.
  Fondane.

When I Read Shakespeare–.
  Lawrence.
Why I Never Went into
  Politics. Shelton.

Languish (ed)
Four Anacreontic Poems, 4.
  Spenser.
Image. Noailles.
Prayer before Execution.
  Mary.
Solomon. Heine.

Languor
Don Juan. Byron.
Hangover Cure. Amphis.
Tropical Weather. Sargent.

Lantern (s)
Blue Ridge. Voigt.
Floating Houses. Wojahn.
Forest without Leaves
  (excerpt). Haines.
Four-Paws. Eden.
A God Once Commanded Us.
  Goldberg.
Late October. Carleton.
Raging Canawl. Anonymous.
Winter Apples. Welles.
The Winter Moon. Kyozo.

Lap (s)
Anno Domini. Walker.
The Apron of Flowers.
  Herrick.
Dorothea. Cleghorn.
In an Old Orchard. Dufault.
Leaf After Leaf..... Landor.
Making Contact. Manifold.
Metamorphoses of M.
  Bishop.
My Dog. Robinson.
Night Watch. Magid.
Outburst from a Little Face.
  Woods.
The Parental Critic. Preston.
Portrait of My Mother on Her
  Wedding Day. Gilbert.
Prayer for Peace. Patrick.
Reconciliation. Lasker-
  Schüler.
Sonnets, II: "The rainbow o'er
  the sea of afternoon."
  Irwin.
The White Dress.
  Zaturenska.

Lapse
Capsule Philosophy.
  Lamport.
Poem on Hampstead Heath.
  Adeane.
Verses on a Cat. Daubeny.

Lares
Why I Can't Write a Poem
  about Lares. Silen.

Large (r)
Aspiration. De Andrade.
Fact. Rexroth.
Fork. Simic.
Greeting from England.
  Anonymous.
I had no time to hate.
  Dickinson.
I took my power in my hand.
  Dickinson.
The Little Toil of Love.
  Dickinson.
Lore. Thomas.
Love is that later thing than
  death. Dickinson.
Savior! I've No One Else to
  Tell. Dickinson.
Solar Creation. Madge.
Was He Married? Smith.

Lark (s)
After Six Thousand Years.
  Hugo.
All Paths Lead to You.
  Wagstaff.
An Anniversary of Death.
  Wieners.
The Commonwealth of Birds.
  Shirley.
For a Little Lady. Saidy.
The Gentle Check.
  Beaumont.
The Grey Friar. Peacock.
How Strangely This Sun
  Reminds Me of My Love.
  Spender.
Johnny Stiles; or, The Wild
  Mustard River.
  Anonymous.
Lilian's Song. Darley.
The Minstrel. Beattie.
Morning, Noon, and...
  Truax.
Over Saleve. Clarke.
The Passing of the Shee after
  Looking at One of A.E.'s
  Pictures. Synge.
Pennines in April. Hughes.
The Plea of the Midsummer
  Fairies. Hood.
The Poem. Merwin.
Portrait. Allen.
Sea Hunger. Mitchell.
Skye Summer. Donaldson.
Spring Doggerel. Coghill.
To a Young Poet. Millay.
To Friends Who Have Also
  Considered Suicide. Webb.
The Ventriloquist. Huff.
The Wild Common.
  Lawrence.

Lash (es)
Carmina Amico. James.
Favour. Fitzgerald.
Of Narrow Streets. Gay.
Simon the Cyrenian Speaks.
  Cullen.
Talking across Kansas.
  Kwon.
Verse Written in the Album
  of Mademoiselle—.
  Dalcour.

Lass (es) (ie)
Ballad of Human Life.
  Beddoes.
The Captain's Feather. Peck.
The Collier Lass.
  Armstrong.
A Cow and a Calf.
  Anonymous.
The Flower. Dodd.
Green Grow the Rashes.
  Burns.
Green Grows the Rashes.
  Anonymous.
The Happy Life (excerpt).
  Thompson.
The Indian Lass.
  Anonymous.
The Jolly Waggoner.
  Anonymous.
The Lass That Made the Bed
  for Me. Burns.
Let the Wind Blow High or
  Low. Anonymous.
The Lucky Sailor.
  Anonymous.
The Pedlar's Song.
  Shakespeare.
Riding Down. Coan.
A Song of Riches. Bates.

To a Child of Fancy.
  Morris.
Unique Among Girls.
  Anonymous.
Villon's Ballade. Lang.
Wine and Cakes for
  Gentlemen. *Anonymous.*

Last
Albatross. Stoddard.
All Service Ranks the Same
  with God. Browning.
The Apprentice Painter.
  Myers.
At Only That Moment.
  Ross.
Auguries of Innocence.
  Blake.
Ballade on Eschatology.
  Madeleva.
Barley-Break; or, Last in Hell.
  Herrick.
Beyond the Presidency.
  Gibson.
Bitter for Sweet. Rossetti.
Calamus. Whitman.
Chryseis. Arensberg.
Comfort thyself, my woeful
  heart. Wyatt.
Concert at the Station.
  Mandelstam.
Contemplations. Bradstreet.
The Cowboy. *Anonymous.*
The Daughter of Jairus.
  Tsvetayeva.
Dead Neck. Standing.
The Death of General
  Uncebunke: A Biography in
  Little. Durrell.
Diary (excerpt). Fuller.
Direct Address. Gerstler.
Dirge of Rory O'More. De
  Vere.
Echo to a Rock. Herbert of
  Cherbury.
Elegy for a Cricket.
  Cunningham.
Elegy: In Spring. Bruce.
Emeritus, n. Coulette.
End of the Affair. Casewit.
Engine 143. *Anonymous.*
Epistle to Augusta. Byron.
Epitaph: "Here cursing
  swearing Burton lies."
  Burns.
Faith. Daley.
Fare Thee Well Blues.
  Calicott.
First Reader. Leary.
Fisbo (excerpt). Nichols.
Flash Crimson. Sandburg.
The Fox and the Crow. La
  Fontaine.
From the Night of Forebeing.
  Thompson.
Gascoigne's Memories.
  Gascoigne.
Glen-Almain, the Narrow
  Glen. Wordsworth.
Golfers. Updike.
Goodbye. De la Mare.
Hail, Tranquil Hour of
  Closing Day. Bacon.
Hearing Steps. Simic.
Holy Spring. Thomas.
Holy Thursday. Wright.
House in Meudon. Aliger.
I Would Like My Love to
  Die. Beckett.
Identity. Aldrich.
The Impossible Dream.
  Darion.
Isis Wanderer. Raine.

The Jam on Gerry's Rock (I).
  Anonymous.
Jamaican Bus Ride.
  Tessimond.
John Hardy. *Anonymous.*
Karl. Spear.
The Lake. Coxe.
Last Affair: Bessie's Blues
  Song. Harper.
The Last Fruit off an Old
  Tree. Landor.
The Last Redoubt. Austin.
Lay of the Last Frontier.
  Hersey.
Letting Go. Shelton.
Liberty Enlightening the
  World. Stedman.
The Life. Wright.
Limerick: "An amateur,
  driving too fast." Wright.
Limerick: "There was a young
  bard of Japan."
  Anonymous.
Limerick: "There was a young
  man from Japan."
  Anonymous.
Limerick: "There was a young
  man of Japan."
  Anonymous.
Lookin' for the Bully of the
  Town. *Anonymous.*
The Lords of Creation.
  Anonymous.
Malediction. Spacks.
Mary in the Silvery Tide.
  Anonymous.
Mercy and Love. Herrick.
Moments of Vision. Hardy.
The Moon Is Distant from the
  Sea. Dickinson.
My Dog Dash. Ruskin.
My Son and I. Levine.
No More Women Blues.
  Alexander.
No Signal for a Crossing.
  Donovan.
North to Milwaukee.
  Vizenor.
O Fond, but Fickle and
  Untrue. Landor.
Ode to the Virgin. Petrarch.
Old Argonaut. Gauldin.
The Old Casa. Connor.
On Colley Cibber's
  Declaration That He Will
  Have the Last Word...
  Pope.
One Thousand Feet of
  Shadow. Craig.
The Orchard-Pit. Rossetti.
Our Country Is Divided.
  Nuur.
The Parting. Jennings.
The Plaudite, or End of Life.
  Herrick.
Poem for Roslyn. Lewisohn.
Poem for the Year Twenty
  Twenty. Lee.
Poems. Drummond.
Poor Grandpa. O'Brien.
The Postman's Bell Is
  Answered Everywhere.
  Gregory.
Rapunzel. Hay.
Residue of Song. Bell.
The Retired Colonel.
  Hughes.
Sally Goodin. *Anonymous.*
Shake Hands with Your Bets,
  Friend. Thomas.
The Silvery Tide.
  Anonymous.

The Simplon Pass.
  Wordsworth.
Sonnets, V: "Into the wood at
  close of rainy day." Irwin.
Soraidh Slan Don Oidhche
  Areir. Mac Muireadach.
A Tale of Drury Lane.
  Smith.
Tangere. Enslin.
Then I'll Believe. Vilakazi.
These Crossings, These
  Words. Troupe.
This Is the Last.
  Waterhouse.
Time, Real and Imaginary.
  Coleridge.
To a Friend Going on a
  Journey. Hassan.
To a Persistent Phantom.
  Horne.
To End Her Fear. Freeman.
To His Watch. Hopkins.
To Italy. Leopardi.
To Julia. Herrick.
Tonight I can write the
  saddest lines. Neruda.
Transfiguration. Barnes.
Two Lives and Others.
  Scott.
The Unpetalled Rose.
  Therese.
Unromantic Song. Brode.
Valley of the Shadow.
  Galsworthy.
Verses on the Prospect of
  Planting Arts and Learning
  in America. Berkeley.
Winter Sign. Eiseley.
The World Is with Me Just
  Enough. Abrams.
You Know. Garrigue.
You Lingering Sparse Leaves
  of Me. Whitman.
Young Girl. Waltner.

Lasting
The Monuments of
  Hiroshima. Enright.
Poem of the Intimate Agony.
  Burgos.
Returning to Roots of First
  Feeling. Duncan.

Lasts
Blue Waves. St. John.
In the Shadowy Whatnot
  Corner. Hillyer.
The Magician. Colby.
Palladium. Arnold.

Late (r) (est)
Amoretti, LXXV. Spenser.
At That Moment. Patterson.
Awake! (parody). Black.
Be Always in Time.
  Anonymous.
The Beech. Young.
Before It Is Too Late.
  Sweet.
Camptown. Ciardi.
Changes around the Bay.
  Palmer.
Don Juan. Byron.
Escape. Graves.
Florine. Campbell.
Grandpa Is Ashamed. Nash.
Grinding Vibrato. Cortez.
Hastings Mill. Fox-Smith.
The High Sailboat.
  Quasimodo.
Homecoming. Dawe.
Late-Flowering Lust.
  Betjeman.

Limerick: "There was a young
  hopeful named Sam."
  Ripley.
Love in Thy Youth.
  Anonymous.
The Loves Who Many Years
  Held All My Mind. Landor.
The New Formalists. Bell.
New Words for an Old Song.
  Deutsch.
The Nightmare. MacLean.
No Country You Remember.
  Mezey.
Old Dan Tucker. Emmit.
The Old Pastor. Tabb.
On History. Hoover.
On the Beach. Cornford.
Orinda to Lucasia. Philips.
Pacified. Nickens.
Penological Study: Southern
  Exposure, 3. Wet Hair...
  Warren.
Point of No Return. Evans.
Princess Elizabeth of
  Bohemia, as Perdita.
  O'Hara.
Pruning. Philips.
See the Crocus' Golden Cup.
  Plunkett.
The Sisters Kastemaloff.
  Talbot.
A Song: "Fair, sweet and
  young, receive a prize."
  Dryden.
Sonnet: "Since I keep only
  what I give away."
  Hetherington.
Supreme Death. Dunn.
T.V. (1). Hollo.
This World. Evans.
The Thousand and Second
  Night. Merrill.
Three Sermons to the Dead.
  Riding.
To an Imaginary Father.
  Rose.
To B. C. Suckling.
To-Night. Thomas.
To One Who Denies the
  Possibility of a Permanent
  Peace. Sackville.
The Undertaker's Horse.
  Kipling.
Van Winkle. Crane.
Wedding. *Anonymous.*
What Voice at Moth-Hour.
  Warren.
When. "Coolidge.
When I am Big, I Mean to
  Buy. Dodge.
Wishes for William. Letts.
The Wreck of the Royal
  Palm. *Anonymous.*
You Will Know When You
  Get There. Curnow.

Lath
The First Lesson. Reiter.

Lattice
Lines for a Feast of Our
  Lady. Maris Stella.
Maytime. *Anonymous.*
On Sturminster Foot-Bridge.
  Hardy.
Very Fair My Lot. Kamzon.

Laud
God of Our Fathers, Whose
  Almighty Hand. Roberts.
Hymn to Night. *Anonymous.*
Troilus and Cressida.
  Shakespeare.

Laugh (ed) (ing) (s)
Aetate XIX.   Merivale.
Album Leaf.   Mallarme.
Amoretti, X.   Spenser.
Anatole France at Eighty.
Oaks.
And of Laughter That Was a
Changeling.   Rendall.
And Three Hundred and
Sixty-Six in Leap Year.
Nash.
April.   Tietjens.
As You Like It.
Shakespeare.
At a Georgia Camp Meeting.
Mills.
At His Father's Grave.
Ormond.
The Bald Cavalier.
Anonymous.
The Beautiful Woman Who
Sings.   Allen.
Beeny Cliff.   Hardy.
A Bestiary.   Rexroth.
Betty at the Party.
Anonymous.
Black Narcissus.   Barrax.
A Boat, a Boat.   Anonymous.
The Bonfire.   Frost.
The Book of Nightmares.
Kinnell.
Bozzy and Piozzi (excerpt).
"Pindar.
Buster Keaton.   McFee.
Caelica, XCIII.   Greville.
The Call.   Kauffman.
Called Away.   Le Gallienne.
Carmina.   Catullus.
The Chickadees.   Hay.
The Contentment of
Willoughby.   Alexander.
Courage.   Frazee-Bower.
The Cowboy.   Antrobus.
The Cynic.   Garrison.
The Dark Cat.   Brown.
A Day of Notes.   Green.
December Day, Hoy Sound.
Brown.
Democritus and Heraclitus.
Prior.
Doney Gal.   Anonymous.
Drink from My Empty Cup.
Mandela.
Dublin Bay.   Milne.
Ducks.   Harvey.
The Duel.   Lovelace.
The Egg Boiler.   Brooks.
The English Labourer.
Anonymous.
Epitaph.   Durrell.
Epitaph: "A great philosopher
did choke."   Butler.
Except I Love.   Parry.
The Faerie Queene.   Spenser.
A Farewell.   Gascoigne.
First Satire of the Second
Book of Horace.   Pope.
From the Joke Shop.   Fuller.
Gascoigne.   Sackville.
The Gipsies.   "Scrace.
A Glimpse of the Body Shop.
Berg.
God's Will.   Munger.
The Harp of David.   Cohen.
He Tries out the Concords
Gently.   "Bagritsky.
The Highway.   Driscoll.
Homesick Blues.   Hughes.
Hot Springs.   Birney.
The House of a Hundred
Lights.   Torrence.

I Come and Stand at Every
Door.   Hikmet.
I've Thirty Months.   Synge.
Idea.   Drayton.
If You Are a Gentleman.
Anonymous.
Isaac and Archibald.
Robinson.
The Jews in Hell.
Goldemberg.
Jonathan.   Fyleman.
A Last Confession.   Rossetti.
The Laughing Faces of Pigs.
Lape.
The Laughing Hyena, by
Hokusai.   Enright.
The Laughing Willow.
Herford.
Laughter.   Waddington.
The Lesson.   Simic.
Let Me Go Warm.   Gongora
y Argote.
Like Gulliver.   Cassian.
Like to the Thundering Tone.
Corbet.
Limerick: "Said the elephant
to the giraffe."   Carter.
Lines to Garcia Lorca.
Jones.
The Little Red Lark.
Graves.
Magical Nature.   Browning.
Making Miso.   Inada.
The Marigold So Likes the
Lovely Sun.   Watson.
Measure for Measure.
Shakespeare.
Medallion.   Plath.
Medieval Norman Songs.
Anonymous.
Merlin, They Say.   Greville.
Modern Love, VI.   Meredith.
Moments.   Allen.
The Mountainy Childer.
Shane.
Mouth of the Amazon.   Gira.
Mrs. Santa Claus' Christmas
Present.   Morris.
My Creed.   Walter.
The Negro's Tragedy.
McKay.
Negroes.   Bodenheim.
New York in the Spring.
Budbill.
Niagara Falls.   Parisi.
Night Slivers.   Turner.
Nocturne of Remembered
Spring.   Aiken.
Nonsense.   Corbett.
O Make Me a Mask.
Thomas.
Ode for a Social Meeting
(With Slight Alterations by
a Teetotaler).   Holmes.
Ogres and Pygmies.   Graves.
On Catullus.   Landor.
Once Upon a Time.   Okara.
One Man Down.   Anthony
("Ai").
One X.   Cummings.
The Only Bar in Dixon.
Welch.
A Phantasy of Heaven.
Kemp.
The Pigs.   Taylor.
Private.   Wormser.
Queen Cleopatra.   Aiken.
The Raquette River, Potsdam,
New York....   Piccone.
Rec Room in Paradise.
Clark.
The Recessional.   Roberts.

Reconciliation.   Russell.
The Revenge.   Ronsard.
Sarah.   Aphek.
Saw God Dead but Laughing.
Villa.
School Is over.   Greenaway.
The Serf's Secret.   Moody.
Shall I Do This.   Purohit
Swami.
She Is More to be Pitied than
Censured.   Gray.
Sholom Aleichem.
Lieberman.
Signature.   Stroud.
Sliding Trombone.
Ribemont-Dessaignes
George.
Some Tyme I Fled the Fyre
That Me Brent.   Wyatt.
The Song of Hiawatha.
Longfellow.
Song of the Darling River.
Lawson.
Song of the Trees of the Black
Forest.   Jabes.
Survivors.   Feinstein.
A Technical Supplement.
Kinsella.
Then Laugh.   Backus.
This Morning.   Galvez.
Three Fitts.   Parker.
Three Spring Notations on
Bipeds.   Sandburg.
Tickly, Tickly, on Your Knee.
Anonymous.
The Time Hath Been.
Skipsey.
Time; or, How the Line
About Chagall's Lovers
Disappears.   Miller.
To A Dark Girl.   Bennett.
Tongues.   Berg.
The Unfortunate Miller; or,
The Country Lasses Witty
Invention.   Anonymous.
A Voyage to Tintern Abbey.
Davies.
The Wait.   Janowitz.
The Waltzer in the House.
Kunitz.
Washyuma Motor Hotel.
Ortiz.
What If Jealousy...   Palmer.
When You Laugh.   Jonker.
Why Can't I Leave You?
Ai.
The Widow of Drynam.
MacDonogh.
The Widower.   Tyler.
The Wife.   Garrison.
Willy, Willy Wilkin.
Anonymous.
Witch.   Tepperman.
Women's Locker Room.
Waniek.
Young Girls.   Souster.

Laughed
Ballade of the Session after
Camarillo.   Galler.
The Barber.   Gray.
The Best Friend.   Davies.
An Evening's Love.   Dryden.
Father.   Kooser.
The Fool of Love.
Anonymous.
Fossils.   Stephens.
God Fashioned the Ship of
the World Carefully.
Crane.
The Happy Night.   Squire.
Her Courage.   Yeats.

I Sought All over the World.
Tagliabue.
If.   Lane.
Interlude.   Smith.
Jack O'Lantern.   Ayre.
A Lawn-Tennisonian Idyll
(parody).   Anonymous.
A Little Person.   Hooker.
Montana Wives.   Haste.
Nightmare.   Emanuel.
Periphery.   Stone.
Policemen Laughing.   Fraser.
Poppies.   Weekes.
Snow-Bound.   Whittier
We Laughed.   Kraut.

Laughter
Adam, Eve and the Big
Apple.   Watkins.
Aubade: Dick, the Donkey-
Boy.   Sitwell.
Back Lane.   Murphy.
Baptism.   Zieroth.
A Battle of Sarsfield.   De
Vere.
The Biglow Papers.   Lowell.
Bundles.   Sandburg.
The Child-King.
Wintchevsky.
Circus.   Farjeon.
The Clarity of Apples.
Perlin.
Dawn Wail for the Dead.
Walker.
Dedicatory Ode: They Say
That in the Unchanging
Place.   Belloc.
The Defence of Guenevere.
Morris.
Ecstasy.   Swarth.
Evening Terrors.   Cheney.
The Execrators.   Galler.
The Fruit Rancher.   Roberts.
Good and Bad.   Stephens.
Good Friday: The Third
Nocturn.   Abelard.
Hyena.   Muske.
Hymn for the Church
Militant.   Chesterton.
A Hymn of Nature.   Bridges.
I Am Not a Camera.
Auden.
If All the Skies.   Van Dyke.
Journal to Stella.   Zabel.
June.   Malloch.
Laugh It Off.   Elliot.
Laughter.   Crawford.
Mellisandra.   Rose.
My Dim-Wit Cousin.
Roethke.
My Grandmother's Love
Letters.   Crane.
My Jack.   O'Donnell.
Nostalgia.   Millard.
Oblique Birth Poem.   Darr.
Old Dog, New Dog.   Lea.
An Old Street.   Cloud.
Omalos.   Warren.
Only Silence.   Bourinot.
Our House.   Thompson.
Pause.   Hamilton.
Retractions.   Cabell.
Return to Sirmio.   Catullus.
Santa Barbara Beach.
Torrence.
Seaward.   Thaxter.
Sirmio.   Catullus.
Song of Breath.   Vidal.
Song of the Intruder.   Jacobs.
Song: "Take it, love!"   Le
Gallienne.
The Spark.   Plunkett.

Speckle-Black Toad and
  Freckle-Green Frog.
  Darley.
Suicide in Trenches.
  Sassoon.
Sunflowers. Scollard.
They Say, and I am Glad
  They Say. Belloc.
This Is Halloween.
  Thompson.
To Puck. Thomas.
To the Memory of Yale
  College. Putnam.
Tune: Endless Union. Li
  Ching-chao.
Twenty-One Love Poems.
  Rich.
Upon a House Shaken by the
  Land Agitation. Yeats.
Waiting for Lilith. Kessler.
Waterfall. Welsh.
Who Calls. Sayers.
Wolves. MacNeice.
Words for a Resurrection.
  Kennedy.
Years Later. Lerner.
You Also, Gaius Valerius
  Catullus. MacLeish.
Your Presence. Diop.
Launch (ed)
George Jones. *Anonymous.*
Great God, Preserver of All
  Things. Pastorius.
Song of the Answerer
  (excerpt). Whitman.
When We Hear the Eye
  Open... Kaufman.
Laundry
Plaque. Ruddick.
Laura
Don Juan. Byron.
Female Glory. Lovelace.
Ode to a Young Lady,
  Somewhat Too Sollicitous
  about Her Manner...
  Shenstone.
Sonnet to Valclusa. Russell.
Laurel (s)
At the Tomb of Washington.
  Scollard.
Corrib. An Emblem. Davie.
Daphne. Rodman.
Daphne and Apollo. Macy.
Dear Old Dad. Shaver.
Europe. Dudek.
Exorcism. Gogarty.
The Herd Boy. Long.
Inspiration. Thoreau.
John Donne's Statue.
  Bishop.
Mercury. On Losing my
  Pocket Milton... Andrews.
A Mother before a Soldier's
  Monument. Rockett.
An Ode for the New Year.
  Gay.
Odes. Horace.
One Thousand Fearful Words
  for Fidel Castro.
  Ferlinghetti.
Orion. Horne.
A Song of Renunciation.
  Seaman.
Sonnet, to the River Loddon.
  Warton, Jr..
The Tears of Scotland.
  Smollett.
The Tears of Scotland Written
  in the Year MDCCXLVI.
  Smollett.

To His Honoured and Most
  Ingenious Friend, Master
  Charles Cotton. Herrick.
To Summer. Blake.
The True Aristocrat.
  Stewart.
Lava
En Passant. Codrescu.
Notes for a Revised Sonnet
  (parody). Pygge.
The Story of Lava. Evans.
Lavender
In an Old Nursery.
  Chalmers.
Lavender's for Ladies.
  Chalmers.
My Donkey. Fyleman.
Silence. Welles.
A Song for My Mother–Her
  Stories. Branch.
That Day You Came. Reese.
Law (s)
Ascension. Devlin.
Athalie: Chorus (excerpt).
  Racine.
Back to Arizona.
  Brininstool.
A Barbed Wire Fence
  Meditates upon the
  Goldfinch. McKay.
Blind-Man's Buff. Blake.
The Builders (excerpt). Van
  Dyke.
Caelica, LXXVII. Greville.
The Chameleon. Prior.
Culloden and After. Smith.
The Death of Meleager.
  Swinburne.
Epitaph on Peter Robinson.
  Jeffrey.
An Essay on Criticism.
  Pope.
Exile. Stroud.
The Faerie Queene. Spenser.
First and Second Law.
  Flanders.
Foundation of Faith.
  Drinkwater.
Greens. Ray.
The Hand and Foot. Very.
Holy Sonnets, XVI. Donne.
Holy Spirit, Truth Divine.
  Longfellow.
Hosanna. Traherne.
Hymn to Zeus. Cleanthes.
I Am Like a Book. Rokeah.
In the Shadows. Gray.
Inscription for the Door of
  the Cell in Newgate...
  Canning.
Inviolable. Hoffman.
Jesse James. *Anonymous.*
Landscape I. Madge.
The Law West of the Pecos.
  Barker.
Let There Be Law. Van
  Doren.
Lobster Cove Shindig.
  Morrison.
Love Enthroned. Lovelace.
Lucifer in Starlight.
  Meredith.
The Marriage of Heaven and
  Hell. Blake.
The Master Spirit.
  Chapman.
A New Catch in Praise of the
  Reverend Bishops.
  Anonymous.
On a Tear. Rogers.

On the Duke of Buckingham,
  Slain by Felton...
  Felltham.
On the Spartan Dead at
  Thermopylae. Simonides
  (of Ceos).
Paradise Regained. Milton.
Plain Dealing. Brome.
The Pleasures of Imagination.
  Akenside.
Poem, 1972. Scroggie.
Poems Chiefly of Early and
  Late Years: Prelude.
  Wordsworth.
Quantum. Johnston.
A Radical Song of 1786.
  Honeywood.
The Reply of Socrates.
  Thomas.
Resurrection. Horne.
The Revolt of Islam.
  Shelley.
Songs of Labor: Dedication.
  Whittier.
The Sonnet. Symonds.
Sonnet I: "If it must be; if it
  must be, O God!" Gray.
A Stanza Put on Westminster
  Hall Gate. *Anonymous.*
Such bitter fruit thy love doth
  yield. *Anonymous.*
The Ten Commandments.
  Anonymous.
Texas Types–"The Bad Man."
  Chittenden.
Tragic Verses. *Anonymous.*
The Tribes. Fuller.
Upon the Curtain of Lucasta's
  Picture It Was Thus
  Wrought. Lovelace.
The Vicar of Bray.
  Anonymous.
Wake, Isles of the South.
  Tappan.
The Wandering Jew. Mezey.
Washington's Monument,
  February, 1885. Whitman.
We. Kirillov.
White-Capped Waves.
  Clarke.
The World Hymn. Lawson.
Ye Simple Men. Blackie.
Young Lincoln. Markham.
Lawn (s)
Chloe. Burns.
The First Snow of the Year.
  Van Doren.
The Golden Age: Hymn to
  Diana. Heywood.
Home Movies. Revard.
How to Fertilize Soil. Scott.
In the Trench. Gellert.
Lady Sara Bunbury Sacrificing
  to the Graces, by Reynolds.
  Hine.
Mowing the Lawn. Bensko.
Singing Death. Rice.
Skyhook. Kizer.
Song for Healing. Hill.
Spitballer. Chappell.
To Dianeme. Herrick.
What Then, Dancer? Smith.
Lawrence
Gross, Coarse, Hideous.
  Lawrence.
D. H. Lawrence and James
  Joyce. Wolfe.
Quantrell (I). *Anonymous.*
Lawyer (s)
Advice to Hotheads. Isaac.
The Beggar's Opera. Gay.

Epigram: "Some people
  admire the work of a Fool."
  Blake.
The Lawyers Know Too
  Much. Sandburg.
Orlando Furioso. Ariosto.
A Vow. Ginsberg.
Lay (ing) (s)
The Aeneid. Virgil (Publius
  Vergilius Maro).
Alba. Pound.
Ars Poetica. Kennedy.
As I Was Laying on the
  Green. *Anonymous.*
Bold Robert Emmet.
  Maguire.
Charley Barley. *Anonymous.*
Come Ye Sons of Art
  (excerpt). Purcell.
Commonplaces (parody).
  Kipling.
The Crowning Gift.
  Cromwell.
Death is a dialogue.
  Dickinson.
The Domicile of John. Pope.
Don Juan. Byron.
The Dumb Soldier.
  Stevenson.
Ella Speed. *Anonymous.*
The Faithful Shepherdess.
  Fletcher.
Ghosts. MacCarthy.
Homosexual Sonnets.
  Pitchford.
Honeysuckle (Chevrefoil).
  Marie de France.
The Human Fold. Muir.
I'm Thankful That My Life
  Doth Not Deceive.
  Thoreau.
I Was Lying Still in a Field
  One Day. Gay.
In Winter. Bretherton.
Lily Munro. *Anonymous.*
The Lonely. Russell.
Making Land. Day.
A Man Called Dante, I Have
  Heard. King.
Meditations. Taylor.
Midsummer. Kinsella.
A Mother's Lament for the
  Death of Her Son. Burns.
A Mother to Her Waking
  Infant. Baillie.
A Necessary Miracle.
  Walton.
Nuptial Sleep. Rossetti.
O, Lay Thy Hand in Mine,
  Dear! Massey.
The Ocean-Fight.
  Anonymous.
Old Christmas. Helton.
The Old Year. Urmy.
The Parental Critic. Preston.
The Poet at Seven.
  Rimbaud.
Psalm XXXII. Wyatt.
Rhode Island. Meredith.
Rocks and Gravel.
  Anonymous.
The Sepulcher. Flint.
Seven Long Years in State
  Prison (with music).
  Anonymous.
She lay all naked in her bed.
  Anonymous.
The Shrouded Stranger.
  Ginsberg.
Song: "I know moon-rise. I
  know star-rise."
  Anonymous.

Song of the Cauld Lad of
  Hylton. *Anonymous.*
Those Not Elect. Adams.
Tryst. Butler.
Twenty Years Ago. Smith.
Unicorn. Smith.
When Doris Danced.
  Eberhart.
Wind, Gentle Evergreen.
  Anonymous.
A Wind Rose in the Night.
  Kilmer.
Ye Wearie Wayfarer: Sun and
  Rain and Dew from
  Heaven. Gordon.

Lay (ing) (s) (laid) (lain)
Africa. Angelou.
Cill Chais. *Anonymous.*
Datur Hora Quieti. Hawker.
Deir El Bahari: Temple of
  Hatshepsut. Enright.
Down-Hall. Prior.
Drowning with Others.
  Dickey.
Egyptian Hieroglyphics.
  Anonymous.
Elegy on Shakespeare. Basse.
Epitaph on the Proofreader of
  the Encyclopedia
  Britannica. Morley.
Glee–The Ghosts. Peacock.
Hamewith. Smith.
Memory. Yeats.
O Brothers, Why Do You
  Talk. Mahadevi
  (Mahadeviyakka).
On the Publication of Diaries
  and Memoirs. Hood.
Song for "The Jaquerie".
  Lanier.
Were You There.
  Anonymous.

Lazarus
The Convent. Chesterton.
In Memory of Arthur
  Winslow. Lowell.

Lazy
The African Trader's
  Complaint. Osadebay.
An Alphabet of Famous
  Goops. Burgess.
Bathing Song. Ridler.
Early Dutch. Palen.
Georgia Boy. *Anonymous.*
The Girl I Left Behind Me.
  Anonymous.
Idyll. Webb.
Lazy Man's Song. Po Chu-i.
On the Road to Gundagai.
  Anonymous.
Poetry Is Happiness.
  Gardiner.
A Schoolmaster's Admonition.
  Anonymous.
Summer Stars. Sandburg.

Lead (led)
After the Movement.
  Oresick.
Ballad of the Lincoln Penny.
  Kreymborg.
Be Still, My Heart.
  Anonymous.
The Beggar's Opera. Gay.
The Best for Us. Burnett.
Bussy d'Ambois. Chapman.
Catching a Horse. Winder.
City of Light. Bomze.
Clare Coast. Lawless.
Commemoration Ode.
  Monroe.
Crocus. Kreymborg.

The Dog Parade.
  Guiterman.
An Epitaph upon That
  Profound and Learned
  Casuist... Brown.
Epitaphs of the War,
  1914-1918. Kipling.
Five Epigrams. Hall.
The Fog. Davies.
The Gate of the Year.
  Haskins.
He Leadeth Me. Barry.
Heaving the Lead Line.
  Anonymous.
The Highwaymen. Gay.
Inscriptio. Pope.
It Was My Choice. Wyatt.
The Jealous Lover (B vers.).
  Anonymous.
Jesus Never Fails. Isenhour.
The Jolly Wagoner.
  Anonymous.
Keeping Victory. Isenhour.
Lead. Cortez.
M-Y T-E-M-P-E-R.
  Anonymous.
The Marginal Field.
  Spender.
Obsequies of Stuart.
  Thompson.
The Pagan Isms. McKay.
The Palace of Truth.
  Langland.
The Star. Smith.
Verses Placed Over the Door
  at the Entrance into the
  Apollo Room... Jonson.
Verses Wrote in a Lady's
  Ivory Table-Book. Swift.
Walken Hwome at Night.
  Barnes.
When I Was Young and
  Foolish (with music).
  Anonymous.

Leaden
The Deserter. Housman.
Ode: "That I have often been
  in love, deep love."
  Wolcot.
The Sunken Garden. De La
  Mare.
To the Lady Margaret,
  Countess of Cumberland.
  Daniel.

Leader (s)
12 O'Clock News. Bishop.
Beauregard. Warfield.
Children of the Heavenly
  King. Cennick.
Copernicus. FitzGerald.
Creide's Lament for Cael.
  Anonymous.
Et Incarnatus Est. Langland.
The Space Child's Mother
  Goose. Winsor.
The Thirty-One Camels.
  Korn.
The Vision of Piers Plowman.
  Langland.

Leaf (leaves)
The African Tramp.
  Haresnape.
Alba: March. Hacker.
American Ash. Plumly.
The American Soldier.
  Freneau.
Amoretti, XXVIII. Spenser.
Amy. Legare.
Animal Songs. *Anonymous.*
Anne and the Peacock.
  Welch.
April. Pastan.

Ascent. Berry
At My Father's Grave.
  Ciardi.
At Night. Akhmadulina.
Auden. Roseliep.
Autumn. Longfellow.
Autumn. Smith.
Autumn Leaves. Webb.
Autumnal Spring Song.
  Miller.
Autumnus. Sylvester.
Back to Life. Gunn.
Before Harvest. Fitzgerald.
The Birds. Blake.
Birthday Gifts. Asquith.
The Blackbird by Belfast
  Lough. *Anonymous.*
Blue Smoke. Frost.
The Brook in February.
  Roberts.
Caelica, LXXIV. Greville.
California Quail in January.
  Jumper.
Catalpa Tree. Colum.
The City of Falling Leaves.
  Lowell.
The Colder the Air. Bishop.
College of Surgeons.
  Stephens.
Commemoration. Newbolt.
The Complacent Cliff-Dweller.
  Fishback.
Contra Mortem. Carruth.
Cut It Down. Coleridge.
Cutting Redbud: An
  Accidental Death.
  Cotterill.
David Ap Gwillam's Mass of
  the Birds. Colum.
Downy Hair. Stryk.
Dream. Bynner.
A Dream of November.
  Gosse.
Drink To-day. Fletcher.
Epigram: Absent-Minded
  Professor. Nemerov.
Evening. Doolittle.
Fall Colors. Mazzaro.
The Fallen Tree. Maybin.
Family. *Anonymous.*
A Farewell. Monroe.
Farewell, Sweet Dust. Wylie.
Farrell O'Reilly. Gogarty.
The Feast of the Snow.
  Chesterton.
Fidelities. Valentine.
A Fine Day. Drayton.
First Love. Kunitz.
Fragment. Robinson.
From Le Havre. Bell.
From My Arm-Chair.
  Longfellow.
From My Thought. Smythe.
Funeral at Ansley. Welch.
The Garden. Grimald.
Gathered at the River.
  Levertov.
The Girl in the Foreign
  Movie. Goedicke.
Greek Archipelagoes. Leigh-
  Fermor.
Green Ice. Finch.
He Comes among. Barker.
Here, as in a Painting, Noon
  Burns Yellow.
  Gorbanyevskaya.
Here Is the Place Where
  Loveliness Keeps House.
  Cawein.
Hillcrest. Robinson.
The House across the Way.
  Hodgson.

The House of the Trees.
  Wetherald.
Impression Japonais. Wilde.
In Cold Storm Light. Silko.
In My Own Album. Lamb.
Independence Day. Berry.
Interior with Mme. Vuillard
  and Son. Fraser.
Invitation Standing.
  Blackburn.
The Italian Air. MacAdams.
July in the Jardin des Plantes.
  McAllister.
The Keeper. *Anonymous.*
Lament of the Jewish Women
  for Tammuz. Reznikoff.
Lamentation. Ezekiel.
Leaf-Eater. Kinsella.
Leaving One of the State
  Parks after a Family
  Outing. Macklin.
Life on Earth (excerpt).
  O'Hara.
Lines: "I followed once a fleet
  and mighty serpent."
  Beddoes.
A Little Song. Hartman.
Liu Ch'e. Wu-Ti.
The Long Small Room.
  Thomas.
Look to the Leaf.
  Anonymous.
Love Fallen to Earth.
  Verlaine.
Love (fragment). Sappho.
A Man of Rain. Barbeitos.
Maple Leaves. Shiko.
Marsh Leaf. Wagoner.
Metric Figure. Williams.
Miners' Wives. Corrie.
Monologue of Two Moons,
  Nudes with Crests. 1938.
  Dubie.
Morgans in October.
  Brabant.
My Babes in the Wood.
  Piatt.
My Butterfly. Frost.
My Fair Lady. *Anonymous.*
Neutral Tones. Hardy.
Ninth Moon. Li Ho.
Now in the Palace Gardens.
  Stickney.
O Amber Day, Amid the
  Autumn Gloom. Allison.
O Sower of Sorrow.
  Plunkett.
Oak. Child.
October. Goren.
October. Hahn.
Of All Plants, the Tree.
  White.
Of Autumn. Porumbacu.
Oh Tannenbaum.
  Anonymous.
Old Age. *Anonymous.*
The Old Ships. Flecker.
On a New Duke.
  Anonymous.
One, the Other, And.
  Wieber.
Orchard Song. Sappho.
The Origins of Escape.
  Tisdale.
Outside Baby Moon's. Violi.
Palm Leaves of Childhood.
  Adali-Mortti.
A Parisian Idyl (excerpt).
  Moore.
Parody. Francescato.
Pennsylvania Academy of
  Fine Arts. Kroll.

Perturbation at Dawn. Ibn Maatuk.
The Piper of Arll. Scott.
Portrait by a Neighbor. Millay.
Possible Love Poem to the Usurer. Armand.
Pound at Spoleto. Ferlinghetti.
The Power of Maples. Stern.
Priapus and the Pool. Aiken.
Promenade. Ignatow.
The Quest of the Orchis. Frost.
Rain. Guri.
Rape Poem. Piercy.
Reply to the Provinces. Kinnell.
Reply to the Question: "How Can You Become a Poet?" Merriam.
Revenge Fable. Hughes.
Robin Hood and Allen A Dale. *Anonymous.*
Rondel for September. Baker.
The Room. Aiken.
The Rose and the Gauntlet. Wilson.
Sea Rose. Doolittle.
The Secret Garden. Kinsella.
The Secret Garden. Nichols.
September 2. Berry.
The Sign. Blackburn.
Simultaneously. Ignatow.
The Singing Bush. Soutar.
A Soft Day. Letts.
Soldier (T. P.). Jarrell.
The Solitary Woodsman. Roberts.
Somewhere or Other. Rossetti.
Song: "I promised Sylvia to be true." Rochester.
Song of Basket-Weaving. Skinner.
A Song of Morning. Sitwell.
Song of the Fucked Duck. Piercy.
Song: "Oh roses for the flush of youth." Rossetti.
Sonnets, XII: "A roadside inn this summer Saturday." Irwin.
Sonnets, XCVII: "How like a winter hath my absence been." Shakespeare.
Spanish Folk Songs. *Anonymous.*
A Speck of Sand. Celan.
Spring Is a Looping-Free Time. Robbins.
Static Autumn. Winters.
Stormy Night in Autumn. Chu Shu-chen.
Summer Garden. Akhmatova.
Summer Resort. Page.
Susanna and the Elders. Gilbert.
Tapestry Trees. Morris.
Then when the Ample Season. Wilbur.
These Leaves. Stafford.
Thomas Trevelyan. Masters.
Thoughts of Thomas Hardy. Blunden.
The Thousand Things. Middleton.
Three Things. Sarton.
To a Lily. Legare.
To Life I Said Yes. Grade.

To the Postmaster General. Redgrove.
Treaties. Ammons.
Tree Poem on My Wife's Birthday. Hanna.
The Truro Bear. Oliver.
Truth. Schaeffer.
A Tryptych for Jan Bockelson. Simon.
The Twilight People. O'Sullivan.
Two Poems. Abrams.
Uncle an' Aunt. Barnes.
The Unquiet Grave. *Anonymous.*
Upon Bishop Andrewes His Picture before His Sermons. Crashaw.
Vittoria Colonna. Marz.
Walking Late. Montague.
The Way to Arcady. Bunner.
West of Your City. Stafford.
When the Lamp Is Shattered. Shelley.
Who Shall Have My Fair Lady? *Anonymous.*
Why Ye Blossome Cometh before Ye Leafe. Herford.
The Wind in the Elms. Miller.
Winter Night. Fairburn.
Woodbines in October. Bates.
Writing to Aaron. Levertov.
The Young Men Come Less Often–Isn't It So? Horace.
The Young Woman from Aenos. *Anonymous.*
Zohara. Hirschman.

League (s)
At last, to be identified! Dickinson.
Elegy for Yards, Pounds, and Gallons. Wagoner.
Envoy. Hovey.
Exultation is the going. Dickinson.
It Is Not Enough. Henderson.
Tecumseh. Mair.

Lean (ed) (ing)
Ancient Historian. Wallace-Crabbe.
The Blackstone Rangers. Brooks.
David in April. Booker.
Division. Ratti.
Feast. Millay.
Feed. Knister.
The Galloway Shore. Tremayne.
The House Was Quiet and the World Was Calm. Stevens.
Hudibras. Butler.
Idea of a Swimmer. Bloch.
In These Dissenting Times. Walker.
The Jesus Infection. Kumin.
Land of Little Sticks, 1945. Tate.
Lines. Ada Sister Mary.
The Mad Scene. Merrill.
Mussels. Oliver.
The New River Head, a Fragment. Dower.
Old Men, White-Haired, beside the Ancestral Graves. Basho (Matsuo Basho).
The Outcast. Russell.
Poems of Night. Kinnell.

Song of the Broad-Ax (excerpt). Whitman.
String Stars for Pearls. Nicolson.
To a Noisy Politician. Freneau.
To Jesus of Nazareth. Knowles.
The Two Old Women of Mumbling Hill. Reeves.
Yes, But... Weiss.

Leander
Across the Straits. Dobson.
A Private Letter to Brazil. Oden.
Shall I Come, If I Swim? Wide Are the Waves, You See. Campion.

Leap (ed) (ing) (s) (t)
Adam on His Way Home. Pack.
As One Who Wanders Into Old Workings. Day-Lewis.
A Bestiary of the Garden for Children Who Should Know Better. Gotlieb.
Catching One Clear Thought Alive. Allen.
The Children's Letters. Livesay.
The Crow-Children Walk My Circles in the Snow. Young Bear.
Days in the Month. *Anonymous.*
Deer at the Roadside. Smith.
Down the Mississippi. Fletcher.
Eclogues. Virgil (Publius Vergilius Maro).
First Dark. Oates.
Health. Thomas.
The Homer Mitchell Place. Engels.
I Walked with My Reason. MacLean.
In All These Acts. Everson.
The Jerboa. Moore.
Little Sticks. Rolls.
The Man in the Ocelot Suit. Brookhouse.
The Midnight Court. Merriman.
Moon Light. Manfred.
The Narrow Doors. Gifford.
Neither Spirit Nor Bird. *Anonymous.*
On Seeing a Fine Frigate at Anchor in a Bay off Mount Edgecumbe. Carrington.
Ontogeny. Ramsey.
Pass to thy Rendezvous of Light. Dickinson.
Private. Wormser.
The Scourge. Kunitz.
Sleep. Naone.
The Trout. Hine.
What Could Be. Gill.

Learn (ed) (ing) (s)
After Reading a Child's Guide to Modern Physics. Auden.
All the Fruit... Holderlin.
America's Answer. Lilliard.
An Ancient Gesture. Millay.
Anecdote for Fathers. Wordsworth.
Astrophel and Stella, XVI. Sidney.
Autant en Emporte le Vent. Marguerite de Navarre.

The Boy Actor. Coward.
By Rail through Istria. Conquest.
Caledonia. McElroy.
The Card-Dealer. Rossetti.
Chain. Lorde.
Dawn and a Woman. Logan.
The Death of Fathers. Weiss.
Desert in the Sea. Swann.
Don Juan. Byron.
The Drunk in the Furnace. Merwin.
Eagle Sonnets. Wood.
Epigram. Trapp.
Evening: an Elegy (parody). Smith.
The Faerie Queene. Spenser.
February. Merwin.
Fire, the Rope... Tikhonov.
First Holes Are Fresh. Shipley.
For Refugio Talamante. Ochester.
Give Me My Work. Whetstone.
Giving the Moon a New Chance. Stokes.
Gnome. Beckett.
Goodbye. Kinnell.
Grandpa Is Ashamed. Nash.
Habitation. Atwood.
He That Ne'er Learns His ABC. *Anonymous.*
The Hill Wife. Frost.
The Human Animal. Mayhall.
A Hundreth Good Poyntes of Husbandry. Tusser.
I Walked Out to the Graveyard to See the Dead. Eberhart.
If You But Knew. *Anonymous.*
In Memoriam A.H.H., XLV. Tennyson.
Journey. Thompson.
Jubilee. *Anonymous.*
Just an Old Man. Goose.
Learning. Chapman.
Lines. Goodman.
Lines on a Bill of Mortality, 1790. Cowper.
The Magician. Miranda.
Millions Are Learning How. Agee.
Mother's Advice. *Anonymous.*
Natural History. Warren.
News from the House. Browne.
Night of Spring. Westwood.
The Notorious Glutton. Taylor.
An Ode on the Despoilers of Learning in an American University (1947). Winters.
Of History More Like Myth. Garrigue.
On a Wednesday. Aliesan.
On Mr. Hearne, the Great Antiquary. *Anonymous.*
On the Breaking-Up of a School. O'Huiginn.
The Other. Fainlight.
Peregrine Prykke's Pilgrimage (parody). James.
A Plain Man's Dream. Keppel.
The Poet's Secret. Stoddard

Porgy, Maria, and Bess. Heyward.
Proof Positive. Taylor.
Relativities (parody). Untermeyer.
Rendez-vous Manque dans la Rue Racine. Synge.
Rich Mine of Knowledge. Chapman.
The Romantic. Ellis.
Roots. Ginsberg.
The Rosary. Rogers.
Safed and I. Levine.
.A Schoolmaster's Precepts. Penkethman.
Seven Years. Crewe.
Sierra Kid. Levine.
Since. Auden.
Sir T. J.'s Speech to his Wife and Children. *Anonymous.*
Six Weeks Old. Morley.
Sky Diving. Reed.
Something. Creeley.
A Song. Hawthorne.
Sonnets, CXVIII: "Like as to make our appetites more keep". Shakespeare.
The Spanish Curate. Fletcher.
Strange Meetings. Monro.
The Surrender of Spain. Hay.
Symon's Lesson of Wisdom for All Manner of Children... *Anonymous.*
These Two. Schwartz.
This Last Pain. Empson.
Three Poems about Children. Clarke.
To a Friend, on Her Examination for the Doctorate in English. Cunningham.
To a Lady on Reading Sherlock upon Death. Chesterfield.
To Madame A. V. Pletneff. Pavlova.
To Mr. Gray. Garrick.
To the Pious Memory of the Accomplisht Young Lady Mrs. Anne Killigrew. Dryden.
The Tree of Silence. Miller.
The Unforeseen. Nale Roxlo.
An Unsaid Word. Rich.
The Waking. Roethke.
What Fifty Said. Frost.
When I Was Still a Child. Harford.
When Land Is Gone and Money Spent. *Anonymous.*
Where Have All the Flowers Gone? (excerpt). Seeger.
White Bear. Griffin.
Woman with Flower. Madgett.
You Jump First. Pietri.
You Say, "I Will Come." Otomo of Sakanoe.
Zone. Bogan.

Least
Adequacy. Browning.
The Ballad of Father Gilligan. Yeats.
The Feast-Time of the Year. *Anonymous.*
The Lion and the Mouse. Taylor.
Part for the Whole. Francis.

Poem Read at Joan Mitchell's. O'Hara.
The Skeleton at the Feast. Roche.
To Spencer. Turberville.
Upon A. M. Suckling.

Leather
An Essay on Man. Pope.
Remembering Lunch. Dunn.
TV. Forbes.

Leaving (s)
Alas! How Should I Sing? *Anonymous.*
Analogy. Higgins.
Animal Fair. Booth.
Another. In Defence of Their Inconstancie. Jonson.
Apologia. Farjeon.
An Appeal. Wyatt.
The Art of Poetry. Horace.
At Early Morn. Dismond.
Behind the Glass Wall. Norse.
The Boar's Head. Anonymous.
Bonny Lizie Baillie. *Anonymous.*
Broke and Hungry. Jefferson.
The Buffalo. Price.
Caelica, XLVIII. Greville.
Caelica, XLIX. Greville.
Careless Love. *Anonymous.*
The Carpet-Weaver's Lament. *Anonymous.*
Christmas at Sea. Stevenson.
Cities #8. Cruz.
Consolation in July. Heppenstall.
Dead on the War Path. *Anonymous.*
Discipleship. Bales.
Divine Abundance. *Anonymous.*
The Divorce of a Lover. Gascoigne.
Doggin' Me around Blues. Pope.
Don't Forget. Berg.
The Door. Tomlinson.
The Earl of Surrey to Geraldine. Drayton.
The Eel. Montale.
Eleven Addresses to the Lord. Berryman.
Epigrams and Epitaphs, VI. Lewis.
Epithalamion. Hopkins.
A Farewell to America. Wilde.
A Farewell to His Mistress. *Anonymous.*
Farewell to Narcissus. Horan.
The Floor Is Dirty. Field.
For the Rebuilding of a House. Berry.
The Gaol Song. *Anonymous.*
Gates. Kooser.
Get You Gone. Sedley.
Give Me Leave. "W.
Glenaradale. Smith.
Go By. Tennyson.
Gone Fishing. Sanders.
The Good Beasts. Barnstone.
Good News. *Anonymous.*
Goodbye, Little Bonny Blue Eyes. *Anonymous.*
Goodnight Ladies. *Anonymous.*
Hard Trials. *Anonymous.*

Have Faith in God. Budzynski.
The High Sailboat. Quasimodo.
Horace, Epistle VII, Book I, Imitated. Swift.
The House of Desire. Williams.
How to Get to New Mexico. Brandi.
In the Planetarium. Fox.
The Inheritors. Geddes.
The Inland Lighthouse. McMichael.
The Jinx Blues. House.
Johnny Todd. *Anonymous.*
Kilroy. McCarthy.
Leave It with Him. *Anonymous.*
Leaving the Dance. Whitaker.
Leaving Town Blues. Bracey.
Letters from Vicksburg, XII. Gildner.
Listens, Too (parody). Berry.
Lochaber No More. Ramsay.
Looking at Power. Woessner.
Lord Randall. *Anonymous.*
The Maid of the Sweet Brown Knowe. *Anonymous.*
The Mariner. Cunningham.
Memory, a Small Brown Bird. Ives.
Mesopotamia. Kipling.
My Days among the Dead Are Past. Southey.
My Love Is Young. Birney.
The Need to Love. Vinner.
Of Angels. Mayo.
Old Ego Song. Minczeski.
On Being a Woman. Parker.
On the Wall. Johnson.
Payday at Coal Creek. *Anonymous.*
Peregrine Prykke's Pilgrimage (parody). James.
Poem of the Mother. Sklarew.
Poetry. O'Hara.
Prayer for the Useless Days. Pierce.
A Quotation from Shakespeare with Slight Improvements. "Carroll.
Residue of Song. Bell.
Resignation–To Faustus. Clough.
Reunion. Cadsby.
Rising High Water Blues. Jefferson.
Samson Agonistes. Milton.
The Second Nimphall. Drayton.
Sermon on the Mount. Wright.
The Shadow Rose. Rogers.
Since so ye please to hear me plain. Wyatt.
A Singer Asleep. Hardy.
Slow Mama Slow. Collins.
Song: "Fond affection, hence, and leave me!" Parry.
Song of Snow-White Heads. Cho Wen-chun.
Sonnets, LXXIII: "That time of year thou mayst in me behold." Shakespeare.

Still Though the One I Sing. Whitman
The Students of Justice. Merwin.
Suburbs on a Hazy Day. Lawrence.
Supplication. Masters.
Sweetheart. Hey.
Tableau Vivant. Gallagher.
Tak' Your Auld Cloak about Ye. *Anonymous.*
Testament. Hughes.
They Closed Her Eyes. Becquer.
This Compost. Whitman.
Time for Us to Leave Her. *Anonymous.*
Time to Leave Her. *Anonymous.*
To an Old Tune. Percy.
To Crinog. *Anonymous.*
To Geron. Jacob.
To His Ever-Loving God. Herrick.
To John Donne. Jonson.
To Summer. Nadel.
Untitled Requiem for Tomorrow. Conyus.
Voices at the Window. Sidney.
Waking Early. Barth.
War Song. *Anonymous.*
What He Took. Anonymous.
Where Are the Ones Who Lived Before? *Anonymous.*
Why Would I Have Survived? Bruck.
Woman with Flower. Madgett.
Work for Small Men (excerpt). Foss.
The Wreck of the Old 97. *Anonymous.*
Your Name in Arezzo. Wright.
Ys Yt Possyble. Wyatt.

Lecture (d)
The Anatomy of Humor. Bishop.
Autumn Morning at Cambridge. Cornford.
Cedar Waxwing. Matchett.
The Snail. Conkling.
Tutor's Dignity. "Carroll.

Ledge (s)
Haarlem Heights. Guiterman.
Intention to Escape from Him. Millay.
Signature for Tempo. MacLeish.
Suicide off Egg Rock. Plath.

Lee
Dame Wiggins of Lee. *Anonymous.*
Gettysburg. Roche.
The Lee Rigg. Fergusson.
Nathaniel Lee to Sir Roger L'Estrange, Who Visited Him in His Madhouse. Lee.
The Ship Rambolee. *Anonymous.*
The Surrender at Appomattox. Melville.

Leech (es)
King Arthur's Dream. *Anonymous.*
The Lost Man: A Crocodile. Beddoes.
The Pastor Speaks Out. Fisher.

Resolution and Independence.
  Wordsworth.
Tlanusi'yi, the Leech Place.
  Cardiff.

Left
Afterword. *Anonymous.*
The Alligator Bride. Hall.
The Ark. Milton.
Ash. MacBeth.
At the Drapers. Hardy.
Ballad: "Of all the Girls that
  e'er were seen." Gay.
The Band. Dennis.
Before the Actual Cold.
  Young Bear.
The Boarder. Feirstein.
The Breeze Is Blowing.
  Anonymous.
Bundles. Sandburg.
The Burial of the Bachelor
  (parody). *Anonymous.*
Caelica, LXXXVII. Greville.
Carved by Obadiah Verity.
  Welch.
The Celebration in the Plaza.
  Rich.
Cocoon. Ishigaki Rin.
Coming Back Home. Young
  Bear.
Conceit upon the Feet
  (parody). Zaranka.
The Connecticut Elm. Swan.
The Curse of Cromwell.
  Yeats.
The Derby Ram.
  Anonymous.
Desire. Cornish.
Dinnshenchas: The Story of
  Macha. *Anonymous.*
Don Juan. Foote.
The Dreadful Has Already
  Happened. Strand.
Epilogue. Singer.
Epitaph on the Fart in the
  Parliament House.
  Hoskyns.
Epitaph...on the Grave of
  Thomas Osborne, Died
  1749. *Anonymous.*
Fires of Driftwood.
  MacKay.
Five Serpents. Burgess.
Flathead and Nez Perce Sin-
  ka-ha. Lewis.
The Floor Is Dirty. Field.
For John Clare. Ashbery.
Gal I Left Behind Me.
  Anonymous.
The Gentle Snorer. Van
  Duyn.
Good-by and Keep Cold.
  Frost.
A Good Thing. Mathew.
The Good Woman.
  MacLean.
Goosey, Goosey, Gander.
  Mother Goose.
Haarlem Heights.
  Guiterman.
I Wish I Were. *Anonymous.*
Inexhaustible. Zangwill.
Instant Coffee. Yau.
Ireland. Shorter.
The Island. Woodcock.
Lady Franklin's Lament (I).
  Anonymous.
The Last Time. Veitch.
The Lay of the Vigilantes.
  Anonymous.
Limerick: "A Phoenician
  called Phlebas forgot."
  Cope.

Little Boy Blue. Lockwood.
A Love Sonnet. Wither.
The Lovemaker. Mezey.
Mantis. McCord.
Mary's Ghost. Hood.
Memorial Day: A
  Collaboration. Berrigan.
Metaphysic of Snow. Finkel.
The Middle-Aged. Rich.
My Angel. Brooks.
My Past Has Gone to Bed.
  Sassoon.
Never Let Your Left Hand
  Know. Johnson.
New Year's Eve. Housman.
Nightletter. Wright.
Nonsense. *Anonymous.*
Not Wanting Myself. Gregg.
O Where Are You Going?
  Auden.
Out of This Life.
  Anonymous.
Parting Gift. Wylie.
Peace. Whitney.
Piney Woods Money Mama.
  Jefferson.
A Quotation from
  Shakespeare with Slight
  Improvements. "Carroll.
The Rat. Davies.
Reflections. MacNeice.
Return. Tillinghast.
Riddle: "Elizabeth, Lizzy,
  Betsy and Bess."
  Anonymous.
Riddle: "Old Mother Twitchet
  had but one eye." Mother
  Goose.
Rubaiyat for Sue Ella Tucker.
  Williams.
The Sermon in the Hospital
  (excerpt). King.
The Seven Hells of the Jigoku
  Zoshi (excerpt).
  Rothenberg.
She Wandered after Strange
  Gods... Benet.
Stepping Outside. Gallagher.
Sweet Willie. *Anonymous.*
The T.E. Lawrence Poems:
  The Void. MacEwen.
Tao in the Yankee Stadium
  Bleachers. Updike.
To Find the Dominical Letter.
  Anonymous.
Uncle Reuben. *Anonymous.*
A Useless Burden upon the
  Earth. Bridges.
Verses Found in Thomas
  Dudley's Pocket after His
  Death. Dudley.
A Waist. Stein.
Waking from Sleep. Bly.
What Is Left? Shakur.
What the Violins Sing in
  Their Baconfat Bed. Arp.
Winter Drive. McAuley.

Leg (s)
Ambulance Call.
  Goldensohn.
Big Woman. Washboard
  Sam.
Bullfrogs. Evans.
The Child Who Walks
  Backwards. Crozier.
Comfortable Strangers.
  Winch.
Dream Songs. Berryman.
Epigram: "Why should
  scribblers discompose."
  Landor.
Finisterra. Winters.

For One Moment. Ignatow.
Frogs. MacCaig.
Gigha. Graham.
How You Get Born. Jong.
The Huckster's Horse.
  Strong.
Knee Lunes. Kelly.
The Last Man. Hood.
A Lesson in Love.
  Hobsbaum.
Limerick: "An elephant sat on
  some kegs." Francis.
Little Song of the Maimed.
  Peret.
Miss Kilmansegg and Her
  Precious Leg. Hood.
Nina. Dienstag.
On Oxford (parody). Keats.
The Oxford and Hampton
  Railway. *Anonymous.*
Party Knee. Updike.
Peg. *Anonymous.*
Poor Dear Grandpapa.
  Thompson.
Reading in Fall Rain. Bly.
Riddle: "Two legs sat upon
  three legs." *Anonymous.*
The Right of Way.
  Williams.
A Sailor's Apology for Bow-
  Legs. Hood.
The Scribblers. Landor.
A Shepherd Kept Sheep on a
  Hill So High. D'Urfey.
The Shropshire Lad's Cousin
  (parody). Hoffenstein.
The Sums. Edmond.
The Swank. Vickers.
Unusual. Eigner.
Wild Swans. Millay.
World's Fare. Stetler.
Young Lambs. Clare.

Legacy
An Elegy Upon My Best
  Friend. King.
Heredity. Ward.
The Legacy. King.
Upon a Braid of Hair in a
  Heart. King.

Legend (s)
The Book of Two Married
  Women and the Widow.
  Dunbar.
The Captain. Varela.
The Captive Stone. Barnes.
Cinque. Hale.
Color Alone Can Speak.
  Nicholl.
Essay on Rime (excerpt).
  Shapiro.
The Figures on the Frieze.
  Reid.
Legend. Crane.
The Legend of the Admen.
  Lord.
Love in Magnolia Cemetery.
  Rankin.
Not Being Oedipus. Heath-
  Stubbs.
Song of Expectancy.
  Hitchcock.
Sunny. Vander Molen.

Leisure
Bird's Nests. Clare.
Davy, the Dicer. More.
Don Juan. Byron.
Henry's Secret. Kilner.
King George V. Hayward.
The Last Night That She
  Lived. Dickinson.
A Peony for Apollo. Eaton.
Secret Pleasures. Morgan.

Solitude. Clare.
The Task. Cowper.
There Is a Charm in Solitude
  That Cheers. Clare.
To Fortune. More.
Wherefore Peep'st Thou,
  Envious Day? *Anonymous.*

Lemon
La Belle Dame sans Merci.
  Fairburn.
Chock House Blues.
  Jefferson.
Julius Caesar. *Anonymous*
The Last Summer. Smith.
Mr. Apollinax. Eliot.
Saratoga Ending. Kees.
A Song for the Spanish
  Anarchists. Read.
Try This Once. *Anonymous.*

Lemonade
The Archaeological Picnic.
  Betjeman.
The Big Rock Candy
  Mountain. *Anonymous.*
The Painters.
  Hemschemeyer.
Six Feet Under. Hale.
Try This Once. *Anonymous.*

Lend
El Hombre. Williams.
Habits. Merwin.
I Had a Little Pony. Mother
  Goose.
In Trust. Dodge.
Submission. Herbert.

Length (s)
Are They Shadows That We
  See? Daniel.
Birthday. Lawrence.
The Marshes of Glynn.
  Lanier.
A Night Watch. *Anonymous.*
On Descending the River Po.
  Parsons.
S.S.R., Lost at Sea–The
  Times. Gustafson.
Scientific Proof. Foley.
To Earthward. Frost. ;

Lenin
The Motive of All of It.
  Rukeyser.
The Skeleton of the Future.
  ""MacDiarmid.

Lens (es)
Citizen. Grudin.
Eye. Burr.
First Photos of Flu Virus.
  Witt.
Lost Contact. Cole.
Some Negatives: X. At the
  Chateau. Merrill.

Lent
Gracey Nugent. Clarke.
My Days Have Been So
  Wondrous Free.
  Anonymous.
To Keep a True Lent.
  Herrick.
To Sir Robert Wroth.
  Jonson.

Leopard
In the Forest of Your Eyes.
  Barbeitos.
Leopard Skin. Stewart.
Limerick: "A leopard when
  told that benzine."
  Herford.
The Protective Grigri. Joans.

Leper
Gehazi. Kipling.
Salute to the Elephant.
  Apolebieji.

The Vocation of St. Francis.
Eleanore.

Leprechaun
Could It Have Been a
Shadow? Shannon.
Faith, I Wish I Were a
Leprechaun. Ritter.

Leprosy
The Leper. Willis.
Spring over the City.
Hebert.
To Women, to Hide Their
Teeth, if They Be Rotten or
Rusty. Herrick.

Lesbos
The Bridegroom Is So Tall.
Sappho.
Fantasy. Carducci.

Less
The Advantages of Washing.
Armstrong.
And Thus in Nineveh.
Pound.
At Ithaca. Doolittle.
The Beginning of the End.
Hopkins.
Caves. Baker.
Cello Entry. Celan.
The Chelsea. Walcott.
Cow Pissing. Morgan.
Heron. Booth.
In Windsor Castle. Surrey.
The Lady in the Pink
Mustang. Erdrich.
Memories of Verdun.
Dugan.
Motels, Hotels, Other People's
Houses. Van Brunt.
New Yeares, Expect New
Gifts. Jonson.
On the Young Statesmen.
Sackville.
Our Coming Countrymen.
Parkes.
Overlooking the River Stout.
Hardy.
Poem for Some Black Women.
Rodgers.
Prisoned in Windsor, He
Recounteth His Pleasure
There Passed. Surrey.
Riddle: "I am within as white
as snow." Anonymous.
Snow Fell with a Will.
Gillman.
A Song in Time of Order
1852. Swinburne.
Song: "Why, lovely charmer,
tell me why." Steele.
Time. Herbert.
To a Bird after a Storm.
Vaughan.
To Ben. Johnson. Upon
Occasion of His Ode of
Defiance. Carew.
To His Girl. Martial
(Marcus Valerius Martialis).
To the Winds. A Song.
Ayres.
Tourist. Van Doren.
Womanisers. Press.

Lesson (s)
America's Answer. Lilliard.
The Balcony Poems. Smith.
Broadway. Whitman.
The Buddha in the Womb.
Jong.
The Bumblebeaver. Cox.
Columbus. Miller.
The Faerie Queene. Spenser.

How the Helpmate of Blue-
Beard Made Free with a
Door. Carryl.
The Lesson. Lowell.
A Lesson in Translation.
Preil.
Music. Nye.
Prince Sumiya. Anonymous.
The Process of Conception.
Quillet.
A Roxbury Garden. Lowell.
The School-Master and the
Truants. "Brownjohn.
Sonnets, CXVIII: "Like as to
make our appetites more
keep". Shakespeare.
The Spider and the Fly.
Howitt.
Survivors. Feinstein.
Two Fishermen. Moss.
The Unteaching. Oles.

Let
2nd Dance–Seeing Lines–6
February 1964. MacLow.
Commination. Landor.
Divorce. Wickham.
Drop the Wires. Seidman.
The Earth Cycle Dream.
Minthorn.
The Face. Stryk.
Getting Out. Mathis.
History Lesson. Van Doren.
Incident at Mossel Bay.
Balazs.
Initiation. Rilke.
Listen. Patterson.
Meet the Supremes.
Trinidad.
Midnight. Stephens.
No-Kings and the Calling of
Spirits. Willard.
Only Joy! Now Here You
Are. Sidney.
Reproof. Anonymous.
Running under Street Lights.
White.
Scaffolding. Heaney.
Sky Diving. Reed.
Suburban Lullaby. Manifold.
Sutra Blues or, This Pain Is
Bliss. Aliesan.
The Teak Forest: For This Is
Wisdom. Hope.

Lethe
Cancelled Stanza of the Ode
on Melancholy. Keats.
Dewdrop, Wind and Sun.
Skipsey.
Fording the River. Deane.
Proust on Noah.
Silberschlag.
The Scarlet Woman.
Johnson.
A Supermarket in California.
Ginsberg.

Letter (s)
Any Man to His Secretary.
Corke.
Big City. Brownstein.
Clausa Germanis Gallia.
Brand.
The Commendations of
Mistress Jane Scrope.
Skelton.
Country Letter. Clare.
Dream Songs. Berryman.
The First Solitude. Gongora
y Argote.
He That Ne'er Learns His
ABC. Anonymous.
I Got a Letter from Jesus
(with music). Anonymous.

Irish Poetry. Longley.
Just before Dawn. Borson.
Lament of a Last Letter.
Harrison.
The Letter. Anonymous.
The Letter Edged in Black.
Anonymous.
Letter from a Working Girl.
Scott.
A Letter to Robert Frost.
Hillyer.
Lives of Great Men.
Anonymous.
A Metrical Index to the Bible.
Chorley.
A New England Church.
Barrett.
Night in the House by the
River. Tu Fu.
Of Three or Four in a Room.
Amichai.
Papa's Letter. Anonymous.
Poet. Pastan.
Sarah Byng. Belloc.
Snow Storm. Tu Fu.
These Two. Schwartz.
To Find the Dominical Letter.
Anonymous.
Too Late. Korn.
Toward the Solstice. Rich.
The True Confession of
George Barker. Barker.
Two Presentations. Duncan.
Unto My Valentine. Brews.
Who's Who. Auden.
A Winter-Piece to a Friend
Away. Berryman.

Lettuce (s)
Ben. Wolfe.
Dietary Advice. Anonymous.
Epitaph: "See here, nice
Death, to please his palate."
Pope.
Inanna's Song. Anonymous.
Tombstone Epitaphs.
Anonymous.

Level (s)
Alpine. Thomas.
Areas. Scalapino.
The Beaver's Story. Watkins.
Deborah as Scion. Dickey.
The Level and the Square.
Morris.
My Grandmother. Adams.
The Outlanders. Glaze.
Safety or Something. Jacobs.
Snow Train. Erdrich.
Solid Mountain. Bowering.

Leviathan
Leviathan. Anonymous.
The Loyal Scot (excerpt).
Marvell.

Lewd (ness)
An Imitation of Martial, Book
II Ep. 105. "H—.
Limerick: "A swimmer whose
clothing was strewed."
Anonymous.
Paradise Lost: V. Hecht.

Liar (s)
The Boy and the Wolf.
Aesop.
The Burning of Books.
Brecht.
Epigrams, CXVIII.
Ausonius.
Knightsbridge of Libya.
MacLean.
Lighten Our Darkness.
Douglas.
Medieval Norman Songs.
Anonymous.

A Plea to Boys and Girls.
Graves.
The Politics of Rich Painters.
Jones.
The Rebel. Pearse.
The Shepherd-Boy and the
Wolf. Aesop.

Libation (s)
At a Potato Digging.
Heaney.
Ceremony. Kunjufu.
Cow Pissing. Morgan.
Recessional for the Class of
1959... Cowen.

Libel
Apocrypha. Kennedy.
On Mr. Edward Howard,
upon His British Princes.
Sackville.

Liberation
Dandelions. Nemerov.
On Death (excerpt).
Sikelianos.
The Road Moves On. Nash.
The Seed-Picture.
McGuckian.

Liberty
A Battle Ballad. Ticknor.
Ben Milam. Wharton.
Brave Paulding and the Spy.
Anonymous.
But Two There Are... Day-
Lewis.
The Conquering Love of
Jesus. Wesley.
Cor Cordium. Swinburne.
Cuba Libre. Miller.
The Dreamer. Gould.
The Electric Telegraph.
Baker.
An Essay on Criticism.
Pope.
The Faithful Friend.
Cowper.
The Foe at the Gates.
Bruns.
France: An Ode. Coleridge.
Full Moon at Tierz: Before
the Storming of Huesca.
Cornford.
General Vallancey's Waltz.
Durcan.
He ate and drank the precious
words. Dickinson.
Her Hair. Anonymous.
Hollin, Green Hollin.
Anonymous.
How Sweet I Roam'd.
Blake.
A Hymn. Nekrasov.
Independence. Smollett.
Inspiration. Johnson.
The Irish Peasant to His
Mistress. Moore.
Jacob Godbey. Masters.
The Jolly Soldier.
Anonymous.
Lincoln and Liberty.
Simpson.
Love's Snare. Wyatt.
Major Andre. Anonymous.
The Man Who Wanted to be
a Seagull. Hervey.
Le Marais du Cygne.
Whittier.
Mare Liberum. Van Dyke.
No Greater Love.
Anonymous.
No Rack Can Torture Me.
Dickinson.
Now Must I Learn to Live at
Rest. Wyatt.

The Nursery. Howe.
Oh! Isn't It a Pity.
  Robinson.
On Independence. Sewall.
One Country. Stanton.
Paul Jones. *Anonymous.*
Pledge of Allegiance.
  Anonymous.
Republic to Republic.
  Bynner.
Robert Fulton. Stanford.
Scholar II. Deane.
So Fast Entangled.
  Anonymous.
Sonnet to Negro Soldiers.
  Cotter, Jr.
Swift's Epitaph. Yeats.
To the Dead of '98.
  Johnson.
To the Returning Brave.
  Johnson.
To the States. Whitman.
The Tree of Liberty. Burns.
Trenton and Princeton.
  Anonymous.
Valley Forge. Read.
Washington. O'Crowley.
Wessex Heights. Hardy.
Where Are the Men Seized in
  This Wind of Madness?
  Espirito Santo.

Lice
How the Doughty Duke of
  Albany Like a Coward
  Knight...(excerpt).
  Skelton.
Mr. Cherry. Newman.
The Old Man's Song.
  Anonymous.
A Terrestrial Cuckoo.
  O'Hara.

License
The Bartholdi Statue.
  Whittier.
Drat My Hateful Birthday.
  Sulpicia.
Learning Experience. Piercy.
The Sandwich Man. Padgett.
Thorns Arm the Rose.
  Claudian.

Lick (ed) (er) (s)
Chantey of Notorious Bibbers.
  Robinson.
Conscience. Ravitch.
Cow-Boy Fun. Coburn.
Evensong. Moffett.
Golden Gate: The Teacher.
  Mastrola.
I Held a Lamb.
  Worthington.
Jack Sprat Could Eat No Fat.
  Mother Goose.
Jack Sprat (parody).
  Hetherington.
Lord Tennyson and Lord
  Melchett. Lawrence.
Night Clouds. Lowell.
Power to the People.
  Nemerov.
So Help Me God. Catullus.
The Turkish Trench Dog.
  Dearmer.
Who Threw the Overalls in
  Mistress Murphy's
  Chowder. Geifer.

Lid (s)
Cruelty. Hummer.
Death of My Aunt.
  Anonymous.
Eyeing the Eyes of One's
  Mistress. Jones.
Goodbye. Knott.

Snakecharmer. Plath.
Song: "Turn, turn thy
  beauteous face away."
  Beaumont.
Street Song. Gunn.
The Tall Toms. Honig.
Then Laugh. Backus.

Lie (d) (s)
Above the Falls at Waimea.
  Johnson.
Adolescence. Schmitz.
All-Knowing Lamp.
  Anonymous.
Antichrist. Muir.
Antrim. Jeffers.
Apocrypha. Moss.
Astrophel and Stella, XLVII.
  Sidney.
At the End of the Affair.
  Kumin.
August Rain. Bly.
A Ballad for Katharine of
  Aragon. Causley.
Ballade of the Grindstones.
  Sherwin.
Battle Won Is Lost. George.
Between Ourselves. Lorde.
A blue-eyed phantom far
  before. Rossetti.
Bohernabreena. Daiken.
The Bongaloo. Milligan.
Burning Hills. Ondaatje.
Caelica, XXI. Greville.
Canticles to Men. Mannes.
A Celebration of Charis.
  Jonson.
Certain Dead. Haines.
A Charm for Spring Flowers.
  Field.
Confession in Holy Week.
  Morley.
Connais-Tu le Pays?
  Shelton.
A Conquest. Pollock.
Consummation. *Anonymous.*
A Cottage in the Wood.
  Edson.
Counting the Beats. Graves.
Crotalus. Harte.
Cruciform. Welles.
Darwin in 1881.
  Schnackenberg.
Definitions. Keith.
The Derby Ram, II.
  Anonymous.
The Difference between a Lie
  and the Truth. Dessus.
The Disordering. Yates.
The Dodger. *Anonymous.*
The Dove. MacColl.
Dream Songs. Berryman.
The Eagle. Blessing.
Eden Revisited. Miller.
Elegy Written on a
  Frontporch. Shapiro.
Elemental. Lawrence.
Eleven Addresses to the Lord.
  Berryman.
The Embankment. Hulme.
Epigram: "Great woe, fire &
  woe." Skythinos.
Epigram: "He drank strong
  waters and his speech was
  coarse." Kipling.
Epigram: The Parson's Looks.
  Burns.
Episode of the Cherry Tree.
  Weston.
Epitaph. *Anonymous.*
An Epitaph for Sir Henry
  Lee... *Anonymous.*

Epitaph: "Here lies I and my
  three daughters."
  Anonymous.
Epitaph: "Here lies my dear
  wife, a sad slattern and a
  shrew." *Anonymous.*
Epitaph on an Infant.
  Crinagoras.
Epitaph on the Earl of
  Strafford. Cleveland.
Epitaph on the World.
  Thoreau.
Epitaph on William Jones.
  Anonymous.
Epitaph to a Dog. Byron.
Eudaimon. Raine.
Eve: Night Thoughts.
  Jerome.
Evil Prayer. Hyde.
Fable. Parker.
The False Heart. Belloc.
Feast. Millay.
The Feral Pioneers. Reed.
Flower of Love. McKay.
Flycatchers. Bridges.
For Chicle & Justina.
  Bickston.
For the Lord's Day Evening.
  Watts.
Foreigners at the Fair.
  Brooks.
Fox. Campbell.
Fragment Thirty-Six.
  Doolittle.
Funny fantasies are never so
  real as oldstyle.
  Ferlinghetti.
The Garden. Wilde.
God Made a Trance.
  Anonymous.
The Grandmother. Berry.
Haiku: "Why is the hail so
  wild..." Wright.
He That Would Thrive.
  Anonymous.
He Thinks of Those Who
  Have Spoken Evil of His
  Beloved. Yeats.
Here and There.
  Stallworthy.
The Holy Innocents. Lowell.
Hot Weather in the Plains–
  India. Tipple.
How Death Came.
  Anonymous.
I Once Loved a Young Man.
  Anonymous.
I Saw a Man Pursuing the
  Horizon. Crane.
Une Idole du Nord. Stuart.
In and Out. Sissman.
The Iron Lung. Plumly.
John Brown's Body. Benét.
The Lake of Gaube.
  Swinburne.
Land of the Wilful Gospel.
  Lanier.
Letter to a Jealous Friend.
  Simmons.
The Liar. *Anonymous.*
Lies and Gossip. Fernandez.
Limerick: "There's a
  Portuguese person named
  Howell." Rossetti.
Little Billy. *Anonymous.*
Little Brown Dog.
  Anonymous.
Lord Rendal. *Anonymous.*
Love Made in the First Age.
  Lovelace.
Mahoney. Jennett.
Mama Knows. Scott.

Man Alone. Bogan.
The Manual. Rubin.
Middle Age. Beer.
The Milk White Doe.
  Anonymous.
Mother the Wardrobe Is Full
  of Infantrymen.
  McGough.
Mummy of a Lady Named
  Jemutesonekh XXI
  Dynasty. James.
A Muse of Water. Kizer.
My Soul Doth Pant towards
  Thee. Taylor.
Not Late Enough. Townson.
Now That My Father Lies
  down Beside Me. Plumly.
Nurse Sharks. Matthews.
Ode on Solitude. Pope.
Of Books. Florio.
Of Women. Edwards.
Oliphaunt. Tolkien.
On a Hand. Belloc.
On John So. *Anonymous.*
On Sir Henry Clinton's
  Recall. *Anonymous.*
On the Death of His Wife.
  O Dalaigh.
On the Spartan Dead at
  Thermopylae. Simonides
  (of Ceos).
Only Thy Dust... Marquis.
Outside the Chancel Door.
  Anonymous.
Pacific Epitaphs. Randall.
The Paper Cutter. Ignatow.
Paradise Lost. Milton.
Parting. Corbin.
Parting. Roscoe.
Pasa Thalassa Thalassa.
  Robinson.
Penological Study: Southern
  Exposure, 3. Wet Hair...
  Warren.
Pier delle Vigne. Dante
  Alighieri.
The Pine of Whiting Wood.
  Sjolander.
Pistol Slapper Blues. Fuller.
Plenary. *Anonymous.*
The Poem That Took the
  Place of a Mountain.
  Stevens.
Poem: "The only response."
  Knott.
The Poet in Old Age Fishing
  at Evening. O'Grady.
The Quiet Life. Pope.
The Rain, It Streams on
  Stone. Housman.
The Ranting Wanton's
  Resolution; 1672.
  Anonymous.
Reasons for Attendance.
  Larkin.
Rimbaud. Auden.
A Sailor's Yarn. Roche.
Saint Coyote. Hogan.
The School Globe. Reaney.
Sea Gods. Doolittle.
Selective Service. Forche.
Self-Criticism in February.
  Jeffers.
The Serpent Muses.
  Henderson.
She Remembers. Aldis.
Sigmund Freud. Nemerov.
Sinnes Heavie Loade.
  Southwell.
Six Questions (A vers.).
  Anonymous.

A Song of Renunciation. Seaman.
Song: "Roses and pinks will be strewn where you go." Davenant.
Song: "What think you of this age now." Anonymous.
Sonnet IX: "As soon as I lie down in my soft bed." Labe.
Sonnets of the Months. San Geminiano.
The Sound of Night. Kumin.
Spring Is at Work with Beginnings of Things. Rose.
Stoklewath; or, The Cymbrian Village. Blamire.
Summer Oracle. Lorde.
Talk to Me Tenderly. Laramore.
Taylor's Travels from London to Prague (excerpt). Taylor.
These Days the Papers in the Street. Reznikoff.
Threnody. Parker.
Ties. Souster.
Time Stands Still, with Gazing on Her Face! Anonymous.
To a Recalcitrant Virgin. Asclepiades.
To Electra. Herrick.
To Shelley. Landor.
To the Thoughtful Reader. Meredith.
To Whom It May Concern. Mitchell.
A True Confession. Stallworthy.
The True Story of Snow White. Bennett.
Twice a Week the Winter Through. Housman.
The Two Brothers. Anonymous.
Two Little Kittens. Anonymous.
Unfortunate Coincidence. Parker.
Variations on a Medieval Theme. Dutton.
Verses Pinn'd to a Sheet, in Which a Lady Stood to Do Penance... Anonymous.
Visiting Day. Young.
War. Shelton.
West-Easterly Divan, IX (excerpt). Goethe.
What Happiness Can Equal Mine. David.
When Green Buds Hang. Housman.
Whitley at Three O'Clock. Worley.
Why from This Her and Him. Cummings.
Why Would I Want. Harris.
The Yoke of Tyranny. Sidney.

Lieutenant
Ballad of Lieutenant Miles. Scollard.
Memories of Verdun. Dugan.
The Summer Story. Lehmann.

Life
1944—On the Invasion Coast. Beeching.
The 90th Year. Levertov.

Absence of Occupation. Cowper.
Absolution. Watson.
Abstinence Sows Sand All Over. Blake.
Abt Vogler. Browning.
Ad Leuconoen. Horace.
Address to My Malay Krees. Leyden.
The Aeneid. Virgil (Publius Vergilius Maro).
After a Parting. Meynell.
Age in Prospect. Jeffers.
Alicante. Prevert.
Alice's Recitation. "Carroll.
All the Scenes of Nature Quicken. Smart.
Aloof. Rossetti.
Always. Neruda.
American against Solitude. Dugan.
Amoretti, VII. Spenser.
Amoretti, XVII. Spenser.
Amoretti, LXXXIX. Spenser.
And If at Last. Labe.
And Is It Night? Anonymous.
The Angels at Hamburg. Jarrell.
The Animal I Wanted. Patchen.
The Annunciation. Tabb.
Another for the Briar Rose. Morris.
Another Life. Bidart.
Anthropology in Fort Morgan, Colorado. Hamod.
Apples. Kaufman.
April Rain. Blind.
Archaic Torso of Apollo. Rilke.
Archilochos:. Tagliabue.
Arm, Arm, Arm, Arm! Fletcher.
Art. Emerson.
Art. Thomson.
Art and Life. Ridge.
Artorius. Heath-Stubbs.
As power and wit will me assist. Wyatt.
Ascension. Devlin.
The Asteroid Light. Anonymous.
At Kenneth Burke's Place. Williams.
At Last. Trask.
At the Comedy. Stringer.
Athletic Employment. Anonymous.
August Was Foggy. Snyder.
Auld Sanct-Aundrians–Brand the Builder. Scott.
An Autobiography. Rhys.
Autumn Flowers. Very.
Autumn Night. Scott.
The Bad Boy. Anonymous.
The Bailey Beareth the Bell Away. Anonymous.
The Bald Spot. McNair.
The Ballad of Charity. Leland.
A Ballad of Past Meridian. Meredith.
Ballad of the Double Bed. Merriam.
Ballade of Expansion. Johnson.
Ballata of Love's Power. Cavalcanti.
The Banjo. Winner.

The Battle. Simpson.
A Battle Ballad. Ticknor.
Because You Prayed. "B.
Bedlam Hills. Smith.
Beyond Recall. Bradley.
Billy the Kid. Anonymous.
Bits of Straw. Clare.
Blight. Emerson.
The Bloody Conquests of Mighty Tamburlaine (excerpt). Marlowe.
A Bob-Tailed Flush. Painter.
Bold Robert Emmet. Maguire.
The Bonnie Banks O Fordie (A vers.). Anonymous.
The Bonnie Banks O Fordie (B vers.). Anonymous.
Boomerang. Perreault.
Boy Wandering in Simms' Valley. Warren.
Breathing the Strong Smell. Norse.
Breughel's Winter. De la Mare.
Brevities. Sassoon.
Brother Green. Anonymous.
The Builders. Wright.
The Bungalows. Ashbery.
The Bunyip and the Whistling Kettle. Manifold.
The Burden of Egypt (excerpt). Milnes.
The Buried Life. Arnold.
Buying a Shop on Dizengoff. Biton.
By an Evolutionist. Tennyson.
The Canal. Huxley.
Canzone: Of His Love, with the Figure of a Sudden Storm. Prinzivalle.
Captain Craig (excerpt). Robinson.
Central Park Some People (3 P.M.). Morejo.
Ceremony. Kunjufu.
Chamonix. Hookham.
A Channel Passage. Swinburne.
Chant for Dark Hours. Parker.
Chant Royal of the Dejected Dipsomaniac. Marquis.
A Child My Choice. Southwell.
Child of Blue. Hogan.
Childe Harold's Pilgrimage: Canto I. Byron.
Childhood. More.
Childhood. Stanton.
The Children. Dyment.
The Choice. Tate.
Christ's Bondservant. Matheson.
A Christmas Prayer. Hines.
A Christopher of the Shenandoah. Thomas.
The City of the Dead. Burton.
A Clock Stopped. Dickinson.
A Collection of Emblemes, Ancient and Moderne (excerpt). Wither.
The Collies. Anthony.
Columbus. Lowell.
Come Holy Spirit, Dove Divine. Judson.
Confessions of the Life Artist. Gunn.
The Convict. Frisch.

The Conviction. Synge.
Coogan's Wood. Stuart.
The Copper Song. Fraser.
Corps d'Esprit. McHugh.
Cosmic Eye. Redwing.
The Coup de Grace. Sill.
Couple. Stone.
The Courtier's Life. Wyatt.
Credo. O'Sullivan.
Creed. Townsend.
The Crucible of Life (excerpt). Guest.
Crucifixion. Booth.
The Crusade. Rinaldo d'Aquino.
A Cry from the Shore. Cortissoz.
The Crystal. Coan.
The Curfew Breakers. Chimsoro.
A Cyprian Woman. Widdemer.
Daddy. Clifton.
The Daisies. Carman.
A Dancer's Life. Justice.
Dante. Duncan.
Daughters Will You Marry? Anonymous.
Dawn on the Headland. Watson.
The Day of Judgement. Young.
Days Were Great as Lakes. Vogel.
A Dead Weasel. Helwig.
Death. Coates.
Death Bells. Hopkins.
Death in Life. Vaux.
The Death of the Gods. An Ode. Ker.
Death, Thou Hast Seized Me. Luzzatto.
Destroyer Life. Anonymous.
Dinosaur. Hearn.
Disillusion. Decker.
Divine Poems. Villa.
The Divorce of a Lover. Gascoigne.
Don Juan. Byron.
Don't Be Sorrowful, Darling. Peale.
The Donzella and the Ceylon. Anonymous.
A Door. Merwin.
The dots of de dondi. Gunnars.
The Dove Apologizes to His God for Being Caught by a Cat. Eaton.
Drat My Hateful Birthday. Sulpicia.
The Dreadful Has Already Happened. Strand.
Dream House. Newell.
Dream Songs. Berryman.
Dreams. Hughes.
Drum. Hughes.
Dryad Song. Fuller.
Duality. Hobson.
The Dump. Kuzma.
During a Chorale by Cesar Franck. Bynner.
Dusk. "Mistral.
Eagles Over the Lambing Paddock. Moll.
Easter. Herbert.
Eddystone Light. Anonymous.
Edmund Pollard. Masters.
Egyptian Hieroglyphics. Anonymous.
An Elegie. Corbett.

Elegy. Fraser.
England. Massey.
The Englishman in Italy. Browning.
Epigram: A Spiral Shell. Nemerov.
Epigrams. Martial (Marcus Valerius Martialis).
Epistle to the Reader. Gibson.
Epitaph for the Poet V. Ficke.
Epitaph: "Here lies the man that madly slain." Hoskyns.
Epitaph on a Vagabond. Gray.
An Epitaph on Master Philip Gray. Jonson.
An Epitaph upon Mr. Ashton a Conformable Citizen. Crashaw.
Escape. Graves.
Esthete in Harlem. Hughes.
Eternal Values. Crowell.
Eurydice. Bourdillon.
An Evasion. Livingstone.
Even in the Darkness. Mullins.
Evensong. Schaumann.
Evolution. Tabb.
Evolution. Zangwill.
Excelsior. Longfellow.
Exchanging Glances. Root.
Exile from God. Wheelock.
The Exile's Return. Lowell.
Experience. Harford.
Facing the Chair. ""MacDiarmid.
Fading-Leaf and Fallen-Leaf. Garnett.
The Faerie Queene. Spenser.
Family/Grove. Goldbarth.
Family History. Bishop.
A Farewell. Fairburn.
Farewell. Kemp.
Farewell and Good. Devlin.
Farewell at the Hour of Parting. Neto.
The Farmer's Curst Wife (A version). Anonymous.
First Love. Olds.
The First Olympionique to Hiero of Syracuse. Pindar.
The First Robin. Leveridge.
The First Song. Burton.
Firstborn (excerpt). Wright.
The Flaming Heart. Crashaw.
The Flea. Donne.
The Flyting o' Life and Daith. Henderson.
The Fog. Coffin.
Folding a Shirt. Levertov.
For a Second Marriage. Merrill.
For Any Beachhead. Joseph.
For February Twelfth. Gessner.
For Kinte. La Grone.
Force. Walcott.
The Forester. Anonymous.
Forgetting God. Harvey.
Form. McHugh.
From Malay. Shapiro.
From Sand Creek (excerpt). Ortiz.
From the Notebooks. Roethke.
Frost-Morning. Alexander.
D.G.C. to J.A. Bronte.
The Garden. Parkwood.

The Gay. Russell.
The Gay Jolly Cowboy Is up with the Sun. Anonymous.
The Ghost. De La Mare.
Ghosts, Places, Stories, Questions. Buckley.
A Gift of God. Anonymous.
Girls. Neruda.
Giving and Forgiving. Springer.
Glauce. De Vere.
The Goat. Saba.
God of the World, Thy Glories Shine. Cutting.
God's Will. Nevin.
God Save Elizabeth! Palgrave.
The Good Man in Hell. Muir.
Good People. Stanton.
The Great Wager. Studdert-Kennedy.
A Greeting. Davies.
Greeting from a Distance. Sahl.
Gull. Smith.
The Hag of Beare. Montague.
The Half-Breed Girl. Scott.
Hamlet in Russia, A Soliloquy. Pasternak.
Happy at 40. Meinke.
Hari, look at me a while. Mira Bai [(or Mirabai)].
Havdolah. Litwack.
Have You Got a Brook. Dickinson.
A Hawthorne Garland: Quick, Sir, the Elixir—"Birthmark." Fogle.
He Lived a Life. Fifer.
He scanned it, staggered, dropped the loop. Dickinson.
He Walks at Peace. Tao Te Ching.
He Would Not Stay for Me. Housman.
Heavenward. Nairne.
Hebe. Lowell.
The Hemingway House in Key West. Schultz.
Here We Were Born. Dos Santos.
The Heritage. Lowell.
The Hermit. Hsu Pen.
Herndon. Mitchell.
Hippolytus. Euripides.
His Life Is Ours. Stroud.
His Sailing from Julia. Herrick.
His Side/Her Side. Skinner.
Holy Spirit, Lead Me. Anonymous.
Homecoming. Szymborska.
Horse. Gluck.
The Horses. Muir.
Horses Graze. Brooks.
The Hour of Magic. Davies.
The House of Pride. Dawson.
House of the Rising Sun. Anonymous.
How Many Nights. Kinnell.
How to Swing Those Obbligatos Around. Fulton.
Hungry China. Cha Liang-cheng.
The Hunter Sees What Is There. Jackson.
Hymn. Key.

Hymn of Joy. Van Dyke.
Hymn to Mary. Zerea Jacob.
A Hymn to My God in a Night of My Late Sicknesse. Wotton.
Hymn to the Holy Cross. Venantius Fortunatus.
A Hymn to the Name and Honour of the Admirable Saint Teresa. Crashaw.
I Am Alone. Bhanot.
I Am Not the Constant Reader. Brownstein.
I Am Sitting Here. Amichai.
I Have a Rendezvous with Life. Cullen.
I Have Been a Forester. Anonymous.
I Heard the Voice of Jesus Say. Bonar.
I Look into the Stars. Draper.
I Love Life. Cassel.
I Love My Life, but Not Too Well. Monroe.
I Never Even Suggested It. Nash.
I Ponder on Life. Ehrmann.
I've Got the World on a String. Koehler.
Icarus. Koopman.
Ice Dragons. Ackerman.
Idea. Drayton.
The Idle Life I Lead. Bridges.
If Chance Assign'd. Wyatt.
If, Jerusalem, I Ever Should Forget Thee. Heine.
If Thou Wilt Mighty Be. Wyatt.
If You Will. Miles.
The Iliad. Homer.
Improvisations: Light and Snow (excerpt). Aiken.
In Blanco County. Fowler.
In Evil Long I Took Delight. Newton.
In Green Old Gardens. "Fane.
In Memoriam A.H.H., XLI. Tennyson.
In Memorium—Leo: A Yellow Cat. Sherwood.
In Memory of Your Body. Shapiro.
In the Heart of Jesus. O Dalaigh.
In the Highlands. Stevenson.
In the House of Idiedaily. Carman.
In the Summer of Sixty. Anonymous.
In Time of Silver Rain. Hughes.
In Time of War. Auden.
Incipit Vita Nova. Payne.
The Incubation. Zolynas.
Indifference. Anonymous.
Indirection. Realf.
The Inevitable. Bolton.
The Inscription. Barker.
The Inward Light. Sutton.
Irish Molly O. Anonymous.
Is Life Worth Living? Austin.
It Is Toward Evening. Anonymous.
It May Be So with Us. Masefield.
Jade Flower Palace. Tu Fu.
Jailhouse Lawyers. Smith.

Jesus a Child His Course Begun. Fuller.
Jesus, I Live to Thee. Harbaugh.
Jesus, My Saviour, Look on Me! MacDuff.
The Jewish Cemetery. Tiempo.
The Jolly Wagoner. Anonymous.
Jonathan. "Rachel" (Rachel Blumstein).
Jonathan Swift Somers. Masters.
Josina, You Are Not Dead. Machel.
Julia's Petticoat. Herrick.
Just after Noon with Fierce Shears. Combs.
Keep Love in Your Life. Clark.
Keno. Wier.
The Key. Oxenham.
Kinchinjunga. Rice.
A King Shall Reign in Righteousness. Streeter.
The Kingdom of God. Trench.
The Knight of Curtesy: The Eaten Heart. Anonymous.
Lachesis. Daley.
Lament of a Man for His Son. Austin.
The Language. Hollo.
Last Quarter. Hollander.
A Last Will and Testament. Winstanley.
Leda. Van Duyn.
Life. Dunbar.
Life and Nature. Lampman.
Life and the Weaver. Dewar.
The Life of St. Cellach: Hail, Fair Morning. Anonymous.
Life on Earth (excerpt). O'Hara.
Life or Death. Dresbach.
Life's Common Things. Allen.
Life's Testament. Baylebridge.
The Life That Counts. "S.
The Lifeboat. Sims.
Lifelines. Hummer.
Like as the bird in the cage enclosed. Wyatt.
Like Those Boats Which Are Returning. Saigyo Hoshi.
Limerick: "A young engine-driver called Hunt." Gray.
Limerick: "There was a young fellow from Fife." Ybarra.
Limerick: "There was an Old Man on some rocks." Lear.
Lincoln. Ditmars.
Lines in Order to Be Slandered. Verlaine.
Lines to a Movement in Mozart's E-Flat Symphony. Hardy.
Lines Written in the Bay of Lerici. Shelley.
Little Sis. Kherdian.
Little Things. Anonymous.
Living. Anonymous.
The Living Chalice. Mitchell.
Lollingdon Downs. Masefield.
Longjaunes His Periplus (excerpt). McCord.

The Lost Angel. Levine.
Lot's Wife. Akhmatova.
Love and Life. Lippmann.
Love and Time. Lloyd.
Love at Large. Patmore.
Lower Court. Baxter.
Lucinda Matlock. Masters.
Madrigal: "Come, sable night." Ward.
Man Is a Weaver. Ibn Ezra.
Mancheser by Night. Blind.
March Hares. Young.
Marie Magdalen's Complaint at Christ's Death. Southwell.
Marriage. Corso.
Mary Hamilton (B version). Anonymous.
Matisse. Hirsch.
Meditation. Salkeld.
The Mermaid (B version). Anonymous.
Message Clear. Morgan.
Middle of the Way. Kinnell.
Middle Passage. Hayden.
The Midnight Court. Merriman.
The Missive. Gosse.
Moments. Schwob.
Moments of Vision. Hardy.
Monna Innominata. Rossetti.
More Than. Fitzpatrick.
Morn. Jackson.
Morning. Ditlevsen.
The Morning Light. Simpson.
The Morning Watch. Vaughan.
Mortality. Devaney.
Mortification. Herbert.
The Mosaic Worker. Peach.
The Mosquito. Jones.
The Most Vital Thing in Life. Kleiser.
The Mother. Ryan.
Musings. Barnes.
My Book of Life. Humphrey.
My Drinking Song. Dehmel.
My Influence. Anonymous.
My Life Like Any Other. Levine.
My Mother's Garden. Allen.
My Name Is Afrika. Kgositsile.
My Portrait. Halpern.
My Prayer. Anonymous.
Mystery. Browning.
Narcissus. Gullans.
Nathan Hale. Partridge.
Nature Notes (excerpt). MacNeice.
Nature's Questioning. Hardy.
The Net-Menders. Vrepont.
New Improved Sonnet XVIII (parody). Titheradge.
New Year Wishes. Sarton.
Next Day. Jarrell.
The Next War. Owen.
The night has a thousand eyes. Bourdillon.
Nightpiece. Turco.
The Ninth of July. Hollander.
No-Man's Land. Knight-Adkin.
The Nobleman's Wedding. Anonymous.
Nobody will open the door for you. Varela.

Northern Boulevard. Denby.
Not in the Guide-Books. Jennings.
The Novel. Levertov.
Now, My Usefulness Over. Honig.
Now That My Father Lies down Beside Me. Plumly.
O Friends! Who Have Accompanied Thus Far. Landor.
O Gracious Father of Mankind. Tweedy.
O, Let Me Kiss––. Gjellerup.
O Lord of Life. Gladden.
O Love, That Wilt Not Let Me Go. Matheson.
O Master Masons. Toller.
Ocean. Jeffers.
Ode. Gilder.
Ode to a Butterfly. Higginson.
Ode to the Alien. Ackerman.
Of a Contented Mind. Vaux.
Of Commerce and Society. Hill.
Oh, Babe, It Ain't No Lie. Cotton.
Oh, My Liver and My Lungs. Anonymous.
Ojibwa War Songs. Anonymous.
Old Damon's Pastoral. Lodge.
The Old Man of Verona. Claudian (Claudius Claudianus).
Omnia Somnia. Watson.
On a Dead Lady. Musset.
On a Ferry Boat. Burton.
On a Whore. Hoskyns.
On Ascending a Hill Leading to a Convent. Mello.
On His Love. Daqiqi.
On Music. Landor.
On the Birth of My Son, Malcolm Coltrane. Lester.
On the Curve-Edge. Evans.
On the Death of Her Mother. Rukeyser.
On the Death of Robert Browning. Swinburne.
On the Meadow. Vala.
On the Universality and Other Attributes of the God of Nature. Freneau.
Once Before. Dodge.
One in Christ. Van Dyke.
One Token. Davies.
The Orient Express. Jarrell.
Orinda to Lucasia. Philips.
Orpheus. Snodgrass.
Other Lives. Hooper.
The Other World. Stowe.
Our Children's Children Will Marvel. Ehrenburg.
An Overture. Knoll.
Oxygen. Swift.
The Paisley Officer. Anonymous.
Panther. Cornish.
Paralytic. Plath.
Part of the 9th Ode of the 4th Book of Horace... Horace.
Passengers. Johnson.
Passing Strange. Bernheimer.
The Pastime of Pleasure. Hawes.
Pastoral. Raab.
Pearl of the White Breast. Anonymous.

The Perfect Life. Richardson.
The Performance. Dickey.
A Personality Sketch: Bill. Davis.
Peter. Moore.
Phantom or Fact. Coleridge.
Philarete Praises Poetry. Wither.
Picture-Show. Sassoon.
The Pier-Glass. Graves.
The Pilgrim. Embury.
The Pilgrims of Hope: Sending to the War. Morris.
The Pillar of Fame. Herrick.
The Place of Pain in the Universe. Hecht.
Pocahontas to her English husband, John Rolfe. Allen.
Poem: "Some are too much at home in the role of wanderer." Levertov.
Poems. Drummond.
The Poet. Clifton.
Poet of Earth. Thayer.
Poetry Is Happiness. Gardiner.
The Point. Jones.
Posthumous. Beers.
Postscript. Hochman.
Prayer. Anonymous.
A Prayer for Every Day. Davies.
Prayer to the Father in Heaven. Skelton.
Prelude. Gibson.
The Princess. Tennyson.
The Princess. Turner.
Privy-Love for my Landlady. Farewell.
Prologue. Symons.
The Prophet. Gibran.
Proverbial Philosophy. Tupper.
Psalm XI. Sidney.
The Punching Clock. Macourek.
Pure Notations. Levine.
The Purification. Cosmas.
Pygmalion. Brockerhoff.
Quand On N'a Pas Ce Que l'on Aime, Il Faut Aimer Ce Que l'on A–. Smith.
The Queen of Paphos, Erycine. Anonymous.
Quick-Falling Dew. Basho (Matsuo Basho).
Quid Sit Futurum Cras Fuge Quaerere. Prior.
The Quiet Hour. Bowman.
Rabbi Yom-Tob of Mayence Petitions His God. Klein.
Rain after a Vaudeville Show. Benét.
Rain Music. Cotter.
The Rainy Day. Longfellow.
Rajpoot Rebels. Lyall.
Rambuncto (parody). Widdemer.
Readings of History. Rich.
Recluse. Camerino.
A Red Glow in the Sky. Blok.
Reference to a Passage in Plutarch's Life of Sulla. Jeffers.
Reflections outside of a Gymnasium. McGinley.
The Remains. Strand.
Remember. Harjo.

Remember, Sinful Youth. Anonymous.
Remembering. Nicoidski.
Report on Experience. Blunden.
Requiem. Lunt
Requiem after Seventeen Years. Ravikovich.
Rescue. Dargan.
Retrospect. Tichborne [(or Tichbourne)].
Reuben and Rachel. Birch.
The Revenant. De la Mare.
Revolutionary Letters. Di Prima.
The Rewards of Farming. Anonymous.
Reynard the Fox (excerpt). Masefield.
Richard Pigott, the Forger (excerpt). McGonagall.
The Ride of Collins Graves. O'Reilly.
The Rise and Fall of Creede. Warman.
Rise with the Lamb of Innocence. Anonymous.
The Rising Sun Blues. Anonymous.
The Ritual of Memories. Gallagher.
The Rival Friends: Have Pity, Grief. Hausted.
Robin Hood's Chase. Anonymous.
Romance of the Cigarette. di Michele.
The Rooftree. Tate.
Rookery. Dauenhauer.
The Room. Harrison.
The Rose of Life. Gongora y Argote.
Roses. Ronsard.
Roses are Beauty, but I Never See. Masefield.
The Royal Way of the Holy Cross. Thomas à Kempis.
The Rubaiyat of Omar Khayyam. Omar Khayyam.
Running Blind. Jones.
Salmon Cycle. Treinin.
Samuel Hoar. Sanborn.
Satires of Circumstance. Hardy.
Satisfied. Mason.
Savage Portraits. Marquis.
The Seed Growing Secretly. Vaughan.
The Sense of Death. Hoyt.
Seventh Eclogue. Radnoti.
Shadow-Evidence. Dodge.
Shaman. Inman.
Share-Croppers. Hughes.
She, to Him. Hardy.
She Took the Dappled Partridge Fleckt with Blood. Tennyson.
The Shock. Eigner.
A Shot in the Park. Plomer.
The Sick Rose. Blake.
Signum Cui Contradicetur. Mary Angelita.
Silence. Morse.
Silent Testimony. Parmenter.
Silex Scintillans. Vaughan.
The Silk Merchant's Daughter (II). Anonymous.
Simplicity Aims Circularly. Walters.
Since We Loved. Bridges.

The Sinew of Our Dreams.
Jackson.
The Slaughter-House. Hayes.
The Slaughter of Grendel by
Beowulf. *Anonymous.*
The Slave Auction. Harper.
Smile, Death. Mew.
So Long Solon. Myers.
So unwarely was never no
man caught. Wyatt.
A Solemn Meditation.
Shenstone.
Song for the Dead, III.
Anonymous.
Song: "If love were but a little
thing." Coates.
The Song of Hungarrda.
Ngunaitponi.
A Song of Living. Burr.
The Song of the Woman-
Drawer. Gilmore.
Song, on Reading That the
Cyclotron has Produced
Cosmic Rays...
Hoffenstein.
Song: "When I lie burning in
thine eye." Stanley.
A Sonnet. Lear.
Sonnet: "O shady vales, O fair
enriched meads." Lodge.
Sonnet: Of Love in Men and
Devils. Angiolieri.
Sonnet: You Were Born; Must
Die. Spender.
Sonnets, XVIII: "Shall I
compare thee to a summer's
day?" Shakespeare.
Sonnets for a Dying Man.
Singer.
Sonnets from China (excerpt).
Auden.
Sonnets from the Portuguese,
XLI. Browning.
The Sons of Our Sons.
Ehrenburg.
The Soul. *Anonymous.*
A Soul's Soliloquy. Abbott.
Spring. Hogan.
A Spring Day on Campus.
Schedler.
Spring Snow and Tui.
Bethell.
Squall. Moss.
Stanzas for Music. Byron.
Starlight Like Intuition
Pierced the Twelve.
Schwartz.
The State of Innocence.
Dryden.
Stigmata. Lane.
Still. Meriluoto.
Still, O LORD, for Thee I
Tarry. Wesley.
The Stockyard. Squire.
The Strong City. Noyes.
Submission in Affliction.
Anonymous.
Success Story. Winch.
The Succession. Mace.
A Suite for Marriage.
Ignatow.
The Sum of All Known
Reverence. Whitman.
Summer. Marshall.
Summer Magic. Hill.
Summer Sabbath. Sampter.
Summer Visitors. Clark.
The Sunflower to the Sun.
Stebbins
Surgeons Must Be Very
Careful. Dickinson.
The Suttee. Skinner.

Sweet Unsure. Ralegh.
Sylvius, your hands near my
mouth are heady flowers.
Burnat-Provins.
Symphony. Horne.
Table Graces, or Prayers for
Adults: Evening Meal.
Anonymous.
Tallahassee (excerpt).
Merkel.
Tally. Miles.
The Task. Campbell.
The Tempest. Shakespeare.
Tenth Elegy. Elegy in Joy.
Rukeyser.
A Terrible Thought.
Steinbarg.
The Test. Tabb.
Testament. Holmes.
The Testament of Beauty.
Bridges.
Thanksgiving. Morgan.
Thanksliving. Piety.
That Time That Mirth Did
Steer My Ship. Wyatt.
That Which You Call "Love
Me." Rosales.
There Is No Death.
McCreery.
Theresienstadt Poem.
Mezey.
Things Going out of My Life.
Adamson.
Think Naught a Trifle.
Anonymous.
Thirty Childbirths. Brand.
This Hour. La Grone.
This Lime-Tree Bower My
Prison. Coleridge.
This Shirt. Trias.
Thou Art the Way. Doane.
Thou Sleepest Fast.
Anonymous.
Three Score and Ten.
Anonymous.
Three Women. Plath.
Thus Spoke My Love.
Hooft.
Time Will Not Grant.
Keyes.
The Tired Petitioner (excerpt).
Wither.
To —. Shelley.
To a Child Trapped in a
Barber Shop. Levine.
To a Musician. Austin.
To America, on Her First
Sons Fallen in the Great
War. Walker.
To Cordelia. Stansbury.
To Graecinus, on Loving Two
Women at Once. Ovid
(Publius Ovidius Naso).
To His Book. Herrick.
To His Ever-Loving God.
Herrick.
To His Muse. Breton.
To His Ring, Given to His
Lady. Turberville.
To Mrs. M. B. on Her Birth-
day. Pope.
To My Dog Blanco.
Holland.
To One. Munch-Petersen.
To Sir Robert Wroth.
Jonson.
To the Departing Spirit of an
Alienated Friend. Seward.
To the Father of the Bride.
Tasso.
To the Modern Man.
Wheelock.

To the Reverend Shade of His
Religious Father. Herrick.
To Think of Time.
Whitman.
A Tombless Epitaph.
Coleridge.
Too soon, too soon comes
Death to show. Patmore.
Travelling Song. McGrath.
The Tree of Life is Also a
Tree of Fire. Norvig.
A Triad. Rossetti.
Troia Fuit. Kauffman.
Trust and Obedience.
Anonymous.
Truth. Cowper.
Truth. Lloyd.
The Twenty-Fifth Year of His
Life. Cavafy.
Two Drinking Songs. Tao
Yuan-Ming.
The Two Mysteries. Dodge.
The Two Wives. Howells.
Unchanging Jesus. Spitta.
Uncle Jack. Kherdian.
The Unremarkable Year.
Fuller.
Untitled Poem. "In the 2
A.M. Club, a working
man's bar." Peterson.
Upon a Second Marriage.
Merrill.
Upon Julia's Petticoat.
Herrick.
Upon the Author's First
Seven Years' Service.
Tusser.
Upon the Image of Death.
Southwell.
An Urban Convalescence.
Merrill.
Vanity (I). Herbert.
A Vision of Judgement.
Southey.
Visit. Outlaw.
La Vita Nuova. Dante
Alighieri.
Vita Nuova. Kunitz.
Voice. Padgett.
Voyager's Song. Wood.
Vulture. Jeffers.
The Wail of Prometheus
Bound. Aeschylus.
Waiting and Peeking. Lang.
Walking Home at Night.
Weissbort.
The Walking Tour. Auden.
Waterfall. Welsh.
The Way, the Truth, and the
Life. Parker.
The Way; The Truth; The
Life. Porter.
We Who Are About to Die.
Fey.
Wedding Anniversary.
Bruner.
Well, World, You Have Kept
Faith with Me. Hardy.
What death is worse than
this." Wyatt.
What is Life? Coleridge.
What Is the Case in Point?
Reisen.
When before those eyes, my
life and light. Stampa.
When I Was Still a Child.
Harford.
The Whirlpool. *Anonymous.*
White Fox. Shepard.
White Magic: An Ode.
Braithwaite.

Whitebeard on Videotape.
Merrill.
Who Loves the Rain. Shaw.
Whoso Would See This Song
of Heavenly Choice.
Wilson.
Why Log Truck Drivers Rise
Earlier Than Students of
Zen. Snyder.
Why Should Vain Mortals
Tremble. Niles.
Wide Walls. *Anonymous.*
Widow. Pollak.
A Widow's Hymn. Wither.
Will ye see what wonders love
hath wrought? Wyatt.
Will You, One Day. Ramie.
Wine. Lebensohn.
The Winter's Walk.
Johnson.
A Wish for the New Year.
Brooks.
Wishes. Child.
With Thee to Soar to the
Skies. *Anonymous.*
Words. Plath.
Words to My Friend.
Vivien.
A Working Party. Sassoon.
Works and Days. Hesiod.
Worried Life Blues.
Anonymous.
Would I Were Chang'd into
That Golden Shower.
Gorges.
Written in Butler's Sermons.
Arnold.
You Growing. Acorn.
Young Washington.
Guiterman.
Your Fair Looks Inflame My
Desire. Campion.

Lifetime
The Big Nasturtiums. Hale.
The Cannibal Hymn.
Anonymous.
The Coward. Spender.
David's Song. Browning.
The Death of an Old Man.
Hamburger.
"For Whom the Bell Tolls".
Ewart.
Go Down, Old Hannah.
Anonymous.
In the Redwood Forest.
Pomeroy.
Leaving Home. Cochrane.
Ol' Hannah. Reese.
Vive Noir! Evans.

Lift (ed) (ing) (s)
Ascension. Devlin.
The Cat and the Moon.
Yeats.
The Crane. Tomlinson.
The Day's March. Nichols.
Died. Browning.
Egyptian Hieroglyphics.
Anonymous.
The Eleventh Commandment
(excerpt). Holmes.
The Enchanted Knight.
Muir.
The End of the World.
Bottomley.
Epigram: "Why should
scribblers discompose."
Landor.
Evening in Paradise. Milton.
Farm Gate. Krige.
The Father's Gold.
Anonymous.

For Everything Give Thanks.
  Tupper.
For Simone Weil. Sister M.
  Therese.
I Have Heard. *Anonymous.*
I Hear That Andromeda.
  Sappho.
In Memoriam. Longley.
Missing. Pudney.
Mole Talk. Kennedy.
My Creed. Walter.
O Thou Whose Gracious
  Presence Shone. Ham.
On a Visit to Ch'ung Chen
  Taoist Temple... Yu
  Hsuan-chi.
Plea For Tolerance. Bruner.
Reading Walt Whitman.
  Forbes.
A Reliable Service. Curnow.
The Serious Merriment of
  Women. Goedicke.
Song: Lift Boy. Graves.
The Summer Days Are Come
  Again. Longfellow.
To W. C. W. M. D.
  Kreymborg.
Winter Apples. Welles.

Light (s)

Africland. La Grone.
After-Song. Gilder.
After the Second Operation.
  Goedicke.
After They Have Tired of the
  Brilliance of Cities.
  Spender.
Ah! Give Me, LORD, the
  Single Eye. Toplady.
Airwaves. Woessner.
Alba: March. Hacker.
Albert Sidney Johnston.
  Ticknor.
The Alchemist. Kelly.
Alone. Shelton.
Alone in an Inn at
  Southampton, April the
  25th, 1737. Hill.
Always, from My First
  Boyhood. Bishop.
Aminta: Chorus I. Tasso.
Among the Ferns.
  Carpenter.
Amoretti, VII. Spenser.
Amoretti, IX. Spenser.
Amoretti, LXVI. Spenser.
Anatole France at Eighty.
  Oaks.
The Angel in the House.
  Patmore.
The Annunciation. Tabb.
Another for the Briar Rose.
  Morris.
Another Night with
  Telescope. Cohen.
Apologia. Swinburne.
April. Belleau.
Ark of the Covenant.
  Nicholl.
Arrival. Wain.
Arriving. Halpern.
As One Who Wanders Into
  Old Workings. Day-Lewis.
Assisi. Noyes.
Astrophel and Stella, XCIX.
  Sidney.
At Camino. Sheehan.
At Swindon. Brett.
At the Museum of Modern
  Art. Swenson.
At the San Francisco Airport.
  Winters.

At the Tomb of Rachel.
  Yehoash.
Atlantis. Auden.
Aubade. Laing.
Aubade. Sitwell.
Baha'u'llah in the Garden of
  Ridwan. Hayden.
The Balcony Poems. Smith.
Ballad of the Flood. Muir.
The Barn. Coatsworth.
The Battle of Lookout
  Mountain. Boker.
Be Still. Kline.
Beach Talk. MacCaig.
Beautiful Woman. Zieroth.
A Beautifull Mistress.
  Carew.
Beethoven's Death Mask.
  Spender.
Besse Bunting. *Anonymous.*
Beyond. Kimball.
The Big Sunflower.
  Newcomb.
Birdwatchers of America.
  Hecht.
A Birthday Poem: for Rachel.
  Simmons.
The Blessed Virgin Mary
  Compared to a Window.
  Merton.
Blindness. Agustini.
Borges. Barnstone.
The Boss's Wife.
  Anonymous.
Boy at the Window. Wilbur.
A Brave-Hearted Maid.
  Anonymous.
Breton Afternoon. Dowson.
Bridge. Ammons.
A Brief Elegie on My Dear
  Son John the Second of
  That Name of Mine.
  Saffin.
The Brook in February.
  Roberts.
Burn out Burn Quick.
  Reisen.
Bus Stop. Justice.
Business as Usual. Vinz.
Buster Keaton. McFee.
But Perhaps. Sachs.
By Moonlight. *Anonymous.*
By the North Sea.
  Swinburne.
Cadaver Politic. Paulin.
The Camera Obscura.
  Symonds.
Canticle. McClure.
Canticle of Darkness.
  Watson.
Cathemerinon: O Noble
  Virgin. Prudentius
  (Aurelius Clemens
  Prudentius).
A Celebration. Sarton.
Chanticleer. Tynan.
The Chanting Cherubs - A
  Group by Greenough.
  Dana.
Charade. Praed.
Chinese Baby Asleep.
  Donnelly.
Chirstographia 35. Warren.
The Chorus Speaks Her
  Words as She Dances.
  Gregg.
Christ and Satan:
  Lamentations of the Fallen
  Angels. *Anonymous.*
Christ in You. *Anonymous.*
The Christians Reply to the
  Phylosopher. Davenant.

A Christmas Package: No. 7
  (excerpt). McCord.
City: San Francisco. Hughes.
The Coal Mine Disaster's Last
  Trapped Man Contemplates
  Salvation. Meissner.
The Cold. Simic.
Come Back. Clough.
Come, O Come. Campion.
Come Turn to Mee, Thou
  Pretty Little One.
  Anonymous.
Commemoration Ode.
  Monroe.
Complaint That His Ladie
  after She Knew of His Love
  Kept Her Face... Surrey.
Conquistador. MacLeish.
Country Club Sunday.
  McGinley.
Country Singer. Nordhaus.
The Cowboy's Life.
  Anonymous.
The Cradle. Robinson.
Credo. Robinson.
A Cry for Light.
  Anonymous.
Curiosity: Fiction. Sprague.
Custer. Stedman.
Daguerreotype Taken in Old
  Age. Atwood.
Dance & Eye Me (Wicked)ly
  My Breath a Fixed Sphere.
  Owens.
A Dancer's Life. Justice.
Dare You See a Soul at the
  White Heat? Dickinson.
Darius Green and his Flying-
  Machine. Trowbridge.
The Darkness. Johnson.
Dawn-Song to Waken the
  Lovers. *Anonymous.*
The Dawning of the Day.
  Anonymous.
Day of Atonement. Myers.
The Day of Judgement.
  Young.
The Day of Judgment.
  Buchanan.
The Death of a Cat (excerpt).
  MacNeice.
The Death of Professor
  Backwards. Kennedy.
A Deserted Barn. Woiwode.
Desire. Traherne.
Dew Sat on Julia's Hair.
  Herrick.
Diana. Constable.
Dieppe. Beckett.
Dino Campana and the Bear.
  Hirsch.
Diretro al Sol. Bell.
Do Not Go Gentle Into That
  Good Night. Thomas.
Do Not Go Gentle (parody).
  Hopkins.
Donald. Abbey.
Dont Worry Yr Hair.
  Bissett.
The Dragon of Red Lights.
  Swickard.
The Dragonfly. Nemerov.
The Dream of Dakiki.
  Firdausi.
Dream the Great Dream.
  Coates.
The Duck Pond at Mini's
  Pasture, a Dozen Years
  Later. Dow.
Dutch Interior. Sarton.
Duty. Hooper.
El Greco. Mayo.

Elegy in Six Sonnets.
  Tuckerman.
Emily Sparks. Masters.
Encounter. Krige.
The Enthusiast. Melville.
Epigram: Invocation.
  Nemerov.
Epigram: "Like when the
  burning sun doth rise."
  Strato.
Epigram: "Loss of our
  learning brought darkness,
  weakenss and woe."
  Anonymous.
Erev Shabbos. Kaminsky.
Escape and Return.
  Jennings.
Europe. Ashbery.
The European Night.
  Vinaver.
Evening Landscape. Mont.
The Evening Star.
  Longfellow.
Evening Star. Poe.
Evening Twilight.
  Baudelaire.
Evening Walk. Akesson.
Eveningsong 1. Wilson.
Eveningsong 2. Wilson.
The Faerie Queene. Spenser.
Family/Grove. Goldbarth.
The Famous Light Brigade.
  Anonymous.
Farewell and Good. Devlin.
Farolita. Berssenbrugge.
February Margins.
  Henderson.
The Field. Huddle.
A Field Poem. Valaitis.
Filling Station. Morin.
Fiorentina. Myers.
First Days. Ruebner.
First Three Verses of an Ode
  to Cary and Morison.
  Jonson.
The First Wedding in the
  World. Rosenberg.
First Winter. Harada.
The Fishers. Pitter.
The Flower Vendor.
  Cabalquinto.
The Flying Fish. Cope.
For a Young South Dakota
  Man. Manfred.
For Annie. Poe.
For Freckle-Faced Gerald.
  Knight.
For He Had Great
  Possessions. Middleton.
For Her. Strand.
For the Children. Snyder.
For the Yiddish Singers in the
  Lakewood Hotels of My
  Childhood. Shapiro.
For Tu Fu. Feng Chih.
Formerly a Slave. Melville.
Four for Sir John Davies.
  Roethke.
Friendship in Perfection.
  Ramsay.
Frolic. Russell.
From. Paulin.
From Bethlehem to Calvary.
  Nicholson.
From the Head. Zukofsky.
From the Notebooks.
  Roethke.
The Frozen Hero. Vance.
Funeral Poem. Jones.
Gallantly within the Ring.
  Reynolds.
The Garden Seat. Hardy.

The Gateway. Hope.
Genesis. Hill.
Getting Up Ahead of
  Someone (Sun). O'Hara.
Getting Up Early. Bly.
The Gifts. Levendosky.
Girandole. Donnelly.
The Girl Writing Her English
  Paper. Wallace.
Give Our Conscience Light.
  Carter.
The Glow-Worm. Shanks.
God and the Soul. Spalding.
The Good Beasts.
  Barnstone.
Good Friday. *Anonymous.*
The Great Lakes Suite.
  Reaney.
The Green Leaf. Zukofsky.
Grey Galloway. Cairncross.
The Grief. Rilke.
The Gutter. Fortini.
Haemorrhage. Fiacc.
Hagar. Adams.
Hall of Ocean Life.
  Hollander.
Hands. Cloud.
Hard Country. Booth.
The Harrowing of Hell.
  Langland.
The Harvest. Aberg.
Having No Ear. Davie.
He Gives His Beloved Certain
  Rhymes. Yeats.
He Maketh Himself One with
  the God Ra. Book of the
  Dead.
He Wore a Crown of Thorns.
  Mortenson.
Hear the Bird of Day.
  Campbell.
Heav'n Boun' Soldier.
  Anonymous.
Heaven's Magnificence.
  Muhlenberg.
Heavenward. Nairne.
The Heir of Linne.
  Anonymous.
Her Going. Kaufman.
Here are fine gifts, children.
  Sappho.
Hermann Ludwig Ferdinand
  von Helmholtz. Meinke.
Holy Innocents. Rossetti.
The Holy Star. Bryant.
Honour. Cowley.
Hope. Carmichael.
Hope's Song. Carlin.
A Horror Story Written for
  the Cover of a Matchbook.
  Wachtel.
The Hotel. Monroe.
The Hounds. Dickinson.
How Night Falls in the
  Courtyard. Rimmer.
The Human Fold. Muir.
Hut Window. Celan.
Hymen: Never More Will the
  Wind. Doolittle.
Hymn. Holmes.
Hymn for Christmas.
  Hemans.
An Hymn on the
  Omnipresence. Byrom.
Hymn to Darkness. Norris.
I am a little church (no great
  cathedral). Cummings.
I Am a Negro. Al-Fituri.
I Believe. Lawrence.
I Bring to You as Offering
  Tonight. Verhaeren.

I Don't Know if Mount Zion.
  Kovner.
I Heard the Voice of Jesus
  Say. Bonar.
"I never saw you, madam, lay
  apart." Surrey.
I Only Am Escaped Alone to
  Tell Thee. Nemerov.
I Pass a Lighted Window.
  Wood.
Icarus. *Anonymous.*
Icons. Waddington.
If Mr. H.W. Longfellow Had
  Written Miss Millay's.
  Adams.
If Thou Wert by My Side, My
  Love. Heber.
An Image from Beckett.
  Mahon.
In a Grave-Yard.
  Braithwaite.
In Dear Detail, by Ideal
  Light. Stafford.
In Dispraise of the Moon.
  Coleridge.
In Memoriam A.H.H.,
  XLVII. Tennyson.
In Memoriam A.H.H., LXII.
  Tennyson.
In Memoriam A.H.H., XCI.
  Tennyson.
In Memorium. Alcott.
In the Beginning. Thomas.
In the Dark. Arnold.
In the Discreet Splendor.
  Strauss.
In the Grass. Garland.
In the Old City. Amichai.
In This City. Brownjohn.
Incandescence. Clifton.
The Incomparable Light.
  Eberhart.
The Indian upon God.
  Yeats.
The Initiate. Merwin.
Insects. Schneider.
The Insusceptibles. Rich.
A Is for Alpha: Alpha Is for
  A. Aiken.
Is It the Morning? Is It the
  Little Morning? Schwartz.
Isabel. Dobell.
It Rains. Thomas.
It Was the Worm.
  Broughton.
Ivy Crest. *Anonymous.*
A Japanese Birthday Wish.
  Swann.
Jogging at Dusk.
  Grossbardt.
John Clare. Anderson.
John Donne's Defiance.
  Hervey.
Jottings of New York.
  McGonagall.
Judas Iscariot. Martin.
Kinneret. Herzberg.
Lalla Rookh. Moore.
Lament for Barney Flanagan.
  Baxter.
The Land of Dreams. Blake.
Laocoon. Gordon.
Last Words. Merrill.
Late Afternoon. Sullam.
Let the Light Enter. Harper.
The Light of Bethlehem.
  Tabb.
The Light of Stars. Furness.
Light's Glittering Morn.
  Neale.
The Lilies. Berry.

Limerick: "Q is a quoter
  who'll cite." Herford.
Lincoln. Turner.
Lines from Catullus. Ralegh.
The Little Red Sled. Bush.
Living in the World. Lau.
Love Poem. Edmond.
Love Poem–1940.
  Hershenson.
Love You Alone Have Been
  with Us. Rumi.
Lovelight. Johnson.
Loving. Kaufman.
Mad Song. Blake.
Madrigal: "Dear, when I did
  from you remove."
  Herbert of Cherbury.
Madrigal: "Why dost thou
  haste away." Sidney.
Mailed to G. B. Derwood.
Make Way! Comfort.
The Master Singers.
  Carpenter.
The Medusa. Davenport.
The Meeting. Hollis.
Memorial Poem. Glatstein.
Microcosmus. Nashe [(or
  Nash(] Thomas.
The Midnight Court.
  Merriman.
Midnight Special.
  Anonymous.
Midnight Special. Patchen.
The Milky Way. Anderson.
Milton. Mifflin.
Mingus. Kaufman.
The Minotaur. Gibb.
Moon Blast. Roberts.
Moon's Ending. Teasdale.
Moonlight on Lake
  Sydenham. MacDonald.
Moonrise. Sherman.
A Morning Hymn.
  Beaumont.
Morning Hymn of Adam and
  Eve. Milton.
The Morning Light.
  Simpson.
Morning Star, O Cheering
  Sight! *Anonymous.*
Mother Earth: Her Whales.
  Snyder.
Motor Cars. Bennett.
Mrs. Applebaum's Sunday
  Dance Class. Schultz.
Music of Colours: the
  Blossom Scattered.
  Watkins.
My Love Sways, Dancing.
  Ibn Ezra.
The Nativity. Vaughan.
The Nature of Love.
  Kirkup.
The New-Come Chief.
  Lowell.
Night. Sutu.
The night has a thousand
  eyes. Bourdillon.
Night Plane. Frost.
Nightfall. Olson.
Nightflight and Sunrise.
  Dutton.
Nightwood. Smith.
No More Destructive Flame.
  Connolly.
Now the People Have the
  Light. Ballard.
O Day of God, Draw Nigh.
  Scott.
Obedience. Macdonald.
October Morning. Piatt.
Ode. Gilder.

Ode to Duty. Wordsworth.
Ode: "Without the evening
  dew and showers."
  Cotton.
Ode Written at Vale-Royal
  Abbey in Cheshire.
  Warton, Jr..
An Officers' Prison Camp
  Seen from a Troop-Train.
  Jarrell.
Oft, in the Stilly Night.
  Moore.
Oh! To Have A Birthday.
  Lenski.
Old Balaam. *Anonymous.*
Old Couple. Simic.
Old Indian Trick. Green.
Old Ships. Morton.
Olney Hymns: The Happy
  Change. Cowper.
On a Picture of Your House.
  Jones.
On a Poet. Parrot.
On Archaeanassa. Plato.
On His Late Espoused Saint.
  Digby.
On Roofs of Terry Street.
  Dunn.
On the Slope of the Desolate
  River. Tagore.
Once by the Pacific. Frost.
Once More. Jonas.
The Only Name Given Under
  Heaven. Steele.
Othello. Shakespeare.
Our Birth Is but a Sleep and a
  Forgetting. Wordsworth.
Out of the Darkness.
  Armstrong.
The Owl and the Pussy-Cat.
  Lear.
The Painter Dreaming in the
  Scholar's House.
  Nemerov.
Pangur Ban. *Anonymous.*
Parting. Massey.
Passages. Walker.
The Pastime of Pleasure.
  Hawes.
Peppergrass. Plumly.
Per Pacem ad Lucem.
  Procter.
The Phi Beta Kappa Poem.
  Lattimore.
Philosophy. Bangs.
The Pilot's Day of Rest.
  Gerlach.
Places of Nestling Green.
  Hunt.
Poem for a Neighbor.
  Francis.
Poem for Hemingway & W.
  C. Williams. Carver.
Poem for J. Berry.
Poem for My Grandfather.
  Jacobs.
Poem to Be Read at 3 a.m.
  Justice.
Poems for the New. Fraser.
The Porpoise. Pape.
Powwow 79, Durango.
  Allen.
Pray! Arnold.
A Prayer. Lampman.
Prayer. Roethke.
Prayer before Sleep. Lucas.
Prayer for Light. Coblentz.
Precursors. MacNeice.
Press Onward. *Anonymous.*
The Prince of Peace.
  Bickersteth.
Prisms (Altea). Dacey.

Private. Wormser.
Professor Kelleher and the Charles River. O'Grady.
The Project. Orr.
Prophecy. Pulci.
Psalm. Hooper.
Psalm. Yehoash.
Psalm CXXXIX. Pembroke.
Psalms, CXLVII. Smart.
The Pysidanthera. Bristol.
Pythagoras. Jones, Jr.
Queen Mab. Shelley.
The Queen of Fairies. *Anonymous.*
Questing. Spencer.
Rain in the Desert. Fletcher.
Red Clay. Hogan.
Reports of Midsummer Girls. Lattimore.
Rest. Segal.
Resurrection. Kaschnitz.
Rise, Happy Morn. Tennyson.
The River. Jones.
Rules and Lessons. Vaughan.
Sadness and Still Life. Ramke.
Saint Coyote. Hogan.
Salutation. Russell.
San Francisco. Austin.
Science for the Young. Irwin.
Sea Lullaby. Wylie.
The Seed-Picture. McGuckian.
The Sensitive Plant. Shelley.
The Sentry. Owen.
September. Huxley.
Seventh Day. Raine.
Shadow. Bruce.
The Shadow of Night. Chapman.
The Shadows. Macdonald.
She lay as if at play. Dickinson.
She Wandered after Strange Gods... Benet.
Shore. Garrigue.
Signatures. Hoffman.
Silex Scintillans. Vaughan.
Sin, Despair, and Lucifer. Fletcher.
A Sitch Cut in April. Dyment.
Slowly, By God's Hand Unfurled. Furness.
The Snow Light. Sarton.
So, We'll Go No More a Roving. Byron.
Some Frenchmen. Updike.
Song for the Sun That Disappeared Behind the Rainclouds. *Anonymous.*
Song of Cradle-Making. Skinner.
The Song of the Bower. Rossetti.
Song: "Something calls and whispers, along the city street." King.
Song: "There's one great bunch of stars in heaven." Marzials.
Songs for the Four Parts of the Night. Owl Woman.
Sonnet: "As when, to one who long hath watched, the morn." Bampfylde.
Sonnet: "O little self, within whose smallness lies." Masefield.

Sonnets, I: "The rough green wealth of wheaten fields that sway." Irwin.
Sonnets, VI: "Awakened, I behold through dewy leaves." Irwin.
A Soul. Rossetti.
Soul-Light. Rossetti.
The Spirit-Land. Very.
The Spirit's Light. Cowper.
Splendor. Shalom.
Spring-Joy Praising God. Praise of the Sun. Greiffenberg.
Spring Song in the City. Buchanan.
Spring Thoughts Sent to Tzuan. Yu Hsuan-chi.
St. Peter's Shadow. Crashaw.
Stanzas–April, 1814. Shelley.
The Star. Weaving.
Star Song. Johnson.
Suilven and the Eagle (excerpt). Bottomley.
Summer. Wilson.
The Summer Countries. Rago.
Summer Garden. Akhmatova.
The Sun Men Call It. Wheelock.
Suppose This Moment Some Stupendous Question. Nowlan.
Swans Mating. Longley.
Sweet Innisfallen. Moore.
The Swerve. Stafford.
Tale of Genji. Seidman.
Talking Myself to Sleep in the Mountains. Ruark.
Tecumseh. Mair.
Ten Sonnets for Today. Stanway.
Terence MacSwiney. Russell.
Terminal. Shapiro.
There Is. Simpson.
There Is No Opera Like "Lohengrin." Wheelwright.
This Feast of the Law. *Anonymous.*
This New Day. Read.
A Thousand Years Have Come. Lynch.
Three Darks Come down Together. Francis.
The Three Kings. Dario.
Three Poems on Morris Graves' Paintings. Logan.
Three Shades of Light on the Windowsill. Griffin.
Through All Your Abstract Reasoning. Patten.
Time in the Sun. Nicholl.
To–-. Morse.
To a Photograph. Tabb.
To a Woman Who Wants Darkness and Time. Barrax.
To Felicity Who Calls Me Mary. Chesterton.
To G.R. Cottam.
To His Father on Praising the Honest Life of the Peasant. E'tesami.
To Lucasta, from Prison. Lovelace.
To Mary. Shelley.
To My Cousin, (C.R.) Marrying My Lady (A.). Carew.

To My Friend. Thompson.
To My Son. *Anonymous.*
To Prote. Simmias.
To the Elephants. Alterman.
To the Mocking-Bird. Pike
To the Postmaster General. Redgrove.
To the Rosella in the Poinsettia Tree. Picot.
To the Unknown Light. Shanks.
To Thee, Eternal Soul, Be Praise. Gilder.
To Wordsworth. Landor.
Tony Get the Boys. Graham.
Too Solemn for Day, Too Sweet for Night. Walker.
The Torch. Forker.
The Total Influence or Outcome of the Matter: THE SUN. Piercy.
Towering O'er the Wrecks of Time. Bowring.
Tragic Love. Turner.
Transformed. Gates.
Try the Uplook. *Anonymous.*
Two Sonnets for a Lost Love. DeWitt.
Tyranny of Moths. Vizenor.
The Unknown Eros. Patmore.
The Unwilling Gypsy. Johnson.
Upon Himself. Herrick.
Vancouver Lights. Birney.
Variation on a Line by Emerson. Merwin.
Vespers. Mitchell.
"Vierge Ouvrante." Palmer.
A View of Montreal (excerpt). Webb.
Viewpoint. Scarbrough.
The Vineyard. Merwin.
The Vision of Piers Plowman. Langland.
The Voice from Galilee. Bonar.
Voice of the Western Wind. Stedman.
Waiting for the Fire. Appleman.
Walking in the Light. Barton.
Walking with God. Cowper.
Waltz. Reich.
Ward Two. Webb.
The Washer-Woman. Bohanan.
Washington. O'Crowley.
The Watcher. Hale.
Water. Larkin.
The Way, the Truth, and the Life. Parker.
We Carry Eggshells. Michaelis.
What Good Poems Are For. Wayman.
What Must (iii). MacLeish.
What the Birds Said. Whittier.
What Was Solomon's Mind? Scott.
When I Came to Israel. Meyers.
When I Want to Speak. Kook.
When the Light Falls. Kunitz.
When the Tree Bares. Aiken.

Where the Slow Fig's Purple Sloth. Warren.
The White City. Gilder.
Who Is It Talks of Ebony? Ghose.
Why I Can't Write My Autobiography. Kamenetz.
Why So Many of Them Die. Wallbank.
The Widow. Ludvigson.
Winter. Akhmadulina.
Winter Sketches. Reznikoff.
Wise Owl. Goedicke.
The Woman's Dream. Horovitz.
Wonders. Kaufman.
The World. Creeley.
A World without Objects Is a Sensible Emptiness. Wilbur.
Written in a Copy of Swift's Poems, for Wayne Burns. Wright.
The Yankee Man-of-War or The Stately Southerner. *Anonymous.*
The Yorkshire Moors. Summers.
The Zodiac, X. Dickey.
A Zong. Barnes.

Lighter
Epitaph on a Well-Known Poet. Moore.
Father and Mother. Kennedy.
Less Lonely. Kreymborg.
My Olson Elegy. Feldman.
Poverty. Theognis.
To Robert Lowell and Osip Mandelstam. Seidel.

Lighthouse
Down by the Station, Early in the Morning. Ashbery.
Epitaph for a Lighthouse-Keeper's Horse. Morton.
I'd Like to Be a Lighthouse. Field.
Six Ten Sixty-Nine. Conyus.

Lightly
A Backwoods Hero (excerpt). McLachlan.
Chamber Music. Joyce.
Goethe and Frederika. Sidgwick.

Lightning (s)
The Ballot. Pierpont.
Before the Storm. Dehmel.
Black Lightning. Sze.
Chloris and Hilas. Made to a Saraban. Waller.
The Cloud-Messenger. Kalidasa.
The Dancer. Campbell.
Dawn Hippo. Clouts.
The Elm's Home. Heyen.
Ethan Boldt. Weingarten.
Flushing Meadows, 1939. Hoffman.
From Life. Eichenrand.
Glanmore Sonnets. Heaney.
If Love's a Yoke. Berry.
Invocation. Stafford.
Is It the Morning? Is It the Little Morning? Schwartz.
Late Spring. Gill.
Lightning. Lawrence.
The Lost History Plays: Savanarola (parody). Beerbohm.
Magic Lantern. Stafford.
Old Ironsides. Holmes.

On the Death of Benjamin
Franklin. Freneau.
On the Unusual Cold and
Rainie Weather in the
Summer, 1648. Heath.
The Painted Hills of Arizona.
Curran.
Paradox. Miller.
The Postilion Has Been
Struck by Lightning. Beer.
The Progress of Poesy.
Gray.
Simaetha. Doolittle.
The Skeleton of the Future.
""MacDiarmid.
Sonnets. Lee.
Sooner or Later. Digby.
To Forget Me. Weiss.
The Usk. Sisson.
Utah. Stevenson.
When I Am Dead. Neihardt.
Without the Herdsman.
Diotimus.

Like (d) (s)
Affection and Desire.
Ralegh.
As an Old Mercer. Fisher.
Beside a Fall. Garrigue.
The Clown. Rose.
Elementary. Tollerud.
The Evening Primrose.
Parker.
First Impressions. Walton.
Folks and Me. Crites.
Fury against the Moslems at
Uhud. Hind bint Utba.
Hence These Rimes. Taylor.
I Have a Place. De Young.
I Love Little Willie.
Anonymous.
I've Been to a Marvellous
Party. Coward.
John Quincy Adams
1767-1848. Benét.
King Pippin. Anonymous.
The Lover Sheweth How He
Is Forsaken of Such as He
Sometime Enjoyed. Wyatt.
Me and Samantha. Johnson,
Jr.
The Melting Pot. Randall.
Menodotis. Leonidas of
Alexandria.
Mr. Minnitt. Fyleman.
My Wishes. Healy.
Never Love. Campion.
On My First Son. Jonson.
Once Upon a Time. Okara.
Our Bow's Bended.
Anonymous.
Patriotism. Scott.
Poem for Flora. Giovanni.
Polarities. Slessor.
A Reunion. Schuyler.
Sonnet: He Will Not Be Too
Deeply in Love.
Angiolieri.
Summer Sky. Gordon.
Tennis Pro. Dessner.
Thomas Jefferson. Benét.
Thoughts at the Museum.
Brennan.
To Cloris. Sedley.
To the Most Fair and Lovely
Mistris, Anne Soame, Now
Lady Abdie. Herrick.
Verses on Daniel Good.
Anonymous.
A Visit to Enniskillen. O
Huiginn.
La Vita Nuova. Dante
Alighieri.

When Shall We See Thy Like
Again? Wingate.
Winnipeg at Christmas.
Fyleman.

Likeness (es)
The Artist as Cuckold.
Anonymous.
Fortunatus the R. A.
Nicarchos [(or Nicarchus)].
I Saw the Winter Weaving.
Rumi.
The Imperfect Artist.
Hamilton.
The Likeness. Gregor.
My Shoes. Simic.
Negative Passage. Newman.
The Old Stories. Frumkin.
The Painter Who Pleased
Nobody and Everybody.
Gay.
Polonius. De La Mare.
Upon Julia's Clothes (parody).
Knox ("Evoe").

Lil (ies) (y)
After Reading Saint Teresa,
Luis De Leon and Ramon
Lull. Lee.
Ballata: One Speaks of the
Beginning of His Love.
Anonymous.
The Birth of Robin Hood.
Anonymous.
A Bulb. Munkittrick.
Childhood. MacDonagh.
The Christ-Child. Gregory
of Narek.
Consider the Lilies. Gannett.
A Cry to Arms. Timrod.
Daphnis Came on a Summer's
Day. Anonymous.
The Dark Night of the Soul.
John of Damascus.
Decoration. Higginson.
Evanescence. Spofford.
Fleur de Lys. Heppenstall.
Four Saints in Three Acts:
"Pigeons on the grass alas."
Stein.
The Gardens of the Sea.
Sterling.
Garlic. Bell.
The Habit of Perfection.
Hopkins.
How on Solemn Fields of
Space. Daryush.
In Galilee. Butts.
The Irish Peasant Girl.
Kickham.
Jump-to-Glory Jane.
Meredith.
The Lily Bed. Crawford.
Lion, Leopard, Lady. Le
Pan.
Lullaby. Holland.
The Maiden and the Lily.
Fraser.
My Friends, This Storm.
Muchemwa.
The Mystery. Whiting.
Noah's Ark. Young.
The Obscure Night of the
Soul. John of Damascus.
On the Death of Dermody,
the Poet. White.
The Poet. Watson.
Premonition. Salverson.
Queen Anne. Anonymous.
The Ratcatcher's Daughter.
Anonymous.
A Room on a Garden.
Stevens.
Sea Gulls. Pratt.

Second Wisdom. Robinson
Song: "Choose now among
this fairest number."
Browne.
Song Set by Nicholas Yonge.
Anonymous.
Sonnets, XCIV: "They that
have power to hurt, and
will do none."
Shakespeare.
Sweet William's Farewell to
Black-Eyed Susan. Gay.
To a Little Girl. Kobbe.
To My Lady Mirriel Howard.
Skelton.
To One of Little Faith.
Flanner.
Two Old Ladies. Sassoon.
Two Points of View.
Watkins.
Upon a Gloomy Night.
Campbell.
Upon the Infant Martyrs.
Crashaw.
Virgin Martyrs. Heath-
Stubbs.
Warning of Winter. Bethell.
What Is the Opposite of a
Prince? Wilbur.
Where the Lilies Used to
Spring. Gray.
The Wind. Morris.
Winter Rain. Rossetti.
Words for a Resurrection.
Kennedy.
The Zebras. Campbell.

Lilac (s)
Ants. Hyde.
For My Son, Born during an
Ice Storm. Jauss.
Green Grow the Lilacs.
Anonymous.
In the Orchard. Stephens.
The Lilac. Wolfe.
Netting. Graham.
Night Flight. Daigon.
Waltz against the Mountains.
Ferril.
With Lilacs in My Eye.
Coleman.

Limb (s)
Aria for Flute and Oboe.
Langland.
The Blue Meridian. Toomer.
The Book of Day-Dreams.
Moore.
Dead Boy. Ransom.
Doric. Sikelianos.
An Epistle Written in the
Country to.... Jenyns.
An Epitaph upon the Right
Honorable Sir Philip
Sidney. Greville.
For Anna. Layton.
He Liked the Dead. Lowry.
The Hearse Song (with
music). Anonymous.
Hyperion. Keats.
Ibant Obscurae. Brown.
Late in Fall. Wilson.
Lines on the Death of
Bismarck. Chapman.
Lines Written on a Very
Boisterous Day in May,
1944. Clare.
A Little Song. Hartman.
The May Tree. Barnes.
Mole Talk. Kennedy.
The Next Table. Cavafy.
November. Coleridge.
Once I Was a Shepherd Boy.
Anonymous.

The Praise of Industry.
Thomson.
The Prophet. Gibran.
Safety. Brooke.
Second Carolina Said-Song.
Ammons.
Simile. Momaday.
The Songs of Bilitis. Louys.
Sonnet: "I saw the object of
my pining thought."
Watson.
Trees and Evening Sky.
Momaday.
When Sadness Fills a Journey.
Waller.

Limbo
Dido to Aeneas. Stanihurst.
Five Poems for Dolls.
Atwood.

Lime (s)
Huxley Hall. Betjeman.
Lovemusic. Kizer.
My Thrush. Collins.
Prothalamion. Kumin.
The Ravaged Villa. Melville.
The Storm. Patmore.
True Knowledge. Panatattu.

Limerick
Limerick: "There was a young
lady of Limerick." Lang.
The Song of the Banjo.
Kipling.

Limestone
Brain Coral. Bassen.
In Praise of Limestone.
Auden.

Limit (ed) (s)
The Cannibal Hymn.
Anonymous.
The Country Man (excerpt).
Farewell.
The Depths of Sorrow.
Anonymous.
February Margins.
Henderson.
Immortality. Greenberg.
In Defense of Metaphysics.
Tomlinson.
Minuet in a Minor Key.
Janowitz.
My Church. G.
Snow Anthology. Bourinot.

Limousines
Funeral. Thompson.
Industrial Size. Wright.

Limp
Bert Kessler. Masters.
The Five-Day Rain.
Levertov.
The Sensualists. Roethke.

Limpid
Hope (excerpt). Shenstone.
O Friendship! Friendship! the
Shell of Aphrodite.
Landor.
O Rose, O Rainbow. Moore.

Lincoln
Grover Cleveland. Benton.
He Leads Us Still.
Guiterman.
Kentucky Birthday. Frost.
Lincoln and Liberty.
Simpson.
Lincoln Leads. Irving.
The Soul of Lincoln. Piety.
The Survival of the Fittest.
Cleghorn.
A Tribute. Anonymous.
Wanted–A Man. Stedman.

Linden (s)
In the Month of Green Fire.
Himmell.

Under the Lindens. Landor.

Line (s)
Achilles Deatheridge.
  Masters.
The Aeneid. Virgil (Publius
  Vergilius Maro).
Afternoon. Bevington.
Ain't No More Cane on This
  Brazos. *Anonymous.*
All Up and Down the Lines.
  Cooperman.
Angel. Merrill.
Angelina. Dunbar.
Art. Thomson.
Band Music. Fuller.
The Black Ball Line.
  Anonymous.
Bridge-Guard in the Karroo.
  Kipling.
Byron: In Men Whom Men
  Condemn as Ill. Miller.
Cardinal. Howes.
Charlie Johnson in
  Kettletown. Smith.
Counry-Western Music.
  Kooser.
A Critic. Landor.
Early Unfinished Sketch.
  Clarke.
Earth. Bryant.
Edvard Munch. Wright.
Enough. Gregor.
Epitaphs of the War, 1914-18.
  Kipling.
The Final Fall. Amprimoz.
Fourth Street, San Rafael.
  Berkson.
A Funeral Oration. Wright.
Hammer Man (with music).
  Anonymous.
Hesitating Ode. Radnoti.
I Followed a Path. Parker.
The Inheritance. Ignatow.
Jerusalem Delivered (excerpt).
  Tasso.
Jessy. Dauenhauer.
Kearny at Seven Pines.
  Stedman.
Keith of Ravelston. Dobell.
Lake. Simpson.
The Late Snow and Lumber
  Strike of the Summer of
  Fifty-Four. Snyder.
A Latter Purification. Guri.
A Letter from Italy.
  Addison.
Letters Found near a Suicide.
  Horne.
Like to the Thundering Tone.
  Corbet.
A Lilliputian Ode on Their
  Majesties' Accession.
  Carey.
Limerick: "A swimmer whose
  clothing was strewed."
  Anonymous.
Limerick: "That the Traylee's
  the best cigarette."
  Rhodes.
The Lines of This New Song
  Are Nothing. Zukofsky.
Lining Track. *Anonymous.*
The Little Pig. Landau.
Lost Garden. "Hale.
Metaphysical Shock while
  Watching a TV Cartoon.
  Rice.
Methinks the Measure.
  Hutchison.
Modern Love, L. Meredith.
Modern Poetry. Skeen.

North of Santa Monica.
  Revard.
A Nuptial Eve. Dobell.
Ode of Wit. Cowley.
On Learning to Play the
  Guitar. Fraser.
Perturbation at Dawn. Ibn
  Maatuk.
Poetics against the Angel of
  Death. Webb.
A Quatrain. Sherman.
Rolled over on Europe.
  Spender.
Searching the Desert for the
  Blues. McTell.
Self-Portrait. Volborth.
Shakespeare Dead. Holland.
Signs. Murphy.
Spring Catch. Keeler.
The Subway Grating Fisher.
  Simpson.
That Day. Kherdian.
These Plaintive Verse, the
  Postes of My Desire.
  Daniel.
Thumbprint. Wright.
Tomorrows. Merrill.
The Unknown Grave.
  Landon.
The Virgin Warrior.
  MacEwen.
Voronezh. Akhmatova.
Wide, Ho? *Anonymous.*
With Cindy at Vallecito.
  McDonald.
Your Catullus Is Depressed.
  Catullus.

Linen
Belfast Linen. *Anonymous.*
Epitaph on Floyd.
  Anonymous.
Hanging Out the Linen
  Clothes (with music).
  Anonymous.
Leda and Her Swan.
  Broumas.
Presumption. Duggan.
Sleep Only with Strangers.
  Jonas.
The Spinning Wheel. Klein.
What Will We Do for Linen?
  Anonymous.

Linger (ed) (s)
Energetic Women.
  Lawrence.
If it is you, there. Ise.
A Little While I Fain Would
  Linger Yet. Hayne.
A Night Full of Nothing.
  Sinclair.
Obit on Parnassus.
  Fitzgerald.
Ode to Anactoria. Sappho.
The Shawls. Gibbon.
Sonnet: "There, on the
  darkened deathbed, dies the
  brain." Masefield.
Stanzas Written in Dejection,
  Near Naples. Shelley.
To John Greenleaf Whittier.
  Ward.
To My Distant Beloved.
  Jeitteles.
To the Mountains. Thoreau.
To wish and want and not
  obtain. Wyatt.
Tolerance. Hardy.
The Vacant Chair. Root.
  George F.
The Vengeance of Finn: The
  Awakening of Dermuid.
  Clarke.

A Viet Cong Sapper Dies.
  Sossaman.
Winter Warfare. Rickword.

Link (ed) (s)
Ad Matrem. Fane.
Certain Maxims of Hafiz.
  Kipling.
Eadwacer. *Anonymous.*
Ezekiel. Stencl.
The Firstborn. Goodchild.
The Gully. Maurice.
The Looks of a Lover
  Enamoured. Gascoigne.
Nature's Hymn to the Deity.
  Clare.
Primary Numbers. Kochek.
Song: "Dorinda's sparkling
  wit, and eyes." Sackville.
Strangers Are We All upon
  the Earth. Werfel.
Woman to Child. Wright.
Women of My Land.
  Armstrong.

Lintel (s)
Invocation. Miller.
Poland/1931.The Wedding.
  Rothenberg.
Skerryvore. Stevenson.

Lion (s)
Afternoon in the Tropics.
  Dario.
Against Unworthy Praise.
  Yeats.
An Ancient Prophecy.
  Freneau.
At the Zoo. Zangwill.
Baseball and Writing.
  Moore.
The Beast with Chrome
  Teeth. Snyder.
Brightness Most Bright I
  Beheld on the Way,
  Forlorn. O Rathaille.
Carolers. Westerfield.
Dandelions. Nemerov.
Dog Alive. Witt.
Dusk. Lopez-Penha.
The Greater Cats. Sackville-
  West.
A History. Williams.
I Am a Lioness. Aisha bint
  Ahmad.
In Nakedness. Pomeroy.
Jerome. Jarrell.
Killed in Action. Tiller.
Kindle the Taper. Lazarus.
Koheleth. Untermeyer.
The Library. Mills.
The Lion and the Cub. Gay.
The Lion's Cub. Thompson.
The Little Girl Found.
  Blake.
Lucky Lion! *Anonymous.*
The Marriage of Heaven and
  Hell. Blake.
Misplaced Sympathy.
  Adams.
Morning at Arnheim. Smith.
Motorcycle. Pray.
Of Baiting the Lion.
  Seaman.
On the Mountains. Alcman.
One Snowy Night in
  December. Morris.
The Sleeping Gypsy–a
  Painting by Rousseau.
  Johnson.
Sunt Leones. Smith.
To a Gnat. *Anonymous.*
To His Wife, for Striking Her
  Dog. Harington.

Upon Umber: Epigram.
  Herrick.
The Victories of Love.
  Patmore.
A Warning. Patmore.
Woman. Layton.
Words for Music Perhaps.
  Yeats.

Lip (s)
Adjectives. Nadir.
Another for the Briar Rose.
  Morris.
"April's amazing meaning".
  Dillon.
As Is the Sea Marvelous.
  Cummings.
Astrophel and Stella, LXXIV.
  Sidney.
Astrophel and Stella, LXXX.
  Sidney.
Attention. Rich.
August 1968. Auden.
The Bands and the Beautiful
  Children. Page.
Basia. Campion.
Berry Picking. Layton.
The Blackbird. Henley.
Blond. De Roche.
Breakfast. Shectman.
Byzantium Burning. Gilbert.
Canopic Jar. Lesser.
The Captived Bee; or, The
  Little Filcher. Herrick.
Change of Life. Urdang.
Charleville. Rimbaud.
The Chimney Sweeper.
  Anonymous.
The Cliff Rose. Fewster.
Come, Landlord, Fill the
  Flowing Bowl.
  Anonymous.
The Day Death Comes.
  Faiz.
A Dream. Keats.
The Dromedary. Campbell.
Drum-Taps. Whitman.
A Drunkard to His Bottle.
  Lefanu.
The Dust of the Overland
  Trail. Adams.
Earth. Wheelock.
Elegy in Six Sonnets.
  Tuckerman.
Elevator Landscapes, Floor:
  Five. Vincent.
Endymion. Wilde.
Enigma. Thomas.
Epigrams. Theocritus.
Evening Song. Lanier.
Fair Margaret and Sweet
  William. *Anonymous.*
The Fall of Hyperion.
  Keats.
The Fifth of May–Napoleon.
  Manzoni.
The Friend of the Fourth
  Decade. Merrill.
Gellius, What Reason Can
  You Give. Catullus.
Golden Gate: The Teacher.
  Mastrolia.
Gulliver. Plath.
The Head Is a Paltry Matter.
  Di Cicco.
Her Lips. *Anonymous.*
Her Lips Are Copper Wire.
  Toomer.
His Are the Thousand
  Sparkling Rills.
  Alexander.
His Wife. Kaufman.
The Horsemen. Baro.

How Can Man Die Better. Tyrtaeus.
How to Choose a Wife. *Anonymous.*
Hymn for Laudes: Feast of Our Lady, Help of Christians. *Anonymous.*
A Hymn to God in Time of Stress. Eastman.
I Died for Beauty. Dickinson.
Impression du Matin. Wilde.
In Hospital. Henley.
Insomnia. Zelvin.
Jove for Europaes Love Tooke Shape of Bull. Barnes.
King Arthur's Waes-Hael. Hawker.
A Lean Day in a Convict's Suit. Wahl.
Liberation. Stone.
Life's Testament. Baylebridge.
Lion. Swenson.
Lips Tongueless. Herrick.
Little Phoebe. *Anonymous.*
A Look into the Gulf. Markham.
Love and Death. Nims.
Love Is Enough. Morris.
The Man to the Angel. Russell.
Mary. Chavez.
A Masque of Life and Death. Bynner.
The Men Are Coming Back! Cole.
Midas: Pan's Song. Lyly.
Midnight. Shakespeare.
Modern Love, XLIX. Meredith.
A Moment. Brooke.
Monarch of the Sea. Starbuck.
A Mustacheless Bard. Coogler.
My Makeup. Kraut.
Now. Browning.
O Dear Life, When Shall It Be? Sidney.
Old Song. Dudek.
On a Dream (after Reading Dante's Episode of Paolo and Francesca). Keats.
On a Rainy Night (excerpt). Mills.
Once I Pass'd Through a Populous City. Whitman.
The Pallid Thunderstricken Sigh for Gain. Tennyson.
A Paradox. Pembroke.
Poem. Lomax.
A Poem about Poems about Vietnam. Stallworthy.
A Poem of Privacy. Symonds.
Poems, XCIII: "Mother, I cannot mind my wheel." Landor.
Poems, XCVIII: "In spring and summer winds may blow." Landor.
The Poet. Grannis.
The Poet's Prothalamion (Excerpt). Scholl.
Poetics. Spire.
Precious Things. *Anonymous.*
The Princess. Turner.
Prothalamium. Sitwell.
A Proud Lady. Wylie.
Rapunzel. Broumas.

Rebels. Crosby.
Reproach. Firdausi.
Return. Cavafy.
The Rose's Cup. Sherman.
Route. Ceravolo.
Screaming Tarn. Bridges.
The Secret Love. Russell.
Sir Launcelot and Queen Guinevere (excerpt). Tennyson.
The Song. Roethke.
Song for a Dancer. Rexroth.
Song: "I went to her who loveth me no more." O'Shaughnessy.
A Song of Praise. Cullen.
Song of the Taste. Snyder.
The Songs of Bilitis. Louys.
Sonnets. Tuckerman.
Sparkling and Bright. Hoffman.
The Speech of the Dead. Ridler.
Spring Night. Mukerji.
The Subject of the Bishop's Miracle. Philip.
Tales of Shatz. Abse.
There Is No Unbelief. Case.
These Things to Come. Butler.
Thisbe. Cone.
Three Variations. Pasternak.
To A Dark Girl. Bennett.
To a Faithless Lover. Greacen.
To a Kiss. Wolcot.
To Azrael. Baudelaire.
To Fanny. Moore.
To George Sand: A Desire. Browning.
Toledo. Gomez Restrepo.
True Love. Johnson.
Two Sonnets from a Sequence. Holt.
Ulysses Returns. Montgomery.
The Unfading Beauty. Carew.
The Unquiet Grave. *Anonymous.*
Watch Repair. Simic.
Whalefeathers. Violi.
Whither. Goetz.
Whitley at Three O'Clock. Worley.
Who Calls. Sayers.
The Window of the Tobacco Shop. Cavafy.
Within a Greenwood Sweet of Myrtle Savour. *Anonymous.*
Woman. *Anonymous.*
The Woman That Had More Babies Than That. Stevens.

Lipstick
A Certain Age. McGinley.
My Makeup. Kraut.
Liquor (s)
The Agonie. Herbert.
Ben Backstay. *Anonymous.*
A Drink with Something in It. Nash.
A drunkard cannot meet a cork. Dickinson.
If You Stick a Stock of Liquor–. Levy.
The Lacquer Liquor Locker. McCord.
Notes for a Revised Sonnet (parody). Pygge.

On a Young Man and an Old Man. May.
Support Your Local Police Dog. Revard.
Lisp
Corn Canon. Stevenson.
Our Insufficiency to Praise God Suitably for His Mercy. Taylor.
List
Give place all ye that doth rejoice. Wyatt.
Hate Whom Ye List. Wyatt.
If with Complaint the Pain Might Be Express'd. Wyatt.
New English Canaan, the Authors Prologue. Morton.
The Old School List. Stephen.
The Queen of Courtesy. *Anonymous.*
The Rime of the Auncient Waggonere (parody). Maginn.
The Visiting Hour. Wagoner.
Listen (ed) (ers) (ing) (s)
The Agents. Conquest.
Among the Pine Trees. Dor.
The Animal That Drank Up Sound. Stafford.
Anti-Memoirs. Schuchat.
At the Party. Auden.
Baptism. Bell.
The Blackbird of Derrycairn. Clarke.
The Coming of His Feet. Allen.
Counry-Western Music. Kooser.
Dead "Wessex" the Dog to the Household. Hardy.
Easter. Coatsworth.
Emilia. Cleghorn.
Evensong. Schaumann.
Expanse Cannot Be Lost. Dickinson.
Fallen Leaves. Tupper.
For Richard Chase. Miller.
Four Preludes on Playthings of the Wind. Sandburg.
The Fury of Flowers and Worms. Sexton.
A Good Start. Moffi.
Halloween. Livingston.
Here Lies a Prisoner. Mew.
The Hill Farmer Speaks. Thomas.
The Homecoming Singer. Wright.
A House of Readers. Miller.
Hyperion. Keats.
I Show the Daffodils to the Retarded Kids. Sharp.
Iambes VIII. Chenier.
If They Spoke. Van Doren.
If You Should Tire of Loving Me. Widdemer.
In Her Song She Is Alone. Swan.
In Memoriam A.H.H., XCIV. Tennyson.
The Iron Lung. Plumly.
Italian Music in Dakota. Whitman.
Knocking at the Door. Freeman.
Letters to Live Poets. Beaver.
Listening. Passy.

Listening to Her. Zach.
Little Theocritus. Paradise.
Loneliness. McPherson.
Mahalia. Harper.
The March Bee. Blunden.
Maxims of a Park Vagrant. Swift.
Middle of the World. Lawrence.
Midsummer. Trowbridge.
New Shoes. Watts.
New Strain. Starbuck.
Night Song for a Woman. Purdy.
Night Thoughts in Age. Wheelock.
Ode to a Skylark. Shelley.
Old Man. Carr.
One-Line Poems from a New Statesman Competition. Prince.
The Orange Tree. Neilson.
Periphery. Stone.
The Photograph of Myself. Anderson.
Poem against the British. Bly.
The Queen. Neruda.
Remorse. Betjeman.
Retractions. Cabell.
Ride the Turtle's Back. Brant.
The Ring. Wakoski.
The Rivals. Stephens.
Smithfield Ham. Smith.
Sonnets. Tuckerman.
The Storm. Hay.
The Swan. Roethke.
Teeth. Holub.
Tennessee. Boyle.
Thieves. Adams.
This Wind. Kryss.
To A. D. Henley.
To Mark Anthony in Heaven. Williams.
Vain Gratuities. Robinson.
The Vindictive Staircase or The Reward of Industry. Gibson.
Whack Fol the Diddle. Kearney.
When I was a good and quick little girl. *Anonymous.*
The Widow Perez. Soto.
The Wild Geese. Jacob.
Winter Sketch. Bourinot.
Woods in Winter. Longfellow.
World's Centre. Dallas.
Lists
Choice. Dickinson.
The Splendid Spur. Quiller-Couch.
Lit
A Dragonfly. Farjeon.
Dream. Ignatow.
Flighting for Duck. Empson.
The Hill Wife. Frost.
Shooting at the Moon. Kim Yo-sop.
Shopkeepers. Leib.
The Starlighter. Guiterman.
Waiting for Nighthawks in Illinois. Pfingston.
Litany
Clerihew. Bentley.
A Madame, Madame B. Beaute Sexagenaire. Sackville.
Literature
Alas! for the South! Coogler.
From the Embassy. Graves.

Misunderstanding. Layton.
The Person from Porlock.
  Graves.

Litter
I Wasn't No Mary Ellen.
  King.
The Master of the Golden
  Glow. Schuyler.
Portrait of a Married Couple.
  Scott.
River Road. Kunitz.
The Rock. Eliot.

Little
Against Meaning. Codrescu.
Alec Yeaton's Son. Aldrich.
All. Slonimski.
April and May. Robinson.
As I Walked in the Woods.
  Anonymous.
The Atheist Buries His Son.
  Abu'l-Atahija.
The Avenue Bearing the
  Initial of Christ into the
  New World. Kinnell.
Awful Fix. Hawkins.
Baby-Land. Cooper.
The Ball Poem. Berryman.
Ballroom Dancing Class.
  McGinley.
Bee Wassail. Anonymous.
Biography. Klein.
Blackberry Winter. Ransom.
The Boat. Pack.
Born Without a Chance.
  Cooke.
The Boy and the Parrot.
  Frere.
Bring Me a Little Water,
  Sylvie. Anonymous.
Buckskin Joe. Anonymous.
The Burden of Decision.
  Everwine.
A Business Man's Prayer.
  Ludlum.
The Calf, the Goat, the Little
  Lamb. Hoffenstein.
The Carpenter's Wife.
  Anonymous.
A Child's Song of Christmas.
  Pickthall.
Childhood. Bradstreet.
The Children. Dickinson.
Christmas Song. Carman.
Circus. Farjeon.
Cows Grazing at Sunrise.
  Matthews.
Cradle Song. Duff.
The Crow and the Nighthawk.
  Kirkconnell.
Cypresses. Francis.
Daphnis to Ganymede.
  Barnfield.
December Blues. Pinsky.
Devilish Mary. Anonymous.
The Dirigible. Bergengren.
Don Juan. Byron.
The Door. Davies.
The Double Tree. Scott.
Each a Part of All.
  Bamberger.
Earth Buried. Mackenzie.
Entoptic Colours. Goethe.
Epitaph on a Tyrant.
  Auden.
Essay on Psychiatrists.
  Pinsky.
The Exercise of Affection.
  Ayton [(or Aytoun)] Sir
  Robert.
Father's Story. Roberts.
Field Sports. Pope.
Fire Island. Swenson.

Firefly. Roberts.
Foal. Miller.
For a Plaque on the Door of
  an Isolated House.
  Stafford.
The Fox. Anonymous.
A Fox Jumped up One
  Winter's Night.
  Anonymous.
From a Very Little Sphinx.
  Millay.
Gascoigne's Woodmanship.
  Gascoigne.
George. Belloc.
Go Fly a Saucer. McCord.
The God of War. Brecht.
Gooseberries. Wild.
The grass so little has to do.
  Dickinson.
Greedy Richard. Taylor.
Haiku: On Her Child's Death.
  Kaga no Chiyo.
Have You Got a Brook.
  Dickinson.
Hey Diddle Diddle.
  Anonymous.
I'm the Police Cop Man, I
  Am. Morrison.
I Would Like You for a
  Comrade. Parry.
Idyll. Macnaghten.
Illi Morituri. Webster.
The Indian Convert.
  Freneau.
Inscription on a Grot.
  Rogers.
Jerked Heartstrings in Town.
  Jones.
The Jolly Pinder of Wakefield
  (A version). Anonymous.
King Henry VIII.
  Shakespeare.
King Richard II.
  Shakespeare.
Lament for the Poets: 1916.
  Ledwidge.
Leaves. Manning.
A Life-Lesson. Riley.
Lilith on the Fate of Man.
  Brennan.
Lincoln. Mitchell.
The Little Boats of Britain.
  Carsley.
The Little Gentleman.
  Anonymous.
Little Things. Stephens.
The Long Race. Robinson.
The Lost Playmate. Brown.
Love Me Little, Love Me
  Long. Anonymous.
Lullaby. Anonymous.
Lullaby for My Dead Child.
  Jallais.
Madam Life. Henley.
Mary's Lullaby. Eastwick.
Me and My Chauffeur Blues.
  Minnie.
Missing. Tabb.
Momotara. Fyleman.
Motels, Hotels, Other People's
  Houses. Van Brunt.
The Mountain That Got
  Little. Stafford.
The Mouse. Coatsworth.
My Uncle Paul of Pimlico.
  Peake.
Naming of Private Parts
  (parody). Williams.
The New Freedom. Dargan.
News. Traherne.
The Nightingale. Petrarch
  (Francesco Petrarca).

Now and Again. Borson.
Old Father Annum.
  Jackson.
On Shooting a Swallow in
  Early Youth. Tennyson.
On the Slope of the Desolate
  River. Tagore.
Once. Widerberg.
Only One. Burns.
Pelicanaries. Lewis.
The Perfect Reactionary.
  Mearns.
The Pettitoes Are Little Feet.
  Anonymous.
Piano Tuner, Untune Me That
  Tune. Nash.
The Pleiades. Coatsworth.
Poets. Flexner.
The Prayer of the Donkey.
  De Gasztold.
Protest. Cullen.
A Rabbit as King of the
  Ghosts. Stevens.
Remember Way Back.
  Green.
The Results of Stealing a Pin.
  Anonymous.
Ringless. Wakoski.
Robin Hood and Little John.
  Anonymous.
Robin's Cross. Darley.
Roll Over. Anonymous.
Roots. Ginsberg.
Round About, Round About,
  Here Sits the Hare.
  Anonymous.
The Rubaiyat of Omar
  Khayyam. Omar
  Khayyam.
The Scaredy. Anonymous.
Sea Shells. Scollard.
Service Supreme.
  Anonymous.
Short'nin' Bread.
  Anonymous.
Sleep, My Child. Aleichem.
Snips and Snails and
  Puppydog Tails.
  Anonymous.
Some Little Bug. Atwell.
Song for a Little Cuckoo
  Clock. Coatsworth.
The Space Child's Mother
  Goose. Winsor.
The Spanish War.
  ""MacDiarmid.
The Star. Taylor.
The Story of the Wild
  Huntsman. Hoffmann.
The Stranger. Gelman.
Sweet and Low. Barnby.
Temperance Song.
  Anonymous.
There's Money in Mother and
  Father. Bishop.
This Little Light of Mine.
  Anonymous.
This Little Pig Had a Rub-a-
  Dub. Anonymous.
This Little Pig Went to
  Market. Anonymous.
Three Streets. Saba.
Tiare Tahiti. Brooke.
Tired Mothers. Smith.
To a Tenting Boy. Turner.
To Any Daddy. Anonymous.
To His Soul. Hadrian.
To Our Lady. Thayer.
A Trapped Fly. Herrick.
Trouble-Shooting. Stafford.
The Turkish Lady.
  Anonymous.

Two Fawns That Didn't See
  the Light This Spring.
  Snyder.
The Unborn. Finch.
Under All Change. Johnson.
The Unknown Color.
  Cullen.
Upon a Dainty Hill Sometime.
  Breton.
The Voice of Ardent Zeal
  Speaks from the Lollard's
  Tower of St. Paul's.
  Farley.
Waking. Pyle.
A Wedgwood Bowl. Taylor.
What Shall I Give? Thomas.
When I Was a Bachelor.
  Anonymous.
The Willows by the Water
  Side. Anonymous.
Woman and Nature. Griffin.
Worry about Money. Raine.
Youghall Harbor.
  Anonymous.
Youth. Shelton.

Littleness
On Descending the River Po.
  Parsons.
You Preach to Me of Laws.
  Tree.

Live (d) (ing) (s)
Absent Creation. Savage.
Ad Matrem. Fane.
Advice against Travel.
  Mangan.
Against the Evidence.
  Ignatow.
The Ailing Parent. Dunetz.
Air: "The Love of a Woman."
  Creeley.
The Alarm. Jacob.
The All-Embracing. Faber.
All for the Cause. Morris.
All Shams. Anonymous.
All Sung. Le Gallienne.
All That Matters. Guest.
L'Allegro. Milton.
Alone am I, and alone I wish
  to be. Pisan.
Along South Inlet. Kuzma.
The Ambrosia of Dionysus
  and Semele. Graves.
America. Newlove.
Amoretti, II. Spenser.
Amoretti, XIV. Spenser.
Amoretti, XXXIII. Spenser.
Amoretti, XLVII. Spenser.
Amoretti, XLVIII. Spenser.
Amoretti, XLIX. Spenser.
Amoretti, LXXV. Spenser.
Another Time. Auden.
The Ant and the Cricket.
  Anonymous.
Appeal. Da.
The Approach of the Storm.
  Anonymous.
An April Day. Cotter.
Arcadia. Sidney.
Armor. Dickey.
Arsenic. Moss.
An Artist. Jeffers.
As One Who Bears beneath
  His Neighbor's Roof.
  Hillyer.
As the Window Darkens.
  Jensen.
At Birth. Thwaite.
At Mexican Springs. Tohe.
At the Tourist Center in
  Boston. Atwood.
Attica Is. Brisby.
Aurora Leigh. Browning.

Autumn Song. Tieck.
Ballad of the Morning Streets. Jones.
Ballade Made in Hot Weather. Henley.
Ballade of Sayings. Merwin.
The Banded Cobra. Leipoldt.
The Bat. Nash.
The Bear. Kinnell.
Because of Clothes. Riding.
Before Disaster. Winters.
Being Forsaken of His Friend He Complaineth. "S.
Bete Humaine. Young.
A Bird's Nest. Biton.
Birthday. Merrill.
Blood Marksman and Kureldei the Marksman. Anonymous.
The Bobolink. Hill.
The Body Politic. Hall.
The Book of Kells. Nemerov.
Bowery. Ignatow.
Boy at Target Practice: A Contemplation. Moses.
The Breeze Is Blowing. Anonymous.
Brief Thunder at Sharpeville. Nortje.
The Broken Bowl. Merrill.
Bunch Grass #37. Sund.
The Burning Bush. Van Dyke.
But Choose. Holmes.
By Frazier Creek Falls. Snyder.
By the Boat House, Oxford. Stevenson.
By the Waterfall. Adler.
By the Waters of Minnetonka. Cavanass.
Caelica, LXXXVII. Greville.
Cardinal Bembo's Epitaph on Raphael. Hardy.
Cecil County. Welburn.
Cedar Mountain. Fields.
Celia Singing. Stanley.
A Chant for Young / Brothas & Sistuhs. Sanchez.
The Chelsea. Walcott.
Children Not Kept at Home. Oates.
The Choice. Pomfret.
Christ Is Arisen. Goethe.
Christmas. Betjeman.
Christmas Eve in France. Fauset.
The Church of the Sacred Heart. Greene.
The City, Lord, Where Thy Dear Life. Dudley.
The Clothes Pit. Dunn.
The Clouds. Mira Bai [(or Mirabai(].
Coasting toward Midnight at the Southeastern Fair. Bottoms.
A Coffee-House Lecture. Mezey.
The Colour of God's Face. Livesay.
Comanche Ghost Dance. Henson.
Come, Chearfull Day, Part of My Life, to Mee. Campion.
A Complaint by Night of the Lover Not Beloved. Petrarch.
The Comrade. Dodd.

Condemnation. Thich Nhat Hanh.
The Conqueror. Williams.
Contented at Forty. Cleghorn.
A Correct Compassion. Kirkup.
Cotton-Mill Colic. Anonymous.
Courage to Live. Crowell.
The Craftsman. Christian.
The Crazy World. Gay.
The Creation. Johnson.
The Cultural Presuppostion. Auden.
Cupid, Thou Naughty Boy. Greville.
The Cyclamen. Bates.
Damon & Pythias. Creeley.
Danebury. Anonymous.
Dangerous Condition: Sign on Inner-City House. Atkins.
Dark Corner. Hough.
David's Song. Browning.
The Dead. Smith.
Death Bells. Hopkins.
The Death of Jefferson. Butterworth.
The Death of Lester Brown, House Painter. Taylor.
The Decoys. Auden.
Description of Holland. Butler.
A Dialogue betwixt GOD and the Soul. Wotton.
Diana. Constable.
The Dinosaur. Junge.
Directions. Matthews.
Discoveries of Bones and Stone. Grigson.
A Dooms-Day Thought Anno 1659. Flatman.
The Double. Feldman.
Dulce et Decorum. Wilson.
Each a Part of All. Bamberger.
The Eagle That Is Forgotten. Lindsay.
Easter Egg. Kieffaber.
Eclipses. Sullivan.
Eclogue. Prokosch.
Eighteen Verse Sung to a Tatar Reed Whistle. Ts'ai Yen.
Eine Kleine Snailmusik. Sarton.
Elegies. Ovid (Publius Ovidius Naso).
An Elegy for Bob Marley. Matthews.
Elegy for Margaret Howard, Lady Buckhurst. Southwell.
Elisa, or an Elegy upon the Unripe Decease... Fletcher.
Endymion, III. Keats.
Envy. Procter.
The Epic of Gilgamesh (excerpt). Anonymous.
Epigram: "My heart still hovering round about you." Nugent.
Epigram: "There are two miseries in human life." Landor.
Epitaph. Corbiere.
An Epitaph. Davies.
Epitaph: "Here lies the man that madly slain." Hoskyns.

An Epitaph: "Interr'd beneath this marble stone." Prior.
Epitaph on Elizabeth, L. H. Jonson.
Epitaphs of the War, 1914-18. Kipling.
Esthetique du Mal. Stevens.
Eternal Life. More.
Except I Love. Parry.
The Eyes of Cantonese Schoolmasters Remembered in Hong Kong. Barnstone.
A Fable for Critics. Lowell.
The Faerie Queene. Spenser.
Fair Iris and Her Swain. Dryden.
The Fairy King. Allingham.
A Farewell. Fairburn.
February. Moffi.
February 14, 22 B. C. Adams.
Felise. Swinburne.
Finders Keepers. Finkel.
Finding the Pistol. Ruark.
Fireflies. Fawcett.
The Fist. Walcott.
Five Ways to Kill a Man. Brock.
The Flight of the Arrow. Stoddard.
The Flood. Lipska.
The Fly. Blake.
A Football-Player. Lefroy.
For all my Grandmothers. Brant.
For Andy Goodman–Michael Schwerner–and James Chaney. Walker.
For Dr. and Mrs. Dresser. Avison.
For Patrick, Aetat: LXX. Betjeman.
For Soldiers. Gifford.
Forest Leaves in Autumn (excerpt). Keble.
The Fox. Clare.
Fragment in Imitation of Wordsworth. Fanshawe.
Fragment of a Pastoral. Schwabsky.
Free Thoughts on Several Eminent Composers. Lamb.
The Friar of Orders Gray. O'Keeffe.
From Creature to Ghost. Hanson.
From the Santa-Fe Trail. Lindsay.
The Fundamental Project of Technology. Kinnell.
Funeral Elegy on the Death of His Very Good Friend Mr. Michael Drayton. Cokayne.
The Gallant Highwayman. De Mille.
The Galley-Slave. Kipling.
Garden. Marvell.
Gentle Jesus. Wesley.
The Geranium. Sheridan.
The Gift of Song. Horace.
Glad World. FitzGerald.
The Glens. Hewitt.
The God of the Living. Ellerton.
God's Work. Cushman.
Good Morning America (excerpt). Sandburg.
Good News Bad News. Abbott.

The Good Shepherd. Gwynne.
Good Thoughts. Haaff.
A Grammarian's Funeral. Browning.
The Grapevine. Ashbery.
A Grave in Ukraine. Tchernichovsky.
A Great Man. Goldsmith.
A Green Refrain. Huss.
Growing Old. Wells.
A Guerrilla Handbook. Jones.
Guilielmus Rex. Aldrich.
The Gypsy Laddie (B vers.). Anonymous.
Hail, Oh Hail to the King. Quickenden.
Hail South Australia. Anonymous.
Half Past Four, October. Hajnal.
Hamlet in Russia, A Soliloquy. Pasternak.
The Hands of God. Lawrence.
The Harp That Once through Tara's Halls. Moore.
The Haymow. Mockett.
He Lives Long Who Lives Well. Randolph.
Head Couples. Matchett.
Heaven in Ordinarie. Wolff.
Help Us to Live. Keble.
Her Courage. Yeats.
Her Eyes Are Wild. Wordsworth.
Here, as in a Painting, Noon Burns Yellow. Gorbanyevskaya.
Herman Altman. Masters.
The Hippo. Roethke.
Hippopotamothalamion. Wheelock.
His Content in the Country. Herrick.
His Lady's Tomb. Ronsard.
Hollin, Green Hollin. Anonymous.
The Holy Ones, the Young Ones. Zeldis.
Homage to Our Leaders. Symons.
Hotel Sierra. St. John.
The Hours of Sleepy Night. Campion.
How Do You Live? Anonymous.
How Oft Has the Banshee Cried. Moore.
Humble Service. Heard.
The Hunt. De La Mare.
Hymn. Young.
Hymn to the Sun. Akhnaton (Amenhotep IV).
Hymn to the Virgin Mary. O'Riordan.
I Accept. Pulsifer.
I Am Now So Weary with Waiting. Stampa.
I Come and Stand at Every Door. Hikmet.
I Had a Dove. Keats.
I Have Bowed before the Sun. Walters.
I Have Fought the Good Fight. Waterbury.
I Have Trod the Upward and the Downward Slope. Stevenson.
I Live Not Where I Love. Anonymous.

I Love Life. Cassel.
I Love, Loved, and So Doth She. Wyatt.
I Love You. Wilcox.
I'm Sad and I'm Lonely. *Anonymous.*
If But One Year. *Anonymous.*
If Ever You Go to Dublin Town. Kavanagh.
If You're Ever Going to Love Me. *Anonymous.*
Il Penseroso. Milton.
Immortality. Ai.
In Evil Long I Took Delight. Newton.
In health and ease am I. Davison.
In Memoriam A.H.H., LXXXII. Tennyson.
In Shame and Humiliation. Wright.
In the Dawn. Shepard.
In the Night Field. Merwin.
Instructions to the Double. Gallagher.
Introspective Reflection. Nash.
Isis Wanderer. Raine.
The Jervis Bay. *Anonymous.*
The Jew of Malta: The Song of Ithamore. Marlowe.
John Riley. *Anonymous.*
Johnny Germany. *Anonymous.*
Joshua's Face. Gilboa.
June. Bryant.
The Keeper. Carpenter.
The Known Soldier. Patchen.
Korea Bound, 1952. Childress.
Lack Wit. *Anonymous.*
Lament for a Husband. *Anonymous.*
Lament of Anastasius. Peabody.
Lamentation. Ezekiel.
Land-Fall. Brady.
Land of the Free. Hosking.
Last Lines. Kennedy.
Late at Night. Stafford.
Late at Night during a Visit of Friends. Bly.
Lead Us, O Father, in the Paths of Peace. Burleigh.
Learning. Chapman.
Learning Experience. Piercy.
A Legend of the Northland. Cary.
Let Us Rise Up and Live. Sherman.
Letters to Live Poets. Beaver.
Lewd Love is Loss. Southwell.
Liadan Laments Cuirithir. Liadan.
Limerick: "There's a Portuguese person named Howell." Rossetti.
The Lines. Jarrell.
Lines Written in Kensington Gardens. Arnold.
The Lion and Albert. Edgar.
The Little Clan. Higgins.
The Little Family. *Anonymous.*
Little Fish. Lawrence.
Little Mousgrove and the Lady Barnet. *Anonymous.*

The Little Poem of Life. Oxenham.
Lives. Dawe.
The Living Dog and the Dead Lion. Moore.
Living with Others. Zolynas.
The Lodger. Longley.
Looking at a Picture on an Anniversary. Hardy.
Looking into History. Wilbur.
Looting. Kessler.
Losers. Sandburg.
Love Is a Place. Cummings.
Love Is Life. Rolle.
Love's Horoscope. Crashaw.
Love's Rosary. Woodberry.
Man and Nature. Weeks.
Man and Wife Is One Flesh. Deacon.
The Man That Lives. *Anonymous.*
Manifest Destiny. Probst.
The Manner of a Poet's Germination. Villa.
Mariana in the South. Tennyson.
A Marriage. Barnett.
Marriage. Lowell.
Mary Mild, Good Maiden. Cille.
The Massacre of the Innocents. Smith.
Meditation in Winter. Dunbar.
Meditations for July 19, 1666. Pain.
Men. MacLeish.
The Merman. Tennyson.
The Miner. King.
Minnie Morse. Starbird.
Miss Millay Says Something Too. Hoffenstein.
The Mistletoe Bough. Bayly.
Moan, Moan, Ye Dying Gales. Neele.
The Monument. Wesley.
Moonset, Gloucester, December 1, 1957, 1:58 AM. Olson.
Morning Worship. Van Doren.
Mountain Top. *Anonymous.*
The Mouse's Petition. Barbauld.
My Evening Prayer. Gabriel.
My Heart Stood Still. Hart.
My Influence. *Anonymous.*
"My Life Has Been the Poem..." Thoreau.
My Mother's Bible. Morris.
My New World. Browne.
My Song. Tagore.
The Mystic. Tennyson.
N.Y. Pound.
Napoli Again. Hugo.
Narrative. Dudek.
Nearer Home. Cary.
New and Old Gospel. Mackey.
The New Ezekial. Lazarus.
News. Schmitz.
Night Boat. Brown.
The Night Is Falling. Mangan.
Night of Sine. Sedar-Senghor.
The Night Wind. Bronte.
No, No, Poor Suffering Heart. Dryden.
No Single Hour Can Stand for Naught. Clare.

Noah's Flood. Drayton.
O God, Though Countless Worlds of Light. Knowles.
O Heaven Indulge. Tilden.
O Living Always, Always Dying. Whitman.
Odes. Horace.
Of Books. Florio.
Of Mistress D.S. Googe.
Of the Loss of Time. Hoskyns.
Oh, Give Me the Hills. *Anonymous.*
Old Black Men. Johnson.
An Old Sweetheart of Mine. Riley.
The Old Women Still Sing. Rowell.
On a Virtuous Young Gentlewoman That Died Suddenly. Cartwright.
On an Insignificant Fellow. Curzon.
On John Donne's Book of Poems. Marriot.
On Reading the Metamorphoses. Garrett.
On the Bleeding Wounds of Our Crucified Lord. Crashaw.
On the Death of a Journalist. Campbell.
On the Decease of the Religious and Honourable Jno Haynes Esqr.... James.
On the Heart's Beginning to Cloud the Mind. Frost.
On the Late Engagement in Charles Town River. *Anonymous.*
On the Late S. T. Coleridge. Allston.
On Two Brothers. Simonides (of Ceos).
The Origin of Didactic Poetry. Lowell.
Others. Meigs.
Our Backs Are to the Cypress. Goldberg.
Our Earth Mother. *Anonymous.*
Out of French. Sedley.
Out of the Vast. Bamberger.
Outside Every Window Is a Flowering Thing. Skeen.
The Owl in the Sarcophagus. Stevens.
Oxford Canal. Flecker.
Parting. Raine.
The Parting Injunctions. Day.
The Passionate Shepherd to His Love. Marlowe.
The Pastime of Pleasure. Hawes.
Patience, Hard Virtue. Berrigan.
Patience With the Living. Sangster.
Patriotic Tour and Postulate of Joy. Warren.
Perhaps. Clifton.
Phantasia for Elvira Shatayev. Rich.
Picture of Seneca Dying in a Bath. Prior.
Pindar's Revenge. Sanders.
Plain-Chant for America. Chapin.
Planetary Exchange. Jones.
Plants Don't Talk, People Say. Castro.

The Pleasant Life in Newfoundland. Hayman.
Plutarch. Agathias.
Poem, 1972. Scroggie.
Poem for a Singer. Acorn.
Poem (I Lived in the First Century). Rukeyser.
A Poem of Broken Pieces. Jones.
Poems. Drummond.
The Poet Lives. Glatstein.
A Poet's Proverbs. Guiterman.
Poland, October. Brasch.
Port of Embarkation. Jarrell.
Portoncini dei Morti. Halpern.
Portraits. Fagg.
The Postcards: A Triptych. Levertov.
Prayer of the Young Stoic. Dunn.
Precious Moments. Sandburg.
President Roosevelt. Williams.
The Prohibition. Donne.
Pure Products. Levertov.
Purgatory. Yeats.
The Python. Belloc.
Qords on the Wind: Fruit of Loneliness. Sarton.
The Quaker of the Olden Time. Whittier.
Queens. Synge.
The Rapid. Sangster.
Readings of History. Rich.
Reflections of a Trout Fisherman. Demon.
Rejoicing at the Arrival of Ch'en Hsiung. Po Chu-i.
Remembering That Island. McGrath.
A Reply to Nancy Hanks. Silberger.
Reservation Special. Blockcolski.
Resume. Parker.
The Resurrection. Brooks.
Retrospect. Tichborne [(or Tichbourne)].
A Return from the Wars. Bock.
Ribh Considers Christian Love Insufficient. Yeats.
Rise, O My Soul! *Anonymous.*
Ritual Three. Ignatow.
The River of Bees. Merwin.
Ron Mason. Tuwhare.
The Room. Day-Lewis.
Rosader's Sonnet. Lodge.
The Rose and the Wind. Marston.
The Sages. Mickiewicz.
Said the Innkeeper. Connolly.
Salomon. Morhange.
Salutation the Second. Pound.
The Secret Love. Russell.
Shackley-Hay. *Anonymous.*
Shall I Compare Thee to a Summer's Day? Moss.
She Died in Beauty. Sillery.
Shearing. Wright.
Shemuel. Bowen.
Signature. Livesay.
Silent in America. Levine.
The Sisters. Whittier.
Sleep, Holy Babe. Caswall.

The Slide at the Empire Mine. Wason.

A Small Elegy. Orten.

The Smooth Divine. Dwight.

The Snowflake Which Is Now and Hence Forever. MacLeish.

So Big! Fatchen.

Soldier, There Is a War between the Mind. Stevens.

A Song: "A song of grass." Yehoash.

Song: "Fond men! whose wretched care the life soon ending." Fletcher.

Song: "Man's a poor deluded bubble." Dodsley.

A Song of Ale. *Anonymous.*

The Song of the Lilies. Wheelock.

Song of the Open Road (excerpt). Whitman.

Song. Set by Mr. Coleman. Cotton.

Sonnet XVII: "I flee the city, temples, and each place." Labe.

Sonnet for My Father. Justice.

Sonnets, V: "Those hours, that with gentle work did frame." Shakespeare.

Sonnets, XVI: "But wherefore do not you a mightier way." Shakespeare.

Sonnets, LV: "Not marble, nor the gilded monuments." Shakespeare.

Sonnets, LXIII: "Against my Love shall be, as I am now." Shakespeare.

Sonnets to Philomel. Davies.

Sonnets Written in the Orillia Woods, VII. Sangster.

The Southern Cross. Hawker.

The Sparkling Bowl. Pierpont.

Sphinx. Hayden.

Spider Reeves. Carlile.

Spoon River Anthology. Robinson.

Spring Street in '58. Walcott.

Still, O LORD, for Thee I Tarry. Wesley.

Stone Walls. Lippmann.

Stopping near Highway 80. Ray.

Strange. Burnshaw.

Strange Meetings. Monro.

Strangeness of Heart. Sassoon.

Strictly for Posterity. Simic.

Stud Groom. Glassco.

Success. *Anonymous.*

Suggested by a Picture of the Bird of Paradise. Wordsworth.

Sunshine and Music. *Anonymous.*

A Survey of the Amphitheatre. Browne.

"Sweet are the thoughts where hope persuadeth hap." Ralegh.

Taking the Train Home. Matthews.

Tenants. Gibson.

That Day. Kherdian.

That such have died enable us. Dickinson.

Theory of Vision: The Green Eye. Merrill.

There Is a Charm in Solitude That Cheers. Clare.

There Is a Woman in This Town. Parker.

There Is Nothing False in Thee. Patchen.

Therefore We Preserve Life. Shen Ch'uan.

These Things to Come. Butler.

They. Thomas.

The Things That Are More Excellent. Watson.

Thomas Jefferson. Benét.

A Thousand Killed. Spencer.

Three Lyrics. Petronius Arbiter (Caius Petronius Arbiter).

Through These Pale Cold Days. Rosenberg.

To a Lady Asking Him How Long He Would Love Her. Etherege.

To a Lock of Hair. Scott.

To a Withered Rose. Bangs.

To Antenor. Philips.

To Anthea, Who May Command Him Anything. Herrick.

To Be a Jew in the Twentieth Century. Rukeyser.

To Delia. Daniel.

To His Coy Love. Drayton.

To His Honoured and Most Ingenious Friend, Master Charles Cotton. Herrick.

To His Mistress in Absence. Tasso.

To Krishna Haunting the Hills. Andal.

To Mr. R.W. Donne.

To My Children, Fearing for Them. Berry.

To My Dear and Loving Husband. Bradstreet.

To Phyllis, to Love and Live With Him. Herrick.

To Richard Wright. Rivers.

To Saffold's Customers. Case.

To the Dandelion. Lowell.

To the Dead of '98. Johnson.

To the Memory of Ben Johnson (excerpt). Mayne.

Tomorrow. Masefield.

Tornado Watch, Bloomington, Indiana. Young.

The Town without a Market. Flecker.

Traveller's Ditty. DeFord.

The Trial. Scholem.

The Truth about My Sister and Me. Probst.

Tune: The Butterfly Woos the Blossoms. Li Ching-chao.

'Twas Like a Maelstrom, with a Notch. Dickinson.

Two Pictures of a Leaf. Bell.

The Uncertain State of a Lover. *Anonymous.*

Under a Hill. *Anonymous.*

Under the Bamboo Tree. Cole.

Understanding. Bliss.

The Unforeseen. Nale Roxlo.

Until Death. Akers.

Upon the Bleeding Crucifix. Crashaw.

Upon the Death of Sir Albert Morton's Wife. Wootton.

Upone Tabacco. Ayton [(or Aytoun)] Sir Robert.

Uselessness. Wilcox.

Utopia TV Store. Chernoff.

Variation on Heraclitus. MacNeice.

The Vedic Hymns: Varuna. *Anonymous.*

Views of Boston Common and Nearby. Blackmur.

Virtue. Herbert.

A Visit to Bridge House. Weber.

W. H. Eheu! Coleridge.

A Walk. Lachmann.

Wang Peng's Recommendation for Improving the People. Eldridge.

Warrior with Shield. Browne.

The Way; The Truth; The Life. Porter.

A Way to Make a Living. Wright.

The Way We Live Now. Dana.

We Must Not Part. *Anonymous.*

We Women. Sodergran.

What If a Much of a Which of a Wind. Cummings.

What the King Has. Fuller.

Where His Lady Keeps His Heart. "W.

White Violet. Osborne.

The Whole Universe Is Full of God. Emre.

Why That's Bob Hope. Hathaway.

The Wife. Dinnies

A Wind from the West. Watt.

The Window. Scarfe.

Winter Mask. Tate.

With a Sliver of Marble from Carrara. Wright.

With Hands Like Leaves. Still.

The Wolf and the Stork. La Fontaine.

A Woman's Sorrow (excerpt). Ho Nansorhon.

Women's Locker Room. Waniek.

The Wonderful Old Man. *Anonymous.*

The World We Make. Walton.

You Are Alms. Thompson.

You Growing. Acorn.

Young Heroes. Horne.

The Young Price and the Young Princess. Ashbery.

Young Reynard. Meredith.

Lively (ier)

Astrophel and Stella, XXXIX. Sidney.

Equals. Untermeyer.

The Forerunners. Herbert.

Leesome Brand (A version). *Anonymous.*

Sonnet: "Sweet secrecy, what tongue can tell thy worth?" Drayton.

To Sleep. Sidney.

Liver

Chandler Nicholas. Masters.

Consolatory! Hankin.

Dr. Dimity Lectures on Unusual Cases. Macdonald.

Limerick: "There's a sensitive man in Toms River." Bishop.

Mirror Images. Speer.

Prometheus. Mastoraki.

Vowel Englyn to the Spider. *Anonymous.*

The Worried Skipper. Irwin.

Livery

Epigram: Fatum Supremum. *Anonymous.*

I'll tell you whence the Rose did first grow red. Strode.

The Last Chapter. De la Mare.

Virgidemiarum: "A Gentle Squire would gladly entertain." Hall.

Livid

Twilight at the Zoo. Rodger.

Liza

Bronc Peeler's Song. *Anonymous.*

Goodbye 'Liza Jane. *Anonymous.*

Sal Got a Meatskin. *Anonymous.*

Liza Jane

Bedbug. *Anonymous.*

Good-By Liza Jane (with music). *Anonymous.*

Li'l Liza Jane. *Anonymous.*

Lizard

Alfred Corning Clark. Lowell.

Arcan Sylvarum. De Kay.

Canto LXXX. Pound.

Four Preludes on Playthings of the Wind. Sandburg.

Haiku: "Eastern guard tower." Knight.

Humanities Lecture. Stafford.

Lines to Dr. Ditmars. Robinson.

Lizard. Lawrence.

Though Ye Suppose. Skelton.

Young Couples Strolling By. Rakosi.

Load (ing) (s)

All This Sunday Long. Johnson.

The Armful. Frost.

Bad Man Ballad. *Anonymous.*

Carmina. Catullus.

Casting All Your Care Upon Him. *Anonymous.*

December Stillness. Sassoon.

Endymion, III (excerpt). Keats.

Erin (Elephant). *Anonymous.*

Farm Cart. Farjeon.

Going. Larkin.

Horse Sense. *Anonymous.*

Life's Joy. *Anonymous.*

The Man with the Hollow Breast. Van Zyl.

No Greater Love. *Anonymous.*

The Priest's Lament. Benson.

Responsibility. *Anonymous.*

Tom the Porter. Byrom.

Waiting for the Doctor. Inez.

Loaf (loaves)
Compensation. Kammeyer.
Miniature. Phillpotts.
Nationality. Gilmore.
The Railroad Corral.
  Anonymous.
Snow by Morning. Swenson.
Two Windows by Magritte. Roston.

Loafer (s)
Amagoduka at Glencoe
  Station. Mtshali.
June Twenty-First.
  Guernsey.
Old Grimes. Greene.
Will you sleep forever.
  Korinna.

Loam
The Body. Herrick.
Fall. Hass.
The Laboratory Midnight.
  Denney.

Loans
Dividends. Creekmore.
Vision. Sidgwick.

Loath ('d) (e) (ed) (ing)
All Those I Love Die Young.
  Bonefonius.
Alma: or, The Progress of the
  Mind. Prior.
Children of Darkness.
  Graves.
Discontents in Devon.
  Herrick.
Doralicia's Song. Graves.
L'Homme Moyhen Sensuel
  (excerpt). Pound.
In the Land of Magic.
  Michaux.
Seek Flowers of Heaven.
  Southwell.
Self Portrait 4. Ditlevsen.
Song: "In mine own
  monument I lie."
  Lovelace.
Words on the Windowpane.
  Rossetti.

Loch
Ante Mortem. Scroggie.
Ante Mortem. Scroggie.
Belfast Lough. *Anonymous.*
The Bothie of Tober-na-
  Vuolich. Clough.
Lachin Y Gair. Byron.
Trout Fisher. Brown.

Lock (ed) (ing) (s)
All Day We've Longed for
  Night. Fabio.
Barbara Allen. *Anonymous.*
Cancion. Levertov.
Christmas Amnesty. Pierce.
Colin Clout. Skelton.
Confession to Settle a Curse.
  Waldrop.
Constancy. O'Reilly.
The Dawning. Vaughan.
The Distant Runners. Van
  Doren.
Eve's Daughter. Sill.
Guardianship. Johnson.
The Humble Petition of Bruar
  Water to the Noble Duke of
  Athole. Burns.
I Dreamed Last Night of My
  True Love (with music).
  Anonymous.
If You Stick a Stock of
  Liquor–. Levy.
Initial. Boyars.
An Italian Chest. Seiffert.
Kitchen Door Blues.
  Williams.

The Lacquer Liquor Locker.
  McCord.
Lines for Michael in the
  Picture. Logan.
The Magnet. Stone.
Meditations in an Emergency.
  O'Hara.
Millom Old Quarry.
  Nicholson.
Mystical Poets. Nervo.
On a Puritanicall Lock-Smith.
  Camden.
The Poem of Joao. De
  Sousa.
Proem to "The Kid." Aiken.
Rowing. Ochester.
Shall These Early Fragrant
  Hours. Vaughan.
She dealt her pretty words
  like blades. Dickinson.
Singing Aloud. Kizer.
The Source. Stallworthy.
Summer Is Ended. Rossetti.
Summerhouse. La Follette.
Waking in the Blue. Lowell.
Walking Home at Night.
  Weissbort.
What Happened? Wieners.
Woman and Nature. Griffin.
The Woman in My Notebook.
  Cervantes.

Locker (s)
After a Game of Squash.
  Albert.
A New Song to an Old Tune.
  Anonymous.
Whom Do You Visualize as
  Your Reader? Pastan.

Locust (s)
August. Howells.
Into the Book. Grossman.
Under the Locust Blossoms.
  Tuckerman.

Lodge (r)
The Difference. O'Huiginn.

Lodging (s)
Amoretti, LXXIII. Spenser.
Lodgers. Tuwim.
The Lodging. Brown.
Mercian Hymns (excerpt).
  Hill.
The One Horse Chay.
  Anonymous.
Prayer of an Unbeliever.
  Reese.
Proffered Love Rejected.
  Suckling.
The Rain. Herbert.

Lofty
Amoretti, XIII. Spenser.
A Barren Soul. Ezobi.
The Bothie of Tober-na-
  Vuolich. Clough.
The Decay of a People.
  Simms
A Degenerate Age. Ibn
  Gabirol.
Epochs. Lazarus.
Self-Discipline. Russell.
Sonnet: Of Beauty and Duty.
  Dante Alighieri.
Spring. Allingham.

Log (s)
All Aboard for Bombay.
  Jackson.
Another Birthday. Jonson.
Breaking Ground in Me.
  Kryss.
Burns's Log Camp.
  Anonymous.
The Dunciad. Pope.

The Fish Will Swim as
  Before. Spence.
The History of Insipids.
  Freke.
The Masque of Christmas.
  Jonson.
Meson Brujo. Lacey.
Ode: To Sir William Sydney,
  on His Birth-Day. Jonson.
The Real Muse. Muratori.
University Curriculum.
  Turner.
When the Drive Goes Down.
  Malloch.

Logic
Clock without Hands. Nims.
Debate: Question, Quarry,
  Dream. Warren.
LXXII A Sonnet for Dick
  Gallup. Berrigan.
Piers the Ploughman.
  Langland.
Record Perpetual Loss.
  Stanley.

Loins
Ages and Ages Returning at
  Intervals. Whitman.
Children of Adam.
  Whitman.
Heroic Heart. Donnelly.
Pent-Up Aching Rivers
  (excerpt). Whitman.
The Royal Mummy to
  Bohemia. Stoddard.
Summum Bonum. Abu-l-Ala
  al-Maarri.
Zimmer's Hard Dream.
  Zimmer.

Loiter (ed)
An Apple Gathering.
  Rossetti.
Beginning My Studies.
  Whitman.
A Schoolmaster's Admonition.
  Anonymous.

London
April Midnight. Symons.
The Bells of London.
  Anonymous.
Cricket. An Heroic Poem.
  Dance.
A Description of London.
  Bancks.
From the Wash the Laundress
  Sends. Housman.
Going up to London.
  Turner.
Homage to Wren.
  MacNeice.
London Voluntaries. Henley.
Picture of Loot. Sillitoe.
Ratcliffe Highway.
  Anonymous.
See-Saw, Sacradown.
  Anonymous.
Simplicity's Song. Wilson.
Thyrsis, Sleep'st Thou?
  Anonymous.
To Maria Gisborne in
  England, from Italy.
  Shelley.
To Pete Atkin: A Letter from
  Paris (excerpt). James.
Upon Paul's Steeple Stands a
  Tree. *Anonymous.*

Lone
Bereft. Hardy.
Looking at a Picture on an
  Anniversary. Hardy.
Lovers. Fullerton.
No-Man's Land. Knight-
  Adkin.

Oh, Bury Me Not on The
  Lone Prairie (with music).
  Anonymous.
The Poor Girl's Meditation.
  Colum.
Prairie Graveyard. Marriott.
A Requiem for Soldiers Lost
  in Ocean Transport.
  Melville.
Seashore. Emerson.

Loneliest
Epitaph. De Vere.
Rich Days. Davies.
Six Days. Petaccia.

Loneliness
Above the Pool. Montague.
Art Thou Lonely? Oxenham.
Buildings. Gioseffi.
Child of Loneliness. Gale.
Cold, Sharp Lamentation.
  Gregory.
The Correspondence School
  Instructor Says Goodbye...
  Kinnell.
A Curse. Rabi'a.
The Disdainful Mistress.
  Anonymous.
The Dove's Loneliness.
  Darley.
Dr. Hu. Mailer.
The Fog. Coffin.
I Explain. Crane.
I walk in loneliness through
  the greenwood.
  Anonymous.
Lalla Rookh. Moore.
Lonely. Modisane.
The Loom of Dreams.
  Symons.
Medlars and Sorb-Apples.
  Lawrence.
No Time Ago. Cummings.
On Myself. Bone.
The Poet. Lowell.
Poetry. Giovanni.
Solitude. Deutsch.
Solitude. Peterson.
Sonnet: "In every dream thy
  lovely features rise."
  Barnes.
Sonnet: You Were Born; Must
  Die. Spender.
Watchmaker God. Lowell.
With a Flower. Dickinson.

Lonely
Acadia (excerpt). Howe.
The Affinity. Wickham.
Antique Glimpses (excerpt).
  Irwin.
Bedtime. Levertov.
The Birch-Tree at Loschwitz.
  Levy.
The Broken Pitcher. Ayton
  [(or Aytoun)] Sir Robert.
Bushed. Lillard.
By the Boat House, Oxford.
  Stevenson.
Canto Cantare Cantavi
  Cantatum. Brown.
The Captain. Tennyson.
The Cat. Church.
The Clown. Bruner.
Comfortable Strangers.
  Winch.
Company in Loneliness.
  Anonymous.
Corner Seat. MacNeice.
Crow's Nest. Armknecht.
The Dark Dialogues, II.
  Graham.
Dimidium Animae Meae.
  Brady.

Dirge on the Death of Art O'Leary. *Anonymous.*
Dull Is My Verse. Landor.
Eleanor Rigby. Beatles.
Elegy. Fraser.
The Escalator. Glasgow.
The Forsaken Merman. Arnold.
The Geranium. Roethke.
Glen-Almain, the Narrow Glen. Wordsworth.
Grammar Lesson. Paston.
His Body. McPherson.
Hope. Hughes.
The House Dog's Grave. Jeffers.
Hughley Steeple. Housman.
The Human Being Is a Lonely Creature. Eberhart.
I Am Lonely. Eliot.
I Met at Eve. De La Mare.
In a Valley of This Restless Mind. Milne.
In Dark Hour. MacManus.
In Memoriam A.H.H., XC. Tennyson.
In the Dark. Jewett.
Iphione. Irwin.
Jackie. Kuka.
Jodrell Bank. Dickinson.
Kearsarge. Mitchell.
Keep a Poem in Your Pocket. De Regniers.
The Late Hour. Strand.
Less Lonely. Kreymborg.
Letter to Garber from Skye. Hugo.
Lifting Illegal Nets by Flashlight. Wright.
The Little Cart. Waley.
The Lonely Street. Williams.
The Long and Lonely Winter. Goulder.
Lost Youth. Casement.
Love. Turner.
Mea Culpa. "Carbery.
Midsummer. Kinsella.
Mirthful Lunacy. Stoddart.
Morning Song. Teasdale.
A Morning to Remember; or, E. Pluribus Unum. Dorn.
The Mother's Prayer. Shorter.
The New Calf. Hearst.
Night-Piece. Patterson.
The Odd Ones. Suckow.
On a Lonely Spray. Stephens.
On the Wide Heath. Millay.
Personal Column. Paulin.
Peter Emberley (III). *Anonymous.*
Poem for Some Black Women. Rodgers.
Poplars. Reed.
Serenade. Timrod.
Sinners. Lawrence.
The Sleeper. Scollard.
The Snow. Keyes.
Soliloquy: South Africa. Nortje.
Sometimes I Wish That I Were Helen-Fair. Harford.
Songs for the Cisco Kid or Singing for the Face. Lyle.
Spirit of Sadness. Le Gallienne.
A Stranger in This Land. Ashby.
Taos Winter. Harjo.
The Teams. Lawson.
Ther's Many a Man Killed on the Railroad (with music). *Anonymous.*
Threnody. Farrar.
To Seem the Stranger Lies My Lot. Hopkins.
A Tree Design. Bontemps.
The Tree of Silence. Miller.
The Two Old Kings. De Tabley.
Two Windows by Magritte. Roston.
Ultimate Exile IV. Currey.
The Victories of Love, II (excerpt). Patmore.
The Villain. Davies.
Voyageur. Rashley.
What Color Is Lonely. Rodgers.
Youth and Age on Beaulieu River, Hants. Betjeman.

Lonesome
August. Pyle.
Down in the Lonesome Garden. *Anonymous.*
Everybody Ought to Make a Change. Estes.
Leaving Here. Philbrick.
Little Mary Cassidy. Fahy.
The Lugubrious Whing-Whang. Riley.
Old Men, White-Haired, beside the Ancestral Graves. Basho (Matsuo Basho).
Red Whiskey. *Anonymous.*
A Shantyman's Life (I). *Anonymous.*
Shorty George. *Anonymous.*
That Lonesome Train Took My Baby Away. McCoy.
An Uninscribed Monument on One of the Battle-Fields of the Wilderness. Melville
What Is-"Paradise". Dickinson.

Long
104 Boulevard Saint-Germain. Pitchford.
About My Poems. Justice.
Abraham Lincoln Walks at Midnight. Lindsay.
Across Kansas. Stafford.
Advice to a Neighbour Girl. Yu Hsuan-chi.
All the Scenes of Nature Quicken. Smart.
American History. Moses.
Among the Worst of Men. Thoreau.
Antigone. Sophocles.
As Freedom Is a Breakfastfood. Cummings.
At Last. Whittier.
Ballad of the Long-Legged Bait. Thomas.
Bearhug. Ondaatje.
Before Life and After. Hardy.
Bird at Night. Hamilton.
A Bird Was Singing. Dietmar von Aist.
Black Jess. Dufault.
Chevaliers de la Table Ronde. *Anonymous.*
A Child's Song of Christmas. Pickthall.
A Child's Song to Her Mother. Welles.
The Christian Pilgrim's Hymn. Williams.
Communication on His Thirtieth Birthday. Bell.
Concerning the Awakening of My Soul. Roland-Holst.
The Corpse-Keeper. *Anonymous.*
A Day in Autumn. Thomas.
The Documentary on Brazil. Corn.
Drinking Alone with the Moon. Li Po.
Dusk in Winter. Merwin.
Easter. Nemerov.
Easter Sunday, 1945. Borgese.
Echo. Rossetti.
English Bards and Scotch Reviewers. Byron.
The Eyes of Cantonese Schoolmasters Remembered in Hong Kong. Barnstone.
Farming. *Anonymous.*
February Twilight. Teasdale.
For My Daughter. Koertge.
Four Choctaw Songs. Barnes.
Funeral. Meyer.
The Gourd Dancer. Momaday.
The Grand Canyon. Merrill.
I Explain. Crane.
I Feel Like My Time Ain't Long. *Anonymous.*
I'm Worried Now but I Won't Be Worried Long. *Anonymous.*
The Indifferent. Beaumont.
Infidelity. Berggolts.
Katie Lee and Willie Grey. *Anonymous.*
Letter to My Mother. Skeen.
Levee Moan (with music). *Anonymous.*
The Lime Avenue. Sitwell.
Little Birdie. *Anonymous.*
Long and Lazy. Herrick.
Long Gone. Brown.
Long John. Anonymous.
Love Me Little, Love Me Long. *Anonymous.*
Man. Wolfe.
A Minor Victorian Painter. Hewitt.
Mister Charlie. Hopkins.
Moon Is to Blood. Duerden.
The Mother of Us All: "We cannot retrace our steps." Stein.
Music. Nye.
My Fiddle. Kwitko.
My Love Is Past. Watson.
My Mother's Birthday: "I used to watch you sleeping." Raine.
Neighbor. Waterman.
Night Song from Backbone Mountain. Epstein.
No No Blues. Baker.
O Atthis. Pound.
One Night Stand. Jones.
Oraga Haru. Issa.
Our Blackness Did Not Come to Us Whole. Bragg.
Out on Santa-Fe–Blues. Petties.
Parole Board. Butler.
Poor Lonesome Cowboy. *Anonymous.*
A Prayer. Gifford.
Progress. *Anonymous.*
The Redingote and the Vamoose. Munkittrick.
Rest. Rossetti.
Riddles and Lies. Zawadiwsky.
Riots and Rituals. Thomas.
The Rise of Man. Chadwick.
Robinson at Home. Kees.
Rural Bliss. Deane.
The Sea-Serpent. Planche.
She Moved through the Fair. Colum.
Small Aircraft. Akhmadulina.
Snatches: "The nightingale singes." *Anonymous.*
So Big! Fatchen.
So Long Ago. Rosenfeld.
Sois Sage O Ma Douleur. Baudelaire.
Song on May Morning. Milton.
Spring Song of a Super-Blake (parody). Untermeyer.
A Story of How a Wall Stands. Ortiz.
The Them Decade. Winch.
Thoughts of a Young Girl. Ashbery.
Time Out. Finkel.
The Tin-Whistle Player. Colum.
To a Scarlatti Passepied. Hillyer.
To a Waterfowl. Bryant.
To St. Mary Magdalen. Hill.
Tour Guide: La Maison des Esclaves. Dixon.
Trivial, Vulgar, and Exalted: 19. Cunningham.
The Turn of the Road. Gifford.
Twice Times Then Is Now. Ibn Hazm Al-Andalusi.
Two Sonnets. Berenberg.
Villanelle of the Poet's Road. Dowson.
Vision. Merwin.
The Weight. Aberg.
The Welsh Marches. Housman.
When the fifth month comes. Ise.
Who Shall Die? Randall, Jr.
The Wide Open Spaces. Lear.
Williams: An Essay. Levertov.
Wings and Seeds. McPherson.
The Woman Who Loved Women. Inez.
Yahrzeit. Schaeffer.

Long Island
Four Spacious Skies. Astor.
Geography: A Song. Moss.
Lake Success. Conquest.

Longed
Eros. Bridges.
My Parents Kept Me from Children Who Were Rough. Spender.
On Becoming Man. Lister.
Sealed Orders. Burton.
The Silver Question. Herford.
Tiresias (excerpt). Clarke.

Longing (s)
All Day We've Longed for Night. Fabio.
Arizona. *Anonymous.*
The Beauty of Things. Jeffers.
The Beloved's Image. *Anonymous.*

Candles. Swarth.
Caterpillar. Rashley.
Distance. Creeley.
Fifth Sunday after Easter.
   Kinsella.
Fulfillment. Muhlenberg.
Goddess. Sherwin.
I Dreamed That I Was Old.
   Kunitz.
I Have a Young Sister.
   Anonymous.
I Took a Hansom on To-Day.
   Henley.
I Will Accept. Rossetti.
If You Are Fire. Rosenberg.
Incognita. Dobson.
It Always Happens. Horace.
The Leaves. Loewinsohn.
Like a Woman. Greenberg.
Lines to a Tree. Teller. J. L.
Longing. Arnold.
A Love Letter to Elizabeth
   Thatcher. Thatcher.
A Man's Love. Ditlevsen.
Nights in Hackett's Cove.
   Strand.
The Odyssey. Homer.
Old Michael. Brady.
One Chord. Sachs.
Reality. Dickinson.
The Sentimentalist. Field.
Sinfonia Eroica. James.
Song: "There stands a lonely
   pine-tree." Heine.
Sweet Voice of the Garb.
   Geilt.
Thrice Welcome First and
   Best of Days. Chanler.
The Tokens of Love: I.
   Anonymous.
The Two Burdens. Marston.
The Wheel. Yeats.

Look (ed) (ing) (s)
29 (A Dream in Two Parts).
   Ai.
999 Call. Bartlett.
Accomplished Facts.
   Sandburg.
Actions. Schwob.
Advice to a Prizefighter.
   Lucilius [or Lucillius].
Amoretti, XXI. Spenser.
Ank'hor Vat. Devlin.
Another Old Song. Bush.
At Eighty. Stanhope.
At the Edge of Town.
   Stafford.
An Athenian Garden.
   Stickney.
Aurora Leigh. Browning.
Autumn. Clare.
Ballade of England.
   MacNeice.
Behold the Lilies of the Field.
   Hecht.
Believe Me, If All Those
   Endearing Young Charms.
   Moore.
Big City. Brownstein.
Black Is a Soul. White.
Blue Homespun. Call.
Bob McKinney. Thomas.
The Bully Song. Trevathan.
Calligram, 15 May 1915.
   Apollinaire.
The Canadian Exile. Gerin-
   Lajoie.
Celebration 1982. Wilkins.
The Centaur Overheard.
   Bowers.
The Church. Muir.

Conversation in Black and
   White. Sarton.
Creeds. Wattles.
Crossing. Oppenheimer.
Cynthia on Horseback.
   Ayres.
Darkness. Campbell.
Death's the Classic Look.
   Ciardi.
Don Juan in Hell.
   Baudelaire.
The Door and the Window.
   Reed.
A Dream. Bronte.
A Drinking Song. Yeats.
The Eagle. Young.
Early Chronology. Sassoon.
East St. Louis Blues.
   Anonymous.
Eros. Bridges.
Finding You. Gilbert.
The Fish. Gustafson.
The Flute of the Lonely.
   Lindsay.
For Stephen. Brookhouse.
Fragment from "Clemo Uti–
   The Water Lilies."
   Lardner.
The Fundamental Project of
   Technology. Kinnell.
Gargoyle. Rabbit.
Getting Up Early. Bly.
Ghazal XII. Ghalib.
Going. Schuyler.
The Grand Guignols of Love.
   Benedikt.
Greeting Descendants.
   Sobin.
Hawk Nailed to a Barn Door.
   Blue Cloud.
Homeward Bound.
   Mphahlele.
The House on Buder Street.
   Gildner.
How to Find Your Way
   Home. Petaccia.
Hyperion. Keats.
I Am in Great Misery
   Tonight. Geilt.
I Dream'd in a Dream.
   Whitman.
I Dreamed I Saw the Crescent
   Moon. Anonymous.
I Have Got to Stop Loving
   You. Anthony ("Ai").
I Walk in the Old Street.
   Zukofsky.
The Iliad. Homer.
In a Cafe. Brautigan.
In Golden Gate Park That
   Day. Ferlinghetti.
In My New Clothing. Basho
   (Matsuo Basho).
In the Mirror. Fleming.
Indian Dance. Niven.
The Invention of New Jersey.
   Anderson.
Jeane Dixon's America.
   Costanzo.
Kangaroos. Anonymous.
The Lady with the Unicorn.
   Watkins.
Late. Bogan.
Leoun. Cocteau.
Let Me Look At Me.
   Martin.
Let the Florid Music Praise.
   Auden.
The Life and Death of Habbie
   Simson, the Piper of
   Kilbarchan. Sempill.

Limerick: "This bird is the
   Keel-billed Toucan."
   Ketcham.
The Little Duck. Joso.
The Little Wee Man.
   Anonymous.
Looking at Each Other.
   Rukeyser.
Looking for a Ship.
   Anonymous.
The Looks of a Lover
   Enamoured. Gascoigne.
Mae West. Field.
Mark You How the Peacock's
   Eye. Hopkins.
May with Its Light Behaving.
   Auden.
The Mermaid. Anonymous.
Movies, Left to Right.
   Sward.
Mr. Wells. Roberts.
My Creed. Walter.
O Child of Beauty Rare.
   Goethe.
Odes. Horace.
Of Loving at First Sight.
   Waller.
Ofay-Watcher Looks Back.
   Serote.
On a Gentleman Marrying
   His Cook. Ellis.
On This Day I Complete My
   Thirty-sixth Year. Byron.
One Home. Stafford.
Origin of Dreams. Bell.
Over the Heather the Wet
   Wind Blows. Auden.
Overcoats. Kramer.
Pigeon. Fuller.
Plans. Brooks.
Poem. Simic.
Poem for Jan. Bruchac.
Poem to Be Read and Sung.
   Vallejo.
The Portrait. Rossetti.
The Purpose of Altar Boys.
   Rios.
The Quest. Cortissoz.
The Rabbit. Roberts.
The Range Rider's Soliloquy.
   Brininstool.
The Reapers. Watt.
Remembering Lutsky.
   Zychlinska.
Remembering My Father.
   Holden.
Ripe, Being Plunged into
   Fire... Holderlin.
The Rising Village.
   Goldsmith.
Rispetti: On the Death of a
   Child. Heyse.
Running Back. Smith.
Saints, and Their Care. Rios.
Samson to His Delilah.
   Crashaw.
Separation. Bunner.
Shaman. Leiper.
The Ships of Arcady.
   Ledwidge.
Ships That Pass in the Night.
   Longfellow.
Sin and Its Cure.
   Anonymous.
The Snake. Corke.
Song: Ah Stay. Congreve.
Song: "I walk'd in the
   lonesome evening."
   Allingham.
Song. Set by Mr. Coleman.
   Cotton.

Song: "She was lyin face down
   in her face." Knott.
Songs from an Evil Wood.
   Plunkett.
Sonic Boom. Updike.
The Sound of Rain.
   Akhmadulina.
The Stable Cat. Norris.
The Stargazer. Anonymous.
Statesboro Blues. McTell.
Strawberries in November.
   Neilson.
The Talking Oak: Olivia.
   Tennyson.
These Stones. Menander.
This Child. Rosten.
This Is a Photograph of Me.
   Atwood.
Three Ballate. Poliziano.
To a Common Prostitute.
   Whitman.
To Helen. Praed.
To Tomas Costello at the
   Wars. O'Higgins.
Tractor Hour. Reid.
Tricks. Moure.
Two. Scott.
Unsent Message to My
   Brother in His Pain.
   Stokesbury.
Verses on a Cat. Daubeny.
The Vestal Virgin. Llwyd.
The Vision of Sir Launfal.
   Lowell.
A Visit to Enniskillen.   O
   Huiginn.
The Walk. Hardy.
The Watergaw.
   ""MacDiarmid.
We do not play on graves.
   Dickinson.
Western Lines. Whitman.
The White Dress. Spear.
Who Can Tell When He Is
   Awake. Tate.
Why Did You Go.
   Cummings.
Wodwo. Hughes.
A Woman Making Advances
   Publicly. Kazantzis.
The Women in Vietnam.
   Paley.

Looking-glass
And the Seventh Dream in
   the Dream of Isis.
   Gascoyne.
Destroyer. Sullivan.
Letter to a Friend.
   Stallworthy.
Tommy Trot. Anonymous.
The World of Fools Has Such
   a Store. Anonymous.

Lookout (s)
The Battle of Lookout
   Mountain. Boker.
Crow's Nest. Armknecht.
The Veteran. Coxe.

Loom (s)
The Creation of My Lady.
   Redi.
Featherstone's Doom.
   Hawker.
The New Bury Loom.
   Anonymous.
Our Lady's Labor. Duffy.
The Scarlet Thread.
   Henderson.
Surely My Soul... Cohen.
Symphony. Dorn.
The Wool Trade. Dyer.

Loon
Clerk Saunders. Anonymous.

The Fruit Rancher. Roberts.
A Jacobite Scot in Satire on England's Unparalleled Loss. *Anonymous.*
Seaward. Thaxter.
Talking to Animals. Howes.

Loose
Aeliana's Ditty. Chettle.
Astrophel and Stella, XVIII. Sidney.
The Castle of Indolence. Thomson.
Eadwacer. *Anonymous.*
Fall Song. Moses.
The Glory Trail. Clark.
Ignorant Men, Who Disclaim. Juana Ines de la Cruz.
The Lane. Young.
Mankind. *Anonymous.*
Real Deal Revelation. Fernandez.
A Song: "Boast no more fond Love, thy Power." D'Urfey.
The Stranger. Rich.
The Tapestry. Nemerov.
Thaw. Broughton.
Till Death Do Us Part. Miccolis.
Upon the Death of G: B. Cotton.
The World So Wide. *Anonymous.*
Zimmer Envying Elephants. Zimmer.

Lord
34 Blues. Patton.
Abiding. Simpson.
Ain't Gonna Grieve My Lord No More. *Anonymous.*
The All-Embracing. Faber.
All That I Am. Arvey.
Alleluia! Alleluia! Let the Holy Anthem Rise. Anonymous.
And Forgive Us Our Trespasses. Behn.
And His Name Shall Be Called Wonderful. Nicholson.
Angels, Roll the Rock Away! Scott.
The Armada, 1588. Wilson.
Astrophel and Stella, XCIX. Sidney.
At Length There Dawns the Glorious Day. Davis.
Attend, Young Friends, While I Relate. *Anonymous.*
Aunt Jane. Nowlan.
Ballade of Faith. MacInnes.
The Band of Gideon. Cotter.
The Bantam Husband. *Anonymous.*
Be Thankful. Bullock.
Before Action. Hodgson.
Beware Fair Maide. *Anonymous.*
The Birthday of the Lord. Carr.
De Blin' Man Stood on de Road an' Cried. *Anonymous.*
Borges. Barnstone.
Canticle of the Sun. Francis of Assisi.
The Chicago Defender Sends a Man to Little Rock, Fall, 1957. Brooks.
Childless. MacConmidhe.
Christ's Resurrection and Ascension. Doddridge.

Christ, the Conqueror. Burder.
Come, All Ye People. Seltzer.
Compensation. Campbell.
Composed on the Eve of the Marriage of a Friend ... Wordsworth.
Conscience. Herbert.
Coronation. Perronet.
The Cosmic Fabric. Polonsky.
The Created. Very.
The Cross and the Tomb. Flint.
The Danger of Writing Defiant Verse. Parker.
Daybreak. Smith.
Death Come to My House He Didn't Stay Long. *Anonymous.*
The Destruction of Sennacherib. Byron.
Do, Lord, Remember Me. *Anonymous.*
Easter Beatitudes. Burkholder.
The Elder, or Bourtree. *Anonymous.*
An Elegie On the Deploreable Departure of ...John Hull. Saffin.
Elegy for a Bad Poet, Taken from Us Not Long Since. Nims.
An Evening Prayer. Kendall.
Ever On. *Anonymous.*
Every Time I Feel the Spirit. *Anonymous.*
Exhortation to Prayer. Cowper.
The Experience. Taylor.
The Fair Flower of Northumberland. *Anonymous.*
Father, Who Mak'st Thy Suff'ring Sons. Coxe.
The Feast o' Saint Stephen. Sawyer.
For Beauty, We Thank Thee. Oxenham.
For Mao Tse-Tung: A Meditation on Flies and Kings. Layton.
For We Are Thy People. *Anonymous.*
Foul Water. Temkin.
Four Christmas Carols (excerpt). *Anonymous.*
Frying Pan Skillet Blues. Tucker.
God Incarnate. Williams.
God's Dominion and Decrees. Watts.
Grace after Meals. *Anonymous.*
Grace at Kirkudbright. Burns.
The Gray Goose. *Anonymous.*
Great and Mighty Wonder. Anatolius.
Hallelujah! Praise the Lord. Hatfield.
The Harrowing of Hell. Langland.
Heriot's Ford. Kipling.
His Name Is at the Top. *Anonymous.*
Hope Springing Up. Wesley.

The Housewife's Prayer. Kelly.
The Hurricane. Crane.
Hymn for the Lighting of the Lamps. Athenogenes.
The Hymn of the World's Creator (excerpt). Caedmon.
I Blow My Pipes. McCrae.
I Don't Want to Be a Gambler (with music). *Anonymous.*
I Love the Lord. *Anonymous.*
I Need Thee. Whitfield.
In Early Spring. Meynell.
In the Garden of the Lord. Keller.
In the Secret Rose Garden. Shabistari.
An Incident. Tennyson.
It's Wonderful. Isenhour.
Jamie Douglas (B vers.). *Anonymous.*
Jesus Spreads His Banner O'er Us. Park.
Jubalee; or, What Is de Matter wid de Mourners. *Anonymous.*
Jubilate Agno. Smart.
The Kingdom of God. Rab.
Lady Maisry. *Anonymous.*
Laus Deo. Whittier.
The Lay of the Last Minstrel. Scott.
Let Us Break Bread Together. *Anonymous.*
The Life of St. Cellach: He Who Forsakes the Clerkly Life. *Anonymous.*
Like Treasure Hidden in the Ground. Mahadevi (Mahadeviyakka).
The Lion for Real. Ginsberg.
Litany for Peace. Clark.
Little Black Man with a Rose in His Hat. Wurdemann.
Locksley Hall Sixty Years After. Tennyson.
The Lord Is King. *Anonymous.*
Lord of the Dance. Carter.
The Lord of the World. Studdert-Kennedy.
Lord Shaftesbury. Dryden.
Lord Thomas and Lady Margaret. *Anonymous.*
Love to My Lord. Van Plettenhaus.
The Majesty of God. Sternhold.
A Man May Live Thrice Nestor's Life. Norton.
Marthy Had a Baby. *Anonymous.*
Meditation on Communion with God. Halevi.
Moanish Lady! (with music). *Anonymous.*
The Monarch. Cowper.
Monasteries. Webb.
Morning Glory. Sassoon.
The Morning Hours. *Anonymous.*
The Morning Light Is Breaking. Smith.
My Jesus, As Thou Wilt. Schmolck.
My Lord's A-Writin' All de Time. *Anonymous.*

My Lord, What a Mourning. *Anonymous.*
The Neighbors Help Him Build His House. *Anonymous.*
Never Weather-Beaten Sail. Campion.
New Lines for Cuscuscaraway and Mirza Murad Ali Beg. Simpson.
Night-Thoughts. Ibn Gabirol.
Nocturne. Hugo.
Not to Us, Not unto Us, Lord. *Anonymous.*
Now I Lay Me Down to Sleep. *Anonymous.*
O Boy Cutting Grass. Hitomaro.
O Brothers, Why Do You Talk. Mahadevi (Mahadeviyakka).
O Deus, Ego Amo Te. Hopkins.
Oh, My Good Lord, Show Me de Way. *Anonymous.*
Omnipresence. Hale.
On a Distinguished Politician. Thorold Rogers.
On a Dog-Collar. *Anonymous.*
On the Death of Emperor Tenji. *Anonymous.*
Other men are thorn. Mahadevi (Mahadeviyakka).
A Paraphrase on Thomas a Kempis. Pope.
The Passions That We Fought With. Stickney.
Praise the Lord and Pass the Ammunition! Loesser.
A Prayer. Oxenham.
Prayer. Stevenson.
A Prayer. Tuwim.
A Prayer to Be Said When Thou Goest to Bed. Seager.
The Precious Blood. *Anonymous.*
The Properties of the Shires of England. *Anonymous.*
Psalm XXIII. Sidney.
A Psalm of Praise (excerpt). Baxter.
Pslam XXIV. Sidney.
The Purification. Cosmas.
Rapture. Carlson.
Revelation. Cook.
Ring Out Your Bells. Sidney.
Rise, Mourner, Rise. *Anonymous.*
The Rising in the North. *Anonymous.*
Roadside Flowers. Carman.
Robin Hood and the Curtal Friar. *Anonymous.*
Samuel Allen. *Anonymous.*
Satan's a Liah (with music). *Anonymous.*
Searching the Desert for the Blues. McTell.
The Sepulcher. Flint.
Sequaire. Godeschalk.
The Shadows. Macdonald.
Silex Scintillans. Vaughan.
Singin' wid a Sword in Ma Han'. *Anonymous.*
A Song in Time of Revolution 1860. Swinburne.
The Song of Mary the Mother of Christ. Walpole.

Songs of Kabir. Kabir.
Soon One Mornin' Death
  Come Creepin'.
  Anonymous.
The Splendid Village. Elliott.
Square-Toed Princes. Coffin.
Summer Magic. Hill.
Suppertime. Burns.
Thanksgiving Day. Bridges.
Thick Grows the Tarragon.
  Anonymous.
Thy Conquering Name.
  Wesley.
Thy Name We Bless and
  Magnify. Power.
Till You've Earned.
  Mahadevi (Mahadeviyakka).
Timber (with music).
  Anonymous.
Too Busy. *Anonymous.*
The Torch. Garrison.
Trooper and Maid, II.
  Anonymous.
The True Apostolate.
  Weyburn.
Truth. McKay.
Truth Brought to Light; or,
  Murder Will Out. College.
The Two Gentlemen of
  Verona. Shakespeare.
Two Graces. *Anonymous.*
Vermont Conversation.
  Hubbell.
The Vision of Piers Plowman.
  Langland.
The Vision of Sir Launfal.
  Lowell.
We Are Watching, We Are
  Waiting. Cushing.
We Plough the Fields.
  Campbell.
We Thank Thee. Oxenham.
Whale. Benet.
What Tidings? Audelay.
When de Good Lord Sets You
  Free. *Anonymous.*
Who but the Lord? Hughes.
Who'll Be a Witness for My
  Lord? *Anonymous.*
The Wild Mustard River.
  Anonymous.
Words from an Old Spanish
  Carol. Sawyer.
Wreck of the Deutschland.
  Hopkins.
You Shall. Stokes.
Your Presence. Temkin.

Lords
Ana(Mary-Army)gram.
  Herbert.
Another Cynical Variation.
  "Helen".
An Aristocratic Trio.
  France.
The Battle of Erie.
  Anonymous.
Buriall. Vaughan.
The Common Sailor.
  Anonymous.
Conquistador. MacLeish.
Conrad. Slonimski.
Crusade. Belloc.
The Death of Nelson.
  Anonymous.
Down in Yon Forest.
  Anonymous.
The Eagle's Nature.
  Anonymous.
Edwin Booth. Brown.
Epitaph. Macdonald.
Epitaph: "Lo worms enjoy the
  seat of bliss." Burns.

Epitaph on the Earl of
  Leicester. Ralegh.
Fair Annie. *Anonymous.*
For Us No Night Can Be
  Happier. Zinzendorf.
The Gardener. Eaton.
Glenfinlas; or, Lord Ronald's
  Coronach. Scott.
The Heir of Linne.
  Anonymous.
Hon. Mr. Sucklethumbkin's
  Story. Barham.
The Hunting of the Cheviot
  (C vers.). *Anonymous.*
In Dessexshire as It Befel.
  Anonymous.
In Memoriam A.H.H., LIII.
  Tennyson.
Irish Antiquities. Moore.
The Knight of Liddesdale.
  Anonymous.
The Lay of the Last Minstrel.
  Scott.
Lord Lovel (D version).
  Anonymous.
The Lords of the Main.
  Stansbury.
Lovers Relentlessly. Kunitz.
May Day. *Anonymous.*
Nelson's Death. *Anonymous.*
A New Song Composed on
  the Death of Lord Nelson.
  Anonymous.
Nocturne. Hugo.
O Whose Are These Children.
  Snyder.
On Christmas Day.
  Anonymous.
The Prophecy of Samuel
  Sewall. Whittier.
Psalm X. Sidney.
The Second Satire of the First
  Book of Horace (excerpt).
  Pope.
The Sun of Grace.
  Anonymous.
The Thousand and One
  Nights: Inscriptions at the
  City of Brass. *Anonymous.*
To Penshurst. Jonson.
A Toast. *Anonymous.*
Upon Christmas Eve.
  Suckling.
The Utopia of Lord Mayor
  Howard. Stow.
The Vedic Hymns: To the
  One God. *Anonymous.*
The Weeper. Crashaw.

Lore
Apology for Youth.
  Madeleva.
April. Emerson.
The Highest Wisdom.
  Jacopone da Todi.
Man Is but a Castaway.
  Day.
Miles Keogh's Horse. Hay.

Lose (s)
Advice to a Blue-Bird.
  Bodenheim.
After the Festival. George.
At Bickford's. Stern.
Big Grave Creek. Corman.
Billy Lyons and Stack O'Lee.
  Lewis.
Christ. Forker.
Christ's Victory and Triumph.
  Fletcher.
Consider. Pico della
  Mirandola.
Damages, Two Hundred
  Pounds. Thackeray.

Dawn and a Woman.
  Logan.
Dry Be That Tear. Sheridan.
Epitaph: "Here lies the man
  that madly slain."
  Hoskyns.
Faint Heart. Linton.
The Fisherman. Wells.
For a Nativity. Mueller.
For Mulatto. Fernandez.
Games. McPherson.
Gather Ye Rosebuds (parody).
  Fowler.
Good Sportsmanship.
  Armour.
Heptonstall Old Church.
  Hughes.
How I Escaped from the
  Labyrinth. Dacey.
Hymn from the French of
  Lamartine (excerpt).
  Whittier.
In Defense of Satire.
  Scroope.
In the Gazebo (parody).
  Appleman.
An Italian Chest. Seiffert.
Keys. Rockwell.
Lalla Rookh. Moore.
Last Week I Took a Wife.
  Kelly.
Limerick: "A camel, with
  practical views." Herford.
Lord! Lead the Way the
  Saviour Went. Croswell.
Love's Labour's Lost.
  Shakespeare.
Love's Lord. Dowden.
The Lovers. Zaturenska.
A Malemute Dog. O'Cotter.
Man. Greenberg.
Montreto to His Mistress.
  Graham.
Mullet Snatching. Glass.
My Father: October 1942.
  Stafford.
No One Talks about This.
  Rakosi.
O Fly My Soul. Shirley.
O Sower of Sorrow.
  Plunkett.
Patty Hearst Hoists the
  Carbine. James.
Persuasions to Love. Carew.
Reflections (excerpt).
  Freneau.
Shakespearean Soliloquy in
  Progress: "To starve, or not
  to..."(parody). Ireland.
Shooting Gallery. Galvin.
A Smile. *Anonymous.*
Songs of Seven. Ingelow.
Sonnet on Death. Walsh.
Sonnet: "So shoots a star as
  doth my mistress glide."
  Davies.
Sonnets, LXIV: "When I have
  seen by Time's fell hand
  defaced." Shakespeare.
Stewball. *Anonymous.*
Such Love Is Like a Smoky
  Fire. Chapman.
The Sunday News. Gioia.
Tamer and Hawk. Gunn.
To the Men Who Lose.
  Scarborough.
Toads. Larkin.
Turn the Glasses Over.
  Anonymous.
Tyne Dock. Scarfe.
Vilanelle. Kerr.
Warriors. Hogan.

Loser (s)
The Elephant to the Girl in
  Bertram Mills' Circus.
  Cronin.
Pleasures, Beauty. Ford.
Winslow Homer, Prisoners
  from the Front. Blakely.
With Cindy at Vallecito.
  McDonald.

Loss (es)
The After-Glow. Blind.
April Fools' Day.
  Komunyakaa.
Arcadia. Sidney.
Arm Wrestling with My
  Father. Driscoll.
The Benjamins' Lamentation
  for Their Sad Loss at Sea,
  by Storms... *Anonymous.*
Blues for an Old Blue.
  Gibson.
Content and Rich.
  Southwell.
The Dead Bride. Hill.
Dear Mrs. McKinney of the
  Sixth Grade:. Kherdian.
Dipsychus. Clough.
Discoveries. Watkins.
Don Juan. Byron.
Flowering Currant.
  MacDonogh.
For Pity, Pretty Eyes,
  Surcease. Lodge.
Gallows and Cross.
  MacDonald.
He Is a Path. Fletcher.
Here Huntington's Ashes
  Long Have Lain. Bierce.
The Hours. Dubie.
How oft have I, my dear and
  cruel foe. Wyatt.
In Memory of the Utah Stars.
  Matthews.
Lessons of the Year.
  Anonymous.
Like as the bird in the cage
  enclosed. Wyatt.
Love's Consolation. Dixon.
Monna Innominata.
  Rossetti.
My Master Was So Very
  Poor. Lee.
A New Song Composed on
  the Death of Lord Nelson.
  Anonymous.
Nine Bean-Rows on the
  Moon. Purdy.
Nonsense Verses. Lamb.
Objects. Auden.
Of Love. Wyatt.
An Old Song Reversed.
  Stoddard.
On the Detraction which
  Followed upon My Writing
  Certain Treatises. Milton.
Overheard in the Louvre.
  Kennedy.
A Pause for Breath. Hughes.
Queen Victoria and Me.
  Cohen.
Qui Perdiderit Animam Suam.
  Crashaw.
Sailboat, Your Secret.
  Francis.
Satires. Wyatt.
Since Nature's Works Be
  Good. Sidney.
The Skeptic. Service.
Sonnets: A Sequence on
  Profane Love. Boker.
Survey of Cornwall. Carew.

Thanksgiving at Snake Butte. Welch.
A Thought. Sangster.
Three Epitaphs. Davison.
To a Lady. Gay.
To His Lute. Drummond.
To L. C. Hawkins.
To the Sun. Bachmann.
To wet your eye withouten tear. Wyatt.
A Valediction. Cartwright.
When Daddy Died. Ackerson.
Whitehall Stairs. Hill.
Why Fear to Die? Sidney.
Yet Listen Now. Carmichael.

Lost
After My Death. Bialik.
An Air by Sammartini. Dudek.
Alas How Long. *Anonymous.*
Alas the grief and deadly woeful smart! Wyatt.
Alice's Recitation. "Carroll.
All That's Bright Must Fade. Moore.
An American Takes a Walk. Whittemore.
The Ancestors. Middleton.
April Midnight. Symons.
The Ascetic. Daley.
At Set of Sun. Eliot.
Australia. Langley.
Baby. Eastman.
Ballad of the Trial of Sodom. Watkins.
The Bath. Graham.
Beauty. *Anonymous.*
Black Sketches, 8. Lee.
Blue Fly. De Assis.
The Bridal Pair. Young.
The Bulldozer. Stauffer.
Calverly's. Robinson.
Camptown. Ciardi.
Captain Kidd. *Anonymous.*
Carentan O Carentan. Simpson.
The Celtic Lyric (parody). Squire.
Changsha Shoe Factory. Barnstone.
Choose. Bishop.
Clementine. Montrose.
Coming Home. Humphries.
The Coming of Dusk upon a Village in Haiti. Rago.
Complaint That His Ladie after She Knew of His Love Kept Her Face... Surrey.
Conflict. Clive.
Consider Well. More.
Count Filippo. Heavysege.
The Dancing Bear. Field.
Dane-Geld. Kipling.
Dare You? Sill.
A Death in the Desert. Browning.
Derelict. Pullen.
Despair. Reed.
Dispossessed Poet. Gibbon.
Dorothy. Lathrop.
Draherin O Machree. *Anonymous.*
Elegy. Trench.
Epigram: "Since I am completely drunk." *Anonymous.*
Epitaph for a Bigot. Johnson.

Epitaph on One Lockyer, Inventor of a Patent Medicine. *Anonymous.*
Epitaph...on the Grave of Thomas Osborne, Died 1749. *Anonymous.*
Eve of Easter. Mayer.
Evening. Doolittle.
An Evening Walk (excerpt). Wordsworth.
Father-in-Law. Mahon.
Feminine. Bunner.
Ferry Hinksey. Binyon.
The Fighting Failure. Appleton.
The First Solitude. Gongora y Argote.
Fish. Williams.
Fog-Horn. Merwin.
For the Lost Generation. Kinnell.
Foreclosure. Van Doren.
From the Notebooks. Roethke.
The Gold-Seekers. Garland.
Golfers. Updike.
A Grafted Tongue. Montague.
Green Light. Fearing.
Green Red Brown and White. Swenson.
Hair Poem. Knott.
Harps Hung Up in Babylon. Colton.
The Heretic's Tragedy. Browning.
Hold-Up. MacNeice.
How a Girl Got Her Chinese Name. Wong.
Human Frailty. Cowper.
Hymn to the Sea. Watson.
I Am in Great Misery Tonight. Geilt.
I don't sleep. Mira Bai [(or Mirabai)].
"I never saw you, madam, lay apart." Surrey.
The Image of Delight. Leonard.
In Computers. Lightman.
In the Secret House. Middleton.
In the Trades. Smith.
In the Wilderness. Pierce.
The Insult. Layzer.
Irish Molly O. *Anonymous.*
It May Not Always Be So. Cummings.
The Lark Ascending. Meredith.
The Leader. Belloc.
A Learned Man. Crane.
Legend. Wheelock.
A Letter from the Caribbean. Howes.
Lines. Brooke.
The Little Brother. Reeves.
The Lochmabyn Harper. *Anonymous.*
The Lost. *Anonymous.*
The Lost Continent. Joseph.
Lost Youth. Casement.
The Mad Lover. Strahan.
The Marriage of Heaven and Earth. Nemerov.
The Marriage of Heaven and Hell. Blake.
The Massacre of the Innocents: The Devil's Doubts. Marino.
Messages. Noyes.

Mexico City Blues: 225th Chorus. Kerouac.
Mile Hill. Schmitz.
Morning. Rios.
Mullet Snatching. Glass.
Murder in the Cathedral. Eliot.
My Dead. "Rachel" (Rachel Blumstein).
My Wish for You. Rabi'a of Balkh.
The Network. Finch.
The Night Moths. Markham.
Night Thoughts While Travelling. Tu Fu.
A Northern Legion. Read.
Notes from a Slave Ship. Field.
Nothing but Image. Swilky.
Now Look What Happened. Peacock.
Of Course I Know. Landau.
Of the Beloved Caravan. Meyer.
Of the Boy and Butterfly. Bunyan.
An Old Maid Early. Blake.
Old Man Hall. Jacobs.
On a Picture of Your House. Jones.
On Her Loving Two Equally. Behn.
On the Death of Captain Nicholas Biddle. Freneau.
On the Slope of the Desolate River. Tagore.
On Top of Old Smoky. *Anonymous.*
One Star Fell and Another. Aiken.
One-Two-Three. Senesh.
Orpheus to Eurydice. Morgan.
The Pack Rat. Pack.
Paradise Lost. Milton.
Parole Denial. Green.
Peschiera. Clough.
The Picture of Little J.A. in a Prospect of Flowers. Ashbery.
Plea for Hope. Carlin.
A Present of Butter. O'Huiginn.
The Rejected "National Hymns". Newell.
Remember, Though the Telescope Extend. Dillon.
Reuben, Reuben. Harper.
A Revel. MacDonagh.
Ross's Poems. Lehmann.
The Runaway. Hicky.
Saint Francis and the Birds. McFadden.
Samson to His Delilah. Crashaw.
Sandpaper, Sandpiper, Sandpit. Slesinger.
Sea-Change. Taggard.
Seagulls on the Serpentine. Noyes.
Seascape with Bookends. Eaton.
Ship-Building Emperors Commanded... Levi.
Simple Faith. Cowper.
Sleepin' at the Foot O' the Bed. Patrick.
The Smell of Old Newspapers Is Always Stronger... Lowery.
Song for a Lost Art. Brasier.

Song: "Though I am dark." *Anonymous.*
Sonnets–Unrealities. Cummings.
Sounding. Ferne.
The South Carolina. *Anonymous.*
South-Folk in Cold Country. *Anonymous.*
Squall. Moore.
Strangers. Stafford.
The Stream's Song. Abercrombie.
Summer Solstice. Keating.
Sun and Moon. Macpherson.
The Sun in Capricorn. Mansour.
Sunset. Bialik.
The Surrender of New Orleans. Manville.
Take Back the Heart. Barnard.
These Are Not Lost. Metcalf.
They Dream Only of America. Ashbery.
Things. Dow.
Tiresias' Lament. Kay.
To a Bed of Tulips. Herrick.
To a Hero Dead at al-Safra. Hind bint Uthatha.
To Dorothy. Bell.
To the Borrower of This Book. Showell, Jr.
To the Virgins, To Make Much of Time. Herrick.
Tripping down the Field-Path. Swain.
Two. Scott.
Two Invocations of Death, II. Raine.
Ula Masondo's Dream. Plomer.
The Unpossessed. Naude.
Upon My Lady Carliles Walking in Hampton-Court Garden. Dialogue. Suckling.
Vetus Flamma. Mezey.
Vision and Prayer. Thomas.
Visions. Petrarch.
Wait On! *Anonymous.*
Wash Me Whiter Than Snow. Wesley.
When We Drive at Night. Pollitt.
Willie Macintosh (B version). *Anonymous.*
With a Nantucket Shell. Webb.
The Womanhood. Brooks.
Yonder Comes My Pretty Girl (B vers.). *Anonymous.*
Yonnondio. Whitman.
Youth and Art. Browning.
The Zucca (excerpt). Shelley.

Lot (s)
Aoibhinn, a leabhrain, do thriall. *Anonymous.*
At the Grave of a Land-Shark. Moll.
The Dying Enthusiast. Mangan.
Enthusiasm. Mangan.
The Hurricane. Freneau.
Lament for Azazel. Landy.
Page from a Diary. O'Grady.
The Pass of Kirkstone. Wordsworth.
Pearl Bryan. *Anonymous.*

Richie Story (A version).
Anonymous.
Samson Agonistes. Milton.
A Smile. Anonymous.
Songs of Seven. Ingelow.
A Summer Night. Arnold.
To a Withered Rose. Bangs.
Verses Supposed to be Written
by Alexander Selkirk.
Cowper.
Whispers of Immortality.
Eliot.
Youth and Age. Mimnermus.

Lotus (es)
A Buddhist Priest. Ho Xuan
Huong.
The Egyptian Lotus. Eaton.
Lotuses. Bynner.
Mountain, Fire, Thornbush.
Shapiro.
Not Yet. Kyger.
Reckoning A. M. Thursday
after an Encounter....
Turner.

Loud (er)
Antaeus: A Fragment.
Owen.
Black Art. Jones.
Doctor Faustus. Hill.
Hillcrest. Robinson.
Inebriates. Brasfield.
Little Ivory Figures Pulled
with String. Lowell.
Prayer. Flecker.
Progress. Douglass.
The Song-Throe. Rossetti.
A White-Throat Sings.
Eaton.
Written in a Time of Crisis.
Benét.

Lounge
Still Pond, No More Moving.
Moss.
Summer. Kulbak.

Louse
Contrast. Nangolo.
My Father Kept a Horse.
Anonymous.
With the Most Susceptible
Element, the Mind, Already
Turned... Benton.

Lousy
The Elizabethans Called It
Dying. Schuyler.
The Elizabethans Called It
Dying. Schuyler.
Lousy Miner. Anonymous.

Louts
Eleventh Song. Sidney.
Gnome. Beckett.
Voices at the Window.
Sidney.

Love (d) (s)
49th & 5th, December 13.
Jacobsen.
98 Degree Blues. Alexander.
Aboriginal Sin. Hay.
Abraham and Isaac. Lasker-
Schüler.
Abroad As I Was Walking.
Anonymous.
The Accountant in His Bath.
Mitchell.
Across the Sky the Daylight
Crept. Patmore.
Acts Passed beyond the
Boundary of Mere Wishing.
Spender.
Ad Domnulam Suam.
Dowson.
Ad Finem. Heine.

Ad Finem. Wilcox.
Ad Matrem. Fane.
Adam on His Way Home.
Pack.
Address to Venus. Lucretius
(Titus Lucretitus Carus).
An Admonition to Young
Lassies. Montgomerie.
Adrift. Dowden.
The Advice. Anonymous.
Advice to a Lover. Jellicoe.
Affection and Desire.
Ralegh.
Affliction. Herbert.
After Aughrim. Lawless.
After-Christmas Poem.
Long.
After Death. Richardson.
After Making Love We Hear
Footsteps. Kinnell.
After Our War. Balaban.
After-Song. Gilder.
After the Quarrel. Gibson.
After the Rain. Crouch.
After Verlaine. Hollo.
Afterthoughts of Donna
Elvira. Kizer.
Afterward. Ward.
Against Indifference. Webbe.
Against Marriage to His
Mistress. Walsh.
Against Quarrelling and
Fighting. Watts.
Age. More.
Aghadoe. Todhunter.
Ah, Be Not False. Gilder.
Ah Yes, When Love Allows.
Hadewijch.
Air. Jones.
Alas, Poor Man, What Hap
Have I. Wyatt.
The Alchemist. Kelly.
Alibi (parody). Guiterman.
All I Ask–. Lawrence.
All on a Summer's Day.
Anonymous.
All-Over Love. Cowley.
All These Birds. Wilbur.
All Those I Love Die Young.
Bonefonius.
All Thro' the Year.
Anonymous.
The Almond Tree.
Stallworthy.
Aloha Oe. Blanding.
Alone am I, and alone I wish
to be. Pisan.
Alpine Spirit's Song.
Beddoes.
The Altar. Untermeyer.
Amantium Irae. Edwards.
Americanized. Dawe.
Amoretti, II. Spenser.
Amoretti, XXVIII. Spenser.
Amoretti, LIX. Spenser.
Amoretti, LXI. Spenser.
Amoretti, LXXV. Spenser.
Amsterdam Letter.
Garrigue.
An Ancient Custom. Steiger.
Ancient Quatrain.
Anonymous.
And Art Thou Come, Blest
Babe? Anonymous.
And Fall Shall Sit in
Judgment. Lorde.
And Is It Night?
Anonymous.
And the Same Words.
Ignatow.
And This Is Love. Reingold.

And While We Are Waiting.
Rodgers.
And Yet–. Rhinow.
Andrea Del Sarto.
Browning.
Andrew Lammie.
Anonymous.
The Angel in the House.
Patmore.
Angels' Song. Causley.
Angels We Have Heard on
High. Anonymous.
The Angler. Bhartrihari.
An Anniversary on the
Hymeneals of My Noble
Kinsman, Thomas Stanley...
Lovelace.
Another. In Defence of Their
Inconstancie. Jonson.
Another Song. Strobel.
Answer to a Child's Question.
Coleridge.
Anticipation. De Tabley.
Antigone I. Martin.
Antipathy. Watkyns.
Any Lover, Any Lass.
Middleton.
Aphrodite Pandemos.
Anonymous.
Apocryphal Apocalypse.
Wheelwright.
Apologia. Swinburne.
Arbor Amoris. Villon.
Arcadia. Sidney.
Are You Born? Rukeyser.
Arethusa. Shelley.
Armorial. Gustafson.
Around Thanksgiving.
Humphries.
The Arsenal at Springfield.
Longfellow.
The Art of Love: Happy the
Man Who Has Two Breasts
to Crush. Koch.
Articles of War. Thompson.
As I Walked Out One
Morning. Anonymous.
As in Their Time.
MacNeice.
As on the Heather. Reinmar
von Hagenau.
As when Some Hungry
Fledgling Hears and Sees.
Colonna.
Ascendancy. Simmons.
Ascension. Devlin.
Ashes. Heine.
Ashore. Hope.
Asleep. Winter.
The Assumption.
Anonymous.
Assurance. Herbert.
Astrophel and Stella, XVI.
Sidney.
Astrophel and Stella, XXV.
Sidney.
Astrophel and Stella, XXVIII.
Sidney.
Astrophel and Stella, XLII.
Sidney.
Astrophel and Stella, LIV.
Sidney.
Astrophel and Stella, LXI.
Sidney.
Astrophel and Stella, LXII.
Sidney.
Astrophel and Stella, LXVI.
Sidney.
Astrophel and Stella, XCI.
Sidney.
Astrophel and Stella, CVII.
Sidney.

At a Calvary Near the Ancre.
Owen.
At Casterbridge Fair.
Hardy.
At Christmas. Duncan.
At Dawning. Eberhart.
At Midnight. Kooser.
At Such a Time, in Such a
Spot. Bronte.
At Sunset. Ledoux.
At Swindon. Brett.
At the Grave of Burns.
Wordsworth.
At the Mermaid Inn.
Hildreth.
At Twilight. Van Rensselaer.
Attack of the Crab Monsters.
Raab.
Aucassin and Nicolete.
Bourdillon.
Auguries of Innocence.
Blake.
August Afternoon. Remaly.
Auld Lang Syne. Chadwick.
Aurora: Sonnet XXVI.
Stirling.
The Author Apologizes to a
Lady for His Being a Little
Man. Smart.
The Authour Still Pursuing
His Invention. Watson.
Autumnal. Dowson.
Ave Caesar. Jeffers.
Awaking. Spender.
Awkward Goodbyes. Miller.
The Aziola. Shelley.
The Azra. Heine.
Baby-Land. Cooper.
Baby's in Jail; the Animal
Day Plays Alone. Ford.
A Bachelor's Life.
Anonymous.
Backgammon. Broumas.
Backyard. Notley.
Ballad. Soutar.
A Ballad in Blank Verse of
the Making of a Poet.
Davidson.
Ballata: Concerning a
Shepherd-Maid.
Cavalcanti.
Barbara Allen. Anonymous.
Barberries. Aldis.
Barcarolle. O'Shaughnessy.
Baroque Comment. Bogan.
Be Thou Then by Beauty
Named. Campion.
Be Ye in Love with April-
Tide? Scollard.
The Bear That Came to the
Wedding. McCord.
The Beast in the Space.
Graham.
Beauty, a Silver Dew.
Anonymous.
Because He Lives. Lathrop.
Because I Liked You Better.
Housman.
Because You're You.
Blossom.
Bedtime. Finlay.
Before and After Marriage.
Campbell.
Before Dawn in the Woods.
Wilkinson.
Before Sunset. Swinburne.
Before the World Was Made.
Yeats.
Before This Loved One.
Auden.
Bega. Pickthall.

Behold Your King! Havergal.
The Beholders. Dickey.
Belgravia. Guest.
Bell Speech. Wilbur.
La Belle Ennemie. Stanley.
Below Hekla. Hill.
Beneath the Shadow of the Cross. Longfellow.
The Bent Sae Brown. Anonymous.
The Bents and Broom. Anonymous.
The Best for Me. Anonymous.
The Best Memory Course. Anonymous.
Betsey and I Are Out. Carleton.
Beyond Labelling Me. Di Cicco.
Beyond the Presidency. Gibson.
Bibliographer. Miles.
Big Thompson Canon. Gower.
Bird-Song. Thayer.
Birth of Venus. Urdang.
Birthday. Emans.
Birthplace. Big Eagle.
Bitter-Sweet. Herbert.
Black Is the Colour. Anonymous.
The Blacksmith. Anonymous.
Bless, Dear Saviour, This Child. Beck.
Bless This House. Taylor.
Bless You, Bless You, Burnie-Bee. Anonymous.
The Blessed Name. Bethune.
Blest Be the Tie That Binds. Fawcett.
The Blind Man's Regret. Anonymous.
The Blue and the Gray. Finch.
Blue and White. Coleridge.
Bluebeard's Wife. Hine.
Bob Anderson, My Beau. Anonymous.
Bobby Shaftoe's Gone to Sea. Mother Goose.
The Body Politic. Hall.
The Bold Soldier. Anonymous.
Bonnets So Blue. Anonymous.
Bony. Ortiz.
Bottom's Dream. Dow.
Bow Down Your Head and Cry. Anonymous.
Boy Wandering in Simms' Valley. Warren.
Breakers over the Sea. Anonymous.
Breakfast. Gunn.
Breath. Strand.
The Breeze Is Blowing. Anonymous.
The Bride. Akhmadulina.
Briggflatts. Bunting.
Britannia's Pastorals. Browne.
The British Church. Herbert.
The Broken Heart. Beedome.
The Broken Heart. Donne.
The Broken Tower. Crane.
Brother. Shelton.
Brown Adam (B version). Anonymous.

Brown of Ossawatomie. Whittier.
Browning at Asolo. Johnson.
Buen Matina. Salusbury.
The Buried Lake. Tate.
Bury Me beneath the Willow. Anonymous.
The Bush Aboon Traquair. Shairp.
But Thou My Deere Sweet-Sounding Lute Be Still. Lynche.
The Butcher Boy. Anonymous.
Buthaina. Jamil.
By the Turnstile. O'Donnell.
Caelica, IV. Greville.
Caelica, V. Greville.
Caelica, IX. Greville.
Caelica, XIV. Greville.
Caelica, XXV. Greville.
Caelica, XXIX. Greville.
Caelica, XLI. Greville.
Caelica, LII. Greville.
Caelica, LIII. Greville.
Caelica, LXI. Greville.
Caelica, LXIII. Greville.
Caelica, LXV. Greville.
Caelica, LXIX. Greville.
Caelica, LXXII. Greville.
Caledonia. McElroy.
California Joe. Anonymous.
The Call. Hall.
The Call of the Christian. Whittier.
Calvary. Hallet.
The Camel-Rider. Anonymous.
The Canary. Turner.
Candle and Book. Walter.
Cantica: Our Lord Christ. Francis of Assisi.
Canticle of Darkness. Watson.
Canzone. Auden.
Canzone: He Perceives His Rashness in Love, but Has No Choice. Guinicelli.
Canzone: Of the Gentle Heart. Guinicelli.
Canzonet. Anonymous.
A Capital Ship. Anonymous.
Careless Love. Anonymous.
The Careless Lover. Suckling.
Carmina. Catullus.
Carmina Amico. James.
Carol for Advent. Heath-Stubbs.
A Carol of St. George. Anonymous.
Carpenter's Son. Flint.
Carry Her over the Water. Auden.
Cascando. Beckett.
Castara. Habington.
The Cause of This I Know Not. Long.
The Causes of Color. Jonas.
Cavalier Lyric. Simmons.
A Celebration of Charis. Jonson.
Celestial Love. Michelangelo.
Celtic Cross. MacCaig.
Centerfold Reflected in a Jet Window. McPherson.
Ceremony for Birth and Naming. Torrence.
Chain. Lorde.
Chalk from Eden. Moss.
Chamber Music. Joyce.

Chameleon. Engle.
A Chaplet of Southernwood (excerpt). Nicholson.
The Charcoal-Burner. Gosse.
Charitas Nimia, or the Deare Bargain. Crashaw.
A Charm for Love and Lasting Affection. Anonymous.
A Chaste Maid in Cheapside: Parting. Middleton.
Chesapeake and Shannon. Anonymous.
Chicago. Harte.
Child and Poet. Swinburne.
Child, Child. Teasdale.
Child of Loneliness. Gale.
The Child's First Grief. Hemans.
Child's Song in Spring. Nesbit.
A Child's Wish. Ryan.
Child with Shell. Everson.
Childe Harold's Pilgrimage: Canto IV. Byron.
The Children. MacDonald.
The Children. Urdang.
Children's Elegy. Rukeyser.
Chiliasm. Eberhart.
Christ Is Here. Lowell.
Christ's Plea to Mankind. Anonymous.
The Christening. De La Mare.
Christian Ethics. Traherne.
Christmas 1944. Levertov.
A Christmas Carol. Behn.
Christmas Eve. Anonymous.
Christmas in Freelands. Stephens.
A Christmas Message. Ewart.
Christmas Song. Long.
Circe. Hope.
The City's Crown. Foulke.
Claiming the Promise. Wesley.
Clear Eyes. De la Mare.
Cleopatra. Story.
Clerk Saunders. Anonymous.
The Clock. Scarfe.
The Clock Tower. Thibaudeau.
Cloistered. Brown.
The Cloud. Lanier.
Cloud and Wind. Rossetti.
Cobweb. Welles.
The Cocks. Pasternak.
Colleen Rue. Anonymous.
Colonel Sharp. Anonymous.
Come away, Come Sweet Love. Anonymous.
Come Hither, My Dear One. Clare.
Come Holy Spirit, Dove Divine. Judson.
Come, You Pretty False-Eyed Wanton. Campion.
Communication. Jennings.
Communion. Gould.
Compel Them to Come In. Dodd.
The Complaint of a Lover Forsaken of his Love. Anonymous.
Complaint of a Lover Rebuked. Surrey.
The Complaint of Troilus. Chaucer.
Complete in Thee, No Work of Mine. Wolfe.
Completion. Tietjens.

Computer. Orban.
Concerning the Dead. Halperin.
Concerning the Nature of Love. Lucretius (Titus Lucretius Carus).
A Conjecture. Richardson.
A Conjuration, to Electra. Herrick.
Connubii Flores, or the Well-Wishes at Weddings. Herrick.
Conon in Alexandria. Durrell.
The Conquering Love of Jesus. Wesley.
The Conquest of Granada. Dryden.
Consummation. Barker.
The Contemplative. Sister M. Therese.
The Convoy. Corretjer.
The Cool, Grey City of Love. Sterling.
The Coquette. Behn.
Cordova. Ibn Zaydun.
Coridon and Phillis. Greene.
A Correct Compassion. Kirkup.
Corydon to His Phyllis. Dyer.
Could I Believe. Milne.
The Counsel. Brome.
Country Statutes. Anonymous.
The Cowboy and His Love. Anonymous.
Crabs. Piercy.
The Crowning Gift. Cromwell.
Crucifixion. Isbell.
Cry from the Battlefield. Menth.
The Crystal Skull. Raine.
The Cuckoo. Anonymous.
Cycles, Cycles. Rioff.
Cyder, I: How to Catch Wasps. Philips.
Cythera. Verlaine.
Daguerreotype of a Grandmother. Wright.
The Dance. Jones.
The Dance of Love. Davies.
The Dance of the Elephants. Harper.
The Dancing Sunshine Lounge. Rabbit.
The Dark Brother. Alexander.
The Dark Girl's Rhyme. Parker.
The Dark Planet. Heath-Stubbs.
Darlin'. Anonymous.
Daughters. Astra.
A Day. Stidger.
A Day in the Life. Beatles.
The Day Is Past and Gone. Leland.
Days of 1964. Merrill.
The Dead. Smith.
Dear Folks. Kavanagh.
Dear Lady, When Thou Frownest. Bridges.
Dear Lord, Behold Thy Servants. Ballou I.
Dear Old Mothers. Ross.
Death and Love. Jonson.
Death and Night. Kenyon.
Death-Bed Reflections of Michel-Angelo. Coleridge.

Death-Bed Song. *Anonymous.*
The Death of the Starling. Coleridge.
Death's Jest Book. Beddoes.
Death Songs. *Anonymous.*
Death Sweet. Beddoes.
The Deaths. Schoultz.
The Deaths at Paragon, Indiana. Woods.
The Debate of the Body and the Soul. *Anonymous.*
The Decoys. Auden.
Dedication. Allison.
Dedicatory Ode: They Say That in the Unchanging Place. Belloc.
Deeds of Kindness. Sargent.
Deep Waters. Sutphen.
Deer Song. Silko.
Definition. Shakely.
Deranged. Fiacc.
Description and Praise of His Love Geraldine. Surrey.
The Description of Castara. Habington.
The Deserter. Taylor.
Desire Knows. Asclepiades.
Despair and Hope. Zangwill.
Despite and Still. Graves.
The Deviator. Warr.
Dialogue. Agathias.
Diana. Constable.
The Diary of Izumi Shikibu (excerpt). Izumi Shikibu.
Die Lotosblume Angstigt. Heine.
Died of Love. *Anonymous.*
The Diggers' Song. Winstanley.
Dinosaur Spring. Waniek.
Dirge. Johnson.
Dirge for Two Veterans. Whitman.
Discourse. Thesen.
Disdain Returned. Carew.
Dispossessed Poet. Gibbon.
The Distances. Olson.
The Distances They Keep. Nemerov.
A Ditty. Jacobs.
The Divine Wooer. Fletcher.
The Divorce. Stanley.
The Divorce of a Lover. Gascoigne.
Do Not Minute. Beddoes.
Do Not Torment Me, Lady. *Anonymous.*
Do Not Torment Me, Woman. *Anonymous.*
Do You Remember. Bayly.
The Dog and the Water-lily. Cowper.
A Dog Day. Field.
Dog Lake with Paula. Hugo.
Dogma. Deutsch.
Don Juan. Byron.
Don't Sit under the Apple Tree with Anyone Else but Me! Pack.
Doralicia's Song. Graves.
Doron's Jigge. Greene.
Dostoievsky's Daughters. Hamburger.
Dove. Farber.
Dover Beach. Arnold.
Draw Me, Saviour, After Thee. Wesley.
Drawing Wildflowers. Graham.
The Dream. Bogan.
The Dream. Roethke.

Dream House. Newell.
A Dream of Death. Jennison.
The Dreams Ahead. Litsey.
Due North. Low.
The Due of the Dead. Thackeray.
Dulnesse. Herbert.
Dust. Brooke.
The Dying Gaul. O'Grady.
The Dying Swan. Moore.
Dying! To be afraid of thee. Dickinson.
Each Day. Ignatow.
Eagles on a Half. Wiley.
Earl Brand. *Anonymous.*
Early in the Spring. *Anonymous.*
Earth's Answer. Blake.
Earthquake. Ford.
Easter Beatitudes. Burkholder.
An Easter Carol. Rossetti.
Easter Hymn. Thwaites.
Easter Song. Alishan.
Ecclesiastes. Langland.
Edna's Hymn. Humphries.
The Eel. Morgan.
Egyptian Dancer. Tiller.
An Elegie. Randolph.
Elegy. Pushkin.
Elegy. Trench.
Elegy for a Puritan Conscience. Dugan.
Elegy for Margaret Howard, Lady Buckhurst. Southwell.
Ellen Bawn. Mangan.
The End of May. Morris.
Endymion. Millay.
England's Triumph. *Anonymous.*
Entoptic Colours. Goethe.
Entropy. Spencer.
Envoi. Causley.
Envoi. Symons.
Envoy. MacLean.
L'Envoy de Chaucer a Scogan. Chaucer.
Epigram: April. Nemerov.
Epigram: "For Hekabe." Plato.
Epigram: "How shall I know if my love lose his youth." Strato.
Epigram: "I don't care for women." *Anonymous.*
Epilogue. Abercrombie.
Epipsychidion. Shelley.
Epitahlamium for Cavorting Ghosts. Rainer.
Epitaph for Himself. Herbert of Cherbury.
Epitaph of Pyramus and Thisbe. Cowley.
Epitaph on a Child Killed by Procured Abortion. *Anonymous.*
Epithalamium. Turner.
Erotic Suite (excerpt). Vega.
Escalade. Symons.
Escape. Rubin.
The Eternal City. Ammons.
Eternal Goodness. Whittier.
Eulogy for Hasdai Ibn Shaprut. *Anonymous.*
Euphoria, Euphoria. DeFoe.
Eurydice. Bourdillon.
Eurymachus's Fancy. Greene.
Even-Song. Herbert.
An Evening. Allingham.

Evening. Keble.
Evening Hymn. Roberts.
Evening Shade. *Anonymous.*
Evening Song. Alexander.
Evolution. Zangwill.
A (excerpt). Zukofsky.
The Excursion. Wordsworth.
The Excuse. Ralegh.
The Exequies. Stanley.
Explanation. Hewitt.
Explanations of Love. Sandburg.
Eyes That Queenly Sit. Daryush.
Fable. Prokosch.
Fable of the Talented Mockingbird. Bates.
Facing the Chair. ""MacDiarmid.
The Fading Rose: Epitaph. Freneau.
The Faerie Queene. Spenser.
Fair and Fair. Peele.
Fair Helen. *Anonymous.*
Fair Iris and Her Swain. Dryden.
The Fair Maid and the Sun. O'Shaughnessy.
The Faithful Lover. Pack.
The Fall. Rochester.
Fall of the Year. Ellison.
The False Bride. *Anonymous.*
False Country of the Zoo. Garrigue.
Fare Well. De La Mare.
Farewell. L'Ouverture.
The Farewell. Stanley.
Farewell to Love. Suckling.
Farewell, Unkind! Farewell! to Me, No More a Father! *Anonymous.*
Farm Wife. Mitchell.
The Farm-Woman's Winter. Hardy.
The Farmer's Daughter. *Anonymous.*
The Fat Budgie. Lennon.
Fatal Love. Prior.
Father. Auslander.
The Father Knows. "H..
Fathomless Is My Love. Kalola.
FayWray to the King. Rechter.
Feathers and Moss. Ingelow.
Feed Still Thyself. Ralegh.
Femina Contra Mundum. Chesterton.
Festus: Proem to the Third Edition. Bailey.
Few Wholly Faithful. *Anonymous.*
Fidelis. Procter.
Fie, Fie on Blind Fancy! Greene.
Fifty-Seventh Street and Fifth. Corn.
Finis. Cuney.
Fiorentina. Myers.
Fire at Murdering Hut. Wright.
Fire Island. Brown.
The First Grief. Hemans.
The First Kiss of Love. Byron.
The Firstborn. Goodchild.
The Fish Come in Dancing. Roberts.
Five Songs. Shapiro.
Flee on Your Donkey. Sexton.

The Flitch of Dunmow. Carnegie.
The Florist Rose. Graves.
Flow, O My Tears! *Anonymous.*
The Flowers. Kipling.
Flowers for the Brave. Thaxter.
Flush or Faunus. Browning.
The Flute of the Lonely. Lindsay.
Foggy Mountain Top. *Anonymous.*
Folk Tale. Mustapaa.
A Fond Greeting, Hillock There. Mac An Bhaird.
The Fool by the Roadside. Yeats.
The Fool of Love. *Anonymous.*
For All Mary Magdalenes. Maksimovic.
For Andy Goodman–Michael Schwerner–and James Chaney. Walker.
For Deeper Life. Bates.
For Elizabeth Madox Roberts. Lewis.
For Every Day. Havergal.
For Her Love I Cark and Care. *Anonymous.*
For My Brother Who Died before I Was Born. Wormser.
For My Mother. Smith.
For One Who Would Not Take His Life in His Hands. Schwartz.
For Perfect Peace. Wesley.
For Simone Weil. Sister M. Therese.
For the Peace of Jerusalem. Wesley.
For the Young Who Want To. Piercy.
Forbearance. Leitner.
Forever. O'Reilly.
Forgotten Island. Hall.
The Fortress. Sexton.
Forty Years Ago. *Anonymous.*
Four Anacreontic Poems, 2. Spenser.
Four Folk-Songs in Hokku Form, 1. *Anonymous.*
Four Folk-Songs in Hokku Form, 4. *Anonymous.*
Four Winds. Teasdale.
Fragment: "Some pretty face remembered in our youth." Clare.
Fragoletta. Swinburne.
Francis Jammes: A Prayer to Go to Paradise with the Donkeys. Wilbur.
Freedom and Love. Campbell.
French Desire. Abbott.
Fresh News from the Past. Bell.
A Friend. De Carrion.
Friendship. Mansfield.
The Friendship. Mezey.
Friendship in Perfection. Ramsay.
Frightened Face. Strobel.
The Frog and the Golden Ball. Graves.
From Heaven High I Come to You. Luther.
From Mistra: A Prospect. Higgs.

From Solitude to Solitude towards Life. Eluard.
From St. Luke's Hospital. L'Engle.
From the German of Uhland. Johnson.
From Thee to Thee. Ibn Gabirol.
Fugato (Coda). Hollander.
Fulfilment. Nichols.
Full Moon. Graves.
Full Well I Know. Coleridge.
The Funeral of Youth: Threnody. Brooke.
The Gambler. Anonymous.
General Wonder in Our Land. Anonymous.
A Gentleman of Fifty Soliloquizes. Marquis.
Gently He Draweth. Anonymous.
Geordie (B vers.). Anonymous.
Georgics. Virgil (Publius Vergilius Maro).
Gerda, My Husband's Wife. Triem.
Getting Serious. Soto.
Giant Decorative Dahlia. Holden.
The Gift of Song. Hecht.
Gill Boy. Schmitz.
Giotto's Campanile. Butler.
Girl in a White Coat. Brinnin.
The Girt Woak Tree That's in the Dell. Barnes.
Gitanjali. Tagore.
Give Love To-Day. Talbot.
Give Me a Lass. Ramsay.
Give Me My Work. Whetstone.
The Glove and the Lions. Hunt.
Glow Worm. Robinson.
Go, Happy Rose. Martial (Marcus Valerius Martialis).
Go, Rose. Gay.
Go Take the World. Macpherson.
God and the Soul: Et Mori Lucrum. Spalding.
God, How I Hate You. West.
God Is Love. Bowring.
God of the Nations, Near and Far. Holmes.
God's Harp. Falke.
God's Mother. Housman.
God's Residence. Dickinson.
God's Sunshine. Oxenham.
God's Trails Lead Home. Clements.
God the Omniscient. Wallace.
Godiva (parody). Berry.
Godspeed. Spofford.
Gold Is the Son of Zeus: Neither Moth Nor Worm May Gnaw It. "Field.
The Golden Elegy. Staff.
The Golden Fish. Arnold.
A Golden Sorrow. Martial (Marcus Valerius Martialis).
Golgotha. Wheelock.
Gone Are the Days. MacCaig.
Good Friday Evening. Rossetti.
Good-Night. Shelley.

Goodby Betty, Don't Remember Me. Cummings.
Graham Bell and the Photophone. Montgomery.
Graves. Sandburg.
The Graves of a Household. Hemans.
The Gray Oak Twilight. Kilgore.
The Great Lover. Brooke.
Great Things Have Happened. Nowlan.
The Green Willow. Anonymous.
Green Willow, Green Willow. Anonymous.
The Groaning Board. "Pink".
A Grotesque Love-Letter. Anonymous.
Growing Old. Anonymous.
Grown and Flown. Rossetti.
Guitar. St. John.
The Hand and Foot. Very.
Hanging Scroll. Stern.
The Happy Countryman. Breton.
Hard, Ain't It Hard. Anonymous.
Hard Is the Fortune of All Womankind. Anonymous.
Harvest. Maino.
The Hate and the Love of the World. Ehrmann.
Hate Whom Ye List. Wyatt.
Have I Done My Best for Jesus? Young.
He Came Too Late. Bogart.
He'd Nothing But His Violin. Dallas.
He Entereth the House of the Goddess Hathor. Book of the Dead.
He Praises Her Hair. Anonymous.
He Said, Lying There. Alta.
The Head-Stone. Barnes.
The Healing of the Leper. Watkins.
A Health at the Ford. Rogers.
Heaven Is Here. Adams.
Hedro's Lamp. Rossetti.
Helen Hunt Jackson. Coolbrith.
Her Eyes Don't Shine Like Diamonds. Marion.
Her Music. Dickinson.
Here's a Poor Widow. Anonymous.
Here We March All Around in a Ring. Anonymous.
The Heretic. Carman.
Heretics All. Belloc.
Hero and Leander. Marlowe.
Hic Jacet. Moulton.
Highland Loves. McOwan.
The Highwayman. Noyes.
Hiking up Hieizan with Alam Lau/Buddha's Birthday 1974. Hongo.
Hiraeth in N.W.3. Vaughan-Thomas.
Hiroshima. Rockwell.
His Banner over Me. Massey.
His Charge to Julia at His Death. Herrick.
His Mother's Joy. Chadwick.
His Plan. Anonymous.

Holy Innocents. Rossetti.
Holy Sonnets, XVI. Donne.
Home. Greenwell.
Home. Harris.
Home Is Where There Is One to Love Us. Swain.
The Homeland. Haweis.
Hope Springing Up. Wesley.
Horses Graze. Brooks.
Hospital. Millard.
The Hostess' Daughter. Uhland.
The Hound of Heaven. Thompson.
The House of Life. Rossetti.
How Are You, Dear World, This Morning? Traubel.
How Happy the Lover. Dryden.
How Many New Years Have Grown Old. Anonymous.
How My Father Died. Ezekiel.
The Hunt. Anonymous.
Husband and Wife. Guiterman.
Hyla Brook. Frost.
An Hymeneal Song on the Nuptials of the Lady Anne Wentworth and... Carew.
Hymn. Nicholl.
Hymn for Christmas Day. Byrom.
Hymn for Second Vespers;Feast of the Apparition of Our Lady of Lourdes. Anonymous.
Hymn of Dedication. Scantlebury.
Hymn: "Thou hidden love of God, whose height." Wesley.
Hymn to Intellectual Beauty. Shelley.
Hymn to Joy. Cunningham.
Hymn to the Creator. Clare.
Hypodermic Release. Corey.
I Am a Leaf. Amichai.
I Am Weary of Straying. York.
I Am with Those. Jonker.
I Bless Thee, Lord, for Sorrows Sent. Johnson.
I Can't Give You Anything but Love. Fields.
I'd Have You, Quoth He. Anonymous.
I Do Not Love to See Your Beauty Fire. Wheelock.
I Don't Know if Mount Zion. Kovner.
I Dreamt I Dwelt in Marble Halls. Bunn.
I Give My Heart to Thee. Palmer.
I Hate to See You Clad. Verlaine.
I Have Set My Heart So High. Anonymous.
I Have Trod the Upward and the Downward Slope. Stevenson.
I Hear an Army. Joyce.
I Hear It Was Charged against Me. Whitman.
I Heard a Linnet Courting. Bridges.
I Know My Love. Anonymous.
I Know That All beneath the Moon Decays. Drummond.

I Live Not Where I Love. Anonymous.
I'll Never Love Thee More. Graham.
I'll Remember You, Love, in My Prayers. Anonymous.
I Love. Chimsoro.
I Love Life. Cassel.
I Love, Loved, and So Doth She. Wyatt.
I Love My Life, but Not Too Well. Monroe.
I Love Snow and All the Forms. Shelley.
I Love Thee, Gracious Lord. Cox.
I Love You. Wilcox.
I Love You Truly. Bond.
I Loved Thee, Atthis, in the Long Ago. Carman.
I loved you; even now I may confess. Pushkin.
I Loved You Once (From the Russian of Alexander Pushkin). Randall.
I Must Go Walk the Wood. Anonymous.
I Once Lov'd a Boy. Anonymous.
I Ought to Weep. Anonymous.
I Said to Love. Hardy.
I Saw from the Beach. Moore.
I saw her crop a rose. Clare.
I Think Table and I Say Chair. Fuertes.
I Thought Joy Went by Me. Wattles.
I've Got the World on a String. Koehler.
I've Learned to Sing. Johnson.
I Walked Out to the Graveyard to See the Dead. Eberhart.
I Will Accept. Rossetti.
I Wish Sometimes, Although a Worthlesse Thing. Fletcher.
I Would Like My Love to Die. Beckett.
Ida, Sweet as Apple Cider. Leonard.
Idea. Drayton.
Identity. Jennings.
Identity. Mary Helen.
Idyl: Sunset. Ray.
Idylls. Moschus.
Idylls of the King. Tennyson.
If fancy would favor. Wyatt.
If I But Knew. Leigh.
If I Should Die before I Wake. Mezey.
If Love, For Love of Long Time Had. Heywood.
If So It Hap, This Of-Spring of My Care. Daniel.
If This Be Love. Eberhart.
If You But Knew. Anonymous.
Il Pastor Fido. Guarini.
Ilicet. Garrison.
Ill Omens. Moore.
Image. Noailles.
Impossibilities, to His Friend. Herrick.
In a Wood. Scovell.
In an Autumn Wood. Percy.
In Autumn. Anderson.
In Despair. Cavafy.

In Her Only Way. Graves.
In Him We Live. Very.
In His Service. Clar.
In Memoriam A.H.H., XLII.
Tennyson.
In Memoriam A.H.H., LX.
Tennyson.
In Memoriam A.H.H.,
XCVII. Tennyson.
In Memoriam A.H.H., CX.
Tennyson.
In Memory. Johnson.
In Memory of a Friend.
Barker.
In Memory of Radio. Jones.
In Misty Blue. Binyon.
In November. Aldrich.
In Orknay. Fowler.
In Praise of Virginity.
Hroswitha von
Grandersheim.
In the Beginning. Thomas.
In the Mines. Swett.
In the Moonlight. Wright.
In the Public Gardens.
Betjeman.
In the Spring. Tennyson.
In the Stable. Goudge.
In the Yellow Light of
Brooklyn. Lee.
In Time of War. Auden.
Incarnate Love. Tillett.
The Incarnation and Passion.
Vaughan.
Indian Education. Louis.
The Indifferent. Beaumont.
The Indifferent. Donne.
Infelice. Smith.
Ingratitude. Thynne.
The Inscription. Barker.
Inscription for the Entrance to
a Wood. Bryant.
Inseparable. Marston.
Insomnia. Bishop.
Insulting Beauty. Rochester.
An International Episode.
Duer.
Interview with a Tourist.
Atwood.
The Intruder. Zaturenska.
The Invention of Comics.
Jones.
Invitation to Youth.
Anonymous.
Invites His Nymph to His
Cottage. Ayres.
Invocation. Little.
Irish Molly O. Anonymous.
A Is for Alpha: Alpha Is for
A. Aiken.
Is There No Balm in
Christian Lands?
Anonymous.
Is This the Time To Sound
Retreat? Hoyt.
Islands. Pomeroy.
Isolation. Peabody.
It Is True. Garcia Lorca.
It Was Not Fate. Moore.
Italian Opera. Miller.
Its Name Is Known.
Kelleher.
Jack the Jolly Tar.
Anonymous.
Javier. Teran.
Je T'Adore. Kinsella.
The Jew of Malta: The Song
of Ithamore. Marlowe.
Johnie Scot. Anonymous.
Johnny German.
Anonymous.

Johnny Shall Have a New
Bonnet. Anonymous.
The Jolly Tester.
Anonymous.
Joy to the World. Watts.
Judas Iscariot. Cullen.
Judas, Peter. Shaw.
A Juggle of Myrtle Twigs.
Codish.
Just. Sherwin.
Just a Few Scenes from an
Autobiography. Tagliabue.
Justine, You Love Me Not!
Saxe.
Juvenal's Sixth Satire.
Dryden.
The Kavanagh. Hovey.
Keep Love in Your Life.
Clark.
Keep Your Kiss to Yourself.
Anonymous.
King Arthur. Dryden.
The King of Denmark's Ride.
Norton.
Kinship. Heaney.
Kirk Lonegren's Home Movie
Taking Place Just North of
Prince George... Thesen.
The Kiss of God. Studdert-
Kennedy.
Kissing the Toad. Kinnell.
Kitty Kline. Anonymous.
The Knowledge That Comes
Through Experience.
Cooper.
Labor and Love. Gosse.
Laboring and Heavy Laden.
Rankin.
Ladies' Eyes Serve Cupid
Both for Darts and Fire.
"W.
A Ladies Prayer to Cupid.
Guarini.
Lady Alice (George Collins),
I. Anonymous.
Lady April. Le Gallienne.
Lady of Castlenoire.
Aldrich.
A Lady of High Degree.
Anonymous.
The Lady of the Lake. Scott.
The Lady with Technique.
Mearns.
Laieikawai's Lament after Her
Husband's Death.
Anonymous.
Laleham: Matthew Arnold's
Grave. Johnson.
The Lamb-Child. Tabb.
Lament City. Lux.
Lament for the Cuckoo.
Alcuin.
The Lamp. Teasdale.
The Land That Is Not.
Sodergran.
The Landfall. Dickey.
The Lark's Song. Blake.
Last Fire. Rossetti.
The Last Invocation.
Whitman.
Last Night They Heard the
Woman Upstairs. Ullman.
Last of the Poet's Car.
Connor.
Last Refuge. Michelangelo.
The Latest Decalogue.
Clough.
Laura's Song. Brown.
Lavender Blue. Anonymous.
Law Like Love. Auden.
The Lay of the Last Minstrel.
Scott.

The Leaders of the Crowd.
Yeats.
A Learned Mistress.
O'Connor.
Leaving Here. Philbrick.
Left Behind. Akers.
Lesbia Railing. Catullus.
Lesbia Sewing. Vinal.
Let Him with Kisses of His
Mouth. Anonymous.
Let Others Sing of Knights
and Palladines. Daniel.
Let's Do It. Porter.
Let There Be New Flowering.
Clifton.
The Letter. Blight.
The Letter. Riddell.
A Letter Catches Up with
Me. Chaet.
Letter Out of the Gray.
Preil.
Letter to P. Friend.
A Letter to William Carlos
Williams. Rexroth.
Lettice. Craik.
Life in the Castle. Hebert.
The Life of St. Cellach: Dear
Was He. Anonymous.
Life's Scars. Wilcox.
Lifesaving. McPherson.
The Light of Asia. Arnold.
Light of the World. Monsell.
Like a Woman. Greenberg.
Like an Adventurous Sea-
Farer Am I. Drayton.
Like Loving Chekhov.
Levertov.
The Lincoln-Child.
Oppenheim.
Line Like. Sachs.
Lines Written in a
Mausoleum. Grant.
The Lion's Bride. Harwood.
The Little Cat Angel.
Stanfield.
Little Cosmic Dust Poem.
Haines.
Little Hands. Binyon.
A Little Page's Song. Percy.
The Little Poem of Life.
Oxenham.
Little Sally Sand.
Anonymous.
Little Sally Waters. Mother
Goose.
The Little Toil of Love.
Dickinson.
Little Willie's My Darlin'.
Anonymous.
Lo Que Digo (with music).
Anonymous.
Lo, what it is to love!
Wyatt.
Lohengrin. Payne.
London City (B vers. with
music). Anonymous.
Long-Line Skinner.
Anonymous.
Long Lines. Goodman.
Long Tom. Gibson.
Longing for the Emperor.
Iwa no Hime.
Look to the Leaf.
Anonymous.
A Looking-Glass. Carew.
Lord Lovel (D version).
Anonymous.
Lord, Save Us, We Perish.
Rossetti.
Lord Thomas Stuart.
Anonymous.
Loss. Madge.

Lost. Alvarez.
Lost But Found. Bonar.
The Lost Children.
Eberhart.
Lost For a Rose's Sake.
Anonymous.
Lost Love. Graves.
Love. Anonymous.
Love. Brooke.
Love. Herbert.
Love. Romanelli.
Love. Untermeyer.
Love and Death. Catullus.
Love and Folly. La
Fontaine.
Love and Hate. O'Connor.
Love and Jealousy. Greene.
Love and Liberation.
Wheelock.
Love and Lust. Rosenberg.
Love and Respect. Jenkyn.
Love and Wine. Shadwell.
Love Continual. Heywood.
Love-Faith. Kemp.
Love for a Beautiful Lady.
Anonymous.
Love has seven names.
Hadewijch.
Love, I Think, Is a Disease.
O Domhnaill.
Love in Dreams. Symonds.
Love in Vain. Johnson.
Love Is a Hunter Boy.
Moore.
Love Is a Secret Feeding Fire.
Anonymous.
Love Is Enough. Morris.
Love Is Life. Rolle.
Love Is of God. Bonar.
Love Laughs at Winter.
Anonymous.
A Love Letter. Anonymous.
The Love-Letter. Rossetti.
Love-Lily. Rossetti.
Love Made Me Such That I
Live in Fire. Stampa.
Love Me! Smith.
Love Me or Not. Campion.
Love Medley: Patrice
Cuchulain. Harper.
The Love-Moon. Rossetti.
Love much. Earth has enough
of bitter in it. Wilcox.
The Love of God. Audelay.
The Love of God. Rascas.
Love Redeemed.
Baylebridge.
Love Rejected. Clifton.
Love's Baubles. Rossetti.
Love's Calendar. Scott.
Love's Deity. Donne.
Love's Fatality. Rossetti.
Love's Grave. Watson.
Love's Old Sweet Song.
Bingham.
Love's Prisoner. Van
Rensselaer.
Love's Resurrection Day.
Alcott.
Love's Servile Lot.
Southwell.
Love's Spite. De Vere.
Love's Tribute. Sturgeon.
Love's Triumph. Jonson.
Love's Wisdom. Deland.
Love's without Reason.
Brome.
Love Serviceable. Patmore.
Love Song. Anonymous.
Love Song. Halevi.
A Love Song. Patterson.
Love Song. Wylie.

Love Song. Zmuda.
Love Song: I and Thou. Dugan.
Love Song to King Shu-Suen. Kubatum.
Love-Songs, At Once Tender and Informative. Hoffenstein.
Love the Ruins. Tussman.
Love, Time and Death. Locker-Lampson.
Love to My Lord. Van Plettenhaus.
The Love Unfeigned. Chaucer.
Love What It Is. Herrick.
Love Who Will, for I'll Love None. Browne.
Love Your Enemy. Iman.
The Lover and the Nightingale. Anonymous.
The Lover and the Syringa Bush. Melville.
The Lover Consults with Reason. Carew.
The Lover's Invitation. Clare.
The Lover's Song. Austin.
The Lover Thinks of His Lady in the North. O'Sheel.
A Lover, upon an Accident Necessitating His Departure.... Carew.
Lovers' Debouchment (parody). Zaranka.
Lower the Standard: That's My Motto. Shapiro.
The Lowest Place. Rossetti.
Luchow's and After. Sissman.
Luck. Epstein.
A Lullaby. Lewis.
Lullaby. Prettyman.
Lunch with Girl Scouts. Bryan.
Lycias. Rochester.
A Lyric. Swinburne.
A Lyric: "How can I sing light-souled." Medici.
A Machine Hand. Ashe.
Madam and Her Madam. Hughes.
The Madman's Song. Webster.
Madonna Mia. Swinburne.
Madrigal. Nims.
Madrigal: "How should I love my best?" Herbert of Cherbury.
Madrigal: "Lady, the birds right fairly." Anonymous.
Madrigal: "My love is neither young nor old." Jones.
Madrigal: "Sweet nymph, come to thy lover." Anonymous.
Madrigal: "The sound of thy sweet name, my dearest treasure." Davison.
Madrigal: "The spring of joy is dry." Peerson.
Madrigal XI: "Love now no fire hath left him." Marino.
The Magic Mirror. Alden.
Maid of Athens, Ere We Part. Byron.
Make Me Hear You. Gibbons.
Making Love, Killing Time. Ridler.

Making Love outside Aras an Uachtarain. Durcan.
Making Miso. Inada.
The Malady of Love Is Nerves. Petronius.
Malcolm's Katie. Crawford.
Male and Female Created He Them. Huxley.
Man to Man. McClure.
Mandala. Boland.
Manong Federico Delos Reyes and His Golden Banjo. Robles.
Many Things. Holmes.
Mariana in the South. Tennyson.
Marie Magdalen's Complaint at Christ's Death. Southwell.
Marriage. Gordett.
Mary an' Martha Jes' Gone 'Long. Anonymous.
Mary Beaton's Song. Swinburne.
Mary Desti's Ass. O'Hara.
Mary Magdalene. Rossetti.
Mary, Queen of Heaven. Anonymous.
Mary's Son. Trent.
The Match. Marvell.
Maternity Gown. Holbrook.
Mathematics or the Gift of Tongues. Branch.
A Matter of Life and Death. Ridler.
May-Day: April and May. Emerson.
A May Song. "Fane.
Mean Mistreater Mama. Carr.
The Meaning of Love. Anonymous.
Measure for Measure. Shakespeare.
The Mechanic. Creeley.
Medieval Norman Songs. Anonymous.
Mediocrity in Love Rejected. Carew.
Meditations. Taylor.
Medusa. Weeks.
Meeting Anais Nin's Elena. Frumkin.
Meeting in Winter. Morris.
Mein Kind, Wir Waren Kinder. Heine.
Memories. Whitman.
Memory. Hoyt.
Menaphon. Greene.
Mendacity. Coppard.
Merced. Rich.
The Mermaid. Tennyson.
The Mess of Love. Lawrence.
Metamorphoses. Ovid (Publius Ovidius Naso).
Metrical Feet. Coleridge.
Mexico Is a Foreign Country, IV: The Mango on the Mango Tree. Warren.
The Mexico Trail. Anonymous.
Midnight. Dryden.
A Midsummer Night's Dream. Shakespeare.
Midway in the Night: Blackman. Redmond.
The Milking Shed. Clare.
Milton. Blake.
Mind Flying Far. Masters.
Mine Eyes Beheld the Blessed Pity. Dante Alighieri.

A Miner Coming Home One Night. Anonymous.
The Minstrel. Beattie.
The Mist over Pukehina. Anonymous.
The Mistress (excerpt). Rochester.
Modern Declaration. Millay.
Modern Love. Keats.
Modern Love, XVII. Meredith.
Modern Love, XXXIII. Meredith.
The Modern Woman to Her Lover. Widdemer.
The Moment of the Rose. Thompson.
Monna Innaminata. Rossetti.
Monna Innominata. Rossetti.
Moon Compasses. Frost.
The Moral Warfare. Whittier.
More Love. Anonymous.
More Love to Thee, O Christ. Prentiss.
More Lovely Grows the Earth. Coleman.
More of Thee. Bonar.
The Morning after...Love. Cumbo.
Morning Prayer. Anonymous.
Morning Star. Ferril.
Mortmain. Warren.
The Mother. Anonymous.
The Mother. Brooks.
Mother darling, I cannot work the loom. Sappho.
Mother/Deer/Lady. Littlebird.
The Mother's Hymn. Bryant.
A Mother's Lament for the Death of Her Son. Burns.
Mother's Love. Montgomery.
Motherhood. Chworowsky.
The Motives of Rhythm. Conquest.
Motown/Smokey Robinson. Hagedorn.
Mulata–to Skinny. Lima.
"Multum Dilexit.'. Coleridge.
Mundus et Infans. Auden.
Mundus Morosus. Faber.
Mural (excerpt). Rodriguez Nietzche.
The Museum. Abrahams.
Music. Herrick.
Muss I Denn. Anonymous.
Muster Out the Rangers. Anonymous.
Mutability. Brooke.
The Mutes. Levertov.
My April Lady. Van Dyke.
My Church. G.
My Creed. Walter.
My Dead. Hosmer.
My Dearest Rival. Suckling.
My Dog. Chute.
My Dream by Henry James. Ryan.
My Father Knows. Tillett.
My Guardian Angel Stein. Schultz.
My Honey, My Love. Harris.
My Lady. Bailey.
My Lady Has the Grace of Death. Plunkett.

My Little Girl. Peck.
My Love I Gave for Hate. Anonymous.
My Love Is Past. Watson.
My Love Was Light. Williams.
My Mother Pieced Quilts. Acosta.
My Own Dark Head (My Own, My Own). Anonymous.
My Portrait. Halpern.
My Queen. Anonymous.
My Ships. Wilcox.
My Silks and Fine Array. Blake.
My Star. Browning.
My Sweetest Lesbia. Campion.
My True Love Hath My Heart and I Have His. Coleridge.
My Trust. Whittier.
My Valentine. Parsons.
Nanny. Davis.
Narcissus. Gullans.
Narrative. Dudek.
Nativity. Sarton.
Natura Naturans. Clough.
Nature and the Poets. Beattie.
The Need to Love. Vinner.
Needs Must I Leave, and Yet Needs Must I Love. Constable.
The Network. Finch.
Never Love. Campion.
A New Ballad, to an Old Tune, Called, I Am the Duke of Norfolk, Etc. Anonymous.
The New Song. Field.
Newark Abbey. Peacock.
The night has a thousand eyes. Bourdillon.
Night Journey. Roethke.
Night Thoughts: Baby & Demon. Harwood.
Nikos Painting. Hanson.
No Sickness Worse Than Secret Love. Anonymous.
No Single Hour Can Stand for Naught. Clare.
No Sufferer for Her Love. Anonymous.
No, Thank You, John. Rossetti.
Not All Sweet Nightingales. Gongora y Argote.
Not Heat Flames Up and Consumes. Whitman.
Not to Be Ministered To. Babcock.
Now Ain't That Love? Rodgers.
Now in my heart. Sappho.
Now Is the Accepted Time. Wesley.
Now Springs the Spray. Anonymous.
Nuptial Song. De Tabley.
A Nymph's Passion. Jonson.
O Cuckoo. Anonymous.
O'er Waiting Harp-Strings of the Mind. Eddy.
O Flame of Living Love. John of Damascus.
O God, in Whom the Flow of Days. Babcock.
O Gracious Father of Mankind. Tweedy.

O Jesus Christ, True Light of God. Ernst.

O Lawd I Went Up on the Mountain. *Anonymous.*

"O loathsome place..." Surrey.

O Love, How Strangely Sweet. Marston.

O Man Unkind. *Anonymous.*

O Mind of God, Broad as the Sky. Huckel.

O My Honey, Take Me Back (with music). *Anonymous.*

O Night, O Jealous Night. *Anonymous.*

O Night O Trembling Night. Spender.

O Sing to Me of Heaven. Dana.

O Softly Singing Lute. Pilkington.

O Son of God, Afflicted. *Anonymous.*

O sweet is love, and sweet is lack! Thompson.

O Western Wind. *Anonymous.*

O, Where Were We before Time Was. Dunn.

The Oblation. Swinburne.

Observation Car and Cigar. Stafford.

An Ode. Herbert of Cherbury.

Ode: "An idea of justice may be precious." O'Hara.

Ode. In Imitation of Pastor Fido Written Abroad, in 1729. Lyttelton.

Ode: "My heart rebels against my generation." Santayana.

An Ode on the Popular Superstitions of the Highlands of Scotland... Collins.

Ode: "Peer of gods he seemeth to me." Sappho.

Ode: Salute to the French Negro Poets. O'Hara.

Ode to a Nightingale (parody). Kelly.

Ode to Cupid. Cotton.

Ode to Psyche. Keats.

Odes. Horace.

The Odyssey. Homer.

Oenone's Complaint. Peele.

Of a Mistress. Cokayne.

Of All the Seas That's Coming. *Anonymous.*

Of an Old Con. Mosby.

Of English Verse. Waller.

Of His Cynthia. Greville.

Of His Majesties Receiving the News of the Duke of Buckingham's Death. Waller.

Of Joan's Youth. Guiney.

Of Love. Sandford.

Oh, No Cross That I May Carry! Mortenson.

Oh, No! We Never Mention Her. Bayly.

Oh send to me an apple that hasn't any kernel. *Anonymous.*

Oh! the time that is past. *Anonymous.*

The Old Astronomer to His Pupil. Williams.

An Old Cat's Confession. Cranch.

An Old Cat's Dying Soliloquy. Seward.

The Old Couple, III, i: Love's Prime. May.

Old Farmer Alone. Coffin.

The Old Hokum Buncombe. Sherwood.

Old-Long-Syne. *Anonymous.*

Old Love. Morris.

An Old Maid Early. Blake.

Old Mothers. Ross.

An Old Street. Cloud.

The Old Year and the New. Flint.

On a World War Battlefield. Clark.

On Being Head of the English Department. Lane.

On Diverse Deviations. Angelou.

On His Exile to Iona. Columcille.

On His Mistress. Donne.

On My First Son. Jonson.

On Shooting a Swallow in Early Youth. Tennyson.

On Snow-Flakes Melting on His Lady's Breast. Johnson.

On Sweet Killen Hill. MacIntyre.

On Sympathisers with the American Revolution. Wesley.

On the Beach at Fontana. Joyce.

On the Crucifix. Michelangelo.

On the Danube. Conquest.

On the Deaths of Thomas Carlyle and George Eliot. Swinburne.

On the Farm. Thomas.

On the Nature of Love. Blunt.

On the Passion. *Anonymous.*

On the Range. Souster.

On the Road There Stands a Tree. Manger.

On the Sea Wall. Day-Lewis.

On the Way to the Island. Ferry.

Once Did My Thoughts. *Anonymous.*

Once on a Time. Banning.

Once on a Time. Benson.

The One. Kavanagh.

The One I Love Is Gone Away. *Anonymous.*

One Immortality. Engels.

One Morning. Miller.

One Morning, Oh! So Early. Ingelow.

One Rose of Stone. Wilson.

One Step Twix't Me and Death. Williams.

Only of Thee and Me. Untermeyer.

Ontogeny. Ramsey.

Origins. Kgositsile.

The Orphan's Song. Dobell.

Ostia Antica. Hecht.

Othello. Shakespeare.

Our Bondage It Shall End. Cartwright.

Our Casuarina Tree. Dutt.

Our Fathers' God. Copeland.

Our Heavenly Father (excerpt). Faber.

Our Lady in the Middle Ages. Faber.

Our School Now Closes Out. Dumas.

Out in the Dark. Thomas.

Out of the Rolling Ocean the Crowd. Whitman.

Out of the Strong, Sweetness. Reznikoff.

Outward Bound. Tylee.

Ovid in the Third Reich. Hill.

The Pains of Sleep. Coleridge.

The Palace of Truth. Langland.

Pamela in Town. Cortissoz.

Panama. Jones.

The Paper Nautilus. Moore.

Paradise Lost. Milton.

The Paradox. Donne.

Paradox: The Birds. Shapiro.

Park Poem. Blackburn.

Pass forth, my wonted cries. Wyatt.

Passing It On. Saner.

The Passing of a Dream. Clare.

The Passion-Flower. Fuller.

The Passionate Professor. Taylor.

The Passionate Shepherd to His Love. Marlowe.

Past Time. Shapiro.

A Pastoral. Byrom.

A Pastoral Ballad in Four Parts. Shenstone.

Pater Vester Pascit Illa. Hawker.

A Pearl, a Girl. Browning.

The Peddler and His Wife. *Anonymous.*

The Peeper. Davison.

Peer Gynt. Sorley.

Peggy. Salkeld.

Perfect Love. *Anonymous.*

Permission to Speak. Orlen.

Peter. *Anonymous.*

Philarete Praises Poetry. Wither.

Philomela's Ode in Her Arbour. Greene.

Philosophers Have Measured Mountains. Herbert.

Phone Call. Crawford.

Photograph. Prettyman.

Phyllida's Love-Call to Her Corydon, and His Replying. *Anonymous.*

Phyllis Corydon clutched to him. Catullus.

Piccadilly. Burke.

Pilgrim Song. Coates.

Pilgrimage. Lennen.

Pity and Love. *Anonymous.*

Pity Not. Simpson.

The Pity of Love. Yeats.

Plain Dealing. Brome.

Platform Goodbye. Mallalieu.

The Platonic Lady. Rochester.

A Plea to Boys and Girls. Graves.

Please Master. Ginsberg.

The Plough-Hands' Song. Harris.

Poem #18. *Anonymous.*

Poem at Equinox. Corke.

Poem/Ditty-Bop. Rodgers.

A Poem (excerpt). Holmes.

A Poem for Diane Wakoski. Young Bear.

Poem: "I loved my friend." Hughes.

Poem: "I Will Always Love You." O'Hara.

A Poem Looking for a Reader. Lee.

Poem: "O gentle queen of the afternoon." Graham.

Poem of Holy Madness, IV. Bremser.

A Poem Put into My Lady Laiton's Pocket. Ralegh.

Poem: "Some are too much at home in the role of wanderer." Levertov.

Poem: "The person who can do." Dugan.

A Poem Written by Sir Henry Wotton, in His Youth. Wotton.

Poems. Drummond.

The Poet. Leitch.

A Poet's Grace. Burns.

The Poor Shammes of Berditchev. Ratner.

Popular Songs of Tuscany. *Anonymous.*

Portrait. Bogan.

Portrait of a Widow. Strauss.

Possessions. Reese.

A Postcard. Denby.

Postman Cheval. Breton.

Postscript to a Pettiness. Tessimond.

The Powers of Love. Horton.

Praise for Mercies Spiritual and Temporal. Watts.

Praxiteles and Phryne. Lowell

Prayer. *Anonymous.*

Prayer. Fowler.

Prayer. Goll.

A Prayer. Noyes.

A Prayer. Rossetti.

Prayer. Wheelock.

Prayer for Living and Dying. La Farge.

Prayer for the Home (excerpt). Guest.

Prayer to Go to Paradise with the Asses. Jammes.

Prayer to Venus. Spenser.

Precious in the Sight of the Lord... *Anonymous.*

Prelude. Aldington.

Prelude. Brentano.

The Presence of the Spirit. Salvadori.

Priapus and the Pool. Aiken.

The Prince of Peace. Bickersteth.

Prince Robert. *Anonymous.*

Proclaim the Lofty Praise. Judson.

Procrastination. Young.

The Progress of Poesy. Gray.

Progression. Scarfe.

The Prohibition. Donne.

Properzia Rossi. Hemans.

Propinquity Needed. Loomis.

Prostration. Semah.

The Protestation, A Sonnet. Carew.

Prothalamion (excerpt). Hillyer.

A Psalm. Blunden.

Psalm for Christmas Day. Pestel.
Psalm to the Holy Spirit. Sullivan.
Psyche to Cupid: Her Ditty. Broughton.
Pure Platonicke. Daniel.
The Purse–Seine. Blackburn.
Pussy Has a Whiskered Face. Rossetti.
Queen and Slave. Collins.
The Queen of Courtesy. Anonymous.
The Queen of Paphos, Erycine. Anonymous.
The Quest. Vinal.
A Question. Anonymous.
The Question to Lisetta. Prior.
A Quintina of Crosses. Walsh.
Race Prejudice. Kreymborg.
The Ragged Wood. Yeats.
Rain, Night, and Wine. Asclepiades.
Rainbow Willow. Anonymous.
Rant Block. McClure.
Rape Poem. Piercy.
Reading Today's Newspaper. Abbott.
Reality. De Vere.
Reality. Dickinson.
Reason for Not Writing Orthodox Nature Poetry. Wain.
The Reason Why. Beddoes.
Recklessly I Cast Myself away. Izumi Shikibu.
Recollection. Carpenter.
Reconciliation. Anonymous.
The Recovery Room: Lying-in. Chasin.
A Red Red Rose. Burns.
Reflection from Rochester. Empson.
The Rejected "National Hymns". Newell.
Reliance. Van Dyke.
Reluctance. Frost.
Remember Not. Johnson.
Remember Way Back. Green.
Remember Your Lovers. Keyes.
Remembering Him. Reccardi.
Remembrance. Kilmer.
The Renewal. Roethke.
Reparation. Hoyt.
Repentance. Stevens.
Resurrexit. Stuart.
Retractions. Cabell.
The Retreat. Vaughan.
The Return. Symons.
The Return from Egypt. Leo XIII.
The Return of Philista. Gallup.
Revelation. Cook.
Revelation. Warren.
The Revival. Vaughan.
Rich Mine of Knowledge. Chapman.
The Rich Old Lady. Anonymous.
Riddles Wisely Expounded. Anonymous.
Rimas. Becquer.
Rise and Shine. Lattimore.
Rissem. Gilbert.

The Rival Friends: Have Pity, Grief. Hausted.
The River Again and Again. Gregg.
The River Walk. Fallon.
Robert G. Shaw. Ray.
The Rocky Island. Anonymous.
Rococo. Payne.
The Rolling Sailor. Anonymous.
Roma. Rutilius.
A Romance. Kallman.
Romeo and Juliet. Putnam.
Romeo and Juliet. Shakespeare.
Ronald Wyn. Bagg.
Rondeau after a Transatlantic Telephone Call. Hacker.
Rondo. Moore.
Rosader's Sonnet. Lodge.
The Rose and God. Stork.
The Rose and the Wind. Marston.
Round Robin. Bhartrihari.
Rowing. Ochester.
The Rubicon. Winter.
Rude Awakenings. Rosenthal.
Runaway. Kurt.
Russian Asylum. Bowering.
The Sabbath Day Was By. Robbins.
Sag', Wo Ist Dein Schones Liebchen. Heine.
The Sailor and the Shark. Powell.
Saints. Garrett.
Samis Idyll. Rainer.
San Francisco Bay. Miller.
Sandpaper, Sandpiper, Sandpit. Slesinger.
Sandwich Man. Johnson.
Sans Souci. Mueller.
Santos: New Mexico. Sarton.
Sapphic Stanzas. Radishchev.
Sather Gate Illumination. Ginsberg.
Saul. Browning.
Savannah Mama. McTell.
The Saviour. Wesley.
Saw You My Father. Anonymous.
Sawney Was Tall. D'Urfey.
Say "Au Revoir," but Not "Good-Bye." Kennedy.
School Days. Cobb.
The Scribe's Prayer. Service.
Sea Canes. Walcott.
Sea-Change. Taggard.
Sea Eclogue. Diaper.
The Sea's Spell. Spalding.
The Search. Clarke.
The Season's Lovers. Waddington.
The Seasons. Thomson.
Seasons of the Soul. Tate.
The Second Pastoral, or, Alexis: The Argument. Virgil (Publius Vergilius Maro).
The Secret of the Cross. Clarkson.
The Secret Place of Prayer. Adams.
Secret Prayer. Belle.
Self-Examination. Anonymous.
Sensitiveness. Newman.
A Separation. Spender.

The September Gale (excerpt). Holmes.
A Serenade. Hood.
A Sestina for Cynthia. Lougee.
Shade. Lynch.
Shadowy Swallows. Becquer.
Shall I Then Hope When Faith Is Fled? Campion.
The Shattering of Love. Anonymous.
She's My Love. Young.
She Scorns Her Husband the Caliph. Maisun.
She Thinks of the Faithful One. Aldis.
She Took the Dappled Partridge Fleckt with Blood. Tennyson.
The Sheffield Apprentice. Anonymous.
Shelley's Arethusa Set to New Measures. Duncan.
The Shepherd and the Shepherdess. Anonymous.
The Shepherd's House. Vigny.
The Shepherd's Wife's Song. Greene.
Sherman. Gilder.
The Shipmen. Hunnis.
The Shiver. Hardy.
Show Me More Love. Anonymous.
Sigh Not for Love. Hay.
Signals. Waldrop.
The Silence. MacLeish.
Silvia. Etherege.
Similes. Moxon.
Simplicity's Song. Wilson.
Since We Loved. Bridges.
Sing, My Soul. Anonymous.
The Singing Cat. Smith.
Sirventes. Blackburn.
Sitting by a River Side. Greene.
Six Jolly Wee Miners. Anonymous.
Six Religious Lyrics: I (excerpt). Shapiro.
Skipping along Alone. Welles.
The Slave and the Iron Lace. Danner.
The Sleep-Song of Grainne Over Dermuid. Anonymous.
The Slide at the Empire Mine. Wason.
Slow Summer Twilight. Wheelock.
Slumber Song. Sassoon.
A Small Boy, Dreaming. Herzing.
Small Song. Shaw.
Snapshot. Garrett.
Snatches: "Joly sheperde of Ascell Down." Anonymous.
The Snowman. Page.
So Close Should Be Our Love. Anonymous.
So Fair, So Sweet, Withal So Sensitive. Wordsworth.
So in Love. Porter.
So Long. Cortez.
So Long. Stafford.
So Sweet Love Seemed. Bridges.
So Touch Our Hearts with Loveliness. Burket.
A Soldier. Suckling.

Soldier's Song. Hume.
The Soldiers Returning. Shelton.
Solomon. Heine.
Solomon to Sheba. Yeats.
Soluble Noughts and Crosses; or, California, Here I Come. Roughton.
Some Tips on Watching Birds. Hudson.
Something. Creeley.
Somewhere I Chanced to Read. Davidson.
Song. Clare.
The Song. Erskine.
Song. Spencer.
Song: "Because I know deep in my own heart." Murray.
Song: "Down the dimpled green-sward dancing." Darley.
Song: "Fair is the night, and fair the day." Morris.
Song: "Flame at the core of the world." Upson.
Song: "Fond men! whose wretched care the life soon ending." Fletcher.
Song for a Birth or a Death. Jennings.
Song for a Country Wedding. Smith.
Song for Autumn. Young.
A Song for the Least of All Saints. Rossetti.
Song: "Four arms, two necks, one wreathing." Anonymous.
A Song from the Italian. Dryden.
Song: "Has summer come without the rose." O'Shaughnessy.
Song: "He that will court a Wench that is coy." Anonymous.
Song: "How many times do I love thee, dear?" Beddoes.
Song: "How pleas'd within my native bowers." Shenstone.
Song: "I've taught thee Love's sweet lesson o'er." Darley.
Song: "If love were but a little thing." Coates.
Song II. The Landskip. Shenstone.
Song: "Lady, you are with beauties so enriched." Davison.
Song: "Leave this gaudy gilded stage." Rochester.
Song: "Love's on the highroad." Burnet.
Song: "Make this night loveable." Auden.
Song: "Misty and dim, a bush in the wilds of Kapa'a." Kaiama.
A Song of Autumn. Rodd.
A Song of Fleet Street. Werner.
A Song of Love. "Carroll.
A Song of My Heart. Bridges.
Song of Myself. Whitman.
A Song of the Four Seasons. Dobson.
Song of the Full Catch. Skinner.
Song of the Last Jewish Child. Jabes.

The Song of the Mean Mary Jean Machine. Hall.

Song of the Sirens. Browne.

Song of Thyrsis. Freneau.

Song: "Oh! say not woman's love is bought." Pocock.

A Song on the South Sea. Winchilsea.

A Song's Worth. Spalding.

Song: "Seek not the tree of silkiest bark." De Vere.

Song Set by John Farmer: "Take Time while Time doth last." *Anonymous.*

Song Set by Robert Jones: "Once did I love and yet I live." *Anonymous.*

Song: "Song is so old." Hagedorn.

Song the Ninth. moore.

Song: "There's one great bunch of stars in heaven." Marzials.

Song: "Thy fingers make early flowers." Cummings.

Song: "Thyrsis, when we parted, swore." Gray.

Song: "'Tis affection but dissembled." Godolphin.

Song to a Fair, Young Lady, Going out of the Town in the Spring. Dryden.

Song to a Lover. *Anonymous.*

Song to His Cynthia. Greville.

Song: "Under a southern wind." Roethke.

Song: "Where did you borrow that last sigh." Berkeley.

Song: "Why, lovely charmer, tell me why." Steele.

Song XI. Auden.

Songs. Deutsch.

Songs. Gilder.

The Songs of Bilitis. Louys.

Songs of Seven. Ingelow.

Sonnet. Brooke.

Sonnet. Duncan.

A Sonnet. Miller.

Sonnet XXI: "What grandeurs make a man seem venerable?" Labe.

Sonnet: "If I might choose where my tired limbs shall lie." Anster.

Sonnet: "In every dream thy lovely features rise." Barnes.

Sonnet: "In heaven there is a star I call my own." McLeod.

Sonnet: Kamikaze. Mayer.

Sonnet: On the Detection of a False Friend. Cavalcanti.

Sonnet Sequence. Turner.

Sonnet: "The Bible says Sennacherib's campaign was spoiled." Lewis.

A Sonnet to My Mother. Heine.

Sonnet: You Were Born; Must Die. Spender.

Sonnets. Hillyer.

Sonnets. Masefield.

Sonnets. Whitman

Sonnets, I: "Deep in a vale where rocks on every side." Rosenhane.

Sonnets, VII: "Sweet Thames I honour thee." Barnfield.

Sonnets, IX: "Is it for fear to wet a widow's eye." Shakespeare.

Sonnets, X: "For shame! deny that thou bear'st love to any." Shakespeare.

Sonnets, X: "Thus was my love, thus was my Ganymed." Barnfield.

Sonnets, X: "When I had turned Catullus into rhyme." Irwin.

Sonnets, XIV: "Here, hold this glove." Barnfield.

Sonnets, XVII: "Cherry-Lipt Adonis in his snowie shape." Barnfield.

Sonnets, XIX: "Devouring Time, blunt thou the lion's paws." Shakespeare.

Sonnets, XIX: "Those former loves wherein our lives have run." Agee.

Sonnets, XX: "A woman's face with nature's own hand painted." Shakespeare.

Sonnets, XXIX: "When in disgrace with fortune and men's eyes." Shakespeare.

Sonnets, XXXII: "If thou survive my well-contented day." Shakespeare.

Sonnets, XXXIV: "Why didst thou promise such a beauteous day." Shakespeare.

Sonnets, XXXVI: "Let me confess that we two must be twain." Shakespeare.

Sonnets, XLII: "Thou that last her, it is not all my grief." Shakespeare.

Sonnets, LVII: "Being your slave, what should I do but tend." Shakespeare.

Sonnets, LXV: "Since brass, nor stone, nor earth, nor boundless sea." Shakespeare.

Sonnets, LXVI: "Tired with all these, for restful death I cry." Shakespeare.

Sonnets, LXXIII: "That time of year thou mayst in me behold." Shakespeare.

Sonnets, LXXVI: "Why is my verse so barren of new pride." Shakespeare.

Sonnets, LXXXIX: "Say that thou didst forsake me for some fault." Shakespeare.

Sonnets, C: "Where art thou, Muse, that thou forget'st so long." Shakespeare.

Sonnets, CXVI: "Let me not to the marriage of true minds." Shakespeare.

Sonnets, CXXX: "My mistress' eyes are nothing like the sun." Shakespeare.

Sonnets, CLI: "Love is too young to know what conscience is." Shakespeare.

Sonnets from the Portuguese, I. Browning.

Sonnets from the Portuguese, X. Browning.

Sonnets from the Portuguese, XVI. Browning.

Sonnets from the Portuguese, XXI. Browning.

Sonnets from the Portuguese, XXII. Browning.

Sonnets from the Portuguese, XXXVIII. Browning.

Sonnets of the Months. San Geminiano.

Sonnets to Aurelia. Nichols.

Sonnets to Karl Theodor German. Platen.

Sonnets to Philomel. Davies.

Soul-Light. Rossetti.

The Soul, Reaching, Throwing Out for Love. Whitman.

The Sound Country Lass. *Anonymous.*

The Source. Stallworthy.

South End. Aiken.

A Space in the Air. Silkin.

The Sparrow's Nest. Wordsworth.

Speak the Word. Wesley.

The Speech of the Dead. Ridler.

The Spell. Addison.

Spinster. Plath.

Spring. Thomson.

Spring 1940. Auden.

A Spring Morning. Clare.

Springfield Mountain (D vers.). *Anonymous.*

St. Ciaran and the Birds. Carson.

Stabat Mater. Jacopone da Todi.

The Stable Cat. Norris.

Stanzas to a Lady, with the Poems of Camoens. Byron.

Stanzas Written on the Road between Florence and Pisa. Byron.

The Star. Conkling.

Starlight. Chadwick.

The Statue. Fuller.

Stay, Time. Watson.

Step on His Head. Laughlin.

Steps. O'Hara.

Still Falls the Rain. Sitwell.

Still Thy Sorrow, Magdalena! Washburn.

Stony Brook Tavern. Reed.

Stony Grey Soil. Kavanagh.

The Story of a Stowaway. Scott.

The Story of Phoebus and Daphne Applied... Waller.

The Stranger. Baudelaire.

The Street of Named Houses. Cohen.

The Strongest. Yehoash.

Such bitter fruit thy love doth yield. *Anonymous.*

Summer Lightning. Moore.

Summer Song I. Barker.

Sunday Morning. Moreland.

Sunday: New Guinea. Shapiro.

Sunday up the River. Thomson.

Surgical Ward: Men. Graves.

Surprise. Cronin.

Sweet Evelina. *Anonymous.*

Sweet Love, If Thou Wilt Gain a Monarch's Glory. *Anonymous.*

Sweet Peril. Macdonald.

Sweet Rosie O'Grady. Nugent.

Sweet Spring Is Your. Cummings.

Sweet Trees Who Shade This Mould. Mabbe.

Sweet Unsure. Ralegh.

Sweeter Far Than the Harp, More Gold Than Gold. "Field.

The Sweetest Story Ever Told. Stults.

The Symphony. Lanier.

Symptom Recital. Parker.

Take a Walk around the Corner. Carr.

Take Home This Heart. Holmes.

The Talker. Appel.

The Talker. Van Duyn.

The Talking Fish. Stone.

Tallahassee (excerpt). Merkel.

Tamerlane. Poe.

Tea Poems: Afternoon Tea. Brown.

A Teacher's Prayer. Havergal.

Tell Me Pretty Maiden. Hall.

The Temper. Herbert.

The Temple of Venus. Jenyns.

A Temple to Friendship. Moore.

Tennyson. Coates.

The Terror of Death. Keats.

The Test. Tabb.

A Thanksgiving. Newman.

There Came a Day at Summer's Full. Dickinson.

There Is a Tavern in the Town. *Anonymous.*

There Is No Name So Sweet on Earth. Bethune.

There is No Trumpet Like the Tomb. Dickinson.

There's Wisdom in Women. Brooke.

There Were an Old and Wealthy Man. *Anonymous.*

These Plaintive Verse, the Postes of My Desire. Daniel.

These Poems, She Said. Bringhurst.

These Words I Write on Crinkled Tin. Roberts.

They Say, and I am Glad They Say. Belloc.

They Say the Sea Is Loveless. Lawrence.

The Thief. Kunitz.

The Things. Aiken.

Thinking of Bookshops. Liddy.

This Blonde Girl. Smithyman.

This Heart That Flutters Near My Heart. Joyce.

This Is My Beloved (excerpt). Benton.

This Is My Love for You. Norton.

This Is What the Watchbird Sings, Who Perches in the Lovetree. Boyd.

This Loneliness for You Is Like the Wound. Thompson.

This Moment. Flint.

Those We Love the Best. Wilcox.

Thou Art Not Fair. Campion.

Thou Hast Wounded the Spirit That Loved Thee. Porter.

Thou Light of Ages. Schloerb.

Though Amaryllis Dance in Green. *Anonymous.*

Though I Thy Mithridates Were. Joyce.

The Thought. Herbert of Cherbury.

A Thousand Martyrs I Have Made. Behn.

The Thraldome. Cowley.

The Three Kingdoms of Nature. Lessing.

Three Loves. Hooper.

Three Poems. Yakamochi.

Three Rimas, 2. Becquer.

Three Shadows. Rossetti.

Three Sweethearts. Heine.

Threes. Sandburg.

Thro' Grief and Thro' Danger. Moore.

Through Amaryllis Dance in Green. *Anonymous.*

Through the Night of Doubt and Sorrow. Baring-Gould.

Thursday. Millay.

Thysia. Luce.

Tickly, Tickly, on Your Knee. *Anonymous.*

The Tide of Faith. Eliot.

Time. Huss.

Time's Times Again. Ammons.

'Tis Now Since I Sate Down. Suckling.

Titian's "Bacchanal" in the Prado at Madrid (excerpt). Moore.

Tityrus to His Fair Phyllis. Dickenson.

To —. Braithwaite.

To—. Hood.

To —. Shelley.

To a Blue Flower. Neilson.

To a Butterfly. Davies.

To a Child. Gardons.

To a Child of Quality. Prior.

To a Cloud. Altolaguirre.

To a Coquet Beauty. Sheffield.

To a Lady on Her Marriage. Bell.

To a New Daughter-in-law. *Anonymous.*

To a Nun. *Anonymous.*

To a Passer-By. Baudelaire.

To a River in the South. Newbolt.

To Amoret. Waller.

To Ariake Kambara. Rosten.

To Art. Rossetti.

To Celia Pleading Want of Merit. Stanley.

To Chloris. Drummond.

To Christ Crucified. *Anonymous.*

To Cynthia. Clifford.

To Delia. Daniel.

To Dionysus. Anacreon.

To G.R. Cottam.

To Hampstead. Hunt.

To Heaven. Jonson.

To Helen. Praed.

To Helen in a Huff. Willis.

To His Forsaken Mistress. Ayton [(or Aytoun)] Sir Robert.

To His Friend Master R.L., in Praise of Music and Poetry. Barnfield.

To His Mistress Desiring to Travel with Him as His Page. Donne.

To His Mistress Objecting to Him Neither Toying or Talking. Herrick.

To His Mistris Confined. Shirley.

To His Noble Friend, Mr. Richard Lovelace, upon His Poems. Marvell.

To His Not-So-Coy Mistress. Vaughan-Thomas.

To Jann, in Her Absence. Driver.

To Keep the Cold Wind away. *Anonymous.*

To Keep the Memory of Charlotte Forten Grimke. Grimke.

To know just how he suffered would be dear. Dickinson.

To Lady Eleanor Butler and the Honourable Miss Ponsonby... Wordsworth.

To Lighten My House. Reid.

To Live in Hell, and Heaven to Behold. Constable.

To Madame A. P. Kern. Pushkin.

To Miss B. Clare.

To Mollidusta. Planche.

To My Dear Friend Mr. Congreve, on His Comedy... Dryden.

To My Valentine. *Anonymous.*

To Naples. Mallalieu.

To Night. *Anonymous.*

To O.E.A. McKay.

To One on Her Waste of Time. Blunt.

To Phoebe. Gilbert.

To Phyllis, to Love and Live With Him. Herrick.

To Pikes Peak. Hills.

To Sycamores. Herrick.

To the Fair Clarinda, Who Made Love to Me, Imagin'd More than Woman. Behn.

To the Harpies. Ficke.

To the Lady of Ch'i. *Anonymous.*

To the Man I Live with. Menebroker.

To the Man Who Watches Spiders. Fox.

To the Modern Man. Wheelock.

To the Most Fair and Lovely Mistris, Anne Soame, Now Lady Abdie. Herrick.

To the Parted One. Goethe.

To the Rosella in the Poinsettia Tree. Picot.

To the Small Celandine. Wordsworth.

To the Spring Sun. Laughton.

To Thee, Eternal Soul, Be Praise. Gilder.

To Tomas Costello at the Wars. O'Higgins.

To Urania on the Death of Her First and Only Child. Colman.

To What Strangers, What Welcome. Cunningham.

A Tombless Epitaph. Coleridge.

Tomorrow Is the Marriage Day. *Anonymous.*

Too Anxious for Rivers. Frost.

Too Busy. *Anonymous.*

Too Soon the Lightest Feet. Hall.

Too soon, too soon comes Death to show. Patmore.

Toujours Amour. Stedman.

Tourists. Muchemwa.

Traditional Charms for Finding the Identity of One's True Love. Gay.

The Train Butcher. Ferril.

The Transfiguration of Beauty. Michelangelo.

Transformation. Troupe.

Travelin' Blues. McTell.

Treat the Woman Tenderly, Tenderly. *Anonymous.*

The Tree. Very.

Triolet. Bridges.

Triolet. Gilbert.

The Triumph of Death. Howes.

Troilus and Criseyde. Chaucer.

The True Confession of George Barker. Barker.

A True Hymn. Herbert.

The True Knight. Hawes.

True Love. Cuney.

A True Love Ditty. Middleton.

The True Lover's Farewell. *Anonymous.*

True Woman. Rossetti.

Truth. Lloyd.

Tune Me, O Lord, into One Harmony. Rossetti.

Turn Back, You Wanton Flyer. Campion.

Turn of the Moon. Graves.

The Turtle Thus with Plaintive Crying. Gay.

The Tutelage. Bell.

Tutto e Sciolto. Joyce.

The Twelve Properties or Conditions of a Lover. More.

Twins. Bulwer-Lytton.

Two Look at Two. Frost.

Two Loves. Douglas.

Two Men in Armour. Heath-Stubbs.

The Two Sisters. *Anonymous.*

Two-Volume Novel. Parker.

The Two Wives. Howells.

Two Young Men, 23 to 24 Years Old. Cavafy.

The Uncertain State of a Lover. *Anonymous.*

Uncle Ananias. Robinson.

Uncourtly Love. Walther von der Vogelweide.

Under Our Own Wings. Wong.

Under the Mountain. MacNeice.

Under the Ruins of Poland. Manger.

Unfriendly Fortune. Skelton.

Unless. Glynes.

Unregenerate. Embry.

Unwanted. Field.

Up Street and Down Street. *Anonymous.*

Upon a Black Twist, Rounding the Arm of the Countess of Carlisle. Herrick.

Upon Drinking in a Bowl. Rochester.

Upon Ford's Two Tragedies... Crashaw.

Upon Hearing His High Sweet Tenor Again. Langland.

Upon His Spaniell Tracie. Herrick.

Upon Julia's Petticoat. Herrick.

Upon Love. Herrick.

Upon Master Fletchers Incomparable Playes. Herrick.

Upon Rook: Epigram. Herrick.

Upon Sir John Lawrence's Bringing Water over the Hills... Suckling.

Upon the Death of George Santayana. Hecht.

An Urban Convalescence. Merrill.

V-Letter. Shapiro.

A Valediction. Browning.

A Valediction. La Follette.

Valentine. Summers.

Valentine for Earth. Frost.

Valentine Promise. *Anonymous.*

Valentine to a Little Girl. Newman.

A Valentine to My Mother. Rossetti.

Vanzetti. Buckmaster.

Variables of Green. Graves.

Variation on Ronsard. Moore.

Vaudeville Dancer. Wheelock.

Vernal Equinox. Lowell.

Verses Copied From the Window of an Obscure Lodging-House. *Anonymous.*

Verses Intended to Be Written below a Noble Earl's Picture. Burns.

A Very Phoenix. Lodge.

The Victories of Love. Patmore.

Victory. *Anonymous.*

Victory comes late. Dickinson.

Virgil: Georgics, Book IV. Schmitz.

The Vision. Herrick.

The Vision of Piers Plowman. Langland.

The Visit. Emerson.

La Vita Nuova. Dante Alighieri.

Vixi. Mackay.

A Vulnerary. Williams.

Vusumzi's Song. Manyase.

Waillie. *Anonymous.*

Waiting in Faith. Michelangelo.

Walking Parker Home. Kaufman.

The Wanton (excerpt). Vidya.

Warren Phinney. Mayer.

Warrior's Song. Austin.

Washington. Turner.
The Wastrel. Kauffman.
The Watering Place.
　Propertius.
Waters of the Sea.
　Goldbeck.
The Wave. Phillips.
The Way. Creeley.
The Wayside. Morse.
We Assume: On the Death of
　Our Son, Reuben Masai
　Harper. Harper.
We'll Never Know.
　Hoellein.
We Meet in the Lives of
　Animals. Everwine.
We Plough the Fields.
　Campbell.
We Reason of These Things.
　Stevens.
Weapons. Wickham.
The Wedding. Kohler.
Wedding. Livesay.
Wedding Song. Meyer.
Welcome, Fortune.
　Anonymous.
Welcome over the Door of an
　Old Inn. *Anonymous.*
Welcome, Ye Hopeful Heirs
　of Heaven. Brown.
The Well: Two Songs.
　Anonymous.
Were My Hart as Some Mens
　Are. Campion.
Wessex Guidebook.
　MacNeice.
The West-Country Damosel's
　Complaint. *Anonymous.*
What Does a Man Think
　About. Holmes.
What God Has Promised.
　Flint.
What Meanest Thou, My
　Fortune. *Anonymous.*
What rage Is this? Wyatt.
What's Hard. Lerner.
What There Is. Patchen.
When a Warlock Dies.
　Gardner.
When I See on Rood.
　Anonymous.
When I Thy Parts Run O'er.
　Herrick.
When I Was Still a Child.
　Harford.
When I went into my garden.
　Bertken.
When Love Meets Love.
　Brown.
When the Curtains of Night
　Are Pinned Back (with
　music). *Anonymous.*
When We Hear the Eye
　Open... Kaufman.
When We in Kind
　Embracements Had Agre'd.
　Anonymous.
When You Are Gone. Van
　Winckel.
Where She Told Her Love.
　Clare.
Where to Seek Love. Blake.
Where You Go When She
　Sleeps. Hummer.
Which Loved Best?
　″Allison.
Which Sword? Pierce.
White as a Paper A-Sail in the
　Air. *Anonymous.*
A White Blossom.
　Lawrence.

White-Haired Lover (excerpt).
　Shapiro.
A White Rose. O'Reilly.
Whitsunday. Keble.
Who knows if the moon's.
　Cummings.
Who of Those Coming After.
　Gottlieb.
Who's Gonna Shoe Your
　Pretty Little Foot?
　Anonymous.
Who's That at My Bedroom
　Window? *Anonymous.*
Whom the Gods Love.
　Howe.
Whose Little Pigs.
　Anonymous.
Why Do I Love You? Croft.
Why I Write Not of Love.
　Jonson.
Wichita Vortex Sutra, II.
　Ginsberg.
A Wife in London. Hardy.
The Wife's Lament.
　Anonymous.
Wild Eden. Woodberry.
Will You Love Me in
　December as You Do in
　May? Walker.
Will You Love Me When I'm
　Old? *Anonymous.*
Will You, One Day. Ramie.
William Wilson. Cowley.
The Willow Tree.
　Anonymous.
The Wind. Creeley.
Wine and Love and Lyre.
　Anonymous.
The Wings of Love. Cousins.
Winter. Wingfield.
The Winter Glass. Cotton.
Winter Love Song.
　Anonymous.
Winter Nights. Campion.
Winter Song. Tollet.
Winter Tryst. Van Doren.
Wisdom. Fallon.
Wisdom. Hicky.
With Lilacs. Crandall.
With Roses. Lloyd.
A Withered Rose. Yehoash.
A Woman's Last Word.
　Browning.
Woman's Love. *Anonymous.*
Woman with Flower.
　Madgett.
Wonders. *Anonymous.*
Wondrous Love. Pembroke.
A Word Made Flesh Is
　Seldom. ″d.
Words. Rutsala.
Words for Love. Berrigan.
Words to My Friend.
　Vivien.
Words Words Words. Krysl.
A Work of Artiface. Piercy.
The Work of Love. Sangster.
A World Beyond. Bowditch
A World for Love. Clare.
The World Is Mine. Coates.
Wrestling Jacob. Wesley.
Written in Exile. Raine.
Written on an Island off the
　Breton Coast. Venantius
　Fortunatus.
Years and Years I Have
　Loved You. Gillett.
Yoke Soft and Dear. Kunze.
You. Clark.
You at the Pump (History of
　North and South).
　O'Hara.

You Do Not Have to Love
　Me. Cohen.
You Got to Love Her with a
　Feeling. Tampa Red.
You Little Stars That Live in
　Skies. Greville.
You'll Love Me Yet!
　Browning.
The Young Laird and
　Edinburgh Katy. Ramsay.
Young Windebank. Woods.
Your Last Drive. Hardy.
The Zodiac, X. Dickey.

Love's
Dusk. MacLeish.
Remember Not. Johnson.

Loveliness
After the War. Le Gallienne.
All That Is Lovely in Men.
　Creeley.
And If at Last. Labe.
Art Thou Poor, Yet Hast
　Thou Golden Slumbers?
　Dekker.
Autumn. Manger.
Autumn Leaves. Heyward.
A Ballade-Catalogue of Lovely
　Things. Le Gallienne.
The Birthnight: To F. De la
　Mare.
Du Bist Wie Eine Blume.
　Heine.
Blue Girls. Ransom.
Calligram, 15 May 1915.
　Apollinaire.
Childe Harold's Pilgrimage:
　Canto IV, XXIX. Byron.
City Trees. Dargan.
Cobweb. Welles.
Dream and the Song.
　Corrothers.
The Dream Queen: Dialogue.
　Bhasa.
Elegy. Guiterman.
Equals. Untermeyer.
Faith. Tabb.
Fast Bundled Is the Firewood.
　Anonymous.
The Finest Thing. Veitch.
For Stephen Dixon. Gilbert.
The Fountain in the Park.
　Haley.
From the Parthenon I Learn.
　Wattles.
Golden Falcon. Coffin.
The Great Lover. Brooke.
Gulls and Dreams.
　Stevenson.
Honesty at a Fire. Squire.
How Glorious Are the
　Morning Stars. Keach.
I Love the Woods. Neidus.
I Met at Eve. De La Mare.
In an Autumn Wood. Percy.
In Death. Bradley.
Laus Virginitatis. Symons.
Let Me Grow Lovely.
　Baker.
Literary Love. Kemp.
The Love-Letter. Rossetti.
Morning. Gallagher.
Mother–a Portrait. Fuller.
The Mother in the House.
　Hagedorn.
Mrs. Albion You've Got a
　Lovely Daughter. Henri.
The Newlyweds. Criswell.
The North of Wales. Morris.
The Only Jealousy of Emer
　(excerpt). Yeats.
Over Saleve. Clarke.
Part of Plenty. Spencer.

Plains. Auden.
Pleasures. Goldbarth.
Portrait. Allen.
A Prayer. Scollard.
The Racer's Widow. Gluck.
The Rose. Ronsard.
Roses on the Breakfast Table.
　Lawrence.
The Rubaiyat of Omar
　Khayyam. Omar
　Khayyam.
Saint Francis and the Sow.
　Kinnell.
Shitty. Amis.
The Shopman. Farjeon.
Small Poem about the Hounds
　and the Hares. Mueller.
Song for the Passing of a
　Beautiful Woman.
　Anonymous.
Sonnets to Miranda.
　Watson.
A Spring Song. *Anonymous.*
St. Philip in Himself.
　Newman.
Things Lovelier. Wolfe.
To Ianthe. Shelley.
Two Voices. Corbin.
Unwritten Poems. Winter.
Upon a House Shaken by the
　Land Agitation. Yeats.
Vanity. Wickham.
A White Tree in Bloom.
　Moreland.
William Street. Slessor.
A Winter Hymn–to the Snow.
　Jones.
Winter Solstice Poem. Scott.
Wishes for a Bridal Couple
　and Their Unborn Child.
　Statius Publius Papinius.

Lover (s)
Agatha. Major.
Agent of Love. Redwing.
And there is nothing at all–
　neither fear.
　Gorbanyevskaya.
Antony and Cleopatra.
　Shakespeare.
As You Like It.
　Shakespeare.
Asking for Ruthie. Grahn.
Barbara Allen. *Anonymous.*
The Bare Branches Tremble.
　Tzu Yeh.
The Beaten Path. Winslow.
Bill and Parson Sim.
　Anonymous.
Blackheads. Skinner.
Bonnie Annie Livieston.
　Anonymous.
The Brown Girl.
　Anonymous.
The Canoe Speaks (excerpt).
　Stevenson.
Carmina. Catullus.
Casuarina. Robinson.
Chances. Stockwell.
Chang'd, Yet Constant.
　Stanley.
Chloris, 'Tis Not in Your
　Power. Etherege.
Clerk Saunders. *Anonymous.*
Confess, Marpessa. Graves.
Cool Tombs. Sandburg.
Country Gods. Cometas.
The Dance. Campion.
Daughters of War.
　Rosenberg.
The Delta. Browne.
The Douglas Tragedy.
　Anonymous

The Dowie Dens of Yarrow. *Anonymous.*

The Drowsy Sleeper (B vers.). *Anonymous.*

Earl Brand; or, The Douglas Tragedy (A vers.). *Anonymous.*

Elegy for Jane. Roethke.

Epigram: "Nicander, ooh..." Alcaeus.

Epitaph in Sirmio. Morton.

The Evening Darkens Over. Bridges.

Fair Ines. Hood.

Fame and Fortune. Drayton.

The First of My Lovers. Carter.

The Fisher Lad of Whitby. *Anonymous.*

For an Obligate Parasite. Dugan.

For Anna. Layton.

For Lover Man, and All the Other Young Men Who Failed to Return... Williams.

Friend and Lover. "Madeline.

A Game of Chance. Moss.

The Garden. Giltinan.

A Garland for Heliodora. Meleager.

Gig at Big Al's. McHugh.

Gondibert. Davenant.

Goodbye, My Lover, Goodbye. *Anonymous.*

Grania. *Anonymous.*

The Great Adventurer. *Anonymous.*

The Great Gatsby: Epitaph. Fitzgerald.

The Green Isle of Lovers. Sands.

Gulf Stream. "Coolidge.

Here/There. Norris.

The Hour-Glass. Herrick.

Hymn to Earth. Wylie.

I Leave Tonight from Euston. *Anonymous.*

In the Wilderness. Graves.

Incidents in Playfair House. Moore.

Infinity. Whitman

Initial. Boyars.

Intermezzo. Hillyer.

Into the Dark. Monette.

Islands. Pomeroy.

A Kiss. Drummond.

A la Claire Fontaine. *Anonymous.*

Lady of Lidice. Chavez.

Lalla Rookh. Moore.

The Last Ascent. Lehmann.

The Last Trail. Coblentz.

Life Story. Tomioka Taeko.

Like Gulliver. Cassian.

Lilly's Song. Zimroth.

Limb and Mind. Waller.

Lonely Lover. Coffin.

Lord Lovel. *Anonymous.*

Lord Lovel (B vers.). *Anonymous.*

Lord Thomas and Fair Annet (B vers.). *Anonymous.*

Love Is Bitter. *Anonymous.*

Love Is Enough. Morris.

Love's Consolation. Dixon.

Love's Despair. O'Curnain.

Love's Epitaph. Newcastle.

Love Song: "I passed by the house of the young man who loves me." *Anonymous.*

Love Songs. *Anonymous.*

The Lover Freed from the Gallows. *Anonymous.*

The Man Who Owned Cars. Fried.

March. Housman.

Medelwold and Sidselille. *Anonymous.*

Medieval Norman Songs. *Anonymous.*

Metamorphoses. Ovid (Publius Ovidius Naso).

A Model for the Laureate. Yeats.

Moonlight. Moxon.

Moonlight. Tahureau.

Mutability. Brooke.

The Nature of the Turtle Dove. *Anonymous.*

Never Such Love. Graves.

Night Harvest. Pence.

Night Song for Two Mystics. Blackburn.

Night Sowing. Campbell.

No Labor-Saving Machine. Whitman.

Non Ti Fidar. Zukofsky.

The North Sea (excerpt). Heine.

Not Wanting Myself. Gregg.

O That My Love Were in My Arms. *Anonymous.*

An Ode Which was Prefixed To a Prayer Booke. Crashaw.

Odes. Santayana.

Old Age. *Anonymous.*

Olden Love-Making. Breton.

On a Prayer Book Sent to Mrs. M. R. (excerpt). Crashaw.

On the Upside. Murray.

The Onion, Memory. Raine.

The Paps of Jura. Young.

Parting. *Anonymous.*

A Pastoral Courtship. Rochester.

The Poet Describes His Love. Nathan.

Prayer. Villiers.

The Primrose. Carew.

The Primrose. Herrick.

Pro Femina. Kizer.

Quantum Est Quod Desit. Moore.

Rain, Rain. Akins.

Remember Your Lovers. Keyes.

Remonstrance. Philodemos of Gadara.

The Repeated Journey. McGrath.

Rome Remember. Keyes.

Romeo and Juliet. Shakespeare.

The Room Above the Square. Spender.

Round Her Neck She Wore a Yellow Ribbon. *Anonymous.*

The Runner in the Skies. James. Oppenheim

Sappho's Reply. Brown.

Saw You My True Love John? *Anonymous.*

Sheer Joy. Cushman.

Shocking Rape and Murder of Two Lovers. *Anonymous.*

Silent Love. Clare.

The Silent Lover. Ralegh.

The Silver Dagger. *Anonymous.*

Sleeping Peasants. Janik.

Song in Spite of Myself. Cullen.

Song of the Taste. Snyder.

Song: One Hard Look. Graves.

Song: "Phillis is my only joy." Sedley.

A Song: "When lovely woman, prone to folly." (parody). *Anonymous.*

Song: "When thy Beauty appears." Parnell.

Sonnet: "When some men gather to talk of Love." McLeod.

Sonnets, XI: "Sighing, and sadly sitting by my Love." Barnfield.

Sonnets, LV: "Not marble, nor the gilded monuments." Shakespeare.

The Spinning Wheel. Waller.

Spinster Song. Tunstall.

Spring. Spire.

Spring in War-Time. Teasdale.

A Stone. Eberhart.

Stragglers. Aretino.

Such Is the Sickness of Many a Good Thing. Duncan.

The Summer Ending. Wescott.

Tableau. Wright.

Tell Me No More. Drummond.

Tenants. Gibson.

Terra Australis. McAuley.

This Lady She Wears a Dark Green Shawl. *Anonymous.*

The Three Arrows. Fitzgerald.

Three Epitaphs on John Hewet and Sarah Drew. Pope.

Three Things. Sarton.

Three Things Jeame Lacks. *Anonymous.*

Thy Heart. *Anonymous.*

Time to Choose a Lover. Horace.

To Delia. Daniel.

To Him That Was Crucified. Whitman.

To His Coy Mistress (parody). Flood.

The Town I Was Born In. Amichai.

The True Lover. Housman.

Twelfth Night. Shakespeare.

Two Lovers Sitting on a Tomb. Hill.

The Two of Cups. Jarrett.

Two Poems. Sosei (Sosei Hoshi).

Under the Waterfall. Hardy.

Vergissmeinicht. Douglas.

The Violin's Complaint. Thayer.

Wake Up, You Drowsy Sleepers. *Anonymous.*

The Wanderer from the Fold. Bronte.

Wedded. Rosenberg.

What Do You Want? Newlove.

What My Lover Said. Greene.

What Sugred Termes, What All-Perswading Arte. Lynche.

What the Animals Said. Serchuk.

When Lovely Woman. Cary.

The Wife of Winter's Tale. Browne.

Winds of Eros. Russell.

Wolf Dream. Lense.

Woman Made of Stars. Thompson.

The Women at the Corners Stand. Golding.

The Word of God. Skjaeraasen.

Young Man's Fancy. Mathew.

A Young Man to an Old Woman Courting Him. Cleveland.

Yugoslav Cemetery. Wright.

Loving

Advice. Hughes.

Arcadia. Sidney.

The Archer. Ainslie.

Are You What Your Faire Lookes Expresse? Campion.

Brother and Sister. Eliot.

Brown Skin Girl. McClennan.

By the Boat House, Oxford. Stevenson.

The Crocuses. Harper.

Crusader's Song. *Anonymous.*

The Curtains Now Are Drawn. Hardy.

Daphne and Apollo. Macy.

Dialogue. Erskine.

Drinking Song. Brome.

Erotic Suite (excerpt). Vega.

The Faerie Queene. Spenser.

The Family Cat. Fuller.

Farewell, Sweet Mary. *Anonymous.*

Flower of Love. McKay.

For Every Day. Havergal.

For My Mother. Jordan.

Georgie Wedlock. *Anonymous.*

Great-Grandma. Shields.

How Shall a Man Fore-Doomed. Coleridge.

I'm Soaked through with You. Korn.

I Want to Tell You. Hochman.

Lady Moon. Milnes.

The Loadstone of His Love. Wesley.

Lost Lover Blues. Fuller.

The Mask the Wearer of the Mask Wears. Bronk.

Motets: "My love, how could your heart consider." *Anonymous.*

Need of Loving. Gillilan.

Nocturne in the Women's Prison. Beneyto.

Obit. Lowell.

Our Light Afflictions. *Anonymous.*

The Poet Loves from Afar. O'Grady.

A Poet's Welcome to His Love-Begotten Daughter. Burns.

The Poet Speaks. Johnson.

Prayer. *Anonymous.*

Sex Play in Four Acts.
Fetherling.
Silent Testimony. Parmenter.
The Song of the Camp.
Taylor.
Song: "Phillis, let's shun the
common Fate." Sedley.
Sonnets, CX: "Alas! 'tis true I
have gone here and there."
Shakespeare.
Sweet Loving Friendship.
Bellamy.
Sylvae, II (excerpt). Statius
Publius Papinius.
Tambourine Song for Soldiers
Going into Battle. Hind
bint Utba.
To His Ever-Loving God.
Herrick.
To My Mother. Heine.
To the United States of
America. Bridges.
Valentine. "T.
Veterans. Johnston.
The Vintage. Cooper.
Ward Two. Webb.
Watching You Walk. Todd.
Why Not? Pastan.
Within the Shelter of Our
Walls. Lennen.
A Woman's Shortcomings.
Browning.
A Young Wife. Lawrence.
Low (er) (ly)
Botany Lesson. Reeve.
Bunker's Hill; or, the Soldier's
Lamentation. Freeth.
Canzo: "Can l'erba fresch'elh
folha par." Bernard de
Ventadour
The Church's One
Foundation. Stone.
The clear water of the
imperial pond. Ise Tayu.
Dirge for a Soldier. Boker.
The Emigrant: Winter in
Lower Canada. O'Grady.
For an Autograph (excerpt).
Lowell.
Forecast. Miles.
The Gate of the Year.
Haskins.
High and Low. Cousins.
Hymn for the Church
Militant. Chesterton.
In Memoriam A.H.H., LX.
Tennyson.
Industrial Size. Wright.
The Insusceptibles. Rich.
The Jovial Tinker; or, The
Willing Couple.
Anonymous.
Lady Geraldine's Courtship.
Browning.
Love, Love! What Nonsense It
Is. Gorbanyevskaya.
The Low-Backed Car.
Lover.
Low down Chariot.
Anonymous.
Lullaby. Rossetti.
A Mother's Lament for the
Death of Her Son. Burns.
No Accident. MacCaig.
Of Boston in New England.
Bradford.
On the Death of a Young and
Favorite Slave. Martial
(Marcus Valerius Martialis).
On the Death of Pym.
Drummond.
The Secret. Stephens.

Shame. Patmore.
A Simile. Prior.
Song: "The feathers of the
willow." Dixon.
There Was a Little Ship.
Anonymous.
To My Love. Saxe.
Tormenting Virgin.
Anonymous.
The Town Betrayed. Muir.
Vale! Noel.
When Each Bright Star Is
Clouded. Callanan.
Wil the Merry Weaver, and
Charity the Chamber-Maid.
Anonymous.
Young Democracy (excerpt).
O'Dowd.
Low-lands
Young Edmondale.
Anonymous.
Lower East Side
Yiddish Speaking Socialists of
the Lower East Side.
Sanders.
Lowlands (s)
The Big Five-Gallon Jar.
Anonymous.
Edwin in the Lowlands Low.
Anonymous.
The Elwha River. Snyder.
The Goulden Vanitie.
Anonymous.
Lowlands. *Anonymous.*
Young Edwin in the Lowlands
Low. *Anonymous.*
Lucid
Henry James. Fadiman.
Letter to Robert. Fabilli.
Resignation. Arnold.
To a Dead Journalist.
Williams.
Voltaire at Ferney. Auden.
Lucifer
The Dream of Gerontius.
Newman.
Godiva (parody). Berry.
Luck (ier) (y)
The Ballad of Billie Potts.
Warren.
Because I Were Shy.
Anonymous.
Bellerophon: There Are No
Gods. Euripides.
Bop Lyrics. Ginsberg.
Bringing Flowers. Spear.
Brother and Sister. Eliot.
The Cave. Dresbach.
Communication. Jennings.
The Crooked Trail to
Holbrook. *Anonymous.*
Despair. Reed.
Devil Got My Woman.
James.
The Douglas Tragedy.
Anonymous
Edenhall. "Coolidge.
Exile Song. Rosenfeld.
The Fall of the House of
Usher. Whittemore.
The Fox Walked Out, B vers.
Anonymous.
Game after Supper. Atwood.
Gipsy Song. Jonson.
Guide to the Perplexed.
Malouf.
How Music's Made. Laing.
A Hundreth Good Poyntes of
Husbandry. Tusser.
The Hunter. Nash.
I Can't Give You Anything
but Love. Fields.

In the Middle of August.
Hirsch.
Inventions. Butler.
A Likeness. Cather.
Lincoln and Liberty.
Simpson.
March the 3rd. Thomas.
The Mariner's Wife. Mickle.
Marriage Couplet. Cole.
Moonlight Night on the Port.
Keyes.
Now Dreary Dawns the
Eastern Light. Yeats.
Oh Lucky Jim. *Anonymous.*
One Perfect Rose. Parker.
Optimism. Salkeld.
Pro Femina. Kizer.
Queen Anne's Musicians.
Hennell.
Rory O'More; or, Good
Omens. Lover.
See a Pin and Pick It Up.
Anonymous.
Shao and the South.
Confucius.
She Was Bred in Old
Kentucky. Braisted.
Song of Myself. Whitman.
Sonnet: "Is there a great green
commonwealth of
Thought." Masefield.
The Surprise. *Anonymous.*
Teddy's Wonderings. Bangs.
Thanksgiving, 1963. Kazan.
The Tramp's Song. O'Neill.
Two Pictures of a Leaf. Bell.
The Undertaking. Gluck.
Wax. Scott.
With a Little Bit of Luck.
Lerner.
Lucy
Energetic Women.
Lawrence.
Four Saints in Three Acts:
"Pigeons on the grass alas."
Stein.
Strange Fits of Passion Have I
Known. Wordsworth.
Lullaby
The Christening. De La
Mare.
Christmas Lullaby.
Troubetzkoy.
Daisy's Song. Keats.
Gascoigne's Lullaby.
Gascoigne.
Golden Slumbers. Dekker.
In the Name of Jesus Christ.
Cranston.
Lullaby, O Lullaby. Bennett.
Mother's Song. *Anonymous.*
The Posy of Thyme.
Anonymous.
Sea-Sleep. Harris
Lumber (ing)
For a New Home. Marinoni.
Hampstead: The Horse
Chestnut Trees. Gunn.
In Trouble and Shame.
Lawrence.
Johnny Carroll's Camp.
Anonymous.
Once More A-Lumbering Go.
Anonymous.
Luminous
The Book of How. Moore.
The Green Afternoon. Rago.
Shadows To-Day. Rossetti.
To What Strangers, What
Welcome. Cunningham.
When a Body. Dawson.

Lump (s)
Lump. Phillips.
On Two Ministers of State.
Belloc.
That Little Lump of Coal.
Anonymous.
Lunar
Annus Mirabilis. Donne.
Capsule Philosophy.
Lamport.
Meditation on a Memoir.
Cunningham.
Moonlight. Apollinaire.
The Supremacy of Bacteria.
Frazier.
Lunatic
Berthe Morisot. Waldman.
The Figure-Head. Garstin.
Lunch
Atheling Grange: or, The
Apotheosis of Lotte
Nussbaum. Plomer.
Canto LXXX. Pound.
Everybody Eats Too Much
Anyhow. Nash.
Hitch Haiku. Snyder.
Listen! Moore.
Lord Lucky. Belloc.
Lunch. Koch.
Macquarie Place.
FitzGerald.
The Things I Say Are True.
Varela.
Tornado Soup. Redwing.
Under Your Voice, among
Legends. Beauvais.
Lungs
Breathless. Noyce.
Coal for Mike. Brecht.
Hello, Hello. Matthews.
Herman Moon's Hourbook.
Middleton.
In the Cabinet. Vinner.
Poems from the Coalfields, 1:
Air Shaft. Healy.
Walrus Hunting. Aua.
Lurch
Epistle to John Hamilton
Reynolds. Keats.
Jane Austen at the Window.
Beer.
Lure
Britannia Rules of
Orthography. "Firth".
Erotion. Swinburne.
A Fish to Feed All Hunger.
Alcosser.
Her Pedigree. Ficke.
Trouvaille. Murphy.
Lurks
The Dog beneath the Skin.
Auden.
Pretty Maids Beware!!!
Anonymous.
Lust (ful) (s) (y)
Alas the grief and deadly
woeful smart! Wyatt.
Ares. Ehrenstein.
The Beauty of Things.
Jeffers.
Betjeman at the Post Office
(parody). Sharpless.
Biography for Traman
(excerpt). Scott.
Caelica, LXXI. Greville.
Chinatown. Mezquida.
Dream Songs. Berryman.
For the Noun C. BL. Tyler.
Hamatreya. Emerson.
Hymns and Spiritual Songs.
Smart.

Little Pretty Nancy Girl. *Anonymous.*
The Lost Ingredient. Sexton.
Love and Lust. Rosenberg.
Marking Time. Steele.
Midnight. Dryden.
Nymphs and Satyrs. Ewart.
Psalm X. Sidney.
A Round. Browne.
The Second Satire of the First Book of Horace (excerpt). Pope.
Sexual Soup. Jong.
Since so ye please to hear me plain. Wyatt.
Soliloquy at Potsdam. Porter.
Stalin. Lowell.
Succubi. Newlove.
The Succubus. Graves.
Three Lyrics. Petronius Arbiter (Caius Petronius Arbiter).
To Barba. May.
The Veteran. Coxe.
You Must Have Been a Sensational Baby (excerpt). Norse.

Lustre
Like a Pearl. Naggid.
Mr. Rockefeller's Hat. Bevington.
On a Bust of Lincoln. Scollard.
On Finding a Small Fly Crushed in a Book. Turner.
Song. Set by Mr. Coleman. Cotton.
Spain's Last Armada. Rice.
Touchstone. Worley.
Tragic Love. Turner.

Lute (s)
Againe. Herrick.
The Argument of Democritus Platonissans. More.
At most mischief. Wyatt.
La Chute. Olson.
From the Turkish. Byron.
I Lay My Lute beside Thy Door. Urmy.
Independence. Fullerton.
The Lover Complaineth the Unkindness of His Love. Wyatt.
On the Death of Phillips. *Anonymous.*
Pallor. Robinson.
The Singing Leaves. Lowell.
Sussyissfriin. Dow.
Upon Julia's Voice. Herrick.
The Virgin Mary to Christ on the Cross. Southwell.

Luxury (ies)
Ave Caesar. Jeffers.
Cyder, I: How to Catch Wasps. Philips.
The Good Rich Man. Chesterton.
Shine, Republic. Jeffers.
The Test. Tabb.
To Leigh Hunt, Esq. Keats.

Lydia
L'Eau Dormante. Aldrich.
Lydia Is Gone This Many a Year. Reese.
Some say cavalry and others claim. Sappho.
Some There Are Who Say That the Fairest Thing Seen. Sappho.
Sweet William. *Anonymous.*

To Lydia Languish. Dobson.

Lynn
The Bells of Lynn. Longfellow.
Limerick: "There lived an old woman at Lynn." *Anonymous.*
Limerick: "There was a gay damsel of Lynn." *Anonymous.*
Oxford. Dorn.

Lyre (s)
Dedication: To Edward John Trelawny. Swinburne.
Epitaph on an Irish Priest. *Anonymous.*
A Gratulatory to Mr. Ben. Johnson for His Adopting of Him... Randolph.
How My Songs of Her Began. Marston.
Israfel. Poe.
My Song of Today. Therese.
Ode on a Sermon against Glory. Akenside.
Ode to Ethiopia. Dunbar.
Returning Home. Du Bellay.
The Sacrifice to Apollo. Drayton.
The Strolling Player. Rimbaud.
Wine and Love and Lyre. *Anonymous.*

Lyric
Comradery. Cawein.
I Like to Quote. Follansbee.
A Kite Is a Victim. Cohen.
Pastel: Masks and Faces. Symons.
The Poets' Paradise. Drayton.
The Scribe. Farkas.

M

Machine (s)
All Watched over by Machines of Loving Grace. Brautigan.
The Boss Machine-Tender after Losing a Son. Corrigan.
The Bulldozer. Stauffer.
The Egg and the Machine. Frost.
Grazing Locomotives. MacLeish.
The Hermit Wakes to Bird Sounds. Kumin.
Highway: Michigan. Roethke.
In New Ross. Iremonger. Sects Gilbert.
In One Battle. Jones.
Into the Book. Grossman.
The New Cows. Waterman.
Running It Backward. Morris.

Mad (man) (ness)
Abelard at Cluny. Rees.
After Reading a Book on Abnormal Psychology. Moll.
Against an Old Lecher. Harington.
Alienation. Kemp.

Alphabetical Song on the Corn Law Bill. *Anonymous.*
An Amorous Dialogue between John and His Mistress. *Anonymous.*
Another Fan Belonging to Mademoiselle Mallarme. Mallarme.
Bits of Straw. Clare.
Caelica, XXVI. Greville.
Cafe in Warsaw. Ginsberg.
Captured Bird. Rachow.
The Chances. Owen.
Christopher Marlowe. Drayton.
City. Biasotti.
Climbing. Fuertes.
Come Dance with Kitty Stobling. Kavanagh.
The Comedy of Billy and Betty. *Anonymous.*
Conversation. Dewey.
Cousins. Cullen.
Cow Dance. Beaver.
The Dream. Byron.
The Dumb Maid. *Anonymous.*
Emblem. Quarles.
Fannie. Aldrich.
A Far Cry after a Close Call. Howard.
Firebrand. Crosby.
For My Contemporaries. Cunningham.
A Franciscan Prayer. Dinnis.
The Greeting of the Roses. Garland.
Hag-Ridden. Graves.
Her Skin Is So White as a Lily. Colum.
Here and There: Nocturnal Landscape. Cowley.
Highway Blues. Hopkins.
The Horse. Levine.
I Heard the Old Song. Vilakazi.
Immensity. Stern.
Impression. Gosse.
In Lombardy. Revell.
Innocent Play. Watts.
Jars. Raboff.
King Lear. Shakespeare.
Lady. Berrigan.
Lady Isabel. *Anonymous.*
The Lake. Stephens.
The Loon. Sarett.
The Lovers Melancholy. Ford.
A Mad Answer of a Madman. Hayman.
Mad Blake. Benet.
Madhouse. Hernton.
The Madman. Urdang.
Madness. Dickey.
Maud. Tennyson.
The Mistress (excerpt). Rochester.
Multiplication Is Vexation. Mother Goose.
My Heart Burns for Him. *Anonymous.*
On Dennis. Pope.
On your dazzling throne, Aphrodite. Sappho.
One Hour of Madness and Joy. Whitman.
Pasquin to the Queen's Statue at St. Paul's, during the Procession... Shippen.
Passing into Storm. Lane.

Peach Orchard Mama. Jefferson.
Perseus. MacNeice.
The Primitive. Lee.
Reason. Tatham.
Reflections. Barrows.
The Seasons. Thomson.
Song. Clare.
Song: "A little onion lay by the fireplace." Moore.
Song: "Desire for a woman took hold of me in the night." *Anonymous.*
The Spring Returns. Moore.
The Storm. Cohen.
That Which We Call a Rose. Dransfield.
There Is No Place to Hide. MacEwen.
They Have Taken It from Me. Corsellis.
This Definition Poetry Doth Fit. Randolph.
To a Lady on Her Marriage. Bell.
The Vietnamese Girl in the Madhouse. Fisher.
You That Are Jealous and Have a Wife. *Anonymous.*

Made
All Things Bright and Beautiful. Alexander.
Bedelia. Jerome.
Comfort in Extremity. Harvey.
The Old Songs. Seaman.
Poem for a Song. Cadsby.
Tyson's Corner. St. John.
The Wheel. Muir.

Madhouse
Let It Go. Empson.
Yellow. Jacobsen.

Madonna
Aspiration. Lamb.
The Frog Prince. Sexton.
Maternal Lady with the Virgin Grace. Lamb.
O Mary Pierced with Sorrow. Kipling.

Maelstrom
Under the Mountain. MacNeice.
Watch Long Enough, and You Will See. Aiken.

Maggie
The Betrothed. Kipling.
Blythsome Bridal. *Anonymous.*
The Cripple for Life. *Anonymous.*
When You and I Were Young, Maggie. Butterfield.

Maggot (s)
The Death Balloon. Goedicke.
God Sour the Milk of the Knacking Wench. Nowlan.
A Simplification. Wilbur.

Magic (al)
Ars Poetica. Vriesland.
Autumn. Shapcott.
The Bad Mother. Griffin.
Byron vs. DiMaggio. Meinke.
Christmas Eve. Davidson.
Cinderella Grass. Fisher.
Dedication to the Generation Knocking at the Door. Davidson.
Dorothea. Cleghorn.

Egyptian Hieroglyphics.
Anonymous.
Enthusiasm. Mangan.
Fairy Story. Todd.
Faust's Servant. Fuller.
The Green Shepherd.
Simpson.
Horse. Benson.
Hump, the Escalator.
Faubion.
An Irish Wind. Dennis.
Javanese Dancers. Symons.
Last Words on Greece.
Byron.
Magic Word. Jackson.
Midsummer Courtship.
Thomson.
La Mort d'Arthur (parody).
Aytoun.
Next Door to Monica's Dance
Studio. Smith.
Ode to a Nightingale: The
Nightingale. Keats.
Pan-Pipes. Chalmers.
Poem for Pat. Allen.
Reflections on a Womb Which
Is Called "Vacant."
Hathaway.
Thanksgiving Magic.
Barrett.
Three Poems for the Indian
Steelworkers in a Bar...
Bruchac.
To a Blind Student Who
Taught Me to See. Hazo.
Vacation Time. Bennett.
A Voice from the Roses.
Kumin.
When I Set out for Lyonnesse.
Hardy.
The Whole Year Christmas.
Morgan.
You Are a Part of Me.
Yerby.

Magician
An Arctic Vision. Harte.
A Death in the Streets.
Petaccia.
Morning Song. Orr.

Magistrates
Advice to Hotheads. Isaac.
The Splendid Village. Elliott.

Magnet (s)
The Fable of the Magnet and
the Churn. Gilbert.
Magnets. Cullen.
The Narrows. Bruchac.
Thou Art the Source. Rumi.

Magnificence
The Connecticut Elm. Swan.
Half-Bent Man. Eberhart.
May Garden. Drinkwater.
To the Ghost of a Kite.
Wright.

Magnolia (s)
Hudson Ferry. Schuyler.
Spring's on the Curb.
Flanner.
Starlings. Olson.

Magpie (s)
Cock-Crow Song.
Anonymous.
Here Lies a Prisoner. Mew.
The Magpies. Glover.
Song of Sixpence.
Anonymous.
Two Magpies Sat on a Garden
Rail. Thompson.

Mahogany
The Funeral Home. Mezey.
The White Dust. Gibson.

Maid (en) (s)
An American Girl.
Matthews.
Annie died the other day.
Cummings.
Another True Maid. Prior.
Apology for Apostasy?
Knight.
Atalanta's Race. Morris.
The Ballad of the Dark Ladie.
Coleridge.
The Beggar Maid. Tennyson.
Behold, the Grave. Crane.
Bid Adieu to Maidenhood.
Joyce.
Blooming Nelly. Burns.
Blow the Winds, I-Ho.
Anonymous.
The Captive's Hymn.
Proctor.
Cashel of Munster.
Anonymous.
The Castle by the Sea.
Uhland.
Come Hither, You That Love.
Fletcher.
The Country Girl's Policy; or,
The Cockney Outwitted.
Anonymous.
Daphne. Jones, Jr.
Easter Zunday. Barnes.
The Eolian Harp. Coleridge.
Epithalamium. Johannes
Secundus.
Fair Annie. *Anonymous.*
Florella. *Anonymous.*
Four Love Poems. Ibn Ezra.
The Friar in the Well (A
version). *Anonymous.*
From Citron-Bower.
Doolithe.
Gascoigne's Praise of His
Mistress. Gascoigne.
Glad and Blithe Might Ye Be.
Anonymous.
The Grape-Vine Swing.
Simms.
Gulls in an Aery Morrice.
Henley.
Have You Been at Carrick?
Anonymous.
A Hymn of the Incarnation.
Anonymous.
I Go by Road. Mendes.
I Have a Young Sister.
Anonymous.
I Shall Be Married on
Monday Morning.
Anonymous.
I Went My Sunday Mornings
Rounds. Clare.
If a Maid Be Fair.
Salverson.
In the Spring. Barnes.
The Irishman and the Lady.
Maginn.
It Always Happens. Horace.
The Lady in the Wood.
Anonymous.
Lalla Rookh. Moore.
The Lexington Miller.
Anonymous.
A Lover's Complaint.
Shakespeare.
The Maiden City. Tonna.
Maiden Eyes. Griffin.
Maids When You're Young,
Never Wed an Old Man.
Anonymous.
The Maple Hangs Its Green
Bee Flowers. Clare.
Marriage. Coleridge.

A Mood. Troubetzkoy.
Morning. Chu Shu-chen.
My Thought Was on a Maid
So Bright. *Anonymous.*
The Nereids. Kingsley.
New Brooms. Wilson.
A Nun to Mary, Virgin. St.
Virginia.
O Stay, Sweet Love.
Anonymous.
The Old Wife's Tale. Peele.
The Old Wives Tale: Song.
Peele.
On a Greek Vase. Sherman.
On a Nightingale in April.
Sharp.
Once on a Time. Banning.
Our Goodman (A version).
Anonymous.
Queen Anne. *Anonymous.*
Rollicking Bill the Sailor.
Anonymous.
The Rose and the Gauntlet.
Wilson.
Sancho. Collin.
The Servant of Rosemary
Lane. *Anonymous.*
Shadows of His Lady.
Tahureau.
Shameful Impotence: Book
III, Elegia VII. Ovid.
The Sign of the Bonny Blue
Bell. *Anonymous.*
Silence Invoked. Flecknoe.
Sing Heigh-Ho! Kingsley.
The Smiths. Murphy.
Song: "How happy were my
days, till now."
Bickerstaffe.
Sorrow. *Anonymous.*
Spring. Loveman.
The Spring Beauties. Cone.
Stanzas Written in My Pocket
Copy of Thomson's "Castle
of Indolence."
Wordsworth.
Sunday up the River.
Thomson.
The Three Captains.
Anonymous.
To Saint Margaret.
Constable.
Tracks. Montague.
Troilus and Criseyde.
Chaucer.
Two Weeks after an April
Frost. Helmling.
Upon One of the Maids of
Honour to Queen Elizabeth.
Hoskyns.
The Ute Lover. Garland.
Where She Told Her Love.
Clare.
Which Road? Barnes.
Why? Crane.
Wild Eden. Woodberry.
Winds. McCrae.
A Woman Is a Branchy Tree.
Stephens.
The Wooing Maid. Parker.
Written in an Ovid. Prior.

Maidenhead
The Bard. Shirley.
How Can I Keep My
Maidenhead. Burns.
Love's Courtship. Carew.
Then Lose in Time Thy
Maidenhead. *Anonymous.*
To Mistress Margery
Wentworth. Skelton.

Mail (s)
The Battle of Harlaw (B
version). *Anonymous.*
The Captain. White.
Correspondence. Chester.
Dostoievsky's Daughters.
Hamburger.
Dynamic Tension. Sanfield.
I Will Write. Graves.
Mamma's Gone to the Mail
Boat. *Anonymous.*
Movies, Left to Right.
Sward.
Paschal Lamb. Hass.
A Postcard to Send to Sumer.
Bronk.
Reflections. Pichaske.
The Six-Horse Limited Mail.
Fuller.
To Robert Lowell and Osip
Mandelstam. Seidel.
Uncertain Sonnets. Johnston.

Main
The Battle of Plattsburg Bay.
Scollard.
The Betrayed Maiden.
Anonymous.
A Cold Front. Williams.
Dragging the Main. Ray.
An Essay on Criticism.
Pope.
An Essay on the Fleet Riding
in the Downes.
Anonymous.
Halieutica. Oppian.
The Heavenly Pilot. Cormac
Mac Cuilenan.
Henry Martyn. *Anonymous.*
Jigsaw III. MacNeice.
A Letter from a Friend.
Morris.
The Lords of the Main.
Stansbury.
The Main-Sheet Song. Day.
A New Song Composed on
the Death of Lord Nelson.
Anonymous.
A New Song on the Total
Defeat of the French Fleet.
Anonymous.
O Billows Bounding Far.
Housman.
Poets to Come. Whitman.
Smooth between Sea and
Land. Housman.
Song: "O'er the waste of
waters cruising." Freneau.
To a Moth Crushed Within
the Leaves of an Iliad.
Thomas.

Maine
Apex. Salsbury.
Battle Song. Wilson.
Battleship of Maine.
Anonymous.
Christening-Day Wishes for
My God-Child Grace Lane
Berkley II. Coffin.
Chrome Babies Eating
Chocolate Snowmen in the
Moonlight. Redwing.
Cows Are Coming Home in
Maine. Coffin.
Half-Mast. Mifflin.
A Leaden Treasury of English
Verse. Dehn.
Marin. Booth.
Quan Lo Ruis De La
Fontana. Rudel.
The Spirit of the Maine.
Jenks.
Stove. Booth.

Uncle Ambrose. Still.
The Word of the Lord from
Havana. Hovey.
Maintain (ance)
A Copy of Verses Composed
by Captain Henry Every.
Anonymous.
Generalization. Capp.
Market Women's Cries.
Swift.
Plain Language from Truthful
James. Harte.
Robins. Bruce.
Majesty
Against Them Who Lay
Unchastity to the Sex of
Women. Habington.
Almighty Sovereign of the
Skies! Strong.
The Apple Dumplings and a
King. Wolcot.
Edward the Second (excerpt).
Marlowe.
Green Grass Growing.
Evans.
Mount Rainier. Bashford.
Now, If You Will Look in My
Brain. Villa.
The Outcast. Russell.
Poem: "The person who can
do." Dugan.
A Prayer. Lampman.
What Called Me to the
Heights? Pilkington.
Who Shined Shoes in Times
Square. Jeffers.
Why the Resurrection Was
Revealed to Women.
Greiffenberg.
With How Sad Steps, O
Moon, Thou Climb'st the
Sky. Wordsworth.
Majorca
In Honor of St. Alphonsus
Rodriguez. Hopkins.
Limerick: "There was a young
girl of Majorca." Lear.
Maker
Amoretti, IX. Spenser.
Amoretti, LIII. Spenser.
Except the Lord, That He for
Us Had Been. Ainsworth.
The Good Great Man.
Coleridge.
Jerusalem Sonnets. Baxter.
The Pagans Wild Confesse the
Bonds. Williams.
The Pauper's Drive. Noel.
Prayer of St. Francis Xavier.
Pope.
Special Starlight. Sandburg.
To Our Lady. Henryson.
Malady
They say that time assuages.
Dickinson.
They say that time assuages.
Dickinson.
Male
The Female of the Species.
Kipling.
A History of Lesbianism.
Grahn.
How to Conceive Boys.
Quillet.
Observation. Herrick.
Of the New Prosody.
Ghiselin.
Palais des Arts. Gluck.
The Picador Bit. Noll.
A Portrait of Henri III.
Aubigne.
Up. Kushner.

Malice
Amoretti, XLIV. Spenser.
Around the Child. Landor.
The Boatswain's Call.
Anonymous.
Caelica, XCV. Greville.
The Divine Passion.
Paravicino y Arteaga.
The Extravagant Drunkard's
Wish. Ward.
The Feeding. Oppenheimer.
Mr. Symons at Richmond,
Mr. Pope at Twickenham.
Symons.
On Censure. Swift.
Twenty-One Sonnets. Stead.
Variation on a Line by
Emerson. Merwin.
Mama
Darlin'. *Anonymous.*
Eight O'Clock. Rossetti.
Go Tell Aunt Rhody.
Anonymous.
Hang It on the Wall.
Patton.
Hmmmm, 8. Scalapino.
I Love Little Willie.
Anonymous.
The Killing of the Birds.
Williams.
The Lass of Roch Royal (B
vers.). *Anonymous.*
A Lesson for Mamma.
Dayre.
Light under the Door.
Waniek.
Misplaced Sympathy.
Adams.
No More Good Water.
Coleman.
Our Polite Parents. Wells.
Paris. Corso.
Red Apple Juice.
Anonymous.
The Talented Man. Praed.
When Brothers Forget.
Boyer.
Mammy
As I Walked Out One
Morning. *Anonymous.*
The Devil's Bag. Stephens.
Go to Sleepy. *Anonymous.*
Gwine to Alabamy.
Anonymous.
I'm O'er Young to Marry Yet.
Burns.
My Boy Tammy. Macneill.
Old Adam (with music).
Anonymous.
Water-Boy. *Anonymous.*
Man (men)
Aaron Burr. Benét.
Abraham Lincoln. Cole.
Adam. Rilke.
Afar in the Desert. Pringle.
Affection and Desire.
Ralegh.
Against Friars. *Anonymous.*
The Agnostic's Creed.
Malone.
Air and Angels. Donne.
All Up and Down the Lines.
Cooperman.
Almost Grown. Ai.
Alphonso of Castile.
Emerson.
America. Taylor.
American Independence.
Hopkinson.
Amoretti, LXI. Spenser.
The Ampler Circumscription.
Baylebridge.

And Jesus Don't Have Much
Use for His Old Suitcase
Anymore. Kryss.
Andraitx–Pomegranate
Flowers. Lawrence.
Angry Dusk. Lindsay.
An Anniversary. Hardy.
Annul Wars. Nahman of
Bratzlav.
Annunciation. Maura.
Another Birthday. Jonson.
Anticipation. Tusiani.
The Aquarium, San Francisco.
Sackville-West.
Arlington Cemetery Looking
toward the Capitol.
Palmer.
The Art of Poetry. Horace.
As Concerning Man.
Radcliffe.
As I Lay Sleeping.
Anonymous.
As I was coming down the
stair. *Anonymous.*
As I Was Standing in the
Street. *Anonymous.*
Ascent to the Sierras. Jeffers.
Asides on the Oboe. Stevens.
Asphodel, That Greeny
Flower. Williams.
Asses. Colum.
Assurance. Herbert.
At last withdraw your cruelty.
Wyatt.
An Autumn Park.
Gascoyne.
Back to Base. Joseph.
Bad Example. Fey.
Ballad: "I put my hat upon
my head." Johnson.
A Ballad in Blank Verse of
the Making of a Poet.
Davidson.
The Ballad of East and West.
Kipling.
Ballad of Human Life.
Beddoes.
The Ballad of Imitation.
Dobson.
The Ballad of Reading Gaol.
Wilde.
Ballade to His Mistress.
Villon.
Band Music. Fuller.
The Bat. Nash.
Battle Cry. Neihardt.
The Beasts' Confession.
Swift.
Beatus Vir. Le Gallienne.
Beaucourt Revisited.
Herbert.
The Bee-Wisp. Turner.
Before the Mirror.
Swinburne.
Beggar to Burgher.
Fairburn.
Benedictio Domini. Dowson.
Benevolence. Akenside.
Bennington. Babcock.
The Better Part. Arnold.
Better to Spit on the Whip
than Stutter Your Love
Like a Worm. Inez.
Between the Traveller and the
Setting Sun. Thoreau.
Big Dog. Hollo.
Big Fat Woman.
Anonymous.
The Birds. Squire.
Birds All Singing. MacCaig.
Birthdays. Driver.
Bits of Straw. Clare.

Black Cat. Dunetz.
Black Fear. Woody.
Black Marble.
O'Shaughnessy.
Blanket Street. Hogan.
Blow the Man Down.
Anonymous.
Blue Hills Beneath the Haze.
Whiting.
Bonfire of Kings. Evans.
Bonny Baby Livingston (A
version). *Anonymous.*
A Boy's Need. Johnson.
The Boy We Want.
Anonymous.
The Boys Brushed By.
Gonick.
The Brave Man. Stevens.
The Bridge. Walcott.
Bridge of the Carousel.
Rilke.
Brief Reflection on the Insect.
Holub.
The Brigg. Skelton.
The Brook. Tennyson.
The Brooklyn at Santiago.
Rice.
Brotherhood. Markham.
The Bull Moose. Nowlan.
Bushes and Briars.
Anonymous.
But How It Came from Earth.
Aiken.
By Blue Ontario's Shore
(excerpt). Whitman.
Caedmon's Hymn.
Caedmon.
Caelica, XXXIX. Greville.
Caelica, XL. Greville.
Caelica, LXVI. Greville.
Caelica, LXVII. Greville.
Caelica, LXXVIII. Greville.
Callypso Speaks. Doolittle.
A Camp in the Prussian
Forest. Jarrell.
Can't. Spofford.
Cape Cod. Santayana.
The Captain of St. Kitts.
May.
Carentan O Carentan.
Simpson.
Carolers. Westerfield.
The Carolinas. Ray.
Cat's Eyes. Scarfe.
Cattle. Skrzynecki.
The Celt in Me. Wilson.
Challengers. Dorn.
The Change. Cowley.
Chant for Dark Hours.
Parker.
Chant Royal of High Virtue.
Quiller-Couch.
Character of the Happy
Warrior. Wordsworth.
Charlie Macpherson.
Anonymous.
Charm for Unfruitful Land.
Anonymous.
A Charm, or an Allay for
Love. Herrick.
The Child Reads an Almanac.
Jammes.
Childe Harold's Pilgrimage:
Canto I. Byron.
Childlike Heart. Catlin.
Children of Auschwitz.
Korzhavin.
Children, the Sandbar, That
Summer. Rukeyser.
The Choice. Pomfret.
Christ 1: Advent Lyrics, III.
Anonymous.

Christchurch Bells. *Anonymous.*
Christmas Eve Service at Midnight at St. Michael's. Bly.
Christmas in the Olden Time. Scott.
Christmas Mourning. Miller.
The City of Baltimore. *Anonymous.*
Cleaning Up, Clearing Out. Bronson.
The Clod. Curran.
Clouds. Brooke.
The Coble o Cargill. *Anonymous.*
The Cock Crows in the Morn. *Anonymous.*
Code of the Cow Country. Barker.
Come, Walk with Me. Bronte.
The Coming American. Foss.
Coming of Age in the County Jail. Revard.
Commemoration Ode. Monroe.
Compozishun–To James Herndon and Others. Goba.
The Confession of Golias (abridged). Archpoet of Cologne.
Consorting with Angels. Sexton.
The Corner Stone. De la Mare.
The Couple. Oppenheimer.
The Cow. Roethke.
A Creed. Markham.
Crimes of Lugalanne. Enheduanna.
The Crucifix. Pushkin.
Cuisine Bourgeoise. Stevens.
Cupid. O'Dowd.
Danny. Synge.
Dark Flows the River. Bourinot.
Darling Corey. *Anonymous.*
The Day of the Night. Scully.
Dead Marine. Coxe.
Dean-Bourn, a Rude River in Devon, by Which Sometimes He Lived. Herrick.
Dear Old Stockholm. Young.
Death. Coates.
Death Killed the Rich. *Anonymous.*
Death of King George V. Betjeman.
The Death of Meleager. Swinburne.
Death's Warning to Beauty. *Anonymous.*
The Death-Wish. MacNeice.
A Decanter of Madeira, Aged 86, to George Bancroft, Aged 86. Mitchell.
December Night. Merwin.
The Decision. Roethke.
Dedication, to Leigh Hunt, Esq. Keats.
Deer Hunt. Jerome.
Deer Song. Confucius.
Deirdre. Stephens.
The Deserted Village. Goldsmith.
The Devil-Dancers. Plomer.

The Dignity of Man–Lesson #1. Kerr.
Dilemma. Bhartrihari.
Dirty Mistreatin' Women. *Anonymous.*
Do You Fear the Wind? Garland.
Doctor Blenn. Bierce.
The Doctor's Story. Carleton.
Don Juan. Byron.
Don't Ask Me Who I Am. Randall, Jr.
Door-Mats. Davies.
A Dressed Man and a Naked Man. Orwell.
Drug Store. Weaver.
The Durham Lock-Out. *Anonymous.*
Eagle Sonnets. Wood.
Easter, 1923. Neihardt.
Elegy for Jack Bowman. Bruchac.
An Elegy on a Lap Dog. Gay.
Emergency Haying. Carruth.
The Emulation. Egerton.
The End of Clonmacnois. *Anonymous.*
England, 1802. Wordsworth.
The Enthusiast: an Ode. Whitehead.
Epigram: "Do you not wish to renounce the Devil?" Lanusse.
Epigram: "O death, thy certainty is such." Luttrell.
Epitaph for the Unknown Soldier. Auden.
Epitaph on Peter Robinson. Jeffrey.
Epitaphs of the War. Kipling.
Eternity's Low Voice. Van Doren.
Everyman. Sassoon.
Evil Days. Pasternak.
Evil Devil Woman. McCoy.
The Exeter Book: Fates of Men. *Anonymous.*
A Fable for Critics. Lowell.
The Faerie Queene. Spenser.
The Family of Nations. Wattles.
Far from the Heart of Culture. Auden.
The Farmer Is the Man. *Anonymous.*
The Faun Tells of the Rout of the Amazons. Moore.
The First of the Emigrants. *Anonymous.*
The First Spousal. Patmore.
The First Thanksgiving. Turner.
Fishing Lines. Hassler.
Five Epigrams. Hall.
Five for the Grace. Scott.
Five Visions of Captain Cook. Slessor.
Flammonde. Robinson.
Flower in the Crannied Wall. Tennyson.
The Fog. Davies.
For a' That and a' That. Burns.
For a War Memorial. Chesterton.
For C. K. Kelleher.
For Edwin R. Embree. Dodson.

For Her Love I Cark and Care. *Anonymous.*
For Though the Caves Were Rabbited. Thoreau.
Ford Madox Ford. Lowell.
Fortune. Madge.
Frankie and Johnny, I (with music). *Anonymous.*
Fraternitas. *Anonymous.*
Fred Apollus at Fava's. Moore.
Friendship. *Anonymous.*
Frog Prince. Pettingell.
From Beyond. Trent.
From Feathers to Iron. Day Lewis.
Frozen Hands. Bruchac.
The Frozen Ocean. Meynell.
The Fugitive. Meynell.
The Galley-Slave. Kipling.
George III. Thackeray.
Georgia Towns. Hicky.
Gimel. Perkoff.
Give Peace, O God, the Nations Cry. Norris.
God's Education. Hardy.
Gold. Hall.
The Golden Voyage. *Anonymous.*
The Golf Links. Cleghorn.
Golfers. Updike.
Good-bye. Emerson.
Goose Pond. Kunitz.
Great Gawd, I'm Feelin' Bad (with music). *Anonymous.*
Great God Paused among Men. Berrigan.
Great Powers Conference. Pierce.
The Great Wave off Kanagwa. Egemo.
Green Lions. Stewart.
The Guinea Pig. *Anonymous.*
Gulls in an Aery Morrice. Henley.
The Gully. Maurice.
Hares on the Mountain. *Anonymous.*
Harvest Poem. Fisher.
Hatteras Calling. Aiken.
He Has Served Eighty Masters. Harford.
He Praises Her Hair. *Anonymous.*
Heart for All Her Children. Hebert, Jr.
The Heart Is Deep. Wolcott.
Helen. Lamb.
Her Dwarf. Elliott.
Here Pause: The Poet Claims at Least This Praise. Wordsworth.
Here We Were Born. Dos Santos.
The Hermit's Song. *Anonymous.*
High Resolve. *Anonymous.*
The Hill Farmer Speaks. Thomas.
His Task–and Ours. Gould.
His Toy, His Dream, His Rest. Berryman.
Hobson and His Men. Loveman.
Holy Night. Benson.
The Homing. Rooney.
Hos Ego Versiculos. Quarles.
Hospital. Millard.
A Hospital. Noyes.
The Hosts. Brady.

The House by the Side of the Road. Foss.
The House That Was. Binyon.
How He Saved St. Michael's. Stansbury.
How Our Forefather Got His Wife. Walton.
How Small Is Man. Blackie.
How to Kill. Douglas.
The Human Heart. Nelson.
Hunt. La Follette.
The Hunters of Men. Whittier.
Hydro Works. Hervey.
Hymn to Adversity. Gray.
I Am Stone of Many Colors. Tauhindauli.
I Enter by the Darkened Door (parody). King.
I Hate Men. Porter.
I Have Felt It as They've Said. Eigner.
I Have Labored Sore. *Anonymous.*
I'll Have You by the Short and Curly Hair. Catullus.
I Saw a Peacock. *Anonymous.*
I Sing the Mighty Power of God. Watts.
I Suppose Her Mother Told Her. Corcos.
I Think I See Him There. Cuney.
Idea. Drayton.
Idol. Driscoll.
Idylls of the King. Tennyson.
If So the Man You Are. Lewis.
Imagination. Davidson.
An Immorality. Pound.
In Bed with a River. Bradley.
In Early Summer Lodging in a Temple to Enjoy the Moonlight. Po Chu-i.
In the Cafe. Borson.
In Time of War. Auden.
Insect Riddle: "Wee man o' leather." *Anonymous.*
Interlude. Wilcox.
Interrupted Romance. *Anonymous.*
Intervals. Ravenel.
Ire. Thomas.
It's Easy to Invent a Life. Dickinson.
It Was in Vegas. Cunningham.
Jehovah Buried, Satan Dead. Cummings.
The Jilted Nymph. Campbell.
Jim Bludso of the Prairie Belle. Hay.
Jodrell Bank. Dickinson.
Joe Tinker. Hall.
John Charles Fremont. Lummis.
Johnny Come Down to Hilo. *Anonymous.*
Joseph Rodman Drake. Halleck.
Josie (with music). *Anonymous.*
Julius Caesar. Shakespeare.
The Kabbalist. Eibel.
The Kid Has Gone to the Colors. Herschell.

The Kindly Neighbor. Guest.

King Lear. Shakespeare.

The Knight of the Burning Pestle. Fletcher.

The Known Soldier. Patchen.

The Ladies' Aid. *Anonymous.*

A Lady Comes to an Inn. Coatsworth.

Lady Diamond. *Anonymous.*

A Lady Stood. Dietmar von Aist.

Lake-Song. Untermeyer.

Lament. Chamberlain.

Lament for Taramoana. Makere.

Lament of Granite. Ross.

Lament while Descending a Shaft. *Anonymous.*

A Lamentation. Rakosi.

Lamentations. Sassoon.

Landscapes. Hugo.

Last Days. Stoddard

The Last Man. Hood.

Last Poems. Housman.

Late Rising. Prevert.

A Learned Mistress. O'Connor.

The Legion. Graves.

Let Us Declare! (excerpt). Morgan.

Let Zulu Be Heard. Shembe.

Letter to My Wife. Rhys.

Letters to Live Poets. Beaver.

The Lexington Miller. *Anonymous.*

A Life. Plath.

Lift Your Glad Voices in Triumph on High. Ware.

Limerick: "There was an old man of Cape Horn." Lear.

Limerick: "There was an Old Man of Dumbree." Lear.

Lincoln. Cheney.

The Line of Beauty. O'Shaughnessy.

Line-Up for Yesterday. Nash.

The Lines. Jarrell.

Lines on the Sea. Laing.

Lines Written in Early Spring. Wordsworth.

Litany For Dictatorships. Benét.

Literary Gruk. Hein.

Little Britain. *Anonymous.*

Little Eclogue. Wylie.

Little Fishes in a Brook. *Anonymous.*

Lizard. Lawrence.

Loitering with a Vacant Eye. Housman.

The Looking-Glass. Kipling.

Lord, Make a Regular Man Out of Me. Guest.

The Lost History Plays: Savanarola (parody). Beerbohm.

A Lost Illusion. Du Maurier.

Love Dislikes Nothing. Herrick.

Love of Nature. Thomson.

The Lover Abused Renounceth Love. Turberville.

The Luciad. Camoens.

The Lucky Coin. Clarke.

Lyttelton Harbor. Cresswell.

Madam, withouten many words. Wyatt.

Madly Singing in the Mountains. Chu-i.

Madonna of the Exiles. Tobin.

Make Way! Comfort.

Malcolm X. Brooks.

Male Rage Poem. Di Cicco.

Man and Cows. Young.

Man and the Ascidian. Lang.

The Man Coming Toward You. Williams.

Man I Thought You Was Talking Another Language That Day. Cruz.

Man Is for Woman Made. Motteux.

Man, Man, Man. *Anonymous.*

A Man of Men. Van Noppen.

The Man of Sorrows. *Anonymous.*

Man's Mortality. Wastell.

The Man Upright. Macdonagh.

The Man Within. Ewing.

Man without Sense of Direction. Ransom.

Mankind. *Anonymous.*

The Manly Man. *Anonymous.*

Mannequins. Epstein.

Manners at Table When away from Home. *Anonymous.*

Many Years Ago. Barbeitos.

Marshall. Macbeth.

The Martin Cat Long Shaged of Courage Good. Clare.

Mary Weeps for Her Child. *Anonymous.*

The Maximus Poems. Olson.

Medieval Norman Songs. *Anonymous.*

Meditation. Shipley.

Meditations in Time of Civil War. Yeats.

Memorial Sonnet. Meeker.

The Men behind the Guns. Rooney.

Men of the North and West. Stoddard.

Men Who March away. Hardy.

Mercury Shew'd Apollo, Bartas Book. Ward.

The Metaphysical Sectarian. Butler.

The Mice at the Door. McHugh.

The Midnight Court. Merriman.

A Midsummer Night's Dream. Shakespeare.

Midwest. Nims.

Midwife. Box.

Milking Before Dawn. Dallas.

The Miller. Cunningham.

The Miller of Dee. *Anonymous.*

Mind Flying Far. Masters.

Minotaur Poems. Mandel.

The Mirror. Gluck.

Miss Twye. Ewart.

Mist Forms. Sandburg.

A Model Sermon. *Anonymous.*

Monna Innominata. Rossetti.

More Prayer. *Anonymous.*

Mother of Man. Parun.

Mouse Night: One of Our Games. Stafford.

The Muse to an Unknown Poet. Potts.

My Lodging It Is on the Cold Ground. D'Avenant.

My Past. Cooper.

The Name. Creeley.

Naseby: Late Autumn. Dowling.

The Nativity of Christ. Southwell.

Nature's Hymn to the Deity. Clare.

New York City. Abbe.

The Next Time You Were There. Hazo.

Nigger. Sanchez.

Night and Morning. Clarke.

No Coward's Song. Flecker.

Not Alone for Mighty Empire. Merrill.

Not Marching away to Be Killed. Fuller.

Now and Then. Hamilton.

O. Villanueva.

O Bruadair. Stephens.

O Glorious Childbearer. Campbell.

O God, How Many Years Ago. Myers.

Ode Sung in the Town Hall. Emerson.

Ode: To Sir William Sydney, on His Birth-Day. Jonson.

Of an Old Con. Mosby.

Ol' Bunk's Band. Williams.

Old Devil. Carter.

The Old Woman Who Bought a Pig. *Anonymous.*

On a Child Beginning to Talk. Bastard.

On a Distant Prospect of an Absconding Bookmaker. Hamilton.

On a Spaniel Called Beau Killing a Young Bird. Cowper.

On Having Piles. Scott.

On Learning That Certain Peat Bogs Contain Perfectly Preserved Bodies. Ludvigson.

On Looking into Henry Moore. Livesay.

On Paunch, A Parasite. Belloc.

On the Crocodile. Heyrick.

On the Death of Joseph Rodman Drake. Halleck.

On the Duke of Buckingham. Shirley.

On the Irish Club. Swift.

Once More, Our God, Vouchsafe to Shine. Sewall.

One's-Self I Sing. Whitman.

One Wife for One Man. Aig-Imoukhuede.

Operation–Souls. *Anonymous.*

Othello. Shakespeare.

Other men are thorn. Mahadevi (Mahadeviyakka).

Out of the Earth. Davies.

The Pagan Isms. McKay.

The Painful Plough. *Anonymous.*

Panama. Jones.

The Parable of the Old Man and the Young. Owen.

Paradise Lost. Milton.

Part of the 9th Ode of the 4th Book of Horace... Horace.

Parting at Morning. Browning.

Paterson. Williams.

Peace. Markham.

The Peasants' Song. *Anonymous.*

Penny Is a Hardy Knight. Anonymous.

The People Has No Obituary. Clark.

The People, Yes. Sandburg.

Personal History: For My Son. Todd.

The Perspective and Limits of Snapshots. Smith.

The Philosopher and Her Father. Brooks.

Piers the Ploughman. Langland.

The Pigs. Lehmann.

The Pity of the Leaves. Robinson.

Pleasure. *Anonymous.*

Plenary. *Anonymous.*

Poem: "I heard of a man." Cohen.

Poem: "We are such stuff as dreams are made of." Hofmannsthal.

The Poet. Randolph.

Poetry Is a Destructive Force. Stevens.

Poetry Reading. Scannell.

Portrait. Bogan.

Prairie. Sandburg.

Prayer. Washbourne.

A Prayer in Time of Blindness. Wood.

Prayer under the Pressure of Violent Anguish. Burns.

The Precept of Silence. Johnson.

Preface. Shauger.

Preludes. Patmore.

Presences. Karelli.

Prince Henry the Navigator. Clouts.

The Princess. Tennyson.

A Problem in Morals. Moss.

The Prophecy Sublime. Hosmer.

The Prophet. Pushkin.

Proud New York. Reed.

Psalm IX. Sidney.

The Quaker's Wooing (with music). *Anonymous.*

The Quest Eternal (excerpt). Seal.

Quiet Work. Arnold.

The Rape of Lucrece. Shakespeare.

Ready. Cary.

The Reaper. Allen.

Rebels from Fairy Tales. Hill.

Reconciliation. Doten.

Reject Jell-O. Day.

The Rejected "National Hymns". Newell.

A Removal from Terry Street. Dunn.

Report from a Planet. Lattimore.

Retrospection. Shaw.

The Return of the Dead (excerpt). Attar.

Reunion. Forche.

The Revenger's Tragedy (excerpt). Tourneur.
The Riddle. Auden.
A Riddle. Martial (Marcus Valerius Martialis).
Riddle: "As I was going o'er London Bridge." *Anonymous.*
Riddles Wisely Expounded. *Anonymous.*
The Rider at the Gate. Masefield.
Ringless. Wakoski.
Rise Up, O Men of God. Merrill.
The Road to the Bow. Corrothers.
Roberta. Leadbelly.
The Rod. Herrick.
Romance VIII. John of Damascus.
Rostov. Fraser.
Sail and Oar. Graves.
Saint Judas. Wright.
Salamis. Aeschylus.
Sanctuary. Boothroyd.
Santa Claus. *Anonymous.*
Sarentino–South Tyrol. Brantingham.
Scissors and String, Scissors and String. *Anonymous.*
The Sea-Limits. Rossetti.
The Seasons. Thomson.
Sedge-Warblers. Thomas.
The Sensualists. Roethke.
Sepulchre. Herbert.
Serenade for Strings. Livesay.
Settin' on de Fence. *Anonymous.*
The Settled Men. Brady.
Seventeen Come Sunday. *Anonymous.*
The Shadow. Jonson.
Shadows. Lawrence.
Shaman. Leiper.
The Shanty Boys and the Pine. *Anonymous.*
She Is More to be Pitied than Censured. Gray.
She Smiled Like a Holiday. *Anonymous.*
The Sheep-Herder. Clark, Jr.
The Shepherd and the Milkmaid. *Anonymous.*
The Shepherd Boys. Saboly.
The Ship and Her Makers. Masefield.
Sic Vita. King.
The Sleepers. Aberg.
The Sluggard. Davies.
A Smile. *Anonymous.*
The Snow-Man. "Douglas.
Snow White. Gillespie.
Soldier, What Did You See? Blanding.
Song. Clare.
A Song of Fleet Street. Werner.
The Song of Lo-Fu. *Anonymous.*
The Song of Quoodle. Chesterton.
The Song of Roland, CL. *Anonymous.*
Song of Seyd Nimetollah of Kuhistan. Emerson.
Song of the Cauld Lad of Hylton. *Anonymous.*
Song Set by Robert Jones: "A woman's looks." *Anonymous.*

Song: "That women are but men's shadows." Jonson.
Sonnet LXXXVI. Greville.
Sonnet–Age. Garnett.
Sonnet: "Not with Libations." Millay.
Sonnets. Masefield.
Sonnets, XVIII: "Shall I compare thee to a summer's day?" Shakespeare.
Sonnets, CXXI: "'Tis better to be vile than vile esteemed." Shakespeare.
Sonnets from a Sequence. Barker.
Sonnets of the Months. San Geminiano.
Soul and Sense. Kimball.
The South Country. Belloc.
The Sower's Song. Carlyle.
Speaking of Television: Robin Hood. McGinley.
Spirits Unchained. Kgositsile.
Spring. McCarriston.
Square-Cap. Cleveland.
St. Anthony's Township. Sheldon.
St. James Infirmary. *Anonymous.*
St. Simon and St. Jude's Day. Alexander.
The Stampede. Miller.
Star Blanket. Young Bear.
Star of the Morning. Johnstone.
Steam Song. Brooks.
Stonefish and Starfish. Blight.
Strange Meetings. Monro.
The Streets of Cairo. Thornton.
The Strike. *Anonymous.*
Success. Lazarus.
Suicide. MacNeice.
A Summer Night. Arnold.
The Surrender of Spain. Hay.
The Switch Blade (or, John's Other Wife.). Williams.
The Talented Man. Praed.
Tamburlaine the Great. Marlowe.
Teddy's Wonderings. Bangs.
Tell All the Truth but Tell It Slant. Dickinson.
Temple. Donne.
Tenebrae. Clarke.
Testament. Sister M. Therese.
The Testament of Beauty. Bridges.
The Texas Song. *Anonymous.*
Thar's More in the Man Than Thar Is in the Land. Lanier.
That All Things Are as They Are Used. Turberville.
Ther's Many a Man Killed on the Railroad (with music). *Anonymous.*
There Are Roughly Zones. Frost.
There Is a Charming Land. Oehlenschlager.
There Is a Man on the Cross. Cheney.
There Is No. Kicknosway.
There Is None, O None But You. Campion.

There was an old owl lived in an oak. *Anonymous.*
These Things Shall Be. Symonds.
They Are Killing All the Young Men. Henderson.
They Pray the Best Who Pray and Watch. Hopper.
A thing which fades. Ono no Komachi.
Things to Come. Reeves.
Think on Yesterday. *Anonymous.*
This Amber Sunstream. Van Doren.
This Compost. Whitman.
This Earthen Body. *Anonymous.*
This Journey. Jonker.
Thou Art Not Lovelier Than Lilacs. Millay.
The Thousand and One Nights: Love. *Anonymous.*
A Thousand Killed. Spencer.
A Thousand Years Have Come. Lynch.
Three Christmas Carols: II. *Anonymous.*
Three Green Trees. Morgan.
Three Hours. Lindsay.
Three Poems. Crane.
Three Poems of the Atomic Age: Dirge for the New Sunrise. Sitwell.
Three Things to Remember. Blake.
Through an Embrace. Eluard.
The Tides. Blackburn.
Time. Collier.
Time and the Garden. Winters.
Times Square Parade. Watson.
To–. Tennyson.
To a Gentleman, Who Desired Proper Materials for a Monody. *Anonymous.*
To a Little Boy Learning to Fish. Hoeft.
To a Lock of Hair. Scott.
To a Visiting Poet in a College Dormitiory. Kizer.
To a Young Gentle-Woman, Councel Concerning Her Choice. Crashaw.
To a Young Poet Who Fled. Logan.
To Bobby Seale. Clifton.
To Dr. Kipling. Porson.
To flee from memory. Dickinson.
To Fletcher Reviv'd. Lovelace.
To Miss B. Clare.
To Mistress Anne. Skelton.
To-Morrow Shall Be My Dancing Day. *Anonymous.*
To Mrs. Diana Cecyll. Herbert of Cherbury.
To Sextus. Sedley.
To Sleep. Fleming.
To the Memory of Yale College. Putnam.
To the Men Who Lose. Scarborough.
To the Reader of Master William Davenant's Play, The Wits. Carew.
To the Soul. Collop.

To William Roe. Jonson.
Tobacco Plant. Gurney.
The Torso: Passages 18. Duncan.
Tottingham Frolic. *Anonymous.*
The Trail Horse. Wagoner.
Trinity Place. McGinley.
Trust the Form of Airy Things. Harington.
A Tryptych for Jan Bockelson. Simon.
Tune: The Butterfly Woos the Blossoms. Li Ching-chao.
Tweed and Till. *Anonymous.*
Twice a Week the Winter Through. Housman.
Two Heavens. Hunt.
Two Jazz Poems. Hines, Jr.
Two Poems About President Harding. Wright.
Two Women. Willis.
Two Years Later. Wieners.
A Typical 6:00 P.M. in the Fun House. Berrigan.
The Uncelestial City (excerpt). Wolfe.
The Undertaking. Lansing.
Uneasy Peace. Blunden.
The Unfortunate Man. *Anonymous.*
Unhappy Bella. *Anonymous.*
Unwelcome. Coleridge.
Vain Men, Whose Follies. Campion.
The Valley. Moss.
Venice. Symonds.
Verses Found in Thomas Dudley's Pocket after His Death. Dudley.
Verses Written at The Hague. Ano 1696. Prior.
The Village. Gashe.
Virginiana. Johnson.
The Visit. Rewak.
The Visitor. Forche.
La Vita Nuova. Dante Alighieri.
Vox Populi, Vox Dei (excerpt). *Anonymous.*
War Blinded. Dunn.
The Warden of the Cinque Ports. Longfellow.
Watt's Improvements to the Steam Engine. Baker.
We Are Four Bums (with music). *Anonymous.*
The Weary Blues. Hughes.
Wedlock. *Anonymous.*
Were Not the Gael Fallen. O'Mulconry.
Western Emigration. Humphreys.
The Whaler's Pig. Brady.
When Adam Was Created. *Anonymous.*
When All Thy Mercies. Addison.
When God Descends with Men to Dwell. Ballou I.
When Indians Heare That Some There Are. Williams.
When There Is Peace. Dobson.
Where I Took Hold of Life. Coffin.
Where Is Our Holy Church? Wilson.
While Shepherds Watched Their Flocks by Night. Tate.

Whistle, Daughter, Whistle. *Anonymous.*
Why. Freeman.
Why, Some of My Best Friends Are Women. McGinley.
The Wild Garden. Pope.
Will to Win. Scott.
Winter Climb. Eunaich.
Winter Night. Fuller.
Woman. Ai.
A Woman I Mix Men Up... Mayer.
A Woman Is a Branchy Tree. Stephens.
Women's Rondo. *Anonymous.*
Wonder–Is Not Precisely Knowing. Dickinson.
Woods Night. Hennen.
Words for Music Perhaps. Yeats.
Words Made of Water. Singer.
Words on the Windowpane. Rossetti.
Written after the Death of Charles Lamb (excerpt). Wordsworth.
The X of the Unknown. Clark.
The Year 1812. Mickiewicz.
You. Masefield.
You Naughty, Naughty Men. Kennick.
Young Democracy (excerpt). O'Dowd.
Young Washington. Guiterman.
Your cheeks flat on the sand. Khoury-Gata.
Youth and Maturity. Greville.
Ys Yt Possyble. Wyatt.

Manage
Astrophel and Stella, XLIX. Sidney.
Progression of the Species. Aldiss.
Sanctuary. Boothroyd.

Manassas
How McClellan Took Manassas. *Anonymous.*
The March into Virginia. Melville.

Manchester
Ellen Taylor. *Anonymous.*
Lancashire Lads. *Anonymous.*

Mane (s)
Another Charme for Stables. Herrick.
Childe Harold's Pilgrimage: Canto IV. Byron.
The Cock Again. *Anonymous.*
Epitaph on a Well-Known Poet. Moore.
The lion is a beast to fight. Quiller-Couch.
The Newborn Colt. Kennedy.
Ta Wa Nee. Dessus.
Unbridled Now. LeGear.

Manger
Advent 1955. Betjeman.
The Blossom of the Branches (excerpt). Gilbert.
The Guest. *Anonymous.*
Jesus Borned in Bethlea. *Anonymous.*

The Kings of the East. Bates.
Shepherd's Song at Christmas. Hughes.

Manhattan
The Indian. Reed.
Manhattan. Hart.
Small Perfect Manhattan. Viereck.
To Desi as Joe as Smoky the Lover of 115th Street. Lorde.
Winter Sketches. Reznikoff.

Manhood
Dauber. Masefield.
The Ghost. Lowell.
King Henry V. Shakespeare.
Lullaby of an Infant Chief. Scott.
The Quick. Jennett.
To the Veld. Cripps.

Mankind
Christ 1: Advent Lyrics, VIII. *Anonymous.*
The Consolation of Philosophy. Boethius.
Davideis. Cowley.
The Dreamers Cry Their Dream. Trent.
The Eagle That Is Forgotten. Lindsay.
Empty Holds a Question. Folk.
Fable IV: The Eagle, and the Assembly of Animals. Gay.
Flight of the Heart. MacNeice.
The Happy Tree. Gould.
History of the Modern World. Coblentz.
Jeremiah. Bynner.
Laura Sleeping. Cotton.
My Country, to Thy Shore. Williams.
O Mind of God, Broad as the Sky. Huckel.
Ode to Peace. *Anonymous.*
On a Distant Prospect of an Absconding Bookmaker. Hamilton.
On the Phrase, "To Kill Time." Voltaire (Francois Marie Arouet).
Radiation Victim. Thiele.
The Secret. Casas.
Slaves Cannot Breathe in England. Cowper.
Song to a Fair, Young Lady, Going out of the Town in the Spring. Dryden.
Song: "Whilst landmen wander, though controlled." *Anonymous.*
Thread Suns. Celan.
To Caelia. *Anonymous.*
Upon Ben. Johnson. Waller.
Venus Accoutered as Mars. *Anonymous.*

Manna
For Every Day. Havergal.
The Name of Jesus. Newton.
The Search. Vaughan.
Silex Scintillans. Vaughan.
Twilight at the Zoo. Rodger.

Manner (ly) (s)
Aborigine. Williams.
Croquet. Huddle.
The Deserted Village. Goldsmith.
Double Ballade of Primitive Man. Lang.

A Goodly Child. *Anonymous.*
It Was Your Song. Kowit.
The Mother Crab and Her Family. Manyase.
Of a Little Take a Little. *Anonymous.*
Pathedy of Manners. Kay.
To the Rose. Davies.
The Vision. Defoe.
The Visitor. Pyle.
William the Bastard. "Lakon".

Mansion (s)
A Child in Prison. O Dalaigh.
Death-Bed Song. *Anonymous.*
Familiar Lines. *Anonymous.*
Farewell This World! *Anonymous.*
High Sheriff Blues. Patton.
Home. Carr.
O'Hussey's Ode to the Maguire. Mangan.
Verses Addressed to a Friend... Henley.
While I Am Young. Ballou.

Mantle (s)
A Cradle Song. Colum.
Dunciad Minor. Hope.
Ichabod! The Glory Has Departed. Uhland.
Spring. d'Orleans.
Sweetest of All. *Anonymous.*
To Mistress Margery Wentworth. Skelton.
Wood Floor Dreams. Henson.

Manuscripts
The Manuscripts of God. Longfellow.
Our Lady of the Libraries. Ignatius.

Map (s)
A Chinese Mural. Baker.
Fame and Fortune. Drayton.
Her True Body. Metz.
The Map. Bishop.
The Map of Places. Riding.
A Mexican Scrapbook. Oliphant.
Six Years. Bloch.
Sonnets, LXVIII: "Thus is his cheek the map of days outworn." Shakespeare.
Timoshenko. Keyes.
We Shall Have Far to Go. Watson.
When Statesmen Gravely Say "We Must Be Realistic." Auden.

Maple (s)
Depressed by a Book of Bad Poetry, I Walk toward an Unused Pasture... Wright.
The Faerie Queene. Spenser.
The Five Little Fairies. Burnham.
Horse. Harrison.
Maple Feast. Frost.
Oxygen. Swift.
The Settlers. Hemschemeyer.
Trees. Carman.
Yonosa House. Smith.

Marble (s)
At the Ocean's Verge. Gustafson.
Boxer. Clancy.
Carrara. Murray.
A Charleston Garden. Bellamann.

David Homindae. Rosenfeld.
A Dirge upon the Death of the Right Valiant Lord, Bernard Stuart. Herrick.
Epitaph. Davenant.
Every Night When the Sun Goes In. *Anonymous.*
The Final Faith. Sterling.
Fishing Harbour towards Evening. Kell.
Ioolas' Epitaph. Drummond.
A Likeness. Cather.
Marmion. Scott.
Misdemeanor. Triem.
A Mother before a Soldier's Monument. Rockett.
On a Bas-Relief. Trimpi.
On Her Dancing. Shirley.
On His Lady's Waking. Ronsard.
The Palace of Humbug. "Carroll.
A Poet Speaks from the Visitors' Gallery. MacLeish.
Pygmalion. Brockerhoff.
Return. Jeffers.
Saint John the Baptist. Drummond.
The Schoolboy Reads His Iliad. Morton.
Sicilian Cyclamens. Lawrence.
Stars. Frost.
To Lucasta. Lovelace.
To Roses in the Bosom of Castara. Habington.
The Toy Horse. Iremonger.

March (ed) (ing)
Ain't Gonna Let Nobody Turn Me Round. *Anonymous.*
Almost. Field.
The Band Played Waltzing Matilda. Bogle.
Blue Horses: West Winds. Endrezze-Danielson.
The Botanist's Vision. Dobell.
A Broadway Pageant. Whitman.
Celestine. Fitzgerald.
Chee Lai! (Arise!). *Anonymous.*
Crispus Attucks McCoy. Brown.
The Dance. Campion.
David and Goliath. Crouch.
Early April. Frost.
Essex Regiment March. Woodberry.
The Exodus from Egypt. Ezekielos.
A Fable for Critics. Lowell.
The Faerie Queene. Spenser.
Faust. Goethe.
Flowering without End. Zweig.
For Black Poets Who Think of Suicide. Knight.
For Those Who Died. Clark.
Freedom. Daniel. Peter
From Age to Age They Gather. Hosmer.
Gibraltar. Blunt.
Glory Hallelujah! or John Brown's Body. Hall.
Hey Diddle Dinkety, Poppety, Pet. *Anonymous.*
In February. Symonds.
In October. Carman.
John Brown's Body. Hall.

The Man Coming Toward You. Williams.
Le Marais du Cygne. Whittier.
The March. Squire.
A March in the Ranks Hard-Prest, and the Road Unknown. Whitman.
Marching Song. Burnet.
Marching through Georgia. Work.
Marching to Pretoria. *Anonymous.*
Mediaeval Appreciations. Gamble.
Memorial Day. Garrison.
Men Who March away. Hardy.
Mount Zion. *Anonymous.*
The Mountain. Frost.
The Mulligan Guard. Harrigan.
On the Late Metamorphosis of an Old Picture.... *Anonymous.*
Pan-Pipes. Chalmers.
Peat Bog Soldiers. *Anonymous.*
Pre-positions. Isaacson.
The Progress of Poesy. Gray.
The Seekers. Sorley.
Skeleton Parade. Prelutsky.
Sousa. Dorn.
To Butterfly. Percy.
The Twelve. Blok.
The Undertakers' Club. *Anonymous.*
Victory March. Joseph.
Whaler's Rhyme. *Anonymous.*
When Johnny Comes Marching Home. Gilmore.
When the Saints Come Marching In. Redding.
Wild March. Woolson.
William Jones. Masters.
The Wizard of Alderley Edge. Coe.
The World, the Devil, and Tom Paine. *Anonymous.*
Would You in Venus' Wars Succeed. *Anonymous.*
Youth. Hughes.

Marco Polo
The Old Figurehead Carver. Cody.

Mardi Gras
Night's Mardi Gras. Wheeler.

Mare
Grotesques. Graves.
The Lochmaben Harper. *Anonymous.*
The Lochmabyn Harper. *Anonymous.*
One to Make Ready. *Anonymous.*
The Road to Hogan's Gap. Paterson.
Tam O'Shanter. Burns.
To a Horse. Hoffman.
Wilt Thou Lend Me Thy Mare? *Anonymous.*
The Zebras. Campbell.

Margaret
Amy Margaret. Allingham.
First Love. Hemschemeyer.
The Souldiers Farewel to his Love. *Anonymous.*
Spring and Fall. Hopkins.

Sweet William and May Marg'ret. Anonymous

Margin (s)
Elegy. Gilbert.
The Made Lake. Nicholl.
New Storefront. Atkins.

Marguerite
The Eve of Crecy. Morris.
Switzerland. Arnold.

Maria
The Murder of Maria Marten. Corder.
Out of the Hurly-Burly. "Adeler.

Marian
Robin Hood and Maid Marian. *Anonymous.*
Sonnet to—. Reynolds.

Marie
All Other Love Is Like the Moon. *Anonymous.*
Comment. Parker.
Lost For a Rose's Sake. *Anonymous.*
Sunset on Calvary. *Anonymous.*
Sweet Marie. Warman.
Untitled. Kuka.

Marigold (s)
Captain Mansfield's Fight with the Turks at Sea. *Anonymous.*
Draw a Pail of Water. *Anonymous.*
Fishing with My Daughter in Miller's Meadow. Stryk.
Jason. Hecht.
Load. Hewitt.
Marigold. Garnett.
The Riddle. *Anonymous.*
A Thought of Marigolds. Farrar.

Mariner (s)
For My Twenty-Fifth Birthday in Nineteen Forty-One. Ciardi.
Henry Martyn. *Anonymous.*
In Cabin'd Ships at Sea. Whitman.
O God! Have Mercy in This Dreadful Hour. Southey.
Parfum Exotique. Baudelaire.

Mark (ed) (s)
Adam's Footprint. Miller.
Afternoon on a Hill. Millay.
Against Quarrelling and Fighting. Watts.
The Call. Mew.
Challenge. Hazo.
Dear, Beazuteous Death! Vaughan.
Episode. Nunes.
The False Favorite's Downfall. *Anonymous.*
Getting On. Sandy.
God's Treasure. "N.
Here Is the Tale. Deane.
Hiatus. Avison.
In the Street. Neilson.
May Day Demonstrators. Lindsay.
An Old Thought. Luders.
On Mr. Pitt's Hair-Powder Tax. Burns.
One Rose of Stone. Wilson.
Prayer to the Hunting Star, Canopus. *Anonymous.*
Returned to Say. Stafford.
Say Who Is This with Silvered Hair. Bridges.

The Scars Remaining. Coleridge.
Sometimes when Night... Sackville-West.
Song for "The Jaquerie". Lanier.
The Stations of the Cross. Colum.
Theme Brown Girl. Hill-Abu Ishak.
Various Ends. Todd.
Virgidemiarum: "A Gentle Squire would gladly entertain." Hall.

Market
I Saw a Delicate Flower Had Grown up 2 Feet High. Thoreau.
The Next Market Day. *Anonymous.*
Shango I. *Anonymous.*
To market, to market. Mother Goose.
Wood and Hill. Young.

Marred
Dugall Quin (A version). *Anonymous.*
Sketch of Lord Byron's Life. Moore.
To My Ill Reader. Herrick.
Tomorrow Is a Birthday. Haste.

Marriage (s)
108 Tales of a Po'Buckra, No. 106. Inman.
The Advice. Flatman.
All the Way from There to Here. Gilbert.
Always We Watch Them. Mariah.
The Applicant. Plath.
Apprenticed. Ingclow.
As I Am Unhappy. Yosano Akiko.
As I Went out for a Ramble. *Anonymous.*
At Christmas. Duncan.
Auction Sale–Household Furnishings. De Leeuw.
The Automobile. Edson.
Ballad of the Cool Fountain. *Anonymous.*
The Bank of the Arkansaw. *Anonymous.*
Beauty in Trouble. Graves.
Big Chief Blues. Lewis.
The Birde's Marriage-Cake. *Anonymous.*
Black Spring. Annensky.
The Bonny Earl of Livingston. *Anonymous.*
The Bridge of Death. *Anonymous.*
The Broken Token. *Anonymous.*
The Butcher. Williams.
Catch. Hughes.
Child Waters. *Anonymous.*
Cindy. *Anonymous.*
Clerk Saunders. *Anonymous.*
Come All You Young Ladies and Gentlemen. *Anonymous.*
Compelled to Love. Stone.
Courtship. Strand.
Daily Courage Doesnt Count. Alta.
A Dark Day. Rossetti.
Early in One Spring. *Anonymous.*
Fairground. Auden.
Fie on Love. Beaumont.

The Fire of Frendraught. *Anonymous.*
The First Love Poem. Schotz.
Five Epigrams. Hall.
For a Second Marriage. Merrill.
For the Time Being. Auden.
From a Lament for Una. Costello.
Fuller and Warren. Whitecotton.
The Girl I Left behind Me (My Parents Raised Me Tenderly). *Anonymous.*
Girl of the Lovely Glance. Praxilla.
Good & Bad Wives. *Anonymous.*
The Goose Girl. Roberts.
Hymeneal. Catullus.
I Know Where I'm Going. *Anonymous.*
I'll Be Fourteen Next Sunday. *Anonymous.*
I'll Not Marry at All. *Anonymous.*
I Mun Be Married a Sunday. Udall.
I Must and I Will Get Married. *Anonymous.*
I Want a Girl. Von Tilzer.
If I Were a Queen. Rossetti.
In the Room of the Bride-Elect. Hardy.
Inst., Ult., and Prox.: Answer. Herbert.
Ithocles, VI (excerpt). Symonds.
Jack Monroe (Jackie's Gone A-Sailing). *Anonymous.*
Jack Wrack. *Anonymous.*
James Hatley. *Anonymous.*
Johnny Todd. *Anonymous.*
The Jolly Young Waterman. Dibdin.
The Joys of Marriage. Cotton.
Kate and the Cowhide. *Anonymous.*
Lamia. Keats.
The Legend of the First Cam-u-el. Guiterman.
The Letters. Tennyson.
Life Is Motion. Stevens.
Limerick: "There was a young man from Elnora." *Anonymous.*
Little Tommy Tucker. Mother Goose.
London. Blake.
Lord Bateman. *Anonymous.*
Lord Ingram and Chiel Wyet. *Anonymous.*
Love's Labour's Lost. Shakespeare.
The Love Token. *Anonymous.*
Lysistrata. Aristophanes.
Marriage and the Care O't. Lochore.
The Marriage Ring. Blake.
Mary Ann. Tabrar.
Maud. Tennyson.
Medea. Seneca.
Men Marry What They Need. I Marry You. Ciardi.
De Mexico Ha Venido. *Anonymous.*
Mirror, Mirror. Graves.
Miss Kilmansegg's Honeymoon. Hood.

Mother of Ten. Strong.
The Muses Elizium. Drayton.
My Thing Is My Own. *Anonymous.*
The New Warden. Baca.
Nothing in Rambling. Minnie.
Nothing to Wear. Butler.
O, the Marriage! Davis.
On an Upright Judge. Swift.
On Saturday Night Shall Be My Care. *Anonymous.*
One I Love. *Anonymous.*
Our Ship She Lies in Harbour. *Anonymous.*
Paper of Pins. *Anonymous.*
The Philanderer. Mendes.
The Plaint of the Wife. Ralston.
A Plea for Trigamy. Seaman.
Pleasure. *Anonymous.*
Prayers of a Christian Bridegroom. Poupo.
Pretty Polly. *Anonymous.*
Prothalamium for Bobolink and His Louisa A Poem. Stein.
A Railroader for Me. *Anonymous.*
The Rambling Cowboy. *Anonymous.*
The Rambling Sailor. *Anonymous.*
Red River Shore. *Anonymous.*
Reincarnation. Jackson.
Reject Jell-O. Day.
The Riddling Knight. *Anonymous.*
Ripperty! Kye! Ahoo! Lawson.
Rise You Up, My True Love. *Anonymous.*
Rosa. *Anonymous.*
The Rover's Apology. Gilbert.
Sailor. Farjeon.
Sally Ann. *Anonymous.*
The Sandgate Girl's Lamentation. *Anonymous.*
Scissors and String, Scissors and String. *Anonymous.*
Searching for Lambs. *Anonymous.*
Sensibility. Simpson.
The Shades of Night Were Falling Fast (parody). Housman.
She Was Bred in Old Kentucky. Braisted.
The Sheep Child. Dickey.
The Silk Merchant's Daughter. *Anonymous.*
Sing Heigh-Ho! Kingsley.
The Single Girl. *Anonymous.*
Soldier Boy for Me. *Anonymous.*
The Soldier's Farewell to Manchester. *Anonymous.*
Somebody (with music). *Anonymous*
Song: "Can love be controll'd by advice?" Gay.
Song to Be Sung by the Father of Infant Female Children. Nash.
Street Chants: I should worry, I should care. *Anonymous.*
Sum. Nolan.
Summer Storm. Simpson.

A Sweetheart in the Army (B vers.). *Anonymous.*
The Swimming Lady. *Anonymous.*
Ten Little Nigger Boys. *Anonymous.*
The Thankful Country Lass. *Anonymous.*
There Came a Day at Summer's Full. Dickinson.
To Be or Not to Be (parody). Edmunds.
To Chuse a Friend, but Never Marry. Rochester.
To Leave the World Serve God. Donzella.
To the Choice Bridegroom. Halevi
Tommy Tucker. *Anonymous.*
Too Candid by Half. Saxe.
The Trance. Spender.
Trooper and Maid, I. *Anonymous.*
Ulysses (excerpt). Joyce.
Upon a Second Marriage. Merrill.
Usage. Thesen.
Waiting at the Church; or, My Wife Won't Let Me. Leigh.
The Wars of Santa Fe. *Anonymous.*
The Wedding Gift. Irving.
Wedding of the Clans. De Vere.
Wedding Song. *Anonymous.*
The Wexford Girl (I). *Anonymous.*
When the Iceworms Nest Again. Service.
The Widow That Keeps the Cock Inn. *Anonymous.*
The Wife Who Would a Wanton Be. *Anonymous.*
William Hall. *Anonymous.*
Woo'd and Married and A'. Ross.
Young Ronald. *Anonymous.*

Marrow
Brave Old World. Lambert.
Don Juan. Byron.
Hungry Grass. MacDonagh.
The Instruments. Smart.
Jealousy. *Anonymous.*
The Marrow. Roethke.
Northern Ireland: Two Comments. Deane.
Put Your Finger in Foxy's Hole. *Anonymous.*

Mars
After the Deformed Woman Is Made Correct. Lietz.
Far Trek. Brady.
Odes. Horace.
The Peasants' Song. *Anonymous.*
The Survivors. Hine.
A Well-Wishing to a Place of Pleasure. *Anonymous.*
What Thing Is Love. Peele.

Marsh (es)
Alternative Endings to an Unwritten Ballad. Dehn.
Evening in England. Ledwidge.
From My Thought. Smythe.
The Marshes. Mayhall.
Marshlands. Johnson.
Mending the Bridge. Stewart.
My Little Love Lies on the Ground. Paraske.

Runoff. Ammons.
The Salt Flats. Roberts.
Swan. Lawrence.
The Widow's Lament in Springtime. Williams.

Martial
Epigram on Elphinstone's Translation of Martial's Epigrams. Burns.
Satires. Juvenal (Decimas Junius Juvenalis).
Ways of War. Johnson.

Martyr (dom) (s)
The Broken Heart. Ford.
Burial of Barber. Whittier.
Calvus to a Fly. Tennyson.
Christmas Prayer. Morse.
Cock-Throwing! Lluellyn.
The Contrary. Brome.
A Dublin Ballad - 1916. "O'Byrne.
Elegy XXIII. Labé.
Fragment. McCrae.
If I Could Believe That Death. Stampa.
J. A. G. Howe.
The King's Missive. Whittier.
Love's Martyrs. Ford.
The Martyrdom of St. Teresa. Hope.
A New Catch in Praise of the Reverend Bishops. *Anonymous.*
President Garfield. Longfellow.
The Prophet. Cowley.
Rolling the Lawn. Empson.
The Sea Hath Many Thousand Sands. *Anonymous.*
Sonnet XXIII: "What good is it to me if long ago." Labe.
Sonnet: "When I was marked for suffering, love forswore." Cervantes Saarvedra.
Stanzas on Mutability. Hofmannsthal.

Marvel (ous) (s)
An African Elegy. Duncan.
Black Sheep. Burton.
Boy at Target Practice: A Contemplation. Moses.
Dain do Eimhir (excerpt). MacLean.
Dream of the Black Mother. Dos Santos.
The Finest Thing. Veitch.
Prospect Beach. Lipsitz.
Shack Poem. Bly.
Soul and Sense. Kimball.
Spring Landscape. Ficke.
That Way. Welsh.
The Wonder-Teacher. Ozick.
XXXVI. Berrigan.

Mary
Baby and Mary. *Anonymous.*
Bessy and Mary. *Anonymous.*
Blue-Eyed Mary. Freeman.
The Canterbury Tales: The Prioress's Tale. Chaucer.
A Cause for Wonder. *Anonymous.*
Cherry Tree Carol. *Anonymous.*
Christ 1: Advent Lyrics, IX. *Anonymous.*
A Christmas Carol. Probyn.
Christmas Morn. Sawyer.

The Constant Farmer's Son. *Anonymous.*
Cowper at Tea. Pain.
The Desire. Hinkson.
Devilish Mary. *Anonymous.*
Duns Scotus's Oxford. Hopkins.
An Epigram to the Queen, Then Lying In. Jonson.
Festum Nativitatis. De Vere.
Gentle Name. Robinson.
Glad and Blithe Might Ye Be. *Anonymous.*
Hail Mary! *Anonymous.*
Hail to the Queen. *Anonymous.*
Harry Semen. ""MacDiarmid.
Highland Mary. Burns.
Hymn: "Hush! oh ye billows." Lefanu.
A Hymn of the Incarnation. *Anonymous.*
I Read, or Write. Sedulius Scottus.
In All the Magic of Christmas Time. Niles.
Irony of God. Warner.
Lisnagade. *Anonymous.*
The Little Dove. *Anonymous.*
Mary Ames. *Anonymous.*
Mary and the Baby, Sweet Lamb. *Anonymous.*
Mary in the Silvery Tide. *Anonymous.*
Mary Jane. *Anonymous.*
Mary Morison. Burns.
Mary's Lamb. Hale.
The Moon behind the Hill. *Anonymous.*
The Moon of Mobile. Chivers.
Newberry (Lonesome Dove). *Anonymous.*
Oh, Mary Don't You Weep. *Anonymous.*
Our Lady in the Middle Ages. Faber.
A Pastoral. Gale.
A Poem to Mary. Mac Con Brettan.
Rice Pudding. Milne.
The Rose of Tralee. Spencer.
Serenade. Callanan.
The Silvery Tide. *Anonymous.*
Song of Praise to Mary. "Angelus Selesius" (Johannes Scheffler).
The Spinner. O'Donnell.
The Stable Cat. Norris.
The Starred Mother. Whitaker.
The Tear. Crashaw.
Telling the Bees. Whittier.
To M.H. Wordsworth.
Twilight Song. Hunter-Duvar.
Two Old Lenten Rhymes: II. *Anonymous.*
Upon an Hermaphrodite. Cleveland.
William and Mary. *Anonymous.*
William Brown. Miller.
The Young Glass-Stainer. Hardy.

Mask (ed) (s)
Appearances. Browning.
Atavism. Wylie.
Chiaroscuro. Berge.

The Cloud. Muir.
The Clown. Bruner.
The Hydra of Birds.
　Engonopoulos.
Karl Heinrich Marx.
　Enzensberger.
Korea Bound, 1952.
　Childress.
The Last Chrysanthemum.
　Hardy.
Letter to My Daughter at the
　End of Her Second Year.
　Finkel.
The Mask. Delany.
Masks. Swann.
One Night Stand. Jones.
Poet. Emerson.
Ripper Collins' Legacy.
　Johnson.
Saadi. Emerson.
Sonnets: A Sequence on
　Profane Love. Boker.
Tonight the City. Cook.
Vanishing Point. Cooley.
We Wear the Mask.
　Dunbar.
Winter Offering. Savage.

Mass (es)
Ars Victrix. Gautier.
The Coral Reef. Blight.
Early Morning Meadow Song.
　Dalmon.
Four Glosses. Anonymous.
The Horse. Ponge.
I Am the People, the Mob.
　Sandburg.
If Frequently to Mass.
　Pisan.
Less and Less Human, O
　Savage Spirit. Stevens.
Moon Man. Valentine.
Rearmament. Jeffers.
Swearing. Fitzsimon.
Truth. Schaeffer.
"Vierge Ouvrante." Palmer.
The Waning Moon. Shelley.
Why, Liquor of Life?
　Carolan.

Massachusetts
The Crossing at
　Fredericksburg. Boker.
Stun. Schuyler.

Massacre (d)
Appleton House (excerpt).
　Marvell
A Bronze Head. Yeats.
Of Autumn. Porumbacu.

Mast
The Death of Peter Esson.
　Brown.
In Summer. Stickney.
Our Lady of Good Voyage.
　Adee.
Sail at the Mast Head.
　Anonymous.
The Veteran. Coxe.

Master
Away. Stryk.
A Ballad of Master McGrath.
　Anonymous.
Be Still. Kline.
Christmas Eve. Field.
Cock a Doodle Doo.
　Anonymous.
Cold Iron. Kipling.
Coleridge. De Vere.
Come up, My Horse, to
　Budleigh Fair.
　Anonymous.
Donkeys. Field.
Eleven Addresses to the Lord.
　Berryman.

Epigram on a Dog. Johnson.
Epigram: The Parson's Looks.
　Burns.
Even though my hands.
　Anonymous.
The Excursion. Wordsworth.
Failures. Upson.
Father Short. Anonymous.
The First Olympionique to
　Hiero of Syracuse. Pindar.
Funny Rigs of Good and
　Tender-Hearted Masters.
　Anonymous.
Ghoul Care. Hodgson.
Go Little Ring. Anonymous.
Grace before Meat.
　FitzGerald.
Guardianship. Johnson.
The Guest. Kimball.
He Has Served Eighty
　Masters. Harford.
The Hired Man on
　Horseback. Rhodes.
History of the Modern World.
　Coblentz.
The Hottentot. Pringle.
How Long Shall I Give?
　Anonymous.
Hymns for the Amusement of
　Children. Smart.
I Know That I Am a Great
　Sinner. Purohit Swami.
I Met the Master.
　Anonymous.
In a Copy of Browning.
　Carman.
In the Valley of the Elwy.
　Hopkins.
The Indomitable. Rakosi.
Is It Nothing to You?
　Kindig.
Jerusalem Sonnets. Baxter.
Kaiser Dead. Arnold.
Limerick: "There once was a
　Master of Arts."
　Monkhouse.
Locksley Hall Sixty Years
　After. Tennyson.
Lord Cozens Hardy.
　Betjeman.
Man of the World.
　Hamburger.
Master Charge Blues.
　Giovanni.
The Morning After. Clark.
My Dog. Bangs.
My Dog Tray. Byrom.
A New Song: "As near
　beauteous Boston lying."
　Anonymous.
O Thou Whose Feet Have
　Climbed Life's Hill.
　Benson.
The Odyssey. Homer.
Oh, Sleep, Fond Fancy.
　Anonymous.
On First Looking into
　Chapman's Homer II
　(parody). Peterson.
A Panegyric. Howe.
Paradise Lost. Milton.
Philomel to Corydon.
　Young.
Piping Peace. Shirley.
Rounded up in Glory.
　Anonymous.
The Scholar and the Cat.
　Anonymous.
The Sheep. Taylor.
Silex Scintillans. Vaughan.
The Song of the Forest
　Ranger. Bashford.

Sonnet: To Brunetto Latini.
　Dante Alighieri.
Sorrow. Phillips.
The Sphinx. Emerson.
Suburban Dream. Muir.
The Summing Up. Simmons.
Swimmers (excerpt).
　Untermeyer.
These Are My People.
　Trent.
The Thracian Filly.
　Anacreon.
Thy Will Be Done. Kerr.
The Time. Fraser.
The Titanic (excerpt). Pratt.
To a Boy. Anonymous.
To All Angels and Saints.
　Herbert.
To Destiny. Anonymous.
To My Son Parker, Asleep in
　the Next Room.
　Kaufman.
The Touch of the Master's
　Hand. Welch.
Transfigured. Piatt.
Triolet. Bridges.
Waking from Sleep. Bly.
Watching Jim Shoulders.
　Connellan.
What's This of Death.
　Millay.
Who Is That A-Walking in
　the Corn? Johnson.
Who Reigns? Shelley.
Who Translates a Poet Badly.
　Prada.
The "Word" of a Watch-Dog.
　Sandag.

Masterpiece
Continuity. Russell.
Nine Nectarines and Other
　Porcelain. Moore.
The Old Masters. Verhaeren.

Mastery
At Tide Water. Roberts.
Dogrose. Stevenson.
The Highest Wisdom.
　Jacopone da Todi.
Of John Bunyans Life &c.
　James.
Les Planches-en-Montagnes.
　Roberts.
The Sunflower. Quennell.

Mastodon (s)
Riding in the Rain. Kumin.
The Rollicking Mastodon.
　Macy.
To a Skull. Irwin.

Masturbate
Letter. Dow.
Scattered Fog. Sanford.

Mat
Hyperion. Keats.
An Unsuspected Fact.
　Cannon.
Western Civilization. Neto.

Match (ed)
The Blessed Match. Senesh.
British Leftish Poetry,
　1930-40. "" MacDiarmid.
Elegy for My Mother.
　Katrovas.
Flowers for the Brave.
　Thaxter.
In Memory of Eva Gore-
　Booth and Con Markiewicz.
　Yeats.
Laid Off. Webb.
March 23, 1982 Tuesday
　Night. Waltner.
Mog the Brunette.
　Anonymous.

On the Friendship betwixt
　Two Ladies. Waller.
The Orange Lily O.
　Anonymous.
Our Wee White Rose.
　Massey.
A Philosopher. Bangs.
Ripper Collins' Legacy.
　Johnson.
'Tis Highly Rational, We
　Can't Dispute. Garnett.
Welcome the Wrath. Kunitz.

Matchless
Mistress of the Matchless
　Mine. Robertson.
Ode to a Fat Cat. Farjeon.
Sonnets to Philomel. Davies.

Mate (d) (s)
Although I Had a Check.
　Surrey.
Captain Stratton's Fancy.
　Masefield.
The Falcon. Anonymous.
Fathomless Is My Love.
　Kalola.
History. Lawrence.
I Am Your Mother, Your
　Mother's Mother. Rumi.
John Winter. Binyon.
Kennedy Airport. Kramer.
The Lonesome Grove.
　Anonymous.
The Lost. Anonymous.
The Lost Orchard. Masters.
The Man in the Dress Suit.
　Wolfe.
The Moon Pond.
　McGuckian.
Moreton Miles, LIV.
　Baylebridge.
The Muddy Rat. Daigaku.
Now I Set Me. Herman
Portait with Background.
　Gogarty.
Portrait of an Indian.
　Rashley.
The Primrose Bed. Graves.
The Reason. Oppenheim.
A Rhapsody (excerpt).
　Vaughan.
Sea-Birds. Akers.
Song of the Queen Bee.
　White.
Spider. Cole.
Study of an Elevation, in
　Indian Ink. Kipling.
Thee, God, I Come from, to
　Thee Go. Hopkins.
To Edom. Heine.
Voyage. Donaghy.

Matter (ed) (s)
After the Battle (1930).
　Viereck.
After the Visit. Hardy.
Age. More.
The Annihilation of Nothing.
　Gunn.
Blue Tropic. Cabalquinto.
Civil Riot. Cole.
Clerihew: "Albert Durer."
　Nicholls.
Dora versus Rose. Dobson.
Elegy (For Himself). Rimos.
Experience. Parker.
God Save Ireland. Sullivan.
I Am Sure of It. Baca.
I Read My Sentence–Steadily.
　Dickinson.
Lynched. Booker.
Marry the Lass? Greig.
The Metaphysical Sectarian.
　Butler.

The News. Saxe.
On the Author of the Treatise of Human Nature. Beattie.
Part of the Vigil. Merrill.
Poem for You. Pack.
Sensationalism. Levis.
Skelton Laureate, Defender, against Lusty Garnesche.... Skelton.
Sundown. Adams.
To His Friend J. H. Brome.
Train Blues. Zimmer.
Valentine. Hall.
Who Will Buy a Poem? O'Heffernan.

Mattresses
Night. Jami.
Poem from Deal. Shapiro.
Vacancy in the Park. Stevens.

Mausoleum (s)
Elegy (excerpt). Bidart.
Marcus Aurelius. Sisson.
Upon the Death of the Lord Hastings. Dryden.

Maw (s)
Cromwell, Our Chief of Men. Milton.
The Fallen Elm. Clare.
The Shipman. Chaucer.
To the Lord General Cromwell. Milton.

May
Almswomen. Blunden.
Alons au Bois le May Cueillir. d'Orleans.
The Altarpiece Finished. Hollander.
Ant-Hills. "Douglas.
Apocalypse. Nims.
As I Walked through the Meadows. Anonymous.
Baby May. Bennett.
Beech Trees. Madeleva.
Bright Clouds. Thomas.
The Canadian Rossignol. Thomson.
Cheddar Pinks. Bridges.
The Cherry Trees. Thomas.
Corinna's Going A-Maying. Herrick.
Count Gismond. Browning.
Dirge for the Year. Shelley.
The Dust. Hall.
Farmer. Fallon.
The Flute of May. Woodbourne.
Fool Song. Lengyel.
The Gladness of May. Wordsworth.
A Glee for Winter. Domett.
The Greedy the People. Cummings.
I Am. Conkling.
I Could Not Though I Would. Gascoigne.
I'm Glad My Birthday Comes in May! Eastwick.
I Want to Be Married and Cannot Tell How. Anonymous.
In November. Aldrich.
In Praise of May. Anonymous.
In Summer. Anonymous.
An Infantryman. Blunden.
Larches. Gurney.
Lines by a Medium. Anonymous.
Lines Written on a Very Boisterous Day in May, 1944. Clare.

The Locust Tree in Flower. Williams.
The Lord of Lorn and the Fals Steward. Anonymous.
Lost in a Norther. Garland.
Love in the Valley. Meredith.
Lovewell's Fight. Anonymous.
Lusty May. Anonymous.
A Lyric: "Into a little close of mine I went." Medici.
March Winds. Mother Goose.
May. Barnes.
A May Burden. Thompson.
May Carol. Anonymous.
May Day. Teasdale.
A May Day Carol. Anonymous.
May in the Green-Wood. Anonymous.
May Morning. Thaxter.
May Poems. Anonymous.
The Mayers' Song. Anonymous.
The Milkmaid. Dobson.
Moon Light. Manfred.
The Naughty Lord & the Gay Young Lady. Anonymous.
Ode on the Spring. Gray.
On Queen Anne's Death. Anonymous.
The Oyster. Nash.
The Padstow Night Song. Anonymous.
A Pastoral. Breton.
Phyllida and Corydon. Breton.
The Pine Bough. Aldridge.
The Poem: "Rise Oedipeus, and if thou canst unfould." Morton.
Since Bonny-Boots Was Dead. Anonymous.
Sing for the Garish Eye. Gilbert.
Sister, Awake! Anonymous.
Song: "Shephard loveth thow me vell?" Passerat.
Spring. Meleager.
Spring. Timrod.
Stock Exchange Wisdom. Anonymous.
Summer Longings. MacCarthy.
Sunday up the River. Thomson.
There Gowans Are Gay. Anonymous.
There Is Snowdrift on the Mountain. Ker.
Three Ballate. Poliziano.
The Thrissil and the Rois. Dunbar.
To the Lady May. Townsend.
The Toad. Locklin.
Tomorrows. Merrill.
The Veterans. MacDonagh.
Watergate. Herschberger.
While April Rain Went By. O'Sheel.
Will You Love Me in December as You Do in May? Walker.
With Poems Already Begun. Korn.

Mayo
The County of Mayo. Fox.
The Tailor That Came from Mayo. McCarthy.

Maze (s)
Joy. Delany.
The Premonition. Roethke.
Sleep-Walking Child. Eybers.
Survival in a Stone Maze. Rachow.
To the Moon. Goethe.
Vincent Van Gogh. Smith.

Mead (s)
Ariosto. Mandelstam.
The Dead Quire. Hardy.
Ebbe Skammelson. Anonymous.
Lady of the Ferry Inn. Mechain.
Lament for Thomas MacDonagh. Ledwidge.
The Old-Fashioned Garden. Hayes.
Spring. Timrod.

Meadow (s)
Between Namur and Liege. Wordsworth.
The Cow. Stevenson.
The Deaths. Schoultz.
Deserted Buildings under Shefford Mountain. Glassco.
The Dove of New Snow. Lindsay.
Haiku, for Cinnamon. Chaffin.
Hippolytus. Euripides.
The Hour of Feeling. Simpson.
In Memoriam. Lowry.
Late Starting Dawn. Brautigan.
March 8, 1840. Thoreau.
The Milkman. O'Sullivan.
Mount Caribou at Night. Wright.
The Mower. Anonymous.
Oh, Susan Blue. Greenaway.
Old Song. Fitzgerald.
Omens. Hamburger.
The Other Voice. Paulin.
The Padda Song. Anonymous.
Pluviose. Bell.
The Poem on Our Mother, Our Mother Rachel. Yeshurun.
Psalm of the Fruitful Field. Klein.
Resurrection. Kemp.
The Salt Flats. Roberts.
Schlof, Bobbeli. Anonymous.
Song: "Only the wanderer." Gurney.
Sonnets. Lee.
Sonnets, XII: "A roadside inn this summer Saturday." Irwin.
Springfield Mountain (B vers.). Anonymous.
Tender Buttons: Objects. Stein.
Terenure. Salkeld.
The Thracian Filly. Anacreon.
We Hurry On, Nor Passing Note. Dolben.
The Wheelbarrow. Edson.

Meadowlark
The Seed of Reality. Von Hartmann.

Meal (S)
After the Storm. Bartlett.
A Breakfast for Barbarians. MacEwen.

A Cat's Conscience. Anonymous.
Darkness. Bacon.
The Eel. Nash.
Envying the Pelican. Weber.
If You Want to Write Me. Anonymous.
An Invitation to Madison County. Wright.
The Lion's Bride. Harwood.
Marble-Top. White.
Mossbawn: Two Poems in Dedication. Heaney.
My Auld Wife. Anonymous.
No Job Blues. Thomas.
Riddle: "A wide mouth, no ears nor eyes." Anonymous.
A Scottish Cat. Anonymous.
Seed Journey. Corso.
The Signal; or, A Satire against Modesty (excerpt). Hawling.
Thanksgiving. Morris.
To Phidyle. Horace.

Mean (ing) (s)
After the War. Le Gallienne.
Alone. Wells.
Antiques. De la Mare.
The Apostate. Coppard.
Apparition. Erskine.
Ars Poetica. MacLeish.
A Birthday in Hospital. Jennings.
Blum. Aldis.
Bones. Morgan.
Canzone. Hacker.
Captain Jinks. Lingard.
A Classic Idyll. Huss.
The Clock. Scarfe.
Comparatives. Momaday.
A Copy of Non Sequitors. Anonymous.
Debora Sleeping. Logan.
The Dog. Anonymous.
La Donna Perpetuum Mobile. Edman.
Edith Sitwell Assumes the Role of Luna. Francis.
The End Is Near the Beginning. Gascoyne.
The Fallen Tree. Maybin.
Felo Da Se. Blackburn.
Fires. Heyen.
Fragment. Lowell.
The Hills of Pomeroy. Milne.
I Think Table and I Say Chair. Fuertes.
Ironic:LL.D. Braithwaite.
It's No Use Raising a Shout. Auden.
Jehu. MacNeice.
The Laurel Tree. Simpson.
Limerick: "A charming young woman named Pat." Anonymous.
List of Prepositions. Kennedy.
The Low Road. Piercy.
A Man-Made World. Spender.
Me List No More to Sing. Wyatt.
Memorandum. Stafford.
The Menagerie. Moody.
The Mental Hospital Garden. Williams.
The Message of the Rain. Russell.
Notes for a Lecture. Ignatow.

The Olive Tree. Baring-
　Gould.
On Donne's Poetry.
　Coleridge.
Out of Sleep. Curnow.
The Owner of My Face.
　Hall.
Pathedy of Manners. Kay.
Peace Is the Mind's Old
　Wilderness. Holmes.
Poem. Tomlinson.
Poet's Protest. Hedges.
The Pool. Creeley.
Prayer in Mid-Passage.
　MacNeice.
Religio Laici. Dryden.
The Resolve. Chudleigh.
Six Rubaiyat. Ibn Abi'l-
　Khayr.
A Small Thought Speaks for
　the Flesh. Drewry.
The Smile of the Walrus.
　Herford.
Snow Country Weavers.
　Welch.
Soul-Severance (parody).
　Hankin.
The Sphinx. Emerson.
Spirit from Whom Our Lives
　Proceed. Robbins.
The Stoic: for Laura von
　Courten. Bowers.
Structure of Rime. Duncan.
Thanksgiving for a Habitat.
　Auden.
The Thirteenth Song.
　Drayton.
To Cypassis, Corinna's Maid.
　Ovid (Publius Ovidius
　Naso).
To His Wife, for Striking Her
　Dog. Harington.
Two Words: A Wedding.
　Nichol.
Unidentified Flying Object.
　Hayden.
Values in Use. Moore.
A Vase of Flowers. Ashbery.
Waiting Both. Hardy.
Why Doubt God's Word?
　Simpson.
The Wind, the Clock, the We.
　Riding.
Yomi, Yomi. *Anonymous.*

Meaningful
Two Dedications, I: The
　Chicago Picasso. Brooks.

Meanness
Epitaphium Vivi Auctoris
　1792. Walpole.
The Historical Judas.
　Nemerov.
Your Animal. Stern.

Measles
Crusoe in England. Bishop.
Old Bill's Memory Book.
　Benet.
The Sow Took the Measles.
　Anonymous.

Measure (d) (s)
Allalu Mo Wauleen (The
　Beggar's Address to His
　Bag). *Anonymous.*
Do Not Torment Me, Lady.
　Anonymous.
El Camino Verde.
　Blackburn.
Epistles. Horace.
Harp Music~. Humphries.
I Sigh, as Sure to Wear the
　Fruit. *Anonymous.*

In Measure Time We'll Row.
　Anonymous.
In the Cafe. Borson.
Is It Nothing to You?
　Probyn.
Knee Lunes. Kelly.
Milton. Blake.
The Minute before Meeting.
　Hardy.
Mountain Vigil. Fraser.
Muirland Meg. Burns.
Mustapha. Greville.
The Others. O'Sullivan.
The Panchatantra: True
　Friendship. *Anonymous.*
A Physics. McHugh.
The Poet's Harvesting.
　O'Malley.
Reconciliation. *Anonymous.*
A Record Stride. Frost.
Roses. Stanley.
Tatiana Kalatschova. Logan.
The Three Taverns: Out of
　Wisdom Has Come Love.
　Robinson.
The Trout. Hine.
The World Hymn. Lawson.

Meat
The Age of the Butcher.
　Friebert.
Another Grace for a Child.
　Herrick.
A Bestiary. Rexroth.
Chops. Dixon.
Dunderbeck. *Anonymous.*
The Everlasting Gospel.
　Blake.
The Fox Walked Out, A vers.
　Anonymous.
Julius Caesar. Shakespeare.
Kreutzer Sonata. Hughes.
The Land of Cokaigne.
　Anonymous.
Last Night in Calcutta.
　Ginsberg.
Lines on Bounce. Pope.
The Maldive Shark.
　Melville.
Nervous Miracles.
　Gustafson.
On Barclay's Apology for the
　Quakers. Green.
The Peasant Declares His
　Love. Roumer.
Personal Song. Arnatkoak.
Prayer before Meat. Harsen.
The Same Old Story.
　Montague.
Transubstantiation. Geddes.
Two Graces. Herrick.
Upon Showbread: Epigram.
　Herrick.
The Wandering Jew. Mezey.

Medal (s)
Dory Miller. Cornish.
The Field Hospital.
　Muldoon.
Gunner. Jarrell.
On a Halfpenny Which a
　Young Lady Gave a
　Beggar... Fielding.

Meddle
I Am Dark and Fair to See.
　Anonymous.
Looking Forward.
　Stevenson.
Sixteen Dead Men. Yeats.
When I am grown to man's
　estate. Stevenson.

Medicine (s)
Caller of the Buffalo. Austin.

The Doctor's Story.
　Carleton.
High-Cool/2. Cunningham.
If God Exists. Lipska.
Moors, Angels, Civil Wars.
　Sinclair.
Les Realites. Guest.
The Staff of Aesculapius.
　Moore.

Meditation
The Infinite. O'Reilly.
To the Right Person. Frost.

Meed (s)
Amoretti, XXV. Spenser.
The Peasants' Song.
　Anonymous.
Song of Coridon and
　Melampus. Peele.

Meek (ness)
Another to Urania. Colman.
The Church's One
　Foundation. Stone.
Lives of the Poet. Miles.
Midnight at Baiae. A Dream
　Fragment of Imperial
　Rome. Symonds.
My Country, Right! Clark.
O Why Was I Born with a
　Different Face? Blake.
One dignity delays for all.
　Dickinson.
A Prayer. Hemans.
Scene in a Madhouse. De
　Vere.
She Walks. Keith.
A Sheep Fair. Hardy.
To the Daisy. Wordsworth.
A Visitor. "Carroll.

Meet (ing) (met)
After the Fair. Hardy.
Another Meeting. Lucas.
Anxiety about Dying.
　Ostriker.
The Apartment-Hunter.
　Schultz.
As Love and I, Late
　Harbour'd in One Inn.
　Drayton.
Ask No Return. Gregory.
At last love has come.
　Sulpicia.
Ballad Written for a
　Bridegroom. Villon.
Between Life and Death.
　Gottlieb.
The Bewildered Guest.
　Howells.
Beyond the Grave. Bruner.
The Bird. Simic.
Botany Bay. *Anonymous.*
The Boys of Sanpete County.
　Anonymous.
By Yon Burn Side.
　Tannahill.
A Child's Song to Her
　Mother. Welles.
Come an' Meet Me wi' the
　Childern on the Road.
　Barnes.
The Country Lovers. Smith.
Daughters. Astra.
The Dawning o' the Year.
　Blake.
The Day You Are Reading
　This. Stafford.
A Different Speech. Nicholl.
Don Juan. Byron.
The Dual Site. Hamburger.
The Dying Mine Brakeman.
　Jenks.
Earl Rothes. *Anonymous.*
Earth Walk. Meredith.

Enfidaville. Douglas.
Epitaph for George Moore.
　Hardy.
The Exequy. To His
　Matchlesse Never to Be
　Forgotten Freind. King.
Face to Face. Cochrane.
Faithless. Lavater.
Five Stanzas on Perfection.
　Jonas.
For a Young South Dakota
　Man. Manfred.
Forever. Carver.
Forty Years Ago.
　Anonymous.
The Gale of August, '27.
　Anonymous.
God Be with You Till We
　Meet Again. Rankin.
God's Call. *Anonymous.*
Good-bye. Emerson.
He Cares. Salway.
Home Is Where There Is One
　to Love Us. Swain.
Home of the Soul. Gates.
I Am He That Aches with
　Love. Whitman.
I, being born a woman and
　distressed. Millay.
I Die; But When the Grave
　Shall Press. Bronte.
I Met Her in the Garden
　Where the Praties Grow
　(with music). *Anonymous.*
I Move the Meeting Be
　Adjourned. Parra.
If Only, When One Heard.
　Anonymous.
Ill Met by Zenith. Nash.
In a Hotel Writing-Room.
　Powys.
In Love with the Bears.
　Kuzma.
Interrupted Romance.
　Anonymous.
It Started. Baca.
John Rogers' Exhortation to
　His Children. *Anonymous.*
Katie May. Hopkins.
A Kiss in the Morning Early.
　Anonymous.
Laundry & School Epigrams.
　Mayer.
The Lea Rig. Burns.
Let's Forget. Wagner.
The Level and the Square.
　Morris.
Lord Thomas and Fair Annet
　(B vers.). *Anonymous.*
A Lost Love. Lyte.
Lovers How They Come and
　Part. Herrick.
Man of Constant Sorrow.
　Anonymous.
Matins, or Morning Prayer.
　Herrick.
McAfee's Confession.
　Anonymous.
Meeting After Long Absence.
　Perry.
Meeting and Passing. Frost.
Meeting Mary. Farjeon.
The Minuet. Dodge.
Morgan Stanwood. Rich.
My Ain Kind Dearie, O.
　Burns.
My Cross. Cocke.
The Newly-Wedded. Praed.
Night Harvest. Pence.
Night Sowing. Campbell.
No Escape. Delafield.
Nocturne. Hillyer.

Not as Wont. Skipsey.
Now Lift Me Close.
  Whitman.
Old Virginny. Bland.
On Visiting the Graves of
  Hawthorne and Thoreau.
  Very.
Only One Life. Bowman.
Our Bondage It Shall End.
  Cartwright.
Part Winter. Bowering.
Parting Friends. *Anonymous.*
A Parting Hymn. Forten.
Pearl Bryan. *Anonymous.*
The Phoenix (excerpt).
  Anonymous.
Phyllis. Randolph.
Prayer. *Anonymous.*
Prayer to the Virgin.
  Anonymous.
Quiescent, a Person Sits Heart
  and Soul. Lardner.
Rendezvous. Hillyer.
Riddle: "I'm a strange
  creature, for I satisfy
  women." *Anonymous.*
The River Merchant's Wife.
  Li Po.
The Sad Lover. Crabbe.
The Search. Shaw.
The Secret Land. Graves.
Should We Legalize Abortion?
  O'Hara.
Sir Walter Ralegh to His Son.
  Ralegh.
Skimbleshanks: the Railway
  Cat. Eliot.
So Fly by Night. Osborne.
Solid Mountain. Bowering.
Some Day or Days. Perry.
A Song. Dunbar.
The Song of the Bower.
  Rossetti.
Song of the Old Love.
  Ingelow.
Song: "We came to Tamichi
  in 1880." Hammond.
  "Doc".
Sons of the Kings. Agnew.
Sorrow. Eden.
Sparkling and Bright.
  Hoffman
Speechless. Marston.
The Spring of the Year.
  Cunningham.
A Storm in the Distance.
  Hayne.
Strange. Burnshaw.
Sun and Moon. Macpherson.
There Is a Man on the Cross.
  Cheney.
To Dante. Alfieri.
To-Day. Low.
To His Lady. Henry VIII.
To My Mistress in Absence.
  Carew.
To the Rev. Mr. Newton.
  Cowper.
The Trimdon Grange
  Explosion. *Anonymous.*
The True Encounter. Millay.
The Vance Song.
  Anonymous.
Walking with Him in White.
  Wesley.
We Shall Walk through the
  Valley. *Anonymous.*
Weeping Sad and Lonely.
  Ucker.
The West Palm Beach Storm.
  Anonymous.

What Shame Forbids to
  Speak. Herrick.
When. Hitomaro.
When Evening Comes.
  Yakamochi.
When First. Thomas.
When Our Earthly Sun Is
  Setting. Nevin.
Who Are My People?
  Marinoni.
The Windows of Waltham.
  Wieners.
Wings and Seeds.
  McPherson.
The Young Fellow Walks
  About. Reznikoff.
Young Training. McGaugh.

Meeting-house
The Captain. Brainard.
The Owl and the Eel and the
  Warming-Pan. Richards.

Meg
Muckle-Mouth Meg.
  Browning.
Muirland Meg. Burns.

Melancholy
The Authors Abstract of
  Melancholy. Burton.
A Dream. Keats.
Il Penseroso. Milton.
The Location of Things.
  Guest.
October. Thomas.
On an Air of Rameau.
  Symons.
Praise-God Barebones.
  Cortissoz.
The Ruins of Rome. Dyer.
Song: "Hence all you vaine
  Delights." Beaumont.
A Song: "If for a woman I
  would die." Winchilsea.
Winter Day. Fried.

Melissa
Melissa. Redl-Hlus.
When Young Melissa Sweeps.
  Turner.

Melodious (ly)
At a Vacation Exercise.
  Milton.
Longfellow's Visit to Venice.
  Betjeman.
Memnon. Scollard.

Melody (ies)
The Arsenal at Springfield.
  Longfellow.
Camp Notes. Yamada.
Church Poem. Thomas.
The Clouds. Aristophanes.
Elegy for Lucy Lloyd. Goch.
Fairy Music. Ledwidge.
God's Will. Nevin.
I Often Want to Let My Lines
  Go. Neidus.
I Would Not Paint a Picture.
  Dickinson.
Ilion, Ilion. Tennyson.
Motif for Mary's Dolors.
  Mary Madeleva.
My Father Is the Nightingale.
  Anonymous.
Nature and the Poets.
  Beattie.
The New Cecilia. Beddoes.
Night. Daley.
Noh Play. Brodey.
The Ovidian Elegiac Metre,
  Described and Exemplified.
  Coleridge.
Plato, a Musician. Leontius.
Poem for Thel–the Very Tops
  of Trees. Major.

The Quest. Cromwell.
The Shell's Song. Keats.
Spring Whistles. Larcom.
Star Dust. Parish.
Title divine–Is mine!
  Dickinson.
To Melody. Allen.
The Tournament of
  Tottenham. *Anonymous.*
Tune Me, O Lord, into One
  Harmony. Rossetti.
Who Shined Shoes in Times
  Square. Jeffers.
The Wool Trade. Dyer.

Melon (s)
The Dancer. Young.
A Hopi Prayer. Conrard.
Melon-Slaughterer; or, A Sick
  Man's Praise for a Well
  Woman (parody). Peters.
Now Philippa Is Gone.
  Ridler.

Melt (ed) (ing) (s)
Admonition to a Traveller.
  Wordsworth.
Ancestors' Graves in
  Kurakawa. Kogawa.
Ancient and Modern Rome
  (excerpt). Keate.
At Liberty. Perlman.
Big City Glissando.
  Christopher.
Boomerang. Hart-Smith.
By Now. Salisbury.
Canto XXIX. Pound.
A Child's Grave Marker.
  Kooser.
Cold Fact. Emmons.
Desert Stone. Waddington.
Event. Plath.
From a Letter. Keats.
Gnosis. Cranch.
The Icc Eagle. Wakoski.
Journey: IV. Lindegren.
The Languages We Are.
  Bryant.
A Looking-Glass. Carew.
Love's Force. Carew.
New Jersey White-Tailed
  Deer. Oates.
The Night Dances. Plath.
On the 25th Anniversary of
  the Liberation of
  Auschwitz... Mandel.
Penal Rock: Altamuskin.
  Montague.
Snowman. Jones.
Sonnet: The Common Grave.
  Dobell.
To Mr C.B. Donne.
To the Etruscan Poets.
  Wilbur.
To You on the Broken
  Iceberg. Gallagher.
The Vestal. Pope.
The Whales off Wales.
  Kennedy.
When Banners Are Waving.
  Anonymous.
White. Krolow.

Member (s)
Act of Love. Scannell.
Conversation between the
  Chevalier de Chamilly and
  Mariana Alcoforado.
  Marias.
Miss Kilmansegg and Her
  Precious Leg. Hood.
Who I Am. Da Gama.

Membrane
Muscae Volitantes. Horne.

Sadness and Still Life.
  Ramke.

Memorial
Boys in October. Layton.
In Memoriam. Jackson.
Memo. Lynch.
Memorials: On the Slain at
  Chickamauga. Melville
Metaphor as Degeneration.
  Stevens.
The Metropolitan Railway.
  Baker Street Station Buffet.
  Betjeman.

Memory (ies)
Among His Books. Nesbit.
Anath. Guri.
The Anniad. Brooks.
At Casterbridge Fair.
  Hardy.
Autumn Journal. MacNeice.
Babylon and Sion (Goa and
  Lisbon). Camoens.
The Battle of Trenton.
  Anonymous.
Bells. Scott.
Bereaved of All, I Went
  Abroad. Dickinson.
Blackberry Winter. Huggins.
By Memory Inspired.
  Anonymous.
Castle Rock. Morgan.
Celan. Barnett.
Clocks. Ginsberg.
The Cracks. Creeley.
Crag Jack's Apostasy.
  Hughes.
Crystals Like Blood.
  " "MacDiarmid.
Days That Have Been.
  Davies.
The Dead Player. Wilson.
The Dead Quire. Hardy.
The Death of a Snake.
  Plomer.
Dirge. Parsons.
Dirge: For One Who Fell in
  Battle. Parsons
Dorothy. Kreymborg.
Dr. Dimity Is Forced to
  Complain. Macdonald.
Dream Girl. Sandburg.
Dream Songs. Berryman.
Dreams. Symons.
Edinburgh. Noyes.
Elegy on Albert Edward the
  Peacemaker. *Anonymous.*
Elegy while Pruning Roses.
  Wagoner.
Epigrams. Theocritus.
An Epitaph. Byron.
Epitaph for the Poet V.
  Ficke.
Etruscan Notebook.
  Clementelli.
Faintly and from Far away.
  Miller.
Fame. More.
Farewell to Anactoria.
  Sappho.
Farewell to Juliet. Blunt.
The First Solitude. Gongora
  y Argote.
For a Parting. Sinclair.
Forgettin'. O'Neill.
The Forging of the Anchor.
  Ferguson.
Frank Drummer. Masters.
The Good Ship. Stephens.
Grandeur of Ghosts.
  Sassoon.
Grandfathers. Shady.

Harlem Gallery: From the Inside. Neal.
Her Hair. Baudelaire.
Housework. Matthews.
Hunter's Morning. Littlebird.
Idiot. Tate.
In After Days. Dobson.
In Memory of John Lothrop Motley. Bryant.
In the Silks. Ackerman.
In Town. Wright.
In Vain. Cooke.
Indian Summer. Burr.
It Is So Long Since My Heart Has Been with Yours. Cummings.
Jardin du Palais Royal. Gascoyne.
John Betjeman's Brighton (parody). Ewart.
Late Rising. Prevert.
Lines Written beneath a Picture. Byron.
Lohengrin. Payne.
London Voluntaries. Henley.
Lost in Translation. Merrill.
Love's Tribute. Sturgeon.
Love-Songs, At Once Tender and Informative. Hoffenstein.
Marriage. Gordett.
May Thirtieth. *Anonymous.*
Memory Air. Dobzynski.
Memory as Memorial in the Last. Marshall.
Minnie and Her Dove. Turner.
Murphy in Manchester. Montague.
The Musician. Lister.
My Bonny Black Bess. *Anonymous.*
Night. Regnier.
Not unto the Forest. Widdemer.
Notes from a Slave Ship. Field.
Ode to Memory. Tennyson.
Oft, in the Stilly Night. Moore.
Oh, Breathe Not His Name. Moore.
The Old Mountaineer. Holmes.
On the Death of Friends in Childhood. Justice.
On the Wallowy. Chester.
Ordeal. Cassian.
The Ordeal by Fire (excerpt). Stedman.
The Other Side. Fuller.
Our Angels. Schwartz.
The Overturned Lake. Ford.
A Painted Fan. Moulton.
The Pearly Everlasting. Fewster.
Penumbra. Rossetti.
A Place in Thy Memory. Griffin.
The Profile on the Pillow. Randall.
Prostration. Semah.
Rachel. "Rachel" (Rachel Blumstein).
Rainy Morning. Rivera-Aviles.
Recollection. Aldrich.
Relics. Gegna.
Remembering. Nicoidski.
Repetition. Prunty.
Robert G. Shaw. Ray.

Rose Aylmer. Landor.
The Rose of May. Howitt.
Round Valley Reflections. Oandasan.
Rumor Laetalis. Abelard.
Sand Dunes and Sea. Moreland.
The Sea. Gorter.
Seven South African Poems. Wright.
The Ships. Maynard.
Simpson's Rest. Simpson.
Song of the Night at Day-Break. Meynell.
Songs of Cheng. Confucius.
Sonnet: Composed after a Journey across the Hamilton Hill, Yorkshire. Wordsworth.
Sorrows Humanize Our Race. Ingelow.
.Spirituality. Greenberg.
Spleen. Dowson.
Stanzas Written in Dejection, Near Naples. Shelley.
Star Dust. Parish.
Sumter's Band. Simmons.
Sweet Genevieve. Cooper.
That We Head Towards. Stephany.
Then Came I to the Shoreless Shore of Silence. Aiken.
They Are All Gone into the World of Light. Vaughan.
Thysia. Luce.
To a Faithless Friend. Arrabey.
To Each His Own. Garvin.
To God. Maurice.
To My Father. Fried.
To Shima sani. Tohe.
Two Strange Worlds. Pereira.
Valediction to My Contemporaries. Gregory.
The Veterans. MacDonagh.
Victorian Grandmother. Lockwood.
White Dusk. Boyd.
Yarrow Revisited. Wordsworth.

Menace
The End. De La Mare.
Outcast. McKay.
The Soldiers Returning. Shelton.
The Trenches. Manning.

Mend (ed) (ing) (s)
At Luca Signorelli's Resurrection of the Body. Graham.
The Bush-Fiddle. Green.
Caelica, LXVII. Greville.
Chairs to Mend. *Anonymous.*
Charing Cross. Roberts.
The Cunning Cobbler Done Over. Anonymous.
Darby and Joan. Honeywood.
Denial. Herbert.
The Elementary Scene. Jarrell.
An Excellent New Ballad Called the Prince of Darkness. *Anonymous.*
Father and Child. Harwood.
Hours of the Passion. Shoreham.
Learn, Lads and Lasses. Pastorius.
Little Mousgrove and the Lady Barnet. *Anonymous.*

Love. Herbert.
On His Mistress Drown'd. Spratt.
On the Decease of the Religious and Honourable Jno Haynes Esqr.... James.
Our Bow's Bended. *Anonymous.*
The Past. Emerson.
Riddle: "As I was going o'er London Bridge." *Anonymous.*
The Tapestry. Nemerov.
Those Trees That Line the Northway. Perreault.
Upon Himself. Herrick.
Walking in a meadow green. *Anonymous.*
Winter Evening Poem. Jensen.

Merchant (s)
A Draft of XXX Cantos, XII: "Said Jim X..." Pound.
Epigram: "Long hair, endless curls." Strato.
Fable of the Water Merchants. Dunn.
The Gouty Merchant and the Stranger. Smith.
Hey Diddle Dinkety, Poppety, Pet. *Anonymous.*
In Memoriam A.H.H., XIII. Tennyson.
The Keeper of the Midnight Gate. Brown.
Seascape. Hughes.

Merciful
Bagman O'Reilly's Curse. Murray.
Compassion. Hardy.
The Pirates of Penzance. Gilbert.
The Tempest. Cotton.

Merciless
Crew-Cuts. Hall.
Girl Betrayed. Hedylos.
Two Poems About President Harding. Wright.

Mercy (ies)
An A.B.C. Chaucer.
Abide, Good Men. *Anonymous.*
The Adventures of Simon Swaugum. Freneau.
All My Luve, Leave Me Not. *Anonymous.*
Altarwise by Owl-Light. Thomas.
Amoretti, XLIX. Spenser.
Amoretti, LV. Spenser.
Andre. Bates.
The Animals. Berg.
Apologia Pro Vita Sua. Sedulius Scottus.
As I Am My Father's. Drachler.
Astraea at the Capitol. Whittier.
Attraction. *Anonymous.*
Balance. Schultz.
Ballat O the Hingit. Villon.
The Best Song As It Seems to Me. *Anonymous.*
The Blessing of St. Francis. Maura.
The Bounty of Jehovah Praise. Sandys.
Breasts. Gallagher.
A Cautionary Tale. Wilkinson.
Cherry Tree Carol. *Anonymous.*

Christ 1: Advent Lyrics, III. *Anonymous.*
Crusty Critics. Crabbe.
The Darkness. Johnson.
The Demon of the Mirror. Taylor.
A Dresscessional. Wells.
The Eel. Morgan.
Elegy for My Mother. Katrovas.
Epitaph for a Tyrannous Governor Who Choked on Wine. Sabir.
The Everlasting Mercy. Masefield.
The Exeter Book: Fates of Men. *Anonymous.*
Far from Our Friends. Belknap.
Father Mapple's Hymn. Melville.
Fire on the Hills. Jeffers.
First Death. Justice.
The Five Joys. *Anonymous.*
Floating Bridge. Estes.
Flying Fish. Taylor.
Follow, Follow. Campion.
Go Far, Come Near. De La Mare.
The Hanging of Sam Archer. *Anonymous.*
Hark the Herald Angels Sing. Beecham.
How Can You? Stevens.
I Heard an Angel Singing. Blake.
If It Were Spring. Cohen.
In This Life. Mezey.
Juliana. Cynewulf.
The Knife. Kaplan.
Let Us Break Bread Together. *Anonymous.*
Let Us with a Gladsome Mind. Milton.
Loony, 29: The Good Folks at the Camp Meeting. Kloefkorn.
The Merchant of Venice. Shakespeare.
Mercy Is Most in My Mind. *Anonymous.*
The Nativity. Wesley.
News from Mount Amiata. Montale.
Notre Dames des Champs. Synge.
O God! Have Mercy in This Dreadful Hour. Southey.
O Lord! My Hiding Place. Raffles.
O Lord, Turn Not Away Thy Face. Marchant.
O Turn Ye, O Turn Ye. Hopkins.
An Old Woman. *Anonymous.*
The Old Woman Who Went to Market. *Anonymous.*
The Poor Old Prurient Interest Blues. Hartford.
A Prayer for the Household. Stevenson.
A Prayer to the Trinity. *Anonymous.*
Psalm 62. Donne Deo. Pembroke.
Recessional. Kipling.
Remember Thy Creator Now. Long.
The Restless Heart. *Anonymous.*
The Scribe's Prayer. Service.

Mercy (continued)

Secret Prayer. Belle.
Slaves Cannot Breathe in
England. Cowper.
So Oft As I Her Beauty Do
Behold. Spenser.
Some wretched creature,
savior take. Dickinson.
Song for an Allegorical Play.
Ciardi.
Sorrow. Trask.
Sticheron for Matins,
Wednesday of Holy Week.
Kassia.
Stigmata. Stoddard.
Summer's Last Will and
Testament: Adieu, Farewell
Earths Blisse. Nashe [(or
Nash[) Thomas.
There Was a Little Woman.
Mother Goose.
Three Roundels of Love
Unreturned. Chaucer.
Truth Brought to Light; or,
Murder Will Out. College.
Two Days. Henley.
A Village Tale. Sarton.
The Virgin Unspotted.
Anonymous.
The Wanderer. *Anonymous.*
Wayfarers in the Wilderness.
Thompson.
Within These Doors
Assembled Now. Holden.
Young Lincoln. Markham.

Merge (d) (s)
Hail! The Glorious Golden
City. Adler.
The Lost Orchard. Masters.
A Poem for Diane Wakoski.
Young Bear.
The Poet in Old Age Fishing
at Evening. O'Grady.
Prospecting. Ammons.
Veni Creator. Carman.
Vuillard: "The Mother and
Sister of the Artist."
Snodgrass.

Merit
The Death of Wolfe.
Anonymous.
Madrigal: "Vain Hope, adieu."
Attey.
The Man and the Weasel.
Phaedrus.
Penmanship. Clark.
To Edward Fitzgerald.
Tennyson.
When Orpheus Went Down.
Lisle.

Mermaid (s)
The Ballad of the Oysterman.
Holmes.
Madness One Monday
Evening. Fields.
Myself when Young (parody).
Donnelly.
Prometheus, with Wings:.
Ondaatje.

Merrily
As I out Rode. *Anonymous.*
The Handcart Song.
Anonymous.
A-Maying, A-Paying. Nashe
[(or Nash[) Thomas.
The Merman. Tennyson.
The Turn of the Road.
Gifford.

Merriment
All Fools' Day. *Anonymous.*
The Mikado. Gilbert.
Summer Mansions.
Herschberger.

Merry
All the Hills and Vales Along.
Sorley.
At a Country Fair. Holmes.
Ballade of the Primitive Jest.
Lang.
But Give Me Holly, Bold and
Jolly. Rossetti.
Caelica, XXXV. Greville.
The Canterbury Tales: The
Merchant's Tale. Chaucer.
Christmas Carol.
Anonymous.
A Christmas Carroll.
Wither.
Christmas Island. Bates.
Christmas Trees. Frost.
De Coenatione Micae.
Martial (Marcus Valerius
Martialis).
The Grasshopper. Lovelace.
Hay, Ay, Hay, Ay.
Anonymous.
I Gave Her Cakes.
Anonymous.
I'm Seventeen Come Sunday.
Anonymous.
Is It Really Worth the While?
Anonymous.
Lambeth Lyric. Johnson.
Laugh and Be Merry.
Masefield.
A Little Girl. *Anonymous.*
Marking Time. Steele.
Memorial Verses for
Travellers. Fitzherbert.
Our Joyful Feast. Wither.
The Quiet Life. Byrd.
Robin Hood and the Beggar.
Anonymous.
Rolling Home. *Anonymous.*
A Song. Hodgson.
Song of the Outlaws. Baillie.
The Sun's Shame. Rossetti.
Three Jolly Fishermen.
Anonymous.
The Way to Arcady.
Bunner.
When You Reach the Hilltop
the Sky Is on Top of You.
Blum.
The Wooden Horse then said.
Mastoraki.

Mess
Beans, Bacon and Gravy.
Anonymous.
Bold Troubleshooters. Veale.
The Creeper. Schmidt.
The Cryptic Streets. Abu-l-
Ala al-Maarri.
Goethe's Death Mask.
Gregg.
The Mess of Love.
Lawrence.
Middle Age. Rankin.
The Monster. Lowbury.
Proud Resignation. Marcus.
Taught to Be Polite. Young.
Timocreon. Simonides (of
Ceos).

Message (s)
Amusing Our Daughters.
Kizer.
Arraignment. Cone.
Before. Goldbarth.
The Cowboy. *Anonymous.*
Desert Bloom. Arnold.
For Gabriel. Firestone.
If You Don't Stay Bitter for
Too Long. Mungoshi.
The Know. Fraser.

The Life of Particles.
Benedikt.
The Message of the Rain.
Russell.
Message to the Bard.
Livingston.
The Messages. Gibson.
The Moon and the Yew Tree.
Plath.
Oak. Child.
On with the Message.
Duewel.
Orange County Plague:
Scenes. Lieberman.
A Preacher's Prayer.
Anonymous.
Prognosis. MacNeice.
Samson Agonistes. Milton.
Sinners, Will You Scorn the
Message? Allen.
Snakes. Wild.
A Song about Major Eatherly.
Wain.
The Waiting Harp. Becquer.

Messenger (S)
A Boy Who Smells Like
Cocoa. Hershon.
Ex Libris. Upson.
Hymn to the Night: II.
"Novalis."
I Told Jesus. Plumpp.
Land of My Heart. Foulke.
The Messenger Song.
Anonymous.
The Peace Message.
Stevenson.
The Second Hymn to the
Night. "Novalis" (George
Friedrich Philipp von
Hardenerg).
Sirocco at Deya. Graves.
A Summer Christmas in
Australia. Sladen.

Messiah
Besieged. Schneour.
God's Language. Fainlight.
In the Ghetto.
Sonnenschein.
The Inn That Missed Its
Chance. Wells.
Our Kind Creator. Howe.
Religious Musings.
Coleridge.

Metal (s)
The Alchemist. Pound.
Brother Malcolm: Waste
Limit. Major.
A Dentist's Window. Baxter.
Free Silver. *Anonymous.*
A Poem Like a Grenade.
Haines.
The Tin Woodsman. Jiles.
Tulip. Wolfe.
V-J Day. Ciardi.
The Whisperer. Bullen.

Metaphor (s)
The Body Politic. Hall.
Coming Down to It (parody).
Glass.
Generation Gap. Wallace.
Hypocrite Auteur.
MacLeish.
Letters & Other Worlds.
Ondaatje.
Myths. Klauck.
Tell Them I'm Struggling to
Sing with Angels. Meltzer.
Very Like a Whale. Nash.

Metaphysics
I Dote Upon Myself.
Whitman.

Whispers of Immortality.
Eliot.

Meteor (ites)
At Camino. Sheehan.
Child with a Cockatoo.
Dobson.
Limerick: "There's a lady in
Washington Heights."
Bishop.

Meter (s)
Lady Jane. Quiller-Couch.
Limerick: "A decrepit old gas
man named Peter."
Anonymous.
The Trip. Jarrett.
The Wide Open Spaces.
Lear.

Metre
Epitaph on Peter Robinson.
Jeffrey.
O You Chorus of Indolent
Reviewers. Tennyson.

Mew (s)
Catch. *Anonymous.*
My Catbird. Venable.
Robin Redbreast.
Anonymous.

Mexico
Dream Record: June 8, 1955.
Ginsberg.
In Mexico. Stein.
The Plains of Mexico; or,
Santa Anna. *Anonymous.*
Santa Anna or The Plains of
Mexico. *Anonymous.*
Santy Anno. *Anonymous.*
The Siege of Chapultepec.
Lytle.
Way Down in Mexico.
Anonymous.

Miaow
Byre. MacCaig.
Sad Memories. Calverley.

Michael
Another Given: The Last Day
of the Year. Dickey.
Lines for Michael in the
Picture. Logan.

Michigan
The Crossing at
Fredericksburg. Boker.
For My Son. Nims.

Microscope
Counting Sheep. Edson.
Stopping by Shadows.
Fulton.

Midas
Cleobulus' Epitaph.
Simonides (of Ceos).
The Ungrateful Garden.
Kizer.

Midday
And It Came to Pass at
Midnight. Yannai.
Mad Dogs and Englishmen.
Coward.

Middle
Case. Janowitz.
The Definition of Beauty.
Herrick.
Ezek'l Saw de Wheel
(excerpt). *Anonymous.*
From the Notebooks.
Roethke.
Just California. McGroarty.
My Father Was a Frenchman.
Anonymous.
Rock, Ball, Fiddle.
Anonymous.
Sally Simpkin's Lament.
Hood.
Time and Eternity. Bunyan.

To Chloe. Hooton.

Middle-age
Milne's Bar. MacCaig.
Ode. Lehman.
On Hearing That the Students
of Our New University
Have Joined... Yeats.
The Patricians. Dunn.
The Tea Shop. Pound.

Middle Ages
Ode. Lehman.

Midnight
The Age of the Butcher.
Friebert.
And It Came to Pass at
Midnight. Yannai.
Apology for Apostasy?
Knight.
The Canterbury Tales: The
Mill at Trumpington.
Chaucer.
The Confessor. Belli.
A Constant Labor.
Thompson.
Dream of a Decent Death.
Borgese.
Dublin: The Old Squares.
Colum.
Earl Mertoun's Song.
Browning.
Elegy on Captain Matthew
Henderson. Burns.
An Excellent Memory.
Curnow.
A Fairy Song. Lyly.
Flowers. *Anonymous.*
The Four Ages of Man.
Yeats.
The Grief of Our Genitals.
Carlile.
The House of Night.
Freneau.
Hurdy-Gurdy Man in Winter.
Watkins.
I Am a Victim of Telephone.
Ginsberg.
If You Should Lightly.
Stickney.
Keep Me As Your Servant, O
Girdhar. Mira Bai [(or
Mirabai)].
The Lion. Turner.
Mountain Convent. Benet.
Night Musick for Therese.
Rainer.
Nocturne. Church.
Nursery Rhymes for the
Tender-Hearted. Morley.
Pastoral Dialogue Castara and
Parthenia. Flatman.
Poem: "I walk at dawn across
the hollow hills." Todd.
Poems, IV. O'Connor.
Portrait. Fox.
Pressure. Waldman.
Pygmalion. Miller.
Seraphion. Baxter.
Skimbleshanks: the Railway
Cat. Eliot.
Sleeper Rise. *Anonymous.*
The Souls of Women at
Night. Stevens.
Spectrum. Evans.
Tales of a Wayside Inn.
Longfellow.
Thoughts in the Gulf Stream.
Morley.
To L.B.S. Scott.
Train Tune. Bogan.
Two Handfuls of Waka for
Thelonious Sphere Monk
(d. Feb. 1982). Lew.

The Urban Experience.
Blockcolski.
When night is almost done.
Dickinson.

Midsummer
Four Years. Craik.
Reports of Midsummer Girls.
Lattimore.

Midwife
The Mirror in Which Two
Are Seen as One. Rich.

Might (y)
America. Smith.
Are Ye Right There, Michael?
French.
Behold the Meads. Poitiers.
Behold the Sea. Kurtz.
Can I Believe. Ariosto.
The Chosen Three, on
Mountain Height. Ela.
Creation. Bhushan.
The Cumberbunce. West.
Do Not Die. Merwin.
Drinking Song: "Drink that
rotgut, drink that rotgut".
Anonymous.
The Eagle's Nature.
Anonymous.
The Eternity of Nature.
Clare.
The Eve of Bunker Hill.
Scollard.
An Excelente Balade of
Charitie. Chatterton.
The Faerie Queene. Spenser.
Festus: Proem to the Third
Edition. Bailey.
The Fox at the Point of
Death. Gay.
Gascoigne's Good Morrow.
Gascoigne.
Land of Hope and Glory.
Benson.
Lines with a Gift of Herbs.
Lewis.
A Little Bird I Am. Guyon.
Little Things. Fletcher.
Might Is Right. Zangwill.
My Inmost Hope. Sullam.
Nearly Everybody Loves
Harvey Martin. Barney.
Night Blessing. *Anonymous.*
The Ocean. Shea.
Paul Veronese. Ferguson.
Psalm XIX. Sidney.
Rekayi Tangwena. Kadhani.
Satires. Wyatt.
Snatches: "Wit hat wonder
and kind ne can."
Anonymous.
Songe betwene the Quenes
Majestie and Englande.
Anonymous.
Sonnet: He Speaks of a Third
Love of His. Cavalcanti.
St. Andrew's Voyage to
Mermedonia. *Anonymous.*
Submarine Mountains. Rice.
This Do in Remembrance of
Me. Bonar.
To Poesy. Tennyson.
Too Late. Perry.
Translation of Horace, Odes,
IV, VII. Horace.
The Vision of Piers Plowman.
Langland.
The Voice of Webster
(excerpt). Johnson.
Wasn't That a Mighty Storm?
Anonymous.
Withstanders. Barnes.
The Year 1812. Mickiewicz.

Mightier
The Pen-Guin. The Sword-
Fish. Wood.
The Story of a Stowaway.
Scott.

Mignonette
Red Geranium and Godly
Mignonette. Lawrence.

Migration
February Margins.
Henderson.
Yachts on the Nile. Spencer.

Mild
Epitaph. Chiabrera.
The Faerie Queene. Spenser.
The Golfer's Rubaiyat
(parody). Boynton.
Noon Quatrains. Cotton.
The Sonnet. Symonds.
To Mr. H. Lawes on His Airs.
Milton.
With a Coin from Syracuse.
Gogarty.

Mile (s)
Abroad Thoughts. Blishen.
Ballad of Springhill. Seeger.
Peggy
Camping Out on Rainy
Mountain. Barnes.
Clifton Chapel. Newbolt.
Cycling to Dublin. Greacen.
Doll's Boy's Asleep.
Cummings.
England. Salter.
A Field Poem. Valaitis.
The Fox. *Anonymous.*
Hitch Haiku. Snyder.
Hunting Song. Burns.
In Death Divided. Hardy.
James Grant. *Anonymous.*
A Jewish Cemetery Near
Leningrad. Brodsky.
Living in the Moment.
Hacker.
Marriage Morning.
Tennyson.
My Own Heart Let Me More
Have Pity On. Hopkins.
Poem for My Father's Ghost.
Oliver.
Stopping by Woods on a
Snowy Evening. Frost.
The Telescope. Hall.
Ten Thousand Miles Away
(with music). *Anonymous.*
Thought for a New Year.
Burket.
Useful Dates. *Anonymous.*
Wag a Leg, Wag a Leg.
Anonymous.
Whoso Draws Nigh to God.
Anonymous.
Wild West. Vinz.
Winter Saint. Ammons.
The Woyi. Blockcolski.

Milk (ing)
The Agricultural Show,
Flemington, Victoria.
Maurice.
An Almanack for the Year of
Our Lord, 1657.
Bradstreet.
The Animals. Simic.
Birthday. Yevtushenko.
A Circus Garland. Field.
Colly, My Cow. *Anonymous.*
Confession in Holy Week.
Morley.
The Cow. Nash.
The Cow. Roethke.
The Cow in Apple Time.
Frost.

The Flowing Summer.
Bruce.
Gift Hour. Banus.
The Good Moolly Cow.
Follen.
Housing Starts. Davison.
How Came She to Such
Poppy-Breath? Volborth.
The Innocent Country-Maid's
Delight. *Anonymous.*
Issues of the Fall. Lea.
Javier. Teran.
Lesotho. Khaketla.
Long Summer (excerpt).
Lowell.
Lost in Translation. Merrill.
Mad Marjory. McCrae.
Mannerly Margery Milk and
Ale. Skelton.
Mexico City Blues. Kerouac.
Milk. Schuyler.
Milkcow's Calf Blues.
Johnson.
The Milkman. Krows.
The Milkman. O'Sullivan.
The Mother and Child.
Watkins.
Not Wanting Myself. Gregg.
The Old Testament (excerpt).
Anonymous.
On Death. Killigrew.
On the Death of a New Born
Child. Mei Yao Ch'en.
Once Upon a Great Holiday.
Wilkinson.
An Otter. Hughes.
Pastourelle. *Anonymous.*
The Servant of Rosemary
Lane. *Anonymous.*
Song of the Milkmaid.
Tennyson.
Sonnet: To the Asshole.
Rimbaud.
Spilt Milk. Yeats.
The Strangers. Brown.
Tennyson at Tea. Pain.
This Cold Nothing Else.
Wier.
To a Dictatorial Sultan.
Anonymous.
To a Sacred Cow.
Anonymous.
To Milk in the Valley Below.
Anonymous.
To the Infant Martyrs.
Crashaw.
The Wake at the Well.
Anonymous.
White Cat. Knister.
Wordsworth at Tea. Pain.

Milkmaid (s)
Anglosaxon Street. Birney.
The Crow Sat on the Willow.
Clare.
Dabbling in the Dew.
Anonymous.
The Milkmaid. *Anonymous.*

Milkman
The Milkman. Krows.

Milkweed
A Storm in April. Wilbur.

Milky Way
For the New Year.
Nicholson.
I Am a Cowboy in the Boat
of Ra. Reed.
In a China Shop. Hellman.
Palm Trees. Warner.
Poetry and Philosophy.
Randolph.
The Urumbula Song.
Anonymous.

Mill (s)
Ah! Leave My Harp and Me Alone. *Anonymous.*
Anastasia McLaughlin. Paulin.
Aunt Rhody. *Anonymous.*
The Brain, Within It's Groove. Dickinson.
Don Quixote. Dobson.
Down by the Old Mill Stream. Read.
Edward Millington. Church.
Grinding. *Anonymous.*
Harvest Song. Dehmel.
The Lass o' Patie's Mill. Ramsay.
Mad Sweeny. Montague.
The Miller. Cunningham.
Omie Wise. *Anonymous.*
Pining for Love. Beaumont.
Sandy. *Anonymous.*
T. S. Eliot. Auden.
Twilights. Wright.
The Upper Skies Are Palest Blue. Bridges.
The Weaver and the Factory Maid. *Anonymous.*
When the Clouds Are upon the Hills. *Anonymous.*
When the Wind Blows. *Anonymous.*
Whither? Muller.

Miller (s)
The Butterfly and the Caterpillar. Lauren.
Farewell. Clare.
The Farmer. Fullerton.
The Miller of Dee. *Anonymous.*
O Merry May the Maid Be. Clerk.
The Pike. Blunden.
Silly. *Anonymous.*
To the Puss Moth. *Anonymous.*
The Two Sisters. *Anonymous.*

Milliner
Taking the Census. Thatcher.

Million (s)
Glory to the Name of Jesus! Simpson.
Harpers Ferry. Rodman.
I Could Not Sleep for Thinking of the Sky. Masefield.
Let Us Smile. Nesbit.
Martial in London. Collins.
A Memory of Earth. Russell.
Mordent for a Melody. Avison.
The Obscured Prince; or, the Black Box Boxed. *Anonymous.*
Rocks. Heide.
Telegram. Wise.
Things That Endure. Olson.

Millionaire
The Little Johnny Mine. Detrick.
A Song of Riches. Bates.
The Story of Ug. Robinson.

Milton
Child's Natural History. Herford.
Faith and Freedom. Wordsworth.
Ill Met by Zenith. Nash.

Limerick: "There was a young lady of Milton." *Anonymous.*
A Willing Suspension. Holmes.

Milwaukee
Bigerlow (with music). *Anonymous.*
The Bigler. *Anonymous.*

Mind (s)
An Acre of Grass. Yeats.
Actual Vision of Morning's Extrusion. Dugan.
Alcestis. Euripides.
All This World's Riches. Spenser.
America Was Schoolmasters. Coffin.
Amores. Ovid (Publius Ovidius Naso).
Amoretti, XV. Spenser.
Appalachian Convalescence. Conquest.
Appeal for Illumination. Pulci.
Ark Astonished. Macpherson.
Artichoke. Taylor.
Astrophel and Stella, CI. Sidney.
At Luca Signorelli's Resurrection of the Body. Graham.
The Atlas. Slessor.
Attica Is. Brisby.
Aunt Gladys's Home Movie No. 31, Albert's Funeral. Miller.
The Bastard. Savage.
Behind the Glass Wall. Norse.
Belief and Unbelief. Freneau.
The Better Bargain. Congreve.
Between the Sunken Sun and the New Moon. Hayne.
The Biglow Papers. Lowell.
Birds and Fishes. Jeffers.
The Birdsville Track. Stewart.
Black Silk. Gallagher.
The Black Tail Range. *Anonymous.*
The Blossom. Donne.
The Blue Swallows. Nemerov.
Bothwell Bridge. *Anonymous.*
Building in Stone. Warner.
Caelica, XCVI. Greville.
The Children's Letters. Livesay.
Children When They're Very Sweet. Ciardi.
Choose Something Like a Star. Frost.
Christmas Shopping. MacNeice.
Clancy. Wagoner.
The Climate of Paradise. Simpson.
The Closed World. Levertov.
Come Ride and Ride to the Garden. Gregory Lady.
Commination. Landor.
The Complaint of Chaucer to His Empty Purse. Chaucer.
The Confirmers. Ammons.

A Considerable Speck. Frost.
Consolatory! Hankin.
Consummation. Traherne.
Contentment. Holmes.
Crow Country. Slessor.
Death. Hood.
Deer. Drinkwater.
Deer at the Roadside. Smith.
Denial. Herbert.
Don't Want No Hungry Woman. Council.
Dreams in Progress. Oyama.
Dupree. *Anonymous.*
Eagles and Isles. Gibson.
Early Influences. Akenside.
East St. Louis Blues. *Anonymous.*
The Elements. Williams.
An English Padlock. Prior.
Enraptured I Gaze. Hopkinson.
Envoy (To King Henry IV). Chaucer.
Epigrams. Martial (Marcus Valerius Martialis).
An Epitaph upon the Right Honorable Sir Philip Sidney. Greville.
Eureka. Maunders.
The Excursion. Wordsworth.
The Factory Hands. Chimedza.
Fairy Tale. Nims.
The First Meeting. Herbert of Cherbury.
The First Olympionique to Hiero of Syracuse. Pindar.
Fishermen, Drowned beyond the West Coast. Smith.
The Fishers. Pitter.
The Flesh and the Spirit. Bradstreet.
For An Allegorical Dance of Women by Andrea Mantegna. Rossetti.
For My Son on the Highways of His Mind. Kumin.
Friendship. Wilcox.
Fulfillment. Miller.
George the Fourth in Ireland. Byron.
Ghazal. Dow.
The Glens. Hewitt.
The Goat Paths. Stephens.
Going to Mass Last Sunday. MacDonagh.
Gothic. Untermeyer.
A Green and Pleasant Land. Bishop.
The Green Hunters. Wilson.
Heart and Mind. Sitwell.
Heat. Anacreon.
High Brow. Fitch.
Home, Sweet Home. Bunner.
Hop Up, My Ladies. *Anonymous.*
Hossolalia. Luton.
Hours I Remember Lonely and Lovely to Me. Irwin.
How Samson Bore Away the Gates of Gaza. Lindsay.
The Human Mind. Ai Shih-te.
"If Cynthia be a Queen..." Ralegh.
If It Be True. Johnson.
Imagine the South. Woodcock.
In Wonted Walks. Sidney.

An Invocation. Cory.
Jacob Godbey. Masters.
Kindness. Davis.
Lad of the Curly Locks. *Anonymous.*
Latter Day Psalms. Ashby.
The Leaves Do Not Mind At All. Wynne.
Like Odysseus under the Ram. Archilochus.
The Lilies. Berry.
Limb and Mind. Waller.
Little Miss and Her Parrot. Marchant.
Little Roads to Happiness. Stitch.
The Loadstone of His Love. Wesley.
Love Poem for Lin Fan. Bowering.
Love's Alchemy. Donne.
Love-Songs, At Once Tender and Informative. Hoffenstein.
Love to Faults Is Always Blind. Blake.
Love Wears Roses' Elegance. Bertken.
Loves Heretick. Stanley.
The Man Coming Toward You. Williams.
The Man in the Recreation Room. Harkness.
Mediaeval Appreciations. Gamble.
The Mental Hospital Garden. Williams.
Mexico. Lowell.
Midnight. Roberts.
A Midnight Interior. Sassoon.
The Mill. Wilbur.
Mira's Will. Leapor.
Modern Love, XIV. Meredith.
The Mower to the Glow-worms. Marvell.
My Mother. Burr.
To a Nightingale. Drummond.
The Norsemen. Whittier.
A North Pole Story. Smedley.
Not Wanting Myself. Gregg.
Novella. Rich.
Of Modern Poetry. Stevens.
Old Crabbed Men. Reeves.
On Hearing the First Cuckoo. Church.
On Mrs. W–. Bentley.
On Portents. Graves.
On the Third Day. Spender.
One Way Gal. Moore.
Ornamental Water. Nicholl.
Our Ship She Lies in Harbour. *Anonymous.*
The Overturned Lake. Ford.
The Passing of a Dream. Clare.
The Passing Strange. Masefield.
Paterson. Williams.
The Peace-Offering. Hardy.
The Picture of Her Mind. Jonson.
Pity Me Not. Millay.
Planetarium. Rich.
The Poor Shammes of Berditchev. Ratner.
Prayer during Battle. Hagedorn.

The Praying Mantis Visits a Penthouse. Williams.
Presences Perfected. Sassoon.
A Prisoner's Song of Jerusalem. *Anonymous.*
The Progress of Poesy. Gray.
Psalm XXXII. Wyatt.
Quiet Days. Mey.
The Quiet Mind. *Anonymous.*
Rededication. Litvinoff.
A Remembrance of a Color inside a Forest. Young Bear.
Residence in France: The Prelude. Wordsworth.
Respectabilities. Silkin.
Reverdure. Berry.
Riddles. Kirby.
Riding across John Lee's Finger. Crouch.
Rogue Pearunners. Everson.
The Saints. Creeley.
Samson Agonistes. Milton.
The Sanctuary. Nemerov.
Scroll-Section. Finch.
The Sea. Frankenberg.
The Secret. Stephens.
Sestina d'Inverno. Hecht.
Sgoran Dhu. Shepherd.
The Ships of Yule. Carman.
Similar Cases. Gilman.
Soldier's Song. Campbell.
Solitudes. Wheelock.
Solomon: To Truth. *Anonymous.*
Some People. Field.
Song of the Bowmen of Shu. *Anonymous.*
Songs. Stoddard.
The Sound. Kelly.
Speech for the Repeal of the McCarran Act. Wilbur.
Stars. Hayden.
Summer Days. Daniells.
The Survivors. Slater.
Sweet Stay-at-Home. Davies.
There Let Thy Bleeding Branch Atone. Bronte.
Three Tanka, 2. Yosano Akiko.
To a Lady on Her Marriage. Bell.
To a Lady Sitting before Her Glass. Fenton.
To Fanny. Keats.
To flee from memory. Dickinson.
To Mary: It Is the Evening Hour. Clare.
To My Mother. Ginsberg.
To Ronge. Whittier.
To the Evening. Bampfylde.
To Toussaint L'Ouverture. Wordsworth.
Toledo. Campbell.
The Tour of Dr. Syntax: In Search of the Picturesque. Combe.
Trying to Sleep. Pomeroy.
Twelfth Raga/for John Wieners. Meltzer.
The Twelve Weapons of Spiritual Battle. More.
Two Things. Babcock.
Upon His Leaving His Mistress. Rochester.
The Upper Canadian. Reaney.

The Useful Plow. *Anonymous.*
The Vanity of Human Wishes. Johnson.
The Village. Thomas.
The Wanderer. Hall.
The Water Lily. Wagoner.
We Thank Thee. Oxenham.
The Well Dressed Man with a Beard. Stevens.
Why Do You Want to Suffer Less. Fisher.
Will You, Won't You? Van Doren.
Wind in the Grass. Van Doren.
World I Have Not Made. Jennings.
Worry. *Anonymous.*
Written in a Thunder Storm July 15th 1841. Clare.
The X of the Unknown. Clark.
Yarrow Visited. Wordsworth.
Years Later. Stone.
Yes, I Could Love if I Could Find. *Anonymous.*
You Never Can Tell. Wilcox.

Mine (r) (rs) (s)
78 Miners in Mannington, West Virginia. Phillips.
African Moonrise. Campbell.
After Death. Parnell.
Afternoon on a Hill. Millay.
All the Things You Are. Hammerstein.
Amoretti, XI. Spenser.
The Angel in the House. Patmore.
Aoibhinn, a leabhrain, do thriall. *Anonymous.*
Back. Mezey.
The Blackleg Miners. *Anonymous.*
Borrowed. *Anonymous.*
Childhood. Santos.
Children, It's Time. Brownstein.
Choosing a Name. Ridler.
A Cleric Courts His Lady. *Anonymous.*
Contented at Forty. Cleghorn.
Cradle Song. Duff.
A Curse on Mine-Owners. *Anonymous.*
Dear Men and Women. Wheelock.
A Dedication. Gordon.
Dry Land Blues. Lewis.
The Dying Lover. Stoddard.
Earl Mertoun's Song. Browning.
Erlinton (B version). *Anonymous.*
Every Thing. Monro.
Every Time I Feel the Spirit. *Anonymous.*
The Flaming Heart. Crashaw.
The Flight of the Heart. Goodale.
The Flyting o' Life and Daith. Henderson.
For Ever, Fortune, Wilt Thou Prove. Thomson.
Girl of Constant Sorrow. Gunning.
Grace before Meat. FitzGerald.

The Happy Swain. Philips.
The Hard-Working Miner. *Anonymous.*
Heliodore. Lang.
High Field–First Day of Winter. Eddy.
Highland Region. Price.
Holy Bible, Book Divine. Burton.
I Came to the New World Empty-Handed. Swift.
I Loved a Lass. Wither.
I Wake and Feel the Fell of Dark. Hopkins.
Instruction from Bly. Macdonald.
Jehovah Our Righteousness. Cowper.
Jesus Himself. Burton.
Jewish Ballad. *Anonymous.*
John J. Curtis. Gallager.
Just from Dawson. *Anonymous.*
The Killing. Muir.
The Lady A. L., My Asylum in a Great Extremity. Lovelace.
Lady Alice (George Collins), IV. *Anonymous.*
Let Mine Eyes See Thee. Theresa of Avila.
Leves Amores. Symons.
Life Study. Orlen.
Lilacs. Lowell.
Lines for Michael in the Picture. Logan.
A Living Memory. Croffut.
Lord! It Is Not Life to Live. Toplady.
Love Me, and the World Is Mine. Reed, Jr.
Lullaby in Bethlehem. Bashford.
Marriage Is a Lovely Thing. Pisan.
Mary's Song. Angus.
The Masochist. Kumin.
May I Feel Said He. Cummings.
May the Men Who Are Born. Hitomaro.
Midnight. Lampman.
My Heart Is Heich Above. *Anonymous.*
My Love and I for Kisses Play'd. Strode.
My Policeman. Fyleman.
The National Miner. *Anonymous.*
Night. Montgomery.
Night Song. Mueller.
No Love, to Love of Man and Wife. Eedes.
No Thanks. Cummings.
Nothing Better. *Anonymous.*
The Nun. Hunt.
Of Love. Wyatt.
On a Certain Engagement South of Seoul. Carruth.
On Mr. G. Herbert's Book. Crashaw.
Only a Miner. *Anonymous.*
Our Lips and Ears. *Anonymous.*
Out of This Life. *Anonymous.*
Palabras Grandiosas. Taylor.
Paradise Regained. Milton.
Pardon, Old Fathers. Yeats.
The Pine. Webster.
A Poet of One Mood. Meynell.

Poetics. Ammons.
Polwart on the Green. Ramsay.
Possession. *Anonymous.*
The Prince of Peace His Banner Spreads. Fosdick.
Psalms of Love. Baum.
The Puritan Hacking away at Oak. Gitlin.
Responsibilities: Prologue. Yeats.
The Right to Life. Morris.
Rosa Nascosa. Hewlett.
The Rural Carrier Stops to Kill a Nine-Foot Cottonmouth. Hummer.
The Sad Child's Song. Van Doren.
Sailing from the United States. Moss.
Saviour, Who Died for Me. Mason.
A Shadow Boat. Bates.
She lay wrapped... Fox.
The Sisters. Whittier.
Six Jolly Wee Miners. *Anonymous.*
Sleep. Doty.
Song: "At setting day and rising morn." Ramsay.
A Song: In the Name of a Lover, to His Mistress... Wycherley.
Sonnets, XXXVI: "Let me confess that we two must be twain." Shakespeare.
The Story of the Rose. "Alice".
The Strong Bond. Ibarbourou.
T.V. (1). Hollo.
Tell Me Not Here, It Needs Not Saying. Housman.
That Time That Mirth Did Steer My Ship. Wyatt.
Things. Simpson.
This Morning. Stallworthy.
Thisbe. Cone.
Those Wedding Bells Shall Not Ring Out. Rosenfield.
The Thraldome. Cowley.
The Three Sisters. Ficke.
Time's Fool. Pitter.
To a Lady To Answer Directly with Yea or Nay. Wyatt.
To an Infant Daughter. Clare.
To Her Againe, She Burning in a Feaver. Carew.
To Morfydd. Johnson.
To My Love. Suckling.
Together. Kumin.
The Trestle Bridge. Wright.
When First Mine Eyes Did View and Mark. Wyatt.
When Israel. Scott.

Mineral (s)
December Fragments. Lattimore.
Irish Poetry. Longley.
Naseby: Late Autumn. Dowling.
Two Armies. Spender.

Minerva
A Celebration of Charis. Jonson.
One Presenting a Rare Book to Madame Hull Senr: His Vallintine. Saffin.

Mingle (s)
The Anti-Symbolist. Keyes.

The Battle of Aughrim:
Rapparees.　Murphy.
The Common Road.
Perkins.
The Disordering.　Yates.
Immortality.　Dana.
In Memoriam A.H.H., XVI.
Tennyson.
The Life of the Blessed.
Leon.
A Night-Piece on Death.
Parnell.
O Saviour of a World
Undone.　Withington.
Only Thy Dust...　Marquis.

Mining (s)
Casey Jones.　*Anonymous.*
Mine.　Hudgins.

Minister
Macbeth.　Shakespeare.
Wanted, a Minister's Wife.
Anonymous.

Minister (s)
Love's Baubles.　Rossetti.
A Tryst in Brobdingnag.
Rich.
The Twelve Properties or
Conditions of a Lover.
More.

Mink
Poem for Mother's Day.
Fishback.
To the Lady Portrayed by
Margaret Dumont.
Hollander.
We Need the Tonic of
Wildness.　Thoreau.

Minor
Critic and Poet.　Murray.
In the Zoo.　Mahaka.
When (parody).　Appleman.

Minor fame
An Afterword: For Gwen
Brooks.　Lee.

Minstrel (s)
A Church Romance.　Hardy.
Fairy Song.　Praed.
The Gully.　Maurice.
Heritage.　Bennett.
Hope's Song.　Carlin.
Hymn to Selene.
Anonymous.
Music of the Night.　Neal.
Nepenthe.　Darley.
Now That the Winter's Gone.
Carew.
The Phoenix.　Darley.
Poetry.　Foote.
Ring Out, Wild Bells.
Tennyson.

Mint
After.　Reese.
Equinox.　Young.
Have You Seen the Lady?
Sousa.
Traveling through Ports That
Begin with "M".　Sanford.

Minuet (s)
The Anniad.　Brooks.
The Minuet.　Dodge.
Miss Nancy's Gown.　Cocke.
Picture People.　Bennett.

Minute (s)
Acceleration near the Point of
Impact.　Oates.
Alas, My God.　Shepherd.
Birthday Poem from Venice.
Beer.
For the Field.　Chock.
A Lecture Upon the Shadow.
Donne.

Letter to an Imaginary
Friend.　McGrath.
Living.　Levertov.
Love and Life.　Rochester.
The Membrane.
Bersssenbrugge.
Mountains.　Auden.
A Paragraph.　Carruth.
River in Spate.　MacNeice.
Sir Toby Matthews.
Suckling.
A Song to Cloris.　Rochester.
Testament.　Zavatsky.
Three Sunrises from Amtrak.
Dolgorukov.
Time of Waiting.　Dutton.
To Miss Lucy F—, with a
New Watch.　Lyttelton.
To Music.　Seymour.
Twenty-Two Minutes.
Martinez.
We Fooled Ourselves.
Gerez.

Miracle (s)
At Darien Bridge.　Dickey.
Bow Down, Mountain.
Farber.
The Boy and the Lantern
(excerpt).　Ribera
Chevremont.
The Cathedral.　Lowell.
Le Chevalier Malheur.
Verlaine.
Chicago.　Whittier.
Conversing with Paradise.
Nemerov.
A Death in the Streets.
Petaccia.
Epilogue to the Outrider.
Livesay.
For the Time Being.　Auden.
Getting inside the Miracle.
Shaw.
The Higher Calling.
Czamanske.
Hospital Poems: Transfusion.
Moore.
Hymns and Spiritual Songs.
Smart.
In the Deep Museum.
Sexton.
In the House of the Dying.
Cooper.
It May Be So with Us.
Masefield.
Leave the Miracle to Him.
Allan.
"Let us suppose the mind."
Moraff.
Love Child–a Black Aesthetic.
Hoagland.
Mamana Saquina.
Craveirinha.
A Miracle for Breakfast.
Bishop.
Miracles.　Whitman.
O Heavy Step of Slow
Monotony.　Toller.
Passover.　Auslander.
Pawnshop Window.
Grenville.
Softening to Heaven.　Filip.
Springtime in Cookham Dean.
Roberts.
Stone Too Can Pray.　Aiken.
Temple.　Donne.
To cause accord or to agree.
Wyatt.
Twilight Thoughts in Israel.
Ravitch.
La Vita Nuova.　Dante
Alighieri.

We Still Must Follow.
Mayo.

Mirage
The Ancient Sage.
Tennyson.
Caravans.　Peabody.
Desert Warfare.　Longley.
Evening Walk.　Akesson.
Marriage of Two.　Day
Lewis.
The Urn.　Crane.
Venice.　Longfellow.

Miranda
At a Summer Hotel.
Gardner.
A Lady Thinks She Is Thirty.
Nash.
Lament for Lost Lodgings.
McGinley.

Mire
The Ageing Hunter.　Avane.
Ballade to His Mistress.
Villon.
Good Master and Mistress...
Anonymous.
The Hawk in the Rain.
Hughes.
Life.　Hare.
Lord Galloway.　Burns.
The Mufaddaliyat: His Camel.
Alqamah.
The Thrush in February.
Meredith.

Miriam
Goodnight.　Smith.
Lullaby for Miriam.　Beer-
Hofmann.

Mirror (ed) (s)
Always, from My First
Boyhood.　Bishop.
Animal Kingdom.　Clouts.
Another Color.　Stewart.
Autumn.　Scannell.
Black Trumpeter.　Dumas.
Brothers Together in Winter.
Elliott.
Chameleon.　LeClaire.
Cleaning Day.　Kozer.
Departure.　Amis.
Doctor Bill Williams.　Walsh.
Dont Tell Bad Dreams Says
Tita's Mother.　Simon.
During the Eichmann Trial
(excerpt).　Levertov.
A Fable for Critics.　Lowell.
The Fat Man in the Mirror.
Lowell.
The Flame.　Pound.
Flaming Creatures.　Elmslie.
From the Ballad of Evil.
Van Wyk Louw.
A Game of Glass.　Reid.
Gift of a Mirror to a Lady.
Wagoner.
Hymn of the Earth.
Channing, II.
I Dream I'm the Death of
Orpheus.　Rich.
I Go to Whiskey Bars.
Thompson.
I Have Come to the
Conclusion.　Fertig.
Landcrab.　Atwood.
Late Reflections.　Deutsch.
Life and Death.　Perry.
Love in Moonlight.
Bhartrihari.
The Lovers' Death.
Baudelaire.
The Madman.　Urdang.
Master Canterel at Locus
Solus.　Shapiro.

Mirror.　Chimako.
Momma's Not Gods Image...
Mitchell.
My Mother's House (excerpt).
Goldberg.
Near Perigord.　Pound.
Now, before Shaving.
Kramer.
On the Fly-Leaf of Manon
Lescaut.　Learned.
One Year Later.　Torgerson.
Picture of Little Letters.
Koethe.
Prayer to Go to Paradise with
the Asses.　Jammes.
The Puddle.　Phillpotts.
Reconciliation.　Rosenmann-
Taub.
Snow White.　Chute.
Snow White and the Seven
Dwarfs.　Sexton.
Song on the Water.　Beddoes.
Song: "She was lyin face down
in her face."　Knott.
Sonnet: "Sweet secrecy, what
tongue can tell thy worth?"
Drayton.
Sunrise at Sea.　Sargent.
This Is the Non-Existent
Beast.　Corman.
Thoughts after Ruskin.
Mitchell.
Three Poems on Morris
Graves' Paintings.　Logan.
To Christ Our Lord.
Kinnell.
The Tree of Diana.　Pizarnik.
The Waiting-Room.　Fuller.
The White Horse.　Mills.

Mirth
An April Adoration.
Roberts.
Ballstown.　*Anonymous.*
The Baron of Brackley (B
version).　*Anonymous.*
The Battle of Monmouth.
Anonymous.
The Earthly Paradise.
Morris.
The Gods of the Earth
Beneath.　Blunden.
The Lovers Melancholy.
Ford.
Lusty May.　*Anonymous.*
Modern Love, XIX.
Meredith.
Nature's Key-Notes.　Irwin.
Ode.　Gilder.
Old Age.　Tennyson.
Sonnets, VII: "Sweet Thames
I honour thee."　Barnfield.
To the Grasshopper and the
Cricket.　Hunt.
The Twins.　Shapiro.

Mischief
The Ceremonies for
Candlemas Day.　Herrick.
An Historical Poem.
Anonymous.
Jack Frost.　Thaxter.
Love and Jealousy.　Greene.
Modesty.　Hill.
The Parson Grocer.
Anonymous.
Robin Hood and the
Scotchman.　*Anonymous.*
Were My Hart as Some Mens
Are.　Campion.
The Wind in a Frolic.
Howitt.

Miser
Gone! Gone! Forever Gone. Griffin.
Miser. Vinal.
Vignette: 1922. Spingarn.

Miserable
Losers. Holden.
We Are Such Stuff As Dreams... Petronius.

Misery
Apology for Vagrants. Langhorne.
The Bad Old Days. Rexroth.
The Calm. Donne.
Complaint. Williams.
Death Sting Me Blues. Martin.
The Deserted Homestead. Eiseley.
The Dream. Byron.
Errors of Ecstasie. Darley.
The Factory Hands. Chimedza.
Go Far, Come Near. De La Mare.
Go Tell Old Nancy. Anonymous.
Grace Abounding. Ammons.
Homage to the New World. Harper.
I Met by Chance. Heine.
I Sing a Song Reluctantly. Die.
If It Were Real. Ono no Komachi.
If This Be All. Bronte.
It Makes No Difference Abroad. Dickinson.
Lalla Rookh. Moore.
Listen. Patterson.
Love. ""MacDiarmid.
My Lodging It Is on the Cold Ground. D'Avenant.
No Voice of Man. Falconer.
Now the Earth, the Skies, the Air. Anonymous.
O God, How Many Years Ago. Myers.
On a Country Road. Elliott.
On King Richard the Third, Who Lies Buried under Leicester Bridge. Suckling.
A Personality Sketch: Bill. Davis.
De Ponto. Ovid (Publius Ovidius Naso).
A Psalm of the Early Buddhist Sisters. Anonymous.
Purgatory. Yeats.
Redbreast, Early in the Morning. Bronte.
The Reed. Lermontov.
A Rondeau of Remorse. Johnson.
Self-Dependence. Arnold.
The Smile. Blake.
Sonnet V: "White Venus limpid wandering in the sky." Labe.
Sonnets, VII: "Sweet Thames I honour thee." Barnfield.
Sorrow. Trask.
Sound of Breaking. Aiken.
South-Wind. Lathrop.
Suffer, Poor Negro. Diop.
Sweet Rivers of Redeeming Love. Granade.
This My Emissary. Dewdney.
The Thorn. Wordsworth.

To His Retired Friend, an Invitation to Brecknock (excerpt). Vaughan.
To White South Africa. Pieterse.

Misfortune (s)
The Art of Wenching (excerpt). Anonymous.
As I Walked Out. Anonymous.
Astrophel and Stella, XXXVII. Sidney.
Charles Gustavus Anderson (I). Anonymous.
Epigram: "A woman working hard and wisely." Kassia.
Fair Margaret and Sweet William. Anonymous.
Molly Bawn. Anonymous.
Run along, You Little Dogies. Anonymous.
Sonnet: "Bird that discoursest from yon poplar bough." Mangan.
The Stargazer. Anonymous.

Mishap (s)
Old Colony Times. Anonymous.
"To make an end of all this strife." Wyatt.
To Sir Hudson Lowe. Moore.

Miss (ed) (es) (ing)
Admonition to the Muse. Taylor.
Air an' Light. Barnes.
The Album. Day Lewis.
The Angel in the House. Patmore.
At the St. Louis Institute of Music. Wallace.
At the Zoo. De La Mare.
The Broken. Merwin.
But We by a Love, So Much Refined. Donne.
The Cat in the Box. Jonas.
Catullus to Lesbia. Reeves.
A Cradle Song. Yeats.
Diana. Constable.
Don't Fish in My Sea. Rainey.
Dream Songs. Berryman.
From a Marriage Broker's Card, 1776. Anonymous.
A Gentleman of the Old School. Dobson.
The Ghost of a Ghost. Leithauser.
Girl. Purdy.
Hector the Dog. Barnes.
Hen Dying. MacLean.
I Shall Not Weep. Ritchey.
The Last Journey. Leonidas.
The Lost Playmate. Brown.
A Love Affair. Bennett.
Love-Songs, At Once Tender and Informative. Hoffenstein.
The Metaphysical Sectarian. Butler.
The Mikado. Gilbert.
Mimma Bella. Lee-Hamilton.
My Father. Chalfi.
Narcissus, Come Kiss Us! Anonymous.
Nightletter. Wright.
Nude Reclining at Word Processor, in Pastel. Conover.

On a Squirrel Crossing the Road in Autumn, in New England. Eberhart.
Open Roads. Donnell.
Pearl Bryan. Anonymous.
The People, Yes. Sandburg.
The Photograph the Cat Licks. Walter.
Prayer to the Hunting Star, Canopus. Anonymous.
Prayer to Venus. Spenser.
Prevision. Murray.
The Profane. Horace.
Rhyme of Rain. Holmes.
A Roman Thank-You Letter. Martial (Marcus Valerius Martialis).
Sent from the Capital to Her Elder Daughter. Otomo of Sakanone [(or Sakanoe)].
She Employed the Familiar "Tu" Form. Fetherling.
Song: "Love, that looks still on your eyes." Browne.
Sonnet: "I envy not Endymion now no more." Stirling.
The Statue. Fuller.
Street Demonstration. Walker.
The Things I Miss. Higginson.
To Silvia. Wilchilsea.
To the Ladies. Kenseth.
Tuesday. Landau.
A Visit from Abroad. Stephens.
Waiting for the Bus. Enright.
White Dove of the Wild Dark Eyes. Plunkett.
The Wolves. Kinnell.
Yiddish. Herzberg.
Youth and Art. Browning.

Mission
The Little Peach. Field.
Shine Just Where You Are. Anonymous.
To Nowhere. Ignatow.

Mississippi
Bound No'th Blues. Hughes.
John Brown's Body. Benét.
Leda and Her Swan. Broumas.
Like Ghosts of Eagles. Francis.
When the Mississippi Flowed in Indiana. Lindsay.

Missouri
Jesse James. Benét.
Like Ghosts of Eagles. Francis.
Little White Schoolhouse Blues. Lennon.
Shenandoah. Anonymous.

Mist (s)
Answering Li Ying Who Showed Me His Poems about Summer Fishing. Yu Hsuan-chi.
At the Entrance. Stewart.
Autumn. Scannell.
Birthday Gifts. Asquith.
The Crow. Page.
The Dream of Aengus Og. Cox.
Early Fall: The Adirondacks. Wright.
Fall Colors. Mazzaro.
The Fleece. Dyer.
From a Car-Window. Harding.
The Gully. Maurice.

Homes of the Cliff Dwellers. Wood.
I Saw a Ghost. Boilleau.
I Stroll. Redgrove.
In Cold Storm Light. Silko.
It Feels Good as It Is Without the Giant. Stevens.
The Kingfisher. Marvell.
The Knot. Rich.
Lion Gate. Rich.
The Lost Heifer. Clarke.
Mahony's Mountain. Stewart.
Mist. Young.
The Mist and All. Willson.
November Eves. Flecker.
River Roads. Sandburg.
The Round Barrow. Young.
Seeking a Mooring. Wang Wei.
Ship's Bell. Dresbach.
Skipping along Alone. Welles.
St. Swithin's Chair. Scott.
Sweet William's Ghost. Anonymous.
Telegram. Lourie.
There Was a Roaring in the Wind All Night. Wordsworth.
Walden. Thoreau.
Wales. Nicholson.
The Witch. Gibson.
Words for Music Perhaps. Yeats.

Mist (s) (y)
The Far Side of Introspection. Lee.
Homage to Arthur Waley. Kees.
The Mists Are Rising Now. Cooperman.
Old Ships. Morton.
Pick-A-Back. Anonymous.
Possession. Aldington.
The Ships of Arcady. Ledwidge.
Starting at Dawn. Sun Yun-feng.
Thomas and Charlie. Wild.
The thought beneath so slight a film. Dickinson.

Mistake (n) (s)
Broad Gold. Akhmatova.
A Comparison. Anonymous.
The Compliment. Habington.
Counting Sheep. Fisher.
A Country Club Romance. Walcott.
The Cuckoo (B vers.). Anonymous.
The Haunch of Venison, A Poetical Epistle to Lord Clare. Goldsmith.
He Maketh No Mistake. Overton.
How Many Miles to Barley-Bridge? Anonymous.
In Winter. Ryan.
The Lover. Duncan.
Luck. Epstein.
Mistakes. Wilcox.
The New Formalists. Bell.
Vaudracour and Julia (excerpt). Wordsworth.
The Younger Van Eyck. Bentley.

Mistletoe
Four Stories. Shapiro.
Mistletoe Sprites. Russell.

A Singular Metamorphosis.
  Nemerov.

Mistress (es)
  Against Constancy.
    Rochester.
  Aunt Helen. Eliot.
  Barney O'Hea. Lover.
  Cavalier. Bruce.
  Circe. MacNeice.
  The Dream. Sherburne.
  Entwined. *Anonymous.*
  Familiarity Breeds
    Indifference. Martial
    (Marcus Valerius Martialis).
  Gascoigne's Praise of His
    Mistress. Gascoigne.
  The Glove. Jonson.
  The Last Trial. *Anonymous.*
  On a Romantic Lady.
    Monck.
  Platonic Love. Cowley.
  The Redshanks. Bell.
  .Room for a Jovial Tinker:
    Old Brass to Mend.
    Anonymous.
  Safety at Forty; or, An
    Abecedarian Takes a Walk.
    Sissman.
  Scenes from Carnac. Arnold.
  The Sheffield Apprentice.
    Anonymous.
  Song: "Would you know
    what's soft?" Carew.
  Sonnet: "The point where
    beauty and intelligence
    meet." Ewart.
  A Spark of Laurel. Kunitz.
  To Fanny. Moore.
  To Labienus. Martial
    (Marcus Valerius Martialis).
  Upon His Leaving His
    Mistress. Rochester.
  A Wealthy Man. Allingham.
  Who Threw the Overalls in
    Mistress Murphy's
    Chowder. Geifer.
  Yes, I Could Love if I Could
    Find. *Anonymous.*
  You Blessed Bowers.
    Anonymous.

Mistrust
  King Henry VI.
    Shakespeare.
  "Too dearly had I bought my
    green and youthful years."
    Surrey.

Misunderstood
  Joe Brainard's Painting
    "Bingo". Padgett.
  To a Young Poet Who Fled.
    Logan.

Mitre
  Doctor Major. Johnson.
  Virgil's Farewell to Dante.
    Binyon.

Mittens
  Presents. Chute.
  Winter. Jaszi.
  The Wood-Cutter's Night
    Song. Clare.

Mix
  Burns at Tea. Pain.
  The Gate's Open. Blight.
  In Memoriam A.H.H., CII.
    Tennyson.
  Laura Cashdollars. Mayer.
  Vain and Careless. Graves.

Moan (ing) (s)
  At most mischief. Wyatt.
  Balder's Wife. Cary.
  The Bells. Poe
  Color. Hughes.

The Dead Quire. Hardy.
An Elegy, or Friend's Passion,
  for His Astrophel (excerpt).
  Anonymous.
Friendless Blues. Gilbert.
Lamentations. Gluck.
Long Distance Moan.
  Jefferson.
My Body in the Walls
  Captived. Ralegh.
The Old Liberals. Betjeman.
On Another's Sorrow. Blake.
Pigeons. Meyers.
Popular Songs of Tuscany.
  Anonymous.
Quarries in Syracuse.
  Goldberg.
Rapist. Teran.
A Savage. O'Reilly.
Sonnet: Of the Grave of
  Selvaggia, on the Monte
  della Sambuca. Cino da
  Pistoia.
Sonnets, LXXI: "No longer
  mourn for me when I am
  dead." Shakespeare.
Soon at Last My Sighs and
  Moans. Ginsberg.
The Strong. Cheney.
The Three Fishers. Kingsley.
Voice in Darkness. Dehmel.

Mob
  A Fable for Critics. Lowell.
  On the Late Metamorphosis
    of an Old Picture....
    Anonymous.

Mobile Bay
  Through Fire in Mobile Bay.
    Anonymous.

Moby Dick
  The Whale and the Essex.
    Sullivan.

Moccasins
  Footwear. Justus.
  If I Were a Pilgrim Child.
    Bennett.
  Navajo Song. Dixon.
  Returned to Say. Stafford.
  Sunflower Moccasins.
    George.
  You, Doctor Martin. Sexton.

Mock (ed) (ing) (s)
  Albi, Ne Doreas. Horace.
  Alone. Laurence.
  The Angel in the House.
    Patmore.
  As If a Phantom Caress'd Me.
    Whitman.
  Bahnhofstrasse. Joyce.
  Blackberry Winter. Huggins.
  Children's Song. Thomas.
  Counting Kisses. Catullus.
  Elegies. Chenier.
  The Family Cat. Fuller.
  Great Is My Envy of You.
    Petrarch (Francesco
    Petrarca).
  The Heart Has Its Reasons.
    Anonymous.
  How Sweet I Roam'd.
    Blake.
  I Do Not Look for Love That
    Is a Dream. Rossetti.
  Limerick: "There was a young
    waitress named Myrtle."
    Herford.
  The Lover, Having Dreamed
    of Enjoying His Love....
    Wyatt.
  A Lover's Plea. Campion.
  Memorial Thresholds.
    Rossetti.

Mima. De la Mare.
Mothers and Daughters.
  Campbell.
The Negro Soldiers.
  Jamison.
No Longer Mourn for Me.
  Shakespeare.
Ode to Jamestown.
  Paulding.
On the Death of His Son
  Vincent. Hunt.
Out of Catullus. Crashaw.
Plowmen. Frost.
Praetorium Scene: Good
  Friday. Lennen.
Rimbaud in Africa.
  Rickword.
The Sea. Lawrence.
Song: "Down the dimpled
  green-sward dancing."
  Darley.
Song of the Turtle and
  Flamingo. Fields.
Sonnets, LXXI: "No longer
  mourn for me when I am
  dead." Shakespeare.
To wet your eye withouten
  tear. Wyatt.
The Torch-Bearers: America.
  Bates.
Vern. Brooks.
Wednesday in Holy Week.
  Rossetti.
Whan the Hert Is Laich.
  Smith.
Wire Monkey. Shiplett.
The Witch. Douglas.

Mocking bird
  Going through. Woodford.
  Listen to the Mocking Bird.
    Hawthorne.

Mock turtle
  Limerick: "There was a young
    waitress named Myrtle."
    Herford.
  Song of the Turtle and
    Flamingo. Fields.

Model (s)
  Aurora Leigh. Browning.
  The Glass Blower. Scully.
  Hold My Hand. Pennant.
  The Love Suicides at Sonezaki
    (excerpt). Monzaemon.
  Mantle. Heyen.
  On William Graham, Esq., of
    Mossknowe. Burns.
  The Pirates of Penzance.
    Gilbert.

Modern
  Always Modern Times.
    Stark.
  Corn. Lanier.
  Don Juan. Byron.
  Hearth and Home. King.
  In Apia Bay. Roberts.
  Lass with a Lump of Land.
    Ramsay.
  A New Simile in the Manner
    of Swift. Goldsmith.
  No More Love Poems #1.
    Shange.
  Other Fabrics, Other Mores!
    Lenngren.

Modest (ies) (y)
  Our little kinsmen.
    Dickinson.
  The Paps of Dana. Stephens.
  Resolution in Four Sonnets.
    Cotton.

Moisture
  A Candle. Suckling.

Don Leon (excerpt).
  Anonymous.
Minnows. Keats.
Princess Sabbath. Heine.

Molasses
  Ain' No Mo' Cane on de
    Brazis. *Anonymous.*
  Bluebird, Bluebird, Fly
    Through My Window.
    Anonymous.
  Little Bird, Go through My
    Window. *Anonymous.*
  The People, Yes. Sandburg.

Mold (s)
  Calling in the Cat.
    Coatsworth.
  The House of Life. Rossetti.
  King Lear. Shakespeare.
  Limerick: "These places
    abound in the old."
    Libaire.
  RIP. Balderston.
  Today. Walker.

Mole
  Absence. Sidney.
  The Battle of Aughrim:
    Rapparees. Murphy.
  How. Sutzkever.
  I Wish I Was a Mole in the
    Ground. *Anonymous.*
  The Plodder Seam.
    Anonymous.
  Shooter's Hill. Bloomfield.
  The Unfortunate Mole.
    Kennedy.
  World, Defined. Weismiller.

Mole (s)
  Maggie's Star. Turner.
  Those of Pure Origin.
    Fuller.

Molecule (s)
  Energy. Fitzgerald.
  The Fisherman. Harrison.
  The Potomac. Shapiro.

Molest
  Epitaph on Dr. Keene's Wife.
    Gray.
  Funeral Elegy on the Death of
    His Very Good Friend Mr.
    Michael Drayton.
    Cokayne.

Molly
  Captain Molly. Collins.
  Handsome Molly.
    Anonymous.
  Mulberry Mountain.
    Anonymous.
  My Last Illusion. Kendall.
  Shooting of His Dear.
    Anonymous.

Molten
  Dreams Old and Nascent.
    Lawrence.
  Hippolytus Temporizes.
    Doolittle.
  The Spell. Roberts.
  Women Transport Corps.
    Anonymous.

Moment (s)
  Aberdeen Train. Morgan.
  Alas, My God. Shepherd.
  All the Things You Are.
    Hammerstein.
  Apparition. Erskine.
  The Banks of Sweet
    Primroses. *Anonymous.*
  The Beautiful Changes.
    Wilbur.
  Breakthrough. Rodgers.
  Closing Prayer. Patrick.
  Danebury. *Anonymous.*

Dawn Amid Scotch Firs.
Sharp.
The Discovery. MacEwen.
Dust. Brooke.
The Ferry. Boker.
The First Olympionique to
Hiero of Syracuse. Pindar.
Five Carols for Christmastide.
Guiney.
The Garden. Strand.
Giving Up on the Shore.
Preil.
The Glass Town. Reid.
Glimmers. Marshall.
Green Apples. Stone.
Homage to Elvis, Homage to
the Fathers. Weigl.
Horas Tempestatis Quoque
Enumero: The Sundial.
Hollander.
I Had to Be Secret. Van
Doren.
The Iliad. Homer.
Indian Woman's Death-Song.
Hemans.
Invisible Landscape. Wright.
Living with Others. Zolynas.
Love. Granville [(or
Grenville(].
Love's Will. Warsh.
The Marriage of Heaven and
Earth. Nemerov.
Meeting Mick Jagger
(parody). Peters.
Mirabell, Book 9 (excerpt).
Merrill.
Monoagram 23. Werner.
Montefiore. Bierce.
My Heart Stood Still. Hart.
O Love, That Dost with
Goodness Crown.
Chadwick.
Ode to a Homemade Coffee
Cup. Warden.
On Such a Day. Coleridge.
An Orchard at Avignon.
Robinson.
The Poem Becomes Canadian.
Di Cicco.
Prologue. Eichenrand.
Sleeping on Horseback. Po
Chu-i.
Snowflakes. Nemerov.
Some Day or Days. Perry.
Some Uses for Poetry.
Merriam.
Stay, Time. Watson.
Step by Step. Ryberg.
Students. Wilkinson.
Suspended Moment.
Davenport.
Ten Definitions of Poetry.
Sandburg.
The Three-Faced. Graves.
Three Poems for Women, 2.
Griffin.
Thus, When Soft Love
Subdues the Heart.
Scarron.
To a Poet. Arensberg.
To Give One's Life. Davies.
To Lighten My House.
Reid.
To My Father Norman Alone
in the Blue Mountains.
Lindsay.
The Turning. Murray.
Under the Locust Blossoms.
Tuckerman.
Uriel. Stead.
Visions. Petrarch.
White. Bouvard.

Monarch (s)
Astraea Redux. Dryden.
Awake, My Soul!
Doddridge.
The Harp of David.
Yehoash.
King Henry V. Shakespeare.
Lord of All I Survey.
Sinclair.
The Medal. Dryden.
The Miller. Cunningham.
My Queen. Winter.
Ode to Mercy. Collins.
The Parliament Dissolved at
Oxford. Ayloffe.
Ralegh's Prizes. Pinsky.
Rulers: Philadelphia.
Johnson.
A Satire on Charles II.
Rochester.
Vaquero. Miller.
Virgidemiarum. Hall.
Written for My Son...at His
First Putting on Breeches.
Barber.
Monastery
A Prophecy. Levenson.
Unlawful Assembly. Enright.
Monday
As Tommy Snooks and Bessy
Brooks. Mother Goose.
The Bold Dragoon.
Anonymous.
Classic Ballroom Dances.
Simic.
How Many Days Has My
Baby to Play? Mother
Goose.
Iron. De La Mare.
On a Monday Morning.
Tawney.
The Schoolmaster.
Anonymous.
Scyros. Shapiro.
Tommy and Bessy.
Anonymous.
West Helena Blues. Sykes.
Money (s)
The 1913 Massacre. Guthrie.
Adieu My Lovely Nancy.
Anonymous.
An Alexandrine Magazine.
Nemerov.
The Artist. Ralegh.
Ballade of the Fair Helm-
Maker. Villon.
Bankers Are Just Like
Anybody Else, Except
Richer. Nash.
Banking Coal. Toomer.
Barney Bodkin. Anonymous.
Basic. Durem.
Baudelaire. Schwartz.
The Beggar on the Beach.
Gregory.
A Bestiary. Rexroth.
Billy Lyons and Stack O'Lee.
Lewis.
The Boarder. Feirstein.
The Boat Sails Away.
Greenaway.
The Bonny Keel Laddie.
Anonymous.
A Busy Man Speaks. Bly.
Christmas Comes but Once a
Year. Anonymous.
Clap Hands, Clap Hands.
Anonymous.
Coming Around the Horn.
Anonymous.
Contemporary Nursery
Rhyme. Anonymous.

The Cormorant in Its
Element. Clampitt.
The Development. Piercy.
Epistle to the Reader.
Gibson.
God Made the Bees. Mother
Goose.
Gwine to Run All Night; or,
De Camptown Races.
Foster.
The Gypsy Countess.
Anonymous.
Hard To Be A Nigger.
Anonymous.
The Holy Ground.
Anonymous.
Homage to a Government.
Larkin.
Home Is the Sailor.
McGinley.
I've Rambled This Country
Both Earlye and Late.
Anonymous.
January 1st. Sexton.
The Last of the Princes.
Ramanujan.
Letter to an Imaginary
Friend. McGrath.
Levant. Durrell.
The Liberty Song.
Dickinson.
London Lickpenny. Lydgate.
The Lost Ingredient. Sexton.
The Maids of Simcoe.
Anonymous.
The Man from Washington.
Welch.
Melissa. Anonymous.
A Mightier Than Mammon.
Carpenter.
The Modes of the Court.
Gay.
The Moon Rises. Garcia
Lorca.
No Money in Art.
Gustafson.
Oraga Haru. Issa.
Pay Me My Money Down.
Anonymous.
The Perfect Gift. Parker.
Poems from a Greek
Anthology (excerpt).
Martial (Marcus Valerius
Martialis).
Poor Man Blues. Townsend.
The Praises of a Countrie
Life. (Horace, Epode 2).
Jonson.
The Rackets around the Blue
Mountain Lake.
Anonymous.
Recuerdo. Millay.
Reuben, Reuben.
Anonymous.
Sally Brown. Anonymous
The Schooner Fred Dunbar.
Hanson.
The Shoulder. Denby.
Some Twenty Years of
Marital Agreement.
Cunningham.
Song for the Squeeze-Box.
Roethke.
Songs for a Colored Singer.
Bishop.
Spectator Ab Extra. Clough.
Spring. McCarriston.
The Thief. Kunitz.
The Three Travelers.
Anonymous.
Tony O! Francis.

Under Your Voice, among
Legends. Beauvais.
We Be Soldiers Three.
Anonymous.
The Wench in the Street.
Anonymous.
What Kin' O Pants Does the
Gambler Wear (with
music). Anonymous.
What's In It For Me?
Guest.
Wind Song. Sandburg.
Writing for Money. Field.
The Youth and the
Northwind. Saxe.
Monk (s)
Animal Fair. Anonymous.
Epigram. Anonymous.
The Eve of Saint John.
Scott.
King Arthur and His Round
Table: Bees and Monks.
Frere.
The Room above the White
Rose. Stroud.
Starlings. MacCaig.
Monkey (s)
The Common Woman.
Grahn.
Darwinity. Merivale.
The Deserted Kingdom.
Dunsany.
The Dying Hogger (with
music). Anonymous.
Letters to Live Poets.
Beaver.
Limerick: "G is for dear little
Gustave." Bellows.
The Monkeys. Thompson.
Oration on the Toes. Brynes.
Pistol Slapper Blues. Fuller.
Primavera. Lima.
So Many Monkeys. Grider.
Song of Abuse. Anonymous.
Tom Fool at Jamaica.
Moore.
Van Amburgh's Menagerie.
Anonymous.
Monotony
In the Sitting Room of the
Opera. Cannady.
Not Any More to Be Lacked.
Dickinson.
Monroe
Gerry's Rocks. Anonymous.
The Jam at Gerry's Rock.
Anonymous.
The Jam on Gerry's Rock (I).
Anonymous.
The Jam on Jerry's Rock (II).
Anonymous.
Young Monroe at Gerry's
Rock. Anonymous.
Monster (s)
Agreeable Monsters.
Clampitt.
The Approach to Thebes.
Kunitz.
The Battel of the Summer-
Islands. Waller.
Continual Conversation with a
Silent Man. Stevens.
Dying. Pinsky.
Hide and Seek. Graves.
If. Hollo.
Love's Triumph. Jonson.
Metamorphoses. Ovid
(Publius Ovidius Naso).
Mythological Sonnets, VIII:
"Suns in a skein." Fuller.
Nell Flaherty's Drake.
Anonymous.

Old Maps and New.
MacCaig.
The Princess. Tennyson.
Rhinoceros. Stoutenburg.
Storm and Quiet. Eberhart.
Under Creag Mhor. Conn.

Monstrous
On Falling. Greig.
Poem of Pathos. Rozewicz.
Poems. Machado.
The Sea-Deeps. Miller.
When Indians Heare That
Some There Are.
Williams.

Monterey
The Maid of Monterey.
Anonymous.
The Mission Bells of
Monterey. Harte.

Month (s)
Before Breakup on the Chena
outside Fairbanks.
McElroy.
The Descent on Middlesex.
St. John.
February. Whitney.
June. Malloch.
The Lonely Month. Todd.
Medieval Norman Songs.
Anonymous.
The Mill. Taylor.
Retro me, Sathana! Rossetti.
The Statesman. Belloc.
Tell Me What Month Was
My Jesus Born in.
Anonymous.
Untimely Thoughts. Aldrich.
Wisdom. Yerby.

Montreal
A Psalm of Montreal.
Butler.

Monument (al) (s)
Armistice. Dehn.
The Battle of Monmouth.
English.
A Black Patch on Lucasta's
Face. Lovelace.
The Bridge from Brooklyn
(excerpt). Henri.
The Broken Bowl. Merrill.
Constancye. Godolphin.
The Coolin Ridge. Bell.
Echo to a Rock. Herbert of
Cherbury.
Gargoyle. Rabbit.
Indian Names. Sigourney.
Inscription for Marye's
Heights, Fredericksburg.
Melville.
Lincoln. Trowbridge.
Meditations in Time of Civil
War. Yeats.
Needle and Thread. Pan
Chao.
The New Victory.
Widdemer.
The Odyssey. Homer.
Old Mother Hubbard.
Anonymous.
President Lincoln's Grave.
Mason.
The Rock. Eliot.
The School for Objects.
Hoover.
A Serio-Comic Elegy.
Whately.
Sholom Aleichem.
Lieberman.
Song by Mr. Cypress.
Peacock.
Song of Gwythno. Peacock.

Sonnet: The Double Rock.
King.
Sonnets, CVII: "Not mine
own fears, nor the prophetic
soul." Shakespeare.
There's No Place to Sleep in
This Bed, Tanguy. Ford.
To Thee, Dear Henry
Morison. Moryson.
Upon the Death of the Lord
Hastings. Dryden.
Yes, the Agency Can Handle
That. Fearing.

Moo (ing)
The Cow. Nash.
Cows. Reeves.
A March Calf. Hughes.
The Pinwheel's Song. Ciardi.
The Plum Tree. Reaney.
When Did the World Begin.
Clairmont.

Mood (s)
Epistle to John Hamilton
Reynolds. Keats.
The Grammar of Love. Pott
and Wright.
Hours I Remember Lonely
and Lovely to Me. Irwin.
In Early Summer Lodging in
a Temple to Enjoy the
Moonlight. Po Chu-i.
The Ivory Gate: Stanzas.
Beddoes.
Lasagna. Kennedy.
Laurence Bloomfield in
Ireland. Allingham.
Madam and the Minister.
Hughes.
October. Thomas.
The Poet. Bryant.
The Shape of a Bird.
Whistler.
Song's Eternity. Clare.
The Wild Swan. Savage.

Moon (light) (lit) (shine) (s)
Absence. Mangan.
Ajanta. Rukeyser.
Always the Melting Moon
Comes. Osborn.
The Angel in the House.
Patmore.
Apollo 8. Berryman.
April. O'Donnell.
The Assignation.
Ibarbourou.
The Assignation. Wright.
At the Edge of the Bay.
Chubb.
Atom from Atom. Emerson.
Auguries of Innocence.
Blake.
The Auroras of Autumn.
Stevens.
Ballad of Davy Crockett.
Anonymous.
The Ballad of Downal Baun.
Colum.
Ballad of the Spanish Civil
Guard. Garcia Lorca.
Ballad of the Three Coins.
Watkins.
Bat Angels. Levis.
Bean Spasms. Berrigan.
Beauty. Whitman.
Being Born Is Important.
Sandburg.
Birch Trees. Moreland.
Blackwater Mountain.
Wright.
The Blood Supply in New
York City Is Low. Stokes.
Bread. Merwin.

The Bunyip. Stewart.
Business as Usual. Vinz.
By Moonlight. Sarton.
The Cabin North of It All.
McMichael.
A Caravan from China
Comes. Le Gallienne.
Elizabethan Days. Irwin.
The End of a Day in the
Provinces. Laforgue.
Epitaph for a Negro Woman.
Dodson.
Euclid. Lindsay.
Evening. Stephens.
Every Saturday He Stands.
Drake.
Fairy Wings. Howard.
Falling Asleep in a Garden.
Wagoner.
Far Rockaway. Schwartz.
Far Trek. Brady.
Father Coyote. Sterling.
Flight. Cawein.
The Flute of the Lonely.
Lindsay.
For Lerida. St. John.
The Fragments. Dale.
From behind the Bars.
Tuquan.
From Sorrow Sorrow Yet Is
Born. Tennyson.
Frost at Midnight.
Coleridge.
Full Moon. Hayden.
Full Moon. Kinnell.
The Gardens of the Sea.
Sterling.
Gebir. Landor.
Ghazals. Harrison.
Glimpses. Helton.
Glints of the Year–from a
Window. Irwin.
Gloaming. Brown.
Grand Finale. Layton.
Haiku: "Sandy shore: and
why." Shiki.
Harbingers. Basho (Matsuo
Basho).
The Hare. De la Mare.
The Haughty Snail-King.
Lindsay.
He Says He Wrote by
Moonlight. Aal.
The Hero (parody). Woddis.
The Hill Above the Mine.
Cowley.
Hills picking up the
moonlight. Cassian.
Hitchhiker. Marshall.
The Homecoming of the
Sheep. Ledwidge.
Honey Dew Falls from the
Tree. Clare.
Honey Moon. Baker.
Hudson Ferry. Schuyler.
I Am the Beginning.
Shembe.
If You Should Lightly.
Stickney.
In the Evening by the
Moonlight. Bland.
In the Moonlight. Wright.
Into the Wind. Scott.
Invocation from a Lawn
Chair. Irion.
The Irish Franciscan.
Mulholland.
It Was the Lovely Moon.
Freeman.
A Japanese Love-Song.
Noyes.

The Jewel Stairs' Grievance.
Li Po.
John Henry (variant).
Anonymous.
The Jolly Beggar. James I,
July in Indiana. Fitzgerald.
Kentucky Moonshiner.
Anonymous.
Lady Moon. Milnes.
Laguna Perdida. Dixon.
The Lake above Santos.
Wilson.
The Last Tournament.
Tennyson.
Levee Camp "Holler."
Anonymous.
Li Po. Gilbert.
Liberty. Thomas.
The Life of.... Weiss.
Looking into a Face. Bly.
Losing a Slave Girl. Po
Chu-i.
Loss! Loss! McMahon.
Louisiana Girls. *Anonymous.*
Love in Moonlight.
Bhartrihari.
Love's Fool. Rosenthal.
Love-Songs, At Once Tender
and Informative.
Hoffenstein.
Madman's Song. Wylie.
The Man Hunt. Cawein.
Mandoline. Verlaine.
Mariners. Morton.
Marriage. Clarke.
Master Hugues of Saxe-Gotha.
Browning.
Memory of Hills (excerpt).
Ingamells.
The Merry Wives of Windsor.
Shakespeare.
Mexico City: 150 Pesos to the
Dollar. Mitsui.
Middle Ages. Sassoon.
Modern Love, XXXIX.
Meredith.
Moon and Candle-Light.
Renton.
The Moon and the Night and
the Men. Berryman.
The Moon-Bone Cycle: New
Moon. *Anonymous.*
Moon Fishing. Mueller.
Moon of the Earth.
Anonymous.
Moon Poem. Sharp.
Moon. Rowe.
The Moon. Sodergran.
Moon Song. Nweke.
Mooncalf I. Keating.
Moonlight. Nance.
Moonlight Night on the Port.
Keyes.
The Morality of Poetry.
Wright.
The New Moon. Teasdale.
Night Airs. Landor.
Night along the Mackinac
Bridge. Hill.
The Night-Blooming Cereus.
Monroe.
The Night Herder. Clark, Jr.
Night Teeth. Brett.
Nocturn Cabbage. Sandburg.
North. Henson.
The Ocean. St. Martin.
Old Mother Goose and the
Golden Egg. *Anonymous.*
Old Scent of the Plum Tree.
Fujiwara Ietaka.
On Certain Days of the Year.
Simpson.

On Moonlit Heath and Lonesome Bank. Housman.
On My Old Ramkiekie. Leipoldt.
Once Only. Snyder.
Orbiter 5 Shows How Earth Looks from the Moon. Swenson.
The Owl and the Pussy-Cat. Lear.
The Owl. Owen.
The Pale Blue Casket. Pitcher.
Parting. *Anonymous.*
Peg-Leg's Fiddle. Adams.
Personality. Lampman.
Photograph of Haymaker, 1890. Holden.
Plague of Dead Sharks. Dugan.
The Play. Judkins.
Plowing at Full Moon. Dangel.
Plowman. Keyes.
Poem for Carroll Descendant of Chiefs. Henson.
Poem, to Jane Wilson on Television. Broley.
Portrait. Cummings.
Prayer to the Young Moon. *Anonymous.*
The Prediction. Strand.
The Progress of Beauty. Swift.
Proposition. Guillen.
Proud New York. Reed.
Pumpkins. Cotton.
Rapunzel. Sexton.
Reality Is an Activity of the Most August Imagination. Stevens.
Returning at Night. Harrison.
Riding with the Fireworks. Darr.
Rigmarole. Williams.
Ringely, Ringely. Follen.
The Rising of the Moon. *Anonymous.*
The River of Heaven. *Anonymous.*
Roads Go Ever Ever On. Tolkien.
Rocket Show. Baxter.
Roses. Miller.
Ryder. Haines.
Sand Paintings. Corbin.
Santorin. Flecker.
Sapientia Lunae. Dowson.
Saw You My Father. *Anonymous.*
Saw You My True Love John? *Anonymous.*
Scattered Fog. Sanford.
Sea Flower. Dorcey.
Sea-Sonnet. Sackville-West.
Sea Words. Leitch.
Serenade. Britt.
Seven Times the Moon Came. Rittenhouse.
Shame Hitherto. Al Mutanabbi.
The Shape of Autumn. Russ.
The Short Night. Buson (Taniguchi Buso).
Sketches of Harlem. Henderson.
Sleepwalkers. Akhmadulina.
The Snake-Charmer. Naidu.

So This Is Our Revolution. Sanchez.
So, We'll Go No More a Roving. Byron.
Son David. *Anonymous.*
Song–Across the Sea. Allingham.
Song for War. Rodgers.
Song of the Rabbits Outside the Tavern. Coatsworth.
The Song of Wandering Aengus. Yeats.
Sonnet: "A wind has blown the rain away." Cummings.
Sonnets, IV: "Remote from smoky cities, aged and grey." Irwin.
Space Travel. Krows.
The Spinning Wheel. Waller.
Spring. Irwin.
The Spring Waters. "Ping Hsin" (Hsieh Wang-ying).
Stars and Planets. MacCaig.
The Statue. Allott.
The Storm. Cohen.
The Story of Samuel Jackson. Leland.
Strawberry Moon. Oliver.
Sur Ma Guzzla Gracile. Stevens.
Surely You Remember. Ravikovich.
Sweet and Low. Barnby.
The Tale of Genji (excerpt). Murasaki Shibiku.
Tears against the Moon. Walsh.
Templeogue. Salkeld.
That's What We'd Do. Dodge.
This New Day. Read.
Three Moments. Sherman.
To a Solitary Disciple. Williams.
To Butterfly. Percy.
To Jane: The Keen Stars Were Twinkling. Shelley.
To My Friends. Berg.
To the Moon. Darley.
Tongues of Fire. Plescoff.
Tor House. Jeffers.
Track. Transtromer.
Trying to Sleep. Pomeroy.
Two Horses. Harjo.
Two Married. Frazee-Bower.
Two Poems. *Anonymous.*
Two Red Roses Across the Moon. Morris.
Two Songs in Praise of Steingerd, 1. Ogmundarson.
Unless We Guard Them Well. Merchant.
The Ute Lover. Garland.
Vacuum. Miles.
The Vagrant. Slender.
Variations on an Old Nursery Rhyme. Sitwell.
The View from a Cab. Taylor.
Wait Till the Darkness is Deep. Wallada.
Walking at Night. Treece.
Wart Hog. Skelton.
Watching the Moon. McCord.
A Water-Party. Bridges.
Watershed. Warren.
Wavelength. St. John.
Western Town. Cannon, Jr..

What's the News? *Anonymous.*
What She Said. Centamputan.
Whaup o' the Rede: The Blades of Harden. Ogilvie.
The Wheel. Hayden.
When I Die. Johnson.
White in the Moon. housman.
Who Shall Speak for the People? Sandburg.
Wings in the Dark. Gray.
Winter Moon. Hughes.
Winter: The Abandoned Nest. Baxter.
Winterscape. Perlman.
The Witches' Wood. Coleridge.
With Thee Conversing. Milton.
The Wolf. Davidson.
Wolfram's Song. Beddoes.
Yarrow Revisited. Wordsworth.
A Year Passes. Lowell.
Yes, What? Francis.

Moonshade
Alone. *Anonymous.*

Moonsick
Baby. Frank.

Moor (ed) (s)
The Cid's Rising. Hemans.
Coroner's Jury. Strong.
Description of Holland. Butler.
From the Day-Book of a Forgotten Prince. Untermeyer.
.Mary of the Wild Moor. *Anonymous.*
More Than People. Fulton.
Motto for a Dog House. Guiterman.
Prelude. Synge.
Resolution and Independence. Wordsworth.
The Seasons in North Cornwall. Causley.
Sheepstor. Strong.
The Shepherd's Calendar. Clare.
The Song of the Galley. *Anonymous.*
Unknown Love. Otomo of Sakanoe.
When Poor Mary Came Wandering Home (with music). *Anonymous.*
Wild nights–wild nights! Dickinson.

Moorland (s)
The Dreary Change. Scott.
Hills o' My Heart. "Carbery.
The Sun upon the Weirdlaw Hill. Scott.
Swansong on the Moorlands. Thorsteinsson.

Moose
The Moose. Bishop.
Poetry, a Natural Thing. Duncan.

Mop
The Clorox Kid. Robertson.
In the Last Few Moments Came the Old German Cleaning Woman. Cooper.

Moral (s)
America Was Schoolmasters. Coffin.

Chevaliers de la Table Ronde. *Anonymous.*
Childe Harold's Pilgrimage: Canto III. Byron.
Divination by a Cat. Hecht.
A Dream of Judgement. Dunn.
Epilogue to a Human Drama. Spender.
Fables: The Shepherd and the Philosopher. Gay.
Faith and Freedom. Wordsworth.
Federation. Goodge.
It Might Be a Lump of Amber. De la Mare.
A Lay of St. Gengulphus (excerpt). Barham.
LLewellyn and the Tree. Robinson.
The Origin of Didactic Poetry. Lowell.
The Portraits. Lenngren.
Salmon Drowns Eagle. Lowry.
The Singing-Lesson. Ingelow.
Ye Wearie Wayfarer: Sun and Rain and Dew from Heaven. Gordon.

More
America, America! Schwartz.
Beggar's Song. Orr.
Caves. Baker.
Cello Entry. Celan.
The Child at Winter Sunset. Van Doren.
Christus Matthaeum et Discipulos Alloquitur. Sherburne.
Crowds of Men and Women. Whitman.
A Curse against the Owner. Sutter.
The Divine Insect. Wheelock.
End of Another Home Holiday. Lawrence.
The Faithful Shepherdess. Fletcher.
Finis. Newbolt.
Get On Board, Little Children. *Anonymous.*
God's Love. *Anonymous.*
Good Friday Evening. Rossetti.
Hymn. Chadwick.
In a Spring Grove. Allingham.
A Life of T. S. Eliot (parody). Frayn.
Love Unchangeable. Dawes
Marble-Top. White.
My Love When This Is Past. Stephany.
The Name. Creeley.
The New Vestments. Lear.
Poem for Some Black Women. Rodgers.
Prayer. Ellwood.
Prometheus Unbound. Shelley.
Remember Dear Mary. Clare.
Slow Summer Twilight. Wheelock.
Song. Miller.
Song: "Why, lovely charmer, tell me why." Steele.
To a Child with Eyes. Van Doren.

Today: The Idea Market. Nicholas.
View. Van Geel.
A Water Glass of Whisky. Kennedy.
We Need a Whole Lot More of Jesus. *Anonymous.*
Woodnotes. Emerson.
Your Need Is Greater Than Mine. Enslin.

Mormon (s)
The Mormon Bishop's Lament. *Anonymous.*
New Mexico and Arizona. Canterbury.

Morn (ing)
28 VIII 69. Chester.
After the Storm. Vaughan.
Algonkian Burial. Bailey.
Alibazan. Richards.
All Morning. Roethke.
All's Well. Kimball.
And in Her Morning. Powers.
The Apple Tree. Brown.
The Arc Inside and Out. Ammons.
Arthur McBride. *Anonymous.*
Aubade. Laing.
Aube Provencale. Hacker.
Auras on the Interstates. Vizenor.
Ballad of the Tempest. Fields.
The Barn in Winter. MacIntosh.
Blasting from Heaven. Levine.
Blind Louise. Dewet
Bombing Casualties: Spain. Read.
Both My Child. Teitoku.
Bout with Burning. Miller.
Break of Day. Clare.
Burges. *Anonymous.*
The Cage. Treinin.
The Captain's Daughter. Fields.
Carol of the Three Kings. Merwin.
Cato. Sisson.
Child of silence and shadow. Caroutch.
The Choristers. Carman.
The Chorus Speaks Her Words as She Dances. Gregg.
A Christmas Carol. Rossetti.
Christmas Song. Carman.
Cicada. Libero.
Clonard. Jones, Jr.
Cocteau's Opium: 2. Finkel.
Cold Blows the Wind. Hamilton.
Come, Let Us Find. Davies.
Come Slowly, Paradise. Kenyon.
A Constant Labor. Thompson.
Convent Cemetery: Mount Carmel. Mary St. Virginia.
Cradle Hymn. Luther.
Dachshunds. Smith.
The Damsel. Omar B. Abi Rabi'a.
The Dawn on the Lievre. Lampman.
Daybreak. Shelley.
Definition of My Brother. Graham.

Devotional Incitements. Wordsworth.
Diary. Solitary Moon. De Clue.
Down in the Meadows. *Anonymous.*
The Drunken Sailor (Early in the Morning). *Anonymous.*
Early in the Morning. *Anonymous.*
An Early Start in Mid-Winter. Sarah.
Elegies. Ovid (Publius Ovidius Naso).
An Epitaph. Wesley.
Epithalamion. Flecker.
An Evening Blessing. Edmeston.
Fable. Pilinszky.
The Fairy Queen. *Anonymous.*
Faith for Tomorrow. Clark.
False Nancy. *Anonymous.*
February. Young.
Fighting South of the Ramparts. *Anonymous.*
The First Day of Creation. Milton.
Five for the Grace. Scott.
Fontenoy. 1745. Lawless.
For He Had Great Possessions. Middleton.
Forebears. Gibbon.
The Four Deer. Jones.
Four Folk-Songs in Hokku Form, 4. *Anonymous.*
Galante Garden. Jimenez.
Getting Through. Coffin.
Gimboling. Gardner.
Go Down, Ol' Hannah. *Anonymous.*
God's Trombones: Listen, Lord. Johnson.
The Golden Net. Blake.
Goodmorning with Light. Ciardi.
Green Sleeves. *Anonymous.*
Guest. Lacey.
Gwineter Harness in de Morning Soon. *Anonymous.*
Haiku: "So the spring has come?" Basho (Matsuo Basho).
Haul on the Bowline. *Anonymous.*
High Summer on the Mountains. Davies.
How Long Will It Last? Horikawa.
I Had a Wife. *Anonymous.*
I'm Seventeen Come Sunday. *Anonymous.*
I Traveled with Them. Mu'tamid.
If It Comes. Booth.
The Iliad. Homer.
In Dat Great Gittin' Up Mornin'. *Anonymous.*
In the Morning. Cortez.
In the Winter of My Thirty-Eighth Year. Merwin.
Indians. Fandel.
The Innocent Breasts. Oppenheimer.
Interior: The Suburbs. Gregory.
It Is the Celestial Ennui of Apartments. Stevens.
John Peel. Graves.
Julian and Maddalo (excerpt). Shelley.

Just Then the Door. Moore.
King Arthur. *Anonymous.*
A Kiss in the Morning Early. *Anonymous.*
The Lady of the Lake. Scott.
A Lamentable Case. Hanbury-Williams.
The Lamps Are Burning. Reznikoff.
Leda, the Lost. Walton.
Like Rousseau. Jones.
The Lodging-House Fuschsias. Hardy.
Loft. Dransfield.
Long Lonely Lover of the Highway. Will.
Lord Thomas and Fair Annet (I version). *Anonymous.*
Lyttelton Harbor. Cresswell.
Madrigal to the City of Santiago. Garcia Lorca.
Man and Machine. Morgan.
The Marriage of Pocahontas. Webster.
May Morning. Thaxter.
Medieval Mirth. *Anonymous.*
Memnon. Scollard.
The Midnight Court. Merriman.
Mighty Day. *Anonymous.*
The Milk-Cart Pony. Farjeon.
The Mistress of Vision. Thompson.
Monserrat. Collin.
Morning. Dickinson.
Morning. Gallagher.
The Morning-Glory. Coates.
Morning Light. Newsome.
The Morning Light. Simpson.
The Moss-Rose. Newbolt.
Neither Here Nor There. Rodgers.
Night. Lovelace.
The Night Watch. Winter.
No One Cares Less Than I. Thomas.
Nothing. Reid.
Now. Monroe.
Now I Lay Me. *Anonymous.*
Nuts an' May. *Anonymous.*
Obermann Once More. Arnold.
Ode to a Homemade Coffee Cup. Warden.
Of Wounds and Sore Defeats. Moody.
Oh, When Shall I See Jesus? *Anonymous.*
Old Bill. *Anonymous.*
On Walt Whitman's Birthday. Waldman.
One Morning the World Woke Up. Williams.
Our Own. Sangster.
Paradise Lost. Milton.
Pharaoh and Joseph. Lasker-Schüler.
Philadelphia. Kipling.
Poem at Thirty. Woods.
A Poem for Trapped Things. Wieners.
Pre Domina. Lipkin.
R-E-M-O-R-S-E. Ade.
The Rabbit. Davies.
The Raisin. Hall.
Raya Brenner. Sadeh.
Red Bird. *Anonymous.*
Resentments Composed Because of the Clamor of Town Topers... Knight.

The Rich Interior Life. Eberhart.
A Riddle. Martial (Marcus Valerius Martialis).
The Road Back and Forth to Ryley. Reid.
The Sack of Deerfield. English.
Salute to Life. Shostakovitch.
The Sea Wind. Martinson.
Search. Alegria.
September. Pastan.
Seraphion. Baxter.
The Sickness. Seidel.
The Sigh That Heaves the Grasses. Housman.
Silex Scintillans. Vaughan.
Sleeping in the Forest. Oliver.
Song for a Camper. Farrar.
Song: "Kiss me and hug me." *Anonymous.*
The Song of the Borderguard. Duncan.
Song. Set by Mr. Coleman. Cotton.
Song: "Woman sits on her porch." Thompson.
Sonnet XV: "This is the way we say it in our time." Scott.
Sonnet XXXVII. Alabaster.
Sonnets. Tuckerman.
Sonnets, XX: "Now stands our love on that still verge of day." Agee.
The Sons of Levi. *Anonymous.*
Stanzas. Ibn Gabirol.
Stanzas Concerning Love. George.
The Summer Countries. Rago.
Summer Morning. Clare.
Sunday Morning. Grahame.
Sunday Morning. Moreland.
Tarry with Me, O My Saviour. Smith.
Tell Me Not Here, It Needs Not Saying. Housman.
Tell Old Bill. *Anonymous.*
That Way. Welsh.
Thefts of the Morning. Thomas.
There Gowans Are Gay. *Anonymous.*
There She Stands a Lovely Creature. *Anonymous.*
The Third Continent. Erulkar.
This Morning. Rukeyser.
Three Ships. *Anonymous.*
Three Songs from the Temple. Domanski.
A Time of Night. Ignatow.
To a Friend. Gullans.
To a Town Poet. Reese.
To the Snake. Levertov.
Towards the Source: Let Us Go Down, the Long Dead Night Is Done. Brennan.
Translating. Whitman.
Translation. Spencer.
The Twilight Shadows Round Me Fall. Ryden.
The Two of Cups. Jarrett.
Unspeakable. Avison.
Unter der Linde. Ellenbogen.
Victory. *Anonymous.*
The Vision. O Rathaille.

The Vision of Delight.
Jonson.
The Water Is Wide.
Anonymous.
We Settled by the Lake.
Reeve.
We Won't Go Home Till
Morning. *Anonymous.*
Weather Wisdom.
Anonymous.
What Is Young Passion.
Coleridge.
When I Went Off to Prospect.
Anonymous.
Wind in the Willows
(excerpt). Grahame.
Woman at the Piano.
Zaturenska.
Working Girls. Sandburg.
The World. Creeley.
The Worm. Souster.
Worship. Jones, Jr.
Your Eyes. Chantikian.
Zoroaster Devoutly Questions
Ormazd. Zoroaster.

Morning Star
Anglosaxon Street. Birney.
Diffugere Nives, 1917.
Baring.
The Djanggawul Cycle, 8.
Anonymous.
The House of Madam Juju.
Mieko.
I Dare Not Pray to Thee.
Baring.
Leiroessa Kalyx. Baring.
Myths and Texts. Snyder.
(...Prelude). Rokwaho.
Shew! Fly, Don't Bother Me.
Reeves.
Sonnet: "Three silences made
him a single word."
Blackmur.
Vigils. Sassoon.

Morrow (s)
The Child. Massey.
The Dowie Dens of Yarrow.
Anonymous.
Fetching the Wounded.
Binyon.
Genesis. Wein.
Interlude. Wilcox.
Nightfall. Trueba.
The Rime of the Ancient
Mariner. Coleridge.
The Sower. Blind.
Time to Go. "Coolidge.

Morsel
Giant Bonaparte.
Anonymous.
Lesbia. Aldington.

Mortal (s)
Alexander's Feast or, the
Power of Music. Dryden.
Du Bartas: His Divine
Weeks...Fifth Day of the
First Week (excerpt).
Sylvester.
Bonner's Ferry. Schjeldahl.
Buthaina. Jamil.
Caelica, XXVIII. Greville.
Caelica, CIV. Greville.
City without Smoke. Denby.
The Coup de Grace. Sill.
Dionysus. Andresen.
The Double Vision of
Manannan. *Anonymous.*
Elegy on Thomas Hood
(parody). Fagg.
Equality, Father! Bruck.
Fairies. Tickell.
Faith. Santayana.

From Certain Bokes of
Virgiles Aeneais. Surrey.
Gethsemane. Tappan.
Gulls and Dreams.
Stevenson.
Hail Man! Morgan
The Human Seasons. Keats.
Hymn on Solitude.
Thomson.
The Last Voyage of the
Fairies. Adams.
Lately, Alas, I Knew a Gentle
Boy. Thoreau.
The Lost Tribe. Finch.
Love. Very.
Malcolm's Katie. Crawford.
Man Is God's Nature.
Eberhart.
Mother Most Powerful.
Dominici.
My Love Is Like the Sun.
Anonymous.
My Son, My Executioner.
Hall.
New-Englands Crisis: The
Prologue. Tompson.
The Night-Apple. Ginsberg.
Ode: "My heart rebels against
my generation."
Santayana.
Odes. Santayana.
The Odyssey. Homer.
Paradise Lost. Milton.
Pelters of Pyramids. Horne.
Peter Emberley (II).
Anonymous.
Poem for the Year Twenty
Twenty. Lee.
Poor Fool. Shute.
Pre Domina. Lipkin.
The Progress of Sir Jack Brag.
Anonymous.
Psalm VIII. Sidney.
The Rising Village.
Goldsmith.
River Sound Remembered.
Merwin.
La Rose des Vents. Wilbur.
She died–this was the way she
died. Dickinson.
Sleep and His Brother Death.
Hayne.
The Small Man Orders His
Wedding. Lewis.
Song for Midsummer Night.
Coatsworth.
Sonnet: "A passing glance, a
lightning long the skies."
Drummond.
The Spectacle of Truth.
Hewitt.
Sweet Muse. Watts.
There Are Gods. Riley.
Tiresias (excerpt). Clarke.
To a Book. Wylie.
To My First Love, My
Mother. Rossetti.
Two Against One.
Anonymous.
Variations on a Theme by
George Herbert.
Zaturenska.
View of the Cathedral.
Henri.
We Shall Have Far to Go.
Watson.
The Wombat. Nash.
Works and Days. Hesiod.

Mortality
An Apologie for the Precedent
Hymnes on Teresa.
Crashaw.

At the Discharge of Cannon
Rise the Drowned.
Witheford.
By Winter Seas. Saul.
Eve's Birth. Chernin.
Figures in a Ruined Ballroom.
Hitchcock.
Her, A Statue. Stoddart.
Inspiration. Gibson.
Mortality. *Anonymous.*
The Recurrence. Muir.
Upper Air. Hill.
What Are Years? Moore.

Mortar
Bussy d'Ambois. Chapman.
Conversations between Here
and Home. Harjo.
How Things Fall. Finkel.
Indian Summer, 1927.
Hussey.

Moscow
L'Aigle a Deux Jambes.
Cassity.
The March to Moscow.
Southey.
Unable by Long and Hard
Travel to Banish Love,
Returns Her Friend.
Turberville.

Moses
At Last. Newcombe.
Black Pride. Burroughs.
Bullocky. Wright.
Moses Supposes His Toeses
Are Roses. *Anonymous.*
A New Order of Chivalry.
Peacock.
Our Polite Parents. Wells.
Three Helpers in Battle.
Coleridge.

Mosquito
Haiku: "Whether I sit or lie."
Ukihashi.
How to Kill. Douglas.
Quick, Henry, the Flit!
Schuyler.
Would a circling surface
vulture. Mahadevi
(Mahadeviyakka).

Moss (y)
Aloha. Griffith.
At the Western Shore.
Youngblood.
Bell-Birds. Kendall.
Fragment: "Near where the
riotous Atlantic surge."
Allingham.
Green. Barnes.
I Died for Beauty.
Dickinson.
The Ice Has Spoken.
Rixson.
In the Home of the Scholar
Wu Su-chiang from Hsin-
an... Wu Tsao.
Life in the Boondocks.
Ammons.
Lines on the Mermaid Tavern.
Keats.
My Friend (parody).
Appleman.
Poet's Wish. Larbaud.
Rhyming with a Friend. Yu
Hsuan-chi.
Rings. Barnes.
Song: "I know that any weed
can tell." Ginsberg.
Surviving a Poetry Circuit.
Stafford.
Who Were before Me.
Drinkwater.

Most
Emblem. Quarles.
Mote (s)
The Barn. Spender.
Bestiary for the Fingers of My
Right Hand. Simic.
Dream Songs. Berryman.
Man's Anxious, but
Ineffectual Guard Against
Death. Beddoes.
Moth (s)
Arriving. Halpern.
The Art of Poetry. Dryden.
Auguries of Innocence.
Blake.
An Autumnal Evening.
Sharp.
The Butterfly and the
Caterpillar. Lauren.
Death. Wright.
Le Jeune Homme Caressant
Sa Chimere. Symonds.
Modern Beauty. Symons.
Montana Remembered from
Albuquerque; 1982.
Rogers.
The Moth and the Flame.
Taggart.
Music in an Empty House.
Davies.
The Quarrel. Swenson.
Though I am Laila of the
Persian romance. Zeb-un-
Nissa.
The Woman Who Loved
Women. Inez.
Mother Earth
The Annunciation. Pritam.
Epitaph. Nathan.
Overlord. Carman.
Sipping Cider through a
Straw. *Anonymous.*
Mother-in-law
Sipping Cider through a
Straw. *Anonymous.*
Mother (s)
Addio a la Mamma. Jitrik.
After Hilary, Age 5.
Kicknosway.
Albemarle Cushing. Roche.
An Alphabet of Famous
Goops. Burgess.
Amagoduka at Glencoe
Station. Mtshali.
Arithmetic. Sandburg.
The Arrival of My Mother.
Wilson.
As All Things Pass.
Bickston.
As I Lay upon a Night.
Anonymous.
As I Was Walkin' Down
Wexford Street (with
music). *Anonymous.*
At Last. Stoddard.
At My Mother's Knee.
Anonymous.
At Night. Eberhart.
At Sunrise. Marinoni.
The Automobile. Edson.
The Automobile. Lewisohn.
The Awful Mother. Griffin.
The Baby. Taylor.
Ballad of the Ten Casino
Dancers. Meireles.
Ballroom Dancing Class.
McGinley.
Bartholomew. Gale.
Battledore. Gray.
Baudelaire in Brussels.
Cronin.

The Beadle's Testimony. Rothenberg.

Bendix. Updike.

Between the Porch and the Altar. Lowell.

The Birds of Bethlehem. Gilder.

Birth of Rainbow. Hughes.

The Biter Bit. Ayton [(or Aytoun)] Sir Robert.

Bonny Lizie Baillie. *Anonymous.*

The Book Our Mothers Read. Whittier.

Boys. Letts.

Breakfast Time. Stephens.

Brothers. Edwards.

Buckaroo Sandman. *Anonymous.*

Bucko-Mate. Schierloh.

Butler's Proclamation. Hayne.

Butterfly. Smith.

Byron. Coogler.

Caelica, XXXII. Greville.

California. Sigourney.

The Captive's Hymn. Proctor.

Carol Naive. McClure.

Chances. Stockwell.

Childhood. Muir.

Childhood. Santos.

The Children Band. De Vere.

Christmas Day Is Come. Wadding.

Clap Hands, Clap Hands. *Anonymous.*

Cleaning Day. Kozer.

Clock on Hancock Street. Jordan.

The Coble o Cargill. *Anonymous.*

Complaynt. Waldman.

The Compliment. Habington.

Cradle Hymn. Watts.

Cradle Song. *Anonymous.*

Cradle Song. Durrell.

Crow, Crow, Get out of My Sight. *Anonymous.*

The Crucifixion. *Anonymous.*

The Cruel Mother. *Anonymous.*

Custer's Last Fierce Charge. *Anonymous.*

Dear Old Mothers. Ross.

Death Come to My House He Didn't Stay Long. *Anonymous.*

Delia Holmes. *Anonymous.*

Down the M4. Abse.

The Drowsy Sleeper (A vers.). *Anonymous.*

Duermete, Nino Lindo. *Anonymous.*

Duo. Dargan.

The Easter Song. Sedulius.

The Eggs. Redgrove.

Elegy. Loney.

Emergency at 8. Hewitt.

Epigram: Lucilius. Nemerov.

Epitaphs of the War, 1914-18. Kipling.

The Evening of the Visitation. Merton.

Ex-Voto. Swinburne.

Execution of Alice Holt. *Anonymous.*

Extracts: from the Journal of Elisa Lynch. Stanton.

Fable XX: The Old Hen and the Cock. Gay.

Fair Annie. *Anonymous.*

The Fairy Book. Brown.

A Father Does His Best. White.

Footpath. Ngatho.

For Each of You. Lorde.

For Those Who Always Fear the Worst. *Anonymous.*

The Four Maries. *Anonymous.*

Four-Paws. Eden.

Frog Hunting. Cooley.

The Frog Prince. Pack.

From a Very Little Sphinx. Millay.

The Fruit Plucker. Coleridge.

The Garden of Olives. Rilke.

The Gay Goshawk (E version). *Anonymous.*

The Ghyrlond of the Blessed Virgin Marie. Jonson.

The Gift. *Anonymous.*

The Great Blue Heron. Kizer.

A Guide to Familiar American Incest: Inventing a Family. Saleh.

Gypsies in the Wood. *Anonymous.*

Haiku: "When the daughter." *Anonymous.*

Hanabi-ko. Rose.

Harriet. Lorde.

He. Koertge.

He Approacheth the Hall of Judgment. Book of the Dead.

Her Eyes Don't Shine Like Diamonds. Marion.

Her Mother. Cary.

Herself a Rose Who Bore the Rose. Rossetti.

The Home Winner. Lindberg.

Homecoming Blues. Miller.

Hopi Woman. Spencer.

The Housecleaner. White.

Housewife. Sexton.

The Hudson. Hellman.

Hullabaloo Belay. *Anonymous.*

If I Only Was the Fellow. Adkin.

In Childbed. Hardy.

The Inquest. Davies.

Insight. Goose.

The Irish Mother in the Penal Days. Banim.

Jack, Afterwards. Dacey.

Jardin de la Chapelle Expiatoire. Finch.

Jellon Grame (A version). *Anonymous.*

Jellon Grame (B version). *Anonymous.*

Jo Jo, My Child. *Anonymous.*

John Webster. Swinburne.

Journey in the Orient. Spaziani.

Jowl, Jowl and Listen. *Anonymous.*

Kaddish. Ginsberg.

Knowledge. *Anonymous.*

Kolendy for Christmas. *Anonymous.*

A Lady Dying in Childbed. Herrick.

The Lamb-Child. Tabb.

A Lament to My Mother. Mhone.

The Last Fierce Charge. *Anonymous.*

The Late Mother. Macdonald.

Lazy Mary. *Anonymous.*

Leaping into the Gulf. Beer.

Limerick: "An amoeba named Sam and his brother." *Anonymous.*

The Little Fish That Would Not Do as It Was Bid. Taylor.

The Little Ghost. Hinkson.

Looking at a Dry Canadian Thistle Brought in from the Snow. Bly.

Lost Anchors. Robinson.

Lunar Paraphrase. Stevens.

Maid, out of Thine Unquarried Mountain-Land. *Anonymous.*

Maine. Nauen.

The Meeting. Spivack.

Mending the Adobe. Carruth.

The Messenger. Valentine.

Mnemosyne Lay in Dust. Clarke.

Mother. Dow.

Mother. Shaul.

Mother. Taylor.

Mother and Child. Eastwick.

Mother Most Powerful. Dominici.

Mother's Advice. *Anonymous.*

Mother's Day. Sala.

Mother's Habits. Giovanni.

Mother's Love. Clapp.

Mother's Love. Montgomery.

A Mother's Name. *Anonymous.*

Motherhood. Bacon.

Motherhood. Lee.

Mothers. *Anonymous.*

Mothers and Children. Johns.

Mothers and Daughters. Campbell.

Mothers of Sons. Saunders.

The Mu'allaqat: Pour Us Wine. Ibn Kolthum.

My Mother. *Anonymous.*

My Mother. Creelman.

My Mother. Ledwidge.

My Mother. Taylor.

My Trust. Whittier.

The Name of Mother. Fetter.

Nativitie. Donne.

The New Bath Guide. Anstey.

New Garden Fields. *Anonymous.*

The New Neighbor. Fyleman.

The New Wife. *Anonymous.*

The New York Woman. Sissman.

The Night Has Twenty-Four Hours. Pietri.

Nobody Knows But Mother. Morrison.

A Northern Spring. Baro.

O. T.'s Blues. Cuney.

The Old Gray Goose. *Anonymous.*

Old Ladies. Dromgoole.

The Old Woman of Berkeley. Southey.

On a Discovery Made Too Late. Coleridge.

On the Death of a Pious Lady. Wexionius.

On the Picture of a "Child Tired of Play." Willis.

The One Who Struggles. Toller.

The Orphan. *Anonymous.*

Our Madonna at Home. Pombo.

Palinode. Stanton.

The Pansy. Hoffenstein.

Parable. Bennett.

Pastourelle. *Anonymous.*

The Patter of the Shingle. *Anonymous.*

The Pavilion on the Pier. Vazakas.

Penitential Psalm to the Goddess Anunit, IV. *Anonymous.*

A Prairie Ride. Moody.

A Prayer. Lampman.

Prayer That an Infant May Not Die. Jammes.

Purification of the Blessed Virgin. Beaumont.

Queen Jane. *Anonymous.*

Rain. Shaw.

Rain to the Tribe. Al-Khansa.

The Reading Mother. Gillilan.

Remember the Ladies. Lifshin.

Rendezvous. Millay.

A Road of Ireland. O'Donnell.

Rock-a-Bye Baby. Canning.

Rosa Mystica. Hopkins.

Rossetti at Tea. Pain.

Saturninus. Conway.

Sausage. Guest.

The Sea. Webb.

Sea-Birds. Chavez.

Seasons of the Soul. Tate.

Seguidilla. Valdivielso.

Seven Long Years in State Prison (with music). *Anonymous.*

The Seven Virgins. *Anonymous.*

She May Have Seen Better Days. Thornton.

The Silver Flask. Montague.

Sing with Your Body. Mirikitani.

The Slacker Apologizes. Viereck.

The Sleepers. Whitman.

Snow White. Broumas.

So Then, I Feel Not Deeply! Landor.

Social Studies. Neville.

Somebody's Mother. Brine.

Somewhere. Mphahlele.

Song of the Sky Loom. *Anonymous.*

The Sonnet-Ballad. Brooks.

Sonnet: He Craves Interpreting of a Dream of His. Maiano.

Sonnet to a Friend... Coleridge.

A Spouse I Do Hate. Wycherley.

The Spring Waters. "Ping Hsin" (Hsieh Wang-ying).

The Star-Song: A Carol to the King; Sung at White-Hall. Herrick.
The Starlight Night. Hopkins.
The Storm-Wind. Barnes.
Stratton Water. *Anonymous.*
Swansong. Muske.
Tashkent Breaks into Blossom. Akhmatova.
Therefore, We Thank Thee, God. Grossman.
Third and Fourth. Rhys.
Thompson Street. McCoy.
A Thought from Cardinal Newman. Russell.
Thoughts in Separation. Meynell.
The Three Captains. *Anonymous.*
To a New-Born Baby Girl. Conkling.
To Mary at Christmas. Brunini.
To My Mother. Moore.
To My Youngest Kinsman, R. L. Chear.
To Sleep. Wordsworth.
Two Hopper. Ikan.
Two Little Children. *Anonymous.*
Unborn. McLeod.
An Unexpected Pleasure. *Anonymous.*
The Unveiling. Bernhardt.
Vigil of the Immaculate Conception. Egan.
The Vision of the Snow. Preston.
Visit. Coccimiglio.
The Voices. Pommy-Vega.
The Welsh Marches. Housman.
Whalen's Fate (George Whalen). *Anonymous.*
What Is Veal? *Anonymous.*
When the Work's All Done This Fall. *Anonymous.*
When Your Cheap Divorce Is Granted. Newell.
Wind and Lyre. Markham.
Wisdom. Yeats.
Wishing. Allingham.
A Wonderful Mother. O'Reilly.
Words Wherein Stinging Bees Lurk. Halevi.
The Yankee's Return from Camp. Bangs.

Mother Tongue
Father Land and Mother Tongue. Lover.
Grinding Vibrato. Cortez.
Lapsus Linguae. Howard.
The Poet. Keats.

Motherhood
Essay in Defense of the Movies. Gibson.
Motherhood. Chworowsky.
Nativity. Hayford.
The Old Mare. Coatsworth.
Wondrous Motherhood. *Anonymous.*

Motion (s)
Amphibian. Clampitt.
At the Museum of Modern Art. Swenson.
Bridges and Tunnels. Bentley.
Classic. Ammons.
The Confirmers. Ammons.
Consummation. Crozier.

Death Looks Down. Gregg.
The First Meeting. Herbert of Cherbury.
Ghost. Bynner.
A Hymn to God in Time of Stress. Eastman.
If My Hands Were Mute. Winkler.
King Wind. Van Doren.
Leaving One of the State Parks after a Family Outing. Macklin.
List of Prepositions. Kennedy.
Loch Luichart. Young.
Man. Vaughan.
Nude Descending a Staircase. Kennedy.
On Lydia Distracted. Ayres.
Pantoum. Ashbery.
Retired Farmer. Evans.
Rules and Lessons. Vaughan.
Sad Strains of a Gay Waltz. Stevens.
Science for the Young. Irwin.
The Sigh of Silence. Keats.
Song of the Screw. *Anonymous.*
Soul. Graham.
Spring Song in the City. Buchanan.
The Storms Are on the Ocean. *Anonymous.*
Sunrise at Sea. Swinburne.
Tales of the Islands, VII. Walcott.
Tommies in the Train. Lawrence.
The Wind in the Tree. Prince.
Young Edwin in the Lowlands Low (B vers.). *Anonymous.*

Motive (s)
The Consolation of Philosophy. Boethius.
If So It Hap, This Of-Spring of My Care. Daniel.
Rainier. Tollerud.
Triple Feature. Levertov.

Motley
The Jester's Sermon. Thornbury.
To the Mocking-Bird. Wilde.

Motor (s)
Coming Home. Stone.
Heroes of the Strip. Cudahy.
Junkyards. Rayford.
Lament for Lost Lodgings. McGinley.

Motto (s)
Part of Mandevil's Travels. Empson.
Sleep and Poetry. Keats.
The Town of Nogood. Penny.
The United States and Macedonian. *Anonymous.*

Mould (ed) (er)
Childe Harold's Pilgrimage: Canto III, XXVII. Byron.
The Dismantled Ship. Whitman.
Epitaph. Peacock.
Farewell, Life. Hood.
For Brother Malcolm. Spriggs.
Gravities. Heaney.
His Plan for Me. Nicholson.

Ho, Everyone That Thirsteth. Housman.
Jonathan Gentry, III: Tom's Sleeping Song. Van Doren.
Lady of Castlenoire. Aldrich.
The Lonesome Dove. *Anonymous.*
The News. Saxe.
Now Is the Accepted Time. Wesley.
One Day. Brooke.
She Weeps over Rahoon. Joyce.
Tottel's Miscellany (excerpt). *Anonymous.*
TV. Forbes.

Mound
The Cynneddf. Humphries.
The Four Winds. Luders.
On the Grave of a Young Cavalry Officer Killed in the Valley... Melville.
Prairie-Dog Town. Austin.
The Shepherd. Gilmore.

Mount
The Assumption. Nerses.
Camel. Miller.
The Dreadful Fate of Naughty Nate. Bangs.
Elegies. Ovid (Publius Ovidius Naso).
Endymion. Keats.
Gradatim. Holland.
The Iliad. Homer.
Land of Our Fathers. Scollard.
Let Me Fly. *Anonymous.*
The Lonely Street. Williams.
Metamorphoses. Ovid (Publius Ovidius Naso).
Returning Home. Du Bellay.
Silex Scintillans. Vaughan.
To Winter. Blake.
The White Horse. Davies.

Mountain (s)
The Aeneid. Virgil (Publius Vergilius Maro).
After Laughter. Sherwood.
Alaskan Mountain Poem #1. Silko.
All Which Isn't Singing Is Mere Talking. Cummings.
Amusing Our Daughters. Kizer.
Ancestry. Crane.
The Apple-Barrel of Johnny Appleseed. Lindsay.
The Art of Love: Happy the Man Who Has Two Breasts to Crush. Koch.
Attraction. Wilcox.
August on Sourdough, a Visit from Dick Brewer. Snyder.
The Bear Went over the Mountain. *Anonymous.*
Behind the Closed Eye. Ledwidge.
Below Mount T'ui K'oy, Home of the Gods.... Stroud.
Benicasim. Warner.
The Black Tower. Yeats.
The Blue Ridge. Monroe.
The Calendar of Oengus: Prologue (excerpt). *Anonymous.*
Cardrona Valley. Wedde.
Christine. Hay.
Coda. MacNeice.

The Cold. Henson.
Cousins. Cullen.
Crossing. Oppenheimer.
Cuchullain's Lament over Fardiad. *Anonymous.*
A Curse on the Cat. Skelton.
The Dancers. Robinson.
Daniel Saw de Stone. *Anonymous.*
The Dark Swimmers. Eigner.
The Dawn on the Lievre. Lampman.
Do It Now! *Anonymous.*
Early Lynching. Sandburg.
Edom. *Anonymous.*
Emigration. Barrows.
The Fairy Harpers. Dollard.
Far from the Heart of Culture. Auden.
Flower Herding on Mount Monadnock. Kinnell.
For Hidden Mist Pavilion. Yu Hsuan-chi.
For Mary. Rexroth.
From Darkness. Izumi Shikibu.
From Mount Nebo. Wolfskehl.
The Frontier. Hewitt.
Gaa-A-Muna, a Mountain Flower. Littlebird.
Go Tell It on the Mountain. *Anonymous.*
Goats. Wood.
God's Blessing on Munster. Patrick.
Goin' 'Cross the Mountain. *Anonymous.*
Good Company, Fine Houses. Newlove.
The Grass on the Mountain. Austin.
The Great Voices. Brooks.
Guide to the Ruins. Nemerov.
Habla Usted Espanol? Reiss.
Here in Katmandu. Justice.
Holding the Sky. Stafford.
The Hour of Feeling. Simpson.
I Go out of Darkness. Izumi Shikibu.
Indian Names. Sigourney.
Indians. Sprague.
Internal. Auslander.
Invocation. Iremonger.
The Isle. Shelley.
Jinny Git Around. *Anonymous.*
The Journey. Middleton.
Kinloch Ainort. MacLean.
Lake, Mountain, Tree. Glover.
The Leaping Laughers. Barker.
Letter to My Daughter at the End of Her Second Year. Finkel.
Like Water Down a Slope. Schneour.
Looking down a Hill. Thompson.
The Man Who Rode to Conemaugh. Brown.
Mandrakes for Supper. Baxter.
Memory. Yeats.
Monument Mountain. Bryant.
Mountain Dew. *Anonymous.*

Mountain

Mountain Lion. Lawrence.
Mountains. Auden.
Mus Ridiculus Non. Welch.
My Grandmother. Adams.
Nightmare on Rhum.
Macmillan.
No Man, If Men Are Gods.
Cummings.
Not Thinking of America.
Kroll.
Notes on a Life to Be Lived.
Warren.
O, Rocks Don't Fall on Me.
Anonymous.
Old Smoky. *Anonymous.*
Olive Grove. MacAdams.
On a Painting by Patient B of
the Independence State
Hospital... Justice.
On Looking into E. V. Rieu's
Homer. Kavanagh.
On the Croun o Bidean.
Annand.
On the Mountain. Joseph.
On the Shore of Nawa.
Hioki no Ko-okima.
Oracle. Mayo.
The Paps of Dana. Stephens.
Perspectives. Randall.
The Platypus. *Anonymous.*
Poem on Canada: Cold
Colloquy. Anderson.
Polly Vaughn (Molly Brawn).
Anonymous.
Postscript. Mills.
Prayer in Time of War.
Treece.
Prayer to the Mountain Spirit.
Anonymous
Prelude. Synge.
The Pretty Girl of Loch Dan.
Ferguson.
Promises. Sherry.
Real Old Mountain Dew.
Anonymous.
Reveille. Ridge.
Roads Go Ever Ever On.
Tolkien.
Round Valley Reflections.
Oandasan.
Route 95 North: New Jersey.
Bowman.
The Scottish Mountaineering
Club Song. Stott.
Sestina from the Home
Gardener. Wakoski.
She'll Be Comin' Round the
Mountain (with music).
Anonymous.
Sleepwalkers' Ballad. Garcia
Lorca.
Song at Santa Cruz. Young.
Song for the Spinning Wheel.
Wordsworth.
The Songs. *Anonymous.*
Songs for the Four Parts of
the Night. Owl Woman.
Songs of the Ghost Dance.
Anonymous.
The Sonnet. Gilder.
Sonnet: Of the Grave of
Selvaggia, on the Monte
della Sambuca. Cino da
Pistoia.
Soul Lifted. Watson.
Sourdough Mountain
Lookout. Whalen.
Southern Liebeslieder.
Retallack.
The Spider. Mackenzie.
The Spiral. Holmes.
A Story. Stafford.

Susiana. *Anonymous.*
Synge's Grave. Letts.
Thalamos. Dufault.
That Dark Other Mountain.
Francis.
Thoughts for You (when She
Came back from the
Mountains). Crosby.
To Frighten a Storm.
Cardiff.
To J. S. Collis. Pitter.
Turtle Lake. Hugo.
Two Scenes. Ashbery.
Under the Pyrenees. Noyes.
An Unseen Fire. Cooke.
An Upper Chamber in a
Darkened House.
Tuckerman.
Utah. Stevenson.
The Wanderer (excerpt).
Robinson.
Water-Lilies. Teasdale.
When Faces Called Flowers.
Cummings.

Mountaineer

Contemplation. Thompson.
From Garden to Garden,
Ridge to Ridge. Muir.

Mourn (ed) (er) (ing) (s)

The Age of a Dream.
Johnson.
Anacreontic, On Parting with
a little Child. Wesley.
The Beads. Jacinto.
Bhagavad Gita (excerpt).
Anonymous.
Bright Be the Place of Thy
Soul! Byron.
Burial. Grigson.
The Burial of Sir John
McKenzie. MacKay.
Caelica, LVIII. Greville.
Cean-Salla. Mangan.
The Christian Life.
Longfellow.
Courtesan with Fan. Spires.
The Courtier's Good-Morrow
to His Mistress.
Anonymous.
Coyote's Daylight Trip.
Allen.
Creation. Nicholl.
Crime. Warren.
The Cuckoo (B vers.).
Anonymous.
Derry Morning. Mahon.
The Deserted Garden.
Stanford.
Don Juan. Byron.
An Elegie Made by Mr.
Aurelian Townshend in
Remembrance of the Ladie..
Townsend.
Elegy for the Wife of a
Friend. Yu Hsuan-chi.
Elegy on Gordon Barber.
Derwood.
Epilogue. Eliyia.
Evening Twilight.
Baudelaire.
For Her Love I Cark and
Care. *Anonymous.*
The Fountain at the Tomb.
Nicias.
George Collins. Anonymous.
Give Me Jesus. *Anonymous.*
The Goldfinches. Jago.
Good Friday. Smith.
Graves of Infants. Clare.
The Gray Mare (Young
Johnny the Miller).
Anonymous.

Hero and Leander. Marlowe.
The House Carpenter.
Anonymous.
I Now Had Only to Retrace.
Bronte.
I Walkt the Other Day (To
Spend My Hour,).
Vaughan.
Idea. Drayton.
If Blood Is Black Then Spirit
Neglects My Unborn Son.
Rivers.
The Iliad. Homer.
In Memory of Ernst Toller.
Auden.
It would be wrong for us.
Sappho.
Joseph Rodman Drake.
Halleck.
The Lament of the Voiceless.
Everett.
Letter with a Black Border.
McPherson.
The Little Clan. Higgins.
Llangollen Vale (excerpt).
Seward.
Looking at a Dead Wren in
My Hand. Bly.
Man's Inhumanity to Man.
Burns.
Man was Made to Mourn, A
Dirge. Burns.
Mater Dolorosa. Barnes.
Merry It Is. *Anonymous*
The Minstrel Responds to
Flattery. Scott.
Mourn for Yourself.
Keating.
The Mourners. Higgons.
My Lord, What a Mourning.
Anonymous.
The Nightingale. Moxon.
O God of My Salvation, Hear.
Barlow.
Oh, How My Love with a
Whirling Power. Tu-kehu
and Wetea.
Old Man Hall. Jacobs.
Old Marse John.
Anonymous.
On the Countess Dowager of
Pembroke. Browne.
On the Death of a Lady's
Dog. Roscommon.
On the Death of Joseph
Rodman Drake. Halleck.
On the Latin Gerunds.
Porson.
Orestes Pursued. Webb.
The Pardon. Wilbur.
A Poem upon the Triumphant
Translation of a Mother in
Our Israel. Danforth.
Polly Williams. *Anonymous.*
The Ruin of Bobtail Bend.
Adams.
Sally Monroe. *Anonymous.*
Silex Scintillans. Vaughan.
Simon Lee the Old Huntsman.
Wordsworth.
Sleep Not, Dream Not.
Bronte.
Some San Francisco Poems.
Oppen.
A Song from Shakespeare's
"Cymbeline". Collins.
The Song of Jed Smith
(excerpt). Neihardt.
Sonnets, CXXXVII: "In the ole
age black was nor counted
fair." Shakespeare.
Sonnets to Aurelia. Nichols.

Spring and Fall. Hopkins.
Stanzas. Wilde.
The Time of the Barmacides.
Mangan.
To His Mistresse on Her
Scorne. Beedome.
Venus of the Louvre.
Lazarus.
La Vita Nuova. Dante
Alighieri.
Weep No More. Fletcher.
Wreathmakertraining.
Patten.

Mouse (mice)

The American Poet–"But
Since It Came to Good..."
Hathaway.
Aylmer's Field. Tennyson.
The Bat. Roethke.
The Bush on Mount Venus.
Finkel.
A Cat. Herrick.
A Change of Heart. Hobbs.
Chanson Naive. McClure.
The Church Mouse. Bullett.
Cruel Clever Cat. Taylor.
Ding, Dong, Bell. Mother
Goose.
The Fieldmouse. Alexander.
The Fury of Hating Eyes.
Sexton.
The Hasty Pudding. Barlow.
Henry Adams. Auden.
Hoddley, Poddley, Puddle and
Fogs. *Anonymous.*
The House of God. Hope.
The Island. Woodcock.
Japanese Beetles. Kennedy.
Little Black Bug. Brown.
A Long Walk before the
Snows Began. Bly.
Mice. Fyleman.
Missing. Milne.
The Monster. Rago.
Mother Tabbyskins. Hart.
Mouse Night: One of Our
Games. Stafford.
No Coward's Song. Flecker.
An Old Cat's Confession.
Cranch.
An Old Woman.
Anonymous.
The Old Woman. Potter.
On a Cat, Ageing. Gray.
The Recovery. Blunden.
Remember September.
Justus.
Riddle: "I am within as white
as snow." *Anonymous.*
Santa Claus and the Mouse.
Poulsson.
Scottsboro. *Anonymous.*
The Silver Racer. Murphey.
The Snow Storm. Millay.
Three Blind Mice.
Anonymous.
The Town Mouse and the
Country Mouse (parody).
Prior.
We Interrupt This Broadcast.
Hemschemeyer.

Moustaches

A Ballad of the Mulberry
Road. Pound.
Lighthearted William.
Williams.

Mouth (s)

Across the Door. Colum.
After Love. Aleixandre.
Apostrophe to a Pram Rider.
White.
Art Work. Wallace.

August 1914. Rosenberg.
Baroque Comment. Bogan.
Beets. Nowlan.
A Bestiary. Rexroth.
Black Rocks. Mar.
Blossom. Plumly.
Candles. Swarth.
A Certain Age. McGinley.
Clams. Ishigaki Rin.
Cleaning Fish. Behm.
The Collector. Behm.
Conceit upon the Feet
    (parody). Zaranka.
Conquistador. MacLeish.
Conversation between the
    Chevalier de Chamilly and
    Mariana Alcoforado.
    Marias.
Cuba. Kearney.
December 21st. Valentine.
Der Blinde Junge. Loy.
Drive Imagining. Vogelsang.
Elliott Hawkins. Masters.
Encounter. Livesay.
The End. Ginsberg.
Eternal Masculine. Benet.
The First Tooth. Rands.
Fish. Witt.
"From sex, this sea...'.
    Jones.
From the Spanish. Towle.
The Garlic. Meyers.
Go Not, Happy Day.
    Tennyson.
A Guard of the Sepulcher.
    Markham.
He Who in His Pocket Hath
    No Money. Anonymous.
Hexameter and Pentameter.
    Anonymous.
Hmmm, 15. Scalapino.
Hmmmm, 8. Scalapino.
Ho, Everyone That Thirsteth.
    Housman.
Homesick Blues. Hughes.
I Can't Figure You Out.
    Fried.
I Hear America Singing.
    Whitman.
In December. Young.
In This Hour. Johnson.
Kissing Natalia. Grier.
Kyran's Christening.
    Nowlan.
A La Promenade. Verlaine.
Landed: A Valentine.
    Howard.
Landscape as a Nude.
    MacLeish.
Like Wings. Schultz.
Lines Inspired by the
    Controversy on the
    Value...of Old English...
    Burgess.
The Little Birds.
    Anonymous.
Living Poetry. Margenat.
Love's Lovers. Rossetti.
Love-Songs, At Once Tender
    and Informative.
    Hoffenstein.
Man's Amazement.
    Anonymous.
The Man under the Bed.
    Jong.
The Marginal Field.
    Spender.
The Married Man. Phillips.
Mothers of Sons. Saunders.
The Mouth and the Ears.
    Palquera.

Mr. East's Feast.
    Anonymous.
My Grief on the Sea.
    Anonymous.
My Grief on the Sea. Hyde.
The Negatives. Levine.
New Season. Levine.
Nina Simone. Jeffers.
No One Ever Walking This
    Our Only Earth.
    Rukeyser.
Not from This Anger.
    Thomas.
Of Pick-Pockets. Gay.
Of You, If Anyone, It Can Be
    Said. Catullus.
Old Fisherman with Guitar.
    Brown.
On May-Day, When the Lark
    Began to Ryse.
    Anonymous.
On the Cards and Dice.
    Ralegh.
Oracle at Delphi. Bagg.
Pacific Sonnets. Barker.
The Past. Hodgson.
The Penalty for Bigamy Is
    Two Wives. Matthews.
Personal Poem. Wendt.
Poem for Marc Chagall.
    Cohen.
Posthumous Coquetry.
    Gautier.
Prophecy. Wylie.
Reasons. James.
The Return. Saleh.
Riddle: "Runs all day and
    never walks." Mother
    Goose.
Robin Red Breast. Weeden.
Running It Backward.
    Morris.
The Sad Story of a Little Boy
    That Cried. Anonymous.
Sappho. Cope.
Scalp Dance Song.
    Anonymous.
The Skull. Young.
The Snake. MacKenzie.
The Snake-Charmer. Hake.
A Song from Armenia. Hill.
Song of the Taste. Snyder.
Spit. Williams.
Spring in Virginia. Wilson.
Stepfather: A Girl's Song.
    Komunyakaa.
Story from Russian Author.
    Redgrove.
Tea. Struthers.
Teeth. Holub.
Their Mouths Full. Ignatow.
There Is a Lady. Walther
    von der Vogelweide.
Theresa. Pass.
This Is a Poem for the
    Fathers and for Michael
    Ryan. Lux.
The Thousand and One
    Nights: Haroun's Favorite
    Song. Anonymous.
To His Mistress for Her True
    Picture. Herbert of
    Cherbury.
To Jesus on His Birthday.
    Millay.
To My Grandmother.
    McGuckian.
Truelove. Anonymous.
Vegas. Bukowski.
The Voice of the Power of
    This World. Hall.

When Dutchy Plays the
    Mouth Harp. Carr.
Who's Most Afraid of Death?
    Cummings.
Yes, the Secret Mind
    Whispers. Young.
You Have the Lovers.
    Cohen.
The Young Man Who Loved
    the Girl Who Took Care of
    Her Aging Father.
    Kuzma.
Your Mouth. Shehabuddin.

Move (d) (s)
All Ignorance Toboggans into
    Know. Cummings.
Alternatives. Amis.
Amoretti, LIV. Spenser.
Armistice Day. Causley.
Astrophel and Stella, XCI.
    Sidney.
At Dante's Grave. Zussman.
Ballad. Ammons.
Black Lotus/a Prayer.
    Johnson.
Country of No Lack.
    Untermeyer.
Cowboy's Salvation Song.
    Carr.
Degrees of Shade. Pinkerton.
Dream Songs. Berryman.
Dream with Fred Astaire.
    Berkson.
Elsewheres. Justice.
Epithalamium. Turner.
Evaporation Poems. Norris.
Five Words for Joe Dunn on
    His 22nd Birthday. Spicer.
Fog. Sandburg.
A Green and Pleasant Land.
    Bishop.
Ground Swell. Koehler.
The Gully. Maurice.
Hai. Perkoff.
I Move the Meeting Be
    Adjourned. Parra.
In Church. Hardy.
In Memoriam A.H.H., LXV.
    Tennyson.
In the Sea of Tears.
    Replansky.
In the Tree House at Night.
    Dickey.
Julius Caesar. Shakespeare.
Keeping Things Whole.
    Strand.
A Lame Beggar. Donne.
The Language. Hollo.
Lines Written at the Grave of
    Alexander Dumas.
    Bennett.
The Lion at Noon. Hugo.
Love's Labour Lost. Tofte.
The Man on the Flying
    Trapeze. Leybourne.
Meeting a Bear. Wagoner.
Meeting Halfway. Hardy.
Mimosa. Mathis.
Miss Creighton. Taylor.
The Mother. Gardons.
Mother. Nagase Kiyoko.
The Need to Love. Vinner.
The New Pieta: For the
    Mothers and Children of
    Detroit. Jordan.
Nightfall. Olson.
Nocturne: Lake Huron.
    Kelly.
The Odyssey. Homer.
Of Dancing. Brownjohn.
Poems. Drummond.
Power. Collier.

Prayer for All Poets at This
    Time. Edman.
Reincarnation (I). Dickey.
River God's Song. Ridler.
Romeo and Juliet.
    Shakespeare.
Sayre. Strongin.
Silent Movies. Pietri.
Song: "I prithee let my heart
    alone." Stanley.
Sonnet: "Madam, 'tis true,
    your beauties move."
    Godolphin.
Sonnets Written in the Orillia
    Woods, VII. Sangster.
The Stone. Vaughan.
Suppliant. Sullivan.
Taunt. Anonymous.
To a Butterfly. Davies.
The Twins. Wright.
The Uninvited. Mundell.
A Valedictory to Standard Oil
    of Indiana. Wagoner.
Variations on a Theme.
    Whitman.
We Shall Not Be Moved.
    Anonymous.
The Whales off Wales.
    Kennedy.
When I Die. Macrow.
Work. Codrescu.
You. Clark.
Movement (s)
The Blue Horses. McAuley.
Chile. Griffin.
Epithalamion. Flecker.
The Glass of Pure Water
    (excerpt). ""MacDiarmid.
The Hill Burns. Shepherd.
Incense. Nicholl.
The Man on the Flying
    Trapeze. Leybourne.
The Movement of Fish.
    Dickey.
On the Appeal From the Race
    of Sheba: II. Senghor.
Reasons for Music.
    MacLeish.
The Seed of Nimrod.
    Harrison.
Venice Recalled. Boyd.
Movie (s)
Buster Keaton. McFee.
Dear Reader. Meinke.
Eclipses. Sullivan.
Shoe Shop. Sutter.
Small Towns. Murguia.
Sunday Afternoon. Levine.
Moving
At Knaresborough. Davie.
Chesapeake. Kennedy.
Corner Seat. MacNeice.
Death of Little Boys. Tate.
For Marianne Moore's
    Birthday. Boyle.
Frank Albert & Viola Benzena
    Owens. Shange.
From the Point. Petrie.
I Love Old Women.
    Kloefkorn.
The Last Landlord. Allen.
Mississippi Mornings. Dent.
Old Song. Scott.
Open and Closed Space.
    Transtromer.
Whalefeathers. Violi.
The Windows. Merwin.
Zennor. Ridler.
Mow (er) (es) (ing) (n) (s)
Adam Lay I-Bowndyn.
    Anonymous.
Bread the Holy. Coatsworth.

Damon the Mower. Marvell.
Epigram: "Neither in idleness consume thy days." Landor.
Examiner. Scott.
Ire. Thomas.
My Maid Mary. *Anonymous.*
Old Man with a Mowing Machine. Lord.
The Recruiting Sergeant. *Anonymous.*
Rose Pogonias. Frost.
Springfield Mountain (B vers.). *Anonymous.*

Mud (dy) (s)
Circe. Gibson.
Depot Blues. Lincoln (Hicks).
Door-Mats. Davies.
Menses. Millay.
On Visiting My Son, Port Angeles, Washington. Niatum.
Three Songs from the Temple. Domanski.

Mud (s)
Attack. Sassoon.
Dream. Edwards.
For a Shetland Pony Brood Mare Who Died in Her Barren Year. Kumin.
Galway. MacDonagh.
I'd Like to Be a Worm. Gay.
I'm a Round-Town Gent. *Anonymous.*
In Carrowdore Churchyard. Mahon.
Kitty, Kitty Casket. *Anonymous.*
Landscape and Figure. Kinsella.
The Marsh. Snodgrass.
Moon Fishing. Mueller.
Mud. Boyden.
On Dreams. Swift.
Stags. Montgomerie.
Sweeney to Mrs. Porter in the Spring. Sissman.
To Daphne and Virginia. Williams.
The Vanity of Existence. Freneau.
Who Likes the Rain? Bates.
Whoopee Blues. Hill.

Mudville
Casey's Daughter at the Bat. Graham.

Muff
The Hind and the Panther. Dryden.
On Lady Anne Hamilton. Sheridan.

Muffle (d)
In Memoriam A.H.H., XLIX. Tennyson.
The Obscure Pleasure of the Indistinct. Ramke.
The Plea of the Midsummer Fairies. Hood.
Recreation. Taylor.
Winter's Dregs. Bowering.

Mulberry
Jennifer Gentle and Rosemary. *Anonymous.*
The Riddling Knight. *Anonymous.*

Mule (s)
Alabama-Bound. *Anonymous.*
Captain Captain. Lipscomb.

Don't Fish in My Sea. Rainey.
The Dustbowl. Elmslie.
The Fight of Paso del Mar! Taylor.
Gee-Up Dar, Mules. Piper.
George. Randall.
The Kicking Mule. *Anonymous.*
Mules. Fox-Smith.
My Relatives for the Most. Hudson.
Oh Oh Blues. Mays.
The Road to Cook's Peak. *Anonymous.*
The Titanic (B vers.). *Anonymous.*

Multiply
Adequacy. Browning.
Counting Kisses. Catullus.
The Female Husband, Who Had Been Married to Another Female.... *Anonymous.*
Necropolis. Shapiro.

Multitude (s)
Be Gone Ye Blockheads. Diogenes Laertius.
The Breastplate of Saint Patrick. *Anonymous.*
Carl Hamblin. Masters.
Fatales Poetae. Parrot.
A Little Scraping. Jeffers.
The Poem of Joao. De Sousa.
Priest Or Poet. Leslie.
Raving Warre, Begot. Campion.
Salamis. Aeschylus.

Mumble
Eclipses. Sullivan.
For Malcolm X. Walker.
The Good Old Days. Fried.
Grandeur of Ghosts. Sassoon.
Some Foreign Letters. Sexton.
Wings in the Dark. Gray.

Mummy
By the Klondike River. Coren.
Love's Alchemy. Donne.
Sonnet to Britain. Ayton [(or Aytoun)] Sir Robert.

Munch (ed)
Pastoral. Creighton.
Third Limick. Nash.
Work Horses. Chase.

Murder (ed) (er) (ing) (s)
Abraham's Knife. Garrett.
Anaesthesia. Valentine.
Andromache. Euripides.
At Last We Killed the Roaches. Clifton.
Autumn. Thomson.
Be Not Silent. *Anonymous.*
The Brockton Murder: A Page out of William James. Skinner.
Captain James. *Anonymous.*
The Cenotaph. Mew.
Cold Water Flat. Booth.
Contest. Victor.
Corpses in the Wood. Toller.
The Cottager's Complaint. Freeth.
Daily the Drum. Wilkinson.
Death Song. Lewis.
The Dirty Word. Shapiro.
Down in the Willow Garden. *Anonymous.*
Dream Songs. Berryman.

The Famine Year. Wilde.
Figure for an Apocalypse. Merton.
The Girl Who Had Borne Too Much. Woods.
Go Down You Murderers. MacColl.
God! How I Long for You... Mackenzie.
The Gosport Tragedy (A vers.). *Anonymous.*
Gunfighter. Locklin.
Harpalus' Complaint. *Anonymous.*
The Hindoo: He Doesn't Hurt a Fly or a Spider Either. Ramanujan.
If I Should Die before I Wake. Mezey.
If You See This Man. Lux.
The Inquest. Davies.
Ireland 1972. Durcan.
Jew. Randall, Jr.
Johnson. *Anonymous.*
The Kent State Massacre. Dane.
Kevin Barry. Ward.
Knoxville Girl. *Anonymous.*
Leda and the Swan. Gogarty.
The Lighthouse Keeper's Offspring. Broughton.
Love between Brothers and Sisters. Watts.
The Man from Strathbogie. FitzGerald.
Mexico City Blues: 179th Chorus. Kerouac.
Modern Critics. Coleridge.
Mosquito. Updike.
Mrs. Asquith Tries to Save the Jacarandas. Witt.
The Murder of Maria Marten. Corder.
My Many-Coated Man. Lee.
Naomi Wise. *Anonymous.*
Nell Flaherty's Drake. *Anonymous.*
Omie Wise. *Anonymous.*
Packet of Letters. Bogan.
Palo Alto: The Marshes. Hass.
Poem Written before Mother's Day for Mrs. Lopez from the South. Hardy.
Poor Omie. *Anonymous.*
The Rabbit. Davies.
Ramble on What in the World Why. Gustafson.
Rigoletto. Levy.
The Ring and the Book. Browning.
Saw God Dead but Laughing. Villa.
Shocking Rape and Murder of Two Lovers. *Anonymous.*
The Song of Crede. *Anonymous.*
The Terrace in the Snow. Su Tung-P'o.
To Death, Castara Being Sicke. Habington.
The Watering Place. Propertius.
When Thou Must Home. Campion.
Why Do You Want to Suffer Less. Fisher.
William Glen. *Anonymous.*

Murmur (ed) (ing) (s)
Amen. Browning.

Before Rereading Shakespeare's Sonnets. Moore.
Birds in Spring. Thomson.
A City Graveyard. Oates.
In Praise of Limestone. Auden.
In Tesla's Laboratory. Johnson.
Mycerinus. Arnold.
Orchestra. Davies.
Pastoral Hymn. Addison.
A Spinning Song. O'Donnell.
The Stormy Hebrides. Collins.
Stray Dog. Mish.
The Thousand and One Nights: Dates. *Anonymous.*
Upon Eckington Bridge, River Avon. Quiller-Couch.
The Wanderings of Oisin. Yeats.
Who'd Be a Hero (Fictional)? Bishop.

Muscle (s)
Canto 5. Weatherly.
A Green and Pleasant Land. Bishop.
High Summer. Jones.
Hmmmm, 10. Scalapino.
The Red Light Saloon. *Anonymous.*

Muse (s)
Astrophel and Stella, I. Sidney.
Astrophel and Stella, LXXVII. Sidney.
The Autumn Wind. Clare.
Blessed Art Thou, O Lord. *Anonymous.*
The Cherry and the Slae (excerpt). Montgomerie.
Collin My Deere and Most Entire Beloved. Smith.
The Court of Charles II. Pope.
Dan Bartholmew's Dolorous Discourses. Gascoigne.
Don Juan. Byron.
Epigram: "All praise your face, your verses none abuse." Walpole.
An Epitaph upon Doctor Brook. Crashaw.
The Faerie Queene. Spenser.
A Farewell to a Fondling. Churchyard.
Fragment. Cowper.
The Great Hunger. Kavanagh.
Green Sunday. Kitasono.
Idea's Mirrour. Drayton.
If by Dull Rhymes Our English Must Be Chained. Keats.
The Illustration–A Footnote. Levertov.
Invocation (parody). Hoffenstein.
The Kirk's Alarm. Burns.
Lakeshore. Scott.
Lilith on the Fate of Man. Brennan.
Lyke Memnons Rocke Toucht, with the Rising Sunne. Fletcher.
Meditation. Rakosi.
Mully of Mountown (excerpt). King.

New Chitons for Old Gods
(excerpt). McCord.
On Harting Down. Moore.
On Lucy Countesse of
Bedford. Jonson.
On the Masquerades. Pitt.
Parrot and Dove. Landor.
The Pillar of Fame. Herrick.
Poeta Loquitur. Swinburne.
Request for Meat and Drink.
Sedulius Scottus.
A Satyretericall Charracter of
a Proud Upstart. Saffin.
The Serpent Muses.
Henderson.
Sonnet I. Alabaster.
Sonnet: Written at
Stonehenge. Warton, Jr..
Those Images. Yeats.
To His Valentine. Drayton.
To King James. Jonson.
To the Prince. Davies.
Uncle Jim. Cullen.
What I Think of Hiawatha
(parody). Morris.

Museum (s)
Calling Home the Scientists.
Rose.
Love Song to Eohippus.
Viereck.
New York Sonnet.
Rodriguez.
Ray. Orban.
Seeds of Lead. Gilboa.
The Story of Zeros. Cruz.
Wind Flowers. Lockwood.

Mushroom (s)
The Circle. Garrigue.
Idylls of the King. Hill.
The Krankenhaus of
Leutkirch. Lattimore.
Rust. Hogan.

Music (al)
Abishag. Fichman.
Afternoons with Baedeker.
Lancaster.
Air. Raine.
The Amorous War: Time.
Mayne.
Antigone I. Martin.
Apocalypse. Enright.
As Yet. Rodgers.
Aspects of Spring in Greater
Boston. Starbuck.
The Battle of Boyne.
Anonymous.
The Battle of the Cowpens.
English.
Below Mount T'ui K'oy,
Home of the Gods....
Stroud.
The Blind Man (excerpt).
Wright.
The Boy and the Flute.
Bjornson.
Boy Playing an Organ.
Sweeney.
Bring the Soul Blocks. Cruz.
Bruckner. Camp.
Chops Are Flyin. Crouch.
Christmas. Herbert.
The Christmas Silence.
Deland.
The Christmas Tree.
Cornelius.
The City. Maddow.
Clearing for the Plough.
Moll.
Clinton South of Polk.
Sandburg.
The Clouds. Aristophanes.
Coleridge. Hellman.

Concert at the Station.
Mandelstam.
The Coyote. Revard.
Dawns I Have Seen.
Gurney.
Dear Old Stockholm.
Young.
The Desert Music (excerpt).
Williams.
Each More Melodious Note I
Hear. Thoreau.
Elegiac. Percival.
End of the Flower-World
(A.D. 2300). Burnshaw.
Endymion's Convoy.
Drayton.
The Enigma Variations.
Petrie.
The Epic. Tennyson.
Evening Ride. Hoffman.
A Fable for Critics. Lowell.
The False Summer.
Zaturenska.
Fifine at the Fair, XCIII
(excerpt). Browning.
The Flute: A Pastoral.
Heredia.
For a Musician. Wither.
For Angela. Gilbert.
For M. S. Singing
Fruhlingsglaube in 1945.
Cornford.
From the Commonwealth.
Esteves.
Golden Oldie. Mariani.
The Greater Music. Weiss.
Ground Swell. Koehler.
Helmet Orchid. Stewart.
Her Beauty. Plowman.
Herbs in the Attic. Waniek.
The Hoofer. Redwing.
How Many Bards Gild the
Lapses of Time! Keats.
How Music's Made. Laing.
Hymn of Joy. Van Dyke.
I Am the Wind. Akins.
I Enter by the Darkened Door
(parody). King.
I Send Our Lady. Mary
Therese.
Iberia. Kirschenbaum.
In Passing. Helton.
In the blue distance. Sachs.
The Investment. Frost.
Love. Tieck.
Love in Age. Bell.
Love the Wild Swan. Jeffers.
Lowriders #2. Cardenas.
Man on Move Despite
Failures. Triggs.
Man's Going Hence. Rogers.
Manong Federico Delos Reyes
and His Golden Banjo.
Robles.
Marble Statuette Harpist.
Allen.
Marginal Music. Meiners.
The Master-Player. Dunbar.
Me, in Kulu Se & Karma.
Rodgers.
Memorial Day. Lent.
A Memory. Knowles.
The Merchant of Venice.
Shakespeare.
Merlin. Emerson.
Merry-Go-Round. Van
Doren.
Microcosmus. Nashe [(or
Nash(] Thomas.
Missa Papae Marcelli.
McAuley.
The Moon. Davies.

Mother. Kelleher.
Mozart Perhaps. Wheelock.
Museum with Chinese
Landscapes. Cybulski.
Music. Anonymous.
Music. Thomas.
Music. Towle.
Music at Twilight. Sterling.
Music of the Dawn.
Harrison.
My Heart Is a Lute.
Barnard.
Near the School for
Handicapped Children.
Shapcott.
Not All Sweet Nightingales.
Gongora y Argote.
Notes for a Movie Script.
Holman.
The Old Summerhouse. De
la Mare.
On a Fly-Leaf of Burn's
Songs. Knowles.
On Christmas Day. Paman.
On the Clerk of a Country
Parish. Shenstone.
On the Coast of Coromandel.
Sitwell.
On the Fifth Anniversary of
Bluma Sach's Death.
D'Ambrosio.
One Morning. Miller.
Our Kind Creator. Howe.
Pediment: Ballet. Nicholl.
Perfect Rhyme. Nims.
A Pindaric on the Grunting of
a Hog. Wesley.
The Pipes at Lucknow.
Whittier.
Places and Ways to Live.
Hugo.
The Poet. Morgan.
Poet's Prayer. Sussman.
The Power of Music. Lisle.
Praise and Love. Rands.
A Prayer from 1936.
Sassoon.
The Precious Name.
Newton.
Prize-Giving. Harwood.
Prologue. Symons.
Proper Clay. Van Doren.
Psalm of the Singing Grave.
Janta.
Rain, Rain. Akins.
Ramble on What in the
World Why. Gustafson.
Recital (excerpt). Nicholl.
Redbreast, Early in the
Morning. Bronte.
Reuben, Reuben. Harper.
The Rich Interior Life.
Eberhart.
Riding with the Fireworks.
Darr.
Robin Hood Rescuing Will
Stutly. Anonymous.
Rosalie. Allston.
Ship-Building Emperors
Commanded... Levi.
A Short History of the Better
Life. Gallagher.
The Silent Piano. Simpson.
Silentium. Tyutchev.
Sion. Herbert.
Sirena. Drayton.
The Snow Lies Sprinkled on
the Beach. Bridges.
A Soldier Poet. Johnson.
A Song of the Seamen and
Land Soldiers.
Anonymous.

The Sonnet. Symonds.
Sonnets, X: "When I had
turned Catullus into
rhyme." Irwin.
Soul. Graham.
The Spirit of Poetry.
Longfellow.
Spring Doggerel. Coghill.
Stanzas–April, 1814. Shelley.
Structure of Rime. Duncan.
Sunshine and Music.
Anonymous.
Then. Rukeyser.
There Is a High Place.
Markham.
There's Music in the Air.
Crosby.
Thomas Hardy. De la Mare.
Though He Slay Me. Miller.
Three-Toed Sloth. Donnelly.
To a Little Sister, Aged Ten.
Cummings.
To Her. Mezey.
To Jane: The Keen Stars
Were Twinkling. Shelley.
To Miss–. Johnson.
Tractor Hour. Reid.
A Tragedy. Marzials.
Tree-Building. Cable.
The Trumpet Shall Sound.
Hicks.
Upon a Wasp Chilled with
Cold. Taylor.
Variations for Two Pianos.
Justice.
Vicksburg. Hayne.
The Vintage to the Dungeon.
Lovelace.
The Wagoner's Lad.
Anonymous.
Walking with Your Eyes Shut.
Stafford.
The Wandering Jew. Mezey.
When a Ring's Around the
Moon. Carr.
When Orpheus Went Down.
Lisle.
When the Tree Bares.
Aiken.
When There Is Music.
Morton.
William of Orange.
Anonymous.
With Lilacs. Crandall.
Woman Painter of Mithila.
Mumford.
Words Spoken Alone. Abse.
The Yankeys' Return from
Camp. Anonymous.
You Will See Your Lord A-
Coming. Anonymous.
Zophiel: Palace of the
Gnomes. Brooks.

Musket (s)
The Death of Queen Jane.
Anonymous.
Epitaph to Thomas Thetcher.
Anonymous.
The Wisconsin Soldier Boy.
Anonymous.

Mustache (s)
The Drunken Fool.
Anonymous.
Grandparents. Lowell.
A Mustacheless Bard.
Coogler.

Mustard
A Baker's Dozen of Wild
Beasts. Wells.
The Good Time Is Now.
Chester.

When Jacky's a Very Good
Boy. Mother Goose.

Mute
The Blindman. Swenson.
Chopping Wood. Smith.
Debts. Rittenhouse.
Flower of Love. McKay.
Midnight at Baiae. A Dream
Fragment of Imperial
Rome. Symonds.
Mute Opinion. Hardy.
The Old Wife's Tale. Peele.
Poetry. Foote.
The Poetry of a Root Crop.
Kingsley.
The Quarrel. Swenson.
Silence. Towne.
Silentium. Tyutchev.
Song. Jewett.
To the Soul. Collop.
The Wedding Coat. Rose.
What Five Books Would You
Pick To Be Marooned
with... Leary.

Mutton
Dandoo. *Anonymous.*
Edmund Burke. Goldsmith.
Limerick: "There was a sick
man of Tobago."
Anonymous.
Mutton and Leather.
Anonymous.
Puss in the Pantry.
Anonymous.

Mutual
Madrigal XI: "Love now no
fire hath left him."
Marino.
The Presbyterian Wedding.
Anonymous.
The Rights of Women.
Barbauld.
Sonnets to Philomel. Davies.
To Marie Osmond. Skelley.
The Tryst. Tabb.

Muzzle (d) (s)
The Ageing Hunter. Avane.
Alphabetical Song on the
Corn Law Bill.
Anonymous.
Beautiful Youth. Benn.
The Shadow of Himself.
Renton.

Myra
Caelica, VII. Greville.
Caelica, XII. Greville.
Caelica, XIV. Greville.
Caelica, XXX. Greville.
Caelica, XXXII. Greville.
Caelica, XLI. Greville.
Caelica, XLIX. Greville.
Sent to Him, as He
Whisper'd. Jacob.

Myrrh
Another on Her. Herrick.
Avarice. Hecht.
A Christmas Carol. Thomas.
Correspondences.
Baudelaire.
The Fossils. Kinnell.
The Perfect Gift. Cooke.
Three Ballate. Poliziano.

Myself
As I Grow Older and Fatten
on Myself. Carson.
The Bird. De.
Caelica, XXXIX. Greville.
Caelica, LX. Greville.
Carmina Burana (excerpt).
Anonymous.
Death Deposed. Allingham.

Dedication of a Mirror.
Plato.
The Dream and the Blood.
Untermeyer.
Easter Eve 1945. Rukeyser.
Everything Has Its History.
Levin.
The Excuse. Ralegh.
Fire in My Meditation
Burned. Ainsworth.
First Dream (Excerpt).
Juana Ines de la Cruz.
The Frost Was Never Seen.
Dickinson.
Frutta Di Mare. Scott.
A Girl's Mood. Reese.
Harbor. Price.
Harvesting. Robinson.
Herbert White. Bidart.
Hymn from the French of
Lamartine (excerpt).
Whittier.
I Looked for a Sounding-
Board. Roland-Holst.
I Went into the Maverick Bar.
Snyder.
In Francum. Davies.
In health and ease am I.
Davison.
Jerusalem Sonnets. Baxter.
Leaves of Grass (excerpt).
Whitman.
Limerick: "There was a young
man with a beard."
Jaffray.
Love Made in the First Age.
Lovelace.
Love Sonnets. Cross.
Mr. Frost Goes South to
Boston (parody).
Houghton.
My Father. Chalfi.
My Playmate. Whittier.
My Shoes. Simic.
On Leaving Ullswater.
Raine.
On the Night Express to
Madrid. Dunetz.
On the South Downs.
Teasdale.
The One Who Struggles.
Toller.
A Pair of Lovers. Foster.
Percolating Highway.
Castro.
The Pillar Perished Is.
Wyatt.
Poem of Angela Yvonne
Davis. Giovanni.
Presaging. Rilke.
Rescue. Stuart.
Return to Life. Evans.
Safety or Something. Jacobs.
Sather Gate Illumination.
Ginsberg.
Sentience. McPherson.
The Serenity in Stones.
Ortiz.
A Shropshire Lad.
Housman.
A Song: "Lord, when the
sense of thy sweet grace."
Crashaw.
Song of Myself. Whitman.
Sorrow. Eden.
Thank God. Rolnik.
Three. Morris.
The Three Mirrors. Muir.
'Tis true—they shut me in the
cold. Dickinson.
Today, Prison Won.
Scarbrough.

Toward Myself. Goldberg.
Translations from the Chinese.
Morley.
What Form or Shape to
Describe? Kabir.
What to Say to the Pasha.
Hitchcock.
Words. Levine.

Mystery (ies) (ious)
108 Tales of a Po'Buckra, No.
106. Inman.
An altered look about the
hills. Dickinson.
Assignment: Descriptive
Essay. Willis.
Aunt Melissa. Smith.
The Birth. Dobson.
The Boy and the Geese.
Fiacc.
Burial of a Fisherman in
Hydra. Schulman.
By Winter Seas. Saul.
The Chalk-Pit. Thomas.
City Pigeons. Chasin.
Clerihew. Bentley.
Constance Kent.
Anonymous.
The Dead Moon. Dandridge.
The Dispensary. Garth.
Dust. Russell.
The Edge. Dobson.
Enter No (Silence is the Blood
Whose Flesh. Cummings.
Epitaph, Found Somewhere in
Space. Ramsaur.
The Flowering Bars.
Donnelly.
Football Field: Evening.
McKellar.
Hands. Untermeyer.
Homage to Vaslav Nijinsky.
Kirkup.
How Many Moments
Must(Amazing Each.
Cummings.
Hymn to the Night: II.
"Novalis."
Idols. Burton.
In Early Spring. Meynell.
In the Palms of Ancient
Bodhisattvas. Tagliabue.
The Incomparable Light.
Eberhart.
The Infinite. O'Reilly.
A Leader. Russell.
Looking for a Country under
Its Original Name.
McElroy.
Love Once Was Like an April
Dawn. Johnson.
Names From the War.
Catton.
New Heaven and Earth.
Lawrence.
Night Blooming Flowers.
Pollitt.
The Offering of the Heart.
Humphries.
One West Coast. Young.
Pass to thy Rendezvous of
Light. Dickinson.
Piano Practice. Moss.
Psyche with the Candle.
MacLeish.
The Scientist. Burroway.
The Second Hymn to the
Night. "Novalis" (George
Friedrich Philipp von
Hardenerg).
The Snail. Hughes.
Spirits of the Dead. Poe.
Thanksgiving. Coates.

The Tourist and the Town.
Rich.

Mystic
Apology of Genius. Loy.
Christ's Nativity. Vaughan.
Hymn to Horus. Blind.
Laurence Bloomfield in
Ireland. Allingham.
Lines. Ewart.
The Martyrdom of St. Teresa.
Hope.
On the Birth of Dan
Goldman. Berrigan.
Piano and Drums. Okara.
The Rosary. Maura.
The Sins of Kalamazoo.
Sandburg.

Myth (s)
Autumn's Mirth. Peck.
Because San Quentin Killed
Two More Today.
Lipman.
Birds All Singing. MacCaig.
Elegy. Johnson.
Empedocles on Etna.
Mallalieu.
Indian Summer. Burr.
Landscape Workers. Elliott.
The Membrane.
Berssenbrugge.
November, 1941. Fuller.
Something Starting Over.
Ferril.
Song to the Tune of
"Somebody Stole My Gal."
Kennedy.
Sunday Evenings. Hollander.
To Brooklyn Bridge. Crane.

N

Nag (ging)
Considering the Death of John
Wayne. Phillips.
Song Ballet (I Was Sixteen
Years of Age).
Anonymous.
Testament. Hughes.

Nail (ed) (s)
Ballad of the Goodly Fere.
Pound.
Blame Not My Cheeks.
Campion.
The Bulldozer. Stauffer.
Busy Carpenters. Tippett.
Carpenter of Eternity. Root.
Country Pastor. Inoue.
Crucifixion. "Marie.
Defense Rests. Miller.
The Ex-Poet. Zavatsky.
The Fakir. Cambridge.
For Fear. Creeley.
Hammer. Funkhouser.
He. Kunitz.
His Father's Hands.
Kinsella.
In-Group. Kearns.
Invitation. Contoski.
Is John Smith Within?
Anonymous.
The James Bond Movie.
Swenson.
Lady of Heaven. Guittone
d'Arezzo.
Life's Work. Kumin.
Limerick: "There was a young
lady of Wales."
Anonymous.

Limerick: "There was an old man of the Nile." Lear.
Lullaby. Owen.
Mothers, Daughter. Kaufman.
The New Ring. Shapiro.
Old January. Spenser.
Prayers of Steel. Sandburg.
Slender Fingers. Chao Luan-luan.
Solitary Confinement. Kennedy.
The Structural Study of Myth. Rothenberg.
To Jesus on the Cross. Tejada.
War and Silence. Bly.
Woodyards in the Rain. Marriott.

Naked (ness)
All Souls. Lawrence.
Alone. Shelton.
Ambition. Willis.
The Ancestors. Barrows.
The Body of Summer. Elytis.
Buddha. Holz.
Ceremony. Miller.
Chugachimute I Love the Name. Owens.
Clothes Make the Man. Conway.
A Coat. Yeats.
Cranach. Read.
The Dance of Saul with the Prophets. Tchernichovsky.
The Death of the Craneman. Hayes.
Defense Rests. Miller.
A Dressed Man and a Naked Man. Orwell.
Epigram: "Wealth covers sin." Kassia.
An Event. Field.
A Fiction of Edvard Munch. di Michele.
For Ruggiero and Angelica by Ingres. Rossetti.
From the Persian. Rexroth.
Giant's Tomb in Georgian Bay. "Hale.
Hero and Leander. Marlowe.
I Am Like a Rose. Lawrence.
I Love You. Farkas.
Illusion. Rak.
In Bertram's Garden. Justice.
In Memoriam Paul Celan. Hollander.
In Memory of Leopardi. Wright.
In Nakedness. Pomeroy.
Indignant Protest. Anonymous.
Into the Glacier. Haines.
King Henry VIII. Shakespeare.
Lenox Avenue. Alexander.
Letters. Spencer.
The Marriage Wig. Whitman.
Masks. Fenton.
Motorcycle Irene. Spence.
Mrs. Severin. Scott.
Myth on Mediterranean Beach: Aphrodite as Logos. Warren.
The Naked and the Nude. Graves.
Nativity. Sarton.

Not because of you, not because of me. Gorbanyevskaya.
Old Crabbed Men. Reeves.
Open Poetry Reading. Melendez.
Pannyra of the Golden Heel. Samain.
Pittsburgh. Bynner.
Pushed to the Scroll. Farrar.
The Race Question. Madgett.
Red Sky at Morning. Thomas.
Remembrances. Clare.
Riddle: "In Spring I look gay." Anonymous.
A Simpler Thing, a Chair. Mezey.
Song at the Skirts of Heaven. Greenberg.
Song for the Newborn. Austin.
The Song of the Borderguard. Duncan.
Song: "The world is full of loss." Rukeyser.
Squid. Blumenthal.
Strip Me Naked, or Royal Gin for Ever. Anonymous.
Style. Bukowski.
That Summer's Shore. Ciardi.
Twins. Bulwer-Lytton.
The Waltz. Corke.
Where to Seek Love. Blake.
The Wooden Chamber. Hebert.

Name (d) (less) (s)
Abdullah Bulbul Amir. Anonymous.
Abou Ben Adhem. Hunt.
Accepting. Miller.
Adam. Booth.
Adam's Race. Sa'di.
The Aeneid. Virgil (Publius Vergilius Maro).
Affirmations: I, II, III. Viereck.
After. Levine.
Akhnaton. Jones, Jr.
The Alchemist. Kelly.
All Is God's. De Haan.
America Prays. Field.
Anchor. Anonymous.
And His Name Shall Be Called Wonderful. Nicholson.
And Through the Caribbean Sea. Danner.
Andre. Bates.
De Angels in Heab'n Gwineter Write My Name. Anonymous.
Anonymous. Tabb.
Anseo. Muldoon.
Arac's Song. Gilbert.
The Artist. Grissom.
As I Am My Father's. Drachler.
As When a Man. Tennyson.
At the Un-National Monument along the Canadian Border. Stafford.
August 12, 1952. Fishman.
Ballade of Ladies' Names. Henley.
The Balloon. Tennyson.
The Bar. Anonymous.
The Bargeman's ABC. Anonymous.

The Battle of Lovell's Pond. Longfellow.
Because we suspected. Ise.
Black All Day. Patterson.
Blackie Thinks of His Brothers. Crouch.
Blacklisted. Sandburg.
Blessed Is God. Anonymous.
Blessing over Food. Bialik.
Blondel. Urmy.
Bordering Manuscript. Applewhite.
Bottom's Dream. Dow.
The Building of the Long Serpent. Longfellow.
By the Salt Margin. Evans.
Caelica, LXXI. Greville.
Caelica, LXXXV. Greville.
Caelica, CIV. Greville.
Can't. Spofford.
Canal Street. Wheelwright.
Cape Ann: A View. Brinnin.
Carmen Genesis. Thompson.
A Cemetery in New Mexico. Alvarez.
The Centennial Ode: Dear Land of All My Love. Lanier.
Ceremony for Birth and Naming. Torrence.
Charm for Burns. Anonymous.
The Child. Popham.
Childhood. Muir.
Choosing Their Names. Hood.
Christmas Eve. Shapiro.
The Church Walking with the World. Edwards.
A City Graveyard. Oates.
The Colour of God's Face. Livesay.
Comin' Thro' the Rye. Burns.
The Constant Bridegrooms. Patchen.
The Constant Swain and Virtuous Maid. Anonymous.
Contact. Livesay.
Contemplations. Bradstreet.
County Sligo. MacNeice.
The Cowboy and the Stork. Carr.
Crime. Warren.
Crow, Straight Flier, but Dark. Firestone.
Culbin Sands. Young.
Cut the Cables. Wilson.
The Death of the Craneman. Hayes.
Deo Gracias. Anonymous.
Dido's Hunting. Surrey.
Dodo. Carlile.
Downy Hair in the Shape of a Flame Moving up the Stomach... Barks.
Dream Songs. Berryman.
Dublinesque. Larkin.
The Dwelling. Dor.
The Eagle That Is Forgotten. Lindsay.
Earth-Visitors. Slessor.
Elegy in a Presbyterian Burying-Ground. Wilson.
The Empty Pain-Killer Bottles. Raworth.
English Bards and Scotch Reviewers. Byron.
Envoi. Causley.

Epigram: "Good Fortune, when I hailed her recently." Cunningham.
Epigram: "Sound, sound the clarion, fill the fife! Scott.
Epilogue. Lowell.
Epistle for Spring. Larsson.
Epistle to Be Left in the Earth. MacLeish.
Epitaph. Cunningham.
Epitaphs of the War, 1914-18. Kipling.
Errata. Simic.
Eternall Mover (excerpt). Wotton.
Etruscan Notebook. Clementelli.
Eugenio Pacelli. Neilson.
Europa. Cory.
Everything We Do. Meinke.
Exits and Entrances. Madgett.
The Fairest He. Bonar.
The Fall of J. W. Beane. Herford.
Fame. Browning.
The Father's Business. Markham.
The Fearless. Adler.
Fire: The People. Corn.
Fleshflower. Root.
The Flirtation. Blumenthal.
The Fog. Coffin.
Footprints on the Glacier. Merwin.
....For They Shall See God. Shaw.
Four Stories. Shapiro.
From the Notebooks. Roethke.
Funeral Notices. Storni.
Garryowen. Anonymous.
Gentle Name. Robinson.
Gethsemane. Bontemps.
The Glorious Name. Wells.
God. Lamartine.
God of Our Fathers. Stryker.
God's Garden. Burton.
God's Language. Fainlight.
God Said, "I Made a Man". Villa.
God, Whom Shall I Compare to Thee? Halevi.
Godiva. Tennyson.
Going Home. Kenny.
De Good Lawd Know My Name. Stanton.
The Gourd Dancer. Momaday.
The Great Summons. Chu Yuan.
Harriet. Lorde.
He Holdeth Fast to the Memory of His Identity. Book of the Dead.
He Told Me His Name Was Sitting Bull. Harjo.
Her Eyes. Ransom.
The Hero of Bridgewater. Jones.
His Name Is at the Top. Anonymous.
Home Folks: The Name of Old Glory. Riley.
Hosanna. Traherne.
How Different! Elliott.
The Human Cry. Tennyson.
A Hundreth Good Poyntes of Husbandry. Tusser.
Hynd Etin. Anonymous.
Hyperion. Keats.

I Died for Beauty. Dickinson.

I Found a Horseshoe (with music). Anonymous.

I Have Bowed before the Sun. Walters.

I Have Sought Thee Daily. Ibn Gabirol.

I like coffee, I like tea. Anonymous.

I'll act out a weird dream. Prager.

I'll Be As True. Beddoes.

I'm nobody! Who are you? Dickinson.

I Rode Southern, I Rode L. & N. Anonymous.

Idea's Mirrour. Drayton.

If I Could Walk out into the Cold Country. Brewster.

If You Happy Would Be. Fernandez.

In a Museum in the Capital. Stafford.

In Memoriam, A.H.H., LIX. Tennyson.

In Memoriam A.H.H., LXXIII. Tennyson.

In Pleasant Lands Have Fallen the Lines. Flint.

Innocent's Song. Causley.

Inseparable. Marston.

An Interlude. Swinburne.

Investor's Soliloquy. Ward.

Invocation. Levi Isaac.

It Was an April Morning. Wordsworth.

John Bright. Gummere.

John Filson. Venable.

Kaddish. Yitzhok.

Keats. Tabb.

The Kilkenny Boy. Shanahan.

King Triumphant. Watts.

The Kingdom of God. Rab.

Kings of France. Lincoln.

The Knight Without a Name. Anonymous.

The Lakers: Prologue (excerpt). Plumptre.

Lalai (Dreamtime). Woolagoodjah.

Lament. Hauroa.

Language of Ancients. Lenski.

Larches. Gurney.

Largo. Thompson.

Late Last Night. Gregor.

The Law. Ibn Ezra.

The Lay of the Last Minstrel. Scott.

Lay Your Weapons Down, Young Lady. Feiritear.

Lecompton's Black Brigade. Halpine.

The Lesson. Bentley.

Let Tyrants Shake Their Iron Rod. Billings.

Letter from Caroline Herschel (1750-1848). Fox.

The Letters of a Name. Inez.

Life's Common Duties. Savage.

Like Wings. Schultz.

Limerick: "The British in branding their betters." McCord.

Lindbergh. Anonymous.

Lines Written near Linton, on Exmoor (parody). Hoffman.

Listening. Passy.

The Living Book. Bates.

Local Note. Guiterman.

The Lodger. Longley.

The Lord of All. Markham.

The Lost Baby Poem. Clifton.

The Louisiana Weekly #4. Henderson.

Love Is the Peace, whereto All Thoughts Doe Strive. Greville.

Love's Protestation. Lodge.

The Lovely Village Fair; or, I Dont Mean to Tell You Her Age. Anonymous.

Lycoris darling, once I burned for you. Martial (Marcus Valerius Martialis).

MacFlecknoe, or a Satire upon the True-Blue Protestant Poet T.S. Dryden.

Madonna: 1936. Bonn.

Mahalia. Harper.

The Maiden. Ratner.

Many Die Here. Jones.

The Marble-Streeted Town. Hardy.

The Meeting. Constanzo.

Mellisandra. Rose.

The Messenger. Gunn.

Midway in the Night: Blackman. Redmond.

The Miracle. Emerson.

Missing My Daughter. Spender.

Modern Love, XV. Meredith.

Molly Pitcher. Richards.

The Monkish Mind of the Speculative Physicist. Ramke.

Mother. Tuwim.

Mother, I Am. Clifton.

Mother's Party. Fisher.

Mr. Pope. Tate.

The Mule-Skinners. Caldwell.

My April Lady. Van Dyke.

My Days among the Dead Are Past. Southey.

My Days of Love Are Over. Byron.

My Soul in the Bundle of Life. Anonymous.

The Name. Anonymous.

The Name. Marquis.

Name Giveaway. George.

The Name of Mother. Fetter.

Nameless Journey (excerpt). Goldberg.

A Nameless Recognition. Gregor.

Names. Enright.

The Names of the Humble. Murray.

The Naming. Hummer.

Naming. Stroud.

The Naming of Cats. Eliot.

The Naming of the Beasts. Sparshott.

Naming Power. Rose.

Naming the Baby. Richstone.

New Canaans Genius: Epilogus. Morton.

A New Poem (for Jack Spicer). Duncan.

New York. Wheelock.

Night. Hesse.

No No Blues. Baker.

Now Israel May Say, and That Truly. Whittingham.

A Nymph's Passion. Jonson.

O Lord, Bow Down Thine Ear. Prince.

O My Saviour and Redeemer. Mortenson.

O Thou Whose Feet Have Climbed Life's Hill. Benson.

Ode to Evening. Collins.

Officers. Miles.

Old English Charm Song. Anonymous.

Olney Hymns: Praise for the Fountain Opened. Cowper.

On a Bust of Lincoln. Scollard.

On a Romantic Lady. Monck.

On an East Wind from the Wars. Dugan.

On the Capture and Imprisonment of Crazy Snake, January, 1900. Posey.

On the Late Metamorphosis of an Old Picture.... Anonymous.

Our Father, Our King. Anonymous.

Passion and Worship. Rossetti.

Pater Vester Pascit Illa. Hawker.

Paul and Virginia. Wheelwright.

Peace. Markham.

Phil. Kooser.

Picture of Little Letters. Koethe.

Please Master. Ginsberg.

The Pleasures of Hope. Campbell.

The Pleiades. Coatsworth.

Po" Boy. Anonymous.

Poem and Message. Abse.

A Poem upon the Death of Oliver Cromwell (excerpt). Marvell.

Poem: "We used to float the paper boats in spring." Olsen.

Poet. Shapiro.

The Poetic Land. Roscoe.

The Politics of Rich Painters. Jones.

The Posy Ring. Marot.

Pot Shot. Fallon.

Praise. Matthews.

Prayer for the Journey. Anonymous.

Prayer of Thanksgiving. Baker.

The Precious Name. Newton.

Prologue to Hugh Kelly's "A Word to the Wise'. Johnson.

Psalm III. Ginsberg.

Psalm VIII. Sidney.

Put My Name Down. Silber.

The Quiet-Eyed Cattle. Norris.

A Quiet Life and a Good Name. Swift.

The Quiet Nights. Hinkson.

Rachel's Lament. Zisquit.

Rambling Gambler. Anonymous.

The Rambling Soldier. Anonymous.

The Rape of Europa. Blackmur.

Raziel. Goll.

Read Me, Please! Graves.

Red Jacket. Halleck.

Republic to Republic. Bynner.

A Riddle. Ozick.

Riddle #14: A Horn. Anonymous.

Riddle 24 (Jay: Higora). Anonymous.

Riddle: "As I was a-walking on Westminster Bridge." Anonymous.

Riddle: "The vase which holds all fat'ning liquor." Anonymous.

Riddle: "There was a man rode through our town." Anonymous.

The Romance of Citrus. Sanford.

The Rosciad. Churchill.

Rumplestiltskin Poems. Hathaway.

The Sailor's Alphabet. Anonymous.

San Francisco Arising. Markham.

Sand Creek. Ballard.

Sappho. Cope.

Scandalize My Name. Anonymous.

A Secret. Anonymous.

Seravezza. Fuller.

Shakespearean Soliloquy in Progress: "To have it out or not?" (parody). "W.

Shakespearean Soliloquy in Progress: "To print, or not to..." (parody). Jago.

Shall Man, O God of Light. Dwight.

She Schools the Flighty Pupils of Her Eyes. Hopkins.

The Ship. MacKay.

Should You Go First. Rowswell.

Signature. Kahn.

Silences: A Dream of Governments. Valentine.

Since Then. Enright.

The Sinking of the Merrimac. Larcom.

Sirventes. Blackburn.

Skerryvore. Stevenson.

Sligo and Mayo. MacNeice.

So Beautiful You Are, Indeed. McLeod.

So it Happens. Feldman.

Soliloquy. Ledwidge.

Someone Knocks. Everwine.

Song for a New Generation. Lutz.

Song: "Mother Mother shave me." Anonymous.

The Song of Lo-Fu. Anonymous.

Song: "Oh the charming month of May!" Addison.

Sonnet: "My Love, I cannot thy rare beauties place." Smith.

Sonnet: "Oh for a poet–for a beacon bright." Robinson.

Sonnet: "Whilst thus my pen strives to eternise thee." Drayton.

Sopolis. Callimachus.

Sorrow. Daniel.
Space-Wanderer's Homecoming. Viereck.
Special Rider Blues. *Anonymous.*
Sporting the Plaid. Wallace-Crabbe.
Stairs. Herford.
A State of Nature. Hollander.
Stocking Feet Blues. Jefferson.
The Stone. Gibson.
The Succubus. Rose.
Suicid/ing Indian Women. Allen.
The Surprise at Ticonderoga. Stansbury.
The Surprising History of Aiken Drum. *Anonymous.*
Surviving a Poetry Circuit. Stafford.
Take a Walk around the Corner. Carr.
Ten Types of Hospital Visitor. Causley.
Thanksgiving Hymn. *Anonymous.*
Thesis, Antithesis, and Nostalgia. Dugan.
They Found Him Sitting in a Chair. Gregory.
Thine Eyes Still Shined. Emerson.
Thistle, Yarrow, Clover. Porter.
Thou Leanest to the Shell of Night. Joyce.
Though Fatherland Be Vast. Cross.
Thrice Blest the Man. Barnard.
Thy Name We Bless and Magnify. Power.
Ticonderoga: A Legend of the West Highlands. Stevenson.
To a God Unknown. Eller.
To a Horse. Hoffman.
To Death. Pearse.
To Felicity Who Calls Me Mary. Chesterton.
To Groves. Herrick.
To His Mistress. Ovid (Publius Ovidius Naso).
To Kurnos. Theognis.
To Mr. George Herbert, with One of My Seals, of the Anchor and Christ. Donne.
To Mr. Jervas, with Fresnoy's Art of Painting, Translated by Dryden. Pope.
To My Daughter. Plutzik.
To My Honoured Friend Mr. George Sandys. King.
To My Sister. Berggolts.
To the Father of the Bride. Tasso.
To W.J.M. G.
Tombstone Epitaphs. *Anonymous.*
Too Late. Korn.
The Tragi-Comedy of Titus Oates. *Anonymous.*
The Train Is off the Track. *Anonymous.*
The Trip. Stafford.
Two Loves. Douglas.
The Umpire. Bracker.
The Umpire. Gibson.

Uncle Mells and the Witches' Tree. Roberts.
Unsatisfied. Holmes.
Upon the Feast of St. Simon and St. Jude. Johnson.
A Vagabond Song. Carman.
Various Beasts. Belloc.
Verses for the 60th Birthday of T. S. Eliot. Barker.
The Vestal in the Forum. Wright.
A Vision. Clare.
The Visiting Hour. Wagoner.
Walk Slowly. Love.
Walk-Up. Merwin.
A Warning to Conquerors. MacDonagh.
Washington's Monument. *Anonymous.*
Watching My Daughter Sew. Privett.
We Never Speak as We Pass By. *Anonymous.*
The Well-Travelled Roadway. Newlove.
What I Have Done. Malanga.
What Was Your Name in The States? (with music). *Anonymous.*
When at Night. Perlberg.
When Senses Fled. Woods.
When Sun Doth Rise. Williams.
When What Hugs Stopping Earth Than Silent Is. Cummings.
White Bear. Griffin.
Who Was It Came. Hoffman.
Who Were before Me. Drinkwater.
Whoe'er This Book, if Lost, Doth Find. *Anonymous.*
The Wise Men. Bowers.
A Wish. *Anonymous.*
With a Lifting of the Head. ""MacDiarmid.
Without Names. Tagami.
Women He Liked. Thomas.
Wood Floor Dreams. Henson.
The Word Man. Moffi.
World Music. Bushnell.
Wrestling Jacob. Wesley.
The Yearbook. Clark.
The Yellow Bird Sings. Tagore.

Nancy
Billy Boy. *Anonymous.*
The Calton Weaver. *Anonymous.*
Going Back to School. Benét.
The Mantle So Green (Lovely Nancy). *Anonymous.*
Neglectful Edward. Graves.
On My Wife's Birth-Day. Smart.
Picnic. Lofting.
William Shakespeare to Mrs. Anne,... Gray.

Nap
Anno Domini. Walker.
Asleep at the. *Anonymous.*
Nothing to Do? Silverstein.
To Sir Hudson Lowe. Moore.
The Wedding. Aiken.
What about You? (parody). Pygge.

Wind Is a Cat. Fuller.
Napalm
Another Late Edition (excerpt). Cabral.
Napoleon
The Bonny Bunch of Roses. *Anonymous.*
Don Juan. Byron.
Macavity: the Mystery Cat. Eliot.
Napoleon Hoped That All the World Would Fall beneath His Sway. *Anonymous.*
Politik. Paulin.
Narcissus
Aurora: Sonnet XXVI. Stirling.
Lines to a Reviewer. Shelley.
Occam's Razor Starts in Massachusetts (parody). Pygge.
On a Beautiful Youth Struck Blind with Lightning. Goldsmith.
Visions. Spivack.
Narrow
Chief Petty Officer. Causley.
Childhood. Vaughan.
Cloister. O'Donnell.
The Country Lovers. Smith.
The Family of Eight. Reisen.
Lady in a Distant Face. Welch.
Leaf. Hewitt.
Limerick: "There was an old lady of Harrow." *Anonymous.*
Moon Tiger. Levertov.
O Atthis. Pound.
On the Death of a Cat. Rossetti.
The Patchwork Quilt. Shorter.
Provincetown, Mass. Shapiro.
Rest Only in the Grave. Mangan.
Solitude. Wilcox.
The Tomb of Crethon. Leonidas.
The Wall of China. Colum.
Nasty
An Adminsitrator. Grigson.
Epigram: "'Reincarnating Pythagoras, say." Ausonius.
Natal
Apostasy. Aus of Kuraiza.
A Birthday Ode to Mr. Alfred Austin. Seaman.
Message from Home. Raine.
Nation (s)
Addressed to Haydon. Keats.
Africa. McKay.
America Prays. Field.
Apology for Love. Boccaccio.
The Axe of the Pioneer. Crawford.
A Ballad of the Boston Tea-Party, December 16, 1773. Holmes.
Battle Songs of the King Tshaka. Anonymous.
Bibliolaters: God Is Not Dumb. Lowell.
Boston. O'Reilly.
British Commerce. Thomson.
Cataldo Mission. Hugo.
Chicago. Sandburg.

Dane-Geld. Kipling.
The Death of Jefferson. Butterworth.
The Dissenters' Thanksgiving for the Late Declaration. *Anonymous.*
Elegy. Slonimski.
The Emancipation Group (excerpt). Whittier.
Epitaph on a Bombing Victim. Fuller.
The Excursion. Wordsworth.
The Faerie Queene. Spenser.
The Flag of the Constellation. Read.
A Hot Day in Sydney. *Anonymous.*
How We Became a Nation. Spofford.
I'll Sail upon the Dog-star. Durfey.
In a Closed Universe. Hayford.
In the Due Honor of the Author Master Robert Norton. Smith.
It's Nation Time. Jones.
The Jewish Cemetery at Newport. Longfellow.
Laus Deo. Whittier.
Life of a Queen. Mueller.
Lincoln. Hill.
The Lunar Probe. Kumin.
The Lusty Fryer of Flanders. *Anonymous.*
MacFlecknoe, or a Satire upon the True-Blue Protestant Poet T.S. Dryden.
The Medal Reversed. Settle.
The Men of the Merrimac. Scollard.
The Message of the Bells. Clark.
The Misses Poar Drive to Church. Pinckney.
A Nation Once Again. Davis.
Near Dover, September, 1802. Wordsworth.
The New-Come Chief. Lowell.
The New World. Engle.
O Lord, Almighty God. *Anonymous.*
Pan and Luna. Browning.
Pastoral. Williams.
Poem of the Future Citizen. Craveirinha.
Prophecy. Pulci.
The Queen's Speech. Mainwaring.
Real Happiness. Goldsmith.
Return of a Reaper. Creighton.
The Sea's Voice. Foster.
The Soul and Body of John Brown. Rukeyser.
Such a Parcel of Rogues in a Nation. Burns.
The Tempest. Smith.
The Traveller: The First, Best Country. Goldsmith.
Troop Train. Shapiro.
Up Rising. Duncan.
Upon a Great Shower of Snow That Fell on May-Day, 1654. Washbourne.
When Israel out of Egypt Came. Housman.
Who Shined Shoes in Times Square. Jeffers.

Nation

The Women of the West. Evans.
The World's Justice. Lazarus.

Native (s)

The Air Sentry. Barrington.
The American Flag. Pise.
Boat-Haven, Co. Mayo. Taylor.
The Boys of Wexford. *Anonymous.*
The Brut. Layamon.
The Final Toast. Veitch.
For a Statue of Chaucer at Woodstock. Akenside.
Hymns and Spiritual Songs. Smart.
The Last Bison: Song. Mair.
Love's Labour's Lost. Shakespeare.
My Land. Davis.
Native-Born. Langley.
Sea-Distances. Noyes.
To a Young Child. Scudder.
To His Friend–. Vaughan.
To Miss L.F.... (parody). Squire.
A Toast to Our Native Land. Bridges.
The Triumph of Forgotten Things. Thomas.
Upon the Works of Ben Jonson (excerpt). Oldham.
We Thank Thee. Clark.
Wellington. Harpur.
The Zoo. Sorrentino.

Nativity

At the Cannon's Mouth. Melville.
Carol of the Brown King. Hughes.
I Worship Thee, O Holy Ghost. Warren.

Natural

Dedication to Hunger. Gluck.
If Thou Wouldest Roses Scent. Pastorius.
The Invention of Zero. Urdang.
Lilies. Colum.
Limerick: "A ghoulish old fellow in Kent." Bishop.
Lives of the Poet. Miles.
Many Things Thou Hast Given Me, Dear Heart. Rollins.
Meditation. Rakosi.
My Heart Leaps Up. Wordsworth.
Oedipus. Muir.
The Protective Grigri. Joans.
Reading Plato. Graham.
Sitting down, Looking up. Ammons.
Worship. Whitaker.

Nature

Ain't Nature Commonplace! Guiterman.
Albinovanus. *Anonymous.*
An Angler's Wish. Van Dyke.
Anticipation. Tusiani.
The Aquarium, San Francisco. Sackville-West.
Art above Nature, to Julia. Herrick.
Bad Dreams. Browning.
Boats in a Fog. Jeffers.
Carmen Genesis. Thompson.
Characters of Women. Young.

The Choice. Wither.
Composed in Spring. Burns.
Consummation. Traherne.
Cynthia's Revels. Jonson.
Death's Lecture at the Funeral of a Young Gentleman. Crashaw.
An Essay on Man. Pope.
Four Fawns. Howes.
Full Be the Year, Abundant Be the Grain. *Anonymous.*
Give Me the Splendid Silent Sun. Whitman.
The Goose and the Swans (excerpt). Moore.
Graves of Infants. Clare.
Heard on the Mountain. Hugo.
Her Dilemma. Hardy.
The Highlands' Swelling Blue. Byron.
The Hittites. Fuller.
Horses Aboard. Hardy.
The House-Top. Melville.
The Human Races. Lister.
In Memory of My Dear Grandchild Elizabeth Bradstreet. Bradstreet.
In New Ross. Iremonger.
Keep in the Heart the Journal. Aiken.
Late Autumn. Sullivan.
Lines. Drayton.
M. Crashaws Answer for Hope. Crashaw.
MacDuff. Tomlinson.
The Match. Marvell.
The Merry Minuet. Harnick.
The Midges Dance Aboon the Burn. Tannahill.
The Month of the Thunder Moon. Doyle.
Music in Camp. Thompson.
Nature at Three. Breeser.
New Zealand. Church.
Night Mists. Hayne.
Ode to Simplicity. Collins.
The Old Cumberland Beggar. Wordsworth.
On Finding the Truth. Very.
On Hope. Crashaw.
On Receiving a Copy of Mr. Austin Dobson's "Old World Idylls". Lowell.
On the Eclipse of the Moon of October 1865. Turner.
An Open Air Performance of "As You Like It." Scovell.
The Opponent Charm Sustained. Greenberg.
The Orb Weaver. Weaver.
The Pagans Wild Confesse the Bonds. Williams.
Pardon. Howe.
Patience. Feinstein.
The Pleasures of Hope. Campbell.
Poly-Olbion. Drayton.
The Power of Innocence. "H.
The Prophecy of Famine. Churchill.
Proverbial Advice on Keeping Healthy. *Anonymous.*
The Quaker Graveyard. Mitchell.
Reformation of Manners. Defoe.
A Remembrance of My Friend Mr. Thomas Morley. Davies.

Returning to the Fields. T'ao Ch'ien.
The Ruin. Tomlinson.
The Seasons. Thomson.
Secret Love. Clare.
Seen in a Glass. Raine.
Sic Transit Gloria Scotia. ""MacDiarmid.
Solar Creation. Madge.
A Song. Coppinger.
Song. Stevenson.
Song: "Again rejoicing Nature sees." Burns.
Sonnet XXI: "What grandeurs make a man seem venerable?" Labe.
Sonnet LXXXVI. Greville.
Sonnets, LXVIII: "Thus is his cheek the map of days outworn." Shakespeare.
Sonnets: A Sequence on Profane Love. Boker.
Sonnets from the Portuguese, X. Browning.
The Spotted Flycatcher. De la Mare.
Tao Teh King. Lao Tse [or Lao Tzu].
The Task. Cowper.
Tecumseh. Mair.
There's Life in a Mussel. A Meditation. Farewell.
Three Blessings (Parody on Dryden). *Anonymous.*
Three Sweethearts. Heine.
Through All the World. *Anonymous.*
To Sleep. Fleming.
To Thee, Then, Let All Beings Bend. Evans.
Trees. Nemerov.
Tunbridge Wells. Rochester.
The Villagers and Death. Graves.
Wealth. Emerson.
Weather. Meredith.
Wrestling Jacob. Wesley.

Naught

All Flesh. Thompson.
Burial of the Spirit. Hughes.
Certain Artists Bring Her Dolls and Drawings. Yeats.
Epitaph. Coppard.
Fifty Years. Johnson.
Flowers I Would Bring. De Vere.
Four Sonnets to Helen, 3. Ronsard.
I Am Dark and Fair to See. *Anonymous.*
The Lark. Bernard de Ventadour
Resurgence. Rumi.

Naughty

The Cruel Naughty Boy. *Anonymous.*
I Don't Like Beetles. Fyleman.

Navajo

Song of the Navajo. Pike.
Story Tellers Summer, 1980. Francisco.

Nave (s)

Barthelemon at Vauxhall. Hardy.
Hamlet. Shakespeare.
The Ice-Floes. Pratt.
On the Nativity of Christ Our Lord. Bennett.

Nay

Atlantic Charter: 1942. Young.
The lively sparks that issue from those eyes. Wyatt.
O Lord, So Sweet. *Anonymous.*
The Quaker's Meeting. Lover.
She That Denies Me. Heywood.
Valerius on Women. Heywood.

Nazareth

The Divine Office of the Kitchen. Hallack.
Four Friends. Ward.
The Garden of Epicurus. Meredith.
Hymn for a Household. Henderson.

Nazi (s)

Binni the Meshuggener. Siegel.
Cubist Blues in Poltergeist Major. Kipp.
Woodchucks. Kumin.

Near (er) (est)

Afar in the Desert. Pringle.
Alien. Frazee-Bower.
Brother, Hast Thou Wandered Far. Clarke.
A Dream. Williams.
Engine 143. *Anonymous.*
Epilogue. Aldington.
A Friend. Talfourd.
Gifts. Stokesbury.
The Giveaway. McGinley.
Gravestones. Stuart.
High Wind at the Battery. Pomeroy.
Homecoming in Storm. Kenyon.
The House of Pain. Coates.
The Irish Wife. McGee.
Janna. Kuka.
The Lady's Resolve. Montagu.
Liberty Tree. Paine.
Limerick: "There was a young Fir-tree of Bosnia." Rossetti.
The Lord God Planted a Garden. Gurney.
The Mahabharata (excerpt). *Anonymous.*
Mizpah. Baker.
My Sun-Killed Tree. Harris.
A New Year Wish. *Anonymous.*
Noel! Noel! Simmons.
On the Death of Dr. Robert Levet. Johnson.
On the Move. Gunn.
Once When You Were Walking. Wynne.
Poem: "Old man in the crystal morning after snow." Schwartz.
Poem: "To go, to leave the classics and the buildings." Ewart.
Postcards from Kodai. Crossley-Holland.
The Praise of Age. Henryson.
Satan Is Following Me. *Anonymous.*
Sing, Brothers, Sing! Rodgers.
Sleeping in a Cave. Nye.

So Close Should Be Our Love.
  Anonymous.
Song: "Because I know deep
  in my own heart."
  Murray.
Sonnets, LXI: "Is it thy wil,
  thy Image should keepe
  open." Shakespeare.
Tenebrae. Celan.
Thou, Our Elder Brother.
  Whittier.
To Lucasta: The Rose.
  Lovelace.
Two Mountains Men Have
  Climbed. Starkweather.
Two Went up to the Temple
  to Pray. Crashaw.
The Wakening. *Anonymous.*
What Mystery Pervades a
  Well! Dickinson.
When You're Away.
  Hoffenstein.
Winter Dusk. De La Mare.
The Work That Saves!
  Bonar.
The World as Meditation.
  Stevens.
Year after year I have
  watched. Li Ch'ing-chao.

Neat (ly)
Ben Backstay. *Anonymous.*
Cats. Francis.
Crucial Stew. Inez.
Decent Burial. Montross.
Quail Walk. Miller.

Nebuchadnezzar
Bestiary. Klein.
Warm Babies. Preston.

Necessary
An American Boyhood.
  Holden.
Julius Caesar. Shakespeare.
Stanzas in Meditation. Stein.
Temperature. Malanga.
Variation on the Word Sleep.
  Atwood.

Necessity
The Excursion. Wordsworth.
Faith–is the Pierless Bridge.
  Dickinson.
Glengormley. Mahon.
The Night There Was
  Dancing in the Streets.
  Olson.
Palamon and Arcite, III:
  "Parts of the whole are we;
  but God the whole.
  Dryden.
Prelude. Whittier.
The Riders. Friend.
These Things Shall Be.
  Symonds.
They might not need me.
  Dickinson.

Neck (s)
Another Kind of Burning.
  Fox.
Archys Last Name.
  Marquis.
Astrophel and Stella,
  LXXXIII. Sidney.
At a Reading. Aldrich.
At the Theater. Herbert.
Barber's Clippers. Baruch.
The Bastard from the Bush.
  Anonymous.
Biography. Jones.
Blue Heron. Welch.
Carol. Wilkinson.
College Yell. *Anonymous.*
Dead Bird (parody). Slavitt.
Deer. No Ch'on-myong.

Epigram: "If thou seekest the
  dread throne of God."
  Anonymous.
The Fertile Valley of the Nile.
  Merriam.
For shamefast harm of great
  and hateful need. Wyatt.
Haiku: "A bitter morning:".
  Hackett.
In the Library. Ochester.
Jacob and the Angel.
  Brother Antoninus.
Kob Antelope. *Anonymous.*
Lachesis. Raine.
The Lesson. Mariani.
Let Your Pastor Know.
  Anonymous.
Nursery Rules from Nannies.
  Anonymous.
Odes (excerpt). Tibullus.
The Odyssey. Homer.
Old Maid's Song.
  Anonymous.
On Bell-Ringers. Voltaire
  (Francois Marie Arouet).
On the Murder of Sir
  Edmund Berry Godfrey.
  Anonymous.
The Progress of Poesy.
  Gray.
A Question. *Anonymous.*
R. I. P. Struther.
Rope and Drum. Currie.
Say That We Saw Spain Die.
  Millay.
The Seasons. Thomson.
A Shot at Random. Lewis.
Swans Mating. Longley.
To See Him Again.
  "Mistral.
To the Pending Year.
  Whitman.
To the Puss Moth.
  Anonymous.
To the Rulers. Nemerov.
Two at Showtime. Brabant.
Vision of 400 Sunrises.
  Schechter.
Walking in the Rain. Saxon.
The Wandering Lunatic Mind.
  Carpenter.
Who Killed Lawless Lean?
  Smith.
The Whummil Bore.
  Anonymous.
Written on a Girl's Table-
  Napkin at Wiesbaden.
  Duncan.

Necklace (s)
Blue Glass. Adcock.
Cressida. Baxter.
Scrimshaw. Hogan.
Sentences (excerpt).
  Harrison.

Nectar
Amoretti, XXXIX. Spenser.
O Dear Life, When Shall It
  Be? Sidney.
On Catullus. Landor.
Rana, why do you treat me.
  Mira Bai [(or Mirabai)].

Need (ed) (s) (y)
Absolution. Sassoon.
After Sex. Kuzma.
All in Due Time.
  Cunningham.
Am I to Lose You?
  Bevington.
And Art Thou Come, Blest
  Babe? *Anonymous.*
Another Easter. Ridland.

Ark Astonished.
  Macpherson.
As a Possible Lover. Jones.
The Awakening. Marquis.
B Stands for Bear. Belloc.
A Black Soldier Remembers.
  Coalman.
The Character of a Good
  Person. Dryden.
Das Schloss. Kirstein.
The Doubter. Gilder.
Ducks. Bly.
Dwell with Me, Lovely
  Images. Maynard.
The Engagement. Clough.
Exiled. Millay.
Guerrilla. Pieterse.
The Halt. Miles.
Hellhound on My Trail.
  Johnson.
Hitherto and Henceforth.
  Flint.
Home Is the Sailor.
  McGinley.
Hunter's Song. Nangolo.
Hymn. Peabody.
A Hymne to Our Saviour on
  the Cross. Chapman.
I Need Not Your Needles.
  Anonymous.
Inscription for a Mirror in a
  Deserted Dwelling. Benet.
Interceding. Gibbs.
Jesus Return. Van Dyke.
Kindness. *Anonymous.*
Leaders. *Anonymous.*
Leaflets. Rich.
Letter to a Dead Father.
  Shelton.
The Little Brother Poem.
  Nye.
Lover to Lover. Morton.
Mary Magdalene. Rossetti.
Masters. Amis.
More Prayer. *Anonymous.*
A Mother's Prayer. Coon.
My life closed twice before its
  close. Dickinson.
A New Song to Sing about
  Jonathan Bing. Brown.
Norembega. Whittier.
O Lord, That Art My God
  and King. Craig.
On Looking at an Old
  Climbing Photograph.
  Fraser.
On Not Being Your Lover.
  McGuckian.
Parting at Morning.
  Browning.
Rainy Night at the Writers'
  Colony. Jacobsen.
Raving Warre, Begot.
  Campion.
Reciprocity. Miller.
Salt. Clifton.
Signals. Amini.
Sing Little Bird. Hastings.
Some Kisses from the Kama
  Sutra. Williams.
The Sprig of Lime. Nichols.
Spring. Larkin.
Thailand Railway. Stow.
Uncle Death. Clark.
Visiting the Oracle. Raab.
Yiddish. Herzberg.
Your Need Is Greater Than
  Mine. Enslin.

Needle (s)
Crow Country. Slessor.
A Dance for Ma Rainey.
  Young.

Great God, Thy Works.
  Byles.
I Need Not Your Needles.
  Anonymous.
In Quest to Have Not.
  Honig.
The Jolly Trades-Men.
  Anonymous.
Leap in the Dark. Hill.
Solo for Bent Spoon. Finkel.
Sonnet. Duncan.
Step father. Fitzgerald.
To Mark Rothko of Untitled
  (Blue, Green), 1969.
  Cherner.

Negative (s)
Aids for Latin. Perry.
Five Epigrams. Hall.
Lament for a Cricket Eleven.
  Allott.
Small Moon. Nemerov.
Sutcliffe and Whitby. Logan.
Though He Slay Me. Miller.

Neglect (ed)
Amynta. Elliot.
At the Un-National
  Monument along the
  Canadian Border. Stafford.
For the Cultural Campaign.
  Jigmed.
In the Tub We Soak Our
  Skin. Horn.
No Foundation. Hollander.
Wildwood Flower.
  Anonymous.

Negotiate
Concerning One Responsible
  Negro with Too Much
  Power. Giovanni.
The Trout. Hine.

Negro (es)
At the Closed Gate of Justice.
  Corrothers.
At the National Black
  Assembly. Jones.
Deep Night. Jimenez.
Down the Mississippi.
  Fletcher.
Echoes of Childhood.
  Corbin.
Hearing Men Shout at Night
  on MacDougal Street. Bly.
The Negro's Tragedy.
  McKay.
Ode to Walt Whitman.
  Garcia Lorca.
On Being Brought from
  Africa to America.
  Wheatley.
The Rooftree. Tate.
Rounding the Cape.
  Campbell.
Suffer, Poor Negro. Diop.
View from the Corner.
  Allen.

Neighbor (s)
Advice from Poor Robin's
  Almanack. *Anonymous.*
Brave Old World. Lambert.
Briggflatts. Bunting.
Contemporary Nursery
  Rhyme. *Anonymous.*
Cross Patch. Mother Goose.
Crosspatch. *Anonymous.*
Eighteen. Mary Honora.
Guard Thy Tongue. Barr.
I before E. *Anonymous.*
In an Arab Town. Tichy.
In the Hole. Ciardi.
Killed at the Ford.
  Longfellow.

The Last Farmer in Queens.
  Karp.
The Latest Decalogue.
  Clough.
Life's Testament.
  Baylebridge.
The Man in the Ocelot Suit.
  Brookhouse.
Mending Wall. Frost.
My Brother Bert. Hughes.
My Daily Creed.
  Anonymous.
Nature's Questioning.
  Hardy.
Near Neighbors. Martial
  (Marcus Valerius Martialis).
Old I Am. Bosman.
A Panegyrick to My Lord
  Protector. Waller.
The Parrot. Lucie-Smith.
The Shoofly. Anonymous.
Tellers of Tales. Kallman.
Theology. Dunbar.
Thoughts on the
  Commandments. Baker.
Twenty-One Sonnets. Stead.
The Twins. Leigh.
Under Glass. Kreymborg.
The World State.
  Chesterton.
Your Neighbor. Biggar.

Neighborhood
Mean Old Twister. Arnold.
Shooting Script (excerpt).
  Rich.
Sonnetto XXXV: "My Lady's
  face it is they worship
  there." Cavalcanti.
Washing Windows. Wild.

Nell
A Ballad upon a Wedding.
  Suckling.
Nell Gwynne's Looking-Glass.
  Blanchard.
Sledburn Fair. Anonymous.
When They Found Giotto.
  Laing.

Nell (ie)
The Bird on Nellie's Hat.
  Lamb.

Nelson
Daniel Defoe. Landor.
Grand Conversation on Brave
  Nelson. Anonymous.
Victory. Anonymous.

Neptune
Hero and Leander. Marlowe.
In Praise of Neptune.
  Campion.
The Lords of the Main.
  Stansbury.
Neptune. Campion.

Nerve (s)
Absence. Jago.
After War. Gurney.
At Night. Proctor.
Dietary Advice. Anonymous.
The Mirror in Which Two
  Are Seen as One. Rich.
Mutations of the Phoenix
  (excerpt). Read.
New Music. Harwood.
Soft Wood. Lowell.
Tonsilectomy. Rivers.
Winter Song. Daiches.

Nervous
At the Tennis Clinic.
  Martin.
Morvin. Fuller.
Prayerwheel/2. Meltzer.

Nest (ed) (s)
Accidia. Beeching.

Alone. Jammes.
Altarwise by Owl-Light.
  Thomas.
Appeal to the Phoenix.
  Untermeyer.
The Begetting of Cain.
  Plutzik.
The Bird. Michelson.
The Birds' Ball. Bardeen.
The Calling. Contardo.
Child's Talk in April.
  Rossetti.
Connoisseur of Chaos.
  Stevens.
Conquistador. McElhaney.
The Container. Corman.
Crows in Spring. Clare.
A Daughter of Admetus.
  Moore.
The Defeated. Merwin.
The Difference. O'Huiginn.
Elegy. Cohen.
Elegy. Dow.
The Emigrant's Child.
  Sproull.
Exaltation. Werfel.
Fall 1961. Lowell.
Free Little Bird. Anonymous.
From a Rise of Land to the
  Sea. Hoffmann.
Good Counsel. Mangan.
Green Jade Plum Trees in
  Spring. Ou Yang Hsiu.
Heavenly Jerusalem,
  Jerusalem of the Earth.
  Goldberg.
Her breast is fit for pearls.
  Dickinson.
Hyperion. Keats.
I Am the Mountainy Singer.
  Campbell.
I Watched a Blackbird.
  Hardy.
An Indian Summer Day on
  the Prairie. Lindsay.
Jason and Medea. Lewis.
King James and Brown.
  Anonymous.
Kriss Kringle. Aldrich.
Lady Isabel and the Elf
  Knight (Pretty Polly).
  Anonymous.
The Land of Indolence.
  Thomson.
Lines: "I followed once a fleet
  and mighty serpent."
  Beddoes.
Lost Beliefs. Howells.
A Memory. Knowles.
Nested. Lulham.
The Pretty Ploughboy.
  Anonymous.
The Rose. Lovelace.
Rus in Urbe. Scott.
Sailor. Hughes.
Sea-Birds. Akers.
The Skull in the Desert.
  Trimpi.
The Skylark's Nest. Long.
The Smooth Divine. Dwight.
Sonnets, II: "And then I sat
  me down, and gave the
  rein." Rosenhane.
Splendid and Terrible.
  O'Sullivan.
Street Kid. Niatum.
The Trail of the Bird.
  Courthope.
Uncle an' Aunt. Barnes.
Walking on Sunday.
  Murphy.

Weaving Love-Knots 2.
  Hsueh T'ao.
When the Iceworms Nest
  Again. Service.
The World's Wanderers.
  Shelley.
The Young Martins. Young.

Net (s)
Ascent. Saunders.
The Delicate, Plummeting
  Bodies. Dobyns.
Drunk as drunk on
  turpentine. Neruda.
Fishing Song. Anonymous.
Hymn to the Virgin Mary.
  O'Riordan.
Love in the Valley.
  Meredith.
My Lord Says He's Gwineter
  Rain Down Fire.
  Anonymous.
The Overthrow of Lucifer.
  Fletcher.
Pains and Gains. De Vere.
Peasant and Geisha Songs.
  Anonymous.
The Poem. Schloss.
Psychoanalysis. Ewart.
Roger Francis. Thorley.
Sheep Country. Pond.
Sunken Evening. Lee.
Swell My Net Full.
  Anonymous
The Zoo in the City. Allen.

Nettles
Bella and the Golem.
  Ombres.
She Weeps over Rahoon.
  Joyce.
The Tin-Whistle Player.
  Colum.

Neurotic
Birthday Card for a
  Psychiatrist. Van Duyn.
Les Etiquettes Jaunes.
  O'Hara.

Never
As Concerning Man.
  Radcliffe.
As If You Had Never Been.
  Eberhart.
Ballad: "Father, through the
  dark that parts us."
  Fuller.
Blow away the Morning Dew.
  Anonymous.
Brummell at Calais. Glassco.
Bulldozers. Dec.
"Don't Care" and "Never
  Mind." Bangs.
Edward. Anonymous.
The Elm. Shepard.
English Girl. Mathers.
Epodes. Horace.
The First Step. Saxton.
For Every Evil under the Sun.
  Anonymous.
For My Students, Returning
  to College. Williams.
Friends. Brown.
Frisbee. Humphries.
From the Point. Petrie.
Grandpa Is Ashamed. Nash.
The Great Hunt. Sandburg.
The Gypsy Girl. Alford.
Hope. Mezquida.
How Firm a Foundation.
  Anonymous.
Kind Words Can Never Die.
  Hutchinson.
The Lost Baby Poem.
  Clifton.

Midsummer. Russell.
The Moral. Weiss.
My Child. Griffin.
My Father's Cot (parody)
  (excerpt). Squire.
The Never Again.
  Dobzynski.
Now. Ken.
Now or Never. Moffett.
Nursery Rhymes for the
  Tender-Hearted. Morley.
Ode: "Love thy Country, wish
  it well." Dodington.
Old Virginny. Bland.
Once When You Were
  Walking. Wynne.
One Goes with Me along the
  Shore. Winkler.
Piano Lessons. Wormser.
A Practical Program for
  Monks. Merton.
Preludes. Aiken.
Prothalamion. Young.
Sabbath. Rosenmann-Taub.
Sacred Formula to Destroy
  Life. Anonymous.
The Satisfying Portion.
  Anonymous.
The Ship in Distress.
  Anonymous.
Sisters. Lowell.
Sonnet: "The master and the
  slave go hand in hand."
  Robinson.
That "Craning of the Neck".
  Gardner.
They Never Taste Who
  Always Drink. Prior.
'Tis the Witching Hour of
  Night. Keats.
Train Blues. Zimmer.
The Walk in the Garden.
  Aiken.
We Cared for Each Other.
  Heine.
A Welcome. Browne.
The Wheel Revolves.
  Rexroth.
Where Are the Ones Who
  Lived Before? Anonymous.
Why Not? Pastan.
A Woman's Shortcomings.
  Browning.
Women Are Not Gentlemen.
  Matthews.

Nevermore
The Raven. Poe
The Reagan (parody).
  Quick.
The Sculptor. Anonymous.

New
Adjustment. Whittier.
Advice. Amichai.
Advice to the Young.
  Waddington.
Amoretti, IV. Spenser.
Amoretti, LXII. Spenser.
Animal Acts. Simic.
Annunciation over the
  Shepherds (excerpt).
  Rilke.
Bells of New Year. Field.
Bleat of Protest. Weston.
The Body. Bronk.
Brave New World.
  MacLeish.
Caelica, CVIII. Greville.
CANDU Can't Do. Filip.
Children Waking: Indian Hill
  Station. Currey.
The Chronicler. Bergman.
Cologne. Domin.

The Common Woman. Grahn.
The Complete Introductory Lectures on Poetry. Mayer.
Confidence. *Anonymous.*
Conquest. Coatsworth.
The Contentment of Willoughby. Alexander.
Corsons Inlet. Ammons.
Crescent Moon. Roberts.
The Cripple for Life. *Anonymous.*
Davening. Ratner.
The Daventry Wonder. Agricola.
Dawn Wail for the Dead. Walker.
Days of the Leaders, 1925: The Deaf. Lamprey.
A Dream about an Aged Humorist. Zeitlin.
Eagle Sonnets. Wood.
Elegy for the Silent Voices and the Joiners of Everything. Patchen.
Enchantment. Alexander.
Entering the Room. Pfingston.
Eye-Witness. Torrence.
Eyesight II. Duncan.
Falltime. Sandburg.
The Fawn. Millay.
Fighter. Zimunya.
Five Little Sisters Walking in a Row. Greenaway.
The Future and the Ancestor. Chedid.
The Hasty Pudding. Barlow.
Heroic Heart. Donnelly.
How Happy the Man. *Anonymous.*
How Shall We Rise to Greet the Dawn? Sitwell.
I Have Seen Black Hands. Wright.
I Like House Cleaning. Thompson.
I like my body when it is with your. Cummings.
Il Pastor Fido. Guarini.
Image from d'Orleans. Pound.
In a U-Haul North of Damascus. Bottoms.
In the Yucca Land. Morris.
In Time of Silver Rain. Hughes.
Italian Woman. Wakoski.
June. Morris.
Let Her Give Her Hand. *Anonymous.*
Libation. Levertov.
Light of the World. Monsell.
Limerick: "Said the spider, in tones of distress." Herford.
Looking at Quilts. Piercy.
A Love-Song. Turner.
Love Unknown. Herbert.
The Magnolia's Shadow. Montale.
Modern Love, XV. Meredith.
Modern Love, XL. Meredith.
Moments. Schwob.
The Moon-Bone Cycle: New Moon. *Anonymous.*
My Beautiful Lady. Woolner.
My Polish Grandma. Field.

Nearer. Herzberg.
The New View. Holmes.
New Year on Dartmoor. Plath.
No Dawns. Perry.
No New Music. Crouch.
Norman Morrison. Mitchell.
O Life That Maketh All Things New. Longfellow.
Observation Car and Cigar. Stafford.
The Odour. Herbert.
Old and New. *Anonymous.*
Old Jewish Cemetery in Worms. Kittner.
The Old Munro Bagger. *Anonymous.*
On a Celtic Mask by Henry Moore. Gregory.
On Linden Street. Ehrlich.
Once I Thought to Die for Love. *Anonymous.*
Outlook Uncertain. Reid.
The Passing of Arthur. Tennyson.
Passion. Kinnell.
Pedlar. Nelson.
The Pilgrim. Wightman.
The Pitch Piles Up in Part. O'Grady.
Poem of Distant Childhood. Sousa.
Poets. Flexner.
Port of Call: Brazil. Lewis.
Public Beach (Long Island Sound). Morley.
Remembering Fannie Lou Hamer. Davis.
Remove the Predicate. Coolidge.
Revving Up La Reve. Dailey.
Sandstone. Marriott.
The Secular Masque. Dryden.
Shadows. Lawrence.
She Asks for New Earth. Hinkson.
Silex Scintillans. Vaughan.
The Skies Cant Keep Their Secret! Dickinson.
Soaps. Witt.
Solomon. Hagedorn.
Sometime I sigh, sometime I sing. Wyatt.
Song of Oenone and Paris. Peele.
Song: "Song is so old." Hagedorn.
Sonnets, XV: "When I consider every thing that grows." Shakespeare.
Sonnets–Actualities. Cummings.
Sonnets after the Italian. Gilder.
That Mulberry Wine. Sylvester.
There Is Nothing New in New York. Pinero.
To a Tenting Boy. Turner.
To Mr. Henry Lawes. Philips.
Tom Cat Blues. *Anonymous.*
Visit. Ammons.
Waillie. *Anonymous.*
We Shall Say. DeFord.
When This Old Hat Was New. *Anonymous.*
Who Knows? Coan.
The "Word" of an Antelope Caught in a Trap. Sandag.

The Work-Out. Movius.
You in Anger. Reeves.

New England
An Elegie upon the Death of the Reverend Mr. Thomas Shepard (excerpt). Oakes.
God's Controversy with New-England. Wigglesworth.
Longfellow's Visit to Venice. Betjeman.
A Painter in New England. Stork.
Praise of New England. Chubb.
Rolling Home. *Anonymous.*
What Is–"Paradise". Dickinson.

New Jerusalem
Kelpius's Hymn. Peterson.
O Christmas Night. Selyns.
The Star. Weaving.
We Are on Our Journey Home. *Anonymous.*

New Mexico
Boggy Creek. *Anonymous.*

New Orleans
Aerial View of Louisiana. Mathis.

New South Wales
Lines on a Mysterious Occurrence. Godley.
There Is a Place in Distant Seas. Whately.

New World (s)
Africland. La Grone.
Big Cars. McNair.
Clarel. Melville.
The Dead Tribune. McCarthy.
Hammerstoke. Domanski.
The Idiot. Naude.
Korf's Enchantment. Morgenstern.
Love Is Enough (excerpt). Morris.
My Feet. Jenkins.
The New World. Engle.
Paradise Lost. Milton.
Prisoners. Jarrell.
Sugar Daddy. Smither.
Tudor Portrait. Lattimore.
We Shall Overcome. *Anonymous.*

New Year
34 Blues. Patton.
Ane Sang of the Birth of Christ, with the Tune of Baw Lula Low. *Anonymous.*
Ceremony. Cumbo.
Comfort and Tidings of Joy. *Anonymous.*
A Dark Day. Rossetti.
Elegy for My Father. Strand.
Forget. *Anonymous.*
Here We Come A-Wassailing. *Anonymous.*
Hymn for the Eve of the New Year. Gerondi.
McKinley. *Anonymous.*
The Moon Shines Bright. *Anonymous.*
The New Year. Craik.
The New Year for Trees. Schwartz.
New Year's Water. *Anonymous.*
On the Circumsision: New Years Day. Wadding.
Sonnet: Of the 20th June 1291. Angiolieri.

Three Ships. *Anonymous.*
Thysia. Luce.
Up the Hill, Down the Hill. Farjeon.
A Vow for New Year's. Davies.
What Cheer? *Anonymous.*

New York
The Bus. Cohen.
Can't They Dance the Polka! *Anonymous.*
The City in the Throes of Despair. Towle.
A Country Boy in Winter. Jewett.
The Good Ship. Stephens.
I Awoke with the Room Cold. Piercy.
I Was Sitting in McSorley's. Cummings.
Jottings of New York. McGonagall.
Limerick: "There was a young lady from Cork." Nash.
Nothing but Image. Swilky.
The Sidewalks of New York. Blake.
Storm on Fifth Avenue. Sassoon.
The Streets of New York. Blossom.
There Is Nothing New in New York. Pinero.
Train to Reflection. O'Neill.
Walking. O'Hara.

New York Central
Tracks. Schwager.

New York Evening/Mail.
Haec Olim Meminise Iuvabait. Taylor.

New York Times
Hot Night on Water Street. Simpson.

New York Tribune
Poetry and Thoughts on Same. Adams.

New Yorker
Under Which Lyre. Auden.

New Zealand
The Burial of Sir John McKenzie. MacKay.
Triumphal Ode MCMXXXIX. Barker.

Newborn
At Wonder Donut. Mar.
Dream Songs. Berryman.
Good Mornin', Blues. *Anonymous.*
Hark! The Herald Angels Sing. Wesley.
My Sister's Sleep. Rossetti.
Night. Lovelace.
A Son Just Born. Miller.
Struggle. Lanier.
Virgin Mary Had One Son. *Anonymous.*
Words from an Old Spanish Carol. Sawyer.

Newbury Street
The Beasts of Boston. Lowry.

Newfoundland
The Banks of Newfoundland (I). *Anonymous.*
The Banks of Newfoundland (II). *Anonymous.*
Bound down to Newfoundland. *Anonymous.*

Newgate
A Friendly Address. Hood.

On Calamy's Imprisonment
  and Wild's Poetry.
  "Hudibras"

News
At First. Sisson.
The Cubistic Lovers. Eaton.
Discomfort in High Places.
  Tremayne.
Ellie Mae Leaves in a Hurry.
  Klappert.
G. K. Chesterton. Wolfe.
Gentian. Crane.
The George Aloe and the
  Sweepstake. *Anonymous.*
Hello! Garnett.
The Hemorrhage. Kunitz.
His Toy, His Dream, His
  Rest. Berryman.
How They Brought the Good
  News by Sea. Farber.
The Late Show. Heyen.
Letter Written on a Ferry
  Crossing Long Island
  Sound. Sexton.
News. Pomeroy.
News! News! Farjeon.
O Night O Trembling Night.
  Spender.
The Only News I Know.
  Dickinson.
A Petition. Aldrich.
A Poem in Praise of Colum
  Cille. Forgaill.
The Print-Out. Nemerov.
Some Bombs (excerpt).
  Padgett.
Sonnet C. Greville.
Stiles. Pudney.
The Telephone. Field.
There's been a death, in the
  opposite house. Dickinson.
When He Thought Himself
  Contemned. Howell.

Newsboys
Aubade. MacNeice.

Newspaper (s)
Daily News. Clark.
Dog's Death. Updike.
Get the Gasworks. Ignatow.
Homecoming. Sanchez.
The Limited. Warren.
Three Women. Edmond.
Twenty-Year Marriage.
  Anthony ("Ai").
Two Hookers. Redwing.

Newton
Death's Vision (excerpt).
  Reynolds.
Letters: With Happiness
  Stretchd Across the Hills.
  Blake.

Next
Answer to Pauper. Hood.
Carry Me Back. Holmes.
"Dover Beach"–a Note to
  That Poem. MacLeish.
Exigencies. Gilbert.
For a Neighbor Girl. Yu
  Hsuan-chi.
From a Survivor. Rich.
Gruesome. McGough.
Havdolah. Litwack.
The Hospital Waiting-Room.
  Davies.
The House of the Trees.
  Wetherald.
A Hymn to Contentment.
  Parnell.
Kings of France. Lincoln.
Limerick: "A clergyman told
  from his text."
  Anonymous.

Meeting the Reincarnation
  Analyst. Gildner.
Phillis. *Anonymous.*
The Revel. Dowling.
Scholfield Huxley. Masters.
The Second Coming.
  Carrington.
The Still Small Voice. Klein.
Susan. *Anonymous.*
There is a soldier on a
  battlefield. *Anonymous.*
The Undertaker's Horse.
  Kipling.
The Virtues of Sid Hamet, the
  Magician's Rod. Swift.
Waiting for the Doctor.
  Inez.

Nice (er) (est)
Ambition. Kilmer.
Bedtime Stories. Moore.
Birthday Cake. Eastwick.
Christmas Dinner. Rosen.
The English Are So Nice!
  Lawrence.
The Finest Thing. Veitch.
The Fire Ship. *Anonymous.*
How the Leaves Came Down.
  "Coolidge.
If I Leave Here Alive.
  Mahaka.
Letter to Scanlon from
  Whitehall. Hugo.
Little Willie. *Anonymous.*
A Local Storm. Justice.
London's Bridge Is A-Burning
  Down. *Anonymous.*
Miss Snooks, Poetess. Smith.
Mr. Pyme. Behn.
Plans. Thompson.
Seumas Beg. Stephens.
Singular Indeed. McCord.
Song of Sukkaartik, the
  Assistant Spirit.
  Anonymous.
Temporary Problems. Rubin.
Two People. Rieu.

Nick
Ballad of Ladies' Love,
  Number Two. Villon.
Song: "Of thee, kind boy, I
  ask no red and white."
  Suckling.

Nickel
In Galleries. Jarrell.
Lemonade Stand.
  Thompson.
Shout, Little Lulu.
  Anonymous.
Wheat Metropolis.
  Hamilton.

Nickle
A Nickle Bet. Knight.

Nicodemus
The Bone That Has No
  Marrow. Dickinson.
Wake Nicodemus. Work.

Niece (s)
Good and Bad Children.
  Stevenson.
Japanesque. Herford.

Nigger (s)
Ain't It Hard to Be a Right
  Black Nigger? *Anonymous.*
Cap'n & Me. Baker.
Cathexis. Bryant, Jr.,
Conversation. Giovanni.
Prime. Hughes.
Run, Nigger, Run!
  Anonymous.
Walky-Talky Jenny (with
  music). *Anonymous.*
Watts. Rivers.

We Raise de Wheat.
  Anonymous.
Whose Old Cow?
  Anonymous.
You're Nothing but a Spanish
  Colored Kid. Luciano.
You've Been a Good Old
  Wagon, But You've Done
  Broke Down. Harney.

Nigh
The Ancient Thought. Kerr.
La Corona. Donne.
God Is Nigh. *Anonymous.*
God the Omniscient.
  Wallace.
The Merchantman.
  Davidson.
My Prayer. *Anonymous.*
On Recrossing the Rocky
  Mountains after Many
  Years. Fremont.
Sweet Loving Friendship.
  Bellamy.
Uncle IV Surveys His Domain
  from His Rocker....
  Williams.

Night (s)
1939 Mercury. Drake.
4th of July. Williams.
Acquainted with the Night.
  Frost.
The Actor. Snapp.
The Acts of Youth. Wieners.
Ad Matrem in Coelis. Van
  Voorhis.
An Additional Poem.
  Ashbery.
Admiral. Allen.
African Dream. Kaufman.
After Reading St. John the
  Divine. Derwood.
After the Party. Cornford.
Ah, Poor Bird. *Anonymous.*
Air. Merwin.
Akiba. Rukeyser.
The Albatross. Reeves.
Alexandria. Durrell.
All Day We've Longed for
  Night. Fabio.
All Night Long. *Anonymous.*
All the while, believe me, I
  prayed. Sappho.
All through the Night.
  Anonymous.
Alone. Manger.
America the Beautiful. Rice.
Amtrak. Fried.
Ancestor. Baca.
Animula. Merwin.
Anthology Poem. Morstein.
The Anti-Semanticist.
  Hoagland.
Apollo's Song. Jonson.
The Apparition of His
  Mistress Calling Him to
  Elysium. Herrick.
April Midnight. Symons.
The Arabian Nights (excerpt).
  Anonymous.
Arise and See the Glorious
  Sun. Hopkinson.
Around You, Your House.
  Stafford.
Artificer. Kennedy.
At Parting. Swinburne.
At the Tomb of Rachel.
  Yehoash.
Autumn Squall–Lake Erie.
  Russo.
Aware. Lawrence.
Ballade of Dead Actors.
  Henley.

Ballade of the Grindstones.
  Sherwin.
A Bar at Night. Hagiwara.
The Battle-Flag. Davis.
The Battle of Bridgewater.
  Anonymous.
A Beautifull Mistress.
  Carew.
Beauty. Whitman.
Before Action. Gellert.
Being Twins. Jackson.
Benediction. Freedman.
The Berkeley Pier. Addiego.
Between the Lines. Gibson.
Biafra. Mack.
Big Fun. Burns.
Bird at Night. Hamilton.
The Birds' Rondel (modern
  version). Chaucer.
The Black Virgin.
  Chesterton.
The Blinded Soldier to His
  Love. Noyes.
Blue Bottle. Hampl.
Blue Calf. *Anonymous.*
The Blue Light. Dent.
Blue Owl Song. Kittner.
A Bon Mot. *Anonymous.*
The Book of the Duchess.
  Chaucer.
Bread and Wine, Part 7.
  Holderlin.
Briggflatts. Bunting.
The Bunyip and the Whistling
  Kettle. Manifold.
The Burial of Saint Brendan.
  Colum.
Burning in the Night. Wolfe.
Burning the Letters. Grew.
Butcher Shop. Simic.
Caelica, LXVIII. Greville.
Cain Shall Not Slay Abel
  Today on Our Good
  Ground. Lowry.
Camel. Derwood.
The Camera Obscura.
  Symonds.
Camp Fire. Bromley.
The Candle A Saint.
  Stevens.
The Captive. Franklin.
Carol of the Russian Children.
  Anonymous.
The Castle of Indolence.
  Thomson.
Cat. Strachey.
The Cave of Night.
  Montague.
Central Heating System.
  Spender.
Chamber Music. Joyce.
Chance Meeting. Griffin.
Chapter Heading.
  Hemingway.
Chez Madame. Harrison.
Childe Harold's Pilgrimage:
  Canto III, XXIV. Byron.
Children of Night. Shelton.
The Choice. Yeats.
Christmas Eve. Clancy.
Cinderella. Ahmed-Ud-Din.
Clams. Ishigaki Rin.
Clickstone. Rokwaho.
The Clock. Jaszi.
The Clouded Morning. Very.
Composed on the Theme
  "Willows by the Riverside."
  Yu Hsuan-chi.
Composed Upon an Evening
  of Extraordinary Splendour
  and Beauty. Wordsworth.
Contemplations. Bradstreet.

The Contented Bachelor. Kendall.
Conversation. McCord.
Corn Rigs Are Bonnie. Burns.
Corner Lot. Bryan.
A Cornish Litany (excerpt). *Anonymous.*
Counsel. Davis.
Courtyards in Delft. Mahon.
Creede. Warman.
Creole Girl. Collins.
Crepuscular. Howard.
Cricket. No Ch'on-myong.
The Cricket Sang. Dickinson.
A Cry from the Ghetto. Rosenfeld.
The Crying of Water. Symons.
Cuvier Light. Wilson.
Daisies. Young.
The Dance of Saul with the Prophets. Tchernichovsky.
The Dancing Bear. Field.
Dark Rosaleen, IX. Wright.
Darling, I won't be your hot love. Sulpicia.
Dawn. *Anonymous.*
Day and Night. Alexander.
Days Too Short. Davies.
Death. Turner.
Death and Night. Kenyon.
Death Songs. Mack.
Death Valley. Lee.
The Deep Dark Night. Tennyson.
Deep in Love. Bhavabhuti.
Deep Night. Jimenez.
A Departure. Mahon.
A Description of an Author's Bedchamber. Goldsmith.
The Desertion of the Women and Seals. Brown.
Dial Tone. Pollak.
Dialogue after Enjoyment. Cowley.
The Dice Were Loaded. Gilmore.
Dinosaur Tracks in Beit Zayit. Kaufman.
Diretro al Sol. Bell.
Dithyramb in Retrospect. Hopegood.
The Divorce Dress. Finley.
Dog. Monro.
Dogskin Rug. Stoutenburg.
Double Ritual. Rainer.
Dover Beach. Arnold.
Dover to Munich. Calverley.
The Dream Called Life. Calderon de la Barca.
Dreams. Breton.
Drinking the Wind. Tan Ying.
The Drummer Boy of Waterloo. *Anonymous.*
The Dysynni Valley (Wales). Holmes.
Ecce Homo. Gascoyne.
The Edge of Day. Lee.
Elegy for an Estrangement. Holloway.
Elegy: In Spring. Bruce.
The Elephant. Hochman.
Empedocles. Jones, Jr.
The Empty House. Hoban.
The End of Man Is His Beauty. Jones.
End Song. Krauss.
Epigram: "O King of the Friday." *Anonymous.*

Epigrams. Martial (Marcus Valerius Martialis).
Epitaph. Nathan.
Epitaphs on Two Piping-Bullfinches of Lady Ossory's. Walpole.
An Escape. Abu Nuwas.
The Escape. Gurney.
Eternal Light. Binney.
Eternity. Herrick.
Eve. Fichman.
Eve in Reflection. Macpherson.
Evening. Matheson.
Evening in Paradise. Milton.
Evening on the Harbor. Tunstall.
Evening Twilight. Baudelaire.
Evensong. Torrence.
Expectant Mother. Shuttle.
Explorations Bronchitis: The Rosario Beach House. Rodriguez.
The Fairies. Hubbell.
The Fairy Queen. *Anonymous.*
Fairy Wings. Howard.
Fatal Interview. Millay.
Fear. Dobyns.
Fields at Evening. Morton.
Fighting South of the Castle. *Anonymous.*
Figure and Ground. Glaser.
Firefly. Uba.
First Cycle of Love Poems. Barker.
The Flower. Warren.
Fog-Horn. Clarke.
Foiled Sleep. "Marie.
Following Van Gogh (Avignon, 1982). Puziss.
Footnote to John ii.4. Mason.
For Sleep, or Death. Pitter.
For Those Who Died. Clark.
The Force of Love. Jones.
Four Folk-Songs in Hokku Form, 2. *Anonymous.*
Four-Paws. Eden.
The Fox. *Anonymous.*
Fragments. Yeats.
From Ghoulies and Ghosties. *Anonymous.*
From the House of Yemanja. Lorde.
The Full Heart. Nichols.
Funeral Toast. Mallarme.
Gabriel Meets Satan. Milton.
A Game of Dice. *Anonymous.*
The Garden of Proserpine. Swinburne.
Gardens Are All My Heart. Triem.
The General Public. Benét.
George III. Lowell.
The Girl with 18 Nightgowns. Orr.
Give Me Not Tears. Lathrop.
The God of Comfort. *Anonymous.*
God's Harp. Falke.
The Good Old Days. Fried.
A Goodnight. Williams.
Gooseberries. Berg.
Grandmother. Young Bear.
The Granite Mountain. Sarett.
The Grave. Blair.

The Green-Gown. *Anonymous.*
The Green Mountain Boys. Bryant.
Green Red Brown and White. Swenson.
Grief Plucked Me out of Sleep. King.
Guilt and Sorrow. Wordsworth.
Half-Light. Waddell.
Halloween. Burns.
The Hamlet of A. MacLeish (excerpt). MacLeish.
Hand-Jive. Castle.
The Happy Husbandman; or, Country Innocence. *Anonymous.*
The Haunted House. Viereck.
He Came to Visit Me. Seymour-Smith.
He Made the Night. Mifflin.
He Who Has Lost All. Diop.
Healing the Wound. Heine.
The Heart of Thomas Hardy. Betjeman.
Helicon. Hollander.
Hematite Lake. Galvin.
Her Kisses. Beddoes.
Here the Trace. Pasternak.
Higher Love. Wright.
His Age. Herrick.
His Parting from Her. Donne.
Hours I Remember Lonely and Lovely to Me. Irwin.
The House of Life. Rossetti.
The House-Wreckers Have Left the Door and a Staircase. Reznikoff.
Human Things. Nemerov.
Hyena. Muske.
A Hymn to Christ at the Author's Last Going into Germany. Donne.
Hymn to Night. Cane.
Hymn to the Night. Longfellow
Hymn to the Sun. Percy.
Hyperion. Keats.
I Believe. Lawrence.
I Caught This Morning at Dawning. Neagle.
I Cut in Two. Hwang Chin-i.
I Don't Know if Mount Zion. Kovner.
I Gazed upon the Cloudless Moon. Bronte.
I Have a Gentle Cock. *Anonymous.*
I Never Asked for More Than Thou Hast Given. Dickinson.
I Rode with My Darling... Smith.
I Say. Tussman.
I Turned On the Hot Water. Canan.
Idea. Drayton.
The Ideal. Baudelaire.
If fancy would favor. Wyatt.
The Iliad. Homer.
Immolated. Melville.
Immortal Israel. Halevi.
The Immortal Part. Housman.
In a Grave-Yard. Braithwaite.

In His Utter Wretchedness. Audelay.
In Memoriam A.H.H., CXXV. Tennyson.
In Memoriam S.C.W., V.C. Sorley.
In New Ross. Iremonger.
In Spite of All This Much Needed Thunder. Gilbert.
In the Discreet Splendor. Strauss.
In the Forest. Edson.
In the Soul Hour. Mezey.
In the Year of Two Thousand. Katz.
Independence. Cato.
Indian Pipes. Welles.
Infallibility. Collier.
Insomnia (excerpt). Tsvetayeva.
The Invaders. Haines.
Invasion. Witheford.
Iron Eyes. Winch.
Is 5. Cummings.
Island of Night. Kinnell.
The Isle of Portland. Housman.
Israel's Duration. Halevi.
It Is When the Tribe Is Gone. Bigger.
It Was a' for Our Rightfu' King. Burns.
It Was Gentle. Harkavi.
Jack Wrack. *Anonymous.*
A Japanese Birthday Wish. Swann.
The Jealous Lovers. Hall.
The Joining. Norvig.
Judas. Miller.
Just as the Small Waves Came Where No Waves Were. Millward.
The Kansas Line. *Anonymous.*
Kelpius's Hymn. Peterson.
Keno. Wier.
Kind Are Her Answers. Campion.
Kitchen Window. Ebberts.
The Kumulipo: Birth of Sea and Land Life. *Anonymous.*
The Ladder of St. Augustine: The Heights. Longfellow.
A Lamentation. Mangan.
Last Look at La Plata, Missouri. Barnes.
The Last Romantic. Laing.
Laundromat. McCord.
Laura Sleeping. Moulton.
Laus Veneris. Swinburne.
Leaf. Hewitt.
A Lecture Upon the Shadow. Donne.
The Legacy. Minty.
A Lementable New Ballad upon the Earle of Essex Death. *Anonymous.*
Lesbian Poem. Morgan.
Letter #8. Brutus.
A Letter from a Friend. Maisel.
Letter to the Night. Frankenberg.
Like Snow. Graves.
Lilium Regis. Thompson.
Limerick: "There was a young lady named Bright." Buller.
The Lincolnshire Poacher. *Anonymous.*

Lines for the Margin of an Old Gospel. Wingfield.
Lines from Catullus. Ralegh.
Listening. Stafford.
Litany for Halloween. *Anonymous.*
Little City. Horan.
Little Roads to Happiness. Stitch.
Little Satellite. Krows.
Living in the Moment. Hacker.
Logging (excerpt). Snyder.
Lollingdon Downs. Masefield.
London Nightfall. Fletcher.
The Lone Biker. Hardy.
Longing. Arnold.
The Look. Teasdale.
Looking for Mountain Beavers. Wagoner.
Los Angeles. Healy.
The Lost Children. Orr.
Lost Light. Akers.
Love, My Machine. Simpson.
A Love Poem for My Country. Chipasula.
Love Song. Ranaivo.
Love Songs. Loy.
Love Was Once Light as Air. Day Lewis.
A Lovely Rose Is Sprung. *Anonymous.*
The Lover. Stoddard.
A Lover's Plea. Campion.
The Lovers. Comfort.
The Lovers' Death. Baudelaire.
Loving She Stood Apart. Lane.
Lucy Taking Birth. Scott.
Maceo. Llorens Torres.
The Mad Gardener's Song. "Carroll.
The Magic Wood. Treece.
The Mahabharata (excerpt). *Anonymous.*
The Malice of Innocence. Levertov.
A Man Called Dante, I Have Heard. King.
Marriage. Gibson.
The Marrowbone Itch. *Anonymous.*
Mary, Mother of Christ. Cullen.
A Masique Presented at Ludlow Castle (Comus). Milton.
Masks. Swann.
The Masters. Widdemer.
May the Ambitious Ever Find. Sackville.
Me Imperturbe. Whitman.
The Meadow. Wieners.
Meditations for August 1, 1666. Pain.
The Meeting. Wilson.
Memory. Stroud.
The Mendicants. Carman.
Mending the Bridge. Stewart.
The Mermaid. *Anonymous.*
Metamorphoses of the Vampire. Baudelaire.
The Middle of the World. Norris.
Midnight on Front Street. Whiteman.
Midnight Patrol. Irvin.

The Milk-Cart Pony. Farjeon.
The Mill-stream, Now that Noises Cease. Housman.
The Miller's Daughter. Tennyson.
Minimum Security. Lewisohn.
Missy Sick. *Anonymous.*
Monkshood XXIX. Gunnars.
Monsieur Qui Passe. Mew.
The Moon. Garnett.
Moon Song. Nweke.
Moonlight. Tahureau.
Morning and Evening. Slonimski.
Moscow Nights. *Anonymous.*
Moth-Song. Cortissoz.
Motto for a Sun Dial. Cunningham.
Mount Caribou at Night. Wright.
The mountains grow unnoticed. Dickinson.
Mr. Cooper. Thwaite.
My Delight. Bradford.
My Husband. *Anonymous.*
My Love's Guardian Angel. Barnes.
My Mother's Shoes. Zychlinska.
My Sweetest Lesbia. Campion.
The Myall in Prison. Gilmore.
Narcissus. Petersen.
Native-Born. Langley.
Negro Dreams. Long.
Neither Here Nor There. Rodgers.
New Year Wishes. Sarton.
News of the World. Barker.
Nicholas Ned. *Anonymous.*
Night. Benet.
Night. Brown.
Night. Southey.
Night and Day. Porter.
Night and the Pines. Scott.
Night Crackles. Woody.
Night Flight. Johnson.
Night for Adventures. Starbuck.
Night Teeth. Brett.
Night Thoughts in Age. Wheelock.
A Night Vigil in the Left Court of the Palace. Tu Fu.
Nightfall in Inishtrahull. O'Sullivan.
Nightflight and Sunrise. Dutton.
No Such Thing. Southwick.
Nocturnal Sounds. Cumbo.
A Nocturne. Blunt.
Nocturne. Camille.
Nocturne. Garnett.
Nocturne–III. Silva.
Nocturne in a Deserted Brickyard. Sandburg.
Norse Sailor's Joy. Thorley.
Nothing Inside and Nothing Out. Amorosi.
November. Rossetti.
Now the Holy Lamp of Love. MacDonogh.
Now while the night her sable veil hath spread. Drummond.
Number 5–December. Henderson.

Nymphing through Car Windows. Keeler.
Odalisque. Coffey.
Ode to Psyche. Keats.
Of All the Gay Birds That E'er I Did See. *Anonymous.*
Of the Night, Let the Bridegroom Sing. Statius Publius Papinius.
Of Women. *Anonymous.*
Officers' Mess. Ewart.
The Old Astronomer to His Pupil. Williams.
Old Men on the Blue. Ferril.
On a Puppy. Feng Chih.
On Growing Old. Masefield.
On Having Grown Old. Moll.
On Recrossing the Rocky Mountains after Many Years. Fremont.
On the Night Train from Oxford. Mayo.
On Waking from a Dreamless Sleep. Fields.
The Orchard and the Heath. Meredith.
Oreads. Raine.
Orpheus. Snodgrass.
Other Lives. Hooper.
The Other World. Book of the Dead.
Out in the Dark. Thomas.
Out of Mourning. Abbott.
Ovedue Balance Sheet. Plantier.
Overnight Guest. Wilson.
Owl. Rokwaho.
Owl Woman's Death Song. *Anonymous.*
The Ownership of the Night. Levis.
Paddy Murphy. *Anonymous.*
Pangur Ban. *Anonymous.*
Paradise Lost. Milton.
Paris in the Snow. Sedar-Senghor.
Paris: The Seine at Night. Divine.
The Peace-Offering. Hardy.
The Pelicans My Father Sees. Maris Stella.
Personal History: For My Son. Todd.
Pete at the Zoo. Brooks.
Pickers. Brett.
The Pilgrim of a Day. Campbell.
The Plains. Fuller.
Poetry. Vigee.
The Poets of the Nineties. Mahon.
The Pointless Pride of Man. *Anonymous.*
Portrait Philippines. Duckett.
A Practical Program for Monks. Merton.
Prayer. Mousley.
Prelude. George.
The Pretty Ploughboy. *Anonymous.*
Primer Lesson. Vinz.
The Protective Grigri. Joans.
Prothalamion. Young.
Psalm. Yehoash.
Psalm CXXXIX. Pembroke.
Pure Nails Brightly Flashing. Mallarme.
Queen Mab. Hood.
The Quiet Night. Heine.

The Quiet Nights. Hinkson.
Quite Forsaken. Lawrence.
Rambunctious Brook. Frost.
The Reason. Oppenheim.
The Recruits. Hamilton.
Regretful Thoughts, II. Yu Hsuan-chi.
Reindeer and Engine. Jacobsen.
The Rejected "National Hymns". Newell.
Remember. Johnson.
The Report. Swan.
Resemblance. *Anonymous.*
Reserved. De La Mare.
A Rhapsody, Written at the Lakes in Westmorland. Brown.
Rocks and Gravel. *Anonymous.*
Rooks. Sorley.
Rose in the Garden. *Anonymous.*
Rules and Lessons. Vaughan.
The Runner in the Skies. James. Oppenheim
Saint Luke the Painter. Rossetti.
Saint Peray. Parsons.
Samarian Nights. Fichman.
Saving the Harvest. Lehmann.
School Days. Stafford.
The Scorpion. Belloc.
The Scribe. Farkas.
The Sea. Stoddard.
Sea Island Miscellany. Blackmur.
Seder, 1944. Torberg.
Seneca. Merton.
The Sentry. Lewis.
A Serenade. Pinkney.
A Serious Poem. Walsh.
Seventeen. Holden.
Shall I Come, Sweet Love, to Thee. Campion.
She Wept, She Railed. Kunitz.
The Shepherd's Star. Jimenez.
A Shining Night; or, Dick Daring, the Poacher. *Anonymous.*
A Shropshire Lad. Housman.
Silence. Bly.
Silence and Stealth of Dayes! Vaughan.
Silex Scintillans. Vaughan.
The Singer. Dowden.
Sir Aldingar. *Anonymous.*
Sittin' on the Porch. Guest.
Six Years Later. Brodsky.
The Skunk. Coffin.
Skyscaper. Sandburg.
The Slaughterhouse Boys. Meissner.
Sleeping on Her Couch. Leigh.
Snatches: "The nightingale singes." *Anonymous.*
Soldier from the Wars Returning. Housman.
Solomon and Morolph, Their Last Encounter. Levertin.
Song: "Do I venture away too far." Douglas.
Song for Past Midnight. Lehmann.
Song of Degrees. Auster.
Song of Despair. Rangiaho.

A Song of Morning. Sitwell.
Song of the Little Villages. Dollard.
The Song of the Pilgrims. Brooke.
Song: "Sergei's a flower." Herschberger.
Song: "The boat is chafing at our long delay." Davidson.
Song: "Turn, turn thy beauteous face away." Beaumont.
Song: "Where in blind files." Boland.
Songs from Cyprus. Doolittle.
Songs of Ch'en. Confucius.
Songs of Joy. Davies.
Sonnet V: "White Venus limpid wandering in the sky." Labe.
Sonnet, XIII: "As long as I continue weeping." Labé.
Sonnet: "Oh, my beloved, have you thought of this." Millay.
Sonnets, IV: "Two stars there are in one faire firmament." Barnfield.
Sonnets, XLIII: "When most I wink, then do mine eyes best see." Shakespeare.
Sonnets, CXLVII: "My love is as a feaver longing still." Shakespeare.
Sonnets to Miranda. Watson.
The Sons of Our Sons. Ehrenburg.
The Sound of Night. Kumin.
South Shore Line. Schlesinger.
Special Starlight. Sandburg.
The Specter. Hardt.
The Sphinx Speaks. Saltus.
The Spirit of Poetry. Longfellow.
Sporting Life Blues. *Anonymous.*
Spring Night. Su Tung-P'o.
Star of Ethiopia. Watkins.
Star Song. Johnson.
The Stars. Dodge.
Stars over the Dordogne. Plath.
Starship. McAleavey.
The Stone. Gibson.
The Stone. Vaughan.
The Storm. Heine.
The Story of Samuel Jackson. Leland.
Street-Walker in March. Albert.
Suburban Dusk. Meyers.
Summary. Sanchez.
The Sun Has Long Been Set. Wordsworth.
Sunday Afternoons. Thwaite.
Sunken Evening. Lee.
Surf-Casting. Merwin.
The Swarm. Moore.
Table-Birds. Mackenzie.
Talking to the Mule. Jensen.
Tennesse Crickets. Outlaw.
The Terrace. Wilbur.
That Corner. Salkeld.
That the Night Come. Yeats.
There Are in Such Moments. Silverstein.

They Went Home. Angelou.
This above All Is Precious and Remarkable. Wain.
This Night. Heyen.
Those Betrayed at Dawn. Wygodski.
Those Guyana Nights. Foerster.
Those Makheta Nights. Chipasula.
Thou Art the Sky. Tagore.
Thoughts on the Shape of the Human Body. Brooke.
The Thousand and One Nights: Tell Him, O Night. *Anonymous.*
A Time of Night. Ignatow.
Timon of Archimedes. Loomis.
To a Lady Who Sent Me a Copy of Verses at My Going to Bed. King.
To an Indian Poet. Harjo.
To Be a Master in Your House. Zach.
To Marie Osmond. Skelley.
To Night: To Judith. Mosby.
To S. M. a Young African Painter, on Seeing His Work. Wheatley.
To the Afternoon Moon, at Sea. Rice.
To the Leanan Shee. Boyd.
To the Memory of Mr. Oldham. Dryden.
To the Moon. Goethe.
To the Muse. Whalen.
To the Nightingale. Davies.
To the Unknown Light. Shanks.
Tom O' Bedlam's Song. *Anonymous.*
Tom Pringle. Simpson.
Too Much. Muir.
Traditional Tune. Fitzgerald.
Tramontana at Lerici. Tomlinson.
Treason of Sand. Roth.
The True Lover. Housman.
Trumpet and Flute. Hernaes.
Truth. Masefield.
Twilight. Custance.
Twilight. Hall.
Two doves upon the selfsame branch. Rossetti.
Two Little Children. *Anonymous.*
The Two Spirits. Shelley.
The Uninvited. Mundell.
The Unsung Heroes. Dunbar.
Upon Visiting His Lady by Moonlight. "W."
Uriel. Stead.
Vacation Song. Millay.
The Valley of Men. Greenberg.
The Vampire. Aiken.
Vancouver Lights. Birney.
The Vanished Night. MacMurray.
Venetian Air. Moore.
Vergier. Pound.
Village in Snowstorm. Krapf.
The Vindictive Staircase or The Reward of Industry. Gibson.
Vision. Merwin.

The Vision to Electra. Herrick.
The Visit. George.
Vistas. Shepard.
Voices from Things Growing in a Churchyard. Hardy.
The Wanderer. Heaney.
The Wandering Knight's Song. Lockhart.
War Swaggers. Litvinoff.
The Watcher. Stone.
Watching Your Gray Eyes. Marcus.
Waterfront. Jenkins.
Waters of Babylon. Untermeyer.
The Wayfarers. Brooke.
Wayne at Stony Point. Scollard.
We Are Such Stuff As Dreams... Petronius.
We Own the Night. Jones.
We Would See Jesus. *Anonymous.*
Welcome, Summer. Chaucer.
Welcome to the Moon. *Anonymous.*
Wellfleet Harbor. Goodman.
Were I in Trouble. Frost.
Western Civilization. Neto.
What Do I Know? Brennan.
What Semiramis Said. Lindsay.
When I Heard at the Close of the Day. Whitman.
When the Cows Come down to Drink. Hoey.
When the Last Riders. Zach.
Where I Am. Dos Santos.
White Attic. Elmslie.
The White-footed Deer. Bryant.
Who Would Have Thought? Herbert.
The Wilderness. Juhasz.
The Windows. Loewinsohn.
Wings in the Dark. Gray.
Winter Nights. Campion.
With I and E. *Anonymous.*
With My God, the Smith. Greenberg.
Witness. Anderson.
Wolves. Haines.
Woman to Child. Wright.
The Word of God. Gwynne.
Work, for the Night Is Coming. Walker.
Working Man Blues. Estes.
Written on Seeing the Flowers, and Remembering My Daughter. Ch'i.
The Wrong Kind of Insurance. Ashbery.
You, Andrew Marvell. MacLeish.
The Young Wife. Stead.

Nightcap
Homecoming. *Anonymous.*
Mr. McGregor's Garden. McGuckian.

Nightingale (s)
Bagley Wood. Johnson.
The Blackbird. Beeching.
The Cat of the House. Ford.
The Deserted Village. Goldsmith.
Dying Thief. Manger.
Early Nightingale. Clare.
Epistle to John Hamilton Reynolds. Keats.
Euthymiae Raptus. Chapman.

Fable. Harris.
Fantoches. Verlaine.
Hast Thou Heard the Nightingale? Gilder.
The House of a Hundred Lights. Torrence.
I Go by Road. Mendes.
In Arcadia. Durrell.
Love's Nightingale. Crashaw.
Malvolio (parody). Landor.
Money Makes the Mirth. Herrick.
The Moon. Davies.
The Nightingale. *Anonymous.*
The Nightingales of Spring. *Anonymous.*
One Morning in May. *Anonymous.*
Painted Head. Ransom.
Peacock and Nightingale. Finch.
The Sailor's Return. *Anonymous.*
Thysia. Luce.
The Valiant Seaman's Happy Return to His Love... *Anonymous.*
When he sailed into the harbor. Korinna.
When in the Woods I Wander All Alone. Hovell-Thurlow.
The Willows. Harte.

Nightmare (s)
The Book of Nightmares. Kinnell.
The Diver. Phocas.
Hob Gobbling's Song. Lowell.
Landcrab. Atwood.
The Note-Book of a European Tramp (excerpt). Hamburger.
Paths They Kept Barren. Garmon.
Upper Family. Bodenheim.

Nile
The Banks of the Nile. *Anonymous.*
Doricha. Robinson.
Kilimandjaro. Taylor.
Leda and Her Swan. Broumas.
Mycerinus. Arnold.
The Queen of the Nile. Smith.
The Sphinx. Brownell

Nimble
The Friar and the Fair Maid. *Anonymous.*
Mother. Kelleher.
San Sepolcro. Graham.

Nimbus
About Children. McGinley.
Look down Fair Moon. Whitman.

Nine
Christmas Birthday. Glaubitz.
Doll's Boy's Asleep. Cummings.
The Doves. Tynan.
He Sports by Himself (parody). Miles.
Hours of Sleep. *Anonymous.*

The Jute Mill Song.
Anonymous.
Methuselah. *Anonymous.*
The Mutual Congratulations
of the Poet's Anna Seward
and Hayley. Porson.
The New Married Couple.
Anonymous.
On Being Much Better Than
Most and Yet Not Quite
Good Enough. Ciardi.

Ninevah
The Burden of Nineveh.
Rossetti.
Fragments. Yeats.
The Impious Feast. Landor.

Nipple (s)
Archilochos:. Tagliabue.
Burning the Root. Gibson.
December 21st. Valentine.
Geisha. Gildner.
The Mind's Liberty. Davies.

No
The Beginning of the End.
Hopkins.
A Bestiary. Rexroth.
Complaint of the Absence of
Her Lover Being Upon the
Sea. Surrey.
Cordial Advice. *Anonymous.*
Counting the Mad. Justice.
La Cucaracha (The
Cockroach). *Anonymous.*
The Egg of Nothing. Taylor.
Essay on Deity. Olson.
A Father Does His Best.
White.
Fire. Wellesley.
I Care Not for These Ladies.
Campion.
Intuition. Delius.
John Henry (E. vers.).
Anonymous.
Lenten Is Come.
Anonymous.
Lighthouse in the Night.
Storni.
LIII. Berrigan.
Love. Jonas.
The Lust for Murder.
Penfold.
No! Cook.
Nothing but No and I, and I
and No. Drayton.
The Outward Man Accused.
Taylor.
A Portrait. Duer.
Report from a Planet.
Lattimore.
The Riddle Song.
Anonymous.
The Rose of Tralee. Spencer.
Salmon Cycle. Treinin.
Seesaw. Diego.
Settler. Lindh.
Song: "Four arms, two necks,
one wreathing."
Anonymous.
Song the Eighth. Moore.
To Lydia Languish. Dobson.
The Too Literal Pupil.
Martial (Marcus Valerius
Martialis).
Tripe. Morton.
The Triumph of Beautie Song
(excerpt). Shirley.
Triumph of Love. Wheelock.
Unrecorded Speech. Adams.
When We Court and Kiss.
Campion.

Noah
Dissatisfaction with
Metaphysics. Empson.
The Loon. Rand.
Old Dog Blue. Jackson.
Sowing on the Mountain.
Anonymous.
Still, Citizen Sparrow.
Wilbur.

Noble (er) (est)
Backward–Forward.
Anonymous.
Bunker Hill. Calvert.
The Call. Hall.
Calm Is the Morn without a
Sound. Tennyson.
The Canterbury Tales:
Prologue. A Knight.
Chaucer.
Casabianca. Hemans.
Chimera. Howes.
Content Thyself with Thy
Estate. *Anonymous.*
The Crooked Gun.
Anonymous.
Deirdre's Lament.
Anonymous.
Echoes from Theocritus.
Lefroy.
An Elegy upon the Death of
That Holy Man...(excerpt).
Taylor.
Epigram: The Mother's
Choice. *Anonymous.*
A Farewell to Fal. Nugent.
The Field of the Grounded
Arms. Halleck.
House in Springfield. Burket.
How many wise men and
heroes. Ch'iu Chin.
The Hunting of the Cheviot
(C vers.). *Anonymous.*
In Memoriam A.H.H., LVIII.
Tennyson.
In the Annals of Tacitus.
Murray.
Influence. Oxenham.
The Lady of the Manor.
Crabbe.
A Lady with a Falcon on Her
Fist. Lovelace.
The Lost Occasion. Whittier.
Love's Force. Carew.
The Maid of Orleans.
Schiller.
Microcosm. Dobell.
The Muses Elizium.
Drayton.
Nobility. Cary.
The Nobleman's Wedding.
Allingham.
O Have You Caught the
Tiger. Housman.
Our Father! While Our Hearts
Unlearn. Holmes.
Remember the Source.
Eberhart.
De Roberval. Hunter-Duvar.
The Rose of May. Howitt.
Scatheless. Wilkinson.
Somebody's Mother. Brine.
A Song: "Chloris, when I to
thee present." *Anonymous.*
Tempora Acta. Meredith."
That's Success! Braley.
Theseus and Ariadne.
Graves.
Tribute to Washington.
Anonymous.
Vox Populi, Vox Dei
(excerpt). *Anonymous.*
Where Is Justice? Steinbarg.

Noblemen
Chevy-Chace. *Anonymous.*
The Geraldine's Daughter
(excerpt). Mangan.
The Jolly Thresherman.
Anonymous.

Noblesse oblige
Belief. Miles.
One-Way Song. Lewis.

Nobody
98 Degree Blues. Alexander.
Don Juan. Byron.
Dream Songs. Berryman.
Dressed Up. Hughes.
England's Difficulty.
Heaney.
Erith, on the Thames.
Anonymous.
Going Away Blues.
Kimbrough.
His Majesty. Brown.
I Saw a Tree That Was
Greater Than All the
Others. Sodergran.
It's nice that though you are
casual about me. Sulpicia.
Kilmeny. Noyes.
A New Song of Wood's
Halfpence. Swift.
Nightmare. Field.
Nobody. Burns.
Poem by a Perfectly Furious
Academician. Brooks.
Roberta. Leadbelly.
Sightseers in a Courtyard.
Guillen.
Springfield Mountain (B
vers.). *Anonymous.*
Sweet Meat Has Sour Sauce.
Cowper.
The Village of Erith.
Anonymous.
When I was a good and quick
little girl. *Anonymous.*

Nod (ded) (ding) (s)
Adam's Apple. Barks.
Anno Domini. Walker.
The Apartment-Hunter.
Schultz.
Ballroom Dancing Class.
McGinley.
The Cedar River. Gibbons.
The Confession. Cooley.
David in April. Booker.
Docteur Foster. *Anonymous.*
Dream Songs. Berryman.
Inspiration. Thoreau.
The Lamplighter. Stevenson.
The Last Fruit off an Old
Tree. Landor.
Love. Ostroff.
Meeting Myself. Lucie-
Smith.
A Moment Please. Allen.
Open. Eigner.
Smithfield Ham. Smith.
The Sparrows at the Airport.
Ostroff.
Springtime. Kreymborg.
Winwick, Lancashire.
Anonymous.
Wynken, Blynken, and Nod.
Field.

Noel
Carol of the Birds. Bas-
Quercy.
Little tree. Cummings.
Man. matron, maiden.
Baden-Powell.
Out of Your Sleep Arise and
Wake. *Anonymous.*

Noise (s) (less) (y)
Although It Is Not Plainly
Visible to the Eye.
Toshiyuki.
Andrew Jackson's Speech.
Bly.
The Approach of the Storm.
Anonymous.
Cape Cod Girls. *Anonymous.*
The Centaur Overheard.
Bowers.
City Walk-Up, Winter 1969.
Forche.
Cockpit in the Clouds.
Dorrance.
Dark Mountains. Lockyer.
The Death of Admiral
Benbow. *Anonymous.*
The Death of General
Uncebunke: A Biography in
Little. Durrell.
The Demagogue. McGinley.
Dorothy. Kreymborg.
God's Word. Clifford.
Hyperion. Keats.
I Have Felt It as They've
Said. Eigner.
I Hope I Don't Have You
Next Semester, But.
Godsey.
Idylls. Theocritus.
In the Huon Valley.
McAuley.
Love Sleeping. Plato.
The Martin Cat Long Shaged
of Courage Good. Clare.
Metric Figure. Williams.
The Mountain Whippoorwill.
Benét.
Neptune. Campion.
November. Rossetti.
The Old. Noel.
On the Marriage of T. K. and
C. C. the Morning Stormy.
Carew.
One Bright Morning...
Anonymous.
Polly, Dolly, Kate and Molly.
Anonymous.
Prayer to the God Thot.
Anonymous.
The Print-Out. Nemerov.
Silence. Turner.
Snoring. Fisher.
Sonnet XLIV. Alabaster.
Sound. Harrison.
The Street. Baro.
Time. Hodgson.
To a Phoebe-Bird. Bynner.
V.D. Clinic. Stoutenburg.

None
Blue Bell. *Anonymous.*
Brave Collier Lads.
Anonymous.
The Chameleon. Merrick.
The Cherry Trees. Thomas.
A Conjuration, to Electra.
Herrick.
Coyote, Coyote, Please Tell
Me. Blue Cloud.
Crash at Leithfield. Curnow.
The Desolate City. Blunt.
Distrust. Herrick.
A Double Ballad of Good
Counsel. Villon.
For Every Evil under the Sun.
Anonymous.
For My Daughter. Kees.
Four Wrens. *Anonymous.*
Give Me Thy Heart.
Procter.

His Content in the Country.
Herrick.
I walk in loneliness through
the greenwood.
Anonymous.
The Impartial Inspection.
Anonymous.
Innocent Play. Watts.
Joan to Her Lady.
Anonymous.
Lady Godiva. Shanks.
Last Poem. Berrigan.
Lavish Kindness. Wylie.
The Leaf. Williams.
Let No Charitable Hope.
Wylie.
The Light and Glory of the
World. Cowper.
The Little Woman and the
Pedlar. *Anonymous.*
Love is Kind. Keech.
Love Who Will, for I'll Love
None. Browne.
Manners in the Dining-Room.
Anonymous.
Marlborough (excerpt).
Sorley.
Memory of a Scholar.
Lattimore.
The Men of the Alamo.
Roche.
The Mikado. Gilbert.
Mother and Poet. Browning.
My Love. Ono-no-Yoshiki.
The Nightingale. Barnfield.
No passenger was known to
flee. Dickinson.
A Northern Legion. Read.
On a Nun. Vittorelli.
On a Picture of a Black
Centaur by Edmund Dulac.
Ycats.
Pluck the Fruit and Taste the
Pleasure. Lodge.
Plutarch. Agathias.
Poly-Olbion. Drayton.
Prospect Beach. Lipsitz.
Provide, Provide. Frost.
Reparation or War.
Anonymous.
Rose Pogonias. Frost.
A Shepherd's Complaint.
Barnfield.
Song: "Old Farmer Oats and
his son Ned." Chapman.
Sonnet: "Oh, if thou knew'st
how thou thyself dost
harm." Stirling.
Sonnets, VIII: "Music to hear,
why hear'st thou music
sadly?" Shakespeare.
Sonnets, LIII: "What is your
substance, whereof are you
made." Shakespeare.
The Spirit's Light. Cowper.
Sunflower Sonnet Number
Two. Jordan.
Thoughts on the Christian
Doctrine of Eternal Hell.
Smith.
To a Painted Lady. Brome.
To a Portrait of Whistler in
the Brooklyn Art Museum.
Cox.
To His Mistress. Herrick.
To Pile Like Thunder to Its
Close. Dickinson.
Truth. Patmore.
The Twelve Properties or
Conditions of a Lover.
More.
Twicknam Garden. Donne.

Valentine. Silverstein.
The Wren. *Anonymous.*
Yung Wind. Confucius.
Nonentity
God and the Holy Ghost.
Lawrence.
Nonsense
The Archer. Ainslie.
Epigrams: "Need from excess–
excess from folly growing."
Bishop.
Upon the Downs. Etherege.
Noodle (s)
Fragment of a Song.
"Carroll.
Old Wichet. *Anonymous.*
Nook (s)
Echoes from the Sabine Farm.
Field.
To the Fountain of Bandusia.
Horace.
Noon
1916 Seen from 1921.
Blunden.
Asides from the Clowns, VII.
Laforgue.
By Loe Pool. Symons.
A Chant out of Doors.
Wilkinson.
Cicada. Stoutenburg.
Country Towns. Slessor.
The Dandelion. Lindsay.
Dawn. Rimbaud.
Drought. Johnson.
Earl Mertoun's Song.
Browning.
An Epitaph. Wesley.
Epitaphs on Two Piping-
Bullfinches of Lady
Ossory's. Walpole.
The Fall of the City: Voice of
the Studio Announcer.
MacLeish.
La Figlia Che Piange. Eliot.
George III. Lowell.
The Harbor of Illusion.
Bernstein.
Hush-a-Ba Birdie, Croon,
Croon. *Anonymous.*
I Found the Phrase.
Dickinson.
I Gave Myself to Him.
Dickinson.
I Look into My Glass.
Hardy.
Labor. Day.
The Last Abbot of Gloucester.
Childe.
A Lecture Upon the Shadow.
Donne.
Legend. Crane.
Life's Evil. Montale.
A long, long sleep.
Dickinson.
Love Was Once Light as Air.
Day Lewis.
On Archaeanassa. Plato.
Pastoral Dialogue Castara and
Parthenia. Flatman.
Poem: "So many pigeons at
Columbus Circle."
Gregor.
Reality. Havergal.
Retrospect. Robinson.
Scroppo's Dog. Swenson.
Spring Morning–Santa Fe.
Riggs.
Those Betrayed at Dawn.
Wygodski.
To a Very Young Lady.
Etherege.

To the Younger Lady Lucy
Sydney. Waller.
Two Poems. Marshall.
Utterance. Dickinson.
The Vision of Lazarus
(excerpt). Johnson.
Works and Days. Hesiod.
Zermatt. Hardy.
Zoroaster Devoutly Questions
Ormazd. Zoroaster.
Noose (s)
Brothers. Currie.
Metaphors. Radnoti.
St. Augustine Contemplating
the Bust of Einstein.
Ackerman.
Normal
One of the Seven Has
Somewhat to Say. Hay.
Policy of the House. Stetler.
Small Town: The Friendly.
Dunn.
North
Blow, Northern Wind.
Anonymous.
Bring the North. Stafford.
The Constant North.
Hendry.
Crossing the Border into
Canada. Harjo.
Drunken Lover. Dodson.
Elegy. Auslander.
Erosion. Graham.
Fifth Avenue Parade. Hecht.
Footprints on the Glacier.
Merwin.
From the North
Saskatchewan. Mandel.
Garden at Heidelberg.
Landor.
Geordie (D version).
Anonymous.
I Now Had Only to Retrace.
Bronte.
I Walk on the River at Dawn.
Hart.
Joined the Blues. Rooney.
Letter: The Japanese, to Her
Husband at War. Walsh.
Love at Large. Patmore.
Men of the North and West.
Stoddard.
Moriturus. Millay
My Mouth Is Very Quiet.
Villa.
The North and the South.
Browning.
The Northern Seas. Howitt.
O Wind, Why Do You Never
Rest. Rossetti.
P.S. Lowell
The Polar Quest. Burton.
A Proclamation.
Anonymous.
The Seasons. Thomson.
The Shorebirds. Reid.
Squall. Moore.
Tennesse Crickets. Outlaw.
Theme and Variations. Ker.
The Things of the North.
McOwan.
Through the Straight Pass of
Suffering. Dickinson.
The Trail of the Bird.
Courthope.
Up There. Auden.
What Music. Harjo.
Wherelings Whenlings.
Cummings.
A Winter Piece. Bryant.
North America
Birth. Bruck.

To the Younger Lady Lucy

Brave Paulding and the Spy.
Anonymous.
Free America. Warren.
Home, Boys, Home.
Anonymous.
On the Late Engagement in
Charles Town River.
Anonymous.
North Carolina
A Poem for a Poet. Lorde.
North Pole
Island Moment. Finlay.
To Poets and Airmen.
Spender.
North Star
D'Avalos' Prayer. Masefield.
London after the Great Fire,
1666. Dryden.
On a Monument to Marti.
Roberts.
North Wind
Nutting Time. Poulsson.
A Spell before Winter.
Nemerov.
Northern Lights
Prison Break. Hogan.
Northumberland
The Duke of Gordon's
Daughter. *Anonymous.*
The Fair Flower of
Northumberland.
Anonymous.
Nose (s)
Amphibious Crocodile.
Ransom.
The Angry Poet. O'Connor.
Annunciation. Maura.
The Apple Dumplings and a
King. Wolcot.
Beneath This Mound.
Bierce.
Carmina. Catullus.
The Cat That Followed His
Nose. Kendall.
Chic Freedom's Reflection.
Walker.
A Child's Pet. Davies.
A Circus Garland. Field.
Close Shave. *Anonymous.*
The Devil and the Governor
(excerpt). Forster.
The Difference. Richards.
A Disagreeable Feature.
Robinson.
A Dog. Zolotow.
Field Path. Clare.
Growing. Frost.
I Had a Little Husband.
Mother Goose.
Intimacy. Young.
The Jolly Woodchuck.
Grider.
A Kitten. Farjeon.
Lament. Williams.
Limerick: "Said the mole:
"You would never
suppose." Herford.
Limerick: "There was a young
man of Montrose."
Bennett.
A Little Pig Asleep.
Jackson.
Many Happy Returns.
Auden.
Murrough Defeats the Danes,
994. *Anonymous.*
Now You're Content. Spire.
Nursery Song in Pidgin
English (parody).
Anonymous.
Old Bandy Legs.
Anonymous.

On Robert Buchanan, Who Attacked Him under the Pseudonym... Rossetti.
Rabbits. Baruch.
A Recent Dialogue. Moore.
Rich and Poor; or, Saint and Sinner. Peacock.
Savage Portraits. Marquis.
Sing a Song of Sixpence. *Anonymous.*
Sing a Song of Sixpence. Mother Goose.
Sniff. Frost.
Song of Sixpence. *Anonymous.*
Song of the Unloved. *Anonymous.*
Song: "Singee songee sick a pence." (parody). *Anonymous.*
Stampede. *Anonymous.*
Tapestry. Simic.
There Was a Man and He Was Mad. *Anonymous.*
There Was an Old Man, on Whose Nose. Lear.
Through a Shop Window. Farjeon.
Tobacco. *Anonymous.*
Unfrocked Priest. Campbell.
Upon Lulls. Herrick.
Walking on Water. Dickey.
What the Engines Said. Harte.
Why I Am Offended By Miracles. Bergman.
The World Is Full of Wonderful Smells. Gay.

Nosegay (s)
Jubilate Agno. Smart.
Morning and Evening. Slonimski.

Nostril (s)
Ambuscade. McCrae.
The Dromedary. Campbell.
A January Morning. Lampman.
Six Sunday. Bibbs.
The Slaughter-House. Hayes.
Thus Crosslegged on Round Pillow Sat in Space. Ginsberg.

Note (s)
After the Broken Arm. Padgett.
Alison. Gold.
All This Everyday (excerpt). Kyger.
Andrew M'Crie. Murray.
At the Mid Hour of Night. Moore.
At the Symphony. Nathan.
Autumn Song. Brettell.
Balsham Bells. Prescot.
The Beloved Person Must I Think. Ki-no-Akimine.
The Blackbird. *Anonymous.*
Carolina Spring Song. Allen.
Close-Ups of Summer. MacCaig.
Colophon for Lan-t'ing Hsiu-Hsi. Peck.
The Cuckoo. Thomas.
The Dead Eagle. Campbell.
Ending. Ewart.
An Epitaph upon the Celebrated Claudy Philips, Musician... Johnson.
Erinna. Antipater of Sidon.
Fair Janet. *Anonymous.*
The Faithful Shepherdess. Fletcher.

High Fidelity. Gunn.
Holy Satyr. Doolittle.
In Memory of Basil, Marquess of Dufferin and Ava. Betjeman.
In Ringlets Curl'd Thy Tresses Flow. Balfour.
In the Secret House. Middleton.
Instant Coffee. Yau.
Is This Africa? Dempster.
Israfel. Poe.
Lament of the Flutes. Okigbo.
The Leaping Fire. Montague.
The Letter. Reznikoff.
Limerick: "No water. dry rocks and dry throats." Cope.
Limerick: "There was an old stupid who wrote." Parke.
Love Letter Postmarked Van Beethoven. Wakoski.
A Love Poem. Ashbery.
A Midsummer Night's Dream. Shakespeare.
The Mocking-bird. Stockard.
Moritura. Davidson.
Much Ado about Nothing in the City (parody). *Anonymous.*
The Musical Lion. Herford.
Notes from an Analyst's Couch. Probst.
Now the Earth, the Skies, the Air. *Anonymous.*
The Panchatantra: The Penalty of Virtue. *Anonymous.*
The Perfectionist. Fleisher.
A Persian Song of Hafiz. Jones.
Riddle: "Close in a cage a bird I'll keep." *Anonymous.*
Robins. Bruce.
Sea-Ward, White Gleaming through the Busy Scud. Coleridge.
The Skylark. Tennyson.
Song and Science. Shinn.
Song for a Dancer. Rexroth.
Songs in Flight (excerpt). Bachmann.
Sonnet: "Not wrongly moved by this dismaying scene." Empson.
Sonnet: To Dante Alighieri (He Reports in a Feigned Vision). Cavalcanti.
The Spruce and Limber Yellow-Hammer. Coleridge.
There Pipes the Wood-Lark. Gray.
To the Muses. Blake.
Water Ouzel. Matchett.
Wrath. Hollander.
Xenophanes. Emerson.

Nothing
All Splendor on Earth. Kiwus.
America. Di Cicco.
Amoretti, LXIII. Spenser.
And He Answered Them Nothing. Crashaw.
Are the Sick in Their Beds as They Should Be? McIntosh.
As It Looked Then. Robinson.

As You Leave the Room. Stevens.
At Sainte-Marguerite. Stickney.
At Such a Time, in Such a Spot. Bronte.
Back Aways. Coolidge.
Ballad of the Three Coins. Watkins.
Beale Street. Hughes.
Big Rock Jail. Bill.
Birth. Urdang.
The Black Angel. Coulette.
A Black Soldier Remembers. Coalman.
Blurt: Master Constable: Song: Love Is Like a Lamb. Middleton.
Bob Stanford. *Anonymous.*
The Book of Mysteries. Barnett.
Brother and Sisters. Wright.
Brummell at Calais. Glassco.
Burial. Van Doren.
Burial of the Spirit. Hughes.
Burning. Snyder.
But. Cummings.
Can I Tempt You to a Pond Walk? Schuyler.
Candida. Kavanagh.
Canzonetta: Of His Lady, and of His Making Her Likeness. Jacopo da Lentino.
Captured Bird. Rachow.
The Careless Gallant. Jordan.
Celia Celia. Mitchell.
Champagne. Dove.
The Character of a Happy Life. Wotton.
Chekhov Comes to Mind at Harvard. Freeman.
A Cocker of Snooks. Gotlieb.
Cockroach. Hoberman.
Cokboy, Part Two. Rothenberg.
Comanche. Gildner.
The Contemporary Muse. Rickword.
Contemporary Song. Spencer.
Contra Mortem. Carruth.
Crime Club. Kees.
Day before Christmas. Chute.
A Day for Anne Frank. Williams.
The Dead. Dudek.
Death Songs. Mack.
Deceased. Corman.
Dedicatory Ode: They Say That in the Unchanging Place. Belloc.
Departure Platform. Allott.
The Disabled Debauchee. Rochester.
Do Something. *Anonymous.*
Don Juan. Byron.
The Ecliptic: Cancer, or, The Crab (excerpt). Macleod.
The End of the World. MacLeish.
Epitaph. Abercrombie.
Epitaph Inscribed on a Small Piece of Marble. Shirley.
Equanimity. Murray.
An Essay on Man. Pope.
Eumares. Asclepiades.
Euridice Saved. Gregg.
Exodus for Oregon. Miller.

Expect Nothing. Walker.
Eyes of Summer. Merwin.
A Failure. Day-Lewis.
Fancy. Creeley.
February. Merwin.
Fires of Driftwood. MacKay.
Flights. McDonald.
For the New Year. Creeley.
Four Preludes on Playthings of the Wind. Sandburg.
From a Cheerful Alphabet. Updike.
From a Hint in the Minor Poets. Wesley.
A Funeral Elogy... Norton II.
Gemwood. Bell.
The Ghost of a Ghost. Leithauser.
Gloucester Moors. Moody.
Glove Glue. Belford.
Going to Sleep in the Country. Moss.
Granma's Words. Palmanteer.
Graves in Queens. Hugo.
Harriet. Lowell.
The Healing of the Leper. Watkins.
Her Husband. Hughes.
Heredity. Guiterman.
Hiawatha. Sandy.
High Windows. Larkin.
The House on the Hill. Robinson.
How to Tell the Wild Animals. Wells.
I asked no other thing. Dickinson.
I Could Not Sleep for Thinking of the Sky. Masefield.
I Knew I'd Sing. McHugh.
I Who Had Been Afraid. Maris Stella.
The Idea of Detroit. Gustafson.
If I should sleep with a lady called death. Cummings.
If I Went Away. O'Grady.
If You Ask Me Who I Am. Guebuza.
Illusion. Wilcox.
In Hardin County, 1809. Thompson.
In Praise of Ivy. *Anonymous.*
In Praise of Limestone. Auden.
In Robin Hood Cove. Hartley.
In the Land Where We Were Dreaming. Lucas.
Incident. Jones.
Incident on a Journey. Gunn.
Incidental Pieces to a Walk: for Conrad. Cunningham.
The Indian Convert. Freneau.
Intimations of Immortality from Recollections of Early Childhood. Wordsworth.
It Is the Season. Jacobsen.
Jesus. McAuley.
Jim the Splitter. Kendall.
Kept for Jesus. Cherry.
Killing No Murder. Warner.
Kind Lovers, Love On. Crowne.
Kind Sir: These Woods. Sexton.

Lady Love. Eluard.
The Last Tournament. Tennyson.
The Last Wish. Lytton.
The Law of Averages. "Troubadour".
Lean Gaius, Who Was Thinner Than a Straw. Lucilius [(or Lucillius)].
Leaving Something Behind. Wagoner.
Let Minions Marshal Every Hair. *Anonymous.*
Letter to a Mute. James.
Letter to the City Clerk. Wright.
Letter VIII. Swingler.
Life Study. Orlen.
Lightning of the Abyss. Laforgue.
Limerick: "O God, inasmuch as without Thee." *Anonymous.*
Lines on Cambridge of 1830. Tennyson.
A Living. Lawrence.
Lollingdon Downs. Masefield.
The Long War. Li Po.
Lost Explorer. Pennant.
Love Hath a Language. Sheridan.
Love Song out of Nothing. Miller.
Lover's Meeting. Mathew.
A Magus. Ciardi.
Malvern Waters. *Anonymous.*
Man's Littleness in Presence of the Stars. White.
The Man with the Blue Guitar. Stevens.
Map of My Country. Holmes.
Martin Luther at Potsdam. Pain.
May Day Demonstrators. Lindsay.
Medusa. Plath.
Memories of Verdun. Dugan.
Metaphysical Shock while Watching a TV Cartoon. Rice.
The Might Buck, the Immigrant Fuck, and Melting Pot Luck. Filip.
Miss Loo. De la Mare.
Monna Innominata. Rossetti.
Monody to the Sound of Zithers. Boyle.
Moon Festival. Tu Fu.
Mother of Fishermen. Roland-Holst.
The Mute City. Eichenrand.
My Babe My Babe. Wilber.
My Sister. Storni.
My Stearine Candles. Henry.
My triumph lasted till the drums. Dickinson.
Natural Law. Deutsch.
No Sense Grieving. Rubin.
Nocturn at the Institute. McElroy.
Northhanger Ridge. Wright.
Notes on a Long Evening. Phillips.
Notes towards a Poem That Can Never Be Written. Atwood.
Nothing Between. Tindley.

Nothing To Be Said. Larkin.
Now and Then. Hamilton.
Old Man. Kicknosway.
On a Clear Day I Can See Forever. Kuo.
On a Dying Boy. Bell.
On a Tired Housewife. *Anonymous.*
On an Houre-Glasse. Hall.
One chip of human bone. Young Bear.
One Star Fell and Another. Aiken.
The ordinary valour only works. Anstey.
Our Angels. Schwartz.
Peace. Jonas.
The People in the Park. Adams.
Perdita. Drennan.
Pledge. Shlonsky.
Pod of the Milkweed. Frost.
Poem: "You are ill and so I lead you away." Purdy.
The Popish Plot. Dryden.
The Powerline Incarnation. Murray.
Prayer. *Anonymous.*
Pretty Polly. *Anonymous.*
Prices. Ginsberg.
The Quiet Fog. Piercy.
Range-Finding. Frost.
Reaching the Horizon. Mezey.
Relativities (parody). Untermeyer.
Resurrection of the Dead. Shenhar.
The Rhyme. Creeley.
Satires of Circumstance. Hardy.
The Saviour Can Solve Every Problem. Smith.
The Sea Fog. Jacobsen.
Sea Hunger. Mitchell.
Seated on her bed legs spread open. Mansour.
Sexual Soup. Jong.
Ship of Death. Lawrence.
Ships in Harbour. Morton.
A Shropshire Lad. Housman.
The Signboard. Creeley.
The Silent Pool. Monro.
Since Nothing Is Impossible. Waters.
Sleeping with One Eye Open. Strand.
Solutions. Barton.
Song: Lift Boy. Graves.
Song, on Reading That the Cyclotron has Produced Cosmic Rays... Hoffenstein.
Song: "She was lyin face down in her face." Knott.
Song: Stop All the Clocks. Auden.
Sonnets, CIX: "O, never say that I was false of heart." Shakespeare.
Stack o' Dollars. Estes.
Stepfathers. Donnell.
The Storm-Cock's Song. ""MacDiarmid.
Storm on the Island. Heaney.
The Strong Are Saying Nothing. Frost.
The Swan–Vain Pleasures. Horton.

The Sweeper of Ways. Nemerov.
Tangier. Dunn.
The Tax-Gatherer. Tabb.
There Is a Box. Greenberg.
There Is Nothing New in New York. Pinero.
There's Nothing Like the Sun. Thomas.
They are rebuilding. Ise.
Thirtieth Anniversary Report of the Class of '41. Nemerov.
This World Is All a Fleeting Show. Moore.
Time Is the Mercy of Eternity. Rexroth.
To Henry Vaughan. Smith.
To Juan at the Winter Solstice. Graves.
To Madame A. V. Pletneff. Pavlova.
To Mr. C, St. James's Place, London, October 22nd. Pope.
To Nearly Everybody in Europe To-Day. ""MacDiarmid.
The Tomtit. De la Mare.
Translation into the Original. Gilbert.
Truth Brought to Light; or, Murder Will Out. College.
Truth Kills Everybody. Hughes.
The Turtle's Belly. Pearce.
Tzu Yeh Songs. *Anonymous.*
Untitled Requiem for Tomorrow. Conyus.
Upon a Ring of Bells. Bunyan.
A Useless Burden upon the Earth. Bridges.
Vanity. Thomson.
Variations, Calypso and Fugue on a Theme of Ella Wheeler Wilcox. Ashbery.
A Vase of Flowers. Ashbery.
The Visitor. Forche.
The Voice. Maris Stella.
Voice in the Crowd. Joans.
Walk-Up. Merwin.
Water. Jabes.
Wet or Fine. Hare.
What Form or Shape to Describe? Kabir.
What Would I Do White? Jordan.
When I Am Not With You. Teasdale.
A White Wall under the Wallpaper. Henderson.
Why Do You Write about Russia? Simpson.
Wild Geese. Hart-Smith.
Wind Secrets. Wakoski.
Winter over Nothing. Coleman.
Winter Sunset. Laforgue.
Winter Trees. Plath.
The Woodlot. Clampitt.
A Word About Woodpiles. Turner.
Yesterday. Merwin.
A Young Man's Song. Bell.
Nothingness
Archne. Foerster.
Calm After Storm. Yerby.
Faust. Goethe.
Five Lyrics from "Good for Nothing Man". Pitchford.

Hast Never Come to Thee an Hour. Whitman.
The Lemmings. Masefield.
Less and Less Human, O Savage Spirit. Stevens.
Lord! Who Art Merciful as Well as Just. Southey.
Memory as Memorial in the Last. Marshall.
She Attempts to Refute the Praises That Truth... Juana Ines de la Cruz.
Song for a Suicide. Hughes.
The Terror of Death. Keats.
They Sing. Roethke.
This Coloured Counterfeit That Thou Beholdest. Juana Ines de la Cruz.
To an Old Lady Dead. Sassoon.
Turn Blind. Celan.
The Way up Is the Way down. Brasch.
Notice (d)
Familiar Faces, Long Departed. Hillyer.
Middle of the Day. Driscoll.
Playing Pocahontas. Blockcolski.
The Reminder. Hardy.
The Row between the Cages. Armstrong.
Spring Ease. Reid.
Notion (s)
Amours de Voyage. Clough.
A Bestiary. Rexroth.
Here Lies... Smith.
More Sonnets at Christmas. Tate.
Sourwood Mountain. *Anonymous.*
When I Am Dead. Stillman.
Notre Dame
The Enigmatic Traveler. Vazakas.
A Paraphrase from the French. Prior.
Nought
The Comin' o' the Spring. Scott.
Eternity. More.
Fear Death by Water. Eberhart.
For An Allegorical Dance of Women by Andrea Mantegna. Rossetti.
The Lookers-On. Heywood.
Love Song out of Nothing. Miller.
Nightfall. Trueba.
Song: "When maidens are young, and in their spring." Behn.
Sonnets of the Months. San Geminiano.
Tamburlaine the Great. Marlowe.
The Things That Are More Excellent. Watson.
Titmouse. De la Mare.
Vow to Love Faithfully, Howsoever He Be Rewarded. Surrey.
Noun (s)
For the Noun C. BL. Tyler.
A Letter to a Live Poet. Brooke.
O Now the Drenched Land Wakes. Patchen.
Nourish (ed) (ing) (ment)
Autumn. Pushkin.
Baking Day. Joseph.

Caelica, XXVII. Greville.
The Cryptic Streets. Abu-l-
Ala al-Maarri.
Death. Bronte.
A Decade. Lowell.
Elegy. Karoniaktatie.
Flora's Lamentable Passion.
Anonymous.
The Huntress. Johnston.
Love's Labour's Lost.
Shakespeare.
Metamorphoses. Ovid
(Publius Ovidius Naso).
Nova. Levendosky.
A Place (Any Place) to
Transcend All Places.
Williams.
Silverthorn Bush. Finch.
Sonnets at Christmas. Tate.

Novel (s)
The Author of Christine.
Howard.
In Spite of His Dangling
Pronoun. Lifshin.
A Meeting of Cultures.
Davie.
On the Same. Campbell.
A Poem. Meltzer.

November
Autumnal. Dowson.
Classic Ballroom Dances.
Simic.
The Dying Garden.
Nemerov.
The Great War. Scannell.
Kevin Barry. Ward.
No! Hood.
Pursuit of an Ideal.
Kavanagh.
The Rooftree. Tate.
The Song of This House.
Vincent.

Now
Alabama Centennial.
Madgett.
All Ignorance Toboggans into
Know. Cummings.
Cancion. Juan II of Castile.
Do It Now! *Anonymous.*
Dulcina. Ralegh.
Eastside Incidents. Corso.
Elegy for My Father. Moss.
The End Is Now. "Marie.
Exchanging Glances. Root.
The Final Mystery.
Newbolt.
First Practice. Gildner.
Girl in a Nightgown.
Stevens.
Her Pedigree. Ficke.
Home. Summers.
In Defense of Black Poets.
Rivers.
Inertia. Chaudhari.
Just Taking Note–. Scott.
Market Day. Cresson.
Now, If You Will Look in My
Brain. Villa.
A Pavane for the Nursery.
Smith.
Portrait of a Marriage.
Abse.
The River of Heaven.
Anonymous.
The Sea Dike. Vasalis.
Song for a Blue Roadster.
Field.
'Tis the Witching Hour of
Night. Keats.
The Trinity. *Anonymous.*
The True Heaven. Hayes.
The West. Muir.

Nowhere
America. Creeley.
Benediction. Freedman.
Birthday. Ciardi.
Border Line. Hughes.
Breath. Dickey.
Bushed. Lillard.
Carrier Indians. Belford.
Circular Roads. Muchemwa.
Friday Evening. Marzan.
Have you heard? The troubles
of the road. Sulpicia.
Letter to the Revolution.
Griffin.
Little Elegy. Wylie.
The Map of Places. Riding.
Now I Have Forgotten All.
Vogel.
The Path That Leads
Nowhere. Robinson.
The Rock. Eliot.
Sailor Man. Bailey.
The Song of Nidderdale.
Ratcliffe.
Tambourine. Cunningham.
To Her Dead Mate: Montana,
1966. Libbey.
To Lighten My House.
Reid.
To Nowhere. Ignatow.
Tzu Yeh Songs. *Anonymous.*
Yesterday. Merwin.

Nude
Corporate Entity. MacLeish.
For Spring. Jones.
Gross, Coarse, Hideous.
Lawrence.
Letter to a Jealous Friend.
Simmons.
Little Air. Mallarme.
Married Three Months.
Nelms.
The Naked and the Nude.
Graves.
Nothing Sacred. Woddis.
O Make Me a Mask.
Thomas.

Numb (ed)
The Addict. Sexton.
Cranes. Davies.
December. Keats.
Elegy: Three. Deane.
I breathed enough to take the
trick. Dickinson.
Stop. Wilbur.

Number (s)
The Abyss. Baudelaire.
The Bastard. Savage.
The Beggar's Opera. Gay.
Chaucer. Brawley.
The Dancer. Waller.
An Evil World. *Anonymous.*
The Faerie Queene. Spenser.
An Heroick Epistle from a
Dog at Twickenham to a
Dog at Court. Pope.
I Consider the Tree. Buber.
Less Nonsense. Herbert.
Life's Testament.
Baylebridge.
Love Poem. Orr.
Message. Raba.
The Million. Redgrove.
Moving Again. Matthews.
Ode for Music on St. Cecilia's
Day. Pope.
Orlando Furioso. Ariosto.
Paradise Lost. Milton.
Poem: "I keep feeling all
space as my image."
Russell.
Prisoner. George.

The Rosy Days Are
Numbered. Ibn Ezra.
Some Semblance of Order.
Wright.
Tiny Catullus. Levine.
To the Same. Jonson.
We Bring No Glittering
Treasures. Phillips.
What's Your Name?
Anonymous.

Nun (s)
The Abbess. Scott.
The Autumn Day Its Course
Has Run. Bronte.
Epistle to George Keats
(excerpt). Keats.
The Eve of Saint John.
Scott.
Love Calls Us to the Things
of This World. Wilbur.
Motets, II. *Anonymous.*
Old Maid. Nicolson.
On the Symbolic
Consideration of Hands and
the Significance of Death.
Williams.
The Reckoning. Friman.
Song: "Since I'm a girl."
Anonymous.
The Young Man and the
Young Nun. Mackie.

Nunnery
Limerick: "There was a young
woman named Plunnery."
Gorey.
Shakespearean Soliloquy in
Progress: "To be, or not to
be..."(parody). Mark.

Nuptial (s)
Ah, Now I Know What Day
This Is. Statius Publius
Papinius.
An Epithalamion upon the
Marquis of Huntilies
Marriage. James I
Epithalamium for Charlotte
Corday and Francis
Ravaillac. Shelley.
The First Olympionique to
Hiero of Syracuse. Pindar.
Had I but Strength Enough,
and Time (parody).
Robinson.
The House of Life. Rossetti.
Love's Courtship. Carew.
Modern Love, XLI.
Meredith.

Nurse (s)
Barren Woman. Plath.
Caelica, XLIII. Greville.
The Cry of the Child
(parody). Zaranka.
The Daughter's Rebellion.
Hopkinson.
Disdain Me Still. Pembroke.
Domestic Duties. Braun.
Elektra on Third Avenue.
Hacker.
Fidelis. Procter.
I Scream You Scream.
McKay.
Lamkin (C vers.).
Anonymous.
Lullaby. Phillip.
Misfortunes Never Come
Singly. Graham.
My Three Wives.
Anonymous.
Ode to the Protestant Poets.
Hoover.
On the Deputy of Ireland's
Child. Davies.

On Tom-O-Combe.
Anonymous.
Richard II. Shakespeare.
The Sherman Cyclone.
Anonymous.
So Then, I Feel Not Deeply!
Landor.
Songs of Seven. Ingelow.
Stroke. Lowery.
There Is Strength in the Soil.
Stringer.
To Robert Louis Stevenson.
Henley.
Two Pieces after Suetonius.
Warren.

Nursery
The Buried Child. Wellesley.
Christina. MacNeice.
The Malefic Surgeon.
Lansing.

Nursery rhyme
Ding Dong (parody). Hilton.
Wild Strawberries. Graves.

Nut (s)
Dawlish Fair. Keats.
I Had a Little Nut Tree.
Mother Goose.
I Sat among the Green
Leaves. Pickthall.
I Saw a Little Squirrel.
Anonymous.
The Lapful of Nuts.
Ferguson.
The Mountain and the
Squirrel. Emerson.
New York–Albany.
Ferlinghetti.
Nutting Time. Poulsson.
Yearning. Kreymborg.

Nutmeg
The American Traveller.
Newell.
The King of China's
Daughter. Sitwell.

Nylon
The Orlando Commercial.
Macbeth.

Nymph (s)
About Children. McGinley.
And to the Young Man.
Moore.
Autobiographies. Mahon.
Caelica, III. Greville.
The Eccho. Leigh.
Endymion's Convoy.
Drayton.
Farewell to the Muses.
Reynolds.
The Golden Age: Hymn to
Diana. Heywood.
In Imitation of Anacreon.
Prior.
Lament. Drummond.
The Luciad. Camoens.
A Note from the Pipes.
Speyer.
A Nymph and a Swain.
Congreve.
Nymphs and Satyrs. Ewart.
A Persian Song of Hafiz.
Hafiz.
A Persian Song of Hafiz.
Jones.
The Progress of Beauty.
Swift.
A Sigh. Wilchilsea.
Sonnets, VI: "Awakened, I
behold through dewy
leaves." Irwin.
Sylvia. Drayton.
The Three Cottage Girls.
Wordsworth.

Thus Bonny-Boots the
Birthday Celebrated.
Anonymous.

Nymphomaniac (s)
The Advantages of Learning.
Martial (Marcus Valerius
Martialis).
Careless Love. Kunitz.

O

Oak (s)
Advice to a Prophet.
Wilbur.
The Ancient Briton: The
Dance of the Sword.
Anonymous.
Ancient of Days. Rudolf.
The Ash and the Oak.
Simpson.
The Battle of Eutaw. Simms.
Beech and Oak. Peacock.
Dodona's Oaks Were Still.
MacDonogh.
Drifting. O'Donnell.
An Essay on the Fleet Riding
in the Downes.
Anonymous.
A Fable for Critics. Lowell.
Faint Yet Pursuing.
Patmore.
The Farmer's Boy.
Bloomfield.
The Gallows. Thomas.
Last Hill in a Vista. Bogan.
Little Epithalamium.
Kallman.
The Meaning. Gustafson.
Misgivings. Melville.
Ode. Freneau.
The Play of the Four P.P.:
The Palmer. Heywood.
Solitude. Clare.
Song: "For the tender beech
and the sapling oak."
Peacock.
Song: "Under the oak tree,
oak tree." *Anonymous.*
Tennyson. Ansen.
There Is a Charm in Solitude
That Cheers. Clare.
To a Friend in the Country.
Gogarty.
To an Oak Tree. Scott.
Weather. MacLeish.
A Wet Sheet. Cunningham.
When Life Is Quite Through
With. Cummings.

Oar (s)
The Galley Slave (excerpt).
Anonymous.
Life's Circumnavigators.
Rodgers.
Loch Luichart. Young.
To His Friend in Elysium.
Du Bellay.
The Willis. Duffield.

Oasis
Memories of West Street and
Lepke. Lowell.
A World without Objects Is a
Sensible Emptiness.
Wilbur.

Oath
Epitaph of a Faithful Man.
Mezey.
The Flying Dutchman.
Anonymous.

Love's Labour's Lost.
Shakespeare.
Queen Eleanor's Confession
(A version). *Anonymous.*
To His Coy Mistress (parody).
Scupham.

Obedience
And Jesus Wept. Brydges.
Interior. Milbauer.
On the Spartan Dead at
Thermopylae. Simonides
(of Ceos).
Preludes. Patmore.
Summer Storm. Montague.
The Times. Manilius.
The Young Bride's Dream.
Coghill.

Obey (ed) (s)
Attainment. Wilcox.
The Broken Heart. Ford.
The Giver of Life.
Unknown.
God's Treasure. "N.
Lately I've felt a grave
concern. Die.
The Law of the Jungle.
Kipling.
The Lords of Creation.
Anonymous.
The Man in the Dream Is
Death. Butler.
The Nut-Brown Maid.
Anonymous.
O Maister Deere and Fader
Reverent! Hoccleve.
On Fortune. Elizabeth I.
Rainer Maria Rilke Returns
from the Dead... Engman.
Riding. Grossman.
The Rights of Women.
Cowper.
To the Memory of a Lady.
Lyttelton.
The Voice of God Is Calling.
Holmes.
Waiting. Davidson.
When the God Returns.
Edson.
Written for My Son...at His
First Putting on Breeches.
Barber.

Object (s)
Envying a Little Bird.
Gregoria Francisca.
Foreplay of the Alphabet.
Gray.
The Higher Empiricism.
Golffing.
A Hub for the Universe.
Whitman.
Life Story. Kates.
Love's Force. Carew.
Saint Mary Magdalene.
Crashaw.
Song: "'Tis true our life is but
a long dis-ease." Philips.
Sonnet in the Mail Coach.
Taylor.
Sonnet. The Cell. Thelwall.
Sonnets to Karl Theodor
German. Platen.

Oblivion
Album. Papenhausen.
An Autograph. Lowell
Defeat O' the Hert. Smith.
Farewell to Juliet. Blunt.
The Final Hunger. Miller.
The Heart Recalcitrant.
Speyer.
Love Poem–1940.
Hershenson.
Memoir. Weingarten.

On the Edition of Mr. Pope's
Works with a Commentary
and Notes. Edwards.
Our Casuarina Tree. Dutt.
Pure Nails Brightly Flashing.
Mallarme.
Ship of Death. Lawrence.
The Undiscovered Country.
Aldrich.
The Winds of Change.
Ballard.
The Zodiac: The Valley of
Sleep. Marsman.

Obscenity (ies)
Fabrication of Ancestors.
Dugan.
The Seventies. Beyer.
Tar. Williams.

Obscure (d)
Ameinias. Simon.
At the Ascension. Leon.
August Night. Swenson.
Eclipse. Roberson.
October. Thomas.
Ode to Memory. Tennyson.
The Sensitive Plant. Shelley.
Spectrum. Dickey.
Ultra-Germano-Criticasterism.
Hunt.

Obsolete
Antiques. De la Mare.
The Biggest Killing. Dorn.
Elegy for the Giant Tortoises.
Atwood.
Last Things. Manhire.

Obvious
Man Carrying Thing.
Stevens.
Translations. Lum.
The Two Deserts. Patmore.
The "Utopia'. Harwood.

Occasion
Academic Moon. Bevington.
Landscape Workers. Elliott.

Occult
Sonnets for Pictures: Our
Lady of the Rocks.
Rossetti.

Ocean (s)
After the Rain. Crouch.
Ants. Hyde.
Arise, Arise. *Anonymous.*
At Mid-Ocean. Bly.
Australia. O'Dowd.
Autumn Squall–Lake Erie.
Russo.
The Beach. Graves.
The Blue-Hole. Bell.
Boundaries. Fleming.
Canoe-Hauling Chant.
Ngata.
Capture of Little York.
Anonymous.
Carmel Point. Jeffers.
Computer. Orban.
The Crystal Lithium.
Schuyler.
Daily the Ocean between Us.
Goedicke.
Don Juan. Byron.
Eight Miles South of Grand
Haven. Kelly.
Eire. Drennan.
Essentials. Greenberg.
The Estate: "Waking by
Night'. Brasch.
Ethelstan: O'er the Wild
Gannet's Bath. Darley.
Evangeline. Longfellow.
Evening. Keble.
Extract. Bowles.
False Dawn. De la Mare.

Faustus Faces His Doom.
Marlowe.
A Field Poem. Valaitis.
For Jan. Wieners.
From Heart to Heart.
Gannett.
The Geraldine's Daughter
(excerpt). Mangan.
German Shepherd.
Livingston.
Goldfish. Nemerov.
Great Titanic. *Anonymous.*
Hatteras Calling. Aiken.
Haunted Country. Jeffers.
Heron's Bay. Galvin.
The Homeric Hexameter,
Described and Exemplified.
Coleridge.
How Many Moments
Must(Amazing Each.
Cummings.
A Hymn of the Sea. Bryant.
I'll Have a Collier for My
Sweetheart. Oliver.
In the Beginning. Monroe.
The Instrument. Raine.
The Jellyfish. Root.
John Henry in Harlem.
Toleson.
John Horace Burleson.
Masters.
The Lemmings. Stauffer.
A Life on the Ocean Wave.
Sargent
Lourenco Marques.
Eglington.
Love in the Wind. Hovey.
Malvern Hills. Cottle.
Message from Home. Raine.
The Miracle of Dawn.
Cawein.
My Johnny. *Anonymous.*
My Ship Is on de Ocean.
Anonymous.
Night Dive. Johnson.
No More the Slow Stream.
McLaren.
Note from an Exhibition.
Goldbarth.
November Day at McClure's.
Bly.
The Ocean. Prentice.
The Ocean Spills.
Hoffenstein.
On the Ocean Floor.
" "MacDiarmid.
On the Struma Massacre.
Gustafson.
Pa, Pa, Build Me a Boat.
Anonymous.
Palm Trees. Warner.
Paradise Lost. Milton.
Putting on My Shoes I Hear
the Floor Cry out beneath
Me (parody). Heffernan.
Rain. Benediktsson.
The Ribbon-Fish. Adamson.
Salt. Clifton.
The Sea-Serpent. Planche.
Seabirds. Smith.
The Seafarer. *Anonymous.*
Seals at High Island.
Murphy.
The Ship Canal from the
Atlantic to the Pacific.
Lieber.
The Soul, Reaching, Throwing
Out for Love. Whitman.
Spawning in Northern
Minnesota. McElroy.
Squall. Moss.
Storm Song. Taylor.

The Strong. Cheney.
Tears. Whitman.
This Ensuing Copy the Late
Printer Hath been Pleased
to Honour... Felltham.
Trying to Believe. Gregg.
Turn the Glasses Over.
Anonymous.
Up out of the African.
Joans.
The Urn. Cowley.
A Vision of the Sea. Shelley.
Voyage West. MacLeish.
Wake, Isles of the South.
Tappan.
The Well-Aimed Stare.
Margenat.
When You and I Must Part.
Anonymous.
Winds of the West, Arise!
Darley.
Ye Sons of Columbia.
Fessenden.

October
Balaclava. *Anonymous.*
The Chestnut Vendor.
Szelki.
Drink To-day. Fletcher.
Drinking Song. Fletcher.
Going A-Nutting. Stedman.
The Great Hunger.
Kavanagh.
Kicking the Leaves. Hall.
Localities. Sandburg.
Looking for a Home. Stern.
October's Bright Blue
Weather. Jackson.
Old October. Constable.
On the First of March.
Anonymous.
A Rose in October. Riley.
September. Lampman.
When the World Ends. Van
Doren.

Odd (s)
The After-Thought. Smith.
Arachne. Kazantzis.
Joan to Her Lady.
Anonymous.
The King of Sunshine.
Silverton.
A lady red upon the hill.
Dickinson.
Mexico City Hand Game.
Green.
Odd to a Krokis.
Anonymous.
Pigs o' Pelton. *Anonymous.*
Prayer. Ewart.
Rory O'More; or, Good
Omens. Lover.
Short Song: "There was an
old crow." *Anonymous.*
Spring and All. Bauer.
To Know If It Be Leap Year.
Anonymous.
The Walrus and the
Carpenter. "Carroll.
What Thing Is Love. Peele.

Ode (s)
The Book-Burning Pit. Lo
Yin.
His Delight. Meilir ap
Gwalchmai.
Lines in Ridicule of Certain
Poems Published in 1777.
Johnson.
Lines on Carmen Sylva.
Lazarus.
Not Lotte. Hoskins.
Poem from Llanybri.
Roberts.

Purchase of a Blue, Green, or
Orange Ode. Miles.
Urceus Exit: Triolet.
Dobson.

Odor (s)
The Angel in the House.
Patmore.
Antigone VI. Martin.
The Blind Girl. Crane.
Chaucer. Longfellow
The Church Mouse. Bullett.
Had I the Choice. Whitman.
Himalayan Balsam.
Stevenson.
Hope and Faith. Peretz.
The Inner Part. Simpson.
The Loves of the Plants.
Darwin.
Matins, or Morning Prayer.
Herrick.
Mock Orange. Gluck.
The Night-Apple. Ginsberg.
No Theory. Ignatow.
The Passengers. Antin.
The Smell of Fish. Meissner.
Solitude Late at Night in the
Woods. Bly.
Song: "Love, that looks still
on your eyes." Browne.
Unprofitablenes. Vaughan.
Widcombe Churchyard.
Landor.

Odysseus
Leda and the Swan. Friman.
The Odyssey. Homer.

Oedipus
Captain's Table. Bynner.
Mother, Mother, Are You All
There? Lamport.

Off
Dictum Sapienti. Webb.
Everything. Paul.
Gila Monster Route. Post.
My Boots. Thoreau.
The Ploughboy. Clare.
Two Hangovers. Wright.

Offend (ed)
An Epigram upon a Young
Gentleman Refusing to
Walk with the Author...
Garrick.
Love's Offence. Suckling.
De Ponto. Ovid (Publius
Ovidius Naso).
Remember the Ladies.
Lifshin.
The School Girl. Venable.
Teamster's Song.
Anonymous.
The Voice of Experience.
Goethe.

Offense
Arizona Boys and Girls.
Anonymous.
Little Boy Blue. Carryl.
On the "Vita Nuova" of
Dante. Rossetti.
Patience Though I Have Not.
Wyatt.
The Wife Takes a Child.
Voigt.
Ye Clerke of Ye Wethere
(parody). *Anonymous.*

Offer (ing) (ings)
The Ampler Circumscription.
Baylebridge.
Anglicized Utopia. Gilbert.
Atalanta's Race. Morris.
Benediction for the Felt.
Anonymous.
Egyptian Hieroglyphics.
Anonymous.

How to Give. *Anonymous.*
The Mother. Palmer.
NN 616410. Tulloch.
The Odyssey. Homer.
Oraga Haru. Issa.
Orchard. Doolittle.
Parting. Raine.
Parting. Yeats.
Pour Down. Holmes.
Resolution in Four Sonnets.
Cotton.
Secret Pleasures. Morgan.
To Destiny. *Anonymous.*
To Leigh Hunt, Esq. Keats.
To the Man I Live with.
Menebroker.
Tortoise. De Longchamps.
What Form or Shape to
Describe? Kabir.

Office (s)
Clancy of the Overflow.
Paterson.
Dreamers. Sassoon.
Flag. Saner.
Getting a Job. Blackburn.
The Questions. Pinsky.
The Seasons. Thomson.
Where I Am Now. Shapiro.
Winter's Onset from an
Alienated Point of View.
Dugan.

Officer (s)
Class Incident from Graves.
Brownjohn.
Gee, Officer Krupke.
Sondheim.
In Memoriam, Private D.
Sutherland. Mackintosh.
My 71st Year. Whitman.
Officers. Miles.
Trenton and Princeton.
Anonymous.
A War Bird's Burlesque (with
music). *Anonymous.*

Offspring
After Five Years. Young.
A Connacht Caoine.
Anonymous.
The Empty Apartment.
Zeitlin.
The Legend of Good Women.
Chaucer.
The Parents of Psychotic
Children. Bell.
The Parish Register. Crabbe.
Shema. Levi.
Verses on the Prospect of
Planting Arts and Learning
in America. Berkeley.
Willie Riley. *Anonymous.*

Often
The Bonnie Cravat. Mother
Goose.
Furnished Lives. Silkin.
How Often (parody). King.
Not Often. Fraser.

Ohio
Banks of the Ohio.
Anonymous.
Labor Day. Pacernick.

Oil
Ank'hor Vat. Devlin.
The Cruse. Nicholl.
The Devil's Dictionary:
Safety-Clutch. Bierce.
The Dying Hogger (with
music). *Anonymous.*
Early Discoveries. Malouf.
The Good Samaritan.
Newman.
The Great Santa Barbara Oil
Disaster OR:. Conyus.

Guy. Emerson.
In the Longhouse, Oneida
Museum. Whiteman.
Killing a Whale. Gill.
The lamp burns sure, within.
Dickinson.
New York. Garcia Lorca.
Oil. Snyder.
The Song of the Good
Samaritan. Watkins.
Spring of Work Storm.
Ceravolo.
Suburban Dusk. Meyers.
Texas. Daugherty.
To Music. Herrick.
Vain and Careless. Graves.
Venezuela. *Anonymous.*
When the Ripe Fruit Falls.
Lawrence.
Worry about Money. Raine.

Oklahoma
Arizona. *Anonymous.*
He Told Me His Name Was
Sitting Bull. Harjo.
Hill Hunger. West.

Old age
Arcadia. Sidney.
The King and the Clown.
Anonymous.
Of Himself. Meleager.
The Secular Masque.
Dryden.
To a Young Lady.
Wordsworth.
Walking Past Paul
Blackburn's Apt. on 7th St.
Wakoski.
Whatever It Was I Was
Saving for My Old Age.
Darr.
The Woman's Labour.
Collier.

Old (en) (er)
Advent. Rossetti.
Age. Winter.
Age Not to Be Rejected.
Anonymous.
All Souls' Night. Cornford.
All to Myself. Nesbit.
Apple Hell. Van Doren.
The Arrow. Yeats.
At the Western Shore.
Youngblood.
Aureng-Zebe. Dryden.
The Barn. Blunden.
Beautiful Hands. Gates.
Being Born Is Important.
Sandburg.
The Bells of London.
Anonymous.
Bird's Nests. Clare.
Birthday. Birney.
Brave New World.
MacLeish.
Britannia's Pastorals.
Browne.
The Bullfinches. Hardy.
But I am Growing Old and
Indolent. Jeffers.
But You, My Darling, Should
Have Married the Prince.
Spivack.
Caelica, XIX. Greville.
The Choirmaster's Burial.
Hardy.
Christmas at Sea. Stevenson.
Connubii Flores, or the Well-
Wishes at Weddings.
Herrick.
Contemplations. Bradstreet.
Cotton-eyed Joe.
Anonymous.

Cynthia, Cynthia. Propertius.
The Deep Dark Night. Tennyson.
Dictum Sapienti. Webb.
Down in the Meadows. *Anonymous.*
The Ebb Tide. Southey.
Elijah Speaking. Fetherling.
Empty Holds a Question. Folk.
The End of the Year. Su Tung-P'o.
Epigram: "I delight in the prime of a boy of twelve." Strato.
Farewell Voyaging World! Aiken.
The Fine Old English Gentleman. *Anonymous.*
The Fish. Moore.
Five-in-June. Borie.
Five Years Old. Borie.
For a Son's Marriage. Martial (Marcus Valerius Martialis).
Friday Night's Dream on a Saturday Told. *Anonymous.*
God of the Earth, the Sky, the Sea. Longfellow.
God, through All and in You All. Longfellow.
Gold Tooth Blues. Williams.
Good-Night, Babette. Dobson.
The Groom's Lament. Peterson.
Growing Old. Learned.
Hard Lines. Robinson.
Harriet. Lowell.
Have You Any Work for a Tinker, Mistris. *Anonymous.*
Helen. Lamb.
Hermit. Baxter.
How Old Are You? Fritsch.
How the Old Horse Won the Bet. Holmes.
I Call the Old Time Back. Whittier.
I Got So Old. Williams.
The Ice. Gibson.
In Cemeteries. Enright.
In His Service. Clar.
In Thine Arms. Holmes.
The Incurables. Upson.
Jeremy's Secrets. Todd.
Joan of Arc to the Tribunal. Frisch.
Jonathan. Fyleman.
June. Rand.
Juvenal's Tenth Satire Translated (excerpt). Vaughan.
The Lads in Their Hundreds. Housman.
A Lady Thinks She Is Thirty. Nash.
Lament for Glasgerion. Wylie.
The Last Memory. Symons.
Leavetaking. Watson.
Let Me Grow Lovely. Baker.
A Letter from a Friend. Morris.
Letter from a State Hospital. Mundorf.
Letter to My Kinder. Gaskin.
Little Things. Strobel.

Living. Savage.
Longing for the Persimmon Tree. Brand.
Lost Companions. Bryant.
Masque of Hymen: Glad Time Is at His Point Arrived. Jonson.
May. Rossetti.
Memory. Browne.
Menaphon. Greene.
Moonlight. Teasdale.
Mother and Son. Tate.
Mother's Love. Montgomery.
My Heart Was Wandering. Brennan.
New Friends and Old Friends. Parry.
The New World. Jones.
The News. Saxe.
No More Than Five. Levinson.
Old Age Sticks. Cummings.
Old and New. *Anonymous.*
Old Maids. *Anonymous.*
The Old Man's Complaint. *Anonymous.*
The Old Wife. Kent.
The Olympic Girl. Betjeman.
On City Streets. Bruner.
On Himself. Oldys.
On Refusal of Aid between Nations. Rossetti.
Once I Thought to Die for Love. *Anonymous.*
Once I Was a Monarch's Daughter. *Anonymous.*
The One to Grieve. Thomas.
The Passing of Lydia. Horace.
Pease Porridge Hot. Mother Goose.
Pedra. Burgon.
Pericles and Aspasia. Landor.
The Pigeon-Feeders in Battery Park. Altrocchi.
The Pitch Piles Up in Part. O'Grady.
Poem on Hampstead Heath. Adeane.
The Priest of Coloony. Yeats.
The Prime of Life. Learned.
Private Means is Dead. Smith.
Promised Land. Engel.
Psalm. Simic.
The Pulse. Van Doren.
A Puzzling Example. Benjamin.
A Quality of Air. Chapin.
The Question. Gibson.
The Quiet Night. Heine.
Remove the Predicate. Coolidge.
Return of a Reaper. Creighton.
A Rhyme of One. Locker-Lampson.
Rhyming Prophecy for a New Year. Cooper.
Riches. *Anonymous.*
Ringely, Ringely. Follen.
The Road to Nijmegen. Birney.
The Ruined Cabin. King.
Scene-Shifter Death. O'Neill.
Sephestia's Song to Her Child. Greene.
Siasconset Song. Booth.

A Sigh. Spofford.
Song. Smith.
A Song: I Thought No More Was Needed. Yeats.
Song: "Me Cupid made a Happy Slave." Steele.
A Song of Ale. *Anonymous.*
Song of the Seasons. Lofton.
A Song: "The nymph in vain bestows her pains." Winchilsea.
Spinners at Willowsleigh. Zaturenska.
Springfield Mountain (C vers.). *Anonymous.*
St. Anthony's Township. Sheldon.
Stealing Trout. Hughes.
The Stone Fleet. Melville.
Strange, Is It Not. Kennedy.
Strokes. Stafford.
Summer Song. Nesbit.
Talk to Me Tenderly. Laramore.
Teatime Variations. Titheradge.
They Go By, Go By, Love, the Days and the Hours. Jesus.
Thomas Dudley Ah! Old Must Dye. *Anonymous.*
Tiger-Cat Tim. Chase.
To a Lady. Piatt.
To an Elderly Virgin. O Brolchain.
To Delia. Daniel.
To My Friends. Schiller.
A Toccata of Galuppi's. Browning.
Toujours Amour. Stedman.
Tune: The Butterfly Woos the Blossoms. Li Ching-chao.
Turning Thirty. Ehrhart.
Unity. Noyes.
Untitled: "fisk is/a/negroid/ institution..." Scott.
Up the Mountain to Pick Mawu. *Anonymous.*
An Upper Chamber. Bannerman.
Waillie, Waillie! (with music). *Anonymous.*
The Wanton (excerpt). Vidya.
The Welcome. Laughton.
Western Magic. Austin.
When I Am Old. Mason.
When the Saints Come Marching In. Lorde.
The White Cat of Trenarren. Rowse.
Why I Write Not of Love. Jonson.
Why They Waged War. Bishop.
Winter is Coming. Carmichael.
The Wonderful Old Man. *Anonymous.*
Youth. Wright.
Youth and Age. Mimnermus.

Old Glory
Home Folks: The Name of Old Glory. Riley.

Old Man
Animal Tranquillity and Decay. Wordsworth.
Autumn. Liliencron.
Bread Loaf to Omaha, Twenty-Eight Hours. Gray.

Clay and Water. Hochman.
Commander Lowell. Lowell.
Dandoo. *Anonymous.*
Distortions. Hutchinson.
Erin (Elephant). *Anonymous.*
Field Day. Rodgers.
Grandfather's Clock. Work.
It's Raining, It's Pouring. *Anonymous.*
Johnny Walk along to Hilo. *Anonymous.*
The Kitchie-Boy. *Anonymous.*
Leonardo's Secret. Bly.
Limerick: "There was an old man in a Barge." Lear.
Limerick: "There was an Old Man in a pew." Lear.
Limerick: "There was an Old Man of Leghorn." Lear.
Limerick: "There was an Old Man of Madras." Lear.
Limerick: "There was an old man of Peru." Lear.
Limerick: "There was an old man of Spithead." Lear.
Limerick: "There was an Old Man of the Dee." Lear.
Limerick: "There was an Old Man of The Hague." Lear.
Limerick: "There was an old man of the West." Lear.
Limerick: "There was an old man of Three Bridges." Lear.
Limerick: "There was an old man with a gong." Lear.
Limerick: "There was an old person of Ewell." Lear.
Madrigal: "Where shall I sorrow great." Peerson.
Maids When You're Young, Never Wed an Old Man. *Anonymous.*
The Moments He Remembers. Van Doren.
My Cow. McCord.
My Good Old Man. *Anonymous.*
My Little Old Man and I Fell Out. *Anonymous.*
A Note Left in Jimmy Leonard's Shack. Wright.
The Old Age of Michelangelo. Prince.
Old Man. Stern.
An Old Man's Advice. *Anonymous.*
Old Witherington. Randall.
On Being Asked for a War Poem. Yeats.
The Pilot. Edson.
Poor Old Man. *Anonymous.*
Shovelling Iron Ore. *Anonymous.*
The Silly Old Man. *Anonymous.*
Small Quiet Song. Smith.
A Symposium: Apples. Pastan.
There Was an Old Man, on Whose Nose. Lear.
Twilight Comes. Carruth.
When We in Kind Embracements Had Agre'd. *Anonymous.*

Oldsmobile
In My Merry Oldsmobile. Bryan.

Olive (s)
Chorus from a Tragedy. Bacon.
Detail. Bethell.
Lament for Ignacio Sanchez Mejias. Garcia Lorca.
Mary's Baby. O'Sheel.
The Olive Tree. Baring-Gould.
Sierran Vigil. Milne.
The Stockdove. Pitter.
A Stopwatch and an Ordanance Map. Spender.
Table-Birds. Mackenzie.
Ultima Ratio Regum. Spender.
Where the Rainbow Ends. Lowell.

Omen (s)
Cattle. Skrzynecki.
Favour. Fitzgerald.
Ghost Pet. Colony.
Often I Am Permitted to Return to a Meadow. Duncan.
An Old Woman Speaks of the Moon. Pitter.
To the King, Upon His Comming with His Army into the West. Herrick.

Omnipotent
The Hymn of the World's Creator (excerpt). Caedmon.
I like to see it lap the miles. Dickinson.
Paradise Lost. Milton.
Sonnets to My Mother. Bourinot.
The Spring Returns. Moore.
Stand by the Flag. Wilder.

One
Additional Verses to Hail Columbia. Holmes.
The Adoration of the Magi. Pilling.
Advent: A Carol. Dickinson.
Andre. Brooks.
Anke von Tharau. Anonymous.
At Dawn of the Year. Klingle.
Ballad of Don Juan Tenorio and the Statue of the Comendador. Campbell.
A Ballad of Orleans. Robinson.
The Beloved. Hinkson.
Beyond Belief. Luhrmann.
Black Is the Color. Anonymous.
Bos'n Hill. Albee.
Bread. "Mistral.
Brother, Lift Your Flag with Mine. Bacon.
Bye Bye Baby Blues. Fuller.
Candle-Lighting Song. Ketchum.
Carol of the Numbers. Anonymous.
Ceylon. Fisher.
Chariots. Bynner.
Crossing with the Light. Okita.
The Deep-Sea Cables. Kipling.
The Dole of the King's Daughter. Anonymous.
The Eagle's Song. Mansfield.
Easter. Herbert.
Echoes. Moore.

An Elegy on Ben Jonson. Cleveland.
Ellen Bawn. Mangan.
The End of a Meaningful Relationship. Fickert.
Enough Not One. Franklin.
Epitaph: "Daniel and Abigail." Barrios.
Epitaph for the Poet. Barker.
An Epitaph on Master Vincent Corbett. Jonson.
Epitaph to a Dog. Byron.
The Faerie Queene. Spenser.
Fair, and Soft, and Gay, and Young. Gould.
For His Sake. Denman.
The Glimpse of a Plain Cap. Anonymous.
The Glory of the Day Was in Her Face. Johnson.
Gnosis. Cranch.
God Gives Them Sleep on Ground, on Straw. Williams.
God's Will. Nevin.
The Good-Morrow. Donne.
The Good Old Days. Fried.
A Grain of Rice. Scott.
Growing Old. Wilcox.
Hawthorn Dyke. Swinburne.
His Being Was in Her Alone. Sidney.
The Holy Earth: In the Immense Cathedral. Wheelock.
Hymn for the Close of the Week. Abelard.
I Am the One. Hardy.
I Must Go Walk the Wood. Anonymous.
I Took Leave of My Beloved One Evening. At Taliq.
If Everything Happens That Can't Be Done. Cummings.
Incarnation Poem. Leax.
Inscription on the Pyramid of Unas. Anonymous.
Iona. Tennyson.
The Kingdom of God. Rab.
Laudate for Christmas. Prudentius (Aurelius Clemens Prudentius).
A Letter to Her Husband, Absent upon Public Employment. Bradstreet.
Lollingdon Downs. Masefield.
Love's Calendar. Scott.
The Lucifer. Glover.
Man. Herbert.
The Men of the Alamo. Roche.
A Midsummer Night's Dream. Shakespeare.
Miss You. Anonymous.
Monna Innominata. Rossetti.
My Country, to Thy Shore. Williams.
My Dad and Mam They Did Agree. Anonymous.
No Love, to Love of Man and Wife. Eedes.
Of Man and Wife. Eedes.
On His Garden Book. Pastorius.
On One Condition. Madge.
One and One. Day Lewis.
One in Christ. Van Dyke.

The People in the Park. Adams.
The People, Yes. Sandburg.
Phallus. Shiraishi Kazuko.
Poem. Strongin.
The Poet Loves a Mistress, But Not to Marry. Herrick.
The Poet Loves from Afar. O'Grady.
A Practical Program for Monks. Merton.
A Rhyme of One. Locker-Lampson.
Riddle: "Elizabeth, Lizzy, Betsy and Bess." Anonymous.
The Rival Sisters, III: Song. Gould.
Rococo. Swinburne.
The Rose. Kennedy.
S. T. Colerige Dismisses a Caller from Porlock. Meyer.
Sagamore. Robinson.
Salt Water Story. Hugo.
The Shade-Seller. Jacobsen.
Simon the Cyrenean. Lyttleton.
The Simple Purification. Anonymous.
Song with Words. Agee.
Sonnet CV. Greville.
A Spark of Laurel. Kunitz.
Stranger. Merton.
Sumter. Brownell.
Take Up the Pen... Anonymous.
There's More Pretty Girls Than One. Anonymous.
Thou One in All, Thou All in One. Beach.
Thought. Cranch.
The Three Sisters. Ficke.
Three Things. Sarton.
To a Wood-Violet. Tabb.
To Chloe, Who Wished Herself Young Enough For Me. Cartwright.
To Jane: The Keen Stars Were Twinkling. Shelley.
To the Rev. F. D. Maurice. Tennyson.
Tora's Song. Hamsun.
Unposted Birthday Card. MacCaig.
The Voice of the Dove. Miller.
Wavelength. St. John.
What needeth these threat'ning words and wasted wind? Wyatt.
What the Serpent Said to Adam. MacLeish.
The White Ships and the Red. Kilmer.
A Woman's Answer to the Vampire. Blake.
Words from a Bottle. Lee.

Onion (s)
At the Lavender Lantern. Divine.
The Avenue Bearing the Initial of Christ into the New World. Kinnell.
Bouzouki. Hanson.
Dietary Advice. Anonymous.
Five Lyrics from "Good for Nothing Man". Pitchford.
Remembering. Toth.
To a Goose. Southey.

Wonders of the World. Shelton.

Onward
Brother and Sister. Eliot.
The Clipper. Day.
Endymion. Keats.
An Evening Revery. Bryant.
True Rest. Goethe.

Ooze
The Buffalo. Price.
Life's Testament. Baylebridge.

Opal (s)
Chinese Baby Asleep. Donnelly.
Glass World. Donnelly.
Life in the City. In Memoriam Edward Gibbon. Whalen.
To Julia. Herrick.

Open (ed) (ing) (ings) (s)
Absence. Meinke.
Another Day. Brown.
As Oyster Nan Stood by Her Tub. Anonymous.
Bad Girl Blues. Borum.
Bert Schultz. Thiele.
The Birds of Tin. Madge.
Black Flags Are Fluttering. Vogel.
A Book of Verses. Marcus.
The Candlelight Fisherman. Anonymous.
Child. MacIntyre.
Clams. Ishigaki Rin.
Coal. Lorde.
The Conqueror's Grave. Bryant.
Cordoba. Mendelssohn.
Correspondences. Duncan.
Daybreak. Meyers.
Destiny. Arnold.
Don't Ask Me Who I Am. Randall, Jr.
Doorman. Galvin.
Elevator Landscapes, Floor: O. Vincent.
Eurydice. Gregg.
Farmer and Sailor. Plato.
For Every Man. Reich.
From Oddity Land. Anthony.
The Hailstorm in June 1831. Clare.
Haunted Odysseus: The Last Testament. Gregory.
The Heart. Ignatow.
A Heart That's Been Broken. Owen.
The Homecoming of Emma Lazarus. Kinnell.
Homesick Blues. Hughes.
How. Marks.
How You Get Born. Jong.
I Accept. Pulsifer.
I Have Heard Them Knock. Hartnett.
I Thank You God for Most This Amazing. Cummings.
The Importance of Mirrors. Sandburg.
In Search of a Short Poem for My Grandmother. Hardeman.
In the Old House. Hall.
In the Open Fields. Sonnenschein.
In Time of Need. Stafford.
The Inflamed Disciple. Kramer.
Invasion on the Farm. Thomas.
Jingle Bells. Pierpont.

A Last Word. Sarton.
Listen. Patterson.
The Longing. Goodreau.
Love Should Grow Up Like a
Wild Iris in the Fields.
Griffin.
Man Is Nothing But.
Tchernichovsky.
The Marriage of Geraint:
Enid's Song. Tennyson.
Martha Graham. Lifshin.
Mr. Flood's Party.
Robinson.
Multitudes Turn in Darkness.
Aiken.
My Grandmother and the
Voice of Tolstoy. Orlen.
My Star. Browning.
The Negatives. Levine.
Night Flight. Daigon.
Nights. Zarco.
Of His Mistress. Hausted.
On a Night of Snow.
Coatsworth.
Passengers. Johnson.
The Penalty for Bigamy Is
Two Wives. Matthews.
Poems, VII. O'Connor.
Poverty. Simic.
A Prayer. Douglas.
Prayer during Battle.
Hagedorn.
Progress. Martin.
Reading Myself. Lowell.
The Rhythm. Creeley.
Serenade. Carnevali.
Shakespearean Soliloquy in
Progress: "To draw, or not
to..." (parody). Anonymous.
Sharks. Lourie.
Simple Song. Piercy.
Sinkholes. McFatter.
Slow Movement. MacNeice.
Song Under Shadow. Benet.
Spring in the Old World.
Levine.
Star Song of the Bushman
Women. Anonymous.
Stigmata. Lane.
Summer, 1960, Minnesota.
Bly.
The Tailor. Garfinkel.
There is a pain—so utter.
Dickinson.
To Flood Stage Again.
Wright.
To the Evening Star: Central
Minnesota. Wright.
To the Hand. Merwin.
The Tool of Fate. Yehoash.
Two Sorrows. St. John.
Two Variations. Levertov.
Tzu Yeh Songs. Anonymous.
The Unscarred Fighter
Remembers France.
Alling.
The Usual Exquisite Boredom
of Patrols. Popham.
The Valley's Singing Day.
Frost.
Walden in July. Junkins.
You Don't Know What Love
Is (parody). Carver.
Young Shepherd Bathing His
Feet. Clarke.
Opera
I cannot dance upon my toes.
Dickinson.
Operation (s)
Consider These, For We Have
Condemned Them. Day
Lewis.

The Crusaders knew the Holy
Places. Mastoraki.
Macavity: the Mystery Cat.
Eliot.
Three Poems. Mastoraki.
Opinion (s)
Caelica, LV. Greville.
Don Juan. Byron.
I Like Them Fluffy.
Herbert.
The Independent. McGinley.
A Jacobite Scot in Satire on
England's Unparalleled
Loss. Anonymous.
An Open Question. Hood.
Opportunity (ies)
The Gnu. Belloc.
John Charles Fremont.
Lummis.
Many Workmen. Crane.
To Chuse a Friend, but Never
Marry. Rochester.
Opposite (s)
5 Poems. Gray.
Animal Song. McHugh.
Butterfly. Conkling.
Presence. Moffit.
Sonnet XIII. Scott.
Sonnet: To Love, in Great
Bitterness. Cino da
Pistoia.
That it will never come again.
Dickinson.
Oppress (ed) (ion) (or)
Apparition of Splendor.
Moore.
The Burning of Paper Instead
of Children. Rich.
Christ, the Man. Davies.
Drink from My Empty Cup.
Mandela.
Happy Britannia. Thomson.
Late at Night during a Visit
of Friends. Bly.
Liberty for All. Garrison.
The Lust of Gold.
Montgomery.
The Marriage of Heaven and
Hell. Blake.
Oh, Ye Censurers. Ibn
Adiya.
The Seasons. Thomson.
To the Memory of J. Horace
Kimball. Ada Sister Mary.
While Cecil Snores: Mom
Drinks Cold Milk.
Cunningham.
Woman's Ruling Passions.
Pope.
Opulence
The Deceptive Present, The
Phoenix Year. Schwartz.
Oracle (s)
Dylan, Who Is Dead. Allen.
My Companion. Wesley.
Oceana and Britannia.
Ayloffe.
Verses Placed Over the Door
at the Entrance into the
Apollo Room... Jonson.
Orange (s)
Apples. Mueller.
Childhood in Jacksonville,
Florida. Cooper.
Color. Rossetti.
Hell Hath No Fury...
Bukowski.
May. Neilson.
The Murdered Girl Is Found
on a Bridge. Hayman.
My Mammy's Maid.
Anonymous.

A New Song of an Orange.
Anonymous.
The Orange Lily.
Anonymous.
The President Slumming.
Tate.
Proof. Ullman.
Radio. O'Hara.
Sierran Vigil. Milne.
Smudging. Wakoski.
Still-Life. Perry.
Trader. Harrison.
What Is Pink? Rossetti.
Orbit (s)
Dark Angel. Bartlett.
Lunar Eclipse. Glancy.
Sungrazer. Greenberg.
Orchard (s)
Because I Live. Ames.
Cider Song. Weston.
Concert. Arvey.
Enigma. Murphy.
Grace for Gardens. Driscoll.
Holiday Inn at Bemidji.
Vizenor.
It is an honorable thought.
Dickinson.
Lightning Bug. Morgan.
My Grandfather Dying.
Kooser.
Never May the Fruit Be
Plucked. Millay.
An Old Habitant. Call.
The Orchard by the Shore: a
Pastoral. Sweetman.
A Pastoral. Hillyer.
Raincoats for the Dead.
Bellg.
Vigils: Down the Glimmering
Staircase. Sassoon.
Orchid (s)
A Girl Combs Her Hair.
Hahn.
Land of the Free. Honora.
Light mist, then dense fog.
Li Ch'ing-chao.
Sea Gulls. Pratt.
Order (ed) (s)
The Affinity. Wickham.
The Astronomers of Mont
Blanc. Bowers.
Before the Pacific. Varela.
Cleopatra: Chorus. Daniel.
A Coal Miner's Goodbye.
Anonymous.
Coyote. Harte.
The Easter Song. Sedulius.
Entropy. Spencer.
The Excursion. Wordsworth.
The Hand and Foot. Very.
In Tenebris. Hardy.
The Instruments. Smart.
The Kirk of the Birds, Beasts
and Fishes. Anonymous.
Lower Court. Baxter.
Ode to the German Drama.
Anonymous.
On the Uniformity and
Perfection of Nature.
Freneau.
The Poet Questions Peace.
Chapman.
Reflections. Gardner.
Refusals. Anderson.
Tanker. Middleton.
To Dives. Belloc.
Tophet. Gray.
A Virtue of Shape. Swiss.
A Waist. Stein.
The Wreck of the Royal
Palm. Anonymous.

Ordinary
Ballet Blanc. Pollitt.
The Epiphany. Strong.
It's A. Robinson.
Night Drive. Heaney.
The thirty eighth year.
Clifton.
Oregon
The Nonpareil's Grave.
McMahon.
The Oregon Trail.
Anonymous.
Poem Composed in Rogue
River Park... Wayman.
The Race of the Oregon.
Meehan.
Organ (s)
The Organ Cactus.
Scarborough.
Potpourri from a Surrey
Garden. Betjeman.
Singing. Stevenson.
Thou Art of All Created
Things. Calderon de la
Barca.
Orgasm
Our Mother's Body Is the
Earth. McAnally.
Orgies
How Things Fall. Finkel.
Metamorphoses. Ovid
(Publius Ovidius Naso).
The Witches' Song. Jonson.
Oriana
Come, Blessed Bird.
Anonymous.
Thus Bonny-Boots the
Birthday Celebrated.
Anonymous.
Orient (al)
Address to Certain Gold
Fishes. Coleridge.
The Prayer Rug. Kennedy.
Reportless subjects, to the
quick. Dickinson.
Skykomish River Running.
Hugo.
Songs of the Sea-Children.
Carman.
Those Flapjacks of Brown's.
Taylor.
Origin (s)
Artorius. Heath-Stubbs.
Every Land Is Exile. Vigee.
A Letter to Ron Silliman on
the Back of a Map of the
Solar System. Schmitz.
The Norsemen. Whittier.
Original
The Consolation of
Philosophy. Boethius.
My Days of Love Are Over.
Byron.
Originality. Aldrich.
Xerox. Belitt.
Oriole (s)
Dancer: Four Poems. Engle.
Dream. Bynner.
Fall 1961. Lowell.
Flute-Priest Song for Rain
(excerpt). Lowell.
Orion
Baseball and Writing.
Moore.
Ceremony. Nemerov.
Final Farewell. Clark.
Hesiod, 1908. Mair.
Ownership. Reese.
Remembered Grace.
Patmore.
Ornament (s)
Beside a Fall. Garrigue.

The Cotter's Saturday Night.
  Burns.
Gothic. Untermeyer.
The Grace-Note. Levertov.
The Houseless Downs.
  Ferebe.
On a Violet in Her Breast.
  Stanley.
Poet's Wish. Larbaud.
The Victors. Levertov.
A Young Birch. Frost.
Orphan (ed) (s)
Alice Fell; or, Poverty.
  Wordsworth.
Chilled by the Blasts of
  Adverse Fate. Duche.
Company in Loneliness.
  Anonymous.
For Myself. Hines.
If No One Ever Marries Me.
  Alma-Tadema.
The Illiterate. Meredith.
Jeremy. Miller.
Lament for the Death of
  Eoghan Ruadh O'Neill.
  Davis.
The New Sun. Wain.
The Orphan Boy's Tale.
  Opie.
Other (s)
Advice to Young Children.
  Smith.
Alibi (parody). Guiterman.
Answer to Master Wither's
  Song, "Shall I, Wasting in
  Despair?" Jonson.
Bar Harbor. Garin.
Basketball. Lewisohn.
Bivouac. Lewis.
The Bride. Bierce.
Bridges. Bacmeister.
Cascando. Beckett.
Coming Back to America.
  Dickey.
The Common Grave.
  Dickey.
The Dead Seal near McClure's
  Beach. Bly.
Deeds of Kindness. Sargent.
A Deposition by John
  Wilmot. McHugh.
The Donner Party (excerpt).
  Keithley.
Eight Miles South of Grand
  Haven. Kelly.
The Elements. Lehrer.
Exercise for the Left Hand.
  Urdang.
The Faithful Wife.
  Greenberg.
False Love. Scott.
Five Vignettes. Toomer.
Foxtail Pine. Snyder.
Girl Sitting Alone at Party.
  Justice.
Harriet. Lowell.
Headsong. Bennett.
I Have No Pain.
  Anonymous.
In Moncur Street. Hewett.
It's the Same at Four A.M.
  Harjo.
Jonah's Gourd Vine: I Vision
  God. Hurston.
Kicking from Centre Field.
  McFadden.
Knole. Sisson.
Leaving the Motel.
  Snodgrass.
Let Me Enjoy. Hardy.
Listening. Stafford.

Man Asleep in the Desert.
  Lux.
The Man Within. Ewing.
The Miller. Anonymous.
A Mother in Egypt.
  Pickthall.
Muckers. Sandburg.
Multitudinous Stars. "Ping
  Hsin" (Hsieh Wang-ying).
My Dad and Mam They Did
  Agree. Anonymous.
My Other Me. Litchfield.
The New Formalists. Bell.
On One Condition. Madge.
The Origins of Life. Carus.
The Other One. Peck.
Our Backs Are to the
  Cypress. Goldberg.
Outbreak. Anderson.
Palindrome. Mueller.
Pedlar. Anonymous.
A Picture from Life's Other
  Side. Anonymous.
Pictures on the Wall.
  Shargel.
Professors. Larrabee.
Psyche with the Candle.
  MacLeish.
Reading the Books Our
  Children Have Written.
  Smith.
Saints Lose Back. Willard.
Sea Born. Vinal.
The Song of Hiawatha.
  Longfellow.
Song: "Why canst thou not, as
  others do." Anonymous.
Sonnets, IX: "Is it for fear to
  wet a widow's eye."
  Shakespeare.
South Inlet. Kuzma.
The Sunlit Vale. Blunden.
This Book Is One Thing.
  Anonymous.
The Torso: Passages 18.
  Duncan.
The Trestle Bridge. Wright.
Two Ways. Weaver.
What needeth these
  threat'ning words and
  wasted wind? Wyatt.
Why Should a Foolish
  Marriage Vow. Dryden.
The Yearbook. Clark.
Otherwise
A Dog's Death. Squire.
The Fifties. Sadoff.
I Live Up Here. Merwin.
My Spirit Will Not Haunt the
  Mound. Hardy.
Prothalamion. Ryan.
Pumas. Sterling.
Our (s) (selves)
Art of the Sonnet: LVI.
  Orlovitz.
As Difference Blends into
  Identity. Miles.
Bony. Ortiz.
The Broom. Leopardi.
Casa d'Amunt. Reid.
Champagne. Dove.
The Couple Upstairs.
  Williams.
Decoration Day. Longfellow.
Defeat. Bynner.
Dirge Written for a Drama.
  Beddoes.
Dreams. Timrod.
Epitaphs of the War, 1914-18.
  Kipling.
The Examination. Snodgrass.

Fathers and Sons.
  Anonymous.
February Margins.
  Henderson.
Fishing, at Coot Shallows.
  Welch.
For All That Ever Has Been
  Ours. Landau.
For Euse, Ayi Kwei & Gwen
  Brooks. Kgositsile.
For My People. Rose.
For the Sleepwalkers.
  Hirsch.
The Garibaldi Hymn.
  Mercantini.
The Heaviest Cross of All.
  Conway.
Heritage. Gilmore.
In the Field. Wilbur.
Inis Fal. O'Rahilly.
Inscribed in Melrose Abbey.
  Anonymous.
Interior Monolgue #666.
  Marshall.
Jew. Shapiro.
King Midas Has Asses' Ears.
  Finkel.
Knowledge after Death.
  Beeching.
Lincoln at Gettysburg.
  Taylor.
Litany of the Lost. Sassoon.
Lost Month. Merwin.
Maggie and milly and molly
  and may. Cummings.
March. Bryant.
Masquerade. Rodgers.
Memorial Day. Wynne.
Movement Song. Lorde.
A New Year's Burden.
  Hopkins.
An Ode in the Praise of Sack.
  Anonymous.
On the Relative Merit of
  Friend and Foe, Being
  Dead. Thompson.
One Star Fell and Another.
  Aiken.
Our Fathers Fought for
  Liberty. Lowell.
Our Mother Tongue; or, An
  Envoy to an American
  Lady. Milnes.
Poetics. Ammons.
Progression of the Species.
  Aldiss.
Reflections on Water.
  Pitchford.
The Smell on the Landing.
  Porter.
Snow Fell with a Will.
  Gillman.
The Song of O'Ruark, Prince
  of Breffni. Moore.
To Her Questioning His
  Estate. Hammond.
Two Shapes. Gregor.
Under the Old Elm. Lowell.
When I Was Growing Up.
  Vogel.
Out
Advice to Young Children.
  Smith.
A Breath. De Vere.
Directions to the Nomad.
  Welch.
Gratitude. Lynch.
The Hourglass. Kees.
Looking West. Stafford.
Love and Jealousy. Walsh.
The Naughty Preposition.
  Bishop.

Not of School Age. Frost.
The Origin of Cities. Hass.
The Rabbit. Durston.
The Refugee. Stuart.
Squeal. McHugh.
Thanksgiving for a Habitat.
  Auden.
To Julia under Lock and Key
  (parody). Seaman.
Translations from the Chinese.
  Morley.
Two Houses. Thomas.
Verse for a Certain Dog.
  Parker.
What to Do. Wise.
Who's In. Fleming.
The Witch, V, i. Middleton.
Outcast (s)
By the Weir. Gibson.
Choosing a Name. Ridler.
.Juan Murray. Anonymous.
A Mile from Eden. Ridler.
Ode to the German Drama.
  Anonymous.
Opportunity. Malone.
Sonnets of the Months. San
  Geminiano.
Where to Seek Love. Blake.
Outcry
Esther's Tomcat. Hughes.
Listening to Foxhounds.
  Dickey.
Outdoor (s)
The Bones of Incontention.
  Cohen.
New Mexico. Boyden.
Sing a Song of Juniper.
  Francis.
Outer
The Defender. Sampley.
Fireflies. Sharp.
Gnat-Psalm. Hughes.
I Shall Not Cry Return.
  Gates.
Midnight. Roberts.
The Self-Hatred of Don L.
  Lee. Lee.
Shakespeare. Blood.
Outlaw
Grizzly. Harte.
I Am a Cowboy in the Boat
  of Ra. Reed.
Jesse James. Benét.
Outlive
All My Pretty Ones. Sexton.
Breakwaters. Walker.
To My Least Favorite
  Reviewer. Nemerov.
To the Learned Critic.
  Jonson.
Outrage
Reflections. Deshoulieres.
Outside
Braddan Vicarage. Brown.
Cromwell. Francis.
The Diver. Howard.
Fence Wire. Dickey.
Hiroshima Exit. Kogawa.
Hunger. Anonymous.
In Harbour. Swinburne.
Japanese Beetles. Kennedy.
The Lights Go On.
  McCloskey.
Oil. Hogan.
Old Age. Keary.
Party Going. Manhire.
The Second Violinist's Son.
  Greger.
The Sleeping-Bag. Ponting.
Sonnet XVII: "I flee the city,
  temples, and each place."
  Labe.

Outward
The Ghost of a Ghost.
Leithauser.
Here I Sit in My Infested
Cubicle. Greenwood.
The Migrations of People.
Leiser.
That Each Thing Is Hurt of
Itself. *Anonymous.*
Thus Crosslegged on Round
Pillow Sat in Space.
Ginsberg.

Outwit (ed)
The Bishop of Canterbury
(King John and the
Bishop). *Anonymous.*
The Hunter. Nash.

Over
Air: "So full of courtly
reverence." North.
Black Taffy. Kenner.
The Bride's Toilette.
Cortissoz.
The Chancellor's Nightmare.
Gilbert.
Duck-Chasing. Kinnell.
The Dying Mine Brakeman.
Jenks.
Emblem. Quarles.
Follow the Leader. Behn.
For Kelley. Belford.
Hunting Song. Burns.
In the Field Forever.
Wallace.
June. Morris.
The Last Time. Veitch.
Laurana's Song. Hovey.
Leg over Leg. *Anonymous.*
Meeting at the Building.
Anonymous.
Mendings. Rukeyser.
The Mill. Wilbur.
Moo! Hillyer.
Moorlands of the Not.
Anonymous.
Night Shift. Shihab.
A Nightmare. Gilbert.
Now I'm Easy. Bogle.
O Tender under Her Right
Breast. Barker.
On the Hill below the
Lighthouse. Dickey.
Postscript. Hochman.
Proclamation/From Sleep,
Arise. Rodgers.
The River Dart. *Anonymous.*
Sky Diving. Lattimore.
Songs of Seven. Ingelow.
A Troop of the Guard.
Hagedorn.
Victory in the Cabarets.
Untermeyer.
The Wasp. Oates.
Watchman, What of the
Night? Swinburne.
Watt (excerpt). Beckett.
Written in March.
Wordsworth.

Overalls
Who Threw the Overalls in
Mistress Murphy's
Chowder. Geifer.

Overboard
Gudveig. Berry.
The Lighthouse Keeper's
Offspring. Broughton.
The Sea and the Mirror.
Auden.

Overcoat
Darwin in 1881.
Schnackenberg.

Overcome (s)
At Masada. Neufeld.
Conscientious Objector.
Millay.
First World War. Alling.
If Along the Highroad.
Anonymous.
Paradise Lost. Milton.
Parchman Farm Blues.
White.
Paths They Kept Barren.
Garmon.
A Rain of Rites. Mahapatra.
The Second Thanksgiving, or
The Reprisal. Herbert.
Song: "Leave this gaudy
gilded stage." Rochester.
We Shall Overcome.
Anonymous.

Overflow (s)
Beginning. Rodriguez Frese.
Pallid Cuckoo. Campbell.
Song for the Sun That
Disappeared Behind the
Rainclouds. *Anonymous.*
To a Dictatorial Sultan.
Anonymous.

Overgrown
A Nobleman's House
(excerpt). Sarton.

Overhead
Desert Shipwreck. Jordan.
The Dust of the Overland
Trail. Adams.
The Girl Writing Her English
Paper. Wallace.
The Last Day. Sargent.
Netting. Graham.
Promenade. Ignatow.
Rose and Root. Piatt.
The Ruined Chapel.
Allingham.
The Sick Stockrider.
Gordon.
The Tree in Pamela's Garden.
Robinson.
Winter Night. Fitzgerald.

Overthrow
Beyond Religion. Lucretius
(Titus Lucretitus Carus).
Caelica, XLIII. Greville.
The Laird of Wariston (B
vers.). *Anonymous.*
Lent Tending. Shepherd.
The Misfortunes of Elphin:
The War-Song of Dinas
Vawr. Peacock.
The Riders. Friend.

Overwhelm (ed) (ing)
Etat (excerpt). Albiach.
The Poor. Williams.
Posthumous Keats. Plumly.

Owe
Behold the Man!
Anonymous.
Jaffar. Hunt.
Mirabell, Book 9 (excerpt).
Merrill.
The Poet's Song to His Wife.
Procter.

Owl (s)
Alice's Recitation. "Carroll.
Asian Peace Offers Rejected
without Publication. Bly.
Ballad. Simic.
The Ballad of Blossom. Van
Duyn.
The Boat. Kelly.
The Country Bedroom.
Cornford.
Dawn. Bottomley.
The Fairies. Allingham.

Glaucopis. Hughes.
The Grey Friar. Peacock.
Hit or Miss. "Carroll.
Holly and Ivy. *Anonymous.*
In Respect of the Elderly.
Peacock.
Notes for Albuquerque.
Whiteman.
"Now you have burned..."
Thompson.
On Himself. Landor.
The Owl. De la Mare.
Owl. Dufault.
A Reflection of Night.
Marietta.
Rev Owl. Klein.
The Shorebirds. Reid.
Stone Trees. Freeman.
A Version of a Song of
Failure. Eigner.
The Waverley Pen.
Anonymous.
When Cats Run Home.
Tennyson.

Own (ed) (er)
At Summer's End.
Benjamin.
The Cynic. Garrison.
Dear gentle soul, who went so
soon away. Camoens.
Drama's vitallest expression is
the common day.
Dickinson.
The Dream. Roethke.
Epitaph on Francis Atterbury,
Bishop of Rochester.
Prior.
Eutaw Springs. Freneau.
A Fever. Donne.
Hard Questions. Tsuda.
If You're Ever Going to Love
Me. *Anonymous.*
January. Godin.
Jesus and His Mother.
Gunn.
Journal of the Storm.
Kuzma.
A Journey to Hell. Ward.
My Child Came Home.
George.
My Elbow Ancestry. Mollin.
Naomi Wise. *Anonymous.*
The North. McKinnon.
O Virtuous Light. Wylie.
Offspring. Madgett.
On the Death of a Recluse.
Darley.
P.S. Kessler.
A Poem (excerpt). Holmes.
Question Not. Gordon.
The Retirement. Norris.
Seele Im Raum. Jarrell.
"Since fortune's wrath envieth
the wealth." Surrey.
Smudging. Wakoski.
Sonnets from the Portuguese,
XXXVIII. Browning.
The Spring Is Late.
Moulton.
Squall. Moore.
A Summer Morning.
Wilbur.
Survival in a Stone Maze.
Rachow.
There Were Ninety and Nine.
Clephane.
They Lie at Rest, Our Blessed
Dead. Rossetti.
Thou Art Coming! Havergal.
Waiting. Burroughs.
We Own the Night. Jones.

When the King Enjoys His
Own Again. Parker.
Where His Lady Keeps His
Heart. "W.

Ox (en)
Auguries of Innocence.
Blake.
Carolers. Westerfield.
Cradle Hymn. Watts.
Cursor Mundi: The Flight
into Egypt. *Anonymous.*
Deranged. Fiacc.
Epigrams. Pastorius.
The Georgiad. Campbell.
How the Bulls Were Begotten:
The Two Bulls.
Anonymous.
Imperious Ox, Imperial Dish:
The Buffalo. Moore.
Jacob. Lasker-Schüler.
March. *Anonymous.*
The Marriage of Heaven and
Hell. Blake.
My Ox Duke. Dyer.
An Old Charcoal Seller. Po
Chu-i.
Ox-Bone Madonna. Duffy.
Ox-Bone Madonna. Galvin.
Starlight Scope Myopia.
Komunyakaa.
Supreme Fortune Falls
Soonest. Herrick.
The Twelve Oxen.
Anonymous
The Witnesses. Kennedy.

Oxford
Adlestrop. Thomas.
English Train, Summer.
Pomeroy.
Miss Gee. Auden.
On the Safe Side. Dunsany.
On Westwell Downs. Strode.
Oxford Bells. Hopkins.
The Spires of Oxford. Letts.
V.D.F. *Anonymous*

Oxford Street
Yesterday in Oxford Street.
Fyleman.

Oyster
As Oyster Nan Stood by Her
Tub. *Anonymous.*
The Ballad of the Oysterman.
Holmes.
Can Zone; or, The Good
Food Guide. Lesser.
Change and Immutability.
Scroggie.
Limerick: "There was an
exclusive old oyster."
Steel.
Mary Had a William Goat
(with music). *Anonymous.*
Observe the Whole of It.
Wolfe.
Ozymandias Revisited.
Bishop.
The Perspective and Limits of
Snapshots. Smith.
The Smacksman.
Anonymous.
Terminal Theater. Sward.
Verbatim from Boileau.
Pope.

Ozarks
Freemon Hawthorne.
Tolson.

Ozone
Aerosol. Witt.
Rain at Wildwood. Swenson.

P

Pace
Affaire d'Amour. Deland.
Altitudes. Wilbur.
John Smith, Fellow Fine. *Anonymous.*
Mules. Walker.
The Progress of Poesy. Gray.
The Third Dimension. Levertov.
Uffia. White.
When Structure Fails Rhyme Attempts to Come to the Rescue. Williams.
The Wind Blows. MacDonagh.

Pacific
In California. Simpson.
On Going to the Wars. Birney.

Pacify
The Friendship. Mezey.
When a Woman Blue (with music). *Anonymous.*

Pack (s)
Anath. Guri.
Don't You Hurry Worry with Me. *Anonymous.*
Here Comes My Lady with Her Little Baby. *Anonymous.*
In the Township. Glover.
The Merry Hay-Makers. *Anonymous.*
Tom's Garland. Hopkins.
The Wolf in the Kennels. Krylov.

Packet
The Homeward Bound. Adams.
The Lisbon Packet. Byron.

Pact
Ark of the Covenant. Nicholl.
With Schoolchildren. Barnstone.

Pad
Application for a Grant. Hecht.
Jersey Cattle. Currey.
The Lost Carnival. Chappell.
Pad, Pad. Smith.

Paddington
Lines on a Mysterious Occurrence. Godley.
Polly Perkins. *Anonymous.*

Paddle (s)
The Djanggawul Cycle, 21. *Anonymous.*
The Djanggawul Cycle, 8. *Anonymous.*
Drifting. Spivack.
The Lake of the Dismal Swamp. Moore.
The Lily Bed. Crawford.
The Ocean Is Like a Wreath. Kuapakaa.
A Simile for Her Smile. Wilbur.
There Won't Be Another. Glancy.

Pagan
The Fate of King Dathi. Davis.
Sheepstor. Strong.
The Visitor. Chalmers.

Page (s)
Abraham Lincoln. Stoddard.

The April of the Ages. Dolben.
Auction. Heyen.
The Author. Churchill.
Centennial Hymn. Bryant.
The Chinese Banyan. Meredith.
Dalyaunce. *Anonymous.*
Diary of a Raccoon. Bennett.
The Escape. Stafford.
The Girl/The Girlie Magazine. Gray.
Gloss. Fiacc.
In These Dissenting Times. Walker.
Mailed to G. B. Derwood.
Memoirs of a Turcoman Diplomat. Devlin.
Old Fellow. Walsh.
On My Fortieth Birthday. Tripp.
On the Edge. Levine.
An Outcry upon Opportunity. Shakespeare.
A Page's Road Song. Percy.
Passage. Crane.
The Plants. Browne.
Shadow of the Old City. Amichai.
Shut Not Your Doors. Whitman.
Sonnet: "Ice over time." Shapiro.
Theme for English B. Hughes.
To the Reader. Levertov.
Waterspout. Camoens.
Whoe'er This Book, if Lost, Doth Find. *Anonymous.*
Young Poets. Parra.

Pail
Greeting Descendants. Sobin.
Ram Time. Heyen.

Pain (ful) (s)
3 A. M. Edmond.
90 North. Jarrell.
Abraham Lincoln Walks at Midnight. Lindsay.
Absence absenting causeth me to complain. Wyatt.
Accused though I be without desert. Wyatt.
Adulthood. Giovanni.
Alexander's Feast or, the Power of Music. Dryden.
The Aloe Plant. Harbaugh.
Amoretti, VI. Spenser.
Amoretti, X. Spenser.
Amoretti, XI. Spenser.
Amoretti, XVI. Spenser.
Amoretti, XLVII. Spenser.
Amoretti, LI. Spenser.
Amoretti, LXIII. Spenser.
An Anodyne. Ken.
April. Linthicum.
Archys Last Name. Marquis.
Ark Articulate. Macpherson.
Astrophel and Stella, XII. Sidney.
Astrophel and Stella, LVII. Sidney.
Astrophel and Stella, LXVII. Sidney.
Austere the Music of My Songs. Sologub.
Beauty. *Anonymous.*
The Bee. Fitzgeffrey.

Beloved, from the Hour That You Were Born. Robinson.
Beyond Feith Buidhe. Brown.
The Bishop of Rum-ti-Foo. Gilbert.
Blacksmith Pain. Bierbaum.
By Night. Cleveland.
Caelica, XLV. Greville.
Christ's Descent into Hell. Rilke.
The Church-Porch. Herbert.
Cleansing Fires. Procter.
The Collector. Souster.
A Complaint by Night of the Lover Not Beloved. Petrarch.
Comrades of the Cross. Wattles.
Condemned Women. Baudelaire.
The Conquest of Granada. Dryden.
Courage for the Pusillanimous. Roche.
Cozzo Grillo. Mallalieu.
Crematorium. Betjeman.
Crickets and Locusts, Cicadas. Castro.
The Cup of Happiness. Thomas.
Cupid the Ploughboy. *Anonymous.*
The Cynic. Tucker.
The Cynotaph. Barham.
Dauber. Masefield.
Death in Life. Vaux.
The Deepest Bow. Takvan.
Dejection. Coleridge.
Desire Is Dead. Lawrence.
The Doll House. Kitzman.
The Dying Words of Stonewall Jackson. Lanier.
Edwardian Hat. Parvin.
The Ejected Wife. *Anonymous.*
Elegy for a Dead Confederate. McGovern.
Elegy on an Australian Schoolboy. Cross.
Emigrant Song. "Ansky.
Emily Bronte. Day Lewis.
An Epitaph of Maister Win Drowned in the Sea. Turberville.
Epitaph: "The fruit of all the service that I serve." Wyatt.
Eternal Reward, Eternal Pain. More.
Eve. *Anonymous.*
Except I Love. Parry.
"The fancy, which that I have served long." Surrey.
Fantasia. Nathan.
Fantoches. Verlaine.
Fare Ye Well, Lovely Nancy. *Anonymous.*
The Ferry. Boker.
The Final Struggle. Block.
Folk Tune. Raab.
Folk Wisdom. Kinsella.
For Hani, Aged Five, That She Be Better Able to Distinguish a Villain. Baro.
Foreboding. Hall.
Full well it may be seen. Wyatt.
Gallows and Cross. MacDonald.

Go Heart, Hurt with Adversity. *Anonymous.*
The Goat. Saba.
Hap. Hardy.
Happy Is the Country Life. *Anonymous.*
The Hock-Cart, or Harvest Home. Herrick.
How Happy the Little Birds. *Anonymous.*
Hymn. Chadwick.
I Awoke with the Room Cold. Piercy.
I'm Soaked through with You. Korn.
I Place Myself. *Anonymous.*
If So It Hap, This Of-Spring of My Care. Daniel.
In a Hard Intellectual Light. Eberhart.
In the Cemetery. Hardy.
The Indian Emperor. Dryden.
Is It Not Sure a Deadly Pain. *Anonymous.*
It Is Well for Small Birds That Can Rise up on High. *Anonymous.*
Joy's Treachery. Blunt.
The Judgment of Paris. Merwin.
Keep in the Heart the Journal. Aiken.
Kiss Me, Dear. Dryden.
The Knight of Curtesy: The Eaten Heart. *Anonymous.*
The knot which first my heart did strain. Wyatt.
The Lads of the Village. Smith.
Lament my loss... Wyatt.
Last Night My Soul Departed. O Dalaigh.
Libation. Levertov.
Life's Scars. Wilcox.
Like Those Sick Folks. Sidney.
Limerick: "A rheumatic old man in White Plains." *Anonymous.*
Limerick: "A well-buggered boy named Delpasse." *Anonymous.*
Lo! how I seek and sue to have. Wyatt.
The Lord of the Isle. George.
The Lover, Having Dreamed of Enjoying His Love.... Wyatt.
Mad Song. Blake.
Mail Call. Bensko.
Make Believe. Cary.
Mary Ann. *Anonymous.*
The Mask. McClaurin.
A Match. Swinburne.
Medieval Norman Songs. *Anonymous.*
Memo. Ballard.
Midnight at Baiae. A Dream Fragment of Imperial Rome. Symonds.
The Midnight Court. Merriman.
Minna. Bodenheim.
Modern Love, II. Meredith.
Motherless Children. *Anonymous.*
Mothers. Giovanni.
The Mouse and the Cake. Cook.
Music and Memory. Albee.

The Musician at His Work. Currie.

My Hand Has a Pain. Columcille.

My Naked Aunt. MacLeish.

My Name Is Afrika. Kgositsile.

My True Love Makes Me Happy. Beatrice de Dia.

My Uninvited Guest. Smith.

Myths and Texts. Snyder.

Nansen. Snyder.

Neaera When I'm There Is Adamant. Buchanan.

Near an Old Prison. Cornford.

The Negatives. Levine.

New England's Growth. Bradford.

The New Physician. Chalmers.

New Year's Carol. *Anonymous.*

New York * December * 1931. Deutsch.

The Night. Al-Khansa.

Night. Bialik.

Night Walkers. Smithyman.

No Pleasure Without Some Pain. Vaux.

Noah's Flood. Drayton.

Not Thou But I. Marston.

O goodly hand. Wyatt.

O, Woman! Scott.

Ode: "Peer of gods he seemeth to me." Sappho.

Old Dog. Souster.

Old Story. Henson.

Over the Great City. Carpenter.

Pain Has an Element of Blank. Dickinson.

Painkillers. Gunn.

Passages. Walker.

Permit Us, Lord, to Consecrate. Green.

Philomela. Arnold.

Piscatorie Eclogues. Fletcher.

Pisgah. Wattles.

A Pleasant New Court Song. *Anonymous.*

Pleasures, Beauty. Ford.

A Poem. Mphahlele.

Poem for J. Berry.

Pomegranate Tree in Jerusalem. Gilead.

Porch. Nowlan.

Prayer by Moonlight. Swartz.

Process. O'Donnell.

Prometheus Unbound. Shelley.

The Race Question. Madgett.

Reckoning. Zwicky.

Renaissance/A Triptych. Minczeski.

The Restless Heart. Surrey.

Return. Naude.

The Riddle. Brome.

Riding Adown the Country Lanes. Bridges.

Rondelay. Dryden.

Rontgen Photograph. Eybers.

Rye Bread. Braithwaite.

The Saviour. Wesley.

The Seasons. Kalidasa.

The Second Life of Lazarus. Harwood.

Self Dirge. Rose.

The Shipmen. Hunnis.

The Ships. Maynard.

Silent Love. *Anonymous.*

Silent, You Say, I'm Grown of Late. Landor.

Sin, Despair, and Lucifer. Fletcher.

Sleep My Child. *Anonymous.*

Soft Wood. Lowell.

Solace. Delany.

Solitude. Wilcox.

Song. Macdonagh.

Song: "I don't want to be a nun." *Anonymous.*

Song: "Know, Celadon, in vain you use." "Ephelia" (Joan Philips).

Sonnet for a Loved One. Joslin.

Sonnet: "In every dream thy lovely features rise." Barnes.

Sonnet: The Army Surgeon. Dobell.

Sonnets, CXLI: "In faith, I do not love thee with mine eyes." Shakespeare.

Souvenirs. Randall.

Spinning Song. *Anonymous.*

Stormy Night in Autumn. Chu Shu-chen.

The Sun Now Risen. Beissel.

Sutra Blues or, This Pain Is Bliss. Aliesan.

Sweet Jesus. Michael of Kildare.

The Swift Bullets. Wells.

The Sword of Tethra. Larminie.

Tears. Khansa.

Then I said to the elegant ladies. Sappho.

There Is a Tide. Kipling.

This Love. Hemschemeyer.

This Yonder Night I Sawe a Sighte. *Anonymous.*

Tho' I Can Not Your Cruelty Constrain. Wyatt.

To a Linnet in a Cage. Ledwidge.

To an Old San Francisco Poet. Abbott.

To Mr. I. L. Donne.

To My Children, Fearing for Them. Berry.

To My Mother at 73. Jennings.

To Our Ladies of Death. Thomson.

To Sleep Easy All Night. *Anonymous.*

To the Jews in Poland. Wittlin.

The Twelve Properties or Conditions of a Lover. More.

Two in the Campagna. Browning.

Two Sonnets for a Lost Love. DeWitt.

The Two Streams. Moore.

Under Stone. Feinstein.

The Vacant Cage. Turner.

A Virile Christ. Boundy.

Visit. Outlaw.

A Visit from Alphonse. Zimmer.

Want of Want of. Szumigalski.

'Way Down in Cuba. *Anonymous.*

Whether Men Do Laugh or Weep. Campion.

While the Summer Trees Were Crying. Iremonger.

Why Has This Ache. Emin.

The Willing Prisoner to His Mistress. Carew.

A Winter Twilight. Bates.

With Timrels. *Anonymous.*

The Woman's Labour. Collier.

Woodrow Wilson. Jeffers.

The Words of Jesus. Benet.

Workmen. Morris.

The World's Desire. Benet.

Your Passing, Fleet Passing. Eliyia.

Paint (ed) (er) (ing) (s)

Ancient Songs of the Women of Fez. *Anonymous.*

And Who Has Seen a Fair Alluring Face. Peele.

L'Art. Feirstein.

Autumn Color. Robinson.

Beauty. *Anonymous.*

The Boy Who Laughed at Santa Claus. Nash.

Caelica, XLIV. Greville.

The Campaign. Addison.

Careless Willie. *Anonymous.*

Cimabuella (parody). Taylor.

Clerihew. Bentley.

Crossing the Park. Moss.

Dancing Gal. Davis.

Don Juan. Byron.

Eloisa to Abelard. Pope.

The Empire Clock. Spencer.

Epiphany: For the Artist. Sewell.

Ghazal: Japanese Paintbrush. Mott.

Good-by, Old Paint. *Anonymous.*

How to Paint a Perfect Christmas. Holub.

Javanese Dancers. Symons.

The Landscape Lies Within My Head. Stewart.

Limerick: "There was a painter named Scott." Rossetti.

Mother Dear, O! Pray for Me. *Anonymous.*

Nimmo. Robinson.

Nocturne: Homage to Whistler. Feldman.

Observing a Vulgar Name on the Plinth of an Ancient Statue. Landor.

An Order for a Picture. Cary.

Outside White Earth. Henry.

The Painters. Hemschemeyer.

Painters. Rukeyser.

Phryne. Donne.

Pictures from Brueghel. Williams.

Plum Blossoms. *Anonymous.*

The Politics of Rich Painters. Jones.

Portrait in Winter. Chapin.

Studies from Life. Dickey.

Teresina's Face. Widdemer.

The Testament of Beauty. Bridges.

The Third Advice to a Painter. Marvell.

This Morning Tom Child, the Painter, Died. Sewall.

To the Painter Preparing to Draw M. M. H. Shirley.

To the Royal Society. Cowley.

The Twins. Van Duyn.

Venice. Moss.

The Young Glass-Stainer. Hardy.

Paintbrush

Independence Day. Smith.

Pair

Another Generation. Squire.

Change. Graves.

The Conformers. Hardy.

Geordie (B vers.). *Anonymous.*

The Hymn to Venus: Venus Goes After Anchises. Homer.

In the Seven Woods. Yeats.

The Jackdaw. Cowper.

The Law of Averages. "Troubadour".

Limerick: "She sat in a mighty fine chair." Cope.

The Man in the Mune Is Making Shune. *Anonymous.*

Modern Love, XLI. Meredith.

The Murder of William Remington. Nemerov.

Nishikigi: The Love-Cave. Motokiyo.

On the Friendship betwixt Two Ladies. Waller.

Synnove's Song. Bjornson.

Paisley

The Paisley Ceiling. Arnold.

Pajamas

The Accountant in His Bath. Mitchell.

Pal (s)

The Erie Canal. Allen.

Erie Canal. *Anonymous.*

Naturally the Foundation Will Bear Your Expenses. Larkin.

Obituary. Fearing.

To Lou Gehrig. Kieran.

Palace (s)

Bubbles. Shorey.

Christmas Day Is Come. Wadding.

Christmas Everywhere. Brooks.

Cock-Crow Song. *Anonymous.*

A Glimpse of Time. Binyon.

Hearing the Early Oriole. Po Chu-i.

Inscriptions at the City of Brass. *Anonymous.*

Most Souls, 'Tis True, but Peep Out Once an Age. Pope.

My Valentine. Stevenson.

Nothing to Wish or to Fear. Newton.

Once More, O Lord. Doane.

Onion Skin in Barn. Alling.

The Ordinary Women. Stevens.

La Priere de Nostre Dame. Chaucer.

Revolution. Harford.

A Rueful Lamentation on the Death of Queen Elizabeth. More.

Second Fig. Millay.

The Serf. Campbell.

Trio for Two Cats and a Trombone. Sitwell.

We Have Seen Her.
Doolittle.
A Wet Sheet. Cunningham.
Palaeolithic
The Titanic (excerpt). Pratt.
Palate
A Dream of Fair Women.
Tennyson.
To the Reader of Master
William Davenant's Play,
The Wits. Carew.
Pale (r) (s)
Bathers. Tiller.
Birch. Simpson.
The Earth in Spring. Halevi.
A Frosty Day. De Tabley.
A Gallop of Fire. Pitt.
Good Counsel to a Young
Maid. Carew.
Impression de Nuit: London.
Douglas.
Invocation. Nakasuk.
Lady Margaret. *Anonymous.*
Laguna Perdida. Dixon.
Late Game. Fairchild.
A Lay of the Famine.
Anonymous.
Lilith. Levi.
Melting in thin mist and
heavy clouds. Li Ch'ing-
chao.
Moon Song. Flanner.
Most Quietly at Times.
Flaischlen.
Now Kindness. Viereck.
Nox. Diaz Miron.
On a Seal. Plato.
Peer of the Gods Is That
Man. Sappho.
Poem: "High on a ridge of
tiles." Craig.
Ryder. Haines.
Salvation Prospect. Smith,
Jr.
Snowdrop. Hughes.
The Soldier. Krige.
Solitary Visions of a
Kaufmanoid...
Cunningham.
Solitude. De la Mare.
Song: "If once I could gather
in song." Gibson.
Sonnets, XCVII: "How like a
winter hath my absence
been." Shakespeare.
The Stirrup Cup. Hay.
They Grow Up Too Fast, She
Said. O Hehir.
To the Rainbow. Campbell.
Villanelle of Acheron.
Dowson.
The Waters of Life. Wolfe.
Watershed. Avison.
A Winter Night. Thomson.
Pall
Beyond the Potomac.
Hayne.
Edinburgh after Flodden
(excerpt). Ayton [(or
Aytoun)] Sir Robert.
In the Old Churchyard at
Fredericksburg. Loring.
Sic Transit. Plunkett.
Pallet
Jack O' Diamonds; or, The
Rabble Soldier.
Anonymous.
Make Me a Pallet on Your
Floor. Yancey.
Pallid
Goosey Goosey Gander.
French.

Hadrian's Address to His Soul
When Dying. Hadrian.
Palm (s)
And Yet–. Sloan.
August. Binyon.
The Candle Flame. Lewis.
Coconut. Satz.
The Container. Corman.
The Donkey. Chesterton.
Elegy for Yards, Pounds, and
Gallons. Wagoner.
England, Unprepared for War.
Akenside.
Epistle, from Algiers, to
Horace Smith. Campbell.
Frascati's. Huxley.
A Lesson in Detachment.
Miller.
Lifelines. Hummer.
Limbo. Heaney.
Love Letters, Unmailed.
Merriam.
Mercedes, Her Aloneness.
Inez.
Musician. Bogan.
O Thou, Who Didst Ordain
the Word. Chapin.
Our Childhood Spilled into
Our Hearts. Vogel.
Palm Sunday: Naples.
Symons.
Preludes. Eliot.
The Queen of the Nile.
Smith.
Royalty. Rimbaud.
Song of Exile. Dias.
Under the Boathouse.
Bottoms.
The Way of the World.
Roche.
You Ask Me, Why, Tho' Ill
at Ease. Tennyson.
Pan
Clorinda and Damon.
Marvell.
The Dancing Faun. Rogers.
Idylls. Theocritus.
The Lady's Song. Dryden.
On the Death of the Great
Chef Alexis Soyer.
Anonymous.
Pan and the Cherries. Fort.
Sonnet: "Not with Libations."
Millay.
Spanish Song. Divine.
Summer Storm. Johnson.
A Vision (excerpt). Procter.
World Music. Bushnell.
Pancakes
The Metamorphosis of Aunt
Jemima. Childress.
Shrovetide. *Anonymous.*
Pane (s)
Amsterdam. Garrigue.
Autumn Chapter in a Novel.
Gunn.
The Candlelight Fisherman.
Anonymous.
The Chestnut Avenue at
Alton House. Tomlinson.
The Frost Pane. McCord.
Interior. Colum.
On the Asylum Road. Mew.
Tracking the Sled, Christmas
1951. Walker.
Pang (s)
Broken Music. Rossetti.
Dido to Aeneas. Stanihurst.
The Excursion. Wordsworth.
The Midnight Court.
Merriman.

On the Death of His Son
Vincent. Hunt.
To an Imperilled Traveller.
Dole.
To Miss * * * * * on the
Death of her Goldfish.
Meredyth.
Panic
Cat. Rosenblatt.
The Clock. Ducic.
I am the sorrow in the wheat
fields. Bass.
Prisoner's Song. Gregory.
Test Drive. Reid.
Pansy (ies)
Man into a Churchyard.
Gutteridge.
Nocturne in a Deserted
Brickyard. Sandburg.
A Prayer after Illness.
Storey.
Pant (ing) (s)
The Battle of Bull Run.
Anonymous.
Emblems. Quarles.
Emma. Goldsmith.
Epipsychidion. Shelley.
French Lisette: A Ballad of
Maida Vale. Plomer.
Ground Hog. Anonymous.
Hero and Leander. Marlowe.
Ignu. Ginsberg.
Limerick: "A cannibal bold of
Penzance." *Anonymous.*
Limerick: "A careless young
lad down in Natchez."
Anonymous.
Limerick: "The poor
benighted Hindoo."
Monkhouse.
Limerick: "There was a young
person named Crockett."
Smith.
Moving. Jarrell.
Poems in Praise of Practically
Nothing. Hoffenstein.
The Return. Fauset.
Those Flapjacks of Brown's.
Taylor.
To Charinus, a Catamite.
Martial (Marcus Valerius
Martialis).
Visitors' Parking.
Szumigalski.
The Voyages of Captain Cock.
Smith.
When Your Pants Begin to
Go. Lawson.
Pantheist
The River Walk. Fallon.
Panther (s)
At a Month's End.
Swinburne.
Bear in the Hill. *Anonymous.*
The Cat. Church.
Here and There: Nocturnal
Landscape. Cowley.
Panties
Familiar Music. Berkson.
Pantomime
Daddy. Fyleman.
Pantyhose
The Great Pretender. Nolan.
Pap
The Last Time I the Well
Woke. *Anonymous.*
The Queen of Scotland.
Anonymous.
The Wake at the Well.
Anonymous.
Papa
Casey Jones. *Anonymous.*

Embraceable You.
Gershwin.
Is It Well-Lighted, Papa?
Bertram.
Proposal. *Anonymous.*
Rumpelstiltskin. Sexton.
Willie's and Nellie's Wish.
Moore.
Paper (s)
The Boarder. Simpson.
Cacoethes Scribendi. Holmes
Correspondence. Chester.
December Fragments.
Lattimore.
Early Bacon. Stodart-
Walker.
Epigram: Absent-Minded
Professor. Nemerov.
Ghazals. Harrison.
Here Lies... Smith.
Household. Jensen.
Inflation. Hartman.
The Katzenjammer Kids.
Reaney.
Lost Moments. Davis.
The Luminous. Guest.
Midnight. Kees.
The Music Crept by Us.
Cohen.
Next Door to Monica's Dance
Studio. Smith.
O Catch Miss Daisy Pinks.
Campbell.
Problems of a Journalist.
Kees.
Rhymes. Steele.
Sensationalism. Levis.
Seven Cent Cotton and Forty
Cent Meat. *Anonymous.*
Song of the Open Road.
Whitman.
Spring. Pasternak.
Spring Signs. Field.
Spring Street Bar.
Berssenbrugge.
Suburban Sonnet. Harwood.
There Is No Opera Like
"Lohengrin."
Wheelwright.
Third Degree. Hughes.
To Shima sani. Tohe.
Water Color. Mooney.
Windy Morning. Behn.
Paperweight
Last Lines. Kennedy.
Papoose
Early Moon. Sandburg.
Little Papoose. Chapman.
Parable (s)
Break of Day. Neilson.
Like an Old Proud King in a
Parable. Smith.
The Spider. Eberhart.
Parachute (s)
After Spending All Day at the
National Museum of Art.
Britt.
Behind the Wheel.
Brownstein.
The City in the Throes of
Despair. Towle.
Departure. Green.
Free Fall. Gordon.
Relativity. Millay.
Paraclete
Deus Immensa Trinitas.
Anonymous.
The Holy Innocents.
Prudentius (Aurelius
Clemens Prudentius).
Nausea. Mayo.

A Sequence with Strophes in Paraphrase Thereof. Burke.
To a Thrush. Daly.

Parade (s)
The Death of a Warrior. Mastoraki.
A Marching Litany to Our Martyrs. Mapanje.
The Parade. Greene.
Poem: "I watched an armory combing its bronze bricks." O'Hara.

Paradise
The Alchemist, 1610. Jonson.
Ambition. Davies.
Astrophel and Stella, LXVIII. Sidney.
Be Present at Our Table, Lord. Cennick.
Behold This Little Bane. Dickinson.
Boy in Ice. Lee.
The Burning of the Birds. Kaufman.
Butterflies. Noyes.
Caelica, LXXVI. Greville.
The Caravan. Blouz.
Christmas Carol. Anonymous.
The Climate of Paradise. Simpson.
Comrade Jesus. Cleghorn.
Corliss Engine-Wheel. Black.
The Creation of My Lady. Redi.
A Death-Bed. Aldrich.
The Death of Grant. Bierce.
Don Juan. Byron.
Drifting. Read.
Effie. Brown.
An Epitaph. Squire.
Eve of Easter. Mayer.
Eve's Advice to the Children of Israel. Neugroschel.
Fair Isle at Sea. Stevenson.
Farewell This World! Anonymous.
Fever 103. Plath.
A Few Lines to Fill up a Vacant Page. Danforth.
Flower of Exile. Dunn.
Forbidden Fruit. Dickinson.
Garden. Marvell.
Good Weather. Belli.
Grasse: The Olive Trees. Wilbur.
Hansom Cabbies. Thorley.
Hunger. Stampa.
I Dwell in Possibility. Dickinson.
I Have a Room whereinto No One Enters. Rossetti.
I Planted My Bright Paradise. Blok.
In Paradise. Bates.
Invocation. Sassoon.
It Cannot Be. Sickels.
Jesus! Thy crucifix. Dickinson.
Julia Miller. Masters.
The Last Coachload. De la Mare.
Light and Love, Hope and Faith. Gray.
The Litany of the Dark People. Cullen.
Love's Justification. Michelangelo.
Love's Labour's Lost. Shakespeare.

Machupuchare. What the Mountain Said. Shaking the Dead Bones... Stroud.
Madrigal: The Beautie, and the Life. Drummond.
The Maiden's Best Adorning. Anonymous.
Measure for Measure. Shakespeare.
Meditations on the Sepulchre in the Garden. Doddridge.
Mendel's Law. Meinke.
Morning Star. Galvin.
My Father's Child. Bloede.
The Nun. Symons.
O Soul, With Storms Beset. Ibn Gabirol.
The Oasis of Sidi Khaled. Blunt.
The Old Road to Paradise. Widdemer.
Old Woman's Song. Cole.
On the Origin of Evil. Byrom.
On Thomas Carew. Anonymous.
One Foot in Eden. Muir.
The Paradigm. Tate.
Partial Comfort. Parker.
Pornographic Poem. Giorno.
The Quest. Wright.
The Raising of the Dead. Dobson.
The Rose of Eden. Phillips.
The Rubaiyat of Omar Khayyam. Omar Khayyam.
A shady friend for torrid days. Dickinson.
The Shed. O'Donnell.
Shepherd and Shepherdess. Breton.
The Song of Roland. Anonymous.
The Song of Roland: The Last Battle. Anonymous.
Stabat Mater. Jacopone da Todi.
Stolen Pleasure. Drummond.
The Sunshine of Paradise Alley. Ford.
Table Graces, or Prayers for Adults: Noon Meal. Anonymous.
Tell Me Now. Wang Chi.
A Tempest. Dickinson.
Thaddeus Stevens. Cary.
There Is a Land Mine Eye Hath Seen. Robins.
There She Is. Gregg.
To—. Morse.
To a Happy Warrior. Blunt.
To "Philomela." Colman.
To the Marchesana of Pescara. Michelangelo.
The Trout. Hine.
Vacation Trip. Babcock.
Winter in Another Country. Anthony ("Ai").
The Woods. Mahon.
You Are Always New. Akhmatova.

Paradox (es)
August Night, 1953. Harrod.
Federation. Goodge.
Reading a Medal. Tiller.

Paragon
The Crystal. Lanier.
No Loathsomeness in Love. Herrick.

Parallel (s)
Dedication to Hunger. Gluck.
Plutarch. Agathias.
Shimmering Pediment. Yau.
Shores of Anguish. Portal.

Parasites
Proper Pride. Lawrence.

Parasol (s)
By the Beautiful Sea. Cole.
When Fishes Set Umbrellas Up. Rossetti.

Paratroop
Invasion Exercise on the Poultry Farm. Betjeman.

Parch (ed) (es)
Ballatetta. Pound.
The Cockney of the North. Graham.
Fading Beauty. Marino.
Repeated Pilgrimage. Brunini.

Pardon (ed) (ing) (s)
After the Deformed Woman Is Made Correct. Lietz.
Amantium Irae. Dowson.
At the Round Earth's Imagin'd Corners, Blow. Donne.
Ave Maris Stella. Anonymous.
The Complaisant Swain. Ovid.
Curse of the Cat Woman. Field.
Divina Commedia. Longfellow.
Elegies. Chenier.
Elegy Against a Latter Day. Smithman.
Farther. Piatt.
For the Goddess Too Well Known. Gidlow.
Forgiveness. Lyte.
The Four Seasons of the Year. Bradstreet.
Friend of Souls. Anonymous.
Goethe and Frederika. Sidgwick.
The Holy Viaticum Comes to Me. Prati.
Hotel Paradiso e Commerciale. Brinnin.
How Sweet Is the Language of Love. Holden.
John Adkins' Farewell. Anonymous.
Journey. Thompson.
The Journey of the Suicides. Bowering.
Joy to the World. Anonymous.
Light-Winged Smoke, Icarian Bird. Thoreau.
Limerick: "A strong-minded lady of Arden." Bishop.
Lux Advenit Veneranda. Adam of St. Victor.
The Man That Hails You Tom or Jack. Cowper.
Marsh Song–At Sunset. Lanier.
Medea in Athens (excerpt). Webster.
Of Impatience Which Brings All Our Gains to Nothing. Jacopone da Todi.
A Prisoner for Life. Anonymous.
The Remorse for Time. Nemerov.

Robin Hood's Chase. Anonymous.
The Romish Lady. Anonymous.
The Sentinel. Flint.
Smoke. Thoreau.
Sonnets, XX: "But now my Muse toyled with continuall care." Barnfield.
Spain 1937. Auden.
The Time Is Ripe and I Repent. Ceile De.
To a Nun. Ormond.
Upon a Great Shower of Snow That Fell on May-Day, 1654. Washbourne.
The Waltz: Hail, Spirit-Stirring Waltz. Byron.
"When reckless youth in an unquiet breast." Surrey.

Paree
If You Want to Know where the Privates Are. Anonymous.

Parent (s)
Childlessness. Merrill.
Conversational. Anonymous.
Dilemma. Ignatow.
Dream Songs. Berryman.
The Fall. Edson.
The House of Life. Rossetti.
Hymn for St. John's Eve. Anonymous.
The Journey and Observations of a Countryman (excerpt). Hawthorn.
Juvenile Court. Hay.
On the Birth of a Posthumous Child, Born in Peculiar Circumstances... Burns.
Persimmon Trees, She Remembers, Not Far Away. Baker.
The Silk Merchant's Daughter. Anonymous.
Taking Care of It. Lee.
To Mr. S. T. Coleridge. Barbauld.
The True-Born Englishman. Defoe.
The Wreck of the Royal Charter. Anonymous.

Parenthesis
The Picture. Lowell.

Paris
As Helen Once. Lee.
The Ballad of the White Horse. Chesterton.
Beyond the Alps. Lowell.
The End of a Day in the Provinces. Laforgue.
Epigram. Moore.
The Farmer and the Farmer's Wife. Herbert.
Four Sheets to the Wind and a One-Way Ticket to France. Rivers.
Homage to Max Jacob. Padgett.
The Iliad. Homer.
Look, Edwin! Millay.
Three Old Brothers. O'Connor.
To a History Professor. Anonymous
Unromantic Song. Brode.

Parish (es)
Epitaph on Will Smith. Anonymous.
Jockie, Thine Hornpipe's Dull. Anonymous.

We miss a kinsman more.
Dickinson.

Park (s)
Central Park South. Revell.
Crossing the Park. Moss.
Driving in the Park.
Anonymous.
Ellis Park. Hoyt.
The Fountain in the Park.
Haley.
Fugue for One Voice. Hecht.
A Gentle Park. Herbert.
Instructions for a Park.
Walker.
Lyarde Is an Old Horse.
Anonymous.
On St. James's Park, as Lately
Improved by His Majesty.
Waller.
P's the Proud Policeman.
McGinley.
The Park at Evening.
Norris.
Poems from the Coalfields, 2:
Advice from a
Nightwatchman. Healy.
Sister, Awake! *Anonymous.*
Spring Rites. Robbins.
Sunday in the Park.
Williams.
To Waken a Small Person.
Justice.
Tourism. Chaffin.
West Paddocks. Davies.
While Strolling through the
Park. Haley.

Parking lot (s)
Chippewa Lake Park.
Woessner.
Heroes of the Strip. Cudahy.
Kora for March 5th.
MacAdams.
Two Years Later. Wieners.

Parliament
A Free Parliament Litany.
Anonymous.
On Entering a Forest.
Lennen.
The Parliament Soldiers.
Anonymous.
The Tired Petitioner (excerpt).
Wither.

Parlor
The Borough. Crabbe.
Invitation to Hsiao Ch'U-
Shih. Po Chu-i.
Pygmalion. Miller.
Tales of the Hall. Crabbe.
The Termite. Nash.

Parrot
I Pull out of the Depths of
the Earth. Rivera.
The Parrot. Skelton.
The Parrot Cry.
""MacDiarmid.

Parsley
Draw a Pail of Water.
Anonymous.
Strawberries. Hughes.

Parson
Acton Beauchamp,
Herefordshire.
Anonymous.
Baucis and Philemon. Swift.
Legsby, Lincolnshire.
Anonymous.
Parson Gray. Goldsmith.
The Raven Visits Rawhide.
Anonymous.
A Vulgar Error. Thorold
Rogers.
Wheelbarrow. Farjeon.

Part (ed) (eth) (ing) (s)
Ad Domnulam Suam.
Dowson.
Against Parting. Zach.
Amaturus. Johnson-Cory.
The Antiquary. Chapt. 10:
Why Sit'st Thou by That
Ruin'd Hall. Scott.
Apollo's Song. Jonson.
Arcadia. Sidney.
As If from Her Nest.
Anonymous.
As Love and I, Late
Harbour'd in One Inn.
Drayton.
Ballad: "Of all the Girls that
e'er were seen." Gay.
The Bird. Simic.
Blue Sparks in Dark Closets.
Snyder.
Breake Now My Heart and
Dye! Campion.
Britannia's Pastorals.
Browne.
A Celebration of Charis.
Jonson.
A Chaste Maid in Cheapside:
Parting. Middleton.
Chicago Poem. Welch.
Cicada. Stoutenburg.
Colin Clout's Come Home
Again. Spenser.
Colorado. Fitzgerald.
Come, Walk with Me.
Bronte.
Could I Say I Touched You.
Littlebird.
Crossing Brooklyn Ferry.
Whitman.
The Dance of Love. Davies.
A Ditty. Spenser.
Dust of Snow. Frost.
The Dying Father's Farewell.
Anonymous.
The Dying Fisherman's Song.
Anonymous.
Elisa. Spenser.
English Courage Displayed.
Anonymous.
Epistle to Davie, a Brother
Poet. Burns.
Epistle to Henry Wriothesley,
Earl of Southhampton.
Daniel.
Ever Since. MacLeish.
The Exequy. To His
Matchlesse Never to Be
Forgotten Freind. King.
A Faded Letter. Fischer.
The Falling of the Leaves.
Yeats.
Family Evening. Huws.
Farewell to the Court
(excerpt). Rochester.
For Bill Hawkins, a Black
Militant. Harris.
The Garden of Shadow.
Dowson.
Give Me Thy Heart.
Procter.
Good People. Stanton.
Green Pastures. Allen.
A Heart Made Full of
Thought. O Domhnaill.
The Hooded Crow.
McOwan.
Hourly I Die. Dryden.
Hymns for Infant Minds
(excerpt). Taylor.
I Could Give All to Time.
Frost.

I Die; But When the Grave
Shall Press. Bronte.
In Exile. Baughan.
Is This Africa? Dempster.
It Is Night Again. Tzu Yeh.
John O'Dwyer of the Glen.
Anonymous.
Junkyards. Rayford.
Last Night. Darley.
Late Comer. Hastings.
Leavetaking. Watson.
Less and Less Human, O
Savage Spirit. Stevens.
Let This Be My Parting
Word. Tagore.
A Letter to Charles Townsend
Copeland (excerpt).
Hillyer.
The Level and the Square.
Morris.
The Lord into His Garden
Comes. *Anonymous.*
Love-Songs, At Once Tender
and Informative.
Hoffenstein.
Lovers How They Come and
Part. Herrick.
Marriage Vow. *Anonymous.*
Meeting. Rossetti.
Meeting After Long Absence.
Perry.
The Meeting of the Ships.
Moore.
Memory. Browne.
Mistrustful Minds Be Moved.
Wyatt.
My Hereafter. De Long.
Naming of Parts. Reed.
Number Song. Waldman.
On My Lord Bacon.
Danforth.
On the Death of an Epicure.
Graves.
On Visiting the Graves of
Hawthorne and Thoreau.
Very.
Once. Ives.
Our Bondage It Shall End.
Cartwright.
Our School Now Closes Out.
Dumas.
Parting at Dawn.
Anonymous.
Poem #18. *Anonymous.*
Poke-Pole Fishing. Schmitz.
Polwart on the Green.
Ramsay.
Polyolbion. Drayton.
The Poor Shammes of
Berditchev. Ratner.
Prayer of Any Husband.
Caruthers.
The Prejudice against the
Past. Stevens.
The Progress of Marriage.
Swift.
Resolution of Dependence.
Barker.
Robin Hood and the Tinker.
Anonymous.
The Rose Is Red, the Rose Is
White. *Anonymous.*
Rowing Early. Peck.
Sacramentum Supremum.
Newbolt.
September Midnight.
Teasdale.
Sir Walter Ralegh to His Son.
Ralegh.
Soap, the Oppressor.
Johnson.
Soggarth Aroon. Banim.

The Soldier That Has Seen
Service. *Anonymous.*
Song: "Fair is the night, and
fair the day." Morris.
Song: "Phillis, let's shun the
common Fate." Sedley.
Sonnet: "What doth it serve to
see sun's burning face."
Drummond.
Sonnets. Tuckerman.
Sonnets, LIII: "What is your
substance, whereof are you
made." Shakespeare.
Spring Hawks. Thomas.
Strange. Burnshaw.
A Strange Passion of a Lover.
Gascoigne.
Such Comfort as the Night
Can Bring to Us. Cooley.
Theophany. Underhill.
'Tis You That Makes My
Friends My Foes.
Anonymous.
To Anthea, Who May
Command Him Anything.
Herrick.
To Julia. Herrick.
To Li Chien. Po Chu-i.
To the River Itchin, near
Winton. Bowles.
Tortoise Shout. Lawrence.
Tow men wrote a lexicon.
Anonymous.
Turn to the Left. Taylor.
The Twelve Properties or
Conditions of a Lover.
More.
Upon His Julia. Herrick.
The Vance Song.
Anonymous.
A Welcome. Browne.
When First. Thomas.
When We Are Parted. Aïdé.
You Are a Part of Me.
Yerby.

Parthenon
The Cathedral of Rheims.
Rostand.
Judeebug's Country.
Johnson.

Particles
The Acts of Youth. Wieners.
The Morning Porches. Hall.
On William Walker, Author
of "A Treatise of English
Particles." *Anonymous.*
Poems from the Coalfields, 1:
Air Shaft. Healy.

Partner (s) (ship)
American Bandstand.
Waters.
Farmers. Percy.
A Heart Made Full of
Thought. O Domhnaill.
The Home Winner.
Lindberg.
Light at Equinox. Adams.
Mississippi Sawyer.
Anonymous.
To an Infant Expiring the
Second Day of its Birth.
Wright.

Partridge (s)
John Brown's Body. Benét.
Solitude Late at Night in the
Woods. Bly.
The White and the Black.
Khaketla.

Party (ies)
Don Juan. Byron.
Frigate Jones, the Pussyfooter.
Burke.

Garland for a Propagandist. Pauker.
Indians at the Guthrie. Vizenor.
The Judgement of Tiresias. Jacob.
June 10. Rodriguez Frese.
Mark Van Doren. Worley.
October's Party. Cooper.
Punk Party. ey Told Me It Was Literary...] Rose.
Reflections at Dawn. McGinley.
A Tale for Husbands. Sidney.
Testing, Testing. Dillon.
To Wordsworth. Clare.
The Widow's Party. Kipling.

Pass (ed) (es) (ing)
All Lovely Things. Aiken.
Anath. Guri.
The Apartment-Hunter. Schultz.
The Bare Arms of Trees. Tagliabue.
Before Dawn in the Woods. Wilkinson.
Building a House. Gallup.
The Burning of the Law. Meir of Rothenburg.
But Still in Israel's Paths They Shine. Revard.
The Camera Obscura. Symonds.
Careless Love. *Anonymous.*
Cinderella Liberated. Hussey.
The Closed Door. Garrison.
Cows. Reeves.
Daisies. Worth.
Darkness. Campbell.
Death of Rimbaud. Fisher.
Delivering Children. Holbrook.
Despair and Hope. Zangwill.
A Dialogue between Thyrsis and Dorinda. Marvell.
Dies Irae. Scott.
The Downright Country-Man; or, The Faithful Dairy Maid. *Anonymous.*
The Dream Called Life. Calderon de la Barca.
Dressing Game. Schmitz.
Dusk. Southwick.
The Egg and the Machine. Frost.
End-of-Summer Poem. Bennett.
Epigram: "Even if I try not to ogle a boy in the street." Strato.
Epithalamium. Sitwell.
The Evening. Gay.
The Flag Goes By. Bennett.
The Goodbye. Sklarew.
Growing Old. Wilcox.
He Fell Among Thieves. Newbolt.
The Head. Fallon.
How Night Falls in the Courtyard. Rimmer.
I Shall Not Pass This Way Again. *Anonymous.*
I Shall Not Pass This Way Again. York.
Idylls of the King. Tennyson.
Image in a Mirror. Goodman.
In a Country Cemetery in Iowa. Kooser.

Indian Summer. Burr.
Inscription for the Entrance to a Wood. Bryant.
Justice. Morstein.
Kitchen Window. MacDonald.
Late, Passing Prairie Farm. Stafford.
Leaves of Grass (excerpt). Whitman.
Leavetaking. Watson.
Lonely Night. Sappho.
A Love-Song. Turner.
Malice Domestic. Nash.
The Money Cry. Davison.
The Most Alluring Clouds That Mount the Sky. Wordsworth.
Most Quietly at Times. Flaischlen.
New York. Field.
North Wind in October. Bridges.
O Living Always, Always Dying. Whitman.
On the Building of Springfield. Lindsay.
On the Island. Brutus.
On the Supposed Author of a Late Poem "In Defense of Satire." Rochester.
Out in the Country, Back Home. Marion.
Parish. Dubie.
Pass It On! *Anonymous.*
Peter Bell, the Third. Shelley.
Pictures on the Wall. Shargel.
Poetry's a Gift Wherein but Few Excell. Ward.
A Popular Personage at Home. Hardy.
Praise the Lord and Pass the Ammunition! Loesser.
Preserves. Waters.
Rain. Lucina.
Reading Plato. Graham.
Reveille. Brown.
Riddle 7 (Mute Swan). *Anonymous.*
Riddle of Night. Langer.
River Afram. Opoku.
The River of Heaven. *Anonymous.*
Road. Merwin.
Sailing to Byzantium. Yeats.
The Sea-Mew. Browning.
Self-Portrait. Jackson.
September. Arnold.
The Serf's Secret. Moody.
Silence. Morse.
Sir Walter Scott at the Tomb of the Stuarts in St. Peter's. Milnes.
Slow Drivers. Barrax.
Song. Killigrew.
Song: "If thou art sleeping." Vicente.
The Sound of Rain. Akhmadulina.
Springfield Mountain (D vers.). *Anonymous.*
Thermopylae. Thwaites.
This, Too, Shall Pass Away. Alexander.
This, Too, Shall Pass Away. Smith.
This Too Will Pass away. *Anonymous.*
Three Rimas, 1. Becquer.
To Evan. Eberhart.

To the Wayfarer. *Anonymous.*
Toyland. MacDonough.
A Tryst. Moulton.
Under Ben Bulben. Yeats.
Under the Shade of the Trees. Preston.
A Very Old Song. Laird.
Water-Front. Salkeld.
We Are a People. Henson.
What the Toys Are Thinking. Wolfe.
When the Dew Is on the Grass. *Anonymous.*
Who Has Seen the Wind? Rossetti.
Why She Moved House. Hardy.
Widow's Lament. *Anonymous.*

Passage (s)
The Aeneid. Virgil (Publius Vergilius Maro).
The All-Night Waitress. Stanton.
The Angler's Wish. Walton.
The Animal Runs, It Passes, It Dies. *Anonymous.*
The Autumn House. Brady.
A Channel Passage. Swinburne.
The Christians Reply to the Phylosopher. Davenant.
The Clouds. Mira Bai [(or Mirabai(].
The Dark Morning. Merton.
The Dead. Morton.
Down by the Old Mill Stream. Read.
Face to Face. Cochrane.
The Harvest Bow. Heaney.
Hello. Corso.
The Holy Well. *Anonymous.*
Horse. Gluck.
In Autumn. Anderson.
In the Children's Hospital. Tennyson.
In Time of War. Auden.
Inscriptions for the Caledonian Canal. Southey.
The Island of the Scots (excerpt). Ayton [(or Aytoun)] Sir Robert.
The Light on Cape May. *Anonymous.*
New England's Dead. McLellan.
The Odyssey. Homer.
Of All the Sounds Despatched Abroad. Dickinson.
Only Waiting. Mace.
The Pink Frock. Hardy.
Placing a $2 Bet for a Man Who Will Never Go to the Horse Races ... Wakoski.
The Room. Orr.
The Sailor's Complaint. *Anonymous.*
Tao and Unfitness at Inistiogue on the River Nore. Kinsella.
Thais. Levy.
To Critics. Learned.
Trains Made of Stone. Young Bear.
Whilst It Is Prime. Spenser.
Wilfred Owen's Photographs. Hughes.
William Jones. Masters.

Passion (s)
Advice to Colonel Valentine. Graves.
Advice to Julia. Luttrell.
Aja's Lament over His Dead Wife. Kalidasa.
The Ancestors. Bishop.
An Ancient Degree. Mayer.
Caelica, XVI. Greville.
Dawn on Mid-Ocean. Wheelock.
Dead Fires. Fauset.
Dedication. Bryant.
Definition. Sarton.
Die Welt Ist Dumm, Die Welt Ist Blind. Heine.
Dream Songs. Berryman.
Epigram: "O King of the Friday." *Anonymous.*
Epithalamium for Honorius and Maria: Palm Tree Mates with Palm. Claudian.
The Estuarial Republic. Dunn.
An Evening's Love. Dryden.
Every morning I get up. Huang O.
Fantoches. Verlaine.
The Fault Is Not Mine. Landor.
Flawless His Heart. Lowell.
Flowers I Would Bring. De Vere.
For a Child Expected. Ridler.
Four Japanese Paintings: III The Wave Symphony. Ficke.
Gascoigne's Passion. Gascoigne.
The Gully. Maurice.
The Half-Breed Girl. Scott.
Hours of the Passion. Shoreham.
How Hardly I Conceal'd My Tears. Wharton.
In Memoriam: John Davidson. Macfie.
Iron Heaven. Alver.
June Rapture. Morgan.
Lady Lost. Ransom.
Love. *Anonymous.*
Madison Square. Glanz-Leyeles. A.
Modern Love, XXVII. Meredith.
The Mountain Heart's-Ease. Harte.
My Dad and Mam They Did Agree. *Anonymous.*
Near the Death of Ovid. Conquest.
No, Never Think. Pushkin.
Normal as Two Ships in the Night. Borawski.
Palm Sunday. Jammes.
Parting with Lucasia: A Song. Philips.
The Passion-Flower. Fuller.
Philomela, the Nightingale (excerpt). Hannay.
The Power of Innocence. "H.
Proud of my broken heart since thou didst break it. Dickinson.
Putney Hymn. *Anonymous.*
Ranolf and Amohia. Domett.
Requiem. Raine.
The Roads Also. Owen.

Passion
The Rustic at the Play.
  Santayana.
Samson Agonistes. Milton.
Second Honeymoon.
  Anonymous.
Song. Meredith.
The Songs of Bilitis. Louys.
Sonnet in the Mail Coach.
  Taylor.
Souls. Gifford.
Speechless. Marston.
A Summing Up. Preil.
Tampico. Conkling.
To a Lady in a Garden.
  Waller.
To a Lady, with a Present of
  a Fan. Brandling.
To a Western Bard Still a
  Whoop and a Holler away
  from English Poetry.
  Meredith.
To the Fair Clarinda, Who
  Made Love to Me, Imagin'd
  More than Woman. Behn.
To Usward. Bennett.
Two in the Campagna.
  Browning.
La Vita Nuova. Dante
  Alighieri.
Winter. Thomson.
Woman's Song. Wright.
You Preach to Me of Laws.
  Tree.
Passive
Apollo 8. Berryman.
Classic Scene. Williams.
On Playwright. Jonson.
Pavlov. Madgett.
The Subalterns. Hardy.
To the Tune of "Ye Commons
  and Peers Pray Lend Me
  Your Ears..." *Anonymous.*
Passover
Pesach Has Come to the
  Ghetto Again. Heller.
Passport
En Passant. Codrescu.
Rib Sandwich. Harris.
Past
Against Marriage to His
  Mistress. Walsh.
Agnosco Veteris Vestigia
  Flammae. Cunningham.
Ali Ben Shufti. Thwaite.
Amagansett Beach Revisited.
  Wheelock.
At an Exhibition of Historical
  Paintings, Hobart. Smith.
At Times I Feel Like a
  Quince Tree. Quinn.
Autobiography. Dipoko.
Becoming Real. Goldensohn.
Blest Retirement.
  Goldsmith.
The Bracelet of Grass.
  Moody.
Brother and Sister. Eliot.
The Captain of St. Kitts.
  May.
Celestine. Fitzgerald.
A Chaplet of Southernwood
  (excerpt). Nicholson.
The Classical Style. Palmer.
Consider These, For We Have
  Condemned Them. Day
  Lewis.
The Cow. Herford.
Cows Grazing at Sunrise.
  Matthews.
Cypress Grove. Clarke.
Darby and Joan.
  Honeywood.

Dawn on the Night-Journey.
  Rossetti.
A Dead Past. Munson.
A Dream. Fullerton.
Enigma. Murphy.
Esthetique du Mal. Stevens.
Ever Since. MacLeish.
Expectancies: The Eleventh
  Hour. Hammond.
False Though She Be to Me.
  Congreve.
Farewell to the Court.
  Ralegh.
Four Quartets. Eliot.
The Future. Tekeyan.
Glass was the street.
  Dickinson.
A Good Life. Watson.
A Harvest to Seduce. Cane.
Have I, This Moment, Led
  Thee from the Beach.
  Landor.
The Heart Flies Up, Erratic as
  a Kite. Schwartz.
Homecoming. Thompson.
I Looked & Saw History
  Caught. Spellman.
The Last Fight. Tooker.
Lollingdon Downs.
  Masefield.
A Man of Words. Ashbery.
The Marsh. Southwick.
May. Edwards.
Meditations for July 19, 1666.
  Pain.
Meeting and Passing. Frost.
A Meeting at the Crossroads.
  Bruchac.
The Music of the Spheres.
  Bell.
My cat and I. McGough.
My God. Ibn Gabirol.
My People. Himel.
Old and New Art. Rossetti.
Old Men. Keesing.
Orpheus and Eurydice.
  Browning.
Piano. Lawrence.
The Pill. Clarke.
Prodigal. Gilbert.
The Room and the Windows.
  Feng Chih.
Sailing to Byzantium. Yeats.
Saturninus. Conway.
The Snow Fall. MacLeish.
So Let Me Hence. Henley.
Solitude. Beattie.
Spring Poem. Ramke.
Stir Me. *Anonymous.*
Tao. Bailey.
Temple Garlands. Robinson.
Think before You Act.
  Elliott.
Thought for a New Year.
  Burket.
Three Poems. Hitomaro.
To Be Quicker... Lee.
To His Ring, Given to His
  Lady. Turberville.
A Trampwoman's Tragedy.
  Hardy.
Upon a Great Shower of
  Snow That Fell on May-
  Day, 1654. Washbourne.
Pastime
Five Epigrams.
  Cunningham.
Stool Ball. *Anonymous.*
Three Ballate. Poliziano.
Pastoral
Improvisations on Aesop.
  Hecht.

Old Homes. Blunden.
The Poets' Paradise.
  Drayton.
Pasture (s)
Afoot. Roberts.
Buffalo. Eglington.
By the North Sea.
  Swinburne.
Lycidas. Milton.
A Mare. Barnes.
Pastoral Song for the Nuptials
  of Charles, Duke of
  Lorraine... de Ronsard.
Song of Napalm. Weigl.
There is a flower that bees
  prefer. Dickinson.
Tornado Watch.
  Shuttleworth.
Patch (ed) (es)
Goodbye. Lewis.
I Gathered Mosses in
  Easedale. Wordsworth.
My "Patch of Blue."
  Carson.
Six Town Eclogues (excerpt).
  Montagu.
That Nature Is a Heraclitean
  Fire... Hopkins.
Walk in the Precepts. Ibn
  Ezra.
Pater Noster.
A Bidding Prayer.
  Anonymous.
The Crafty Miss of London;
  or, The Fryar Well Fitted.
  Anonymous.
The Peter-Penny. Herrick.
A Second Epitaph.
  Anonymous.
The Wee May o'Caledon.
  Spence.
Paterson
Preface to Paterson: Book
  One. Williams.
Path (s) (way)
Absence. Knies.
After a Journey. Hardy.
Afterwards. Havergal.
Aimless. Palagyi.
Arise, My Soul! With Rapture
  Rise! Smith.
Behold This Dreamer.
  Bartlett.
Beyond the Chagres.
  Gilbert.
Blue Juniata: The Streets of
  Air. Cowley.
Chinese Poems: Arthur
  Waley. Fair.
Chrysalides. Kinsella.
Convention. Lee.
Dante at Verona. Rossetti.
Emblem. Quarles.
The End of Sorrow. Fleg.
An English Wood. Graves.
The Garden. Doolittle.
Glow Worm. Robinson.
Grass on the Prayer Path.
  Anonymous.
The Haunter. Hardy.
Ho! Ye Sun, Moon, Stars.
  Anonymous.
The Homing Heart.
  Henderson.
Hope. Theognis.
How Easily Men's Cheeks Are
  Hot. Heidenstam.
I Know That I Must Die
  Soon. Lasker-Schüler.
In Memoriam A.H.H., XL.
  Tennyson.

In the Beginning Was the
  Bird. Treece.
The Land behind the Wind.
  Wagoner.
Leavetaking. Reape.
The Light of Asia. Arnold.
Love Unsought. Embury.
Maggie's Star. Turner.
Mignon. Goethe.
My Peace I Give unto You.
  Kennedy.
Norah. Akins.
Obedience. Macdonald.
On the Discoveries of Captain
  Lewis. Barlow.
On the Path. Strauss.
The Origin of Centaurs.
  Hecht.
The Path. Bryant.
The Path of the Padres.
  Osborne.
The Path That Leads
  Nowhere. Robinson.
The Personified Sentimental.
  Harte.
The Pilgrimage. Ralegh.
The Quarrel. Swenson.
Red River Valley.
  Anonymous.
The Ribbon-Fish. Adamson.
Saint. Merilaas.
September Evening, 1938.
  Plomer.
Stone Song (Zen Rock) the
  Seer & the Unbeliever.
  Karoniaktatie.
"The Straight Road.
  Hooper.
Strength, Love, Light.
  Robert II.
Tableau. Cullen.
Thysia. Luce.
The Unseen Bridge.
  Thomas.
The Valley of the Heavens.
  Leon.
Vitae Summa Brevis Spem
  Nos Vetat Incohare
  Longam. Dowson.
Walk. Horne.
Words Wherein Stinging Bees
  Lurk. Halevi.
Pathos
Eagle Valor, Chicken Mind.
  Jeffers.
Epistle to Dr. Blacklock.
  Burns.
Lunar Paraphrase. Stevens.
A Pauper. Tate.
Patience
Aside. Thomas.
Bani. Dadu.
Barmenissa's Song. Greene.
Bruce and the Spider.
  Barton.
Caelica, XLVI. Greville.
Camouflage. Manifold.
Carol of Patience. Graves.
The Church-Porch. Herbert.
Cuckoo. Lister.
Customs. Gelman.
The Doomed Man.
  Alexander.
Epitaph for a Lighthouse-
  Keeper's Horse. Morton.
Extract the Quint-essence.
  Pastorius.
Extras. Burton.
Fairground. Auden.
His Answer. Thompson.
The Holy Land of
  Walsingham. Musser.

Hounslow Heath.
Anonymous.
International Conference.
Ellis.
Jack and Jill (parody).
Loomis.
My Shoes. Simic.
One Almost Might.
Tessimond.
The Pulverized Screen.
Jabes.
Redo, 1-5. Hejinian.
Samson Agonistes. Milton.
The Solsequium.
Montgomerie.
Sonnet I: "If it must be; if it
must be, O God!" Gray.
A Summer Night. Auden.
The Third Wonder.
Markham.
Will God's Patience Hold Out
for You? Johnson.
Patient (s)
Another to Urania. Colman.
Buttercups and Daisies.
Howitt.
Cancer's a Funny Thing.
Haldane.
Crossing the Colorado River
into Yuma. Ortiz.
Day on Kind Continent.
Cohen.
Driftwood Dybbuk.
Lefcowitz.
Good Riddance to Bad
Rubbish O at Last!
Goodman.
Last Letter to Pablo.
Lowther.
London Voluntaries. Henley.
Macbeth. Shakespeare.
Omniscience. Kelly.
Patience With the Living.
Sangster.
Spring Song. Nahum.
Tempora Mutantur. Brasch.
Thaba Bosio. Sutu.
The Timid Gazelle.
Kasmuneh.
The Tired Man. Wickham.
The Toiler (excerpt).
Markham.
Patria
Dulce et Decorum Est.
Owen.
Patrick
Ossian (excerpt). O'Donnell.
The Plain of Adoration.
Anonymous.
Prayer to St. Patrick.
Ninine.
Patriot (ism) (s)
Arnold at Stillwater.
English.
Colonial Nomenclature.
Lang.
Irish History. Allingham.
Lamentations. Sassoon.
The Patriot Game.
Anonymous.
To A Polish Mother.
Mickiewicz.
To an Oak Tree. Scott.
To the National Arts Council.
Schjeldahl.
Washington's Statue.
Tuckerman.
Patron (s)
Come Ye Sons of Art
(excerpt). Purcell.
Debutantrum. Benet.
Ingratitude. Thynne.

A Reply to an Imitation of
the Second Ode....of
Horace. Bentley.
Vergidemiarum: Prologue: "I
first adventure, with
foolhardy might."
Barnfield.
Verses. Bentley.
Pattern (s)
The End Bit. Burns.
His Plan for Me. Nicholson.
Maker of Songs. Hall.
Of the Mathematician.
Matthews.
The Owner of My Face.
Hall.
Patterns. Lowell.
Rain on the Roof. Kinney.
Ration Party. Manifold.
Relics. Gegna.
Thou Knowest. Bates.
View. Munro.
Woman through the Window.
Falk.
Paul
For Your Inferiority Complex.
O'Rourke.
The Revolving Door. Levy.
The Spanish Descent. Defoe.
Tales of a Wayside Inn.
Longfellow.
The Twins. Jackson.
The Yankee Man-of-War.
Anonymous.
Pauper
The One Thing Needful.
Reich.
The Pauper's Drive. Noel.
To Our House-Dog Captain.
Landor.
Pause (d)
The Anthill. Babcock.
Are We Thankful?
Anonymous.
Because of Clothes. Riding.
Bloody Pause. Astra.
Call It a Louse. Corman.
The Convoy. Corretjer.
The Deserted Village.
Goldsmith.
The Discovery of the Pacific.
Gunn.
Earliest Spring. Levertov.
Horses at Valley Store.
Silko.
The Iliad. Homer.
In the Time of the Rose.
Savant.
Ode to Moderation (excerpt).
Plumptre.
Philomela's Second Ode.
Greene.
Plans. Brooks.
Rhinoceros. Stoutenburg.
Substitution. Browning.
Washing Windows. Spacks.
Why She Moved House.
Hardy.
Pavement (s)
The Beginning of the End.
Stallworthy.
The Cockney of the North.
Graham.
A Dream. Jackson.
The Fate of a Broom–An
Anticipation. Peacock.
London Pavement Artist.
Schevill.
To a Flea in a Glass of
Water. Greig.
Woman, Gallup, N.M.
Swenson.

Paw (s)
A Cloud in Trousers:
Prologue. Mayakovsky.
Hoosen Johnny.
Anonymous.
A Kitten. Farjeon.
Koala. Ross.
The Lion at Noon. Hugo.
To the Lord General
Cromwell. Milton.
Whym Chow. "Field."
Pawn (s)
Autumn Poem. Cronin.
Black Bear. Lepan.
He Fumbles at Your Soul.
Dickinson.
On the Young Statesmen.
Sackville.
The Pawns. Betts.
The Wolf and the Stork. La
Fontaine.
Pax Romana
A History of Peace. Graves.
Pay (s) (paid)
Advertisement. *Anonymous.*
And. Gonsalves.
Aurora Leigh. Browning.
Autumn Poem. Cronin.
Behold the Man!
Anonymous.
Carrier's Address.
Anonymous.
Covet. Bierce.
The Dance. *Anonymous.*
Deo Opt. Max. Sandys.
Driving Saw-Logs on the
Plover (with music).
Anonymous.
The Earl of Mar's Daughter.
Anonymous.
An Elegy on Ben Jonson.
Cleveland.
The Empress Brand Trim:
Ruby Reminisces.
Williams.
Epilogue to Mithridates, King
of Pontus. Dryden.
Epitaph on an Army of
Mercenaries. Housman.
Epitaphs of the War, 1914-18.
Kipling.
Excerpts from the Notebook
of the Poet of Santo Tomas.
Shelton.
The Fairies Break Their
Dances. Housman.
Fear. Hajnal.
Flesh Coupon. Wright.
Footnote to Enright's
"Apocalypse." Bell.
From a Connecticut
Newspaper. Rockwell.
Harpers Ferry. Rodman.
How Happy the Soldier.
Anonymous.
I Stood with the Dead.
Sassoon.
Interview with Doctor Drink.
Cunningham.
Invocation to the Muse.
Hughes.
Jonathan. "Rachel" (Rachel
Blumstein).
The Land. Kipling.
The Last Families in the
Cabins. Brand.
Life's Little Things.
Anonymous.
Limerick: "There was a young
man of Montrose."
Bennett.
The Lodging. Brown.

Matter of Taste. *Anonymous.*
The Mountain Cemetery.
Bowers.
My Wage. Rittenhouse.
New Jersey Turnpike.
Cumbie.
The New Vicar of Bray.
Ellis.
No Accident. MacCaig.
Now. Ken.
On Himself. Swift.
On the Death of an Epicure.
Graves.
Our Insufficiency to Praise
God Suitably for His
Mercy. Taylor.
Po' Laz'us. *Anonymous.*
The Poor Man Pays for All.
Anonymous.
Pursuit. Rutsala.
Scazons. Lewis.
De Se. Weever.
Sh-Ta-Ra-Dah-Dey (Irish
Lullaby). (with music).
Anonymous.
Sonnets, CXXXIV: "So, now
I have confessed that he is
thine." Shakespeare.
Thoughts from a Bottle.
Clark.
Tiger Bay. *Anonymous.*
To Fine Grand. Jonson.
To Sextus. Pott and Wright.
To Spain–A Last Word.
Thomas.
To the Most Virtuous
Mistress Pot, Who Many
Times Entertained Him.
Herrick.
To the Rev. F. D. Maurice.
Tennyson.
Upon the Dramatick Poems of
Mr. John Fletcher.
Cartwright.
Why I Sing the Blues. King.
Peace.
After the Killing. Randall.
Against Unworthy Praise.
Yeats.
The Aloe Plant. Harbaugh.
America's Task. Lincoln.
America to England.
Woodberry.
Amoretti, XI. Spenser.
Amoretti, XLIV. Spenser.
Amoretti, LVII. Spenser.
Amoretti, LXXI. Spenser.
An Ancient Virgin. Crabbe.
Angels' Song. Causley.
Anne Sexton. Juergensen.
Apollo and Daphne.
Rodgers.
Apology for Love.
Boccaccio.
Arise, My Soul! With Rapture
Rise! Smith.
Arizona Village. Davieau.
At the Band Concert.
Brinnin.
At Vshchizh. Tyutchev.
The Atheist's Tragedy.
Tourneur.
Athene's Song. Boland.
The Avenues. St. John.
The Babiaantje. Prince.
Barbara. Smith.
The Battle Autumn of 1862.
Whittier.
Beauty's Hands Are Cool.
Baker.
Beecher Island. Chapman.
Beggars. Higginson.

Bells of New Year. Field.
A Benedictine Garden. Brown.
Bid Me Sin No More. Wesley.
The Birth of Galahad: Ylen's Song. Hovey.
A Birthday Wish. Mcdonald.
The Blessing of St. Francis. Maura.
Blessing of the Priests. *Anonymous.*
Blessings on Doneraile. O'Kelly.
The Blind Man's Regret. *Anonymous.*
Bordello. Turco.
The Bower of Peace. Southey.
By the Pool at the Third Rosses. Symons.
The Cable Hymn. Whittier.
Calm After Storm. Yerby.
Canticle of Darkness. Watson.
Canzone: Of His Dead Lady. Pugliesi.
Captain Glen's Unhappy Voyage to New Barbary. *Anonymous.*
The Card-Players. Larkin.
Carol for His Darling on Christmas Day. Stanford.
A Chip on His Shoulder. *Anonymous.*
Christ's Victory and Triumph. Fletcher.
Christ the Consoler. Baker.
Christmas 1898 (excerpt). Morris.
A Christmas Carol. Behn.
Christmas Prayer. Morse.
Chromis. Fletcher.
Columbia. *Anonymous.*
Communication in Whi-te. Lee.
Compensation. Brainard.
Complaint of the Common Weill of Scotland. Lyndsay.
Comrade, Remember. Kresensky.
The Contretemps. Hardy.
The Cost. Hecht.
The Cowboy. *Anonymous.*
Cradle Song. Blake.
Danny Boy. *Anonymous.*
Dante. Longfellow.
Darling of Gods and Men, beneath the Gliding Stars. Bunting.
Day's End. Binyon.
The Death of Moses. *Anonymous.*
Declaration of Independence. Brownstein.
Die Not, Fond Man. *Anonymous.*
Dionysus. Layton.
The Disappointment. Taylor.
Disarm the Hearts. Jordan.
Disarmament (excerpt). Whittier.
Distant View. Krige.
Divina Commedia. Longfellow.
Dixie. Pike
Dream-Land. Rossetti.
The Dreme: Of the Realme of Scotland. Lindsay.

A Drum for Ben Boyd. Webb.
Earth Listens. Bates.
Eating Lechon, with my Brothers and Sisters. Cabalquinto.
El Greco: Espolio. Birney.
End of Summer. Pomerantz.
Epigram: "Paddy, I have but stol'n your living." Elliott.
Epigram: "Since first you knew my am'rous smart." Nugent.
An Epistle from a Half-Pay Officer in the Country. Pack.
Epitaph for Himself. Herbert of Cherbury.
Eternal God, Whose Power Upholds. Tweedy.
Evening. Manger.
Evening Hymn. Roberts.
Evening Prayer. *Anonymous.*
An Evening Revery. Bryant.
An Evening Walk in Bengal. Heber.
The Excursion. Wordsworth.
Fable II: The Vulture, the Sparrow, and Other Birds. Gay.
Faint Falls the Gentle Voice. Timrod.
The Fairy Wood. Symons.
Falling Asleep. Sassoon.
The Farmer. Shove.
Fatherland Song. Bjornson.
Firebell for Peace. Lee.
The First Olympionique to Hiero. Pindar.
The Flying Wheel. Hinkson.
For All in Pain. Carmichael.
For All Things Black and Beautiful. Rivers.
For Beauty Being the Best of All We Know. Bridges.
For One Who Is Serene. Bruner.
For the Gifts of the Spirit. Sill.
Forty Years Peace. Sivan.
The French Revolution. Blake.
From a Full Heart. Milne.
From Battle Clamour. Romanelli.
From Countless Hearts. Burket.
From Heraclitus. Dugan.
The Gale of August, '27. *Anonymous.*
Garrison. Alcott.
God Cares. Farningham.
God of the Nations, Near and Far. Holmes.
God Save the Nation. Tilton.
The Grave. Winters.
The Haunter. Hardy.
He Asketh Absolution of God. Book of the Dead.
He Kindleth a Fire. Book of the Dead.
He Knoweth the Souls of the East. Book of the Dead.
He Shall Speak Peace. Clark.
He Shall Speak Peace Unto the Nations. Walters.
He Walks at Peace. Tao Te Ching.
Hear, Hear, O Ye Nations. Hosmer.

Heaven Is Here. Adams.
Here Lies My Wife. Cunningham.
The Hermit. Parnell.
Hill Love. Macmillan.
His Glory Tell. Bonar.
Home, Sweet Home. Bunner.
The Hostage and His Takers. Olds.
The House. Scott.
Hugh Spencer's Feats in France (A version). *Anonymous.*
Hymn to Amen Ra, the Sun God. *Anonymous.*
Hymn to Christ the Saviour. Clement of Alexandria (Titus Flavius Clemens).
Hymn to Science. Akenside.
I Am a King. Rimon. I. Z.
I Hear and See Not Strips of Cloth Alone. Whitman.
I Heard an Angel Singing. Blake.
I Heard the Bells on Christmas Day. Longfellow.
Idylls of the King. Tennyson.
In Memoriam. Fortini.
In Memoriam. Jackson.
In My Father's House (with music). *Anonymous.*
In Our Boat. Craik.
In the Morning I Will Pray. Furness.
The Indians Count of Men as Dogs. Williams.
Inisgallun. Figgis.
International Brigade Dead. O'Brien.
Invocation and Prelude. George.
It Was Not Fate. Moore.
The Ivory Bed. Scott.
Jack-in-the-Box. Olson.
Joculator Domini. Mary John Frederick
Keep the Sea. *Anonymous.*
A Kitchen Prayer. Petersen.
The Land Called Scotia. Donatus.
Lao-Tse. Jones, Jr.
The Last Communion. Ward.
The Last Instructions to a Painter. Marvell.
Lauda. Beneveni.
A Legend of Versailles. Tolson.
Lessons. Weber.
Let the Dead Depart in Peace. *Anonymous.*
Let There Be Law. Van Doren.
Let There Be Light. Vories.
Let Us Have Peace. Turner.
Life at War. Levertov.
Life's Evening. Foulke.
Life's Testament. Baylebridge.
Light, 2. Eberhart.
The Light of Asia. Arnold.
The Light Yoke and Easy Burden. Wesley.
Limerick: "The daughter of debate." Elizabeth I.
Lines Written in the Bay of Lerici. Shelley.
Love. Herbert.

Man As He Shall Be. Owens.
Marian. Meredith.
The Mariner's Dream. Dimond.
The martyr poets–did not tell–. Dickinson.
The Meaning of a Letter. *Anonymous.*
Meeting of the Waters. Moore.
The Men behind the Guns. Rooney.
A Message of Peace. O'Reilly.
The Middle-Aged. Rich.
Midwinter. Bruner.
Minot's Ledge. O'Brien.
The Minute-Men of North-Boro'. Rice.
Moods of Rain. Scannell.
A Morning Hymn. Smart.
Mother of Fishermen. Roland-Holst.
Mother's Hands. Wedgefarth.
Mourning. Van Fossan.
My Fathers Came from Kentucky. Lindsay.
My Peace I Give unto You. Kennedy.
Netley Abbey. Midnight. Sotheby.
The New Mars. Coates.
A New-Yeares-Gift Sung to King Charles, 1635. Jonson.
News of the World. Barker.
The Noble Fisherman, or Robin Hood's Preferment. *Anonymous.*
Not Thou But I. Marston.
November Afternoons. Mary Madeleva.
O God of Bethel. Logan. John
O Risen Lord upon the Throne. Benson.
O Sion, Haste, Thy Mission High Fulfilling. Thomson.
O Sons of Earth. Pope.
O Star of Galilee. Savonarola.
Ode to the Virgin. Petrarch.
Oedipus to the Oracle. Trimpi.
The Old House. Woodberry.
The Old Woman. Bunker.
The Old Woman Remembers. Gregory, Augusta Gregory.
The Omnipresence of the Deity. Montgomery.
On the Height. Tietjens.
On the Smooth Brow and Clustering Hair. Landor.
One-and-Twenty. *Anonymous.*
One Careless Look. Clare.
One Morning, Oh! So Early. Ingelow.
Our Father, by Whose Name. Tucker.
Our Flag Was Still There. Tillinghast.
Our Tense and Wintry Minds. Carruth.
Out of the Frying Pan into the Fire. Henry.
The Page of Illustrations. Schjeldahl.
The Palace of Art. Tennyson.

Pan Cogito's Thoughts on Hell. Herbert.
A Panegyric on Geese. Mahony.
Paradise Lost. Milton.
The Paths of Prayer. Roditi.
Patience. Feinstein.
Patmos. Thomas.
Patty, 1949-1961. Libera.
Peace. Bhartrihari.
Peace. Edman.
Peace. Longley.
Peace. Markham.
Peace. Pulsifer.
Peace Is the Mind's Old Wilderness. Holmes.
Peace Is the Tranquillity of Order. Wilberforce.
The Peace Message. Stevenson.
The Peace of Christ. La Trobe.
The Peddler and His Wife. *Anonymous.*
Per Pacem ad Lucem. Procter.
The Pioneer. Guiterman.
Pleading Voices. Katav.
The Poet to the Birds. Meynell.
Portrait. Fearing.
A Post-Mortem. Sassoon.
Power and Peace. Herrick.
Prayer. Moricke.
Prayer for Peace. Patrick.
Prayer in a Country Church. Van Dusen.
Prayer on Fourth of July. Turner.
Prayer to the Trinity. Edmeston.
President Garfield. Longfellow.
The Prince of Peace. Bickersteth.
The Promised Land. Sampter.
Prophet and Fool. Golding.
Psalm XXIX. Sidney.
Psalm for Christmas Day. Pestel.
Purity. Lenski.
Queen Sabbath. Bialik.
Quiet Things. Crowell.
Rainy Season Love Song. Hayford.
Raleigh Was Right. Williams.
Ranch at Twilight. *Anonymous.*
Reconciliation. Mason.
Reconciliation. Nicolson.
Return. Sussman.
The Return (excerpt). Woods.
Reynard the Fox (excerpt). Masefield.
Robert Fulton. Stanford.
Robin Hood and the Scotchman. *Anonymous.*
Rondeau: "Of Eden lost." Ellis.
The Sages. Mickiewicz.
A Sail. Lermontov.
Saint Brendan's Prophecy. *Anonymous.*
Salaam Alaikum. *Anonymous.*
San Juan Capistrano. Cooper.
Satires. Horace.

The Second Advice to a Painter. Marvell.
Second of August. *Anonymous.*
See in the Midst of Fair Leaves. Moore.
The Sentinel. Flint.
The Shepherd's Dog. Norris.
Shooter's Hill. Bloomfield.
Sick Love. Graves.
The Sick Nought. Jarrell.
Silver Lamps. Dix.
Sing, Sing for Christmas. Egar.
Sleep, Angry Beauty. Campion.
Sleep! Sleep! Beauty Bright. Blake.
The Sleeper. Scollard.
The Sleeping Fury. Bogan.
The Snare. MacDonogh.
So Sr. Henry Vane the Younger. Milton.
Solitude. More.
A Song. Barlow.
Song for Memorial Day. Scollard.
The Song of Hiawatha. Longfellow.
The Song of the Derelict. McCrae.
Sonnet: "Cry, crow." Carruth.
Sonnet: Death Is Not without but within Him. Cino da Pistoia.
The Spell of the Yukon. Service.
Stanzas from the Grande Chartreuse. Arnold.
Stone Angel. Ridler.
The Succession. Mace.
Summary of the Distance between the Bomber and the Objective. Benton.
Sunset. Mickle.
Surrender. Grimke.
Swedenborg's Skull. Watkins.
Switzerland. Arnold.
The Tears of Scotland. Smollett.
The Tears of Scotland Written in the Year MDCCXLVI. Smollett.
Tecumseh. Mair.
Thank Thee, Lord. Adams.
Theseus: A Trilogy. Winters.
They Cast Their Nets in Galilee. Percy.
Thy Sea So Great. Garrison.
Time's Hand is Kind. Bruner.
To a Captain in Sinai. Aharoni.
To Holy Jesus. Philipa.
To Jane: The Recollection. Shelley.
To Look at Any Thing. Moffit.
To Make the People Happy. Hugo.
To My Brother. Bogan.
To Naples. Mallalieu.
To Sleep. Kochanowski.
To the Rainbow. Campbell.
To the Virgin Mary. Petrarch.
To This Hill Again. Macmillan.
Traveling America. Struther.
Trees. De la Mare.

A Triplet on the Reign of the Great Sultan. Mangan.
The True Encounter. Millay.
'Twas at the Matin Hour. *Anonymous.*
The Two Neighbours. Hay.
Two Points of View. Watkins.
The Two Wives. Howells.
The Unemployed. Roberts.
The Urn. Crane.
Vain Questioning. De la Mare.
Valley of the Shadow. Galsworthy.
Verbatim from Boileau. Pope.
Verona. Wright.
La Vita Nuova. Dante Alighieri.
The Volunteer's Thanksgiving. Larcom.
The Wall. Phelps.
War. Hall.
War in Chang-An City. Wang Tsan.
Washing Windows. Spacks.
Waters of the Sea. Goldbeck.
The Way to Heaven. Whiting.
We See Jesus. Flint.
A Wedding-Song. Chadwick.
The Well of Living Water. Wesley.
Well Pleaseth Me the Sweet Time of Easter. Pound.
Whan the Hert Is Laich. Smith.
When I Am Old. Mason.
When the Great Gray Ships Come in. Carryl.
When There Is Peace. Dobson.
While to Bethlehem We Are Going. Violante Do Ceo.
The White Canoe. Sullivan.
Who Has Known Heights. Whiteside.
Wild Eden. Woodberry.
Wilt Thou Not Visit Me? Very.
The Windmill. Longfellow.
Wisdom. Yerby.
Woodrow Wilson. Jeffers.
Wordsworth's Grave. Watson.
A World of Light. Jennings.
The Young Recruit. Fiche.
Your Glory, Lincoln. Goodman.
Youth. Rittenhouse.

Peaceful (ly) (ness)
Abdolonymus the Sidonian. Very.
At Chappaqua. Benton.
Bantry Bay. Molloy.
The Blackbird. *Anonymous.*
Caroline and Her Young Sailor Bold. *Anonymous.*
Cleopatra and Antony. Dryden.
The Close of Day. Curtwright.
The Hills. Cornford.
The Lake. Arnold.
Lincoln. Riley.
Ninety-Fifth. *Anonymous.*
Opinions of the New Student. Pedroso.
Peace Delegate. Livingstone.

Rest Only in the Grave. Mangan.
Samson Agonistes. Milton.
Since Nature's Works Be Good. Sidney.
Tiresias. Tennyson.
What the Stone Dreams. Hathaway.
Who Are They? *Anonymous.*

Peach (es)
Among the Orchards. Lampman.
Another Sunset. Minczeski.
The Blue-Fly. Graves.
Death and the Cobbler. *Anonymous.*
A Fine, a Private Place. Ackerman.
Flower Women. Keating.
Four Women. Simone.
Limerick: "Miss Minnie McFinney of Butte." Wells.
The Painted Lady. Danner.
The Peaches. Oppenheimer.
Ryokan. Heyen.

Peacock (s)
Another Sunset. Minczeski.
Apples. Hall.
Arthur Mitchell. Moore.
Domination of Black. Stevens.
The Faerie Queene. Spenser.
The Loves of the Birds. *Anonymous.*
Meditations in Time of Civil War. Yeats.
Nineteen Hundred and Nineteen. Yeats.
Rigor Viris. Avison.
Things Kept. Dickey.
Vihio Images. Volborth.
World Enough. Hathaway.

Peak (s)
The Conversion of the Magdalene. Malon de Chaide.
The Cumberland and the Merrimac. *Anonymous.*
The Dying Eagle. Pratt.
Eagles and Isles. Gibson.
God's Blessing on Munster. Patrick.
Hymn of the Angels and Sibyls. Vicente.
I passed by the beach. Akahito (Yamabe no Akahito).
Lady Anne Bathing. Delius.
On a Ledge. Bell.
The Peaks. Crane.
Rare Moments. Phelps.
Sonnet: "If I could get within this changing I." Masefield.
Today Beneath Benignant Skies. Wortman.

Peal (s)
General Wonder in Our Land. *Anonymous.*
Mole Catcher. Blunden.

Peanut Butter
Being Adult. Zavatsky.

Peanuts
Children's Rhymes. Hughes.
Peanuts. *Anonymous.*
Peanuts. Belford.

Pear (s)
Daydreamers. Davis.
Fragments. Praxilla.
The Fruit of the Tree. Wagoner.

Little Friend. *Anonymous.*
Most beutiful of things I leave
 is sunlight. Praxilla.
Poem: "In the early evening,
 as now, a man is bending."
 Gluck.
Song: "Dress me in green."
 Anonymous.
Song: "Rose and grape, pear
 and bean." *Anonymous.*
Spring Goeth All in White.
 Bridges.
The Twelve Days of
 Christmas. *Anonymous.*

Pearl (s)
Arcturus Is His Other Name.
 Dickinson.
Art. Flax.
Avenue Y. Barrows.
The Burial. Thalman.
Columbus. Hutchison.
The Consolation of
 Philosophy. Boethius.
Consummation. Barker.
Diving for Pearls.
 Yamamoto.
Dorothea. Cleghorn.
Eve. Gascoyne.
Fat Tuesday. Di Piero.
Five Songs. Shapiro.
The Flight of the Duchess.
 Browning.
Florida Hillocks. Elmslie.
Friends. Ashbery.
Georges Bank. Older.
Gethsemane. Droste-
 Hulshoff.
Godly Casuistry. Butler.
Going for Water. Frost.
Hanging from the branches of
 a green willow tree. Ise.
The Heap of Rags. Davies.
In a Copy of Omar Khayyam.
 Lowell
Janis Joplin and the Folding
 Company. Winters.
Like a Pearl. Naggid.
Limerick: "Said a lachrymose
 Labrador seal." Herford.
Lips and Eyes. Carew.
Lips and Eyes. Marino.
The Lonely Shell. Perry.
Oh Lovely Fishermaiden.
 Heine.
The Pearl. Andersen.
The Perspective and Limits of
 Snapshots. Smith.
The Portrait. Lytton.
Portrait of an Artist. Howes.
The Powerful Eyes O' Jeremy
 Tait. Irwin.
Rain. Guri.
Song: "If she be not as kind
 as fair." Etherege.
Sonnets, XXXIV: "Why didst
 thou promise such a
 beauteous day."
 Shakespeare.
To Christopher Smart.
 Stroud.
Troilus and Cressida.
 Shakespeare.
The Zodiac Song. Ruskin.

Peasant (s)
Georgics. Virgil (Publius
 Vergilius Maro).
Louis XV. Sterling.
Poet and Peasant. Long.
Robert Burns. Alexander.
Sleeping Peasants. Janik.
Sweet Auburn. Goldsmith.
Why? Chima.

Pebble (s)
Ancestors' Graves in
 Kurakawa. Kogawa.
At Dieppe: Green and Grey.
 Symons.
Danger. Jackson.
For Once, Then, Something.
 Frost.
In the Heartland. Vinz.
The Law. Haynes.
The Narrow Door. Mew.
Nevada. Gurney.
The Practice of Absence.
 Friend.
Preexistence. Cornford.
September 7. Bass.
Time. Graves.
Wind and Wave. Patmore.
You Can Get Despondent.
 Careme.
You're Not the Only Pebble
 on the Beach. Braisted.

Peck (ed)
The Eye. Tate.
Fable of the Speckled Cow.
 Opperman.
Hens. Nowlan.
I Wanted to Die in the
 Desert. *Anonymous.*
Metagnomy. Pritchard.
Peter Piper. *Anonymous.*
The Poet Lives. Glatstein.
Poultry. Der Hovanessian.
Sing a Song of Sixpence.
 Mother Goose.

Pecos
The Law West of the Pecos.
 Barker.

Peculiar
The Buffalo Hunters.
 Anonymous.
Faith. Dunkels.
Limerick: "There was a young
 lady of Ealing."
 Anonymous.

Pedestals
Monument to Pushkin.
 Brodsky.
Women. Swenson.

Peel
The Far Country. Greacen.
The Skull. Young.
Songs of the Squatters, I.
 Lowe.

Peep (ed) (ing)
As Soon as Ever Twilight
 Comes. De la Mare.
Conversion. Hulme.
December Eclipse.
 Lockwood.
Friends in Paradise.
 Vaughan.
The Grey Linnet.
 McCarroll.
Lady Godiva. Shanks.
Limerick: "Said old Peeping
 Tom of Fort Lee."
 Bishop.
Say Who Is This with Silvered
 Hair. Bridges.
Slepynge Long in Greet
 Quiete is Eek a Greet
 Norice to Leccherie.
 Hollander.
The Stampede. Brininstool.

Peer
At Newmarket. Bishop.
Epitaph: "Tread softly; bid a
 solemn music sound."
 Morton.
Hawk and Snake. Silko.

It's Three No Trumps.
 Innes.
Lord Heygate. Belloc.
A Mare. Barnes.
Tomorrow's Men. Johnson.

Peevishness
The Poetaster. Jonson.
Song: "If I freely may
 discover." Jonson.

Peggy
It Was Miss Scarlet with the
 Candlestick in the Billiard
 Room. Mayer.
Love Is Like a Dizziness.
 Hogg.
To couple is a custom.
 Anonymous.
The True Ballad of the Great
 Race to Gilmore City.
 Hey.

Pekinese
The Extraordinary Dog.
 Turner.
An Invitation to the
 Zoological Gardens.
 Anonymous.
The Ordinary Dog. Turner.

Pelican
The Frigate Pelican. Moore.
The Northern Seas. Howitt.
The Shanty Boys and the
 Pine. *Anonymous.*

Pellet (s)
A Balanced Bait in Handy
 Pellet Form. Curnow.
Past and Present.
 Warburton.
A Plea for a Plural.
 Lehmann.

Pelt
Erris Coast, 1943. Connell.
An Otter. Hughes.
The Thatcher. Kennelly.

Pen (s)
An Allusion to Horace. The
 Tenth Satire of the First
 Book. Rochester.
Aunt Beulah's Wisdom.
 Box.
The Author's Reply.
 Scroope.
Been in the Pen So Long
 (with music). *Anonymous.*
The Broken Oar.
 Longfellow.
Cacoethes Scribendi. Holmes
A Dirge. Croffut.
The Dog. Davies.
Elsewhere. Pastan.
Epistle to the President, Vice-
 President, and
 Members...(excerpt).
 Geddes.
Epistles to Mr. Pope (excerpt).
 Young.
Evening: an Elegy (parody).
 Smith.
A Fancy. Lodge.
A Flemish Madonna. Stork.
The Gift. Ciardi.
The Hen. Herford.
Here Lies... Smith.
How to Write a Letter.
 Turner.
Iter Boreale. Wild.
Koala. Ross.
Lawyer Clark Blues. Estes.
Letters to My Daughters.
 Minty.
The Lust for Murder.
 Penfold.

A Messe of Nonsense.
 Anonymous.
Next Door to Monica's Dance
 Studio. Smith.
Pen Hy Cane. Mason.
River Skater. Welles.
The Scholar's Life.
 Anonymous.
The Scribe's Prayer.
 Guiterman.
The Song of the Pen. Al-
 Harizi.
Sonnets to Laura. Petrarch.
The Thresher's Labour.
 Duck.
To Oxford. Hopkins.
To the Learned and Reverend
 Mr. Cotton Mather...
 Rawson.
To the Prince. Davies.
The Twa Mariit Wemen and
 the Wedo. Dunbar.
The Waverley Pen.
 Anonymous.
We Object. *Anonymous.*
Weapons. Wickham.
Will Yer Write It Down for
 Me? Lawson.

Penance
Amoretti, LII. Spenser.
The Avenging Daughters.
 Anonymous.
The Grief of Our Genitals.
 Carlile.
The Lass and the Friar.
 Burns.
The Maid and the Palmer.
 Anonymous.
Troilus and Criseyde.
 Chaucer.
Young Benjie. *Anonymous.*

Pencil (s)
Ghost Boy. Van Doren.
A He as O. Cummings.
To My Friends. Schiller.

Penelope
An Ancient Gesture. Millay.
The Fatal Dream; or, The
 Unhappy Favourite.
 Collins.
Odysseus' Song to Calypso.
 Dufault.
Ulysses Returns.
 Montgomery.

Penguin
The Pen-Guin. The Sword-
 Fish. Wood.

Penicillin
Birth. Raine.

Penis
Along History. Rukeyser.
Limerick: "A smooth-
 bottomed fellow named
 Fritz." *Anonymous.*
Limerick: "In a high-fashion
 journal for queers."
 Anonymous.
A Sheeprancher Named John.
 Ehrlich.
To Philaenis. Martial
 (Marcus Valerius Martialis).

Penitent (s)
An A.B.C. Chaucer.
December Storm. Hay.
An Epitaph. Wesley.
La Priere de Nostre Dame.
 Chaucer.
The Spanish Friar. Dryden.

Penitentiary
The Boston Burglar.
 Anonymous.
Judge Harsh Blues. Lewis.

Midnight Special (with music).
Anonymous.
Penknife
Lady, Weeping at the
Crossroads. Auden.
Little Sir Hugh. Anonymous.
Newgate's Garland.
Anonymous.
Pennsylvania
Clerihew: "William Penn."
Smith.
Philadelphia. Kipling.
Ten Thousand Miles From
Home. Anonymous.
Penny (ies)
Ann Grenville, Countess
Temple, Appointed Poet
Laureate... Walpole.
Black Your Honour's Shoes?
Anonymous.
Gold Watch. Kavanagh.
He Said He Had Been a
Soldier. Wordsworth.
Hunger. Davies.
Ideal and Reality. Campbell.
June Twenty-First.
Guernsey.
Limerick: "B was a beggarly
bear." Wells.
Money Is What Matters.
Anonymous.
The Mouse's Lullaby. Cox.
My Ship and I. Stevenson.
An Old Woman. Ross.
Penny and Penny.
Anonymous.
The Peter-Penny. Herrick.
Rain. Harrison.
The Silver Penny. de la
Mare.
Snatches: "Spende, and God
shal sende." Anonymous.
To a Covetous Churl. May.
Pension
Casey Jones (D vers.).
Anonymous.
An Epitaph on William
Whitehead... Anonymous.
Mama Have You Heard the
News?(B vers. with music).
Anonymous.
Off Brighton Pier. Ross.
Pensive (ly)
Amoretti, XXXIV. Spenser.
The Coliseum. Byron.
Decay of Piety.
Wordsworth.
The Earth, Late Choked with
Showers. Lodge.
The Pewee. Trowbridge.
Solitude. Lampman.
Sonnet: "If I might choose
where my tired limbs shall
lie." Anster.
Pentagon
Here Lies Fierce Strephon.
Hecht.
Pentagonia (parody). Bates.
Pentecost
Channing. Alcott.
I Worship Thee, O Holy
Ghost. Warren.
Just the Same Today.
Anonymous.
Miss Euphemia. Ransom.
The National Gallery.
MacNeice.
Oh, for a Pentecost!
Anonymous.
Tulips. Colum.

Penury
Frigid and sweet her parting
face. Dickinson.
Measure for Measure.
Shakespeare.
A Plea for Mercy. Brew.
The Spider. Littleton.
People (s)
An Address to the
Vacationers at Cape
Lookout. Stafford.
Aged Fisherman. Bynner.
Animal Songs: Giraffe.
Anonymous.
Arrivals at a Watering-Place.
Praed.
At Cove on the Crooked
River. Stafford.
At the Un-National
Monument along the
Canadian Border. Stafford.
A Baby Sardine. Milligan.
A Bestiary. Rexroth.
Birmingham 1963.
Patterson.
Brother... Amini.
Bunch Grass #37. Sund.
Burial. Sarton.
But I Do Not Need Kindness.
Corso.
City-Storm. Monro.
The Cry of the Peoples.
Brody.
The Crystal Gazer.
Teasdale.
A Curse on Uruk.
Enheduanna.
Dark Symphony. Tolson.
Day's End. Harford.
Docteur Foster. Anonymous.
Doubting. Simpson.
Driving toward the Lac Qui
Parle River. Bly.
Eighteen-Forty-Three.
Anonymous.
Eleanor Rigby. Beatles.
The Empty House. Monro.
Eye of God. Tollerud.
For a Young South Dakota
Man. Manfred.
For Tom Numkena, Hopi/
Spokane. Littlebird.
For We Are Thy People.
Anonymous.
The Fortification of New Ross
(excerpt). Anonymous.
Friends. Durem.
From Greenland to Iceland.
Anonymous.
The Gardens of Alcinous.
Pope.
Gauley Bridge. Rukeyser.
The Glen of Silence.
""MacDiarmid.
God of Our Fathers.
Stryker.
God of the Nations. Bowie.
God Save the People. Elliott.
God That Doest Wondrously.
Ibn Ezra.
Granite and Cypress. Jeffers.
Gubbinal. Stevens.
He Is Coming, Adzed-Head.
Anonymous.
Hominization. Holub.
Hymn of Gratitude.
Anonymous.
I Like Americans. Boyd.
I the People. Notley.
Imagine the South.
Woodcock.

In a Chain-Store Cafeteria.
Grano.
Independence. Faleti.
Indian Camp. McFatter.
An Invitation to Madison
County. Wright.
Ireland. Piatt.
Ja, Ja, Ja! Anonymous.
Jesus Is Coming Soon.
Johnson.
Jewish Arabic Liturgies.
Anonymous.
Joan Miro. Todd.
Johnny Went to Church One
Day. Anonymous.
Lament for Banba.
O'Rahilly.
Legend. Waller.
Legsby, Lincolnshire.
Anonymous.
Limerick: "I have often been
told," said the horse."
Herford.
Limerick: "There was an old
lady of Chertsey." Lear.
Limerick: "There was an old
person of Brussels." Lear.
Limerick: "There was an Old
Person of Shoreham."
Lear.
A Little More About the
Brothers and Sisters.
Scott.
Loneliness. Jenkins.
The Lost Tribe. Pitter.
Love Pictures You as Black
and Long-Faced. Jeffers.
The Malfeasance. Bold.
The Man Who Invented Las
Vegas. Costanzo.
Many Die Here. Jones.
The Masterful Man. Tyrrell.
Meadowland. Anonymous.
The Movies. Gilbert.
Mummy of a Lady Named
Jemutesonekh XXI
Dynasty. James.
"My days' delight, my
springtime joys fordone."
Ralegh.
My Face. Euwer.
The New Integrationist. Lee.
The New Vicar of Bray.
Ellis.
Now the People Have the
Light. Ballard.
Nude in a Fountain.
MacCaig.
O By the By. Cummings.
O for the Happy Hour.
Bethune.
On the Duke of Buckingham,
Slain by Felton...
Felltham.
Passing Remark. Stafford.
People. Kanik.
The People. Roberts.
The People Went to War.
Jacinto.
Peyote Poem. McClure.
Pleading Voices. Katav.
Poem. Hughes.
The Point. Jones.
The Preacher's Mistake.
Doane.
The Raging Generation.
Mtshali.
Recessional. Kipling.
Regenesis. Welburn.
The Ride of Collins Graves.
O'Reilly.

The Right Kind of People.
Markham.
The Rock Crumbles. Lasker-
Schüler.
The Romish Lady.
Anonymous.
Rosh Pina. Knut.
The Rusted Chain. Ben
Yeshaq.
San Francisco Poem. Logan.
Seeing Oloalok. Bowering.
Sir Hugh; or The Jew's
Daughter (D vers.).
Anonymous.
Sir Menenius Agrippa, the
Friend of the People.
Brough.
Sleeping Beauty: August.
Knight.
Some Blesseds. Oxenham.
Sonnet to the Prince Regent.
Byron.
The Sound of Rain.
Akhmadulina.
Sound the Loud Timbrel.
Moore.
Sunday in Glastonbury. Bly.
The Taxis. MacNeice.
Tecumseh. Mair.
Th Unifying Principle.
Ammons.
The Three Tall Men.
Anonymous.
The Titans. Alver.
To Fez Cobra. Joans.
Token. Bacon.
Town I Left. Sorrells.
Translations. Lum.
Trombone Solo. King.
The Unpredicted. Heath-
Stubbs.
Whatever Comes. Stafford.
When We Were Very Silly.
Morton.
Windows in Providence.
Barnstone.
You Growing. Acorn.
Perceive (s)
Before the Pacific. Varela.
The Hind and the Panther.
Dryden.
Return to Spring. Mastin.
Perdition
The Dangers of Sexual Excess.
Armstrong.
A Lost Soul. Macpherson.
Sacrifice. Emerson.
To the University of
Cambridge, in New-
England. Wheatley.
The Zealous Puritan.
Anonymous.
Perfect (ed) (ion)
Adam's Song to Heaven.
Bowers.
Amoretti, LXXXIV.
Spenser.
Archaeology. Pollitt.
Archilochos:. Tagliabue.
The Canterbury Tales:
Prologue. A Knight.
Chaucer.
The Critic's Rules. Lloyd.
Dance Hymn. Shembe.
The Doom of Beauty.
Michelangelo.
The Dress. Strand.
Elegy V. Barker.
Envoi. Wickham.
Epitaph. Abercrombie.
Epithalamion Made at
Lincolnes Inne. Donne.

The Eternal City. Ammons.
Everyone in the World.
 Dailey.
Fire-Queen. Fainlight.
First to Throw a Stone.
 Anonymous.
For Nijinsky's Tomb.
 Cornford.
The Gift. Williams.
Gift to a Jade. Wickham.
Good Weather. Belli.
The Hand and Foot. Very.
Heartsearch. Gibson.
I live on this depraved and
 lonely cliff. Colonna.
I Want to Die while You
 Love Me. Johnson.
Infinity. Savage.
The Lake. Coxe.
Lead Us, O Father, in the
 Paths of Peace. Burleigh.
Let Not One Sparke of Filthy
 Lustfull Fyre. Spenser.
Looking for a Country under
 Its Original Name.
 McElroy.
Margaret and Dora.
 Campbell.
Misunderstanding. Layton.
New Construction: Bath Iron
 Works. Koehler.
Ode: "Love thy Country, wish
 it well." Dodington.
On the Eclipse of the Moon of
 October 1865. Turner.
Pacific Sonnets. Barker.
Patience. Studdert-Kennedy.
Per Pacem ad Lucem.
 Procter.
A Perfect Day. Bond.
The Planster's Vision.
 Betjeman.
Plenty. Jones.
Poetry of Departures.
 Larkin.
Pretty Twinkling Starry Eyes.
 Breton.
Resignation–To Faustus.
 Clough.
The Rise of Man. Chadwick.
Rose-Cheeked Laura.
 Campion.
Rowland's Rhyme. Drayton.
The Secretary. Redgrove.
The Sermon in the Hospital
 (excerpt). King.
Still Life. Raine.
Theseus: A Trilogy. Winters.
To Our Saviour. Agostinho
 da Cruz.
Tom Pringle. Simpson.
The Tray. Cole.
The Twilight Shadows Round
 Me Fall. Ryden.
Verses Made Sometime Since
 upon the Picture....
 Josselyn.
Watchmaker God. Lowell.
We Three Kings of Orient
 Are. Hopkins, Jr.
Whatever Is, Is Right. Gaik.
Whose Hand. Anonymous.
With Lilacs. Crandall.
The Word of God. Gwynne.
The Young Cordwainer.
 Graves.
Perform (ed) (ing) (ance)
The Bedbug. Harrison.
Carnegie Hall: Rescued.
 Moore.
A Correct Compassion.
 Kirkup.

Glory. Moore.
Light Shining Out of
 Darkness. Borthwick.
Now That the Truth Is Tried.
 Whythorne.
Over. Thomas.
To Juan at the Winter
 Solstice. Graves.
Vaudeville. Kirstein.
Wanting Out. Ewart.
Wasted Night. Anonymous.
Perfume (d) (s)
Above Salerno. Murray.
After the Shower.
 Lampman.
Autobiography. Dube.
The Balcony. Baudelaire.
Butchery. McPherson.
David and Bethsabe. Peele.
News Report. Ignatow.
Not of Itself but Thee.
 Anonymous.
The Perfume. Donne.
The Perfume. Herrick.
The Retort Discourteous.
 Benét.
The Reward of Innocent
 Love. Habington.
Smell My Fingers. Axelrod.
To My Cousin, (C.R.)
 Marrying My Lady (A.).
 Carew.
Peril (s)
Awake! Walther von der
 Vogelweide.
The Consolation of
 Philosophy. Boethius.
The Gunner. Webb.
Jacques Cartier. McGee.
On the Danger of War.
 Meredith.
The Wreck of the Northfleet.
 Anonymous.
Perilous
Columbus and the Mayflower.
 Milnes.
The Equilibrists. Ransom.
Infidelity. Untermeyer.
The Little Girl with Bands on
 Her Teeth. Taggard.
The Migration of the Grey
 Squirrels. Howitt.
Period (s)
Above It All. Levine.
The Crusaders knew the Holy
 Places. Mastoraki.
Great Streets of Silence Led
 Away. Dickinson.
In Despair He Orders a New
 Typewriter. Olson.
Pain Has an Element of
 Blank. Dickinson.
Proclamation/From Sleep,
 Arise. Rodgers.
Sonnet. I. Suckling.
Three Poems. Mastoraki.
Periphery
Three Brown Girls Singing.
 Holman.
True Enough: To the Physicist
 (1820). Goethe.
Perish (ed) (es) (ing)
The Agony in the Garden.
 Hemans.
The Ailing Parent. Dunetz.
Amoretti, II. Spenser.
Andre's Request to
 Washington. Willis.
The Azra. Heine.
Birmingham 1963.
 Patterson.

The Bitter Withy.
 Anonymous.
Cargoes of the Radanites.
 Potamkin.
Casabianca. Hemans.
Daisy. Thompson.
The Death of Lincoln.
 Bryant.
A Description of Beauty,
 Translated out of Marino.
 Daniel.
Epigrams. Theocritus.
I Should Not Dare to Be So
 Sad. Dickinson.
Lament to Nana of Erech.
 Anonymous.
The Little Dark Rose.
 MacWard.
The Little Knight in Green.
 Bates.
Love Speaks at Last.
 Herbert of Cherbury.
Mary Lifted from the Dead.
 Alfred.
Messengers. Towne.
Miles Keogh's Horse. Hay.
My Days among the Dead
 Are Past. Southey.
Mysterious Landscape.
 Carossa.
Nostalgia. Lawrence.
O Fearfull, Frowning
 Nemesis. Daniel.
Ode for a Master Mariner
 Ashore. Guiney.
Old Gardens. Upson.
Passer Mortuus Est. Millay.
A Perverse Custom.
 Anonymous.
Promises Like Pie-Crust.
 Rossetti.
Psalm I. Sidney.
The Rhyme of Joyous Garde
 (excerpt). Gordon.
A Royal Princess. Rossetti.
Satire. Donne.
Song: "Come, rest in this
 bosom, my own stricken
 deer." Moore.
Sonnet: "Evening, as slow thy
 placid shades descend."
 Bowles.
Tamerlane. Daley.
There Is Nothing False in
 Thee. Patchen.
They Will Look for a Few
 Words. Turner.
'Twas Like a Maelstrom, with
 a Notch. Dickinson.
Under a Lady's Picture.
 Waller.
Upon the Troublesome Times.
 Herrick.
A View of the Town
 (excerpt). Gilbert.
The Worthless Heart. Di
 Roma.
Perjury
I Have a King. Dickinson.
Lad of Athens, faithful be.
 Dickinson.
Permanent
Actions. Schwob.
August Night, 1953. Harrod.
Caelica, XIV. Greville.
Limerick: "When you think of
 the hosts without No."
 Anonymous.
Nox Nocti Indicat Scientiam.
 Habington.
The Put-Down Come On.
 Ammons.

Rondel: "Love, love, what wilt
 thou with this heart of
 mine?" Froissart.
Sea-Hawk. Eberhart.
The Them Decade. Winch.
Things. Kilmer.
Two Sonnets for a Lost Love.
 DeWitt.
Perpetual
In Exile. Lazarus.
The Place of the Solitaires.
 Stevens.
Prayer. Pierce.
Question and Answer.
 Raine.
A Sky of Late Summer
 (excerpt). Rago.
To the Lord Love. "Field.
Perplex (ed)
As Concerning Man.
 Radcliffe.
Limerick: "There was an old
 person of Cassel." Lear.
To His Book. Herrick.
Persecute (d)
El Ropero. Montoro.
Once I Was a Monarch's
 Daughter. Anonymous.
Persephone
At a Summer Hotel.
 Gardner.
Leo to His Mistress.
 Sedgwick.
Troubadours. Ficke.
Persian
The Fall of the Leaf.
 Thoreau.
New Year's Day. Crashaw.
Vision of Belshazzar. Byron.
We Are Keeping an Eye on
 the Girls. Tsvetayeva.
Person (s)
Any Man's Advice to His
 Son. Fearing.
Baudelaire in Brussels.
 Cronin.
Calypsomania. Brode.
Crucial Stew. Inez.
The Day the Winds. Miles.
Four Prayers, IV.
 Anonymous.
The Happy Man.
 Chesterton.
Here Lies Fierce Strephon.
 Hecht.
How to Get There. O'Hara.
The Knight and Shepherd's
 Daughter (A version).
 Anonymous.
Limerick: "There was an old
 person of Cromer." Lear.
Limerick: "There was an old
 person of Diss." Lear.
Limerick: "There was an old
 stupid who wrote." Parke.
Memories. Whitman.
Places, Loved Ones. Larkin.
The Rann of the Three.
 Anonymous.
Rattan bed, paper netting.
 Li Ch'ing-chao.
A Recollection. Cornford.
A Song of a Young Lady to
 Her Ancient Lover.
 Rochester.
To the Holy Trinity.
 Anonymous.
Zachary Zed. Reeves.
Personal
Goat Dance. Loewinsohn.
In the Public Garden.
 Moore.

The True-Born Englishman.
Defoe.
Peru
In Praise of Llamas.
Guiterman.
Limerick: "There was an old
man of Peru." Lear.
Pest
Savage Portraits. Marquis.
Yaw, Dot Is So! Adams.
Pestilence
Autumn. Nashe [(or Nash)]
Thomas.
The Canterbury Tales: The
Wife of Bath's Tale.
Chaucer.
The Marriage of Heaven and
Hell. Blake.
On Seeing an Officer's Widow
Distracted. Barber.
Things Dead. Schwob.
Pet (s)
According to eternal laws.
Landor.
If You. Creeley.
My House. Krows.
Ode of Odium on Aquariums.
Guiterman.
The Princess Addresses the
Frog Prince. Brewster.
Riven Doggeries. Tate.
To a Young Brother.
Jewsbury.
'Twas Ever Thus (parody).
Anonymous.
Two at Showtime. Brabant.
Petal (s)
Almond Blossom in Wartime.
Spender.
Caresses. Barker.
The Day of the Night.
Scully.
Epigram: "The breath of my
life." Meleager.
Faustina, or Rock Roses.
Bishop.
Feri's Dream. Cornford.
Fireworks. Reeve.
The Four Winds. Luders.
Joy of Knowledge.
Schneider.
Lesbian. Jennings.
Letter from a Black Soldier.
Anderson.
The Orchard. Spence.
The Poet Prays. Crowell.
Portrait of a Lady. Williams.
Sodom's Sister City.
Amichai.
Solution. Emerson.
A Tough Generation.
Gascoyne.
An Upper Chamber in a
Darkened House.
Tuckerman.
Villanelle of Marguerites.
Dowson.
The Wild Dog Rose.
Montague.
Peter
Blue Sparks in Dark Closets.
Snyder.
A Cock Crowing in a
Poulterer's Shop.
Ferguson.
Father Malloy. Masters.
Immolation. Farren.
Lament of the Mangaire
Sugach. Magrath.
Limerick: "There was a bright
fellow named Peter."
MacDonald.

Slovenly Peter. Hoffmann.
The Trappist Abbey: Matins.
Merton.
The Twins. Jackson.
Wishmakers' Town. Young.
Peter Pan
Pantomime Diseases. Abse.
The Tree-Top Road. Smith.
Peter Piper
Peter Piper. Anonymous.
Peter the Great
Peterhof. Wilson.
Petitioners
The Petition of the
Orangemen of Ireland.
Moore.
To the Right Hon. Henry
Pelham... Moore.
Petrarch
Don Juan. Byron.
Sonnet: "Keen, fitful gusts are
whisp'ring here and there."
Keats.
Sonnet to Valclusa. Russell.
Petticoat (s)
The Art of Dancing. Jenyns.
Did You See My Wife?
Anonymous.
I'm Going to California.
Mossman.
Lent. Rodgers.
Pussy Cat Mole.
Anonymous.
A Tawnymoor. Anonymous.
Petty
O, Let Me Kiss--. Gjellerup.
O Merry May the Maid Be.
Clerk.
The Results of Stealing a Pin.
Anonymous.
Think Small. Equi.
Pew (s)
Limerick: "There was an Old
Man in a pew." Lear.
Love of Fame, The Universal
Passion. Young.
Synnove's Song. Bjornson.
Phaeton
On Thomas, Second Earl of
Onslow. Anonymous.
On Tom Onslow, Earl of
Onslow. Anonymous.
Spoken Extempore.
Rochester.
Phantom (s)
Apologia Pro Vita Sua.
Coleridge.
The Coup de Grace. Sill.
Explorations Bronchitis: The
Rosario Beach House.
Rodriguez.
Hold. Chalmers.
Idylls of the King.
Tennyson.
The Lateshow Diorama.
Dewdney.
Lines Where Beauty Lingers.
Adams.
Low Barometer. Bridges.
The Man with the Hoe: A
Reply. Cheney.
Ode on Indolence. Keats.
Rontgen Photograph.
Eybers.
Thailand Railway. Stow.
Pharaoh
A Classic Ode. Loomis.
Didn't Old Pharaoh Get Los'?
Anonymous.
First Days. Ruebner.
In Time of Gold. Doolittle.

Three Sonnets on Oblivion.
Sterling.
With You Here at Mertu.
Anonymous.
Pharmacy
Chaplin's Sad Speech.
Alberti.
Les Realites. Guest.
Pheasant (s)
The Bofors A.A. Gun.
Ewart.
King George V. Hayward.
Miss Pheasant. De la Mare.
The Reading Lesson.
Murphy.
A Rule for Shooting.
Anonymous.
Philadelphia
In Columbus, Ohio.
Matthias.
Rulers: Philadelphia.
Johnson.
Philip
The Praise of Philip Sparrow.
Gascoigne.
Upon an Hermaphrodite.
Cleveland.
Phillis
The Conquest of Granada.
Dryden.
To the Honorable Charles
Montague, Esq. Prior.
Philomel (s)
The Plea of the Midsummer
Fairies. Hood.
Waltz. Sitwell.
Whither Is Gone the Wisdom
and the Power. Coleridge.
Philosopher (s)
Epigram. Garnett.
Moral Essays. Pope.
On Philosophers.
Anonymous.
The Philosopher's Scales.
Taylor.
The Political Orlando.
Macbeth.
Winter Rune. Coatsworth.
Philosophy
Is 5. Cummings.
On Philosophy. Goldstein.
On the Heights. Holmes.
The Refugees. Muir.
Snow Crystals on Meall Glas.
Wilson.
They Meet Again. Aldis.
Phlox
Fishing with My Daughter in
Miller's Meadow. Stryk.
Scribe. Auster.
Song for a Little House.
Morley.
Phoebe
Anniversary in September.
Brown.
Madrigal: "Stay, nymph."
Pilkington.
The Need of Being Versed in
Country Things. Frost.
To Phoebe. Gilbert.
Phoebus
The Bore. Horace.
Evening Quatrains. Cotton.
From a Beggarman's Song.
Anonymous.
Phoenix
Appeal to the Phoenix.
Untermeyer.
Chelmsfords Fate. Tompson.
Epitaph. Rose.
Evening in Camp. Ledward.

Forty-Five Years Since the
Fall of the Ch'ing Dynasty.
Whalen.
On Sitting Down to Read
"King Lear" Once Again.
Keats.
The Phoenix. Fisher.
Poem from London, 1941.
Woodcock.
Roses Red. Holz.
Season Ticket. Frym.
Song: "When I lie burning in
thine eye." Stanley.
Welcome My World. Devlin.
Westering. Kane.
Phone
Emergency at 8. Hewitt.
Letter to My Mother. Skeen.
Long Distance. Naone.
Photograph (ed)
Before the Mountain.
Libbey.
Cedar. Morgan.
Epilogue. Lowell.
Hold My Hand. Pennant.
Hut. Dutton.
In a Cafe. Brautigan.
Lamentations. Brody.
The Oneness of the
Philosopher with Nature.
Chesterton.
The Pavilion on the Pier.
Vazakas.
Punk Party. ey Told Me It
Was Literary...] Rose.
Phyllis
Don't. Roche.
Honeymoon. Albert.
Lydia Is Gone This Many a
Year. Reese.
Phyllis's Age. Prior.
William and Phyllis.
Anonymous.
Physic
Beauty. Anonymous.
David Garrick, the Actor, to
Sir John Hill, a Physician...
Garrick.
Epigram: "Fair Ursly, in a
merry mood." Anonymous.
On Sir John Hill, M.D.,
Playwright. Garrick.
Physician (s)
The Citizen and the Red Lion
of Brentford. Smart.
Doctor Blenn. Bierce.
The Remedy Worse Than the
Disease. Prior.
Tempora Mutantur. Brasch.
To Be a Nurse. Lawrence.
Piano
A Gothic Gesture. Levine.
Home Is So Sad. Larkin.
The Light Passages. Greger.
Links. Dempster.
Piano at Evening. Palea.
Piazza
Piazzas. Guest.
Saint's Parade. Layzer.
Picardy
The Bohemians. Gurney.
Marching Song. Burnet.
Pick (ed) (s)
Americana. Rakosi.
B Negative. Kennedy.
Children, It's Time.
Brownstein.
Clinic: Examination.
Conard.
A Copy of Non Sequitors.
Anonymous.
Crocuses. Josa.

The Devil's Dictionary: Body-Snatcher. Bierce.
Elektra on Third Avenue. Hacker.
Half-Bent Man. Eberhart.
Lad's Love. Duff.
Limerick: "A thrifty young fellow of Shoreham." *Anonymous.*
The Moon Ground. Dickey.
Music by the Waters. Hay.
Peter Piper. *Anonymous.*
Pick a Bale of Cotton. *Anonymous.*
The Pickety Fence. McCord.
Reward of Virtue. Guiterman.
Road Hazard. Green.
A Silver Lantern. Baker.
Sketch for a Morning in Muncie, Indiana. Murray.
Two Translatons from Villon. Synge.
Where the Fight Was. Corbin.
Whore. King.

Picket (s)
After Midnight. Jones.
The Jews. Jastrun.
New Romance. Wong.
Relieving Guard. Harte.
Street Scene–1946. Porter.

Pickle (d)
Lady Isabel and the Elf Knight (H version). *Anonymous.*
Liquor and Longevity. *Anonymous.*
Miss Millay Says Something Too. Hoffenstein.
Ode on a Jar of Pickles (parody). Taylor.
Peter Piper. *Anonymous.*
Roger Francis. Thorley.

Picture (d) (s)
An Aestuary. Croly.
Because I Paced My Thought. Hewitt.
Childe Rolandine. Smith.
The Conspiracy. Creeley.
The Crystal Gazer. Teasdale.
The Dance. Williams.
Double Exposure. Young.
Euclid. Lindsay.
The Face Upon the Floor. D'Arcy.
Faces (parody). Berry.
A Floridian Museum of Art. Whittemore.
Gibraltar. Trench.
Haymaking. Thomas.
Hippocrene. Lowell.
How the Death of a City Is Never More Than the Sum of the Deaths... Coleman.
Intaglio. Coulette.
The Keekin' Glass. Burns.
Laus Veneris. Moulton.
The Likeness. Martial (Marcus Valerius Martialis).
Lord Abbott. Belloc.
The Man She Called Honey, and Married. Rios.
Maps to Nowhere. Rosenberg.
The Most Expensive Picture in the World. Nemerov.
Old Man. Henry.
An Order for a Picture. Cary.

A Picture from Life's Other Side. *Anonymous.*
Picture-Show. Sassoon.
Pictures from Brueghel. Williams.
Progress? Auden.
Secrecy Protested. Carew.
To Lucasta: Her Reserved Looks. Lovelace.
To Miss Charlotte Pulteney in Her Mother's Arms. Philips.
To the Muse. Stevenson.
To the Reader. Jonson.
Worry. *Anonymous.*

Pie (s)
Anacreon's Dove. Johnson.
The Derby Ram. *Anonymous.*
Fragment of a Character. Moore.
The Glutton. Oakman.
Grandmother's Apple Pies. Munro.
The Lay of the Ettercap (parody). Leyden.
Limerick: "A heathen named Min, passing by." Herford.
A Melton Mowbray Pork-Pie (parody). Le Gallienne.
Old Christmas. *Anonymous.*
On the Planet of Flies. Morgenstern.
The Pumpkin. Whittier.
Riddle: "First it was a pretty flower." Rossetti.
Riddle: "Higgledy-piggledy here we lie." *Anonymous.*
Thanksgiving Time. *Anonymous.*
This Is the Life. MacNeice.
The Value of Pi. *Anonymous.*
A Was an Apple Pie, B Bit It, C Cut It. *Anonymous.*
William Shakespeare to Mrs. Anne,... Gray.

Piece (s)
The Adhesive Autopsy of Walt Whitman. Williams.
Around You, Your House. Stafford.
At Camino. Sheehan.
Bloody Pause. Astra.
Driftwood Dybbuk. Lefcowitz.
Everything: Eloy, Arizona, 1956. Anthony ("AI").
Fingers in the Door. Holbrook.
Haec Olim Meminise Iuvabait. Taylor.
Landscape with Little Figures. Justice.
Mind. Graham.
Nightbreak. Rich.
The Nottinghamshire Poacher. *Anonymous.*
The Offensive. Douglas.
On Falling Asleep to Birdsong. Meredith.
A Poem for a Poet. Lorde.
Times Square Parade. Watson.
Tregardock. Betjeman.
Upon the Works of Ben Jonson (excerpt). Oldham.

Pier (s)
The Berkeley Pier. Addiego.
Eliza Telefair. Sloan.
The Fisherman. Bruce.

Rome. Hardy.

Pierce (d) (s)
Balinda's Dance. Erdrich.
The Bayonet and the Needle. Steinbarg.
Caelica, CVI. Greville.
Hot Day at the Races. Raworth.
The House of Life. Rossetti.
Kicking from Centre Field. McFadden.
Prayer of a Modern Thomas. Shillito.
The Rose and the Thorn. Hayne.
Scissor-Man. MacBeth.
Sorrow. Eden.
Walking to Dedham. Wright.

Piety (pious)
Brother and Sister. Eliot.
An Elegy in Memory of the Worshipful Major Thomas Leonard Esq.... Danforth II.
The End of Being. Seneca.
The Hermit. Parnell.
Heroique Stanzas, Consecrated to the Glorious Memory... Dryden.
Rich and Poor; or, Saint and Sinner. Peacock.
To the King on His Navy. Waller.
To William Camden. Jonson.
View of the Cathedral. Henri.

Pig (s)
Ambition. Agnew.
Animals Are Passing from Our Lives. Levine.
Any Part of Piggy. Coward.
Apres le Bain. Williams.
Artillery Shoot. Forsyth.
Autumn. Clare.
Betty Pringle's Pig. *Anonymous.*
The Boar of Badenoch and the Sow of Atholl. Mitchison.
The Boasting Drunk in Dodge City. *Anonymous.*
Definition for Blk/Children. Sanchez.
First in a Carriage. *Anonymous.*
Food of the North. Lawrence.
Hernando de Soto. Benét.
The Hunt of Sliabh Truim (excerpt). *Anonymous.*
If Pigs Could Fly. Reeves.
Johnny Morgan. *Anonymous.*
Judged by the Company One Keeps. *Anonymous.*
The Laughing Faces of Pigs. Lape.
Learning the Spells: A Diptych. Probst.
Let's Go to the Wood, Says This Pig. *Anonymous.*
Little Jack Dandy-Prat. *Anonymous.*
Little Piggy. Hood.
Mary Middling. Fyleman.
Mystic. Lawrence.
The Old Woman Who Bought a Pig. *Anonymous.*
On the Relinquishment of a Title. Grigson.
Pigs. Cotton.

St. Anthony and His Pig. A Cantata. Forrest.
This Town. Paul.
"The Time Has Come," the Walrus Said. "Carroll.
To a Boy-Poet of the Decadence. Seaman.
'Twas an evening in November. *Anonymous.*
The Whaler's Pig. Brady.
Where Are You Going. Follen.

Pigeon (s)
All of a Row. *Anonymous.*
Birthday Poem from Venice. Beer.
Lady Luck. Gottlieb.
Letter Across Doubt and Distance. Holman.
The Lost. *Anonymous.*
The Magician. Ramke.
Pigeons. Whisler.
The Pilot's Day of Rest. Gerlach.
Poems, III. O'Connor.
Possibilities. Dufault.
The Power of Love He Wants Shih (Everything). Owens.
She Stoops to Conquer. Goldsmith.
Spring Poem. Symons.
The Statue. Finch.
Trinity Place. McGinley.
Wild Oats. MacCaig.

Pike (s)
The Cropper Lads. *Anonymous.*
The Death of General Pike. Osborn.
The Death of Queen Jane. *Anonymous.*
The Fox and the Goose. *Anonymous.*
From Plane to Plane. Frost.
The Gold Seeker's Song. *Anonymous.*
Good Men Afflicted Most. Herrick.
The Guttural Muse. Heaney.
He Understands the Great Cruelty of Death. Synge.
His Cavalier. Herrick.
Lancashire Winter. Connor.
New National Anthem. *Anonymous.*
The Rising of the Moon. *Anonymous.*
To a Hedgehog. Thompson.

Pike's Peak
The Gold Seeker's Song. *Anonymous.*

Pile (d) (s)
Down and Out. Hay.
Evil Is No Black Thing. Fabio.
The Fools of Forty-Nine. *Anonymous.*
The Gold Seeker's Song. *Anonymous.*
Horoscope. Cunningham.
Limerick: "I saw Nelson at the Battle of the Nile." *Anonymous.*
Longing. Herbert.
Ravings (parody). Hood.
Ten Thousand Cattle. Wister.
To a Millionaire. Lampman.
Windharp. Montague.

Pilgrim (age) (s)
Asian Desert. Wellesley.

At My Mother's Knee.
Anonymous.
Autumn Flowers. Very.
Cockle-Shell and Sandal-
Shoon. Coleman.
The Coming of Christ.
Anonymous.
The Decision. Dodson.
Farewell to My Mother.
"Placido" (Gabriel de la
Conception Valdes).
For Life I Had Never Cared
Greatly. Hardy.
Hap. Hardy.
In Canterbury Cathedral.
Oldenburg.
In the Azure Night.
Galindez.
It Cannot Be. Sickels.
Leap in the Smoke. Buchan.
Life Is Like a Mountain
Railroad. Anonymous.
Lough Bray. O'Grady.
The Man of Life Upright.
Campion.
Marston. Spender.
O Fly My Soul. Shirley.
One by One. Procter.
The Pilgrimage. Ralegh.
The Pilgrims Came. Wynne.
Present. Sanchez.
Puer Aeternus. Raine.
Recollections of a Day's
Journey in Spain. Southey.
Song Set by Thomas Ford:
"Unto the temple of thy
Beauty." Anonymous.
Song: "Under the oak tree,
oak tree." Anonymous.
The Songs of the Birds.
Carpenter.
To a Young Girl Dying.
Parsons
To My Father. Tree.
To the Moon. Smith.
The Twenty-Second of
December. Bryant.
Watchman, Tell Me.
Anonymous
Yattendon. Newbolt.

Pillage
A Poem to Show the Trouble
That Befell Him When He
Was at Sea. Prys.
The Poor of London.
Forster.

Pillar (s)
The Arrow of Desire.
Anonymous.
Brazilian Fazenda. Page.
Canzone: Of His Love, with
the Figure of a Sudden
Storm. Prinzivalle.
The Cloud. Muir.
Patience. Horne.
The Pleasure of Ruins.
McClatchy.
A Row of Thick Pillars.
Crane.

Pillow (s)
Death. Herbert.
The Dying Ranger.
Anonymous.
Emily Dickinson. Hagerup.
Fall Comes in Back-Country
Vermont. Warren.
Four Heads & How to Do
Them. Forbes.
Good Wish. Anonymous.
A Hundred Collars. Frost.
In the Night Watches.
Roberts.

The Instructions of King
Cormac (excerpt).
Anonymous.
Light. Coates.
Limerick: "There once was a
kind armadillo." Herford.
Lullaby. Adams.
Man's Pillow. Browne.
Morning. McCrae.
The Night Mirror.
Hollander.
On a Monday Morning.
Tawney.
On the Victory of Poland and
Her Allies over the Sultan
Osman, 1621. Sarbiewski.
Sleeping with Someone Who
Came in Secret. Ise.
Song: "If love were but a little
thing." Coates.
The Storm. Alcaeus.
Stroke. Lowery.
Survivor. MacLeish.
Tears against the Moon.
Walsh.
To Tan Ch'iu. Li Po.
Where Be You Going, You
Devon Maid? Keats.
The Wisconsin Soldier Boy.
Anonymous.

Pills
Brigham Young.
Anonymous.
Disguised. Perreault.
The Happy Pair (excerpt).
Sedley.
Though a Soldier at Present.
Moore.

Pilot (s)
Crossing the Bar. Tennyson.
The Dead Wingman. Jarrell.
The Last Instructions to a
Painter. Marvell.
The Plantation. Heaney.
Rhododaphne. Peacock.
The River Boats. Hicky.
Sonnet: "Ice over time."
Shapiro.
Time Zones for Forty-Four.
Stauffer.
Wind of the Prairie. Howes.

Pimps
The Last Instructions to a
Painter. Marvell.
On Authors and Booksellers.
Pope.

Pin (s)
Ane Satire of the Three
Estaitis (excerpt).
Lyndsay.
Betwixt and Between.
Lofting.
Cupid's Darts. Herbert.
Delphine. Anderson.
Epigram: "Wealth covers sin."
Kassia.
Limerick: "A thrifty young
fellow of Shoreham."
Anonymous.
A Song: "I'll sing you a
song." Anonymous.
Ten Week Wife. Donovan.

Pinch (ed)
Abdication Street Song.
Anonymous.
Coma. Schmitz.
The Fairies. Herrick.
Party. Justice.

Pindar
Although I was her pupil.
Korinna.
Fragments. Corinna.

I Disapprove Even of
Eloquent Myrtis.
"Corinna".

Pine (s)
Among the Pine Trees. Dor.
And there is nothing at all—
neither fear.
Gorbanyevskaya.
Cold Water. Hall.
Countersign. Ketchum.
Do Not Accompany Me.
Halkin.
Drum-Taps. Whitman.
Eight Sandbars on the Takano
River. Snyder.
Fable XLV: The Poet and the
Rose. Gay.
Family Trees. Malloch.
The Farmer and the Shanty
Boy (Trenton Town).
Anonymous.
The Flowering of the Rod.
Doolittle.
Funeral in Hungary. Boyle.
Halcyon Days. Barnes.
Have Sky. MacAdams.
Hawthorne. Alcott.
The Hill Pines Were Sighing.
Bridges.
In the Mountains on a
Summer Day. Li Po.
Infinity. Whitman
John Smith's Approach to
Jamestown. Hope.
Lines to a Reviewer. Shelley.
The Little Donkey. Jammes.
The Man with the Blue
Guitar. Stevens.
Moonrise. Doolittle.
My Land Is Fair for Any
Eyes to See. Stuart.
On a Horse Carved in Wood.
Hall.
Our Sunday morning when
dawn-priests were applying.
Berryman.
Petit, the Poet. Masters.
The Pleasant Comedie of Old
Fortunatus. Dekker.
A Poem for the Meeting of
the American Medical
Association. Holmes.
Poem: "This life like no
other." Orr.
Returning. Harding.
Roger Williams.
Butterworth.
Self-Dependence. Arnold.
Since to Be Loved Endures.
Bridges.
Sleep. Winters.
Song: "Virtue's branches
wither, virtue pines."
Dekker.
The Storm. Roethke.
Tammuz. Alterman.
These Purists. Williams.
Time to Myself. Jiles.
Vapor Trails. Snyder.
Visit. Welch.
We Walked among the
Whispering Pines. Boner.
Why She Says No. Voigt.
Wind Gardens (parody).
Untermeyer.

Pinions
The Aeneid. Virgil (Publius
Vergilius Maro).
The Bullfinches. Hardy.
A Judgment in Heaven.
Thompson.
Spring (excerpt). Gisborne.

Summer. Davidson.

Pink (s)
Air Travel in Arabia.
Johnston.
Brazilian Fazenda. Page.
Come down, You Bunch of
Roses, Come down.
Anonymous.
Nymphs and Satyrs. Ewart.
Photographs: A Vision of
Massacre. Harper.
Plum Blossoms. Basho
(Matsuo Basho).

Pint
At the Ship. Lister.
To Mr. Alexander Ross.
Beattie.
To the Blacksmith with a
Spade. O'Sullivan.

Pioneer (s)
All the Past We Leave
Behind. Whitman.
Babies of the Pioneers.
Luckey.
Farther. Piatt.
The Home Winner.
Lindberg.
Pioneers! O Pioneers!
Whitman.

Pious
The Bounty of Our Age.
Farley.
Haleluiah; or, Britain's Second
Remembrancer: Hymne I.
Wither.
The Renegado (Act V, Scene
I). Massinger.
To Phidyle. Horace.
A Tribute to the Founder.
Amis.

Pipe (s)
As I out Rode. Anonymous.
The Difference. King.
Driving to Sauk City.
Woessner.
Fall Days. Conger.
Faun-Taken. O'Neill.
The Firetail's Nest. Clare.
Forcing House. Roethke.
How Night Falls in the
Courtyard. Rimmer.
Indoors. Johnston.
Inter Sodales. Henley.
The Merry Bagpipes.
Anonymous.
Moon-Madness. Starbuck.
Pindar. Antipater of Sidon.
The Pipes. Lipsitz.
The Relief of Lucknow.
Lowell.
The Seven Ages of Elf-Hood.
Field.
The She Wolf. Spark.
The Shepherd. Anonymous.
Snakecharmer. Plath.
Tom Long. Anonymous.
The Walk Home.
Whittemore.
With Pipe and Flute.
Dobson.

Piper (s)
The Barricades. Levertov.
Change and Immutability.
Scroggie.
The Cow Ate the Piper.
Anonymous.
The Dance. Anonymous.
The Harvest Moon.
Longfellow.
The Host of the Air. Yeats.
Hymn of Pan. Shelley.
In June. Perry.

Piper

Lament for the Great Music
(excerpt). ""MacDiarmid.
The Life and Death of Habbie
Simson, the Piper of
Kilbarchan. Sempill.
The Magic Piper. Marsh.
Mr. Molony's Account of the
Ball. Thackeray.
The Musician. Lister.
The Piper o' Dundee.
Anonymous.
Switzerland. Thwaite.
To William Blake. Dargan.

Pirate

Bold Princess Royal.
Anonymous.
The Downfall of Piracy.
Franklin.
The Flying Cloud.
Anonymous.
Freedom. Barlow.
Nor'Easter. Bradbury.
Roughchin, the Pirate.
Boswell.
Upon Kinde and True Love.
Townsend.

Piss

Anadarko John. Arnett.
Coptic Poem. Durrell.
The Garden of Earthly
Delights. Simic.
The Painters.
Hemschemeyer.
To an Alcoholic.
McPherson.
The Virtues of Sid Hamet, the
Magician's Rod. Swift.

Pistol (s)

The Dream about Junior High
School in America.
Lourie.
The Huntsman.
Wheelwright.
On His Publisher. Tennyson.
Sarajevo. Durrell.
Tell Us No More.
Anonymous.
Texas Types–"The Bad Man."
Chittenden.

Pit

Afternoon 3. Kuroda.
Artemis. Nerval.
A Ballad of the Strange and
Wonderful Storm of Hail.
Anonymous.
Cherry-Pit. Herrick.
The Dreamers and the Sea.
Wilkins.
The Lame One. Anderson.
Let Me Not Die. Pierce.
An Outdoor Litany. Guiney.
A Plum. Leib.
Poem: "O who can ever praise
enough." Auden.
Ranolf and Amohia.
Domett.
Upon the Death of George
Santayana. Hecht.

Pitcher

The Annunciation. Duffy.
The Double Play. Wallace.
The Old-Fashioned Pitcher.
Phair.
The Story of Abraham and
Hagar. Aphek.

Pitchfork

The Riot; or, Half a Loaf is
Better Than No Bread.
More.

Pitiful

Desideravi. Maynard.
Madness. Yoshihara.

The Worshiper. Miller.

Pitt

Fort Duquesne. Plimpton.
George II. Thackeray.
On Imitation. Coleridge.

Pity (ied) (ies) (ing)

Aeliana's Ditty. Chettle.
The Aeneid. Virgil (Publius
Vergilius Maro).
American Twilights, 1957.
Wright.
Armistice Day. Trent.
Astrophel and Stella, XLV.
Sidney.
At Night. Cornford.
Baja. Stern.
The Ballad of Father Gilligan.
Yeats.
The Bishop and His
Portmanteau. *Anonymous.*
Caelica, IX. Greville.
The Case of Thomas More.
Mary St. Virginia.
Charlotte Corday.
Tomlinson.
Christmas 1942. Irvin.
The Compassionate Fool.
Cameron.
The Coward. Spender.
Cradle Song. MacNeice.
Crowds. Baudelaire.
Crustaceans. Fuller.
A Dark Country. Mahon.
The Darned Mounseer.
Gilbert.
A Dead Weasel. Helwig.
A Dream of Artemis.
Ledwidge.
Ephelia to Bajazet. Etherege.
Express. Rodgers.
The Faithful. Cooper.
False Country of the Zoo.
Garrigue.
The Galloping Cat. Smith.
Giotto's Campanile. Butler.
The Graveyard. Bialik.
Her Sister. O'Neill.
Holstenwall. Keyes.
I Heard an Angel Singing.
Blake.
I Read, or Write. Sedulius
Scottus.
The Indictment (excerpt).
Ayer.
Inscription for the Tank.
Wright.
The Intruder. Kizer.
Intrusion. Levertov.
Judgment Day. Howells.
The Killing. MacBeth.
A La Promenade. Verlaine.
A Leave-taking. Swinburne.
Love. Graham.
Lunar Paraphrase. Stevens.
A Machine Hand. Ashe.
Medieval Norman Songs.
Anonymous.
The Membrane.
Berssenbrugge.
The Milkmaid's
Epithalamium. Randolph.
The Mistake. *Anonymous.*
Modern Love, XLIV.
Meredith.
The Moon. Shelley.
Myths and Texts. Snyder.
The Nightingale. Barnfield.
O Pity Our Small Size.
Rosenbaum.
O Youth with Blossoms
Laden. Peach.

Old Maid's Song.
Anonymous.
The Old Men. Javitz.
Old Men's Ward. Dean.
One of Us Two. Wilcox.
Pacific Sonnets. Barker.
Philomel. Barnfield.
Piscatorie Eclogues.
Fletcher.
Pity and Love. *Anonymous.*
The Pool. Mayo.
Poor Kings. Davies.
Poor Little Jesus.
Anonymous.
A Post-Mortem. Sassoon.
Prayer for Fine Weather.
Leslie.
Prayer in Affliction. Storey.
President Parker.
Anonymous.
Priam and Achilles. Pope.
A Prisoner for Life.
Anonymous.
Psalme CXXXVII. Sandys.
Regret. *Anonymous.*
The Road to Hate.
Kavanagh.
The Seaman's Compass.
Anonymous.
Sleep, Angry Beauty.
Campion.
A Song for the Ragged
Schools of London.
Browning.
Song from the Bride of
Smithfield. Warner.
Song: "Know, Celadon, in
vain you use." "Ephelia"
(Joan Philips).
Song Set by Thomas Ford:
"Unto the temple of thy
Beauty." *Anonymous.*
Sonnets, XX: "But now my
Muse toyled with continuall
care." Barnfield.
The Sounds of Dawn.
Huerta.
The Spring Vacation.
Mahon.
A Storm of Love. Corke.
Sweet Violets. *Anonymous.*
The Terrible Dead. Davies.
These Are the Chosen People.
Nathan.
Three Memorial Sonnets.
Barker.
Thysia. Luce.
To My Worthy Friend, Mr.
James Bayley... Noyes.
To Poets and Airmen.
Spender.
To Stella. Swift.
Tragic Guilt. Rhys.
Troynovant. Dekker.
Tunes for Bears to Dance To.
Wallace.
Upon Jone and Jane.
Herrick.
Upon Moon. Herrick.
Upon One of the Maids of
Honour to Queen Elizabeth.
Hoskyns.
When Doris Danced.
Eberhart.
When I See the Earth Ornate
and Lovely. Gambara.
While the Summer Trees
Were Crying. Iremonger.
Wisdom. Hanson.
Women, whoever wishes to
know my lord. Stampa.
The Wooing Maid. Parker.

Yourself and Myself.
Anonymous.

Place (d) (s)

1614 Boren. Hugo.
Achilles in Scyros (excerpt).
Bainbridge.
Ambition. Pope.
And Through the Caribbean
Sea. Danner.
At half-past three.
Dickinson.
At the Place of the Sea.
Flint.
A Bachelor's Life.
Anonymous.
The Bailey Beareth the Bell
Away. *Anonymous.*
A Ballad of London. Le
Gallienne.
Be Wise, and Fly Not.
Campion.
Bear Song. Swanton.
The Birth of a Shark.
Wevill.
The Book. Vaughan.
Caelica, LXXX. Greville.
The Closing Album.
MacNeice.
Colley's Run-I-O.
Anonymous.
Coming to This. Strand.
The Constant Lover.
Suckling.
A Cow Camp on the Range.
Anonymous.
Crossing with the Light.
Okita.
Cumberland Station. Smith.
The Descent on Middlesex.
St. John.
The Deviator. Warr.
A Devonshire Song.
Anonymous.
Discovering My Daughter.
Stuart.
Eat and Walk. Hall.
Elegy. Ibn Ezra.
Epigram: "Loss of our
learning brought darkness,
weakenss and woe."
Anonymous.
Epilogue (parody). Byron.
Epitaph of a Sailor.
Leonidas of Tarentum
Evaporation Poems. Norris.
Evening Hymn. Roberts.
Everything Has Its History.
Levin.
The Exact Same Places.
Vandersee.
Explanations of Love.
Sandburg.
The Faerie Queene. Spenser.
Fair Maiden, Who Is This
Bairn? *Anonymous.*
The Faithful Shepherdess.
Fletcher.
Follower. Arvey.
For the Rebuilding of a
House. Berry.
For Want I Will in Woe I
Plain. Wyatt.
The Fountain of Tears.
O'Shaughnessy.
Four-Leaf Clover.
Higginson.
From the Garden of Heaven.
Hafiz.
From the Roof. Levertov.
G. K. Chesterton. Wolfe.

Go, Grieving Rimes of Mine. Petrarch (Francesco Petrarca).
God's-Acre. Longfellow.
The Gulf. Levertov.
Happiness Amidst Troubles. Di Roma.
He accepts the circle, speech and so. Albiach.
Here Is a Toast That I Want to Drink. Lathrop.
Highway Construction. Chapin.
Homing. Bowman.
The Hour of Prayer. Adams.
Hymns for the Amusement of Children. Smart.
In a Country Museum. Beer.
In eternum I was once determed. Wyatt.
In the Henry James Country. Abrahams.
In the Marble Quarry. Dickey.
Initiation. Cortez.
Inland Passages, I: The Long Hunter. Berry.
Joy o' Living. Hall.
Just Keep On. Abbott.
The Labyrinth. Muir.
Las Trampas U.S.A. Tomlinson.
The Late Show. Sylvester.
The Letter. Tatham.
The Life of San Millan (excerpt). Berceo.
Life or Death. Dresbach.
Lines Written near Linton, on Exmoor (parody). Hoffman.
Madly Singing in the Mountains. Chu-i.
A Manifesto for the Faint-Hearted. Oles.
The Map. Soto.
The Mormon Bishop's Lament. Anonymous.
A Morning. Strand.
Mountain Creed. Nutter.
Moving: New York–New Haven Line. Corn.
My Dark Fathers. Kennelly.
My Place. Ignatow.
The Mystery. Hyde.
Oh No. Creeley.
On Certain Ladies. Pope.
The Onion. Thompson.
The Other Side of This World. Forbes.
Over Case's Door. Case.
The Owslebury Lads. Anonymous.
A Painful Love Song. Amichai.
Paradise Lost. Milton.
Parting as Descent. Berryman.
Penelope. Laederach.
The Pink Locust. Williams.
A Place in Thy Memory. Griffin.
The Place of the Solitaires. Stevens.
Places I Have Been. Volk.
Places, Loved Ones. Larkin.
Pleasure Reconciled to Vertue: A Masque. Jonson.
The Poem You Asked For. Levis.
Process of time worketh such wonder. Wyatt.

Prospero on the Mountain Gathering Wood. Gilbert.
Puppy. Lape.
Recollections of a Day's Journey in Spain. Southey.
The Savage Beast. Williams.
Scotch Rhapsody. Sitwell.
Shall I Be Silent? Herbert.
Some Things You Cannot Will to Men. Isenhour.
Song of Texas. Hosmer.
Sonnet: "So shoots a star as doth my mistress glide." Davies.
The Spires of Oxford. Letts.
Spirit Song. Anonymous.
The Spring. Fyleman.
The Spring Offensive of the Snail. Piercy.
St. George. Anonymous
The Statesman in Retirement. Cowper.
Suggested by a Picture of the Bird of Paradise. Wordsworth.
Take Your Place. Anonymous.
Tanks. McMaster.
There Is a Grey Thing That Lives in the Tree-Tops. Crane.
There Is Always a Place for You. Campbell.
Ticonderoga: A Legend of the West Highlands. Stevenson.
To London the Train Gallops, Its Shrill Steel Hooves'. Dyment.
To My Most Gracious Dread Sovereign. Davics.
To Queen Elizabeth. Davies.
Triphammer Bridge. Ammons.
Twenty Stars to Match His Face. Braithwaite.
A View of Jersey. Field.
Visit to a Hospital. Chace.
The Voyage. Muir.
We'll Never Know. Hoellein.
The Well Rising. Stafford.
Where? Patchen.
Will there really be a morning? Dickinson.
The Window Frames the Moon. Mar.
Winter Evening Poem. Jensen.
Winter Wakens All My Care. Anonymous.
Wofully Araide. Anonymous.
Woman Blues. Anonymous.
The Working Man. Donovan.
Working the Skeet House. Eastman.
The World's Miser. Maynard.
Wrap Me Up in My Tarpaulin Jacket. Anonymous.
Years of Indiscretion. Ashbery.
The Yellowhammer. Clare.
You Must Have Been a Sensational Baby (excerpt). Norse.

Placid
The Ant. Nash.
A Bought Embrace. Fraser.

Characteristics of a Child Three Years Old. Wordsworth.
For Lucas Cranach's Eve. Crapsey.
Plague (s)
Autumn. Nashe [(or Nash)] Thomas.
Burnet's Character. Anonymous.
Cataclysm. Catullus.
The Duenna (excerpt). Sheridan.
Invocation. Horace.
London. Blake.
Look up to Pentland's Tow'ring Tap. Ramsay.
Moderation: Odes. Horace.
The Poet and the Dun. Shenstone.
Song. Sheridan.
Song Set by Robert Jones: "She whose matchless beauty staineth." Anonymous.
Plaid
Ca' the Yowes to the Knowes. Anonymous.
The Elfin Knight. Anonymous
The Ould Plaid Shawl. Fahy.
Recreation. Taylor.
Plain (s)
Ah, necromancy sweet! Dickinson.
At My Whisper. Donaghy.
The Avon. Jacobs.
Behind the Wheel. Brownstein.
The Black Mesa. Merrill.
Bronc Peeler's Song. Anonymous.
Chances "R". Ginsberg.
Clean Hands. Dobson.
Colin Clout at Court. Spenser.
Commemoration. Newbolt.
The Comparison (excerpt). Anonymous.
The Dancers. Robinson.
A Disagreeable Feature. Robinson.
The Discovery. MacEwen.
A Dream. Arnold.
England and America. Stephen.
The Exile of Erin. Anonymous.
The Faerie Queene. Spenser.
Figure of Eight. MacNeice.
Gebir. Landor.
God's Blessing on Munster. Patrick.
Haiku: "The long, long river." Boncho.
The Hour of Feeling. Simpson.
The Iliad. Homer.
In Dispraise of the Moon. Coleridge.
In Spite of Sorrow. Judson.
The Inca Tupac Upanqui. Hart-Smith.
Independence. Cato.
The Joy of a Singer. Piuvkaq.
The Legend of Grand Lake. Westcott.
Light Shining Out of Darkness. Cowper.

A Long Walk before the Snows Began. Bly.
The Makers. Kell.
March Winds. Lloyd.
McAfee's Confession. Anonymous.
Not Quite Fair. Leigh.
Ode to Evening. Warton.
Off Riviere Du Loup. Scott.
On Certain Wits. Nemerov.
On the Night. Gurney.
The Plains. Dixon.
The Plains of Mexico; or, Santa Anna. Anonymous.
Population Drifts. Sandburg.
The Rambling Cowboy. Anonymous.
The Raven Days. Lanier.
Santy Anno. Anonymous.
Sea and Land Victories. Anonymous.
Singing the Reapers Homeward Come. Anonymous.
The Sleep of Spring. Clare.
The Smoke-Blue Plains. Clark.
Sonnet: The Army Surgeon. Dobell.
Summer. Aiken.
Texas. Lowell.
The Thousand and One Nights: Death. Anonymous.
To a Jilt. Armstrong.
To Her Body, Against Time. Kelly.
Variations on a Time Theme. Muir.
Verses Written at Montauban in France, 1750. Warton.
The Wagon Train. Simpson.
Who Has Not Walked Upon the Shore. Bridges.
Plaint (s)
How Goodly Is Thy House. Jacobs.
Like to These Unmeasurable Mountains. Wyatt.
Stanzas from Saint Peter's Complaint. Southwell.
Plan (ned) (s)
And When I Am Entombed. Emerson.
Barriers Burned. Field.
Deer Song. Confucius.
The Down-Pullers. Isenhour.
Exhortation. Bogan.
A Fable for Critics. Lowell.
Forget It. Anonymous.
Happy Birthday. Bidart.
I Heard a Young Man Saying. Fields.
In Memoriam A.H.H., XVI. Tennyson.
The Last Republicans. Clarke.
Looking for a Country under Its Original Name. McElroy.
The Mugger. Pack.
Nature's Hymn to the Deity. Clare.
Observation Car. Hope.
The Pagan Isms. McKay.
Probity. Swanger.
Summer Visitors. Clark.
Watt's Improvements to the Steam Engine. Baker.
A Woman. Thayer.
Yung Wind. Confucius.

Plane (s)
As a Plane Tree by the Water.
 Lowell.
Battle Hymn of the Spanish
 Rebellion. Mackey.
Epithalamium for Honorius
 and Maria: Palm Tree
 Mates with Palm.
 Claudian.
Feet, a Sermon. Paul.
Instant Coffee. Yau.
A Leg in a Plaster Cast.
 Rukeyser.
The Levelled Churchyard.
 Hardy.
Nightmare at Noon. Benét.
The Plane: Earth. Sun-Ra.
This Is My Death-Dream.
 Salisbury.

Planet (s)
After Grey Vigils.
 Santayana.
Amoretti, LX. Spenser.
Aphorisms. "Novalis"
 (George Friedrich Philipp
 von Hardenerg).
The Book of Day-Dreams.
 Moore.
Caelica, XLIV. Greville.
End of the World. Lasker-
 Schüler.
Epitaphs of the War, 1914-18.
 Kipling.
First Kiss. Holden.
Fourth Act. Jeffers.
Jim the Splitter. Kendall.
Lady Day. Fallon.
Leaves Like Fish. Cardiff.
The Man Who Dreamt He
 Was Turquoise. Rose.
Nuclear Land. Tuft.
On a Tear. Rogers.
The Planet. Jacobsen.
Planetary Exchange. Jones.
A Pulpit to Be Let.
 Anonymous.
Pumpkin. Morgan.
The Rejected "National
 Hymns". Newell.
The Shadow of Night.
 Chapman.
Song: "Something calls and
 whispers, along the city
 street." King.
Valentine for Earth. Frost.
Verses on Accepting the
 World. Brodsky.

Plant (ed) (ing) (s)
Adams and Liberty. Paine.
After Annunciation.
 Wickham.
The Annunciation. Kriel.
Apple-Seed John. Child.
Bill Venero. *Anonymous.*
A Child's Thought of Harvest.
 "Coolidge.
Death of a Young Son by
 Drowning. Atwood.
A Dream. Sackville-West.
The Dying Man in His
 Garden. Sewell.
Epitaph on a Fir-Tree.
 Murphy.
Eve. Wolf.
The First Love Poem.
 Schotz.
Foxfire. Willard.
Fraility. Herbert.
The Gardener. Housman.
The Ivy Green. Dickens.
On the Eve of Our
 Anniversary. Margolis.

Peace. Speed.
Ross's Poems. Lehmann.
Solomon: To Truth.
 Anonymous.
Soul-Sickness. Very.
The Unfading. "Marie.
A Woman Waits for Me.
 Whitman.

Plantation
A Charm against the Tooth-
 Ache. Heath-Stubbs.
Florida Hillocks. Elmslie.

Plate (s)
Conservancies. Miles.
Jack Sprat (parody).
 Hetherington.
Oil. Snyder.
Portrait of a Senator.
 Norman.
Recipe for a Pleasant Dinner-
 Party. *Anonymous.*
The Renaming. Sinason.
Strawberries. Morgan.
Unhappy Boston. Revere.
Xerox. Belitt.

Plato
A Night-Piece; or, Modern
 Philosophy. Smart.
The Village. Thomas.

Platter (s)
As You Like It. Weiss.
Dog (parody). Berry.
John the Baptist. Simpson.

Play (ed) (ers) (ing) (s)
About a Year after He Got
 Married He Would Sit
 Alone... Whitehead.
Above the Dock. Hulme.
According to eternal laws.
 Landor.
The Aeneid. Virgil (Publius
 Vergilius Maro).
After Tennyson: "To watch
 the tipsy cripples on the
 beach." Lear.
Ago. Jennings.
Aiken Drum. *Anonymous.*
Air: "So full of courtly
 reverence." North.
Alciphron and Leucippe.
 Landor.
All Work and No Play Makes
 Jack a Dull Boy.
 Anonymous.
Allie. Graves.
Anacreontic, On Parting with
 a little Child. Wesley.
Animula Vagula. Campbell.
Bad Girl Blues. Borum.
Bard. Black.
Bobby's First Poem. Gale.
The Brothers. Muir.
A Bunch of Roses. Tabb.
Butterfly in the Fields.
 Campbell.
Caelica, XIII. Greville.
Caelica, XXV. Greville.
Caelica, LXX. Greville.
Caelica, LXXXIV. Greville.
Caesar, when that the traitor
 of Egypt. Wyatt.
The Cat and the Lute.
 Master.
The Chess-Board. Lytton.
The Child's First Grief.
 Hemans.
A Children's Don't.
 Graham.
Christmas Eve. *Anonymous.*
Clever Peter and the Ogress.
 Pyle.
Conversation. Malley.

A Copy of Verses Sent by
 Cleone to Aspasia.
 Landor.
The Cottage Hospital.
 Betjeman.
The Cottager. Clare.
Could I Believe. Milne.
Critic. White.
Croquet. Huddle.
Cut It Down. Coleridge.
A Dance for Ma Rainey.
 Young.
Discovery. Keech.
The Dumb World. Davies.
The End of Day. Yeats.
English Courage Displayed.
 Anonymous.
Epiderm. Dransfield.
Epigram: "Why should
 scribblers discompose."
 Landor.
Epigrams in Distich, I: The
 Fine Lady Reform'd.
 Anonymous.
Epitaph on an Irish Priest.
 Anonymous.
Epitaph: "What is our life?"
 Anonymous.
Epitaphs of the War, 1914-18.
 Kipling.
Evening Song. Alexander.
Everything Is Round.
 "Mistral.
Fern House at Kew. Dehn.
First Fight. Then Fiddle.
 Brooks.
The Flute of May.
 Woodbourne.
Foal. Watkins.
The Fountains. Rodgers.
Four for Sir John Davies.
 Roethke.
Fragments. Cotton.
From the Commonwealth.
 Esteves.
Fun in a Garret. Dowd.
Galway. O'Neill.
God is indeed a jealous God.
 Dickinson.
The Golf Links. Cleghorn.
Goliath and David.
 Untermeyer.
The Green Tree. Reiss.
The Guitarist Tunes Up.
 Cornford.
Hamlet. Shakespeare.
Harmonica Man. Wolny.
Henry's Secret. Kilner.
Hey Fella Would You Mind
 Holding This Piano a
 Moment. Harris.
Hope. Hughes.
How McDougal Topped the
 Score. Spencer.
The Hunt. *Anonymous.*
I Come and Stand at Every
 Door. Hikmet.
I Love Little Pussy. Taylor.
I Was Lying Still in a Field
 One Day. Gay.
I Wish I Were. *Anonymous.*
If Women Could Be Fair.
 De Vere.
Kelly. Hershon.
Kentucky Blues. Jones.
King Henry V. Shakespeare.
The Kirkyaird by the Sea
 (excerpt). Valery.
Laugh and Be Merry.
 Masefield.
Legacy. Ford.

Limerick: "There was a young
 fellow named Hatch."
 Anonymous.
Liszt. Bentley.
The Long Garden.
 Kavanagh.
The Lost Children. Jarrell.
Love-Song. Lasker-Schüler.
A Lyric to Mirth. Herrick.
MacPherson's Farewell.
 Anonymous.
Medieval Norman Songs.
 Anonymous.
Modern Love, XIV.
 Meredith.
A Mongoloid Child Handling
 Shells on the Beach.
 Snyder.
Morning. McCrae.
A Mother to Her Waking
 Infant. Baillie.
My Mistress Makes Music.
 Anonymous.
My Purse. *Anonymous.*
My Zipper Suit. Allen.
Nelly Bly. Foster.
The New Hellas. Edman.
No More Words.
 Lushington.
Nothing Sacred. Woddis.
Ode to Pornography.
 Anderson.
Of My Lady Isabella Playing
 on the Lute. Waller.
Old I Am. Stanley.
On My Old Ramkiekie.
 Leipoldt.
One Thing at a Time.
 Stodart.
Opossum. Smith.
The Palatine. Cather.
A Pastoral. *Anonymous.*
Pete at the Seashore.
 Marquis.
The Philanderer. Mendes.
Phyllis. *Anonymous.*
Picture People. Bennett.
The Plaudite, or End of Life.
 Herrick.
Poem for Black Boys.
 Giovanni.
A Poem for Players. Young.
Poem: "The only response."
 Knott.
Polo Grounds. Humphries.
Porgy, Maria, and Bess.
 Heyward.
The Purpose of Fable-Writing.
 Phaedrus.
Rain on the Roof. Kinney.
The Rainbow. McCord.
Rink Keeper's Sestina.
 Draper.
Robin Good-Fellow's Song.
 Anonymous.
Romance. Howells.
Rondel for Middle Age.
 Nicholl.
Rosalynde. Lodge.
A Roundel of Rest. Symons.
The Show is not the Show.
 Dickinson.
Skipping along Alone.
 Welles.
Some Ruthless Rhymes.
 Graham.
The Song. Very.
Sonnets, XCVIII: "From you
 have I been absent in the
 spring." Shakespeare.
Sparrows in College Ivy.
 Wolfe.

Stamp Blues. Hollins.
The Story of Good. Janik.
Summons. Ficke.
The Swallow. Aiken.
Table Talk. Cowper.
The Tape. Livingston.
Ten Brothers. *Anonymous.*
Thumbing Old Magazines.
Vizenor.
To Avisa. Willoby.
To Betsey-Jane, on Her
Desiring to Go
Incontinently to Heaven.
Eden.
To Dr. F. B. on His Book of
Chess. Lovelace.
To His Soul. Hadrian.
To Sextus. Sedley.
The Toilette. A Town
Eclogue. Gay.
The Trumpeter. *Anonymous.*
The Turtle-Doves' Nest.
Anonymous.
Two Pictures. *Anonymous.*
Up-Tails All. *Anonymous.*
Upon Appleton House, to My
Lord Fairfax. Marvell.
A Vision (excerpt). Procter.
Vitai Lampada. Newbolt.
Walking on Water. Petaccia.
Warm rain, sunny wind. Li
Ch'ing-chao.
Wasted Night. *Anonymous.*
We Used to Play. Welch.
When a Fellow's Four. Carr.
When I Was Otherwise Than
Now I Am. *Anonymous.*
When you Love, or speak of
it. Behn.
Who Taught Caddies to
Count? or; A Burnt Golfer
Fears the Child. Nash.
Youth. *Anonymous.*

Playground
Mimma Bella. Lee-
Hamilton.
P's the Proud Policeman.
McGinley.
Visitations. Crewe.

Playmate (s)
The Burman Lover. Baker.
Endymion. Keats.
For Two Girls Setting out in
Life. Viereck.
Love in the Wind. Hovey.
Ossian's Serenade. Campbell.
Pirates. Noyes.
The Revolt of Islam.
Shelley.

Plaything (s)
The City: Midnight. Dawe.
Cops and Robbers.
Middleton.
Foreign Lands. Stevenson.

Plaza
In the Plaza We Walk. De
Leon.

Plead (ing) (s)
The All-Sufficient Christ.
Lubke.
Ave! Nero Imperator.
Osborne.
Bacon's Epitaph, Made by His
Man. *Anonymous.*
Come Hither, You That Love.
Fletcher.
Lines to His Son on Reaching
Adolescence. Logan.
Mother. Shaul.
Nimbus. Le Pan.
Storm. Nagy.

Their height in heaven
comforts not. Dickinson.
Truth. McKay.

Pleasant
The Dark-Eyed Sailor.
Anonymous.
Death and the Bridge.
Lowell.
The Deserted Mountain.
Anonymous.
Evolutionary Hymn. Lewis.
Farm Implements and
Rutabagas in a Landscape.
Ashbery.
The Flower and the Leaf.
Anonymous.
I Accept. Pulsifer.
If in Beginning Twilight.
Cummings.
Light, Light of My Eyes.
Propertius.
May. Edwards.
The Meadow Lark. Garland.
The Message. Heywood.
The Old Settler's Song.
Henry.
A Parisian Idyl (excerpt).
Moore.
Reflections outside of a
Gymnasium. McGinley.
The Sheep. Taylor.
Some Things That Easter
Brings. Parrish.
"The soote season..." Surrey.
Spectator Ab Extra. Clough.

Please (d) (s)
The Acquiescence of Pure
Love. Cowper.
Advice to the Ladies of
London in the Choice of
Their Husbands.
Anonymous.
Against Love. Philips.
Browning. Stevenson.
Caelica, LXXXIV. Greville.
The Climate. Denby.
A Countrywoman of Mine.
Eastman.
A Death. Jennings.
Dedication, to Leigh Hunt,
Esq. Keats.
Driven by desire I did this
deed. Wyatt.
Edward the Second (excerpt).
Marlowe.
Elegy on Coleman.
Anonymous.
Epigram on a Dog. Johnson.
Epitaph on the Lap-Dog of
Lady Frail. Wilkes.
An Epitaph upon My Dear
Brother, Francis Beaumont.
Beaumont.
The Faerie Queene. Spenser.
The Female God.
Rosenberg.
Foeda Est In Coitu.
Petronius Arbiter (Caius
Petronius Arbiter).
For Her Sake. Reid.
The Gift of Song. Horace.
A Greek Gift. Dobson.
Hence These Rimes. Taylor.
Holy Spirit, Lead Me.
Anonymous.
I Pressed Her Rebel Lips.
Anonymous.
It Pleases. Snyder.
Limerick: "There was an Old
Person of Shoreham."
Lear.

Madrigal: "Sweet Philomel in
groves and deserts
haunting." *Anonymous.*
A Mountain Heritage.
Ellison.
Naso, You're All Men's Man.
Catullus.
The Old Man Dreams.
Holmes.
On the Death of Mr. Purcell.
Dryden.
The Pleasing Constraint.
Sheridan.
Polly Oliver's Rambles.
Anonymous.
Pretext. Rodefer.
Random Reflections on a
Cloudless Sunday.
Wheelock.
The Redwoods. Simpson.
Song: "Give me leave to rail
at you." Rochester.
Song Set by Thomas Weelkes:
"Three times a day my
prayer is." *Anonymous.*
The Songs of Bilitis. Louys.
Sonnet. The Cell. Thelwall.
Stanzas Written in My Pocket
Copy of Thomson's "Castle
of Indolence."
Wordsworth.
Tellers of Tales. Kallman.
To My Grandmother.
Locker-Lampson
To Nysus. Sedley.
The True-Born Englishman.
Defoe.
The Unfortunate Miller; or,
The Country Lasses Witty
Invention. *Anonymous.*
Upon His Julia. Herrick.
The Way It Is. Oden.
You Simple Bostonians.
Anonymous.

Pleasing
Aglaia. Breton.
The Apron of Flowers.
Herrick.
Heart's Music. *Anonymous.*
Holy Sonnets, XVIII.
Donne.
If I should die. Dickinson.
Invocation. Eastman.
My Aunt. Wood.
Old Crabbed Men. Reeves.
The Path of Wisdom.
Anonymous.
Sonnet to Byron. Keats.

Pleasure (s)
Absence absenting causeth me
to complain. Wyatt.
Against Botticelli. Hass.
Alexander's Feast or, the
Power of Music. Dryden.
Amoretti, XLVII. Spenser.
Amoretti, LXV. Spenser.
Another Way. Bierce.
Arcadia. Sidney.
The Ass. Mendes.
Before Parting. Swinburne.
The Beggar's Opera. Gay.
Behold, O Man. Spenser.
Beneath a Cool Shade.
Behn.
Big, Fat Summer—and the
Lean and Hard. Bock.
A Bird Was Singing.
Dietmar von Aist.
The Blue-Bird. Wilson.
Brave Wolfe. *Anonymous.*
Chorus. Daniel.

The City Rat and the Country
Rat. La Fontaine.
A Common Poem. Rodgers.
Condemned Women.
Baudelaire.
Direct Song. Merriam.
The Disappointment. Taylor.
Don Juan. Byron.
The Dream. Money-Coutts.
The End of Being. Seneca.
Evening Song. Alexander.
Experience. O'Reilly.
Farewell to Cuba. Brooks.
The Father and His Children.
Anonymous.
The Ferry. Boker.
Fie, Pleasure, Fie!
Gascoigne.
For Communion with God
(excerpt). Shepherd.
Gifts of Rain. Heaney.
The Grace of Cynthia's
Maidenhood. D'Ambrosio.
Hero and Leander. Marlowe.
The Hunters of Men.
Whittier.
Hymn. Chadwick.
I Sigh, as Sure to Wear the
Fruit. *Anonymous.*
I Wandered Lonely as a
Cloud. Wordsworth.
I Would in Rich and Golden
Coloured Raine. Lodge.
If the Heart of a Man. Gay.
Il Penseroso. Milton.
The Indian Emperor.
Dryden.
The Jolly Trades-Men.
Anonymous.
Kind Miss (with music).
Anonymous.
The Kitten and the Falling
Leaves. Wordsworth.
Lament for the Woodlands.
Anonymous.
Langley Lane. Buchanan.
The Lee Rigg. Fergusson.
Limerick. *Anonymous.*
Limerick: "There was a young
lady of Oakham."
Anonymous.
The Little Dancers. Binyon.
The Little Family.
Anonymous.
A Logical Song. *Anonymous.*
The Long River. Hall.
Love in May. Passerat.
Madrigal: "Sing we and chant
it." Morley.
Mothers. Giovanni.
The Mouse and the Cake.
Cook.
A Nocturnal Reverie.
Wilchilsea.
O Miserable Sorrow,
withouten Cure. Wyatt.
Ode I Allusion to Horace.
Akenside.
Odes. Santayana.
Old Maps. Tietjens.
On the Loss of U.S.
Submarine S4 (excerpt).
Canfield.
Parson's Pleasure. Higgs.
Pluck the Fruit and Taste the
Pleasure. Lodge.
Poet-Hearts. Eichendorff.
Psalm XVI. Sidney.
The Ranting Wanton's
Resolution; 1672.
Anonymous.

Reynard the Fox (excerpt). Masefield.
A Riddle. Cowper.
Rink Keeper's Sestina. Draper.
She Was All That You Loved. Laxness.
Shouting Song. *Anonymous.*
Since Youth Is All for Gladness. Dresbach.
The Smile of the Goat. Herford.
Solon's Song. D"Urfey.
Song: "The engine screams and Murphy, isolate." Kinsella.
Songs Set by Thomas Morley: "Sing we and chant it." *Anonymous.*
Still, O LORD, for Thee I Tarry. Wesley.
The Swallows: An Elegy. Jago.
Three Songs from the Temple. Domanski.
To Charinus, a Catamite. Martial (Marcus Valerius Martialis).
To Edward Fitzgerald. Tennyson.
To Papilus. Martial (Marcus Valerius Martialis).
To Spenser. Keats.
To the Moon. Winters.
To William (Whom We Have Missed). Wodehouse.
Trust Not the Treason. Spenser.
Twa Bonny Lads. Burns.
The Twelve Weapons of Spiritual Battle. More.
Two Paintings by Gustav Klimt. Graham.
Two Smiles. Herford.
Untitled Poem. Dugan.
Up at a Villa–Down in the City. Browning.
Upon Julia's Ribband. Herrick.
Upon Love Fondly Refus'd for Conscience Sake. Randolph.
Visions. Petrarch.
Volpone. Jonson.
Water. Emerson.
Whole and Without Blessing. Gregg.
Why Are Our Summer Sports So Brittle? *Anonymous.*
Winter Nights. Campion.
The Word Plum. Chasin.
The Young Rhymer Snubbed. Barnes.

Pledge (d)
A Battle Ballad. Ticknor.
Brown Adam (A version). *Anonymous.*
Come Hither, My Dear One. Clare.
The Cudgelled but Contented Cuckold. La Fontaine.
Epistle to the President, Vice-President, and Members...(excerpt). Geddes.
Haarlem Heights. Guiterman.
Memorial Sonnet. Meeker.
The Oeconomy of Love (excerpt). Armstrong.
The Queen of Seasons. Newman.

To My Son. Byron.
The Vow of Washington. Whittier.
We Be Three Poor Mariners. *Anonymous.*
We Praise Thee, God, for Harvests Earned. Adams.

Pleiades
Ceremony. Nemerov.
Epitaph of Cleonicus. Calverley.
Hasidim Dance. Sachs.
O Ye Sweet Heavens! Parsons
Per Aspera. Coates.

Plenty
August. Spenser.
The Banks of the Sacramento. *Anonymous.*
Bessy and Mary. *Anonymous.*
California (with music). *Anonymous.*
An Elegy on Ben Jonson. Cleveland.
The First Olympionique to Hiero. Pindar.
The Happy Miner. *Anonymous.*
How to Get to Canada. Berrigan.
In the Year of Many Conversions and the Private Soul. Ciardi.
The Jerboa. Moore.
Larry M'Hale. Lever.
Madrigal: "Ladies, you see time flieth." Morley.
Old Grandpaw Yet. *Anonymous.*
De Rerum Natura. Lucretius (Titus Lucretius Carus).
To His Love When He Had Obtained Her. Ralegh.

Plight (ed)
Canaan. Spark.
Christmas 1898 (excerpt). Morris.
The Double Autumn. Reeves.
The Dynasts. Hardy.
Families. Blackburn.
Flowers. Hood.
Ode to a Lady Whose Lover Was Killed by a Ball... Byron.
Or Ever God Created Adam. *Anonymous.*

Plod
The Greatest Person In the Universe. Marsh.
Rock Pilgrim. Palmer.
To an Indian Skull (excerpt). McLachlan.

Plot
Antrim. Jeffers.
Carta Canadensis. Gustafson.
Life of the Letters. Borenstein.
On the Murder of Sir Edmund Berry Godfrey. *Anonymous.*
Walking to Bellrock. Ondaatje.

Plough (ed) (ing) (s)
Abundance. Borson.
Air: "A flaxen-headed cowboy, as simple as may be." O'Keefe.
Beyond Wars. Morrow.

Bishop Blougram's Apology. Browning.
Braddock's Fate, with an Incitement to Revenge. Tilden.
Chaucer. Longfellow
The Crow Sat on the Willow. Clare.
Cupid the Ploughboy. *Anonymous.*
Edwin in the Lowlands Low. *Anonymous.*
Epitaph for Mael Mhuru. *Anonymous.*
Eve. Wolf.
A Failure. Day-Lewis.
Fair and Softly. Ayres.
Farm Child. Thomas.
God Save the Plough. Sigourney.
Hell. *Anonymous.*
Hold On. *Anonymous.*
The India Guide.... Dallas.
John Grumlie. *Anonymous.*
The Jolly Farmer. *Anonymous.*
The Land. Sackville-West.
The Minute-Men of North-Boro'. Rice.
On Christmas Day. *Anonymous.*
On the Loss of the "Royal George." Cowper.
On the Poet's Leer. Ray.
The Painful Plough. *Anonymous.*
Pastoral. Magowan.
The Ploughboy. Clare.
The Ploughman. *Anonymous.*
The Ploughman. Thomas.
The Plowman. Burns.
The Plowman. Harris.
Plowman's Song. Knister.
Recitative. McCuaig.
Richard Dick upon a Stick. *Anonymous.*
Robert Burns. Alexander.
The Royal George. Cowper.
The Schooner Fred Dunbar. Hanson.
The Simple Ploughboy. *Anonymous.*
Tubal Cain. Mackay.
Untrodden Ways. Machar.
The Useful Plow. *Anonymous.*
The Vampire. Aiken.
Where I Took Hold of Life. Coffin.

Ploughshare (s)
As the Team's Head-Brass. Thomas.
The Law. Haynes.
Matrimony. Williams.
My Heart, How Very Hard It's Grown! Mather.
Two Generations. Strong.

Plover
Driving Saw-Logs on the Plover (with music). *Anonymous.*
The Escape. Van Doren.

Pluck (ed)
As I Walked through the Meadows. *Anonymous.*
Four Sonnets to Helen, 4. Ronsard.
Hares on the Mountain. *Anonymous.*
The Honeysuckle. Rossetti.
The Hunter. Nash.

I Am but a Little Woman. Kivkarjuk.
It Was the Time of Roses. Hood.
James Rigg (parody). Hogg.
Letters to Walt Whitman. Johnson.
Love's Emblems. Fletcher.
The Lover Exhorteth His Lady to Take Time, While Time Is. Turberville.
Missing. *Anonymous.*
Old Gardens. Upson.
The Proffered Rose. Wenceslas.
Prostration. Semah.
Riddle: "Higgledy-piggledy here we lie." *Anonymous.*
Simple Nature. Romanes.

Plum (s)
Bring Daddy Home. *Anonymous.*
Ceremonies for Christmas. Herrick.
Christmas. Hunt.
Dips or Counting Out Rhymes: "Eachie, peachie, pearie, plum." *Anonymous.*
Gardener. Emerson.
Haiku: "The piano man." Knight.
Helen's Scar. Nowlan.
In War. Mason.
Last Breath. Chester.
The Lion and the Unicorn. Mother Goose.
March. Hopper.
Morning. Chu Shu-chen.
New Season. Levine.
O Love, how thou art. Newcastle.
Ode on His Majesty's Proclamation, Commanding the Gentry... Fanshawe.
Of the Theme of Love. Newcastle.
Song: Fie My Fum. Ginsberg.
Song: "Heron is harsh with despair." Chamberlain.

Plumage
Absence. Jago.
Atavism. Wylie.
Auspice of Jewels. Riding.
Buffel's Kop. Campbell.
Fern. Hughes.
The Great Moth. Gittings.
Leda Reconsidered. Van Duyn.
Marmion. Scott.
No More, O Maidens. Alcman.
The Poplar's Shadow. Swenson.
The Purple Blemish. Lagerkvist.
Unity. Russell.

Plunge (d) (s)
Dogwood Blossoms. Blue Cloud.
Dolphin Seen Alone. Lattimore.
Ever Watchful. Ta' Abbata Sharra.
Frankenstein. Field.
In a Dream, the Automobile. Marcus.
Mistral. Howes.
Moonlight among the Pines. ""MacDiarmid.

The Mother's Malison, or,
Clyde's Water.
Anonymous.
Salutamus. Brown.
Some Uses for Poetry.
Merriam.
A Son of the Sea. Carman.
Surrender to Christ. Myers.
Te Deum. Le Fort.
The Way Through.
Levertov.
West of Alice. Harney.

Plural
Grammar Lesson. Paston.
Singular Singulars, Peculiar
Plurals. Espy.

Pluto
The Character of Holland.
Marvell.
The Curse of Doneraile.
O'Kelly.
In Cnidus Born, the Consort I
Became. Heraclides.
Ternissa! You Are Fled.
Landor.

Plymouth
The Courtship of Miles
Standish. Longfellow.
Ode to Jamestown.
Paulding.
Thoughts for St. Stephen.
Morley.
The Wreck of the Rambler.
Anonymous.

Pocahontas
You at the Pump (History of
North and South).
O'Hara.

Pocket (s)
The Fairies Break Their
Dances. Housman.
Fire Island Poem. Wakoski.
Hi, Hi, Curlywig.
Anonymous.
The Highwayman's Ghost.
Garnett.
Inspiration. Service.
Itiskit, Itaskit. *Anonymous.*
The Laureate (parody).
Aytoun.
Limerick: "There was a young
person named Crockett."
Smith.
Master Hugues of Saxe-Gotha.
Browning.
The Moon Rises. Garcia
Lorca.
Pockets. Nemerov.
The Reason for Skylarks.
Patchen.
Reflections on a Womb Which
Is Called "Vacant."
Hathaway.
Reward of Virtue.
Guiterman.
Song: Lift Boy. Graves.
Sooner or Later. Cornish.
The Subway Witnesses.
Thomas.
Treasure. Long.
Trinidad, 1958. Mondy.
Twelfth Night. *Anonymous.*
A Way Up on Clinch
Mountain (A vers. with
music). *Anonymous.*
Ye Tourists and Travellers,
Bound to the Rhine.
Hood.

Pod (s)
Three Memorial Sonnets.
Barker.

A Warm Winter Day.
Cooper.

Poem (s)
After My Death. Bialik.
An Afternoon in the Garden.
Edmond.
The Alphabet Came to Me.
Rothenberg.
Apologia. Gascoyne.
Autobiographia Literaria.
O'Hara.
Barbara's Land Revisited–
August 1978. Hobson.
Batches of New Leaves.
London.
Becoming a Nun. Jong.
Black Art. Jones.
Black Holes. Perkins.
Boogie with O. O. Gabugah.
Young.
The Caucasus. Pasternak.
The Change. O'Bruadair.
Colophon for Lan-t'ing Hsiu-
Hsi. Peck.
Come, holy tortoise shell.
Sappho.
Composition in Late Spring.
Layton.
The Correspondence School
Instructor Says Goodbye...
Kinnell.
The Cottage at Chigasaki.
Blunden.
Dawn. Pizarnik.
Dead Center. Whitman.
The Death of the Epileptic
Poet Yesenin. Boyajian.
A Decision. Sodergran.
Doesn't It Seem to You.
Emin.
The Double Play. Wallace.
Economics. Van Duyn.
Elegy and Kaddish.
Rosenmann-Taub.
Entering the Desert: Big
Circles Running. Rose.
Epilogue to a Book of Verse.
Guiterman.
Essay on Rime (excerpt).
Shapiro.
Father-in-Law. Mahon.
Five Visions of Captain Cook.
Slessor.
Frangipanni. *Anonymous.*
A Ghazel of Absence.
Lansing.
Ghosts, Places, Stories,
Questions. Buckley.
The Great Lakes Suite.
Reaney.
Here the Frailest Leaves of
Me. Whitman.
Homage to Literature.
Rukeyser.
The House. Marietta.
Hymn to St. Geryon, I.
McClure.
I Am 25. Corso.
I Can Give Myself to Her.
Yosano Akiko.
I Have Seen the Robins Fall.
Dudek.
I Sing an Old Song.
Williams.
I write to make you suffer.
Kegels.
If It All Went up in Smoke.
Oppen.
Illegitimate Things.
Williams.
Image in a Lilac Tree.
Tiller.

In a Spring Still Not Written
Of. Wallace.
In Sylvia Plath Country.
Jong.
Inspiration. Service.
January 1st. Sexton.
Knowing I Live in a Dark
Age. Acorn.
Lecture Note: Elizabethan
Period. Grigson.
Letter to My Daughter at the
End of Her Second Year.
Finkel.
Lines for a Dead Poet.
Ferry.
The Long Word. Ballantyne.
Looking at Your Face.
Kinnell.
Love's Own Form Is Sufficient
Unto. Vliet.
Love U.S.A. Spivack.
The Man Coming Toward
You. Williams.
The Meadow. Wieners.
Memo from the Desk of X.
Justice.
Metaphysical Shock while
Watching a TV Cartoon.
Rice.
Modern Poetry. Skeen.
My Own House. Ignatow.
My Son, Forsake Your Art.
O'Heffernan.
Natural History. Fargas.
New Numbers: Foreword.
Logue.
The Newly Pressed Suit.
McGough.
Nine Years after Viet Nam.
Quintana.
Notes towards a Poem That
Can Never Be Written.
Atwood.
Notice What This Poem Is
Not Doing. Stafford.
Nude. Witt.
Ode:"Mistah Berrybones, you
daid?" (parody). Zaranka.
Of Modern Poetry. Stevens.
Of Sir Philip Sidney.
Beaumont.
Old Dog. Souster.
On the Death of Ho Chi
Minh. Mandel.
On the Lake Poets.
Townsend.
One Inch Tall. Silverstein.
Ovid on the Dacian Coast.
Thompson.
Paradox. Bennett.
Passin Ben Dorain. Mackie.
Poem. Brodey.
The Poem. Deutsch.
The Poem Becomes Canadian.
Di Cicco.
Poem Called Poem.
Whitehead.
A Poem, in Defence of the
Decent Ornaments of
Christ-Church..(excerpt).
Anonymous.
The Poem in the Park.
Davison.
Poem near the Sea. Frelimo.
Poem to Be Read at 3 a.m.
Justice.
Prayer. Mak.
The Quick and the Dead.
Voronca.
The Rapist. Dunn.
Rhymes. Segal.
Scrimshaw. Hogan.

Shall I Compare Thee to a
Summer's Day? Moss.
Simplicity. Simpson.
Smile. Thomas.
Song for My Little Friends.
Adame.
Stone Hammer Poem.
Kroetsch.
Stonetalk. Hamelin.
Sweet Diane. Barlow.
Talk with a Poet. Bevington.
That Poem. Saez Burgos.
There's Been Some Sort of
Mistake. Gilfillan.
The Thief. Kunitz.
To a Visiting Poet in a
College Dormitiory.
Kizer.
To Build a Poem. Hemp.
To Christian Montpelier.
Jonas.
To Dr. Delany (excerpt).
Swift.
To My Friends. Levi.
Today. Fuller.
Trinity Churchyard.
Rukeyser.
True Confessional.
Ferlinghetti.
Untitled. Randall, Jr.
Verses Written on Sand.
Ravitch.
Villanelle of a Villaness.
Robinson.
Waiting. Cooper.
What Curious Dresses All
Men Wear. Schwartz.
Whom Do You Visualize as
Your Reader? Pastan.
Why Don't I Write in the
Language of Air? Sa'udi.
Why Write Poetry? Davis.
Windfall. Scott.
Wmffre the Sweep.
Humphries.
Writing for Money. Field.
Written on a Leaf.
Anonymous.
You. Tagliabue.
You Hated Spain. Hughes.
Your Phone Call at Eight
A.M. Harjo.

Poesy (ies)
Comradery. Cawein.
In February. Simpson.
Santa Lucia. *Anonymous.*
Speeches at the Barriers
(excerpt). Howe.
To Detraction I Present My
Poesie. Marston.

Poet (ic) (s)
Auspex. Lowell.
Ballade of the Poetic Life.
Squire.
The Beginning of the End.
Hopkins.
Behaviorally. Hollo.
Break, Break, Break (parody).
Squire.
The Bridegroom Is So Tall.
Sappho.
Bring Home the Poet.
MacDonogh.
Calypsomania. Brode.
Childless. MacConmidhe.
Christopher Marlowe.
Drayton.
Cliques and Critics. Sa'ib of
Isfahan.
Coleridge. Watts-Dunton.
The Cow-Chace. André.

The Daughter of Jairus. Tsvetayeva.
Deirdre and the Poets. Milne.
A Description. Herbert of Cherbury.
The Description of Sir Geoffrey Chaucer. Greene.
Dunbar. Spencer.
Early Spring. Tennyson.
The End. Ginsberg.
An Epigram: "Great Charles, among the holy gifts of grace." Jonson.
Epigram: "Loss of our learning brought darkness, weakenss and woe." Anonymous.
Epigram: "Yes, every poet is a fool." Prior.
Epistle to a Lady: Of the Characters of Women. Pope.
Europe. Dudek.
Evanescence. Myers.
Every Critic in the Town. Murray.
Fatales Poetae. Parrot.
First Flight. Wellesley.
Flowers. Mallarme.
For Some Poets. Jackson.
For the Lady Olivia Porter; a Present upon a New-years Day. Davenant.
Glasgow Street. Montgomerie.
Go, Forget Me. Wolfe.
Gormley's Laments (excerpt). Gormley.
The Great Poet. Mu'tamid.
Hanukah. De Haan.
Harangue on the Death of Hayyim Nahman Bialik. Tiempo.
The Harp of David. Yehoash.
Honeysuckle Was the Saddest Odor of All, I Think. Davis.
The Humble Petition of Poor Ben to the Best of Monarchs... Jonson.
If Thou Indeed Derive Thy Light from Heaven. Wordsworth.
The Immortality of Verse. Horace.
In Memorial. Coogler.
In My Old Verses. Guerin.
In the Garden. Schmidt.
In Time of War. Auden.
The Lads of the Village. Smith.
Lamentations of an Au Pair Girl. Feldman.
Laudanum. Anonymous.
Lines Left at Mr. Theodore Hook's House in June, 1834. Barham.
Lost. Fisher.
Mary Hynes. Fallon.
The Masterpiece. Arensberg.
Mending Crab Pots. Smith.
Message to the Bard. Livingston.
The Mistress of Vision. Thompson.
The Motives of Rhythm. Conquest.
Mountain Days. Fraser.
Namby-Pamby. Carey.

The New Physician. Chalmers.
Nights Primarily III. Lipman.
O My Swallows. Toller.
Ode to Quinbus Flestrin. Pope.
Ode to Terminus. Auden.
Of One Who Neither Sees Nor Hears. Gilder.
Of the Confident Stranger. Coolidge.
Of the Mathematician. Matthews.
On a Portrait of Wordsworth by B. R. Haydon. Browning.
On Hearing Mrs. Woodhouse Play the Harpsichord. Davies.
On Poets. Pope.
On the New Laureate. Anonymous.
Onan. Leary.
The Petition of Tom Dermondy to the Three Fates in Council Sitting. Dermody.
Pilgrims. Brodsky.
A Poem of Broken Pieces. Jones.
Poem to My Death. Burgos.
The Poet. Tennyson.
Poet and Peasant. Long.
Poetry. Giovanni.
Poets and Their Bibliographies. Tennyson.
Postscript. Thomas.
Proem. Cawein.
Quite Apart from the Holy Ghost. Mitchell.
De Rerum Natura. Codrescu.
Saadabad. Flecker.
A Sailor at Midnight. Sargent.
San Francisco County Jail Cell B-6. Conyus.
Satire. Geddes.
A Satire. Oldham.
De Senectute. Adams.
A Sessions of the Poets. Suckling.
Soliloquy. Ledwidge.
Song: "Trip it Gipsies, trip it fine." Rowley.
Sonnet: After Dark Vapors. Keats.
Sonnet Sonnet. Engle, Jr.
Sonnets, XII: "Some talke of Ganymede th' Idalian Boy." Barnfield.
Sonnets, XXXII: "If thou survive my well-contented day." Shakespeare.
The Spider. Littleton.
The Storm. Alcaeus.
Talking Bronco. Campbell.
Teaching about Arthropods. Holub.
Tears for Sale. Speyer.
Testing Ground. Hammond.
Theory of Poetry. MacLeish.
"These are the live." Fearing.
The Thrush. Austin.
To a Scottish Poet. Fraser.
To a Swallow. Euenos.
To a Young Poet Who Fled. Logan.

To His Kinswoman, Mistress Penelope Wheeler. Herrick.
To My Children Unknown, Produced by Artificial Insemination. Kirkup.
To Poets. Landor.
To the Thawing Wind. Frost.
Trip It Gipsies, Trip It Fine. Middleton.
Twist-Rime on Spring. Guiterman.
Two Triolets. Robertson.
The Unknown Grave. Landon.
Viewpoint. Scarbrough.
Villanelle. Skeat.
Voice. Spofford.
Voice in the Crowd. Joans.
When Heaven Would Strive to Do the Best She Can. Drayton.
Why Should I Wander Sadly. Susskind.
A Wish. Nicolas.
The Wits. Suckling.
Words to Remind Me of Grandmother. Castro Rios.

Poetry
Advice. Landor.
Alas! 'Tis Very Sad to Hear. Landor.
Art McCooey. Kavanagh.
Be Drunken. Baudelaire.
The Bear. Kinnell.
Before the Poetry Reading. Simpson.
Buster Keaton. McFee.
Childe Roland, etc. Olson.
The Contagiousness of Dreams. Middlebrook.
Erotic Suite (excerpt). Vega.
The External Element. McFadden.
Five Words for Joe Dunn on His 22nd Birthday. Spicer.
It would be wrong for us. Sappho.
Kiss. Young.
Letter to Reed from Lolo. Hugo.
Letter to Tina Koyama from Elliot Bay Park. Mitsui.
Meanwhile. Dailey.
Mugging (excerpt). Ginsberg.
The Mutes. Levertov.
Naked Poetry. Cooley.
No Answer. Whistler.
No Time for Poetry. Fields.
The Observatory Ode. Nims.
On a Portrait of Wordsworth by B. R. Haydon. Browning.
Orchestra. Davies.
Plains. Auden.
Poetry. Moore.
S. T. Colerige Dismisses a Caller from Porlock. Meyer.
Satire. Geddes.
The Secret of Poetry. Anderson.
The Song of the Borderguard. Duncan.
Song Tournament: New Style. Untermeyer.
To A Child. Morley.
To Hear My Head Roar. Taylor.

To Hell with It. O'Hara.
To My Nephew, J.B. Barksdale.
To Remain. Cavafy.

Pogrom
Red White & Another Ism. Otey.

Point (ing) (s)
The Black Finger. Grimke.
Books. Baer.
The Fork of the Road. Renton.
Geometry. Dove.
Good Friday and the Present Crucifixion. Buckley.
How to Catch a Trout. Barker.
A Hundreth Good Poyntes of Husbandry. Tusser.
Liberal or Innocent by Definition. McAuley.
Losing Track. Song.
Metaphysics. Herford.
No Signal for a Crossing. Donovan.
On Visiting My Son, Port Angeles, Washington. Niatum.
P's the Proud Policeman. McGinley.
Shoplifter. Edwards.
A Snapshot of Uig in Montana. Hugo.
Still. Clifton.
Sylvia. Leopardi.

Poise (d)
Burial in the Sand. Sullivan.
Chapel Deacon. Thomas.
Green Rain. Webb.
King Henry VI. Shakespeare.
The Ocotillo in Bloom. Guild.
Relearning the Alphabet. Levertov.
Trees, Who Are Distant. Warr.
The Watcher. Peck.

Poison (ed) (s)
An Angry Word. Bruner.
Astrophel and Stella, XVI. Sidney.
The Bird. Greacen.
Christmas 1924. Hardy.
Distich. Shuraikh.
Ears in the Turrets Hear. Thomas.
From Trollope's Journal. Bishop.
Hunter's Song. Nangolo.
The Life of Service. Davie.
Miss Fogerty's Cake. Anonymous.
Money. Contoski.
On W. R–, Esq. Burns.
The Parting Injunctions. Day.
Quills. Gafford.
Rana, why do you treat me. Mira Bai [(or Mirabai].
Roisin Dubh. De Vere.
Rumor Laetalis. Abelard.
A Sense of Coolness. Troupe.
Seven South African Poems. Wright.
Song for a Lost Art. Brasier.
Sonnets, CXVIII: "Like as to make our appetites more keep". Shakespeare.
Spirit's Song. Bogan.
The Tribes. Fuller.

Poke (s)
Coach into Pumpkin. Reid.
The Lizard. Roethke.
Some Ruthless Rhymes.
  Graham.

Poker
Limerick: "There was an Old
  Man with a poker." Lear.
With Cindy at Vallecito.
  McDonald.

Polar
The Ice King. Demille.
The Season's Lovers.
  Waddington.
Through the Straight Pass of
  Suffering. Dickinson.

Pole (s)
Astronomy. Housman.
The Ballad of Yukon Jake.
  Paramore.
The Circulation.
  Washbourne.
A Dialogue between the
  Resolved Soul and Created
  Pleasure. Marvell.
Fetching Cows. MacCaig.
Great God, Thy Works.
  Byles.
Haircut. Packard.
I See the Boys of Summer.
  Thomas.
The Latin Tongue. Daly.
A Life. Woodberry.
M'Fingal. Trumbull.
Men Working. Millay.
On the Eve of the Feast of the
  Immaculate Conception:
  1942. Lowell.
Pain. Brown.
Sea Burial. Monkman.

Police (man) (men)
Central Park. Lowell.
The Comman Man. Smith.
First Party at Ken Keseys
  with Hell's Angels.
  Ginsberg.
Frisco Whistle Blues. Bell.
Homage to Our Leaders.
  Symons.
In Laughter. Hughes.
James Powell on Imagination.
  Neal.
One Bright Morning...
  Anonymous.
Outlaw. Giorno.
To a Red-Headed Do-Good
  Waitress. Dugan.

Polish
Around the Kitchen Table.
  Gildner.
An Egyptian Pulled Glass
  Bottle in the Shape of a
  Fish. Moore.
The Good Shepherd. Rhys.
Jerusalem. Slonimski.
Philatelic Lessons: The
  German Collection.
  Spingarn.
Preparations. Silko.
There Is No Country.
  Tuwim.

Polite (ness)
Dressed to Kill. Major.
El Gusano. Layton.
Opinions of the New Student.
  Pedroso.
Principal and Principle.
  Anonymous.

Toujours la Politesse.
  Anonymous.
The Visitor. Pyle.

Politics
The Crows. Ghose.
The Rise of Shivaji. Ghose.
Second Hymn to Lenin.
  ""MacDiarmid.

Polka (s)
Can't They Dance the Polka!
  Anonymous.
My Cousin German Came
  From France. *Anonymous.*
The Wooyeo Ball.
  Anonymous.

Poll (s)
The Doubt of Future Foes.
  Elizabeth I.
His Heart Was True to Poll.
  Burnand.
Jack's Fidelity. Dibdin.
On Oliver Goldsmith.
  Garrick.
Portrait. D'Orge.

Pollen
Gathered at the River.
  Levertov.
Lambs Frolicking Home.
  Lape.
The Poems Come Easier.
  Mathew.
Vigil of the Wounded.
  Minthorn.

Polly
Green Corn. *Anonymous.*
A Midsummer Song. Gilder.
Morning. Calverley.
Pretty Polly of Topsham.
  Anonymous.
Wicked Polly. *Anonymous.*

Pomegranates
After Tennyson: "Spoonmeat
  at Bill Porter's in the Hall."
  Lear.
When You Laugh. Jonker.

Pomp
An Angel Describes Truth.
  Jonson.
Idiom of the Hero. Stevens.
Jack and Joan. Campion
New Prince, New Pomp.
  Southwell.
Othello. Shakespeare.
A Palinode. Bolton.
Translator to Translated.
  Pound.

Pond (s)
Central Park, 1916. Stewart.
Coleridge Crossing the Plain
  of Jars: 1833. Dubie.
The Duck. King.
The Elm Beetle. Young.
In Hellbrunn. Trakl.
Little Ponds. Guiterman.
Neutral Tones. Hardy.
Nursery Rhyme. Burke.
The Sand Martin. Clare.
The Snapper. Heyen.
The Upper Canadian.
  Reaney.

Ponder (ed) (s)
Delay Has Danger. Crabbe.
The Image. Hughes.
In These Dissenting Times.
  Walker.
The Mountain. Lermontov.
New Things and Old. Mary
  Madeleva.
Third and Fourth. Rhys.
World's Centre. Dallas.
Written on a Sunday
  Morning. Southey.

Pont-du-lac
Andre's Ride. Beesly.

Pony (ies)
Home, Sweet Home.
  Anonymous.
I Had a Little Pony. Mother
  Goose.
Love Song. Sexton.
The Wandering Cowboy.
  Anonymous.
Windharp. Montague.
The Wooden Horse then said.
  Mastoraki.

Pool (s)
The Ancient Couple on Lu
  Mountain. Van Doren.
August. Wylie.
The Buffalo. Price.
By Loe Pool. Symons.
Cafe Tableau. Swenson.
A Circle, a Square, a Triangle
  and a Ripple of Water.
  Cooper.
Crow's Way. Niatum.
Crumbs. De la Mare.
Falling from the ridge.
  Yozei.
Five Lives. Sill.
Folk Song. *Anonymous.*
God to Man. Talmud.
Going for Water. Frost.
Invocation. Sassoon.
The King o' Spain's Daughter.
  Foster.
The Kingfisher. Davies.
No Empty Hands.
  Brownstein.
On the Third Day. Spender.
Oread. Doolittle.
Pool. Sandburg.
Portrait of the Artist with
  Hart Crane. Wright.
The Ship. Mifflin.
The Sign. Blackburn.
Skunks (excerpt). Jeffers.
A Song of Enchantment. De
  la Mare.
Sonnets, IX: "An isle of trees
  full foliaged in a meadow."
  Irwin.
To Daphne and Virginia.
  Williams.
Villa Thermidor. Hitchcock.
Watching You Sleep under
  Monet's Water Lilies.
  Ruark.
Words. Plath.

Poor
Aberdeen, Mississippi Blues.
  White.
Alas, Poor Man, What Hap
  Have I. Wyatt.
All Things Be Dear but Poor
  Mens Labour. *Anonymous.*
The Anger That Breaks a
  Man Down into Boys.
  Vallejo.
An Apology. Morris.
The Author to Her Book.
  Bradstreet.
Ave! Nero Imperator.
  Osborne.
Back Water Blues.
  Anonymous.
A Bad Joke. Martial
  (Marcus Valerius Martialis).
The Blasted Herb. Weare.
Carol. Short.
A Choctaw Chief Helps Plan
  a Festival... Barnes.
Christ, the Man. Davies.

Christmas in the Olden Time.
  Scott.
A Complaint. Wordsworth.
The Cypress Curtain of the
  Night. Campion.
Dakota Land. *Anonymous.*
The Dean. Porter.
Dear Lady, When Thou
  Frownest. Bridges.
Decision. *Anonymous.*
Dedication, to Leigh Hunt,
  Esq. Keats.
Desolation Is a Delicate
  Thing. Wylie.
El Ropero. Montoro.
Epigrams in Distich, III: The
  Purse-Proud. *Anonymous.*
Et Sa Pauvre Chair.
  Stevenson.
Eternities. Mailer.
Fair Iris and Her Swain.
  Dryden.
Father, Who Mak'st Thy
  Suff'ring Sons. Coxe.
The Flower Market. Po
  Chu-i.
Flowers for the Altar.
  Dolben.
The Frowardness of the Elect
  in the Work of Conversion.
  Taylor.
The Gombeen. Campbell.
The Gourmand (parody).
  Graham.
The Grasshopper. Lovelace.
Hawks. Stephens.
Hymn: "Brightest and best of
  the sons of the morning."
  Heber.
I never lost as much but
  twice. Dickinson.
In Memory of Arthur
  Winslow. Lowell.
Jim Fisk. *Anonymous.*
Joy of Life. Ibn Ezra.
Lady Flower. *Anonymous.*
Lord of Life, All Praise
  Excelling. Moore.
Love Is Like a Dizziness.
  Hogg.
The Madman's Wife. Orlen.
The Marriage of Geraint:
  Enid's Song. Tennyson.
Masters in This Hall.
  Morris.
The Modern World. Ellis.
Mozart. Glatstein.
My God, How Wonderful
  Thou Art. Faber.
Night. Young.
No Bread for the Poor (with
  music). *Anonymous.*
Old Christmas. Howitt.
On an Anniversary after
  Reading the Dates in a
  Book of Lyrics. Synge.
Once I Was a Monarch's
  Daughter. *Anonymous.*
The Orphan Girl.
  Anonymous.
Othello. Shakespeare.
Our Heavenly Father
  (excerpt). Faber.
Our Lady, Help of Christians.
  Claudel.
Our Village. Hood.
The Owl. Thomas.
The Panchatantra: Poverty.
  Anonymous.
The Panther. *Anonymous.*

The Pilgrims of Hope: Sending to the War. Morris.

Poem against the British. Bly.

A Poem upon the Imprisonment of Mr. Calamy in Newgate. Wild.

Poor Kings. Davies.

The Poor Man Pays for All. *Anonymous.*

The Poor Man's Province. Wright.

The Reckoning. Roethke.

The Relapse. Stanley.

Reserve. Reese.

Rock Water Blues. Smith.

Round and Round Hitler's Grave. *Anonymous.*

Seizure. Sappho.

She's Like the Swallow. *Anonymous.*

The Ship That Never Returned (with music). *Anonymous.*

The Silent Lover. Ralegh.

Sleep That Like the Couched Dove. Griffin.

The Small Lady. Smith.

A Song: "While a thousand fine projects are planned ev'ry day." *Anonymous.*

A Soul. Jarrell.

The Splendid Village. Elliott.

Squire and Milkmaid. *Anonymous.*

Sure a Poor Man. *Anonymous.*

System. Stevenson.

That Nature Is a Heraclitean Fire... Hopkins.

The Third Wonder. Markham.

Time's Fool. Pitter.

To His Love When He Had Obtained Her. Ralegh.

To me he seems like a god. Sappho.

To My Daughter Betty, the Gift of God. Kettle.

To Nature. Coleridge.

Tommy's Dead. Dobell.

Tony O! Francis.

Two Birds. *Anonymous.*

Two White Horses in a Line. Two Poor Boys.

The Vietnamese Girl in the Madhouse. Fisher.

While Stars of Christmas Shine. Poulsson.

While We Slept. Wolff.

A Wreath. Herbert.

Popcorn

Pacified. Nickens.

The Popcorn-Popper. Baruch.

Triple Feature. Levertov.

You Take My Hand And. Atwood.

Pope

Alehouse Sonnets: The Dressing Station. Dubie.

Amours de Voyage. Clough.

Commanders of the Faithful. Thackeray.

On the Death of Doctor Swift. Swift.

The Procession: A New Protestant Ballad. *Anonymous.*

Spoken Extempore on the Death of Mr. Pope. *Anonymous.*

Written at Mr. Pope's House at Twickenham. Lyttelton.

Poplars

For My Son. Nims.

In the Dordogne. Bishop.

Last Hill in a Vista. Bogan.

The Poplars. Trotter.

Poppy (ies)

Acon. Doolittle.

After Summer. Marston.

Aftermath. Longfellow.

The Alchemy of Day. Hebert.

The Dirty Dozens. Speckled Red.

Dream Song. Middleton.

In Flanders Fields. McCrae.

Lost City. Jonker.

The Man of Taste. Bramston.

Poppies on the Wheat. Jackson.

Reply to In Flanders Fields. Mitchell.

The Sentry. Lewis.

Spots of Blood. Webb.

There Is Sweet Music Here. Tennyson.

The Thousand and One Nights: The Sleeper. *Anonymous.*

The Village of Reason. Palmer.

Porch (es)

Ben Bolt. *Anonymous.*

Hellenics: Blue Sleep. Bryher.

In Ohio. Wright.

The Lord of All. Markham.

The Poet at Night-Fall. Wescott.

A Poet's Household. Kizer.

Prelude. Benson.

Sittin' on the Porch. Guest.

Porcupine

Porcupines. Wilson, Jr.

Portrait of a Cree. "Hale.

Some Feelings. Benedikt.

Pore (s)

Back to Griggsby's Station. Riley.

The Beginning of the End. Hopkins.

Earthly Love. Bennett.

Jacob Tonson, His Publisher. Dryden.

Pork

Hog Meat. Davis.

A Melton Mowbray Pork-Pie (parody). Le Gallienne.

Mutton (parody). *Anonymous.*

Porridge

Greed. *Anonymous.*

The Man in the Moon. Anonymous.

A Shrewish, Barren, Bony, Nosy Servant. O Bruadair.

Ward Two. Webb.

The Wheel of Fortune. Gunn.

Port (s)

Across the Fields to Anne. Burton.

D'Avalos' Prayer. Masefield.

The Cotton Boll. Timrod.

The Djanggawul Cycle, 11. *Anonymous.*

The Djanggawul Cycle, 12. *Anonymous.*

Earthborn. McArthur.

Echoes from Theocritus. Lefroy.

An Exchange of Hats. Moss.

Four Sonnets to Helen, 1. Ronsard.

The Hope of the World. Watson.

Invocation and Prelude. George.

Jam Fa Jamaica. Lynch.

A Letter to Lord Middleton. Etherege.

The Lover Compareth His State to a Ship... Wyatt.

McAndrew's Hymn. Kipling.

My Father's at the Helm. *Anonymous.*

My Galley. Wyatt.

Now Strike Your Sailes Ye Jolly Mariners! Spenser.

Old Ship Riggers. Cody.

On Board the Leicester Castle. *Anonymous.*

The Pilot. Chapman.

The Port. Mayer.

Sailors' Harbour. Reed.

Sea Voyage. Empson.

Song about My Father. Smither.

To-Day I Saw Bright Ships. Robinson.

To Mr. Newton on His Return from Ramsgate. Cowper.

When the Troubled Sea Swells and Surrounds. Colonna.

Portal

The Night Is Falling. Mangan.

Snowflake on Asphodel. Aiken.

Porter (s)

Ballad of Mistress Death. Devlin.

Running the Batteries. Melville.

Song: "There's a barrel of porter at Tammany Hall." Halleck.

Vox Clero, Lilliburlero. *Anonymous.*

Portion

All Things Wait upon Thee. Rossetti.

Blessed... Soné.

The Crafty Farmer. *Anonymous.*

Fair Annie. *Anonymous.*

Herons. Blaser.

Many Indeed Must Perish in the Keel. Hofmannsthal.

A Nameless Epitaph. Arnold.

Ortus. Pound.

The Pass of Kirkstone. Wordsworth.

This Is the Life. MacNeice.

Time-Servers. Halevi.

To His Retired Friend, an Invitation to Brecknock (excerpt). Vaughan.

Portrait

Christmas Thoughts, by a Modern Thinker. Mallock.

Portrait in Available Light. Miles.

Portrait in Winter. Chapin.

Portugal

Limerick: "There was a young lady of Portugal." Lear.

The Portrait of Prince Henry. Clouts.

Pose (s)

Carnal Knowledge. Gunn.

Come down, You Bunch of Roses, Come down. *Anonymous.*

High Fidelity. Gunn.

Hint from Voiture. Shenstone.

Horse-Girl. Petroski.

Introduction. Parsons.

Photographs. Wright.

Warning to a Guest. Holloway.

Position

The Keyhole in the Door. *Anonymous.*

Limerick: "A new servant maid named Maria." *Anonymous.*

Those Not Confused Are Prisoners of War... Mitchell.

Possess (ed)

Autumn. Lowell.

A Boon. Meredith.

Love. Granville [(or Grenville(].

My Dead. "Rachel" (Rachel Blumstein).

An Ode upon a Question Moved, Whether Love Should Continue For Ever? Herbert of Cherbury.

Portrait. Bogan.

Since Love Is Such That as Ye Wot. Wyatt.

The Swatche Uncut. Hewitt.

Two Voices in a Meadow. Wilbur.

The Village Atheist. Masters.

Possession (s)

Babylon. Russell.

A Bob-Tailed Flush. Painter.

Crows. Booth.

The Dwarf of the Hill Caves. Mphande.

I Dreamed a Dream. Clough.

In Consort to Wednesday, Jan. 1st. 1701... Henchman.

The Lady A. L., My Asylum in a Great Extremity. Lovelace.

Loot. Gunn.

O people who live in the world. Andal.

The Old Bullock Dray. *Anonymous.*

The Old Hymns. Stanton.

Possibility

Ballet. Kaplan.

From a Survivor. Rich.

Girl in Front of the Bank. Wallace.

The Grand Inquisitor's Song. Gilbert.

Linen Town. Heaney.

To a Child. Gardons.

Varium et Mutabile. Wyatt.

Post

The Geraldines. Davis.

I Am a Wild Young Irish Boy. *Anonymous.*

A New Song to Sing about Jonathan Bing. Brown.

Nicholas Nye. De La Mare.

Posterity
A Hint from Herrick.
Aldrich.
John Barleycorn. Burns.
"My days' delight, my
springtime joys fordone."
Ralegh.
To My Dead Friend Ben:
Johnson. King.

Posture (s)
All Hungers Pass Away.
Nortje.
Coriolanus. Shakespeare.
Notes to the Reader.
Bringhurst.
The Sigh. Wanley.

Pot (s)
Baby and I. *Anonymous.*
The Bards. Graves.
Could It Have Been a
Shadow? Shannon.
Crabe dans Calalou.
Anonymous.
Don't Care. *Anonymous.*
Epitaph to Thomas Thetcher.
Anonymous.
Fairyland. Tagore.
Five Little Sisters Walking in
a Row. Greenaway.
Forcing House. Roethke.
The General Elliott. Graves.
Love's Labour's Lost.
Shakespeare.
Modern Love, XXIX.
Meredith.
Nocturne: Homage to
Whistler. Feldman.
On the University of
Cambridge's Burning the
Duke of Monmouth's...
Stepney.
The Pot of Flowers.
Williams.
Problem in Social Geometry–
The Inverted Square!
Durem.
The Reading Lesson.
Murphy.

Potato
Mr. East's Feast.
Anonymous.
Sonnet Found in a Deserted
Mad-House. *Anonymous.*
Vegetables. Farjeon.

Pound (ing) (s)
Asses. Colum.
Bird of Power. Tollerud.
The Grocer and the Gold-
Fish. Thorley.
Had I a Golden Pound.
Ledwidge.
Limerick: "Once a pound-
keeper chanced to
impound." Herford.
Nursery Rhyme: "Judge,
judge, tell the judge."
Anonymous.
A Pint of Water.
Anonymous.
A Satire against Wit.
Blackmore.
Solomon to Sheba. Yeats.
Sweet Riley. *Anonymous.*
Swimmers (excerpt).
Untermeyer.
Willie of Winsbury.
Anonymous.

Pour (ed)
Golgotha. Wheelock.
London Nightfall. Fletcher.

The Night-Piece, to Julia.
Herrick.
Professor Drinking Wine.
Clayre.
The Seasons. Thomson.
Vacation. Stafford.

Poverty
Abdolonymus the Sidonian.
Very.
Bargain. Stone.
Childhood in Jacksonville,
Florida. Cooper.
Computer. Orban.
The Faerie Queene. Spenser.
Francis Jammes: A Prayer to
Go to Paradise with the
Donkeys. Wilbur.
Holy Thursday. Blake.
Is This a Holy Thing to See.
Blake.
Lean Street. Fraser.
Love and Poverty. Pullen.
Market Day. Webb.
May Bright Mushrooms
Grow. Banda.
Poverty, in Imitation of
Milton. Jones.
Poverty Knock. *Anonymous.*
Prayer to Go to Paradise with
the Asses. Jammes.
The Ramble-eer.
Anonymous.
Talking Nothin'.
Anonymous.
The Woman's Labour.
Collier.

Powder (s)
The Ballad of Bunker Hill.
Hale.
Brigham Young.
Anonymous.
Dynamite Song. *Anonymous.*
Fare Ye Well, My Darlin'.
Anonymous.
The Garden of Appleton
House, Laid Out by Lord
Fairfax... Marvell.
The Injured Moon.
Baudelaire.
Primitives. Randall.

Power (ful) (s)
Acts Passed beyond the
Boundary of Mere Wishing.
Spender.
All Hushed and Still Within
the House. Bronte.
All-Souls' Day. Sassoon.
Among the Coffee Cups and
Soup Toureens Walked
Beauty. Spicer.
Armida, the Sorceress.
Tasso.
Ars Poetica. Horace.
Astrophel and Stella, XXXIV.
Sidney.
The Ballad of New Orleans.
Broker.
.Blackfoot Sin-ka-ha. Lewis.
Bottle Up and Go.
Anonymous.
Brasilia. Plath.
Britannia's Pastorals.
Browne.
Columbus and the Mayflower.
Milnes.
Come Love or Death.
Thompson.
Come, Thou Almighty King.
Wesley.
Communal. Fullerton.
The Conquest of Granada.
Dryden.

Consecration of the House.
Fairbridge.
The Country Justice.
Langhorne.
Creatrix. Wickham.
Daphne and Apollo. Prior.
The Death of Richard
Wagner. Swinburne.
The Death of the Gods. An
Ode. Ker.
Defenceless Children, Your
Great Enemy. Smithyman.
The Diggers' Song.
Winstanley.
Disdain Returned. Carew.
Dogrose. Stevenson.
Don Juan. Byron.
English Poetry. Daniel.
An Essay on the Fleet Riding
in the Downes.
Anonymous.
Eternity's Speech against
Time. Greville.
An Excelente Balade of
Charitie. Chatterton.
The Excesses of God.
Jeffers.
The Excursion. Wordsworth.
Fainne Gael An Lae.
Milligan.
The Farewell. Stanley.
Father Mapple's Hymn.
Melville.
A Flemish Madonna. Stork.
Freedom. Ibn Ezra.
From an Irish-Latin
Macaronic. Taylor.
Give Me Leave. "W.
God and the Soul: Nature and
the Child. Spalding.
God Is with Me. Smith.
Golgotha. Kennedy.
The Hills. Cornford.
The Hills. Grenfell.
The House of Life. Rossetti.
How Strange Love Is, in
Every State of
Consciousness. Schwartz.
I Bless Thee, Lord, for
Sorrows Sent. Johnson.
I Grieved for Buonaparte.
Wordsworth.
I Have Not So Much
Emulated the Birds that
Musically Sing. Whitman.
Immanence. Hovey.
The Inscription. Barker.
Invites His Nymph to His
Cottage. Ayres.
Is This the Time To Sound
Retreat? Hoyt.
The Jungle (excerpt).
Fleming.
Lake Leman. Byron.
Let Me Lift Jesus, Lord.
Gardner.
Letter to Manlius Torquatus.
Catullus.
Love's Labour Lost. Tofte.
Love's Triumph. Jonson.
The Lover to the Thames of
London. Turberville.
Memo. Sahl.
A Miracle Indeed. Purohit
Swami.
More Reformation. Defoe.
My Life had stood–a Loaded
Gun. Dickinson.
My Teeth. Ochester.
News of the World. Ridler.
Norris Dam. Rodman.
Not Drunk Is He. Peacock.

O Lord, So Sweet.
Anonymous.
Ode to Naples (excerpt).
Shelley.
On a Pair of Shoes Presented
to Him (excerpt).
O'Rahilly.
On Mercenary and Unjust
Bailiffs. Selyns.
On the Receipt of My
Mother's Picture Out of
Norfolk. Cowper.
Our Father, God. Judson.
Our Times Are in His Hands.
Freeze.
The Passions That We Fought
With. Stickney.
The Plow. Horne.
Power. Rich.
The Power of Music. Lisle.
Psalm XXI. Sidney.
Psalm XXXVI. Sidney.
Psalm–People Power at the
Die-In. Levertov.
Pure Products. Levertov.
The Quiet Tide near
Ardrossan. Turner.
A Rebel. Fletcher.
Reference to a Passage in
Plutarch's Life of Sulla.
Jeffers.
Revolutionary Letters. Di
Prima.
Riches. *Anonymous.*
The Riddle. Brome.
Rome. Hardy.
San Francisco Falling.
Markham.
Santa Caterina. Schotz.
Sapphics Against Anger.
Steele.
Satire. Donne.
Say This of Horses. Moody.
The Sea–in Calm.
"Cornwall.
Service. Browning.
The Shadow of Night.
Chapman.
Shakespearean Soliloquy in
Progress: "To starve, or not
to..."(parody). Ireland.
Silex Scintillans. Vaughan.
Since Love Is Such That as
Ye Wot. Wyatt.
Some San Francisco Poems.
Oppen.
Song of a Jewish Boy. J.M.
Song of Nexahualcoyotl.
Anonymous.
The Song of Roland, XCIX.
Anonymous.
Song: "'Tis said that absence
conquers love!" Thomas.
Songe betwene the Quenes
Majestie and Englande.
Anonymous.
Spirits Unchained.
Kgositsile.
A Summer Noon at Sea.
Sargent.
Summons. Ficke.
The Teacher Sees a Boy.
Morningstar.
The Temper. Herbert.
Temple. Donne.
Their Last Will and
Testament. MacNeice.
Then I Saw What the Calling
Was. Rukeyser.
Thou Art Coming to a King.
Newton.
To a Military Rifle. Winters.

Power

To a Young Poet. Bennett.
To Charinus, a Catamite. Martial (Marcus Valerius Martialis).
To God, on His Sickness. Herrick.
To God, Ye Choir above. Skelton.
To the King on His Navy. Waller.
To the Memory of Sir Isaac Newton (excerpt). Thomson.
To William Camden. Jonson.
Tree-Planting. Smith.
The Triumphs of Thy Conquering Power. Bathurst.
Two Prayers. Gilman.
The Visionary. Bronte.
Waiting and Peeking. Lang.
The Wind. *Anonymous.*
A Winter Hymn–to the Snow. Jones.
The Wisdom of the World. Sassoon.
A World Beyond. Bowditch
Your World. Johnson.

Powerless

Never Again, Orpheus. Antipater of Sidon.
Personal Poem. Smithyman.
The Wooden Tiger. Yellen.

Pox

Elegy XIII. Smith.
A New Simile in the Manner of Swift. Goldsmith.
Of Kate's Baldness. Davies.
The Progress of Marriage. Swift.
To Scilla. Sedley.

Practice (s)

The Animal That Drank Up Sound. Stafford.
Art of the Sonnet: LVI. Orlovitz.
The Birth of St. Patrick. Lover.
Cavalier Lyric. Simmons.
The Double Autumn. Reeves.
An Epistle to Sir Edward Sackville, Now Earl of Dorset. Jonson.
A Ladies Prayer to Cupid. Guarini.
Limerick: "There was a young poet of Thusis." *Anonymous.*
A New Bundling Song. *Anonymous.*
Trees Lose Parts of Themselves inside a Circle of Fog. Ponge.
A Waist. Stein.

Prado

How It Strikes a Contemporary. Browning.

Prague

The City of Prague. Prowse.
Limerick: "There was an old person of Prague." Lear.

Prairie (s)

Big Dam. Moses.
Consummation. Crozier.
Cowboy Jack. *Anonymous.*
The Dying Cowboy. *Anonymous.*
ESP. Revard.
Good-by, Old Paint. *Anonymous.*

The Last Quatrain of the Ballad of Emmet Till. Brooks.
Letters to Walt Whitman. Johnson.
The Lone Prairie. *Anonymous.*
Marie Curie Contemplating the Role of Women Scientists... Frazier.
Paths They Kept Barren. Garmon.
Prairie Lullaby. *Anonymous.*
Prairie Spring. Fallis.
Rosalie, the Prairie Flower. Root.
Saskatchewan Dusk. Buckaway.
A Siding Near Chillicothe. Lattimore.
The Western Trail. Carr.

Praise (d) (s)

After. Grayson.
The American Soldier's Hymn. *Anonymous.*
The Annunciation. Nerses.
As Gentle Dews Distill. Rogers.
As when Some Hungry Fledgling Hears and Sees. Colonna.
Ascension. Donne.
Astrophel and Stella, XXXV. Sidney.
The Bathtub. Pound.
The Beautiful World. Childress.
Behold, the Shade of Night Is Now Receding. Gregory the Great.
Benedicite. Brackett.
Blessed Be the Holy Will of God. *Anonymous.*
Brother Astolfo Sated Appetite. Aretino.
The burning–at first–would be probably worst. Stephen.
Caelica, XCIII. Greville.
The Campaign. Addison.
Canzone: He Beseeches Death for the Life of Beatrice. Dante Alighieri.
The Cell. Rostrevor.
Christ for the World! We Sing. Wolcott.
The Christian Life. Longfellow.
Christmas Day. Young.
Christopher Marlowe. Swinburne.
The Church the Garden of Christ. Watts.
Columbus at the Convent. Trowbridge.
Commendatory Sonnet to Hoby's Courtier. Sackville.
Courage Means Running. Empson.
Critics. Martial (Marcus Valerius Martialis).
Crowded Ways of Life. Gresham.
Dear Brethren, Are Your Harps in Tune? Smith.
Dear March, come in! Dickinson.
Deirdre (excerpt). Yeats.
Dejection. Bridges.
A Description. Herbert of Cherbury.
Diana. Constable.

Dog, Dog in My Manger. Barker.
Echoes of Love's House. Morris.
Edge-Hill. Jago.
Elegy for a Bad Poet, Taken from Us Not Long Since. Nims.
Elegy for a Diver. Meinke.
Elegy on Albert Edward the Peacemaker. *Anonymous.*
Ellis Park. Hoyt.
Emblems. Quarles.
En Passant. Codrescu.
England's Triumph. *Anonymous.*
Epigram: "I dreamt that I was God Himself." Pound.
Epigram: "Neither in idleness consume thy days." Landor.
The Epitaph. Hinkson.
Epithalamium for the Dedication of a Church. *Anonymous.*
The Everlasting Contenders. Patchen.
The Experience. Taylor.
Facing the New Year. Pearse.
Fain Would My Thoughts. Austin.
First Praise. Williams.
The Flea Circus at Tivoli. Willard.
Floods Swell Around Me, Angry, Appalling. Eddy.
For Every Day. Havergal.
For Her Sake. Reid.
For Inspiration. Michelangelo.
Four Prayers, II. *Anonymous.*
A Friend. Johnson.
From All That Dwell below the Skies. Watts.
From the Crag. Leib.
The Georges. Landor.
Georgics. Virgil (Publius Vergilius Maro).
God Everywhere. Ibn Ezra.
The God of Galaxies. Van Doren.
God of Our Fathers, Whose Almighty Hand. Roberts.
The Good-Natur'd Man: Prologue. Johnson.
The Goods She Can Carry: Canticle of Her Basket Made of Reeds. Ruark.
Guide to the Perplexed. Malouf.
Hail, Thou Once Despised Jesus! Bakewell.
Haleluiah; or, Britain's Second Remembrancer: Hymne I. Wither.
Hamlet. Shakespeare.
A Heart to Praise Thee. Herbert.
The Heavenly Aeroplane. *Anonymous.*
Hiking up Hieizan with Alam Lau/Buddha's Birthday 1974. Hongo.
How Glorious Are the Morning Stars. Keach.
Hurrah for Greer County. *Anonymous.*
Hush, Honey. Saunders.
Hymn. Call.
Hymn. Key.

Hymn for Easter Morn. *Anonymous.*
Hymn of Apollo. Shelley.
Hymn to Athena. *Anonymous.*
I Yield Thee Praise. Cleveland.
In God's Eternity. Ballou I.
In Search of a Short Poem for My Grandmother. Hardeman.
Instruction in the Art. Booth.
It Started. Baca.
Je T'Adore. Kinsella.
Jerusalem Delivered (excerpt). Tasso.
A Joyful Sound It Is. Strebeck.
Jubilate Canis. Jong.
Judgment. Channing-Stetson.
The King of Love. Baker.
A Lark's Nest. Smart.
A Last Word. Sarton.
The Lay of the Last Minstrel. Scott.
Lecompton's Black Brigade. Halpine.
Lemons, Lemons. Young.
Let Tyrants Shake Their Iron Rod. Billings.
Let Us Gather at the River. Piercy.
Letter from a Death Bed. Ciardi.
Letter to the Front. Rukeyser.
Light and Rejoicing to Israel. *Anonymous.*
Lines on Being Refused a Guggenheim Fellowship. Whittemore.
A Little Page's Song. Percy.
A Little While to Love and Rave. Hoffenstein.
The Living God. Ben Judah.
Lo, What Enraptured Songs of Praise. Streeter.
London, Hast Thou Accused Me. Surrey.
The Loss of the Due Dispatch. *Anonymous.*
The Lover Exhorteth His Lady to Be Constant. *Anonymous.*
The Lucky Coin. Clarke.
May 20: Very Early Morning. Shaw.
Meditations. Taylor.
Moonlight in Italy. Kinney
Much Ado about Nothing. Shakespeare.
My Dog Dash. Ruskin.
My November Guest. Frost.
My Song Is Love Unknown. Crossman.
Mysterious Presence! Source of All. Beach.
Neptune. Campion.
New Prince, New Pomp. Southwell.
Non Nobis Domine. Kipling.
Now Is Farewell. Salkeld.
O Holy, Holy, Holy Lord. Eastburn.
O How I Love Thy Law. Watts.
O Lord of Life. Gladden.
Ode to Nea. Moore.
The Old Cottagers. Clare.
The Old Hundredth. Kethe.

On a Fortification at Boston Begun By Women. Tompson.
On His Friend, Joseph Rodman Drake. Halleck.
On the Big Horn. Whittier.
The Opening Year. *Anonymous.*
Other Sheep I Have, Which Are Not of This Fold. Bryant.
Our Lady of the Libraries. Ignatius.
Our States, O Lord. Mycall.
A Palinode. Bolton.
Paradise Lost. Milton.
The Pariah's Prayer. Goethe.
The Parliament of Bees. Day.
Peter Quince at the Clavier. Stevens.
Petition. Drinkwater.
Petition to the Queen. Ralegh.
Pewter. Gilbert.
The Phoenix Answered. Ridler.
Pied Beauty. Hopkins.
A Poet. Hardy.
Praise. Rilke.
Praise to Jesus! Ball.
Prayer at Dawn. O'Shea.
Prayer of Thanksgiving. Baker.
A Prayer to Be Said When Thou Goest to Bed. Seager.
Precious Child, So Sweetly Sleeping. Hoppe.
Preludes. Patmore.
Pretty Twinkling Starry Eyes. Breton.
The Pride of a Jew. Halevi.
Proclaim the Lofty Praise. Judson.
Psalm VII. Sidney.
Psalm XXVI. Sidney.
Psalm XXXV. Sidney.
A Psalm of Praise (excerpt). Baxter.
A Psalm Praising the Hair of Man's Body. Levertov.
Published Correspondence: Epistle to the Rapalloan. MacLeish.
Question to Life. Kavanagh.
The Rape of the Lock. Pope.
Reconciliation. Doten.
Relearning the Alphabet. Levertov.
Reminder. *Anonymous.*
The Resolve. Chudleigh.
The Rise of Shivaji. Ghose.
Samson Agonistes. Milton.
Self-Examination. *Anonymous.*
Send Forth, O God, Thy Light and Truth. Adams.
Sent Ahead. Hay.
Silex Scintillans. Vaughan.
Sincere Praise. Watts.
So Fair, So Sweet, Withal So Sensitive. Wordsworth.
Some Day. Addison.
Song of Praise to Mary. "Angelus Selesius" (Johannes Scheffler).
A Song: "When lovely woman, prone to folly." (parody). *Anonymous.*

Songs for a Three-String Guitar. Sedar-Senghor.
Sonnet. Wolf.
Sonnets, LIX: "If there be. Shakespeare.
Sonnets, CVI: "When in the chronicle of wasted time." Shakespeare.
Speak This Kindly to Her. Bagg.
Success. Empson.
A Teacher's Prayer. Havergal.
Thanksgiving. Ketchum.
Thanksgiving. Sangster.
Thanksgivings for the Beauty of His Providence. Traherne.
That Summer's Shore. Ciardi.
Thou Art of All Created Things. Calderon de la Barca.
Thou Beautiful Sabbath. *Anonymous.*
Thy Garden, Orchard, Fields. Pastorius.
To a Bird after a Storm. Vaughan.
To a Certain Lady, in Her Garden. Brown.
To Bulow–2. Platen.
To Edward Fitzgerald. Tennyson.
To God, Ye Choir above. Skelton.
To His Honoured and Most Ingenious Friend, Master Charles Cotton. Herrick.
To Li Po from Tu Fu. Kizer.
To M. E. W. Chesterton.
To Mary Unwin. Cowper.
To My Booke. Jonson.
To My Father. Ray.
To the Immortal Memory of the Halibut on Which I Dined This Day. Cowper.
Translation. Lesser.
Trusting Jesus. Renfrow.
Tune Me, O Lord, into One Harmony. Rossetti.
The Twenty-Third Psalm. Herbert.
The Unawkward Singers. Ferry.
An Unpraised Picture. Burton.
Variations on a Theme by George Herbert. Zaturenska.
Verbum Supernum. Ambrose of Milan.
The Virtuous Wife. Susskind.
The Vow of Washington. Whittier.
Watching Gymnasts. Francis.
While the Bells Ring. Dunetz.
Who Here Can Cast His Eyes Abroad. Holmes.
Widsith, the Minstrel. Anonymous.
William Shakespeare to Mrs. Anne,... Gray.
With Christ and All His Shining Train. Prince.
With God and His Mercy. Rosenius.

The Works of God. Ibn Ezra.
A Wreath. Herbert.
Your Last Drive. Hardy.

Pray (ed) (er) (ers) (ing) (s)
25 December 1960. Jonker.
Address to a Haggis. Burns.
Adultery. Dugan.
After. Grayson.
After the Pleasure Party. Melville.
Alcoholic. Berryman.
The Aliscamp. Mistral.
Amoretti, XX. Spenser.
The Ancestors. Barrows.
Annie died the other day. Cummings.
An Ante-Bellum Sermon. Dunbar.
An Antipastoral Memory of One Summer. Smith.
Ascension. Donne.
At the Edge of the Day. Urmy.
Aunt Jane. Nowlan.
Be Kind to Me. Sappho.
Because You Prayed. "B.
Blooming Nelly. Burns.
The Bohemian Hymn. Emerson.
Broken Music. Rossetti.
The Buoy-Bell. Turner.
A Butterfly in Church. McClellan.
Buy Us a Little Grain. Lavant.
A Call to Pentecost. Tyler.
Candle-Lighting Song. Ketchum.
A Cathedral. Vinaver.
Christian, Be Up. Nathan.
The Christian's New-Year Prayer (excerpt). Wilcox.
A Christmas Dawn at Sea. Morgan.
Clonmel Jail. *Anonymous.*
The Coconut. Milne.
Cole Younger. *Anonymous.*
The Coweta County Courthouse. Robinson.
The Croppy Boy. McBurney.
The Cuckoo and the Nightingale. Clanvowe.
The Curse: A Song. Herrick.
The Dark Scent of Prayer. Drachler.
The Day Is Gone. Keats.
The Dead Make Rules. Davies.
December Night. Merwin.
A Devout Lover. Randolph.
The Dispensary. Garth.
The Distracted Puritan. Corbet.
Don Juan. Byron.
The Donkey. *Anonymous.*
The Dream of Gerontius. Newman.
Dream Songs. Berryman.
The Drummer Boy of Shiloh. *Anonymous.*
The Dying Cowboy. *Anonymous.*
Earth. Wheelock.
Elegy: to Delia. Hammond.
Eleven Addresses to the Lord. Berryman.
Ensamples of Our Saviour. Southwell.
Epitaphs of the War, 1914-18. Kipling.

Ev'ry Time I Feel de Spirit. *Anonymous.*
Evangeline. Longfellow.
Evening Prayer. *Anonymous.*
The Excursion. Wordsworth.
Facing the New Year. Pearse.
The Feast of Stephen. Hecht.
Fir Forest. Fuller.
For the Marriage of Faustus and Helen. Crane.
Founder's Day. Bridges.
Four Prayers, IV. *Anonymous.*
Friends. Johnson.
From Countless Hearts. Burket.
From St. Luke's Hospital. L'Engle.
Give Us Sober Men. Isenhour.
God Knows the Answer. Whitney.
God Moves on the Water. *Anonymous.*
God Prays. Morgan.
Graven on the Palms of His Hands. Wesley.
Hands up. Rudolf.
Haverhill, 1640-1890. Whittier.
Help Us to Live. Keble.
The Hermit's Song. *Anonymous.*
Hertza. Fondane.
Himself (excerpt). Ellis.
The History of the U.S. Stoner.
Home, Sweet Home. Bunner.
The Hour of Prayer. Elliott.
The House of Life. Rossetti.
How Can I See You, Love. Vogel.
Hugh Spencer's Feats in France (B version). *Anonymous.*
I Couldn't Hear Nobody Pray. *Anonymous.*
I loved you; even now I may confess. Pushkin.
I Loved You Once (From the Russian of Alexander Pushkin). Randall.
The Iliad. Homer.
In Brittany. Weekes.
The Incantation. Amergin.
The Indian Ghost Dance and War. Prather.
Inscape. Litwack.
Inscription on a Shrine Near Ischl. Elizabeth.
It's Me, O, Lord. *Anonymous.*
Joculator Domini. Mary John Frederick
John-John. Macdonagh.
Journey. Thompson.
The Judas Goat. Musgrave.
The Land of Cokaygne. *Anonymous.*
Landscape of Violence. Currey.
The Larger Prayer. Cheney.
The Leaves of Life. *Anonymous.*
A Legend. Procter.
Lilith. Goll.
Lives. Mahon.
Locusts of Silence. Mayne.

The Lord in the Wind.
Picot.
Louise. Smith.
Madrigal: "Penelope, that
longed for the sight."
Byrd.
Manchan's Prayer.
Anonymous.
Mary Mild, Good Maiden.
Cille.
Mary Shepherdess. Pickthall.
Master's in the Garden Again.
Ransom.
Maumee Ruth. Brown.
Memo. Flanner.
The Merry-ma-Tanzie.
Anonymous.
Midnight Prayer. Bialik.
The Misses Poar Drive to
Church. Pinckney.
More Prayer. *Anonymous.*
A Morning Prayer.
Perpetuo.
Mother of Men. Southwold.
Mrs. Frances Harris's
Petition. Swift.
Muhammedan Call to Prayer.
Bilal.
My Father's Voice in Prayer.
Nottage.
My Period Had Come for
Prayer. Dickinson.
The Negro's Tragedy.
McKay.
A Negro Soldier's Viet Nam
Diary. Martin.
Night. Jami.
The Night Has Twenty-Four
Hours. Pietri.
No Doubt. Adams.
Now I Lay Me Down to
Sleep. *Anonymous.*
O Gracious Father of
Mankind. Tweedy.
O Martyred Spirit.
Santayana.
Of Pardons, Presidents, and
Whiskey Labels. Snyder.
Oh, Hear Me Prayin'(Lord,
Feed My Lam's).
Anonymous.
Ole Moke... Littlebird.
On the Day of Atonement.
Amichai.
Orange County Plague:
Scenes. Lieberman.
Our Prayer of Thanks
(excerpt). Sandburg.
Pagett, M. P. Kipling.
Parting as Descent.
Berryman.
The Passing of the Unknown
Soldier. Owens.
Pastourelle. *Anonymous.*
The Petition of the
Orangemen of Ireland.
Moore.
The Phoenix and the Turtle.
Shakespeare.
Pocahontas. Morris.
The Poetry of a Root Crop.
Kingsley.
Powers and Times Are Not
Gods. Auden.
Pray! Wells.
Pray, Christian, Pray!
Anonymous.
Pray-Give-Go. Flint.
Prayer. *Anonymous.*
Prayer. Bilderdijk.
A Prayer. Tuwim.
Prayer–Answer. Cheney.

A Prayer for Faith.
Sangster.
Prayer in a Country Church.
Van Dusen.
Prayer of a Patriot. Von
Schlichten.
A Prayer of the Peoples.
MacKaye.
Prayer to Isis. Walsh.
Prayer to St. Patrick.
Ninine.
Prayer to the Virgin.
Anonymous.
The Quaker of the Olden
Time. Whittier.
Qui Laborat, Orat. Clough.
Religion Is a Fortune I Really
Do Believe. *Anonymous.*
The Return. Strong.
Riddle: "What God never
sees." *Anonymous.*
Rising High Water Blues.
Jefferson.
Rolling John (excerpt).
Wood.
A Roman Officer Writes.
Doughty.
Rookhope Ryde.
Anonymous.
Roslin and Hawthornden.
Van Dyke.
Sabbath Reflection. Wrafter.
Salami. Levine.
Scroll. Moss.
Seaconk Plain Engagement.
Tompson.
The Secret Place. Pollard.
The Secret Place of Prayer.
Adams.
The Semblables. Williams.
The Sentinel. Flint.
Shadows. Claudel.
Shame. Rimbaud.
She was my staff and I am
blind. Jana Bai.
Sheltering the Same Needs.
Kuo.
Sheriff. Bierce.
The Ship Rambolee.
Anonymous.
Sir Walter Ralegh to His Son.
Ralegh.
The Sisters. Tabb.
Skin the Goat's Curse on
Carey. *Anonymous.*
So Young Ane King.
Lindsay.
Song: "Dark was de night an'
col' was de groun'."
Anonymous.
Songs of Labor: Dedication.
Whittier.
Sonnet VII. Sharp.
Sonnets, CXLIII: "Lo, as a
careful housewife runs to
catch." Shakespeare.
The Speech of the Dead.
Ridler.
Supplication. Pierce.
Sweeney, Old and Phthisic,
among the Hippopotami
(parody). Cummings.
Sweet Hour of Prayer.
Walford.
Tales of a Wayside Inn.
Longfellow.
The Temple. Sisson.
The Testament of Beauty.
Bridges.
That Holy Thing.
Macdonald.

They Cast Their Nets in
Galilee. Percy.
Three Helpers in Battle.
Coleridge.
Three Songs from the Temple.
Domanski.
To a Bird after a Storm.
Vaughan.
To Eros. Anacreon.
To the Right Hon. Henry
Pelham... Moore.
To the Wayfarer.
Anonymous.
To William Wordsworth.
Coleridge.
Tom Dunstan, or, The
Politician. Buchanan.
The Tree of Silence. Miller.
Two Old Lenten Rhymes: II.
Anonymous.
An Unpraised Picture.
Burton.
Upon Parson Beanes.
Herrick.
A Valediction. La Follette.
The Varuna. Boker.
Waiting for the Rain.
Mnthali.
Weakness of Nature.
Froude.
Week-Seek. Tollerud.
Whack Fol the Diddle.
Kearney.
What Is Prayer?
Montgomery.
What Schoolmasters Say.
Seymour-Smith.
When I Admire the
Greatness. Steendam.
When Nobody Prays.
Clapper.
When Ol' Sis' Judy Pray.
Campbell.
Who Has Our Redeemer
Heard. Foster.
Who Prayed? *Anonymous.*
Who Shapes a Balustrade?
Aiken.
Windigo. Jiles.
Wish of Manchin of Liath.
Anonymous.
Wishmakers' Town. Young.
Without Ceremony. Miller.
Yawcob Strauss. Adams.
Ye Old Mule. Wyatt.
You Do Not Have to Love
Me. Cohen.
The Young Man and the
Young Nun. Mackie.

Prayer-book
Sir Hugh, or, The Jew's
Daughter (N version).
Anonymous.

Prayer's Effect
Romeo and Juliet.
Shakespeare.

Prayer Shawls
Benediction. Sklarew.

Prayer Sticks
Offering. *Anonymous.*

Prayere
What Tidings? Audelay.

Prayerful Mood
Kibbutz Sabbath. Levi ben
Amittai.

Prayerless
Goosey Goosey Gander.
French.

Prayers
Annie and Willie's Prayer.
Snow.

At Her Fair Hands.
Davison.
Beneath Thy Wing. Bialik.
Chomei at Toyama. Bunting.
Debussy and Proust.
Tagliabue.
Divine Songs to Ahura
Mazda. Zoroaster.
Epigram: "Passing the flower-
stalls." Strato.
For David Shapiro. Lehman.
Here Is the Church, and Here
Is the Steeple. *Anonymous.*
Homesick. Lasker-Schüler.
Honolulu and Back. Logan.
Hymn: "Brightest and best of
the sons of the morning."
Heber.
Hymn for the Dedication of a
Church. Norton.
I'll Remember You, Love, in
My Prayers. *Anonymous.*
In All the Argosy of Your
Bright Hair. Thompson.
Last Night We Had a
Thunderstorm in Style.
Stevenson.
Little Fred. *Anonymous.*
Looking for Maimonides:
Tiberias. Kaufman.
Lord, Hear My Prayer.
Clare.
Motley. De La Mare.
My Little Girl. Peck.
Now and Afterwards. Craik.
Old Man Mountain. Noyes.
Outward Bound. Tylee.
The Powerline Incarnation.
Murray.
Praise of Zeus. Aratus of
Soli.
Prayer to the Virgin of
Chartres. Adams.
Psalm XX. Sidney.
A Rat. *Anonymous.*
A Solis Ortus Cardine.
Ford.
To Heaven. Jonson.
Victimae Paschali Laudes.
Wipo.
Westland Row. Stephens.
When the Curtains of Night
Are Pinned Back (with
music). *Anonymous.*
Ye Scattered Nations.
Cradock.

Praysed
Amoretti, XXXVIII.
Spenser.

Preach (er) (ers)
The Atheist Buries His Son.
Abu'l-Atahija.
Did any bird come flying.
Rossetti.
Ha Ha This-a-Way.
Anonymous.
Mother Country. Rossetti.
My Love, She's but a Lassie
Yet. Burns.
My Owen. Downing.
The Old Chartist. Meredith.
The Parish Register. Crabbe.
Phoebe Dawson. Crabbe.
The Preacher's Prayer.
Macdonald.
The Preacher's Wife.
Anonymous.
Sonnet: "Lift not the painted
veil which those who live."
Shelley.
This Sun Is Hot.
Anonymous.

Upon Parson Beanes. Herrick.
We're a' Dry wi' the Drinkin' o't. *Anonymous.*
The Windy Bishop. Watson.

Precious
August 13, 1966. Hine.
Be Kind. Courtney.
The Canterbury Tales: The Knight's Interruption of the Monk's Tale. Chaucer.
Charlotte Bronte. "Coolidge.
The End of Man Is Death. Ibn Ezra.
The Faithful Few. Shuler.
An Irish Lullaby. Graves.
The Letter. *Anonymous.*
A Marching Litany to Our Martyrs. Mapanje.
Mothers. *Anonymous.*
The Odyssey. Homer.
On Roofs of Terry Street. Dunn.
People Hide Their Love. Wu-Ti.
Poem Ending with an Old Cliche. Zimmer.
R. W. Gold.
A Sonnet to My Mother. Heine.
Sweet Rivers of Redeeming Love. Granade.

Precision
Death of Little Boys. Tate.
In Cold Hell, In Thicket. Olson.
La Reproduction Interdite / Not to Be Reproduced. Fraser.
The Steam Threshing-Machine. Turner.
Watching Gymnasts. Francis.

Prefer
Epigram: "Of virtues I most warmly bless." Hopkins.
Helen. Lamb.
I Can Fly. Holman.
Juventius, Could You Not Find in This Great Crowd of Men. Catullus.
Modern Love, XXXI. Meredith.
The One Who Runs Away. Callimachus.
Parisian Nectar. Burgess.
Said Aristotle Unto Plato. Wister.
Sentimental Lines to a Young Man Who Favors Pink Wallpaper... Fishback.
Violins in Repose. Plescoff.

Pregnant
The City Mouse and the Garden Mouse. Rossetti.
Folds of a White Dress/Shaft of Light. Keenan.
Long History of the Short Poem. Hoover.
Men tell and talk. Francisco.
Tracks. Torain.

Presence (s)
Absence. McKay.
Animal Magnetism. Halloran.
At half-past three. Dickinson.
Awake My Soul, Betimes Awake. Chanler.
Ballata: Concerning a Shepherd-Maid. Cavalcanti.

Beyond the Wall. Maloney.
The Gascon Punished. La Fontaine.
God's Presence Makes My Heaven. Smith.
The Horses. Muir.
Hymn to Artemis, the Destroyer. Zaturenska.
In an Empty Window. Fraser.
Letter to the Revolution. Griffin.
The Life of San Millan (excerpt). Berceo.
Lilies of the Valley. Gardner.
The Lion for Real. Ginsberg.
Ode: Solitude, at an Inn. Warton, Jr..
On My Stand. Scott.
Presences. Karelli.
Punch, Brothers, Punch! *Anonymous.*
Room Poems. Bachar.
Sailing in Crosslight. Skeen.
See How the Rising Sun. Scott.
A Solitude. Levertov.
Song for a Transformation (excerpt). Arrivi.
Sonnets from the Portuguese, XX. Browning.
The Sun Now Risen. Beissel.
Tellus. Huntington.
To the Child Jesus. Van Dyke.
Tree-Planting. Smith.
When Winds Are Raging. Stowe.

Present (s)
Alma Mater's Roll. Hale.
At the Nursing Home. Cain.
Bologna, and Byron. Rogers.
Britannia's Pastorals. Browne.
Castle Rock. Morgan.
Christmas Tree. Cook.
The Conquerors. Dunbar.
Enough. Moore.
For a Birthday. Emans.
Glass was the street. Dickinson.
Have I, This Moment, Led Thee from the Beach. Landor.
Henry K. Sawyer. *Anonymous.*
I in Thee, and Thou in Me. Cranch.
I Sing the Mighty Power of God. Watts.
Little Tommy Yesterday. Glasgow.
Loulou and Her Cat. Locker-Lampson.
The Man Coming Toward You. Williams.
O Miserable Sorrow, withouten Cure. Wyatt.
On Leaving Ullswater. Raine.
Persuasions to Love. Carew.
A Plea for Promiscuity. Waller.
Proust on Noah. Silberschlag.
The Question. Shelley.
September. Arnold.
Shores of Anguish. Portal.
Soliloquy by the Shore. Scholten.

Solitude. Beattie.
Song for Seven Parts of the Body, 7. Kumin.
Song: "Me Cupid made a Happy Slave." Steele.
Sunday at the State Hospital. Ignatow.
Temperature. Malanga.
To George Pulling Buds. O'Keeffe.
To Phillis. Waller.
Waking in Nice. Traxler.
The Zucca (excerpt). Shelley.

Preserve (d)
The Progress of a Divine (excerpt). Savage.
The Shash. *Anonymous.*
To Mr. Jervas, with Fresnoy's Art of Painting, Translated by Dryden. Pope.
Why Should Vain Mortals Tremble. Niles.

President (s)
God Save Our President. Janvier.
Leetla Giorgio Washeenton. Daly.
Mulberry Street. Herschberger.
Nothing New. Herrick.
Old Zip Coon (Turkey in the Straw). Farrell.
The Professor Waking. Tate.
She Was a Beauty. Bunner.
To Marie Osmond. Skelley.
Tornado Soup. Redwing.
Trumpet Voluntary. Hoover.
Up Rising. Duncan.

Press (ed) (ing)
Critics. Swift.
Days through Starch and Bluing. Fulton.
A Fable. Frere.
Fill a Glass with Golden Wine. Henley.
The Indian Serenade. Shelley
The Letter. Blight.
The Lonesome Dove. *Anonymous.*
New and Old Gospel. Mackey.
An Ode to Master Endymion Porter, upon His Brother's Death. Herrick.
On Donne's Poetry. Coleridge.
The Only Jealousy of Emer (excerpt). Yeats.
The Reporters. Levy.
Satire. Pope.

Pressure
In Memoriam A.H.H., CXIX. Tennyson.
The Seesaw. Williams.
The Verdict. Cameron.

Prester John
On the Edge of the Pacific. Maynard.
Sonnets of the Months. San Geminiano.

Presume
I Kissed You. *Anonymous.*
On Seeming to Presume. Durrell.

Pretend (s)
Absent Star. Duval.
The Busy Body. Field.
Dido's Hunting. Surrey.
Epigram: "Hetero-sex is best." Marcus Argentarious.

Happy New Year, Anyway. Cole.
The Hawk. Yeats.
Innocent Landscape. Wylie.
Love U.S.A. Spivack.
Take My Song of Love to Heart. *Anonymous.*
To Nowhere. Ignatow.
The Traveler. Lindsay.
The Two Parents. ""MacDiarmid.
Virgidemiarum. Hall.

Pretty
All My Pretty Ones. Sexton.
The Balloon Man. Fyleman.
Benjamin Franklin. Benét.
Budgie Finds His Voice (parody). Cope.
Fain Would I Have a Prettie Thing to Give unto My Ladie. *Anonymous.*
Falling Snow. *Anonymous.*
Haiku: "Death it can bring." Issa.
Hair Ribbons. *Anonymous.*
I Lived in a Town. *Anonymous.*
It's Almost Done. *Anonymous.*
John Kinsella's Lament for Mrs. Mary Moore. Yeats.
The Jolly Soldier. *Anonymous.*
Leicester Chambermaid. *Anonymous.*
Nichols Fountain. Miner.
The Nine. Sheffield.
Patience Is a Virtue. *Anonymous.*
Philadelphia. *Anonymous.*
A Pretty Woman. Ortiz.
Sweet and Low. Barnby.
There's More Pretty Girls Than One. *Anonymous.*
To and on Other Intellectual Poets.... Guthrie.
The Trees So High. *Anonymous.*
Two Englishmen. Stewart.
Upon a Girl of Seven Years Old. Pope.

Prevail (ed) (ing) (s)
Encouraged. Dunbar.
The Lass and the Friar. Burns.
The Patient Church. Newman.
A Storm from the East. Whittemore.
Truth. Patmore.

Prey
The African Chief. Bryant.
The Art of Poetry. Dryden.
As He Lay Dying. Stow.
Cadenus and Vanessa (excerpt). Swift.
Fly-Fishing. Gay.
Gastrology (excerpt). Archestratus.
The Hunt of the Poem. Behm.
A Letter to John Donne. Sisson.
Man and Beast. Dyment.
Miser. LeClaire.
The Nightingale. *Anonymous.*
On Foinaven. Saunders.
Soliloquy on Death. Fiawoo.
Tamer and Hawk. Gunn.
The Undreamed. Emans.

The Wounded Man and the
Swarm of Flies. Somervile.
The Wry Rowan.
Anonymous.

Price
Amoretti, XI. Spenser.
The Bear. Hughes.
Bear, Cat and Dove.
Greenberg.
Beginners. Whitman
Customs Change.
Anonymous.
Epitaphs of the War, 1914-18.
Kipling.
Judaism. Newman.
Limerick: "A bugler named
Douglas MacDougal."
Nash.
A Mother before a Soldier's
Monument. Rockett.
No Greater Love.
Anonymous.
The Offender. Levertov.
The Other Side. Heaney.
Poem for My Mother.
Jaeger.
Portrait of the Autist as a
New World Driver.
Murray.
Publication Is the Auction.
Dickinson.
The Second Life of Lazarus.
Harwood.
This Is the Horror That,
Night after Night. Gould.
To the Blacksmith with a
Spade. O'Sullivan.
Your Thoughts Don't Have
Words Every Day.
Dickinson.

Prick (s)
Epitaph on a Willing Girl.
Rowlandson.
I Have Something for You to
Laugh at, Cato. Catullus.
On Mr. Pricke. *Anonymous.*
The Opponent Charm
Sustained. Greenberg.
To Bellinus. *Anonymous.*
To Polycharmus. Martial
(Marcus Valerius Martialis).

Pride
Adam and Eve. Sisson.
The Alley. An Imitation of
Spenser. Pope.
Amantium Irae. Dowson.
Amoretti, V. Spenser.
At Cambridge. McGaffin.
The Battle of Plattsburg Bay.
Scollard.
Called Proud. Landor.
Cervera. Shadwell.
The Cow Wandering in the
Bare Field. Jarrell.
David. Davies.
Decoration Day. Barbour.
Dewdrop, Wind and Sun.
Skipsey.
Do They Whisper behind My
Back? Schwartz.
Elegy on the Death of Mme.
Anna Pavlova (excerpt).
Meyerstein.
Epigram: "Of virtues I most
warmly bless." Hopkins.
Epigrams. Martial (Marcus
Valerius Martialis).
Eternity. More.
The Extravagant Drunkard's
Wish. Ward.
The Faerie Queene. Spenser.

The First Solitude. Gongora
y Argote.
Forgiveness. Whittier.
Going the Rounds: A Sort of
Love Poem. Hecht.
A Graveyard in Queens.
Montague.
He Came Too Late. Bogart.
Honest, Wouldn't You?
Anonymous.
Hound on the Church Porch.
Coffin.
Hypatia (excerpt). Tollet.
I Sing a Song Reluctantly.
Die.
Icarus. Bottrall.
An Idler's Calendar: January.
Blunt.
In Memoriam Roy Campbell.
Currey.
In the Old Theatre, Fiesole.
Hardy.
An Irish Lamentation.
Goethe.
Jealosie. Donne.
Juvenal's Sixth Satire.
Dryden.
The Lesson. Lucie-Smith.
The Lilly in a Christal.
Herrick.
A Madame, Madame B.
Beaute Sexagenaire.
Sackville.
A Man Young and Old: The
Friends of his Youth.
Yeats.
Model T. Stoutenburg.
The Motives of Rhythm.
Conquest.
Nightmare Inspection Tour
for American Generals.
Ruark.
O What Pleasure 'Tis to Find.
Behn.
Of a Woman, Dead Young.
Parker.
The Parrot. Skelton.
The Peasants' Song.
Anonymous.
Pride. Jacob.
Pride Is Out. *Anonymous.*
The Priesthood. Herbert.
Recitative. Crane.
Rivets. Olds.
Robin Hood's Golden Prize.
Anonymous.
Running Vines in a Field.
Brown.
Somebody's Mother. Brine.
Somewhere I Chanced to
Read. Davidson.
Sonnet: The Wild Duck's
Nest. Wordsworth.
Sorrow Shatters My Heart.
Ibn Ezra.
Take This Hammer.
Anonymous.
Tamping Ties. *Anonymous.*
Thomas Winterbottom Hance.
Gilbert.
'Tis Now Since I Sate Down.
Suckling.
To a Lady, with a Present of
a Walking-Stick. Frere.
To My Nose. Forrester.
The Twa Magicians.
Anonymous.
Undertakers. Bierce.
Variations on Sappho.
"Field.

Verses under a Peacock
Portrayed in Her Left
Hand. Greene.
Virgil: Georgics, Book IV.
Schmitz.
What Are Outward Forms.
Bickerstaffe.
What Is Truth? (excerpt).
Manning.
The White Steed of the
Prairies. Barber.
The Woman of Three Cows.
Mangan.
The World Turned Upside
Down. *Anonymous.*

Priest (ess) (s)
Autumn. Untermeyer.
Avalon. McGaffin.
Bagman O'Reilly's Curse.
Murray.
The Bandit Peter Mancino's
Death. *Anonymous.*
Brebeuf and His Brethren.
Scott.
Chambers of Jerusalem.
Karni.
The Covenant of His Grace.
Wesley.
Credo. Cohen.
Danny's Wooing. Wright.
Deserted Shrine. Treinin.
Dundonnel Mountains.
Young.
An Elegy upon the Death of
the Dean of St. Paul's, Dr.
John Donne. Carew.
Epigram. Dodsley.
Epigram: "Gold priests,
wooden chalices."
Anonymous.
Glorious Things of Thee Are
Spoken. Newton.
Harriet Beecher Stowe.
Dunbar.
The Helmets, a Fragment.
Penrose.
Hind Etin. *Anonymous.*
Love and Liberty. A Cantata.
Burns.
The Masque of the Inner-
Temple and Gray's Inne.
Beaumont.
Missouri Sequence: Nightfall.
Coffey.
Of a Zealous Lady.
Harington.
On the New Forcers of
Conscience Under the Long
Parliament. Milton.
The Small Silver-Coloured
Bookworm. Parnell.
The Telephone Operator.
Francis of Assisi.
To Marie Osmond. Skelley.
To Mary: At the Thirteenth
Station. Roseliep.
To Nature. Coleridge.
A Year of Sorrow. De Vere.

Prime
Amoret. Akenside.
The Bermondsey Tragedy.
Anonymous.
Cadenus and Vanessa
(excerpt). Swift.
The Evening-Watch.
Vaughan.
In Robin Hood Cove.
Hartley.
Johnny Raw and Polly Clark.
Anonymous.
Kellyburnbraes. *Anonymous.*

The Lattice at Sunrise.
Turner.
The Little Farm; or, The
Weary Ploughman.
Anonymous.
O It's Best Be a Total Boor.
O Bruadair.
Saint Francis and Saint
Benedight. *Anonymous.*
There's Life in a Mussel. A
Meditation. Farewell.
To a Weak Gamester in
Poetry. Jonson.
To His Not-So-Coy Mistress.
Vaughan-Thomas.
To the Virgins, To Make
Much of Time. Herrick.
Whilst It Is Prime. Spenser.
The Young Sailor Cut down
in His Prime.
Anonymous.

Primitive
The Aging Poet, on a Reading
Trip to Dayton... Snyder.
Double Ballade of Primitive
Man. Lang.
Grid Erectile. Dewdney.
In Praise of Robert Penn
Warren. Lehman.
The Toil of the Trail.
Garland.

Primrose (s)
Fairies. Conkling.
Henceforth I Will Not Set My
Love. Gorges.
The Memory of Kent.
Blunden.
Minnie and Mattie. Rossetti.
Threshold. Blunden.

Prince
Against Love. Denham.
Ali. Djangatolum.
Andrew. Parsons
Baron Renfrew's Ball.
Halpine.
A Christmas Carol.
Coleridge.
A Christmas Carol. Lowell.
The Common's Petition to
King Charles II.
Anonymous.
Dream Data. Duncan.
Elizabethan Tragedy: A
Footnote. Moss.
Even the Best. Kizer.
The Faithful Few. Shuler.
Heralds of Christ.
Copenhaver.
His Glory Tell. Bonar.
The History of Prince Edward
Island. *Anonymous.*
Jubilate Agno. Smart.
Love by the Water-Reeds.
Anonymous.
The Morning After. Clark.
The New Day. Johnson.
Noblesse Oblige. Wright.
Old England Forever and Do
It No More. *Anonymous.*
Papermill Graveyard. Belitt.
The Phoenix (excerpt).
Anonymous.
Plain Dealing. Brome.
Praetorium Scene: Good
Friday. Lennen.
Prince of Wales' Marriage.
Anonymous.
Royal Education. Praed.
Sargent's Portrait of Edwin
Booth at "The Players".
Aldrich.

Shine Out, Fair Sun.
Anonymous.
Smudging. Wakoski.
Song: "Shine out, fair Sun,
with all your heat."
Anonymous.
The Stirrup Cup. Ainslie.
Ten Thousand Times Ten
Thousand. Alford.
The Triumph of the Whale.
Lamb.
The True Story of Snow
White. Bennett.
Uccello. Corso.
Upon Kinde and True Love.
Townsend.
The Warrior's Lament.
Seaman.
What Is the Rhyme for
Porringer? *Anonymous.*
Young Paris. Crabbe.

Princess
Bold Princess Royal.
Anonymous.
The Duchess of York's Ghost.
Anonymous.
Frog Prince. Pettingell.
Love by the Water-Reeds.
Anonymous.
Peter. Benet.
The Princess of Dreams.
Dowson.
Tyrannic Love. Dryden

Principal
Zimmer in Grade School.
Zimmer.

Principle (s)
Clerihews. Bentley.
A Levantine. Plomer.
Principal and Principle.
Anonymous.
Upon Looking at a Book of
Astrology. McFadden.

Print (ed) (er) (s)
The Flight into Egypt.
Quennell.
Fossil. Blodgett.
The Lion. Turner.
Living by the Red River.
Wright.
Mrs. Seymour Fentolin.
Herford.
A Nice Correspondent.
Locker-Lampson.
Night Mail. Auden.
Old Fellow. Walsh.
Poetry. Sutzkever.
Printer's Error. Wodehouse.
Second Reading. Beyer.
The Snitterjipe. Reeves.
The Thought-Fox. Hughes.
To a Bicycle (parody).
Anonymous.
To a Lady Sitting before Her
Glass. Fenton.
To Stephen Spender.
Corsellis.
Tomlinson. Kipling.
White Spider. Garin.

Prism
Leaving Smoke's. Henry.
New Every Morning.
Anonymous.

Prison (er) (ers) (s)
The Animal Runs, It Passes,
It Dies. *Anonymous.*
Archie of Cafield.
Anonymous.
The Artist. Brisby.
Broughty Wa's. *Anonymous.*
Cell Song. Knight.

A Child in Prison. O
Dalaigh.
Confab. Rosen.
The Courtier's Life. Wyatt.
The Dark Morning. Merton.
Dopefiends Trip. Angulo.
Early Morning at Bargis.
Hagedorn.
The Fair Thief. Wyndham.
The Flint Hills. Blockcolski.
The Genius of Death. Croly.
Gravel. Mariah.
Grey Him. Mariah.
He Came Unlook'd For.
Coleridge.
I Remember. Sanchez.
Korea Bound, 1952.
Childress.
A Letter from Home.
Minarik.
M'Fingal. Trumbull.
Nothing to Wish or to Fear.
Newton.
Of Difference Does It Make.
Paulin.
On Amaryllis A Tortoyse.
Pickthall.
One-and-Twenty.
Anonymous.
Our Lady of France.
Johnson.
Passive Resistance. Bruchac.
Pick upon Pick... Comfort.
A Prayer for a Preacher.
Shillito.
Prayer to Santa Maria Del
Vade. Ruiz.
A Prisoner for Life.
Anonymous.
Requiem 1935-1940.
Akhmatova.
Solitary. Olds.
Stay, Shade of My Shy
Treasure! Juana Ines de la
Cruz.
To Aaron Burr, under Trial
for High Treason.
Morton.
To Carry the Child. Smith.
To Speak of Chile. Gibson.
Upon a Ribband. Carew.
Utrillo's World. Glassco.
Wall, Cave, and Pillar
Statements, After Asoka.
Dugan.
Winter Twilight. Lipsitz.

Private
Adultery. Dugan.
Anteroom: Geneva. Devlin.
Blood to Blood. Aubert.
A Bully. *Anonymous.*
A Dedication to My Wife.
Eliot.
Dissembler. Shaw.
Dr. Coppelius. Gardiner.
Epigram: "Private faces in
public places." Auden.
Flooded Mind. MacCaig.
Gypsy. Miles.
Love Song. Ewart.
On a Painting by Patient B of
the Independence State
Hospital... Justice.
The Second Man. Symons.
Standing on the Streetcorner.
Denby.
Taxis. Field.
What Curious Dresses All
Men Wear. Schwartz.
Wild Sports of the West.
Montague.
The Young Recruit. Fiche.

Prize (s)
At Casterbridge Fair.
Hardy.
Atalanta. Ovid (Publius
Ovidius Naso).
Bel M'es Quan Lo Vens
M'Alena. Daniel.
The Cherry Boy (excerpt).
Ellis.
Credo. Kreymborg.
The Discovery of America.
Robertson.
The Dreamer. Gould.
Earl Brand. *Anonymous.*
The Finder Found. Muir.
Firstfruits in 1812. Rice.
God and the Soul: Et Mori
Lucrum. Spalding.
The Gymnasiad, or Boxing
Match (excerpt).
Whitehead.
The Hen. Herford.
If Easter Be Not True.
Barstow.
The Indians Prize Not English
Gold. Williams.
Instruction in the Art.
Booth.
Junk. Zaranka.
Keep Your Eyes on the Prize.
Anonymous.
Lady of Carlisle.
Anonymous.
Limerick: "There was a young
man of Devizes."
Marshall.
The Market Town. Carlin.
Miss Snooks, Poetess. Smith.
The Nightingale and Glow-
Worm. Cowper.
A Northern Suburb.
Davidson.
Ordinance on Winning.
Lazard.
Phoenix. Oliver.
Poem: "I take four devils with
me when I ride." Stewart.
Praise of Mary. *Anonymous.*
Silex Scintillans. Vaughan.
The Streets of Forbes.
McGuire.
A Young Man's Epigram on
Existence. Hardy.

Problem (s)
Aids to Composition.
Conquest.
Ballade of the Back Road.
Block.
Dinner Guest: Me. Hughes.
Dwarf of Disintegration.
Williams.
High to Low. Hughes.
Landscapeople. Ashbery.
Man of Letters. Knox.
Milton. Ray.
Our Presidents. *Anonymous.*
Our Youth. Ashbery.
Problems. Scott.

Procession
Girls on Saddleless Horses.
Vliet.
Moods. Kwitko.
The Strayed Reveller.
Arnold.

Proclaim (ed)
Amanda Barker. Masters.
The City of Dreadful Night.
Thomson.
The Democratic Barber; or,
Country Gentleman's
Surprise. Parrish.

Drinking Alone in the
Moonlight. Li T'ai-po.
Proclamation
The Poem: "Rise Oedipeus,
and if thou canst unfould."
Morton.
The Second Anniversarie.
Donne.
Prodigal
Birthday Sonnet. Wylie.
Phantasus. Holz.
Product
A Consumer's Report.
Porter.
A Garden Song. Sims.
Professor
Epigram on an Academic
Visit to the Continent.
Porson.
Heliotrope. Peck.
Profit (s)
The Angel in the House.
Patmore.
A bright moon illumines the
night-prospect.
Anonymous.
Investor's Soliloquy. Ward.
My Son, Forsake Your Art.
O'Heffernan.
Nicolas Gatineau. Bourinot.
On the Island. Sissman.
Sailboat, Your Secret.
Francis.
Seasong. George.
The Sleepers. Aberg.
The Spring Equinox. Ridler.
The Undertaking. Lansing.
Profound
At Rochdale. Young.
The Inverted Torch.
Thomas.
Three City Cantos. Wagner.
La Vita Nuova. Dante
Alighieri.
Progeny
Lilith. Feldman.
Murder of a Community.
Weissbort.
November, 1941. Fuller.
Progress
Considering the Snail. Gunn.
Dinosaurs. Stoloff.
English History in
Rhyme...(excerpt).
Goodwin.
If All the Thermo-Nuclear
Warheads. Burke.
In the Palms of Ancient
Bodhisattvas. Tagliabue.
John Brown. Koopman.
Mr. Attila. Sandburg.
Songs of Education.
Chesterton.
We All Have a Bench in the
Park to Reach. Jonas.
Project (s)
Desires of Men and Women.
Berryman.
Limerick: "A large, colored
dyke from Atlanta."
Anonymous.
O Realm Bejewelled.
Farrokhzad.
Prolific
I Knew a Cappadocian.
Housman.
In Praise of Water-Gruel.
Green.
Limerick: "There was a young
lady of Venice."
Anonymous.
Thanksgiving. Koch.

Promenade
At a Cowboy Dance.
  Adams.
Idaho Cowboy Dance.
  Anonymous.
Rhymed Dance Calls.
  Anonymous.
Promise (d) (s)
Ascension Day. Kaye-Smith.
The Belongings. Enslin.
Birth of Love. Warren.
Blue Waves. St. John.
The Bulldozer. Stauffer.
Christ's Coming to Judgment.
  Dekker.
Columbus. Schiller.
The Coming of the Lord.
  Very.
The Death of a Negro Poet.
  Rivers.
The Duke of Athole's Nurse
  (A version). *Anonymous.*
Ecce in Deserto. Beers.
The Emigrant. O'Grady.
Estat ai en greu cossirier.
  Dia.
Even during War. Rukeyser.
Everyman: The Desertion of
  Beauty and Strength.
  Anonymous.
Explanations. Clifton.
False Prophet. O'Malley.
The Fight at Nevadaville.
  Anonymous.
The Fortress. Sexton.
A Friend's Passing. Sheaks.
The Gentle Check.
  Beaumont.
Graduation Day, 1965.
  Marzan.
Harold at Two Years Old.
  Myers.
I Am Weary of Straying.
  York.
John Otto. Merwin.
Levant. Durrell.
Like Smoke. Mririda n'Ait
  Attik.
Margaret Love Peacock.
  Peacock.
Marrying the Hangman.
  Atwood.
More Than Flowers We Have
  Brought. Turner.
My Master and I.
  Anonymous.
Noah's Raven. Merwin.
Norfolk. Betjeman.
Oh Promise Me. Scott.
The Pied Piper of Hamelin.
  Browning.
Promise! Gwala.
Relics. Wagoner.
She Proves the Inconsistency
  of the Desires and Criticism
  of Men... Juana Ines de la
  Cruz.
Song: "I promised Sylvia to be
  true." Rochester.
Steer, Bold Mariner, On!
  Schiller.
Their Lonely Betters.
  Auden.
Thoralf and Synnov.
  Boyeson.
To a Girl. Waller.
Trading Chicago. Hartman.
True Love. Shelley.
Tyson's Corner. St. John.
We Long to See Jesus.
  Hamilton.

Wearing of the Green.
  Fisher.
Weeds. Stanford.
When Father Slept.
  Anderson.
With Poems Already Begun.
  Korn.
The Wrecker Driver Foresees
  Your Death. Baker.
Promised Land
Bullocky. Wright.
Casey Jones. *Anonymous.*
Darkened Windows.
  Bottrall.
If You Want to Go to Heben.
  Anonymous.
Madonna Natura. "Macleod.
Moses' Account. Fuest.
The Promised Land.
  Anonymous.
Rock and Roll. James.
Sonnet: To the Asshole.
  Rimbaud.
Variations on a Time Theme.
  Muir.
Where Are the Hebrew
  Children? Cartwright.
Where Now Are the Hebrew
  Children? *Anonymous.*
Where O Where Is Old
  Elijah? (with music).
  Anonymous.
Where, Oh Where Are the
  Hebrew Children?
  Anonymous.
Proper
The Character of a Good
  Person. Dryden.
Darky Sunday School.
  Anonymous.
A Letter from School.
  Peacock.
Prayer for Fish. Wallace.
The Swan and the Goose.
  Aesop.
What I Have Done.
  Malanga.
Prophecy
The Conflict of Convictions.
  Melville.
Elsewhere. Pastan.
Explanations. Clifton.
Farther. Piatt.
In the Beginning Was the
  Bird. Treece.
Morning Glory. Pitter.
Red Sky at Morning.
  Thomas.
Refracted Lights. Wooley.
The Rise of Man. Chadwick.
Therefore Is the Name of It
  Called Babel. Sitwell.
To John C. Fremont.
  Whittier.
Prophet (ess) (s)
Chambers of Jerusalem.
  Karni.
I, Lord of All Mortals.
  Anonymous.
Lyon. Melville.
Michael Angelo: A Fragment
  (excerpt). Longfellow.
Milton. Blake.
The Morning Prayers of the
  Hasid, Rabbi Levi Yitzhok.
  Gotlieb.
Primary Lesson: The Second
  Class Citizens. Sun-Ra.
To the Right Honourable
  William, Earl of
  Dartmouth. Wheatley.

Prose
Dreambooks. Corn.
English Poetry. Daniel.
Epistle to John Hamilton
  Reynolds (excerpt). Keats.
Give Us This Day Our Daily
  Day. Levy.
Love and Poetry. Simpson.
Poetry for Supper. Thomas.
Self-Criticism in February.
  Jeffers.
Thy Garden, Orchard, Fields.
  Pastorius.
Vice. Hecht.
Prospect (s)
Astrophel and Stella, XXIX.
  Sidney.
Crack in the Wall Holds
  Flowers. Miller.
The Devil's Dictionary:
  Prospect. Bierce.
Me and Prunes. Sherwood.
Thoughts on the Sight of the
  Moon. Knight.
The Woman's Labour.
  Collier.
Prosper (ed) (ity)
America's Prosperity. Van
  Dyke.
Beowulf: The Tale of
  Sigemund. *Anonymous.*
Fighter. Zimunya.
Fragment. Vaughan.
Kill a Robin or a Wren.
  Anonymous.
The Letter. Tatham.
Satires. Wyatt.
Song for Unbound Hair.
  Taggard.
Transport. Meredith.
Wedding Celebration. Kono.
Protect (ed) (ion) (or) (s)
Caelica, LXXVII. Greville.
Chrysothemis. Reed.
The Country Justice.
  Langhorne.
Down by the Station, Early in
  the Morning. Ashbery.
Elegy. Karoniaktatie.
God Has Pity on
  Kindergarten Children.
  Amichai.
Hipporhinostricow. Milligan.
In a Child's Album.
  Wordsworth.
The Little Star. *Anonymous.*
Mira is dancing with bells
  tied. Mira Bai [(or
  Mirabai)].
Mount Vernon. *Anonymous.*
Night Song for a Child!
  Williams.
A Poem on England's
  Happiness. *Anonymous.*
Tara. *Anonymous.*
To the Right Noble,
  Valourous, and Learned
  Prince Henry... Davies.
Who but the Lord? Hughes.
The Wreck of the Northfleet.
  Anonymous.
The Wren. *Anonymous.*
Protestant (s)
Birth Report. Kennedy.
The Cardinal and the Dog.
  Browning.
The Old Orange Flute.
  Anonymous.
The Teeth Mother Naked at
  Last. Bly.

Proteus
On This Sea-Floor.
  Gustafson.
The Shape-Changer.
  Wallace-Crabbe.
Proud
224 Stoop. Cruz.
Accusation. Utahania.
Amoretti, XXVII. Spenser.
Appeal. Da.
Beasts and Birds. O'Keeffe.
A Brown Girl Dead. Cullen.
Bunky Boy Bunky Boy Who's
  My Little Bunky Boy.
  Mollin.
Chicago. Sandburg.
Chronicle. Berssenbrugge.
A Dance for Ma Rainey.
  Young.
Dublin Made Me.
  MacDonagh.
Elegy in a Presbyterian
  Burying-Ground. Wilson.
Epigrams. Theocritus.
For Steve. Birney.
Going or Gone (parody).
  Lamb.
Homo Sapiens. Rochester.
The Invention of the
  Telephone. Klappert.
Kate o' Belashanny.
  Allingham.
King of the Belgians. Smith.
Lonely. Spire.
Mabel Kelly. O'Carolan.
Man. Davies.
Masters in This Hall.
  Morris.
The Mysterious Cat.
  Lindsay.
Now in the Bloom. Frank.
Old Father Annum.
  Jackson.
Poem for My Father. West.
Poem: "I met Mother on the
  street." Bruce.
Primer Lesson. Sandburg.
Quarrel. McDougall.
Red. Cullen.
The Rights of Women.
  Cowper.
Rock and Hawk. Jeffers.
Samuel Hall. *Anonymous.*
A Satire against Reason and
  Mankind. Rochester.
Sea-Change. Masefield.
Sonnets from the Portuguese,
  XXXVIII. Browning.
Swordy Well. Clare.
Teddy Bear. Milne.
To the Ladies. Chudleigh.
Virgidemiarum. Hall.
Were I, Who to My Cost
  Already Am. Rochester.
Prove (d)
Beyond Recall. Bradley.
The Golden Vanity.
  Anonymous.
I Love a Flower. Philipps.
Roses. *Anonymous.*
Sea Monster. Merwin.
Written with a Diamond on
  Her Window at Woodstock.
  Elizabeth I.
Prove (d) (proof)
Ark of the Covenant.
  Nicholl.
The Challenge. Kleiser.
Desire Is a Witch. Day-
  Lewis.
Fabrication of Ancestors.
  Dugan.

For My Brother Who Died
before I Was Born.
Wormser.
Much Ado about Nothing.
Shakespeare.
My Love Is Past. Watson.
Nydia's Song. Lytton.
On Queen Caroline's
Deathbed. Pope.
Reading Time: 1 Minute 26
Seconds. Rukeyser.
The Saddled Ass. Taylor.

Prove (d) (s)
Absence of Occupation.
Cowper.
Basia, VIII. Johannes
Secundus.
Blow the Candle Out.
Anonymous.
Caelica, XXXIV. Greville.
Capability Brown. Cowper.
Don Juan. Byron.
For a War Memorial.
Chesterton.
The Hour of Magic. Davies.
I Am a Book I Neither Wrote
Nor Read. Schwartz.
I Do Not Love to See Your
Beauty Fire. Wheelock.
Limerick: "A farmer's boy,
starting to plough."
Martin.
The Message. Donne.
Omnia Somnia. Sylvester.
Pardon, Old Fathers. Yeats.
A Poet's Proverbs.
Guiterman.
Remorse. Lattimore.
Responsibilities: Prologue.
Yeats.
Single Sonnet. Bogan.
Song: "'Tis said that absence
conquers love!" Thomas.
Thysia. Luce.
To Phillis. Waller.
Too Dark. McCloskey.
The Trick. Davies.

Provence
Ma Provence. Koch.
To Ford Madox Ford in
Heaven. Williams.

Proverb
Counsel to Unreason.
Adams.
The Maid of the Moor, or
The Water-Fiends.
Colman.
To That Most Senseless
Scoundrel, the Author of
Legion's Humble...
Brown.

Provide (s)
In Some Way or Other the
Lord Will Provide. Cook.
Narcissus. Gullans.
The Poets' Paradise.
Drayton.
Provide, Provide. Frost.

Providence
The Bee-Wisp. Turner.
The Caesar's Victory.
Anonymous.
Inebriety (parody). Crabbe.
The Light of Faith. Dupree.
A Moral Poem.
Cunningham.
Resolution. More.
The Ring and the Book.
Browning.

Provision (s)
A Dooms-Day Thought Anno
1659. Flatman.

A Projection. Whittemore.
Some Murmur When Their
Sky Is Clear. Trench.

Provoke (d)
The flaming sighs that boil
within my breast. Wyatt.
Mary Ames. *Anonymous.*
Wild Provoke of the
Endurance Sky. Ceravolo.

Prow
Loch Luichart. Young.
On the Lake. Sackville-West.
A Passer By. Bridges.
Postlude. Williams.
Purpose. Piatt.
Shortening Sail. Falconer.

Prudence
A Blue Ribbon at Amesbury.
Frost.
The Case of Thomas More.
Mary St. Virginia.
A Dream of Jealousy.
Heaney.

Psalm (s)
The Auld Seceder Cat.
Anonymous.
King David and King
Solomon. Naylor.
Luss Village. Smith.
Meditations. Taylor.
Miniatures IV. Mute the
Hand Moves from the
Heart. Strongin.
Mysterious Presence! Source
of All. Beach.
The Opponent Charm
Sustained. Greenberg.
The Presbyterian Wedding.
Anonymous.
The Psalm. Bridges.
Psalm. Simic.
Roslin and Hawthornden.
Van Dyke.

Puberty
Limerick: "Though the music
of love is Schuberty."
Anonymous.
To the New Annex to the
Detroit County Jail.
Thomas.

Public
After Horace. Godley.
After the Last Bulletins.
Wilbur.
April 1962. Goodman.
Cynical Ode to an Ultra-
Cynical Public. Mackay.
A Dedication to My Wife.
Eliot.
Dressed to Kill. Major.
Epigram: "Private faces in
public places." Auden.
For Cal. Cunningham.
From V.C. (a Gentleman of
Verona). Ewart.
The God of War. Brecht.
Harvesting Wheat for the
Public Share. Li Chu.
Nocturne: Homage to
Whistler. Feldman.
On a Painting by Patient B of
the Independence State
Hospital... Justice.
The Second Man. Symons.
To His Book. Herrick.
Two Poems About President
Harding, I. Wright.

Publicity
Mousemeal. Nemerov.
To the Unknown Warrior.
Chesterton.

Publish (ed) (ing)
A Judezmo Writer in Turkey
Angry. Levy.
Note on Modern Journalism
during the Last Campaign.
Mayo.
Opportunity. Graham.

Pudding (s)
Charlie Wag. *Anonymous.*
Girls and Boys, Come out to
Play. Mother Goose.
The Glutton. Oakman.
Lace Tell. *Anonymous.*
Ladybird, Ladybird. Mother
Goose.
Little Pudding (parody).
Roberts.
On Ladies' Accomplishments.
Anonymous.
The Pot-Bellied Anachronism.
Darr.
Sing, Sing. *Anonymous.*
Stroke. Lowery.
William Shakespeare to Mrs.
Anne,... Gray.

Puddle
Our "Civilization." Morgan.
Poem to the Sun. Sklar.
Trail End. *Anonymous.*

Puff
Absolute and Abitofhell.
Knox.
Ad Persephonen. Adams.
Limerick: "There was an old
cat named Macduff."
Francis.
Nights Passed on Ward's
Island, Toronto Harbour.
Fetherling.
Snow. Stone.
Sporting the Plaid. Wallace-
Crabbe.

Pull (ed) (ing)
Eight Oars and a Coxswain.
Guiterman.
The End of a Leave. Fuller.
The Everlasting Forests.
Ravikovich.
Extensions of Linear Mobility.
Hathaway.
Fame. *Anonymous.*
The Four Dears. Elliott.
From Here to There.
Anonymous.
Good-By er Howdy-Do.
Riley.
The Last Man. Hood.
The Lives of Famous Men.
Gilbert.
On Portents. Graves.
She. Roethke.
Shooting Script (excerpt).
Rich.
Summit Lake. Thalman.
Upon the Double Murther of
King Charles I... Philips.

Pulse (s)
The. Underwood.
Bianca. Symons.
Brown Boy to Brown Girl.
Cullen.
A Cat's Conscience.
Anonymous.
Clocks. Sandburg.
A Dedication. Boye.
For An Allegorical Dance of
Women by Andrea
Mantegna. Rossetti.
A Heart to Praise Thee.
Herbert.

I Heard You Solemn-Sweet
Pipes of the Organ.
Whitman.
In the Hospital of the Holy
Physician. Willard.
Kitty Bhan. Walsh.
Measure. Hass.
Meditation. Pain.
Midwest Town. Peterson.
The Secret of the Sea.
Longfellow.
She listen'd like a cushat
dove. Rossetti.
Sonnets on the Sea's Voice.
Sterling.
Spinster's Lullaby. Miller.
Summer Resort. Page.
Sunday Evening. Guest.
Village and Factory.
Bezymensky.
Zola. Robinson.

Pumpkin (s)
Coach. Farjeon.
The Drifter. *Anonymous.*
A Prayer in Late Autumn.
Storey.
The Pumpkin. Whittier.
Thinking of You. Lourie.

Punch
The Crooked Trail to
Holbrook. *Anonymous.*
The Dorchester Giant.
Holmes.
The Jug of Punch.
Anonymous.

Punchinello
The Monkey. Howitt.
To Mr. Punchinello.
Anonymous.

Punctual
Lightly stepped a yellow star.
Dickinson.
The True Weather for
Women. Simpson.

Punish (ed) (ment)
Astrophel and Stella, XXXIII.
Sidney.
The Cold Heaven. Yeats.
The Culprit Fay. Drake.
Early Rising. Saxe.
The Indignation of Taliesin.
Peacock.
Jerusalem. Blake.
The Poet's Journal (excerpt).
Taylor.
The Ship of Fools. Barclay.
The Vedic Hymns: Forgive,
Lord, Have Mercy.
Anonymous.
With Two Fair Girls.
MacGregor.
The Wreath. Graves.

Pup (py) (s)
Dame. Astor.
Dog Wanted. MacKay.
Familiar Friends. Tippett.
Growing. Frost.
Growing Up. *Anonymous.*
My Dog. Chute.
My Puppy. Fisher.
The Ordinary Dog. Turner.
Shop Windows. Fyleman.
The Span of Life. Frost.

Pupils
Ballata: Of True and False
Singing. *Anonymous.*
Song: "The engine screams
and Murphy, isolate."
Kinsella.
The Sun Spirit. Chubb.

Puppet (s)
All Service Ranks the Same
   with God. Browning.
Gardeners. Ignatow.
The Little Lady. Edson.
A Poem for Anton Schmidt.
   Pillen.
Purchase (d)
Beginners. Whitman
The Divorce of a Lover.
   Gascoigne.
His Plan. *Anonymous.*
In Praise of Seafaring Men, in
   Hopes of Good Fortune.
   Grenville.
Pure (r) (st)
The Aesthete. Gilbert.
Are You What Your Faire
   Lookes Expresse?
   Campion.
Beauty. Rosenberg.
Because. Vilakazi.
Before a Saint's Picture.
   Landor.
Before Thy Throne.
   Carpenter.
Du Bist Wie Eine Blume.
   Heine.
Congal: Simile. Ferguson.
Death as a Lotus Flower.
   Anonymous.
The Defence of Night.
   Michelangelo.
Each Day. Ignatow.
Epitaph. Chiabrera.
The Fall of the Plum
   Blossoms. Banko.
Further Instructions.
   O'Sullivan.
A Girl of Pompeii. Martin.
The Grotto. Scarfe.
Hendecasyllables, Help!
   Catullus.
Heth. Montemayor.
I Come to Supplicate. Ben
   Abun.
In Memoriam A.H.H., CII.
   Tennyson.
In Shame and Humiliation.
   Wright.
Infirmity. Roethke.
A Kite Is a Victim. Cohen.
The Landrail. De Vere.
Legends of Christmas.
   Fisher.
Limerick: "Said the Reverend
   Jabez McCotton." Flagg.
Limerick: "There once was a
   sculptor called Phidias."
   Herford.
The Line of an American
   Poet. Whittemore.
My Comrade. Roche.
My Mind Keeps out the Host
   of Sin. Elys.
Nanny. Davis.
The Nightmare. Kessler.
Old Smoky. *Anonymous.*
On the Margins of a Poem.
   Langer.
Patience: Bunthorne's
   Recitative and Song.
   Gilbert.
The Pearl. *Anonymous.*
A Prayer. Butler the Second.
Purity of Heart. Keble.
The Quiet Hour. Bowman.
The Refiner's Fire.
   Anonymous.
Running Back. Smith.
Sonnets to Philomel. Davies.
Star Morals. Nietzsche.

Sumter–A Ballad of 1861.
   Anonymous.
Sunday up the River.
   Thomson.
That Pure Place. Moriarty.
To a Painted Lady. Brome.
To His Wife. Deniehy.
To the Evening. Bampfylde.
Tormenting Virgin.
   Anonymous.
The Translated Way.
   Adams.
The Unity of God.
   Panatattu.
Variations: The Air Is
   Sweetest That a Thistle
   Guards. Merrill.
Where Is She Now?
   Anonymous.
The White Anemone.
   Meredith."
A White Rose. O'Reilly.
The Witnesses. Kennedy.
Words to My Friend.
   Vivien.
Zong Belegt Baatar.
   Anonymous.
Purgatory
On Donne's Poem "To a
   Flea." Coleridge.
Sonnet XIII: "Harry whose
   tuneful and well measur'd
   Song." Milton.
To Mr. H. Lawes on His Airs.
   Milton.
Puritan
The Masterful Man. Tyrrell.
The Penurious Quaker; or,
   The High Priz'd Harlot.
   Anonymous.
Thoughts for St. Stephen.
   Morley.
Purity
At a Bach Concert. Rich.
Author's Entreaty for His
   Lay. Asgrimsson.
Ballata: In Exile at Sarzana.
   Cavalcanti.
Five Epigrams. Hall.
Founder's Day. Bridges.
Herman Moon's Hourbook.
   Middleton.
How of the Virgin Mother
   Shall I Sing? Ennodius.
Hymns and Spiritual Songs.
   Smart.
Midwinter. Trowbridge.
Song for Memorial Day.
   Scollard.
Tartar. Brown.
Thou Who Taught the
   Thronging People. Minde.
When You Will Walk in the
   Field. Goldberg.
Purple
The Abbot of Inisfalen.
   Allingham.
As a Bell in a Chime.
   Johnson.
Bygones (parody). Taylor.
Dark Phrases. Shange.
The Last Romantic. Laing.
The Lesson. Rubin.
Life-Hook. Ibarbourou.
No More, O Maidens.
   Alcman.
On Hampstead Heath.
   Gibson.
The Poster Girl. Wells.
Quebec Liquor Commission
   Store. Klein.
Sonnets. Tuckerman.

This Is the Last Night.
   Borson.
Upon Lazarus His Teres.
   Crashaw.
Upon Prue, His Maid.
   Herrick.
The Vanity of Human Wishes.
   Juvenal (Decimas Junius
   Juvenalis)
Purpose (s)
Almada Hill: An Epistle from
   Lisbon (excerpt). Mickle.
A Death to Us. Silkin.
Envoy. Hovey.
The Eyes of Flesh.
   Hochman.
He Hides Within the Lily.
   Gannett.
Indian School. Russell.
Michelangelo: "The Creation
   of Adam." Djanikian.
O Son of Man, Thou Madest
   Known. Littlefield.
Realization. Acharya.
Security. Sandell.
Selah. Thomas.
Sonnets, XXI: "So is it not
   with me as with that
   Muse." Shakespeare.
Vanzetti. Buckmaster.
Wilderness Rivers.
   Coatsworth.
Purr (s)
For the Book of Love.
   Laforgue.
See That One? Bagg.
Wind Is a Cat. Fuller.
Purse (s)
Convention Song.
   Anonymous.
The Daughter's Rebellion.
   Hopkinson.
Distressed Men of War.
   Anonymous.
The Gallant Highwayman.
   De Mille.
The Ghost in the Martini.
   Hecht.
Hog at the Manger. Farber.
The Knight and Shepherd's
   Daughter (A version).
   Anonymous.
On a Poet. Parrot.
Storm Over Rockefeller
   Center. Holden.
Pursue (d)
Absence of Occupation.
   Cowper.
Ascendancy. Simmons.
Barrage. Aldington.
By a Rich Fast Moving
   Stream. Tagliabue.
The Crow and the Crane.
   Anonymous.
The Dalliance of Eagles.
   Whitman.
The Dean's Lady. Crabbe.
The Haunter. Hardy.
A Life's Parallels. Rossetti.
Love's Pursuit. Browning.
Partial Draft. Shaw.
Peace. Herbert.
Recessional for the Class of
   1959... Cowen.
The Street. Paz.
Ten Sonnets for Today.
   Stanway.
Valse Oubliee. Heath-Stubbs.
Ways of Pronouncing "Ough'.
   Anonymous.
Push (ed) (er) (ing)
Fame. *Anonymous.*

Father's Story. Roberts.
For deLawd. Clifton.
Mainline. Ditsky.
Parentage. Stafford.
Wild Bill Jones. *Anonymous.*
Puss (y)
A Cat's Conscience.
   Anonymous.
Cats and Dogs. Moss.
Chickitten Gitten! Joans.
Gray Thrums. Bates.
Loulou and Her Cat.
   Locker-Lampson.
Pussy. *Anonymous.*
Stopping the Swing.
   Anonymous.
Visitor. *Anonymous.*
Who's That Ringing At My
   Door Bell? *Anonymous.*
Puzzle (d)
Benediction. Freedman.
Meditatio. Pound.
Puzzled. Wells.
A Vilna Puzzle. Chorny.
The Way the Bird Sat.
   Young Bear.
Pygmalion
Hagiograph. Heppenstall.
Pygmies
Dear Folks. Kavanagh.
Pyjamas
Zalinka. MacInnes.
Pyramid
The Egyptian Lotus. Eaton.
His Poetry His Pillar.
   Herrick.
Pyramis or The House of
   Ascent. Hope.
Reflexions on the Seizure of
   the Suez.... Nemerov.
To My Honoured Friend Mr.
   George Sandys. King.
Pyramus
Dyvers Thy Death Doo
   Dyverslye Bemone.
   Surrey.

Q

Quack (s)
The Bat. Sitwell.
Ducks. Harvey.
I Saw a Ship A-Sailing.
   Mother Goose.
Sent to a Patient, with the
   Present of a Couple of
   Ducks. Jenner.
When Did the World Begin.
   Clairmont.
Who Likes the Rain? Bates.
Quaff (ing)
Original Epitaph on a
   Drunkard. Tyler.
The Poet to the Sleeping Saki.
   Goethe.
Stanzas Occasioned by the
   Ruins of a Country Inn.
   Freneau.
Quail
Cuttings. Roethke.
The Harvest Moon.
   Longfellow.
The Hunt. Halpern.
Quake
The Advice. *Anonymous.*
George the Third. Byron.
Hitler, Frothy-Mouth.
   Anonymous.

Om. *Anonymous.*

Quaker (s)
The Four-Legg'd Quaker.
Anonymous.
Merrily Danced the Quaker's
Wife. *Anonymous.*
Miss Kilmansegg and Her
Precious Leg. Hood.
My Country 'Tis of Thee.
Bierce.

Quality (ies)
Birds and Fishes. Jeffers.
Go not too near a house of
rose. Dickinson.
One Way Down. Craig.
Science in God. Herrick.
Thing Poem. Morstein.

Quarrel (ed) (ing) (s)
Accusation. Utahania.
Betsey and I Are Out.
Carleton.
Dum and Dee. *Anonymous.*
The Entailed Farm. Glassco.
The Epitaph upon Gilbert
Glanvill... Prior.
Haiku: "Being newly-married
before all the world."
Anonymous.
I Never Even Suggested It.
Nash.
Jeannette and Jeannot.
Jeffries.
The Lesson for Today.
Frost.
A Party. Richards.
Portia. Wilde.
The Token. Prince.
Tweedle-Dum and Tweedle-
Dee. *Anonymous.*
Two Little Kittens.
Anonymous.

Quarry
Annus Mirabilis. Dryden.
Coriolanus. Shakespeare.
The Falconer of God. Benet.
Green Slates. Hardy.
Hawking. Drayton.
In Obitum Ben. Jons.
Westmoreland.
Love Song. *Anonymous.*
Pittsburgh. Sobiloff.
Quarries in Syracuse.
Goldberg.
Snake Hill. Parini.
To the Mutable Fair. Waller

Quart (s)
Father and Mother.
Kennedy.
I Have No Pain.
Anonymous.
The Milkman. Gardner.

Quarter (s)
Epitaphs of the War, 1914-18.
Kipling.
From Far, from Eve and
Morning. Housman.
A Pint of Water.
Anonymous.
W.L.M.K. Scott.

Quartz
Beinn Naomh, IV: The
Summit. Raine.
I know a place where summer
strives. Dickinson.
Sandpiper. Bishop.

Quebec
Brebeuf and His Brethren.
Pratt.

Queen (s)
As Concerning Man.
Radcliffe.

Ballade Tragique a Double
Refrain. Beerbohm.
The Battle of Plattsburg Bay.
Scollard.
The Beggar Maid. Tennyson.
Boatman's Hymn. Magrath.
The Bride. Hope.
The Candle A Saint.
Stevens.
City Butterfly. Siebert.
Craqueodoom. Riley.
Dear Body. Canan.
The Death of Queen Jane.
Anonymous.
Deirdre. Stephens.
Depression before Spring.
Stevens.
Diptych. Sykes.
The Ditty of the Six Virgins.
Watson.
The Duke of Grafton.
Anonymous.
Earl Bothwell. *Anonymous.*
Edmund's Song. Scott.
Eire. Drennan.
The Elves' Dance.
Anonymous.
The English Queen. Lawson.
Epigram: "No more of your
titled acquaintances boast."
Burns.
An Epitaph on the
Marchioness of Winchester.
Milton.
Fantasy. Bennett.
The First Lord's Song.
Gilbert.
The Fleece. Dyer.
A Forced Music. Graves.
Gone. De la Mare.
Grace: "God bless our meat."
Anonymous.
Henry and Mary. Graves.
Homage. Kahn.
I Know a Lady. Thomas.
If I Were a Queen. Rossetti.
In the Queen's Bedroom.
Cameron.
An Invective Against the
Wicked of the World.
Breton.
Jealousy. Coleridge.
The Jolly Young Sailor and
the Beautiful Queen.
Anonymous.
The Journeyman Tailor.
Anonymous.
The Kinkaiders. *Anonymous.*
Labor Day. Pomeroy.
Lament to Nana of Erech.
Anonymous.
The Lark. *Anonymous.*
The Last Meeting of
Pocahontas and the Great
Captain. Preston.
Life of a Queen. Mueller.
The Little Knight in Green.
Bates.
Love's Resume. Heine.
Mad Marjory. McCrae.
The Marigold. Ford.
My Queen. *Anonymous.*
A New Ballade of the
Marigolde. *Anonymous.*
Ode to Mercy. Collins.
Ode to the Human Heart.
Blanchard.
On a Piece of Tapestry.
Santayana.
One Saturday. Robinson.
Our Lady on Calvary.
Michael Marie.

Out of Whack. Edson.
Pangloss's Song. Wilbur.
Paracelsus. Browning.
Petition to the Queen.
Ralegh.
The Queen of Courtesy.
Anonymous.
Queen of the World.
Anonymous.
Red. Cullen.
The Rich Lady from Dublin.
Anonymous.
Robin Hood and Queen
Katherine. *Anonymous.*
The Roses of Queens. White.
The Ruler of the Queen's
Navee. Gilbert.
Shillin' a Day. Kipling.
Since We Loved. Bridges.
The Singing Leaves. Lowell.
Sleeping Beauty. Shore.
Song of the Factory Girls.
Anonymous.
Sonnet: "When Phoebe form'd
a wanton smile." Collins.
The Soul. Barlow.
The Star-Song: A Carol to the
King; Sung at White-Hall.
Herrick.
Supreme Surrender. Rossetti.
Theseus and Ariadne.
Graves.
Time to Be Wise. Landor.
To Dinah Washington.
Knight.
To Naso. Catullus.
To Our Lady. Henryson.
To the Looking-Glass World
It Was Alice That Said
(parody). "Carroll.
To the Moonflower. Betts.
To W.L.G. on Reading His
Chosen Queen. Forten.
The Toad-Eater. Burns.
Trio for Two Cats and a
Trombone. Sitwell.
The Waltz: Hail, Spirit-
Stirring Waltz. Byron.
Was Worm. Swenson.
Yes: I Write Verses. Landor.
Young Waters. *Anonymous.*

Queer
Limerick: "I is for Ignorant
Ida." Bellows.
Limerick: "The treatment by
old Mr. Mears."
Anonymous.
The Lodging. Brown.
The Thinker. Delius.
Wodwo. Hughes.

Quench (ed)
The Aeneid. Virgil (Publius
Vergilius Maro).
I sighed and owned my love.
Anonymous.
"If he that erst the form so
lively drew." Surrey.
Missing. Auden.
The Rock. Eliot.
To Her Againe, She Burning
in a Feaver. Carew.
Two Puritans. *Anonymous.*

Quest
A'Chuilionn. Hutchison.
Fragrant Thy Memories.
Anonymous.
Hierarchie of the Blessed
Angels (excerpt).
Heywood.
Idylls of the King.
Tennyson.

Let Me Live but from Year to
Year. Van Dyke.
O Mariners! Rutledge.
Prayer. *Anonymous.*
Ultima Thule. Longfellow.

Question (ed) (ing) (s)
Address to an Absolute.
McFadden.
The Affliction of Richard.
Bridges.
Alfonso Churchill. Masters.
Anecdote of 2 A.M. Wain.
The Anti-Symbolist. Keyes.
Before the War. Pendergast.
Bleak Season Was It,
Turbulent and Wild.
Wordsworth.
The Brockton Murder: A
Page out of William James.
Skinner.
Cultural Notes. Fearing.
The Day before Christmas.
Souster.
The Dinosaur. Taylor.
Dr. Sigmund Freud Discovers
the Sea Shell. MacLeish.
Driving through Minnesota
during the Hanoi Bombings.
Bly.
An Early Illinois Winter.
Kuo.
Evensong. Stevenson.
The Feast of Padre Chala.
Walsh.
Funnel. Sexton.
Great Man. Johnson.
His Side/Her Side. Skinner.
The History of the World as
Pictures. Sullivan.
An Inspiration. Wilcox.
Lethe. Doolittle.
Living with You. Langfield.
Mine old dear enemy...
Wyatt.
Mother, among the Dustbins.
Smith.
Murgatroyd. Wright.
Next. Koyama.
The Night Has Twenty-Four
Hours. Pietri.
Of Tact. Guiterman.
On the Death of the
Evansville University
Basketball Team...
Hamblin.
Original Child Bomb
(excerpt). Merton.
Promised Land. Engel.
The Redeemer. Muchemwa.
Return. Tillinghast.
The Sleeping-Bag. Ponting.
The Sunshine of the Gods
(excerpt). Taylor.
Te Judice. Scott.
Thinking of Iceland. Paulin.
The Thousand and Second
Night. Merrill.
To You. Koch.
Trees Once Walked and
Stood. Tan Pai.
Walk-Up. Merwin.

Question mark (s)
Archaeologists. Faucher.
Casting. Nemerov.
Christ Walking on the Water.
Rodgers.

Quick (ly)
Before the Statue of a
Laughing Man. Bowie.
Castoff Skin. Whitman.
The Engagement. Clough.

For Guillaume Apollinaire.
  Meredith.
Frustration.   Parker.
Gardener Janus Catches a
  Naiad.   Sitwell.
The Lives of Gulls and
  Children.   Nemerov.
Louise.   Smith.
Love Unknown.   Herbert.
Politics.   Tennyson.
Shelter.   Derwood.
Silex Scintillans.   Vaughan.
The Silver Leaf.   Hay.
Town Owl.   Lee.
What It Means, Living in the
  City.   Dickey.

Quiet (er) (ly) (ness)
Advice.   Landor.
Agnus Dei.   Kinon.
All.   Beers.
Aridity.   "Field.
Birds in the Flax.   Snaith.
The Breathing.   Levertov.
Bus Stop.   Justice.
The Cap and Bells.   Yeats.
Choice.   Cunningham.
Colenso Rhymes for Orthodox
  Children.   Harte.
Columcille's Greeting to
  Ireland.   Columcille.
The Conversation in the
  Drawingroom.   Kees.
Coroner's Jury.   Strong.
The Creation of Man.
  Anonymous.
The Day of Wrath.   Waddell.
Daybreak.   Longfellow.
Death and the Arkansas
  River.   Stanford.
The Deep.   Brainard.
The Dog of Art.   Levertov.
Duck.   Donaghy.
Easter Song.   Leslie.
Elegy, Montreal Morgue.
  MacDonald.
Emergency at 8.   Hewitt.
The Enquiry.   Dyer.
The Epitaph upon Gilbert
  Glanvill...   Prior.
A Fable for Critics.   Lowell.
The Faerie Queene.   Spenser.
The Figures.   Creeley.
The Ghost.   De La Mare.
Good Advice.   Montagu.
The Grass, Alas.   Emmons.
A Happy Man.   Carphyllides
Henry Adams.   Auden.
A Hymn of Trust.   Sargent.
Hymn to Castor and Pollux.
  Anonymous.
Joy.   Jeffers.
Lament for Turlough
  O'Carolan.   Hopes.
Leoun.   Cocteau.
Lucy Lavender.   Eastwick.
Man Thinking about Woman.
  Lee.
Mashkin Hill.   Simpson.
Memorial Rain.   MacLeish.
A Midsummer Noon in the
  Australian Forest.   Harpur.
The Mountain Lake.
  Church.
Music God.   Van Doren.
My Mouth Is Very Quiet.
  Villa.
Myths and Texts.   Snyder.
Night.   Brown.
Now You're Content.   Spire.
An Old Woman.
  Anonymous.
On Ellson Fell.   Landles.

On Wearing Ears.   Harris.
Park.   Ignatow.
Pastoral Poesy.   Clare.
Pawnbrokers.   Wilkinson.
Philotas: Chorus.   Daniel.
Poem to Negro and Whites.
  Bodenheim.
Quaker Ladies.   Cortissoz.
Quiet.   Swann.
Quiet By Hillsides in the
  Afternoon.   Lifson.
Quiet Desperation.   Simpson.
The Quiet Life.   Byrd.
The Quiet of the Dead.
  Webster.
The Reapers.   Watt.
Return.   Brown.
The Revelation.   Williams.
A Rhapsody, Written at the
  Lakes in Westmorland.
  Brown.
Sketch.   O'Sullivan.
Song on the Water.   Beddoes.
Sonnets, XXVII: "Weary with
  toil, I haste me to my bed."
  Shakespeare.
A Sparrow-Hawk Proud.
  Anonymous.
The Starling Lake.
  O'Sullivan.
There Was an Old Woman,
  and What Do You Think?
  Mother Goose.
Three Kings.   Vaughn.
Three Part Invention.
  Blackburn.
Three Sweethearts.   Heine.
To a Sleeping Friend.
  Cocteau.
Treason of Sand.   Roth.
Twin Aces.   Wilson.
The Visit.   Gauer.
Visit to the Hermitage.
  Anderson.
What Was Solomon's Mind?
  Scott.
Whither.   Cheney.
Wild Weather.   Bates.
A Wintering Moon.   Hardy.

Quietude
The Battle of King's
  Mountain.   *Anonymous.*
Choricos.   Aldington.
Mari Magno.   Clough.

Quill (s)
His Desire.   Herrick.
A Judicious Observation of
  That Dreadful Comet.
  Wiswall.
News from Mount Amiata.
  Montale.
The Peacock "At Home'.
  Dorset.
Visions of Mexico While at a
  Writing Symposium in Port
  Townsend...   Cervantes.

Quilt (s)
Angina Pectoris.   Moses.
For Stephen Drawing Birds.
  Rogers.
The Leaves in a Frolic.
  Anonymous.
My Mother Pieced Quilts.
  Acosta.

Quit (s)
Alas the grief and deadly
  woeful smart!   Wyatt.
At a Georgia Camp Meeting.
  Mills.
The Consolation of
  Philosophy.   Boethius.
Don't Quit.   *Anonymous.*

Dupree (B vers.).
  Anonymous.
Easy Rider Blues.   Jefferson.
The Farmer's Boy.
  Bloomfield.
The Function Room.
  Phillips.
The Jolly Cowboy.
  Anonymous.
Montcalm and Wolfe.
  Anonymous.
The Mower.   *Anonymous.*
A New Ballad, to an Old
  Tune, Called, I Am the
  Duke of Norfolk, Etc.
  Anonymous.
Now all of change.   Wyatt.
The Quitter.   *Anonymous.*
The Royal Adventurer.
  Freneau.
The Shed.   O'Donnell.
Some Opposites.   Wilbur.
The Water-Truck.   Lane.
We Love the Name of Texas.
  Anonymous.

Quiver (ing)
The autumn made colors
  burn.   Khoury-Gata.
In the Seven Woods.   Yeats.
Let the Dead Depart in Peace.
  Anonymous.
A Picture.   Cuthbertson.
Where Avalanches Wail.
  Anonymous.

R

Rabbit (s)
Agamemnon.   Aeschylus.
All Out and Down.
  Leadbelly.
Birthdays.   Chute.
Dream Songs.   Berryman.
Great-Aunt Rebecca.
  Brewster.
July Meadow.   Driscoll.
Lenox Christmas Eve 68.
  Cornish.
Lion and Rabbit.   Greenberg.
Market Square.   Milne.
Morals.   Thurber.
My Other Chinee Cook.
  Stephens.
The Rabbit Man.
  Anonymous.
To Henrietta, on Her
  Departure for Calais.
  Hood.
Tour de Force.   Dufault.

Race (r) (s)
The Aeneid.   Virgil (Publius
  Vergilius Maro).
The African Affair.   Wright.
As Like the Woman as You
  Can.   Henley.
Astrophel and Stella, XXVI.
  Sidney.
Astrophel and Stella, XLI.
  Sidney.
At Fredericksburg.   O'Reilly.
At the Last.   Engels.
Autumn Love.   Ibycus.
Battle-Song of the Oregon.
  Rice.
Bruce and the Spider.
  Barton.
Country Statutes.
  Anonymous.

The Crimson Cherry Tree.
  Treece.
Experience.   Emerson.
An Explanaton of the
  Grasshopper.   Lindsay.
Fable XXIV: The Butterfly
  and the Snail.   Gay.
For My People.   Walker.
Gipsies.   Clare.
The Hand of Lincoln.
  Stedman.
Harriet Beecher Stowe.
  Dunbar.
In My Place.   Archibald.
In Pleasant Lands Have
  Fallen the Lines.   Flint.
The Invitation.   MacDonagh.
The King's Own Regulars.
  Anonymous.
The Last Instructions to a
  Painter.   Marvell.
The Last Longhorn's
  Farewell.   Sjolander.
The Lust of Gold.
  Montgomery.
Metrical Feet.   Coleridge.
More of a Corpse than a
  Woman.   Rukeyser.
Mr. Hosea Biglow to the
  Editor of "The Atlantic
  Monthly."   Lowell
Mr. Z.   Holman.
The Murder of Moses.
  Shapiro.
O Black and Unknown Bards.
  Johnson.
Old Timbrook Blues.   Byrd.
On a Cat, Ageing.   Gray.
On a Stupendous Leg of
  Granite, Discovered
  Standing by Itself...   Smith.
On Amaryllis A Tortoyse.
  Pickthall.
On the Death of Southey.
  Landor.
Paradise Lost.   Milton.
The Peaceable Race.   Daly.
The Pinto.   Wister.
Poem: "At night Chinamen
  jump."   O'Hara.
Poet.   Emerson.
The Pony Express.
  Thompson.
A Prairie Ride.   Moody.
A Prehistoric Camp.   Young.
A Racing Eight.
  Cuthbertson.
The Song of the Colorado.
  Hall.
Sonnet: September 1, 1802.
  Wordsworth.
Tangmalangaloo.   Hartigan.
To My Generation.   Galai.
The Tomb of Michael Collins.
  Devlin.
Too Late.   Thomas.
The True Ballad of the Great
  Race to Gilmore City.
  Hey.
The Vision.   Burns.
Voyage.   Schramm.

Rack (s)
In a Dream.   Synge.
King Lear.   Shakespeare.
Limerick: "Now the ears, so I
  always had thunk."
  Euwer.
Snaps for Dinner, Snaps for
  Breakfast, and Snaps for
  Supper.   Horton.

Radiance
Annunciation Night.
Hemenway.
Bread. Merwin.
Buffalo. Coates.
Catechism Elegy. Gibson.
Epitaph of a Courtesan.
Asclepiades.
An Evening Walk (excerpt).
Wordsworth.
Father. Ficke.
The Flowers of Politics.
McClure.
For the Sun Declined.
Lamdan.
The Guide. Gregor.
His Dream of the Sky-Land:
A Farewell Poem (excerpt).
Li Po.
If. Collins.
O Virtuous Light. Wylie.
On Earth There Is a Lamb So
Small. Zinzendorf.
Pauper Woodland. Everson.
Pilgrimage. Lennen.
Portrait of the Artist with
Hart Crane. Wright.
Reading Time: 1 Minute 26
Seconds. Rukeyser.
Santa Barbara. Browne.
Socrates Prays a Day and a
Night. O'Neil.
Sonnets: A Sequence on
Profane Love. Boker.
These Images Remain.
Sarton.
This Flock So Small.
Nitschmann.
To My Soul. Fletcher.
Today I Have Touched the
Earth. Smith.
Upanishads: Second Khanda.
Anonymous.
Radio (s)
Afternoons with Baedeker.
Lancaster.
Faith Healer Come to Rabun
County. Bottoms.
Mr. Vachel Lindsay Discovers
Radio (parody).
Hoffenstein.
Numbers. Elliott.
She Employed the Familiar
"Tu" Form. Fetherling.
Radish
The Mole. Schmitz.
Spring Arithmetic.
Anonymous.
Radium
Artificial Death, II. James.
Raft (s)
Forever Ambrosia. Morley.
Rain. Haines.
Time Zones for Forty-Four.
Stauffer.
Rafter (s)
Bat Angels. Levis.
Crime. Warren.
For Wilma. Johnson.
The Friendly Beast.
Anonymous.
John Webster. Swinburne.
Misgivings. Melville.
Only Silence. Bourinot.
Rag (s)
Alone. Shelton.
Apologue. Connor.
As for Me, I Delight in the
Everyday Way. Stroud.
The Beauty of Dawn.
Mnthali.

Cast Our Caps and Cares
Away. Fletcher.
Drug Store. Shapiro.
Festubert: The Old German
Line. Blunden.
For Us No Night Can Be
Happier. Zinzendorf.
Haiku: "Don't dress for it."
Chiyo.
Lakeside Incident. Skelton.
Maple Leaf Rag. Brown.
Neighbors. Evans.
The Rejected "National
Hymns". Newell.
Running through Sleep.
Norris.
Song: "Whipped by sorrow
now." Radnoti.
Southern Blues. Rainey.
To a Lady Friend. Davies.
Rage
Adventure. Norton.
Blessed Mary. *Anonymous.*
Brothers (I). Reiss.
Caelica, LIV. Greville.
Codicil. Walcott.
The Destiny of Nations.
Coleridge.
Do Not Go Gentle (parody).
Hopkins.
Epitaph. Chiabrera.
For My Son Noah, Ten Years
Old. Bly.
God from His Throne with
Piercing Eye. Steward.
The Harvesting of the Roses.
Ben Jacob.
The Horse. Levine.
The Innocents. Macpherson.
Inscription for a Headstone.
Clarke.
The Lass of Roch Royal (C
vers.). *Anonymous.*
The Magnolia Tree.
Witheford.
My Master and I.
Anonymous.
Mye Love Toke Skorne My
Servise to Retaine. Wyatt.
Poem About Waking. Ferry.
The Same Old Story.
Montague.
The Thief. Kunitz.
To an Athlete Turned Poet.
Meinke.
Under the Pot. Graves.
Vaquero. Miller.
The White Stallion. Owen.
A Winter Piece. Bryant.
Ragged
The Children of the Poor.
Hugo.
If I Have Made, My Lady,
Intricate. Cummings.
Old Red Hoss Mountain.
Warman.
The Plea of the Midsummer
Fairies. Hood.
Southern Blues. Rainey.
Rail (s)
The Broomstick Train.
Holmes.
Farewell to the Court
(excerpt). Rochester.
The First Epistle of the
Second Book of Horace.
Pope.
On the Irish Club. Swift.
On Those That Hated "The
Playboy of the Western
World", 1907. Yeats.

Payday at Coal Creek.
Anonymous.
Railroad Song. Chivers.
The Roaring Days. Lawson.
Song: "Lovers in ladies'
magazines." McGrath.
Railroad (s)
Before Invasion, 1940.
Betjeman.
Careless Love. *Anonymous.*
Casey Jones. *Anonymous.*
Chicago. Sandburg.
Doing Railroads for the
"Rocky Mountain News."
Warman.
English History in
Rhyme...(excerpt).
Goodwin.
I Don't Like No Railroad
Man (with music).
Anonymous.
I Once Loved a Young Man.
Anonymous.
Out Goes She. *Anonymous.*
Pat Works on the Railway.
Anonymous.
Railroad Bill. *Anonymous.*
The Railroad Corral.
Anonymous.
A Railroader for Me.
Anonymous.
The Scissors-Grinder.
Lindsay.
Seance. Roditi.
Ther's Many a Man Killed on
the Railroad (with music).
Anonymous.
Words from the Window of a
Railway Car. Steiger.
Raiment
Advent Meditation. Meynell.
The Ballad of Adam's First.
Davis.
Sri Rama's Raiment.
Anonymous.
Waking an Angel. Levine.
When the Fairies. Dorn.
Rain (ed) (ing) (s) (y)
Above the Falls at Waimea.
Johnson.
After Rain. Thomas.
Ain't Gonna Rain (with
music). *Anonymous.*
Ain't It Fine Today!
Malloch.
American Letter. MacLeish.
Amoretti, XLVI. Spenser.
Analyst. Fisher.
And So the Day Drops By.
Tuckerman.
And When the Green Man
Comes. Haines.
Anishinabe Grandmothers.
Vizenor.
The Anniversary. Spear.
April 1940. Maybin.
The Arkansas Traveler.
Anonymous.
Around You, Your House.
Stafford.
The Artist. Brisby.
At Sea. Trowbridge.
At Thomas Hardy's
Birthplace, 1953. Wright.
Auditory Hallucinations.
Mansour.
Autumn Rain. Lawrence.
Bay Poem. Henson.
Beckon Me, Ye Cuillins.
Hendrie.
Before Harvest. Fitzgerald.
Before the Rain. Aldrich.

Before the Rain.
Troubetzkoy.
Biography of Southern Rain.
Patchen.
Black Poplar-Boughs.
Freeman.
Bouncing Ball. Watson.
Builders. Flexner.
A Burial, Green. Southwick.
Burning Off. Dutton.
Butterfly Song. *Anonymous.*
Calamity. Scott.
Calm and Full the Ocean.
Jeffers.
Can-Opener. McAleavey.
The Cat and the Rain. Swift.
Cat's Cradle. Sarah.
Charm. Radnoti.
Chenille. Dickey.
Chimes. Rossetti.
City Rain. Field.
The Cloud-Flower Lullaby.
Anonymous.
The Cocks. Pasternak.
Come On in My Kitchen.
Johnson.
The Comforters. Shorter.
Composed on the Theme
"Willows by the Riverside."
Yu Hsuan-chi.
Corrymeela. O'Neill.
Cortege for Colette.
Garrigue.
The Cows at Night.
Carruth.
Cuckoo, Cherry Tree.
Anonymous.
Dafydd Ap Gwilym Resents
the Winter. Humphries.
Daydream. Tessimond.
The Death Watchers.
Ryerson.
Desert Song. Galsworthy.
Desolate. Dobell.
Dictum: For a Masque of
Deluge. Merwin.
Domestic Quarrel.
McInerney.
Drought. Holbrook.
The Dynasts. Hardy.
Elegy for an Estrangement.
Holloway.
Epigram: April. Nemerov.
Epos. Rosenberg.
Evening Red and Morning
Gray. *Anonymous.*
The Falls of Glomach.
Young.
Farmer. Bailey.
The Farmer. Herbert.
Farmers. Lux.
A Fence. Sandburg.
Flute-Priest Song for Rain
(excerpt). Lowell.
A Footnote to a Gray Bird's
Pause. Cunningham.
For an Autumn Festival
(excerpt). Whittier.
For Cal. Cunningham.
For My Brother and Sister
Southwestern Indian Poets.
Hobson.
For My Daughter. Ochester.
For Sleep, or Death. Pitter.
Fragment: Rain. Shelley.
Freedom. Green.
From Life. Eichenrand.
From Life. Hooker.
Fun in a Garret. Dowd.
The Garland. Vaughan.
The General's Death.
O'Connor.

Geography. Dransfield.
Georgics. Virgil (Publius Vergilius Maro).
Getting Drunk with Daughter. Huff.
Goin' Home. *Anonymous.*
Good Friday and the Present Crucifixion. Buckley.
The Green Corn Dance. Corbin.
Harvest Hymn. Whittier.
The Haymow. Mockett.
Hide in the Heart. Frankenberg.
Hilo, Hanakahi, Rain Rustling Lehua. *Anonymous.*
Hitch Haiku. Snyder.
The House of Falling Leaves. Braithwaite.
The House of Life. Rossetti.
The Husbandman. Taylor.
I wrung my hands under my dark veil... Akhmatova.
In Memoriam A.H.H., XCVIII. Tennyson.
In Time of Grief. Reese.
Independence. Cato.
Indulgences. Hogan.
Interior. Parker.
Invocation for a Storm. *Anonymous.*
An Irish Picture. Bigg.
It's Raining, It's Pouring. *Anonymous.*
Jack. Goldberg.
Jack-in-the-Pulpit. Eastwick.
The Jealous Brothers. *Anonymous.*
Job Hunting. Hennen.
John Garfield. Christopher.
A Junkie with a Flute in the Rain. Fisher.
Kingfisher Flat. Empson.
A Kiss in the Rain. Peck.
The Knife. Tillinghast.
The Last Furrow. Markham.
The Latter Rain. Very.
Lean Street. Fraser.
Letter to My Wife. Radnoti.
Lichtenberg. Kipling.
The Life and Death of Jason. Morris.
Light Rain. Buckley.
Limerick: "There was a young man of Fort Blainy." Anonymous.
The Lion's Skeleton. Turner.
The Little Cart. Waley.
Little Rain. Roberts.
Little Wind. Greenaway.
London Rain. MacNeice.
Lost Beliefs. Howells.
The Lost Heifer. Clarke.
Love Poem. Silko.
A Man of Rain. Barbeitos.
Marching. Rosenberg.
May Day. Teasdale.
May You Always Be the Darling of Fortune. Miller.
Meditation in Winter. Mann.
Melissa. Redl-Hlus.
Memo. Fearing.
Memorial Rain. MacLeish.
Memory of Another Climate. Preil.
The Message of the Rain. Russell.
Michaelmas. Nicholson.
Mnemosyne. Stickney.
Moods of Rain. Scannell.

The Moon Pond. McGuckian.
A Night in June. Scott.
Noah. Hagedorn.
Nox Benigna. Reeves.
O Lyric Love. Scott.
The Old Boast. Merwin.
Old Emily. Hill.
Old Iron. Stewart.
Old Man Rain. Cawein.
An Old Woman of the Roads. Colum.
On Gay Wallpaper. Williams.
On the Edge. Levine.
On the Edge at Santorini. Blumenthal.
On the First of March. *Anonymous.*
The Origins of Escape. Tisdale.
Orpheus. Hendry.
Out-Dated Poem. Gallup.
The Palm. Campbell.
The Palm Tree. Abd-ar-Rahman I.
Party Piece. Patten.
Phaedra. Doolittle.
The Phantom Bark. Crane.
The Plaidie. Sibley.
Poem for Pat. Allen.
Prayer. Brown.
Prayer for Rain. Palmer.
Proud Songsters. Hardy.
Psittachus Eois Imitatrix Ales Ab Indis. Sitwell.
Queen. Moraes.
Rain. Kirby.
Rain. Murray.
Rain. O'Sullivan.
The Rain, It Streams on Stone. Housman.
A Rain of Rites. Mahapatra.
Rain on the Down. Symons.
Rain on the Roof. Kinney.
Rain Sizes. Ciardi.
The Rain Song. Rogers.
The Rainbow. Davies.
The Rainy Day. Longfellow.
Rainy Day Song. Storey.
Rainy Morning. Rivera-Aviles.
Les Realites. Guest.
Renewal by Her Element. Devlin.
Reprieve. Cormack.
Retrospect. Pilibin.
Return of Autumn. Neruda.
Return to Astolat. White.
Roadside near Moscow. Ford.
A Room on a Garden. Stevens.
Rooms. Mew.
The Rosy Bosom'd Hours. Patmore.
Samurai and Hustlers. Johnson.
The Sand Painters. Belitt.
Scotland. Gray.
Sensibility. Simpson.
The Shadow of Cain. Sitwell.
She Weeps over Rahoon. Joyce.
Silex Scintillans. Vaughan.
Singing. Stevenson.
Sleep. Simic.
The Smoky Smirr o' Rain. Hay.

Somewhere I Have Never Travelled, Gladly Beyond. Cummings.
The Song of the Ancient People. Hay.
Song of the Rain Chant. *Anonymous.*
Song of the Wind and the Rain. Ibn Gabirol.
Sonnets, VII: "Upon an upland orchard's sunny side." Irwin.
Sorrow. De Vere.
Star Child Suite. Allen.
The Storm. Coatsworth.
Summer Images. Clare.
Sunset. Gwala.
Tales of the Islands, X. Walcott.
That the Neighborhood Might Be Covered. Eigner.
The Thatcher. Kennelly.
Then and Now. Murray.
There's a Feeling. Bullwinkle.
Therese. Nowlan.
Time Reminded Me. Uceda.
To a Print of Queen Victoria. Baxter.
To an Elder Poet. Williams.
To Germany. Sorley.
To His Coy Mistress (parody). Scupham.
To Ibn Zaidun. Wallada.
To K. de M. Stevenson.
Towards the Vanishing Point. Lehman.
Transfigured Life. Rossetti.
The Trip. Dennis.
The Tumble. Taylor.
Twice. Finlay.
Twilight Song. Robinson.
The Two Old Women of Mumbling Hill. Reeves.
Two Rivers. Emerson.
Two Variations. Levertov.
Tyrannic Love. Dryden
Uptown. Ginsberg.
Utah. Stevenson.
A Valediction. La Follette.
The Visitor. Browne.
Voices in the Winter. McCullough.
Waiting for the Rain. Mnthali.
Waking Up. Schmidt.
Watchers. Merwin.
The Way the Bird Sat. Young Bear.
Weather Rhymes. Brown.
What Have They Done to the Rain. Reynolds.
Whatever Comes. Stafford.
When I Went out. Kuskin.
When Sun Came to Riverwoman. Silko.
Who Shall Speak for the People? Sandburg.
Why Must You Know? Wheelwright.
The Wind of Our Enemy (excerpt). Marriott.
Windmill in March. Privett.
Winter Journey. Wygodski.
The Witch. Gibson.
Working against Time. Wagoner.
You Could Say. Mezey.
You Made It Rain. Allah.
Your Birds Build Sun-Castles with Song. Sloate.
Yugoslav Cemetery. Wright.

Rainbow (s)
April Fool. Hammond.
The Caged Skylark. Hopkins.
Day and Night. Alexander.
A Factory Rainbow. Sa'di.
Fragment. Lowell.
Hooking the Rainbow. Baldwin.
Indian Song: Survival. Silko.
Infant Noah. Watkins.
Lake Harvest. Knister.
Legend. Wright.
Leila. Hill.
NHR. Hirschman.
A Non Sequitor. Corbett.
Pancho Villa. Lipsitz.
Paradise Lost. Milton.
The Quaker Graveyard in Nantucket. Lowell.
The Rain and the Rainbow. Fredericks.
The Rainbow. McCord.
Reason Has Moons. Hodgson.
Silver Ships. Meigs.
Sonnet LXX. Alabaster.
Sowing on the Mountain. *Anonymous.*
To Waken a Small Person. Justice.
Two Somewhat Different Epigrams. Hughes.
The Vestal. Crane.
Whales Weep Not! Lawrence.
Wind and Wave. Patmore.

Raincoat (s)
Art Gallery. Dickson.
Lobsters in the Window. Snodgrass.
Nausicaa. Layton.

Raindrop (s)
April, Glengarry. Coxon.
A Dream of Suffocation. Bly.
During Wind and Rain. Hardy.
I'd Like to Mark Myself. Acorn.
Prayer to the Pacific. Silko.
Rain. Benediktsson.

Rainforest
Once the Striped Quagga. Tallmountain.

Raise (d) (s)
B's the Bus. McGinley.
Can I Say. Bird.
The Conclusion. Ralegh.
For a Christening. Watkins.
Giovanni da Fiesole on the Sublime or Fra Angelico's "Last Judgment." Howard.
His Metrical Prayer: Before Execution. Graham.
How to Murder Your Best Friend. O Hehir.
Joshua's Face. Gilboa.
Journal. Ciardi.
Look at All Those Monkeys. Milligan.
Lord Gorbals. Graham.
The Marriage of Pocahontas. Webster.
The Mother's Malison, or, Clyde's Water. Anonymous.
Old Black Men Say. Emanuel.

On Watching Politicians
Perform at Martin Luther
King's Funeral. Knight.
Poem from Llanybri.
Roberts.
Psalm XXXVI. Sidney.
Raise a Ruckus Tonight.
Anonymous.
Silence. Akhmadulina.
A Supplement. Tompson.
To Cheer Our Minds.
Ronksley.
To My Ingenious and Worthy
Friend William Lowndes,
Esq. Gay.
A Treatie of Human Learning.
Greville.
The Trooper's Horse.
Anonymous.
Watch Repair. Simic.
Zimmer's Hard Dream.
Zimmer.

Raisin (s)
Bread. Urdang.
Brief Autumnal. *Anonymous.*
Dunce Song 6. Van Doren.

Rake (s)
The Creeper. Schmidt.
In a Garden. Babcock.
Obituary. Brode.
The Pleasure of Walking
through an Alley. Gay.
Raking Walnuts in the Rain.
Shannon.
The Ramble-eer.
Anonymous.

Rally (ing)
The Fire-bringer. Moody.
The Monkey's Wedding (with
music). *Anonymous.*
Operation–Souls.
Anonymous.
Shoot the Buffalo.
Anonymous.

Ram (s)
Brigham Young.
Anonymous.
The City and the Trucks.
Thompson.
Lancashire Born.
Anonymous.

Rambling
Didn't He Ramble. Handy.
The Girl I Left behind Me
(My Parents Raised Me
Tenderly). *Anonymous.*
My Ramblin' Boy. Paxton.
The Ram of Darby.
Anonymous.
Rambling, Gambling Man.
Anonymous.
The Rambling Sailor.
Anonymous.
The Reek and the Rambling
Blade. *Anonymous.*
Spencer the Rover.
Anonymous.
Spilt Milk. Yeats.
YGreen Grows the Laurel.
Anonymous.

Rampart
Living. Monro.
On Hearing a Symphony of
Beethoven. Millay.
The Passing Strange.
Masefield.

Range (d) (r) (s)
The Bushrangers.
Harrington.
The Butterfly. Burr.
Canterbury. Dowling.

A Cow Camp on the Range.
Anonymous.
Curly Joe. *Anonymous.*
Emus. Fullerton.
The Faerie Queene. Spenser.
The Last Whiskey Cup.
Engle.
Lay of the Last Frontier.
Hersey.
Lord Beichan and Susie Pye.
Anonymous.
The Man of the Open West.
Monroe.
Oil Painting of the Artist As
the Artist. MacLeish.
Pattonio, the Pride of the
Plain. *Anonymous.*
The Rancher. Wilson.
Roll a Rock Down. Burton.
Specialist. Roethke.

Rank (s)
At Midnight's Hour.
Thoreau.
Jock the Leg and the Merry
Merchant. *Anonymous.*
Odes. Horace.
One dignity delays for all.
Dickinson.
The Progress of Man.
Canning.
Pruners: Conca di Marini.
Langland.
Saint. Merilaas.

Ransom (ed) (s)
I Saw One Hanging.
Anonymous.
I Shall Be Satisfied. Behemb.
The Lantern out of Doors.
Hopkins.
Mary Tired. Pickthall.
Saviour, Thy Dying Love.
Phelps.
Sonnets, XXXIV: "Why didst
thou promise such a
beauteous day."
Shakespeare.
Sonnets, CXX: "That you
were once unkind befriends
me now." Shakespeare.
Sunset Horn. O'Higgins.
We Praise Thee, If One
Rescued Soul. Sigourney.

Rape (d)
Autumn Journal. MacNeice.
Lost Contact. Wheeler.
O Artemis and your virgin
girls. Telesilla.
Pacific Epitaphs. Randall.
The Pueblo Women I
Watched Get down in
Brooklyn. Rose.
Unto Adam, His Own
Scriveyn. Chaucer.
Upon the Lark and the
Fowler. Bunyan.
Vision of 400 Sunrises.
Schechter.
The Voices Inescapable.
Stanford.

Rapture (d) (s)
The Abduction. Kunitz.
The Adventurous Muse.
Watts.
The Beauties of Santa Cruz.
Freneau.
A bee his burnished carriage.
Dickinson.
A Channel Passage.
Swinburne.
Christian Ethics. Traherne.
The Everlasting Mercy.
Masefield.

Fatal Interview. Millay.
Incognita of Raphael.
Butler.
Invention. Watson.
Jesus, Keep Me Near the
Cross. Crosby.
Let Me Enjoy. Hardy.
Life. Coleridge.
Lines Written Immediately
after Parting from a Lady.
Brydges.
The Monochord. Rossetti.
Music. Herrick.
A Painter in New England.
Stork.
Paradise. Faber.
Poems. Drummond.
Pomegranates. Valery.
Read the Bible Through.
Wells.
A Receipt for Stewing Veal.
Gay.
Resurgam. Burt.
The Romantic. Ellis.
Saul. Browning.
Sights and Sounds of the
Night. Wilcox.
Singing on the Moon.
Hughes.
Sonnet against the Too-Facile
Mystic. Harrod.
Sonnet: "Could then the Babes
from yon unshelter'd cot."
Russell.
A Sonnet to Opium;
Celebrating Its Virtues.
"Orestes".
The Soul's Travelling
(excerpt). Browning.
To Mrs. M. B. on Her Birth-
day. Pope.
When Wild Confusion Wrecks
the Air. Byles.
Your World. Johnson.

Rare
Amores. Parini.
Britannia's Pastorals.
Browne.
The Confirmation. Muir.
Constancy. Daniel.
John Smith of His Friend
Master John Taylor.
Smith.
Lately, Alas, I Knew a Gentle
Boy. Thoreau.
On an Indian Tomineois, the
Least of Birds. Heyrick.
The Panchatantra: The
Penalty of Virtue.
Anonymous.
Senile. Folk.
Sonnets, LVI: "Sweet love,
renew thy force."
Shakespeare.
The Tapestry. George.
Verbal Critics. Pope.

Rascal (s)
Jumbled in the Common Box.
Auden.
Tom Southerne's Birth-Day
Dinner at Ld. Orrery's.
Pope.
Tricksters. Benet.

Rat (s)
Arizona Village. Davieau.
Artificer. Kennedy.
Assailant. Raven.
Bullfrog. Hughes.
Chez-Nous. Austin.
The Church of San Antonio
de la Florida. Petrie.

The Doctor Who Sits at the
Bedside of a Rat. Miles.
Family Evening. Huws.
For a Little Girl Mourning
Her Favorite Cat.
Whittier.
Four Preludes on Playthings
of the Wind. Sandburg.
Hoddley, Poddley, Puddle and
Fogs. *Anonymous.*
How a Good Greyhound Is
Shaped. *Anonymous.*
The Intoxicated Rat.
Anonymous.
The Man from Changi.
Hetherington.
The Rat and the Elephant.
La Fontaine.
Short Haired Woman.
Hopkins.
Slides. Maiden.
The Three Little Kittens.
Anonymous.
Three Little Kittens. Cook.
Tin Cup Blues. Jefferson.
Trench Poets. Rickword.
Water Color of Granchester
Meadows. Plath.
With Mercy for the Greedy.
Sexton.

Rattle (s)
At Grand Canyon's Edge.
Ray.
The Cambridge Ladies.
Cummings.
Edgehill Fight. Kipling.
It Is Winter, I Know.
Moore.
On Scafell Pike. Walker.
The Rattlesnake.
Anonymous.
To a Friend Concerning
Several Ladies. Williams.
Tongue River Psalm.
Gildner.
The Transparent Man.
Hecht.
Whispering Clouds. Platov.

Rattlesnake
A California Idyl. McGaffey.
Ella, in a Square Apron, along
Highway 80. Grahn.
John Henry (variant).
Anonymous.
Old Rattler. *Anonymous.*
The Rattlesnake Band.
Conley.
Springfield Mountain (C
vers.). *Anonymous.*

Ravage (d)
The Gash. Everson.
Malediction. McGinley.
O Pioneers! Bishop.

Rave (s)
A Dedication. Gordon.
Hurry Me Nymphs. Darley.
I'll always dress in black and
rave. Pisan.
Mozart Perhaps. Wheelock.
A Question. Synge.

Raven (s)
The Beauty of the Stars. Ibn
Ezra.
Connubii Flores, or the Well-
Wishes at Weddings.
Herrick.
Course Bread and Water's
Most Their Fare.
Williams.
The Grave. Donaghy.
High Up on Suilven.
MacCaig.

Imperfect Sestina. Webb.
The Lovely Youth. Aneirin.
Ninth Moon. Li Ho.
Noah's Song. Jones.
Novembers or Straight Life.
  Owen.
Prayer for Messiah. Cohen.
Soaring. Clothier.
They Were Welcome to Their
  Belief. Frost.
To Eliza, Duchess of Dorset.
  Bennett.

Ravished
Beneath a Cool Shade.
  Behn.
A Lodging for the Night.
  Wylie.
A Question. *Anonymous.*
Sonnet: To the Lady
  Beaumont. Wordsworth.

Ray (s)
Alma Mater. Quiller-Couch.
The Djanggawul Cycle, 84.
  Anonymous.
Don Juan. Byron.
The Double Vision. Day.
La Fayette. Coleridge.
God Be With You.
  Anonymous.
It Will Not Shine Again.
  Bronte.
The Landfall. Dickey.
Long Lonely Lover of the
  Highway. Will.
Noon Quatrains. Cotton.
Pure is the Dewy Gem.
  Callanan.
Religious Musings.
  Coleridge.
Sigh. Mallarme.
Stanzas. Thoreau.
The Times. Manilius.
To a Young Leader of the
  First World War. George.

Razor
Aiken Drum. *Anonymous.*
Belfast Linen. *Anonymous.*
Brothers (I). Reiss.
Edmund Burke. Goldsmith.
Punk Pantoum. Stewart.
Sonnet: "Ice over time."
  Shapiro.

Reach (ed) (es) (ing)
Adam. Hecht.
Air Is. Brennan.
The Author, of His Own
  Fortune. Harington.
The Coach of Time.
  Pushkin.
The Crazed Moon. Yeats.
The Gnomes. Bentley.
The Gossip. Halpern.
The Greedy Fox and the
  Elusive Grapes. Aesop.
I felt a cleavage in my mind.
  Dickinson.
I Kissed Pa Twice after His
  Death. Peterson.
Identities. Young.
If. Bangs.
In a Railway Compartment.
  Fuller.
In the Dawn. Shepard.
In the Old Theatre, Fiesole.
  Hardy.
A Mother in Egypt.
  Pickthall.
Of Life and Death (excerpt).
  Vaughan.
Old Couple. Simic.
Parting. Preil.
Point Grey. Hine.

Poor Omie. *Anonymous.*
Prison Walls–Red Brick
  Crevices. Wilkins.
Return to a Place Lit by a
  Glass of Milk. Simic.
The Road Moves On. Nash.
The Sea-God's Address to
  Bran. Anonymous.
Shade. Lynch.
The Spider. Eberhart.
St. Roach. Rukeyser.
The Swimmer's Moment.
  Avison.
Tending. Rankin.
There's a Fire in the Forest.
  Ross.
To a Lady That Desired Me I
  Would Bear My Part with
  Her in a Song. Lovelace.
To the Nightingale.
  Wilchilsea.
A Woman to Her Lover.
  Walsh.

Read (er) (ing) (s)
Abraham's Knife. Garrett.
Acceptance Speech. Bell.
Adventures. Kramer.
After Horace. Godley.
The Art of Eyes. Spenser.
The Author to the Reader.
  Jarrell.
Beauty's Pageant. Rossetti.
Belshazzar. Dickinson.
Books Fall Open. McCord.
Can Zone; or, The Good
  Food Guide. Lesser.
Cat's Eyes. Scarfe.
Le Chariot. Wieners.
Clio's Protest. Sheridan.
The Company of Scholars.
  Bevington.
The Complete Introductory
  Lectures on Poetry.
  Mayer.
The Corpse. Moore.
Darling of Gods and Men,
  beneath the Gliding Stars.
  Bunting.
Dere's a Han'writin' on de
  Wall. *Anonymous.*
The Disgrace. di Michele.
Do It Now. Braley.
During Music. Symons.
An Elegie. Corbett.
Epigram: "Cu Chuimne in
  youth." *Anonymous.*
Epigram on One who Made
  Long Epitaphs. Pope.
Epitaph at Hadleigh, Suffolk.
  Anonymous.
Epitaph: "O flower of all that
  springs from gentle blood."
  Chaibrera.
Epitaph on a Well-Known
  Poet. Moore.
Etruscan Tombs. Robinson.
Fable. Mills.
The Faerie Queene. Spenser.
February Margins.
  Henderson.
The Flag. Roche.
The Flaming Heart.
  Crashaw.
Gaspara Stampa. Benet.
Generation Gap. Wallace.
The Gospel According to
  You. *Anonymous.*
Greens. Ray.
Growing Up. Gregg.
Hallowed Places. Palmer.
The Hemorrhage. Kunitz.
Hossolalia. Luton.

The House Was Quiet and the
  World Was Calm.
  Stevens.
Hymns for the Amusement of
  Children. Smart.
I in the Grayness Rose.
  Phillips.
I Saw Thee. Palmer.
If You See This Man. Lux.
An Image from Beckett.
  Mahon.
In Sepia. Anderson.
Japanese Beetles. Kennedy.
Letter to Lord Byron.
  Auden.
Limerick: "There was an old
  person who said." Smith.
A Long & Happy Life.
  Schuchat.
Looking at Your Face.
  Kinnell.
Mother. Libera.
Musophilus. Daniel.
News. Pomeroy.
October. Spacks.
Of All Things for You to Go
  Away Mad. Kyger.
On a Baltimore Bus. Bell.
On a Visit to Ch'ung Chen
  Taoist Temple... Yu
  Hsuan-chi.
On His Books. Belloc.
On the Death of Old Bennet
  the News-Crier.
  Anonymous.
On When McCarthy Was a
  Wolf among a Nation of
  Queer-Queers. Dugan.
One Desiring Me to Read, but
  Slept It out, Wakening.
  Daniel.
The Oracle. Ficke.
Paradise Lost. Milton.
A Patch of Old Snow. Frost.
Peace. Calverley.
R is for the Restaurant.
  McGinley.
The Reading Mother.
  Gillilan.
The Respectable Burgher.
  Hardy.
Sapientia Lunae. Dowson.
The Season's Lovers.
  Waddington.
Sense and Spirit. Meredith.
Serious Readers. Redgrove.
A Sigh. Wilchilsea.
Sir Walter Scott's Tribute.
  Scott.
The Sluggard. Watts.
Sonnets, XXIII: "As an
  unperfect actor on the
  stage." Shakespeare.
The Story of Rimini. Hunt.
Sunday Funnies. Keiter.
The Sunday News. Gioia.
These Two. Schwartz.
They Say My Verse Is Sad:
  No Wonder. Housman.
To a Certain Most Certainly
  Certain Critic. McCord.
To a Poet a Thousand Years
  Hence. Heath-Stubbs.
To the Reader. Baudelaire.
Trastevere. Denby.
True Confessional.
  Ferlinghetti.
Two Presentations. Duncan.
The Verb "To Think'.
  Enright.
Volcano. Walcott.
Warm Tea. MacAdams.

The Way to the River.
  Merwin.
When We Were Very Silly.
  Morton.
The White Stallion. Owen.
Wil the Merry Weaver, and
  Charity the Chamber-Maid.
  Anonymous.
With a China Chamberpot, to
  the Countess of
  Hillsborough. Holland.
Writing in England Now.
  O'Connor.
You Call That a Ts'ing: A
  Letter (parody). Barrow.

Ready
The Angler's Reveille. Van
  Dyke.
The Boy Washington.
  Thompson.
The Cenci. Shelley.
Eleven Addresses to the Lord.
  Berryman.
For Real. Cortez.
A Good Life. Watson.
He Raise a Poor Lazarus.
  Anonymous.
I Have Got My Leave.
  Tagore.
I to My Perils. Housman.
Look. Stafford.
Mis' Smith. Paine.
One for Money. *Anonymous.*
Prelude. George.
Quick Now, Here, Now,
  Always–. Rewak.
The Santa Barbara
  Earthquake. *Anonymous.*
Starting Rhymes for Hide-
  and-Seek: "Green lady,
  green lady." *Anonymous.*
Tract. Williams.
Upland. Ammons.
Upon My Lord Brohall's
  Wedding. Suckling.
The Virginia Song.
  Anonymous.
Walk in Jerusalem Jus' Like
  John. *Anonymous.*
Words Most Often
  Mispronouncd in Poetry.
  Kuo.

Reaffirm
The Searching. Cobb.

Real
All Hushed and Still Within
  the House. Bronte.
All Too Little on Pictures.
  Black.
Ambushed by Angels.
  Davidson.
At Night. Montgomery.
Auburn. Verlaine.
The Banjo. Winner.
Death May Leap on a Sunny
  Day. Thompson.
Discourse on the Real.
  Yellen.
Doggerel by a Senior Citizen.
  Auden.
Ellora. Nathan.
The Exchanges II. Kelly.
Five for the Grace. Scott.
Her sweet weight on my heart
  a night. Dickinson.
I Know He Is Real.
  Anonymous.
I Went into the Maverick Bar.
  Snyder.
James Powell on Imagination.
  Neal.

A Lost God (excerpt).
Bourdillon.
The Man under the Bed.
Jong.
Moving. Gray.
My Father's Eye. Vakalo.
A Natural History of Dragons
and Unicorns My Daughter
and I Have Known. Root.
Once in a While a Protest
Poem. Axelrod.
Paradise. Sargent.
The Pipes. Lipsitz.
Pleasures. Goldbarth.
Proverbial Philosophy: Of
Reading. Calverley.
The Reactionary Poet. Reed.
A Real Story. Pastan.
The Rhododendron Plant.
Katzman.
The Room. Day-Lewis.
Salut Au Monde! Whitman.
Some of Us Are Exiles from
No Land. O Hehir.
Song for a Blue Roadster.
Field.
Still Life. Austin.
Stopping the Heart.
Edmond.
Superbull. Witt.
Terminal Theater. Sward.
That Everything Moves Its
Bowels (parody). Slavitt.
This Decoration. Carruth.
To Be of Use. Piercy.
To the Shore. Swenson.
The Water-Wheel. Clemo.
What's in a Name?
Munkittrick.
Woman Poem. Giovanni.

Reality (ies)
As I Look Out. St. Martin.
The Basement Watch.
Tolnay.
Drugged. De la Mare.
Evergreen. Milne.
Exit Line. Ciardi.
Hurt Hawks. Jeffers.
I Am a Book I Neither Wrote
Nor Read. Schwartz.
I am so lost. Narihira
(Ariwara no Narihira).
I'm a Dreamer. Cumbo.
The Master. Merwin.
On Ascending a Hill Leading
to a Convent. Mello.
Spring 1943. Fuller.
Sunday Night Walk.
Souster.
These Trees Are No Forest of
Mourners. Jones.
Tim. Montague.
The Tree of Death. Vigee.
What Sanguine Beast?
Smith, Jr.
While I Have Vision.
Quennell.

Realize
First Sight of Her and After.
Hardy.
He Asked about the Quality.
Cavafy.
Immortality. Horne
Realization. Acharya.
Salamis. Durrell.

Realm (s)
As Yet. Rodgers.
The Book of Hours (excerpt).
Rilke.
Christ's Resurrection and
Ascension. Doddridge.

Commemoration Ode.
Monroe.
Don Juan. Byron.
An Epigram to the Queen,
Then Lying In. Jonson.
Fates of the Apostles.
Cynewulf.
A Grave. Moreland.
The History of Arizona: How
It Was Made and Who
Made It. Brown.
Messiah. Pope.
The Mother. Palmer.
The Nature of the Turtle
Dove. Anonymous.
O Thou Whose Gracious
Presence Shone. Ham.
Ode for Decoration Day
(excerpt). Peterson
On a Poet. Luttrell.
The Sages. Mickiewicz.
So Young Ane King.
Lindsay.
To Forget Me. Weiss.
Today I Have Touched the
Earth. Smith.
The Word of God to Leyden
Came. Rankin.

Reap (ed) (ing) (s)
Afternoon in a Tree. Maris
Stella.
Basia. Campion.
Before Olympus. Fletcher.
Calm. Camerino.
Ezekiel, You and Me (with
music). Anonymous.
The Faerie Queene. Spenser.
Golden Silences. Rossetti.
A Good Creed. Anonymous.
He Singeth a Hymn to Osiris,
the Lord of Eternity.
Book of the Dead.
I Bore with Thee, Long,
Weary Days. Rossetti.
In Spite of Sorrow. Judson.
Lines Written in a Country
Parson's Orchard. Daiken.
Martyrdom of Father
Campion. Walpole.
Reapers. Blind.
The Reapers. Watt.
The Seed Growing Secretly.
Vaughan.
Trilby. Du Maurier.
Turn Back, You Wanton
Flyer. Campion.
Weeping and Singing.
Tiempo.
You're Going to Reap Just
What You Sow.
Anonymous.

Rear (ed) (ing) (s)
All Over the World.
Johnson.
A Fit of Rime against Rime.
Jonson.
A Happy New Year (excerpt).
Auden.
Rookie's Lament.
Anonymous.
Song of Allegiance. Mason.
Songs of Seven. Ingelow.
This Be Our Revenge.
Tchernichovsky.

Reason (s)
All Things Drink. Stanley.
Almanac Verse. Danforth.
The Apology Addressed to the
Critical Reviewers.
Churchill.
Astrophel and Stella, X.
Sidney.

At Last the Secret Is Out.
Auden.
The Beauty of Things.
Jeffers.
The Bride. Bierce.
Caelica, XIV. Greville.
The Case for Miners.
Sassoon.
Charm for Corns.
Anonymous.
Coming to This. Strand.
The Cormorant in Its
Element. Clampitt.
Cullen. Page.
The Dead Marten. Landor.
Dear Fanny. Moore.
The Destiny of Nations.
Coleridge.
Don Juan. Byron.
The Doppelganger. Hine.
Eclipse. Fagg.
Empedocles. Meredith.
The English Garden (excerpt).
Mason.
Epigram: "What makes all
subjects discontent."
Butler.
An Essay on Man. Pope.
For No Clear Reason.
Creeley.
Gascoigne's Woodmanship.
Gascoigne.
Houseplant. Napier.
Hymn to Proust. Ewart.
I, being born a woman and
distressed. Millay.
I Have Sought Long with
Steadfastness. Wyatt.
In a Mirror. Stubbs.
In Wonted Walks. Sidney.
The Indian Burying Ground.
Freneau.
Indifference to Fortune.
Thomson.
Jerusalem. Kanalenstein.
John Button Birthday.
O'Hara.
Justice Is Reason Enough.
Wakoski.
"Love Not Me for Comely
Grace." Anonymous
Lying Down with Men and
Women. Woods.
Manhood. More.
Mimnermus in Church.
Cory.
Moonshine. Williamson.
The Nature of Man. Sisson.
Near the Death of Ovid.
Conquest.
O Love, How Strangely Sweet.
Marston.
On Walking Back to the Bus.
Gardner.
The One Thing Needful.
Miller.
Poem from the Empire State.
Jordan.
The Quiet Glen. Fraser.
A Reason Fair to Fill My
Glass. Morris.
Religio Laici. Dryden.
De Sade. Fuller.
The Same Old Story.
Montague.
Sarah. Hyde.
The Scales of Love.
Hartmann von Aue.
The School-Mistress. In
Imitation of Spenser.
Shenstone.

The Song of the Western
Men. Hawker.
The Sound of the Sea.
Longfellow.
Swordy Well. Clare.
There Was a Crimson Clash
of War. Crane.
To His Love That Sent Him a
Ring. Turberville.
To His Mistress. Rochester.
The Traveller. Goldsmith.
The Tribes. Fuller.
Valley Blood. Sternlieb.
Voices at the Window.
Sidney.
Your Eyes Have Their
Silence. Barrax.

Reasoning
Heredity. Aldrich.
Recessional. Johnson.

Reave
As Life What Is So Sweet?
Anonymous.

Reawakening
Near the Border of Insanities.
Abse.

Rebecca
Three Sisters. De la Mare.

Rebel (s)
Amoretti, XIX. Spenser.
The Battle-Cry of Freedom.
Root.
Brother Green. Anonymous.
He "Digesteth Harde Yron".
Moore.
Jefferson D. Cornwell.
The Litttle Black-Eyed Rebel.
Carleton.
Paradise Lost. Milton.
The Rebel Soldier.
Anonymous.
Strange Monsters. Watkyns.
Throw away the Flowers.
Daryush.
Tin-Ore. Anonymous.
To the Ghost of John Milton.
Sandburg.

Reborn
Born Again. Farrokhzad.
Caedmon. Garrett.
Countee Cullen. Maleska.
Epitaph. Rose.
Grape-Gathering. Shlonsky.
Abraham
In Memoriam. Fortini.
Inside, Outside, and Beyond.
Ratti.
Light. Hagedorn.
Mexico City Blues: 229th
Chorus. Kerouac.
Reborn. Amis.
Semele Recycled. Kizer.
A Small Bird's Nest Made of
White Reed Fiber. Bly.
Speak to the Sun. Wilson.
Spirits Unchained.
Kgositsile.
Toroi Bandi. Anonymous.

Recall (ed)
The Argument. Moreland.
The Dream. Allingham.
Glass Dialectic. Nemerov.
Haiku: "A balmy spring
wind..." Wright.
The House. Nelson.
Late Light. Blunden.
Love and Age. Landor.
Neckwear. Silverton.
Reading Faust. Goldin.
The Sea Serpent. Irwin.
To the Holy Spirit. Winters.

With Whom Is No
Variableness, Neither
Shadow of Turning.
Clough.
Receive (d) (r) (s)
Lament for a Cricket Eleven.
Allott.
Natural Architecture. Hay.
A New-Years-Gift to Brian
Lord Bishop of Sarum...
Cartwright.
Orange County Plague:
Scenes. Lieberman.
The Pet Lamb. Wordsworth.
Rowing Early. Peck.
Samson Agonistes. Milton.
The Tables Turned.
Wordsworth.
Reckless
The Cowboy's Meditation.
Anonymous.
It's Cold in China Blues.
Nettles.
Reckon (ed) (ing)
Cain Shall Not Slay Abel
Today on Our Good
Ground. Lowry.
An English Mother.
Johnson.
An Epistle to Sir Edward
Sackville, Now Earl of
Dorset. Jonson.
I Have a Roof. Jackson.
Last Things. Meredith.
Old Voyager. Blackstock.
Rembrandt's Late Self-
Portraits. Jennings.
The Righteous Man. Butler.
Recognize (d) (s)
Change of Address. Fraser.
Christ. Holmes.
The Day after Sunday.
McGinley.
The Englishman on the
French Stage. Seaman.
A Farewell. Patmore.
Grace at Evening. Poteat.
How Did He Get Here?
Leivick.
Image in a Mirror.
Goodman.
Leit. Rodriguez Frese.
Lullaby for Ann-Lucian.
Forbes.
My Strawlike Hair. Asya
(Asya Gray).
On First Looking into
Chapman's Homer II
(parody). Peterson.
Paring the Apple.
Tomlinson.
Poem: "I keep feeling all
space as my image."
Russell.
Sisters. Rich.
Strange Meetings. Monro.
Transit. Rich.
Recollection (s)
Dead Dog. Scannell.
Disaster. Mangan.
Epigram: "Good Fortune,
when I hailed her recently."
Cunningham.
Hardy's Plymouth. Grigson.
John Betjeman's Brighton
(parody). Ewart.
Limerick: "There was an old
man of Khartoum." Inge.
A Terrible Infant. Locker-
Lampson.
Reconcile (d) (s)
A Christmas Hymn. Wilbur.

Model. Ammons.
The Nativity. Wesley.
Rest O Sun I Cannot.
Tusiani.
Thought for the Winter
Season. Osborn.
Verses Supposed to be Written
by Alexander Selkirk.
Cowper.
Winter Stars. Levis.
Record (s)
The Business. Creeley.
Centennial Hymn. Bryant.
Conversation in Avila.
McGinley.
The Desert Music (excerpt).
Williams.
Excerpt from a Report to the
Galactic Council.
Conquest.
Lines Left at Mr. Theodore
Hook's House in June,
1834. Barham.
Phantom or Fact. Coleridge.
The Rhyme of the Chivalrous
Shark. Irwin.
Steamboat Bill. *Anonymous.*
Writing. Allingham.
Recover
The Damage You Have Done.
Komey.
Idea. Drayton.
If God Exists. Lipska.
Lament after Her Husband
Bishr's Murder. Al-
Khirniq.
Langaig. Hugo.
The Lovers. Zaturenska.
Poem after Apollinaire.
Sadoff.
Recreation
The Fox. Hesketh.
O'Tuomy's Drinking Song.
O'Tuomy.
Recruit (ed)
Seventeen. Holden.
Verses on Accepting the
World. Brodsky.
Red
Alabama. Simmons.
Alone in April. Cabell.
Altarwise by Owl-Light.
Thomas.
Arab Love-Song. Thompson.
The Armada: A Fragment.
Macaulay.
Barbara Allen. *Anonymous.*
A Beautiful Young Nymph
Going to Bed. Swift.
The Betrayal of the Rose.
Thomas.
Birdwatcher. Treece.
Bolsum Brown (with music).
Anonymous.
Carved on an Areca Nut...
Ho Xuan Huong.
Charlie Cherry. Jackson.
Cherry Tree. Rossetti.
Childhood. Read.
Circles. Sandburg.
Columbia the Gem of the
Ocean. Becket.
Comrade Jesus. Cleghorn.
Degrees of Gray in
Philipsburg. Hugo.
Devon to Me. Galsworthy.
Dinnshenchas: The Story of
Macha. *Anonymous.*
Drinking Time. O'Sullivan.
Eighteen-Seventy. Rimbaud.
Elegy. McFadden.
England. Montgomery.

Errant. Godfrey.
Eurydice. Doolittle.
The Fashionable Heart.
Gilbert.
A Fauxbourg. Croly.
Five Little Sisters Walking in
a Row. Greenaway.
Flag Song. Ward.
The Flowers. Rands.
Gibraltar. Blunt.
The Gray Plume. Carlin.
Green Grow the Lilacs.
Anonymous.
The Gull. Nakasuk.
Haroun al-Rachid for Heart's-
Life. *Anonymous.*
Headline History. Plomer.
The Heart's Low Door.
Mitchell.
Here's the Tender Coming.
Anonymous.
History and Abstraction.
Lux.
How Roses Came Red.
Herrick.
How to Choose a Wife.
Anonymous.
I Have Seen Black Hands.
Wright.
Idaho Jack. Lee.
In the Home of the Scholar
Wu Su-chiang from Hsin-
an... Wu Tsao.
In Yellow Meadows I Take
No Delight. Browne.
Inquisitive Barn. Frost.
Isaac Leybush Peretz.
Halpern.
Jane Was a Neighbor.
Anonymous.
Joe Bowers. *Anonymous.*
July 4th. Swenson.
The Keys of the Jail.
Anonymous.
Late Lights in Minnesota.
Kooser.
Life the Beloved. Rossetti.
The Lights in the Hallway.
Wright.
The Little Red Ribbon.
Riley.
Many Red Devils. Crane.
March Snow. McKay.
Mary Was a Red Bird.
Anonymous.
Mass at Dawn. Campbell.
Mercian Hymns (excerpt).
Hill.
Middle Ages. Sassoon.
The Missel-Thrush's Nest.
Clare.
My Old True Love.
Anonymous.
New Proverb. Brooks.
Nineteen Hundred and
Nineteen. Yeats.
Note on Local Flora.
Empson.
The Novelty Shop. Niatum.
Ode to the Spirit of Earth in
Autumn. Meredith.
Of the Pythagorean
Philosophy. Dryden.
Of Your Father's Indiscretions
and the Train to California.
Emanuel.
An Old Charcoal Seller. Po
Chu-i.
Old World, New World.
Roskolenko.
Otoe County in Nebraska.
Kloefkorn.

The Pact. Rubin.
Phaedra. Doolittle.
Poems. Conkling.
Prevarication. *Anonymous.*
The Puddle. Phillpotts.
Put Down. Damas.
Rain Forest. Rolls.
Red Clay. Hogan.
The Red Flag. Connell.
The Red Man's Wife. Hyde.
Red Right Returning. Coxe.
The Red, White and Blue.
Shaw.
The Red, White and Red.
Anonymous.
Riddle: "Four and twenty
white bulls." *Anonymous.*
Rodin to Rilke. Grosholz.
The Rose. Howell.
The Roses on the Terrace.
Tennyson.
Salvation Prospect. Smith,
Jr.
The Second Coming. Abse.
Sentences (excerpt).
Harrison.
She'll Be Comin' Round the
Mountain. *Anonymous.*
The Ship of Fools. Barclay.
Sleepyhead. De la Mare.
Soldiers Bathing. Prince.
Song of the Trees of the Black
Forest. Jabes.
Spectrum. Dickey.
Spring Landscape. La
Follette.
The Streets of Laredo.
MacNeice.
The Sun Drops Red. Miller.
Sweet William. *Anonymous.*
The Tantanoola Tiger.
Harris.
Th Gypsy Countess.
Anonymous.
They Went Forth to Battle,
but They Always Fell.
O'Sheel.
They Who Wait. Going.
The Tin Woodsman. Jiles.
A Toast to the Flag. Daly.
The Tombstone Told When
She Died. Thomas.
Treaty-Trip from Shulus
Reservation. Lane.
Utah Carroll. *Anonymous.*
Vlamertinghe: Passing the
Chateau. Blunden.
Walt Whitman at Bear
Mountain. Simpson.
Wandering Chorus. Alquit.
War Comes. Schneour.
Weather Rhymes. Brown.
What Semiramis Said.
Lindsay.
What the Red-haired Bo'sun
Said. Souter.
What though the Green Leaf
Grow? Fleming.
When Almonds Bloom.
Shinn.
Who among You Knows the
Essence of Garlic? Hongo.
Who Is My Brother? Lane.
Will the Weaver.
Anonymous.
Wolves for Company.
Anonymous.
Wounds. Minty.
Your Flag and My Flag.
Nesbit.

Redeem (ed) (er) (ing) (s)
Come to Calvary's Holy
  Mountain. Montgomery.
Dostoievsky's Daughters.
  Hamburger.
Game Out of Hand. Ross.
Government Official. Dehn.
Help from History. Stafford.
An Hymne of the Ascension.
  Drummond.
In God's Eternity. Ballou I.
Melons. Yungman.
The Messiah. Frishman.
Not There. *Anonymous.*
Now Kindness. Viereck.
Psalm CXXX, De Profundis.
  O.T.
The Redeemer. "Macleod.
Spirit from Whom Our Lives
  Proceed. Robbins.
Sumter–A Ballad of 1861.
  Anonymous.
To the River Isca (the Usk).
  Vaughan.
Twin. Haring.
The Virgin Unspotted.
  Anonymous.

Redemption
The Cherry Fair.
  Anonymous.
Farewell This World!
  Anonymous.
For Innocents Day.
  Wadding.
Sonnet: A Rapture
  Concerning His Lady.
  Cavalcanti.
Spring Song. Nahum.
To Julia, the Flaminica Dialis,
  or Queen-Priest. Herrick.
We Would See Jesus.
  Anonymous.
Wicked Polly. *Anonymous.*

Redress
To Whom Shall the World
  Henceforth Belong?
  Oxenham.
When that I call unto my
  mind. Wyatt.

Red River
Idaho Jack. Lee.
Red River Shore.
  Anonymous.

Red Sea
Glee–The Ghosts. Peacock.
Silex Scintillans. Vaughan.

Reed (s)
Bay Bank. Ammons.
Employment. Herbert.
Epigram: "I celebrate
  Rhegion." *Anonymous.*
Exorcism. Gogarty.
The Fall of Hyperion.
  Keats.
Florence MacCarthy's
  Farewell to Her English
  Lover. De Vere.
Ghazal: Japanese Paintbrush.
  Mott.
Heron in Swamp. Howard.
Homage to Chagall. Niatum.
Idylls. Moschus.
Indian Rock, Bainbridge
  Island, Washington.
  Niatum.
It Is the Reed. Maris Stella.
Keats. Longfellow.
Lamentations. Gluck.
Love-Song. Lasker-Schüler.
Madrigal: "Since just disdain."
  Peerson.
A Mirage. Setterberg.

Morning Fancy. Fenollosa.
Museum with Chinese
  Landscapes. Cybulski.
Nocturne in G Minor.
  Vollmoeller.
On a Fowler. Isidorus.
Pan and Syrinx. Rodgers.
"Picciola". Newell.
Silver. De La Mare.
Stanley Meets Mutesa.
  Rubadiri.
To a Friend Concerning
  Several Ladies. Williams.
To a Lady: She Refusing to
  Continue a Dispute with
  Me... Prior.
Variation on a Theme by John
  Lyly. Sitwell.
The Vision of Piers Plowman.
  Langland.
Winter Burn. Hill.

Reef
The Ground-Swell. Pratt.
Homecoming. Baxter.
In Memoriam A.H.H.,
  XXXVI. Tennyson.
Let Go the Reef Tackle.
  Anonymous.
Sea School. Howes.
Song: "My dreams were
  doleful and drear." Irwin.
Sonnets. Tuckerman.
The Wreck of the Hesperus.
  Longfellow.

Reek (ing)
Civil Defense. Burke.
Diary. Moon of the Hiding
  Doe. De Clue.
Fragment from the
  Elizabethans. Bridges-
  Adams.

Reels
The Satirist. Koopman.
To the Film Industry in
  Crisis. O'Hara.

Reference
Analogue of Unity in
  Multeity. Eberhart.
Landscape I. Madge.
Literary Criticism.
  Gopaleen.
Sidewalk Orgy. O'Connell.

Refine (d) (ment) (s)
An Apology for the Foregoing
  Hymn.... Crashaw.
English Bards and Scotch
  Reviewers. Byron.
Here are fine gifts, children.
  Sappho.
Of Astraea. Davies.

Reflect (ed) (ion) (s)
At the Loom. Duncan.
Change of Venue.
  Clockadale.
Corner Seat. MacNeice.
Cuisine Bourgeoise. Stevens.
Fast. Tagliabue.
The Father and His Children.
  Anonymous.
For Haroun al Raschid.
  Abu'l-Atahija.
Letters to Live Poets.
  Beaver.
Looking Up at Leaves.
  Howes.
The Mirror. Gluck.
Morning. Reed.
Narcissus. Press.
On the Night Express to
  Madrid. Dunetz.
One Almost Might.
  Tessimond.

Paris by Night. Milbauer.
Pure Nails Brightly Flashing.
  Mallarme.
Stanzas to Mr. Bentley.
  Gray.
Strains of Sight. Duncan.
Thoughts on Pausing at a
  Cottage near the Paukataug
  River. Knight.
The Waiting-Room. Fuller.
A Way of Looking.
  Jennings.
Written on a Sunday
  Morning. Southey.

Reflex
Amoretti, LXVI. Spenser.
Laus Infantium. Canton.
Speech for the Repeal of the
  McCarran Act. Wilbur.

Reform (er)
More Reformation. Defoe.
An Old Man's Advice.
  Anonymous.
The Reformed Pirate.
  Roberts.

Refraction
Departure. Amis.
Gibbs (excerpt). Rukeyser.
In Memoriam A.H.H., XCII.
  Tennyson.

Refrain
Hilo, Hanakahi, Rain Rustling
  Lehua. *Anonymous.*
Motif for Mary's Dolors.
  Mary Madeleva.
What Frenzy Has of Late
  Possess'd the Brain!
  Garth.

Refreshed
Limerick: "There was an old
  person of Ewell." Lear.
One Step Twix't Me and
  Death. Williams.
To the Trinity. Stanyhurst.

Refuge
Because He Was Tempted.
  Anonymous.
Epistle to John Hamilton
  Reynolds (excerpt). Keats.
Fire. Carpenter.
The Granite Mountain.
  Sarett.
Lord, while for All Mankind.
  Wreford.
Lyve Thowe Gladly, Yff So
  Thowe May. Wyatt.
O Lord! My Hiding Place.
  Raffles.
On the Death of Sylvia Plath.
  Herzberg.
Rooftop Winter. Thorpe.
Thirteenth Station.
  Donaghy.
The Voice of Webster
  (excerpt). Johnson.
When Structure Fails Rhyme
  Attempts to Come to the
  Rescue. Williams.

Refugee (s)
The British Museum Reading
  Room. MacNeice.
Epitaph for a Bigot.
  Johnson.
Our Lady of the Refugees.
  Maura.

Refuse (d)
Advice to the Old Beaux.
  Sedley.
Cleanliness. Lamb.
Cycle. Miller.
The Disordering. Yates.

Epistles to Mr. Pope (excerpt).
  Young.
Good Company. Henry
  VIII.
Heart Oppress'd with
  Desperate Thought.
  Wyatt.
Lend a Hand. Hale.
Love's Torment. *Anonymous.*
My Garden, My Daylight.
  Graham.
Sextus the Usurer. Martial
  (Marcus Valerius Martialis).
Song: "Is it dirty." O'Hara.
Sonnet I. Alabaster.
Sonnet: "My God, where is
  that ancient heat towards
  thee." Herbert.
Sonnets from Walton's Life of
  Herbert, 1670. Herbert.
Stanzas Written on Battersea
  Bridge during a
  Southwesterly Gale.
  Belloc.
The Truth the Dead Know.
  Sexton.
Under the Scub Oak, a Red
  Shoe. Smith.
The Winter Twilight, Glowing
  Black and Gold.
  Schwartz.

Regard (s)
Dream. Miles.
The Faerie Queene. Spenser.
Give My Regards to
  Broadway. Cohan.
Lines Descriptive of
  Thomson's Island. Lynde.

Regeneration
Fashion. Cambridge.
Inter Sodales. Henley.
Milton. Blake.

Region (s)
Fates of the Apostles.
  Cynewulf.
A Happy Man. Carphyllides
Mary and the Lamb.
  Sherman.
To the Sister of Elia.
  Landor.

Regions
Crane. Langland.
Evangeline. Longfellow.
The Home of the Naiads.
  Armstrong.
Ode: "Bards of Passion and of
  Mirth." Keats.
To Helen. Poe.

Regret (s) (ted)
Autumn. Watson.
Before Parting. Swinburne.
Beneath the Cypress Shade.
  Peacock.
Bewick Finzer. Robinson.
Captain Craig (excerpt).
  Robinson.
Caterpillars. Freeman.
Counsel. Davis.
Distich. Hay.
An Elegy on the Late King of
  Patagonia. Hankin.
Epitaph: "Here lies my dear
  wife, a sad slattern and a
  shrew." *Anonymous.*
Epitaph on Washington.
  Anonymous.
The Eyes of My Regret.
  Grimke.
Fiddler Jones. Masters.
For an Officer. *Anonymous.*
The Grave of Love.
  Peacock.

Have I, This Moment, Led
   Thee from the Beach.
   Landor.
In Memoriam A.H.H., CII.
   Tennyson.
Incident on a Journey.
   Gunn.
Jim Jones. *Anonymous.*
Lament in Autumn. Stewart.
Memo from the Desk of X.
   Justice.
Mr. Roosevelt Regrets.
   Murray.
Murphy in Manchester.
   Montague.
One Thing. Meredith.
Parting. Patmore.
Portrait of the Artist as an
   Old Man. Dransfield.
The Spirit of the Cairngorms.
   Firsoff.
Thirty-Eight. Smith.
The Three Arrows.
   Fitzgerald.
Two Travelers. Day.
Virgilia (excerpt). Markham.
When in My Arms.
   Pushkin.
Would I Be Shrived? Swain.

Rehabilitate
Posthumous Rehabilitation.
   Rozewicz.

Rehearse (s)
Incident. Shapiro.
Lame Angel. Finkel.
Opening of Eyes. Riding.
Retractions. Cabell.
The Sleeper. Clouts.

Reign (ed) (s)
Ah! Why, Because the
   Dazzling Sun. Bronte.
Bless the Blessed Morn.
   Bonar.
Blessing, and Honor. Bonar.
By Babel's Streams.
   Freneau.
Centennial Hymn. Bryant.
The Chronicle. Cowley.
Come, Let Us Tune Our
   Loftiest Song. West.
The Day of Doom.
   Wigglesworth.
God of the Prophets! Bless the
   Prophets' Sons. Wortman.
The Golden Age.
   Anonymous.
Great Shepherd of the Sheep.
   Wesley.
Guilielmus Rex. Aldrich.
Her Rambling. Lodge.
Homage to the British
   Museum. Empson.
In the Beginning Was a
   Word. Graves.
Inscription for the Door of
   the Cell in Newgate...
   Canning.
Jealousy. Johnson.
King Cahal Mor of the Wine-
   Red Hand. Mangan.
The King of Brentford.
   Thackeray.
Laus Deo. Whittier.
Let War's Tempests Cease.
   Longfellow.
MacFlecknoe. Dryden.
The Majesty of God.
   Sternhold.
Nations That Long in
   Darkness Walked.
   Barnard.

Ode to Walt Whitman.
   Garcia Lorca.
Of History More Like Myth.
   Garrigue.
On Leaving Holland (excerpt).
   Akenside.
Paradise Lost. Milton.
A Poem on England's
   Happiness. *Anonymous.*
Psalm XV. Sidney.
Put Forth, O God, Thy
   Spirit's Might. Robbins.
Sardis. *Anonymous.*
Summer Evening and Night.
   Thomson.
To Francelia. Duffett.
The Tune to the Devonshire
   Cant. Ayloffe.
The Vicar of Bray.
   Anonymous.
Vitality. Fonte Boa.
When This Old Hat Was
   New. *Anonymous.*

Rein (s)
All These Birds. Wilbur.
At a Child's Baptism.
   Miller.
The Brass Horse. Allison.
Cantica: Our Lord Christ.
   Francis of Assisi.
Georgics. Virgil (Publius
   Vergilius Maro).
The Last Campaign.
   Lehmann.
Phaeton. Mandel.
Riding. Grossman.
She Contrasts with Herself
   Hippolyta. Doolittle.
To My Blood Sister. Hemp.

Reject (ed) (ion)
Arthur Ridgewood, M.D.
   Davis.
From the Highest Camp.
   Gunn.
If She Be Made of White and
   Red. Horne.
Mona Lisa. Dowden.
On Evolution. Ciardi.
Resurrection. Pack.
A Test of Competence.
   Forker.
Thoughts of God.
   Anonymous.

Rejoice (d)
Astrophel and Stella, LVII.
   Sidney.
Bitter-Sweet: Hymn.
   Holland.
Bringing in the Sheaves.
   Anonymous.
Canto Amor. Berryman.
The Carpenter's Son. Peck.
Childe Harold's Pilgrimage:
   Canto III. Byron.
Elegy on Gordon Barber.
   Derwood.
The Expedition to
   Wessagusset. Longfellow.
The First Spring Day.
   Rossetti.
The Four Zoas. Blake.
Graffiti. Bold.
The Homeless. Hall.
I Heard Immanuel Singing.
   Lindsay.
I Wakened to a Calling.
   Schwartz.
The Irish Language.
   Mangan.
The King Enjoys His Own
   Again. Parker.

The Mechanical Optimist.
   Stevens.
Midsummer. Trowbridge.
The Owl. Thomas.
The Pastor. Summers.
Poem for the Year Twenty
   Twenty. Lee.
The Poet. Markham.
Responsibilities. Hall.
Saul's Song of Love.
   Tchernichovsky.
Since you will needs that I
   shall sing. Wyatt.
Somewhere. Mphahlele.
The Sow of Feeling.
   Fergusson.
Tho' I Can Not Your Cruelty
   Constrain. Wyatt.
Thy Praise, O God, in Zion
   Waits. Kimball.
The Two Voices. Tennyson.
Vernal Sentiment. Roethke.
Whispering Hope.
   Hawthorne.

Relation (s) (ship)
Aaron. Denby.
Despisals. Rukeyser.
Friendship. *Anonymous.*
Husbands and Wives.
   Hershenson.
I Consider the Tree. Buber.
A New Song to Sing about
   Jonathan Bing. Brown.
On Trinity Sunday. Byrom.
Relationships. Di Cicco.

Relative (s)
The Sea Fog. Jacobsen.
Tongue-Tied in Black and
   White. Harper.

Relativity
Newton to Einstein.
   Chappell.

Relax (ation)
La Grande Jatte: Sunday
   Afternoon. Cole.
Journey. Hall.
Let Go: Once. Fleming.
One Man Down. Anthony
   ("Ai").

Release (d)
The Climber Surveys His
   Mountain. Ouston.
The Flagpole Sitter. Finkel.
For You. Berrigan.
How Robin Hood Rescued
   the Widow's Sons.
   Anonymous.
The Last of the Fire Kings.
   Mahon.
Lost, But Won. Von
   Schlichten.
Lowly Bethlehem.
   Zinzendorf.
The Men behind the Guns.
   Rooney.
Robin Hood and the Widow's
   Three Sons. *Anonymous.*
Shir Ma'alot/A Song of
   Degrees. Flantz.
Song: "If I had only loved
   your flesh." Sackville-
   West.
Sonnet: "Leave me, all sweet
   refrains my lip hath made."
   Camoens.
The Spring. Voigt.
Stones: Avesbury. Aldan.
Whoever You Are Holding
   Me Now in Hand.
   Whitman.
The Widow. Southey.
The Woods. Mahon.

Relent
The Faerie Queene. Spenser.
The Metamorphosis of
   Pygmalion's Image
   (excerpt). Marston.

Relic (s)
His Return to London.
   Herrick.
The Last Gloucesterman.
   Grant.
Love's Franciscan.
   Constable.
Mussel Hunter at Rock
   Harbor. Plath.
The Twelve Properties or
   Conditions of a Lover.
   More.

Relief (ieve) (ieved)
Antonio and Mellida
   (excerpt). Marston.
The Beggar. Moss.
Caelica, LIV. Greville.
Canal Street, Chicago.
   Fixmer.
The Coal-Owner and the
   Pitman's Wife.
   Anonymous.
Confide in a Friend.
   Anonymous.
Cote d'Azure. Hoskins.
A Dark Country. Mahon.
The Dusk of Horses.
   Dickey.
Fear Not, Poor Weary One.
   Upham.
Je Suis une Table. Hall.
Limerick: "There was an old
   man of Three Bridges."
   Lear.
Lost Love. Graves.
Maria. Stevens.
Negro Servant. Hughes.
A Parodie. Herbert.
Planetarium. Rich.
Prisoned in Windsor, He
   Recounteth His Pleasure
   There Passed. Surrey.
Religio Laici. Dryden.
Sighs and Groans. Herbert.
Stack Arms! Alston.
The Storm (excerpt).
   O'Rahilly.
There Was an Old Man, on
   Whose Nose. Lear.

Religion (s)
At Length the Busy Day Is
   Done. Hopkinson.
Castara. Habington.
A Conversation. Shelley.
Hansel and Gretel. Sexton.
Homeless Blues. Jackson.
Inscription at Mount Vernon.
   Anonymous.
John Landless Leads the
   Caravan. Goll.
Leave Us Religion. Salkeld.
Legem Tuam Dilexi.
   Patmore.
Love of Fame, The Universal
   Passion. Young.
The Lusty Fryer of Flanders.
   Anonymous.
The Minister. Johnson.
Night the Ninth Being the
   Last Judgment. Blake.
Ode Written at Vale-Royal
   Abbey in Cheshire.
   Warton, Jr..
On the Religion of Nature.
   Freneau.
Phyllidula. Pound.

Reformation of Manners.
Defoe.
Salt Lake City. Carruth.
So Sr. Henry Vane the
Younger. Milton.
This Tokyo. Snyder.
To a Friend. Cooper, Jr.
Relish
And This Is My Father.
Grapes.
The Sovereign Poet. Watson.
Relives
The Fire Burns Low. Leax.
Reluctance
If My Hands Were Mute.
Winkler.
Remain (der) (ed) (s)
Basketball. Lewisohn.
The Cornelian. Byron.
Credo. Jeffers.
The Dark Chamber.
Untermeyer.
The Day of Doom.
Wigglesworth.
Father, How Wide Thy
Glories Shine. Wesley.
Four Folk-Songs in Hokku
Form, 4. *Anonymous.*
Goliath of Gath. Wheatley.
Inis Fal. O'Rahilly.
Love's Pains. Clare.
Metamorphoses. Ovid
(Publius Ovidius Naso).
The Middle of a War.
Fuller.
Missing Dates. Empson.
Modern Love. Stern.
The Moon Bird. Vickers.
Mountaineering Bus.
McOwan.
The Mute City. Eichenrand.
Names. Guillen.
On Hearing a Beautiful
Young Woman Describe
Her Class... Hovde.
On My Dear Grand-Child
Simon Bradstreet...
Bradstreet.
A Plum. Leib.
Prairie. Llewellyn.
Respectable People. Clarke.
River God's Song. Ridler.
Salamis. Durrell.
Serenade of Angels. Lasnier.
Sonnets, LXXIV: "But be
contented: when that fell
arrest." Shakespeare.
To Delia. Daniel.
Turn (a poem in 4 parts).
Belford.
A Warning to Conquerors.
MacDonagh.
Winter Holding Off the Coast
of North America.
Momaday.
Remedy
Brightness Most Bright I
Beheld on the Way,
Forlorn. O Rathaille.
Comparison of Love to a
Streame Falling from the
Alpes. Wyatt.
From these high hills...
Wyatt.
God and the Holy Ghost.
Lawrence.
The Great Magicians. Day
Lewis.
No Remedy. Allison.
An Ode to the Framers of the
Frame Bill. Byron.

To Pass the Place where
Pleasure Is. *Anonymous.*
Remember (ed) (ing) (s)
Academic Moon. Bevington.
After the Pow-Wow (excerpt).
Littlebird.
Alien. MacLeish.
Amnesiac. Osaki.
Antipater of Thessalonica.
Rexroth.
Apoem I. Pichette.
An Armoury. Alcaeus.
Awakening. Haines.
Baby's Awake Now.
Berkson.
Ballad of the Golden Bowl.
Hay.
Be Wise, and Fly Not.
Campion.
Bee-Master. Sackville-West.
Before Sleep. Prudentius
(Aurelius Clemens
Prudentius).
Believe the Bible. Simpson.
The Bethlehem Star Shines
On! Mortenson.
Bloom Street. McCabe.
A Call to Arms. Andrews.
Certified Copy. Deacon.
Changsha Shoe Factory.
Barnstone.
Christmas Songs. Kennedy.
The Coal Mine Disaster's Last
Trapped Man Contemplates
Salvation. Meissner.
The Cost. Hecht.
Cows Grazing at Sunrise.
Matthews.
Cradle Song for Miriam.
MacNeice.
The Cuckoo. *Anonymous.*
Dartmoor: Sunset at
Chagford. Brown.
The Dead. Strand.
Death's Warning to Beauty.
Anonymous.
Do, Lord, Remember Me.
Anonymous.
The Dog beneath the Skin.
Auden.
The Eagle. Blessing.
Edward Weston in Mexico
City. Dacey.
Elegy for Mr. Goodbeare.
Sitwell.
Envoy. MacLean.
An Epitaph. de la Mare.
Epitaphs of the War, 1914-18.
Kipling.
Escapade. Leslie.
Esther. Blunt.
Evelyn Hope. Browning.
Evening. Tzara.
Face-Paintings of the Caduveo
Indians. Dickey.
Failure. Wilkins.
Fantasy. Nerval.
Farewell. Tynan.
Farmers. Lux.
Fingernail Sunrise. Watkins.
For a Parting. Sinclair.
For Nothing. Castro Rios.
Four Ducks on a Pond.
Allingham.
Friends, you are lucky you
can talk. Vidya.
The Gift to Be Simple.
Moss.
Go where Glory Waits Thee.
Moore.
The Green Door. Drake.
Greystone Cottage. Hugo.

Harden Now Thy Tired
Heart. Campion.
He Holdeth Fast to the
Memory of His Identity.
Book of the Dead.
Heart! We will forget him!
Dickinson.
Helen in Egypt. Doolittle.
Helen's Scar. Nowlan.
The Horse. Merwin.
I Dreamed That I Was Old.
Kunitz.
I'll Remember You, Love, in
My Prayers. *Anonymous.*
I Took Leave of My Beloved
One Evening. At Taliq.
If You Want to Write Me.
Anonymous.
Improved Farm Land.
Sandburg.
Improvising. Nicholl.
In Memoriam A.H.H., LXIV.
Tennyson.
The Inheritance. Ignatow.
It Might Be a Lump of
Amber. De la Mare.
Jarama Valley. *Anonymous.*
Jesus Spreads His Banner O'er
Us. Park.
Joe Gillon Hypnotizes His
Son. Goldbarth.
John Smith Is My Name.
Anonymous.
Juana. Musset.
Kissing Natalia. Grier.
Lament for a Poor Poet.
Connolly.
Lament for the Cuckoo.
Alcuin.
The Land War. O'Sullivan.
Light under the Door.
Waniek.
Long Since Last. Miller.
Love-Letter Two.
Anonymous.
Love Songs. *Anonymous.*
Loveliness. Conkling.
Lupine Dew. Ramsey.
Mary's Son. Trent.
Meeting of a Poetry Society.
Rago.
Memory. Hoyt.
Mending the Adobe.
Carruth.
Midnight, Walking the
Wakeful Daughter.
Meredith.
Mr. Apollinax. Eliot.
My Mother's House.
Tietjens.
Mystery Story. Nemerov.
Name Giveaway. George.
The Nights Remembered.
Vinal.
Note from an Intimate Diary.
Litvinoff.
November the Fifth. Clark.
O Youth with Blossoms
Laden. Peach.
Old Loves. Murger.
On a Summer Day, 1972.
Murry.
On a Thrush Singing in
Autumn. Morris.
On Such a Day. Coleridge.
One Sea-Side Grave.
Rossetti.
Orchestra. Saner.
The Patient. Moore.
Pleasant Memories: The
Meadow-Field. Sangster.

Red River Valley.
Anonymous.
Regret and Refusal.
Anonymous.
Remember. Rossetti.
Remember Me! Haweis.
Remember (parody).
Anonymous.
Rhyme for Remembrance of
May. Burton.
Rococo. Swinburne.
Roses in December.
Studdert-Kennedy.
Rude Awakenings.
Rosenthal.
Saadabad. Flecker.
The Sacrifice. Bloch.
Saturday Market. Mew.
Sea Owl. Smith.
Seagulls on the Serpentine.
Noyes.
Seascape. Bishop.
Self in 1958. Sexton.
Simple Sam. Jackson.
Smile, Death. Mew.
Song. Griffin.
Song: "I saw the day's white
rapture." Towne.
A Song of Faith. Holland.
Southern Ships and Settlers,
1606-1732. Benét.
The Span of Life. Frost.
The Statesman. Belloc.
The Temple of the Trees.
Pellow.
Testament. Holmes.
Those Were the Days.
Anonymous.
Three Poems. Hitomaro.
Time Does Not Bring Relief.
Millay.
'Tis Sweet to Rest in Lively
Hope. *Anonymous.*
To a June Breeze. Bunner.
To Ausonius. Paulinus of
Nola.
To Butterfly. Percy.
To Diane. Whitney.
To Groves. Herrick.
To Those Who Sing America.
Davis.
Tonight Everyone in the
World Is Dreaming the
Same Dream. Litwack.
Tonight when You Leave...
Harvey.
The Trip. Stafford.
The True Romance. Jones.
Two Childhood Memories.
Zolynas.
Wall Shadows. Sandburg.
What the Toys Are Thinking.
Wolfe.
When Moonlike Ore the
Hazure Seas. Thackeray.
When My Blood Runs Chilly
and Col'. *Anonymous.*
When Other Lips and Other
Hearts. Bunn.
When the Curtains of Night
Are Pinned Back (with
music). *Anonymous.*
When There Were Trees.
Willard.
Why Would I Have Survived?
Bruck.
Wild Geese. Hart-Smith.
With Schoolchildren.
Barnstone.
A Woman's Question.
Procter.
Words. Brooks.

Writing. Nemerov.
The Young Dead Soldiers.
  MacLeish.
Remembrance (s)
Ah Woe Is Me. Propertius.
Augusto Ngangula.
  Andrade.
A Ballad of Remembrance.
  Hayden.
Forgotten Dreams. Silvera.
Friendship. Blair.
The Grave. Blair.
His Sailing from Julia.
  Herrick.
I held a jewel in my fingers.
  Dickinson.
Ireland. Gwynne.
Lucy. De la Mare.
Piano. Lawrence.
Priam and Achilles. Pope.
The Recessional. Roberts.
Self-Portrait in a Convex
  Mirror. Ashbery.
Time Long Past. Shelley.
Two Angels. Milnes.
The Wanderer. Williams.
What Once I Was. Wyatt.
The Wild. Berry.
Remind (ed) (er)
Beach House. Hurley.
Grandmother and Grandson.
  Merwin.
Identikit. Brodey.
Oh, Would That I Knew.
  Ibn Adiya.
Parable. Auden.
Sepia Fashion Show.
  Angelou.
Sonnet: Death Warnings.
  Quevedo y Villegas.
This Journey. Jonker.
Remnant (s)
The Ants. Clare.
Cry Faugh! Graves.
He Made the Night. Mifflin.
The Marsh. Southwick.
Remorse
Childe Harold's Pilgrimage:
  Canto IV. Byron.
Mosquito. Updike.
Purgatory. Yeats.
Shadows. Milnes.
Sweet Violets. *Anonymous.*
Remote
Eagle Sonnets. Wood.
Loam Norton. Brooks.
Majuba Hill. MacNab.
The Old Summerhouse. De
  la Mare.
Search for Love. Johnson.
Sonnets on the Sea's Voice.
  Sterling.
Remove (d) (s)
Batte's Song. Drayton.
Escape Me?–Never.
  Browning.
Fine Knacks for Ladies.
  Dowland.
Lines. Mary Ada, Sister.
Old King Cabbage.
  Munkittrick.
Sabbatical. Zisquit.
They Are All Gone into the
  World of Light. Vaughan.
The Twenty-Third Psalm.
  Herbert.
Rend (er) (ing)
The Crazed Moon. Yeats.
The Impartial Inspection.
  Anonymous.
Lines Written in the Front of
  a Well-Read Copy of

Burns's Songs.
  Anonymous.
A Miltonic Sonnet for Mr.
  Johnson... Wilbur.
Paradise Regained. Milton.
Prayer of a Soldier in France.
  Kilmer.
A Question. Synge.
The Tree of Rivelin. Elliott.
Rendezvous
Beaver Sign. Porter.
I Have a Rendezvous with
  Death. Seeger.
West Fifty-Seventh Street.
  Vazakas.
Renew (ed) (ing)
Aesop at Play. Phaedrus.
After an Eclipse of the Sun.
  Heimler.
Amantium Irae. Edwards.
Amoretti, LXXV. Spenser.
Modern Love, XIII.
  Meredith.
To My Lady Mirriel Howard.
  Skelton.
Wino. Hughes.
Renounce (d)
Clay. Lucas.
Inscription at Mount Vernon.
  Anonymous.
To a Vagabond. Woodrow.
Renown (ed)
And Who Has Seen a Fair
  Alluring Face. Peele.
Be Kind. Courtney.
Custer. Stedman.
A Grey Eye Weeping.
  O'Rahilly.
The Iliad. Homer.
King Arthur. Dryden.
Sing a Song of Joy!
  Campion.
St. Michael the Weigher.
  Lowell.
To the Trinity. Stanyhurst.
Rent (s)
The Age of Bronze: Rent,
  Rent, Rent! Byron.
The Constellation. Vaughan.
Down in the Jungle.
  Anonymous.
Epitaph for Jean Maillard.
  Anonymous.
Essay. Mayer.
The Fisher's Life.
  Anonymous.
Gascoigne's Memories.
  Gascoigne.
The Grimsby Fisherman.
  Anonymous.
I Want a Tenant: A Satire.
  O'Keefe.
Limerick: "There was an old
  man of Tarentum."
  Monkhouse.
Lord Gorbals. Graham.
Pity the Down-Trodden
  Landlord. Clayton.
A Poem of Broken Pieces.
  Jones.
The Sally from Coventry.
  Thornbury.
Silex Scintillans. Vaughan.
The Tenancy. Gilmore.
Travelling Song. McGrath.
Words for Music Perhaps.
  Yeats.
Repair (s)
The Constellation. Vaughan.
The Great Adventure.
  Thoreau.
Handyman. Phillips.

How Sleep the Brave!
  Collins.
In New Ross. Iremonger.
Softened by time's
  consummate plush.
  Dickinson.
Soldier's Dream. Owen.
To the Daisy. Wordsworth.
Will ye see what wonders love
  hath wrought? Wyatt.
Repay
From Generation to
  Generation. Newbolt.
The Patriot. Browning.
Widcombe Churchyard.
  Landor.
Repeat (ed) (ing) (s)
Advice from Poor Robin's
  Almanack. *Anonymous.*
Auditory Hallucinations.
  Mansour.
Burnt. Slutsky.
An Early Illinois Winter.
  Kuo.
Epigram, in a Maid of
  Honour's Prayer-Book.
  Pope.
Evening. Simic.
Ezekiel. Binyon.
Faces from a Bestiary.
  Kennedy.
The Family Meeting.
  Sprague.
From One Who Stays.
  Lowell.
A Hint to the Wise. Barret.
January 25th. Kumin.
The Ladder Has No Steps.
  Plescoff.
Little Musgrave and Lady
  Barnard (B version).
  Anonymous.
Love Made Me Such That I
  Live in Fire. Stampa.
Love Me or Not. Campion.
A Love Poem. Ashbery.
Mone, Member, Mone.
  Anonymous.
Reminiscent Reflection.
  Nash.
Ruston, Louisiana: 1952.
  Mathis.
Saint John the Baptist.
  Drummond.
Sea-Wash. Sandburg.
Since Ye Delight to Know.
  Wyatt.
Sonnets from the Portuguese,
  XXVIII. Browning.
Thanksgiving. Melo.
Tho' You May Boast You're
  Fairer. *Anonymous.*
The Time Is Ripe and I
  Repent. Ceile De.
Wet Casements. Ashbery.
When I Hear Your Name.
  Fuertes.
When Men Shall Find.
  Daniel.
Repent (ance) (ed) (ing) (s)
Caelica, XI. Greville.
The Candidate. Gray.
The Crow. Creeley.
Dispraise of a Courtly Life.
  Sidney.
Dives and Lazarus.
  Anonymous.
The Legend of Good Women.
  Chaucer.
A Logical Song. *Anonymous.*

Look on Him Whom They
  Pierced, and Mourn.
  Watts.
Repentance. Stevens.
Song: "Whenever, Chloe, I
  begin." Chesterfield.
The Three Arrows.
  Fitzgerald.
Times without Number Have
  I Pray'd. Wesley.
To My Mother. Brock.
Underneath a Cypress Shade,
  The Queen of Love Sat
  Mourning. *Anonymous.*
White Christmas. Rogers.
Repetition (s)
A Letter. Hecht.
The Odyssey. Homer.
On Lavater's Song of a
  Christian to Christ.
  Goethe.
Whistle Aloud, Too Weedy
  Wren. Stevens.
Repine
The Dead Marten. Landor.
Girl to Soldier on Leave.
  Rosenberg.
The Power of Time. Swift.
Shall I Repine? Swift.
Replace (d) (s)
Doors. Clark.
River Road Studio. Guest.
Superballs. Clark.
That Radio Religion.
  Ludlum.
Reply (ing)
The Answer. Herbert.
Cante Hondo. Kay.
Creation. Nicholl.
Dial Call. Morley.
Give Me Not Tears.
  Lathrop.
Letter from Pretoria Central
  Prison. Nortje.
The Message. Heywood.
Nightfall. Trueba.
O Son of God, Afflicted.
  Anonymous.
Poet to Dancer. Kavinoky.
The Question Is Proof.
  Bartlett.
Sometimes. Hesse.
The Sunshine of the Gods
  (excerpt). Taylor.
The Temple. Sisson.
The True Facts of the Case.
  Euwer.
The waters chased him as he
  fled. Dickinson.
Within my Garden, rides a
  Bird. Dickinson.
Report (s)
Brummell at Calais. Glassco.
Europe. Dudek.
Go, Sad Complaint. Orleans.
It Was Not Death, for I Stood
  Up. Dickinson.
The Mother. *Anonymous.*
The Newspaper. Crabbe.
The Patrol. Knight-Adkin.
The Thespians at
  Theermopylae. Cameron.
Repose (d)
Advice to a Raven in Russia
  December 1812. Barlow.
Babyhood. Holland
The Beggar's Opera. Gay.
Blind Girl. Merwin.
Canopus. Taylor.
Don Juan. Byron.
A Dream. Bronte.
The Emigrant. O'Grady.

Enough of Thought,
Philosopher. Bronte.
Epigram. *Anonymous.*
Everyman. Sassoon.
Fever. Gunn.
Haworth Churchyard
(excerpt). Arnold.
Health Counsel. Harington.
If the Heart of a Man. Gay.
Ill Omens. Moore.
Lear. Williams.
Man Carrying Bale. Monro.
Nubia. Taylor.
Ode to Fanny. Keats.
Question to Life. Kavanagh.
Reflections, Written on
Visiting the Grave of a
Venerated Friend. Plato.
Les Salaziennes (excerpt).
Lacaussade.
Seicheprey. *Anonymous.*
Seventh Day. Raine.
The Shadows of the Evening
Hours. Procter.
Snowfall. Carducci.
A Soldier's Grave. Albee.
Soliloquy II. Aldington.
Tywater. Wilbur.

Reprieve
A Song: "Fair, sweet and
young, receive a prize."
Dryden.

Reprimand
Of God We Ask One Favor.
Dickinson.

Reproach
Cashel of Munster.
Anonymous.
Cormac Mac Airt Presiding at
Tara. *Anonymous.*
A Hymn to the Pillory.
Defoe.
Love. Davies.
Salmon Draught at Inveraray.
Nunley.
Song: "So large a morning, so
itself, to lean." Auden.
A Viet Cong Sapper Dies.
Sossaman.
Watchers. Merwin.

Republic (ans)
Ave Imperatrix! Wilde.
Claustrophobia. O Riordain.
Faithful unto Death.
Titherington.
The Last Republicans.
Clarke.
Master McGrath.
Anonymous.
Presumption. Duggan.
Siena. Swinburne.
Spring in Washington. Boer.
The Stone Gentleman.
Reeves.
The Universal Republic.
Hugo.
War. Channing-Stetson.

Repulsed
A Letter to the Countess of
Denbigh. Crashaw.
To the Noblest and Best of
Ladies, the Countess of
Denbigh. Crashaw.

Reputation
The Complaint of Tarpeia's
Door. Propertius.
Lines to Be Embroidered on a
Bib.... Nash.
Richard II. Shakespeare.
Since "The Pillow Knows
All." Ise.

Request (s)
The Answered Prayer. Flint.
Limerick: "There was an old
man of Dunblane." Lear.
Poem for Edie Sedgwick.
Brisby.
Request for Meat and Drink.
Sedulius Scottus.
Tho' I Can Not Your Cruelty
Constrain. Wyatt.

Require (d) (s)
Inscription of a Chemise.
ErPo 06
Know Thyself. Burke.
Lycoris darling, once I burned
for you. Martial (Marcus
Valerius Martialis).
Of Perfect Friendship.
Cheke.
Two Mornings. McGaugh.
Upon the Decease of Mrs.
Anne Griffin... Fiske.
A Woman Defending Herself
Examines Her Own
Character Witness.
Griffin.

Requite
Amoretti, XLVIII. Spenser.
Phyllis Corydon clutched to
him. Catullus.
Upstairs Downstairs. Allen.

Rescue (s)
Beyond the Firehouse. Gray.
Composition for a Nativity.
Ciardi.
Could We. *Anonymous.*
Glory. Moore.
The Lantern out of Doors.
Hopkins.
Poem to Negro and Whites.
Bodenheim.
Rescue the Dead. Ignatow.
Song: "Poppies paramour the
girls." Long.

Resent (ed)
1,000 Illustrations & a
Complete Concordance.
André.
Here Is Your Realism.
Bodenheim.
Post Mortem. Harden.

Reservation
The Last Reservation.
Learned.
Space Travel. Krows.

Resign (ed)
The Aeneid. Virgil (Publius
Vergilius Maro).
Another to Urania. Colman.
At Day's End. *Anonymous.*
Dirge without Music.
Millay.
Great God, How Frail a
Thing Is Man. Byles.
The Happy Swain. Philips.
The Lady A. L., My Asylum
in a Great Extremity.
Lovelace.
Light, 4. Zukofsky
Men of the Rocks. Drinan.
Mimnermus Incert. Landor.
Netley Abbey. Midnight.
Sotheby.
Operative No. 174 Resigns.
Fearing.
The Sow of Feeling.
Fergusson.
Tentative Description of a
Dinner to Promote the
Impeachment...
Ferlinghetti.
Willy Wet-Leg. Lawrence.

Winter. Burns.

Resist (s)
Apparition of Splendor.
Moore.
Epigram. *Anonymous.*
London Is a Fine Town.
Anonymous.
Paradise Lost. Milton.
Resolution in Four Sonnets.
Cotton.
The Vamp Passes.
Montague.

Resolution
Hot Afternoons Have Been in
West 15th Street.
Blackburn.
Mine old dear enemy...
Wyatt.
Mine Old Dear Enemy, My
Froward Master. Petrarch
(Francesco Petrarca).
New Year's Eve. Mallalieu.
On the Birth of Dan
Goldman. Berrigan.
Paradise Lost. Milton.
Prayer under the Pressure of
Violent Anguish. Burns.
Procrastination. Young.
The Retreat. King.

Resonance
A Conversation. Howes.
Upon Hearing His High Sweet
Tenor Again. Langland.

Respect (s)
Courtesy. Patmore.
A Defence of Poetry.
Macconmidhe.
The Domineering Eagle and
the Inventive Bratling.
Carryl.
Eagles Over the Lambing
Paddock. Moll.
Heredity. Guiterman.
Lamentation. Otey.
Misadventures at Margate.
Barham.
Money. Nemerov.
"Oxford is a Stage." Nolan.
Pocket Guide for Servicemen.
Creekmore.

Respectable
An Election Address.
Stephen.

Response
The Voice of Experience.
Goethe.
When Oats Were Reaped.
Hardy.
Yom Kippur. Day.

Responsibility
Nightmare Begins
Responsibility. Harper.
The Sea Fog. Jacobsen.
Tryst. Merriam.

Rest (ed) (ing) (s)
Absence. Jago.
The Advice. Ralegh.
After a Little While.
Randall.
After Frost. Patten.
Agamemnon. Aeschylus.
Airs of Pei. Confucius.
Ambition. Kilmer.
Amoretti, XXXIII. Spenser.
Amoretti, LV. Spenser.
Amoretti, LIX. Spenser.
Amoretti, LXXVI. Spenser.
The Answer. Herbert.
Apostrophe to the Island of
Cuba. Percival.
Arabia. Falkner.

Arise and See the Glorious
Sun. Hopkinson.
The Art of Love. Ovid
(Publius Ovidius Naso).
Arthur. Winter.
As I Laye A-Thynkynge.
Barham.
Astrophel and Stella, XCVI.
Sidney.
At a Chinaman's Grave.
Lum.
At the Worst. Zangwill.
Autolycus' Song (parody).
Greene.
The Barn. Berry.
Beauty. "E.-Yeh.-Shure"
(Louise Abeita).
Bereavement of the Fields.
Campbell.
Blacksmiths. *Anonymous.*
The Blantyre Explosion.
Anonymous.
The Breakfast Song.
Poulsson.
Bright Was the Morning.
D'Urfey.
Brother, Though from Yonder
Sky. Bancroft.
The Brown Girl.
Anonymous.
Caelica, XLI. Greville.
Caelica, LXXIV. Greville.
The Call to the Strong.
Merrill.
Calm as the Cloudless
Heaven. Wilson.
The Canterbury Tales: The
Mill at Trumpington.
Chaucer.
The Cardinal and the Dog.
Browning.
A Celebration of Charis.
Jonson.
A Cellebration of Charis.
Jonson.
Chairs. Worth.
Charity. *Anonymous.*
The Chipmunk's Day.
Jarrell.
The Circulation.
Washbourne.
The Clock. Holman.
Colin Clout's Come Home
Again. Spenser.
Come, Gentle Death!
Watson.
Come, O Lord, Like Morning
Sunlight. Littlefield.
Come, O Sabbath Day.
Gottheil.
Come unto Me. Osgood.
Come unto Me, When
Shadows Darkly Gather.
Watterman.
Company. Howells.
Comrades. Housman.
The Confession Stone.
Dodson.
The Cooleen. Hyde.
The Cornelian. Byron.
The Creation of Man.
Anonymous.
The Cross of Gold. Gray.
The Crossed Apple. Bogan.
Crown of Days. *Anonymous.*
Crucifix. Olson.
The Day Is Past and Gone.
Leland.
The Dead Child. Dowson.
The Death of Nelson.
Anonymous.
Depression. Bly.

Depression. Burwell.
Devotional Incitements. Wordsworth.
Dew on a Dusty Heart. Untermeyer.
Different Winter. Nicholl.
The Divorce of a Lover. Gascoigne.
A Dream. Tomlinson.
The Dreamers. Garrison.
A Drizzling Easter Morning. Hardy.
Duermete, Nino Lindo. *Anonymous.*
Easter Song. Leslie.
Edith. Channing
Eleventh Sunday after Trinity. Keble.
Enigma. Fauset.
Epigram: "No charm can stay, no medicine can assuage." Landor.
An Epistle from Mr. Pope to Dr. Arbuthnot. Pope.
An Essay on Man. Pope.
Even-Song. Herbert.
Evening Hymn. Roberts.
Evening of the Rose. Rudolf.
Evening Quatrains. Cotton.
Evening Shade. *Anonymous.*
Exaggerator. Van Doren.
The Excursion. Wordsworth.
The Faerie Queene. Spenser.
Fall 1961. Lowell.
Felixstowe, or The Last of Her Order. Betjeman.
The Female Sailor. *Anonymous.*
The Final Word. Moraes.
Fire at Murdering Hut. Wright.
First Lessons in Musical Time. *Anonymous.*
A Flower. Nangolo.
Fly from the World. *Anonymous.*
For Every Day. Havergal.
For Her Heart Only. *Anonymous.*
For Them All. Wheelock.
Four Prayers, I. *Anonymous.*
Francis Beaumont's Letter from the Country to Jonson. Jonson.
Fraternitas. *Anonymous.*
From a Street Corner. Hammond.
From Mount Nebo. Wolfskehl.
The Funeral of Philip Sparrow. Skelton.
Gardens Are All My Heart. Triem.
George Jones. *Anonymous.*
Go Down Death. Johnson.
God Cares. Farningham.
God Is Nigh. *Anonymous.*
God's Dark. Martin.
God's Funeral. Hardy.
Going Home with Jesus. Isenhour.
The Gospel of Labor. Van Dyke.
Grand Rapids Cricket Club (excerpt). Moore.
The Grasshopper. Cowley.
The Great St. Bernard. Rogers.
Green. Verlaine.
Hail, Tranquil Hour of Closing Day. Bacon.

The Happiest Heart. Cheney.
Happiness in the Trees. Ceravolo.
He Careth. Farningham.
He Puts Me to Rest. Ignatow.
Hellas: Chorus. Shelley.
High O'er the Hills. Walker.
The Hind and the Panther. Dryden.
Home. Van Dyke.
Home-Sickness. Kerner.
How Dear to Me the Hour. Moore.
An Hymn of Heavenly Beauty (excerpt). Spenser.
Hymn to Darkness. Norris.
I Know That My Redeemer Lives. Wesley.
I Would I Were a Careless Child. Byron.
If I Should Die Tonight. Smith.
Imagined Happiness. Karlfeldt.
In a Cathedral City. Hardy.
In eternum I was once determed. Wyatt.
In Memory of G. K. Chesterton. De la Mare.
In Rain. Berry.
The Innocent Gazer. Cutts.
Inscription for an Old Bed. Morris.
International Brigade Dead. O'Brien.
An Irish Blessing. Murray.
Is My Lover on the Sea? "Cornwall.
Jacob. Reznikoff.
Jesus, Enthroned and Glorified. Eddy.
Jesus, Keep Me Near the Cross. Crosby.
John Rogers' Exhortation to His Children. *Anonymous.*
Keep Ye Holy Sabbath Rest. *Anonymous.*
Kneeling Here, I Feel Good. Piercy.
Knowledge. Grutzmacher.
Lady Moon. Rossetti.
Laleham: Matthew Arnold's Grave. Johnson.
Lalla Rookh. Moore.
A Lamentation on My Dear Son Simon Who Dyed of the Small Pox... Saffin.
Last Light. Kelly.
Last Lines. Barham.
The Last Reservation. Learned.
Legacy. Turner.
A Legend of Camelot. Du Maurier.
Lennox Island. McFadden.
Limerick: "An epicure, dining at Crewe." *Anonymous.*
Limerick: "There once was a kind armadillo." Herford.
Lines for a Drawing of Our Lady of the Night. Thompson.
Lines Written on a Very Boisterous Day in May, 1944. Clare.
The Lone Wild Fowl. MacFayden.
Lounge in the shade of the luxuriant laurel's/beautiful foliage. Anyte.

Love Letter. Pastan.
Lovelye William. *Anonymous.*
The Lovers Melancholy. Ford.
Lucifer in the Train. Rich.
Lullaby. Adams.
Lullaby. Barnes.
The Lullaby. Lope de Vega Carpio.
Mademoiselle Richarde. Sitwell.
The Madman's Song. Webster.
The Maimed Debauchee. Pope.
Man. Vaughan.
The Man of Calvary. *Anonymous.*
Man Thinking about Woman. Lee.
The Mantis Friend. McHugh.
Maurice de Guerin. Egan.
Meeting After Long Absence. Perry.
Memorabilia. Browning.
Memorial Day. Lent.
Memorial Rain. MacLeish.
Midnight. Dryden.
Midnight–September 19, 1881. O'Reilly.
Mongan Laments the Change That Has Come upon Him and His Beloved. Yeats.
The Moon at the Fortified Pass. Li Po.
Moonlight...Scattered Clouds. Bloomfield.
A Mother's Lament for the Death of Her Son. Burns.
My Daughter Louise. Greene.
My Faith. Acharya.
My Father's at the Helm. *Anonymous.*
The Name of Jesus. Newton.
A New Year's Promise. *Anonymous.*
No Speech from the Scaffold. Gunn.
The Noble Fisherman, or Robin Hood's Preferment. *Anonymous.*
A Nosegay Always Sweet, for Lovers to Send for Tokens of Love... Hunnis.
November. Coatsworth.
Now Let Our Hearts Their Glory Wake. Scott.
O Day of Rest and Gladness. Wordsworth.
O Powers Celestial, with What Sophistry. Barnes.
O That I Had Wings Like a Dove. *Anonymous.*
The Oasis of Sidi Khaled. Blunt.
Ode to a Nightingale (parody). Kelly.
The Odyssey. Homer.
The Odyssey, VII. Virgil (Publius Vergilius Maro).
Of Fortune. Kyd.
Oh, Earlier Shall the Rosebuds Blow. Cory.
Oh, Sleep, Fond Fancy. *Anonymous.*
The Old Grey Wall. Carman.
Old Homes. Blunden.

The Old-Time Cowboy. *Anonymous.*
An Old-World Thicket. Rossetti.
Ollie, Answer Me. Berg.
On Seeing Swift in Laracor. MacNamara.
On the Needle of a Sun-Dial. Quarles.
On This Day I Complete My Thirty-sixth Year. Byron.
The Onondaga Madonna. Scott.
The Orange Bough. Hemans.
The Ossianic Cycle: The Song of Finn. *Anonymous.*
Parted Souls. Herbert of Cherbury.
The Peace of Wild Things. Berry.
The Poem. Schloss.
The Poetess's Bouts-Rimes. *Anonymous.*
Poetry's a Gift Wherein but Few Excell. Ward.
A Prayer. McLeod.
Press'd by the Moon, Mute Arbitress of Tides. Smith.
Prospice. Browning.
A Quiet Soul. Oldham.
Rest Is Not Here. Nairne.
A Rhapsody, Written at the Lakes in Westmorland. Brown.
Riddle: "Black I am and much admired." *Anonymous.*
Riddle: "Two brothers we are." *Anonymous.*
Roll Out, O Song. Sewall.
Round Our Restlessness. Browning.
A Roundel of Rest. Symons.
Rural Bliss. Deane.
Samson Agonistes. Milton.
Send Forth the High Falcon. Adams.
Sept. 1957. Marshall.
The Seventh Hell... Rothenberg.
The Ship. Doran.
A Shropshire Lad. Housman.
Sioux Indians. *Anonymous.*
Sir Gawaine and the Green Knight. Winters.
Six Weeks Old. Morley.
A Sleeping Beauty. Watson.
The Snow-Shower. Bryant.
So Let Me Hence. Henley.
So Tir'd Are All My Thoughts. Campion.
Some Day, Some Day. Castillejo.
Song. Clare.
Song: "Child, Is Thy Father Dead?" Elliott.
Song for a Suicide. Hughes.
Song for the Spinning Wheel. Wordsworth.
The Song of the Jellicles. Eliot.
Sonnet: "Could then the Babes from yon unshelter'd cot." Russell.
Sonnet: In Absence from Becchina. Angiolieri.
Sonnets, XI: "Ye two fair trees that I so long have known." Irwin.
The Stampede. Brininstool.

Stanzas. Bronte.
Stanzas to--. Bronte.
The Storm-Cock's Song.
   ""MacDiarmid.
Studies at Delhi. Lyall.
Such Stuff as Dreams Are
   Made Of. Higginson.
A Summer Wish. Rossetti.
Swans. Wordsworth.
Thick Grows the Tarragon.
   Anonymous.
Through the Year. Cutler.
To a Living Author.
   Anonymous.
To Hope. Williams.
To Lady, When about Five
   Years Old, with a Present
   of Shells. Walpole.
To Midnight. *Anonymous.*
To the Sister of Elia.
   Landor.
The Tombe. Stanley.
The Trance of Time.
   Newman.
Trinity Sunday. Herbert.
The Trosachs. Wordsworth.
Troubles of the Day. Barnes.
Try Smiling. *Anonymous.*
Tryst. Butler.
Two Points of View.
   Watkins.
Ultima Thule. Longfellow.
The Unfailing One.
   Havergal.
The Unillumined Verge.
   Bridges.
The Unquiet Grave.
   Anonymous.
Upon Julia Washing Herself
   in the River. Herrick.
Upon the Crucifix.
   Alabaster.
A Veteran Cowboy's
   Ruminations. Kuykendall.
Visions. Petrarch.
The Visit. George.
Vo'k a-Comen into Church.
   Barnes.
Wait. Steele.
Wanderer's Night Song.
   Goethe.
Wash-Day Wonder.
   Faubion.
Water Fowl. Wordsworth.
We Need Not Bid, for
   Cloistered Cell. Keble.
Weep Not for a Warrior.
   Mtshali.
Went up a year this evening!
   Dickinson.
When I Was Growing Up.
   Vogel.
Where I Took Hold of Life.
   Coffin.
Which Shall It Be? Beers.
Why We Bombed Haiphong.
   Holden.
The Wife to Her Husband.
   Anonymous.
The Wilderness. Juhasz.
The Willing Mistress. Behn.
Winged Mariner. Howes.
Wisdom Is the Finest Beauty
   of a Person. *Anonymous.*
With My God, the Smith.
   Greenberg.
The Word of God. Flint.
Wordsworth's Grave.
   Watson.
Young Edwin in the Lowlands
   Low (B vers.).
   Anonymous.

Zaydee. Levine.
Restless
The Constant North.
   Hendry.
Fable IV: The Eagle, and the
   Assembly of Animals.
   Gay.
The Faerie Queene. Spenser.
"The fancy, which that I have
   served long." Surrey.
Frost. Hewitt.
The Hour-Glass. Herrick.
The Lovemaker. Mezey.
My Heart Was Wandering.
   Brennan.
November. Morris.
Round Our Restlessness.
   Browning.
The Sliprails and the Spur.
   Lawson.
Songs of Ch'en. Confucius.
The Soul of Jesus Is Restless.
   Mitchell.
Star of the Western Skies.
   Anonymous.
Versailles (Petit Trianon).
   Rich.
When I strip. Kegels.
Restore (d) (s)
Christ, the Good Physician.
   Wesley.
The Fair Maid of the West.
   Anonymous.
The Harvesting of the Roses.
   Ben Jacob.
Inscription for a Wayside
   Spring. Cornford.
Mary Weeps for Her Child.
   Anonymous.
Paradise Regained. Milton.
Restrained
Dearest, Do Not You Delay
   Me. Fletcher.
If There Be Sorrow. Evans.
Result (s)
Eagle Valor, Chicken Mind.
   Jeffers.
A Farewell to English
   (excerpt). Hartnett.
A Hand-Mirror. Whitman.
In Memoriam A.H.H.,
   LXXIII. Tennyson.
The Mystery of Life.
   Gambold.
Three Gates. Day.
Resurrect (ed) (ion)
Antrim. Jeffers.
At Communion. L'Engle.
The Author to His Book.
   Alsop.
The Beirut–Hell Express.
   Adnan.
The Black Rock of Kiltearn.
   Young.
Churchyard of St. Mary
   Magdalene, Old Milton.
   Heath-Stubbs.
Death. Hood.
Domaine Public. Hill.
Dream after Touring the
   Tokyo Tokei. Kogawa.
Edlesborough. Ridler.
The Elegy. Hope.
Epitaph. Heath-Stubbs.
I Know That My Redeemer
   Liveth. Boyle.
The Island. Muir.
Knole. Sisson.
A lady red upon the hill.
   Dickinson.
Magdalene. Pasternak.

The Mediatix of Grace.
   Burke.
Message Clear. Morgan.
O Christ of Calvary, This
   Lent. Mortenson.
Out of the corpse-warm
   vestibule of heaven steps the
   sun. Bachmann.
The Poetry of a Root Crop.
   Kingsley.
The Smell of Death Is So
   Powerful. Marguerite de
   Navarre.
The Song of Chess. Ibn
   Ezra.
Sonnet: "It is not death, that
   sometime in a sigh."
   Hood.
Upon M. Ben Jonson–
   Epigram. Herrick.
Voice of the Crocus. Hoyer.
Vox Oppressi to the Lady
   Phipps. Henchman.
Wang Peng's
   Recommendation for
   Improving the People.
   Eldridge.
The Yew-Tree. Watkins.
Reticence
Paired Lives. Rodgers.
The Truest Poetry Is the Most
   Feigning; or, Ars Poetica
   for Hard Times. Auden.
Retina (l) (s)
The limb of forests rises up.
   Carouth.
My Mother's Life. Meredith.
Poem: "Love being what it is,
   full of betrayals."
   Herschberger.
The Unblinding. Lieberman.
Retire (d)
The Aeneid. Virgil (Publius
   Vergilius Maro).
Hail, Tranquil Hour of
   Closing Day. Bacon.
He May Be Envied, Who with
   Tranquil Breast. Smith.
On Harting Down. Moore.
On Myselfe. Winchilsea.
Written in the Beginning of
   Mezeray's History of
   France. Prior.
Retreat (ing)
Behold the Manly
   Mesomorph. Auden.
The Calling. Contardo.
Fable II: The Vulture, the
   Sparrow, and Other Birds.
   Gay.
In Winter in the Woods
   Alone. Frost.
The Last Lap. Kipling.
The Ode on St. Cecilia's Day.
   Dryden.
Quite Forsaken. Lawrence.
Sun and Moon. Macpherson.
Through Binoculars.
   Tomlinson.
The Travel Bureau.
   Mitchell.
Vers La Vie. Upson.
Western Emigration.
   Humphreys.
What's the Use. Nash.
Within My Breast. Wyatt.
Retribution
The Fight at Sumter.
   Anonymous.
I Like to Think of Harriet
   Tubman. Griffin.

Retrospective
The Edward Hopper
   Retrospective. Quagliano.
Return (ed) (ing) (s)
Abraham. Silberschlag.
After the Hurricane. Hazo.
Amen. Mutis.
Atomic Courtesy. Jacobson.
Away! Frost.
The Band. Dennis.
The Battle of New Orleans.
   Anonymous.
The Beggar to Mab, the Fairie
   Queen. Herrick.
The Broken Token.
   Anonymous.
Bufo. Pope.
Burn Down the Icons.
   Schulman.
Burr Oaks: The Attic.
   Eberhart.
Cat into Lady. La Fontaine.
The Caughnawaga Beadwork
   Seller. Lighthall.
A Charm for Our Time.
   Merriam.
Closing Time. Michie.
Cynthia, Cynthia.
   Propertius.
Damn the Filipinos.
   Anonymous.
The Death of a Negro Poet.
   Rivers.
The Death of Dermid.
   Ferguson.
Deliverance. Dawson.
The Despairing Lover.
   Walsh.
Diaduminius. Benoit.
The Difference. Scott.
Dreaming America. Oates.
El Greco: Espolio. Birney.
Epilogue Spoken by Mrs.
   Boutell. Dryden.
Epitaph on the Lady Mary
   Villers. Carew.
Epitaphs of the War, 1914-18.
   Kipling.
The Exile's Song. Gilfillan.
The Faerie Queene. Spenser.
The Fiftieth Birthday of
   Agassiz. Longfellow.
Fighting South of the Castle.
   Anonymous.
For a College Yearbook.
   Cunningham.
For Love. Creeley.
A Form of Epitaph.
   Whistler.
The Gate. Jamal.
The Grave. Blair.
The Harper. Campbell.
Hippocrene. Lowell.
Hooker's Across. Boker.
Hope. Bronte.
The Hunter of the Prairies.
   Bryant.
Images. Aldington.
In the Evening. Hardy.
Invocation. Levertov.
Is Love Not Everlasting?
   McCuaig.
Jesus Return. Van Dyke.
Junker Schmidt. Prutkov.
The Knight in the Wood.
   De Tabley.
Lady Franklin's Lament (I).
   Anonymous.
Landscape with Minute
   Wildflowers. Maxton.
Letter to a Friend.
   Thompson.

A Letter to Dafnis April: 2d 1685. Winchilsea.
Lisbon. *Anonymous.*
Little Satellite. Krows.
Love Once Was Like an April Dawn. Johnson.
Lula Vires. *Anonymous.*
Marigolds. Graves.
Marriage. Van Doren.
The Million. Redgrove.
Muss I Denn. *Anonymous.*
My Love behind Walls. Spears.
The New Year's Gift to Phyllis. Prior.
Night Scenes. Duncan.
Nine Men out of a Minyan. Guri.
November. Daryush.
October Maples, Portland. Wilbur.
Off the Back of a Lorry. Paulin.
Off to Patagonia. Weiss.
Oft have I sigh'd for him that heares me not. Campion.
Oisin in the Land of Youth. Comyn.
Olivia. Pollock.
On an Indian Tomineois, the Least of Birds. Heyrick.
On Leander's Swimming over the Hellespont to Hero. Warton, Jr..
On No Work of Words. Thomas.
Once More Fields and Gardens. T'ao Ch'ien.
Opportunity. Ingalls.
The Origin of Cities. Hass.
.Our Dead. Nichols.
Ourobouros. Plescoff.
Painting by Chimes. Mayer.
The Palace of Art. Tennyson.
Pastoral Song for the Nuptials of Charles, Duke of Lorraine... de Ronsard.
Pirouette. Lorde.
Pleasant and Delightful. *Anonymous.*
Prisoner's Song. Gregory.
Re-Birth. *Anonymous.*
Resurgence. Rumi.
Return. Sussman.
The Revenant. Siegel.
Revolt. "Rachel" (Rachel Blumstein).
The Ritual. Ashley.
Robin Hood's Golden Prize. *Anonymous.*
Route 29. Brosman.
The Sacred Hearth. Gascoyne.
The San Francisco Company. Baker.
The Scrutiny. Lovelace.
A Sea Dirge. "Carroll.
Serio-Comic History of Bridgwater. Burrington.
The Sisseton Indian Reservation. Lyons.
The Sleepers. Whitman.
Solomon on the Vanity of the World. Prior.
Son David. *Anonymous.*
Song: "Distil not poison in mine ears." Hall.
Song of Despair. Rangiaho.
Sonnets, CXIX: "What potions have I drunk of Siren Tears." Shakespeare.

The Statue. Creeley.
Stepping Outside. Gallagher.
Suicide. Stevenson.
The Summer Rentals. Halpern.
There Was a Monkey. *Anonymous.*
Things I Didn't Know I Loved. Hikmet.
To My Distant Beloved. Jeitteles.
To My Mother. Rosenberg.
To the Snake. Levertov.
To William Shelley. Shelley.
Today Is Armistice, a Holiday. Schwartz.
Toe Queen Poems (excerpt). Sanders.
Toyland. MacDonough.
A View of Montreal (excerpt). Webb.
Vigil of the Wounded. Minthorn.
Vixi. Mackay.
The Walk. Hardy.
The Walker River Night. Louis.
The Way Down: They Return. Macpherson.
When Spring Came. *Anonymous.*
When the Dews Are Earliest Falling. Clough.
When the Tree Bares. Aiken.
When the Troubled Sea Swells and Surrounds. Colonna.
Where Unimaginably Bright. Hale.
While Waiting for Kohoutek. Erb.
The Whistling Boy. Crabbe.
The Winchester Wedding. D'Urfey.
The Wind Was There. Imbs.
The Winding Banks of Erne. Allingham.
Winter Solstice Poem. Scott.
The World's Bible. Flint.
The Wreck of the Old 97. *Anonymous.*
The Year's Ending. Yako.
Reveal (ed) (s)
Fortune. Madge.
His Winding-Sheet. Herrick.
Japan That Sank under the Sea. Satoru Sato.
Jesus, These Eyes Have Never Seen. Palmer.
Lady Franklin's Lament (II). *Anonymous.*
A Man Was Drawing Near to Me. Hardy.
Merlin. Emerson.
The Moment. Smithyman.
Peter Hath Lost His Purse. *Anonymous.*
Snow-Flakes. Longfellow.
Sonnets, XIX: "Those former loves wherein our lives have run." Agee.
Revel (ling) (ry) (s)
The Buccaneer: The Island. Dana.
A Christmas Caroll, Sung to the King in the Presence at White-Hall. Herrick.
In Answer of an Elegiacall Letter upon the Death of the King of Sweden. Carew.
In the Orchard. Ibsen.

Invasion. Witheford.
To John Keats, Poet, at Springtime. Cullen.
Revelation (s)
All Revelation. Frost.
Confessio Fidei. Dryden.
Fourth Sation. Colum.
The Hind and the Panther. Dryden.
The Matin Pandemoniums. Eberhart.
Memoria Technica for the Books of the Bible. Braybrooke.
Sea Lavender. Bowman.
Revenge.
Autobiography. Pagis.
Basia, VIII. Johannes Secundus.
The Cat and the Lute. Master.
Condone. Bierce.
Disdain Returned. Carew.
Epigram: "Just as he is growing a beard." Flaccus.
Ode upon Doctor Harvey. Cowley.
The Raven. Coleridge.
Sonnet: The Double Rock. King.
To Scilla. Sedley.
Vengeance. Kunene.
Reverence
At Lulworth Cove a Century Back. Hardy.
Character. Emerson.
The City in the Sea. Poe.
In Memoriam A.H.H., CXIV. Tennyson.
Sonnets to Karl Theodor German. Platen.
A Tale Told by a Head. Moyles.
Tennyson. Aldrich.
Reverie (s)
From Mistra: A Prospect. Higgs.
The Giant Tortoise. Lucie-Smith.
Pomegranates. Campbell.
To My Cat. Tomson.
Revive (d)
Childhood. Traherne.
Madrigal Macabre. Hoffenstein.
Queen Anne's Lace. Jordan.
Revolt (ing) (s)
The Canary. Nash.
Limerick: "I don't give a...." Burgess.
Still Though the One I Sing. Whitman
They Are Ours. Magil.
Revolution
About Women's Liberation. Saucedo.
For the Truth. Spriggs.
Get Stuffed. Alurista.
Huey. Knight.
Josina, You Are Not Dead. Machel.
Reflections in Bed. Symons.
Regenesis. Welburn.
Revolutionary Dreams. Giovanni.
Saying Goodbye. Juhasz.
This Is the Time. Machel.
This Tokyo. Snyder.
Why I Like Movies. Jones.

Revolutionary
Down Wind against the Highest Peaks. Major.
Just Taking Note-. Scott.
Memorial. Sanchez.
The Revolutionary Screw. Lee.
To L. Perry.
Revolving
The Giant Squid of Tsurai. Robertson.
Girls Working in Banks. Shapiro.
Habitue. Stickney.
How Copernicus Stopped the Sun. Dillard.
Wading at Wellfleet. Bishop.
When West Comes East. Ford.
Reward (ed) (s)
1st Dance–Making Things New–6 February 1964. MacLow.
A Bad Joke. Martial (Marcus Valerius Martialis).
A Chasm. Silverton.
Christ's Coming to Judgment. Dekker.
Disdain Me Still. Pembroke.
Epitaphs of the War, 1914-18. Kipling.
Inspiration. Thoreau.
Intimations. Koenig.
The Isolation of Genius. Byron.
Lord! Lead the Way the Saviour Went. Croswell.
The Man Who Married Magdalene... Hecht.
Mexico City Blues: 230th Chorus. Kerouac.
Mythics. Chasin.
Ode to Joy. Schiller.
Of Fortune. More.
The Picture of Little J.A. in a Prospect of Flowers. Ashbery.
Plant a Tree. Larcom.
Reflection and Advice. Pound.
Rondeau: "By two black eyes my heart was won." *Anonymous.*
Sonnet: "Madam, 'tis true, your beauties move." Godolphin.
Stanzas to a Lady, with the Poems of Camoens. Byron.
The Story of Cruel Psamtek. *Anonymous.*
Teach Us to Serve Thee, Lord. Ignatius Loyola.
Thus Spake the Saviour. Belknap.
The Tide of Life. Kirkconnell.
The Twa Books. Ramsay.
Two Travelers. Day.
The Uncertain State of a Lover. *Anonymous.*
Women Don't Travel in Clubcars. Jonas.
Yeats in Dublin (excerpt). Watkins.
Rhine
Bingen on the Rhine. Norton.
The Puzzled Census Taker. Saxe.

Rhododendron
Limerick: "A major, with wonderful force."
Anonymous.
There is a flower that bees prefer. Dickinson.
Rhyme (s)
Admonition to the Muse. Taylor.
The Aesthete Weasel. Morgenstern.
After Ever Happily. Serraillier.
Almanac Verse. Danforth.
Altars and Sacrifice. Wright.
Arkansas. Young.
Autumn. Tagore.
A Bagatelle. Reeves.
Ballad of the Despairing Husband. Creeley.
Bathymeter. Hart-Smith.
Builders. Flexner.
Carried Away. Elder.
A Catch. Hood.
The Chances of Rhyme. Tomlinson.
Daphne and Apollo. Macy.
Davy, the Dicer. More.
December. Keats.
A Dedication. Boye.
Denial. Herbert.
A Domestic Cat. Denby.
Don Juan. Byron.
A Drawing-Room Ballad. Traill.
The Exchanges II. Kelly.
Fishing Harbour towards Evening. Kell.
Gascoigne's Woodmanship. Gascoigne.
The Great Poet. Mu'tamid.
The Heart's Location. Meinke.
Hello Goodbye. Thesen.
How Many Seconds in a Minute? Rossetti.
Hustle and Grin. Anonymous.
In My Lifetime. Welch.
The Kiss. O'Gorman.
Lilliputian's Beer Song. Winner.
Lines on Being Refused a Guggenheim Fellowship. Whittemore.
Local Note. Guiterman.
The Louse-Catchers. Rimbaud.
Mother. Helburn.
The Motives of Rhythm. Conquest.
Noh Play. Brodey.
A Note from the Pipes. Speyer.
The One Thing Needful. Miller.
The Origin of Didactic Poetry. Lowell.
A Pastoral. Hillyer.
Poem from the Empire State. Jordan.
Poet. Emerson.
A Poet to His Beloved. Yeats.
The Poetess's Bouts-Rimes. Anonymous.
The Practice of Magical Evocation. Di Prima.
Published Correspondence: Epistle to the Rapalloan. MacLeish.
Quietly. Rexroth.

A Red Glow in the Sky. Blok.
The Road to School. Lane.
The Room. Harrison.
Scel Lem Duib. Anonymous.
Snowflakes. Sansom.
Song for Peace. Rodgers.
Song of a Factory Girl. Zaturenska.
A Sonnet: "O lovely O most charming pug." Fleming.
Sonnets, XVII: "Who will believe my verse in time to come." Shakespeare.
Spring Signs. Field.
Supreme Fiction. Winn.
Tell Me Not in Joyous Numbers. Crane.
To a Photograph. Tyler.
To a Poet a Thousand Years Hence. Heath-Stubbs.
To Edward Fitzgerald. Tennyson.
To Fortune. More.
Variations on a Late October Day. Mosby.
Vice. Hecht.
The Watchers. Spear.
The Wide Open Spaces. Lear.
Word. Spender.
Ribbon (s)
Concerning the Dead Women: The Munitions Plant Explosion: June, 1918. Libbey.
Distribution of Honours for Literature. Landor.
End of the Picnic. Webb.
Epigram: "Why do the Graces now desert the Muse?" Landor.
Evening on the Harbor. Tunstall.
The Life of the Wolf. Gildner.
Limerick: "There was an old man with a ribbon." Lear.
Little Blue Ribbons. Dobson.
Little Viennese Waltz. Garcia Lorca.
Lucy and Kitty. Anonymous.
Notes from an Analyst's Couch. Probst.
Poem; or, Beauty Hurts Mr. Vinal. Cummings.
Possessions. Smith.
The Shan Van Vocht. Anonymous.
Silence. Welles.
The Trooper and the Maid. Anonymous.
The Unknown Beloved. Wheelock.
Ribs
The Body. Herrick.
The Cunning Clerk. Anonymous.
Dido's Farewell. Pastan.
Snow. Wright.
Whispers of Immortality. Eliot.
Why? Chima.
Rice
Bone China. Lister.
How Do You Do? Jones.
Hunting. Snyder.
Ode for the American Dead in Korea. McGrath.
A Sometimes Love Poem. Leong.

Sumo Wrestlers. Kirkup.
To My Grandmother. McGuckian.
Rich (er) (es)
Against Proud Poor Phryna. Davies.
The Amber Bead. Herrick.
Appearances. Browning.
Astrophel and Stella, XXXVII. Sidney.
Ballad of Bedlam. Anonymous.
Charity. Lathrop.
A Christmas Thought. Breck.
The Coal Miner's Child. Anonymous.
Come, Captain Age. Cleghorn.
Compared with Christ. Toplady.
The Consolation of Philosophy. Boethius.
Contention between Four Maids... Davies.
Discovery of the New World. Revard.
Early in One Spring. Anonymous.
Epigrams in Distich, III: The Purse-Proud. Anonymous.
Epitaph Inscribed on a Small Piece of Marble. Shirley.
For My Mother. Smith.
For the Market. Mayhall.
Harlem, Montana: Just Off the Reservation. Welch.
Home Is the Sailor. McGinley.
I Have a Roof. Jackson.
The Idea of Entropy at Maenporth Beach. Redgrove.
Idle Chatter. Cooper.
If Christ Were Here To-Night. Sangster.
The Illiterate. Meredith.
Joseph Mary Plunkett. Meynell.
Labor Day. Pomeroy.
Lord, Thou Hast Promised. Cox.
Love Hath a Language. Sheridan.
The Maid Freed from the Gallows (C vers.). Anonymous.
Mind. Graham.
On Authors and Booksellers. Pope.
On the Death of the Giraffe. Hood.
Our Lady. Coleridge.
Overseer of the Poor. Hayford.
The Parrot. Skelton.
Poor for Our Sakes. Smith.
A Post Card out of Panama. Barney.
Proem. Cawein.
Quantity and Quality. Letts.
The Rainy Season. Meredith.
Rhododaphne. Peacock.
The Shanty-Man's Life (with music). Anonymous.
The Silent Lover. Ralegh.
Some Contemplations of the Poor, and Desolate State of the Church... Williams.
Song of the Poor Man. Anonymous.

Sonnet: He Argues His Case with Death. Angiolieri.
Sonnets. Hillyer.
A Spider Danced a Cosy Jig. Layton.
Street Chants; Old Daddy Witch. Anonymous.
The Suicides of the Rich. Contoski.
A Sweetheart in the Army (A vers.). Anonymous.
The Task. Cowper.
A Terrestrial Cuckoo. O'Hara.
Thus Spake the Saviour. Belknap.
To Thee, O God, the Shepherd Kings. Brainard.
Train to Dublin. MacNeice.
A Trapped Fly. Herrick.
True Riches. Martin.
Verbal Critics. Pope.
Visions. Petrarch.
Walking with Your Eyes Shut. Stafford.
Westward Ho. Anonymous.
What Is to Come. Henley.
Whispers. Hill.
William Wallace. Adams.
Winter Fairyland in Vermont. Osgood.
Winter Memories. Thoreau.
Worldly Wealth. Watkyns.
You're in the Army Now. Anonymous.
Your Money and Mine. Anonymous.
Richmond
Mr. Symons at Richmond, Mr. Pope at Twickenham. Symons.
My Correspondent's Last Ride. Townsend.
On to Richmond. Thompson.
Rid (den)
The Bewick and the Graeme. Anonymous.
A Fountain, a Bottle, a Donkey's Ears and Some Books. Frost.
Hangover Cure. Nicochares.
'Spacially Jim. Morgan.
Wanted. Silverstein.
Wild Horse. Olson.
Riddle (s)
Bird Riddle: "As I went out, so I came in."
Anonymous.
The Day before Christmas. Souster.
The Massacre of the Innocents: The Devil's Doubts. Marino.
The Monkey's Wedding. Anonymous.
The New Married Couple. Anonymous.
On Beauty. A Riddle. Prior.
Riddle: "As I went through a garden gap." Anonymous.
Riddle: "I sat wi' my love, and I drank wi' my love." Anonymous.
Riddle: "Purple, yellow, red, and green." Anonymous.
Riddle: "Red and blue and delicate green." Anonymous.
Riddle: "The land was white." Anonymous.

Riddle: "What God never sees." *Anonymous.*
Some Things That Fly There Be. Dickinson.
Trinitas. Whittier.
What Riddle Asked the Sphinx. MacLeish.
Why Does It Snow? Richards.

Ride (r) (s)
17. IV. 71. Blackburn.
Alabama Bus. Hairston.
An Apology. Wakoski.
D'Artagnan's Ride. Morris.
Artemis. Davidson.
The Automobile. Lewisohn.
Baby Toes. Sandburg.
Big Cars. McNair.
Billy Could Ride. Riley.
Boots and Saddles. Saboly.
Chasing the Paper-Shamans. Rose.
Considering the Death of John Wayne. Phillips.
Conventicle. Lansing.
The Death of Parcy Reed. *Anonymous.*
The Dentist. Fyleman.
Dink's Blues. *Anonymous.*
The Diverting History of John Gilpin. Cowper.
Driving in the Park. *Anonymous.*
The Dying Cowboy of Rim Rock Ranch. *Anonymous.*
Emergency Poem 1973. Zarco.
Epigram: "Though riders be thrown in black disgrace." *Anonymous.*
Fairy Tale. Nims.
The Farmer's Daughter. *Anonymous.*
Ferry-Boats. Tippett.
For Jack Chatham. Carter.
Janie Swecker and Me and Gone with the Wind. Huddle.
Jingle Bells. Pierpont.
Judith. Young.
Jump Cabling. Pastan.
Just for the Ride. *Anonymous.*
The King of Denmark's Ride. Norton.
Lady Elspat. *Anonymous.*
Love Poem. Comfort.
Me Alone. Weeden.
My Feet. Burgess.
My Feet They Haul Me 'Round the House. Burgess.
O, the Marriage! Davis.
Old Mother Goose. *Anonymous.*
An Oration, Entitled "Old, Old, Old, Old Andrew Jackson." Lindsay.
The Panama Limited. White.
Pegasus. Day.
A Poem for the Insane. Wieners.
Prayer for a Pilot. Roberts.
Railroad Bill. *Anonymous.*
Railroad Bill (with music). *Anonymous.*
The Railroad Blues. *Anonymous.*
Railroad Song. Chivers.
Raisins and Nuts. Reznikoff.

Reasons to Go Home. Forker.
Ride a Cock Horse (parody). Pain.
Rodney's Ride. *Anonymous.*
A route of evanescence. Dickinson.
Shall I Go Bound and You Go Free? Colum.
Shon a Morgan. *Anonymous.*
Slave. Hughes.
Sometimes Heaven Is a Mean Machine. Root.
Song: Time Drawes Neere. Waldman.
The Statue. Belloc.
Th Wundrfulness uv th Mountees Our Secret Police. Bissett.
Thomas Iron-Eyes Born Circa 1840. Died 1919, Rosebud Agency, S.D. Walsh.
Through the Metidja to Abd-el-Kadr. Browning.
Trailer Park. MacAdams.
Uneasy Rider. Wakoski.
Untitled. Tohee.
Wait for the Wagon. Buckley.
White Horse of the Father, White Horse of the Son. Root.
Will to Win. Scott.
Young Billy Crane. *Anonymous.*
Your Air of My Air. Margenat.

Ride (r) (s) (rode)
Bicycalamity. Peters.
Big Fat Woman. *Anonymous.*
The Canterbury Tales: The Pardoner's Tale. Chaucer.
Commuter. White.
The Covered Wagon. Blakeney.
Death Rode a Pinto Pony. Montgomery.
Epigram: Mythological Beast. Nemerov.
I Once Knew a Man. Clifton.
If Life's a Lousy Picture, Why Not Leave before the End. McGough.
In Lincoln Lane. *Anonymous.*
The Journey. Johnson.
The Knight's Leap. Kingsley.
Landscape of Violence. Currey.
The Last Campaign. Lehmann.
Male Rain. Tohe.
The Man from Strathbogie. FitzGerald.
Moon Going Down. Patton.
The Night Herder. Clark, Jr.
On the Road to Chorrera. Bates.
The Outlandish Knight. *Anonymous.*
Parcy Reed. *Anonymous.*
Pastoral. Ewart.
Pattonio, the Pride of the Plain. *Anonymous.*
Payday at Coal Creek. *Anonymous.*
Riders of the Stars. Knibbs.
Riding with Kilpatrick. Scollard.

The Stampede. Brininstool.
Stately Verse. *Anonymous.*
The Traveller. Dennis.
Upon the Horse and Rider. Bunyan.
White Horse of the Father, White Horse of the Son. Root.
Who. Halpern.

Ridge (s)
Dalmatian Nocturne. Santic.
The Death of an Elephant. Pagnucci.
Gettysburg. Stedman.
Metrical Feet. Coleridge.
Rock Pilgrim. Palmer.
The Sharp Ridge. Graves.
The World Looks On. Newman.

Ridiculous
The Humble-Bee. Emerson.
Letter to a Jealous Friend. Simmons.
Our Kind. Stafford.
To the Girls of My Graduating Class. Layton.

Rifle (s)
Dangerous Condition: Sign on Inner-City House. Atkins.
The Donner Party (excerpt). Keithley.
The Dying Ranger. *Anonymous.*
The 'Eathen. Kipling.
Homage to the New World. Harper.
Human Relations. Sisson.
I Heard a Soldier. Trench.
Inspiration. Knox.
The Patriot Game. *Anonymous.*
Poem Beginning with a Line by Cavafy. Mahon.
The Rifleman's Song at Bennington. *Anonymous.*
The Soldier's Song. Kearney.
Turista. Osaki.
The Victory of the Battle of Wounded Knee. Parson.
Why I Can't Write a Poem about Lares. Silen.

Right (s)
Absalom and Achitophel. Dryden.
All Those Hymnings Up to God. Evans.
Apollo's Song. Jonson.
Apostasy. Aus of Kuraiza.
Armistice Day Vow. Gould.
The Armless. Welch.
Astrophel and Stella, XLIX. Sidney.
At It. Thomas.
Autumn. Beeton.
Ballad: "Of all the Girls that e'er were seen." Gay.
Before Sentence Is Passed. Blackmur.
A Brief Elegie on My Dear Son John the Second of That Name of Mine. Saffin.
The Call. Clark.
Cat & the Weather. Swenson.
Clerical Oppressors. Whittier.
The Code. Frost.
The Collier Lad's Lament. *Anonymous.*
The Collier's Wife. Lawrence.

Come Back. Clough.
Comfort for the Sleepless. Bradby.
Conversation. McCord.
Court of Sapience. Lydgate.
The D.L. and W.'s Phoebe Snow. *Anonymous.*
The Death of Lincoln. Bryant.
Do It Right. Buckner.
A Double Standard. Harper.
Dry-Point. Larkin.
Eighteen-Seventy. Rimbaud.
The Eighties Becoming. Rosenthal.
The Enchanted Halibut. Nickerson.
Entirely. MacNeice.
An Epistle from Mr. Pope to Dr. Arbuthnot. Pope.
Epistle to Davie, a Brother Poet. Burns.
The Ernest Liberal's Lament. Hemingway.
An Essay on Man. Pope.
Eve's Version. Harrison.
For Every Man. Reich.
Fountain of Tears, River of Grief. Pisan.
The Fringes. Lenowitz.
Fugue. Spivack.
God Our Help. *Anonymous.*
Gracious Goodness. Piercy.
Home for Thanksgiving. Merwin.
Hunchbacked and Corrected. Belford.
I Grieved for Buonaparte. Wordsworth.
The Ideal Husband to His Wife. Foss.
In the Neolithic Age. Kipling.
In the "Old South." Whittier.
The Island. Southey.
The Jolly Soldier. *Anonymous.*
Juanita. Miller.
Just Keep On. Abbott.
Land of the Free. Hosking.
The Leper. Swinburne.
Life. *Anonymous.*
Life's Lesson. Wilcox.
A Little Talk wid Jesus Makes It Right. *Anonymous.*
The Maimed Debauchee. Pope.
The Melmac Year. Hilton.
Metaphysic of Snow. Finkel.
Midsummer. Kinsella.
Might Is Right. Zangwill.
Mixed Media. Schevill.
The Mother's Hymn. Bryant.
Murgatroyd. Wright.
My Mother's Life. Meredith.
Nashville Stonewall Blues. Wilkins.
The New World. Very.
Night Blessing. *Anonymous.*
The Nineteenth of April. Larcom.
Not of School Age. Frost.
On Mercenary and Unjust Bailiffs. Selyns.
On the Uniformity and Perfection of Nature. Freneau.
One-Night Fair. Price.

One, Two, Three, Four, Five.
Anonymous.
The Optimist. Anonymous.
Pippa Passes. Browning.
The Planster's Vision.
Betjeman.
Poem for Nana. Jordan.
A Poem on England's
Happiness. Anonymous.
A Poet's Proverbs.
Guiterman.
The Poor of London.
Forster.
Porson on His Majesty's
Government. Porson.
Preface ShrinkLit: Elements of
Style William Strunk, Jr. &
E. B. White. Sagoff.
A Prophecy. Lee.
Rabbi Yussel Luksh of Chelm.
Glatstein.
Regarding (1) the U. S. and
(2) New York. Adams.
Retreat. Bushnell.
Return. Tillinghast.
Robert Frost's Left-Leaning
TRESPASSERS WILL BE
SHOT Sign (parody).
Zaranka.
Rooming House. Kooser.
Roosters. Coatsworth.
The Royal Stag.
""MacDiarmid.
The Rule of the Road.
Anonymous.
Sales Talk for Annie.
Bishop.
A Salesman Is an It That
Stinks Excuse. Cummings.
Sam Bass. Anonymous.
The Seasons. Thomson.
Shakespearean Soliloquy in
Progress: "To draw, or not
to..."(parody). Anonymous.
A Sonet: "His Golden lockes,
Time hath to Silver turn'd."
Peele.
The Song of Roland, XCIII.
Anonymous.
The Song of the Jellicles.
Eliot.
Songe betwene the Quenes
Majestie and Englande.
Anonymous.
Sonnets, II: "Our doom is in
our being." Agee.
Squatter's Children. Bishop.
A Stanza on Freedom.
Lowell
Stanzas on Freedom. Lowell.
The Starfish. Coffin.
Strength, Love, Light.
Robert II.
The Swiss Peasant.
Wordsworth.
Talk. Perreault.
Teasing. Anonymous.
The Tempest. Anonymous.
That All Things Are as They
Are Used. Turberville.
That Brings Us to the
Woodstove in the Wilds, at
Night. Hall.
That Woman Down There
beneath the Sea.
Anonymous.
Themes for Country-Western
Singers (excerpt). Kooser.
'Tis the Gift To Be Simple.
Anonymous.
A Trip to Four or Five
Towns. Logan.

The Two Anchors.
Stoddard.
Ultimate Equality. Durem.
Waking in the Dark.
Livesay.
We Who Were Born. Lewis.
Wedding Song. Anonymous.
What a Court Hath Old
England. Anonymous.
When that I call unto my
mind. Wyatt.
Whitsunday. Herbert.
Withstanders. Barnes.
A Word to Husbands. Nash.
World's Bliss, Have Good
Day! Anonymous.
The Year's at the Spring.
Browning.
A Year's Burden.
Swinburne.
You Got a Right.
Anonymous.
Righteous (ness)
Cleanness (excerpt).
Anonymous.
An Epistle to the Right Hon.
Charles James Fox
(excerpt). Maurice.
Jehovah Our Righteousness.
Cowper.
No Harm to Lovers.
Tibullus.
No Sect in Heaven.
Cleaveland.
Paradise Lost. Milton.
Psalm XXII. Sidney.
Religio Laici. Dryden.
Though I Should Seek.
Onderdonk.
Thy Kingdom Come.
Hosmer.
Thy Mercies, Lord, to Heaven
Reach. Kethe.
To a Political Poet. Heine.
To the Memory of a Lady.
Lyttelton.
Unseen. Crosby.
Waiting for the Morning.
Anonymous.
Right Hand (s)
The Beloved. Probyn.
Charlie Rutledge.
Anonymous.
The Chimney Sweeper.
Anonymous.
Flag. Saner.
Ford Pickup. Evans.
Isaac. Gilboa.
Lakshmi. Fallon.
Never Let Your Left Hand
Know. Johnson.
On Laying the Corner-Stone
of the Bunker Hill
Monument. Pierpont.
Peace. Whitney.
To-Morrow Shall Be My
Dancing Day. Anonymous.
Wes Hardin: From a
Photograph. Carver.
Rigor Mortis
The Martyr and the Army.
Henderson.
My Uncle Joe. Smith.
Rim
The Edge of the World.
Youngs.
The Fish-Hawk. Wheelock.
Mailed to G. B. Derwood.
To an Old Venetian Wine-
Glass. Mifflin.
Urania. De Vere.

Ring (ing) (s)
The Alexandrite Ring.
Ryan.
All Gold. Anonymous.
Assembly: Harlem School.
Maleska.
Back Again from Yucca Flats.
Kelley.
Bitter Question. Macdougall.
Carmen. Levy.
Caterpillars. Freeman.
A Clock in the Square.
Rich.
Constancy. Daniel.
Curfew Must Not Ring To-
Night. Thorpe.
Daybreak. Meyers.
Dead Hand. Merwin.
The Death of the Starling.
Coleridge.
The Door-Bell. Becker.
Doorbells. Field.
Down by the River.
Anonymous.
The Dragon of Red Lights.
Swickard.
Driving Carl's '56 Chevy.
Woessner.
Easter Song. Leslie.
The Faerie Queene. Spenser.
From Government Buildings.
Devlin.
Glen Lough. Grigson.
The Green Gnome.
Buchanan.
Hammer, Ring. Anonymous.
Hope. Herbert.
How Strangely This Sun
Reminds Me of My Love.
Spender.
If He'd Be a Buckaroo.
Anonymous.
Jealousy. Anonymous.
Kiss in the Ring.
Anonymous.
The Lake in the Sky.
Haines.
The Lay of Thrym.
Anonymous.
The Little Golden Ring.
Anonymous.
The Little Red Ribbon.
Riley.
More Sonnets at Christmas.
Tate.
Mother of the Groom.
Heaney.
My Father Kept His Cats
Well Fed. Sherman.
Not Thinking of America.
Kroll.
Occupational Hazards.
Young.
The Old Gospel Ship.
Anonymous.
On Christmas-Day.
Traherne.
On the Eve of Our
Anniversary. Margolis.
The Phoenix of Mozart.
Vigee.
Please to Ring the Belle.
Hood.
Poet to His Love.
Bodenheim.
Pre-Existence. Hayne.
The Raftsmen. Anonymous.
Riddle: "Flour of England,
fruit of Spain."
Anonymous.
Ring around the World.
Wynne.

The Ring Poem: A Husband
Loses His Wedding Band...
Dacey.
Ringless. Wakoski.
Rosewood Casket.
Anonymous.
Snow. Avison.
Song of the Hanged. Vakalo.
Songs of the Ghost Dance.
Anonymous.
Songs of Seven. Ingelow.
Squabbling Blues. Bill.
Sunday in South Carolina.
Parham.
The Temple by the Sea.
Dutton.
'Tis but a Little Faded
Flower. Howarth.
To a Young Leader of the
First World War. George.
The Two Wives. Henderson.
Upon a Dainty Hill Sometime.
Breton.
Valse Jeune. Guiney.
The World. Vaughan.
Wrestlers. Drayton.
You want the summer
lightning, throw the knives.
Bachmann.
Rip (s)
Homage to Elvis, Homage to
the Fathers. Weigl.
An Old Malediction. Hecht.
Snow. Stone.
The Thatcher. Kennelly.
Ripe (ness)
As on the Heather. Reinmar
von Hagenau.
August 1914. Rosenberg.
Brittle Beauty. Surrey.
The Bull. Laughton.
Catechism Elegy. Gibson.
Connubii Flores, or the Well-
Wishes at Weddings.
Herrick.
Drum-Taps. Whitman.
Dutch April. Halpern.
Face. Toomer.
The Flowers. Rands.
Happy Are Those Who Have
Died. Peguy.
Mickleham Way. Eastwick.
Native African
Revolutionaries. Jones.
The Night There Was
Dancing in the Streets.
Olson.
The Nurse-Life Wheat.
Greville.
Poem of Explanations.
Ravikovich.
Poem: something broke the
dream. Gill.
Preface. Auden.
The Ripe and Bearded Barley.
Anonymous.
The Sea and the Mirror.
Auden.
Song: "Dress me in green."
Anonymous.
Two Young Maids.
Anonymous.
Ripple (s)
The Cachalot. Pratt.
The Crane Is My Neighbour.
Neilson.
Growing Old. Henderson.
Maps. Hass.
Swimming Chenango Lake.
Tomlinson.

Rise (n) (s) (th)
An Additional Poem. Ashbery.
After the Night Hunt. Dickey.
Alleluia! Alleluia! Let the Holy Anthem Rise. Anonymous.
The Alliance of Education and Govenment. Gray.
And So Should You. Anonymous.
Angels, Roll the Rock Away! Scott.
Apartment Cats. Gunn.
Assurance. Munson.
At Easter Time. Richards.
Aunt Eliza. Anonymous.
The Author, of His Own Fortune. Harington.
The Banks of Sweet Dundee. Anonymous.
The Betrayed Maiden. Anonymous.
Christ Our Example in Suffering. Montgomery.
Christ's Resurrection and Ascension. Doddridge.
The Coast: Norfolk. Cornford.
Crocus. Murray.
The Cross and the Tomb. Flint.
Declension. Sandy.
Dese Bones Gwine to Rise Again. Anonymous.
Diffugere Nives, 1917. Baring.
The Diver. Hayden.
Don'ts. Lawrence.
A Drizzling Easter Morning. Hardy.
The Drunken Sailor (Early in the Morning). Anonymous.
Easter Carol. Lovejoy.
Eclogue. Drayton.
Epigram. Field.
An Epistle to a Friend, to Persuade Him to the Wars. Jonson.
Epithalamion. Schulman.
Even during War. Rukeyser.
Evening in Camp. Ledward.
Fables for the Female Sex, V: The Poet and His Patron. Moore.
Faith. Moreland.
Festal Song. Merrill.
For My People. Walker.
For Sleep, or Death. Pitter.
Forced March. Radnoti.
Four Epitaphs. Warner.
From Thy Fair Face I Learn. Michelangelo.
Get Up and Bar the Door (B version). Anonymous.
Go Down, Ol' Hannah. Anonymous.
Go Tell Them That Jesus Is Living. Anonymous.
Good Friday in My Heart. Coleridge.
The Great Speckled Bird. Anonymous.
Harry Carey's General Reply... Carey.
He Made Us Free. Egan.
The Heaven of Animals. Dickey.
The Heavenly Tree Grows Downward. Lansing.
High and Low. Cousins.

Hosanna to Christ. Watts.
Hymn, to Light. Cowley.
I Have Fought the Good Fight. Waterbury.
In Come de Animuls Two by Two. Anonymous.
In Memory of Bryan Lathrop. Masters.
In Parenthesis. Jones.
In Solitary Confinement, Sea Point Police Cells. Driver.
In the Forest. Sadeh.
In the Mountain Tent. Dickey.
Isis Wanderer. Raine.
Jacob and the Angel. Mitchell.
The Jewish Cemetery at Newport. Longfellow.
Johnny Armstrong. Anonymous.
Kitchen Window. MacDonald.
The Landfall. Dickey.
Landscapes. Eliot.
Let Us Rise Up and Live. Sherman.
Light's Glittering Morn. Neale.
London Night. Raine.
The Lover is Near. Goethe.
Marriage. Sklarew.
Midnight–September 19, 1881. O'Reilly.
Mirror. Plath.
Mounds of Human Heads Are Wandering into the Distance. Mandelstam.
Not Drunk Is He. Peacock.
On Eleanor Freeman. Anonymous.
On the Death of Parents. Barson.
Open the Door to Me, O. Burns.
Pity Not. Simpson.
Poor Angels. Hirsch.
A Prayer for Thanksgiving. Auslander.
Preachment for Preachers. Barclay.
The Raising of Lazarus. Clifton.
Refuge. McCartney.
Repeated Pilgrimage. Brunini.
De Rerum Natura. Lucretius (Titus Lucretitus Carus).
The Resurrection. Wanley.
Resurrexit. Stuart.
Reveille. Untermeyer.
Rise, Mourner, Rise. Anonymous.
Le Roi Est Mort. Robinson.
Rolling Thunder. Wolf.
The Room and the Windows. Feng Chih.
Schoolgirl on Speech-Day in the Open Air. Smith.
The Seeds of Love. Anonymous.
The Sheaves. Robinson.
The Ship of Fools. Barclay.
Sonnet: The Army Surgeon. Dobell.
Sonnets. Masefield.
Stealing Trout. Hughes.
Still I Rise. Angelou.
Stonewall Jackson. Flash.
Sunday in the Country. Swenson.

Thammuz. Moody.
Thou Grace Divine, Encircling All. Scudder.
Three Sunrises from Amtrak. Dolgorukov.
To a Departing Favorite. Horton.
To a Tyrant. Brodsky.
Trinity Sunday. Herbert.
Views of Boston Common and Nearby. Blackmur.
The Warnings. Furlong.
West Helena Blues. Sykes.
Written in a Lady's Prayer Book. Rochester.
Xantippe. Levy.
Ye Heavens, Uplift Your Voice. Anonymous.
Rising (s)
At the Setting of the Sun. Anonymous.
Aubade. McBride.
Blessing, and Honor. Bonar.
Cocteau's Opium: 2. Finkel.
Early Rising. Saxe.
Father. Weston.
The Fight of the Armstrong Privateer. Roche.
Her Sweet Voice. Carew.
House of the Rising Sun. Anonymous.
Hurrying away from the Earth. Bly.
Jumbo Jee. Richards.
Last Antiphon: To Mary. Donohue.
The Liar. Anonymous.
A Mermaiden. Hennell.
The Mole. Haines.
My Former Hopes Are Fled. Cowper.
Old King Cole. Robinson.
Poem in Which My Legs Are Accepted. Fraser.
A Simple Pastoral. Stevens.
The Slough of Despond. Lowell.
The Song of a Happy Rising. Thewlis.
Song of the New World. Morgan.
Tauhid. Toure.
To the First of August. Plato.
Tractatus. Mahon.
What Wild Dawns There Were. Levertov.
When the World Was in Building. Ford.
Wishful Thinking. Blumenthal.
The Wolfman. Kuzma.
The Young Fenians. Fallon.
Risk (s)
The Acrobat from Xanadu Disdained All Nets. Georgakas.
Conjugation of the Verb, "To Hope." Lipsitz.
The Day the Winds. Miles.
Dipsychus. Clough.
Having Read Books. McHugh.
His Mother-in-Law. Parke.
The Little Girl with Bands on Her Teeth. Taggard.
Santa Claus in a Department Store. Hassall.
Suckers for Truth. Sarah.
Waiting. Creeley.

Rite (s)
The Grave of King ARthur. Warton, Jr..
The New-Yeeres Gift, Sung to the King in the Presence at White Hall. Herrick.
Winter. De Vere.
A Year of Sorrow. De Vere.
Ritual (s)
After the Hurricane. Hazo.
All the Death-Room Needs... Hartnett.
Bread. Klein.
The Death of Digenes Akritas. Heath-Stubbs.
Folding a Shirt. Levertov.
Rune. Brasfield.
Second Avenue Winter. Simic.
Three Cheers for the Black, White and Blue. Pitter.
The Trick Is Consciousness. Allen.
Two Pieces after Suetonius. Warren.
Rival (s)
The Betrothed. Kipling.
Colebrook Dale (excerpt). Seward.
Eclogues. Virgil (Publius Vergilius Maro).
Love Is Bitter. Anonymous.
Obsequies to the Lady Anne Hay. Carew.
Old Age. Anonymous.
La Promessa Sposa. Landor.
Song: "You wrong me, Strephon." "Ephelia" (Joan Philips).
The Truth. Davies.
River (s)
The Age of Sheen. Hughes.
Animal Songs: Zebra. Anonymous.
Anteros. Cory.
The Apple Trees. Gluck.
Arrowtown. Glover.
As Sun, As Sea. Sullivan.
Ask Me. Stafford.
Atalanta in Calydon. Swinburne.
The Avocado Pit. Rakosi.
The Beggar Wind. Austin.
Beyond Possession. Jennings.
Beyond the Potomac. Hayne.
Boatman's Dance. Emmett.
The Brazos River. Anonymous.
Breaking Green. Ondaatje.
The Bridge. Walcott.
Bring Back. Ridler.
Britannia's Pastorals. Browne.
By the Beautiful Ohio. LaBombard.
The Call of the River Nun. Okara.
Ceremony. Stafford.
Charlie, He's a Young Man. Anonymous.
Charon's Cosmology. Simic.
Chicago. Ridge.
Christ's Victory and Triumph. Fletcher.
City. Bruchac.
Climbing. Maiden.
Cock-Crow. Anonymous.
Conjuring Roethke. Tate.
Days That Have Been. Davies.

Dean-Bourn, a Rude River in Devon, by Which Sometimes He Lived. Herrick.
The Dear Ladies of Cincinnati. Stevenson.
December 24, 1979. Weaver.
The Diary of Amanda McFadden. Hogan.
Dicky Dilver. *Anonymous.*
The Dipper. Hesketh.
Drinking Alone with the Moon. Li Po.
Eli, Eli. Wright.
Epigram: "Oh! Trouble not Menedemos by guile." Strato.
The Estuary. Pitter.
Exit Line. Nemerov.
The Faithless Wife. Garcia Lorca.
Ford O' Kabul River. Kipling.
Fountain of Tears, River of Grief. Pisan.
From the North Saskatchewan. Mandel.
From the Other Shore. Root.
Ganga. Blackburn.
Girl's Song. Zaturenska.
The Grave of Rulry. Rolleston.
Growing Wild. Miller.
The Gulf Stream. Bellamann.
The Heavenly City. Smith.
The Hermit's Song. *Anonymous.*
How I Got Ovah. Rodgers.
Howl, II. Ginsberg.
I Remember. Glover.
In Arcadia. Durrell.
In the Deep Channel. Stafford.
In the Hellgate Wind. Defrees.
In the Highlands. Stevenson.
In the Wicker Fish-Trap. *Anonymous.*
The International Brigade Arrives at Madrid. Neruda.
Johnny Stiles; or, The Wild Mustard River. *Anonymous.*
A Journey through the Moonlight. Edson.
Keine Lazarovitch. Layton.
Know Ye Not That Lovely River. Griffin.
Koina ta ton Philon. Symonds.
Kree. Gordon.
A Lake. Beddoes.
Landscapes. Eliot.
Letter to an Imaginary Friend. McGrath.
The Light of Asia (excerpt). Arnold.
Limbo. Rugo.
Living Poetry. Margenat.
Love Is Not Solace. Maris Stella.
The Lover: A Ballad. Montagu.
Madwoman at Rodmell. Roberts.
Map Reading. Citino.
Men Fade Like Rocks. Turner.

Men Fishing in the Arno. Jennings.
Midnight. Tennyson.
Moon Light. Manfred.
Mortally. Kirkup.
The Mountains. Dudek.
Mr. Symons at Richmond, Mr. Pope at Twickenham. Symons.
The Murder of the Tsarevich Dimitri by Boris Godunov. *Anonymous.*
A Musical Instrument. Browning.
My Pretty Little Miss. *Anonymous.*
My Sister, My Self. Filip.
Noah an' Jonah an' Cap'n John Smith. Marquis.
The Noonday April Sun. Love.
Norah. Akins.
O, Wasn't Dat a Wide River! *Anonymous.*
Odes. Horace.
Of Swimming in Lakes and Rivers. Brecht.
Oh There Is Blessing in This Gentle Breeze. Wordsworth.
Ol' Man River. Hammerstein.
On the Wings of a Dove. Miller.
One Foot in the River. Stern.
One More River to Cross. *Anonymous.*
Orara. Kendall.
Party at Hydra. Layton.
The Permanent Tourists. Page.
Poem in Time of Winter. Mathew.
Prayer. *Anonymous.*
A Psalm Praising the Hair of Man's Body. Levertov.
Queen. Moraes.
Requiem after Seventeen Years. Ravikovich.
Riven Doggeries. Tate.
The River. MacDonogh.
The River. MacNab.
River-Mates. Colum.
River Sound Remembered. Merwin.
Round about Me (fragment). Sappho.
Roustabout Holler. *Anonymous.*
Rushing. Young Bear.
Salutation. Russell.
Saviour, Who Thy Flock Art Feeding. Muhlenberg.
Sea-Monster. Kolmar.
Shadow Dirge. Dexter.
Sharks, Caloosahatchee River. Pape.
The Snowflake Which Is Now and Hence Forever. MacLeish.
Soaring. Clothier.
Solitude. Rilke.
Song. Newbolt.
A Song of Dagger-Dancing (excerpt). Tu Fu.
Song of Praise for an Ox. Sutzkever.
A Song-Offering. Tagore.
Sonnet to Seabrook. Ray.
Sonnets. Tuckerman.
Spring Rain. Chute.

Stars. Nowlan.
The Stringer. Brasfield.
Summer. Asch.
Summer, 1960, Minnesota. Bly.
Summer Near the River. Kizer.
Sunday Evenings. Hollander.
Supreme Death. Dunn.
The Thousand and One Nights: Psalm of the Bottle. *Anonymous.*
The Three Fates. Dobson.
Three Sentences for a Dead Swan. Wright.
The Tides Run Up the Wairau. Duggan.
To Dean Bourn, a Rude River in Devon, by Which Sometimes He Lived. Herrick.
To Her Dead Mate: Montana, 1966. Libbey.
To the Hand. Merwin.
Tropic Rain. Stevenson.
Two Songs, II. Kabir.
Tzu Yeh Songs. *Anonymous.*
Under the Shade of the Trees. Preston.
Valediction to My Contemporaries. Gregory.
The Village of the Presents. McMichael.
Waiting to Be Fed. Young Bear.
The Waters of Tyne. *Anonymous.*
When Howitzers Began. Carruth.
When I Am Dead and Sister to the Dust. Barker.
When I Went out. Kuskin.
When We Are Like Two Drunken Suns. Caroutch.
Where the River Shannon Flows. Russell.
Who's in Charge Here? Bell.
The Widow's Party. Kipling.
Widow to Her Son. Smith.
You Can't Go Home Again (excerpt). Wolfe.

Roach (es)
Aubade: N.Y.C. Wallace.
Starry Sky. Simic.
Vigils: Down the Glimmering Staircase. Sassoon.

Road (s) (side) (way)
Against Romanticism. Amis.
Answering Li Ying Who Showed Me His Poems about Summer Fishing. Yu Hsuan-chi.
At Cockcrow. Reese.
The Best Road of All. Towne.
The Bird. Simic.
The Black Vulture. Sterling.
De Blin' Man Stood on de Road an' Cried. *Anonymous.*
Bogac Ban. Figgis.
Broom at Twilight. Sarah.
Buzzard. Daugherty.
The Call of the Spring (excerpt). Noyes.
Circular Roads. Muchemwa.
Corporal Stare. Graves.
Crowded Ways of Life. Gresham.
The D.L. and W.'s Phoebe Snow. *Anonymous.*

Dawn. "Rachel" (Rachel Blumstein).
The Dead by the Side of the Road. Snyder.
Death of a Poet. Causley.
Deirdre and the Poets. Milne.
Descending. Pack.
Echoes of Wheels. Maurice.
The End of the Way. Cole.
Entirely. MacNeice.
The Entrepreneur Chicken Shed His Tail Feathers, Surplus. Miles.
Farewell to Town. Housman.
First Death in Nova Scotia. Bishop.
Fishing in Air. Crozier.
Floating. Brownstein.
Florida Road Workers. Hughes.
Forest without Leaves (excerpt). Haines.
Frankie Silvers. Silvers.
From Romany to Rome. Irwin.
Gravelly Run. Ammons.
The Gypsies' Road. Shorter.
Her Way. Benet.
The Home Fire. Johns.
The House and the Road. Peabody.
I Love a Hill. Hodgson.
I Recognized You Because When I Saw the Print. Jimenez.
I watched the moon around the house. Dickinson.
Ida Red. *Anonymous.*
If All the Voices of Men. Traubel.
In the Footsteps of the Walking Air. Patchen.
Irish Lords. Souter.
June. Ledwidge.
June Morning. McCrae.
The Killing. Muir.
Landscapes. Eliot.
Limerick: "There was an old man of El Hums." Lear.
Local Habitation: On Inhabiting an Orange. Miles.
The Long Road West. Knibbs.
Lost Johnny. *Anonymous.*
Love. Langland.
A Maltese Dog. *Anonymous.*
Man Is Nothing But. Tchernichovsky.
A March in the Ranks Hard-Prest, and the Road Unknown. Whitman.
The March to Moscow. Southey.
Mary Hynes. Raftery.
Mignon. Goethe.
The Mirrors of Jerusalem. Lefcowitz.
My House, I Say. But Hark to the Sunny Doves. Stevenson.
My Road. Opdyke.
Night Fishing for Blues. Smith.
Night Out. Simpson.
Of Pardons, Presidents, and Whiskey Labels. Snyder.
Oh, Sing to God. Steendam.
An Old Cracked Tune. Kunitz.

Road

The Old Road to Paradise. Widdemer.
On a Lady Who P-ssed at the Tragedy of Cato. Pope.
On Exodus, III, 14, I Am That I Am. Prior.
On the Meadow. Vala.
The Origin of the Praise of God. Bly.
An Otter. Hughes.
Out on Santa-Fe–Blues. Petties.
Plainness. Borges.
Praises of the Train. Segooa.
A Prayer in Time of Blindness. Wood.
A Prayer to Escape from the Market Place. Wright.
Preference. Sargent.
The Queen of Elfan's Nourice. Anonymous.
The Railroad Corral. Anonymous.
Remembrances. Clare.
Ride. Miles.
The Road. Fletcher.
The Road. Schneour.
Road Hazard. Green.
The Road to Anywhere. Taylor.
The Road to Babylon. Wilson.
The Road to the Pool. Conkling.
The Rock. Eliot.
The Roman Road. Hardy.
Romany Gold. Burr.
The Rose of the World. Yeats.
The Seekers. Masefield.
September. Pasternak.
Six Variations. Levertov.
The Sleepers. Kocan.
Song of the Breed. Arnett.
Sonnet: In Absence from Becchina. Angiolieri.
The Stab. Harney.
Stars Climb Girders of Light. Meyers.
Suicide. MacNeice.
Ten Thousand Miles Away (with music). Anonymous.
Threnody. Harding.
Tinker's Moon. Milne.
To S. T. C. on His 179th Birthday, October 12th, 1951. Carpenter.
Tomah Stream. Anonymous.
A Trucker. Gunn.
Twilight Song. Robinson.
Tyranny of Moths. Vizenor.
Unemployment. Mills.
The Vagabond. Stevenson.
Waking on a Greyhound. Henry.
Walking at Night. Hare.
Walking with God. Cowper.
The Way Through the Woods. Kipling.
The Wayfarer. Crane.
White in the Moon. housman.
Will You Be as Hard? Gregory.
Work to Do Toward Town. Snyder.
The Wounded. Louis.
Yellow. Wright.
The Young Calves. Coffin.
The Zest of Life. Van Dyke.

Roam (ed)

Egyptian Hieroglyphics. Anonymous.
The Gamboling Man (C vers.). Anonymous.
In Praise of Seafaring Men, in Hopes of Good Fortune. Grenville.
In the Silence. Stephany.
The Investiture. Sassoon.
Love-Songs, At Once Tender and Informative. Hoffenstein.
Paradise Regained. Milton.
Preference. Sargent.
The Progress of Error. Cowper.
The Road to Babylon. Wilson.
Run along, You Little Dogies. Anonymous.
The Sea-Captain. Anonymous.
Self-Acquaintance. Cowper.
A Shantyman's Life (II). Anonymous.
Way Down in Mexico. Anonymous.

Roan

The Strawberry Roan. Anonymous.

Roar (ed) (ing) (s)

Afternoon in the Tropics. Dario.
Ancient Lights. Clarke.
Baby Song. Gunn.
The Djanggawul Cycle, 6. Anonymous.
Dog Alive. Witt.
From the Notebooks. Roethke.
In a Railway Compartment. Fuller.
In Memoriam A.H.H., XXXVI. Tennyson.
In Romney Marsh. Davidson.
In the Evening from My Window. Anonymous.
Lament over the Ruins of the Abbey of Teach Molaga. Mangan.
Limerick: "There was an Old Lady named Crockett." Smith.
Mother Goose Up-to-Date. Untermeyer.
Old Fashioned Fun. Thackeray.
On Death (excerpt). Sikelianos.
Paphos. Durrell.
Paterson. Williams.
Prayer. Schlonsky.
The Progress of Poesy. Gray.
Recessional. MacGreevy.
The Seasons. Holcroft.
Storm Tide on Mejit. Anonymous.
A Wife's Song. Bennett.
Wild Beasts. Stein.
The Winter Lakes. Campbell.
Woman. Layton.

Roast (ed) (ing)

10:X:57, 45 Years Since the Fall of the Ch'ing Dynasty. Whalen.
A Dish for a Poet. Anonymous.

"Don't Touch Me!" I Scream at Passers-By. Gorbanyevskaya.
The Flying Bum: 1944. Plomer.
Old Christmas Returned. Anonymous.
Rufus's Mare. Anonymous.
A Song in Praise of Old English Roast Beef. Leveridge.
Steam in Sacrifice. Herrick.
Yaddo. Herschberger.

Rob (ber) (bed) (bing) (s)

Black Bart, PO8. Bierce.
The Clear Air of October. Bly.
Defeat of the Rebels. Graves.
The Demon Lover. Anonymous.
Dick Turpin and the Lawyer. Anonymous.
The Four Dears. Elliott.
He Understands the Great Cruelty of Death. Synge.
The House Carpenter (with music). Anonymous.
The Innocent Gazer. Cutts.
The Letter. Tatham.
Newgate's Garland. Anonymous.
Robbing and Stealing Blues. Campbell.
Rye Whiskey. Anonymous.
The Sheffield Apprentice. Anonymous.
Sir Andrew Barton (Andrew Batann). Anonymous.
The Terrible Robber Men. Colum.
Three Presidents: Theodore Roosevelt. Bly.
A Way Up on Clinch Mountain (A vers. with music). Anonymous.
With You a Part of Me. Santayana.

Robe (s)

The April Snow. Very.
The Coliseum. Poe.
Crimson Tent. Dos Passos.
For Thee, O Dear Dear Country! Neale.
Funeral Hymn. Anonymous.
Heaven's Magnificence. Muhlenberg.
Henry C. Calhoun. Masters.
How I wish I had known. Anonymous.
The King in His Beauty. Deck.
Lens. Wilkinson.
Loyalty. Davies.
O Thou, Who Didst Ordain the Word. Chapin.
Oh, Yes! Oh, Yes! Wait 'Til I Git on My Robe. Anonymous.
Palm-Sunday. Vaughan.
Praetorium Scene: Good Friday. Lennen.
Romeo and Juliet. Shakespeare.
Song: Under the Bronze Leaves. Perse.
Symphony. Dorn.
Woo Not the World. Mu'tamid.
A Word to Peter Olds. Brasch.

Robert

Burns. Halleck.
The Call to a Scot. Harding.
Hallelujah: A Sestina. Francis.
I'll Never Use Tobacco. Anonymous.
The Pear-Tree. Anonymous.
The Reader Writes. Crane.
Steamboat Bill. Anonymous.
That English Weather: After Browning (parody). Anonymous.

Robin (s)

Auld Robin Gray. Barnard.
The Blossom. Blake.
Bread and Milk. Rossetti.
Catch. Anonymous.
The Death of Robin Hood (excerpt). Anonymous.
Fifty Faggots. Thomas.
For My Newborn Son. Smith.
Goodbat Nightman. McGough.
Happy Were He. Essex.
Kind Robin Lo'es Me. Anonymous.
Late Autumn. Young.
Little Brother. Fisher.
Little John a Begging (B version). Anonymous.
Love Poem. Orr.
Midsummer Morn. Davis.
Robin Hood and the Beggar. Anonymous.
Robin Redbreast. Allingham.
Robin Redbreast. Anonymous.
Sonnet to—-. Reynolds.
Sonnet Written at the End of "The Floure and the Lefe." Keats.
A Spring Lilt. Anonymous.
To Robin Red-Breast. Herrick.
Twenty Foolish Fairies. Turner.
What Robin Told. Cooper.
Winter in the Wood. Eastwick.

Robot (s)

Butch Is Back. Box.
From a Venetian Sequence. Naude.
Lecture. Hollo.
A Poem for Anton Schmidt. Pillen.

Robs (bed) (ber) (bing) (s)

Sonnets, XXXV: "No more be grieved at that which thou hast done." Shakespeare.
Virgidemiarum. Hall.

Rock (ed) (ing) (s) (y)

Age. Jones.
All the Dead Dears. Plath.
All the Fruit... Holderlin.
Along Shore. Bashford.
Amtrak. Fried.
Another Face. Young Bear.
Appalachian Front. Weeks.
Ark Articulate. Macpherson.
At a Summer Hotel. Gardner.
At the Western Shore. Youngblood.
At White River. Haines.
Autumn Rain. Rexroth.
Back Road. Guernsey.
The Backward Look. Nemerov.

Baha'u'llah in the Garden of Ridwan. Hayden.
The Ballad of Downal Baun. Colum.
Bard's Chant. Shirley.
Biographical Note. Preil.
The Bird with the Coppery, Keen Claws. Stevens.
A bright moon illumines the night-prospect. *Anonymous.*
Bright Sparkles in de Churchyard. *Anonymous.*
Bring Back. Ridler.
Buachaille Etive Mor and Buachaille Etive Beag. Mitchison.
A Busy Man Speaks. Bly.
Butterfly on Rock. Layton.
Carmel Point. Jeffers.
Carpenter. Brown.
Casting at Night. Hoey.
A Child Accepts. Hamburger.
Childe Harold's Pilgrimage: Canto IV. Byron.
The David Jazz. Robinson.
The Dawning of the Day. Mangan.
The Deserted Village. Goldsmith.
The Dipper. Hesketh.
Downwards. Williams.
Dream. Ignatow.
Dream of Winter. Brown.
Eagle. Skelton.
Eddystone Light. *Anonymous.*
Epilog (to Lost Copper). Rose.
An Epistle to My Friend J. B. Dodsley.
The Eye. Wilkins.
Faith. Whittier.
The Faith Came First. Carter.
The Far Side of Introspection. Lee.
Father Malloy. Masters.
Father's Voice. Stafford.
A Footnote to a Gray Bird's Pause. Cunningham.
The Four Zoas. Blake.
The Galloway Shore. Tremayne.
The Gardens of Cymodoce. Swinburne.
Genesis. Ingham.
Gideon at the Well. Hill.
Girl Athletes. Long.
The Gods. Merwin.
The Grey Cock. *Anonymous.*
Ham Hound Crave. Lacy.
A Handful of Small Secret Stones. Bursk.
Hatteras Calling. Aiken.
Hawk and Snake. Silko.
High Island. Murphy.
Home in That Rock. *Anonymous.*
Horatio Alger Uses Scag. Jones.
Hosanna to Christ. Watts.
A Hymn of Nature. Bridges.
I Am the Mountainy Singer. Campbell.
I Came from Salem City. *Anonymous.*
I Got a Home in-a Dat Rock. *Anonymous.*
I Will Bow and Be Simple. *Anonymous.*

In Cold Storm Light. Silko.
Jars. Raboff.
John Hardy (A vers.). *Anonymous.*
Kithairon sang of cunning Kronos. Korinna.
Last Poems. Housman.
The Leaves That Rustled on This Oak-Crowned Hill. Wordsworth.
Little Fan. Reeves.
Looking for My Old Indian Grandmother in the Summer Heat of 1980. Glancy.
Los Mineros. Dorn.
Loss in Delay. Southwell.
Love Me! Smith.
Love's Labour Lost. Tofte.
Lucy. Wordsworth.
Mater Amabilis. Lazarus.
Matlock Bath. Betjeman.
Morning on the Lievre. Lampman.
The Mountain Tree. Connell.
My People. Lasker-Schüler.
My Soul Shall Cling to Thee. Elliot.
Nearer Home. Cary.
Noah. Bloch.
The Oleaster. Graves.
On Calamy's Imprisonment and Wild's Poetry. "Hudibras"
One Morning in May. *Anonymous.*
Only a Little Litter. Livingston.
Orpheus in the Underworld. Gascoyne.
The Pass. Logan.
Pittsburgh. Bynner.
Prayer in Time of War. Treece.
The Red-Gold Rain. Sitwell.
Requiem for the Plantagenet Kings. Hill.
Ripe, Being Plunged into Fire... Holderlin.
The Rock. Stevens.
Rock-a My Soul. *Anonymous.*
Rock 'n' Row Me over. *Anonymous.*
Rockingchair. Morgan.
The Rocky Road to Dublin. *Anonymous.*
Ronald Wyn. Bagg.
Saagin. Smith.
The Sea. Davies.
Sea Dawn. Hackett.
Sea Dirge. Scott.
Sea Flower. Dorcey.
A Sea-Spell. Rossetti.
The Shadow of the Rock. Faber.
Signpost. Jeffers.
Sirens. Coleman.
Slim Man Canyon. Silko.
Sometimes a Little House Will Please. Coatsworth.
A Song of Degrees. Ker.
Sonnet: "Shall I be fearful thus to speak my mind." McLeod.
Sonnet: The Double Rock. King.
A Sort of a Song. Williams.
Spider Crystal Ascension. Wright.
Spring. Smart.

The Sugar-Plum Tree. Field.
Survival in a Stone Maze. Rachow.
Sweet Was the Song the Virgin Sung. *Anonymous.*
Three Mile Island. Owen.
Touches. Stafford.
Travellers Turning over Borders (parody). Ransome.
Turn the Glasses Over. *Anonymous.*
The View of Rangitoto. Brasch.
Villanelle with a Line by Yeats. Bennett.
Warren's Address at Bunker Hill. Pierpont.
The Weary Blues. Hughes.
Wedding. Lipska.
Welcome. Thomas.
When the Troubled Sea Swells and Surrounds. Colonna.
When Thickly Beat the Storms of Life. Robins.
The Winter Lakes. Campbell.

Rock of Ages
Bryan's Last Battle (The Scopes Trial). *Anonymous.*
Hide Thou Me. *Anonymous.*

Rocker (s)
Br'er Sterling and the Rocker. Harper.
Katie Lee and Willie Grey. *Anonymous.*
Titus, Son of Rembrandt: 1665. Lyons.

Rocket (s)
Enough. Masson.
Limerick: "A young kangaroo, Miss Hocket." *Anonymous.*
Limerick: "There was an Old Lady named Crockett." Smith.
Miss Kilmansegg's Birth. Hood.
A Projection. Whittemore.
A Prophecy. Ginsberg.
Space Travel. Krows.
The Witch's Cat. Serraillier.

Rod
At Last. Newcombe.
By Mrs. Hopley, on Seeing Her Children Say Goodnight to Their Father. Hopkins.
Caelica, XXXIV. Greville.
He Establisheth His Triumph. Book of the Dead.
Hickory Stick Hierarchy. Selle.
The Lord Is My Shepherd. Knox.
Pere Lalement. Pickthall.
The Pole-Vaulter. *Anonymous.*
The Reed. Carpenter.
Risen Matters. Coolidge.
Roger Francis. Thorley.
Sources of Good Counsel. Idley.
Still Century. Paulin.
Symbols. Rossetti.
Thanksgiving. Best.
To Urania on the Death of Her First and Only Child. Colman.
The Virtues of Sid Hamet, the Magician's Rod. Swift.

Rodent
But There Was Once a Time When the Bones. Vakalo.
If Some Grim Tragedy. Smith.

Rogue (s)
An Epigram on Scolding. Swift.
Epigram: "Our fathers took oaths as of old they took wives." Brown.
Epilogue to the Satires. Pope.
A Health to the Tackers. *Anonymous.*
Insect Riddle: "I was round and small like a pearl." *Anonymous.*
The Jolly Sailor's True Description of a Man-of-War. *Anonymous.*
London Adulterations. *Anonymous.*
Phyllis; or, The Progress of Love. Swift.
The Speculators. Thackeray.
A Strong Hand. Hill.
Such a Parcel of Rogues in a Nation. Burns.
To the Respective Judges. *Anonymous.*
The Vision of Piers Plowman. Langland.
When I Solidly Do Ponder. Pastorius.

Roland
The Last Tourney. Van de Water.
The Song of Roland. *Anonymous.*
The Sound of the Horn. Vigny.

Roll (ed) (ing) (s)
The Alabama. *Anonymous.*
Beetle Bemused. Lister.
The Caisson Song. Gruber.
The Charge by the Ford. English.
Diamond Joe. *Anonymous.*
The Dove of Dacca. Kipling.
Dry Loaf. Stevens.
Eddystone Light. *Anonymous.*
Eighteen-Ninety. Shipp.
An Epitaph: On Elizabeth Chute. Jonson.
Fiascherino. Tomlinson.
For Elizabeth Bishop. McPherson.
From Heart to Heart. Gannett.
Funeral. Thompson.
I Got to Roll. *Anonymous.*
Investiture. Henderson.
Let the Wind Blow High or Low. *Anonymous.*
Lord Cozens Hardy. Betjeman.
Mary Speaks to Jesus. Dempster.
Mimma Bella. Lee-Hamilton.
The Mouse's Lullaby. Cox.
My Bonnie Highland Laddie. Burns.
Naming the Rain. West.
Nine Pound Hammer. *Anonymous.*
Oh, Roll on, Babe. *Anonymous.*
Pater's Bathe. Parry.

The Pedestrian's Plaint. Lucas.
Return to Lane's Island. Matchett.
Robert Rowley Rolled a Round Roll Round. *Anonymous.*
Roll, Jordan, Roll. *Anonymous.*
Roll, Julia, Roll. *Anonymous.*
Roll the Union On. Hays.
Rolling the Lawn. Empson.
Salutation. Russell.
Shaggy Dog Story. Steele.
The Sinking of the Graf Spee. *Anonymous.*
This Night. Hai-Jew.
A Trot, and a Canter, a Gallop, and Over. *Anonymous.*
View from My Window. MacLean.
When the Roll Is Called up Yonder. Black.

Rollers
The Landlubber's Chantey. Montgomery.
Only Years. Rexroth.
Tristram of Lyoness: Swimming. Swinburne.

Roman (s)
After a Lecture on Keats. Holmes.
Amours de Voyage. Clough.
Invisible Trumpets Blowing. Pratt.
A Shropshire Lad. Housman.
A Sonnet: "O lovely O most charming pug." Fleming.
Talk. Stalker.
To a Contemporary Bunkshooter. Sandburg.
To My Nose. Forrester.
Triumph. Ransom.

Romance
America. Di Cicco.
Ballade of the Old-Time Engine. Vines.
Old Susan. De la Mare.
A Song of Diligence. Frazee-Bower.

Rome
Antony and Cleopatra. Lytle.
Arlington Cemetery Looking toward the Capitol. Palmer.
At Night. Montgomery.
Caelica, XXX. Greville.
Cleopatra to the Asp. Hughes.
Country Pleasures. Martial (Marcus Valerius Martialis).
Domine Quo Vadis? Watson.
Forty Days (excerpt). Wheelwright.
Goosey Goosey Gander. French.
The Holy Land of Walsingham. Musser.
A Hundreth Good Poyntes of Husbandry. Tusser.
In the Old Theatre, Fiesole. Hardy.
Julius Caesar. Shakespeare.
Non Dolet. Gogarty.
Of My Lady Isabella Playing on the Lute. Waller.
On the Campagna. Stoddard
Petrarch. Carducci.

A Road in the Weald. Church.
The Sentiments. *Anonymous.*
Sleet Storm on the Merritt Parkway. Bly.
Song of Hannibal: Rome. Christian.
The Third Satire of Juvenal. Dryden.
A True Story. Bell.
Two Pictures. *Anonymous.*
When in Rome. Evans.
A Word of Warning. *Anonymous.*

Romp (ed) (ing)
Eating Poetry. Strand.
O Pioneers! Bishop.
October. Goren.
The Sick Stockrider. Gordon.

Roof (s)
3rd Dance–Making a Structure with a Roof or under a Roof... MacLow.
After Chagall. Wenger.
The Ascension. Beaumont.
Calais Sands. Arnold.
Celebration. Cohen.
The Cemetery by the Sea. Valery.
City Butterfly. Siebert.
City Roofs. Towne.
The Destroyers (excerpt). Fleming.
Esther's Tomcat. Hughes.
For Wilma. Johnson.
Fragment: "–you see." Allingham.
A Frolic. Herrick.
Genesis (excerpt). *Anonymous.*
The Gifts. Levendosky.
Heavy, Heavy–What Hangs Over? Burke.
Hymn: "The Church's Restoration." (parody). Betjeman.
The Man of the House. Hinkson.
Morning at the Window. Eliot.
Moving In. Shapiro.
Prayer Against Indifference. Davidman.
Returning to the World. Chester.
The Roofwalker. Rich.
The Secret of the Deeps. Lysaght.
She Hears the Storm. Hardy.
Summons for the Undead. Keating.
Synthesizing Several Abstruse Concepts with an Experience (parody). Poster.
Training. Herrera.
U is for Umbrellas. McGinley.
Unitarian Easter. McPherson.
The Vision of Mac Conglinne. *Anonymous.*
Waking in New York. Ginsberg.
The Young Man. MacAdams.

Rooks
Erinna. Antipater of Sidon.
The Life of Hubert, I (excerpt). Cole.

Weathers. Hardy.
Room (s)
Abortion. Anthony ("Ai").
Above Machu Picchu, 129 Baker Street, San Francisco. Stroud.
After a Game of Squash. Albert.
After Reading Certain Books. Coleridge.
Angels in the House. Metz.
The Animals. MacAdams.
As Soon as Ever Twilight Comes. De la Mare.
Bean Spasms. Berrigan.
Because He Liked to Be at Home. Patchen.
Caelica, LXIV. Greville.
Car Episode. Gordon.
Childhood. Stanton.
Close Quarters. Tabb.
Coming and Going. Johnson.
Construction. Schonborg.
A Dead King. Swinburne.
Depression. Cope.
Development. Enright.
Did our best moment last. Dickinson.
Dinner at the Hotel de la Tigresse Verte. Evans.
Elegy. Layzer.
Fall Letter. Kelly.
Far from Africa. Danner.
Fish. Hogan.
The Furnished Room. Merrill.
Get On Board, Little Children. *Anonymous.*
Gitanjali. Tagore.
The Gold Country: Hotel Leger, Mokelumne Hill, Revisited. Stroud.
Goodbye Now, or, Pardon My Gauntlet. Nash.
The Gospel Train. *Anonymous.*
Halcyon. Doolittle.
Historical Museum, Manitoulin Island. Mueller.
House Blessing. Guiterman.
How the Joy of It Was Used Up Long Ago. Gregg.
I Am. Kushner.
I Dreamed I Saw the Crescent Moon. *Anonymous.*
An Inconvenience. Raven.
Johnnie Bought a Ham. *Anonymous.*
A Late Spring: Eastport. Booth.
The Lodge Room over Simpkins' Store. Greenleaf.
Loss. Davis.
Loving. Kaufman.
A Man Walks in the Wind. Lesemann.
Moon as Medusa. D'Ambrosio.
Moon Blast. Roberts.
Morning Light. Dudek.
Mrs. Malone. Farjeon.
The Myall in Prison. Gilmore.
Neoplatonic Soliloquy. Babcock.
The New House. McDougall.
New Jersey. Bennett.
Niagara Falls. Parisi.

Night. Hayes.
No Bread for the Poor (with music). *Anonymous.*
No Laws. Allwood.
On the Death of Squire Christopher, a Remarkably Fat Sportsman. Wigson.
Out of Chaos Out of Order Out. Roberts.
The Pear Tree. Longwell.
Physical Geography. Nicholl.
The Pilot. Edson.
Poem: "I watched an armory combing its bronze bricks." O'Hara.
The Poolhall. Burt.
Popular Songs of Tuscany. *Anonymous.*
A Prayer. Laird.
Readymade. Perreault.
Resurrection of Arp. Smith.
Returning to the World. Chester.
The Room. Orr.
The Room. Soutar.
The Room's Width. Ward.
Room Service. Moser.
S. T. Colerige Dismisses a Caller from Porlock. Meyer.
Sappho's Tomb. Stringer.
Soaping Down for Saint Francis of Assisi: The Canticle of Sister Soap. Ruark.
Song: "I came to the door of the House of Love." Noyes.
Song of Hope. Lathbury.
The Song of the Sons of Esau. Runkle.
Suicid/ing Indian Women. Allen.
Summerhouse. La Follette.
Tenant at Number 9. Blight.
Tour Guide: La Maison des Esclaves. Dixon.
A Trapped Fly. Herrick.
Triolet against Sisters. McGinley.
The Truth Is Quite Messy. Harris.
Twilight on Sumter. Stoddard.
Untitled. Naone.
Variation on Heraclitus. MacNeice.
Victory. Johnson.
Virgo Descending. Wright.
The Wake. Prunty.
Waking Early. Barth.
The Walk. Hardy.
Where the Slow Fig's Purple Sloth. Warren.
Why Would I Want. Harris.
The Wind. Rendall.
With My Grandfather. Zelda.
The Young Man Who Loved the Girl Who Took Care of Her Aging Father. Kuzma.

Roost
The Canterbury Tales: A Monk. Chaucer.
First Confession. Kennedy.
The Gangster's Death. Reed.

Rooster (s)
At the Cantina. Soto.
The Birthplace. Heaney.

The Eggplants Have Pins and
Needles. Matveyeva.
I Had a Rooster.
Anonymous.
Old Boards. Bly.
Rocking. Ammons.
To France. Chaplin.
Root Hog
The Bullwhacker.
Anonymous.
The California Stage
Company. Anonymous.
A Hit at the Times.
McGrew.
Root Hog or Die. Small.
Root (s)
After Laughter. Sherwood.
All the Dead Dears. Plath.
And This of All My Hopes.
Dickinson.
At Dawn. Synge.
At the Nature-Strip.
Rodriguez.
The Atoll in the Mind.
Comfort.
Autonomous. Van Doren.
The Bats. Hillyer.
Birth. Lyon.
The Boy with a Cart
(excerpt). Fry.
Brooklyn Summer. Lipsitz.
Caelica, CVI. Greville.
Corrib. An Emblem. Davie.
The Creek of the Four Graves
(excerpt). Harpur.
The Day of the Night.
Scully.
Drinking. Terris.
Drinking Cold Water.
Everwine.
The Dusting of the Books.
Hughes.
Eleven. MacLeish.
The Farmer. Herbert.
From a Litany. Strand.
From the Notebooks.
Roethke.
Green Song. Booth.
The Hesperides. Tennyson.
In Vistas of Stone.
Stoltzenberg.
The Interpreters. Enright.
John Chapman. Wilbur.
Joy Is the Blossom. Landor.
The Judgment of Paris.
Merwin.
Life-Hook. Ibarbourou.
London. Ghose.
Lone Gentleman. Neruda.
Lord Barrenstock. Smith.
Message. Pallottini.
Most Weeds, Whilst Young.
Pastorius.
New Life. Burr.
November. Cary.
The Olive. Housman.
On Thomas Carew.
Anonymous.
The Palace for Teeth.
Luttinger.
A Place (Any Place) to
Transcend All Places.
Williams.
Poem: "Some are too much at
home in the role of
wanderer." Levertov.
The Progress of Learning:
Preface. Denham.
Recipe. Goldbarth.
Rehearsal. Dabydeen.
Riddle: "Lives in winter."
Mother Goose.

Ritual of Departure.
Kinsella.
The Room Above the Square.
Spender.
Running the Trotline.
Elledge.
Shooting Script (excerpt).
Rich.
Silverthorn Bush. Finch.
Since I've Felt This Pain.
Ono no Komachi.
Snake Doctor Blues. Short.
The Song of the Woman-
Drawer. Gilmore.
Sonnets from the Portuguese,
XLIV. Browning.
The Sons of Levi.
Anonymous.
The Storm. Imr el Kais.
The Sunflower to the Sun.
Stebbins
Tanka I–VIII. Alexander.
Thaw. Untermeyer.
There Is Good News.
Jacobsen.
This Is What the Watchbird
Sings, Who Perches in the
Lovetree. Boyd.
The Three Bushes. Yeats.
To Paint a Water Lily.
Hughes.
Trees and Cattle. Dickey.
Visit. Ammons.
Where She Was Not Born.
Yvonne.
Rope (s)
As I Step over a Puddle at the
End of Winter. Wright.
A Book of Music. Spicer.
The Boss. Lowell.
Buachaille Etive Mor and
Buachaille Etive Beag.
Mitchison.
Contentment. Osaki.
Did I Ever Think. Ono no
Takamura.
Distance. Everwine.
Dobbin. Bowering.
Etruscan Notebook.
Clementelli.
Exchange. Hamilton.
How Paddy Stole the Rope.
Anonymous.
I Want to Be a Cowboy.
Anonymous.
The Lives of Famous Men.
Gilbert.
Lord Randall. Anonymous.
A Nonsense Carol.
Anonymous.
An Ode to the Framers of the
Frame Bill. Byron.
On a Rope Maker Hanged.
Browne.
A Rat. Anonymous.
Rock Leader. Bathgate.
The Same Continued. Blunt.
Schoolroom on a Wet
Afternoon. Scannell.
To the Bell-Ringer. Farren.
Treehouse. Kooser.
The World. Rutsala.
Rosary
The House of Love: Pride of
Youth. Rossetti.
Post-Meridian. Garrison.
To an Old Lady Dead.
Sassoon.
Rose (s)
All through the Stranger's
Wood. Peretz.

Anacreon to the Sophist.
"H.
Anacreontic. Clarke.
The Angel in the House.
Patmore.
Anteroom: Geneva. Devlin.
Ants. Hyde.
Apologia Addressed to Ireland
in the Coming Days.
Yeats.
Apology for Bad Dreams.
Jeffers.
As in a Rose-Jar. Jones, Jr.
Ashes of Roses. Eastman.
At Ecelin. Browning.
Attainment. Tassin.
Autumn Twilight. Regnier.
Ave Eva. Wheelwright.
B-52s. Kenseth.
The Babe. Gibbon.
Ballade of the Dreamland
Rose. Hooker.
The Banks of the Roses.
Anonymous.
Barbara Allen. Anonymous.
The Battle. Davies.
Be Beautiful. Villa.
Be Still As You Are Beautiful.
MacDonogh.
Beachcomber. Oliver.
Believe Me, If All Those
Endearing Young Charms.
Moore.
Ben Bolt. Anonymous.
Between the Lines. Gibson.
Beyond Possession. Jennings.
Big Wind. Roethke.
Birthing: 2000. Aguila.
The Blind Girl. Crane.
Blood Red Roses.
Anonymous.
Blue Mason Jars. Abbott.
The Bonny Bunch of Roses.
Anonymous.
The Buried Life. Arnold.
Cat in the Snow. Fisher.
A Colonist in His Garden.
Reeves.
Come All You Fair and
Tender Ladies.
Anonymous.
Come down, You Bunch of
Roses, Come down.
Anonymous.
Confidence. Hartley.
Conversation. MacNeice.
The Dance of the Daughters
of Herodias. Symons.
Dear Old Mothers. Ross.
Dogrose. Stevenson.
The Dowie Houms o' Yarrow.
Anonymous.
The Dream of the Cross.
Anonymous.
Earl Brand (B vers.).
Anonymous.
Easter Song. Lathbury.
Etruscan Warrior's Head.
Henze.
Evanescence. Spofford.
Eve. Bull.
The Faerie Queene. Spenser.
False Love. Burns.
A Fancy. Lodge.
Farewell!–but Whenever You
Welcome the Hour.
Moore.
Farewell, Life. Hood.
Fatal Interview. Millay.
The Flowers. Rands.

For Colored Girls Who Have
Considered
Suicide...(excerpt). Shange.
Four Sonnets to Helen, 4.
Ronsard.
From Grenoble. Flecker.
Frost. Benson.
A Garland for Heliodora.
Meleager.
The Gift of God. Robinson.
God's Garden. Burton.
Grandmither, Think Not I
Forget. Cather.
The Grave and the Rose.
Hugo.
He Liked the Dead. Lowry.
Henry the Fifth's Conquest of
France. Anonymous.
Her Lips. Anonymous.
His Lady's Tomb. Ronsard.
How can you look at the
Neva. Akhmatova.
I Am Like a Rose.
Lawrence.
I Love the Blue Violet.
Clare.
I Love You and the
Rosebush. Uribe.
Idyl. Mombert.
If Crossed with All Mishaps.
Drummond.
If You Had Known. Hardy.
Impression. Symons.
In Crisis. Durrell.
In Hospital. Flecker.
In Memoriam A.H.H.,
CXXII. Tennyson.
In Pursuit of Love. Norris.
The Innocent Spring.
Sitwell.
Inscription. Hamilton.
Is It Far to Go. Day.
The Island. Muir.
It Is at Moments after I Have
Dreamed. Cummings.
June. Ledwidge.
Keats. Reese.
Kindness. Plath.
A Knight of Ghosts and
Shadows. Thompson.
Lat Noman Booste of
Konnyng Nor Vertu.
Lydgate.
Lecture Noir. Thesen.
A Legend. Tschaikovsky.
Let All Created Things.
Seagrave.
Like a Midsummer Rose.
Lydgate.
The Lilacs and the Roses.
Aragon.
Lines for a Feast of Our
Lady. Maris Stella.
The Little Red Ribbon.
Riley.
The Lonely Shell. Perry.
Love and Death.
Mulholland.
The Lover Tells of the Rose
in His Heart. Yeats.
A Lyric: "Into a little close of
mine I went." Medici.
Ma Provence. Koch.
Madonna of the Exiles.
Tobin.
Madrigal: "I always loved to
call my lady Rose."
Anonymous.
Maiden in the Mor.
Anonymous.
The Maidens Came.
Anonymous.

Rose

Mandoline. Verlaine.
Mary Passes. *Anonymous.*
The Meeting. Louys.
Midsummer. Spender.
The Miracle of Dawn.
  Cawein.
Moonlight. Apollinaire.
Morning Compliments.
  Dayre.
Mother, Mother, Make My
  Bed. *Anonymous.*
Mouth to mouth recitation.
  Fitzgerald.
Mozart. Heath-Stubbs.
My Aunt. Holmes.
My Mother's Garden. Allen.
My Regrets. André.
My Rose. Hawthorne.
The name—of it—is "Autumn."
  Dickinson.
Nijinsky. Tyler.
A Nocturnal Sketch. Hood.
Nonsense. Schauffler.
November. Cary.
Nude in a Fountain.
  MacCaig.
The Nurse Believed the Sick
  Man Slept. Bronte.
O Youth with Blossoms
  Laden. Peach.
Of a Spider. Thorley.
Of His Lady's Old Age.
  Ronsard.
Off Molokai. Hindley.
Old Gardens. Upson.
Old Mothers. Ross.
Old Woman's Song. Cole.
On a Damaske Rose Sticking
  upon a Ladies Breast.
  Carew.
On a Rosebud Sent to Her
  Lover. *Anonymous.*
On Growing Old. Masefield.
On the Death of Dermody,
  the Poet. White.
On Waking. Gulick.
One Perfect Rose. Parker.
Only Thy Dust... Marquis.
Originality. Aldrich.
Orlando Furioso. Ariosto.
Orphans. Ray.
Out There Somewhere.
  Knibbs.
Overnight, a Rose. Giltinan.
The Ovibos. Hale.
The Painted Lady. Danner.
Paraphrase. Crane.
Perdita. Coates.
A Poem for the Meeting of
  the American Medical
  Association. Holmes.
The Poet. Watson.
Popular Songs of Tuscany.
  Anonymous.
A Portrait. Hooker.
Praxis. Thesen.
Prelude. Benson.
A Pretty Ambition.
  Freeman.
Prisoners. Mavity.
The Proffered Rose.
  Wenceslas.
Quid Non Speremus,
  Amantes? Dowson.
The Rain and the Rainbow.
  Fredericks.
Reading Sign. Anderson.
A Responsory, 1948.
  Merton.
The Reversible Metaphor.
  "Troubadour".
The Rise of Shivaji. Ghose.

Rococo. Payne.
Ronsard to His Mistress.
  Thackeray.
A Rose. Bates.
The Rose. Herbert.
The Rose. Kennedy.
The Rose. Lodge.
The Rose. Lovelace.
The Rose. Ronsard.
Rose and Root. Piatt.
The Rose-Bud To a Young
  Lady. Broome.
The Rose of Eden. Phillips.
The Rose Tree. Yeats.
The Rosebush and the Trinity.
  Barrett.
Roses. Campion.
Roses. Miller.
Roses. Ronsard.
The Roses of Queens. White.
The Sandman. Janvier.
Sapientia Lunae. Dowson.
Scatter Seeds of Kindness.
  Smith.
The Schreckhorn. Hardy.
Sea-Distances. Noyes.
Seville. Walters.
The Shadow-Child. Monroe.
Simple Nature. Romanes.
The Slave. Very.
The Sleeping. Emanuel.
The Sleeping Beauty. Sitwell.
Song: "Choose now among
  this fairest number."
  Browne.
Songs of the Pixies.
  Coleridge.
Sonnet: "Say what you will."
  Millay.
Sonnets, CIX: "O, never say
  that I was false of heart."
  Shakespeare.
Southern Gothic. Justice.
Spiritual Isolation.
  Rosenberg.
Sprinkling. Pierce.
The Swans. Sitwell.
The Tailor. Garfinkel.
There She Stands a Lovely
  Creature. *Anonymous.*
Thine Eyes Still Shined.
  Emerson.
This Poem Will Never Be
  Finished. Souster.
Thoughts after Ruskin.
  Mitchell.
To a Rose. Sherman.
To a Withered Rose. Bangs.
To Autumn. Blake.
To Be Recited to Flossie on
  Her Birthday. Williams.
To Bring Spring. Keithley.
To Her Love. May.
To Miss Eleanor Ambrose...
  Chesterfield.
To My Lady Mirriel Howard.
  Skelton.
To Poets. Landor.
To Rose. Teasdale.
To Sir William, of
  Hawthornden Alexander.
  Drummond.
To the Newborn. Toth.
To Vera Thompson. Haines.
To William Wordsworth.
  Coleridge.
Today I Am Envying the
  Glorious Mexicans.
  Blumenthal.
The Tragic Mary Queen of
  Scot. "Field.

The Travail of Passion.
  Yeats.
A True Account of Talking to
  the Sun at Fire Island.
  O'Hara.
Truelove. *Anonymous.*
The Tumble. Taylor.
Two Birds. Linnell.
Two Red Roses Across the
  Moon. Morris.
Under My Window.
  Westwood.
Under the Rose. *Anonymous.*
The Vase. Tiller.
The Vision of Delight.
  Jonson.
The Vision of Sin.
  Tennyson.
A Vision of Truth. Squire.
The Wars of the Roses.
  Anonymous.
When Life Is Quite Through
  With. Cummings.
Where Do I Love You,
  Lovely Maid? Roseliep.
The White Flag. Hay.
White World. Doolittle.
Wild Eden. Woodberry.
The Window Sill. Graves.
With a Rose from Conway
  Castle. Dorr.
With Roses. Lloyd.
With Rue My Heart Is Laden.
  Housman.
Within a Greenwood Sweet of
  Myrtle Savour.
  Anonymous.
Women and Roses.
  Browning.
Woods. MacNeice.
The World-Soul. Emerson.
The World Well Lost.
  Stedman.

Rosemary

The Dying Man in His
  Garden. Sewell.
Essential oils—are wrung.
  Dickinson.
Essential Oils—are wrung—675.
  Dickinson.
Good Frend. Doolittle.
The Rock. *Anonymous.*
A Song for My Mother—Her
  Stories. Branch.

Rosy

A Bunch of Roses. Tabb.
Design for a Bowl.
  Anacreon.
Garden. Marvell.
The Reflection. Taylor.
To an Old Venetian Wine-
  Glass. Mifflin.
Wee Davie Daylicht.
  Tennant.

Rot (s) (ten)

Apple Offering. *Anonymous.*
Arrows. Heyen.
The Burden of Junk.
  Glassco.
Death Songs. *Anonymous.*
Flying Foxes and Others.
  Boyle.
Limerick: "A Phoenician
  called Phlebas forgot."
  Cope.
Limerick: "Said the Reverend
  Jabez McCotton." Flagg.
Oh, Bury Me Not on The
  Lone Prairie (with music).
  Anonymous.
An Old Folks Home. Lake.

Per Amica Silentia Lunae.
  Carvalho.
Poem: "You, who in April
  laughed, a green god in the
  sun." Chamberlain.
A Renouncing of Love.
  Wyatt.
Spoon River Anthology.
  Robinson.
Turn on the Footlights: The
  Perils of Pedagogy.
  Carter.
Upon the Bankruptcy of a
  Physician. Selyns.
The War Year. Ts'ao Sung.
Winter Sunset. Laforgue.

Rouge

The Aphrodisiac.
  McGuckian.
Don Juan. Byron.

Rough

The Canadian Prairies View of
  Literature. Donnell.
Country Dance. Sitwell.
First Pathways. Lysaght.
I Have Heard. *Anonymous.*
Jeremiah, Blow the Fire.
  Anonymous.
The New-Chum's First Trip.
  Anonymous.
O-U-G-H. Loomis.
The Pluralist and Old Soldier.
  Collier.
Poem about a Seashell.
  Crosby.
The Pot of Flowers.
  Williams.
Sonnet Written in a Blank
  Leaf of Dugdale's
  Monasticon. Warton, Jr..
To Sleep. Casa.

Round (s)

12 October. Livingston.
Apple Peeler. Francis.
Apples. Hall.
At Bickford's. Stern.
The Death of Harrison.
  Willis.
Drinking Song: "Drink that
  rotgut, drink that rotgut".
  Anonymous.
Engineers. Garthwaite.
Escape. Johnson.
Feud. Sarett.
God's Goin' to Set This
  World On Fire (B vers.)
  (with music). *Anonymous.*
Gradatim. Holland.
The Healer (excerpt).
  Whittier.
Hey, My Kitten, My Kitten.
  Anonymous.
How to Build a Ha-Ha.
  Mason.
Hymn of the Earth.
  Channing, II.
A Masique Presented at
  Ludlow Castle (Comus).
  Milton.
Microcosmus. Nashe [(or
  Nash(] Thomas.
My Birth-Day. Moore.
Pastoral. Wright.
The Pleasures of Merely
  Circulating. Stevens.
The Rabbit. Durston.
The Ronan Robe Series.
  Quick-To-See-Smith.
The Round Table. Kenner.
Rounded up in Glory.
  Anonymous.

'Tis the Gift To Be Simple.
Anonymous.
Todlen Butt, and Todlen Ben.
Anonymous.
Upland. Ammons.

Round-up
I'd Like to Be in Texas when
They Round-Up in the
Spring. Anonymous.
Utah Carroll. Anonymous.

Roundelay (s)
A Blith and Bonny Country
Lass. Lodge.
It Fell upon a Holy Eve.
Spenser.
Perigot and Willye. Spenser.
To an Autumn Leaf.
Mathews.
Whither Is Gone the Wisdom
and the Power. Coleridge.

Rouse
The British Lyon Roused.
Tilden.
Cavalier Tunes. Browning.
Green Sleeves. Anonymous.
Men of the High North.
Service.
To a Sleeping Friend.
Cocteau.

Rout
The Last Lap. Kipling.
Metamorphoses. Ovid
(Publius Ovidius Naso).
The Moods. Yeats.
The Poem: "I sing th'
adventures of mine worthy
wights." Morton.
Song for Peace. Rodgers.

Route (s)
The Changes. Pinsky.
Evening in the Country.
Ashbery.
Is It Really Worth the While?
Anonymous.
The Southeast Ramparts of
the Seine. Toth.
Tracking the Sled, Christmas
1951. Walker.

Rove
Epigram: "Glad youth had
come thy sixteenth year to
crown." Ausonius.
False Love. Scott.
The Jolly Beggar.
Anonymous.
Marian Drury. Carman.
O God, in Whom the Flow of
Days. Babcock.
Roving Gambler Blues.
Anonymous.
The Sliprails and the Spur.
Lawson.
So, We'll Go No More a
Roving. Byron.
A Thousand Martyrs I Have
Made. Behn.

Rover
The Lost War-Sloop.
Proctor.
The Roving Worker.
Anonymous.
Wild Rover. Anonymous.

Row (ed) (ing) (s)
As I Came O'er Cairney
Mount. Anonymous.
The Barcarole of James Smith.
Gorman.
The Big Swing-Tree Is Green
Again. Carr.
Bridal Song. Brentano.
The Drunk in the Furnace.
Merwin.

The Faerie Queene. Spenser.
A House of Readers. Miller.
If You See My Mother.
Maze.
In Measure Time We'll Row.
Anonymous.
Limerick: There once was a
man who said, "How."
Anonymous.
The Lotus Flowers. Voigt.
Michael, Row the Boat
Ashore. Anonymous.
The Natural Order of Things.
Elliott.
The Old Miner's Refrain.
Anonymous.
The Oldest Soldier. Graves.
Poplars. Reed.
A Racing Eight.
Cuthbertson.
Rake. Ratcliffe.
Rapunzel. Broumas.
Rivets. Olds.
Robin Hood's Progress to
Nottingham. Anonymous.
Rock 'n' Row Me over.
Anonymous.
Row of Houses. Quinn.
The Strong Swimmer. Benet.
You, Doctor Martin. Sexton.

Rowboat
Hero and Leander.
Newman.
Undersea Fever. Cole.

Royal
The Banished Duke of
Grantham. Anonymous.
Farewell to Earth. Doten.
Geordie (C vers.).
Anonymous.
An Ironical Encomium.
Anonymous.
Limerick: "An old East End
worker called Jock."
Gray.
The Room. Day-Lewis.
Six Dukes Went a-Fishing.
Anonymous.
Tiger. Hope.
The Wreck of the Royal
Charter. Anonymous.

Rub (bed)
A Beautiful Young Nymph
Going to Bed. Swift.
Cressida. Baxter.
Limerick: "While visiting
Arundel Castle." Gray.
My Boots. Thoreau.
Touching Shoulders.
Anonymous.

Rubber
The Boy. Field.
Brown Like Us. Soto.
Chicago, Summer Past.
Snyder.
Hymn in Columbus Circle.
Benét.
A Little Pig Asleep.
Jackson.
Psychological Prediction.
Brasier.
Street Fire. Halpern.

Rubbish
Every Thing. Monro.
Flycatchers. Bridges.
The Great Statue of the
General Du Puy. Stevens.
In a Bed-Sitter. Porter.
The Moon Bird. Vickers.
A Sonnet: "Two voices are
there." Stephen.
The Warning. Longfellow.

Rubble
Birmingham 1963.
Patterson.
Primitives. Randall.
Variations on a Time Theme.
Muir.
Villages Demolis. Read.

Rubicon
Fording the River. Deane.
The Lost Leader. Fraser.
A Thought of Death.
Flatman.

Ruby (ies)
Beltway. McLaughlin.
A Chanted Calendar.
Dobell.
John of Hazelgreen (C vers.).
Anonymous.
A Nuptial Verse to Mistress
Elizabeth Lee Now Lady
Tracy. Herrick.
Song: "It was a friar of orders
free." Peacock.

Ruby (rubies)
Buddha. Holz.
In the Dark None Dainty.
Herrick.
Lucifer. Lawrence.

Rudder
A Home without a Bible
(excerpt). Meigs.
The Temple of Venus.
Jenyns.

Ruddy
Maud. Tennyson.
The Shedpherd's Week.
Gay.
The Tumble. Taylor.

Rude (ness)
Bracken Hills in Autumn.
""MacDiarmid.
Characters of Women.
Young.
The Dog. Anonymous.
The Embarrassing Episode of
Little Miss Muffet. Carryl.
Excuse Us, Animals in the
Zoo. Wynne.
For a Statue of Chaucer at
Woodstock. Akenside.
A Hymn to Mary. Dunbar.
The Lesser Lynx. Rieu.
Limerick: "There once was a
sensitive cat." Brown.
The Return of Eve.
Chesterton.
The Sailor's Grave. Cook.
Tee-Vee Enigma. Raskin.

Rue (d)
Army Bugle Calls: Stable Call.
Anonymous.
Bothwell Bridge.
Anonymous.
Bouquet in Dog Time.
Carruth.
Busy with love, the bumble
bee. Meleager.
Crowned. Lowell.
Dust of Snow. Frost.
Grandmither, Think Not I
Forget. Cather.
Jephthah's Daughter.
Yehoash.
Kellyburnbraes. Anonymous.
My Heart Is Heich Above.
Anonymous.
The New-Slain Knight.
Anonymous.
Poem: "Entombed in my
heart." Dodson.
The Seeds of Love.
Anonymous.

Tiggady Rue. McCord.
Tommy Was a Silly Boy.
Greenway.

Ruffle (d)
The Bwoat. Barnes.
Free Little Bird. Anonymous.
The Laundress. Kinsella.

Rug (s)
Melkon. Kherdian.
Money (with music).
Anonymous.
Mr. Hughes. Campbell.
Signs. Murphy.
The Silver Racer. Murphey.

Ruin (ed) (s)
Absalom and Achitophel.
Dryden.
All Ruin Is the Same.
Litvinoff.
Amoretti, LVI. Spenser.
Australia 1970. Wright.
Belfast. Revell.
Blennerhassett's Island.
Read.
Boadicea. Cowper.
The Book Rises Out of the
Fire. Jabes.
The Burning of Jamestown.
English.
The Carpenter's Wife.
Anonymous.
Cataclysm. Catullus.
Christ Walks in This Infernal
District Too. Lowry.
Climb in Torridon. Macrow.
Concord Hymn. Emerson.
Continuity. Russell.
Death. Cawein.
The Descent of Odin. Gray.
Dirge. Troupe.
Eileen Aroon. O'Daly.
Enoch. Very.
Evangeline. Longfellow.
The Faerie Queene. Spenser.
Farewell, Sweet Mary.
Anonymous.
The Four Zoas. Blake.
From a Lament for Una.
Costello.
Garrison. Alcott.
The Good Town. Muir.
The Gulistan. Sa'di.
The Horse. Eguren.
I Pray You. Moore.
In Memoriam
A.H.H.,LXXVI.
Tennyson.
In the Cabinet. Vinner.
In the Hospital of the Holy
Physician. Willard.
Inscribed upon a Rock.
Wordsworth.
Irish Hymn to Mary.
Anonymous.
Job's Ancient Lament.
Dodson.
Lament for Corc and Niall of
the Nine Hostages. Torna.
A Letter from Aragon.
Cornford.
Letter in Winter. Patterson.
Limerick: "There was a
professor called
Chesterton." Gilbert.
Limerick: "There was an Old
Person of Philae." Lear.
Love the Ruins. Tussman.
The Making of Man.
Chadwick.
The Mask and the Poem.
Pizarnik.
Mortally. Kirkup.

October. Pape.
Ode to Nea. Moore.
On the Death of Captain
  Nicholas Biddle. Freneau.
On the Death of Catarina de
  Attayda. Camoens.
Passing Out. Levine.
The Permanent Tourists.
  Page.
Pharsalia: The Rivalry
  between Caesar and
  Pompey. Lucan (Marcus
  Annaeus Lucanus).
Psalm XXXIV. Sidney.
The Queen's Speech.
  Mainwaring.
The Ruined Maid. Hardy.
Safe Places. Urdang.
The Sailor Cut down in His
  Prime. *Anonymous.*
South Carolina to the States
  of the North. Hayne.
Survey of Cornwall. Carew.
To Be Carved on a Stone at
  Thoor Ballylee. Yeats.
To My Native Land.
  Mangan.
To Nature Seekers.
  Chambers.
Tom Dooley. *Anonymous.*
Tristium. Ovid (Publius
  Ovidius Naso).
Trooper and Maid, II.
  Anonymous.
Two Days. Henley.
Two Pictures of a Leaf. Bell.
Vanbrug's House. Swift.
Voice and Address. Palmer.
A Voyage to Tintern Abbey.
  Davies.
The War Horse. Boland.
Way-Out Morgan. Brooks.
Wedded Memories. Marston.

Rule (d) (r) (s)
Absalom and Achitophel.
  Dryden.
Against Them Who Lay
  Unchastity to the Sex of
  Women. Habington.
And Lo, the Star! Haley.
The Answer that Ye Made to
  Me, My Dear. Wyatt.
The Ballade of the
  Incompetent Ballade-
  Monger. Stephen.
The Burning of Jamestown.
  English.
Caelica, XLIV. Greville.
Come unto Me. Stuart.
Compassion So Divine.
  Steele.
Complaint of the Common
  Weill of Scotland.
  Lyndsay.
The Dead Make Rules.
  Davies.
Dialogue between a Squeamish
  Cotting Mechanic and his
  Sluttish Wife... Ward.
The Dove. Daley.
A Father's Testament. Ibn
  Tibbon.
The First Lord's Song.
  Gilbert.
Flux. Eberhart.
Generalization. Capp.
He Is Our Peace. Haley.
How to Keep Accounts.
  Anonymous.
The Humours of the King's
  Bench Prison, a Ballad.
  Howard.

An Hymeneal Song on the
  Nuptials of the Lady Anne
  Wentworth and... Carew.
Keep a Good Tongue in Your
  Head... Parker.
The Last Instructions to a
  Painter. Marvell.
The Lord of Heaven to Earth
  Came Down. Peck.
The Lost History Plays: King
  Canute (parody).
  Sharpless.
The Marchen. Jarrell.
Methods of Cooking Trout.
  Barker.
The Native Irishman.
  Anonymous.
The New Ancient of Days.
  Melville.
Now When So Much Has
  Passed. Seferis.
The Old Man Who Lived in a
  Wood. *Anonymous.*
Old Maps. Tietjens.
One Step at a Time.
  Anonymous.
Paradise Regained. Milton.
Peace Is the Tranquillity of
  Order. Wilberforce.
Plow. *Anonymous.*
Pray to What Earth Does
  This Sweet Cold Belong.
  Thoreau.
Prayer. *Anonymous.*
Presidents of the United
  States. *Anonymous.*
The Prophecy of Famine.
  Churchill.
Resignation. Longfellow.
Thoughts of Chairman Mao.
  Young.
What Has Happened.
  Angoff.

Rum
Away with Rum.
  Anonymous.
The Boston Burglar.
  Anonymous.
The Convicts' Rum Song.
  Anonymous.
Derelict. Allison.
The Drove-Road. Gibson.
Dupree (A vers.).
  Anonymous.
Eleazar Wheelock. Hovey.
Go-d'ling. *Anonymous.*
Oh, My Geraldine. Burnand.
The Old Keg of Rum.
  Anonymous.
Solioquy I. Aldington.
When Sir Beelzebub. Sitwell.

Rumor
Back Road Farm. Bruce.
The Ballad of Tonopah Bill.
  Anonymous.
The Road Back. Sexton.

Rump
On Having Piles, Scott.
On Hedylus. Martial
  (Marcus Valerius Martialis).

Rumpelstiltskin
Needles and Pins. Van
  Doren.

Rumple
Blow away the Morning Dew.
  Anonymous.
The Coy Lass Dress's Up in
  Her Best. *Anonymous.*
Moles. Stafford.
Out of the Sea, Early.
  Swenson.

There Was a Knight and He
  Was Young. *Anonymous.*
Run (ning) (s) (ran)
Acts Passed beyond the
  Boundary of Mere Wishing.
  Spender.
Alone in the House. Bogin.
Antelope. Smith.
Autobiography: Last Chapter.
  Barnes.
Awake, Arise, You Drowsy
  Sleeper. *Anonymous.*
Barn Fire. Lux.
The Battle of Plattsburg.
  Anonymous.
Before Action. Gellert.
Big Night Blues. Jefferson.
Blessing the Hounds.
  Winter.
The Boy and the Snake.
  Lamb.
Boy in the Roman Zoo.
  MacLeish.
The Broomfield Hill.
  Anonymous.
Caelica, XIII. Greville.
Camptown. Ciardi.
Cape Ann. *Anonymous.*
Cave Sedem! MacManus.
A Centipede Was Happy
  Quite. *Anonymous.*
Chance Meeting. Griffin.
The Contemplative Quarry.
  Wickham.
Country Dance. Sitwell.
A Day at the Races.
  Phillips.
"The Day is Done " (Parody
  on Longfellow). Cary.
Do What You Will. Hobson.
Double-Header. Stone.
Eclogues. Virgil (Publius
  Vergilius Maro).
Eleventh Song. Sidney.
Escape. Rubin.
The Evening Wind. Bryant.
The Examination of His
  Mistress' Perfections.
  Beaumont.
The Faun. Pound.
The Faun Sees Snow for the
  First Time. Aldington.
The Fence. McHugh.
Fight. *Anonymous.*
The Flower. Holmes.
Glimpse. Lomax.
The Gofongo. Milligan.
Golden Pheasant. Hart-
  Smith.
Grandser. Brown.
The Hind and the Panther.
  Dryden.
The History of
  Communications and a
  Running Account. Pien
  Chih-lin.
Housewife. Miles.
I'm Gonna Run to the City of
  Refuge. Johnson.
Indian Song: Survival. Silko.
John Henry (E. vers.).
  Anonymous.
Labor and Capital:
  Impression. Howells.
Leave Cancelled. Berkson.
Letter to Myself (parody).
  Reid.
The lion is a beast to fight.
  Quiller-Couch.
The Midnight Train (with
  music). *Anonymous.*

My Former Hopes Are Fled.
  Cowper.
Nature Note. Guiterman.
Nightmare. Field.
The Noonday April Sun.
  Love.
Now I Have Forgotten All.
  Vogel.
O. Wilbur.
O All You Little Blackey-
  Tops. *Anonymous.*
Old Farmer Giles.
  Anonymous.
On the Couch. Williams.
Partly to My Cat. Bass.
Percolating Highway.
  Castro.
Pet Panther. Ammons.
A Picture. Nemerov.
Pigeon. Loftin.
Pirate Wind. Carr.
Pretty Molly. *Anonymous.*
Professional Amnesia.
  Moure.
Redo, 1-5. Hejinian.
Remembrances. Clare.
Renouncement. Meynell.
The Rescue. Creeley.
The Return (excerpt).
  Woods.
Riddle: "Two bodies have I."
  Anonymous.
Rock Leader. Bathgate.
Romp. Etter.
Shango II. *Anonymous.*
Smoke. McGuckian.
The Snake. Suknaski.
The Song of Samuel Sweet.
  Causley.
The Song of the Ungirt
  Runners. Sorley.
Songs about Life and Brighter
  Things Yet. Hoffenstein.
Songs for Fragoletta. Le
  Gallienne.
Sonnet: Dolce Stil Novo.
  Ewart.
The Spooniad. Masters.
The Stream. Weeden.
Strip Mining Pit. Gillespie.
Taking Care of It. Lee.
Talking to Myself. McTell.
Three Presidents: Andrew
  Jackson. Bly.
Thyrsis and Milla, Arm in
  Arm Together.
  Anonymous.
To His Book. Herrick.
To His Coy Mistress.
  Marvell.
Touches. Stafford.
Trinity Sunday. Herbert.
Twilight Calm. Rossetti.
Two Sonnets from a Sequence.
  Holt.
The Unfinished Race.
  Cameron.
Venus, with Young Adonis.
  Griffin.
Voices at the Window.
  Sidney.
The Warden Said to Me the
  Other Day. Knight.
We'll All Feel Gay. Scott.
Well, Wanton Eye. Orleans.
A Winter Scene.
  Whittemore.
Winter Streams. Carman.
The Woman. Lima.
The Woyi. Blockcolski.
You Kicked and Stomped and
  Beat Me. *Anonymous.*

Rune (s)
The Collector. Behm.
Nodes. Henderson.
Sapientia Lunae. Dowson.

Rung (s)
The Crow Sat on the Willow.
Clare.
God's Promises. *Anonymous.*
My Wife's a Wanton Wee
Thing. *Anonymous.*
The Psychonaut Sonnets:
Jones. Goldbarth.

Runner (s)
Early Pregnancy. Shuttle.
Liverpool Girls. *Anonymous.*

Rural
Arcades: O'er the Smooth
Enamelled Green. Milton.
Binsey Poplars. Hopkins.
He May Be Envied, Who with
Tranquil Breast. Smith.
Lines Descriptive of
Thomson's Island. Lynde.

Rush (es)
An Ancient to Ancients.
Hardy.
Diretro al Sol. Bell.
In All These Acts. Everson.
In the Selkirks. Scott.
Nobody Riding the Roads
Today. Jordan.
Out of Question & Mind...
Mitchell.
Plucking the Rushes.
Anonymous.
The Rush of the Oregon.
Guiterman.
Sailing after Lunch. Stevens.
Son of the King of May.
Anonymous.
The Soul's Travelling
(excerpt). Browning.
The Spring. Voigt.
Three Poems. *Anonymous.*
Winter Has At Last Come.
Shigeyuki.

Russia (n)
Grandparents. Lowell.
A Happy New Year (excerpt).
Auden.
Limerick: "There was a young
lady of Russia." Lear.
Morning Poem. Beenen.

Rust (ing) (s)
The Black Knight.
Todhunter.
Blacksmith Pain. Bierbaum.
Childe Harold's Pilgrimage:
Canto III. Byron.
Dead in the Sierras. Miller.
Emily Dickinson. Longley.
Food Strike. Hogan.
Hunger. Rimbaud.
The News. Saxe.
Nurse No Long Grief.
Gilmore.
Romeo and Juliet.
Shakespeare.
The Sinking of the Graf Spee.
Anonymous.
Some Good Things to Be Said
for the Iron Age. Snyder.
The Tenancy. Gilmore.

Rustic (s)
Constancy to an Ideal Object.
Coleridge.
The Dismantled Ship.
Whitman.
His Statement of the Case.
Morse.
In That Dark Cave.
Silverstein.

Junkyards. Rayford.
Lady Sara Bunbury Sacrificing
to the Graces, by Reynolds.
Hine.
Wild Roses. Fawcett.

Rustle (d) (s)
The Empty Woman. Brooks.
The Evening Wind. Bryant.
The Flower. Warren.
Folk Song. *Anonymous.*
Glanmore Sonnets. Heaney.
In the Cool of the Evening.
Noyes.
.Juan Murray. *Anonymous.*
November Wears a Paisley
Shawl. Morris.
Souls. Wertheimer.
Ten Thousand Cattle.
Wister.
Tramp Miner's Song.
Anonymous.

Ruth
Bring Tem Not Back.
Kenyon.
Diana. Constable.
To Demeter. Fleming.
A True Confession.
Stallworthy.

Ruthless
Flood. Joyce.
Watergate. Herschberger.

S

Sabbath
All Last Night...
Abercrombie.
Cleansing. Waldeck.
Giles Corey of the Salem
Farms: Prologue.
Longfellow.
Hymn. Stowe.
In Saram. Cotton.
Macaffie's Confession.
Anonymous.
Monday's child is fair of face.
Mother Goose.
The Organist. Stevens.
Riddle: "Once hairy scenter
did transgress."
Anonymous.
A Sabbath of Rest. Luria.
Shattered Sabbath.
Goldstein.
Softly Fades the Twilight Ray.
Smith.
Song of the Sabbath.
Molodovsky.
To My Honour'd Kinsman,
John Driden... Dryden.
Welcome, Queen Sabbath.
Schneour.
With Due Deference to
Thomas Wolfe. Townsend.

Sable
Changeful Beauty. Lang.
Clouds. Reaney.
Negro Spiritual. Trott.
Poem for Mother's Day.
Fishback.
Shop and Freedom.
Anonymous.

Sack (ed) (s)
The Barn. Heaney.
Brooms. Simic.
The Editor's Tragedy.
Hankin.
The Geranium. Roethke.

How Our Forefather Got His
Wife. Walton.
On the Candidates for the
Laurel. Pope.
Raking Walnuts in the Rain.
Shannon.
The Sensualists. Roethke.
Southward Bound. Burt.
There Was a Maid Went to
the Mill. *Anonymous.*

Sackcloth
Incognita. Dobson.
Renunciants. Dowden.
Simchas Torah. Rosenfeld.

Sacrament (al) (s)
The Envy of Poor Lovers.
Clarke.
The Holy Eucharist.
Calderon de la Barca.
The House of Pride.
Dawson.
A Letter to William Carlos
Williams. Rexroth.
My Grandfather's Funeral.
Applewhite.
Peter Quince at the Clavier.
Stevens.
Shacked Up at the Ritz.
Fetherling.
Sunday in the Country.
Swenson.
The Temple of the Trees.
Pellow.
Three Phases of Africa.
Parkes.
The Zen of Housework.
Zolynas.

Sacramento
The Banks of Sacramento
(with music). *Anonymous.*
California (with music).
Anonymous.

Sacred
After Sunset. Allingham.
Amoretti, LXV. Spenser.
At Lanier's Grave. Tabb.
Carriers of the Dream Wheel.
Momaday.
Come, Says Jesus' Voice.
Barbauld.
A Curse on Uruk.
Enheduanna.
The Day Duke Raised; May
24th, 1974. Troupe.
The Dead in Europe.
Lowell.
The Djanggawul Cycle, 1.
Anonymous
The Djanggawul Cycle, 166.
Anonymous.
Ellsworth. *Anonymous.*
Epilogue to the Satires.
Pope.
Essay in Defense of the
Movies. Gibson.
A Fancy. Lodge.
The Flying Lesson. Petrarch.
The Glory of Toil. Proctor.
The Hind and the Panther.
Dryden.
In the Backs. Cornford.
Invocation. Eastman.
Llangollen Vale (excerpt).
Seward.
Look down Fair Moon.
Whitman.
The Midshipman. Falconer.
Morality. Garrigue.
Musica No. Duerden.
O How Sweet Are Thy
Words! Steele.
Peter. Marlatt.

The Promise in Disturbance.
Meredith.
Psalm XV. Sidney.
Rosa Nascosa. Hewlett.
Tarquin and Tullia.
Mainwaring.
Tell Me, O Love.
Hammond.
That Reminds Me. Nash.
To Africa. Kunene.
To His Dying Brother, Master
William Herrick. Herrick.
Towering O'er the Wrecks of
Time. Bowring.
Whence Had They Come?
Yeats.
The White Isle of Leuce.
Read.

Sacrifice (d)
The Aeneid. Virgil (Publius
Vergilius Maro).
Call to Conflict. *Anonymous.*
A Christmas Carol. Thomas.
Dundonnel Mountains.
Young.
Epitaph on Pegasus, a
Limping Gay. Beccadelli.
The Exequies. Stanley.
Friendship's Mystery.
Philips.
How Shall I Build. Blunt.
Hunger. *Anonymous.*
Hymn for the Slain in Battle.
Braithwaite.
Hymn: "O Thou who camest
from above." Wesley.
In the Holy Nativity of Our
Lord God. Crashaw.
Isaac. Burnshaw.
Ivanhoe. Chapt. 39: Rebecca's
Hymn. Scott.
Like a Beach. Shapiro.
Lincoln. Riley.
Living Bread. Sefton.
The Masque of the Inner-
Temple and Gray's Inne.
Beaumont.
Mi Y'Malel. *Anonymous.*
Old Man Hall. Jacobs.
Pentucket. Whittier.
Preludes. Patmore.
Sign for My Father, Who
Stressed the Bunt.
Bottoms.
Sleep and Poetry. Keats.
Song: "O faire sweet face, O
eyes celestiall bright."
Beaumont.
Sonnet: "Tell me no more
how fair she is." King.
The Sugaring. Klein.
Tales of the Islands, V.
Walcott.
Upon Ford's Two Tragedies...
Crashaw.
The Vine to the Goat.
Euenos.
The Way of the Cross.
Clarke.
When Israel. Scott.
Wisdom. Sobiloff.
Wisdom Is the Finest Beauty
of a Person. *Anonymous.*
Women Pleased. Fletcher.
Written in Juice of Lemmon.
Cowley.

Sad (den) (der) (dest)
An African Elegy. Duncan.
Against Botticelli. Hass.
Anchises. Salkeld.
At the Grave of Walker.
Miller.

Ballad of the Golden Bowl. Hay.
Barney Bodkin. *Anonymous.*
Being Sad. Kanik.
A Black Soldier Remembers. Coalman.
Childhood. Tabb.
Cleaning Up, Clearing Out. Bronson.
The Clerks. Robinson.
Composed in Spring. Burns.
The Dead Man Dragged from the Sea. Gardner.
The Deserted Home. Meyer.
Don Juan. Byron.
The Earth, Late Choked with Showers. Lodge.
An Easter Song. "Coolidge.
Ebbe Skammelson. *Anonymous.*
Evening Music. Smithyman.
Fannie. Aldrich.
Father to the Man. Knight.
The Flying Cloud (I). *Anonymous.*
From a Lament for Una. Costello.
The Garden. Shirley.
Getting Serious. Soto.
Grab-Bag. Jackson.
Gubbinal. Stevens.
He Will Give Them Back. Klingle.
Henry Martyn. *Anonymous.*
Home-Thoughts from France. Rosenberg.
Impenitentia Ultima. Dowson.
In Memorial. Coogler.
In the Old City. Fichman.
Inebriates. Brasfield.
Inertia. Finch.
Inviting a Friend to Supper. Jonson.
Ireland, Ireland. Newbolt.
Judaeus Errans. Golding.
Lament for Ignacio Sanchez Mejias. Garcia Lorca.
Lancelot and Guinevere. Gould.
The Lay of the Last Minstrel. Scott.
Limerick: "A lady track star from Toccoa." Blount Roy.
Loss. Madge.
The Magic Mirror. Alden.
A Maori Girl's Song. Domett.
The Mask. Browning.
The Mu'allaqat: Pour Us Wine. Ibn Kolthum.
My Camping Ground. Rosenfeld.
Nobody Lives on Arthur Godfrey Boulevard. Costanzo.
Nocturne–III. Silva.
Notes for a Speech. Jones.
O I Won't Lead a Homely Life. Hardy.
The Objects of the Summer Scene. Irwin.
The Odyssey. Homer.
Oh, Who Regards. *Anonymous.*
Once. Ives.
Patty-Poem. Kenny.
Poem against the Rich. Bly.
Rains on the Island. Preil.
Realization. Fisher.
Relocation. Mura.

Remember. Rossetti.
Remember (parody). *Anonymous.*
Rhyming a Friend's Poem. Yu Hsuan-chi.
The Seasons. Kalidasa.
Seaward. Thaxter.
Sion. Herbert.
Sir Walter Scott at the Tomb of the Stuarts in St. Peter's. Milnes.
Song: "Music, thou queen of souls, get up and string." Randolph.
Song of Expectancy. Hitchcock.
The Song of Roland, CL. *Anonymous.*
Sonnets. Woodberry.
Spring Song. Conkling.
They Are All Gone into the World of Light. Vaughan.
Time's Balm. Shaw.
Tired Tim. De la Mare.
The Titanic. *Anonymous.*
Tristan and Isolda. Levy.
Two in August. Ransom.
Under the Wood. *Anonymous.*
The Voiceless. Holmes.
Waiting for the Rain. Mnthali.
Water Without Sound. Tussman.
What Is the Opposite of a Prince? Wilbur.
When the Dawn Comes. *Anonymous.*
While Stars of Christmas Shine. Poulsson.
Wind and Rain. *Anonymous.*
The Windmill. Johnson.
Winter and Red Berries. Moore.
The Wisdom of Folly. Fowler.
With every note. *Anonymous.*
Your Catullus Is Depressed. Catullus.
Saddle (d) (s)
Bonnie George Campbell. *Anonymous.*
Braggin' Bill's Fortytude. Hallock.
The Cowboy's Life. *Anonymous.*
A Dream of Burial. Wright.
The Dying Ranger. *Anonymous.*
Empty Saddles. *Anonymous.*
Evening Ride. Hoffman.
The Newmarket Song. D'Urfey.
Ol' Dynamite. Le Noir.
The Rancher. Wilson.
The Skew-Ball Black. *Anonymous.*
Some Day. Silverstein.
The Stallion. Merrill, Jr.
The Superfluous Saddle. La Fontaine.
A Trot, and a Canter, a Gallop, and Over. *Anonymous.*
Sadness
Album. Miles.
Autumn. Akhmadulina.
Awake. Coleridge.
The Borough. Crabbe.
Driving through Belgium. Brownstein.

The Evening of the Feast-Day. Leopardi.
First Song. Kinnell.
From Here to There. Korn.
In All the Argosy of Your Bright Hair. Thompson.
Jesus, in Sickness and in Pain. Gallaudet.
Lonely Road. Abrahams.
My Sadness Sits Around Me. Jordan.
On the Picture of the Three Fates in the Palazzo Pitti, at Florence. Hallam.
Sing On, Blithe Bird! Motherwell.
Sonnets, II: "The rainbow o'er the sea of afternoon." Irwin.
The Tree of Diana. Pizarnik.
Safe (ly) (r) (est) (ty)
The Acquiescence of Pure Love. Cowper.
After the Night Hunt. Dickey.
All That You Have Given Me, Africa. Kanie.
And When the Prince Came. Hillyer.
Burn Down the Icons. Schulman.
The Children. Heyen.
Christmas Night. Sail.
Civil Defense. Burke.
The Cloud of Carmel. Powers.
The Death of a Negro Poet. Rivers.
A Desolate Shore. Henley.
Discovery of the New World. Revard.
The Doubter's Prayer. Bronte.
An Epigram to the Queen, Then Lying In. Jonson.
Epitaph. *Anonymous.*
A Fable for Critics. Lowell.
The Garden of Proserpine. Swinburne.
God Bless You. *Anonymous.*
The Great River. Van Dyke.
Hail and Farewell. Spicer.
The Hailstorm in June 1831. Clare.
Hats. Dillard.
Here's to the Ranger! *Anonymous.*
The Hills of Tsa la gi. Conley.
Hobbes, 1651. Hollander.
I Place Myself. *Anonymous.*
Keep Thou My Way, O Lord. Crosby.
Love Song. *Anonymous.*
Monologue through Bars. Hubbell.
Night Out. Simpson.
The Old Ladies. Ellis.
On Looking up by Chance at the Constellations. Frost.
The Painters. Hemschemeyer.
Peace on Earth. Williams.
Playwright. Woods.
A Prayer. Le Gallienne.
Psalm IV. Sidney.
The Rabbit. Durston.
Sacrifice. Emerson.
Safe for Democracy. Strong.
Simple Faith. Cowper.
Song: "Can love be controll'd by advice?" Gay.

Table Graces, or Prayers for Children. *Anonymous.*
The Teasers. Empson.
There is a pain–so utter. Dickinson.
This Book Is Mine. *Anonymous.*
Three Children. *Anonymous.*
To a Shade. Yeats.
To Sir Toby. Freneau.
To the Evening Star: Central Minnesota. Wright.
To William Earle of Pembroke. Jonson.
Tom's Angel. De La Mare.
The Unconcerned. Flatman.
The Valiant Sailor. *Anonymous.*
The Wall. Merriam.
When All Thy Mercies. Addison.
A Willing Suspension. Holmes.
Saga
The Building of the Long Serpent. Longfellow.
The Great Hunger. Kavanagh.
Sage (s)
An Adage. Byron.
Being to Timelessness as It's to Time. Cummings.
The Book Our Mothers Read. Whittier.
Civilization. Yuan Chen.
Half Hours with the Classics. DeBurgh.
Homage to Edward Hopper. George.
House in Springfield. Burket.
Kinfauns Castle (excerpt). Montgomerie.
Thanksgiving for the Body. Traherne.
To a Goose. Southey.
Tumbleweed. Wagoner.
Why I Voted the Socialist Ticket. Lindsay.
Sahara
Country Roads. Jacobsen.
Noon Glare. Brennan.
Sail (ed) (ing) (s)
Al Capone in Alaska. Reed.
Anti-Nostalgia. Grynberg.
Arcady Revisited. Funge.
As Ocean's Stream. Tyutchev.
At Best. O'Reilly.
At the Discharge of Cannon Rise the Drowned. Witheford.
Battery Park, High Noon. Belitt.
Beachhead Preachment. Zu-Bolton.
Beg-Innish. Synge.
Ben Alder 1963-1977. Hannigan.
Betty and Dupree. *Anonymous.*
Blood on the Sails. Colclough.
Caelica, XCVI. Greville.
A Call on Sir Walter Raleigh. Piatt.
A Coconut for Katerina. McPherson.
Columbus. Miller.
Commentaries on the Song of Songs. Herzberg.
Contentment. Cotton.
Cordial Advice. *Anonymous.*

The County of Mayo. *Anonymous.*
The County of Mayo. Fox.
Crazed. De la Mare.
The Cruise of the Mystery. Thaxter.
Essex Regiment March. Woodberry.
Experience. Hofmannsthal.
The Fairies in New Ross. *Anonymous.*
The Falcon. Blunt.
The False Lover. *Anonymous.*
Fiddler's Green. Roberts.
Foggy Mountain Top. *Anonymous.*
For John Clare. Ashbery.
A Grain of Salt. Irwin.
He Commandeth a Fair Wind. Book of the Dead.
Heroism. Emerson.
Hidden Valley. Burrows.
The Hope of the World. Watson.
Human Frailty. Cowper.
The Island of the Blest. West.
Jack Is Every Inch a Sailor. *Anonymous.*
Jottings of New York. McGonagall.
Kindness. Moore.
Kites. Brownstein.
The Lame Soldier. *Anonymous.*
The Last Voyage. Hinkson.
The Leaving of Liverpool. *Anonymous.*
Leda, the Lost. Walton.
Lord Arnaldos. Flecker.
A Myth. Kingsley.
A Note on Wyatt. Amis.
November Day at McClure's. Bly.
O Gentle Ships. Meleager.
Odysseus. Merwin.
The Old Gospel Ship. *Anonymous.*
Old Hundred. Van Doren.
Old Ships. Morton.
Our Lady of Good Voyage. Adee.
Panegyrick upon O. Cromwell. Waller.
Passage to India. Whitman.
Poem on His Birthday. Thomas.
The Poet at Seven. Rimbaud.
The Poet on the Island. Murphy.
Poets Seven Years Old. Rimbaud.
Private Rooms. O Hehir.
Put Off Thy Bark from Shore, Though Near the Night. Tuckerman.
The Raven. Rich.
Resurrection. Blackmur.
Rooftop. Barnstone.
The Sailor. MacDonald.
A Sailor's Song. Harri.
A Sea-Song from the Shore. Riley.
A Seaman's Confession of Faith. Kemp.
Sheep. Davies.
The Ship A-Raging. *Anonymous.*
A Ship, an Isle, a Sickle Moon. Flecker.

The Ship That Sails. *Anonymous.*
The Shoals of Herring. *Anonymous.*
Sir Patrick Spens. *Anonymous.*
The Spark. Plunkett.
Strike the Bell. Anonymous.
The Swan. Gosse.
Thaw in the City. Lipsitz.
Theocritus. Fields.
There Was a Little Ship. *Anonymous.*
To Manon, Comparing Her to a Falcon. Blunt.
The Tree-Top Road. Smith.
The Unfortunate Miller. Coppard.
The Unquiet Grave. *Anonymous.*
A Vision. Hofmannsthal.
The Voyage of Jimmy Poo. Emanuel.
What the Old Man Said. Smith.
When You and I Must Part. *Anonymous.*
Wild Eden. Woodberry.
Yachting in Arkansas. Weeden.
Yachts on the Nile. Spencer.
Sailor (s)
A British Man-of-War. *Anonymous.*
Columbus. Jackson.
The Dom Pedro. *Anonymous.*
Hand-Clapping Rhyme. *Anonymous.*
Jack the Guinea Pig. *Anonymous.*
Jack the Jolly Tar. *Anonymous.*
Jackie Tar. *Anonymous.*
The Jolly Young Sailor and the Beautiful Queen. *Anonymous.*
The Last Chantey. Kipling.
Leaving Inishmore. Longley.
My Sailor of Seven. Brenan.
Off to Sea Once More. *Anonymous.*
One Year After. Kizer.
Ramon. Lacey.
Sailor. Farjeon.
The Sailor Boy. *Anonymous.*
The Sailor's Consolation. Dibdin.
Sailor's Consolation. Pitt.
The Sailor's Grave. *Anonymous.*
Sailor's Woman. Cornell.
Sailor, What of the Isles? Sitwell.
The Sea. *Anonymous.*
Sea Turtle. Pope.
Sea-Wind. Mallarme.
The Shepherdess and the Sailor. *Anonymous.*
The Ship Rambolee. *Anonymous.*
Snowfall in the Afternoon. Bly.
Soldier an' Sailor Too. Kipling.
The Stillness of the Poem. Loewinsohn.
Traveller's Hope. Granville.
Weather Wisdom. *Anonymous.*
William Glen. *Anonymous.*

The Yarn of the Loch Achray. Masefield.
Ye Parliament of England. *Anonymous.*
Saint (s)
Alcestis on the Poetry Circuit. Jong.
The Blind Man's Regret. *Anonymous.*
Bride Song. Rossetti.
A Brief Elegie on My Dear Son John the Second of That Name of Mine. Saffin.
Caelica, X. Greville.
Caelica, LII. Greville.
Christmas Island. Bates.
Civilization. Yuan Chen.
Dover to Munich. Calverley.
The Figure-Head. Garstin.
Franciscan Aspiration. Lindsay.
Hagiograph. Heppenstall.
Her Courtesy. Yeats.
House in Springfield. Burket.
The House of a Hundred Lights. Torrence.
Hymn of the Waldenses. Bryant.
In the Beginning Was a Word. Graves.
Iona. Tennyson.
Keeping Victory. Isenhour.
The Knight's Tomb. Coleridge.
Lincoln. Trowbridge.
Loves End. Herbert of Cherbury.
The Maid of Honour. Massinger.
A Masque of Reason: God's Thanks to Job. Frost.
Moon Landing. Auden.
The Muted Screen of Graham Greene. McGinley.
O Holy, Holy, Holy Lord. Eastburn.
Old Man in the Park. Osborn.
On the Death of a Journalist. Campbell.
The Only Bar in Dixon. Welch.
Parliament of Cats. Enright.
Post-Meridian. Garrison.
Rejoicing in Hope. Toplady.
Riding Together. Morris.
The Road to Hate. Kavanagh.
Rosalind's Scroll. Browning.
Silex Scintillans. Vaughan.
The Sinner-Saint. Blunt.
The Song of Mary the Mother of Christ. Walpole.
Song: "This is the song." Justema.
The Spell. Herrick.
This Flock So Small. Nitschmann.
To a Nun. Ormond.
To Theodora. *Anonymous.*
Troilus and Criseyde. Chaucer.
True and Joyful News. *Anonymous.*
The Tyrant Apple Is Eaten. MacCaig.
Upon Faireford Windowes. Corbett.
A Valentine to My Mother. Rossetti.
Virgidemiarum. Hall.

The Vision of Piers Plowman. Langland.
Waiting for Breakfast, While She Brushed Her Hair. Larkin.
The Way-Side Well. Cotter.
The West Palm Beach Storm. *Anonymous.*
When the Saints Come Marching In. Redding.
Why Do We Mourn Departing Friends? Watts.
Salad (s)
Lusty Juventus. Madge.
Tombstone Epitaphs. *Anonymous.*
The Universal Favorite. Wells.
Salary
On the Candidates for the Laurel. Pope.
You're in the Army Now. *Anonymous.*
Sale (s)
Absolute and Abitofhell. Knox.
For Sale. Silverstein.
Last of the Poet's Car. Connor.
Queen Mab. Shelley.
Stupidity Street. Hodgson.
Salesman
Everything We Do. Meinke.
Rap Sheet. Shiplett.
Sally
Blooming Sally. *Anonymous.*
The Dolls' Wash. Ewing.
A Rich Irish Lady (Sally). *Anonymous.*
The Rich Lady from Dublin. *Anonymous.*
Walk, Jaw-Bone. Steele.
Salmon
Around the Fish: After Paul Klee. Moss.
Goldfish. Monro.
Sunset. Montague.
Salt
Attack of the Squash People. Piercy.
Before. Goldbarth.
Being Born Is Important. Sandburg.
Calypso. Kell.
The Candle Indoors. Hopkins.
The Caulker. Lewis.
The Child Reads an Almanac. Jammes.
Dialogue. Nemerov.
Dinosaur Spring. Waniek.
Discretions of Alcibiades. Pinsky.
Dreams of the Sea. Davies.
Elegy on My Father. Curnow.
Estuary. Walker.
The Exorcism. Roethke.
The Fishvendor. Meredith.
Here She Stands. Rabearivelo.
Hills of Salt. Ravikovich.
His Wife. Kaufman.
January. Dutton.
Kyran's Christening. Nowlan.
Leonardo's Secret. Bly.
The Lost Ingredient. Sexton.
Love Poem. Craig.
Maritimes. Shuttle.
May He Lose His Way on the Cold Sea. Archilochus.

A Memory of the Players in a
Mirror at Midnight.
Joyce.
Moon Man.   Valentine.
Nightingales Are Not Singing.
Dor.
The Old Swimmer.   Morley.
One Year After.   Kizer.
Places and Ways to Live.
Hugo.
Prayer for a Second Flood.
MacDiarmid.
Regret.   *Anonymous.*
Returning Home.   Du Bellay.
The Salt Garden.   Nemerov.
Salt of the Earth.   Lawrence.
The Sea Birds.   Brock.
Sheep Dipping.   MacCaig.
Silver.   Ammons.
Sir Andrew Barton (Andrew
Batann).   *Anonymous.*
Slick.   Hoffman.
Sometimes I Walk where the
Deep Water Dips.
Tuckerman.
Sonnets.   Tuckerman.
Stars, I Have Seen Them Fall.
Housman.
Stony Brook Tavern.   Reed.
Sunny.   Vander Molen.
Testament.   Holmes.
A Tropical Morning at Sea.
Sill.
Wash Well the Fresh Fish.
Anonymous.

Salutation (s)
A Chant out of Doors.
Wilkinson.
The Lady of Life.   Kettle.
Shadow to Shadow.   Allen.
Shunting.   Dowling.
The Skein.   Kizer.

Salute
The Ballad of Private Chadd.
Milne.
In Memory of George
Whitby, Architect.
Betjeman.
Iron Landscapes (and the
Statue of Liberty).   Gunn.
Overripe Fruit.   Kasmuneh.
Peekaboo, I Almost See You.
Nash.
To a Common Prostitute.
Whitman.
Variations Done for Gerald
Van de Wiele.   Olson.

Salvage
History.   Lowell.
In These Dissenting Times.
Walker.

Salvation
Balance.   Schultz.
Bishop Butler of Kilcash.
Anonymous.
Blues for Sister Sally.
Kandel.
Eyewash.   Montgomery.
Fulfillment.   Muhlenberg.
God and the Holy Ghost.
Lawrence.
How Fevered Is the Man.
Keats.
Hymn: "Sing, my tongue, the
Saviour's glory."   Thomas
Aquinas.
I to the Lord from My
Distress.   *Anonymous.*
Lines: I Praise God's
Mankind in an Old Woman.
Watson.

Man, Not His Arms.
Rodman.
Marmion.   Scott.
The May Magnificat.
Hopkins.
My Blackness Is the Beauty of
This Land.   Jeffers.
Our Rock.   Key.
A Panegyric upon Oates.
Duke.
Prayer Moves the Hand That
Moves the World.
Wallace.
Psalm XXXVIII.   Sidney.
Rejoice and Be Merry.
Anonymous.
Risen with Healing in His
Wings.   John of Damascus.
Saying Goodbye.   Juhasz.
The Shortness and Misery of
Life.   Watts.
A Song for Simeon.   Eliot.
Sonnets: A Sequence on
Profane Love.   Boker.
St. Patrick's Hymn before
Tara.   Mangan.
The Sun and Moon So High
and Bright.   *Anonymous.*
To Our Lord in the
Sacrament.   Anselm.
Wake Up, Dear Boy That
Holds the Flute!   Mira Bai
[(or Mirabai)].
The Wanderer.   *Anonymous.*

Salvation Army
Away with Rum.
Anonymous.
Hope Is a Tattered Flag.
Sandburg.

Sam
The Cabin Creek Flood.
Anonymous.
The Cremation of Sam
McGee.   Service.
English Liberal.   Taylor.

Same
Against the Fear of Death.
Lucretius (Titus Lucretius
Carus).
Ah (You Say), This Is Holy
Wisdom.   Doolittle.
Ain't Nature Commonplace!
Guiterman.
All Ruin Is the Same.
Litvinoff.
And Fall Shall Sit in
Judgment.   Lorde.
Another and the Same.
Rogers.
Apology.   Williams.
Archy Confesses.   Marquis.
Art Thou the Same.   Tatnall.
As I Was Laying on the
Green.   *Anonymous.*
At Casterbridge Fair.
Hardy.
Ballade of the Grindstones.
Sherwin.
A Bestiary of the Garden for
Children Who Should
Know Better.   Gotlieb.
But Still in Israel's Paths
They Shine.   Revard.
Captain Arthur Phillip and
the Birds.   Banning.
Come Back.   Merwin.
The Complaint of Henrie
Duke of Buckinghame.
Sackville.
Desert.   Gergely.
Duel in the Park.   Grenelle.
An Essay on Man.   Pope.

Evening.   Simic.
Growing Old.   *Anonymous.*
In the Marble Quarry.
Dickey.
Inconstancy's the Greatest of
Sins.   Herbert of Cherbury.
A Love Poem.   Ashbery.
Mutual Problem.   Cole.
One More Time.   Shelton.
The Other Side.   Reiter.
Plain Language from Truthful
James.   Harte.
Rabbi Ben Ezra.   Browning.
Russian New Year.   Berkson.
Schoolgirl on Speech-Day in
the Open Air.   Smith.
Sorrow.   Daniel.
Stumbling.   Lourie.
This May Be Your Captain
Speaking.   Stead.
To Mr. Bays.   Sackville.
Today: The Idea Market.
Nicholas.
The Tower.   Booth.
A Weekday.   Eigner.
When You're Away.
Hoffenstein.

Samela
Doron's Description of
Samela.   Greene.
Menaphon.   Greene.
Samela.   Greene.

Sanctify
The Altar.   Herbert.
For the Peace of Jerusalem.
Wesley.
Slain Lamb of God.
Zinzendorf.

Sanctity
The Life of San Millan
(excerpt).   Berceo.
The Robin Is the One.
Dickinson.

Sanctuary
Moon-Man.   Hewett.
Zillebeke Brook.   Blunden.

Sand piper
Madaket Beach.   Barr.
Surrealism in the Middle
Ages.   Lamantia.

Sand (s)
The African Desert (excerpt).
Tupper.
America.   McKay.
Assignation with a
Somnambulist.   Manifold.
At Staufen.   Hamburger.
The Ballad of Dead Men's
Bay.   Swinburne.
Ballad of No Proper Man.
Hoffman.
The Ballad of the Boat.
Garnett.
Ballad of the Spanish Civil
Guard.   Garcia Lorca.
Camel.   Miller.
The Children Band.   De
Vere.
Collaboration.   Towle.
A Concert Party.   Sassoon.
Cook County.   MacLeish.
Cycle.   Jennett.
Danger.   Paine.
Dead Embryos.   Toth.
Don't You Hurry Worry with
Me.   *Anonymous.*
The Easter Song.   Sedulius.
El Alamein Revisited.
MacNab.
Epilogue of the Wandering
Jew.   Newbury.
Eternal Masculine.   Benet.

Evening.   Kuka.
Farewell.   Wilson.
The Flight into Egypt.
Quennell.
Franklin Hyde.   Belloc.
Gebir.   Landor.
Hagar and Ishmael.   Lasker-
Schüler.
Here We Come A-Piping.
Anonymous.
In a City Square.   Wallis.
The Inflammable Woman.
Baxter.
The Katzenjammer Kids.
Reaney.
The Lamp Now Flickers.
Grunewald.
The Last Tournament.
Tennyson.
Lawrence: The Last Crusade
(excerpt).   Rodman.
Mexican Quarter.   Fletcher.
Moenkopi.   Sze.
Morning Song.   Blakely.
My heart I gave thee...
Wyatt.
A Nobleman's House
(excerpt).   Sarton.
Oh Beach Love Blossom.
Crews.
Omnia Vanitas.   Buchanan.
On Waking from a Dreamless
Sleep.   Fields.
Only One King.   Moreland.
The Other Journey.   Chapin.
Ozymandias.   Shelley.
A Paris Nocturne.   Sharp.
Pelters of Pyramids.   Horne.
The Powte's Complaint.
Anonymous.
Rock (excerpt).   Raine.
The Sands of Dee.   Kingsley.
Sappho.   Carman.
'Scaped.   Crane.
Sea Dirge.   Scott.
Second Fig.   Millay.
The Shack.   Miller.
The Ship of Rio.   De La
Mare.
Siberia.   Mangan.
Skipping along Alone.
Welles.
Softly the Evening (parody).
Mallock.
Some San Francisco Poems.
Oppen.
Sonnets, VIII: "The apples
ripen under yellowing
leaves.   Irwin.
The Stars.   "Ping Hsin"
(Hsieh Wang-ying).
Sunny.   Vander Molen.
Tears of the World.
Mu'tamid.
There Is a Dream Dreaming
Us.   Dubie.
To Woman.   Byron.
A Traveller.   Rowland.
Twilight Calm.   Rossetti.
Two Songs on the Economy
of Abundance.   Agee.
United States.   Keble.
Voice from Danang.
Redshaw.
Water.   Jabes.
We Play at Paste.
Dickinson.
What's the Railroad.
Thoreau.
White Sand and Grey Sand.
Anonymous.
Yves Tanguy.   Gascoyne.

Sandal (s)
The Avengers. Markham.
Early Waking. Adams.
Euclid Alone Has Looked on
Beauty Bare. Millay.
Felix Randal. Hopkins.
Free Enterprise. Stetler.
Nuit Blanche: North End.
Aiken.
Songs of Kabir. Kabir.
To Potapovitch. Crane.

Sane
Fall Letter. Kelly.
Getting Experience.
Williams.
Ross's Poems. Lehmann.
Talking to Her. O'Sullivan.

Santa Claus
For Allan. Frost.
For the Children or the
Grown-Ups? Anonymous.
A Real Santa Claus.
Sherman.
The Skeptic. Service.
When Santa Claus Comes.
Anonymous.

Santa Fe
Oh But It Was Good...
Littlebird.

Santiago
Dogs of Santiago.
McCarthy.
Song of Black Cubans.
Garcia Lorca.

Sap
At Candlemas. Causley.
Bark. Welch.
The Danger of Writing
Defiant Verse. Parker.
The Glacier. MacNeice.
I Was Made Erect and Lone.
Thoreau.
Morning Dialogue. Aiken.
Nevertheless. Moore.
The Secular. Wallace-
Crabbe.
Spring Song. Carman.
Sugar Weather. McArthur.

Saraband (s)
To Lucasta. Lovelace.
Vacation Exercise. Joseph.
The Witch's Ballad. Scott.

Sarcophagi
Among the Anthropophagi.
Nash.
Funebrial Reflections. Nash.

Sark
A Border Forecast. Landles.
Insularum Ocelle.
Swinburne.
The Patriarch. Burns.

Sassafras
In the Corn Land. Howard.
Witchwood. Justus.

Satan
The Extravagant Drunkard's
Wish. Ward.
The Hare. De la Mare.
Jerusalem. Blake.
Modern Love, XXVIII.
Meredith.
Paradise Lost. Milton.
Within These Doors
Assembled Now. Holden.

Satchels
The Blackbird of Derrycairn.
Anonymous.
A Description of the Morning.
Swift.

Satin
The Cruel Mother (C vers.).
Anonymous.

Escapist's Song. Spencer.
The Queens. Fitzgerald.
They Have Turned the
Church Where I Ate God.
Gildner.

Satire
The Contemporary Muse.
Rickword.
Horace I. Field.
On Tobacco. Cotton.
Six Poets in Search of a
Lawyer. Hall.

Satisfaction (s)
Citizen. Schjeldahl.
Dust. Spivack.
The House of Madam Juju.
Mieko.

Satisfy (ied)
Aesop's Fable of the Frogs.
La Fontaine.
Dr. Donne. Alling.
Friendship. Wilcox.
God's Presence Makes My
Heaven. Smith.
Got the Blues, Can't Be
Satisfied. Hurt.
If Only the Dreams Abide.
Scollard.
The Limits of Submission.
Nuur.
A Local Man Remembers
Betty Fuller. Whitehead.
Losses. Jarrell.
Of the Terrible Doubt of
Appearances. Whitman.
Pesci Misti. Aaronson.
Spiral Landscape.
Brownstein.
Star of the Western Skies.
Anonymous.
An Undefined Tenderness.
Oppenheimer.

Saturday (s)
Death Comes to the Salesman.
Brodsky.
Everybody Loves Saturday
Night. Anonymous.
From a Full Heart. Milne.
Here We Go Looby Loo.
Anonymous.
Linstead Market.
Anonymous.
Marry Monday, Marry for
Wealth. Anonymous.
Minotaur Poems. Mandel.
Open the Door. Grider.
Poems about Playmates.
Davis.
Sally Go Round the Sun.
Anonymous.
Sunflowers and Saturdays.
Boyd.
They That Wash on Monday.
Anonymous.
West Helena Blues. Sykes.

Saturn
Caelica, XLIV. Greville.
Hyperion. Keats.

Satyr (s)
The Golden Age: Hymn to
Diana. Heywood.
Idylls. Theocritus.
News for the Delphic Oracle.
Yeats.
Nymphs and Satyrs. Ewart.
Small Park in East Germany:
1969. Mayer.
Vacation Exercise. Joseph.

Sauce
As You Like It.
Shakespeare.
Owen Seaman. Untermeyer.

A Wish. Synge.
Saucepan
After the Gentle Poet
Kobayashi Issa. Hass.

Saucer
Four Stories. Shapiro.
I Peeped through the
Window. Anonymous.

Saul
Dead Fly. Chuilleanain.
The Feast of Stephen.
Nichols.
King Saul. Horvitz.
Ressaif My Saul. Saunders.
Saul. Browning.
To a Flea in a Glass of
Water. Greig.

Saunter (ing)
Emerson. Dodge.
September Evening, 1938.
Plomer.
That Strain Again.
Hambleton.

Savage (s)
Assynt. Gilchrist.
The Boy; or, Son of Rip-Off
(parody). Glass.
Brebeuf and His Brethren.
Scott.
The Farmer's Boy.
Bloomfield.
Here's to the Ranger!
Anonymous.
Limerick: "There was a fair
maid from Decatur."
Anonymous.
The Pioneer Mother. Fuller.
Song of the Dark Ages.
Young.
A Suggestion Made by the
Posters of the "Globe."
Thorold Rogers.
The Warrior Maid. Branch.
When the Five Prominent
Poets. Jacobsen.

Save (d) (s)
The Anchorsmiths. Dibdin.
Andromeda. Browning.
The Ant. Lovelace.
Any Wife to Any Husband.
Browning.
The Armada, 1588. Wilson.
As I Gird on for Fighting.
Housman.
At First. Sisson.
Ballade of Expansion.
Johnson.
The Canterbury Tales: The
Knight's Tale. Chaucer.
Charlton Heston. Fried.
Cities and Seas. Jordan.
Come, Every Soul. Stockton.
Comrades. McGlennon.
The Dead Tribune.
McCarthy.
Desire. Arnold.
Distraction. Vaughan.
Diversity. Thompson.
Eager Spring. Bottomley.
Easter Hymn. Housman.
Emergency. Conant.
Epigram: "Cibber! write all
thy verses upon glasses."
Pope.
Epitaph on an Army of
Mercenaries. Housman.
Epitaphs of the War, 1914-18.
Kipling.
The Flood. Lipska.
For James Baldwin. Boyle.
The Glorious Name. Wells.

Horologium: The Mother of
God. Anonymous.
Hymn. Crane.
I Want God's Heab'n to Be
Mine. Anonymous.
The Idea of Detroit.
Gustafson.
Inside and Out. Phillips.
"It Out-Herods Herod, Pray
You Avoid It." Hecht.
Khristna and His Flute.
Hope.
Liberty for All. Garrison.
The Light Now Shineth.
Anonymous
The Loss of the Birkenhead.
Doyle.
Love's Assize. Cavalcanti.
The Maid Freed from the
Gallows. Anonymous.
The Man Freed from the
Gallows. Anonymous.
Massachusetts Song of
Liberty. Warren.
May 30, 1893. Bangs.
The Mood. Prettyman.
Nothing Better. Anonymous.
Ode on Lord Macartney's
Embassy to China.
Shepherd.
The Odyssey. Homer.
The Old Sailor. Milne.
On a Beautiful Youth Struck
Blind with Lightning.
Goldsmith.
On Sympathisers with the
American Revolution.
Wesley.
On the Candidates for the
Laurel. Pope.
Opportunity. Sill.
Our Left. Tichnor.
Our National Banner. Smith.
Pacelli and the Ethiop.
Cassity.
The Painter in the Lion Cage.
Alver.
Paracelsus. Browning.
The Passion of Our Lady.
Peguy.
Peace with Honor.
Appleman.
Penny and Penny.
Anonymous.
Physical for My Son. Smith.
Poem for Friends. Troupe.
Qui Perdiderit Animam Suam.
Crashaw.
Rain to the Tribe. Al-
Khansa.
Rescue. Stuart.
Richard Pigott, the Forger
(excerpt). McGonagall.
The Rising Village.
Goldsmith.
Saved. Horta.
Seamas, Light-Hearted and
Loving Friend of My Breast
(excerpt). O Suilleabhain.
A Slant of Sun on Dull
Brown Walls. Crane.
Snatches: "The formest of
these bestes three."
Anonymous.
Someone, I tell you. Sappho.
Song: "Come, rest in this
bosom, my own stricken
deer." Moore.
Soon One Mornin' Death
Come Creepin'.
Anonymous.
The Suez Crisis. Anonymous.

Sweet Diane. Barlow.
Thou Alone Canst Save. Wakeford.
To the Christ. Tabb.
Vers de Societe (parody). Traill.
Views from the High Camp. Merwin.
Wake, child. Mira Bai [(or Mirabai[).
Wellington Letter: XI. Edmond.
Whatever It Was I Was Saving for My Old Age. Darr.
When Wilt Thou Teach the People—? Lawrence.
While O'er Our Guilty Land, O Lord. Davies.
Why, Liquor of Life? Carolan.

Saving
The Accountings. Goldbarth.
Ethics. Pastan.
Festus: Proem to the Third Edition. Bailey.
The Gypsy Bible. Tuwim.
Modern American Nursing. Hricz.
The Shapes of Death. Spender.
Spleen. Gray.
To Li Po from Tu Fu. Kizer.

Savior
The Adoration of the Wise Men. Alexander.
Beautiful Savior. Kruger.
The Bible. Stroud.
Blessed Assurance, Jesus Is Mine. Crosby.
The Blue Booby. Tate.
Brother, Though from Yonder Sky. Bancroft.
The Burial of an Infant. Vaughan.
The Charge. Wright.
Christmas Legends. McCarthy.
Communion Hymn of the Ancient Irish Church. Anonymous.
Covetousness. Idley.
Deeply Repentant of My Sinful Ways. Stampa.
The Execution of Luke Hutton. Anonymous.
The Firstborn. Goodchild.
For Dr. and Mrs. Dresser. Avison.
Gentle Jesus. Wesley.
Gethsemane. Tappan.
Glory to the Name of Jesus! Simpson.
H.Scriptures. Vaughan.
Hail Our Incarnate God! Duke.
Hail to the Joyous Day. Tyler.
The Happy Tree. Gould.
Hark! Hark! With Harps of Gold. Chapin.
Have I Done My Best for Jesus? Young.
He Died for Me. Bethune.
The Heavenly Aeroplane. Anonymous.
He's Come! The Saviour Has Come! Mortenson.
I Said Sometimes with Tears. Crossman.

The Lady Venetia Digby. Jonson.
Letter from the Vieux Carre. Russell.
Lines to the Blessed Sacrament. Callanan.
Lord! Lead the Way the Saviour Went. Croswell.
Missouri Sequence: Nightfall. Coffey.
Moment by Moment. Whittle.
My Companion. Ramage.
My Soul Shall Cling to Thee. Elliot.
O How Sweet Are Thy Words! Steele.
On the Death of His Son Vincent. Hunt.
Only the Beards Are Different. Dawe.
Pass It On! Anonymous.
The Passion and Exaltation of Christ. Watts.
Peter Emberley (I). Anonymous.
A Poem, upon the Caelestial Embassy Perform'd by Angels... Steere.
A Prayer. Bronte.
Prayer before Execution. Mary.
A Preacher's Prayer. Anonymous.
Proclaim the Lofty Praise. Judson.
Quatrains. Quirk.
Quid Petis, O Fily? Anonymous.
Rest of the Weary. Anonymous.
The Salamanca Doctor's Farewell. Anonymous.
Send Forth, O God, Thy Light and Truth. Adams.
The Song of Mary the Mother of Christ. Walpole.
Sonnet. Petrarch.
Tannhauser. Payne.
Tempt Me No More. Day-Lewis.
Ten Thousand Times Ten Thousand. Alford.
'Tis Midnight and on Olive's Brow. Tappan.
To Thee. Anonymous.
Worship. Jones, Jr.

Sawing
A Day in the Life... Pixner.
Driving Saw-Logs on the Plover (with music). Anonymous.
I Saw Esau Sawing Wood. Anonymous.

Saxon (s)
The Anglo-Saxon Race. Tupper.
The Dark Palace. Milligan.
Eire. O'Bruadair.
The Irish Hurrah. Davis.
O Say, My Brown Drimin. Anonymous.
The Song of O'Ruark, Prince of Breffni. Moore.

Say (s) (said)
Adder's Epigrams. Ellis.
America. Newlove.
America, America! Schwartz.
April 68. Cornish.
Away to Twiver, Away, Away! Anonymous.

Before Day. Sassoon.
A Bird in Search of a Cage. Pack.
Brief Encounter. Scott.
The Campus on the Hill. Snodgrass.
Can I Tempt You to a Pond Walk? Schuyler.
Chicken. Etter.
Childhood. Bradstreet.
Contemporary Song. Spencer.
The Cowman's Prayer. Anonymous.
Cuckoo, Scabbed Gowk. Anonymous.
The Curse of Cromwell. Yeats.
The Deacon's Masterpiece Or, The Wonderful "One-Hoss Shay." Holmes.
Departing Words to a Son. Pack.
The Duchess of York's Ghost. Anonymous.
Elegy for Two Banjos. Shapiro.
Eminent Critic. Nims.
Expounding the Torah. Zukofsky.
Faith. Browning.
Faults, Male and Female. Anonymous.
Fidelities. Valentine.
Five Roses. Verdaguer.
For My Students, Returning to College. Williams.
Four Translations from the English of Robert Hershon. Hershon.
Furnished Lives. Silkin.
Gethsemane. Bontemps.
Gloucester Moors. Moody.
Gnat on My Paper. Eberhart.
Grandeur of Ghosts. Sassoon.
The Gymnasiad, or Boxing Match (excerpt). Whitehead.
Hartico. Walters.
Here and Now. Levine.
Homecoming. Sanchez.
Hospital for Defectives. Blackburn.
The House on the Hill. Robinson.
Hudibras. Butler.
I Been a Bad, Bad Girl. Anonymous.
I Like Americans. Boyd.
I'm Going to Break Out. Valle.
In Praise of Commonplace. Seaman.
Letter for Melville 1951. Olson.
Life Is a Jest, and All Things Show It. Gay.
The Likeness. Nathan.
Lilac Time. Hein.
The Lord Sits with Me Out in Front. Gilbert.
Lydia. Reese.
Modern Ode to the Modern School. Erskine.
Motels, Hotels, Other People's Houses. Van Brunt.
My Creed. Gilder.
My Mother. Mezey.
Old Man. Booth.

The Old Walking Song. Tolkien.
On a Bright and Summer's Morning. Anonymous.
On a Clear Day I Can See Forever. Kuo.
On Poet Ninny. Rochester.
On Prince Frederick. Anonymous.
Our Silly Little Sister. Aldis.
The Patter of the Shingle. Anonymous.
Pedlar. Anonymous.
Philatelist Royal. Graves.
Poem: "I believe the yellow flowers think with me." Notley.
Portrait of a Man. Bernheimer.
The Priest and the Mulberry Tree. Peacock.
Prologue. MacLeish.
Reformed Drunkard. Scannell.
Relativities (parody). Untermeyer.
Retrospection. Quiller-Couch.
The Return of the Native. Matthews.
Robin Hood's Death. Anonymous.
Sally Simpkin's Lament. Hood.
Seal Rock. Baugh.
Simple. Madgett.
Since You Seem Intent... Locklin.
Singe We Alle and Say We Thus. Anonymous.
Some San Francisco Poems. Oppen.
Sometime. Smith.
The Song of the Mad Prince. De La Mare.
Sonnets from the Portuguese, XXVIII. Browning.
Sonnets of a Portrait Painter. Ficke.
The Soul of Time. Stickney.
The Sound of the Trees. Frost.
Stocking Fairy. Welles.
The Storm-Cock's Song. ""MacDiarmid.
Stumpfoot on 42nd Street. Simpson.
That There Are Powers above Us I Admit. Clough.
Think as I Think. Crane.
Thirtieth Anniversary Report of the Class of '41. Nemerov.
Though I get home how late, how late! Dickinson.
Time Is the Mercy of Eternity. Rexroth.
The Time Is Today. Farrar.
To Himself. Anacreon.
The Twins. Roberts.
The Two Old Women of Mumbling Hill. Reeves.
W. S. Landor. Moore.
The Waiting Harp. Becquer.
West-Running Brook. Frost.
What Are You Doing for Jesus? Nicholson.
What Kind of a Guy Was He? Nemerov.
When I Awoke. Patterson.
The Whip. Creeley.

Why Doubt God's Word?
Simpson.
Why Not? Pastan.
Witchcraft: New Style.
Abercrombie.
WOMEN OPEN
CAUTIOUSLY. Lee.
Words! Words! Fauset.
You Go, I'll Go wid You.
Anonymous.
You Serve the Best Wines
Always, My Dear Sir.
Martial (Marcus Valerius
Martialis).
Saying (s)
Bouquets. Francis.
The Death Bed. Cuney.
I'm a Baby. Corman.
The Letters of Summer.
Buckley.
Lines Left at Mr. Theodore
Hook's House in June,
1834. Barham.
Mad Song. Sigerson.
Scab (s)
Dido: Swarming. Spivack.
For Laurence Jones. Kizer.
Ice Handler. Sandburg.
Song of Myself. Whitman.
Scaffold (ing) (s)
Charles Guiteau, I.
Anonymous.
Saint-Just 1767-93. Lowell.
Scaffolding. Heaney.
Song about My Father.
Smither.
St. Augustine Contemplating
the Bust of Einstein.
Ackerman.
Scald (ed)
Bacchus. Empson.
The Balance of Europe.
Pope.
An Egyptian Pulled Glass
Bottle in the Shape of a
Fish. Moore.
Feast of the Ram's Horn.
Shapiro.
His Mother's Love. Stern.
Links. Pau-Llosa.
Mene, Mene, Tekel, Upharsin.
Cawein.
Morning Glory Pool.
McPherson.
New York Bird.
Voznesensky.
No Sense Grieving. Rubin.
This Cold Nothing Else.
Wier.
When Satan Fell. Lawrence.
The Winds. Williams.
Scale (s)
A Feather's Weight.
Lathrop.
Man's Littleness in Presence
of the Stars. White.
A Miner's Life. *Anonymous.*
Odes. Horace.
On a Certain Effeminate Peer.
Winstanley.
The Philosopher's Scales.
Taylor.
To Alan. Fraser.
Scalp
Blackfoot Sin-ka-ha. Lewis.
The Disheartened Ranger.
Anonymous.
The Dreary Black Hills.
Anonymous.
Scaly
Lizards and Snakes. Hecht.
Mythics. Chasin.

The Poet and the Wood-
Louse. Eden.
Scan
Fighting Words. Parker.
The Office of Poetry.
Whiting.
The Red Men. Sangster.
To a Photograph. Tyler.
Scandal (ous)
God Don't Like It.
Anonymous.
A Journey to Hell. Ward.
The Scurrilous Scribe.
Freneau.
The Twenty-Fifth Year of His
Life. Cavafy.
Scant
Breathless. Noyce.
Dear Lady, When Thou
Frownest. Bridges.
Scar (d) (s)
Leap in the Dark. Hill.
Leda Forgets the Wings of the
Swan. Keating.
Old Man with a Mowing
Machine. Lord.
Periods of Adjustment.
Wong.
The Wrangler Kid.
Anonymous.
Scar (red) (s)
Age in Youth. Stickney.
Black Rocks. Mar.
Blue Squills. Teasdale.
Certainties. Widdemer.
Forgive and Forget.
"Totius" [(J. D. Du Toit)].
The Girl I Call Alma.
Gregg.
Green Breeks. Dunn.
Plea to Eros. *Anonymous.*
To Chicago at Night.
Merryman.
The Western Trail. Carr.
Scare (d) (s)
A Change of Heart. Hobbs.
Desert Places. Frost.
The Dream-Follower.
Hardy.
Dreaming about Freedom.
Baca.
Epilogue. Spender.
The Faun. Pound.
Hiding in the Cucumber
Garden. Vidya.
Hitler, Frothy-Mouth.
Anonymous.
Homosexual Sonnets.
Pitchford.
The House of Desire.
Williams.
I'm Tired of Being Scared.
Giorno.
The Man in the Mirror.
Strand.
Possession. Lawner.
A Riddle. Zolotow.
Robert Lowell Is Dead.
Gray.
The Silken Snake. Herrick.
Situation. Hughes.
Skunk Hour. Lowell.
To Poem. Lifshin.
Wardance. George.
Scarecrows
The Late, Last Rook.
Hodgson.
That's Our Lot. Halpern.
Scarf
The Power of Silence.
Davies.
Rise and Shine. Lattimore.

Scarlet
Before the Carnival. Gunn.
Eighteen-Seventy. Rimbaud.
The Grave-Tree. Carman.
I Gathered Mosses in
Easedale. Wordsworth.
On His Books. Belloc.
The Poppy. Corman.
Ravngard and Memering.
Anonymous.
Slender Fingers. Chao Luan-
luan.
Strange, All-Absorbing Love.
Dolben.
To Any M.F.H. Sackville-
West.
Upon Scarlet and Blush-
Coloured Ribbands, Given
by Two Ladies. Shirley.
Scatter (ed) (ing) (s)
Battle Songs of the King
Tshaka. Anonymous.
Ben Bolt. *Anonymous.*
The Bicycle Rider. Shapcott.
The Blood-Letting. Harjo.
Coming Home from Camp.
Kaneko.
Family. *Anonymous.*
Fuimus Fumus. Sylvester.
Green Haven Halls.
Culhane.
Herman Moon's Hourbook.
Middleton.
Lament of the Jewish Women
for Tammuz. Reznikoff.
Shepherd and Shepherdess.
Hennell.
Snow Geese in the Wind.
Dow.
The Tower of Babel.
Crouch.
Scavenger
For My Twenty-Fifth
Birthday in Nineteen Forty-
One. Ciardi.
The Tarry Buccaneer.
Masefield.
Scene (s)
Afternoons with Baedeker.
Lancaster.
All Night Long. Cassian.
Anonymous Drawing.
Justice.
The Bricklayer's Labours.
Tatersal.
Converstion with Three
Women of New England.
Stevens.
Credences of Summer.
Stevens.
Danebury. *Anonymous.*
Down to the Sacred Wave.
Smith.
Epigram: "My soul, sit thou a
patient looker-on."
Quarles.
Garage Sale. Shapiro.
The Highlands' Swelling Blue.
Byron.
In a Hotel Writing-Room.
Powys.
The Lay of the Last Minstrel.
Scott.
Love Dislikes Nothing.
Herrick.
Muse, June, Related. Coffey.
A Night-Piece. Wordsworth.
Ode on the Poetical
Character. Collins.
On His Own Agamemnon and
Iphigenia. Landor.

On the Queen's Visit to
London. Cowper.
Pure Nails Brightly Flashing.
Mallarme.
To the Memory of Ben
Johnson (excerpt). Mayne.
To the Tune "The Fall of a
Little Wild Goose."
Huang O.
Verses Written during the
War 1756–1763.
Mordaunt.
Scent (ed) (s)
After. Reese.
Alien. Hayes.
Amid the Myrtles. Halevi
Anabasis, IV. Perse.
Bagley Wood. Johnson.
The Dark Scent of Prayer.
Drachler.
Folding the Sheets. Dobson.
Haiku: "The bride puts them
away." *Anonymous.*
I Bring to You as Offering
Tonight. Verhaeren.
If my nipples were to drip
milk. Sappho.
In the Dry Riverbed. Zelda.
Lent. Rodgers.
Life. Herbert.
Meeting by the Gjulika
Meadow. Grigson.
Mild the Mist upon the Hill.
Bronte.
Nursing the Hide. Dunne.
Paralytic. Plath.
Piere Vidal Old. Pound.
Plum Blossoms. *Anonymous.*
Prowling the Ridge. Minty.
Reading Sign. Anderson.
Sleep. Doty.
Song: "My spirit like a
shepherd boy." Sackville-
West.
Songs of Kabir. Kabir.
Spring Nocturne. Liessin.
They Live in Parallel Worlds.
Harris.
Trembling. Shenhar.
Scepter
Booze Turns Men into
Women. Mayer.
Cradle and Throne.
Anonymous.
Down the Nile. Lowell.
An Epithalamium upon the
Marriage of Captain
William Bedloe. Duke.
Exiles. Russell.
Great and Mighty Wonder.
Anatolius.
Lines on Succession of the
Kings of England.
Anonymous.
News from the Court.
Wagoner.
Paradise Regained. Milton.
Song: "O'er the waste of
waters cruising." Freneau.
You That Have Been Often
Invited. *Anonymous.*
Schedule
The Anathemata. Jones.
Two Scenes. Ashbery.
Scheme (rs) (s)
A Bad Joke. Martial
(Marcus Valerius Martialis).
Clerihew. Bentley.
The Ghaists: A Kirk-Yard
Eclogue. Fergusson.
Horses Aboard. Hardy.
Is. Kavanagh.

Lines on the Celebrated
   Picture by Leonardo Da
   Vinci... Lamb.
Scholar (s)
Circle. Dobson.
Epitaph on Dr. Johnson.
   Jenyns.
The Funeral. Spender.
The Original Lamb.
   Anonymous.
Riddle: "As I was a-walking
   on Westminster Bridge."
   Anonymous.
Riddle: "The land was white."
   Anonymous.
Thyrsis. Arnold.
To learn the transport by the
   pain. Dickinson.
A Treasure. Whittemore.
School (s)
Acceptance Speech. Bell.
American Commencement.
   Boyajian.
Black Sketches, 1. Lee.
The Bulldog on the Bank.
   Anonymous.
The Bush on Mount Venus.
   Finkel.
Churchyard. Hass.
Circle. Dobson.
The Corral. Thompson.
Daisy Fraser. Masters.
Dead Dog. Scannell.
A Description of the Morning.
   Swift.
Epigram: "Loss of our
   learning brought darkness,
   weakenss and woe."
   Anonymous.
Fables: The Shepherd and the
   Philosopher. Gay.
First Departure. Frost.
A Fit of Rime against Rime.
   Jonson.
Getting Through. Merrill.
The Ghoul. Prelutsky.
Haiku. Vizenor.
In the Days of Rin-Tin-Tin.
   Hoffman.
Indian Education. Louis.
The Lament for Art O
   Laoghaire (excerpt).
   O'Connell.
Mending Crab Pots. Smith.
Michael Robartes and the
   Dancer. Yeats.
O Thou Whose Feet Have
   Climbed Life's Hill.
   Benson.
Of One Self-Slain. Towne.
The Old Brown Schoolhouse.
   Anonymous.
An Old Man's Thought of
   School. Whitman.
Osmund Toulmin. Sitwell.
Pedagogical Principles.
   Amoss.
The Picnic. Logan.
Pronouns. Baker.
Schoolgirls Hastening.
   Neilson.
Sedge-Warblers. Thomas.
The Shepherd and His Flock.
   Mtshali.
Sing a Song of Sunshine.
   Eastwick.
Slightly before the Middle of
   Congressman Pudd.
   Cummings.
Still Do I Keep My Look, My
   Identity... Brooks.
What Fifty Said. Frost.

The Wonder Clock. Pyle.
Schooner (s)
A Finished Gentleman.
   Dutton.
The Prairie Schooner. Dale.
Science
Charing Cross. Roberts.
Deus Ex Machina. Armour.
An Essay on Criticism.
   Pope.
Even Though. Stone.
Night the Ninth Being the
   Last Judgment. Blake.
The Observatory Ode. Nims.
Proem to the Parlement of
   Foules. Chaucer.
There Was a Young Man
   from Trinity. *Anonymous.*
Time's Song. Praed.
Verses on a Cat. Daubeny.
Whatever It Was I Was
   Saving for My Old Age.
   Darr.
Scissors
The Afterwake. Rich.
My Face Is My Own, I
   Thought. Raworth.
The Tailor's Wedding.
   Simpson.
Une Vie. Saarikoski.
Scold (ing)
Californy Stage. *Anonymous.*
The Dumb Wife Cured.
   Anonymous.
Old Man Pondered.
   Ransom.
The Wakers. Freeman.
Scope
Consummation. Traherne.
Motorcycle. Pray.
Scorched
The Dynasts. Hardy.
A Fly about a Glass of Burnt
   Claret. Lovelace.
Nearer. Herzberg.
Staying Ahead. Glass.
Score (s)
The Grey Hair. Halevi.
The Smell of Old Newspapers
   Is Always Stronger...
   Lowery.
Telling the Cousins. Murray.
Scorn (e) (ed) (es)
Be Gone Ye Blockheads.
   Diogenes Laertius.
Caelica, XCIII. Greville.
Days. Emerson.
Disdain Me Still. Pembroke.
The Dromedary. Campbell.
The Eccho. Leigh.
Farewell to the World of
   Richard Bishop.
   Anonymous.
The Gift. Russell.
I Wish Sometimes, Although
   a Worthlesse Thing.
   Fletcher.
Idyllis. Theocritus.
In Memoriam A.H.H., XXVI.
   Tennyson.
It May Be. Jacob.
Jack Donahoe. *Anonymous.*
Lords of the Wilderness.
   Leyden.
Marsyas. Roberts.
The Range Riders.
   Anonymous.
Sir Walter Scott's Tribute.
   Scott.
Some Tyme I Fled the Fyre
   That Me Brent. Wyatt.

Song: "I prithee let my heart
   alone." Stanley.
Song: "Or love mee lesse, or
   love mee more."
   Godolphin.
Sonnet–To the Critic.
   Drayton.
Strive No More. Peele.
To a Lady across the Way.
   White.
To His Late Majesty
   Concerning the True Form
   of English Poetry.
   Beaumont.
To His Mistresse on Her
   Scorne. Beedome.
Tolerance. Morris.
Underneath a Cypress Shade,
   The Queen of Love Sat
   Mourning. *Anonymous.*
Upon Lazarus His Teres.
   Crashaw.
Water Fowl. Wordsworth.
When Men Shall Find.
   Daniel.
The Wild Flower's Song.
   Blake.
The Witch. Hinkson.
The World's Justice.
   Lazarus.
Scorpion (s)
Fragments. Praxilla.
The Modern Fine Lady.
   Jenyns.
Monsoon. Wevill.
On Fell. Lessing.
The Walls Do Not Fall.
   Doolittle.
We have seen how the most
   amiable. Doolittle.
Scotland
The Ballad of Sir Patrick
   Spens. *Anonymous.*
The Day of the Crucifixion.
   ""MacDiarmid.
The Fire. Scott.
Five Visions of Captain Cook.
   Slessor.
The Gay Gos-hawk.
   Anonymous.
Gude Wallace (G version).
   Anonymous.
John Barleycorn. Burns.
Leave Cancelled. Berkson.
Lord Derwentwater (D
   version). *Anonymous.*
The Mariner. Cunningham.
McNaughtan (Johnny Scot).
   Anonymous.
The Old Scottish Cavalier.
   Ayton [(or Aytoun)] Sir
   Robert.
On the Hill. Soutar.
Rumba of the Three Lost
   Souls. Madge.
Scotland Yet. Riddell.
Sir Patrick Spens.
   Anonymous.
Snatches: "Maidenes of
   Engelande, sare may ye
   morne." *Anonymous.*
Twenty-One Sonnets. Stead.
The Wind. *Anonymous.*
Scottsboro
The Trial. Rukeyser.
Scout (ing) (s)
The Horseman on the Skyline.
   Lawson.
Memorial Day. Ching.
Tonto. Koertge.
Scratch (ed) (ing)
The Chickens. *Anonymous.*

Choosing Their Names.
   Hood.
Elegy. Nemerov.
Hard Daddy. Hughes.
The Marrowbone Itch.
   Anonymous.
The Old Gray Goose.
   Anonymous.
On Dr. Keene, Bishop of
   Chester. Gray.
Renewal. Kowit.
Reply. McCabe.
Taboo to Boot. Nash.
To a Squirrel at Kyle-Na-No.
   Yeats.
To and on Other Intellectual
   Poets.... Guthrie.
We Object. *Anonymous.*
Scream (ed) (er) (ing) (s)
African Dream. Kaufman.
Assimilation. Feldman.
The Ballad of Sister Anne.
   Sitwell.
Burning Oneself In. Rich.
But, Still, He. Lucas.
The City. Maddow.
Drama. Hart-Smith.
The Election. Pack.
Emily Dickinson. Hagerup.
A Fairy Tale. Mackenzie.
Fixing to Die. White.
The Good Woman.
   MacLean.
Grog-an'-Grumble
   Steeplechase. Lawson.
The Happy Family. Ciardi.
He Was Formidable.
   Warren.
Homing. Bontemps.
The Idea of San Francisco.
   Gustafson.
In My Own Twentieth
   Century. Gorbanyevskaya.
Just Making It. Thomas.
Minotaur Poems. Mandel.
Nerves. Symons.
A Northern Hoard. Heaney.
On Diverse Deviations.
   Angelou.
Out of Whack. Edson.
Poem. Blaser.
The Railway Stationery.
   Koch.
The Recruits. Hamilton.
Rothiemurchus. Lamont.
The Sacrilege. Hardy.
A Screamer Discusses
   Methods of Screaming.
   Schevill.
Shoplifter. Edwards.
Sirens in Bad Weather.
   Santos.
Sonnet V: "White Venus
   limpid wandering in the
   sky." Labe.
Sound Advice. *Anonymous.*
This Is Pioneer Weather.
   Williams.
A Vision. Winters.
Winter Warfare. Rickword.
The Witch. Southey.
Witch. Tepperman.
Woman's Liberation. Maura.
Words, Like Spiders. Wolny.
Screen (ing) (s)
The Absence. Levertov.
Bijou. Rutsala.
Euclid Avenue. Simic.
Evening Ebb. Jeffers.
The Flicker. Blockcolski.
Going Away. Nemerov.
Midnight. Roberts.

The Pulverized Screen. Jabes.
Shitty. Amis.
Three Part Invention. Blackburn.
Western Movies. Jensen.

Screw (ed)
Frankenstein Gets His Man. Carr.
Mental Health. Fried.
On Donne's Poetry. Coleridge.
Taste. Updike.
To Corydon. Beccadelli.

Scribble (d)
Limerick: "A senator, Rex Asinorum." Anonymous.
Post Early For Space. Henniker-Heaton.

Scripture (s)
A Case at Sessions. Landor.
Caught in the Pocket. Barney.
The Copulating Gods. Kizer.
To My Daughter Betty, the Gift of God. Kettle.
The Wisdom of Old Jelly Roll. Smith.

Scythe (s)
Apology of Genius. Loy.
The Fox-Hunters. Elliott.
The May Day Garland. Blunden.
The Mower. Anonymous.
The Mower in Ohio. Piatt.
Mowing. Frost.
The Ripe and Bearded Barley. Anonymous.
Scythe Song. Lang.
Sonnets, C: "Where art thou, Muse, that thou forget'st so long." Shakespeare.
Sonnets, CXXIII: "No, Time, thou shalt not boast that I do change." Shakespeare.

Sea
Evening Refrain. Santos.
Girl at the Seaside. Murphy.

Sea (s)
Adam. Booth.
Adams and Liberty. Paine.
Adelaide Crapsey. Sandburg.
Adieu My Lovely Nancy. Anonymous.
Albatross. Burgess.
Albert Sidney Johnson. Sherwood.
Alien. Hayes.
All That Is Perfection in Woman. Williams.
All the Fruit... Holderlin.
Amber Beads. Brown.
The Ambitious Ant. Wells.
America the Beautiful. Bates.
Anactoria (excerpt). Swinburne.
Analyst. Fisher.
Andrew Bardeen. Anonymous.
Annabel Lee. Poe.
Another of Seafarers, Describing Evil Fortune. Anonymous.
Answers to the Snails. Solway.
Antwerp Musee des Beaux-Arts. Ross.
Ark Artefact. Macpherson.
As Sun, As Sea. Sullivan.

Aspects of the World Like Coral Reefs. Bronk.
At Best. O'Reilly.
At Melville's Tomb. Crane.
At Sea. Rogers.
At the Band Concert. Brinnin.
At the Grave of Walker. Miller.
At the Sea's Edge. Harwood.
At the Slackening of the Tide. Wright.
Aubade. O'Hara.
The Auld Matrons. Anonymous.
Aunt Zillah Speaks. Palmer.
An Autumn Garden. Carman.
Back Road Farm. Bruce.
Bahamas. Oppen.
A Ballad of the Captains. Brady.
Ballad of the Two Tapsters. Watkins.
The Battel of the Summer-Islands. Waller.
The Battle of Erie. Anonymous.
The Battle of Manila. Hovey.
Beach House. Hurley.
Beachcomber. Brown.
The Beatific Sea. Campbell.
Beauty Is Ever to the Lonely Mind. Nathan.
Beech Leaves. Reeves.
Before. Stanford.
Before Sunrise in Winter. Sill.
Betty by the Sea. McCuaig.
Beyond Kerguelen. Kendall.
The Birth of Galahad: Ylen's Song. Hovey.
The Birth of Venus. Anonymous.
The Black Horse Rider. Loving.
Blue Mountain. Hill.
The Blue Wing. Hall.
Bold Princess Royal. Anonymous.
Bones. Sandburg.
Braemar. Kinnell.
The Bride's Song. Cory.
The Broken Oar. Longfellow.
The Brooklyn Bridge. Proctor.
Burd Ellen and Young Tamlane. Anonymous.
The Buried Life. Arnold.
By the North Sea. Swinburne.
Byzantium. Yeats.
Cadaver Politic. Paulin.
Cadgwith. Johnson.
Caelica, XCVI. Greville.
The Campanero. Anonymous.
Can Ye Sew Cushions? Anonymous.
The Captain. Varela.
Captain Jones' Invitation. Freneau.
Captain Ward and the Rainbow. Anonymous.
Carlyle and Emerson. Schuyler.
Child of Blue. Hogan.
The Choristers. Carman.
Christ. Forker.

The Christ of the Andes (excerpt). Markham.
La Ci Darem La Mano. Nims.
Cino. Pound.
The Clipper. Day.
Columbus. Jackson.
The Coming of Night. Wade.
Commemorative of a Naval Victory. Melville.
Cormorants. Blight.
The Coromandel Fishers. Naidu.
Darwinity. Merivale.
The Dead Man Dragged from the Sea. Gardner.
Dedication: To Edward John Trelawny. Swinburne.
Deep Blue Sea. Anonymous.
The Deeper Seas. Bellamann.
The Defeat of the Norsemen (excerpt). Sedulius Scottus.
The Demon Lover. Anonymous.
The Demon Lover. Rich.
Der Mond Ist Aufgegangen. Heine.
Die My Shriek. Kushniroff.
Dinosaur Spring. Waniek.
Dirge. De Vere.
Dirge. Fearing.
The Distances. Merwin.
The Djanggawul Cycle, 182. Anonymous
The Djanggawul Cycle, 4. Anonymous
The Djanggawul Cycle, 6. Anonymous.
The Dockyard Gate. Anonymous.
Dorothy. Kreymborg.
A Dream. Arnold.
Dream. Edwards.
Dream Songs. Berryman.
A Drover. Colum.
Duet. Tennyson.
Early. Bennett.
Early Summer Sea-Tryst. Macartney.
Earlye, Earlye, in the Spring. Anonymous.
East Coast–Canada. Brewster.
Ebbtide at Sundown. "Field.
Endymion, II. Keats.
England. Day.
Enigma. McCrae.
Enoch Arden. Tennyson.
Enueg. Beckett.
Epigram: "O Diodorus." Anonymous.
Epitaph on Achilles. Anonymous.
Especially When the October Wind. Thomas.
Etruscan Notebook. Clementelli.
Evarra and His Gods. Kipling.
Evening on Howth Head. Brennan.
Events. O'Neil.
The Faerie Queene. Spenser.
Farewell. Plato.
The Farm Near Norman's Lane. Finnin.
The Feather. Watkins.
Fern Hill. Thomas.

The Fiddler of Dooney. Yeats.
Fiddler's Green. Roberts.
Fife Tune. Manifold.
Figurehead. Paul.
Finisterra. Winters.
Fire Burial. McInnis.
The Fisher Lad of Whitby. Anonymous.
The Fisher's Life. Anonymous.
The Fisherman. Leonidas.
Fishermen. Bunting.
Five Lyrics from "Good for Nothing Man". Pitchford.
Flake Diamond of/the Sea. Eigner.
Flora MacDonald and the King. Anonymous.
Flying Fish. Fenollosa.
Fog. Reed.
For Summer's Here. Barnett.
For the Wine of Circe. Rossetti.
For Thomas Hardy. Cooper.
The Forsaken Merman. Arnold.
Four in the Morning. Sitwell.
The Four Maries. Anonymous.
The Fourth of July. Pierpont.
From My Lai the Thunder Went West. Ryan.
From Russian Hill. Coolbrith.
The Future. Arnold.
A Garden by the Sea. Morris.
The Garden of Proserpine. Swinburne.
The Gardens of the Sea. Sterling.
Gigha. Graham.
God Is Working His Purpose Out. Ainger.
Going Towards Spain. Googe.
The Good Dream. Levertov.
Grasmere Sonnets. Wright.
Gray Shore. Rorty.
A Great Favourite Song, Entitled The Sailor's Hornpipe. Anonymous.
Hallelujah! Anonymous.
Heaven-Haven. Hopkins.
Henceforth, from the Mind. Bogan.
Henley on Taieri. Brasch.
Henry Martyn (E version). Anonymous.
Her Dead Brother. owell.
Her Longing. Roethke.
Hermes of the Ways. Doolittle.
The Hero of Bridgewater. Jones.
Hic Me, Pater Optime, Fessam Deseris. Robinson.
Hieroglyphic. Sklarew.
High Island. Murphy.
The Holy Ground. Anonymous.
The Hounds. Freeman.
The House Carpenter's Wife. Anonymous.
The House in the Green Well. Wheelock.

The House Next Door. Dunn.
The House of Falling Leaves. Braithwaite.
How Many Heavens... Sitwell.
Hurricane. MacLeish.
Hymn. Stowe.
The Iceberg. Roberts.
In and Out: Severance of Connections, 1946. Sissman.
In Him. Blake.
In Orknay. Fowler.
In Pace In Idipsum Dormiam Et Requiescam. O'Connor.
In This World's Raging Sea. Drummond.
Incident at Mossel Bay. Balazs.
The Indian Mohee. *Anonymous.*
Inishkeel Parish Church. Paulin.
Insomnia. Bishop.
The Inspection. Watt.
Intimacy. Young.
Irish Hotel. Wevill.
The Island. Dickey.
Island of Giglio. Norse.
The Islands. Jarrell.
Jack the Guinea Pig. *Anonymous.*
Jack Wrack. *Anonymous.*
Jacques Cartier. McGee.
January. Dutton.
The Jealous Brothers. *Anonymous.*
A Jew Walks in Westminster Abbey. Hodes.
John Hardy (A vers.). *Anonymous.*
Keine Lazarovitch. Layton.
The Knight Without a Name. *Anonymous.*
Lament for a Dead Lover. Haad.
Lament for Richard Rolston. Sitwell.
The Lark. *Anonymous.*
The Lass of Roch Royal (C vers.). *Anonymous.*
The Last Chantey. Kipling.
The Last Galway Hooker. Murphy.
The Laureate. Graves.
Laus Veneris. Swinburne.
The Leak in the Dike. Cary.
Leander Stormbound. Smith.
Leaving Barra. MacNeice.
Lethe. Johnson.
The Lido. Wilson.
The Life. Dow.
A Life. Plath.
A Life. Woodberry.
Life of Life. Edfelt.
Light. Silkin.
Light Lover. Kilmer.
Like Noah's Weary Dove. Muhlenberg.
Limerick: "O was an ossified oyster." Wells.
Little Fish. Lawrence.
The Loss of the Evelyn Marie. *Anonymous.*
The Lost War-Sloop. Proctor.
Love Song. MacLeod.
The Loving Ballad of Lord Bateman. Dickens.
The Lowlands o' Holland. *Anonymous.*

The Lowlands of Holland. *Anonymous.*
Lyric. Child.
Magellan. Curnow.
Maggie and milly and molly and may. Cummings.
A Man's Woman. Davies.
The Man Whom the Sea Kept Awake. Bly.
Manos Karastefanis. Merrill.
The Mares of the Camargue. Mistral.
The Mariner's Song. Davies.
The Mariners. Woods.
Mary Beaton's Song. Swinburne.
The Master Mariner. Sterling.
The Master's Call. Smith.
Meditation. Pain.
The Medusa. Davenport.
Mein Liebchen, Wir Sassen Zusammen. Heine.
Memoirs of a Spinach-Picker. Plath.
The Mermaid. *Anonymous.*
The Mermaid (B version). *Anonymous.*
Message from Ohanapecosh Glacier. Ransom.
Mid-Country Blow. Roethke.
Milton. Longfellow
Miracles. Bontemps.
The Mirror. Morris.
Missions. *Anonymous.*
The Moon-Bone Cycle: New Moon. *Anonymous.*
The Moon Is Teaching Bible. Zelda.
The Morality of Poetry. Wright.
More Sonnets at Christmas. Tate.
Morning Swim. Kumin.
Musica No. Duerden.
My Atthis, although our dear Anaktoria. Sappho.
My Doves. Browning.
My Playmate. Whittier.
My Valentine. Stevenson.
My Voice. Wilde.
The Nabara. Day Lewis.
Nebraska. Swan.
Night Fishing for Blues. Smith.
Night's Fall. Graham.
Nightmares. Fox.
Nightwalker. Kinsella.
No Change in Me. *Anonymous.*
Nocturne. Frost.
The Noonday April Sun. Love.
Norah. Akins.
North Atlantic. Sandburg.
The Novelty Shop. Niatum.
Now Is Farewell. Salkeld.
Now Strike Your Sailes Ye Jolly Mariners! Spenser.
O Carib Isle! Crane.
O Christ, Thou Art within Me Like a Sea. Pierce.
O'er Continent and Ocean. Holmes.
O Pioneers! Bishop.
O Sailor, Come Ashore. Rossetti.
The Objects of the Summer Scene. Irwin.
The Ocean. St. Martin.

The Ocean Burial. *Anonymous.*
An Ocean Lullaby. Keeler.
Ode to a Nightingale: The Nightingale. Keats.
Oedipus at Colonus. Sophocles.
Of Little Faith. Pulsifer.
Of the Lost Ship. White.
Off Molokai. Hindley.
Off to Sea Once More. *Anonymous.*
Oh, Come to Me when Daylight Sets. Moore.
The Old Flagman. Sandburg.
On a View of Pasadena from the Hills. Winters.
On an Italian Hillside. Weber.
On First Entering Westminster Abbey. Guiney.
On First Looking into Chapman's Homer (parody). Brownlie.
On Galveston Beach. Howes.
On Independence. Sewall.
On Leaving Bruges. Rossetti.
On Seeing a Poet of the First World War on the Station at Abbeville. Causley.
On the Athenian Dead at Ecbatana. Plato.
On the Discoveries of Captain Lewis. Barlow.
On the Edge at Santorini. Blumenthal.
On the Night. Gurney.
On the South Coast of Cornwall. Gray.
Orpheus. Hendry.
Our Lady of the Waves. Brown.
Out of That Sea. Ferry.
Outward. Neihardt.
Over All the Face of Earth Main Ocean Flowed. Milton.
Ovid's Metamorphosis: Sixth Book. Sandys.
Owning. Lane.
Pacific Door. Birney.
Paddy West. *Anonymous.*
Pain. Storni.
Paradise Lost. Milton.
The Parrot Fish. Merrill.
Pater Vester Pascit Illa. Hawker.
Patmos. Thomas.
The Pear-Tree. Goll.
Peg-Leg's Fiddle. Adams.
Perspectives. Randall.
Pete at the Seashore. Marquis.
Phenomenal Survivals of Death in Nantucket. Gluck.
Piano Practice. Walcott.
Pick upon Pick... Comfort.
The Place at Alert Bay. Rukeyser.
The Play. Judkins.
Play-Song. *Anonymous.*
Plymouth Harbor. Radford.
Poem near the Sea. Frelimo.
Poem without a Main Verb. Wain.

A Poem Written in Time of Trouble by an Irish Priest... Gregory.
The Poet Is Dead. Everson.
A Poet's Hope. Channing
Poetry Is... Bennett.
Poetry Is in the Darkness. Boyajian.
Polifemo y Galatea: The Love Song of Polyphemus. Gongora y Argote.
Polyolbion. Drayton.
Portmanteau Parodies: After Algernon Charles Swinburne. Chesterton.
Portrait of the Poet as Landscape. Klein.
Postscript. Mills.
Prairie. Bates.
Presentation Piece. Hacker.
Prison Graveyard. Knight.
Prologue to General Hamley. Tennyson.
Prometheus Unbound. Shelley.
Promises. Sherry.
The Promontory Moment. Swenson.
Public Beach (Long Island Sound). Morley.
The Queen of Crete. Grimes.
Quiet Waters. Wagstaff.
Radio. Tessimond.
Ragged Island. Millay.
The Railway Junction. de la Mare.
Rain. Hollo.
The Rape of the Lock. Pope.
Reason Has Moons. Hodgson.
Reasons for Music. MacLeish.
Requiem after Seventeen Years. Ravikovich.
Response to Rimbaud's Latter Manner. Moore.
Return. Jeffers.
Returning to Store Bay. Howes.
Riddle 7 (Mute Swan). *Anonymous.*
Ringsend. Gogarty.
Ripe, Being Plunged into Fire... Holderlin.
Rise, Ye Children. Falckner.
The River. MacNab.
Rock (excerpt). Raine.
Rondel: Beside the Idle Summer Sea. Henley.
The Room of My Life. Sexton.
Room of Return. Kinnell.
Rosabelle. Scott.
Round Dance, & Canticle. Kelly.
Rousecastle. Wright.
Sailing at Dawn. Newbolt.
The Sailing of the Sword. Morris.
Sailor. Farjeon.
A Sailor's Prayer. Morris.
A Sailor's Wife. Bernhardt.
Sailors. Simpson.
Sailors for My Money. *Anonymous.*
The Salt Flats. Roberts.
Salt of the Earth. Lawrence.
Santorin. Flecker.
The Sea. Webb.
Sea Born. Vinal.
Sea-Change. Masefield.

A Sea Child. Carman.
A Sea Dirge. "Carroll.
Sea Dirge. Scott.
Sea-Grief. O'Reilly.
Sea Gulls. Pratt.
The Sea Hath Its Pearls. Heine.
The Sea-Limits. Rossetti.
The Sea Serpent Chantey. Lindsay.
A Sea Song. Cunningham.
Sea Song. Holland.
Sea Words. Leitch.
The Seafarer. *Anonymous.*
The Seagull. Howitt.
Seagulls on the Serpentine. Noyes.
Seascape with Bookends. Eaton.
The Seasons. Thomson.
The Seasons in North Cornwall. Causley.
Seaway. Wilson.
Sent from Egypt with a Fair Robe of Tissue to a Sicilian Vinedresser. Moore.
A Sermon. Sackville.
Seven South African Poems. Wright.
Seymour and Chantelle or Un Peu de Vice. Smith.
The Shannon and the Chesapeake. Bouve.
Shells in Rock. Roberts.
The Ship A-Raging. *Anonymous.*
The Ship and the Sea. Baughan.
The Ship-Builders. Whittier.
The Ship of Fools. Barclay.
The Ship of State. Horace.
Shore Tullye. Rendall.
Shortening Sail. Falconer.
Silences. Pratt.
The Simple Ploughboy. *Anonymous.*
Sing to the Lord Most High. Dwight.
Sir Andrew Barton (Andrew Batann). *Anonymous.*
So I Said I Am Ezra. Ammons.
Someplace Else. Piercy.
Son and Surf. Strong.
Song–Across the Sea. Allingham.
Song against Women. Wright.
Song at the Skirts of Heaven. Greenberg.
A Song Before Grief. Lathrop.
Song for All Seas, All Ships. Whitman.
Song: "Gold wings across the sea!" Morris.
Song: "I walk'd in the lonesome evening." Allingham.
The Song of a Heathen. Gilder.
A Song of Dagger-Dancing (excerpt). Tu Fu.
A Song of Freedom. Milligan.
The Song of the Colorado. Hall.
The Song of the Derelict. McCrae.
Song of the Sea. Burton.
Song: "The bells of Sunday rang us down." Ciardi.

Song: "To all you ladies now at land." Sackville.
Songs Before Sunrise: Prelude. Swinburne.
Songs for the Four Parts of the Night. Owl Woman.
Sonnet–Age. Garnett.
Sonnet: "High on the wall that holds Jerusalem." Chesterton.
The Sonnet's Voice. Watts-Dunton.
Sonnets. Tuckerman.
Sonnets, V: "Into the wood at close of rainy day." Irwin.
Sonnets, VIII: "The apples ripen under yellowing leaves." Irwin.
Sonnets of the Triple-Headed Manichee: II. Barker.
Sonnets to Miranda. Watson.
The Soul. Barlow.
The Souls of the Slain. Hardy.
St Enda. Lerner.
St. Govan. Prys-Jones.
Stages on a Journey Westward. Wright.
Still-Life. Hughes.
Still Pond, No More Moving. Moss.
The Storm Cone. Kipling.
Such is Holland! Genestet.
Summer's Early End at Hudson Bay. Carruth.
The Summer Story. Lehmann.
The Sun Has Set. Bronte.
Sunday up the River. Thomson.
Sunlight and Sea. Noyes.
Sutcliffe and Whitby. Logan.
Swamp. Hill.
Swimmer. Francis.
Swimmers (excerpt). Untermeyer.
Switzerland. Arnold.
Te Deum. Le Fort.
Teneriffe (excerpt). Myers.
Thalassius. Swinburne.
Thalatta. Allen.
That Summer's Shore. Ciardi.
Theme and Variations. Ker.
Themes. Glover.
There Was a Little Ship. *Anonymous.*
They Lie at Rest, Our Blessed Dead. Rossetti.
They Say the Sea Is Loveless. Lawrence.
This Air That Blows in from the Sea. Coatsworth.
Three Sonnets on Oblivion. Sterling.
Three White Birds of Angus. Cox.
Through Binoculars. Tomlinson.
The Tides Run Up the Wairau. Duggan.
Till the Sea Runs Dry. *Anonymous.*
Time. Shelley.
"The Time Has Come," the Walrus Said. "Carroll.
To —. Shelley.
To a Pretty Girl. Zangwill.
To a Sea-Bird. Harte.
To a Seaman Dead on Land. Boyle.

To a Young Lady, with Some Lampreys. Gay.
To Be a Master in Your House. Zach.
To Christopher Smart. Stroud.
To E.L., on His Travels in Greece. Tennyson.
To My Friend Butts I Write. Blake.
To Pyrrha. Horace.
To Sea. Beddoes.
To the Nile. Keats.
To the Western Wind. Halevi.
Told by Seafareres. Kinnell.
Tongues of Fire. Plescoff.
Transcendence. Hovey.
The Triangle Ladies. Montgomery.
The Triumph of Time. Swinburne.
The Troika. Simpson.
True and False. Crawford.
Two Musics. MacCaig.
Two Old Men Look at the Sea. Hervey.
Two Pieces after Suetonius. Warren.
The Two Selves. Avison.
The Two Streams. Holmes.
Underground. Mudie.
Vaticide. O'Higgins.
Veneta. Coleridge.
Voyage. Schramm.
W o m a n. Portal.
Waitaki Dam. Glover.
The Wanderings of Oisin. Yeats.
Watch the Lights Fade. Jeffers.
The Weepers Tower in Amsterdam. Goodman.
Welcome to the Nations. Holmes.
A Wet Sheet. Cunningham.
The Whale. *Anonymous.*
When I Was Dying. Hathaway.
Where Is the Sea? Hemans.
Whistles. Field.
The White Birds. Yeats.
Why Linger Yet upon the Strand? Benson.
Will Beauty Come. Nathan.
Wind and Wave. Stoddard.
Wishes. Ault.
The Witch's Whelp. Stoddard.
With a Nantucket Shell. Webb.
Wobbly Rock. Welch.
The Woman of Beare. *Anonymous.*
Wreaths. Hill.
The Wreck of the Northfleet. *Anonymous.*
The Yarn of the Loch Achray. Masefield.
Year's End. Benson.
The Young Men Come Less Often–Isn't It So? Horace.

Seabird
The Echoing Cliff. Young.
Loss of an Oil Tanker. Causley.
The Old Boat. Pratt.
Training. Herrera.

Seagull (s)
Confidence. Hartley.
I'm 92, Joe Said. Weber.

Numerous Celts (parody). Squire.
Storm Warning. Bardsley.
Seahorse
The Horses of the Sea. Rossetti.
The Turtle. *Anonymous.*
Seal (ed) (s)
At the Round Earth's Imagin'd Corners, Blow. Donne.
The Butcher. Williams.
Come to Calvary's Holy Mountain. Montgomery.
Damnation of Vancouver: Speech of the Salish Chief. Birney.
Deportation. Glanz-Leyeles.
Extraordinary Will. Jackett.
.The Fire Side. A Pastoral Soliloquy. Browne.
Four Years Were Mine at Princeton. Bishop.
Hamlet. Shakespeare.
Hmmmm, 9. Scalapino.
If a Man Die–. Moreland.
Is There a Voice (parody). Appleman.
Lady Franklin's Lament (II). *Anonymous.*
A Marriage Charm. Hopper.
A Martyr's Mass. Barrett.
The Nineteenth of April. Larcom.
Paradise Lost. Milton.
The Scarecrow. De la Mare.
Sent to a Lady, with a Seal. Lloyd.
Smiles. Schjeldahl.
A Song of Praise. Cullen.
Thomas Wolfe's Tombstone (excerpt). Wolfe.
To S. M. a Young African Painter, on Seeing His Work. Wheatley.
A Warm Winter Day. Cooper.
Where Shall the Baby's Dimple Be? Holland.
Seam (s)
The Cobbler. Chaffee.
The Cumberland. Longfellow.
The Dress of Spring. Justus.
The Long White Seam. Ingelow.
White Earth Reservation 1980. Vizenor.
Seaman
The Child and the Mariner. Davies.
Don Juan. Byron.
Forty Singing Seamen. Noyes.
Heaving the Lead. Pearce.
The Lovers of Marchaid. Pickthall.
The Old Sailor. Dresbach.
On the Capture of the Guerriere. Freneau.
Sea-Gulls. Holland.
A Seaman's Confession of Faith. Kemp.
Sonnet. Squire.
There Was an Indian. Squire.
The Wreck of the Royal Charter. *Anonymous.*
Search (ed) (ing)
The Asylum, II. Carruth.
Behind the Plough. Cousins.
Brother. Shelton.

Casida of the Rose. Garcia
Lorca.
The Dreadful Has Already
Happened. Strand.
Egg-and-Dart. Finch.
Farewell at the Hour of
Parting. Neto.
Found in a Storm. Stafford.
His Quest. Tooker.
Horizon without Landscape.
Lowenstein.
The India Guide.... Dallas.
Infants of Summer. Raphael.
Kind Sir: These Woods.
Sexton.
The Laundress. Kinsella.
A Lone Striker. Frost.
Loneliness. Werfel.
Pastoral. Creighton.
The Praying Mantis Visits a
Penthouse. Williams.
The Revelation. Williams.
The Snare. Stephens.
Song: "In the air there are no
coral-reefs or ambergris."
Scott.
St. James Infirmary.
Anonymous.
Stray Dog, near Ecully.
Avison.
To His Muse. Herrick.
To the Elephants. Alterman.
The Trenches. Manning.
Variations on a Time Theme.
Muir.
Wedlock. A Satire. Wright.
Wilderness Theme. Mudie.
The Window. Smith.
You. Clark.

Seashell
Lines. Meredith.
Parachute. Okita.

Seashore
Don Juan. Byron.
Luscious and Sorrowful.
Rossetti.

Seasick
For God While Sleeping.
Sexton.
Put Off Thy Bark from Shore,
Though Near the Night.
Tuckerman.

Season (s)
The Ancient Mansion.
Crabbe.
And Fall Shall Sit in
Judgment. Lorde.
Aristotle to Phyllis.
Hollander.
The Burden of Junk.
Glassco.
Canzone: To the Lady Pietra,
of Sienna. Dante Alighieri.
Celebrating the Mass of
Christian Burial. Mathis.
Counterparts. Dobyns.
The Couriers. Plath.
The Cross of Snow.
Longfellow.
A Fable for Critics. Lowell.
The Falling of the Leaves.
Yeats.
For Every Day. Havergal.
Good-Night to the Season.
Praed.
Guide to the Perplexed.
Malouf.
Hamlet. Shakespeare.
Harvest Time. Powers.
Hotel Sierra. St. John.
The House Beautiful.
Stevenson.

I Bring You News.
Anonymous.
In June and Gentle Oven.
Wilkinson.
The Lament of Saint Ann.
Anonymous.
Late at Night. Stafford.
Late Autumn. Sullivan.
The Lincolnshire Poacher.
Anonymous.
The Merchant of Venice.
Shakespeare.
My Grandfather's Funeral.
Applewhite.
On Laying up Treasure.
Hiers.
Pastoral. Raab.
Plowman. Keyes.
Poems: Birmingham
1962-1964. Fields.
The Prophet. Gibran.
Reluctance. Frost.
The Repeated Journey.
McGrath.
A Shining Night; or, Dick
Daring, the Poacher.
Anonymous.
The Shorebirds. Reid.
Song of the Seasons. Lofton.
The Sportsman. McCord.
Spring Sequence. Minty.
Thanksgiving at Snake Butte.
Welch.
To His Maid Prew. Herrick.
The Tray. Cole.
Triolet on a Dark Day.
Fishback.
Valediction to My
Contemporaries. Gregory.
Variations Done for Gerald
Van de Wiele. Olson.
Vigil of the Immaculate
Conception. Egan.
Wet Summer: Botanic
Gardens. McDonald.
Winter in Etienburgh.
Parker.
Wrap Me in Blankets of
Momentary Winds.
Littlebird.

Seat (ed) (s)
America Was Schoolmasters.
Coffin.
Angelo Orders His Dinner
(parody). Taylor.
Caelica, LXXXI. Greville.
Choose You a Seat 'n' Set
Down. *Anonymous.*
Daisy Bell (A Bicycle Built
for Two). Dacre.
Don Juan. Byron.
Heavens Bright Lamp, Shine
Forth Some of Thy Light.
Alsop.
Jubilate Agno. Smart.
Jubilation T. Cornpone.
Mercer.
Lost in a Corridor of Power.
Brownstein.
Mozart, 1935. Stevens.
On the Death of M. D'Ossoli
and His Wife, Margaret
Fuller. Landor.
Once upon a Nag.
McMahon.
Place-Names of China.
Bennett.
The Poem in the Park.
Davison.
Salute Your Partner.
Anonymous.
Te Deum. Reznikoff.

Thoughts on One's Head.
Meredith.

Seattle
Chrome Babies Eating
Chocolate Snowmen in the
Moonlight. Redwing.
The Harbor at Seattle. Hass.
The Late Snow and Lumber
Strike of the Summer of
Fifty-Four. Snyder.

Seaward
Earth-Canonized. Robinson.
Jake's Wharf. Booth.
Locksley Hall. Tennyson.
The Slow Pacific Swell.
Winters.

Seaweed
Doesn't he realize. Ono no
Komachi.
Extreme Unction in Pa.
Ray.
For the Wine of Circe.
Rossetti.
Here She Stands.
Rabearivelo.
The Skipper-Hermit. Rich.
The Vanity of Existence.
Freneau.
The Vow. Rakosi.

Second
Adam and Eve. Sisson.
An Autobiography. Bairam
at Tunisie.
Chamber Music. Ditsky.
Christ Climbed Down.
Ferlinghetti.
Clear Bright. Li Ch'ing-
chao.
Cousin Jack Song.
Tregonning.
Distich. Hay.
Emblem. Quarles.
The English Succession.
Anonymous.
In Festubert. Blunden.
In Memoriam A.H.H., XLV.
Tennyson.
The Knight's Ghost.
Anonymous.
Midweek. Miles.
My Garden. Davies.
One Almost Might.
Tessimond.
A Paragraph. Carruth.
Phenomenal Survivals of
Death in Nantucket.
Gluck.
A Poet's Proverbs.
Guiterman.
Rediscovery. Awoonor.
Requiem for "Bird" Parker.
Corso.
Robin Hood Newly Revived.
Anonymous.
The Second Mate. O'Brien.
Seventh Station. Claudel.
Sonnet: He Speaks of a Third
Love of His. Cavalcanti.
Sorrow. Santayana.
The Soup of Venus. Tate.
Spring Comes to Murray Hill.
Nash.
Strawberries. Hughes.
Swansong. Muske.
Woman's Ruling Passions.
Pope.

Seconds
The People's Choice: The
Dream Poems II. Jones.
The Punching Clock.
Macourek.

Rumplestiltskin Poems.
Hathaway.

Secret (s)
Air. Denby.
Amsterdam Street Scene,
1972. Rudnik.
At Last the Secret Is Out.
Auden.
The Ballad of Dreamland.
Swinburne.
Be Beautiful. Villa.
Bones in the Desert. White.
Caelica, XXXIII. Greville.
Canopic Jar. Lesser.
Cleaning the Well. Ruffin.
Concert at Sea. Creekmore.
Corn Canon. Stevenson.
Deer in the Bush. Bloch.
The Dragonfly. Rand.
Dream Songs. Berryman.
Dreams. Timrod.
Duality. Hardy.
Ego. MacCaig.
Elegy. Layzer.
Epitaph. Aleichem.
Epithalamium for Stella and
Violentilla: Why Do You
Dally So? Statius Publius
Papinius.
Fan. Lew.
A Fortune-Teller. Bynner.
A fuzzy fellow, without feet.
Dickinson.
The Goldfinches. Jago.
The Hour of Prayer. Hoy.
Hymn for St. John's Eve.
Anonymous.
I Held a Shelley Manuscript.
Corso.
I Saw Thee. Palmer.
If the Birds Knew. Ashbery.
In Terror of Hospital Bills.
Wright.
In the Bayou. Marquis.
The Jogger: Denver to Kansas
City. Ray.
Knowledge, Acquaintance.
Skelton.
A Land Not Mine.
Akhmatova.
The Lattice at Sunrise.
Turner.
The Lingam and the Yoni.
Hope.
Lock the Place in Your Heart.
Mandela.
Losers. Holden.
Love Sonnets. Cross.
Mask-Maker. Jackson.
Montgomery. Evans.
Moonlight. De la Mare.
Morning Song. Stokebury.
Mother Carey's Chicken.
Watts-Dunton.
Mountain Vigil. Fraser.
The Mud Turtle. Nemerov.
Music of Colours–White
Blossom. Watkins.
My Love Sways, Dancing.
Ibn Ezra.
Mythics. Chasin.
Names in Monterchi: To
Rachel. Wright.
Netley Abbey. Midnight.
Sotheby.
New Season. Levine.
O God, in Restless Living.
Fosdick.
October Hill. Hardy.
Of One Who Seemed to Have
Failed. Mitchell.

Once in an Ancient Book.
Zaturenska.
One for Sorrow, Two for Joy.
Anonymous.
An Open Secret. Mason.
The Other. Fainlight.
The Outer from the Inner.
Dickinson.
Passing It On. Saner.
Photographic Plate, Partly
Spidered, Hampton Roads,
Virginia... Smith.
Portrait of the Poet as
Landscape. Klein.
A Private. Thomas.
Psalm LXXIII. Surrey.
The Quick and the Dead.
Voronca.
The Red-Haired Man's Wife.
Stephens.
Riches. Blake.
Runes. Nemerov.
Sandy Star. Braithwaite.
Satire Septimus Contra
Sollistam. Rankins.
Second Avenue Winter.
Simic.
A Secret. *Anonymous.*
Secret Love. Clare.
The Secret Place of Prayer.
Adams.
Secrets. Fowler.
Sister Bernardo. Wilde.
Sloops in the Bay. Tate.
A Song of Degrees. Ker.
Song: "The little Black Rose
shall be red at last!" De
Vere.
Sonnet XV: "To honor the
return of sparkling sun."
Labe.
Speaking. Ryan.
The Stranger. De la Mare.
Sundays Visiting. Rios.
The Thinker. Williams.
Thou Shalt Not. Tussman.
To know thy bent and then
pursue. Wilcox.
To Modigliani to Prove to
Him That I Am a Poet.
Jacob.
To Nobodaddy. Blake.
Tourists. Muchemwa.
An Unseen Fire. Cooke.
La Vita Nuova. Dante
Alighieri.
What Is Good. O'Reilly.
When Geometric Diagrams...
"Novalis" (George
Friedrich Philipp von
Hardenerg).
When Winds Are Raging.
Stowe.
Where Children Live. Nye.
Yeats' Tower. Watkins.
Yosemite. Shinn.
Zohara. Hirschman.

Security
Contemplations. Bradstreet.
Death and the Plowman.
Keyes.
Epitaph: On the Favourite
Dog of a Politician.
Belloc.
A Free Nation. Markham.
Helen in Egypt: Thetis Is the
Moon-Goddess. Doolittle.
Invasion Song. *Anonymous.*
Just Beguiler. Campion.
The Man without a Road: X.
Lindegren.
Meditation. Pain.

My House. Bruce.
My Love behind Walls.
Spears.
Noah's Carpenters.
Anonymous.
Open the Gates. *Anonymous.*
Seduce (d)
The Naughty Lord & the Gay
Young Lady. *Anonymous.*
The Voice of Experience.
Goethe.
See (ing) (n) (s) (saw)
The Addict. Rubin.
Addio a la Mamma. Jitrik.
Air Raid. Wild.
All Our Griefs to Tell.
Newton.
The Altarpiece Finished.
Hollander.
America, America!
Schwartz.
American Heritage. Sward.
American History. Harper.
Amoretti, IX. Spenser.
Amoretti, XLV. Spenser.
Amoretti, LIII. Spenser.
The Apostasy. Traherne.
Aran Islands. Layton.
Astrophel and Stella, XVIII.
Sidney.
Ballata V: "Light do I see
within my Lady's eyes."
Cavalcanti.
The Bear Went over the
Mountain. *Anonymous.*
Beautiful Brown Eyes.
Anonymous.
The Beauty of the Ship.
Whitman.
The Beaver's Story. Watkins.
The Bee. Fandel.
Bunny. Fahy.
Cages. Solomon.
Car Wash. Livingston.
The Celestial City. Fletcher.
Chamber-Pot Rhyme.
Anonymous.
Chant-Pagan. Kipling.
The Children. Vinz.
The Chums. Roethke.
The Couple. Blandiana.
The Crooked Footpath.
Holmes.
Crossing the Bar. Tennyson.
The Cynneddf. Humphries.
Differences. Young Bear.
The Diggers. Merwin.
Dilemma. Parker.
Diver. Francis.
Diversions of the Re-Echo
Club. Wells.
The Djanggawul Cycle, 22.
Anonymous.
Do Not Minute. Beddoes.
Don Juan. Byron.
The Door to the Future.
Gallup.
Dream Songs. Berryman.
Easter Hymn. Housman.
Edith and Harold. Butler.
The English Retort.
Anonymous.
Epigram. Du Guillet.
Epigram: "A fool much bit by
fleas put out the light."
Lovelace.
The Epiphany. Strong.
Epitaph. *Anonymous.*
Epitaph for the Unknown
Soldier. Auden.
Europa. Thayer.
The Ex-Poet. Zavatsky.

Eyes and Tears. Marvell.
The Fairy Lough. O'Neill.
Falling down to bed.
NorthSun.
Farewell. Plato.
For Dan Berrigan. Knight.
For He Had Great
Possessions. Middleton.
For the Conjunction of Two
Planets. Rich.
The Gap in the Cedar.
Scheele.
A Garden by the Sea.
Morris.
Ghost Story. Thomas.
The Glass Door. Watson.
Glenfinlas; or, Lord Ronald's
Coronach. Scott.
Glenkindie. Scott.
The Grave. *Anonymous.*
Green. De la Mare.
The Gulistan. Sa'di.
The Hand That Held It.
Elmslie.
Hawthorn Dyke. Swinburne.
He Knows the Way.
Anonymous.
He Says He Wrote by
Moonlight. Aal.
He Sees Through Stone.
Knight.
Her Praises. Skoloker.
Hero and Leander.
Chapman.
Hide and Seek. Pagis.
The Higher Pantheism.
Tennyson.
Hogarth. Churchill.
Home Thoughts. Glover.
How Tuesday Began. Fraser.
I am furious with myself.
Tio.
I Heard a Fly Buzz–When I
Died. Dickinson.
I've seen a dying eye.
Dickinson.
I Will Go Away. Shargal.
"I Would," Says Fox, "A Tax
Devise." Sheridan.
Idylls of the King.
Tennyson.
"If Cynthia be a Queen..."
Ralegh.
Impossibilities, to His Friend.
Herrick.
In Freiburg Station. Brooke.
In Your Absence. Baxter.
Infirm. Martin.
Is It True? Williams.
The Islands. Jarrell.
It's Almost Done.
Anonymous.
John Smith Is My Name.
Anonymous.
King Henry VIII.
Shakespeare.
The King of the
Hobbledygoblins.
Richards.
The Lace Curtains.
MacAdams.
Lady Alice (B version).
Anonymous.
The Lady Who Offers Her
Looking Glass. Prior.
Lais to Aphrodite.
Robinson.
Lamentation on the Death of
the Duke of Wellington.
Anonymous.
Langley Lane. Buchanan.
Lantern. Soto.

Little Snail. Conkling.
The Lord of All. Markham.
The Lost History Plays:
Savanarola (parody).
Beerbohm.
Love Lies Sleeping. Bishop.
Love-Songs, At Once Tender
and Informative.
Hoffenstein.
The Lowest Trees Have Tops.
Dyer.
LXX. Berrigan.
Magnificat in Transit from the
Toledo Airport. Starbuck.
Make Me Hear You.
Gibbons.
The Man Hidden behind the
Drapes. Rogers.
Marx, the Sign Painter.
Masters.
Mary Ames. *Anonymous.*
Midsummer Night. Edey.
Miracles. Aiken.
Moon Mattress. Di Prima.
Moonlight. Longfellow.
Mr 'Gater. Bodecker.
Musgrove. *Anonymous.*
My Father's Watch. Ciardi.
My Home's across the
Smokey Mountains.
Anonymous.
My Son Doesn't See a Thing.
Rivera.
The Nettles. Hardy.
News of the palace. Ise.
No Escape. Delafield.
Of purpose love chose first for
to be blind. Wyatt.
The Old Songs. Seaman.
On a Proud Fellow.
Anonymous.
On Noman, a Guest. Belloc.
On the Death of Emperor
Tenji. *Anonymous.*
One Morning in May.
Anonymous.
Orinda to Lucasia Parting,
October, 1661, at London.
Philips.
The Others Hunters in the
North The Cree.
Rothenberg.
Out of That Sea. Ferry.
The Owl and the Jay Bush.
Anonymous.
Passage. Eberhart.
Paterson. Williams.
Peace. Hughes.
Petition. Drinkwater.
Philippine Madonna. Ray.
Philosophy Is Born.
Morgenstern.
The Poet's Welcome to His
Illegitimate Child. Burns.
Porson on His Majesty's
Government. Porson.
Potomac Town in February.
Sandburg.
Pray On! *Anonymous.*
The Princess Who Fled to the
Castle. Landy.
Private Worship. Van
Doren.
Psalm XVII. Sidney.
The Purple Cow. Burgess.
Radar. Ross.
The Ragged Robin Opens.
Radnoti.
Rains for the Harvest.
Anonymous.
The Rat. Davies.

Recollections of the Arabian Nights. Tennyson.
Remainder. Blankner.
The Reversible Metaphor. "Troubadour".
The Right of Way. Williams.
Ritratto. Pound.
The Sabbath Day Was By. Robbins.
The Sea. Noyle.
Seeing St. James's. Mathew.
The Shadow Dance. Moulton.
She Is My Dear. Anonymous.
The Shepherd's House. Vigny.
Shorty George. Anonymous.
Silvia. Etherege.
Similia Similibus. Morgan.
The Sleep of Spring. Clare.
Some Refrains at the Charles River. Viereck.
Some Ruthless Rhymes. Graham.
Some There Are Who Say That the Fairest Thing Seen. Sappho.
Song. Philips.
Song of the Leadville Mine Boss. Cameron.
Song: Paper. Waldrop.
Song To Celia. Jonson.
Sonnet: "This infant world has taken long to make." Macdonald.
Sonnet: To Homer. Keats.
Sonnets, XVIII: "Shall I compare thee to a summer's day?" Shakespeare.
Sonnets, XXIV: "Mine eye hath play'd the painter, and hath steel'd. Shakespeare.
Soul's Liberty. Wickham.
The Southern Cross. Hawker.
Spider. Lattimore.
The Spider and the Ghost of the Fly. Lindsay.
Spooks. Crane.
The Star. Taylor.
A Star There Fell. Schneour.
The Statue. Fuller.
The Story of the Shepherd. Anonymous.
The Strong Are Saying Nothing. Frost.
Such Soft Ideas All My Pains Beguile. Montagu.
Sunday Morning. Fitzgerald.
Switzerland. Arnold.
Tango. Jordana.
The Task. Cowper.
Thanksgiving. Coates.
Theory of Vision: The Green Eye. Merrill.
There Lived a Lady in Milan. Benet.
A Thing Remembered. Anonymous.
Three Cezannes. Whipple.
Through These Pale Cold Days. Rosenberg.
Time of fish dying. Melinescu.
The Tint I Cannot Take Is Best. Dickinson.
To a Mouse. Burns.
To Be in Love. Brooks.

To His Forsaken Mistress. Ayton [(or Aytoun)] Sir Robert.
To Lucasta, from Prison. Lovelace.
To Miss B. Clare.
To the Man Who Watches Spiders. Fox.
To the Memory of Ben Johnson (excerpt). Mayne.
The Torch. Forker.
The Truth about My Sister and Me. Probst.
Try (parody). Appleman.
Two Sonnets for a Lost Love. DeWitt.
The Unknown God. Russell.
Upon Being Awakened at Night by My Four Year Old Daughter. Rainer.
Visions. Petrarch.
The Visitor. Bogin.
The Watchman. Reisen.
We Are Standing Facing Each Other. Atwood.
We Need a King. Macdougall.
What Is That in Thine Hand? Gray.
What We See Is What We Think. Stevens.
When I Awoke. Patterson.
When Shall We See Thy Like Again? Wingate.
Where? Tessimond.
The White Peacock. Mills.
Why Do I Hate That Lone Green Dell? Bronte.
Winter's End. Moss.
Winter Twilight. Lipsitz.
The Witch o' Fife. Hogg.
The Witch of Atlas. Shelley.
Woman. Loftin.
Ye Walls! Sole Witnesses of Happy Sighs. Landor.
You Ask Me, Why, Tho' Ill at Ease. Tennyson.
Zalka Peetruza. Dandridge.

Seed (ed) (ing) (s)
Aftermath. Longfellow.
The Anxious Farmer. Johnson.
Aunt Jane Allen. Johnson.
Benediction. Turbyfill.
A Child's Thought of Harvest. "Coolidge.
Deserted Buildings under Shefford Mountain. Glassco.
Diving for Pearls. Yamamoto.
Emily's Haunted Housman (parody). Cummings.
Epitaph for the Tomb of Adolfo Baez Bone. Cardenal.
Fall To. Jones.
Fragment: "The wing'd seeds with decaying wings." Allingham.
The Garden of Shadow. Dowson.
God of the Strong, God of the Weak. Gilder.
A Hard Frost. Day Lewis.
Hearts and Flowers. Brine.
The Holy Spirit. Underhill.
The Husbandman. Taylor.
In the Surgery. Ditta.
Influence. Oxenham.
Joseph, Jesus and Mary. Anonymous.

The Lunar Games. Manner.
Nam Semen Est Verbum Dei. Guiney.
Of Love. Wyatt.
Open. Bruchac.
The Patient Church. Newman.
The Point, the Line, the Surface and Sphere. Bragdon.
The Pruned Tree. Moss.
Psalm XVIII. Sidney.
The Psalm of St. Priapus. Broughton.
Puberty. Wallace.
A Quilled Quilt, a Needle Bed. Leithauser.
The Road. Muir.
The Roots of Revolution in the Vegetable Kingdom. Urdang.
Seed Journey. Corso.
She. Winkler.
Silence. Orr.
Silkweed. Savage.
Song of a Factory Girl. Zaturenska.
The Song of the Old Mother. Yeats.
The Sower. Cowper.
Spell of Creation. Raine.
Starlings. Jensen.
Tansy for August. Enslin.
Three Barrows Down. Brooke.
To the Faithful. Ana.
To the Father of the Bride. Tasso.
To the Mothers. Toller.
To the Queen of Dolors. Maura.
Upon Wedlock, and Death of Children. Taylor.
Vernal Paradox. Kurt.
The Wanton Seed. Anonymous.

Seek (ers) (ing) (s)
Amoretti, LXXVIII. Spenser.
Azrael. Longfellow.
Bird Shadows Mounting. Eigner.
The Blind. Baudelaire.
Childhood Fled. Lamb.
The Conversational Reformer. Graham.
Differences. Young Bear.
Early One Morning. Anonymous.
Eldorado. Poe.
Emblem. Quarles.
Epigram: "I delight in the prime of a boy of twelve." Strato.
Fisherman's Luck. Gibson.
The Flying Fish. Gray.
Goats. Wood.
Home. Sepamla.
The Hooded Crow. McOwan.
How Far? Miller.
I Shall Forget You Presently, My Dear. Millay.
Ideal Beauty. Herrera.
In the Stable. Goudge.
In the Third Year of War. Treece.
The martyr poets–did not tell–. Dickinson.
Mimma Bella. Lee-Hamilton.
The Mirror. Rossetti.

New England's Growth. Bradford.
The New Man. Very.
Old Walt. Hughes.
On Philosophers. Anonymous.
Paradise Regained. Milton.
The Peak. Gibson.
A Poet's Wish: An Ode. Ramsay.
Pompey and Cornelia. Rowe.
The Quest. Vinal.
Sensuality. Patmore.
She Wandered after Strange Gods... Benet.
The Shiver. Hardy.
Snails. Blodgett.
Some Things You Cannot Will to Men. Isenhour.
The Song of the Forest Ranger. Bashford.
Squall. Moore.
Sunset. Bialik.
The Task. Cowper.
Throwing the Racetrack Cats at Saratoga. Ray.
Understanding. Soroka.
The Unerring Guide. Shipton.
The Untold Want. Whitman.
With Hands Like Leaves. Still.
World Planners. Steece.
The World's Illusion. Ibn Ezra.

Self (selves)
Africa. Alexander.
After Nightfall. Renton.
Against Dark's Harm. Halley.
Aleph. Perkoff.
Amoretti, XLV. Spenser.
Amoretti, LXXVIII. Spenser.
Amours de Voyage. Clough.
Argent Solipsism. Blake.
Artist and Ape. Link.
Astrophel and Stella, CIII. Sidney.
At 21. Belisle.
Autumn Song. Stepanchev.
Babylon. Sassoon.
Before the Statue of a Laughing Man. Bowie.
Beneath the Shadow of the Cross. Longfellow.
Boat Poem. Spencer.
Bussy d'Ambois. Chapman.
Christ Alone. Monod.
The Dance. Jones.
Deaf School. Hughes.
Down from the Country. Blight.
Elements. Link.
The End of It. Thompson.
Epitaph for George Moore. Hardy.
An Essay on Man. Pope.
Family Plot. Singer.
A Fantasy of Little Waters. Scully.
Fine! Barker.
First Day of Teaching. Overstreet.
For A' That and A' That (parody). Anonymous.
The Forgiven Past. Riding.
The Greater Trial. Winchilsea.
I am the sorrow in the wheat fields. Bass.

In the Holy Nativity of Our Lord God. Crashaw.

The Just Vengeance (excerpt). Sayers.

Love Enthroned. Lovelace.

Love's Apparition and Evanishment. Coleridge.

The Loyal General: Prologue. Dryden.

Malediction. Spacks.

The Merry Window. Scarfe.

Murder in the Cathedral. Eliot.

Myself. Guest.

None of Self and All of Thee. Monod.

Now That I Am Forever with Child. Lorde.

An Ode in the Praise of Sack. Anonymous.

Oh, If They Only Knew! Mapes.

The Ongoing Story. Ashbery.

The People's Choice: The Dream Poems II. Jones.

The Poet Haunted. Rose.

Poetics. Ammons.

A Prayer for the Self. Berryman.

Prothalamion. Schwartz.

Pythagoras. Jones, Jr.

A Queen Wasp. De La Mare.

Resurrection: Fragments. Mnthali.

Roses on the Breakfast Table. Lawrence.

Self-Projection. Ammons.

The Sickness of Friends. Coulette.

The Solitary. Teasdale.

Some Twenty Years of Marital Agreement. Cunningham.

Sonnets, VI: "Then let not winter's ragged hand deface." Shakespeare.

Things. De la Mare.

Thoughts for My Grandmother. Firestone.

The Tourists. Day-Lewis.

The Triumph of Chastity. Howes.

Valediction. Heaney.

Verses under a Peacock Portrayed in Her Left Hand. Greene.

A Vulgar Error. Thorold Rogers.

When West Comes East. Ford.

You Growing. Acorn.

Selfish (ness)

Catalogue. Untermeyer.

Charity. Lathrop.

The English Queen. Lawson.

I Would Not Ask. Troy.

The New-Come Chief. Lowell.

On Being Head of the English Department. Lane.

Sell (ing) (s) (sold)

Advice to a Painter. Anonymous.

Are You Glad. Anonymous.

Banbury Fair. Anonymous.

Buying a Record (parody). Peters.

Charcoal Man. Anonymous.

Christus Matthaeum et Discipulos Alloquitur. Sherburne.

Emblem. Quarles.

Fish Crier. Sandburg.

Fish Riddle: "Although it's cold no clothes I wear." Anonymous.

For the Market. Mayhall.

Geordie. Anonymous.

If I had as much money as I could/spend. Mother Goose.

The Inheritance. Ignatow.

Jonathan to John. Lowell.

Kentucky Bootlegger. Anonymous.

Key West. Crane.

The Lady in the Pink Mustang. Erdrich.

Landscapes. Hugo.

Letter to the City Clerk. Wright.

Love Poem Investigation for A.T. Frate.

Lydia Pinkham (with music). Anonymous.

Mr. Tom Narrow. Reeves.

My Stars. Ibn Ezra.

Not Her, She Aint No Gypsy. Young.

The Patriot Game. Anonymous.

Skin Man. Brown.

Sonnets, XXI: "So is it not with me as with that Muse." Shakespeare.

The Starred Mother. Whitaker.

Such a Parcel of Rogues in a Nation. Burns.

The Tale of the Dixie-Belle. Chase.

Tears for Sale. Speyer.

Three Jolly Fishermen. Anonymous.

Tie Your Tongue, Sir? Smith.

The Toy Lamb Seller. Anonymous.

Varick Street. Bishop.

The Word Man. Moffi.

Writing for Money. Field.

Semblance

At the Zoo. De La Mare.

Duck in Central Park. Savage.

The Hand of Lincoln. Stedman.

Shadows of His Lady. Tahureau.

Senate

The French Revolution. Blake.

A Veld Eclogue: The Pioneers. Campbell.

Senator (s)

A Man Named Hods. Anonymous.

Remembering That Island. McGrath.

Remonstrance. Philodemos of Gadara.

Send (sent)

The Author to Her Book. Bradstreet.

Autumn Even. Andriello.

By Return Mail. Aldridge.

Coast to Coast. Rich.

The Conspiracy. Creeley.

The Fabulous Teamsters. Sherwin.

Form Rejection Letter. Dacey.

From Heaven High I Come to You. Luther.

Idea. Drayton.

Jehovah-Rophi. Cowper.

A Kiss. Anonymous.

Letter to the Front. Rukeyser.

Limerick: "A maiden caught stealing a dahlia." Anonymous.

Little Maid, Pretty Maid. Anonymous.

Love-Letter One. Anonymous.

The Maids Conjuring Book. Anonymous.

Money in the Bank. Ehrhart.

Noah's Song. Jones.

Paradise Regained. Milton.

Portrait of a Married Couple. Scott.

Rattan bed, paper netting. Li Ch'ing-chao.

Saved, but–. Anonymous.

Something You Can Do. Anonymous.

A Thought of Marigolds. Farrar.

Traditional Funeral Songs. Anonymous.

The True Confession of George Barker. Barker.

The Tupelo Destruction. Anonymous.

A Wartime Exchange: Letter to an American Visitor. Comfort.

When Heaven Would Strive to Do the Best She Can. Drayton.

Sensation (s)

Light in the Open Air. Dillard.

On the Disadvantages of Central Heating. Clampitt.

The Raspberry in the Pudding. O'Connor.

Trumpet and Flute. Hernaes.

Sense (s)

Aphorisms. "Novalis" (George Friedrich Philipp von Hardenerg).

A Beautiful Night. Beddoes.

Because of Clothes. Riding.

The Business Life. Ignatow.

Caelica, LV. Greville.

Caelica, LXXIX. Greville.

A Channel Passage. Swinburne.

The Child's Sight. Sobiloff.

Correspondences. Baudelaire.

Dante's Angels: The Angels of Protection. Dante Alighieri.

Epistle to a Lady: Of the Characters of Women. Pope.

Erotica. Farkas.

An Essay on Criticism. Pope.

The Ethnic Life. Halpern.

Even as the Others Mock. Dante Alighieri.

An Excellent New Ballad Giving a True Account of the Birth... Sackville.

Extreme Unction. Dowson.

The Face. Wade.

The Far Side of Introspection. Lee.

Fata Morgana. Brenner.

For An Allegorical Dance of Women by Andrea Mantegna. Rossetti.

For My Contemporaries. Cunningham.

Go Bring Me Back My Blue-Eyed Boy (with music). Anonymous.

Goodbye. Akhmadulina.

Green. Verlaine.

The Hind and the Panther. Dryden.

The House of Life. Rossetti.

A Hymn of Touch. Bottomley.

I don't sleep. Mira Bai [(or Mirabai)].

In Me Two Worlds. Day Lewis.

In Wonted Walks. Sidney.

Limerick: "Wrote the clergy: "Our Dear Madame Prynne:". Fogle.

Loss. Aldington.

Love Redeemed. Baylebridge.

A Man of Sense. Eberhart.

The Man with the Blue Guitar. Stevens.

The Marriage of Heaven and Hell. Blake.

O Sons of Earth. Pope.

October Poems: The Garden. Warren.

On Tobacco. Cotton.

A Pastoral Ballad. By John Bull. Moore.

Peter Bell, the Third. Shelley.

Prefatory Sonnet. Kendall.

The Prophecy of Famine. Churchill.

Psycholophon. Burgess.

The Quarrelsome Trio. G.

Recognition. Chadwick.

Reward of Service. Browning.

The Rise of Shivaji. Ghose.

The Song of the Borderguard. Duncan.

Sonnet: To Dante Alighieri (On the Last Sonnet of the Vita Nuova). Angiolieri.

A Sonnet to Opium; Celebrating Its Virtues. "Orestes".

Spiritual Isolation. Rosenberg.

Upon an Ingenious Friend, Over-Vain. Fitzgerald.

A Venetian Night. Hofmannsthal.

Wake. Hughes.

The Walk. Hardy.

Wildfire. Toth.

Yankee Poet. Wilson, Jr.

You, Neighbor God. Rilke.

Senseless

Caelica, XLVI. Greville.

Delusions VI. Madge.

Of This World's Theater in Which We Stay. Spenser.

To Pikes Peak. Hills.

Youth! Thou Wear'st to Manhood Now. Scott.

Sensual

Afternoon at Cannes. Davis.

Afterwards, They Shall Dance. Kaufman.
The Deepest Sensuality. Lawrence.
A Lesson in Hammocks. Schevill.
My Winter Past. Grier.
The Nude on the Bathroom Wall. Ford.
On the Street. Cavafy.
Return. Montague.

Sentence
The Emergency Room. Fisher.
Exile. Stroud.
On the Farm. Thomas.
The Prisoner. Bronte.
Soldiers. Bodenheim.
Two Old Men Look at the Sea. Hervey.
When I Hear Your Name. Fuertes.

Separate (d) (ly) (ness)
Chinese Poems: Arthur Waley. Fair.
The Continuing City. Housman.
Deaf School. Hughes.
God of Mercy. Molodovsky.
The Harvesters. Gilmore.
Hymn. Ammons.
Islands. Rukeyser.
Marriage. Sklarew.
No Less Than Prisoners. Macartney.
Novella. Rich.
The Rights of Women. Barbauld.
The Seasons. Kalidasa.
The Songs of Bilitis. Louys.
Summer Island. Logan.
To His Dear Friend, Bones. Parini.
Villanelle. Hacker.
Young Girl: Annam. Colum.

Separation
Prayer. Mak.
To My Wife. Forsyth.
Written in Exile. Raine.
You came. And you did well to come. Sappho.

September
Biftek aux Champignons. Beers.
I Wish. Turner.
Sunday Evening. Guest.
When All of Tem Ran Off. Hollander.

Sepulcher (s)
Absence. Knies.
The Blindness of Samson. Milton.
The Devil's Dictionary: Orthography. Bierce.
Funeral Toast. Mallarme.
How Much Longer Will I Be Able to Inhabit the Divine Sepulcher... Ashbery.
If a Man Die–. Moreland.
Linota Rufescens. Donaghy.
Little Viennese Waltz. Garcia Lorca.
Meditations on the Sepulchre in the Garden. Doddridge.
Obituary. "Adeler."

Sequel
The Second Volume. Bell.

Sequence
Beads from Blackpool. Ridler.

Sequestered
In Memory of W. B. Yeats. Auden.

Seraphim
At the Grave of Burns. Wordsworth.
The Solemn Noon of Night. Warton, Jr..
Song: "Three little maidens they have slain." Maeterlinck.

Serenade
Hello. Corso.
O'Connor the Bad Traveler. Klappert.
Soul's Kiss. Greenberg.

Serene
The Borough. Crabbe.
Gray Days. Lawlor.
Let Me Speak of Pure Things. Ho Chih-Fang.
The Light of Stars. Furness.
Lines Addressed to a Seagull. Griffin.
News of the World. Ridler.
Off Womanheid Ane Flour Delice. Anonymous.
The Old Mountaineer. Holmes.
Orpheus and Eurydice. Hill.
Pastoral Song for the Nuptials of Charles, Duke of Lorraine... de Ronsard.
The Refugees. Read.
Solace. Delany.
Woof of the Sun, Ethereal Gauze. Thoreau.
The Year's End. Cole.
Years. Anderson.

Serious
Aurora Leigh. Browning.
Clerihew. Bentley.
Conversation Galante. Eliot.
Houses Burning: Quebec. Anderson.
Letter from an Island. Brinnin.
Signals. Waldrop.
Song (October 1969). Fraser.
The Spanish Friar. Dryden.
Why Mira Can't Go Back to Her Old House. Mira Bai [(or Mirabai)].

Sermon (s)
The Bible Is an Antique Volume. Dickinson.
Clonfeacle. Muldoon.
Memorandum for Minos. Kell.
Mozart. Glatstein.

Serpent (s)
A Bad Break. Goodge.
Black Marble. O'Shaughnessy.
The Book of Kells. Nemerov.
Bucket of Sea-Serpents. Ant.
The Cultural Presuppostion. Auden.
The Dark and the Fair. Kunitz.
The Elder Edda: The Beginning and the End (abridged). Anonymous.
Epigram: "A golden casket I designed." Drennan.
The Everlasting Gospel. Blake.
Family. MacCaig.
For the Holy Family by Michelangelo. Rossetti.

Goodbye to Serpents. Dickey.
In a Garden. Babcock.
In Memory of My Feelings. O'Hara.
A Lesson from Van Gogh. Moss.
O Crimson Blood. Hildegard von Bingen.
On Falling Asleep by Firelight. Meredith.
On the Snake. Anonymous.
Penetration and Trust. Meredith.
Prayer for Peace: II. Senghor.
Quatrina. Bennett.
Returning, We Hear the Larks. Rosenberg.
A Shropshire Lad. Housman.
The St. Lawrence and the Saguenay. Sangster.
Thanks, Gentle Moon, for Thy Obscured Light. Anonymous.
War Cry: To Mary. Leo XIII.
The Woman with the Serpent's Tongue. Watson.

Servant (s)
Abdelfatteh. Lacey.
Alone. Witheford.
Are We Not the People. Ibn Adiya.
Bani. Dadu.
The Battle of Harlaw (B version). Anonymous.
The Curse. Synge.
Domine Exaudi. Wyatt.
Doris: A Pastoral. Munby.
Elinda's Glove. Lovelace.
Epitaphs of the War. Kipling.
Eternity's Speech against Time. Greville.
How Many New Years Have Grown Old. Anonymous.
I Am So Far from Pitying Thee. Anonymous.
In Hoc Signo. Bradby.
Invitation. Ibn Gabirol.
A Letter to Sir Robert Walpole. Fielding.
Man. Herbert.
The Master. Robbins.
Now the Laborer's Task Is O'er. Ellerton.
Nunc Viridant Segetes. Sedulius Scottus.
O King, I Know You Gave Me Poison. Mira Bai [(or Mirabai)].
Ode for a Social Meeting (With Slight Alterations by a Teetotaler). Holmes.
Paradise Lost. Milton.
A Paraphrase on Thomas a Kempis. Pope.
The Pearl. Anonymous.
Pet Crane. Anonymous.
A Prayer. Dolben.
Psalm. Heimler.
The Resolve. Brome.
The Skeleton in the Cupboard. Locker-Lampson.
A Song for Simeon. Eliot.
The Soul Longs to Return Whence It Came. Eberhart.
Think. Weekes.
The Three Woes. De Vere.

To My More Than Meritorious Wife. Rochester.
Uppon the First Sight of New-England June 29, 1638. Tillam.

Serve (d) (s)
Be Just (Domestick Monarchs) unto Them. Alsop.
Be Thou Then by Beauty Named. Campion.
Business Is Business. Braley.
Canticle of the Sun. Francis of Assisi.
Daily I Fall in Love with Waitresses. Fried.
A Dish for a Poet. Anonymous.
Double Monologue. Rich.
A Driver's Prayer. Anonymous.
Epitaphs of the War, 1914-18. Kipling.
Father, Teach Me. Lee.
The Grandiloquent Goat. Wells.
He Doeth All Things Well. Bronte.
Her Face Her Tongue Her Wit. Gorges.
The Holy Earth: In the Immense Cathedral. Wheelock.
I Serve a Mistress. Munday.
The Last Instructions to a Painter. Marvell.
The Linen Weaver. Anonymous.
Man of Derby. Anonymous.
The Midnight Tennis Match. Lux.
The Muses. Thomas.
The Nut-Brown Maid. Anonymous.
O, That I Had Some Secret Place. Anonymous.
Of Mistress D.S. Googe.
One Year to Live. Reed.
The Parting of the Ways. Gilder.
A Poem for Heroes. Fields.
Praise for Mercies Spiritual and Temporal. Watts.
Put Forth, O God, Thy Spirit's Might. Robbins.
Reward of Service. Browning.
The Road. Sassoon.
The Sentiments. Anonymous.
Serve in Thy Post. Clough.
Shore Birds. Gale.
Since Love Will Needs That I Shall Love. Wyatt.
Sonnet on His Blindness. Milton.
Suffering in sorrow in hope to attain. Wyatt.
"Sweet are the thoughts where hope persuadeth hap." Ralegh.
To Lucasta, from Prison. Lovelace.
To the Unknown God. Nietzsche.
Ur Burial. Eberhart.

Service (d) (s)
The Blessed Task. Kimball.
Cruel You Be. Puttenham.
Expectans Expectavi. Sorley.
From the Triads of Ireland. Anonymous.

Grace at Evening. Guest.
Hottest Brand Goin'. Smoky Babe.
In Christ. Oxenham.
In Cipres Springes (Wheras Dame Venus Dwelt). Surrey.
In Parenthesis. Jones.
Last Poem. Donnelly.
A Little Rhyme and a Little Reason. Anstadt.
Lord of All Pots and Pans and Things. Hallack.
The Mariner's Song. Davies.
A Mistress without Compare. Orleans.
Musicians wrestle everywhere. Dickinson.
The Parliament of Bees. Day.
The Perfect Gift. Parker.
The Poet: A Rhapsody. Akenside.
Reward of Service. Browning.
Sonnet: "To rail or jest, ye know I use it not." Wyatt.
You Will Find a Joy in Service. Stroud.

Servile
Deep Down the Blackman's Mind. Armattoe.
For the Union Dead. Lowell.
The Market-Square's Admiring Throngs. Goethe.
Savonarola. Bentley.
Sticheron for Matins, Wednesday of Holy Week. Kassia.
We Thank Thee, Lord. Laufer.

Setting
Day: A Pastoral. Cunningham.
Eclogue. Drayton.
How Well for the Birds. Anonymous.
The King's Men. Heyen.
Man's Going Hence. Rogers.
The Objects of the Summer Scene. Irwin.
The Sin of Omission. Sangster.
Spring Waters (excerpt). Wolcot.
Thermopylae. Hillyer.
When All Is Done. Dunbar.

Settle (d) (ment)
Astronaut's Choice. Darcy.
Binding Arbitration. Wrigley.
Domicilium. Hardy.
Fair Sylvia. Anonymous.
The Gathering on the Plains. Butler.
An Inspiration. Wilcox.
Milkcow's Calf Blues. Johnson.
Nothing in Rambling. Minnie.
Plans for Altering the River. Hugo.
Putting on My Shoes I Hear the Floor Cry out beneath Me (parody). Heffernan.
Riot. Brooks.
A Rub. Tabb.
The Tin Woodsman. Jiles.
Tittery-Irie-Aye. Anonymous.

Seven (th)
The Angels Came A-Mustering. Zangwill.
The Art of Cookery. King.
Black Pony Eating Grass. Bly.
Blackfriars. Farjeon.
The Book of Merlin. Spicer.
Burbank with a Baedeker: Bleistein with a Cigar. Eliot.
Cape Coloured Batman. Butler.
The Celebration. Mezey.
Le Chariot. Wieners.
A Child's Laughter. Swinburne.
Colin Clout. Skelton.
The Dancing Bear. Southey.
Devotional Incitements. Wordsworth.
The Dole of the King's Daughter. Anonymous.
Duty. Markham.
Ever Since. Coatsworth.
Father Grumble. Anonymous.
The Flowers. Kipling.
"For Whom the Bell Tolls". Ewart.
Into the Salient. Blunden.
Lessons of the War. Reed.
Limerick: "There was a young fellow from Fife." Ybarra.
My Atlas Poet. Bowering.
The Mystic. Bynner.
New York. Senghor.
Oh, the Funniest Thing... Anonymous.
Old Man in the Wood. Anonymous.
The Old Man Who Lived in the Woods. Anonymous.
Old-Time Service. Churchyard.
One Winter Night in August. Kennedy.
Rites of the Eastern Star. Pommy-Vega.
Sabbath, My Love. Halevi.
Seven Years. Crewe.
Seven Years Old. Swinburne.
Sing, Woods and Rivers All. Claudian.
Song to Beta. Drayton.
St. Gervais. Roberts.
To Find the Dominical Letter. Anonymous.
To New York. Senghor.
We Are Seven. Wordsworth.
Which Shall It Be? Beers.
Why I Didn't Go to Delphi. Welch.

Seventeen
L'Eau Dormante. Aldrich.
For Stephen. Brookhouse.
Her Dancing Days. Adams.

Seventy (ies)
Confidential. Scott.
Hookerlumps in the Love Canal. Sylvester.
Little Billee. Thackeray.
A Proposal for Recycling Wastes. Piercy.
The Sorcerer: Mr. Wells. Gilbert.
The Wasp's Frolic. Anonymous.
When the Ambulance Came. Morgan.

Sever (ed) (s)
Fish in River. Anonymous.

In Death Divided. Hardy.
Love-Songs, At Once Tender and Informative. Hoffenstein.
Modern Love, I. Meredith.
Perhaps It's Only Music. Zach.
The Submarine Bed. Bishop.
Sweetness. Anonymous.
To the Earl of Warwick. Tickell.

Sew (ed) (ing) (s)
Beyond Wars. Morrow.
The Bison. Belloc.
Goodbye. Lewis.
I Came A-Riding. Reinmar von Zweter.
I Sit and Sew. Nelson.
The Long White Seam. Ingelow.
Old Ben Golliday. Van Doren.
The Tapestry. Nemerov.
That Day. Kherdian.
Ulysses Returns. Montgomery.

Sex
The American Dream. Scott.
A Fairy Tale. Thompson.
Games, Hard Press and Bruise of the Flesh. Vliet.
History of Ideas. Cunningham.
An Indian Mother about to Destroy Her Child. Montgomery.
The Judgement of Tiresias. Jacob.
Near the Death of Ovid. Conquest.
Pernicious Weed. Cowper.
Polar Exploration. Spender.
The Rosciad. Churchill.
The School Hockey Team in Amsterdam. Ormsby.
Some Twenty Years of Marital Agreement. Cunningham.
Too Young for Love. Horace.
Without the Moon. Laforgue.
Women. Cartwright.

Shabby
Broken Heart, Broken Machine. Grant.

Shack (s)
A Dream of Women. Maisel.
Horatian Variation. Bacon.
Negro Dreams. Long.

Shade (s)
The Afternoon of a Faun: Eclogue. Mallarme.
All through the Rains. Snyder.
The Animal Runs, It Passes, It Dies. Anonymous.
The Apple. Smith.
Approach of Evening. Croly.
Aria. Humphries.
At a Summer Hotel. Gardner.
August Night. Swenson.
The Ballad of New Orleans. Broker.
Behind the Line. Blunden.
A Bird Comes. Yosano Akiko.
Casualty. Witherby.
Charlotte Corday. Tomlinson.

Cleitagoras. Leonidas.
Clifton Grove (excerpt). White.
Color Blind. Paine.
Composed Upon an Evening of Extraordinary Splendour and Beauty. Wordsworth.
The Crackling Twig. Stephens.
Cuchullain's Lament over Fardiad. Anonymous.
Dangers of the Journey to the Happy Land. Ceravolo.
Defiance. Landor.
Do Not Accompany Me. Halkin.
The Dog in the River. Phaedrus.
The Dream of Dakiki. Firdausi.
The Dying Stockman. Anonymous.
Elver Fishers. Gurney.
Endymion. Keats.
The Faerie Queene. Spenser.
Gabriel Meets Satan. Milton.
Gathered at the River. Levertov.
Graceful Acacia. Landor.
Hawk and Snake. Silko.
Her Shadow. Pullen.
Horror. Treece.
The Horses of Marini. Van Zyl.
A Hymne to Our Saviour on the Cross. Chapman.
In the Shade of the Old Apple Tree. Williams.
Indolence. Watkins.
The Introduction. Winchilsea.
Italian Rhapsody. Johnson.
Kunai-Mai-Pa Mo. Anderson.
Light at Equinox. Adams.
Locus. Hayden.
Looking Back (excerpt). Vaughan.
Lost in Translation. Merrill.
The Lost Parasol (excerpt). Weores.
MacFlecknoe. Dryden.
A Meeting of Cultures. Davie.
Memory. Stagnelius.
Le Monocle de Mon Oncle. Stevens.
A Moth. Baildon.
The Murderer. Petrie.
My Ox Duke. Dyer.
Ode for Music on St. Cecilia's Day. Pope.
Ode: To the Nightingale. Warton.
An Old Woman Laments in Spring-Time. Sitwell.
On Liberty and Slavery. Horton.
On Man. Landor.
On My Late Dear Wife. Richardson.
On Myselfe. Winchilsea.
On the Extinction of the Venetian Republic. Wordsworth.
Orion. Horne.
Palinode. Gogarty.
Pericles and Aspasia. Landor.
A Poem for Max Nordau. Robinson.
Polyolbion. Drayton.

Reapers. Toomer.
Report from the Correspondent They Fired. McElroy.
The Rising Village. Goldsmith.
San Sabas. Palés Matos.
Second Shadow. Roethke.
She Attempts to Refute the Praises That Truth... Juana Ines de la Cruz.
The Siesta. *Anonymous.*
The Sigh of Silence. Keats.
Sis Joe. *Anonymous.*
Slain. Crosland.
Snowfall. Carducci.
A Solitary Life. Drummond.
Song: "Poppies paramour the girls." Long.
Song: "When Love at first did move." Jonson.
The Spirit of the Cairngorms. Firsoff.
Still Life. Outlaw.
Sun and Cloud. Cane.
Thrice Happy He. Drummond.
To Lindsay. Ginsberg.
To My Father. Baxter.
The Tower. Yeats.
Two Sonnets. Berenberg.
Under the Shade of the Trees. Preston.
The Upper Skies Are Palest Blue. Bridges.
When the World is Burning. Jones.
Winter the Huntsman. Sitwell.

Shadow (s) (y)
Afternoon, with Just Enough of a Breeze. Sund.
The Ambience of Love. Schneider.
And on This Shore. Holman.
Andromeda. Aldrich.
Around the Block. Waldrop.
At Melville's Tomb. Crane.
Bear Dance. Rogers.
Behind the Line. Blunden.
The Belfry of Bruges. Longfellow.
Bird-Song. Thayer.
Birds and Roses Are Birds and Roses. Heyen.
The Blazing Heart. Brotherton.
Blue Ridge. Hodges.
Boundaries. Spear.
Braque. Joseph.
Caelica, XC. Greville.
Camping Out on Rainy Mountain. Barnes.
Central Park. Nemerov.
A Changeling Grateful. Peabody.
Charity, Thou Art a Lie. Crane.
Chelsea Churchyard. Mills, Jr.
The Child and the Shadow. Jennings.
A Child's Winter Evening. John.
Christus Triumphans. Pallen.
Clickstone. Rokwaho.
Clouds. Hill.
The Clouds Have Left the Sky. Bridges.

The Colors of Night. Momaday.
Compensation. Emerson.
Concordance. Violi.
Constancy to an Ideal Object. Coleridge.
The Corner Stone. De la Mare.
The Crucifix. Lamartine.
Cypresses. Francis.
The Day Is Dying in the West. Lathbury.
The Death of Vitellozzo Vitelli. Feldman.
The Deaths. Schoultz.
A Defeat. Levertov.
Diogenes. Eastman.
Dog Hospital. Wild.
Dream. Eliyia.
Eagle Sonnets. Wood.
Early Morning. Dow.
Easter Sunday, 1945. Borgese.
Eclogues. Virgil (Publius Vergilius Maro).
The Eggplants Have Pins and Needles. Matveyeva.
Elegy for Chief Sealth (1786–1866). Niatum.
Encounter in Jerusalem. Lipshitz.
Epilogue of the Wandering Jew. Newbury.
Eve. Fichman.
Evening. Doolittle.
An Evening Walk (excerpt). Wordsworth.
The Exiles. Auden.
Farmyard. Dallas.
The Field. Huddle.
The Fifteen Days of Judgement. Evans.
The First Voyage of John Cabot. *Anonymous.*
For Posterity. Raine.
From Far away. Agustini.
Funeral of Rufino Contreras. Schuler.
Girl Sitting Alone at Party. Justice.
Greece. Haygarth.
Greek Archipelagoes. Leigh-Fermor.
Guernica. Lewisohn.
Hallowe'en. Frost.
Hard Country. Booth.
Haunted Odysseus: The Last Testament. Gregory.
Hills o' My Heart. "Carbery.
Horse. Benson.
Hospital Evening. Harwood.
The House-Builders. Das.
A Hundred Years from Now. Ford.
A Hymn. Shirley.
I Saw Thee, Child, One Summer's Day. Bronte.
Image of City. Henson.
L'Imprevisibilite. Hippius.
In Green Old Gardens. "Fane.
In Old Tucson. Beghtol.
In the Caves of Auvergne. Turner.
The Indian Burying Ground. Freneau.
Indirection. Realf.
Interior with Mme. Vuillard and Son. Fraser.
Irradiations. Fletcher.
January Is Here. Fawcett.

Kick a Little Stone. Aldis.
The King of Connacht. *Anonymous.*
King of Ireland's Son. Hopper.
Lament for Ignacio Sanchez Mejias. Garcia Lorca.
Landscape. Paz.
Little Birches. Newsome.
Loss. Aldington.
Love Is Life. Rolle.
The Lover to Himself. Phillips.
The Manzanita. Winters.
Metamorphoses. Ovid (Publius Ovidius Naso).
Midrigal: "I heard a noise." Bateson.
Midwest. Nims.
Midwinter Stars. Whiteman.
The Mirabeau Bridge. Apollinaire.
Morning. Reed.
The Morrow's Message. Rossetti.
A Moth. Baildon.
Mwilu/ or Poem for the Living. Lee.
My Grace Is Sufficient for Thee. *Anonymous.*
The New Faces. Yeats.
Night at Gettysburg. Seitz.
Nights on the Indian Ocean. Rice.
Nocht o' Mortal Sicht. Macarthur.
Nocturne–III. Silva.
Northhanger Ridge. Wright.
Not Here. Wilson.
Not Yet Dead, Not Yet Alone. Mandelstam.
O Fly My Soul. Shirley.
October, Hanson's Field. Borson.
Oisin. *Anonymous.*
On Eastnor Knoll. Masefield.
On My Late Dear Wife. Richardson.
On the Death of Robert Browning. Swinburne.
The One Who Grew to Be a Wolf. Monaghan.
Orange Chiffon. Cortez.
Orchestra. Davies.
Palace. Johnson.
Panic. MacLeish.
The Parklands. Smith.
A Part-Sequence for Change. Duncan.
The Passengers. Antin.
Perdita. Drennan.
Perspectives Are Precipices. Bishop.
Plaint. Elliot.
Poem for My Grandfather. Jacobs.
A Poem in Black and White. Serote.
Poems. Machado.
The Poetaster. Jonson.
The Political Prisoner. Kunene.
Polo Match. Ciardi.
A Prairie Water Colour. Scott.
Privilege. Pizarnik.
Professor Kelleher and the Charles River. O'Grady.
Promises, VIII. Founding Fathers.... Warren.

Quiet By Hillsides in the Afternoon. Lifson.
Rag Doll and Summer Birds. Dodson.
Recollection. Donnelly.
Rock Carving. Stewart.
A Room in the Villa. Smith.
A Row of Thick Pillars. Crane.
Sad Strains of a Gay Waltz. Stevens.
Samadhi. Aiken.
The Sea. Lawrence.
Sea-Weed. Lawrence.
A Serenade for Two Poplars. Raab.
The Seven-League Boots. Voronca.
Seventh Day. Raine.
Shadow. Bruce.
The Shadow. Jonson.
Shadow-Bride. Tolkien.
Shadow River. Johnson.
The Shadow Rose. Rogers.
Sheep Country. Pond.
The Shepherd's Despair. Dermody.
Sketch. Sandburg.
The Snow-Gum. Stewart.
Snowfall. Carducci.
Song for a Dark Girl. Hughes.
Song: "If once I could gather in song." Gibson.
Song of a Jewish Boy. J.M.
Song: "That women are but men's shadows." Jonson.
Song: "There is no joy in water apart from the sun." Currey.
Song: "What binds the atom together." Dow.
Sonnets, XCVIII: "From you have I been absent in the spring." Shakespeare.
St. Peter's Shadow. Crashaw.
Stanzas. Goodman.
The Storm. Jennings.
The Story. Simic.
Sunday. Rungren.
A Sunday in Cambridge. Linden.
Survey Our Progress from Our Birth. Webster.
Sweet Peas. Keats.
Tenebris. Grimke.
Teresa of Avila. Jennings.
Thank You. Koch.
That Is Not Indifference. Hanson.
This Coloured Counterfeit That Thou Beholdest. Juana Ines de la Cruz.
Timber Line Trees. Holme.
A Time of Light, a Time of Shadow. Yellen.
The Tin Woodsman. Jiles.
'/Tis a Little Journey. *Anonymous.*
To a Rose. Tabb.
To Avisa. Willoby.
To Beachey, 1912. Sandburg.
To Her Portrait. Juana Ines de la Cruz.
To S.A. Lawrence.
To—-, with an Ivory Hand-Glass. Douglas.
Tolerance. Hardy.
The Torch. Forker.

Trees Once Walked and Stood. Tan Pai.
The Twelve Weapons of Spiritual Battle. More.
Twilights. Wright.
Under Cancer. Hollander.
Upon His Picture. Randolph.
Upon the Curtain of Lucasta's Picture It Was Thus Wrought. Lovelace.
Vala; or, The Four Zoas. Blake.
Views. Susskind.
The Vigil. Levertov.
Vihio Images. Volborth.
Villa Sciarra: Rome. Curtis.
Visions. Petrarch.
Wall Shadows. Sandburg.
Walt Whitman. Carnevali.
Water-Lilies. Teasdale.
The Water-Ousel. Webb.
When We Drive at Night. Pollitt.
Whim Alley. Allen.
The Whisperers. Gibson.
Wild West. Vinz.
Windfall. Arsenault.
Winter. Akhmadulina.
With Eyes at the Back of Our Heads. Levertov.
Wolf-Boy. Malouf.
Words to the Wind. Di Cicco.
Writ on the Eve of My 32nd Birthday. Corso.
You, Andrew Marvell. MacLeish.
Yucca in the Moonlight. Dresbach.

Shady
A Hedge before Me. Columcille.
The Hymn to Venus: Venus Goes After Anchises. Homer.
The One Thing That Can Save America. Ashbery.
Sadie's Playhouse. Danner.

Shaft (s)
Always the Following Wind. Auden.
At the Woodpile. Henri.
Breake Now My Heart and Dye! Campion.
The Children's Letters. Livesay.
Concord Hymn. Emerson.
For Cora Lightbody, R.N. Glassco.
How McClellan Took Manassas. Anonymous.
The Progress of Poesy. Gray.
Vegetable Loves. Darwin.
You Tell Me to Sit Quiet. Jordan.
The Zen Archer. Kirkup.

Shake (n) (s)
Absent Star. Duval.
The Aeneid. Virgil (Publius Vergilius Maro).
Agitato Ma Non Troppo. Ransom.
Aubade. Laing.
Betsy Baker. Anonymous.
Blackberry Sweet. Randall.
The Blues Don't Change. Young.
Brittle Beauty. Surrey.

The Cricket and the Greshope Wenten Hem to Fight. Anonymous.
Deceitful Brownskin Blues. Jefferson.
Fare Thee Well Blues. Calicott.
Granite and Cypress. Jeffers.
Grey October. "The Critics."
The Hike. Weiss.
How Do You Do? Jones.
The Jew at Christmas Eve. Shapiro.
King Lear. Shakespeare.
The Knot. Kunitz.
Listening to Grownups Quarreling. Whitman.
Lord of the World. Anonymous.
Maud. Tennyson.
Nearing Winter. Sandeen.
Nonsense. Anonymous.
The Ode on St. Cecilia's Day. Dryden.
The Quaker's Wooing. Anonymous.
To an Elder Poet. Williams.
The Transformed Metamorphosis: Awake, Oh Heaven. Tourneur.
Veneris Venefica Agrestis. Piccolo.
Villa Sciarra: Rome. Curtis.
The Woodman's Dog. Cowper.

Shakespeare
Critics and Poets. Grigson.
Dogs are Shakespearean, Children Are Strangers. Schwartz.
Easier. Harrison.
From Plane to Plane. Frost.
House. Browning.
In the Old Churchyard at Fredericksburg. Loring.
The Informing Spirit. Emerson.
On Shakespeare and Voltaire. Holcroft.
On the Erection of Shakespeare's Statue in Westminster Abbey. Pope.
Rehearsal. Fisher.
Sasha and the Poet. Valentine.
They Don't Speak English in Paris. Nash.
William Shakespeare to Mrs. Anne,... Gray.

Shale
Calm and Full the Ocean. Jeffers.
Diesel and Shale. Anonymous.
Sonnet to Seabrook. Ray.

Shallow (er) (s)
Insomnia. Bishop.
On the Death of Karl Barth. Clemo.
One Time. Livingstone.
One Way Down. Craig.
Some San Francisco Poems. Oppen.
Sonnet for the End of a Sequence. Parker.
Why, Lord? Van Doren.

Shame (d) (s)
Adventure. Norton.
Ain't It a Shame. Anonymous.
Alone. Joyce.

The Atheist's Tragedy. Tourneur.
The Authors of the Town (excerpt). Savage.
Bagley Wood. Johnson.
A Ballad Called Perkin's Figary. Anonymous.
Ballade to My Psychoanalyst. Lillington.
A Beginning and an End. Roditi.
Beowulf. Anonymous.
Butler's Proclamation. Hayne.
Canzone: Of the Gentle Heart. Guinicelli.
The Cathedral of Rheims. Rostand.
The Church's Testimony. Dryden.
Cock-Crow: Woodstock. Robinson.
Cupid Ungodded. Shirley.
Death. Williams.
Death's Songsters. Rossetti.
Died. Browning.
The Dying Sergeant. Anonymous.
Epigram: A Spiral Shell. Nemerov.
Epitaphs of the War. Kipling.
Epitaphs of the War, 1914-18. Kipling.
Fable XIII: The Tame Stag. Gay.
Fear. Camerino.
The Flirt. Davies.
The Glory of Lincoln. Clark.
God Don't Like It. Anonymous.
His Life Is Ours. Stroud.
Ichabod. Whittier.
The Impious Feast. Landor.
In the Restaurant. Hardy.
Ireland. Holyday.
Kit Logan and Lady Helen. Graves.
The Lass and the Friar. Burns.
Life's Chequer-Board. Oxenham.
Lines Written on Hearing the News of the Death of Napoleon. Shelley.
Love Is Strong. Burton.
A Lovely Lass to a Friar Came. Rochester.
Mary Hamilton (B version). Anonymous.
A Name in the Sand. Gould.
Noble Sisters. Rossetti.
Not Even in Dreams. Ise.
On the Proposal to Erect a Monument in England to Lord Byron. Lazarus.
The "Pater Noster". Anonymous.
Peter Hath Lost His Purse. Anonymous.
The Pony Blues. House.
Poor but Honest. Anonymous.
Poor Little Jesus. Anonymous.
Prometheus Bound. Aeschylus.
Query. Weston.
A Rhapsody of Old Men, VII. Tsaloumas.

Sally Free and Easy. Tawney.
She Is More to be Pitied than Censured. Gray.
She Was Poor but She Was Honest. Anonymous.
Sonnets, IX: "Is it for fear to wet a widow's eye." Shakespeare.
Sonnets, LXXII: "O, lest your true love may seem false in this." Shakespeare.
Straus Park. Stern.
This Flock So Small. Nitschmann.
Time to Rise. Stevenson.
Tolerance. Morris.
Vashti. Harper.
Waiting. Henley.
White Center. Hugo.
Your Chase Had a Beast in View. Bishop.
Yucca in the Moonlight. Dresbach.
Zimmer in Grade School. Zimmer.

Shameless
Dancing-Girl's Song. Kshetrayya.
A Mask Presented at Ludlow Castle (Comus). Milton

Shamrock
Clare's Dragoons. Davis.
The Green Little Shamrock of Ireland. Cherry.

Shape (d) (s)
America Was Schoolmasters. Coffin.
Between Two Furious Oceans. Diespecker.
Castilian. Wylie.
A Celebration of Charis. Jonson.
The Changes. Pinsky.
The Cicada (excerpt). Aiken.
The Common Street. Cone.
Fealty. Wolfram von
Field Day. Rodgers.
For Sale. Anonymous.
Four for Sir John Davies. Roethke.
The Glens. Hewitt.
Her Going. Kaufman.
The Image of Delight. Leonard.
John Webster. Swinburne.
Knockmany. Ryan.
Leviathan. Quennell.
The Likeness. Gregor.
Limerick: "There was an old man of the Cape." Anonymous.
The Marshes of Glynn. Lanier.
A Memento for Mortality. Basse.
Metamorphoses. Ovid (Publius Ovidius Naso).
Nothing. De la Mare.
Nude Descending a Staircase. Kennedy.
On the Tombs in Westminster Abbey. Beaumont.
The Overgrown Back Yard. Holmes.
The Pot-Bellied Anachronism. Darr.
The Power to Change Geography. O Hehir.
The Refugees. Muir.
Sacred Poetry. Wilson.

Shape

The Supper after the Last.
Kinnell.
Tally. Miles.
This Runner. Webb.
The Titanic (excerpt). Pratt.
To—. Tennyson.
To a Military Rifle. Winters.
To a Skull. Irwin.
Twelfth Night. Shakespeare.
Unit. Fullerton.
A Virtue of Shape. Swiss.
Visit. Ammons.
Walk Past Those Houses on a
Sunday Morning.
Smithyman.
When the Loneliness of the
Tomb Went down into the
Marketplace. Sa'udi.
Witches' Spells. Edmondson.

Share (d)

After You, Madam.
Comfort.
Air. Denby.
Alone. Chu Shu-chen.
The Anatomy of Angels.
Nowlan.
Cambrian (excerpt). Manner.
The Carpenter's Son. Peck.
Christmas Chant. Shaw.
Christmas Eve. Parmenter.
The Counsels of O'Riordan,
the Rann Maker.
O'Bolger.
A Cry for Light.
Anonymous.
Early Morning. Dow.
An Evening Thought.
Hammon.
Fair Thou Art. Ben Isaac.
Fear. Peacock.
Friends. Clark.
From the Gulf. Ogilvie.
George the Third's Soliloquy.
Freneau.
The Hard Lovers. Dillon.
Here Lies Fierce Strephon.
Hecht.
His Further Resolution.
Anonymous.
Holly and Mistletoe.
Farjeon.
The House. Nelson.
The Indian. Reed.
Johnny and the Highwayman.
Anonymous.
The Lament for Yellow-
Haired Donough.
Anonymous.
Lines. Drayton.
Love Beleagured. Chapin.
My Legacy. Jackson.
No, Never Think. Pushkin.
O Child of Lowly Manger
Birth. Blanchard.
Ode to a Homemade Coffee
Cup. Warden.
On a Monday Morning.
Tawney.
Only a Smile. Anonymous.
Reports of Midsummer Girls.
Lattimore.
The Robin. Very.
Ruth. Hood.
Sharing Eve's Apple. Keats.
Someone Like No One Else.
Farrokhzad.
The Song of the Lilies.
Wheelock.
Sonnet for a Loved One.
Joslin.
The Surprise. Anonymous.
The Sympathizers. Miles.

This I Can Do. Lefevre.
Those Who Come What Will
They Say of Us. Knoepfle.
To a Republican Friend.
Arnold.
To Miss L.F.... (parody).
Squire.
Today. Very.
Translations. Rich.
Welcome Morning. Sexton.
What Is to Come. Henley.
Where Have You Been Dear?
Kuskin.
The Woman at the Washtub.
Daley.
The Women's Marseillaise.
Macaulay.
The Wooing of Etain.
Anonymous.

Shark (s)

Anti-Love Poems. Brewster.
The Chivalrous Shark.
Anonymous.
Cornwallis. Beyer.
Handlining Tockers &
Gizmos. Planz.
The Leg. Shapiro.
Love Is a Shark.
Anonymous.
The Nightingale.
Anonymous.
The Rhyme of the Chivalrous
Shark. Irwin.
The Sea-Turtle and the Shark.
Tolson.
Storm at Sea. Anonymous

Sharp

The Cancer Cells. Eberhart.
Dogskin Rug. Stoutenburg.
How to Build a Ha-Ha.
Mason.
Summer. Page.

Shatter (ed) (s)

Charing Cross. Roberts.
Gift of a Mirror to a Lady.
Wagoner.
The Old Song. Chesterton.
The Scarlet Thread.
Henderson.
The Shattering of Love.
Anonymous.
The Sleeping Beauty. De
Ford.
Temptation. Cowper.
To—? Dehmel.
Tohub. Hoddis.
Woman, Gallup, N.M.
Swenson.

Shave (s)

Commuter. White.
Lyric Barber. Romano.
Prolonged Sonnet: When the
Troops Were Returning
from Milan. Niccolo.
Revised Notes for a Sonnet
(parody). Pygge.
Tapestry. Simic.

Shaving (s)

Inscription for the Sign of
"The Jolly Barber',...
Swift.
A Way of Life. Nemerov.
When through the Whirl of
Wheels. Kennedy.

Shawl (s)

Byrontown. Anonymous.
Friday Night. Smithyman.
Furchte Nichts, Geliebte
Seele. Untermeyer.
Gift. Hemschemeyer.
Indian Sky. Kreymborg.
Precaution. Heine.

The Shawls. Gibbon.
Wrapped Hair Bundles.
LaPena.

She

98 Degree Blues. Alexander.
Birthday. Birney.
A Celebration of Charis.
Jonson.
The Celts. Smith.
Chloe. Mordaunt.
The Courteous Knight.
Anonymous.
Dawn. Anonymous.
Epitaph. Anonymous.
The Feast. Hass.
Fidelia: Shall I, Wasting in
Despair. Wither.
Foxfire. Willard.
Girl Betrayed. Hedylos.
Grieve Not for Me.
Anonymous.
He Runs into an Old
Acquaintance. Nowlan.
Hymn of the Angels and
Sibyls. Vicente.
I'd Want Her Eyes to Fill
with Wonder. Patchen.
I Know a Lady. Thomas.
In an Artist's Studio.
Rossetti.
Limerick: "There was a young
lady of Munich."
Anonymous.
The Little Ghost. Hinkson.
Love's Resume. Heine.
The Lover's Resolution.
Wither.
The Lover's Song. Sill.
Meeting Point. MacNeice.
Miss Kilmansegg's
Honeymoon. Hood.
The Mother. Anonymous.
My Grandmother Green.
Anonymous.
Never the Time and the Place.
Browning.
One of the Principal Causes of
War. ""MacDiarmid.
The Other Side of a Mirror.
Coleridge.
Paradise Lost. Milton.
Phyllidula. Pound.
Pleasure Reconciled to Vertue:
A Masque. Jonson.
Poison Ivy! Gallagher.
Punto Final. Witt.
The Queen of Courtesy.
Anonymous.
Rain on the Down. Symons.
Snatches: "A man may a
while." Anonymous.
Sonnet: "Let others of the
world's decaying tell."
Stirling.
Sonnets, CXLI: "In faith, I do
not love thee with mine
eyes." Shakespeare.
Sonnets to Philomel. Davies.
Souvenirs. Randall.
The Spirit of Night. Rogers.
Sway. Johnson.
That Time That Mirth Did
Steer My Ship. Wyatt.
A Virgin Declares Her
Beauties. Barberino.
Waiting for Her. Nowlan.
The Watercress Seller.
Miller.
A Well-Wishing to a Place of
Pleasure. Anonymous.
West Wind. Anonymous.

With Ships the Sea Was
Sprinkled. Wordsworth.

Sheaf

Celanta at the Well of Life.
Peele.
The Fugitive. Meynell.
A Love Letter to Elizabeth
Thatcher. Thatcher.

Shear (ed) (s)

By Plain Analogy We're Told.
Bierce.
The Dust of Time (fragment).
Sappho.
Moderation. Herrick.
A Scottish Proverb.
Anonymous.
The Willows. Harte.

Sheath (ed)

Against Gaudy-Bragging-
Undoughty Daccus.
Davies.
At the Door. Merriam.
Cuttings. Roethke.
Cuttings, later. Roethke.
Deus Noster Ignis
Consumens. Housman.
Guerrilla Promise. Nangolo.
Late Spring. Gill.
Leesome Brand (B version).
Anonymous.
Make Way! Negri.
Romeo and Juliet.
Shakespeare.

Sheave (s)

Bringing in the Sheaves.
Anonymous.
Bringing Our Sheaves.
Akers.
The Harvest Moon.
Longfellow.
Laus Mortis. Knowles.
A Memory. Tynan.
The Myth. Muir.
An Old Man's Idyl. Realf.
The Old Wife's Tale. Peele.
On Bertrand Russell's
"Portraits from Memory'.
Davie.

Shed (s)

The Balloon of the Mind.
Yeats.
Epitaph at Hadleigh, Suffolk.
Anonymous.
Paphnutius (excerpt).
Hroswitha von
Grandersheim.
The Plowman. Burns.
Scene-Shifter Death. O'Neill.
Sixth-Month Song in the
Foothills. Snyder.
They Grow Up Too Fast, She
Said. O Hehir.
Under the Woods. Thomas.

Sheen

Epilogue to Lessing's
Laocoon. Arnold.
Willie Macintosh.
Anonymous.

Sheep

Arcadia. Sidney.
At Carmel. Austin.
The Blind Sheep. Jarrell.
The Blood-Strained Banders.
Anonymous.
A Child's Nativity. Morris.
A Child's Pet. Davies.
Complaint. Bennett.
Cupid. O'Dowd.
Done Foun' My Los' Sheep.
Anonymous.
Dusk Chant. Volborth.
Eighteen-Ninety. Shipp.

The Fallen Zulu Commander. Van Den Heever.
The Friar in the Well (B version). *Anonymous.*
From his flock stray'd Coridon. Greene.
Growing Wild. Miller.
The Holy Eclogue. del Castillo.
How Low Is the Lowing Herd. Kelly.
I Am Glad Daylong. Braithwaite.
In Memory of Leopardi. Wright.
In the Trench. Gellert.
Let Thy Kingdom. *Anonymous.*
A Lincolnshire Shepherd. *Anonymous.*
The Little Black Sheep. Dunbar.
Love Letter Postmarked Van Beethoven. Wakoski.
The Maiden's Complaint. *Anonymous.*
Moderation. Herrick.
O Gracious Shepherd. Constable.
De Ol' Sheep Done Know De Road. *Anonymous.*
An Old Song. Yehoash.
On the Wing. Rossetti.
The Peasant. Wolf.
The Pentland Hills. *Anonymous.*
Philosophy Is Born. Morgenstern.
Piano Practice. Walcott.
Poor Lil' Brack Sheep. Brazelton.
A Rich Tuft of Ivy. Geilt.
Riddle: "White sheep, white sheep, on a blue hill." *Anonymous.*
Sheep. Davies.
Sheep. Francis.
Sheep and Lambs. Hinkson.
The Sheep-Herder's Lament. Chapman.
Sheepherder blues. Tapahonso.
The Shepherd's Ode. Greene.
The Shepherdess. Meynell.
Shop of Dreams. Carr.
The Sick Child. Stevenson.
Silex Scintillans. Vaughan.
Slumber Song. Ledoux.
Somewhere Near Phu Bai. Komunyakaa.
The Testament of Beauty. Bridges.
Those I Love. Contoski.
The Three Poplars. Little.
Virgidemiarum. Hall.
What Are They Thinking... Guinness.
Whistle, Daughter, Whistle. *Anonymous.*

Sheet (s)
Ad Librum. Danforth II.
Alba. Beckett.
A Considerable Speck. Frost.
The Crystal Lithium. Schuyler.
A Drop of Ink. Whitney.
The Force That through the Green Fuse Drives the Flower. Thomas.

I am the sorrow in the wheat fields. Bass.
Idiot. Tate.
An Island. Wong.
Let Go the Reef Tackle. *Anonymous.*
The Lonely Death. Crapsey.
The Lovers. Smith.
Mythmaking. Spivack.
Song of the Sheet (parody). Anonymous.
Spring. Verlaine.
Strung out with Elgar on a Hill (excerpt). Williams.
Undergraduate. Moore.

Shelf
Dream Songs. Berryman.
Duck. Worth.
The Dumb Soldier. Stevenson.
The Little Maid. Wells.
The Miner's Helmet. Macbeth.
Mister Frog Went A-Courting (with music). *Anonymous.*
Shopping. Nitzche.

Shell (s)
Bell Tower. Adams.
Blue Lantern. Song.
Breakfast. Gibson.
Canning Time. Morgan.
The Children. Vinz.
The Crocodile. *Anonymous.*
Double Ritual. Rainer.
Earliness at the Cape. Deutsch.
An Epistle to R. Dunkin.
The Event. Moore.
For Richard Chase. Miller.
For This, the Tide. Vallis.
Fragment 113. Doolittle.
From a Street Corner. Hammond.
He Praises His Wife When She Had Gone from Him. Flower.
Helen in Egypt. Doolittle.
Homecoming Celebration. Catacalos.
In a Cafe. Dobson.
In Memoriam A.H.H., X. Tennyson.
The Incubation. Zolynas.
Italian Woman. Wakoski.
Letters to Live Poets. Beaver.
Limerick: "There once was a kind armadillo." Herford.
The Lonely Shell. Perry.
Man on Wheels. Shapiro.
Manos Karastefanis. Merrill.
Marriage Contract. Rutsala.
Martin Buber in the Pub. Harris.
Miss Crustacean. Phillips.
Not in the Poet. Barker.
Nude in a Fountain. MacCaig.
Peanuts. Belford.
Portrait of an Artist. Howes.
The Possibility of New Poetry. Bly.
Pregnant Teenager on the Beach. Balazs.
Reproduction of Life. Darwin.
Right On: White America. Sanchez.
The Roosters Will Crow. Meireles.
The Shellpicker. Perry.
Shells in Rock. Roberts.

Shelly Beach. Koch.
The Smacksman. *Anonymous.*
A Tall Tale; or, A Moral Song. Webb.
To Lydia, with a Coloured Egg, on Easter Monday. Jones.
Walking the Beach. Youngblood.
Why Then (Quod I) Old Proverbs Never Fail. Gascoigne.

Shelley
A Man Whom Men Deplore. Kreymborg.
To Jane: The Recollection. Shelley.

Shelter (d) (s)
Abraham Sutskever. Mayne.
Art of the Sonnet: LVI. Orlovitz.
The Christ of the Andes (excerpt). Markham.
Evening Prayer. *Anonymous.*
Ex Nihilo. Gascoyne.
Furniture. Harris.
The Good Shepherd. Tuck.
Ireland. Stuart.
Jeronimo's House. Bishop.
Juniper. Duggan.
Limerick: "When they go out walking the Sioux." *Anonymous.*
The Mountaineer. Nathan.
Old House Place. Sanders.
The Orphan Boy. *Anonymous.*
Packing in with a Man. McCombs.
Pilgrims in Mexico. *Anonymous.*
The Ploughman, in Imitation of Milton. Jones.
Sea Gods. Doolittle.
Secret. Bennett.
The Sixth Pastoral. Philips.
Sonnets: A Sequence on Profane Love. Boker.
The Strange People. Erdrich.
The Sun in Capricorn. Mansour.
To a Young Friend. Coleridge.
The Wedding Poem (excerpt). Russ.
Winter Nights. Dunetz.
Your Attention Please. Porter.

Shepherd (ess) (s)
Among the Millet. Lampman.
As I out Rode. *Anonymous.*
The Bishop of Canterbury (King John and the Bishop). *Anonymous.*
The Blood-Strained Banders. *Anonymous.*
Break of Day. Clare.
Brebeuf and His Brethren. Pratt.
The Carnival of Animals (excerpt). Nash.
A Carol. Bolton.
Cassamen and Dowsabell. Drayton.
Christmas Myth, 1973. McGovern.
The Death of Moses. *Anonymous.*
Death Swoops. Pitchford.
December. Rossetti.

Eclogue. Drayton.
Fair and Fair. Peele.
.The Fire Side. A Pastoral Soliloquy. Browne.
Gorbo and Batte. Drayton.
The Inca Tupac Upanqui. Hart-Smith.
The Island. Ungaretti.
It May Be. Jacob.
Jack Rabbit. Stoutenburg.
A Jig. Greene.
Kate of Aberdeen. Cunningham.
King John and the Bishop. *Anonymous.*
Lament for Daphnaida. Spenser.
The Lamentation of Chloris. *Anonymous.*
Let Thy Kingdom. *Anonymous.*
Madrigal: "Crabbed age and youth." Shakespeare.
Mary Shepherdess. Pickthall.
Masques. Jonson.
Menaphon. Greene.
Mercies and Blessings. *Anonymous.*
Mr. Thomas Shepheard...Hee a Man of a Thousand. Johnson.
Ned Vaughan. De la Mare.
The North Country Collier. *Anonymous.*
O Gracious Shepherd. Constable.
Pans Anniversarie. Jonson.
The Pastoral on the King's Death. Written in 1648. Brome.
Pastoral Song for the Nuptials of Charles, Duke of Lorraine... de Ronsard.
Pastoral: The Tenth Eclogue. Drayton.
A Poem to Show the Trouble That Befell Him When He Was at Sea. Prys.
Proverbially Useful for Weather Forecasts. *Anonymous.*
Rise Up, Shepherd, and Follow. *Anonymous.*
Roads. Brown.
Robin Hood and the Shepherd. *Anonymous.*
Rock of My Salvation. Ben Isaac.
The Shepherd. Blake.
The Shepherd's Calendar. Clare.
The Shepherd's Lament. Goethe.
The Shepherd's Wife's Song. Greene.
Silex Scintillans. Vaughan.
Stir the Wallaby Stew. *Anonymous.*
Summer Storm. Johnson.
A Supplication. Breton.
Sylvia. Drayton.
Thus Bonny-Boots the Birthday Celebrated. *Anonymous.*
To Certain Critics. Cullen.
The Wandering Shepherdess. *Anonymous.*
Whilst Alexis Lay Prest. Dryden.

Sheriff
Big Rock Jail. Bill.
Eviction. Brewster.

How Robin Hood Rescued the Widow's Sons. *Anonymous.*
Robin Hood and the Widow's Three Sons. *Anonymous.*

Sherman
First Monday Scottsboro Alabama. Weatherly.
The Song of Sherman's Army. Halpine.

Sherry
A Boat, a Boat. *Anonymous.*
Golden Grain. Wright.

Sherwood
Robin Hood and the Scotchman. *Anonymous.*
A Song of Sherwood. Noyes.

Shield (s)
At the Loom. Duncan.
The Compasses. MacBeth.
Creide's Lament for Cael. *Anonymous.*
The Fair Hills of Eire, O! Mangan.
Hymn on Solitude. Thomson.
I Have No Strength for Mine. Kyger.
In State (excerpt). Willson.
The King of Connacht. *Anonymous.*
Lo, Who Could Stand. *Anonymous.*
Marmion. Scott.
The Name of Jesus. Flint.
The Nineteenth of April. Larcom.
To the Returning Brave. Johnson.
What a Friend We Have in Jesus. Scriven.

Shift (ed) (ing)
An Appeal to John Harralson. *Anonymous.*
At Dawn of the Year. Klingle.
Epitaphs of the War. Kipling.
Featherstone's Doom. Hawker.
A Great Favourite Song, Entitled The Sailor's Hornpipe. *Anonymous.*
Human Relations. Jarrett.
Miss Kilmansegg's Birth. Hood.
The Ploughman, in Imitation of Milton. Jones.
Prometheus Bound. Aeschylus.
Retaliation. Goldsmith.
A Sestina for Cynthia. Lougee.

Shilling (s)
The Five Best Doctors. Hoffman.
The Gospel of Mr. Pepys. Morley.
How Five and Twenty Shillings Were Expended in a Week. *Anonymous.*
Little Jack Dandy-Prat. *Anonymous.*
My Dream. *Anonymous.*

Shiloh
The Battle of Shiloh. *Anonymous.*
Shiloh, A Requiem. Melville.

Shimmer (ing)
Haiku: "Green weeds of summer." Basho (Matsuo Basho).

Journey: IV. Lindegren.
The Long Parenthesis. Whiteman.
Song: "I make my shroud but no one knows." Crapsey.

Shine (s) (shone)
After X-Ray. Pastan.
An Allegory. Ignatow.
Apple Blight. Zimmer.
The Armorer's Daughter. Greger.
Aubade. Laing.
Autumn 1940. Auden.
The Barber's. De la Mare.
Bingen on the Rhine. Norton.
The Bridge: Three Songs. Crane.
Calvinist Autumnal. Harrod.
Candles. *Anonymous*
The Chance. Sze.
The Character of a Good Person. Dryden.
Christmas. Herbert.
The Cobbler. Chaffee.
A Contemplation on Night. Gay.
Contemplations. Bradstreet.
The Djanggawul Cycle, 166. *Anonymous.*
The Djanggawul Cycle, 8. *Anonymous.*
Doris. Congreve.
Elephant. McFadden.
Etude Realiste. Swinburne.
Evening. Shelley.
Explanation, on Coming Home Late. Hughes.
Fairest Lord Jesus. *Anonymous.*
Fawnia. Greene.
Firelight. Robinson.
The Flash Colonial Barman. Coxon.
The Flattered Flying Fish. Rieu.
Flute Song. Masaveimah.
For My Wife. Lautermilch.
For Sleep, or Death. Pitter.
God's Sunshine. Oxenham.
The Groves of Blarney. Millikin.
Hame, Hame, Hame. Cunningham.
Her Application to Elysium. Norris.
Holy Night. Clifton.
House Plants. McFadden.
I Kissed Pa Twice after His Death. Peterson.
I'll Give My Love a Light and Friendly Kiss. *Anonymous.*
The Iliad. Homer.
Immortal Nature. Darwin.
It Was the Lovely Moon. Freeman.
King of the Belgians. Smith.
Kings Came Riding. Williams.
A Lament. Avison.
Last Words. Plath.
Lessons. Untermeyer.
The Light of Stars. Furness.
Looking at Henry Moore's Elephant Skull Etchings in Jerusalem... Kaufman.
Love Poem. Rea.
The Lover's Choice. Bedingfield.
Low Tide. Woessner.
Made Shine. Miles.

Madrigal: "Dear, when I did from you remove." Herbert of Cherbury.
Magaica. De Sousa.
Magnolia Tree in Summer. Sitwell.
Mariners' Carol. Merwin.
May Day. Teasdale.
Mock On, Mock On, Voltaire, Rousseau. Blake.
Mockery. Blake.
My Days Are Gliding Swiftly By. Nelson.
My Mother's Feet. Plumly.
My Spirit. Traherne.
My Springs. Lanier.
My Thoughts Are Winged with Hopes. Clifford.
The Natives. Mura.
Night Catch. McHugh.
O Dream, Where Art Thou Now? Bronte.
Of Kings and Things. Morrison.
Oh, Day of Days. Brant.
Olney Hymns: The Happy Change. Cowper.
On Mistress Nicely, a Pattern for Housekeepers. Hood.
On the Countess of Dorchester. Sackville.
Our Lady of the Waves. Brown.
Out. Burt.
Over the Phone. McBride.
Patience. Cattafi.
The Pearl. *Anonymous.*
Phantom. Coleridge.
The Planet. Jacobsen.
Psalm VIII. Sidney.
Resignation. *Anonymous.*
Resignation. Landor.
A Revivalist in Boston. Rich.
The Secret Heart. Coffin.
September. Huxley.
Sherburne. *Anonymous.*
Shine Just Where You Are. *Anonymous.*
Sleeping Beauty. Drummond.
Sometimes Heaven Is a Mean Machine. Root.
A Song of Love for Jesus. Rolle.
Sonnet: "Since I keep only what I give away." Hetherington.
Sonnets, LXV: "Since brass, nor stone, nor earth, nor boundless sea." Shakespeare.
Spring in Virginia. Wilson.
The Statesman in Retirement. Cowper.
Surely My Soul... Cohen.
Sweet Caroline. *Anonymous.*
Table Manners for the Hostess (excerpt). Meung.
Tall Windows. Hass.
Tarquin and Tullia. Mainwaring.
Thy Kingdom Come. Bernard of Clairvaux
Titian's "Bacchanal" in the Prado at Madrid (excerpt). Moore.
To Cynthia. Clifford.
To the Rev. Mr. Newton. Cowper.
Twilight Song. Robinson.
A Valediction. Cartwright.

A Very Minor Poet Speaks. Valle.
The Washer-Woman. Bohanan.
West Helena Blues. Sykes.
Where Fled. Wieners.
A White Blossom. Lawrence.

Shingle (s)
Noah in New England. Lowenstein.
The Patter of the Shingle. *Anonymous.*
Rain. Haines.
Rain on the Roof. Kinney.

Ship (ed)
The Acquiescence of Pure Love. Cowper.
Don Juan. Byron.
The Fisher's Boy. Thoreau.
L'Infinito. Leopardi.
The Pilot. Chapman.

Ship (s)
After the Sea-Ship. Whitman.
All Is Well. Clough.
Amoretti, LVI. Spenser.
Amoris Exsul. Symons.
The Animals in the Ark. *Anonymous.*
Anti-Love Poems. Brewster.
August Rain. Bly.
The Balena. *Anonymous.*
The Bead Mat. de la Mare.
The Beauty of the Ship. Whitman.
Becalmed. Blight.
The Bonnie Ship the Diamond. *Anonymous.*
The Brave Old Ship, the Orient. Lowell.
The Brooklyn at Santiago. Rice.
The Cachalot. Pratt.
The Carpenter's Wife (The Daemon Lover). *Anonymous.*
Chester. Billings.
Christopher Columbus (excerpt). Hart-Smith.
The Cocoa-Tree. Stoddard.
Coming Around the Horn. *Anonymous.*
The Dead Ship of Harpswell. Whittier.
Defeat and Victory. Rice.
The Dhows. Young.
Dublin Bay. *Anonymous.*
The End of His Work. Herrick.
An Endless Chain. Reisen.
Epitaph. Comfort.
Even during War. Rukeyser.
The Flying Cloud. *Anonymous.*
The Glorious Victory of Navarino! *Anonymous.*
Handlining Tockers & Gizmos. Planz.
The Historie of Squyer William Meldrum: Squire Meldrum at..... Lindsay.
I'd Like to Be a Lighthouse. Field.
I, Who Fade with the Lilacs. Griffith.
In a Boat. Belloc.
In Cabin'd Ships at Sea. Whitman.
The Inspection. Watt.
James Harris (C vers.). *Anonymous.*

Jubilate. Arnold.
Lament for Richard Rolston. Sitwell.
The Last Voyage. Hinkson.
Leaving Forever. Levertov.
The Legend of Walbach Tower. Houghton.
Let Zeus Record. Doolittle.
Mainsail Haul. *Anonymous.*
Mariners. Morton.
The Mayflower. Ellsworth
Mayflower. O'Reilly.
Merry May the Keel Row. *Anonymous.*
Messmates. Newbolt.
Mr. Kurtz. McGovern.
My Ship Is on de Ocean. *Anonymous.*
Not Gone Yet. Drennan.
Nude with Green Chair. Oldknow.
Ode for a Master Mariner Ashore. Guiney.
Old Counsel of the Young Master of a Wrecked California Clipper. Melville.
The Old Saint. Stuart.
On Leaving Cuba, Her Native Land. Gomez de Avellaneda Gertrudis.
On the Verge. Winter.
Paddy, Get Back. *Anonymous.*
Pater's Bathe. Parry.
Pictures. Smith.
Pilgrimage. Clarke.
Rain. Stevenson.
Riding Double. Wild.
The Sailor. MacDonald.
The Sappa Creek. Snyder.
Say That He Loved Old Ships. Hicky.
A Seaman's Confession of Faith. Kemp.
A Ship, an Isle, a Sickle Moon. Flecker.
The Ship in the Midst of the Sea. Wordsworth.
Ship's Bell. Dresbach.
The Ship That Never Returned. Work.
The Ship That Sails. *Anonymous.*
Shore. Miller.
Shore Roads of April. Adams.
The Sinking of the Merrimac. Larcom.
Sir Patrick Spens. *Anonymous.*
Sketch. Sandburg.
Song for All Seas, All Ships. Whitman.
Standin' on the Walls of Zion (with music). *Anonymous.*
The Thanksgiving in Boston Harbor. Butterworth.
This Is My Hour. Akins.
Thoughts upon a Walk with Natalie, My Niece, at Houghton Farm. Pulsifer.
The Titanic. *Anonymous.*
To You on the Broken Iceberg. Gallagher.
Tranquil Sea. Thomson.
Treasure Boat. Fujino.
Troilus and Criseyde. Chaucer.
The Unseaworthy Ship. *Anonymous.*
The Way to the Sea. Lerner.

What Ship Is This? Hauser.
Whate'er You Dream with Doubt Possest. Clough.
When My Ship Comes In. Burdette.
The Wind Has Such a Rainy Sound. Rossetti.
With the Nuns at Cape May Point. Anderson.
Shipmate
Joy, Shipmate, Joy! Whitman.
Shipwreck (ed)
The Acquiescence of Pure Love. Cowper.
Don Juan. Byron.
The Fisher's Boy. Thoreau.
L'Infinito. Leopardi.
The Pilot. Chapman.
Shirt (s)
Bath. Kirstein.
Bill Groggin's Goat. *Anonymous.*
The Canadian Prairies View of Literature. Donnell.
The Clothing's New Emperor. Finkel.
The Collier's Rant. *Anonymous.*
Dilly Dilly Piccalilli. Watson.
Epitaph: "Hic jacet Tom Shorthose." *Anonymous.*
Et Quid Amabo Nisi Quod Aenigma Est. Sandy.
The Glazier. Mallarme.
I'd Like to Be a Worm. Gay.
My Papa's Waltz. Roethke.
A New Shirt! Why? Grano.
Old Boniface. Anonymous.
On the Uncleanly Habits of Sir Charles Wetherell. *Anonymous.*
Portrait of a Poet. Masters.
Salesman. Roston.
Song: "Kiss me and hug me." *Anonymous.*
Song of the All-Wool Shirt. Field.
The Song of the Shirt. Hood.
Upon Pagget. Herrick.
Walking Around. Neruda.
What Is Being Forgotten. Healy.
Shit (s) (ting)
A Dance for Militant Dilettantes. Young.
Don't Answer the Phone for Me the Same. Locklin.
Easter. O'Hara.
The Excrement Poem. Kumin.
Family Life. *Anonymous.*
The Garden Boy. Motaung.
The Grotto. Fraser.
The Hustler. *Anonymous.*
Hygiene Sonnet. Gallup.
Ode: To My Lovers. Verlaine.
The Old Athens of the West Is Now a Blue Grass Tour. Hall.
To Fez Cobra. Joans.
Shiver (ed) (ing) (s)
The Bottle of Chianti. Souster.
The Bubble: A Song. Herrick.
Common Sense and Genius. Moore.

The Curse. Francis.
Dawn-Angels. Robinson.
Decayed Time. Wahl.
Domestic Didactics by an Old Servant: The Broken Dish. Hood.
Ella of the Cinders. French.
Emblems. Tate.
The Farmer. Shove.
Five Degrees South. Young.
In the Pines. *Anonymous.*
Iron Heaven. Alver.
Lady Anne Bathing. Delius.
Long-Distance. Burnes.
Marriage. Carver.
May the man who gained my trust yet did not come. Ryojin Hisho.
The Midnight Court. Merryman.
Nocturne in G Minor. Vollmoeller.
To the Pines. *Anonymous.*
Touching the River. Kinsella.
Whose Voice. Bush.
Shoal (s)
Halieutica. Oppian.
Heron. Walker.
Message from Home. Raine.
The Shoals of Herring. *Anonymous.*
Shock (ed) (s)
Captain Kid's Farewell to the Seas. *Anonymous.*
Catching Soft Craws. Vernon.
Drama. Hart-Smith.
Epitaph (Inscription from Anticyra). *Anonymous.*
An Epithalamy to Sir Thomas Southwell and His Lady. Herrick.
For Allen Ginsberg, Who Cut Off His Beard. Pinsker.
Limerick: "There once was a sculptor called Phidias." Herford.
One to Destroy, Is Murder by the Law. Young.
When the Frost Is on the Punkin. Riley.
You Are a Jew! Schwartz.
Shoe (s)
An Accommodating Lion. Jenks.
Ann Grenville, Countess Temple, Appointed Poet Laureate... Walpole.
Aubade. Hollo.
Burning Sand of Sinai. Sachs.
The Centipede. Adams.
A Certain Age. McGinley.
Cosmogony (parody). Berry.
Dark. Healy.
A Devonshire Rhyme. *Anonymous.*
Disintegration. Shelton.
The Door-Keeper Has Big Feet. Sappho.
Eclogue IV. The Poet (excerpt). Jenner.
Epigram. *Anonymous.*
An Epigram: "A member of the modern great." Cunningham.
The Gazelle Calf. Lawrence.
Gift for the Queen. *Anonymous.*
The Good Shepherd. Rhys.

Hannah Binding Shoes. Larcom.
Hen and Cock. *Anonymous.*
Hob, Shoe, Hob; Hob, Shoe, Hob. *Anonymous.*
I Found a Horseshoe (with music). *Anonymous.*
I'm a Round-Town Gent. *Anonymous.*
It's Fun to Go out and Buy New Shoes to Wear. Hoberman.
Little Blue Shoes. Greenaway.
The Little Shoes That Died. Gilmore.
Looking for Work. Carver.
The Lost Shoe. De la Mare.
The Mad Yak. Corso.
Martyrdom of Two Pagans. Whalen.
Mothers. Sexton.
My Donkey. Fyleman.
New Shoes. Wilkins.
Old Men Pitching Horseshoes. Kennedy.
Old Shoes and Leggin's. *Anonymous.*
Orpheus and Eurydice. Valentine.
Question. Craig.
Reality. Souster.
Resolution. Merwin.
The Sailor's Grace. *Anonymous.*
Sale. Miles.
The Shoemakker. *Anonymous.*
A Song About Myself, st. 4. Keats.
The Strolling Player. Rimbaud.
Water. Sexton.
We Were Permitted to Meet Together in Prison to Prepare for Trial. Berrigan.
Shook
Building Bridges. Mahaka.
The Poet. Tennyson.
Sleigh Bells at Night. Coatsworth.
"Somedays now". Rickert.
Spring Oak. Kinnell.
Tales of the Islands, VII. Walcott.
Uriel. Emerson.
Shoot (ing) (s)
Al Capone in Alaska. Reed.
At First I Was Given Centuries. Atwood.
Blossom. Plumly.
A Choice of Weapons. Kunitz.
The Dying Desperado. *Anonymous.*
Fireflies. Hall.
Graffiti. Field.
The Great Silkie of Sule Skerrie. *Anonymous.*
Hot Springs. Birney.
Hunting at Dusk. Cockrell.
The Huntsman. Wheelwright.
Inspiration. Knox.
Long Barren. Rossetti.
Love Song. Parker.
Mule-Train. Sellers.
My Home. *Anonymous.*
An Owl in an Oak. *Anonymous.*

Shoot
Shoot the Buffalo.
  Anonymous.
Those Guyana Nights.
  Foerster.
To My Child. Sutzkever.
Translations from the Chinese.
  Morley.
Windigo. Jiles.
Shop (ping)
Bundles. Farrar.
Canteen Pimpin'. Jamal.
Dances of Death. Blok.
December. Heath-Stubbs.
He Asked about the Quality.
  Cavafy.
The Inheritance. Ignatow.
It's Fun to Go out and Buy
  New Shoes to Wear.
  Hoberman.
Leopard Skin. Stewart.
Shore (s)
Africa. Naude.
And in That Drowning
  Instant. Klein.
Ariosto. Mandelstam.
At Dieppe: Green and Grey.
  Symons.
Ave Atque Vale. Swinburne.
Ballad of the Two Tapsters.
  Watkins.
Bathed Is My Blood. La
  Grone.
The Battle of the Jarama.
  Neruda.
Birds. Jeffers.
Bounty. Miles.
Come Home, Come Home!
  Clough.
The Coming of Night.
  Wade.
Crowds of Men and Women.
  Whitman.
Dixie's Green Shore.
  Anonymous.
The Dying Mine Brakeman.
  Jenks.
Epitaph. Comfort.
The Event. Moore.
The Excursion. Tu Fu.
The Fair Maid by the Shore.
  Anonymous.
Fairy Song. Hemans.
Far in the West. Fraser.
Fires of Driftwood.
  MacKay.
First Prelude. Dream in Ohio:
  The Father. Logan.
The Flying Cloud (II).
  Anonymous.
From Gloucester Out. Dorn.
From the Window Down.
  Coxe.
Gathering the Bones Together.
  Orr.
The General Armstrong.
  Anonymous.
Give No White Flower.
  Chamberlain.
The Gravedigger. Carman.
Heat. Mackenzie.
Hermes of the Ways.
  Doolittle.
High Poetry and Low.
  Stevens.
How Many Heavens...
  Sitwell.
The Hymn of Hate. Miller.
A Hymn of the Sea. Bryant.
I Hear the Wave.
  Anonymous.
I Many Times Thought Peace
  Had Come. Dickinson.

I Stand as on Some Mighty
  Eagle's Beak. Whitman.
Immortal. Teasdale.
In the Home of the Scholar
  Wu Su-chiang from Hsin-
  an... Wu Tsao.
Just a Closer Walk with Thee.
  Anonymous.
The Katzenjammer Kids.
  Reaney.
Lament. Drummond.
Liberation. Mark.
Life's Testament.
  Baylebridge.
Little Fan. Reeves.
The Long Harbour. Bethell.
Melancholy. Habington.
Middle Passage. Hayden.
Mimma Bella. Lee-
  Hamilton.
Modern Love, L. Meredith.
A Monument. Madge.
Noah's Prayer. Gastold.
Now Our Meeting's Over.
  Anonymous.
O'er Continent and Ocean.
  Holmes.
Ode on Advancing Age.
  Dixon.
Ode to Nea. Moore.
Open Heart. Salcman.
The Orchard by the Shore: a
  Pastoral. Sweetman.
Other Shore. *Anonymous.*
Pirate Story. Stevenson.
The Quiet Nights. Hinkson.
Rolling Home. *Anonymous.*
Satisfied. Mason.
Sea-Birds. Thomson.
The Sea-Captain.
  Anonymous.
The Ship in the Midst of the
  Sea. Wordsworth.
A Small Bird's Nest Made of
  White Reed Fiber. Bly.
Song of Marion's Men.
  Bryant.
A Song of Sickness.
  Tangikuku.
Sonnet. Squire.
Spirit of Freedom, Thou Dost
  Love the Sea. Dodge.
The Swan. Rodgers.
Sweet By and By. Bennett.
Switzerland. Arnold.
Thalatta! Thalatta! Brown.
There Is a Land. Watts.
Time Passing, Beloved.
  Davie.
To a Sea-Bird. Harte.
Trans Canada. Scott.
Tristram of Lyoness:
  Swimming. Swinburne.
Tunnel Beach. Baxter.
The Unknown Bird.
  Thomas.
Until I Saw the Sea. Moore.
Vers La Vie. Upson.
Vigil. Campbell.
The Volunteers. Lytle.
War Song of O'Driscol.
  Griffin.
The White Canoe. Sullivan.
With a Nantucket Shell.
  Webb.
Short (en) (er) (est)
Amoretti, LXIII. Spenser.
Apparition. Henley.
At the Corner of Muck and
  Myer. Violi.
At the Nadir. Kennedy.

The Bloody Conquests of
  Mighty Tamburlaine
  (excerpt). Marlowe.
A Celebration of Charis.
  Jonson.
Clocks. Ginsberg.
The Discoverer. Field.
Epigram: "If true that notion,
  which but few contest."
  Anonymous.
Epithalamion. Spenser.
February. Whitney.
For Bill. Hewitt.
January. Kees.
Life. Herbert.
Little Birdie. *Anonymous.*
Now while the night her sable
  veil hath spread.
  Drummond.
On a Fly Drinking out of His
  Cup. Oldys.
The Painted Ceiling. Lowell.
Prayer for the Little Daughter
  between Death and Burial.
  Scott.
Response. Bethell.
The Retirement. Norris.
Samson Agonistes. Milton.
The Song against Grocers.
  Chesterton.
Song: "Shepherd, who can
  pass such wrong." Young.
Sonnet Written in Tintern
  Abbey, Monmouthshire.
  Gardner.
Teddy Bear. Milne.
To a Certain Most Certainly
  Certain Critic. McCord.
To His Watch. Hopkins.
Toast to a Departing Duchess.
  Marot.
A Triad. Rossetti.
Under Which Lyre. Auden.
Shortcomings
Modern Love Poems.
  Anonymous.
The Signal. Ignatow.
Shot (s)
Annie Breen. *Anonymous.*
But We Shall Bloom. Guri.
Civil War. Clarke.
Comanche. Gildner.
The Donner Party (excerpt).
  Keithley.
Driving to Sauk City.
  Woessner.
The Duel. *Anonymous.*
Epitaph: "Here he lies
  moulding." Mellichamp.
A Friend. Power.
Ho, Brother Teig.
  Anonymous.
I'll find My Self-Belief.
  Glatstein.
In India. Shapiro.
In Snow. Allingham.
In the Beginning. Thomas.
Little Britain. *Anonymous.*
No More Words! To the
  Field, to Arms! Franco.
On Zacchaeus. Quarles.
Plot Improbable, Character
  Unsympathetic. Olson.
Road Runner. Hall.
The Shooting. Pack.
Shooting of His Dear.
  Anonymous.
Sir Henry Clinton's Invitation
  to the Refugees. Freneau.
The Snail. Lovelace.
Soccer. Voznesensky.
The Sportsman. McCord.

A Street in Bronzeville:
  Southeast Corner. Brooks.
The Virgin Sturgeon.
  Anonymous.
Shotgun
Almost Grown. Ai.
Usually an Old Female Is the
  Leader. Hennen.
Should
The Bird. Hoffenstein.
The Invisible Bridge.
  Burgess.
Lines by a Medium.
  Anonymous.
Look Home. Southwell.
Seminary. Carrier.
Shrine to What Should Be.
  Evans.
Subway Psalm. Nowlan.
Sundays. Rugo.
Shoulder (s)
The Aeneid. Virgil (Publius
  Vergilius Maro).
August/Fresno 1973. Spear.
An Autumn Day. MacLean.
Because He Is Young.
  Okura.
The Boxcar Poem. Young.
Bridesmaid. Wilson, Jr.
Childlessness. Merrill.
The Day Concludes Burning.
  O'Grady.
Divination. Metz.
Fellowship. *Anonymous.*
Field-Glasses. Young.
Hair-Dressing. Untermeyer.
Hazard. Petersen.
Jacob's Destiny. Beer-
  Hofmann.
Jane Retreat. Honig.
Legend. Wright.
Light Baggage. Walker.
Love-Song. Lasker-Schüler.
Merits of Laughter and Lust.
  Mandel.
Mugging (excerpt).
  Ginsberg.
The Natives. Mura.
Noise Grimaced. Eigner.
Ode to Aphrodite. Sappho.
The Old Grey Wall.
  Carman.
On Solomon Lazarus Lee,
  Exhibitioner of Balliol.
  Beeching.
Pole Vault. Murano.
The Priest's Lament.
  Benson.
Rain Journal: London: June
  65. Harwood.
The Spider. Mackenzie.
A Statue in a Garden. Lee.
To the Swallows of Viterbo.
  Ruark.
War Blinded. Dunn.
Shout (ed) (ing) (s)
Aideen's Grave. Ferguson.
Burges. *Anonymous.*
Captain Jinks. *Anonymous.*
Carol of the Birds. Bas-
  Quercy.
The Chestnut Vendor.
  Szelki.
Child on Top of a
  Greenhouse. Roethke.
Cow Dance. Beaver.
Crew Cut. McCord.
The Crow. Boumi-Pappas.
A Dream of Surreal Science.
  Ghose.
Errata. Simic.
The Farmer's Head. Padgett.

Forced March. Radnoti.
Free America. Warren.
Friday. Wet Dusk. Logue.
Glory, Glory to the Sun.
  Alford.
Heroes of the Strip. Cudahy.
Human Relations. Jarrett.
I Talk to You. Newlove.
In God's Eternity. Ballou I.
Judean Summer. Lipshitz.
The Miner's Progress.
  Delano.
Now Our Meeting's Over.
  Anonymous.
The Old Gospel Ship.
  Anonymous.
On Shooting Particles beyond
  the World. Eberhart.
Roundel in the Rain.
  Anonymous.
Sound Advice. *Anonymous.*
Sukkot. Lachman.
Te Deum. Le Fort.
To a God Unknown. Eller.
Underwear. Ferlinghetti.
We Are Watching, We Are
  Waiting. Cushing.
When a Warlock Dies.
  Gardner.
Shovel
In the Township. Glover.
The Last Supper. Rice.
Professor Noctutus.
  Macdonald.
We Must Make a Kingdom of
  It. Orr.
Show (ed) (s)
Ain't It Hard to Be a Right
  Black Nigger? *Anonymous.*
And if an eye may save or
  slay. Wyatt.
Beginning by Example.
  Gilbert.
Best of Show. Howes.
La Bete Humaine. Kirkup.
Broadway. Whitman.
The Butcher Boy.
  Anonymous.
The Cid: Two Lovers in the
  Toils of Honor. Corneille.
Clocks. Locker.
The Clown's Baby.
  Thomson.
The Dance of Love. Davies.
The Dog and the Water-lily.
  Cowper.
Elegy. Merwin.
Epigram: "Do you not wish to
  renounce the Devil?"
  Lanusse.
Even in my dreams. Ise.
Fat Cat. Ronan.
The Harp That Once through
  Tara's Halls. Moore.
Heaven. *Anonymous.*
Herndon. Mitchell.
The Hind and the Panther.
  Dryden.
The Horn. Reaney.
The Humours of Donnybrook
  Fair. O'Flaherty.
In Memoriam, A.C.M.L.
  (excerpt). Spring-Rice.
Jim the Splitter. Kendall.
Love's Labour's Lost.
  Shakespeare.
M & O Blues. Brown.
Maps to Nowhere.
  Rosenberg.
The Masters. Hope.
Midsummer Magic.
  Eastwick.

The Only News I Know.
  Dickinson.
Person, or A Hymn on and to
  the Holy Ghost. Avison.
A Present to a Lady.
  Anonymous.
The Question. Duncan.
Romance of the Swan's Nest.
  Browning.
Sarah Hazard's Love Letter.
  Ellis.
Show Me Thyself. Sangster.
Sonnets, V: "Those hours,
  that with gentle work did
  frame." Shakespeare.
Sonnets, XCIII: "So shall I
  live, supposing thou art
  true." Shakespeare.
Still Do I Keep My Look, My
  Identity... Brooks.
Third Enemy Speaks. Day
  Lewis.
To My More Than
  Meritorious Wife.
  Rochester.
To the White Fiends.
  McKay.
Visionary Oklahoma Sunday
  Beer. Whitehead.
A Wondrous Show.
  Thomson.
Shower (s)
After a Game of Squash.
  Albert.
Anger's Freeing Power.
  Smith.
Athletes. Gibson.
Beethoven. Wheelock.
Cathleen. *Anonymous.*
Help Thy Servant.
  Broaddus.
Love's Servile Lot.
  Southwell.
May Carols. De Vere.
Ode on the Departing Year.
  Coleridge.
On the Dark, Still, Dry,
  Warm Weather ... White.
The Phoenix. Darley.
Snow White and the Seven
  Dwarfs. Dahl.
Song: "Hither haste, and
  gently strew." Beddoes.
Tall Nettles. Thomas.
The Thunder Mutters Louder
  and More Loud. Clare.
The Whitsun Weddings.
  Larkin.
Shrapnel
The Bus-Stop on the Somme.
  Rowbotham.
On a Photo of a Baby Killed
  in the War. Defoe.
Shreds
The Garden. Wilde.
Upon Some Women.
  Herrick.
Shrew
The Masked Shrew.
  Gardner.
The Shrew. Nash.
Shrewd
And Dust to Dust. Webb.
Astrophel and Stella, XVII.
  Sidney.
Vignette: 1922. Spingarn.
Shriek (ed) (ing) (s)
Bad Dream. MacNeice.
A Common Inference.
  Gilman.
The Face Upon the Floor.
  D'Arcy.

Fear. Schjeldahl.
The Frost Spirit. Whittier.
Hyperion. Keats.
Little Miss Muffet (parody).
  Anonymous.
On the Marriage of T. K. and
  C. C. the Morning Stormy.
  Carew.
Quebec Farmhouse. Glassco.
Redbreast, Early in the
  Morning. Bronte.
Ulysses' Library. Daiches.
The Wedding of Alcmane and
  Mya. Chapman.
Young Edwin in the Lowlands
  Low. *Anonymous.*
Shrine (s)
Amours de Voyage. Clough.
The Ancient Sacrifice.
  Fisher.
Art Thou Afraid the Adorer's
  Prayer. Landor.
Caelica, III. Greville.
Epigram: "God scatters
  beauty as he scatters
  flowers." Landor.
An Epitaph upon the
  Celebrated Claudy Philips,
  Musician... Johnson.
The Eve of St. Mark. Keats.
Fame. Rutsala.
The Geraldine's Daughter
  (excerpt). Mangan.
Jefferson Davis. Bell.
Kinchinjunga. Rice.
More Than Most Fair.
  Greville.
On Mr. G. Herbert's Book.
  Crashaw.
Proem. Whittier.
The Small Silver-Coloured
  Bookworm. Parnell.
Song to the Virgin Mary.
  Lopez de Ayala.
Trail All Your Pikes.
  Winchilsea.
Troilus and Criseyde.
  Chaucer.
We Praise Thee, If One
  Rescued Soul. Sigourney.
Shriner
A Disappearance in West
  Cedar Street. Sissman.
Shrink
He Visits a Hospital.
  Humphries.
The Jovial Marriner; or, The
  Sea-Man's Renown.
  Playford.
The Trees of the Garden.
  Rossetti.
Upon the Author; by a
  Known Friend.
  Woodbridge.
Weak Is the Will of Man, His
  Judgment Blind.
  Wordsworth.
Shrivel (ed) (s)
Art. Thomson.
Dried Fruit (parody). Dow.
A Freshet. Antiphilus of
  Byzantium.
The Playboy of the Demi-
  World: 1938. Plomer.
String. Schmitz.
Shroud (s)
The African Desert (excerpt).
  Tupper.
Arachne. Cooke.
The Child-Bride. Oates.
A Dream. Sackville-West.
Eliza Telefair. Sloan.

The Falcon. Stoddard.
Five Degrees South. Young.
Flax. Bunin.
Funeral Hymn. *Anonymous.*
Highland Shooting Lodge.
  Lindsay.
Hymn of the Moravian Nuns
  of Bethlehem. Longfellow.
Hyperion. Keats.
In Memoriam A.H.H., XXVI.
  Tennyson.
July 1914. Akhmatova.
Last Cargo. Bellows.
Mid-Ocean in War-Time.
  Kilmer.
My Stars. Ibn Ezra.
Night Quarters. Brownell.
Oblivion. Fauset.
Out of Luck. Ibn Ezra.
Resurrection. Blackmur.
Rites for a Demagogue.
  Thwaite.
Song: "I make my shroud but
  no one knows." Crapsey.
Sweeney Among the
  Nightingales. Eliot.
The Vision of Judgement.
  Byron.
Shrub (s)
Central Park. Lowell.
Sonnets. Tuckerman.
Shrug (s)
Birthday. Ciardi.
An Israeli Soldier's
  Nightmare. Carb.
Poem for People Who Are
  Understandably Too Busy
  to Read Poetry. Dunn.
Shrunk (en)
Coogan's Wood. Stuart.
The Fairies Feast. Doughty.
How It Is. Greenberg.
The palm of my hand. Saito.
Shudder (ed) (ing)
Brussels in Winter. Auden.
Early Summer Night. Wen
  I-to.
Grief and God. Phillips.
Singing on the Moon.
  Hughes.
Six O'Clock. Stickney.
Sonnets. Tuckerman.
Stanzas. Ibn Gabirol.
Throughout the Day We Are
  Able to Ban the Voices.
  Roland-Holst.
Shun (ned)
Botany Bay. *Anonymous.*
Come, All Ye Youths.
  Otway.
Drowning is Not so Pitiful.
  Dickinson.
Little Mousgrove and the
  Lady Barnet. *Anonymous.*
Lust. Shakespeare.
Song: The Hopeless Comfort.
  Gould.
Sonnets, CXXIX: "Th'
  expense of spirit in a waste
  of shame." Shakespeare.
Springfield Mountain (C
  vers.). *Anonymous.*
A Wild Rattling Cowboy.
  Anonymous.
Shut (ting) (s)
As Oyster Nan Stood by Her
  Tub. *Anonymous.*
A Bestiary. Rexroth.
Boast Not Proud English, of
  Thy Birth and Blood.
  Williams.

Shut
Cardinal Ideograms.
  Swenson.
Doors. Hagedorn.
Five Were Foolish. Hodge.
For Every Man. Reich.
Get Up and Bar the Door.
  Anonymous.
A Heart That's Been Broken.
  Owen.
I Am the Door. Crashaw.
Invasion on the Farm.
  Thomas.
The Jealous Lovers. Hall.
Jittery Jim. Smith.
Music. Phillips.
Pull My Daisy. Kerouac.
The Sandman. Janvier.
Sonnets. Tuckerman.
Where the Picnic Was.
  Hardy.
Your Body Is Stars.
  Spender.

Shut up
Flashback. Ginsberg.
Letter to Garber from Skye.
  Hugo.
To the Moon. Hardy.
Where I'll Be Good. Ryan.
A Word to Husbands. Nash.

Shutter (s)
Berceuse. Clampitt.
Christmas Amnesty. Pierce.
On the Day of Atonement.
  Amichai.
Passover Eve. Kruger.
Profile. Wallace.
Winter Saint. Ammons.

Shuttle (s)
The Bat. Voigt.
Poverty Knock. *Anonymous.*
The Scarlet Thread.
  Henderson.

Shy (ness)
An Artist Draws a Peach.
  Hampl.
Because I Were Shy.
  Anonymous.
The Distances They Keep.
  Nemerov.
Easter in the Woods. Frost.
False Friends-Like. Barnes.
The Grace of Cynthia's
  Maidenhood. D'Ambrosio.
Growing Old. Learned.
The Jungle. Williams.
A Nameless Recognition.
  Gregor.
Nightingales. Conkling.
On Yes Tor. Gosse.
A Pretty a Day. Cummings.
Song. Macdonagh.
Suicide. MacNeice.
Walking for That Cake.
  Harrigan.

Siberia
Exiles. Hayne.

Siblings
The Djanggawul Cycle, 172.
  Anonymous.
To My Wife Asleep. Tick.

Sicily
Last Sheet. Fuller.
Theocritus. Wilde.

Sick (er) (ness)
The Aesthete to the Rose
  (parody). *Anonymous.*
After the Agony in the Guest
  Bedroom. Atwood.
As I Came O'er Cairney
  Mount. *Anonymous.*
Commissary Report. King.

Dirty Mistreatin' Women.
  Anonymous.
Do you have a sweet thought,
  Cerinthus. Sulpicia.
A Doctor Fell in a Deep
  Well. *Anonymous.*
Euch, Are You Having Your
  Period? Alta.
A Far Cry after a Close Call.
  Howard.
From Summer Hours.
  Samain.
From the Notebooks.
  Roethke.
From Trollope's Journal.
  Bishop.
Green and Yellow.
  Anonymous.
Inebriates. Brasfield.
Ipecacuanha. Canning.
Journal. Ciardi.
Joy of Life. Ibn Ezra.
Keeping Their World Large.
  Moore.
Leaving Inishmore. Longley.
Limerick: "There was a young
  lady of Twickenham."
  Herford.
Men. Parker.
Mother Superior. MacBeth.
No Theory. Ignatow.
Now Springs the Spray.
  Anonymous.
Office Party. McGinley.
Oh, England. Sick in Head
  and Sick in Heart.
  Anonymous.
On One That Lived
  Ingloriously. Hoskyns.
A Prayer. McLeod.
Sonnet: He Will Not Be Too
  Deeply in Love.
  Angiolieri.
Sonnets, CXVIII: "Like as to
  make our appetites more
  keep". Shakespeare.
'Tis Summer Time on Bredon
  (parody). Kingsmill.
To Meet, or Otherwise.
  Hardy.
Tragedy. Russell.
Troilus and Cressida.
  Shakespeare.
A True Maid. Prior.
The Willing Prisoner to His
  Mistress. Carew.

Sickle
Babel. Pacernick.
Caelica, XXVIII. Greville.
The Employee. Holzapfel.
Harvest Time. Watermeyer.
Hope. Fanshawe.
New Mexican Mountain.
  Jeffers.
Pauca Mea: I Said, This
  Misery Must End.
  Brennan.
Poems from a Greek
  Anthology (excerpt).
  Palladas.
The Sword and the Sickle.
  Blake.
To Helen. Praed.

Side
Alone. Witheford.
Bear Hunting. Aua.
Black Jack Davy.
  Anonymous.
The Brothers. Sprague.
Christ Is Crucified Anew.
  Moreland.

The Dead by the Side of the
  Road. Snyder.
The Dream. Bogan.
Elfer Hill. *Anonymous.*
Environ S. Eigner.
Father, Hear the Prayer We
  Offer. Willis.
Fear Not, Poor Weary One.
  Upham.
For a Shetland Pony Brood
  Mare Who Died in Her
  Barren Year. Kumin.
A Game of Glass. Reid.
Headsong. Bennett.
I Got to Roll. *Anonymous.*
Innocence. Spencer.
Jesu, Come on Board.
  Pyrlaeus.
Long, Long Ago. Bayly.
Love Me and Never Leave
  Me. McCuaig.
The Miller and His Sons.
  Anonymous.
The Most Beautiful Girl in
  the World. Hart.
My Lady Has the Grace of
  Death. Plunkett.
Narcissus, Come Kiss Us!
  Anonymous.
Never. Reavey.
O, Open the Door to Me, O!
  Burns.
Old Christmas. Helton.
One Immortality. Engels.
Painted Passages. Harada.
Pastoral. Tate.
The Permanence of the Young
  Men. Soutar.
The Pines. Lippmann.
Sailor Man. Bailey.
Seven Long Years in State
  Prison (with music).
  Anonymous.
Stafford in Kansas (parody).
  Hall.
Strange Tree. Roberts.
We Greet Each Other in the
  Side (parody) (excerpt).
  Anonymous.
We Need a King.
  Macdougall.
Which Side Are You On?
  Reese.

Sidewalk (s)
Chalk from Eden. Moss.
I Done Got So Thirsty That
  My Mouth Waters at the
  Thought of Rain. Jones.
Ordinary Women. Hacker.
Tar. Williams.
The Wives. Hall.

Siege
At Belle Isle. *Anonymous.*
Leningrad Cemetery, Winter
  of 1941. Olds.
Woodcut. Wilson.

Sieve
Fragment: The Furl of Fresh-
  Leaved Dog-Rose Down.
  Hopkins.
Looking for the Melungeon.
  Smith.
Satires. Wyatt.
The White Ship. Hill.

Sift
Last Rite. Hicks.
Madrigal: To His Lady
  Selvaggia Vergiolesi...
  Cino da Pistoia.

Sigh (ed) (ing) (s)
Ae Fond Kiss. Burns.
April Love. Dowson.

At Her Fair Hands.
  Davison.
At most mischief. Wyatt.
Bird and the Muse.
  Zaturenska.
The Burning of the Temple.
  Rosenberg.
Caelica, VIII. Greville.
Childe Harold's Pilgrimage:
  Canto III. Byron.
The Clover. Deland.
Coda. Johnson.
Cowper's Three Hares.
  Turner.
A Dirge. Rossetti.
Dixie's Green Shore.
  Anonymous.
A Drinking Song. Yeats.
Drinking the Wind. Tan
  Ying.
The Duenna (excerpt).
  Sheridan.
Even though my hands.
  Anonymous.
Fall Song. Moses.
Fantasy. Nerval.
Far in a Western Brookland.
  Housman.
Fingal: an Ancient Epic Poem
  (excerpt). MacPherson.
The Flying Tailor (parody).
  Hogg.
The Fury of Flowers and
  Worms. Sexton.
The Galley Slave (excerpt).
  Anonymous.
The Garden That I Love.
  Henderson.
Houdini. Mandel.
I Love My Love in the
  Morning. Griffin.
The Iliad. Homer.
In These Fair Vales.
  Wordsworth.
Inanna and Ishkur.
  Enheduanna.
Into Blackness Softly. Evans.
The Kingfisher. Davies.
Labor and Love. Gosse.
The Lady of the Lake.
  Anonymous.
The Lass of Roch Royal (D
  version). *Anonymous.*
Last Rite. Hicks.
Lise. Cooke.
The Look. Daryush.
The Lowest Trees Have Tops.
  Dyer.
March Evening. Strong.
The Master Mariner.
  Sterling.
Medieval Christ Speaks on a
  Spanish Sculpture of
  Himself. Owens.
The Monks of Bangor's
  March. Scott.
The Moon at the Fortified
  Pass. Li Po.
The Moon-Child. "Macleod.
My Days Have Been So
  Wondrous Free.
  Anonymous.
My Lute and I. Wyatt.
My Song. Bialik.
Negro Serenade. Campbell.
Night-Wind. Lloyd.
Now That the Flowers.
  Jones.
On the Way to Language.
  Palmer.

A Poem Written in Time of Trouble by an Irish Priest... Gregory.

Popular Songs of Tuscany. *Anonymous.*

Praise. O'Sullivan.

The Prisoner of Chillon. Byron.

The Roman Earl. *Anonymous.*

Rose Aylmer. Landor.

The Scholar. Cornford.

Seascape. Spender.

Silences. O'Shaughnessy.

Smothered Fires. Johnson.

Solitude. Peterson.

Sonnet: "I must now grieve my Love, whose eyes would read." Daniel.

Sonnet: To the Same Ladies; with Their Answer. Dante Alighieri.

Stanzas. Bronte.

Storm at Sea. Davenant.

Sylvia the Fair. Dryden.

The Taj. Keene.

To Mary: I Sleep with Thee, and Wake with Thee. Clare.

To R. B. Hopkins.

To Sycamores. Herrick.

To the Virgin Mary. Petrarch.

Tutto e Sciolto. Joyce.

The Unutterable Beauty. Studdert-Kennedy.

Vala; or, The Four Zoas. Blake.

A Valediction: of Weeping. Donne.

Variation on a Theme by John Lyly. Sitwell.

Villa Sciarra: Rome. Curtis.

Visions of the Daughters of Albion. Blake.

La Vita Nuova. Dante Alighieri.

Waking. MacDonogh.

Wash-Day Wonder. Faubion.

The Way I Read a Letter's— This. Dickinson.

When Damon First Began to Love. Behn.

When Two Are Parted. Heine.

While I walked in the moonlight. Murasaki Shibiku.

Wild Cherry Tree. Blunden.

Winter Life and Scenery. Irwin.

Written at an Inn at Henley. Shenstone.

Sight

Afreet. McCord.

Allah. Mahlmann.

An Apologie for Having Loved Before. Waller.

Artificial Teeth. Brown.

At the Ball Game. Field.

At the Smithsonian. Haley.

Ballad of the Ten Casino Dancers. Meireles.

Bingo Has an Enemy. Fyleman.

Captain's Table. Bynner.

Cease, Then, My Tongue! Spenser.

Chester. Billings.

A Child's Song of Christmas. Pickthall.

The Christmas Tree. Cornelius.

A Copy of Verses on Jefferys the Seaman. *Anonymous.*

Cupid's Pastime. Davison.

Dandelions. Albee.

Dawning. Dixon.

The Dead Singer. Townsend.

The Dirty-Billed Freeze Footy. Hemschemeyer.

Dithyramb in Retrospect. Hopegood.

The Fair-Haired Girl. *Anonymous.*

Fire Island. Swenson.

The Glens. Hewitt.

How Glorious Are the Morning Stars. Keach.

I Saw a Peacock. *Anonymous.*

Inishkeel Parish Church. Paulin.

Journey. Harrison.

Lightning. Bynner.

Little Satellite. Krows.

Love-Songs, At Once Tender and Informative. Hoffenstein.

A Lover's Words. Watkins.

A Lyric from a Play. *Anonymous.*

Malcolm. Cumbo.

Marmion. Scott.

The Marrowbone Itch. *Anonymous.*

A Midnight Interior. Sassoon.

The Mill. Robinson.

A Miltonic Sonnet for Mr. Johnson... Wilbur.

Morgans in October. Brabant.

My Grandmother. Adams.

New Mexican Desert. Bynner.

October's Song. Farjeon.

Oh Bright Oh Black Singbeast Lovebeast Catkin Sleek. McClure.

On the Porch at the Frost Place, Franconia, NH. Matthews.

Paradox. Miller.

Places of Nestling Green. Hunt.

The Postilion Has Been Struck by Lightning. Beer.

Pride. Holyday.

The Rain. Davies.

The Sanctuary. Nemerov.

Shall I Come, If I Swim? Wide Are the Waves, You See. Campion.

Ships That Pass in the Night. Dunbar.

Sockeye Salmon. Hambleton.

Something. Creeley.

Song for Midsummer Night. Coatsworth.

A Song of Love for Jesus. Rolle.

Song of the All-Wool Shirt. Field.

The Song of the Bower. Rossetti.

Sonnets, IV: "Two stars there are in one faire firmament." Barnfield.

Spiral Landscape. Brownstein.

St. Isaac's Chruch, Petrograd. McKay.

Stars. Frost.

Tears. Reese.

The Testament of Beauty. Bridges.

Three Blind Mice. *Anonymous.*

Three Trees at Solstice. Finnin.

To My Cousin, (C.R.) Marrying My Lady (A.). Carew.

To the Sun. Bachmann.

Twilight. Lawrence.

The Unblinding. Lieberman.

Visions. Petrarch.

La Vita Nuova. Dante Alighieri.

Voice. Moss.

The Winter's Walk. Johnson.

Sightless

Hands. Cloud.

Hector the Collector. Silverstein.

A Trucker. Gunn.

Sights

Engine Failure. Corsellis.

Haitian Suite. Orr.

Maturity. Owen.

Sightseers

In Canterbury Cathedral. Oldenburg.

Sign (s)

After Tennyson: "To watch the tipsy cripples on the beach." Lear.

The Amputee Soldier. Dacey.

An Argument–Of the Passion of Christ. Merton.

Artist. Mercer.

At the Roman Baths, Bath. Lucie-Smith.

Bahnhofstrasse. Joyce.

The Battle of Bunker Hill. *Anonymous.*

Burlesque Translation of Lines from Lope de Vega's "Arcadia'. Butler.

The Death of a Warrior. Mastoraki.

Domine, Quo Vadis? *Anonymous.*

An Epithalamion upon the Marquis of Huntilies Marriage. James I

Extraordinary Will. Jackett.

The Faerie Queene. Spenser.

Fear. Simic.

Fling Out the Banner! Doane.

The Gangrel Rymour and the Pairdon of Sanct Anne. Corbiere.

Gone Fishing. Sanders.

Harvest. Sitwell.

I'll act out a weird dream. Prager.

In Hoc Signo. Bradby.

Insularum Ocelle. Swinburne.

Kaiser Dead. Arnold.

Lost Month. Merwin.

Marm Grayson's Guests. Freeman.

Marx, the Sign Painter. Masters.

May Day Demonstrators. Lindsay.

Minuet in a Minor Key. Janowitz.

The Month of the Thunder Moon. Doyle.

Night. Montgomery.

Not the Arms Race. Abrams.

Ode: "As it fell upon a day." Barnfield.

An Ode in Time of Hesitation: Robert Gould Shaw. Moody.

The Once-Over. Blackburn.

One Is a Sign of Mischief. *Anonymous.*

Parish. Dubie.

Peace Walk. Stafford.

The Policeman. Watts.

The Postcards: A Triptych. Levertov.

Refracted Lights. Wooley.

Rise and Fall of Valentines. Downey.

Scene from a Play, Acted at Oxford, Called "Matriculation." Moore.

The Setting of the Moon. Leopardi.

Special Delivery. Montague.

Third Degree. Hughes.

The Wise Men. Bowers.

Signal (s)

Bill the Whaler. Lawson.

Dante. Duncan.

Dog Fight. Rolls.

Failures. Upson.

Isolation. Peabody.

Revelation. Markham.

Theocritus. Fields.

To Be Sung. Viereck.

'Twas Warm at First, Like Us. Dickinson.

Signature

Look, How Beautiful. Jeffers.

Melchior Vulpius. Moore.

The Pact. Rubin.

River Skater. Welles.

Writing on the Wall. Fallon.

Significant

An Epitaph Upon–. Marvell.

Peterhead in May. Singer.

Succumbing. Reeve.

Silence (d) (s)

Abiku. Soyinka.

After Commencement. Nemerov.

Aftermath. Longfellow.

Against Seasons. Mezey.

Air. Raine.

All Which Isn't Singing Is Mere Talking. Cummings.

Alone. Witheford.

Aprons of Silence. Sandburg.

The Argument of Democritus Platonissans. More.

The Arid Lands. Bashford.

Artemis Prologizes. Browning.

At It. Thomas.

Australian Transcripts, IX: The Bell-Bird. Sharp.

Autumn. Clare.

Away from You. Meireles.

The Bird at Dawn. Monro.

Black-Out. Jeffers.

Blue Owl Song. Kittner.

The Bride's Prelude. Rossetti.

Building in Stone. Warner.

Bullfrog. Hughes.

The Bush (excerpt). O'Dowd.

Cancer Research. Parlatore.

A "Case of Assault."
  Stephanou.
Child Bearing. Ghigna.
Clowns' Houses. Sitwell.
Coal Miner's Grace. Divine.
The Coastwise Lights.
  Kipling.
Cold Is the Winter.
  Anonymous.
The Collector. Flynn.
Colonial Set. Bailey.
The Complaisant Friend.
  Louys.
Conscience. Ravitch.
Convalescence. McAuley.
Conversing with Paradise.
  Nemerov.
Crossing the Water. Plath.
Daphne. Flanner.
The Dark Chamber.
  Untermeyer.
The Demagogue. McGinley.
Depression. Bly.
The Descent of Winter
  (Section 10/30). Williams.
Dinosaur Tracks in Beit Zayit.
  Kaufman.
Distance. Everwine.
Eagle Sonnets. Wood.
Echo. De la Mare.
Eclogue. Diaper.
Elegy for an Unknown
  Soldier. Baxter.
Elliott Hawkins. Masters.
Encounter. Hammond.
Evening. Sangster.
Evening Song. Cheney.
Evening Song of Senlin.
  Aiken.
Faint Music. De La Mare.
Father and Son. Higgins.
Fear of Death. Ashbery.
Fireworks. Deutsch.
First Communion. Silva.
Foreboding. Hall.
Fourteenth Birthday.
  McGinley.
From Life. Eichenrand.
The Fruit Rancher. Roberts.
A Fugue. Church.
Full Fathom Five. Fairburn.
Full Valleys. Scott.
Funeral Toast. Mallarme.
Gethsemane. Bontemps.
Ghazals. Harrison.
Gods in Vietnam. Redmond.
The Gray Folk. Nesbit.
A Guard of the Sepulcher.
  Markham.
The Heart Mountain Japanese
  Relocation Camp: 30 Years
  Later. Levendosky.
The Heavens Are Our Riddle.
  Bates.
Hello Goodbye. Thesen.
Herman Moon's Hourbook.
  Middleton.
Hosanna to Christ. Watts.
The House of Life. Rossetti.
I Have Come Far to Have
  Found Nothing. Corman.
I Hear It Said. Young.
I'll find My Self-Belief.
  Glatstein.
Illustrious Ancestors.
  Levertov.
In the City of Bogota. Pape.
In the Garden of the Turkish
  Consulate. Sadeh.
The Indwelling God.
  Hosmer.

A Judicious Observation of
  That Dreadful Comet.
  Wiswall.
Juniper. Francis.
Kiss. Young.
Knee Lunes. Kelly.
The Last Fire. Steingart.
The Legend of the Organ-
  Builder. Dorr.
Lights Out. Thomas.
Like an Ideal Tenant.
  Daigon.
Listening. Corbin.
Loneliness. Essex.
Losing the Straight Way.
  Wedde.
Love Poem on Theme by
  Whitman. Ginsberg.
Love's Wisdom. Deland.
Mad Sweeny. Montague.
The Man with the Hoe.
  Markham.
Mary's Assumption. Barrett.
Meet Me in the Primrose
  Lane. Clare.
Memorial to the Great Big
  Beautiful Self-Sacrificing
  Advertisers. Ebright.
The Memory of Elena.
  Forche.
Midnight and Ten Minutes.
  Vinner.
A Minor Bird. Frost.
Mont Blanc. Shelley.
Moon. Walcott.
Moving in Winter. Rich.
Music at Twilight. Sterling.
Nanye'hi (Nancy Ward), the
  Last Beloved Woman of the
  Cherokees... Green.
Ndaaya's Kasala (excerpt).
  Citeku Ndaaya.
Night in the House by the
  River. Tu Fu.
Night opens like an almond.
  Caroutch.
Night Song at Amalfi.
  Teasdale.
Nocturne of the Self-Evident
  Presence. MacGreevy.
Noel: Christmas Eve, 1913.
  Bridges.
Notes for a History of Poetry.
  Daiches.
Now Is the High-Tide of the
  Year. Lowell.
O Realm Bejewelled.
  Farrokhzad.
Objects. Auden.
Of Late. Starbuck.
Of Snow. Brick.
Old Man. Carr.
The Old Woman. Bunker.
On the Eclipse of the Moon of
  October 1865. Turner.
Oreads. Raine.
The Parachutist. Anderson.
Paradise Lost. Milton.
Partings. Guerin.
The Peepers in Our Meadow.
  MacLeish.
Pelters of Pyramids. Horne.
Persephone. Longley.
The Pilgrim of a Day.
  Campbell.
Poem for the Atomic Age.
  Litvinoff.
Poem with the Final Tune.
  Burgos.
Poet in Residence at a
  Country School. Welch.
Praise. O'Sullivan.

Prayer. Bro.
The Pueblo Women I
  Watched Get down in
  Brooklyn. Rose.
The Queen's Last Ride.
  Wilcox.
Quick and Bitter. Amichai.
Repose. Lichtenstein.
Requiescat. Porter.
Reuben's Cabin. Morgan.
Roarers in a Ring. Hughes.
The Rose. Roethke.
The Sacrifice. Bloch.
Sagacity. Benet.
Saint. Mallarme.
The Sea and the Mirror.
  Auden.
Seasons of the Soul. Tate.
Seaward Bound. Brown.
Sermon in a Churchyard.
  Macaulay.
Ships That Pass in the Night.
  Longfellow.
A Short Treatise upon Our
  Failures. Norris.
The Silence. MacLeish.
Silence. Masters.
Silences. Pratt.
Silent Love. Clare.
The Silent Piano. Simpson.
The Slaughterhouse Boys.
  Meissner.
The Snow Party. Mahon.
Snowfall. Carducci.
A Soldier Poet. Johnson.
Sonnet of Departure.
  Hervey.
Sonnets at Christmas. Tate.
Sonnets from the Portuguese,
  XXI. Browning.
Speechless. Marston.
St. Simon and St. Jude's Day.
  Alexander.
The Stones. Berry.
Sub Specie Aeternitatis.
  Hayden.
The Swan. Roethke.
Sweet Silence after Bells!
  Brennan.
Tatiana Kalatschova. Logan.
Teresa of Avila. Jennings.
This Is My Hour. Akins.
This One Heart-Shaken.
  Maris Stella.
Threnody. Ignatow.
Thy Sea So Great. Garrison.
To a Baseball. *Anonymous.*
To the Nightingale. Ayres.
The Tomboy. Burford.
The Trial. Rukeyser.
Tunes for Bears to Dance To.
  Wallace.
Twenty-One Sonnets. Stead.
The Two Stars. Davies.
Untitled: "Words do not grow
  on the landscape." Malley.
Vers La Vie. Upson.
Vicissitudes of the Creator.
  MacLeish.
Voyage a L'Infini.
  Arensberg.
Walking on Water. Petaccia.
The Water-Hole. Wood.
Were I to Choose. Okara.
When I Heard the Learn'd
  Astronomer. Whitman.
When in the Crowd I
  Suddenly Behold. Nathan.
When We Two Parted.
  Byron.
The White Bird. McFadden.

The Widow of Drynam.
  MacDonogh.
Wild Eden. Woodberry.
Winter Sketch. Bourinot.
Winter Sleep. Thomas.
Woman and Nature. Griffin.
You Are My Sisters.
  Rodenbach.
Your Eyes Have Their
  Silence. Barrax.
Your Songs. Bennett.

Silent Land
Song of the Silent Land.
  Salis-Seewis.

Silent (ly) (ness)
As Animals. Spivak.
Be Still As You Are Beautiful.
  MacDonogh.
Benighted to the Foothills of
  the Cairngorms. Fraser.
Between Life and Death.
  Gottlieb.
Black and White. Adame.
Buffalo Creek. Brereton.
Burial. Sarton.
Castle Rock. Morgan.
Channel Crossing. Barker.
Corporal Stare. Graves.
Creed. Spencer.
Creide's Lament for Cael.
  Anonymous.
"The Day is Done " (Parody
  on Longfellow). Cary.
Delicate Mother Kangaroo.
  Lawrence.
Desolation. Lowell.
Elevation. Baudelaire.
Ere the Golden Bowl Is
  Broken. Branch.
Feathers and Moss. Ingelow.
Florella. *Anonymous.*
Fragment. McCrae.
Fragments of Ancient Poetry
  (excerpt). Macpherson.
Harp in the Rigging.
  Maclaren.
He Drunken Rose. Amarou.
The Hermit Wakes to Bird
  Sounds. Kumin.
Homage to Edward Hopper.
  George.
How to Write a Letter.
  Turner.
I Love. Chimsoro.
I Rode with My Darling...
  Smith.
In a Valley of This Restless
  Mind. Milne.
In This Hour. Johnson.
Inishkeel Parish Church.
  Paulin.
Leaves of Grass. Whitman
The Meeting of the Ships.
  Moore.
Mouth. Nicoidski.
An Ode on the Death of Mr.
  Henry Purcell (excerpt).
  Dryden.
On Sunday in the Sunlight.
  Benet.
Out of the Sea. Bynner.
Pacific Epitaphs. Randall.
The Paradox. Pereira.
Pasa Thalassa Thalassa.
  Robinson.
The Pointed People. Field.
A Prayer: "Give me work to
  do." *Anonymous.*
Prolonged Sonnet: When the
  Troops Were Returning
  from Milan. Niccolo.
Redemption. Cooperman.

Revolution. Housman.
Sea Food Thought. Moser.
Sea Sonnet. Lay.
The Second Poem the Night-Walker Wrote. Goethe.
September Evening, 1938. Plomer.
Seven Poems. Niedecker.
Silent Hill. Snyder.
Silent in America. Levine.
Simultaneously. Ignatow.
The Smoky Smirr o' Rain. Hay.
The Snowstorm. Scott.
Sonnets, XXIII: "As an unperfect actor on the stage." Shakespeare.
Spring Nocturne. Liessin.
Sunday on Hampstead Heath. Woodcock.
Tennesse Crickets. Outlaw.
Thrushes. Hughes.
Thus Crosslegged on Round Pillow Sat in Space. Ginsberg.
To a Friend. Gullans.
To Boris Pasternak. Kushner.
To Potapovitch. Crane.
Too Late. Marston.
Unsaid. Ammons.
Upanishads: Seventh Brahmana. *Anonymous.*
What Were They Like? Levertov.
The White Horse. Lawrence.
Winter-Solitude. Lampman.
The World Is Not a Fenced-Off Garden. Steinberg.
You Are the Brave. Patterson.

Silent Night
Come, Holy Babe! Bangham.
Oft in the Silent Night. Bierbaum.
Then Twist the Neck of This Delusive Swan. Gonzales Martinez.

Silhouette
The Poet in Old Age Fishing at Evening. O'Grady.
Widow's Walk. Spires.

Silk (en) (s)
As for Me, I Delight in the Everyday Way. Stroud.
Baby Running Barefoot. Lawrence.
Boudoir Lament. Yu Hsuan-chi.
Caelica, L. Greville.
Cocoon. Ishigaki Rin.
Dislike of Tasks. Lattimore.
Enueg. Beckett.
The Field. Valentine.
For a Poet. Cullen.
For a Shetland Pony Brood Mare Who Died in Her Barren Year. Kumin.
Great-Aunt Rebecca. Brewster.
Lalique. Porter.
Lamia. Keats.
The Lost Parasol (excerpt). Weores.
Love and Debt Alike Troublesom. Suckling.
Modern Love. Stern.
Out of the Sea, Early. Swenson.
Pussy Cat Mole. *Anonymous.*
Rain Clouds. Long.

The Ship. Squire.
Three Poems. "Ping Hsin" (Hsieh Wang-ying).
Turn Blind. Celan.

Silkworms
Tzu Yeh Songs. *Anonymous.*

Silly
Carmina. Catullus.
The Critic on the Hearth. Sissman.
Felo de Se. Hughes.
Hipporhinostricow. Milligan.
July 1st, French Creek. Roberts.
Limerick: "There was a young man named Achilles." Robinson.
The Man Who Sang the Sillies. Ciardi.
Mullion. Herbert.
On a Very Young, Very Dead Soldier. Gillman.
An Owl in an Oak. *Anonymous.*
Warning to One. Moore.

Silt
Arrowtown. Glover.
Not in Narrow Seas. Curnow.

Silver
Adelina, the Yale Boola Girl. Loomis.
America A Prophecy. Blake.
The Ark and the Dove. Sargent.
The Autumnal Moon. Thomson.
Banks of Marble. Rice.
Before the Dive. Kempf.
The Brook (excerpt). Wright.
The Bunyip. Stewart.
The Burman Lover. Baker.
Death's Transfiguration. Zangwill.
A Doubting Heart. Procter.
The Dream of the Rood. *Anonymous.*
Elements of Grammar. Hernton.
An Esthetic of Imitation. Finkel.
The Fable of the Magnet and the Churn. Gilbert.
The Faithful Shepherdess. Fletcher.
Fishermen at Dawn. Meissner.
Fishing Harbour towards Evening. Kell.
Five Things White. May.
The Flood. Bell.
The Gamblers. Delius.
A Garden Song. Moore.
The glow and beauty of the stars. Sappho.
Go Take the World. Macpherson.
Going for Water. Frost.
Golden Moonrise. Braithwaite.
Graves at Elkhorn. Hugo.
The Great Divide. Sarett.
The Greenland Men. *Anonymous.*
Halieutica. Oppian.
The Harlot's House. Wilde.
The Heavenly City. Smith.
How a Girl Was Too Reckless of Grammar. Carryl.
Hudson Ferry. Schuyler.
The Hunt. *Anonymous.*

In Memoriam: A.C., R.J.O., K.S. Betjeman.
In Memory of Garcia Lorca. Grier.
Inflation. Hartman.
Inquietude. Murray.
Interruption. Graves.
It Dropped So Low—in My Regard. Dickinson.
Jesus Drum. Lomax.
June. Reaney.
Labor Day. Pomeroy.
A Lament. Avison.
Lamentations. Gluck.
Linota Rufescens. Donaghy.
Love in a Cottage. Willis.
Malediction upon Myself. Wylie.
Marriage. Carver.
Mary in the Silvery Tide. *Anonymous.*
Medoro's Inscription for a Cave. Stewart of Baldynnis.
The Navigators. Turner.
New Friends and Old Friends. Parry.
New Leaves. Jimenez.
New Storefront. Atkins.
Next unto Him Was Neptune Pictured. Spenser.
Ode to the Moon. Hood.
Of a Spider. Thorley.
Oh, I Would Be a Cowboy and with the Cowboys Stand. *Anonymous.*
Pacelli and the Ethiop. Cassity.
Paradise Lost. Milton.
The Persistence of Memory, the Failure of Poetry. Phillips.
A Pilot from the Carrier. Jarrell.
Raid on the Market. Chimedza.
The Return. Bishop.
The Ride-by-Nights. De la Mare.
The River in March. Hughes.
Rye Whiskey. *Anonymous.*
Sharks, Caloosahatchee River. Papc.
The Sharpbreasted Snake (Hokpe Fuske). Oliver.
The Silent Walls. Strachan.
Silver in the Wind. Strachan.
The Silver Question. Herford.
The Skaters. Fletcher.
Song: "How pleas'd within my native bowers." Shenstone.
Sonnets to Orpheus. Rilke.
Summer Night. Bialik.
Teahouse. Rinaldi.
Tecumseh. Mair.
Ticonderoga. Wilson.
Tiger Lily. McCord.
Treasure Boat. Fujino.
Trooper and Maid, I. *Anonymous.*
The Tusks of Blood. Greenberg.
The Virgins. Walcott.
The Waif. De la Mare.
Water. Conkling.
A Way Up on Clinch Mountain (A vers. with music). *Anonymous.*
What He Took. Anonymous.

White Fear. Welles.
Winds A-Blowing. Justus.
Wings at Dawn. Auslander.
Words for Music Perhaps. Yeats.

Simile (s)
Footnote. Delius.
Monody on a Century. Birney.
Very Like a Whale. Nash.

Similitude
Aurora Leigh. Browning.
On the Esplanade des Invalides. Fisher.

Simon
Simple Simon. *Anonymous.*
Simple Simon. Morgridge.

Simple (r)
The Amish. Updike.
The Angel in the House. Patmore.
Content. Whitney.
The Court We Live On. Tremblay.
Darwinity. Merivale.
Each Day. Ignatow.
The Fire. Creeley.
The Good Rich Man. Chesterton.
Grandfather's Heaven. Nye.
Hen Woman. Kinsella.
In the Orpheum Building. Robinson.
Jack and Jill. Morgridge.
Jack and Jill (parody). Powell.
Kinaxixi. Neto.
Love Poem. Rea.
Naples Again. Freeman.
New Maths. Lehrer.
Nothing but a man. Tueni.
One Word More. Browning.
Poem: "Geranium, houseleek, laid in oblong beds." Gray.
Progression. Scarfe.
Psalm XII. Sidney.
Quick-Step. Creeley.
Rural Simplicity. Byron.
Scylla and Charybdis. Kinsella.
The Snake. Moore.
Thoughts after Work. Rubadiri.
To a Daisy. Meynell.
Valentine. Summers.
Way out West. Jones.

Simplicity
Canberra in April. Rowland.
A Fire-Truck. Wilbur.
How Happy Is the Little Stone. Dickinson.
Idleness. Mitchell.
Implicit Faith. De Vere.
London Despair. Cornford.
A Maiden and Her Hair. Davies.
A Midnight Interior. Sassoon.
"Nature" Is What We See. Dickinson.
New Guinea. McAuley.
Right Apprehension. Traherne.
Simple Faith. Cowper.
Simplicity. Dickinson.
So Graven. Miles.

Sin (ful) (ned) (ner) (ners) (ning) (s)
Alma Redemptoris Mater. Contractus.

Almighty! What Is Man?
  Ibn Gabirol.
Annie Shore and Johnnie
  Doon. Orr.
An Appeal to My
  Countrywomen. Harper.
Astrophel and Stella, XIV.
  Sidney.
At One Glance. Mihri
  Hatun.
Attend, Young Friends, While
  I Relate. Anonymous.
Awake My Soul, Betimes
  Awake. Chanler.
Baby. Eastman.
The Ballad of Reading Gaol.
  Wilde.
Balm in Gilead. Anonymous.
The Bank Thief. Farrell.
Beauty. Rosenberg.
Bid Me Sin No More.
  Wesley.
The Black Riders. Crane.
Caelica, LXVI. Greville.
Chinatown. Mezquida.
Christ Speaks. Hopkins.
College of Flunkeys, and a
  Few Gentlemen.
  Berryman.
Come and Welcome.
  Haweis.
Come Here Lord!
  Anonymous.
The Coming and the
  Appearing. Anonymous.
The Complaisant Swain.
  Ovid.
The Conscience. Wickham.
The Cross. Calderon de la
  Barca.
The Cure. McGuckian.
The Debate of the Body and
  the Soul. Anonymous.
Dedication. Eugenius III.
Dirge for a Bad Boy. Rieu.
The Dole of the King's
  Daughter. Anonymous.
Dream Songs. Berryman.
An Election. Marcus.
Elegy for a Puritan
  Conscience. Dugan.
English Counties.
  Anonymous.
Epigram on Voltaire. Young.
Epitaph. Ignatow.
Eves Apologie. Lanier.
Experience. Harford.
The Factory Girl. Phillips.
Fall. Melinescu.
A Farewell Ballad of Poppies.
  Brudne.
Flowers. Anonymous.
For a Blind Beggar's Sign.
  Biondi.
Forest Leaves in Autumn
  (excerpt). Keble.
Four Wise Men on Edward
  II's Reign. Anonymous.
Gallows and Cross.
  MacDonald.
Ganymede and Helen.
  Anonymous.
The Garden. Very.
A General Summary.
  Kipling.
Go Far, Come Near. De La
  Mare.
God's Goin' to Set This
  World on Fire (A vers.)
  (with music). Anonymous.
The Gresford Disaster.
  Anonymous.

Hand Me Down My Walking
  Cane. Anonymous.
A Hawthorne Garland:
  Pastoral Letter. Fogle.
Heart of Oak. Luders.
Heredity. Ward.
How Shall a Man Fore-
  Doomed. Coleridge.
Huxley Hall. Betjeman.
Hymn to Mary. Zerea
  Jacob.
I Have Heard Ingenuous
  Indians Say. Williams.
I Sigh when I Sing.
  Anonymous.
If I Go Not, Pray Not, Give
  Not. Anonymous.
If I Have Sinn'd in Act.
  Coleridge.
In Answer to a Question.
  Blunt.
In Memoriam A.H.H.,
  XXXIII. Tennyson.
In the Beginning Was a
  Word. Graves.
In the Churchyard at
  Cambridge. Longfellow.
Jesus, How Much Thy Name
  Unfolds! Peters.
Judgement Day. Anonymous.
Just As Thou Art. Cook.
The Kind of Act of. Creeley.
Lady Sara Bunbury Sacrificing
  to the Graces, by Reynolds.
  Hine.
The Lay of the Last Minstrel.
  Scott.
Letter Containing a Panegyric
  on Bath. Anstey.
The Light from Within.
  Very.
The Litanie. Donne.
Lo! As the Potter Mouldeth.
  Anonymous.
A Logical Song. Anonymous.
Looking Back (excerpt).
  Vaughan.
Lord! Who Art Merciful as
  Well as Just. Southey.
Madam and the Minister.
  Hughes.
Marius Victor. Raleigh.
Mary Wore Three Links of
  Chain (with music).
  Anonymous.
The Methodist. Lloyd.
Mirth. Herrick.
My Soul Would Fain Indulge
  a Hope. Steward.
The Nativity. Wesley.
The News. Saxe.
The Norsemen. Whittier.
O God, Though Countless
  Worlds of Light. Knowles.
Ode to Peace. Anonymous.
Old Inn on the Eastern Shore.
  Matchett.
On a Soldier Fallen in the
  Philippines. Moody.
On His Books. Belloc.
One Thing I of the Lord
  Desire. Anonymous.
Orchids. Wratislaw.
Out of My Soul's Depth.
  Campion.
The Outward Man Accused.
  Taylor.
Paean to Eve's Apple.
  Liddy.
Peeping Tom. Hope.
The Penitent Palmer's Ode.
  Greene.

Persicos Odi. Merrill, Jr.
Philosophers Have Measured
  Mountains. Herbert.
Pig. Hecht.
Poem for a Christmas
  Broadcast. Ridler.
The Price He Paid. Wilcox.
Pride. Jacob.
Pride Is Out. Anonymous.
Punkydoodle and Jollapin.
  Richards.
The Quaker's Song.
  Anonymous.
The Question. Taylor.
Quoniam Ego in Flagella
  Paratus Sum. Habington.
Reformation of Manners.
  Defoe.
Riddle: "Fatherless an'
  motherless." Anonymous.
Right Is Right. Faber.
The Righteous Man. Butler.
The Rubaiyat of Omar
  Khayyam. Omar
  Khayyam.
The Rubicon. Winter.
She Was All That You Loved.
  Laxness.
Sin. Herbert.
Sinner, Is Thy Heart at Rest?
  Waterbury.
Sinners, Will You Scorn the
  Message? Allen.
Snatches: "Marie, thou
  queen." Anonymous.
Some Folks in Looks Take So
  Much Pride. Anonymous.
Sonnet. Malon de Chaide.
Sonnets, CXLI: "In faith, I do
  not love thee with mine
  eyes." Shakespeare.
Stand-To: Good Friday
  Morning. Sassoon.
The Sting of Death. Scott.
The Stranger. Clare.
Sumter. Stedman.
Taedium Vitae. Wilde.
Tales of a Wayside Inn.
  Longfellow.
Tales of the Islands, IV.
  Walcott.
Taliesin: A Masque: Voices of
  Unseen Spirits. Hovey.
Tamerton Church-Tower; or,
  First Love. Patmore.
The Telephone Operator.
  Francis of Assisi.
The Third Century.
  Traherne.
This Is a Sin-Tryin' World.
  Anonymous.
Tho' You May Boast You're
  Fairer. Anonymous.
Thou Grace Divine,
  Encircling All. Scudder.
Times without Number Have
  I Pray'd. Wesley.
To a Pope. Pasolini.
Tonight at Least, My Sinner.
  Anonymous.
Truth. Cowper.
The Two Angels. Whittier.
Ubi Sunt Qui Ante Nos
  Fuerunt? Anonymous.
The Unfading. "Marie.
Unknown Girl in the
  Maternity Ward. Sexton.
Upon the Decease of Mrs.
  Anne Griffin... Fiske.
Vivisection (excerpt).
  Fowler.
Votive Ode. Erasmus.

Wind. Brown.
The Word of God. Gwynne.
You Preach to Me of Laws.
  Tree.
Sincere
At Length the Busy Day Is
  Done. Hopkinson.
Deer Song. Confucius.
Fraternitas. Anonymous.
Sinew (s)
Corn. Lanier.
Fencing School. Manifold.
Greed. Blazek.
The Presence. Kumin.
The Seasons. Thomson.
The Sinew of Our Dreams.
  Jackson.
We Are Living, We Are
  Dwelling. Coxe.
Sing (ing) (s) (sang) (sung)
Accidia. Beeching.
Across the Fields to Anne.
  Burton.
Ad Leuconoen. Mahony.
After the Pow-Wow (excerpt).
  Littlebird.
After the Speech to the
  Librarians. Wagoner.
The After Woman.
  Thompson.
Afterword: Song of Song.
  Broughton.
Air. Merwin.
The Airy Christ. Smith.
Alabama. Fields.
Alle Vogel Sind Schon Da.
  Chesterton.
Altarwise by Owl-Light.
  Thomas.
America. Mayer.
Anasazi at Mesa Verde.
  Saner.
And So Men Say, I Love
  Thee! Coleridge.
The Angels for the Nativity of
  Our Lord. Drummond.
The Angels' Song. Sears.
Anishinabe Grandmothers.
  Vizenor.
Appreciation. Aldrich.
The Argument of His Book.
  Herrick.
Arrivals and Departures. La
  Follette.
As with Gladness Men of Old.
  Dix.
Assay a Friend. Anonymous.
Assembly. Merwin.
Atomic Pantoum. Meinke.
The Auld Seceder Cat.
  Anonymous.
The Bailey Beareth the Bell
  Away. Anonymous.
Bamboo. Rolls.
Be Like the Bird. Hugo.
The Bear's Song.
  Anonymous.
The Beautiful Woman Who
  Sings. Allen.
The Beauty of Dawn.
  Mnthali.
Beginning My Studies.
  Whitman.
The Belly Dancer in the
  Nursing Home. Wallace.
Beneath the Mound. Smith.
Benny Havens, Oh!
  Anonymous.
Beyond Wars. Morrow.
Big Fun. Burns.
Bile Them Cabbage Down.
  Anonymous.

The Blackbird. Wolfe.
Blessed Lord, What It Is to Be Young. McCord.
The Blessed Name. Bethune.
The Blind Boy. Cibber.
The Blue Flag (parody). Miller.
Blue Tanganyika. Bethune.
The Blues Today. Jackson.
The Bride. Lawrence.
Brother of My Heart. Kinnell.
A Brown Girl Dead. Cullen.
The Bullfinches. Hardy.
Burning Bush. Baker.
Bushed. McKinnon.
Butterfly Maidens. Lahpu.
The Captain. Varela.
Carriers of the Dream Wheel. Momaday.
The Carter. Anonymous.
The Children's Carol. Farjeon.
Choir Practice. Crosby.
Christ. Burdette.
Christmas. Herbert.
Christmas Day. Young.
Christmas Song. Ward.
Chromis. Fletcher.
Clabe Mott. Still.
The Clearing. Jones.
Coda. Tate.
Collin My Deere and Most Entire Beloved. Smith.
Comatas. Mathews.
Come Not near My Songs. Anonymous.
A Common Ground. Levertov.
Complete in Thee, No Work of Mine. Wolfe.
Conversations from Childhood: The Victrola. Langland.
Counting-Out Rhyme for March. Frost.
The Court We Live On. Tremblay.
The Courteous Knight. Anonymous.
The Coventry Carol. Anonymous.
Cricket. Scollard.
The Cricket's Story. Nason.
The Cuckoo. Locker-Lampson.
The Dancing Faun. Rogers.
Dawn: God. Monro.
Daydream. Tessimond.
The Dead Sparrow. Cartwright.
Dear Brethren, Are Your Harps in Tune? Smith.
Death Chant. Blue Cloud.
Debts. Rittenhouse.
A Description of His Ugly Lady. Hoccleve.
Diana. Constable.
Ditty to an Air from Bach. Stevenson.
The Djanggawul Cycle, 51. Anonymous.
Domine ne in Furore. Wyatt.
Don Baty, the Draft Resister. Rukeyser.
Don Giovanni on His Way to Hell. Gilbert.
Down in Yonder Meadow. Anonymous.
The Dream of Aengus Og. Cox.

A Dream of Judgement. Dunn.
Driving in Oklahoma. Revard.
Duermete, Nino Lindo. Anonymous.
Dull Is My Verse. Landor.
Duncton Hill. Belloc.
Each Day Is Anxious. Akhmatova.
The Eagle-Feather Fan. Momaday.
Easter. Kilmer.
Easter Joy. Turner.
Easter Week. Kingsley.
Eggs. Asquith.
Eighteen Verses Sung to a Tartar Reed Whistle. Ts'ai Yen.
Elegy on Albert Edward the Peacemaker. Anonymous.
The Emigrant's Child. Sproull.
The Empty House. Hoban.
Empty Kettle. Oliver.
English Bards and Scotch Reviewers. Byron.
Envying the Pelican. Weber.
Epistle to John Hamilton Reynolds. Keats.
Es Fallt Ein Stern Herunter. Heine.
Everyone Sang. Sassoon.
The Execution of Cornelius Vane. Read.
Fair Janet. Anonymous.
Fealty. Wolfram von
Fern Hill. Thomas.
Festum Nativitatis. De Vere.
First Miracle. Taggard.
The First Olympionique to Hiero of Syracuse. Pindar.
First Satire: Prologue.. Persius (Aulus Persius Flaccus).
The First Spring Day. Rossetti.
Five Degrees South. Young.
Flail. Dalton.
Floods Swell Around Me, Angry, Appalling. Eddy.
The Flying Fish. Cope.
The Food of Love. di Michele.
For the Coming Year. Everwine.
The Four Zoas. Blake.
The Fowler. Gibson.
Frank Sinatra. Waters.
A Friend. Johnson.
The Frogs' Singing-School. Carbell.
From the Day-Book of a Forgotten Prince. Untermeyer.
The Garden. Grimald.
Garden Lore. Ewing.
Ghetto Lovesong–Migration. Clemmons.
Glory. Wise.
Great Day (Union Version). Anonymous.
The Greatest Person In the Universe. Marsh.
The Green Family. Thibaudeau.
Greystone Cottage. Hugo.
A Guerrilla Handbook. Jones.
Gwinter Sing All along de Way. Anonymous.

Hail to the Joyous Day. Tyler.
The Handloom. Rodriguez.
Hay-Time; or The Constant Lovers. A Pastoral. Relph.
He Gave Himself for Me. Anonymous.
Hearing the Early Oriole. Po Chu-i.
The Heart Has Its Reasons. Anonymous.
Heart-of-the-Daybreak. Marais.
High O'er the Hills. Walker.
Hoc Cygno Vinces. Hawkins.
Holiday. Horace.
The Holly and the Ivy. Anonymous.
Homage. Kahn.
Home, Sweet Home. Bunner.
Homecoming Celebration. Catacalos.
The Homecoming Singer. Wright.
Homesick Song. Simpson.
The Horse Show at Midnight. Taylor.
Hours I Remember Lonely and Lovely to Me. Irwin.
House in St. Petersburg. Burnshaw.
The House of a Hundred Lights. Torrence.
How Can I Keep from Singing? (excerpt). Lowry.
A Huguenot. Coleridge.
Hummingbird. Littlebird.
Hunting-Song. Anonymous.
Hymn for Christmas Day. Byrom.
Hymn to Darkness. Norris.
"I Am a Sioux Brave," He Said in Minneapolis. Wright.
I'll Go with Her Blues. Wilkins.
I Looked for a Sounding-Board. Roland-Holst.
The Idea of Entropy at Maenporth Beach. Redgrove.
If All the World Were Paper. Anonymous.
If the Black Frog Will Not Ring. Roberson.
Iliad. Wolfe.
The Immortal. Pickthall.
In Grato Jubilo. McCord.
In Memoriam A.H.H., XXXVIII. Tennyson.
In Populated. Clifton.
In the Evening by the Moonlight. Bland.
In the Suburbs. Simpson.
Independence. McFadden.
Infelice. Smith.
Inspirations. Dawson.
The Island. Jennett.
It Couldn't Be Done. Guest.
It Is the Reed. Maris Stella.
It May Not Always Be So. Cummings.
Jesu, Joy of Man's Desiring. Fitzgerald.
Johnny Stiles; or, The Wild Mustard River. Anonymous.
The Jolly Shepherd Wat. Anonymous.
Joseph's Suspicion. Rilke.

Joy and Pleasure. Davies.
The Joy of Church Fellowship Rightly Attended. Taylor.
Judas Iscariot. Mason.
Keeping You Alive. Gallagher.
The Kings From the East. Gray.
Lament for a Husband. Anonymous.
Land Where the Columbines Grow. Fynn.
Last May. Arnett.
The Last Song. Duggan.
The Last Will and Testament of the Grey Mare. Anonymous.
The Last Word of a Bluebird. Frost.
Lauds. Auden.
Laughing Song. Blake.
Leap in the Dark. Hill.
Letters to Walt Whitman. Johnson.
A Light Breather. Roethke.
Lilium Regis. Thompson.
Lilliputian's Beer Song. Winner.
The Lily-white Rose. Anonymous.
Lines. Ewart.
Lines. Meredith.
Lines Written at the Grave of Alexander Dumas. Bennett.
Listen to the Mocking Bird. Hawthorne.
The Little Beach-Bird. Dana.
Little Songs. Pickthall.
Little Theocritus. Paradise.
Little tree. Cummings.
Local Places. Moss.
Long Tail Blue. Anonymous.
Loo-Wit. Rose.
Love's Fool. Rosenthal.
Love's Nightingale. Crashaw.
Loving Henry. Anonymous.
Loyalty. Davies.
A Lyric to Mirth. Herrick.
Mad Day in March. Levine.
Madrigal: "Dainty sweet bird." Vautor.
Madrigal: "No, no, Nigella!" Morley.
Magic. Wolfe.
The Magic Flute. Snodgrass.
The Magician Suspends the Children. Oles.
Mama Don't 'Low. Anonymous.
The Meaning of Africa. Nicol.
Meditations. Taylor.
Merie Sungen the Muneches. Anonymous.
Metric Figure. Williams.
Midsummer Night. Edey.
Mockingbird, Copy This. Myers.
The Monks of Bangor's March. Scott.
Morning Swim. Kumin.
Morning Vigil. George.
The Mosquito. Jones.
A Music. Berry.
Music. Emerson.
Music. Farjeon.
Music and Words. Jennings.
Music by the Waters. Hay.

The Music of the Spheres. Bell.

My Camping Ground. Rosenfeld.

My Father Is the Nightingale. *Anonymous.*

My Lady Takes the Sunlight for Her Gown. Cole.

My Maid Mary. *Anonymous.*

My Song. Kuka.

My Song of Today. Therese.

Nelly Bly. Foster.

Nemea 11 (excerpt). Pindar.

New Lines for Cuscuscaraway and Mirza Murad Ali Beg. Simpson.

New Shoes. Wilkins.

New Year Wishes. Sarton.

New Yeares, Expect New Gifts. Jonson.

Night Song. Mueller.

No White Bird Sings. Ciardi.

North Shore. Davison.

Not in the Poet. Barker.

Not with a club. Dickinson.

Now Does Our World Descend. Cummings.

O Bruadair. Stephens.

O'Duffy's Ironsides. *Anonymous.*

Obligatory Love Poem. Jacobs.

Oblique Birth Poem. Darr.

Ode to a Fat Cat. Farjeon.

Of A' the Airts the Wind Can Blaw. Burns.

Of the Night, Let the Bridegroom Sing. Statius Publius Papinius.

Oh, Lawd, How Long? *Anonymous.*

Oh, Let Us Howl Some Heavy Note. Webster.

Old Colony Times. *Anonymous.*

The Old Gospel Ship. *Anonymous.*

An Old Song. Blumgarten (Yehoash)

The Old Violin. Egan.

On a Poetess. Hopkins.

On Board the Leicester Castle. *Anonymous.*

On the Death of Mary. Rilke.

On the Death of Mr. Crashaw. Cowley.

On the South Downs. Teasdale.

One's-Self I Sing. Whitman.

The One Song. Hanzlicek.

Orestes Pursued. Webb.

Our Singing Strength. Frost.

Out of the Depths. Knowles.

Out of the Vast. Bamberger.

Owl and Rooster. Cardiff.

The Owl and the Nightingale (excerpt). *Anonymous.*

The Palm. Campbell.

The Parents of Psychotic Children. Bell.

The Pariah's Prayer. Goethe.

The Parliament of Bees. Day.

Peg of Limavaddy. Thackeray.

Penitential Psalms: Introduction. Wyatt.

Pennsylvania Winter Indian 1974. Littlebird.

Permanence in Change. Goethe.

Pervigilium Veneris. Noguere.

The Phantom Horsewoman. Hardy.

The Phantom-Wooer. Beddoes.

Phoebe's Sonnet. Lodge.

Piano at Evening. Palea.

The Pit of Bliss. Stephens.

Place Me in the Breach. Karni.

The Pleasant Comedie of Old Fortunatus. Dekker.

The Pleiades. Barnard.

The Plum Gatherer. Millay.

Poet and Lark. De Vere.

Poet's Prayer. Love.

Poetics. Spire.

Poets. Kilmer.

Poor Howard. *Anonymous.*

A Prayer. Ham.

The Preacher's Prayer. Macdonald.

The Princess Addresses the Frog Prince. Brewster.

The Prophet. Gibran.

Prospectus. Huffstickler.

Protagonist. Henrich.

Psalm XXX. Sidney.

Psychometrist. Stephens.

The Quartette. De La Mare.

A Quatrain. Sherman.

Queen Victoria. *Anonymous.*

Rabbits. Schmitz.

Raccoon's Got a Bushy Tail. *Anonymous.*

Rain Forest. Smith.

Rebel. McLeod.

The Recall. Lowell.

Recollection. Mumford.

Recruiting Drive. Causley.

Resurrection Hymn. Weiss.

The Retarded Children Find a World Built Just for Them. O Hehir.

A Return to the Tree of Time. Parun.

Reunion. Forche.

Risselty-Rosselty. *Anonymous.*

The Rivals. Stephens.

Robert Louis Stevenson. Reese.

The Robin. Daniel.

Robin Good-Fellow's Song. *Anonymous.*

Rock, Rock, Sleep, My Baby. Watson.

Roma Aeterna. Crapsey.

Round Trip. Rice.

A Sacred Grove. Winant.

Sang: "There's a reid lowe in yer cheek." MacLellan.

Sappho Rehung. Smith, Jr.

The Second Shepherds' Play. *Anonymous.*

The Secret. Peach.

The Serpent. Langland.

The Seven-League Boots. Voronca.

Shore Roads of April. Adams.

Sightseers in a Courtyard. Guillen.

The Silk Merchant's Daughter (I). *Anonymous.*

Since you will needs that I shall sing. Wyatt.

Singing. Stevenson.

The Singing Bush. Soutar.

Sleepless Night. O'Rahilly.

Sleepyhead. De la Mare.

The Sod-Breaker. Stringer.

Some Painful Butterflies Pass Through. Gallagher.

Somebody. *Anonymous.*

Sometime I Loved. *Anonymous.*

The Song. Erskine.

Song against Women. Wright.

A Song as Yet Unsung. Yehoash.

Song: "I know that any weed can tell." Ginsberg.

Song in the Songless. Meredith.

Song My. Griffin.

Song: "O fair! O sweet! when I do look on thee." Sidney.

Song: "O faire sweet face, O eyes celestiall bright." Beaumont.

Song of Sukkaartik, the Assistant Spirit. *Anonymous.*

The Song of the Christmas Tree. Wade.

The Song of the Reed Sparrow. *Anonymous.*

Song of the Strange Young Duckling. Munro.

Song Set by Thomas Weelkes: "In pride of May." *Anonymous.*

Song, to the Gods, is Sweetest Sacrifice. Fields.

Song to the Mountains. *Anonymous.*

A Song to the Wind. Taliesin.

Song: "Yes, the book of Revelations will be brought forth dat/day." *Anonymous.*

Songs My Mother Taught Me. Wagoner.

The Songs of Maximus: 3. Olson.

Sonnet XLIV. Alabaster.

Sonnets. Tuckerman.

Sonnets, XCVII: "How like a winter hath my absence been." Shakespeare.

Sonnets to Orpheus. Rilke.

Spanish Song. Divine.

The Sparrow-Hawk's Complaint. *Anonymous.*

The Spell. Addison.

Spider. Lattimore.

Splinter. Sandburg.

Spring. *Anonymous.*

A Star. MacBeth.

Stark County Holidays. Oliver.

Stone Song (Zen Rock) the Seer & the Unbeliever. Karoniaktatie.

Supremacy. Robinson.

Sweet Clover. Rice.

Sympathy. Dunbar.

A Temple. Patchen.

Then Sings My Soul. Mariani.

There Is a Name I Love to Hear. Whitfield.

There Is No Name So Sweet on Earth. Bethune.

Those Images. Yeats.

Thoughts from a Bottle. Clark.

Threnody. Hayes.

Thrice Welcome First and Best of Days. Chanler.

The Thrush. Benet.

Thus Bonny-Boots the Birthday Celebrated. *Anonymous.*

Thy Praise, O God, in Zion Waits. Kimball.

To A. D. Henley.

To a Gone Era. McClaurin.

To a Western Bard Still a Whoop and a Holler away from English Poetry. Meredith.

To a Young Woman on the World Staff. Adams.

To Robert Browning. Landor.

To the Fountain of Bandusia. Horace.

To the Small Celandine. Wordsworth.

Translation into the Original. Gilbert.

The Tree of Liberty. Burns.

'Twas Jolly, Jolly Wat. Stubbs.

Two Simpleton Songs, II. *Anonymous.*

The Uninvited. Livesay.

Unrest. Marquis.

Upon Her Voice. Herrick.

Upon the Swallow. Bunyan.

The Velvet Sonneteers. MacInnes.

Verifying the Dead. Welch.

The Village Choir (parody). *Anonymous*

The Violent Space. Knight.

The Vow of Washington. Whittier.

The Waits. Nightingale.

Wednesday, January 1, 1701. Sewall.

Weeping and Singing. Tiempo.

Welcome. Waldo.

West of Alice. Harney.

West Sussex Drinking Song. Belloc.

What Black Elk Said. Smith.

What Is a Jewish Poem? Sklarew.

What Then? Yeats.

When Christ Was Born of Mary Free. *Anonymous.*

Which Is the Bow? *Anonymous.*

Whit Sunday. Beaumont.

The White Dove Sat on the Castle Wall. Wager.

Why Should I Wander Sadly. Susskind.

The Wind. Stevenson.

Windsor-Forest To the Right Honourable George Lord Lansdown. Pope.

Winter Song. Jimenez.

The Wise Men Ask the Children the Way. Heine.

Women of My Land. Armstrong.

Wondrous Love. Means.

The Woods Are Still. Field.

The Works of God. Ibn Ezra.

Worried Man Blues. *Anonymous.*

Wulf. Manhire.

Yardbird's Skull. Dodson.

Yet Another Song. Rubadiri.

Yiddish Poet. Jacobs.
Young Hunting. *Anonymous.*
Young Hunting (Loving
　Henry). *Anonymous.*
Youth and Maidenhood.
　Williams.
Singer (s)
L'Envoi. Morris.
Good Morning America
　(excerpt). Sandburg.
The Makers. McDonald.
The Moment of Vision.
　Eberhart.
Moritura. Davidson.
My Mother. Ledwidge.
An Old-Fashioned Poet.
　Murray.
On Learning to Play the
　Guitar. Fraser.
People Buy a Lot of Things.
　Wynne.
Rhymes to Be Traded for
　Bread: Prologue. Lindsay.
Rookhope Ryde.
　Anonymous.
The Rubaiyat of Omar
　Khayyam. Omar
　Khayyam.
There Was a Man with a
　Tongue of Wood. Crane.
To John Greenleaf Whittier.
　Ward.
William Yeats in Limbo.
　Keyes.
Young Companions.
　Anonymous.
Single
After Midnight. Simpson.
After Passing the
　Examination. Meng
　Chiao.
Aleph. Perkoff.
As the World Turns. Mollin.
Call All. *Anonymous.*
The Children's Carol.
　Farjeon.
Come All You Young Ladies
　and Gentlemen.
　Anonymous.
Death Warnings. Quevedo y
　Villegas.
Deep Well. Robinson.
Elegy in a Theatrical
　Warehouse. Fearing.
Freud: Dying in London, He
　Recalls the Smoke of His
　Cigar... Schevill.
Gift from Kenya. Miller.
The Grey Cock. *Anonymous.*
Growing Together. Oates.
Heart of My Heart.
　Anonymous.
I Go to Whiskey Bars.
　Thompson.
I'm Not a Single Man.
　Hood.
In and Out: Severance of
　Connections, 1946.
　Sissman.
Jacky Jingle. *Anonymous.*
Letters: With Happiness
　Stretchd Across the Hills.
　Blake.
Light. Silkin.
The Marriage. Winters.
The Monument and the
　Shrine. Logan.
Mrs. Kriss Kringle. Thomas.
　O. Villanueva.
Oh, I Wish I Were Single
　Again. *Anonymous.*

Outside the Supermarket.
　Fuller.
Registered at the Bordello
　Hotel (Vienna). Rubin.
The Relationship. Vincent.
The River. Welch.
The Sidewalk Racer.
　Morrison.
Six Young Men. Hughes.
Sonnets, VIII: "Music to hear,
　why hear'st thou music
　sadly?" Shakespeare.
Spassky at Reykjavik.
　Fisher.
Sweet Boy, Gentle Boy.
　Pushkin.
Symphony in Gray Major.
　Dario.
To Lovers of Earth: Fair
　Warning. Cullen.
Tree Man. McQuilkin.
When I Was Single.
　Anonymous.
World without Peculiarity.
　Stevens.
Singular (ly) (ity)
Bedtime. Levertov.
Mercedes, Her Aloneness.
　Inez.
A Plea for a Plural.
　Lehmann.
The Poet. Kirkup.
Poet and Critic. Daniel.
Sleeping on the Wing.
　O'Hara.
Tiny Catullus. Levine.
Sink (ing) (s) (sank)
Aged Ninety Years. Snow.
Alas, Alack. De La Mare.
The Attack. Read.
The Bramble Briar.
　Anonymous.
Chimney Swallows. Powers.
A Cry from the Ghetto.
　Rosenfeld.
Death in the Corn.
　Liliencron.
The Demon Lover.
　Anonymous.
The Duff. Wright.
The Elder Edda: The
　Beginning and the End
　(abridged). *Anonymous.*
Epipsychidion. Shelley.
An Epistle to My Friend J. B.
　Dodsley.
Epitaph of Cleonicus.
　Calverley.
The Escapade. Ignatow.
Ezra Shank. *Anonymous.*
Fall In. Kirstein.
Family Evening. Huws.
The Female Warrior.
　Anonymous.
First Dark. Oates.
First Vision. O'Huiginn.
Flying Letters. Gilead.
For Cora Lightbody, R.N.
　Glassco.
From "The River-Fight."
　Brownell.
The Garden of Earthly
　Delights. Simic.
I Carried Statues. Nagy.
Incident Characteristic of a
　Favourite Dog.
　Wordsworth.
Inquietude. Murray.
The Journeyman.
　Anonymous.
The Legend of the Organ-
　Builder. Dorr.

Lethe. Johnson.
Life and Thought. Arnold.
The Mermaid (B version).
　Anonymous.
Metaphysics. Herford.
The Moon-Bone Cycle: The
　Evening Star. *Anonymous.*
The Name of Our Country.
　Schmitz.
A Necessitarian's Epitaph.
　Hardy.
Night of Sine. Sedar-
　Senghor.
O, Open the Door to Me, O!
　Burns.
Old Furniture. Hardy.
An Old Song Re-sung.
　Masefield.
On His Seventy-Fifth
　Birthday. Landor.
The People. Yeats.
The Pilgrim of a Day.
　Campbell.
A Poet's Hope. Channing
Priest Or Poet. Leslie.
Prometheus Unbound.
　Shelley.
Quicksands (parody).
　Zaranka.
A Room in the Past.
　Kooser.
Sails. Sterling.
Santorin. Flecker.
The Shipwreck. Palmer.
The Sinking of the Merrimac.
　Larcom.
The Splendid Shilling
　(parody). Phillips.
Storm. Doolittle.
The Storm (excerpt).
　O'Rahilly.
The Terror of Death. Keats.
Throw out the Lifeline.
　Ufford.
To His Book. Stokesbury.
True and False. Crawford.
The Tundra. Haines.
The United States and
　Macedonian. *Anonymous.*
Unto Jehovah Sing Will I.
　Ainsworth.
Veni Creator. Carman.
Voluspo. *Anonymous.*
Sip (ped) (ping) (s)
Antipater of Thessalonica.
　Rexroth.
The Enchanted Spring.
　Darley.
The Five Little Fairies.
　Burnham.
Indifference. *Anonymous.*
The Night Sits in This Chair.
　Notley.
On Time. Hughes.
The Phoenix. Darley.
Six Feet Under. Hale.
To His Not-So-Coy Mistress.
　Vaughan-Thomas.
To Mr. Gray. Garrick.
Sir
Apostrophic Notes from the
　New-World Physics.
　White.
As I Went up the Humber
　Jumber. *Anonymous.*
At the Gate of Heaven.
　Byron.
The Avenging Daughters.
　Anonymous.
The Canterbury Tales: The
　Knight's Interruption of the
　Monk's Tale. Chaucer.

The County Ball (excerpt).
　Praed.
Growing Old. Learned.
Lady Isabel and the Elf-
　Knight (B vers.).
　Anonymous.
Limerick: "There was a young
　Fellow of Wadham."
　Anonymous.
A New-Years-Gift to Brian
　Lord Bishop of Sarum...
　Cartwright.
On a Day's Stint. Scott.
Pink Dominoes. Kipling.
The Royal Line. Hunt.
Sir Cawline. *Anonymous.*
The Tithe: To the Bride.
　Herrick.
The Vision of Sir Launfal.
　Lowell.
The Wolf and the Dog. La
　Fontaine.
Sire (s)
An Account of the Cruelty of
　the Papists... Harris.
An Evening Walk in Bengal.
　Heber.
Idylls. Theocritus.
Priam and Achilles. Pope.
Siren (s)
Lamarck Elaborated.
　Wilbur.
A Nuptial Song, or
　Epithalamie, on Sir Clipseby
　Crew and His Lady.
　Herrick.
The Odyssey. Homer.
Pocahontas. Thackeray.
The Romaunt of the Rose.
　Anonymous.
Science Fiction. Amis.
Scroppo's Dog. Swenson.
The Sirens. Manifold.
The Sounds Begin Again.
　Brutus.
To the Queen of Dolors.
　Maura.
The Welder. Lima.
With Freedom's Seed.
　Pushkin.
Sister (s)
As I Set down to Play Tin-
　Can. *Anonymous.*
Brother and Sister. "Carroll.
Cats Climb Trees. Veitch.
The Dance of the Rain.
　Marais.
Der Mond Ist Aufgegangen.
　Heine.
The Desert Lark. Marais.
Dumpy Ducky. Larcom.
The Early Morning. Belloc.
The Eel. De La Mare.
The Eel. Montale.
Epithalamium. Kennedy.
Fair Annie. *Anonymous.*
For Sale. Silverstein.
Frost. Davies.
Ghazal. Dow.
A Guide to Familiar
　American Incest: Inventing
　a Family. Saleh.
Herself a Rose Who Bore the
　Rose. Rossetti.
Hippety Hop to the Barber
　Shop. Mother Goose.
I, Woman. McClaurin.
The Ladies. Kipling.
Little Red Riding Hood.
　Broumas.
Little Rosewood Casket.
　Anonymous.

Sister

Lord Thomas and Lady Margaret. *Anonymous.*
Nine Times a Night. *Anonymous.*
The Orphan. *Anonymous.*
Painting of a White Gate and Sky. Erdrich.
The Paper Lantern. Williams.
A Paragraph. Carruth.
Plain, Humble Letters. Vogel.
Random Generation of English Sentences; or, The Revenge of the Poets. Smith.
Redesdale and Wise William. *Anonymous.*
Sharon Will Be No/Where on Nobody's Best-Selling List. Scott.
The Sphere of Glass. Lehmann.
To All Brothers. Sanchez.
To the Ladies. Kenseth.
To the Moon. Shelley.
The Two Sisters. *Anonymous.*
What Color Is Lonely. Rodgers.
The Woman and the Aloe. Adams.

Sisyphus

Arrival in Hell. Huch.
Aviemore. Waller.
Ghazal. Dow.
Idea. Drayton.
The Journey. Middleton.

Sit (ting) (s) (sat)

Addressing His Deaf Wife, Kansas, 1916. Olsen.
The Affectionate Shepherd (excerpt). Barnfield.
Alone. *Anonymous.*
Angelo Orders His Dinner (parody). Taylor.
The Animal I Wanted. Patchen.
Arches and Shadows. Dillard.
The Argument. Moreland.
The Assumption. Beaumont.
August 13, 1966. Hine.
Captive. Hirshbein.
Choice. Morgan.
The Cold. Henson.
Come All Ye Fair and Tender Maidens. *Anonymous.*
A Copy of Non Sequitors. *Anonymous.*
Denunciation; or, Unfrock'd Again. Whalen.
The Dockyard Gate. *Anonymous.*
Docteur Foster. *Anonymous.*
Elegy for the Monastery Barn. Merton.
Elephants in the Circus. Lawrence.
Evening. Miller.
A Fairy Voyage. *Anonymous.*
Fall Letter. Kelly.
The Fortunes of Men (excerpt). *Anonymous.*
Friendless Blues. Gilbert.
The Frog. *Anonymous.*
Garden Lore. Ewing.
Get Up, Jack! John, Sit Down! *Anonymous.*
The Grand Canyon. Merrill.

Grandma's Lost Balance. Dayre.
Hakluyt Unpurchased. McDuffee.
The Helmet. Levine.
Henry Adams. Auden.
I Sit and Sew. Nelson.
I stood on the bridge at midnight. *Anonymous.*
I've Gone and Stained with the Color of Love. Acorn.
Ice. Roberts.
Illusion. Gosse.
The Image. Hughes.
In Jerusalem Are Women. Sivan.
The Intellectual. Shapiro.
Is Love, Then, So Simple. McLeod.
Japanese Beetles. Kennedy.
Kansas Boys. *Anonymous.*
Kitchen Tables. Huddle.
Lady, of Anonymous Flesh and Face. Cunningham.
Late. Halpern.
Let Us All Be Unhappy on Sunday. Neaves.
Limerick: "There was a young girl of Lahore." Monkhouse.
Limerick: "There was, in the village of Patton." *Anonymous.*
Long Are the Hours the Sun Is Above. Bridges.
The Lord Sits with Me Out in Front. Gilbert.
Love. Herbert.
Loving Henry. *Anonymous.*
The Lowest Place. Rossetti.
The Lyricism of the Weak. Viereck.
Matmiya. Tallmountain.
Meeting My Best Friend from the Eighth Grade. Gildner.
The Microbe's Serenade. Ade.
My Cats. Smith.
My Little Wife. *Anonymous.*
No Country You Remember. Mezey.
November Sunday Morning. Feinman.
The Old Anguish. Chu Shu-chen.
Old Winter. Noel.
On Another's Sorrow. Blake.
On the Lawn at the Villa. Simpson.
Paradise Lost. Milton.
Peace. Hopkins.
A Pig-Tale. "Carroll.
Portrait of a Lady. Eliot.
Prize for Good Conduct. Allott.
Rest. *Anonymous.*
Round about the Rosebush. *Anonymous.*
Sacred Objects. Simpson.
The Same Side of the Canoe. Espirito Santo.
Song: "I'd much rather sit there in the sun." Krauss.
Song of Myself. Whitman.
Songs of Seven. Ingelow.
Spider. Lattimore.
Summer Comes. Agnew.
Swans. Durrell.
Then Laugh. Backus.
This Is My Hour. Akins.
The Tired Man. Wickham.

To a Husband. Angelou.
To His Muse. Herrick.
Turn on the Footlights: The Perils of Pedagogy. Carter.
Undersea Fever. Cole.
Untitled: "Words do not grow on the landscape." Malley.
Visit to the Hermitage. Anderson.
The Waiting-Room. Fuller.
The Warm of Heart Shall Never Lack a Fire. Coatsworth.
Wasp. Nowlan.
We Greet Each Other in the Side (parody) (excerpt). *Anonymous.*
The Weight. Aberg.
Where's Mary? Eastwick.
Windy Trees. Ammons.
A Winter Daybreak above Vence. Wright.
Young Hunting (Loving Henry). *Anonymous.*

Situation

A Later Note on Letter #15. Olson.
This Form of Life Needs Sex. Ginsberg.

Six

Antoine and I Go Fishing. Budbill.
Back to Arizona. Brininstool.
Beginnings (excerpt). Hayden.
Berthe Morisot. Waldman.
Birthday Garden. Eastwick.
The Charge of the Light Brigade. Tennyson.
The End. Milne.
Fair Annie. *Anonymous.*
Garden Party. Mills.
Here Lies a Lady. Ransom.
Hold on, Abraham. *Anonymous.*
Ignu. Ginsberg.
Jubilate Agno. Smart.
The Loss of the Evelyn Marie. *Anonymous.*
My Birthday's in Winter. Gay.
Old Man. Henry.
Our Birthday. Edey.
Riddle 24 (Jay: Higora). *Anonymous.*
Sabbath. Burden.
A Satire on the O'Haras. O Huiginn.
Six in June. Davies.
Some Ruthless Rhymes. Graham.
Swansong. Muske.
To Stew a Rump-Steak. *Anonymous.*
Tomorrows. Merrill.
When I Was Six. Cross.

Sixteen

Glenlogie, or, Jean o Bethelnie (B version). *Anonymous.*
Growing Old. Learned.
Love Somebody, Yes I Do (with music). *Anonymous.*
Printing Jenny. Mitchell.
To His Love in Middle-Age. Brock.

Size

The Ballad of the Harp-Weaver. Millay.

For Every Last Batch When the Next One Comes Along. Dickey.
The Fort of Ard Ruide. *Anonymous.*
The Leith Police Dismisseth Us. *Anonymous.*
Museum of Man. Birney.
Something Very Elegant. Fisher.
Tall Windows. Hass.
To Ailsa Rock. Keats.

Skeeter (s)

Highly Educated Man. *Anonymous.*
I Was Born about Ten Thousand Years Ago. *Anonymous.*
Limerick: "There was a bright fellow named Peter." MacDonald.

Skeleton (s)

The Dead Sheep. Young.
Drunken Streets. Locker.
In the Flight of the Blue Heron: To Montezuma. Probst.
In the Study. Hardy.
The Knowledge That Comes Through Experience. Cooper.
Lament of the Jewish Women for Tammuz. Reznikoff.
The Round Barrow. Young.
A Serious and a Curious Night-Meditation. Traherne.

Skeptic

Archys Autobiography. Marquis.
Proof Positive. Taylor.

Skier

Transit. Rich.

Skiff

En Bateau. Verlaine.
Poem by the Bridge at Ten-Shin. Li Po.

Skill (ed) (s)

Amoretti, L. Spenser.
Challenge. Hazo.
Columbus to Ferdinand. Freneau.
Commendatory Sonnet to Hoby's Courtier. Sackville.
The Coral Reef. Lieberman.
Cupid and Death: Victorious Men of Earth. Shirley.
Cypresses. Francis.
The Desert Music (excerpt). Williams.
Elegy for a Diver. Meinke.
An Essay on the Genius of Pope (excerpt). Lloyd.
The Evangelist. Sinclair.
For My Contemporaries. Cunningham.
In Praise of Winchester. *Anonymous.*
The Market Town. Carlin.
Milton's Prayer for Patience. Howell.
Once Alien Here. Hewitt.
The Question, Is It? Bailey.
Snatches: "Wit hat wonder and kind ne can." *Anonymous.*
Sonnets, XVI: "But wherefore do not you a mightier way." Shakespeare.
"Sweet are the thoughts where hope persuadeth hap." Ralegh.

To a Lady: She Refusing to
Continue a Dispute with
Me... Prior.
The World's Way. Aldrich.
Skin (s)
Adolescence. Orr.
Autonomous. Van Doren.
Bent Tree. Serchuk.
Biotherm. O'Hara.
Certified Copy. Deacon.
The Circumcision. Zisquit.
Cottonmouth Country.
Gluck.
Deaf School. Hughes.
Dear John Wayne. Erdrich.
Elegy for Drowned Children.
Dawe.
Escapist's Song. Spencer.
Four Choctaw Songs.
Barnes.
I Am Ham Melanite.
Millett.
I Have Seen. McCracken.
I Think of Housman Who
Said the Poem Is a Morbid
Secretion... Kroll.
The Jewels. Baudelaire.
Lilies of the Valley. Silkin.
The Little Man and the Little
Maid. *Anonymous.*
Moderation. Herrick.
Night Songs. Kinsella.
One Morning. Levine.
Original Sin. Laing.
Paradigms of Fire. Swann.
The Peasant and the Sheep.
Kriloff.
A Plum. Leib.
Proof. Ullman.
Reflection: After Visiting Old
Friends. Allison.
Rhymes. Steele.
September. Kyger.
September 30. Lourie.
Shadows in the Water.
Traherne.
The Shirt. Morley.
Signature. Orlock.
Skin. Jason.
Skin Man. Brown.
Special Bulletin. Hughes.
Summons for the Undead.
Keating.
Surprised by Evening. Bly.
A Symposium: Apples.
Pastan.
Tetrachordon (excerpt).
Milton.
Trouble. Wright.
Two Childhood Memories.
Zolynas.
The Waltz. Corke.
Was It All Worth While?
Anonymous.
What Will We Do for Linen?
Anonymous.
Winter Love. Jennings.
Woman with Girdle. Sexton.
Skinflint
Old Skinflint. Gibson.
What Changes, My Love.
Honig.
Skip (ping) (s)
Curtain! Dunbar.
Lion & Honeycomb.
Nemerov.
The Ship of Rio. De La
Mare.
Skipping along Alone.
Welles.
Whales. Bates.
Windy Wash Day. Aldis.

Skirt (s)
Advice to Country Girls.
Anonymous.
Ch'in Chia's Wife's Reply.
Anonymous.
I Hear That Andromeda.
Sappho.
I'm Going to California.
Mossman.
In Memoriam. Longley.
The Insect Kitchen.
Jackowska.
Out of the Past. Wallace.
Red Stockings, Blue
Stockings. *Anonymous.*
Sagimusume: The White
Heron Maiden. Sullivan.
Sonnet: True Ambition.
Stillingfleet.
Spring in the Old World.
Levine.
The Words, the Words, the
Words. Williams.
Skittles
Chicago Analogue. Preston.
A House and Grounds.
Hunt.
Skull (s)
Axioms. Hollander.
The Balance. Sherwin.
The Battle of the Cowpens.
English.
Beethoven's Death Mask.
Spender.
The Blue Flag (parody).
Miller.
Cinco de Mayo, 1862. Rios.
Considering the Bleakness.
Halpern.
Cortes. Rios.
Fag-End. O'Connor.
For the Man Who Stole a
Rose. Elliott.
Gnat-Psalm. Hughes.
I'm Lucky. Mandel.
Laguna Perdida. Dixon.
Letters for the New England
Dead. Baron.
Letters to Live Poets.
Beaver.
Looking at Henry Moore's
Elephant Skull Etchings in
Jerusalem... Kaufman.
Love and Death. Nims.
Mahoney. Jennett.
A Maiden Lies in Her
Chamber. Heine.
Nightmare of Mouse.
Warren.
Noah's Ark. Young.
A Poet Recognizing the Echo
of the Voice. Wakoski.
Serenade. Britt.
South Country. Slessor.
Spleen. Baudelaire.
Stony Limits.
""MacDiarmid.
Suffering. Ehrenstein.
Tattooed. Plomer.
Three Sonnets on Oblivion.
Sterling.
Skunk
A History of the Pets.
Huddle.
Maps. Hass.
Sky (skies)
14 July 1956. Lerner.
About the Cool Water.
Rexroth.
Above Ben Loyal. Ball.
Advice to a Blue-Bird.
Bodenheim.

De Aegypto. Pound.
After Dinner We Take a
Drive into the Night.
Towle.
After Midsummer. Scovell.
After the Rain. Janeczko.
Agbor Dancer. Clark.
Alfred-Seeable Philadelphia
Sky. Siegel.
Almost. Field.
Another Night with
Telescope. Cohen.
Armistice. Daryush.
At Carbis Bay. Symons.
The Balloon Man. Fyleman.
Bathing Song. Ridler.
Beach Queen. Campbell.
Beata L'Alma. Read.
Beauty. Whitman.
Because river-fog. Kiyowara
Fukuyabu.
Before the Mirror.
Swinburne.
Beginning to Squall.
Swenson.
Behind me–dips eternity–.
Dickinson.
Bell Tower. Adams.
Bells of Grey Crystal.
Sitwell.
Betty by the Sea. McCuaig.
Birthday. Stafford.
The Blackberry. Nicholson.
The blossoms have fallen.
Shikishi.
The Blue Church. Balakian.
Blue Homespun. Call.
The Boy with a Cart
(excerpt). Fry.
The Bracelet of Grass.
Moody.
Breaking Ground in Me.
Kryss.
The Builders. Longfellow.
Building a Skyscraper.
Tippett.
The Butterfly. James.
Bygones (parody). Taylor.
Caelica, LXII. Greville.
Can the Circle Be Unbroken?
Anonymous.
Carmen Miranda. Polite.
Casual Meeting. Bradley.
The Cats of Campagnatico.
Porter.
Change Is Not Always
Progress. Madhubuti.
The Child in the Rug.
Haines.
Chinoiseries. Lowell.
The City Tree. Crawford.
Clouds. Chapman.
Comcomly's Skull. Barnes.
The Commonwealth of Birds.
Shirley.
Contentment. Estes.
The Coromandel Fishers.
Naidu.
Cowboy Jack. *Anonymous.*
Daisies. Young.
A Day in a Long Hot
Summer. Kageyama.
Dead of Winter. Towne.
Death-Bed Song.
Anonymous.
Deep Night. Jimenez.
The Deserted Village.
Goldsmith.
The Distant Runners. Van
Doren.
Doorman. Galvin.

The Downfall of Heathendom.
Anonymous.
Draft of a Reparations
Agreement. Pagis.
Drifting. Bushby.
Drum-Taps. Whitman.
Drunken Winter. Ceravolo.
Eagles. Woody.
Easter. Kilmer.
Easter Hymn. John of
Damascus.
Ego Tripping. Giovanni.
The Empty House. Williams.
End of a Year. Lowell.
Epigrams. Theocritus.
Epitaph on an Engraver.
Thoreau.
The Eye. Herrick.
Familiar Lines. *Anonymous.*
The Far North. Savoie.
The Farmer's Clothes Are
Soaked Through and Never
Dried. Ise Tayu.
Father and I in the Woods.
McCord.
Feast of the Ram's Horn.
Shapiro.
Fifteen Ships on George's
Banks. *Anonymous.*
The First Hunt. Anderson.
Flora MacDonald and the
King. *Anonymous.*
Food. Valle.
For Avi Killed in Lebanon.
Osaki.
For Sleep, or Death. Pitter.
For You, Falling Asleep after
a Quarrel. Middlebrook.
Four Choctaw Songs.
Barnes.
Frank O'Hara. Berrigan.
From the Spanish. Towle.
A Front. jarrell.
Garment. Hughes.
The General's Death.
O'Connor.
Gift of Sight. Graves.
Glyph. *Anonymous.*
The Gorse. Gibson.
Graffiti. Field.
Great Shepherd of the Sheep.
Wesley.
Greenwich Observatory.
Keyes.
The Grief. Rilke.
Halieutica. Oppian.
Halloween Witches.
Holman.
Have Sky. MacAdams.
Heaven and Earth.
Thompson.
The Heron. Donaghy.
Hobbes, 1651. Hollander.
Holding On. Jackson.
Home on the Range.
Anonymous.
The Homeric Hexameter,
Described and Exemplified.
Coleridge.
Horizontal World. Saunders.
How to Get to Canada.
Berrigan.
How to Tell the Top of a Hill.
Ciardi.
How to Write a Poem about
the Sky. Silko.
Hymns for the Amusement of
Children. Smart.
I Break the Sky. Dodson.
I Now Had Only to Retrace.
Bronte.

I Once Loved a Young Man. *Anonymous.*
I've Lost My—. Cholmondeley-Pennell.
I Wonder as I Wander. *Anonymous.*
The Iliad. Homer.
Immortality. Mitchell.
In a Province. Prince.
In Autumn When the Woods Are Red. Stevenson.
In Dream: The Privacy of Sequence. Young Bear.
In Its Place. Stager.
In the Grass. Garland.
Independence Day. Smith.
Inland Passages, I: The Long Hunter. Berry.
Interview. Lieberman.
Introduction of the Shopping Cart. Costanzo.
The Iris. Gasetsu.
Irradiations. Fletcher.
The Island of the Blest. West.
Israfel. Poe.
It Is Better to Be Together. Miller.
It's Over Now; I've Known It All. Bronte.
Job Hunting. Hennen.
Kings Came Riding. Williams.
A la Bourbon. Lovelace.
Labor. Day.
Lament. Rilke.
The Landing of the British Settlers of 1820 (excerpt). Wilmot.
A Landscape. Cunningham.
The Lark. Reese.
Late Abed. MacLeish.
Life from the Lifeless. Jeffers.
Like the Prime Mover. Seljouk.
Lineage. Terry.
Lion, Leopard, Lady. Le Pan.
A Little Song of Life. Reese.
Lost on September Trail, 1967. Rios.
Lost Ships. Ferril.
Love Is More Thicker Than Forget. Cummings.
Love Should Grow Up Like a Wild Iris in the Fields. Griffin.
Lullabye. Stripling.
Lunar Baedeker. Loy.
Mallee in October. Hudson.
A Man's Woman. Davies.
Memento Mori. Halpern.
Merits of Laughter and Lust. Mandel.
Mile Hill. Schmitz.
A Moment of War. Lee.
Moon. Horovitz.
Moon Man. Valentine.
Morning. Keats.
Moth. Henson.
Mythological Sonnets, VIII: "Suns in a skein." Fuller.
The Name. Duggan.
Nekros. Tabb.
New England Greenhouse. McQuilkin.
The News & the Weather. Lesser.
November. Binyon.
Nuclear Racial Lockdowns. Aguila.

Ode: On the Death of William Butler Yeats. Smith.
Ode to Quinbus Flestrin. Pope.
Oedipus. Muir.
The Old Gospel Ship. *Anonymous.*
The Old Liberals. Betjeman.
An Old Woman's Song. Akjartoq.
On Mites, To a Lady. Duck.
Once More, O Lord. Doane.
Once Only. Snyder.
One Foot in Eden. Muir.
Ordinary Women. Hacker.
Our History. Coblentz.
Outward. Neihardt.
Over the Heather the Wet Wind Blows. Auden.
The Oxford Girl (Expert Town). *Anonymous.*
The Paisley Officer. *Anonymous.*
Parachute Descent. Bourne.
Parisian Dream. Baudelaire.
Part Winter. Bowering.
The Party. Sala.
Pine Trees and the Sky: Evening. Brooke.
Poor Omie. *Anonymous.*
Prairie Graveyard. Marriott.
Proverbially Useful for Weather Forecasts. *Anonymous.*
The Pythoness. Raine.
Rabbit Cry. Lucie-Smith.
Remembering. Akjartoq.
The Renaming. Sinason.
Renascence. Millay.
Resignation—To Faustus. Clough.
Room of Return. Kinnell.
Ross's Poems. Lehmann.
Sea Dawn. Hackett.
Sea Sonnet. Lay.
The Seals in Penobscot Bay. Hoffman.
Seed Leaves. Wilbur.
The Serenity in Stones. Ortiz.
Silver Sheep. Payne.
Since "The Pillow Knows All." Ise.
Sinnes Heavie Loade. Southwell.
Skywriting. Maxtone.
Sleep. Berssenbrugge.
Sleep on the Fraser. Lane.
Sleet. MacCaig.
Snowfall: Four Variations. Amabile.
Solitude. Sill.
Song. Lowell
A Song of Degrees. Ker.
A Song of Honor. Hodgson.
Song of the Sky Loom. *Anonymous.*
Song of the Thunders. *Anonymous.*
Spirit of Sadness. Le Gallienne.
Spring Street Bar. Berssenbrugge.
Starfish. Welles.
The Storm. Shanks.
Summer Mansions. Herschberger.
Surfaces. Meinke.
Sylvia. Croxall.
A Temple. Patchen.
The Temple by the Sea. Dutton.

That's June. Butts.
To —. Shelley.
To a Skeleton. Vardhill.
To Gabriel of the Annunciation. Abelard.
To Mary Magdalen. Argensola.
To My Father. Graham.
To One Who Died in Autumn. McCormick.
To Robert Lowell and Osip Mandelstam. Seidel.
Tongues of Fire. Plescoff.
Traditional Red. Huff.
Trip: San Francisco. Hughes.
Ts'eekkaayah. Tallmountain.
The Turn of the Road. Gifford.
Twilit Revelation. Adams.
Two Chorale-Preludes. Hill.
Two Loves. Eberhart.
Usually an Old Female Is the Leader. Hennen.
Vaquero. Dorn.
Vestigia Restrorsum: The Vales of the Medway. Munby.
Wagon Wheels. LaMoure.
A Walk on Snow. Viereck.
Walking through the Door. Henderson.
The Walking Tour. Auden.
War Requiem. Rogers.
A Warning. Nicolson.
Water. Conkling.
We like March—his shoes are purple. Dickinson.
We Reached Out Far. Markish.
Wet Weather. Low.
What Are You Thinking About? Macmillan.
What Could Be Lovelier Than to Hear. Coatsworth.
What It Was. Sward.
When Nature Hath Betrayed the Heart That Loved Her. Jewett.
Who. Honig.
Why Do We Mourn Departing Friends? Watts.
Wild Provoke of the Endurance Sky. Ceravolo.
The Wind. Corbin.
The Wind Carries Me Free. Shady.
Winter. Thomson.
Winter Circus. Fisher.
Wisdom. Hughes.
Wolfram's Dirge. Beddoes.
Women at the Market. Aymrich.
Wood-cut. Sackville-West.
The Ziz. Hollander.

Skylark
At the Salon. Wilkinson.
How Looks the Night? Hopkins.

Skyline (s)
The Horseman on the Skyline. Lawson.
Metroliner. Du Vall.

Skyscraper (s)
Drink. Williams.
The Magistrate's Escape. Fulton.
Prayers of Steel. Sandburg.
Skyscaper. Sandburg.

Slab
On Having Grown Old. Moll.

What I Have Done. Malanga.

Slack (en)
Evensong. Drewry.
The Good-Morrow. Donne.
Hard Times, But Carrying On. Smith.
Homeward Bound. Rogers.
Lyke Memnons Rocke Toucht, with the Rising Sunne. Fletcher.
Pitch Seven. Brown.
Prince Charming. Miller.
Spiders. Ackerman.

Slake
Tiger. McKay.
To Himselfe and the Harpe. Drayton.

Slam (med)
The City and the Trucks. Thompson.
Docker. Heaney.
Rebecca, Who Slammed Doors for Fun and Perished Miserably. Belloc.
When the Ambulance Came. Morgan.

Slander (ing) (s)
Old Age in His Ailing. Melville.
Summing Up in Italy. Browning.
Woe to Him Who Slanders Women. Mac Gearailt.

Slant (ed) (ing)
Harvest. Maino.
Nine Years after Viet Nam. Quintana.
Private Rooms. O Hehir.
The Sigh of Silence. Keats.

Slapped
In Memoriam. Weber.
Indifference. Graham.

Slate (s)
Ireland with Emily. Betjeman.
School Days. Cobb.
You're. Plath.

Slaughter (ed)
An Idler's Calendar: January. Blunt.
Lee-ers of Hew... Cunningham.
The Man from the Top of the Mind. Wagoner.
Melon-Slaughterer; or, A Sick Man's Praise for a Well Woman (parody). Peters.
Through Baltimore. Taylor.
To Daisies. Thompson.
The Vine to the Goat. Euenos.

Slaughterhouse
Eau-Forte. Flint.
Radcliff, Kentucky. Nickens.
The Temple of Nature. Darwin.

Slave (ry) (s)
Actaeon. Bewe.
After Aughrim. Geoghegan.
Aladdin and the Jinn. Lindsay.
All the Slaves. Lux.
As You Like It. Shakespeare.
Astrophel and Stella, XXIX. Sidney.
At the Holi festival of color. Mira Bai [(or Mirabai)].
The Battle of Aughrim. Murphy.
Black Cat. Dunetz.

Black Soldier's Civil War Chant. *Anonymous.*
Bold Jack Donahue. *Anonymous.*
Botany Lesson. Reeve.
Breath in My Nostrils. Jeffers.
Bryan, Bryan, Bryan, Bryan. Lindsay.
Bury Me In a Free Land. Harper.
Caelica, LXXVIII. Greville.
A Child's Future. Swinburne.
Colonial Nomenclature. Lang.
Coriolanus. Shakespeare.
Coronation. Jackson.
Cupid. *Anonymous.*
Dear Body. Canan.
December 1970. Tagliabue.
E. B. B. Thomson.
Edward Millington. Church.
Elegy: On Delia's Being in the Country. Hammond.
An Essay on Woman. Leapor.
A Fable for Critics. Lowell.
Fair Hebe. West.
La Fayette. Coleridge.
Freedom. Ibn Ezra.
Girls from Home. Reisen.
Hearing Men Shout at Night on MacDougal Street. Bly.
How He Saved St. Michael's. Stansbury.
I Know That I Am a Great Sinner. Purohit Swami.
In Bondage. McKay.
In Harmony with Nature. Arnold.
Italy. Filicaja.
Jack Donahoe. *Anonymous.*
Lament for the Death of Eoghan Ruadh O'Neill. Davis.
The lamp burns sure, within. Dickinson.
The Liberty Song. Dickinson.
Love Constraining to Obedience. Cowper.
Mary Magdalene. Kassia.
Massachusetts to Virginia. Whittier.
The Minstrel-Boy. Moore.
My eyes are thirsty. Mira Bai [(or Mirabai)].
Oh! Isn't It a Pity. Robinson.
On Hearing Mrs. Woodhouse Play the Harpsichord. Davies.
On Scaring Some Waterfowl in Loch Turit... Burns.
On the Lord Mayor and Court of Aldermen... Marvell.
Osip Mandelshtam. Layton.
Pennsylvania Song. *Anonymous.*
Phillis's Resolution. Walsh.
Philomel to Corydon. Young.
Poem: "It's a dull poem." Jonas.
Portrait of a Machine. Untermeyer.
A Proclamation. *Anonymous.*
The Proclamation. Whittier.

Reparation or War. *Anonymous.*
The Rhyme of the Three Captains. Kipling.
Rosh Pina. Knut.
Rule Britannia. Thomson.
Samson Agonistes. Milton.
The Search. Brew.
She's Free! Harper.
The Slave Chase. *Anonymous.*
Slave Story. Carter.
A Song for the Spanish Anarchists. Read.
Song: "Give me leave to rail at you." Rochester.
Song of the Factory Girls. *Anonymous.*
Song of the Poor Man. *Anonymous.*
Song of the Son. Toomer.
A Special Moment. Phillips.
Squaring the Circle. Coxe.
Stanzas on Freedom. Lowell.
The Summing Up. Simmons.
Swimmers (excerpt). Untermeyer.
These Are My People. Trent.
To an Anti-poetical Priest. MacNamee.
To the Memory of J. Horace Kimball. Ada Sister Mary.
Toilet Bowl Congregation. Baxter.
Upon His Majesty's Being Made Free of the City. Marvell.
Who Reigns? Shelley.
Why Should I Care for the Men of Thames? Blake.
The Wind Is Blind. Meynell.
Slay (s) (slain)
Abel. Lasker-Schüler.
Amoretti, XVI. Spenser.
Anticipation. De Tabley.
Arachne. Empson.
The Battle of Bridgewater. *Anonymous.*
Bete Humaine. Young.
Boston in Distress. *Anonymous.*
Bronzeville Man with a Belt in the Back. Brooks.
The Camelopard. Belloc.
Casuarina. Robinson.
Child Maurice (B version). *Anonymous.*
The Duke of Athole's Nurse (A version). *Anonymous.*
Epitaphs of the War, 1914-18. Kipling.
The Frailty. Cowley.
Golden Wings. Morris.
Good Friday. *Anonymous.*
Joy May Kill. Michelangelo.
Just behind the Battle, Mother. *Anonymous.*
Lady Diamond. *Anonymous.*
Lady Isabel and the Elf-Knight (A vers.). *Anonymous.*
Liberty. Hay.
Madonna of the Exiles. Tobin.
Mohammed and Seid. Morris.
Moreton Miles, LIV. Baylebridge.
My Luve's in Germany. *Anonymous.*

Of the Nativity of the Lady Rich's Daughter. Constable.
Parentage. Meynell.
A Poem To Be Said on Hearing The Birds Sing. *Anonymous.*
The Riders Held Back. Simpson.
Sainclaire's Defeat. *Anonymous.*
Saul. Heavysege.
Shall I Abide This Jesting? *Anonymous.*
Silences. Pratt.
The Silent Slain. MacLeish.
Sonnets, XXII: "My glass shall not persuade me I am old." Shakespeare.
The stars are old, that stood for me. Dickinson.
The Summer Landscape; or, The Dragon's Teeth. Humphries.
Thus Speak the Slain. Holliday.
The Tombe. Stanley.
Trafalgar. Palgrave.
The Unhappy Lover. Al-Harizi.
Victory. Duggan.
Young Barnswell. *Anonymous.*
Youth. Cloud.
Sled
Blue Bog Children. Weingarten.
Sled (s)
First Winter's Day. Aldis.
Sleek
Bells of Grey Crystal. Sitwell.
Surfers at Santa Cruz. Goodman.
Sleep (er) (ing) (s) (y)
Abandoned Copper Refinery. Gillespie.
About the Phoenix. Merrill.
Abraham Lincoln Walks at Midnight. Lindsay.
Absent Daughter. Toerien.
Abt Vogler. Browning.
Across the Sky the Daylight Crept. Patmore.
Adam's Song to Heaven. Bowers.
Admiral Death. Newbolt.
Aedh Hears the Cry of the Sedge. Yeats.
Afoot. Roberts.
After. Marston.
After All These Years. Sarton.
After Apple-Picking. Frost.
After Sunday Dinner We Uncles Snooze. Ciardi.
After the Agony in the Garden. Hine.
Afterglow. Borges.
The Age of the Butcher. Friebert.
Ah! Why, Because the Dazzling Sun. Bronte.
Aideen. *Anonymous.*
Albuera. Hardy.
All the Pretty Little Horses. *Anonymous.*
Alone with the Dawn. Sweeney.
Aminta: Chorus I. Tasso.

Among the Coffee Cups and Soup Toureens Walked Beauty. Spicer.
And So Men Say, I Love Thee! Coleridge.
Anecdote of the Prince of Peacocks. Stevens.
Anguish. Mallarme.
Another Song. Ross.
The Anxious Dead. McCrae.
The Apron. Friebert.
Ars Poetica. Trias.
Ascension. Devlin.
Asleep. Owen.
Aubade: N.Y.C. Wallace.
Auld Sang. Soutar.
Autumn Poem. Cronin.
Bags Packed and We Expected This. Wilson.
Ballad of the Icondic. Ciardi.
The Banjo. Winner.
Barbarossa. Rueckert.
The Battle of Antietam Creek. *Anonymous.*
The Battle of Valparaiso. *Anonymous.*
Beach Fire. Frost.
A Beautiful Night. Beddoes.
Beautiful Things. Allerton.
Becalmed. Tabb.
The Bed. Merrill.
Bed-Time Song. Poulsson.
A Bed without a Woman. Souster.
Bedtime Stories. Moore.
Before Sleep. Prudentius (Aurelius Clemens Prudentius).
Behold This Dreamer. Bartlett.
Ben Allah Achmet. Gilbert.
Beside the Bed. Mew.
The Birds Do Thus. Frost.
Birmingham. MacNeice.
The Blind Man. Lewisohn.
Blond. De Roche.
A blue-eyed phantom far before. Rossetti.
Blue Island Intersection. Sandburg.
Blue Squills. Teasdale.
The Bog Lands. Byrne.
The Bored Mirror. Nagayasu.
Bridal Piece. Gluck.
Broken Sky. Sandburg.
A Brook in the City. Frost.
Bucolic. Merwin.
Bury Me beneath the Willow. *Anonymous.*
But That Is Another Story. Justice.
Byron in Greece. Rosten.
Call Me Not Back from the Echoless Shore. *Anonymous.*
Cantico del Sole. Pound.
Cat & the Weather. Swenson.
Cats. Farjeon.
Cell-Mates. Untermeyer.
Chanticleer. Irvin.
Charm: "Bring the holy crust of Bread." Herrick.
Charm: "Let the superstitious wife." Herrick.
Child's Game. Jerome.
The Child Who Walks Backwards. Crozier.
Christmas Eve in Whitneyville, 1955. Hall.

Christopher at Birth.
  Longley.
Clamour of the Wind Making
  Music. Columcille.
Clams. Ishigaki Rin.
A Clear Midnight.
  Whitman.
Clinton South of Polk.
  Sandburg.
Close to Me. "Mistral.
A Cloud in Trousers:
  Prologue. Mayakovsky.
A Colloquy with God.
  Browne.
The Columbine. Very.
Come, Come, What Doe I
  Here? Vaughan.
Come Out, Come Out, Ye
  Souls That Serve.
  Brennan.
Come Slowly, Paradise.
  Kenyon.
Comfort. Browning.
Conestoga. Murphy, Jr.
The Confession. Cooley.
The Conversation in the
  Drawingroom. Kees.
The Cottage at Chigasaki.
  Blunden.
Courtyards in Delft. Mahon.
The Critic. Farrar.
The Crucifix. Lamartine.
Curiosity: Fiction. Sprague.
The D Minor. Mayo.
Danny Boy. Anonymous.
Dante. Duncan.
The Dark Cavalier.
  Widdemer.
Davis Matlock. Masters.
The Day Is Gone. Keats.
The Day Returns.
  Stevenson.
The Dead Wingman. Jarrell.
The Death of Nick Charles.
  Jones.
Death's Head. Gotlieb.
Death Snips Proud Men.
  Sandburg.
Depot Blues. Lincoln
  (Hicks).
Description of a Summer's
  Eve. White.
A Dialogue between Thyrsis
  and Dorinda. Marvell.
Dinnshenchas: The Enchanted
  Fawn. Anonymous.
Dirge for the Year. Shelley.
Do You Not Hear? Picot.
Doctor Drink. Cunningham.
A Dog Sleeping on My Feet.
  Dickey.
Don't Sing Love Songs.
  Anonymous.
Down the Mississippi.
  Fletcher.
Down to Sleep. Jackson.
Dream Fantasy. "Macleod.
The Drunkard. Levine.
The Dug-Out. Sassoon.
The Dynasts. Hardy.
East Texas. Stokesbury.
Eclogue. Prokosch.
Eighteen-Seventy. Rimbaud.
Elfer Hill. Anonymous.
The Emigrant's Child.
  Sproull.
The End. Rice.
The Enduring Music. Vinal.
Endymion. Keats.
The Epicurean. Doyle.
An Epitaph. Sackville.

Epitaph for a Judge.
  Jeitteles.
Epitaph of a Faithful Man.
  Mezey.
Epitaph of Hipponax.
  Calverley.
Epitaph on a Well-Known
  Poet. Moore.
Epitaphs of the War, 1914-18.
  Kipling.
Ernest Dowson. Wheelock.
The Estate: "Waking by
  Night". Brasch.
Evangeline. Longfellow.
Evening. Miller.
Evening Harbour. Paulin.
Evening Song of Senlin.
  Aiken.
Evensong. Drewry.
Evensong. Stevenson.
Exhortation: Summer, 1919.
  McKay.
Exile. Yeatman.
Experience. Wharton.
An Extra Joyful Chorus for
  Those Who Have Read
  This Far. Transtromer.
The Fairies. Hubbell.
The Fairies' Shopping.
  Deland.
Fallen Leaves. Tupper.
False Enchantment.
  Untermeyer.
The Farm Hands. Laing.
Father and Son. Wallace.
Fever. Gunn.
First Cycle of Love Poems.
  Barker.
The Fishes' Lamentation.
  Anonymous.
Five Songs. Shapiro.
Foiled Sleep. "Marie.
For Bill. Hewitt.
For Colored Girls Who Have
  Considered
  Suicide...(excerpt). Shange.
For God While Sleeping.
  Sexton.
For the Briar Rose. Morris.
For the Record. Blount Roy.
Forms, LXXVII. Enslin.
Forza D'Agro. Denby.
Four Sides to a House.
  Lowell.
Free Martin. Hopegood.
Freight Train. Anonymous.
From the Antique. Rossetti.
From the Santa-Fe Trail.
  Lindsay.
Funeral Elegy on the Death of
  His Very Good Friend Mr.
  Michael Drayton.
  Cokayne.
Furry Bear. Milne.
The Galliass. De la Mare.
The Garden of Proserpine.
  Swinburne.
The Gardener. Symons.
Gaspara Stampa. Benet.
Gautama in the Deer Park at
  Benares. Patchen.
Genius Loci of the Morning.
  Fetherling.
Georgia Towns. Hicky.
Getting out of Bed. Farjeon.
Gimboling. Gardner.
Ginevra (excerpt). Shelley.
Girl Betrayed. Hedylos.
A Girl's Song. Hinkson.
God Bless This House from
  Thatch to Floor.
  Anonymous.

God, Give Us Men!
  Holland.
The Gold Country: Hotel
  Leger, Mokelumne Hill,
  Revisited. Stroud.
The Gossip. Halpern.
Gossip Grows Like Weeds.
  Hitomaro.
Graveyard by the Sea. Lux.
Greeting. Young.
The Gunner. Webb.
Halloween. Pomeroy.
Handlining Tockers &
  Gizmos. Planz.
The Harbor Dawn. Crane.
Hawthorne. Alcott.
He Hears the Cry of the
  Sedge. Yeats.
He Said. Valentine.
Hearing the Wind at Night.
  Swenson.
Hell's Pavement. Masefield.
Homosexual Sonnets.
  Pitchford.
Hoping All the Time.
  Anonymous.
The Horse Show at Midnight.
  Taylor.
The Hour. Greenberg.
House on a Cliff. MacNeice.
Housework. Matthews.
Human Life. Prior.
The Humble-Bee. Emerson.
Hushed by the Hands of
  Sleep. Grimke.
Hymn to Proserpine.
  Swinburne.
I Can Give Myself to Her.
  Yosano Akiko.
I Can't Think What He Sees
  in Her. Herbert.
I Left. Ruebner.
I'm a Dreamer. Cumbo.
I Scream You Scream.
  McKay.
Idylls. Moschus.
Idylls. Theocritus.
If You Can't Eat You Got
  To. Cummings.
Ilicet. Swinburne.
Imitation of Julia A. Moore.
  "Twain.
In a Gondola. Browning.
In Dream. Synge.
In Flanders Fields. McCrae.
In Harbour. Swinburne.
In Memoriam A.H.H., CVIII.
  Tennyson.
In Memory of a Friend.
  Barker.
In Pace In Idipsum Dormiam
  Et Requiescam. O'Connor.
In Praise of Wyatt's Psalms.
  Surrey.
In Procession. Graves.
In Tall Grass. Sandburg.
In the Firelight. Field.
In the Footsteps of the
  Walking Air. Patchen.
In the Henry James Country.
  Abrahams.
In the Name of Jesus Christ.
  Cranston.
In the Old House. Aiken.
In the Silent Night. Peretz.
An Indian Song. Yeats.
Inner-City Lullaby. Atkins.
Insomnia. MacCarthy.
It Fell on a Summer's Day.
  Campion.
It was a Special Treat.
  Tapahonso.

John Carey's Second Song.
  McGrath.
John Standish, Artist.
  Fearing.
The Jolly Woodchuck.
  Grider.
Journey toward Evening.
  McGinley.
Juncture. Duncan.
Just About Asleep Together.
  Peacock.
Keeping You Alive.
  Gallagher.
Kentucky Babe. Buck.
A Kitten. Farjeon.
Knole. Sisson.
Knoxville, Tennessee.
  Giovanni.
Lalla Rookh. Moore.
The Lamp of Poor Souls.
  Pickthall.
Lancer. Housman.
The Last Word. Knowles.
A Late Spring. Scully.
Laziness and Silence. Bly.
Let Not the Sluggish Sleep.
  Anonymous.
Letter for Duncan. Eigner.
Letter to Anne Ridler.
  Fraser.
Light. Coates.
Lines for a Drawing of Our
  Lady of the Night.
  Thompson.
Lines: "When youthful faith
  hath fled." Lockhart.
Listening to Her. Zach.
Little Boy Blue. Ransom.
A Little Carol of the Virgin.
  Lope de Vega Carpio.
The Little Girl Lost. Blake.
The Little Land. Stevenson.
Little Pagan Rain Song.
  Shaw.
Little Tiny Puppy Dog.
  Milligan.
Living in the Present. Lott.
Living Marble.
  O'Shaughnessy.
Locks. Koch.
Lodging with the Old Man of
  the Stream. Po Chu-i.
Long Pursuit. Anonymous.
Lord, How Shall I Me
  Complain. Anonymous.
Lotuses. Bynner.
Love by the Water-Reeds.
  Anonymous.
Love Poem. Williams.
The Lovely Etan.
  Anonymous.
The Lovesleep. Ewart.
Lullaby. Anonymous.
Lullaby. Eckman.
Lullaby. Hoffenstein.
Lullaby. Moraes.
Lullaby. Vinner.
Lullaby for Miriam. Beer-
  Hofmann.
Lullaby Town. Diller.
The Lunar Probe. Kumin.
Made Shine. Miles.
Madrigal: "Lady, the birds
  right fairly." Anonymous.
Mammy Hums. Sandburg.
Man Asleep in the Desert.
  Lux.
A Man's Bread. Peabody.
Marian Drury. Carman.
The Mariners. Woods.
The Marshes of Glynn.
  Lanier.

A Masique Presented at Ludlow Castle (Comus). Milton.
Mater Amabilis. Lazarus.
Maumee Ruth. Brown.
Memorial Rain. MacLeish.
Mexican Serenade. Guiterman.
The Middleaged Man. Simpson.
The Midnight Court. Merriman.
Midnight on Front Street. Whiteman.
Minimum Security. Lewisohn.
Moods of Rain. Scannell.
Moon at Three a.m. Henson.
Moon, So Round and Yellow. Barr.
Morning Fog. Duval.
Morning Glory. Sassoon.
Mosquito. Updike.
Most Souls, 'Tis True, but Peep Out Once an Age. Pope.
Mother. Ehrmann.
The Mother. Mendes.
Mother. Montoya.
Mountain Evenings. Holme.
Music. Lowell.
Mutability. Shelley.
My Little Buckaroo. Anonymous.
My Young Mother. Cooper.
The Nearest Friend. Faber.
Nebuchadnezzar. Wylie.
Never. Reavey.
Never More, Sailor. De la Mare.
Never the Time and the Place. Browning.
New Graveyard: Jerusalem. Kaufman.
New York. Senghor.
Next of Kin. Rossetti.
Night Feeding. Rukeyser.
Night Interpreted. Hoagland.
Night of Sine. Sedar-Senghor.
Night Piece. Strand.
Night Plane. Frost.
Night Storm. Simms.
Nightmare at Noon. Benét.
A Nocturne. Blunt.
Nooksack Valley. Snyder.
The North Country. Lawrence.
Northhanger Ridge. Wright.
Not Quite Spring. Lifshin.
Now Springs the Spray. Anonymous.
Now the Laborer's Task Is O'er. Ellerton.
La Nuit Blanche. Kipling.
The Nymphs (excerpt). Hunt.
O Jesu Parvule. Anonymous.
O Sleep. Norton.
O That My Love Were in My Arms. Anonymous.
The Obsequies of the Lord Harrington. Donne.
Ode on a Jar of Pickles (parody). Taylor.
Ode: "Sire of the rising day." De Tabley.
Odes, V. Hafiz.
The Odyssey. Homer.
Off to the Fishing Ground. Montgomery.

Oh, Sleep, Fond Fancy. Anonymous.
Old Ego Song. Minczeski.
The Old King. Heath-Stubbs.
Old Lizette on Sleep. Lee.
Old Moon My Eyes Are New Moon. Ginsberg.
An Old Song. Blumgarten (Yehoash)
An Old Song. Yehoash.
The Old Woman. Seiffert.
On a Poetess. Hopkins.
On a Watchman Asleep at Midnight. Field.
On the Death of Emperor Tenji. Anonymous.
On the Edge of a Safe Sleep. Cader.
On the Picture of a "Child Tired of Play." Willis.
On the Wall. Di Roma.
On Waking. Campbell.
Once More. Jonas.
One Winter Night in August. Kennedy.
Only a Cowboy. Anonymous.
Only the Beards Are Different. Dawe.
Our "Civilization." Morgan.
The Outlaw of Loch Lene. Callanan.
Paradise Lost. Milton.
Park Avenue. Fitzgerald.
Parks and Ponds. Emerson.
Parta Quies. Housman.
Parting. Corbin.
Patience of a People. Bryant, Jr.,
Pelicanaries. Lewis.
Peregrine's Sunday Song. Wylie.
Peter Emberley (III). Anonymous.
Philosophy. Bangs.
Physical Universe. Simpson.
Piano. Russ.
The Plum Tree by the House. Gogarty.
Poem in May. Hewitt.
Poem Rocket. Ginsberg.
Poems. Machado.
The Poet. Benton.
The Poet's Lot. Holmes.
Poetry Paper. Codrescu.
The Pointless Pride of Man. Anonymous.
Polyolbion. Drayton.
The Poor Ghost. Rossetti.
Possessions. Gurney.
Prairie Lullaby. Anonymous.
Praise. Matthews.
A Prayer for Peace. Sill.
Prayer on the Night Before Easter. Holmes.
Prettiest Little Baby in the County-o. Anonymous.
Prince Lucifer: Mother-Song. Austin.
Prison Cell Blues. Jefferson.
Prison Walls–Red Brick Crevices. Wilkins.
A Prophecy. Levenson.
Pyramus and Thisbe. Dakin.
Quatrain: "Good-looking, I'll never stoop for you." Mahsati.
The Quest of the Sangraal: The Coming of the Sangraal. Hawker.
The Quiet Nights. Hinkson.
The Rampage. Williams.

The Reaper. Tabb.
Reflections, Written on Visiting the Grave of a Venerated Friend. Plato.
Registered at the Bordello Hotel (Vienna). Rubin.
Remembering Fire. Jones.
Reply to In Flanders Fields. Mitchell.
Requiem. Lee.
Requiem for a Young Soldier. Coates.
Rhyme for Night. Aiken.
The Riddle Song. Anonymous.
Rispetto. Robinson.
The River. Leitch.
The Rock. Stevens.
Rock Me to Sleep. Allen.
The Rod. Herrick.
Rose in the Garden. Anonymous.
Rose Red to Snow White. Colby.
Rounding the Cape. Campbell.
The Rubaiyat: A book of verses underneath the bough. Omar Khayyam.
Saturday Night in the Parthenon. Patchen.
Schlof, Bobbeli. Anonymous.
Scissor-Man. MacBeth.
The Sea and the Mirror. Auden.
Sea Burial. Monkman.
The Sea-Deeps. Miller.
Sea-Fever. Masefield.
The Sea–in Calm. "Cornwall.
The Sea Princess. Pyle.
Seafarer. MacLeish.
Seaweed, Seaweed. Tatana.
September 2. Berry.
The Setting Sun. Horton.
The Shadows. Sherman.
Shellbrook. Barnes.
The Shepherd. Gilmore.
The Shepherds. Van Slyke.
The Sherman Cyclone. Anonymous.
Shira. Schwartz.
Shooting Whales. Strand.
A Short History of British India. Hill.
The Siesta. Anonymous.
The Silent Ranges. Bird.
Sir Hugh, or, The Jew's Daughter (N version). Anonymous.
Six-Forty-Two Farm Commune Struggle Poem. Leifer.
Sleep. Aldrich.
Sleep. Martin.
Sleep Brings No Joy. Bronte.
Sleep Is a Suspension. Sandburg.
Sleep, Madame, Sleep. Ewing.
The Sleep Song of Diarmaid and Grainne. Anonymous.
Sleep Watch. Henson.
The Sleeper. Hume.
The Sleeper. Scollard.
Sleeping Alone. Fickert.
The Sleeping House. Tennyson.
Sleeping on Horseback. Po Chu-i.
Sleeping on the Ceiling. Bishop.

Sleeping with Women. Koch.
Slow Movement. MacNeice.
Slow Movement. Williams.
The Sluggard. Lucilius [(or Lucillius)].
The Snake. Berry.
Snow. Pomeroy.
Song for a Child. Davis.
Song for the Spinning Wheel. Wordsworth.
Song: "Let's sing a song together once." Simpson.
Song: "Life with her weary eyes." Zaturenska.
The Song of Crede. Anonymous.
Song of the Springbok Does. Anonymous.
Song: "The moth's kiss, first!" Browning.
Song: "There is many a love in the land, my love." Miller.
Songs of Ch'en. Confucius.
Sonnet: "In heaven there is a star I call my own." McLeod.
Sonnet: "Now keep that long revolver at your side." Hetherington.
Sonnet: "She is so young, and never never before." Davison.
Sonnets. Tuckerman.
Sonnets: A Sequence on Profane Love. Boker.
Sonnets of the Months. San Geminiano.
Sops of Light. Shove.
South of My Days. Wright.
Spleen. Dowson.
Spring in New Hampshire. McKay.
Spring Whistles. Larcom.
Standing on the Streetcorner. Denby.
Staying Up on Jack's Fork Near Eminence, Missouri. Salsich.
Stopping by Woods on a Snowy Evening. Frost.
The Stories in the Light. Waters.
The Storm Is Over. Bridges.
The Summons. Ross.
The Sun Wields Mercy. Bukowski.
Sunsets. Sandburg.
Sweet and Low. Barnby.
Table-Birds. Mackenzie.
Tall and Singularly Dark You Pass among the Breakers. Zukofsky.
Telephoning It. Edmond.
The Tempest. Shakespeare.
Ten Days Leave. Snodgrass.
Tenant Farmer. Ward.
Tenants. Gibson.
Tenement Room: Chicago. Davis.
The Texas Cowboy. Anonymous.
Thailand Railway. Stow.
That Which Hath Wings Shall Tell. Van Voorhis.
Things. Smith.
Things to Do in Providence. Berrigan.
The Thousand and One Nights: Dates. Anonymous.

Three. Kitchell.
Three Presidents: Andrew
  Jackson. Bly.
The Three Seamstresses.
  Peretz.
Three Women Blues.
  McTell.
Ticonderoga: A Legend of the
  West Highlands.
  Stevenson.
Time to Rise. Stevenson.
To a Defeated Saviour.
  Wright.
To a Friend's Child.
  Barnstone.
To a Happy Warrior. Blunt.
To Allegra Florence in
  Heaven. Chivers.
To Critics. Learned.
To Dorothy. Bell.
To Everlasting Oblivion.
  Marston.
To My Son (excerpt).
  Barker.
To New York. Senghor.
To Sleep. Graves.
To Summer. Nadel.
To the Generous Reader.
  Herrick.
Traverse City Zoo. Harrison.
Tribal Memories. Duncan.
The True Story of Snow
  White. Bennett.
Turn the Key Deftly. Brock.
Twilight. Bevington.
Twins. Matthews.
The Two Brothers.
  Anonymous.
Two Little Kittens.
  Anonymous.
Two Wise Generals. Hughes.
The Ugstabuggle. Wesley-
  Smith.
Under the Casuarina.
  Riddell.
The Unillumined Verge.
  Bridges.
Upon a Dainty Hill Sometime.
  Breton.
Upon Eckington Bridge, River
  Avon. Quiller-Couch.
Ur Burial. Eberhart.
The Usk. Sisson.
Verses to Miss —-. Wilde.
Victory March. Joseph.
The Virgin's Slumber Song.
  Carlin.
A Visit. Anderson.
The Visit. George.
Visitations. Durrell.
Visiting Emily Dickinson's
  Grave with Robert Francis.
  Bly.
Wagon Train. Mayo.
Waking Early. Barth.
Waldere 2. Anonymous.
The Wall. Merriam.
Wanderer's Song. Symons.
War Poem. Ehrenburg.
Watching You Sleep under
  Monet's Water Lilies.
  Ruark.
A Water-Colour of Venice.
  Durrell.
We Are a People. Henson.
The Welsh Marches.
  Housman.
What Profit? Di Roma.
When from the Calyx-Canopy
  of Night. Laughton.
When the Orient Is Lit by the
  Great Light. Colonna.

Whirring Wheels. Oxenham.
Whistles. Field.
The Whole Duty of Berkshire
  Brooks. Conkling.
Wild Peaches. Wylie.
Will You Be as Hard?
  Gregory.
Willie Macintosh.
  Anonymous.
Winter Night. Fitzgerald.
Winter Song. Tollet.
A Wintering Moon. Hardy.
The Wisdom of Merlyn.
  Blunt.
With Happiness Stretched
  Across the Hills. Blake.
With I and E. Anonymous.
With Rue My Heart Is Laden.
  Housman.
The Wonder Clock. Pyle.
Woods Night. Hennen.
Words for a Picture of
  Newlyweds. T'ang Yin.
Written on the Banks of
  Wastwater during a Calm.
  Wilson.
You and It. Strand.
You Know Not How Deep
  Was the Love Your Eyes
  Did Kindle. Ibn al-Abbar.
Your Glory, Lincoln.
  Goodman.
Youth, Day, Old Age, and
  Night. Whitman.
Sleepless
The Beloved's Image.
  Anonymous.
Insomnia. Tabb.
Lament for Better or Worse.
  Baro.
My Nightingale. Auslander.
Night-Piece. Patterson.
Sea Dirge. Archias.
Sentinel Songs. Ryan.
Waiting for Death. Gebirtig.
Sleet
In the Surgery. Ditta.
A Puritan Lady. Reese.
The Slushy Snow Splashes and
  Sploshes. Hoberman.
Sleeve (s)
The Clothing's New Emperor.
  Finkel.
Correspondence:. Ise.
Death's Blue-Eyed Girl.
  Pastan.
Grandfather. Barnstone.
I Know the Reputation. Kii.
June. Reaney.
King's College Chapel.
  Causley.
Lee-ers of Hew...
  Cunningham.
Letter: The Japanese, to Her
  Husband at War. Walsh.
Lubber Breeze. Moore.
Missouri Town. Palen.
North to Milwaukee.
  Vizenor.
Ray Charles. Cornish.
Seeing the Plum Blossoms by
  the River. Ise.
There Is Something. Pope.
Through the thatched roof.
  Tenchi.
Sleigh
Jingle Bells. Pierpont.
Slender
Child of the Romans.
  Sandburg.
Love Song. Anonymous.

Many Indeed Must Perish in
  the Keel. Hofmannsthal.
Oppian's Halieuticks (parody).
  Diaper.
Slept
1916 Seen from 1921.
  Blunden.
Abraham Lincoln. Brownell.
After Love. Kumin.
All Night Long. Cassian.
Angina Pectoris. Moses.
The Animals' Arrival.
  Jennings.
The Author Loving These
  Homely Meats... Davies.
Awake! Walther von der
  Vogelweide.
Burglar Bill. Anstey.
The Carnal and the Crane.
  Anonymous.
Chimney Swallows. Powers.
Deliverance. Dawson.
Earthy Anecdote. Stevens.
Epitaphs of the War, 1914-18.
  Kipling.
The Eve of St. Agnes.
  Keats.
From That First Night.
  Izumi Shikibu.
Good Company, Fine Houses.
  Newlove.
The House of Night (excerpt).
  Freneau.
In Memoriam A.H.H., CIII.
  Tennyson.
The Kiss. Patmore.
The Knell. Al-Fituri.
The Mendicants. Carman.
Mother of Men. Southwold.
Museum Piece. Wilbur.
The Net-Menders. Vrepont.
The Nut-Gathering Lass.
  Burns.
Old Boniface. Anonymous.
Old I Am. Bosman.
On a Certain Alderman.
  Cunningham.
Rachel. Gilbert.
The Sleepers. Untermeyer.
Spring Poem. Ramke.
A True Account of Talking to
  the Sun at Fire Island.
  O'Hara.
Under the Arc de Triomphe:
  October 17. Hacker.
The Unfortunate Reminder.
  Pattison.
The View from an Attic
  Window. Nemerov.
The Weary Blues. Hughes.
Zalinka. MacInnes.
Slew
Amanda Barker. Masters.
Anathema of Cats. Skelton.
The Conquerors. McGinley.
The Cross. Lanier.
Epitaphs of the War, 1914-18.
  Kipling.
Fause Foodrage (B version).
  Anonymous.
A Prairie Water Colour.
  Scott.
To a Lady: She Refusing to
  Continue a Dispute with
  Me... Prior.
Slice (s)
The Alphabet. Greenaway.
Butcher's Wife. Scott.
A Common Light. Orlen.
How to Murder Your Best
  Friend. O Hehir.
Kitchen Song. Dobbs.

Sausage. Axionicus.
Slid (e) (es)
Achitophel: the Earl of
  Shaftesbury. Dryden.
First Winter's Day. Aldis.
For the Union Dead.
  Lowell.
The Fury of Flowers and
  Worms. Sexton.
Give Way, Ye Gates.
  Roethke.
I don't have the energy...
  Gold.
The Indian Queen: Song of
  Aerial Spirits. Dryden.
The Jellyfish. Root.
Limerick: "There was a young
  curate of Kidderminster."
  Anonymous.
Mein Liebchen, Wir Sassen
  Zusammen. Heine.
The Spouse to the Younglings.
  Baldwin.
Waiting. Yevtushenko.
Slight (ed)
The D.L. and W.'s Phoebe
  Snow. Anonymous.
Evening. Cowper.
Lady Flower. Anonymous.
Of Common Devotion.
  Quarles.
Oh! the time that is past.
  Anonymous.
Slim
Defiance. Landor.
Limerick: "There was a gay
  damsel of Lynn."
  Anonymous.
A Pastel. Verlaine.
Portrait in Georgia. Toomer.
The Song of the Pen. Al-
  Harizi.
Slime
Citizen. Grudin.
I Break the Sky. Dodson.
Memory. Rimbaud.
The Navigators. Turner.
The Sea and the Skylark.
  Hopkins.
Sling
Danger. Jackson.
The David Jazz. Robinson.
A Metrical Version of the
  Bible....(excerpt).
  Anonymous.
Slip (s)
Artificer. Kennedy.
The Bastard from the Bush.
  Anonymous.
Close to Me. "Mistral.
The Dance. Duncan.
He Shot at Lee Wing.
  Anonymous.
How Did It Seem to Sylvia?
  Schnackenberg.
The Last Trail. Coblentz.
Limerick: "A housewife called
  out with a frown."
  Anonymous.
No Fault in Women.
  Herrick.
On the Meetings of the Scotch
  Covenanters. Anonymous.
Out of You. Phillips.
Over Bright Summer Seas.
  Hillyer.
Reading Plato. Graham.
Sea-Weed. Lawrence.
The Sky. Roberts.
Specimen of an Induction to a
  Poem. Bernheimer.
Templeogue. Salkeld.

Thomas and Charlie. Wild.
To-Day. Carlyle.
Wires. Bassett.
With Whom Is No
Variableness, Neither
Shadow of Turning.
Clough.
A Year without Seasons.
Williams.

Slipper (s)
Baron Renfrew's Ball.
Halpine.
The Epistle of Othea to
Hector (excerpt). Pisan.
Hakluyt Unpurchased.
McDuffee.
Juan Belmonte, Torero.
Finkel.

Slippery
Frost at Night. Thomson.
Twenty Years After. Shute.

Slit
The Little Ones' A.B.C.
Coward.
Romeo and Juliet. Putnam.
Upon Scobble. Epigram.
Herrick.

Slogans
Afternoons with Baedeker.
Lancaster.
Beach Queen. Campbell.

Slope (s)
Bare Almond-Trees.
Lawrence.
Brevard Fault. Morgan.
Campi Flegrei. Toerien.
Earth-Canonized. Robinson.
Father. Weston.
A Fond Greeting, Hillock
There. Mac An Bhaird.
God's Blessing on Munster.
Patrick.
Hyena. Muske.
Never. Reavey.
Precarious Ground. Drake.

Sloth
The Butterfly and the Bee.
Bowles.
Day-Dreams. Canton.
Defeat of the Rebels.
Graves.

Slouch (es)
The Australian. Adams.
Desires. Bensley.
The Second Coming. Yeats.

Slow (er) (ly) (ness)
An Alphabet of Famous
Goops. Burgess.
Aunt Alice in April.
Matchett.
Builder Kachina: Home-
Going. Rose.
Catching One Clear Thought
Alive. Allen.
The Cloud-Mobile. Swenson.
Coin in the Fist. Brownell.
Considering the Snail. Gunn.
Ding Dong (parody). Hilton.
"Don't Touch Me!" I Scream
at Passers-By.
Gorbanyevskaya.
Elm. Plath.
Full Moon: Santa Barbara.
Teasdale.
Girod Street Cemetery: New
Orleans. Morris.
Hal's Birthday. Larcom.
The Harvest. Aberg.
Head Couples. Matchett.
Here We March All Around
in a Ring. *Anonymous.*

High Wind at the Battery.
Pomeroy.
The Horse and the Mule.
Wynne.
How Morning Glories Could
Bloom at Dusk. Graham.
I Was the Child. Warren.
Instead of a Journey.
Hamburger.
Juncture. Duncan.
The Louse-Catchers.
Rimbaud.
Midnight. Tennyson.
New York City–1935.
Corso.
Ode to the Protestant Poets.
Hoover.
On Riding to See Dean Swift
in the Mist of the Morning.
Parnell.
The Operation. Snodgrass.
Paradise Lost. Milton.
Politics. Tennyson.
Progress of Evening.
Landor.
Quatrains. Bennett.
Rendez-vous Manque dans la
Rue Racine. Synge.
The Ritualists. Williams.
Saturday Night in the Village.
Leopardi.
The Sequel. Roethke.
Ship's Bell. Dresbach.
Snail. Eybers.
Sonnets, XVII: "Cherry-Lipt
Adonis in his snowie
shape." Barnfield.
Still and All. Singer.
Subalterns. Daryush.
Thus Crosslegged on Round
Pillow Sat in Space.
Ginsberg.
The Tortoise. Corman.
Tortoise-Shell. Lawrence.
Tragedy. Russell.
The True Weather for
Women. Simpson.
White Cat. Knister.

Slug (s)
The Berg. Melville.
A Curse. Feldman.
To the Fly in My Drink.
Wagoner.

Slum (s)
Ah Fading Joy. Dryden.
The Ashtabula Disaster.
Moore.
A Ballad of the Boston Tea-
Party, December 16, 1773.
Holmes.
Boy's Day. Henderson.
The Day of Denial. Very.
A Departed Friend. Moore.
Dusk in the Domain.
Mackellar.
The Dustman. Weatherly.
Epigrams. Theocritus.
Epitaph: "Here, time
concurring (and it does)."
Ciardi.
Goya. Aiken.
Hamasah: His Children.
Hittan of Tayyi.
Her Fairness, Wedded to a
Star. O'Brien.
The Iliad. Homer.
The Landscape Lies Within
My Head. Stewart.
Love Song. Leon.
Mary Wyatt and Henry
Green. Anonymous.
Midnight. Dryden.

Music (after Sully
Prudhomme). Du
Maurier.
Night. "Mistral.
Omnia Somnia. Sylvester.
Orchard Song. Sappho.
Refrigerium. Tuckerman.
Regret Not Me. Hardy.
A Second Review of the
Grand Army. Harte.
Song: "Awake thee, my Bessy,
the morning is fair."
Callanan.
The Spirit's Odyssey.
Krishnamurti.
Stevedore. Collins.
Three Fragments.
Allingham.
Trastevere. Denby.
Two Angels. Milnes.
Unknown Soldier. Dunn.
A Vow. Ginsberg.
War-Baby. Lawrence.
The Whaleman's Song.
Anonymous.
Without the Herdsman.
Diotimus.

Sly
Crematorium. Betjeman.
Fannie. Aldrich.
Lady Tactics. Waldman.

Smack (ed)
Blond Hair at the Edge of the
Pavement. Smith.
Bring the War Home.
Matthews.
Limerick: "Charlotte Bronte
said, "Wow, sister! What a
man!" Gray.
Woman. *Anonymous.*

Small (er) (est)
The All-Night Waitress.
Stanton.
Arcadia. Sidney.
Arrival. Wain.
At Nine O'Clock in the
Spring. Bishop.
August Night. Roberts.
Burning Bush. Untermeyer.
Carol: "We saw him sleeping
in his manger bed."
Bullett.
A Century of Couplets
(excerpt). Trench.
Coma. Schmitz.
Crossing Brooklyn Ferry.
Whitman.
Design. Frost.
Find. Miles.
Graveyard. Coffin.
The Homecoming of the
Sheep. Ledwidge.
How Small Is Man. Blackie.
I took my power in my hand.
Dickinson.
Lady of Lidice. Chavez.
Lament. Roberts.
The Little Searcher. Bowen.
The Lotus Flowers. Voigt.
A May Day Carol.
Anonymous.
The Mountain in Labor.
Aesop.
Notre Dame des Petits.
Mercier.
O Pity Our Small Size.
Rosenbaum.
One for the Ladies at the
Troy Laundry Who Cooled
Themselves... Zimmer.
People. Kanik.

Postcard to a Foetus.
Robertson.
Rest Only in the Grave.
Mangan.
The Shanty-Man's Life (with
music). *Anonymous.*
Silent Is the Night. Glick.
The Smoked Herring. Cros.
A Solemn Thing–It Was–I
Said. Dickinson.
A Song in Humility.
Drewry.
St. Simon and St. Jude's Day.
Alexander.
String Stars for Pearls.
Nicolson.
Then. Aldis.
They might not need me.
Dickinson.
Traverse City Zoo. Harrison.
Voyagers. Van Dyke.
A Wind Rose in the Night.
Kilmer.
The Window Frames the
Moon. Mar.
Wishes for My Son.
Macdonagh.
Work for Small Men
(excerpt). Foss.
Yang-Se-Fu. Yehoash.

Smallpox
Meeting the British.
Muldoon.

Smart
Absence absenting causeth me
to complain. Wyatt.
Against Mosquitoes.
Meleager.
Celia Bleeding, to the
Surgeon. Carew.
Farewell the reign of cruelty!
Wyatt.
Getting Experience.
Williams.
I Love, Loved, and So Doth
She. Wyatt.
Limerick: "The life boat that's
kept at Torquay."
Anonymous.
The Lover Abused
Renounceth Love.
Turberville.
The Rainy Season.
Meredith.
The Silent Lover. Ralegh.
Sir Walter Ralegh to the
Queen. Ralegh.
The Song-Throe. Rossetti.
Sweet Violets. *Anonymous.*
Upon a Diamond Cut in
Forme of a Heart... Ayton
[(or Aytoun)] Sir Robert.
Upon a Mole in Celia's
Bosom. Carew.

Smash (ed)
After Reading Twenty Years
of Grantland Rice. Skene.
A Backwards Journey. Page.
A Brick Not Used in
Building. Replansky.
The Crucifix. Read.
Delirium in Vera Cruz.
Lowry.
How We Drove the Trotter.
Goodge.
Limerick: "There was an old
man with a gong." Lear.
The Old O. O. Blues.
Young.
Thoughts. Ignatow.

Smell (ed) (ing) (s)
The Adventures of Simon Swaugum. Freneau.
After the Party. Cornford.
Although I Remember the Sound. Huff.
At the Zoo. Thackeray.
Balgu Song. *Anonymous.*
The Beach. Graves.
De Black Girl. *Anonymous.*
Blood River Day. Brutus.
Burning Shit at An Khe. Weigl.
Butchery. McPherson.
Camel. Merwin.
The Canticle of the Rose. Sitwell.
Carmina. Catullus.
The Cinnamon Peeler. Ondaatje.
The City. Ignatow.
Clerihews. Bentley.
A Day in the Life... Pixner.
The Elwha River. Snyder.
Explaining about the Dachshund. Stone.
Fall. Hass.
Farewell, Life. Hood.
The Fields. Merwin.
Fod. *Anonymous.*
Friday Night after Bathing. Levy.
The Goat. Young.
Haitian Suite. Orr.
His Fare-well to Sack. Herrick.
I Can Tell by the Way You Smell. Davis.
In the Garden. Crosby.
Jack. Goldberg.
Julius Caesar. Shakespeare.
The Kingly Lyon, and the Strong Arm'd Beare. Wood.
Manhood End. Thwaite.
Minor Elegy. Lisboa.
The Moose. Bishop.
Mothy Monologue. Gustafson.
Mud. Boyden.
Neither Here Nor There. Rodgers.
Night Flight. Daigon.
Old Men and Old Women Going Home on the Street Car. Moore.
Old Pudding-Pie Woman. *Anonymous.*
On Apples. Ross.
Opening the Season. Lewandowski.
Poems about Playmates. Davis.
Population Drifts. Sandburg.
Quicksands (parody). Zaranka.
Radcliff, Kentucky. Nickens.
Ravenna. MacNeice.
Roan Stallion. Jeffers.
The Shirt. Morley.
The Skipper-Hermit. Rich.
The Smell of Death Is So Powerful. Marguerite de Navarre.
Smells. Morley.
Song To Celia. Jonson.
Sonnets, XCIV: "They that have power to hurt, and will do none." Shakespeare.
Spring Poem. Ramke.
Steam in Sacrifice. Herrick.

Summer in a Small Town. Gregg.
A Table Richly Spread. Milton.
The Taste of Space. Smith.
The Three Little Kittens. *Anonymous.*
Three Little Kittens. Cook.
To My Cousin, (C.R.) Marrying My Lady (A.). Carew.
To Noel Coward. Coward.
Unharvested. Frost.
The World Is Full of Wonderful Smells. Gay.
Smile (d) (s)
The Affectionate Shepherd (excerpt). Barnfield.
After Bombardment. Pudney.
After the Dentist. Swenson.
Against an Old Lecher. Harington.
The Allegorical Figure of Brooklyn. Towle.
Amasis. Binyon.
The Angel in the House. Patmore.
Apocrypha. Deutsch.
April Love. Dowson.
Art. Gautier.
As Well as They Can. Hope.
As You Leave Me. Knight.
At Midsummer. Dubie.
Ave Atque Vale. Watson.
Away. Stryk.
Before Action. Gellert.
Bibliotheca Bodleiana. Grigson.
Bring a Torch, Jeanette, Isabella. Saboly.
The Butcher. Williams.
Butterflies. Noyes.
Caelica, LXXVI. Greville.
The Canary. Turner.
Carmarthen Bar. Brinnin.
Cesar Franck. Auslander.
Chain Gang Blues. *Anonymous.*
Chamber Music. Ditsky.
A Classical Quatrain. Goodman.
Clerihew: "Instead of blushing cherry hue." Laing.
Collin My Deere and Most Entire Beloved. Smith.
Consecration. Hoppe.
The Corner of the Field. Cornford.
Courage. Frazee-Bower.
Creation. Bierce.
Creation Myths. Raffel.
The day began with dismal doubt. *Anonymous.*
The Day's March. Nichols.
The Dead Child. Barlow.
The Death of Dermid. Ferguson.
The Death of the Novel. Young.
Declension. Sandy.
The Departure from Hydra. Koch.
The Description of a Good Boy. Dixon.
Developing a Wife. Taylor.
The Dew Each Trembling Leaf Inwreath'd. Balfour.
Dirge for the Year. Shelley.
Down to the Sacred Wave. Smith.

A Dream as Reported. Earle.
The Dream Feast. Endrezze-Probst.
Duck in Central Park. Savage.
The Dying Reservist. Baring.
Envoy. Thompson.
Epigram: "On parent knees, a naked new-born child." Jones.
Epipsychidion. Shelley.
Every Saturday He Stands. Drake.
The Fall. Barnes.
False Love. Scott.
Fantasy Under the Moon. Boundzekei-Dongala.
Far from Africa. Danner.
Farewell, Peace. *Anonymous.*
Fiction: A Message. Ewart.
The Flag. Flash.
The Foggy Dew. *Anonymous.*
For a Father. Cronin.
Forza D'Agro. Denby.
Four Pictures by Juan, Age 5. McKain.
From Here to There. Korn.
The Frowning Cliff. Asquith.
Getting On. Sandy.
Gioconda. MacGreevy.
The Gladness of Nature. Bryant.
Growing Old. Henderson.
Growing Smiles. *Anonymous.*
Hands. Untermeyer.
He Never Smiled Again. Hemans.
He Runs into an Old Acquaintance. Nowlan.
Heart's Compass. Rossetti.
Hello, Sister. Saylor.
Hereafter. Spofford.
Heritage. Bennett.
Hill-Side Tree. Bodenheim.
The House of Hospitalities. Hardy.
How Grand and How Bright. *Anonymous.*
The Hut. Van Stockum.
I Saw My Darling. Morgan.
Idyl. Mombert.
If You Are a Gentleman. *Anonymous.*
In Memoriam A.H.H., LXII. Tennyson.
In Memory of James T. Fields. Whittier.
In Memory of My Mother. Kavanagh.
Integer Vitae. Horace.
Is 5. Cummings.
Jacob. Lasker-Schüler.
Jeannie Marsh. Morris.
Junk. Zaranka.
Keep Smiling. *Anonymous.*
The King. Livingstone.
Lady Godiva. Shanks.
The Last Job I Held in Bridgeport. Donzella.
The Leaves. Loewinsohn.
The Lesser Lynx. Rieu.
Let No Charitable Hope. Wylie.
A Letter to Charles Townsend Copeland (excerpt). Hillyer.
Lincoln. Mitchell.

Lines Addressed to a Seagull. Griffin.
A Lyric: "How can I sing light-souled." Medici.
The Maiden of the Smile. Austin.
Maidenhood. Longfellow.
A Man by the Name of Bolus. Riley.
The Man Who Hid His Own Front Door. MacKinstry.
The Man Who Wanted to be a Seagull. Hervey.
Matins. Levertov.
Metaphors. Radnoti.
Modern Love, VII. Meredith.
The Mother in the Snow-Storm. Smith.
Mr. Hughes. Campbell.
My Many-Coated Man. Lee.
My Parents Kept Me from Children Who Were Rough. Spender.
My sweet old etcetera. Cummings.
My Uncle Paul of Pimlico. Peake.
Naphtha. O'Hara.
A New Poet. Canton.
New York Sonnet. Rodriguez.
Not Dead. Graves.
Not from This Anger. Thomas.
Notes for a Movie Script. Holman.
Objects. Wilbur.
Odes. Horace.
Of His Lady. *Anonymous.*
Old Photographs. Harsent.
On a Scooter. Greig.
On Being Asked for a Peace Poem. Nemerov.
On the House of a Friend. Logan.
On the Road to the Sea. Mew.
Once Upon a Time. Okara.
The Oranges. Abu Dharr.
The Peacock Room. Hayden.
Pensionnaires. Verlaine.
Phyllis Knotting. Sedley.
Portrait by Alice Neel. Kramer.
Portrait of a Lady. Eliot.
The Prime of Life. Learned.
The Quest. Cortissoz.
The Rape of the Lock. Pope.
The Rapist's Villanelle. Disch.
Refuge. McCartney.
Remember. Rossetti.
Remembrance. Boner.
Rest in Peace. Funk.
Rivalry. Nowlan.
A Runic Ode. Warton, Sr..
The Serpent. Langland.
The Sexual Life of the Camel. *Anonymous.*
Shall Then Another. Mackenzie.
She Was a Pretty Horse. Harjo.
The Sickness. Seidel.
Sleep! Sleep! Beauty Bright. Blake.
The Small Hotel. Longley.
A Smile. *Anonymous.*

Some Small Shells from the Windward Islands. Swenson.
Song: "Hears not my Phillis how the birds." Sedley.
Song: "My spirit like a shepherd boy." Sackville-West.
Song of Three Smiles. Merwin.
Sonnet: "Evening, as slow thy placid shades descend." Bowles.
Sonnet to a Tyrant. Ellis.
Spring on the Ochils. Robertson.
Standardization. Hope.
Stanzas–April, 1814. Shelley.
Steamboats, Viaducts, and Railways. Wordsworth.
Still Century. Paulin.
String Quartet. Deutsch.
The Sunlit Vale. Blunden.
Temple of the Muses. Bentley.
The Temptation of Saint Anthony. Symons.
Thompson Street. McCoy.
The Thousand and One Nights: Pearls Seen through Amber. Anonymous.
Tim, the Fairy. Livesay.
Time of Waiting in Amsterdam. Jonker.
Time to Go. "Coolidge.
'Tis Late and Cold. Fletcher.
To a Friend in Love during the Riots. Parsons.
To a Print of Queen Victoria. Baxter.
To an Old Tune. Percy.
To His Lovely Mistresses. Herrick.
To the King's Most Excellent Majesty. Wheatley.
To the Lady May. Townsend.
To Thine Eternal Arms, O God. Higginson.
The Town of Don't-You-Worry. Bartlett.
The Transandean Railway. Kretz.
Trus' an' Smile. Williams.
The Twa Books. Ramsay.
The Two Lovers. Hovey.
The Underground Stream. Dickey.
Upon Her Soothing Breast. Bronte.
Upon the Priory Grove, His Usual Retirement. Vaughan.
The Victors. Levertov.
A Vision of the Sea. Shelley.
Walking in the Rain. Saxon.
Was It You? Long.
Washing Windows. Spacks.
Washington Heights, 1959. Blumenthal.
Watermelons. Simic.
Wayfarers. Burnet.
What a Proud Dreamhorse. Cummings.
Whereat Erewhile I Wept, I Laugh. Greene.
White Roses. Fabbri.
The White Witch. Johnson.
Why? Boyd.
Women Don't Travel in Clubcars. Jonas.

Smiling
As a Great Prince. Honig.
August Smiles. Coatsworth.
Before the Mountain. Libbey.
Brass Tacks. Levertov.
A Child of To-Day. Buckham.
Content. Crane.
The Dark Cavalier. Widdemer.
In a Season of Unemployment. Avison.
Jenny's Ribbons. Barnes.
Lips and Eyes. Marino.
The Making of Man. Chadwick.
La Melinite: Moulin-Rouge. Symons.
Memphis Minnie-Jitis Blues. Minnie.
Neighbors. Evans.
On Mother's Day. Fisher.
Poem. Lomax.
The Ripe and Bearded Barley. Anonymous.
Self-Consciousness Makes All Changes Happy. Richardson.
A Short History of British India. Hill.
A Song the Grass Sings. Blanden.
To Hafiz. Aldrich.
To Sally. Adams.
La Tricoteuse. Thornbury.
Try Smiling. Anonymous.
The Tryst. Morley.
Variation on a Theme by Francis Kilvert. Humphries.

Smirk
For the Book of Love. Laforgue.
Slow Drivers. Barrax.

Smite (smote)
Abraham Lincoln. Stedman.
The Bartholdi Statue. Whittier.
Last Came, and Last Did Go. Milton.
Leaving Troy. Irwin.
Othello. Shakespeare.
When Banners Are Waving. Anonymous.

Smith
Altars and Sacrifice. Wright.
Antichrist; or, The Reunion of Christendom: An Ode. Chesterton.
Chicago Boy Baby. Sandburg.

Smock
Blow the Fire, Blacksmith. Anonymous.
Distances (excerpt). Okigbo.

Smoke
3rd Dance–Making a Structure with a Roof or under a Roof... MacLow.
Academic Affair. Stockwell.
And All the While the Sky Is Falling... Dunetz.
Ashes. Levine.
The Chase (excerpt). Somervile.
Chinoiseries. Lowell.
City. Bruchac.
The Depot. Turco.
Dunedin Revisited. Glover.
Encounter in Jerusalem. Lipshitz.

Field Work. Cockrell.
Fighting Her. Phillips.
The First Hunt. Anderson.
The Fishes' Lamentation. Anonymous.
He Liked the Dead. Lowry.
Hello, Hello. Matthews.
The Inspection. Watt.
Irradiations. Fletcher.
Lady in a Distant Face. Welch.
Last Hill in a Vista. Bogan.
Like Smoke. Mririda n'Ait Attik.
Limerick. Anonymous.
Limerick: "There was a young lady of Oakham." Anonymous.
Lord, Grant Us Calm. Rossetti.
Lost Silvertip. Reed.
"Luckies". Gibbons.
Man Has No Smokestack. Anonymous.
Ned's Delicate Way. Lawson.
Neighbors. Francis.
November Sunday Morning. Feinman.
The Old. Mosby.
On the Hazards of Smoking. Goldberg.
Paradise Lost. Milton.
The People, Yes. Sandburg.
Prelude. Benson.
Restless as a Wolf. Halpern.
Sailing in Crosslight. Skeen.
Shelby County, Ohio. November 1974. Murray.
Shunting. Dowling.
Sin and Death. Milton.
Such Love Is Like a Smoky Fire. Chapman.
The Third Light. Longley.
The Trumpet-Vine Arbour. Lowell.
Waders and Swimmers. Plumly.
You Owe Them Everything. Allman.

Smoking
An Exchange of Hats. Moss.
Old Man Told Me. Henson.
Precious Mettle. Warsh.
The President Slumming. Tate.
To the Driving Cloud. Longfellow.
A Way of Life. Nemerov.

Smooth
At Night. Cornford.
Birch. Simpson.
Boy at a Certain Age. Francis.
Fragmenti. Pound.
Friday Night after Bathing. Levy.
Ho! Ye Sun, Moon, Stars. Anonymous.
Little Father Poem. Bell.
My Mistress. Warner.
Night. Camerino.
A Song: "Hark! 'tis Freedom that calls, come, patriots, awake!" Anonymous.
To Music. Herrick.
The World's a Well Strung Fidle, Mans Tongue the Quill. Ward.

Smothered
Britannia's Pastorals. Browne.

The Nigga Section. Smith.

Snail (s)
After the Gentle Poet Kobayashi Issa. Hass.
Death on a Live Wire. Baldwin.
Driving Home after a Funeral. Orr.
The Four Friends. Milne.
In Praise of Blur. Chandra.
In the Madison Zoo. Hill.
Otoe County in Nebraska. Kloefkorn.
Sonnets for a Dying Man. Singer.
The Spider's Nest. MacBeth.
Upon a Snail. Bunyan.
White Serpent. Sachs.

Snake (s)
The Book of Hours of Sister Clotilde. Lowell.
Bucket of Sea-Serpents. Ant.
The Carver. Aiken.
Castoff Skin. Whitman.
The Catch. Ghiselin.
Drunken Heracles. Gould.
Genesis. Higgins.
Gioconda. MacGreevy.
Grotesque. Graves.
A History of the Pets. Huddle.
In Hospital: Poona (I). Lewis.
In Praise of a Gentlewoman. Gascoigne.
Jason and Medea. Lewis.
Le Jeune Homme Caressant Sa Chimere. Symonds.
June. Reaney.
A Lake. Beddoes.
Like Gulliver. Cassian.
Madonna: 1936. Bonn.
Merlin and the Snake's Egg. Norris.
My Angeline. Smith.
My Home. Anonymous.
Oil and Blood. Kizer.
Priapus and the Pool. Aiken.
The Silent Slain. MacLeish.
Snakeskin and Stone. Douglas.
A Temple. Patchen.
That Black Snake Mama. Jefferson.
Thermometer Wine. Morgan.
Two Lovers Sitting on a Tomb. Hill.
When I Vexed You. Browning.
Who Be Kind To. Ginsberg.
Working Song. Anonymous.

Snap (s)
Desires. Bensley.
Fishing the Big Hole. Holbrook.
Heaven and Hell. Anonymous.
I'll Build My House. Hall.
Load. Hewitt.

Snapshots
A Family Man. Kumin.

Snare (s)
At the End of the Affair. Kumin.
Boy Breaking Glass. Brooks.
Come, All Ye Youths. Otway.
Happy Is the Country Life. Anonymous.
Katharine. Heine.

Snare
The Man in the Dress Suit.
Wolfe.
O Girl, You Torment Me...
Anonymous.
On a Fowler. Isidorus.
On Waking. Campbell.
A Rondel of Love. Scott.
The Spring Equinox. Ridler.
Van Dieman's Land (A vers.).
Anonymous.

Snark
The Hunting of the Snark.
"Carroll.

Snatch (ed) (s)
The Desperado. *Anonymous.*
The Farm-Woman's Winter.
Hardy.
Fraulein Reads Instructive
Rhymes. Kumin.
He Made the Night. Mifflin.
Limerick: "There was a young
fellow named Hatch."
Anonymous.
On Alexis. Plato.
Song: "Stay Phoebus, stay."
Waller.

Sneaker (s)
Foots It (parody). Berry.
Hope. Anderson.
SM. Moss.

Sneer (ed) (s)
The Jew. Rosenberg.
The Kiss-Fest. Edman.
A Solemn Thing–It Was–I
Said. Dickinson.

Sneeze (d) (s)
Big Friend of the Stones.
Orlen.
The big trimmer. Tanaka.
The Humorist. Preston.
The Lupracaun, or Fairy
Shoemaker. Allingham.
Saragossa. Leigh.
Visitors. Behn.

Sniff
Cocaine Bill and Morphine
Sue. *Anonymous.*
Tune: Crimson Lips Adorned.
Li Ching-chao.

Snore (r) (s)
An Attorney General.
Bierce.
Away with Bloodshed.
Housman.
Eclipse. Fagg.
The Jolly Woodchuck.
Grider.
Limerick: "There was a young
man from Elnora."
Anonymous.
Necessity. Graham.
The Owl. De la Mare.
Paradise. Di Roma.
To the Eternal Feminine.
Corbiere.

Snout
Ego. Siegel.
In Praise of Blur. Chandra.
Learning the Spells: A
Diptych. Probst.
Reversion. Higgs.
Sausage. Axionicus.

Snow (s) (y)
Abundance. Borson.
Advice from Euterpe.
Revard.
After They Have Tired of the
Brilliance of Cities.
Spender.
Among the Heather.
Allingham.
The Amorist. *Anonymous.*

Apple Blossoms. Larcom.
The April Snow. Very.
Are You There, Mrs. Goose?
Hicks.
Around the Rough and
Rugged Rocks the Ragged
Rascal Rudely Ran.
Ashbery.
As birds are fitted to the
boughs. Simpson.
As on Serena's Panting Breast.
Anonymous.
At Times I Feel Like a
Quince Tree. Quinn.
Aubade. Lechlitner.
Autumn. Levine.
The Ballad of Dead Ladies.
Villon.
Battles of the Centaurs:
Centaurs and Lapithae.
Sitwell.
Before the Actual Cold.
Young Bear.
Bend as the Bow Bends.
Aiken.
The Call. Mew.
Camel. Stallworthy.
Casement's Funeral.
Murphy.
Cauld Cornwood.
Anonymous.
The Cherokee Dean. Russell.
The Child. Tabb.
Child of My Winter.
Snodgrass.
Circumstance. Stroblas.
Claus Von Stauffenberg.
Gunn.
The Composition of Distances.
Pien Chih-lin.
Cressida. Baxter.
The Cubical Domes.
Gascoyne.
Cuckoo, Cherry Tree.
Anonymous.
Daffodils. Harding.
The Dance of Gray Raccoon.
Guiterman.
The Dead Cities Speak to the
Living Cities. Fleg.
Dead in Bloody Snow. Le
Sueur.
A Dead Leaf. Moss.
Deadfall. Keller.
The Death of Crazy Horse.
Neihardt.
Death of Rimbaud. Fisher.
The Decision. Roethke.
The Destruction of
Sennacherib. Byron.
Different Winter. Nicholl.
Dogwood Blossoms.
McClellan.
Dreams. Hughes.
Duchess. Lyon.
Dunce Song 6. Van Doren.
The Dwarf. Locklin.
Early Winter. Kees.
Elizabeth at the Piano.
Gregory.
Epilogue. Falkner.
Epithalamium. Fairburn.
Fall Letter. Kelly.
The Fall of the Plum
Blossoms. Banko.
Farm Boy after Summer.
Francis.
Father Damien. Tabb.
Father, the Year Is Fallen.
Lorde.
February: The Boy Breughel.
Dubie.

First Death in Nova Scotia.
Bishop.
First Sight. Larkin.
First Snow. Eastwick.
The First Snow-Fall. Lowell.
First Snow in Alsace.
Wilbur.
The First Snow of the Year.
Van Doren.
Footwear. Justus.
For Snow. Farjeon.
For Years. Mills, Jr.
Foxgloves and Snow. Angus.
From a Childhood. Rilke.
From the Rain Down.
Espaillat.
Frost. Davies.
The Frozen Heart. Herrick.
The Funeral. Dubie.
Geneva. Reid.
Going to Remake This World.
Welch.
A Good Resolution.
Campbell.
A Green Place. Smith.
Green World Two.
Waddington.
Haiku: "A bare pecan tree."
Knight.
The Harlot. Brown.
The Heavenly Foreigner.
Devlin.
Hedges Freaked with Snow.
Graves.
Herons. *Anonymous.*
The Holly. King.
Hospital Evening. Harwood.
How can you look at the
Neva. Akhmatova.
The Howling of Wolves.
Hughes.
I Awoke with the Room Cold.
Piercy.
I Never Shall Love the Snow
Again. Bridges.
I Was Sitting in McSorley's.
Cummings.
Ice River. Baker.
The Idle Flowers. Bridges.
In March. Martin.
In Memory of Kathleen.
Patchen.
In the Hospital. Jensen.
In the Streets of Catania.
Casement.
In Winter. Blackburn.
The Innocent Country-Maid's
Delight. *Anonymous.*
The Insomniac Sleeps Well for
Once and. Carruth.
Instant Coffee. Yau.
It's Raining, It's Pouring.
Anonymous.
January Is Here. Fawcett.
Jealousy. DeVries.
The Jew at Christmas Eve.
Shapiro.
Job Hunting. Hennen.
Katherine's Dream. Lowell.
Landscape. Purdy.
Last Rite. Hicks.
Last Rites. Rossetti.
A Leaf-Treader. Frost.
Leaps over the Aisle of
Syllogism (parody). Berry.
Lester Tells of Wanda and the
Big Snow. Zimmer.
Loveliest of Trees.
Housman.
Lullaby. Vigneault.
Lullaby. Waddington.
The May Tree. Barnes.

Meditations in Time of Civil
War. Yeats.
Milk at the Bottom of the
Sea. Williams.
A Mill. Allingham.
Miss Ada. Fahy.
Molly Bond. *Anonymous.*
Moss. Willard.
The Mountains. De la Mare.
The Mudtower. Stevenson.
Murrough Defeats the Danes,
994. *Anonymous.*
My Feet. Jenkins.
My Latest Sun Is Sinking
Fast. Haskell.
Nam Semen Est Verbum Dei.
Guiney.
Nature: The Artist.
Knowles.
New Feet Within My Garden
Go–. Dickinson.
New Snow. Rowles.
News. Schmitz.
Night Thoughts over a Sick
Child. Levine.
November. Cary.
November through a Giant
Copper Beech. Honig.
Now Is the High-Tide of the
Year. Lowell.
O Bird, So Lovely. Golding.
O Wind, Why Do You Never
Rest. Rossetti.
Old Countryside. Bogan.
The Old Flame. Lowell.
On Burning a Dull Poem.
Swift.
On the Death of an Emperor
Penguin in Regent's Park,
London. Wright.
One A.M. Levertov.
One Snowy Night in
December. Morris.
Our Lady of the Snows.
Kipling.
Over! The Sweet Summer
Closes. Tennyson.
Painting of a White Gate and
Sky. Erdrich.
A Palinode. Bolton.
Pantoum. Ashbery.
Partly to My Cat. Bass.
Passing into Storm. Lane.
Penal Rock: Altamuskin.
Montague.
Persephone. Longley.
The Phenomenon. Shapiro.
The Plum-Blossom. Akahito
(Yamabe no Akahito).
Poems for the New. Fraser.
Prague Spring. Harrison.
The Procession. Widdemer.
Propertian. MacKay.
The Rehearsal. Gregory.
Remembering Snow. Currey.
The Retrieval System.
Kumin.
Roadside near Moscow.
Ford.
The Runner. Gildner.
Rural Lines after Breughel.
Krapf.
Safe in Their Alabaster
Chambers. Dickinson.
Sailor's Carol. Causley.
The Same Gesture.
Montague.
Says Something, Too (parody).
Taylor.
The Seasons. Humphries.
Seasons. Rossetti.

Self-Pity Is a Kind of Lying, Too. Schuylr.
Sestina d'Inverno. Hecht.
The Shadow. De la Mare.
Shh! The Professor Is Sleeping. Morris.
Silence. Cummings.
Silent Poem. Francis.
The Six-Quart Basket. Souster.
Six Winter Privacy Poems. Bly.
Sleep. Simic.
Snail. Shinkichi.
Snow. Crapsey.
The Snow. Dyment.
Snow. Thomas.
The Snow-Ball. Stanley.
Snow Crystals on Meall Glas. Wilson.
The Snow Fall. MacLeish.
The Snow-Filled Nest. Cooke.
Snow in the City. Field.
The Snow Storm. Millay.
The Snowfish. Field.
The Snowing of the Pines. Higginson.
So Handy, Me Boys, So Handy. *Anonymous.*
Soho. Brodsky.
Song: "Let it be forgotten, as a flower is forgotten." Teasdale.
Song: "Let's sing a song together once." Simpson.
Song: "We came to Tamichi in 1880." Hammond.
"Doc"
The Sonnet of the Mountain. Saint-Gelais.
Spring Goeth All in White. Bridges.
Spring Pools. Frost.
Still. Zeidner.
Story from Russian Author. Redgrove.
Sudden Frost. Wagoner.
A Suit of Nettles. Reaney.
The Swans. Sitwell.
Tales of a Wayside Inn. Longfellow.
Tasmania. Smith.
Tattoo. Stevens.
Than(By Yon Sunset's Wintry Glow. Cummings.
Things to Do around a Lookout. Snyder.
This Poem Is for Nadine. Janeczko.
To a Sparrow. Ledwidge.
To F. C. Collins.
To Vera Thompson. Haines.
Tracks. Shurmantine.
A Traveller. *Anonymous.*
Travels With the Band-Aid Army. Henson.
Twelfth Night. Scupham.
Two Lives and Others. Scott.
Two Mornings and Two Evenings. Bishop.
Upon a Delaying Lady. Herrick.
Valentine's Day. Fisher.
Variations on a Theme by Sidney Keyes. Wilkins.
Velvet Shoes. Wylie.
The Victory of the Battle of Wounded Knee. Parson.
The Walls Do Not Fall. Doolittle.

Watering the Horse. Bly.
Watkwenies. Scott.
Wednesday at North Hatley. Gustafson.
A White City. Schuyler.
The White Hare. Lyon.
White Season. Frost.
The Whummil Bore. *Anonymous.*
The Wife of Winter's Tale. Browne.
Wild Strawberry. Kenny.
Willows in the Snow. Tsuru.
The Wind Carol. Turco.
Winter. Williams.
Winter and Summer. Spender.
Winter Circus. Fisher.
Winter in the Sierras. Austin.
Winter Noon. Teasdale.
A Winter's Tale. Thomas.
Winter Scene. Young.
Winter Streams. Carman.
Wintered Sunflowers. Snyder.
With a Spray of Apple Blossoms. Learned.
Words for Music Perhaps. Yeats.
Years Later. Stone.
Young Molly Ban. *Anonymous.*
Zaydee. Levine.
Snowdrop (s)
After Christmas. Richards.
Death. Clare.
Epigram: "I ran upon life unknowing, without or science or art." Tennyson.
Snowflake (s)
At Nine O'Clock in the Spring. Bishop.
Blue Springs, Georgia. Young.
The Case. Hays.
The Doll. Orr.
First Snow. Kooser.
In a Valley of This Restless Mind. Milne.
Long Lines. Goodman.
Love Letters, Unmailed. Merriam.
O Bird, So Lovely. Golding.
Quilt Song. Vinz.
When What Hugs Stopping Earth Than Silent Is. Cummings.
Winter Love. Jennings.
Snowman
I'm not here never was. Buzea.
I remember... Jackson.
My Birthday's in Winter. Gay.
Winter News. Haines.
Snuff
Cherry Blossoms. "Lewis.
The County Ball (excerpt). Praed.
Frau Bauman, Frau Schmidt, and Frau Schwartze. Roethke.
Morning Star. Galvin.
On the Snuff of a Candle. Ralegh.
Retaliation. Goldsmith.
West Texas. *Anonymous.*
Snug
Covered Bridge. Coffin.
Settlers. Paulin.

Soak (ed) (ing)
February. Savage.
If the Oak Is out before the Ash. *Anonymous.*
Jersey Bait Shack. Balakian.
My Christmas: Mum's Christmas. Forsyth.
Soap
Commanding Elephants. Levine.
How Come? Ignatow.
Keep It Clean. Jordan.
Lion & Honeycomb. Nemerov.
Soar (ed) (ing) (s)
The Beauty of the Friend It Was That Taught Me. Makhfi.
The Bird with a Broken Wing. Butterworth.
Circle of Struggle. Root.
A Documentary on Airplane Glue. Henderson.
I Have Not So Much Emulated the Birds that Musically Sing. Whitman.
Life's Evil. Montale.
Little Satellite. Krows.
The Making of Birds. Tynan.
Nike. Wazyk.
On the Road There Stands a Tree. Manger.
Psyche. Very.
Royal Palm. Crane.
Soaring. Clothier.
To a Very Wise Man. Sassoon.
To Althea from Prison. Lovelace.
The Wasp. Davidson.
Whales. Bates.
Wild Swan. *Anonymous.*
Sob (bed) (bing) (s)
Again. Stallworthy.
Anzac Cove. Gellert.
Arraignment. Cone.
Breaths. Diop.
The Captain. White.
The Cry of the Children. Browning.
Eighteen Verses Sung to a Tatar Reed Whistle. Ts'ai Yen.
Eliza. Darwin.
For Thomas Hardy. Cooper.
The Harvest of the Sea. McCrae.
In the Silent Night. Peretz.
Jealous Adam. Manger.
The Lady of the Lake. *Anonymous.*
The Rain Comes Sobbing to the Door. Kendall.
Song of Songs. Owen.
The Songs of Bilitis. Louys.
To a Madonna. Baudelaire.
Sober
Drink To-day. Fletcher.
Drinking Alone in the Moonlight. Li T'ai-po.
Dromedary. Dodat.
Epitaph. Jeffrey.
Epitaph on a Party Girl. Usborne.
The Horatians. Auden.
The Intoxicated Rat. *Anonymous.*
Miss Millay Says Something Too. Hoffenstein.
No Great Matter. Lawson.

On Rachmaninoff's Birthday. O'Hara.
On the Translation of Anacreon. Walpole.
A Prayer for the Self. Berryman.
Social
An Essay on Man. Pope.
Fashion. Cambridge.
Her Garden. Downie.
In the Heat of the Morning. Szumigalski.
The Kiwi Bird in the Kiwi Tree. Bernstein.
Marmion. Scott.
The Seasons. Thomson.
Socialists
Yiddish Speaking Socialists of the Lower East Side. Sanders.
Society
Abraham:. Schwartz.
Inishkeel Parish Church. Paulin.
The Mute Phenomena. Mahon.
The Seasons. Thomson.
Song: "I've taught thee Love's sweet lesson o'er." Darley.
Sociologist
At the Klamath Berry Festival. Stafford.
Sock (s)
A Border Forecast. Landles.
Inventory. Parker.
Strawberry Blond. Berkson.
The Three Foxes. Milne.
Socrates
Io Victis. Story.
Sod
The Angel in the House. Patmore.
The Battle of Antietam Creek. *Anonymous.*
The Brave at Home. Read.
A Common Inference. Gilman.
Couplets for WCW. Christina.
Dirge. Percy.
Garden Party. Mills.
The Green Tree. Reiss.
Lorena. *Anonymous.*
The Servants. Wightman.
The Sherman Cyclone. *Anonymous.*
Soda
Don Juan. Byron.
Feast on Wine or Fast on Water. Chesterton.
Roll on the Ground. *Anonymous.*
You Too? Me Too–Why Not? Soda Pop. Hollander.
Sodium
Sir Humphry Davy. Bentley.
Sodom
The Psalter of Avram Haktani. Klein.
Sodom. Grade.
Upon the Heavenly Scarp. Klein.
Sofa
Analysands. Randall.
Soft (en) (er) (ly) (ness)
At Quebec. Blewett.
The Blackbird. *Anonymous.*
Broken Treaties: Teeth. Contoski.
Brooklyn Bridge at Dawn. Le Gallienne.
The Cloud-Mobile. Swenson.

A Dark Day. Rossetti.
Epigram: "A woman working hard and wisely." Kassia.
Epigram: "No charm can stay, no medicine can assuage." Landor.
Grape Daiquiri. Koyama.
The Hardness Scale. Peseroff.
He's Coming. Van Doren.
He Wishes for the Cloths of Heaven. Yeats.
Her Voice Could Not Be Softer. Clarke.
The Legend of the Organ-Builder. Dorr.
Limerick: "There was an Old Man who said: "How." Lear.
Little Father Poem. Bell.
Love Is Enough. Morris.
Minuet in a Minor Key. Janowitz.
My Love, Oh, She Is My Love. Anonymous.
My Mistress. Warner.
Piano after War. Brooks.
Prince Lucifer: Mother-Song. Austin.
Prothalamion. Spenser.
Quatrains. Bennett.
Ravens. Hughes.
Robin's Come! Caldwell.
The Roosters Will Crow. Meireles.
A Snowfall. Eberhart.
Songs of Cheng. Confucius.
A Sprig of Rosemary. Lowell.
The Storm-Wind. Barnes.
Suppositions. Faulkner.
Tales of the Islands, III. Walcott.
To Mrs. Reynold's Cat. Keats.
Too Solemn for Day, Too Sweet for Night. Walker.
Two Fawns That Didn't See the Light This Spring. Snyder.
Ute Pass. Whitney.
Where He Hangs His Hat. Lee.
Within the Veil. Sangster.
Young Strephon and Phillis. Anonymous.

Soho
The First Epistle of the Second Book of Horace. Pope.

Soil (ed) (ing)
The Advice. Ralegh.
The Art of Making Puddings. King.
The Atlantides. Thoreau.
Before/and After... Amini.
Definition. Rolfe.
Drunken Americans. Ashbery.
Four Quartets. Eliot.
From Harvest to January. Tennyson.
How to Fertilize Soil. Grainger.
How to Get On in Society. Betjeman.
In City Streets. Smith.
June. Feinstein.
Lincoln. Lowell.
Marriage. Gordett.
Mully of Mountown (excerpt). King.

On Some Humming-Birds in a Glass Case. Turner.
On Zion and on Lebanon. Onderdonk.
Return to the Valley. Read.
The Shield of War. Sackville.
Sumter–A Ballad of 1861. Anonymous.
Tanka I–VIII. Alexander.
To a Detainee. Zimunya.
To the Mothers. Toller.
Yet Dish. Stein.

Solace
All of Us Always Turning away for Solace. Schwartz.
At a Hasty Wedding. Hardy.
Birthday. Lawrence.
Davideis. Cowley.
In the Woods. Scott.
Mirth. Herrick.
Morning. Savage.
Odes. Santayana.
Pastoral Ballad: Absence. Shenstone.
A Pastoral Ballad in Four Parts. Shenstone.
The Pewee. Trowbridge.
Song: "Poppies paramour the girls." Long.
Sonnet: "Nuns fret not at their convent's narrow room." Wordsworth.
Sorrow. Phillips.
The Unfailing Friend. Scriven.
The Unpetalled Rose. Therese.
What a Friend We Have in Jesus. Scriven.
When Christ Was Born of Mary Free. Anonymous.

Solar
Alphonso of Castile. Emerson.
Giffen's Debt. Kipling.
Shadow. Delius.
Song of the Evil Spirit of the Woods. Moore.

Soldier (s)
Ah, Poverties, Wincings, and Sulky Retreats. Whitman.
The Alphabet. Anonymous.
The American Soldier. Freneau.
Andre's Request to Washington. Willis.
Buttermilk Hill. Anonymous.
Carrickfergus. MacNeice.
Charade. Praed.
Dead Soldier. Guillen.
The Deserter. Taylor.
Dirge for Fajuyi. Arowa. Omobayode
A Domestic Cat. Denby.
Don Juan. Byron.
Elegy for a Dead Soldier. Shapiro.
Esthetique du Mal. Stevens.
Fare You Well, My Darling. Anonymous.
Faust. Goethe.
From Trollope's Journal. Bishop.
Grace. Wilbur.
The Green Estaminet. Herbert.
Heav'n Boun' Soldier. Anonymous.
Hohenlinden. Campbell.

Homage to Jack Yeats. MacGreevy.
Homecoming. Shapiro.
Hush'd Be the Camps To-Day. Whitman.
I Give My Soldier Boy a Blade. Anonymous.
I Heard a Soldier. Trench.
I'm a Soldier in the Army of the Lord. Anonymous.
If I Were King. Milne.
In Memory of Basil, Marquess of Dufferin and Ava. Betjeman.
It's Wonderful. Isenhour.
The Jolly Soldier. Anonymous.
Kent State, May 4, 1970. Goodman.
Lady Flower. Anonymous.
The Lame Soldier. Anonymous.
Moll-in-the-Wad and I Fell Out. Anonymous.
Moon Festival. Tu Fu.
The Moon of Brooklyn. Crane.
The Mutilated Soldier. Fisher.
Of Common Devotion. Quarles.
Old Soldier. Colum.
Old Soldiers Never Die. Anonymous.
The Oldest Soldier. Graves.
The Orphan Boy. Anonymous.
The Parliament Soldiers. Anonymous.
Pilgrims. Brodsky.
Place Pigalle. Wilbur.
The Royal Light Dragoon. Anonymous.
Soldier an' Sailor Too. Kipling.
Soldier Boy for Me. Anonymous.
The Soldier Is Home. Neilson.
The Soldier's Grave. Muir.
Some San Francisco Poems. Oppen.
Song My. Griffin.
Stragglers. Aretino.
Such Is the Death the Soldier Dies. Wilson.
A Sweetheart in the Army (B vers.). Anonymous.
Terror. O'Brien.
Thanks in Old Age. Whitman.
Training on the Shore. Vinner.
Trench Blues. Anonymous.
Two Veterans. Whitman.
Vergissmeinicht. Douglas.
We Am Clim'in' Jacob's Ladder. Anonymous.
A Yankee View. Anonymous.

Solemn
The Battle in the Clouds. Howells.
The Common Woman. Grahn.
Evening. Sangster.
Father and Sons. Shapiro.
In a Hard Intellectual Light. Eberhart.
One Word More. Browning.
A Poe–'em of Passion. Lummis.
Solitude. Grainger.

When Adam Was Created. Anonymous.

Soliloquies
Desert Warfare. Longley.
Hamlet (parody). Sharpless.

Solitude (s)
After Long Busyness. Bly.
The Auroras of Autumn. Stevens.
Autumn, Dark Wanderer. Daryush.
The Autumn Wind. Clare.
Birds in the Flax. Snaith.
Compensation. Jeffers.
The Correspondence School Instructor Says Goodbye... Kinnell.
Delusions VI. Madge.
Echoes. Lazarus.
Escape. Johnson.
Evening. Vriesland.
The Founts of Song. "Macleod.
Give Me the Splendid Silent Sun. Whitman
The Great Fountains. Hebert.
In High Places. Monroe.
Lauds. Auden.
Lines Written at Bridgwater, 27 July 1797 (excerpt). Thelwall.
The Lychee. Wang I.
Milton. Mifflin.
Mont Blanc. Shelley.
Muse-Haunted. McCrae.
Napoleon. De La Mare.
Next Day. Jarrell.
Night in the House by the River. Tu Fu.
No One So Much As You. Thomas.
Now all that sound of laughter, sound of singing. Castro.
O Fairest of the Rural Maids. Bryant.
Ode: Solitude, at an Inn. Warton, Jr..
Of Solitude. Cowley.
The Offender. Levertov.
Older Now. Gingell.
On Leaving Prison. Leon.
Pain. Sodergran.
Paradise Lost. Milton.
Poets Observed. Rosenberger.
Psalm–People Power at the Die-In. Levertov.
The Quantocks. Wordsworth.
The Quarry Pool. Levertov.
Retirement. Cowper.
The Seven Sleepers. Read.
Solitude. Rilke.
Stanzas to Augusta. Byron.
Terenure. Salkeld.
There Is a Mystery in Human Hearts. Anonymous.
To a Deaf and Dumb Little Girl. Coleridge.
To One in Bedlam. Dowson.
To Walk on Hills. Graves.
Under the Edge of February. Cortez.
Woman Alone. Levertov.

Solomon
The Destruction of Jerusalem by the Babylonian Hordes. Rosenberg.
Go to the Ant. Sharpless.
God Provides. Bible, N.T..

Jack and Jill (parody).
  Loomis.
The Space Childs' Mother
  Goose. Winsor.
A Worm Fed on the Heart of
  Corinth. Rosenberg.
Solution (s)
Human Cylinders. Loy.
The Rock. Fabilli.
Where Are You Now
  Superman? Patten.
World Planners. Steece.
Solve (d)
Crime Club. Kees.
Milton. Ray.
A Riddle. Ozick.
Somber
For the Sun Declined.
  Lamdan.
Somebody (one)
Ballad for the Unknown
  Soldier. Taylor.
Being Somebody. Honig.
Christmas Eve. Berkson.
Dreaming with a Friend.
  Berg.
Drinking Song. Stephen.
For Elizabeth Bishop.
  McPherson.
For the Sake O' Somebody.
  Burns.
Hegel. Jones.
Hello, Somebody.
  Anonymous.
How Gray the Rain.
  Coatsworth.
I've Had Many an Aching
  Pain. Clare.
In Laughter. Hughes.
Love Somebody, Yes I Do.
  Anonymous.
Marking Time. Steele.
Marrow of My Bone. Evans.
She Sees Another Door
  Opening (parody).
  Houghton.
There Lived a King. Gilbert.
To a Lady Holding the Floor.
  Weston.
To the Man Who Watches
  Spiders. Fox.
The Two Coyotes. Marietta.
Wanderer. Powers.
West Fifty-Seventh Street.
  Vazakas.
A Withered Rose. Yehoash.
The World's Last Unnamed
  Poem. Redwing.
Somersault (s)
For Kai Snyder. Whalen.
His Mother-in-Law. Parke.
An Historic Moment.
  Harris.
Somewhere
Aphrodite Metropolis.
  Fearing.
Ask, and Ye Shall Receive.
  Flint.
Autograph Book/Prophecy.
  Halley.
Delay. Jennings.
First of All. Hanson.
First Snow. Allen.
The Fools' Adventure: The
  Seeker. Abercrombie.
Halfway Down. Milne.
Lives. Dawe.
Ponder, Darling, These Busted
  Statues. Cummings.
Pray Without Ceasing.
  Browning.
Sailor Man. Bailey.

Stars Climb Girders of Light.
  Meyers.
Where? Patchen.
Somnolent
First Winter Storm.
  Everson.
Son-of-a-gun
Rag Time Cowboy Joe.
  Muir.
The Ramble-eer.
  Anonymous.
World War I. *Anonymous.*
Son of God
A Hundred Thousand
  Welcomes. *Anonymous.*
The Master of Laborers.
  Day.
Watchman, Tell us of the
  Night. Bowring.
Wondrous Son of God.
  Goertz.
Son of Man
Young and Radiant, He Is
  Standing. Cross.
Son of Mary
What Child Is This? Dix.
Son (s)
Adoration of the Disk by
  King Akhn-Aten and
  Princess Nefer Neferiu..
  Book of the Dead.
Advice. Bierce.
Aftermath. McCulloch.
The Agony in the Garden.
  Hemans.
All Over the World.
  Johnson.
Annul Wars. Nahman of
  Bratzlav.
The Annunciation. Conway.
Answering Dance. Root.
Aunt Jane Allen. Johnson.
Austriad. Latino.
Avalon. Chivers.
The Betrayed Maiden.
  Anonymous.
Brave Paulding and the Spy.
  Anonymous.
The Bridge: Indiana. Crane.
The British Lyon Roused.
  Tilden.
Bucolic Eclogues: Waking,
  Child, While You Slept.
  Anderson.
Caelica, XXXII. Greville.
Calvary. Stopple.
Carolina. Timrod.
The Celebration. Dickey.
The Chamber Over the Gate.
  Longfellow.
Charm for Burns.
  Anonymous.
Child Maurice (B version).
  Anonymous.
The Children March.
  Riddell.
Christmas Day. Young.
Come Up from the Fields
  Father. Whitman.
Daddy. Clifton.
Das Schloss. Kirstein.
David's Lamentation.
  Anonymous.
David's Lamentation.
  Billings.
Dawn and a Woman.
  Logan.
The Devil and the Angel.
  Dobson.
Divorce. Widerberg.
Door and Window Bolted
  Fast. Leib.

Double Take at Relais de
  l'Espadon. Davis.
Dream of the Black Mother.
  Dos Santos.
Ecce Puer. Joyce.
Eighteen Verses Sung to a
  Tatar Reed Whistle. Ts'ai
  Yen.
The Elderly Gentleman.
  Canning.
Elegy for a Diver. Booth.
Epigram: "Broad and ample
  he warms himself."
  Anonymous.
Epitaph at Upton-on-Severn.
  Anonymous.
Epitaph on a Quack.
  Anonymous.
Esther. Chavez.
Even the Best. Kizer.
Family 8. Lifshin.
La Fayette. Madison.
The Fire of Frendraught (C
  version). *Anonymous.*
For the Family of
  Cuchonnacht O Dalaigh.
  O Bruadair.
Fourth Poem. Andrade.
Funeral Hymn. Howe.
The Gardener. Wheelock.
The Geraldines. Davis.
Gil Morrice. *Anonymous.*
Grace before Meat.
  FitzGerald.
Grandser. Brown.
The Great Silkie of Sule
  Skerrie. *Anonymous.*
The Grimsby Lads.
  Anonymous.
Hot-Cross Buns. Mother
  Goose.
The Hurt of Love.
  Macdonald.
Hush Thee, Princeling.
  Bennett.
If. Kipling.
Is This Africa? Dempster.
Jesus Shall Reign. Watts.
John Brown's Body. Benét.
The Joys of Mary.
  Anonymous.
Juanita, Wife of Manuelito.
  Ortiz.
The Lady's Song. Dryden.
The Lament of the Voiceless.
  Everett.
The Land War. O'Sullivan.
The Last Fierce Charge.
  Anonymous.
Let Us Learn. Ravitch.
Lines for a Hard Time.
  Ford.
Lines to His Son on Reaching
  Adolescence. Logan.
Lines to My Father. Daiken.
The Little House in Lithuania.
  Marshak.
Living among the Dead.
  Matthews.
La Llorona. Pape.
The Lonely Mother.
  Johnson.
The Loss of the New
  Columbia. *Anonymous.*
Lost Anchors. Robinson.
Lost, But Won. Von
  Schlichten.
M'Fingal. Trumbull.
Madonna of the Hills. Allen.
Manly Diversion. Kopp.
Marm Grayson's Guests.
  Freeman.

Midwife. Box.
Miscarriage. Longley.
Momma's Not Gods Image...
  Mitchell.
Morning Hymn. Ken.
Mosby at Hamilton. Cawein.
The Mother. Pearse.
Mothers of Sons. Saunders.
The Mu'allaqat: Pour Us
  Wine. Ibn Kolthum.
My Lord Tomnoddy.
  Brough.
Mythology. Durrell.
The New Calf. Hearst.
North Atlantic. Sandburg.
Ode to Simplicity. Collins.
Oh, Absalom, My Son.
  Anonymous.
On the Bridge of Athlone: A
  Prophecy. MacDonagh.
On the Death of My Son
  Charles. Webster.
The Only Son. Newbolt.
Open the Gates. *Anonymous.*
Out of Our Shame. Rosten.
The Parable of the Old Man
  and the Young. Owen.
The Passions. Collins.
Patmos. Holderlin.
The Phoenix. Nemerov.
The Plan of Salvation.
  Milton.
Po' Laz'us (Poor Lazarus).
  Anonymous.
Poem: "I met Mother on the
  street." Bruce.
Prayer for the Journey.
  Anonymous.
A Prayer in Time of
  Blindness. Wood.
Prodigal's Return. Eberly.
The Pytheness. Raine.
The Queen of Scotland.
  Anonymous.
The Queen of the Angels.
  Boccaccio.
The Rebel. Belloc.
The Return of the Dead
  (excerpt). Attar.
Reuben, Reuben. Harper.
The Revenge of America.
  Warton.
The River Don. *Anonymous.*
Rodney's Ride. *Anonymous.*
Romance VIII. John of
  Damascus.
Rose Connoley. *Anonymous.*
San Lorenzo Giustiniani's
  Mother. Meynell.
Saul. Heavysege.
Secret Laughter. Morley.
The Sergeant, He Is the Worst
  of All (with music).
  Anonymous.
Sleep and Poetry. Keats.
Sleeping with Foxes. Hill.
Somebody's Mother. Brine.
The Son of a Gambolier (with
  music). *Anonymous.*
Song for Dov Shamir. Abse.
Sonnets, XIII: "O! that you
  were yourself; but, love,
  you/are." Shakespeare.
Sons. Polson.
Source of News. *Anonymous.*
Spain. Livesay.
The Spider. Coffin.
The Spirit of the Maine.
  Jenks.
Spiv Song. Ellis.
Stratton Water. *Anonymous.*
That Day. Kherdian.

The Theology of Jonathan Edwards. McGinley.
There Is None to Help. Walsh.
This Is a Poem to My Son Peter. Meinke.
A Thought. Lermontov.
To a Young Gentle-Woman, Councel Concerning Her Choice. Crashaw.
To My Son (excerpt). Barker.
The Town I Was Born In. Amichai.
True Son of God, Eternal Light. Cormican.
Ubi Sunt Qui Ante Nos Fuerunt? *Anonymous.*
Under the Wood. *Anonymous.*
Unknown Soldier. Dunn.
Upon a Funeral. Beaumont.
Waiting for Lilith. Kessler.
We'll Never Know. Hoellein.
We Pity Our Bosses Five. *Anonymous.*
Welcome O Great Mary. O'Gallagher.
Welcome! Our Messiah. *Anonymous.*
What Does It Mean to Be American? Montgomery.
Willie's Lady. *Anonymous.*
Yaqui Women: Three Generations. Casillas.
The Yielded Life. W.A..

Song (s)
Accidia. Beeching.
Adieu to the Stone Walls. *Anonymous.*
The Aeneid. Virgil (Publius Vergilius Maro).
The After Woman. Thompson.
Afterword: Song of Song. Broughton.
Again for Hephaistos, the Last Time. Howard.
Air: "The Love of a Woman." Creeley.
All Day It Has Rained. Lewis.
All Night I Heard. Moffat.
All Which Isn't Singing Is Mere Talking. Cummings.
Alone by the Road's Edge. O Hehir.
Answer. Speyer.
The Apology. Emerson.
April. Auringer.
Arcadia. Sidney.
Ardor. Bradford.
The Ark and the Dove. Sargent.
Arraignment. Cone.
At Bedtime. Van Rensseleaer.
At the St. Louis Institute of Music. Wallace.
Auditory Hallucinations. Mansour.
Auspex. Lowell.
The Ballad of Dreamland. Swinburne.
Bay Bank. Ammons.
Be Strong. Babcock.
The Bear's Song. *Anonymous.*
The Beautiful World. Childress.
Beethoven. Wheelock.

Beginning My Studies. Whitman.
Beyond Possession. Jennings.
Bide a Wee! Oxenham.
Big Thompson Canon. Gower.
Bile Them Cabbage Down. *Anonymous.*
Birds Waking. Merwin.
Bitter Bread. Mandelstam.
A Black Girl Goes By. Roumer.
The Blackbird of Derrycairn. *Anonymous.*
Blanaid's Song. Campbell.
Blessed Lord, What It Is to Be Young. McCord.
The Blind Psalmist. Kinney
The Blue Closet. Morris.
The Brahms. Morris.
Breath. McHugh.
The Bush (excerpt). O'Dowd.
Bushed. McKinnon.
By the North Sea. Swinburne.
Caelica, LXVIII. Greville.
The Camel-Rider. *Anonymous.*
Camilla. Keeler.
Camoens. Melville.
The Canadian Rossignol. Thomson.
Canto Amor. Berryman.
Celestial Queen. Sannazaro.
The Celts. McGee.
Chanting the Square Deific. Whitman.
A Child Accepts. Hamburger.
Child and Boatman (excerpt). Ingelow.
The Child's Dream. Ludvigson.
Chorale. Hope.
Christmas Is Remembering. Binns.
Chromis. Fletcher.
The Clearing. Jones.
Compensation. Thaxter.
A Consecration. Masefield.
A Credo. Thackeray.
A Crowned Poet. Aldrich.
Daffodils. Reese.
David. Davies.
Daw's Dinner. Kilmer.
The Days. Blocklyn.
Death's Songsters. Rossetti.
Death Sweet. Beddoes.
Debts. Rittenhouse.
Dedication. Gogarty.
A Dedication. Gordon.
The Derby Ram, II. *Anonymous.*
Detroit City. Boyer.
Diana Enamorada: Ring Forth, Fair Nymphs, Your Joyful Songs. Gil Polo.
Domine ne in Furore. Wyatt.
Doom-Devoted. Golding.
Dream and the Song. Corrothers.
The Drowned. MacCaig.
Drum-Taps. Whitman.
Drummer Boy. Stafford.
The Durham Lock-Out. *Anonymous.*
During Thoughts after Ofay-Watching. Serote.
Dusk. Heyward.
The Dying Swan. Tennyson.

The Earliest Christian Hymn. Clement of Alexandria (Titus Flavius Clemens).
Echoes. Lazarus.
Elegy. Bell.
Eletelephony. Richards.
End of the Flower-World (A.D. 2300). Burnshaw.
Envoi. Mandel.
Epithalamium. Crashaw.
Erosion. Graham.
Eutopia. Palgrave.
Evening in Paradise. Milton.
Everyone Sang. Sassoon.
Evoe! Thomas.
An Excellent New Song upon His Grace...Lord Archbishop of Dublin. Swift.
Factory Windows Are Always Broken. Lindsay.
The Fair Morning. Very.
Fantasy. Bennett.
Farewell. Kemp.
A Farewell. Kingsley.
Father Takes to the Road and Lets His Hair down. Lau.
'Fiddler's Green. *Anonymous.*
The First and the Last. Bonar.
The First Olympionique to Hiero of Syracuse. Pindar.
Fisherman's Blunder off New Bedford, Massachusetts. Ewing.
Flail. "Dalton.
Flavius, If Your Girl Friend. Catullus.
Flute Players. Rabearivelo.
A Footnote to a Famous Lyric. Guiney.
For Our Lady. Sanchez.
For You, O Democracy. Whitman.
Foreboding. Hall.
From My Arm-Chair. Longfellow.
Frost. Hewitt.
The Gift of Song. Hecht.
Gipsy Love Song. Smith.
The Girl Who Learned to Sing in Crow. Mariani.
The God of Comfort. *Anonymous.*
The Green Roads. Thomas.
Haiku: "The piano man." Knight.
The Heart of the World. Nahman of Bratzlav.
The Heather. Blicher.
His Delight. Meilir ap Gwalchmai.
The History of Prince Edward Island. *Anonymous.*
Hosanna to Christ. Watts.
The Hosts of Faery. *Anonymous.*
House in St. Petersburg. Burnshaw.
The House of Life. Rossetti.
How Gentle God's Commands. Doddridge.
How Glorious Are the Morning Stars. Keach.
How to the Singer Comes the Song? Gilder.
Hugging the Jukebox. Nye.
Hymn. Larcom.
"I Broke the Spell That Held Me Long." Bryant.
I Come Again. Foeth.

I Expected My Skin and My Blood to Ripen. Rose.
I Hear America Singing. Whitman.
I Lay My Sines on Jesus. Bonar.
I'll Build My House. Hall.
I'll Go with Her Blues. Wilkins.
I Praise the Tender Flower. Bridges.
I Saw the Clouds. White.
Icarus. Smithyman.
Idylls. Theocritus.
The Impious Feast. Landor.
In a Museum. Hardy.
In Cabin'd Ships at Sea. Whitman.
In Memoriam A.H.H., XXXVII. Tennyson.
In Memoriam A.H.H., XXXVIII. Tennyson.
In Memoriam: John Davidson. Macfie.
In Memory of W. H. Auden. Slavitt.
In the Swamp in Secluded Recesses. Whitman.
The Indifferent. Beaumont.
Inexhaustible. Zangwill.
The Invitation. Godfrey.
Iolanthe. Gilbert.
An Irish Satire. *Anonymous.*
Irradiations. Fletcher.
It Was Your Song. Kowit.
January. Gibson.
Jesus, the Soul of Our Joys. Wesley.
Jim Farrow. *Anonymous.*
John Bright. Gummere.
Judge Me, O God. Barlow.
The King on the Tower. Thackeray.
Kitchen Song. Dobbs.
Lady of the Ferry Inn. Mechain.
Lament for a Poor Poet. Connolly.
A Lament for Bion. Moschus.
Last Songs. Kinnell.
A Leave-Taking. Broome.
Lethe. Millay.
Letter to the Night. Frankenberg.
Light Another Candle. Chaikin.
Like Barley Bending. Teasdale.
Limerick: "An anal erotic named Herman." *Anonymous.*
Local Places. Moss.
The Long Night. Smith.
Long Tail Blue. *Anonymous.*
Lord Arnaldos. Flecker.
Love. Davies.
Love and Hate. O'Connor.
Love Me Little, Love Me Long. *Anonymous.*
A Love Poem for My Country. Chipasula.
Love Redeemed. Baylebridge.
Love's Old Sweet Song. Bingham.
Love Song for a Tyrant. Rewey.
The Lover in Liberty Smileth at Them in Thraldom. *Anonymous.*

The Loves of the Plants. Darwin.
Lovesong. Rilke.
The Lyre-Bird. Robinson.
Mad Blake. Benet.
Maine. Nauen.
The Makers. McDonald.
The Man from Porlock. Bevington.
Man Holding Boy. Dixon.
A Man Walking and Singing. Berry.
The Masque of the Inner-Temple and Gray's Inne. Beaumont.
The Masters. Hope.
Meeting Mick Jagger (parody). Peters.
Melissa. Redl-Hlus.
Melody. Moreh.
The Military Harpist. Pitter.
Milton. Blake.
A Minor Bird. Frost.
Miserere mei, Domine. Wyatt.
Monday, Monday. Trinidad.
The Monkey's Wedding (with music). *Anonymous.*
The Monks of Ely. *Anonymous.*
Monna Innominata. Rossetti.
Morning. Cunningham.
Morning Song. Foeth.
Moschus Moschiferus. Hope.
Mother Carey's Chicken. Watts-Dunton.
A Mother's Prayer. Sangster.
Mother Sarah's Lullaby. Manger.
The Music. Hoagland.
Music. Ryan.
Musical Shuttle. Shapiro.
My Buried Friends. *Anonymous.*
My Flying Machine. Brodsky.
My Little Cow. *Anonymous.*
My Song. Tagore.
My Subtle and Proclamant Song. Jennett.
The Negro Singer. Corrothers.
Neni, Coronaberis. *Anonymous.*
None Other Fame Mine Unambitious Muse. Daniel.
Nonsense. Schauffler.
Noon's Dream-Song. Lee-Hamilton.
Not Heaving from My Ribb'd Breast Only. Whitman.
The Nyum-Nyum. *Anonymous.*
O Bruadair. Stephens.
O'Connor the Bad Traveler. Klappert.
O Nightingale! Thou Surely Art. Wordsworth.
Ode: On the Death of William Butler Yeats. Smith.
Odes. Horace.
The Odyssey. Homer.
Oh, Lawd, How Long? *Anonymous.*
Omnia Somnia. Watson.
On Imagination. Wheatley.
On Liberty and Slavery. Horton.
Once Alien Here. Hewitt.

Only Seven (parody). Leigh.
Oppression. Hughes.
Orara. Kendall.
The Other. Fainlight.
Our Burden Bearer. Brooks.
Our Country. Howe.
Our States, O Lord. Mycall.
The Outlaw of Loch Lene. Callanan.
Oystercatchers. Middleton.
Pain. Speyer.
Paradox: The Birds. Shapiro.
A Paragraph. Carruth.
Parfum Exotique. Baudelaire.
The Passionate Pilgrim. Shakespeare.
A Pastoral. Breton.
A Pastoral Ballad in Four Parts. Shenstone.
Paul Laurence Dunbar. Corrothers.
Peace on Earth. Sears.
Percussions. Welburn.
Pervigilium Veneris. Noguere.
Piano Recital. Deutsch.
Poem for Marc Chagall. Cohen.
Poem: "Hasten on your childhood to the hour." Picasso.
The Poems Come Easier. Mathew.
The Poet Prays. Crowell.
The Poet's Use. Pope.
A Poet Speaks from the Visitors' Gallery. MacLeish.
Poly-Olbion. Drayton.
The Pontoon Bridge Miracle. Lindsay.
Poor Howard. *Anonymous.*
Poor Man Blues. *Anonymous.*
The Praise of Sailors. *Anonymous.*
Proem to Hellenics. Landor.
The Prophet. Gibran.
Prothalamion. Spenser.
Psycholophon. Burgess.
Quatrain: "Gone are the games we played all night." Mahsati.
The Quest of Silence: Fire in the Heavens, and Fire Along the Hills. Brennan.
The Ration Card. Bahe.
The Reaper. Duncan.
Recollections of "Lalla Rookh." Trowbridge.
Request for a Song. Tuwim.
The Return of Eve. Chesterton.
Return to Ritual. Van Doren.
Riddle: The Swan: "Silent my robe, when I rest on earth." *Anonymous.*
Rise, Ye Children. Falckner.
Robin Hood and the Tinker. *Anonymous.*
Rock, Rock, Sleep, My Baby. Watson.
Rookhope Ryde. *Anonymous.*
Roy Bean. *Anonymous.*
The Rubaiyat of Omar Khayyam. Omar Khayyam.
Sailing Homeward. Chan Fang-sheng.

Saints. Garrett.
A Satire on the People of Kildare. *Anonymous.*
Secret. Bennett.
The Secret. Peach.
The Seed of Reality. Von Hartmann.
The Selfsame Song. Hardy.
She Was Young and Blithe and Fair. Monro.
The Shepheardes Calender:. Spenser.
The Ships. Maynard.
The Shooting of the Cup. Neihardt.
The Shortest and. Macdonald.
Sightseers in a Courtyard. Guillen.
Sigil. Doolittle.
Silence. Akhmadulina.
Skating. Asquith.
The Skylark's Nest. Long.
The Slacker Apologizes. Viereck.
The Sleeping Beauty. Sitwell.
The Sleeping Gypsy–a Painting by Rousseau. Johnson.
Sleepless Night. O'Rahilly.
Slim Man Canyon. Silko.
Some Lines in Three Parts. Viereck.
Sometime I Loved. *Anonymous.*
Sometimes With One I Love. Whitman.
The Song. Erskine.
A Song. Schwartz.
A Song as Yet Unsung. Yehoash.
Song-Maker. Endrezze-Danielson.
Song Making. Teasdale.
A Song of Desire. Knowles.
Song of Myself. Whitman.
The Song of the Robin. Bergquist.
Song of the Sea. Burton.
The Song of the Shirt. Hood.
The Song of the Trout Fisher. Ikinilik.
A Song's Worth. Spalding.
Song: "She sat and sang alway." Rossetti.
Song–Talysarn. Chamberlain.
Song: "The little Black Rose shall be red at last!" De Vere.
Song: "This is the song." Justema.
Song to the Mountains. *Anonymous.*
Sonnets, V: "Into the wood at close of rainy day." Irwin.
Sonnets, CII: "My love is strengthen'd." Shakespeare.
Sonnets to Miranda. Watson.
The Sparrow-Hawk's Complaint. *Anonymous.*
Spectral Lovers. Ransom.
Speech to the Court. Lowenfels.
Spirit of Freedom, Thou Dost Love the Sea. Dodge.
The Spirit of Wine. Henley.
Spring. Behn.
The Spur. Yeats.

Stories Relate Life. Shady.
A Street in April. Dudek.
The Subject of the Bishop's Miracle. Philip.
The Succession. Mace.
The Summer Days Are Come Again. Longfellow.
Sun Song. Hughes.
Table Talk. Cowper.
Tales of the Islands, VIII. Walcott.
Tell Us No More. *Anonymous.*
Thanks from Earth to Heaven. Wheelock.
That Is Not Indifference. Hanson.
That's Jesus. Renfrow.
There Is a Name I Love to Hear. Whitfield.
This Poem Will Never Be Finished. Souster.
Thou Beautiful Sabbath. *Anonymous.*
Thread Suns. Celan.
Three City Cantos. Wagner.
Three Holy Kings from Morgenland. Heine.
Three Modes of History and Culture. Jones.
Three wise men of Gotham. Mother Goose.
Thy Garden, Orchard, Fields. Pastorius.
Thysia. Luce.
The Time-Clock. Towne.
To a Caty-Did. Freneau.
To a Wasp Caught in the Storm Sash... Cooley.
To John Greenleaf Whittier. Ward.
To Little Renee on First Seeing Her Lying in Her Cradle. Bradley.
To Love A Sonnet. Ayres.
To Phyllis. Field.
To Sir William, of Hawthornden Alexander. Drummond.
To Speak of Chile. Gibson.
To Stella. Sidney.
To the Jews in Poland. Wittlin.
To the Mocking-Bird. Pike.
Toll the Bell for Damon. Anderson.
The Trail Up Wu Gorge. Sun Yun-feng.
The Tree-Toad. Johns.
The Troubadour of God. Stork.
True Child. Hodge.
The Two Angels. Whittier
Two Generations. Strong.
The Unfailing One. Brooks.
Urn I: Silent for Twenty-Five Years, The Father of My Mother Advises. Lew.
Vendor's Song. Crapsey.
The Virgin's Slumber Song. Carlin.
Vita Nuova. Watson.
Voice. Spofford.
The Voice of Thought. Chivers.
Walrus Hunting. Aua.
The Wandering One Makes Music. Aldis.
Water Ouzel. Matchett.
The Wedding (1957). Pasternak.

Wednesday, January 1, 1701. Sewall.
Welsh Landscape. Thomas.
What Do I Care. Teasdale.
When I See Another's Pain. Leib.
When the Nightingale Sings. *Anonymous.*
Whither. Goetz.
Wild Eden. Woodberry.
The Wind. Stevenson.
A Wish. Nicolas.
Women Are Not Gentlemen. Matthews.
Women of My Land. Armstrong.
Work Gangs. Sandburg.
The World's a Well Strung Fidle, Mans Tongue the Quill. Ward.
World Youth Song. *Anonymous.*
Wulf and Eadwacer. Ryan.
Yet Another Song. Rubadiri.
Young Companions. *Anonymous.*
Youth. Cloud.

Sonnet (s)
Auf Meiner Herzliebsten Augelein. Heine.
Don Juan. Byron.
Lines in Ridicule of Certain Poems Published in 1777. Johnson.
Notes for a Sonnet (parody). Pygge.
Odd to a Krokis. *Anonymous.*
Quickening. Morley.
Rope's End. Neumeyer.
Roses, Revisited, in a Paradoxical Autumn. Cullum.
Sonnet: He Is Past All Help. Angiolieri.
To the Poet T. J. Mathias. Landor.
Urceus Exit: Triolet. Dobson.
What Is a Sonnet? Watkins.

Sons-of-bitches
French Poets. Saroyan.
I've Labored Long and Hard for Bread. Black Bart.

Soon (er)
Afraid? Of whom am I afraid? Dickinson.
Cat-Goddesses. Graves.
Don Juan. Byron.
Dulcina. Ralegh.
Haiku: "Tow-head dandelions." Phillips.
A Note of Humility. Bontemps.
Out of Tune. Henley.
The Pennycandystore beyond the El. Ferlinghetti.
Red Beauty. *Anonymous.*
Song: "If I had only loved your flesh." Sackville-West.
Sonnet: A Lady Laments for Her Lost Lover... *Anonymous.*
Time's Mutability. Brecht.
A Timepiece. Merrill.
To Night. Shelley.
The Undertaker's Horse. Kipling.
When Fog Come Creepin' over Beccles (parody). Fitton.

Sooth (ed) (es)
Airey-Force Valley. Wordsworth.
Call Me Not Back from the Echoless Shore. *Anonymous.*
The Conviction. Synge.
Crack in the Wall Holds Flowers. Miller.
The Draught of Life. Abu-l-Ala al-Maarri.
Gethsemane. Tappan.
I.H.B. Winter.
Ianthe. Landor.
Long Summer (excerpt). Lowell.
On the Receipt of My Mother's Picture Out of Norfolk. Cowper.
Sleep and Poetry. Keats.
Snatches: "Who so cometh to any hous." *Anonymous.*
The Song of the Happy Shepherd. Yeats.
'Tis Midnight and on Olive's Brow. Tappan.
To Our Ladies of Death. Thomson.

Sore (s)
Against Women. Juvenal (Decimas Junius Juvenalis).
Ah My Dere. *Anonymous.*
Almond Blossom. Lawrence.
Concerning the Nature of Love. Lucretius (Titus Lucretius Carus).
Garlic. Bell.
The Grey Ones. MacNeice.
The Guttural Muse. Heaney.
Justice. Hughes.
Last Poems. Housman.
Poet Woman's Mitosis: Dividing All the Cells Apart. Rose.
Precedent. Dunbar.
Punch and Judy. *Anonymous.*
The Shepherd's Lament. Goethe.
What Wourde Is That That Chaungeth Not. Wyatt.

Sorrow (ful) (s)
9 Verses of the Same Song. Berry.
Ah, Poor Bird. *Anonymous.*
Amoretti, XXXIV. Spenser.
Amoretti, LXIII. Spenser.
Amoretti, LXXXVII. Spenser.
The Answer. Teasdale.
Any Human to Another. Cullen.
Astrophel and Stella, XVIII. Sidney.
Ballad. Seiffert.
Barbara Allen. *Anonymous.*
A Baroque Gravure. Merton.
Behold Your King! Havergal.
The Benefactors. Hay.
Big, Fat Summer–and the Lean and Hard. Bock.
A Bird Was Singing. Dietmar von Aist.
Birth and Death. Swinburne.
Black Mammies. Holloway.
The Bride of Abydos. Byron.
Bring Me the Cup. Ibn Ezra.

The British Museum Reading Room. MacNeice.
By Cobequid Bay. Fraser.
By Coelia's Arbor. Sheridan.
Caelica, XXV. Greville.
Caelica, XCIV. Greville.
Canzone. Auden.
Cape Coloured Batman. Butler.
Chorus of the Unborn. Sachs.
Clearing for the Plough. Moll.
Cologne. Bate.
Come All Ye Fair and Tender Maidens. *Anonymous.*
Come, Ye Disconsolate. Moore.
Consolation. Darley.
The Constant Farmer's Son. *Anonymous.*
Cricket. No Ch'on-myong.
Deem Not. Santayana.
The Depths of Sorrow. *Anonymous.*
A Dialogue. Ignatow.
Diary. Moon of the Hiding Doe. De Clue.
Earl Brand (Sweet William). *Anonymous.*
The Elected Knight. *Anonymous.*
Epitaph: "Come knock your heads against this stone." Blake.
Faith. Clark.
Faith's Difficulty. Maynard.
The Fall of Hyperion. Keats.
Family Cups. Orlen.
Fergus and the Druid. Yeats.
Flute Players. Rabearivelo.
A Fond Greeting, Hillock There. Mac An Bhaird.
Forgetfulness. Bodenheim.
The Ghost. De La Mare.
Goodnight. Smith.
Hangover Cure. Nicochares.
Hart Crane. Symons.
Head of Medusa. Zaturenska.
Humaine Cares. Wanley.
Hymn of Pan. Shelley.
I Am Not a Camera. Auden.
I Had a Hippopotamus. Barrington.
I let the incense grow cold. Li Ch'ing-chao.
Icarus. Smithyman.
Idylls. Moschus.
If It Is Not My Portion. Tagore.
Imitated from Sonetto in Morte 42. Petrarch (Francesco Petrarca).
Immensity. Stern.
In Memoriam F. A. S. Stevenson.
In Sickness. Swift.
In the Dusk the Path. Izumi Shikibu.
In the Time of Trouble. Clark.
Incognita. Dobson.
Inertia. Finch.
Judgment Day. Oxenham.
July 1914. Akhmatova.
The Kingfisher. Clampitt.
The Lady of the Manor. Crabbe.

Lassitude. Blind.
Like Barley Bending. Teasdale.
A Likeness. Cather.
The Lonely Mother. Johnson.
Love in Thy Youth. *Anonymous.*
Love Poem: "Less the dog begged to die in the sky." Barker.
Love Song. *Anonymous.*
A Lover's Lament. *Anonymous.*
Lucasia, Rosania and Orinda Parting at a Fountain, July 1663. Philips.
The Malefic Return. Velarde.
Medieval Norman Songs. *Anonymous.*
Mists and Rain. Baudelaire.
Mog the Brunette. *Anonymous.*
Moles. Stafford.
Moon Song. Nweke.
Motherless Children. *Anonymous.*
The Naked World. Sully-Prudhomme.
Nature in War-Time. Palmer.
The New View. Holmes.
The Night Will Never Stay. Farjeon.
No Time. Tiller.
Noon. "Field.
Not Changed, But Glorified. *Anonymous.*
A Nuptial Eve. Dobell.
O Sing to Me of Heaven. Dana.
October 1803. Wordsworth.
The Old Man. Fisher.
On a Certain Engagement South of Seoul. Carruth.
On My Sorrowful Life. Ibn Ezra.
Orchids. Wratislaw.
Pain. Lucas.
Pan-Asian Holiday Tour. Syquia.
Paradise Lost. Milton.
The Parish Register. Crabbe.
Philomel. Barnfield.
Poems. Drummond.
Popular Songs of Tuscany. *Anonymous.*
Prescience. Aldrich.
A Procession at Candlemas. Clampitt.
Prognostic. Yellen.
Prospero on the Mountain Gathering Wood. Gilbert.
A Roman Officer Writes. Doughty.
The Rubicon. Winter.
Selfishness. Bruner.
A Shantyman's Life (I). *Anonymous.*
The Shrubbery. Cowper.
A Song of Morning. Sitwell.
Song of the Bowmen of Shu. *Anonymous.*
The Song of the Ghost. Graves.
Song Set by John Dowland: "Come, ye heavy states of night." *Anonymous.*
Sonnet XCIV. Greville.
"The soote season..." Surrey.
The Spleen. Green.

The Spring. O'Donnell.
Sympathy. Gyles.
Sympathy. Heber.
The Task. Cowper.
Think before You Act.
  Elliott.
Though I've a Clever Head.
  Anonymous.
Three Christmas Carols: III.
  Anonymous.
Three Tanka, 2. Yosano
  Akiko.
Threnody. Ignatow.
Time. Wilkinson.
Time to Go. "Coolidge.
To a Gone Era. McClaurin.
To Heliodora, Dead.
  Meleager.
To His Muse. Breton.
To L. C. Hawkins.
Tom O' Bedlam's Song.
  Anonymous.
The Triad of Things Not
  Decreed. Furlong.
A Twilight in Middle March.
  Ledwidge.
Two Folk Songs, 2.
  Anonymous.
Upon the Losse of His
  Mistresses. Herrick.
Vala; or, The Four Zoas.
  Blake.
Villanelle. Simpson.
The Violet. Scott.
The Virgin Mary to Christ on
  the Cross. Southwell.
A Vision of Judgement.
  Southey.
The Wayfarer. Pearse.
We Are Such Stuff As
  Dreams... Petronius.
Weak Is the Will of Man, His
  Judgment Blind.
  Wordsworth.
The Weaver. Forrester.
Were You on the Mountain?
  Anonymous.
Whispering Hope.
  Hawthorne.
Who Can Tell? *Anonymous.*
The Whole Duty of Berkshire
  Brooks. Conkling.
Yarrow Visited.
  Wordsworth.

Sorry
Artillery Shoot. Forsyth.
Clementine. Montrose.
The Dolls' Wash. Ewing.
Epigram. *Anonymous.*
Errore. Di Cicco.
Ferry-Boats. Tippett.
Go Down, Old Hannah.
  Anonymous.
I'd Like to Be a Worm.
  Gay.
Ice Handler. Sandburg.
Margaret Are You Drug.
  Starbuck.
A Mother Speaks: The Algiers
  Motel Incident, Detroit.
  Harper.
No More Love Poems #1.
  Shange.
Now Look What Happened.
  Peacock.
The Patriot Game.
  Anonymous.
The Penitent. Millay.
The Perfect Child. Porter.
Poppies. McPherson.
Self-Pity. Lawrence.

Special Rider Blues.
  Anonymous.
Spring Song. Conkling.
The Streets of Cairo.
  Thornton.
Tableau Vivant. Gallagher.
W. Reeves.
Waking. Higgins.

Sort (s)
Choosing Shoes. Wolfe.
The Great Beam of the Milky
  Way. *Anonymous.*
Point Grey. Hine.
To the God of Love. Knox.

Sought
Arcadia. Sidney.
The Frightened Man. Bogan.
I Follow, Lo, the Footing.
  Jonson.
The Search. Crosby.
Search. Marriott.

Soul (s)
Advertisement of a Lost Day.
  Sigourney.
An African Song.
  Chatterton.
After the Dazzle of Day.
  Whitman.
After the Flight of the Earls.
  O Gnimh.
All Hallows. Gluck.
All Is Vanity, Saith the
  Preacher. Byron.
Alone. Joyce.
Amen. Benson.
Amendment. Traherne.
America First! Oldham.
America's Gospel. Lowell.
An American to France.
  Miller.
Ancestral Weight. Storni.
The Ancient Speech. Raine.
And Did the Animals? Van
  Doren.
And Would You See My
  Mistress' Face? Campion.
Animal Song. McHugh.
Any Lover, Any Lass.
  Middleton.
Apollo 113. Finne.
As Flows the Rapid River.
  Smith.
As Is the Sea Marvelous.
  Cummings.
Asleep in the Bosom of
  Youth. Halevi.
At Ease. De La Mare.
Attainment. Cawein.
Autobiography of a
  Lungworm. Fuller.
Autumn. Hood.
The Ballad of Barnaby.
  Auden.
Ballad of Douglas Bridge.
  Carlin.
Ballata: In Exile at Sarzana.
  Cavalcanti.
Baptism. McKay.
Barthram's Dirge.
  Anonymous.
A Bathing Girl. Jensen.
The Battle in the Clouds.
  Howells.
The Battle of the Baltic.
  Campbell.
Be Still, My Soul. Schlegel.
Be Still. The Hanging
  Gardens Were a Dream.
  Stickney.
A Beam of Light. Rooney.
Beauty. Hille.
Beauty. Spenser.

Bed Charm. *Anonymous.*
Before a Statue of Achilles.
  Santayana.
Before Rereading
  Shakespeare's Sonnets.
  Moore.
Before Sleeping. *Anonymous.*
The Beggar's Opera. Gay.
Beyond the Nigger. Plumpp.
The Blade of Grass Sings to
  the River. Goldberg.
Blessed Nearness. Bullock.
Blind. Bangs.
The Boarding. Johnson.
Bodily Beauty. Rostrevor.
Bonny Bee Hom.
  Anonymous.
Boston, Lincolnshire.
  Anonymous.
The Bridge of Death.
  Anonymous.
The Brut. Layamon.
A Bulb. Munkittrick.
The Burning Bush. Van
  Dyke.
By the Sea. Dixon.
Caedmon. Garrett.
Caelica, XCIX. Greville.
Calvary's Cry. Cunningham.
Canned Heat Blues.
  Johnson.
Canonicus and Roger
  Williams. *Anonymous.*
Captain Kidd. *Anonymous.*
Carry On! Service.
The Cedars of Lebanon.
  Lamartine.
Champ de Manoeuvres.
  Read.
The Child Reads an Almanac.
  Jammes.
A Child's Question. Nason.
Childe Harold's Pilgrimage:
  Canto III. Byron.
The Circuit Judge. Masters.
The Circulation.
  Washbourne.
The City Church. "K..
Claiming the Promise.
  Wesley.
A Classical Quatrain.
  Goodman.
Cleator Moor. Nicholson.
Closing Prayer. Patrick.
The Clue. Bates.
The College Cat. Godley.
Columbus Dying. Proctor.
Come, O Lord, Like Morning
  Sunlight. Littlefield.
Come, Said My Soul.
  Whitman.
Communism. Wilcox.
Comrades. Woodberry.
The Conquering Love of
  Jesus. Wesley.
Conscience. Sherburne.
The Contemplative. Sister
  M. Therese.
A Conversation. Howes.
Could'st Thou (O Earth) Live
  Thus Obscure. Alsop.
Could We. *Anonymous.*
Crass Times Redeemed by
  Dignity of Souls. Viereck.
Crazy Bill to the Bishop
  (parody). Peters.
Crossing Brooklyn Ferry.
  Whitman.
Crow, Straight Flier, but
  Dark. Firestone.
Crucifixion. Booth.
Crucifying. Donne.

Damned Women.
  Baudelaire.
Darest Thou Now O Soul.
  Whitman
Davideis. Cowley.
Dear Brethren, Are Your
  Harps in Tune? Smith.
Death and the Arkansas
  River. Stanford.
Death at Daybreak. Aldrich.
The Death of Don Pedro.
  Anonymous.
The Death of Grant. Bierce.
The Death of Jefferson.
  Butterworth.
Debout (excerpt). Tam'si.
The Demon of the Mirror.
  Taylor.
Departed–to the Judgment.
  Dickinson.
Der Heilige Mantel Von
  Aachen. Musser.
Did our best moment last.
  Dickinson.
Diversity. Thompson.
Do Not Torment Me,
  Woman. *Anonymous.*
The Dole of the King's
  Daughter. *Anonymous.*
The Dream of Dakiki.
  Firdausi.
A Drifting Petal. Fenollosa.
Due North. Low.
Dulce Ridentem. Benét.
The Dying Cowboy.
  Anonymous.
The Eagle's Nature.
  Anonymous.
Eagles and Isles. Gibson.
Earth's Night. Allingham.
Ellen Flannery. *Anonymous.*
The Emigrant's Child.
  Sproull.
Endymion. Keats.
Energy for a New Thang.
  Mkalimoto.
Ensamples of Our Saviour.
  Southwell.
Epigram: "At even, when the
  hour drew nigh." Strato.
Epigram: "One boy alone."
  Meleager.
Epitaph. *Anonymous.*
Epitaph. Da Modena.
Epitaph for Himself. Herbert
  of Cherbury.
An Epitaph: On Elizabeth
  Chute. Jonson.
Eternal Spirit, Source of
  Light. Davies.
The Eugenist. Graves.
Evangeline. Longfellow.
Everyman. *Anonymous.*
Exiles. Hayne.
A Faithless Shepherd. Clare.
The Falconer of God. Benet.
Family Life. Laing.
Fantasia. Chesterton.
Far in a Western Brookland.
  Housman.
Farewell. L'Ouverture.
The Fatal Spell. Byron.
Fire and Ice. Pettit.
The First Olympionique to
  Hiero of Syracuse. Pindar.
Flight of the Earls.
  Anonymous.
Flood-Time on the Marshes.
  Stein.
Fly from the World.
  Anonymous.

Footnote to "Howl."
  Ginsberg.
For Zorro. Bickston.
The Fountain of Youth.
  Butterworth.
Four for Sir John Davies.
  Roethke.
Freedom in Mah Soul.
  Cannon, Jr..
From Disciple to Master.
  Gibbon.
The Funeral of Philip
  Sparrow. Skelton.
The Future. Tekeyan.
Georgics. Virgil (Publius
  Vergilius Maro).
The Gift. Bruner.
The Glory of Nature.
  Tennyson.
God and the Soul: At the
  Ninth Hour. Spalding.
God Give to Men.
  Bontemps.
The God of the Living.
  Ellerton.
God's World. Millay.
Godmother. Parker.
Goliath of Gath. Wheatley.
The Grave-Yard. Very.
Greyport Legend. Harte.
Gulf-Weed. Fenner.
Ha Ha This-a-Way.
  Anonymous.
Hail, Tranquil Hour of
  Closing Day. Bacon.
Hamlet. Shakespeare.
Harps Hung Up in Babylon.
  Colton.
Harvest. Booth.
He Commandeth a Fair Wind.
  Book of the Dead.
The Heart of God.
  Littlewood.
Heart of Oak. Luders.
The Heart of the Night.
  Rossetti.
A Heavenly Friend. Tucker.
The Heretic's Tragedy.
  Browning.
Hermit. Baxter.
A Hex on the Mexican X.
  McCord.
The High Priest.
  Anonymous.
Hollywood. Shapiro.
The Holy Office. Joyce.
Home. Van Dyke.
Home-Sickness. Lachmann.
Home, Sweet Home.
  Bunner.
Homecoming. Shapiro.
Horatian Ode. Beach.
Hot Weather in the Plains–
  India. Tipple.
The Hour of Prayer. Elliott.
House and Land. Curnow.
The House of Life. Rossetti.
How Shall We Honor Them?
  Markham.
How to the Singer Comes the
  Song? Gilder.
How We Burned the
  Philadelphia. Eastman.
How We Learn. Bonar.
"Hullo!" Foss.
The Human Touch. Free.
Hyacinths to Feed Thy Soul.
  Sa'di.
Hymn. Browning.
Hymn (excerpt). Gilder.
Hymn for the Church
  Militant. Chesterton.

Hymns for the Amusement of
  Children. Smart.
Hymns of the Marshes:
  Sunrise. Lanier.
I Am the Poet Davies,
  William. Davies.
I Didn't Know My Soul.
  Ben-Yitzhak.
I.H.B. Winter.
I Have Folded My Sorrows.
  Kaufman.
I Know de Moonlight.
  Anonymous.
I Know My Soul. McKay.
I Love Thee, Lord.
  Calenberg.
I Sigh when I Sing.
  Anonymous.
I Sing the Body Electric.
  Whitman.
If I Have Made, My Lady,
  Intricate. Cummings.
If i should sleep with a lady
  called death. Cummings.
Immortality. Arnold.
In Cemeteries. Enright.
In God's Eternal Studios.
  Shivell.
In Memory of Francois
  Rabelais. Moritz.
In Spain. Wyatt.
In the Dock. De La Mare.
In the Night. Stephens.
In the Pantry.
  ""MacDiarmid.
In the Shadows. Gray.
Incarnatio Est Maximum
  Donum Dei. Alabaster.
Inclusions. Browning.
Inscape. Litwack.
Inscription for a Wayside
  Spring. Cornford.
Intellect. Emerson.
Intimate Associations.
  Baudelaire.
The Isle of the Long Ago.
  Taylor.
Isolation. Symons.
Iter Supremum. Hardy.
Japanese Fan. Kirkup.
Jehovah. Zangwill.
Jesus Understands.
  Anonymous.
Jimmy Judge. Anonymous.
A Jog-Trot Pair. Hardy.
John Brown. Proctor.
Joy May Kill. Michelangelo.
The Joys of Art. Taylor.
Keep on Pushing.
  Henderson.
The King's Missive.
  Whittier.
King Saul. Horvitz.
The Knight's Leap.
  Kingsley.
The Knight's Tomb.
  Coleridge.
The Lake of Gaube.
  Swinburne.
The Land. Sackville-West.
The Lark. Anonymous.
The Lass of Roch Royal (D
  version). Anonymous.
The Last Guest. Shaw.
A Last Will and Testament.
  Anonymous.
The Lay of the Last Minstrel.
  Scott.
A Lementable New Ballad
  upon the Earle of Essex
  Death. Anonymous.
Let Me Be a Giver. Davies.

Letters. Bukowski.
Letters from Birmingham.
  Bond.
The Lie. Ralegh.
Life. Deland.
Life's Chequer-Board.
  Oxenham.
Life's Evening. Foulke.
Limerick: "A camel, with
  practical views." Herford.
Linen Bands. Thompson.
Lines in Order to Be
  Slandered. Verlaine.
A Little Dog-Angel.
  Holland.
Little Pagan Rain Song.
  Shaw.
A Lodging for the Night.
  Wylie.
The Looking Glass. Shirley.
Lord of the World.
  Anonymous.
Lost and Found.
  Macdonald.
Love. Trask.
Love and Language.
  Bevington.
Love and Sleep. Swinburne.
Love-Lily. Rossetti.
The Love-Moon. Rossetti.
Love's Flight. Lasker-
  Schüler.
Love's Testament. Rossetti.
The Love-Talker. "Carbery.
Lovers. Fullerton.
Lying in a Yuma Saloon.
  Barnes.
A Lyke-Wake Dirge.
  Anonymous.
Mad Blake. Benet.
Madrigal: "What is life."
  Byrd.
The Magic Mirror. Alden.
The Maiden's Best Adorning.
  Anonymous.
Makhno's Philosophers.
  Manifold.
Malacoda. Beckett.
The Man of the Open West.
  Monroe.
The Marathon Runner.
  Johnson.
The Mariner's Dream.
  Dimond.
Mary Immaculate. Donnelly.
Matrix (excerpt). Wellesley.
Matthew, Mark, Luke and
  John. Anonymous.
May. Bird.
May, 1840. Coleridge.
The Meaning of Love.
  Anonymous.
Meditation. Pain.
A Meditation for Christmas.
  Image.
Meditations Seven. Taylor.
Meeting. Rossetti.
Milton. Longfellow
Miracles at the Birth of
  Christ. Watts.
Modern Love, XII.
  Meredith.
Modern Love, XXXII.
  Meredith.
Modern Love, XLVI.
  Meredith.
The Monasteries Lift Gold
  Domes. Bat-Miriam.
More Strong Than Time.
  Hugo.
Moses and Joshua. Lasker-
  Schüler.

Moses on Mount Nebo.
  Regelson.
Mother of Men. Southwold.
Mulford. Whittier
The Murder of Goins.
  Anonymous.
Musgrove. Anonymous.
Music. Dunbar-Nelson.
Music of Hungary. Aldrich.
My Captain. Day.
My Soul Would Fain Indulge
  a Hope. Steward.
My Star. Browning.
The Mystic's Prayer. Sharp.
The Name of Jesus. Newton.
The Nameless One. Mangan.
Narcissus. Valery.
Natura Naturans. Raine.
Nature. Clare.
The Nature of the Eagle.
  Anonymous.
Nature's Influence on Man.
  Akenside.
Negro Poets. Johnson.
Neighbors. Spencer.
Netley Abbey. Midnight.
  Sotheby.
New National Hymn.
  Crawford.
New York City. Bodenheim.
Night. Sidney.
Night. Symonds.
Night and the Pines. Scott.
A Night in a Village.
  Nikitin.
Night Piece. Joyce.
The Night-Piece, to Julia.
  Herrick.
The Nightingale. Strada.
No Friend Like Music.
  Hicky.
None of Self and All of Thee.
  Monod.
Not to March. Hackleman.
Nothing Better. Anonymous.
Now Does Our World
  Descend. Cummings.
Now I Have Found a Friend.
  Hope.
Now I Lay Me Down to
  Sleep. Anonymous.
O Could I Find from Day to
  Day. Cleavland.
O Glorious Christ of God; I
  Live. Mather.
O God, in Restless Living.
  Fosdick.
O Jesus! Sweet the Tears I
  Shed. Palmer.
O Son of God, Afflicted.
  Anonymous.
O Thou to Whom the Musical
  White Spring. Cummings.
Obedience. Herbert.
October 14. 1644. Herbert of
  Cherbury.
The Octopus.
  ""MacDiarmid.
Ode for Music on St. Cecilia's
  Day. Pope.
Ode: "How are thy Servants
  blest, O Lord!" Addison.
The Odyssey. Homer.
Of One Who Seemed to Have
  Failed. Mitchell.
Of Seals and Arms. Taylor.
Oft in My Thoughts.
  Orleans.
Often I Compare My Lord to
  Heaven. Stampa.
Oh, Breathe Not His Name.
  Moore.

Oh, Let Thy Teachings. Di
Roma.
Old Arm-Chair. Cook.
Old Forty-Five Per Cent.
Anonymous.
Old Men's Ward. Dean.
The Old Violin. Egan.
An Old Woman.
Anonymous.
On a Contentious Companion.
Hoskyns.
On a Greek Vase. Sherman.
On Sir William Anson, Fellow
of All Souls. *Anonymous.*
On the Death of Dr. Robert
Levet. Johnson.
On the Death of Robert
Browning. Swinburne.
On the Site of a Mulberry-
Tree. Rossetti.
On the Wide Stairs.
Amichai.
On Writing for the Stage.
Sheffield.
Only Waiting. Mace.
The Orphan Girl.
Anonymous.
Othello. Shakespeare.
Our Madonna at Home.
Pombo.
Over Sir John's Hill.
Thomas.
Pain. Russell.
Pale Is Death. Du Bellay.
A Panegyric. Howe.
The Pangolin. Moore.
Parfum Exotique.
Baudelaire.
The Parrot. Gibson.
Partings. Guerin.
The Path That Leads
Nowhere. Robinson.
Paudeen. Yeats.
Peace. *Anonymous.*
A Perfect Day. Bond.
Peter Bell, the Third.
Shelley.
The Petrified Leaf. Branch.
Pilgrims in Mexico.
Anonymous.
The Pity of the Leaves.
Robinson.
Poem. Hughes.
Poem. Sinclair.
A Poem for Christmas.
Snodgrass.
Poem for the Year Twenty
Twenty. Lee.
Poet and Peasant. Long.
The Poet Confides. Coleman.
The Poet's Harvesting.
O'Malley.
Poet Songs. Baker.
Point of No Return. Graves.
Portrait. Fearing.
The Postern Gate (excerpt).
Rauschenbusch.
Povre Ame Amoureuse.
Labe.
Praise of God. *Anonymous.*
Praise Ye the Lord, O
Celebrate His Fame.
Folger.
Praises of God. *Anonymous.*
Prayer. *Anonymous.*
A Prayer. Le Gallienne.
A Prayer for My Son.
Winters.
Prayer for Peace. Patrick.
A Prayer for the Old
Courage. Towne.

Prayer to St. Helena.
Anonymous.
Prayer under the Pressure of
Violent Anguish. Burns.
The Precious Name.
Newton.
The Preparative. Traherne.
Prescience. Widdemer.
The Prince of Peace His
Banner Spreads. Fosdick.
The Princess. Tennyson.
A "Prize' Poem. Brooks.
De Profundis.
""MacDiarmid.
Protea. Mattera.
Psalm of the Fruitful Field.
Klein.
Pure is the Dewy Gem.
Callanan.
The Question. Taylor.
Racing, Reckoning Fingers
Flick. Palladas.
Rapture: An Ode. Dixon.
The Reformed Pirate.
Roberts.
Remembering. Angelou.
Remembering Home.
Petrykewycz.
Renascence. Millay.
Resignation. Arnold.
Richard Somers. Eastman.
Riddle 7 (Mute Swan).
Anonymous.
The Ride to the Lady. Cone.
Rio Grande de Loiza.
Burgos.
Rock-a My Soul.
Anonymous.
Rockferns. Nicholson.
Romance. Turner.
Rondeau for You. De
Andrade.
Rosalie. Allston.
The Rowan County Crew
(Tolliver-Martin Feud
Song). *Anonymous.*
Ruth. Murray.
Sacred Formula to Attract
Affection. *Anonymous.*
The Sailor and His Bride.
Anonymous.
Salt. Gibbon.
The Salutation of the Blessed
Virgin. Byrom.
Satire. Donne.
Saul. Heavysege.
Saul. Rosenberg.
Sea Dirge. Archias.
The Seafarer. *Anonymous.*
The Seasons. Thomson.
A Second Epitaph.
Anonymous.
Seeing. Donaghy.
Segovia and Madrid. Cooke.
Self-Dependence. Arnold.
Servant Girl and Grocer's
Boy. Kilmer.
Set Down, Servant.
Anonymous.
The Seven Old Men.
Baudelaire.
The Seven Wonders of
England. Sidney.
Shadows. Yehoash.
Shalom. Levertov.
She. Gippius.
The Sheep-Herder's Lament.
Chapman.
Shine on Me, Secret Splendor.
Markham.
A Short Prayer to Mary.
Anonymous.

Silex Scintillans. Vaughan.
The Singer in the Prison.
Whitman.
Singing My Doubts Away.
Anonymous.
Skyscaper. Sandburg.
A Soldier: His Prayer.
Kersh.
Solon's Song. D"Urfey.
The Song Against Songs.
Chesterton.
Song for Dov Shamir. Abse.
Song from "Chartivel."
Marie de France.
Song: "O fair! O sweet! when
I do look on thee."
Sidney.
Song of Degrees. Auster.
Song of the Forest Trees.
Anonymous.
Song: "Oh! that we two were
Maying." Kingsley.
Song Set by Philip Rosseter:
"And would you see my
mistress' face?"
Anonymous.
Song Set by Philip Rosseter:
"What is a day.."
Anonymous.
Sonnet: "I envy not Endymion
now no more." Stirling.
Sonnet XXIV. Alabaster.
Sonnet: "Blest Spirit of Calm
that dwellest in these
woods!" Sangster.
Sonnets from the Portuguese,
XXI. Browning.
Sonnets from the Portuguese,
XXXII. Browning.
Sonnets from the Portuguese,
XLIV. Browning.
Sonnets to Miranda.
Watson.
Sops of Light. Shove.
Soul and Sense. Kimball.
The Soul and the Body.
Davies.
Soul-Light. Rossetti.
The Soul of Lincoln. Piety.
The Soul of the World.
Crosby.
The Soul, Reaching, Throwing
Out for Love. Whitman.
The Soul's Desire. Hull.
The Soul's Expression.
Browning.
The Soul's Garment.
Newcastre.
Souls. Gifford.
Souvenir. Musset.
Spirit Song. *Anonymous.*
A Sprig of Rosemary.
Lowell.
Stanzas. Bronte.
Star Journey. Madgett.
Still, O LORD, for Thee I
Tarry. Wesley.
The Stranger's Song. Hardy.
The Strayed Reveller.
Arnold.
Street Kid. Niatum.
The Stricken South to the
North. Hayne.
Studies at Delhi. Lyall.
Suave Mari Magno.
Lucretius (Titus Lucretitus
Carus).
Summons. Ficke.
The Sun Now Risen. Beissel.
The Swan. Gosse.
Taedium Vitae. Wilde.

The Tailor That Came from
Mayo. McCarthy.
Teach Us to Mark This, God.
Werfel.
Tecumseh. Mair.
Tempted. Sill.
Thalassius. Swinburne.
Thalatta! Thalatta! Brown.
A Thankful Acknowledgment
of God's Providence.
Cotton.
There Is No Vacancy.
Scarbrough.
There's a Light upon the
Mountains. Burton.
There Was One I Met upon
the Road. Crane.
These Two. Schwartz.
The Third Century.
Traherne.
This dirty little heart.
Dickinson.
This Night Sees Ireland
Desolate. MacMarcuis.
This World Is Not
Conclusion. Dickinson.
Those Not Elect. Adams.
The Three Enemies.
Rossetti.
The Three Silences of
Molinos. Longfellow.
Through Willing Heart and
Helping Hand. Hosmer.
The Tide of Faith. Eliot.
Time-Servers. Halevi.
To a Linnet in a Cage.
Ledwidge.
To a Little Girl. Eden.
To a Little Girl. Kobbe.
To a Poet a Thousand Years
Hence. Flecker.
To a Pretty Girl. Zangwill.
To a Wasp Caught in the
Storm Sash... Cooley.
To a Wood-Violet. Tabb.
To Borglum's Seated Statue of
Abraham Lincoln. Jordan.
To Midnight. *Anonymous.*
To Music: A Song. Herrick.
To My Excellent Lucasia, on
Our Friendship. Philips.
To My Mistress in Absence.
Carew.
To My Mother. Poe.
To Saint Margaret.
Constable.
To Sleep. Keats.
To the University of
Cambridge, in New-
England. Wheatley.
To—-, with an Ivory Hand-
Glass. Douglas.
Toast. Horne.
Tom Bowling. Dibdin.
Tombstone Epitaphs.
Anonymous.
The Tongue. Strong.
The Trial. Longfellow.
A Tribute to Dante.
Boccaccio.
A Tryst. Moulton.
Twelve P.M. Howells.
The Twelve Properties or
Conditions of a Lover.
More.
Twenty-One Love Poems.
Rich.
Twilight. Masefield.
Twilight Song. Hunter-
Duvar.
The Two Rabbins. Whittier.
Two Temples. Hall.

The Uncelestial City (excerpt).
Wolfe.
The Unforeseen. Nale
Roxlo.
The Unquiet Grave.
Anonymous.
Upon Castara's Absence.
Habington.
Valentine. Summers.
Variations of Greek Themes.
Robinson.
Variations on a Late October
Day. Mosby.
Vast Light. Eberhart.
Villiers de L'Isle-Adam.
Huxley.
The Violin's Complaint.
Thayer.
The Virgin Mother (excerpt).
Lawrence.
The Vision of Piers Plowman.
Langland.
The Vision of Sir Launfal.
Lowell.
Volpone. Jonson.
The Waiting Harp. Becquer.
The Wakening. *Anonymous.*
The Wander-Lovers. Hovey.
Wanderers. Clark.
The Washer-Woman.
Bohanan.
What Guardian Counsels?
March.
What Have We Done Today?
Waterman.
What Is an Epigram?
Coleridge.
What the Sonnet Is.
Hamilton.
When I Would Image.
Meredith.
Whispers of Heavenly Death.
Whitman.
Who? Jaffe.
Who'll Be a Witness for My
Lord? *Anonymous.*
Wild Eden. Woodberry.
The Wild Mustard River.
Anonymous.
William and Helen. Scott.
Wind and Lyre. Markham.
The Wine Cup. Meleager.
A Winter Hymn–to the Snow.
Jones.
Winter's Dregs. Bowering.
Winter Westerlies. Devaney.
The Wisdom of Insecurity.
Eberhart.
With Wordsworth at Rydal.
Fields
Within These Doors
Assembled Now. Holden.
The Woman at the Washtub.
Daley.
Worship. Lord
Writ on the Eve of My 32nd
Birthday. Corso.
Written Forty Miles South of
a Spreading City. Bly.
Written in a Little Lady's
Little Album. Faber.
Young Edwin in the Lowlands
Low (B vers.).
Anonymous.
Young Love. Massey.
The Young Woman of Beare.
Clarke.
Your Passing, Fleet Passing.
Eliyia.
The Zeal of Jehu. Newman.

Sound (ing) (s)
3rd Migration, Third Series.
Henderson.
Ancient Lullaby. Griffin.
The Ascension. Beaumont.
Aside. Dugan.
Australian Transcripts, V:
Mid-Noon in January.
Sharp.
Balalaika. Dubie.
Ballad in Blonde Hair
Foretold. Bagg.
Ballad of Faith. Williams.
Before Good-Bye. Wolny.
Bethou Me, Said Sparrow.
Stevens.
Betrothed. Bogan.
Black Jess. Dufault.
Bloom Street. McCabe.
Boudoir Lament. Yu Hsuan-
chi.
The Brain–Is Wider than the
Sky. Dickinson.
The Brut. Layamon.
By Night. Francis.
The Charms of Nature.
Warton.
Childe Harold's Pilgrimage:
Canto III, XXI. Byron.
City Trees. Millay.
The Coming of the Plague.
Kees.
Compromise. McKinney.
Confrontions of March.
Dillow.
Daily the Drum. Wilkinson.
Dawn on the Headland.
Watson.
The Day You Are Born.
Song.
The Dead Eagle. Campbell.
The Deep Dark Night.
Tennyson.
The deer on pine mountain.
Onakatomi Yoshinobu.
Deja Vu. Mulligan.
Dream. Dobyns.
Ducks. Harvey.
Epithalamium. Sitwell.
Evening Song. Cheney.
Every Christian Born of God.
Anonymous.
The Executive's Death. Bly.
Faint Music. De La Mare.
The First Year (excerpt).
Scovell.
For Inspiration.
Michelangelo.
A Girl's Song. Hinkson.
Glyph. *Anonymous.*
The Gully. Maurice.
Helen Grown Old. Lewis.
Hmmmm, 8. Scalapino.
Honestly I wish I were dead!
Sappho.
Hunger. Stone.
The Hunter's Song.
"Cornwall.
I Hear the Wave.
Anonymous.
The Idea of Order at Key
West. Stevens.
In the Children's Hospital.
""MacDiarmid.
It's Over a(See Just.
Cummings.
Jerusalem. Blake.
The Jungle. Dudek.
King Hart: Hart's Castle.
Douglas.
Knowledge. Bogan.

Late, Passing Prairie Farm.
Stafford.
Late Winter. McAuley(
The Letters. Tennyson.
Limerick: "There was a frank
lady of Dedham." "Z.
Loch Coruisk (Skye). Sharp.
Lost Letter to James Wright,
with Thanks for a Map of
Fano. Ruark.
A May Sunday. Irwin.
Mid-Country Blow.
Roethke.
Modern Love, XVI.
Meredith.
A Mystic as Soldier.
Sassoon.
The Names. Edmond.
New Music. Harwood.
Not for That City. Mew.
November. Fisher.
An Old Inmate. Mackenzie.
On the Wing. Rossetti.
Pilgrimage. Duggan.
The Pleasures of Merely
Circulating. Stevens.
The Poems of Our Climate.
Stevens.
Poetry is Death Cast Out.
Clouts.
A Private. Thomas.
"Rake" Windermere.
Pounds.
Rebirth. Machado.
The Red Dog. Jensen.
The Rescued Year. Stafford.
Robin. Allen.
The Rose. Roethke.
Rushing. Young Bear.
Sacred Poetry. Wilson.
Sects. Gilbert.
Shelly Beach. Koch.
Ships That Pass in the Night.
Dunbar.
Sleep and Poetry. Keats.
Snow. Wilkins.
Somewhere Down below Me
Is a Street. Maloney.
Sonnet: "I saw magic on a
green country road."
Hartnett.
Sonnets. Tuckerman.
The Sounds Begin Again.
Brutus.
The Spleen. Green.
A Spring Morning. Clare.
Starting at Dawn. Sun Yun-
feng.
The Stripper. Probst.
The Testament of Beauty.
Bridges.
This Lime-Tree Bower My
Prison. Coleridge.
To Be Sung on the Water.
Bogan.
To the Bell-Ringer. Farren.
To the Muses. Blake.
To the Wife of a Sick Friend.
Millay.
The Trackless Deeps.
Shelley.
Transfigured Life. Rossetti.
Triphammer Bridge.
Ammons.
Two Musics. MacCaig.
The Two Selves. Avison.
Two Sonnets. Ashbery.
Umbilical. Merriam.
Untitled. Crowne.
The Voices. Pommy-Vega.
Voices of the Air. Mansfield.

The Wandering One Makes
Music. Aldis.
Water Without Sound.
Tussman.
Whales. Bates.
The White Window.
Stephens.
Why Do You Write about
Russia? Simpson.
Woman. Patmore.
Your Songs. Bennett.
Soundless
Cat on the Porch at Dusk.
Harriman.
Dirge. Troupe.
Soup
13 Ways of Eradicating
Blackbirds (parody).
DeFoe.
African in Louisiana. Kyei.
A Dreamed Realization.
Corso.
Haiku: "Winter rain at
night..." Wright.
Limerick: "There was a young
lady from Cork." Nash.
Queen Elizabeth.
Anonymous.
The Soup of Venus. Tate.
Soup Song. Sugar.
Turtle Soup. "Carroll.
Vers de Societe (parody).
Traill.
Sour
Blackberry Winter. Huggins.
First Hymn. Gill.
Lancashire Born.
Anonymous.
Mumps. Roberts.
My Grandfather Dying.
Kooser.
Poietes Apoietes. Coleridge.
The Villagers and Death.
Graves.
When the Bells Justle in the
Tower. Housman.
Who'd Be a Hero (Fictional)?
Bishop.
Winter Coming On. Bell.
Source (s)
Against Winter. Feinstein.
April, Glengarry. Coxon.
The Beauty of the Friend It
Was That Taught Me.
Makhfi.
A Chinaman's Chance.
Chin.
The Clovers. Garrigue.
History of My Heart.
Pinsky.
In October.... Hamburger.
In Praise of Wisdom. Ibn
Gabirol.
The Progress of Poesy.
Gray.
The Sign of the Cross.
Newman.
Soldier's Song. Campbell.
Who? Jaffe.
Xantippe. Levy.
South (ern) (ward)
Antwerp Musee des Beaux-
Arts. Ross.
Anzac Cove. Gellert.
Approach of Winter.
Thomson.
A Ballad of John Silver.
Masefield.
Beyond Kerguelen. Kendall.
Blow Ye Winds Westerly.
Anonymous.

Chou and the South.
  Confucius.
Christ in Alabama. Hughes.
Corn-Grinding Song.
  Anonymous.
Distant View. Krige.
Down South on the Rio
  Grande. *Anonymous.*
Down the Mississippi.
  Fletcher.
Fanny. Aldrich.
The Fight at Sumter.
  Anonymous.
The Gar. Bell.
Garden at Heidelberg.
  Landor.
Going to the North.
  Wygodski.
Grasse: The Olive Trees.
  Wilbur.
The Great Scarf of Birds.
  Updike.
Holy-Cross Day. Browning.
Indigo Pete's J. B. Kibbs.
Joined the Blues. Rooney.
Killer Diller. Minnie.
The Lost Shipmate. Roberts.
The Man of the North
  Countrie. McGee.
Moriturus. Millay.
Morning at Arnheim. Smith.
Mosby at Hamilton. Cawein.
My Horses. Jaszi.
My Mouth Is Very Quiet.
  Villa.
The North and the South.
  Browning.
P.S. Lowell
Sois Sage O Ma Douleur.
  Baudelaire.
Something in Common.
  Church.
Song: "From whence cometh
  song?–". Roethke.
Song of the Border. Norris.
Song of the Fishes.
  Anonymous.
South Wind. Yonathan.
The Spanish Needle.
  McKay.
Sumter. Stedman.
Tennesse Crickets. Outlaw.
Tired as I Can Be. Jackson.
Two Voices. Blunden.
The Vision of Lazarus
  (excerpt). Johnson.
We Are Building a Strong
  Union. *Anonymous.*
You Ask Me, Why, Tho' Ill
  at Ease. Tennyson.
South Africa
Echo of Mandela. Mandela.
Protea. Mattera.
South Sea
A Reply to an Imitation of
  the Second Ode....of
  Horace. Bentley.
The South. Wang Chien.
Verses. Bentley.
Southern Cross
On a Monument to Marti.
  Roberts.
On a Sea-Grape Leaf.
  Chapin.
Southwest
The Monarche: After the
  Flood. Lindsay.
Southwind
Eating Bamboo-Shoots. Po
  Chu-i.
He's Coming. Van Doren.
Heart. Black.

The Little Cradle Rocks
  Tonight in Glory.
  Anonymous.
Man Thinking about Woman.
  Lee.
The Recantation. Tibullus.
Souvenir (s)
A Ballad of Remembrance.
  Hayden.
From Colony to Nation.
  Layton.
From the Domain of
  Arnheim. Morgan.
They Part. Parker.
Sovereign (s)
Above the Stable. Duffy.
The Boy Serving at Table.
  Lydgate.
Gilderoy. Anonymous.
Give Beauty All Her Right.
  Campion.
Leonardo Da Vinci's.
  Moore.
The Lover Rejoiceth the
  Enjoying of His Love.
  Wyatt.
The Majesty of God.
  Sternhold.
Off Womanheid Ane Flour
  Delice. *Anonymous.*
The Saga of Gisli (excerpt).
  Anonymous.
Shadows. Claudel.
Sovereign Queen. Padeshah
  Khatun.
The Spinning Girl.
  Alterman.
Wellington. Disraeli.
What Are Outward Forms.
  Bickerstaffe.
Soviet (s)
Building Society Blues.
  Roughton.
Meadowland. *Anonymous.*
Sow (ed) (er) (ing) (s)
Aeglamour's Lament.
  Jonson.
Afternoon in a Tree. Maris
  Stella.
Basia. Campion.
The Bird and the Tree.
  Torrence.
A Black Man Talks of
  Reaping. Bontemps.
The Boar of Badenoch and
  the Sow of Atholl.
  Mitchison.
Ezekiel, You and Me (with
  music). *Anonymous.*
Fighter. Zimunya.
God and the Strong Ones.
  Widdemer.
A Good Creed. *Anonymous.*
He Singeth a Hymn to Osiris,
  the Lord of Eternity.
  Book of the Dead.
Hell. *Anonymous.*
Lines Written in a Country
  Parson's Orchard. Daiken.
Nightmare, with Angels.
  Benét.
A Part of an Ode. Jonson.
The River in March.
  Hughes.
Saint Francis and the Sow.
  Kinnell.
Satire upon the Licentious
  Age of Charles II. Butler.
Shanty-Boy and the Farmer's
  Son. *Anonymous.*
Trilby. Du Maurier.

You're Going to Reap Just
  What You Sow.
  Anonymous.
Zeimbekiko. Magowan.
Space (s)
Arriving. Preil.
Aspects. MacCaig.
August 1914. Rosenberg.
A Backwards Journey. Page.
Bathtubs. Lattimore.
Before Sunrise in Winter.
  Sill.
Beware : Do Not Read This
  Poem. Reed.
Bitter Bread. Mandelstam.
Butterflies. Sansom.
Catherine Kinrade. Brown.
Coloratura. Page.
Coming across. Mehri.
Concert. Sward.
Credo (excerpt). Gilder.
Day Twenty-Three.
  Coleman.
Death on the Farm.
  Waterman.
Don Juan. Byron.
The Double Play. Wallace.
The Dragon of Red Lights.
  Swickard.
Drawings by Children.
  Mueller.
East Coast–Canada.
  Brewster.
The Egoist Dead. Brewster.
For Kinte. La Grone.
The Ghost of the Cargo Boat.
  Neruda.
Glitter of Pebbles. Moraes.
The Green Train. Rieu.
Hand. Roditi.
The Hanging of the Crane.
  Longfellow.
Here Lies a Lady. Ransom.
High Up on Suilven.
  MacCaig.
I Am the Beginning.
  Shembe.
The Idea of Ancestry.
  Knight.
If I Had Ridden Horses.
  Maynard.
In Memoriam A.H.H.,
  CXXV. Tennyson.
In the Planetarium. Fox.
The Jungle. Dudek.
The Letter. Tatham.
Letter from Pretoria Central
  Prison. Nortje.
Life's Testament.
  Baylebridge.
Limerick: "The ladies
  inhabiting Venus."
  Graham.
The Man Awakened by a
  Song Above His Roof.
  Transtromer.
Megalometropolitan Carnival
  (excerpt). Gascoyne.
Metonymy as an Approach to
  a Real World. Bronk.
Milton. Blake.
Muscae Volitantes. Horne.
My Way Is in the Sand
  Flowing. Beckett.
The Naked Land. Patchen.
Nappy Edges (A Cross
  Country Sojourn). Shange.
New York in the Spring.
  Budbill.
Not for Its Own Sake...
  Littlefield.
Nude. Halpern.

Ode to Arnold Schoenberg.
  Tomlinson.
On a Portrait of Columbus.
  Woodberry.
One, Two, Three. Albert.
Our Lives. Scott.
Panther and Peacock.
  Harwood.
Parachute. Snaith.
Party. Carrier.
Plenty. Jones.
Poem about People. Pinsky.
Poem: "Some who are
  uncertain compel me."
  Lange.
Poplar. Benn.
Pre-Existence. Hayne.
Relativity. Millay.
Sleeping on the Wing.
  O'Hara.
Sometimes I Go to Camarillo
  & Sit in the Lounge. Lyle.
Song Set by Robert Jones:
  "Life is a poet's fable."
  Anonymous.
Songs Before Sunrise: Prelude.
  Swinburne.
Sonnet of Brotherhood.
  Mason.
Speak Like Rain. Metz.
Sundays. Rugo.
The Swallows. Agathias.
Systole and Diastole. Aiken.
Taking Long Views.
  Kendall.
To George Barker.
  Derwood.
To My Honoured Patron
  Humphrey Davie...
  Tompson.
Too Many Miles of Sunlight
  between Us. Myers.
Twilit Revelation. Adams.
Victory in Defeat.
  Markham.
Vision. Devaney.
Ward Two. Webb.
A Wish for Waving Goodbye.
  Hill.
Spade (s)
Bereaved of All, I Went
  Abroad. Dickinson.
Caesar Remembers.
  Seymour.
The Devil's Dictionary: Body-
  Snatcher. Bierce.
Lemonade. *Anonymous.*
Life's a Game. *Anonymous.*
Peat Bog Soldiers.
  Anonymous.
Professor Noctutus.
  Macdonald.
Song: "A woman's face is full
  of wiles." Gifford.
A Spade Is Just a Spade.
  Hawkins.
Summer Beach. Cornford.
The Welsh Marches.
  Housman.
Why Tomas Cam Was
  Grumpy. Stephens.
Spain
Aladdin. Lowell.
The Andalusian Sereno.
  Saltus.
A Ballad to Queen Elizabeth.
  Dobson.
The Carpenter's Wife (The
  Daemon Lover).
  Anonymous.
Eisenhower's Visit to Franco,
  1959. Wright.

Epigram: "With favour and fortune fastidiously blest." Swift.
An Excellent New Song Called "Mat's Peace," or The Downfall of Trade. Mainwaring.
Iberia. Kirschenbaum.
Lines to Garcia Lorca. Jones.
Mene, Mene, Tekel, Upharsin. Cawein.
Miss Lavender. Stallworthy.
Neither This Nor That. Palés Matos.
A New Ballad. *Anonymous.*
Phantoms All. Spofford.
Ponce de Leon: A Morning Walk. Young.
Robert's Rules of Order. Peterson.
The Rollicking Mastodon. Macy.
Rounding the Horn. *Anonymous.*
Skirt Dance. Reed.
There Was a Monkey. *Anonymous.*
To Aunt Rose. Ginsberg.

Span
Clocks. Ginsberg.
Feel Like a Bird. Swenson.
Good Counsel. James I King of Scotland.
Granite and Steel. Moore.
Man. Wolfe.
On Startling Some Pigeons. Turner.
On the Death of Mistress Mary Prideaux. Strode.
The Royal Stag. ""MacDiarmid.
The Temple. Po Chu-i.
Three Score and Ten. *Anonymous.*

Spangle (s)
Birdsong. Singer.
Horses. MacNeice.
The Man in the Dress Suit. Wolfe.
Song of Texas. Hosmer.
A Tryptych for Jan Bockelson. Simon.

Spaniel
Epigram: "With favour and fortune fastidiously blest." Swift.
Polly. Gay.

Spank (ed)
Limerick: "A young lady of fair Mytilene." *Anonymous.*
My Heart Belongs to Daddy. Porter.
There Was a Little Girl. Longfellow.
When a Feller's Itchin' to Be Spanked. Dunbar.

Spare (d) (s)
The Aesthete to the Rose (parody). *Anonymous.*
The Auld Man's Mear's Dead. Birnie.
The Battel of the Summer-Islands. Waller.
Boys. Letts.
Death Is Awful. Hall, Vera.
Epigram: "Thy eyes and eyebrows I could spare." *Anonymous.*
Hickory Stick Hierarchy. Selle.

On Leander's Swimming over the Hellespont to Hero. Warton, Jr..
Oxford. Douglas.
Please Tell Me Just the Fabuli. Silverstein.
Rosalynde. Lodge.
Songs Set by Thomas Morley: "Sing we and chant it." *Anonymous.*
Subject. Ponsot.
Theodosia Burr. Terrell.
To Mother Fairie. Cary.
The "Word" of a Wolf Encircled by the Hunt. Sandag.

Spark (s)
Behind the Stove. Hearst.
Camera. Kooser.
Come Up, Methuselah. Day-Lewis.
Death of a Cat. Schevill.
Elegy on Thomas Hood (parody). Fagg.
Femme et Chatte. Verlaine.
The Fire. Bell.
For Eros II. Wurdemann.
The Forge. Gogarty.
In the Shelter. Day Lewis.
The Gathering. Thorpe.
He Renounceth All the Effects of Love. Vaux.
The Incentive. Cleghorn.
January. Gibson.
Our Children's Children Will Marvel. Ehrenburg.
The Recruit. Chambers.
Reuben Pantier. Masters.
Second Horn. Di Piero.
Sonnet II: "O handsome chestnut eyes, evasive gaze." Labe.
The Sons of Our Sons. Ehrenburg.
Static. Sutter.
Stud Groom. Glassco.
Upon Prue, His Maid. Herrick.
When Youth Had Fled. Surrey.

Sparkle (d)
Audley Court. Tennyson.
The Cloud of Unknowing. Murray.
Dans l'Allee. Verlaine.
A Frosty Morning. Davidson.
A Lady. Lowell.
The Museum of the Second Creation. McPherson.

Sparrow (s)
Anathema of Cats. Skelton.
The Augsburg Adoration. Jarrell.
The Birds. Posner.
The Chaste Arabian Bird. Rochester.
Church of the Holy Innocents, Dunedin. Hyde.
Deities and Beasts. Updike.
Did you Ever Hear an English Sparrow Sing? Johnston.
The Escape. Gurney.
Georgian Spring. Campbell.
Ghostly Story. Acorn.
The Last Flight of the Great Wallenda. Hyett.
Old and New. *Anonymous.*
Paul. Wright.
Per Iter Tenebricosum. Gogarty

Powwow Remnants. Blockcolski.
Sagesse. Doolittle.
Says Robin to Jenny, "If you will be mine.". *Anonymous.*
Sent to Wen T'ing-Yun on a Winter Night. Yu Hsuan-chi.
Shoreham: Twilight Time. Palmer.
The Sparrow's Dirge. Skelton.
Thaw in the City. Lipsitz.
The Vacant Farm House. De La Mare.
A White-Throat Sings. Eaton.

Spars
Fair Weather. Parker.
Ships in Harbour. Morton.

Sparta (n)
On Hurricane Jackson. Dugan.
On the Army of Spartans Who Died at Thermopylai. *Anonymous.*

Spasm
Adam on His Way Home. Pack.

Spastic
Oil and Blood. Kizer.
Phraseology. Cortez.

Spat
Recrimination. Wilcox.
Tuesday. Landau.

Spawn (ing)
After the Surprising Conversions. Lowell.
Coming Out. Lapidus.
The Fisherman. Stuart.

Speak (ing) (s) (spake) (spoke)
Absent Creation. Savage.
Archaic Apollo. Plomer.
All Legendary Obstacles. Montague.
Almighty Lord, with One Accord. Stryker.
Amoretti, III. Spenser.
Another of the Same. Ralegh.
April. Valentine.
As I Am My Father's. Drachler.
The Bad Apple. Bennett.
Ballad of Don Juan Tenorio and the Statue of the Comendador. Campbell.
The Beak. Smither.
Beneath the Mound. Smith.
Beverly Hills, Chicago. Brooks.
The Birth. Dobson.
The Bustan. Sa'di.
But Choose. Holmes.
The Bystander. Dobson.
The Card-Dealer. Rossetti.
Cartoon. Simmerman.
A Celebration of Charis. Jonson.
The Celestial City (Excerpt). Wolfe.
Chekhov Comes to Mind at Harvard. Freeman.
The Clearing. Everwine.
The Coastwise Lights. Kipling.
The Condition. Carmi.
The Constant Bridegrooms. Patchen.
The Contrast. Cone.
A Contempt for Dylan Thomas. Watson.

Dear Maiden. Heine.
The Deserter. Smith.
Despair. Levertov.
Diana. Constable.
Distrust. Herrick.
Doubt. Deland.
Eastward I Stand, Mercies I Beg. *Anonymous.*
Effort at Speech between Two People. Rukeyser.
Eight Volunteers. Bailey.
Elegy for a Countryman. Fallon.
Epitaph for the Poet V. Ficke.
Epithalamium. Turner.
The Flowering Urn. Riding.
For One Who Died Young. Hays.
From the Righteous Man Even the Wild Beasts Run away. Bromwich.
Games. McPherson.
Get Up and Bar the Door. *Anonymous.*
Ghosts. Reid.
The "Gloria Patri." Heywood.
The Green Lake. Roberts.
Gull Lake Reunion. Ivie.
A Handful of Dust. Oppenheim.
Hero and Leander. Marlowe.
How to Write a Letter. Turner.
A Hymn of Form. Bottomley.
I Wage Not Any Feud with Death. Tennyson.
If She Be Made of White and Red. Horne.
The Iliad. Homer.
In Memoriam A.H.H., XIX. Tennyson.
In Memoriam A.H.H., LXXXII. Tennyson.
Introversion. Underhill.
It Was an April Morning. Wordsworth.
Juniper. Francis.
A Letter. Mu'tamid.
Madeleine in Church (excerpt). Mew.
Meditation on a Bone. Hope.
The Message. Heine.
The Minstrel's Song. Chatterton.
The Mixer. MacNeice.
Mother. Taylor.
Mourn Not the Dead. Chaplin.
Mrs. Golightly. Hall.
My Love's Guardian Angel. Barnes.
Mynstrelles Songe. Chatterton.
The Names of the Humble. Murray.
Nani. Rios.
Neighbour. Hervey.
Next to of Course God America I. Cummings.
The Night-Blooming Cereus. Hayden.
Night on Clinton. Mezey.
O, Thou Eternal One! Derzhavin.
Oh, Stop Being Thankful All Over the Place. Nash.
On a Cast from an Antique. Pellew.

On Buying a Dog. Klauber.
Paradise Lost. Milton.
Partings. Jewsbury.
Paul's Wife. Frost.
Perugia. Burr.
The Photograph of Myself.
  Anderson.
Picture of Seneca Dying in a
  Bath. Prior.
Poet. Shapiro.
Post Mortem. Munby.
The Precept of Silence.
  Johnson.
Precious Moments.
  Sandburg.
Protagonist. Henrich.
Quatrain: "I knew like a song
  your vows weren't strong."
  Mahsati.
The Quiet Hour. Bowman.
Rain Forest. Smith.
Revelation. Frost.
Revenge. Nugent.
The Robin. Daniel.
The Rusted Chain. Ben
  Yeshaq.
Saffold's Cures. Saffold.
Salt Man. West.
The Seaman's Compass.
  Anonymous.
She listen'd like a cushat
  dove. Rossetti.
Silence. Towne.
Sir Roland; a Fragment.
  Merry.
Smile, Death. Mew.
Soliloquy: South Africa.
  Nortje.
Sonnet: To Certain Ladies.
  Dante Alighieri.
Speak Out for Jesus.
  Anonymous.
The Speed of Darkness.
  Rukeyser.
Still, O LORD, for Thee I
  Tarry. Wesley.
(The Syl La Ble Speaks En
  Erg y/Sound). Sanchez.
Three Epigrams.
  Cunningham.
To Azrael. Baudelaire.
To His Lovely Mistresses.
  Herrick.
To His Mistress Objecting to
  Him Neither Toying or
  Talking. Herrick.
To My Love. Saxe.
To Sally. Adams.
To the Rt. Hon. the Lady C.
  Tufton. Winchilsea.
To the Soul. Collop.
To You. Whitman.
The Toys Talk of the World.
  Pyle.
The Tryst after Death.
  Anonymous.
Two Women with Mangoes.
  Cramer.
Upon Ben Johnson. Herrick.
The Vestal Virgin. Llwyd.
Voting Machine. Nathan.
Voyager's Song. Wood.
Warriors. Hogan.
What Does a Man Think
  About. Holmes.
What Shame Forbids to
  Speak. Herrick.
What Wild Dawns There
  Were. Levertov.
When Geometric Diagrams...
  "Novalis" (George

Friedrich Philipp von
  Hardenerg).
Winds of Africa. Obi.
Winter Twilight. Schiff.
The Woman Poet. Kolmar.
Yourself. Very.
Zen Buddhism and
  Psychoanalysis
  Psychoanalysis and Zen
  Buddhism. MacLow.

Spear (s)
Autobiography: Hollywood.
  Reznikoff.
Bear Hunting. Aua.
Christ Is Crucified Anew.
  Moreland.
A Classic Ode. Loomis.
Corruption. Simoko.
Cressid. Perry.
A Dead Soldier.
  Montgomery.
Essay on Psychiatrists.
  Pinsky.
The Garden. Solomon.
Historical Incidents. Day.
The Iliad. Homer.
The Lady of the Lake. Scott.
Marmion. Scott.
Our Love Was a Grim
  Citadel. Mason.
Proud Hollyhock. Buller.
A Skilful Spearman!
  Anonymous.
The Storming of Stony Point.
  Guiterman.
To a Contemporary
  Bunkshooter. Sandburg.
The Wind Sprang up at Four
  O'Clock. Eliot.

Spearmint
Does the Spearmint Lose Its
  Flavor on the Bedpost
  Overnight? Rose.

Special
Gifts. Harris.
Marriage: To K. Hall.
Portrait of a Jew Old Country
  Style. Rothenberg.
The Sleeper. Field.
There Was a Knight and He
  Was Young. *Anonymous.*

Specialist (s)
April Inventory. Snodgrass.
To the Heart. Rozewicz.

Species
The Female of the Species.
  Kipling.
How to Conceive Boys.
  Quillet.
Letter to Ben, 1972. Durcan.
Ode to Pornography.
  Anderson.

Spectacle (s)
A Classic Idyll. Huss.
The Faerie Queene. Spenser.
The Life and Lucubrations of
  Crispinus Scriblerus
  (excerpt). Woodhouse.
Love. Moore.

Spectral
An Infantryman. Blunden.
Inscription. Hayes.
Jezreel. Hardy.
The Rooftree. Tate.

Spectre
Andrew M'Crie. Murray.
One Need Not Be a
  Chamber-To Be Haunted.
  Dickinson.

Spectrum
The African Affair. Wright.
To a Chameleon. Moore.

Speculate
Financial Wisdom.
  Anonymous.
January 1st. Sexton.
One blessing had I.
  Dickinson.

Speech (es)
At Carmel Highlands.
  Lewis.
Belgravia. Guest.
Blessed Are Those Who Sow
  and Do Not Reap. Ben-
  Yitzhak.
Cesar Franck. Auslander.
The Chinese Graves in
  Beechworth Cemetery.
  Mead.
Cripples. Reed.
Dew. Reznikoff.
Emigration. Barrows.
England's Difficulty.
  Heaney.
Ghost. Bynner.
Historical Museum,
  Manitoulin Island.
  Mueller.
I Love a Flower. Nichols.
I'r hen Iaith A'i Chanedon
  (To the Old Tongue and its
  Songs). Dowding.
The Imprisoned. Fitzgerald.
Imprisoned. Tietjens.
Inflation. Hartman.
The Irish Schoolmaster
  (parody). Hood.
King of the Belgians. Smith.
Lacrimae Musarum. Watson.
Lara. Byron.
The Maltworm's Madrigal.
  Dobson.
The Offended. Hebert.
Old Age. Al-Aswad.
On J. W. Ward. Rogers.
The Orator's Epitaph.
  Brougham.
Paterson. Williams.
Ruins under the Stars.
  Kinnell.
Sent to Him, as He
  Whisper'd. Jacob.
Shakespeare. Arnold.
The Shapes of Death.
  Spender.
Silence Spoke with Your
  Voice. Goodman.
Sleep and His Brother Death.
  Hayne.
Sonnet: He Is Past All Help.
  Angiolieri.
Spikenard. Housman.
Three Gates. Day.
To the Memory of Yale
  College. Putnam.
To the Red Lory. Neilson.
The Yule Log. Hayne.

Speechless
After Picking Rosehips.
  Elliott.
Day after Day. Tagore.
A Death in the Desert.
  Tomlinson.
Epitaph on the Earl of
  Strafford. Cleveland.
The House of Life. Rossetti.
Tho We All Speak. Ort.

Speed (ing) (s) (sped)
Against Witches.
  Anonymous.
Anno 1829. Heine.
Asolando. Browning.
Ballade of the Old-Time
  Engine. Vines.

Canzo: "Can l'erba fresch'elh
  folha par." Bernard de
  Ventadour
Dawn on the Headland.
  Watson.
Dreaming America. Oates.
Envoy. Johnson.
The Fishermen. Whittier.
The Green Knight's Farewell
  to Fancy. Gascoigne.
The Harvest of Time.
  Pulsifer.
The Hope of the World.
  Watson.
London Lickpenny. Lydgate.
The Maids Conjuring Book.
  Anonymous.
The Merchant of Venice.
  Shakespeare.
Merritt Parkway. Levertov.
Ode: "An idea of justice may
  be precious." O'Hara.
Park Avenue. Fitzgerald.
Pony Girl. Moreland.
Prometheus Unbound.
  Shelley.
Rising in the Morning.
  Rhodes.
River Rhyme. Williams.
Sir Francis Drake; or Eighty-
  Eight. *Anonymous.*
Sonnets. Tuckerman.
Sonnets, VI: "Sweet Corrall
  lips, where Nature's
  treasure lies." Barnfield.
Street Song. Gunn.
This Day. Raab.
Vergidemiarum: Prologue: "I
  first adventure, with
  foolhardy might."
  Barnfield.
Wellington. Disraeli.
The Wheel. Sully-
  Prudhomme.

Speedometer
1948 Plymouth Abandoned on
  the Ice. Meissner.

Spell (s)
Amanda Is Shod. Kumin.
Between Leaps. Leithauser.
Cheers. Merriam.
Claud Halcro's Invocation.
  Scott.
The Crystal. Coan.
Egyptian Hieroglyphics.
  Anonymous.
Fable. Aiken.
From a Beggarman's Song.
  Anonymous.
Government Injunction.
  Miles.
He Could Have Found His
  Way. Dalziel.
The Herald Crane. Garland.
Hermann Ludwig Ferdinand
  von Helmholtz. Meinke.
I Find My Love Fishing.
  Anonymous.
In Memory of My Mother.
  Kavanagh.
Mater Desiderata. Praed.
The Mowing. Roberts.
Peter Bell, the Third.
  Shelley.
Sancta Silvarum. Johnson.
Spraying the Potatoes.
  Kavanagh.
Tacita. Kenyon.
Time Out. Jenkins.
The Waiting Chords.
  Thayer.

When There Is Peace.
Dobson.
Young Girl. Waltner.
Spellbound
Autumn Music. Preil.
Intimates. Lawrence.
Progress Report. Simic.
Spend (ing) (spent)
And Now a Fig for the Lower
House. Cary.
The Animal Store. Field.
Another and the Same.
Rogers.
As I Was Going up Pippen
Hill. *Anonymous.*
A Ballad upon a Wedding:
The Bride. Suckling.
Becky Deem. Leadbelly.
Ding Dong Dollar.
Henderson.
The Diver. Howard.
Early Losses: A Requiem.
Walker.
From Generation to
Generation. Newbolt.
The Grimsby Fisherman.
Anonymous.
Heart Specialist. Lieberman.
House of the Rising Sun.
Anonymous.
Lightning of the Abyss.
Laforgue.
Love Unknown. Crossman.
Monna Innaminata. Rossetti.
Mr. Davis's Experience.
Anonymous.
My Song Is Love Unknown.
Crossman.
New Sea Song. *Anonymous.*
On the Decease of the
Religious and Honourable
Jno Haynes Esqr.... James.
Orlando Furioso. Ariosto.
Pass around Your Bottle.
Anonymous.
Sonnets, CXIX: "What
potions have I drunk of
Siren Tears." Shakespeare.
Spendthrift. Richards.
Two Translatons from Villon.
Synge.
Sperm
Girl in a Black Bikini.
Brown.
Greed. Blazek.
Resurrection. Pack.
Sonnet. Clark.
Whose Scene? Stone.
A Woman's Song. McElroy.
Sphere (s)
Afternoons with Baedeker.
Lancaster.
Alphonso of Castile.
Emerson.
The Amorous War: Time.
Mayne.
The Archangel. Byron.
Back to Base. Joseph.
A Ballad of Heaven.
Davidson.
A Canticle to Apollo.
Herrick.
Eppur Si Muove? Hillyer.
The Hand and Foot. Very.
Invocation. Randolph.
Letters from the Astronomers,
I: Nicholas Copernicus
(1473-1543). Fox.
The Lost Pleiad. Simms
The Lover Consults with
Reason. Carew.

The Mole and the Eagle.
Hale.
Mother Carey's Chicken.
Watts-Dunton.
Night. Symonds.
The Ode on St. Cecilia's Day.
Dryden.
Odes, XII. Hafiz.
On a Tear. Rogers.
Prudence. Emerson.
Satires. Boileau-Despréaux.
Structure of Rime. Duncan.
To a Nightingale.
Drummond.
To Meet, or Otherwise.
Hardy.
The Windmill of Evening.
Reich.
"The world below the brine".
Whitman.
Zophiel: Palace of the
Gnomes. Brooks.
Sphinx (es)
The Egyptian Lotus. Eaton.
Four Legs, Two Legs, Three
Legs. Empson.
The Sexual Life of the Camel.
Anonymous.
Sospetto d'Herode. Crashaw.
Spice (s)
An Elegy for D. H. Lawrence.
Williams.
Limerick: "There was a young
fellow named Dice."
Anonymous.
Of Her Breath. Herrick.
Silex Scintillans. Vaughan.
Spider (s)
Amoretti, XXIII. Spenser.
Amoretti, LXXI. Spenser.
The Detail. Corman.
The Drunkards. Lowry.
For a Dewdrop. Farjeon.
The Gold Nest. Wallace.
High Up on Suilven.
MacCaig.
Ipsey Wipsey. *Anonymous.*
Little City. Horan.
Love. Jammes.
Moving. McFatter.
My Grandfather in Search of
Moonshine. Lyon.
Parson's Pleasure. Higgs.
Pepys Bar, West Forty-Eight
Street, 8 a.m. Sissman.
Re-Forming the Crystal.
Rich.
The Sirens. Lipsitz.
The Spider. Littleton.
The Stone Gentleman.
Reeves.
Tiger Lily. McCord.
Under the Williamsburg
Bridge. Kinnell.
White Spider. Garin.
Spike (s)
City Afternoon. Howes.
Ice Cream. Wild.
Man Is in Pain. Lamantia.
Mike. *Anonymous.*
On First Looking into the
Dark Future. Green.
Sea Owl. Smith.
Spill (ed) (ing)
Any Time, What May Hit
You. Hummer.
Haiku: "The dew of the
rouge-flower." Kaga no
Chiyo.
If. Howells.
Immortality. Reese.

The Journey and Observations
of a Countryman (excerpt).
Hawthorn.
The Man in the Moon.
Mother Goose.
O Thou to Whom the Musical
White Spring. Cummings.
Poppies. Scheele.
"The storms are past, these
clouds are overblown."
Surrey.
Verses. Lowell.
Water Tap. MacCaig.
Wild Geese, Wild Geese,
Ganging to the Sea.
Anonymous.
Spin
The Boar. Kelly.
Buckeye Jim. *Anonymous.*
Lunar Eclipse. Scarbrough.
Miracle Play: The Lament of
Eve. *Anonymous.*
Posterity. Dabydeen.
Song of the Weaving Woman.
Yuan Chen.
Sonnet: "Between my love and
me there runs a thread."
McLeod.
That Beauty I Ador'd Before.
Behn.
Westminster Drollery, 1671.
Behn.
Spine (s)
The Copperhead. Bottoms.
The Little Hunchback.
Riley.
The Patient Is Rallying.
Kees.
Watching Jim Shoulders.
Connellan.
Spinning
Bacchanal. Layton.
The Flight. Haines.
Fragments. Yeats.
Laundromat. McCord.
Leaving Mendota, 1956.
Locke.
Love. Jammes.
Night of Frost in May.
Meredith.
Personal History: For My
Son. Todd.
The Ropewalk. Longfellow.
Wash-Day Wonder.
Faubion.
Spinningwheel
As I Sat at My Spinning-
Wheel. *Anonymous.*
Bess and Her Spinning-Wheel.
Burns.
Sonnet: "My soul surcharged
with grief now loud
complains." Morpurgo.
Spinning in April. Peabody.
Spinster
Family Chronicle. Parlatore.
There Once Was a Wicked
Young Minister. Aiken.
Spire (s)
The Alley. An Imitation of
Spenser. Pope.
The Avon. Jacobs.
Giotto's Tower. Longfellow.
God's Saints. Vaughan.
Power Station. Ramsey.
Secret Parting. Rossetti.
Victoria Market. Brabazon.
Spirit (s) (ual)
The Aeneid. Virgil (Publius
Vergilius Maro).
Aesop at Play. Phaedrus.
After the Seance. Clewell.

Again as Evening's Shadow
Falls. Longfellow.
America. Coxe.
Anatomy of Monotony.
Stevens.
The Appeasement of Demeter.
Meredith.
An Art of Poetry. McAuley.
At Day's End. *Anonymous.*
At Masada. Neufeld.
The Bacchai: The Home of
Aphrodite. Euripides.
Beachy Head (excerpt).
Smith.
The Beacon. Gregor.
The Beggar. Bruner.
The Blue Meridian. Toomer.
Brothers. Johnson.
The Bulwark of Liberty.
Lincoln.
Bury Me In a Free Land.
Harper.
Caelica, XL. Greville.
Canoe. Douglas.
The Canterbury Tales: The
Franklin's Prologue.
Chaucer.
The Cascade. Rickword.
The Chambermaid's Second
Song. Yeats.
Chavez. Sweeney.
Cheerio My Deario.
Marquis.
Childe Rolandine. Smith.
The Chosen Three, on
Mountain Height. Ela.
The Collector. Flynn.
Come, Thou Almighty King.
Wesley.
Correspondences.
Baudelaire.
La Crosse at Ninety Miles an
Hour. Eberhart.
Dam Neck, Virginia.
Eberhart.
Dawn. Scott.
Deaf. Bunner.
Death. Harjo.
The Defence of Night.
Michelangelo.
The Djanggawul Cycle, 182.
Anonymous
Drop Me the Seed.
Masefield.
The Earth. Mann.
Epitaph. *Anonymous.*
Eternal Masculine. Benet.
Ev'ry Time I Feel de Spirit.
Anonymous.
Evening in Tyringham Valley.
Gilder.
An Evil Spirit, Your Beauty
Haunts Me Still. Drayton.
The Execution of Luke
Hutton. *Anonymous.*
Favonius. Church.
The First Kiss. Watts-
Dunton.
First Vision. O'Huiginn.
For Deeper Life. Bates.
Forgotten Island. Hall.
France: An Ode. Coleridge.
The Friar. Peacock.
The Genie. Stanford.
Geography. Dransfield.
The Ghostly Crew.
Anonymous.
The Ghostly Father.
Redgrove.
The God of the Living.
Ellerton.
Golden Lines. Nerval.

Grace after Dinner.   Burns.
Great God, How Frail a
   Thing Is Man.   Byles.
Grey Woman.   Cardiff.
Hanging Scroll.   Stern.
He Walketh by Day.   Book
   of the Dead.
Her, A Statue.   Stoddart.
Her Fair Inflaming Eyes.
   Campion.
Hermontimus.   Ayton [(or
   Aytoun)] Sir Robert.
Holes in the Sky (excerpt).
   MacNeice.
Holy Numbers Litany to the
   Holy Spirit (excerpt).
   Herrick.
How Could We, Beforehand,
   Live in Quiet.   Gumilev.
Hymn for Second
   Vespers;Feast of the
   Apparition of Our Lady of
   Lourdes.   Anonymous.
Hymn for the Close of the
   Week.   Abelard.
Hymn to God the Father.
   Wesley.
I Have Heard.   Anonymous.
I Lost the Love of Heaven.
   Clare.
I'm Happiest When Most
   Away.   Bronte.
I Stood Tip-Toe.   Keats.
If Spirits Walk.   Jewett.
In Memoriam A.H.H., XLIII.
   Tennyson.
In the Marble Quarry.
   Dickey.
In the Still, Star-Lit Night.
   Stoddard
The Irish Peasant to His
   Mistress.   Moore.
It Is Not Beauty I Demand.
   Darley.
Jane Smith (parody).
   Kipling.
John Fitzgerald Kennedy.
   Masefield.
The Laurel Tree.   Simpson.
The Lay of the Captive
   Count.   Goethe.
Legerdemain.   MacKenzie.
The Lighthouse Invites the
   Storm.   Lowry.
Litany to the Holy Spirit
   (excerpt).   Herrick.
The Lone Wild Fowl.
   MacFayden.
The Lord of Heaven to Earth
   Came Down.   Peck.
Lost after All.   Tillman.
Love Redeemed.
   Baylebridge.
Love's Lord.   Dowden.
A Magic Mist.   O
   Suilleabhain.
Malachi.   Marlatt.
The Marriage.   Winters.
Martyrdom.   Learsi.
Me.   de la Mare.
Metamorphoses.   Ovid
   (Publius Ovidius Naso).
Midnight.   Vaughan.
A Mood.   Howells.
Mrs. Asquith Tries to Save
   the Jacarandas.   Witt.
My Doves.   Browning.
My Father's Cot (parody)
   (excerpt).   Squire.
Naked in Borneo.   Swenson.
The New Heart.   Anonymous.
November.   Daryush.

Now Is the Accepted Time.
   Wesley.
O Day of Rest and Gladness.
   Wordsworth.
O God, the Rock of Ages.
   Bickersteth.
O Lord, I Come Pleading.
   Lawson.
O Thought!   Susskind.
Ode.   Gilder.
The Odyssey.   Homer.
Old Indian Trick.   Green.
The Old Mountaineer.
   Holmes.
On How the Cobler.
   Anonymous.
On the Death of Commodore
   Oliver H. Perry.   Brainard.
On the Tower.   Droste-
   Hulshoff.
Original Epitaph on a
   Drunkard.   Tyler.
The Other Voice.   Paulin.
Our Dead, Overseas.
   Markham.
Overlord.   Carman.
Permanence in Change.
   Goethe.
The Pieta, Rhenish, 14th C.,
   the Cloisters.   Van Duyn.
Placing a $2 Bet for a Man
   Who Will Never Go to the
   Horse Races ...   Wakoski.
Poll Star.   Lamport.
Post Mortem.   Jeffers.
A Prayer to the Trinity.
   Stanyhurst.
Preachin' the Blues.   House.
Precious Words.   Dickinson.
Prison Graveyard.   Knight.
The Professional.   Ignatow.
Publication Is the Auction.
   Dickinson.
Quaker Ladies.   Cortissoz.
The Question.   Duncan.
The Recapitulation.
   Eberhart.
Renewal.   Cromwell.
The Revolt of Islam.
   Shelley.
The Riven Quarry.   Oden.
Sancte Confessor.   Rhabanus
   Maurus.
Sanctimony.   Anonymous.
Seventh Station.   Claudel.
She Was a Phantom of
   Delight.   Wordsworth.
Solitude.   Keats.
Song and Wine.   Bacchylides.
Song: "O spirit of the
   Summertime!"   Allingham.
Song of Fionnuala.   Moore.
Song: "The primrose in the
   green forest."   Deloney.
Speechless.   Marston.
The Spirit of the Fall.
   Dandridge.
The Spirit of the Maine.
   Jenks.
The Spirit's Grace.
   Heyward.
Spiritual Love.   Roscoe.
Stanzas to Augusta.   Byron.
They May Rail at This Life.
   Moore.
Though Mine Eye Sleep Not.
   Anonymous.
Thoughts.   Benedikt.
To a Child Running with
   Outstretched Arms in
   Canyon de Chelly.
   Momaday.

To a Highland Girl.
   Wordsworth.
To Auden on His Fiftieth.
   Eberhart.
To God the Father.
   Constable.
To My Brothers.   Keats.
To Our Lord.   Galvam.
To Scott.   Letts.
To the Moon.   Shelley.
To the Reverend W.L.
   Bowles.   Coleridge.
To the River Beach: Stalks of
   Wild Hay.   Davis.
To the Trinity.   Stanyhurst.
Tom Thomson.   Bourinot.
Two Puritans.   Anonymous.
Under the Pot.   Graves.
Upon a Wife that Dyed Mad
   with Jealousie.   Herrick.
Vain Questioning.   De la
   Mare.
View from the Gorge.   Belitt.
A Vision.   Clare.
Waking.   MacDonogh.
Walking on Water.   Dickey.
Washyuma Motor Hotel.
   Ortiz.
We're Gonna Move When the
   Spirit Says Move!
   Anonymous.
We Who Build Visions.
   Coblentz.
Welcome O Great Mary.
   O'Gallagher.
Weltschmerz.   Yerby.
When Aurelia First I Courted.
   Anonymous.
When the Seed of Thy Word
   Is Cast.   Mather.
Whither Is Gone the Wisdom
   and the Power.   Coleridge.
"Who Are You?" Asked the
   Cat of the Bear.
   Coatsworth.
Why?   Crane.
Wild Eden.   Woodberry.
Wild Swan.   Anonymous.
William and Helen.   Scott.
Wilt Thou Not Visit Me?
   Very.
The Window-Glance.   Heine.
Winter Night.   Day-Lewis.
The Winter's Spring.   Clare.
A Wish.   Arnold.
Within Us, Too.   Grenville.
Wrap Me in Blankets of
   Momentary Winds.
   Littlebird.
Written on an Island off the
   Breton Coast.   Venantius
   Fortunatus.
The Young Martins.   Young.
Youth and Maturity.
   Greville.

Spit (s)
74th Street.   Livingston.
Aubade for Hope.   Warren.
A Dark Hand.   Manger.
Desert Holy Man.   Beecher.
Driving the Mule.
   Anonymous.
Higher Love.   Wright.
Ja, Ja, Ja!   Anonymous.
The Lamentation of the Old
   Pensioner.   Yeats.
Meditations in an Emergency.
   O'Hara.
The Midnight Court.
   Merryman.
My Sweetheart's the Mule in
   the Mines.   Anonymous.

The Second Iron Age
   (1939-1945).   Harrington.
Silex Scintillans.   Vaughan.
Tanker.   Middleton.
Tudor Aspersions.
   Piddington.
Two Somewhat Different
   Epigrams.   Hughes.
War Bride.   Worth.
Watermelons.   Simic.
Spite (ful) (s)
Caelica, XII.   Greville.
My Inmost Hope.   Sullam.
An Ode.   Updike.
To One Who Is Too Gay.
   Baudelaire.
What rage Is this?   Wyatt.
Splash (ing)
Lament for the Non-
   Swimmer.   Wagoner.
A Loon I Thought It Was.
   Anonymous.
On a Spring-Board.   Lefroy.
Play-Song.   Anonymous.
Raccoon Poem.   Palmer.
Song: "Woman sits on her
   porch."   Thompson.
These.   Williams.
Spleen (s)
The Fan.   Gay.
In Praise of Water-Gruel.
   Green.
Measure for Measure.
   Shakespeare.
Orange March.   Murphy.
Splendid
Come, Captain Age.
   Cleghorn.
Euphoria, Euphoria.   DeFoe.
Road-Song of the Bandar-Log.
   Kipling.
Robben Island.   Dederick.
Sonnet to A Negro in Harlem.
   Johnson.
The Wicked Neighbor.
   Shneurson.
Splendor (s)
And Have the Bright
   Immensities.   Robbins.
Bhagavadgita: The One.
   Anonymous.
The Claim That Has the
   Canker on the Rose.
   Plunkett.
Elegy in Six Sonnets.
   Tuckerman.
Epilogue.   Abercrombie.
The Geese.   Plutzik.
Hail! The Glorious Golden
   City.   Adler.
Intimations of Immortality
   from Recollections of Early
   Childhood.   Wordsworth.
The Islands of the Ever
   Living.   Anonymous.
Love You Alone Have Been
   with Us.   Rumi.
Mary Immaculate.   Donnelly.
Most Lovely Shade.   Sitwell.
Notes of an Interview.   Cory.
Nothing.   Burgos.
Poem: "The rose fades."
   Williams.
Riverton.   Wilson.
Satan.   Dutt.
Schoolboys in Winter.   Clare.
Sea-Voyage.   Wheelock.
Shrouds and Away.   Bailey.
St. Michael the Weigher.
   Lowell.
The Sumach Leaves.   Very.

Splendor

Sur Ma Guzzla Gracile. Stevens.
To One Who Denies the Possibility of a Permanent Peace. Sackville.
To Stella. Shelley.
Trail Breakers. Daugherty.
Triple Feature. Levertov.
Truth in Poetry. Crabbe.
Why I Can't Write My Autobiography. Kamenetz.
Work: A Song of Triumph. Morgan.

Splinters

Fair Weather. Parker.
Love the Ruins. Tussman.
Mother. Nagase Kiyoko.
Prayer. Mak.
Summer Solstice. Keating.
Tide Pools. Smith.

Split (ting)

At War. Madge.
Beethoven's Death Mask. Spender.
Carmen Miranda. Polite.
An Epistle to My Friend J. B. Dodsley.
How Death Came. Anonymous.
Hypocrite Women. Levertov.
The Nature of Love. Kirkup.
No Remedy. Allison.
On the Thirteenth Day of Christmas. Causley.
Party Knee. Updike.
Reuben, Reuben. Anonymous.
We Greet Each Other in the Side (parody) (excerpt). Anonymous.
A Working Party. Sassoon.

Spoil (ed) (ers) (ing) (s)

Behind the Plough. Cousins.
Come, Captain Age. Cleghorn.
Epistle to John Hamilton Reynolds. Keats.
Epithalamium for Helen: Song of the Sleepy Bridegroom. Theocritus.
Gifts. Snow.
Hickory Stick Hierarchy. Selle.
In the Queen's Bedroom. Cameron.
Lines Written in the Front of a Well-Read Copy of Burns's Songs. Anonymous.
Shakespeare's Mourners. Tabb.
The Song of the Lower Classes. Jones.
Sunday in the Country. Swenson.
A Thought from Porpertius. Yeats.
The Ticket. Ashbery.
To a Child. Herrick.
The Voyeur. Pickard.
The Wooing Frog. Reeves.

Sponge

The Bath. Graham.
Fireworks. Deutsch.
The Last Supper. Rice.
The Russian Soul II. Hollander.

Spoon (ful) (s)

The Big One. Morin.
Clouds. Levine.

Conservancies. Miles.
The Dancer. Young.
Poussin. MacNeice.
Riddle: "House full, yard full." Anonymous.
The Story of the Wild Huntsman. Hoffmann.

Spoon river

Daisy Fraser. Masters.
Mrs. Williams. Masters.
Rhoda Pitkin. Masters.

Sport (ing) (s)

Address to Plenty. Clare.
Amoretti, X. Spenser.
Caesar, when that the traitor of Egypt. Wyatt.
Dupree (A vers.). Anonymous.
The Echoing Green. Blake.
Epitaph for My Cat. Garrigue.
A Fisher's Apology. Johnstone.
Forty-Five Minutes from Broadway. Cohan.
Games, Hard Press and Bruise of the Flesh. Vliet.
Hold Hard, These Ancient Minutes. Thomas.
Innocent Play. Watts.
Landscape with Figures. Fairburn.
Leicester Chambermaid. Anonymous.
Madrigal: "Sweet Cupid, ripen her desire." Corkine.
Madrigal: "The spring of joy is dry." Peerson.
My Bonny Black Bess. Anonymous.
O Aa the Manly Sports. Annand.
On the Banks of Salee. Anonymous.
Our English Gamesters Scorne to Stake. Williams.
Piers Gaveston. Drayton.
The Presence. Graves.
Puck Goes to Court. Johnson.
Song: "If she be not as kind as fair." Etherege.
Sporting Life Blues. Anonymous.
Stag-Hunt. Anonymous.
Table Talk. Cowper.
To Friend and Foe. Anonymous.
To George Pulling Buds. O'Keeffe.
Villanelle. Feld.
When you Love, or speak of it. Behn.
Whom Do You Visualize as Your Reader? Pastan.
Womanisers. Press.

Spot (s)

Beth Gelert. Spencer.
Crescent Moon. Renton.
Enlightenment. Carr.
For Mack C. Parker. Murray.
How Long Hast Thou Been a Gravemaker? Perkins.
Limerick: "A leopard when told that benzine." Herford.
Little Brown Church in the Vale. Pitts.
Looking at a Dead Wren in My Hand. Bly.

The Missel-Thrush's Nest. Clare.
De Naevo in Facie Faustinae. Bastard.
New World of Will. Shapiro.
Our Lives. Scott.
A Petticoat. Stein.
Rag Doll and Summer Birds. Dodson.
Resignation. Landor.
The Schoolmaster Abroad. Seaman.
The Seasons. Kalidasa.
The Song of the MicMac. Howe.
Sonnet upon a Swedish Cottage. Carr.
Stranger Call This Not. Anonymous.
To the State of Love. Cleveland.
Two Fawns That Didn't See the Light This Spring. Snyder.
The World's Miser. Maynard.

Spouse (s)

Alas, That Ever That Speche Was Spoken. Anonymous.
The Betrothed. Kipling.
A City Eclogue. "J.
England's Prayer. Blundell of Crosby.
The Ghyrlond of the Blessed Virgin Marie. Jonson.
Limerick: "There was a young fellow named Dice." Anonymous.
Love. Beaumont.
Mary Gulliver to Captain Lemuel Gulliver. Swift.
My Old Wife's a Good Old Cratur. Anonymous.
The One-Eyed Bridegroom. Urdang.
Our Lady with Two Angels. Childe.
A Perverse Custom. Anonymous.
To Our Blessed Lady. Constable.
Two or Three: A Recipe to Make a Cuckold. Pope.

Spray (ing)

The Artist on Penmaenmawr. Turner.
The Bead Mat. de la Mare.
The Beautiful Lawn Sprinkler. Nemerov.
Boats. Bennett.
Cino. Pound.
Departure. Strong.
Dickens in Camp. Harte.
The Djanggawul Cycle, 6. Anonymous.
From My Thought. Smythe.
Heliotrope. Peck.
I Watched a Blackbird. Hardy.
Irradiations. Fletcher.
Keepsake from Quinault. Alyea.
The Milkmaid. Dobson.
The Rapid. Sangster.
Rock-Lily. Robinson.
Silence Spoke with Your Voice. Goodman.
Tales of the Islands, I. Walcott.
The Thousand Things. Middleton.
Two Sonnets. Ashbery.

Writing on the Wall. Fallon.

Spread (s)

Barthelemon at Vauxhall. Hardy.
The Caterpillar and the Ant. Ramsay.
The Crazed Moon. Yeats.
Hops. Pasternak.
The Kumulipo: The Dawn of Day. Anonymous.
Lord Jesus Christ, We Humbly Pray. Jacobs.
Love Is a Law. Anonymous.

Spree

Champagne Charlie. Leybourne.
Picnic. Lofting.

Spring (s) (itme)

18 West 11th Street. Merrill.
Abishag. Fichman.
Act II. Davis.
Aftermath. Sassoon.
Ah, Sweet Is Tipperary. McCarthy.
Altarwise by Owl-Light. Thomas.
Anacreontics. Cowley.
Andonis, My Daughter. Peacock.
Anticipation. De Tabley.
An Apple Orchard in the Spring. Martin.
The Apple-Tree. Vrepont.
Approach of Winter. Thomson.
April, Glengarry. Coxon.
As Joseph Was A-Walking. Anonymous.
As You Like It. Shakespeare.
At a Private Showing in 1982. Kumin.
At Mrs. Appleby's. McWebb.
The Beech. Young.
Before the Cashier's Window in a Department Store. Wright.
Benediction for the Tent. Anonymous.
The Birch-Tree at Loschwitz. Levy.
The Blackbird. Tennyson.
The blossoms have fallen. Shikishi.
Bucking Bronco. Anonymous.
The Burning of the Leaves. Binyon.
Buxom Lass. Anonymous.
The Call. Kauffman.
Cardinal. Howes.
Casual Gold. Uschold.
Certainty. Hardy.
Cleaning the Candelabrum. Sassoon.
The Cloud of Unknowing. Murray.
The Clouds. Aristophanes.
Collin My Deere and Most Entire Beloved. Smith.
The Comin' o' the Spring. Scott.
The Death-Wish. MacNeice.
The Delights of the Door. Ponge.
Dirge. Naidu.
Dismissal. Campion.
The Doubter's Prayer. Bronte.
Dream Songs. Berryman.

Dying: An Introduction. Sissman.
Eager Spring. Bottomley.
Easter. Sabin.
The Easter Song. Sedulius.
An Epitaph on a Robin-Redbreast. Rogers.
Eve. Bull.
Evergreen. Milne.
Fading Beauty. Marino.
The Faithful Lover. Pack.
Fall Lightly on Me. Gaess.
The Farmer and the Shanty Boy (Trenton Town). Anonymous.
February. Savage.
February. Whitney.
February. Young.
February Thaw. Dutton.
Ferry Hinksey. Binyon.
First Love. Kunitz.
The First Robin. Leveridge.
The Flowers That Bloom in the Spring. Gilbert.
Force. Sill.
Fragment: "Near where the riotous Atlantic surge." Allingham.
France. Mitchell.
Getting at the Root of the Matter (parody). Taylor.
Ghosts. Munkittrick.
Giving Up Butterflies. Kudaka.
Glad Earth. Forbes.
Gone Were but the Winter Cold. Cunningham.
Ground Hog Day. Pomeroy.
The Groundhog Foreshadowed. Sher.
Haiku: "Things long forgotten–". Shiki.
Health. Thomas.
Hero and Leander. Marlowe.
The Hock-Cart, or Harvest Home. Herrick.
Hold Hard, These Ancient Minutes. Thomas.
The Hound. Deutsch.
The Hours of Sleepy Night. Campion.
The House of Life. Rossetti.
How to Fly by Standing Still (excerpt). Baxter.
I'd Like to Be in Texas when They Round-Up in the Spring. Anonymous.
I Had Not Fastened My Sash over My Gown. Tzu Yeh.
I Have Had Not One Word from Her. Sappho.
I, Hermes, Have Been Set Up. Anyte [(or Anytes)].
I So Liked Spring. Mew.
If Buttercups Buzz'd after the Bee. Anonymous.
If I Consider. Ise.
If It Were Not for the Voice. Nakatsukasa.
Impression de Paris. Wilde.
In April. Wetherald.
In Memoriam A.H.H., LXXXV. Tennyson.
In Springtime. Kipling.
In the Cemetery of the Sun. Watson.
In the Fields. Mew.
In the Lake Country. Wissinger.
In the Ringwood. Kinsella.
In the Spring. Barnes.
In the Spring. Tennyson.

In the Trenches. Aldington.
In Time of Silver Rain. Hughes.
It Is in the Winter That We Dream of Spring. Wilson.
January. Gibson.
Jess's Dilemma. Anonymous.
Kite Days. Sawyer.
Lady of Castlenoire. Aldrich.
A Lady Thinks She Is Thirty. Nash.
The Lambs of Grasmere, 1860. Rossetti.
The Last Word of a Bluebird. Frost.
The Lawyer's Invocation to Spring. Brownell.
Leavetaking. Reape.
Limerick: "There was a young fellow named Hall." Wilson.
Lines Occasioned by the Burning of Some Letters. Dixon.
Little Songs. Pickthall.
The Lover Freed from the Gallows. Anonymous.
Madrigal: "Flow not so fast." Dowland.
Malvern Hill. Melville.
The Man-Moth. Bishop.
March Wind. Uschold.
Mardi Gras. Keithley.
Margaret Love Peacock. Peacock.
Mary and the Lamb. Sherman.
Master Skylark. Bennett.
Men Are the Devil. Davies.
Merce of Egypt. Olson.
Miss Betty's Singing-Bird. Winstanley.
Mollesse. Jacobsen.
The Mower in Ohio. Piatt.
My Country 'Tis of Thee. Bierce.
My Love-Song. Lasker-Schüler.
My Old Straw Hat. Cook.
Myths. Butler.
News. Lima.
The Nightingales of Spring. Anonymous.
Norway. Dubie.
November. Coatsworth.
November. Turner.
Now That the Winter's Gone. Carew.
O Nightingale. Nakatsukasa.
O Spring, Come Prettily In. Strodtmann.
O Sweet Spontaneous. Cummings.
Occasioned by Seeing a Walk of Bay Trees. Westmoreland.
Ode: To the Cuckoo. Bruce.
Ode to the West Wind. Shelley.
Old Scent of the Plum Tree. Fujiwara Ietaka.
Omnia Somnia. Watson.
On Ben Dorain. MacIntyre.
On Seeing the Field Being Singed. Ise.
On the Danube. Conquest.
On the Eve of Our Anniversary. Margolis.
On the Hazards of Smoking. Goldberg.

The Organ Grinders' Garden. Merryman.
Oxford Bells. Hopkins.
A Page's Road Song. Percy.
The Pageant. Whittier.
The Palm Willow. Bridges.
Paradise Lost. Milton.
A Pastoral. Hillyer.
The Pine. Webster.
A Pipe of Tobacco. Browne.
Piping Peace. Shirley.
A Place of Burial in the South of Scotland. Wordsworth.
Poem: "In the early evening, as now, a man is bending." Gluck.
Poem: "The tiny new emotions." Clark.
Poem: "These grasses, ancient enemies." Douglas.
Poem Written before Mother's Day for Mrs. Lopez from the South. Hardy.
Prague Spring. Harrison.
Prevision. Murray.
Privation. Carruth.
The Process. Kelly.
Rain on the Cumberlands. Still.
The Resurrection. Brooks.
Return to Spring. Mastin.
Returning. Harding.
Returning Spring. Eichendorff.
Rural Dumpheap. Cane.
The Sailor's Return. Anonymous.
Satori. Jones.
The Sea-Elephant. Williams.
The Seasons. Thomson.
September. Huxley.
Sestina to the Common Glass of Beer: I Do Not Drink Beer. Wakoski.
Silex Scintillans. Vaughan.
Smell My Fingers. Axelrod.
Snow. Pomeroy.
Snow-Girl. Mortiz.
Song: "Bone-aged is my white horse." Chamberlain.
Song for a Jewess. Goll.
Song from a Country Fair. Adams.
Song: "Heron is harsh with despair." Chamberlain.
Song of the Hesitations. Blackburn.
Song Set by John Dowland: "Come, ye heavy states of night." Anonymous.
Song: "Shine out, fair Sun, with all your heat." Anonymous.
Song: "With whomsoever I share the spring." Burroway.
Songs for the Cisco Kid or Singing for the Face. Lyle.
Sonnet: "If ever Sorrow spoke from soul that loves." Constable.
Sonnet: Of Love in Men and Devils. Angiolieri.
Sonnet: To the Lady Beaumont. Wordsworth.
Sonnet Written at the Close of Spring. Smith.
Sonnets. Tuckerman.
Soon with the Lilac Fades Another Spring. MacDonogh.

The Sow Took the Measles. Anonymous.
Spring. Thomas Nash.
Spring and Death. Hopkins.
Spring Death. Marano.
Spring in Washington. Boer.
Spring Is in the Making. Duffy.
The Spring of the Year. Cunningham.
A Spring Song. Anonymous.
Spring Song. Conkling.
Spring Song. O'Brien.
The Spring Trip of the Schooner Ambition. Anonymous.
Spring Wind. Turner.
The Springtime. Levertov.
Springtime in Cookham Dean. Roberts.
Stay, Spring. Young.
The Stone and the Blade of Grass in the Warsaw Ghetto. Scheinert.
The Sun's Shame. Rossetti.
Sushi-Okashi and Green Tea with Mitsu Yashima. Robles.
Sussyissfriin. Dow.
The Swallow. Cowley.
The Swallow (parody) (excerpt). Squire.
The Swallows: An Elegy. Jago.
Swedes. Thomas.
Sweeney to Mrs. Porter in the Spring. Sissman.
Sweet Spring Is Your. Cummings.
The Tall Sky. Ball.
Tears in Spring. Channing.
That Sharp Knife. Wolfe.
Thenot Protests. S."
There Goes a Girl Walking. Meeks.
Those Trees That Line the Northway. Perreault.
Time of the Mad Atom. Brasier.
To a Blue Flower. Neilson.
To a Girl. Waller.
To a School-Girl. Neilson.
To a Very Young Lady. Waller.
To Favonius. Bolton.
To God, on His Sickness. Herrick.
To Life I Said Yes. Grade.
To Spring: On the Banks of the Cam. Roscoe.
To the Best and Most Accomplished Couple—. Vaughan.
To the Lady May. Townsend.
The Tree Sleeps in the Winter. Russell.
Trico's Song. Lyly.
Turner's Camp on the Chippewa. Anonymous.
Twist-Rime on Spring. Guiterman.
Two Springs. Li Ch'ing-chao.
Tzu Yeh Songs. Anonymous.
The Undertaking. Donne.
The Unquiet Grave. Anonymous.
Upon Eckington Bridge, River Avon. Quiller-Couch.
Upon Roses. Herrick.

The Valiant Seaman's Happy Return to His Love... *Anonymous.*
Vernal Sentiment. Roethke.
Villanelle of Washington Square. Roberts.
War Walking Near. Young Bear.
Wearing of the Green. Fisher.
A Welcome. Browne.
Where It Is Winter. O'Neil.
Who Calls. Sayers.
Wild Geese. Peterson.
Winter in the Fens. Clare.
Winter, New Hampshire. Kherdian.
The Winter's Spring. Clare.
Wintering. Plath.
The Wistful Days. Johnson.
With Garments Flowing. Clare.
The Women in Old Parkas. Tallmountain.
Written at the White Sulphur Springs. Key.
Yom Kippur. Pastan.
You Are Like the Snow Only. Cummings.
You Cannot Go down to the Spring. Neilson.
You within Love. MacCaig.
Young Virgins Plucked Suddenly. Pomerantz.

Sprite (s)
Arcadia. Sidney.
Caelica, V. Greville.
Epigrams. Theocritus.
Government Injunction. Miles.
Never Weather-Beaten Sail. Campion.
O Hear My Prayer, Lord. Craig.

Spur (s)
Ad Johannuelem Leporem, Lepidissimum, Carmen Heroicum. *Anonymous.*
Budmouth Dears. Hardy.
Crecy. Palgrave.
Dr. Wild's Ghost. *Anonymous.*
Golden Spurs. Miner.
Idaho Cowboy Dance. *Anonymous.*
The Spur. Yeats.
What Is Truth? (excerpt). Manning.
Ye Simple Men. Blackie.

Spurn (ed)
The Holy Office. Joyce.
The Nettles. Hardy.
To the One of Fictive Music. Stevens.
Women, whoever wishes to know my lord. Stampa.

Spy (ing)
An Essay on Criticism. Pope.
For Sale. Silverstein.
November 2 A.M. Conspiracy. Field.
Three Dreams. Michie.
A wounded deer leaps highest. Dickinson.

Squadron (s)
The Aeneid. Virgil (Publius Vergilius Maro).
Fredericksburg. Aldrich.
Herve Riel. Browning.

Square
Anniversary. Wain.

The Belfry of Bruges. Longfellow.
Eastward to Eden. Bogardus.
Gotta' Smoke? Franklin.
Haiku: "Making jazz swing in." Knight.
Jam Fa Jamaica. Lynch.
The Level and the Square. Morris.
The New Bury Loom. *Anonymous.*
Prothalamion. Kumin.
Red May. Robinson.
The Snuff-Boxes. *Anonymous.*
Ten Brothers. *Anonymous.*

Squash (ed)
And Again (parody). Evans.
A Hopi Prayer. Conrard.
How Old's the Moon? *Anonymous.*
I Don't Like You. Wright.
Limerick: "There once was a peach on a tree." Brown.

Squat (s)
The Broken-Down Squatter. *Anonymous.*
A Buddhist Priest. Ho Xuan Huong.
End of Steel. Saunders.
Interview with Doctor Drink. Cunningham.
The Legion of Iron. Ridge.
The Little Fox. Grider.
The Old Angler. De La Mare.
Song for the Cattle. Campbell.
Uncle Simon and Uncle Jim. Ward.

Squaw
Red Cloud. Neihardt.

Squeak (ed)
Beautiful Youth. Benn.
First Satire: Prologue.. Persius (Aulus Persius Flaccus).
New Shoes. Watts.
The Organ-Grinder. Garthwaite.

Squeal (ing)
Easter Zunday. Barnes.
Love for a Hare. La Follette.
Maiden Lane. Lee.
Many Workmen. Crane.

Squeeze
Chicago, Summer Past. Snyder.
If It Would All Please Hurry. Tate.
Parade's End. Guest.
To Chloe. Hooton.

Squire
Bishop Blomfield's First Charge to His Clergy. Smith.
Jack the Jolly Tar. *Anonymous.*
Kit Logan and Lady Helen. Graves.
The Nimble Stag. Knox.

Squirrel (s)
The Graduate. Stetler.
How She Resolved to Act. Moore.
You Can Get Despondent. Careme.

Stab (bed) (bing)
All through the Stranger's Wood. Peretz.

Considerations of Norfolk Island (excerpt). Smithyman.
A Dentist's Window. Baxter.
Dying under a Fall of Stars. Shapiro.
The Lie. Ralegh.
Praises of the King Dingana (Vesi). *Anonymous.*
Prelude. Mason.
Prophets for a New Day. Walker.
Romeo and Juliet. Scott.
They Live. Swingler.
To an Old Tune. Percy.
Two Poems. Abrams.
Young Edmondale. *Anonymous.*

Stability
Mortality. *Anonymous.*
O Realm Bejewelled. Farrokhzad.
Park. Ignatow.

Stable (d)
Brooklyn Bridge. Roberts.
The Fascination of What's Difficult. Yeats.
For Us No Night Can Be Happier. Zinzendorf.
I like to see it lap the miles. Dickinson.
More to It Than Riding. Lindon.
Oh Oh Blues. Mays.
The Quiet-Eyed Cattle. Norris.
Tam o' the linn cam up the gait. *Anonymous.*
Together. Sassoon.
The Witnesses: The Innkeeper's Wife. Sansom.

Stack
The Armful. Frost.
Epigram: "No more of your titled acquaintances boast." Burns.

Staff
A Book. Reese.
The Lord Is My Shepherd. Knox.
The New River Head, a Fragment. Dower.
Thanksgiving. Best.
The Three Poplars. Little.

Stag
Caenlochan. Cruickshank.
The Dark Stag. Crawford.
Goddess of Wisdom Whose Substance Is Desire. Waldman.
In the Rut. Brown.
The Starry Frost Descends. Geilt.

Stage
Goodbye, Sally. Simmons.
Guest Lecturer. Turner.
Inscription in a Hermitage. Warton, Jr..
Jack the Giant Queller. An Antique History. Brooke.
King Henry V. Shakespeare.
Lament. Burgess.

Stagger (ed) (ing) (s)
The Blue Light. Dent.
Childbirth. Hughes.
The Four-Legg'd Quaker. *Anonymous.*
King Harald's Trance. Meredith.
Mortality. Madgett.
Sleeping They Bear Me. Mombert.

Tarras Moon. Baxter.

Stain (ed) (s)
Art Thou Afraid the Adorer's Prayer. Landor.
Beale Street, Memphis. Snyder.
Epigrams. Martial (Marcus Valerius Martialis).
Field Work. Heaney.
The Flute. Taylor.
Forest Leaves in Autumn (excerpt). Keble.
The Garden. Very.
God Save the Flag. Holmes.
I'm Not Rich. Rolnik.
Jacket So Blue. *Anonymous.*
The Jackfruit. Ho Xuan Huong.
Madrigal: "Why dost thou haste away." Sidney.
Off from Boston. *Anonymous.*
The Pedigree. Hardy.
A Plea for Flood Ireson. Brooks.
Room Poems. Bachar.
Sonnets, XXXIII: "Full many a glorious morning have I seen." Shakespeare.
Sonnets: A Sequence on Profane Love. Boker.
Sundown. Adams.
Sweeney Among the Nightingales. Eliot.
Thy Brother's Blood. Very.
To Dear Daniel. Greenberg.
To Spain–A Last Word. Thomas.
Tuskegee. Hill.
The Wakening. Hamill.
What Would I Give? Rossetti.

Stair (s)
Alone in the House. Bogin.
The Apartment-Hunter. Schultz.
At Thomas Hardy's Birthplace, 1953. Wright.
A Child Asleep. Roberts.
Confession. Pomeroy.
The Demolition. Stevenson.
Down in Yonder Meadow. *Anonymous.*
The Drum: the Narrative of the Drummer of Tedworth. Sitwell.
Eight O'Clock Bells. *Anonymous.*
Epigram: "Had we two met, blythe-hearted Burns." Landor.
The Flood. Mak.
The Gift of God. Robinson.
Goosey Gander. *Anonymous.*
Goosey, Goosey, Gander. Mother Goose.
Haunted Odysseus: The Last Testament. Gregory.
The Huntsmen. De La Mare.
Larks. Hinkson.
Last Night They Heard the Woman Upstairs. Ullman.
Late Winter. McAuley(
The Location of Things. Guest.
Mima. De la Mare.
The New House. McDougall.
Poem: "I heard of a man." Cohen.
Prelude. Benson.

Proceedings of the Wars.
Moure.
The Spider. Eiseley.
Still Life. Whittemore.
The Treehouse. Emanuel.
Venus and the Rain.
McGuckian.
When We Were Very Silly.
Morton.

Staircase (s)
Love in Labrador. Sandburg.
On the Staircase. Farjeon.
Somebody's Gone. Ford.
Twins. Matthews.

Stake (s)
Age. Cowley.
The Cruel Sister.
Anonymous.
Despair. Tennyson.
Epigram: "The arctic raven
tracks the caribou."
Wilson.
Faithless Nellie Gray. Hood.
Lamkin (A version).
Anonymous.
Lamkin (C vers.).
Anonymous.
Six O'Clock. Stickney.
Some of Wordsworth.
Landor.
The Two Sisters.
Anonymous.

Stale
Epigram: "Kissing
Hippomenes." Paulus
Silentiarius.
Impressions, Number III.
Cummings.
It Is the Celestial Ennui of
Apartments. Stevens.
The Nut-Brown Ale.
Marston.
Once I Thought to Die for
Love. Anonymous.

Stalk (s)
Apartment Cats. Gunn.
The Beasts of Boston.
Lowry.
The Cedar River. Gibbons.
Contrary Theses (I). Stevens.
The Golden Shower.
Campbell.
I Grieved for Buonaparte.
Wordsworth.
Jump or Jiggle. Beyer.
Letters to Walt Whitman.
Johnson.
The Lover Exhorteth His
Lady to Take Time, While
Time Is. Turberville.
The Messenger. Gunn.
Miser. LeClaire.
The Moon Now Rises to Her
Absolute Rule. Thoreau.
The Ocean. Ralegh.
Over and Over Stitch.
Graham.
Please keep an eye on my
house for a few moments.
Vidya.
Spraying the Potatoes.
Kavanagh.
This Is the Hay That No Man
Planted. Coatsworth.
To a Friend Concerning
Several Ladies. Williams.

Stall (s)
But Art Thou Come, Dear
Saviour? Anonymous.
Carol. Anonymous.
The Cherry-Tree Carol, IV.
Anonymous.

Christmas Day Is Come.
Wadding.
Corydon and Tityrus.
Anonymous.
The Loan of a Stall. Duff.
The Mother's Tale. Farjeon.
Three Men. Moore.
To Speak of Woe That Is in
Marriage. Lowell.
Tourist Guide: How You Can
Tell for Sure When You're
in South Dakota. Heynen.

Stallion (s)
Ambuscade. McCrae.
Bacchus. Empson.
Letter to Pasternak.
Pomeroy.
The White Stallion. Owen.

Stamp (ed) (s)
Caelica, LXXX. Greville.
A Concise History of the
World. Sadoff.
An Execration against
Whores. Webster.
In Lucas, Kansas. Williams.
King George V. Hayward.
The Printer, to Her Majesty.
Lichfield.
Rain after a Vaudeville Show.
Benét.
Rumplestiltskin Poems.
Hathaway.

Stand (ing) (s) (stood)
Achitophel: the Earl of
Shaftesbury. Dryden.
The Aged Pilot Man.
"Twain.
The Agnostic's Creed.
Malone.
Apology of Genius. Loy.
Architects of Dream. Trent.
At an Inn. Hardy.
At the Grave of Henry
Vaughan. Sassoon.
Attitudes of a New Zealand
Poet. Curnow.
Autumnal Ode. De Vere.
Bacchus. Empson.
Ballad of the Days of the
Messiah. Klein.
A Ballad of the Mulberry
Road. Pound.
The Barren Moors.
Channing
Bearhug. Ondaatje.
The Beatific Vision.
Chesterton.
Beautiful Sunday. Falstaff.
Before Sentence Is Passed.
Blackmur.
Birds in the Flax. Snaith.
Black Silk. Gallagher.
The Bungalows. Ashbery.
By a Lake in Minnesota.
Wright.
Calvin in the Attic Cleans.
Weeden.
Canzone: Of His Love, with
the Figure of a Sudden
Storm. Prinzivalle.
Carol. Rodgers.
Cash Only, No Refund, No
Return. Epstein.
Changes. Heaney.
Christ's Descent into Hell.
Rilke.
The Church of the
Revolution. Butterworth.
Civilization. Yuan Chen.
Cogitabo Pro Peccato Meo.
Habington.
Conemaugh. Ward.

The Crab Tree. Gogarty.
The Dance. Campion.
A Dark Hand. Manger.
Dawn. Dudek.
December: Of Aphrodite.
Merwin.
A Dedication. Chesterton.
Desks. Smith.
Don Giovanni on His Way to
Hell. Gilbert.
Downwards. Williams.
Epitaph: "Here lies John Trot,
the friend of all mankind."
Blake.
Epitaph: Snake River.
Henson.
Evening. Miller.
The False Knight on the
Road. Anonymous.
Fifteen. Stafford.
A Fighting-Man. Campbell.
The Fire. Burford.
Fishermen. Emanuel.
The Flowering of the Rod.
Doolittle.
For A' That and A' That
(parody). Anonymous.
For My Daughter. Ochester.
Free Fall. Gordon.
The General Armstrong.
Anonymous.
Gitanjali. Tagore.
Goblin Market. Rossetti.
The Good Old Days. Fried.
Hare. Holden.
Heavenly Vision.
Anonymous.
A Hill. Hecht.
The Hound. Francis.
I Look at My Hand.
Gonzalez.
In Front of a Japanese
Photograph. Peck.
In Fur. Stafford.
In Galilee. MacKay.
An Incident. LePan.
Injured Maple. Everson.
A Lame Beggar. Donne.
Late Starting Dawn.
Brautigan.
Leisure. Davies.
Lights among Redwood.
Gunn.
Lines Composed a Few Miles
above Tintern Abbey.
Wordsworth.
The Little Cart. Waley.
A Living. Di Piero.
A March Calf. Hughes.
The Mirror. Bowers.
Miss Kilmansegg and Her
Precious Leg. Hood.
Miss Rosie. Clifton.
A Mountain Heritage.
Ellison.
The Mystic. Rice.
The New Cows. Waterman.
Not One Is Turned away from
God. Stroud.
The Ocean Said to Me Once.
Crane.
The Old Girl. Lenhart.
The Old Wharves. Field.
On the Slope of the Desolate
River. Tagore.
Patience. Studdert-Kennedy.
Peace. Whitney.
Peter White. Anonymous.
The Pines. Lippmann.
Poem for My Twentieth
Birthday. Koch.

Popular Songs of Tuscany.
Anonymous.
A Portrait of Rudy.
Cunningham.
The Premonition. Roethke.
The Purple Island. Fletcher.
R. W. Gold.
Riddle: "Thirty white horses."
Mother Goose.
Ringless. Wakoski.
Round Trip. Rice.
The Scarlet Tanager.
Benton.
The Search. Clarke.
A Serio-Comic Elegy.
Whately.
Shimmering Pediment. Yau.
The Shirts. Gallagher.
Simultaneously. Ignatow.
Sindhi Woman. Stallworthy.
A Song About Myself, st. 4.
Keats.
Sonnet on His Blindness.
Milton.
Sonnets from the Portuguese,
XXII. Browning.
Start Where You Stand.
Braley.
Te Judice. Scott.
Terenure. Salkeld.
They Also Stand... Moore.
They Can't Do That.
Anonymous.
This Is the Way the Ladies
Ride. Mother Goose.
Thomas at Chickamauga.
Sherwood.
To a Scottish Poet. Fraser.
To Be in Love While in
Prison. Minarik.
To Hafiz. Aldrich.
Tzu Yeh Songs. Anonymous.
Voices in the Winter.
McCullough.
The Wagoner's Lad.
Anonymous.
The Waiting Watchers.
Treece.
The Wall Test. Simpson.
The War God's Horse Song.
Anonymous.
Watch Yourself Go By.
Gillilan.
Western Lines. Whitman.
What My Child Learns of the
Sea. Lorde.
What Then? Anonymous.
Wintered Sunflowers.
Snyder.
Woman and Nature. Griffin.
The Worst. Silverstein.
A Young Fir-Wood.
Rossetti.
Zimmer in Fall. Zimmer.

Standard (s)
The Black Narrator.
Alhamisi.
Evolutionary Hymn. Lewis.
The Horrible Decree (excerpt).
Wesley.

Stanza (s)
3 Stanzas about a Tree. Bell.
Stanzas in Meditation. Stein.
Translations from the Chinese.
Morley.
What about You? (parody).
Pygge.

Star (d) (s)
The Collector of the Sun.
Smith.
The Double Autumn.
Reeves.

Ecstasy. Turner.
The Photographer Whose
  Shutter Died. Meissner.
The Stuffed Owl.
  Wordsworth.
Star (ry) (s)
2nd Dance–Seeing Lines–6
  February 1964. MacLow.
Ad Matrem in Coelis. Van
  Voorhis.
The Adventurer. Shepard.
After Reading Saint Teresa,
  Luis De Leon and Ramon
  Lull. Lee.
Alpine Spirit's Song.
  Beddoes.
America for Me. Van Dyke.
America Resurgent. Stafford.
Amtrak. Fried.
Andromeda. Browning.
The Angels at Hamburg.
  Jarrell.
The Angels for the Nativity of
  Our Lord. Drummond.
Apology for Bad Dreams.
  Jeffers.
Apple. Fry.
Arm Wrestling with My
  Father. Driscoll.
As an Old Mercer. Fisher.
An Astrologer's Song.
  Kipling.
Astronaut's Choice. Darcy.
At Dante's Grave. Zussman.
At the Ball Game. Field.
At the Telephone Club.
  Coulette.
Atom from Atom. Emerson.
Aunt Zillah Speaks. Palmer.
The Bad Season Makes the
  Poet Sad. Herrick.
Bagley Wood. Johnson.
Barbara Frietchie. Whittier.
The Barn. Coatsworth.
Baseball and Writing.
  Moore.
Bathtubs. Lattimore.
The Battle-Flag. Davis.
Beauty. Whitman.
The Bethlehem Star Shines
  On! Mortenson.
Beyond Rathkelly. Carlin.
Bird Shadows Mounting.
  Eigner.
Birth of the Foal. Juhasz.
Bitter Bread. Mandelstam.
Bloom. Kreymborg.
The Blue-Hole. Bell.
The Blue Light. Dent.
Blue Winter. Francis.
The Bonnie Blue Flag.
  Ketchum.
Bow Down, Mountain.
  Farber.
Bread. Urdang.
Buffalo Trace. Morgan.
Caelica, LXXVIII. Greville.
Caliban in the Coal Mines.
  Untermeyer.
Calverly's. Robinson.
The Camp Within the West.
  Quinn.
Candle and Star.
  Coatsworth.
The Carol of the Poor
  Children. Middleton.
The Carpenter. Whiteside.
Centaur Song. Doolittle.
The Centuries Are His.
  Ebeling.
Child. Plath.

Chinese Serenade for the Ut-
  Kam and Tong-Koo.
  Chivers.
Chrismas Carol. *Anonymous.*
Christmas Carol.
  Anonymous.
A Christmas Carol.
  Chesterton.
Christmas Lights. Worth.
Christmas Lullaby for a New-
  Born Child. Gregory.
Christmas Night. Sail.
Christmas Rede. Barlow.
The Circumcision. Zisquit.
The City by the Sea.
  Sterling.
A Clear Midnight.
  Whitman.
Coasting toward Midnight at
  the Southeastern Fair.
  Bottoms.
Come Christmas. McCord.
The Coming of Night.
  Wade.
Communion. Gould.
Comrades. Woodberry.
Confession. Barker.
Continuum. Levertov.
The Cot. Amen.
Country Reverie. Coates.
Creeds. Wattles.
Daisies. Young.
The Dancers. Deutsch.
The Dandelion. Lindsay.
Darkness Music. Rukeyser.
Daybreak. Kinnell.
The Dead Singer. Townsend.
Delivering Children.
  Holbrook.
Delos. Durrell.
Denmark. Wolfe.
Description of a View.
  Empson.
The Desert. Wood.
Desert Shipwreck. Jordan.
Die My Shriek. Kushniroff.
Dirge. Parsons.
Discarded Christmas Tree.
  Long.
Distribution of Honours for
  Literature. Landor.
Don Juan. Byron.
Don Juan's Address to the
  Sunset. Nichols.
Dream the Great Dream.
  Coates.
Dream Tryst. Le Gallienne.
Driving through the Pima
  Indian Reservation. Cook.
Drummer Hodge. Hardy.
Dwell with Me, Lovely
  Images. Maynard.
The Dying Patriot. Flecker.
Early in the Springtime.
  Anonymous.
The Earth. Emerson
The Earth in Spring. Halevi.
The Earth Will Stay the
  Same. Hill.
East River (New York).
  Thomas.
Easter. O'Hara.
Eclipse. Sheehan.
Elements of Grammar.
  Hernton.
Eleven Addresses to the Lord.
  Berryman.
Emigravit. Jackson.
Emily Bronte. Day Lewis.
Empedocles. Jones, Jr.
Epigram: "The boys of Tyre
  are beautiful." Meleager.

An Epistle to a Friend, to
  Persuade Him to the Wars.
  Jonson.
Epitaph on Prince Henry.
  Holland.
The Escape. Gurney.
Escape at Bedtime.
  Stevenson.
Europa. Walcott.
Even the Best. Kizer.
Evening Ceremony: Dream for
  G.V. Rose.
Evening on the Harbor.
  Tunstall.
Evolution. Blight.
Excelsior. Longfellow.
The Excursion. Wordsworth.
Facts. "Carroll.
The Fall of the City: Voice of
  the Studio Announcer.
  MacLeish.
Fame. Tabb.
Fecundity. Keating.
The Fire. Bell.
Fireworks. Worth.
First Frost. Curran.
Fish. Levis.
The Fish-Hawk. Wheelock.
Five Words for Joe Dunn on
  His 22nd Birthday. Spicer.
Fledglings. Harris.
The Flight of Apollo.
  Kunitz.
For Sue. Hey.
Fragment: I Saw His Round
  Mouth's Crimson... Owen.
Freedom For the Mind.
  Garrison
From Bethlehem Blown.
  Leitch.
From Jerusalem: A First
  Poem. Preil.
From Russian Hill.
  Coolbrith.
From the Sea. Teasdale.
Frost. Johnson.
The Full Heart. Nichols.
Gertrude Stein at Snails Bay.
  Porter.
Gitanjali. Tagore.
God, the Artist. Morgan.
The Golden Journey to
  Samarkand. Flecker.
Grand Finale. Layton.
The Great Bear. Hollander.
Grover Cleveland. Benton.
Haiku: "Pluck a daisy here–."
  Phillips.
Haiku: "Under moon
  shadows." Knight.
Happy Christmases (excerpt).
  O'Donnell.
Harlem in January. Fields.
Has Been. Worsley.
He Made the Night. Mifflin.
The Heart of Herakles.
  Rexroth.
Heart-Summoned. Stuart.
Heartbreak Camp.
  Campbell.
The Herd. Cornford.
Herman Moon's Hourbook.
  Middleton.
High Island. Murphy.
Holy Night. Benson.
Home. Beaumont.
Hope. Carmichael.
Horat. Ode 29. Book 3.
  Paraphras'd in Pindarique
  Verse. Dryden.
How Stars and Hearts Grow
  in Apples. Elson.

How to Reach the Moon.
  Pomerantz.
The Howling of Wolves.
  Hughes.
Hymn. Dunbar.
Hymn to the Sun. Doughty.
I Am Goya. Voznesensky.
I Once Loved a Young Man.
  Anonymous.
I Traveled with Them.
  Mu'tamid.
I Walk in the Old Street.
  Zukofsky.
I was born under a kind star.
  Tynan.
Idol. Driscoll.
Idylls. Theocritus.
The Immortal. Pickthall.
In God's Eternal Studios.
  Shivell.
In the Fall. ""MacDiarmid.
In the First House. Keith.
In the Hospital. Howland.
Incident on a Front Not Far
  from Castel di Sangro.
  Brown.
Indian Song. Johnson.
The Indian Women Are
  Listening: To the Nuke
  Devils. Rose.
Insects. Schneider.
Interlude: The Casement.
  Brennan.
The Invention of Astronomy.
  Matthews.
Invitation to a Sabbath.
  Mathews.
Is It a Month. Synge.
The Island of Geological
  Time. Fargas.
Journey from New Zealand.
  Hyde.
Julian Grenfell. Baring.
King Alfred Answers the
  Danes. Chesterton.
Kings Came Riding.
  Williams.
The Kings of the East.
  Bates.
The Land of Dreams. Blake.
Last Cargo. Bellows.
The Last Good-By.
  Moulton.
Last Words. Droste-
  Hulshoff.
Leaves. Davies.
Leonidas. Croly.
Levee Camp "Holler."
  Anonymous.
Life's Common Duties.
  Savage.
Life's Testament.
  Baylebridge.
The Light Year. Ridland.
The Linebacker at Forty.
  Wallace.
The Lone Biker. Hardy.
Love in Labrador. Sandburg.
Love Unsought. Embury.
Lumen de Lumine. Shelley.
Lute Music. Rexroth.
Magaica. De Sousa.
Magic Fox. Welch.
A Man Called Dante, I Have
  Heard. King.
The Man Hunt. Cawein.
A Man Who Had Fallen
  Among Thieves.
  Cummings.
Maps to Nowhere.
  Rosenberg.
Mary Immaculate. Donnelly.

Masque of Cupid: Up, Youths and Virgins, Up, and Praise. Jonson.
The Mendicants. Carman.
Microcosmos. Heseltine.
Mirthful Lunacy. Stoddart.
Modern Love, XXII. Meredith.
The Moon. Follen.
The Moon. Garnett.
Moon Watching by Lake Chapala. Young.
Moonbeam. Conkling.
Moonlight. Moxon.
Morituri Salutamus. Longfellow.
Morning Star. Galvin.
Mother. Sinclair.
The Mother and Child. Watkins.
The Mountain Afterglow. Laughlin.
The Mountain to the Pine. Hawkes.
Music in the Night. Spofford.
My Cheap Lifestyle. Myles.
My Lord, What a Mourning. *Anonymous.*
My Penis. Ochester.
Nancy Lee. *Anonymous.*
New Year Wishes. Sarton.
Night. Daley.
Night and Love. Lytton.
The Night Journey. Brooke.
The Night Long. Imr el Kais.
No Friend Like Music. Hicky.
Noel! Noel! Simmons.
"Noone" Autumnal This Great Lady's Gaze. Cummings.
Nothing. Reid.
Novella. Rich.
O Night Flower. Barbeitos.
O What Transparent Waves, What a Tranquil Sea. Colonna.
October Night. Dean.
Ode to Joy. Schiller.
The Odyssey. Homer.
Oh, Sweet Content. Davies.
The Old Astronomer to His Pupil. Williams.
On Earth. Farrokhzad.
On Eleanor Freeman. *Anonymous.*
On Having Grown Old. Moll.
On Hearing the Marsh Bird's Water Cry. Niatum.
On Middleton Edge. Young.
On My Pretty Marten. Cotton.
On One Who Died in May. Cook.
On the Esplanade des Invalides. Fisher.
On the Lake. Sackville-West.
On the Nativity of Our Saviour. Philipott.
Once in Royal David's City. Alexander.
Opportunity. Malone.
The Oregon Trail. Guiterman.
Oriflamme. Fauset.
The Other World. Book of the Dead.
Others. *Anonymous.*

Our Dead, Overseas. Markham.
Outward. Simpson.
Paean to Eve's Apple. Liddy.
Paradise Lost. Milton.
Paradise Regained. Milton.
The Part of Fortune. Sanfedele.
Passion. Kinnell.
Peace by Night. Mary Madeleva.
The Peaceable Kingdom. Piercy.
The Pear-Tree. Goll.
The People, Yes. Sandburg.
Photograph at the Cloisters: April 1972. Chasin.
Pibroch. Hughes.
The Pilgrim. Wightman.
Pinay. Cerenio.
Planetary Exchange. Jones.
The Pleiades. Barnard.
The Poem Circling Hamtramck, Michigan All Night in Search of You. Levine.
The Poets of the Nineties. Mahon.
Presence of an External Master of Knowledge. Stevens.
Prison Break. Hogan.
Prometheus Unbound. Shelley.
The Protagonist. Hopegood.
Psalm of the Jealous God. Abramovitch.
A Pulpit to Be Let. *Anonymous.*
Queen. Moraes.
Queen Mab. Shelley.
R.M.S. Titanic. Cronin.
The Rape of the Lock. Pope.
Reciprocity. Drinkwater.
Reconciliation. Doten.
Reconciliation. Lasker-Schüler.
Remember Sabbath Days. Eigner.
Remember That Country. Garrigue.
Resignation. *Anonymous.*
Response. Kaufman.
Riders of the Stars. Knibbs.
Rides. Derwood.
The Roads Also. Owen.
Ruaumoko–The Earthquake God. Turei.
Saddle. Simpson.
Sails. Sterling.
Satires. Boileau-Despréaux.
Sea Island Miscellany. Blackmur.
Sea Lyric. Braithwaite.
Sea Pieces. Fitzgerald.
Sea Violet. Doolittle.
The Secret. Russell.
Senlin. Aiken.
Sent Ahead. Hay.
September. Kyger.
Sequence for a Young Widow Passing. Munro.
The Seven Sleepers. Van Doren.
The Sextant. Sullivan.
She Warns Him. Cornford.
Shepherds' Carol. Nicholson.
Sherman's March to the Sea. Byers.

A Ship Burning and a Comet All in One Day. Eberhart.
Ships in Harbour. Morton.
Skins. Spires.
Slow Riff for Billy. Cunningham.
Sohrab and Rustum. Arnold.
Solitude. Mollineux.
Some Last Questions. Merwin.
Song: "I kept neat my virginity." Jones.
A Song of Honor. Hodgson.
Song of the Moderns. Fletcher.
Sonnet. Berryman.
Sonnet in a Garden. Peabody.
Sonnet: "The understanding of a medical man." Warner.
Sonnets: A Sequence on Profane Love. Boker.
Sonnets of the Triple-Headed Manichee: II. Barker.
The Sons of Levi. *Anonymous.*
Soul Lifted. Watson.
Speak With the Sun. Campbell.
Special Starlight. Sandburg.
Speculation. Nemerov.
Standing on Tiptoe. Cameron.
The Star. Smith.
Star. Whitebird.
Star-Fear. Speyer.
Star Journey. Madgett.
Stars. Hayden.
Stars. Moss.
Stone. Mayo.
Stone. Simic.
Street Corner College. Patchen.
Street Scene. Mezey.
The Sun Men Call It. Wheelock.
Sunflower Sonnet Number Two. Jordan.
Sunset after Rain. Merwin.
Survival. Coates.
Swamp. Hill.
Swimming by Night. Merrill.
Symbols. Thompson.
Tact. Robinson.
Ten Sonnets for Today. Stanway.
Tenth Elegy. Elegy in Joy. Rukeyser.
Text. Zeitlin.
These Two. Schwartz.
A Thing Remembered. *Anonymous.*
This House. Young Bear.
This Night. Heyen.
Thomas Iron-Eyes Born Circa 1840. Died 1919, Rosebud Agency, S.D. Walsh.
Though Fatherland Be Vast. Cross.
Three Elements. Benét.
A Time to Dance: The Flight. Day-Lewis.
To a Child. Montgomery.
To a Friend. Cooper, Jr.
To a Traveler. Johnson.
To Chicago at Night. Merryman.
To-Day I Saw Bright Ships. Robinson.
To Dick, on His Sixth Birthday. Teasdale.

To Etesia Looking from Her Casement at the Full Moon. Vaughan.
To Imagination. Thomas.
To My Father. Pomeroy.
To the Choice Bridegroom. Halevi
To Women. Hugo.
The Tomb of Diogenes. *Anonymous.*
The Tomb of Honey Snaps Its Marble Chains. Stanford.
Track. Transtromer.
The Tree. Very.
Triad. Foster.
Two Chorale-Preludes. Hill.
The Two-Headed Calf. Gilpin.
Two Heavens. Hunt.
Two Mornings and Two Evenings. Bishop.
Two Songs from a Play. Yeats.
Under the Stars. Rice.
Unity. Russell.
Unrelenting Flood. Matthews.
Unrest. Marquis.
Until We Built a Cabin. Fisher.
The Unwilling Gypsy. Johnson.
V.D.F. *Anonymous*
The Vagrant. Slender.
Vain Advice at the Year's End. Wright.
Very Early. Kuskin.
Vilna. Kulbak.
Violet Twilights. Sodergran.
Virginia's Bloody Soil. *Anonymous.*
The Vision. Dante Alighieri.
Voltaire at Ferney. Auden.
Wait Till the Darkness is Deep. Wallada.
Walking Westward (excerpt). Stead.
War Cry: To Mary. Leo XIII.
Washington's Tomb. Lawrence.
Water (excerpt). Raine.
Waterloo. De Vere.
We Reached Out Far. Markish.
We Will Watch the Northern Lights. *Anonymous.*
Wedded Memories. Marston.
Welcome to the Moon. *Anonymous.*
Western Lines. Whitman.
What Are You Thinking About? Macmillan.
What Do I Know? Brennan.
What She Wished. Throne.
Wheels. Donnelly.
When I Heard the Learn'd Astronomer. Whitman.
When Last Seen. Flexner.
When Sun Doth Rise. Williams.
When This Cruel War Is Over. *Anonymous.*
When Young Hearts Break. Heine.
Who Goes with Fergus? Yeats.
Who Has Known Heights. Whiteside.
William Shakespeare. Swinburne.

Winter Night, Cold Spell.
Nelson.
A Winter Twilight. Grimke.
Wisdom. Middleton.
The Wit. Bishop.
With the Shell of a Hermit
Crab. Wright.
Without You. Corman.
Witness. Anderson.
The Witnesses. Kennedy.
Woman Made of Stars.
Thompson.
Woman Seed Player.
Whiteman.
Wooden Ships. Morton.
Word of Art. Bernheimer.
Yet Vain, Perhaps, the Fruits.
Tuckerman.
You Shall Above All Things
Be Glad and Young.
Cummings.
Young Sea. Sandburg.
Zarathustra. Jones, Jr.
Star Spangled Banner
The Rejected "National
Hymns". Newell.
Stare (d) (s)
Advice to Julia. Luttrell.
Antipater of Thessalonica.
Rexroth.
"L'Apparition" of Gustave
Moreau. Bottomley.
Brazilian Fazenda. Page.
Christmas Carol. Opperman.
Circle of Struggle. Root.
The Cit's Country Box.
Lloyd.
Concerning the Dead.
Halperin.
Crazy Horse Returns to South
Dakota. Elliott.
A Dream of Jealousy.
Heaney.
Ducks. Hesketh.
End of Play. Graves.
The Ex-Queen among the
Astronomers. Adcock.
False Dawn. De la Mare.
Family. MacCaig.
Fishermen. Bunting.
For Delphine. Simmons.
Form Was the World.
English.
Hakluyt Unpurchased.
McDuffee.
The Hunt. Deutsch.
Judas Iscariot. Spender.
Leisure. Davies.
Lights among Redwood.
Gunn.
Look, in the Labyrinth of
Memory. Schwartz.
The Lovers. Smith.
Mahony's Mountain.
Stewart.
Meditations in Time of Civil
War. Yeats.
Michael's Room. Gibbons.
Modern Love, XLVI.
Meredith.
Morning on the Shore.
Campbell.
Multitudes Turn in Darkness.
Aiken.
My Mate Bill. Gibson
("Ironbark").
On the Coast near Sausalito.
Hass.
On the Night Express to
Madrid. Dunetz.
Patrol. Pomeroy.
Phyllis. Russell.

Psalm. Oppen.
Retinue. Verlaine.
The Rhinoceros. Nash.
Sitting. Griffin.
Snatches: "What! why didest
thou wink." *Anonymous.*
A Song of Honor. Hodgson.
A Starling and a Willow-
Wren. Auden.
The Storm. Heine.
Three Poems, II.
Castellânos.
To a Spanish Poet. Spender.
The Triumph of Chastity.
Howes.
Upon Shaving Off One's
Beard. Updike.
Why? De La Mare.
The Years. Wheelock.
Starless
Ballad. Kendall.
Flowers. Mallarme.
In Sepia. Anderson.
A Walk in March.
Reynolds.
Whoroscope. Beckett.
Starlight
The Access. Kanabus.
BC : AD. Fanthorpe.
Endymion. Keats.
The Eyes, the Blood.
Meltzer.
The Final Faith. Sterling.
Hill Love. Macmillan.
Is It a Sin to Love Thee?
Anonymous.
The Lover is Near. Goethe.
The Merry Wives of Windsor.
Shakespeare.
Migration as a Passage in
Time. Bolz.
The Old and the New.
Mills.
She Comes Not When Noon
Is on the Roses. Trench.
Silent Poem. Francis.
Song: "I saw the day's white
rapture." Towne.
Sonnets. Hillyer.
The Soul in the Body.
Thomas.
Words and Music (excerpt).
Beckett.
Starling (s)
The Barn. Thomas.
Jenny Wren. Davies.
Mineral Point. Dana.
With Thee Conversing.
Milton.
Start (ed) (er) (ing) (s)
Afternoon on a Hill. Millay.
Ancient History. Guiterman.
Before Chilembwe Tree.
Mapanje.
Black Sketches, 1. Lee.
Buckinghamshire.
Anonymous.
Buffalo–Isle of Wight Power
Cable. Hollo.
Common Dust. Johnson.
Considerations. Helwig.
The Dirty-Billed Freeze
Footy. Hemschemeyer.
Dream Songs. Berryman.
The Future. Oppenheim.
The Homes. Pitkin.
The Jovial Marriner; or, The
Sea-Man's Renown.
Playford.
The Kaleidoscope. Gill.
Leap-Centuries. Celan.

Limerick: "There once was a
pious young priest."
Anonymous.
The Master City. Orente.
Merlin in the Cave: He
Speculates without a Book.
Gunn.
Midnight, Walking the
Wakeful Daughter.
Meredith.
Nobody Loses All the Time.
Cummings.
The Panchatantra: Fool and
False. *Anonymous.*
Question Time. Lindsay.
Red-Herring. Lawrence.
The Sea Dike. Vasalis.
The Spring Offensive of the
Snail. Piercy.
Terraplane Blues. Johnson.
Think of Eight Numbers.
Silverstein.
To Sherrie. Matuzak.
A Toast. *Anonymous.*
Startle (d)
Britannia's Pastorals.
Browne.
Dejection. Coleridge.
Four III "here's a little
mouse." Cummings.
The Golden Stallion.
Thompson.
How to Cure Hops and
Prepare Them for Sale.
Smart.
Our Father's Hand. Flint.
Psalm. Oppen.
She Schools the Flighty Pupils
of Her Eyes. Hopkins.
The Star. Redpath.
Sunthin' in the Pastoral Line.
Lowell.
This Is Halloween.
Thompson.
Starve (d) (s)
Amoretti, XXCVIII.
Spenser.
Amoretti, LXXXVIII.
Spenser.
Big Steamers. Kipling.
Bread. Thomas.
Children's Crusade, 1939.
Brecht.
The Crocodile. Herford.
The Diet. Burge.
An Epistle from Mr. Pope to
Dr. Arbuthnot. Pope.
The Farewell. Churchill.
A Farewell to London In the
Year 1715. Pope.
For a Blind Beggar's Sign.
Biondi.
The Gourmet's Love-Song.
Wodehouse.
Hurrah for Greer County.
Anonymous.
Japanese Beetles. Kennedy.
Manyoshu: To Love Someone.
Kasa.
One-and-Twenty.
Anonymous.
Plea. Ciardi.
Sealed Bags of Ducats.
Martial (Marcus Valerius
Martialis).
The Shoofly. *Anonymous.*
'Tis Now Since I Sate Down.
Suckling.
Two Refugees. Marcus.
Up from the Wheelbarrow.
Nash.

Upon de Mountain.
Anonymous.
An Utter Passion Uttered
Utterly (parody).
Todhunter.
Victory comes late.
Dickinson.
State (s)
Across Kansas. Stafford.
Affidavit in Platitudes.
White.
At the Lincoln Tomb.
Bryant.
The Children of the State.
Lewisohn.
Climbing. Clark.
Coming Around the Horn.
Anonymous.
English Thornton. Masters.
The Excursion. Wordsworth.
The Founders of Ohio.
Venable.
God Send Us Men. Gillman.
Horatian Ode. Beach.
In the States. Stevenson.
Let America Be America
Again. Hughes.
Limbo. Coleridge.
List of Prepositions.
Kennedy.
A Man of Experience. Mac
an Bhaird.
The Moone-Calfe. Drayton.
Ned Braddock. Palmer.
The Oak. Dryden.
Omniscience. Kelly.
Paradise Lost. Milton.
Serve in Thy Post. Clough.
Sketch of his Own Character.
Gray.
Sonnets, XXIX: "When in
disgrace with fortune and
men's eyes." Shakespeare.
The Sudbury Fight. Rice.
Supposed Confessions of a
Second-Rate Sensitive Mind.
Tennyson.
To Mr. Henry Lawes.
Philips.
A Toast to Our Native Land.
Bridges.
Upon the Death of the
Viscount of Dundee.
Dryden.
Were My Hart as Some Mens
Are. Campion.
What Constitutes a State?
Jones.
What Was Your Name in The
States? (with music).
Anonymous.
Wide, Ho? *Anonymous.*
Stately
Alceste in the Wilderness.
Hecht.
The Angel in the House, VIII.
Patmore.
Old Roadside Resorts.
Peacock.
The Stately Homes of England
(parody). Coward.
The Stranger. Garrigue.
Statesman (men)
The Beggar's Opera. Gay.
An Epitaph on True, Her
Majesty's Dog. Prior.
If I Were a Voice. Mackay.
Static
Making Music. Minty.
Ohio. Updike.
Ross's Poems. Lehmann.

Stars Shine So Faithfully.
Flanders.
Station (s)
Are the Sick in Their Beds as
They Should Be?
McIntosh.
A Bird's Nest. Biton.
Divina Commedia. Dante
Alighieri.
Failure. Wilkins.
Figure of Eight. MacNeice.
Get a Transfer. *Anonymous.*
Odes. Horace.
The Possibility of New Poetry.
Bly.
To Dr. Swift on His Birthday,
30th November 1721.
Johnson.
Statistics
Thanks to Industrial Essex.
Davie.
Statue (d) (s)
The African Affair. Wright.
For Zbigniew Herbert,
Summer, 1971, Los
Angeles. Levis.
High Poetry and Low.
Stevens.
Ideal Landscape. Rich.
The Labourer in the Vineyard.
Spender.
The Lady of Life. Kettle.
Landscape. Gascoyne.
Laocoon. Gordon.
Last Sheet. Fuller.
Life's Evil. Montale.
On Marcus the Physician.
Nicarchos [(or Nicarchus)].
A Pastel. Verlaine.
Paul and Virginia.
Wheelwright.
Pygmalion. Miller.
Rushmore. Witt.
The World's Worst Boxer.
Lucilius [(or Lucillius)].
They Came This Evening.
Damas.
Statue of Liberty
Thanksgiving (1956).
Cummings.
Stature
In Manchester Square.
Meynell.
Magdalene. Pasternak.
Our First Century.
Woodberry.
Statutes
Country Statutes.
Anonymous.
We Two Boys together
Clinging. Whitman.
Stay (ed) (ing) (s)
After He Had Gone.
Warner.
Against Marriage to His
Mistress. Walsh.
Are You Just Back for a Visit
or Are You Going to Stay?
Rosenberger.
At Early Morn. Dismond.
Autumn Sequel, IV.
MacNeice.
A Ballad upon a Wedding.
Suckling.
Be off! Smith.
Bedtime. Farjeon.
Ben. Johnsons Sociable Rules
for the Apollo. Jonson.
Birlinn Chlann-Raghnaill.
MacDonald.
Choose Something Like a
Star. Frost.

Clara. Pound.
Cock-Crowing. Vaughan.
Come Out, Come Out, Ye
Souls That Serve.
Brennan.
Content. Whitney.
Death Deposed. Allingham.
The Emigrant's Child.
Sproull.
The End of the World.
Bottomley.
Ending. Ewart.
Endymion. Longfellow
Epitaphs of the War, 1914-18.
Kipling.
Executive. Betjeman.
Explanation, on Coming
Home Late. Hughes.
Fair Annet's Song. Wylie.
The Familie. Herbert.
For Sale. Lowell.
Form. McHugh.
Generations. Simmons.
God of Abraham, of Isaac,
and of Jacob. *Anonymous.*
Grief. Berry.
Handyman. Phillips.
Hardy's Plymouth. Grigson.
He Lifted from the Dust.
Smith.
Here. Thomas.
Heron in Swamp. Howard.
The High Sailboat.
Quasimodo.
A Hillside Thaw. Frost.
I Wish I Was a Little Bird
(with music). *Anonymous.*
The Ides of March. Fuller.
De Imagine Mundi.
Ashbery.
In the Park. Hoyt.
In the Rut. Brown.
An Instance. Reid.
John Henry (D vers.).
Anonymous.
Kimono. Graham.
Kit Hath Lost Her Key.
Anonymous.
Limerick: "There was an old
man of Dunblane." Lear.
Maine. Booth.
The Man in the Mirror.
Strand.
Many Wagons Ago.
Ashbery.
The Master City. Orente.
Metamorphoses. Ovid
(Publius Ovidius Naso).
Mojo Hiding Woman.
Fuller.
Moonlight (with music).
Anonymous.
My Love Wants to Park.
Healy.
My Picture. Procter.
Natural History. Warren.
New Jail. *Anonymous*
A Night Full of Nothing.
Sinclair.
Not This Leaf Haunts Me.
Cosier.
Nothing Gold Can Stay.
Frost.
O'Reilly's Reply. Weber.
On the Power of Sound.
Wordsworth.
On the World. Quarles.
Parachute Descent. Bourne.
Passing Love. Hughes.
The Passionate Pilgrim.
Shakespeare.

A Person, a Mexican.
Martinez.
Philomela's Second Ode.
Greene.
The Pleaders. Davison.
Poem Composed in Rogue
River Park... Wayman.
Questions of Travel. Bishop.
A Raccoon. Fox.
Rome. Du Bellay.
The Scholar. Cornford.
Sentence. Bynner.
A Separation. Spender.
Sitting in the Woods: A
Contemplation. Moses.
Someday Baby. Williams.
A Song of Twilight.
Anonymous.
Spencer the Rover.
Anonymous.
Stay All Night, Stay a Little
Longer. *Anonymous.*
Stay, Spring. Young.
Stay, Time. Watson.
Steal away. *Anonymous.*
Surviving. Welch.
Thou Lord of Hosts, Whose
Guiding Hand.
Frothingham.
To Heliodora: A Fretful
Monody. Meleager.
To Lydia Languish. Dobson.
Tongues. Berg.
Traveling America. Struther.
Trying to Stay. Chang.
The White Cliffs. Miller.
Wild Thyme. Farjeon.
The Wind. *Anonymous.*
Winter. Donaghy.
You Can Dig My Grave.
Anonymous.
Young Heroes, III· Walter
Bradford. Brooks.
Your Looks So Often Cast.
Wyatt.
Steadfast
The Flag. Flash.
I Am Like a Book. Rokeah.
On One Who Died in May.
Cook.
On the Heights. Foote.
Solomon. Hagedorn.
Steady
After a Death. Orr.
Blow Ye Winds Westerly.
Anonymous.
For one who says he feels.
Morstein.
Idylls. Theocritus.
Intimate Parnassus.
Kavanagh.
Song of the Fishes.
Anonymous.
Verses. Lowell.
The Virginia Song.
Anonymous.
Steal (ing) (s) (stole) (stolen)
Across the Western Ocean.
Anonymous.
After Summer. Marston.
Arabia. De la Mare.
At Summer's End.
Benjamin.
The Ballad of the Ivanhoe.
Adams.
Bedelia. Jerome.
The Beggar's Opera. Gay.
Being Refused Local Credit.
Rankin.
Big Dog. Booth.
A Call to the Wild.
Dunsany.

The Day Is Done.
Longfellow.
Deborah Lee. Yvonne.
December. Keats.
Don Juan. Byron.
Don't Anybody Move.
Epstein.
Epigram: On Inclosures.
Anonymous.
Fairies' Song. Hunt.
For C. Whalen.
Gypsies. Nowlan.
Here Do I Put My Name for
to Betraye. *Anonymous.*
History. Liddy.
I Am 25. Corso.
The Indian Convert.
Freneau.
Isabella, or The Pot of Basil.
Keats.
Jehovah. Zangwill.
Katharine Jaffray (C version).
Anonymous.
The Killing. MacBeth.
Kleptomaniac. Speyer.
The Man in the Tree.
Strand.
The Man on the Flying
Trapeze. Leybourne.
The March to Moscow.
Southey.
A Misconception. Lowell.
My Mammy's Maid.
Anonymous.
No Sickness Worse Than
Secret Love. *Anonymous.*
On Sir Henry Clinton's
Recall. *Anonymous.*
Outside the Window. Hardy.
Peter Hath Lost His Purse.
Anonymous.
Riddle: "In marble halls as
white as milk."
Anonymous.
The Robber. Eastwick.
Robbing and Stealing Blues.
Campbell.
The Rock-A-By Lady. Field.
The Sheep Beezness. Barker.
Shopping for Midnight.
Murray.
Someday Baby. Williams.
Song of Fairies Robbing an
Orchard (excerpt). Hunt.
The Song of Nu-Numma-
Kwiten. *Anonymous.*
Song to the Tune of
"Somebody Stole My Gal."
Kennedy.
Sonnet: He Jests Concerning
His Poverty. Sant' Angelo.
Three Thousand Dollar Death
Song. Rose.
To a Living Author.
Anonymous.
To Modigliani to Prove to
Him That I Am a Poet.
Jacob.
To My New Mistress.
Bowie.
To Saxham. Carew.
Tropical Weather. Sargent.
Visiting Day. Young.
The West-Country Lover.
Brown.
Wizard Frost. Sherman.
The Women at the Corners
Stand. Golding.
Stealth
He Is a Path. Fletcher.

Steam
Brand Fire New Whaling
Song Right from the Pacific
Ocean. *Anonymous.*
Childhood. Bruck.
Cloud. Hoffenstein.
Cressida. Baxter.
Motherhood. Ludvigson.
Nantucket / Mussels /
October. Lewandowski.
Train. Smith.
Steamboat (s)
Away Above a Harborful.
Ferlinghetti.
The Reactionary Poet. Reed.
Trinity Place. Sandburg.
Stedfast
Lak of Stedfastnesse.
Chaucer.
Steed (s)
Bunker Hill. Calvert.
Burial of the Minnisink.
Longfellow.
The English Language.
Story.
The Faerie Queene. Spenser.
The King of Denmark's Ride.
Norton.
Lord Derwentwater (The
King's Love-Letter).
Anonymous.
Odes, VII. Hafiz.
Pony Girl. Moreland.
The Reaper. Allen.
Song of the Navajo. Pike.
The Song of the Valkyries.
Anonymous.
Songs of the Squatters, I.
Lowe.
The St. Lawrence and the
Saguenay. Sangster.
Young Man of Alien Beauty.
O Dalaigh.
Steel
2 Poems for Black Relocation
Centers. Knight.
49th & 5th, December 13.
Jacobsen.
Before Disaster. Winters.
Between Two Furious Oceans.
Diespecker.
A Busy Man Speaks. Bly.
Camouflage. Manifold.
Death Comes for the Old
Cowboy. Clark.
Edgehill Fight. Kipling.
Fencing School. Manifold.
A Fieldmouse. Sund.
Five Men Against the Theme
"My Name is Red Hot....."
Brooks.
The Fountain. Mu'tamid.
Fragment 113. Doolittle.
Hand Saw. Funkhouser.
Heart's Needle. Snodgrass.
Looking Down on West
Virginia. Dickson.
The Magnet. Stanley.
Metropolitan Nightmare.
Benét.
Not Honey. Doolittle.
The Odyssey. Homer.
The Power of Thought.
Susskind.
Prayer for a Pilot. Roberts.
The Rape of the Lock.
Pope.
Scrap Iron. Durgnat.
Smoke and Steel (excerpt).
Sandburg.
Somewhere You Exist.
Winkler.

Song: "John Henry tol' his
Cap'n." *Anonymous.*
South Shore Line.
Schlesinger.
Summer. Kulbak.
A Sword. Boye.
The Tinder. Carew.
To Some Builders of Cities.
Snaith.
Steep
Ashboughs. Hopkins.
In a Mirror. Stubbs.
Not of All My Eyes See.
Hopkins.
Vermont. Cleghorn.
The White Horse of
Westbury. Turner.
White Magic: An Ode.
Braithwaite.
Steeple (s)
A Bell in the Orthodox
Steeple. Waltner.
Little Dunkeld. *Anonymous.*
Pan in Wall Street. Stedman.
Preston. *Anonymous.*
The Steeple-Jack. Moore.
Veni Coronaberis. Hill.
What Are They Thinking...
Guinness.
Steer (ing) (s)
Being Herded Past the
Prison's Honor Farm.
Wagoner.
Erith. *Anonymous.*
Erith, on the Thames.
Anonymous.
Flute Notes from a Reedy
Pond. Plath.
In Memoriam A.H.H., CIII.
Tennyson.
A Letter to Lord Middleton.
Etherege.
Love at Sea. Gautier.
My Elbow Ancestry. Mollin.
My Feet They Haul Me
'Round the House.
Burgess.
The Sailor. Allingham.
The Texas Cowboy.
Anonymous.
The Village of Erith.
Anonymous.
The Voice of America 1961.
Liddy.
Stella
Ah, Now I Know What Day
This Is. Statius Publius
Papinius.
Astrophel and Stella, XVIII.
Sidney.
Astrophel and Stella, XXI.
Sidney.
Astrophel and Stella, XXIII.
Sidney.
Astrophel and Stella, XXVI.
Sidney.
Astrophel and Stella, XXXII.
Sidney.
Astrophel and Stella, XXXIV.
Sidney.
Astrophel and Stella, L.
Sidney.
Astrophel and Stella, LXXIV.
Sidney.
Astrophel and Stella,
LXXXIV. Sidney.
Astrophel and Stella, CIV.
Sidney.
Hypocrite Swift. Bogan.
To Dr. Swift on His Birthday,
30th November 1721.
Johnson.

To Sleep. Sidney.
Stem (s)
Cawsand Bay. *Anonymous.*
Epigram: "The scentless laurel
a broad leaf displays."
Landor.
A Fairy Voyage.
Anonymous.
Flowers By the Sea.
Williams.
Late Dandelions. Belitt.
Loss. Ammons.
The Lough. Allingham.
Pastoral. Dyment.
Paul Laurence Dunbar.
Hayden.
Progress of Unbelief.
Newman.
Ribald Romeos Less and Less
Berattle. Nims.
A Shallot. Wilbur.
The Shape of the Fire.
Roethke.
To His Child. Bullokar.
Woman to Child. Wright.
Stench
Sonnets. Tuckerman.
Unprofitablenes. Vaughan.
Step (s)
Almada Hill: An Epistle from
Lisbon (excerpt). Mickle.
At the Tombs of the House of
Savoy. Smith.
Beauty. Binyon.
Caelica, LXXXII. Greville.
Caesura. MacKenzie.
A Circular Cry. Jabes.
A Dawn Horse. Harmon.
Dieppe. Beckett.
Dundonnel Mountains.
Young.
Easter Sunday, 1945.
Borgese.
The End of Sorrow. Fleg.
Epithalamium on a Late
Happy Marriage. Smart.
The Gentle Hill. Quasimodo.
God. Slutsky.
God's Promises. *Anonymous.*
The Golden Sequence.
Innocent III.
How to Tell the Top of a Hill.
Ciardi.
I Am the Autumn. Manger.
I Am with You Alway.
Nevin.
In My Dreams I Searched for
You. *Anonymous.*
In the Dark. Higginson.
Investiture. Henderson.
An Irish Blessing. Murray.
Kicking the Leaves. Hall.
The Loss of Strength.
Clarke.
The Man Whom the Sea Kept
Awake. Bly.
The Misfit-1939-1945. Day
Lewis.
Moving Day. Horne.
My Mother's Feet. Plumly.
O Lord, Thou Hast Been to
the Land. *Anonymous.*
Overland to the Islands.
Levertov.
The Ownership of the Night.
Levis.
Popular Songs of Tuscany.
Anonymous.
A Prayer. Yehoash.
The Prisoner. Plomer.
Raven at Lemon Creek Jail.
Waltner.

Solitude. Clare.
Step It Up and Go.
Anonymous.
To a Waterfowl. Bryant.
The Torrent. Robinson.
Touch Thou Mine eyes.
Ham.
Triptych. Heaney.
The Trout. Hine.
The Unpetalled Rose.
Therese.
Vicksburg. Hayne.
The Wall of China. Colum.
Written in a Lady's Prayer
Book. Rochester.
The Yankeys' Return from
Camp. *Anonymous.*
Stern
The Complaint. Akenside.
The Sailor's Alphabet.
Anonymous.
To Jesus on the Cross.
Tejada.
Two Smiles. Herford.
Stew (ed)
At the Lavender Lantern.
Divine.
Brother and Sister. "Carroll.
Celery. Nash.
A Farewell to English
(excerpt). Hartnett.
The Land of Cockayne.
Anonymous.
Persicos Odi. Adams.
To Henrietta, on Her
Departure for Calais.
Hood.
The Young Wife. Stead.
Stick (ing) (s)
Beaver Pond. Marriott.
A Bestiary. Rexroth.
Blok Let Me Learn the Poem.
Boyajian.
Blond Hair at the Edge of the
Pavement. Smith.
The Candid Man. Crane.
Change the Can Cheerily.
Anonymous.
Children When They're Very
Sweet. Ciardi.
Darling! Because My Blood
Can Sing. Cummings.
A Hazel Stick for Catherine
Ann. Heaney.
Icicles. Pinsky.
In the Children's Hospital.
""MacDiarmid.
IT. Lattimore.
Less and Less Human, O
Savage Spirit. Stevens.
Mswaki. Brodey.
Mule Skinner's Song (with
music). *Anonymous.*
Penal Servitude for Mrs.
Maybrick. *Anonymous.*
The Postage Stamp Lesson.
Anonymous.
Ribald Romeos Less and Less
Berattle. Nims.
Song of the Open Road
(excerpt). Whitman.
The Stick. Bennett.
Three Dreams. Michie.
To Ping-Ku, Asleep.
Durrell.
Union Maid. Guthrie.
Wiltshire Downs. Young.
Stiff (en)
Donkey. Van Doren.
I know a place where summer
strives. Dickinson.

Limerick: "A well-bred young girl of Gomorrah." *Anonymous.*
Mankind. *Anonymous.*
Post-Modern Literature. Moure.
Rodin to Rilke. Grosholz.
Seance. King.
The Sword of Tethra. Larminie.
Winter Holding Off the Coast of North America. Momaday.

Stifle (d)
Awake. Coleridge.
The Songs of Bilitis. Louys.
To a Golden Heart, Worn Round His Neck. Goethe.

Stile
Arcturus Is His Other Name. Dickinson.
Literary Importation. Freneau.
Though He That Ever Kind and True. Stevenson.
To A Skull. Jones.
Verses Written In 1872. Stevenson.

Still (ed) (ness)
Answer. Speyer.
Any April. Beard.
Arabesque. Johnson.
The Argument Begins with A. Thesen.
At Majority. Rich.
A Baby-Sermon. Macdonald.
Bacchanalia (excerpt). Arnold.
Be Still, My Heart. *Anonymous.*
Be Still, My Soul. Schlegel.
Before the Stuff Comes down. Snyder.
The Bush-Fiddle. Green.
The Canterbury Tales: Prologue to the Pardoner's Tale. Chaucer.
The Catfish. Waters.
A Charm for Bees. *Anonymous.*
The Clavichord. Sarton.
Crumbs. De la Mare.
Daily Trials. Holmes.
Dead. Johnson.
Dirge. Cawein.
Easter. Coatsworth.
Evensong. Schaumann.
The Everlasting Voices. Yeats.
The Excursion. Wordsworth.
Falling from the ridge. Yozei.
A Farewell. Brown.
The Farmer. Shove.
Father Death Blues. Ginsberg.
The Figures. Creeley.
The First Autumn. Schacht.
The Firstling. Davison.
The Fisherman. Fawcett.
Four Quartets. Eliot.
The Gothic Dusk. Prokosch.
Green Moth. Simic.
Haiku: "The falling snow flakes." Knight.
Haiku: "Why is the hail so wild..." Wright.
I Am Disquieted When I See Many Hills. Plutzik.
I Flung up My Arm Half from Sleep. Combs.
The Idler. Jennings.

In January, 1962. Kooser.
In the Backs. Cornford.
Inland Passages, I: The Long Hunter. Berry.
Ipswich Bar. Bates.
Kinship. Roberts.
Last Poems. Housman.
A Legend of Paul Bunyan. Bourinot.
The Light of Stars. Furness.
Limerick: "At a modernist school in Park Hill." Bishop.
Lincoln. Turner.
Lines Written in a Mausoleum. Grant.
Looking Both Ways before Crossing. Woods.
Merlin Enthralled. Wilbur.
The Mind Is Still. Le Guin.
The Moment of the Rose. Thompson.
The Monks at Ards. Maybin.
The Morning Track. Parone.
Moses on Mount Nebo. Regelson.
Mouths. Dudek.
Music. Ryan.
Myxomatosis. Larkin.
Name Giveaway. George.
Narcissa. Brooks.
Nicholas Nye. De La Mare.
Night. Bialik.
Night. Brown.
An Ode Written in the Peak. Drayton.
On the Cliff. Summers.
On the Move. Gunn.
Over and Over Stitch. Graham.
Perhaps. Spender.
The Practice of Magical Evocation. Di Prima.
Put Forth Thy Leaf, Thou Lofty Plane. Clough.
Pyramus and Thisbe. Dakin.
Quiet Days. Mey.
Reflections. Becker.
Riddle. Storm: "At times I am fast confined by my Master." *Anonymous.*
Rumination. Eberhart.
Sea Calm. Hughes.
Sea-Way. Cortissoz.
Sea Words. Leitch.
She being Brand. Cummings.
Silence, an Eloquent Applause. Gregory.
Sleep. Winters.
Solar Creation. Madge.
Song: "Woman sits on her porch." Thompson.
Sonnets from a Sequence. Barker.
Sourdough Mountain Lookout. Whalen.
Southern Mansion. Bontemps.
Spanish Blue. Morris.
The Spell of the Yukon. Service.
Starvation Camp near Jaslo. Szymborska.
The Stepping Stones. Aiken.
Storm. Wright.
Surfaces. Mayhall.
A Timepiece. Merrill.
To His Coy Mistress. Marvell.
To M.H. Wordsworth.

To Mary: It Is the Evening Hour. Clare.
To Nature. Fisher.
To Perilla. Herrick.
To the Newborn. Toth.
A Tree Design. Bontemps.
The Visitation. Le Compte.
Waiting for the Post. Auchterlonie.
The Walking Road. Hughes.
Water Island. Moss.
When Nature Hath Betrayed the Heart That Loved Her. Jewett.
Whym Chow. "Field.
A Wind Rose in the Night. Kilmer.
Winter. De Vere.
The World. Raine.
The Yachts. Williams.

Sting (s)
All Is Vanity, Saith the Preacher. Byron.
April 1940. Maybin.
The Bottle. Levine.
Death Sting Me Blues. Martin.
Delight in Books from Evening. Pastorius.
The Dumb Maid. *Anonymous.*
Epigram: "An epigram should be–if right." Walsh.
For Tony, Dougal, Mick, Bugs, Nick et al. Bathgate.
Georgics. Virgil (Publius Vergilius Maro).
If to Die–. Romilu.
If You Were Coming in the Fall. Dickinson.
The Impulse of October. Moses.
Irish History. Allingham.
The Kisse: A Dialogue. Herrick.
The Lethal Thought. Wagner.
Lines Written after the Discovery ... of the Germ of Yellow Fever. Ross.
Man and Wife Is One Flesh. Deacon.
The Marriage Ring. Blake.
Mojo Hiding Woman. Fuller.
Pretty Words. Wylie.
The Snake. Moore.
The Snake-Charmer. Hake.
To a Pet Cobra. Campbell.
To Himself. Aldridge.
Upon a Mole in Celia's Bosom. Carew.
Vegetable Loves. Darwin.
The Wandering Gadling. Wyatt.
A Winter Twilight. Bates.
With Seed the Sowers Scatter. Housman.

Stink (s)
Arnold. *Anonymous.*
Ask Not to Know This Man. Jonson.
Aubade: The Desert. Bock.
The Author. Churchill.
The Beggar's Opera. Gay.
Earth out of Earth. *Anomymous*
The First Epistle of the First Book of Horace Imitated (excerpt). Pope.

Memento Homo quod Cinis Es Et in Cinerem Reverteris. *Anonymous.*
On the Countess of Dorchester. Sackville.
To Poets. Landor.
Two Poems against His Rival, II. Catullus.
The Walk Home. Whittemore.

Stir (red) (s)
Absence. McKay.
As Well as They Can. Hope.
Ask Not to Know This Man. Jonson.
Auschwitz from Colombo. Ranasinghe.
The Bards. Graves.
A Beauty That All Night Long. Julal ed-Din Rumi.
Caelica, LXXI. Greville.
Epigram: "When Graphicus sat by the baths." Strato.
Failure. Brooke.
Fallen Leaves. Tupper.
Feather or Fur. Becker.
The Heart of the Tree. Bunner.
In Memoriam. Gingell.
Man Holding Boy. Dixon.
My Morning Song. Macdonald.
Noon. Clare.
Out of Chaos Out of Order Out. Roberts.
Portrait. Pound.
The Pruned Tree. Moss.
The Quickening. Tuttle.
Song of a Factory Girl. Zaturenska.
Sonnets: A Sequence on Profane Love. Boker.
Spring Song. Carman.
Supper. De La Mare.
Switzerland. Arnold.
The Three Silences of Molinos. Longfellow.
To Lygdus. Martial (Marcus Valerius Martialis).
Upon a Child That Died. Herrick.
The Vision. O Rathaille.
Willows. Schreiber.

Stitches
The Candidate. Gray.
The Tailor. Leftwich.
To My Cousin Mary, for Mending My Tobacco Pouch. Key.

Stock (s)
A Congratulatory Poem to the Honoured Edmund Morris, Esq.... Settle.
Iron. De La Mare.
Letters to Live Poets. Beaver.
The Lusty Fryer of Flanders. *Anonymous.*
My Dearest Rival. Suckling.
The Rose. Browne.
The Vine. Herrick.
When I Solidly Do Ponder. Pastorius.

Stocking (s)
A Description of an Author's Bedchamber. Goldsmith.
Hang up the Baby's Stocking! *Anonymous.*
The Man. Browne.
Santa Claus and the Mouse. Poulsson.

Sermon in a Stocking. Jewett.
Sonnet: "Idly she yawned, and threw her heavy hair." Moore.
Thinking of "The Autumn Fields." Bly.
The Three Foxes. Milne.
Women. Rich.

Stockman (men)
The Dying Stockman. *Anonymous.*
The Man from Snowy River. Paterson.

Stomach
Love's Progress. Donne.
Parole Denial. Green.
A Pizza Joint in Cranston (parody). Weeden.
Recall. Whittemore.
Robin the Bobbin. *Anonymous.*
Stomach. Norris.
To Sleep Easy All Night. *Anonymous.*

Stone Age
An Elegy. Winters.
More (parody). Appleman.

Stone (d) (s)
The After-Comers. Lowell.
After the Martyrdom. Iris.
The Air of June Sings. Dorn.
The Alexandrite Ring. Ryan.
All Songs. Page.
Amoretti, XXXII. Spenser.
Amoretti, LIV. Spenser.
The Anatomy of Angels. Nowlan.
The Angel and the Anchorite. Shelton.
De Angel Roll de Stone Away. *Anonymous.*
Animal Songs: Baboon 2. *Anonymous.*
Answer. Goldberg.
Aran Islands. Layton.
As You Like It. Shakespeare.
At Saint Patrick's Purgatory. O'Dala.
At the Jewish Cemetery in Prague. Levertin.
Audubon, Drafted. Jones.
Augusto Ngangula. Andrade.
Auto Wreck. Shapiro.
Back Road Farm. Bruce.
Baiamai's Never-failing Stream. Hart-Smith.
Ballywaire. Paulin.
Beaver Pond. Marriott.
Bedlam Hills. Smith.
The Black Bottom Bootlegger. Leiper.
Black Magdalens. Cullen.
The Boar of Badenoch and the Sow of Atholl. Mitchison.
Break My Heart of Stone. Wesley.
The Brigg. Skelton.
Burial in the Sand. Sullivan.
The Camelopard. Belloc.
A Cathedral. Vinaver.
Celia Singing. Carew.
Cherry-Pit. Herrick.
Chilled by Different Winds. Swaim.
Church Lock and Key. Herbert.

A Circle, a Square, a Triangle and a Ripple of Water. Cooper.
The City's Crown. Foulke.
Cockley Moor, Dockray, Penrith. Nicholson.
Come to the Stone. Jarrell.
Conserving the Magnitude of Uselessness. Ammons.
Contemplations. Bradstreet.
Correspondences. Duncan.
The Cruel Falcon. Jeffers.
Crumbs. De la Mare.
A Curse on a Closed Gate. Cousins.
The Cutting Edge. Levine.
Daniel Saw de Stone. *Anonymous.*
Dead. Coghill.
The Dead Sparrow. Cartwright.
Death of a Son. Silkin.
Desert Stone. Waddington.
Despair. Merwin.
Dipsychus. Clough.
Dirge. Cawein.
The Distances. Olson.
The Drunkeness of Pain. Shenhar.
Easter Flood. Stockwell.
Elegy Before Death. Millay.
Elegy in Six Sonnets. Tuckerman.
Elegy on the L.C. Donne.
The End. De La Mare.
Envoi. Mayo.
Epigram. *Anonymous.*
Epigram: "When 'mongst the youths." *Anonymous.*
An Epitaph. Benjacob.
Epitaph of Sarah Sexton. *Anonymous.*
Epitaph on a Party Girl. Usborne.
Epitaph on Erotion. Hunt.
An Epitaph upon the Right Honorable Sir Philip Sidney. Greville.
Euclid Alone Has Looked on Beauty Bare. Millay.
Evolution. Swenson.
Ex Nihilo. Gascoyne.
The Example. Davies.
Exile of the Sons of Uisliu (excerpt). *Anonymous.*
The Exiled Heart. Lindsay.
First to Throw a Stone. *Anonymous.*
Five Songs. Shapiro.
For a New Home. Marinoni.
Fragment. Robinson.
Fragments. Praxilla.
The Friar of Orders Grey. *Anonymous.*
Galatea Again. Taggard.
The Gathering. Thorpe.
The Gift. Stanford.
Gipsy Queen. Chapman.
A Girl's Song. Hinkson.
Girls. Rosen.
Glitter of Pebbles. Moraes.
God's Little Mountain. Hill.
Golden Lines. Nerval.
The Great Canzon. Rexroth.
Green Mountain Boy. Smyth.
Guinea. Roumain.
Hamlet. Shakespeare.
He Bare Him Up, He Bare Him Down. *Anonymous.*
He Sees Through Stone. Knight.

The Hellenics. Landor.
Heron. Plumly.
Hill People. Blackwell.
His Being Was in Her Alone. Sidney.
Hoc Est Corpus. Comfort.
A Holy Hill. Russell.
Homage to Paul Mellon, I. M. Pei, Their Gallery, and Washington City. Meredith.
Hosanna to Christ. Watts.
How Things Fall. Finkel.
I, Lord of All Mortals. *Anonymous.*
I Wish I Were by That Dim Lake. Moore.
Idea. Drayton.
The Iliad. Homer.
Impression du Matin. Wilde.
In This Hour. Johnson.
In Time of Crisis. Patterson.
Indian Painting, Probably Paiute, in a Cave near Madras, Oregon. Ramsey.
Indian Summer: Vermont. Stevenson.
Inniskeen Road: July Evening. Kavanagh.
The Interpreter. Johns.
Jesus. Pimentel Coronel.
John Standish, Artist. Fearing.
Julius Caesar. Shakespeare.
Junction. Pass.
Kingfisher Flat. Empson.
The Kingfishers. Olson.
Kiph. De la Mare.
Kohoutek. Ryan.
The Lament for Art O Laoghaire (excerpt). O'Connell.
Lapidary. Alexander.
The Leader. Livesay.
Leaving Mexico One More Time. Urdang.
Letter to a Friend. Warren.
Life from the Lifeless. Jeffers.
Little Things. Johns.
Long Island Springs. Moss.
The Loss of Strength. Clarke.
Love Me at Last. Corbin.
Lucy. Wordsworth.
Luzzato. Reznikoff.
Lyell's Hypothesis Again. Rexroth.
The Magnet. Stanley.
The Malcontent. Marston.
Meditations in Time of Civil War. Yeats.
Meditations of an Old Woman. Roethke.
Medusa. Weeks.
The Melancholy Year. Stickney.
A Metrical Version of the Bible....(excerpt). *Anonymous.*
Micromutations. Wright.
The Mill-stream, Now that Noises Cease. Housman.
Minor Key. Teller. J. L.
Montana Eclogue. Stafford.
The Moon Ground. Dickey.
Morality. Garrigue.
Morgain Le Fay. Crozier.
A Mountain Wind. Russell.
My Hands Are Withered. *Anonymous.*
N. Seidman.

Nativity. Hogan.
Nature. Herbert.
A New Dress. Korn.
A New Simile in the Manner of Swift. Goldsmith.
Newness. Paulin.
No Names. *Anonymous.*
Not Three–But One. Duff.
Not with a club. Dickinson.
Notes for Echo Lake 11. Palmer.
Notre Dame Perfected by Reflection. Witt.
Now I Have Nothing. Benson.
Nude in a Fountain. MacCaig.
Observation. Wynard.
October. Berkson.
Ode against St. Cecilia's Day. Barker.
Ode on Solitude. Pope.
Old. Hoyt
The Old Prison. Wright.
On a Stone Thrown at a Very Great Man, but Which Missed Him. Wolcot.
On Foinaven. Saunders.
Open Earth. Nicoidski.
Orion. Horne.
Orphic Interior. Sinisgalli.
Ox-Bone Madonna. Galvin.
Parnell. Yeats.
Paros. Macgowan.
Pastoral. Voigt.
Paul Laurence Dunbar. Hayden.
Piano Practice. Walcott.
The Piper's Progress. Mahony.
The Plain of Adoration. *Anonymous.*
Plainness. Borges.
The Playboy of the Demi-World: 1938. Plomer.
Poem About Your Face. Alterman.
Poems from a Greek Anthology (excerpt). Martial (Marcus Valerius Martialis).
Post Mortem. Jeffers.
The Power of Thought. Susskind.
Pregnant Teenager on the Beach. Balazs.
Private Worship. Van Doren.
Putting on My Shoes I Hear the Floor Cry out beneath Me (parody). Heffernan.
The Quiet of the Dead. Webster.
Rain. Henson.
Rainy Mountain Cemetery. Momaday.
Ramon. Harte.
The Rape of Lucrece. Shakespeare.
Red Lilies. Guest.
Reflecting on the Aging-Process (parody). Peters.
The Return. Cox.
The Rider. Drake.
The Ring Poem: A Husband Loses His Wedding Band... Dacey.
The River in the Meadows. Adams.
The Roadmenders' Song. *Anonymous.*

Roads Go Ever Ever On.
Tolkien.
The Rock. Merwin.
Rock Painting. Arnett.
Rock Tumbler. Reid.
The Room Above the Square.
Spender.
The Scorpion. Plomer.
Scribe. Auster.
The Secret Garden. Nichols.
Sestina: Of the Lady Pietra
degli Scrovigni. Dante
Alighieri.
She. Wilbur.
The Sheiling. Thomas.
Simon the Cyrenian Speaks.
Cullen.
The Skaian Gate (excerpt).
Scott.
Skara Brae. Longley.
The Small. Roethke.
A Small Faculty Stag for the
Visiting Poet. Birney.
A Soldier. Frost.
Soliloquy II. Aldington.
The Solitary. Teasdale.
The Song. Roethke.
Song: "I placed my dream in
a boat." Meireles.
Sonnets. Tuckerman.
The Soul Selects Her Own
Society. Dickinson.
St. Isaac's Chruch, Petrograd.
McKay.
Stanzas for My Daughter.
Gregory.
The Stone. Gibson.
The Stone Fleet. Melville.
Stone from the Gods.
Wassall.
Stone Giant. Bruchac.
The Street. Baro.
Suicide Pond. McLaughlin.
Summer Street. Ilce.
There Was a Strife 'Twixt
Man and Maid. Kipling.
They Who Tread the Path of
Labor. Van Dyke.
The Three Hills. Squire.
The Three Kingdoms of
Nature. Lessing.
Three Spring Notations on
Bipeds. Sandburg.
Three Women. Plath.
To a Young Girl Leaving the
Hill Country. Bontemps.
To Laura Phelan: 1880-1906.
Stokesbury.
To Some Builders of Cities.
Snaith.
To Vera Thompson. Haines.
Ts'ai Chi'h. Pound.
Two Birds. Linnell.
Two Pieces after Suetonius.
Warren.
Unto Jehovah Sing Will I.
Ainsworth.
Unusual Things. Hennen.
Upon This Rock. Todd.
Us Potes. Adams.
Valediction. Wheelock.
Volubilis, North Africa.
Currey.
Wake Cry. Cuney.
The Wanderer. Yehoash.
Watching a Cloud. Abse.
Waterfalls. Watkins.
Welcome to This House.
George.
Were I to Choose. Okara.
Wind. Hughes.

With a Posthumous Medal.
Brinnin.
The Words of the All-Wise
(excerpt). *Anonymous.*
Words Spoken by Pasternak
during a Bombing.
Akhmadulina.
The Years. Wheelock.
Stone wall
A Time to Talk. Frost.
A Tribe Searching. Reich.
Stonington
The Battle of Stonington on
the Seaboard of
Connecticut. Freneau.
Stony Point
Wayne at Stony Point.
Scollard.
Stool (s)
The Busy Body. Field.
A Charge to the Poets
(excerpt). Whitehead.
Cinderella's Song. Roberts.
The Inner Significance of the
Statues Seated Outside the
Boston... Arensberg.
R. I. P. Struther.
Sum, Es, Est. *Anonymous.*
Stoop (ed) (s)
Astraea. Emerson.
The Falcon. Lovelace.
My Blessing Be on Waterford.
Letts.
Our Heavenly Father
(excerpt). Faber.
Piano Recital. Deutsch.
So proud she was to die.
Dickinson.
The Soul. *Anonymous.*
Stop (ped) (ping) (s)
The Aga Khan. Orlen.
As in the Land of Darkness.
Miklitsch.
B's the Bus. McGinley.
Baedeker for Metaphysicians.
Higgins.
The Black Army. Mqhayi.
The Call of the Eastern Quail.
Hitchcock.
Clerihew: "The Empress
Poppaea." *Anonymous.*
The Concert. McGinley.
Crossing West Texas (1966).
Robertson.
Descending. Iremonger.
An Evasion. Livingstone.
Everything. Paul.
First Lessons in Musical
Time. *Anonymous.*
The Flint Hills. Blockcolski.
The Flower Vendor.
Cabalquinto.
Four. Gibbs.
Girl at the Seaside. Murphy.
Going down the Mountain.
Iremonger.
Golden Pheasant. Hart-
Smith.
The Good Woman.
MacLean.
Grandfather's Clock. Work.
Happiness. Dickey.
The Hired Man's Way.
Bangs.
The Iliad. Homer.
Invocation for the New Year.
Armstrong.
It Was in Vegas.
Cunningham.
The Line to Heaven by Christ
Was Made. *Anonymous.*
Madaket Beach. Barr.

Making up for a Soul.
Wagoner.
Morning Bus. Coulter.
The Mugger. Pack.
My Father's Leaving. Sadoff.
Mystic. Plath.
An Old Lady Watching TV.
Skinner.
Out of Body. Moore.
The Photographer Whose
Shutter Died. Meissner.
The Policeman. Watts.
Rain Forest. Smith.
Ringed Plover by a Water's
Edge. MacCaig.
San Sepolcro. Graham.
Scalp Dance Song.
Anonymous.
She Is Carefully Stepping over
the Important
Communications. Canan.
Song. Clare.
Song of Myself. Whitman.
There's Somethin'. Small.
This Cold Nothing Else.
Wier.
Thomas Carlyle.
Anonymous.
The Turn. Creeley.
Twentieth-Century Blues.
Fearing.
Underground Poetry. Pietri.
Upanishads: Third Adhyaya.
Anonymous.
Voices Answering Back: The
Vampires. Raab.
Wake. Spires.
What a Proud Dreamhorse.
Cummings.
Your Neighbor. Biggar.
Store (s)
Across the Western Ocean.
Anonymous.
As an Old Mercer. Fisher.
The Beggar. Moss.
Bouncing Ball. Watson.
A Dialogue between the
Resolved Soul and Created
Pleasure. Marvell.
The Faerie Queene. Spenser.
Freedom. Green.
The Gift. Bruner.
Hiroshima Exit. Kogawa.
The Hongo Store 29 Miles
Volcano Hilo, Hawaii.
Hongo.
A Present from the Emperor's
New Concubine. Pan
Chieh-yu.
The Sailor's Lamentation.
Anonymous.
The Seed. Fisher.
Shopkeepers. Leib.
Song of the Harvest.
Washburn.
Sonnets, LXVII: "Ah
wherefore with infection
should he live."
Shakespeare.
Sunday. Coatsworth.
Times o' Year. Barnes.
To Favonius. Bolton.
To Plautia. Cokayne.
The Vision of Sir Launfal.
Lowell.
Stork (s)
Among Those Killed in the
Dawn Raid Was a Man
Aged One Hundred.
Thomas.
The History of Insipids.
Freke.

Lament of Hsi-Chun. Hsi-
chun.
Storm (s) (y)
Andromache. Euripides.
At Midsummer. Dubie.
Barnacle Geese. Higham.
The Campaign. Addison.
Chorus. Godolphin.
The Cotton Cat. Newsome.
Courtship. Strand.
Dauber. Masefield.
The Disinherited, IX.
Gilmore.
The Drowned Mariner.
Smith
Drumochter. Murray.
The Face against the Pane.
Aldrich.
Faeryland. Pinsky.
Farmer. Bailey.
Georgics. Virgil (Publius
Vergilius Maro).
Gondibert (excerpt).
Davenant.
Her Longing. Roethke.
Hills of the Middle Distance.
Mitchell.
Horat. Ode 29. Book 3.
Paraphras'd in Pindarique
Verse. Dryden.
I Didn't Know My Soul.
Ben-Yitzhak.
I Live My Life. Rilke.
I Love Snow and All the
Forms. Shelley.
Inanna and Ebih.
Enheduanna.
The Jovial Marriner; or, The
Sea-Man's Renown.
Playford.
The Last Buccaneer.
Macaulay.
Leda. Van Duyn.
Life's Lessons. *Anonymous.*
Like Those Boats Which Are
Returning. Saigyo Hoshi.
Limerick: "When they go out
walking the Sioux."
Anonymous.
Lines Written on a Very
Boisterous Day in May,
1944. Clare.
Lost Beliefs. Howells.
The Lost Colors. Ward.
Lullaby. Harris.
Metamorphoses of the
Vampire. Baudelaire.
Mighty Day. *Anonymous.*
The Mother's Lullaby.
Clare.
The New House. Rutsala.
Nocturne in G Minor.
Vollmoeller.
Odes. Horace.
Of Little Faith. Pulsifer.
Old Ironsides. Holmes.
The Old Parish Church,
Whitby. Rawnsley.
On a Dream (after Reading
Dante's Episode of Paolo
and Francesca). Keats.
On a Sea-Storm Nigh the
Coast. Steere.
On the Slain Collegians.
Melville.
On Top of Troubled Waters.
Langford.
Pasa Thalassa Thalassa.
Robinson.
Paths They Kept Barren.
Garmon.

People Who Went by in
   Winter. Stafford.
Prayer after World War.
   Sandburg.
A Prayer for a Marriage.
   Davies.
Prayer on Making a Canoe.
   Anonymous.
Presaging. Rilke.
The Rainy Summer.
   Meynell.
Reconnaissance. Bontemps.
The Reformed Pirate.
   Roberts.
The Rhyme of the Rain
   Machine. Clarke.
Rothiemurchus. Lamont.
A Sail. Lermontov.
The Sailor. Warner.
Significant Fevers. Fell.
Song from the Waters.
   Beddoes.
Song: "O ruddier than the
   cherry." Gay.
Song of Eros. Woodberry.
Sonnet: "An open wound
   which has been healed
   anew." Trench.
Sonnets for a Dying Man.
   Singer.
Stewball. *Anonymous.*
A Stormy Day. *Anonymous.*
The Story of a Stowaway.
   Scott.
Strawberries. Morgan.
Studies from Life. Dickey.
Summoned by Bells: Cornwall
   in Childhood. Betjeman.
Theodosia Burr. Palmer.
This Place in the Ways.
   Rukeyser.
To a Town Poet. Reese.
The True Lovers Bold.
   Anonymous.
U is for Umbrellas.
   McGinley.
Venice. Symonds.
The Wakeupworld. Cullen.
Whispers. Hill.
The Wound. Gunn.
Writing on the Wall. Fallon.
Ye Mariners of England.
   Campbell.
Young Sea. Sandburg.
Story (stories)
After Her Death. Stevenson.
The Approach to Thebes.
   Kunitz.
Aunt Sue's Stories. Hughes.
Barber, Spare Those Hairs.
   Love.
Christmas Eve. Kooser.
Cinderella. Sexton.
Columbus. Hale.
The Coplas on the Death of
   His Father, the
   Grandmaster of Santiago.
   Manrique.
The Darby Ram.
   Anonymous.
A Dirge upon the Death of
   the Right Valiant Lord,
   Bernard Stuart. Herrick.
Don Juan. Byron.
The Electric Cop. Cruz.
The Enchanted Castle.
   D'Orge.
The End of Fall. Ponge.
Footnote to John ii.4.
   Mason.
Freely Espousing. Schuyler.
Herman Melville. Auden.

A Hymne on the Nativitie of
   My Saviour. Jonson.
I Love to Tell the Story.
   Hankey.
The Idiot. Wilson.
In an Old House. Brown.
Iter Boreale. Wild.
Let Not Thy Beauty.
   Townsend.
Literary Life in the Golden
   West. Whalen.
Little Tee-Wee. *Anonymous.*
Lost Light. Akers.
Mother Carey's Chicken.
   Watts-Dunton.
My Aunt. Hughes.
The Nameless Doon.
   Larminie.
Naomi Wise. *Anonymous.*
Nature, That Washed Her
   Hands in Milk. Ralegh.
The Odyssey. Homer.
The Old Story over Again.
   Kenney.
An Overture. Knoll.
The Owl and the Nightingale.
   Anonymous.
A Poem of Sir Walter
   Rawleighs. Ralegh.
Rejoicing at the Arrival of
   Ch'en Hsiung. Po Chu-i.
Rubaiyat for Sue Ella Tucker.
   Williams.
Satellites. Lenhart.
A Second Molting.
   Salisbury.
Slim Man Canyon. Silko.
Song: "Too late, alas! I must
   confess." Rochester.
Spring in England. Going.
The Story We Know.
   Collins.
Stratagem. Curnow.
Street Window. Sandburg.
The Tale of Jorkyns and
   Gertie; or, Vice Rewarded.
   Lister.
That Idiot, Wordsworth.
   Byron.
To Groves. Herrick.
A Toad. Allen.
Under the Moon. Yeats.
Washyuma Motor Hotel.
   Ortiz.
The Wave. Hine.
We'll Meet Again. Smith.
The Whole Story. Stafford.
Winter Watch. Marion.
Wishes to His Supposed
   Mistress. Crashaw.
You Lovely People. Cerenio.
Stout
A New Catch in Praise of the
   Reverend Bishops.
   Anonymous.
The Red Cockatoo. Po Chu-
   i.
Song of Duke William.
   Belloc.
Teddy Bear. Milne.
Under Milk Wood (excerpt).
   Thomas.
Stove
Don't Copy Cat. "Twain.
Indoors. Johnston.
Two Lines from the Brothers
   Grimm. Orr.
Warmth. Sutter.
Straight
After Drinking All Night with
   a Friend... Bly.
Blood. Bremser.

Drinking Song: "Drink that
   rotgut, drink that rotgut".
   Anonymous.
Grandfather Yoneh.
   Borenstein.
The Helmet. Levine.
Japanese Beetles. Kennedy.
Love in a Cottage.
   McKellar.
November 1967. Durcan.
Our Bias. Auden.
The Plow. Horne.
Sindhi Woman. Stallworthy.
Washington. Meyrich.
Strain (s)
Anthony Wayne.
   Guiterman.
The Best Time for
   Conception. Quillet.
Betty Zane. English.
The Cattle of His Hand.
   Underwood.
Childe Harold's Pilgrimage:
   Canto III. Byron.
The Flute of the Lonely.
   Lindsay.
Gesture. Welles.
Gethsemane. Tappan.
The Legion Club (excerpt).
   Swift.
Madrigal: "Surcharged with
   discontent." *Anonymous.*
The Making of Man.
   Chadwick.
The Old General. Williams.
The Pines and the Sea.
   Cranch
Poem: "Geranium, houseleek,
   laid in oblong beds."
   Gray.
De Profundis. Rossetti.
The Seamy Side of Motley.
   Seaman.
Sonnets, XC: "Then hate me
   when thou wilt; if ever,
   now." Shakespeare.
There Is a Pool on Garda.
   Scollard.
Tree-Building. Cable.
The Whisperer. Stephens.
Strait (s)
The Gulistan. Sa'di.
A Hot Engagement between a
   French Privateer and an
   English Fireship.
   Anonymous.
A Thanksgiving. Newman.
Strait jacket
Between Me and Anyone Who
   Can Understand–. Scott.
Strand (s)
All That Is Left. Hartnett.
Autumn. Rossetti.
The Father's Gold.
   Anonymous.
Inspiration. Tabb.
The Mystic. Rice.
Sonnets on the Sea's Voice.
   Sterling.
Strange
The 20th Century. Gray.
After the Visit. Hardy.
All Souls' Night. Cornford.
American Dreams. Simpson.
Antiquary. Donne.
Ball Game. Eberhart.
Brobdingnag. Stoutenburg.
Caelica, LXXII. Greville.
Comrades As We Rest
   Within. Hambleton.
The Dam, Glen Garry.
   Symmons.

Dark Room. Zydek.
Davideis. Cowley.
Deare, If You Change.
   Anonymous.
Dreamtime. Domanski.
The Dykes. Kipling.
Folded Power. Cromwell.
For Guillaume Apollinaire.
   Meredith.
God's Ways Are Strange.
   Bruner.
Greeting. Young.
Haiku: "That duck, bobbing
   up". Joso.
Hotel de l'Univers et Portugal.
   Merrill.
In Childbed. Hardy.
Janna. Kuka.
The Life and Lucubrations of
   Crispinus Scriblerus
   (excerpt). Woodhouse.
Long Term Suffering.
   Eberhart.
Madrigal: "Dear, if you
   change." Dowland.
The Magic Apple Tree.
   Feinstein.
Meditation under Stars.
   Meredith.
Memorial Rain. MacLeish.
Moments. Schwob.
My Soul Is Robbed.
   Rosenberg.
Nathaniel Lee to Sir Roger
   L'Estrange, Who Visited
   Him in His Madhouse.
   Lee.
The Negatives. Levine.
Neural Folds. Day.
On Leaving Ullswater.
   Raine.
The Oracle. Ficke.
Ortho's Epitaph. Calverlcy.
Plankton. Miller.
The Poet. Long.
The Praise of Ben Dorain.
   MacIntyre.
Rain. Wright.
Report from a Far Place.
   Stafford.
A Self Accuser. Donne.
The Sleeping Beauty. Sitwell.
Sometimes When I Sit Musing
   All Alone. Robinson.
Song for a Cracked Voice.
   Irwin.
Song of a Man about to Die
   in a Strange Land.
   Anonymous.
Songs. Gilder.
Sonnet: "Oh, my beloved,
   have you thought of this."
   Millay.
The Story of Pyramid
   Thothmes. *Anonymous.*
Strange Meetings. Monro.
There Is a Place in Distant
   Seas. Whately.
Travelling Song. McGrath.
Trees, Who Are Distant.
   Warr.
Urgency. Sholl.
Vision. Zangwill.
The Voice. Wilson.
Waterchew! Corso.
Why the British Girls Give in
   So Easily. Moore.
A Winter Daybreak above
   Vence. Wright.
The Wise. Cullen.
A Woman Making Advances
   Publicly. Kazantzis.

Stranger (s)
Another Death.   Borrell.
At the Battery Sea-Wall.
  Laube.
Beneath This Mound.
  Bierce.
The Birds of Scotland
  (excerpt).   Grahame.
Brave Donahue.   Donahue.
The Bride's Farewell: Two
  Songs.   *Anonymous.*
Cafe in Warsaw.   Ginsberg.
Chamber Music.   Joyce.
The Choice.   Norris.
Chorus from the Rock–III.
  Eliot.
Consumed.   Tate.
The Country North of
  Belleville.   Purdy.
Daughter.   Hahn.
Dogs are Shakespearean,
  Children Are Strangers.
  Schwartz.
Elegy.   Ignatow.
Emily Hardcastle, Spinster.
  Ransom.
Etude for Voice and Hand.
  Levin.
Ever Since.   MacLeish.
Finite.   "Dalton.
For an Emigrant.   Jarrell.
The Friend of the Fourth
  Decade.   Merrill.
Gaeltacht.   Hutchinson.
Geography.   Farjeon.
Gerda, My Husband's Wife.
  Triem.
The Ghost of an Education.
  Michie.
The Gulistan.   Sa'di.
The Home Fire.   Johns.
I never hear that one is dead.
  Dickinson.
Inscription for Arthur
  Rackham's Rip Van
  Winkle.   Flecker.
Jacob's Well.   *Anonymous.*
Landfall.   *Anonymous.*
Leda Reconsidered.   Van
  Duyn.
Love's Guerdons.   Nesbit.
Meeting After Long Absence.
  Perry.
Memorial Day.   Gilder.
Parachutes, My Love, Could
  Carry Us Higher.   Guest.
Passage of an August.
  Wilkins.
Pastoral.   Dyment.
Piccante.   Di Michele.
A Poem for the Old Man.
  Wieners.
Power-Cut.   McGuckian.
Prelude.   Aidoo.
The Prisoner of Zenda.
  Wilbur.
Reasons.   James.
The Rune of Hospitality.
  Anonymous.
Seance.   Roditi.
Separation.   Arnold.
Singles.   Waters.
Stranger, Why Do You
  Wonder So?   Jones-
  Quartey.
Sudan.   Jackson.
The Sword of Surprise.
  Chesterton.
The Table.   Heffernan.
Time to Myself.   Jiles.
To a Lady.   Scott.
To an Artist.   Burns.

Too Young for Love.
  Horace.
Trees in the Garden.
  Lawrence.
The Triumph of Forgotten
  Things.   Thomas.
Under the Casuarina.
  Riddell.
Undertone.   Stanford.
The Vowels of Another
  Language.   Disch.
The Wickedest Man in
  Memphis.   Brown.
A Woman of Words.   Hall.
Wonder.   Raymund.
Young Man of Alien Beauty.
  O Dalaigh.
Yourself.   Very.
Strangle (d)
Eighteen Verses Sung to a
  Tatar Reed Whistle.   Ts'ai
  Yen.
In Days of New.   Bartlett.
In Santa Maria del Popolo.
  Gunn.
Providence.   Rice.
The Sleeper.   Hay.
William Wilson.   Cowley.
Straps
Before the Statue of Apollo.
  Tchernichovsky.
The New Saddhus.   Pinsky.
Stratford
Ben Jonson Entertains a Man
  from Stratford.   Robinson.
Stratophon
Advice to a Prizefighter.
  Lucilius [or Lucillius].
Straw
The Bards.   Graves.
Christmas Morning.
  Lautermilch.
Conversations between Here
  and Home.   Harjo.
Epigram: "You were a pretty
  boy once."   Philip of
  Thessaloni.
Fragment: The Furl of Fresh-
  Leaved Dog-Rose Down.
  Hopkins.
The Gipsy Laddie.
  Anonymous.
Grey Him.   Mariah.
Haitian Suite.   Orr.
Hangman.   Anthony ("Ai").
A Hundreth Good Poyntes of
  Husbandry.   Tusser.
Limerick: "There was a young
  lady of Lynn."
  Anonymous.
The Name.   Hay.
The Saucy Sailor.
  Anonymous.
Sipping Cider through a
  Straw.   *Anonymous.*
Spring.   Giltinan.
Sucking Cider Through a
  Straw.   *Anonymous.*
To William Allen White.
  Ferber.
Strawberries
Ave Eva.   Wheelwright.
Curly Locks.   Mother Goose.
Epigram: "The son of the
  King of the Moy."
  Anonymous.
Fresh Cheese and Cream.
  Herrick.
Hexameter and Pentameter.
  Anonymous.
Housing Starts.   Davison.

Son of the King of May.
  Anonymous.
Song: "Smooth was the Water,
  calm the Air."   Sedley.
With Strawberries.   Henley.
Stray (ed) (ing)
Chamber Music.   Joyce.
The Crier.   Drayton.
Eclogue IV. The Poet
  (excerpt).   Jenner.
The Faerie Queene.   Spenser.
The Holy Eclogue.   del
  Castillo.
An Hymn of Heavenly Beauty
  (excerpt).   Spenser.
In the Garden of the Lord.
  Keller.
The Life of the Blessed.
  Leon.
Mr. Thomas Shcpheard...Hee
  a Man of a Thousand.
  Johnson.
One.   Rodgers.
The Plantation.   Heaney.
The Seasons.   Thomson.
Snowstorm.   Clare.
To Chloe.   Horace.
You're Sorry, Your Mother Is
  Crazy, & I'm a Chinese
  Shiksa.   Lee.
Streak (s)
Deserts.   Hanes.
Forecast.   Miles.
London Interior.   Monro.
Stream (s)
The Alley. An Imitation of
  Spenser.   Pope.
Anasazi at Mesa Verde.
  Saner.
The Ancestors.   Wright.
And the Old Folks Said.
  Mark.
Auras of Delight.   Patmore.
Below the Surface-Stream,
  Shallow and Light.
  Arnold.
Braddock's Defeat.
  Anonymous.
Breathe on the Glass.
  Stineford.
The Brook.   Lord
Casting at Night.   Hoey.
Cattle.   *Anonymous.*
Childe Harold's Pilgrimage:
  Canto IV, XXVIII.
  Byron.
Christmas Creek.   Kendall.
Circus Elephant.   Worth.
Confession.   Clifton.
Corries.   Smith.
Dat Lonesome Stream.
  Anonymous.
Describes the Place Where
  Cynthia Is Sporting Herself.
  Ayres.
Dew Sat on Julia's Hair.
  Herrick.
Dressing Game.   Schmitz.
An Evening Walk (excerpt).
  Wordsworth.
Falsehood.   Cartwright.
The First Day Out.   Reiter.
The Gardens of Alcinous.
  Pope.
Halieutica.   Oppian.
The Heavenly City.   Smith.
The Hidden Truth.   Jami.
I Am a Peach Tree.   Li Po.
I Wept as I Lay Dreaming.
  Heine.
In Between the Curve.
  Bacon.

In the Ravine.   Ross.
In the Redwood Forest.
  Pomeroy.
Indian Woman's Death-Song.
  Hemans.
Karoo Town.   Dederick.
A Late Manuscript at the
  Schocken Institute.   Preil.
Lethe.   Millay.
Lines Composed a Few Miles
  above Tintern Abbey.
  Wordsworth.
Lines to the Blessed
  Sacrament.   Callanan.
Lucina Schynning in Silence
  of the Night...
  Chuilleanain.
Madrigal: To His Lady
  Selvaggia Vergiolesi...
  Cino da Pistoia.
Madrigal: "Wake, sleepy
  Thyrsis."   Pilkington.
Men Improve with the Years.
  Yeats.
Message from Ohanapecosh
  Glacier.   Ransom.
Mi Abuelo.   Rios.
Midnight.   Tennyson.
The Mother.   Coleridge.
On Lisa's Golden Hair.
  Campbell.
On the Discoveries of Captain
  Lewis.   Barlow.
On the Inconstancy of
  Women: From the Latin of
  Catullus.   Lamb.
On the Road to California.
  Anonymous.
Orpheus.   Winters.
Poetry is Death Cast Out.
  Clouts.
The River That Is East.
  Kinnell.
Rural Sports.   Gay.
Salutation.   Russell.
Shall I Be Silent?   Herbert.
Shall I Come, If I Swim?
  Wide Are the Waves, You
  See.   Campion.
A Short History of the
  Teaching Profession.
  Maura.
Sierra Kid.   Levine.
Silver.   De La Mare.
Song from the Maker of
  Totems.   Niatum.
Spring Pastoral.   Wylie.
Starting at Dawn.   Sun Yun-
  feng.
The Stepping Stones.   Aiken.
There's a Fire in the Forest.
  Ross.
To Be Sung on the Water.
  Bogan.
To Venus.   Horace.
The Triumph of Time.
  Swinburne.
Upon Julia's Hair Filled with
  Dew.   Herrick.
Street-car (s)
I Walked over the Grave of
  Henry James.   Eberhart.
The Songs of Maximus, 1.
  Olson.
Street (s)
2nd Dance–Seeing Lines–6
  February 1964.   MacLow.
The Art of Love: Life Is Full
  of Horrors and Hormones.
  Koch.
An Aspect of Love, Alive in
  the Ice and Fire.   Brooks.

Babylon. Taylor.
Behaviour of Money.
  Spencer.
Bess. Stafford.
Blue Juniata: The Streets of
  Air. Cowley.
A Catch of Shy Fish.
  Brooks.
Central Park South. Revell.
A Charge to the Poets
  (excerpt). Whitehead.
Clear. Lewis.
The Cottage Hospital.
  Betjeman.
Dances of Death. Blok.
The Dog Parade.
  Guiterman.
Dogs of Santiago.
  McCarthy.
An Egyptian Tomb. Bowles.
The Friar in the Well (B
  version). Anonymous.
Girls Working in Banks.
  Shapiro.
A God Once Commanded Us.
  Goldberg.
Harlem Shadows. McKay.
Howl, II. Ginsberg.
I'm the Police Cop Man, I
  Am. Morrison.
In Old Tucson. Hall.
The Investiture. Sassoon.
Jane Austen at the Window.
  Beer.
Limerick: "One evening a
  goose, for a treat."
  Herford.
Lines for a Young Wanderer
  in Mexico. Logan.
The Marines' Hymn.
  Anonymous.
May Evening. Brennan.
The Morning. Gay.
Not without Beauty.
  McLeish.
On Linden Street. Ehrlich.
Parts Man. West.
Pedlar. Nelson.
The Perturbations of Uranus.
  Fuller.
The Plodder Seam.
  Anonymous.
Poem in Karori. Johnson.
The Purpose of the
  Chesapeake & Ohio Canal.
  Smith.
Quivira. Guiterman.
Revelation. Bullis.
Sale. Miles.
Samuel Brown. Cary.
The Shell. Stephens.
Somewhere Down below Me
  Is a Street. Maloney.
A Song in the Front Yard.
  Brooks.
The Songs. Bell.
Sonnet to A Negro in Harlem.
  Johnson.
The Streets of New York.
  Blossom.
Sweet Ethel. Piper.
The Sword of Surprise.
  Chesterton.
These Purists. Williams.
Toys. Sutzkever.
Tradition. Guiterman.
Trippers. Sitwell.
Two Pictures. Anonymous.
Waiting for the Post.
  Auchterlonie.
Watershed. Avison.
Weather Ear. Nicholson.

Who Makes the Journey.
  Song.
Zaydee. Levine.
Strength (s)
Anticipaton. Bronte.
As Thy Days. Tullar.
The Author's Apology.
  Carmi.
A Battle. Crawford.
Buttercups and Daisies.
  Howitt.
Canticle. McClure.
Christchurch, N.Z. Birney.
The Christian's New-Year
  Prayer (excerpt). Wilcox.
Come Back. Herbert.
Come to Me, Beloved.
  Dolben.
Convention. Kreymborg.
The Crowning Gift.
  Cromwell.
Day by Day. Winward.
The Dream of Gerontius.
  Newman.
Dryad Song. Fuller.
Fair England. Cone.
Fidelity. Wordsworth.
The First and the Last.
  Bonar.
First-Day Thoughts.
  Whittier.
For Strength. Tagore.
The Gatineaus. Watson.
Gone Is the Sleepgiver.
  Shuttle.
Grandmother and Child.
  Dallas.
Gratitude for Work.
  Oxenham.
Hills. Guiterman.
History Lesson. Van Doren.
Homestead-Winter Morning.
  Duryee.
House Sonnet. Wylie.
A Hymn of Trust. Sargent.
A Hymn to My God in a
  Night of My Late Sicknesse.
  Wotton.
I See God. Anonymous.
If This Be All. Bronte.
The Iliad. Homer.
Introducing a Madman.
  Waldrop.
John Landless Leads the
  Caravan. Goll.
A Juggle of Myrtle Twigs.
  Codish.
Kula...A Homecoming.
  Mark.
The Lay of the Captive
  Count. Goethe.
Lear. Williams.
Letter from a Wife. Reese.
Love Letter. Gregory.
Love Song: "The little
  sycamore." Anonymous.
The Man's Prayer. Daly.
Mandrakes for Supper.
  Baxter.
A Midnight Interior.
  Sassoon.
Midstream. Enright.
Miracle Play: Satan and
  Pilate's Wife. Anonymous.
The Modern Fine Gentleman
  (excerpt). Jenyns.
Mount Vernon. Anonymous.
My Soul Shall Cling to Thee.
  Elliot.
Narrative. Eybers.
Night-Music: Time Exposures.
  Rukeyser.

No Snake in Springtime.
  Coatsworth.
O God, in Whose Great
  Purpose. Gilkey.
The Oak. Tennyson.
Ode for a Master Mariner
  Ashore. Guiney.
The Old Man's Wish. Pope.
On Descending the River Po.
  Parsons.
Our Heroes. Cary.
Outside the Holy City.
  Gilkey.
The Perfect Garden.
  Robertson.
Prayer. Trench.
Prayer. Washbourne.
Psalm XXIX. Sidney.
Psalm XXXIX. Sidney.
The Quarry. Boscan.
Real Life. Berrigan.
Rekayi Tangwena. Kadhani.
Single Sonnet. Bogan.
The Song of the Body
  Dreamed in the Spirit's
  Mad Behest. Antoninus.
The Spartan Wrestler.
  Damagetus.
Survivors. Hogan.
The Testament of a Man
  Forbid. Davidson.
Thanksgiving. Nichols.
Thanksgiving After
  Communion. Anonymous.
Their Beginning. Cavafy.
This Do in Remembrance of
  Me. Bonar.
The Thousand and One
  Nights: Pearls Seen through
  Amber. Anonymous.
Tiger. McKay.
To the World: a Farewell for
  a Gentlewoman, Virtuous
  and Noble. Jonson.
The Vintage. Cooper.
Washington. Goodman.
Wealth. Emerson.
When the Dead Men Die.
  O'Neill.
Within the Shelter of Our
  Walls. Lennen.
Strengthen (ed)
Easter Communion.
  Hopkins.
Goblin Market. Rossetti.
Silex Scintillans. Vaughan.
Songs of Joy. Davies.
Stress (es)
Credit. Anonymous.
Voronezh. Akhmatova.
Written on the Sense of
  Isolation in Contemporary
  Ireland. Greacen.
Stretch (ed)
Absence. Jago.
The Boss. Lowell.
A Christmas Dawn at Sea.
  Morgan.
I Cut in Two. Hwang Chin-
  i.
Let America Be America
  Again. Hughes.
Outer Space, Inner Space.
  Cardiff.
De Profundis. Rossetti.
Sandstone. Marriott.
The Unloved to His Beloved.
  Percy.
Victory in Defeat.
  Markham.
Walking. Glaubitz.

Strew
Decoration. Higginson.
Inspiration. Tabb.
Stricken
Time Does Not Bring Relief.
  Millay.
The Wizard of Alderley Edge.
  Coe.
Stride (s)
Africa. Angelou.
Break, Break, Break (parody).
  Squire.
Catching Up. Walker.
The Foal. Renton.
For Mulatto. Fernandez.
On the Doorstep. Hardy.
Summer Solstice. Bowering.
To Walk on Hills. Graves.
Tristan da Cunha. Campbell.
Strife
The Banquet. Herbert.
Blow, Bugle! Clark.
The Breath of Night. Jarrell.
Cresophontes: Prayer to
  Peace. Euripides.
The Day of Wrath. Waddell.
Disillusion. Decker.
Every Christian Born of God.
  Anonymous.
The Harder Task.
  Anonymous.
It Is Finished. Bonar.
Kind Hearts. Anonymous.
Lullaby of an Infant Chief.
  Scott.
On the Death of Anne Bronte.
  Bronte.
Pain. Brown.
The Rakes of Mallow.
  Anonymous.
Rhythm. Waddell.
Robin Hood's Chase.
  Anonymous.
Roma. Rutilius.
The Rooftree. Tate.
A Russian Cradle Song.
  Nomberg.
Tao. Bailey.
Thy Will Be Done. Kerr.
The Undersong. Emerson
The Way. Morse.
We Are the Burden-Bearers
  (excerpt). Stidger.
The Winds of Fate. Wilcox.
The World Needs.
  Anonymous.
Strike (s) (struck)
Age. Landor.
At Dawn of the Year.
  Klingle.
The Avengers. Markham.
The Barn. Spender.
Battle Songs of the King
  Tshaka. Anonymous.
Binding Arbitration.
  Wrigley.
The Birdsville Track.
  Stewart.
Casey's Daughter at the Bat.
  Graham.
Casey-Twenty Years Later.
  McDonald.
Change the Can Cheerily.
  Anonymous.
The Diaspora. Auden.
D.G.C. to J.A. Bronte.
Elegy for My Mother.
  Katrovas.
Experience. Simmons.
The Fear. Frost.

It Was the Morning.
Petrarch (Francesco
Petrarca).

Madrigal: "The greedy hawk
with sudden sight of lure."
Anonymous.

March 23, 1982 Tuesday
Night. Waltner.

Modern Love, III. Meredith.

O Hark to the Herald. Ben
Kalir.

Ojibwa War Songs.
Anonymous.

Once for Candy Cook Had
Stolen. Auden.

Othello. Shakespeare.

Parable. Soutar.

Poems, XCVIII: "In spring
and summer winds may
blow." Landor.

Rhyming Prophecy for a New
Year. Cooper.

The Silent Woman:
Clerimont's Song. Jonson.

The Son, Condemned.
Rubin.

To Fool, or Knave. Jonson.

The United States and
Macedonian. *Anonymous.*

The Workers Rose on May
Day or Postscript to Karl
Marx. Lorde.

Strikeout (struck out)

From the Batter's Box.
Harford.

String (s)

Balloon Man. North.

The Birds' Courting Song.
Anonymous.

Childhood in Jacksonville,
Florida. Cooper.

Corinna. Campion.

The Djanggawul Cycle, 144.
Anonymous.

Dust to Dust. De La Mare.

The Face. Stryk.

Father and Son. Stafford.

Jack the Jolly Tar.
Anonymous.

The Kite. Behn.

Lent in a Year of War.
Merton.

Like Gulliver. Cassian.

Limerick: "Our Vicar is good
Mr. Inge." *Anonymous.*

Love Flows from God.
Mechtild of Magdeburg.

Musician. Bogan.

My Heart Is a Lute.
Barnard.

O Sheriffs. Allison.

Play. Asch.

The Puppet Player. Grimke.

A Receipt to Cure a Love Fit.
Anonymous.

Romance. Poe.

Rondel for Middle Age.
Nicholl.

The String of My Ancestors.
Nyhart.

They Tell Me I Am Lost.
Kenny.

To the Carp, and Those Who
Hunt Her. Hazard.

Warning to Children.
Graves.

When There Is Music.
Morton.

When to Her Lute Corinna
Sings. Campion.

Stripes

The Cumberland and the
Merrimac. *Anonymous.*

In the Hospital. Howland.

Virginia's Bloody Soil.
Anonymous.

Strive (s)

The Anglers Song. Basse.

An Answer to Another
Persuading a Lady to
Marriage. Philips.

Ballad of the Two Tapsters.
Watkins.

The British Lyon Roused.
Tilden.

The Dream. Allingham.

Enamored Architect of Airy
Rhyme. Aldrich.

The Gentle Check.
Beaumont.

I See My Plaint. Harington.

Nevertheless. Davidson.

The Rosary. Rogers.

The Statue and the Bust.
Browning.

Take Time to Talk with God.
Frazee-Bower.

Truth. Masefield.

Twelfth Night. Shakespeare.

The Weaver. *Anonymous.*

Stroke (d) (s)

The Assassination of President
McKinley. Blackburn.

At Least. Mattera.

Belfast: High Street. Colum.

A Child's Pet. Davies.

Elegy. Nemerov.

Esthetique du Mal. Stevens.

The flaming sighs that boil
within my breast. Wyatt.

Harriet Beecher Stowe.
Dunbar.

In a Poem. Frost.

Jack Rose. Bodenheim.

Old Doc. Vinz.

Painting by Chimes. Mayer.

Perversity. Griffin.

Poems of the Arabic (excerpt).
Anonymous.

Prayer for Pain. Neihardt.

Rockingchair. Morgan.

Sea-Ruck. Eberhart.

The Secret in the Cat.
Swenson.

Song at Summer's End.
Fairburn.

Spring Song. Nahum.

Tender Buttons: Objects.
Stein.

To Fool, or Knave. Jonson.

Tropisms on John Berryman.
Vizenor.

When I Solidly Do Ponder.
Pastorius.

Stroll (ing)

Bread and Wine, Part 7.
Holderlin.

Guadalupe, W.I. Guillen.

Road Fellows. Young.

Two X "16 heures l'Etoile."
Cummings.

Strong (er) (est)

Another Cynical Variation.
"Helen".

Arawata Bill. Glover.

Be Thou My Guide. Coates.

Begin the Day with God.
Anonymous.

Boy with a Hammer.
Hoban.

Cowper at Tea. Pain.

Dead. Johnson.

Dream Songs. Berryman.

Drum-Taps. Whitman.

Elder Tree. Aiken.

The End of the Year. Su
Tung-P'o.

An Essay on the Genius of
Pope (excerpt). Lloyd.

The Eve of Bunker Hill.
Scollard.

Eye of God. Tollerud.

The Faithful Shepherdess.
Fletcher.

February. Winder.

A Fence or an Ambulance.
Malins.

The Fire of Love. Sackville.

Forbearance. Leitner.

A Freedom Song for the
Black Woman. Gregory.

From William Tyndale to
John Frith. Bowers.

The Gar. Bell.

The Garden of Ships.
Stewart.

George. Randall.

Golden Lines. Nerval.

The Good Time Coming.
Mackay.

Granma's Words.
Palmanteer.

He's Coming. Van Doren.

Heritage. Gilmore.

The Hills and the Sea.
Campbell.

Hogyn cam to bower's dore.
Anonymous.

Hymn to St. Geryon, I.
McClure.

In a Garden. Jennings.

In Memoriam A.H.H., CXVI.
Tennyson.

The Invisible Woman.
Morgan.

Last Words on Greece.
Byron.

Letter. Empson.

Limerick: "Once a Frenchman
who'd promptly said "oui'."
Anonymous.

The Lonely Land. Smith.

Macbeth. Shakespeare.

Madonna Mia. Swinburne.

Man and Nature. Weeks.

The Man of Peace. Carman.

Monna Innaminata. Rossetti.

Motown/Smokey Robinson.
Hagedorn.

My Comrade. Roche.

My Lord, What a Morning.
Cuney.

Nativity Song. Jacopone da
Todi.

Now Poem. For Us.
Sanchez.

O, Love Is Not a Summer
Mood. Gilder.

On the Road Home.
Stevens.

Once. Batterham.

Orator. Emerson.

Our Smoke Has Gone Four
Ways. Henson.

Peter. Marlatt.

The Poets at Tea. Pain.

Power Failure. Jacobsen.

A Prayer. Watkins.

Repentance. Herbert.

Seduced Girl. Hedylos.

The Serpent of God.
Farallon.

The Singer. Wickham.

The Sleeping Fury. Bogan.

Solidarity Forever. Chaplin.

A Song for the Least of All
Saints. Rossetti.

Sonnet IV: "From that first
flash when awful Love took
flame." Labe.

Spider. Cole.

The Story of a Stowaway.
Scott.

The Strong Are Saying
Nothing. Frost.

Three wise men of Gotham.
Mother Goose.

To a Friend on His Nuptials.
Prior.

To America. Austin.

To Himself. Catullus.

To Sally. Horace.

The Unquiet Grave.
Anonymous.

Variations on a Line from
Shakespeare's Fifty-Sixth
Sonnet. Mayo.

War Song. Davidson.

Woman to Man. Ai.

Ye Simple Men. Blackie.

Ye Sorrowers. Werfel.

Strophe

Make Way! Negri.

Still the Mind Smiles.
Jeffers.

Structure (s)

3rd Dance–Making a
Structure with a Roof or
under a Roof... MacLow.

Arriving. Preil.

Beach Glass. Clampitt.

The City Rises.
Cunningham.

Failure. Mayo.

The Great St. Bernard.
Rogers.

It Feels Good as It Is
Without the Giant.
Stevens.

To a Skull. Irwin.

Struggle (d) (s)

Against Negritude. Corgo.

Ajanta. Rukeyser.

Anchor. *Anonymous.*

The Composer's Winter
Dream. Dubie.

Corruption. Simoko.

Credit. *Anonymous.*

Epilogue to the Outrider.
Livesay.

The Hands. Harrison.

If Easter Be Not True.
Barstow.

On Dressing to Go Hunting.
Anonymous.

The Rock. Eliot.

They Are Ours. Magil.

The Women's Marseillaise.
Macaulay.

Strumpet

The Dream. Bendo.

Stubble

Epitaph at Great Torrington,
Devon. *Anonymous.*

Nonsense. Schauffler.

Stubborn

Ancient and Modern Rome
(excerpt). Keate.

Crabs. Piercy.

The Old Beauty. McGinley.

A Thought for My Love.
Williamson.

Stuck

Baby's Awake Now.
Berkson.

Epitaph. *Anonymous.*

Limerick: "There once was a happy hyena." Wells.
Trees, Effigies, Moving Objects. Curnow.
World's Fare. Stetler.

Student (s)
Going to School in France or America. Clark.
On Lady Gregory's Search for Talent. Joyce.

Studio
Honeysuckle. Paul.
A Story About the Body. Hass.

Study (studies)
Aesop at Play. Phaedrus.
As You Like It. Shakespeare.
At the Louvre. Mayo.
Bishop Blougram's Apology. Browning.
Butter's Etymological Spelling Book, &c. Coleridge.
Epitaph for Cu Chuimne. Anonymous.
I'm Agoing to Lay Down My Sword. Anonymous.
It Is Not Sweet Content, Be Sure. Clough.
Limerick: "When an All-American gd." Anonymous.
New Students. Bell.
The Old Age Home. Holmes.
On a Distant Prospect of an Absconding Bookmaker. Hamilton.
Philosopher, Whom Dost Thou Most Affect." Garnett.
Silex Scintillans. Vaughan.
Sing Me a New Song. Clarke.
Two Drinking Songs. Tao Yuan-Ming.
Verses Written During a Sleepless Night. Pushkin.
The White Rat. Young.

Stuff (ed) (s)
As I Grow Older and Fatten on Myself. Carson.
By the Ford. Thomas.
Cleaning Up. Dyson.
Diary. The Deer Break Their Horns. De Clue.
Dilly Dilly. Anonymous.
Helpmate. Chapin.
I Come to Bury Caesar. Harris.
The Money Cry. Davison.
Polyolbion. Drayton.
Stew Meat Blues. Jackson.
The Tale of the Dixie-Belle. Chase.
The Tempest. Shakespeare.
Theme and Variation. De Vries.
The Tower of Babel. Crouch.
Trombone Solo. King.
Twelfth Night. Shakespeare.
Verses to Miss —-. Wilde.
What a Friend We have in Cheeses! Cole.

Stumble (d)
Catching Up. Walker.
Conclusion. Nims.
Goodwill, Inc. Schmitz.
Ignu. Ginsberg.
Joy. Delany.

On a Soldier Fallen in the Philippines. Moody.
The Potter. Anonymous.
Prayer of an Unbeliever. Reese.
Wheelbarrow. Farjeon.

Stump (s)
Cut. Plath.
Girls. Rosen.
Yankee Doodle's Expedition to Rhode Island. Anonymous.

Stun (ned)
Daughter. Voigt.
I Would Not Paint a Picture. Dickinson.
The Poet Is Dead. Everson.

Stung
The Bee. Anonymous.
Four Anacreontic Poems, 1. Spenser.
In Praise of a Gentlewoman. Gascoigne.

Stunt
Maple Leaf Rag. Brown.
Osculation. Harrison.

Stupid (ity)
Air. Jones.
Ar(chibald')s Poetica (parody). Ribback.
Devil's Cauldron. Gibbon.
Hibiscus on the Sleeping Shores. Stevens.
Homage to Jack Yeats. MacGreevy.
Limerick: "Curiosity's not in me head." Livingston.
Morning. Chu Shu-chen.
New Proverb. Brooks.
Ritual Not Religion. Indian.

Stutter (ing)
Better to Spit on the Whip than Stutter Your Love Like a Worm. Inez.
Elegy. Loney.
Neighbors. Lennox.

Sty
Brent: A Poem to Thomas Palmer, Esq. Diaper.
Circe. Gibson.
I Saw a Chapel All of Gold. Blake.
Muckish Mountain (The Pig's Back). Leslie.

Stygian
The Dispensary. Garth.
Epitaph: "See, one physician, like a sculler, plies." Jekyll.
The Fate of a Broom—An Anticipation. Peacock.

Style (s)
And Through the Caribbean Sea. Danner.
Captain Jinks. Anonymous.
Executive. Betjeman.
Family History. Bishop.
God in the Nation's Life. Anonymous.
L'Homme Moyhen Sensuel (excerpt). Pound.
An Insult. Anonymous.
On Don Surly. Jonson.
Petition. Auden.
Poem: "on getting a card." Williams.
Ross's Poems. Lehmann.
Shifting Colors. Lowell.
Sonnets, XXXII: "If thou survive my well-contented day." Shakespeare.
This Last Pain. Empson.

To the River Isca (the Usk). Vaughan.

Styx
A Walk by the Charles. Rich.

Subdue (d) (s)
Ascension-Hymn. Vaughan.
Beauty. Stanley.
The Hyperboreans. Paulin.
Mars and Venus. Greene.
The Stricken South to the North. Hayne.
The Trumpet. Ehrenburg.
The Woman in My Notebook. Cervantes.

Subject (s)
The Advice. Anonymous.
Among the Coffee Cups and Soup Toureens Walked Beauty. Spicer.
The Angler's Ballad. Cotton.
Caelica, LXXVIII. Greville.
Colonel B. Carrier.
Dear Mrs. McKinney of the Sixth Grade:. Kherdian.
A Dialogue between King William and the Late King James... Blount.
England's Sovereigns in Verse. Anonymous.
A Funeral Elogy... Norton II.
A Hit at the Times. McGrew.
The Junk Shop. Coulette.
A Minor Victorian Painter. Hewitt.
Parthenope. Barnes.
The Power in the People. Herrick.
A Prophecy. Lee.
Seascape. Bishop.
Sonnets, LIX: "If there bc." Shakespeare.

Sublime
Apologia Pro Vita Sua. Coleridge.
Aurora Leigh. Browning.
Epistle to Dr. Blacklock. Burns.
The Floating Candles. Lea.
The Flock at Evening. Shepard.
God of the Prophets! Bless the Prophets' Sons. Wortman.
The Instalment (excerpt). Young.
Steamboats, Viaducts, and Railways. Wordsworth.
The Trees. Larcom.

Submarine
Maiden Lane. Lee.
Sparrow in Winter. Shinkichi.

Substance
Age of Gold. Metastasio.
Five Birds Rise. Hayward.
Friends. Perreault.
How to Give. Anonymous.
The Lion's Skeleton. Turner.
Man's Amazement. Anonymous.
The Maunding Soldier. Parker.
Nightflight and Sunrise. Dutton.
The Presence. Graves.
Pretty Beads. Gallup.
Rain. Hollo.
Sonnets, V: "Those hours, that with gentle work did frame." Shakespeare.

Spring 1940. Auden.
When It Burns before the Harps and Freezes behind the Easels. Arp.

Suburb (an) (s)
Childhood. Justice.
Delaying Tactics. Wiseman.
Evening Walk. Akesson.
Funnel. Sexton.
A Jew Walks in Westminster Abbey. Hodes.
Kilroy. Viereck.
Portrait of a Young Girl Raped at a Suburban Party. Patten.
Suburban. Ciardi.
To the Little House. Morley.

Subway
Life. Adams.
Nuit Blanche: North End. Aiken.
Recuerdo. Millay.
The Report. Swan.
The Sloth. Gardner.

Succeed (ed) (s)
Base Words Are Uttered. Auden.
Jealousy. Johnson.
My Style. Bukowski.
Names. Enright.
Paddle Your Own Canoe. Bolton.
Pandora and the Moon. Moore.
Sunday Review Section. Wormser.
To the Rose. Davies.

Success
At the Treatment Center. Sala.
Barney's Invitation. Freneau.
The Beast with Chrome Teeth. Snyder.
Cheers. Merriam.
Judgment. Anonymous.
Lines on the Back of a Confederate Note. Jonas.
Lisbon. Anonymous.
Measure of Success. Anonymous.
On Don Juan del Norte, Not Don Juan Tenorio del Sur. Dugan.
On First Looking into Loeb's Horace. Durrell.
The Rewards of Farming. Anonymous.
Rock and Hawk. Jeffers.
Success. Anonymous.
That's Success! Braley.
To Sir William Davenant, Upon His Two First Books of Gondibert. Lovelace.
Ways of Loving. Weiss.

Succession
The Country Fiddler. Montague.
Crows. Clark.
Silex Scintillans. Vaughan.

Suck (ed) (ing) (s)
But Perhaps. Sachs.
Commercial Traveller. Edmond.
The Complete Cynic. Preston.
Far in the West. Fraser.
Fighting Her. Phillips.
He Saw Far in the Concave Green of the Sea. Keats.
House and Shutter. Turco.

Limerick: "That famous old
   pederast, Wilde."
   Anonymous.
Lincoln and Liberty.
   Simpson.
Northern Ireland: Two
   Comments. Deane.
The Octopus. Merrill.
Relationships. Van Duyn.
Self-Congratulatory Ode on
   Mr Auden's Election
   (parody). Mason.
Silenus in Proteus. Beddoes.
South Street. Silvera.
The Story of Little Suck-a-
   Thumb. Hoffmann.
To Philaenis. Martial
   (Marcus Valerius Martialis).
To Phoebus. Martial
   (Marcus Valerius Martialis).
A Valedictory to Standard Oil
   of Indiana. Wagoner.

Suckle
Battle Cry. Neihardt.
The Child Compassion.
   Ruddock.
Long Division: A Tribal
   History. Rose.

Sudden (ly)
Autumn Change. Clare.
For Under the Volcano.
   Lowry.
From Bethlehem Blown.
   Leitch.
Fulfillment. Miller.
A Learned Mistress.
   O'Connor.
Lecture Hall. Kavanagh.
The Lesson. Lucie-Smith.
March. Williams.
November Cotton Flower.
   Toomer.
Of an Old Song. Lecky.
Our Lucy. Goodman.
Rosa Rosarum. Robinson.
September. Huxley.
Three Lyrics. Petronius
   Arbiter (Caius Petronius
   Arbiter).
Violets in Thaumantia's
   Bosome. Sherburne.

Sue (s)
Driving into Enid. Van
   Walleghen.
She Was Bred in Old
   Kentucky. Braisted.
The Silent Lover. Ralegh.
Sir Walter Ralegh to the
   Queen. Ralegh.

Suffer (ed) (es) (ing) (s)
Beauty I Would Suffer for.
   Piercy.
Bei Hennef. Lawrence.
Benedictio Domini. Dowson.
Burning Oneself In. Rich.
Cambrian (excerpt). Manner.
A Conversation. Shelley.
Courage for the
   Pusillanimous. Roche.
A Dark Country. Mahon.
The Doll. Friend.
Elegy. Slonimski.
Elk Ghosts: A Birth Memory.
   Smith.
England. Newman.
Epitaph. Aleichem.
For My Father: Two Poems.
   Kherdian.
The Hem of His Garment.
   Hamilton.
History: Madness. Rice.
The Homeless. Hall.

Hymn of Trust. Holmes.
In the Forest. Petofi.
Jesus, Child and Lord.
   Faber.
Kinchinjunga. Rice.
Limerick: "There's a vaporish
   maiden in Harrison."
   Bishop.
The Man of Sorrows.
   Anonymous.
Milne's Bar. MacCaig.
Minutes. Johnson.
Moreton Bay. *Anonymous.*
My Child. Griffin.
No Sufferer for Her Love.
   Anonymous.
Nonsense. *Anonymous.*
Oh, for the Time When I
   Shall Sleep. Bronte.
Over the Hill to the Poor-
   House. Carleton.
Pentecost. Anthony ("Ai").
Poem: "The rose fades."
   Williams.
Queen Anne's Lace. Jordan.
Rebirth. Bruner.
The Reed. Lermontov.
Revolutionary Letters. Di
   Prima.
The Royal Way of the Holy
   Cross. Thomas à Kempis.
A Sailor's Wife. Bernhardt.
Seizure. Sappho.
Shore Leave Lorry. Fuller.
Since Love Will Needs That I
   Shall Love. Wyatt.
Sonnet II. Alabaster.
The Stranger. Clare.
Suffering in sorrow in hope to
   attain. Wyatt.
To an Imperilled Traveller.
   Dole.
The Troops. Sassoon.
Untitled. Randall, Jr.
Wedding Song. Meyer.
Why Do You Want to Suffer
   Less. Fisher.
A Word about Freedom and
   Identity in Tel Aviv.
   Silkin.
Words for the Raker of
   Leaves. Adams.

Suffice (d) (s)
Bottle Should Be Plainly
   Labeled Poison. Hay.
Dundonnel Mountains.
   Young.
Fire and Ice. Frost.
Follow Your Saint.
   Campion.
Nothing Move Thee.
   Theresa of Avila.
Seeking God. Dowden.
Spite hath no power to make
   me sad. Wyatt.
St. Teresa's Book Mark.
   Theresa of Avila.

Sufficient
The Precious Blood.
   Anonymous.
To a Certain Lady, in Her
   Garden. Brown.

Suffocate
Labour of the Brain, Ballad of
   the Body. Forman.

Sugar
As You Like It.
   Shakespeare.
Crawdad. *Anonymous.*
Harlem Sweeties. Hughes.
If. Bangs.

My Pretty Little Pink (with
   music). *Anonymous.*
The Shearer's Song.
   Anonymous.
Song for February. Paulin.
Song: "Smooth was the Water,
   calm the Air." Sedley.
Tom's Little Dog. De la
   Mare.

Sugarhill
Harlem Sweeties. Hughes.

Sugarplums
Husband and Heathen. Foss.
Naming the Baby.
   Richstone.

Suicide (s)
The Break-Up. Klein.
Call It a Good Marriage.
   Graves.
Exeat. Smith.
Political Poem. Jones.
Suicide Pond. McLaughlin.

Suit
All heavy minds. Wyatt.
The Courser and the Jennet.
   Shakespeare.
Cowboy Song. Causley.
Do You Plan to Speak Bantu?
   Nash.
Hero and Leander. Marlowe.
The Merchant of Venice.
   Shakespeare.
De Profundis. Wyatt.
Redemption. Herbert.
A Sea-Chaplain's Petition.
   "T.
Song Set by Thomas Weelkes:
   "Three times a day my
   prayer is." *Anonymous.*

Suitcase (s)
The Clock Works.
   MacAdams.
Possessions. Smith.

Suitor
Goddess of Wisdom Whose
   Substance Is Desire.
   Waldman.
Satire. Donne.

Sulk (y)
Senex. Betjeman.
The World's Music.
   "Setoun. Gabriel"

Sullen
Georgics. Virgil (Publius
   Vergilius Maro).
Hudibras. Butler.
Song of Breath. Vidal.
The Tower of the Dream
   (excerpt). Harpur.
Walking in Beech Leaves.
   Young.

Sultry
Autumn. Irwin.
The Man in Black. Strand.
The Turkish Bakery.
   Anonymous.

Sum
Brightness. McHugh.
Deservings. *Anonymous*
Epitaph on an Army of
   Mercenaries. Housman.
Fame. Herrick.
Man's Amazement.
   Anonymous.
Sea Voyage. Empson.

Summer
1930's. Lowell.
3:16 and One Half...
   Bukowski.
About the Cool Water.
   Rexroth.
Above the Pool. Montague.

Accident at Three Mile
   Island. Barnes.
After the Show. Harrison.
Against Death. Redgrove.
All on a Summer's Day.
   Anonymous.
Ant-Hills. "Douglas.
Apple Season. Frost.
Apple Song. Frost.
As imperceptibly as grief.
   Dickinson.
Astrophel and Stella,
   LXXXIX. Sidney.
August. Howells.
The Auroras of Autumn.
   Stevens.
Autumn Daybreak. Millay.
Autumn Song. Tieck.
Barefoot Days. Field.
Beans in Blossom. Clare.
The Bee Is Not Afraid of Me.
   Dickinson.
The Birth of Galahad: Ylen's
   Song. Hovey.
Black Water and Bright Air.
   Carrier.
The Bobolink. Hill.
The Broom Flower. Howitt.
By a Rich Fast Moving
   Stream. Tagliabue.
Candle. Segal.
Cauld Cornwood.
   Anonymous.
The Circus. Koch.
A Cold Spring. Bishop.
Conrad in Twilight.
   Ransom.
Consolations of Philosophy.
   Mahon.
The Cornet. Surrey.
Cornfield Myth. Goose.
The Cowboy's Life. Adams.
The Cuckoo. *Anonymous.*
Cut Grass. Larkin.
Daphne. Sitwell.
The Deceptive Present, The
   Phoenix Year. Schwartz.
Descent to Bohannon Lake.
   Barnes.
A Difference. Clark.
Digging Out the Roots.
   Niatum.
Dolor. Miles.
The Dragonfly. Bogan.
The Drummer. Robinson.
Dust. Spivack.
Dvonya. Simpson.
Earthborn. McArthur.
Elegy. Bell.
Ellen Taylor. *Anonymous.*
The End of Summer. Millay.
End-of-Summer Poem.
   Bennett.
Essential oils—are wrung.
   Dickinson.
Ethnogenesis. Timrod.
The Falls of Glomach.
   Young.
Farewell to Summer.
   Arnold.
First of Summer, Lovely
   Sight. *Anonymous.*
Firwood. Clare.
Fishing. Wordsworth.
Fly away, Fly away over the
   Sea. Rossetti.
Follow the Leader. Behn.
For Ann Scott-Moncrieff.
   Muir.
For Music. Byron.
From the Notebooks.
   Roethke.

Glen Lough. Grigson.
God Hasn't Made Room.
  Mririda n'Ait Attik.
The Good Humor Man.
  McGinley.
Gunnar's Howe above the
  House at Lithend. Morris.
Haiku. Vizenor.
Harvest Home. Guiterman.
The Heart's Summer.
  Sargent
Hemlock Mountain.
  Cleghorn.
Heritage. Mackellar.
Hitch Haiku. Snyder.
Hold Hard, These Ancient
  Minutes. Thomas.
I Hear a River. Stickney.
I Loved Thee, Atthis, in the
  Long Ago. Carman.
I'm Going to Rocky Island.
  Anonymous.
Une Idole du Nord. Stuart.
If Buttercups Buzz'd after the
  Bee. Anonymous.
In Memorabilia Mortis.
  Sherman.
In the Beach House. Sexton.
In the Cathedral. Beer.
In the Doorway. Browning.
In the Good Old Summer
  Time. Shields.
In the Hamptons. Morris.
Influence of Natural Objects.
  Wordsworth.
Invocation to Rain in
  Summer. Bennett.
The Inward Morning.
  Thoreau.
January. Dutton.
January. Heath-Stubbs.
Jeanie with the Light Brown
  Hair. Foster.
June. Feinstein.
Kingcups. Sitwell.
Lady Elspat. Anonymous.
The Last Hour. Clifford.
Late Leaves. Landor.
Lavender's for Ladies.
  Chalmers.
Little Ah Sid (with music).
  Anonymous.
Little Red Riding Hood.
  Carryl.
Loch Ossian. Scroggie.
The Long Picnic. Edson.
Long Summer Day.
  Anonymous.
Love and Death.
  Mulholland.
Love Lifted Me. Leary.
Malaga. Hutchinson.
Master Skylark. Bennett.
Merry-Go-Round. Jenkins.
Midsummer. Scully.
Milton by Firelight. Snyder.
The Mirror. Morris.
Modern Love, XLV.
  Meredith.
Monaghan. Leslie.
Musk Oxen. Igjugarjuk.
My Heart Shall Be Thy
  Garden. Meynell.
Names. Aldis.
Of the Day Estivall. Hume.
Old Nick in Sorel. O'Grady.
On a Fly Drinking out of His
  Cup. Oldys.
One-Eyed Gunner.
  Anonymous.
Open Casket. McPherson.
Passing Love. Hughes.

Pastoral. Ewart.
Patience of a People. Bryant,
  Jr.,
Peach Tree with Fruit.
  Colum.
Pear Tree. Doolittle.
The Pine. Webster.
Poem in June. Acorn.
Poetry. Vigee.
Polyolbion. Drayton.
Portrait. Allen.
Portrait of the Father.
  Hough.
Pray to What Earth Does
  This Sweet Cold Belong.
  Thoreau.
Precious to me–she still shall
  be. Dickinson.
Prevision. Murray.
Privation. Carruth.
Professional Amnesia.
  Moure.
The Quest of the Orchis.
  Frost.
A Return from the Wars.
  Bock.
Reynard the Fox (excerpt).
  Masefield.
Richard Cory. Robinson.
The River Glideth in a Secret
  Tongue. Ostroff.
Roman Fountain. Bogan.
Route Six. Kunitz.
Sailing after Lunch. Stevens.
Santa Barbara. Browne.
Secret. Doolittle.
The Sedge-Warbler.
  Hodgson.
September. Arnold.
September. Fallis.
September Afternoon.
  Carpenter.
The Shepherd Boy. Clare.
The Shepherd of Meriador.
  Childe.
Sing a Song of Sunshine.
  Eastwick.
Snow-Flakes. Dodge.
Snowflakes. Eliot.
The Soldier in the Park.
  Riddell.
Song: "Now let us honor with
  violin and flute." Sarton.
Song: "O, it was out by
  Donncarney." Joyce.
Song: "O spirit of the
  Summertime!" Allingham.
Song:"Once my heart was a
  summer rose." Sitwell.
Song: "The fringed vallance of
  your eyes advance."
  Shadwell.
Sonnet: "I know I am but
  summer to your heart."
  Millay.
Sonnet: September, 1815.
  Wordsworth.
Sonnet–To Silence. Poe.
Sonnets. Tuckerman.
Sonnets, II: "The rainbow o'er
  the sea of afternoon."
  Irwin.
Sonnets, LVI: "Sweet love,
  renew thy force."
  Shakespeare.
Sonnets to Orpheus. Rilke.
The Spirit of Poetry.
  Longfellow.
Spring Rites. Robbins.
A Spring Song. Anonymous.
Stanzas. Thoreau.
Stanzas (excerpt). Newton.

Stanzas for Music. Byron.
Summer. Clare.
Summer Afternoon.
  Dowling.
Summer Comes. Agnew.
Summer Has Come.
  Anonymous.
Summer's Farewell. Nashe
  [(or Nash[) Thomas.
A Sunset. Hugo.
Surely You Remember.
  Ravikovich.
Syringa. Ashbery.
That Was Summer. Ridlon.
These Apple Trees.
  Iremonger.
Thieves. Adams.
To a Friend in the Wilderness
  (excerpt). Fairburn.
To Harriett. Clare.
To Spenser. Keats.
To the Ghost of a Kite.
  Wright.
To the Grasshopper and the
  Cricket. Hunt.
To the Nightingale. Davies.
Touring. Morton.
The Track into the Swamp.
  Morse.
Tree Felling. Woodcock.
Tulip Tree. Sitwell.
Vermont: Indian Summer.
  Booth.
The Voice. Roethke.
The Waking. Roethke.
We Did It. Amichai.
Westgate-on-Sea. Betjeman.
When the fifth month comes.
  Ise.
Why Are Our Summer Sports
  So Brittle? Anonymous.
Winter's End. Moss.
With Me My Lover Makes.
  Day-Lewis.

Summit (s)
Ascent. Saunders.
Barter. Blake.
The Book Rises Out of the
  Fire. Jabes.
The Buzzards. Armstrong.
Crown of Happiness.
  Hebert.
Irish Music. Levis.
The Isolation of Genius.
  Byron.
Middle-Aged Conversation.
  Tessimond.
Mountain Sculpture. Will.
Voyageur. Rashley.

Summons
An Adobe House. Bynner.
Asleep in Jesus. MacKay.
A Creed. Anonymous.
Paradise Lost. Milton.

Sun
Abraham Lincoln, the Master.
  Clark.
Additional Verses to Hail
  Columbia. Holmes.
Adonais. Harney.
Africa. McKay.
Alfred Corning Clark.
  Lowell.
Allie. Graves.
Among the Firs. Lee-
  Hamilton.
Aphorisms. "Novalis"
  (George Friedrich Philipp
  von Hardenerg).
The Apple-Barrel of Johnny
  Appleseed. Lindsay.
An April Morning. Carman.

Aranda Song. Anonymous.
The Arc Inside and Out.
  Ammons.
The Archaeology of Love.
  Murphy.
As I Grew Older. Hughes.
As You Come In. Marriott.
The Assumption. Beaumont.
Astrophel and Stella, LXXVI.
  Sidney.
At Dante's Grave. Zussman.
At Nightfall. Towne.
At the Setting of the Sun.
  Anonymous.
Auguries of Innocence.
  Blake.
August from My Desk.
  Flint.
Aurora Borealis. Roditi.
The Authour's Dreame.
  Quarles.
Ave Imperatrix! Wilde.
Baha'u'llah in the Garden of
  Ridwan. Hayden.
Ballad of Another Ophelia.
  Lawrence.
Banalbufar, A Brazier,
  Relativity, Cloud
  Formations... Blackburn.
Beauty. Whitman.
The Beauty of My Land Peers
  Warily. Brutus.
Beethoven's Death Mask.
  Spender.
Beetle on the Shasta Daylight.
  Kaufman.
Before I got my eye put out.
  Dickinson.
Before the War. Hacker.
Begging on North Main.
  Stuart.
Begin Summer. Jonker.
Being a Giant. Mezey.
Beyond. Kimball.
The Bicycle Rider. Shapcott.
Big City Glissando.
  Christopher.
Bird Riddle: "What is it more
  eyes doth wear."
  Anonymous.
A Black November Turkey.
  Wilbur.
The Black Vulture. Sterling.
"Blue Is the Hero...
  Berkson.
The Book of Persephone.
  Kelly.
The Boomerang. Nichols.
Boy Breaking Glass. Brooks.
Boy in the Roman Zoo.
  MacLeish.
Break of Day. Neilson.
Breakers of Broncos. Sarett.
Bricklayer Love. Sandburg.
A Bridal Song. Shelley.
Bridge. Damon.
Brother... Amini.
Bullfrog Blues. Harris.
By the Bridge. Walker.
Canada. Roberts.
CANDU Can't Do. Filip.
Celia Singing. Carew.
The Celtic Lyric (parody).
  Squire.
Changelings. Higginson.
The Charge at Santiago.
  Hayne.
Cherry Tree Carol.
  Anonymous.
Child of silence and shadow.
  Caroutch.

Child with a Cockatoo. Dobson.
Children of Darkness. Graves.
Civil Elegies (excerpt). Lee.
The Class. Jacobsen.
Cloud Country. Merrill.
Cock before Dawn. MacCaig.
Coins and Coffins under My Bed. Wakoski.
The Collier. Watkins.
Come All You Fair and Tender Ladies. Anonymous.
Come Out into the Sun. Francis.
Comrade, Remember. Kresensky.
Country Dance. Sitwell.
The Crane's Ascent. Bozanic.
Crow Voices. Tremblay.
The Crystal Skull. Raine.
The Curse. Francis.
Dauber. Masefield.
David Ap Gwillam's Mass of the Birds. Colum.
Dawn. Anonymous.
Dawn. "Rachel" (Rachel Blumstein).
The Day after Trinity. Oyama.
The Days. Blocklyn.
The Dead Brother. Anonymous.
Dead Man's Song, Dreamed by One Who Is Alive. Anonymous.
Death. Vaughan.
Decay of Piety. Wordsworth.
The Deer. Asya (Asya Gray).
Dial Tone. Pollak.
Dialogue. Nemerov.
Diana. Constable.
Dog Sacrifice at Lake Ronkonkoma. Heyen.
The Double Tree. Scott.
Down the Mississippi. Fletcher.
The Dream of Aengus Og. Cox.
Drum-Taps. Whitman.
Duet. Tennyson.
Earth, Sky. Clouts.
Earth Trembles Waiting. Wagstaff.
East Bronx. Ignatow.
Ebbtide at Sundown. "Field.
Eclipses. Sullivan.
Edward (C vers.). Anonymous.
An Egyptian Pulled Glass Bottle in the Shape of a Fish. Moore.
Epitaph. Driscoll.
Epitaph of a Young Man. Anonymous.
Escape. Graves.
Evening Dance of the Grey Flies. Page.
Evening in Camp. Ledward.
The Fair Singer. Marvell.
Field Trip. Miranda.
The Fight of the Armstrong Privateer. Roche.
Fires. Heyen.
First Winter Storm. Everson.
Fool's Song. Holcroft.

For Alan Blanchard. Simon.
For Marianne Moore's Birthday. Boyle.
Forecast. Miles.
Forest without Leaves (excerpt). Haines.
Four Glimpses of Night. Davis.
The Fox. Scheuer.
Freedom. Green.
A Freshet. Antiphilus of Byzantium.
Friend Who Never Came. Stafford.
From behind the Bars. Tuquan.
From Skye, Early Autumn. Michal.
A General Communion. Meynell.
Generations. Steingart.
A Girl's Mood. Reese.
Girl's Song. Zaturenska.
Give Place, Ye Lovers. Surrey.
Give Us This Day Our Daily Bread. Babcock.
The Glass Eaters. Jonas.
A Gnarled Riverina Gum-Tree. Moll.
Go, Ploughman, Plough. Campbell.
Going In. Piercy.
The Golden Sestina. Pico della Mirandola
The Gorse. Gibson.
Grapes. Maris Stella.
The Grapevine. Brockman.
The Great Lakes Suite. Reaney.
The Green Family. Thibaudeau.
Greener Grass. Steele.
The Greenland Voyage. Anonymous.
The Greeting of the Roses. Garland.
Guadalupe, W.I. Guillen.
Guide to Jerusalem. Silk.
The Gulf Stream. Bellamann.
The Guns in the Grass. Frost.
H.M.S. Glory at Sydney. Causley.
Hard Frost. Young.
Hay Scuttle. Morgan.
He Liked the Dead. Lowry.
Hebrew Letters in the Trees. Williams.
Helios. Spingarn.
Her Window. Leigh.
Here. Larkin.
Here are fine gifts, children. Sappho.
The Hero (parody). Woddis.
The Heron. Donaghy.
Hialmar Speaks to the Raven. Leconte de Lisle.
Homes of the Cliff Dwellers. Wood.
Hope. Johnson.
Hopeless Desire Soon Withers and Dies. "W.
Hours I Remember Lonely and Lovely to Me. Irwin.
How Copernicus Stopped the Sun. Dillard.
How Goes the Night? Anonymous.
Human Needs. Walker.
Hunting at Dusk. Cockrell.

Hunting for Blueberries. James.
Hymn of Joy. Van Dyke.
Hysteria. Chu Shu chen.
I ran for a catch. Kernahan.
I Served in a Great Cause. Traubel.
I taste a liquor never brewed. Dickinson.
I Was a Brook. Coleridge.
In a Child's Album. Wordsworth.
In Bed. Sklarew.
In Memorabilia Mortis. Sherman.
In the Badlands. Wagoner.
In the Beginning. Monroe.
In the Emptied Rest Home. Akhmadulina.
In the Glorious Epiphanie of Our Lord God. Crashaw.
The Incentive. Cleghorn.
Inquisitive Barn. Frost.
The Insomniacs. Rich.
Intimacy. Young.
The Island. Dickey.
It Will Not Shine Again. Bronte.
Jealousy. DeVries.
Jephthah's Daughter. Heavysege.
A Jerusalem Notebook. Shapiro.
Joy of Knowledge. Schneider.
A Joyful Noise. Finkel.
June Morning. McCrae.
Keeping Their World Large. Moore.
Kitchen Song. Dobbs.
Lake Chemo. Rowe.
A Lament. Avison.
Lament for Pasiphae. Graves.
The Landfall. Dickey.
Legend. Laforgue.
The Legend of Montrose. Chapt. 6: Annot Lyle's Song: "Birds of Omen". Scott.
Letter to Karl Shapiro. Mayo.
Light a Candle. Zelda.
Like David. Preil.
Little Saling. Baker.
Liverpool John. Anonymous.
Lobster Cove Shindig. Morrison.
The Long Garden. Kavanagh.
The Lord of All. Markham.
Lost Dog. Rodman.
Love Dirge. Anonymous.
Love in Action. Patmore.
Love, the Light-Giver. Michelangelo.
Lullaby of the Woman of the Mountain. Pearse.
The March Bee. Blunden.
The Marriage of a Virgin. Thomas.
A Mask Presented at Ludlow Castle (Comus). Milton.
Master Canterel at Locus Solus. Shapiro.
May (excerpt). O'Donnell.
Meditation in Winter. Mann.
Meeting by the Gjulika Meadow. Grigson.
Mexican Market Woman. Hughes.
Midnight Patrol. Irvin.

Minotaur Poems. Mandel.
Mishka. Gray.
Monna Innominata. Rossetti.
The Moon Is Up. Anonymous.
More Sonnets at Christmas. Tate.
Mother. Sinclair.
Mounds of Human Heads Are Wandering into the Distance. Mandelstam.
The Mouth of the Hudson. Lowell.
Mussel Hunter at Rock Harbor. Plath.
My Father Dragged by Horses. Broughton.
Night. Daley.
Night and the Child. Wright.
Night Crackles. Woody.
Night in Martindale. Raine.
Nilotic Elegy. Fraser.
Non Piangere, Liu. Porter.
North Labrador. Crane.
O Carib Isle! Crane.
O Holy City Seen of John. Bowie.
The Odyssey. Homer.
Off Viareggio. Pitchford.
Oh, Roll on, Babe. Anonymous.
Old King Cole. Robinson.
The Old Wife. Kent.
An Old Woman's Song. Akjartoq.
On a Drop of Dew. Marvell.
On a Girdle. Waller.
On Certain Days of the Year. Simpson.
On the Bright Side. Revard.
On the holy day of your going out to war. Mahodahi.
On the Marriage of a Virgin. Thomas.
On the Nativity of Our Saviour. Philipott.
On the Porch of the Antique Dealer. Ramsey.
One of the Regiment. Le Pan.
Out-of-Doors. Whitaker.
The Pageant of Seaman. Byron.
Pantisocracy. Coleridge.
Park Pigeons. Cane.
The Parklands. Smith.
Pastoral. Strobel.
Pearl Diver. Benet.
Perspectives Are Precipices. Bishop.
The Phoenix (excerpt). Anonymous.
Pioneer Woman. Crawford.
Plague of Dead Sharks. Dugan.
A Poem for a Poet. Lee.
Poem to the Sun. Sklar.
Polyolbion. Drayton.
The Poor. Verhaeren.
A Postcard from the Volcano. Stevens.
Praise for an Urn. Crane.
A Prayer for a Marriage. Davies.
Prophecy. Pulci.
Psalm. Ben-Yitzhak.
The Pythoness. Raine.
Quatorzain. Timrod.
Queen Anne's Musicians. Hennell.

Question and Answer.
  Raine.
Rain. Fry.
Rain. Nabokov.
Rannoch Moor. MacGregor.
Rapunzel. Mandel.
The Real People Loves One
  Another. Penny.
Reconciliation. Doten.
Reflection. Turner.
Remembering. Akjartoq.
Remembering Snow. Currey.
Requiem. Fearing.
Resignation. Chatterton.
Response to Rimbaud's Latter
  Manner. Moore.
The Return. Aiken.
Revelation. Markham.
The Revenge of Hamish.
  Lanier.
The Riddle. *Anonymous.*
Rollo's Miracle. Zimmer.
Rooftop. Barnstone.
Rooms. Mew.
The Sadness of the Moon.
  Baudelaire.
Samson Rends His Clothes.
  Eldan.
Schemmelfennig. Harte.
Schoolboys in Winter. Clare.
A Sea Child. Carman.
The Sea-God's Address to
  Bran. Anonymous.
Sea Owl. Smith.
Secret. Doolittle.
Seeds. De la Mare.
Self-Portrait, as a Bear. Hall.
The Shadow-Child. Monroe.
She Died in Beauty. Sillery.
She Tied Up Her Few Things.
  Clare.
She Waited. Van Zyl.
The Shedpherd's Week.
  Gay.
The Shepherd and His Flock.
  Mtshali.
The Ship and the Sea.
  Baughan.
Silex Scintillans. Vaughan.
The Sin of Omission.
  Sangster.
Since to Be Loved Endures.
  Bridges.
Sir Cawline. *Anonymous.*
The Sleepers. Harvey.
The Slough of Despond.
  Lowell.
Smelling the End of Green
  July. Yates.
Snapshot of Hue. Halpern.
The Snowman's Resolution.
  Fisher.
Solar Myth. Taggard.
Solo for Bent Spoon. Finkel.
Son David. *Anonymous.*
Song for September.
  Fitzgerald.
Song for the Divine Bride and
  Mother. Lope de Vega
  Carpio.
Song: "I'd much rather sit
  there in the sun." Krauss.
Song: "Love, by that loosened
  hair." Carman.
A Song of Praise. Cullen.
The Song of Wandering
  Aengus. Yeats.
Song: "Poppies paramour the
  girls." Long.
The Sonne. Herbert.
Sonnet LXX. Alabaster.

Sonnets, IV: "Two stars there
  are in one faire firmament."
  Barnfield.
The Soul and Body of John
  Brown. Rukeyser.
St. Michael's Mount.
  Davidson.
Stable-Talk. Knister.
Stanzas. Thoreau.
State Fair Pigs. Pfingston.
Stones. Jeffrey.
A Storm in the Distance.
  Hayne.
The Sun. Drinkwater.
Sun of the Center. Kelly.
Sunday Stroll. Pettit.
Sunset on Calvary.
  Anonymous.
Supremacy. Robinson.
The Supreme Sacrifice.
  Maurice.
Sur Ma Guzzla Gracile.
  Stevens.
Susan. Magowan.
Sweet Innisfallen. Moore.
Taking Long Views.
  Kendall.
Tears. Sitwell.
The Telephone. Belloc.
Thanksgiving. Koch.
There's Nothing Like the Sun.
  Thomas.
There Was a Roaring in the
  Wind All Night.
  Wordsworth.
These Days the Papers in the
  Street. Reznikoff.
Thesis. Dorn.
Though Bodies Are Apart.
  Day-Lewis.
Thought. Emerson.
Three Sonnets on Oblivion.
  Sterling.
To a Brown Girl. Davis.
To a Wild Rose Found in
  October. Hayes.
To Harriett. Clare.
To His Coy Mistress.
  Marvell.
To His Lady. Davies.
To see her is a picture.
  Dickinson.
Today. Schuyler.
The Train Out. Lea.
Transfiguration. Barnes.
Troubadours. Ficke.
Truth. Donne.
A Tryptych for Jan
  Bockelson. Simon.
Turning Fifty. Wright.
Upon Phillis Walking in a
  Morning before Sun-rising.
  Cleveland.
The Upper Skies Are Palest
  Blue. Bridges.
Ur Burial. Eberhart.
A Valley where I Don't
  Belong. Piercy.
Variations on an Old Nursery
  Rhyme. Sitwell.
Vernon Castle. Monroe.
The View from a Cab.
  Taylor.
The Vision. Dante Alighieri.
Vision and Prayer. Thomas.
Voice from Danang.
  Redshaw.
Walt Whitman. Carnevali.
War. Joseph.
The Waste Places. Stephens.
Weldon Kees. Levis.
Western Town. Cannon, Jr..

Wet Through. Summers.
What to Do. Wise.
What Triumph Moves on the
  Billows So Blue? Lewis.
What Wild Dawns There
  Were. Levertov.
The Wheel. Hayden.
When Fishes Set Umbrellas
  Up. Rossetti.
When the Orient Is Lit by the
  Great Light. Colonna.
Where the Dropwort Springs
  up Lithe and Tall.
  Donaghy.
White Autumn. Morgan.
The White Eagle.
  McDonald.
William Shakespeare.
  Swinburne.
The Wind on the Hills.
  Shorter.
Winter Garden. Gascoyne.
Winter Noon. Teasdale.
Winter Streams. Carman.
Winter with the Gulf Stream.
  Hopkins.
Wizard Frost. Sherman.
The Woman. Keithley.
The Woman with Child.
  Laughton.
Woodbird. Bell.
The Woolworth Philodendron.
  Sandy.
Words at Farewell. Derian.
Work. Block.
Written in Prison. Clare.
Yellow. Jacobsen.
You Tell Me to Sit Quiet.
  Jordan.
Youth. Lodge.
Youth, Day, Old Age, and
  Night. Whitman.
Sunbeam (s)
The Coming of Good Luck.
  Herrick.
The Crocus. Crane.
The End. Wilkinson.
The Glance. Herbert.
The Lone Prairie.
  Anonymous.
Man's Anxious, but
  Ineffectual Guard Against
  Death. Beddoes.
Mattens. Herbert.
On a Sunbeam. Heyrick.
Sunday (s)
Aside. Dugan.
At Church Next Sunday.
  Anonymous.
Canzone. Thomas.
Christ Church Meadows,
  Oxford. Hall.
The Cit's Country Box.
  Lloyd.
Courtship. *Anonymous.*
Diary. Wagoner.
For a Child. Glover.
How Many Days Has My
  Baby to Play? Mother
  Goose.
Hudson Hornet. Cook.
I Mun Be Married a Sunday.
  Udall.
Not on Sunday Night.
  Anonymous.
On a Sunday Afternoon.
  Sterling.
The Planter's Daughter.
  Clarke.
Poem: "Time and the weather
  wear away." Justice.
The Rock. Eliot.

The Snuff-Boxes.
  Anonymous.
Spring Is a Looping-Free
  Time. Robbins.
Street Car Blues. Estes.
Sunday Bells. Allingham.
Swell My Net Full.
  Anonymous
Watching the Out-Door
  Movie Show. Struthers.
West Helena Blues. Sykes.
Sundown
Out of the Rolling Ocean the
  Crowd. Whitman.
Pachuta, Mississippi / A
  Memoir. Young.
Sunflower (s)
Ah, Sun-Flower. Blake.
Sunflowers and Saturdays.
  Boyd.
Sunk (en)
An Anniversary. Hardy.
Emblems of Evening. Horan.
Fragment of Sappho.
  Philips.
The Golden Vanity (B vers.).
  Anonymous.
On a Bust of Dante. Parsons
Sunday Evenings. Hollander.
Thoughts of Loved Ones.
  Fishback.
Sunless
Ballad. Kendall.
The Laborer. Heredia.
November. Bridges.
The Sea of Death. Hood.
She, to Him. Hardy.
Sunlight
The. MacNeice.
America for Me. Van Dyke.
Calypso's Island. MacLeish.
The Children's Letters.
  Livesay.
Daniel Webster. Holmes.
The Fair Hills of Eire, O!
  Mangan.
Fire Burial. McInnis.
Fishin' Blues. Ramirez.
From a Beggarman's Song.
  Anonymous.
The Great Man. Tietjens.
The growth of Sym. Dennis.
The Homeward Journey.
  Aaronson.
Hymn to the Sea. Roberts.
Hymn to the Sun. Roberts.
If There Are Any Heavens.
  Cummings.
In Bohemia. Symons.
Inscription. Hamilton.
Into & At. Pennant.
A Leave-Taking. Broome.
Little Roach Poem.
  Truesdale.
Lovebirds. Smith.
Moving. Steele.
No. Zach.
The Poets of the Nineties.
  Mahon.
The Proof. Auden.
Repetitions. Sandburg.
Samadhi. Aiken.
Snapshots of the Cotton
  South. Davis.
Songs of Divorce. Green.
Spring Doggerel. Coghill.
Spring in These Hills.
  MacLeish.
Sunlight and Sea. Noyes.
To a Sleeping Friend.
  Cocteau.
To the Red Lory. Neilson.

The Trial. Auden.
Walking in Bush. Dowling.
Watching a Cloud. Abse.
A Winter Daybreak above
Vence. Wright.
Your Name in Arezzo.
Wright.
Sunrise
Alma to Her Sister. Gregg.
The Arabian Nights (excerpt).
Anonymous.
Australian Transcripts, X: The
Wood-Swallows. Sharp.
Berceuse. Clampitt.
I know some lonely houses off
the road. Dickinson.
Lonely House. Dickinson.
October Elegy. Gibson.
Of Women. *Anonymous.*
Out of the Darkness.
Kolmar.
Presentation Piece. Hacker.
Sunrise. Sangster.
Sunrise Trumpets.
Auslander.
Voices That Have Filled My
Day. Chiang.
Winter Count of Sean Spotted
Wolf. Thompson.
Ya Se Van Los Pastores.
Fitts.
Sunset (s)
Alma to Her Sister. Gregg.
Another and Another and
Another. Henry.
Beauty Is Ever to the Lonely
Mind. Nathan.
A Chasm. Silverton.
Comfort. Widdemer.
Coruisk. Smith.
The Dead Prospector.
Chapman.
The First Day of the Hunting
Moon. Low.
Immanence. Hovey.
The Last Post. Graves.
The Morning Drum-Call on
My Eager Ear. Stevenson.
The Musician. Lister.
The Narrows. Bruchac.
October, Hanson's Field.
Borson.
An Old-World Thicket.
Rossetti.
Oregon Trail: 1851.
Marshall.
Perspective. Vorpahl.
Riding with the Fireworks.
Darr.
The Rooftree. Tate.
Sandhill People. Sandburg.
Sea Food Thought. Moser.
Serengeti Sunset. Oerke.
Song of Basket-Weaving.
Skinner.
Steps. Hill.
The Story of Vinland.
Lanier.
Temagami. Lampman.
This Amber Sunstream. Van
Doren.
Twilight. Pagaza.
The Vanishers. Whittier
When I Am Dead. Barrie.
The Word. Realf.
Sunshine
The All-Embracing. Faber.
All's Well. Whittier.
Amoretti, XL. Spenser.
A Bather in a Painting.
Greene.

The Blossom of the Soul.
Johnson.
The Blue-Bird. Wilson.
A Factory Rainbow. Sa'di.
France. Mitchell.
Hast Thou Seen Reversed the
Prophet's Miracle.
Tuckerman.
A Hundred Years to Come.
Brown.
I Was the Child. Warren.
Life's Lessons. *Anonymous.*
A Little Word. *Anonymous.*
Lucasta's World. Lovelace.
Ophra. Halevi.
Red River Valley.
Anonymous.
Silex Scintillans. Vaughan.
Sweet Peril. Macdonald.
To the Memory of the Brave
Americans. Freneau.
The Two Old Women of
Mumbling Hill. Reeves.
Wild Weather. Bates.
Windshield Wipers. Lee.
Sup (ped)
Bed Time. *Anonymous.*
Come, Let's to Bed.
Anonymous.
Greedy Tom. Anonymous.
Lancashire Born.
Anonymous.
Superlative
A Fable for Critics. Lowell.
Petition. Slater.
Superman
While the Bells Ring.
Dunetz.
Superstition
The Destiny of Nations.
Coleridge.
The People vs. the People.
Fearing.
A Ribbon Two Yards Wide.
Kreymborg.
Supper
Accept Our Tribute. Watts.
Busy Old Fool (parody).
Kelso.
A Croon on Hennacliff.
Hawker.
Domestic Science.
Anonymous.
The Dream of a Boy Who
Lived at Nine Elms.
Rands.
The Dream of a Girl Who
Lived at Sevenoaks.
Rands.
Lot Later. Nemerov.
The Mendicants. Carman.
More Scraps of Lear: "Hassall
irritates me." Lear.
Paper Matches. Jiles.
The Peaches. Oppenheimer.
Suppertime. Burns.
Twenty-third Street Runs into
Heaven. Patchen.
Suppliant (s)
At the Grave of Henry
Vaughan. Sassoon.
Good-By. Bruner.
To an Infant Expiring the
Second Day of its Birth.
Wright.
Supply (supplies)
Blues for Sister Sally.
Kandel.
The Dutchess of Monmouth's
Lamentation for the Loss of
her Duke. *Anonymous.*
The Rose. Browne.

Under the Willow-Shades.
Davenant.
Ye Beauties, Beaux, Ye
Pleaders at the Bar.
Anonymous.
Support
Goodbye to Serpents.
Dickey.
To a Lady, with a Present of
a Walking-Stick. Frere.
Waiting Inside. Ignatow.
Suppose
The Crocodile. Herford.
The Mantis Friend.
McHugh.
Postcards from Kodai.
Crossley-Holland.
Supremacy
Contributions: For Instance.
McAlmon.
The Last Turn. Williams.
News of the World. Ridler.
Poor Vaunting Earth, Gloss'd
with Uncertain Pride.
Alsop.
This Too Will Pass away.
Anonymous.
Supreme Court
The Hustler. *Anonymous.*
Sure
As the Holly Groweth Green.
Henry VIII.
The Camel. Nash.
Certainty Enough. Burr.
Come, Says Jesus' Voice.
Barbauld.
Consecration of the House.
Fairbridge.
Corruption. Vaughan.
Cuba. Stedman.
Eagle Sonnets. Wood.
An Epitaph on Master Philip
Gray. Jonson.
Et Cetera. Walker.
Fearful Symmetry. Bunting.
A Flower of Mullein. Reese.
The Fourth Option. Rasof.
The Frolicksome Farmer.
Anonymous.
A Garage in Co. Cork.
Mahon.
The Horse and the Mule.
Wynne.
Laying By. Williams.
Let Us with a Gladsome
Mind. Milton.
Medium Poem. Myles.
The Melmac Year. Hilton.
My Letter. Litchfield.
Porson on His Majesty's
Government. Porson.
Praise the Lord. Milton.
The Retarded Class at F.A.O.
Schwarz's Celebrates
Christmas. Fisher.
Road-Song of the Bandar-Log.
Kipling.
Rondel: "Love, love, what wilt
thou with this heart of
mine?" Froissart.
A Shadow of the Night.
Aldrich.
Suche Waywarde Wais Hath
Love. Surrey.
Up in the Morning Early.
Burns.
Upon the Same. Herrick.
Vale. Ciardi.
The Valley. Moss.
Victorian Grandmother.
Lockwood.

Waiting for the Bus.
Enright.
Watching My Daughter Sew.
Privett.
Surf
Listening to Beethoven on the
Oregon Coast. Carlile.
North of Santa Monica.
Revard.
Spanish Waters. Masefield.
Suicide off Egg Rock. Plath.
They Who Possess the Sea.
Adams.
Surface (s)
Ballydavid Pier. Kinsella.
Bordering Manuscript.
Applewhite.
The Donibristle Moss Moran
Disaster. *Anonymous.*
From My Window.
Williams.
The Name of Our Country.
Schmitz.
Pentucket. Whittier.
Revolution. Zimunya.
San Francisco Poem. Logan.
Stone. Chayat.
Surfaces. Madden.
Technique. Eaton.
Telephoning It. Edmond.
Useless Day. Castellânos.
Surfeit
Against Absence. Suckling.
Murdering Beauty. Carew.
Surge (s)
Boatman's Hymn. Magrath.
Dr. Sigmund Freud Discovers
the Sea Shell. MacLeish.
George Washington.
Ingham.
Greece. Haygarth.
Monday. Stafford.
The Pine to the Mariner.
Turberville.
The thought beneath so slight
a film. Dickinson.
To William Sharp. Scollard.
Verses Written at Montauban
in France, 1750. Warton.
Surgeon (s)
Bring Your Own Victim.
Curnow.
Cancer's a Funny Thing.
Haldane.
God's Little Mountain. Hill.
O Doctor Dear My Love.
Halley.
Ulster. Adler.
The Unblinding. Lieberman.
Surmise (d)
Cornfield. Cox.
Epitaph on Francis Atterbury,
Bishop of Rochester.
Prior.
Footnotes to "The
Autobiography of Bertrand
Russell." Van Duyn.
Modern Love, XLVIII.
Meredith.
Sam Bass. *Anonymous.*
Surpass (es)
The Bridegroom Is So Tall.
Sappho.
The Impious Feast. Landor.
A Summer Night. Auden.
Surprise (d) (s)
Acceptance. Hughes.
Apparition. Erskine.
At the Aquarium. Eastman.
Bayard Taylor. Whittier.
Busts and Bosoms Have I
Known. *Anonymous.*

Change. Graves.
Conclusion. Nims.
Condone. Bierce.
Environment. Kearns.
Familiar Friends. Tippett.
For the Opening of the
Hunting Season. Bishop.
For the Sleepwalkers.
Hirsch.
Hiding. Aldis.
If You Saw a Negro Lady.
Jordan.
Kiss Me Quick and Go.
Steele.
Life's Made up of Little
Things. Hartman.
Limerick: "A Lesbian born
under Pisces."
Anonymous.
Limerick: "Your verses, dear
friend, I surmise."
Anonymous.
Metamorphoses of M.
Bishop.
Ode in Honour. Scarfe.
The Oranges. Abu Dharr.
People on Sunday. Denby.
The Petrified Fern. Branch.
The Petrified Leaf. Branch.
Plus Ultra. Swinburne.
Poem for Half-White College
Students. Jones.
The Quiet Life. Seneca
(Lucius Annaeus Seneca).
R-and-R Centre: An Incident
from the Vietnam War.
Enright.
Somehow, Somewhere,
Sometime. Letts.
The Sound of Rain.
Akhmadulina.
Stained Glass. Barnstone.
Surprises. Soule.
Tiresias (excerpt). Clarke.
Walk with De Mayor of
Harlem. Henderson.
The Warning. Creeley.
Surrender (ed) (ing) (s)
All That I Am. Arvey.
The Dispraise of Absalom.
Anonymous.
Epitaph. Davenant.
For Strength. Tagore.
Higher Love. Wright.
How Are You, Dear World,
This Morning? Traubel.
Knight Olaf. Heine.
The Love Song. Gurney.
Nature Notes (excerpt).
MacNeice.
Newsletter from My Mother.
Harper.
Spring. Kulbak.
Sunset. Bayldon.
Triumphalis. Carman.
What to Say to the Pasha.
Hitchcock.
That Which You Call "Love
Me." Rosales.
The White Flag. Hay.
Surround (ed) (ings) (s)
In the Garden of the Turkish
Consulate. Sadeh.
Letters to Walt Whitman.
Johnson.
Poetry Paper. Codrescu.
Survey
Lord of All I Survey.
Sinclair.
Survive (d) (s) (survival)
The accident has occurred.
Atwood.

Akiba. Rukeyser.
Album. Miles.
All the World Moved.
Jordan.
The Aztec City. Ware.
Blood-Sister. Rich.
California, This Is Minnesota
Speaking. Dunn.
Chant Royal. Morgan.
A Chinaman's Chance. Kuo.
Conversation. Anthony
("Ai").
Cornfields in Accra. Aidoo.
The Cost of Pretending.
Davison.
Cradle Song. Hoffenstein.
Daughter. Voigt.
Driving; Driven. McAleavey.
The Enigma. Eberhart.
Generations. Simmons.
Gill Boy. Schmitz.
Henry VIII. *Anonymous.*
The Hinge. Cowing.
In Apia Bay. Roberts.
In Defense of Black Poets.
Rivers.
Limerick: "A lady track star
from Toccoa." Blount
Roy.
Lucy Taking Birth. Scott.
Masada. Mozeson.
Massachusetts Song of
Liberty. Warren.
An Old Cracked Tune.
Kunitz.
Onwardness. Hedges.
Painting. Jacobs.
Planting a Magnolia.
Snodgrass.
Poem after a Speech by Chief
Seattle, 1855. Brashers.
Poems Chiefly of Early and
Late Years: Prelude.
Wordsworth.
Poets Observed.
Rosenberger.
Potato. Wilbur.
Radical Coherency. Antin.
The Rath in Front of the Oak
Wood. *Anonymous.*
Return. Naude.
The River of Bees. Merwin.
She of the Garden.
Verhaeren.
The Significance of a
Veteran's Day. Ortiz.
Survival This Way. Ortiz.
The Test. Emerson.
This Morning. Clifton.
To My Fellow-Mariners,
March, '53. Whitbread.
Watching Salmon Jump.
Ortiz.
We Survive! Glick.
Woman and Nature. Griffin.
Words from a Bottle. Lee.
Survivor (s)
Lobo. Lillard.
Marginalia (excerpt). Auden.
North to Milwaukee.
Vizenor.
So Live, So Love, So Use
That Fragile Hour.
Stevenson.
Time-Travel. Olds.
Susan
The Best Line Yet. Allen.
A British Man-of-War.
Anonymous.
I Love the Blue Violet.
Clare.

The Pride of Kildare.
Anonymous.
Suspicious
Christmas Carol. Opperman.
My Father's Eye. Vakalo.
Testimony to an Inquisitor.
Stafford.
Written in Her French
Psalter. Elizabeth I.
Sustain (s)
Amoretti, XLVI. Spenser.
Coming Back to America.
Dickey.
Whither Is Gone the Wisdom
and the Power. Coleridge.
Sustenance
I Cannot Live With You.
Dickinson.
Song from the Gulf.
Humphries.
A Trial. Dugan.
Swain (s)
As Chloris Full of Harmless
Thought. Rochester.
The Comparison (excerpt).
Anonymous.
Jack and Joan. Campion
A Pastoral. Byrom.
Pastoral: The Tenth Eclogue.
Drayton.
The Question to Lisetta.
Prior.
The Seasons. Thomson.
Written at Mr. Pope's House
at Twickenham. Lyttelton.
Swallow (ed) (ing) (s)
Adam's Death. Levin.
All of a Sudden. Jesus.
The Bard's Song. Stapylton.
The Book I Held Grew Cold.
Toller.
The Cummerbund. Lear.
Didymus. MacNeice.
Disaster (parody). Calverley.
The Finished Course. Joseph
of the Studium.
From a Rise of Land to the
Sea. Hoffmann.
From Sunset to Star Rise.
Rossetti.
Grotesque. Graves.
I've Known a Heaven Like a
Tent. Dickinson.
Ingestion. McDonald.
Kinship. Heaney.
Limerick: "A big bull-dyke,
surly and sallow."
Anonymous.
The Lion. Nash.
Little Red Riding Hood.
Carryl.
Madwoman at Rodmell.
Roberts.
Misericordia! Lipton.
My Garden. Davies.
My Song. Bialik.
Night. Bly.
O My Swallows. Toller.
The Old Lady Who
Swallowed a Fly.
Anonymous.
On the Planet of Flies.
Morgenstern.
Orgy. Labriola.
Praise. *Anonymous.*
The Preiching of the Swallow.
Henryson.
Quiet. Ungaretti.
The Singular Sangfroid of
Baby Bunting. Carryl.
Slides. Maiden.

The Song of Nu-Numma-
Kwiten. *Anonymous.*
Soup on a Cold Day. Hill.
Speaking for Them. Carruth.
Swallow the Lake. Major.
Swallows. Ferril.
Swallows over the Camp.
Krige.
Three Landscapes (excerpt).
Rothenberg.
Transit. Avison.
Unanswered. Dickinson.
Waltz. Sitwell.
What Are You Thinking
About? Macmillan.
Yes, the Secret Mind
Whispers. Young.
Swamp (ed)
The Butterfly. Avison.
Heron in Swamp. Howard.
Maps. Hass.
The Path. Bryant.
Poets and Their
Bibliographies. Tennyson.
Wake Nicodemus. Work.
Swan (s)
Academic Discourse at
Havana. Stevens.
The Black Swan. Merrill.
The Canterbury Tales: A
Monk. Chaucer.
Canticle. McAuley.
Central Park, 1916. Stewart.
A Conversation. Thomas.
Erinna. Antipater of Sidon.
Erris Coast, 1943. Connell.
The Falcon. Lovelace.
Hidden Valley. Burrows.
A High-Toned Old Fascist
Gentleman (parody).
Zaranka.
Ione. De Vere.
Leda. Doolittle.
Leda. Rilke.
Love Is a Keeper of Swans.
Wolfe.
The Made Lake. Nicholl.
Madrigal: "The silver swan."
Gibbons.
Modern Love, XLVII.
Meredith.
Mother. Vincent.
Name Giveaway. George.
A New Siege: An Historical
Meditation (excerpt).
Montague.
Of Commerce and Society.
Hill.
Oh, Let Us Howl Some Heavy
Note. Webster.
Peace. Greenberg.
The Pleiades. Barnard.
Portrait of a Cree. "Hale.
Program Note on Sibelius.
Babcock.
Romance of the Swan's Nest.
Browning.
Season Ticket. Frym.
The Sisters. Jackowska.
The Sleeping Beauty. Cohen.
Snow Storm. Mary
Madeleva.
A Son Just Born. Miller.
Sonnet: "This virgin, beautiful
and lively day." Mallarme.
Summer Idyll. Barker.
Swan. Hall.
Swan Swam over the Sea.
Anonymous.
Swans. Durrell.
The Swans. Sitwell.
Swans at Night. Gilmore.

Swansong on the Moorlands.
  Thorsteinsson.
Three Poems on Morris
  Graves' Paintings. Logan.
Venice. Wright.
Whilst I Beheld the Neck o'
  th' Dove. Cary.

Swank
Some Scribbles for a
  Lumpfish. Johnson.

Swansong
Days in White. Bachmann.
Dead at Clonmacnois.
  O'Gillan.
It Must Be Summer. Csoori.
The Psychonaut Sonnets:
  Jones. Goldbarth.
The Pylons. Spender.

Swarm (ed) (s)
Edward Lear. Auden.
Evening Quatrains. Cotton.
The Fleece. Dyer.
Herman Moon's Hourbook.
  Middleton.
Into the Book. Grossman.
The Sense of Responsibility.
  Mathews.

Swat
The Akond of Swat. Lear.
On the Road to Vicenza.
  Gustafson.
Poems of Passion, Carefully
  Restrained So as to Offend
  Nobody. Hoffenstein.
A Threnody. Lanigan.

Sway (ed) (ing)
All the Fruit... Holderlin.
The Day Thou Gavest.
  Ellerton.
Epigram: "Perchance some
  coming after." Strato.
In Scorching Time. Stevens.
May the man who gained my
  trust yet did not come.
  Ryojin Hisho.
The Midnight Court.
  Merriman.
Oceana and Britannia.
  Ayloffe.
The Poet. Bryant.
The Power in the People.
  Herrick.
The Rookery at Sunrise.
  Sharp.
A Sacred Grove. Winant.
The Visitant. Roethke.

Swear (swore)
The Belly Dancer in the
  Nursing Home. Wallace.
Caelica, XXI. Greville.
The Common Woman.
  Grahn.
A Conquest. Pollock.
Conversation. MacNeice.
Empty Dwelling Places.
  Patchen.
Friends, you are lucky you
  can talk. Vidya.
I Knew I'd Sing. McHugh.
I'm Gonna Move to the
  Outskirts of Town.
  Broonzy.
Incidental Pieces to a Walk:
  for Conrad. Cunningham.
A Little Pretty Bonny Lass.
  Anonymous.
Nymph of the Garden where
  All Beauties Be. Sidney.
O, Be Not Too Hasty, My
  Dearest. Newell.
The Old Man Who Lived in
  the Woods. Anonymous.

The Parrot. Lucie-Smith.
Robin Hood and the Ranger.
  Anonymous.
Satan, No Woman. Greville.
She's My Love. Young.
Tom Tiler; or,The Nurse.
  Anonymous.
Upon the Curtain of Lucasta's
  Picture It Was Thus
  Wrought. Lovelace.
When Your Pants Begin to
  Go. Lawson.

Sweat
Appendix to the Anniad.
  Brooks.
Boy's Will, Joyful Labor
  without Pay, and Harvest
  Home (excerpt). Warren.
Cadenza. Hughes.
Defense Rests. Miller.
Frascati's. Huxley.
Girl in a Black Bikini.
  Brown.
Gitanjali. Tagore.
Go, Ploughman, Plough.
  Campbell.
Good Memory. Rivera-
  Aviles.
Hermetic Bird. Lamantia.
I Wake and Feel the Fell of
  Dark. Hopkins.
The Iliad. Homer.
The Ladies' Aid.
  Anonymous.
Lilith. Finkel.
Midewiwan. Wolf.
Old Man, the Sweat Lodge.
  George.
On St. Winefred. Hopkins.
On Those That Hated "The
  Playboy of the Western
  World", 1907. Yeats.
Registered at the Bordello
  Hotel (Vienna). Rubin.
Savage Portraits. Marquis.
Shoplifters. Stanton.
Sophistication. Miller.
The Teeth Mother Naked at
  Last. Bly.
Testament. Sister M.
  Therese.
This Shirt. Trias.
What about You? (parody).
  Pygge.
What Music. Harjo.
Women Transport Corps.
  Anonymous.

Sweater
Sisters. McPherson.
The Sweater. Orr.
Two Lovers Sitting on a
  Tomb. Hill.

Sweden
Limerick: "There was a young
  lady of Sweden." Lear.

Sweep (ing) (s)
Brooms. Aldis.
The Fate of a Broom–An
  Anticipation. Peacock.
Gargoyle. Rabbit.
Halloween Witches.
  Holman.
The Lady in the Barbershop.
  Rudnik.
The Minute. Shapiro.
The Plodder Seam.
  Anonymous.
Roof Garden. Filip.
Telling My Feelings. Yu
  Hsuan-chi.
Three Poems on Morris
  Graves' Paintings. Logan.

Two Clouds. Raab.
When Young Melissa Sweeps.
  Turner.

Sweet (er) (es) (s)
Absence. Landor.
Ad Chloen, M.A. Collins.
Alas! How Should I Sing?
  Anonymous.
All That's Bright Must Fade.
  Moore.
Amor Mysticus. Marcela de
  Carpio.
The Angel in the House.
  Patmore.
Are You What Your Faire
  Lookes Expresse?
  Campion.
Assynt. Gilchrist.
Astrophel and Stella, LVII.
  Sidney.
At the Nadir. Kennedy.
Backward–Forward.
  Anonymous.
The Ballad of Charity.
  Leland.
Bartholomew. Gale.
Because of You. Hensley.
The Beginning of the End.
  Hopkins.
Benediction. Kunitz.
A Bewilderment at the
  Entrance of the Fat Boy
  into Eden. Hine.
Big Dog. Booth.
Blackberry Winter. Huggins.
Brendan Gone. Fiacc.
Brother and Sister. Eliot.
But What Is the Reader to
  Make of This? Ashbery.
Came to me–/Who? Rudaki.
Carol: "We saw him sleeping
  in his manger bed."
  Bullett.
Che Sara Sara. Plarr.
Cherry. Baro.
Childe Harold's Pilgrimage:
  Canto III, XXIV. Byron.
Chorus. Jonson.
Circus. Farjeon.
The Compound Eye.
  Davison.
The Confession of Golias
  (abridged). Archpoet of
  Cologne.
Confessions. Browning.
The Crab Tree. Gogarty.
Daisy Bell (A Bicycle Built
  for Two). Dacre.
The Death of Warren.
  Sargent.
The Demagogue. McGinley.
Dishonor. Denby.
Doubt. Chipp.
Dressed Up. Hughes.
Dulce et Decorum. Wilson.
Epigram: "If true that notion,
  which but few contest."
  Anonymous.
Epilogue. Heine.
Equality. Shirley.
Extras. Burton.
The Fairies' Shopping.
  Deland.
The Faithful Shepherdess.
  Fletcher.
Farm Cart. Farjeon.
The First Kiss of Love.
  Byron.
The First Olympionique to
  Hiero of Syracuse. Pindar.
The Flitting. Clare.

For We Are All Madwomen.
  Sweeney.
Give Beauty All Her Right.
  Campion.
The Good Humor Man.
  McGinley.
He Has Fallen from the
  Height of His Love.
  Blunt.
Hester. Lamb.
The Hibakusha's Letter
  (1955). Mura.
Holy Cross. Anonymous.
Home Is Where There Is One
  to Love Us. Swain.
Homeric Hymns: Hymn to
  Mercury. Anonymous.
Honey Bee. Perkins.
Hunger. Stampa.
I Saw from the Beach.
  Moore.
Ideals. Greene.
In the City. Zangwill.
In the Garden. Crosby.
Judah in Exile Wanders.
  Sandys.
Keep Sweet. Anonymous.
Kentucky Moonshiner.
  Anonymous.
Life and Nature. Lampman.
Lion. Swenson.
A Little Word. Anonymous.
Living. Anonymous.
Love and Death. Catullus.
Love Is a Hunter Boy.
  Moore.
The Love Song. Gurney.
Lying in State. Mitchell.
The Man of Peace. Carman.
The Man Who Sang the
  Sillies. Ciardi.
Many Things. Holmes.
Market Women's Cries.
  Swift.
Meditation under Stars.
  Meredith.
Mickleham Way. Eastwick.
Monna Lisa. Lowell.
A Mustacheless Bard.
  Coogler.
My Pretty Little Pink (with
  music). Anonymous.
New Year's Day. Crashaw.
Nikolina. Thaxter.
Old Ellen Sullivan. Welles.
Old Men and Old Women
  Going Home on the Street
  Car. Moore.
On Clarastella Walking in Her
  Garden. Heath.
On the Queen's Visit to
  London. Cowper.
Out of the Sea. Bynner.
Pain. Russell.
Pass It On! Anonymous.
A Persian Song of Hafiz.
  Hafiz.
A Persian Song of Hafiz.
  Jones.
Philomela's Ode in Her
  Arbour. Greene.
The Pillar-Box. Wolker.
The Platonic Lady.
  Rochester.
Poems, XCIII: "Mother, I
  cannot mind my wheel."
  Landor.
The Praise of Derry.
  Columcille.
Prometheus Unbound.
  Shelley.
The Queen's Song. Flecker.

Sweet

Quid Non Speremus,
Amantes? Dowson.
The Raven. Coleridge.
Red Wine. Richardson.
Retirement. Cowper.
Romeo and Juliet.
Shakespeare.
A Roundel of Rest. Symons.
The Ruins of Rome. Dyer.
Sanary. Mansfield.
The Shadowgraphs.
Lattimore.
A Shepherd's Gift. Anyte
[(or Anytes)].
The Shortest and.
Macdonald.
Simon and Susan.
Anonymous.
A Song for My Mother–Her
Stories. Branch.
A Song. Hawthorne.
The Song of Love. Rilke.
Song of Praise for an Ox.
Sutzkever.
Song: "Sing the old song,
amid the sounds
dispersing." De Vere.
Sonnet VII: "We see each
living thing finally die."
Labe.
A Sonnet. Lear.
Sonnet upon a Swedish
Cottage. Carr.
Sonnets, XCIX: "The forward
violet thus did I chide."
Shakespeare.
Spring at Fort Okanogan.
Wilson.
St. James Infirmary.
Anonymous.
The Stately Structure of This
Earth. Brewster.
The Sweet o' the Year.
Meredith.
The Sweetest Story Ever Told.
Stults.
The Test. McAlpine.
Testament. Holmes.
There's Life in a Mussel. A
Meditation. Farewell.
To a Kiss. Wolcot.
To Jesus on the Cross.
Tejada.
To One Admiring Her Selfe in
a Looking-Glasse.
Randolph.
Visions of the Daughters of
Albion. Blake.
The Voiceless. Holmes
Water Ouzel. Matchett.
A White Rose. O'Reilly.
Wild Eden. Woodberry.
Woman's Constancy.
Suckling.
The World's a Well Strung
Fidle, Mans Tongue the
Quill. Ward.
Written to a Young Lady.
Callanan.
You Shall Be Queen.
Anonymous.

Sweetheart (s)

The Bedpost. Graves.
Driving the Mule.
Anonymous.
Green Grow the Lilacs.
Anonymous.
Her Eyes Don't Shine Like
Diamonds. Marion.
Lord Randall. *Anonymous.*
A Lost Jewel. Graves.

A New Song on the Blandford
Privateer. *Anonymous.*
O Ease My Spirit.
""MacDiarmid.
An Old Sweetheart of Mine.
Riley.
Poor Lonesome Cowboy (with
music). *Anonymous.*
The Rose Is Red, the Rose Is
White. *Anonymous.*
The Smuggler's Victory.
Anonymous.
Song: "This peach is pink
with such a pink." Gale.
The Tale of a Tart.
Weatherly.
Ten Thousand Miles.
Anonymous.
With Strawberries. Henley.
The Wren She Lies in Care's
Bed. *Anonymous.*

Sweetness (es)

The All-Embracing. Faber.
And What Sordello Would
See There. Browning.
Aubade: The Desert. Bock.
Bees Inside Me. Chester.
Choice. Farrar.
Days of 1978. Stern.
Edith. Channing
Flowers for the Brave.
Thaxter.
Friends. Yeats.
Hast Thou Not Seen an Aged
Rifted Tower. Coleridge.
Inside of King's College
Chapel, Cambridge.
Wordsworth.
Lonesome in the Country.
Young.
Love's Alchemy. Donne.
Marriage Is a Lovely Thing.
Pisan.
Noble Love. Flecknoe.
Not Saying Much. Gregg.
Pharaoh and Joseph. Lasker-
Schüler.
Poietes Apoietes. Coleridge.
The River of Life. Campbell.
Rose. Thompson.
The Shirts. Gallagher.
A Spray of Honeysuckle.
Bradley.
A Spring Journey. Palmer.
St. Stephen's Word.
Heppenstall.
The Sugaring. Klein.
Sweetness. *Anonymous.*
The Sweetness of Nature.
Anonymous.
Unharvested. Frost.
The Violet and the Rose.
Webster.

Swell (ed) (ing) (s)

The Character of a Certain
Whig. Shippen.
The Cherwell Water Lily.
Faber.
Ezra Pound. Lowell.
February. Savage.
For Music. Byron.
Go, Forget Me. Wolfe.
Lo, What Enraptured Songs
of Praise. Streeter.
Lobsters in the Window.
Snodgrass.
The Song of the Flume.
Fitch.
Tall Windows. Hass.
Upper Lambourne.
Betjeman.

Young Billy Crane.
Anonymous.

Swift (ly)

Click o' the Latch. Turner.
The Cloud-Mobile. Swenson.
Come, O Come. Campion.
Epitaph: "See, one physician,
like a sculler, plies."
Jekyll.
The Fable of Acis,
Polyphemus, and Galatea.
Dryden.
Flying Crooked. Graves.
The Golden Stallion.
Thompson.
The Homing Heart.
Henderson.
A Jew Walks in Westminster
Abbey. Hodes.
My Letter. Litchfield.
On the Height. Tietjens.
The Owl. Sackville-West.
The Power of Music (excerpt).
Pindar.
The Singer. Wickham.
War Song. Davidson.
The Yoke. Ben Kalonymos.

Swig

A Ballad in "G". Ware.
The Boothbay Whale.
Anonymous.
Said the monkey to the
donkey. *Anonymous.*

Swim (mer) (ming) (s) (swam)

Above These Cares. Millay.
The Boats Are Afloat. Chu
Hsi.
Cock-Crow. *Anonymous.*
Don Juan. Byron.
The Drunken Boat.
Rimbaud.
The Duck. King.
Epigram: "O Diodorus."
Anonymous.
Epigram: "When Pontius
wished an edict might be
passed." Prior.
Exercise in a Meadow.
Elliot.
Fall In. Kirstein.
The Female Warrior.
Anonymous.
Fish Story. Kinnick.
From the Wave. Gunn.
The Guttural Muse. Heaney.
Hero and Leander.
Chapman.
I Never Will Marry.
Anonymous.
The Immortal. Blake.
In Prague. Celan.
Leah. Kaufman.
The Lesson. Krows.
Let Go: Once. Fleming.
The Marshes of Glynn.
Lanier.
Meditation. Pain.
Meditations. Taylor.
Memorandum / The
Accountant's Notebook.
Norris.
Niagara. Braun.
Of Swimming in Lakes and
Rivers. Brecht.
The Old Swimmer. Morley.
The Old Swimmin'-Hole.
Riley.
On Being Much Better Than
Most and Yet Not Quite
Good Enough. Ciardi.
Outward. Simpson.
A Pair. Swenson.

The Poet of Bray. Heath-
Stubbs.
The Possibility That Has Been
Overlooked Is the Future.
Hartnett.
The Preacher Sought to Find
Out Acceptable Words.
Eberhart.
San Francisco Poem. Logan.
Sensational Relatives.
Krasilovsky.
Song of Expectancy.
Hitchcock.
Song of the White Lady of
Avenel. Scott.
The Spirit of Wrath. Heyen.
Telephoning It. Edmond.
To My Mistris Sitting by a
Rivers Side. An Eddy.
Carew.
Under. Bowering.
Winter Pond. Belitt.
With Kit, Age 7, at the
Beach. Stafford.
Zoe and the Ghosts.
Weslowski.

Swind (lers)

Another on the Same.
Belloc.
I meant to have but modest
needs. Dickinson.

Swine

I Saw a Chapel All of Gold.
Blake.
The Odyssey. Homer.
Soliloquy of the Spanish
Cloister. Browning.
The Sow of Feeling.
Fergusson.
To a Young Poet Who Fled.
Logan.
The Wry Rowan.
Anonymous.

Swineheard

Summer Night. Bialik.
To a Young Poet Who Fled.
Logan.

Swing (er) (ing) (s)

Ambition. Bishop.
Atlantis. Crane.
Birches. Frost.
The Carolinas. Ray.
The Circle. Coates.
Conversation Piece.
Freeman.
Deprecating Parrots. May.
The Foiled Reaper.
Seymour.
Heaven-Haven. Hopkins.
Legend. Wright.
Luriana, Lurilee. Elton.
Murder in the Cathedral.
Eliot.
The Neighbors. Garrison.
Our Dead, Overseas.
Markham.
Prayer. Pierce.
The Professionals. Grigson.
Rings. Barnes.
Spanish Johnny. Cather.
Spring Night. Su Tung-P'o.
Trellis. Chester.
The Trial. Abse.
Tropisms on John Berryman.
Vizenor.
Walking on the Green Grass.
Anonymous.
Weary Will. Paterson.

Swirl (ing) (s)

At Times I Feel Like a
Quince Tree. Quinn.

The Gap in the Cedar.
Scheele.
Isolation Ward. Koenig.
Luath. Burns.
Switch (ed)
America Was Schoolmasters.
Coffin.
Asleep at the. *Anonymous.*
Asleep at the Switch. Hoey.
Feeling That Way Too.
Vogelsang.
The Huckster's Horse.
Strong.
Witch Hazel. Enslin.
Swollen
Look Out There.
Anonymous.
Up Rising. Duncan.
Swoon (ed) (s)
Alone. Joyce.
Aunt Nerissa's Muffin.
Irwin.
Medieval Norman Songs.
Anonymous.
Moonlight Night: Carmel.
Hughes.
Space Being(Don't Forget to
Remember)Curved.
Cummings.
Swoop (s)
The Bird. Michelson.
The Energy of Light. Hay.
Faintly and from Far away.
Miller.
The Sea and the Eagle.
Clouts.
Sword (s)
Abraham Lincoln. Brownell.
Alone. Laurence.
Amours de Voyage. Clough.
The Antiplatonick.
Cleveland.
Arabic Script. Thwaite.
As I Gird on for Fighting.
Housman.
The Author's Reply.
Scroope.
The Ballad of Reading Gaol.
Wilde.
Beauty. Stanley.
The Compasses. MacBeth.
Cresophontes: Prayer to
Peace. Euripides.
The Destruction of Troy:
Aeneid II. Denham.
Deus Noster Ignis
Consumens. Housman.
Disarmament (excerpt).
Whittier.
The Duel. Pulsifer.
Elizabethan Days. Irwin.
End of the Comedy.
Untermeyer.
Enfant Perdu. Heine.
Epithalamium. Housman.
The Female Warrior.
Anonymous.
Figurehead. Paul.
For an Ex-Far East Prisoner
of War. Causley.
Guitar. Garcia Lorca.
The Gulistan. Sa'di.
Halcyon Days. Barnes.
Immortality. Hardy.
John the Baptist. Simpson.
King Arthur and King
Cornwall. Anonymous.
The Knight Fallen on Evil
Days. Wylie.
The Knight in Disguise.
Lindsay.

Lament after Her Husband
Bishr's Murder. Al-
Khirniq.
The Lost History Plays: King
Ethelred the Unready
(parody). Greenwell.
Love between Brothers and
Sisters. Watts.
Love-Songs, At Once Tender
and Informative.
Hoffenstein.
Matty Groves. *Anonymous.*
Merlin. Emerson.
Message to Siberia. Pushkin.
Miami. Epstein.
Modern Love, I. Meredith.
My Lady Has the Grace of
Death. Plunkett.
Ned Braddock. Palmer.
New Moses. Joseph.
Poem: "I do not want to be
your weeping woman."
Boodson.
Pogroms. Spire.
Prayer. Chesterton.
The Prayer of Beaten Men.
Woods.
Reveille. Brown.
The Sailing of the Sword.
Morris.
Saul. Sterling.
The Scales of Love.
Hartmann von Aue.
Singin' wid a Sword in Ma
Han'. *Anonymous.*
Solomon on the Vanity of the
World. Prior.
The Song of the Valkyries.
Anonymous.
A Sword. Boye.
The Terrace in the Snow. Su
Tung-P'o.
Terror Conduction.
Lamantia.
This Beast That Rends Me.
Millay.
Though a Soldier at Present.
Moore.
To Henry Constable and
Henry Keir. Montgomerie.
To My Truly Valiant, Learned
Friend.... Lovelace.
Tour 5. Hayden.
Tubal Cain. Mackay.
Upon Pagget. Herrick.
A Very Heroical Epistle in
Answer to Ephelia.
Rochester.
The Viking. Stokes.
Waldere 2. *Anonymous.*
The Western Rebel.
Anonymous.
Which Sword? Pierce.
Would You in Venus' Wars
Succeed. *Anonymous.*
The Young Cordwainer.
Graves.
Sycamore
Go, Little Book. Stevenson.
It Is Winter, I Know.
Moore.
Syllable (s)
Axioms. Hollander.
The Brain–Is Wider than the
Sky. Dickinson.
Close, Mortal Eyes. Pitter.
The Empress. Wakoski.
Pictures of a Gone World.
Ferlinghetti.
Serpent Knowledge. Pinsky.
Step lightly on this narrow
spot! Dickinson.

Table Talk. Cowper.
Writing to Aaron. Levertov.
Sylvan
An Autumn Breeze. Hayne.
The Poet of Gardens.
Henderson.
Poly-Olbion. Drayton.
To the Maiden in the East.
Thoreau.
A Vision (excerpt). Procter.
Windsor-Forest To the Right
Honourable George Lord
Lansdown. Pope.
Sylvia
Dove's Nest. Taylor.
A Roundelay. Drayton.
Symbol (s)
Arctic Tern in a Museum.
Newsome.
Candle and Book. Walter.
Childhood Church. Wilson.
Elegy for the Giant Tortoises.
Atwood.
Jig for Sackbuts. Lewis.
Leonardo Da Vinci's.
Moore.
Philander. Hall.
The Plane: Earth. Sun-Ra.
The Tree of Death. Vigee.
Two Sonnets: Harvard.
Holmes.
Symbolized
Money. Nemerov.
Symmetry
I'm Lucky. Mandel.
On the Dates of Poets.
Johnson.
On the Portrait of a Woman
About to be Hanged.
Hardy.
The Tiger. Blake.
Sympathy
It Is Not Beauty I Demand.
Darley.
Lately, Alas, I Knew a Gentle
Boy. Thoreau.
The Loveliness of Love.
Darley.
Once in a While a Protest
Poem. Axelrod.
The Other Person's Place.
Hover.
Prayer for a Day's Walk.
Crowell.
Sonnet: The Double Rock.
King.
What God Has Promised.
Flint.
Symphony
After the Dazzle of Day.
Whitman.
Fragments. Cotton.
The Organ Cactus.
Scarborough.
The Skunk. Coffin.
System (s)
Limerick: "There was a young
man of Mauritius."
Lindsay.
On the Emigration to
America. Freneau.
Sleet Storm on the Merritt
Parkway. Bly.

T

Table (s)
Amoretti, LXXVII. Spenser.

The Art of Cookery. King.
As in the Old Days: Passages
8. Duncan.
Baby's Drinking Song.
Kirkup.
Ballad of an Empty Table.
Kryss.
Blest Winter Nights.
Armstrong.
The Blood. Cassian.
Child of the Romans.
Sandburg.
A Collection of Hymns...of
the Moravian Brethern
(excerpt). *Anonymous.*
A Comparison of the Life of
Man. Barnfield.
Epodes. Horace.
The Garden. Gluck.
Genesis. Kramer.
The House of Cards.
Rossetti.
In the Operating Room.
Nowlan.
January 1939. Thomas.
Jupiter and Ganimede.
Heywood.
Kitchen Tables. Huddle.
Lighting the Night Sky.
Hanson.
May He Lose His Way on the
Cold Sea. Archilochus.
Nations. Brownstein.
A New Song on the Birth of
the Prince of Wales.
Anonymous.
New York. Towle.
The Power of Maples. Stern.
The Quarrel. Swenson.
Song of Myself. Whitman.
They Two. Breck.
The Two Glasses. Wilcox.
Where Two O'Clock Came
From. Patchen.
Winter Night. Pasternak.
Tablet (s)
Bordello, Revisited. Triem.
Elegy Written at the Sea-Side,
and Addressed to Miss
Honoria Sneyd. Seward.
The Eleventh Commandment
(excerpt). Holmes.
Tadpole (s)
A Big Turtle. *Anonymous.*
Evolution. Smith.
Rebels from Fairy Tales.
Hill.
Tail (s)
The Angry Poet. O'Connor.
The Animals. Berg.
An Appeal to Cats in the
Business of Love.
Flatman.
Basking Shark. MacCaig.
The Cat and the Rain. Swift.
Children. Edson.
Christmas Ornaments.
Worth.
An Epitaph. Watson.
Farewell to Love. Donne.
From Oddity Land.
Anthony.
Fulani Cattle. Clark.
A Garden Lyric. Locker-
Lampson.
Holding Hands. Link.
How a Good Greyhound Is
Shaped. *Anonymous.*
Jack Was Every Inch a Sailor.
Anonymous.
Jonah and the Whale.
Anonymous.

The Little Bird. *Anonymous.*
Little Bo-Peep. Mother Goose.
Lizards and Snakes. Hecht.
The Malfeasance. Bold.
On Rears. Hedin.
P Is for Paleontology. Bracker.
Perigoo's Horse. *Anonymous.*
Poem of the Conscripted Warrior. Nogar.
Pride. Holyday.
Rat Riddles. Sandburg.
Riddle: "Old Mother Twitchet had but one eye." Mother Goose.
Riddle: "See, see, what shall I see?" *Anonymous.*
The Run from Manassas Junction. *Anonymous.*
A Scot, a Welsh and an Irish Man. *Anonymous.*
Shaggy Dog Story. Steele.
A Ship Burning and a Comet All in One Day. Eberhart.
So to Tell the Truth. Dube.
The Southern Snow-Bird. Hayne.
The Spirk Troll-Derisive. Riley.
The Tale of a Pony. Harte.
Tip-Toe Tail. Willson.
Titus, Son of Rembrandt: 1665. Lyons.
To The Magpie. *Anonymous.*
The Tom-Cat. Marquis.
Tommie Makes My Tail Toddle. Burns.
Tyin' a Knot in the Devil's Tail. Gardner.
The Whale. Buson.
The Zodiac Rhyme. *Anonymous.*

Tailor
The Clever Skipper. *Anonymous.*
Illustrious Ancestors. Levertov.
The Journeyman Tailor. *Anonymous.*
My Father, Who's Still Alive. Kozer.
The Oviparous Tailor. Beddoes.
The Tailor That Came from Mayo. McCarthy.

Taint (s)
Amelia Street. Ormsby.
A Method of Preserving Hay from Being Mow-Burnt, or Taking Fire. Dodsley.
Suburbs on a Hazy Day. Lawrence.

Take (n) (s)
The Ant. Herford.
The Better Bargain. Congreve.
Cherry Blossoms. "Lewis.
Conquistador. MacLeish.
Dare Quam Accipere. Blind.
Elegy for My Father. Moss.
Ex-Voto. Swinburne.
Garcia Lorca. Dudek.
Hurting. Gale.
I'd like a little. *Anonymous.*
I'll Take You Home Again, Kathleen. Westendorf.
Incident in a Rose Garden. Justice.
The Inundation. Sergeant.
The Jolly Pinder of Wakefield (B version). *Anonymous.*

Leichhardt in Theatre: The Room. Webb.
Letter to an Imaginary Friend. McGrath.
A Likeness. Browning.
Lines to a Friend in Trouble. Di Piero.
Lump. Phillips.
The Mask and the Poem. Pizarnik.
Masters. Amis.
Meditation. Pain.
Miners' Wives. Corrie.
My Blessing Be on Waterford. Letts.
New Mexico and Arizona. Canterbury.
The North and the South. Browning.
Not Wholly Lost. Souster.
Of the Holy Eucharist. *Anonymous.*
Once I Played and Danced in My Parents' Kingdom. *Anonymous.*
Our Saviour's Golden Rule. Watts.
Postscript to Die Schone Mullerin. Llster.
A Prayer for Faith. Norris.
The Quidditie. Herbert.
Riddle: "Stiff standing on the bed." *Anonymous.*
The Rival Friends: Have Pity, Grief. Hausted.
Rue. *Anonymous.*
The Runaway. Frost.
Siege at Stony Point. Gregory.
Snow in the Suburbs. Hardy.
Soggarth Aroon. Banim.
Sonnets, XV: "When I consider every thing that grows." Shakespeare.
Suicid/ing Indian Women. Allen.
The Task. Cowper.
Tattoos. Wright.
The Withdrawal. Lowell.
Wizard Oil (with music). *Anonymous.*
The Working Man. Donovan.

Tale (s)
Astrophel and Stella, XLV. Sidney.
Autumn on the Upper Thames. Morris.
Bear a Horn and Blow It Not. *Anonymous.*
The Canterbury Tales: The Franklin's Prologue. Chaucer.
The Canterbury Tales: The Franklin's Tale. Chaucer.
The Cheer of the Trenton. Mitchell.
Chipeta's Ride. Taylor.
A Consecration. Masefield.
The Dumb Soldier. Stevenson.
The Durable Bon Mot. Preston.
Epitaphs of the War, 1914-18. Kipling.
A Fable. Frere.
The Faerie Queene. Spenser.
The Fallen Tower of Siloam. Graves.
The First One Drew Me. Kook.
Focus. Rich.

The Foretelling of Cathbad the Druid at Deirdre's Birth. *Anonymous.*
Garland for a Storyteller. Farnham.
Gascoigne's Woodmanship. Gascoigne.
Homage to Max Jacob. Padgett.
Household Remedies. *Anonymous.*
I thought that Love had been a boy. *Anonymous.*
Ivy and Holly. Meyerstein.
Little Birds. "Carroll.
Marmion. Scott.
The Moth and the Flame. Taggart.
My Little Wife. *Anonymous.*
The Mystery of Cro-A-Tan. Preston.
Nell Flaherty's Drake. *Anonymous.*
Ode to Simplicity. Collins.
On Beauty. A Riddle. Prior.
One We Knew. Hardy.
The Passions. Collins.
A Pig Tale. Reeves.
The Portraits. Lenngren.
The Second Volume. Bell.
Snatches: "There was a man that hadde nought." *Anonymous.*
Song: "Under the lime-tree, on the daisied ground." Walther von der Vogelweide.
Sonnet to Byron. Keats.
Sonnet: Written at Stonehenge. Warton, Jr..
The Thousand and Second Night. Merrill.
Three Gates. Day.
The Three Warnings. Thrale Piozzio.
To the Young Man Jesus. Dalton.
We Are Keeping an Eye on the Girls. Tsvetayeva.
The Wooing Frog. Reeves.

Talent (s)
Envy. Lamb.
The Perfect Gift. Parker.
Rhyme from Grandma Goose. Ewing.
Sir Francis Bacon. Bierce.
To the Minister Liu. Yu Hsuan-chi.
The Truth Made Breakfast. Miller.

Talisman
The Bridge of Heraclitus. Reavey.
Lost Explorer. Pennant.

Talk (ed) (ers) (ing) (s)
720 Gabriel St. Outlaw.
Absalom and Achitophel. Dryden.
Ajax. Sophocles.
Arches and Shadows. Dillard.
Assailant. Raven.
At a Georgia Camp Meeting. Mills.
A Boisterous Poem about Poetry (excerpt). Wain.
A Celebration of Charis. Jonson.
Clock on Hancock Street. Jordan.
The Closing Album. MacNeice.

Come Laugh with Me. *Anonymous.*
Converstion with Three Women of New England. Stevens.
The Dancers Inherit the Party. Finlay.
A Dancing Girl. Osgood
Death in the Home. Moore.
Deep in Love. Bhavabhuti.
Distinctions. Tomlinson.
Down the Rain Falls. Coatsworth.
Driving toward the Lac Qui Parle River. Bly.
East Texas. Stokesbury.
The Emancipation of George-Hector (a colored turtle). Evans.
An Empty Threat. Frost.
A Family Man. Kumin.
The Fighter. Etter.
France Blues. Sunny Boy.
The greatest bore is boredom. *Anonymous.*
Guilt. Thomas.
Hansel and Gretel Return. Ray.
He Met Her at the Green Horse... Levi.
Hegel. Jones.
Hell and Heaven. *Anonymous.*
Helpmate. Chapin.
The Hired Man's Way. Bangs.
Hitch Haiku. Snyder.
Husbands and Wives. Hershenson.
I Speak, I Say, I Talk. Shapiro.
De Imagine Mundi. Ashbery.
Imitation of Chaucer (parody). Pope.
In the Subway. Jimenez.
In the Yucca Land. Morris.
The Intellectuals. Randall.
Interim. Ormsby.
Interrupted Romance. *Anonymous.*
Intervals. Ravenel.
Late. Halpern.
Life Story. Tomioka Taeko.
A Little Talk wid Jesus Makes It Right. *Anonymous.*
The Long Season. Haug.
Look Down That Lonesome Road. *Anonymous.*
Lydia Is Gone This Many a Year. Reese.
Me, Colored. Abrahams.
The Medium. Feinstein.
Meeting at the Local. Parson.
Mendax. Lessing.
Michael Walked in the Wood. Greacen.
Moose Lake State Hospital. Shady.
Mrs. Kriss Kringle. Thomas.
My cat and I. McGough.
Newton to Einstein. Chappell.
Not Saying Much. Gregg.
The Old Folk. Ditlevsen.
Old Men Working Concrete. Hey.
On Bertrand Russell's "Portraits from Memory'. Davie.

On Buying a Dog. Klauber.
On Censure. Swift.
On Oliver Goldsmith.
Garrick.
One More New Botched
Beginning. Spender.
Peace. Jonas.
People Will Talk. Dodge.
Poetry for Supper. Thomas.
Postcard from London,
23.l0.1972. Salkey.
The Praise of Ben Dorain.
MacIntyre.
Prayerwheel/2. Meltzer.
Reflections at Dawn.
McGinley.
Rest. Segal.
The Rooks. Browne (Aunt
Effie).
Sea Bells. Eberhart.
She and I. Cameron.
Sic Transit Gloria Scotia.
""MacDiarmid.
The Significance of a
Veteran's Day. Ortiz.
A Sinner's Lament. Herbert
of Cherbury.
Slow Me Down. Anonymous.
Sound from Leopardi.
Berkson.
A Store-House. Dudek.
Streets of Glory.
Anonymous.
The Suicide. Lang.
The Sun Used to Shine.
Thomas.
Surview. Hardy.
Take Nothing for Granite.
Salsbury.
That spring night I spent.
Suwo.
The Thinker. Williams.
To My Friend, Grown
Famous. Tietjens.
Tune: Endless Union. Li
Ching-chao.
Two Little Dogs.
Anonymous.
A Valediction: Of My Name
in the Window. Donne.
W. S. Landor. Moore.
We're Gonna Move When the
Spirit Says Move!
Anonymous.
What Schoolmasters Say.
Seymour-Smith.
When the Tree Bares.
Aiken.
When You with Hogh Dutch
Heeren Dine. Prior.
The Will to Change. Rich.
Wires. Bassett.
Wolves. MacNeice.

Tall
1916 Seen from 1921.
Blunden.
Auguries for Three Women.
Crews.
The Brigg. Skelton.
The Californians. Spencer.
A Child's Song to Her
Mother. Welles.
Christmas Morn. Sawyer.
Dining out with Doug and
Frank. Schuyler.
The Down-Pullers. Isenhour.
Dream Songs. Berryman.
Fragment in Imitation of
Wordsworth. Fanshawe.
Go to Bed Late. Anonymous.
The Grave of Shelley. Wilde.

Great-Great Grandma, Don't
Sleep in Your Treehouse
Tonight. Kennedy.
Loving Henry. Anonymous.
Madrigal: "Some there are as
fair to see to." Davison.
The Maids of Elfin-Mere.
Allingham.
Mana Aboda. Hulme.
Playgrounds. Alma-Tadema.
The Quiet Fog. Piercy.
Ravenglass Railway Station,
Cumberland. Nicholson.
Tall Men Riding. Barker.
There Is Good News.
Jacobsen.
Trust. Reese.
The Victim of Aulis. Abse.
Wishes for Her. Devlin.
Wooden Ships. Morton.
The World in Making.
Parker.
The Wounded. Louis.
Young Hunting (Loving
Henry). Anonymous.

Tally
The Cheerful Horn.
Anonymous
Cowboy's Dream.
Anonymous.
Magellan. Curnow.
The Plumber Arrives at Three
Mile Island. Stewart.

Talons
A Decision. Sodergran.
Ganymede. Bynner.

Tambourine
The Cocooning. Mistral.
Near the School for
Handicapped Children.
Shapcott.

Tame (d) (s)
Ain't Nature Commonplace!
Guiterman.
Angels in Winter. Willard.
At the Un-National
Monument along the
Canadian Border. Stafford.
Chesspieces. Campbell.
Ecclesiastes. Langland.
The Escape. Van Doren.
For a Statue of Chaucer at
Woodstock. Akenside.
Love's Flight. Lasker-
Schüler.
Of Loving at First Sight.
Waller.
(Poem) (Chicago) (The Were-
Age). Knott.
Pot Shot. Fallon.
Rapid Transit. Agee.
Tamer and Hawk. Gunn.
Verses for the 60th Birthday
of T. S. Eliot. Barker.
Whoso liest to hunt, I know
where is an hind..
Petrarch (Francesco
Petrarca).
With a Coin from Syracuse.
Gogarty.

Tammany Hall
Song: "There's a barrel of
porter at Tammany Hall."
Halleck.

Tangent
Cold Glow: Icehouses.
Wojahn.
The Daily Round. McCuaig.

Tangerine
In the Plaza We Walk. De
Leon.

The Romance of Citrus.
Sanford.
Two Childhood Memories.
Zolynas.

Tangiers
I Thought It Was Tangiers I
Wanted. Hughes.

Tangle (d)
He Praises the Trees.
Anonymous.
How Can One E'er Be Sure.
Horikawa.
If You Want to Go A-
Courting. Anonymous.
Netted Strawberries.
Bottomley.
To a Woman. Glover.
Water Picture. Swenson.

Tango
Conjuring Roethke. Tate.

Tank (s)
Ballad of the Days of the
Messiah. Klein.
On a Lover of Books.
Grigson.
Tin-Ore. Anonymous.
Wallace Stevens Gives a
Reading. Zinnes.
War Horses. Cole.

Tantalus
Epitaph: "The fruit of all the
service that I serve."
Wyatt.
On Lisa's Golden Hair.
Campbell.

Tap (ping)
Braille. Costanzo.
The Cobbler in Willow Street.
O'Neil.
Elegy for Dylan Thomas.
Sitwell.
Open the Door. Anonymous.
Otters. Hart-Smith.
The Poet. Clifton.
Sight. Gibson.
To a Blind Student Who
Taught Me to See. Hazo.

Tape (d)
Langston Hughes.
Blockcolski.
Letters Found near a Suicide.
Horne.
More Letters Found Near a
Suicide. Horne.
Plexus and Nexus. Jerome.
This Runner. Webb.

Taper (s)
The Eve of St. Mark. Keats.
Immortalis. Morton.
The Maid. Bregy.
Many Indeed Must Perish in
the Keel. Hofmannsthal.
Moonlight on Lake
Sydenham. MacDonald.
Relics. Cameron.
San Marco Museum, Florence.
Maris Stella.
To a Segar. Low.
A Wish. Rogers.

Tapestry (tries)
Music in an Empty House.
Davies.
My Lady Takes the Sunlight
for Her Gown. Cole.
The Puritan Hacking away at
Oak. Gitlin.

Tar (s)
The Beach. Graves.
The Constitution and
Guerriere. Anonymous.
Pine Cones. Smith.
Pourquoi. Anonymous.

Riddle: "White as snow and
snow it isn't." Anonymous.
The Shannon and the
Chesapeake. Anonymous.
The Tars of the Blanche.
Anonymous.
Through Fire in Mobile Bay.
Anonymous.
The Trees. Morley.

Target
Pacific Epitaphs. Randall.
Riddle: "I'm called by the
name of a man."
Anonymous.
A Soldier. Frost.

Tarnish
Advice to Julia. Luttrell.
Armour's Undermining
Modesty. Moore.

Tarry (ied) (ies)
A Christmas Ghost-Story.
Hardy.
Epistles. Horace.
I Say I'll Seek Her. Hardy.
In Obitum Ben. Jons.
Westmoreland.
The Market-Square's
Admiring Throngs.
Goethe.
A Nursery Song. Richards.
To the Virgins, To Make
Much of Time. Herrick.
Troubadour Song. Bernard
of Ventadour

Tart
Chickory. Gal'ed.
The Judgment. Spivack.
Shut Out That Moon.
Hardy.
The Tale of a Tart.
Weatherly.

Tartan
Were You Ever in
Dumbarton? Anonymous.

Tarzan
Arroyo. Weatherly.

Task (s)
Abraham Lincoln, the Master.
Clark.
All That You Have Given
Me, Africa. Kanie.
Beneath the Shadow of the
Cross. Longfellow.
The Blessed Task. Kimball.
Challenge. Hazo.
A Christmas Sermon: To Be
Honest, To Be Kind.
Stevenson.
The Crowing of the Red
Cock. Lazarus.
For the One Who Would
Take Man's Life in His
Hands. Schwartz.
The Glove and the Lions.
Hunt.
I Shall Not Cry Return.
Gates.
Limerick: "Consider the
lowering Lynx." Reed.
Mother-Prayer. Widdemer.
The Mowers. Allingham.
The Muses. Thomas.
My Grandmother. Shapiro.
The New-Come Chief.
Lowell.
Praise. Smart.
Prayer of a Teacher.
Littlewort.
Salamis. Durrell.
A Short Winter Tale. Zach.
The Song of Songs. Heine.
Summer Sabbath. Sampter.

Th Child's Purchase.
Patmore.
Tudor Church Music.
Warner.
Ultimatum. Church.
Work. Lowell.
Taste (d) (less) (s)
Alone. Holden.
Anonymous. Cruz.
The Apple. Sackville.
Apple Season. Frost.
Apple Song. Frost.
As You Like It.
Shakespeare.
The Ascetic. Daley.
At the Well. Tussman.
The Barberry-Bush. Very.
The Claim. Nesbit.
Clouds. Aldis.
Contentment. Holmes.
Dakota: Five Times Six.
Hansen.
Deadsong. Domanski.
A Donkey Will Carry You.
Steinberg.
The English Garden (excerpt).
Mason.
A Fable for Critics. Lowell.
Family Prime. Van Doren.
Food and Drink (excerpt).
Untermeyer.
Freedom of the Hills.
Fraser.
The Gifts. Heath-Stubbs.
The Great Nebula in
Andromeda. Seidman.
The Harvester. Lawrence.
Her Praises. Skoloker.
Hogarth. Churchill.
Hymn: "Thou hidden love of
God, whose height."
Wesley.
I Had a Duck. Stodart-
Walker.
I Know That My Redeemer
Lives. Wesley.
I Planted My Bright Paradise.
Blok.
I've Tasted My Blood.
Acorn.
It. Snyder.
Jonathan. "Rachel" (Rachel
Blumstein).
The Legend of Success, the
Salesman's Story.
Simpson.
Madrigal: "My dearest
mistress." Corkine.
The Magical Mouse.
Patchen.
Modern Love, VIII.
Meredith.
Modern Love, XVI.
Meredith.
The Mole. Clare.
My Dreams, My Works, Must
Wait Till after Hell.
Brooks.
My Teeth. Ochester.
The Nativity of Christ.
Southwell.
The Night-Apple. Ginsberg.
Ode on the Pleasure Arising
from Vicissitude. Gray.
Old Men and Old Women
Going Home on the Street
Car. Moore.
"Oxford is a Stage." Nolan.
Paphos. Durrell.
Paradise Lost. Milton.
Persimmons and Plums.
Hodges.

The Poet of Bray. Heath-
Stubbs.
A Present of Butter.
O'Huiginn.
Quarrel. *Anonymous.*
Quatrain. Toerien.
Ragout (parody). Zaranka.
The Ration Card. Bahe.
The Ravine. Applewhite.
Recipe. Goldbarth.
Reply to a Marriage Proposal.
Irihapeti Rangi te Apakura.
Robin Hood and the Beggar.
Anonymous.
Schedules. Dean.
The Singing Bones. Stow.
So What (parody).
Appleman.
Sonnet: To Love, in Great
Bitterness. Cino da
Pistoia.
Spring Poem. Ramke.
Taste. Updike.
The Teacher. Young.
To a Poor Old Woman.
Williams.
To a Woman Who Wants
Darkness and Time.
Barrax.
To an Author. Freneau.
To the Wife of a Sick Friend.
Millay.
The Truth Is Blind.
Gascoyne.
A Vegetarian Sings. Conard.
Visions of the Daughters of
Albion. Blake.
Voice. Moss.
Vulture. Kennedy.
The West-Country Lover.
Brown.
When the Bells Justle in the
Tower. Housman.
Tatters
The Caroline. Crabbe.
Foreclosure. Van Doren.
Prince Tatters. Richards.
Tom Tatter's Birthday Ode.
Hood.
Under the Window: Ouro
Preto. Bishop.
Tattoo
The Tattooed Man. Smith.
Taunt (s)
In Rebellion. Synge.
My country need not change
her gown. Dickinson.
Seraphion. Baxter.
Settling In. Stuart.
Tavern (s)
The Bold Pedlar and Robin
Hood. *Anonymous.*
Epitaph. Durrell.
The Moving Finger. Omar
Khayyam.
Villon's Ballade. Lang.
Tawdry
Jerked Heartstrings in Town.
Jones.
Sunday Evening in the
Common. Wheelock.
Tax (ed) (es)
At Cheyenne. Field.
Doctor Bill Williams. Walsh.
The Flower Market. Po
Chu-i.
Godiva. Tennyson.
The Land. Kipling.
The Modern World. Ellis.
A New Song on the Taxes.
Anonymous.
Taxes. Lee.

Taxi (s)
The Birth of My Father.
Dempster.
Errant. Godfrey.
Nocturne, Central Park South.
Sissman.
Our Visit to the Zoo. Pope.
Songs about Life and Brighter
Things Yet. Hoffenstein.
Te Deum (s)
Bishop Winterbourne. De la
Mare.
Eugenio Pacelli. Neilson.
Ireland with Emily.
Betjeman.
Madonna of the Evening
Flowers. Lowell.
A Paraphrase from the
French. Prior.
To the Archbishop of Tuam.
Anonymous.
Tea
Animal Crackers. Morley.
Anno Domini. Walker.
Billy and Me. *Anonymous.*
The boy stood in the supper-
room. *Anonymous.*
Buckingham Palace. Milne.
Departure. Millay.
Extremely Naughty Children.
Godley.
The Fastidious Serpent.
Johnstone.
Fish. Satz.
The Gossips. *Anonymous.*
Impetuous Samuel. Graham.
In a Chain-Store Cafeteria.
Grano.
Inspiration. Service.
Miss Bitter. Bodecker.
The New Neighbor.
Fyleman.
Now Philippa Is Gone.
Ridler.
The Old Vicarage,
Grantchester. Brooke.
Poe at Tea. Pain.
Polly Put the Kettle On.
Mother Goose.
Rhymes on the Road
(excerpt). Moore.
Send for Lord Timothy.
Heath-Stubbs.
The Shearer's Song.
Anonymous.
Small and Early. Jenks.
The Soldier Loves His Rifle.
Auden.
Starting Rhymes for Hide-
and-Seek: "Green lady,
green lady." *Anonymous.*
Tea-Time. *Anonymous.*
Teatime Variations.
Titheradge.
Visitor. *Anonymous.*
When a Goose Meets a
Moose. Gay.
Teacakes
How to Get On in Society.
Betjeman.
Teach (es) (ing) (taught)
Advice to the Young.
Waddington.
After he stripped off my
clothes. Vallana.
Although I put away his life.
Dickinson.
Amoretti, XXI. Spenser.
Ancient and Modern Rome
(excerpt). Keate.
Anecdote for Fathers.
Wordsworth.

Beech and Oak. Peacock.
Caelica, LIV. Greville.
Christ Our Example in
Suffering. Montgomery.
Cypresses. Francis.
The Dark and the Fair.
Kunitz.
Dead Dog. Scannell.
December 24, 1979. Weaver.
A Dream of Venus. Bion.
The Dying Swan. Moore.
Education. Lee.
Epigram: "I dined with
Demetrios." Automedon.
An Essay on Criticism.
Pope.
Forbearance. Emerson
God's Education. Hardy.
Journey to a Parallel.
Wright.
Juanita, Wife of Manuelito.
Ortiz.
Learning. Chapman.
A Little Sequence (excerpt).
Money-Coutts.
Lord, I Know Thy Grace Is
Nigh Me. Ganse.
My Mother's Bible. Morris.
The Mystery. Hyde.
No teacher I of boys or
smaller fry. Ramsey.
O-U-G-H. Loomis.
The Paps of Dana. Stephens.
Pedagogy. Locklin.
A Plain Man's Dream.
Keppel.
The Poet. Whitman.
.A Schoolmaster's Precepts.
Penkethman.
Self-Congratulatory Ode on
Mr Auden's Election
(parody). Mason.
The Sluggard. Watts.
Small Town. Joyce.
Snapshot. Garrett.
Solitude. Grainger.
Song: "For the tender beech
and the sapling oak."
Peacock.
Song: "Where did you borrow
that last sigh." Berkeley.
Stanza from an Early Poem.
Cranch
A Teacher. Whittemore.
To a Little Girl. Eden.
To Cupid. Drayton.
Traveller's Ditty. DeFord.
Wedding-Hymn. Lanier.
What Is Prayer?
Montgomery.
When Wilt Thou Teach the
People—? Lawrence.
Whilst I Beheld the Neck o'
th' Dove. Cary.
Woman. *Anonymous.*
Writing in England Now.
O'Connor.
You Shall Above All Things
Be Glad and Young.
Cummings.
You've Got to be Carefully
Taught. Hammerstein.
Teacher (s)
End of Term. *Anonymous.*
An Old Man's Thought of
School. Whitman.
The Original Lamb.
Anonymous.
Tao. Bailey.
The Unteaching. Oles.

Teacups
The Cats' Tea-Party.
Weatherly.
Conversation. Dewey.
The Deserted Village.
Goldsmith.
Haiku: "In the August grass."
Knight.
In a Surrealist Year.
Ferlinghetti.
The Little Maid. Wells.

Team (work)
As the Team's Head-Brass.
Thomas.
Co-operation. Knox.
Horses. Wellesley.
The Scholar's Life.
Anonymous.

Teaparty
Siege of Plattsburg.
Anonymous.

Teapot
Cowper at Tea. Pain.
Macaulay at Tea. Pain.
The Poets at Tea. Pain.

Tear (s)
8:00 a.m. Monday Morning.
Welsh.
Abishag. Fichman.
Aftermath. Plath.
Agamemnon. Aeschylus.
Age Not to Be Rejected.
Anonymous.
The Aloe Plant. Harbaugh.
Alone. Bialik.
Although I Do Not Know.
Saigyo Hoshi.
Ancient Songs of the Women
of Fez. *Anonymous.*
And She Washed His Feet
with Her Tears,...
Sherburne.
The Angel in the House.
Patmore.
Anger's Freeing Power.
Smith.
The Anniverse: An Elegy.
King.
Another. Thorold Rogers.
Apologia Pro Poemate Meo.
Owen.
Apology for Vagrants.
Langhorne.
At Bungendore. McAuley.
At Casterbridge Fair.
Hardy.
At Dawn. Synge.
At Delos. Scott.
At the Well. Tussman.
Autumn. Shelley.
Autumn Healing. Ward.
Bags of Meat. Hardy.
Baptism. Bell.
Beale Street, Memphis.
Snyder.
Before the Birth of One of
Her Children. Bradstreet.
Beginning the Year at
Rosebud, S.D. Whiteman.
Bill and Parson Sim.
Anonymous.
Bill Peters, the Stage Driver.
Anonymous.
A Blackbird Singing.
Thomas.
The Blantyre Explosion.
Anonymous.
The Blessed Damozel.
Rossetti.
Blowing Bubbles. Allingham.
The Bones of Chuang Tzu.
Chang Heng.

Brest Left behind. Farrar.
Bundles. Sandburg.
Caelica, VIII. Greville.
Cherry Robbers. Lawrence.
The Childless Father.
Wordsworth.
Chinoiseries. Lowell.
The Christian's New-Year
Prayer (excerpt). Wilcox.
The Clock. Scarfe.
The Comb. De la Mare.
Comrades. Johnson.
Condemned Women.
Baudelaire.
Confidence. *Anonymous.*
Consummation. Barker.
The Coplas on the Death of
His Father, the
Grandmaster of Santiago.
Manrique.
Correspondence:. Ise.
Corydon's Farewell, on Sailing
in the Late Expedition
Fleet. *Anonymous.*
The Covered Wagon.
Blakeney.
Crazy Jane on the Mountain.
Yeats.
Crocodiles. Kurka.
Cwmrhydyceirw Elegiacs.
Watkins.
The Dawn in Britain.
Doughty.
The Dead. Very
Death of a Son. Silkin.
Del Cascar. Braithwaite.
Departure. Smith.
Desert River. Benton.
Desert Stone. Waddington.
Diana. Constable.
Down by the Salley Gardens.
Yeats.
Dry Be That Tear. Sheridan.
The Duchess of York's Ghost.
Anonymous.
Duchesses. Campbell.
The Dutchess of Monmouth's
Lamentation for the Loss of
her Duke. *Anonymous.*
The Ecstasy. Al-Hallaj.
Eighteen Verses Sung to a
Tatar Reed Whistle. Ts'ai
Yen.
The Election. Pack.
Elegy: "Child, your white face
is chanting memories."
Woestijne.
Epigram: "Our youth was
happy: why repine."
Landor.
Epitaph at Hadleigh, Suffolk.
Anonymous.
Epitaph: "O flower of all that
springs from gentle blood."
Chaibrera.
An Epitaph of Sir Thomas
Gravener, Knight. Wyatt.
An Epitaph upon Doctor
Brook. Crashaw.
Eyam (excerpt). Seward.
Face to Face. Cochrane.
The Fair Maid and the Sun.
O'Shaughnessy.
The Falling of the Leaves.
Yeats.
Fantasy Street. Glaze.
A Farewell. Patmore.
Farewell. Tynan.
Fate! I Have Asked. Landor.
Father and Child. Harwood.
The Festal Board.
Anonymous.

Flash. Booker.
Flow Not So Fast.
Anonymous.
The Flying Tailor (parody).
Hogg.
Fond Youth. Rogers.
Footsteps of Spring. Bialik.
For an Epitaph at Fiesole.
Landor.
For Beauty Being the Best of
All We Know. Bridges.
A Forced Music. Graves.
The Forest Fire. Monroe.
The Fortunate One. Monroe.
The Fountain of Tears.
O'Shaughnessy.
Four Ducks on a Pond.
Allingham.
Fresh Spring. Daryush.
From Here to There. Korn.
From the Epigrams of
Martial. Michie.
From the Notebooks.
Roethke.
Funeral Song for Mamie
Eisenhower. Wong.
A Funerall Song (Lamenting
Syr Phillip Sidney).
Anonymous.
The Gaelic. Kelly.
"Go Bring Me," Said the
Dying Fair. Hunter.
God's Trails Lead Home.
Clements.
Going to Norway.
Anderson.
Gray Silk Twisting. Lane.
Grieve Not the Holy Spirit.
Herbert.
Had There Been Falsehood in
My Breast. Bronte.
The Hand That Signed the
Paper. Thomas.
Has Sorrow Thy Young Days
Shaded? Moore.
The Heap of Rags. Davies.
Hendecasyllabics.
Swinburne.
Hours of Idleness. Byron.
The House of Life. Rossetti.
How Grand and How Bright.
Anonymous.
Hymn: Crucifixus Pro Nobis.
Carey.
Hymn to the Supreme Being
on Recovery (excerpt).
Smart.
I Could Not Sleep for
Thinking of the Sky.
Masefield.
I Have Loved Flowers.
Bridges.
I Knew a Boy with Hair Like
Gold. La Follette.
Idea. Drayton.
If I Had My Way. Johnson.
If You Trap the Moment.
Blake.
The Iliad. Homer.
In Leinster. Guiney.
In Memoriam A.H.H.,
XLVIII. Tennyson.
In Memory of V. R. Lang.
Hammond.
In the Name of Our Sons.
Gould.
In the Night. Stephens.
In the Night of the Full
Moon. Busse.
In the Night Watches.
Roberts.
In the Street. Neilson.

The Indigestion of the
Vampire. Merwin.
Insensibility. Owen.
Intimations of Immortality
from Recollections of Early
Childhood. Wordsworth.
The Irish Mother in the Penal
Days. Banim.
Is It Because of Some Dear
Grace... Golding.
Is This Africa? Dempster.
It Says. Silkin.
Jane Retreat. Honig.
Janette's Hair. Halpine.
January Wraps up the Wound
of His Arm. Ford.
John Sutter. Winters.
Jungle. Smith.
The King of the Cradle.
Ashby-Sterry.
Knife and Sap. Leslie.
The Knight of Liddesdale.
Anonymous.
Lachrymae. Gascoyne.
Lake-Song. Untermeyer.
Lament for the Alamo.
Guiterman.
The Lass That Died of Love.
Middleton.
A Leader. Russell.
Lessons from the Gorse.
Browning.
Life. Treasone.
Light Casualties. Francis.
Limerick: "A pretty young
school mistress named
Beauchamp." *Anonymous.*
The Little Cart. Waley.
Little Gray Songs from St.
Joseph's, XXX. Norton.
Little Theocritus. Paradise.
Live Not, Poor Bloom, but
Perish. *Anonymous.*
Lollingdon Downs.
Masefield.
Lost. Chu Shu-chen.
Mad Maid's Whim. Stow.
Madchen Mit Dem Rothen
Mundchen. Heine.
Madrigal: "Flow not so fast."
Dowland.
The Man. Browne.
Man and Woman. Conquest.
Masks. Aldrich.
May Margaret. Marzials.
Meetings and Absences.
Fuller.
The Memorial Pillar.
Hemans.
A Memory of the Players in a
Mirror at Midnight.
Joyce.
Metamorphoses. Ovid
(Publius Ovidius Naso).
The Miner's Progress.
Delano.
The Mockery of Life. Blunt.
Morning. Blake.
Moses and Jesus. Zangwill.
Mother Marie Therese.
Lowell.
The Mountain. Lermontov.
Mr. Whittier. Scott.
"Multum Dilexit.'.
Coleridge.
My Sins in Their
Completeness. O
Brolchain.
My spouse, Chunaychunay.
Anonymous.
A Nameless One. Avison.
Negro Woman. Alexander.

A New Dress. Korn.
Night. Bialik.
Nightmare. Emanuel.
Nocturne. Bennett.
Nocturne–III. Silva.
Not Changed, But Glorified. *Anonymous.*
Not Knowing. Brainard.
Nothing in Heaven Functions As It Ought. Kennedy.
O Saviour of a World Undone. Withington.
O, Thou Eternal One! Derzhavin.
Ode–Imitated from the Psalms. Gilbert.
Odes, VI. Hafiz.
The Odyssey. Homer.
On Dreams and Mexican Songs. Dent.
On His Mistress Drown'd. Spratt.
On the Death of President Garfield. Holmes.
One Thousand Feet of Shadow. Craig.
Orpheus I Am, Come from the Deeps Below. Fletcher.
The Passing of the Unknown Soldier. Owens.
A Pastorall Dialogue. Carew.
The Philosophic Apology. Greenberg.
...Plashes the Fountain. Celan.
Poem: "I do not want to be your weeping woman." Boodson.
A Poem in Black and White. Serote.
The Poem in the Park. Davison.
A Poem Written in Time of Trouble by an Irish Priest... Gregory.
Poem: "Your face." St. John.
Poems from a Greek Anthology (excerpt). Martial (Marcus Valerius Martialis).
A Poet of One Mood. Meynell.
Poet's Bread. Mary Philip.
Polyolbion. Drayton.
Portrait of a Poet. Masters.
The Power of Innocence. "H.
A Prayer. Braley.
Prince Robert. *Anonymous.*
Private Worship. Van Doren.
The Progress of Poesy. Gray.
A Psalm to the Son. Wilkinson.
Put Your Word to My Lips. Korn.
The Quest. Cortissoz.
Quoniam Ego in Flagella Paratus Sum. Habington.
Reading and Talking. Zukofsky.
Red Anger. Smith.
The Resolute Courtier. Shipman.
The restful place, reviver of my smart. Wyatt.
Return. *Anonymous.*
The Return. Bontemps.

The Return. MacBeth.
Return to Ararat. Halsall.
Riding. Amoss.
The Rosary of My Tears. Ryan.
Round. Boimwall.
The Rubaiyat of Omar Khayyam. Omar Khayyam.
Sad Love and Sad Song. Iwano.
Saint Harmony My Patroness. Goodman.
Santa Barbara Beach. Torrence.
Sappho's Tomb. Stringer.
The Sea Horse. Graves.
Self in 1958. Sexton.
Separation. Bunner.
Seymour and Chantelle or Un Peu de Vice. Smith.
The Shamrock. Egan.
Sierra. Storni.
The Sigh That Heaves the Grasses. Housman.
Silex Scintillans. Vaughan.
Snow Harvest. Young.
So Have I Spent on the Banks of Ysca Many a Serious Hour. Vaughan.
Song. Manifold.
Song: "I have loved flowers that fade." Bridges.
Sonnet XV. Alabaster.
Sonnet LXX. Alabaster.
Sonnet LXXI. Alabaster.
Sonnet to Chatterton. Keats.
Sonnets. Hillyer.
Sonnets. Tuckerman.
Sonnets, XXXIV: "Why didst thou promise such a beauteous day." Shakespeare.
Sonnets, XLIV: "If the dull substance of my flesh were thought." Shakespeare.
Sonnets: A Sequence on Profane Love. Boker.
Sowing. Thomas.
The Spinner. O'Donnell.
Spring Thoughts Sent to Tzu-an. Yu Hsuan-chi.
A Star There Fell. Schneour.
The Statute of Liberty. Field.
The Stirrup Cup. Kilmer.
A Storm in Summer. Blunt.
The Survivor. Thomas.
Sweet Violets. *Anonymous.*
Swift Floods. Petroczi.
The Tear. Crashaw.
Tear. Kinsella.
Tears. Whitman.
Tears, Flow No More. Herbert of Cherbury.
Tears for Sale. Speyer.
A Temple. Patchen.
These Images Remain. Sarton.
These Lacustrine Cities. Ashbery.
Time! Where Dist Thou Those Years Inter. Habington.
To–. Tennyson.
To an Icicle. Dickinson.
To Emily Dickinson. Crane.
To Jesus on His Birthday. Millay.
To Madame A. P. Kern. Pushkin.
To Monsieur de la Mothe le Vayer. Moliere.

To Pikes Peak. Hills.
To Primroses Fill'd with Morning-Dew. Herrick.
To the Rev. Mr. Newton. Cowper.
To the Spirit Great and Good. Hunt.
To the Wife of a Sick Friend. Millay.
To Usward. Bennett.
The Tombstone Told When She Died. Thomas.
Traditional Funeral Songs. *Anonymous.*
Truth Is a Native, Naked Beauty. Williams.
The Twelve Properties or Conditions of a Lover. More.
Uncourtly Love. Walther von der Vogelweide.
Undine. Layton.
Untitled. Hine.
Upon His Spaniell Tracie. Herrick.
Upon Julia Weeping. Herrick.
Upon the Double Murther of King Charles I... Philips.
The Valley of Unrest. Poe.
Vaunting Oak. Ransom.
Vern. Brooks.
The Village Blacksmith. *Anonymous.*
The Violet. Scott.
Virgin and Unicorn. Heath-Stubbs.
Vision. Zangwill.
Votive Song. Pinkney.
Walking Around. Neruda.
The War of the Worlds. Rutsala.
A Wasted Sympathy. Howells.
Water Song. Ibn Gabirol.
What Winter Floods, What Showers of Spring. Bronte.
When Men Shall Find. Daniel.
When We Two Parted. Byron.
Which Are You? *Anonymous.*
Will Yer Write It Down for Me? Lawson.
The Wreck of the Rambler. *Anonymous.*
Yahrzeit. Jaffe.
Your Tears. Markham.

Teardrop
Judas. Miller.
Why? Boyd.

Tearooms
For the Truth. Spriggs.

Tease (d)
The Little Brother. Reeves.
Pussy. *Anonymous.*
Teasing. Mack.

Teaspoon
Of Difference Does It Make. Paulin.

Teatime
For Posterity. Raine.

Teatray
The Mad Hatter's Song. "Carroll.

Teeth
After Reading Nelly Sachs. Pastan.
Appearance and Reality. Hollander.

As I Went over the Water. *Anonymous.*
As You Like It. Shakespeare.
At the End of the Day. Hovey.
Bald. Zavatsky.
Big Momma. Lee.
Bitten. Van Doren.
Bridgework. Lynch.
But Since I Know Thy Falsehood and Thy Pride. Cowley.
Cinco de Mayo, 1862. Rios.
Day of These Days. Lee.
Down the Mississippi. Fletcher.
Dr. Potatohead Talks to Mothers. Sherwin.
East Coast Journey. Baxter.
Epilog (to Lost Copper). Rose.
Evening Ceremony: Dream for G.V. Rose.
A Failure. Day-Lewis.
Final Soliloquy on a Randy Rooster (in a Key of Yellow) (parody). Peters.
A Fine, a Private Place. Ackerman.
Fire Island. Brown.
Frightened. Ferlinghetti.
Getting On. Sandy.
Goody Blake and Harry Gill (excerpt). Wordsworth.
The Gorilla at Twenty Nine Years. Reed.
Hagar and Ishmael. Lasker-Schüler.
Halcyon Days. Barnes.
How Can Man Die Better. Tyrtaeus.
Kalaloch. Forche.
Killing Rabbits. Ochester.
Kindertotenlieder. Longley.
The Linen Workers. Longley.
Love (excerpt). Walker.
Making an Impression. Jackson.
Metal Fatigue. Le Fevre.
Moon-Witches. Hughes.
Mr. Muscle-On. Kicknosway.
New York in the Spring. Budbill.
Nightmare of Mouse. Warren.
Nina Simone. Jeffers.
Of One That Had a Great Nose. Turberville.
On the Miracle of Loaves. Crashaw.
Our Country Is Divided. Nuur.
Overture to Strangers. Haring.
Pastoral. Patchen.
Portrait. Landor.
The Problem of Wild Horses. Winder.
A Question. Synge.
Refusing What Would Bind You to Me Irrevocably. Koertge.
Roast Swan Song. *Anonymous.*
A Scholder Indian Poem. Harjo.
A Seamark. Carman.
The Springtime. Levertov.
Testimony. Rodgers.

They Have Turned the
Church Where I Ate God.
Gildner.
To Women, to Hide Their
Teeth, if They Be Rotten or
Rusty. Herrick.
Two Simpleton Songs, I.
Anonymous.
Watermelons. Simic.
Wicked Polly. *Anonymous.*
You and I Will Go to
Finegall. *Anonymous.*
Zimmer's Head Thudding
against the Blackboard.
Zimmer.
Tel-Aviv
Harangue on the Death of
Hayyim Nahman Bialik.
Tiempo.
Telegram.
How I Brought the Good
News from Aix to Ghent or
Vice Versa (parody).
Yeatman.
Telegraph
The Line-Gang. Frost.
A Strong Wind. Clarke.
Telephone
Bachelor. Meredith.
Depot Blues. *Anonymous.*
Eletelephony. Richards.
The Gramophone. Reaney.
Hello, Ma Baby. Emerson.
Ida.
The Invention of the
Telephone. Klappert.
Lily Flower. Brownstein.
The Line-Gang. Frost.
Love Poem. Orr.
Man Thinking about Woman.
Lee.
A Motorbike. Hughes.
Room Service. Moser.
Tombstone with Cherubim.
Gregory.
The Woodpecker. Roberts.
Telescope
The Arkansaw Traveler.
Anonymous.
The Jews in Hell.
Goldemberg.
A Letter. Emerson.
The State of Arkansas.
Anonymous.
Television
The Last Refuge. Young.
May. Updike.
One No. 7. Frank.
Pine Point, you are:. Henry.
Rec Room in Paradise.
Clark.
Room Service. Moser.
Tell (ing) (s)
Ain't No Tellin. Hurt.
The Anniversary. Dickey.
Arrogance Repressed.
Betjeman.
Ash Wednesday. Rossetti.
At Mexican Springs. Tohe.
A Ballad of Abbreviations.
Chesterton.
The Ballad of Reading Gaol.
Wilde.
Ballade of a Talked-Off Ear.
Parker.
The Birth of the Poet.
Prettyman.
The Birthday. Dacey.
The Boarding. Johnson.
Branches Back Into. Belford.
The Brickster. *Anonymous.*
Cante Hondo. Kay.

The Captain's Feather. Peck.
Carrier's Address.
Anonymous.
Cleobulus' Epitaph.
Simonides (of Ceos).
Endurance. Forche.
An Epicurean Ode. Hall.
Epigrams. Martial (Marcus
Valerius Martialis).
Epitaph on Elizabeth, L. H.
Jonson.
Even in the Moment of Our
Earliest Kiss. Millay.
Everyday Dirt. *Anonymous.*
Fatal Interview. Millay.
The Flea. Young.
Friendship. Silverstein.
From the Journals of the Frog
Prince. Mitchell.
A fuzzy fellow, without feet.
Dickinson.
Hymn to Selene.
Anonymous.
I Had Two Pigeons Bright
and Gay. *Anonymous.*
I Love to Tell the Story.
Hankey.
I'm nobody! Who are you?
Dickinson.
I Meant to Tell You.
Haldane.
The Idiot. Wilson.
If You Ask Me Who I Am.
Guebuza.
Improvisations: Light and
Snow (excerpt). Aiken.
In Springtime. Kipling.
Intimations of Mortality.
McGinley.
It's in Your Face.
Anonymous.
John Gorham. Robinson.
John Henry (E. vers.).
Anonymous.
Johnny Dyers. *Anonymous.*
Kite. Jensen.
The Last Fierce Charge.
Anonymous.
Last Words. Merrill.
Letter. Merwin.
Limerick: "There was an old
man of Tarentum."
Monkhouse.
A Little While. Rossetti.
Lord Arnaldos. Flecker.
Mabel, in New Hampshire.
Fields.
The Market. Snyder.
Marlborough (excerpt).
Sorley.
The Meanings in the Pattern.
Grahn.
The Murmur of a Bee.
Dickinson.
My Fatherland. Lawton.
Naomi Wise. *Anonymous.*
O Lord of Life. Gladden.
The Old Story over Again.
Kenney.
On a Honey Bee. Freneau.
On Clarastella Walking in Her
Garden. Heath.
On His Mistress, the Queen of
Bohemia. Wotton.
Once More A-Lumbering Go.
Anonymous.
The People. Campanella.
Pewter. Gilbert.
Plato Told. Cummings.
The Poetess's Bouts-Rimes.
Anonymous.

Portrait in Available Light.
Miles.
Potomac Town in February.
Sandburg.
Prelude. Yamamoto.
Riddle: "As I went through a
garden gap." *Anonymous.*
Riddle: "There was a king
met a king." *Anonymous.*
Robin's Secret. Bates.
Ross's Poems. Lehmann.
Round and Round the
Rugged Rock.
Anonymous.
Roy Bean. *Anonymous.*
The Secret. Webster.
Secrets. Pastan.
The Silent. Very.
Sir Hugh; or, The Jew's
Daughter (B vers.).
Anonymous.
Song of the Strange Young
Duckling. Munro.
Song: "Under the lime-tree,
on the daisied ground."
Walther von der
Vogelweide.
The Songs of Bilitis. Louys.
Sonnet: On the Detection of a
False Friend. Cavalcanti.
Sonnets from the Portuguese,
XLIV. Browning.
The Sorrow of Kodio.
Anonymous.
The Speaking Tree.
Rukeyser.
Springtime in Cookham Dean.
Roberts.
Student. Cheng Min.
Telling It. Sullivan.
Those Two Boys. Adams.
Three Gates. Day.
To a Skylark. Meredith.
To Robert Earl of Oxford,
and Earl Mortimer. Pope.
The Too Literal Pupil.
Martial (Marcus Valerius
Martialis).
Tourist. Van Doren.
Upon Ben Johnson. Herrick.
Verses on Blenheim. Martial
(Marcus Valerius Martialis).
Waiting for a Second Time.
LaPena.
The Wanderer. Heaney.
A War. Jarrell.
Was She a Witch? Richards.
The Watchman. Reisen.
Water-Boy. *Anonymous.*
What I Tell Him. Ortiz.
When Thou Must Home.
Campion.
Whistles. Field.
Yesterday. Sanchez.
You Tell On Yourself.
Anonymous.
Your Absence Has Not
Taught Me. Fetherling.
Temper (ed) (s)
Alice's Recitation. "Carroll.
Elver Fishers. Gurney.
For Miriam. Macgoye.
Hagar. Eybers.
Matilda. Evans.
A Sword. Boye.
The Times. Manilius.
Wise Men in Their Bad
Hours. Jeffers.
Temperance
Beware of Dogmas. Elliott.
Christian Ethics. Traherne.
Health Counsel. Harington.

Lines. Goodman.
Temperance Song.
Anonymous.
Temperature
Glacier. Nicholson.
Homer. Gallup.
Tempest (s)
The Albatross. Reeves.
The Broken Heart. Ford.
A Dedication. Gordon.
Four Folk-Songs in Hokku
Form, 2. *Anonymous.*
Horses on the Camargue.
Campbell.
If This Be Love. Eberhart.
Rain. Thomas.
Rude Boreas. *Anonymous.*
Song of the Sea.
MacColmain.
St. Michael's Mount.
Davidson.
The Tempest. Zaturenska.
To Mr. Newton on His
Return from Ramsgate.
Cowper.
Who Would Have Thought?
Herbert.
A Winter Night. Burns.
Template (s)
The Harbor of Illusion.
Bernstein.
Marie Curie Contemplating
the Role of Women
Scientists... Frazier.
This Is after All Vacation.
Zukofsky.
Temple Bar
Colin Clout. Skelton.
Temple (s)
Astrophel and Stella, XL.
Sidney.
Because I Paced My Thought.
Hewitt.
Bedlam: A Poem on His
Majesty's Happy
Escape...(excerpt).
Anonymous.
Birth. Melinescu.
Boy with His Hair Cut Short.
Rukeyser.
The Covenanter's Lament for
Bothwell Brigg. Praed.
A Cruell Mistris. Carew.
Dream Songs. Berryman.
Enoch. Very.
Epilogue to the Satires.
Pope.
The Forced Bridal.
Anonymous.
Forcing a Way. *Anonymous.*
Gentlemen. Taylor.
Her Sacred Bower.
Campion.
In the Suburbs. Simpson.
An Incident. LePan.
Investiture. Henderson.
Jesus, Enthroned and
Glorified. Eddy.
Little Things. Johns.
Loves End. Herbert of
Cherbury.
The Mask and the Poem.
Pizarnik.
Metamorphoses. Ovid
(Publius Ovidius Naso).
Mutual Love. Hammond.
Of Dying Beauty. Zukofsky.
On Jordan's Bank. Byron.
Sequaire. Godeschalk.
Sonnet Written in Tintern
Abbey, Monmouthshire.
Gardner.

To Egypt. Davis
To God the Father. Constable.
Two Temples. Hall.
Why Should Men Love the Church? Eliot.
Yom Kippur. Day.
You Ask Me, Why, Tho' Ill at Ease. Tennyson.
Your Woods. Holley.

Temptation (s)
At Mass. Lindsay.
The Bloodhound. Anthony.
Brother Green. *Anonymous.*
Conscience. Sherburne.

Ten
At Cheyenne. Field.
The Battle of Stonington on the Seaboard of Connecticut. Freneau.
The Bonny Lass of Anglesey. *Anonymous.*
The Bulldog on the Bank. *Anonymous.*
A Capital Ship. *Anonymous.*
A Christmas Package: No. 7 (excerpt). McCord.
Come on In. *Anonymous.*
The Devil. *Anonymous.*
The Dove Says, Coo, Coo. *Anonymous.*
The Doves. Tynan.
For Carole. Burns.
How to Murder Your Best Friend. O Hehir.
The Jute Mill Song. *Anonymous.*
King Midas. Moss.
The Lament of the Damned in Hell. Young.
Letter to Derek Mahon. Longley.
Lord Thomas and Fair Annet (I version). *Anonymous.*
Mr. Artesian's Conscientiousness. Nash.
Mr. Billings of Louisville. Field.
My Luve's Like a Red, Red Rose. Burns.
On a Mistress of Whose Affections He Was Doubtful. Nabbes.
On Being Much Better Than Most and Yet Not Quite Good Enough. Ciardi.
Rococo. Swinburne.
The Sampler. Turner.
The School-Master and the Truants. "Brownjohn.
Starting Early from the Ch'U-Ch'eng Inn. Po Chu-i.
Sweet Slug-a-Bed. *Anonymous.*
Ten Little Indian Boys. Hutchinson.
Ten Thousand Miles away. *Anonymous.*
The Tithe: To the Bride. Herrick.
Title of a Swift Horse. *Anonymous.*
To His Unconstant Friend. King.
Twilight of Freedom. Mandelstam.
Waking. Maxton.
Weaving at the Window. Wang Chien.
Wee Willie Winkie. Mother Goose.

Willie of Winsbury. *Anonymous.*

Ten Commandments
Precepts He Gave His Folk. Hazaken.

Tenant (s)
The Skeleton in the Cupboard. Locker-Lampson.
The Things. Aiken.
The Town I Was Born In. Amichai.

Tender (ness)
Carravagio. Hamill.
Cutting Wood on Shell Creek. Ehrlich.
The Elephant to the Girl in Bertram Mills' Circus. Cronin.
First or Last. Hardy.
Flags. Brooks.
Focus. Norris.
For Mary. Rexroth.
Here's the Tender Coming. *Anonymous.*
Holy Sonnets, XVII. Donne.
I See God. *Anonymous.*
It Scarcely Seems Worth While. Khodasevich.
King of the Belgians. Smith.
Love Unknown. Herbert.
The Musmee. Arnold.
The Mutilated Soldier. Fisher.
Omnia Vincit. Cochrane.
Quaker Ladies. Cortissoz.
The Shepherd's Home. Shenstone.
Somehow We Survive. Brutus.
The Spring Waters. "Ping Hsin" (Hsieh Wang-ying).
Swallows over the Camp. Krige.
Thailand Railway. Stow.
Three American Women and a German Bayonet. Scott.
To an Olde Gentlewoman, That Painted Hir Face. Turberville.
To William Blake. Dargan.
Unclench Yourself. Piercy.
Woodtown Manor. Montague.

Tendrils
Uncourtly Love. Walther von der Vogelweide.
The Vines. Gray.

Tenement (s)
Canal Street, Chicago. Fixmer.
A Pitcher of Mignonette. Bunner.
To a Fighter Killed in the Ring. Lipsitz.
To a Gone Era. McClaurin.
Walk with De Mayor of Harlem. Henderson.

Tennessee
Anecdote of the Jar. Stevens.
Bad Luck Blues. Jefferson.
Highly Educated Man. *Anonymous.*
O Magnet-South. Whitman.
Tom Dooley. *Anonymous.*
The Yellow Rose of Texas. *Anonymous.*

Tennis
A Ballade of Lawn Tennis. Adams.
Old Dominion. Hass.
Tennis in San Juan. Denney.

Tennyson
La Belle Dame sans Merci. Fairburn.
Lotos Eating. Collins.
The Menu. Aldrich.

Tenor
The Choirmaster's Burial. Hardy.
Poems, X. O'Connor.

Tent (s)
Ana(Mary-Army)gram. Herbert.
Autumn, Dark Wanderer. Daryush.
Benediction. Sklarew.
The Black Regiment. Boker.
The Butterbean Tent. Roberts.
The Deserted Pasture. Carman.
Evening Prayer. *Anonymous.*
Her, A Statue. Stoddart.
In Iceland. McCord.
An Invitation to an Invitation. Catullus.
The Knee on Its Own. Morgenstern.
Last Night in Sisseton, S. D. Goose.
Sheep. Hoffenstein.
Traveller's Guide to Antarctica. Stoutenburg.

Term (s)
Epitaphs of the War, 1914-18. Kipling.
Exhortation. Bogan.
Explorations. MacNeice.
Limerick: "W was a wild worm." Wells.
The Middle-Aged. Rich.
Poet. Emerson.
You Are a Jew! Schwartz.

Terrace (d) (s)
Adultery at a Las Vegas Bookstore. Liu.
Fairyland. Tagore.
Flight to Italy. Day-Lewis.
La Madonna di Lorenzetti. Andrews.
Walking Westward (excerpt). Stead.

Terrain
The Singing Bones. Stow.
Six Years. Bloch.
Terrain. Ammons.
Translation. Fuller.

Terrapin
Terrapin War. *Anonymous.*

Terre
Acadian Lane. St. John.

Terrible
Adventure. Fullerton.
Auf Dem Wasser Zu Singen. Spender.
For a Christening. Ridler.
Gare du Midi. Auden.
Great-Granddad. *Anonymous.*
Hotel in Paris. Trudell.
In That Dim Monument Where Tybalt Lies. Ficke.
It's a Terrible Thing! Hoagland.
The Leopard. Thomas.
The Lions of Fire Shall Have Their Hunting. Patchen.
Love Is a Terrible Thing. Norton.
O Love, Answer. Ridler.
The Old Women. Brown.
Pumas. Sterling.

Tennyson
To Xanadu, Which Is Beth Shaul. Sivan.
When the Saints Come Marching In. Lorde.
A Woman Came to Me. Silverton.

Terrify (ing)
From Which War. Minthorn.
The Hairs in My Nose. Boyajian.
In the Night. Stephens.
Upon Being Awakened at Night by My Four Year Old Daughter. Rainer.

Terror (s)
After Sunset. Conkling.
Allatoona. *Anonymous.*
Analyst. Fisher.
The Black Man's Son. Durand.
Condone. Bierce.
Conversation between the Chevalier de Chamilly and Mariana Alcoforado. Marias.
Dead Dog. Scannell.
Epitaph (Inscription from Anticyra). *Anonymous.*
Eve. *Anonymous.*
Eve Am I, Great Adam's Wife. *Anonymous.*
Famine. Heym.
The Frailty of Beauty. "C.
Grania. *Anonymous.*
Hatteras Calling. Aiken.
In the Churchyard at Cambridge. Longfellow.
Iona: The Graves of the Kings. Jeffers.
A July Storm: Johnson, Nemaha Country, Nebraska. Hahn.
Kinship. Heaney.
Lady Ralegh's Lament. Lowell.
Late Autumn. Allingham.
Man's World Dissolving. Butler.
Meditations for July 26, 1666. Pain.
NW5 & N6. Betjeman.
Old Indian Trick. Green.
One Night away from Day. Digby.
Ordinary Women. Hacker.
Patrico's Song. Jonson.
Poem About Your Face. Alterman.
Praise of Ibikunle. *Anonymous.*
The Reformed Pirate. Roberts.
Rimbaud Fire Letter to Jim Applewhite. Chappell.
Roma. Rutilius.
Send Forth the High Falcon. Adams.
The Sparrow's Skull. Pitter.
Survey of Cornwall. Carew.
Terror. Warren.
The Third Century. Traherne.
To Mary. Gottfried von Strasburg.
The Trance. Spender.
Treasure Hunt. Warren.
Trembling. Shenhar.

Test (ed) (ing)
Alexander. Morgan.
Apprentices. Munro.

Bishop Blougram's Apology.
Browning.
The Clouds. Mira Bai [(or
Mirabai(].
Dauber. Masefield.
Hills. Munro.
Life, A Question. Robinson.
Pigmeat. Leadbelly.
Poem for John My Brother.
Aberg.
Splendor. Shalom.
True Woman. Rossetti.

Test tube
Scientia Vincit Omnia?
Moore.

Testament
Chanson de Chateaulaire.
Gorman.
I Lift My Heart to Thee.
Sternhold.
In Paris. Macdonagh.
Testament. Holmes.

Tether
Down on My Luck.
Fairburn.
Mules. Walker.
On Clergymen Preaching
Politics. Byrom.

Texas
College Song. Anthony.
The Eyes of Texas.
Anonymous.
I'd Like to Be in Texas when
They Round-Up in the
Spring. *Anonymous.*
In Texas Grass. Troupe.
Lasca. Desprez.
The Road to Texas. Nance.

Text (s)
The Church-Porch. Herbert.
Double Duty. Farbstein.
For Angus MacLeod. Smith.
The Interpreters. Enright.
Jutaculla Rock. Morgan.
Patience of all my smart.
Wyatt.
Religion. Butler.
Seascape with Bookends.
Eaton.

Thames
A Charge to the Poets
(excerpt). Whitehead.
The Fall of Tecumseh.
Anonymous.
Jealosie. Donne.
None Other Fame Mine
Unambitious Muse.
Daniel.
Prothalamion. Spenser.
The Retired Colonel.
Hughes.
Rivers. Storer.
Rivers Arise. Milton.
Social Science. Brown.
Whitmonday. MacNeice.

Thank (ed) (s)
The Abbey Walk. Henryson.
Accept My Full Heart's
Thanks. Wilcox.
Accidents of Birth.
Meredith.
Archie O Cawfield (B vers.).
Anonymous.
Are We Thankful?
Anonymous.
Baby's Breakfast. Poulsson.
Because of Thy Great Bounty.
Crowell.
Blind. Pearce.
A Boy's Prayer. Beeching.
Canticle of the Sun. Francis
of Assisi.

Catherine. Kuskin.
A Change in Style. O
Heoghusa.
Cleitagoras. Leonidas.
The Cliff. Rowbotham.
The Conquerors. Dunbar.
The Corn-Song. Whittier.
The Crow and the Nighthawk.
Kirkconnell.
The Deaf Woman's Courtship.
Anonymous.
Dream Songs. Berryman.
Dubrovnik Poem (Emilio
Tolentino). Rudolf.
Evangeline. Longfellow.
Face to Face with Reality.
Oxenham.
Fain Would My Thoughts.
Austin.
Fair Annie. *Anonymous.*
The Faith of Abraham
Lincoln. Lincoln.
Faithfully Tinying at Twilight
Voice. Cummings.
The Fallen. Scott.
The flaming sighs that boil
within my breast. Wyatt.
For Beauty, We Thank Thee.
Oxenham.
For Everything Give Thanks.
Tupper.
Give Thanks. Tupper.
Grace Before Sleep.
Teasdale.
Gratitude. McGee.
Gratitude for Work.
Oxenham.
I Give Thee Thanks, My
King. O Brolchain.
I Give You Thanks My God.
Dadie.
In Every Thing Give Thanks.
Anonymous.
A Jacobite Scot in Satire on
England's Unparalleled
Loss. *Anonymous.*
Kibbutz Sabbath. Levi ben
Amittai.
A Kodak; Tregantle. Brown.
Lady Isabel and the Elf
Knight (B version).
Anonymous.
Long Lines. Goodman.
The Managers. Auden.
Morning Song. Ibn Gabirol.
New Years and Old.
Jackson.
The Norfolk Rebellion: The
Rebels' Rhyme.
Anonymous.
Now. Ken.
October Flies. Kessler.
Ode on a Plastic Stapes.
Walsh.
Old Man, the Sweat Lodge.
George.
One Winter Afternoon.
Cummings.
The Open Sea. Meredith.
Our Prayer of Thanks
(excerpt). Sandburg.
The Pilgrims Came. Wynne.
Planting Trees. Friedlaender.
A Pleasant New Court Song.
Anonymous.
Pleasure It Is. Cornish.
Poems in Praise of Practically
Nothing. Hoffenstein.
A Prayer for Thanksgiving.
Auslander.
De Produndis (excerpt).
Browning.

Proposals for Building a
Cottage. Clare.
Psalm XXX. Sidney.
The Radical. Cuney.
The Rain. Herbert.
Requiem. Connell.
The Rev. Nicholas Noyes to
the Rev. Cotton Mather...
Noyes.
A Sailor's Prayer. Morris.
Send Forth, O God, Thy
Light and Truth. Adams.
Sensuality. Patmore.
Solioquy I. Aldington.
A Song of Thanks. Jones.
Song of Thanksgiving.
Moreland.
Stacking Up. Rosenfeld.
Sunset Song. *Anonymous.*
Thanks from Earth to
Heaven. Wheelock.
Thanksgiving. Driscoll.
Thanksgiving. Emerson.
A Thanksgiving. Larcom.
Thanksgiving Day. Bridges.
There Is a Tide. Kipling.
The Things I Miss.
Higginson.
To God. Blake.
To His Books. Vaughan.
Tubal Cain. Mackay.
The Twa Books. Ramsay.
The Unfortunate Male. Ben
Kalonymos.
Voices That Have Filled My
Day. Chiang.
A Wasted Sympathy.
Howells.
We Plough the Fields.
Campbell.
We Thank Thee. Oxenham.
William Gifford. Landor.
With God and His Mercy.
Rosenius.
Yonosa House. Smith.

Thankful (ly) (ness)
Common Blessings. Clark.
The First Thanksgiving.
Prelutsky.
G. Belloc.
Home Alone These Last
Hours of the Afternoon...
Levy.
Jonathan Swift Somers.
Masters.
The Last of the Fire Kings.
Mahon.
Simhat Torah. Gordon.
Sonnet: Composed by the Side
of Grasmere Lake.
Wordsworth.
Thanksgiving Day. Wynne.
Upon a Spider Catching a
Fly. Taylor.

Thanksgiving
Every Day Thanksgiving Day.
Spofford.
The Excursion. Wordsworth.
The Exeter Book: Fates of
Men. *Anonymous.*
The First Thanksgiving.
Turner.
First Thanksgiving of All.
Turner.
Five Kernels of Corn.
Butterworth.
A Monumental Memorial of
Marine Mercy &c. Steere.
My Triumph. Whittier.
Riddle: "First it was a pretty
flower." Rossetti.
Thankful Heart. Davis.

The Volunteer's Thanksgiving.
Larcom.

Thatch (ed) (er) (ing)
The Christmas Tree. Beer.
Laurence Bloomfield in
Ireland. Allingham.
A Love Letter to Elizabeth
Thatcher. Thatcher.
On Edward Seymour, Duke of
Somerset. *Anonymous.*
A Thatcher of Thatchwood
Went to Thatchet A-
Thatching. *Anonymous.*

Thaw (ed) (ing) (s)
Before the Thaw. Gill.
The Frozen Heart. Herrick.
Immortal. Van Doren.
Prague Spring. Harrison.
Raccoon Poem. Palmer.
Russians. Douglas.
Spring in Hiding. Frost.
To a Wall of Flame in a Steel
Mill, Syracuse, New York,
1969. Levis.
Victory. Duggan.

Theater (s)
The Aeneid. Virgil (Publius
Vergilius Maro).
A Dancer's Life. Justice.
Drama's vitallest expression is
the common day.
Dickinson.
Horror Comic. Conquest.
Stumptown Attends the
Picture Show. Bottoms.
Unsleeping City. Garcia
Lorca.

Thebes
The Aeneid. Virgil (Publius
Vergilius Maro).
The Rock of Cashel. De
Vere.

Theft
On an Ill-Managed House.
Swift.
Prometheus Unbound. Hope.
Unharvested. Frost.

Theme (s)
The Double Vision. Day.
Epigram for the Dead at
Tegea. *Anonymous.*
In the Distance. Van Brunt.
An Invitation to Madison
County. Wright.
Johnny Carroll's Camp.
Anonymous.
A Martian Sends a Postcard
Home. Raine.
Meditation on a Memoir.
Cunningham.
On Mr. Milton's Paradise
Lost. Marvell.
Passin Ben Dorain. Mackie.
Poets and Their
Bibliographies. Tennyson.

Theory (theories)
Anthropology. Hollo.
Creation Myths. Raffel.
The Ex-Poet. Zavatsky.
Golfers. Layton.
No Theory. Ignatow.
Transducing. Dickenson.

Therapy
At the Treatment Center.
Sala.

Thermodynamics
First and Second Law.
Flanders.

Thermopylae
Limerick: "There was an Old
Man of Thermopylae."
Lear.

Thermopylae

On Installing an American Kitchen in Lower Austria. Auden.

The Thespians at Theermopylae. Cameron.

Thesaurus

Letter to Kafka. Stanton.

Thespians

The Thespians at Theermopylae. Cameron.

Thick (er) (ness)

Blood Is Thicker Than Water. Rice.

The Book of the People. Lamennais.

Boy and the Wandering Recluse. Robles.

Confession. Herbert.

Lobsters in the Window. Snodgrass.

The Painters. Hemschemeyer.

Quodlibets. Hayman.

Root Hog or Die. Small.

The Unawkward Singers. Ferry.

The Wives of Spittal. Anonymous.

Thicket (s)

Arms and the Boy. Owen.

In the Black Camaro. Bottoms.

Judas Iscariot. Mason.

Location. Skinner.

The Middle Ages: Two Views. Drake.

Preliminary Poem. Heath-Stubbs.

Sleeping Beauty. Nemerov.

There Goes a Girl Walking. Meeks.

Thief (thieves)

Aubade after the Party. O'Grady.

Aurora Borealis. Roditi.

A Bestiary. Rexroth.

The Bishop and His Portmanteau. Anonymous.

Buckinghamshire. Anonymous.

The Cattle Thief. Tekahionwake.

Childe Harold's Pilgrimage: Canto IV. Byron.

Epigram on a Lawyer's Desiring One of the Tribe to Look.... Fergusson.

Five Lyrics from "Good for Nothing Man". Pitchford.

Hagiograph. Heppenstall.

Idea. Drayton.

In gold sandals. Sappho.

The Murder of William Remington. Nemerov.

Night's Fall. Graham.

On a Nomination to the Legion of Honour. Anonymous.

A Pastoral. Hillyer.

The Peddler and His Wife. Anonymous.

Riddle #29: The Moon and the Sun. Anonymous.

Riddle: "In marble halls as white as milk." Anonymous.

Riddle: The Book-Worm: "A moth ate a word." Anonymous.

Solitary Confinement. Kennedy.

Sonnet: He Jests Concerning His Poverty. Sant' Angelo.

Sonnets, XXXV: "No more be grieved at that which thou hast done." Shakespeare.

The Spinning Girl. Alterman.

Stoklewath; or, The Cymbrian Village. Blamire.

The Thieves. Graves.

Time. Taylor.

Trials of a Tourist. Tibble.

A Vision Upon This Conceipt of the Faerie Queene. Ralegh.

Why I Never Went into Politics. Shelton.

Zapata & the Landlord. Spellman.

Thigh (s)

America A Prophecy. Blake.

"L'Apparition" of Gustave Moreau. Bottomley.

Bathers. Tiller.

Egyptian Hieroglyphics. Anonymous.

Gellius, What Reason Can You Give. Catullus.

Hostia. Layton.

In Kerry. Synge.

Love Poem. Comfort.

My Spring Thing. Hoagland.

Nova. Levendosky.

On Oxford (parody). Keats.

On Those That Hated "The Playboy of the Western World", 1907. Yeats.

The One Whose Reproach I Cannot Evade. Hitchcock.

Praise for Sick Women. Snyder.

Quietly. Rexroth.

The Return to Work. Williams.

The Shrouded Stranger. Ginsberg.

To a Dead Elephant. Livingstone.

We Dressed Each Other. Eifuku.

Wedding. Livesay.

You. Clark.

You gaze at me teasingly through the window. Praxilla.

Thimble

Diodorus Siculus. Anonymous.

Thin

After the War. Naggid.

The Beggar's Opera. Gay.

The Depot. Turco.

Easter Poem. Raine.

Fair Days; or, Dawns Deceitful. Herrick.

Fall Wind. Stafford.

A Gnarled Riverina Gum-Tree. Moll.

Great-Aunt Rebecca. Brewster.

I need only fall asleep. Blandiana.

Letters Found near a Suicide. Horne.

Little Tiny Puppy Dog. Milligan.

Man and Woman. Lee.

NHR. Hirschman.

November. Harvey.

An Officers' Prison Camp Seen from a Troop-Train. Jarrell.

Oil. Hogan.

Retreat. Collins.

Snow in the Suburbs. Hardy.

Songs of Cheng. Confucius.

Splinter. Sandburg.

V-Letter to Karl Shapiro in Australia. Rodman.

Veni Creator. Carman.

Winter Ploughing. Everson.

The Woman I Met. Hardy.

Think (ing) (s)

Acres of Clams. Anonymous.

Address to the Deil. Burns.

The Aim of Life: A Country Town. Bailey.

Alphabet. Lear.

The Amputation. Sorrells.

The Arctic Ox. Moore.

Aspens. Thomas.

At Night. Proctor.

At North Farm. Ashbery.

The Banks of the Gaspereaux. Anonymous.

The Barge. Fyleman.

Because They Were Very Poor That Winter. Patchen.

Believe Not. Peretz.

A Bestiary. Rexroth.

Birth. Urdang.

The Blacksmith. Anonymous.

Blow Me Eyes! Irwin.

Bow Down Your Head and Cry. Anonymous.

Breakings. Taylor.

Cake. Potter.

Call It Goofus. Berkson.

Canticles to Men. Mannes.

Celia Celia. Mitchell.

Ceremony. Wilbur.

Climbing. Fuertes.

Codicil. Stone.

The Concept of Force. Sargent.

Conquerors. Treece.

Could Man Be Drunk for Ever. Housman.

The Country House. Simpson.

Country Towns. Slessor.

Creeds. Wattles.

Custer (2). Baker.

Darling of Gods and Men, beneath the Gliding Stars. Bunting.

Days through Starch and Bluing. Fulton.

Dear Companion. Anonymous.

Desolation Row. Dylan.

The Dinosaur. Taylor.

Do They Think of Me at Home. Carpenter.

The Doubter. Gilder.

The Elephant. Asquith.

Endymion, III. Keats.

Evidence. Kober.

Existentialism. Frankenberg.

A Farewell to English (excerpt). Hartnett.

Five Domestic Interiors. Scannell.

For Muh' Dear. Rodgers.

Forthfaring. Howells.

Gaily I Lived. Anonymous.

The Gambler. Anonymous.

Ghost. Weaver.

Glee–The Ghosts. Peacock.

Goddess. Sherwin.

The Golden Shower. Campbell.

Harriet. Lowell.

High Germany. Anonymous.

Homosexual Sonnets. Pitchford.

Honey Moon. Baker.

Hope and Despair. Abercrombie.

The Horrid Voice of Science. Lindsay.

How to Meditate. Kerouac.

I Have a Room whereinto No One Enters. Rossetti.

If you go away. Anonymous.

In My Dreams. Smith.

The Inefficacious Egg. Bishop.

An Invitation to an Invitation. Catullus.

Jack the Guinea Pig. Anonymous.

A Jealous Man. Anonymous.

Julius Caesar. Shakespeare.

King Henry IV. Shakespeare.

Late Abed. MacLeish.

Light Rain. Buckley.

The Little Golden Ring. Anonymous.

Love-Songs, At Once Tender and Informative. Hoffenstein.

A Man in Our Village. Norris.

Moan, Moan, Ye Dying Gales. Neele.

Modern Midnight Conversation: Between a Contractor and His Wife. Anonymous.

Music and Words. Jennings.

My Daily Creed. Anonymous.

My Mother's Life. Meredith.

Nameless Journey (excerpt). Goldberg.

Ned's Delicate Way. Lawson.

The Newlyweds' Separation. Tu Fu.

A Nymph's Disdain of Love. Anonymous.

O Bury Me Beneath the Willow (with music). Anonymous.

October. Wolfe.

Ode to a Pig While His Nose Was Being Bored. Southey.

Of a Contented Mind. Vaux.

The Old Settler's Song. Henry.

On Monsieur Coue. Inge.

On the Following Work and Its Author. Mitchell.

Once. Walker.

Our Silly Little Sister. Aldis.

The Paperweight. Schnackenberg.

The Paps of Dana. Stephens.

Parting. Hogan.

The Pelican Chorus. Lear.

A Photo of Miners. Galvin.

Plato Instructs a Midwest Farmer. Palmer.

Precious Stones. Calverley.

Printer's Error. Wodehouse.

Rainscapes, Hydrangeas, Roses, and Singing Birds. Eberhart.

The Reason. Bacon.

Red Light. Jones.

Reformed Drunkard. Scannell.

A Religious Use of Taking
Tobacco. Wisdome.
Reserve. Aldington.
Retractions. Cabell.
Reuben's Cabin. Morgan.
Rhyme of Rain. Holmes.
Rift Tide. Walsh.
Rumors of War in Wyoming.
Rea.
Senex to Matt. Prior.
Stephen.
The Sluggard. Watts.
Sometime. Smith.
The Song of the Mischievous
Dog. Thomas.
Song: "Reading about the
Wisconsin Weeping
Willow." Krauss.
Song Set by Robert Jones: "A
woman's looks."
Anonymous.
A Sonnet. Aiken.
Sonnet: "How that vast
heaven intitled First is
rolled." Drummond.
Sonnets: A Sequence on
Profane Love. Boker.
Stanzas for Music. Byron.
The Streams of Bunclody.
Anonymous.
Strike the Bell. Anonymous.
The Talker. Van Duyn.
Tamburlaine the Great.
Marlowe.
The Terror of Death. Keats.
That Reminds Me. Nash.
There's Nothing Polite about
a Tank. Minarik.
They Never Taste Who
Always Drink. Prior.
Think No More, Lad.
Housman.
Thought and the Poet.
Yates.
Thoughts on the Cosmos.
Adams.
To an Old Philosopher in
Rome. Stevens.
To Celia, upon Love's
Ubiquity. Carew.
To J.S. Misch.
To Maynard on the Long
Road Home. Ehrhart.
To Soulfolk. Burroughs.
Two Lives. Leonard.
Two Mountains Men Have
Climbed. Starkweather.
A Valediction. Cartwright.
Voice in Darkness. Dehmel.
Wagtail and Baby. Hardy.
Wasp. Nowlan.
What the Sixties Were Really
Like. Abrams.
What We See Is What We
Think. Stevens.
When I strip. Kegels.
When the Nightingale Sings.
Anonymous.
When You with Hogh Dutch
Heeren Dine. Prior.
Whose Voice. Bush.
The Woman of the House.
Murphy.
The Yawn. Blackburn.

Third
Alluding to the One-Armed
Bandit (parody). Berry.
And in That Drowning
Instant. Klein.
At Their Place. Mariah.
An Autobiography. Bairam
at Tunisie.

Ballad of the Three Spectres.
Gurney.
Hotel. Wazyk.
The Impartial Inspection.
Anonymous.
Les Jours Gigantesques / The
Titanic Days. Fraser.
The Knight's Ghost.
Anonymous.
Lines Printed under the
Engraved Portrait of
Milton. Dryden.
Lives of the Poet. Miles.
Oyster-Crabs (parody).
Wells.
Requiem for "Bird" Parker.
Corso.
Returning at Night.
Harrison.
Scylla and Charybdis.
Kinsella.
De Se. Weever.
The Second Coming. Clark.
Spring Comes to Murray Hill.
Nash.
Star Blanket. Young Bear.
Zoo You Too! Joans.

Third Alley
Third Alley Blues. Smith.

Third Avenue
Agreeable Monsters.
Clampitt.

Thirst (ing) (s) (y)
Age in Prospect. Jeffers.
All Things Drink. Stanley.
The April of the Ages.
Dolben.
The Broken Bowl. Very.
Customs. Gelman.
Defense Rests. Miller.
Epitaph for Liberal Poets.
MacNeice.
Feast. Millay.
God. Bradford.
His Are the Thousand
Sparkling Rills.
Alexander.
Last Lines (excerpt).
Meredith.
Meditation. Rakosi.
Men are Children of This
World. Ibn Ezra.
Modern Love, XXIV.
Meredith.
The Mountains. De la Mare.
Nepenthe. Darley.
O briar-scents, on yon wet
wing. Meredith.
The Odyssey. Homer.
Priest Or Poet. Leslie.
Psalter of the Blessed Virgin
Mary. Bonaventure.
The Roadmenders' Song.
Anonymous.
Sailor. Page.
The Shepherd's Calendar.
Clare.
Sonnet XXXII. Alabaster.
Tiger. McKay.
Toulouse Lautrec. Tollefsen.
Transfiguration. Barnes.
Wallflower to a Moonbeam
(parody). Untermeyer.
Water-Girl. *Anonymous.*
The Water Tower. Paul.
When We Are Like Two
Drunken Suns. Caroutch.
The Yellow Bittern.
Macdonagh.

Thirty
A Ballad of Redhead's Day.
Glaenzer.

The Battle of New Orleans.
Anonymous.
Betrayal. Cholmondeley.
Dauber. Masefield.
Fading Beauty. *Anonymous.*
The Fat Budgie. Lennon.
Fifty Years Spent. Burt.
Go-d'ling. *Anonymous.*
The Months of the Year.
Grafton.
Now. Stafford.
On My Thirty-Third Birthday
January 22, 1821. Byron.
The Private Dining Room.
Nash.
Riddle: "I saw five birds all in
a cage." *Anonymous.*
Scene from a Play, Acted at
Oxford, Called
"Matriculation." Moore.
Thirty-Eight. Smith.
To Mrs. Thrale on Her
Thirty-Fifth Birthday.
Johnson.

This be
Dyvers Thy Death Doo
Dyverslye Bemone.
Surrey.

Thistle (s)
Beleaguered Cities. Lucas.
Death. Scott.
The Fairies. Hubbell.
Holding-paddock. Hart-
Smith.
House in Denver. Ferril.
Imogen–In Wales. Irwin.
James Rigg (parody). Hogg.
Simple Verses. Marti.
St. Michael the Weigher.
Lowell.
Theophilus Thistledown, the
Successful Thistle Sifter.
Anonymous.
Thistle-Down. Bates.
Thistledown. Glover.
Thistledown. Monro.

Thorn (s)
Absalom. Gilead.
Ah Were She Pitiful.
Greene.
Autumnal Consummation.
Stevenson.
The Brome Abraham and
Isaac. *Anonymous.*
The Choice of the Cross.
Sayers.
Comparisons. Rossetti.
Corpus Christi (B vers.).
Anonymous.
Etruscan Warrior's Head.
Henze.
An Even-Song. Dobell.
The Funeral Home. Mezey.
God Sour the Milk of the
Knacking Wench.
Nowlan.
The Gossamer. Smith.
The Little Child. Paine.
Mary Passes. *Anonymous.*
My Limbs I Will Fling.
Strode.
My Pretty Rose Tree. Blake.
O Faithless Thorn.
Anonymous.
Old Miniatures. Vroman.
Orgy. Labriola.
Psalm. Celan.
Quatrain. Blanden.
Quid Non Speremus,
Amantes? Dowson.
Reading Sign. Anderson.
Roses Only. Moore.

Scatter Seeds of Kindness.
Smith.
Simple Nature. Romanes.
Simple Verses. Marti.
Sir Gawain and the Green
Knight. *Anonymous.*
Sleeping Beauty. Nemerov.
Sonnets. Tuckerman.
Spring Ecstasy. Reese.
There Are Sweet Flowers.
Landor.
To My Worthy Friend Master
George Sands.... Carew.
To Sleep. Casa.
To William Blake. Dargan.
Why the Robin's Breast Was
Red. Randall.
Written in the Visitors' Book
at the Birthplace of Robert
Burns. Cable.
Ye Flowery Banks. Burns.

Thought (s)
Aardvark. Fields.
After the Rain. Collier.
The Age of Sheen. Hughes.
Airey-Force Valley.
Wordsworth.
Alone. Chu Shu-chen.
Altitudes. Wilbur.
Amoretti, LXXVI. Spenser.
Amoretti, LXXVII. Spenser.
Amoretti, LXXVIII.
Spenser.
Andrew Magrath's Reply to
John O'Tuomy. Magrath.
Another Academy.
Bukowski.
Antigone. Sophocles.
April Fool. Hunt.
Art of the Sonnet: LVI.
Orlovitz.
As Night Comes On.
Wesley.
As When a Man. Tennyson.
At the Ball Game. Williams.
Autobiography. Dipoko.
Autumn. Pushkin.
The Avengers. Graves.
Baby. Macdonald.
Be Thou My Guide. Coates.
Beauty. Alling.
Black Silk. Gallagher.
Blest Be the Day. Petrarch
(Francesco Petrarca).
Bobber. Carver.
The Bothie of Tober-na-
Vuolich. Clough.
The Bridge. Peterson.
Caelica, XVIII. Greville.
Caelica, LXX. Greville.
Caelica, LXXXVII. Greville.
The Catholic Faith. Digby.
Chiaroscuro: Rose. Aiken.
Chile. Griffin.
Chloe. Mordaunt.
Christ, the Man. Davies.
A Christmas Prayer.
Stevenson.
Common Bill. *Anonymous.*
Confusion (parody). Hervey.
The Crane Is My Neighbour.
Neilson.
The Crow-Children Walk My
Circles in the Snow.
Young Bear.
The Dancer. Campbell.
The Dark-Red Shadow-Spots.
Kanbara.
Dedicatory. Gilmore.
The Della Cruscans. Gifford.
Divided. Ingelow.
Donna. Allen.

Down from the Country.
Blight.
The Editor's Wooing.
Newell.
The Effigy. Cavalcanti.
An Elegy Upon My Best
Friend. King.
Elisa, or an Elegy upon the
Unripe Decease...
Fletcher.
The English Language.
Story.
English Liberal. Taylor.
Enigma. Thomas.
Epitaph on Himself.
Regnier.
Epithalamium for Stella and
Violentilla: Why Do You
Dally So? Statius Publius
Papinius.
Evanescence. Myers.
The Evans Country. Amis.
Evening in Paradise. Milton.
Eye. Burr.
Fain I Would. *Anonymous.*
Fears in Solitude. Coleridge.
The Fire of Drift-Wood.
Longfellow.
Firelight. Robinson.
The First Fathers. Hawker.
A Flemish Madonna. Stork.
The Food Drops Off a Fork.
Silverton.
For Annie. Poe.
For Every Day. Havergal.
Four Haiku. Wright.
From a Car-Window.
Harding.
The Frozen Girl (with music).
Anonymous.
Garadh. Colum.
The Generous Years.
Spender.
God Everywhere. Ibn Ezra.
God's Unspeakable Gift.
Sealey.
The Good Town. Muir.
The Great Scarf of Birds.
Updike.
The Hand of Lincoln.
Stedman.
Hat Bar. Weston.
Haunted Houses.
Longfellow.
Heat. Lampman.
Homer. Ehrenstein.
A Hot-Weather Song.
Marquis.
How Long Will It Last?
Horikawa.
I Am a Peach Tree. Li Po.
I'm Ashamed of My
Thoughts. *Anonymous.*
I Thought It Was Tangiers I
Wanted. Hughes.
I Walked over the Grave of
Henry James. Eberhart.
Impression de Nuit: London.
Douglas.
In eternum I was once
determed. Wyatt.
In Memoriam A.H.H., CXIX.
Tennyson.
In Memoriam A.H.H.,
CXXII. Tennyson.
In Memory of Major Robert
Gregory. Yeats.
In Summer. Stickney.
The Inner Silence. Monroe.
Inside of King's College
Chapel, Cambridge.
Wordsworth.

The Insusceptibles. Rich.
Interior Landscape. Fuertes.
It Is No Dream of Mine.
Thoreau.
It Seems That God Bestowed
Somehow. Hall.
Ivanhoe. Chapt. 39: Rebecca's
Hymn. Scott.
Jonah and the Whale.
Meynell.
The Junk Shop. Coulette.
The Kiss. Patmore.
Lady Godiva. Shanks.
Lament for the Dorsets.
Purdy.
Lamorna Cove. Davies.
Lara. Byron.
Laurence Bloomfield in
Ireland. Allingham.
Lie on the Sand. Campbell.
Life. Coleridge.
Lines on Hearing the Organ.
Calverley.
Lines on Seeing a Lock of
Milton's Hair. Keats.
The Lone Star Trail.
Anonymous.
Lough Bray. O'Grady.
Love and fortune and my
mind... Wyatt.
Love's Labour's Lost.
Shakespeare.
The Lover and Birds.
Allingham.
The Lucky Coin. Clarke.
Madrigal: "The swans, whose
pens as white as ivory"
(excerpt). Greene.
Mater Desiderata. Praed.
The Metre Columbian
(parody). *Anonymous.*
The Miracle. De La Mare.
The Mouse. McCrae.
Mute Opinion. Hardy.
My Lost Youth. Longfellow
Napoleon Hoped That All the
World Would Fall beneath
His Sway. *Anonymous.*
Never Could I Think. Izumi
Shikibu.
Night at an Airport.
Ignatow.
Not I. *Anonymous.*
Not Such Your Burden.
Agathias.
Nothing to Say, You Say?
Aiken.
Notre Dame. Mandelstam.
O God of My Salvation, Hear.
Barlow.
O Heart, Small Urn.
Doolithe.
O Lord, My Best Desire
Fulfil. Cowper.
Of Late. Starbuck.
Of Love and Time.
Henderson.
Old Balaam. *Anonymous.*
On Another. Belloc.
On Dr. Samuel Ogden.
Arden.
On Love. Tamekane.
On Seeing a Lady's Garter.
Anonymous.
On the Following Work and
Its Author. Mitchell.
On the South Coast of
Cornwall. Gray.
Out of Doors. Arensberg.
Oxford Nights. Johnson.

The Painter Who Pleased
Nobody and Everybody.
Gay.
The Pelican Chorus. Lear.
Perpetual Christmas. Field.
Please Say Something.
Tomioka Taeko.
The Portrait. Winchilsea.
The Praise of Industry.
Thomson.
Prayer. Lewis.
The Priest and the Mulberry
Tree. Peacock.
The Prince of Life.
Oxenham.
The Private Dining Room.
Nash.
Problem in Social Geometry–
The Inverted Square!
Durem.
Procrastination. Young.
A Quality of Air. Chapin.
Rain. Williams.
The Rapture. Baker.
A Real Question Calling for
Solution. Warren.
Realization. Fisher.
The Red Men. Sangster.
Riprap. Snyder.
A Satire Addressed to a
Friend (excerpt). Oldham.
Shack Poem. Bly.
The Ship and Her Makers.
Masefield.
Silence. Masters.
Since I Heard. Mitsune
(Oshikochi no Mitsune).
The Singer in the Prison.
Whitman.
Sleep and Poetry. Keats.
Solitudes. Wheelock.
Solomon: To Truth.
Anonymous.
Some People. Field.
Song: "Day will rise and the
sun from eastward." Hay.
Songs to Survive the Summer.
Hass.
Sonnet I. Alabaster.
Sonnet LXX. Alabaster.
Sonnet against the Too-Facile
Mystic. Harrod.
Sonnet: "How that vast
heaven intitled First is
rolled." Drummond.
Sonnets: A Sequence on
Profane Love. Boker.
Sorrow. De Vere.
The Sparrow's Nest.
Wordsworth.
The Spring. Fyleman.
Standing on the Streetcorner.
Denby.
Star Song. Johnson.
The Stick. O'Rourke.
Submarine Mountains. Rice.
The Sunshade. Hardy.
The Swallow's Flight. Levy.
Tamburlaine the Great.
Marlowe.
The Task. Cowper.
There Is a Nook Among the
Alders. Frost.
They. Thomas.
This Is My Hour. Akins.
Though I Regarded Not.
Surrey.
Thought. Emerson.
A Thought of Marigolds.
Farrar.
Thoughts about the Person
from Porlock. Smith.

Thro' Grief and Thro'
Danger. Moore.
Thunderstorms. Davies.
The Time Is Today. Farrar.
The Times. Manilius.
To a Blind Student Who
Taught Me to See. Hazo.
To a Writer of the Day.
Mitchell.
To a Young Lady. Savage.
To My Friend. Thompson.
To Sleep. Wordsworth.
Transformation.
Rittenhouse.
The Truth. Lampman.
Tune Thou My Harp.
Carmichael.
Two doves upon the selfsame
branch. Rossetti.
Tzu Yeh Songs. *Anonymous.*
Undo Your Heart.
Anonymous.
Unity. Russell.
University Examinations in
Egypt. Enright.
Upon the Crucifix.
Alabaster.
The Upper Canadian.
Reaney.
Venice Recalled. Boyd.
A Violinist. Bourdillon.
Vow to Love Faithfully,
Howsoever He Be
Rewarded. Surrey.
Waiting. Freeman.
War. Brownstein.
Was It a Dream. Spenser.
Washing and Dressing.
Taylor.
When as a Lad. Mackay.
When Israel. Scott.
When We in Kind
Embracements Had Agre'd.
Anonymous.
Where Have You Been Dear?
Kuskin.
White. Woodcock.
Who Is Not a Stranger Still.
Stephany.
Who Would Have Thought.
Howell.
Wise Men in Their Bad
Hours. Jeffers.
Within the Shelter of Our
Walls. Lennen.
Words Made of Water.
Singer.
Wreck of the Deutschland.
Hopkins.
Written upon the Top of Ben
Nevis. Keats.
Yom Kippur: Fasting.
Whitman.
Young Blondes. Ewart.
Young Charlottie. Smith.
Yung Wind. Confucius.
Zimbabwe. Sinclair.
Thousand (s)
At Mass. Lindsay.
At the End of Spring. Yu
Hsuan-chi.
The Biglow Papers. Lowell.
The City of the Moon
(excerpt). Rexroth.
Exile's Letter. Li Po.
The Faerie Queene. Spenser.
Glass Houses. Robinson.
The Goatherd. Conkling.
The Heart's Proof.
Buckham.
Howl, I. Ginsberg.

I go to this window.
Cummings.
I Lie on the Chilled Stones of
the Great Wall. Liu.
If Justice Moved. Sellers.
The Iliad. Homer.
In the Silence. Stephany.
Jesus, How Much Thy Name
Unfolds! Peters.
The Little Drummer.
Anonymous.
The Mahratta Ghats. Lewis.
Mediterranean. Pincas.
The Motion of the Earth.
Nicholson.
My Love, She Passed Me By.
Anonymous.
No Madam Butterfly. Hajek.
O Girl, You Torment Me...
Anonymous.
Old Bangum. *Anonymous.*
Once on a Time a Thousand
Different Men. Henry.
The One Girl at the Boys
Party. Olds.
Owning. Lane.
Piano Tuner, Untune Me That
Tune. Nash.
Poem for My Father's Ghost.
Oliver.
Resurrection. Blackmur.
The Sedge-Warbler.
Hodgson.
The Sheaves. Robinson.
The Sod-Breaker. Stringer.
Spring in England. Going.
The Water-Witch. Perry.
A Wave of Coldness.
Yosano Akiko.
When I Held You to My
Chest, You Fit. Myers.
Why the Robin's Breast Was
Red. Randall.
Will You Be as Hard?
Gregory.
Winter. Wingfield.
Thrall (dom)
The Arraignment of a Lover.
Gascoigne.
Ballade to Rosamund.
Chaucer.
Behold with Joy.
Winchester.
A Cause for Wonder.
Anonymous.
I Bind My Heart. Watt.
The One Lost. Rosenberg.
Our Lady's Salutation.
Southwell.
A Vision of Judgement.
Southey.
Thrash (ing)
Nine Inch Will Please a Lady.
Burns.
The Pike. Bruce.
There Are in Such Moments.
Silverstein.
Thread (s)
Across Space and Time.
Olson.
Between the Walls of the
Valley. Peck.
Departure. Hitchcock.
February. Heath-Stubbs.
Gemini Elegy. Gibson.
In the Dusk the Path. Izumi
Shikibu.
Leave the Thread with God.
Anonymous.
The Lover's Gifts.
Anonymous.
Maintenance. Sarah.

My Lady Takes the Sunlight
for Her Gown. Cole.
My Thread. Hofstein.
Nevertheless. Moore.
Rear Vision. Smith.
Rebirth. Stamp.
The Red Thread of Honor.
Doyle.
Riddle: "There is one that has
a head without an eye."
Rossetti.
Sister Songs (excerpt).
Thompson.
Sleep-Walking Child.
Eybers.
Song of a Prison Guard.
Mphande.
A Spool of Thread.
Eastman.
Threadbare
The Crowd. Masefield.
Threat (en) (s)
The Apparition. Donne.
The Impious Feast. Landor.
Landscape. Purdy.
On a Piece of Unwrought
Pipeclay. Bryant.
The Pity of Love. Yeats.
The Seventies. Beyer.
Varitalk. Holbrook.
Three
After a Death. Orr.
Amoretti, LXXIV. Spenser.
The Art of Cookery. King.
The Ashland Tragedy, II.
Anonymous.
Baudelaire. Schwartz.
Bell Horses, Bell Horses,
What Time of Day?
Mother Goose.
Bird Riddle: "One day I went
down in the golden harvest
field." *Anonymous.*
Bold Adventures of Captain
Ross. *Anonymous.*
Cantemus Cuncti Melodum.
Notker Balbulus.
Cape Ann. *Anonymous.*
A Christmas Childhood.
Kavanagh.
Cocoon. McCord.
The Collier's March.
Anonymous.
The Duke of Athole's Nurse
(A version). *Anonymous.*
Eight O'Clock. Rossetti.
An Elder's Reproof to His
Wife. Muuse.
Flannan Isle. Gibson.
Fly in December. Wallace.
Gets Hung up on a Dirty, of
All Things, Joke (parody).
Taylor.
Give Me Three Grains of
Corn, Mother. Edwards.
The Great Summons. Chu
Yuan.
How Robin Hood Rescued
the Widow's Sons.
Anonymous.
I Am the captain of the
Pinafore. Gilbert.
I Love a Flower. Philipps.
I picked up my mother.
Ishikawa Takuboku.
I Went My Sunday Mornings
Rounds. Clare.
Isabelle (parody). Hogg.
Johnson's Motor Car.
Anonymous.

Lady Isabel and the Elf
Knight (H version).
Anonymous.
Laudate for Christmas.
Prudentius (Aurelius
Clemens Prudentius).
Limerick: "There was an old
man of Three Bridges."
Lear.
A Literary Squabble.
Planché.
Little Brother. Fisher.
March 23, 1982 Tuesday
Night. Waltner.
The Meanings in the Pattern.
Grahn.
Nansen. Snyder.
Narcissus in a Cocktail Glass.
Howard.
Of All the Men. Moore.
The Old Woman Who Bought
a Pig. *Anonymous.*
On Being Sixty. Po Chu-i.
Our Clock. Eakman.
The Outlandish Knight.
Anonymous.
Poem: "We are such stuff as
dreams are made of."
Hofmannsthal.
The Poet Loves a Mistress,
But Not to Marry.
Herrick.
Prayer for the Speedy End of
Three Great Misfortunes.
O'Connor.
Riddle: "The fiddler and his
wife." *Anonymous.*
Riddle: "There were three
sisters in a hall."
Anonymous.
Robin Hood and the Widow's
Three Sons. *Anonymous.*
Robin Hood's Delight.
Anonymous.
Roses. *Anonymous.*
Rub-a-Dub-Dub. Mother
Goose.
The Search. Crosby.
A Seat for Three: Written on
a Settle. Crane.
The Shade-Seller. Jacobsen.
Sky links cloud waves. Li
Ch'ing-chao.
Sleeping Heroes. Shanks.
The Snake. Suknaski.
Song about Whiskers.
Wodehouse.
A Song in Time of Order
1852. Swinburne.
A Stanza on Freedom.
Lowell.
Stanzas on Freedom. Lowell.
The Start. *Anonymous.*
Take Me Out to the Ball
Game. Norworth.
Thanksgiving, 1963. Kazan.
This Pretty Woman.
Anonymous.
Three Loves. Hooper.
A Toast. Stetler.
Valentine Browne. O
Rathaille.
When a Fellow's Four. Carr.
When a Goose Meets a
Moose. Gay.
Willie Brew'd a Peck o' Maut.
Burns.
With a Rod No Man Alive.
Walther von der
Vogelweide.
The Woodspurge. Rossetti.

The Young Gray Head.
Southey.
Young Training. McGaugh.
Threshold (s)
The Dispossessed. Kinsella.
Elegy for Drowned Children.
Dawe.
For Simone Weil. Sister M.
Therese.
The Gulistan. Sa'di.
Home. Gibson.
The Porch. Thomas.
Protest in Passing. Speyer.
Sun in the East. *Anonymous.*
A Triad. Rossetti.
West-Easterly Divan, IX
(excerpt). Goethe.
A Wish for Waving Goodbye.
Hill.
Thrill (ed) (ing) (s)
Buildings. Gioseffi.
The Door-Bell. Becker.
The Doorstep. Stedman.
The Fleet at Santiago.
Russell.
Holy Was Demeter Walking
th' Corn Furrow. Sanders.
In the Heart of the Hills...
Anonymous.
Living. *Anonymous.*
Martyrdom. Learsi.
The Mosquito. Jones.
My Heart Stood Still. Hart.
Shut Not Your Doors.
Whitman.
Song of the Corsairs. Byron.
Sonnets–Actualities.
Cummings.
There's No Lust Like to
Poetry. *Anonymous.*
To Certain Critics. Cullen.
Thrive (d) (s)
Asolando. Browning.
Epitaph for a Negro Woman.
Dodson.
He That Would Thrive.
Anonymous.
Madrigal Macabre.
Hoffenstein.
The Orb Weaver. Weaver.
Promises Like Pie-Crust.
Rossetti.
Transitional Poem. Day.
A Warning. *Anonymous.*
Throat (s)
Alternatives. Amis.
The Boar. Kelly.
Burial at Sea. Pratt.
Butterfly. Armstrong.
Cancion. Levertov.
Corner Lot. Bryan.
Cuchulain Comforted. Yeats.
A Curse on Mine-Owners.
Anonymous.
Destiny of the Poet. Vigee.
Doe. Dow.
Don Juan. Byron.
The Drenching Night Drags
On. O Rathaille.
An Early Bluebird.
Thompson.
Edge. Fitzgerald.
Epigrams. Martial (Marcus
Valerius Martialis).
Faustus. Hope.
Gary Gotow. Uba.
Gift. Hemschemeyer.
Going Back Again. Lytton.
A Hand of Solo. Kinsella.
Hieroglyph. Auster.
Honeysuckle. Paul.

The Horse Wrangler.
  O'Malley.
Lady of Shrouding Hair.
  Anonymous.
The Legion Club (excerpt).
  Swift.
Like to These Unmeasurable
  Mountains. Wyatt.
The Little Black Dog Ran
  Round the House.
  Anonymous.
The Little Ones' A.B.C.
  Coward.
Lupus in Fabula. Lowry.
Madrigal: "Pretty wantons,
  sweetly sing." *Anonymous.*
A Man of Action. Stetler.
Meditation. Rakosi.
The Mocking-Bird. Hayes.
Mother. Heaney.
Negro Spiritual. Trott.
Observation at Dawn.
  Kovner.
On an Upright Judge. Swift.
Othello. Shakespeare.
A Penguin. Herford.
Pretty Wantons. *Anonymous.*
Prisoner's Song. Gregory.
Real Old Mountain Dew.
  Anonymous.
The Room of My Life.
  Sexton.
Snow-Bound. Whittier
St. Julien's Eve: For Dennis
  Cross. Cunningham.
This Place in the Ways.
  Rukeyser.
To My Father. Curtis.
To the Boston Women.
  Anonymous.
The Truth the Dead Know.
  Sexton.
Vision by Sweetwater.
  Ransom.
Winter Swan. Bogan.
Your Back Is Rough.
  Atwood.

Throb (bing) (s)
Departure. Strong.
Hand Saw. Funkhouser.
I Found Her Out There.
  Hardy.
The Poet's Harvesting.
  O'Malley.
Psychology Today. Jerome.
The Secret Love. Russell.
Sonnet in the Mail Coach.
  Taylor.

Throne (s)
Ah! Give Me, LORD, the
  Single Eye. Toplady.
Alley Blues. Holmes.
At Florence. Wordsworth.
Autumn. Tagore.
Before the Anaesthetic; or, A
  Real Fright. Betjeman.
The Blackbird by Belfast
  Lough. *Anonymous.*
C. G. Jung's First Years.
  Kinsella.
Carol. *Anonymous.*
Charlie Rutledge.
  Anonymous.
The City in the Sea. Poe.
Cradle and Throne.
  Anonymous.
Cross and Throne. Bonar.
The Destiny of Nations.
  Coleridge.
The Dream of the Rood.
  Anonymous.
The Excursion. Wordsworth.

Exiles. Russell.
Failure. Brooke.
George the Third. Byron.
Great Lord of All, Whose
  Work of Love. Duche.
Heavens Bright Lamp, Shine
  Forth Some of Thy Light.
  Alsop.
Hospital. Funk.
A Hundred Years from Now.
  Ford.
I Heard Immanuel Singing.
  Lindsay.
The Iliad. Homer.
The King of Kings.
  Woodrum.
The Lake: Coda. Clark.
The Lost Leader. Browning.
M-Y T-E-M-P-E-R.
  Anonymous.
The Maiden City. Tonna.
Mary, Queen of Scots. Bell.
Maud. Tennyson.
Molly Moor. Farewell.
Ne Plus Ultra. Coleridge.
Old Grimes. Greene.
The Paradox. *Anonymous.*
The Plougher. Colum.
Red Jacket. Halleck.
The Return. Fields.
The Scarlet Tanager.
  Benton.
Secret Prayer. Belle.
Sesostris. Mifflin.
Shakespeare. Longfellow.
The Sovereigns. Mifflin.
These Things I Do
  Remember. Solomon ben
  Aaron.
To Aaron Burr, under Trial
  for High Treason.
  Morton.
To My Friend, Dr. Charleton,
  on His Learned and Useful
  Works. Dryden.
The Value of Dentistry.
  Brown.
Vision of Belshazzar. Byron.
What Is Charm? Thomas.
What Is White? Macdonagh.
William Blake. Thomson.

Throng
The American Patriot's
  Prayer. *Anonymous.*
Beauty and the Bird.
  Rossetti.
Civil Elegies (excerpt). Lee.
The Crowning of Dreaming
  John. Drinkwater.
Hustle and Grin.
  Anonymous.
Ode: On the Death of William
  Butler Yeats. Smith.
On the Death of Squire
  Christopher, a Remarkably
  Fat Sportsman. Wigson.
Song of Texas. Hosmer.
To Usward. Bennett.
We Whom the Dead Have
  Not Forgiven. Field.
What Would I Do without
  This World Faceless
  Incurious. Beckett.
Zito the Magician. Holub.

Throw (n)
Boomerang. Perreault.
Doubt. Jackson.
First to Throw a Stone.
  Anonymous.
Four Translations from the
  English of Robert Hershon.
  Hershon.

If So the Man You Are.
  Lewis.
The Legend of Paper Plates.
  Haines.
Love's Pains. Clare.
Machupuchare. What the
  Mountain Said. Shaking the
  Dead Bones... Stroud.
Markings. Steele.
The Old Man Said. Arnett.
The Origin of Baseball.
  Patchen.
Our English Gamesters Scorne
  to Stake. Williams.
The Slave's Dream.
  Longfellow.
Summer. Asch.
Three Poems about Children.
  Clarke.
To Make an Amblongus Pie.
  Lear.
Upon the King's Voyage to
  Chatham.... *Anonymous.*
Wake Up, Jacob.
  Anonymous.

Thrush (es)
The Bride. Lawrence.
David Ap Gwillam's Mass of
  the Birds. Colum.
Four Stories. Shapiro.
The Green Roads. Thomas.
Happy Were He. Essex.
Inspiration. Knox.
Judas Iscariot. Mason.
The King's Ballad. Kilmer.
My Thrush. Collins.
Old Woman. Pastan.
The Relic. Hillyer.
The Squire of Low Degree
  (excerpt). *Anonymous.*
To Cheer Our Minds.
  Ronksley.
Unless We Guard Them Well.
  Merchant.
Yonosa House. Smith.

Thrust
Bear Hunting. Aua.
The Knight in Disguise.
  Lindsay.
The Lass of Lochroyan.
  Anonymous
Restoration. Spears.
Say That We Saw Spain Die.
  Millay.
Sextains. Baylebridge.

Thucydides
In Humbleness. Hoffman.

Thud
The Last Flight of the Great
  Wallenda. Hyett.
Separation. Savage.

Thule
Dream-Land. Poe.
Lament. Drummond.

Thumb (s)
The Cigarette. Laforgue.
Commercial Traveller.
  Edmond.
Curses. Duemer.
Epitaph for the Race of Man.
  Millay.
Father Greybeard.
  Anonymous.
How Do You Spell
  "Missile"?: Preliminary
  Instructions... Uba.
How One-Thumb Willie Got
  His Name. Sellers.
Passage. Roderick.
Pity Poor Labourers.
  Anonymous.
Trench Poets. Rickword.

Thumbnails
On When McCarthy Was a
  Wolf among a Nation of
  Queer-Queers. Dugan.

Thump (s)
Clams. Moss.
Drum-Taps. Whitman.
Limerick: "There was a
  composer named Bong."
  Anonymous.
Power to the People.
  Nemerov.
To a Loudmouth Pontificator.
  Mizer.
Treaty-Trip from Shulus
  Reservation. Lane.
Washing Day. *Anonymous.*

Thunder (ed) (s)
Africa. Naude.
And So the Day Drops By.
  Tuckerman.
Andromeda. Browning.
The Black Vulture. Sterling.
Brooklyn Bridge at Dawn.
  Le Gallienne.
By the Sea. Wordsworth.
Caesar. Valery.
Clabe Mott. Still.
Conflict. Fitzell.
Dan Dunder. Ciardi.
Dawn on the Headland.
  Watson.
Death for the Dark Stranger.
  McGrath.
Direction. Hill.
The Double Axe.
  Hazlewood-Brady.
Dream Songs. Berryman.
Europa. Plomer.
The Everlastings. Dubie.
Flushing Meadows, 1939.
  Hoffman.
The Fourth of July.
  Pierpont.
The Genius of Death. Croly.
Giving the Moon a New
  Chance. Stokes.
The Hag. Herrick.
The Higher Pantheism.
  Tennyson.
Hiram Powers' "Greek Slave."
  Browning.
I Went Out into the Garden.
  Ibn Ezra.
In the Catacombs. Ballard.
In the Children's Hospital.
  ""MacDiarmid.
Instructions to a Celebrated
  Laureat (excerpt). Wolcot.
Instructions to a Painter.
  Waller.
The Labors of Thor.
  Wagoner.
Laus Veneris. Swinburne.
A Letter. Ridler.
My Mother, Who Came from
  China, Where She Never
  Saw Snow. Mar.
New York in August. Davie.
The Odyssey. Lang.
Over and Under. Smith.
Pancho Villa. Lipsitz.
Paradox. Miller.
Precursors. MacNeice.
Rain on the Cumberlands.
  Still.
Rapture. George.
Rise, Ye Children. Falckner.
Romance. Henley.
Song of the Thunder.
  Anonymous.

Spirit of Freedom, Thou Dost
  Love the Sea. Dodge.
Thunder Pools. Coffin.
A Time of Turquoise.
  Volborth.
To Germany. Sorley.
The Tree of Rivelin. Elliott.
Views of the Favorite
  Colleges. Brinnin.
La Vita Nuova. Kees.
Walleye. Hoey.
Wesley in Heaven. Brown.
What Could Be Lovelier Than
  to Hear. Coatsworth.
The Wild Geese. Morse.
Year's End. Antoninus.
Thunderbolt (s)
The Eagle. Tennyson.
Farragut. Meredith.
The Flaming Terrapin.
  Campbell.
Make Way! Negri.
The Suez Crisis. *Anonymous.*
Thyme
Concertmaster. Burgin.
The Posy of Thyme.
  Anonymous.
Sleeping at Last. Rossetti.
Thyme. *Anonymous.*
Thyself
Arcadia. Sidney.
As I Walked By My Self.
  Anonymous.
The Counsel. Brome.
An Essay on Man. Pope.
Hail, Thou Head! Bernard of
  Clairvaux.
The Latest Decalogue.
  Clough.
Ode to Beauty. Emerson.
Prayer. Stevenson.
Self-Knowledge. Coleridge.
To Shakespeare. Day.
Trust Only Yourself.
  Anonymous.
Virgil's Farewell to Dante.
  Binyon.
Tick (ing)
The Big Clock. *Anonymous.*
The Busy Body. Field.
Cinderella. Plath.
Kaddish. Ginsberg.
Recall. Whittemore.
Similes. *Anonymous.*
Time Passes. Lister.
To Judith Asleep. Ciardi.
White Serpent. Sachs.
The Widow Perez. Soto.
Ticket (s)
Back to Dublin. Ford.
How to Walk in a Crowd.
  Hershon.
Mexico City Hand Game.
  Green.
The Rock Island Line.
  Anonymous.
The Traveler. Bottoms.
Tickle
Ardor. Bradford.
Belsnickel. Guiterman.
Building Society Blues.
  Roughton.
Contentment. Johnson.
Epigrams. Theocritus.
An Old Maid, an Old Maid.
  Anonymous.
A Westminster Wedding.
  Anonymous.
Tide (s)
The Absinthe-Drinker.
  Symons.

Address to Children.
  Anonymous.
Age. Jones.
The Alliance of Education
  and Govenment. Gray.
Am Driven Mad. Polite.
Arrival and Departure.
  Eglington.
The Autumnal Moon.
  Thomson.
The Book of Day-Dreams.
  Moore.
The Borough. Crabbe.
Caedmon. Nicholson.
Cities Drowned. Newbolt.
Continent's End. Jeffers.
Craqueodoom. Riley.
Cuchulains's Fight with the
  Sea. Yeats.
The Dead Knight. Masefield.
The Distances. Carroll.
Domestic Quarrel.
  McInerney.
Donald. Abbey.
Dream Songs. Berryman.
Ebb. Donaghy.
The Estuary. Pitter.
The Fall. Raine.
Fields Where We Slept.
  Rukeyser.
The Fisherman. Bruce.
Freighter. Ruddick.
George Washington.
  Ingham.
Give No White Flower.
  Chamberlain.
Growing Gray. Dobson.
Haiku: "Seaweed..." Kito.
The Home Front. Bell.
Hunger Strike. Franklin.
Icarus. Bottrall.
Just as the Tide Was A-
  Flowing. *Anonymous.*
Juvenal's Tenth Satire
  Translated (excerpt).
  Vaughan.
Liberation. Mark.
The Logs. Roberts.
Lucy Answers. Ehrlich.
The Masque of Queen Bersabe
  (excerpt). Swinburne.
My Language. Politzer.
North of Berwick.
  Tremayne.
Nursery Rhyme: "Yellow-
  belly, yellow-belly, come
  and take a swim."
  Anonymous.
Ode on Advancing Age.
  Dixon.
Off Banks Peninsula. Glover.
Old Woman of Beare.
  Anonymous.
On the American Rivers.
  Smith.
The Phantom Horsewoman.
  Hardy.
The Pilot's Day of Rest.
  Gerlach.
Proud New York. Reed.
Psalm to My Beloved.
  Tietjens.
The Ritual. Pratt.
Sandstone. Marriott.
Sea Flower. Dorcey.
The Shipwreck. Falconer.
Song: "Where in blind files."
  Boland.
Sonnet at Dover Cliffs.
  Bowles.

Sonnet Suppos'd to Be
  Written at Lemnos.
  Russell.
The St. Lawrence and the
  Saguenay: The Thousand
  Islands. Sangster.
Stone Giant. Bruchac.
Summer Storm. Montague.
Ticking Clocks. Field.
The Tide in the River.
  Farjeon.
Tide Turning. Nims.
Time and Tide. Lamarre.
To William Sharp. Scollard.
The Town of Passage.
  Anonymous.
Trouvaille. Murphy.
The Waning of the Harvest
  Moon. Wieners.
The Water-Lily. Tabb.
Tidings
Annette Myers; or, A Murder
  in St. James's Park.
  Anonymous.
Aspiration. Thomson.
The Dolphin's Return.
  Anonymous.
The Excursion. Wordsworth.
Fleet Street. Leslie.
Henry Martyn. *Anonymous.*
The Light in the Temple.
  Benet.
Marmion. Scott.
The Smallest Angel. Binns.
Summer Is Gone.
  Anonymous.
Th' Almighty Spake, and
  Gabriel Sped. Richards.
Tidy
Epitaph: "Here lie my
  husbands One Two Three."
  Anonymous.
It Was All Very Tidy.
  Graves.
Tie (d)
As I Was Standing in the
  Street. *Anonymous.*
Barbara Allen. *Anonymous.*
The Bonnie Cravat. Mother
  Goose.
The Evans Country. Amis.
The Exile of Erin.
  Anonymous.
Hot Line. Dunann.
I wanted to see you.
  Miccolis.
Othello Jones Dresses for
  Dinner. Roberson.
Towser Shall Be Tied Tonight.
  Anonymous.
Tiger-lily
Intermezzo: At Glan-Y-Wern.
  Symons.
Song: A Spirit Haunts the
  Year's Last Hours.
  Tennyson.
Tiger (s)
Ceremony. Wilbur.
Cupid. O'Dowd.
Disillusionment of Ten
  O'Clock. Stevens.
Euroclydon. Evans.
Growing Up. Behn.
The Gulistan. Sa'di.
Here She Is. Miller.
The Hermit. Davies.
In the Field. Janik.
India. Turner.
The Kiss. O'Gorman.
Lament of the Frontier
  Guard. Li Po.

The Last of the Grand Old
  Masters. Patey.
Limerick: "There was a young
  lady of Riga."
  Anonymous.
The Mimshi Maiden.
  McCrae.
Mr. Hughes. Campbell.
Of Iron Am I. *Anonymous.*
Paper Words. Franklin.
Sad Day in Berlin. Kirsch.
Tiger. *Anonymous.*
The Train Runs Late to
  Harlem. Rivers.
The Way of Cape Race.
  Pratt.
Where's the Poet? Keats.
Tight
Angel. Skelton.
Handlining Tockers &
  Gizmos. Planz.
One-Line Poems from a New
  Statesman Competition.
  Southgate.
The Painters.
  Hemschemeyer.
The Perforated Spirit.
  Bishop.
Tailor. Farjeon.
The Yarn of the "Nancy Bell'.
  Gilbert.
Tightrope
The Circus. Kaplan.
Reflections. Smith.
Tiles
Ku Li. Hyde.
My Six Toothbrushes.
  McGinley.
The Pell Mell Celebrated.
  Gay.
Tilt (ing)
Beetle on the Shasta Daylight.
  Kaufman.
Mater Dei. Fallon.
Perfect. ""MacDiarmid.
Running. Wilbur.
Timber (s)
Air Is. Brennan.
The Ritual. Pratt.
Timber. Jerry the Mule.
When the Drive Goes Down.
  Malloch.
Time (s)
Absence. Kemble.
The Advice. Sackville.
Advice to the Same. Sidney.
After Reading Nelly Sachs.
  Pastan.
After the War. Le Gallienne.
An Afternoon in the Garden.
  Edmond.
Aging. Jarrell.
The Alarm. Jacob.
Allalu Mo Wauleen (The
  Beggar's Address to His
  Bag). *Anonymous.*
Allegory of the Adolescent
  and the Adult. Barker.
Almanac Verse. Danforth.
Along Shore. Bashford.
Amoretti, LXX. Spenser.
An Ancient to Ancients.
  Hardy.
Another Time. Auden.
Anti-Love Poems. Brewster.
The Antiquary. Chapt. 10:
  Why Sit'st Thou by That
  Ruin'd Hall. Scott.
Approaching America.
  Squire.
Armistice Day. Freeman.
The Art of Picasso. Dali.

The Artist. Ralegh.
As Long as the Heart Beats.
  Zawadiwsky.
Ashore. Hope.
Ask of the Sun. Zukofsky.
Aspects. MacCaig.
At Casterbridge Fair.
  Hardy.
At Lincoln. Adams.
Audiences. Hollander.
Autumn Twilight. Regnier.
Awake, Awake! Campion.
Awakening. Robinson.
Ay or Nay? Schomberg.
A Backwards Journey. Page.
The Ballad of Nat Turner.
  Hayden.
Ballad of the Despairing
  Husband. Creeley.
The Barber. Fuller.
Be Still. Kline.
Beetle Bemused. Lister.
Behind the Stove. Hearst.
Beside the Blackwater.
  O'Conor.
Between the Tides.
  Councilman.
Between Two Furious Oceans.
  Diespecker.
The Black Ball Line.
  Anonymous.
Black Boy. Rosten.
Blow the Man Down.
  Anonymous.
Blue Sleigh. Scott.
The Book of Persephone.
  Kelly.
Bread. "Mistral.
Brief Farewell. Delius.
Buckingham Palace. Milne.
Bugger Burns. Anonymous.
The Buke of the Howlat.
  Holland.
Burbank with a Baedeker:
  Bleistein with a Cigar.
  Eliot.
By the North Sea.
  Swinburne.
Cadenus and Vanessa
  (excerpt). Swift.
Caelica, XXCII. Greville.
Caelica, LXXXII. Greville.
Caelica, CIX. Greville.
Cat's Eyes. Scarfe.
Child with Shell. Everson.
Christ, the Man. Davies.
Christian, Be Up. Nathan.
Christmas Bills. Hatton.
Clandestine Work. Goll.
Clock-a-clay. Clare.
Closing Cadence. Moffit.
The Coach of Time.
  Pushkin.
Coastline. Feinstein.
A Cold Night. Spencer.
Come Turn to Mee, Thou
  Pretty Little One.
  Anonymous.
Concertmaster. Burgin.
Confession of a Glutton.
  Marquis.
Conversation with Rain.
  Gunn.
Corona. Celan.
Counting. Sandburg.
The Country Clergy.
  Thomas.
Crossing with the Light.
  Okita.
Dead on the War Path.
  Anonymous.

Dear Mrs. McKinney of the
  Sixth Grade:. Kherdian.
Death of a Vermont Farm
  Woman. Howes.
The Divine Narcissus. Juana
  Ines de la Cruz.
The Divine Tragedy: The Fate
  of the Prophets.
  Longfellow.
Domus Caedet Arborem.
  Mew.
The Doomed City. Poe.
Doralicia's Song. Graves.
Down by the Old Mill
  Stream. Read.
Driving to Town Late to Mail
  a Letter. Bly.
Drop Me the Seed.
  Masefield.
The Dumbfounding. Avison.
The Dynasts. Hardy.
Ear Is Not Deaf. Dayton.
Early Dutch. Palen.
"Earth's Holocaust."
  Schuyler.
An Easter Carol. Rossetti.
The Enigma Variations.
  Petrie.
Epitaph on a Dormouse,
  Which Some Children Were
  to Bury. Anonymous.
Epitaphs of the War, 1914-18.
  Kipling.
Epithalamion. Spenser.
Escape. Jones.
Essay on Memory.
  Fitzgerald.
Esthetique du Mal. Stevens.
The Evening-Watch.
  Vaughan.
Everybody Eats Too Much
  Anyhow. Nash.
Evolution. Smith.
Expectation. Stanley.
The Eye of Humility. Smith.
Fable. Mills.
Fable XIII: Plutus, Cupid,
  and Time. Gay.
The Fairies' Farewell.
  Corbet.
Faith Healing. Larkin.
Fall Wind. Stafford.
Family Prime. Van Doren.
Faust. Goethe.
La Fayette. Madison.
Fidelity. Stickney.
Finding a Poem. Merriam.
Fire and Ice. Pettit.
First Spring Morning.
  Bridges.
The First Time Ever I Saw
  Your Face. MacColl.
Five Visions of Captain Cook.
  Slessor.
Flesh. Fullerton.
The Flowing Summer.
  Bruce.
The Flying Change. Taylor.
For Kinte. La Grone.
For My Grandfather. Webb.
For Nicholas, Born in
  September. Perry.
For Righteousness' Sake.
  Whittier.
The Fortress. Sexton.
Four Quartets. Eliot.
Four Translations from the
  English of Robert Hershon.
  Hershon.
The Fourth Dimension.
  Nathan.
The Fox. Hesketh.

The Future. Benedikt.
The Gar. Bell.
George. Randall.
Georgia Towns. Hicky.
The Georgiad (excerpt).
  Campbell.
Girl Friday. Equi.
The God of War. Brecht.
Gold Watch. Kavanagh.
The Grand Duke of New
  York. Pagis.
Graphemics (excerpt).
  Spicer.
The Grave. Tchernichovsky.
Great God, Preserver of All
  Things. Pastorius.
Green Mountain Boy.
  Smyth.
The Grey Wolf. Symons.
Growing Gray. Dobson.
The Gude and Godlie Ballatis:
  The Reid in the Loch Sayis.
  Anonymous.
Guide to the Ruins.
  Nemerov.
Hamlet. Shakespeare.
Harry Pearce. Campbell.
The Harvest Waits. Mifflin.
Heart. LaBombard.
Heaven in Ordinarie. Wolff.
Here Lies... Smith.
High Wonders (parody).
  Marks.
Homage to Sextus Propertius,
  VII. Pound.
How It Strikes a
  Contemporary. Browning.
Humanity. Dixon.
The Hunt. Deutsch.
The Hurrier. Monro.
I am furious with myself.
  Tio.
I Am Like a Book. Rokeah.
I Am the Way. Meynell.
I Done Got So Thirsty That
  My Mouth Waters at the
  Thought of Rain. Jones.
I Feel Like My Time Ain't
  Long. Anonymous.
I Like Christmas. Tippett.
I Sing America Now! Stuart.
I Was Fair Beat. "Garioch.
Idyll of the Rose. Ausonius.
If It Be True. Johnson.
An Image from Beckett.
  Mahon.
Impiety (excerpt). Margaret.
In a Poem. Frost.
In Death's Field. Al-
  Khansa.
In Distrust of Merits.
  Moore.
In Old Tucson. Conrard.
In Rama. Townsend.
In Time. Graves.
In Time Like Glass. Turner.
In Wonted Walks. Sidney.
The Incomparable Light.
  Eberhart.
Indictment. Ritter.
An Introduction to Some
  Poems. Stafford.
The Inverted Torch.
  Thomas.
Irish-American Dignitary.
  Clarke.
It's a Long Way.
  Braithwaite.
Jobson's Amen. Kipling.
John Garner's Trail Herd.
  Anonymous.

The Journey to Golgotha.
  Rao.
The Kicking Mule.
  Anonymous.
The Lamentation of the Old
  Pensioner. Yeats.
Last Letter to Pablo.
  Lowther.
Last Verses. Motherwell.
Leaves of Grass. Whitman
Legend. Wheelock.
Leisure. Davies.
Let Erin Remember the Days
  of Old. Moore.
Life's Testament.
  Baylebridge.
Lifelong. Boimwall.
LII. Berrigan.
Like an Adventurous Sea-
  Farer Am I. Drayton.
Limerick: "There was a trim
  maiden named Wood."
  Lockwood.
Lines. Martin.
Listen. Patterson.
Little Steamboat. Williams.
Lives of the Saints.
  Anderson.
Living in the Moment.
  Hacker.
Looking at Quilts. Piercy.
Love's Language.
  MacDonagh.
Love's Remorse. Muir.
Lutea Allison. Suckling.
Macdonald's Raid. Hayne.
Madaket Beach. Barr.
Make Way. Lavoie.
The Man from the Top of the
  Mind. Wagoner.
The Man's Prayer. Daly.
March Twilight. Bogan.
Marcus Antoninus Cui
  Cognomen Erat Aurelius.
  Singer.
Marrakech. Eberhart.
Mary on Her Way to the
  Temple. Schaumann.
Mary's Girlhood. Rossetti.
Maud Muller Mutatur
  (parody). Adams.
May-June, 1940. Jeffers.
Memory. Rossetti.
Merlin. Muir.
Milton. Blake.
A Miltonic Sonnet for Mr.
  Johnson... Wilbur.
Mine Old Dear Enemy, My
  Froward Master. Petrarch
  (Francesco Petrarca).
Mockingbird in Winter.
  Kroll.
A Moment Please. Allen.
Monkshood XXIII.
  Gunnars.
Moonlight. Harjo.
The More Loving One.
  Auden.
Movement Song. Lorde.
Mutations: Midsummer.
  Fitzgerald.
Mye Love Toke Skorne My
  Servise to Retaine. Wyatt.
The Mystery of Emily
  Dickinson. Bell.
Nahant. Emerson.
Near the Ocean. Lowell.
Night Light. Willard.
A Night Vigil in the Left
  Court of the Palace. Tu
  Fu.
No Time. Tiller.

Nocturne, Central Park South. Sissman.
The Noodle-Vendor's Flute. Enright.
North Labrador. Crane.
Northward. Lepore.
Not Saying Much. Gregg.
O Day of Light and Gladness. Hosmer.
October 1803. Wordsworth.
Of a Contented Mind. Vaux.
Of an Old Song. Lecky.
The Old Couple, III, i: Love's Prime. May.
Old Damon's Pastoral. Lodge.
Old Mortality. Scott.
Old Woman Awaiting the Greyhound Bus. Niatum.
On Ascending a Hill Leading to a Convent. Mello.
On the Death of a Nightingale. Randolph.
On the Defeat of Henry Clay. Lord.
On the Duke of Buckingham. Shirley.
On Time with God. Nutter.
On Two Brothers. Simonides (of Ceos).
Open Dream Sequence. Sanchez.
Our Backs Are to the Cypress. Goldberg.
A Palinode. Greene.
The Pancake Collector. Prelutsky.
The Paradox of Time. Ronsard.
Partings. Jewsbury.
The Party. Dunbar.
A Pastoral. Hillyer.
The Pedigree of Honey. Dickinson.
Pedra. Burgon.
Pennsylvania Places. Daly.
The Perfect Gift. Parker.
Phyllis. *Anonymous.*
Pictures from Brueghel. Williams.
The Pilot in the Jungle. Ciardi.
Player. Dunning.
A Plea for Haste. Petronius Arbiter (Caius Petronius Arbiter).
Poem for My Thirty-Second Birthday. Ciardi.
Poem for Vladimir. Ripley.
Poem in the Matukituki Valley. Baxter.
Poem of the Mother. Sklarew.
Poem: "This room is very old and very wise." Harrison.
Poems. Drummond.
The Poet. Day-Lewis.
Poet. Emerson.
The Poet Laments the Coming of Old Age. Sitwell.
The Poet's Song to His Wife. Procter.
Poetry. O'Hara.
Poets. Akenside.
Poll Star. Lamport.
Polly Oliver's Rambles. *Anonymous.*
The Pool. Creeley.
The Poolhall. Burt.
Portrait. Bogan.
Postscript, on a Name. Ratcliffe.

Prayer by Moonlight. Swartz.
A Prayer for Rivers. Wilson.
Prescription of Painful Ends. Jeffers.
The Prism. Pinkerton.
Process of time worketh such wonder. Wyatt.
De Profundis Clamavi. Baudelaire.
The Progress of Dulness. Trumbull.
Psalm. Heimler.
Pyramus and Thisbe. Dakin.
The Queen's Song. Flecker.
The Quiet Light of Flies. Zach.
Quod Tegit Omnia. Winters.
Raccoon Poem. Palmer.
The Rape of Lucrece. Shakespeare.
Rapunzel Song. Meyer.
The Rebellious Vine. Monro.
Recollection. Mumford.
Recollections of "Lalla Rookh." Trowbridge.
Relativity. Millay.
Remembering Apple Times. Hitchner.
Reminiscences of a Day: Wicklow. O'Donnell.
The Respite. Bachmann.
Rest O Sun I Cannot. Tusiani.
Retreat. Bushnell.
Reunion. Cadsby.
Riddle: "There was a man rode through our town." *Anonymous.*
Right Now. Stafford.
The Ringers. Peck.
The Rite. Dale.
The River. Welch.
The River God. Sitwell.
Rivulose. Ammons.
The Robin. Scott.
Roll, Johnny Booger. *Anonymous.*
Rome. Du Bellay.
Rome, Conqueror, Conquered. Sylvester.
Roof Garden. Schuyler.
The Rubaiyat of Omar Khayyam. Omar Khayyam.
Rural Simplicity. Byron.
The Sakiyeh. Blind.
The Santa Barbara Earthquake. *Anonymous.*
Satires. Alamanni.
Satires. Wyatt.
Scel Lem Duib. *Anonymous.*
The Seafarer. *Anonymous.*
The Second Life. Morgan.
The Secular Masque. Dryden.
Self-Portrait in a Convex Mirror. Ashbery.
A Short Winter Tale. Zach.
The Sighing Time. Blunden.
So, So. Clerke.
Sometimes I Go to Camarillo & Sit in the Lounge. Lyle.
The Song against Grocers. Chesterton.
Song: "How many times do I love thee, dear?" Beddoes.
A Song of Greatness. Austin.
Song Set by John Dowland: "What poor astronomers are they." *Anonymous.*

Song Set by Robert Jones: "She whose matchless beauty staineth." *Anonymous.*
Song: "Sweet are the Charms of her I love." Booth.
Sonnet: "So shoots a star as doth my mistress glide." Davies.
Sonnet: To Guido Cavalcanti. Dante Alighieri.
Sonnets. Tuckerman.
Sonnets, LX: "Like as the waves make towards the pebbled shore." Shakespeare.
Sonnets, C: "Where art thou, Muse, that thou forget'st so long." Shakespeare.
Sonnets of a Portrait Painter. Ficke.
Space and Time. Scroggie.
Spring Signs. Field.
Stevenson's Birthday. Miller.
Stop a Minute! *Anonymous.*
The Sun. Oerke.
Sunday Afternoons. Thwaite.
Sunday Morning, King's Cambridge. Betjeman.
Sweet William and May Marg'ret. Anonymous.
Systole and Diastole. Aiken.
The Temper of Aristippus. Cooper.
Tenth Symphony. Ashbery.
Thais. Levy.
That the Night Come. Yeats.
Theme Brown Girl. Hill-Abu Ishak.
There Are Delicacies. Birney.
There Is Yet Time. Steece.
These People. Corning.
They Grow Up Too Fast, She Said. O Hehir.
This Solitude of Cataracts. Stevens.
This Was a Poet. Dickinson.
This World. Abu-l-Ala al-Maarri.
Three Green Windows. Sexton.
The Three Wise Monkeys. Davis.
Threshold. Blunden.
Thy Beauty Fades. Very.
Ticking Clocks. Field.
Time for Us to Leave Her. *Anonymous.*
Time Long Past. Shelley.
Time Recover'd. Casone.
Time's Bright Sand. Finch.
Time's Dedication. Schwartz.
Time's Fool. Updike.
Time to Choose a Lover. Horace.
The Time to Trust. *Anonymous.*
To a Bed of Tulips. Herrick.
To a Lofty Beauty, from Her Poor Kinsman. Coleridge.
To a Republican. Freneau.
To His Watch, When He Could Not Sleep. Herbert of Cherbury.
To Lady Eleanor Butler and the Honourable Miss Ponsonby... Wordsworth.
To My First Love, My Mother. Rossetti.

To My Son Parker, Asleep in the Next Room. Kaufman.
To the Most Beautiful Lady, the Lady Bridget Manners. Barnes.
To the South. Ghiselin.
To William Sharp. Scollard.
Tonight the Famous Psychiatrist. Simpson.
Tottenham Court: Song: "What a dainty life the milkmaid leads." Nabbes.
Towards the Last Spike. Pratt.
Trala Trala Trala La-Le-La. Williams.
Two. Aliger.
The Unbeseechable. Cornford.
The Unrealities. Schiller.
Ursa Major. Kirkup.
Verses on a Cat. Daubeny.
A Vision of Judgement. Southey.
Wait On! *Anonymous.*
Waiting. Behn.
Warren Phinney. Mayer.
Washington. Roche.
Waves. Emerson
The Wayside Station. Muir.
The Wedding Night. Sexton.
Welt. Johnson.
What about You? (parody). Pygge.
What Secret Desires of the Blood. Sachs.
What Shall I Give? Thomas.
What Winter Floods, What Showers of Spring. Bronte.
Wheeler's Brigade at Santiago. Rice.
When I Get Time. Masson.
When I Saw You Last, Rose. Dobson.
A Wife's Song. Bennett.
Will you sleep forever. Korinna.
Wives in the Sere. Hardy.
A Woman. Johnson.
Wonders. Kaufman.
The Writer. Jacob.
Written on a Fly-Leaf of Theocritus. Thompson.
Yardley-Oak. Cowper.

Timid (ly)
A Bunny Romance. Herford.
Doubt me, my dim companion! Dickinson.
The Goshawk. Haines.
Lines Written in Dejection. Yeats.

Tin
Alle Vogel Sind Schon Da. Chesterton.
At Grandfather's. Bates.
Aunt Jemima of the Ocean Waves. Hayden.
A Baby Sardine. Milligan.
The Desert of Love. Pilinszky.
Domestic Quarrel. McInerney.
Field Work. Cockrell.
Little Steamboat. Williams.

Tinkling
The Kasidah. Burton.
A Trucker. Gunn.

Tinsel
African Christmas. Press.

Tinsel
Clock Symphony. Nims.
Epigram: "Me Polytimus
  vexes and provokes."
  Martial (Marcus Valerius
  Martialis).
Tint
The Ballant o' the Laird's
  Bath. Young.
Tintinnabulum
Lyre. White.
Tiny
3 More Things. Nauen.
Adam in Love. Mitchell.
Combe Florey. Durcan.
The Death of the Bird.
  Hope.
Disaster (parody). Calverley.
Infant Spring. Shove.
Psalm. Mendes.
The Spring Waters. "Ping
  Hsin" (Hsieh Wang-ying).
To His Coy Mistress (parody).
  Flood.
A Wife Talks to Herself.
  Berg.
Tip (s)
Begging A.I.D. Rubadiri.
Gay Epiphany. Mitchell.
I Am Too Near.
  Szymborska.
If Not (parody). Evans.
Limerick: "A taxi-cab whore
  out at Iver." Gray.
Once. Walker.
Recollection. Mumford.
Sketch for a Morning in
  Muncie, Indiana. Murray.
You Gotta Have Your Tips
  on Fire. Cruz.
Tippecanoe
Old Tippecanoe. *Anonymous.*
Tipperary
Ah, Sweet Is Tipperary.
  McCarthy.
Tipple (r)
I taste a liquor never brewed.
  Dickinson.
Limerick: "Once a Frenchman
  who'd promptly said "oui'."
  Anonymous.
Riddle; "As I was going o'er
  Tipple Tine." *Anonymous.*
The Royalist. Brome.
Tiptoe
Christmas Morning.
  Roberts.
Country Reverie. Coates.
The Fallow Deer at the
  Lonely House. Hardy.
Hey Betty Martin.
  Anonymous.
Tanker. Middleton.
Tire (d) (s)
The 90th Year. Levertov.
Astrophel and Stella, XCVI.
  Sidney.
The Bonny Lass of Anglesey.
  Anonymous.
A Clash with Cliches.
  Miller.
Clouds. Ault.
Colonialism. Qarshe.
The Couch. Wright, Jr.
Deep Sea Tug. *Anonymous.*
Descent for the Lost. Child.
The Disconnection. Brown.
The Djanggawul Cycle, 51.
  Anonymous.
Doubt. Rogers.
Emblem. Quarles.
An Essay on Criticism.
  Pope.

Eye and Tooth. Lowell.
The Fairies of the Caldon
  Low. Howitt.
Father. Kaffka.
The Funeral. De la Mare.
The Happy Wanderer.
  Addleshaw.
A Heart Made Full of
  Thought. O Domhnaill.
Hitch Haiku. Snyder.
I Like to Sing Also. Updike.
Kinaxixi. Neto.
The Last Words of My
  English Grandmother.
  Williams.
The Lazy People. Silverstein.
Limerick: "An elephant sat on
  some kegs." Francis.
Love Me Little, Love Me
  Long. Herrick.
Love's Flight. Lasker-
  Schüler.
Men. Parker.
The Mermaidens. Richards.
The Moor. Hodgson.
Mrs. Hamer. Stembridge.
On a Seven-Day Diary.
  Dugan.
Outburst from a Little Face.
  Woods.
Preludes. Patmore.
Prison Cell Blues. Jefferson.
Problem in Social Geometry–
  The Inverted Square!
  Durem.
The Quilt. Newsome.
Rain-in-the-Face. Crow.
A Rhapsody (excerpt).
  Vaughan.
Richard II. Shakespeare.
Solstice. Weekes.
Sonnet VII. Sharp.
Sunday Night Walk.
  Souster.
To a Butterfly. Davies.
Tree Planting. *Anonymous.*
Two Nocturnes. Mansfield.
Wind in the Grass. Van
  Doren.
Tissue (s)
At a Parade. Prince.
Merchant Marine. Miles.
Those Various Scalpels.
  Moore.
Tissue. Griffin.
Titan (s)
The Master. Robinson.
Three Sonnets on Oblivion.
  Sterling.
The Vision. O Rathaille.
Titanic
Great Titanic. *Anonymous.*
R.M.S. Titanic. Cronin.
Tithe (s)
Alma Mater, Forget Me.
  Cole.
Tamlane. *Anonymous.*
The Voyage of Maeldune.
  Tennyson.
Titian
Renaissance. Avrett.
Title (s)
A Bunny Romance.
  Herford.
The Complete Introductory
  Lectures on Poetry.
  Mayer.
Modern Poetry. Skeen.
Old Man Travelling.
  Wordsworth.
The Politics of Rich Painters.
  Jones.

The Scow on Cowden Shore.
  Anonymous.
Spectator's Guide to
  Contemporary Art.
  McGinley.
To Delia. Daniel.
The Value of Dentistry.
  Brown.
The Wolfman. Kuzma.
You. Tagliabue.
Titter (s)
Epitaph for a Funny Fellow.
  Bishop.
The Haunted Oven.
  Kennedy.
Titwillow
The Suicide's Grave.
  Gilbert.
Toad (s)
As into the Garden Elizabeth
  Ran. Housman.
Bound No'th Blues. Hughes.
Events. O'Neil.
A Friend in the Garden.
  Ewing.
Think as I Think. Crane.
Toast
Bundaberg Rum. Scott.
The Cost-of-Living Mother
  Goose. Richardson.
Limerick: "There was an Old
  Man of the Coast." Lear.
Misfortunes Never Come
  Singly. Graham.
O Thou That Sleep'st.
  Davenant.
Of Pardons, Presidents, and
  Whiskey Labels. Snyder.
Rhymes on the Road
  (excerpt). Moore.
The Times. *Anonymous.*
To Amy. Coogler.
Tobacco
Boy! Bring an Ounce of
  Freeman's Best (parody).
  Browne.
The Cook. Young Bear.
Goin' Down to Town (with
  music). *Anonymous.*
Lynchburg Town.
  Anonymous.
The Pipe of Tobacco. Usher.
A Religious Use of Taking
  Tobacco. Wisdome.
Says the Miner to the
  Mucker. *Anonymous.*
Upone Tabacco. Ayton [(or
  Aytoun)] Sir Robert.
The Way & the Way Things
  Are. NorthSun.
The Wolves. Kinnell.
Today
Are We Thankful?
  Anonymous.
At the End of the Day.
  Hovey.
Barbara Allen. *Anonymous.*
Birthday on Deathrow.
  Otey.
A Child Is Born.
  Anonymous.
Epigram: "How shall I know
  if my love lose his youth."
  Strato.
Evening Hymn (excerpt).
  Macdonald.
Finale. Picot.
Garlic. Richardson.
General Store. Field.
Glimpses # xii (excerpt).
  McGaugh.
Help Me Today. Robinson.

Her Answer. Bennett.
The Horse. Coppard.
I knew quite well that some
  day. Narihira (Ariwara no
  Narihira).
Irritable Song. Atkins.
Killers. Sandburg.
My Song of Today. Therese.
Naming of Parts. Reed.
Our Jack's Come Home
  Today. *Anonymous.*
Over the Hill to the Poor-
  House. Carleton.
Quatrain. *Anonymous.*
Quid Sit Futurum Cras Fuge
  Quaerere. Prior.
Rhymes to Be Traded for
  Bread: Prologue. Lindsay.
The Rosemary Spray.
  Gongora y Argote.
Saints in Glory, We Together.
  Adams.
She Is No Liar. Graves.
To My Daughter. Spender.
Today. Bangs.
Today: The Idea Market.
  Nicholas.
Tomorrow. Collins.
Tomorrow. Leitner.
Undertones. Sims.
The Voice of the Dove.
  Miller.
Watching the Sun Rise over
  Mount Zion. Whitman.
Wedding Day at Nagasaki.
  Hall.
While Dissecting Frogs in
  Biology Class Scrut
  Discovers... Roberts.
With Flowers. Dickinson.
Toddle
Alison Gross. *Anonymous.*
The Fathers. Sassoon.
Toe (s)
Boy at a Certain Age.
  Francis.
The Children and Sir
  Nameless. Hardy.
A Copy of the Last Verses
  Made by Dr. Wild...
  (excerpt). Wild.
The Fairies. Herrick.
The False Fox Came into Our
  Croft. *Anonymous.*
Grass Fingers. Grimke.
Hakluyt Unpurchased.
  McDuffee.
Hang up the Baby's Stocking!
  Anonymous.
Johnson's Cabinet Watched by
  Ants. Bly.
Learning to Count. Turner.
The Man Hidden behind the
  Drapes. Rogers.
The More It Snows. Milne.
Moses Supposes His Toeses
  Are Roses. *Anonymous.*
Oiseaurie (parody).
  Widdemer.
One in the Gout Wishing for
  King Pyrrhus His Toe...
  Browne.
The Pobble Who Has No
  Toes. Lear.
Robinson Crusoe. Carryl.
Since Robin Hood.
  Anonymous.
The Testament of John
  Davidson: The Last
  Journey. Davidson.
Till Death Do Us Part.
  Miccolis.

Two Stories. Wright.
Up in the Lift Go We. *Anonymous.*
Well I Never. *Anonymous.*
Whenas in Jeans. Dehn.
The Willow Cats. Widdemer.

Together
28 VIII 69. Chester.
The Accomplices. Aiken.
The Aged Lover Discourses in the Flat Style. Cunningham.
Animal Songs: Giraffe. *Anonymous.*
Asphodel, That Greeny Flower. Williams.
Aunt Laura Moves Toward the Open Grave of Her Father. De Roche.
Barriers Burned. Field.
Carved on an Areca Nut... Ho Xuan Huong.
Chorus of the Rescued. Sachs.
Cold, Sharp Lamentation. Gregory.
The Cornfield. Roberts.
The Course. Huff.
Dialectique. Maxton.
Discovery of This Time. MacLeish.
Drift. Glover.
The Dual Site. Hamburger.
Eadwacer. *Anonymous.*
The Ecclesiast. Ashbery.
Erotica. Farkas.
Eton Boating Song. Cory.
An Evening's Love. Dryden.
Fair Margaret and Sweet William. *Anonymous.*
For the Children. Snyder.
For We Are All Madwomen. Sweeney.
Foreplay of the Alphabet. Gray.
The Garret. Pound.
Getting Back. Thompson.
The Hard Lovers. Dillon.
Hell Hath No Fury... Bukowski.
The Hosts. Merwin.
How will you cross. Oku.
How Will You Manage. Daihaku.
Humpty Dumpty Sat on a Wall. Mother Goose.
Hymn to Priapus. Lawrence.
I Have a Room whereinto No One Enters. Rossetti.
In Fur. Stafford.
The Indigo Glass in the Grass. Stevens.
Interlude. Smith.
An Invitation to Lubberland. *Anonymous.*
Jigsaw Puzzle. Hoban.
John Riley. *Anonymous.*
Johnny Germany. *Anonymous.*
Jump Cabling. Pastan.
The Last Ride Together. Browning.
The Leaf-Picking. Mistral.
Long I Thought That Knowledge Alone Would Suffice. Whitman.
Lord, Many Times Thou Pleased Art. Wither.
Love-Songs, At Once Tender and Informative. Hoffenstein.

The Mitten Song. Allen.
More Power. O'Rahilly.
The Mountain Tree. Connell.
The Mowers. Allingham.
My Son, My Executioner. Hall.
No More Words! To the Field, to Arms! Franco.
O, Lay Thy Hand in Mine, Dear! Massey.
Observation. Weber.
On the Seventh Anniversary of the Death of My Father. Pack.
Portoncini dei Morti. Halpern.
Prayer at Dawn. Poteat.
Quail in Autumn. Smith.
Quick and Bitter. Amichai.
Reasons. James.
Riddle: "Humpty Dumpty sat on a wall." *Anonymous.*
Romance VIII. John of Damascus.
The Self-Slaved. Kavanagh.
The Sinking of the Merrimac. Larcom.
The Song of Cove Creek Dam. Anonymous.
Song of Resignation. Amichai.
The Song on the Way. *Anonymous.*
Soul and Body. Waddington.
Sublimation. Comfort.
The sweat. NorthSun.
There is a soldier on a battlefield. *Anonymous.*
Time's Dedication. Schwartz.
To My Setter, Scout. Seldon.
To the Christ. Tabb.
Today. Hughes.
Trellis. Chester.
The Tuft of Flowers. Frost.
Two Nocturnes. Mansfield.
United. Paulus Silentiarius.
Villanelle with a Line by Yeats. Bennett.
The Way Sun Keeps Falling Away from Every Window. Lifshin.
We Go out Together. Patchen.
What's Good for the Soul Is Good for Sales. Wilbur.
Where Fire Burns. Cardiff.
The White Cat of Trenarren. Rowse.
You and I. Alford.

Toil (ed) (ers) (s)
Amoretti, LXIX. Spenser.
Art and Life. Ridge.
The Carpenter. Whiteside.
The Commonwealth of Toil. Chaplin.
The Dry-Landers. *Anonymous.*
Epigram: "Cease your labours, lovers of boys." *Anonymous.*
The Fair Maid and the Sun. O'Shaughnessy.
Fragrant Thy Memories. *Anonymous.*
The Galley-Slave. Kipling.
Gitanjali. Tagore.
The Gospel of Labor. Van Dyke.
Human Frailty. Cowper.

I Will Be What God Made Me, Nor Protest. Bridges.
In Memoriam A.H.H., CXXVIII. Tennyson.
The Isolation of Genius. Byron.
Jack Tar. *Anonymous.*
The Ladder of St. Augustine: The Heights. Longfellow.
The Ladies' Aid. *Anonymous.*
The Little Toil of Love. Dickinson.
Lounge in the shade of the luxuriant laurel's/beautiful foliage. Anyte.
La Madonna di Lorenzetti. Andrews.
Margaret to Dolcino. Kingsley.
A Net to Snare the Moonlight. Lindsay.
Nuremberg. Longfellow.
O Come with Me, Thus Ran the Song. Bronte.
Ode X: The First of April (excerpt). Warton, Jr..
Old Age. Al-Aswad.
Over in the Meadow. Wadsworth.
The Ploughman. Thomas.
Prayer for Rain. Kalevala.
Seneca Lake. Percival.
The Servants. Wightman.
Sordello's Birth-Place. Browning.
The Spinner. De Vere.
To an Indian Skull (excerpt). McLachlan.
To the Right Honourable Robert Walpole, Esq. Philips.
Whirlwinds of Danger. *Anonymous.*
Widows. Masters.
The Witching Song. Thomson.
The Young Workman. Frear.

Toilet
Anniversary. Kooser.
The Great Poet. King.
Late Lights in Minnesota. Kooser.
LXXVI. Berrigan.
The Rape of the Lock. Pope.

Token
The Ashtabula Disaster. Moore.
The Death of the Gods. An Ode. Ker.
One Year to Life on the Grand Central Shuttle. Lorde.
Precious in the Sight of the Lord... *Anonymous.*
The Silver Dagger. *Anonymous.*
The Suire. Irwin.
The Surrender at Appomattox. Melville.

Told
108 Tales of a Po'Buckra, No. 106. Inman.
Age Not to Be Rejected. *Anonymous.*
Autumn Orchard. Jacobs.
The Ballad of Minepit Shaw. Kipling.
The Boat. Pack.

The Burial of the Bachelor (parody). *Anonymous.*
Dark Pines under Water. MacEwen.
Do You Love Me. *Anonymous.*
The Elixir. Herbert.
I Know. Barker.
Langston. Evans.
Letter. Empson.
Little Birds. "Carroll.
Lost Light. Akers.
Man's Amazement. *Anonymous.*
My Little Wife. *Anonymous.*
Navajo. Simpson.
The Night a Sailor Came to Me in a Dream. Wakoski.
A Night in the Red Sea. Lyall.
Old Houses. Romano.
The Oracle. Ficke.
Riddle: "There was a king met a king." *Anonymous.*
The Runaway. Frost.
The Tomboy. Burford.
The Whole Duty of a Poem. Guiterman.

Toleration
Two Sonnets. Berenberg.
Washington's Monument, February, 1885. Whitman.

Toll (ing) (s)
Devotions. Donne.
For Whom the Bell Tolls. Donne.
Guilt and Sorrow. Wordsworth.
Idolatry. Bontemps.
Leaves. Hughes.
A Mermaiden. Hennell.
An Old Woman. *Anonymous.*
Oxford Bells. Maris Stella.
Theme. Spitteler.
They're Tearing down a Town. Strunk.
To Sherrie. Matuzak.

Tom (my)
Christ Church Bells. Aldrich.
Christchurch Bells. *Anonymous.*
Drifters. Dawe.
Heigh Ho! My Heart Is Low. *Anonymous.*
Men in Green. Campbell.
Mr. Merry's Lament for "Long Tom". Brainard.
Pat-a-Cake, Pat-a-Cake, Baker's Man. *Anonymous.*
Poor Dear Grandpapa. Thompson.
Tom Tatter's Birthday Ode. Hood.
Too Candid by Half. Saxe.
When the Mississippi Flowed in Indiana. Lindsay.
Widdecombe Fair. *Anonymous.*
Wild Strawberries. Graves.

Tomahawks
Fancy Dress. Sassoon.

Tomato
In Response to Executive Order 9066: ALL AMERICANS OF JAPANESE... Okita.

Tomato juice
Country Club Sunday. McGinley.

Tomb (s)

Advent. Antoninus.
Aerial View of Louisiana. Mathis.
Ah! Lovely Appearance of Death! Wesley.
Anath. Guri.
Annabel Lee. Poe.
Cenotaph of Lincoln. McKay.
Charleston. Timrod.
Cool Tombs. Sandburg.
County Sligo. MacNeice.
Creed. Lowenfels.
Dawn. Shevin.
A Departed Friend. Moore.
Echoes from Theocritus. Lefroy.
Epigrams. Theocritus.
Epitaph Inscribed on a Small Piece of Marble. Shirley.
Epitaph on Erotion. Hunt.
Epitaph on the Stanton Harcourt Lovers. Montagu.
First Philosopher's Song. Huxley.
The Fisherman. Leonidas.
Florella. Anonymous.
A Fly That Flew into My Mistress's Eye. Carew.
Fort McHenry. Anonymous.
From William Tyndale to John Frith. Bowers.
Frontispiece. Swenson.
Glasgow. Smith.
The Gray Plume. Carlin.
The Great Hunger. Kavanagh.
A Great Time. Davies.
Green Symphony. Fletcher.
The Green Willow. Anonymous.
The Gulistan. Sa'di.
Haufi. Anonymous.
His Being Was in Her Alone. Sidney.
Home. Chalmers.
I Saw Thee, Child, One Summer's Day. Bronte.
In Front of the Landscape. Hardy.
In Praise of a Gentlewoman. Gascoigne.
In the Shelter. Day Lewis.
Inscriptions at the City of Brass. Anonymous.
Invasion Weather. Newton.
The Killer Too. Gibson.
Lamentation on the Death of the Duke of Wellington. Anonymous.
The Leaders of the Crowd. Yeats.
Lullaby. Fearing.
Memory. Lincoln.
The Mistress (excerpt). Rochester.
Mone, Member, Mone. Anonymous.
Monument. Sullivan.
The Mourners Came at Break of Day. Adams.
Much Ado about Nothing. Shakespeare.
A New England Bachelor. Eberhart.
An Ode: "Awake, faire Muse; for I intend." Browne.
On Some Humming-Birds in a Glass Case. Turner.

On the Countess Dowager of Pembroke. Browne.
On the Death of a Lady's Owl. Mendes.
On the Death of a Young and Favorite Slave. Martial (Marcus Valerius Martialis).
Orpheus to Woods. Lovelace.
Pacific Door. Birney.
Palm House, Botanic Gardens. Hetherington.
A Pastoral. Hill.
Peter Emberley (III). Anonymous.
The Pill. Clarke.
The Poetry of a Root Crop. Kingsley.
Poly-Olbion. Drayton.
The Portrait. Rossetti.
Pyramus and Thisbe. Ovid (Publius Ovidius Naso).
The Sea-Ritual. Darley.
The Setting of the Moon. Leopardi.
Sick unto Death of Love. Anonymous.
Sister Songs (excerpt). Thompson.
Sligo and Mayo. MacNeice.
Some we see no more, tenements of wonder. Dickinson.
Song for "The Jaquerie". Lanier.
Song: "There is many a love in the land, my love." Miller.
Sonnet: "Sweet Spring, thou turn'st with all thy goodly train." Drummond.
Sonnets, CVII: "Not mine own fears, nor the prophetic soul." Shakespeare.
Spring Bereaved. Drummond.
Stranger Call This Not. Anonymous.
The Talmud. Frug.
There Is an Hour of Peaceful Rest. Tappan.
This Amber Sunstream. Van Doren.
Three Sentences for a Dead Swan. Wright.
Timas. Sappho.
To a Rose. Sherman.
To a Shade. Yeats.
To an Old Lady Dead. Sassoon.
To Fine Lady Would-Be. Jonson.
To Lucasta. Lovelace.
To Robin Red-Breast. Herrick.
To the Departing Spirit of an Alienated Friend. Seward.
The Tomb of the Brave. Hutton.
Tone's Grave. Davis.
Unearthing. Rosenberg.
Upon a Young Mother of Many Children. Herrick.
Upon the Death of His Sparrow an Elegie. Herrick.
Upon the Double Murther of King Charles I... Philips.
Urania. Pitter.
View of Louisiana. Mathis.
Were You There. Anonymous.

What Am I Who Dare. Habington.
What Is Young Passion. Coleridge.
What Profit? Di Roma.
The Wheel. Yeats.
Woman's Love. Anonymous.
Young Charlottie. Carter.

Tombstone (s)

At a Chinaman's Grave. Lum.
The Broken Bowl. Merrill.
Do It Now. Braley.
Last Rites. Rossetti.
My Cats. Smith.
On an East Wind from the Wars. Dugan.

Tomorrow (s)

Amores. Ovid (Publius Ovidius Naso).
At the End of the Day. Hovey.
Barbara Allen. Anonymous.
Blackmen: Who Make Morning. Jackson.
Broken Home. Stafford.
Corsons Inlet. Ammons.
The Dust. Reese.
The Dynasts. Hardy.
Envoy. Thompson.
Evening Hymn (excerpt). Macdonald.
Finale. Picot.
From a Diary. Morgan.
The Future Is for Tomorrow. Greki.
Galway. O'Neill.
Garlic. Richardson.
The Gentle Check. Beaumont.
Girl in a Nightgown. Stevens.
Green Song. Booth.
Heaven Overarches Earth and Sea. Rossetti.
Herman Moon's Hourbook. Middleton.
His Majesty the Letter-Carrier. Carnevali.
Holy Innocents. Rossetti.
Hurry Tomorrow. Eastwick.
I'm Thankful That My Life Doth Not Deceive. Thoreau.
In Go-Cart So Tiny. Greenway.
In Sickness. Swift.
Into the Future. Witt.
Irish. Celan.
Is It Really Worth the While? Anonymous.
Katie May. Hopkins.
The King of the Cradle. Ashby-Sterry.
A Kiss. Dobson.
The Last of the Grand Old Masters. Patey.
Let Other People Come as Streams. Reznikoff.
Let Us Forget. Robinson.
The Lily of Torrow. Van Dyke.
Little Mathiue Grove. Anonymous.
Little Musgrave and Lady Barnard (Little Matthy Groves). Anonymous.
Make Me a Garment. Anonymous.
Malawi. Banda.
Maria. Stevens.
Moments. Allen.

A Night Watch. Anonymous.
Not Going with It. Gurevitch.
Ode on a Plastic Stapes. Walsh.
Oystering. Howard.
Peace on Earth. Williams.
Per Diem et per Noctem. Stanley.
Phyllis. Randolph.
Potomac Town in February. Sandburg.
Quatrain. Anonymous.
Reading the Books Our Children Have Written. Smith.
Right On: White America. Sanchez.
The Rosemary Spray. Gongora y Argote.
The Roses of Thy Cheeks. Rafi of Merv.
A Scene. Davies.
Security. Hamburger.
September. Fallis.
Sheer Joy. Cushman.
The Shepherd's Week:. Gay.
Signs of Rain. Jenner.
Sire. Merwin.
Soliloquy in a Motel. Gibson.
Solitary Travel. MacNeice.
Song for Tomorrow. Trent.
Song of Thyrsis. Freneau.
Song: "'Tis sweet to hear the merry lark." Coleridge.
Spouse. Bynner.
Though You Are Young. Campion.
To a Magnolia Flower in the Garden of the Armenian Convent in Venice. Mitchell.
To Leuconoe. Field.
To My Retired Friend Wei. Tu Fu.
Tomorrow. Collins.
Tomorrow. Leitner.
Venus Vigils (excerpt). Anonymous.
Westphalian Song. Anonymous.
Whenever I Go There. Merwin.
Where Have You Gone, Little Boy. Harjo.
Woman's Constancy. Donne.
Woman Seed Player. Whiteman.
The Year Ahead. Powers.

Tone (s)

The Family Cat. Fuller.
Flying Crow. King.
God's Harp. Falke.
Music God. Van Doren.
Our Father. Swartz.
Poet of Earth. Thayer.
Senlin. Aiken.
Song's Eternity. Clare.
To Disraeli. Brooks.
To Helen. Praed.

Tong (s)

He Shot at Lee Wing. Anonymous.
The Iliad. Homer.
In the Round. Weiss.
Keep a Good Tongue in Your Head... Parker.
The Midnight Court. Merriman.
Wag a Leg, Wag a Leg. Anonymous.

Tongue (s)
The Aeolian Harp. Melville.
Alien. Turner.
Amanda, Playing. Truesdale.
The Animals. MacAdams.
Arcadia. Sidney.
Art of Love (excerpt). Ovid.
Assumption. Fallon.
Astrophel and Stella, XLVII. Sidney.
Before Harvest. Fitzgerald.
Bobber. Carver.
Caelica, II. Greville.
The Card-Dealer. Rossetti.
Chomei at Toyama. Bunting.
The Church the Garden of Christ. Watts.
Corn Canon. Stevenson.
Crusoe's Island. Walcott.
Desert Flowers. Douglas.
The Domestic Stones. Arp.
Duel with Verses over a Great Man. *Anonymous.*
Dumb, Dumb, Dumb. *Anonymous.*
The Dumb Maid. *Anonymous.*
The Dumb Wife Cured. *Anonymous.*
Earth Song. Peacock.
Eureka. Maunders.
Eve. Rossetti.
Ex Ore Infantium. Thompson.
Finisterra. Winters.
First Love. Kunitz.
Food and Drink (excerpt). Untermeyer.
For Miriam. Macgoye.
Fragment. Clare.
The Gaelic. Kelly.
God Sour the Milk of the Knacking Wench. Nowlan.
Gravel. Mariah.
Grog-an'-Grumble Steeplechase. Lawson.
Hare in Winter. Piercy.
Hope. Cowper.
How She Resolved to Act. Moore.
How to Write a Letter. Turner.
I Muse Not. Davison.
If I Stand in My Window. Clifton.
In Allusion to the French Song, N'entendez Vous Pas ce Language. Lovelace.
In Memory of Colonel Charles Young. Cullen.
Invocation of Silence. Flecknoe.
Isolation Cell Poem. Green.
Ivy and Holly. Meyerstein.
Japanese Beetles. Kennedy.
The Jewels. Clarke.
Johnny Dyers. *Anonymous.*
The Lady in Kicking Horse Reservoir. Hugo.
Lesbia. Congreve.
A Lesson in Oblivion. Stuart.
Let Not Thy Beauty. Townsend.
Like Any Other Man. Orr.
Love's Labour's Lost. Shakespeare.
The Lowveld. Eglington.
Lynched Negro. Bodenheim.
The Maltworm's Madrigal. Dobson.

Manomin. Wolf.
Mothers, Daughter. Kaufman.
My Atthis, although our dear Anaktoria. Sappho.
My Grandmother. Shapiro.
The New Style. O'Bruadair.
Next. Koyama.
Night Clouds. Lowell.
Not Her, She Aint No Gypsy. Young.
O Holy, Holy, Holy Lord. Eastburn.
Ode to a Country Hoyden. Wolcot.
On a Slanderer. Martial (Marcus Valerius Martialis).
On Mrs. W–. Bentley.
On My Lord Bacon. Danforth.
Parrot and Dove. Landor.
A Poem Containing Some Remarks on the Present War. *Anonymous.*
The Poet. Dunbar.
The Prairie Schooner. Dale.
Prayer of Columbus. Whitman.
The Precious Pearl. Wilson.
Psalm XXXV. Sidney.
The Range in the Desert. Jarrell.
The Real Thing. Wallace.
Resentments Composed Because of the Clamor of Town Topers... Knight.
Saints. Garrett.
Saying Dante Aloud. Wright.
The Seduction. Rioff.
Shake'nbake Ballad. Van Toorn.
Song of Hate. Frances.
Sonnets, CII: "My love is strengthen'd." Shakespeare.
Sonnets, CVI: "When in the chronicle of wasted time." Shakespeare.
The Soul Has Bandaged Moments. Dickinson.
The Stammerers. Kent.
Sweeney to Mrs. Porter in the Spring. Sissman.
Tales from a Family Album. Justice.
Telephone Ghosts. Frazier.
Theophilus Thistledown, the Successful Thistle Sifter. *Anonymous.*
There's Wisdom in Women. Brooke.
To His Friend, on the Untunable Times. Herrick.
The Tomb of Honey Snaps Its Marble Chains. Stanford.
The Tongue. Strong.
Trainwrecked Soldiers. Nims.
Tramp. Hughes.
Transport. George.
The United States Prepare for the Permanent Revolution. Hitchcock.
The Unknown City. Roberts.
An Unsuspected Fact. Cannon.
Up Time. *Anonymous.*
Upon His Timorous Silence in Her Presence. Davison.
Vaquero. Miller.

Vert-Vert, the Parrot. Gresset.
The War of the Secret Agents. Coulette.
When He Spoke to Me of Love. Mokhomo.
When the Bells Justle in the Tower. Housman.
When the Storms Come. Mphande.
Why the Soup Tastes Like the Daily News. Piercy.
Wishes for My Son. Macdonagh.
...With Its Quiet Tongue. Das.
With Mercy for the Greedy. Sexton.
A Year without Seasons. Williams.
The Yoke of Tyranny. Sidney.
Tonight
Anastasis. Smythe.
And Tomorrow Wend Our Ways. *Anonymous.*
Ballad of Douglas Bridge. Carlin.
Birth of a Country. Gergely.
Cherry Blossoms. "Lewis.
Cold Is the Winter. *Anonymous.*
A Crown of Wildflowers. Rossetti.
The Dance. Halpern.
A Dream of Fair Women. Amis.
Eating Lechon, with my Brothers and Sisters. Cabalquinto.
Edward Weston in Mexico City. Dacey.
The Fairy Folk. Bird.
The Happy Night. Squire.
Heaven Overarches Earth and Sea. Rossetti.
Holiday. Horace.
A Hot Time in the Old Town. Hayden.
Ivory Masks in Orbit. Kgositsile.
The Little Black Train. *Anonymous.*
Lullaby of the Woman of the Mountain. Pearse.
The Mahogany Tree. Thackeray.
The Most Beautiful Woman at My Highschool Reunion. Bissert.
The Move Continuing. Young.
The Newmarket Song. D'Urfey.
A Night Watch. *Anonymous.*
Not Tonight, Josephine. Curzon.
Old Smoky. *Anonymous.*
On Looking up by Chance at the Constellations. Frost.
Raise a Ruckus Tonight. *Anonymous.*
Six-Forty-Two Farm Commune Struggle Poem. Leifer.
Star-Fear. Speyer.
Star Wish. *Anonymous.*
Starry Sky. *Anonymous.*
A Theory of Wind. Goldbarth.
Tonight at Least, My Sinner. *Anonymous.*

Villanelle of Washington Square. Roberts.
Wedding-Hymn. Lanier.
Where Is My Wandering Boy Tonight? Lowry.
Where Is Your Boy Tonight? *Anonymous.*
Tool (s)
By Frazier Creek Falls. Snyder.
The Objection to Being Stepped On. Frost.
The Tool of Fate. Yehoash.
The Tower of Babel. Crouch.
Tooth
August 1914. Rosenberg.
The Best Dance Hall in Iuka, Mississippi. Johnson.
Modern Love, XXVI. Meredith.
Pisces. Thomas.
Second Honeymoon. *Anonymous.*
This World Is Not Conclusion. Dickinson.
Two Songs of a Fool. Yeats.
Toothache
A Meditation upon the Toothache. Lerner.
Sam, Sam the butcher man. *Anonymous.*
Toothbrush
The Horse Named Bill (with music). *Anonymous.*
Toothless
A Bad Break. Goodge.
Tootsey wootsey
In the Good Old Summer Time. Shields.
Top (s)
At Dunwich. Thwaite.
The Calculation. Wagoner.
The Doubt of Future Foes. Elizabeth I.
English Bards and Scotch Reviewers. Byron.
First Steps up Parnassus. Drayton.
The Hang-Glider's Daughter. Hacker.
Hang up the Baby's Stocking! *Anonymous.*
His Name Is at the Top. *Anonymous.*
I've Got a Dog as Thin as a Rail. *Anonymous.*
The Kite. Behn.
Loving Henry. *Anonymous.*
The Man Hidden behind the Drapes. Rogers.
Montgomery. Evans.
The Pine to the Mariner. Turberville.
Prescription of Painful Ends. Jeffers.
The Purpose of Altar Boys. Rios.
Putting on Nightgown. *Anonymous.*
Revolution. Zimunya.
The Schoolboy Reads His Iliad. Morton.
The Swimmer. Ransom.
Top Hand. *Anonymous.*
You're the Top. Porter.
Young Sycamore. Williams.
Topaz
To Julia. Herrick.
Topknot
Tom, He Was a Piper's Son. *Anonymous.*

Torah
  The Angels Came A-
    Mustering. Zangwill.
Torch (es)
  The April Earth. Eastman.
  Bavarian Gentians.
    Lawrence.
  Chee Lai! (Arise!).
    Anonymous.
  Confession. Clifton.
  Modern Beauty. Symons.
  Ode to Psyche. Keats.
  Puer Aeternus. Raine.
  Radiation Victim. Thiele.
  A Song Before Grief.
    Lathrop.
  Speaking of Poetry. Bishop.
  Thou Light of Ages.
    Schloerb.
  The Torch. Garrison.
  The Wall-Flower.
    Wergeland.
  You See the Worst of Love,
    but Not the Best. Landor.
Torchlight
  Don't Ask Me What to Wear.
    Sappho.
  Thus Saith My Chloris Bright.
    Guarini.
Tore
  Conversation. Dewey.
  The Gosport Tragedy (A
    vers.). *Anonymous.*
  I Went to the Toad That Lies
    under the Wall.
    Anonymous.
  In the Garden of the Turkish
    Consulate. Sadeh.
Torment (or) (s)
  Boys. Letts.
  Correspondences. Duncan.
  The Farmer's Curst Wife (A
    version). *Anonymous.*
  Feast on Wine or Fast on
    Water. Chesterton.
  Gethsemane, Illinois.
    Allwood.
  I Place Myself. *Anonymous.*
  If I Could Believe That
    Death. Stampa.
  Later Life, VII. Rossetti.
  Love's Arithmetic.
    Sherburne.
  My Thirty Years. Manzano.
  On His Mistress Going from
    Home. *Anonymous.*
  Song Set by Robert Jones:
    "She whose matchless
    beauty staineth."
    Anonymous.
  The Thief. Cowley.
  To Lesbia. Catullus.
Torn
  Actaeon. Heppenstall.
  Doctor Faustus. Hill.
  Draft of a Reparations
    Agreement. Pagis.
  Fishermen. Preil.
  Forgiven? Gillespy.
  Friend, how can I meet my
    lord? Mira Bai [(or
    Mirabai)].
  Guest. Lacey.
  The Pine to the Mariner.
    Turberville.
  The Quarrel. Swenson.
  Sleep: and between the Closed
    Eyelids of Sleep. Aiken.
  Sonnet to Be Written from
    Prison. Adamson.

Tornado (es)
  Physical Geography.
    Nicholl.
  The Tornado. Russell.
Torpedoes
  Resigning from a Job in a
    Defense Industry.
    McPherson.
Torrent (s)
  The Chase (excerpt).
    Somervile.
  The Iliad. Homer.
  The Imprisoned. Fitzgerald.
  Night up There. Valentine.
  On the Projected Kendal and
    Windermere Railway.
    Wordsworth.
  The Paltry Nude Starts on a
    Spring Voyage. Stevens.
  Symphony in Blue. Roseliep.
  The Torrent. Robinson.
Torture (d) (s)
  Children of Auschwitz.
    Korzhavin.
  Eutychides. Lucilius [(or
    Lucillius)].
  Evil Prayer. Hyde.
  The Fakir. Cambridge.
  From a Museum Man's
    Album. Hewitt.
  I Think of Him as One Who
    Fights. Branch.
  The Innocent Gazer. Cutts.
  New England. Robinson.
  The Passions That We Fought
    With. Stickney.
  The Signal. Ignatow.
  Something about It.
    Hollander.
  Upon Boys Diverting
    Themselves in the River.
    Foxton.
Tory (Tories)
  Don Juan. Byron.
  Italy Versus England.
    Byron.
  A Primrose Dame. White.
  To the Tune of "Ye Commons
    and Peers Pray Lend Me
    Your Ears..." *Anonymous.*
  The Whigs' Lamentation for
    the Death of Their Dear
    Brother College....
    Anonymous.
Toss (ed) (es) (ing)
  Boats. Bennett.
  Definition of the Soul.
    Pasternak.
  Hic Me, Pater Optime,
    Fessam Deseris. Robinson.
  In Memoriam A.H.H., X.
    Tennyson.
  Michael Robartes Bids His
    Beloved Be at Peace.
    Yeats.
  The Moon at the Fortified
    Pass. Li Po.
  The Old Flame. Lowell.
  Plans. Brooks.
  Plymouth Harbor. Radford.
  Puss in the Pantry.
    Anonymous.
  Song: "Trip it Gipsies, trip it
    fine." Rowley.
  Songs of Ch'en. Confucius.
  Spontaneous Me. Whitman.
  Sunday. Herbert.
  To-Day. Low.
  To Felicity Who Calls Me
    Mary. Chesterton.
  Trip It Gipsies, Trip It Fine.
    Middleton.

  The Wind of January.
    Rossetti.
Tot (s)
  Time Out. Butterfield.
  What's Going to Happen to
    the Tots? Coward.
Total
  Hope's Okay. Ammons.
  Lover That I Hope You Are.
    Acorn.
  The "Utopia'. Harwood.
Tottered
  Epitaph for a Funny Fellow.
    Bishop.
Toucan (s)
  The Pecan. The Toucan.
    Wood.
  September. Hacker.
  The Toucan. Johnson, Jr.
  Toucannery. Prelutsky.
Touch (ed) (es) (ing)
  Admonition to a Traveller.
    Wordsworth.
  The Amphora. Sologub.
  Arcan Sylvarum. De Kay.
  Astrophel and Stella, IX.
    Sidney.
  At Baia. Doolittle.
  Auction. Heyen.
  B-52s. Kenseth.
  The Ballad of the Angel.
    Garrison.
  The Battle of Trenton.
    Anonymous.
  Black Magic. Sanchez.
  The Blind Leading the Blind.
    Mueller.
  Boom. Rayford.
  The Burning of Paper Instead
    of Children. Rich.
  The Carnation. Hannigan.
  The Comedian. Layton.
  A Confession. Mezey.
  Country Reverie. Coates.
  The Cows near the
    Graveyard. Nelson.
  Daddy Shot a Bear.
    Anonymous.
  Degli Sposi. Lesser.
  A Dentist's Window. Baxter.
  The Dungeon. Coleridge.
  Eagle Plain. Francis.
  The Elephant Is Slow to
    Mate. Lawrence.
  The Elixir. Herbert.
  L'Envoi. Robinson.
  Episode. Nunes.
  Fall Comes in Back-Country
    Vermont. Warren.
  The Fifth Sense. Beer.
  The First Kiss. Watts-
    Dunton.
  First Light. Kinsella.
  Fish. Halpern.
  Flights. McDonald.
  For a Masseuse and
    Prostitute. Rexroth.
  The Girl in the Willow Tree.
    Maisel.
  Gravestones. Stuart.
  Greater Love. Owen.
  Green Enravishment of
    Human Life. Juana Ines
    de la Cruz.
  The Hemingway Syndrome.
    Louis.
  Horatian Ode. Beach.
  House Poem. Cooper.
  I Done Got So Thirsty That
    My Mouth Waters at the
    Thought of Rain. Jones.

  I Wake, My Friend, I.
    Kicknosway.
  Imagine the South.
    Woodcock.
  In Which She Satisfies a Fear
    with the Rhetoric of Tears.
    Juana Ines de la Cruz.
  Islanders, Inlanders. Mott.
  Just About Asleep Together.
    Peacock.
  Kate Temple's Song. Collins.
  Kiss. Young.
  Like Rousseau. Jones.
  Listening. Stafford.
  Living with Children. Miller.
  A Masique Presented at
    Ludlow Castle (Comus).
    Milton.
  Mexico. Lowell.
  Michael Angelo: A Fragment
    (excerpt). Longfellow.
  Michelangelo: "The Creation
    of Adam." Djanikian.
  Montrose to His Mistress.
    Graham.
  Mother's Hands.
    Wedgefarth.
  Music in Camp. Thompson.
  My Daughter Considers Her
    Body. Skloot.
  My Love. Shelton.
  My Love Is Sleeping. Leslie.
  The Name. Duggan.
  New Potatoes. Belford.
  Night. McKay.
  Ode to Quinbus Flestrin.
    Pope.
  Of Nicolette. Cummings.
  On the Death of Ho Chi
    Minh. Mandel.
  On the Death of Phillips.
    Anonymous.
  Oshun, the River Goddess.
    Anonymous.
  Out of Mourning. Abbott.
  Out of the Deepness.
    Jackson.
  The Overtakelessness of
    Those. Dickinson.
  Painting. Jacobs.
  Paradigms of Fire. Swann.
  People Trying to Love.
    Berg.
  Permanence. Meynell.
  Playing House. Gilbert.
  Precious Things.
    Anonymous.
  The Princess. Tennyson.
  Promontory Moon. Kinnell.
  Pulling Out. Lifshin.
  The Reconciliation.
    MacLeish.
  Red Stockings, Blue
    Stockings. *Anonymous.*
  Rigmarole. Williams.
  The Robin and the Redbreast.
    Anonymous.
  Romeo and Juliet.
    Shakespeare.
  The Rubicon. Winter.
  Shade. Lynch.
  Song of the Bride. Mernit.
  The Song of the Lower
    Classes. Jones.
  Song to the Masquers.
    Shirley.
  Sonnet: "There is no God, as
    I was taught in youth."
    Masefield.
  Spectral Lovers. Ransom.
  St. Roach. Rukeyser.

Story from Another World.
Petrie.
The Talking Oak: Olivia.
Tennyson.
Technique. Eaton.
That No Man Should Write
But Such as Do Excel.
Turberville.
That We Head Towards.
Stephany.
To Delia. Daniel.
To Himself. Aldridge.
To Lucasta. Lovelace.
The Touch of the Master's
Hand. Welch.
Trim's Song: The Fair
Kitchen-Maid. Steele.
Under Stars. Gallagher.
Upon Being Awakened at
Night by My Four Year
Old Daughter. Rainer.
The Valley. Moss.
Virtuosa. Townsend.
Voice. Moss.
What Am I to Do With My
Sister? Yuhara.
With Seed the Sowers Scatter.
Housman.
Within the Veil. Sangster.
A Work of Artifice. Piercy.
Written in Very Early Youth.
Wordsworth.

Touch (es) (ed) (ing)
Afternoon, with Just Enough
of a Breeze. Sund.
A Bather in a Painting.
Greene.
Brief Encounter. Scott.
Club 82: Lisa. Genser.
Cortege for Colette.
Garrigue.
Credo. Gale.
Dispersion and Convergence.
Clark.
Dusk. Southwick.
Eclipse. Rashidd.
The Evans Country. Amis.
The Fear. Frost.
For the El Paso Weather
Bureau. Wild.
High Flight. Magee, Jr.
The Hippopotamus.
Durston.
The Iliad. Homer.
Love Song. Chantikian.
Midnight, Walking the
Wakeful Daughter.
Meredith.
My Influence. *Anonymous.*
The Porch. Gildner.
The Quarrel. Aiken.
Sonnets. Tuckerman.
The Toil of the Trail.
Garland.
Walking on the Prayerstick.
Rose.
Wax. Scott.
What You Need. Fraser.
When I Cut My Hair.
Green.
White Violets. Low.

Touchdown
Dream. Witt.

Tough
Great-Aunt Rebecca.
Brewster.
His Picture. Donne.
Jersey Belle Blues. Johnson.
King Lear. Shakespeare.
Semen. Francescato.
Tin Cup Blues. Jefferson.

A Tough Cuss from Bitter
Creek. Adams.
XXXVI. Berrigan.

Toulon
Limerick: "There was an old
man of Toulon. Smith.

Tour (ist)
Amours de Voyage. Clough.
Public Aid for Niagara Falls.
Bishop.
Queen Victoria and Me.
Cohen.
Shut Up, I Said. Bennett.
Tours. Liu.

Tow
Aran Islands. Layton.
Homeward Bound. Rogers.
Warren Phinney. Mayer.
Whipping Cheare.
Anonymous.

Towels
Walking Around. Neruda.

Tower (s)
Alma Mater. Quiller-Couch.
The Apollyonists. Fletcher.
The Bells of San Gabriel.
Stoddard.
Bitter rain in my courtyard.
Wu Tsao.
The Brigg. Skelton.
The Builders (excerpt). Van
Dyke.
Building a Skyscraper.
Tippett.
Burragorang. McDonald.
Chateau Papineau. Harrison.
Crow's Last Stand. Hughes.
Cumnor Hall. Mickle.
George III. Thackeray.
In Memory of Bryan Lathrop.
Masters.
Iowa, June. Browne.
Lament for Better or Worse.
Baro.
The Princess of Dreams.
Dowson.
The Purple Island. Fletcher.
The Red-Gold Rain. Sitwell.
The Serf. Campbell.
Sermon on the Mount.
Wright.
Skerryvore. Stevenson.
Song of the Builders.
Murton.
A Street Melody. Cooper.
'Tis Merry in Greenwood.
Scott.
To Lizard Head. Laube.
United States. Keble.
Venice. Longfellow.

Town (s)
Above the High. Grigson.
Adieu to Old England.
Anonymous.
The Aeneid. Virgil (Publius
Vergilius Maro).
After Tsang Chih. Notley.
Anno 1829. Heine.
Autumn. Hulme.
The Ballad of Longwood
Glen. Nabokov.
Battle Royal. *Anonymous.*
The Bonny Earl of Murray (A
vers.). *Anonymous.*
The Bonny Earl of Murray (B
vers.). *Anonymous.*
The Burial of the Bachelor
(parody). *Anonymous.*
The Canterbury Tales: A
Miller. Chaucer.
The Carpet-Weaver's Lament.
Anonymous.

The Chaunt of the Brazen
Head (excerpt). Praed.
Christmas at Vail: On Staying
Indoors. Monaghan.
City Roofs. Towne.
Clerihews. Bentley.
Clonakilty. *Anonymous.*
The Comparison (excerpt).
Anonymous.
A Country Wedding.
Anonymous.
Dappled Grey. *Anonymous.*
The Dark Lady. *Anonymous.*
The Disused Temple.
Cameron.
Eagle of Pengwern.
Anonymous.
Elegy for an Estrangement.
Holloway.
Explanation. Hewitt.
Finite. "Dalton.
Five Stanzas on Perfection.
Jonas.
The Fox. *Anonymous.*
Fragment of an Anti-Papist
Ballad. *Anonymous.*
Good-By, Pretty Mama.
Anonymous.
Goodbye, Little Bonny Blue
Eyes. *Anonymous.*
Grand Rapids. Moore.
Hardy's Plymouth. Grigson.
Haverhill, 1640-1890.
Whittier.
Honeysuckle. Paul.
I Point Out a Bird. Duval.
In Procession. Graves.
Incident at Imuris. Rios.
The Insomniacs. Rich.
It Isn't the Town, It's You.
Glover.
The Kilfenora Teaboy.
Durcan.
Lady Day in Harvest. Kaye-
Smith.
Lineage. Farren.
Little Nag. *Anonymous.*
Matronita. Silk.
Mrs. Hen. *Anonymous.*
November Wears a Paisley
Shawl. Morris.
People. Lenski.
Pickin Em Up and Layin Em
Down. Angelou.
Pisanello's Studies of Men
Hanging on Gallows.
Wheatcroft.
The Pressures. Jones.
Quits. Aldrich.
The Railroad Corral.
Anonymous.
Ratcliffe Highway.
Anonymous.
The Recruit. Housman.
Riddle: "The vase which holds
all fat'ning liquor."
Anonymous.
Right Now. Stafford.
The Sandman. Janvier.
A Sessions of the Poets.
Suckling.
Shall I Charge Like a Bull.
Auvaiyar.
The Sloth. Gardner.
Slow Mama Slow. Collins.
Small Town. Joyce.
Soap (II). Rothenberg.
Song in a Siege. Heath.
A Song of Two Wanderers.
Wilkinson.
Syringa. Ashbery.
Thistledown. Reese.

To the Boston Women.
Anonymous.
To the Mountains. Thoreau.
To W.B.Yeats Who Says That
His Castle of Ballylee Is His
Monument. Gogarty.
Trains at Night. Frost.
The Trojan Horse.
Drummond.
Villanelle of Washington
Square. Roberts.
We Go out Together.
Patchen.
Which Are You?
Anonymous.
The Winning of Cales.
Anonymous.
Work to Do Toward Town.
Snyder.

Toy (s)
All Work and No Play Makes
Jack a Dull Boy.
Anonymous.
The Angler. Chalkhill.
Begging A.I.D. Rubadiri.
Blight. Emerson.
Certain Artists Bring Her
Dolls and Drawings.
Yeats.
Cops and Robbers.
Middleton.
Dance. Weeden.
Deo Optimo Maximo.
Guiney.
A Dialogue betwixt GOD and
the Soul. Wotton.
Epigram: "Time was when
once upon a time."
Glaucus.
Fie, Fie on Blind Fancy!
Greene.
George. Belloc.
Jill Came from the Fair.
Farjeon.
Looking Forward.
Stevenson.
Love Poem. Nims.
The New Nutcracker Suite
(excerpt). Nash.
The Ocean Said to Me Once.
Crane.
October XXIX, 1795.
Braithwaite.
Odes. Horace.
The Philanderer. Mendes.
A Ruined House. Aldington.
Sonnets from a Sequence.
Barker.
Travel. Stevenson.
When I am grown to man's
estate. Stevenson.
Windy Morning. Behn.
Winter Nights. Campion.

Toyko
Come, Ride with Me to
Toyland. Bennett.
In a Bar near Shibuya Station,
Tokyo. Engle.

Trace (d) (s)
Afterword. *Anonymous.*
Beauty Is Most at Twilight's
Close. Lagerkvist.
The Beast That Rode the
Unicorn. Meyer.
The Dance. Lehmann.
Death Killed the Rich.
Anonymous.
The Death of Will.
Tomlinson.
The Dedication to a Book of
Stories Selected from the
Irish Novelists. Yeats.

Epilogue. Russell.
Icarus. Bottrall.
The Lateshow Diorama.
  Dewdney.
Playmates. Everts.
Soho. Brodsky.
Summer Solstice. Bowering.
Tema con Variazioni.
  "Carroll.
They. Leib.
To My Little Son. Davis.
Wheatlet Son of Milklet.
  MacConglinne.

Track (s)
The Beaten Path. Winslow.
Beauty Is Most at Twilight's
  Close. Lagerkvist.
Bolsum Brown (with music).
  Anonymous.
Calling Trains. *Anonymous.*
Depot in Rapid City. Hill.
The Desert. Knibbs.
Dream of the Lynx. Haines.
Engine. Tippett.
Epigram: The Hunt Goes By.
  Nemerov.
The Fear. Abercrombie.
Fish. Shinkichi.
For Freckle-Faced Gerald.
  Knight.
The Goose Fish. Nemerov.
I Taught the Talented.
  Sappho.
In the Forest. Wilde.
The Landmark. Rossetti.
Leaps over the Aisle of
  Syllogism (parody). Berry.
Like Snow. Graves.
Memoir. Weingarten.
Railway Station. Hay.
The Red Flag. Jackson.
Riddle: "Goes through the
  mud." *Anonymous.*
The Russian Soul II.
  Hollander.
The Shack. Miller.
The Sixties. Listmann.
Sleep. Simic.
Variations on a Theme.
  Whitman.
Variations on a Theme.
  Williams.
A White Wall under the
  Wallpaper. Henderson.
The Womanhood. Brooks.

Tractor
Drive a Tractor. *Anonymous.*
Wagon Wheels. LaMoure.
Yachting in Arkansas.
  Weeden.

Trade (s)
Battle of the King's Mill.
  English.
The Beggar's Opera. Gay.
Coronary Thrombosis.
  Turner.
Dugall Quin (B version).
  Anonymous.
Epigram: "The greatest saints
  and sinners have been
  made." Butler.
Goldenhair. Waller.
Hearing Russian Spoken.
  Davie.
I Was a Bustle-Maker Once,
  Girls. Barrington.
It's Such a Little Thing to
  Weep. Dickinson.
A light exists in spring.
  Dickinson.
Marginalia. Wilbur.
Mary Hynes. Fallon.

On a Monday Morning.
  Tawney.
The Ploughman.
  Anonymous.
The Refugees. Jarrell.
Retrospection. Shaw.
The Rhyme of the Three
  Captains. Kipling.
The Scholar and the Cat.
  Anonymous.
Shop and Freedom.
  Anonymous.

Tradition
Breaking Tradition.
  Mirikitani.
The Discovery of Tradition.
  Inada.
Generations. Simmons.
In Memory of George
  Whitby, Architect.
  Betjeman.
The Latest Decalogue.
  Clough.
The Woodchuck Who Lives
  on Top of Mt. Ritter.
  Simon.

Trafalgar
The National Gallery.
  MacNeice.

Traffic
Caelica, XIX. Greville.
County Roads. Rabbit.
Eternal Contour. Smyth.
Fear. Wier.
My Father's Martial Art.
  Liu.
On the "Sievering" Tram.
  Spencer.
Slipping out of Intensive Care.
  Trefethen.
Surfaces. Mayhall.
Trafique Is Earth's Great
  Atlas. Alsop.
Wheels. Donnelly.

Tragedy
Adriatic. Conquest.
All Human Things (parody).
  Schroeder.
The Beautiful Negress.
  Pitter.
The Beginning. Stevens.
Captain Glen's Unhappy
  Voyage to New Barbary.
  Anonymous.
On His Own Agamemnon and
  Iphigeneia. Landor.
Orpheus. Hendry.
Poem from "The Revolution."
  Rubin.
Puerto Ricans in New York.
  Reznikoff.
Tales of the Islands, II.
  Walcott.
"These are the live."
  Fearing.
This Life a Theater.
  Palladas.
Tristan and Isolda. Levy.
The Wail of Archy (excerpt).
  Marquis.

Trail
The Brother Eagles.
  Anonymous.
Bucking Bronco.
  Anonymous.
Dawn Boy's Song.
  Anonymous.
Dogie Song. *Anonymous.*
Doney Gal. *Anonymous.*
Frozen Fire. McLaren.
The Grave-Tree. Carman.

Hymns and Spiritual Songs.
  Smart.
Jess's Dilemma. *Anonymous.*
John Garner's Trail Herd.
  Anonymous.
Laramie Trail. Hanson.
Message from Ohanapecosh
  Glacier. Ransom.
Milton by Firelight. Snyder.
The Pioneer. Guiterman.
The Red Men. Sangster.
A Snapshot of Uig in
  Montana. Hugo.
The Texas Ranger. Boswell.
The Trail. Weismiller.
We Love the Name of Texas.
  Anonymous.
Woodlore. Kurt.

Trailers
The City and the Trucks.
  Thompson.

Train (s)
900 Miles. *Anonymous.*
Acts Passed beyond the
  Boundary of Mere Wishing.
  Spender.
Alabama-Bound.
  Anonymous.
The Angel of Patience.
  Whittier.
At Devlin's Siding. Boake.
Big Fat Woman.
  Anonymous.
Bill Groggin's Goat.
  Anonymous.
The Broomstick Train.
  Holmes.
Burying Ground by the Ties.
  MacLeish.
Charley Snyder. *Anonymous.*
The Chosen–Kalgoorlie, 1894.
  Zwicky.
The City in the Throes of
  Despair. Towle.
A Dream. Jones.
Dreamers. Sassoon.
Eric. Barford.
The Escalator. Glasgow.
The Farmer's Ingle.
  Fergusson.
For Sale. Lowell.
Goodbye 'Liza Jane.
  Anonymous.
The Green Train. Rieu.
The Hell-Bound Train.
  Anonymous.
In Texas Grass. Troupe.
Jack and Joan. Campion
The Journey. Hansbrough.
Liza Jane. *Anonymous.*
A Local Train of Thought.
  Sassoon.
Mary Had a Baby.
  Anonymous.
Observation Car. Hope.
Passenger Train. Chase.
The Rescued Year. Stafford.
Rouen. Cannan.
Same Train. *Anonymous.*
Seems Like We Must Be
  Somewhere Else.
  Levertov.
September: Last Day at the
  Beach. Tillinghast.
Signs of Christmas. Lees.
Skimbleshanks: the Railway
  Cat. Eliot.
Sleep. Statius Publius
  Papinius.
Snow Country. Etter.
Song of a Train. Davidson.
Squabbling Blues. Bill.

Hymns and Spiritual Songs.
The Stationmaster's Lament.
  Rothenberg.
To Guillaume Appollinaire.
  Brodey.
The Train of Religion
  (excerpt). Tupper.
The Train to Glasgow.
  Horsburgh.
Train Window. Finch.
Trains. Tippett.
Travel. Millay.
The Traveller. Berryman.
Unsent Message to My
  Brother in His Pain.
  Stokesbury.
A Vision. Vaughan.
Visit of Hope to Sydney Cove,
  near Botany-Bay. Darwin.
Volleyball Teacher Ends the
  Game. Teran.
Western Town. Shapiro.
Where the Single Men Go in
  Summer. Bourne.
Who Follows in His Train?
  Heber.
Who's Gonna Shoe Your
  Pretty Little Foot?
  Anonymous.
Windy Morning. Behn.
Within My Breast. Wyatt.
The Wreck on the Somerset
  Road. *Anonymous.*

Traitor (s)
The Ballad of Helmut Franze.
  Sala.
Day of Renewal. MacNeice.
The Death of Ben Hall.
  Ogilvie.
Hobie Noble. *Anonymous.*
Julius Caesar. Shakespeare.
The River Fight. Brownell.
To Sir Toby. Freneau.
The Turtle-Dove.
  Anonymous.
Upon the Death of George
  Santayana. Hecht.
Wendell Phillips (excerpt).
  O'Reilly.
Wine and Love and Lyre.
  Anonymous.

Tralee
The Rose of Tralee. Spencer.

Tram
A Jewish Cemetery Near
  Leningrad. Brodsky.
Limerick:"There once was a
  man who said: "Damn!"
  Hare.

Tramp
Just Lost, When I Was Saved!
  Dickinson.
The Lady Is a Tramp. Hart.
Rain Riders. Scollard.

Trample (d)
Buffalo. Brodsky.
Credo. Cohen.
Envoy. MacLean.
Fleur de Lys. Heppenstall.
Golden Stockings. Gogarty.
Like a sweet apple reddening
  on the high. Sappho.

Trampoline
Dancers at the Moy.
  Muldoon.
Movement. Levertov.

Trance
Idylls. Theocritus.
Life. Coleridge.
The Sleeping Beauty. De
  Ford.

Tranquil (ity)
The College Cat. Godley.

From My Window.
  Coleridge.
In Praise of Blur. Chandra.
Influence of Natural Objects.
  Wordsworth.
The Lonely Isle. Claudian
  (Claudius Claudianus).
The Old. Noel.
On the Birth of His Son. Su
  Tung-p'o.
On the Frozen Lake.
  Wordsworth.
Refuge. Sarett.
Sohrab and Rustum. Arnold.
Sonnet: Composed by the Side
  of Grasmere Lake.
  Wordsworth.
The Stars on Shabbat.
  Schlonsky.
'Tis Said the Gods Lower
  Down That Chain Above.
  Alsop.
A Vision. "Field.
Winter Twilight. Rlliot.

Transcend (ence) (ental) (ing) (s)
80-Proof. Ammons.
Asolando. Browning.
Equal Troth. Rossetti.
The Flesh-Fly and the Bee.
  Patmore.

Transfer
Get a Transfer. *Anonymous.*
Journey. Wakoski.

Transfiguration
Mythics. Chasin.

Transfigured
The Lamentation of the Old
  Pensioner. Yeats.
Prayer. Wilder.
The Transfiguration of Beauty.
  Michelangelo.

Transformation (s)
The Anteroom. Levertov.
Cider and Vesalius. Peck.
From the Journals of the Frog
  Prince. Mitchell.
On a Damaske Rose Sticking
  upon a Ladies Breast.
  Carew.
The Statue of Medusa.
  Drummond.

Transgress (ion)
Letter Containing a Panegyric
  on Bath. Anstey.
Lo, I Am Stricken Dumb.
  Anonymous.
O Heaven Indulge. Tilden.

Transient
Credo. Kreymborg.
Daisies of Florence. Raine.
The Image-Maker. Gogarty.
The Put-Down Come On.
  Ammons.
To the Earl of Dorset.
  Philips.

Translate (d)
Epitaph on an Engraver.
  Thoreau.
Letter to Tina Koyama from
  Elliot Bay Park. Mitsui.
Prospero on the Mountain
  Gathering Wood. Gilbert.

Translation
Destiny of the Poet. Vigee.
Japanese Fan. Veley.
A Lesson in Translation.
  Preil.

Transparent
Like Water Down a Slope.
  Schneour.
Washing Windows. Wild.

Transport (ed) (ing) (s)
2nd Dance–Seeing Lines–6
  February 1964. MacLow.
An African Song.
  Chatterton.
Against Love. Philips.
As Down a Valley. Dwight.
Chilled by the Blasts of
  Adverse Fate. Duche.
For Under the Volcano.
  Lowry.
The Invitation. Godfrey.
The Seasons. Thomson.

Trap (ped)
Attis. Catullus.
Cultural Notes. Fearing.
Dead Center. Whitman.
O Lamb Give Me My Salt.
  Anonymous.
Riddle: "Old Mother Twitchet
  had but one eye." Mother
  Goose.
Traps. Davies.

Trash
Critics. Swift.
The Food of Love. di
  Michele.
A Quarrel with Fortune.
  Colman.
September Sun: 1947.
  Gascoyne.
Tattle. Turner.

Travel (ed) (er) (ing) (s)
Arches and Shadows.
  Dillard.
Black Bart, P08. Bierce.
The Book of Day-Dreams.
  Moore.
The Bridge. Kohler.
Caelica, LXXV. Greville.
Cities behind Glass. Hogan.
The Comparison and
  Complaint. Watts.
Dark Flows the River.
  Bourinot.
December Stillness. Sassoon.
The Delinquent Travellers.
  Coleridge.
The Faerie Queene. Spenser.
Freeborn Man. MacColl.
The Gamboling Man (C
  vers.). *Anonymous.*
God's Saints. Vaughan.
The Gone Dead Train. Hill.
Good Memory. Rivera-
  Aviles.
Haiku: "Even in my village..."
  Kyorai.
He Embarketh in the Boat of
  Ra. Book of the Dead.
Hesperus. Clare.
Hitch Haiku. Snyder.
I Heard the Voice of Jesus
  Say. Bonar.
The Idiot Boy. Wordsworth.
John Clare. Anderson.
The Journey of the Suicides.
  Bowering.
Just Forget. Dryden.
Late, Passing Prairie Farm.
  Stafford.
A Letter Is a Gypsy Elf.
  Wynne.
Like an Adventurous Sea-
  Farer Am I. Drayton.
The Little Girl with Bands on
  Her Teeth. Taggard.
Mary Desti's Ass. O'Hara.
The MJQ. Thomas.
The Mufadaliyat: Gone Is
  Youth. Salamah.
The New House. Rutsala.

Now the Leaves Are Falling
  Fast. Auden.
Outside Dunsandle. Sitwell.
Permission to Speak. Orlen.
Phoenix. Rodgers.
Poem out of Childhood.
  Rukeyser.
The Pony Blues. House.
Promise. Russell.
The Queen's Marie.
  Anonymous.
Silence. Wheelock.
Silex Scintillans. Vaughan.
The Spire Cranes. Thomas.
The Stethoscope. Abse.
Swift's Epitaph. Yeats.
Thanks in Old Age.
  Whitman.
Thyrsis. Arnold.
Traveling on My Knees.
  Goodwin.
Traveller's Guide to
  Antarctica. Stoutenburg.
Unable by Long and Hard
  Travel to Banish Love,
  Returns Her Friend.
  Turberville.
The Unexplorer. Millay.
Walking at Night. Hare.
What need I travel, since I
  may. Hall.
Whoopee Blues. Hill.
The Winners. Kipling.
The Witch Doctor's Magic
  Flight. Narautjarri.
X, Oh X. Simpson.

Trawl (er)
Deep Sea Tug. *Anonymous.*
The Final Trawl.
  Anonymous.
Fourteenth Birthday.
  McGinley.
The Loss of the Evelyn Marie.
  Anonymous.
Sunken Evening. Lee.

Treachery (ies)
Hawks. Stephens.
The Odyssey. Homer.
The People's Choice: The
  Dream Poems II. Jones.
Young Paris. Crabbe.

Tread (ing) (s)
Ad Infinitum. Aronsten.
As into the Garden Elizabeth
  Ran. Housman.
At Dunwich. Thwaite.
Fragment: "Near where the
  riotous Atlantic surge."
  Allingham.
Hope. Theognis.
Learning Destiny. Bosman.
The Man of Kerioth (excerpt).
  Norwood.
Mary Hamilton. *Anonymous.*
Mr. Brunt. Siegel.
On the Death of a Cat.
  Rossetti.
The Pyre of My Indian
  Summer. Leib.
Resolution. Berrigan.
The Slave Chase.
  Anonymous.
The Sower. Binyon.
The Wish. Stanley.
Years Later. Stone.

Treadmill
Crystals Like Blood.
  ""MacDiarmid.

Treason
Christmas 1944. Levertov.
Fishermen. Bunting.

Gunpowder Plot Day.
  Anonymous.
King Henry VI.
  Shakespeare.
Ode: "Now I find thy looks
  were feigned." Lodge.
The Purple Island. Fletcher.
Thanks, Gentle Moon, for
  Thy Obscured Light.
  Anonymous.
Were My Hart as Some Mens
  Are. Campion.

Treasure (d) (s)
America. McKay.
The Apple Tree. Baxter.
The Bargain. Neidhart von
Carmina Amico. James.
Clouds. Chapman.
Don't. *Anonymous.*
Early Losses: A Requiem.
  Walker.
Gallery of My Heart. Kuka.
The Gombeen. Campbell.
He Is a Path. Fletcher.
Holy Bible, Book Divine.
  Burton.
I Sigh, as Sure to Wear the
  Fruit. *Anonymous.*
If You're Ever Going to Love
  Me. *Anonymous.*
The Island Boatman's Love-
  Croon. Farren.
The Journey nears the Road-
  End. Tagore.
The Kitten and the Falling
  Leaves. Wordsworth.
Lines with a Gift of Herbs.
  Lewis.
Lolo Died Yesterday. Zarco.
Lord of Life, All Praise
  Excelling. Moore.
Madrigal: "Shall a frown."
  Corkine.
Madrigal: "Sing we and chant
  it." Morley.
Our Life Is Hid with Christ in
  God. Herbert.
Pater Filio. Bridges.
Promise of Peace. Jeffers.
The Rope. Van Zyl.
Saint R. L. S. Cleghorn.
The Seafarer. Pound.
Six Epigrams (excerpt).
  Hopkins.
Some Verses Upon the
  Burning of Our House, July
  10th, 1666. Bradstreet.
A Song: "Chloris, when I to
  thee present." *Anonymous.*
Song Set by Robert Jones: "O!
  How my thoughts do beat
  me. *Anonymous.*
Songs Set by Thomas Morley:
  "Sing we and chant it."
  Anonymous.
Sonnets, XX: "A woman's
  face with nature's own hand
  painted." Shakespeare.
Sons of Promise. Clark.
Souvenir. Musset.
Surely You Remember.
  Ravikovich.
A Treasure. Whittemore.
Treasure Boat. Fujino.
Troy. Muir.
The Vedic Hymns: To the
  One God. *Anonymous.*
What Makes a Home?
  Anonymous.
Woodbines in October.
  Bates.

Treasury
A Hymn of Thanksgiving.
  Nesbit.
Riches. Blake.

Treat (ed)
Blow Me Eyes! Irwin.
Catastrophe. Brock.
Ease It to Me Blues. Hicks.
I'm Going Down This Road
  Feeling Bad. *Anonymous.*
If You Saw a Negro Lady.
  Jordan.
A Letter to Her Mother.
  Eristi-Aya.
O Fearfull, Frowning
  Nemesis. Daniel.
One Fish Ball. *Anonymous.*
To His Friend J. H. Brome.

Treatises
On a Portrait of Mme.
  Rimsky-Korsakov. Amis.
To a Child. McCord.

Treaty
In Death's Field. Al-
  Khansa.
The Trophy. Muir.

Treblinka
Golda. Wolfert.

Tree (s)
3 Stanzas about a Tree. Bell.
An ABC. *Anonymous.*
An Abortion. O'Hara.
Above the Rocking Heads of
  the Mothers. Sachs.
Against the Thieves of
  Liddesdale. Maitland.
Ah My Dere. *Anonymous.*
Alison Gross. *Anonymous.*
All Hallows. Gluck.
Allison Gross. *Anonymous*
Amoretti, LVI. Spenser.
Annunciation. Rilke.
The Apple. Smith.
Apple-Seed John. Child.
Apples in New Hampshire.
  Gilchrist.
Arbor Amoris. Villon.
Arbor Day. Thompson.
Ark Articulate. Macpherson.
Aspens. Thomas.
At Torrey Pines State Park.
  Mazzaro.
Atheist. Harburg.
Aunt Mary. Hawker.
Autumn Color. Robinson.
Autumnal Spring Song.
  Miller.
Ballad of the Goodly Fere.
  Pound.
A Ballad of the Rising in the
  North. *Anonymous.*
Best of Two Worlds.
  Boothroyd.
A Bird Comes. Yosano
  Akiko.
The Bitter Withy.
  Anonymous.
Blessing Mrs. Larkin.
  Mansfield.
Boy Riding Forward
  Backward. Francis.
Breaking Point. Auxier.
Breasts. Unger.
The Brereton Omen (excerpt).
  Hemans.
Brother Juniper. Kelly.
The Cage. Bartlett.
The Call. Dickey.
Can-Opener. McAleavey.
The Carolinas. Ray.
Chou and the South.
  Confucius.

The Circus. Koch.
Citizen. Wallace-Crabbe.
Collaboration. Towle.
Come Christmas. McCord.
The Comfort of the Trees.
  Gilder.
The Coming of Good Luck.
  Herrick.
Coppersmith. Murphy.
The Cradle. Robinson.
Crescent Moon. Roberts.
The Cross. Lanier.
Dad and the Cat and the
  Tree. Wright.
The Dancers. Robinson.
A Dangerous Music. Knoll.
Daphne. Flanner.
Daphne. Jones, Jr.
Death of Rimbaud. Fisher.
The Demiurge's Laugh.
  Frost.
Denials 1. Somerville.
Desire Is Dead. Lawrence.
Detroit City. Boyer.
The Devil's Thoughts
  (excerpt). Porson.
Dirge in the Woods.
  Meredith.
Don't Break It. Ceravolo.
Dream Songs. Berryman.
The Drummer-Boy and the
  Shepherdess. Rands.
E Questo Il Nido in Che la
  Mia Fenice? Hope.
The Earth-Spirit. Channing,
  II.
Echoes of Wheels. Maurice.
The Empty House. De la
  Mare.
Eve's Song in the Garden.
  Gottlieb.
Every One to His Own Way.
  Cheney.
Evolution. Swenson.
Execution of Alice Holt.
  Anonymous.
A Fallen Yew. Thompson.
Farewell to the Glen.
  Rossetti.
Farmyard. Dallas.
Father and I in the Woods.
  McCord.
The Felled Plane Tree.
  Hajnal.
Fireworks. Reeve.
First Love. Kunitz.
The Flowering of the Rod.
  Doolittle.
For Allan. Frost.
For No Clear Reason.
  Creeley.
For Spring. Jones.
Fourteen Men. Gilmore.
Funeral in Hungary. Boyle.
The Garden. Grimald.
Genesis. Ingham.
Getting Out. Maloney.
Giraffe and Tree. Turner.
The Girt Woak Tree That's in
  the Dell. Barnes.
The Golden Fleece.
  Williams.
The Happy Tree. Gould.
Harbingers. Basho (Matsuo
  Basho).
The Haunted Oak. Dunbar.
Hazlitt Sups. Little.
Head and Bottle. Thomas.
The Heart of the Tree.
  Bunner.
Heavy, Heavy–What Hangs
  Over? Burke.

Heresy for a Class-Room.
  Humphries.
The Hero. Jackson.
Hiking. Bruchac.
Hippolytus. Euripides.
Honolulu and Back. Logan.
Hope. Carmichael.
How to Tell the Wild
  Animals. Wells.
I Had a Dove. Keats.
I See His Blood upon the
  Rose. Plunkett.
I Sought All over the World.
  Tagliabue.
Improved Farm Land.
  Sandburg.
In a Country Church.
  Thomas.
In the Deep Channel.
  Stafford.
In the Forest. Bowering.
Injured Maple. Everson.
The Insular Celts. Carson.
Invisible, indivisible Spirit.
  Doolittle.
Invitation to Juno. Empson.
Jack-in-the-Box. Olson.
A Journey through the
  Moonlight. Edson.
The Journey to the Insane
  Asylum. Lichtenstein.
Juniper. Duggan.
The Kabbalist. Eibel.
Kind Lovers, Love On.
  Crowne.
The Kingfisher. Davies.
The Kite. Behn.
The Knee on Its Own.
  Morgenstern.
Lake, Mountain, Tree.
  Glover.
Landeys. *Anonymous.*
Late in Fall. Wilson.
The Leaf-Makers. Stewart.
A Legend of the Northland.
  Cary.
A Lesson from Van Gogh.
  Moss.
Lilly Dale. Thompson.
Limerick: "There is little in
  afternoon tea." Burgess.
The Little Cradle Rocks
  Tonight in Glory.
  Anonymous.
The Lost Orchard. Masters.
Love Speaks at Last.
  Herbert of Cherbury.
The Lover: A Ballad.
  Montagu.
Lucy. Wordsworth.
MACV Advisor. Gray.
Manhattan Menagerie.
  Cherwinski.
March Hares. Young.
Mason Jar. Steinberg.
Matisse. Hirsch.
Me Imperturbe. Whitman.
Midsummer Jingle. Levy.
Monkey. Miles.
The Moon. Hall.
Moschatel. O'Sullivan.
Mountain Top. *Anonymous.*
The Mouse That Gnawed the
  Oak-Tree Down. Lindsay.
Mrs. Asquith Tries to Save
  the Jacarandas. Witt.
The New View. Holmes.
No Possum, No Sop, No
  Taters. Stevens.
November Night. Crapsey.
O Brother Man. Whittier.
The Odd Ones. Suckow.

Of the Theme of Love.
  Newcastle.
The Oft-Repeated Dream.
  Frost.
On Corwen Road. Ames.
On Dr. Evans Cutting down a
  Row of Trees at St. John's
  College... *Anonymous.*
On Dwelling. Graves.
Once I Was a Shepherd Boy.
  Anonymous.
Or Wren or Linnet.
  Coleridge.
Overtones. Percy.
Paradise Lost. Milton.
The Park. Blaser.
Parks and Ponds. Emerson.
A Pastel. Verlaine.
Paul. Wright.
Peking Man, Raining. Lorr.
Pictures of a Gone World.
  Ferlinghetti.
Piney Woods. Cowley.
Plainness. Borges.
Planting a Tree. Turner.
Planting Trees. Friedlaender.
Playgrounds. Alma-Tadema.
Poem for Hemingway & W.
  C. Williams. Carver.
Poem in June. Acorn.
Poem: "We used to float the
  paper boats in spring."
  Olsen.
The Postures of Love.
  Comfort.
Protective Colors. Logan.
Psalm. Schwartz.
Rain. Murray.
Red May. Robinson.
Reflection in a Green Arena.
  Corso.
Restless as a Wolf. Halpern.
Resurgam. Burt.
Riddle: "A white bird
  featherless floats down
  through the air."
  Anonymous. Peterson
Rinaldo. Peterson
The Ring. Pack.
The Rivals. Stephens.
Roads. Dallas.
Robin Hood and the Beggar.
  Anonymous.
Ruston, Louisiana: 1952.
  Mathis.
The Same Continued. Blunt.
San Sabas. Palés Matos.
Saturday Market. Mew.
La Selva. Corman.
Shade. Garrison.
A Silent Wood. Siddal.
Sleeping Beauty. De La
  Mare.
The Sleeping Beauty. Sitwell.
Snow. Aldis.
The Snow-Gum. Stewart.
Softly, White and Pure.
  Fulton.
Some Modern Good Turns.
  Dibben.
Song for a Dark Girl.
  Hughes.
Song: "Music, thou queen of
  souls, get up and string."
  Randolph.
Song: "Now let us honor with
  violin and flute." Sarton.
A Song of Enchantment. De
  la Mare.
Song of the Fucked Duck.
  Piercy.

Song of the Open Road.
Nash.
Song: "Those rivers run from
that land." Creeley.
Soon at Last My Sighs and
Moans. Ginsberg.
Sophistication. Miller.
Sound. Harrison.
Spanish Folk Songs.
Anonymous.
Spirits of the Dead. Poe.
The Stockdoves. Young.
The Stone Garden. Shelton.
A Stopwatch and an
Ordanance Map. Spender.
The Sun Came Out in April.
Day-Lewis.
Symbols. Thompson.
Talking with Soldiers.
Turner.
Tam Lin. *Anonymous.*
They. Leib.
This Is What the Watchbird
Sings, Who Perches in the
Lovetree. Boyd.
The Thousand and One
Nights: Love. *Anonymous.*
Three Green Windows.
Sexton.
The Three Ladies. Creeley.
Thunderstorm. Mitchell.
To God. Herrick.
To Her Love. May.
To Laurels. Herrick.
To Life I Said Yes. Grade.
To the Faithful. Ana.
The Torrent. Robinson.
The Tree. Bjornson.
The Tree in the Desert.
Hebbel.
The Tree-Top Road. Smith.
Trees. Clark.
Trees. Kilmer.
The Trees. Morley.
The Trees Are Down. Mew.
Trees at the Arctic Circle.
Purdy.
Trees Both in Hills and
Plaines, in Plenty Be.
Wood.
Trees Lose Parts of
Themselves inside a Circle
of Fog. Ponge.
Tropical Towns. Selva.
A Typical 6:00 P.M. in the
Fun House. Berrigan.
Uncle Mells and the Witches'
Tree. Roberts.
Under the Shade of the Trees.
Preston.
The Underside of Trees. De
Clue.
University Curriculum.
Turner.
The Unquiet Grave.
Anonymous.
Vacation Trip. Babcock.
Variations on a Still Morning.
Cole.
The Village of the Presents.
McMichael.
The Visions. Du Bellay.
Voice from Danang.
Redshaw.
War and Silence. Bly.
Watertower. Bellg.
The Way the Bird Sat.
Young Bear.
We Become New. Piercy.
When I See Another's Pain.
Leib.

When There Were Trees.
Willard.
Who Has Seen the Wind?
Rossetti.
The Wife's Tale. Heaney.
Wild Cherry Tree. Blunden.
Willows. Schreiber.
The wind begun to knead the
grass. Dickinson.
Winter Trees. Diekmann.
Witness. Miles.
A Woman Is a Branchy Tree.
Stephens.
The Woman Who Combed.
Rankin.
Wood Music. King.
The World's Wanderers.
Shelley.
The Wry Rowan.
Anonymous.
You Got a Right.
Anonymous.
The Zilver-Weed. Barnes.

Trellis
At the Indian Killer's Grave.
Lowell.

Tremble (d) (s)
The Bonhomme Richard and
Serapis. Freneau.
Compline. Scott.
Desideravi. Maynard.
Design for a Bowl.
Anacreon.
The Drunkeness of Pain.
Shenhar.
The Edge. Dobson.
Epipsychidion. Shelley.
Explorations Bronchitis: The
Rosario Beach House.
Rodriguez.
The Fear. Gibson.
Homecoming. Margolin.
In Me, Past, Present, Future
Meet. Sassoon.
Incident. MacCaig.
October 1803. Wordsworth.
On the Wallowy. Chester.
Rainer Maria Rilke Returns
from the Dead... Engman.
Romance. Poe.
Sad Memories. Calverley.
The Sailor. Warner.
Songs of the Priestess.
Tussman.
Station Island (excerpt).
Heaney.
To Julia in Shooting Togs
(parody). Seaman.
To Make the People Happy.
Hugo.
Unbeliever. Dow.
Vernal Equinox. Stone.
The Vestal Virgin. Llwyd.
The Voice. Gale.
You Must Have Been a
Sensational Baby (excerpt).
Norse.

Trembling
Almeria. Neruda.
At Swindon. Brett.
The City Rat and the Country
Rat. La Fontaine.
Jack-in-the-Box. Olson.
Jerked Heartstrings in Town.
Jones.
Johnson's Cabinet Watched by
Ants. Bly.
The Morning of the Red-
Tailed Hawk. Sellers.
The Rape of the Lock.
Pope.
The Sorcerer. Smith.

Welcome Every Guest.
Anonymous.
Wind and Lyre. Markham.
The Yule Log. Hayne.

Tremont Street
A Revivalist in Boston.
Rich.

Tremor
The California Phrasebook.
Schmitz.
The Clock. Ducic.
Fencing School. Manifold.

Trench
Battle: Hit. Gibson.
The Little White Cat.
Anonymous.

Trenton Falls
Fitz Adam's Story. Lowell.

Trespass (ers) (es)
And Forgive Us Our
Trespasses. Behn.
Durer: Innsbruck, 1495.
Malley.
Little Things. Stephens.
The Penance. Tate.
Sonnets, CXX: "That you
were once unkind befriends
me now." Shakespeare.
The Specialist. Perlman.

Tress (es)
I'll Twine White Violets.
Meleager.
Love in the Valley.
Meredith.
No and Yes. Ashe.
The Painter's Mistress.
Flecker.
A South Coast Idyll.
Watson.
'Tis but a Little Faded
Flower. Howarth.

Trial (s)
All My Trials. *Anonymous.*
Ballyhoo for a Mendicant.
Talbott.
Christ and the Little Ones.
Gill.
The Christian's New-Year
Prayer (excerpt). Wilcox.
Dream Songs. Berryman.
Highway Patrol Stops Me,
Going Too Slow.
Peterson.
Homecoming. Szymborska.
The Last Trial. *Anonymous.*
Lula Vires. *Anonymous.*
The Ship in Distress.
Anonymous.
Zeal and Love. Newman.

Tribe (s)
The Birds of Scotland
(excerpt). Grahame.
The Butterfly and the Bee.
Bowles.
Death Song. Lewis.
Deer in the Bush. Bloch.
The Dove. Halevi.
The Enormous Aquarium.
Santos.
Finders Keepers. Finkel.
An Indian at the Burial-Place
of His Fathers. Bryant.
Nepenthe. Darley.
Nostalgias. Mahon.
Oh, How My Love with a
Whirling Power. Tu-kehu
and Wetea.
Rachel's Lament. Zisquit.
The Surrender at
Appomattox. Melville.

Tribulation
The Dissenters' Thanksgiving
for the Late Declaration.
Anonymous.
Glazunoviana. Ashbery.
Peace and Joy in Jesus Christ.
Franck

Tribunal
The Trial. Scholem.

Tribute (s)
The Dolphin's Return.
Anonymous.
An Epitaph. Byron.
For Nijinsky's Tomb.
Cornford.
In Passing. Shepherd.
An Interlude. Bishop.
Like the Prime Mover.
Seljouk.
Lines on Mountain Villages.
"Sunset Joe".
Love's Tribute. Sturgeon.
Nijinsky. Ferne.
The Three Kings. Field.
We Praise Thee, If One
Rescued Soul. Sigourney.
Women of My Land.
Armstrong.

Trick (ed) (s)
April Fool. Hunt.
Denouement. Stone.
The Inflatable Globe.
Spencer.
Links. Cassity.
The Magician. Miranda.
Old Rowley the King.
Anonymous.
Sea-Fever. Masefield.
So Graven. Miles.
Song: "Of thee, kind boy, I
ask no red and white."
Suckling.
Sonnet: "Of thee (kind boy) I
ask no red and white."
Suckling.
To Poets and Airmen.
Spender.
Village of Winter Carols.
Lee.
The Wanton Trick.
Anonymous.

Trifle (d) (s)
Last Week I Took a Wife.
Kelly.
Limerick Town (excerpt).
O'Donnell.
To Clio. From Rome. Dyer.

Trigger
Annie Breen. *Anonymous.*
He scanned it, staggered,
dropped the loop.
Dickinson.
Honest Abe Lincoln.
Shulman.
Light, 2. Eberhart.
The Verdict. Cameron.

Trim
The Faerie Queene. Spenser.
Indolence. Bridges.
Sailors' Harbour. Reed.
Song: "Farewell, adieu, that
court-like life!" Pickering.

Trinity
The Assassination of President
McKinley. Blackburn.
Christmas Now Is Drawing
Near. *Anonymous.*
Epiphany. Shanahan.
The Gift of a Skull. Skelton.
Look, You Have Cast Out
Love! Kipling.

Trinity

On a Doctor of Divinity.
Porson.
On a Fellow of Trinity
College, Cambridge.
Porson.
Patroling Barnegat.
Whitman.
Rillons, Rillettes. Wilbur.
Sighed a Dear Little
Shipboard Divinity.
Aiken.
Upon a Dead Man's Head.
Skelton.

Trinket (s)

The moon was but a chin of
gold. Dickinson.

Trio

Number Song. Waldman.

Trip (s)

Abroad Thoughts from Home.
Hall.
Bigerlow (with music).
Anonymous.
The Bigler. Anonymous.
The Golden Age: Hymn to
Diana. Heywood.
In Go-Cart So Tiny.
Greenway.
Little Elegy. Kennedy.
A-Maying, A-Paying. Nashe
[(or Nash(] Thomas.
The Nurse's Dole in the
Medea. Euripides.
One West Coast. Young.
Sea-Chill. Guiterman.
Since Robin Hood.
Anonymous.
Tea Poems: Afternoon Tea.
Brown.
Ten Thousand Miles away.
Anonymous.

Tripe (s)

Sausage. Axionicus.
These Obituaries of
Rattlesnakes Being Eaten by
the Hogs. Weingarten.

Triste

All Human Things (parody).
Schroeder.
Snatches: "The lovedy
Fortune is bothe frend and
fo." Anonymous.

Trite

A Sparrow's Feather.
Barker.
With a First Reader.
Hughes.

Triumph (ed) (ing) (s)

Astrophel and Stella, XLII.
Sidney.
At the Wedding March.
Hopkins.
The Battle-Field. Bryant.
The Battle of Lookout
Mountain. Boker.
The British Prison Ship:
Canto III. The Hospital
Prison Ship. Freneau.
Call All. Anonymous.
Captain Molly. Collins.
Character of the Happy
Warrior. Wordsworth.
Charleston. Timrod.
Chorus. Jonson.
A Creed. McLeod.
An Elegie on the Lady Jane
Pawlet, Marchion: of
Winton. Jonson.
Etruscan Warrior's Head.
Henze.
For Randolph Bourne.
Oppenheim.

Green Plumes of Royal
Palms. Brant.
Hymn of Joy. Van Dyke.
If to Die–. Romilu.
In a Dream. Ignatow.
In October. Carman.
In Winter. Bretherton.
The Last Day. Derosier.
Last Speech to the Court.
Vanzetti.
Letter to a Friend. Warren.
Loving and Beloved.
Suckling.
The Needle. Tall.
A Note of Humility.
Bontemps.
Old Amusement Park.
Moore.
On a Travelling Speculator.
Freneau.
On Time. Milton.
One to Destroy, Is Murder by
the Law. Young.
Our Country's Call. Bryant.
Paradise Lost. Milton.
A Soldier: His Prayer.
Kersh.
Some in Their Harts Their
Mistris Colours Bears.
Smith.
The Song of the MicMac.
Howe.
Sousa. Dorn.
Spring Thoughts. Huang-fu
Jan.
Tell Forth His Fame.
Anonymous.
The Temptation of Saint
Anthony. Symons.
There's a Light upon the
Mountains. Burton.
The Tombe. Stanley.
The Train Will Fight to the
Pass. Pitter.
The Triumphs of Thy
Conquering Power.
Bathurst.
What Am I Who Dare.
Habington.
Will Yer Write It Down for
Me? Lawson.

Triumphant

Description of a Ninety Gun
Ship. Falconer.
Easter Hymn. John of
Damascus.
Elliott Hawkins. Masters.
Judge Me, O God. Barlow.

Trivial (ity)

3 A. M. Edmond.
Treasures. Thomas.

Trod (den)

A Fable for Critics. Lowell.
The Flute. Taylor.
God. Slutsky.
Levavi Oculos. Campbell.

Troilus

But Whan the Cok: Troilus
and Criseide. Chaucer.

Trojan

The Iliad. Homer.
Walking in a meadow green.
Anonymous.

Troop (s)

Expanse Cannot Be Lost.
Dickinson.
Gastrology (excerpt).
Archestratus.
Ode to the Inhabitants of
Pennsylvania. Anonymous.
Reinforcements. Lynch.

Trophy (ies)

In a Garret. Melville.
An Ode: "Thou Dome, where
Edward first enroll'd."
Tickell.
A Satyretericall Charracter of
a Proud Upstart. Saffin.

Trot (ted)

Busby, Whose Verse No
Piercing Beams, No Rays.
Moore.
Dogs and Weather. Welles.
How the Old Horse Won the
Bet. Holmes.

Troth

The Doom-Well of St.
Madron. Hawker.
The Siller Croun. Blamire.
Till the Sea Runs Dry.
Anonymous.

Troubadour (s)

The Banjo Player. Johnson.
Bryan, Bryan, Bryan, Bryan.
Lindsay.

Trouble (d) (s)

After the Quarrel. Gordon.
Black Mountain Blues.
Smith.
Come All Ye Fair and Tender
Maidens. Anonymous.
Corn Canon. Stevenson.
The Crib. Finch.
Darling Corey. Anonymous.
A Day in My Union Suit.
Pettit.
A Dead Child. Lucian [(or
Lucianus)].
Diogenes. Bishop.
A Dog's Death. Squire.
Don't Trouble Trouble.
Pearse.
Dough Roller Blues. Akers.
Dry Land Blues. Lewis.
The Elder Edda: Part of the
Lay of Sigrdrifa.
Anonymous.
An Elegy. Yuan Chen.
Epigram: The World Is Full
of Care." Ward.
An Execration against
Whores. Webster.
Fair/Boy Christian Takes a
Break. Harrison.
La Figlia Che Piange. Eliot.
The First Time I Met You.
Montgomery.
The Flying Wheel. Hinkson.
For Every Day. Havergal.
For Just Men Light Is Sown.
Wigglesworth.
For the Earth God.
Anonymous.
God's A-Gwineter Trouble de
Water. Anonymous.
High Price Blues. Sykes.
A Hint to the Wise. Barret.
How Old Brown Took
Harper's Ferry. Stedman.
I'm Sad and I'm Lonely.
Anonymous.
I to My Perils. Housman.
In Vain Was I Born.
Nezalhualcoyotl.
Lights in the Quarters Burnin'
Mighty Dim. Anonymous.
Little Sparrow (Come All You
Young and Handsome
Ladies). Anonymous.
Love It Is Pleasing.
Anonymous.
The Maiden Hind.
Anonymous.

Man Frail, and God Eternal.
Watts.
My Black Mama. House.
My Heart Moves as Heavy as
the Horse That Climbs the
Hill. Anonymous.
The Nameless One. Mangan.
Ninety-Fifth. Anonymous.
Nobody Knows de Trouble I
See. Anonymous.
Oatmeal Deluxe. Dobyns.
Of All the Sayings in This
World. Anonymous.
On Christmas Eve. Pierce.
On William Wilson, Tailor.
Anonymous.
Peter Bell. Reynolds.
A Poor Man's Work Is Never
Done. Anonymous.
Porson on His Majesty's
Government. Porson.
Prologue to a Saga. Parker.
Psalm XXV. Sidney.
The Railroad Blues.
Anonymous.
The Rebel. Evans.
The Revenant. Siegel.
Roberta. Leadbelly.
The Sad Day. Flatman.
Scissors and String, Scissors
and String. Anonymous.
Senzangakhona. Anonymous.
A Shantyman's Life (I).
Anonymous.
A Shropshire Lad.
Housman.
The Silent Pool. Monro.
Slavery Chain Done Broke at
Last. Anonymous.
Song for the Wandering Jew.
Wordsworth.
Spell of Sleep. Raine.
Spenser's Ireland. Moore.
They Say My Verse Is Sad:
No Wonder. Housman.
This Beast That Rends Me.
Millay.
To My Body. Sullivan.
To the River Beach: Stalks of
Wild Hay. Davis.
Toe, Trip and Go.
Anonymous.
The Toy-Maker. Colum.
The Troubled Soldier.
Anonymous.
Visitations. Durrell.
Vo'k a-Comen into Church.
Barnes.
W. Reeves.
Wade in the Water.
Anonymous.
Wartime Blues. Jefferson.
Were I in Trouble. Frost.
The White Canoe. Sullivan.
The Wife-Hater. Anonymous.

Troubleshooters

Bold Troubleshooters. Veale.

Trousers

Apples Be Ripe. Anonymous.
Coplas. Anonymous.
A Fragment: "The boy stood
on the burning deck."
(parody). Anonymous.
Jackie Tar. Anonymous.
The Jam-Pot. Kipling.
My Specialty Is Living Said.
Cummings.
Ode to Popularity. Praed.
Remember Suez? Mitchell.
Taffy. Anonymous.
Taffy Was a Welshman.
Anonymous.

Trout
And Angling, Too. Byron.
Ballade: To a Fish of the Brooke. Wolcot.
Dips or Counting Out Rhymes: "I saw a doo flee our the dam." *Anonymous.*
Flyfisherman in Wartime. Bacon.
Gateposts. McGuckian.
An Irish Lake. Rodgers.
Mac Diarmod's Daughter. Carlin.
Poem: "Disturbing to have a person." Guest.
Skunks (excerpt). Jeffers.
Spring. Hogan.
Water. Snyder.

Troy
Aeneas at Washington. Tate.
Ballad of Hector in Hades. Muir.
The Ditty of the Six Virgins. Watson.
Helen–Old. MacKay.
The Iliad. Homer.
In a Bed-Sitter. Porter.
Of Ballad-Singers. Gay.
Venus. Rossetti.

Truant
Clever Peter and the Ogress. Pyle.
The Rain-Crow. Cawein.

Truck (s)
The City and the Trucks. Thompson.
Country Trucks. Shannon.
Hunting. Snyder.
Julio. Robertson.
Kindness during Life. *Anonymous.*
Who's in Charge Here? Bell.

Truckdriver
The Trouble with Truck Drivers. Treitel.

True
Always Battling. O'Brien.
Always True to You in My Fashion (excerpt). Porter.
American Muse. Benét.
Amphimachos the Dandy. McHugh.
The Anchor's Aweigh. *Anonymous.*
Annan Water. *Anonymous*
Annie of Lochroyan. *Anonymous.*
Antichrist. Muir.
As I Went out for a Ramble. *Anonymous.*
At Her Fair Hands. Davison.
At the Setting of the Sun. *Anonymous.*
Aurora Leigh. Browning.
Autumn. Winwar.
The Bailiff's Daughter of Islington. *Anonymous*
The Ballad of Minepit Shaw. Kipling.
Barbara Allen. *Anonymous.*
Beautiful Isle of Somewhere. Pounds.
Beauty in Trouble. Graves.
Because My Faltering Feet. Belloc.
Before Thy Throne. Carpenter.
Bird Song. Rosenberg.
Bonny Barbara Allen (B vers.). *Anonymous.*

A Border Ballad (parody). Peacock.
Bouquet in Dog Time. Carruth.
The Broomfield Wager. *Anonymous.*
Chang'd, Yet Constant. Stanley.
Charlie Macpherson. *Anonymous.*
The Chimney Sweeper. *Anonymous.*
The Church of the Sacred Heart. Greene.
Colonel Sharp. *Anonymous.*
Come All Ye Fair and Tender Ladies. *Anonymous.*
The Comparison. Carew.
Crossedroads. Shockley.
Dead Love. Siddal.
Death. Oppenheim.
The Douglas Tragedy. *Anonymous*
Dover Beach. Arnold.
Down in the Willow Garden. *Anonymous.*
Dreaming in the Trenches. McCabe.
Dropping Your Aitches. Beach.
The Drunkard. Johnson.
Dunkirk. Nathan.
Earl Brand (B vers.). *Anonymous.*
An Elegy on the Death of Furuhi. Yamanoue Okura.
England's Heart. Tupper.
Epistemology. Wilbur.
An Epitaph on True, Her Majesty's Dog. Prior.
An Esthetic of Imitation. Finkel.
An Excellent New Song, Being the Intended Speech of a Famous Orator... Swift.
Extraordinary Will. Jackett.
The Fair Beauty Bride. *Anonymous.*
The Fair Flower of Northumberland. *Anonymous.*
Faith of Our Fathers. Faber.
The Fire i' the Flint. Robinson.
Five Domestic Interiors. Scannell.
Fragment for the Dark. Jennings.
Friday Night's Dream on a Saturday Told. *Anonymous.*
The Garden. Shirley.
Geometry. Dove.
George Collins. Anonymous.
Gerry's Rocks. *Anonymous.*
Gipsy Love Song. Smith.
The Girl in the Carriage. *Anonymous.*
God Gives Them Sleep on Ground, on Straw. Williams.
A Grey Day. Moody.
Hail, Holy Land. Tillam.
Hamlet. Shakespeare.
Hard, Ain't It Hard. *Anonymous.*
Her Faith. Belloc.
High Germany. *Anonymous.*
Hind Horn (In Scotland Town). *Anonymous.*

The House of a Hundred Lights. Torrence.
I Came A-Riding. Reinmar von Zweter.
I Did Not Know the Truth of Growing Trees. Schwartz.
I'll Remember You, Love, in My Prayers. *Anonymous.*
I Take Thee Life. Ruddock.
I Think I See Him There. Cuney.
Ideals. Greene.
In Memoriam, A. H. 1916. Baring.
In Memoriam A.H.H., XVI. Tennyson.
In Memoriam Francis Ledwidge. Heaney.
The Indifferent. Donne.
Ivy and Holly. Meyerstein.
James Hatley. *Anonymous.*
Jerusalem Sonnets. Baxter.
John Henry (B vers.). *Anonymous.*
King Henry V. Shakespeare.
The Knight of the Burning Pestle. Fletcher.
Lady Alice (A version). *Anonymous.*
Lady Alice (C version). *Anonymous.*
Lady Alice (George Collins), I. *Anonymous.*
The Lass of Roch Royal (A vers.). *Anonymous.*
Legend. Laforgue.
Let Her Give Her Hand. *Anonymous.*
The Lexington Miller. *Anonymous.*
Little Musgrave and Lady Barnard (Little Matthy Groves). *Anonymous.*
Lord Lovel. *Anonymous.*
Lord Lovel (A vers.). *Anonymous.*
Lord Thomas and Fair Ellinor. *Anonymous.*
Love. Tasso.
Love and Life. Rochester.
Love Letter from an Impossible Land. Meredith.
The Love Suicides at Sonezaki (excerpt). Monzaemon.
The Lover Freed from the Gallows. *Anonymous.*
The Lucifer. Glover.
A Maiden's Ideal of a Husband. Carey.
Make Me a Garment. *Anonymous.*
The Man from the Woods. Ciardi.
The Man of Taste. Bramston.
The Martyrdom of St. Teresa. Hope.
The Mexico Trail. *Anonymous.*
Mountain Medicine. Long.
Murder Mystery. Steele.
My Dancing Day. *Anonymous.*
Newark Abbey. Peacock.
The Night Nurse Goes Her Round. Gray.
Nothing. Singer.
O, Open the Door to Me, O! Burns.
Odysseus. Merwin.

Oh, Think Not I Am Faithful to a Vow! Millay.
An Old Man from Peru. *Anonymous.*
Old Smoky. *Anonymous.*
Old Voyager. Blackstock.
On Falling Asleep to Birdsong. Meredith.
On Sunday in the Sunlight. Benet.
On Top of Old Smoky. *Anonymous.*
The Only Way to Have a Friend. *Anonymous.*
Optimism. Wilcox.
Our True Beginnings. Gardiner.
The Passer. Abbe.
A Pastoral. Breton.
The Peaceful Western Wind. Campion.
Le Pere Severe. *Anonymous.*
Poop. Locklin.
Poor Omie. *Anonymous.*
The Postage Stamp Lesson. *Anonymous.*
Praise of New England. Chubb.
Prayer of a Beginning Teacher. Dunnam.
Red River Valley. *Anonymous.*
Remorse. Lattimore.
Riddle: "Every lady in the land." *Anonymous.*
The Rifles. *Anonymous.*
Ring Out, Wild Bells. Tennyson.
The Road's End. Garrison.
La Rose des Vents. Wilbur.
Rydal. Coleridge.
Satyrus Peregrinana. Rankins.
Scarborough Fair. *Anonymous.*
The Second Rapture. Carew.
Seth Compton. Masters.
She Is Overheard Singing. Millay.
A Shropshire Lad. Housman.
A Soldier's Prayer. Freeman.
Solomon. Hagedorn.
Something to Eat. Veitch.
Song. Clare.
The Song of the Bow. Doyle.
Song Under Shadow. Benet.
Sonnet: He Is Past All Help. Angiolieri.
Sonnet: "My soul surcharged with grief now loud complains." Morpurgo.
Sonnets, LVII: "Being your slave, what should I do but tend." Shakespeare.
Sonnets, CXIII: "Since I left you, mine eye is in my mind." Shakespeare.
Sonnets, CXXIII: "No, Time, thou shalt not boast that I do change." Shakespeare.
Still Growing. *Anonymous.*
Stopping by Shadows. Fulton.
Sweethairt, Rejoice in Mind. Montgomerie.
Switzerland. Godley.
Talking in Bed. Larkin.
The Tattooed Man. Smith.
Ten Thousand Miles. *Anonymous.*

Ten Thousand Miles Away (with music). *Anonymous.*
Thoreau. Alcott.
Thou Joy'st, Fond Boy. Campion.
To cause accord or to agree. Wyatt.
To His Mistris Confined. Shirley.
To His Unconstant Friend. King.
The Trees They Do Grow High. *Anonymous.*
Treizaine. Wyatt.
The Tri-Coloured Ribbon. Kearney.
True Love. Cuney.
True Night. Char.
True Rest. Goethe.
Twicknam Garden. Donne.
The Unquiet Grave. *Anonymous.*
Until Death. Akers.
Upon Some Women. Herrick.
Upon the Most Useful Knowledge, Craft or Cunning... Wycherley.
Verses Made the Night before He Died. Drayton.
The Virgin. *Anonymous.*
Wardrobe. Mary Madeleva.
The Western Rebel. *Anonymous.*
Whittingham Fair. *Anonymous.*
Wild Eden. Woodberry.
The Wreck of Number Nine. *Anonymous.*
You Never Miss the Water. Williams.

Truly
I Love You Truly. Bond.
Nothing Fair on Earth I See. "Angelus Selesius" (Johannes Scheffler).

Trump
Amoretti, LXXXV. Spenser.
Latimer's Light. *Anonymous.*
Life's a Game. *Anonymous.*

Trumpery
The Apologist's Evening Prayer. Lewis.

Trumpet (s)
Airship. Sobiloff.
And When I Lamented. Heine.
And Yet We Are Here! Wolfskehl.
Ballade d'une Grande Dame. Chesterton.
The Bands and the Beautiful Children. Page.
Beethoven's Death Mask. Spender.
Child with a Cockatoo. Dobson.
Columbus the World-Giver. Egan.
Dakota Land. *Anonymous.*
Domestic Duties. Braun.
Epilogue for a Masque of Purcell. Rich.
Fabien Dei Franchi. Wilde.
False Prophet. O'Malley.
Far Trumpets Blowing. Benson.
The Fight at the Bridge. Macaulay.
His Metrical Vow. Graham.
In Memoriam A.H.H., XCVI. Tennyson.

Laus Veneris. Swinburne.
A Letter to a Live Poet. Brooke.
Logic. Murry.
Oh, When Shall I See Jesus? *Anonymous.*
A Piece of Black Bread. "Bagritsky.
The Promised Land. Sampter.
Retaliation. Goldsmith.
The Second Anniversarie. Donne.
Sheep. Hoffenstein.
Slievenamon. *Anonymous.*
Song: "Sometimes I feel like an eagle in de air." *Anonymous.*
The Storm. Coatsworth.
Toward a True Peace. Cheyney.
You May Bury Me in de Eas'. *Anonymous.*

Trundle Bed
My Mother's Prayer. O'Kane.

Trunk (s)
The Alphabet. *Anonymous.*
Between Leaps. Leithauser.
Birch. Simpson.
The Elephant. Belloc.
End of Play. Graves.
For You I Have Emptied the Meaning. Zukofsky.
The Golden Fleece. Williams.
The Haunted Oak. Dunbar.
I Wilp Turn Your Money Green. Lewis.
Places of Nestling Green. Hunt.
The Railroad Corral. *Anonymous.*
The Silver Flask. Montague.
This Morning I Wakened among Loud Cries of Seagulls. MacDonogh.

Trust (ed) (ing) (s)
Accused though I be without desert. Wyatt.
Afterward. Ward.
All Those Hymnings Up to God. Evans.
The Art of Politics. Bramston.
"...As When Emotion Too Far Exceeds its Cause"– Elizabeth Bishop. Oden.
Beatrice Has Gone up into High Heaven. Dante Alighieri.
The Best for Me. *Anonymous.*
The Blessed Virgin's Expostulation. Tate.
Caelica, XLVIII. Greville.
Cast Down, but Not Destroyed. *Anonymous.*
The Child's Heritage. Neihardt.
The Conclusion. Ralegh.
Crow and Pie. *Anonymous.*
Cuba. Rice.
Cupid's Indictment. Lyly.
A Development of Idiotcy. Jones.
Discouraged. Stanaback.
Driven by desire I did this deed. Wyatt.
Elegy. Di Roma.
English Bards and Scotch Reviewers. Byron.

Epitaphs of the War, 1914-18. Kipling.
Eulogy for Hasdai Ibn Shaprut. *Anonymous.*
Face to Face with Trouble (excerpt). Sangster.
Fair Days; or, Dawns Deceitful. Herrick.
Fair Florella (B vers.). *Anonymous.*
A Fairy Tale. Mackenzie.
Famine Song. *Anonymous.*
The First Dandelion. Whitman.
First-Day Thoughts. Whittier.
For the Lady Olivia Porter; a Present upon a New-years Day. Davenant.
A Form of Adaptation. Creeley.
Four Things. Van Dyke.
The Girl on the Greenbriar Shore. *Anonymous.*
"Girt in my guiltless gown..." Surrey.
God's Eye Is on the Sparrow. Meyer.
Hedgehog. Muldoon.
Her Face Her Tongue Her Wit. Gorges.
How? *Anonymous.*
Imitation of Chaucer (parody). Pope.
In Some Way or Other the Lord Will Provide. Cook.
In the Forest. Petofi.
It Was My Choice. Wyatt.
Jay Gould's Daughter (with music). *Anonymous.*
The Jealous Lover (B vers.). *Anonymous.*
Jesus, I Come to Thee. Beman.
The Lady Fortune. *Anonymous.*
The Last Man. Campbell.
Liberty. Hay.
Lilith on the Fate of Man. Brennan.
The Lincoln Statue. Collins.
Lyve Thowe Gladly, Yff So Thowe May. Wyatt.
Mount Vernon. *Anonymous.*
Mundus Morosus. Faber.
Mundus Qualis. Sylvester.
My Love, She Passed Me By. *Anonymous.*
Old Damon's Pastoral. Lodge.
One, the Other, And. Wieber.
One Way of Trusting. Kimball.
The Paper Nautilus. Moore.
A Poet's Grace. Burns.
Poly-Olbion. Drayton.
Possession. Lawner.
A Prayer. Ham.
Psalm XXXIII. Sidney.
Psalm XXXIV. Sidney.
Psalm XXXVII. Sidney.
Recipe for Living. Walton.
Renewal. "Field.
Rime LVII: "Ever myn happe is slack and slo in commyng." Petrarch (Francesco Petrarca).
Satire. Donne.
The Sea-Captain. Gould.
Security. Sandell.
Sense and Spirit. Meredith.

Sing, My Soul. *Anonymous.*
The Soldier Thought Dead Returns Home. *Anonymous.*
A Song of Diana's Nymphs. Lyly.
Spaniel's Sermon. Ellis.
Summum Bonum. Browning.
Te Deum Laudamus. *Anonymous.*
Thy Will Be Done. Reitz.
The Time to Trust. *Anonymous.*
To Laura W—, Two Years Old. Willis.
To Lucasta, from Prison. Lovelace.
To the King on His Navy. Waller.
Trust Him. *Anonymous.*
Trust in Women. *Anonymous.*
Under Which Lyre. Auden.
Vers de Societe (parody). Traill.
Virgin and Unicorn. Heath-Stubbs.
A Volume of Chopin. Picot.
Wait for the Hour. Soutar.
Whan netilles in wynter bere rosis rede. *Anonymous.*
Which Shall It Be? Beers.
Wisdom. Middleton.

Truth (ful) (s)
After the Murder of Jimmy Walsh. Murray.
Alcestis. Euripides.
Another Given: The Last Day of the Year. Dickey.
Another September. Kinsella.
The Archer. Ainslie.
Armistice Day Vow. Gould.
As Tranquil Streams. Ham.
Assurance. Herbert.
Astrophel and Stella, LXVII. Sidney.
At the Bottom of the Well. Untermeyer.
Babylon. Taylor.
Beale Street, Memphis. Snyder.
Benedicite, What Dreamed I This Night? *Anonymous.*
Betweens. MacCaig.
Black and Glossy as a Bee and Curled Was My Hair. Ambapali.
The Boy and the Wolf. Aesop.
Bus Stop. O'Sullivan.
By Gentle Love. *Anonymous.*
Caelica, XXXVI. Greville.
Caelica, LXVI. Greville.
Caelica, LXXVII. Greville.
The Call. Clark.
A Catch-22 Test. Sellers.
The City of the Moon (excerpt). Rexroth.
Claudius Gilbert Anagram. Tis Braul I Cudgel. Wilson.
Cockies of Bungaree. *Anonymous.* ?
The College Colonel. Melville.
The Coming of Wisdom with Time. Yeats.
Country Walk. Taylor.
Crossing the County Line. Randall-Mills.
Crusty Critics. Crabbe.

Dead in Wars and in Revolutions. O'Neill.
A Death in the Desert. Browning.
The Derby Ram. *Anonymous.*
Diehard. Moffett.
The Difference between a Lie and the Truth. Dessus.
The Dream of Gerontius. Newman.
Dream the Great Dream. Coates.
Duty. Hooper.
Eden Revisited. Miller.
The Elder Edda: The Short Lay of Sigurd (excerpt). *Anonymous.*
Epilogue to a Human Drama. Spender.
Epitaph for Himself. Herbert of Cherbury.
An Essay on Man. Pope.
An Essay on Translated Verse (excerpt). Roscommon.
For Righteousness' Sake. Whittier.
Founder's Day. Bridges.
Fragment: "Some pretty face remembered in our youth." Clare.
G.M.B. Davie.
Goat's-Leaf. Marie de France.
Godly Casuistry. Butler.
Habakkuk. Roditi.
Halfway. Kumin.
The Hand. Feldman.
The Hidden Truth. Jami.
The Hills. Grenfell.
I Came to Jesus. White.
I Lift My Heart to Thee. Sternhold.
I've Worked for a Silver Shilling. Kennedy.
I Was Washing outside in the Darkness. Mandelstam.
In a Hard Intellectual Light. Eberhart.
In a World of Change. Awad.
In Memoriam A.H.H., XLII. Tennyson.
In the Mood of Blake. Soutar.
It Rolls On. Bishop.
It Was My Choice. Wyatt.
Laid in My Quiet Bed. Surrey.
Laocoon. Hall.
Last Refuge. Michelangelo.
A Last World. Ashbery.
A Letter from When. Bernadine.
Life's Testament. Baylebridge.
The Light That Came. Clifton.
Lobotomy. Pitchford.
The Locus. Corman.
Loneliness. Werfel.
Lost Illusions. Johnson.
Lying. Moore.
Magna Est Veritas. Smith.
The Maid of the Moor, or The Water-Fiends. Colman.
Malachi. Marlatt.
The Man Christ. Lindsey.
The Man on the Dump. Stevens.

Maymie's Story of Red Riding-Hood. Riley.
Mazeppa. Campbell.
A Meditation on John Constable. Tomlinson.
Mein Kind, Wir Waren Kinder. Heine.
Mexico City Blues. Kerouac.
Modern Love, XLIV. Meredith.
Modern Love, XLVIII. Meredith.
The Moral Warfare. Whittier.
More of Thee. Bonar.
Morning. Kavanagh.
The Mother's Hymn. Bryant.
My Ace of Spades. Joans.
Nature and the Poets. Beattie.
A Nautical Extravaganza. Irwin.
Night Flight. Johnson.
No Sweeter Thing. Love.
O Lord of Life. Gladden.
Ode on a Grecian Urn (parody). Parrott.
Of the Mathematician. Matthews.
Omnia Vincit. Cochrane.
On a Frightful Dream. Bampfylde.
On Approaching My Birthday. Miller.
On Behalf of Some Irishmen Not Followers of Tradition. Russell.
Our Orders. Lowe.
Outside. Stafford.
Paradise Regained. Milton.
The People. Campanella.
Petition. Thomas.
Picture of a Castle. Meredith.
The Pilgrim. Embury.
The Poets at Tea. Pain.
Portrait in Available Light. Miles.
The Powerful Eyes O' Jeremy Tait. Irwin.
A Prayer. Sill.
A Prayer for the Self. Berryman.
The Prize of the Margaretta. Carleton.
Psalms, CXLVII. Smart.
The Purpose of Fable-Writing. Phaedrus.
Queen Mab. Shelley.
A Remonstrance. Gerrard.
Revenge. Nugent.
Rimbaud. Auden.
Robin Hood and Little John. *Anonymous.*
The Rose of Tralee. Spencer.
Sacrifice. Emerson.
Satire. Pope.
Scholar I. Deane.
Scotch Te Deum. Kethe.
The Search. Brew.
Secret Prayer. Belle.
Send No Money. Larkin.
Sexsmith the Dentist. Masters.
Shadows. Milnes.
Shakespeare, an Epistle to David Garrick, Esq.. Lloyd.
Shells. Moore.
The Shepherd-Boy and the Wolf. Aesop.

"So Quietly". Hill.
Sonnet: "Lift not the painted veil which those who live." Shelley.
Sonnet Sonnet. Engle, Jr.
Sonnets, XIV: "Not from the stars do I my judgement pluck." Shakespeare.
Sonnets, XIX: "Those former loves wherein our lives have run." Agee.
Sonnets, LIV: "O, how much more doth beauty beauteous seem." Shakespeare.
Sonnets of the Months. San Geminiano.
Sonnets to Aurelia. Nichols.
Sound from Leopardi. Berkson.
The Spelling Bee at Angels. Harte.
Swearing. Fitzsimon.
A Tabernacle Thought. Zangwill.
Tales of the Islands, V. Walcott.
Telling It. Sullivan.
There Is No Balm in Birmingham. Deacon.
Think Not When You Gather to Zion. Snow.
This Discord in the Pact of Things. Boethius.
Thou Art the Way. Doane.
Thou Lord of Hosts, Whose Guiding Hand. Frothingham.
Threnody. Scherzo.
To Purity and Truth. *Anonymous.*
A Tribute to Dante. Boccaccio.
The True Knight. Hawes.
The True, the Good and the Beautiful. Schwartz.
Truth. McKay.
Ulysses Hears the Prophecies of Tiresias. Homer.
Voice in the Crowd. Joans.
Wedlock. A Satire. Wright.
The Whale. *Anonymous.*
What Dreamed I? *Anonymous.*
Wild Bees. Baxter.
Women Singing. Taylor.
Wordsworth at Tea. Pain.
Work. Block.
Youth. Shelton.

Try (tried) (tries)
After Some Day of Decision. Whittemore.
The Beast Section. Smith.
The Bookworm. De la Mare.
Canto XIII. Pound.
Courage to Live. Crowell.
The Death of Europe. Olson.
Evil Devil Woman. McCoy.
The Flying Dutchman. *Anonymous.*
A Hoggie Dead! *Anonymous.*
How the Little Kite Learned to Fly. *Anonymous.*
Limerick: "There was a young maid who said, "Why." *Anonymous.*
The Modes of Vallejo Street San Diego, Los Angeles (excerpt). Seidman.
The Newlyweds' Cuisine. Wang Chien.
Pact. Fearing.

Prospero Dreams of Arnaud Daniel Inventing Love in the Twelfth Century. Gilbert.
Sky Pictures. Newsome.
Solomon and the Witch. Yeats.
Song: "'Tis said that absence conquers love!" Thomas.
To a Child. Gardons.
Tragedy. Van Doren.
The Urban Experience. Blockcolski.
War. Ostroff.
Winter Drive. McAuley.
Trying
Dream Songs. Berryman.
I Am Going to Sleep. Storni.
Important Matters. Mungoshi.
Sonnets to Philomel. Davies.
Tryst
Aaron Burr's Wooing. Stedman.
The Bell of the Hermitage. *Anonymous.*
Carrier Letter. Crane.
Church Bell in the Night. *Anonymous.*
If Spirits Walk. Jewett.
The Moth. De la Mare.
Two Paths. Dorr.
Tuck (ed)
Footnote to John ii.4. Mason.
Index. Mayer.
Limerick: "A jolly young artist called Bruno." *Anonymous.*
Trains at Night. Frost.
When You Go Away. Merwin.
Tucson
Bronco Busting, Event #1. Swenson.
In Old Tucson. Beghtol.
Tuesday
An Auctioneer's Handbill. Hall.
I Shall Be Married on Monday Morning. *Anonymous.*
Spouse. Bynner.
Tuft (s)
Feathered Dancers. Elmslie.
Haiku: "Once upon a time". Issa.
Homecoming. *Anonymous.*
The Song Called "His Hide Is Covered with Hair.'. Belloc.
Tug (ged) (ging) (s)
Father and Son. Stafford.
I never hear the word "escape'. Dickinson.
In the Deep Channel. Stafford.
The Last Resort. Willson.
Running the Trotline. Elledge.
The Sentiments. *Anonymous.*
Tulip (s)
The Lady's Dressing Room. Swift.
March Snow. McKay.
Nightfall in Dordrecht. Field.
To a Young Lover. Mu'izzi.
Tulips. McGuckian.

Tumble (d) (s)
The Domineering Eagle and the Inventive Bratling. Carryl.
In Kansas. *Anonymous.*
It's nice that though you are casual about me. Sulpicia.
It troubled me as once I was. Dickinson.
Jack and Jill. Mother Goose.
Limerick: "There was a young man at St. Kitts." *Anonymous.*
Little Blue Betty. *Anonymous.*
My Childhood's Bedroom. Tisdale.
Ode to Fortune. Drake.
The Portrait of a Florentine Lady. Reese.
Softly, Drowsily. De la Mare.
The Tower of Babel. Crouch.
Truth. North.
Tumbling. *Anonymous.*
Youth. Toerien.

Tumult
Another True Maid. Prior.
In Memoriam A.H.H., LXXV. Tennyson.
Letter. Empson.
Waterfall. Heaney.

Tuna
Limerick: "A coloratura named Luna." Wilson.

Tundra
Back to Base. Joseph.
The Tundra. Haines.

Tune (d) (s)
Al Fitnah Muhajir. Sudan.
All Sung. Le Gallienne.
Astrophel and Stella, XLIV. Sidney.
Australia's on the Wallaby. *Anonymous.*
Back from the Paved Way. FitzGerald.
Collin My Deere and Most Entire Beloved. Smith.
Fallen Leaves. *Anonymous.*
Finland. Graves.
For Walter Lowenfels. Rose.
Great Day (Union Version). *Anonymous.*
Greystone Cottage. Hugo.
His Metrical Vow. Graham.
I Won't Be My Father's Jack. *Anonymous.*
In the Isle of Dogs. Davidson.
Italian Opera. Miller.
Letter. Empson.
MacPherson's Farewell. Anonymous.
Moment Musicale. Gould.
The Next Market Day. *Anonymous.*
The Night Will Never Stay. Farjeon.
Player Piano. Updike.
Psalm XXXII. Wyatt.
Query. Ebon.
The Reason for Skylarks. Patchen.
The Scorner. Tam'si.
Scotch Song. D"Urfey.
Snow. De la Mare.
A Song of the Road. Stevenson.

Sonnet: "Not wrongly moved by this dismaying scene." Empson.
Troubador. Simmons.
Turkey in the Straw. *Anonymous.*
The Village Choir (parody). *Anonymous*
The Voyage of Life. Bernstein.
Wheeler's Brigade at Santiago. Rice.

Tunnel (s)
Coda. MacNeice.
In the Evening from My Window. *Anonymous.*
Travellers Turning over Borders (parody). Ransome.

Turbulence
Discomfort in High Places. Tremayne.
London and Bristol Delineated. Savage.

Turf
A Backwoods Hero (excerpt). McLachlan.
The Father. O'Grady.
Ortho's Epitaph. Calverley.

Turk
Ad Coelum. Romaine.
Commanders of the Faithful. Thackeray.

Turkey
A Melancholy Lay. Fleming.
This Is the Life. MacNeice.

Turmoil
Eye and Tooth. Lowell.
Little Son. Johnson.
A Sailor's Prayer. Morris.

Turn (ed) (ing) (s)
Ad Infinitum. Aronsten.
The Aged Pilot Man. "Twain.
Alas, Alack. De La Mare.
Amoretti, XIX. Spenser.
And That Will Be Heaven. Paterson.
Anna Elise. *Anonymous.*
Aridity. Lewis.
Arm Wrestling with My Father. Driscoll.
At the Grave of a Land-Shark. Moll.
Aunt Alice in April. Matchett.
Autobiography. Causley.
The Balloon Man. Aldis.
Beside the Road. Belford.
The Big Swing-Tree Is Green Again. Carr.
Blind Geronimo. Berkson.
Blue Homespun. Call.
Canto CXIII. Pound.
Castles in the Air. Ballantine.
Childe Harold's Pilgrimage: Canto III. Byron.
Cleavage. Nicholl.
A Day in the Life. Beatles.
Death Rode a Pinto Pony. Montgomery.
Deep Night. Jimenez.
Domine Quo Vadis? Watson.
Dressed to Kill. Major.
The Eel. Morgan.
Elegy Written on a Frontporch. Shapiro.
Everything. Paul.
Father and Son. Kunitz.
A Feather's Weight. Lathrop.

First Day of Teaching. Overstreet.
Foetal Song. Oates.
The Garden. Dolben.
Gnome. Beckett.
Good Friday, 1613. Riding Westward. Donne.
Good Tradition. *Anonymous.*
A Grave. Moore.
Growing Up. Gregg.
Happening. Honig.
Harvesting Wheat for the Public Share. Li Chu.
The Hill. Brooke.
Hotel. Wazyk.
Hunchbacked and Corrected. Belford.
I Dreamed Last Night of My True Love (with music). *Anonymous.*
I'm On My Way. *Anonymous.*
I turn you out of doors. Chartier.
Iceland First Seen. Morris.
In Hades. Brackett.
In Moncur Street. Hewett.
In the Night. Jennings.
Incident. Kopp.
An Israeli Soldier's Nightmare. Carb.
It May Not Always Be So. Cummings.
It's Hard to See but Think of a Sea. Zukofsky.
Jerked Heartstrings in Town. Jones.
The Kiss. Yau.
The Landmark. Rossetti.
The Lesser Evil. Orwell.
Let Me Look At Me. Martin.
Linen Town. Heaney.
The Little Wee Man. *Anonymous.*
Looby Loo. *Anonymous.*
Lullaby in Auschwitz. Morhange.
Lunar Eclipse. Scarbrough.
The Man Who Named Children. Rios.
The Mask. Delany.
The Mill. Wilbur.
The Miller and His Sons. *Anonymous.*
Mirror. De Vries.
Miss Creighton. Taylor.
Mothers. Tzara.
Mountain Convent. Benet.
Nights in Hackett's Cove. Strand.
Nooksack Valley. Snyder.
Northwind. Baro.
Not Even in Dreams. Ise.
O Turn Once More. Scott.
Ode: "To orisons, the midnight bell." Beckford.
Ode: "Who can support the anguish of love?" Ibn al-Arabi.
The Odyssey. Homer.
Old Moon My Eyes Are New Moon. Ginsberg.
On the Ineffable Inspiration of the Holy Spirit. Greiffenberg.
Once More. Jonas.
The One-Horned Ewe. *Anonymous.*
Out of the Deepness. Jackson.

Overlooking the River Stout. Hardy.
The Oyster-Eaters. Blight.
Paradox: The Birds. Shapiro.
People on Sunday. Denby.
Perhaps. Clifton.
Pity Me Not. Millay.
A Place to Live. Grossman.
A Poem beginning with a Line by Pindar. Duncan.
Poppies. Weekes.
Raccoon on the Road. Brennan.
A Renunciation. King.
Requiem. Maynard.
Robinson Crusoe. Carryl.
The Run from Manassas Junction. *Anonymous.*
The Sea. Webb.
Seen from the Train. Day Lewis.
A Sleeping Beauty. Riley.
Snowbanks North of the House. Bly.
Sodom; or, The Quintessence of Debauchery (excerpt). Rochester.
Song for Ireland. Colclough.
Song the Ninth. moore.
Songs of Ch'en. Confucius.
Sonnets. Tuckerman.
The Sower. Binyon.
The Strath of Kildonan. Morris.
Summer on the Great American Desert. Sage.
Summer Visitors. Clark.
Sunrise in Summer. Clare.
Takes All Kinds. Dickey.
Though My Thoughts. Pastorius.
'Tis the Gift To Be Simple. *Anonymous.*
To Grosphus. Godfrey the Satirist
To One Far Away, Dancing. Finley.
The Triumph of Doubt. Bishop.
The Tropics in New York. McKay.
Trot along Pony. Grider.
Turning. Finch.
The Unloved to His Beloved. Percy.
Upon Glass: Epigram. Herrick.
Wake. Spires.
Washington. Goodman.
Wedding Song. Goethe.
What No Man Knoweth. Blunt.
The Wheelbarrow. Edson.
When Diamonds, Nibbling in my Ears. Davies.
When Geometric Diagrams... "Novalis" (George Friedrich Philipp von Hardenerg).
When I Grow Up. Wise.
When I Was Growing Up. Vogel.
When the Tree Bares. Aiken.
Who Will Endure. Auden.
The Widow. Ludvigson.
The Wizard's Funeral. Dixon.
The Woman I Met. Hardy.
"The world goes turning". Dillon.

You Turn for Sugar an' Tea.
Anonymous.
Youth in Arms: IV. Carrion.
Monro.
The Zest of Life. Van Dyke.

Turnip
If the Man Who Turnips
Cries. Johnson.

Turntable
Old Gramophone Records.
Kirkup.

Turret
Coruisk. Smith.
The Death of the Ball Turret
Gunner. Jarrell.
Water Color of Granchester
Meadows. Plath.

Turtle dove (s)
I'm Going to Georgia.
Anonymous.
London City (B vers. with
music). Anonymous.
A Miner Coming Home One
Night. Anonymous.
Sliding Trombone.
Ribemont-Dessaignes
George.
There Is a Tavern in the
Town. Anonymous.

Turtle (s)
Aboriginal Sin. Hay.
Death Chant. Blue Cloud.
Etiquette. Gilbert.
Limerick: "There was a young
waitress named Myrtle."
Herford.
On His Mistris that Lov'd
Hunting. Anonymous.
Tony the Turtle. Rieu.
The Turtle. Nash.

Tusk (s)
Birth. Melinescu.
The Death of Adonis.
Theocritus.
The Thrifty Elephant.
Holmes.

Tutor (s)
The Learning Soul.
Whittemore.
The Tutor. Wells.

Twain
Ballad Written for a
Bridegroom. Villon.
Love's Calendar. Scott.
Next of Kin. Rossetti.
O Child of Beauty Rare.
Goethe.
Sonnet: "Then whilst that
Latmos did contain her
bliss." Stirling.
Take Up the Pen...
Anonymous.
Youth and Age. Arnold.

Twelve
Angelus-Time near Dublin.
Stanford.
Fortitude. Eeinmar von
Zweter.
Growing Up. Guiterman.
If I Forget Thee. Litvinoff.
The Iliad. Homer.
My Twelve Oxen.
Anonymous.
The Science of the Night.
Kunitz.
Sheep Shearing. Anonymous.

Twenty
Collect Calls. Bickston.
Columbia College, 1796.
Shippey.
Days of the Month.
Anonymous.

Dream 2: Brian the Still-
Hunter. Atwood.
Empty Holds a Question.
Folk.
Epitaph. Wolker.
The Fight of the Armstrong
Privateer. Roche.
The Garrett. Thackeray.
Labor Not in Vain.
Anonymous.
The Legs. Graves.
Love Somebody, Yes I Do
(with music). Anonymous.
Maria Jane. Scott-Gatty.
Milton's Wife on Her Twenty-
Third Birthday. Conant-
Bissell.
Old Testament Contents.
Anonymous.
Peggy. Salkeld.
The Petition of Tom
Dermondy to the Three
Fates in Council Sitting.
Dermody.
Prattle. Ciardi.
Reflecting on the Aging-
Process (parody). Peters.
Roll-Call. Shepherd.
The Sirens. Manifold.
Slightly Old. Rosenthal.
Twenty Years Ago. Smith.
Youth's Progress. Updike.

Twice
Done For. Cooke.
The Hare and the Tortoise.
Serraillier.
Katharine Jaffray (B vers.).
Anonymous.
London's Bridge Is A-Burning
Down. Anonymous.
North. Booth.
The Other Side. Reiter.
The Shepherd's House.
Vigny.
Sonnets, XVII: "Who will
believe my verse in time to
come." Shakespeare.
Variation on Heraclitus.
MacNeice.

Twig (s)
As Night Comes On.
Wesley.
The Clearing. Graves.
The Coral Grove. Percival.
Darling! Because My Blood
Can Sing. Cummings.
Desertmartin. Paulin.
Difficult Times. Brecht.
Henry VIII. Farjeon.
Her breast is fit for pearls.
Dickinson.
The Heron. Donaghy.
I'm not here never was.
Buzea.
Koala. Ross.
Men's Impotence.
Anonymous.
Moral Essays. Pope.
My Grandfather in Search of
Moonshine. Lyon.

Twilight (s)
Aubade. MacNeice.
Chanson Naive. McClure.
Don Juan. Byron.
Epos. Rosenberg.
The First Note, Simple; the
Second Note, Distinct.
Aiken.
From Four Lakes' Days.
Eberhart.
Hopeless Desire Soon Withers
and Dies. "W.

The Little Searcher. Bowen.
Love's Old Sweet Song.
Bingham.
Man and Dog. Thomas.
Merlin. Emerson.
Midsummer. Allingham.
Moonlight. De la Mare.
My Birth. Savage.
The New Freedom. Dargan.
The One Certainty. Rossetti.
The One Whose Reproach I
Cannot Evade. Hitchcock.
Pastorale. Davis.
Raya Brenner. Sadeh.
Sails. Sterling.
Song: "Where is the nymph,
whose azure eye." Moore.
Songs for a Three-String
Guitar. Sedar-Senghor.
Sonnet Written after Seeing
Wilton-House. Warton,
Jr..
Star of the Evening. Sayles.
The Toadstool Wood.
Reeves.
Twilight. Custance.
Vespers. Mitchell.
What Will Remain after Me?
Naigreshel.

Twin (s)
Country Singer. Nordhaus.
Droving Man. Astley.
Dwell with Me, Lovely
Images. Maynard.
For My Grandfather.
Robbins.
For Those Who Fail. Miller.
KRAA. Root.
Leda and the Swan.
Gogarty.
Obon by the Hudson.
Oyama.
Poem for My Thirty-Second
Birthday. Ciardi.
To the Liffey with the Swans.
Gogarty.
The Twins. Aldis.
What I Have. North.

Twine (d)
Bonny Barbara Allen (B
vers.). Anonymous.
Disturbing the Sallies Forth.
Coolidge.
Fishing Season. Vallis.
Her breast is fit for pearls.
Dickinson.
London. Ghose.
O, Lay Thy Hand in Mine,
Dear! Massey.
Sonnet: "Between my love and
me there runs a thread."
McLeod.

Twinkle (d)
The Litttle Black-Eyed Rebel.
Carleton.
Past. Galsworthy.
A Prayer. Bailey.
The Star. Taylor.

Twinkling
The Authour's Dreame.
Quarles.
A Starscape. Bellenden.
Tirocinium; or, A Review of
Schools. Cowper.
Twinkle, Twinkle, Little Star
(parody). Dehn.
Vuillard: "The Mother and
Sister of the Artist."
Snodgrass.
The Wee Wee Man.
Anonymous.

Twirl
C Was Papa's Gray Cat.
Lear.

Twist (ed) (s)
A Crown of Wildflowers.
Rossetti.
Epigram: "The scentless laurel
a broad leaf displays."
Landor.
The Gold Nest. Wallace.
A Grave. Moore.
Harper. Anonymous.
Moving. Matthews.
The Outlaw of Loch Lene.
Callanan.
Rhapsody on a Windy Night.
Eliot.
Saint Nicholas,. Moore.
Samuel Hearne in Wintertime.
Newlove.
Song for Ireland. Colclough.
To Auden on His Fiftieth.
Eberhart.
The Walking Road. Hughes.
When a Twister, A-Twisting,
Will Twist Him a Twist.
Wallis.
When Geometric Diagrams...
"Novalis" (George
Friedrich Philipp von
Hardenerg).
Woke Up This Morning with
My Mind on Freedom.
Anonymous.

Twitch (es) (ing)
Defensive Position.
Manifold.
Geeandess. Cole.
Knockmany. Ryan.
Oil and Blood. Kizer.
Rookery. Dauenhauer.

Two
527 Cathedral Parkway.
Lesser.
Ah Me, Do You Remember
Still. Robinson.
All the Smoke. Siegel.
And One Shall Live in Two.
Brooks.
–Answer to Yo/Question of
Am I Not Yo/Woman...
Sanchez.
At the Klamath Berry
Festival. Stafford.
The auctioneer of parting.
Dickinson.
Ballade de Marguerite.
Anonymous.
Ballade of Big Plans. Parker.
The Beach at Veracruz.
Bowering.
Being Twins. Jackson.
Bell Horses, Bell Horses,
What Time of Day?
Mother Goose.
Black Spring. Annensky.
The Blind Leading the Blind.
Mueller.
Byron: In Men Whom Men
Condemn as Ill. Miller.
Caelica, LX. Greville.
California Joe. Anonymous.
Central Park Tourney.
Weston.
Chariots. Bynner.
The Children of Greenock.
Graham.
A Children's Don't.
Graham.
La Ci Darem La Mano.
Nims.

The Cows near the Graveyard. Nelson.
Crawl, Laugh. Issa.
Crossing. MacLeish.
Damages, Two Hundred Pounds. Thackeray.
Duality. Abse.
The Eagle's Song. Mansfield.
El Capitan-General. Leland.
The End of a Meaningful Relationship. Fickert.
Epigram. Byron.
Epitaph on a Fir-Tree. Murphy.
Faith and Works. Spark.
A Glimpse. Whitman.
The Glimpse of a Plain Cap. Anonymous.
The Glory of Hanalei Is Heavy Rain. Alohikea.
The Good-Morrow. Donne.
Green Enravishment of Human Life. Juana Ines de la Cruz.
Growing Old. Wilcox.
Hands. Finkel.
Hearts-Ease. Landor.
Homage to the Weather. Hamburger.
Hoo, Suffolk. Anonymous.
The Horny-Goloch. Anonymous.
Houses, Past and Present. Bachar.
How Do You Do? Jones.
The Ideal Age for a Man. Shannon.
The Indigo Glass in the Grass. Stevens.
The Intruder. Reeves.
Jockie, Thine Hornpipe's Dull. Anonymous.
John Gorham. Robinson.
The Kilkenny Cats. Anonymous.
The Lavender Cowboy. Hersey.
Limerick: "There once were two cats of Kilkenny." Anonymous.
Limerick: "When twins came, their father, Dan Dunn." Braley.
Little Mary Cassidy. Fahy.
The Man Hidden behind the Drapes. Rogers.
Meeting at Night. Browning.
Mime. Allen.
Mists and Rain. Baudelaire.
Modern Love, XXXVI. Meredith.
My Father's Wedding 1924. Bly.
My Home. Anonymous.
A New Poet. Canton.
Nothing. Singer.
A Nuptial Song, or Epithalamie, on Sir Clipseby Crew and His Lady. Herrick.
Of Time and the Line. Bernstein.
Oh But It Was Good... Littlebird.
Oh moon, oh moon! Anonymous.
On a Whore. Hoskyns.
Once at Swanage. Hardy.
One Bright Morning... Anonymous.
Oyster-Crabs (parody). Wells.

The Plowman. Anonymous.
The Poet Loves a Mistress, But Not to Marry. Herrick.
Prayer. Anonymous.
Prayer of Any Husband. Caruthers.
Rachel Goes to the Well for Water. Manger.
Reconciliation. Nicolson.
Reformation of Manners. Defoe.
Relativity of Spring. Gold.
Robin Hood. Keats.
The Same Old Jazz. Whalen.
De Se. Weever.
Secret. Jacobs.
A Shropshire Lad. Housman.
The Silence. MacLeish.
A Silent Wood. Siddal.
Sonnet XIII. Scott.
Spirits Everywhere. Uhland.
Spring Song of a Super-Blake (parody). Untermeyer.
A Stanza on Freedom. Lowell
Stanzas on Freedom. Lowell.
Stoklewath; or, The Cymbrian Village. Blamire.
The String of My Ancestors. Nyhart.
Sweetest of All. Anonymous.
They Two. Breck.
This Afternoon... Saez Burgos.
To Chloe, Who Wished Herself Young Enough For Me. Cartwright.
To His Maid Prew. Herrick.
Tongue River Psalm. Gildner.
Traps. Davies.
Tune: Magnolia Blossom. Li Ching-chao.
Turn Blind. Celan.
Twenty-One Love Poems. Rich.
Two-An'-Six. McKay.
Two-Cent Coal. Anonymous.
Under the Bamboo Tree. Cole.
What's Your Fancy. Anonymous.
What the Serpent Said to Adam. MacLeish.
When I Was Growing Up. Vogel.

Tybalt
Anna-Marie, Love, Up Is the Sun. Scott.
In That Dim Monument Where Tybalt Lies. Ficke.
Tyburn
A Ballad upon the Popish Plot. Gadbury.
The Beggar's Opera. Gay.
Tybrun and Westminster. Heywood.
Type (s)
Ballade of Youth and Age. Henley.
The Cubistic Lovers. Eaton.
Harriet. Lowell.
One Old Ox. Anonymous.
Resurrection. Crabbe.
To the Rainbow. Campbell.
Tyranny
Columbia the Gem of the Ocean. Becket.
Death Invoked. Massinger.

Here Pause: The Poet Claims at Least This Praise. Wordsworth.
The Hunting of the Hare. Newcastle.
A Maiden's Ideal of a Husband. Carey.
Paradise Lost. Milton.
Poem: "O men, walk on the hills." Bodenheim.
Reparation or War. Anonymous.
Sonnet on Chillon. Byron.
Votive Ode. Erasmus.
The Wyoming Massacre. Terry.
Tyrant (s)
The Battle of Navarino. Anonymous.
Britannia and Raleigh. Ayloffe.
Caelica, LXXVIII. Greville.
A Convict's Lament on the Death of Captain Logan. Anonymous.
Epitaph. Anonymous.
The Fleece. Dyer.
Happy Britannia. Thomson.
Hope. Fanshawe.
Independence. Smollett.
An Indian Mother about to Destroy Her Child. Montgomery.
Jealousy. Johnson.
Lord North's Recantation. Anonymous.
My Political Faith. Cameron.
Ode on Science. Sumner.
Of Narrow Streets. Gay.
On the Prorogation. Anonymous.
Peace. Kavanagh.
The Rebel. Pearse.
A Rose. Fanshawe.
The Rose of Life. Gongora y Argote.
Summer Solstice. Bowering.
Tribute to Washington. Anonymous.

U

Udder
The Animals. Simic.
The Cow in Apple Time. Frost.
Ugly (ier) (est)
Audubon, Drafted. Jones.
Becky Deem. Leadbelly.
Blue-Eyed Girl. Anonymous.
A Cat May Look at a King. Anonymous.
Dragging in Winter. McElroy.
The Dwarf. Locklin.
Fashion in the 70's. Swenson.
Frisbee. Humphries.
Goethe's Death Mask. Gregg.
Gubbinal. Stevens.
The Hen and the Oriole. Marquis.
A Jealous Man. Anonymous.
Justice Is Reason Enough. Wakoski.

Madrigal: "To be a whore, despite of grace." Cotton.
Masquerade. Rodgers.
The Princess Addresses the Frog Prince. Brewster.
Reunion. Dehn.
Song: "Me Cupid made a Happy Slave." Steele.
Three Bad Ones. Anonymous.
An Untitled Poem, about an Uncompleted Sonnet. Pinsker.
William Street. Slessor.
Written in Her French Psalter. Elizabeth I.
Ukulele
Begin Summer. Jonker.
Ulcers
The Hypocrite. Caryll.
Ulysses
Delilah. Kipling.
The Odyssey. Homer.
Youth. Toerien.
Umbrella (s)
The Cure's Progress. Dobson.
The Elf and the Dormouse. Herford.
End of the Seers' Convention. Fearing.
Haiku: "Just enough of rain..." Wright.
Little Snail. Conkling.
The Outcast. Sanford.
Probity. Swanger.
The rain it raineth on the just. Bowen.
Unborn
Bonnie James Campbell. Anonymous.
Cloris and Mertilla. Drayton.
Counting. Johnson.
Endless. Rukeyser.
From the Sea. Teasdale.
March. Webb.
Mother Superior. MacBeth.
Quickening. Morley.
Remembering Fire. Jones.
Stray Animals. Tate.
Toast. Horne.
The Unwanted. Gordon.
Unbroken
An Epistle Written in the Country to.... Jenyns.
Epitaph of a Faithful Man. Mezey.
The Firstborn. Goodchild.
The Old Ladies. Ellis.
Truth. Russell.
Unbutton (ed)
Freely, from a Song Sung by Jewish Women of Yemen. Levy.
On the New Road. Lifshin.
The Wife's Tale. Heaney.
Uncertain (ties)
The Continuance. Bronk.
Edmond Halley. Fuller.
A Garden of Situations. Anderson.
One Night Stand. Jones.
There Was a Boy. Wordsworth.
Unchanged
Art Thou the Same. Tatnall.
For M. S. Singing Fruhlingsglaube in 1945. Cornford.
Hammers and Anvil. Clifford.

I Shall Go Back. Millay.
A Separation. Spender.

Uncle (s)
The Banks of Dundee.
Anonymous.
Call the Horse, Marrow.
Anonymous.
Game after Supper. Atwood.
The Garlic. Meyers.
Grandpa Bear. Eisenberg.
Ichthycide. Rosenblatt.
Limerick: "Once a grasshoper
(food being scant)."
Herford.
Lions and Gruel and Uncles.
"Carroll.
Obituary. "Adeler.
Rainuv: A Romantic Ballad
from the Early Basque
(parody). Widdemer.
Song for the Old Ones.
Angelou.
The Sun and the Moon and
Fear of Loneliness.
Anonymous.
Time Like an Ever-rolling
Stream. Wodehouse.
What He Saw. Currie.
When My Uncle Willie Saw.
Freeman.

Unconscious (ness)
Dreams Old and Nascent.
Lawrence.
In a Cathedral City. Hardy.
Milk for the Cat. Monro.
A Policeman's Lot. Cope.

Uncover
Cloud River. Wright.
Gold. Hall.

Unction
Come Holy Spirit, Dove
Divine. Judson.

Undefeated
The Fighter. Kiser.

Under
The Butterfly. Avison.
The Flight. Roethke.
I like my body when it is with
your. Cummings.
Paradise Lost. Milton.
Plowman's Song. Knister.
Regent's Park. Fyleman.
Song with Words. Agee.
A Stopwatch and an
Ordanance Map. Spender.
Through the Waters. Flint.

Underground
At the Executed Murderer's
Grave. Wright.
Bereft. Hardy.
Calling Myself Home.
Hogan.
The Chimney-Sweeper's
Complaint. Alcock.
The Horrid Voice of Science.
Lindsay.
In Memoriam Francis
Ledwidge. Heaney.
In Praise of Limestone.
Auden.
Miners. Wright.
A Poem of a Maid Forsaken.
Anonymous.
Such Is the Sickness of Many
a Good Thing. Duncan.
Think No More, Lad.
Housman.
'Tis Late and Cold. Fletcher.
Wonder and a Thousand
Springs. Percy.

Underneath
Geraldine's Garden.
O'Donnell.
The Holy Field. Milman.
Limerick: "There was an old
man of Blackheath."
Anonymous.

Underpass
Father. Carroll.

Undersea
Crabbing. Daniel.

Undersong
Lament for Daphnaida.
Spenser.
Personal Talk. Wordsworth.
Undersong. Van Doren.

Understand (ing) (s)
And Ut Pictura Poesis Is Her
Name. Ashbery.
Ask No Return. Gregory.
Beowulf. Wilbur.
A Bouquet for Jerry Ford.
Marcus.
A Boy Thirteen. Irish.
Caelica, XXXIX. Greville.
Celtic Cross. MacCaig.
Comfort of the Fields.
Lampman.
Confession. Barker.
Conversation with
Washington. Livingston.
Earth Song. Peacock.
Epilogue. Baudelaire.
Estuary. Montgomerie.
Evelyn Hope. Browning.
An Evening. Mezey.
The Excesses of God.
Jeffers.
Falling down to bed.
NorthSun.
Farther Along. *Anonymous.*
Felo Da Se. Blackburn.
The Flowers. Kipling.
Force. Walcott.
Forgiveness. Sewell.
Go, Then. Bruck.
God Know What He's About.
Anonymous.
Graffiti in a University
Restroom... Mitsui.
Hatred. Bennett.
Here Is the Tale. Deane.
How They Came from the
Blue Snows. Kenseth.
I Have a Big Favor to Ask
You, Brothers. Landau.
I Hear the Wave.
Anonymous.
I'm Here. Ignatow.
I should have been too glad.
Dickinson.
Ifa. *Anonymous.*
In Broken Images. Graves.
In Memoriam A.H.H.,
XCVII. Tennyson.
Inanna and An.
Enheduanna.
The Invisible Man.
Matthews.
Lines for a Wedding Gift.
Trimpi.
Loneliness. Jenkins.
The Lover Remembereth Such
as He Sometimes Enjoyed...
Stokesbury.
Murder in the Cathedral.
Eliot.
My Dog. Robinson.
Mythology. Thompson.
Needle and Thread. Pan
Chao.

Of the Incomparable Treasure
of the Scriptures.
Anonymous.
Ollie, Answer Me. Berg.
Omphalos: The Well.
Jennett.
On a Catholic Childhood.
Hale.
On the Subject of Poetry.
Merwin.
Organ Solo. Skinner.
Passing Remark. Stafford.
The Poet. Morgan.
A Primary Ground. Rich.
The Ram's Horn. Hewitt.
Rededication. Litvinoff.
The Seekers. Starbuck.
The Sleeping Beauty. Sitwell.
The Sparrows at the Airport.
Ostroff.
Spring MCMXL. Gascoyne.
The Statue. Fuller.
The Stolen Child. Yeats.
The Tarantula. Whittemore.
The Technique of Love.
Kessler.
To a Cat. Swinburne.
To a Poet a Thousand Years
Hence. Heath-Stubbs.
Understanding. Bliss.
The Vampire. Kipling.
Virginia. Loftin.
W. S. Landor. Moore.
Where Art Is a Midwife.
Paulin.
Who Is Not a Stranger Still.
Stephany.
Why Stone Does Not Sing by
Itself. Endrezze-Danielson.
The Wise Woman.
Untermeyer.
A Woman's Answer to the
Vampire. Blake.
The Woman Who
Understands. Appleton.
Words to the Wind. Di
Cicco.
The Words Will Resurrect.
De Lima.
Working with Tools.
Ammons.
The World's Last Unnamed
Poem. Redwing.

Understood
The Causes of Color. Jonas.
Comedy. Van Doren.
The Copernican System.
Chatterton.
The Cumberbunce. West.
Elegy for N. N. Milosz.
The Emancipators. Jarrell.
Epigram: To English
Connoisseurs. Blake.
How Did It Seem to Sylvia?
Schnackenberg.
If Only We Understood.
Anonymous.
Ithaca. Cavafy.
Not Understood. Bracken.
On a Cast from an Antique.
Pellew.
Poem to Negro and Whites.
Bodenheim.
Seeing St. James's. Mathew.
The Seven Sages. Yeats.
Sidrophel, the Rosicrucian
Conjurer. Butler.
To Mrs. Diana Cecyll.
Herbert of Cherbury.
Two Englishmen. Stewart.
Upon the Decease of Mrs.
Anne Griffin... Fiske.

Wili Woyi, Shaman, also
known as Billy Pigeon.
Conley.

Undertake (n)
The Jilted Funeral. Burgess.
To Make a Bridge. Madge.

Undertow
Inheritance. Higginson.

Underwear
Carol Took Her Clothes Off.
Messenger.
Street Preacher. MacCaig.

Underwood
In Memory of Captain
Underwood, Who Was
Drowned. *Anonymous.*
Summer. Davidson.

Underworld
Freethinkers. Eibel.

Undo (ing) (ne)
And Ut Pictura Poesis Is Her
Name. Ashbery.
Anonymous Gravestone.
Kastner.
At a Welsh Waterfall.
Hopkins.
Bid Adieu to Maidenhood.
Joyce.
Bundles. Farrar.
Dialogue after Enjoyment.
Cowley.
Don Juan. Byron.
Doom. O'Shaughnessy.
Fair, and Soft, and Gay, and
Young. Gould.
The Fair Singer. Marvell.
The Gay. Russell.
Killing No Murder. Warner.
A Letter to the Countess of
Denbigh. Crashaw.
London Sad London.
Anonymous.
Looking for a Country under
Its Original Name.
McElroy.
The Metaphysical Amorist.
Cunningham.
On Authors and Booksellers.
Pope.
On His Mistresse Going to
Sea. Cary.
Only a Little Thing. Handy.
Our Own. Sangster.
A Palinode. Greene.
Permanently. Koch.
The Plot against the Giant.
Stevens.
The Straw. Graves.
To Little or No Purpose.
Etherege.
To the Noblest and Best of
Ladies, the Countess of
Denbigh. Crashaw.
Ulysses and the Siren.
Daniel.
With Serving Still. Wyatt.
The Young Man Thinks of
Sons. Mason.

Undress (ed)
Good Night, God Bless You.
Anonymous.
New York. Gunn.
Passing the Graveyard.
Young.
The Resurrection. Wanley.
Song: "Life with her weary
eyes." Zaturenska.

Uneasy
At the Roman Baths, Bath.
Lucie-Smith.
The Joys of Marriage.
Cotton.

Unfinished
The Deserted Garden.
Stanford.
Enoch. Very.
Hawthorne. Longfellow.
Kindergarten. Schmitz.
The Middle of the World.
Norris.

Unfit
Three Epitaphs. Davison.
Wasted Night. *Anonymous.*

Unfold
The Book of Pilgrimage.
Rilke.
A Dedication. Coleridge.
Man's Amazement.
Anonymous.

Unforgiven
In the Naked Bed, in Plato's
Cave. Schwartz.
The People. Campanella.

Unfortunate
Young Man Cut Down in His
Prime. *Anonymous.*

Ungrateful (ness)
Astrophel and Stella, XXXI.
Sidney.
In Memoriam A.H.H.,
XXXVIII. Tennyson.
The Ladybirds. Lucie-Smith.
Seguidilla. Valdivielso.
To a Beautiful but Heartless
Coquette. Terrazas.

Unguessed
Apology. Lowell.
Magnets. Binyon.
Sonnet: "If I could get within
this changing I."
Masefield.

Unhappy
I see that chance hath chosen
me. Wyatt.
The Man in the Recreation
Room. Harkness.
St Enda. Lerner.

Unharmed
The Anvil of God's Word.
Clifford.
London. Wilson.

Unheard
The Celestial City. Fletcher.
Listening to Her. Zach.

Unholy
Dark Rapture. Russell.
The Devil's Dictionary: Body-
Snatcher. Bierce.
Sonnet: Composed by the Side
of Grasmere Lake.
Wordsworth.
They Make a Pretty Pair of
Debauchees. Catullus.

Unhonored
The Lay of the Last Minstrel.
Scott.
The Traveller; or, A Prospect
of Society. Goldsmith.

Unicorn (s)
About Children. McGinley.
The Beast That Rode the
Unicorn. Meyer.
A Bestiary. Rexroth.
Caelica, XX. Greville.
Dance Song. *Anonymous.*
Inhuman Henry or Cruelty to
Fabulous Animals.
Housman.
The Late Passenger. Lewis.
The Middle Ages: Two Views.
Drake.
The Paint Box. Rieu.

Uniform
Baseball Note. Adams.

Lan Nguyen: The Uniform of
Death 1971. Mura.

Uninvited
The Seaside and the Fireside:
Dedication. Longfellow.

Union
The Columbiad: One Centred
System. Barlow.
Get Thee Behind Me, Satan.
Lampell.
Glory Hallelujah! or John
Brown's Body. Hall.
He's a Fool. Anonymous.
Its a Good Thing to Join a
Union. *Anonymous.*
Ludwig's Death Mask.
Hughes.
Raggedy. *Anonymous.*
The Rejected "National
Hymns". Newell.
Roll the Union On. Hays.
Solidarity Forever. Chaplin.
Spiritual Passion. Barlow.
To Jesus on the Cross.
Tejada.
Union Maid. Guthrie.
The Utah Iron Horse.
Anonymous.
Wendell Phillips (excerpt).
O'Reilly.
You Gotta Go Down (And
Join the Union).
Anonymous.

Unique
The Bibliomaniac's Prayer.
Field.
I Don't Want Any More
Visitors. Jonker.
I Went to Heaven.
Dickinson.

Unison
The Lemmings. Stauffer.
A Unison. Williams.

Unite (d)
The Downfall of the Gael.
O'Gnive.
The Knot. Vaughan.
Liberty Tree. Paine.
Marriage Song. Halevi.
O Lord, Bow Down Thine
Ear. Prince.
Qua Cursum Ventus.
Clough.
Written in a Time of Crisis.
Benét.

United States
A Record Stride. Frost.

United States Marines
The Marines' Hymn.
Anonymous.

Unity
Complaint of the Common
Weill of Scotland.
Lyndsay.
The Earl of Mar's Daughter.
Anonymous.
Einstein (1929). MacLeish.
Things Not of This Union.
Gregg.
Vanguardia. Esteves.

Universal
All Hail the Power of Jesus'
Name. Perronet.
To Jane: The Invitation.
Shelley.

Universal Church
Religio Laici. Dryden.

Universe
All Tropic Places Smell of
Mold. Shapiro.
An Astronomer's Journal.
Shore.

Aurora Leigh. Browning.
A Beam of Light. Rooney.
Beyond the Nigger. Plumpp.
The Carpenter's Real
Anguish. Gardner.
Clerihew. Bentley.
Darkness. Byron.
The Destroyers (excerpt).
Fleming.
Dramatis Personae: Epilogue.
Browning.
Eichmann. Blazek.
Evening Hymn. Furness.
Failure. Mayo.
A Fine Thing. Veitch.
Gypsy-Heart. Bates.
He Fumbles at Your Soul.
Dickinson.
Hokusai's Wave. Cabral.
Human Cylinders. Loy.
In a Museum. Hardy.
In the Wide Awe and Wisdom
of the Night. Roberts.
Man's Littleness in Presence
of the Stars. White.
My Sun-Killed Tree. Harris.
On Frozen Fields. Kinnell.
Pity this busy monster,
manunkind. Cummings.
Revolutionary Letters. Di
Prima.
Richard Tolman's Universe.
Bacon.
The Seesaw. Williams.
Sonnets, CIX: "O, never say
that I was false of heart."
Shakespeare.
Soul-Drift. Blind.
Surrender to Christ. Myers.
Terra Cotta. Lyle.
There Is No Death.
McCreery.
They Live in Parallel Worlds.
Harris.
To My Friends. Schiller.
To Rich Givers. Whitman.
To the Moon, 1969.
Deutsch.
Tortoise Shout. Lawrence.
The Weakest Thing.
Browning.
West Wind. Koch.
The Woodchuck Who Lives
on Top of Mt. Ritter.
Simon.

University
Dog Prospectus. Redgrove.
Emerson. Alcott.

Unjust
Jacob's Winning. Sherwin.
Lucasta Laughing. Lovelace.
Sarah. Schwartz.

Unkind
Alberta. *Anonymous.*
Bright Was the Morning.
D'Urfey.
The Conquest of Granada.
Dryden.
Fragment of a Love Lament.
Anonymous.
Heaven and earth and all that
hear me plain. Wyatt.
Ode to a Young Lady,
Somewhat Too Sollicitous
about Her Manner...
Shenstone.
Of Rosalind. Lodge.
A Prayer for Charity.
Kennedy.
Sonnet: "If chaste and pure
devotion of my youth."
Drayton.

Sonnet: "My Love, I cannot
thy rare beauties place."
Smith.
Sonnets, CXXXV: "Whoever
hath her wish, thou hast
thy Will." Shakespeare.
Talking in Bed. Larkin.

Unkiss (ed)
Courtship. Brome.
What Should I Say. Wyatt.

Unknown
Because We Do Not See.
Anonymous.
The Bibliomaniac's Prayer.
Field.
Brother and Sister. Eliot.
Epitaph: "How fair a flower is
sown." Patmore.
The Flesh and the Spirit.
Bradstreet.
The Flight of the Geese.
Roberts.
Four trees upon a solitary
acre. Dickinson.
God's Trails Lead Home.
Clements.
Haiku: "Autumn's bright
moon." Kaga no Chiyo.
Happy He. *Anonymous.*
The Helmsman: An Ode.
Cunningham.
The Incomprehensible.
Watts.
The Lay of the Last Minstrel.
Scott.
The Man to the Angel.
Russell.
May 30, 1893. Bangs.
The Minstrel Responds to
Flattery. Scott.
Muse Poem. Van
Spanckeren.
Nature. Longfellow.
O Powers Celestial, with
What Sophistry. Barnes.
On the Death of Neruda.
Van Brunt.
Prothalamion (excerpt).
Hillyer.
Scene with Figure. Deutsch.
Shadow. Mars.
"So Quietly". Hill.
The Soldier. Aiken.
Some Time at Eve. Hardy.
Song: "The boat is chafing at
our long delay."
Davidson.
Stond Who So List upon the
Slipper Toppe. Wyatt.
There's an Unknown River in
Soweto. Mandela.
To Manon, on His Fortune in
Loving Her. Blunt.
The Tragedy of Pompey the
Great (excerpt). Masefield.

Unlearn (ed) (ing)
First Grade. George.
Letter from Paparua.
Newbury.
My Past Has Gone to Bed.
Sassoon.
Whenever I Have. Maurice.

Unlimited
Ceiling Unlimited. Rukeyser.

Unlock (ed)
Like Any Other Man. Orr.
To a Lady That Desired I
Would Love Her. Carew.

Unloved
The Room. Nabokov.
Search for Love. Johnson.

Unlucky
Fine Body. Clare.
Unmarked
Hymn. Synesius.
Malcolm. Smith.
Ways of Seeing. Stafford.
Unmarried
The Relationship. Vincent.
Unmeaning
Orpheus. Winters.
Submarine Mountains. Rice.
Unmeasured
Art McCooey. Kavanagh.
What Called Me to the
Heights? Pilkington.
Unnecessary
To the Pay Toilet. Piercy.
To the Rulers. Nemerov.
Unnoticed
Pictures from Brueghel.
Williams.
Variation on the Word Sleep.
Atwood.
Unopened
Separation. Wolny.
Song of the Open Road.
Whitman.
Unpleasant
Limerick. *Anonymous.*
Unpopular
Popular. Tennyson.
Unpossessed
The Unpossessed. Naude.
Unproven
Geometry. Dove.
Unreal
Correspondences. Duncan.
On the Death of Lisa Lyman.
Burt.
Unreason
Black Earth. Moore.
Melancthon. Moore.
Unreliable
Experts on Woman.
Guiterman.
The Lie. Lee.
Sometime during Eternity.
Ferlinghetti.
Unremember (ed)
Cups of Illusion. Bellamann.
Hymn to Athena.
Anonymous.
June. MacDonald.
Unremembrance
Blessed Are Those Who Sow
and Do Not Reap. Ben-
Yitzhak.
To Celio. Juana Ines de la
Cruz.
Unrest
As Oft as I Behold and See.
Surrey.
Bought. Davison.
The Land of Indolence.
Thomson.
The Lucky Chance: Song.
Behn.
Madrigal: "What is life."
Byrd.
The Pyre of My Indian
Summer. Leib.
A Sea Lyric. Hayne.
Wind and Wave. Patmore.
Unrivalled
By Babel's Streams.
Freneau.
The First Olympionique to
Hiero of Syracuse. Pindar.
He Praises His Wife When
She Has Left Him.
Anonymous.

Unsaid
Birds in Snow. Doolittle.
The Middle-Aged. Rich.
Words. Finch.
Unsatisfactory
Hit or Miss. "Carroll."
Unsatisfied
Fate. Spalding.
Prayer. Untermeyer.
To the Tune "Red
Embroiderd Shoes'.
Huang O.
Unseen
The Celestial City. Fletcher.
The Complaint of Rosamond.
Daniel.
Mistletoe. De la Mare.
Persephone. Abbott.
Sequel to Finality. Kirby.
Some Time at Eve. Hardy.
To Clarissa Scott Delany.
Grimke.
Variations on a Time Theme.
Muir.
When All Thy Mercies.
Addison.
Unselfishness
The Joy of Love. Dowling.
Unsex (ed)
Limerick: "A lady who signs
herself "Vexed.'". Gorey.
Unshared
The Bottle. De la Mare.
Unsheathed
Hurt Hawks. Jeffers.
Late Spring. Gill.
Unsigned
The Stump Is Not the
Tombstone. Seager.
Unsought
Interlude. Duggan.
The Seaside and the Fireside:
Dedication. Longfellow.
Unspoken
I Would That Even Now.
Shoku.
My Friends, This Storm.
Muchemwa.
Poem for the Atomic Age.
Litvinoff.
The Servant in Literature.
Welish.
Unsung
Hearth and Home. King.
The Lay of the Last Minstrel.
Scott.
The Minstrel Responds to
Flattery. Scott.
Rumplestiltskin Poems.
Hathaway.
A Song as Yet Unsung.
Yehoash.
The Unknown City. Roberts.
Unsure
For the New Year. Creeley.
The Young Ones. Jennings.
Unsuspecting
Afternoon's Angel. Mayne.
Untidy
Miriam Tazewell. Ransom.
Untold
The Battle of Waterloo.
Byron.
Sonnet: "If I could get within
this changing I."
Masefield.
Untroubled
Charleston. Timrod.
Sonnets, I. Hillyer.
Untrue
Change Thy Mind Since She
Doth Change. Essex.

Note on Intelligence. Auden.
Sonnets, CXIII: "Since I left
you, mine eye is in my
mind." Shakespeare.
Talking in Bed. Larkin.
Unusual
Eyewitness. Hall.
Unusual conversation
Chocolates. Simpson.
Unwanted
In the Tub We Soak Our
Skin. Horn.
My Mother's Birthday: "I
used to watch you
sleeping." Raine.
Unwed
The Faithless Wife. Garcia
Lorca.
Unwilling
Sea Eclogue. Diaper.
To the Ship in Which Virgil
Sailed to Athens (Odes, I,
3). Horace.
Unworthy
Amours de Voyage. Clough.
Colonel Chartres.
Arbuthnot.
Dear Lady, When Thou
Frownest. Bridges.
Epilogue (excerpt). Percy.
Epitaph on Colonel Francis
Chartres. Arbuthnot.
Good Friday. Smith.
Unwritten
Song of the Open Road.
Whitman.
Stray Animals. Tate.
Up
Advice to Country Girls.
Anonymous.
The Bonfire. Frost.
Child on Top of a
Greenhouse. Roethke.
The Drunken Sailor (Early in
the Morning). *Anonymous.*
Fourteen Men. Gilmore.
The Grand Old Duke of
York. Mother Goose.
Grandfather's Heaven. Nye.
A July Dawn (excerpt).
O'Donnell.
The Liftman. Evans.
Little Red Riding Hood.
Sexton.
The Noble Duke of York.
Anonymous.
Northboun'. Holloway.
Ode to a Vanished Operator
in an Automatized Elevator.
Rosenfield.
The Square at Dawn. Tate.
The T.V.A. *Anonymous.*
Up-Tails All. *Anonymous.*
World's End. Chettur.
Uplift (ed) (ing)
Grandma Fire. Ballard.
Two Shapes. Gregor.
The Way, the Truth, and the
Life. Parker.
Upper
The Fascinating Chill That
Music Leaves. Dickinson.
The Garden Seat. Hardy.
The Justice of the Peace.
Belloc.
The Lexington Murder.
Anonymous.
Upright (s)
The Fence. McHugh.
Unto the Upright Praise:
Chorus. Luzzatto.

Walking in a Swamp.
Wagoner.
Uprising
Customs Change.
Anonymous.
Hymn to the Sun. Doughty.
The Message of the March
Wind. Morris.
Uproar
How Many Bards Gild the
Lapses of Time! Keats.
The Moths. O Riordain.
Upset
Eastward I Stand, Mercies I
Beg. *Anonymous.*
For the Poet Who Said Poets
Are Struck by Lightning
Only... Klappert.
The Young Fenians. Fallon.
Upside-down
Bats. Newsome.
Casting. Nemerov.
If Buttercups Buzz'd after the
Bee. *Anonymous.*
The Manatee. Blyton.
The Parliament of Bees.
Day.
The Ride of Tench Tilghman.
Scollard.
To My Friend, behind Walls.
Kizer.
Zephyr. Ware.
Upstairs
Direct Address. Gerstler.
During a Bombardment by V-
Weapons. Fuller.
Little Miss Pitt. Wise.
Nothing to Do? Silverstein.
Upstate
Eastside Chick with Drive.
Spector.
Upstream
Coming Out. Lapidus.
Feeling the Quiet Strike.
Minor.
The Hours of a Bridge.
Merwin.
Upward (s)
A'Chuilionn. Hutchison.
The Dancing Ploughmen.
Joseph.
The Fountain. Lowell.
The Ladder of St. Augustine:
The Heights. Longfellow.
A Nocturnal Sketch. Hood.
The Poet. Noguchi.
Schubertiana. Transtromer.
To Our Lady, the Ark of the
Covenants. Larsson.
To the Right Honourable
William, Earl of
Dartmouth. Wheatley.
The White Kite. *Anonymous.*
Uranium
In the Longhouse, Oneida
Museum. Whiteman.
Urchin
It Is the Sinners' Dust-
Tongued Bell Claps Me to
Churches. Thomas.
Urge (s)
Boatman's Hymn. Magrath.
Creatrix. Wickham.
In Memoriam. Gingell.
Urgent
Japanese Beetles. Kennedy.
Trees at Night. Johnson.
Urine
The Picador Bit. Noll.
Urn (e) (s)
The Accursed. Baudelaire.
Ashes. Heine.

Epitaph on the Lady Mary
  Villers. Carew.
Epitaph on the Lady Mary
  Villiers. Carew.
Eternity of Love Protested.
  Carew.
In Mutual Time. Lavoie.
The Legacy. King.
Marvell's Ghost. Ayloffe.
Power. Prior.
Reminiscence. Aldrich.
Sag', Wo Ist Dein Schones
  Liebchen. Heine.
Sestina in Time of Winter.
  Anderson.
Silex Scintillans. Vaughan.
Solomon on the Vanity of the
  World. Prior.
To Her Lover's Complaint.
  Barker.
To One of Little Faith.
  Flanner.
The Tree. Winchilsea.
Youth and Beauty.
  Townsend.

Us

And Now Farley Is Going to
  Sing While I Drink a Glass
  of Water! Goldbarth.
Ducks down in the Meadow.
  Stafford.
For Euse, Ayi Kwei & Gwen
  Brooks. Kgositsile.
Four Preludes on Playthings
  of the Wind. Sandburg.
The Helmsman. Doolittle.
In Time. Raine.
The K.K.K. Disco...
  Mitchell.
The Liberator. Coleman.
The Lonesome Dream.
  Mueller.
Medusa. Plath.
Mrs. Hamer. Stembridge.
The Night Court. Mitchell.
The Octopus. Nash.
Our House. Thompson.
Poem about People. Pinsky.
The Universe. Swenson.
Us. Wyatt.
Valentine. Hall.
A Woman Defending Herself
  Examines Her Own
  Character Witness.
  Griffin.
You Understand the
  Requirements. Lifshin.

Use (d) (s)

Aurora Leigh. Browning.
Balow. *Anonymous.*
The Bustle in a House.
  Dickinson.
England and America.
  Stephen.
The Gardens of Alcinous.
  Pope.
Good Company. Henry
  VIII.
The Great Swamp Fight.
  Hazard.
Happy Endings. White.
Leaflets. Rich.
Moment. Creeley.
Money. Armour.
No Use. Snodgrass.
Opposition. Lanier.
Photographs: A Vision of
  Massacre. Harper.
The Poet's Final Instructions.
  Berryman.

Sonnet: "Flesh, I have
  knocked at many a dusty
  door." Masefield.
Stealin', Stealin'.
  Anonymous.
Wardour Street. Wolfe.
Women's Longing. Fletcher.

Useful (ness)

A Bestiary. Rexroth.
The Burro. Gibbons.
Camoens in the Hospital.
  Melville.
The Cow. *Anonymous.*
The School Bus. Eigner.
Thank You. Koch.
Uselessness. Wilcox.
Vulture. Kennedy.

Useless

Death of an Irishwoman.
  Hartnett.
Jean. Potts.
Moral Essays. Pope.
Snow Storm. Tu Fu.
To a Jack Rabbit. Barker.

Usurper

The Defiance. Flatman.
I Will Enjoy Thee Now.
  Carew.
The Reckoning. Roethke.

Utah

Marching to Utah.
  Anonymous.

Utmost

An Elegy. Gascoyne.
Woodland Worship.
  Wetherald.

Utter (most) (s)

All the World. *Anonymous.*
Joy-Month. Wasson.
Letter to P. Friend.
October. Wolfe.
Painting. Jacobs.
Tales from a Family Album.
  Justice.
Tramp. Hughes.

Utterance

In the Isle of Dogs.
  Davidson.
Prayer. Lewis.

V

Vacancy

A Friend. Snodgrass.
Inertia. Chaudhari.
Kings of France. Lincoln.
Mont Blanc. Shelley.
More Foreign Cities.
  Tomlinson.
Preludes. Eliot.
She Said. De la Mare.
Unsaid. Ammons.
Vison of Rotterdam. Corso.
The Wanderer. Dobson.

Vacation

Limerick: "A schoolma'am of
  much reputation." Upton.
Open Casket. McPherson.
Peace and Joy. Silverstein.
The Preacher's Vacation.
  Anonymous.
The Song of Songs. Heine.

Vacuum

Christmas Shopping.
  MacNeice.
Elegy for My Father. Moss.
In a Dream. Ignatow.
Strange Kind (II). Reed.

Vagabond (s)

Envoy. Hovey.
Maps. Thompson.
The Road to Vagabondia.
  Burnet.
A Vagabond Song. Carman.

Vagina

The Contribution. Shapiro.
In the Baggage Room at
  Greyhound. Ginsberg.

Vagrancy

Eclogue IV. The Poet
  (excerpt). Jenner.
Fraternity. Tabb.
Resurrection. Kemp.
Washing Windows. Wild.

Vague

Autumn. Scannell.
The Obscure Pleasure of the
  Indistinct. Ramke.
Vast Light. Eberhart.
World-Secret. Hofmannsthal.

Vain

Choice. Cunningham.
The Conflict of Convictions.
  Melville.
The Cuckoo. Locker-
  Lampson.
Dodo. Carlile.
An Essay on Criticism.
  Pope.
Hence, Away, You Sirens!
  Wither.
I Wept as I Lay Dreaming.
  Heine.
A Letter to John Donne.
  Sisson.
Lost Desire. Meleager.
Love in Vain. Johnson.
Mary at the Cross. McGee.
Measure for Measure.
  Shakespeare.
The New Physician.
  Chalmers.
O, Let Me Kiss—. Gjellerup.
Paradise Lost. Milton.
A Prayer. Hemans.
Simple Faith. Cowper.
A Song: "Hast thou seen the
  Down in the Air."
  Suckling.
Song to a Lute. Suckling.
Sonnet on the Death of
  Richard West. Gray.
The Sparrow's Song.
  Anonymous.
Supplication. Johnson.
The Thousand and One
  Nights: The Power of Love.
  Anonymous.
To a Beautiful but Heartless
  Coquette. Terrazas.
Vain and Careless. Graves.
What Is That Music High in
  the Air? Smith.
The Wife's Lament.
  Anonymous.

Vale (s)

The Ashtabula Disaster.
  Moore.
The Book of Thel. Blake.
The Brown Jug. Fawkes.
The Chase (excerpt).
  Somervile.
Constancy. Daniel.
Evening in Tyringham Valley.
  Gilder.
The Irish Girl's Lament.
  Anonymous.
Little Brown Church in the
  Vale. Pitts.
The Night Serene. Leon.

Night up There. Valentine.
The Norfolk Rebellion: The
  Slaughter of the Rebels.
  Anonymous.
Ode: To the Nightingale.
  Warton.
Rivers of the West. "Sunset
  Joe".
Robin Good-Fellow.
  Anonymous.
Song of Longing.
  Anonymous.
Tartary. De La Mare.
Thy Praise, O God, in Zion
  Waits. Kimball.
The Watershed. Meynell.
The Wool Trade. Dyer.

Valediction

Little Gidding. Eliot.

Valentine Brown

A Grey Eye Weeping.
  O'Rahilly.

Valentine (s)

An Epithalamion, or Marriage
  Song. Donne.
February 14, 22 B. C.
  Adams.
Hearts Were Made to Give
  Away. Wynne.
Letter from a Coward to a
  Hero. Warren.
The Lovable Child.
  Poulsson.
Mare Nostrum.
  Oppenheimer.
A New Orleans Balcony–1880.
  Haight.
Rise and Fall of Valentines.
  Downey.
Shepherdess' Valentine.
  Andrewes.
St. Valentine's Day.
  Anonymous.
A Sure Sign. Turner.
Valentine. Gasparini.
The Wine Menagerie. Crane.
You. Clark.

Valet

The End of a Dynasty.
  Herbert.

Valiant

Choral Symphony Conductor.
  Coates.
Great Day. *Anonymous.*
A Man! Scollard.
Morte Arthur (excerpt).
  Anonymous.

Valid

Thou Shalt Surely Die...: No
  Ghost Is True. Fiedler.

Valium

Tea for Two. Nolan.

Valley Forges

George Washington. Tippett.

Valley (s)

Anastasis. Smythe.
Apocalypse. Lipkin.
April. Auringer.
Ave, Vita Nostra! Laure.
Between the Walls of the
  Valley. Peck.
Birds Are Drowsing on the
  Branches. Rudnitsky.
The Calendar of Oengus:
  Prologue (excerpt).
  Anonymous.
The Call. Kauffman.
Cardrona Valley. Wedde.
Chamber Music. Joyce.
A Common Ground.
  Levertov.
Death Valley. Lee.

Dem Bones. *Anonymous.*
The Downfall of Heathendom. *Anonymous.*
Dream Fantasy. "Macleod.
Earth Has Shrunk in the Wash. Empson.
Edom. *Anonymous.*
Effigy. McElhaney.
Flowers in the Valley. *Anonymous.*
Full Valleys. Scott.
I Met at Eve. De La Mare.
In Mutual Time. Lavoie.
Lalla Rookh. Moore.
Lament for the Woodlands. *Anonymous.*
The Lent Lily. Housman.
Little Black Rose. *Anonymous.*
Memento Vivendi. Brudne.
The Mountains. Dudek.
Mririda. Mririda n'Ait Attik.
Nevada. Noyes.
The Novice. Davison.
Pennsylvania Winter Indian 1974. Littlebird.
The Plain Golden Band. *Anonymous.*
Questions and Answers. O Hehir.
Rain. Wright.
Sally Goodin. *Anonymous.*
Sleet Storm. Tippett.
Song of the Chattahoochee. Lanier.
Song: "There is no joy in water apart from the sun." Currey.
Summer Journey. Rodgers.
To Milk in the Valley Below. *Anonymous.*
The Walker of the Snow. Shanly.
Westering. Kane.
The Wound. Gunn.

Valor
Decoration Day. Barbour.
For a Picture Where a Queen Laments over the Tomb of a Slain Knight. Carew.
Guilty. Wilkinson.
Her Race. Yeats.
Heroique Stanzas, Consecrated to the Glorious Memory... Dryden.
In Apia Bay. Roberts.
On the Lord Gen. Fairfax at the Siege of Colchester. Milton.
A Song: "Smile, Massachusetts, smile." *Anonymous.*
Sonnet: Of Becchina in a Rage. Angiolieri.

Valuable
A Proposal for Recycling Wastes. Piercy.
Valuable. Smith.

Value (d) (s)
The Apostasy. Traherne.
The Bloody Sire. Jeffers.
Boy-Man. Shapiro.
The Death of Admiral Benbow. *Anonymous.*
If I Went Away. O'Grady.
A Likeness. Browning.
Making. Webb.
Praise of New England. Chubb.
Song: "If she be not as kind as fair." Etherege.

Vampire (s)
The Conger Eel. MacGill.
To Pius IX. Whittier.
An Utter Passion Uttered Utterly (parody). Todhunter.

Van Dyck
The Strong Heroic Line. Holmes

Van Gogh
The Flowers of Politics. McClure.
It Is When the Tribe Is Gone. Bigger.

Vandal (s)
Qua Song. Inez.
Subterranean Homesick Blues. Dylan.
The Temple at Segesta. Henri.

Vanilla
The Bachelor's Ballade. Parry.
Dark Romance. Corpi.
The Gerbil Who Got Away. Root.

Vanish (ed) (es) (ing)
The Alchemist. Church.
The Animal Runs, It Passes, It Dies. *Anonymous.*
Bernie's Quick-Shave (1968). Lea.
Black Absence Hides upon the Past. Clare.
Bum's Rush. Dransfield.
Butterfly. Lawrence.
Cat. Rosenblatt.
The Constant One. Dillon.
Die Heimkehr (excerpt). Heine.
Dino Campana and the Bear. Hirsch.
Early Morn. Davies.
Extinct Birds. Wright.
The Faerie Queene. Spenser.
Full Moon. De La Mare.
Gabriel. Wattles.
Gifts. Stokesbury.
Give Me Not Tears. Lathrop.
Haiku: "Tow-head dandelions." Phillips.
Jack Frost. Davis.
Midpoint. Simic.
Moonlight Song of the Mocking-bird. Hayne
Morning at the Window. Eliot.
Mum and the Sothsegger: A Dream. *Anonymous.*
Music in the Night. Spofford.
My Father after Work. Gildner.
Not Being Oedipus. Heath-Stubbs.
Ode: "To orisons, the midnight bell." Beckford.
Out of the Sea. Bynner.
Parish. Dubie.
Party at Hydra. Layton.
Poem for Dorothy Holt. Rea.
The Poem Rising by Its Own Weight. Levertov.
Pontoosuce. Melville.
A Prayer to Escape from the Market Place. Wright.
Sir Humphrey Gilbert. Longfellow.
The Snowflake. De la Mare.

The Snowflake Which Is Now and Hence Forever. MacLeish.
Song of the All-Wool Shirt. Field.
Suddenly Afraid. *Anonymous.*
Tao and Unfitness at Inistioge on the River Nore. Kinsella.
Tear. Kinsella.
To a Scarlatti Passepied. Hillyer.
The Wood-Dove's Note. Miller.

Vanity (ies)
As in the Midst of Battle There Is Room. Santayana.
The Butterfly and the Bee. Bowles.
Ecclesiastes. Chesterton.
The Glove and the Lions. Hunt.
Night Comes Apace. Shute.
Ode to Wisdom. Carter.
Odes. Santayana.
On a Certain Poet. *Anonymous.*
On an Infant Dying as Soon as Born. Lamb.
Putney Hymn. *Anonymous.*
The Spring Beauties. Cone.
Timon's Villa. Pope.
Upon Rook: Epigram. Herrick.
The Vanity of All Worldly Things. Bradstreet.

Vanquish (ed)
The Battle of Philiphaugh. *Anonymous.*
In the Balance. *Anonymous.*
Italy. Filicaja.
Last Refuge. Michelangelo.
Poem: "The haven and last refuge of my pain." Machiavelli.
The Two Lovers. Hovey.

Vapor (s)
Don Juan. Byron.
Eighteen-Seventy. Rimbaud.
The Fleece. Dyer.
Jeanie with the Light Brown Hair. Foster.
A Little Boy Lost. Blake.
Marshlands. Johnson.
The Sons of Indolence. Thomson.

Variation (s)
The Origin of Species. Sklarew.
Passin Ben Dorain. Mackie.

Variety
Day and Night Handball. Dunn.
Ode: "That I have often been in love, deep love." Wolcot.

Vase
Home Is So Sad. Larkin.
Poppies. McPherson.
Recessional. Johnson.
The Vase of Tears. Spender.

Vast
The Angel. Hayes.
Cloister. O'Donnell.
The Coral Reef. Blight.
Fiat Lux. Mifflin.
Flood. Joyce.
How Small Is Man. Blackie.
A Mantelpiece of Shells. Todd.

The Old Conservative. Tooker.
Unreturning. Stoddard
Victory Parade. Hoffman.
We Are All Workmen. Rilke.

Vatican
I Woke Up Revenge. Poulin, Jr.
The Lost History Plays: Savanarola (parody). Beerbohm.

Vaudeville
Confirmation. Lange.

Vault (ed) (s)
Banks of Marble. Rice.
Doctrinal Point. Empson.
Epitaph. *Anonymous.*
Epitaph: "Here lies I and my three daughters." *Anonymous.*
Hallowe'en. Hecht.
I Am. Clare.
The Knell. Al-Fituri.
Poem on the Suicide of My Teacher. Stroud.

Vegetable (s)
Cerne Abbas. Summers.
The Glacier. MacNeice.
In the Emptied Rest Home. Akhmadulina.
The King in May. Browne.
Sonnet Made upon the Groves near Merlou Castle. Herbert of Cherbury.
Tummy Ache. Fisher.

Vegetarian
The Logical Vegetarian. Chesterton.

Veil (ed)
Arthur Mitchell. Moore.
Daisies of Florence. Raine.
Drifting Sands and a Caravan. Langworthy.
For Communion with God (excerpt). Shepherd.
The Hymn of Saint Thomas in Adoration of the Blessed Sacrament. Crashaw.
Idylls of the King. Tennyson.
Impressions. Wilde.
Jesus Only. Simpson.
Jesus, These Eyes Have Never Seen. Palmer.
Mully of Mountown (excerpt). King.
Odes, II. Hafiz.
Plum Blossoms. Basho (Matsuo Basho).
Sappho. Catullus.
The Stuffed Owl. Wordsworth.
They Say She Is Veiled. Grahn.

Vein (ed) (s)
Ambuscade. McCrae.
Arbor Vitae. Sassoon.
Boy with His Hair Cut Short. Rukeyser.
The Cave-Drawing. Watkins.
Confession. Savage.
A Dance for Ma Rainey. Young.
David Homindae. Rosenfeld.
A Day Begins. Levertov.
The Flesh. Yamanaka.
Fragment of a Sonnet. Ronsard.
The Glacier. MacNeice.
Hippolytus Temporizes. Doolittle.

In Praise of Cocoa, Cupid's
Nightcap. Sharpless.
In the Barrio. Alurista.
Jane Retreat. Honig.
Keine Lazarovitch. Layton.
Landscape I. Madge.
Nunc Scio, Quid Sit Amor.
Mackay.
O, Beautiful They Move.
Pillen.
Respectabilities. Silkin.
Survival Kit. Slater.
The Train Dogs. Johnson.
Variations on a Theme.
Williams.
The Waking. Roethke.
Velasquez
The Strong Heroic Line.
Holmes
Veldt
Camp Fire. Bromley.
Far from Africa. Danner.
I Heard a Soldier. Trench.
Velvet
The Dentist. Fyleman.
Hark, Hark! The Dogs Do
Bark. Mother Goose.
Images. Campbell.
Mare. Thurman.
Sunday Afternoon. Levertov.
The Velvet Sonneteers.
MacInnes.
When I Am Dead. Barrie.
Vengeance
The Constancy of a Lover.
Gascoigne.
The Gold Seekers.
Richardson.
Horned Lizard. Molesworth.
Idyllis. Theocritus.
Odes. Horace.
Of a Woman, Dead Young.
Parker.
Verses in the Style of the
Druids (excerpt). Scott.
The Welshmen of Tirawley.
Ferguson.
Yellow Woman Speaks.
Woo.
Venice
The City of Falling Leaves.
Lowell.
The Eve of St. Mark. Keats.
From a Venetian Sequence.
Naude.
Jerusalem, Port City.
Amichai.
Julian and Maddalo (excerpt).
Shelley.
The Love-Making: His and
Hers. Merriam.
Venom
Limerick: "Said an asp to an
adder named Rhea."
Newman.
Modern Love, XXVI.
Meredith.
Snake Hunt. Wagoner.
To One Who Is Too Gay.
Baudelaire.
Venus
Astrophel and Stella, CII.
Sidney.
Atalanta's Race. Morris.
Dedication. Gogarty.
Earth-Visitors. Slessor.
Father Mat. Kavanagh.
For Travelers Going Sidereal.
Frost.
Hymn to Her Unknown.
Turner.
In the Balance. *Anonymous.*

The Judgement of Tiresias.
Jacob.
The Love-Making: His and
Hers. Merriam.
My Loves. Blackie.
The New Litany. Brown.
O Gentle Love. Peele.
On Sight of a Gentlewoman's
Face in the Water. Carew.
Phyllis Corydon clutched to
him. Catullus.
A Song of Pleasure.
Massinger.
A Sonnet, to the Noble Lady,
the Lady Mary Worth.
Jonson.
Stars. Brown.
The Survivors. Hine.
Veranda
At a Summer Hotel.
Gardner.
Limerick: "A lady who lived
in Uganda." Smith.
There Were Fierce Animals in
Africa. Aubert.
Verandahs. Brissenden.
Verb
For the Noun C. BL. Tyler.
Verbena
In the Proscenium.
Derwood.
Limerick: "There once was a
happy hyena." Wells.
Periphery. Ammons.
Variations on Southern
Themes. Justice.
Verdant
The Kind of Waters, the Sea
Shouldering Whale.
Wood.
Song: "How pleas'd within my
native bowers." Shenstone.
Verdict (s)
The Death of Samuel Adams.
Anonymous.
Drilling Missed Holes.
Cameron.
The Nyum-Nyum.
Anonymous.
Verdure
Ode to Arnold Schoenberg.
Tomlinson.
Portrait of the Father.
Hough.
Summer Morning. Thomson.
Verge
Arizona. Hall.
The Coromandel Fishers.
Naidu.
The Iliad. Homer.
Verity
Ballad of the Three Spectres.
Gurney.
Companionship. Coleridge.
Proof. Bird.
Twelve P.M. Howells.
Vermilion
The name—of it–is "Autumn."
Dickinson.
Soliloquy in an Air-Raid.
Fuller.
Vermin
By the Ford. Thomas.
How the Doughty Duke of
Albany Like a Coward
Knight...(excerpt).
Skelton.
Thinking of Holderlin.
Middleton.
Vermont
Limerick: "Evangelical Vicar
in want." Knox.

Vernal
Do Nothing till You Hear
from Me. Henderson.
Rhyme for Remembering the
Date of Easter.
Richardson.
The Stormy Hebrides.
Collins.
Verse (d) (s)
A Ballad to the Tune of "The
Cut-Purse." Swift.
The Ballade of the
Incompetent Ballade-
Monger. Stephen.
Beau's Reply. Cowper.
Bourbons. Landor.
Bufo. Pope.
By Return Mail. Aldridge.
A Cardinal. Snodgrass.
Cimabuella (parody). Taylor.
Clerihew: "Edmund Clerihew
Bentley." Smith.
A Crucifix. Verlaine.
Dismissing Progress and its
Progenitors. Reavey.
A Dream of Jealousy.
Heaney.
English Poetry. Daniel.
Epigram: "I dreamt that I was
God Himself." Pound.
Epilogue. Singer.
Epitaph on One Lockyer,
Inventor of a Patent
Medicine. *Anonymous.*
Fighting Words. Parker.
Had I the Choice. Whitman.
The High Bridge above the
Tagus River at Toledo.
Williams.
The History of Prince Edward
Island. *Anonymous.*
The Hundred Best Books.
Pigott.
I, Lessimus, of Salt Lake City
(parody). Peters.
Impression. Gosse.
In February. Simpson.
Lovers, and a Reflection.
Calverley.
Meeting Mick Jagger
(parody). Peters.
Mercy to Animals. Tupper.
The New Castalia. Ward.
An Ode: "Awake, faire Muse;
for I intend." Browne.
On a Midsummer Eve.
Hardy.
On Mr. Milton's Paradise
Lost. Marvell.
On the Death of Mr. Pope.
Anonymous.
On the Death of Mr. William
Hervey. Cowley.
Opening of Eyes. Riding.
Perpetuum Mobile. Sitwell.
Pick-up at Chef Rizal
Restaurant. Cerenio.
Poem: "So they begin."
Pasternak.
The Request. Cowley.
Ronald Wyn. Bagg.
Seal Rocks: San Francisco.
Conquest.
The Shepheardes Calender:.
Spenser.
Solution. Emerson.
Sonnets. Tuckerman.
Sonnets, XIX: "Devouring
Time, blunt thou the lion's
paws." Shakespeare.
Sonnets, LX: "Like as the
waves make towards the

pebbled shore."
Shakespeare.
St. Valentine,. Moore.
Starlight. Meredith.
The Steele Glas. Gascoigne.
Three Poems. "Ping Hsin"
(Hsieh Wang-ying).
The Three Ravens (C vers.).
Anonymous.
To His Darrest Freind.
Stewart.
To Mr. T. W. Donne.
To Natalie. Ryskind.
To the Immortal Memory of
the Halibut on Which I
Dined This Day. Cowper.
To the Reader. Oakes.
To the Reverend Shade of His
Religious Father. Herrick.
To Those Who Sing America.
Davis.
Two Poems against His Rival,
II. Catullus.
Young Reynard. Meredith.
Vertical
Apologia. Farjeon.
Lines on the Sea. Laing.
Sunday Rain. Updike.
What I Saw Passages 3.
Duncan.
Vertigo
Do Not Accompany Me.
Halkin.
Mother Goose's Garland.
MacLeish.
Vessel (s)
British Commerce. Dyer.
Down among the Wharves.
Jewett.
The False Lover.
Anonymous.
L'Imprevisibilite. Hippius.
The Inchcape Rock.
Southey.
Letters. Emerson.
Of Commerce and Society.
Hill.
Panegyrick upon O.
Cromwell. Waller.
The Reed. Carpenter.
Song: "The boat is chafing at
our long delay."
Davidson.
Storm and Quiet. Eberhart.
Vestal
Urania. Pitter.
Vestal moon
At the Shelter-Stone.
Macrow.
Vestibule
The Contribution. Shapiro.
Talking to Myself. McHugh.
Vesture
Arbor Vitae. Sassoon.
Epigram: "Dear, my familiar
hand in love's own gesture."
Cunningham.
In February. Simpson.
Vex (ation) (ed) (es)
The Fall of Hyperion.
Keats.
Limerick: "As a little fat man
of Bombay." *Anonymous.*
Limerick: "There was an Old
Man on the Border."
Lear.
On a Vase of Gold-Fish.
Tennyson.
Rejoice, O Youth, in the
Lovely Hind. Ibn Ezra.
Vicar
The Lady of the Lake. Scott.

Limerick: "There was a young
curate of Salisbury."
Libaire.
The Nimble Stag. Knox.
The Spanish Curate.
Fletcher.
Vice
The Authors of the Town
(excerpt). Savage.
Caelica, CVI. Greville.
Carmina. Catullus.
The Character of a Certain
Whig. Shippen.
Elegy for Doctor Dunn.
Herbert of Cherbury.
The Fable of Acis,
Polyphemus, and Galatea.
Dryden.
The Happy Nightingale.
Anonymous.
How the Doughty Duke of
Albany Like a Coward
Knight...(excerpt).
Skelton.
Invocation. Byron.
Marius Victor. Raleigh.
On the Loss of U.S.
Submarine S4 (excerpt).
Canfield.
A Remonstrance. Gerrard.
The Resolve. Chudleigh.
Sir Francis Bacon. Bierce.
A Sonnet to Opium;
Celebrating Its Virtues.
"Orestes".
When Wilt Thou Save the
People? Elliott.
The Young Conquistador.
Peterson.
Vicinity
Limerick: "There was an old
Fellow of Trinity." Hilton.
Oh, Noa, Noa! Cole.
Vicious
Limerick: "There was a young
man of Mauritius."
Lindsay.
London Voluntaries. Henley.
Paradise Lost. Milton.
The Song of the Mischievous
Dog. Thomas.
The Soviet Union.
Berryman.
Verses Written in the Chiosk
at Pera, Overlooking
Constantinople. Montagu.
Vicissitudes
To a Depraved Lying Woman.
MacLean.
Victim (s)
Abstrosophy. Burgess.
The Blantyre Explosion.
Anonymous.
The Dying Desperado.
Anonymous.
The Grauballe Man.
Heaney.
The Milwaukee Fire.
Anonymous.
Namby-Pamby. Carey.
Ode to Moderation (excerpt).
Plumptre.
Pentucket. Whittier.
Song to a Fair, Young Lady,
Going out of the Town in
the Spring. Dryden.
A Soldier from Missouri.
Anonymous.
The Praying Mantis Visits a
Penthouse. Williams.

Victor
Cotton Manuscript: Maxims.
Anonymous.
Cupid. O'Dowd.
The Duke of Buckingham.
Pope.
Grubber's Day. Sigmund.
John Pelham. Randall.
Lines Addressed to a Seagull.
Griffin.
Love in Fantastic Triumph.
Behn.
The Mecklenburg Declaration.
Elam.
Nancy Hanks. Monroe.
A Prayer for St. Innocent's
Day. Eden.
The Praying Mantis Visits a
Penthouse. Williams.
The Ride to Cherokee.
Carpenter.
Song. Love Arm'd. Behn.
The Victor. Young.
Victoria
The Bold Dragoon.
Anonymous.
Queen Victoria. *Anonymous.*
Victory (ies)
Ah, Poverties, Wincings, and
Sulky Retreats. Whitman.
All-Souls' Day. Sassoon.
American Independence.
Hopkinson.
As I Lay with My Head in
Your Lap Camerado.
Whitman.
Awake, My Soul!
Doddridge.
The Ballad of Paco Town.
Scollard.
A Ballad of the Good Lord
Nelson. Durrell.
Basic Communication.
Ferril.
The Battle of Blenheim.
Southey.
Because He Lives. Lathrop.
The Bed. Marino.
The Boasting of Sir Peter
Parker. Scollard.
Byron in Greece. Rosten.
The Captain Stood on the
Carronade. Marryat.
The Constitution's Last Fight.
Roche.
David and Bethsabe. Peele.
Death's Songsters. Rossetti.
The Dreaded Task. Bruner.
The Faerie Queene. Spenser.
The Fight at the Bridge.
Macaulay.
The First Olympionique to
Hiero of Syracuse. Pindar.
God to Thee We Humbly
Bow. Boker.
Henry Before Agincourt.
Lydgate.
Hold the Fort. *Anonymous.*
Hound Voice. Yeats.
If You Happy Would Be.
Fernandez.
Inscription for Marye's
Heights, Fredericksburg.
Melville.
It's G-L-O-R-Y to Know I'm
S-A-V-E-D. *Anonymous.*
It Is Finished. Bonar.
Joyce Kilmer. Burr.
Judgment. Channing-Stetson.
King Christian. Evald.
The Last Communion.
Ward.

Letters Found near a Suicide.
Horne.
Lines Written after the
Discovery ... of the Germ of
Yellow Fever. Ross.
The Marseillaise. Rouget de
Lisle.
Masque of the Virtues against
Love. From Guarini.
Monck.
More Letters Found Near a
Suicide. Horne.
The Nineteenth of April.
Larcom.
Now as Then. Ridler.
O What Pleasure 'Tis to Find.
Behn.
Obsequies of Stuart.
Thompson.
Ombre at Hampton Court.
Pope.
On Gustavus Adolphus, King
of Sweden. Roe.
Onward, Onward, Men of
Heaven. Sigourney.
Our Nation Forever. Bruce.
Overheard in a Barbershop.
Layton.
Peace. Hughes.
The Pro. Swenson.
Prometheus. Byron.
Religious Musings.
Coleridge.
Resurrection. John of
Damascus.
Resuscitation Team.
Fanthorpe.
The Riders. Friend.
Smothered Fires. Johnson.
The Song of Roland, CUV.
Anonymous.
Sonnet VI: "The coming of
that limpid Star is twice."
Labe.
The stars are old, that stood
for me. Dickinson.
Survival. Coates.
There's A Regret. Henley.
The Trumpet. Ehrenburg.
Upon the Hill before
Centreville. Boker.
A Victory Dance. Noyes.
Waking an Angel. Levine.
Your Animal. Stern.
Your Pain. Guebuza.
Zagonyi. Boker.
Viet Cong
Who Needs Charlie Manson?
Thompson.
Vietnam
Bring the War Home.
Matthews.
Kilroy. McCarthy.
Norman Morrison. Mitchell.
To Whom It May Concern.
Mitchell.
Vision of 400 Sunrises.
Schechter.
View (s)
Absolute and Abitofhell.
Knox.
Corruption. Vaughan.
From Childhood's Hour.
Poe.
The Instalment (excerpt).
Young.
Mr. Rockefeller's Hat.
Bevington.
Ode on the Poetical
Character. Collins.
Old Women of Toronto.
Waddington.

Samson Agonistes. Milton.
Shaggy Dog Story. Steele.
Sonnets, XXXI: "Thy bosom
is endeared with all hearts."
Shakespeare.
To Clelia. Coppinger.
Very Old Man. Henry.
What Glorious Vision.
Cradock.
The World I Am Passing
Through. Child.
Vigil (s)
The American Book of the
Dead: Six Selections.
Giorno.
The Battle of the Jarama.
Neruda.
Shakespeare's Mourners.
Tabb.
This Quiet Dust. Wheelock.
Vigil. Campbell.
Vigilant
Annunciations. Hill.
Climbing Zero Gully.
Morley.
The Rod. Herrick.
Two Variations. Levertov.
Village (rs) (s)
Dear as the Moon.
Anonymous.
Evangeline. Longfellow.
The Excursion. Wordsworth.
For Her. Strand.
From Jerusalem: A First
Poem. Preil.
Inscriptions on Chinese
Paintings: Lines To Do
With Youth. Bynner.
Lines on Mountain Villages.
"Sunset Joe".
Marching Song. Stevenson.
Metaphors of a Magnifico.
Stevens.
The Noise of the Village.
Anonymous.
O Christ of Bethlehem.
Lanier.
The Old Cottagers. Clare.
Patapan. De La Monnoye.
The Poets. Wevill.
Sleeping Peasants. Janik.
Song of the Little Villages.
Dollard.
The Sound of the Drum.
Anonymous.
The Two Villages. Cooke.
The Village of
Balmaquhapple. Hogg.
The Villagers and Death.
Graves.
The Vulture. Hoh.
Villain (y)
Naomi Wise. *Anonymous.*
Village-Born Beauty.
Anonymous.
Villan (y)
Carol in Praise of the Holly
and Ivy. *Anonymous.*
Epilogue to the Satires.
Pope.
Holly and Ivy. *Anonymous.*
The Sally from Coventry.
Thornbury.
Satire. Marston.
To Everlasting Oblivion.
Marston.
Villas
Aurora Leigh. Browning.
Vine (s)
After the Annunciation.
Duggan.

American Vineyard.
  Cousens.
Amours de Voyage. Clough.
Bacchus on Beverages. Redi.
The Creeper. Schmidt.
Even in the Moment of Our
  Earliest Kiss. Millay.
Harvest Poem. Fisher.
The Mediterranean. Tate.
Monody. Melville.
My Neighbor's Roses.
  Gruber.
The Mysteries Remain.
  Doolittle.
An Ode to Master Endymion
  Porter, upon His Brother's
  Death. Herrick.
On the Marriage. Beaumont.
Pictures of the Rhine.
  Meredith.
Praise of Earth. Browning.
The Preference Declared.
  Field.
Rare Moments. Phelps.
Vacancy in the Park.
  Stevens.
Variations on a Theme.
  Williams.
The Vine. Herrick.

Vinegar
Buy Us a Little Grain.
  Lavant.
Damis, an Author Cold and
  Weak. *Anonymous.*
Early Discoveries. Malouf.
Jack and Jill. Mother Goose.
Sausage. Axionicus.
Sidrophel, the Rosicrucian
  Conjurer. Butler.

Vineyards
Epigram: "As honey in wine."
  Meleager.
Love Poem. Lewis.

Vintage
For a Wine Festival.
  Watkins.
In Celebration. Bass.

Violence (ent)
At the Hammersmith Palais...
  Riddell.
The Bloody Sire. Jeffers.
The Book of Kells. Colum.
The House. Scott.
Lesbian Play on T.V.
  Gilfillan.
Love Me Little, Love Me
  Long. Herrick.
On Lavater's Song of a
  Christian to Christ.
  Goethe.
Paradise Lost. Milton.
The Poet's Use. Pope.
The Storm. Donne.
Sunset Horn. O'Higgins.
This Morning. Rukeyser.
To Mars. Chapman.
Tywater. Wilbur.

Violet (s)
April Rain. Loveman.
Down a Woodland Way.
  Howells.
Doxology. Taylor.
Endymion. Keats.
Eulalie. A Song. Poe.
Henceforth I Will Not Set My
  Love. Gorges.
Her Music. Dickinson.
I Am. Conkling.
If my nipples were to drip
  milk. Sappho.
In the Spring. Meleager.
Lament. Binyon.

Life in the Boondocks.
  Ammons.
Mark You How the Peacock's
  Eye. Hopkins.
Morning. Waddington.
Night Singers. Sappho.
Nothing to Save. Lawrence.
On the Death of Keats.
  Logan.
The Passing of March.
  Wilson.
Pliny Jane. Luton.
The Rainbow. Hopkins.
Rainy Day Song. Storey.
Then the Ermine. Moore.
To Miss Arundell. Landor.
Under the Violets. Holmes.
Vowels. Rimbaud.

Violin (ist) (s)
Always Before Your Voice
  My Soul. Cummings.
Cadenza. Hughes.
The Composer's Winter
  Dream. Dubie.
First Fight. Then Fiddle.
  Brooks.
I Love You. Farkas.
Songs. Cummings.
South of the Border.
  Nicholas.
Stradivarius: Working with
  God. Eliot.
Symphony in Gray Major.
  Dario.
Under the Earth. Sutzkever.
Violins in Repose. Plescoff.

Virgil
Epitaph for One Who Would
  Not Be Buried in
  Westminster Abbey. Pope.
Upon the Death of His
  Sparrow an Elegie.
  Herrick.

Virgin
Echoes. Henley.

Virgin (al) (ity) (s)
August. Spenser.
The Bed. Marino.
The Benedictine Ultima.
  Anonymous.
The Carnal and the Crane.
  Anonymous.
Caution. *Anonymous.*
Corinna in Vendome.
  Ronsard.
Euch, Are You Having Your
  Period? Alta.
Fie, Fie on Blind Fancy!
  Greene.
Girl of the Lovely Glance.
  Praxilla.
How of the Virgin Mother
  Shall I Sing? Ennodius.
I Lie Down with God.
  Anonymous.
Lunar Baedeker. Loy.
The Merry Hay-Makers.
  Anonymous.
November. Keble.
The Oeconomy of Love
  (excerpt). Armstrong.
Of the Confident Stranger.
  Coolidge.
Poor Is the Life That Misses.
  Anonymous.
La Preciosa. Walsh.
Ramble on What in the
  World Why. Gustafson.
Saul's Song of Love.
  Tchernichovsky.
Strephon. Smyth.

Two Songs from a Play.
  Yeats.
Valediction. MacNeice.
The Ways and the Peoples.
  Jarrell.
The White Anemone.
  Meredith."
Young Virgins Plucked
  Suddenly. Pomerantz.

Virgin Mary
Blackheads. Skinner.
O Virgin. *Anonymous.*
Poem for Unwed Mothers.
  Giovanni.
Prewar Late October Sea
  Breeze. Grenier.
Salve Regina. *Anonymous.*
Spring. Loveman.
"Through the Open Door..."
  Kavanagh.

Virginia (ns)
The Ambassadors. Lawson.
The Bachelor's Ballade.
  Parry.
First Families Move Over!
  Nash.
Foxgloves. Hughes.
Robert E. Lee. Howe.
Virginiana. Johnson.

Virginny
Clare De Kitchen.
  Anonymous.
A Net for a Night Raven.
  Anonymous.

Virtue (s)
Abraham Lincoln. Stoddard.
Achitophel: the Earl of
  Shaftesbury. Dryden.
Advice to the Same. Sidney.
All This World's Riches.
  Spenser.
Amoretti, XV. Spenser.
Apologia pro Vita Sua.
  Pope.
Armida, the Sorceress.
  Tasso.
Astrophel and Stella, IV.
  Sidney.
Astrophel and Stella, LII.
  Sidney.
Astrophel and Stella, LXIV.
  Sidney.
Ballata V: "Light do I see
  within my Lady's eyes."
  Cavalcanti.
Be Drunken. Baudelaire.
Character of the Happy
  Warrior. Wordsworth.
The Conscience. Wickham.
Crime at Its Best. King.
Death and Love. Jonson.
The Earl of Surrey to
  Geraldine. Drayton.
Elegy for Doctor Dunn.
  Herbert of Cherbury.
Fortune and Virtue. Dekker.
Full Be the Year, Abundant
  Be the Grain. *Anonymous.*
In Tyme the Strong and
  Statlie Turrets Fall.
  Fletcher.
Indifference to Fortune.
  Thomson.
The Inscription on the Tombe
  of the Lady Mary
  Wentworth. Carew.
An Invective Against the
  Wicked of the World.
  Breton.
Jansenist Journey. Devlin.
Lament. Thomas.

Let Not Thy Beauty.
  Townsend.
Lines Written near Richmond,
  upon the Thames, at
  Evening. Wordsworth.
Llangollen Vale (excerpt).
  Seward.
Love's Triumph. Jonson.
Marginalia (excerpt). Auden.
Mary Gulliver to Captain
  Lemuel Gulliver. Swift.
Maystress Jane Scroupe.
  Skelton.
Melancholy. Habington.
A Moral Poem Freely
  Accepted from Sappho.
  Wright.
Nature and the Poets.
  Beattie.
A Nuptial Song, or
  Epithalamie, on Sir Clipseby
  Crew and His Lady.
  Herrick.
O Rose, O Rainbow. Moore.
Ode to Wisdom. Carter.
On Fortune. Elizabeth I.
On Philosophers.
  Anonymous.
Palamon and Arcite, III:
  "Parts of the whole are we;
  but God the whole.
  Dryden.
The Pilot. Chapman.
Poem: "on getting a card."
  Williams.
Potato. Wilbur.
Preludes. Patmore.
Rachel's Lament. Zisquit.
A Remonstrance. Gerrard.
Report on Experience.
  Blunden.
The Shadow of Night.
  Chapman.
The Song of O'Ruark, Prince
  of Breffni. Moore.
Song Set by Philip Rosseter:
  "What is a day.."
  Anonymous.
Song: "Virtue's branches
  wither, virtue pines."
  Dekker.
Sonnet: "I fear to me such
  fortune be assign'd."
  Drummond.
Sonnet, X: "When I catch
  sight of your fair head."
  Labé.
Sonnet: Of Virtue. San
  Geminiano.
Spring Bereaved.
  Drummond.
Streets. Goldring.
Summing Up in Italy.
  Browning.
Tamburlaine the Great.
  Marlowe.
Time. Fletcher.
To a Lady, with a Compass.
  Napier.
To an Enemy. Bodenheim.
To Mistress Gertrude
  Statham. Skelton.
To Mistress Margaret Tilney.
  Skelton.
Transformation. Catullus.
Verses Written in the Chiosk
  at Pera, Overlooking
  Constantinople. Montagu.
A Virtue of Shape. Swiss.
The Vision. Burns.

Virtuous
The Constant Swain and
Virtuous Maid.
Anonymous.
The Duke of Benevento.
Moore.
On a Horse and a Goat.
Lister.
The 'Prentice Boy.
Anonymous.
The Princess of Dreams.
Dowson.
Virus
Miss Kilmansegg and Her
Precious Leg. Hood.
Visage
Chambers of Jerusalem.
Karni.
Sonnet: He Will Not Be Too
Deeply in Love.
Angiolieri.
Visibility
Ceiling Unlimited. Rukeyser.
Visible
The Battle of Waterloo.
Byron.
A Dance Chant. *Anonymous.*
In the Flowering Season.
Roberts.
Look You, My Simple Friend.
Clough.
Person, or A Hymn on and to
the Holy Ghost. Avison.
The Three Movements. Hall.
To My Quick Ear.
Dickinson.
Vision (ary) (ing) (s)
Air (parody). Dow.
All-Souls' Day. Sassoon.
Begin the Day with God.
Anonymous.
Bell-Birds. Kendall.
The Brothers. Muir.
Buddha. Holmes.
Cader Idris at Sunset.
Turner.
Circe. MacNeice.
The Complaisant Friend.
Louys.
Cry Faugh! Graves.
The Duchess of York's Ghost.
Anonymous.
Enigma. McCrae.
Essay. Mayer.
The Eternal City. Ammons.
An Exeter Riddle. Ewart.
The Higher Pantheism.
Tennyson.
In Time of Gold. Doolittle.
Joses, the Brother of Jesus.
Kemp.
Keep Me As Your Servant, O
Girdhar. Mira Bai [(or
Mirabai)].
Love-Songs, At Once Tender
and Informative.
Hoffenstein.
Mary's Vision. *Anonymous.*
Milton. Blake.
A Miltonic Sonnet for Mr.
Johnson... Wilbur.
Miserere. Gascoyne.
Mors et Vita. Waddington.
Notre Dame Perfected by
Reflection. Witt.
Oh Bright Oh Black Singbeast
Lovebeast Catkin Sleek.
McClure.
On Writing Asian-American
Poetry. Kudaka.
Oriflamme. Fauset.
Plead for Me. Bronte.

Poem Touching the Gestapo.
Heyen.
Poetry. Soutar.
Prayer. *Anonymous.*
Prayer. Flint.
Recalling War. Graves.
The Sacred Hearth.
Gascoyne.
Sonnets. Tuckerman.
Sonnets, First Series.
Tuckerman.
Spring. Larkin.
St. Gervais. Roberts.
Sunflower Sutra. Ginsberg.
Surfaces. Mayhall.
To —. Praed.
To Liebig-7. Platen.
To My Friend Butts I Write.
Blake.
Troy. Flower.
Two Sonnets. Berenberg.
The Undreamed. Emans.
A Vision. "Field.
A Vision. Herbert of
Cherbury.
With Happiness Stretched
Across the Hills. Blake.
Woolworth's. Hall.
Visit (ed) (or) (ors)
Are You Just Back for a Visit
or Are You Going to Stay?
Rosenberger.
A Card of Invitation to Mr.
Gibbon, at Brighthelmstone.
Hayley.
The Chimpanzee. Sly.
Christ Church Meadows,
Oxford. Hall.
The Corpse-Keeper.
Anonymous.
Days Ago. Hai-Jew.
The Evening Wind. Bryant.
Five Roses. Verdaguer.
Hibernia. Howard-Jones.
Hunger for Me. Alta.
In a Mountain Cabin in
Norway. Bly.
On Riding to See Dean Swift
in the Mist of the Morning.
Parnell.
Peyote Poem. McClure.
Post Mortem. Harden.
Prologue. Sanchez.
The Ragged Robin Opens.
Radnoti.
Santa Claus. Moraes.
Second Sight. Longley.
The Sonnet. Hoffman.
The Strand. MacNeice.
Ten Types of Hospital Visitor.
Causley.
The Visiting Hour.
Wagoner.
Your Neighbor. Biggar.
Vista (s)
A Farm Picture. Whitman.
To Alan. Fraser.
Words for the Raker of
Leaves. Adams.
Vital (ity)
America's Prosperity. Van
Dyke.
The Deceptive Present, The
Phoenix Year. Schwartz.
The Most Vital Thing in Life.
Kleiser.
A Poet!—He Hath Put His
Heart to School.
Wordsworth.
Vivid (ly) (ness)
Lecture Hall. Kavanagh.

A Little Morning Music.
Schwartz.
Lyre! Though Such Power Do
in Thy Magic Live.
Wordsworth.
Vocabulary
Casting at Night. Hoey.
Discourse. Thesen.
Stations. Hughes.
Vodka
In Iceland. McCord.
Voice (s)
Adam–The First Kiss.
Porter.
The Age Is Great and Strong.
Hugo.
The Alchemical Cupboard.
Benveniste.
Andrew Jackson's Speech.
Bly.
The Angel Michael. Bental.
The Anniversary. Dickey.
Anniversary Poem for the
Cheyennes Who Fell at
Sand Creek. Henson.
April. Shorter.
Aridity. "Field.
At Mass. Lindsay.
At Night. Guidacci.
Autobiography, Chapter XII.
Barnes.
An Autumn Breeze. Hayne.
Autumn Song on Perry Street.
Frankenberg.
The Band in the Pines.
Cooke.
Base Words Are Uttered.
Auden.
Beverly Hills, Chicago.
Brooks.
Birds. Lawrence.
Black Absence Hides upon the
Past. Clare.
The Blind Man (excerpt).
Wright.
Blizzard. Garfinkel.
Bloom Street. McCabe.
The Brewing of Soma.
Whittier.
Butcher Shop. Simic.
The Cage. Treinin.
Catherine Kinrade. Brown.
Change of Life. Urdang.
The Child. Ormsby.
The Churchyard. Buchanan.
A City Graveyard. Oates.
Codex. Rodefer.
Components. McDonald.
Conrad. Slonimski.
The Country Clown.
Trumbull.
The Court Historian.
Thornbury.
The Crack. Hall.
Cressida. Baxter.
Cry for a Disused Synagogue
in Booysens. Hirsch.
The Cuckoo. Thomas.
The Culprit Fay. Drake.
A Dangerous Music. Knoll.
Dante. Longfellow.
The deer on pine mountain.
Onakatomi Yoshinobu.
Discord in Childhood.
Lawrence.
Do You Remember Me?
Landor.
Doctor Faustus. Hill.
Domine ne in Furore.
Wyatt.
The Doors. Mifflin.
The Drill. Brown.

Earthly. Wedde.
El Sueno de la Razon.
Cooper.
The Enthusiast; or, The Lover
of Nature. Warton.
Epilogue. Heine.
Etude for Voice and Hand.
Levin.
Evangeline. Longfellow.
The Everlasting Voices.
Yeats.
The Exile at Rest. Pierpont.
The Fall of Hyperion.
Keats.
The Food of Love. di
Michele.
For a Father. Cronin.
For My Brother Jesus.
Layton.
....For They Shall See God.
Shaw.
Fragments of Ancient Poetry
(excerpt). Macpherson.
The Future. Tekeyan.
The Garden. Solomon.
General Wonder in Our Land.
Anonymous.
God's Call. *Anonymous.*
Gods in Vietnam. Redmond.
Gone on the Wind. Mangan.
The Grave of Rulry.
Rolleston.
The Gray Folk. Nesbit.
The Green Lake. Roberts.
Haiku: "into a forest."
Otsuji.
The Haunted House.
Viereck.
He Fell Among Thieves.
Newbolt.
He Said, Lying There. Alta.
The Heavenly Aeroplane.
Anonymous.
Hem and Haw. Carman.
Her Voice Could Not Be
Softer. Clarke.
The Higher Pantheism.
Tennyson.
His Lachrimae or Mirth,
Turn'd to Mourning.
Herrick.
Homage to the New World.
Harper.
The Hospital Waiting-Room.
Davies.
How Strangely This Sun
Reminds Me of My Love.
Spender.
The Hunter of the Prairies.
Bryant.
Hymn before Sunrise, in the
Vale of Chamouni.
Coleridge.
I Cannot Sing the Old Songs.
Anonymous.
I Korinna am here to sing the
courage. Korinna.
I Turned On the Hot Water.
Canan.
Idylls of the King.
Tennyson.
In Allusion to the French
Song, N'entendez Vous Pas
ce Language. Lovelace.
In Hospital: Poona (II).
Lewis.
In Like a Lion. Hewitt.
In Populated. Clifton.
In the Garden. Miles.
An Inconclusive Evening.
Bellerby.
Indirection. Realf.

Integer Vitae. Horace.
J. Milton Miles. Masters.
The Jam Fish. Parry.
John's Song. Aiken.
June. Bryant.
The King Enjoys His Own
   Again. Parker.
The Lame One. Anderson.
The Last. Zussman.
A Letter to David Campbell
   on the Birthday of W. B.
   Yeats, 1965. Hope.
Limerick: "An extinct old
   ichthyosaurus."
   Anonymous.
The Limits of Equitation.
   Winder.
Listening. Fisher.
Little Cosmic Dust Poem.
   Haines.
A London Plane-Tree. Levy.
Loneliness. McPherson.
The Long Season. Haug.
The Lost Heifer. Clarke.
The Love Song of J. Alfred
   Prufrock. Eliot.
The Lovely Shall Be Choosers.
   Frost.
Madrigal: "Come, woeful
   Orpheus." Byrd.
Mastrim: A Meditation
   (excerpt). Maxton.
Maud. Tennyson.
The Men behind the Guns.
   Rooney.
The Missal. Dobson.
Monkeys. Colum.
Moon Poems. Wieners.
Mr. Over. Smith.
My Kin Talk. Margolin.
Mystery. Yehoash.
The Names of Georgian
   Women. Akhmadulina.
Night and Wind. Symons.
Night Letter. Piercy.
Now Help Us, Lord.
   Anonymous.
Nudities. Spire.
Obscene Phone Call #2.
   Harjo.
Ode: The Spirit Wooed.
   Dixon.
Odes. Horace.
The Odyssey. Homer.
On a Little Bird.
   Armstrong.
On Some Buttercups.
   Sherman.
On the Death of Commodore
   Oliver H. Perry. Brainard.
Oracle. Mayo.
Pantomime. Verlaine.
Parodies of Cole Porter's
   "Night and Day"
   Lardner.
The Poet. Markham.
Poet of Earth. Thayer.
The Poet's Call. Clarke.
Poetry. Kuzma.
Portrait. Pound.
Pound at Spoleto.
   Ferlinghetti.
Prayer for the Royal
   Marriage. Masefield.
Rabbits. Schmitz.
Rain Journal: London: June
   65. Harwood.
Reminder. Anonymous.
The Reply of Socrates.
   Thomas.

A Rhapsody, Written at the
   Lakes in Westmorland.
   Brown.
Riding. Grossman.
Roundel in the Rain.
   Anonymous.
September in Australia.
   Kendall.
Ships That Pass in the Night.
   Longfellow.
Small Birds. Quennell.
The Soldier's Dream.
   Campbell.
Some Day. Addison.
Someone Talking. Harjo.
A Song. Schwartz.
Song and Science. Shinn.
A Song: "Come, cheer up, my
   lads, like a true British
   band." Anonymous.
Song for a Lyre. Bogan.
Song: "Love, Love today, my
   dear." Mew.
Song of the Captured Woman.
   Devaney.
Song: "The sun is mine."
   Hogg.
Sonnet: A sound of many
   waters!–now I know."
   Trench.
Sonnet: "An open wound
   which has been healed
   anew." Trench.
Sonnets to Aurelia. Nichols.
Souvenir. Robinson.
Stanzas. Clare.
Stanzas–April, 1814. Shelley.
Such Soft Ideas All My Pains
   Beguile. Montagu.
Suggestions by Steam. Hood.
Summum Bonum. Abu-l-Ala
   al-Maarri.
Surview. Hardy.
Swimmer. Cardiff.
Tak for Sidst. Deutsch.
The Talking Fish. Stone.
Tamburlaine. Marlowe.
Tennyson. Van Dyke.
Theme One: The Variations.
   Wilson.
There's Music in the Air.
   Crosby.
Thought of a Briton on the
   Subjugation of Switzerland.
   Wordsworth.
Three Holy Kings from
   Morgenland. Heine.
Threnody. Beddoes.
To a Boy. Anonymous.
To a Cricket. Bennett.
To a Friend. Gullans.
To an Old Danish Song-Book.
   Longfellow.
To Joan. Clifton.
To Song. Jones, Jr.
To the Lady with a Book.
   Anonymous.
To the Painter Preparing to
   Draw M. M. H. Shirley.
The Tone of Voice.
   Anonymous.
The Tree. Sloman.
Two Girls Singing. Smith.
The Two Poets. Meynell.
The Unbidden Wedding
   Guest. Marti.
The Uninvited. Livesay.
A Unison. Williams.
Upon a Notorious Shrew.
   Anonymous.
Village before Sunset.
   Cornford.

Virginia Beach. Plumly.
The Voice of God. Stephens.
The Voices. Anonymous.
Waiting for Lilith. Kessler.
War Poet. Fuller.
Watch and Pray. Elliott.
The Weaving of the Wing.
   Hodgson.
What the Devil Said.
   Stephens.
What Would I Do without
   This World Faceless
   Incurious. Beckett.
Where Is Heaven? Carman.
Why Hast Thou Forsaken
   Me? Walsh.
The Witch's Whelp.
   Stoddard.
Woman at the Piano.
   Zaturenska.
Wood Flower. Le Gallienne.
Your Little Voice.
   Cummings.
Your Name in Arezzo.
   Wright.

Void
Apocalypse in Springtime.
   Banning.
Clear After Rain. Tu Fu.
Come Up, Methuselah. Day-
   Lewis.
Death. Fuller.
The Egotist. Evans.
The End of It. Thompson.
Equation. Read.
Faith. Whittier.
Fulfillment. Miller.
The Harvest Waits. Mifflin.
How on Solemn Fields of
   Space. Daryush.
I Just Walk around, around,
   around. Kulbak.
Jean. Potts.
Lamentations. Gluck.
None. Miles.
Ode on a Jar of Pickles
   (parody). Taylor.
Quien Sabe? Morris.
The Seed of Nimrod.
   Harrison.
Separation. Savage.
Song of the Weaving Woman.
   Yuan Chen.
Tell Them I'm Struggling to
   Sing with Angels. Meltzer.
The World. Raine.

Volcanic
Incipience. Rich.
Pittsburgh. Sobiloff.

Voltaire
The Respectable Burgher.
   Hardy.
Sunday in the Country.
   Swenson.

Volume (s)
The Glutton. Shapiro.
Lovers, and a Reflection.
   Calverley.
The Pleasures of Imagination.
   Akenside.
A Precious–Mouldering
   Pleasure–'tis–. Dickinson.
Then Twist the Neck of This
   Delusive Swan. Gonzales
   Martinez.

Volunteer (s)
Ballad of Lieutenant Miles.
   Scollard.
A Bestiary. Rexroth.
The Cripple for Life.
   Anonymous.

Football and Rowing–An
   Eclogue. Godley.
A Georgia Volunteer.
   Townsend.
The Surprise at Ticonderoga.
   Stansbury.

Voluptuous
The Eyes of Children at the
   Brink of the Sea's Grasp.
   Jacobsen.
Paradise Lost. Milton.
Prothalamium. Smith.

Voracity
The Ballad of the Emeu.
   Harte.

Vote (d) (s)
Bears. Guiterman.
By-Election Idyll. Dickinson.
Chicago Boy Baby.
   Sandburg.
The Everlasting Mercy
   (parody). Squire.
The Legion Club (excerpt).
   Swift.
The Morning Star. St. John.
My Candidate. Crowell.
The Need of the Hour.
   Markham.
Walt Whitman at the Reburial
   of Poe. Christopher.

Vow (ed) (s)
The Aeneid. Virgil (Publius
   Vergilius Maro).
The Balcony. Baudelaire.
Blooming Nelly. Burns.
Caelica, IV. Greville.
Castara. Habington.
Cloris and Mertilla.
   Drayton.
Daphne. Carman.
Les Estreines. Prior.
The First Wedding in the
   World. Rosenberg.
From his flock stray'd
   Coridon. Greene.
Ghost-Flowers. Higginson.
The Happy Swain. Philips.
His Tears to Thamasis.
   Herrick.
In the Name of Our Sons.
   Gould.
James Hatley. Anonymous.
Let the Florid Music Praise.
   Auden.
The Lexington Miller.
   Anonymous.
Lycoris darling, once I burned
   for you. Martial (Marcus
   Valerius Martialis).
The Night of the Dance.
   Hardy.
The Palm-Tree and the Pine.
   Milnes.
A Soldier's Prayer. Freeman.
Solemn Rondeau. Bell.
Song: "In vain you tell your
   parting lover." Prior.
To a Comrade in Arms.
   Lewis.
To a Young Gentleman in
   Love: A Tale. Prior.
To Woman. Byron.
The True Lover. Housman.
The Vision of Sir Launfal.
   Lowell.
Votive Ode. Erasmus.
Westward on the High-Hilled
   Plains. Housman.
The Winds. Clemo.

Vowel (s)
Anglo-Saxon. Mayo.
A Day in France. Holbrook.

The Letters at School.
Dodge.
Oft have I sigh'd for him that
heares me not.　Campion.
Sonnets, XIX: "Ah no; nor I
my selfe: though my pure
love."　Barnfield.
Survey of Literature.
Ransom.

Voyage (r) (s)
An Address to His Elbow-
Chair, New Cloath'd.
Somervile.
Death from Cancer.　Lowell.
Frontispiece.　Swenson.
The India Guide....　Dallas.
Intimate Associations.
Baudelaire.
Memories.　Whitman.
My Sailor of Seven.　Brenan.
Permit Me Voyage.　Agee.
The Staircase with a Hundred
Steps.　Peret.
The Tempest.　Smith.
The Untold Want.　Whitman.

Vulgar
Architectural Masks.　Hardy.
Death's Transfiguration.
Zangwill.
Epitaph on a Tuft-Hunter.
Moore.
Hudibras.　Butler.
One-Line Poems from a New
Statesman Competition.
Fitton.
Song: "Soules joy, now I am
gone."　Herbert.

Vulnerable
House Poem.　Cooper.
I Am Stone of Many Colors.
Tauhindauli.
Slug.　Head.
You Are Reading This Too
Fast.　Norris.

Vulture (s)
The Battle-Field.　Mifflin.
The Battle of Eutaw.　Simms.
Chandler Nicholas.　Masters.
Epigram: "Those snooty boys
in all their purple drag."
Strato.
The Poets.　Wevill.
Prometheus.　Swift.
The Shark.　Pratt.
Spring in the Desert.
Merrill.

W

Wabash
On the Banks of the Wabash,
Far Away.　Dresser.

Waddles
Ground Hog Day.　Pomeroy.
Quack!　De la Mare.
To Daphne and Virginia.
Williams.

Wade (s)
Abruptly All the Palm Trees.
Smith.
Feeling for Fish.　Trawick.
Fishing Blue Creek.　Scheele.
Mud.　Boyden.
Perspective He Would Mutter
Going to Bed.　Gilbert.
Silex Scintillans.　Vaughan.

Wafer (s)
A Coney Island of the Mind.
Ferlinghetti.
Woods Gets Religion.
Woods.

Waft (ing)
Peace in the World.
Galsworthy.
Rolling Home.　Anonymous.
The Unquiet Grave.
Anonymous.

Wag (s)
Astrophel and Stella, XVII.
Sidney.
Caelica, XIII.　Greville.
The Durable Bon Mot.
Preston.
So Wags the World.
Cortissoz.
The Stammerers.　Kent.

Wage (s)
Bed-Time.　Erskine.
Limerick: "One morning old
Wilfrid Scawen Blunt."
Gray.
A Miner's Life.　Anonymous.
The New-Fashioned Farmer.
Anonymous.
Nigger.　Shapiro.
Striking Times.　Anonymous.
Tales of the Islands, IV.
Walcott.
Wages.　Tennyson.

Wagon (s)
The Curate's Kindness.
Hardy.
Epitaph: "Here lies I, no
wonder I'm dead."
Anonymous.
The Gold-Tinted Dragon.
Kuskin.
Meditations.　Taylor.
Oliver Wiggins.　Vestal.
The Oregon Trail.
Guiterman.
Santa Fe Trail.　Guest.
This Night.　Alterman.
Wait for the Wagon.
Buckley.

Waif (s)
As Consequent, etc.
Whitman.
The Road.　Morris.

Wail (ed) (ing)
Antonina.　Mnthali.
As Spring the Winter Doth
Succeed.　Bradstreet.
The "Duke" and the "Count."
Fewell.
Evangeline.　Longfellow.
Evening in England.
Ledwidge.
The Fly.　Googe.
For Her on the First Day
Out.　Bagg.
The Iliad.　Homer.
Laila Boasting.　Akhyaliyya.
Le Livre Est sur la Table.
Ashbery.
Morte d'Arthur.　Tennyson.
Once Musing as I Sat.
Googe.
Patient Griselda.　Chaucer.
Prairie Wolves.　Carr.
The Shooting of the Cup.
Neihardt.
To Xanadu, Which Is Beth
Shaul.　Sivan.
The War Dance.　Carr.
Where the Fight Was.
Corbin.
White Queen.　Fuller.

Wait (ed) (ing) (s)
The Adorable Paratroopess.
Silverton.
After the Last Dynasty.
Kunitz.
After Tschaikowsky.　Gould.
And While We Are Waiting.
Rodgers.
The Angel in the House.
Patmore.
The Animals' Arrival.
Jennings.
Arrows.　Heyen.
At Casterbridge Fair.
Hardy.
Austere the Music of My
Songs.　Sologub.
Barren.　"Rachel" (Rachel
Blumstein).
Be Still, My Heart.
Anonymous.
Beach House.　Hurley.
Bessy and Mary.
Anonymous.
Beyond Words.　Frost.
A Black Poetry Day.
Johnson.
Blackbird's Song.
Anonymous.
Boadicea.　Cowper.
Bordering Manuscript.
Applewhite.
Bushed.　Birney.
Cake.　Potter.
Call from the Afterworld.
Gerez.
A Call to Pentecost.　Tyler.
Calm.　Coblentz.
Cato.　Sisson.
A Cemetery in New Mexico.
Alvarez.
Ceremony.　Cumbo.
Chant for Dark Hours.
Parker.
The Child.　Massey.
The Children's Crusade.
Levine.
A Christmas Hymn.
Alexander.
The Christmas Trees.　Butts.
Click o' the Latch.　Turner.
The Coast of Peru.
Anonymous.
Cock before Dawn.
MacCaig.
The Cod-Fisher.　Lincoln.
Columbia's Agony.　Newell.
Creation.　Nicholl.
Crossing the Colorado River
into Yuma.　Ortiz.
The Cup.　Wright.
The Dance of Dust (parody).
Untermeyer.
Dark in the Reich of the
Blond.　Heyen.
Day before Christmas.
Chute.
Death & Empedocles 444 B.C.
Gregory.
The Desperado.　Anonymous.
Dinner Guest: Me.　Hughes.
Doorbells.　Field.
A Dream of Burial.　Wright.
Dream the Great Dream.
Coates.
Dreams in War Time
(excerpt).　Lowell.
Driftwood Dybbuk.
Lefcowitz.
The Drowned Children.
Gluck.

Earth Trembles Waiting.
Wagstaff.
Echo.　Hardy.
Elsewheres.　Justice.
Empire Builders.　MacLeish.
En Route.　Mayo.
Epitaph.　Corbiere.
Epithalamium.　Halpern.
Equestrienne.　Colby.
Eros Turannos.　Robinson.
Explanation.　Hewitt.
Extremum Tanain.　Horace.
Farewell.　Bahe.
The Farmer.　Stokes.
The Fisherman.　Stuart.
Foetal Song.　Oates.
Four-Leaf Clover.
Higginson.
From the Wave.　Gunn.
God's Trombones: Listen,
Lord.　Johnson.
Going through Changes.
Tepperman.
The Good Time Coming.
Mackay.
Grandmother Sleeps.　Bahe.
The Grey Cock (A vers.).
Anonymous.
Hagar to Ishmael.　Eibel.
Hail Our Incarnate God!
Duke.
The Hard Listener.
Williams.
A Harrow Grave in Flanders.
Ashburton.
Haunted Odysseus: The Last
Testament.　Gregory.
He Cares.　Salway.
"He Didn't Oughter..."
Herbert.
Home.　Anonymous.
Horses at Valley Store.
Silko.
The Hound.　Francis.
I Never Asked for More Than
Thou Hast Given.
Dickinson.
I Wait My Lord.
Anonymous.
Idyl: Sunrise.　Ray.
If I Felt Less.　Wintchevsky.
In Harbor.　Reese.
In the Shade of the Old Apple
Tree.　Williams.
In the Sitting Room of the
Opera.　Cannady.
In These Dissenting Times.
Walker.
In Winter.　Symons.
Invasion Exercise on the
Poultry Farm.　Betjeman.
Invitation to a Mistress.
Anonymous.
Jersey Bait Shack.　Balakian.
John Plans.　Pierce.
The Jungle.　Williams.
Jupiter and Ganimede.
Heywood.
Keep A-Pluggin' Away.
Dunbar.
Late.　Halpern.
Learn to Wait.　Anonymous.
Leningrad.　Mandelstam.
The Leopard.　Thomas.
Leviathan.　Merwin.
Like Children of the
Summertime Playing at
Cards.　White.
Like Rousseau.　Jones.
Lines for the Planned
Parenthood Clinic.
Spurrier.

The Little Green Orchard.
De La Mare.
The Lover's Prayer.
Anonymous.
Magnificat in Transit from the
Toledo Airport. Starbuck.
Mary on Her Way to the
Temple. Schaumann.
A Masique Presented at
Ludlow Castle (Comus).
Milton.
Meeting Together of Poles &
Latitudes: in Prospect.
Avison.
The Mermaid. *Anonymous.*
Mimma Bella. Lee-
Hamilton.
Minotaur. Fisher.
Misdemeanor. Triem.
Moment Musicale. Gould.
The Moon. Creeley.
A Morning Prayer.
Perpetuo.
The Most Beautiful Woman at
My Highschool Reunion.
Bissert.
The Moths. Merwin.
Mount Saint Helens/Loowit:
An Indian Woman's Song.
Rose.
Mountain Evenings. Holme.
My Mother's Childhood.
Spacks.
Myxomatosis. Larkin.
Napa, California. Castillo.
Native Origin. Brant.
Naughty Boy. Creeley.
Niagara Falls. Parisi.
Night on the Prairies.
Whitman.
Night Poem in an Abandoned
Music Room. Pillen.
Now, before Shaving.
Kramer.
O Canada! Routhier.
Odiham. Gray.
An Old Man's Idyl. Realf.
On an Ill-Managed House.
Swift.
On His Royal Blindness
Paramount Chief Kwangala.
Mapanje.
Ordinance on Winning.
Lazard.
Orgy. Labriola.
Ossian (excerpt). O'Donnell.
Patience. Graham.
Pendulum Rhyme.
Robinson.
Persephone. Duncan.
Philomena Andronico.
Williams.
A Plantation Ditty. Stanton.
The Poor. Strahan.
Port Authority Terminal: 9
A.M. Monday. Walsh.
Portrait. Cummings.
A Psalm of Life. Lang.
A Psalm of Life. Longfellow
Put Forth Thy Leaf, Thou
Lofty Plane. Clough.
Python. *Anonymous.*
Quilt Song. Vinz.
Remembrance. Bruner.
Rescue. Voigt.
Residential Rhymes (excerpt).
Edwards.
Reunion. Tawney.
The Rime of the Ancient
Feminist (excerpt).
Markman.
Robin. Allen.

The Sacrifice. Bloch.
Sad-Eyed Lady of the
Lowlands. Dylan.
Sailor's Woman. Cornell.
Sea and Shore. Koopman.
Second Vision. O'Huiginn.
Seeing in the Dark.
Brennan.
Shango II. *Anonymous.*
Shemuel. Bowen.
Slow Waker. Gunn.
Somebody Prayed.
Anonymous.
Song of Myself. Whitman.
The Song of This House.
Vincent.
Sonnet: "A wind has blown
the rain away."
Cummings.
Sonnet on His Blindness.
Milton.
Standing on the Corner.
Levine.
Starting Rhymes for Hide-
and-Seek: "Green lady,
green lady." *Anonymous.*
Summer Longings.
MacCarthy.
A Summer Night. Stoddard
Sweeping the Skies. Hart.
Symbols. Rossetti.
Tardy George. *Anonymous.*
Then. Cooke.
There Are Children in the
Dusk. Warr.
There Is No. Kicknosway.
This Is an African Worm.
Danner.
This Is the Place to Wait.
Gregory.
To Atalanta. Dow.
To Cheer Our Minds.
Ronksley.
To His Coy Mistress (parody).
Bird.
To the Sun. Gezelle.
Traveling Boy. Meredith.
Travis, the Kid Was All
Heart. Stokes.
Twilight Thoughts in Israel.
Ravitch.
Unborn. McLeod.
Verse for a Certain Dog.
Parker.
Verses Written In 1872.
Stevenson.
Wait. Steele.
Waiting. Stout.
Waiting for You to Come By.
Ortiz.
Waitress. Brownstein.
Whalan of Waitin' a While.
Gordon.
What a Friend We Have in
Mother. Roat.
What I'm Doing Here.
Cohen.
When Love Comes Knocking.
Gardner.
When My Brothers Come
Home. Santos.
The Whole Story. Stafford.
The Wife's Complaint.
Anonymous
The Wife's Lament.
Anonymous.
A Wish. Arnold.
Work. Lowell.
Worldly Wealth. Watkyns.
The Wreck on the Somerset
Road. *Anonymous.*

You Have What I Look For.
Sabines.
Young Man's Fancy.
Mathew.
Young Men You Are So
Beautiful up There.
Goedicke.
Waive
The Lost History Plays: King
Canute (parody).
Sharpless.
Wake (d) (ful) (n) (ned) (ning)
(ns) (s)
After Grief. Plumly.
After the Night Hunt.
Dickey.
After the Sea-Ship.
Whitman.
Again. Stallworthy.
Ah! Why, Because the
Dazzling Sun. Bronte.
The Alarm Clock. Evans.
And Again (parody). Evans.
Any Wife to Any Husband.
Browning.
As Ocean's Stream.
Tyutchev.
As We Are So Wonderfully
Done with Each Other.
Patchen.
Ballet Blanc. Pollitt.
The Bird. Hoffenstein.
Bout with Burning. Miller.
Breakfast Time. Stephens.
Cadenza. Waddington.
Christmas Legend. Worrell.
The Clouds. Vogelsang.
Coleridge. De Vere.
A Colloquy with God.
Browne.
Come, Come, What Doe I
Here? Vaughan.
Come Slowly, Paradise.
Kenyon.
The Cottager to Her Infant.
Wordsworth.
Counting the Beats. Graves.
Dante. Duncan.
Death and the Arkansas
River. Stanford.
The Death of Nick Charles.
Jones.
The Diakka. Massey.
The Distances. Olson.
The Divorce Dress. Finley.
Don't Say. Yungman.
The Dragon of the Seas.
Page.
The Dream. Symons.
The Dream of Gerontius.
Newman.
Evelyn Hope. Browning.
Fairy Song. Praed.
Finnegan's Wake.
Anonymous.
Fire at Murdering Hut.
Wright.
First Sight. Larkin.
For the Lord's Day Evening.
Watts.
Forms, LXXVII. Enslin.
Grandmother Sleeps. Bahe.
Holy Innocents. Rossetti.
I Need No Sky. Bynner.
Ice. Driscoll.
If It Comes. Booth.
In the Tree-Top. Larcom.
Iris. St. John.
Jack Frost. "Setoun.
Gabriel"
Jesus, Child and Lord.
Faber.

The Kite. Strand.
Lachrimae Amantis. Hill.
The Lady of the Lake. Scott.
Laser. Ammons.
Letter for Duncan. Eigner.
Lines in Order to Be
Slandered. Verlaine.
Lines: "When youthful faith
hath fled." Lockhart.
London Spring. Slonimski.
Lord, How Shall I Me
Complain. *Anonymous.*
Loving. Kaufman.
Lullaby. Nairne.
A Man Whom Men Deplore.
Kreymborg.
Men's Voices. Christensen.
Mimma Bella. Lee-
Hamilton.
The Moon behind High
Tranquil Leaves. Nichols.
Morning Fog. Duval.
Mrs. Walpurga. Rukeyser.
The Mystic's Prayer. Sharp.
Next, Please. Larkin.
The Night before Larry Was
Stretched. *Anonymous.*
The Nine Little Goblins.
Riley.
Now I Lay Me Down to
Sleep. *Anonymous.*
Now through Night's
Caressing Grip. Auden.
Now while the night her sable
veil hath spread.
Drummond.
Olive Grove. Merrill.
Othello. Shakespeare.
Out of Hearing. Barlow.
The Path of the Stars. Jones,
Jr.
Peggy Browne. O'Carolan.
Poem Following Discussion of
Brain. Rice.
Poem from Deal. Shapiro.
Pomegranate Tree in
Jerusalem. Gilead.
Prayer for a Very New Angel.
Storey.
Preachment for Preachers.
Barclay.
Rain, Rain. Akins.
Rest. Rossetti.
The Ribbon-Fish. Adamson.
Ripening. Caskey.
Rune. Rukeyser.
Scenes from the Life of the
Peppertrees. Levertov.
Security. Sangster.
The Seven Sleepers. Read.
The Ship of Fools. Barclay.
The Sidewinder. Lummis.
Silex Scintillans. Vaughan.
Sir Dilberry Diddle, Captain
of Militia. *Anonymous.*
Sleep, Angry Beauty.
Campion.
So Live, So Love, So Use
That Fragile Hour.
Stevenson.
Song. Lowell
Song for a Child. Davis.
Songs of Ch'en. Confucius.
Sonnets, LXI: "Is it thy wil,
thy Image should keepe
open." Shakespeare.
The Star-Tribes. *Anonymous.*
The Stones of Sleep. Mayo.
The Swallows. Dickinson.
Taking the Train Home.
Matthews.
Tapwater. Jensen.

The Tempest. Shakespeare.
To * * * * *. Callanan.
To Lighten My House. Reid.
To Marie Osmond. Skelley.
To Mrs. M. B. on Her Birthday. Pope.
Tribal Memories. Duncan.
Troopship for France, War II. Bogin.
Two Campers in Cloud Country. Plath.
Two Sonnets from a Sequence. Holt.
The Unfortunate Reminder. Pattison.
Upon a Dainty Hill Sometime. Breton.
Visit by Water. McLaren.
Waiting. Behn.
The Watchers. Rukeyser.
We Lay Un Down to Sleep. Moulton.
What Winter Floods, What Showers of Spring. Bronte.
When My Beloved Sleeping Lies. McLeod.
The White Dream. Doney.
A Widow in Wintertime. Kizer.
Wild Eden. Woodberry.
Woman Asleep on a Banana Leaf. Pollitt.
Wonderland. Peck.
Wood Flower. Le Gallienne.
The Worm in the Whirling Cross. Brinnin.
Writing. Nemerov.

Waking
Albuera. Hardy.
Barcarolle. O'Shaughnessy.
Cosmogony. Rickword.
Daughter. Hahn.
Dream Fantasy. "Macleod.
For Under the Volcano. Lowry.
The Garret. Pound.
Heaven. *Anonymous.*
Hunting at Dusk. Cockrell.
Infidelity. Berggolts.
Just About Asleep Together. Peacock.
The Kiss of God. Studdert-Kennedy.
Lagoons, Hanlan's Point. Souster.
Love Is Loathing & Why. Ford.
Lullaby of an Infant Chief. Scott.
The Moon Pond. McGuckian.
Nerves. Symons.
Not for That City. Mew.
One Desiring Me to Read, but Slept It out, Wakening. Daniel.
The Poet to the Sleeping Saki. Goethe.
Sleep, Baby Mine, Desire. Sidney.
Up Early. Robinson.
The Washers of the Shroud. Lowell.
Wood Floor Dreams. Henson.

Wales
English Bards and Scotch Reviewers. Byron.

Walk (ed) (er) (ing) (s)
The Abominable Baseball Bat. Kennedy.
The Access. Kanabus.
An Advancement of Learning. Heaney.
Adventure. Mason.
After a Death. Orr.
After the Storm. Bartlett.
Afternoon. Hall.
The Aged Pilot Man. "Twain.
The Albatross. Baudelaire.
Almost Human. Day-Lewis.
Along the Road. Hamilton.
The Angel in the House. Patmore.
Arthur McBride. *Anonymous.*
Ascension Day. Kaye-Smith.
At a Georgia Camp Meeting. Mills.
At the Sea's Edge. Harwood.
The Bard. Blake.
The Bare Arms of Trees. Tagliabue.
Betty Blue. *Anonymous.*
Billy Grimes. *Anonymous.*
The Blind Man. Lewisohn.
Brief Encounter. Scott.
The Calculation. Wagoner.
Calenture. Reid.
Carmarthen Bar. Brinnin.
A Caution to Everybody. Nash.
A Celebration of Charis. Jonson.
A Choctaw Chief Helps Plan a Festival... Barnes.
Christmas Eve. Clancy.
Clock on Hancock Street. Jordan.
Close Your Eyes! Bontemps.
Coleridge. De Vere.
Collaboration. Towle.
Concert. Sward.
Consider the Auk. Nash.
Conversation. Buson.
Counsel. Davis.
Couple. Swope.
Courtesy. Dodge.
Crazy Jane and Jack the Journeyman. Yeats.
The Cuckoo. *Anonymous.*
Damnation of Vancouver: Speech of the Salish Chief. Birney.
A Death-Bed. Aldrich.
The Desolate Lover. Shanahan.
Dew. Maiden.
Dink's Blues. *Anonymous.*
Dinosaurs. Worth.
The Djanggawul Cycle, 30. *Anonymous.*
Do You Fear the Wind? Garland.
Eat and Walk. Hall.
An Elegy. Scovell.
The Elephant I. *Anonymous.*
Encounter. Krige.
Epigram: April. Nemerov.
Epitaph on a Fir-Tree. Murphy.
Erlington. *Anonymous.*
Evangeline. Smith.
Eyes. Nicoidski.
Fallen Majesty. Yeats.
February Morning. Kuka.
Fifteen Boys, or Perhaps Even More. Akhmadulina.

The Folk Who Live in Backward Town. Hoberman.
Food. Chute.
For Eager Lovers. Taggard.
For Mary McLeod Bethune. Walker.
For Mulatto. Fernandez.
The Forms of Love. Oppen.
Forty Years Peace. Sivan.
The Fugs. Sanders.
Gare du Midi. Auden.
Gates of Damascus. Flecker.
A Gentle Park. Herbert.
Glimpse. Lomax.
God Wants a Man. *Anonymous.*
The Good Town. Muir.
The Grey-Eyed King. Akhmatova.
Hawk's Eyes. Winters.
He Met Her at the Green Horse... Levi.
The Healer (excerpt). Whittier.
Healing Song. *Anonymous.*
Heartbreak Road. Cone.
The Heaven of Animals. Dickey
Hog Rogues on the Harricane. *Anonymous.*
Holiday. Rich.
The Horse. Kicknosway.
Hospital Evening. Harwood.
Hyena. *Anonymous*
I Can Fly. Holman.
I Have to Have It. Aldis.
I haven't told my garden yet. Dickinson.
I Heard the Voice of Jesus Say. Bonar.
I Know Not Where the Road Will Lead. Cummins.
I'll Have a Collier for My Sweetheart. Oliver.
I Pray You. Moore.
I Spread Out unto Thee My Hand. Ainsworth.
I walk in loneliness through the greenwood. *Anonymous.*
I Will Enjoy Thee Now. Carew.
I Wonder How My Home Is. *Anonymous.*
In the Footsteps of the Walking Air. Patchen.
In the Open Fields. Sonnenschein.
Innocence. Kavanagh.
Jephthah's Daughter. Heavysege.
Johnny Walk along to Hilo. *Anonymous.*
Jump or Jiggle. Beyer.
The Keys of Canterbury. *Anonymous.*
Kinaxixi. Neto.
Klaxon. Reaney.
A la Claire Fontaine. *Anonymous.*
Lady and Crocodile. Burgess.
Lady Luck. Gottlieb.
Lake Walk at New Year's. Perez-Diotima.
The Lamb. Wilson.
Last Born. Kirkwood.
Limerick: "There once was a girl of New York." Monkhouse.

Look Down That Lonesome Road. *Anonymous.*
Lord of the Far Horizons. Carman.
Lost Acres. Graves.
Lost Moment. Fuller.
Mad Sonnet 1. McClure.
Man of Galilee. Deissler.
The Man Upright. Macdonagh.
May God Give Strength. Van Wynen.
May the man who gained my trust yet did not come. Ryojin Hisho.
Michael Walked in the Wood. Greacen.
Modern Love, XLV. Meredith.
The Morning after...Love. Cumbo.
Mrs. Green. Huddle.
Mrs. Smith. Locker-Lampson.
Mwilu/ or Poem for the Living. Lee.
My Books. Longfellow
My Heart Was Wandering. Brennan.
The Myall in Prison. Gilmore.
Nest Eggs. Stevenson.
New Romance. Wong.
No More Women Blues. Alexander.
Not Seeing Is Believing. Petrie.
Number 29. Wallace.
The Obsession. Liggett.
Of Watchmen. Gay.
The Old Man at the Crossing. Strong.
The Old Road. Very
The Old Sailor. Dresbach.
On a Child Beginning to Talk. Bastard.
On the Path. Strauss.
Onion Bucket. Thomas.
Open Range. Mitchell.
The Pass. Logan.
Pathedy of Manners. Kay.
Peregrine's Sunday Song. Wylie.
Pilgrim's Problem. Lewis.
The Place of V. Young Bear.
Poem for My Father's Ghost. Oliver.
Poem: "I walk at dawn across the hollow hills." Todd.
Poem to My Father. Stroud.
The Power of Fancy. Freneau.
The Pretty Girl of Loch Dan. Ferguson.
Recitative. Crane.
The Return. Moss.
Riddle: "In Mornigan's park there is a deer." *Anonymous.*
The Road's End. Garrison.
Sea-Grape Tree and the Miraculous. Root.
A Second Birthday. Kayper-Mensah
The Shadow of Cain. Sitwell.
She and I. Cameron.
The Shepherdess. Meynell.
Shine, Perishing Republic. Jeffers.
The Shudder. Hall.

Walk

Sindhi Woman. Stallworthy.
Sings a Bird. Nist.
The Snow-Man. "Douglas.
Solid Mountain. Bowering.
Some Sound Advice from
   Singapore. Ciardi.
Sonnets, I: "Deep in a vale
   where rocks on every side."
   Rosenhane.
Sonnets. Tuckerman.
The Sorrows of Sunday: An
   Elegy (excerpt). Wolcot.
South of My Days. Wright.
The Spoon. Simic.
Spring Night. Aldridge.
Spring Song. Smith, Jr.
Stabat Mater. Hunt.
The Stallion. Merrill, Jr.
Star & Garter Theater.
   Schmitz.
Staying Ahead. Glass.
Stones. Jeffrey.
Style. Bukowski.
The Subway Grating Fisher.
   Simpson.
Tales of a Wayside Inn.
   Longfellow.
These Leaves. Stafford.
This Golden Summer.
   Lowell.
Through You. Honig.
To a Negro Boy Graduating.
   Maleska.
To Fortune. Herrick.
To Perilla. Herrick.
To the Maids Not to Walk in
   the Wind. Gogarty.
Training on the Shore.
   Vinner.
Transformation.
   Rittenhouse.
Two Drinking Songs. Tao
   Yuan-Ming.
Upon the Priory Grove, His
   Usual Retirement.
   Vaughan.
Variations on a Time Theme.
   Muir.
Velvet Shoes. Wylie.
Vessels. Schwartz.
The Village Coddled in the
   Valley. Barker.
The Vision of Piers Plowman.
   Langland.
Walk in Jerusalem Jus' Like
   John. Anonymous.
Walking for That Cake.
   Harrigan.
We Walked among the
   Whispering Pines. Boner.
We Who Were Born. Lewis.
What Can You Expect.
   Maryam bint Abi.
What If Jealousy... Palmer.
When I Peruse the Conquer'd
   Fame. Whitman.
Whitman in Black. Berrigan.
With Thee Conversing.
   Milton.
Words for Music Perhaps.
   Yeats.
The Worm in the Whirling
   Cross. Brinnin.
Your Church and Mine.
   Lord.
Youth. Rittenhouse.

Walk out

Elegy. St. John.
Morning Song. Dugan.
Situation. Hughes.
The Sweet. Ai.

Wall (ed) (s)

And That's All. Anonymous.
Anniversary. Kooser.
At the Hacienda. Harte.
A Bar at Night. Hagiwara.
Barnfire during Church. Bly.
Because. Johnson.
The Berg. Melville.
A Bridge Instead of a Wall.
   Anonymous.
British Leftish Poetry,
   1930-40. ""MacDiarmid.
Chalk from Eden. Moss.
Cock-Crow Song.
   Anonymous.
The Color. Haines.
Coloratura. Page.
Come Visit My Garden.
   Dent.
Comes Winter, the Sea
   Hunting. Dubie.
Comfort. Doney.
Content. Whitney.
Country School. Curnow.
Cover. Frost.
The Crane. Tomlinson.
Crawl Blues. McHugh.
Dancer: Four Poems. Engle.
Death Is a Door. Turner.
The Decay of a People.
   Simms
Dedication. Bryant.
Dere's a Han'writin' on de
   Wall. Anonymous.
The Double Fortress. Noyes.
Drifting. Read.
Drunk. Arnett.
Father Father Son and Son.
   Swan.
Hamlet. Shakespeare.
The Handwriting on the Wall.
   Shaw.
Hart Crane. Symons.
Home Life. Nolan.
Hope. Fanshawe.
House in Denver. Ferril.
The Hurricane. Crane.
If We Must Die. McKay.
In an Old Nursery.
   Chalmers.
In Jail. Corretjer.
In Old Tucson. Hall.
In the Morning All Over.
   Stafford.
Jericho. Wattles.
Jerusalem. Blake.
Landscape. Mason.
Leaflight. Donnelly.
The Leaping Laughers.
   Barker.
Lincoln Monument:
   Washington. Hughes.
Many a Mickle. De La
   Mare.
A Map of the Western Part of
   the County of Essex in
   England. Levertov.
Meditation on the BMT.
   Blackburn.
Metaphors of a Magnifico.
   Stevens.
Midnight. Kees.
Midnight. "Mistral.
Night Watch. Magid.
Novelettes III: The Gardener.
   MacNeice.
October. Frost.
Of Commerce and Society.
   Hill.
Olive Trees. Colum.
On a School-Teacher.
   Anonymous.

On a Summer Day, 1972.
   Murry.
One A. M. Kennedy.
One of the Boys. Dacey.
Parable. Soutar.
Paraphrase. Crane.
Phoenix. Auslander.
The Picture That Is Turned
   toward the Wall. Graham.
Poem for My Grandfather.
   Jacobs.
Porous. Williams.
Prisoners. Mavity.
The Purpose of the
   Chesapeake & Ohio Canal.
   Smith.
Pyramus and Thisbe. Saxe.
Rant Block. McClure.
Rome. Hardy.
Scaffolding. Heaney.
Screw Spring. Hoffman.
The Shadow Remains.
   Roberts.
Six Questions (A vers.).
   Anonymous.
Song: "Joshua fit de battle ob
   Jerico." Anonymous.
Song of Degrees. Auster.
Speak when you're spoken to.
   Anonymous.
Spitting on Ira Rosenblatt.
   Hershon.
Standard Forgings Plant.
   Stephens.
Street Kid. Niatum.
Sulky Sue. Anonymous.
A Tale: "There was an old
   woman sat spinning."
   Anonymous.
Tenants. Gibson.
Terra Cotta. Lyle.
To Mrs. Reynold's Cat.
   Keats.
To My Friend, behind Walls.
   Kizer.
A Troop of the Guard.
   Hagedorn.
The Twelve Weapons of
   Spiritual Battle. More.
Untitled. Hine.
Up against the Wall (parody).
   Berry.
The Wall. Reed.
The Wall Test. Simpson.
The Walls of Jericho.
   Dickinson.
Wide Walls. Anonymous.

Wall of China

Rhymes on the Road
   (excerpt). Moore.

Wall Street

That Poem. Saez Burgos.
The Workers Rose on May
   Day or Postscript to Karl
   Marx. Lorde.

Wallpaper

Mother and Son. Tate.
Vuillard: "The Mother and
   Sister of the Artist."
   Snodgrass.

Walnut tree (s)

August Afternoon. Edey.
The Walnut Tree. McCord.

Waltz (ed) (ing)

All Night! Baker.
Little Viennese Waltz.
   Garcia Lorca.
My Papa's Waltz. Roethke.
The Scorner. Tam'si.
The Waltz: Hail, Spirit-
   Stirring Waltz. Byron.
The Wedding Coat. Rose.

Waltzing Matilda

Waltzing Matilda.
   Anonymous.

Wan

Captain Car, or, Edom o
   Gordon (H version).
   Anonymous.
The Dream of the Rood.
   Anonymous.
How It Is. Greenberg.
Masks. Aldrich.
Sonnet: To the Same Ladies;
   with Their Answer. Dante
   Alighieri.
Wheeler at Santiago.
   Gordon.
Woefully Arrayed. Skelton.

Wand

The Queens. Fitzgerald.
A Shropshire Lad.
   Housman.
Sleep. Statius Publius
   Papinius.

Wand'ring

Paradise Lost. Milton.

Wander (ed) (ing) (s)

About the Heavenly Life.
   Leon.
Another. Lovelace.
The Apple Trees at Olema.
   Hass.
Autumn Day. Rilke.
Base Chapel, Lejeune 4/79.
   Hobson.
Behind the Line. Blunden.
Billy the Kid. Anonymous.
Bitter Sanctuary. Monro.
Climb in Torridon. Macrow.
Codes. Montross.
Dawn Boy's Song.
   Anonymous.
The Demon Speaks.
   Calderon de la Barca.
Down among the Wharves.
   Jewett.
An Excuse of Absence.
   Carew.
Father Fisheye. Balakian.
For Miriam. Macgoye.
Gadoshkibos. Burns.
Good Master and Mistress...
   Anonymous.
Heaven and Earth.
   Thompson.
Home Alone These Last
   Hours of the Afternoon...
   Levy.
Hot Weather in the Plains–
   India. Tipple.
The House of Life. Rossetti.
Hunt the Buffalo.
   Anonymous.
I Met at Eve. De La Mare.
I Need No Sky. Bynner.
I Wonder as I Wander.
   Anonymous.
The Iliad. Homer.
Lonely Are the Fields of
   Sleep. Baldwin.
Mignon. Goethe.
Moorburn in Spring.
   Anonymous.
Morning in Spring.
   Ginsberg.
Naples. Rogers.
O Magnet-South. Whitman.
Peregrine's Sunday Song.
   Wylie.
Piano and Drums. Okara.
Poem: "Look at Me 8th
   Grade." Sanchez.

A Poem Written in Time of Trouble by an Irish Priest... Gregory.
Realism. Aldrich.
Renascence. Dooher.
Ridin'. Clark, Jr.
Robin. A Pastoral Elegy. Dobson.
The Scissors-Grinder. Lindsay.
The Sheepherder. Sarett.
Shepherd and Shepherdess. Hennell.
The Song of the MicMac. Howe.
The Song of the Sons of Esau. Runkle.
Spring. Spire.
Taking Long Views. Kendall.
To the Moon. Goethe.
The Torn Hat. Willis.
The Wander-Lovers. Hovey.
The Wanderer. Williams.
With Garments Flowing. Clare.
Written on a Leaf. *Anonymous.*

Wanderer (s)
The Ajax Samples. Jensen.
Awake, My Soul! In Grateful Songs. Fowler.
The Beggar Boy. Alexander.
Christmas Eve under Hooker's Statue. Lowell.
A Dream. Blake.
Fair Sylvia. *Anonymous.*
Good-By. Litchfield.
The Heath. Boyd.
Migrants. Anderson.
Riddle: The Swan: "Silent my robe, when I rest on earth." *Anonymous.*
Shepherd. Stafford.
Song for the Wandering Jew. Wordsworth.
Song of the Corsairs. Byron.
The Tree in the Desert. Hebbel.
The Unerring Guide. Shipton.

Wane (s)
As I Look Out. St. Martin.
The Bedpost. Graves.
Easter Monday. Rossetti.
No Room. Stroud.
Scenes de la Vie de Boheme. Symons.

Want (ed) (ing) (s)
Action Would Kill It/A Gamble. Adamson.
The Angel in the House. Patmore.
Another Poem on Absalom. Yonathan.
The Bells Are Ringing for Me and Chagall. Winch.
Bury Me in America. Karlen.
The Controls. Fisher.
The Crazy World. Gay.
Drums in Scotland. Hugo.
Elegy (excerpt). Bidart.
The End. Thesen.
The End of Summer. Minty.
Epigram. Butler.
Epigram: "I delight in the prime of a boy of twelve." Strato.
Epigram: "Prepare to meet the King of Terrors." Elliott.
Exigencies. Gilbert.

Ford Madox Ford. Lowell.
Four Christmas Carols (excerpt). *Anonymous.*
Freedom. Hughes.
A Friendly Address. Hood.
The Frog and the Mouse. *Anonymous.*
Fungo. Plumly.
Give Me My Infant Now. Te-whaka-io-roa.
Grandma Chooses Her Plot at the County Cemetery. Ruffin.
Green and Yellow. *Anonymous.*
H–y P–tt. *Anonymous.*
Harriet. Lowell.
Hearthstone. Monro.
How Totally Unpredictable We Are to One Another. Sward.
I Have Got to Stop Loving You. Anthony ("Ai").
I Want a Girl. Von Tilzer.
I Want to Die Easy when I Die. *Anonymous.*
I Want You. Gillom.
In Memoriam A.H.H., LXXIX. Tennyson.
Jesus Shall Reign. Watts.
July 4th. Swenson.
The Last Will and Testament of the Grey Mare. *Anonymous.*
The Late Show. Sylvester.
Limerick: "A Clergyman out in Dumont." Bishop.
Lord Thomas and Fair Ellender. *Anonymous.*
Meeting of a Poetry Society. Rago.
Miners' Wives. Corrie.
Motive for Mercy. Milburn.
My Death. Smith.
Neo-Thomist Poem. Hemingway.
On Dennis. Pope.
Pocket Poem. Kooser.
Poem for Flora. Giovanni.
Poem: "I do not want only." Thibaudeau.
Poems from a Greek Anthology (excerpt). Ausonius.
Profit and Loss: An Elegy upon the Decease of Mrs. Mary Gerrish... Danforth.
Returning to the Town Where We Used to Live. Musgrave.
Risselty-Rosselty. *Anonymous.*
She Is Carefully Stepping over the Important Communications. Canan.
Since Nothing Is Impossible. Waters.
A Small Dragon. Patten.
Somebody Almost Walked Off Wid Alla My Stuff. Shange.
Stories from Kansas. Stafford.
T. B. Blues. Leadbelly.
Tant' Amare. *Anonymous.*
There Is Only One of Everything. Atwood.
To an Old San Francisco Poet. Abbott.
To Anne. Stirling-Maxwell.
To the Young Rebels. Mayo.
Tutankhamen. Dickey.

Two Gifts. *Anonymous.*
Unaccompanied. Andrews.
Up against the Wall (parody). Berry.
Variations on a Theme by William Carlos Williams. Koch.
Walk in Jerusalem Jus' Like John. *Anonymous.*
The Wants of Man. Adams.
We Who Are Dead. Benjamin.
What Do You Want? Newlove.

Wanton (s)
Aunt Beulah's Wisdom. Box.
Between Ourselves. Lorde.
The Dawn. Yeats.
Evening. Aldington.
Four Winds. Porter.
The Gipsy Laddie. *Anonymous.*
Kissing and Bussing. Herrick.
The Laird of Logie. *Anonymous.*
Lord! Who Art Merciful as Well as Just. Southey.
Magic. Johnson.
Papio. Chock.
She That Denies Me. Heywood.
Sonnet: Of Love in Men and Devils. Angiolieri.
'Tis but a Wanton Trick. *Anonymous.*
To Dr. F. B. on His Book of Chess. Lovelace.
Valerius on Women. Heywood.
The Way a Ghost Dissolves. Hugo.
The White City. McKay.

War (red) (ring) (s)
After Our War. Balaban.
After Sunset. Conkling.
The Aged Stranger. Harte.
Airliner. Webb.
American Heritage. Sward.
Amoretti, XI. Spenser.
The Ancient Sacrifice. Fisher.
Another Dying Chieftain. Green.
At a March against the Vietnam War. Bly.
The Atheist's Tragedy. Tourneur.
Aubade. MacNeice.
Ave Imperatrix! Wilde.
The Battle of Brunanburh (excerpt). *Anonymous.*
Beauty Eternal: To-Day I Saw a Butterfly. Hooley.
Between Two Prisoners. Dickey.
Big Dream, Little Dream. Simpson.
The Biglow Papers. Lowell.
Bitter Question. Macdougall.
Blow, Bugle! Clark.
Bookra. Warner.
Boots. Kipling.
Caelica, LXXVI. Greville.
The Christian Soldier (excerpt). Studdert-Kennedy.
The Closing Album. MacNeice.
Concert at Sea. Creekmore.

Conquistador: The Argument. Stevens.
Crime Club. Kees.
Cycle. Jennett.
The Dark Hills. Robinson.
The Day the Beatles Lost One to the Flesh-Eating Horse. Kelly.
The Dead Wingman. Jarrell.
December 24, 1979. Weaver.
The Desperado. *Anonymous.*
A Dirge for McPherson. Melville.
A Domestic Cat. Denby.
The Dutch Seamen and New Holland. Reeves.
Endless. Rukeyser.
An English Mother. Johnson.
Epistles. Horace.
Epitaph (Inscription from Anticyra). *Anonymous.*
The Eye. Jeffers.
Fabrication of Ancestors. Dugan.
The Faerie Queene. Spenser.
Fairground. Auden.
Flathead and Nez Perce Sin-ka-ha. Lewis.
For Myself. Hines.
The Fourth of July. Pierpont.
From Which War. Minthorn.
Funeral of Napoleon I. Hagarty.
Georgics. Virgil (Publius Vergilius Maro).
Hard Frost. Young.
Helena Embarks for Palestine. Cynewulf.
High Germany. *Anonymous.*
High Germany. Shanks.
The Horse and His Rider. Baillie.
Hugh Spencer's Feats in France (A version). *Anonymous.*
I'm Agoing to Lay Down My Sword. *Anonymous.*
The Iliad. Homer.
In Me Two Worlds. Day Lewis.
In the Pink. Sassoon.
In White Tie. Huddle.
The Inspection. Watt.
Investigation. Vinograd.
Invocation. Horace.
It Was the Last of the Parades. Simpson.
James Gerard. Shiplett.
A Jealous Man. Graves.
Jeannot's Answer. Jeffries.
King Henry VI. Shakespeare.
The Knowledge That Comes Through Experience. Cooper.
The Land Called Scotia. Donatus.
Late Wisdom. Crabbe.
A Legend of Versailles. Tolson.
Lesbian Poem. Morgan.
Marian. Meredith.
The Miracle. Grade.
The Mothers of Men. Miller.
The New Crusade. Bates.
The New World. Engle.
Nigerian Unity/or little niggers killing little niggers. Lee.

Nocturne. Frost.
Ode to Peace. *Anonymous.*
On the Sea Wall. Day-Lewis.
Othello. Shakespeare.
The Pacific Highway. Ballard.
Picasso and Matisse. Francis.
Poem for the Young White Man Who Asked Me How I, an Intelligent... Cervantes.
Poem (I Lived in the First Century). Rukeyser.
Poem to My Sister, Ethel Ennis.... Jordan.
The Portent. Melville.
Private Means is Dead. Smith.
The Progress of Poesy. Gray.
The Quick. Jennett.
Radcliff, Kentucky. Nickens.
Rain Inters Maggiore. Kreymborg.
The Recruiting Sergeant. *Anonymous.*
Reinforcements. Lynch.
Remembering That Island. McGrath.
Rides. Derwood.
Rite of Passage. Olds.
Robin Hood and the Scotchman. *Anonymous.*
Roses of Memory. Gordon.
Rumors. Arkell.
The Sage in Unison. Stewart.
Seaman, 1941. Holden.
The Second Advice to a Painter. Marvell.
Shield. *Anonymous.*
The Sick Nought. Jarrell.
Silent Testimony. Parmenter.
Sing Me a New Song. Clarke.
Soldier's Dove. Forsyth.
The Song-Maker. Fairbridge.
The Song of the Borderguard. Duncan.
Song: "The pints and the pistols, the pike-staves and pottles." Praed.
Source of News. *Anonymous.*
A Spool of Thread. Eastman.
St Mary's Loch. Faber.
Strength to War. Stepanchev.
Study War No More. *Anonymous.*
The Surrender at Appomattox. Melville.
The Surrender of Cornwallis. *Anonymous.*
Tamburlaine the Great. Marlowe.
Terrapin War. *Anonymous.*
That Crazy War. *Anonymous.*
This Is the Last. Waterhouse.
This Loneliness for You Is Like the Wound. Thompson.
This Tokyo. Snyder.
Three Migrations. Salisbury.
Time Out. Butterfield.
The Times. Madge.
Timoshenko. Keyes.

To a Sleeping Friend. Cocteau.
To a Writer of the Day. Mitchell.
To Make the People Happy. Hugo.
To My Wife. Forsyth.
Tom Gage's Proclamation... *Anonymous.*
Troop Train. Shapiro.
Uccello. Corso.
The Unemployed. Roberts.
Venus Accoutered as Mars. *Anonymous.*
Vine and Fig Tree. Altman.
Voices of Heroes. Gregory.
War. Channing-Stetson.
War. Hall.
The War. Merwin.
War Song. *Anonymous.*
War. Wallace.
Warriors. Dunn.
The Way to Heaven. Whiting.
The Wayside Station. Muir.
We Who Are Dead. Benjamin.
Weeping Sad and Lonely. Ucker.
What's That Smell in the Kitchen? Piercy.
Why That's Bob Hope. Hathaway.
Winter Love. Doolittle.
Woman Guard. Aguila.
Written in Ireland. Alcock.
The Year 1812. Mickiewicz.

Warble (d) (s)
The Enthusiast; or, The Lover of Nature. Warton.
On Sivori's Violin. Osgood
Religious Musings. Coleridge.

Warbling (s)
Lines on Carmen Sylva. Lazarus.
Pretty Wantons. *Anonymous.*
Ye Little Birds That Sit and Sing. Heywood.

Ward (s)
Captain Ward and the Rainbow. *Anonymous.*
A Game of Consequences. Dehn.
Variations on a Theme by William Carlos Williams. Koch.
Verses Intended to Be Written below a Noble Earl's Picture. Burns.

Warden
Coon Can (Poor Boy) (with music). *Anonymous.*
Fidessa, More Chaste Than Kind, XXXVII. Griffin.
The Wheelchair Butterfly. Tate.

Warm (ed) (er) (est) (s)
About an Allegory. Arensberg.
The Addict. Rubin.
After Death. Rossetti.
Among the Heather. Allingham.
And Forgetful of Europe. Grigson.
And If I Turn. Bowering.
Angina Pectoris. Moses.
At Knaresborough. Davie.
Before the Big Storm. Stafford.

Ben. Johnsons Sociable Rules for the Apollo. Jonson.
Beside the Sea. Johnston.
Birthday Poem for Thomas Hardy. Day-Lewis.
Byron in Greece. Rosten.
Cats and Egypt. Hughes.
The Center of the Garden. Stanford.
Christmas Tree. Smith.
The Contented Bachelor. Kendall.
December. Schuyler.
English Girl. Mathers.
Envoi. Lewis.
The Fairies' Shopping. Deland.
For Anna. Layton.
Four Choctaw Songs. Barnes.
The Frozen Girl (with music). *Anonymous.*
Girls in Their Seasons. Mahon.
The Harvest Bow. Heaney.
Hope. Reeve.
The Horn. Reeves.
Horoscope. Cunningham.
The Humble Petition of Poor Ben to the Best of Monarchs... Jonson.
Hunter's Moon. Sandy.
If the Robin Sings in the Bush. *Anonymous.*
Lament for the Dorsets. Purdy.
Leda. Doolittle.
Love. Herbert.
May-Day. Hill.
Miramar Beach. Cunningham.
My House. Bruce.
The New-Yeeres Gift, Sung to the King in the Presence at White Hall. Herrick.
Ode. In Imitation of Pastor Fido Written Abroad, in 1729. Lyttelton.
Ode to a Beautiful Woman. Clark.
On Elizabeth Ireland. *Anonymous.*
One Time Henry Dreamed the Number. Long.
The Opportune Overthrow of Humpty Dumpty. Carryl.
Paradox: That Fruition Destroys Love (excerpt). King.
Pocket Poem. Kooser.
A Praefatory Poem to the Little Book, Entituled, Christianus per Ignem. Noyes.
Quite Shy Actually but Obsessed. Miller.
A Robyn Joly Robyn. Wyatt.
Sleep. Viau.
Softly, Drowsily. De la Mare.
Someone Talking. Harjo.
Sonnet: "A warm rain whispers, but the earth knows best." Leslie.
That Brings Us to the Woodstove in the Wilds, at Night. Hall.
Welcome to This House. George.

While the leaves of the bamboo rustle. *Anonymous.*
The White Eagle. McDonald.

Warming-pan
My Three Wives. *Anonymous.*
To the Ladybird. *Anonymous.*

Warmth
Around Thanksgiving. Humphries.
As Well as They Can. Hope.
Baptism. Zieroth.
Boy at the Window. Wilbur.
Epigram: "Broad and ample he warms himself." *Anonymous.*
Ethnogenesis. Timrod.
Father, the Year Is Fallen. Lorde.
Holy Innocents. Rossetti.
House and Shutter. Turco.
A House of Mercy. Smith.
In Memoriam A.H.H., XLVI. Tennyson.
In the Beginning. Porter.
The Ladder Has No Steps. Plescoff.
Lake Harriet: Wind. Taylor.
The Languages We Are. Bryant.
Ode Written at Vale-Royal Abbey in Cheshire. Warton, Jr..
The Old Woman Sits. Davis.
The Touch of Human Hands. Clark.
The Unknown Eros. Patmore.
Watching Your Gray Eyes. Marcus.
Winter Encounters. Tomlinson.

Warn (ed) (ing) (s)
The Angel in the House. Patmore.
Angels. Hall.
A Ballad from the Seven Dials Press... *Anonymous.*
Ballad of the Oedipus Complex. Durrell.
Censorship. Brasfield.
Come All Ye Fair and Tender Ladies. *Anonymous.*
The Death of Slavery. Bryant.
Don't Sing Love Songs. *Anonymous.*
Earthquake. Ford.
First Rain. Akins.
The Flying Cloud. *Anonymous.*
The Flying Cloud (I). *Anonymous.*
Gather Ye Rosebuds (parody). Fowler.
Hob Gobbling's Song. Lowell.
A Hue and Cry after Blood and Murder. *Anonymous.*
The Last Frontier. Thomas.
The Lexington Miller. *Anonymous.*
Limerick: "A Fire Island pixie called "Mary.'". *Anonymous.*
The Limits of Departure. Weigl.
The Poet: A Rhapsody. Akenside.

Rainbow at Night.
Anonymous.
Red Sky at Night.
Anonymous.
The Road the Crows Own.
Astor.
The Silver Dagger.
Anonymous.
Springfield Mountain.
Anonymous.
Springfield Mountain (C
vers.). *Anonymous.*
That Summer. Treece.
Weather Rhymes. Brown.
Weather Wisdom.
Anonymous.
What I Did Last Summer.
Ikan.

Warp
The Chronicle of Meola
Creek. Sinclair.
Warp and Woof. Halbisch.

Warrant (ed)
The Lily of the Valley.
Beddoes.
Lydford Journey. Browne.
Mr. Bleaney. Larkin.

Warrior (s)
The Battle of Finnsburg.
Anonymous.
Battle Pledge. *Anonymous.*
Blood Marksman and
Kureldei the Marksman.
Anonymous.
Character of the Happy
Warrior. Wordsworth.
The Cow-Chace. André.
Fern. Hughes.
Gadoshkibos. Burns.
January Is Here. Fawcett.
Lines Written after a Battle.
Anonymous.
Ortiz. Butterworth.
Sunrise. Tollerud.
The Vikings. *Anonymous.*
"When reckless youth in an
unquiet breast." Surrey.

Warsaw
Conversation with a
Countryman. Slonimski.

Wart (s)
Toad. Cotton.
Washrags. Rutsala.

Wary
Limerick: "A Fire Island pixie
called "Mary.'".
Anonymous.
Veterans. Johnston.

Wash (ed) (ing) (es)
At the Slackening of the Tide.
Wright.
A Battle of Similes.
Anonymous.
Babysitter's Song.
Anonymous.
Cleaning Up. Dyson.
The First Proclamation of
Miles Standish. Preston.
For a Friend. Steingass.
Hope. Reeve.
Hunger. *Anonymous.*
I Am Your Loaf, Lord.
Ross.
In the House of the Dying.
Cooper.
In a Wood Clearing.
MacDonald.
The Intruder. Kizer.
The Leper Cleansed. Collop.
Lord High-Bo. Belloc.
Marie Magdalene. Herbert.
Me, Colored. Abrahams.

Metaphysics. Herford.
Nursery Rules from Nannies.
Anonymous.
On the Uncleanly Habits of
Sir Charles Wetherell.
Anonymous.
Oxford. Dorn.
Peter Rabbit. McPherson.
The Ploughman.
Anonymous.
The Plumber Arrives at Three
Mile Island. Stewart.
A Psalm to the Son.
Wilkinson.
Rats. De La Mare.
The Remorse for Time.
Nemerov.
Saturday Morning at the
Laundry. Gilbert.
Sea Lullaby. Wylie.
Shepherd, Show Me How to
Go. Eddy.
Silex Scintillans. Vaughan.
The Smell of Fish. Meissner.
Snow in New York.
Swenson.
Sonnet XV: "This is the way
we say it in our time."
Scott.
They That Wash on Monday.
Anonymous.
To Manon. Blunt.
Tree Planting. Farkas.
Wash. Chuilleanain.
The Washing Machine.
Davies.
Wet Weather. Low.
What Would I Give?
Rossetti.

Washboards
Boudoir Lament. Yu Hsuan-
chi.

Washbowl
I Come from Salem City.
Anonymous.

Washington
Abraham's Daughter.
Winner.
Evacuation of New York by
the British. Anonymous.
The Federal Constitution.
Milns.
Grand Opening of the
People's Theatre.
Goldrick.
Grover Cleveland. Benton.
The Name of Washington.
Field.
Old Song Written during
Washington's Life.
Anonymous.
The Rivers Remember.
Turner.
Shakespearean Soliloquy in
Progress: "Tubby or not
tubby-" (parody).
Burnand.
The Trip to Cambridge.
Sewall.
Under the Old Elm. Lowell.
Watergate. Herschberger.
Whisperin' Bill. Bacheller.

Washington Square
I Took a Bow and Arrow.
Ciardi.

Washrag
Washrags. Rutsala.

Wasp
The Book of Job and a Draft
of a Poem to Praise the
Paths... Oppen.

The Dark Scent of Prayer.
Drachler.
Escape. Wylie.
The Fear of Flowers. Clare.
Transition. Sarton.
The Wasp. Hine.

Waspish
Delight in Books from
Evening. Pastorius.
The Honest Whore, I, 1604.
Dekker.

Wasselling
The Wassail Song.
Anonymous.

Waste (d) (s)
Across the Fens. Thomas.
The Aged Lover Renounceth
Love. Vaux.
Amen. Mutis.
Autumn Woods. Bryant.
A Bob-Tailed Flush. Painter.
Coffee. Cunningham.
A Comparison. Cowper.
Confined Love. Donne.
The Crusade. Rinaldo
d'Aquino.
Driving to Town Late to Mail
a Letter. Bly.
Fog-Horn. Clarke.
Forebears. Gibbon.
The Future Verdict.
Cambridge.
Gascoigne's Memories.
Gascoigne.
The Heather. Blicher.
Light Breaks Where No Sun
Shines. Thomas.
The Lion and Albert. Edgar.
Lost in Translation. Merrill.
Morning. Taylor.
Movement Song. Lorde.
Night Piece. Joyce.
The Old Man Said. Arnett.
On a Bas-Relief. Trimpi.
On the Big Horn. Whittier.
On the Detraction which
Followed upon My Writing
Certain Treatises. Milton.
The Pin. Taylor.
Prognostic. Yellen.
Sextains. Baylebridge.
Someone Could Certainly Be
Found. Scott.
There Pipes the Wood-Lark.
Gray.
To a Pet Cobra. Campbell.
To a Poet I Knew. Amini.
The Wayfarers. Brooke.
What the Bones Know.
Kizer.
Written in a Copy of The
Earthly Paradise. Morris.

Wastebasket
My Physics Teacher.
Wagoner.

Wastefulness
A Meeting. Day Lewis.
To Whom It May Concern.
Cunningham.

Wasting
Pocahontas to her English
husband, John Rolfe.
Allen.
She Attempts to Refute the
Praises That Truth...
Juana Ines de la Cruz.

Watch (ed) (er) (ers) (s)
The 49 Stomp. Blockcolski.
Arm Wrestling with My
Father. Driscoll.
Ars Poetica. Kennedy.

At Grand Canyon's Edge.
Ray.
Awake, Awake! Campion.
Birthday. Stafford.
Brahma, the World Idea.
Anonymous.
A Burnt Offering to Your
Greenstone Eyes, Tangaroa.
Tuwhare.
By Rail through the Earthly
Paradise, Perhaps
Bedfordshire. Levertov.
Catastrophe. Brock.
Child with Six Fingers.
Muske.
The Cotton Cat. Newsome.
Country Stars. Meredith.
The Death of Professor
Backwards. Kennedy.
Dirge. Cawein.
Drinking Alone with the
Moon. Li Po.
Early Winter. Kees.
The Egg Boiler. Brooks.
End of The Affair. Grigson.
Epitaphs of the War, 1914-18.
Kipling.
The Eye. Jeffers.
The Fathers. Sassoon.
February Twilight. Teasdale.
Four Lovely Sisters.
Trypanis.
Foxgloves and Snow. Angus.
Fraulein Reads Instructive
Rhymes. Kumin.
Freedom For the Mind.
Garrison
From a Venetian Sequence.
Naude.
Give Us Sober Men.
Isenhour.
God Bless This House from
Thatch to Floor.
Anonymous.
God's Dark. Martin.
Heart. LaBombard.
Hell's Pavement. Masefield.
Her Birthday. Witt.
How the Flowers Grow.
"Setoun. Gabriel"
The Hundred-Yard Dash.
Lindsey.
Hysteria. Chu Shu chen.
I threw a penny in the air.
Anonymous.
Ice. Roberts.
In Time. Raine.
It Is at Moments after I Have
Dreamed. Cummings.
Journal of the Storm.
Kuzma.
The Lady of the Lake. Scott.
Lake Superior. Niedecker.
The Leaf. Fagg.
Like Rousseau. Jones.
London Spring. Slonimski.
Looking for a Home. Stern.
My Former Hopes Are Fled.
Cowper.
The Myth. Muir.
The Name. Creeley.
The Natural History of Pliny.
McHugh.
The Neighbors. Garrison.
Neither Out Far Nor In Deep.
Frost.
The Night-Blooming Cereus.
Hayden.
The Observer. Yates.
On Scratchbury Camp.
Sassoon.

One of Wally's Yarns.
Masefield.
People. Kanik.
Peyote Vision. Blockcolski.
The Pigs. Lehmann.
A Poem for Trapped Things.
Wieners.
Prayer. *Anonymous.*
Rondel. Dacey.
The Routine. Blackburn.
Sanctuary. Boyd.
The Scarecrow. De la Mare.
Scenes de la Vie de Boheme.
Symons.
Sea School. Howes.
Seeing Oloalok. Bowering.
Shakespeare. Watson.
The Singing-Woman from the
Wood's Edge. Millay.
Snakebite. James.
Sonnet: "As when, to one who
long hath watched, the
morn." Bampfylde.
Sonnets. Hillyer.
Sonnets, I. Hillyer.
Sorrow. Lawrence.
The Spanish Gypsy (excerpt).
Eliot.
The Stars Are Lit. Bialik.
The Tables Turned.
Wordsworth.
Their Cone-Like Cabins.
Ballard.
There Are Delicacies.
Birney.
Umbrellas. Bennett.
A Visitation. Snodgrass.
War Cry: To Mary. Leo
XIII.
Watch and Pray. Elliott.
The West's Asleep. Davis.
The Wife. Creeley.
Winter Song. Tollet.
The Woman's Dream.
Horovitz.
Words to My Mother.
Storni.
Zionist Marching Song.
Imber.

Watch out (ed) (er) (ers) (s)
Instamatic. Morgan.
Limerick: "Now the sneeze is
a joy-vent, I s'pose."
Euwer.
Turn the Glasses Over.
Anonymous.

Watchdog
Maytime. *Anonymous.*
A Pastoral. Hillyer.

Watchfire
The Inquisitors. Jeffers.

Watching
Also Watches (parody).
Berry.
Anniversary Poem for the
Cheyennes Who Fell at
Sand Creek. Henson.
Ballad of Luna, Luna.
Garcia Lorca.
The Bird's Nest.
Drinkwater.
Daffodils. Heffernan.
Dick and Will. Roberts.
The Distant Winter. Levine.
The Heavenly Banquet.
Brigid.
Late Abed. MacLeish.
Leoun. Cocteau.
The Little Green Orchard.
De La Mare.
A Supermarket in California.
Ginsberg.

This Day Be with Me.
Macdonald.
Those before Us. Lowell.
Where Is Your Boy Tonight?
Anonymous.

Watchman (men)
Eleven Addresses to the Lord.
Berryman.
The Town Mouse and the
Country Mouse (parody).
Prior.

Watchtower
Little Things. *Anonymous.*
McKinley. *Anonymous.*

Watchword
Sumter's Band. Simmons.
The Way to Heaven.
Whiting.
We Conquer or Die.
Pierpont.

Water-pistol
A Choice of Weapons.
Kunitz.

Water (s)
The Abandoned. Symons.
An Aboriginal Mother's
Lament. Harpur.
Actaeon. Clough.
After. Levine.
The Alchemist. Church.
Alpheus and Arethusa.
Daly.
American Falls. Keeler.
Amusing Our Daughters.
Kizer.
And the Gas Chamber Drones
in the Distance. Forker.
The Angel in the House.
Patmore.
Animal Songs: Lion.
Anonymous.
Antipater of Thessalonica.
Rexroth.
Apollo 113. Finne.
Appoggiatura. Hayes.
Aquarium. Wright.
Ardan Mor. Ledwidge.
As I Was Going to Saint Ives.
Hoffman.
As the Window Darkens.
Jensen.
At a Child's Baptism.
Miller.
At Her Step the Water-Hen.
Rossetti.
At Only That Moment.
Ross.
The Atoll in the Mind.
Comfort.
August Rain. Bly.
Ave Atque Vale. Swinburne.
The Avenging Daughters.
Anonymous.
The Ballad of O'Bruadir.
Higgins.
The Bath. Oppenheimer.
The Bathers. Crane.
The Battle of Aughrim:
Rapparees. Murphy.
A Beauty That All Night
Long. Julal ed-Din Rumi.
Before. Goldbarth.
Birds. Jeffers.
Birth. Lyon.
Blood Is Thicker Than Water.
Rice.
The Boat. Pack.
Bonac. Wheelock.
The Brazos River.
Anonymous.
The Briefless Barrister. Saxe.
Bums, on Waking. Dickey.

The Cachalot. Pratt.
Calenture. Reid.
Calm Morning at Sea.
Teasdale.
Camel. Merwin.
Cana Revisited. Heaney.
Carrier's Address.
Anonymous.
The Caulker. Lewis.
Caution. *Anonymous.*
Change of Venue.
Clockadale.
Chilly Water. *Anonymous.*
Cleanliness. Lamb.
A Coast View (excerpt).
Harpur.
The Collection. Manhire.
Come Ride and Ride to the
Garden. Gregory Lady.
Connais-Tu le Pays?
Shelton.
Continent's End. Jeffers.
Corries. Smith.
Crab Orchard Sanctuary: Late
October. Kinsella.
Cross Ties. Kennedy.
The Crying of Water.
Symons.
The Culprit Fay. Drake.
A Dark World. Scovell.
Daysleep. Smith.
Dear Friend, Whose Presence
in the House. Clarke.
Death from Cancer. Lowell.
The Death of the Sailor's
Wife. Barton.
Death on the Farm.
Waterman.
The Deep Calling. Rothfork.
Description of a New England
Spring. Josselyn.
Dingman's Marsh. Moore.
Dirge for Small Wilddeath.
Moffett.
Discomfort in High Places.
Tremayne.
Discovery of San Francisco
Bay. White.
A Distance from the Sea.
Kees.
The Djanggawul Cycle, 67.
Anonymous.
Documentary. Stroud.
The Driver. Dickey.
Drop a Pebble in the Water.
Foley.
The Drunken Fisherman.
Lowell.
L'Elisir d'Amore. Wiebe.
The Enduring Music. Vinal.
Epitaph: "If fruits are fed on
any beast." Synge.
Ere the Golden Bowl Is
Broken. Branch.
Etruscan Notebook.
Clementelli.
Even during War. Rukeyser.
The Everlasting Forests.
Ravikovich.
Exile. Dowson.
Exiled. Millay.
Fairest of Freedom's
Daughters. Rankin.
Fairy Tales. Flanders.
Fancy. Smedley.
Far from the Heart of
Culture. Auden.
The Faun. Long.
A Film. Goldbarth.
A Fire a Simple Fire. Will.
First Rain. Akins.
Fish. Ross.

Fishing. Wellesley.
Fishing with Buddies. Eddy.
The Flight. Roethke.
A Flight of Wild Ducks.
Harpur.
Flood. Charles.
Folding the Sheets. Dobson.
Food. Valle.
The Forms of Love. Oppen.
Fountain. Jennings.
The Fountain. Mu'tamid.
Four Folk-Songs in Hokku
Form, 1. *Anonymous.*
The Full Heart. Nichols.
Gastric. "T.
Getting at the Root of the
Matter (parody). Taylor.
The Gift of Water. Garland.
The Glass Bubbles.
Greenberg.
God Is Working His Purpose
Out. Ainger.
God Moves on the Water.
Anonymous.
God's A-Gwineter Trouble de
Water. *Anonymous.*
Godamighty Drag.
Anonymous.
Going Up and Down.
Daniels.
Great Bacchus: from the
Greek. Prior.
Green, Green is El Aghir.
Cameron.
Grey Him. Mariah.
The Grimsby Lads.
Anonymous.
Haiku: "The dew of the
rouge-flower." Kaga no
Chiyo.
Hermann Ludwig Ferdinand
von Helmholtz. Meinke.
The Herons. Ledwidge.
His mansion in the pool.
Dickinson.
Hooking the Rainbow.
Baldwin.
Hy-Brasail–The Isle of the
Blest. Griffin.
I am Hermes. Anyte.
I Korinna am here to sing the
courage. Korinna.
Images. Raine.
In a Warm Bath. Rakosi.
In an Hour the Sun. Freed.
In March. Martin.
In the Soul Hour. Mezey.
In the Twilight (excerpt).
O'Donnell.
Inanna's Song. *Anonymous.*
Instruction sore long time I
bore. Kingsley.
Intimations of Immortality
from Recollections of Early
Childhood. Wordsworth.
Isabel. *Anonymous.*
Island Moment. Finlay.
Jug Brook. Voigt.
Just Friends. Creeley.
Keep It Clean. Jordan.
Kinmont Willie. *Anonymous.*
Kitchenette Building. Brooks
Landscape I. Madge.
The Last Utterance of the
Delphic Oracle.
Anonymous.
Late Afternoon on a Good
Lake. Wier.
A Late Spring. Scully.
A Legend of Alhambra.
Trench.

A Legend of Lake Okeefinokee. Richards.
The Lesson of the Water-Mill. Doudney.
Liard Hot Springs. Massman.
Life from the Lifeless. Jeffers.
The Lifeguard. Dickey.
Like Water Down a Slope. Schneour.
Lilium Regis. Thompson.
Long Song. Ejong.
Long Trip. Hughes.
Looking into History. Wilbur.
Lord of the Winds. Coleridge.
The Lovers. Comfort.
Luss Village. Smith.
M and A, R and I. *Anonymous.*
The Magic Apple Tree. Feinstein.
The Magnolia's Shadow. Montale.
The Man That Waters the Workers' Beer. *Anonymous.*
Marriage. Sklarew.
The Marshes of Glynn. Lanier.
Materia Nupcial. Neruda.
Matronita. Silk.
A Merry Ballad of Vintners. Payne.
Midnight. Vaughan.
The Mill. Heyen.
A Muse of Water. Kizer.
My Cabinets Are Oyster-Shells. Newcastre.
My heart I gave thee... Wyatt.
My Mother Takes a Bath. Kageyama.
Needs. Rendall.
A New Song of Mary. *Anonymous.*
Next, Please. Larkin.
Night Flight. Whalley.
Nightfall. Tyutchev.
The Nike of Samothrace. Morley.
Noah. Bloch.
Not Being Wise. Elson.
O Brazil, the Isle of the Blest. Griffin.
Observation. Wynard.
Off Manilly. Cooke.
The Old Age Home. Holmes.
The Old Girl. Lenhart.
The Old Man Who Is Gone Now. Reyes.
The Old Pond. Basho (Matsuo Basho).
Old Triton Time. Watkins.
On a Prohibitionist Poem. Chesterton.
On a Quaker's Tankard. Landor.
On King Richard the Third, Who Lies Buried under Leicester Bridge. Suckling.
On the Lake. Sackville-West.
On the Lake Poets. Townsend.
One Morning in May. *Anonymous.*
Ornamental Water. Nicholl.

Over All the Face of Earth Main Ocean Flowed. Milton.
Owl and Rooster. Cardiff.
The Palace of Art. Tennyson.
Parade's End. Guest.
The Passion. Knevet.
Piano Practice. Serraillier.
Piazza Di Spagna. Grimes.
Pictor Ignotus. Browning.
The Pike. Blunden.
Plans for Altering the River. Hugo.
Poem in Which My Legs Are Accepted. Fraser.
Postscript to Die Schone Mullerin. Llster.
Praise. Grenville.
The Predicter of Famine. Williams.
The Premonition. Roethke.
Pretty Vomit. Rosenthal.
The Problem of Wild Horses. Winder.
Psalm. Schwartz.
The Public Garden. Lowell.
The Rape of Lucrece. Shakespeare.
Reality Is an Activity of the Most August Imagination. Stevens.
Reasons For and Against Marrying Widows. Selyns.
Rebirth. Machado.
Recipe. Goldbarth.
The Red Dog. Jensen.
The Red-Gold Rain. Sitwell.
Refuge. Allen.
Resigning from a Job in a Defense Industry. McPherson.
The Right True End. *Anonymous.*
Rip. Wright.
The River. Stuart.
Roots Go Down. Frankenberg.
The Rubaiyat of Omar Khayyam. Fitzgerald.
Salmon-Fishing. Jeffers.
Sanctuary. Boyd.
Satires. Wyatt.
Scotland's Burning. *Anonymous.*
The Sea and the Eagle. Clouts.
Sea Burial from the Cruiser "Reve." Eberhart.
Sea Calm. Hughes.
Second Sight. Longley.
The Sedges. O'Sullivan.
Sestina with Refrain. Shapcott.
The Shallows of the Ford. Knibbs.
Shameful Impotence: Book III, Elegia VII. Ovid.
Shooting Whales. Strand.
The Sieve. Sa'di.
Silex Scintillans. Vaughan.
Singing Water. Lehmann.
The Sixties. Listmann.
The Small Towns of Ireland. Betjeman.
The Snow-Ball. Petronius Arbiter (Caius Petronius Arbiter).
Snow in New York. Swenson.
Solomon: Inspiration. *Anonymous.*

Some Magic. Koller.
Sonet XXV. Stirling.
Song–Across the Sea. Allingham.
Song: "If thou art sleeping." Vicente.
Song of a Common Lover. Ranaivo.
Song of Poverty. *Anonymous.*
Song of the Lioness for Her Cub. *Anonymous.*
Song of the Three Angels. Vicente.
Song of the Turkey Buzzard. Welch.
Sonnet XVI: "After an age when thunderbolts and hail." Labe.
Sonnet: "Cry, crow." Carruth.
Sonnet to Chatterton. Keats.
South Street. Falkenbury.
Sparkling Water. Schaaf.
Spitballer. Chappell.
Stone and the Obliging Pond. Ackerson.
Sub Rosa. Domanski.
Sudan. Jackson.
The Suicides. Macbeth.
Summer Wind. Bryant.
Super Flumina Babylonis. Swinburne.
The Swan. Rodgers.
Swans Mating. Longley.
Talking with Soldiers. Turner.
Terce. McMichael.
A Testimony. Lyon.
There Are Oceans. Harjo.
There Were Some Summers. Lux.
This Evening, My Love, Even as I Spoke Vainly. Juana Ines de la Cruz.
Tho We All Speak. Ort.
The Thousand and One Nights: The Power of Love. *Anonymous.*
The Thousand and One Nights: The Song of the Narcissus. *Anonymous.*
The Thousand and One Nights: To Lighten My Darkness. *Anonymous.*
Three Green Windows. Sexton.
Three Things. Sarton.
Through Binoculars. Tomlinson.
To Drink. "Mistral.
To Jane: The Recollection. Shelley.
To K. H. Brown.
To My Mother. Rosenberg.
To Sir Francis Brian. Wyatt.
To the Water Nymphs, Drinking at the Fountain. Herrick.
Twice Shy. Heaney.
Two Campers in Cloud Country. Plath.
Underground. Mudie.
The Unremitting Voice of Nightly Streams. Wordsworth.
The View of Rangitoto. Brasch.
The Viking Terror. *Anonymous.*
Virgins. Carlin.
The Voyage. Shapiro.

Voyagers' Prayer. *Anonymous.*
Wade in the Water. *Anonymous.*
Wash. Chuilleanain.
Washing the Coins. Dunn.
Water. Conkling.
Water Color. Mooney.
Water-Images. Osborn.
The Water Mill. Doudney.
Water on the Highway. Simpson.
Water Tap. MacCaig.
The Water-Witch. Perry.
Water Without Sound. Tussman.
The Watered Lilies. *Anonymous.*
We thirst at first. Dickinson.
Welcome. Thomas.
Weldon Kees in Mexico, 1965. Wojahn.
The Well. Levertov.
Wet Summer. Ward.
When I Went out. Kuskin.
When the Loneliness of the Tomb Went down into the Marketplace. Sa'udi.
Whitmonday. MacNeice.
Who. Honig.
The Wilderness. Raine.
Willow Poem. Williams.
Wine and Water. Chesterton.
Winter Rain. Rossetti.
Winter Sunrise (excerpt). Binyon.
Woodyards in the Rain. Marriott.
Wounds. Minty.
Young Waters. *Anonymous.*
Zebra. "Dinesen.

Waterdogs
Hunting. Snyder.

Waterfall (s)
And Then It Rained. Van Doren.
Behind the Waterfall. Welles.
The Canoe. Crawford.
Fireworks. Worth.
Louisa. Wordsworth.
Nature's Charms. Beattie.
Nocturn Cabbage. Sandburg.
Said the Canoe. Crawford.
Spring. Sitwell.
Tarantella. Belloc.

Waterford
The Praise of Waterford (excerpt). *Anonymous.*

Waterlilies
The Dream Queen: Dialogue. Bhasa.
The Gods! The Gods! Lawrence.
The Song of Hiawatha. Longfellow.

Waterloo
Distinction. Howe.
The Drummer Boy of Waterloo. *Anonymous.*
The Plains of Waterloo. *Anonymous.*

Waterman
The Jolly Young Waterman. Dibdin.

Watermelon
The Body Is the Victory and the Defeat of Dreams. Anghelaki-Rooke.
The Old Men. Reznikoff.
To be a mistress. Tsuda.

Warden's Day. Baxter.
Watersprite
The Hurrying Brook.
Blunden.
Waterways
A Kind Inn. Dillon.
Watery
The Day the House Sank.
Urdang.
Grandpa's .45. Ransom.
His Hope or Sheet-Anchor.
Herrick.
History. Gregor.
The Jealous Brothers.
Anonymous.
The Loon. Street.
The Mysterious Music of
Ocean. *Anonymous.*
Roll, Alabama, Roll.
Anonymous.
Spider Crystal Ascension.
Wright.
Three Score and Ten.
Anonymous.
The Wreck of the Royal
Charter. *Anonymous.*
Wattle (s)
Airliner. Webb.
Lichtenberg. Kipling.
Under the Wattle. Sladen.
Wave (d) (s)
The. Underwood.
Adore We the Lord.
Anonymous.
Aeolian Harp. Allingham.
The Anchorsmiths. Dibdin.
Answering a Letter from a
Younger Poet. Ghiselin.
The Assignation. Wright.
Autumn. Tagore.
Autumn Along the Beaches.
Wheelock.
The Balloon Man. Aldis.
The Banks of Newfoundland
(1). *Anonymous.*
The Battle of Valparaiso.
Anonymous.
Battle-Song of the Oregon.
Rice.
Beech Leaves. Reeves.
Bonac. Wheelock.
The Bramble Briar.
Anonymous.
Burn Down the Icons.
Schulman.
A Call to Action. Ch'iu
Chin.
Calm as the Cloudless
Heaven. Wilson.
Christmas 1930. Scruggs.
Clevedon Church. Lang.
Clock. Monro.
Cold Wave Blues. Hicks.
The Columbiad: One Centred
System. Barlow.
A Cyclone at Sea. Hayne.
The Day the House Sank.
Urdang.
The Death of Cuchulain.
Yeats.
The Death of Peter Esson.
Brown.
Death's Blue-Eyed Girl.
Pastan.
The Diary of the Waning
Moon (excerpt). Abutsu.
Elemental. Dillon.
Epigram for the Dead at
Tegea. *Anonymous.*
Erotic Suite (excerpt). Vega.
Eye of God. Tollerud.

The Fall of Niagara.
Brainard.
Father Fisheye. Balakian.
The Fiddler of Dooney.
Yeats.
Freedom. Barlow.
From the Wave. Gunn.
Going to Norway.
Anderson.
The Goldfish. Brown.
Headland. Ghiselin.
Hero and Leander. Marlowe.
Homage to Marcel Proust.
MacGreevy.
I Love Snow and All the
Forms. Shelley.
Icarus. Smithyman.
Impressions. Wilde.
In a Cafe. Dobson.
In Memoriam A.H.H.,
XXXVI. Tennyson.
In the Depths of Night.
Gutierrez Najera.
Indian. Doriot.
The Instrument. Raine.
Izaac Walton, Cotton, and
William Oldways. Landor.
John Webster. Swinburne.
Julian Grenfell. Baring.
July 4th. Waldman.
Keep Thou My Way, O Lord.
Crosby.
Kelp. Dauenhauer.
Lalla Rookh. Moore.
Lament over the Ruins of the
Abbey of Teach Molaga.
Mangan.
Land's End. Coblentz.
Lear. Williams.
The Little Waves of Breffny.
Gore-Booth.
The Living Statue.
Anonymous.
Le Livre Est sur la Table.
Ashbery.
The Lost History Plays: King
Canute (parody).
Sharpless.
The Lovers. Rodgers.
Lullaby. *Anonymous.*
Martyr. Fullerton.
Memento Mori. Halpern.
The Mermaid. *Anonymous.*
Mid-Ocean in War-Time.
Kilmer.
Mighty Sea! Cameleon-Like
Thou Changest. Campbell.
The Morality of Poetry.
Wright.
Morning Express. Sassoon.
A Mourning-Song for
Rangiaho. Herea.
My Woman. Catullus.
The Nameless Doon.
Larminie.
The New Notebook. Banus.
The Nineteenth Century and
After. Yeats.
Ninety-Fifth. *Anonymous.*
Nod. Bennett.
The Northern Star.
Anonymous.
Notes Made in the Piazza San
Marco. Swenson.
Ode to Liberty. Shelley.
Off Saguenay. Bailey.
Old Woman. Smith.
On the Loss of the "Royal
George." Cowper.
On the Subject of Waves...
Grier.
Pilgrimage. Clarke.

Poems of Night. Kinnell.
Postcard from Zamboanga.
Esbensen.
Progress of Evening. Landor.
The Rejected Member's Wife.
Hardy.
Rolling Home. *Anonymous.*
Ronsard. DeFord.
Rosa Rosarum. Robinson.
The Royal George. Cowper.
The Sailor and His Bride.
Anonymous.
The Sailor's Grave. Cook.
Sally My Dear. *Anonymous.*
Salt Water Story. Hugo.
The Seafarer. *Anonymous.*
Seal Rock. Baugh.
Seeing Auden off. Booth.
Sexy Food Stamps. Miller.
Shabbat Morning. Strahan.
The Ships of Arcady.
Ledwidge.
Shore. Miller.
Signature for Tempo.
MacLeish.
Snow. Fry.
The Snow Lies Sprinkled on
the Beach. Bridges.
Song: Time Drawes Neere.
Waldman.
Sonnet: "I watched the sea for
hours blind with sun."
Scott.
Spot-Check at Fifty.
Scannell.
The Swan Song of Parson
Avery. Whittier
The Swimmer. Layton.
Tahola. Hugo.
Terminus. Emerson
To a Courtesan a Thousand
Years Dead. Eldridge.
To Mackinnon of Strath.
Lom.
To the Poet Wordsworth.
Hemans.
To the Returning Brave.
Johnson.
Toward Winter. *Anonymous.*
Upon Julia Washing Herself
in the River. Herrick.
Venus Transiens. Lowell.
Voice and Address. Palmer.
Voice from Danang.
Redshaw.
Walking Along the Sea of
Galilee. Knut.
The Whaleman's Song.
Anonymous.
The White Canoe. Sullivan.
Wind and Wave. Stoddard.
Winter Has Come.
Anonymous.
The Yachts. Williams.
Waving
B. Eigner.
Chicken. Etter.
The Inside Chance. Piercy.
Morning from My Office
Window. Wood.
Neighbors. Evans.
The Scythe. Kanabus.
The Waving of the Corn.
Lanier.
Wax (ed) (en) (y)
49th & 5th, December 13.
Jacobsen.
Easter Monday. Rossetti.
Jason and Medea. Gower.
Jubilate Herbis. Farber.
Kindergarten. Schmitz.

Lenin (excerpt). Wellesley.
A Poem against Rats.
Levinson.
The Sirens. Finkel.
Stings. Plath.
When the Nightingale Sings.
Anonymous.
Way (s)
Aerosol. Witt.
After Reading Twenty Years
of Grantland Rice. Skene.
After the Quarrel. Dunbar.
After Tsang Chih. Notley.
Alabaster Boxes.
Anonymous.
Alcohol. MacNeice.
The Alphabet of Aristotle.
Benet.
Arabs. Kreymborg.
The Ass in the Lion's Skin.
Aesop.
At the Tomb of Rachel.
Yehoash.
Ballad. Simic.
Ballata of Love's Power.
Cavalcanti.
Bar Not the Door. Campion.
Be Patient. Klingle.
Boundaries. Spear.
Caelica, XCVI. Greville.
Cape Coast Castle Revisited.
Hall-Evans.
Certain Choices. Shelton.
The Child. Popham.
Choice. Morgan.
Chorus: "If I drink water
while this doth last."
Peacock.
The Christ. Oxenham.
A City Eclogue. "J.
Clear the Way. Montague.
The Cloud-Mobile. Swenson.
Columbus at the Convent.
Trowbridge.
Contrast. Duggan.
The Country North of
Belleville. Purdy.
The Creditor. MacNeice.
Death and Doctor Hornbook.
Burns.
Death and the Bridge.
Lowell.
Domestic: Climax. Moore.
The Draft Horse. Frost.
The Eel. Nash.
Eli the Thatcher.
Rothenstein.
Emblem. Quarles.
The End of the Way. Cole.
Epigram: "If you see someone
beautiful." Adaios.
Epitaph. Logue.
Epitaph for the Race of Man.
Millay.
Eurydice. Gregg.
The Exhortation of a Father
to His Children. Smith.
Ezekiel Saw the Wheel.
Anonymous.
A Faded Letter. Fischer.
The Fall of Richmond.
Melville.
The Fear. Abercrombie.
First Pathways. Lysaght.
The Fist. Walcott.
The Footpath Way.
Hinkson.
Four Folk-Songs in Hokku
Form, 1. *Anonymous.*
Four for Sir John Davies.
Roethke.
Free Will. Clark.

From Far, from Eve and Morning. Housman.
God's Ways Are Strange. Bruner.
Grandmother, Rocking. Merriam.
Harvest. Cortissoz.
Hay Scuttle. Morgan.
He Lifted from the Dust. Smith.
He Singeth in the Underworld. Book of the Dead.
I Have a King. Dickinson.
I Set Forth Hopeful. Lalleswari.
I Spread Out unto Thee My Hand. Ainsworth.
I Think of Him as One Who Fights. Branch.
Impotence. Knight.
In a Motion. Chester.
In Hardwood Groves. Frost.
In Passing. Jonas.
In the Dark. Higginson.
In the Heart of Jesus. O Dalaigh.
In the Morning All Over. Stafford.
The Injury. Williams.
Inscription. Elliott.
January Morning. Williams.
Journeys. Snyder.
June. Hopper.
Keeping Victory. Isenhour.
Kindly Unhitch That Star, Buddy. Nash.
Lazy Lou. Dodge.
Life after Death. Thomas.
Lights Out. Thomas.
Limerick: "There was a young lady from Cork." Nash.
Liszt. Bentley.
Little Thomas. Evans.
Long Walks in the Afternoon. Gibson.
Looking for a Country under Its Original Name. McElroy.
Love Will Find Out the Way. Anonymous.
The Lyttel Boy. Field.
Magic Worlds. Nalungiaq.
Man and Wife Is One Flesh. Deacon.
Le Marais du Cygne. Whittier.
The Marigold. Wither.
May Trees in a Storm. Grigson.
Mexico City Blues: 225th Chorus. Kerouac.
A Morning Hymn. Beaumont.
Mother Dear, O! Pray for Me. Anonymous.
The Mother's Hymn. Bryant.
My Cousin German Came From France. Anonymous.
My Cross. Cocke.
My Horses. Jaszi.
Not My Best Side. Fanthorpe.
Notes on a Life to Be Lived. Warren.
Nothing Between. Tindley.
Now the Holy Lamp of Love. MacDonogh.
Number 29. Wallace.
O Fly My Soul. Shirley.

Oh, My Good Lord, Show Me de Way. Anonymous.
The Old Stories. Frumkin.
The Olive Tree. Baring-Gould.
On City Streets. Bruner.
On His Mistress Drown'd. Spratt.
The Open Door. Coolidge.
An Open Secret. Mason.
Paradise Lost. Milton.
The Pastor. Summers.
The Phi Beta Kappa Poem. Lattimore.
The Pilgrim. Embury.
A Poem of Sir Walter Rawleighs. Ralegh.
Poems, X. O'Connor.
The Pony Blues. House.
Prayer. Bynner.
Psalms, CXLVII. Smart.
Quiet Things. Crowell.
Recompense. Waterman.
The Resident Worm. Hayford.
Resignation. Longfellow.
Resolve. Gilman.
The River of Stars. Noyes.
Sam Bass. Anonymous.
See-Saw, Sacradown. Anonymous.
A Sergeant's Prayer. Brodie.
Sestina. Justice.
Shelley's Arethusa Set to New Measures. Duncan.
A Shooting Song. Rands.
The Sins of Youth. Vaux.
The Snow. Dyment.
Something in Common. Church.
Sometimes on My Way Back Down to the Block. Cruz.
A Song: "Hark! 'tis Freedom that calls, come, patriots, awake!" Anonymous.
Song in the Wood. Fletcher.
Sonnet: "Patience, hard thing! the hard thing but to pray." Hopkins.
Sorrow seldom killeth any. Davison.
Southern Summer. Stuart.
Spring. Johns.
The Star. Taylor.
Stepping Westward. Wordsworth.
Still Century. Paulin.
Strength, Love, Light. Robert II.
Superballs. Clark.
There Were an Old and Wealthy Man. Anonymous.
These Green-Going-to-Yellow. Bell.
They. Sassoon.
The Thirty-One Camels. Korn.
This Is the Way the Ladies Ride. Mother Goose.
Thoughts of a Young Girl. Ashbery.
The Tint I Cannot Take Is Best. Dickinson.
To a Child. O'Conor.
To Our Lady, the Ark of the Covenants. Larsson.
Toe'osh: A Laguna Coyote Story. Silko.
The Torch of Love Dispels the Gloom. Landor.
Translation. Lesser.

Trials. Troy.
Troubles of the Day. Barnes.
The Truth from Above. Anonymous.
Try the Uplook. Anonymous.
The Twa Dogs. Burns.
Two Sons. Mac An Bhaird.
The Unforgiven. Robinson.
The Unknown. Davidson.
A View of Jersey. Field.
The Way My Ideas Think Me. Villa.
The Way, the Truth, and the Life. Parker.
The Way to Arcady. Bunner.
The Way We Live Now. Dana.
When Any Mortal. Cummings.
Where There's a Will There's a Way. Cook.
The Wild Garden. Pope.
The Wisdom of Folly. Fowler.
With the Most Susceptible Element, the Mind, Already Turned... Benton.
You Want to Go Back. Atwood.
Zagonyi. Boker.

Wayfarer (s)
I Am the Way. Meynell.
The Question Whither. Meredith.

Wayside
The Milking-Maid. Rossetti.
Old. Hoyt.

Wayward
Advice to a Lover. Jellicoe.
Let There Be Light. Vories.
To Jesus of Nazareth. Knowles.
Wedlock. Grahame.
The Witch in the Glass. Piatt.

We
Communion. Snider.
The Day. Bynner.
The Emancipators. Jarrell.
For Our Sakes. Wilde.
A Glimpse. Whitman.
Lord, Many Times Thou Pleased Art. Wither.
The Monk in the Kitchen. Branch.
One More New Botched Beginning. Spender.
Ring-a-Ring o' Roses. Anonymous.
Snow in the Suburbs. Hardy.
Vale. Ciardi.

Weak (est) (ness)
Blessing, and Honor. Bonar.
Californy Stage. Anonymous.
Come to Me, Beloved. Dolben.
The Doubter's Prayer. Bronte.
A Drinking-Song... Wycherley.
An Early Christian. Brough.
English Poetry. Daniel.
Flowers for the Altar. Dolben.
The Frailty. Cowley.
Jesus. Parker.
Joy May Kill. Michelangelo.
Last Words on Greece. Byron.
Letter from Paparua. Newbury.

Limerick: "I know a young girl who can speak." Webber.
The Loss of the Birkenhead. Doyle.
A Miltonic Sonnet for Mr. Johnson... Wilbur.
Myfanwy. Betjeman.
O Pity Our Small Size. Rosenbaum.
Pacifists. Woodcock.
Peer Gynt. Sorley.
A Penguin. Herford.
Pick a Quarrel, Go to War. Auden.
Sonnet VII. Sharp.
They Never Quite Leave Us. Sangster.
To a Severe Nun. Merton.
La Vita Nuova. Dante Alighieri.
The Waste of War. Stidger.
The Weakest Thing. Browning.
With All My Heart, Jehovah, I'll Confess. Ainsworth.
Ye Simple Men. Blackie.

Weal
Fortune. Anonymous.
Jesus, in Sickness and in Pain. Gallaudet.

Wealth (y)
Advice to Hotheads. Isaac.
Ambition. Pope.
The Battle of King's Mountain. Anonymous.
Be Kind. Courtney.
Bowery. Ignatow.
The Cock Crows in the Morn. Anonymous.
Columbus and the Mayflower. Milnes.
The Contentment of Willoughby. Alexander.
The Deserted Village. Goldsmith.
Freedom. Ibn Ezra.
Goldenrod. Eastman.
Joy of Life. Ibn Ezra.
The Kitten and the Falling Leaves. Wordsworth.
A Little Brother of the Rich. Martin.
Lord Finchley. Belloc.
The Mouldering Vine. Anonymous.
Night's Fall. Graham.
None Can Experience Stint. Dickinson.
Of a Rich Miser. Turberville.
On the Detraction which Followed upon My Writing Certain Treatises. Milton.
On Vital Statistics. Belloc.
Pindarick Elegy upon the Renowned Mr. Samuel Willard. Danforth.
Prince Alfrid's Itinerary (excerpt). Anonymous.
The Quiet Mind. Anonymous.
Right Apprehension. Traherne.
Rune of Riches. Converse.
Scum o' the Earth. Schauffler.
Some Things You Cannot Will to Men. Isenhour.
Songe betwene the Quenes Majestie and Englande. Anonymous.

Wealth

Sonnets, LXVII: "Ah
  wherefore with infection
  should he live."
  Shakespeare.
To a Covetous Churl.   May.
To My Friend.   Campbell.
Two Songs in Praise of
  Steingerd, 2.
  Ogmundarson.
Venomous thorns that are so
  sharp and keen.   Wyatt.
What She Said.   Okkur
  Macatti.
Youth.   Salkeld.

Wean (ed)

At the Altar-Rail.   Hardy.
God and the Soul: Nature and
  the Child.   Spalding.

Weapon (s)

Beauty.   Stanley.
Homosexual Sonnets.
  Pitchford.
Jack and Roger.   Franklin.
Luchow's and After.
  Sissman.
Nearly Everybody Loves
  Harvey Martin.   Barney.
The Objection to Being
  Stepped On.   Frost.
Poems from the Greek
  Anthology (excerpt).
  Asclepiades.
Poetry Workshop in a Reform
  School.   Adcock.
Scissor-Man.   MacBeth.
Sound from Leopardi.
  Berkson.
To Pertinax Cob.   Jonson.
A Way of Life.   Nemerov.

Wear (ing) (s)

Beer.   Arnold.
Bonnie Wee Thing.   Burns.
Courtship.   Corbin.
A Day in Autumn.   Thomas.
Dedicatory Ode: They Say
  That in the Unchanging
  Place.   Belloc.
Dreams of Auschwitz.
  Slutsky.
Freaks of Fashion.   Rossetti.
I Hoed and Trenched and
  Weeded.   Housman.
If my nipples were to drip
  milk.   Sappho.
If Wishes Were Horses.
  Anonymous.
The Lamenting Maid.
  Anonymous.
Lan Nguyen: The Uniform of
  Death 1971.   Mura.
The Leaf-Makers.   Stewart.
Limerick: "I don't give a...."
  Burgess.
Limerick: "There was an
  Archdeacon who said."
  Anonymous.
Lower Forms of Life.
  Winter.
The Mould.   Cromwell.
New Shoes.   Wilkins.
The Night is Freezing Fast.
  Housman.
Nothing to Wear.   Butler.
On a Fair Woman.   Money-
  Coutts.
Red Riding Hood at the
  Acropolis.   Sklarew.
Regina Confessorum.
  Anonymous.
Said the Rose.   Miles.
Sam's World.   Cornish.
Shoes.   Robinson.

Six Divine Circles.   Ghai.
Vocation.   Herzberg.
Wc Wear the Mask.
  Dunbar.
Were You Ever in
  Dumbarton?   Anonymous.
With a Gift of Rings.
  Graves.
Wonder.   Traherne.

Weary

Adam's Curse.   Yeats.
Adjuration.   Wheeler.
Armageddon.   Ransom.
The Ashtabula Disaster.
  Moore.
Asleep.   Winter.
At Delos.   Scott.
Autumn.   Anonymous.
Caelica, CVII.   Greville.
Death and Night.   Kenyon.
Don't Grow Weary, Boys.
  Anonymous.
A Dubious Night.   Wilbur.
A Fable for Critics.   Lowell.
The Faerie's Child.   Irwin.
Fall.   Melinescu.
Flathead and Nez Perce Sin-
  ka-ha.   Lewis.
Flowers for the Altar.
  Dolben.
For Every Day.   Havergal.
Fox.   Dyment.
Freedom For the Mind.
  Garrison
The Garden of Proserpine.
  Swinburne.
Heartbreak Road.   Cone.
Helen of Kirconnell.
  Anonymous.
Hmmm, 15.   Scalapino.
Hymn to Darkness.   Norris.
"If care do cause men cry..."
  Surrey.
Letter of a Mother.   Warren.
Like Weary Trees.   Glatstein.
A Little While, a Little While.
  Bronte.
The Name of Jesus.   Newton.
Night Flight.   Whalley.
O Earth! Art Thou Not
  Weary?   Dorr.
Oh! Weary Mother.   Pain.
The Old-Time Cowboy.
  Anonymous.
Our Light Afflictions.
  Anonymous.
The Pipe.   Squire.
Poets.   Flexner.
Resolution.   More.
Safety at Forty; or, An
  Abecedarian Takes a Walk.
  Sissman.
Scorned.   Smith.
Soft Falls the Sweet Evening.
  Clare.
Song: "I was so chill, and
  overworn, and sad."
  Wickham.
Summer Longings.
  MacCarthy.
Tears in My Heart That
  Weeps.   Verlaine.
The Thrusting of It.   Burns.
To a Lady Troubled by
  Insomnia.   Adams.
To Heaven.   Jonson.
To My Father.   Tree.
Vala; or, The Four Zoas.
  Blake.
Venice.   Symons.
A Veteran Cowboy's
  Ruminations.   Kuykendall.

Victory Bells.   Conkling.
Waiting for Death.   Gebirtig.
When the Sleepy Man Comes.
  Roberts.
Written at Florence.   Blunt.
Written in the Beginning of
  Mezeray's History of
  France.   Prior.

Weather (s)

Altarwise by Owl-Light.
  Thomas.
Bagpipe Music.   MacNeice.
The Ballad of Halfmoon Bay
  (excerpt).   Sinclair.
Buffalo Boy.   Anonymous.
The Butterfly.   Spenser.
Cold's the Wind.   Dekker.
Country Hirings.
  Anonymous.
Covered Bridge.   Coffin.
The Cure All.   Lee
Deck the Halls.   Anonymous.
Disillusionment of Ten
  O'Clock.   Stevens.
A Fanfare for the Makers.
  MacNeice.
Garment.   Hughes.
The Great Bear Lake
  Meditations (excerpt).
  Yates.
Hop Up, My Ladies.
  Anonymous.
Hopper's "Nighthawks."
  (1942).   Sadoff.
I Come Home Wanting to
  Touch Everyone.   Dunn.
If the Robin Sings in the
  Bush.   Anonymous.
In a Shuttered Room I Roast.
  Thomas.
Internal Injuries.   Warren.
Ironwood.   Domanski.
Links.   Pau-Llosa.
The Miner's Lament.
  "Twain.
New York in August.   Davie.
The Night There Was
  Dancing in the Streets.
  Olson.
The North of Wales.   Morris.
Now Christmas Is Come.
  Anonymous.
October's Bright Blue
  Weather.   Jackson.
Ode to the Norther.
  Chittenden.
Old Man at a Cricket Match.
  Nicholson.
The Other Side.   Heaney.
A Poem to Explain
  Everything about a Certain
  Day in Vermont.   Taggard.
Post-Modern Literature.
  Moure.
Riding Song.   Schneider.
Rock (excerpt).   Raine.
Scenario.   Savage.
Security.   Hamburger.
The Self-Slaved.   Kavanagh.
Southern Exposures.
  Murray.
A Summer Gone.   Moss.
Telephone Directory.
  Crosby.
To Helen Frankenthaler of
  Circe, 1974.   Cherner.
Towards the Vanishing Point.
  Lehman.
Tree at My Window.   Frost.
The Unwilling Guest: An
  Urban Dialogue.   Gregory.

Views of Our Sphere.
  Sandeen.
Where I Walk in Nebraska.
  Westerfield.
Winter's Onset from an
  Alienated Point of View.
  Dugan.
Work Room.   Elmslie.
Yuki.   Fenollosa.

Weathercock (s)

Evangeline.   Longfellow.
Squall.   Moore.

Weathervanes

Horse-Girl.   Petroski.

Weave (r) (s)

Buckeye Jim.   Anonymous.
The Clavichord.   Sarton.
Death Bed.   Kinsella.
The Devil's Nine Questions.
  Anonymous.
Electra.   Williams.
Fishing Season.   Vallis.
Goodwill, Inc.   Schmitz.
A Is for Alpha: Alpha Is for
  A.   Aiken.
The Master Weaver.
  Anonymous.
Silex Scintillans.   Vaughan.
Spider.   Lattimore.
Two Lovers Sitting on a
  Tomb.   Hill.
The Weaver.   Burleigh.
Weaver's Life.   Anonymous.
Wil the Merry Weaver, and
  Charity the Chamber-Maid.
  Anonymous.
The Work of the Weavers.
  Anonymous.

Weaving

The Loom of Dreams.
  Symons.
The Small Square.
  Andresen.
Weavers.   Heine.

Web (s)

Abiku.   Soyinka.
Featherstone's Doom.
  Hawker.
For the Sun Declined.
  Lamdan.
The Journal of Albion
  Moonlight (excerpt).
  Patchen.
Liberation.   Stone.
Moving.   McFatter.
My Grandfather in Search of
  Moonshine.   Lyon.
Personal History: For My
  Son.   Todd.
Snow Country Weavers.
  Welch.
South Shore Line.
  Schlesinger.
Speech for the Repeal of the
  McCarran Act.   Wilbur.
Spider.   Farber.
That Is Not Indifference.
  Hanson.
The Weaver.   Burleigh.
The Witch.   Gibson.

Wed (ded) (ding)

Abenamar, Abenamar.
  Anonymous.
The Aged Wino's Counsel to
  a Young Man on the Brink
  of Marriage.   Kennedy.
Although Tormented.   Ben
  Judah.
The Angel in the House.
  Patmore.
Autumn Imagined.   Davie.
Bagpipes.   Anonymous.

The Ballad of Sally in our
Alley. Carey.
Bingo. *Anonymous.*
A Black Wedding Song.
Brooks.
Blancheflour and Jellyflorice.
Anonymous.
The Book Rises Out of the
Fire. Jabes.
The Cherry Trees. Thomas.
A Country Wedding.
Anonymous.
The Crafty Farmer.
Anonymous.
Dion of Tarsus. *Anonymous.*
The Drowsy Sleeper (B vers.).
Anonymous.
Elegy. Maclaurin.
Epigram: "Now art thou fair,
Diodorus." Strato.
The Faery Reaper.
Buchanan.
Fair Annie. *Anonymous.*
I Peeped through the
Window. *Anonymous.*
I Went My Sunday Mornings
Rounds. Clare.
In the Spring. Barnes.
Jack Tar. *Anonymous.*
The Jolly Young Sailor and
the Beautiful Queen.
Anonymous.
Last May a Braw Wooer.
Burns.
Like a Laverock in the Lift.
Ingelow.
Love and Marriage.
Mathew.
The Lover Freed from the
Gallows. *Anonymous.*
Modern Love, XXXV.
Meredith.
Molly Bawn and Brian Oge.
Anonymous.
My True Love. Eastwick.
A Pastoral. Marzials.
Peggu's Wedding. Brown.
Pontoosuce. Melville.
The proverb reporteth, no
man can deny...
Anonymous.
A Question of Form and
Content. Stallworthy.
The Ring. Pack.
Robin Hood and the Prince of
Aragon. *Anonymous.*
The Rock. Eliot.
Searching for Lambs.
Anonymous.
She Moved through the Fair.
Colum.
Siilenboor. *Anonymous.*
The Simple Ploughboy.
Anonymous.
Sir Helmer Blaa and His
Bride's Brothers.
Anonymous.
Snow in the City. Siegel.
The Souldiers Farewel to his
Love. *Anonymous.*
Spring. Rodgers.
They Came to the Wedding.
Deutsch.
Thomas o Yonderdale.
Anonymous.
Thro' Grief and Thro'
Danger. Moore.
To Clarissa. Nugent.
The Touch-Stone. Bishop.
A Tryst. Moulton.
Two Words: A Wedding.
Nichol.

Young Peggy. *Anonymous.*
Wed (ded) (ding) (s)
Moggy's Wedding. Thatcher.
Wedding cake
Winter Time. Stevenson.
Wedding gown
The Long White Seam.
Ingelow.
Wedding ring (s)
Good Bishop Valentine.
Farjeon.
The Lucky Marriage.
Blackburn.
The Single Girl. *Anonymous.*
Yes. Blackmore.
Wedge
At the Woodpile. Henri.
The Drenching Night Drags
On. O Rathaille.
Fall Again. Coursen.
Wedlock
At the Wedding March.
Hopkins.
Epithalamium for Stella and
Violentilla: Why Do You
Dally So? Statius Publius
Papinius.
A Farmer's Son So Sweet.
Anonymous.
The Lightning Flash.
Anonymous.
Ode: "That I have often been
in love, deep love."
Wolcot.
Shakespearean Soliloquy in
Progress: "To wed or not to
wed?" (parody).
Anonymous.
The Swimming Lady.
Anonymous.
Two Lovers Discoursing.
Anonymous.
Wednesday
Could You Spare Some Time
for Jesus? Knickman.
The Sign of the Bonny Blue
Bell. *Anonymous.*
Spouse. Bynner.
Summer Concert.
Whittemore
Thursday. Millay.
Wee
Birds. O'Neill.
Chanson Innocent.
Cummings.
The False Knight on the
Road. *Anonymous.*
The Fause Knicht upon the
Road. *Anonymous.*
Madchen Mit Dem Rothen
Mundchen. Heine.
Round About, Round About.
Anonymous.
This Little Pig Went to
Market. *Anonymous.*
The Three Little Pigs.
Gatty.
Thumb Bold. *Anonymous.*
Tommy Tibule. *Anonymous.*
When a Ring's Around the
Moon. Carr.
Weed (s)
Above These Cares. Millay.
The Actor. Snapp.
The Auld House. Nairne.
The Birth of a Shark.
Wevill.
Coming Suddenly to the Sea.
Dudek.
Continuum. Levertov.
Corn Canon. Stevenson.
Dead. Coghill.

The Disordering. Yates.
Easily onward, thorough
flowers and weed... Keats.
Endymion. Keats.
Epigram: "Neither in idleness
consume thy days."
Landor.
Fair Weather. Parker.
The Flower. Speed.
The Flower. Tennyson.
For Whom, Pyrrha? Horace.
A Gentle Heart: Two.
Sherwin.
A Gentle Wind. Fu Hsuan.
Gone. Pomeroy.
I'm Just a Stranger Here,
Heaven Is My Home.
Clemmons.
In These Dissenting Times.
Walker.
Incantation to Get Rid of a
Sometime Friend.
DiPasquale.
Inversnaid. Hopkins.
Invocation. Drewry.
Judge Somers. Masters.
A Lament. Avison.
Lament. Chamberlain.
The Letter. Reznikoff.
My Aunt. Hughes.
My Birthday. Crabbe.
Old Miniatures. Vroman.
On an Old Muff. Locker-
Lampson.
Reapers. Toomer.
Reflective. Ammons.
Sailing upon the River.
Crabbe.
Seeds. Snyder.
Song: "I know that any weed
can tell." Ginsberg.
A Song of Sickness.
Tangikuku.
Sonnets, XCIV: "They that
have power to hurt, and
will do none."
Shakespeare.
Stepfather Blues. Williams.
Supervising Examinations.
Lucy.
To the Laggards. Bovshover.
The Unknown Soldier.
Wagner.
The Untended Field. Hillyer.
War-Baby. Lawrence.
We Hurry On, Nor Passing
Note. Dolben.
What Do They Say. Snyder.
Where or When. Whalen.
A Widow's Weeds. De La
Mare.
The Womanhood. Brooks.
Week (s)
Forever and a Day. Aldrich.
In the Week When Christmas
Comes. Farjeon.
Miriam Tazewell. Ransom.
My Name Is George
Nathaniel Curzon.
Anonymous.
On the Island. Brutus.
On the Meanness of Lord
Eldon. *Anonymous.*
Pedro. Hoffman.
Sneeze on a Monday, You
Sneeze for Danger.
Anonymous.
Speech to Those Who Say
Comrade. MacLeish.
The Statesman. Belloc.
Week-End. Munro.

A Week of Doodle.
Whittemore.
You Take My Hand And.
Atwood.
Weekend (s)
On a Seven-Day Diary.
Dugan.
Signs. Martin.
Weep (ing) (s) (wept)
Abdullah Bulbul Amir.
Anonymous.
Adjuration. Wheeler.
After Tschaikowsky. Gould.
Age Not to Be Rejected.
Anonymous.
Allergy. Gibson.
Alone. Bialik.
Amoretti, XVIII. Spenser.
And Jesus Wept. Brydges.
Another Song of the Same
Woman, to Some
Partridges... Florencia del
Pinar.
Armistice Day.
Montgomery.
The Arrow. Yeats.
At Dawn. Symons.
At Dawn the Light Will
Come. Van Wyk Louw.
At Last. Stoddard.
Autumn. Rodgers.
Back to the Ghetto.
Glatstein.
Ballad of the Ten Casino
Dancers. Meireles.
Ballata: Of His Lady among
Other Ladies. Cavalcanti.
The Banks of Dee.
Anonymous.
Bar Mitzvah. Orlen.
The Barber. Gray.
The Beast. Roethke.
Behold, the Grave. Crane.
Berries. De La Mare.
The Blessed Damozel.
Rossetti.
The Blithe Mask. Fuguet.
Bubba Esther, 1888.
Whitman.
Bufo. Pope.
But I Shall Weep. Redpath.
Cafe in Warsaw. Ginsberg.
The Children of the Poor.
Hugo.
Chivalry. Russell.
Christmas 1930. Scruggs.
Christmas Eve. Kooser.
Clerk Saunders. *Anonymous.*
Closing Piece. Rilke.
Cock-Crow. Herrick.
Comforting Lines.
Anonymous.
A Considered Reply to a
Child. Price.
Cradle Song. *Anonymous.*
Crying. Kinnell.
The Dark Memory.
Wheelock.
David's Lament for Jonathan.
Abelard.
The Dead Bride. Hill.
A Death in Hospital.
Lehmann.
Diana. Constable.
Diary. Solitary Moon. De
Clue.
Dirge Written for a Drama.
Beddoes.
Disarmed. Searing.
Divine Compassion.
Whittier.

Don't You Weep after Me. *Anonymous.*
Dorcas. Macdonald.
The Duke of Grafton. *Anonymous.*
Embarcation. Hardy.
Epigram: "On parent knees, a naked new-born child." Jones.
Epipsychidion. Shelley.
Epitaph: "I was buried near this dyke." Blake.
Epitaph on the Politician Himself. Belloc.
Esthonian Bridal Song. Herder.
Eyes and Tears. Marvell.
Falling Asleep. Serraillier.
The Felled Plane Tree. Hajnal.
Field Day. Rodgers.
For Peter. Gerlach.
Gethsemane. Betham-Edwards.
Go Tell Aunt Rhody. *Anonymous.*
God's Will. Munger.
Goya. Aiken.
Greater Love. Owen.
Grief. Browning.
Hark, All Ye Lovely Saints. *Anonymous.*
The Harvest of the Sea. McCrae.
Has Sorrow Thy Young Days Shaded? Moore.
He and I. Rossetti.
Headlined in Heaven. Grano.
Helen Grown Old. Lewis.
Her Epitaph. Parsons
House-Mates. Gellert.
How Sleep the Brave! Collins.
How We Learn. Bonar.
The Hunting of the Snark. "Carroll.
Hymns for the Amusement of Children. Smart.
I Dreamed That I Was Old. Kunitz.
I Love but Thee. Heine.
I Walk on the River at Dawn. Hart.
I Weep. Grimke.
In Lombardy. Revell.
In Mortem Venerabilis Andreae Prout Carmen. Mahony.
Intrusion. Levertov.
Irish History. Allingham.
The Irish Mother in the Penal Days. Banim.
It Was a' for Our Rightfu' King. Burns.
January Eclogue. Spenser.
Jesus, Child and Lord. Faber.
Joe Tinker. Hall.
The Jokesmith's Vacation. Marquis.
Keen Thyself, Poor Wight. Keating.
King Lear. Shakespeare.
Kolendy for Christmas. *Anonymous.*
Kore. Pound.
Lalla Rookh. Moore.
Lament. Stroud.
Lament for Adonis. Browning.

The Last Words. Maeterlinck.
The Legend of Waukulla. Butterworth.
The Light of the World. Alquit.
Lines for a Drawing of Our Lady of the Night. Thompson.
Little Gray Songs from St. Joseph's, XLVII. Norton.
Little Rosewood Casket. *Anonymous.*
The Lonely. Russell.
A Lost World. Graves.
Love Song. Wylie.
The Lover Mourns for the Loss of Love. Yeats.
The Maiden's Complaint. *Anonymous.*
Making Contact. Manifold.
Margaret to Dolcino. Kingsley.
Marvell's Garden. Webb.
Mason Jar. Steinberg.
Meditations of a Hindu Prince. Lyall.
The Messenger. Noyes.
Micheal Mac Liammoir. Durcan.
Mine Eyes Beheld the Blessed Pity. Dante Alighieri.
Moon-Madness. Starbuck.
Mother Wept. Skipsey.
The Mountain Woman. Heyward.
Mourning. Marvell.
Mutability. Shelley.
My Best Clothes. Netser.
The Need of Being Versed in Country Things. Frost.
The New Jewish Hospital at Hamburg. Heine.
Night Winds. Crapsey.
O Grief! *Anonymous.*
O Holy Water. Ruddock.
O Mary, Don't You Weep, Don't You Mourn. *Anonymous.*
O What if the Fowler. Dalmon.
Oh, Mary Don't You Weep. *Anonymous.*
Old Man Told Me. Henson.
On a Child. Landor.
On a Wife. Coutts.
On Friendship. Whitehead.
On Gustavus Adolphus, King of Sweden. Roe.
On the Death of a Lady's Owl. Mendes.
On the Death of Sir Philip Sidney. Constable.
On the Fifth Anniversary of Bluma Sach's Death. D'Ambrosio.
Orphic Interior. Sinisgalli.
Outside the Supermarket. Fuller.
Penitential Psalm. *Anonymous.*
Pharaoh's Army Got Drownded (with music). *Anonymous.*
Phyllis. Russell.
Piano. Lawrence.
Piers Plowman (excerpt). *Anonymous.*
The Place of the Fian Is Bare Tonight. *Anonymous.*
The Portrait. Lytton.
Pretty Molly. *Anonymous.*

Pruning. Philips.
The Recessional. Roberts.
La Rue de la Montagne Sainte-Genevieve. Dudley.
The Runaway. Hicky.
Saturn Fallen. Keats.
She Dried Her Tears. Bronte.
Silex Scintillans. Vaughan.
Sleet. MacCaig.
So Live, So Love, So Use That Fragile Hour. Stevenson.
Song: "Shepherd, who can pass such wrong." Young.
Sonnet, XXIV: "Don't scold me, Ladies, if I have loved." Labé.
Sonnet: "As when, to one who long hath watched, the morn." Bampfylde.
Sonnet: Oft o'er My Brain. Coleridge.
Sonnets. Hillyer.
Spring 1940. Auden.
The Stolen Child. Yeats.
Summer Is Ended. Rossetti.
Synekdechestai. Schmid.
Tears for Sale. Speyer.
There Is No Nearer Nearness. Cha Liang-cheng.
The Thousand and One Nights: Her Rival for Aziza. *Anonymous.*
Three Rimas, 3. Becquer.
To a Spaniel. Landor.
To His Wife. Skelton.
To Manon. Blunt.
To the Reader. Oakes.
To the River Itchin, near Winton. Bowles.
To You Building the New House. Sachs.
The Tropics in New York. McKay.
Twelfth Night. Shakespeare.
Two. Canzoneri.
Upon Julia Weeping. Herrick.
Vagabonds. Hughes.
The Village Tudda. Patchen.
The Violet and the Rose. Skipsey.
La Vita Nuova. Dante Alighieri.
Voices in the Winter. McCullough.
Walking Around. Neruda.
Warrior's Song. Austin.
The Watchers. Rukeyser.
We Lay Un Down to Sleep. Moulton.
We'll Go No More A-Roving. Henley.
We Woke Together. Brennan.
The Weeping Willow. *Anonymous.*
The Well. Brown.
Whereat Erewhile I Wept, I Laugh. Dickinson.
Whilst Eccho Cryes, What Shall Become of Mee. Constable.
White Roses. Fabbri.
Wild Cherry. Nicholl.
Willow Bend and Weep. Johnson.
With Timrels. *Anonymous.*
Woman. *Anonymous.*
Your Passing, Fleet Passing. Eliyia.

Weeping willow (s)
The Laughing Willow. Herford.
Listen to the Mocking Bird. Hawthorne.
Vernal Equinox. Stone.
Weigh (ed) (ing) (s)
Equipment. Dunbar.
Farewell to Van Gogh. Tomlinson.
I before E. *Anonymous.*
Man O'War Bird. Walcott.
Mary, Queen of Scots. Bell.
Mene, Mene, Tekel, Upharsin. Cawein.
Nursery Rhyme: "Judge, judge, tell the judge." *Anonymous.*
Red lotus incense fades on the jewelled curtain. Li Ch'ing-chao.
Weight (ed) (less) (s)
Ancestral Weight. Storni.
The Argument Begins with A. Thesen.
Breaking Point. Auxier.
A Chinese Vase. Hirsch.
Conquistador. MacLeish.
Could Mortal Lip Divine. Dickinson.
The Country of a Thousand Years of Peace. Merrill.
The Crane. Tomlinson.
The Enchanted Knight. Muir.
The Grauballe Man. Heaney.
The Hands. Harrison.
Hoc Est Corpus. Comfort.
A Hot-Weather Song. Marquis.
I Keep to Myself Such Measures. Creeley.
In a Season of Unemployment. Avison.
In Spain. Wyatt.
Juggler. Wilbur.
Listens, Too (parody). Berry.
No Sense Grieving. Rubin.
Now That Your Shoulders Reach My Shoulders. Francis.
On the Edition of Mr. Pope's Works with a Commentary and Notes. Edwards.
Paul Laurence Dunbar. Hayden.
Plantation Bitters. *Anonymous.*
Prayers Must Have Poise. Herrick.
Recollection. Donnelly.
Science as Art. Seidman.
Sindhi Woman. Stallworthy.
The Slave Auction. Harper.
The Song against Grocers. Chesterton.
A Tail of the See. Corbett.
Too happy time dissolves itself. Dickinson.
A Typical 6:00 P.M. in the Fun House. Berrigan.
Urn Burial. Hughes.
Variations on a Theme. Williams.
Weight (s)
The Garden. Gluck.
Weird
Limerick: "There was a young man with a beard." Jaffray.

The Radiance. Kabir.
Welcome (d) (r) (s)
Another Year. Smith.
Contented wi' Little. Burns.
A Dainty Song. Ramsay.
Dame Wiggins of Lee.
    Anonymous.
Deacon Morgan. Madgett.
December 26. Hoffman.
Elegy for Former Students.
    Miner.
Epitaph on James Grieve,
    Laird of Boghead. Burns.
Evening. Cowper.
The Farm on the Links.
    Watson.
For Gabriel. Firestone.
Have You Been at Carrick?
    Anonymous.
Homeward Bound. Tooker.
The Indian's Welcome to the
    Pilgrim Fathers.
    Sigourney.
Inland Passages, I: The Long
    Hunter. Berry.
Ire. Thomas.
Jack Frost. Thaxter.
Jacques Cartier. McGee.
Lachrimae Amantis. Hill.
A Letter from the Country to
    a Friend in Town.
    Oldham.
Life Is Like a Mountain
    Railroad. Anonymous.
Limerick: "There was a young
    lady whose bonnet." Lear.
Little Libbie. Moore.
A Mery Gest How a
    Sergeaunt Wolde Lerne to
    Be a Frere. More.
The Moneyless Man.
    Stanton.
Mundus Morosus. Faber.
Now That Your Shoulders
    Reach My Shoulders.
    Francis.
Ode to the Spirit of Earth in
    Autumn. Meredith.
Older Grown. Greenaway.
On the Death of His Son.
    Wesley.
The Restoration of
    Enheduanna to Her Former
    Station. Enheduanna.
The Rifles. Anonymous.
Song on May Morning.
    Milton.
Sonnets, CX: "Alas! 'tis true I
    have gone here and there."
    Shakespeare.
The Soul Has Bandaged
    Moments. Dickinson.
Spring. Blake.
That after horror that was Us.
    Dickinson.
To—. Tennyson.
To the Thirty-Ninth Congress.
    Whittier.
Trico's Song. Lyly.
Welcome, Queen Sabbath.
    Schneour.
A Welcome to Dr. Benjamin
    Apthorp Gould. Holmes.
What Thou Lovest Well,
    Remains American. Hugo.
When Each Bright Star Is
    Clouded. Callanan.
The Wizard's Funeral.
    Dixon.
Welfare
Corn-Planter. Kenny.
Tecumseh. Mair.

Welkin
The Book of the Duchesse.
    Chaucer.
The Canadian Authors Meet.
    Scott.
The Dream of the Rood.
    Anonymous.
Pluto's Council. Fairfax.
Well
All Being Well. Gibson.
Always Finish. Anonymous.
An Amorous Dialogue
    between John and His
    Mistress. Anonymous.
A and B. Sisson.
Being to Timelessness as It's
    to Time. Cummings.
By the Fire. Anonymous.
A Coast View (excerpt).
    Harpur.
A Doctor Fell in a Deep
    Well. Anonymous.
A Father in Tennessee.
    Simmons.
Fire Down Below.
    Anonymous.
Frustration. Parker.
A Health Note. Hard.
A Heavenly Friend. Tucker.
Hebrews. Oppenheim.
I'm Here. Ignatow.
In Memoriam A.H.H.,
    CXXV. Tennyson.
In Reference to Her Children,
    23. June, 1656. Bradstreet.
It Happens, Often.
    Robinson.
Julian Grenfell. Baring.
Keeping You Alive.
    Gallagher.
Lines on a Certain Friend's
    Remarkable Faculty...
    Beerbohm.
Mag's Song (with music).
    Anonymous.
The Maid of the Moor, or
    The Water-Fiends.
    Colman.
The Missionary Visits Our
    Church in Scranton.
    Parini.
Morning Swim. Kumin.
A Nativity. Kipling.
Ninth Moon. Li Ho.
Old Beard A-Shakin'.
    Anonymous.
The Old Oaken Bucket.
    Woodworth.
Omnia Vanitas. Buchanan.
On Fell. Lessing.
Out of Sorts. Gilbert.
The Philosopher. Millay.
Photograph in a Stockholm
    Newspaper for March 13,
    1910. Coles.
Poetry Is... Bennett.
Poggio. Durrell.
A Removal from Terry Street.
    Dunn.
Say Well and Do Well.
    Anonymous.
Sonnets to Philomel. Davies.
"Tollable Well." Stanton.
Upon the Bleeding Crucifix.
    Crashaw.
Village in Snowstorm.
    Krapf.
Vita Benefica. Rollins.
Wells. Hall.
Wishes for Her. Devlin.
With Long Black Wings.
    Stickney.

Yahrzeit. Schaeffer.
Wells
Limerick: "There was an old
    man of Cape Race."
    Anonymous.
O Risen Lord upon the
    Throne. Benson.
Ponce de Leon. Thomas.
The Romance of Imprinting.
    Sanford.
Santa Barbara Beach.
    Torrence.
The Water-Witch. Perry.
The Wells of Jesus Wounds.
    Anonymous.
Welsh
The Battle of Brunanburh.
    Anonymous.
Epigram: "It is true that I
    held Thero fair."
    Meleager.
Jackdaw. Earley.
Weltschmerz
A Gothic Gesture. Levine.
Wench (es)
God Made Trees.
    Anonymous.
In Francum. Davies.
Nostalgia. Millard.
Plaint. Anonymous.
Southern Cop. Brown.
Werewolf
Wellfleet Harbor. Goodman.
West
Aeroplane. Pudjipangu.
The Anathemata. Jones.
August on Sourdough, a Visit
    from Dick Brewer.
    Snyder.
Away Out West. Hall.
Burial of Barber. Whittier.
By the Pacific Ocean. Miller.
The Camp Within the West.
    Quinn.
Changelings. Higginson.
Charlie Macpherson.
    Anonymous.
Come All You Fair and
    Tender Ladies.
    Anonymous.
Dawn-Angels. Robinson.
The Djanggawul Cycle, 24.
    Anonymous.
Dog Yoga. Wright.
Drama. Hart-Smith.
The Dying Hobo.
    Anonymous.
Early Moon. Sandburg.
Eire. Drennan.
An Epitaph. de la Mare.
The Far, Far West.
    Anonymous.
Grand Rapids. Moore.
The Harbor Dawn. Crane.
If All the Voices of Men.
    Traubel.
In Spain. Lawless.
July the First. Currie.
Kit Carson's Last Smoke.
    Vestal.
The Lamp in the West.
    Higginson.
Legend. Laforgue.
The Legend of Boastful Bill.
    Clark, Jr.
Limerick: "There was an old
    man of the West." Lear.
Limerick: "There was an old
    man of West Dumpet."
    Lear.
Little Sally Sand.
    Anonymous.

Lounge in the shade of the
    luxuriant laurel's/beautiful
    foliage. Anyte.
Love on the Mountain.
    Boyd.
The Man of the Open West.
    Monroe.
The Maryland Battalion.
    Palmer.
Men of the North and West.
    Stoddard.
Moonlight...Scattered Clouds.
    Bloomfield.
My Africa. Dei-Anang.
Neutrality. MacNeice.
New Hymns for Solitude.
    Dowden.
Ode to a Lebanese Crock of
    Olives. Wakoski.
Ohio. Updike.
The Old Scout's Lament.
    Anonymous.
Poem near midway truck stop.
    Henson.
The Prairie Schooner. Dale.
Prayers to Liberty. Shaul.
Proverbial Weather Rhymes.
    Anonymous.
Robin Hood and the Butcher.
    Anonymous.
Sails. Sterling.
Somewhere West. Jones.
The Sonnets. Berrigan.
The Springfield Calibre Fifty.
    Hanson.
The Stampede. Miller.
Stanley Meets Mutesa.
    Rubadiri.
Tauhid. Toure.
The Texas Ranger. Boswell.
Thomas Hood. Robinson.
Three Trees at Solstice.
    Finnin.
The Tide That from the West
    Washes Africa to the Bone.
    Rubadiri.
To a Jack Rabbit. Barker.
To Some Few Hopi Ancestors.
    Rose.
To the Driving Cloud.
    Longfellow.
The Triumph. Lanier.
Villanelle of Sunset.
    Dowson.
Wandering Chorus. Alquit.
Western Wagons. Benét.
What Needeth All This
    Travail. Anonymous.
The Wind on the Hills.
    Shorter.
The Woman in the Wagon.
    Robertson.
The Women of the West.
    Evans.
You Are on U.S. 40 Headed
    West. White.
Western
Across the Western Ocean.
    Anonymous.
Aubade: Lake Erie. Merton.
Christmas 1914. Harding.
The Cotton Boll. Timrod.
Cuba to Columbia. Carleton.
Dickens in Camp. Harte.
The Grave of Rulry.
    Rolleston.
The Haschish. Whittier.
Ho! Westward Ho!. Dodge.
Humanities Course. Updike.
A Map of Montana in Italy.
    Hugo.

Metamorphoses. Ovid
  (Publius Ovidius Naso).
Moon Festival. Tu Fu.
Prophecy. Pulci.
The Sea-King. Tooker.
Star of the Western Skies.
  Anonymous.
Talbrager. Lawson.
This Amber Sunstream. Van
  Doren.
A Trampwoman's Tragedy.
  Hardy.
Two Dedications, I: The
  Chicago Picasso. Brooks.
Western Formula.
  Anonymous.
When I Was a Brave Cowboy.
  Anonymous.

Westminster
The Abbey Mason. Hardy.

Westward
Ballad. Kingsley.
Easter Sunday, 1945.
  Borgese.
Empire Builders. MacLeish.
Exodus to Connacht. O
  Meallain.
Ho! Westward Ho!. Dodge.
A Missouri Traveller Writes
  Home: 1830. Bly.
The Pipe of Peace. Lucas.
To England. Boker.
A Trip to the Grand Banks.
  Hanson.
The Waterwitch.
  Anonymous.
Wild Eden. Woodberry.

Westwind
Dana Point. Ghiselin.

Wet
Black Hawk in Hiding.
  Keithley.
Ch'in Chia's Wife's Reply.
  Anonymous.
The Cold Irish Earth.
  Skinner.
The Edge of Town.
  Clamurro.
Epitaph for a Timid Lady.
  Cornford.
The Falls of Glomach.
  Young.
The Forms of Love. Oppen.
Haiku: "Spring rain! And as
  yet." Buson (Taniguchi
  Buso).
The Home. Axelrod.
I Have No Pain.
  Anonymous.
January. Hass.
London. Rowland.
Love's Prisoner. Van
  Rensselaer.
Mad Sweeny. Montague.
May 10th. Kumin.
Modern Architecture.
  Nathan.
Nymphs and Satyrs. Ewart.
On a Wet Day. Sacchetti.
The Palmer. Langland.
The Pike. Bruce.
(Poem) (Chicago) (The Were-
  Age). Knott.
Poem: "Look at Me 8th
  Grade." Sanchez.
Rain. Henley.
Reading in Fall Rain. Bly.
Return of Autumn. Neruda.
Rite of Spring. Heaney.
Roots and Leaves Themselves
  Alone. Whitman.

Seeing the Plum Blossoms by
  the River. Ise.
The Self and the Weather.
  Whittemore.
September. Pastan.
Thomas in the Fields.
  Moyles.
Two Poems. Hitomaro.
Vanitas Vanitatum.
  Zangwill.
The Vision of Piers Plowman.
  Langland.
Westgate-on-Sea. Betjeman.
What Is Liquid. Newcastle.

Whale (s)
Blow Ye Winds. *Anonymous.*
The Blue Whale. Watson.
The Bonnie Ship the
  Diamond. *Anonymous.*
The Boothbay Whale.
  Anonymous.
The Cachalot. Pratt.
Captain Bunker. *Anonymous.*
The Coast of Peru.
  Anonymous.
Darwin on Species.
  Anonymous.
Dog Lake with Paula. Hugo.
Genocide. Dauenhauer.
Jack Was Every Inch a Sailor.
  Anonymous.
The Lady in Kicking Horse
  Reservoir. Hugo.
A Mother's Song. Ledwidge.
Naughty Boy. Creeley.
The Nightingale.
  Anonymous.
A Perilous Life. *Anonymous.*
The Ploughboy. Clare.
The Seafarer. *Anonymous.*
A Song of the Hatteras
  Whale. *Anonymous.*
Song: The Railway Train.
  Anonymous.
They Say the Sea Is Loveless.
  Lawrence.
Whale. Benet.
The Whale and the Essex.
  Sullivan.
The Whaler's Pig. Brady.
White Whales Specked Black.
  Outlaw.

Wharf (wharves)
Then they paraded Pompey's
  urn. Mastoraki.
Waterfront. Jenkins.
Where Ships of Purple—Gently
  Toss. Dickinson.
The White City. McKay.

Wheat
Color in the Wheat.
  Garland.
He Singeth a Hymn to Osiris,
  the Lord of Eternity.
  Book of the Dead.
A Hundreth Good Poyntes of
  Husbandry. Tusser.
Kneading. Crooker.
Meadowsweet. Allingham.
Nebraska. Swan.
Pharaoh and Joseph. Lasker-
  Schüler.
Poppies on the Wheat.
  Jackson.
Questions and Answers. O
  Hehir.
Sifting. Beck.
Summer, 1960, Minnesota.
  Bly.
The Wind-Swept. De Vere.
Windmill in March. Privett.

The Youth with Red-Gold
  Hair. Sitwell.

Wheel (s)
Blue-Butterfly Day. Frost.
The Colder the Air. Bishop.
Cut. Feela.
The Dancing Ploughmen.
  Joseph.
Dead Man's Dump.
  Rosenberg.
DOA in Dulse. Burns.
Empires. Money-Coutts.
Engineers. Garthwaite.
Faith. Cambridge.
The Figured Wheel. Pinsky.
Form Was the World.
  English.
Fortune. *Anonymous.*
Freya's Spinning Wheel.
  Oehlenschlager.
The Gaol Song. *Anonymous.*
The Gol-Darned Wheel.
  Anonymous.
Idea. Drayton.
Limerick: "There was an old
  person of Harrow." Lear.
Love for a Hare. La
  Follette.
A Lover, upon an Accident
  Necessitating His
  Departure.... Carew.
Model T. Stoutenburg.
The Monument and the
  Shrine. Logan.
New York. Russell.
Nine Pound Hammer.
  Anonymous.
The Old Mill. English
The One-Horned Ewe.
  Anonymous.
Paradox: The Birds. Shapiro.
Parts Man. West.
Passenger Train. Chase.
Private Transport. Mitchell.
A. R. U. (with music).
  Anonymous.
Rural Sports. Gay.
Sheet Lightning. Blunden.
Sonnets. Tuckerman.
Sparkles from the Wheel.
  Whitman.
A Spinning Song.
  O'Donnell.
The Steam Threshing-
  Machine. Turner.
Tat for Tit. De la Mare.
Thrown. Hodgson.
Tithonus. Tennyson.
To Beachey, 1912.
  Sandburg.
Wading at Wellfleet. Bishop.
The Wheel. Berry.
Yule's Come, and Yule's
  Gane. *Anonymous.*

Wheelbarrow
The Bachelor's Lament.
  Anonymous.
When I Was a Bachelor.
  Anonymous.

Whelp
The Four-Legg'd Elder.
  Birkenhead.
To His Wife, for Striking Her
  Dog. Harington.

Where
All Is Well. Clough.
Chant. Williams.
Clipper Ships. Anderson.
The Dead Men. Andresen.
The Duke of York's Statue.
  Landor.
Eleanor Rigby. Beatles.

Fable of the Speckled Cow.
  Opperman.
Housewife. Schaeffer.
John Clare. Halperin.
Maud. Tennyson.
My Past. Cooper.
Old Virginny. Bland.
A Philosopher. Bangs.
The Pleasant Life in
  Newfoundland. Hayman.
A Pool. Whitbread.
Progress. McCord.
The Rubaiyat of Omar
  Khayyam. Omar
  Khayyam.
Salangadou. *Anonymous.*
Solitude. Traherne.
Stance. Enslin.
Still Barred Thy Doors.
  Dutt.
Suspira. *Anonymous.*
Those Old Zen Blues.
  Broughton.
Whate'er You Dream with
  Doubt Possest. Clough.
Where Is He? *Anonymous.*
Who Knows Where.
  Liliencron.
Winter. Menashe.
The Wood-Dove's Note.
  Miller.
The World As Wave and
  Idea. Coxe.

Wherever
Friends. Brown.
Last Song. Guthrie.
When I Was Single.
  Anonymous.

Whigs
The Humble Address.
  Anonymous.
Oxford & Cambridge.
  Browne.

Whim (s)
An Elegy. To an Old Beauty.
  Parnell.
An Elegy. To an Old Beauty.
  Parnell.
Lord Lucky. Belloc.
Of Rama. Melville.
To a Young Lady. Savage.
Whimper of Awakening
  Passion. Jones.

Whimper (s)
Elegies. Chenier.
The Hollow Men. Eliot.
To a Spaniel. Landor.

Whine (s)
Forgive Me When I Whine.
  Anonymous.
The Fox and the Grapes.
  Moore.
Jill, Afterwards. Dacey.
The Rats. Trakl.

Whip (ped) (ping) (s)
And "I Know Why the Caged
  Bird Sings": A Villanelle.
  Mosby.
April 1940. Maybin.
The Beasts Are Very Wise.
  Kipling.
Caelica, XLIII. Greville.
The Complaints of Poetry
  (excerpt). James.
December Storm. Hay.
Doctor Faustus. *Anonymous.*
Dr. Wild's Ghost.
  Anonymous.
Dreams of Snakes, Chocolate
  and Men. Sanford.

Epigram: "Thy nags (the leanest things alive)." Prior.
Genius. Perkins.
In the Silks. Ackerman.
Limerick: "There was a young lady whose dream." Jordan.
March Weather. Swan.
The Masque of Queenes. Jonson.
The Old Woman in a Shoe. Anonymous.
The Team. Maurice.
Transit. Wilbur.
Upon Fone a School-master. Epigram. Herrick.
Winter the Huntsman. Sitwell.

Whippoorwill (s)
Johnny Stiles; or, The Wild Mustard River. Anonymous.
Poet's Prayer. Sussman.

Whirl (ed) (ing) (s)
At dawn of the day the Creator. Stampa.
Canto Amor. Berryman.
Cincophrenicpoet. Kaufman.
An Elegy. To an Old Beauty. Parnell.
News from the Court. Wagoner.
The Pike. Blunden.
The Sad Shepherd. Yeats.

Whirlpool
Dorothy. Kreymborg.
Frankenstein. Field.
Nessa. Durcan.
Route 95 North: New Jersey. Bowman.
Tlanusi'yi, the Leech Place. Cardiff.

Whirlwind (s)
Boolee, the Bringer of Life. Gilmore.
California Quail in January. Jumper.
The Campaign. Addison.
Tauhid. Toure.

Whiskers
Dream Songs. Berryman.
Moire. McClure.
Mr. McGregor's Garden. McGuckian.
The Nude Republic. Perreault.
Rats. De La Mare.
Tuscaloosa Sam. Newell.
Woman Par Excellence. Owens.

Whiskey
After the Industrial Revolution, All Things Happen at Once. Bly.
Bad Day on the Boulder. Davis.
Depression. Burwell.
Fat Tuesday. Di Piero.
Fourth of July in Maine. Lowell.
I Don't Let the Girls Worry My Mind. Anonymous.
Packin' Trunk Blues. Leadbelly.
The Roving Shanty Boy. Anonymous.
Sunflower Rock. Blackburn.
The Wisdom of Old Jelly Roll. Smith.

Whisper (ed) (ers) (ing) (s)
At Midnight's Hour. Thoreau.
At the Jewish Museum. Cabral.
Atropos. O'Hara.
Aubade. McBride.
The Belly Dancer in the Nursing Home. Wallace.
Bird and the Muse. Zaturenska.
Brindabella. Stewart.
The Brook in February. Roberts.
The Cable Hymn. Whittier.
Epistemology. Wilbur.
The Explorer. Kipling.
Fatigues. Aldington.
Finding a Friend Home. Hamm.
A Foreign Country. Zach.
Gallantry. Douglas.
A Game at Salzburg. Jarrell.
Hill-Side Tree. Bodenheim.
I Know Not Why, but All This Weary Day. Timrod.
I Talk to You. Newlove.
If in Beginning Twilight. Cummings.
In a Museum in the Capital. Stafford.
In Memoriam A.H.H., CXXV. Tennyson.
In Ohio. Wright.
The Inner Light. Myers.
Je Ne Veux de Personne aupres de ma Tristesse. Regnier.
Kentucky Mountain Farm. Warren.
Lest Thou Forget. Stidger.
Letters to a Stranger. James.
The Magic Words. Koertge.
Nausicaa with Some Attendants. Lowenstein.
The Night before the Battle of Waterloo. Byron.
The Night-Blooming Cereus. Hayden.
On the Desert. Crane.
One Goes with Me along the Shore. Winkler.
Overture to Strangers. Haring.
Pericles. Shakespeare.
Poem to a Redskin. Rose.
A Prayer. Noyes.
Retirement. Cowper.
Retreat. Collins.
S. S. City of Benares. Fraser.
A Slight Confusion. Reiss.
Song for Seven Parts of the Body, 5. Kumin.
Threnody for a Poet. Carman.
To a God Unknown. Eller.
Tree Felling. Woodcock.
The Unreturning. Scollard.
Upon the Lake. Lenski.
The Villagers and Death. Graves.

Whist
Dis Alitr Visum; or, le Byron de nos Jours. Browning.

Whistle (d) (r) (s)
Ah Blackbird, Giving Thanks. Anonymous.
Air: "A flaxen-headed cowboy, as simple as may be." O'Keefe.
As You Leave Me. Knight.
The Blithe Mask. Fuguet.

Carried Away. Elder.
Down the M4. Abse.
The Friar. Casal.
Hitch Haiku. Snyder.
In Just-. Cummings.
Independence Day. Berry.
Inducements. Anonymous.
Issues of the Fall. Lea.
The Jump Shooter. Trudell.
Limerick: "There is a young artist named Whistler." Rossetti.
Limerick: "There's a combative Artist named Whistler." Rossetti.
The Little Whistler. Frost.
Mr. Edwards and the Spider. Lowell.
My Country. Lermontov.
Oh, oh, you will be sorry for that word! Millay.
Resolution. "Wiolar".
Simple Simon. Anonymous.
Soliloquy by the Shore. Scholten.
A Song for New Orleans. Keithley.
Storm at Sea. Davenant.
Summer. Page.
What the Engines Said. Harte.
The Whistle. Murray.
Whistle, Daughter, Whistle. Anonymous.
Young Girls. Souster.

Whistling
Barnyard Melodies. Brooks.
The Blackbird of Derrycairn. Clarke.
Catching a Horse. Winder.
Departure. Blunden.
The Djanggawul Cycle, 22. Anonymous.
The Jolly Farmer. Anonymous.
Verses Written In 1872. Stevenson.
Whistling Boy. Quinn.

White
An Age. Jensen.
The Animals Sick of the Plague. Moore.
Apocalypse and Resurrection. Bayliss.
April Moment. Ficke.
At Devlin's Siding. Boake.
At the Beginnings of the Andes. Ras.
Aubade. Lechlitner.
Autumn. Hulme.
Baby Toes. Sandburg.
Ballad of John Cable and Three Gentlemen. Merwin.
A Beautiful Young Nymph Going to Bed. Swift.
Behaviour of Fish in an Egyptian Tea Garden. Douglas.
Black and White. Adame.
Blue Smoke. Frost.
Bone Thoughts on a Dry Day. Starbuck.
The Canoe. Crawford.
Canoe Song at Twilight. McCully.
A Cautionary Tale. Wilkinson.
Chipeta. Field.
A Christmas Hymn. Alexander.

Columbia the Gem of the Ocean. Becket.
Consumer's Report. Kennedy.
The Cowboy's Life. Anonymous.
Cross. Hughes.
The Crow-Children Walk My Circles in the Snow. Young Bear.
Cyclamens. "Field.
Dandelions. Mayer.
The Dead Liebknecht. ""MacDiarmid.
Deaf-and-Dumb School. Delius.
The Death of the Moon. Wagoner.
Dedication to the Final Confrontation. Djangatolum.
Deserted. Cawein.
Dirge. Aragon.
Discovery. Flanner.
Dog Creek Mainline. Wright.
The Dove. Daley.
The Dream Queen: Dialogue. Bhasa.
Dreams in War Time (excerpt). Lowell.
Egnatius, Because His Teeth Are White. Catullus.
Elegy. Gilbert.
Epigram: "Peace is made with a warlike man–." Anonymous.
Etat (excerpt). Albiach.
Europa. Plomer.
The Everlasting Gospel. Blake.
The Fair Agnete. Miegel.
Far inland go my sad thoughts. Anonymous.
The Fawn. Millay.
The Field. Lawder.
The First Autumn. Schacht.
First Praise. Williams.
The First Thanksgiving Day. Preston.
Flag Song. Ward.
Footnote. Delius.
For England, in Grateful Appreciation (excerpt). Vogt.
For Her on the First Day Out. Bagg.
For Summer's Here. Barnett.
For Thee, O Dear Dear Country! Neale.
Fresh Paint. Pasternak.
From a Childhood. Rilke.
George Robinson: Blues. Rukeyser.
The Goose and the Gander. Anonymous.
The Gospel of Peace. Roche.
Green Grow the Lilacs. Anonymous.
The Grief. Rilke.
Hammerin' Hank. Martin.
Harlem Gallery (excerpt). Tolson.
He's Doing Natural Life. Conyus.
Her Legs. Herrick.
The Hero. Sassoon.
Hiram Powers' "Greek Slave." Browning.
His Swans. Grigson.
History. Tanaquil.

Hoc Cygno Vinces. Hawkins.
Hokku: In the Falling Snow. Wright.
The Holly. King.
How Lillies Came White. Herrick.
I Awoke with the Room Cold. Piercy.
I Shall Not Die for Thee. Hyde.
I Went to the Sea. *Anonymous.*
The Idiot. Randall.
The Iliad. Homer.
In Assisi. Blumenthal.
In Yellow Meadows I Take No Delight. Browne.
Inland Passages, I: The Long Hunter. Berry.
Invocation. Nakasuk.
Le Jeune Homme Caressant Sa Chimere. Symonds.
John Burns of Gettysburg. Harte.
June. McGuckian.
Kaddish. Ginsberg.
The Lapful of Nuts. Ferguson.
Lawd, Dese Colored Chillum. Allah.
Let Me Love Bright Things. Choyce.
Like a Silkworm Weaving. Mahadevi (Mahadeviyakka).
Like a wave crest. Uda.
Like Treasure Hidden in the Ground. Mahadevi (Mahadeviyakka).
Limerick: "There was a young lady called Starky." *Anonymous.*
Limerick: "There was a young lady in White." Lear.
A Little Girl on Her Way to School. Wright.
Little Marble Boy. Wright.
The Little White Cat. *Anonymous.*
Little White Lily. Macdonald.
Low Tide. Woessner.
Manos Karastefanis. Merrill.
Mass at Dawn. Campbell.
May-Day at Sea. Finerty.
May You Always Be the Darling of Fortune. Miller.
Le Medecin Malgre Lui. Williams.
Mending Crab Pots. Smith.
The Mermaid. King.
The Moon-Bone Cycle: The Evening Star. *Anonymous.*
Mrs. Johnson Objects. Thompson.
Near a Waterfall at Ryumon. Ise.
Negro Servant. Hughes.
News. Pomeroy.
Night Airs. Landor.
The Night before the Battle of Waterloo. Byron.
Not Seeing Is Believing. Petrie.
Now in This Long-Deferred Spring. Warner.
Now the Leaves Are Falling Fast. Auden.
Ode: Salute to the French Negro Poets. O'Hara.

Old Woman Awaiting the Greyhound Bus. Niatum.
On a World War Battlefield. Clark.
On Catching a Dog-Daisy in the Mower. Redgrove.
On Mr. G. Herbert's Book. Crashaw.
On the Esplanade des Invalides. Fisher.
On the Height. Tietjens.
On the Pole. Greenberg.
Once. Walker.
Once in Royal David's City. Alexander.
One Snowy Night in December. Morris.
Over the Water to Charlie. *Anonymous.*
The Palace of Art. Tennyson.
Part Winter. Bowering.
A Passer By. Bridges.
A Petticoat. Stein.
Play-Song. *Anonymous.*
Poem: "In the corner a violet jug." Picasso.
Poem: "It's a dull poem." Jonas.
Port Bou. Spender.
A Prayer for the Old Courage. Towne.
The Purpose of Altar Boys. Rios.
The Quiet Flower. Johnson.
Rag Doll and Summer Birds. Dodson.
The Real Muse. Muratori.
The Red, White and Blue. Shaw.
The Red, White and Red. *Anonymous.*
Remembrance of Things Past. Coleman.
Reply to the Committed Intellectual. Sparshott.
Resurgam. *Anonymous.*
Return. Brown.
The Return. Silkin.
Rip. Wright.
Robertin Tush. *Anonymous.*
Roll On, Sad World! Tuckerman.
Said the Canoe. Crawford.
The Shadow. De la Mare.
The Ship-Builders. Whittier.
Simple Verses. Marti.
The Six-Quart Basket. Souster.
The Skater. Roberts.
Skier. Francis.
The Snow Light. Sarton.
Snow Storm. Mary Madeleva.
Snow White. Gillespie.
Snowflakes. Behrend.
Song for a Girl on Her First Menstruation. *Anonymous.*
Song in White. Le Dressay.
Song of Snow-White Heads. Cho Wen-chun.
The Song of the Pilgrims. Brooke.
Song of the Rejected Woman. Kibkarjuk.
Song to the Masquers. Shirley.
Sonnets. Tuckerman.
Sonnets, VII: "Upon an upland orchard's sunny side." Irwin.

South-Folk in Cold Country. *Anonymous.*
A Sugar-Candy Bird. Young.
Swan. Hall.
Theme and Variations. Ker.
There Has to Be a Jail for Ladies. Merton.
Therese. Nowlan.
Three Women. Dempster.
Through the Dark Aisles of the Wood. Treece.
Time Poem. Hill.
To a Little Girl. Kobbe.
A Toast to the Flag. Daly.
Tom Starr. Conley.
Tongues of Fire. Plescoff.
.Train Journey. Wright.
The Troika. Simpson.
Trout Fisher. Brown.
Two Fawns That Didn't See the Light This Spring. Snyder.
A Virginal. Pound.
Vive Noir! Evans.
Wandering Chorus. Alquit.
Wheeler at Santiago. Gordon.
Where Shall Wisdom Be Found. Euripides.
White Azaleas. Kimball.
The White Cockade. *Anonymous.*
The White Dress. Spear.
White Dusk. Boyd.
The White Man Pressed the Locks. Kilgore.
White Roses. Ashbery.
The White Sand. Wilson.
The White Women. Coleridge.
Wichita Vortex Sutra, II. Ginsberg.
Winter Scene. Young.
Wordspinning. Kirsch.
Your Flag and My Flag. Nesbit.

White man (men)
At Grand Canyon's Edge. Ray.
Burke and Wills. Barratt.
The Castle. Alexander.
Circles. Sandburg.
For Dan Berrigan. Knight.
Geronimo: Old Man Lives On. Dessus.
The Indian Hunter. Cook.
Pulling Weeds. Chock.
Sleeping Beauty. Johnson.
Someone Gave Him Some Plastic Flowers Once. Shady.
Street Scene–1946. Porter.
The United States of America We. Abrams.
Upstairs Downstairs. Allen.
Work Song. Kunene.
Whitecaps
Praise Doubt. Van Doren.
Whiteness
Ancient. Russell.
The Brahms. Morris.
Camel. Derwood.
The Corpse-Plant. Rich.
Countess Laura. Boker.
Prayer to the Snowy Owl. Haines.
Salesman. Roston.
Stories of Snow. Page.
We Are Transmitters–. Lawrence.

Whites
Baptism. Bell.
In Westminster Abbey. Betjeman.
Ode to Walt Whitman. Garcia Lorca.
Walam Olum; or, Red Score (excerpt). *Anonymous.*
Whitsun
Dancing at Whitsun. Marshall.
Who
Burial of an Irish President. Clarke.
Clad All in White. Cowley.
Following the Sun. Kessler.
The Geranium. Sheridan.
Hotel Transylvanie. O'Hara.
Man Cannot Name Himself. Shaw.
Self-Employed. Ignatow.
A Song off Clover. Holm.
Sonnets to Aurelia. Nichols.
To Thee, Then, Let All Beings Bend. Evans.
Whole
Artemis. Deamer.
Autumn Apples. Lee.
The Babe of Bethlehem. Beer.
The Blanket around Her. Harjo.
Canzonetta: Of His Lady in Absence. Pugliesi.
Chanson of the Bells of Oseney. Rice.
The Cloud Factory. Haines.
Dauber. Masefield.
Directive. Frost.
Discovering God Is Waking One Morning. L'Heureux.
Distraction. Vaughan.
English Bards and Scotch Reviewers. Byron.
The Ever-Touring Englishmen... *Anonymous.*
Foggy Mountain Top. *Anonymous.*
From the Rain Forest. Flynn.
God of the World, Thy Glories Shine. Cutting.
He's Got the Whole World in His Hands. Anonymous.
The Hospital–Retrospections. Mackenzie.
I Am a Pilgrim. *Anonymous.*
I Break the Sky. Dodson.
I Walked with My Reason. MacLean.
In Hades. Brackett.
Karl Marx. Lee.
Keeping Things Whole. Strand.
Knowledge after Death. Beeching.
The Landscape of the Heart. Grigson.
Last Day of the Trip. Davis.
Lifelong. Boimwall.
A Little Song. Grosseteste.
The Lost Ingredient. Sexton.
Love Letter from an Impossible Land. Meredith.
Marrakech. Eberhart.
Married Man Blues. Reynolds.
Mathematics or the Gift of Tongues. Branch.
Migration. Bruchac.
Morning Once More. Harjo.

The Murmurers. Jacobsen.
My Father's Cot (parody)
  (excerpt). Squire.
The New World: The New
  God. Bynner.
No Marvel Is It. Bernard de
  Ventadour
Ode in May. Watson.
Old Men. Keesing.
Old Men's Ward. Dean.
One Year After. Kizer.
Part for the Whole. Francis.
Peace on Earth. Sears.
Phineas within and without.
  Zimmer.
Picture of Seneca Dying in a
  Bath. Prior.
Prayer. Marr.
Presence. Moffit.
Progress. Wilcox.
Remember Way Back.
  Green.
Reply. McCabe.
Restricted. Waddington.
A Satyre Entituled the Witch.
  Anonymous.
Sent with a Rose to a Young
  Lady. Deland.
Sneeze on a Monday, You
  Sneeze for Danger.
  Anonymous.
Sonnet: Of Why He Is
  Unhanged. Angiolieri.
Sonnets, CXXXIV: "So, now
  I have confessed that he is
  thine." Shakespeare.
Theophany. Underhill.
Tortoise Shout. Lawrence.
The Two Gretels. Morgan.
Up against the Wall (parody).
  Berry.
Virtue. Herbert.
The Way of Pain. Berry.
A Way Up on Clinch
  Mountain (B vers. with
  music). *Anonymous.*
Wild Eden. Woodberry.

Wholesome
Okeechobee. Allison.
An Old Buffer. Locker-
  Lampson.
The Stones of Sleep. Mayo.
Up in the North.
  Anonymous.

Whore (s)
Apocalypse. Nims.
Captain Barton's Distress on
  Board the Lichfield.
  Anonymous.
An Epigram on Scolding.
  Swift.
Fish Peddler and Cobbler.
  Rexroth.
Greasy Spoon Blues.
  Gasparini.
Hard Is the Fortune of All
  Womankind. *Anonymous.*
In Fuscum. Davies.
Lassitude. Verlaine.
Liverpool Girls. *Anonymous.*
Madrigal: "To be a whore,
  despite of grace." Cotton.
Phyllis; or, The Progress of
  Love. Swift.
Queen Mother to New Queen.
  Graves.
A Rapture. Carew.
Sam Hall. *Anonymous.*
The Spanish Friar. Dryden.
Squire and Milkmaid.
  Anonymous.

Street Corner College.
  Patchen.
Street-Walker in March.
  Albert.
Thoughts from a Bottle.
  Clark.
To the Honorable Charles
  Montague, Esq. Prior.
Wedlock. A Satire. Wright.

Why?"
And There Was a Great
  Calm. Hardy.
Dead of Winter. Towne.
The Disagreeable Man.
  Gilbert.
The Flower of Flame
  (excerpt). Nichols.
Graffiti. Bold.
Here I Am. Sutzkever.
Homecoming. Margolin.
Horses Aboard. Hardy.
Hotel Transylvanie. O'Hara.
Lament. Millay.
Limerick: "There was a young
  man of Madrid."
  Anonymous.
Medieval Norman Songs.
  Anonymous.
The Modes of Vallejo Street
  San Diego, Los Angeles
  (excerpt). Seidman.
The Negatives. Levine.
The Net and the Sword.
  LePan.
The Newt. McCord.
O Earth, Turn! Johnston.
A Reply from the Akond of
  Swat. Scheffauer.
Rilke. Webb.
The Rubaiyat of Omar
  Khayyam. Omar
  Khayyam.
Two. Canzoneri.
Why. Freeman.
Winter Song. Macdonald.
Yesterday. Sanchez.

Wichita
Chances "R". Ginsberg.
Wichita Vortex Sutra, II.
  Ginsberg.

Wick (s)
February. Heath-Stubbs.
For Eros II. Wurdemann.
Limerick: "There was an old
  person of Wick." Lear.
My Thread. Hofstein.
Warm rain, sunny wind. Li
  Ch'ing-chao.

Wicked
Abracadabra. Livesay.
An Adieu to My Landlady.
  Farewell.
Ballad of Another Ophelia.
  Lawrence.
Echo Canyon. *Anonymous.*
Holstenwall. Keyes.
How Big Was Alexander?
  Jones.
If I Had My Way. Johnson.
Legsby, Lincolnshire.
  Anonymous.
Limerick: "With a conscience
  we're able to see." Euwer.
Little Mousgrove and the
  Lady Barnet. *Anonymous.*
Now Israel May Say, and
  That Truly. Whittingham.
The Old-Time Cowboy.
  Anonymous.
Pachuco Remembered.
  Villanueva.

Prize for Good Conduct.
  Allott.
The Queen of Elfan's Nourice.
  Anonymous.
The Rambling Boy.
  Anonymous.
A Sweet Little Bell.
  Anonymous.
A Veteran Cowboy's
  Ruminations. Kuykendall.
Was It Not Curious? Smith.

Wide
Don Juan. Foote.
The Elephant. Asquith.
Exile. Beecham.
The Fisher Cat. Eberhart.
From the Day-Book of a
  Forgotten Prince.
  Untermeyer.
Gesture. Welles.
A Grave. Moreland.
I Am a Horse. Arp.
Jim Desterland. Plutzik.
Kingcups. Sitwell.
The Lord. Gabriel y Galan.
Lost Jimmie Whalen.
  Anonymous.
The Midnight Court.
  Merryman.
Moonlight...Scattered Clouds.
  Bloomfield.
A Nation's Wealth. Dyer.
On Fanny Godwin. Shelley.
Snow in the Suburbs. Hardy.
Soil Searcher. Joyce.
Songs. Gilder.
Sonnets for a Dying Man.
  Singer.
Sonnets of the Months. San
  Geminiano.
The Terror of Death. Keats.
To a Crow. Wilson.
Troia Fuit. Kauffman.
Woman Blues. *Anonymous.*

Widow (s)
Aaron Burr's Wooing.
  Stedman.
A Brisk Young Widow.
  Anonymous.
Coleridge Crossing the Plain
  of Jars: 1833. Dubie.
A Contention betwixt a Wife,
  a Widow, and a Maid.
  Davies.
Fly, Love, That Art So
  Sprightly. *Anonymous.*
Four Love Poems. Ibn Ezra.
Fourth Station. Donaghy.
Gloucester Harbor. Ward.
Hard Times, But Carrying
  On. Smith.
Harp Song of the Dane
  Women. Kipling.
Henry K. Sawyer.
  Anonymous.
I am a widow, robed in black,
  alone. Pisan.
In Memoriam A.H.H., XVII.
  Tennyson.
Jubilate Agno. Smart.
Keen. Millay.
Lady Maisry (B version).
  Anonymous.
Pennsylvania Deutsch.
  Morley.
To His Lute. Drummond.
Two Countries. Marti.
Undertakers. Bierce.
The Widow. Ramsay.
A Widow's Weeds. De La
  Mare.

The Widow That Keeps the
  Cock Inn. *Anonymous.*

Wife (wives)
108 Tales of a Po'Buckra, No.
  106. Inman.
Abroad and at Home. Swift.
All's Well That Ends Well.
  Anonymous.
All Shams. *Anonymous.*
An Ancient Degree. Mayer.
And What About the
  Children. Lorde.
Andante, Ma Non Assai.
  Rufinus Domesticus.
Another True Maid. Prior.
Antiphonal Hymn in Praise of
  Inanna. Enheduanna.
Antiquary. Donne.
The Bachelor's Complaint.
  Anonymous.
The Bachelor's Lament.
  Anonymous.
Bad Man Ballad.
  Anonymous.
Ballad of Human Life.
  Beddoes.
The Bat. Nash.
The Bath. Oppenheimer.
The Battle of Harlaw (A
  version). *Anonymous.*
The Blacksmith's Serenade.
  Lindsay.
Bluebeard's Wife. Hine.
Brigham Young.
  Anonymous.
Brother Green. *Anonymous.*
The Bullwhacker.
  Anonymous.
Business Trips. Taylor.
The Card-Players. Ray.
The Carpenter's Wife.
  Anonymous.
Child and Boatman (excerpt).
  Ingelow.
Cod Liver Ile. *Anonymous.*
Composed on the Eve of the
  Marriage of a Friend ...
  Wordsworth.
Concerning Mme. Robert.
  Taylor.
The Conservative Shepherd to
  His Love. D'Arcy.
A Contention betwixt a Wife,
  a Widow, and a Maid.
  Davies.
The Cow. Roethke.
The Cowboy's Life Is a Very
  Dreary Life. *Anonymous.*
Dance-Song of the Lightning.
  Anonymous.
Daniel at Breakfast.
  McGinley.
Decoy. Ashbery.
The Demon Lover.
  Anonymous.
Don't Be Sorrowful, Darling.
  Peale.
The Double Transformation.
  Goldsmith.
The Drunkard. Johnson.
The Drunken Man. Orlen.
Dumb, Dumb, Dumb.
  Anonymous.
Emblems. Tate.
An Encomium upon a
  Parliament. Defoe.
The Engineer's Story. Hall.
Epigram. Moore.
Epigram. Pott and Wright.
Epigram: "Me Polytimus
  vexes and provokes."

Martial (Marcus Valerius Martialis).
Epigram: "Milo's from home; and, Milo being gone." Martial (Marcus Valerius Martialis).
Epigram: "There are two miseries in human life." Landor.
An Execration upon Vulcan. Jonson.
The Fair Lady of the Plains. *Anonymous.*
Farewell, Peace. *Anonymous.*
The Farmer's Curst Wife (A version). *Anonymous.*
Father Grumble. *Anonymous.*
The First Lawcase. *Anonymous.*
The Fisherman. Leonidas.
Five Epigrams. Hall.
Freedom of Love. Breton.
From a Churchyard in Wales. *Anonymous.*
Frost Warning. McFarland.
The Gulistan. Sa'di.
Hand-Clapping Rhyme. *Anonymous.*
The Handloom. Rodriguez.
Herve Riel. Browning.
Hind Etin (B version). *Anonymous.*
His Own True Wife. Wolfram
The Home Winner. Lindberg.
Hope. Hughes.
The House Carpenter (with music). *Anonymous.*
The Hunt Is Up. *Anonymous.*
Husbands and Wives. *Anonymous.*
I Am Your Wife. *Anonymous.*
I Have Always Heard of These Old Men. *Anonymous.*
I Hear That Lycoris Has Buried. Martial (Marcus Valerius Martialis).
I'm Wife—I've Finished That. Dickinson.
I Point Out a Bird. Duval.
I Think Sometimes... Hartnett.
I Went to the Sea. *Anonymous.*
Inscription in a Garden. Gascoigne.
Is There Life across the Street? Watson.
Jack in the Pulpit. *Anonymous*
Jacky Jingle. *Anonymous.*
Jacob. Cary.
Johann Gaertner (1793-1887). Gildner.
Johnny Faa, the Lord of Little Egypt. *Anonymous.*
The Jolly Cowboy. *Anonymous.*
The Jolly Shilling. *Anonymous.*
The Jolly Tester. *Anonymous.*
The Joys of Marriage. Cotton.
Julius Caesar. *Anonymous*
Just a Few Scenes from an Autobiography. Tagliabue.

The Kentucky Thoroughbred. Riley.
Kissing and Bussing. Herrick.
Last Week I Took a Wife. Kelly.
A Lay of St. Gengulphus (excerpt). Barham.
The Legend of the First Cam-u-el. Guiterman.
Let Me Go. *Anonymous.*
Life of the Mannings. *Anonymous.*
The Light of Life. ""MacDiarmid.
Lilith. Fainlight.
Little Tommy Tucker. Mother Goose.
Locks and Bolts. *Anonymous.*
Love Song: I and Thou. Dugan.
The Market. Snyder.
Marriage. *Anonymous.*
Miriam: Chorus. Carew.
The Mistress. Barton.
The Modern Chinese History Professor Plays Pool Every Tuesday... Hall.
Modern Love, XXXIII. Meredith.
Movies, Left to Right. Sward.
My Ain Wife. Laing.
My Estate. Drinkwater.
My Wife's a Winsome Wee Thing. Burns.
Nancy Lee. *Anonymous.*
The New Married Couple. *Anonymous.*
The Nobleman and Thresherman. *Anonymous.*
Note in a Sanitorium. Amorosi.
Note in Lieu of a Suicide. Finkel.
Note on Intelligence. Auden.
O. T.'s Blues. Cuney.
October. Spacks.
Old Man in the Wood. *Anonymous.*
On a Window at the Four Crosses. Swift.
Once More A-Lumbering Go. *Anonymous.*
One Wife for One Man. Aig-Imoukhuede.
Over the Coffin. Hardy.
The Oyster. Nash.
Parable. Bennett.
The Passionate Shepherd to His Love. Schwartz.
The Perfect Child. Porter.
A Plea for Trigamy. Seaman.
Pleasure. *Anonymous.*
Poor Devil That I Am, Being So Attacked. Palladas.
A Poor Man's Work Is Never Done. *Anonymous.*
A Popular Functionary. Dibdin.
Prayer for the Great Family. Snyder.
The Process of Conception. Quillet.
Proposal. Sward.
A Reasonable Affliction. Prior.
The Red Man's Wife. Hyde.
Robin Hood and the Butcher. *Anonymous.*

Robin Hood and the Tanner. *Anonymous.*
A Rose in October. Riley.
Scrimshaw. Hogan.
The Seasons. Kalidasa.
September 30. Lourie.
Shameful Death. Morris.
A Shantyman's Life (II). *Anonymous.*
Skin Man. Brown.
The Smuggler's Victory. *Anonymous.*
Soldier, Soldier, Won't You Marry Me? *Anonymous.*
Song. Clare.
A Song of Ale. *Anonymous.*
Songs to a Lady Moonwalker. Sutzkever.
The Sonnet. Hoffman.
Sonnet: "The point where beauty and intelligence meet." Ewart.
A Southern Girl. Peck.
Spencer the Rover. *Anonymous.*
The Sweater. Orr.
Sweet Jane. *Anonymous.*
Thespian in Jerusalem. Schotz.
To Mr. C, St. James's Place, London, October 22nd. Pope.
To the Landlord. Swift.
Toll the Bell for Damon. Anderson.
Tommy Tucker. *Anonymous.*
Upon Batt. Herrick.
Waiting at the Church; or, My Wife Won't Let Me. Leigh.
Waiting for Lilith. Kessler.
War Swaggers. Litvinoff.
We Love the Name of Texas. *Anonymous.*
Wedlock. *Anonymous.*
The Well of Life. Read.
When Adam Was Created. *Anonymous.*
While the leaves of the bamboo rustle. *Anonymous.*
Who Drags the Fiery Artist Down? Day.
Whose Little Pigs. *Anonymous.*
The Widower. Tyler.
The Wife-Hater. *Anonymous.*
Willie's Lyke-Wake. *Anonymous.*
The Winds. Williams.
The Wives of Mafiosi. Jong.
Work and Play. Martial (Marcus Valerius Martialis).
Worsening Situation. Ashbery.

Wig
Doctor Major. Johnson.
The Elderly Gentleman. Canning.
Hickety, Pickety, I-Silicity. *Anonymous.*
On Halloween. Silverstein.
Orator Prigg. Blake.
The Song Called "His Hide Is Covered with Hair.'. Belloc.
Where Are You Going. Follen.

Wight
Ballad of Our Lady. Dunbar.

Christ's Triumph after Death. Fletcher.
Old Mortality. Scott.
Wild
An Adage. Byron.
Ain't Nature Commonplace! Guiterman.
And in the Hanging Gardens. Aiken.
Beauty Rohtraut. Moricke.
The Burman Lover. Baker.
The Call of the Wild. Service.
The Cedar River. Gibbons.
The Child Is Father to the Man. Hopkins.
Dear Harp of My Country. Moore.
Domicilium. Hardy.
The Escape. Van Doren.
Everything is Plundered. Akhmatova.
Flowers of the Foothills & Mountain Valleys. Notley.
The Gay. Russell.
Go to the Shine That's on a Tree. Eberhart.
The Hawthorn Hedge. Wright.
I Want a Tenant: A Satire. O'Keefe.
In My Boat That Goes. Saigyo Hoshi.
In the Corn Land. Howard.
The Island. Muir.
It Was an April Morning. Wordsworth.
The Kite. O'Keeffe.
Lament, with Flesh and Blood. McPherson.
Lilly Dale. Thompson.
Little Wild Baby. Janvier.
Loch Coruisk (Skye). Sharp.
Love the Wild Swan. Jeffers.
Mares of Night. Long.
Melancholy. Habington.
The Mind Is an Ancient and Famous Capital. Schwartz.
My Wild Irish Rose. Olcott.
Night Flight. Whalley.
Nijinsky. Ferne.
Of the Scythians. Pollitt.
The Old Boat. Pratt.
On a Subway Express. Firkins.
An Open Air Performance of "As You Like It." Scovell.
People Do Gossip. Sappho.
Poem for Epiphany. Nicholson.
Preliminary Poem. Heath-Stubbs.
Publishing 2001. Rosenthal.
The Rambling Boy. *Anonymous.*
Rapid Transit. Agee.
Remembering the Winter. Bennett.
The Sailor's Grave. *Anonymous.*
The Sea. "Cornwall.
The Shadow People. Ledwidge.
Song to My Love. McKinney.
Sonnet upon a Swedish Cottage. Carr.
Stanzas. Bronte.
Surfaces. Mayhall.
There Will Be Peace. Pettengill.

Unguarded. Murray.
Whoso List to Hunt. Wyatt.
Wild Ass. Colum.
Wild Oats. Davies.
Wildness. Wagstaff.
With a Coin from Syracuse.
  Gogarty.
Wild beasts
Canto XLVII. Pound.
Darkness Music. Rukeyser.
The Rocky Mountains.
  Anonymous.
To Corydon. Beccadelli.
Wild bird (s)
A Bird inside a Box.
  Stafford.
Down the Bayou. Townsend.
I Am a Wild Young Irish
  Boy. *Anonymous.*
I'm Going to Georgia.
  Anonymous.
In Memoriam A.H.H.,
  XXXVI. Tennyson.
Love Song. *Anonymous.*
Middle of the Way. Kinnell.
My Home. *Anonymous.*
Old Bangum. *Anonymous.*
On Top of Old Smoky.
  Anonymous.
Owre the Hill. Soutar.
Psalm. Oppen.
The Snakes of September.
  Kunitz.
Soliloquy of the Returned
  Gold Adventurer.
  "Syntax".
The St. Lawrence and the
  Saguenay: The Thousand
  Islands. Sangster.
The Stars Go over the Lonely
  Ocean. Jeffers.
The Truth Made Breakfast.
  Miller.
Untitled Poem. "A swim in
  Ohuira Bay." Peterson.
Wilderness
Adulteries, Murthers,
  Robberies, Thefts.
  Williams.
Belden Hollow. Jennings.
Canaan. Spark.
Chaplinesque. Crane.
Confounded Nonsense.
  Hood.
Down in Alabam'. Warner.
Grant at Appomattox.
  Claytor.
Inversnaid. Hopkins.
Out of the Wilderness.
  Troubetzkoy.
The People at the Party.
  Mueller.
The Prairies. Bryant.
The Rehearsal. Gregory.
The Rubaiyat of Omar
  Khayyam. Omar
  Khayyam.
Temagami. Lampman.
Thrushes. Hughes.
True Love. Shelley.
Variations on a Time Theme.
  Muir.
The Voortrekker. Kipling.
Wilderness. Sandburg.
Wildfire
Dewey and His Men. Rice.
Wildflower (s)
An Anecdote of Love. Clare.
No Regret. Kraut.
Our Singing Strength. Frost.
A Prelude. Thompson.
Rain Clouds. Long.

Resounding. Soniat.
Spring Market. Driscoll.
Wilding
The Two April Mornings.
  Wordsworth.
Wildman
Wash Day. Mollin.
Wilds
Christmas Eve. Clancy.
Inscriptions for the
  Caledonian Canal.
  Southey.
Wildwood
Hunt the Buffalo.
  Anonymous.
Waking in the Dark. Rich.
Yonder Comes My Pretty Girl
  (B vers.). *Anonymous.*
Wile (s)
Autumn. O'Connor.
Hymn to Mercury. Homer.
O Woman Full of Wile.
  Keating.
Sleep! Sleep! Beauty Bright.
  Blake.
Wilful (ness)
December 1970. Tagliabue.
Koskiusko. Coleridge.
Sonnet: "Women have loved
  before as I love now."
  Millay.
Will (ed) (ing) (s)
Addressed to Lady ****, Who
  Asked What the Passion of
  Love Was? Morris.
After Sex. Kuzma.
Against Friars. *Anonymous.*
Alcestis. Verry.
The Alchemist. Bogan.
Alcoholic. Berryman.
Amen. Browning.
Amy Wentworth. Whittier.
Ars Poetica. Horace.
As a Great Prince. Honig.
The Authour Still Pursuing
  His Invention. Watson.
The Ballad of the Children of
  the Czar. Schwartz.
The Ballot. Pierpont.
Blest Is the Man Whose
  Tender Breast. Davis.
By the Statue of King Charles
  at Charing Cross.
  Johnson.
Calvin in the Casino.
  Cassity.
Can I Believe. Ariosto.
Christ, My Beloved.
  Baldwin.
The Circle. Coates.
Columbus the World-Giver.
  Egan.
Construction # 13.
  Sherwin.
Convention. Kreymborg.
La Corona. Donne.
Creator of Infinities. Hansen.
The Crosse. Herbert.
The Death of Will.
  Tomlinson.
Desiderium. Fletcher.
Disappointment. *Anonymous.*
The Drowned Seaman.
  Goldring.
Early Spring. Tennyson.
Egrets. Eastman.
Epigram: "Cloe's the wonder
  of her sex." Sackville.
Epitaph for a Sailor Buried
  Ashore. Roberts.
Epitaphs: For a Fickle Man.
  Van Doren.

Epitaphs of the War, 1914-18.
  Kipling.
Essay on Deity. Olson.
An Excelente Balade of
  Charitie. Chatterton.
Explorers as Seen by the
  Natives. Fetherling.
Fire. Wellesley.
Fisherman. Francis.
For an Obligate Parasite.
  Dugan.
For Strength. Tagore.
A Fragment. Winters.
Georgics. Virgil (Publius
  Vergilius Maro).
Glen Rosa. Jeffrey.
God's Will for Us.
  Anonymous.
God's Will is Best.
  Anonymous.
God's Will Is Best. Curtis.
Harry Pearce. Campbell.
Hart and Hare. *Anonymous.*
A Heathen Hymn (excerpt).
  Morris.
Heinrich Heine. Lewisohn.
The Herald Crane. Garland.
His Will Be Done. Flint.
The Holy Man. *Anonymous.*
How My Songs of Her Began.
  Marston.
An Humble Wish (excerpt).
  Thompson.
Hydro Works. Hervey.
I Do Not Ask Thee, Lord.
  Anonymous.
I Have a King. Dickinson.
I Lie Down with God.
  Anonymous.
I Yield Thee Praise.
  Cleveland.
In Harbor. Reese.
In Heavy Mind I Strayed the
  Field. Agee.
In Memoriam A.H.H., CX.
  Tennyson.
Jesus a Child His Course
  Begun. Fuller.
The Kangarcoster. Cox.
The Kingis Quhair: The
  Coming of Love. James I.
Laid on Thine Altar.
  Anonymous.
Letter I. Swingler.
Like as a Huntsman.
  Spenser.
Love in Time's Despite.
  Muir.
A Lover Left Alone.
  Anonymous.
Lulla La, Lulla Lulla Lullaby.
  Byrd.
Machine Out of the God.
  Sanders.
The Malady of Love Is
  Nerves. Petronius.
A Man May Live Thrice
  Nestor's Life. Norton.
Mill Girl. Baxter.
My Hairt Is Heich Aboif.
  Anonymous.
My Jesus, As Thou Wilt.
  Schmolck.
My Son and I. Norman.
The Necessity of Rejection.
  Schevill.
Non Que Je Veuille Oter La
  Liberte. Guillet.
Not in Dumb Resignation.
  Hay.
Now Evening Puts Amen to
  Day. Horgan.

An Old Atheist Pauses by the
  Sea. Kinsella.
Old Man of Tennessee. Hay.
On Being Told That One's
  Ideas Are Victorian. Hay.
On Leaving Bruges.
  Rossetti.
On the Instability of Youth.
  Vaux.
On the Triumph of
  Rationalism. Ainger.
Overtures to Death. Day
  Lewis.
The Pearl. *Anonymous.*
Playboy. Wilbur.
The Poet. Bryant.
Poet. Viereck.
A Prayer for Pentecost.
  Brown.
The Progress of Photography.
  Vazakas.
The Quaker Graveyard in
  Nantucket. Lowell.
The Quaker Widow. Taylor.
Reflections. Smith.
The Restless Heart. Surrey.
Return. Naude.
The Riders. Friend.
Salutation to Jesus Christ.
  Calvin.
Sea and Shore. Koopman.
Song: "Hang sorrow, cast
  away care." *Anonymous.*
The Song of the Colorado.
  Hall.
A Song of Winter. Davis.
Sonnet: "The azured vault, the
  crystal circles bright."
  James I.
Sonnets, CXXXV: "Whoever
  hath her wish, thou hast
  thy Will." Shakespeare.
Sonnets, CXLIII: "Lo, as a
  careful housewife runs to
  catch." Shakespeare.
A Soul. Rossetti.
The Spouse to the Younglings.
  Baldwin.
Teach Us to Serve Thee,
  Lord. Ignatius Loyola.
The Testament of Cathaeir
  Mor. *Anonymous.*
The Thoughts That Move the
  Heart of Man. Oakley.
Thy Will Be Done. Flint.
To a Dead Elephant.
  Livingstone.
Toward a True Peace.
  Cheyney.
The Unborn. Hardy.
We Heart. Chester.
What Is That in Thine Hand?
  Gray.
When I Am Dead. Macbeth.
Where There's a Will There's
  a Way. Cook.
Why? Talmud.
Wilderness Rivers.
  Coatsworth.
Will. Wilcox.
Wind. Stephens.
William
Earl Brand (Sweet William).
  Anonymous.
Lines on the Succession of the
  Kings of England
  (reversed). *Anonymous.*
The Plains of Waterloo.
  Anonymous.
A Sailor's Life. *Anonymous.*
The Tarantula. Whittemore.

William Morris
Rondel (parody).
Anonymous.
William the Norman
The Lay of St. Cuthbert
(excerpt). Barham.
Willie
Bird in a Cage (with music).
Anonymous.
Brennan on the Moor.
Anonymous.
Careless Willie. *Anonymous.*
Deep Blue Sea. *Anonymous.*
In Memoriam. "Adeler.
We Love You the Way You
Are. McFadden.
Whistling Willie. Starbird.
Willow (s)
The Aliscamp. Mistral.
The Ash and the Oak.
Simpson.
Balder's Wife. Cary.
Betrothed. Bogan.
Brook Song. Morse.
Buen Matina. Salusbury.
The Cobbler in Willow Street.
O'Neil.
Counting-Out Rhyme.
Millay.
Farewell, Sweet Dust. Wylie.
The Fish. Brooke.
Haiku: "I would like a bell..."
Wright.
He is not dead that sometime
hath a fall. Wyatt.
The House of Life. Rossetti.
I Am but a Little Woman.
Kivkarjuk.
Inscriptions on Chinese
Paintings: Lines To Do
With Youth. Bynner.
Keeping Hair. Wilson.
Lady Isabel and the Elf
Knight. *Anonymous.*
The Lady of the Lake.
Anonymous.
Little Catkins. Blok.
The Long Small Room.
Thomas.
Neither Spirit Nor Bird.
Anonymous.
O Sing unto my Roundelay.
Chatterton.
An Old Polish Lesson.
Pickard.
Repose of Rivers. Crane.
Saint George of England.
Fox-Smith.
Scene in a Madhouse. De
Vere.
See Where My Love A-
Maying Goes. *Anonymous.*
A Song: "My head on moss
reclining." *Anonymous.*
Song: "Roses and pinks will
be strewn where you go."
Davenant.
The Suicide's Grave.
Gilbert.
There Is a Tavern in the
Town. *Anonymous.*
Under the Drooping Willow
Tree. *Anonymous.*
The Visitant. Roethke.
Washing the Dishes. Morley.
The Willow-Man. Ewing.
Win (ner) (ners) (ning) (s)
13 Ways of Eradicating
Blackbirds (parody).
DeFoe.
Afterthoughts of Donna
Elvira. Kizer.

And the World's Face.
Symons.
Atalanta. Ovid (Publius
Ovidius Naso).
Be Hopeful. Gillilan.
The Beautiful Horses. Hall.
Between You and Me. Hazo.
The Cancer Match. Dickey.
Chick! My Naggie.
Anonymous.
Contest. Victor.
Creation's Lord, We Give
Thee Thanks. Hyde.
Cynisca. *Anonymous.*
Dedicatory Ode: They Say
That in the Unchanging
Place. Belloc.
Dragon Lesson. Hearst.
The Fight of the Year.
McGough.
For the Running of the New
York City Marathon.
Dickey.
Funky Football. Allah.
Georgics. Virgil (Publius
Vergilius Maro).
Good Friday: The Third
Nocturn. Abelard.
The Historical Judas.
Nemerov.
The Hobbit (excerpt).
Tolkien.
If Grief for Grief Can Touch
Thee. Bronte.
If You Happy Would Be.
Fernandez.
In My Place. Archibald.
It's Simply Great. Mase.
James Grant. *Anonymous.*
Limerick: "God's plan had a
hopeful beginning."
Anonymous.
Limerick: "Should a plan we
suggest, just that minute."
Anonymous.
Making a Man. Waterman.
Montrose to His Mistress.
Graham.
The Mould. Cromwell.
My Father: October 1942.
Stafford.
An Old Song Resung.
Graves.
Overheard in the Louvre.
Kennedy.
Pact. Fearing.
Poem: "In the earnest path of
duty." Forten.
The Secular Masque.
Dryden.
A Serious Poem. Walsh.
Shooting Gallery. Galvin.
A Smile. *Anonymous.*
Snow White and the Seven
Dwarfs. Dahl.
A Song: "When lovely
woman, prone to folly."
(parody). *Anonymous.*
Spring. Hopkins.
Success. Cameron.
Take Tools Our Strength...
Simmons, Jr.
Talking Union. Lampell.
The Tide Will Win.
Leonard.
To an Avenue Sport.
Collins.
To Arms. Benjamin.
To Flavia. Waller.
To Our Daughter. Armitage.
To Whistler, American.
Pound.

The Track. Christopher.
Vilanelle. Kerr.
Winslow Homer, Prisoners
from the Front. Blakely.
Wooing Song. Fletcher.
Would You in Venus' Wars
Succeed. *Anonymous.*
Winchester
The Dream about Junior High
School in America.
Lourie.
Sheridan's Ride. Read.
Wind (s) (y)
Abolitionist Hymn.
Anonymous.
Absolute and Abitofhell.
Knox.
An Additional Poem.
Ashbery.
An Adobe House. Bynner.
De Aegypto. Pound.
The Aeneid. Virgil (Publius
Vergilius Maro).
Afterward. Matheson.
Against the Age. Simpson.
Ah Me, If I Grew Sweet to
Man. "Field.
Alcestis in Ely. Moore.
All That Time. Swenson.
Allah's Tent. Colton.
Although It Is Not Plainly
Visible to the Eye.
Toshiyuki.
Among Iron Fragments.
Ruebner.
Anabasis. Nelson.
The Anchorsmiths. Dibdin.
And There Will I Be Buried.
Davidson.
Appearance. Russell.
April. Tietjens.
April 1940. Maybin.
Are You There, Mrs. Goose?
Hicks.
The Arrogant Frog and the
Superior Bull. Carryl.
As birds are fitted to the
boughs. Simpson.
At the Crossroads. Hovey.
The Auld House. Nairne.
Auschwitz from Colombo.
Ranasinghe.
Autumn Morning at
Cambridge. Cornford.
Backyard. Notley.
Backyard Swing. Hale.
The Balloon of the Mind.
Yeats.
The Banks of Sweet
Primroses. *Anonymous.*
The Bat. Spear.
Bay Bank. Ammons.
The Beautiful Ruined
Orchard. Berrigan.
Beauty. Rosenberg.
Beauty and Love. Young.
Beauty of This Earth. Opitz.
Beckon Me, Ye Cuillins.
Hendrie.
Bedtime Story. MacBeth.
Beggars. Carpenter.
Besides the autumn poets sing.
Dickinson.
Beyond. Kimball.
Big Road Blues. Johnson.
The Birdsville Track.
Stewart.
Blow Ye Winds. *Anonymous.*
Botany Lesson. Reeve.
The Bower of Bliss. Spenser.
Breaths. Diop.

The Bridegroom of Cana.
Pickthall.
Brook Song. Morse.
The Buckle. De la Mare.
Burning against the Wind.
Minty.
The Butterfly. Burr.
By the North Sea.
Swinburne.
The Cachalot. Pratt.
The Captive Stone. Barnes.
The Card-Players. Larkin.
Cherry Blossoms. "Lewis.
Christmas Dawn. Adcock.
The Circus. Koch.
Clearing at Dawn. Li Po.
The Coasters. Day.
Codes. Montross.
The Coming of the Plague.
Kees.
Composed on the Theme
"Willows by the Riverside."
Yu Hsuan-chi.
Conserving the Magnitude of
Uselessness. Ammons.
The Cot. Amen.
Councils. Piercy.
Crazed. De la Mare.
The Crystal Cabinet. Blake.
Cupidon. Smith.
The Curse: A Song. Herrick.
Dauber. Masefield.
The Day the Winds. Miles.
Deadfall. Keller.
Deaf. Higgs.
The Death of a Snake.
Plomer.
The Death of Old Joe Yazzie.
Rogers.
Deck the Halls. *Anonymous.*
Definitions of the Word Gout.
Koyama.
Descending. Iremonger.
Diana. Constable.
Dictum: For a Masque of
Deluge. Merwin.
Dithyramb in Retrospect.
Hopegood.
The Dog beneath the Skin.
Auden.
Dolphins in Blue Water.
Lowell.
Down in the Valley.
Anonymous.
Drawings by Children.
Mueller.
Drum-Taps. Whitman.
Drumochter. Murray.
Drunken Lover. Dodson.
East Coast–Canada.
Brewster.
El Alamein Revisited.
MacNab.
Elegy for Her Brother Sakhr.
Al-Khansa.
End of Summer. Kunitz.
Enigmas. Neruda.
The Enkindled Spring.
Lawrence.
L'Envoy. Herbert.
Epitaphs: For a Fickle Man.
Van Doren.
The Equinox. Heyward.
Esyllt. Jones.
The Exile at Rest. Pierpont.
Failure. Brooke.
Failure. Lattimore.
Faint Yet Pursuing.
Patmore.
The Fair Singer. Marvell.
The Falls of Glomach.
Young.

Fatal Interview. Millay.
The Fathers. Saltman.
Fatigues. Aldington.
The Faun. Long.
Fear. Simic.
'Fiddler's Green.
  Anonymous.
First Rain. Akins.
First Star. Smith.
The Firstborn. Soto.
Flying Noises. Lux.
For Michael. Mitchell.
For Nicholas, Born in
  September. Perry.
For St. Bartholomew's Eve.
  Cowley.
Four Choctaw Songs.
  Barnes.
Four Things Choctaw.
  Barnes.
Fragment: Rain. Shelley.
From Far, from Eve and
  Morning. Housman.
From the Notebooks.
  Roethke.
Fuimus Fumus. Sylvester.
The Full Heart. Nichols.
Funeral. Thompson.
The Garland. Vaughan.
The General Armstrong.
  Anonymous.
Genius. Perkins.
Georgics. Virgil (Publius
  Vergilius Maro).
Getting Out. Maloney.
Gibraltar. Trench.
The Gods. Merwin.
Going down the Mountain.
  Iremonger.
Gone on the Wind. Mangan.
Graduation Day, 1965.
  Marzan.
Grasmere Sonnets. Wright.
Grasses. Mills, Jr.
Guy. Emerson.
The Half of Life. Hoelderlin.
He Fumbles at Your Soul.
  Dickinson.
He is not dead that sometime
  hath a fall. Wyatt.
He Praises the Trees.
  Anonymous.
The Heritage. Reed.
Les Hiboux. Baudelaire.
Hide in the Heart.
  Frankenberg.
The Hind and the Panther.
  Dryden.
Homeward Bound. Southey.
Homing. Bontemps.
Hop Up, My Ladies.
  Anonymous.
Hurricane. MacLeish.
A Hymn of the Sea. Bryant.
I Am Not Yours. Teasdale.
I Feel an Apparition. Le
  Roy.
I Hear You've Let Go.
  Ferre.
I Know You Rider.
  Anonymous.
I Love a Flower. Nichols.
I Love Old Women.
  Kloefkorn.
I Love Snow and All the
  Forms. Shelley.
I Walk on the River at Dawn.
  Hart.
I Wish I Was Where I Would
  Be. Clare.
If I Had Ridden Horses.
  Maynard.

Immortalis. Morton.
In the Highlands. Stevenson.
In the Monastery. O'Conor.
In the Morning All Over.
  Stafford.
In the Name of Jesus Christ.
  Cranston.
In the Park. Harwood.
In the Turkish Ward.
  Balakian.
Indian Song. Johnson.
The Innocent Country-Maid's
  Delight. *Anonymous.*
The Innocent Spring.
  Sitwell.
Intuition. Delius.
Invocation for a Storm.
  Anonymous.
An Irish Wind. Dennis.
A Jacobite's Exile.
  Swinburne.
Jesse James. (Version B).
  Anonymous.
The Journey to Golgotha.
  Rao.
Joy. Bantock.
The Kabbalist. Eibel.
The Land behind the Wind.
  Wagoner.
The Last Gloucesterman.
  Grant.
The Last Tournament.
  Tennyson.
Leavetaking. Reape.
Let the Wind Blow High or
  Low. *Anonymous.*
Let Zeus Record. Doolittle.
A Letter to Lord Middleton.
  Etherege.
Lindedi Singing. Banda.
The Lion's Skeleton. Turner.
The Little Lough. Hewitt.
The Little Rose Is Dust, My
  Dear. Conkling.
Little Wind. Greenaway.
Locksley Hall. Tennyson.
The Long Parenthesis.
  Whiteman.
A Long Prologue to a Short
  Play... Sheers.
Love Poem. Silko.
The Lowlands of Holland.
  Anonymous.
Lucy Gray. Wordsworth.
The Lyricism of the Weak.
  Viereck.
Magpie. Davison.
Man Thinking about Woman.
  Lee.
Manerathiak's Song.
  Anonymous.
The Manoeuvre. Williams.
Manyoshu: Waiting for the
  Emperor Tenji. Nukada.
  Princess.
March Weather. Swan.
March Winds. Lloyd.
The Measure. Lane.
Medieval Norman Songs.
  Anonymous.
A Meditation. Eberhart.
Meditations of an Old
  Woman. Roethke.
The Message of the Rain.
  Russell.
Metric Figure. Williams.
Milkweed. Levine.
The Mill. Taylor.
Mirror. Chimako.
Modern Grimm.
  Richardson.
Monaghan. Leslie.

Moon-Madness. Starbuck.
The Moon's the North Wind's
  Cooky. Lindsay.
Moonlight. Apollinaire.
Moving. Crooker.
Museum with Chinese
  Landscapes. Cybulski.
My Father in the Night
  Commanding No.
  Simpson.
My Johnny. *Anonymous.*
My Woman. Catullus.
Myrtle. Kooser.
The New House. Thomas.
Night and a Distant Church.
  Atkins.
Night and Wind. Symons.
No End of No-Story.
  Macdonald.
North. Henson.
North Atlantic. Sandburg.
Nostalgia. Shapiro.
November 1968. Rich.
Now Christmas Is Come.
  Anonymous.
Now Close the Windows.
  Frost.
Now That the Flowers.
  Jones.
O City, Cities! (excerpt),.
  Larsson.
Oblivion! Sachs.
Odes. Horace.
Of His Returne from Spaine.
  Wyatt.
Of the Scythians. Pollitt.
The Old Couple. Green.
Old Man Rain. Cawein.
The Old Prison. Wright.
An Old Woman of the Roads.
  Colum.
Olive Grove. MacAdams.
On Such a Windy Afternoon.
  Enslin.
On the First of March.
  Anonymous.
On the Projected Kendal and
  Windermere Railway.
  Wordsworth.
On the Tower. Droste-
  Hulshoff.
One Poet Visits Another.
  Davies.
Opium Clippers. Henderson.
Our Sunday morning when
  dawn-priests were applying.
  Berryman.
Outside the Door. Wynne.
Outward. Neihardt.
Parable. Auden.
Pastures of Plenty. Guthrie.
Penelope, for Her Ulysses'
  Sake. Spenser.
The People, Yes. Sandburg.
Peter Gray. *Anonymous.*
The Phoenix of Mozart.
  Vigee.
Poem about People. Pinsky.
Poem against the British.
  Bly.
Poem for Good Friday.
  Jones.
Poem for Pat. Allen.
The Poet at Night-Fall.
  Wescott.
Poetry Is... Bennett.
The Poor. Verhaeren.
Population Drifts. Sandburg.
Portrait of an Indian.
  Rashley.
Possessions. Gurney.
Praises of God. *Anonymous.*

Preparations. Silko.
Prison Graveyard. Knight.
Proverbial Weather Rhymes.
  Anonymous.
Rain Has Fallen on the
  History Books. Rosenberg.
The Rats. Trakl.
Recognition. Perry.
The Red-Gold Rain. Sitwell.
Resolution. "Wiolar".
The Revenge of Hamish.
  Lanier.
The Road of Remembrance.
  Reese.
Rosabelle. Scott.
The Rose and the Wind.
  Marston.
The Rubaiyat of Omar
  Khayyam. Fitzgerald.
A Sacred Grove. Winant.
Sail at the Mast Head.
  Anonymous.
Sailors for My Money.
  Anonymous.
(San Ysidro, Cabezon).
  Allen.
Scattered Leaves. Henson.
Scotland. Gray.
The Sea-Lands. Johns.
Sea Love. Mew.
The Seasons. Thomson.
Seaway. Wilson.
Second Skins–A Peyote Song.
  Bruchac.
The Secret of the Deeps.
  Lysaght.
The Sedges. O'Sullivan.
The Seven Fiddlers. Evans.
She Comes Majestic with Her
  Swelling Sails. Southey.
Sheltered Garden. Doolittle.
Sicelides: Woman's
  Inconstancy. Fletcher.
Silex Scintillans. Vaughan.
Silver in the Wind.
  Strachan.
The Silver Leaf. Hay.
Sir Gawain and the Green
  Knight (excerpt).
  Anonymous.
Sirocco at Deya. Graves.
The Sleeping Beauty. Sitwell.
Sleepless at Crown Point.
  Wilbur.
Small Dark Song. Dacey.
Snow Country Weavers.
  Welch.
Snowgoose. Allen.
Some Negatives: X. At the
  Chateau. Merrill.
Some San Francisco Poems.
  Oppen.
Song. Thaxter.
Song-Maker. Endrezze-
  Danielson.
A Song of Freedom.
  Milligan.
The Song of the Ancient
  People. Hay.
Song of the Fishes.
  Anonymous.
Song of the Three Angels.
  Vicente.
Song of the Thunders.
  Anonymous.
Song: "The sun is mine."
  Hogg.
Sonnet at Dover Cliffs.
  Bowles.
Sonnet: "Go, thou that vainly
  dost mine eyes invite."
  King.

Sonnets. Masefield.
Sonnets. Tuckerman.
Sonnets to Miranda.
  Watson.
The Sorceress. Marais.
The Soul. Barlow.
The Sounding Portage.
  Dalton.
A South Coast Idyll.
  Watson.
South Wind. Yonathan.
Southerly Wind. *Anonymous.*
Speak Like Rain. Metz.
The Spider. Eiseley.
Spring. Shikishi.
The Spring Waters. "Ping
  Hsin" (Hsieh Wang-ying).
The Statute of Liberty.
  Field.
Staying in the Mountains in
  Summer. Yu Hsuan-chi.
The Story of a Well-Made
  Shield. Momaday.
Street-Walker in March.
  Albert.
The Struggle with the Angel.
  Vigee.
Suddenly. Blaser.
The Sun Has Set. Bronte.
Sundays Visiting. Rios.
Temptation. Cowper.
The Ten-Fifteen Community
  Poems (excerpt).
  Knoepfle.
Tennyson. Ansen.
The Term. Williams.
The Terrace in the Snow. Su
  Tung-P'o.
The Thatcher. Kennelly.
There Is a Dream Dreaming
  Us. Dubie.
They Who Possess the Sea.
  Adams.
Thistledown. Glover.
Thomas Trevelyan. Masters.
Three in Transition.
  Ignatow.
Three Songs: Thessalian.
  Bryher.
To a Snowflake. Thompson.
To a Young Gentleman in
  Love: A Tale. Prior.
To Ellen at the South.
  Emerson.
To the Maids Not to Walk in
  the Wind. Gogarty.
To the Western Wind.
  Halevi.
Tomorrow. Fearing.
The Tragic Mary Queen of
  Scot. "Field.
Train Ride. Wheelwright.
Tranquil Sea. Thomson.
The Trial. Abse.
The Twa Corbies.
  Anonymous.
The Two Old Women of
  Mumbling Hill. Reeves.
Under Restless Clouds.
  Michaelis.
The Unknown Color.
  Cullen.
The Unquiet Grave.
  Anonymous.
Upone Tabacco. Ayton [(or
  Aytoun)] Sir Robert.
La Vita Nuova. Kees.
Waiting. Corke.
Waiting for the Bus.
  Enright.
A Walk in Kyoto. Birney.

Washing between the
  Buildings. Eigner.
Watch Hill. Scott.
The Way a Ghost Dissolves.
  Hugo.
Weak Is the Will of Man, His
  Judgment Blind.
  Wordsworth.
Weather Ear. Nicholson.
West of Chicago. Dimoff.
When he sailed into the
  harbor. Korinna.
When Poor Mary Came
  Wandering Home (with
  music). *Anonymous.*
When the Lamp Is Shattered.
  Shelley.
When the spent day begins to
  frail. Cummings.
When Yon Full Moon.
  Davies.
While I walked in the
  moonlight. Murasaki
  Shibiku.
White Bird. Megged.
Who Has Seen the Wind?
  Rossetti.
Who Will Stop His Hand
  from Giving Warmth.
  Pizarnik.
The Wind. Creeley.
The Wind. Miller.
Wind and Impulse. Big
  Eagle.
The Wind and the Bird.
  Anonymous.
The Wind at Penistone.
  Davie.
The Wind Blow East.
  Anonymous.
The Wind Carol. Turco.
The Wind Has Such a Rainy
  Sound. Rossetti.
The Wind in the Tree.
  Prince.
The Wind It Blew Up the
  Railroad Track (with
  music). *Anonymous.*
The Wind Like an Ocean.
  Eigner.
The Wind of Our Enemy
  (excerpt). Marriott.
Wind of the Prairie. Howes.
The Wind on the Hills.
  Shorter.
The Wind's Way. Conkling.
Winds A-Blowing. Justus.
Winter Encounters.
  Tomlinson.
Winter Moon. Spaziani.
Winter Night. Fitzgerald.
Wires. Bassett.
Woman from the West Coast.
  Crozier.
A Woman Is a Branchy Tree.
  Stephens.
Words for Music Perhaps.
  Yeats.
The World in Making.
  Parker.
Wrack. Feldman.
Writing. Nemerov.
A Yellow Pansy. Cone.
The Young Girl and the
  Beach. Andresen.
Your Eyes. Chantikian.
Windbell
The Poet at Night-Fall.
  Wescott.
Windfalls
Charity. Bensley.
In an Old Orchard. Dufault.

Windharp
Black Bagatelles. Hall.
Winding
Poly-Olbion. Drayton.
The Winding Banks of Erne.
  Allingham.
Windingsheet
Christus Triumphans.
  Pallen.
Elegy. Cohen.
The Exile. Rubin.
A House in Taos. Hughes.
Nothing. Simic.
Sonnet Written in a Blank
  Leaf of Dugdale's
  Monasticon. Warton, Jr..
The Spinner. De Vere.
Sun Moon Kelp Flower or
  Goat. Gregg.
Written in a Copy of The
  Earthly Paradise. Morris.
Windmill (s)
Men against the Sky.
  Haines.
Telephone Directory.
  Crosby.
A Tune. Symons.
The Windmill. De Tabley.
Window (s)
The Adepts. Durrell.
Akriel's Consolation. Pillen.
Another November. Plumly.
Anxiety Pastorale. Schaefer.
Beginning by Example.
  Gilbert.
Les Belles Roses sans Mercie.
  Cripps.
The Black Cottage. Frost.
The Book of Nightmares.
  Kinnell.
Canzone. Waldman.
Cat into Lady. La Fontaine.
Chamber Music. Joyce.
Clay and Water. Hochman.
Cold Feet in Columbus.
  Heath.
Crabbing. Levine.
Diagnosis. Canan.
Drought. Holbrook.
Drunken Lover. Dodson.
Eclogues. Schmitz.
The Evening Star.
  Longfellow.
Eyes That Queenly Sit.
  Daryush.
Fate in Incognito. Benedikt.
Fifth & 94th. Plumly.
The Flirtation. Blumenthal.
For the Altarpiece of the
  Roseau Valley Church,
  Saint Lucia. Walcott.
Fourth Street, San Rafael.
  Berkson.
Hannah Binding Shoes.
  Larcom.
Hawthorne. Longfellow.
Hospital Observation.
  Symons.
In Like a Lion. Hewitt.
In the Fall. Rivero.
Japanese Fan. Kirkup.
The Lace Curtains.
  MacAdams.
Late. Halpern.
Limerick: "I must eat an
  apple," said Link." Blair.
Listening to the Music of
  Arsenio Rodriguez Is
  Moving Closer... Cruz.
Little Bird, Go through My
  Window. *Anonymous.*
Long Lines. Goodman.

Los Mineros. Dorn.
The Magnet. Stone.
Man Asleep in the Desert.
  Lux.
Manhattan. Hays.
Minor Key. Teller. J. L.
Near Helikon. Stickney.
Night Flight. Daigon.
Night of Rain. Kenyon.
North Sea Off Carnoustie.
  Stevenson.
Poem for Half-White College
  Students. Jones.
Postcard to D--. Ginsberg.
Red May. Robinson.
Sacred Objects. Simpson.
Schoolyard in April. Koch.
Serenade. Carnevali.
Sleeping Beauty. Sheck.
Sleeping Beauty. Shore.
The Song of a Factory
  Worker. Collins.
Standard Forgings Plant.
  Stephens.
Storm Windows. Nemerov.
The Theory of the Flower.
  Palmer.
There Isn't Enough Bread.
  Culhane.
This Morning. Wright.
To Make an Amblongus Pie.
  Lear.
To Ultima Thule.
  Dangerfield.
Tulips and Addresses. Field.
Walls Breathe. Mariah.
Waters of Babylon.
  Untermeyer.
Wellington. Manhire.
What It Was. Sward.
Window. Cherner.
The Window. Muir.
Window to the East. Evans.
Words. Burden.
Windowpane (s)
A Brick Not Used in
  Building. Replansky.
Candle. Segal.
Dutch Interior. Sarton.
Gooseberries. Berg.
Pipings. Paget-Fredericks.
Who Is Tapping at My
  Window. Deming.
Windowshade
Puerto Ricans in New York.
  Reznikoff.
Windowsill
Into & At. Pennant.
Questioning Faces. Frost.
Tiptoe Night. Drinkwater.
Windshield
Long Summer (excerpt).
  Lowell.
Prosser. Carver.
Windsor
Dappled Grey. *Anonymous.*
George III. Thackeray.
The Great Lakes Suite.
  Reaney.
Wine
After the Persian. Bogan.
After Work. Snyder.
The Age of Wisdom.
  Thackeray.
The Agonie. Herbert.
And in the Hanging Gardens.
  Aiken.
And Thus in Nineveh.
  Pound.
The Angel. Hayes.
Angelus. Blumgarten
  (Yehoash)

The Antiquary. Martial (Marcus Valerius Martialis).
The Appeasement of Demeter. Meredith.
At a Private Showing in 1982. Kumin.
Au Tombeau de Mon Pere. McCuaig.
Bacchus on Beverages. Redi.
Be Drunken. Baudelaire.
Bold Reynard the Fox. *Anonymous.*
Cherry Tree. Sitwell.
Chickory. Gal'ed.
Chorus: "If I drink water while this doth last." Peacock.
Christmas. Betjeman.
Clarel. Melville.
Come Out of Crete. Sappho.
Consummation. Barker.
A Credo. Thackeray.
Crotchet Castle. Peacock.
The Cup. Oldham.
Damis, an Author Cold and Weak. *Anonymous.*
The Dandelion Gatherer. Francis.
Days Were Great as Lakes. Vogel.
Dear Friend, Whose Presence in the House. Clarke.
Departure. Smith.
Divination. Metz.
A Drinking-Song. Carey.
Ebbe Skammelson. *Anonymous.*
Ecce Homunculus. Mason.
Enjoyment. Theognis.
Epigram: "Drink, unhappy lover." Meleager.
Epitaph in a Churchyard at Thetford, in Norfolk. *Anonymous.*
Exchange. Mary Dorothy Ann.
Farewell, Sweet Dust. Wylie.
Five Arabic Verses in Praise of Wine. *Anonymous.*
The Fly. Quevedo y Villegas.
Frippery. Horace.
The Fugitive. Meynell.
Ganymede. Bynner.
Garden at Heidelberg. Landor.
Glencoe. Chesterton.
The Good Day. Bashford.
The Good Samaritan. Newman.
Great Bacchus: from the Greek. Prior.
Haiku: "The bride." *Anonymous.*
The Harvester. Lawrence.
I Am Forsaken. *Anonymous.*
I Don't Let the Girls Worry My Mind. *Anonymous.*
I Planted My Bright Paradise. Blok.
If. Collins.
In a Wine Cellar. Daley.
In the Gold Room. Wilde.
Indian Summer. Dickinson.
Indifference. *Anonymous.*
Introductory Lines (excerpt). Yeats.
The Jar. Stoddard.
The Laborer. Chimsoro.
Last Lines (excerpt). Meredith.
The Lesson. Rubin.

Lines to Mr. Hodgson. Byron.
Logic. *Anonymous.*
Lustily, Lustily. *Anonymous.*
Mass at Dawn. Campbell.
Medieval Norman Songs. *Anonymous.*
A Merry Ballad of Vintners. Payne.
The Miracle. Sedulius.
The Mither's Lament. Smith.
Modern Love, XXXII. Meredith.
Monangamba. Jacinto.
The Muse. Davies.
Music. *Anonymous.*
My Spectre around Me Night & Day. Blake.
Nantucket / Mussels / October. Lewandowski.
The Night Sits in This Chair. Notley.
An Ode to Master Endymion Porter, upon His Brother's Death. Herrick.
Odes. Horace.
On Himselfe. Herrick.
On the Way. Trakl.
Plum Blossoms. Chu Shu-chen.
Prayer by Moonlight. Swartz.
Proverbial Advice on Eating and Drinking. *Anonymous.*
A Responsory, 1948. Merton.
Riddle: "I sat wi' my love, and I drank wi' my love." *Anonymous.*
Roan Stallion. Jeffers.
Robin Hood's Delight. *Anonymous.*
The Rosy Days Are Numbered. Ibn Ezra.
The Rubaiyat of Omar Khayyam. Omar Khayyam.
Rude Boreas. *Anonymous.*
The Shooting of Werfel. Watkins.
Silex Scintillans. Vaughan.
Sir Halewyn. *Anonymous.*
Song and Wine. Bacchylides.
Song of the Cape of Good Hope. Schubart.
The Song of the Good Samaritan. Watkins.
A Song of the Moon. McKay.
Stanzas Occasioned by the Ruins of a Country Inn. Freneau.
Summer Journey. Rodgers.
The Sunbeam. *Anonymous.*
This Bread I Break Was Once the Oat. Thomas.
Though All the Fates Should Prove Unkind. Thoreau.
A Thought from Porpertius. Yeats.
The Thousand and One Nights: To Lighten My Darkness. *Anonymous.*
The Three Kingdoms of Nature. Lessing.
Three Phases of Africa. Parkes.
To a Friend on His Marriage. Prince.
To Master Davenant for Absence. Suckling.

To Our Lord, upon the Water Made Wine. Crashaw.
To the Water Nymphs, Drinking at the Fountain. Herrick.
Trying to Believe. Gregg.
Twilight in California. Dow.
Two Gardens. De Bevoise.
Upon Drinking in a Bowl. Rochester.
The Victor of Antietam. Melville.
Warning to a Guest. Holloway.
We Go out Together. Patchen.
When I Came to London. Castelete.
Wine and Love and Lyre. *Anonymous.*
Wine and Water. Chesterton.
Wine Bowl. Doolittle.
Wine O Living. Marshall.
The Winter Glass. Cotton.
A Winter Wish. Messinger.
The Young Cordwainer. Graves.
Zong Belegt Baatar. *Anonymous.*

Wine-cup (s)
Alcibiades to a Jealous Girl. Ficke.
The Dandelion Gatherer. Francis.
The Minstrel. Goethe.
On the Bridge of Athlone: A Prophecy. MacDonagh.
Song: "The pints and the pistols, the pike-staves and pottles." Praed.

Winepress
Grape-Gathering. Shlonsky. Abraham
Milton. Blake.

Wing (ed) (s)
Absent Lover. *Anonymous.*
Advice from Euterpe. Revard.
After. Hodgson.
After Alcman. Gallup.
Again My Fond Circle of Doves. Hathaway.
Angels. Abse.
Antique Glimpses (excerpt). Irwin.
The Argument Begins with A. Thesen.
As I Came Down Mount Tamalpais. Urmy.
Assumption. Fallon.
An Australian Symphony. Evans.
Autumn. Wolfe.
The Bat. Roethke.
Be Like the Bird. Hugo.
Beachhead Preachment. Zu-Bolton.
The Beauty of the Stars. Ibn Ezra.
A Bestiary of the Garden for Children Who Should Know Better. Gotlieb.
Beware the Cuckoo. Moll.
Bicycling Song. Beeching.
Big City Glissando. Christopher.
The Bird. Greacen.
The Bird. Tagore.
The Bird, Let Loose in Eastern Skies. Moore.
Birds. Miller.

The Birds of Tin. Madge.
The Blackcock. Baillie.
The Bonny Moorhen. *Anonymous.*
The Book of Job and a Draft of a Poem to Praise the Paths... Oppen.
Broncho Versus Bicycle. Crawford.
Buffel's Kop. Campbell.
The Burial. Davis.
The Butterfly. Spenser.
Carolina Spring Song. Allen.
The Caterpillar and the Ant. Ramsay.
Child with Six Fingers. Muske.
The Children of the Poor. Hugo.
Christmas Eve Service at Midnight at St. Michael's. Bly.
Conceits. Bates.
Confusion. Cruz.
A Cottage in the Wood. Edson.
Dawn. Scott.
The Day of the Night. Scully.
Days. Baker.
The Dead Butterfly. Levertov.
Dear, Do Not Your Fair Beauty Wrong. May.
Death for the Dark Stranger. McGrath.
The Death of the Starling. Coleridge.
Delight in Books from Evening. Pastorius.
Diretro al Sol. Bell.
Discovered in Mid-Ocean. Spender.
The Double Fortress. Noyes.
The Duck Pond at Mini's Pasture, a Dozen Years Later. Dow.
The Eagle. Young.
The Easter Song. Sedulius.
The Egg. Bowering.
The Elder Edda: The Beginning and the End (abridged). *Anonymous.*
Elemental. Dillon.
The Faerie Queene. Spenser.
The Falcon. Stoddard.
Fiat Lux. Mifflin.
For a Homecoming. Randall.
Forgiven? Gillespy.
Fountains. Sitwell.
Geological Faults. Unger.
Gibberish. Coleridge.
Glazunoviana. Ashbery.
God's Grandeur. Hopkins.
Godspeed. Spofford.
Going Down Hill on a Bicycle. Beeching.
The Grave. Blair.
The Great Man. Tietjens.
Guardian Angel. Newman.
The Gull. Nakasuk.
A Gull Goes Up. Adams.
The Gully. Maurice.
Heron Weather. Crase.
The House of Life. Rossetti.
Hugh Stuart Boyd: His Blindness. Browning.
Icarus. Spender.
Ideal and Reality. Campbell.
Images. Schaukal.
Impression. Symons.

In Grandfather's Glasses.
  Peters.
In Her Song She Is Alone.
  Swan.
In Memoriam A.H.H.,
  XLVIII. Tennyson.
In Weather. Hass.
Iron Heaven. Alver.
Janitor Working on
  Threshold. Avison.
Johnie Cock (K version).
  Anonymous.
Judith Recalls Holofernes.
  Stanton.
Kissing the Dancer. Sward.
The Knot. Kunitz.
Lament of a Last Letter.
  Harrison.
Let Us Declare! (excerpt).
  Morgan.
Letter to Alex Comfort.
  Abse.
Light of the World. Judd.
Little Cock Robin.
  Anonymous.
A Little Cock Sparrow Sat on
  a Green Tree. *Anonymous.*
Long-Billed Gannets.
  Emery.
Love. Trask.
Love Is Life. Rolle.
Love Songs. Loy.
Love the Wild Swan. Jeffers.
The Man on the Bed.
  Greger.
Many Wings. Conant.
Meditations. Taylor.
A Meeting. Hoffman.
Mellowness & Flight.
  Barlow.
Minnie and Her Dove.
  Turner.
Mother's Song. *Anonymous.*
Murder in the Cathedral.
  Eliot.
Nightgown, Wife's Gown.
  Sward.
A Note on Lizards' Feet.
  Van Rensselaer.
O Whither Shall I Fly?
  Quarles.
Of Life and Death (excerpt).
  Vaughan.
The Old Couple, III, i: Love's
  Prime. May.
The Old Pilot. Hall.
On Measure. Waldrop.
On Startling Some Pigeons.
  Turner.
On the Height. Tietjens.
Our History. Coblentz.
The Owl. Davison.
The Owl in the Rabbi's Barn.
  Jaffe.
Parting. Roscoe.
Peace in the World.
  Galsworthy.
Perdita. MacNeice.
Perfect. ""MacDiarmid.
The Phoenix. Megged.
Pigeons in Prison. Butler.
The Play of the Weather: The
  English Schoolboy.
  Heywood.
The Plea of the Midsummer
  Fairies. Hood.
Poem for Myself and Mei:
  Abortion. Silko.
Poems, LVIII: "Twenty years
  hence my eyes may grow."
  Landor.

The Poplar's Shadow.
  Swenson.
A Prayer. Noyes.
The Rape of the Lock.
  Pope.
Raven at Lemon Creek Jail.
  Waltner.
Red Lilies. Guest.
Resting Place. Silkin.
The Road the Crows Own.
  Astor.
The Road to Pengya. Tu Fu.
The Rubaiyat of Omar
  Khayyam. Omar
  Khayyam.
Sacco-Vanzetti. Halpern.
Sea-Birds. Thomson.
Seagulls on the Serpentine.
  Noyes.
The Serious Merriment of
  Women. Goedicke.
The Shadow and the Light
  (excerpt). Whittier.
Shag Rookery. Hart-Smith.
Signs Everywhere of Birds
  Nesting, While. Williams.
Silex Scintillans. Vaughan.
The Silkworms. Stewart.
The Singers. Bruce.
Sir Lark and King Sun: A
  Parable. Macdonald.
The Small. Roethke.
Small Song. Shaw.
Song: "Gold wings across the
  sea!" Morris.
Song: "My dreams were
  doleful and drear." Irwin.
Song of the Fallen Deer.
  Anonymous.
Song of the Murdered Child
  Whose Bones Grew into a
  Milk-white Dove.
  Anonymous.
Sonnet: "I stood beside a pool,
  from whence ascended."
  Trench.
Sonnet: A Trance of Love.
  Cino da Pistoia.
Sonnets. Tuckerman.
Sonnets from the Portuguese,
  XXXV. Browning.
The Soul's Travelling
  (excerpt). Browning.
Star. Derwood.
The Stormy Petrel.
  "Cornwall.
The Story of Vinland.
  Lanier.
Sunset. Bashford.
A Table Richly Spread.
  Milton.
The Therapeutist. Bentley.
There Isn't Enough Bread.
  Culhane.
Thou Art the Source. Rumi.
Three Poems on Morris
  Graves' Paintings. Logan.
The Three Ravens (C vers.).
  Anonymous.
Three Songs. Beaumont.
"The Time Has Come," the
  Walrus Said. "Carroll.
Time's Song. Praed.
To a Mosquito. Bryant.
To a Sea Eagle.
  ""MacDiarmid.
To God. Maurice.
To His Mistress. Rochester.
To My Friend, behind Walls.
  Kizer.
To the Western Wind.
  Herrick.

Tor House. Jeffers.
The Trail Horse. Wagoner.
Under Our Own Wings.
  Wong.
The Unerring Guide.
  Shipton.
Untitled. Naone.
Warning to Cupid.
  Anonymous.
The Wasp. Sharp.
Where Is My Butterfly Net?
  McCord.
Where She Was Not Born.
  Yvonne.
Whit Sunday. Beaumont.
The Windmill of Evening.
  Reich.
Winged Man. Benét.
Winged Mariner. Howes.
Wings. Holub.
Wings. Hugo.
The Wings. Levertov.
Wings at Dawn. Auslander.
Without That Once Clear
  Aim. Spender.
Written in a Little Lady's
  Little Album. Faber.
Yachts on the Nile. Spencer.
Wink (ed) (ing) (s)
Amores. Ovid (Publius
  Ovidius Naso).
At Lucky Moments We Seem
  on the Brink. Auden.
Ballad of Another Ophelia.
  Lawrence.
End of Season. Warren.
A Face. Browning.
Handicapped. Berrigan.
A Pair of Fireflies. Liu.
The Raising of the Dead.
  Dobson.
Some Negatives: X. At the
  Chateau. Merrill.
Temptation in Harvest.
  Kavanagh.
When 'omer Smote 'is
  Bloomin' Lyre. Kipling.
Winter
Above the Rocking Heads of
  the Mothers. Sachs.
Address to Plenty. Clare.
Affaire d'Amour. Deland.
Aging. Wakoski.
Ago. Jennings.
All for Love. Dryden.
Alone. De la Mare.
An Anniversary of Death.
  Wieners.
Apostasy. Mills.
Apple Season. Frost.
Autumn. Carpenter.
Autumn. Nashe [(or Nash)]
  Thomas.
Autumn Poem. Cronin.
Beautiful. Bixler.
Beauty and Sadness. Song.
The Beekeeper's Daughter.
  Plath.
Big Friend of the Stones.
  Orlen.
Blizzard. Garfinkel.
Blue Winter. Francis.
The Braes o' Gleniffer.
  Tannahill.
Canning Time. Morgan.
Cardinal. Howes.
Cauld Cornwood.
  Anonymous.
Certainty. Hardy.
Chickens. Hewitt.
Chorus for Survival (excerpt).
  Gregory.

The Climate of Paradise.
  Simpson.
The Closing Scene. Read.
Comanche Ghost Dance.
  Henson.
The Coming of Spring.
  Perry.
Composed near Calais, on the
  Road Leading to Ardres,
  August 7, 1802.
  Wordsworth.
Conrad in Twilight.
  Ransom.
Contemplations. Bradstreet.
Crows in Spring. Clare.
The Dance. Lehmann.
A Day of Notes. Green.
Daydream. Tessimond.
Death of Rimbaud. Fisher.
Don Juan. Byron.
Edith. Channing
Elegy for My Father.
  Strand.
Epilogue. Falkner.
Epitaph: "Lais now old, that
  erst attempting lass."
  Anonymous.
Epithalamium. Cluysenaar.
Eskimo Chant. *Anonymous.*
ESP. Revard.
Farm Wife. Field.
The Farmer and the Shanty
  Boy (Trenton Town).
  Anonymous.
First Snow. Eastwick.
The Firstborn. Soto.
For Musia's Grandchildren.
  Layton.
Force. Sill.
Fort Robinson. Kooser.
The Frost Pane. McCord.
Furry Bear. Milne.
Georgics. Virgil (Publius
  Vergilius Maro).
A Glee for Winter. Domett.
"Grandfather" in. Feirstein.
Greedy Seasons. Myles.
The Ground-Swell. Pratt.
Haiku: "An empty sickbed..."
  Wright.
Hamlet. Shakespeare.
Harlem in January. Fields.
A Hill. Hecht.
Himalayan Balsam.
  Stevenson.
Holiday. Rich.
The Holly Tree. Southey.
Impression de Paris. Wilde.
In the Doorway. Browning.
In the New Sun. Levine.
It Is in the Winter That We
  Dream of Spring. Wilson.
Jephthah's Daughter.
  Heavysege.
A Knight of Ghosts and
  Shadows. Thompson.
Ladies and Gentlemen This
  Little Girl. Cummings.
Lament of a Mocking-Bird.
  Kemble
Langsyne, When Life Was
  Bonnie. Anderson.
Last Look at La Plata,
  Missouri. Barnes.
Last Snow. Young.
Leningrad Cemetery, Winter
  of 1941. Olds.
Lent Tending. Shepherd.
Loft. Dransfield.
The Long and Lonely Winter.
  Goulder.

Love Laughs at Winter.
  Anonymous.
Lynx. Howard.
Mid-Winter Walking.
  Graves.
Midcentury Love Letter.
  McGinley.
Miramar Beach.
  Cunningham.
Misericordia. Mead.
The Misogynist. Morgan.
Monaghan. Leslie.
A More Ancient Mariner.
  Carman.
My Feet. Jenkins.
My Nannie's Awa'. Burns.
My Penis. Ochester.
New Snow. Rowles.
A Nightly Deed. Madge.
NTo R. B. Hopkins.
Nursing the Hide. Dunne.
October. Very.
October Winds. Randall.
Ode to the West Wind.
  Shelley.
Often I Compare My Lord to
  Heaven. Stampa.
An Old Man's Winter Night.
  Frost.
Old May Song. *Anonymous.*
Old Winter. Noel.
The Old Woman Sits. Davis.
On Being Asked for a War
  Poem. Yeats.
The Paperweight.
  Schnackenberg.
Paradise. Sargent.
Passing the Masonic Home for
  the Aged. Scott.
Pearl Diver. Benet.
The Pelicans My Father Secs.
  Maris Stella.
The Phantom Light of the
  Baie des Chaleurs. Eaton.
Pilgrimage to Hennessey's.
  Sher.
Polyolbion. Drayton.
Portrait of an Indian.
  Rashley.
The Private Meeting Place.
  Wright.
Privation. Carruth.
The Procession. Widdemer.
Pruners: Conca di Marini.
  Langland.
The Quiet of the Dead.
  Webster.
Raisins and Nuts. Reznikoff.
Remembering the Winter.
  Bennett.
Riddle: "In Spring I look
  gay." *Anonymous.*
The Riding Stable in Winter.
  Tagliabue.
The Roadmenders' Song.
  Anonymous.
Robin's Song. King.
Rondeau. Orleans.
The Schoolboy. Blake.
Scraps. Fried.
The Snowstorm. Scott.
Soft White. Harwood.
Song: "Shine out, fair Sun,
  with all your heat."
  Anonymous.
Sonnets, XCVII: "How like a
  winter hath my absence
  been." Shakespeare.
Sonnets, XCVIII: "From you
  have I been absent in the
  spring." Shakespeare.

The Spirit of the Fall.
  Dandridge.
Spring in These Hills.
  MacLeish.
A Spring Journey. Palmer.
Staying Alive. Wagoner.
Sugar in the Cane. Williams.
A Sunset. Hugo.
Surely You Remember.
  Ravikovich.
Swedes. Thomas.
Tarantula or the Dance of
  Death. Hecht.
Thesis. Dorn.
They Return. Macpherson.
The Throstle. Tennyson.
Through the Year. Cutler.
To Delia. Daniel.
To the Grasshopper and the
  Cricket. Hunt.
Tracking the Sled, Christmas
  1951. Walker.
Tramp Miner's Song.
  Anonymous.
Up in the Morning Early.
  Burns.
Vain Advice at the Year's
  End. Wright.
Walk on a Winter Day.
  Allen.
Walter Lesly. *Anonymous.*
The Way Down: They Return.
  Macpherson.
What Music. Harjo.
When Men Shall Find.
  Daniel.
Wild Bees. Baxter.
Wild Peaches. Wylie.
Winter. Mair.
Winter. Sackville.
Winter Burn. Hill.
Winter Day. Fried.
Winter Days. Owen.
Winter: East Anglia.
  Blunden.
Winter Memories. Thoreau.
Winter Trout. Dickey.
A Wintering Moon. Hardy.
The Year of Winter.
  LaPena.
Your Mother. Cornish.
Zummer Thoughts in Winter
  Time. Barnes.

Wintry
A Child That Has a Cold We
  May Suppose. Dibdin.
Death and Birth. Swinburne.
December. Rossetti.
The Seasons. Thomson.
Snow. Crapsey.
'Tis Winter Now.
  Longfellow.
To a Sparrow. Ledwidge.

Wipe (d) (s)
Autumn Evening. Anthony.
Bruton Town. *Anonymous.*
Come! Ignatow.
Heedless o' My Love.
  Barnes.
Hmmm, 15. Scalapino.
I Had a Little Husband.
  Mother Goose.
If You Trap the Moment.
  Blake.
A Lady. Snodgrass.
The Little Maid. Wells.
Lost. Chu Shu-chen.
Minotaur Poems. Mandel.
Pause. Bethell.
The Poet's Fate. Hood.

Wire (d) (s)
Afternoons with Baedeker.
  Lancaster.
The Captive Stone. Barnes.
Composition in Black and
  White. Pollitt.
The Ever-Touring
  Englishmen... *Anonymous.*
In Parenthesis. Jones.
The Leaf. Fagg.
Looking at Power.
  Woessner.
The Middleaged Man.
  Simpson.
On Autumn Lake. Ashbery.
Passive Resistance. Bruchac.
The Sage in Unison.
  Stewart.
Song: "And can the physician
  make sick men well?"
  Anonymous.
Sonnet: "Matte brandy bottle,
  adjacent voices, skin."
  Hacker.
Tombstone with Cherubim.
  Gregory.

Wisdom
90 North. Jarrell.
Address to the Scholars of
  New England. Ransom.
After the Burial. Lowell
Alajire. *Anonymous.*
Anacreontic, On Parting with
  a little Child. Wesley.
The Ashland Tragedy, I.
  Anonymous.
Berrying. Emerson.
Better to Spit on the Whip
  than Stutter Your Love
  Like a Worm. Inez.
The Butterfly. O'Keeffe.
Caelica, LXVI. Greville.
The Chemistry of Character.
  Dorney.
Child of Loneliness. Gale.
The Commonplace.
  Whitman.
Confessio Amantis. Gower.
The Counsels of O'Riordan,
  the Rann Maker.
  O'Bolger.
A Dutch Proverb. Prior.
Eastern Tempest. Blunden.
An Elegy. To an Old Beauty.
  Parnell.
The Emigrant. O'Grady.
The Eternity of Nature.
  Clare.
Eyes. Davies.
The Flying Fish. Gray.
Gascoigne's Memories.
  Gascoigne.
George Levison. Allingham.
Girl in a White Coat.
  Brinnin.
Go Take the World.
  Macpherson.
God Is Love. Bowring.
He Leadeth Me. Barry.
Helen. "Coolidge.
Hero and Leander. Marlowe.
The Horn. Adams.
The Housewife. Coblentz
I Have a Big Favor to Ask
  You, Brothers. Landau.
In Memoriam A.H.H., CVIII.
  Tennyson.
Kinship. Roberts.
Little Hands. Binyon.
Look Not to Me for Wisdom.
  Divine.

Lord, My Weak Thought in
  Vain Would Climb.
  Palmer.
Love's Wisdom. Deland.
The Marathon Runner.
  Johnson.
Mrs. Jaypher. Lear.
"Nature" Is What We See.
  Dickinson.
Of Perfect Friendship.
  Cheke.
Old Men. Keesing.
On Reading Aloud My Early
  Poems. Williams.
On the Road. Jenks.
One Step at a Time.
  Anonymous.
Pangur Ban. *Anonymous.*
The Praise of Fionn.
  Anonymous.
Praises of King George VI.
  Ngani.
Prayer for Serenity.
  Niebuhr.
Proust on Noah.
  Silberschlag.
Right Apprehension.
  Traherne.
The Secret. Casas.
The Seven Sages. Yeats.
Solomon and the Bees. Saxe.
Summum Bonum. Abu-l-Ala
  al-Maarri.
The Swarthmore Phi Beta
  Kappa Poem. Lattimore.
Talking to Animals. Howes.
To God, Ye Choir above.
  Skelton.
To One That Desired to
  Know My Mistris. Carew.
"Too dearly had I bought my
  green and youthful years."
  Surrey.
The Train Butcher. Ferril.
The Trees in the Garden
  Rained Flowers. Crane.
The Vanity of Human Wishes.
  Johnson.
A Vault inside the Castle at
  Goito. Browning.
Wisdom. Peavy.
With Kathy at Wisdom.
  Hugo.
Woo Not the World.
  Mu'tamid.
A Word to the Wise. Duer.
A World Beyond. Bowditch

Wise (r) (st) (ly)
African Dream. Kaufman.
Arabian Proverb.
  Anonymous.
Astrophel and Stella, XXXIII.
  Sidney.
At the Cavour. Symons.
At Tide Water. Roberts.
The Bacchante to Her Babe.
  Tietjens.
The Bait. Donne.
Beautiful Sunday. Falstaff.
Before Thy Throne.
  Carpenter.
Biography (excerpt).
  Masefield.
Boy at Target Practice: A
  Contemplation. Moses.
Caelica, LI. Greville.
Chelmsfords Fate. Tompson.
Le Chevalier Malheur.
  Verlaine.
A Christmas Carol.
  Swinburne.

Christmas Morning. Roberts.
The Cock Crows in the Morn. *Anonymous.*
Columbus. Wynne.
The Complaint, or Night Thoughts on Life, Death and Immortality. Young.
Deaf. Bunner.
The Disabled Debauchee. Rochester.
The Dunce. De la Mare.
An English Elegy. Hine.
Epigram. Del Medigo.
Epigrams. Martial (Marcus Valerius Martialis).
An Epitaph of the Death of Nicholas Grimald. Googe.
Epitaph on Charles II. Rochester.
An Essay on Man. Pope.
Fables: The Shepherd and the Philosopher. Gay.
Farewell Advent! Ryman.
Farewell Voyaging World! Aiken.
Fuller and Warren. Whitecotton.
The Gipsies. "Scrace.
Habitations. Belloc.
The Handmaid of Religion. Rickword.
The Happy Wanderer. Addleshaw.
He Who Knows. *Anonymous.*
The Heron. Hovell-Thurlow.
The Hills and the Sea. Campbell.
Homo Sapiens. Rochester.
Hose and Iron. Kuzma.
The House of a Hundred Lights. Torrence.
Hunting Song. Finkel.
I Hardly Ever Ope My Lips. Garnett.
If a Maid Be Fair. Salverson.
Indian School. Russell.
The Insidious Dr. Fu Man Chu. Jones.
Leaf After Leaf..... Landor.
Little Boys of Texas. Coffin.
Locale. Shuttle.
The Locus. Corman.
Love's Fool. Rosenthal.
Love's Labour's Lost. Shakespeare.
Lullaby. Hoffenstein.
Madrigal: "The silver swan." Gibbons.
Marcus Argentarius. Rexroth.
Morning in the Hills. Carman.
My Owen. Downing.
The New World. Jones.
The Newspaper. Crabbe.
Not Being Wise. Elson.
O, Love Is Not a Summer Mood. Gilder.
Ode on a Distant Prospect of Eton College. Gray.
Oh Light Was My Head. Day Lewis.
Old Wichet. *Anonymous.*
On a Picture of Lincoln. Cheney.
Open Your Eyes. Whisenand.
Over in the Meadow. Wadsworth.

A Panegyric to Sir Lewis Pemberton. Herrick.
The Philosopher. Millay.
Remembering the Winter. Bennett.
Riddle. Bookworm: "A moth ate a word." *Anonymous.*
Riddle: The Book-Worm: "A moth ate a word." *Anonymous.*
The Riddles. *Anonymous.*
The Rime of the Ancient Mariner. Coleridge.
A Satire against Reason and Mankind. Rochester.
The Scholar in the Narrow Street. Tso Ssu.
Second Wisdom. Robinson
The Snowfish. Field.
Sonnet: "Chloris, whilst thou and I were free." Cotton.
Sonnet: "When some men gather to talk of Love." McLeod.
Spell of Sleep. Raine.
Sweeping the Skies. Hart.
Take the World as It Is (excerpt). Swain.
Temper. *Anonymous.*
There was an old owl lived in an oak. *Anonymous.*
This Heart That Flutters Near My Heart. Joyce.
Thoreau. Alcott.
The Three Sisters. Ficke.
The Three Wise Monkeys. Davis.
Tiare Tahiti. Brooke.
To the Ladies. Chudleigh.
Tomorrow You Will Live. Martial (Marcus Valerius Martialis).
The Triple Fool. Donne.
Trust Only Yourself. *Anonymous.*
Tunbridge Wells. Rochester.
Two Voices. Corbin.
A Valentine. Gillespy.
A Word to the Wise. Duer.

Wish (ed) (es) (ing)
The Advice. Sackville.
After the Rain. Janeczko.
After the Revolution. Hacker.
Air XXIII: "Sleep, O sleep." Gay.
The Airy Christ. Smith.
Alcestis. Verry.
The Antarctic Muse. Perry.
The Aquarium, San Francisco. Sackville-West.
Ariana. Sanborn.
Armaments Race. Paterson.
Armour's Undermining Modesty. Moore.
As I was coming down the stair. *Anonymous.*
At Annika's Place. Widerberg.
At Dawn the Light Will Come. Van Wyk Louw.
The Author's Epitaph. *Anonymous.*
Avoidances. Welburn.
Ballad against the Enemies of France. Villon.
Barley-Break; or, Last in Hell. Herrick.
Beginning the Year at Rosebud, S.D. Whiteman.
Benediction for the Felt. *Anonymous.*

Beyond Rathkelly. Carlin.
The Birthday. Dacey.
The Blue Bells of Scotland. Jordan.
Cake. Potter.
A Case. *Anonymous.*
The Chaperon. Bunner.
Children's Runes and Omens. *Anonymous.*
Clay. Lucas.
Comfort and Tidings of Joy. *Anonymous.*
The Concept of Force. Sargent.
The Cottager's Complaint. Freeth.
A Country Life: To His Brother, M. Tho: Herrick. Herrick.
Cradle Hymn. Watts.
The Crust of Bread. *Anonymous.*
Cumberland Station. Smith.
Despair. Reed.
The Desponding Soul's Wish. Byrom.
Diddie Wa Diddie. Blake.
Dispraise of a Courtly Life. Sidney.
Don Juan. Byron.
Drifters. Dawe.
Earl Brand; or, The Douglas Tragedy (B vers.) (excerpt). *Anonymous.*
Ennui. Viereck.
Epigram: "Grown old in Love from Seven till seven times Seven." Blake.
Epigrams. Martial (Marcus Valerius Martialis).
Epitaph for a Timid Lady. Cornford.
Everglade. Cherner.
Faith, I Wish I Were a Leprechaun. Ritter.
First Holes Are Fresh. Shipley.
Fish. Rosenblatt.
The Fish Sonata. Scott.
The Fisherman. McCord.
Foreign Children. Stevenson.
Four. Gibbs.
Gluggity Glug. Coleman the Younger.
The Gold-Tinted Dragon. Kuskin.
The Gowden Locks of Anna. Burns.
The Great Pretender. Nolan.
A Grievance (parody). Stephen.
Growing Gray. Dobson.
Guide to the Perplexed. Malouf.
The Haughty Snail-King. Lindsay.
He Satisfies. Faber.
Hmmmm, 19. Scalapino.
Homecoming Blues. Miller.
The Horse Show. Williams.
Hours of Idleness. Byron.
The House I Go to in My Dream. Barker.
A Hunt in the Black Forest. Jarrell.
Hymn. Chadwick.
I Met a Man. *Anonymous.*
I Wish I Was a Mole in the Ground. *Anonymous.*
In Memoriam A.H.H., XC. Tennyson.

In the Garden: Villa Cleobolus. Durrell.
Keep a Good Tongue in Your Head... Parker.
The Labyrinth. Auden.
The Lice-Finders. Rimbaud.
Little Girl, Be Careful What You Say. Sandburg.
The Little Man Who Wasn't There. Mearns.
Lord Delamere. *Anonymous.*
Love Song. Parker.
Loving. Stembridge.
Lullabye. Stripling.
The Maid Freed from the Gallows (I version). *Anonymous.*
Mary Speaks to Jesus. Dempster.
May Carol. *Anonymous.*
The Missionary Visits Our Church in Scranton. Parini.
Modern Love, I. Meredith.
The Monuments of Hiroshima. Enright.
The Mountains. Gibson.
My Heart Leaps Up. Wordsworth.
My Naked Aunt. MacLeish.
The Nightingale. Brathwaite.
Non Que Je Veuille Oter La Liberte. Guillet.
Nostalgia. Lawrence.
Oh Fair Enough Are Sky and Plain. Housman.
On New-Years Day 1640 to the King. Suckling.
On the Decease of the Religious and Honourable Jno Haynes Esqr.... James.
The Ordinary Dog. Turner.
Paul Klee. Todd.
Phallus. Shiraishi Kazuko.
Playgrounds. Alma-Tadema.
Port of Many Ships. Masefield.
The Postman. Richards.
A Primrose Dame. White.
A Projection. Whittemore.
Prothalamion. Schwartz.
Reflections at Dawn. McGinley.
A Removal from Terry Street. Dunn.
Rendezvous. Millay.
Riddle; "Formed long ago, yet made today." *Anonymous.*
Riddles Wisely Expounded. *Anonymous.*
Runaway. Coghill.
Satire. Young.
School after Christmas. Garthwaite.
Sleep Brings No Joy. Bronte.
The Smack in School. Palmer.
Song. Parnell.
Song: "How happy were my days, till now." Bickerstaffe.
Song: "O, that joy so soon should waste!". Jonson.
Song of the Queen Bee. White.
Sonnets, LVI: "Sweet love, renew thy force." Shakespeare.
Star-Light, Star-Bright. Mother Goose.
Star Wish. *Anonymous.*

There Are Three Who Await My Death. *Anonymous.*
To an Oriole. Fawcett.
To Clarissa. Nugent.
To J.F.K. 14 Years after. Weaver.
To Mother Nature. Knowles.
To My Children, Fearing for Them. Berry.
To Parker. Turberville.
Triolet. Chesterton.
Turner's Sunrise. Bevington.
Understanding. Soroka.
The Value of Pi. *Anonymous.*
La Vie C'est La Vie. Fauset.
Villanelle. Laing.
Voice. Padgett.
Vota Amico Facta, Fol. 160. Gazaeus.
Waiting. Jacob.
When I Was Single. *Anonymous.*
When These Old Barns Lost Their Inhabitants.... Kherdian.
Who Shapes a Balustrade? Aiken.
Wilful Waste Brings Woeful Want. *Anonymous.*
Wishes for Her. Devlin.
Would That I Were. Clough.
The Writer. Wilbur.
Zinnias. Worth.
Wishbone
Thanksgiving Wishes. Guiterman.
Wisp
Lilith. Levi.
Rain in the Desert. Fletcher.
Wistful (ness)
Autumn. Hulme.
The Mould. Cromwell.
Wit (s) (ty)
An Allusion to Horace. The Tenth Satire of the First Book. Rochester.
Amoretti, III. Spenser.
The Apple. Sackville.
Arabia. De la Mare.
Astrophel and Stella, XII. Sidney.
Astrophel and Stella, LIX. Sidney.
Astrophel and Stella, LXIV. Sidney.
Conquest. Desportes.
Dr. Johnson. Jenyns.
Dream Songs. Berryman.
The Dunciad. Pope.
The Emulation. Egerton.
Epitaph on Laurence Sterne. Garrick.
An Essay on Criticism. Pope.
The Exercise of Affection. Ayton [(or Aytoun)] Sir Robert.
The Friar in the Well (A version). *Anonymous.*
The Green Autumn Stubble. Browne.
The Hawk. Yeats.
Hercules Oetaeus, II: Chorus. Seneca (Lucius Annaeus Seneca).
Homo Sapiens. Rochester.
Idea. Drayton.
If. Collins.
Love. Herbert.

Madrigal: "Some there are as fair to see to." Davison.
My Little Soul, My Vagrant Charmer. Hadrian.
No Mean City. MacDonogh.
Ode on Leaving the Great Town. Randolph.
An Ode to Mr. Anthony Stafford to Hasten Him into the Country. Randolph.
Of Three Damsels in a Meadow. Payne.
On Mr. Hobbs, and His Writings. Sheffield.
The Poet's Prayer. *Anonymous.*
The Rabbit-Hunter. Frost.
Religio Laici. Dryden.
Resolution in Four Sonnets. Cotton.
A Satire against Reason and Mankind. Rochester.
Self-Defense. De Carrion.
Sir T. J.'s Speech to his Wife and Children. *Anonymous.*
Song: Wit and Beauty. Gould.
Sonnets, XX: "But now my Muse toyled with continuall care." Barnfield.
Sonnets, XXIII: "As an unperfect actor on the stage." Shakespeare.
Sonnets, LIX: "If there be. Shakespeare.
A Spouse I Do Hate. Wycherley.
That All Things Are as They Are Used. Turberville.
This Definition Poetry Doth Fit. Randolph.
Three Epitaphs. Davison.
To a Witty Man of Wealth and Quality... Wycherley.
To the Reader of Master William Davenant's Play, The Wits. Carew.
To the Virginian Voyage. Drayton.
Tristium. Ovid (Publius Ovidius Naso).
The Twelve Properties or Conditions of a Lover. More.
Two Songs in Praise of Steingerd, 2. Ogmundarson.
Upon an Ingenious Friend, Over-Vain. Fitzgerald.
What Is an Epigram? Coleridge.
When before those eyes, my life and light. Stampa.
Wit's-End Corner. *Anonymous.*
Witch (es)
Against Witches. *Anonymous.*
Charm for a Sudden Stitch. *Anonymous.*
Giles Corey of the Salem Farms: Prologue. Longfellow.
The House in the Wood. Jarrell.
Jeremy's Secrets. Todd.
The Little Creature. De La Mare.
The Maryland Yellow-Throat. Van Dyke.
Papa John. De Lima.

Sonnet: "When I was marked for suffering, love forswore." Cervantes Saarvedra.
To a Wanton. Habington.
The Tunning of Elinor Rumming. Skelton.
The Turn of the Road. Stephens.
Two Kitchen Songs. Sitwell.
The Witch-Bride. Allingham.
Wither (ed) (ing) (s)
The Coming of Wisdom with Time. Yeats.
Dialogue. Nemerov.
Double Gift. *Anonymous.*
The Dragonfly. Nemerov.
Evening Primrose. Clare.
Fable XLV: The Poet and the Rose. Gay.
Fear Has Cast Out Love. Blunt.
The Herons. Ledwidge.
In Stone Settlements When the Moon Is Stone. Levi.
Kohoutek. Ryan.
Lament for Glasgerion. Wylie.
Love in Time's Despite. Muir.
Love Is a Law. *Anonymous.*
My Hands Are Withered. *Anonymous.*
O Crimson Blood. Hildegard von Bingen.
Odes. Horace.
On Approaching My Birthday. Miller.
The Ripe Fruit. *Anonymous.*
The Robin in Winter. Cowper.
The Son, Condemned. Rubin.
Suddenly. Speyer.
To Crinog. *Anonymous.*
Under the Violets. Holmes
We Carry Eggshells. Michaelis.
What's the Life of a Man? *Anonymous.*
When Youth and Beauty Meet Together. *Anonymous.*
Withhold (ing) (s)
I Thank Thee, Lord. *Anonymous.*
Over to God. Harrigan.
Reserve. Townsend.
Two Prayers. Adawiyya. Rabi'a al-.
Within
At Ballyshannon, Co. Donegal. Allingham.
For Both of Us at Fisk. Scott.
Happiness. Isenhour.
The Melancholy Knight: The Poetaster. Rowlands.
Modern Love: XLIII. Meredith.
NHR. Hirschman.
A Painted Whore, the Mask of Deadly Sin. Lithgow.
Rainy Season Love Song. Hayford.
Sun. Rowe.
Tamburlaine the Great. Marlowe.
Without
The Antagonist. Ferry.
Any Soul to Any Body. Monkhouse.

At Ballyshannon, Co. Donegal. Allingham.
Dividing the House. Richardson.
Hell in Texas. *Anonymous.*;
A Painted Whore, the Mask of Deadly Sin. Lithgow.
Rainy Season Love Song. Hayford.
Seventh Eclogue. Radnoti.
A Ship, an Isle, a Sickle Moon. Flecker.
Witness (ed) (es)
Ascension-Day. Vaughan.
Ash-Glory. Celan.
Benedicite, What Dreamed I This Night? *Anonymous.*
The Choice of the Cross. Sayers.
Cornelia's Window. Kane.
Eleven Addresses to the Lord. Berryman.
Etched away From. Celan.
Giovanni da Fiesole on the Sublime or Fra Angelico's "Last Judgment." Howard.
Her face was in a bed of hair. Dickinson.
Ibycus. Heath-Stubbs.
An Invitation to the Zoological Gardens. *Anonymous.*
Moving Out. Oates.
Othello. Shakespeare.
The Owner of My Face. Hall.
Paradise Regained. Milton.
Pelvic Meditation. Smith.
A Separation Deed. Morris.
The Slaughterhouse Boys. Meissner.
A Song of Winter. Davis.
What Dreamed I? *Anonymous.*
Who'll Be a Witness for My Lord? *Anonymous.*
The Witnesses. Longfellow.
The Wrestling. Evans.
Wizard (ry)
Come Wary One. Manning-Sanders.
Mimma Bella. Lee-Hamilton.
Say Who Is This with Silvered Hair. Bridges.
Woe (s)
Anacreontic, On Parting with a little Child. Wesley.
An Appeal to My Countrywomen. Harper.
Astrophel and Stella, LI. Sidney.
Astrophel and Stella, CV. Sidney.
Astrophel and Stella, CVIII. Sidney.
Behold Your King! Havergal.
The Bride's Tragedy: Poor Old Pilgrim Misery. Beddoes.
Caelica, XXIV. Greville.
Carmina. Catullus.
The Cause of This I Know Not. Long.
Charleston in the 1860s. Rich.
The Crystal Cabinet. Blake.
The Curse of Doneraile. O'Kelly.
Davideis. Cowley.

A Deposition from Love.
   Carew.
The Dictionary Is an
   Historian. McCombs.
The Effect of Example.
   Keble.
Elegies. Chenier.
Epigram: "Queen,/thou
   holdest in thine arms."
   Anonymous.
Evil Prayer. Hyde.
Fancy, Farewell. Dyer.
The Fatal Spell. Byron.
First Vision. O'Huiginn.
Guy Mannering. Chapt. 4:
   Twist Ye, Twine Ye! Even
   So. Scott.
Honey from the Lion.
   Drake.
The Humble-Bee. Emerson.
Hymn to the Holy Spirit.
   Langton.
Hymn to the Supreme Being
   on Recovery (excerpt).
   Smart.
I Saw My Lady Weep.
   Anonymous.
If You Trap the Moment.
   Blake.
In the Garden. Miles.
Jesus, in Sickness and in Pain.
   Gallaudet.
The Knight of Curtesy: The
   Eaten Heart. *Anonymous.*
Madrigal: "Oft thou hast with
   greedy ear." Cooper.
Medieval Norman Songs.
   Anonymous.
Moan, Moan, Ye Dying
   Gales. Neele.
Modern Midnight
   Conversation: Between an
   Unemployed Artist...
   Anonymous.
The Mourners. Higgons.
Mr. Housman's Message.
   Pound.
Much Ado about Nothing.
   Shakespeare.
Much Ado about Nothing in
   the City (parody).
   Anonymous.
My Love Is Like the Sun.
   Anonymous.
Nativitie. Donne.
The Nereids. Kingsley.
The Norsemen. Whittier.
Ode to Wisdom. Carter.
The Odyssey. Homer.
Of purpose love chose first for
   to be blind. Wyatt.
Oh, Give Us Back the Days
   of Old. Neale.
Ol' Clothes. *Anonymous.*
On the Late Massacre in
   Piedmont. Milton.
On the Sale By Auction of
   Keats' Love Letters.
   Wilde.
Our Lady of the Passion.
   Mauropus.
Paradise Lost. Milton.
The Pessimist. King.
Poem: "He watched with all
   his organs of concern."
   Auden.
Prayer to Santa Maria Del
   Vade. Ruiz.
Prelude to Space. Lewis.
Psalm XII. Sidney.
The Seven Wonders of
   England. Sidney.

The Shepheardes Calender:.
   Spenser.
Sir Roland; a Fragment.
   Merry.
Some in Their Harts Their
   Mistris Colours Bears.
   Smith.
Sonnets, XC: "Then hate me
   when thou wilt; if ever,
   now." Shakespeare.
Stanzas to Edward Williams.
   Shelley.
Tears in My Heart That
   Weeps. Verlaine.
Thank God. Rolnik.
The Thorn. Wordsworth.
To the Memory of Lord
   Halifax (excerpt). Philips.
Translation of Lines by
   Benerade. Johnson.
The Twelve Properties or
   Conditions of a Lover.
   More.
Two Folk Songs, 1.
   Anonymous.
Venomous thorns that are so
   sharp and keen. Wyatt.
Visions of the Daughters of
   Albion. Blake.
The Voyage. Heine.
What death is worse than
   this." Wyatt.
Wit, Whither Wilt Thou?
   Anonymous.
Woe Be Unto You.
   Anonymous.
The Worst Horror.
   Euripides.
Woke
A Belated Violet. Herford.
A Convict's Tour to Hell.
   MacNamara.
Creation. Bierce.
The Dead Poet. Douglas.
Goya. Aiken.
The Journey. Hansbrough.
A July Dawn (excerpt).
   O'Donnell.
Limerick: "There was an old
   person of Woking." Lear.
The Lone Star Trail.
   Anonymous.
The Midnight Court.
   Merriman.
My Dream. Blockcolski.
Nuptial Sleep. Rossetti.
One Morning the World
   Woke Up. Williams.
One Winter Night in August.
   Kennedy.
Shango I. *Anonymous.*
Soldier's Dream. Owen.
Spring. Rosenberg.
Sunthin' in the Pastoral Line.
   Lowell.
.Train Journey. Wright.
Transfigured Bird. Merrill.
Under the Arc de Triomphe:
   October 17. Hacker.
Vita Benefica. Rollins.
Years. Anderson.
Wolf (wolves)
Arrows. Heyen.
Ascent to the Sierras. Jeffers.
Awake! Awake! Ruskin.
The Battle of Brunanburh
   (excerpt). *Anonymous.*
Burial at Sea. Pratt.
By Plain Analogy We're Told.
   Bierce.
A Child's Nativity. Morris.
The Cold. Henson.

Cominus, You Reprobate Old
   Goat. Catullus.
Cromwell, Our Chief of Men.
   Milton.
The Gulistan. Sa'di.
In Chagall's Village.
   Auslander.
Last Words before Winter.
   Untermeyer.
Little Red Riding Hood.
   Broumas.
The Marriage of Heaven and
   Hell. Blake.
Night, Stars, Glow-Worms.
   Leivick.
Nightwood. Smith.
On the Death of Sylvia Plath.
   Herzberg.
The One Who Grew to Be a
   Wolf. Monaghan.
The Shark. Pratt.
'Tis Sweet to Roam.
   Anonymous.
To the Lord General
   Cromwell. Milton.
The True Encounter. Millay.
Unguarded Gates. Aldrich.
Woman (women)
About Women. Putnam.
Adults Only. Stafford.
Advice to the Same. Sidney.
The Affinity. Wickham.
Against a Second Coming:
   The Walking Woman.
   Keyes.
Against Blame of Woman.
   Desmond.
Aidenn. Trask.
Ain't I a Woman? Truth.
Air and Angels. Donne.
Aisling. Clarke.
Alexander the Great.
   Anonymous.
Alison. *Anonymous.*
Amoretti, LIV. Spenser.
Andraitx–Pomegranate
   Flowers. Lawrence.
Angel. Skelton.
Animal Songs: Zebra Stallion.
   Anonymous.
Another Poem about the
   Madness of Women.
   Wayman.
Another September.
   Kinsella.
An Ape, Lion, Fox and Ass.
   Anonymous.
The Apple Trees. Gluck.
Archaeology. Pollitt.
Aristophanes' Symposium.
   Brown.
As All Things Pass.
   Bickston.
As the Window Darkens.
   Jensen.
Auguries of Innocence.
   Blake.
Baith Gud and Fair and
   Womanlie. *Anonymous.*
A Ballad in Blank Verse of
   the Making of a Poet.
   Davidson.
Barbie Doll. Piercy.
Battle Cry. Neihardt.
The Beauty of Job's
   Daughters. Macpherson.
Berthe Morisot. Waldman.
Beyond Wars. Morrow.
Birds. O'Sullivan.
Birthplace. Big Eagle.
Bitter Herbs. Alta.

A Black Girl Goes By.
   Roumer.
The Blood-Letting. Harjo.
Caelica, XXI. Greville.
Caelica, XXVI. Greville.
The Captain. White.
Carmina. Catullus.
The Change. Cowley.
Children, the Sandbar, That
   Summer. Rukeyser.
The Chivalrous Shark.
   Anonymous.
"Cholly" Blues. *Anonymous.*
Closer First to Earth.
   Hazlewood-Brady.
Codes. Chang.
The Common Woman.
   Grahn.
The Conscience. Wickham.
Consorting with Angels.
   Sexton.
Cosmetic. Herbkersman.
The Cowboy's Lament (II).
   Anonymous.
A Credo. Thackeray.
Cynicus to W. Shakspere.
   Stephen.
Cynisca. *Anonymous.*
Cynthia. Dyer.
Dance Instructions for a
   Young Girl. Hahn.
Darling Cora. *Anonymous.*
Dawn of Womanhood.
   Monro.
The Day of Inverlochy.
   Lom.
Death. O Riordain.
The Death of Marilyn
   Monroe. Olds.
The Death-Wish. MacNeice.
Deirdre and the Poets.
   Milne.
Deliverance. Harper.
The Disappointed Sailor.
   Anonymous.
Double Semi-Sestina.
   Starbuck.
A Double Standard. Harper.
Duriesdyke. *Anonymous.*
Dusk. Welshimer.
Early Morning Woman.
   Harjo.
Elegy on Any Lady by
   George Moore. Beerbohm.
Elegy to Sports. Shapiro.
Ella, in a Square Apron, along
   Highway 80. Grahn.
Emergency Haying. Carruth.
An English Mother.
   Johnson.
The English Queen. Lawson.
Epitaph for Cu Chuimne.
   Anonymous.
Epitaph of Sarah Sexton.
   Anonymous.
Epitaph V On Mrs. Corbet,
   Who Dyed of a Cancer in
   her Breast. Pope.
Epithalamion Made at
   Lincolnes Inne. Donne.
Erosion. Pratt.
An Essay on Woman.
   Leapor.
Evening Harbour. Paulin.
Farm Wife. Mitchell.
Fields at Evening. Morton.
Fire. Harjo.
Five Lyrics from "Good for
   Nothing Man". Ptichford.
For Hollis Sigler. Equi.
For Ruggiero and Angelica by
   Ingres. Rossetti.

For the Book of Love. Laforgue.
For the Holy Family by Michelangelo. Rossetti.
From an Old House in America. Rich.
From: First Aspen. Strongin.
From the Ice Age. Bloom.
From the Notebooks. Roethke.
From the Other Shore. Root.
The Fury of Cocks. Sexton.
Future Blues. Brown.
The Gambler. *Anonymous*.
Gamesters All. Heyward.
A Gentle Echo on Woman. Swift.
Gil, the Toreador. Webb.
Gold Tooth Blues. Williams.
The Gown. Davies.
The Grand Match. O'Neill.
Great Man. Johnson.
Green Grass Growing. Evans.
Grinding Vibrato. Cortez.
Gudveig. Berry.
Hair Poem. Knott.
A Hate-Song. Shelley.
Helen. Harrison.
Hellhound on My Trail. Johnson.
Heritage. Mackellar.
The Hero. Sassoon.
Heroic Heart. Donnelly.
Hiawatha's Wooing. Longfellow.
History. Tanaquil.
Home-Coming. Ehrenstein.
Hysteria. Chu Shu chen.
I Am a Hunchback. Stevenson.
I Disapprove Even of Eloquent Myrtis. "Corinna".
I Want to Tell You. Hochman.
Ice Cold. O Riordain.
Idol. Driscoll.
Idylls of the King. Tennyson.
If Blood Is Black Then Spirit Neglects My Unborn Son. Rivers.
The Iliad. Homer.
The Impatient Poet. Cresswell.
In Memory of My Mother. Kavanagh.
Inscape. Litwack.
Iris. St. John.
Irish Hymn to Mary. *Anonymous*.
Joe Tinker. Hall.
Keep Your Kiss to Yourself. *Anonymous*.
Lady Isabel. *Anonymous*.
The Lady Jane: A Humorous Novel in Rhyme (excerpt). Willis.
Lady Maria, in You Merit and Distinction. Bieiris de Romans.
Lake-Song. Untermeyer.
Lay Your Arms Aside. Ferriter.
Lear. Williams.
Lines from an Orchard Once Surveyed by Thoreau. Booth.
Long-Line Skinner. *Anonymous*.

Look to the Back of the Hand. Minty.
The Lost Continent. Joseph.
Lough Derg. Devlin.
Love's Alchemy. Donne.
Love-Songs, At Once Tender and Informative. Hoffenstein.
Love, the Delight of All Well-Thinking Minds. Greville.
The Lowly Peasant. *Anonymous*.
Lunar Eclipse. Scarbrough.
The Lure. O'Reilly.
A Maid's Complaint. Campion.
Man Is for Woman Made. Motteux.
Man, Man, Man. *Anonymous*.
Man without Sense of Direction. Ransom.
The Marriage of Heaven and Hell. Blake.
Mars and Venus. Greene.
Mary Magdalene. Speyer.
The Maximus Poems. Olson.
Medieval Norman Songs. *Anonymous*.
Meditations of a Hindu Prince. Lyall.
Men tell and talk. Francisco.
Mercury Shew'd Apollo, Bartas Book. Ward.
Mist Forms. Sandburg.
Monna Innominata. Rossetti.
More Distant Than the Dead Sea. Tueni.
The Most Beautiful Woman at My Highschool Reunion. Bissert.
Mother. Montoya.
Mother–a Portrait. Fuller.
Mourning. Marvell.
My Father's Leaving. Sadoff.
My Woman. Winans.
Naming Power. Rose.
Nashville Stonewall Blues. Wilkins.
Natural History (excerpt). Monro.
New Minglewood Blues. Lewis's.
News! News! Farjeon.
No Child. Colum.
Nothing to Wear. Butler.
O Gongyla, my darling rose. Sappho.
Oatmeal Deluxe. Dobyns.
Ode to Cupid. Cotton.
Old Humpy. *Anonymous*.
The Old Woman Who Bought a Pig. *Anonymous*.
Old Women. Deutsch.
On Growing Old. Rayaprol.
On the Death of His Wife. O'Connor.
Ordinary Women. Hacker.
Orpheus I Am, Come from the Deeps Below. Fletcher.
Othello. Shakespeare.
Otis. Thomas.
The Parts of a Poet. Rose.
Pericles. Shakespeare.
Philomel to Corydon. Young.
Picasso's Women. Cabral.
Poetry Reading. Scannell.
Poppies. Weekes.
The Portrait. Graves.

Portrait in Available Light. Miles.
A Portrait of Henri III. Aubigne.
The Practice of Absence. Friend.
Praise of Little Women. Ruiz.
The Primrose, Being at Montgomery Castle, upon the Hill... Donne.
A Problem in Morals. Moss.
Prologue to The Tempest. Dryden.
Promenades and Interiors. Coppee.
Proust's Madeleine. Rexroth.
A Question. Livingston.
Recapitulations. Shapiro.
Reunion. Forche.
Revenge to Come. Propertius.
The Rhyme of the Chivalrous Shark. Irwin.
The Riddle. Auden.
The River. Cornish.
The Saginaw Song. Roethke.
Sail and Oar. Graves.
Satan, No Woman. Greville.
Saturday Blues. Bracey.
The Searching. Cobb.
Seated on her bed legs spread open. Mansour.
The Shadow. Jonson.
Signpost. Jeffers.
Skipper Ireson's Ride. Whittier.
Sleeping with Women. Koch.
Slow Dancer That No One Hears but You. Niatum.
Someday Baby. Williams.
Song: "It is all one in Venus' wanton school." Lyly.
Song: "O, like a queen's her happy tread." Watson.
Song of the Fisherman's Lover. Lloyd.
Song of the Full Catch. Skinner.
Song to Imogen (parody). Greene.
Song: "When thy Beauty appears." Parnell.
Song: "With my frailty don't upbraid me." Congreve.
Sonnet: "My soul surcharged with grief now loud complains." Morpurgo.
Sonnet: "Not with Libations." Millay.
A Sonnet on a Monkey. Fleming.
Sourwood Mountain. *Anonymous*.
St. Kilda. Reid.
Steam Song. Brooks.
Strawberry Moon. Oliver.
Swift. Irwin.
The Switch Blade (or, John's Other Wife.). Williams.
Tale of a Little Pig. *Anonymous*.
Talk to Me Tenderly. Laramore.
Talking Blues. *Anonymous*.
Talking to Myself. McTell.
Telephone Arguin' Blues. Short.
Tell Me, O Love. Hammond.

Th Church Bell at Night. *Anonymous*.
That Crawling Baby Blues. Jefferson.
There Is None, O None But You. Campion.
There Was an Old Woman, and What Do You Think? Mother Goose.
Third Alley Blues. Smith.
This Particular Christian. Johnson.
This Pretty Woman. *Anonymous*.
Three Poems. Crane.
Three Poems for Women, 2. Griffin.
The Tides. Blackburn.
Tight Rope. Jones.
To Art. Rossetti.
To Delia. Daniel.
To His Wife. Deniehy.
To Mistress Gertrude Statham. Skelton.
To My Mouse-Colored Mare. Corbiere.
To Olivia. Thompson.
The Token. Prince.
Tom Dooley. *Anonymous*.
"Too dearly had I bought my green and youthful years." Surrey.
The Torso: Passages 18. Duncan.
Trust in Women. *Anonymous*.
Trust the Form of Airy Things. Harington.
The Truth about My Sister and Me. Probst.
The Tryst after Death. *Anonymous*.
Tulips. McGuckian.
The Twa Knights. *Anonymous*.
Two Loves. Housman.
Uncle Henry. Auden.
Under the Moon. Yeats.
The Unfortunate Male. Ben Kalonymos.
The Unhappy Lover. Al-Harizi.
Untitled Poem. Dugan.
Vain Men, Whose Follies. Campion.
Venetian Air. Moore.
Vision of 400 Sunrises. Schechter.
Visual Memory. Martinson.
The Voice. Hardy.
Wasp Sex Myth (One). Hollo.
A Wasted Sympathy. Howells.
The Well of Vertew and Flour of Womanheid. *Anonymous*.
West Texas. *Anonymous*.
Whan netilles in wynter bere rosis rede. *Anonymous*.
The Wife of Bath Her Prologue, from Chaucer (excerpt). Pope.
Window. Cherner.
Woe Is Me, My Soul Says, How Bitter Is My Fate. Morpurgo.
Woe to Him Who Slanders Women. Mac Gearailt.
Woman. *Anonymous*.
The Woman I Am. Allen.

The Woman in the Wagon.
Robertson.
The Women of the Better
Class. Herford.
The Women of the West.
Evans.
Women's Locker Room.
Waniek.
Written in an Ovid. Prior.
Ye Sons of Columbia.
Anonymous.
Youth and Age on Beaulieu
River, Hants. Betjeman.
Womb (s)
Adoramus Te, Christe. O
Bruadair.
Advice to Young Ladies.
Hope.
Annunciation. Donne.
Ave Maria. Charasson.
The Bee. Hawkins.
Birthsong. Scarbrough.
Bread. Keesing.
The Children Look at the
Parents. Tessimond.
Early Pregnancy. Shuttle.
Epigram: "Hail, blissfulest
maiden." *Anonymous.*
Epitaph. Morton.
The Eye of Humility. Smith.
The Frog Prince. Sexton.
God and Nature. Farhi.
The Journal of Albion
Moonlight (excerpt).
Patchen.
Life and Death. Henley.
Locale. Shuttle.
Malcolm. Sanchez.
Mary and the Bramble.
Abercrombie.
Momist. Groesbeck.
O Wha's the Bride?
""MacDiarmid.
On Looking into Henry
Moore. Livesay.
Orpheus to Woods.
Lovelace.
Pregnancy. McPherson.
Reflections. Barrows.
Rest from Loving and Be
Living. Day-Lewis.
Richard II. Shakespeare.
Those Guyana Nights.
Foerster.
To Fine Lady Would-Be.
Jonson.
To the Bridegroom. Halevi
The Visitation. Le Compte.
Won
Angela Davis. Cobb.
Benediction. Johnson.
Conflict. Clive.
Curse of the Cat Woman.
Field.
Daniel Defoe. Landor.
Explorations. MacNeice.
Gettysburg. Stedman.
The Great Lakes Suite.
Reaney.
Grog-an'-Grumble
Steeplechase. Lawson.
Hometown Piece for Messrs.
Alston and Reese. Moore.
Inscription at Mount Vernon.
Anonymous.
Juggler. Wilbur.
My Love. Shelton.
Nocturne. Aldrich.
Nothing Better. *Anonymous.*
Of the Boy and Butterfly.
Bunyan.
Postlude: for Goya. Guthrie.

Remembrances. Clare.
Santiago. Janvier.
Secret. Jacobs.
Tamlane. *Anonymous.*
To Plautia. Cokayne.
Walt Whitman at the Reburial
of Poe. Christopher.
Wildwood Flower.
Anonymous.
The Winning of the TV West.
Alexander.
A Woman's Question.
Lathrop.
Written in Prison. Clare.
Wonder Bread
You Owe Them Everything.
Allman.
Wonder'd
A Song About Myself, st. 4.
Keats.
Wonder (ed) (er) (ing) (s)
Advice to Julia. Luttrell.
Against Fulfillment of Desire.
Anonymous.
Amoretti, LXXXV. Spenser.
Anne. Reese.
Anti-Love Poems. Brewster.
As in a Dusky and
Tempestuous Night.
Drummond.
At the Grave of a Land-
Shark. Moll.
Autosonic Door. Thompson.
Back Yard, July Night.
Cole.
The Barcarole of James Smith.
Gorman.
The Beautiful Changes.
Wilbur.
The Biglow Papers. Lowell.
Black Sheep. Burton.
Boy Wandering in Simms'
Valley. Warren.
The Bystander. Dobson.
Carmina. Catullus.
Civilization. Yuan Chen.
Cocteau's Opium: 1. Finkel.
Coloring Margarine.
Hathaway.
Columbus. Clough.
Conjectured to Be upon the
Death of Sir Walter Ralegh.
King.
Conquered. Akins.
Cry from the Battlefield.
Menth.
The Cynneddf. Humphries.
The Death Bed. Cuney.
Death of a Fair Girl. Butler.
The Desk. Bottoms.
Diana. Constable.
Dirge. Townson.
Dividing the House.
Richardson.
The Divine Paradox.
Anonymous.
Down in the Hollow. Fisher.
Droving Man. Astley.
Early Evening Quarrel.
Hughes.
Eden. Traherne.
Epigram: "My heart still
hovering round about you."
Nugent.
A Face. Browning.
The Factory Girl. Phillips.
Fall. Fisher.
Fifth Birthday Gift. Lederer.
For Sapphires. Rodgers.
For the Man Who Stole a
Rose. Elliott.

The Foretelling of Cathbad
the Druid at Deirdre's
Birth. *Anonymous.*
Fountain. Jennings.
The Frailty. Cowley.
The Freedom of the Moon.
Frost.
Graffito Inscribed on a Wall
of the Taj Mahal.
Anonymous.
A Grain of Rice. Scott.
Graveyard. Coffin.
Great Things Have Happened.
Nowlan.
Greenwich Observatory.
Keyes.
The Groundhog. Shaw.
A Guard of the Sepulcher.
Markham.
The Hemingway House in
Key West. Schultz.
Hogyn. *Anonymous.*
Household Remedies.
Anonymous.
I Am Waiting. Ferlinghetti.
I Can't Help but Wonder
Where I'm Bound. Paxton.
I'll Be Your Epitaph. Speyer.
I Wonder as I Wander.
Anonymous.
I Wonder How Many People
in This City. Cohen.
I Wonder What It Feels Like
to Be Drowned? Graves.
The Immoral Arctic. Bishop.
In a Hotel Writing-Room.
Powys.
In Coventry. Daly.
Instructions to a Celebrated
Laureat (excerpt). Wolcot.
An Irishman's Christening.
Anonymous.
J.B. (excerpt). MacLeish.
The Joy of Love. Dowling.
Just after Noon with Fierce
Shears. Combs.
Kochia. Ferril.
Lagoons, Hanlan's Point.
Souster.
Lamorna Cove. Davies.
The Last Instructions to a
Painter. Marvell.
A Letter. Ridler.
The lively sparks that issue
from those eyes. Wyatt.
Love's Insight. *Anonymous.*
A Meditation for Christmas.
Image.
The Memory. Creeley.
Muskrat. *Anonymous.*
My Grandfather's Church
Goes Up. Chappell.
My Last Illusion. Kendall.
Nuptial Sleep. Rossetti.
Of London Bridge, and the
Stupendous Sight, and
Structure Thereof. Howell.
The Old Maid Factory.
Urdang.
On the Reed of Our Lord's
Passion. Alabaster.
On the Sale By Auction of
Keats' Love Letters.
Wilde.
One for the Ladies at the
Troy Laundry Who Cooled
Themselves... Zimmer.
Orders. Klein.
The Pariah's Prayer.
Goethe.

Prayer of the Maidens to
Mary. Rilke.
Prosit Neujahr. Santayana.
Rose the Red and White
Lilly. *Anonymous.*
Sea Words. Leitch.
Sleep. Simic.
Song: "Soules joy, now I am
gone." Herbert.
Song with Words. Agee.
Sonnets, CVI: "When in the
chronicle of wasted time."
Shakespeare.
Sonnets to Miranda.
Watson.
Stove. Belford.
Stranger, Why Do You
Wonder So? Jones-
Quartey.
Sunflakes. Asch.
Tamburlaine the Great.
Marlowe.
Ten Days Leave. Snodgrass.
There Is None to Help.
Walsh.
They See Gods Wonders That
Are Call'd. Williams.
Thomas in the Fields.
Moyles.
Threnody. Parker.
To His Late Majesty
Concerning the True Form
of English Poetry.
Beaumont.
To Jesus of Nazareth.
Knowles.
To the Right Honourable the
Countesse of C.
Habington.
Umbrellas. Bennett.
Walt Whitman at the Reburial
of Poe. Christopher.
Watching Clouds. Farrar.
When a Goose Meets a
Moose. Gay.
Whistling Willie. Starbird.
The Window Has Four Little
Panes. Burgess.
Wit Wonders. *Anonymous.*
Woman from the West Coast.
Crozier.
Women Pleased. Fletcher.
Wonders. Thomas.
Your Dog Dies. Carver.
Your Light. Lee.
Wonder Lake
Lake Walk at New Year's.
Perez-Diotima.
Wonderful
Eyesight II. Duncan.
If Everything Happens That
Can't Be Done.
Cummings.
Limerick: "His figure's not
noted for grace." Cox.
Song at Santa Cruz. Young.
Three American Women and
a German Bayonet. Scott.
Twenty-third Street Runs into
Heaven. Patchen.
Wonderland
Wonderland. Peck.
Wonderment
Endymion, IV. Keats.
Fancy's Home. Davies.
Wondrous
Cana Revisited. Heaney.
The Divine Wooer. Fletcher.
Easter, Day of Christ Eternal.
Moore.
The Great Victory. Gilbert.

Now Evening Puts Amen to
Day. Horgan.
The Old Garden.
Eichendorff.
Second Vision. O'Huiginn.
Woo (ed) (er) (ing) (s)
Ad Chloen, M.A. Collins.
Cripple Dick upon a Stick.
Anonymous.
Endymion. Keats.
From his flock stray'd
Coridon. Greene.
Jephthah's Daughter.
Heavysege.
Pursuit of an Ideal.
Kavanagh.
A Radical War Song.
Macaulay.
Sir Colin. Anonymous.
Sonnet XIII: "Harry whose
tuneful and well measur'd
Song." Milton.
Star Journey. Madgett.
Subject to All Pain.
Anonymous.
To His Mistress. Herrick.
Villanelle of a Villaness.
Robinson.
Woo'd and Married and A'.
Ross.
Wooing Song. Fletcher.
Written on a Sunday
Morning. Southey.
Wood (en) (s)
After the Festival. George.
After the Shower.
Lampman.
L'Aigle a Deux Jambes.
Cassity.
Alons au Bois le May Cueillir.
d'Orleans.
Amen. Mutis.
Aunt Jemima of the Ocean
Waves. Hayden.
Awful Fix. Hawkins.
The Axe in the Wood.
Dyment.
The Babes in the Wood.
Anonymous.
A Ballad of Trees and the
Master. Lanier.
Barnfloor and Winepress.
Hopkins.
The Battle of Brunanburh
(excerpt). *Anonymous.*
Bold Rangers. *Anonymous.*
The Busy Body. Field.
The Byrnies. Gunn.
A Cabin in Minnesota. Bell.
Carpenter of Eternity. Root.
The Centaurs. Stephens.
Ceremony. Wilbur.
Charm for a Sudden Stitch.
Anonymous.
The Child-King.
Wintchevsky.
Christ's Victory and Triumph.
Fletcher.
The Circle. Garrigue.
The Cross. Lanier.
Cuckoo! Belloc.
The Dancing Bear. Field.
Dark Wood. Wedde.
The Death of the Flowers.
Bryant.
Defeated Farmer. Van
Doren.
The Elder Edda: The First
Lay of Gudrun.
Anonymous.
Emerson. Dodge.
Endymion, IV. Keats.

Epigram: "When Graphicus
sat by the baths." Strato.
Epigram: "Why do the Graces
now desert the Muse?"
Landor.
Epithalamion. Spenser.
Erlington. *Anonymous.*
Eve in Reflection.
Macpherson.
An Evening Walk (excerpt).
Wordsworth.
A Fable for Critics. Cooper.
The Fair Morning. Very.
The Fairy King. Allingham.
The Famous Ballad of the
Jubilee Cup. Quiller-
Couch.
Farmer. Stryk.
The Farmer's Boy.
Bloomfield.
The Fisherman's Wife.
Lowell.
Four Stories. Shapiro.
The Fox. Scheuer.
Gadoshkibos. Burns.
Good Appetite. Van Doren.
Good Christians. Herrick.
The Great Voices. Brooks.
Harry Dunne (I).
Anonymous.
He is not dead that sometime
hath a fall. Wyatt.
Heart of the Woods.
Curtright.
Here, where the Red Man
Swept the Leaves away.
Tuckerman.
History of France. Elmslie.
Hoarded Joy. Rossetti.
The House in the Wood.
Jarrell.
Housing Starts. Davison.
How Much Wood Would a
Wood-Chuck Chuck.
Mother Goose.
Hymn on Solitude.
Thomson.
I Fear No Power a Woman
Wields. McGaffey.
I Have Cut an Eagle.
Koller.
I Rode with My Darling...
Smith.
In Autumn When the Woods
Are Red. Stevenson.
In Defense of Satire.
Scroope.
In Detroit. Cuscaden.
In October. Carman.
In the Dream of the Body.
Keller.
In the Emptied Rest Home.
Akhmadulina.
Iscah. Schwartz.
It's Spring Returning, It's
Spring and Love.
Anonymous.
Jabberwocky. Cooper.
Jacklight. Erdrich.
Jacob and Esau. Lasker-
Schüler.
Kind Sir: These Woods.
Sexton.
Lavinia. Thomson.
Limerick: "There was a queer
fellow named Woodin."
"Bede.
The Long River. Hall.
The Lumberman's Alphabet.
Anonymous.
Luzzato. Reznikoff.
The Magic Wood. Treece.

The Maids of Simcoe.
Anonymous.
Man and Dog. Thomas.
The Man in the Wilderness.
Anonymous.
Manufactured Gods.
Sandburg.
Marina. Eliot.
A Masique Presented at
Ludlow Castle (Comus).
Milton.
May. Bird.
Melampus. Meredith.
The Monuments of
Hiroshima. Enright.
Morning Dialogue. Aiken.
My Cheap Lifestyle. Myles.
A Natural History of
Southwestern Ontario, III.
Dewdney.
New York 1962: Fragment.
Lowell.
Not Dead. Graves.
A Note from the Pipes.
Speyer.
Nutting. Wordsworth.
An Old Air. Higgins.
Old Log House. Tippett.
Out of the Earth. Davies.
The Oxyrhyncus Sayings of
Jesus. *Anonymous.*
Paradise Regained. Milton.
The Poem in the Park.
Davison.
Polonged Sonnet. Antella.
The Puritan Hacking away at
Oak. Gitlin.
Pygmalion. Brockerhoff.
The Ride to the Lady. Cone.
Robin Hood and Little John.
Anonymous.
The Scourge. Kunitz.
La Selva. Corman.
September. Lampman.
Sestina. Justice.
Sidrophel, the Rosicrucian
Conjurer. Butler.
A Silent Wood. Siddal.
Sir Turlough; or, The
Churchyard Bride.
Carleton.
The Sleep of Spring. Clare.
Snow-Flakes. Longfellow.
Snow White. Ochester.
A Song of Early Autumn.
Gilder.
A Song of Enchantment. De
la Mare.
Spring Rites. Robbins.
Stars. Nowlan.
These Words I Write on
Crinkled Tin. Roberts.
They Who Tread the Path of
Labor. Van Dyke.
The Third Advice to a
Painter. Marvell.
To Corydon. Beccadelli.
To Deck a Woman, XI
(excerpt). Hodgson.
Two Married. Frazee-Bower.
The Villain. Davies.
Volto Sciolto e Pensieri
Stretti. Mangan.
The Water-Wheel. Clemo.
The Way Through the Woods.
Kipling.
The Wilding. Booth.
The Willow-Man. Ewing.
The Wind in the Pines.
Cawein.
Wood and Hill. Young.
Woodcut. Wilson.

Woodworker's Ballad.
Palmer.
A Word About Woodpiles.
Turner.
Working near Lake Traverse.
Hennen.
The Yellow Violet. Bryant.
Wood Shady
All, All A-lonely.
Anonymous.
Wood Wind
Oboe. McKinney.
Woodbine
Henceforth I Will Not Set My
Love. Gorges.
The Third Light. Longley.
Woodchuck
How Much Wood Would a
Wood-Chuck Chuck.
Mother Goose.
Woodland
The Clovers. Garrigue.
Cowper's Three Hares.
Turner.
Dissonance. Whitman.
Evangeline. Longfellow.
The Funnels. Morgenstern.
Inscription for a Tablet on the
Banks of a Stream.
Southey.
The Poet. Noguchi.
Seven Woodland Crows.
Vizenor.
Sonnets. Tuckerman.
Storm Warning. Bardsley.
Sunset. Mickle.
Woodlark
Sheepbells. Blunden.
Woodwind (s)
Aubade: Lake Erie. Merton.
Woof
Warp and Woof. Halbisch.
Wool (ly)
Apology. Miller.
Arcadia. Sidney.
The Child in the Rug.
Haines.
Colin Clout. Skelton.
The Gone Years. Fulton.
Last Words before Winter.
Untermeyer.
The Lover's Gifts.
Anonymous.
The Nativity. Lewis.
You Read Us Your Verse.
Martial (Marcus Valerius
Martialis).
Word (s)
3rd Migration, Third Series.
Henderson.
Abraham Sutskever. Mayne.
Absence. Barnes.
Academic Curse: An Epitaph.
Court.
Adam. Booth.
Adam's Death. Levin.
The Aeolian Harp. Melville.
After Jericho. Thomas.
After Spending All Day at the
National Museum of Art.
Britt.
Air XXXV: "How happy
could I be with either."
Gay.
The Alchemy of Day.
Hebert.
All Friends Together.
Simpson.
Although he has no form.
Mukta Bai.
Analyst. Fisher.
The Ancient Speech. Raine.

And the Same Words. Ignatow.
The Angel in the House. Patmore.
The Animal Howl. J. M.
The Annunciation. Merwin.
Archaic Apollo. Plomer.
The Art of Love: Life Is Full of Horrors and Hormones. Koch.
The Art of Politics. Bramston.
As All Things Pass. Bickston.
As I Went to Bonner. *Anonymous.*
As Rivers of Water in a Dry Place. Bary.
At Lake Geneva. Eberhart.
At Night. Meynell.
Baby Toodles. Newman.
Beauty's Pageant. Rossetti.
Beaver Pond. Marriott.
Because I Liked You Better. Housman.
Below Bald Mountain. Moore.
The Best of All. Crosby.
Birth. Hughes.
A Birthday in Hospital. Jennings.
Book-Moth. *Anonymous.*
The Book of Lies. Tate.
The Botticellian Trees. Williams.
The Bourgeois Poet–67. Shapiro.
The Brook. Thomas.
A Burial, Green. Southwick.
Burning Shit at An Khe. Weigl.
The Buzz Plane. Francis.
Cartoon. Simmerman.
Casual Meeting. Bruner.
The Child Is Father to the Man. Hopkins.
Christmas 1930. Scruggs.
The Clearing. Jones.
The Cliff. Rowbotham.
The Clock. Scarfe.
The Collector. Whisler.
Colosseum. Norse.
The Coming of the Lord. Very.
Communion. Dowden.
Conon in Alexandria. Durrell.
Coppersmith. Murphy.
Corner Meeting. Hughes.
The Crosse. Herbert.
Danny's Wooing. Wright.
The Day before April. Davies.
The Dead Poet. Purdy.
The Death of Richard Wagner. Swinburne.
Declension. Sandy.
Definition. Crowell.
Definition. Rolfe.
Definitions of the Word Gout. Koyama.
The Diver. Mayo.
Do I Really Pray? Burton.
The Dog beneath the Skin. Auden.
The Dragon of Red Lights. Swickard.
Driftwood. Smythe.
The Dusting of the Books. Hughes.
Dynamic Tension. Sanfield.

The Earthly Paradise. Morris.
Eastward I Stand, Mercies I Beg. *Anonymous.*
The Effect of Snow. Finch.
Elegy. Gilbert.
Elegy for a Nature Poet. Nemerov.
Elegy for Our Dead. Rolfe.
The Eleventh Commandment (excerpt). Holmes.
The End. Ginsberg.
Enemy, Enemy. Mullins.
The English Language. Story.
The Englishman. Cook.
Envoi. Mandel.
Epigram: "Stolen kisses, wary eyes." Strato.
Fair Isabell of Rochroyall. *Anonymous.*
Father and Child. Harwood.
Fear of Death. Ashbery.
Fire, the Rope... Tikhonov.
The First Autumn. Schacht.
Flail. "Dalton.
Flight. Hemschemeyer.
Fly. Merwin.
The Fog Dream. Gilbert.
For Every Day. Havergal.
For Nothing. Castro Rios.
....For They Shall See God. Shaw.
A Foreign Country. Zach.
Fourth Station. Claudel.
The Free Woman. Garrison.
Fresh News from the Past. Bell.
The Future. Cameron.
Gaspara Stampa. Benet.
Gathering the Sparks. Schwartz.
A Gazelle. Stoddard.
Generalities. Conquest.
Genesis. Higgins.
Genesis. Kramer.
Geneva. Reid.
A Gentle Word. *Anonymous.*
George Allen. *Anonymous.*
God's Unspeakable Gift. Sealey.
The Gods Are Mighty. Van Wyk Louw.
The Golden Vanity. *Anonymous.*
Graphemics (excerpt). Spicer.
The Greater Gift. Bruner.
Hail, Holy Land. Tillam.
Happiness. Dickey.
Hark, and Hear My Trumpet Sounding. *Anonymous.*
He Could Have Found His Way. Dalziel.
The Heart's Location. Meinke.
Hello Goodbye. Thesen.
The Heron. Watkins.
His Ejaculation to God. Herrick.
His Last Week. Lennen.
His Promises. Nicholson.
How My Father Died. Ezekiel.
Hunger. *Anonymous.*
Hymn to God the Father. Wesley.
Hyperion. Keats.
I Am Weary of Straying. York.
I Built My Hut. T'ao Chi'en.

I Come to Supplicate. Ben Abun.
I Dream'd in a Dream. Whitman.
I Know Not Whether I Am Proud. Landor.
I'll Be Your Epitaph. Speyer.
If Any Be Pleased to Walk into My Poor Garden... Pastorius.
The Illiterate. Meredith.
Immanence. Hovey.
Immortality Conferred in Vain. Theognis.
In Canterbury Cathedral. Oldenburg.
In Cold Hell, In Thicket. Olson.
In Memorium–Leo: A Yellow Cat. Sherwood.
In Memory of Radio. Jones.
In Shadow. Crane.
In the City of Bogota. Pape.
Inseparable. Marston.
The Instruments. Smart.
It is her cousin's death... Fox.
It Started. Baca.
Jailhouse Blues. Smith.
Japanese Beetles. Kennedy.
Jeff Buckner. Beddo.
John Gilbert Was a Bushranger. *Anonymous.*
Johnny Appleseed. Venable.
Jutaculla Rock. Morgan.
Kate Temple's Song. Collins.
Kearny at Seven Pines. Stedman.
Kind Words Can Never Die. Hutchinson.
Ku Klux. Cawein.
Lady of Letters. Roseliep.
The Laird o Drum. *Anonymous.*
Lamentation of Nippur. *Anonymous.*
Landed: A Valentine. Howard.
Last Days. Stoddard
Late Tutorial. Buckley.
Leave the Miracle to Him. Allan.
Lector Aere Perennior. Cunningham.
A Lesson in Handwriting. Reid.
Letter for Melville 1951. Olson.
Letters. Emerson.
Life. Very.
Life and Nature. Lampman.
Life of the Letters. Borenstein.
Like Groping Fingers. Sutzkever.
Lilith: The Anguish'd Doubt Broods over Eden. Brennan.
Limerick: "There was a young bard of Japan." *Anonymous.*
Limerick: "There was a young man from Japan." *Anonymous.*
Limerick: "There was a young man of Japan." *Anonymous.*
The Lion's Nature. *Anonymous.*
Little Miss and Her Parrot. Marchant.

The Lost Continent. Joseph.
Love. Tasso.
Love Came Back at Fall o' Dew. Reese.
Love Once Was Like an April Dawn. Johnson.
Love's Caution. Davies.
Love's Witness. Behn.
A Lover's Anger. Prior.
Madonna of the Dons. MacGillvray.
Mahabalipuram. MacNeice.
The Man Closing Up. Justice.
The Man in the Tree. Strand.
Manchouli. Empson.
Merops. Emerson.
Message. Pallottini.
The Missal. Dobson.
Mistakes. Swarberg.
Monkey. Miles.
Moonlit Night in Kansas. Contoski.
More Truth and Light. Robinson.
Morning Dialogue. Aiken.
The Muscovy Drake. Lesoro.
My Companion. Wesley.
My Father's Leaving. Sadoff.
My Letter. Litchfield.
My Spring Thing. Hoagland.
The Negatives. Levine.
New Life. Burr.
No One Cares Less Than I. Thomas.
Noh Play. Brodey.
Not I. *Anonymous.*
Nothing Better. *Anonymous.*
Now in the Time of This Mortal Life. Nicholson.
O Lord of Life. Gladden.
October. Berkson.
October. Wolfe.
Of Autumn. Porumbacu.
Of Impatience Which Brings All Our Gains to Nothing. Jacopone da Todi.
Of Myself. Goldberg.
Off from Swing Shift. Hongo.
Old Bibles. Waniek.
The Old-Marrieds. Brooks.
On a Dead Poet. Osgood
On Death. Landor.
On the Power of Sound. Wordsworth.
On Trust in the Heart. Seng-Ts'an.
Once Did My Thoughts. *Anonymous.*
One Thought for My Lady. Modisane.
Optimism. Wilcox.
An Ordinary Day beyond Kaitaia. Smithyman.
The Other Voice. Paulin.
Out of the Sea. Bynner.
Parsley. Dove.
Paterson. Williams.
The Patter of the Shingle. *Anonymous.*
Peri Poietikes. Zukofsky.
The Phoenix. Nemerov.
Photograph at the Cloisters: April 1972. Chasin.
Piers the Plowman's Creed. *Anonymous.*
Pine Boat a-Shift. *Anonymous.*

A Place in Thy Memory. Griffin.
Poem. Blaser.
Poem for the Atomic Age. Litvinoff.
The Poems of Our Climate. Stevens.
A Poet. Hardy.
A Poet's Household. Kizer.
Poet to Dancer. Kavinoky.
Poetry Defined. Holmes.
Porphyria's Lover. Browning.
Portrait of the Artist with Hart Crane. Wright.
A Prayer. Cotter.
A Prayer. Rossetti.
Priam and Achilles. Pope.
The Prince of Peace His Banner Spreads. Fosdick.
Prison Letter. Knoll.
The Prophet. Pushkin.
Public Library. Stevenson.
Published Correspondence: Epistle to the Rapalloan. MacLeish.
The Quarrel. Aiken.
The Question. Rukeyser.
The Quick and the Dead. Voronca.
The Quiet Hour. Bowman.
Rain Has Fallen on the History Books. Rosenberg.
Rain in Summer. Longfellow.
Red Rock Ceremonies. Endrezze-Probst.
A Refusal. Googe.
Repetition of Words and Weather. Stone.
Reserve. Reese.
The Return. Bontemps.
Riddle. Bookworm: "A moth ate a word." Anonymous.
Riddle: The Book-Worm: "A moth ate a word." Anonymous.
The Riddles. Anonymous.
Rissem. Gilbert.
The Rubaiyat of Omar Khayyam. Omar Khayyam.
Saint Malcolm. Amini.
Satire. Donne.
The Scarecrow. Franklin.
The Scribe. De La Mare.
Seaweed. Longfellow.
The Second Hymn to the Night. "Novalis" (George Friedrich Philipp von Hardeneng).
Seizure. Warren, Jr.
A Series 5.8. Wieners.
Shall I Be Silent? Herbert.
The Silent Lover. Ralegh.
Sirens. Coleman.
Snow Country Weavers. Welch.
Soldier: Twentieth Century. Rosenberg.
Some Day. Addison.
Somebody Prayed. Anonymous.
Someone Sits at the Harp. Lang.
The Song of Hiawatha. Longfellow.
Song to a Negro Wash-Woman. Hughes.
Song: "We break the glass, whose sacred wine." Pinkney.

Sonnet LXX. Alabaster.
Sonnet: To Certain Ladies. Dante Alighieri.
Sonnet: To Dante Alighieri (On the Last Sonnet of the Vita Nuova). Angiolieri.
Sophia Nichols. Blaser.
Speaking. Ryan.
The Speech of the Dead. Ridler.
Speech to Those Who Say Comrade. MacLeish.
Speeches at the Barriers (excerpt). Howe.
Spelling. Atwood.
State Prison 4:00 p.m. Nickens.
Stone Words for Robert Lowell. Eberhart.
Strategies. Smith.
Succumbing. Reeve.
Suddenly Afraid. Anonymous.
Summary. Sanchez.
Summer Rain. Tillinghast.
The Symphony. Lanier.
A Tail of the See. Corbett.
Take Time to Be Holy. Longstaff.
Take Time to Talk with God. Frazee-Bower.
Talk. Stalker.
There Is a Box. Greenberg.
Therefore I Must Tell the Truth. Torlino.
These Men. Booth.
The Threat. Codrescu.
The Three Enemies. Rossetti.
Thrice Blest the Man. Barnard.
A Time of Change. O'Rahilly.
To a Cactus Seller. Shaul.
To A Polish Mother. Mickiewicz.
To a Young Lady Swinging Upside Down on a Birch Limb... Koch.
To an Athlete Turned Poet. Meinke.
To an Old Philosopher in Rome. Stevens.
To His Lovely Mistresses. Herrick.
To His Tomb-Maker. Herrick.
To John C. Fremont. Whittier.
To T. S. Eliot. Litvinoff.
To Thee, Eternal Soul, Be Praise. Gilder.
Today I Have Touched the Earth. Smith.
Tramp. Hughes.
A Translation from Petrarch. Synge.
The Traveler. Anonymous.
Travels With the Band-Aid Army. Henson.
The Tree Stands Very Straight and Still. Wynne.
A True Love Ditty. Middleton.
Twelfth Raga/for John Wieners. Meltzer.
Two Armies. Spender.
Two in August. Ransom.
The Two Poets. Meynell.
Uncertain Sonnets. Johnston.
Under the Earth. Sutzkever.
Unison. Wheelock.

Upon Julia's Voice. Herrick.
A Venetian Night. Hofmannsthal.
A Visit. Anderson.
La Vita Nuova. Dante Alighieri.
Waiting. Davidson.
Waking, the Love Poem Sighs. Hall.
Walls of Ice. Hale.
Week-End by the Sea. Masters.
The Wharf, May 1978. Segal.
Whispering Clouds. Platov.
William and Margaret. Mallet.
Winter. Anonymous.
Wish. Henson.
The Woman That Had More Babies Than That. Stevens.
The Word. Weiss.
The Word of God. Flint.
The Word of Water. Mayo.
Wynken De Worde. Ende.
Yaddo. Herschberger.
The Yew-Tree. Watkins.
You Call That a Ts'ing: A Letter (parody). Barrow.
Young Waters. Anonymous.

Wordless
Brevities. Sassoon.
Catalpa Tree. Waddington.
Everyone Sang. Sassoon.

Wordsworth
Period Piece. Berlind.
Thou Strainest through the Mountain Fern. Stevenson.

Work (ed) (er) (ing) (s)
Abraham Lincoln. Ames.
Aecclesiae et Reipub. Strachey.
The Aeneid. Virgil (Publius Vergilius Maro).
After Two Thousand Years. ""MacDiarmid.
Ain't Workin' Song. Anonymous.
All Work and No Play Makes Jack a Dull Boy. Anonymous.
Alluding to the One-Armed Bandit (parody). Berry.
And Truly It Is a Most Glorious Thing. Bradford.
The Animals. Berg.
The Ant and the Cricket. Anonymous.
An Appeal by Unemployed Ex-Service Men. Anonymous.
As Often as Some Where before My Feet. Pastorius.
Aurora Leigh. Browning.
Automobile Mechanics. Baruch.
The Barnyard. Burnham.
Beauty. "E.-Yeh.-Shure" (Louise Abeita).
Bed-Time. Jones.
Belle de Jour (parody). Melly.
Beowulf. Anonymous.
Blue Monday. Anonymous.
Blueprint. Steinman.
The Book. Garrison.
The Book. Vaughan.
Boxer. Clancy.
The Boy We Want. Anonymous.

A Brook in the City. Frost.
Butcherboy. Schmidt.
Cancel My Subscription. Hines.
Car Episode. Gordon.
The Carpenter. Whiteside.
Carpenter of Eternity. Root.
The Carpenter of Galilee. Smith.
Cave of Staffa, I. Wordsworth.
Chain Gang Blues. Anonymous.
The Chosen Three, on Mountain Height. Ela.
Christ the Carpenter. Haskin.
Cities and Thrones and Powers. Kipling.
Clandestine Work. Goll.
Click Go the Shears. Anonymous.
The Collector. Whisler.
The Common Tasks. Crowell.
The Counselor. Parker.
The Curse upon Edward. Gray.
The Damage You Have Done. Komey.
Dear Lord, Behold Thy Servants. Ballou I.
Dedication of the Chronicles of England and France. Fabyan.
Discovery. Keech.
A Dollar and a Half a Day. Anonymous.
A Dream. Akhmadulina.
Early Meadow-Rue. Plumly.
(End) of Summer (1966). Knott.
Epistles. Horace.
The Epitaph. Hinkson.
An Essay on Man. Pope.
The Exhortation of a Father to His Children. Smith.
A Fable. Frere.
Facing the New Year. Anonymous.
Farmers. Percy.
Father Grumble. Anonymous.
Faust. Goethe.
Fear Not. Bullock.
Femina Contra Mundum. Chesterton.
Fifty-Seventh Street and Fifth. Corn.
For Angus MacLeod. Smith.
For the Company Underground. MacNamara.
Four-Leaf Clover. Higginson.
Galway. O'Neill.
Generations. Clark.
Get Somebody Else. Dunbar.
Give to the Winds Thy Fears. Gehardt.
The Gleaner. Taylor.
God. Lamartine.
Good Night and Good Morning. Milnes.
Grass. Sandburg.
Gratitude for Work. Oxenham.
The Great American Bum. Anonymous.
Habeas Corpus. Jackson.
Hard Heart of Mine. Alline.

The Harp. Weigl.
Heaven Will Protect the
   Working Girl. Smith.
The Hired Man on
   Horseback. Rhodes.
The Hired Man's Way.
   Bangs.
His Prayer for Absolution.
   Herrick.
The House of Life. Rossetti.
How the First Hielandman of
   God Was Made of Ane
   Horse Turd... Anonymous.
Human Debasement. A
   Fragment. Rushton.
Human Needs. Walker.
I Have Not Lingered in
   European Monasteries.
   Cohen.
I'm a Round-Town Gent.
   Anonymous.
I Saw a New World. Rands.
The Iliad. Homer.
In Pilgrim Life Our Rest.
   Sandys.
Inquests Extraordinary, III:
   On the Same. Anonymous.
Invocation (excerpt).
   Spencer.
It's Simply Great. Mase.
Jesus a Child His Course
   Begun. Fuller.
Kassie Jones. Lewis.
Laborers Together with God.
   Perkins.
A Letter from Aragon.
   Cornford.
Light Shining Out of
   Darkness. Borthwick.
Lincolnshire Remembered.
   Cornford.
The Little Factory Girl to a
   More Fortunate Playmate.
   Anonymous.
A Little Song of Work.
   Sprouse.
Love and Sacrifice. O'Dowd.
Loyal. Matthews.
The Lust of Gold.
   Montgomery.
Man-Making. Markham.
Man May Work from Sun to
   Sun. Anonymous.
The Marriage of Heaven and
   Hell. Blake.
Me and My Dog.
   Anonymous.
Mendings. Rukeyser.
The Midnight March.
   Gilbert.
Mihailovich. McFadden.
Model. Ammons.
Monday. Stafford.
The Monk and His Pet Cat.
   Anonymous.
Monument to a Boxer.
   Lucilius [(or Lucillius)].
Moon Man. Valentine.
The moon of Id came.
   Jahan.
Mr. Roger Harlackenden.
   Johnson.
My Son. Hughes.
Necessity. Hughes.
Nehi Blues. Reynolds.
New Year's Eve. Hardy.
Newes from Virginia. Rich.
Night (excerpt). Oppenheim.
No Job Blues. Thomas.
O! Start a Revolution.
   Lawrence.
Of Watchmen. Gay.

Old Man in the Wood.
   Anonymous.
The Old Man Who Lived in
   the Woods. Anonymous.
The Old Mother.
   Anonymous.
Old Ship Riggers. Cody.
On an Indian Tomineois, the
   Least of Birds. Heyrick.
On the Death of Mr. Pope.
   Anonymous.
On the Hurry of This Time.
   Dobson.
One Thing at a Time.
   Stodart.
Our Hunting Fathers.
   Auden.
Our Own. Sangster.
Pat Works on the Railway.
   Anonymous.
Penelope, for Her Ulysses'
   Sake. Spenser.
Pentagonia (parody). Bates.
Percy/68. Myles.
Personal Poem. O'Hara.
Photogenes and Apelles.
   Prior.
Plant a Tree. Larcom.
Poetry Defined. Holmes.
Poor Movies. Bennett.
Portland County Jail.
   Anonymous.
A Prayer. Garrison.
The Pretty Maid. Powell.
Psalm V. Sidney.
Psalm 62. Donne Deo.
   Pembroke.
Pygmalion. Doolittle.
Ranchers. Lesemann.
A Receipt to Cure a Love Fit.
   Anonymous.
Remember the Source.
   Eberhart.
The Renegado (Act V, Scene
   I). Massinger.
Resurrection. Fearing.
Reverdure. Berry.
Riddle: "Little bird of
   paradise." Anonymous.
The Riot; or, Half a Loaf is
   Better Than No Bread.
   More.
Ron Mason. Tuwhare.
A Roundel of Rest. Symons.
Sailing from the United States.
   Moss.
Saint Luke the Painter.
   Rossetti.
Salutation the Second.
   Pound.
Satire. Donne.
A Satirical Poem about Drink.
   Jigmed.
The Scarecrow. Doak.
The Scissor-Man.
   Nightingale.
The Self-Deceaver.
   Montalvan.
Send Me. Rossetti.
Sh-Ta-Ra-Dah-Dey (Irish
   Lullaby). (with music).
   Anonymous.
Shekhinah. Wolfskehl.
Silhouette in Sepia. Carr.
The Sluggard. Watts.
Small Game. Levine.
The Social Future. Ingram.
Some Pieces. Forbes.
Song of the Leadville Mine
   Boss. Cameron.
Song: "Sometimes in the fast
   food kitchen." Lane.

Songs of the Transformed:
   Siren Song. Atwood.
Spontaneous Me. Whitman.
The Stampede. Miller.
Story of a Hotel Room.
   Tonks.
The Straw Men. Culhane.
There Is a Green Hill.
   Alexander.
The Three Taverns: Out of
   Wisdom Has Come Love.
   Robinson.
Through the Barber Shop
   Window. Anderson.
The Ticket Agent. Leamy.
Times Square Parade.
   Watson.
To a Young Woman on the
   World Staff. Adams.
To Be of Use. Piercy.
To the Generous Reader.
   Herrick.
Tokens. Barnes.
Tractor. Sellers.
The Tuft of Flowers. Frost.
United Front. Eisler.
Unwasted Days. Lowell.
Us Potes. Adams.
The View from the Window.
   Thomas.
The Vineyard. Anonymous.
The Voice of God. Barnard.
Waking, the Love Poem Sighs.
   Hall.
We Are Four Bums (with
   music). Anonymous.
What Is That in Thine Hand?
   Gray.
What the Chairman Told
   Tom. Bunting.
When I First Came to This
   Land. Anonymous
When the Work's All Done
   This Fall. Anonymous.
When Youth and Beauty Meet
   Together. Anonymous.
Which Shall It Be? Beers.
Whose Hand. Anonymous.
Why Tomas Cam Was
   Grumpy. Stephens.
A Wish. Arnold.
With My Crowbar Key.
   Stafford.
The Wooden Horse then said.
   Mastoraki.
Work. Thompson.
Work. Van Dyke.
Work: A Song of Triumph.
   Morgan.
The Work of the Weavers.
   Anonymous.
Work Room. Elmslie.
Would You Be a Man of
   Fashion? Anonymous.

Workhouse
Eclogue. Barnes.
Little Willie. Massey.
Rosemary Lane. Anonymous.

World (s)
Above Salerno. Murray.
Abraham Lincoln.
   Auslander.
Abruptly All the Palm Trees.
   Smith.
Adam. Booth.
An Address to His Elbow-
   Chair, New Cloath'd.
   Somervile.
Advice to a Raven in Russia
   December 1812. Barlow.
After Plotinus. Stafford.

After the Annunciation.
   Duggan.
After the Hurricane. Hazo.
After Tsang Chih. Notley.
Against the Age. Simpson.
Alexander Graham Bell Did
   Not Invent the Telephone.
   Coffin.
All That Summer. Dunetz.
Almeria. Neruda.
Amends to Nature. Symons.
An American Boyhood.
   Holden.
American Jump.
   Anonymous.
Amoretti, XXIX. Spenser.
Amoretti, LXXXV. Spenser.
The Ancient Speech. Raine.
The Anglo-Saxon Race.
   Tupper.
Angry Dusk. Lindsay.
Anishinabe Grandmothers.
   Vizenor.
Annunciation Night.
   Conway.
Another Color. Stewart.
Answer to Pauper. Hood.
Antiquitez de Rome. Du
   Bellay.
Anywhere Out of the World.
   Baudelaire.
April Rise. Lee.
The Ark. Feldman.
The Ark and the Dove.
   Sargent.
The Armless. Welch.
The Armorer's Daughter.
   Greger.
Artificer. Kennedy.
Astrophel and Stella, CI.
   Sidney.
At Gibraltar. Woodberry.
At Home in Heaven.
   Southwell.
At the Roadside. Knoepfle.
Aurora Leigh. Browning.
The Author to His Booke.
   Heywood.
Autumn Journey. Levertov.
The Autumnal Moon.
   Thomson.
Awake, Awake to Love and
   Work. Studdert-Kennedy.
Baby Mine. Anonymous.
Ballad of Davy Crockett.
   Anonymous.
Ballad of the Two Tapsters.
   Watkins.
The Ballad of the White
   Horse. Chesterton.
Ballade of Youth and Age.
   Henley.
Battle Hymn. Adolphus.
Before Sunrise in Winter.
   Sill.
Before the World Was Made.
   Yeats.
Behaviour of Money.
   Spencer.
Behold. Pukui.
Belief in Plan of Thee.
   Whitman.
Bells of New Year. Field.
Beloved, Let Us Once More
   Praise the Rain. Aiken.
Beowulf. Anonymous.
Bethlehem of Judea.
   Anonymous.
Bitter Question. Macdougall.
Black and Gold. Turner.
Black People: This Is Our
   Destiny. Jones.

The Blade of Grass Sings to the River. Goldberg.
Blest Retirement. Goldsmith.
Blind Steersmen. Parkes.
Blindness. Agustini.
The Boatman. Macpherson.
The Bonnie Blue Flag. Ketchum.
The Botanist's Vision. Dobell.
Boundaries. Spear.
Brave New World. MacLeish.
Bread Is Born. Hebert.
The Bride. Hodgson.
Brother Ass. Irvin.
The Brut. Layamon.
Burr Oaks: The Attic. Eberhart.
Buster Keaton & the Cops. Keithley.
The Butcher Boy. Anonymous.
Caelica, XCVI. Greville.
Calamiterror, VI. Barker.
California (with music). Anonymous.
The Calyx of the Oboe Breaks. Aiken.
Camels of the Kings. Norris.
A Capstan Chantey. Brady.
Care. Cloud.
Carthusians. Dowson.
Casting. Nemerov.
The Cat. Matthews.
Child of Our Time. Boland.
Childhood Fled. Lamb.
Childhood, IV. Rimbaud.
Chorus: "If I drink water while this doth last." Peacock.
Chorus of the Elements. Newman.
Chosen of God. Zweig.
Christmas Is Remembering. Binns.
City Walk-Up, Winter 1969. Forche.
Climb in Torridon. Macrow.
A Clock in the Square. Rich.
Clonard. Jones, Jr.
Clorinda and Damon. Marvell.
The Coat of Fire. Sitwell.
The Colour of God's Face. Livesay.
The Columbiad: One Centred System. Barlow.
Columbus. Hale.
Columbus. Lowell.
Columbus. Miller.
Come Let Us Make Love Deathless. Trench.
The Complaint of Rosamond. Daniel.
The Condor. Hogan.
Conjectured to Be upon the Death of Sir Walter Ralegh. King.
The Constant Bridegrooms. Patchen.
Contra Mortem. Carruth.
Could I Believe. Milne.
A Countrywoman of Mine. Eastman.
Cousins. Cullen.
The Coyote. Revard.
Credo (excerpt). Gilder.
Cristina. Browning.

La Crosse at Ninety Miles an Hour. Eberhart.
Cupid, Thou Naughty Boy. Greville.
The Custom of the World. Simpson.
Darkness. Bacon.
The Daughter of Jairus. Tsvetayeva.
Davideis. Cowley.
Dawn and Dark. Gale.
Dawn of the Space Age. Ciardi.
Dawn on the Headland. Watson.
Day and Night. Dhingra.
Day Begins at Governor's Square Mall. Stokesbury.
The Dead. Wright.
The Dead Water. Wen I-to.
The Dearest Spot on Earth. Wrighton.
The Death of Richard Wagner. Swinburne.
Definition. Rolfe.
The Democratic Barber; or, Country Gentleman's Surprise. Parrish.
Departed–to the Judgment. Dickinson.
The Descent of Odin. Gray.
Desert Stone. Waddington.
Diana. Constable.
The Discoverer. Field.
Disillusionment. Alegria.
Diversity. Thompson.
The Divine Narcissus. Juana Ines de la Cruz.
Do Not Die. Merwin.
Dock Rats. Moore.
Don Juan. Byron.
The Donkey. Anonymous.
"Dover Beach"–a Note to That Poem. MacLeish.
Dream-Song. De la Mare.
The Dreamers Cry Their Dream. Trent.
Dreams. Herrick.
Drink that Rot Gut. Anonymous.
Drinking Song: "Drink that rotgut, drink that rotgut". Anonymous.
The Dumb World. Davies.
The Edge. Dobson.
Edgehill Fight. Kipling.
The Effect of Example. Keble.
The Egyptian Lotus. Eaton.
The Elements. Newman.
Elephants from the Sea. Young.
Emily Dickinson Postage Stamp. Strongin.
The End of the World. McGrath.
Epitaph. Coppard.
An Epitaph. Heywood.
Epitaphs of the War, 1914-18. Kipling.
Epithalamion. Broumas.
Esther. Blunt.
Everything Is Round. "Mistral.
The Ex-Poet. Zavatsky.
Exercise for the Left Hand. Urdang.
Eyesight II. Duncan.
The Fall of Hyperion. Keats.
Fantastic World's End. Moure.

Farewell. Symonds.
The Fat Man. Rutsala.
Fate. Cooper, Jr..
The Female God. Rosenberg.
The Female Phaeton. Prior.
Feuerzauber. Untermeyer.
First Love. Anonymous.
The Flesh and the Spirit. Bradstreet.
The Flight. Mifflin.
The Flight of the Duchess. Browning.
A Flight Shot. Thompson.
Florine. Campbell.
Following Van Gogh (Avignon, 1982). Puziss.
The Fools of Forty-Nine. Anonymous.
For February Twelfth. Gessner.
For He Had Great Possessions. Middleton.
For James Baldwin. Boyle.
For Steve. Birney.
For Zorro. Bickston.
Found in a Storm. Stafford.
Four for Sir John Davies. Roethke.
Four Quartets. Eliot.
Fr Anselm Williams and Br Leander Neville Hanged by Lutheran... Smither.
Friend Who Never Came. Stafford.
From Vice, 1966. Brodey.
Gasbags. Anonymous.
Georgiques Chretiennes (excerpt). Jammes.
Gifts. Piety.
Girandole. Donnelly.
Give to the Living. Morris.
Glass. Lento.
Gnome. Beckett.
Go Down, Ol' Hannah. Anonymous.
God (excerpt). McLachlan.
God of the Prophets! Bless the Prophets' Sons. Wortman.
Going up to London. Turner.
The Golden Shower. Campbell.
The Gordian Knot. Tomkis.
Graffito Inscribed on a Wall of the Taj Mahal. Anonymous.
Great God Paused among Men. Berrigan.
The Gulistan. Sa'di.
Guy. Emerson.
Gypsy-Heart. Bates.
Hamlet. Shakespeare.
Hard Trials. Anonymous.
Hart Crane. Creeley.
The Hate and the Love of the World. Ehrmann.
He Saw Far in the Concave Green of the Sea. Keats.
Heart's Compass. Rossetti.
Heaven's Magnificence. Muhlenberg.
The Hecatomb to His Mistress. Cleveland.
Hedgehog. Muldoon.
Her Hair. Chester.
The Hermit Cackleberry Brown, on Human Vanity:. Williams.
Heroes. Proctor.
Himself (excerpt). Ellis.
Hiroshima. Rockwell.

His Task–and Ours. Gould.
Hold the Wind. Anonymous.
Homage to Elvis, Homage to the Fathers. Weigl.
Homage to the New World. Harper.
Home. Heidenstam.
The Home. Tagore.
The Hooded Crow. McOwan.
The Horse Trader's Song. Anonymous.
The Hotel. Monroe.
A House of the Eighties. Wilson.
How Small Is Man. Blackie.
Hungering Hearts. Anonymous.
A Hymn for Canada. Watson.
Hymn for the Lighting of the Lamps. Athenogenes.
A Hymn to the Sea. Stoddard.
Hymns and Spiritual Songs. Smart.
I Am a Horse. Arp.
I Breathed into the Ash. Robinson.
I Don't Want to Get Adjusted. Anonymous.
I Dream a World. Hughes.
I Like Americans. Boyd.
I.M.H. Baring.
I'm on an Island. Clark.
I've Got the World on a String. Koehler.
Identity. Mary Helen.
If Birds That Neither Sow Nor Reap. Williams.
If Buttercups Buzz'd after the Bee. Anonymous.
If the Owl Calls Again. Haines.
If They Spoke. Van Doren.
If You Made Gentler the Churlish World. Ehrmann.
Ightham Woods. Sisson.
Illusion. Rak.
Imagination. Davidson.
In Back of the Real. Ginsberg.
In Death. Bradley.
In Honour of That High and Mighty Princess Queen Elizabeth... Bradstreet.
In Hospital. Henley.
In Memoriam A.H.H., XXXIII. Tennyson.
In Memoriam A.H.H., CXXIX. Tennyson.
In Small Townlands. Heaney.
In the Night. Jennings.
In the Secret Rose Garden. Shabistari.
In the Shadowy Whatnot Corner. Hillyer.
In the Tree House at Night. Dickey.
Inscription in a Hermitage. Warton, Jr..
Irish Hymn to Mary. Anonymous.
Is Love Not Everlasting? McCuaig.
It Is a Distinct Pleasure. Veitch.
It Is Not Too Late. Trent.
January 18, 1979. Yau.
Jim at the Corner. Farjeon.

Journey through the Night. Holloway.
Judas Iscariot. Martin.
Just before Dawn. Borson.
Just California. McGroarty.
Kicking from Centre Field. McFadden.
The Kid: The Awakening (excerpt). Aiken.
Kind Miss (with music). *Anonymous.*
Known. Dailey.
Labor Not in Vain. *Anonymous.*
The Ladies of St. James's. Dobson.
Lalla Rookh. Moore.
Lamia. Keats.
Last Journey. Davidson.
The Last Picnic. Kunitz.
Last Statement. Mayakovsky.
The Last Turn. Williams.
The Last Whiskey Cup. Engle.
A Last Word. Sarton.
Legacy II. Quintana.
Let the Rest of the World Go By. Brennan.
Letter to Graham and Anna. MacNeice.
Letters from a Father. Van Duyn.
Leviathan. Merwin.
Life Cycle of Common Man. Nemerov.
Light and Dark. Howes.
Light Baggage. Walker.
The Likeness. Martial (Marcus Valerius Martialis).
Lincoln. Hill.
Lines Addressed to a Seagull. Griffin.
Lines on Leaving a Scene in Bavaria. Campbell.
Little Son. Johnson.
Loch Lomond. Scott.
London City (B vers. with music). *Anonymous.*
The Lord of the World. Studdert-Kennedy.
The Lost Mr. Blake. Gilbert.
Love, as a Warrior Lord. Ovid (Publius Ovidius Naso).
Love in May. Passerat.
Love Is a Place. Cummings.
Love Me, and the World Is Mine. Reed, Jr.
Love, My Machine. Simpson.
Love-Song. Lasker-Schüler.
Luminous Night. Simpson.
Mad Sweeny. Montague.
Madam Mouse Trots. Sitwell.
The Making of Color. Seidman.
Man O'War Bird. Walcott.
The Man without a Road: X. Lindegren.
Mantis. Zukofsky.
Mary's Song. Causley.
Mary Tired. Pickthall.
May Garden. Drinkwater.
The Mediatix of Grace. Burke.
Meeting at the Building. *Anonymous.*
Menodotis. Leonidas of Alexandria.

A Message from Space. Stafford.
Metaphors. McNall.
The Middle of the World. Norris.
The Mighty Heart. Emerson.
Mihailovich. McFadden.
Mock Orange. Gluck.
The Moment. Rowbotham.
Monet Refused the Operation. Mueller.
Morning in Spring. Ginsberg.
A Morning Letter. Duncan.
Mountain Born. Bost.
The Mud Turtle. Nemerov.
My Body. Korn.
My Grandmother and the Voice of Tolstoy. Orlen.
My Heart Shall Be Thy Garden. Meynell.
My Name Was Legion. Swift.
My New World. Browne.
Mythmaking. Spivack.
Narcissus. Petersen.
Nature in War-Time. Palmer.
Nelson's Death. *Anonymous.*
The New Song. Field.
The New Victory. Widdemer.
A New Year. Davies.
New Year on Dartmoor. Plath.
Night. Lovelace.
No. Schorb.
Nocturnal Sounds. Cumbo.
Nocturne. Burr.
Note. Lima.
November. Tuckerman.
The Novices. Levertov.
Now. Monroe.
Now Is the Cherry in Blossom. Wilkins.
O Dirty Bird Yr Gizzard's Too Big & Full of Sand. Koller.
O Son of Man, Thou Madest Known. Littlefield.
O Tan-Faced Prairie-Boy. Whitman.
O Thou Whose Gracious Presence Shone. Ham.
Ode on Solitude. Pope.
Ode to the Day. Norris.
Oenone's Complaint. Peele.
Of Thomas Traherne and the Pebble outside. Clouts.
The Old One and the Wind. Short.
Old People Working (Garden, Car). Brooks.
Old Witherington. Randall.
On a Monday Morning. Tawney.
On a Picture by Michele da Verona, of Arion as a Boy Riding... Ridler.
On a Proud Fellow. *Anonymous.*
On Fanny Godwin. Shelley.
On Mites, To a Lady. Duck.
On No Work of Words. Thomas.
On the Death of an Emperor Penguin in Regent's Park, London. Wright.
On the Ridgeway. Young.
On Wearing Ears. Harris.
One Morning the World Woke Up. Williams.

The Operation. Snodgrass.
Original Epitaph on a Drunkard. Tyler.
Our Country Is Divided. Nuur.
Our Lady of the Skies. Hayes.
A Painful Love Song. Amichai.
A Pair. Gjellerup.
Panegyric. Lenowitz.
Parisian Dream. Baudelaire.
Parochial Theme. Stevens.
Parting at Morning. Browning.
Passage Steamer. MacNeice.
The Passion of Christ. Devlin.
The Passion of Our Lady. Peguy.
Paul's Wife. Frost.
The Peace of Wild Things. Berry.
Peewits on the Hills. Stuart.
Permission to Speak. Orlen.
Permit Us, Lord, to Consecrate. Green.
The Perspective and Limits of Snapshots. Smith.
Pippa Passes. Browning.
Poem H. Rodriguez Nietzche.
The Poet. Browning.
Poet. Emerson.
The Poet. Tennyson.
The Poet's Song. Tennyson.
Poetry. Markham.
Poland, October. Brasch.
The Pomegranate. Dudek.
The Porpoise. Pape.
A Portrait of Rudy. Cunningham.
Pot Shot. Fallon.
The Power of Malt. Housman.
Praise and Love. Rands.
Prayer. Wilder.
Prayer for Dreadful Morning. Root.
Prayer Moves the Hand That Moves the World. Wallace.
Prayer to Hermes. Creeley.
Proem. Cawein.
Proportions. Stroud.
Purer Than Purest Pure. Cummings.
Quarrel. *Anonymous.*
Queen of the World. *Anonymous.*
A Question. *Anonymous.*
Questions. Hilarova.
Questions and Answers. Muhringer.
The Quick. Jennett.
The Rainbow. *Anonymous.*
Remarks of Soul to Body. Warren.
Remember, Though the Telescope Extend. Dillon.
De Rerum Natura. Lucretius (Titus Lucretius Carus).
Resignation. *Anonymous.*
Resignation. Arnold.
The Retreat. Read.
Rilke Speaks of Angels. Donnelly.
Ring around the World. Wynne.
The Ritual. Gwillim.

Rome, Conqueror, Conquered. Sylvester.
The Rose of the World. Yeats.
The Rural Lass. Jemmat.
The Sad Day. Flatman.
Sally's Garden. *Anonymous.*
The Sapphire. Merwin.
Satires. Wyatt.
The Saucy Sailor. *Anonymous.*
Sea. Gordon.
The Sea of Silence Exhales Secrets. Bialik.
The Second-Fated. Graves.
The Sensualists. Roethke.
A Sermon on Swift. Clarke.
Sermon on the Mount. Wright.
Shadows. Claudel.
Shakespeare. Watson.
The Shark's Parlor. Dickey.
She Turns the Dolls' Faces to the Wall. Yeats.
Ship Bottom. Lattimore.
Shop Talk. Fuller.
Significant Fevers. Fell.
Sing Little Bird. Hastings.
Sleep Will Come Singly. Oliver.
Slepynge Long in Greet Quiete is Eek a Greet Norice to Leccherie. Hollander.
Snakebite. James.
Snow Train. Erdrich.
So Wags the World. Cortissoz.
Solemn Hour. Rilke.
Song (2). Rolfe.
Song: "How do I love you?" McLeod.
A Song of Faith. Holland.
The Song of the Good Samaritan. Watkins.
Sonnet at Dover Cliffs. Bowles.
Sonnet: "This infant world has taken long to make." Macdonald.
Sonnets. Lee.
Sonnets, I: "From fairest creatures we desire increase." Shakespeare.
Sonnets, LXXI: "No longer mourn for me when I am dead." Shakespeare.
Sonnets of a Portrait Painter. Ficke.
Sonnets of the Months. San Geminiano.
Sonnets to Miranda. Watson.
Sorting, Wrapping, Packing, Stuffing. Schuyler.
Speak Like Rain. Metz.
Speakers, Columbus Circle. Souster.
The Spoilers and the Spoils. Sherwin.
Spring Morning. Lawrence.
Spring Omnipotent Goddess. Cummings.
St. Alphonsus Rodriguez. Hopkins.
St. James Infirmary. *Anonymous.*
The Stars. "Ping Hsin" (Hsieh Wang-ying).
Stealing Trout. Hughes.
The Stolen Child. Yeats.

The Storms Are on the Ocean.
Anonymous.
Summer Sun. Stevenson.
A Summing Up. Preil.
The Sums. Edmond.
Sunday Night Walk.
Souster.
Switzerland. Arnold.
Symphony: First Movement.
Wheelock.
'Tain't Nobody's Business.
Stokes.
Take the World as It Is
(excerpt). Swain.
Teaching Swift to Young
Ladies. Dickey.
Ten Week Wife. Donovan.
The Testament of John
Davidson: The Last
Journey. Davidson.
A Text for These Distracted
Times. Hall.
A Thanksgiving. Newman.
That Man in Manhattan.
Kelley.
Theme Brown Girl. Hill-
Abu Ishak.
There Came A Wind Like A
Bugle. Dickinson.
There's Gowd in the Breast.
Hogg.
This Is the Garden.
Cummings.
This Is Your Hour.
Kaufman.
This Only Do I Know.
Anonymous.
Thought and the Poet.
Yates.
Thought's End. Adams.
Three Poems, I. Castellânos.
Throbs the Night with Mystic
Silence. Bialik.
Thy Kingdom Come.
Bernard of Clairvaux
Tidying Up. Weber.
Time. More.
'Tis the Last Rose of Summer.
Moore.
To a Linnet in a Cage.
Ledwidge.
To a Spanish Poet. Spender.
To a Vagabond. Woodrow.
To Charlotte Corday.
Sitwell.
To Colman Returning.
Colman.
To Columbus. Dario.
To Dianeme. Herrick.
To Forget Me. Weiss.
To France. Chaplin.
To Liebig–6. Platen.
To Lighten My House.
Reid.
To Pius IX. Whittier.
Today's News. Berrigan.
Tombstone Epitaphs.
Anonymous.
Tourist Guide: How You Can
Tell for Sure When You're
in South Dakota. Heynen.
Toward a True Peace.
Cheney.
The Tragedy of the Leaves.
Bukowski.
Training for the Apocalypse.
Frym.
Tricks. Moure.
The Trouble with Angels.
Norris.
Turn on Your Side and Bear
the Day to Me. Barker.

Twenty-One Love Poems.
Rich.
Twenty-One Sonnets. Stead.
The Twinkling Earn.
Davidson.
Two Dogs. Davidson.
Ultima Ratio Regum.
Spender.
The Uncouth Knight.
McCrae.
Unity. Noyes.
Univac to Univac. Salomon.
The Universal Republic.
Hugo.
Up Silver Stairsteps. Stuart.
Upanishads: Second Khanda.
Anonymous.
Upon Julia's Ribband.
Herrick.
Upper Family. Bodenheim.
Urania. De Vere.
Urban Roses. Isaac.
Us. Ignatow.
Us Tasting the Air. Shapiro.
Vain World Adieu.
Anonymous.
The Vance Song.
Anonymous.
Vapour and Blue. Campbell.
Variations. Jarrell.
Variations on a Theme. Hay.
Venus Abandoned.
Shakespeare.
The Vigil. Levertov.
A Village Tale. Sarton.
A Visitation. Snodgrass.
Voices of Heroes. Gregory.
W'en you see a man in woe.
Foss.
Wake. Spires.
A Walk in Kyoto. Birney.
Walls. Cavafy.
The War Horse. Boland.
Warrior Nation Trilogy.
Henson.
The Way to Live.
Anonymous.
We Men Are of Two Worlds.
Colman.
We Woke Together.
Brennan.
Webster: An Ode (excerpt).
Wilkinson.
The Well Rising. Stafford.
What Is the World? Dryden.
What need I travel, since I
may. Hall.
When a Man Turns
Homeward. Hicky.
When Green Buds Hang.
Housman.
When Heaven Would Strive to
Do the Best She Can.
Drayton.
When I Was Six. Cross.
Whirlwinds of Danger.
Anonymous.
The White Horse. Lawrence.
Who Knows? Coan.
The Widower. Tyler.
Wild Eden. Woodberry.
The Window. Aiken.
The Window Frames the
Moon. Mar.
Wires. Bassett.
With Mercy for the Greedy.
Sexton.
Wonders. Thomas.
Words. Eberhart.
The Work of Love. Sangster.
The World an Illusion.
Anonymous.

"The world goes turning".
Dillon.
The World I Am Passing
Through. Child.
The World Is Mine. Coates.
The World Looks On.
Newman.
World of Darkness. Chatain.
World's Worth. Rossetti.
The World We Make.
Walton.
World Winter. Birney.
World within a World.
Bender.
Written on a Sunday
Morning. Southey.
The Year's at the Spring.
Browning.
Years and Years I Have
Loved You. Gillett.
You Can't Keep No Brown.
Jackson.
Young Heroes. Horne.
Youth. Bates.

World War
The End of World War One.
Olds.
Safe for Democracy. Strong.
World War III. Anonymous.

Worldly
Astrophel and Stella,
XXXVII. Sidney.
Lough Bray. O'Grady.
The Parrot. Skelton.
Seek Flowers of Heaven.
Southwell.
To God. Blake.

Worm (s)
After Wings. Piatt.
Against Constancy.
Rochester.
And This of All My Hopes.
Dickinson.
The Art of Poetry. Dryden.
Bagman O'Reilly's Curse.
Murray.
Blind Steersmen. Parkes.
Christmas Dinner. Rosen.
Conflict. Fitzell.
Couplets for WCW.
Christina.
Cupid. O'Dowd.
Eternity's Low Voice. Van
Doren.
Face. Toomer.
Farewell to Love. Donne.
Father. Pack.
Fisherman. Francis.
The Foreman's Wife.
Tagami.
Genesis. Ingham.
The growth of Sym. Dennis.
The Hambone and the Heart.
Sitwell.
The Hearse Song (with
music). Anonymous.
I Move to Random
Consolations. Heyen.
It Was the Worm.
Broughton.
The Lion's Skeleton. Turner.
The Moral Bully. Holmes.
Nobody Loses All the Time.
Cummings.
Nobody will open the door for
you. Varela.
On Ryneveld, an Unpopular
Dutch Judge at the Cape of
Good Hope. Anonymous.
Pelleas and Ettarre (excerpt).
Tennyson.

The Princess in the Ivory
Tower. Davidman.
The Revenger's Tragedy
(excerpt). Tourneur.
Scholfield Huxley. Masters.
The Snake. Palmer.
Song of Myself. Whitman.
Song of the Three Hundred
Thousand
Drunkards...(excerpt).
Tappan.
Sonnet: "My God, where is
that ancient heat towards
thee." Herbert.
Sonnets from Walton's Life of
Herbert, 1670. Herbert.
The Staircase. Allen.
Summit Lake. Thalman.
They Have Turned the
Church Where I Ate God.
Gildner.
To a Worm Which the
Author Accidentally Trode
Upon. Hawkins.
Treason. Dunetz.
Tyranny. Lanier.
Were I to Choose. Okara.
The Whaler's Pig. Brady.
The Yellow Bittern.
MacIntyre.
You. Masefield.

Worn
Beautiful Things. Allerton.
Junk. Wilbur.
Kin. Harper.
Let Me Go down to Dust.
Sarett.
Limerick: "An extinct old
ichthyosaurus."
Anonymous.
On Hedylus. Martial
(Marcus Valerius Martialis).
A Suicide. Kryss.
There is a flower that bees
prefer. Dickinson.
Tomorrow. Collins.
A Valley where I Don't
Belong. Piercy.
Walk in the Precepts. Ibn
Ezra.
You Take My Hand And.
Atwood.

Worry (ied)
After the First Frost.
Blockcolski.
Afterwards (excerpt). Stein.
As the Window Darkens.
Jensen.
The Birth of My Father.
Dempster.
Does It Matter? Sassoon.
Family Matters. Grass.
High Water Everywhere.
Patton.
I Don't Let the Girls Worry
My Mind. Anonymous.
I'm Worried Now but I Won't
Be Worried Long.
Anonymous.
Lifting and Leaning. Wilcox.
Mind Reader Blues. Lee.
Never, Never Can
Nothingness Come.
Keating.
Pussy. Anonymous.
Two Kinds of People.
Wilcox.
Worried Life Blues.
Anonymous.

Worse (worst)
Ataraxia. Taylor.

The Best and the Worst.
Anonymous.
Birches. Frost.
The Chosen. Dennis.
Cradle Song. Hoffenstein.
The Crowned Heart.
Anonymous.
Don't Quit. *Anonymous.*
Ecce Homunculus. Mason.
Emblem. Quarles.
Fie on Love. Beaumont.
Fisbo (excerpt). Nichols.
Flash Crimson. Sandburg.
Fod. *Anonymous.*
For Hire. Rosenfeld.
The Frogs Who Wanted a
King. Aesop.
I Came to This Country in
1865. *Anonymous.*
I Wake and Feel the Fell of
Dark. Hopkins.
In Memory of Kathleen.
Patchen.
Jewish Ballad. *Anonymous.*
Lord, Many Times. Trench.
Love, I Think, Is a Disease.
O Domhnaill.
Microcosm. Dobell.
My Ladies Haire Is Threeds
of Beaten Gold. Griffin.
November. Hughes.
The Nude on the Bathroom
Wall. Ford.
Old Man at a Cricket Match.
Nicholson.
On Gaulstown House. Swift.
Pedlar. *Anonymous.*
Reflexes. Bell.
Resolution in Four Sonnets.
Cotton.
The Revolutionaries. Lister.
A Rodomontade on His Cruel
Mistress. Rochester.
The Saddest Words
(Addendum). *Anonymous.*
A Satire on Samuel Butler
(excerpt). Oldham.
Song of Oenone and Paris.
Peele.
A Sonnet: "Two voices are
there." Stephen.
Surnames to Be Avoided in
Marriage. *Anonymous.*
Two Hundred Men and
Eighteen Killed. Henry.
Upon Julia (parody).
Radford.
Wei Wind. Confucius.
Where Are the War Poets?
Day-Lewis.
Worship (ped) (per) (ping) (s)
The Acts of Youth. Wieners.
Adonis. Doolittle.
African Christmas. Press.
Aspiration. Lamb.
Aubade: Donna Anna to Juan,
Still Asleep. Howard.
Bereavement of the Fields.
Campbell.
Bread. Klein.
The Common Living Dirt.
Piercy.
Diver. Simpson.
The Eagles. Very.
Flowers for the Altar.
Dolben.
Fragment of an Ode to Maia.
Keats.
The Gift. Williams.
Hail to the Sabbath Day.
Bulfinch.

Homage to the Carracci.
Disch.
Hymn of Gratitude.
Anonymous.
Hymn of Sivaite Puritans.
Anonymous.
I Fear Thy Kisses, Gentle
Maiden. Shelley.
I Have Sought Thee Daily.
Ibn Gabirol.
I Turn to Jesus. Smith.
I Want to Write a Jewish
Poem. Pacernick.
Inanna and the City of Uruk.
Enheduanna.
Invocation. Walsh.
An Invocation (excerpt).
Iqbal.
Isaac. Burnshaw.
The Landing of the Pilgrim
Fathers. Hemans.
The Lyre Player. George.
Malachi. Marlatt.
A Marriage Prospect.
Mallock.
Maternal Lady with the
Virgin Grace. Lamb.
Mice in the Hay. Norris.
Midnight in Bonnie's Stall.
Johnson.
The Moon. Davies.
Moonlight in Italy. Kinney
My Morning Song.
Macdonald.
My Period Had Come for
Prayer. Dickinson.
Ode to Nea. Moore.
Once More, Our God,
Vouchsafe to Shine.
Sewall.
Quatrain. Sarmed the
Yahud.
Sincere Praise. Watts.
A Song for Beauty. Lal.
Tell Me You Wandering
Spirits. *Anonymous.*
A Thankful Acknowledgment
of God's Providence.
Cotton.
Three Christmas Carols: I.
Anonymous.
To Clelia. Coppinger.
To England. Moore.
To God. Blake.
True Love. Cary.
Whaddaya Do for Action in
This Place? Starbuck.
When Mahalia Sings.
Prettyman.
Worsted
Lachesis. Daley.
What Would You Fight For?
Lawrence.
Worth (y)
Astrophel and Stella, LXXV.
Sidney.
At last love has come.
Sulpicia.
Aurora Leigh. Browning.
Because of You. Hensley.
The Birds. Dracontius.
The Bruce. Barbour.
Caelica, XIV. Greville.
Caelica, LII. Greville.
Canzonetta: Of His Lady, and
of His Making Her
Likeness. Jacopo da
Lentino.
Castile. Unamuno.
Christmas at a Decade's End.
Snyder.

The Cid: Two Lovers in the
Toils of Honor. Corneille.
A Curse. Rabi'a.
A Description. Herbert of
Cherbury.
A Ditty. Jacobs.
A Dream, or the Type of the
Rising Sun. Adams.
Eagle Sonnets. Wood.
First Love. Campion.
Gondibert. Davenant.
Gun Teams. Frankau.
The Heritage. Lowell.
Homage to Theodore Dreiser
on the Centennial of His
Birth (excerpt). Warren.
A Kite Is a Victim. Cohen.
Limerick: "Said the crab:
"'Tis not beauty or birth."
Herford.
Lizard. Lawrence.
My Way Is Not Thy Way.
Lawrence.
My Wish for You. Rabi'a of
Balkh.
New Construction: Bath Iron
Works. Koehler.
An Old Story. Robinson.
The Poor Shammes of
Berditchev. Ratner.
A Pretty Fair Maid (with
music). *Anonymous.*
Song to His Cynthia.
Greville.
Sonnets, LX: "Like as the
waves make towards the
pebbled shore."
Shakespeare.
Sonnets from the Portuguese,
XVI. Browning.
Sonnets of the Months. San
Geminiano.
Success. Guest.
Tell Her So. *Anonymous.*
The Virtuous Wife.
Susskind.
La Vita Nuova. Dante
Alighieri.
What needeth these
threat'ning words and
wasted wind? Wyatt.
When Youth and Beauty Meet
Together. *Anonymous.*
Worthiest
Another. In Defence of Their
Inconstancie. Jonson.
Astrophel and Stella, XCV.
Sidney.
Prince Alfrid's Itinerary
(excerpt). *Anonymous.*
Worthless
A Song of Emptiness to Fill
up the Empty Pages
Following. Wigglesworth.
Wound (ed) (s)
Address to an Absolute.
McFadden.
After the fiercest pangs of hot
desire. Duke.
Among Iron Fragments.
Ruebner.
Amoretti, LVII. Spenser.
Arrogance. De la Mare.
At the Badr Trench. Safiya
bint Musafir.
Blok Let Me Learn the Poem.
Boyajian.
The Cathedral of Rheims.
Verhaeren.
Christmas Eve Service at
Midnight at St. Michael's.
Bly.

Christmas Mourning. Miller.
The Cloud Factory. Haines.
Content. Crane.
The Corpus Christi Carol
(from Scotland).
Anonymous.
Cozzo Grillo. Mallalieu.
The Dainty Young Heiress of
Lincoln's Inn Fields.
Sackville.
The Dearest Poets. Hunt.
The Duel. Pulsifer.
Earl Brand (Sweet William).
Anonymous.
Epilogue. Levertov.
Fair Isabell of Rochroyall.
Anonymous.
Gesture. Welles.
Gift from Kenya. Miller.
The Good Samaritan.
Newman.
Guitar. Garcia Lorca.
The Homecoming of Emma
Lazarus. Kinnell.
Horace Kephart. Morgan.
In Summer. Towne.
In the Land of Magic.
Michaux.
In Vinculis: The Deeds That
Might Have Been. Blunt.
Jamila. Mala'ika.
January. Thomas.
Jesus to Those Who Pass By.
Anonymous.
The Lament for O'Sullivan
Beare. *Anonymous.*
The Lost Tribe. Finch.
Matinal. McQueen.
May Bright Mushrooms
Grow. Banda.
Merciless Beauty. Chaucer.
Messengers. Gluck.
Morte d'Arthur. Tennyson.
My Daughter Considers Her
Body. Skloot.
Next Time. Simmons.
No Pains Comparable to His
Attempt. *Anonymous.*
O Gentle Love. Peele.
October 1942. Fuller.
Oh Yes. Matthews.
One of the Principal Causes of
War. ""MacDiarmid.
The Only Jealousy of Emer
(excerpt). Yeats.
Our People. Burns.
Paradise Lost. Milton.
Paradise Regained. Milton.
The Passion. Knevet.
Power. Rich.
The Praying Mantis Visits a
Penthouse. Williams.
The Request. Cowley.
The Rising in the North.
Anonymous.
Romantic. Garrett.
A Rondel of Merciless Beauty.
Chaucer.
Saturday Morning. Howard.
Seasons of the Soul. Tate.
Shattered Sabbath.
Goldstein.
She Used to Let Her Golden
Hair Fly Free. Petrarch
(Francesco Petrarca).
Slick. Hoffman.
Small Prayer. Kees.
Song of Myself. Whitman.
Song: "Of thee, kind boy, I
ask no red and white."
Suckling.

The Stations of the Cross.
  Colum.
Strephon. Smyth.
The Stricken South to the
  North. Hayne.
A Terre. Owen.
Thank You for the Valentine.
  Wakoski.
Thou Who Createdst
  Everything. *Anonymous.*
To a Crucifix. Wickham.
To Cupid. Davison.
The Triple Dream.
  Lermontov.
An Unbeliever. Branch.
Untitled. Mueller.
Washington in Love.
  Berryman.
We Are Such Stuff As
  Dreams... Petronius.
The Western Trail. Carr.
The Willing Prisoner to His
  Mistress. Carew.
The Wounded Breakfast.
  Edson.

Wounded Knee
American Names. Benét.

Wove (n)
The Climbing Rope. Stuart.
Crowned. Lowell.
The Curse upon Edward.
  Gray.
Her Pedigree. Ficke.
Merlin Enthralled. Wilbur.
Our Lady's Labor. Duffy.
Riddle: "I washed my face in
  water." *Anonymous.*
The Shirt. Silkin.
The Spinning Wheel. Klein.
Upon Julia's Ribband.
  Herrick.
Vala; or, The Four Zoas.
  Blake.

Wrack
The Ark. Feldman.
Venus of the Salty Shell.
  Devlin.
Vox Populi, Vox Dei
  (excerpt). *Anonymous.*
The Wrecker's Prayer.
  Roberts.

Wraith (s)
The Dance of Gray Raccoon.
  Guiterman.
The Lover. Duncan.
The Prophet Lost in the Hills
  at Evening. Belloc.
Victor Galbraith.
  Longfellow.

Wrap (ped) (s) (t)
Christmas Night.
  MacCawell.
For a Poet. Cullen.
Hushie Ba, Burdie Beeton.
  Anonymous.
Like an Ideal Tenant.
  Daigon.
A New Song to Sing about
  Jonathan Bing. Brown.
On Dr. Samuel Ogden.
  Arden.
The Storm Is Over. Bridges.
To Bring the Dead to Life.
  Graves.
Vision. Augustini.
Woman. Chambers.

Wrath (s)
The Aeneid. Virgil (Publius
  Vergilius Maro).
The Akathistos Hymn.
  Anonymous.

Apostrophe to the Island of
  Cuba. Percival.
Auguries of Innocence.
  Blake.
Childe Harold's Pilgrimage:
  Canto I. Byron.
Childe Maurice. *Anonymous.*
Chiliasm. Eberhart.
The Cry of the Children.
  Browning.
Discipline. Herbert.
The Doomed Man.
  Alexander.
Doors of the Temple.
  Huxley.
Fear Has Cast Out Love.
  Blunt.
The Fugitive Slaves. Very.
Give Peace, O God, the
  Nations Cry. Norris.
If, on Account of the Political
  Situation. Auden.
It's No Good! Lawrence.
Letters for the New England
  Dead. Baron.
Meditations 6. Taylor.
The Meek and the Proud.
  Ibn Chasdai.
A Mother in Egypt.
  Pickthall.
My God. Ibn Gabirol.
Of a Lady That Refused to
  Dance with Him. Surrey.
Paradise Lost. Milton.
Poem: "O who can ever praise
  enough." Auden.
Psalm XXXIX. Sidney.
The School Girl. Venable.
The Song of the Flume.
  Fitch.
Song of the Mariner's Needle.
  Clarke.
Sonnets, II: "Our doom is in
  our being." Agee.
Th Unifying Principle.
  Ammons.
Thrice Blest the Man.
  Barnard.
A Wanderer's Litany.
  Stringer.

Wreath (ed) (es) (ing) (s)
Anklet Song. *Anonymous.*
Between You and Me. Hazo.
The Clavichord. Sarton.
Credo. Tchernichovsky.
Cyclops. Euripides.
An Evening Walk (excerpt).
  Wordsworth.
The Expensive Wife. Ibn
  Sabbatai.
The Fear of Dying. Holmes.
For Randolph Bourne.
  Oppenheim.
I'll Twine White Violets.
  Meleager.
Llangollen Vale (excerpt).
  Seward.
The Moon of Brooklyn.
  Crane.
Mr. Pope. Tate.
Obituary. Kees.
Poem: "In the earnest path of
  duty." Forten.
A Rose to the Living.
  Waterman.
Sonnet: "Innumerable
  Beauties, thou white haire."
  Herbert of Cherbury.
Stonewall Jackson. Melville.
To a Friend on His Marriage.
  Prince.
To a Lady. Scott.

To His Honoured and Most
  Ingenious Friend, Master
  Charles Cotton. Herrick.
To My Worthy Friend Master
  George Sands.... Carew.
The Unknown Beloved.
  Wheelock.
Walking in the Rain. Saxon.
A Wedgwood Bowl. Taylor.
Winter. Thomson.

Wreck (ed) (er) (s)
Amoretti, LVI. Spenser.
The Buccaneer: The Island.
  Dana.
A Child Accepts.
  Hamburger.
China. Empson.
Housemates. Shepard.
Lament. Walsh.
Mother, Mother, Are You All
  There? Lamport.
Newstead Abbey. Byron.
An Old Song Re-sung.
  Masefield.
The Palatine. Whittier.
The Sea's Spell. Spalding.
Song: "O, strew the way with
  rosy flowers." Mangan.
To Mr. Newton on His
  Return from Ramsgate.
  Cowper.
The Warning. Longfellow.
Which Are You?
  Anonymous.
The Winds. "Eglinton.
With a Nantucket Shell.
  Webb.

Wren (s)
The Businessman of Alicante.
  Levine.
Fifty Faggots. Thomas.
The growth of Sym. Dennis.
Jubilate Agno. Smart.
The Merchant of Venice.
  Shakespeare.
The Reading Lesson.
  Murphy.
The Stack. Snaith.
Three Things to Remember.
  Blake.

Wrestle (d) (s)
Apocrypha. Moss.
Art. Melville.
The Bride. Hodgson.
Carrion Comfort. Hopkins.
For Every Day. Havergal.
Reflections on Water.
  Pitchford.
Still Wrestling. Boiarski.
Two Wrestlers. Francis.
Vetus Flamma. Mezey.
What is Life? Coleridge.
Your Light. Lee.

Wretch (es) (ed)
Christ 1: Advent Lyrics, III.
  Anonymous.
The History of Insipids.
  Freke.
I, a Most Wretched Atlas.
  Heine.
Last Verses. Chatterton.
Lulla La, Lulla Lulla Lullaby.
  Byrd.
Man. Davies.
The Monument. Wesley.
On the Sentence Passed by the
  House of Lords on Dr.
  Sacheverell. *Anonymous.*
Song of the Evil Spirit of the
  Woods. Moore.

Sonnets, XCI: "Some glory in
  their birth, some in their
  skill." Shakespeare.
St. Francis of Assisi and the
  Miserable Jews. Wittlin.
Sylvoe: A Song. Dryden.
They Closed Her Eyes.
  Becquer.
Written over a Gate.
  Sheffield.

Wring (ing) (s)
Dead Bird (parody). Slavitt.
The Dreamers and the Sea.
  Wilkins.
The Stranger Not Ourselves.
  Stafford.
Upon the King's Return from
  Flanders. Hall.
Venice. Wright.
The Vicar of Wakefield.
  Goldsmith.
Who Killed Lawless Lean?
  Smith.

Wrinkle (d) (s)
Abishag. Spire.
April Fourth. Mezey.
Canadian Farmer. Bartole.
Cotton-eyed Joe.
  Anonymous.
Fill the Bumper Fair.
  Moore.
Harriet. Lowell.
Quiet. Swann.
Virtue. Di Roma.

Wrist (s)
Et Quid Amabo Nisi Quod
  Aenigma Est. Sandy.
Fencing School. Manifold.
Hugh Maguire. O'Hussey.
Lobsters in the Window.
  Snodgrass.
My Grandmother Had Bones.
  Hemschemeyer.
The Phoenix of Mozart.
  Vigee.
Roses, Revisited, in a
  Paradoxical Autumn.
  Cullum.
The Serving Maid. Munby.
The Statue and the Perturbed
  Burghers. Devlin.
Three Part Invention.
  Blackburn.
The Watch. Swenson.
The Withdrawal. Lowell.

Wristwatch
The Withdrawal. Lowell.

Writ (s)
Epigram: "Some people
  admire the work of a Fool."
  Blake.
The Prows o' Reekie.
  Spence.
The Romance of the Rose.
  Guillaume de Lorris
Satire. Donne.
Sonnets, CXVI: "Let me not
  to the marriage of true
  minds." Shakespeare.
To Sextus. Sedley.
To the Learned and Reverend
  Mr. Cotton Mather...
  Rawson.

Write (r) (s) (wrote)
Advice to a Young Man (of
  Letters)... Edman.
All This Everyday (excerpt).
  Kyger.
Amoretti, III. Spenser.
Apologia. Gascoyne.
The Argument of His Book.
  Herrick.

Astrophel and Stella, I.
Sidney.
A Ballad to the Tune of "The
Cut-Purse." Swift.
Bio-Poetic Statement:
Instruction to Warriors on
Security. Arnett.
Boogie with O. O. Gabugah.
Young.
A Bookshop Idyll. Amis.
Clerihew. Bentley.
The Clouds. Vogelsang.
Columbus. Hale.
The Cottage at Chigasaki.
Blunden.
The Country House.
Simpson.
A Critic. Landor.
A Crucifix. Verlaine.
The Cruise of the P.C.
Anonymous.
A Curse for a Nation.
Browning.
Darling of Gods and Men,
beneath the Gliding Stars.
Bunting.
Death of a Poet. Causley.
Der Brief, Den Du
Geshrieben. Untermeyer.
A Dirge. Croffut.
Eclogue IV. The Poet
(excerpt). Jenner.
Elegy Written at the Sea-Side,
and Addressed to Miss
Honoria Sneyd. Seward.
Emily Dickinson Postage
Stamp. Strongin.
Epilogue. Singer.
An Epistolary Essay from
M.G. to O.B. upon Their
Mutual Poems. Rochester.
An Essay upon Satire.
Sheffield.
Evening: an Elegy (parody).
Smith.
The External Element.
McFadden.
Fall Letter. Kelly.
Force. Walcott.
Fragment. Clare.
The Fresh Start. Wickham.
The Future. Cameron.
Geordie (D version).
Anonymous.
The George Aloe and the
Sweepstake. Anonymous.
Green Grow the Lilacs.
Anonymous.
A Hedge before Me.
Columcille.
The Height of the Ridiculous.
Holmes.
I Know That All beneath the
Moon Decays.
Drummond.
I Wonder How Many People
in This City. Cohen.
It is her cousin's death...
Fox.
John Baynham's Epitaph.
Dermody.
John Was A-Writin'.
Anonymous.
Journey to Iceland. Auden.
The Lamp Now Flickers.
Grunewald.
A Letter. Mu'tamid.
Letter from Smyrna to His
Sisters at Crux-Easton,
1733. Lisle.
Letter to Reed from Lolo.
Hugo.

A Letter to Robert Frost.
Hillyer.
Letters to Live Poets.
Beaver.
Love. Herbert.
Lyke Memnons Rocke
Toucht, with the Rising
Sunne. Fletcher.
Many Red Devils. Crane.
Melody. Moreh.
Musophilus. Daniel.
Night in Martindale. Raine.
Not Going with It.
Gurevitch.
A Note on The Hunted City,
1939-1967. Patchen.
Now That Can Never Be
Done. Maris Stella.
On Christopher Wordsworth,
Master of Trinity.
Kennedy.
On Oliver Goldsmith.
Garrick.
On Poet Ninny. Rochester.
Only One King. Moreland.
People of the Future.
Berrigan.
Piazza Di Spagna. Grimes.
A Plea to Boys and Girls.
Graves.
Poems. Drummond.
The Postman's Bell Is
Answered Everywhere.
Gregory.
Praise. Cooper.
Questions for the Candidate.
Holmes.
Rainbow Writing. Merriam.
Savage Portraits. Marquis.
The Scribe. Anonymous.
Secret-Love. Dryden.
"So Quietly". Hill.
Sonnet: "Like Memnon's rock,
touched with the rising
sun." Fletcher.
A Sonnet: "Two voices are
there." Stephen.
Spring Street Bar.
Berssenbrugge.
Success Story. Bennett.
The T.E. Lawrence Poems:
The Void. MacEwen.
The Ten Commandments.
Anonymous.
Testament. Zavatsky.
There Is No Reason Why Not
to Look at Death. Sward.
There's Been Some Sort of
Mistake. Gilfillan.
There's Money in Mother and
Father. Bishop.
To Fletcher Reviv'd.
Lovelace.
Upon the Dramatick Poems of
Mr. John Fletcher.
Cartwright.
The Van Gogh Influence.
Silverstein.
Walt Whitman. Robinson.
What Frenzy Has of Late
Possess'd the Brain!
Garth.
When Klopstock England
Defied. Blake.
The Whisperer. Stephens.
With a China Chamberpot, to
the Countess of
Hillsborough. Holland.
The Writer. Jacob.
Written on a Leaf.
Anonymous.

Writhes
The Brass Horse. Allison.
My Arkansas. Angelou.
River Rhyme. Williams.
War Swaggers. Litvinoff.
Writing (s)
Archys Last Name.
Marquis.
The Ballad of the Billycock.
Deane.
December 24 and George
McBride is Dead. Hugo.
Dedication. Gustafson.
Four Preludes on Playthings
of the Wind. Sandburg.
Ghetto Summer School.
Worth.
The Handwriting on the Wall.
Shaw.
The Lake Isle. Pound.
Letter to "M'. Anonymous.
Mouth. Nicoidski.
Musophilus. Daniel.
My Life by Somebody Else.
Strand.
Notes on a Certain Terribly
Critical Piece.
Whittemore.
Shifting Colors. Lowell.
Squeal (parody). Simpson.
Stone. Simic.
The Story of Johnny Head-in-
Air. Hoffmann.
The Talk of The Town.
Fisher.
Teaching the Ape to Write
Poems. Tate.
To Francis Beaumont.
Jonson.
Writing for Money. Field.
Writing in England Now.
O'Connor.
Written
The 90th Year. Levertov.
The After-Comers. Lowell.
Aldfrid's Itinerary Through
Ireland. Fionn.
Doubt. Nolan.
An Elegie. Corbett.
Flail. "Dalton.
He Prayeth for Ink and
Palette That He May Write.
Book of the Dead.
Lecture Note: Elizabethan
Period. Grigson.
The Long Picnic. Edson.
My True Sailor Boy.
Anonymous.
A Nice Correspondent.
Locker-Lampson.
Printer's Error. Wodehouse.
To the Reverend Joseph
Trapp, on the First
Volume... Evans.
What hundred books are best.
Bangs.
What I Have Written I Have
Written. Porter.
What Is There. Bell.
Wrong (s)
Abandoned Farmhouse.
Kooser.
Alajire. Anonymous.
As a Boy with a Richness of
Needs I Wandered.
Dyment.
At It. Thomas.
The Bad Girl's Lament; or,
St. James Hospital.
Anonymous.
The Banshee. Todhunter.

Bring Tem Not Back.
Kenyon.
Caelica, XLVI. Greville.
The Cowboy's Lament; or,
The Streets of Laredo (B
vers.). Anonymous.
Crisis. Fraser.
Death's Jest Book. Beddoes.
Dichterliebe. Engler.
The Earthly Paradise.
Morris.
An Easter Garland.
Rumens.
Elegy: to Delia. Hammond.
The Engine: A Manual.
Dobberstein.
Epigrams. Theocritus.
Epitaph: "Here lies a poet,
briefly known as Hecht."
Hecht.
Errore. Di Cicco.
Expression. Rosenberg.
Frankie and Johnny, I (with
music). Anonymous.
Garage Sale. Shapiro.
The Gospel of Peace. Roche.
Grandmother. Carlile.
Gwendolyn Brooks. Lee.
Hegel. Jones.
The Herd. Cornford.
How to Forget. Foresman.
Hymn to the Virgin.
William.
I Am Not Bound to Win.
Lincoln.
I Been a Bad, Bad Girl.
Anonymous.
I Dream I'm the Death of
Orpheus. Rich.
The Ideal Husband to His
Wife. Foss.
An Idyl in Idleness. Pack.
In My Lifetime. Welch.
In Perspective. Graves.
In Prison. Morris.
Innocence. Chappell.
Isaac. Burnshaw.
Langaig. Hugo.
A Leaden Treasury of English
Verse. Dehn.
Love Me Again. Anonymous.
Mary Le More. Reynolds.
A Miracle for Breakfast.
Bishop.
Money and a Friend.
Anonymous.
Mourn Not the Dead.
Chaplin.
The New Balow.
Anonymous.
Night Mail. Auden.
Nonsense. Anonymous.
The Obscured Prince; or, the
Black Box Boxed.
Anonymous.
Ode to a Nightingale
(parody). Kelly.
Of Those Who Walk Alone.
Burton.
Old Hannah. Anonymous.
On Hearing the Airlines Will
Use a Psychological
Profile... Dunn.
On the Projected Kendal and
Windermere Railway.
Wordsworth.
Overflow. Tabb.
Parting at Dawn. Ransom.
The Planster's Vision.
Betjeman.
Prayer for Song. Noble.

Prometheus Bound.
Aeschylus.
A Psalm. Blunden.
Rain. Moss.
The Riddle. Hodgson.
The Rule of the Road.
Anonymous.
Sadie (with music).
Anonymous.
The Same Old Jazz. Whalen.
Satyrus Peregrinana.
Rankins.
The Shadow of Night.
Patmore.
The Shoemaker's Holiday.
Dekker.
The Song-Maker. Wickham.
The Song of Roland, XCIII.
Anonymous.
Spite hath no power to make
me sad. Wyatt.
Stepfather Blues. Williams.
Teamster's Song.
Anonymous.
Thought on June 26.
Kunene.
The Thrush. Corsellis.
To a Red-Headed Do-Good
Waitress. Dugan.
To Delia. Daniel.
To God. Maurice.
Undying Thirst. Antipater of
Sidon.
Upon a Diamond Cut in
Forme of a Heart... Ayton
[(or Aytoun)] Sir Robert.
We Whom the Dead Have
Not Forgiven. Field.
Windows. Husid.

Wrought
Commemoration Ode.
Monroe.
Cuckoo, Scabbed Gowk.
Anonymous.
Epilogue. Russell.
Give to the Winds Thy Fears.
Gehardt.
Lessons. Untermeyer.
Ode to the Medieval Poets.
Auden.
Petition for a Miracle.
Morton.
A Remembrance of My
Friend Mr. Thomas Morley.
Davies.

X

X
The Motive for Metaphor.
Stevens.
Ultimate Anthology. Bell.

Y

Yacht
Christmas Eve. Beer.
Off Banks Peninsula. Glover.
Squaring the Circle. Coxe.
Yale
Monkey. Miles.
Mother of Men. Hooker.
Yankee
An American Girl.
Matthews.

An Appeal to John Harralson.
Anonymous.
The Armstrong at Fayal.
Rice.
The Constellation and the
Insurgente. *Anonymous.*
Blackpool Breezes.
Anonymous.
Death of the Lincoln
Despotism. *Anonymous.*
For Decoration Day:
1898-1899. Hughes.
Dewey in Manila Bay.
Risley.
A Fable for Critics. Lowell.
Humbug Steamship
Companies. *Anonymous.*
A New Ballad. *Anonymous.*
The New Hellas. Edman.
A New War Song by Sir Peter
Parker. *Anonymous.*
Running the Blockade.
Perry.
To Lou Gehrig. Kieran.
Treason's Last Device.
Stedman.
The United States and
Macedonian. *Anonymous.*
Yankee Thunders.
Anonymous.
Yankee Doodle
Barnyard Melodies. Brooks.
The Last Appendix to Yankee
Doodle. *Anonymous.*
Yard (s)
After Midnight. Jones.
Art and Reality. Simmons.
The Ballad of Reading Gaol.
Wilde.
The Comman Man. Smith.
Dancer. Scheele.
The Emigres. Walker.
Epistles. Horace.
Head and Bottle. Thomas.
To Our House-Dog Captain.
Landor.
Useful Dates. *Anonymous.*
Yarn (s)
Little Ball of Yarn.
Anonymous.
A Nautical Extravaganza.
Irwin.
Noah an' Jonah an' Cap'n
John Smith. Marquis.
The Yarn of the Loch
Achray. Masefield.
Yarrow
Bonnie Annie (B version).
Anonymous.
Bouquet in Dog Time.
Carruth.
The Dowie Houms o' Yarrow.
Anonymous.
In the Month of Green Fire.
Himmell.
The Occasional Yarrow.
Smith.
Rare Willie Drowned in
Yarrow, or, The Water o
Gamrie (A version).
Anonymous.
Rare Willie Drowned in
Yarrow, or, The Water o
Gamrie (B version).
Anonymous.
Yarrow Unvisited.
Wordsworth.
Yawn ('d) (ing)
Evening Song. Fearing.
Horatian Epode to the
Duchess of Malfi. Tate.

Metamorphoses. Ovid
(Publius Ovidius Naso).
The Return. Saleh.
Year (s)
Above Pate Valley. Snyder.
Age in Youth. Stickney.
Alabama Centennial.
Madgett.
Alas, My God. Shepherd.
The Anniverse: An Elegy.
King.
Antigone I. Martin.
Autumn Burial: A Meditation.
Gullans.
The Ballad of Paco Town.
Scollard.
The Beekeeper's Daughter.
Plath.
Birthday. Merrill.
Blackberry-Picking. Heaney.
The Book of Pilgrimage.
Rilke.
Briggflatts. Bunting.
Brother and Sister. Eliot.
By Cobequid Bay. Fraser.
The Careless Gallant.
Jordan.
Chant for Skippers.
Gallagher.
Cherry-Ripe. Herrick.
A Cherry Year. *Anonymous.*
Childhood. Stanton.
Christ's Nativity. Vaughan.
Christmas in the Olden Time.
Scott.
Comets and Princes.
Johnson.
Cypresses. Francis.
The Dagger. Borges.
The Dart. *Anonymous.*
Daughters of War.
Rosenberg.
The Dead Man Ariseth and
Singeth a Hymn to the Sun.
Book of the Dead.
Death Is Awful. Hall, Vera.
December 26. Hoffman.
Desert in the Sea. Swann.
Dirge. Naidu.
The Ebb Tide. Southey.
Echo. Hardy.
Elegy. Keyes.
Entrance Exams. "Bede.
Epigram: "Nicander, ooh..."
Alcaeus.
A Faery Song. Yeats.
Faustus. Hope.
February. Whitney.
Feminine. Bunner.
Finding a Friend Home.
Hamm.
The First Olympionique to
Hiero of Syracuse. Pindar.
Fish Story. Kinnick.
For No One. McCartney.
For the West. Snyder.
Give Ear, O God, to My
Loud Cry. Prince.
Gratitude. McGee.
Hard Rock Returns to Prison
from the Hospital for the
Criminal Insane. Knight.
Historical Museum,
Manitoulin Island.
Mueller.
Hounslow Heath.
Anonymous.
House and Home. Hugo.
How to Swing Those
Obbligatos Around.
Fulton.

A Hundred Years Ago (with
music). *Anonymous.*
Idle Verse. Vaughan.
In February. Symonds.
In October. Carman.
In the Carpenter's Shop.
Teasdale.
The Influence of Local
Attachment (excerpt).
Polwhele.
Invocation to Sappho.
Gidlow.
Ivesiana. Berkson.
January Man. Goulder.
June. Malloch.
Just Be Glad. Riley.
Kicking the Leaves. Hall.
The Lady of the Lake. Scott.
Land of Our Fathers.
Scollard.
Last Light. Kelly.
Like Any Other Man. Orr.
Lilith. Finkel.
The Lincolnshire Poacher.
Anonymous.
Living. Savage.
Long Time a Child.
Coleridge.
Love's Nightingale.
Crashaw.
The Masked Shrew.
Gardner.
Melhill Feast. Barnes.
Memories. Stringer.
Mimma Bella. Lee-
Hamilton.
Mimosa. Mathis.
National Cold Storage
Company. Shapiro.
The New Year. Cotton.
A New Year. Davies.
New Year. Harada.
New Year's Eve in Troy.
Rich.
A Night in the Red Sea.
Lyall.
No Answer. Whistler.
A Nocturnal upon St Lucy's
Day, Being the Shortest
Day. Donne.
Not Only in the Christmas-
Tide. Dodge.
Old Mortality. Scott.
Older Grown. Greenaway.
On His 86th Birthday.
Hardy.
Parting. *Anonymous.*
Pause. Livesay.
Poem. Towle.
The Poet's Song. Tennyson.
Poet Wondering What He Is
Up To. Enright.
Post-Meridian. Garrison.
The Quiet Pilgrim. Thomas.
Rain. Lindsay.
Reconsecration. Gould.
Red Dust. Levine.
Respice Finem. Proctor.
Resurgam. *Anonymous.*
Resurrection. Crabbe.
Retro me, Sathana! Rossetti.
The Sad Years. Gore-Booth.
Sifting. Beck.
Sleeping on Horseback. Po
Chu-i.
So That Even a Lover.
Zukofsky.
Some Day or Days. Perry.
Spring. Blake.
Spring Death. Marano.
St. Alphonsus Rodriguez.
Hopkins.

Year

Sunrise. Sangster.
Sweet Clover. Rice.
The Sweet o' the Year.
  Meredith.
Tell Me What Month Was
  My Jesus Born in.
  Anonymous.
Times o' Year. Barnes.
To a Salesgirl, Weary of
  Artificial Holiday Trees.
  Wright.
To His Wife. Ausonius.
To Mistress Isabel Pennell.
  Skelton.
To the King, Upon his
  welcome to Hampton-
  Court. Herrick.
To Vera Thompson. Haines.
Unposted Birthday Card.
  MacCaig.
Untitled: "fisk is/a/negroid/
  institution..." Scott.
La Vita Nuova. Dante
  Alighieri.
Waiting for the Doctor.
  Inez.
Waiting in Front of the
  Columnar High School.
  Shapiro.
A Walk in March.
  Reynolds.
The Welsh Sea. Flecker.
What the Light Was Like.
  Clampitt.
Winter. Hurnard.
The World Well Lost.
  Stedman.
The Year Ahead. Powers.
Year's End. Antoninus.
Your Hand Full of Hours.
  Celan.

Yearbook

Class of 19–. Dec.

Yearling (s)

Lion. Swenson.
The Lone Star Trail.
  Anonymous.
O-Bar Cowboy. *Anonymous.*
Youth of the Mountain.
  Hand.

Yearn (ed) (ing)

A Cantor's Dream before the
  High Holy Days. Robbins.
The Dromedary. Campbell.
In Memoriam A.H.H., CXVI.
  Tennyson.
The Lark. Bernard de
  Ventadour
Partings. Jewsbury.
Razor. Smith.
Song of Despair. Rangiaho.
Survival. Coates.
There's a Fire in the Forest.
  Ross.
To Sleep. Kochanowski.
Two in the Campagna.
  Browning.
Violins in Repose. Plescoff.
Water Music. Lewis.
Zebaoth. Lasker-Schüler.

Yeats

Dream Songs. Berryman.
Four for Sir John Davies.
  Roethke.

Yell (ed) (ing)

As I Walked Out.
  Anonymous.
A Disappointment. Baillie.
An Evening Walk (excerpt).
  Wordsworth.
GraceAnAnne. Borie.
Hunting at Dusk. Cockrell.

A Joyful Noise. Finkel.

Yellow

1930's. Lowell.
The Alchemist in the City.
  Hopkins.
Apples. Mueller.
At Least. Mattera.
Autobiography. Akesson.
The Blindman. Swenson.
The Buildings. Berry.
The Cauliflower. Haines.
Crocuses in the Grass. Gray.
The Cry of the Lovelorn.
  Martin.
An Essay on Criticism.
  Pope.
Eulogy to the Bow and
  Arrow. *Anonymous.*
Evadne. Doolittle.
The Fairies in New Ross.
  Anonymous.
The Fashionable Heart.
  Gilbert.
The Fathers. Saltman.
Five Little Sisters Walking in
  a Row. Greenaway.
For Anne Gregory. Yeats.
Four Glosses. *Anonymous.*
From a Bus. Wangara.
The Good Time Is Now.
  Chester.
The Green Eye of the Yellow
  God. Hayes.
The Green Leaves All Turn
  Yellow. Kenney.
The Haughty Snail-King.
  Lindsay.
Heave Away. *Anonymous.*
Heave away, My Johnny.
  Anonymous.
The Humble Petition of Bruar
  Water to the Noble Duke of
  Athole. Burns.
I Show the Daffodils to the
  Retarded Kids. Sharp.
The Lament of the Border
  Widow. *Anonymous.*
The Legend of Good Women.
  Chaucer.
Lie Closed, My Lately Loved.
  Woods.
Limerick: "There once was a
  guy named Othello."
  Robinson.
Lost Love. *Anonymous.*
Mahony's Mountain.
  Stewart.
Melting in thin mist and
  heavy clouds. Li Ch'ing-
  chao.
Mud. Boyden.
Near Avalon. Morris.
The Nigga Section. Smith.
Of Nicolette. Cummings.
On the Thirteenth Day of
  Christmas. Causley.
One Kingfisher and One
  Yellow Rose. Brennan.
The Physics of Ochun. Cruz.
The Pleiades. Barnard.
Red Wing Hawk.
  Applewhite.
Saratoga Ending. Kees.
Song of Grief. Liu Hsi-
  Chun.
Sonnets, XIII: "I walk of grey
  noons by the old canal."
  Irwin.
Times Gettin' Hard, Boys
  (with music). *Anonymous.*
To Bring Spring. Keithley.
Ward Two. Webb.

The Wasp's Song. "Carroll.
We Go out Together.
  Patchen.
Willie's Fatal Visit.
  Anonymous.
The Words, the Words, the
  Words. Williams.
Yearning. Kreymborg.
Yellow. Kilmer.
The Yellow-haired Laddie.
  Anonymous.
Yellow Light. Hongo.
Yellow Meal. *Anonymous.*
The Yellowhammer. Clare.

Yellowstone National Park

Further Notice. Whalen.

Yelp (ed) (s)

Fantasia. Nathan.
Hmmmm, 19. Scalapino.
Rain Falls. It Dries...
  Radnoti.

Yes

And Yet We Are Here!
  Wolfskehl.
Art Thou Weary? Neale.
Darling, Tell Me Yes. Saxe.
Document. Ruebner.
Emily Dickinson's Sestina for
  Molly Bloom. Lefcowitz.
The Examination. Snodgrass.
The First Time. Newlove.
For My Daughter. Koertge.
Fragments. Praxilla.
Himalayan Balsam.
  Stevenson.
I Been Treated Wrong.
  Washboard Sam.
In Celebration of My Uterus.
  Sexton.
It's Three No Trumps.
  Innes.
Letter to Scanlon from
  Whitehall. Hugo.
Limerick: "A schoolma'am of
  much reputation." Upton.
Love Is a Place. Cummings.
The People, Yes. Sandburg.
Seesaw. Diego.
The Soldier Is Home.
  Neilson.
Some San Francisco Poems.
  Oppen.
Sonnet: Of Becchina, the
  Shoemaker's Daughter.
  Angiolieri.
The Story of Rimini. Hunt.
Sukey, You Shall Be My
  Wife. *Anonymous.*
Surprise. Behn.
To a Tyrant. Brodsky.
Tzu Yeh Songs. *Anonymous.*
Woman. Rakosi.

Yesterday (s)

The Amaranth. Patmore.
Ancestor. Baca.
Don Larsen's Perfect Game.
  Goodman.
Epigrams. Martial (Marcus
  Valerius Martialis).
Fairy Story. Todd.
I Cry to You as I Pass Your
  Windows. Brennan.
In an Old Library. Yuan
  Mei.
Inscription on a Grot.
  Rogers.
The King. Kipling.
The Last of the Grand Old
  Masters. Patey.
Let Us Forget. Robinson.
Loss. Madge.

A Maudle-In Ballad (parody).
  Anonymous.
On Trust in the Heart. Seng-
  Ts'an.
Opinions of the New Student.
  Pedroso.
The Political Prisoner.
  Kunene.
The Prophet. Gibran.
A Song of Impossibilities.
  Praed.
Under a Stagnant Sky.
  Henley.
Where Have You Gone, Little
  Boy. Harjo.

Yew (s)

Baucis and Philemon. Swift.
Enigma. Murphy.
Florence MacCarthy's
  Farewell to Her English
  Lover. De Vere.
The Gnu Wooing. Johnson.
In the Oregon Country.
  Stafford.
The Moon and the Yew Tree.
  Plath.
My Fixed Abode Is Glen
  Bolcain. Geilt.

Yiddish

Down the M4. Abse.
Where the Cedars. Glatstein.

Yield (ed) (ing) (s)

Bulldozers. Dec.
The Circumcision. Zisquit.
Dialogue at the Cross. Spee.
The Eighteenth Song.
  Hadewijch.
Elegy Written at the Sea-Side,
  and Addressed to Miss
  Honoria Sneyd. Seward.
Lords of the Wilderness.
  Leyden.
Meeting a Bear. Wagoner.
The Mower. *Anonymous.*
Night Thought. Jonas.
Ode to England. Lord
Poem: "Geranium, houseleek,
  laid in oblong beds."
  Gray.
Reflections in a Hospital.
  Eisenberg.
Resolutions?–New and Old.
  Rolfe.
Robin Hood and the Curtal
  Friar. *Anonymous.*
To Chloris, upon a Favour
  Received. Waller.
To His Child. Bullokar.
Tutto e Sciolto. Joyce.
When Damon First Began to
  Love. Behn.
The Year 1812. Mickiewicz.

Yoke

The Battle Within. Rossetti.
Be Still. Ayer.
Caelica, XXXI. Greville.
The Carpenter's Son. Peck.
Enslaved. McKay.
Jesus a Child His Course
  Begun. Fuller.
Spring Song. Nahum.
Sumter–A Ballad of 1861.
  Anonymous.
What Am I? Stoltzenberg.
With Freedom's Seed.
  Pushkin.

Yolk

Abiku. Soyinka.
It's in the Egg. Rosenblatt.
The Wounded Breakfast.
  Edson.

Yonder
Glasgow. Smith.
I Have Some Friends Before Me Gone. *Anonymous.*
The Leaden Echo and the Golden Echo. Hopkins.
Paw-Paw Patch. *Anonymous.*
The Sun Shines over the Mountain. *Anonymous.*
Who Dat A-Comin' ovah Yondah? *Anonymous.*

Yorrick
The Island of Yorrick. Bodecker.

You
110 Year Old House. Ochester.
After Storm. Morton.
An Afternoon in the Garden. Edmond.
Again for Hephaistos, the Last Time. Howard.
Ah! Why, Because the Dazzling Sun. Bronte.
Alas! 'Tis Very Sad to Hear. Landor.
America. Creeley.
April Fool's Day. Pomeroy.
As I Was Going up Pippen Hill. *Anonymous.*
Astraea Redux. Dryden.
Astrophel and Stella, XCI. Sidney.
At the Dark Hour. Dehn.
Baby. Macdonald.
Ballad for the Unknown Soldier. Taylor.
The Barrel-Organ. Symons.
Bean Spasms. Berrigan.
Because of You. Hensley.
Because You're You. Blossom.
Beyond Recall. Bradley.
A Blackbird Suddenly. Auslander.
Blue Like Death. Welch.
Boadicea. Cowper.
Bobbie's Cat. Locklin.
Body of the Queen. Evans.
The Book of Mysterics. Barnett.
A Bowl of Roses. Henley.
Bricklayer Love. Sandburg.
Broad Gold. Akhmatova.
Caelica, LX. Greville.
The Calf, the Goat, the Little Lamb. Hoffenstein.
Carnal Knowledge. Harwood.
Caught by Chance. Ramsey.
Celia Celia. Mitchell.
Christmas Singing. Chandler.
Circumstance. Shelley.
Clerihew. Bentley.
Codicil. Stone.
Confessions of a Born Spectator. Nash.
Constant. Dickinson.
The Crucifix. Read.
Dagger. Lermontov.
Deare, If You Change. *Anonymous.*
Death's Lecture at the Funeral of a Young Gentleman. Crashaw.
The Dial Tone. Nemerov.
Dining-Room Tea. Brooke.
The Dirty-Billed Freeze Footy. Hemschemeyer.
Dream. Bynner.

Dream Sequence, Part 9. Madgett.
Dreamtime. Domanski.
The Dying Lover. Stoddard.
Egyptian Hieroglyphics. *Anonymous.*
An Elegie. Randolph.
The Emancipators. Jarrell.
The Ending. Engle.
England. Salter.
Enigma. Fauset.
Escalade. Symons.
An Evening Walk. Stafford.
Faberge. Schuyler.
A Fancy. Lodge.
Feud. Sarett.
Finding You. Thayer.
First Love. Calverley.
Following the Sun. Kessler.
For a Friend. Kooser.
For an Obligate Parasite. Dugan.
For You, O Democracy. Whitman.
The Fortune-Teller To a Young Lady in Search of Her Destiny. Prior.
Friend, don't be angry. Mira Bai [(or Mirabai)].
The Ghoul. Prelutsky.
Goddess. Sherwin.
The Golden Rule. Wells.
The Gospel According to You. *Anonymous.*
The Hands. Moses.
Hearing That His Friend Was Coming Back from the War. Wang Chien.
Heart's Needle. Snodgrass.
Heaven's Last Best Work. Pope.
Herman Moon's Hourbook. Middleton.
I Am Here. Mezey.
I can't break with the Dark One. Mira Bai [(or Mirabai)].
I Know Something Good About You. Shimon.
I'll Buy You a Tartan Bonnet. *Anonymous.*
I Shall Not Care. Teasdale.
Idea. Drayton.
In a Cathedral City. Hardy.
In Death Divided. Hardy.
In former days we'd both agree. Bhartrihari.
In health and ease am I. Davison.
Indian Death. Walton.
Infidelity. Untermeyer.
Is This Land Your Land? *Anonymous.*
It Isn't the Church—It's You. *Anonymous.*
It Isn't the Town, It's You. Glover.
It's You. McDonald.
The K.K.K. Disco... Mitchell.
The Lady of the Pearls (excerpt). Dumas.
The Last Word. Knowles.
Late Last Night. Hughes.
Leaving Ithaca. Snodgrass.
Limerick: "Said a saucy young skunk to a gnu." Neyroud.
Lindeman. White.
Lines Written on November 15, 1933 by a Man Born

November 14, 1881... Hamilton.
The Little Elf. Bangs.
A Little Person. Hooker.
The Little Rose Is Dust, My Dear. Conkling.
The Locomotive to the Little Boy. Low.
Look, I Have Thrown All Right. MacKay.
Love Song. Chantikian.
Love Song: I and Thou. Dugan.
Madrigal: "Dear, when I did from you remove." Herbert of Cherbury.
Madrigal: "Some there are as fair to see to." Davison.
Miss You. *Anonymous.*
Miss You. Cory.
The Mouse. McCrae.
My Life Is a Bowl. Smith.
My Love. Shelton.
My Road. Opdyke.
The Mysteries Remain. Doolittle.
Near. Kovner.
Nessa. Durcan.
The Next Time You Were There. Hazo.
No Madam Butterfly. Hajek.
Nocturne. Weaver.
Noises. Johnson.
Now Is the Cherry in Blossom. Wilkins.
Now That I Am Forever with Child. Lorde.
An Ode on Miss Harriet Hanbury. Williams.
An Old Woman. *Anonymous.*
On Buying a Dog. Klauber.
On Noman, a Guest. Belloc.
One Year Later. Torgerson.
Oxford Nights. Johnson.
Paradoxes and Oxymorons. Ashbery.
Paterson. Williams.
Penmanship. Clark.
A Poem for Players. Young.
Poem Wondering If I'm Pregnant. Fraser.
Poet-Tree. Birney.
Portrait d'une Femme. Pound.
Prayer for Rain. Jama.
Priapus and the Pool. Aiken.
The Queen. Neruda.
Refugee Blues. Auden.
Resolving Doubts. Dickey.
Retractions. Cabell.
Return to a Place Lit by a Glass of Milk. Simic.
Rhyme for Remembrance of May. Burton.
The Robin's Song. Fraser.
Rondeau for You. De Andrade.
Roots and Leaves Themselves Alone. Whitman.
The Rose. Lodge.
The Rose Is Red, the Violet's Blue. *Anonymous.*
Sacred and Profane Love, or, There's Nothing New under the Moon Either. De Vries.
Several Voices out of a Cloud. Bogan.
Sloe Gin. Heaney.
Snowfall: A Poem about Spring. Wright.

Somebody. *Anonymous.*
Song: "Dew on the bamboos." *Anonymous.*
Song: "Fool, take up thy shaft again." Stanley.
Song of Myself. Whitman.
Song: "Reading about the Wisconsin Weeping Willow." Krauss.
Songs for a Three-String Guitar. Sedar-Senghor.
Sonnet: "Dead men of 'ninety-two, also of 'ninety-three." Rimbaud.
Spring Day. Ashbery.
Starlight. Meredith.
The Stars. "Ping Hsin" (Hsieh Wang-ying).
Stella at Wood-Park. Swift.
Still He Sings. Taylor.
The Still Voice of Harlem. Rivers.
The Strange Visitor. *Anonymous.*
The Sum of All Known Reverence. Whitman.
Sweeping the Sky. *Anonymous.*
A Tardy Epithalamium for E. and N. Pomeroy.
Tell Me Pretty Maiden. Hall.
That We Head Towards. Stephany.
There Once Was a Puffin. Jaques.
To a Lady Friend. Davies.
To Blossoms. Herrick.
To-Day. Low.
To J.S. Misch.
To L. C. Hawkins.
To Maynard on the Long Road Home. Ehrhart.
To Men. Wickham.
To Mr. George Herbert, with One of My Seals, of the Anchor and Christ. Donne.
To Myself, after Forty Years. White.
To T. H., a Lady Resembling My Mistress. Carew.
To the Harbormaster. O'Hara.
Together. Kumin.
Two Sonnets. Sorley.
Unborn. Brereton.
Unwelcome. Dovey.
Warning to a Guest. Holloway.
Wearyin' fer You. Stanton.
What the Serpent Said to Adam. MacLeish.
When I strip. Kegels.
When To My Deadlie Pleasure. Sidney.
Who Is It Talks of Ebony? Ghose.
Who Is Not a Stranger Still. Stephany.
The Wife-Woman. Spencer.
Years. Margolin.
Yom Kippur: Fasting. Whitman.
You Shall Be Queen. *Anonymous.*

Young
An Adage. Byron.
Afternoon's Angel. Mayne.
Album. Miles.
Alibi. Tilghman.
Along the River. Enright.

Another Cynical Variation. "Helen".
Aubade. Lechlitner.
Aureng-Zebe. Dryden.
Autumn. Beeton.
Ave Maria. O'Hara.
The Bad Girl's Lament; or, St. James Hospital. *Anonymous.*
Baucis and Philemon. Hoskins.
Beautiful Hands. Gates.
Ben. Wolfe.
Billy Boy. *Anonymous.*
Brendan Gone. Fiacc.
Caelica, XIX. Greville.
Casanova. Usborne.
The Chaperon. Bunner.
Childhood. Cornford.
A Childhood. Spender.
Christenings. Porter.
The City. Russell.
Clonard. Jones, Jr.
Could I Believe. Milne.
County Mayo. Raftery,
Death Songs. *Anonymous.*
A Dis, a Dis, a Green Grass. *Anonymous.*
Down by the Salley Gardens. Yeats.
Draw a Pail of Water. *Anonymous.*
Dream Songs. Berryman.
The Duchess of Malfi. Webster.
Early Thoughts. Lecky.
The Earth and Man. Brooke.
Egan O Rahilly. Stephens.
Epitaphs of the War. Kipling.
Epitaphs of the War, 1914-18. Kipling.
Erin (Elephant). *Anonymous.*
Esther. Blunt.
Evening Meal in the Twentieth Century. Holmes.
Fair Florella (B vers.). *Anonymous.*
February 11, 1977. Morgan.
The Finnesburh Fragment. *Anonymous.*
The Fire i' the Flint. Robinson.
For Lucas Cranach's Eve. Crapsey.
Good-Bye Old Paint. *Anonymous.*
Green Lions. Stewart.
Half Moon. Garcia Lorca.
Hares on the Mountain. *Anonymous.*
Hen's Nest. Clare.
His Toy, His Dream, His Rest. Berryman.
Homework for Annabelle. McGinley.
Hunting Pheasants in a Cornfield. Bly.
Hymn to the Sun. Akhnaton (Amenhotep IV).
I'm O'er Young to Marry Yet. Burns.
I Shall Go Back. Millay.
I used to wrap my white doll up in. Jackson.
I Want to Be Married and Cannot Tell How. *Anonymous.*
In a Spring Still Not Written Of. Wallace.

In the Old House. Hall.
The Incurables. Upson.
June. Rand.
The Kilkenny Boy. Shanahan.
Laly, Laly. Van Doren.
The Last Memory. Symons.
Late Sonnet. Carruth.
Learn, Lads and Lasses. Pastorius.
Limerick: "The S & M bar, oh my dears." *Anonymous.*
Limerick: "There was a young lady of Corsica." Lear.
Limerick: "There was a young lady of Milton." *Anonymous.*
Lines Written among the Euganean Hills. Shelley.
The Little Farm; or, The Weary Ploughman. *Anonymous.*
Love and Age. Peacock.
The Love of Older Men. Kirkup.
Love's Remorse. Muir.
Made in Heaven. Porter.
Maids When You're Young, Never Wed an Old Man. *Anonymous.*
Mary Ackerman, 1938, Eugene Buechel Photograph Museum of Modern Art... Glancy.
A Masique Presented at Ludlow Castle (Comus). Milton.
The Merry Hoastess. *Anonymous.*
The Modern Chinese History Professor Plays Pool Every Tuesday... Hall.
Modern Love, XLVII. Meredith.
Monday. Stafford.
Month of January. Armstrong.
Mountain Days. Fraser.
My Boy Tammy. Macneill.
My Love, She Passed Me By. *Anonymous.*
Natural History. *Anonymous.*
Nehi Blues. Reynolds.
New King Arrives in His Capital by Air... Betjeman.
The Newlyweds' Cuisine. Wang Chien.
The Nobleman's Wedding. Allingham.
"Noone" Autumnal This Great Lady's Gaze. Cummings.
Novelettes III: The Gardener. MacNeice.
An Old Man. Wordsworth.
Old Triton Time. Watkins.
On Reading Aloud My Early Poems. Williams.
On the Mountain. Neidhart von
Once and Future. Chang.
Padraic O'Conaire—Gaelic Storyteller. Higgins.
The Palm-Tree and the Pine. Milnes.
Paracelsus. Browning.
The Permanence of the Young Men. Soutar.
Philomela. Ransom.

Phyllis. *Anonymous.*
Piazza Piece. Ransom.
Poem. Blaser.
The Poet. Grannis.
The Poet at Fifty. Lerner.
A Pretty Fair Maid (with music). *Anonymous.*
The Pulse. Van Doren.
The Puzzled Game Birds. Hardy.
The Renowned Generations. Yeats.
Retractions. Cabell.
Revolutionary. Friel.
The Road. Aiken.
The Road to Nijmegen. Birney.
Sally's Garden. *Anonymous.*
Shellbrook. Barnes.
Shepherd. Blunden.
Shore Roads of April. Adams.
Slow Summer Twilight. Wheelock.
So Sweet Love Seemed. Bridges.
So Young Ane King. Lindsay.
Song. Sheridan.
Song: "Had I a heart for falsehood fram'd." Sheridan.
Song: "Me Cupid made a Happy Slave." Steele.
A Song of Ale. *Anonymous.*
Sonnets, XIX: "Devouring Time, blunt thou the lion's paws." Shakespeare.
Soon with the Lilac Fades Another Spring. MacDonogh.
Spawning in Northern Minnesota. McElroy.
The Spoils of War. Watkins.
Springfield Mountain (C vers.). *Anonymous.*
State Prison 5:00 p.m. Nickens.
Stay Beautiful. Wright.
Stories Relate Life. Shady.
Summer Song. Nesbit.
Sunday up the River. Thomson.
Thanksgiving. Booth.
Theory. Parker.
Three Epitaphs. Davison.
Three Sermons to the Dead. Riding.
To a Golden-Haired Girl in a Louisiana Town. Lindsay.
To Mr. Hobbes. Cowley.
To One Older. Boyd.
The Toy Lamb Seller. *Anonymous.*
Tree-Sleeping. Coffin.
Vapour and Blue. Campbell.
A Visit to Bridge House. Weber.
The Vocation of St. Francis. Eleanore.
War-Time. Rodgers.
Warriors. Hogan.
Welcome Morning. Sexton.
When Boys Go A-Courting. *Anonymous.*
When You and I Were Young, Maggie. Butterfield.
A Wild Romantic Dell. Mickle.
Wind and Mist. Thomas.

Wishes for My Son. Macdonagh.
Written at Florence. Blunt.
The Young Sailor Cut down in His Prime. Anonymous.
Youth. Wright.

Your (s)
The Album. Day Lewis.
Another Letter to Lord Byron. Slavitt.
Chaste Florimel. Prior.
A Contemplation upon Flowers. King.
Epitaph on a Dormouse, Which Some Children Were to Bury. *Anonymous.*
First Coffin Poem. Ignatow.
First, Goodbye. Smith.
The Flowers of Apollo. Flanner.
For Tu Fu. Feng Chih.
The House. Williams.
The House Dog's Grave. Jeffers.
How to Own Land. Farley.
I Am Here. Mezey.
The Imagination of Necessity. Codrescu.
The Indian's Grave. Mountain.
Instruction from Bly. Macdonald.
Letter. Strand.
Lines for Michael in the Picture. Logan.
Lost. Alvarez.
Madam, withouten many words. Wyatt.
Need Is Our Name. Shaw.
Our Mother Tongue; or, An Envoy to an American Lady. Milnes.
The Question. Beattie.
R. B. Gorton.
Saved. Horta.
A Song of Impossibilities. Praed.
Surrender. Burr.
T.V. (1). Hollo.
Temporal. Jonas.
To a Lady To Answer Directly with Yea or Nay. Wyatt.
To a Republican Friend. Arnold.
To Italy. Leopardi.
To the Last Wedding Guest. Gregory.
Translation. Lesser.
Upon Lesbia—Arguing. Cochrane.
Voice. Merwin.
Where? Tessimond.
William Gifford. Landor.
With Thee. Pinkham.
Your Place. Oxenham.

Yourself (selves)
Amoretti, LVIII. Spenser.
Autobiography: Last Chapter. Barnes.
Calypso's Song to Ulysses. Mitchell.
The Confirmation. Muir.
Dear Child Whom I Begot. Cunningham.
Epigrams and Epitaphs, VI. Lewis.
Harriet. Lowell.
In Sylvia Plath Country. Jong.
Last Poem. Donnelly.

The Last Will and Testament of the Grey Mare. *Anonymous.*
Love Sonnets. Cross.
The Maximus Poems. Olson.
Poem for Friends. Troupe.
A Poet's Proverbs. Guiterman.
Prepare. Bynner.
Real Deal Revelation. Fernandez.
Risselty-Rosselty. *Anonymous.*
She's All My Fancy Painted Him. "Carroll.
Silent Movies. Pietri.
Tattoos. Wright.
To the Modern Man. Wheelock.
True Enough: To the Physicist (1820). Goethe.
What She Wanted. Koertge.
The White Dove Sat on the Castle Wall. Wager.
You Tell On Yourself. *Anonymous.*

Youth
Alas for Youth. Firdausi.
Allen-a-Dale. Scott.
Almighty Sovereign of the Skies! Strong.
Amen. Sabines.
At the Mermaid Inn. Hildreth.
Autumn. Wolfe.
The Best Memory Course. *Anonymous.*
Chicago. Sandburg.
The County Ball (excerpt). Praed.
The Doorstep. Stedman.
Epigram: "Most inexplicable the wiles of boys I deem." Rhianus.
Epithalamium. Johannes Secundus.
Founder's Day. Bridges.
The Garden Party. Davie.
God Lyaeus. Fletcher.
Happy Is the Country Life. *Anonymous.*
Hialmar. Campbell.
The House of Love: Pride of Youth. Rossetti.
Hymn to Marriage, for Manlius and Junia. Catullus.
I Dreamed That I Was Old. Kunitz.
Image-Nation 3. Blaser.
Invitation to the Dance. *Anonymous*
Jessie Mitchell's Mother. Brooks.
The Kerry Dance. Molloy.
Legend. Crane.
Let Others Sing of Knights and Palladines. Daniel.
Lightly Like Music Running. Garrigue.
Little Dirge. Untermeyer.
The Lost Genius. Piatt.
Lying. Moore.

Mary Wyatt and Henry Green. Anonymous.
Milton. Blake.
The Moss-Rose. Newbolt.
The Mouldering Vine. *Anonymous.*
My Lost Youth. Longfellow
The Noble Balm. Jonson.
O Friends! Who Have Accompanied Thus Far. Landor.
O Little Well. *Anonymous.*
Ode to Zion. Halevi.
Odes. Horace.
On My Sweet Mother. Sappho.
Once on a Time. Banning.
Outgrown. Dorr.
A Perverse Custom. *Anonymous.*
Poems: Birmingham 1962-1964. Fields.
The Poet. Leitch.
The Purpose of Fable-Writing. Phaedrus.
Rabbi Ben Ezra. Browning.
The Rambling Boy. *Anonymous.*
The River of Life. Campbell.
Ronsard to His Mistress. Thackeray.
Sagesse. Verlaine.
Les Salaziennes (excerpt). Lacaussade.
Shelly. McIntyre.
Silex Scintillans. Vaughan.
Since Youth Is All for Gladness. Dresbach.
The Singers in a Cloud. Torrence.
The Sins of Youth. Vaux.
The Sky Is up above the Roof. Verlaine.
The Small Celandine. Wordsworth.
Song: "Bone-aged is my white horse." Chamberlain.
Song of Loneliness. Halevi.
Song: "When I lie burning in thine eye." Stanley.
Sonnet: "I have not spent the April of my time." Griffin.
Spring Song. Hesse.
The Star. Smith.
Suicide in Trenches. Sassoon.
Susan to Diana. Cornford.
Sweet Clover. Rice.
Sweeter Far Than the Harp, More Gold Than Gold. "Field.
To —. Braithwaite.
To a Cat. Keats.
To Age. Landor.
To the Bridegroom. Halevi
To the Memory of Yale College. Putnam.
Triumph of Bacchus and Ariadne. Medici.
Two Long Vacations: Grasmere. Butler.
Under Leafy Bowers. Al-Harizi.
Underneath a Cypress Shade,

The Queen of Love Sat Mourning. *Anonymous.*
Upon Love Fondly Refus'd for Conscience Sake. Randolph.
View from Heights. Ficke.
Village of Winter Carols. Lee.
Westward on the High-Hilled Plains. Housman.
What Fifty Said. Frost.
What Is White? Macdonagh.
A White Blossom. Lawrence.
Whom the Gods Love. Howe.
Young Forbest. *Anonymous.*
Youth. *Anonymous.*
Youth's Agitations. Arnold.

Yule
If Candlemas Day Be Dry and Fair. *Anonymous.*
The Ships of Yule. Carman.

Z

Zeal
The Comparison and Complaint. Watts.
Holy Sonnets, V. Donne.
Muse. Wagoner.
One Step Twix't Me and Death. Williams.
Sequaire. Godeschalk.
The Winter Glass. Cotton.

Zebra (s)
An Alphabet. Carryl.
An Apology. Wakoski.
Koko. Downer.

Zechariah
Direction from Zulu. Halpern.

Zen
Geo-Politics. Cardona-Hine.
La Misere (parody). Appleman.

Zenith
The Stars on Shabbat. Schlonsky.

Zenocrate
The Bloody Conquests of Mighty Tamburlaine (excerpt). Marlowe.
Tamburlaine. Marlowe.

Zenophile
The Little Love-God. Meleager.

Zepheria
Sonnet: "When, from the tower whence I derive love's heaven." *Anonymous.*

Zephyr (s)
Madrigal: "Poor turtle, thou bemoans." Drummond.
Uprising See the Fitful Lark. *Anonymous.*
Within the Veil. Sangster.

Zero (s)
The ABC Bunny. Gag.
After the Hurricane. Hazo.
The Alphabet. Calverley.

The Lumberman's Alphabet. *Anonymous.*
A More Ancient Mariner. Carman.
Ode on Zero. Pettingell.
The Story of Zeros. Cruz.

Zest
Peter Cooper. Miller.

Zeus
O Gentle Ships. Meleager.
The Odyssey. Homer.
Youth. Toerien.

Zinc
A Nonsense Alphabet. Lear.

Zion
Evening Prayer. Fitger.
Great Day. *Anonymous.*
In Spite of Sorrow. Judson.
The Lamps Are Burning. Reznikoff.
Mear. *Anonymous.*
The Prophet Jeremiah and the Personification of Israel. Ben Kalir.
The Temple. Kahn.
What Ship Is This? Hauser.
Woodworker's Ballad. Palmer.

Zodiac (s)
Epos. Tuwim.
The Goose Fish. Nemerov.
The Thing Is Violent. MacEwen.

Zombie
Request Numbers. Sprod.

Zone (s)
Mechanophilus (excerpt). Tennyson.
N. B., Symmetrians. Derwood.

Zoo
Aquellos Vatos. Villanueva.
Excuse Us, Animals in the Zoo. Wynne.
Famous Poet. Hughes.
Five Songs. Shapiro.
The Gorilla. Hathaway.
In the Zoo. Mahaka.
The Miscegenous Zebra. Young.
The Monkeys. Thompson.
Poems from Prison. Maloney.
The Prodigy. Herbert.
The Sloth. Gardner.
The Toucan. Johnson, Jr.
The Zoo of You. Freeman.

Zooks
Fra Lippo Lippi. Browning.
Sledburn Fair. *Anonymous.*

Zoroaster
Direction from Zulu. Halpern.
Z Is for Zoroaster. Farjeon.

Zulus
New Orleans. Carruth.

Zun
Zun-Zet. Barnes.

Zuni
The Songs. *Anonymous.*

Zuyder Zee
A Single-Rhyme Alphabet. *Anonymous.*